BOOKS IN PRINT®

1997–98

50th EDITION
BOOKS IN PRINT
1948-1998

This edition of
BOOKS IN PRINT 1997-98
was prepared by the R.R. Bowker's
Database Publishing Group in
collaboration with the Publication Systems Department

Database Publishing Group
Leigh C. Yuster-Freeman, Vice President, Database Production
Andrew Grabois, Senior Managing Director

International Standard Book Number/Standard Address Number Agency
Don Riseborough, Senior Managing Editor
Lynn Ann Sahner, Senior Editor
Margot Cronin, Adeyinka Fagbongbe, and Brenda Joseph, Assistant Editors
Diana Fumando, SAN Coordinator

Publishers Authority Database
William D. McCahery, Senior Editor
Janet Weiss, Assistant Editor

Editorial
Roy Crego , Managing Director
Samuel J. Dempsey, Editorial Director
Constance Harbison, Managing Editor
Edward Han, George Krubski, Annamaria Lalevee, Raymond Padilla, Senior Editors
Daniel Dickholtz, Senior Associate Editor
Kathleen Keiderling, Associate Editor, Enhancements
Sheri Falzarano, Lisa Heft, Ila Joseph-Corley, Thomas Lucas, Sean O'Dell, and Steven Zaffuto, Assistant Editors

Electronic Data Transfer Group
Frank Accurso, Senior Managing Editor
Mary Craig Daley, Managing Editor
Jennifer Fountain, Richard Whalen, and William Zavorskas, Senior Editors
David Gerridge, Associate Editor

Data Collection & Processing Group
Valerie Harris, Director
Mervaine Ricks, Production Manager
Cheryl Patrick, Lead Project Coordinator
Rhonda McKendrick and Karen Santana, Project Coordinators
Rita Phillips, Sally Snelling, Janet Foltz, and Denise Styers, Assistant Coordinators

Subject Guide
Elsa Meyers, Senior Editor
Angela Barrett, Senior Associate Editor
Mark D. MacDonald, Joseph V. Tondi, Assistant Editors

Production
Doreen Gravesande, Production Director
Myriam Nunez, Managing Editor
Barbara Holton, Frank McDermott, Senior Editors
Megan Roxberry, Senior Associate Editor
Monalisa Massiah, Associate Editor
Clarice D. Isaacs, Assistant Editor

Editorial Systems Group
Gary Aiello, Director, Bibliographical and Advertising Systems
Rhonda Vollbrecht, Project Manager
Mark Heinzelman, Project Leader
Rita Hrycak, Analyst

Computer Operations Group
Nick Wikowski, Director, Network/Computer Operations
Michael DeLuca, Production Control Manager
Jack Murphy, Supervisor

Reed Technology and Information Services
Dilma Kalbfleisch, Production Service Manager

BOOKS IN PRINT®

1997–98

VOLUME 8

TITLES ♦ R-Z

R.R. BOWKER
A Unit of Reed Elsevier Business Information
New Providence, New Jersey

Published by
R.R. Bowker
A Unit of Reed Elsevier Business Information
121 Chanlon Rd., New Providence
New Jersey 07974

Neal Goff, Chief Operating Officer

Telephone: 908-464-6800, Toll-free: 1-888-BOWKER2 (1-888-269-5372); Fax: 908-665-6688
E-mail address: info@bowker.com
URL: http://www.bowker.com

International Standard Book Numbers
Set: 0-8352-3935-7
Volume 1: 0-8352-3936-5
Volume 2: 0-8352-3937-3
Volume 3: 0-8352-3938-1
Volume 4: 0-8352-3940-3
Volume 5: 0-8352-3941-1
Volume 6: 0-8352-3943-8
Volume 7: 0-8352-3944-6
Volume 8: 0-8352-3945-4
Volume 9: 0-8352-3946-2

International Standard Serial Number
0068-0214

Library of Congress Catalog Card Number
4-12648

Printed in the United States of America

ISBN 0-8352-3935-7

9 780835 239356

Contents of Volume 1

Contents of Volume 2

Contents of Volume 3

Contents of Volume 4

Contents of Volume 5

Contents of Volume 6

Contents of Volume 7

Contents of Volume 8

Contents of Volume 9

BOOKS IN PRINT®

1997-98

Volume 8

TITLES

R-Z

R

R: BASE 3.1 Project Book. Sanford. 1992. pap. text ed. write for info. (*0-07-054929-X*) McGraw.

R - C Boat How To's. Intro. by Gerry Yarrish. (Illus.). 98p. (Orig.). 1993. pap. 14.95 (*0-911295-26-7*) Air Age.

R. A. F. Kenley. Peter Flint. 192p. 1994. 120.00 (*0-86138-036-3*, Pub. by T Dalton UK) St Mut.

R. A. Fisher: An Appreciation. Ed. by Stephen E. Fienberg & D. H. Hinkley. (Lecture Notes in Statistics Ser.: Vol. 1). 208p. 1990. 42.95 (*0-387-90476-X*) Spr-Verlag.

R. A. Fisher: The Life of a Scientist. Joan F. Box. (Probability & Mathematical Statistics Ser.). 512p. 1985. pap. text ed. 64.95 (*0-471-83898-5*) Wiley.

R. A. I. D. Alan E. Gonzalez. (Illus.). 64p. 1992. 12.95 (*1-880798-00-X*) Centurion Pub & Mgt.

R. A. S. P. E. C. T. - 1: Reading Allah - Jah's Signs Prophesies, Envisioning Coming Tribulations. Ricardo A. Scott. (Ras Cardo Book of Light Ser.). (Illus.). 100p. (Orig.). pap. text ed. write for info. (*1-883427-46-0*) Crnerstone GA.

R. A. Weeks International Symposium on Science & Technology of SiO2 & Related Materials. Ed. by David L. Griscom & Hideo Hosono. (Illus.). 380p. 1994. 83.00 (*0-944904-85-8*, 1GBK00D) Am Ceramic.

R & B. Bruce Andrews. (Segue Bks.). 32p. (Orig.). 1983. pap. text ed. 5.00 (*0-937804-05-3*) Segue NYC.

R & B JamTrax for Guitar. Ralph Agresta. (Illus.). 1993. pap. 9.95 (*0-8256-1348-5*, AM91045) Music Sales.

R & D As an Economic Development Strategy: The Microelectronic & Computer Technology Corporation Comes to Austin. Josh Farley & Norman J. Glickman. (Working Paper Ser.: No. 35). 26p. 1985. pap. 5.00 (*0-89940-515-0*) LBJ Sch Pub Aff.

R & D Career Path. Technical Association of the Pulp & Paper Industry Staff. 78p. reprint ed. pap. 25.00 (*0-317-30114-4*, 2025299) Bks Demand.

R & D Catalog. (Paranoia Ser.). 96p. 10.00 (*0-87431-157-8*, 12024) West End Games.

R & D Collaboration on Trial: The Microelectronics & Computer Technology Corporation. David V. Gibson & Everett M. Rogers. LC 93-1374. 608p. 1994. 35.00 (*0-87584-364-6*) Harvard Busn.

R & D Cooperation among Marketplace Competitors. William J. Murphy. LC 90-8919. 272p. 1990. text ed. 55.00 (*0-89930-489-3*, MRD/, Quorum Bks) Greenwood.

R & D for Industry: A Century of Technical Innovation at Alcoa. Margaret B. Graham & Bettye H. Pruitt. (Illus.). 640p. (C). 1990. 69.95 (*0-521-39413-9*) Cambridge U Pr.

R & D for Small & Medium-Sized Firms: Proceedings of a Symposium at the University of Michigan, October 25, 1966. Michigan University, Institute of Science & Technology, Industrial Development Division Staff. Ed. by John M. Armstrong. LC 67-20367. (Illus.). 112p. reprint ed. pap. 32.00 (*0-317-10638-4*, 2012297) Bks Demand.

R & D, Innovation & Industrial Structure: Essays on the Theory of Technological Competition. B. Maurer. (Contributions to Economics Ser.). 158p. 1996. 59.00 (*3-7908-0900-4*) Spr-Verlag.

R & D One Hundred Awards to NIST: Seventy-One Outstanding Technical Developments with Significant Commercial Potential. 52p. (Orig.). (C). 1992. pap. text ed. 30.00 (*1-56806-097-1*) DIANE Pub.

R & D, Patents, & Productivity. Zvi Griliches. LC 83-18121. (National Bureau of Economic Research Conference Report Ser.). 524p. (C). 1987. pap. text ed. 23.00 (*0-226-30884-7*) U Ch Pr.

R & D Ratios & Budgets. 200p. 1992. pap. text ed. 325.00 (*1-878339-16-8*) Schonfeld & Assocs.

R & D Ratios & Budgets. 200p. 1993. pap. text ed. 325.00 (*1-878339-23-0*) Schonfeld & Assocs.

R & D Ratios & Budgets. 216p. 1995. pap. text ed. 325.00 (*1-878339-38-9*) Schonfeld & Assocs.

R & D Ratios & Budgets: 1990 Edition. Schonfeld & Associates Staff. 200p. (C). 1990. pap. text ed. 295.00 (*1-878339-06-0*) Schonfeld & Assocs.

R & D Ratios & Budgets: 1996 Edition. 220p. 1996. pap. text ed. 325.00 (*1-878339-45-1*) Schonfeld & Assocs.

***R & D Ratios & Budgets: 1997 Edition.** 216p. 1997. pap. text ed. 345.00 (*1-878339-54-0*) Schonfeld & Assocs.

R & D Ratios & Budgets, 1989. Schonfeld & Associates Staff. 207p. (C). 1989. pap. text ed. 295.00 (*1-878339-01-X*) Schonfeld & Assocs.

R & D Ratios & Budgets, 1991. Schonfeld & Associates Staff. 200p. (C). 1991. pap. text ed. 295.00 (*1-878339-11-7*) Schonfeld & Assocs.

R & D Statistics & Output Measurement in the Higher Education Sector "Frascati Manual" Supplement. OECD Staff. (Measurement of Scientific & Technical Activities Ser.). 72p. (Orig.). 1989. pap. 12.00 (*92-64-13193-0*) OECD.

R & D Tactics. Harold R. Kaufman. 147p. (Orig.). (C). 1989. pap. 7.95 (*0-9623587-0-3*) Front Range Rsch.

R & D Workers: Managing Innovation in Britain, Germany, Japan, & the United States. Ed. by Philip Shapira. LC 94-45278. 184p. 1995. text ed. 55.00 (*0-89930-891-0*, Quorum Bks) Greenwood.

R & D's Role in Product Liability. Frank C. Jose. LC 75-109525. 64p. reprint ed. pap. 25.00 (*0-317-09579-X*, 2051516) Bks Demand.

R & R: A Story about Two Alphabets. Chris Raschka. LC 90-7082. (Illus.). 82p. (J). 1989. 4.95 (*0-87178-731-8*, 8318) Brethren.

R. Atkinson Fox & William M. Thompson: Identification & Price Guide. Patricia L. Gibson. LC 94-70639. (Illus.). 256p. (Orig.). 1995. pap. 19.95 (*0-9635202-1-0*) Collectors Pr.

R. Atkinson Fox, His Life & Work. Rita Mortenson. LC 84-52506. 159p. 17.95 (*0-87069-437-5*) L-W Inc.

R. B. Bennett: The Calgary Years. James H. Gray. 336p. 1991. 29.95 (*0-8020-5975-9*) U of Toronto Pr.

R B E for High-LET Radiations with Respect to Mutagenesis. International Commission on Radiological Protection. (International Commission of Radiological Protection Ser.: No. 18). 50p. 1972. pap. 13.75 (*0-08-017008-0*, Pergamon Pr) Elsevier.

R. B. Schueller. Irene Ledwith. (Illus.). 48p. (Orig.). 1992. pap. 12.00 (*0-89822-101-3*) Visual Studies.

R. B. Woodward Remembered: A Collection of Papers in Honour of Robert Burns Woodward 1917-1979. Ed. by F. R. Barton. (Illus.). 542p. 1982. 125.00 (*0-08-029238-0*, Pergamon Pr) Elsevier.

***R. B.-169-Navigation Rules for International & Inland Waters Including the Great Lakes & Western Rivers: Revised Edition "E"** rev. ed. Ed. by Richard A. Block. (Illus.). 260p. 1996. pap. text ed. 30.00 (*1-879778-48-3*, BK-234) Marine Educ.

R: BASE 3.1: Relational Database Concepts in Practice. Jan L. Harrington. (Illus.). 584p. (C). 1991. pap. text ed. 54.95 incl. disk (*1-878748-15-7*); pap. text ed. 35.25 incl. disk (*1-878748-17-3*); pap. text ed. 54.95 incl. disk (*1-878748-16-5*); pap. text ed. 31.25 incl. disk (*1-878748-18-1*) Course Tech.

R-C Airplane Building Techniques. Randy Randolph. (Illus.). 146p. 1991. 14.95 (*0-911295-13-5*) Air Age.

R-C Car Painting & Finishing Techniques. Richard Muise. (Illus.). 29p. (Orig.). 1992. pap. 7.95 (*0-911295-19-4*) Air Age.

R-C Car Troubleshooting: Two Hundred Tech Tricks, Vol. 1. Illus. by Jim Newman & Gerry Yarrish. 74p. (Orig.). 1992. pap. 12.95 (*0-911295-22-4*) Air Age.

R C D C (Regional Cooperation among Developing Countries) The New Imperative of Development in the 1980's. Ervin Laszlo et al. 75p. 1981. pap. 25.00 (*0-08-027556-7*, Pergamon Pr) Elsevier.

R. C. Gorman: Chinle to Taos. Virginia Dooley. (Illus.). 63p. (Orig.). 1988. pap. 10.00 (*0-9622721-0-8*) Navajo Gallery.

***R. C. Gorman: Navajo Artist.** Spring Hermann. LC 95-8807. (Multicultural Junior Biographies Ser.). (Illus.). 104p. (J). (gr. 4-10). 1995. lib. bdg. 18.95 (*0-89490-638-0*) Enslow Pubs.

R. C. Gorman, Vol. 2: Nudes & Foods. Virginia Dooley. (Illus.). 96p. (Orig.). 1989. pap. 20.00 (*0-9622721-1-6*) Navajo Gallery.

R. C. Gorman's Nudes & Foods, Vol. II. Virginia Dooley. (Illus.). (Orig.). 1989. write for info. (*0-318-65110-6*) Navajo Gallery.

R. C. Gorman's Nudes & Foods: In Good Taste. Ed. & Compiled by Virginia Dooley. LC 94-28417. (Illus.). 112p. 1994. 34.95 (*0-940666-41-3*) Clear Light.

R Complete. Marilyn M. Toomey & Paula Carmel. (Illus.). 204p. 1988. vinyl bd. 28.00 (*0-923573-07-0*) Circuit Pubns.

R Coronae Borealis Light Curves, 1843-1990. Janet A. Mattei et al. (AAVSO Monograph: No. 4). (Illus.). 40p. 1991. pap. text ed. 7.50 (*1-878174-03-7*) Am Assn Var Star.

R Coronae Borealis Light Curves 1991-1995: AAVSO Monograph 4, Supplement 1. Janet A. Mattei et al. (Illus.). 14p. 1996. pap. text ed. 10.00 (*1-878174-17-7*) Am Assn Var Star.

***R. Crumb Coffee Table Art Book.** R. Crumb & Peter Poplaski. LC 97-16339. 1997. 40.00 (*0-316-16306-6*) Little.

R. Crumb Draws the Blues. Robert Crumb. 1993. pap. 16.95 (*0-86719-401-4*) Last Gasp.

R. Crumb Postcard Book: Drawings from the Secret Sketchbook of the Artist! Robert Crumb. Ed. by Peter Poplaski. (Illus.). 24p. 1993. pap. 11.95 (*0-87816-184-8*) Kitchen Sink.

R. Crumb Sketchbook, Vol. 3. Robert Crumb. Ed. by Gary Groth. (Illus.). 144p. (Orig.). 1993. 39.95 (*1-56097-128-2*); pap. 19.95 (*1-56097-127-4*) Fantagraph Bks.

R. Crumb Sketchbook, 1964-1965, Vol. 1. Robert Crumb. 176p. 1992. 39.95 (*1-56097-083-9*); pap. 19.95 (*1-56097-082-0*) Fantagraph Bks.

R. Crumb Sketchbook, 1965-1966, Vol. 2. Robert Crumb. 176p. 1992. 39.95 (*1-56097-105-3*); pap. 19.95 (*1-56097-104-5*) Fantagraph Bks.

R. Crumb's America. Robert Crumb. 1995. pap. text ed. 16.95 (*0-86719-433-2*) Last Gasp.

R. D. Culver Memoranda & Letters: With Principals in the Murray Harris Affair of Trinity Evangelica - Divinity School. Robert D. Culver. 19p. 1992. reprint ed. pap. 0.95 (*1-883858-55-0*) Witness CA.

R. D. Laing: A Biography. Adrian C. Laing. LC 95-118981. 248p. 9500. 50.00 (*0-7206-0934-8*, Pub. by P Owen Ltd UK) Dufour.

***R. D. Laing: A Biography.** Adrian C. Laing. 1997. pap. text ed. 12.95 (*1-56025-105-0*) Thunders Mouth.

R. D. Laing & Me: Lessons in Love. Roberta Russell & R. D. Laing. Ed. by Suzanne Smith. LC 92-70905. (Illus.). 292p. 1992. 25.95 (*0-940106-61-2*, Baker & Taylor); pap. 16.95 (*0-940106-50-7*, Baker & Taylor) Hillgarth Pr.

R-DAT. John Watkinson. 240p. 1991. 79.95 (*0-240-51306-1*, Focal) Buttrwrth-Heinemann.

R. E. A. D. Reading Enhancement & Development. 4th ed. Rhonda H. Atkinson & Debbie G. Longman. Ed. by Baxter. 525p. (C). 1992. pap. text ed. 31.50 (*0-314-93357-3*) West Pub.

***R. E. M.** Istvan Banya. LC 96-53853. (J). 1997. pap. 14.99 (*0-670-87492-2*) Viking Penguin.

***R. E. M.** Istvan Banyai. 1997. 14.99 (*0-614-29141-0*) Viking Penguin.

R. E. M. Behind the Mask. Jim Greer. 1994. pap. 15.95 (*0-316-32732-8*) Little.

R. E. M. From Chronic Town to Monster. Dave Bowler & Bryan Dray. LC 95-22310. (Illus.). 216p. 1995. pap. 12.95 (*0-8065-1724-7*, Citadel Pr) Carol Pub Group.

R. E. M. Monster. 14.95 (*0-7935-4440-8*, 00306030) H Leonard.

R. F. D. Bill Knight. (Illus.). 96p. (Orig.). 1992. pap. 4.99 (*0-9624613-1-8*) Mayfly Prodns.

R. F. D. Charles A. Smart. 1993. reprint ed. lib. bdg. 89.00 (*0-7812-5403-5*) Rprt Serv.

R. F. D. Journal. Bill Knight. (Illus.). 112p. (Orig.). 1993. pap. 5.99 (*0-9624613-2-6*) Mayfly Prodns.

R. F. D. Notebook. Bill Knight. (Illus.). 96p. 1994. 4.99 (*0-9624613-3-4*) Mayfly Prodns.

R. F. Delderfield. Sanford Sternlicht. (English Authors Ser.: No. 463). 152p. 1988. 22.95 (*0-8057-6967-6*, Twayne) Scribnrs Ref.

R. F. Grigsby's Sierra Madre Journal: 1864: An American Prospector's Adventures. Robert F. Grisby. Ed. by Eugene H. Boudreau. LC 76-43601. 1976. pap. 10.00 (*0-686-16316-8*) Redbud Press.

R-Factors: Their Properties & Possible Control: Symposium, Baden Near Vienna, April 27-29, 1977. Ed. by J. Drews. (Topics in Infectious Diseases Ser.: Vol. 2). 1978. 53.95 (*0-387-81455-8*) Spr-Verlag.

***R for Revenge.** Created by Francine Pascal. (Sweet Valley High Super Edition Ser.: No. 24). 240p. (Orig.). (YA). (gr. 7 up). 1997. mass mkt. 4.50 (*0-553-57072-2*) BDD Bks Young Read.

R. G. A. History of the Plantation: Industry in the Malay Peninsula. D. J. Tate. (Illus.). 688p. 1996. 85.00 (*983-56-0004-X*) OUP.

R. G. Collingwood: A Bibliographical Checklist. Ed. by Christopher Dreisbach. 139p. 1993. 29.00 (*0-912632-93-3*) Philos Document.

R. G. Dun & Co., Eighteen Forty-One to Nineteen Hundred: The Development of Credit-Reporting in the Nineteenth Century. James D. Norris. LC 77-95359. (Contributions in Economics & Economic History Ser.: No. 20). (Illus.). 206p. 1978. text ed. 55.00 (*0-313-20326-1*, NDC/) Greenwood.

R. G. Hawtrey & the Development of Macroeconomics. Patrick Deutscher. LC 89-20404. 300p. 1990. reprint ed. text ed. 49.50 (*0-472-10179-X*) U of Mich Pr.

R. G. Talks about: Nuggets from the Writings of R. G. LeTourneau Provide the Only Way to Live. Ed. by Louise L. Dick & Richard H. LeTourneau. LC 86-91106. (LeTourneau One-Way Ser.: Vol. 9). 317p. (Orig.). 1986. pap. 6.95 (*0-935899-05-7*) LeTourneau Pr.

R. H. Puzzlemaker's Handbook. Stan Kurzban & Mel Rosen. 1995. pap. 14.00 (*0-8129-2544-0*, Times Bks) Random.

R. H. Tawney. Anthony Wright. (Lives of the Left Ser.). 192p. 1988. text ed. 55.00 (*0-7190-1998-2*, Pub. by Manchester Univ Pr UK) St Martin.

R. H. Tawney & His Times: Socialism As Fellowship. Ross Terrill. LC 72-188350. 320p. 1974. pap. 14.95 (*0-674-74377-6*) HUP.

R. Hittleman's Yoga. Richard L. Hittleman. 192p. 1984. mass mkt. 5.99 (*0-553-27428-7*) Bantam.

An Asterisk (*) at the beginning of an entry indicates that the title is appearing in BIP for the first time.

R. Holmes & Co. Being the Remarkable Adventure of Raffles Holmes. John K. Bangs. LC 78-91073. (American Humorists Ser.). reprint ed. lib. bdg. 44.50 (*0-8398-0151-3*) Irvington.

R. I. C. A. Rito Para Iniciar los Cristianos Adultos. M.A. C.C. Team Staff. (Illus.). 68p. (SPA.). 1989. write for info. (*0-614-04886-9*) Mex Am Cult.

R. I. O. T. Devotional, Vol. 1. Carman. 1996. pap. text ed. 4.99 (*1-880089-38-6*) Albury Pub.

R. I. O. T. Devotional, Vol. 2. Carman. 1996. pap. text ed. 4.99 (*1-880089-39-4*) Albury Pub.

***R. I. P. The Complete Book of Death & Dying.** Constance Jones. LC 96-30420. 304p. 1997. 25.00 (*0-06-270140-1*, Harper Ref) HarpC.

R. L., the Most Pleasant History of Tom A Lincolne. Ed. by Richard S. Hirsch. (Renaissance English Text Society Ser.: Vol. 7). 144p. 1978. 25.00 (*0-87249-358-X*, MRET7, Renaiss Eng Text Soc) MRTS.

R. I., the Most Pleasant History of Tom A. Lincolne. Richard Johnson. Ed. by Richard S. Hirsch. (Renaissance English Text Society Ser.: Vol. 7-8). 121p. 1978. 7.50 (*0-911028-21-8*) Newberry.

***R Is for Radish.** Molly Coxe. LC 97-10046. (Early Step into Reading Ser.). (J). 1998. lib. bdg. 11.99 (*0-679-98574-3*) Random.

***R Is for Radish.** Molly Coxe. LC 97-10046. (Early Step into Reading Ser.). (J). 1998. pap. 3.99 (*0-679-88574-9*) Random.

R Is for Rainbow: Developing Young Children's Thinking Skills Through the Alphabet. Sandra Anselmo. 1986. text ed. 28.00 (*0-201-20199-2*) Addison-Wesley.

R Is for Rocket. Ray Bradbury. 1994. lib. bdg. 24.95 (*1-56849-449-1*) Buccaneer Bks.

R. J. Reynolds Tobacco Company. Nannie M. Tilley. LC 84-20811. (Illus.). xxi, 706p. 1985. text ed. 55.00 (*0-8078-1642-6*) U of NC Pr.

R. Juspa, Shammash of Warmaisa (Worms) Jewish Life in 17th Century Worms. Shlomo Eidelberg. (Illus.). 217p. 1991. 22.00 (*965-223-762-0*, Pub. by Magnes Press IS) Eisenbrauns.

R K F D V: German Resettlement & Population Policy, 1939-1945: A History of the Reich Commission for the Strengthening of Germandom. Robert B. Koehl. LC 57-8625. (Historical Monographs: No. 31). 274p. 1957. 20. 00 (*0-674-77326-8*) HUP.

R. K. Narayan: A Critical Appreciation. William Walsh. LC 82-40320. (Illus.). 184p. (C). 1982. 15.00 (*0-226-87213-0*) U Ch Pr.

R. K. Narayan: A Painter of Modern India, Vol. 4. Michel Pousse. (Studies of World Literature in English). 232p. (C). 1995. text ed. 49.95 (*0-8204-2768-3*) P Lang Pubng.

R. K. Narayan: Contemporary Critical Perspectives. Ed. by Geoffrey R. Kain. 200p. (C). 1993. 27.95 (*0-87013-330-6*) Mich St U Pr.

R. L. S. A Centenary Exhibition at the Beinecke Rare Book & Manuscript Library Commemorating the Death of Robert Louis Stevenson. Vincent Giroud. (Illus.). 60p. (C). 1994. pap. text ed. write for info. (*0-8457-3129-7*) Yale U Lib.

R. L. Stevenson: A Critical Study. Frank A. Swinnerton. (BCL1-PR English Literature Ser.). 195p. 1992. reprint ed. lib. bdg. 69.00 (*0-7812-7672-1*) Rprt Serv.

R. L. Stevenson Trail Through the Cevennes. GTBS Publications Staff. (C). 1990. pap. text ed. 45.00 (*0-9515828-0-1*, Pub. by GTBS Pubns UK) St Mut.

R. L. Stevenson Trail Through the Cevennes. George Osborn. (C). 1989. pap. text ed. 55.00 (*0-9515838-0-8*, Pub. by GTBS Pubns UK) St Mut.

R. L. Stine. Jill C. Wheeler. LC 95-41217. (Young at Heart Ser.). (J). 1996. lib. bdg. 14.98 (*1-56239-521-1*) Abdo & Dghtrs.

R. L. Stine: Indiana Jones & the Giants of Silver Tower, Indiana Jones & the Curse of Horror Island, Indiana Jones & the Cult of the Mummy's Crypt, & Indiana Jones & the Ape Slaves of Howling Island, Set. R. L. Stine. 1995. boxed 14.00 (*0-345-39260-4*) Ballantine.

R-Linear Endomorphisms of R(n) Preserving Invariants. Bernard R. McDonald. LC 83-15648. (Memoirs Ser.: No. 46/287). 67p. 1983. pap. 17.00 (*0-8218-2287-X*, MEMO/46/287) Am Math.

R. L.'s Dream. Walter Mosley. 1996. pap. 12.00 (*0-614-97796-7*, WSP) PB.

R. L.'s Dream: A Novel. Walter Mosley. 288p. 1995. 22.00 (*0-393-03802-5*) Norton.

R. M. Fischer. Elisabeth Kirsch & Susan Feagin. Ed. by Craig Subler. (Illus.). 15p. (Orig.). 1984. pap. 4.00 (*0-914489-02-X*) Univ Miss-KC Art.

R. M. Rilke: Aspects of His Mind & Poetry. Ranier M. Rilke et al. Ed. by G. C. Houston. LC 72-6484. (Studies in German Literature: No. 13). (Illus.). 190p. 1972. reprint ed. lib. bdg. 39.95 (*0-8383-1617-4*) M S G Haskell Hse.

R. M. S. Titanic. Anthony Cronin. (Raven Long Poems Ser.). 1981. 8.95 (*0-906897-31-9*) Dufour.

R. M. S. Titanic. Sue Hamilton. Ed. by John Hamilton. LC 88-71722. (Day of Disaster Ser.). (Illus.). 32p. (J). (gr. 4). 1989. lib. bdg. 12.98 (*0-939179-42-3*) Abdo & Dghtrs.

R. M. Schinder: Composition & Construction. Ed. by Lionel March & Judith Sheine. (Illus.). 264p. 1995. pap. 38.00 (*1-85490-423-X*) Academy Ed UK.

R. M. Schindler: An International Survey. Ed. by Lionel March & Judith Sheine. (Illus.). 244p. 1993. 85.00 (*1-85490-159-1*) Academy Ed UK.

R. M. Wade & Co. & Family: Four Generations. Wade Newbegin. Ed. by Helen W. Bledsoe. 112p. (Orig.). 1991. write for info. (*0-9630153-0-3*) R M Wade.

R. Madison Mitchell: His Life & Decoys. Charles L. Robbins. (Illus.). 1988. 24.95 (*0-9620028-0-1*) C L Robbins.

R. N. S. Webb. 1985. pap. 3.50 (*0-8217-1665-4*) Kensgtn Pub Corp.

R. N. Sharon Webb. (Orig.). 1982. mass mkt. 2.95 (*0-89083-915-8*, Zebra Kensgtn) Kensgtn Pub Corp.

R. N. Elliott's Market Letters (1938-1946) Robert R. Prechter, Jr. (Illus.). 234p. 1993. 55.00 (*0-932750-20-6*) New Classics Lib.

R. N. Elliott's Masterworks: The Definitive Collection. R. N. Elliott. Ed. by Robert R. Prechter, Jr. LC 93-87631. (Illus.). 308p. 1994. 34.00 (*0-932750-37-0*) New Classics Lib.

R. Nathaniel Dett: His Life & Works (1882-1943) Vivian F. McBrier. (YA). 1990. 15.95 (*0-87498-092-5*) Assoc Pubs DC.

R-oneR-twoCSO-x Structures in the Conversion of Thiocarbonyl Compounds into the Corresponding Oxo Derivatives, Vol. 3. L. Carlsen. 44p. 1983. pap. text ed. 70.00 (*3-7186-0184-2*) Gordon & Breach.

R. P. Blackmur, Poet-Critic: Toward a View of Poetic Objects. Robert Boyers. LC 80-15414. (Literary Frontiers Editions Ser.). 96p. 1980. pap. 9.95 (*0-8262-0315-9*) U of Mo Pr.

R. R. A. S. Field List of the Birds of Nevada. Compiled by M. Vincent Mobray. 8p. 1989. pap. 2.00 (*0-9635550-1-4*) Red Rock Audubon.

R. R. Lyrae Stars. Horace A. Smith. (Astrophysics Ser.: No. 27). (Illus.). 208p. (C). text ed. 66.95 (*0-521-32180-8*) Cambridge U Pr.

R-r-rhubarb: From Soup to Nuts. Camille McDonald. 34p. (Orig.). 1988. pap. 3.35 (*0-9625416-0-5*) Cynthia Promos.

R. S. Thomas: Poet of the Hidden God. D. Z. Phillips. LC 85-31998. (Princeton Theological Monographs: No. 2). 192p. (Orig.). 1986. pap. 15.00 (*0-915138-83-2*) Pickwick.

R. S. Thomas: Selected Prose. R. S. Thomas. Ed. by Sandra Anstey. LC 84-71579. 187p. (C). 1987. pap. 18.95 (*0-685-09628-9*, Pub. by Poetry Wales Pr UK) Dufour.

R. S. Thomas: Selected Prose. 3rd ed. R. S. Thomas. Ed. by Sandra Anstey. 164p. 1995. pap. 24.95 (*1-85411-104-3*, Pub. by Seren Bks UK) Dufour.

R Scuti Light Curves, 1985-1990. Janet A. Mattei et al. (AAVSO Monograph: No. 3, Supplement 1). (Illus.). 22p. 1991. pap. text ed. 7.50 (*1-878174-07-X*) Am Assn Var Star.

R Scuti Light Curves 1991-1995: AAVSO Monograph 3, Supplement 2. Janet A. Mattei et al. (Illus.). 15p. 1996. pap. text ed. 10.00 (*1-878174-16-9*) Am Assn Var Star.

***R. T. K. L.** (Illus.). 256p. 1996. 59.95 (*1-875498-53-2*) AIA Press.

R-T, Margaret, & the Rats of NIMH. Jane L. Conly. (J). 1990. lib. bdg. 15.89 (*0-06-023647-7*) HarpC Child Bks.

R-T, Margaret, & the Rats of NIMH. Jane L. Conly. LC 89-19968. (Trophy Bk.). (Illus.). 272p. (J). (gr. 4-7). 1991. pap. 4.50 (*0-06-440387-4*, Trophy) HarpC Child Bks.

R-Ticulation. Mary Zellmer. (Illus.). (J). (ps-4). 1986. 19.00 (*0-930599-23-3*) Thinking Pubns.

R. U. R. Josef Capek & Karel Capek. Bd. with Insect Play. 188p. 1961. Set pap. 14.95 (*0-19-281010-3*) OUP.

R. V. H. Manual on Palliative-Hospice Care: A Resource Book. Ed. by Ina Ajemian & Balfour M. Mount. pap. 37.95 (*0-405-13934-9*) Ayer.

R-V Pillsbury Deep-Sea Biological Expedition to the Gulf of Guinea, 1964-1965: Parts 1 & 2. (Studies in Tropical Oceanography Ser.). 1970. 32.50 (*0-87024-190-7*) U of Miami Pr.

R. V. W. A Biography of Ralph Vaughan Williams. Ursula V. Williams. (Illus.). 464p. 1993. pap. 21.00 (*0-19-282082-6*) OUP.

R. W. Emerson, Tourist. limited ed. Lois Rather. (Illus.). 1979. 35.00 (*0-686-26147-X*) Rather Pr.

R. W. Seton-Watson & the Yugoslavs: Correspondence 1906-1941, 2 vols. G. H. Seton-Watson et al. 468p. 1979. 259.00 (*0-685-04770-9*) St Mut.

***R. W. Seton-Watson & the Yugoslavs, Correspondence 1906-1941, 2 vols.** 1946. 29.98 (*0-85672-151-4*) David Brown.

***"R" Word: Retention is OK.** Georgiann Lanier. LC 94-80244. (Illus.). 30p. (Orig.). (J). (gr. 1-5). 1995. pap. 7.95 (*1-884063-50-0*) Mar Co Prods.

R. Young's Guide to Entering Sweepstakes. R. Young. 32p. 1991. pap. 6.95 (*0-9631443-5-9*) R Young Enter.

***R-3 Administration.** Liane Will. (C). 1997. text ed. 45.14 (*0-201-92469-2*) Addison-Wesley.

***R-3 Process Oriented Implementations: Iteractive Process Prototyping.** Gerhard Keller. (C). 1997. text ed. 45.14 (*0-201-92470-6*) Addison-Wesley.

RA Material: An Ancient Astronaut Speaks. Don Elkins et al. Ed. by Hank Stine. LC 82-12967. (Illus.). 229p. (Orig.). 1984. pap. 6.95 (*0-89865-260-X*) Donning Co.

RAAF in Vietnam Vol. 4: Australian Air Operations in the Vietnam War 1962-1975. Chris Coulthard-Clark. (Illus.). 352p. 1995. 59.95 (*1-86373-305-1*) Paul & Co Pubs.

R.A.A.P. Responsibilitating African American Parents. Ida V. St Hill. Ed. by Joyce Johnson. 110p. (Orig.). pap. 5.95 (*0-9640736-0-9*) Simountainhill.

Rab. Mark Dunster. 14p. (Orig.). 1987. pap. 4.00 (*0-89642-150-3*) Linden Pubs.

Rab & Dab. limited ed. Elizabeth A. Pringle. Ed. & Intro. by Anne Blythe. 1985. 27.50 (*0-685-13973-5*) Seajay Society.

Rab & His Friends. John Brown. LC 72-5910. (Short Story Index Reprint Ser.). 1977. reprint ed. 21.95 (*0-8369-4193-4*) Ayer.

Rab Saadia Gaon: Studies in His Honor. Ed. by Louis Finkelstein & Steven Katz. LC 79-7169. (Jewish Philosophy, Mysticism & History of Ideas Ser.). 1980. reprint ed. lib. bdg. 21.95 (*0-405-12250-0*) Ayer.

Rabad of Posquieres: A Twelfth-Century Talmudist. Isadore Twersky. LC 62-7192. (Semitic Ser.: No. 18). 348p. 1962. 22.50 (*0-674-74550-7*) HUP.

Rabat: Urban Apartheid in Morocco. Janet L. Abu-Lughod. LC 80-7508. (Princeton Studies on the Near East). 405p. reprint ed. pap. 115.50 (*0-7837-1405-X*, 2041759) Bks Demand.

Rabban Gamaliel II: The Legal Traditions. Shamai Kanter. LC 80-12229. (Brown Judaic Studies: No. 8). 362p. reprint ed. pap. 103.20 (*0-7837-5433-7*, 2045198) Bks Demand.

Rabbenu Yisrael Abuchatzira: The Story of His Life & His Wonders. A. Y. Harel. 1991. 15.95 (*0-685-53656-4*) Feldheim.

Rabbi. Noah Gordon. 408p. 1987. mass mkt. 5.99 (*0-449-21454-0*, Crest) Fawcett.

***Rabbi, 3 vols.** Noah Gordon. 30.00 (*0-89064-052-1*) NAVH.

Rabbi Abraham Ibn Ezra: Studies in the Writings of a Twelfth-Century Jewish Polymath. Ed. by Isadore Twersky & Jay M. Harris. LC 93-26130. (Harvard Judaic Texts & Studies: Vol. 10). 224p. (C). 1994. text ed. 29.95 (*0-674-74554-X*); pap. text ed. 14.95 (*0-674-74555-8*) HUP.

***Rabbi Abraham Ibn Ezra's Commentary on the Creation.** Michael Linetsky. LC 97-23850. 1998. write for info. (*0-7657-9982-0*) Aronson.

Rabbi Abraham Isaac Kook & Jewish Spirituality. Ed. by Lawrence J. Kaplan & David Shatz. LC 94-17494. (Reappraisals in Jewish Social & Intellectual History Ser.). (C). 1994. 55.00 (*0-8147-4652-7*); pap. 20.00 (*0-8147-4653-5*) NYU Pr.

***Rabbi Akiba & His Contemporaries.** Judah Nadich. LC 97-2410. 1997. write for info. (*0-7657-5975-6*) Aronson.

Rabbi & His Driver. David A. Adler. (J). 14.95 (*0-06-020421-4*, HarpT); lib. bdg. 14.89 (*0-06-020422-2*, HarpT) HarpC.

Rabbi & the Nun. Mordecai Schreiber. LC 91-60448. 253p. 1991. 18.95 (*0-88400-150-4*) Shengold.

Rabbi & the Poet: Victor Reichert & Robert Frost. Andrew R. Marks. LC 93-72556. (Illus.). 64p. (Orig.). 1994. pap. 14.00 (*1-885934-01-7*) Andover Green.

Rabbi & the Priest. Y. B. Arrarat. 1988. 12.95 (*0-318-36110-8*) Feldheim.

***Rabbi & the Priest.** Y. B. Arrarat. 1988. pap. 9.95 (*0-614-25808-1*) Feldheim.

Rabbi & the Priest. Y. B. Arrarat. 224p. 1988. 12.95 (*0-944070-02-7*) Targum Pr.

Rabbi Confesses. Bob Alper. (Illus.). 112p. (Orig.). 1995. pap. 14.95 (*1-888016-18-3*) Finkstrom Prods.

Rabbi Eizik: Hasidic Stories about the Zaddik of Kallo. Ed. & Tr. by Andrew Handler. LC 75-5245. 195p. (C). 1976. 32.50 (*0-8386-1739-5*) Fairleigh Dickinson.

Rabbi Esriel Hildesheimer & the Creation of a Modern Jewish Orthodoxy. David Ellenson. LC 89-20554. (Judaic Studies). 232p. 1991. text ed. 37.95 (*0-8173-0485-1*) U of Ala Pr.

Rabbi in the Attic. Eileen Pollack. 239p. 1991. 20.00 (*1-883285-08-9*) Delphinium.

Rabbi Israel Salanter & the Mussar Movement: Seeking the Torah of Truth. Immanuel Etkes. Tr. by Jonathan Chipman from HEB. LC 93-9277. 400p. (ENG & HEB.). 1993. 39.95 (*0-8276-0438-6*) JPS Phila.

Rabbi Jacob Danglow: The Uncrowned Monarch of Australian Jews. John Levi. 340p. 1995. 49.95 (*0-522-84645-9*, Pub. by Melbourne Univ Pr AT) Paul & Co Pubs.

***Rabbi Jesus: Learning from the Master Teacher.** Stephen D. Jones. LC 96-37170. 96p. (Orig.). 1997. pap. 9.95 (*1-57312-099-5*) Smyth & Helwys.

***Rabbi Max Heller: Reformer, Zionist, Southerner, 1860-1929.** Bobbie Malone. LC 96-48359. (Judaic Studies). 1997. write for info. (*0-8173-0875-X*) U of Ala Pr.

Rabbi Menachem Mendel of Kotzk. Joseph Fox. 180p. 1988. 12.95 (*0-932351-21-2*) Besad Prodns.

Rabbi Moshe Chaim Luzzatto: His Life & Works. Yirmeyahu Bindman. LC 94-12660. 200p. 1995. 25.00 (*1-56821-293-3*) Aronson.

Rabbi Nachman De Breslov. Rabbi Nachman of Breslov et al. (Illus.). 442p. 1986. pap. 15.00 (*0-930213-20-3*) Breslov Res Inst.

Rabbi Nachman's Stories. Nachman of Breslov. Tr. by Aryeh Kaplan from HEB. LC 83-70201. 552p. 1983. 21. 00 (*0-930213-02-5*) Breslov Res Inst.

Rabbi Nachman's Stories: Skazocnniji Histori Rabbi Nechman iz Bratzlav. Nachman of Breslov. Tr. by Baruch Avni from HEB. (Illus.). 332p. (Orig.). (C). 1987. pap. 10.00 (*0-930213-29-7*) Breslov Res Inst.

Rabbi Nachman's Tikkun: The Comprehensive Remedy. Nachman of Breslov. Tr. by Avraham Greenbaum from HEB. 256p. 1984. 12.00 (*0-930213-06-8*) Breslov Res Inst.

***Rabbi Nachman's Tikun: The Tikun Haklali.** Rabbi Nachman of Breslov. Tr. by Avraham Greenbaum from HEB. 128p. 1982. pap. 5.00 (*0-930213-07-6*) Breslov Res Inst.

Rabbi Nachman's Wisdom. Nachman of Breslov. Ed. by Zvi A. Rosenfeld. Tr. by Aryeh Kaplan from HEB. (Illus.). 510p. 1984. reprint ed. 16.00 (*0-930213-00-9*) Breslov Res Inst.

***Rabbi of Light.** Yitta Halberstam. Date not set. 24.95 (*1-57322-037-X*, Riverhead Books) Putnam Pub Group.

Rabbi Plotkin: A Memoir. Albert Plotkin. Ed. by Gordon A. Sabine. 160p. (Orig.). 1992. lib. bdg. write for info. (*1-879286-02-5*) AZ Bd Regents.

Rabbi, Rabbi. Andrew Kane. 1995. 22.95 (*0-312-11879-1*) St Martin.

Rabbi Reads the Psalms. Jonathan Magonet. 192p. (Orig.). 1994. pap. 16.00 (*0-334-01364-X*, SCM Pr) TPI PA.

***Rabbi Samson Raphael Hirsch: Architect of Judaism for the Modern World.** Eliyahu M. Klugman. 26.99 (*0-89906-632-1*, RSRP); pap. 20.99 (*0-89906-633-X*, RSRP) Mesorah Pubns.

Rabbi Samuel Ben Meir's Commentary on Genesis: An Annotated Translation. Samuel Ben Meir. Tr. by Martin I. Lockshin from HEB. LC 89-33529. 440p. 1989. lib. bdg. 109.95 (*0-88946-256-9*) E Mellen.

Rabbi Schneur Zalman of Liadi, Vol. 2. Nissan Mindel. (Philosophy of Chabad Ser.). 256p. 1973. reprint ed. 12. 00 (*0-8266-0417-X*) Kehot Pubn Soc.

***Rabbi Small, Bk. 2.** Harry Kemelman. Date not set. write for info. (*0-688-05617-2*) Morrow.

Rabbi Talks with Jesus: An Intermillennial, Interfaith Exchange. Jacob Neusner. LC 93-36807. 176p. 1994. pap. 9.00 (*0-385-47306-0*, Image Bks) Doubleday.

Rabbi Tarfon: The Tradition, the Man, & Early Rabbinic Judaism. Joel D. Gereboff. LC 78-15220. (Brown Judaic Studies: No. 7). 507p. reprint ed. pap. 144.50 (*0-7837-5453-1*, 2045218) Bks Demand.

Rabbi Yisroel Baal Shem Tov. Moshe Prager. (Illus.). (HEB.). 2.00 (*0-914131-51-6*, D500) Torah Umesorah.

Rabbi Yisroel Baal Shem Tov. Moshe Prager. (Illus.). 1987. 2.00 (*0-914131-50-8*, D510) Torah Umesorah.

***Rabbi Yissocher Frand: In Print.** Yonoson Rosenblum. 18. 99 (*0-89906-630-5*, FIPH); pap. 15.99 (*0-89906-631-3*, FIPP) Mesorah Pubns.

Rabbinate As Calling & Vocation: Models of Rabbinic Leadership. Ed. by Basil Herring. LC 90-1247. 320p. 1991. 40.00 (*0-87668-735-4*) Aronson.

Rabbinate in America: Reshaping an Ancient Calling. Ed. by Jacob Neusner. LC 92-37068. (Judaism in Cold War America, 1945-1990 Ser.: Vol. 10). 256p. 1993. text ed. 20.00 (*0-8153-0082-4*) Garland.

Rabbinic Authority. Ed. by Elliot L. Stevens. 118p. 1982. 15.00 (*0-916694-88-7*) Central Conf.

Rabbinic Authority & Personal Autonomy. Ed. by Moshe Z. Sokol. LC 91-25301. 264p. 1992. 30.00 (*0-87668-581-5*) Aronson.

Rabbinic Commentary on the New Testament: The Gospels of Matthew, Mark & Luke. Samuel T. Lachs. 600p. 1987. 39.50 (*0-88125-089-9*); pap. 24.95 (*0-88125-115-1*) Ktav.

Rabbinic Essays. Jacob Z. Lauterbach. LC 52-18170. 586p. reprint ed. pap. 167.10 (*0-317-42031-3*, 2025693) Bks Demand.

Rabbinic Judaism: Debates & Disputes, First Series. Jacob Neusner. LC 94-27844. (USF Studies in the History of Judaism: No. 107). 310p. 1994. 79.95 (*0-7885-0006-6*, 240107) Scholars Pr GA.

Rabbinic Judaism: Structure & System. Jacob Neusner. LC 95-30693. 1995. pap. 24.00 (*0-8006-2909-4*) Augsburg Fortress.

Rabbinic Judaism: The Documentary History of Its Formative Age 70-600 C. E. Jacob Neusner. 413p. (C). 1994. 42.00 (*1-883053-06-4*) CDL Pr.

Rabbinic Judaism in the Making: A Chapter in the History of the Halakhah from Ezra to Judah I. Alexander Guttmann. LC 69-10525. 344p. reprint ed. pap. 98.10 (*0-7837-3620-7*, 2043486) Bks Demand.

Rabbinic Lay Confrontations in Jewish Law. Ed. by Walter Jacob & Moshe Zemer. ix, 128p. (Orig.). 1993. pap. 9.50 (*0-929699-04-1*) Rodef Shalom Pr.

Rabbinic Literature & the New Testament: What We Cannot Show, We Do Not Know. Jacob Neusner. LC 94-15415. 208p. (Orig.). (C). 1994. pap. 17.00 (*1-56338-074-9*) TPI PA.

***Rabbinic Manuscripts in the Cambridge Genizah Collection: The New Series of the Taylor-Schechter Collection.** Ed. by Robert Brody & E. J. Wiesenberg. (Cambridge Genizah Ser.: No. 5). 320p. 1997. text ed. 145.00 (*0-521-58400-0*) Cambridge U Pr.

Rabbinic Mind. 3rd ed. Max Kadushin. LC 75-189016. 1972. 27.50 (*0-8197-0566-7*); pap. 16.95 (*0-8197-0007-X*) Bloch.

Rabbinic Perspectives on the New Testament. Daniel Cohn-Sherbok. LC 90-21375. (Studies in the Bible & Early Christianity: Vol. 28). 140p. 1990. lib. bdg. 69.95 (*0-88946-689-0*) E Mellen.

Rabbinic Political Theory: Religion & Politics in the Mishnah. Jacob Neusner. (Chicago Studies in the History of Judaism). 284p. 1991. pap. text ed. 27.00 (*0-226-57651-5*) U Ch Pr.

Rabbinic Psychology. W. Hirsch. LC 73-2208. (Jewish People; History, Religion, Literature Ser.). 1973. reprint ed. 26.95 (*0-405-05272-3*) Ayer.

Rabbinical Assembly Mahzor. 12.00 (*0-686-96025-4*) USCJE.

Rabbinical Mathematics & Astronomy. rev. ed. W. M. Feldman. LC 78-60816. (Judaic Studies: No. SHP4). 1978. pap. text ed. 14.95 (*0-87203-026-1*) Hermon.

***Rabbinische Responsen Zum Synagogenbau Teil 1: Die Responsentexte, Ubersetzt und Eingeleitet von brigitte Kern-Ulmer.** (Studien Zur Kunstgeschichte Ser.: Bd. 56). xii, 234p. (GER.). 1990. write for info. (*3-487-09397-9*) G Olms Pubs.

Rabbis & Jewish Communities in Renaissance Italy. Ed. by Robert Bonfil. (Illus.). 380p. 1993. reprint ed. pap. 24.95 (*1-874774-17-X*) Bnai Brith Bk.

Rabbis & Lawyers: The Journey from Torah to Constitution. Jerold S. Auerbach. LC 89-46008. 272p. 1990. 12.95 (*0-253-31085-7*) Ind U Pr.

Rabbis & Lawyers: The Journey from Torah to Constitution. Jerold S. Auerbach. LC 89-46008. 272p. 1993. pap. 10.95 (*0-253-20843-2*) Ind U Pr.

Rabbis & Vegetarianism: An Evolving Tradition. unabridged ed. Ed. by Roberta Kalechofsky. 104p. 1996. pap. 10.00 (*0-916288-42-0*) Micah Pubns.

An Asterisk (*) at the beginning of an entry indicates that the title is appearing in BIP for the first time.

Rabbi's Bible Vol. 1: Torah, 2 pts. Solomon Simon & Morrison D. Bial. teacher ed., pap. 14.95 (*0-87441-021-5*); teacher ed., pap. 14.95 (*0-87441-022-3*) Behrman.

Rabbi's Bible Vol. 1: Torah, 2 pts. Solomon Simon & Morrison D. Bial. (J). (gr. 5-6). 7.95 (*0-87441-020-7*); student ed. 3.50 (*0-317-70152-5*) Behrman.

Rabbi's Bible Vol. 1: Torah, Wkbk. 1. Solomon Simon & Morrison D. Bial. (J). (gr. 5-6). student ed., pap. 3.50 (*0-87441-319-2*) Behrman.

Rabbi's Bible Vol. 1: Torah, Wkbk. 2. Solomon Simon & Morrison D. Bial. (J). (gr. 5-6). student ed., pap. 3.50 (*0-87441-320-6*) Behrman.

Rabbi's Bible Vol. 2: Early Prophets. Solomon Simon & Morrison D. Bial. teacher ed., pap. 14.95 (*0-87441-025-8*) Behrman.

Rabbi's Bible Vol. 2: Early Prophets. Solomon Simon & Morrison D. Bial. (J). (gr. 6-7). pap. 7.95 (*0-87441-023-1*) Behrman.

Rabbi's Bible Vol. 3: Later Prophets. Solomon Simon & Abraham Rothberg. (J). (gr. 7-8). pap. 7.95 (*0-87441-026-6*) Behrman.

Rabbi's Bible Vol. 3: Later Prophets. Solomon Simon et al. teacher ed., pap. 14.95 (*0-87441-028-2*) Behrman.

Rabbi's Girls. Johanna Hurwitz. LC 82-2102. (Illus.). 192p. (J). (gr. 4-6). 1982. 15.00 (*0-688-01089-X*, Morrow Junior) Morrow.

Rabbis, Lawyers, Immigrants, & Thieves: Exploring Women's Roles. Rita J. Simon. LC 92-41618. 272p. 1993. text ed. 52.95 (*0-275-94410-7*, C4410, Praeger Pubs) Greenwood.

Rabbi's Rovings. Israel Mowshowitz. 385p. 1985. 20.00 (*0-88125-069-4*) Ktav.

Rabbi's Tarot: Spiritual Secrets of the Tarot. Daphna Moore. LC 89-2489. (New Age Tarot Ser.). (Illus.). 408p. (Orig.). 1989. pap. 12.95 (*0-87542-572-0*) Llewellyn Pubns.

Rabbi's Vision, a Century of Proclaiming the Messiah: A History of Chosen People Ministries. Chosen People Ministries Staff. 708p. (Orig.). 1994. pap. 39.00 (*1-882675-04-5*) Chosen People.

Rabbit. Alison Catley. (Illus.). 32p. (J). (ps-1). 1993. 15.95 (*0-09-174408-3*, Pub. by Hutchinson UK) Trafalgar.

Rabbit. Mark Evans. LC 92-52829. (ASPCA Pet Care Guides for Kids Ser.). (Illus.). 48p. (J). (gr. 2 up). 1992. 9.95 (*1-56458-128-4*) DK Pub Inc.

Rabbit. Kwok Man-Ho. LC 93-48006. (Chinese Horoscopes Library). (Illus.). 48p. 1994. 8.95 (*1-56458-606-5*) DK Pub Inc.

***Rabbit.** Christine Morley & Carole Orbell. LC 96-50420. (Me & My Pet Ser.). (Illus.). (J). 1997. 9.95 (*0-7166-1797-8*); pap. 5.95 (*0-7166-1798-6*) World Bk.

Rabbit. Photos by Barrie Watts. (See How They Grow Ser.). (Illus.). 24p. (J). (gr. k-3). 1992. pap. 6.95 (*0-525-67356-3*, Lodestar Bks) Dutton Child Bks.

Rabbit: An Owner's Guide to a Happy, Healthy Pet. Audrey Pavia. 1996. 12.95 (*0-87605-489-0*) Howell Bk.

Rabbit & the Moon. Wood & Baker. LC 96-31651. (J). 1998. 16.00 (*0-689-80769-4*, S&S Bks Young Read) S&S Childrens.

Rabbit & the Tigerdile. W. W. Rowe. (Illus.). 25p. (J). (ps-2). 1996. pap. 8.95 (*1-55939-067-0*) Snow Lion Pubns.

Rabbit & the Turnip. Addison-Wesley Staff. (ESL Ser.). (Illus.). 16p. (J). (gr. k-2). 1989. lib. bdg. 16.00 (*0-201-19367-1*); ring bd. 4.33 (*0-201-19360-4*) Addison-Wesley.

Rabbit & the Turnip. Addison-Wesley Staff. (ESL Ser.). (Illus.). 16p. (J). (gr. k-2). 1989. 31.75 (*0-201-19326-4*) Addison-Wesley.

Rabbit & the Turtle: A Story in Dance. Katherine Goodale. (Illus.). 20p. (Orig.). (J). (ps-2). 1995. pap. 9.95 (*0-9609662-1-8*) Goodale Pub.

Rabbit & the Turtle & The Boy Who Cried Wolf, 2 bks., 2 cassettes, Set. (Stepping into English Ser.: Level 2). (YA). 1990. 39.50 incl. audio (*1-57970-010-1*, AFE442) Audio-Forum.

Rabbit Angstrom: The Four Novels. John Updike. 1516p. 1995. 30.00 (*0-679-44459-9*, Everymans Lib) Knopf.

Rabbit at Rest. John Updike. 448p. 1991. mass mkt. 5.99 (*0-449-21962-3*, Crest) Fawcett.

***Rabbit At Rest.** John Updike. 1996. pap. 12.95 (*0-449-91194-2*) Fawcett.

Rabbit at Rest. large type ed. John Updike. 1990. 30.00 (*0-394-58815-0*) Knopf.

Rabbit at Rest. large type ed. John Updike. 1990. 24.95 (*0-394-58936-X*) Random Hse Lrg Prnt.

Rabbit Blue. Marie-Louise Gay. (Illus.). 32p. (J). (gr. k-3). 1993. 12.95 (*0-7737-2750-7*, Pub. by Stoddart Pubng CN) Genl Dist Srvs.

Rabbit Boss. Thomas Sanchez. (Vintage Contemporaries Ser.). 1989. pap. 16.00 (*0-679-72621-7*, Vin) Random.

Rabbit Cadabra! James Howe. LC 91-34656. (Illus.). 48p. (J). (gr. k up). 1993. 15.00 (*0-688-10402-9*, Morrow Junior); lib. bdg. 14.93 (*0-688-10403-7*, Morrow Junior) Morrow.

Rabbit-Cadabra! James Howe. 48p. (J). 1994. pap. 5.99 (*0-380-71336-5*, Camelot Young) Avon.

Rabbit Dissection Manual. Bruce D. Wingerd. LC 84-15761. 80p. 1985. 12.95 (*0-8018-2470-2*) Johns Hopkins.

Rabbit Feeding & Nutrition. Peter R. Cheeke. (Animal Feeding & Nutrition Ser.). 376p. 1987. text ed. 89.00 (*0-12-170605-2*) Acad Pr.

Rabbit Gets Ready. Claire Fletcher. (Illus.). 32p. (J). (ps-k). 1996. 19.95 (*0-370-31960-5*, Pub. by Bodley Head UK) Trafalgar.

Rabbit Hill. Robert Lawson. (Illus.). (J). (gr. 1-3). 1977. pap. 3.99 (*0-14-031010-X*, Puffin) Puffin Bks.

Rabbit Hill. Robert Lawson. (Illus.). (J). (gr. 4-6). 1944. pap. 15.99 (*0-670-58675-7*) Viking Child Bks.

Rabbit Hill. large type ed. Robert Lawson. (J). (gr. 4-6). reprint ed. 10.00 (*0-89064-076-9*) NAVH.

Rabbit Hunting. Paul Jukes et al. LC 85-72451. 1985. reprint ed. pap. 9.95 (*0-910042-50-0*) Allegheny.

Rabbit in the Moon. LC 88-33456. (Jataka Tales Ser.). (Illus.). 32p. (Orig.). (J). (ps-4). 1989. pap. 7.95 (*0-89800-191-9*) Dharma Pub.

Rabbit in the Moon: A Garden Tale for the Young & the Young at Heart. Alice Van Trease. (Illus.). 80p. (J). (gr. k-8). 1996. pap. 12.00 (*0-9651578-0-6*) Pele Pubng.

Rabbit in the Moon: Haiku. Raymond Roesliep. LC 83-6445. (Illus.). 128p. 1983. 15.00 (*0-934184-15-1*); pap. 9.00 (*0-934184-16-X*) Alembic Pr.

Rabbit Inn, Vol. 1. Patience Brewster. (J). (ps-3). 1991. 14.95 (*0-316-10747-6*) Little.

Rabbit Is Rich. John Updike. LC 81-1287. 480p. 1981. 30.00 (*0-394-52087-4*) Knopf.

Rabbit Is Rich. John Updike. 448p. 1982. mass mkt. 5.99 (*0-449-24548-9*, Crest) Fawcett.

***Rabbit Is Rich.** John Updike. 1996. pap. 12.95 (*0-449-91182-9*) Fawcett.

Rabbit Loses His Tail. Ann Rompert. LC 96-21513. (J). 1997. 14.95 (*0-395-82281-5*) HM.

Rabbit Loses His Tail. Ann Rompert. LC 96-21513. (Illus.). 1997. 14.95 (*0-395-82264-5*) HM.

Rabbit Magic. Susie Jenkin-Pearce & Julia Malim. (Illus.). 32p. (J). (ps-k). 1994. 18.95 (*0-370-31813-7*, Pub. by Bodley Head UK) Trafalgar.

Rabbit Makes a Monkey of Lion. Verna Aardema. LC 86-11523. (Illus.). 32p. (J). (ps-3). 1989. pap. 11.95 (*0-8037-0297-3*); pap. 11.89 (*0-8037-0298-1*) Dial Bks Young.

Rabbit Makes a Monkey of Lion: A Swahili Tale. Illus. by Jerry Pinkney. 32p. (J). (ps-3). 1993. pap. 5.99 (*0-14-054593-X*) Puffin Bks.

Rabbit Moon. John Rowe. LC 92-6047. (Illus.). 28p. (J). 1992. pap. 14.95 (*0-88708-246-7*, Picture Book Studio) S&S Childrens.

***Rabbit Moon.** John A. Rowe. LC 96-47343. (Illus.). 32p. (J). (gr. k-3). 1997. pap. 6.95 (*1-55858-724-1*) North-South Bks NYC.

Rabbit on Bear Mountain. (J). Date not set. pap. 1.95 (*0-590-31257-X*) Scholastic Inc.

Rabbit on the Face of the Moon: Mythology in the Mesoamerican Tradition. Alfred L. Austin. Tr. by Bernard R. Ortiz De Montellano & Thelma Ortiz De Montellano. (Illus.). 144p. 1996. pap. 14.95 (*0-87480-527-9*) U of Utah Pr.

Rabbit on the Face of the Moon: Mythology in the Mesoamerican Tradition. Alfredo L. Austin. Tr. by Bernard R. Ortiz De Montellano & Thelma Ortiz De Montellano. (Illus.). 144p. 1996. text ed. 35.00 (*0-87480-521-X*) U of Utah Pr.

Rabbit Pancakes: A Century of Family Recipes. Joy J. Daymon. LC 95-92066. (Illus.). 434p. 1995. spiral bd. 24.95 (*0-9645110-0-2*) J Daymon.
A unique story-book cookbook. I wanted to pass our family recipes on to my children & grandchildren, but I wanted them to know where they came from & why. This book is a result. It tells what was happening during each decade of the 1900s & how it affected what & how we ate. The second part is a basic cookbook of about 700 recipes from the turn-of-the-century Boiled Fresh Ham & Poke Sallet to Mother's Egg Custard to Tamale Pie & Thanksgiving Turkey to today's quicker healthier recipes. These recipes I cooked for my family, & my mother & grandmother before me. The third section consists of useful tips & helps, including menus for every day of the year. The book is 6 1/2" X 9 1/2" hardcover, spiral bound with over 400 pages including about 25 color pages. Delightful cover. Great for beginning cooks, but useful for anyone. Coded to indicate low-cost, low-fat, time-saver, etc. For information write: Rabbit Pancakes; 108 Randolph, El Dorado, AR 71730, or send $24.95 plus $3.00 S/H for each book. Make check payable to Joy Daymon. Great Gift. ***Publisher Provided Annotation.***

***Rabbit Party Book.** Beatrix Potter. (J). 1998. pap. 6.99 (*0-7232-4367-0*) Warne.

Rabbit Production. 7th ed. Peter R. Cheeke et al. LC 94-77802. (Illus.). xiv, 474p. 1996. text ed. 27.95 (*0-8134-3034-8*) Interstate.

Rabbit Rambles On. Susanna Gretz. LC 91-17069. (Illus.). 32p. (J). (ps-1). 1992. lib. bdg. 12.95 (*0-02-737325-8*, Four Winds Pr) S&S Childrens.

***Rabbit Read Play.** Beatrix Potter. (J). 1997. pap. 4.99 (*0-7232-4373-5*) Warne.

***Rabbit Rebound: Space Jam Eye Illusion.** (J). 1996. 4.00 (*1-56144-886-9*) Pubns Intl Ltd.

Rabbit Redux. John Updike. 1971. 27.50 (*0-394-47273-X*) Knopf.

Rabbit Redux. John Updike. 352p. 1985. mass mkt. 5.99 (*0-449-20934-2*, Crest) Fawcett.

***Rabbit Redux.** John Updike. 1996. pap. 12.95 (*0-449-91193-4*) Fawcett.

Rabbit Run. John Updike. 1960. 25.00 (*0-394-44206-7*) Knopf.

Rabbit Run. John Updike. 288p. 1983. mass mkt. 5.99 (*0-449-20506-1*, Crest) Fawcett.

***Rabbit Run.** John Updike. 1996. pap. 12.95 (*0-449-91165-9*) Fawcett.

Rabbit Run. large type ed. John Updike. 1996. lib. bdg. 20.00 (*0-7838-1823-8*, GK Hall) Thorndike Pr.

Rabbit Seeds. Bijou Le Tord. 32p. (J). (ps-3). 1993. pap. 3.99 (*0-440-40767-2*) Dell.

***Rabbit Story.** Alvin Tresselt & Carolyn Ewing. (FRE.). (J). pap. 6.99 (*0-590-74143-8*) Scholastic Inc.

Rabbit Who Overcame Fear: A Jataka Tale. Illus. by Eric Meller. LC 90-48400. (Jataka Tales Ser.). 32p. (Orig.). (J). (gr. k-4). 1991. 15.95 (*0-89800-212-5*); pap. 7.95 (*0-89800-211-7*) Dharma Pub.

Rabbit Who Wanted Red Wings. Nellie McCaslin. 28p. 1963. reprint ed. pap. 3.45 (*0-87129-023-5*, R44) Dramatic Pub.

Rabbit Wishes: A Cuban Folktale. Linda Shute. LC 93-45895. (Illus.). 32p. (J). (ps up). 1995. 16.00 (*0-688-13180-8*); lib. bdg. 15.93 (*0-688-13181-6*) Lothrop.

Rabbiter's Bounty: Collected Poems. Les A. Murray. 300p. 1992. 25.00 (*0-374-12622-4*) FS&G.

Rabbiteye Blueberries: Development, Production, & Marketing. Max E. Austin. LC 94-10048. (Illus.). 160p. (C). 1994. 54.00 (*0-9631397-2-X*) AgScience.

Rabbits. (Colorguide Ser.). 1982. pap. 6.95 (*0-940842-18-1*) South Group.

Rabbits. Jason Cooper. LC 94-39533. (Barn Yard Friends Ser.). (J). (gr. 2-6). 1995. write for info. (*1-55916-090-X*) Rourke Bk Co.

Rabbits. Tina Hearne. (Responsible Pet Care Ser.). (Illus.). 32p. (J). (gr. 2-5). 1989. 11.95 (*0-685-58609-X*); lib. bdg. 15.94 (*0-86625-187-1*) Rourke Corp.

Rabbits. Paul R. Paradise. (Illus.). 1979. 9.95 (*0-86622-832-2*, KW-021) TFH Pubns.

Rabbits. Kate Petty. (First Pets Ser.). (Illus.). 24p. (J). (ps-3). 1993. pap. 3.95 (*0-8120-1473-1*) Barron.

Rabbits: A Complete Pet Owner's Manual. Monika A. Wegler. 64p. 1990. pap. 6.95 (*0-8120-4440-1*) Barron.

***Rabbits: Look-&-Learn.** Marcy Myerovich. (Illus.). 64p. pap. 6.95 (*0-7938-0171-0*, KD-004S) TFH Pubns.

Rabbits & Hares. Annette Barkhausen & Franz Geiser. Tr. by Jamie Daniel from GER. LC 93-15932. (Animal Families Ser.). (J). 1994. lib. bdg. 19.93 (*0-8368-1004-X*) Gareth Stevens Inc.

Rabbits & Hares. Emilie U. Lepthien. LC 93-33514. (New True Bks.). (Illus.). 48p. (J). (gr. k-4). 1994. lib. bdg. 19.00 (*0-516-01058-1*) Childrens.

Rabbits & Hares. Emilie U. Lepthien. LC 93-33514. (Illus.). 48p. (J). (gr. k-4). 1994. pap. 5.50 (*0-516-41058-X*) Childrens.

Rabbits & Hares. Annie McBride. (Illus.). 128p. text ed. 19.95 (*0-905483-67-7*, Pub. by Whittet Bks UK) Diamond Farm Bk.

Rabbits & Raindrops. Jim Arnosky. (J). 1997. 15.95 (*0-399-22635-4*, Putnam) Putnam Pub Group.

Rabbits Are Coming. Kathleen Bullock. (J). (ps). 1991. pap. 13.95 (*0-671-72963-2*, S&S Bks Young Read) S&S Childrens.

Rabbits Are Coming! Kathleen Bullock. LC 90-49830. (Illus.). 40p. (J). (ps-1). 1993. pap. 4.95 (*0-671-79609-7*, Litl Simon S&S) S&S Childrens.

Rabbits As a Hobby. Bob Bennett. (Save Our Planet Ser.). (Illus.). 98p. 1991. pap. 8.95 (*0-86622-417-3*, TT003) TFH Pubns.

Rabbits As a New Pet. Barry Martin. (Illus.). 64p. (Orig.). 1990. pap. 6.95 (*0-86622-618-4*, TU-010) TFH Pubns.

Rabbit's Carnival. Annie Ingle. LC 92-29930. (Picturebacks Ser.). (Illus.). 24p. (J). (ps-3). 1995. pap. 2.50 (*0-679-85337-5*) Random Bks Yng Read.

Rabbits, Crabs, Etc. Stories by Japanese Women. Tr. by Phyllis Birnbaum. LC 82-8365. 160p. 1984. pap. 9.95 (*0-8248-0817-7*) UH Pr.

Rabbit's Escape. Suzanne C. Han. LC 94-36516. (Illus.). (J). (gr. k-3). 1995. 15.95 (*0-8050-2675-4*) H Holt & Co.

Rabbits Everywhere. Alicia Ezpeleta. 1996. 24.95 (*0-614-14718-2*) Abrams.

Rabbits Everywhere. Alicia Ezpeleta. LC 95-620. (Illus.). 128p. 1996. 24.95 (*0-8109-3781-6*) Abrams.

Rabbits for Food & Profit. 1995. 12.95 (*0-944079-19-9*) Lessiter Pubns.

Rabbits for Those Who Care. Anmarie Barrie. (Illus.). 32p. 1994. pap. 4.95 (*0-7938-1377-8*, B117) TFH Pubns.

Rabbits Golden Rule Book. Pam Adams & Michael Twin. LC 90-2677. (J). 1989. 9.99 (*0-85953-298-4*) Childs Play.

***Rabbit's Golden Rule Book.** Pam Adams & Michael Twinn. (ITA.). (J). 1989. 9.99 (*0-85953-562-2*) Childs Play.

***Rabbit's Good News.** Ruth Bornstein. 1997. pap. 4.95 (*0-395-84514-9*, Clarion Bks) HM.

Rabbit's Good News. Ruth L. Bornstein. LC 93-30719. (J). (gr. 4 up). 1995. 13.95 (*0-395-68700-4*, Clarion Bks) HM.

Rabbits' Habits. Jane B. Moncure. LC 87-12841. (Magic Castle Readers Ser.). (Illus.). 32p. (J). (ps-2). 1987. lib. bdg. 21.36 (*0-89565-406-7*) Childs World.

Rabbits, Hares & Pikas: Status Survey & Conservation Plan. Ed. by Joseph A. Chapman & John E. Flux. (Illus.). 168p. (Orig.). 1991. pap. 25.00 (*2-8317-0019-1*, Pub. by IUCN SZ) Island Pr.

Rabbit's Judgment. Suzanne C. Han. LC 93-11031. (Illus.). (ENG & KOR.). (J). 1994. 15.95 (*0-8050-2674-6*) H Holt & Co.

Rabbit's New Rug. Judy Delton. LC 93-15453. (Parents Magazine Read Aloud Original Ser.). (Illus.). (J). 1993. lib. bdg. 17.27 (*0-8368-0972-6*) Gareth Stevens Inc.

Rabbit's New Rug. Judy Delton. LC 79-16639. (Illus.). 40p. (J). (ps-3). 1980. 5.95 (*0-8193-1009-3*); lib. bdg. 5.95 (*0-8193-1010-7*) Parents.

***Rabbit's Spring Cleaning.** Gaby Goldsack. (Little Spring Window Bks.). 1998. 3.99 (*1-57584-072-3*) Rdrs Dgst Yng Fam.

Rabbits, Squirrels, & Chipmunks. Mel Boring. LC 96-11582. (Take-Along Guide Ser.). (Illus.). 48p. (J). (gr. 3-7). 1996. pap. 6.95 (*1-55971-579-0*) NorthWord.

Rabbits Today. Horst Schmidt. (Illus.). 64p. 1996. 12.95 (*0-7938-0105-2*, WW006) TFH Pubns.

***Rabbits Today: A Complete & Up-to-Date Guide.** Horst Schmidt & American Society for the Prevention of Cruelty to Animals Staff. LC 97-3632. (Basic Domestic Pet Library). 1997. write for info. (*0-7910-4617-6*) Chelsea Hse.

Rabbits' Wedding. Garth Williams. LC 58-5285. (Illus.). 30p. (J). (ps-1). 1958. 15.00 (*0-06-026495-0*) HarpC Child Bks.

Rabbit's Wish for Snow. Tchin. LC 96-24746. (Hello Reader! Ser.). (J). 1996. write for info. (*0-590-69767-6*) Scholastic Inc.

Rabble in Arms. Kenneth Roberts. LC 96-19617. (Illus.). 592p. 1996. reprint ed. pap. 16.95 (*0-89272-386-6*) Down East.

Rabble Starkey. Lois Lowry. 208p. (J). (gr. k-6). 1988. pap. 3.99 (*0-440-40056-2*, YB BDD) BDD Bks Young Read.

Rabble Starkey. Lois Lowry. (J). (gr. 5 up). 1987. 14.95 (*0-395-43607-9*) HM.

Rabble Starkey. large type ed. Lois Lowry. 1989. lib. bdg. 14.95 (*0-8161-4776-0*, GK Hall) Thorndike Pr.

Rabdology. John Napier. Tr. by William F. Richardson from GAE. (Charles Babbage Institute Reprint Series for the History of Computing). 138p. 1990. 40.00 (*0-262-14046-2*) MIT Pr.

Rabeinu Bachya Ben Asher "Kad Hakemach" see **Encyclopedia of Torah Thoughts**

Rabelais. Michael J. Heath. Ed. by Richard J. Schoeck. (Medieval & Renaissance Texts & Studies: Vol. 130). 144p. 1996. 22.00 (*0-86698-181-0*, MR130) MRTS.

Rabelais. Jean-Marie Laclavetine. (Maison D'Ecrivain Collection). (Illus.). (FRE.). 1995. 49.95 (*2-86808-065-0*) Intl Scholars.

Rabelais & Bakhtin: Popular Culture in "Gargantua & Pantagruel" Richard M. Berrong. LC 85-21773. xiv, 156p. 1986. text ed. 35.00 (*0-8032-1191-0*) U of Nebr Pr.

Rabelais & His World. Mikhail Bakhtin. Tr. by Helene Iswolsky from RUS. LC 84-47792. 510p. 1984. 39.95 (*0-253-34830-7*); pap. 15.95 (*0-253-20341-4*, MB 341) Ind U Pr.

Rabelais' Carnival: Text, Context, Metatext. Samuel Kinser. 1990. 45.00 (*0-520-06522-0*) U CA Pr.

Rabelais et Montaigne: Chapitres Choisis. Intro. by Camilla J. Nilles. LC 91-29802. 596p. 1991. lib. bdg. 119.95 (*0-7734-9704-8*) E Mellen.

Rabelais in Context: Proceedings of the 1991 Vanderbilt Conference. Ed. by Barbara Bowen. LC 93-85166. (Illus.). 210p. 1994. lib. bdg. 39.95 (*0-917786-95-5*) Summa Pubns.

Rabelais in English Literature. H. Brown. 1972. 59.95 (*0-8490-0923-5*) Gordon Pr.

Rabelais in English Literature. Huntington Brown. 254p. 1967. reprint ed. 35.00 (*0-7146-2051-3*, Pub. by F Cass Pubs UK) Intl Spec Bk.

Rabelais in Glasgow: Proceedings of the 1993 Colloquium. Ed. by J. Coleman & C. Jimack. 1993. 40.00 (*0-9509831-0-1*, Pub. by Univ of Glasgow UK) St Mut.

***Rabelais Ressuscite, EFT XX.** N. Horry. Ed. by N. Goodley. 98p. (FRE.). (C). pap. 19.95 (*0-85989-006-6*, Pub. by Univ Exeter Pr UK) Northwestern U Pr.

Rabelais Revisited. Elizabeth Zegura & Marcel Tetel. (Twayne's World Authors Ser.). 208p. 1993. 23.95 (*0-8057-8294-X*, Twayne) Scribnrs Ref.

Rabelaisian Mythologies. Max Gauna. 296p. 1996. write for info. (*0-8386-3631-4*) Fairleigh Dickinson.

Rabelais's Incomparable Book: Essays on His Art. Ed. by Raymond C. La Charite. LC 85-80421. (French Forum Monographs: No. 62). 247p. (Orig.). 1986. pap. 17.95 (*0-917058-63-1*) French Forum.

***Rabelais's Laughers & Joubert's Trait du Ris.** Gergory D. Rocher. LC 78-15341. (Illus.). 176p. pap. 50.20 (*0-608-05123-3*, 2065682) Bks Demand.

Rabi'a: The Life & Work of Rabi'a & Other Women Mystics in Islam. Margaret Smith. 246p. 1995. pap. 12.95 (*1-85168-085-3*) Onewrld Pubns.

Rabia the Mystic. Margaret Smith. 212p. 1996. 19.95 (*1-56744-475-X*) Kazi Pubns.

Rabid Beasts. Carlos Miralejos. LC 93-61697. 216p. (Orig.). 1994. pap. 14.95 (*0-9625266-3-0*) Outer Space Pr.

Rabid Eye: The Dream Art of Rick Veitch. Rick Veitch. (Collected Rare Bit Fiends Ser.: Vol. 1). 200p. (Orig.). 1995. pap. 14.95 (*0-9624864-1-8*) King Hell Pr.

Rabies. Ed. by J. B. Campbell & K. M. Charlton. (Developments in Veterinary Virology Ser.). (C). 1988. lib. bdg. 206.50 (*0-89838-390-0*) Kluwer Ac.

Rabies. Elaine Landau. LC 92-26117. 64p. (J). (gr. 2-5). 1993. pap. 14.99 (*0-525-67403-9*, Lodestar Bks) Dutton Child Bks.

Rabies. Virginia B. Silverstein et al. LC 93-21417. (Diseases & People Ser.). 128p. (YA). (gr. 6 up). 1994. lib. bdg. 18.95 (*0-89490-465-5*) Enslow Pubs.

Rabies & Wildlife: A Biologist's Perspective. David W. MacDonald. (Illus.). 1980. write for info. (*0-318-54886-0*) OUP.

Rabies in Bats: Natural History & Public Health Implications. Danny A. Brass. (Illus.). 335p. 1994. 49.95 (*0-9637045-1-6*) Livia Pr CT.

Rabies in the Tropics. Ed. by E. Kuwert et al. (Illus.). 804p. 1985. 118.00 (*0-387-13826-9*) Spr-Verlag.

***Rabies, Lyme Disease, Hanta Virus: And Other Animal-Borne Human Diseases in the U. S. & Canada.** E. Lendell Cockrum. (Illus.). 176p. 1997. pap. 14.95 (*1-55561-138-9*) Fisher Bks.

R

R

Rabin: Our Life, His Legacy. Leah Rabin. LC 96-36743. (Illus.). 320p. 1997. 24.95 (0-399-14217-7, Putnam) Putnam Pub Group.

Rabin Memoirs: An Expanded Edition with Recent Speeches, New Photographs, & an Afterword. Yitzak Rabin. (Illus.). 400p. (C). 1996. 40.00 (0-520-20776-9) U CA Pr.

Rabin Memoirs: An Expanded Edition with Recent Speeches, New Photographs, & an Afterword. Yitzak Rabin. (Illus.). 400p. (C). 1996. pap. 16.95 (0-520-20766-1) U CA Pr.

Rabin of Israel: Warrior for Peace. Robert Slater. 640p. 1996. mass mkt. 6.99 (0-06-101066-9, Harp PBks) HarpC.

Rabindranath: The Man Behind His Poetry. Maitreyi Devi. (Illus.). 1978. 8.00 (0-86578-122-2); pap. 4.00 (0-86578-123-0) Ind-US Inc.

Rabindranath Tagore. B. Roy. 1972. 59.95 (0-8490-0924-3) Gordon Pr.

***Rabindranath Tagore.** Tagore. Date not set. 27.95 (0-312-16973-6) St Martin.

Rabindranath Tagore. Ernest Rhys. LC 78-133286. (Studies in Asiatic Literature: No. 57). 1970. reprint ed. lib. bdg. 75.00 (0-8383-1185-7) M S G Haskell Hse.

Rabindranath Tagore: A Bibliography. Katherine Henn. LC 85-1768. (American Theological Library Association Monograph: No. 13). 1985. 37.50 (0-8108-1790-X) Scarecrow.

Rabindranath Tagore: A Study of Women Characters in His Novels. M. Sarada. 160p. 1989. text ed. 20.00 (81-207-0800-8, Pub. by Sterling Pubs II) Apt Bks.

***Rabindranath Tagore: Great Short Stories from Around the World I.** Illus. by James Balkovek. LC 94-75347. (Classic Short Stories Ser.). 80p. 1994. pap. 5.95 (0-7854-0654-9, 40068) Am Guidance.

Rabindranath Tagore: His Impact on Indian Education. K. R. Salkar. 192p. 1990. text ed. 25.00 (81-207-0521-1, Pub. by Sterling Pubs II) Apt Bks.

Rabindranath Tagore: Life & Work. E. Thompson. LC 74-7119. (Studies in Asiatic Literature: No. 57). 1974. lib. bdg. 75.00 (0-8383-1980-7) M S G Haskell Hse.

Rabindranath Tagore: Poet & Dramatist. Edward Thompson. LC 74-30343. (Studies in Asiatic Literature: No. 57). 1974. lib. bdg. 55.95 (0-8383-1982-3) M S G Haskell Hse.

Rabindranath Tagore: Poet & Dramatist. Edward J. Thompson. (Oxford India Paperbacks Ser.). 380p. 1992. pap. 14.95 (0-19-562645-1) OUP.

Rabindranath Tagore: The Myriad-Minded Man. Krishna Dutta & Andrew Robinson. LC 95-39735. 512p. 1995. 35.00 (0-312-14030-4) St Martin.

Rabindranath Tagore No. 25: Political Thinkers of Modern India. Ed. by Verinder Grover. (C). 1995. 52.00 (81-7100-571-3) S Asia.

Rabindranath Tagore - Builders of Modern India. Hiranmay Banerjee. 195p. 1981. 9.95 (0-318-36913-3) Asia Bk Corp.

Rabindranath Tagore & Modern Sensibility. Bhabatosh Chatterjee. 200p. (C). 1996. 19.95 (0-19-563796-8) OUP.

Rabindranath Tagore et Romain Rolland: Lettres et Autres Ecrits. Romain Rolland & Rabindranath Tagore. (Illus.). 208p. (FRE.). 1961. pap. 8.95 (0-7859-5460-0) Fr & Eur.

Rabindranath Tagore's Aesthetics. K. K. Sharma. 1988. 12.50 (81-7017-237-3, Pub. by Abhinav II) S Asia.

Rabindranath Tagore's Visit to Canada. P. C. Mahalanobis. LC 76-52432. (Studies in Asiatic Literature: No. 57). 1977. lib. bdg. 75.00 (0-8383-2130-5) M S G Haskell Hse.

Rabindranath Tagore: The Poet of India. A. K. Basu. (C). 1993. 14.00 (81-85182-92-2, Pub. by Indus Pub II) S Asia.

Rabo de Lagartija de Aquel Famoso Senor Rector & Otros Cuentos de Orilla. Felix Cordova-Iturregui. LC 85-72325. 109p. (SPA.). 1986. pap. 6.95 (0-940238-84-5) Ediciones Huracan.

Rabotiagi: Perestroika & after Viewed from Below. David Mandel. 288p. (C). 1993. text ed. 30.00 (0-85345-879-0) Monthly Rev.

Rabotiagi: Perestroika & after Viewed from Below. David Mandel. 288p. (C). 1994. pap. text ed. 19.00 (0-85345-878-2) Monthly Rev.

Rabouilleuse. Honore De Balzac. 1960. 10.95 (0-685-58346-5, 2070361632) Fr & Eur.

Rabouilleuse. Honore De Balzac. (Folio Ser.: No. 163). (FRE.). 1960. pap. 9.95 (2-07-036163-2) Schoenhof.

Rabouilleuse. Honore De Balzac. 448p. (FRE.). 1972. pap. 12.95 (0-7859-1705-5, 2070361632) Fr & Eur.

Rabouilleuse. unabridged ed. Honore De Balzac. (FRE.). pap. 7.95 (2-87714-223-X, Pub. by Bookking Intl FR) Distribks Inc.

Raccolta Di Lettre Sulla Pittura, Scultura Ed Architettura, 8 vols. Giovanni G. Bottari & Stefano Ticozzi. (Bibliotheca Scelta Di Opere Italiane Antiche E Moderne Ser.: Vol. VI, 1). xvi, 4282p. 1976. reprint ed. Set. 785.00 (3-487-06013-2) G Olms Pubs.

Raccolta di un Amatore: D'arte Primtiva. Paolo Morigi. (Illus.). 475p. (ENG, FRE, GER & ITA.). 1980. lib. bdg. 195.00 (0-87817-286-6) Hacker.

Raccomandazione. Nat Scammacca. Ed. by Stanley H. Barkan. (Cross-Cultural Review Chapbook Ser.: No. 1: Shorty Story 1). 24p. (ENG & ITA.). 1980. 15.00 (0-89304-831-3, CCC126); pap. 5.00 (0-89304-800-3) Cross-Cultrl NY.

Racconti Del Novecento: Realta Regionali. Ilene T. Olken & Claudio Mazzola. 320p. (C). 1990. pap. text ed. 42.00 (0-13-750001-7) P-H.

Racconti di Alberto Moravia. Alberto Moravia. Ed. by Vincenzo Traversa. LC 68-11595. (Illus.). (Orig.). (ITA.). (C). 1979. reprint ed. pap. text ed. 12.95 (0-89197-368-0) Irvington.

Racconti di oggi. Franca C. Merlonghi. (C). 1991. pap. 27.56 (0-395-55423-3) HM Soft Schl Col Div.

Raccontini Divertenti see Lecturas Italianas

Raccoon at Clear Creek Road. Carolyn B. Otto. (Smithsonian's Backyard Ser.). (Illus.). 32p. (J). (ps-3). 1995. 15.95 (1-56899-175-4); 4.95 (1-56899-176-2); 19.95 incl. audio (1-56899-179-7); 29.95 (1-56899-177-0) Soundprints.

Raccoon at Clear Creek Road, Incl. toy. Carolyn B. Otto. (Smithsonian's Backyard Ser.). (Illus.). 32p. (J). (ps-3). 1995. 12.95 (1-56899-178-9); 29.95 incl. audio (1-56899-181-9) Soundprints.

Raccoon Book. Katharyn M. Aal. LC 82-7831. (Illus.). 88p. 1982. pap. 5.95 (0-935526-05-6) McBooks Pr.

Raccoon Connection. rev. ed. Grace E. Lassik. Ed. by G. M. Carolock et al. (Illus.). 15p. (J). (ps-2). 1992. reprint ed. pap. 9.95 (1-880926-00-8) Four Star SC.

Raccoon John Smith. 2nd ed. Louis Cochran. (Heritage of a Movement Book Club Ser.). 370p. 1985. reprint ed. pap. text ed. 10.99 (0-89900-277-3) College Pr Pub.

Raccoon John Smith: Frontiersman & Reformer. 2nd ed. Everett Donaldson. LC 93-72516. (Illus.). 1993. reprint ed. pap. 9.95 (0-9636545-1-9) Wind Pubns.

Raccoon Magic for Kids. Jeff Fair. LC 95-16317. (Animal Magic for Kids Ser.). (Illus.). (J). 1995. lib. bdg. 18.60 (0-8368-1377-4) Gareth Stevens Inc.

Raccoon on the Moon. Barbara Gregorich. Ed. by Joan Hoffman. (Start to Read! Ser.). (Illus.). 16p. (Orig.). (J). (gr. k-2). 1991. pap. 2.25 (0-88743-024-4, 06024) Sch Zone Pub Co.

Raccoon on the Moon. Bruce Witty. (Start to Read! Ser.). (Illus.). 32p. (J). (gr. k-2). 1992. 3.95 (0-88743-418-5) Sch Zone Pub Co.

Raccoons. Karen M. Kostyal & National Geographic Society Staff. Ed. by Donald J. Crump. (Books for Young Explorers: Set 14, No. 1). (Illus.). 32p. (J). (ps-3). 1993. Set. 8.00 (0-87044-677-0) Natl Geog.

Raccoons. Lynn M. Stone. (North American Animal Discovery Library). (Illus.). 24p. (J). (gr. k-5). 1990. lib. bdg. 11.94 (0-86593-045-7); lib. bdg. 8.95 (0-685-46450-4) Rourke Corp.

Raccoons: In Folklore, History & Today's Backyards. Virginia C. Holmgren. (Illus.). 208p. (Orig.). (C). 1989. reprint ed. lib. bdg. 31.00 (0-8095-4073-8) Borgo Pr.

Raccoon's Adventure in Alphabet Town. Janet McDonnell. LC 92-1066. (Read Around Alphabet Town Ser.). (Illus.). 32p. (J). (ps-2). 1992. lib. bdg. 17.50 (0-516-05418-X) Childrens.

Raccoons & Ripe Corn. Jim Arnosky. LC 87-4243. (Illus.). 32p. (J). (ps up). 1991. reprint ed. pap. 4.95 (0-688-10489-4, Mulberry) Morrow.

Raccoons for Kids. Jeff Fair. LC 93-47298. (Wildlife for Kids Ser.). (Illus.). 48p. (J). (gr. k-8). 1994. pap. 6.95 (1-55971-229-5) NorthWord.

Raccoon's Hide & Seek. Dick McCue. (Animal Shape Board Bks.). (Illus.). 12p. (J). (ps). 1985. 2.95 (0-671-55854-4, Litl Simon S&S) S&S Childrens.

Raccoon's Tale. Justine Korman. (J). (ps-3). 1996. pap. text ed. 3.95 (0-307-10002-2, Golden Pr) Western Pub.

Race. John R. Baker. 1984. lib. bdg. 79.95 (0-87700-637-7) Revisionist Pr.

***Race.** Hunter R. Clark. 304p. Date not set. 23.00 (0-465-06808-1); pap. write for info. (0-465-06809-X) Basic.

Race. David M. Cooper. LC 87-50096. 100p. (Orig.). 1987. pap. 6.95 (0-933571-02-X) Ure Pr.

Race. Eliyahu M. Goldratt & Robert E. Fox. LC 86-18197. (Illus.). 179p. (Orig.). 1986. pap. 15.00 (0-88427-062-9) North River.

Race. Ed. by Steven Gregory & Roger Sanjek. LC 94-534. 400p. (C). 1994. text ed. 48.00 (0-8135-2108-4); pap. text ed. 17.95 (0-8135-2109-2) Rutgers U Pr.

Race. David Guinn. (Great Race Ser.). 170p. (Orig.). (YA). (gr. 6 up). 1994. pap. 9.95 (1-887002-16-2) Cross Trng.

Race. Bob Judd. 272p. 1992. mass mkt. 4.99 (0-380-71556-2) Avon.

Race. Loreen Leedy. (Let Me Read Ser.). (Illus.). (J). (ps-k). 1995. 2.95 (0-673-36277-9, GoodYrBooks) Addson-Wesley Educ.

Race. Deborah Shine. (Whole-Language Big Bks.). 16p. (J). (ps-2). 1992. pap. 14.95 (1-56784-051-5) Newbridge Comms.

Race. Lauraine Snelling. (Golden Filly Ser.: Bk. 1). 160p. (Orig.). (J). (gr. 7-9). 1991. pap. 5.99 (1-55661-161-7) Bethany Hse.

Race. John R. Baker. (Illus.). (C). 1989. reprint ed. 25.00 (0-936396-04-0) Foun Human GA.

Race: A Study in Superstition. rev. ed. Jacques Barzun. LC 78-63649. (Studies in Fascism: Ideology & Practice). 288p. reprint ed. 34.50 (0-404-16899-X) AMS Pr.

Race: An Anthology in the First Person. Bart Schneider. 1997. pap. 14.00 (0-517-88728-2) Random.

Race: Ethnicity & Nation International Perspectives on Social Conflict. Ed. by Peter Ratcliffe. 256p. 1996. pap. 27.50 (1-85728-661-8, Pub. by UCL Pr UK) Taylor & Francis.

Race: How Blacks & Whites Think & Feel about the American Obsession. Studs Terkel. LC 92-31260. 416p. 1993. pap. 14.00 (0-385-46889-X, Anchor NY) Doubleday.

Race: How Blacks & Whites Think & Feel about the American Obsession. Studs Terkel. 416p. 1992. 24.95 (1-56584-000-3) New Press NY.

***Race: Jean Toomer's Swan Song.** Ronald Dorris. (Occasional Publications: Vol. 7). xii, 86p. (Orig.). 1997. pap. 8.95 (1-883275-06-7) Xavier Rev.

Race: Matters Concerning Pan Afrikan History, Culture & Genocide. Ed. by Kiarri T-H. Cheatwood. LC 90-63873. 560p. 1991. 24.98 (0-9625169-4-5); pap. 16.98 (0-9625169-5-3) Native Sun Pubs.

***Race: The History of an Idea in America.** Thomas F. Gossett. (Race & American Culture Ser.). 560p. 1997. 45.00 (0-19-509777-7); pap. 19.95 (0-19-509778-5) OUP.

Race: The History of an Idea in the West. Ivan Hannaford. 500p. 1996. pap. 19.95 (0-8018-5223-4); text ed. 60.00 (0-8018-5222-6) Johns Hopkins.

Race: The Origins of an Idea, 1760-1850. Ed. & Intro. by Hannah Augstein. (Key Issues Ser.: No. 14). 240p. Date not set. 72.00 (1-85506-455-3); pap. 24.95 (1-85506-454-5) Bks Intl VA.

Race: Twentieth Century Dilemmas--Twenty-First Century Prognoses. Ed. by Winston A. Van Horne. LC 89-51910. (Ethnicity & Public Policy Ser.: Vol. 8). xiii, 314p. (Orig.). (C). 1989. 30.00 (0-942672-14-3); pap. 14.95 (0-942672-15-1) UWI IRE.

***Race Ace Roger.** John Light. (ITA.). (J). 1991. pap. 3.99 (0-85953-604-1) Childs Play.

Race Ace Roger. John Light. LC 91-33417. (Light Reading Ser.). (J). (gr. 4 up). 1991. 3.99 (0-85953-501-0) Childs Play.

Race Across Alaska: First Woman to Win the Iditarod Tells Her Story. Libby Riddles & Tim Jones. LC 87-25273. (Illus.). 240p. (Orig.). 1988. pap. 14.95 (0-8117-2253-8) Stackpole.

Race Adjustment. Kelly Miller. Incl. Essays on the Negro in America. LC 68-29012. 1968. (0-318-50875-3); Everlasting Stain. LC 68-29012. 1968. (0-318-50876-1); LC 68-29012. (American Negro: His History & Literature, Ser. 1). 688p. 1969. reprint ed. 19.95 (0-405-01831-2) Ayer.

Race Adjustment: Essays on the Negro in America. Kelly Miller. LC 77-89389. (Black Heritage Library Collection). 1977. 18.95 (0-8369-8634-2) Ayer.

Race Adjustment: Essays on the Negro in America. Kelly Miller. 15.00 (1-56675-020-2) Mnemosyne.

Race Against Empire: Black Americans & Anticolonialism, 1937-1957. Penny M. Von Eschen. LC 96-22283. (Illus.). 296p. 1996. 35.00 (0-8014-3197-2); pap. write for info. (0-8014-8292-5) Cornell U Pr.

Race Against the Court: The Supreme Court & Minorities in Contemporary America. Girardeau A. Spann. 256p. (C). 1993. 45.00 (0-8147-7963-8) NYU Pr.

Race Against the Court: The Supreme Court & Minorities in Contemporary America. Girardeau A. Spann. (C). 1994. pap. 19.00 (0-8147-7993-X) NYU Pr.

Race Against the Machine: With Notes & Tablature. 80p. 1994. otabind 19.95 (0-7935-3015-6, 00694910) H Leonard.

Race Against Time. 1980. pap. 10.00 (0-317-52425-9) Work Women Educ.

***Race Against Time.** Michael Coleman. LC 94-79399. (Ten-Minute Mysteries Ser.). 32p. (YA). (gr. 6-12). 1994. pap. 2.95 (0-7854-0847-9, 40772) Am Guidance.

Race Against Time. Lynn Turner. 384p. 1995. mass mkt. 4.99 (0-8217-0154-1, Zebra Kensgtn) Kensgtn Pub Corp.

Race Against Time. Piers Anthony. 256p. 1986. reprint ed. pap. 3.50 (0-8125-3101-9) Tor Bks.

***Race Against Time, Vol. 3.** Gilbert Morris. LC 97-21024. (The Time Navigators Ser.). (J). 1997. pap. 5.99 (1-55661-397-0) Bethany Hse.

Race Against Time: Psychotherapy & Psychoanalysis in the Second Half of Life. Ed. by Robert A. Nemiroff & Calvin A. Colarusso. LC 84-17683. (Critical Issues in Psychiatry Ser.). 350p. 1985. 52.50 (0-306-41753-7, Plenum Pr) Plenum.

***Race Against Time Readalong.** Michael Coleman. LC 94-79399. (Ten-Minute Mysteries Ser.). 32p. (YA). (gr. 6-12). 1994. pap. 12.95 incl. audio (0-7854-1056-2, 40774) Am Guidance.

Race & Authority in Urban Politics. David Greenstone. 392p. 1976. pap. text ed. 7.95 (0-226-30713-1, P696) U Ch Pr.

Race & Authority in Urban Politics: Community Participation & the War on Poverty. J. David Greenstone & Paul E. Peterson. LC 73-76763. 326p. 1974. 45.00 (0-87154-373-7) Russell Sage.

Race & Borough Politics. Frank W. Reeves. 318p. 1989. text ed. 58.95 (0-566-05573-2, Pub. by Avebury Pub UK) Ashgate Pub Co.

Race & Class in American Society. rev. ed. Edward H. Ransford. 1994. pap. 18.95 (0-87047-069-8) Schenkman Bks Inc.

Race & Class in American Society. 2nd rev. ed. Edward H. Ransford. 1994. 29.95 (0-87047-068-X) Schenkman Bks Inc.

Race & Class in American Society: Black, Chicano, Anglo. H. Edward Ransford. LC 74-84674. 200p. 1977. pap. text ed. 11.95 (0-87073-041-X) Schenkman Bks Inc.

Race & Class in Colonial Oaxaca. John K. Chance. LC 76-48011. xviii, 250p. 1978. 39.50 (0-8047-0937-8) Stanford U Pr.

Race & Class in Texas Politics. Chandler Davidson. (Illus.). 372p. 1990. text ed. 49.50 (0-691-07861-0); pap. text ed. 16.95 (0-691-02539-8) Princeton U Pr.

Race & Class in the American South since 1890. Ed. by Melvyn Stokes & Rick Halpern. LC 94-18351. 288p. 1994. 45.95 (1-85973-031-0); pap. 19.95 (1-85973-036-1) Berg Pubs.

Race & Class in the Southwest: A Theory of Racial Inequality. Mario Barrera. LC 78-62970. 261p. (C). 1980. pap. text ed. 14.00 (0-268-01601-1) U of Notre Dame Pr.

***Race & Class on Campus: Conversations with Ricardo's Daughter.** Jay Rochlin. LC 96-45817. 175p. 1997. 24.95 (0-8165-1670-7) U of Ariz Pr.

***Race & Class Politics in New York City Before the Civil War.** Anthony Gronowicz. LC 97-10292. 1998. write for info. (1-55553-327-2); pap. write for info. (1-55553-326-4) NE U Pr.

Race & Color in Brazilian Literature. David Brookshaw. LC 86-961. 356p. 1986. 39.50 (0-8108-1880-9) Scarecrow.

***Race & Colour.** (Who Cares Ser.). (ITA.). (J). 1992. pap. 3.99 (0-85953-583-5) Childs Play.

***Race & Colour: Who Cares about Them.** Child's Play Staff. (J). 1996. lib. bdg. 11.95 (0-85953-874-5) Childs Play.

Race & Community Care. Ed. by Waqar I. Ahmad & Karl Atkin. LC 95-50908. ("Race", Health & Social Care Ser.). 160p. 1996. 85.00 (0-335-19463-X, Open Univ Pr); pap. 23.95 (0-335-19462-1, Open Univ Pr) Taylor & Francis.

Race & Crime. Delores Jones. (Crime, Justice, & Punishment Ser.). (YA). 1997. 19.95 (0-7910-4273-1) Chelsea Hse.

Race & Crime. Willem A. Bonger. Tr. by Margaret M. Hordyk. LC 69-14912. (Criminology, Law Enforcement, & Social Problems Ser.: No. 34). 1969. reprint ed. 20.00 (0-87585-034-0); reprint ed. pap. 10.00 (0-87585-907-0) Patterson Smith.

Race & Criminal Justice. Ed. by Michael J. Lynch & E. Britt Patterson. LC 91-20028. (Orig.). (C). 1991. pap. text ed. 21.50 (0-911577-20-3) Harrow & Heston.

Race & Culture: A World View. Thomas Sowell. 352p. 1995. pap. 14.00 (0-465-06797-2) Basic.

Race & Culture Contacts in the Modern World. E. Franklin Frazier. LC 78-17087. 338p. 1978. reprint ed. text ed. 38.50 (0-313-20579-5, FRRC, Greenwood Pr) Greenwood.

Race & Culture in America: Readings in Racial & Ethnic Relations. 3rd ed. Ed. by Carl E. Jackson & Emory J. Tolbert. 360p. (C). 1989. pap. text ed. 32.95 (0-8087-7015-2) Burgess MN Intl.

Race & Culture in Psychiatry. Suman Fernando. 200p. 1988. lib. bdg. 49.95 (0-7099-4912-X, Pub. by Croom Helm UK) Routledge Chapman & Hall.

Race & Curriculum: Social Inequality & the Theories & Politics of Difference in Contemporary Research on Schooling. Cameron McCarthy. 224p. 1990. 60.00 (1-85000-682-2, Falmer Pr); pap. 28.00 (1-85000-683-0, Falmer Pr) Taylor & Francis.

***Race & Default in Credit Markets: A Colloquy.** Ed. by Michael A. Stegman. (Illus.). 126p. (Orig.). (C). 1996. pap. 35.00 (0-7881-3131-1) DIANE Pub.

Race & Democracy: The Civil Rights Struggle in Louisiana, 1915-1972. Adam Fairclough. LC 94-22563. 1995. 34.95 (0-8203-1700-4) U of Ga Pr.

Race & Democratic Society. Franz Boas. 15.00 (0-685-71709-7) J J Augustin.

Race & Democratic Society. Franz Boas. LC 70-86641. 1969. reprint ed. 30.00 (0-8196-0248-5) Biblo.

***Race & Education: Narrative Essays, Oral Histories, & Documentary Photography.** Alan Wieder. (Counterpoints Ser.: Vol. 47). 216p. (C). 1997. pap. text ed. 29.95 (0-8204-3690-9) P Lang Pubng.

Race & Educational Reform in the American Metropolis: A Study of School Decentralization. Dan A. Lewis & Kathryn Nakagawa. (SUNY Series, Frontiers in Education). 176p. (C). 1994. pap. text ed. 18.95 (0-7914-2134-1) State U NY Pr.

Race & Educational Reform in the American Metropolis: A Study of School Decentralization. Dan A. Lewis & Kathryn Nakagawa. (SUNY Series, Frontiers in Education). 176p. (C). 1995. text ed. 57.50 (0-7914-2133-3) State U NY Pr.

Race & Ethnic Conflict: Contending Views on Prejudice & Ethnoviolence. Fred L. Pincus. 332p. (C). 1994. pap. text ed. 26.50 (0-8133-1662-6) Westview.

Race & Ethnic Relations. Hubert M. Blalock, Jr. (Foundations of Modern Sociology Ser.). (Illus.). 160p. (C). 1981. pap. text ed. 25.80 (0-13-750174-9) P-H.

Race & Ethnic Relations: American & Global Perspectives. 2nd ed. Martin N. Marger. 591p. (C). 1991. text ed. 43.95 (0-534-13950-7) Wadsworth Pub.

Race & Ethnic Relations: American & Global Perspectives. 3rd ed. Martin N. Marger. 607p. 1994. text ed. 44.75 (0-534-20809-6) Wadsworth Pub.

Race & Ethnic Relations: American & Global Perspectives. 4th ed. Martin N. Marger. LC 96-18143. (Sociology Ser.). (C). 1997. text ed. 61.95 (0-534-50563-5) Wadsworth Pub.

Race & Ethnic Relations: An Annotated Bibliography. Graham C. Kinloch. LC 83-49297. (Library of Sociology). 278p. 1984. text ed. 56.00 (0-8240-8971-5, SS226) Garland.

Race & Ethnic Relations: 1996-1997. annuals 6th ed. John A. Kromkowski. 256p. (C). 1996. per. write for info. (0-697-31716-1) Brown & Benchmark.

***Race & Ethnic Relations in America, 2 vols.** Kenneth Stewart. 425p. (Orig.). (C). 1996. pap. text ed. 26.00 (0-922914-28-1) MicroCase.

Race & Ethnic Relations in Latin America & the Caribbean: An Historical Dictionary & Bibliography. Robert M. Levine. LC 80-15179. 260p. 1980. 22.50 (0-8108-1324-6) Scarecrow.

***Race & Ethnic Relations in the Contemporary United States: Reading for the 21st Century.** Ed. by Christopher Ellison & Allen Martin. LC 96-49904. 410p. (Orig.). (C). 1997. pap. text ed. write for info. (0-935732-80-2) Roxbury Pub Co.

***Race & Ethnic Relations in the First Person.** Alfred T. Kisubi & Michael A. Burayidi. 1998. text ed. write for info. (0-275-96069-2, Praeger Pubs) Greenwood.

Race & Ethnicity. John Rex. LC 86-5197. (Concepts in Social Sciences Ser.). 160p. 1986. pap. 22.00 (0-335-15385-2, Open Univ Pr) Taylor & Francis.

An Asterisk (*) at the beginning of an entry indicates that the title is appearing in BIP for the first time.

Race & Ethnicity: A Study of Intracultural Socialization Patterns. Smith & Jackson. 400p. 1989. per. 39.84 (*0-8403-5653-6*) Kendall-Hunt.

Race & Ethnicity in America: Meeting the Challenge in the 21st Century. Ed. by Gail E. Thomas. LC 95-12576. 1995. pap. write for info. (*1-56032-328-0*); boxed 59.95 (*1-56032-327-2*) Taylor & Francis.

Race & Ethnicity in Chicago Politics: A Reexamination of Pluralist Theory. Dianne M. Pinderhughes. LC 86-19297. 339p. reprint ed. pap. 96.70 (*0-8357-3297-5*, 2039520) Bks Demand.

Race & Ethnicity in Latin America. Intro. by Jorge I. Dominquez. LC 93-47174. (Essays on Mexico, Central & South America Ser.: Vol. 7). 384p. 1994. text ed. 70.00 (*0-8153-1491-4*) Garland.

***Race & Ethnicity in Latin America.** Peter Wade. LC 96-51820. (Critical Studies on Latin America). 1997. write for info. (*0-7453-0988-7*, Pub. by Pluto Pr UK) LPC InBook.

***Race & Ethnicity in Latin America.** Peter Wade. (Critical Studies on Latin America). 1997. pap. text ed. 14.95 (*0-7453-0987-9*, Pub. by Pluto Pr UK) LPC InBook.

Race & Ethnicity in Modern Britain. David Mason. (Oxford Modern Britain Ser.). (Illus.). 144p. 1995. text ed. 39.95 (*0-19-878098-2*) OUP.

Race & Ethnicity in Research Methods. John H. Stanfield, II & Rutledge M. Dennis. (Focus Editions Ser.: Vol. 157). (Illus.). 320p. (C). 1993. text ed. 54.00 (*0-8039-5006-3*); pap. text ed. 24.95 (*0-8039-5007-1*) Sage.

Race & Ethnicity in the United States. Richard T. Schaefer. LC 94-18921. (C). 1995. text ed. 22.95 (*0-673-46949-2*) Addson-Wesley Educ.

Race & Family in the Colonial South. Ed. by Winthrop D. Jordan & Sheila L. Skemp. LC 87-23157. (Chancellor's Symposium on Southern History Ser.). 174p. 1987. 35.00 (*0-87805-333-6*); pap. 15.95 (*0-87805-334-4*) U Pr of Miss.

Race & Gender: Equal Opportunities Policies in Education. Ed. by Madeleine Arnot. 154p. 1985. 27.95 (*0-08-032675-7*, M110, M115, M12, Prgamon Press); pap. text ed. 18.95 (*0-08-032674-9*, Prgamon Press) Buttrwrth-Heinemann.

Race & Gender Discrimination Across Urban Labor Markets. Susanne Schmitz. LC 96-17462. (Studies in the History of American Labor). (Illus.). 196p. 1996. text ed. 55.00 (*0-8153-2392-1*) Garland.

Race & Gender in the American Economy: Views from Across the Spectrum. Ed. by Susan F. Feiner. LC 93-38937. 1994. pap. text ed. 33.60 (*0-13-670092-6*) P-H Gen Ref & Trav.

Race & Health in Contemporary Britain. Ed. by Waqar I. Ahmad. LC 93-25331. 192p. 1993. 90.00 (*0-335-15698-3*, Open Univ Pr); pap. 29.00 (*0-335-15697-5*, Open Univ Pr) Taylor & Francis.

Race & Health Policy. Allan McNaught. 160p. 1987. lib. bdg. 45.00 (*0-7099-4673-2*, Pub. by Croom Helm UK) Routledge Chapman & Hall.

Race & History: Selected Essays, 1938-1988. John H. Franklin. LC 89-32613. 464p. 1990. 29.95 (*0-8071-1547-9*) La State U Pr.

Race & History: Selected Essays, 1938-1988. John H. Franklin. LC 89-32613. 450p. (C). 1991. pap. 16.95 (*0-8071-1764-1*) La State U Pr.

Race & Human Evolution: A Fatal Attraction. Rachel Caspari & Milford H. Wolpoff. (Illus.). 448p. 1997. 26.00 (*0-684-81013-1*, S&S) S&S Trade.

Race & IQ. expanded ed. Ashley Montagu. 400p. 1997. 30.00 (*0-19-510220-7*) OUP.

Race & Justice: Rodney King & O. J. Simpson in a House Divided. Jewelle T. Gibbs. 348p. 1996. 25.00 (*0-7879-0264-0*) Jossey-Bass.

Race & Labour in Twentieth-Century Britain. Ed. by Kenneth Lunn. 192p. 1986. 32.00 (*0-7146-3238-4*, Pub. by F Cass Pubs UK); pap. 17.50 (*0-7146-4052-2*, Pub. by F Cass Pubs UK) Intl Spec Bk.

Race & Manifest Destiny: The Origins of American Racial Anglo-Saxonism. Reginald Horsman. LC 81-4293. 376p. (C). 1981. 37.00 (*0-674-74572-8*) HUP.

Race & Manifest Destiny: The Origins of American Racial Anglo-Saxonism. Reginald Horsman. 376p. (C). 1986. pap. 16.95 (*0-674-94805-X*) HUP.

Race & Mixed Race. Naomi Zack. LC 92-44252. 232p. 1993. 49.95 (*1-56639-064-8*) Temple U Pr.

Race & Mixed Race. Naomi Zack. LC 92-44252. 232p. 1994. pap. 19.95 (*1-56639-265-9*) Temple U Pr.

Race & Nationalism: The Struggle for Power in Rhodesia - Nyasaland. Thomas M. Franck. LC 60-10738. 381p. reprint ed. pap. 108.60 (*0-7837-0447-X*, 2040770) Bks Demand.

Race & Nationalism: The Struggle for Power in Rhodesia-Nyasaland. Thomas M. Franck. LC 73-11853. 369p. 1973. reprint ed. text ed. 35.00 (*0-8371-7074-5*, FRRN, Greenwood Pr) Greenwood.

Race & Nationalism in Trinidad & Tobago: A Study of Decolonization in Multiracial Society. Selwyn D. Ryan. LC 70-185735. 525p. reprint ed. pap. 149.70 (*0-317-55731-9*, 2029348) Bks Demand.

Race & Other Misadventures: Essays in Honor of Ashley Montagu in His Ninetieth Year. Ed. by Larry T. Reynolds & Leonard Lieberman. LC 95-82132. (Illus.). 432p. 1996. text ed. 65.95 (*1-882289-35-8*) Gen Hall.

Race & Place: A Legal History of the Neighborhood School. Meyer Weinberg. 1968. pap. 3.60 (*0-912008-06-7*) Equity & Excel.

Race & Political Strategy. Ed. by Thomas E. Cavanagh. LC 83-22189. 60p. (Orig.). 1983. pap. 12.25 (*0-941410-33-1*) Jt Ctr Pol Studies.

Race & Politics. Muhammad Anwar. 256p. 1986. 32.50 (*0-422-79840-1*, 9913, Pub. by Tavistock UK) Routledge Chapman & Hall.

***Race & Politics.** James Jennings. Date not set. pap. 18.00 (*1-85984-198-8*, Pub. by Verso UK) Routledge Chapman & Hall.

***Race & Politics.** James Jennings. (C). Date not set. text ed. 60.00 (*1-85984-862-1*, Pub. by Verso UK) Routledge Chapman & Hall.

Race & Politics: Partnership in the Federation of Rhodesia & Nyasaland. Edward Clegg. LC 75-3731. 280p. 1975. reprint ed. text ed. 35.00 (*0-8371-8061-9*, CLRPO, Greenwood Pr) Greenwood.

Race & Politics in South Africa. Ed. by Ian Robertson & Phillip Whitten. LC 76-50334. 274p. 1978. text ed. 34.95 (*0-87855-137-9*) Transaction Pubs.

Race & Public Policy: A Study of Local Politics & Government. Shamit Saggar. 213p. 1991. text ed. 55.95 (*1-85628-097-7*, Pub. by Avebury Pub UK) Ashgate Pub Co.

Race & Racism. 3rd ed. Bell. 1992. 48.00 (*0-316-08822-6*) Little.

Race & Racism: Essays in Social Geography. Ed. by Peter Jackson. 320p. (C). 1987. text ed. 49.95 (*0-04-305002-6*) Routledge Chapman & Hall.

Race & Racism in Britain. 2nd ed. John Solomos. LC 93-15200. 1993. pap. 18.95 (*0-312-09980-0*) St Martin.

***Race & Rally Car: A DIY Guide to Building or Modifying a Racing or Rally Car.** 4th ed. Allan Staniforth. (Illus.). 256p. 1997. 39.95 (*0-85429-984-X*, Pub. by G T Foulis Ltd) Haynes Pubns.

Race & Rally Source Book: A DIY Guide to Building or Modifying a Race or Rally Car. Allan Staniforth. (Illus.). 256p. 1992. 32.95 (*0-85429-848-7*, Pub. by G T Foulis Ltd) Haynes Pubns.

Race & Rapprochement. Stuart Anderson. LC 79-24185. 240p. 1981. 33.50 (*0-8386-3001-4*) Fairleigh Dickinson.

Race & Reality. Carleton Putnam. LC 67-19407. 192p. 1980. pap. 12.00 (*0-914576-14-3*) Howard Allen.

Race & Reason. Carleton Putnam. LC 61-8447. 125p. 1977. pap. 12.00 (*0-914576-08-9*) Howard Allen.

Race & Reconciliation: Healing the Wounds, Winning the Harvest. Ed. by Jack W. Hayford. (Spirit-Filled Life Bible Ser.). 160p. 1996. pap. 6.99 (*0-7852-1131-4*) Nelson.

Race & Religion in Early Nineteenth Century America, 1800-1850: Constitution, Conscience, & Calvinist Compromise, 2 vols. Joseph R. Washington, Jr. LC 88-32752. (Studies in American Religion). 1016p. 1989. lib. bdg. 159.95 (*0-88946-682-3*) E Mellen.

Race & Religion in Mid-Nineteenth Century America, 1850-1877: Protestant Philanthropists. Joseph R. Washington, Jr. LC 88-32751. (Studies in American Religion: Vol. 40). 736p. 1989. lib. bdg. 139.95 (*0-88946-683-1*) E Mellen.

Race & Reparations: A Black Perspective for the Twenty-First Century. Clarence J. Munford. LC 96-10811. 576p. 1996. 79.95 (*0-86543-510-3*); pap. 21.95 (*0-86543-511-1*) Africa World.

Race & Residence: An Analysis of Property Values in Transitional Areas, Atlanta, Georgia, 1960-1971. Howard Openshaw. LC 74-620726. (Research Monograph: No. 53). 132p. 1973. spiral bd. 19.95 (*0-88406-019-5*) GA St U Busn Pr.

Race & Revolution. Gary B. Nash. 224p. 1990. 29.95 (*0-945612-11-7*); pap. 15.95 (*0-945612-21-4*) Madison Hse.

Race & Revolutionary Consciousness: A Documentary Interpretation of the 1970 Black Revolt in Trinidad. Ivar Oxaal. 96p. 1971. boxed 32.95 (*0-87073-066-5*) Transaction Pubs.

***Race & Rumors of Race: White Nightmares of Black Revolt, 1941-1945.** Howard W. Odum. LC 97-14450. 1998. write for info. (*0-8018-5757-0*) Johns Hopkins.

Race & Schooling in the City. Adam Yarmolinsky et al. LC 80-20424. 291p. (C). 1981. 29.00 (*0-674-74577-9*) HUP.

Race & Schooling in the South, Eighteen Eighty to Nineteen Fifty: An Economic History. Robert A. Margo. LC 90-11249. (National Bureau of Economic Research Long Term Factors in Economic Development Ser.). (Illus.). 176p. 1990. 29.95 (*0-226-50510-3*) U Ch Pr.

Race & Schooling in the South, 1880-1950: An Economic History. Robert A. Margo. (National Bureau of Economic Research Long Term Factors in Economic Development Ser.). (Illus.). x, 174p. 1994. pap. text ed. 12.95 (*0-226-50511-1*) U Ch Pr.

Race & Sentencing: A Study in the Crown Court: a Report for the Commission for Racial Equality. Roger G. Hood. LC 92-26724. 150p. 1993. pap. 24.95 (*0-19-825840-2*, Clarendon Pr) OUP.

Race & Sex Effects in the Conformity Behavior of Children. Gordon N. Cantor. (Augustana College Library Occasional Papers, Wallin Lecture: No. 14). 16p. 1978. pap. 1.00 (*0-910182-37-X*) Augustana Coll.

Race & Slavery in the Middle East: A Historical Enquiry. Bernard Lewis. (Illus.). 194p. 1992. pap. 10.95 (*0-19-505326-5*) OUP.

Race & Slavery in the Middle East: An Historical Enquiry. Bernard Lewis. (Illus.). 200p. 1990. 30.00 (*0-19-506283-3*) OUP.

***Race & State: The Collected Works of Eric Voegelin, Vol. 2.** Ed. by Klaus Vondung. Tr. by Ruth Hein. LC 97-19444. 272p. 1997. text ed. 35.00 (*0-8071-1842-7*) La State U Pr.

Race & Sterilization & Eugenics: A Nazi Reply to the Pope. 1991. lib. bdg. 67.96 (*0-8490-4425-1*) Gordon Pr.

Race & the City: Work, Community, & Protest in Cincinnati, 1820-1970. Ed. by Henry L. Taylor, Jr. LC 92-37088. (Greater Cincinnati Bicentennial History Ser.). 336p. (C). 1993. text ed. 44.95 (*0-252-01986-5*) U of Ill Pr.

***Race & the Construction of Modern American Nationalism.** Rennie Childress. Ed. by William Cain. (Wellesley Studies in Critical Theory, Literary History & Culture). 300p. 1998. text ed. 45.00 (*0-8153-2016-7*) Garland.

Race & the Decline of Class in American Politics. Robert Huckfeldt & Carol W. Kohfeld. LC 88-26109. 224p. 1989. text ed. 27.50 (*0-252-01600-9*) U of Ill Pr.

Race & the Education of Desire: Foucault's History of Sexuality & the Colonial Order of Things. Ann L. Stoler. LC 95-14487. 248p. 1995. text ed. 45.95 (*0-8223-1678-1*); pap. text ed. 15.95 (*0-8223-1690-0*) Duke.

Race & the Enlightenment: A Reader. Emmanuel C. Eze. 200p. (C). Date not set. 49.95 (*0-631-20136-X*); pap. 19.95 (*0-631-20137-8*) Blackwell Pubs.

Race & the Incidence of Environmental Hazards: A Time for Discourse. Ed. by Bunyan Bryant & Paul Mohai. 251p. (C). 1992. pap. text ed. 30.00 (*0-8133-8513-X*) Westview.

Race & the Jury: Racial Disenfranchisement & the Search for Justice. H. Fukurai et al. (Crime & Justice Ser.). (Illus.). 266p. 1992. 37.50 (*0-306-44144-6*, Plenum Pr) Plenum.

Race & the Naming of the White House. David L. Hancock. 90p. (Orig.). 1992. pap. 6.95 (*1-56411-046-X*) Untd Bros & Sis.

Race & the Rise of the Republican Party, 1848-1865. James D. Bilotta. LC 91-35924. (American University Studies: History: Ser. IX, Vols. 123). 524p. (C). 1992. text ed. 75.95 (*0-8204-1762-9*) P Lang Pubng.

Race & the Runner see To Be a Doctor

Race & the Shaping of Twentieth-Century Atlanta. Ronald H. Bayor. LC 95-39552. (Fred W. Morrison Series in Southern Studies). (Illus.). 380p. (C). 1996. 29.95 (*0-8078-2270-1*) U of NC Pr.

Race & the South: Two Studies, 1914-1922, 2 bks. Lily H. Hammond. Incl. In Black & White. LC 72-38448. 1972. (*0-318-50877-X*); In the Vanguard of a Race. LC 72-38448. 1972. (*0-318-50878-8*); LC 72-38448. (Religion in America, Ser. 2). 486p. 1975. reprint ed. 35.95 (*0-405-04067-9*) Ayer.

***Race & the Subject of Masculinities.** Ed. by Harry Stecopoulos & Michael Uebel. LC 96-49942. (New Americanists Ser.). (Illus.). 448p. 1997. pap. text ed. 18.95 (*0-8223-1966-7*); lib. bdg. 54.95 (*0-8223-1958-6*) Duke.

Race as a Revolutionary Idea: Physical Race, Spiritual Race, Soul Race. 1991. lib. bdg. 74.00 (*0-8490-4433-2*) Gordon Pr.

Race at Bay: New York Times Editorials on the "Indian Problem," 1860-1900. Robert G. Hays. LC 96-22191. 304p. (C). 1997. 39.95 (*0-8093-2067-3*) S Ill U Pr.

Race Bomb. Paul R. Ehrlich. 1980. write for info. (*0-394-59581-5*) Random.

Race, Campaign Politics, & the Realignment in the South. James M. Glaser. LC 95-32636. 1996. write for info. (*0-300-06398-9*) Yale U Pr.

Race Car. (Mighty Machines Ser.). 24p. (J). (gr. k-3). 1996. 9.95 (*0-7894-0574-1*) DK Pub Inc.

Race Car Aerodynamics: Designing for Speed. Joseph Katz. LC 95-34326. 1995. write for info. (*0-8376-0142-8*) Bentley.

***Race Car Chassis Design & Tuning.** Forbes Aird. LC 97-14012. (PowerPro Ser.). (Illus.). 160p. 1997. pap. 19.95 (*0-7603-0283-9*) Motorbooks Intl.

Race Car Engineering & Mechanics. Paul Van Valkenburg. (Illus.). 176p. 1992. pap. 16.95 (*1-55788-064-6*, HP Books) Berkley Pub.

Race Car Engineering & Mechanics. 2nd ed. Paul Van Valkenburgh. (Illus.). 176p. (C). 1986. pap. 18.95 (*0-9617425-0-X*) Van Valkenburgh.

Race Car Flashback: A Celebration of America's Affair with Auto Racing. John Gunnell. LC 94-77499. (Illus.). 304p. 1994. pap. 19.95 (*0-87341-309-1*, RC01) Krause Pubns.

Race Car Graphics - The Professional Touch. Gary Smith. (Illus.). 64p. (Orig.). 1979. pap. text ed. 10.95 (*0-936834-18-8*) S S Autosports.

***Race Car Legends, 12 bks.** (Illus.). (J). (gr. 3 up). 179.40 (*0-7910-3175-6*) Chelsea Hse.

Race Car Vehicle Dynamics. William F. Milliken & Douglas L. Milliken. (Illus.). 922p. 1994. 85.00 (*1-56091-526-9*, R146) Soc Auto Engineers.

***Race Card: White Guilt, Black Resentment.** Peter Collier & David Horowitz. LC 96-52393. 240p. 1997. boxed 24.00 (*0-7615-0942-9*) Prima Pub.

Race Cars. Sallie Stephenson. (Cruisin' Ser.). 48p. (J). (gr. 3-4). 1991. lib. bdg. 17.80 (*1-56065-068-0*) Capstone Pr.

***Race Cars.** Sallie Stephenson. (Cruisin' Ser.). (Illus.). 48p. (J). (gr. 3-6). 1991. 18.40 (*0-516-35068-4*) Childrens.

Race Cars. rev. ed. Jeff Savage. (Rollin' Ser.). 48p. (J). (gr. 3-9). 1996. lib. bdg. 17.80 (*1-56065-368-X*) Capstone Pr.

Race Cars & Roadsters. (Pop-Out & Drive Away Ser.). (J). 1996. 9.95 (*0-614-15613-0*) DK Pub Inc.

Race, Change & Urban Society. Ed. by Peter Orleans & William R. Ellis, Jr. LC 70-127992. (Urban Affairs Annual Reviews Ser.: Vol. 5). 640p. reprint ed. pap. 180.00 (*0-317-08723-1*, 2021939) Bks Demand.

Race, Class, & Community in Southern Labor History. Ed. by Gary M Fink & Merl E. Reed. LC 93-32301. 320p. 1994. text ed. 39.95 (*0-8173-0719-2*) U of Ala Pr.

Race, Class & Conservatism. Thomas D. Boston. LC 88-982. 192p. (C). 1988. pap. 19.95 (*0-04-330369-2*) Routledge Chapman & Hall.

Race, Class & Conservatism. Thomas D. Boston. 1988. 34.95 (*0-04-330368-4*) Routledge Chapman & Hall.

Race, Class, & Culture: A Study in Afro-American Mass Opinion. Robert C. Smith & Richard Seltzer. LC 91-8824. (SUNY Series in Afro-American Studies). 203p. (C). 1992. text ed. 57.50 (*0-7914-0945-7*); pap. text ed. 18.95 (*0-7914-0946-5*) State U NY Pr.

Race, Class, & Education: The Politics of Second Generation Discrimination. Kenneth J. Meier et al. LC 89-40262. 240p. (Orig.). (C). 1990. pap. text ed. 15.95 (*0-299-12214-X*) U of Wis Pr.

***Race Class & Gender.** 4th ed. Rothenberg. Date not set. pap. text ed. write for info. (*0-312-17961-8*) St Martin.

Race, Class, & Gender: An Anthology. Margaret L. Andersen & Patricia H. Collins. 518p. (C). 1992. pap. 24.95 (*0-534-13566-8*) Wadsworth Pub.

Race, Class, & Gender: An Anthology. 2nd ed. Margaret L. Andersen & Patricia H. Collins. LC 94-19800. 640p. 1995. pap. 31.95 (*0-534-24768-7*) Wadsworth Pub.

Race, Class, & Gender: An Anthology. 2nd ed. Margaret L. Anderson & Patricia H. Collins. 1995. teacher ed. write for info. (*0-534-24770-9*) Brooks-Cole.

***Race, Class & Gender: An Anthology.** 3rd ed. Andersen & Hill. (Sociology Ser.). (C). 1998. pap. 31.95 (*0-534-52879-1*) Wadsworth Pub.

Race, Class & Gender: Common Bonds, Different Voices. Doris Y. Wilkinson. (Gender & Society Readers Ser.). 384p. (C). 1996. 48.00 (*0-8039-7056-0*); pap. 24.95 (*0-8039-7057-9*) Sage.

Race, Class & Gender in a Diverse Society. Kendall. 544p. 1996. pap. 38.00 (*0-205-19828-7*) Allyn.

Race, Class & Gender in Nineteenth-Century Culture. Ed. by Maryanne C. Horowitz. (Library of the History of Ideas: No. III). 335p. 1991. 55.00 (*1-878822-02-0*) Univ Rochester Pr.

Race, Class, & Gender in the United States. 2nd ed. Paula S. Rothenberg. LC 90-63537. 416p. (C). 1992. pap. text ed. 19.00 (*0-312-05667-2*) St Martin.

Race, Class, & Gender in the United States. 3rd ed. Paula S. Rothenberg. 528p. 1994. pap. text ed. 22.00 (*0-312-09652-6*) St Martin.

Race, Class, & Gender in the United States: An Integrated Study. 2nd ed. Paula S. Rothenberg. 463p. (C). 1992. text ed. 45.00 (*0-312-08578-8*) St Martin.

***Race, Class & Gender in the United States: An Integrated Study.** 4th ed. Paula S. Rothenberg. 1997. 39.95 (*0-312-17429-2*) St Martin.

Race, Class & Political Consciousness. John Leggett. 243p. 1972. pap. 11.95 (*0-87073-257-9*) Schenkman Bks Inc.

Race, Class, & Political Consciousness. John Leggett. 243p. 1972. boxed 34.95 (*0-87073-256-0*) Transaction Pubs.

Race, Class & Political Symbols: Rastafari & Reggae in Jamaican Politics. Anita M. Waters. 224p. 1989. pap. 21.95 (*0-88738-632-6*) Transaction Pubs.

Race, Class, & Politics in Southern History: Essays in Honor of Robert F. Durden. Ed. by Jeffrey J. Crow et al. LC 89-30172. 297p. 1990. text ed. 37.50 (*0-8071-1512-6*) La State U Pr.

Race, Class, & Power in Brazil. Ed. by Pierre-Michel Fontaine. (Special Publications: Vol. 7). 160p. 1985. pap. 10.95 (*0-934934-23-1*) CAAS Pubns.

Race Class & the Apartheid State. Harold Wolpe. LC 89-81237. (UNESCO Apartheid & Society Ser.). 130p. (C). 1990. 29.95 (*0-86543-141-8*); pap. 9.95 (*0-86543-142-6*) Africa World.

Race, Class, & the Changing Division of Labour under Apartheid. Owen Crankshaw. 240p. (C). 1994. text ed. 69.95 (*0-415-14613-5*) Routledge.

Race (Colombia) Reading Level 2. (Fitting In Ser.). 1993. 2.95 (*0-88336-995-8*); audio 6.95 (*0-88336-771-8*) New Readers.

Race, Color, & the Young Child. John E. Williams & J. Kenneth Morland. LC 76-812. 374p. reprint ed. pap. 106.60 (*0-8357-4416-7*, 2037236) Bks Demand.

Race Conflict in New Zealand, 1814-1865. Harold G. Miller. LC 81-20183. (Illus.). xxvii, 328p. 1982. reprint ed. text ed. 52.50 (*0-313-23443-4*, MIRC, Greenwood Pr) Greenwood.

Race Consciousness: African-American Studies for the New Century. Ed. by Judith J. Fossett & Jeffrey A. Tucker. 268p. (C). 1997. 50.00 (*0-8147-4227-0*); pap. 18.95 (*0-8147-4228-9*) NYU Pr.

Race Contacts & Interracial Relations. Alain L. Locke. Ed. by Jeffrey Stewart. LC 91-43415. 114p. 1992. 22.95 (*0-88258-137-6*); pap. 14.95 (*0-88258-158-9*) Howard U Pr.

Race, Crime & Justice. Barbara A. Hudson. (International Library of Criminology, Criminal Justice & Penology). (Illus.). 450p. 1996. text ed. 129.95 (*1-85521-660-4*, Pub. by Dartmth Pub UK) Ashgate Pub Co.

***Race, Crime & the Criminal Justice System: A Bibliography.** Ed. & Compiled by Joan Nordquist. (Contemporary Social Issues: Vol. 45). 72p. (Orig.). 1997. pap. 15.00 (*0-937855-88-X*) Ref Rsch Serv.

Race, Crime, & the Law. Randall Kennedy. LC 96-46534. 624p. 1997. 30.00 (*0-679-43881-5*) Random.

Race Crossing in Jamaica. Charles B. Davenport. LC 77-106833. 516p. 1970. reprint ed. text ed. 65.00 (*0-8371-3455-2*, DRC&, Greenwood Pr) Greenwood.

Race, Culture, & Counselling. Colin Lago & Joyce Thompson. LC 95-24920. 192p. 1996. 79.00 (*0-335-19295-5*, Open Univ Pr); pap. 24.95 (*0-335-19294-7*, Open Univ Pr) Taylor & Francis.

Race, Culture & Difference. James Donald & Ali Rattansi. 336p. (C). 1992. text ed. 59.95 (*0-8039-8579-7*); pap. text ed. 21.95 (*0-8039-8580-0*) Sage.

Race, Culture, & Evolution: Essays in the History of Anthropology. George W. Stocking, Jr. LC 81-23154. (Phoenix Ser.). xviii, 408p. 1982. pap. text ed. 19.95 (*0-226-77494-5*) U Ch Pr.

Race, Culture, & Mental Disorder. Philip Rack. 300p. 1982. 33.00 (*0-422-78160-6*, NO. 3801, Pub. by Tavistock UK) Routledge Chapman & Hall.

An Asterisk (*) at the beginning of an entry indicates that the title is appearing in BIP for the first time.

R

Race, Culture & Portuguese Colonialism in Cabo Verde. Deirdre Meintel. (Foreign & Comparative Studies Program, African Ser.: No. 41). (Orig.). 1984. pap. text ed. 12.50 (*0-915984-66-0*) Syracuse U Foreign Comp.

Race, Culture, & the City: A Pedagogy for Black Urban Struggle. Stephen N. Haymes. LC 94-11213. (SUNY Series, Teacher Empowerment & School Reform). 185p. (C). 1995. text ed. 39.50 (*0-7914-2383-2*); pap. text ed. 12.95 (*0-7914-2384-0*) State U NY Pr.

Race Decadence: An Examination of the Causes of Racial Degeneration in the United States. William S. Sadler. 1973. 75.00 (*0-87968-343-0*) Gordon Pr.

Race des Hommes, L'Empire et la Trappe. Jacques Audiberti. 224p. (FRE.). 1968. pap. 12.95 (*0-7859-0366-6*, F83890) Fr & Eur.

Race Differences. Otto Klineberg. LC 74-5777. 367p. 1974. reprint ed. text ed. 59.75 (*0-8371-7519-4*, KLRD, Greenwood Pr) Greenwood.

Race, Discourse & Labourism. Caroline Knowles. LC 92-4311. (International Library of Sociology). 192p. (C). (gr. 13). 1992. text ed. 89.95 (*0-415-05012-X*, A9578) Routledge.

Race, Discourse & Power in France. Maxim Silverman. (Research in Ethnic Relations Ser.). 137p. 1991. text ed. 51.95 (*1-85628-103-5*, Pub. by Avebury Pub UK) Ashgate Pub Co.

Race, Discourse, & the Origin of the Americas: A New World View. Ed. by Vera L. Hyatt & Rex Nettleford. (Illus.). 448p. 1995. text ed. 42.00 (*1-56098-507-0*) Smithsonian.

***Race Discrimination in Public Higher Education: Interpreting Federal Civil Rights Enforcement, 1964-1996.** John B. Williams. LC 97-5595. 1997. text ed. write for info. (*0-275-95983-X*, Praeger Pubs); pap. text ed. write for info. (*0-275-95984-8*, Praeger Pubs) Greenwood.

Race Distinctions in American Law. G. T. Stephenson. 1977. lib. bdg. 69.95 (*0-8490-2496-X*) Gordon Pr.

Race Distinctions in American Law. Gilbert T. Stephenson. LC 71-89445. (Black Heritage Library Collection). 1977. 27.95 (*0-8369-8656-3*) Ayer.

Race Distinctions in American Law. Gilbert T. Stephenson. LC 70-99889. reprint ed. 31.50 (*0-404-00215-3*) AMS Pr.

Race Distinctions in American Law. Gilbert T. Stephenson. LC 76-84694. xiv, 388p. 1970. reprint ed. text ed. 52.50 (*0-8371-1669-4*, STR&, Negro U Pr) Greenwood.

Race, Economics, & Corporate America. John W. Work. LC 84-1233. 324p. 1984. lib. bdg. 40.00 (*0-8420-2217-1*) Scholarly Res Inc.

Race, Education, & Work. David Drew. 232p. 1995. 59.95 (*1-85972-111-7*, Pub. by Avebury Pub UK) Ashgate Pub Co.

Race, Equality & Planning: Policies & Procedures. Huw Thomas & Vijay Krishnarayan. LC 94-231162. 200p. 1994. 59.95 (*1-85628-486-7*, Pub. by Avebury Pub UK) Ashgate Pub Co.

***Race Equality in Health Care.** Baxter. 1997. pap. text ed. 35.00 (*0-7020-2031-1*, Bailliere-Tindall) Saunders.

Race et Histoire. Claude Levi-Strauss. (FRE.). 1987. pap. 12.95 (*0-7859-3970-9*) Fr & Eur.

Race et Histoire. Claude Levi-Strauss. (Folio Essais Ser.: No. 58). 127p. (FRE.). 1987. pap. 9.95 (*2-07-032413-3*) Schoenhof.

Race, Ethnicity, & Applied Bioanthropology. Ed. by Claire C. Gordon. LC 93-35791. (NAPA Bulletin Ser.: Vol. 13). 1993. write for info. (*0-913167-59-2*) Am Anthro Assn.

Race, Ethnicity, & Class: Forging the Plural Society in Latin America & the Caribbean. unabridged ed. Franklin W. Knight. LC 96-76628. (Charles Edmondson Historical Lectures: No. 17). 51p. (Orig.). 1996. pap. 5.95 (*0-918954-64-9*) Baylor Univ Pr.

Race, Ethnicity, & Class in American Social Thought, 1865-1919. Glenn C. Altschuler. Ed. by John H. Franklin & A. S. Eisenstadt. LC 81-173970. (American History Ser.). 168p. (C). 1982. pap. text ed. write for info. (*0-88295-808-9*) Harlan Davidson.

Race, Ethnicity, & Entrepreneurship in Urban America. Ivan H. Light & Carolyn Rosenstein. LC 95-3418. (Sociology & Economics Ser.). 266p. 1995. pap. text ed. 24.95 (*0-202-30506-6*); lib. bdg. 49.95 (*0-202-30505-8*) Aldine de Gruyter.

***Race, Ethnicity & Gender: A Global Perspective.** Oliner & Gay. 464p. (C). 1997. 42.44 (*0-7872-3678-0*) Kendall-Hunt.

Race, Ethnicity, & Gender in Early Twentieth-Century American Socialism. Ed. by Sally M. Miller. LC 95-40447. (Garland Reference Library of Social Science: Vol. 880). 303p. 1996. text ed. 60.00 (*0-8153-1163-X*) Garland.

Race, Ethnicity, & Gender in the United States: Inequality, Group Conflict, & Power. Joseph F. Healey. LC 96-15614. (Illus.). 368p. (Orig.). (C). 1996. pap. 39.95 (*0-7619-8520-4*) Pine Forge.

Race, Ethnicity, & Minority Housing in the United States. Ed. by Jamshid A. Momeni. LC 86-9971. (Contributions in Ethnic Studies: No. 16). (Illus.). 249p. 1986. text ed. 55.00 (*0-313-24848-6*, MRY/, Greenwood Pr) Greenwood.

Race, Ethnicity & Multiculturalism: Issues in Domination, Resistance & Diversity. Maulana Karenga. (C). 1994. text ed. 39.95 (*0-943412-17-X*) Univ Sankore Pr.

***Race, Ethnicity, & Multiculturalism: Policy & Practice.** Curators of University of Missouri Staff. Ed. by Peter Hall. LC 96-40991. (Missouri Symposium on Research & Educational Policy Ser.: Vol. 1). (Illus.). 242p. 1997. pap. text ed. 18.95 (*0-8153-2442-1*) Garland.

***Race, Ethnicity, & Multiculturalism: Policy & Practice.** Ed. by Peter Hall. LC 96-40991. (Missouri Symposium on Research & Educational Policy Ser.: Vol. 1). (Illus.). 242p. 1997. text ed. 42.00 (*0-8153-2011-6*) Garland.

Race, Ethnicity & Nation: International Perspectives on Social Conflict. Ed. by Peter Ratcliffe. LC 94-12567. 1994. 75.00 (*1-85728-099-7*, Pub. by UCL Pr UK) Taylor & Francis.

***Race, Ethnicity & National Origin.** Ed. by Ferrante. LC 97-17604. (C). 1998. text ed. write for info. (*0-321-01133-3*) Addson-Wesley Educ.

Race, Ethnicity, & Participation in the Arts: Patterns of Participation by Hispanics, Whites, & African-Americans in Selected Activities from the 1982 & 1985 Surveys of Public Participation in the Arts. Paul DiMaggio & Francie Ostrower. LC 92-31145. (Research Division Report, National Endowment for the Arts Ser.: No. 25). 112p. 1992. pap. text ed. 11.95 (*0-929765-03-6*) Seven Locks Pr.

Race, Ethnicity, & Power in the Renaissance. Ed. by Joyce G. MacDonald. LC 96-14655. (Illus.). 192p. 1997. 34.50 (*0-8386-3656-X*) Fairleigh Dickinson.

Race, Ethnicity, & Power in the Renaissance. Joyce G. MacDonald. 1996. write for info. (*0-318-61237-2*) Fairleigh Dickinson.

Race, Ethnicity & Self: Identity in Multicultural Perspective. Ed. by Elizabeth P. Salett & Diane R. Koslow. 224p. (Orig.). 1994. pap. 19.95 (*1-885077-20-3*) NMCI Pubns.

Race, Ethnicity, & Society. Benjamin B. Ringer & Elinor R. Lawless. 256p. (C). 1989. pap. 14.95 (*0-415-90035-2*, A1591, Routledge NY); text ed. 35.00 (*0-415-90034-4*, A1587, Routledge NY) Routledge.

Race, Ethnicity & Socioeconomic Status: A Theoretical Analysis of Their Interrelationship. Charles V. Willie. LC 83-80157. 279p. (Orig.). 1983. lib. bdg. 38.95 (*0-930390-48-2*) Gen Hall.

Race, Ethnicity, & Urbanization: Selected Essays. Howard N. Rabinowitz. 376p. 1993. text ed. 42.50 (*0-8262-0930-0*) U of Mo Pr.

Race, Ethnicity, Gender & Class: The Sociology of Group Conflict & Change. Joseph F. Healey. 1995. 49.95 (*0-8039-9027-8*) Pine Forge.

***Race, Evolution, & Behavior: A Life History Perspective.** LC 96-39197. 1996. 39.95 (*1-56000-320-0*) Transaction Pubs.

***Race, Evolution, & Behavior: A Life History Perspective.** LC 96-39197. 1996. pap. 24.95 (*1-56000-943-8*) Transaction Pubs.

Race, Evolution, & Behavior: A Life History Perspective. J. Phillipe Rushton. LC 93-21282. 398p. (C). 1994. 39.95 (*1-56000-146-1*) Transaction Pubs.

Race Fans Reference: Understanding Winston Cup Racing. William Burt. 1995. pap. 29.95 (*0-9648129-0-8*) Alastra Corp.

Race First: The Ideological & Organizational Struggles of Marcus Garvey & the Universal Negro Improvement Association. Tony Martin. (New Marcus Garvey Library: No. 8). (Illus.). x, 421p. (Orig.). (C). 1986. reprint ed. pap. text ed. 12.95 (*0-912469-23-4*) Majority Pr.

Race, Folk, Individuality & Mankind. Albert Steffen. Tr. by Arvia MacKaye. 30p. 1982. pap. 3.50 (*0-932776-04-3*) Adonis Pr.

Race for a Change in Continuing & Higher Education. Mal Leicester. LC 93-1895. (Cutting Edge Ser.). 1993. 79.00 (*0-335-09768-5*, Open Univ Pr); pap. 29.00 (*0-335-09767-7*, Open Univ Pr) Taylor & Francis.

***Race for Autumn's Glory.** Doris Elaine Fell. LC 96-53869. (Seasons of Intrigue Ser.: 6). 272p. (Orig.). 1997. pap. 9.99 (*0-89107-926-2*) Crossway Bks.

Race for Freedom. Lois W. Johnson. (Riverboat Adventures Ser.: Vol. 2). 192p. (Orig.). (J). (gr. 3-8). 1996. pap. 5.99 (*1-55661-352-0*, Hampshire MN) Bethany Hse.

Race for Justice: Mumia Abu-Jamal's Fight Against the Death Penalty. Leonard Weinglass & Defense Team Staff. LC 95-34216. 272p. (Orig.). 1995. 29.95 (*1-56751-071-X*); pap. 15.00 (*1-56751-070-1*) Common Courage.

Race for Land. Esther L. Vogt. LC 91-36787. 112p. (Orig.). (J). (gr. 4-7). 1992. pap. 5.99 (*0-8361-3575-X*) Herald Pr.

Race for Life: From Cancer to the Ironman. Ruth Heidrich. (Illus.). 200p. (Orig.). 1990. pap. 14.95 (*0-9604190-1-2*) Hawaii Hlth Pubs.

Race for Life: The Joel Sonnenberg Story. Janet Sonnenberg. 1983. 9.95 (*0-310-25930-4*) Phoenix Soc.

Race for Life Cookbook. Ruth Heidrich. 102p. 1994. pap. 14.95 (*1-960419-01-3*) Hawaii Hlth Pubs.

***Race for Love.** large type ed. Shirely Allen. (Ulverscroft Large Print Ser.). 544p. 1997. 27.50 (*0-7089-3767-5*) Ulverscroft.

Race for Modernization: Britain & Germany Since the Industrial Revolution. Ed. by Adlof Birke et al. (Prince Albert Studies: Vol. 6). 155p. 1988. 42.00 (*3-598-21406-5*) K G Saur.

Race for Safe Schools: A Staff Development Curriculum. Miriam S. McLaughlin & Sandra P. Hazouri. Ed. by Don L. Sorenson. LC 94-70339. (Illus.). 144p. 1994. teacher ed. 49.95 (*0-932796-59-1*) Ed Media Corp.

***Race for Success.** George Fraser. Date not set. write for info. (*0-688-15248-1*) Morrow.

Race for the Championship. Jane Kidd & John Oaksey. 96p. 1990. 32.00 (*0-85131-325-6*, Pub. by J A Allen & Co UK) St Mut.

Race for the Park Street Treasure. Sigmund Brouwer. (Accidental Detective Ser.: Vol. 7). 132p. (J). (gr. 3-7). 1995. pap. 5.99 (*1-56476-376-5*, 6-3376, Victor Bks) Chariot Victor.

Race for the Part Street Treasure. Sigmund Brouwer. (Accidental Detective Ser.). 132p. (J). (gr. 3-7). 1991. pap. 4.99 (*0-89693-859-X*) SP Pubns.

Race for the Planet: The U. S. & the New World Order. Gerald Horne. 112p. (C). 1994. per. 26.10 (*0-8403-9389-X*) Kendall-Hunt.

Race for the Presidency: The Media & the Nominating Process. Ed. by James D. Barber. LC 78-111878. (American Assembly Guides Ser.). 1978. 11.95 (*0-13-750141-2*) Am Assembly.

Race for Tomorrow. Elaine Barbieri. (Orig.). 1993. mass mkt. 3.99 (*0-373-83243-5*, 1-83243-5) Harlequin Bks.

Race Forever. large type ed. Raymond A. Montgomery. (Choose Your Own Adventure Ser.). 116p. (J). (gr. 3-7). 1987. reprint ed. 8.95 (*0-942545-12-5*); reprint ed. lib. bdg. 9.95 (*0-942545-17-6*) Grey Castle.

Race Gallery. Marek Kohn. 1996. 35.00 (*0-224-03958-X*, Pub. by Jonathan Cape UK) Trafalgar.

Race, Gender, & Class. Larry Davis & Enola Proctor. 368p. (C). 1989. pap. text ed. 50.00 (*0-13-750118-8*) P-H.

Race, Gender, & Class in Criminology: The Intersection. Ed. by Martin D. Schwartz et al. LC 96-17322. (Current Issues in Criminal Justice Ser.: Vol. 19). (Illus.). 328p. 1996. text ed. 55.00 (*0-8153-2136-8*, SS1072) Garland.

Race, Gender, & Desire: Narrative Strategies in the Fiction Of Toni Cade Bambara, Toni Morrison & Alice Walker. Elliott Butler-Evans. 232p. 1991. pap. 19.95 (*0-87722-831-0*) Temple U Pr.

Race, Gender, & Health. Marcia Bayne-Smith. LC 95-35483. (Series on Race & Ethnic Relations: Vol. 15). (Illus.). 240p. 1995. 52.00 (*0-8039-5504-9*); pap. 24.00 (*0-8039-5505-7*) Sage.

Race, Gender, & Power in America: The Legacy of the Hill-Thomas Hearings. Ed. by Anita F. Hill & Emma C. Jordan. 302p. 1995. 25.00 (*0-19-508774-7*) OUP.

Race, Gender, & Rank: Early Modern Ideas of Humanity. Ed. by Maryanne C. Horowitz. LC 92-23111. (Library of the History of Ideas: Vol. 8). 421p. (C). 1992. 65.00 (*1-878822-15-2*) Univ Rochester Pr.

Race, Gender & the Education of Teachers. Ed. by Iram Siraj-Blatchford. LC 92-29884. (Gender & Education Ser.). 1993. 27.50 (*0-335-19017-0*, Open Univ Pr) Taylor & Francis.

Race, Gender, & Work: A Multi-Cultural Economic History of Women in the United States. Teresa Amott & Julie A. Mattaei. 420p. (Orig.). 1991. 38.95 (*0-921689-91-8*, Pub. by Black Rose Bks CN); pap. 19.95 (*0-921689-90-X*, Pub. by Black Rose Bks CN) Consort Bk Sales.

Race, Gender, & Work: A Multicultural Economic History of Women in the United States. rev. ed. Teresa Amott & Julie A. Mattaei. LC 96-10382. 444p. 1996. 40.00 (*0-89608-538-4*) South End Pr.

Race, Gender & Work: A Multicultural Economic History of Women in the United States. rev. ed. Teresa Amott & Julia A. Mattaei. 444p. 1996. pap. 21.00 (*0-89608-537-6*) South End Pr.

Race Horse. Bob Buess. 1978. pap. 2.50 (*0-934244-08-1*) Sweeter Than Honey.

Race Horses at Risk: Overnutrition, Drugs, Breakdowns. Lennart Krook & George A. Maylin. (Illus.). 205p. 1989. 49.95 (*0-9621868-0-5*) L Krook G A Maylin.

Race Hygiene & National Efficiency: The Eugenics of Wilhelm Schallmayer. Sheila F. Weiss. LC 86-24895. (Illus.). 244p. 1987. 48.00 (*0-520-05823-2*) U CA Pr.

Race, I. Q. & Jensen. James R. Flynn. 320p. 1980. 32.50 (*0-7100-0651-9*, RKP) Routledge.

Race, Identity & Representation in Education. Ed. by Cameron McCarthy & Warren Crichlow. (Critical Social Thought Ser.). 416p. (C). (gr. 13). 1993. pap. 17.95 (*0-415-90558-3*, A6869, Routledge NY); text ed. 62.95 (*0-415-90557-5*, A6865, Routledge NY) Routledge.

Race in America: The Struggle for Equality. Ed. by Herbert Hill & James E. Jones, Jr. LC 92-37501. 476p. (Orig.). (C). 1993. pap. 17.95 (*0-299-13424-5*) U of Wis Pr.

Race in Ancient Egypt & the Old Testament. Archibald H. Sayce. 160p. 1993. pap. 15.00 (*1-878465-08-2*) Scott-Townsend Pubs.

Race in Britain. Christopher T. Husbands. (Conflict & Change in Britain - A New Audit Ser.). 240p. (C). pap. 19.95 (*0-485-80104-3*, Pub. by Athlone Pr UK); text ed. 60.00 (*0-485-80004-7*, Pub. by Athlone Pr UK) Humanities.

Race in Britain Today. Richard Skellington & Paulette Morris. (Informal Open University Mini-Series on Race, Education & Society). (Illus.). 160p. (C). 1992. 49.95 (*0-8039-8689-0*); pap. 18.95 (*0-8039-8690-4*) Sage.

Race in North America: Origins & Evolution of a Worldview. Audrey Smedley. 340p. (C). 1993. pap. text ed. 24.00 (*0-8133-0622-1*) Westview.

Race in Post White America. Reed. 1996. write for info. (*0-201-62464-8*) Addison-Wesley.

***Race in Space: The Representation of Ethnicity in Star Trek & Star Trek, the Next Generation.** Michael C. Pounds. LC 97-9554. 1997. write for info. (*0-8108-3322-0*) Scarecrow.

***Race in the Global Era: African Americans at the Millenium.** Clarence Lusane. 228p. (Orig.). 1997. pap. 15.00 (*0-89608-573-2*) South End Pr.

***Race in the Global Era: African Americans at the Millenium.** Clarence Lusane. 228p. 1997. 40.00 (*0-89608-574-0*) South End Pr.

***Race in the Hood: Conflict & Violence among Urban Youth.** Howard Pinderhughes. LC 97-13526. 1997. write for info. (*0-8166-2918-8*); pap. write for info. (*0-8166-2919-6*) U of Minn Pr.

Race in the Making: Cognition, Culture, & the Child's Construction of Human Kinds. Lawrence A. Hirschfeld. LC 95-40230. (Learning, Development, & Conceptual Change Ser.). (Illus.). 256p. (C). 1996. 35.00 (*0-262-08247-0*, Bradford Bks) MIT Pr.

Race-ing Justice, En-Gendering Power: Essays on Anita Hill, Clarence Thomas, & the Construction of Social Reality. Intro. by Toni Morrison. LC 92-54119. 512p. (Orig.). 1992. pap. 15.00 (*0-679-74145-3*) Pantheon.

***Race, Intelligence & Bias in Academe.** 2nd rev. ed. Roger Pearson. Orig. Title: Race, Intelligence & Bias in Academe. (Illus.). 340p. 1997. pap. 28.00 (*1-878465-23-6*) Scott-Townsend Pubs.

Race, Intelligence & Bias in Academe see Race, Intelligence & Bias in Academe

Race Is a Nice Thing to Have: A Guide to Being a White Person or Understanding the White Persons in Your Life. Janet E. Helms. 108p. 1992. pap. write for info. (*0-9633036-0-0*, CC102) Content Comms.

Race Is a Nice Thing to Have: A Guide to Being a White Person or Understanding the White Persons in Your Life. Janet E. Helms. 1994. audio 11.95 (*0-9633036-2-7*) Content Comms.

Race Is Run One Step at a Time: Every Woman's Guide to Taking Charge of Breast Cancer. Nancy Brinker & Catherine M. Harris. LC 95-24204. 1995. pap. 13.95 (*1-56530-182-X*) Summit TX.

Race, Language & Culture. Franz Boas. LC 81-21998. (Illus.). xx, 648p. (C). 1982. reprint ed. pap. text ed. 22.50 (*0-226-06241-4*) U Ch Pr.

***Race, Law, & Culture: Reflections on Brown vs. Board of Education.** Austin Sarat. 256p. 1997. 45.00 (*0-19-510621-0*); pap. 16.95 (*0-19-510622-9*) OUP.

Race Management Handbook. 1994. pap. text ed. 40.00 (*0-685-71327-X*) US Sail Assn.

***Race, Markets, & Social Outcomes.** Patrick L. Mason & Rhonda M. Williams. LC 97-7145. (Recent Economic Thought Ser.). 1997. lib. bdg. 95.00 (*0-7923-9893-9*) Kluwer Ac.

Race Matters. Cornel West. LC 92-35170. 112p. 1993. 15.00 (*0-8070-0918-0*) Beacon Pr.

Race Matters. Cornel West. 1994. pap. 10.00 (*0-679-74986-1*, Vin) Random.

Race Mixing in Public Schools. Charles V. Willie & Jerome Beker. LC 73-10947. (Special Studies in U. S. Economic, Social & Political Issues). 1973. 29.50 (*0-275-28812-9*) Irvington.

Race, Modernity, Postmodernity: A Look at the History & the Literatures of People of Color since the 1960s. W. Lawrence Hogue. LC 95-49336. 222p. 1996. text ed. 49.50 (*0-7914-3095-2*); pap. text ed. 16.95 (*0-7914-3096-0*) State U NY Pr.

Race, Multiculturalism & the Media: From Mass to Class Communication. rev. ed. Clint C. Wilson, II & Felix Gutierrez. LC 95-13492. Orig. Title: Minorities & Media: Diversity & the End of Mass Communication. 224p. (C). 1995. 45.00 (*0-8039-4628-7*); pap. 19.95 (*0-8039-4629-5*) Sage.

Race, Myth & the News. Christopher P. Campbell. 170p. 1995. text ed. 42.00 (*0-8039-5871-4*); pap. text ed. 19.50 (*0-8039-5872-2*) Sage.

Race, Nation & Class. Etienne Balibar. LC 91-27500. 232p. (C). 1991. pap. text ed. 19.00 (*0-86091-542-5*, A5525, Pub. by Vrso UK) Norton.

Race, Nation & Class. Etienne Balibar. LC 91-27500. 232p. (C). (gr. 13). 1991. text ed. 60.00 (*0-86091-327-9*, A5521, Pub. by Vrso UK) Norton.

Race, Nation, Person: Total Aspects of the Race Problem. LC 70-128291. (Essay Index Reprint Ser.). 1977. 24.95 (*0-8369-2019-8*) Ayer.

Race of Angels: The Genesis of U2. John Waters. 306p. 1996. pap. 17.95 (*1-85702-210-6*, Pub. by Fourth Estate UK) Trafalgar.

***Race of My Life.** Compiled by Sean Magee. (Illus.). 168p. 1997. 40.00 (*0-7472-1259-7*, Pub. by Headline UK) Trafalgar.

Race of Prisoners Admitted To State - Federal Institutions. (Illus.). 50p. (Orig.). (C). 1993. pap. text ed. 20.00 (*1-56806-827-1*) DIANE Pub.

***Race of the Golden Apples.** Claire Martin. (Illus.). 32p. (J). 3.98 (*0-8317-4518-5*) Smithmark.

Race of the Soil: "The Ninth New Hampshire Regiment in the Civil War" William Marvel. (Illus.). 534p. 1988. 35.00 (*0-916107-67-1*) Broadfoot.

Race of Time: Three Lectures on Renaissance Historiography. Herschel C. Baker. LC 66-29031. (Alexander Lectures: No. 1965). 110p. reprint ed. pap. 31.40 (*0-685-23635-8*, 2014122) Bks Demand.

Race of Toad & Deer. Illus. by Maya I. Brooks. LC 94-45919. 32p. (J). (ps-1). 1996. 14.95 (*0-531-09477-4*); lib. bdg. 15.99 (*0-531-08777-8*) Orchard Bks Watts.

Race or Mongrel. Alfred P. Schultz. 1977. lib. bdg. 69.95 (*0-8490-2497-8*) Gordon Pr.

Race or Mongrel: History of the Rise & Fall of the Ancient Races of Earth. Alfred P. Schultz. Ed. by Gerald Grob. LC 76-46103. (Anti-Movements in America Ser.). 1977. reprint ed. lib. bdg. 31.95 (*0-405-09974-6*) Ayer.

Race or Nation: Conflict of Divided Loyalties. Gino Speranza. LC 74-17955. (Italian American Experience Ser.). 284p. 1975. reprint ed. 23.95 (*0-405-06424-1*) Ayer.

Race Orthodoxy in the South & Other Aspects of the Negro Question. Thomas P. Bailey. reprint ed. 27.50 (*0-404-00136-X*) AMS Pr.

Race, Place, & Risk: Black Homicide in Urban America. Harold M. Rose & Paula D. McClain. LC 89-48538. (SUNY Series in Afro-American Studies). 297p. 1990. text ed. 64.50 (*0-7914-0393-9*); pap. text ed. 23.95 (*0-7914-0394-7*) State U NY Pr.

Race, Politics & Culture: Critical Essays on the Radicalism of the 1960s. Ed. by Adolph Reed, Jr. LC 85-27162. (Contributions in Afro-American & African Studies: No. 95). 304p. 1986. text ed. 59.95 (*0-313-24480-4*, RRA/, Greenwood Pr) Greenwood.

An Asterisk (*) at the beginning of an entry indicates that the title is appearing in BIP for the first time.

Race, Politics & Economic Development: Community Perspectives. James Jennings. LC 92-27545. (Haymarket Ser.). 300p. (C). 1992. pap. text ed. 18.00 (*0-86091-589-1*, A9711, Pub. by Vrso UK) Norton.

Race, Politics & Economic Development: Community Perspectives. James Jennings. LC 92-27545. (Haymarket Ser.). 300p. (C). (gr. 13). 1992. text ed. 60.00 (*0-86091-388-0*, A9707, Pub. by Vrso UK) Norton.

Race, Politics, & Governance in the United States. Ed. by Huey L. Perry. LC 96-19925. (Illus.). 240p. 1997. lib. bdg. 49.95 (*0-8130-1456-5*) U Press Fla.

Race, Politics, & Governance in the United States. Ed. by Huey L. Perry. LC 96-19925. (Illus.). 240p. 1997. pap. 21.95 (*0-8130-1481-6*) U Press Fla.

Race, Politics & Social Change. John Solomos & Les Back. 240p. (Orig.). (C). 1995. pap. 19.95 (*0-415-08578-0*, B3577) Routledge.

Race, Politics & Social Change. John Solomos & Les Back. LC 94-35566. 240p. (Orig.). (C). (gr. 13). 1995. text ed. 62.95 (*0-415-08577-2*, B3573) Routledge.

Race, Politics & the White Media: The Jesse Jackson Campaigns. Arnold Gibbons. 162p. (C). 1993. pap. text ed. 22.00 (*0-8191-8977-4*) U Pr of Amer.

Race, Politics & the White Media: The Jesse Jackson Campaigns. Arnold Gibbons. 162p. (C). 1993. lib. bdg. 48.00 (*0-8191-8976-6*) U Pr of Amer.

Race, Poverty, & American Cities. Ed. by John C. Boger & Judith W. Wegner. LC 95-45056. 528p. (C). 1996. pap. text ed. 24.95 (*0-8078-4578-7*) U of NC Pr.

Race, Poverty, & American Cities. Ed. by John C. Boger & Judith W. Wegner. LC 95-45056. 528p. (C). (gr. 13). 1996. lib. bdg. 59.95 (*0-8078-2274-4*) U of NC Pr.

Race, Power & Resistance. Chris Mullard. 256p. 1985. 42.50 (*0-7100-9774-3*, RKP) Routledge.

Race, Power & Social Segmentation in Colonial Society. Brian L. Moore. 320p. 1987. 48.00 (*2-88124-203-0*) Gordon & Breach.

Race, Power, & Social Segmentation in Colonial Society: Plantation Guyana After Slavery 1838-1891, Vol. 4. Brian L. Moore. (Caribbean Studies: Vol. 4). 310, xvip. 1987. text ed. 55.00 (*0-677-21980-6*) Gordon & Breach.

Race Prejudice. Jean Finot. Tr. by Florence Wade-Evans. LC 72-89413. (Black Heritage Library Collection). 1977. 22.95 (*0-8369-8570-2*) Ayer.

Race Prejudice. Jean Finot. Tr. by Florence Wade-Evans. LC 75-100290. 320p. 1970. reprint ed. text ed. 35.00 (*0-8371-2909-5*, FIP&, Greenwood Pr) Greenwood.

Race, Prejudice & the Origins of Slavery in America. Ed. by Raymond Starr & Robert Detweiler. 165p. 1975. pap. text ed. 16.95 (*0-87073-665-5*) Schenkman Bks Inc.

***Race, Prejudice, & the Origins of Slavery in America.** Ed. by Raymond Starr & Robert Detweiler. LC 72-92683. 174p. reprint ed. pap. 49.60 (*0-608-05333-3*, 2065038) Bks Demand.

***Race Pride & the American Identity.** Joseph T. Rhea. LC 97-22046. 1997. 25.00 (*0-674-56681-5*) HUP.

Race Problem in the South. Joseph Le Conte. LC 78-81123. (Black Heritage Library Collection). 1977. 11.95 (*0-8369-8619-9*) Ayer.

Race Questions, Provincialism, & Other American Problems. Josiah Royce. LC 67-23266. (Essay Index Reprint Ser.). 1977. 25.95 (*0-8369-0842-2*) Ayer.

***Race Racism & Psychology: Towards a Reflexive History.** Graham Richards. 392p. (C). 1997. text ed. 79.95 (*0-415-10140-9*) Routledge.

***Race, Racism & Psychology: Towards a Reflexive History.** Graham Richards. 392p. (C). 1997. pap. 24.95 (*0-415-10141-7*) Routledge.

Race, Racism & Rhyme. Greg C. Lawson. (Illus.). (Orig.). 1990. 8.00 (*0-9623750-0-4*) SunLaw Pubns.

Race, Racism & the Death Penalty in the United States. Adalberto Aquirre et al. (Illus.). 130p. (C). 1991. text ed. 29.95 (*0-9628916-5-7*) Vande Vere.

Race, Radicalism, & Reform: Selected Papers of Abram L. Harris. Abram L. Harris. 500p. 1988. 49.95 (*0-88738-210-X*) Transaction Pubs.

Race, Rape, & Lynching: The Red Record of American Literature, 1890-1912. Sandra Gunning. (Race & American Culture Ser.). 208p. (C). 1996. 35.00 (*0-19-509990-7*) OUP.

Race Rebels. Kelley. 1996. pap. 23.00 (*0-02-874124-2*) Free Pr.

Race Rebels: Culture, Politics, & the Black Working Class. Robin D. Kelley. 250p. 1994. 24.95 (*0-02-916706-X*, Free Press) Free Pr.

Race Rebels: Culture, Politics, & the Black Working Class. Robin D. Kelley. (Illus.). 368p. 1996. pap. 17.95 (*0-684-82639-9*) Free Pr.

Race, Redevelopment, & the New Company Town. Daniel J. Monti. LC 89-21829. (SUNY Series in Urban Public Policy). 250p. 1990. text ed. 64.50 (*0-7914-0325-4*); pap. text ed. 21.95 (*0-7914-0326-2*) State U NY Pr.

Race Redistricting in the U.S. House of Representatives. Canon. 1996. lib. bdg. 46.00 (*0-226-09270-4*) U Ch Pr.

Race Redistricting in the U.S. House of Representatives. Canon. 1996. pap. text ed. 17.95 (*0-226-09271-2*) U Ch Pr.

Race, Reform, & Rebellion: The Second Reconstruction in Black America, 1945-1990. rev. ed. Manning Marable. LC 90-19215. 1991. pap. 15.95 (*0-87805-493-6*) U Pr of Miss.

Race, Reform, & Rebellion: The Second Reconstruction in Black America, 1945-1990. 2nd rev. ed. Manning Marable. LC 90-19215. 1991. 37.50 (*0-87805-505-3*) U Pr of Miss.

***Race Reform & Rebellion 2.** Marable. 1997. text ed. 17.95 (*0-333-56433-2*) St Martin.

Race Relations. 5th ed. Kitano. 336p. (C). 1996. text ed. 44.67 (*0-13-011677-7*) P-H.

Race Relations. Ed. by Jitsuichi Masuoka & P. Valien. (New Reprints in Essay & General Literature Index Ser.). 1977. reprint ed. 26.95 (*0-518-10205-X*, 10205) Ayer.

Race Relations: Elements & Social Dynamics. Oliver C. Cox. LC 75-38572. 354p. reprint ed. pap. 100.90 (*0-317-30024-5*, 2025022) Bks Demand.

Race Relations: Opposing Viewpoints. rev. ed. Ed. by Paul A. Winters. LC 95-9016. (Opposing Viewpoints Ser.). (Illus.). 239p. (YA). (gr. 9-12). 1996. pap. text ed. 12.96 (*1-56510-356-4*); lib. bdg. 20.96 (*1-56510-357-2*) Greenhaven.

Race Relations - New Wine & Old Bottles: Creating a Newer Vision. Danielle Levy. Ed. by Diane Parker. LC 92-50878. 200p. 1993. pap. 11.95 (*0-88247-980-6*, 980) R & E Pubs.

Race Relations & American Law. Jack Greenberg. LC 59-11179. 493p. reprint ed. pap. 140.60 (*0-317-26579-2*, 2023967) Bks Demand.

Race Relations & the Race Problem, a Definition & an Analysis. Edgar T. Thompson. (History - United States Ser.). 338p. 1993. reprint ed. lib. bdg. 89.00 (*0-7812-4867-1*) Rprt Serv.

Race Relations & Urban Education. Gajendra K. Verma & Peter D. Pumfrey. 1990. 75.00 (*1-85000-710-1*, Falmer Pr); pap. 35.00 (*1-85000-711-X*, Falmer Pr) Taylor & Francis.

Race Relations in British North America, 1607-1783. Bruce A. Glasrud & Alan M. Smith. LC 81-18824. 368p. 1982. 38.95 (*0-88229-388-5*) Nelson-Hall.

Race Relations in Sociological Theory. John Rex. 180p. (Orig.). (C). 1982. pap. text ed. 13.95 (*0-7100-9299-7*, RKP) Routledge.

Race Relations in the Portuguese Colonial Empire 1415-1825. Charles R. Boxer. LC 85-740. vii, 136p. 1985. reprint ed. text ed. 49.75 (*0-313-24733-1*, BORR, Greenwood Pr) Greenwood.

Race Relations in the Primary School. Cecile Wright. 144p. 1992. pap. 27.50 (*1-85346-142-3*, Pub. by D Fulton UK) Taylor & Francis.

Race Relations in the Urban South, 1865-1890. Howard N. Rabinowitz. LC 96-19848. 1996. pap. 24.95 (*0-8203-1880-9*) U of Ga Pr.

Race Relations in Virginia & Miscegenation in the South: 1776-1860. James H. Johnston. LC 78-87833. 376p. 1970. 37.50 (*0-87023-050-6*) U of Mass Pr.

Race Relations in World Perspective: Papers. Conference on Race Relations in World Perspective, Honolulu, 1954. Ed. by Andrew W. Lind. LC 73-7074. 488p. 1973. reprint ed. text ed. 65.00 (*0-8371-6907-0*, RRWP, Greenwood Pr) Greenwood.

Race Relations Litigation in an Age of Complexity. Stephen L. Wasby. LC 94-47132. (Constitutionalism & Democracy Ser.). 480p. (C). 1995. text ed. 65.00 (*0-8139-1572-4*); pap. text ed. 22.50 (*0-8139-1573-2*) U Pr of Va.

Race Relations on Campus: Stanford Students Speak. John H. Bunzel. (Portable Stanford Bks.). 192p. (Orig.). 1992. pap. 12.95 (*0-916318-49-4*) Stanford Alumni Assn.

Race Relations Rights. Paul Gordon et al. (C). 1988. 21.00 (*0-946088-02-0*, Pub. by NCCL UK) St Mut.

Race Relations Within Western Expansion. Alan J. Levine. LC 95-43772. 176p. 1996. text ed. 49.95 (*0-275-95037-9*, Praeger Pubs) Greenwood.

Race, Religion, & Ethnicity in Disaster Recovery. Robert C. Bolin & Patricia Bolton. (Program on Environment & Behavior Monograph Ser.: No. 42). 400p. (Orig.). (C). 1986. pap. 10.00 (*0-685-28116-7*) Natural Hazards.

Race, Research, & Reason: Social Work Perspectives: Report. Institute on Research Toward Improving Race Relations (1967: Warrenton, VA). Ed. by Roger R. Miller. LC 68-59483. 190p. reprint ed. pap. 54.20 (*0-317-55746-7*, 2029277) Bks Demand.

***Race Resistance & the Ainu of Japan.** Richard M. Siddle. 288p. (C). 1996. text ed. 69.95 (*0-415-13228-2*) Routledge.

***Race, Rights & the Asian American Experience.** Angelo N. Ancheta. LC 97-24855. 224p. 1998. 47.00 (*0-8135-2463-6*); pap. 18.00 (*0-8135-2464-4*) Rutgers U Pr.

***Race, Rights & the Law in the Supreme Court of Canada: Historical Case Studies.** James W. Walker. (Illus.). 448p. 1997. 39.95 (*0-88920-289-3*) Wilfrid Laurier.

Race Riot: Chicago in the Red Summer of 1919. William M. Tuttle, Jr. LC 71-130983. (Illus.). 1972. 8.95 (*0-689-10372-7*, Atheneum S&S) S&S Trade.

Race Riot: Chicago in the Red Summer of 1919. William M. Tuttle, Jr. (Blacks in the New World Ser.). 320p. 1996. pap. text ed. 14.95 (*0-252-06586-7*) U of Ill Pr.

***Race Riot after a Verdict: Role Play Peacegame.** David W. Felder. 58p. 1997. pap. text ed. 8.95 (*1-57501-101-8*, 20E) Wellington Pr.

Race Riot at East St. Louis, July 2, 1917. Elliott M. Rudwick. LC 82-1940. (Blacks in the New World Ser.). 322p. reprint ed. pap. 91.80 (*0-8357-7503-8*, 2034461) Bks Demand.

Race, Riots & Policing: Lore & Disorder in a Multi-Racist Society. Michael C. Keith. 288p. 1993. 75.00 (*1-85728-109-8*, Pub. by UCL Pr UK); pap. 25.00 (*1-85728-110-1*, Pub. by UCL Pr UK) Taylor & Francis.

Race Rock. Peter Matthiessen. LC 87-40096. 320p. 1988. pap. 8.95 (*0-394-74538-8*, Vin) Random.

***Race Rules.** Michael E. Dyson. LC 97-5433. 1997. pap. 12.00 (*0-679-78156-0*, Vin) Random.

Race Rules: Navigating the Color Line. Michael E. Dyson. Ed. by Elizabeth Maguire. 224p. 1996. 20.00 (*0-201-91186-8*) Addison-Wesley.

***Race, Self-Employment & Upward Mobility: An Illusive American Dream.** Timothy Bates. LC 97-17782. 1997. pap. text ed. 16.95 (*0-8018-5799-6*) Johns Hopkins.

***Race, Self-Employment & Upward Mobility : An Illusive American Dream.** Timothy M. Bates. LC 97-17782. 1997. write for info. (*0-8018-5798-8*) Johns Hopkins.

***Race Sex: Their Sameness, Differences & Interplay.** Naomi Zack. LC 96-21091. (Thinking Gender Ser.). 256p. (C). 1997. pap. 17.95 (*0-415-91590-2*); text ed. 59.95 (*0-415-91589-9*) Routledge.

Race, Sex, & Gender in Contemporary Art: The Rise of Minority Culture. Edward Lucie-Smith. LC 93-29218. 1994. 45.00 (*0-8109-3767-0*) Abrams.

Race, Sex & National Origin: Public Attitudes of Desegregation see Readings on Equal Education, Vol. 10: Critical Issues for a New Administration and Congress

Race Skills for Alpine Skiing. Ellen P. Foster. 98p. 1994. pap. 14.95 (*0-9647390-1-1*) Turning Pt Ski Found.

Race, Social Class & Individual Differences in I. Q. Sandra W. Scarr. 560p. (C). 1981. 99.95 (*0-89859-055-8*) L Erlbaum Assocs.

Race, the City & the State. Ed. by Malcolm Cross & Michael C. Keith. LC 92-9286. 256p. (C). 1992. pap. 18.95 (*0-415-08432-6*, A9644) Routledge.

Race, the City & the State. Ed. by Malcolm Cross & Michael C. Keith. LC 92-9286. 256p. (C). (gr. 13). 1992. text ed. 79.95 (*0-415-08431-8*, A9640) Routledge.

***Race the Dawn.** Katherine Kincaid. 384p. 1997. mass mkt. 4.99 (*0-8217-5807-1*, Zebra Kensgtn) Kensgtn Pub Corp.

Race the Tide. Leigh A. Latham-Bass. 1995. 10.95 (*0-533-11084-X*) Vantage.

***Race Theory & the Biophobia Hypothesis: Humanics, Humanimals & Macroanthropology.** Melvin D. Williams. 1998. text ed. write for info. (*0-275-96076-5*, Praeger Pubs) Greenwood.

Race to European Eminence: Who are the Coming Tele-service Multinationals? Ed. by Erik Bohlin & Ove Grandstrand. LC 94-3800. 572p. 1994. 142.75 (*0-444-81961-4*) Elsevier.

Race to Fashoda: Colonialism & African Resistance. David L. Lewis. LC 94-36013. 1995. pap. 13.95 (*0-8050-3556-7*, Owl) H Holt & Co.

Race to Justice: A Racial Justice & Diversity Program for Junior High. Robin F. Gray & Jose A. Ballester y Marquez. 1995. pap. 30.00 (*1-55896-293-X*) Unitarian Univ.

Race to Nome. Kenneth A. Ungermann. Ed. by Walter Lord. (Illus.). 192p. 1993. reprint ed. pap. 9.95 (*0-938271-04-0*) Press N Amer.

Race to Pearl Harbor: The Failure of the Second London Naval Conference & the Onset of World War II. Stephen E. Pelz. LC 73-89711. (Studies in American-East Asian Relations: No. 5). 416p. 1974. text ed. 25.50 (*0-685-02135-1*) HUP.

***Race to Recruit: Strategies for Successful Business Attraction (Caled)** Maury Forman & James Mooney. 216p. 1996. per., pap. text ed. 29.95 (*0-7872-2781-1*) Kendall-Hunt.

***Race to Recruit: Strategies for Successful Business Attraction (Indiana)** Maury Forman & James Mooney. 216p. 1996. per., pap. text ed. 29.95 (*0-7872-2779-X*) Kendall-Hunt.

***Race to Recruit: Strategies for Successful Business Attraction (Washington)** Maury Forman & James Mooney. 216p. 1996. per., pap. text ed. 29.95 (*0-7872-2780-3*) Kendall-Hunt.

Race to Save Christmas. Richard Conant. LC 91-65291. (Illus.). 44p. (J). (gr. k-3). 1991. pap. 5.95 (*1-55523-432-1*) Winston-Derek.

***Race to Save the Planet.** Wolf. 1998. pap. 20.95 (*0-534-53703-0*) Brooks-Cole.

Race to Save the Planet: 1995 Edition. Wolf. (Biology Ser.). 1995. student ed., pap. 14.50 (*0-534-25038-6*) Wadsworth Pub.

Race to Save the Planet: 1996 Edition. Wolf. (Biology Ser.). 1996. student ed., pap. 20.95 (*0-534-25039-4*) Wadsworth Pub.

Race to Save the Planet, 1997. Wolf. 1997. student ed., pap. 15.00 (*0-534-52407-9*) Course Tech.

Race to Save the Tropics: Ecology & Economics for a Sustained Future. Robert J. Goodland. LC 89-71677. 216p. (Orig.). (C). 1990. pap. 24.95 (*1-55963-040-X*) Island Pr.

Race to Space. Stuart A. Kallen. LC 95-38344. (Giant Leaps Ser.). (J). 1996. lib. bdg. 14.98 (*1-56239-564-5*) Abdo & Dghtrs.

Race to the Altar. Patricia Thayer. (Silhouette Romance Ser.). 1994. pap. 2.75 (*0-373-19009-3*, 5-19009-5) Harlequin Bks.

Race to the Altar. Patricia Thayer. 1994. 2.75 (*0-373-91009-6*) Silhouette.

Race to the Finish. Gayle Roper. LC 90-21160. (Sports Stories for Boys Ser.). 128p. (J). (gr. 3-7). 1991. pap. 4.99 (*1-55513-816-0*, 38166, Chariot Bks) Chariot Victor.

Race to the Moon. (Babar Story Bks.). (Illus.). 48p. (J). 1990. 6.99 (*0-517-05208-3*) Random Hse Value.

Race to the Moon: America's Duel with the Soviets. William B. Breuer. LC 92-31849. 232p. 1993. text ed. 24.95 (*0-275-94481-6*, C4481, Praeger Pubs) Greenwood.

Race to the Stratosphere. D. H. De Vorkin. (Illus.). xiii, 406p. 1989. 65.95 (*0-387-96953-5*) Spr-Verlag.

Race to the Swift: State & Finance in Korean Industrialization. Jung-En Woo. 280p. (C). 1992. pap. text ed. 17.50 (*0-231-07147-7*) Col U Pr.

Race to Velasco. Paul N. Spellman. LC 95-606. (Orig.). (YA). (gr. 4 up). 1995. pap. 7.95 (*1-885777-01-9*) Hendrick-Long.

Race, Training & Employment. Ed. by Gajendra K. Verma & D. S. Darby. 150p. 1987. 55.00 (*1-85000-243-6*, Falmer Pr); pap. 31.00 (*1-85000-244-4*, Falmer Pr) Taylor & Francis.

Race Traitor. Ed. by Noel Ignatiev & John Garvey. 256p. (C). 1996. pap. 16.95 (*0-415-91393-4*, Routledge NY); text ed. 59.95 (*0-415-91392-6*, Routledge NY) Routledge.

Race Traits & Tendencies of the American Negro. Frederick L. Hoffman. LC 70-169474. reprint ed. 45.00 (*0-404-00065-7*) AMS Pr.

Race Versus Class: The New Affirmative Action Debate. Ed. by Carol M. Swain. LC 96-21837. 298p. 1996. pap. text ed. 29.00 (*0-7618-0413-7*); lib. bdg. 49.00 (*0-7618-0412-9*) U Pr of Amer.

Race Winning Strategies: Smart Lessons with Deep Dakron. Tom Linskey. (Illus.). 250p. 1995. pap. 17.95 (*0-924486-88-0*) Sheridan.

Race with Buffalo: And Other Native American Stories for Young Readers. Richard Young & Judy D. Young. 1994. pap. 12.95 (*0-87483-342-6*) August Hse.

Race with Death. Gilbert Morris. LC 94-14532. (Danielle Ross Mystery Ser.: No. 6). 288p. (Orig.). (gr. 10). 1994. pap. 8.99 (*0-8007-5498-0*) Revell.

Race with the Buffalo & Other Native American Stories for Young Readers. Richard Young & Judy D. Young. 176p. (J). 1993. 19.95 (*0-87483-343-4*) August Hse.

Race Without a Finish Line: America's Quest for Total Quality. Warren H. Schmidt & Jerome P. Finnigan. LC 92-16530. (Management Ser.). 428p. text ed. 29.00 (*1-55542-462-7*) Jossey-Bass.

Race Without End: The Grind Behind the Glamour of the Sasol Jordon Grand Prix Team. Maurice Hamilton. (Illus.). 232p. 1994. 32.95 (*1-85260-500-6*, Pub. by J H Haynes & Co UK) Motorbooks Intl.

Race, Writing, & Difference. Ed. by Henry Louis Gates, Jr. LC 86-6921. (Illus.). 432p. (C). 1987. pap. text ed. 19.50 (*0-226-28435-2*) U Ch Pr.

***Racechanges: White Skin, Black Face in American Culture.** Susan Gubar. (Race & American Culture). (Illus.). 356p. 1997. 37.50 (*0-19-511002-1*) OUP.

***Race/Ethnicity & Treatment of Children & Adolescents in Hospitals by Diagnosis.** D. Robert Harris et al. (Illus.). 107p. (Orig.). (C). 1997. pap. text ed. 35.00 (*0-7881-3852-9*) DIANE Pub.

Racehorse Caper. Mary Crawford. 96p. (Orig.). (J). (gr. 4-7). 1997. pap. 7.00 (*0-88092-068-8*) Royal Fireworks.

Racehoss: Big Emma's Boy. Albert R. Sample. 160p. 1986. mass mkt. 5.99 (*0-345-32807-8*, Ballantine Epiphany) Ballantine.

Racehoss: Big Emma's Boy. Albert R. Sample. 272p. 1984. 14.95 (*0-89015-442-2*) Sunbelt Media.

Racers. (Mighty Machines Ser.). (J). 1996. 9.95 (*0-614-15615-7*) DK Pub Inc.

Racer's Dictionary. Don Alexander & John Block. (Illus.). 96p. (Orig.). 1980. pap. text ed. 10.50 (*0-936834-27-7*) S S Autosports.

Racer's Encyclopedia of Metals, Fibers & Materials. Forbes Aird. (Power Pro Ser.). (Illus.). 128p. 1994. pap. 19.95 (*0-87938-916-8*) Motorbooks Intl.

Racer's Guide to Fabricating Shop Equipment. John Block. (Illus.). 56p. (Orig.). 1985. pap. text ed. 12.95 (*0-936834-45-5*) S S Autosports.

Racer's Math Handbook. Bob Emmons. (Illus.). 48p. (Orig.). 1993. pap. text ed. 22.95 (*0-936834-93-5*) S S Autosports.

Racers, Whipsnakes & Indigos. W. P. Mara. (Illus.). 64p. 1996. pap. 9.95 (*0-7938-2062-6*, RE142) TFH Pubns.

Races: A Study of the Problems of Race Formation in Man. Carleton S. Coon et al. LC 80-24479. (American Lecture Ser.: No. 77). (Illus.). xiv, 153p. 1981. reprint ed. text ed. 49.75 (*0-313-22878-7*, CORA, Greenwood Pr) Greenwood.

Races & Immigrants in America. 2nd ed. John R. Commons. LC 67-27834. xxiv, 242p. 1967. reprint ed. 39.50 (*0-678-00321-1*) Kelley.

Races, Chases & Crashes: A Complete Guide to Car Movies & Biker Flicks. David Mann & Ron Main. (Illus.). 144p. 1994. pap. text ed. 14.95 (*0-87938-859-5*) Motorbooks Intl.

Races of Britain. John Beddoe. 300p. 1983. reprint ed. 40.00 (*0-941694-13-5*) Cliveden Pr.

Races of Burma. 2nd ed. Collin M. Enriquez. LC 77-87013. (Illus.). 152p. reprint ed. 29.50 (*0-404-16816-7*) AMS Pr.

Races of Central Europe: A Footnote to History. Geoffrey M. Morant. LC 77-87532. reprint ed. 32.50 (*0-404-16598-2*) AMS Pr.

Races of Europe. Carleton S. Coon. LC 76-184840. (Illus.). 739p. 1972. reprint ed. text ed. 69.50 (*0-8371-6328-5*, CORE, Greenwood Pr) Greenwood.

Races of Maize in Peru: Their Origins, Evolution & Classification. Alexander Grobman & Ricardo Sevilla. LC 61-60080. (National Research Council, Publication Ser.: 915). 384p. reprint ed. pap. 109.50 (*0-317-28682-X*, 2055288) Bks Demand.

Races of Man: Outline of Anthropology & Ethnography. Joseph Deniker. (Select Bibliographies Reprint Ser.). 1977. reprint ed. 49.95 (*0-8369-5932-9*) Ayer.

Races of Man & Their Distribution. A. C. Haddon. 1981. 250.00 (*0-87968-288-4*) Gordon Pr.

Races of Mankind: Theosophy & Secret Doctrine Condensed. Harriet L. Henderson. 49p. 1994. reprint ed. spiral bd. 7.00 (*0-7873-1283-5*) Hlth Research.

Races of Men. Robert Knox. LC 78-89401. (Black Heritage Library Collection). 1977. 18.95 (*0-8369-8617-2*) Ayer.

***Races of Rice in India.** Reporter on Economic Products to the Government of India Staff. 594p. 1996. pap. 300.00 (*81-85880-91-3*, Pub. by Print Hse II) St Mut.

Racetrack Betting: The Professor's Guide to Strategies. Peter Asch & Richard E. Quandt. LC 91-13947. 206p. 1991. pap. text ed. 12.95 (*0-275-94103-5*, B4103, Praeger Pubs) Greenwood.

R

Racetrack Betting: The Professors' Guide to Strategies. Richard E. Quandt & Peter Asch. LC 86-7871. 206p. 1986. text ed. 55.00 (*0-86569-147-9*, Auburn Hse) Greenwood.

Racetrack Robbery. Ellen Leroe. LC 95-8912. (Illus.). 64p. (J). (gr. 2-4). 1996. 13.95 (*0-7868-0093-3*) Hyprn Child.

Racetrack Robbery. Ellen Leroe. LC 95-8912. (Illus.). 64p. (J). (gr. 2-4). 1996. pap. 3.95 (*0-7868-1092-0*) Hyprn Child.

Racewalking for Fun & Fitness. John Gray. 176p. 1985. 15.95 (*0-13-944711-3*); pap. 7.95 (*0-13-944703-2*) P-H.

Raceways: Having Fun with Balls & Tracks. Bernie Zubrowski. LC 84-20600. (Illus.). 80p. (J). (gr. 3-7). 1985. pap. 6.95 (*0-688-04160-4*) Morrow.

***Rachael Low's History of British Cinema.** Rachael Low & Jeffrey Richards. LC 96-51734. 2590p. (C). 1997. text ed. write for info. (*0-415-15451-0*) Routledge.

Rachael's Splendifilous Adventure. Daryl May & Roger Bansemer. Ed. by Carl Little. LC 91-66032. (Illus.). 40p. (Orig.). (J). (ps-4). 1992. 10.95 (*0-932433-83-9*) Windswept Hse.

Rache Bartmoss' Guide to the Net. Ed Bolme. (Illus.). 152p. (Orig.). 1993. pap. 16.00 (*0-937279-39-0*, CP3241) R Talsorian.

Rachel. James Agate. LC 72-84504. 1972. 18.95 (*0-405-08192-8*, Pub. by Blom Pubns UK) Ayer.

Rachel. Mary C. Borntrager. LC 90-45033. (Ellie's People Ser.: Vol. 3). (Orig.). 1990. pap. 7.99 (*0-8361-3539-3*) Herald Pr.

Rachel. Samuel H. Dresner. LC 94-2826. 1994. pap. 20.00 (*0-8006-2777-6*, Fortress Pr) Augsburg Fortress.

Rachel. Elfman. Date not set. write for info. (*0-395-32505-6*) HM.

Rachel. Ivan Southall. LC 86-45509. 147p. (J). (gr. 5 up). 1986. 14.00 (*0-374-36163-0*) FS&G.

Rachel. Lynda Trent. (Historical Ser.: No. 719). 1992. mass mkt. 3.99 (*0-373-28719-4*, 1-28719-2) Harlequin Bks.

Rachel. large type ed. Mary C. Borntrager. (Ellie's People Ser.: Vol. 3). 160p. 1993. pap. 8.99 (*0-8361-3638-1*) Herald Pr.

Rachel: Her Stage Life & Her Real Life. Francis Gribble. LC 70-93163. (Illus.). 1972. reprint ed. lib. bdg. 24.95 (*0-405-08582-6*, Pub. by Blom Pubns UK) Ayer.

Rachel & Her Children: Homeless Families in America. Jonathan Kozol. 320p. 1987. 16.95 (*0-517-56730-X*, Crown) Crown Pub Group.

Rachel & Her Children: Homeless Families in America. Jonathan Kozol. 272p. 1989. pap. 10.00 (*0-449-90339-7*, Columbine) Fawcett.

***Rachel & Her Grandma: A Program on Grief & Loss.** Denise B. Kern. LC 96-77599. (Illus.). 25p. (Orig.). (J). (ps-5). 1996. pap. 9.95 (*1-884063-92-6*) Mar Co Prods.

Rachel & Obadiah. Brinton Turkle. LC 77-15661. (Illus.). (J). (gr. k-3). 1978. pap. 15.00 (*0-525-38020-5*) Dutton Child Bks.

Rachel & the Pink & Green Dragon. Margaret Alexander. (Illus.). 44p. (J). (gr. k-3). 1992. 6.95 (*1-55523-518-2*) Winston-Derek.

Rachel & the Rabbi Jesus. Rosario De Bello. 1989. pap. 2.95 (*0-8091-6580-5*) Paulist Pr.

***Rachel & the Royal Garden.** Lynda Dumas. Ed. by John Dumas. LC 96-86146. (Illus.). 99p. (J). (gr. k-4). 1997. 14.95 (*1-888934-82-4*) Central OR Coast.

Rachel Calof's Story: Jewish Homesteader on the Northern Plains. Rachel Calof. LC 95-5742. (Illus.). 176p. 1995. 20.00 (*0-253-32942-6*) Ind U Pr.

Rachel Calof's Story: Jewish Homesteader on the Northern Plains. J. Sanford Rikoon. 176p. 1995. pap. 12.95 (*0-253-20986-2*) Ind U Pr.

***Rachel Carson.** Liza N. Burby. LC 96-41731. (Making Their Mark Ser.). (J). 1996. write for info. (*0-8239-5023-9*) Rosen Group.

Rachel Carson. Houghton Mifflin Company Staff. 1992. pap. 5.44 (*0-395-63568-3*) HM.

Rachel Carson. Mary A. McCay. (Twayne's United States Authors Ser.). 160p. 1993. 21.95 (*0-8057-3988-2*, Twayne) Scribnrs Ref.

Rachel Carson. Judith J. Presnall. LC 93-49487. (Importance of... Biographies Ser.). (Illus.). 112p. (J). (gr. 5-8). 1995. lib. bdg. 17.96 (*1-56006-052-2*) Lucent Bks.

Rachel Carson. Leslie A. Wheeler. (Pioneers in Change Ser.). (Illus.). 144p. (J). (gr. 5-9). 1991. pap. 6.95 (*0-382-24174-6*); lib. bdg. 13.95 (*0-382-24167-3*) Silver Burdett Pr.

Rachel Carson: Caring for the Earth. Elizabeth Ring. (J). (gr. 4-7). 1992. pap. 6.56 (*0-395-64730-4*) HM.

Rachel Carson: Caring for the Earth. Elizabeth Ring. LC 91-37644. (Gateway Green Biography Ser.). (Illus.). 48p. (J). (gr. 2-4). 1992. pap. 5.95 (*1-56294-798-2*); lib. bdg. 14.90 (*1-56294-056-2*) Millbrook Pr.

Rachel Carson: Friend of Nature. Carol Greene. LC 91-39446. (Rookie Biographies Ser.). (Illus.). 48p. (J). (gr. k-3). 1992. lib. bdg. 18.30 (*0-516-04229-7*) Childrens.

Rachel Carson: Friend of Nature. Carol Greene. LC 91-39446. (Rookie Biographies Ser.). (Illus.). 48p. (J). (gr. k-3). 1993. pap. 4.95 (*0-516-44229-5*) Childrens.

Rachel Carson: Friend of the Earth. Francene Sabin. LC 92-5825. (Illus.). 48p. (J). (gr. 4-6). 1992. lib. bdg. 12.95 (*0-8167-2821-6*) Troll Communs.

Rachel Carson: Friend of the Earth. Francene Sabin. LC 92-5825. (Illus.). 48p. (J). (gr. 4-6). 1997. pap. 3.95 (*0-8167-2822-4*) Troll Communs.

Rachel Carson: Pioneer of Ecology. Kathleen V. Kudlinski. (Women of Our Time Ser.). (Illus.). 64p. (J). (gr. 2-6). 1989. pap. 4.99 (*0-14-032242-6*, Puffin) Puffin Bks.

Rachel Carson: Sounding the Alarm: A Biography of Rachel Carson. Judith Harlan. LC 88-35909. (People in Focus Ser.). (Illus.). 128p. (J). (gr. 5 up). 1989. lib. bdg. 13.95 (*0-87518-407-3*, Dillon Silver Burdett) Silver Burdett Pr.

Rachel Carson: The Environmental Movement. John Henricksson. (New Directions Ser.). (Illus.). 96p. (YA). (gr. 7 up). 1991. pap. 5.95 (*1-56294-833-4*) Millbrook Pr.

Rachel Carson: The Wonder of Nature. Catherine Reef. (Earth Keepers Ser.). (Illus.). 68p. (J). (gr. 4-7). 1992. lib. bdg. 14.98 (*0-941477-38-X*) TFC Bks NY.

Rachel Carson: Voice for the Earth. Ginger Wadsworth. (Lerner Biography Ser.). (Illus.). 128p. (J). (gr. 5 up). 1992. lib. bdg. 22.95 (*0-8225-4907-7*, Lerner Publctns) Lerner Group.

***Rachel Carson: Witness for Nature.** Linda Lear. LC 97-8324. 1997. 35.00 (*0-8050-3427-7*) H Holt & Co.

Rachel Carson: Biologist & Author see American Women of Achievement

Rachel Carson: Biologist & Author see Junior World Biographies

Rachel Carson, Gentle Crusader. Barbara Ravage. LC 96-20313. (Innovative Minds Ser.). (J). 1997. lib. bdg. 27.11 (*0-8172-4406-9*) Raintree Steck-V.

Rachel Carson: Who Loved the Sea see Discovery Biographies

Rachel Carson, Writer & Scientist. Carol Alexander. (Illus.). (J). (gr. 1-4). 1995. pap. 4.95 (*0-8136-5738-5*); lib. bdg. 10.60 (*0-8136-5732-6*) Modern Curr.

Rachel Chance. Jean Thesman. 192p. (YA). 1992. pap. 3.50 (*0-380-71378-0*, Flare) Avon.

Rachel Chance. Jean Thesman. 180p. (J). (gr. 5-9). 1990. 13.95 (*0-395-50934-3*) HM.

Rachel Crothers: A Research & Production Sourcebook. Colette Lindroth & James Lindroth. LC 94-41267. (Modern Dramatists Research & Production Sourcebooks Ser.: Vol. 8). 160p. 1995. text ed. 59.95 (*0-313-27815-6*, Greenwood Pr) Greenwood.

Rachel, Crying for Her Children: Secrets of the Third Reich. Athina Cavelaris. (Illus.). 257p. 1994. pap. write for info. (*0-9642706-3-3*) A Cavelaris.

The bells of PANAYIAS (Madonna's) were ringing mournfully as we walked to school. It was the twenty-eighth of October & soon we would find out that the Italians had declared war with Greece. That year, 1941, was the beginning of our ten year tribulations, the exodus from North East Greece to North West. We lost our home, our money became inflated, we lived on roots & dandelions. The Communist Guerrillas killed my father with ninety eight others. They buried them all in a great big hole. The Best Citizens. I fled alone to Athens. They were after me. I lived homeless in the streets. I was abducted by the Germans & ended up in a home in Austria, where Hitler had gathered European girls, the youngest & the best looking he could find. They were the brides to be of the selected German officers. The New Aryan Race. I rebelled, & was put in the Gestapo jail, then I was taken to Paris. I left Paris the day that the Americans liberated the town. I ended up in Salzburg, where I was raped by the liberating U.S. Army. The Americans moved us to Munich, at the old Nazi officers quarters. There I married, at 18, a Greek medical student, in the Greek Orthodox Church. They flew us in the Old Dakotas to Athens, where my son was born. More Civil War, more hunger. My husband was in the Army & was a prisoner of war, out of Greece. In 1951 My uncle sent me papers to come to America. Constantly I was mourning for all the Jews in the Holocaust, our friends, our neighbors. The kids I went to school with...no one came back to our hometown. I mourned for the Greek mothers who lost their sons & mothers in Europe & the U.S. That's where the title of my book came from. Jeremiah 31:15, "A voice was heard in Ramah, 'RACHEL, WEEPING FOR HER CHILDREN' & refused to be comforted because THEY were not."
Publisher Provided Annotation.

Rachel Dyer. John Neal. 276p. 1996. pap. text ed. 6.95 (*1-57392-049-5*) Prometheus Bks.

Rachel Dyer. John Neal. LC 64-10667. 1979. reprint ed. 50.00 (*0-8201-1263-1*) Schol Facsimiles.

Rachel Dyer, a North American Story. John Neal. 1988. reprint ed. lib. bdg. 49.00 (*0-7812-0003-2*) Rprt Serv.

***Rachel Field's Hitty: Her First Hundred Years with New Adventures.** Rosemary Wells & Rachel Field. LC 97-18683. (Illus.). (J). 1999. 19.95 (*0-689-81716-9*) S&S Childrens.

Rachel Fister's Blister. Amy MacDonald. (Illus.). 32p. (J). (ps-3). 1990. 13.95 (*0-395-52152-1*) HM.

Rachel Fister's Blister. Amy MacDonald. (Illus.). 32p. (J). (gr. k-3). 1993. pap. 4.95 (*0-395-65744-X*) HM.

Rachel Fister's Blister. Amy MacDonald. (Illus.). 32p. (J). (ps-3). 1996. pap. 8.95 incl. audio (*0-395-77978-2*) HM.

Rachel Giese: The Donegal Pictures. Rachel Giese. LC 87-50534. (Illus.). 104p. 1987. 20.00 (*0-916390-27-6*) Wake Forest.

Rachel McMasters Miller Hunt Botanical Library. (Illus.). viii, 35p. 1961. 5.00 (*0-913196-37-1*) Hunt Inst Botanical.

Rachel, Meet Your Angel! Fran Manushkin. 96p. (J). 1995. pap. 3.99 (*0-14-037198-2*) Puffin Bks.

Rachel of Old Louisiana. Avery O. Craven. LC 74-15921. (Illus.). 122p. 1995. pap. 9.95 (*0-8071-2016-2*) La State U Pr.

Rachel Papers. Martin Amis. LC 92-50078. 1992. pap. 11.00 (*0-679-73458-9*, Vin) Random.

Rachel Parker, Kindergarten Show-Off. Ann M. Martin. LC 91-25793. (Illus.). 40p. (J). (ps-3). 1992. lib. bdg. 15.95 (*0-8234-0935-X*) Holiday.

Rachel Parker Kindergarten Show-Off. Ann M. Martin. LC 91-25793. (Illus.). 40p. (J). (ps-3). 1993. pap. 6.95 (*0-8234-1067-6*) Holiday.

Rachel Ray. Anthony Trollope. Ed. by Rose D'Agostino. (Harding Grange Library). (Illus.). 557p. 1986. 25.00 (*0-932282-50-4*) Caledonia Pr.

Rachel Ray. Anthony Trollope. (World's Classics Ser.). 464p. 1989. pap. 9.95 (*0-19-281809-0*) OUP.

Rachel Ray. Anthony Trollope. Ed. & Intro. by John Sutherland. 368p. 1996. pap. 9.95 (*0-14-043410-0*) Penguin.

Rachel Ray, 2 Vols. Anthony Trollope. Ed. by N. John Hall. LC 80-1881. (Selected Works of Anthony Trollope). 1981. reprint ed. lib. bdg. 71.95 (*0-405-14140-8*) Ayer.

Rachel Ray. Anthony Trollope. 1980. reprint ed. pap. 7.95 (*0-486-23930-6*) Dover.

Rachel Ray (1863) Anthony Trollope. 416p. 1993. 7.95 (*0-14-043815-7*, Penguin Classics) Viking Penguin.

Rachel Rosary: Intercessory Prayer for Victims of Post-Abortion Syndrome. Larry Kupferman. (Spirit Life Ser.). 40p. (Orig.). (C). 1994. pap. 3.95 (*1-878718-21-5*) Resurrection.

***Rachel Rosenthal.** Moira Roth. LC 97-9332. (PAJ Publications). 1997. write for info. (*0-8018-5628-0*); pap. write for info. (*0-8018-5629-9*) Johns Hopkins.

Rachel the Clever & Other Jewish Folktales. Josepha Sherman. 171p. (J). 1993. 18.95 (*0-87483-306-X*); pap. 10.95 (*0-87483-307-8*) August Hse.

Rachel the Immortal: Stage-Queen, Grande Amoureuse, Street Urchin, & Fine Lady. Bernard Falk. LC 70-91900. 1972. 24.95 (*0-405-08495-1*, Pub. by Blom Pubns UK) Ayer.

Rachel Weeping: And Other Essays on Abortion. James T. Burtchaell. 383p. (C). 1991. reprint ed. pap. 11.95 (*0-919225-34-9*) Life Cycle Bks.

***Rachel Whiteread.** Ed. by Fiona Bradley. LC 96-61179. (Illus.). 132p. (Orig.). 1997. pap. 24.95 (*0-500-27936-5*) Thames Hudson.

Rachel Whiteread: House. Jon Bird et al. Ed. by James Lingwood. (Illus.). 144p. (Orig.). 1995. pap. 24.95 (*0-7148-3459-9*, Pub. by Phaidon Press UK) Chronicle Bks.

Rachela's Story: From Out of the Firestorm. Rachela Walshaw. 154p. (J). (gr. 5-8). 1994. pap. 7.95 (*1-56171-021-0*) Sure Seller.

***Rachel's Burning Bush: Surviving Loss & Abandonment from Members of the Opposite Sex.** 2nd rev. ed. Lucho-ben Alexander. LC 94-96520. 256p. 1997. pap. 21.95 (*0-9643782-2-1*) Luvo Pubs.

Rachel's Burning Bush: The Story of a Man's Painful Relationship with A Borderline Personality. Lucho Ben Alexander. LC 94-96520. 224p. 1996. pap. 12.95 (*0-9643782-1-3*); lib. bdg. 21.95 (*0-9643782-0-5*) Luvo Pubs.

Rachel's Children. Harriet Hassell. LC 90-32564. (Library of Alabama Classics). 336p. 1990. reprint ed. pap. 19.95 (*0-8173-0499-1*) U of Ala Pr.

Rachel's Children: Margaret Laurence's A Jest of God. Nora F. Stovel. (Canadian Fiction Studies: No. 12). 109p. (C). 1992. pap. text ed. 14.95 (*1-55022-126-4*, Pub. by ECW Press CN) Genl Dist Srvs.

Rachel's Daughters: Newly Orthodox Jewish Women. Debra R. Kaufman. LC 90-42040. 240p. (C). 1991. text ed. 35.00 (*0-8135-1637-4*); pap. text ed. 16.00 (*0-8135-1638-2*) Rutgers U Pr.

***Rachel's In, Lila's Out.** Francine Pascal. (Unicorn Club Ser.: No. 18). (J). 1997. pap. 3.50 (*0-553-48446-X*) BDD Bks Young Read.

Rachel's Island. Kris Sullivan. 427p. 1992. pap. 5.95 (*0-9630193-2-5*) Van Allen Enter.

Rachel's Song. Miguel Barnet. Tr. by W. Nick Hill from SPA. LC 91-55412. 128p. (Orig.). 1991. pap. 9.95 (*0-915306-87-5*) Curbstone.

Rachel's Star. Betty McCutchan. LC 91-75205. 97p. (YA). (gr. 6 up). 1992. 8.95 (*1-55523-464-X*) Winston-Derek.

Rachel's Vineyard: A Psych. & Spirit. Journey of Post-Abortion Healing. Theresa K. Burke & Barbara Cullen. LC 95-20262. 167p. (Orig.). 1995. pap. 12.95 (*0-8189-0719-3*) Alba.

Rachel's Walk. 2nd ed. Jonathan Berman. 150p. 1989. pap. write for info. (*0-318-64795-8*) JMPS Pubs.

Rachel's Way. large type ed. Connie Monk. 1991. 25.99 (*0-7089-2521-9*) Ulverscroft.

Rachmaninoff. (Dent Master Musicians Ser.). (Illus.). (C). pap. write for info. (*0-19-816488-2*) OUP.

Rachmaninoff. Geoffrey Norris. (Master Musicians Ser.). 194p. 1994. 30.00 (*0-02-870685-8*) Schirmer Bks.

Rachmaninoff. Robert Walker. (Illustrated Lives of the Great Composers Ser.). (Illus.). 144p. 1996. 14.95 (*0-7119-0253-4*, OP 42339) Omnibus NY.

Rachmaninoff. Watson Lyle. LC 74-24140. 1976. reprint ed. 42.50 (*0-404-13003-8*) AMS Pr.

Rachmaninoff. Victor I. Seroff. (Biography Index Reprint Ser.). 1977. reprint ed. 23.95 (*0-8369-8034-4*) Ayer.

Rachmaninoff: Composer, Pianist, Conductor. Barrie Martyn. (Illus.). 672p. 1990. text ed. 69.95 (*0-85967-809-1*, Pub. by Scolar Pr UK) Ashgate Pub Co.

Rachmaninoff: The Illustrated Lives of the Great Composers. Robert Walker. 1980. pap. text ed. 14.95 (*0-89524-208-7*) Music Sales.

Rachmaninoff Very Best for Piano. Ed. by John L. Haag. (Illus.). 160p. (Orig.). 1995. pap. 14.95 (*1-56922-070-0*, 07-2032) Creat Cncpts.

Rachmaninoff's Recollections Told to Oskar Von Riesemann. Sergei Rachmaninoff. LC 74-111100. (Select Bibliographies Reprint Ser.). 1977. 31.95 (*0-8369-5232-4*) Ayer.

Rachmaninov Orchestral Music. Patrick Piggott. (BBC Music Guides Ser.). 64p. 1996. 2.95 (*0-563-12468-7*, BB 11147, BBC-Parkwest) Parkwest Pubns.

RACI National Convention, 8th, August 1987. Ed. by P. R. Andrews & J. S. Morley. (Drug Design & Delivery Ser.: Vol. 3, No. 2). 108p. 1988. pap. text ed. 180.00 (*3-7186-4836-9*) Gordon & Breach.

Racial & Cultural Minorities: An Analysis of Prejudice & Discrimination. 5th ed. George E. Simpson & J. Milton Yinger. (Environment, Development, & Public Policy: Public Policy & Social Services Ser.). 506p. 39.50 (*0-306-41777-4*, Plenum Pr) Plenum.

***Racial & Ethnic Classifications Use by Public Schools.** 1997. lib. bdg. 250.95 (*0-8490-6210-1*) Gordon Pr.

***Racial & Ethnic Classifications Used by Public Schools.** 1997. lib. bdg. 254.95 (*0-8490-6084-2*) Gordon Pr.

Racial & Ethnic Competition. Michael P. Banton. (Modern Revivals in Sociology Ser.). 1993. 69.95 (*0-7512-0110-3*, Pub. by Gregg Pub UK) Ashgate Pub Co.

Racial & Ethnic Differences in Disease. Anthony P. Polednak. (Illus.). 376p. 1989. 59.95 (*0-19-505970-0*) OUP.

Racial & Ethnic Differences in the Health of Older Americans. National Research Council, Committee on Vision Staff. 450p. (Orig.). (C). 1997. pap. 45.00 (*0-309-05489-3*) Natl Acad Pr.

Racial & Ethnic Diversity in Academic Libraries: Multicultural Issues. Ed. by Deborah A. Curry et al. LC 94-5445. (Reference Librarian Ser.: Nos. 45 & 46). (Illus.). 374p. 1994. lib. bdg. 49.95 (*1-56024-656-1*) Haworth Pr.

Racial & Ethnic Families in America. 2nd ed. Juan L. Gonzales. (C). 1994. student ed. 28.95 (*0-8403-9480-2*) Kendall-Hunt.

Racial & Ethnic Groups. Richard T. Schaefer. LC 92-20465. (C). 1992. text ed. 39.00 (*0-673-52241-5*) Addson-Wesley Educ.

Racial & Ethnic Groups. 6th ed. Schaefer. (C). 1995. teacher ed. write for info. (*0-673-54252-1*) Addson-Wesley Educ.

Racial & Ethnic Groups. 6th ed. Schaefer. 608p. (C). 1996. text ed. 55.95 (*0-673-52363-2*) Addson-Wesley Educ.

***Racial & Ethnic Groups.** 7th ed. Richard T. Schaefer. LC 97-20518. 1997. write for info. (*0-673-52556-2*) Addison-Wesley.

***Racial & Ethnic Groups.** 7th ed. Richard T. Schaeffer. (C). 1998. wbk. ed., pap. text ed. write for info. (*0-321-00207-5*) Addson-Wesley Educ.

***Racial & Ethnic Groups.** 7th ed. Ed. by Schaffer. (C). 1998. text ed. write for info. (*0-321-01371-9*) Addson-Wesley Educ.

Racial & Ethnic Identity: Psychological Development & Creative Expression. Ed. by Ezra E. Griffith et al. (Illus.). 288p. (C). (gr. 13). 1994. text ed. 62.95 (*0-415-90867-1*, B2978) Routledge.

Racial & Ethnic Identity: Psychological Development & Creative Expression. Ed. by Ezra E. Griffith et al. (Illus.). 288p. (C). (gr. 13). 1994. pap. 18.95 (*0-415-90868-X*, B2982) Routledge.

Racial & Ethnic Patterns of Mortality in New Mexico. Ed. by Thomas M. Becker et al. LC 92-29585. 256p. 1993. 16.95 (*0-8263-1405-8*) U of NM Pr.

Racial & Ethnic Politics in California. Ed. by Bryan O. Jackson & Michael B. Preston. 405p. (Orig.). (C). 1991. pap. 19.95 (*0-87772-328-1*) UCB IGS.

Racial & Ethnic Presence in American Methodism: A Bibliography. Compiled by C. Jarrett Gray. 89p. 1992. pap. text ed. 5.00 (*1-880927-14-4*) Gen Comm Arch.

Racial & Ethnic Relations. 5th ed. Joe R. Feagin & Clairece B. Feagin. LC 95-18296. 1995. text ed. 57.00 (*0-13-186552-8*) P-H.

Racial & Ethnic Relations in America. 4th ed. S. Dale McLemore. LC 93-2934. 1993. text ed. 59.00 (*0-205-14346-6*) Allyn.

***Racial & Ethnic Relations in America.** 5th ed. S. Dale Mclemore & Harriett Romo. LC 96-37717. 1997. 52.00 (*0-205-19956-9*) Allyn.

***Racial & Ethnic Tensions in American Communities: Poverty, Inequality, & Discrimination -- a National Perspective.** Ed. by Mary F. Berry et al. 204p. (C). 1997. reprint ed. pap. text ed. 40.00 (*0-7881-4168-6*) DIANE Pub.

Racial Attitude Survey: PC Windows 1.0 Version. unabridged ed. Ed. by Thomas J. Rundquist. (Illus.). 45p. (Orig.). 1996. teacher ed., pap. 39.95 incl. disk (*1-884239-03-X*) Nova Media.

Racial Attitudes in America: Trends & Interpretations. Howard Schuman et al. (Social Trends in the United States Ser.). (Illus.). 288p. 1985. text ed. 35.00 (*0-674-74574-4*) HUP.

Racial Attitudes in America: Trends & Interpretations. Howard Schuman et al. (Social Trends in the United States Ser.). 276p. (C). 1988. pap. text ed. 14.95 (*0-674-74573-6*) HUP.

***Racial Attitudes in America: Trends & Interpretations.** Howard Schuman. 1997. pap. text ed. 19.95 (*0-674-74569-8*) HUP.

Racial Attitudes in America: Trends & Interpretations. Howard Schuman et al. (Social Trends in the United States Ser.). 344p. 1990. reprint ed. 37.50 (*0-674-74575-2*) HUP.

*__Racial Attitudes in the 1990s: Continuity & Change.__ Ed. by Steven A. Tuch & Jack K. Martin. LC 97-11075. 1997. text ed. write for info. (*0-275-95015-8*, Praeger Pubs); pap. text ed. write for info. (*0-275-96037-4*, Praeger Pubs) Greenwood.

Racial Biology of the Jews. Otmar Von Verschuer. 1987. lib. bdg. 75.00 (*0-8490-3945-2*) Gordon Pr.

Racial Biology of the Jews. Otmar Von Verschuer. (Illus.). 1984. lib. bdg. 250.00 (*0-87700-560-5*) Revisionist Pr.

Racial Change & Community Crisis: St. Augustine, Florida, 1877-1980. David R. Colburn. 320p. 1985. text ed. 52.50 (*0-231-06046-7*) Col U Pr.

Racial Change & Community Crisis: St. Augustine, Florida, 1877-1980. David R. Colburn. (Florida Sand Dollar Bks.). 280p. (C). 1991. reprint ed. pap. 19.95 (*0-8130-1066-7*) U Press Fla.

Racial Chaos & Criminal Anarchy: The Prelude to Black Revolution. W. J. Davis. 1982. lib. bdg. 59.95 (*0-87700-412-9*) Revisionist Pr.

Racial Characteristics of Syrians & Armenians. Carl C. Seltzer. (HU PMP Ser.). 1936. 25.00 (*0-527-01230-0*) Periodicals Srv.

Racial Classification & History see American Contributions

Racial Classification & History see Critical Race Theory: Essays on the Social Construction & Reproduction of "Race"

Racial Compact: A Call for Racial Rights, Preservation & Independence. Richard McCulloch. 135p. (Orig.). 1994. pap. 7.95 (*0-9608928-3-4*) Towncourt Ent.

Racial Conditions: Politics, Theory, Comparisons. Howard Winant. LC 93-30445. 1994. pap. 17.95 (*0-8166-2387-2*) U of Minn Pr.

Racial Conditions: Politics, Theory, Comparisons. Howard Winant. LC 93-30445. 232p. 1994. 44.95 (*0-8166-2386-4*) U of Minn Pr.

Racial Conflict & Economic Development. W. Arthur Lewis. (Illus.). 128p. 1985. 19.95 (*0-674-74579-5*) HUP.

Racial Conflict & Healing: An Asian-American Theological Perspective. Andrew S. Park. 176p. (Orig.). 1996. pap. 18.00 (*1-57075-078-5*) Orbis Bks.

Racial Conflict & Negotiations: Perspectives & First Case Studies. Ed. by W. E. Chalmers & G. W. Cormick. LC 72-634167. (Orig.). 1971. 12.00 (*0-87736-313-7*); pap. 5.95 (*0-87736-314-5*) U of Mich Inst Labor.

Racial Conflict, Discrimination, & Power: Historical & Contemporary Studies. Ed. by William Barclay et al. LC 75-11964. (Studies in Modern Society: Political & Social Issues: No. 9). 1976. pap. 11.95 (*0-404-13144-1*); lib. bdg. 32.50 (*0-404-13140-9*) AMS Pr.

Racial Conflict in Contemporary Society. John Stone. 192p. 1986. 26.50 (*0-674-74565-5*); pap. 12.95 (*0-674-74566-3*) HUP.

Racial Consciousness. Michael P. Banton. (Illus.). 176p. (Orig.). (C). 1988. pap. text ed. 31.95 (*0-582-02384-X*, 70445) Longman.

*__Racial Contract.__ Charles Mills. LC 97-15840. 192p. 1997. 19.95 (*0-8014-3454-8*) Cornell U Pr.

*__Racial Contract.__ Charles W. Mills. LC 97-15840. 1997. pap. write for info. (*0-8014-8463-4*) Cornell U Pr.

Racial Crisis in American Higher Education. Ed. by Kofi Lomotey & Philip G. Altbach. LC 90-33700. (SUNY Series, Frontiers in Education). 275p. (C). 1991. text ed. 74.50 (*0-7914-0520-6*); pap. text ed. 24.95 (*0-7914-0521-4*) State U NY Pr.

Racial Decay: A Compilation of Evidence from World Sources. O. C. Beale. 1976. lib. bdg. 59.95 (*0-8490-2498-6*) Gordon Pr.

Racial Determinism & the Fear of Miscegenation Post-1900: Race & "The Negro Problem", Pt. II. 9,301th ed. Ed. by John D. Smith. LC 92-32109. (Anti-Black Thought, 1863-1925 Ser.: Vol. 8). 440p. 1993. text ed. 71.00 (*0-8153-0980-5*) Garland.

Racial Determinism & the Fear of Miscegenation Pre-1900: Race & "The Negro Problem", Pt. I. 9,302th ed. Ed. by John D. Smith. LC 92-32108. (Anti-Black Thought, 1863-1925 Ser.: Vol. 7). 496p. 1993. text ed. 74.00 (*0-8153-0979-1*) Garland.

*__Racial Differences in Life Expectancy among Elderly African Americans & Whites: The Surprising Truth about Comparisons.__ rev. ed. Laura B. Shrestha. LC 96-30016. (Studies on the Elderly in America). (Illus.). 184p. 1997. text ed. 48.00 (*0-8153-2764-1*) Garland.

*__Racial Differences in Perceptions of Access to Health Care among the Elderly.__ rev. ed. Shulamit L. Bernard. LC 96-39994. (Studies on the Elderly in America). (Illus.). 183p. 1997. text ed. 53.00 (*0-8153-2646-7*) Garland.

*__Racial Dimension of American Overseas Colonial Policy.__ Hazel M. McFerson. LC 97-2233. (Contributions in Comparative Colonial Studies: Vol. 33). 1997. text ed. write for info. (*0-313-28996-4*, Greenwood Pr) Greenwood.

Racial Discrimination. D. J. Walker & Michael Redman. 1977. pap. 80.00 (*0-7219-0770-9*, Pub. by Scientific UK) St Mut.

Racial Discrimination Against Overseas Indians: A Class Analysis. Prakash C. Jain. (C). 1990. text ed. 23.00 (*81-7022-288-5*, Pub. by Concept II) S Asia.

Racial Disparities in the Criminal Justice System. Joan Petersilia. LC 83-9777. 128p. 1983. pap. 10.00 (*0-8330-0506-5*, R-2947-NIC) Rand Corp.

Racial Economy of Science: Toward a Democratic Future. Ed. by Sandra Harding. LC 92-31286. (Race, Gender, & Science Ser.). (Illus.). 544p. 1993. 39.95 (*0-253-32693-1*) Ind U Pr.

Racial Elements of European History. Hans F. Gunther. 1973. 59.95 (*0-8490-0926-X*) Gordon Pr.

Racial Equality. L. McDonald. Ed. by Franklyn S. Haiman. (To Protect These Rights Ser.). 168p. 1991. pap. 12.95 (*0-8442-6004-5*, Natl Textbk) NTC Pub Grp.

Racial Equality in America. John H. Franklin. LC 93-19766. 136p. (C). 1993. pap. 12.95 (*0-8262-0912-2*) U of Mo Pr.

Racial Equality in America & the Color Line - Legacy for the Twenty-First Century. John H. Franklin. LC 93-36622. 224p. 1994. 150.00 (*0-8262-0913-0*) U of Mo Pr.

Racial Equality in the Church: A Critique of the Homogeneous Unit Principle in Light of a Practical Theology Perspective. Bruce W. Fong. LC 96-24604. 314p. 1996. lib. bdg. 46.00 (*0-7618-0437-4*) U Pr of Amer.

Racial Equation: Pontius Pilate Plus Judus Iscariot Equals Crucification. Arthur T. Davidson. 1986. write for info. (*0-933389-00-0*) Northeastern Pub.

Racial Exclusionism & the City: The Urban Support of the National Front. Christopher T. Husbands. 240p. 1983. text ed. 55.00 (*0-04-329045-0*) Routledge Chapman & Hall.

Racial Fault Lines: The Historical Origins of White Supremacy in California. Tomas Almaguer. LC 93-42513. 1994. 40.00 (*0-520-07597-8*); pap. 15.00 (*0-520-08947-2*) U CA Pr.

Racial Formation in the United States: 1960-1990. 2nd ed. Michael Omi & Howard A. Winant. LC 93-336254. 224p. (C). 1994. pap. 15.95 (*0-415-90864-7*, Routledge NY) Routledge.

Racial Formation in the United States from the 1960's to the 1980's. Michael Omi & Howard A. Winant. 224p. 1986. pap. 13.95 (*0-7102-0970-3*, 09703, RKP) Routledge.

Racial Formations - Critical Transformations: Articulations of Power in Ethnic & Racial Studies in the United States. E. San Juan, Jr. LC 91-33426. 176p. (C). 1994. pap. 15.00 (*0-391-03858-3*) Humanities.

Racial Healing: Confronting the Fear Between Blacks & Whites. Harlon L. Dalton. 256p. 1996. pap. 12.00 (*0-385-47517-9*, Anchor NY) Doubleday.

Racial History of Man, 2 vols. Roland Dixon. 1973. Set. 250.00 (*0-87968-273-6*) Gordon Pr.

Racial Hybridity: The Origin of Races & Racial Mixture. 1991. lib. bdg. 61.00 (*0-8490-4431-6*) Gordon Pr.

Racial Hygiene: Medicine under the Nazis. Robert N. Proctor. (Illus.). 496p. 1990. pap. text ed. 18.95 (*0-674-74578-7*) HUP.

*__Racial Identity Theory: Applications to Individual, Group, & Organizational Interventions.__ Ed. by Chalmer E. Thompson & Robert T. Carter. LC 96-47293. 275p. 1997. write for info. (*0-8058-2080-9*); pap. 32.50 (*0-8058-2081-7*) L Erlbaum Assocs.

Racial Inequality: A Political-Economic Analysis. Michael Reich. LC 80-8573. (Illus.). 358p. 1981. reprint ed. pap. 102.10 (*0-7837-8181-4*, 2047886) Bks Demand.

Racial Integration in American Neighborhoods: A Comparative Study. Norman M Bradburn et al. (Report Ser.: No. IIIB). 1970. 6.50 (*0-932132-08-1*) Natl Opinion Res.

Racial Integrity - A Plea for the Establishment of a Chair of Negro History in Our Schools & Colleges, Etc. Arthur Schomburg. (African Studies). reprint ed. 10.00 (*0-938818-42-2*) ECA Assoc.

Racial Integrity & Other Features of the Negro Problem. Alexander H. Shannon. LC 70-38024. (Black Heritage Library Collection). 1977. reprint ed. 22.95 (*0-8369-8990-2*) Ayer.

Racial Matching in Fostering: The Challenge to Social Work Practice. Penny J. Rhodes. 225p. 1992. 59.95 (*1-85628-264-3*, Pub. by Avebury Pub UK) Ashgate Pub Co.

Racial Matters: The FBI's Secret File on Black America 1960-1972. Kenneth Oreilly. 1991. pap. 16.95 (*0-02-923682-7*, Free Press) Free Pr.

Racial Minorities in Banking: New Workers in the Banking Industry. R. D. Corwin. 1971. pap. 16.95 (*0-8084-0042-8*) NCUP.

Racial Myths. Juan Comas. LC 76-5909. (Race Question in Modern Science Ser.). 51p. 1976. reprint ed. text ed. 35.00 (*0-8371-8801-6*, CORM, Greenwood Pr) Greenwood.

Racial Negotiations: Potentials & Limitations. W. Ellison Chalmers. LC 74-78509. 1974. 15.00 (*0-87736-321-8*) U of Mich Inst Labor.

Racial Origin & Earliest Racial History of the Hebrews. Eugen Fischer. 1987. lib. bdg. 75.00 (*0-8490-3931-2*) Gordon Pr.

Racial Origins of the Founders of America: Extracted from the Works of Madison Grant & Ales Hrdlicka. Ed. by R. Peterson. (Illus.). 124p. (Orig.). 1995. pap. 15.00 (*1-878465-11-2*) Scott-Townsend Pubs.

Racial Patterns in 1994 D.C. Mayoral Primary: Beyond the Handwringing. Jeffrey Henig. (Occasional Papers: No. 013). 14p. (Orig.). Date not set. pap. 4.00 (*1-888028-25-4*) GWU Ctr WAS.

Racial Policies & Practices of Real Estate Brokers. Rose Helper. LC 73-81398. 403p. reprint ed. pap. 114.90 (*0-317-41746-0*, 2055874) Bks Demand.

Racial Politics & Urban Planning: Gary, Indiana, 1980-1989. Robert A. Catlin. LC 92-43016. (Illus.). 256p. (C). 1993. text ed. 35.00 (*0-8131-1798-4*) U Pr of Ky.

Racial Politics at the Crossroads: Memphis Elects Dr. W. W. Herenton. Marcus D. Pohlman & Michael P. Kirby. LC 95-32505. (Illus.). 288p. (C). 1996. pap. text ed. 17.00 (*0-87049-927-0*); lib. bdg. 34.00 (*0-87049-926-2*) U of Tenn Pr.

Racial Politics in American Cities. Ed. by Rufus P. Browning et al. LC 89-36784. 243p. (Orig.). (C). 1990. pap. text ed. 29.95 (*0-8013-0178-5*, 75837) Longman.

Racial Politics in American Cities. 2nd ed. Rufus P. Browning. LC 96-30443. (C). 1997. pap. text ed. 31.95 (*0-8013-1535-2*); pap. text ed. write for info. (*0-8013-1691-X*) Addison-Wesley.

Racial Preference & Racial Justice: The New Affirmative Action Controversy. Ed. by Russell Nieli. 544p. (C). 1991. 25.95 (*0-89633-147-4*) Ethics & Public Policy.

Racial Prehistory in the Southwest & the Hawikuh Zunis. Carl C. Seltzer. (HU PMP Ser.). 1944. pap. 25.00 (*0-527-01256-4*) Periodicals Srv.

*__Racial Prejudice: Why Can't We Overcome?__ Elaine Pascoe. LC 96-36913. (Impact Bks.). 1997. lib. bdg. 22.70 (*0-531-11402-3*) Watts.

Racial Pride & Prejudice. Frwd. by Eric J. Dingwall. LC 78-32177. 246p. 1979. reprint ed. text ed. 52.50 (*0-8371-5940-7*, DIR&, Greenwood Pr) Greenwood.

Racial Problem in the Works of Richard Wright & James Baldwin. Jean-Francois Gounard. Tr. by Joseph J. Rodgers, Jr. LC 90-43379. (Contributions in Afro-American & African Studies: No. 140). 324p. 1992. text ed. 55.00 (*0-313-27308-1*, GRL/, Greenwood Pr) Greenwood.

Racial Segregation & the Origins of Apartheid in South Africa, 1919-36. Saul Dubow. 272p. 1989. text ed. 45.00 (*0-312-02774-5*) St Martin.

Racial State: Germany, 1933-1945. Michael Burleigh & Wolfgang Wipperman. (Illus.). 416p. (C). 1991. 54.95 (*0-521-39114-8*) Cambridge U Pr.

Racial State: Germany, 1933-1945. Michael Burleigh & Wolfgang Wipperman. (Illus.). 416p. (C). 1993. pap. text ed. 19.95 (*0-521-39802-9*) Cambridge U Pr.

Racial Stratification As Accident & As Policy. 1989. 5.00 (*0-685-43621-7*) U VA Ctr Pub Serv.

*__Racial Subjects: Writing on Race in America.__ David T. Goldberg. LC 96-39653. 224p. (C). 1997. text ed. 59.95 (*0-415-91830-8*, Routledge NY) Routledge.

*__Racial Subjects: Writing on Race in America.__ David T. Goldberg. LC 96-39653. 224p. 1997. pap. 16.95 (*0-415-91831-6*, Routledge NY) Routledge.

*__Racial Tension in High School: Role Play Peacegame.__ David W. Felder. 58p. 1997. pap. text ed. 8.95 (*1-57501-108-5*, 22B) Wellington Pr.

Racial Theories. Michael P. Banton. LC 86-32734. 250p. 1987. text ed. 54.95 (*0-521-33456-X*) Cambridge U Pr.

Racial Theories. Michael P. Banton. LC 86-32734. 250p. 1987. pap. text ed. 17.95 (*0-521-33675-9*) Cambridge U Pr.

Racial Violence & Law Enforcement in the South. Ed. by Michal R. Belknap. LC 91-3628. (Civil Rights, White House & Justice Dept. Ser.: Vol. 10). 544p. 1991. text ed. 160.00 (*0-8240-3379-5*) Garland.

Racial Violence in Britain, 1840-1950. Ed. by Panikos Panayi. LC 92-36259. 256p. 1993. 59.00 (*0-7185-1397-5*, Pub. by Leicester Univ Pr) St Martin.

Racial Violence in Kentucky, 1865-1940: Lynchings, Mob Rule, & "Legal Lynchings" George C. Wright. LC 89-38651. (Illus.). 368p. (C). 1996. pap. 14.95 (*0-8071-2073-1*) La State U Pr.

Racialisation of British Policing. Simon Holdaway. 1996. text ed. 49.95 (*0-312-12939-4*) St Martin.

Racialization of America. Yehudi O. Webster. 224p. 1992. 22.95 (*0-312-07557-X*) St Martin.

Racialization of America. Yehudi O. Webster. 320p. 1993. pap. 16.95 (*0-312-10354-9*) St Martin.

Racialized Barriers: The Black Experience in the United States & England in the 1980s. Stephen Small. LC 94-5584. (Critical Studies in Racism & Migration). 256p. (C). 1994. pap. 16.95 (*0-415-07726-5*, B4320) Routledge.

Racialized Boundaries: Race, Nation, Gender, Colour & Class & the Anti-Racist Struggle. Floya Anthias & Nira Yuval-Davis. 240p. (C). 1993. pap. 17.95 (*0-415-10388-6*) Routledge.

Racially Mixed People in America: Within, Between & Beyond Race. Maria P. Root. (Illus.). 400p. 1992. 58.00 (*0-8039-4101-3*); pap. 26.00 (*0-8039-4102-1*) Sage.

Racin' The NASCAR/Winston Cup Stock Car Racing Series. Mark Gilliam. LC 88-62456. (Illus.). 200p. 1989. 45.00 (*0-943231-18-3*) Howell Pr VA.

Racine. Lucien Goldmann. Tr. by Alastair Hamilton from FRE. (Orig.). 1981. pap. 4.95 (*0-906495-77-6*) Writers & Readers.

Racine: A Theatrical Reading. David Meskell. (Illus.). 296p. 1991. 80.00 (*0-19-815161-6*) OUP.

Racine: Mithridate. Jean-Baptiste Racine. Ed. by Gustave Rudler. (Bristol French Texts Ser.). 150p. (FRE.). 1979. pap. 15.95 (*0-631-00440-8*, Pub. by Blckwell Pubs UK) Focus Pub-R Pullins.

Racine: Phedre. Ed. by R. Parish. (French Texts Ser.). 144p. (FRE.). 1996. pap. 18.95 (*1-85399-459-6*, Pub. by Brstl Class Pr UK) Focus Pub-R Pullins.

Racine et Shakespeare: Etudes sur le Romantisme. Stendhal. (Coll. GF). pap. 3.95 (*0-685-35016-9*) Fr & Eur.

Racine, Phedre. Edward D. James & Gillian Jondorf. LC 93-49361. (Landmarks of World Literature Ser.). 128p. (C). 1994. text ed. 34.95 (*0-521-39319-1*) Cambridge U Pr.

Racine, Phedre. Edward D. James & Gillian Jondorf. LC 93-49361. (Landmarks of World Literature Ser.). 128p. (C). 1995. pap. text ed. 12.95 (*0-521-39721-9*) Cambridge U Pr.

Racines du Ciel. Romain Gary. (Folio Ser.: No. 242). (FRE.). 1956. pap. 10.95 (*2-07-036242-6*) Schoenhof.

Racines du Ciel. Romain Gary. 512p. (FRE.). 1972. pap. 11.95 (*0-7859-2289-X*, 2070362426) Fr & Eur.

*__Racine's Phaedra.__ Derek Mahon. 66p. 1996. pap. 12.95 (*1-85235-165-9*) Dufour.

Racine's Theatre: The Politics of Love. William J. Cloonan. LC 77-8683. (Romance Monographs: No. 28). 1978. 22.00 (*84-399-7422-1*) Romance.

Racinet's Full-Color Pictorial History of Western Costume: With 92 Plates Showing Over 950 Authentic Costumes from the Middle Ages to 1800. Auguste Racinet. (Fine Arts Ser.). (Illus.). iv, 92p. (Orig.). 1987. reprint ed. pap. 14.95 (*0-486-25464-X*) Dover.

Racinet's Historic Ornament in Full Color. Auguste Racinet. 112p. 1988. pap. 14.95 (*0-486-25787-8*) Dover.

Racing: A Beginner's Manual. John Craig & Tim Davison. 64p. (C). 1990. text ed. 59.00 (*0-906754-37-2*, Pub. by Fernhurst Bks UK) St Mut.

Racing a Ghost Ship: The Incredible Journey of the Great American II. Rich Wilson. Ed. by JoAnn B. Guernsey. LC 96-1914. (Illus.). (J). 1996. 16.95 (*0-8027-8415-1*); lib. bdg. 17.85 (*0-8027-8417-8*) Walker & Co.

Racing Against Time: Surviving an Organ Transplant & Living a Healthy Life. Anthony C. Anjoubault. 1995. pap. 14.95 (*0-935016-29-5*) Zinn Communs.

Racing Ahead - a Competitors Guide to Motorsport: A Racing Driver's Textbook to Greater Success in Motorsport. Glyn Thomas. (Illus.). 256p. 1995. pap. 19.95 (*0-947981-89-6*, Pub. by Motor Racing UK) Motorbooks Intl.

*__Racing Alone: Fire & Earth, a Visionary Architests Passionate Quest.__ 3rd ed. Nader Khalili. (Illus.). x, 243p. 1983. reprint ed. 14.95 (*1-889625-00-0*) Cal-Earth.

Racing & Wagering Assistant. Jack Rudman. (Career Examination Ser.: C-2714). 1994. pap. 23.95 (*0-8373-2714-8*) Nat Learn.

Racing Around Kentucky. limited ed. Lynn S. Renau. (Illus.). 218p. (Orig.). 1995. pap. 16.95 (*0-9646111-0-4*) Herr Hse.

*__Racing Bike Book.__ Steve Thomas. 1997. pap. text ed. 29.95 (*1-85960-319-X*, Pub. by J H Haynes & Co UK) Motorbooks Intl.

Racing Bikes. J. Kent. (Superskills Ser.). (Illus.). 48p. (YA). (gr. 6-10). 1990. pap. 5.95 (*0-7460-0518-0*, Usborne) EDC.

Racing Breed. Helen Ueltzen. LC 83-20706. (Illus.). 233p. 1984. 34.95 (*0-915309-00-9*) GFI Assocs.

Racing Car Design & Development. Len Terry & Alan Baker. LC 73-85159. 272p. 1973. 14.95 (*0-8376-0080-4*) Bentley.

Racing Cars. Clive Gifford. (Young Machines Ser.). (Illus.). 32p. (J). (ps-3). 1994. pap. 6.95 (*0-7460-1654-9*, Usborne) EDC.

Racing Cars. Clive Gifford. (Machines Board Bks.). (Illus.). 12p. (J). (ps). 1994. bds. 4.95 (*0-7460-1979-3*, Usborne) EDC.

Racing Cars. Clive Gifford. (Machines Board Book Ser.). (Illus.). 32p. (J). (ps-3). 1994. lib. bdg. 14.95 (*0-88110-701-8*, Usborne) EDC.

Racing Cars. Ian Graham. LC 94-17294. (How it Goes Ser.). (J). 1995. lib. bdg. 10.95 (*0-8120-6472-0*) Barron.

Racing Cars. Ian Graham. (How It Goes Ser.). (J). 1995. pap. text ed. 4.95 (*0-8120-9083-7*) Barron.

*__Racing Cars.__ Jeff Savage. (Rollin' Ser.). (Illus.). 48p. (J). (gr. 3-7). 1996. 18.40 (*0-516-20091-7*) Childrens.

Racing Certainties. Brough Scott. (Illus.). 192p. 1996. 39.95 (*0-575-06211-8*, Pub. by V Gollancz UK) Trafalgar.

Racing Crew. Malcolm McKeag. 96p. (C). 1990. text ed. 59.00 (*0-906754-68-2*, Pub. by Fernhurst Bks UK) St Mut.

Racing Days. Brendan Boyd. 1995. pap. 22.50 (*0-8050-4293-8*) H Holt & Co.

Racing Demon. David Hare. 88p. (Orig.). pap. 9.95 (*0-571-16106-5*) Faber & Faber.

Racing Driver: The Theory & Practice of Fast Driving. Denis Jenkinson. LC 59-3790. (Illus.). (J). 1959. 14.95 (*0-8376-0200-9*) Bentley.

*__Racing Driver: The Theory & Practice of Fast Driving.__ Denis Jenkinson. LC 97-17012. 1997. write for info. (*0-8376-0201-7*) Bentley.

Racing Drivers. Tim Wood. Ed. by Rebecca Stefoff. LC 91-39098. (Living Dangerously Ser.). (Illus.). 32p. (J). (gr. 5-9). 1992. lib. bdg. 17.26 (*1-56074-042-6*) Garrett Ed Corp.

Racing Failure: What It Takes to Become an Entrepreneur... & Make It! Bill D. Freiberg. LC 88-92756. 192p. (Orig.). 1989. pap. 8.95 (*0-9622450-0-3*) Freiberg Pub Co.

Racing for Keeneland. Elizabeth H. Sutton. LC 93-43385. 96p. (J). (gr. 5-12). 1994. 14.95 (*1-56566-051-X*) Lickle Pubng.

Racing for the Stars. Maggie Dana. LC 87-16246. (Best Friends Ser.). (Illus.). 128p. (J). (gr. 4-8). 1988. pap. text ed. 2.95 (*0-8167-1196-8*) Troll Communs.

Racing Hearts. Francine Pascal. (SVH Ser.: No. 9). 160p. (YA). 1984. mass mkt. 3.99 (*0-553-27878-9*) Bantam.

*__Racing Hondas.__ Colin MacKellar. (Illus.). 200p. 1997. 35.95 (*1-86126-073-3*, Pub. by Crowood UK) Motorbooks Intl.

Racing Is Everything: Images from the Track. Stephen H. Baker. LC 95-1429. (Illus.). 144p. 1995. pap. 24.95 (*0-253-20982-X*) Ind U Pr.

Racing Kinsers: America's First Family of Sprint Car Racing. Philip Le Vrier. (Illus.). 205p. 1989. lib. bdg. 29.95 (*0-915088-48-7*) C Hungness.

*__Racing Machines.__ Charlie Webster. (Pocket Gems Ser.). (J). 1997. 3.95 (*0-7641-5018-9*) Barron.

Racing Men of TV. Miles Napier. 128p. 1990. pap. 21.00 (*0-85131-301-9*, Pub. by J A Allen & Co UK) St Mut.

Racing Numerology: A Standard System of the Science of Numbers Applied to Horse Racing. 2nd ed. Mozan. 103p. 1993. reprint ed. spiral bd. 21.00 (*0-7873-0628-2*) Hlth Research.

*__Racing on the Rim: A History of the Annual Automobile Racing Tournaments Held on the Sands of the Ormond/Daytona Beach, Florida 1903-1910.__ Dick Punnett. Ed. by Yvonne Punnett. LC 97-90095. (Illus.). vi, 106p. (Orig.). 1997. pap. 22.95 (*0-9657211-0-8*) Tomoka.

R

An Asterisk (*) at the beginning of an entry indicates that the title is appearing in BIP for the first time.

R

Racing on the Tour de France: And Other Stories of Sports. (Illus.). 63p. (J). (gr. 4-6). 1989. 10.95 (0-88309-546-7) Zaner-Bloser.

Racing Planes & Pilots. Joe Christy. (Illus.). 208p. 1982. pap. 8.95 (0-8306-2322-1, 2322) McGraw-Hill Prof.

Racing School Directory. Ed. by Jeffrey Willerth. 100p. 1994. lib. bdg. 9.95 (0-9644044-0-0) Wilston Ent.

Racing School Directory. 6th rev. ed. Jeffrey Willerth. lib. bdg. 11.95 (0-9644044-1-9) Wilston Ent.

***Racing Silver Arrows: Mercedes Benz vs. Auto Union 1934-1939.** Chris Nixon. (Illus.). 362p. 1997. 75.00 (0-85184-055-8, Pub. by Transport Bookman UK) Motorbooks Intl.

Racing Skipper. Robin Aisher. 96p. (C). 1990. text ed. 59. 00 (0-906754-69-0, Pub. by Fernhurst Bks UK) St Mut.

Racing Sled Dogs: An Original North American Sport. Michael Cooper. LC 87-25007. (Illus.). 96p. (J). (gr. 4-7). 1988. 13.95 (0-89919-499-0, Clarion Bks) HM.

Racing the Iditarod Trail. Ruth Crisman. LC 92-25870. (Illus.). 72p. (J). (gr. 5 up). 1993. lib. bdg. 14.95 (0-87518-523-1, Dillon Silver Burdett) Silver Burdett Pr.

***Racing the Iditarod Trail.** Ruth Crisman. 72p. (J). 1996. pap. 7.95 (0-382-39229-9, Dillon Silver Burdett) Silver Burdett Pr.

Racing the IMCA Modified. Steve Smith. (Illus.). 120p. (Orig.). 1990. pap. text ed. 15.95 (0-936834-73-0) S S Autosports.

Racing the Small Block Chevy. John Thawley. (Illus.). 152p. (Orig.). 1990. pap. text ed. 11.95 (0-936834-12-9) S S Autosports.

Racing the Sun. Paul Pitts. 160p. (J). 1988. pap. 4.50 (0-380-75496-7, Camelot) Avon.

Racing the Wind. Wauneta Hackleman. (Illus.). 96p. (Orig.). 1989. pap. 15.00 (0-9622846-0-2); lib. bdg. 23.50 (0-9622846-1-0) Portal AZ.

Racing the Yamaha KT 100-S Engine. Jean Genibrel. (Illus.). 64p. (Orig.). 1986. pap. text ed. 12.95 (0-936834-51-X) S S Autosports.

Racing Through Paradise: A Pacific Passage. limited ed. William F. Buckley, Jr. LC 86-26209. (Illus.). 384p. 1987. 150.00 (0-394-56128-7) Random.

Racing Tides. Martin Kevan. 283p. 1985. pap. 4.95 (0-7736-7092-0) Genl Dist Srvs.

Racing to Love. Martha Ambrose. 192p. 1994. 17.95 (0-8034-9064-X) Bouregy.

Racing to the Beginning of the Road: The Search for the Origin of Cancer. Robert A. Weinberg. 270p. 1996. 27. 50 (0-517-59118-9, Harmony) Crown Pub Group.

Racing to the Moon. Val M. Morelli. Ed. by Spoon. (Renee Romance Ser.). 266p. (Orig.). pap. 5.95 (0-9637810-1-4) Not Aver Mind.

Racing to Win: A Handbook for Serious Racers. Jay A. Hall & George N. Zoros. Ed. by Kay Cleary. 65p. (Orig.). 1990. pap. text ed. 19.95 (0-9626428-0-0) Winning Systems.

Racing Toward Two Thousand One: The Forces Shaping America's Religious Future. Russell Chandler. LC 91-50588. 272p. 1992. 18.00 (0-685-55367-1) Harper SF.

Racing with Catastrophe: Rescuing Higher Education in America. Richard Gambino. 145p. (C). 1990. pap. text ed. 20.00 (0-932088-50-3, Freedom Hse) U Pr of Amer.

Racing with Disaster. Franklin W. Dixon. (Hardy Boys Ser.: No. 126). 160p. (Orig.). (YA). (gr. 3-6). 1994. pap. 3.99 (0-671-87210-9, Minstrel Bks) PB.

***Racing with the Clock: Making Time for Teaching & Learning in School.** Nancy E. Adelman et al. LC 97-15313. 185p. (Orig.). 1997. pap. text ed. 17.95 (0-8077-3648-1) Tchrs Coll.

***Racing with the Clock: Making Time for Teaching & Learning in School.** Nancy E. Adelman et al. LC 97-15313. 185p. 1997. text ed. 39.00 (0-8077-3649-X) Tchrs Coll.

***Racing with the Moon, Bk. 29.** Muriel Jensen. (Born in the U. S. A. Ser.). 1997. 4.50 (0-373-47179-3, 1-47179-6) Harlequin Bks.

Racing with the World: How States Can Build a 21st Century Workforce. Scott Liddell. 37p. 1994. 20.00 (1-55516-807-8, 3912) Natl Conf State Legis.

Racing Without Tears: Horses. Caroline Ramsden. (Illus.). 10.00 (0-87556-247-7) Saifer.

Racism. Maurianne Adams. 160p. (C). 1995. 22.97 (0-7872-1678-X) Kendall-Hunt.

Racism. Christopher B. Doob. (C). 1992. 24.50 (0-06-041720-X) Addson-Wesley Educ.

Racism. Samidha Garg & Jan Hardy. LC 96-16163. (Global Issues Ser.). (J). 1997. lib. bdg. write for info. (0-8172-4548-0) Raintree Steck-V.

Racism. Leonard Harris. LC 97-24857. (Key Concepts in Critical Theory Ser.). 360p. (C). 1997. pap. 19.95 (0-391-03792-7) Humanities.

Racism. Ann T. Keene. LC 94-30540. (Teen Hotline Ser.). (YA). 1995. lib. bdg. 25.68 (0-8114-3815-5) Raintree Steck-V.

Racism. Robert Miles. 158p. (C). 1989. pap. 11.95 (0-415-01809-9) Routledge.

Racism. Linda Mizell. (Think Ser.). 160p. (YA). (gr. 7 up). 1992. pap. 9.95 (0-8027-7365-6); lib. bdg. 15.85 (0-8027-8113-6) Walker & Co.

Racism. Pete Sanders & Steve Myers. (What Do You Know About...Ser.). (Illus.). 32p. (J). (gr. 4-6). 1995. lib. bdg. 15.40 (1-56294-941-1, Copper Beech Bks) Millbrook Pr.

Racism: American Style-A Corporate Gift. Dempsey J. Travis. 250p. 1991. 22.50 (0-941484-09-2) Urban Res Pr.

Racism: An American Cauldron. 2nd ed. Christopher B. Doob. (C). 1995. teacher ed. write for info. (0-614-08611-6) Addson-Wesley Educ.

Racism: An American Cauldron. 2nd ed. Christopher B. Doob. 272p. (C). 1996. text ed. 25.50 (0-673-99485-6) Addson-Wesley Educ.

Racism: Divided by Color. Gerald Newman & Eleanor N. Layfield. LC 94-38963. (Multicultural Issues Ser.). (Illus.). 112p. (YA). (gr. 6 up). 1995. lib. bdg. 18.95 (0-89490-641-0) Enslow Pubs.

Racism: From Slavery to Advanced Capitalism. Carter A. Wilson. LC 96-10053. (Sage Series on Race & Ethnic Relations: Vol. 17). 256p. 1996. 44.00 (0-8039-7336-5); pap. 21.95 (0-8039-7337-3) Sage.

Racism: The Nation's Most Dangerous Pollutant. Gus Hall. 1971. pap. 0.50 (0-87898-064-4) New Outlook.

Racism see Life Issues - Group 2

Racism, a World Issue. Edward D. Soper. LC 75-98731. 304p. 1970. reprint ed. text ed. 52.50 (0-8371-2788-2, SOR&, Greenwood Pr) Greenwood.

Racism after 'Race' Relations. Robert Miles. LC 92-47079. 256p. (C). 1993. pap. 17.95 (0-415-10034-8, Routledge NY) Routledge.

Racism after 'Race' Relations. Robert Miles. LC 92-47079. 256p. (C). (gr. 13). 1993. text ed. 62.95 (0-415-07453-3, Routledge NY) Routledge.

Racism & America's Economic Elite: A Critica Review of Andrew Hacker's Two Nations. Sidney M. Willhelm. 45p. (Orig.). 1994. pap. 5.00 (1-56411-105-9) Untd Bros & Sis.

Racism & Anti-Racism in Probation. David Denney. LC 92-2795. 192p. (C). (gr. 13). 1992. text ed. 79.95 (0-415-06156-3, A7060) Routledge.

Racism & Anti-Racism in Probation. David Denney. LC 92-2795. 224p. (C). (gr. 13). 1993. pap. text ed. 16.95 (0-415-06157-1, A7064) Routledge.

Racism & Anti-Racism in World Perspective. Ed. by Benjamin P. Bowser. LC 95-16620. (Race & Ethnic Relations Ser.: Vol. 13). 304p. 1995. 52.00 (0-8039-4953-7); pap. 24.00 (0-8039-4954-5) Sage.

Racism & Antiracism: Inequalities, Opportunities & Policies. Ed. by Peter Braham et al. 320p. (C). 1992. 55.00 (0-8039-8581-9); pap. 19.95 (0-8039-8582-7) Sage.

Racism & AntiRacism in Real Schools. David Gillborn. LC 94-25726. 496p. 1995. 79.00 (0-335-19093-6, Open Univ Pr); pap. 24.95 (0-335-19092-8, Open Univ Pr) Taylor & Francis.

***Racism & Child Protection: The Black Experience of Child Sexual Abuse.** Valerie Jackson. (Illus.). 128p. 1996. pap. 21.95 (0-304-33276-3); text ed. 60.00 (0-304-33274-7) Cassell.

Racism & Criminology. Dee Cook & Barbara A. Hudson. (C). 1994. text ed. 59.95 (0-8039-8762-5); pap. text ed. 19.95 (0-8039-8763-3) Sage.

Racism & Education: Research Perspectives. Barry Troyna. LC 93-8506. (Modern Educational Thought Ser.). 1993. 79.00 (0-335-15779-3, Open Univ Pr); pap. 27.50 (0-335-15778-5, Open Univ Pr) Taylor & Francis.

Racism & Education: Structures & Strategies. Ed. by Dawn Gill et al. 336p. 1992. 69.95 (0-8039-8577-0); pap. 19.95 (0-8039-8578-9) Sage.

Racism & Equal Opportunity Policies in the 1980s. 2nd ed. Ed. by Richard Jenkins & John Solomos. (Comparative Ethnic & Race Relations Ser.). (Illus.). 256p. (C). 1990. pap. text ed. 22.95 (0-521-38968-2) Cambridge U Pr.

Racism & Human Survival: Lessons of Nazi Germany for Today's World. Claude M. Lightfoot. LC 72-82082. (Illus.). 304p. reprint ed. pap. 86.70 (0-8357-3510-9, 2034255) Bks Demand.

Racism & Justice: The Case for Affirmative Action. Gertrude Ezorsky. LC 91-55062. 136p. 1991. pap. 9.95 (0-8014-9922-4) Cornell U Pr.

Racism & Mental Health: Essays. Ed. by Charles V. Willie et al. LC 72-78933. (Contemporary Community Health Ser.). 624p. reprint ed. pap. 177.90 (0-7837-2472-1, 2042626) Bks Demand.

Racism & Migrant Labour: A Critical Text. Robert Miles. 206p. (Orig.). 1983. pap. 14.95 (0-7100-9212-1, RKP) Routledge.

Racism & Migration in Western Europe. John Wrench & John Solomos. LC 93-1679. 294p. 1993. 45.95 (0-85496-332-4) Berg Pubs.

Racism & Migration in Western Europe. Ed. by John Wrench & John Solomos. LC 93-1679. 293p. 1993. pap. 19.95 (1-85973-007-8) Berg Pubs.

Racism & Psychiatry. Alexander Thomas & Samuel Sillen. 180p. 1974. reprint ed. pap. 9.95 (0-8065-0409-9, Citadel Pr) Carol Pub Group.

Racism & Race Relations: Index & Reference Book of New Information. Neal H. Howell. 150p. 1996. 47.50 (0-7883-0954-4) ABBE Pubs Assn.

Racism & Race Relations: Index & Reference Book of New Information. Neal H. Howell. 150p. 1996. pap. 44.50 (0-7883-0955-2) ABBE Pubs Assn.

Racism & the Class Struggle: Further Pages from a Black Worker's Notebook. James Boggs. LC 74-105314. 188p. reprint ed. pap. 53.60 (0-7837-3916-8, 2043764) Bks Demand.

Racism & the Incorporation of Foreign Labour: Farm Labour Migration to Canada. Vic Satzewich. (Critical Studies in Racism & Migration). 244p. (C). (gr. 13). 1991. text ed. 89.95 (0-415-04396-4, A6140) Routledge.

***Racism & the Law the Legacy & Lessons of Plessy.** Date not set. text ed. 100.00 (0-7923-4665-3) Kluwer Ac.

Racism & the Underclass: State Policy & Discrimination Against Minorities. Ed. by George W. Shepherd, Jr. & David Penna. LC 91-9547. (Studies in Human Rights: No. 13). 192p. 1991. text ed. 49.95 (0-313-27863-6, SZJ, Greenwood Pr) Greenwood.

Racism As a Factor in the 1989 Gubernatorial Election of Doug Wilder. David R. Jones. 104p. 1991. lib. bdg. 59. 95 (0-7734-9432-4) E Mellen.

Racism, Culture, Markets. Gabriel. LC 94-11023. 240p. (Orig.). (C). 1994. pap. 16.95 (0-415-09492-5, B3954) Routledge.

Racism, Culture, Markets. Gabriel. LC 94-11023. 240p. (Orig.). (C). (gr. 13). 1994. text ed. 62.95 (0-415-09491-7, B3950) Routledge.

Racism, Dissent, & Asian Americans: A Documentary History. Ed. by Phillip S. Foner & Daniel Rosenberg. LC 92-38451. (Contributions in American History Ser.: No. 148). 320p. 1993. text ed. 59.95 (0-313-27913-6, FUE/) Greenwood.

Racism, Ethnicity & Politics in Contemporary Europe. Ed. by Alec G. Hargreaves & Jeremy Leaman. 296p. 1995. text ed. 70.00 (1-85278-838-0) E Elgar.

Racism, Ethnicity, & Social Policy. Ian Law. LC 96-498. (Contemporary Social Policy Ser.). 1996. 24.95 (0-13-354093-6) P-H.

Racism, Health, & Post-Industrialism: A Theory of African-American Health. Clovis E. Semmes. LC 95-34440. 200p. 1996. pap. text ed. 18.95 (0-275-95428-5, Greenwood Pr) Greenwood.

Racism, Health, & Post-Industrialism: A Theory of African-American Health. Clovis E. Semmes. LC 95-34440. 200p. 1996. text ed. 59.95 (0-275-94945-1, Praeger Pubs) Greenwood.

Racism, Imperialism, & Peace. Herbert Aptheker. Ed. by Marvin J. Berlowitz & Carol E. Morgan. LC 87-2984. (Studies in Marxism: Vol. 21). 210p. 1987. 22.95 (0-930656-49-0); pap. 9.95 (0-930656-50-4) MEP Pubns.

***Racism in a Racial Democracy: The Maintenance of White Supremacy in Brazil.** Frances W. Twine. LC 97-10768. 1997. write for info. (0-8135-2364-8); pap. write for info. (0-8135-2365-6) Rutgers U Pr.

Racism in America. Ed. by Allan Johnson. 66p. (C). 1984. reprint ed. 26.00 (0-86828-164-6, Pub. by Deakin Univ AT) St Mut.

Racism in American Education: A Model for Change. William E. Sedlacek & Glenwood C. Brooks, Jr. LC 76-6909. 250p. 1976. pap. 25.95 (0-88229-585-3) Nelson-Hall.

Racism in College Athletics. Ed. by Dana D. Brooks & Ronald C. Althouse. LC 92-73667. 319p. (C). 1993. 38. 00 (0-9627926-2-4) Fit Info Tech.

Racism in Contemporary America. Compiled by Meyer Weinberg. LC 95-38637. (Bibliographies & Indexes in Ethnic Studies: No. 6). 864p. 1996. text ed. 125.00 (0-313-29659-6, Greenwood Pr) Greenwood.

Racism in Society. John Solomos & Les Back. 1996. text ed. 49.95 (0-312-16113-1) St Martin.

Racism in Society. John Solomos & Les Back. 1996. text ed. 18.95 (0-312-16114-X) St Martin.

Racism in the Academic Marketplace. David C. Johnson. 160p. 1990. 14.95 (0-533-08573-X) Vantage.

Racism in the Lives of Women: Testimony, Theory & Guides to Antiracist Practice. Ed. by Jeanne Adleman & Gloria Enguidanos. LC 94-20592. 382p. (C). 1995. lib. bdg. 49.95 (1-56024-918-8) Harrington Pk.

Racism in the Lives of Women: Testimony, Theory & Guides to Antiracist Practice. Jeanne Adleman. Ed. by Gloria M. Enguidanos-Clark. LC 94-20592. 1995. pap. 29.95 (1-56023-863-1) Harrington Pk.

Racism in the Post-Civil Rights Era: Now You See It, Now You Don't. Robert C. Smith. LC 94-21493. (SUNY Series in Afro-American Studies). 203p. (C). 1995. text ed. 57.50 (0-7914-2437-5); pap. text ed. 19.95 (0-7914-2438-3) State U NY Pr.

Racism in the United States: A Comprehensive Classified Bibliography. Compiled by Meyer Weinberg. LC 89-78118. (Bibliographies & Indexes in Ethnic Studies: No. 2). 672p. 1990. text ed. 89.50 (0-313-27390-1, WRK/, Greenwood Pr) Greenwood.

Racism in the Western Film from D. W. Griffith to John Ford: Indians & Blacks. Jean-Jacques Sadoux. (Cinema Ser.). 1980. lib. bdg. 250.00 (0-87700-272-X) Revisionist Pr.

Racism is a Myth. Willie Richey. 96p. 1996. per., pap. text ed. 19.95 (0-7872-2011-6) Kendall-Hunt.

Racism Modernity & Identity on the Western Front. Ed. by Ali Rattansi & Sallie Westwood. 350p. 1995. 60.95 (0-7456-0941-4) Blackwell Pubs.

Racism Modernity & Identity on the Western Front. Ed. by Ali Rattansi & Sallie Westwood. 350p. 1995. pap. 24. 95 (0-7456-0942-2) Blackwell Pubs.

Racism of Psychology. Dennis Howitt & J. Owusu-Bampah. (Illus.). 224p. 1994. pap. write for info. (0-13-320680-7) P-H.

Racism of Psychology: Time for Change. Dennis Howitt & J. Owusu-Bempah. 218p. 1995. pap. 29.95 (0-7450-1352-X) P-H.

Racism on Campus: Confronting Racial Bias Through Peer Interventions. Ed. by Jon C. Dalton. LC 85-644751. (New Directions for Student Services Ser.: No. 56). 1991. 19.00 (1-55542-780-4) Jossey-Bass.

Racism 101. Nikki Giovanni. 1995. pap. 11.00 (0-688-14234-6, Quill) Morrow.

Racism or Attitude? The Ongoing Struggle for Black Liberation & Self-Esteem. James L. Robinson. 260p. 1995. 24.95 (0-306-44945-5) Da Capo.

Racism Problematic: Contemporary Sociological Debates on Race & Ethnicity. Ed. by Rohit Barot. LC 96-16101. (Studies in Sociology: Vol. 11). 288p. 1996. 89.95 (0-7734-8818-9) E Mellen.

Racism, Report 3, No. RC3: The Destruction of Civil & Political Liberties. 1993. text ed. 20.00 (0-946088-43-8, Pub. by NCCL UK) St Mut.

Racism, Revolution, Reaction 1861-1877: The Rise & Fall of Radical Reconstruction. Peter Camejo. LC 76-24184. (Illus.). 269p. 1976. lib. bdg. 50.00 (0-913460-49-4) Pathfinder NY.

Racism, Revolution, Reaction 1861-1877: The Rise & Fall of Radical Reconstruction. Peter Camejo. LC 76-24184. (Illus.). 266p. 1976. pap. 17.95 (0-87348-821-0) Pathfinder NY.

***Racism, Sexism, & the University: The Political Science Affair at the Univeristy of British Columbia.** M. Patricia Marchak. 272p. 1996. 42.95 (0-7735-1514-3, Pub. by McGill CN) U of Toronto Pr.

***Racism, Sexism, & the University: The Political Science Affair at the University of British Columbia.** M. Patricia Marchak. 272p. 1996. pap. 16.95 (0-7735-1515-1, Pub. by McGill CN) U of Toronto Pr.

Racism, Sexism, & the World-System: Studies in the Political Economy of the World-System. Ed. by Joan Smith et al. LC 88-10248. (Contributions in Economics & Economic History Ser.: No. 84). 233p. 1988. text ed. 55.00 (0-313-26331-0, SRX/) Greenwood.

Racism, Sexism, Power & Ideology. Colette Guillaumin. LC 94-12149. (Critical Studies in Racism & Migration). 288p. (C). 1995. pap. 16.95 (0-415-09385-6, B4784) Routledge.

Racism, Sexism, Power & Ideology. Colette Guillaumin. LC 94-12149. (Critical Studies in Racism & Migration). 288p. (C). (gr. 13). 1995. text ed. 62.95 (0-415-09384-8, B4779) Routledge.

Racism under Cover in the Suburbs. Elsie F. Keeley. (Illus.). 214p. (Orig.). 1996. pap. 18.95 (0-9648568-0-8) Divrsty Dialogue.

Racist & Sexist Quotations: "Some of the Most Outrageous Things Ever Said" Robert Fikes, Jr. Ed. by Diane Parker. LC 90-60449. 200p. 1992. text ed. 12.95 (0-88247-845-1) R & E Pubs.

Racist Culture: Philosophy & the Politics of Meaning. David T. Goldberg. LC 92-36107. 1993. pap. 22.95 (0-631-18078-8) Blackwell Pubs.

Racist Mind: Portraits of American New-Nazis & Klansmen. Ezekiel Raphael. 368p. 1996. pap. 12.95 (0-14-023449-7, Penguin Bks) Viking Penguin.

Racist Mind: Portraits of Neo-Nazis & Klansmen. Raphael S. Ezekiel. LC 94-45177. 1995. pap. 24.95 (0-670-83958-2, Viking) Viking Penguin.

***Racist Symbols & Reparations: Philosophical Reflections on Vestiges of the American Civil War.** George Schedler. LC 97-25037. (Studies in Social, Political, & Legal Philosophy). 160p. 1997. 53.00 (0-8476-8675-2); pap. 19.95 (0-8476-8676-0) Rowman.

Racist Violence & the State: A Comparative Analysis of Britain, France, & the Netherlands. Rob Witte. LC 95-48378. 232p. (C). 1996. pap. text ed. 15.50 (0-582-27799-X, Pub. by Longman UK) Longman.

Racist Violence in Europe. Ed. by Tore Bjorgo & Rob Witte. 272p. 1994. text ed. 20.95 (0-312-12409-0) St Martin.

Rack, Rope & Red-Hot Pincers: A History of Torture & Its Instruments. Geoffrey Abbott. (Illus.). 243p. 1995. pap. 13.95 (0-7472-3984-3, Pub. by Headline UK) Trafalgar.

Rack Storage of Materials. National Fire Protection Association Staff. 57p. 1991. 22.25 (0-317-63340-6, 231C-91) Natl Fire Prot.

Rack up a Victory. Thomas D. Rossman. (Illus.). 182p. (Orig.). 1988. pap. 7.00 (0-9626414-0-5) T D Rossman.

Racket & Paddle Games: A Guide to Information Sources. Ed. by David A. Peele. LC 80-23977. (Sports, Games, & Pastimes Information Guide Ser.: Vol. 9). 264p. 1980. 68.00 (0-8103-1480-0) Gale.

Racket-Ridden Longshoreman. Daniel Bell. (Reprint Series in Social Sciences). (C). 1993. reprint ed. pap. text ed. 1.00 (0-8290-3813-2, S-13) Irvington.

Racketeering & Organized Crime in the Bingo Industry. (Illus.). 78p. (Orig.). (C). 1994. pap. text ed. 20.00 (0-7881-0234-6) DIANE Pub.

Racketeering in Legitimate Industries. 57p. (Orig.). (C). 1993. pap. text ed. 25.00 (1-56806-835-2) DIANE Pub.

Racketeering in Medicine. J. P. Carter. 392p. 1992. pap. 12. 95 (1-878901-32-X) Hampton Roads Pub Co.

Racketeering in Northern Ireland: A New Version of the Patriot Game. Paul K. Clare. 55p. (C). 1989. pap. text ed. 5.00 (0-942511-19-0) OICJ.

Racketeering in Washington: An Account of the Grafting in Small & Great Things by Our Senators & Members of the House of Representatives & Executives in Public Departments. Raymond Clapper. LC 73-19138. (Politics & People Ser.). 356p. 1974. reprint ed. 26.95 (0-405-05863-2) Ayer.

Rackham's Color Illustrations for Wagner's Ring. Illus. by Arthur Rackham & James Spero. LC 78-73985. 1979. pap. 9.95 (0-486-23779-6) Dover.

Rackman's Fairy Tales Coloring Book. Arthur Rackman. (Illus.). (J). (gr. k-3). 1980. pap. 2.95 (0-486-23844-X) Dover.

Racks: The Natural History of Antlers & the Animals that Wear Them. David Peterson. (Illus.). 208p. (C). 1991. reprint ed. lib. bdg. 35.00 (0-8095-4084-3) Borgo Pr.

Rackstraw: The Magical Thoughts & Adventures of A Brilliant Young Art Mouse. James Drew. Ed. by Mary G. George. LC 93-71718. (Illus.). 168p. (J). (gr. 2-9). 18. 95 (0-9625023-9-1) Art Pr Intl.

Racky. Sadie H. Hawthorne. (True Tales from Hootin' Hollow Ser.). (Illus.). 60p. (J). (gr. k-7). 1992. 10.00 (0-931647-03-7) S & B Pubs.

Racquet. George Hitchcock. 220p. 19.95 (0-934257-54-X) Story Line.

Racquet Sports: An Illustrated Guide. Elinor Nickerson. LC 82-17180. (Illus.). 192p. 1982. lib. bdg. 37.50 (0-89950-051-X) McFarland & Co.

***Racquetball.** Brown & Benchmark Staff. LC 97-12269. (Elements of Learning Ser.). 120p. (C). 1997. per. write for info. (0-697-29453-6) Brown & Benchmark.

Racquetball. Dewayne J. Johnson & Robert A. Oliver. (Illus.). 75p. (Orig.). (C). 1980. pap. text ed. 8.95 (0-89641-045-5) American Pr.

Racquetball. Richard Trestrail. 144p. (C). 1995. pap. text ed. 14.43 (0-7872-1261-X) Kendall-Hunt.

An Asterisk (*) at the beginning of an entry indicates that the title is appearing in BIP for the first time.

Racquetball. 2nd ed. Linus J. Dowell & William A. Grice. (Illus.). 128p. (C). 1983. pap. text ed. 11.95 (*0-89641-123-0*) American Pr.

Racquetball. 2nd ed. Larry R. Edwards. 120p. (Orig.). (C). 1992. pap. text ed. 14.95 (*0-89787-621-0*) Gorsuch Scarisbrick.

Racquetball. 5th ed. Philip E. Allsen & Alan R. Witbeck. 112p. (C). 1991. per. write for info. (*0-697-10060-X*) Brown & Benchmark.

Racquetball. 6th ed. Philip E. Allsen & Alan R. Witbeck. 128p. (C). 1996. per. write for info. (*0-697-25627-8*) Brown & Benchmark.

Racquetball: Basic Skills & Drills. 3rd rev. ed. Bill Verner. LC 91-22393. 136p. (C). 1992. pap. text ed. 14.95 (*1-55934-073-8*, 1073) Mayfield Pub.

Racquetball: Steps to Success. Stan Kittleson. LC 91-11908. 160p. (Orig.). 1992. pap. 14.95 (*0-88011-440-1*, PKIT0440) Human Kinetics.

Racquetball: Strategies for Winning. Lou Fabian. (Illus.). 120p. 1986. text ed. 13.95 (*0-912855-65-7*) E Bowers Pub.

Racquetball: Teaching the Technique-The Technique of Teaching. Rod Anfenson. 88p. (Orig.). 1989. pap. 8.95 (*0-317-93247-0*) R Anfenson.

Racquetball: Ten Beginning Keys to Success. Lou Fabian et al. 124p. 1988. pap. text ed. 13.95 (*0-912855-79-7*) E Bowers Pub.

Racquetball Book. Steve Strandemo. 1990. pap. 8.95 (*0-671-72518-1*) PB.

Racquetball Everyone. 3rd ed. Larry D. Isaacs et al. 176p. 1992. pap. text ed. 14.95 (*0-88725-181-1*) Hunter Textbks.

Racquetball for Everyone: Technique & Strategy. James Sylvis. (Illus.). 128p. 1986. 13.50 (*0-13-750324-5*) P-H.

Racquetball for Men & Women. John W. Reznik et al. (Illus.). 1984. pap. 7.40 (*0-87563-246-7*) Stipes.

Racquetball for Women. Toni Hudson et al. 1980. pap. 3.00 (*0-87980-384-3*) Wilshire.

Racquetball for Women. Joyce R. Weckstein. LC 75-39392. (Illus.). 1975. 2.50 (*0-686-12301-8*) Lincoln Pr MI.

Racquetball Primer. Mitch Henkin. Ed. by Brian P. Jenny. 134p. (Orig.). 1984. pap. 5.95 (*0-915765-03-9*, Full Court Pr Bks.) Natl Pr Bks.

Racquetball Today. Lynn Adams & Erwin Goldbloom. Ed. by Clyde Perlee. 230p. (C). 1991. pap. text ed. 21.75 (*0-314-76958-7*) West Pub.

Racso & the Rats of NIMH. Jane L. Conly. LC 85-42634. (Trophy Bk.). (Illus.). 288p. (J). (gr. 4-7). 1991. pap. 4.50 (*0-06-440245-2*, Trophy) HarpC Child Bks.

Rad Barrier. (Illus.). 1996. 9.95 (*1-889155-15-2*, ODS 3500) Optimus Design.

Radar. P. S. Hall et al. Ed. by R. G. Lee & Frank Hartley. (Land Warfare Ser.: Vol. 9). 170p. 1991. 40.00 (*0-08-037710-6*, Pub. by Brasseys UK); 25.00 (*0-08-037711-4*, Pub. by Brasseys UK) Brasseys Inc.

Radar: A Wartime Miracle. Colin Latham & Anne Stobbs. (Illus.). 256p. 1996. 31.95 (*0-7509-1114-X*, Pub. by Sutton Pubng UK) Bks Intl VA.

***Radar: A Wartime Miracle.** Colin Latham & Anne Stobbs. (Illus.). 256p. (Orig.). 1997. pap. 22.95 (*0-7509-1480-7*, Pub. by Sutton Pubng UK) Bks Intl VA.

Radar: Principles, Technology, Applications. Byron Edde. 816p. 1992. text ed. 72.00 (*0-13-752346-7*) P-H.

Radar - How It All Began. J. Brown. (Illus.). 180p. 1996. pap. 15.95 (*1-85756-212-7*, Pub. by Janus Pubng UK) Paul & Co Pubs.

Radar - Present & Future, London, 23-25, October, 1973. International Conference on Radar Staff. LC 74-169985. (Institution of Electrical Engineers Conference Report Ser.: No. 105). 446p. reprint ed. pap. 127.20 (*0-317-10077-7*, 2012134) Bks Demand.

***Radar Absorbing Materials: From Theory to Design & Characterization.** K. J. Vinoy. 208p. (C). 1996. lib. bdg. 120.00 (*0-7923-9753-3*) Kluwer Ac.

Radar & Arpa Manual. A. G. Bole & W. O. Dineley. (Illus.). 430p. 1993. pap. 58.95 (*0-7506-0818-8*) Buttrwrth-Heinemann.

Radar & Sonar, Pt. 1. Richard E. Blahut et al. (IMA Volumes in Mathematics & Its Applications Ser.: Vol. 32). (Illus.). xi, 260p. 1991. 49.95 (*0-387-97516-0*) Spr-Verlag.

Radar & Sonar: Part 2. (IMA Volumes in Mathematics & Its Applications Ser.: Vol. 39). 155p. 1991. 47.95 (*0-387-97746-5*) Spr-Verlag.

Radar & the Atmosphere. Alfred J. Bogush, Jr. (Radar Library). 375p. 1989. text ed. write for info. (*0-89006-222-6*) Artech Hse.

Radar & the Atmosphere. Alfred J. Bogush. LC 88-35003. (Artech House Radar Library). (Illus.). 470p. reprint ed. pap. 134.00 (*0-7837-5395-0*, 2045159) Bks Demand.

Radar Applications. Merrill I. Skolnik. LC 87-3150. 488p. 1988. 69.95 (*0-87942-223-8*, PCO2212) Inst Electrical.

Radar Array Processing: With Contributions by Numerous Experts. Ed. by Simon Haykin et al. LC 92-10763. (Information Sciences Ser.: Vol. 25). (Illus.). 234p. 1992. 98.00 (*3-540-55224-3*); 108.95 (*0-387-55224-3*) Spr-Verlag.

Radar at Sea: The Royal Navy in World War II. H. Derek Howse. (Illus.). 383p. 1993. 44.95 (*1-55750-704-X*) Naval Inst Pr.

Radar Book. Samuel M. Van Wyck & Max H. Carpenter. LC 84-45261. (Illus.). 106p. (Orig.). 1984. pap. text ed. 20.00 (*0-87033-326-7*) Cornell Maritime.

Radar Calculations Using Personal Computers: Supplement to Radar Calculations Using the TI-59 Programmable Calculator. William A. Skillman. LC 84-70226. (Illus.). 164p. reprint ed. pap. 46.80 (*0-318-39754-4*, 2033128) Bks Demand.

Radar Calculations Using the TI-59 Programmable Calculator. William A. Skillman. LC 81-71047. (Illus.). 417p. reprint ed. pap. 118.90 (*0-685-20805-2*, 2030131) Bks Demand.

Radar Characteristics of Aircrafts. Aleksandr A. Kostylev. LC 93-19658. 400p. 1994. 180.95 (*0-8493-9324-8*) CRC Pr.

Radar Clutter. David K. Barton. LC 82-215301. (Radars Ser.: No. 5). 430p. reprint ed. pap. 122.60 (*0-318-35024-6*, 2030921) Bks Demand.

Radar Cross Section. 2nd ed. Eugene F. Knott et al. LC 92-37802. (Radar Library). 575p. 1993. text ed. write for info. (*0-89006-618-3*) Artech Hse.

Radar Cross Section Analysis & Control. Asoke K. Bhattacharyya & Dipak L. Sengupta. (Radar Library). 356p. 1991. text ed. 49.00 (*0-89006-371-0*) Artech Hse.

Radar Cross Section Handbook, 2 vols. George Ruck et al. LC 68-26774. 949p. 1970. 72.00 (*0-306-30343-4*) Peninsula CA.

Radar Cross Section Measurement. Eugene F. Knott. LC 92-43286. (Electrical Engineering Ser.). 1993. text ed. 99.95 (*0-442-00536-9*) Van Nos Reinhold.

Radar Cross Sections of Complex Objects. Ed. by W. Ross Stone. LC 89-26962. (Illus.). 544p. 1990. text ed. 79.95 (*0-87942-254-8*, PC02485) Inst Electrical.

Radar Days. E. G. Bowen. (Illus.). 248p. 1987. 39.00 (*0-85274-590-7*) IOP Pub.

Radar Design Principles. 2nd ed. Fred E. Nathanson. 1991. text ed. 70.00 (*0-07-046052-3*) McGraw.

Radar Detection. fac. ed. J. V. DiFranco & W. L. Rubin. LC 68-18248. (Artech Radar Library). (Illus.). 670p. 1980. pap. 180.00 (*0-7837-7627-6*, 2047379) Bks Demand.

Radar Detection & Tracking Systems. Shahen A. Hovanessian. LC 73-81238. (Modern Frontiers in Applied Science Ser.). 412p. reprint ed. pap. 117.50 (*0-685-15311-8*, 2027159) Bks Demand.

Radar Electronic Counter-Countermeasures. Ed. by Stephen L. Johnston. LC 79-18873. (Artech Radar Library). 558p. reprint ed. pap. 159.10 (*0-317-27643-3*, 2025062) Bks Demand.

Radar Engineer's Sourcebook. William C. Morchin. LC 92-18686. 1992. write for info. (*0-89006-559-4*) Artech Hse.

Radar Engineer's Sourcebook. William C. Morchin. LC 92-18686. (Artech House Radar Library). 493p. 1993. reprint ed. pap. 140.80 (*0-608-02081-8*, 2062734) Bks Demand.

Radar Equation. David K. Barton. LC 74-82597. (Radars Ser.: No. 2). 248p. reprint ed. pap. 70.70 (*0-318-35025-4*, 2030923) Bks Demand.

Radar Evaluation Handbook. Ed. by Anro Engineering, Inc. Staff et al. (Artech House Radar Library). 450p. 1991. text ed. 77.00 (*0-89006-488-1*) Artech Hse.

Radar for Meteorologists. Ronald E. Rinehart. (Illus.). 218p. (Orig.). (C). 1990. pap. text ed. 15.95 (*0-9608700-5-9*) U NDak Pres.

Radar for Meteorologists. 2nd ed. Ronald E. Rinehart. 334p. (Orig.). (C). 1991. pap. text ed. 25.00 (*0-9608700-7-5*) U NDak Pres.

Radar for Technicians: Installation, Maintenance & Repair. Frederick L. Gould. LC 94-47270. 1995. text ed. 45.00 (*0-07-024062-0*) McGraw-Hill Prof.

Radar Handbook. 2nd ed. Merrill I. Skolnik. 1232p. 1990. text ed. 99.50 (*0-07-057913-X*) McGraw.

Radar in Meteorology: Battan Memorial & 40th Aniversary Radar Meteorology Conference. Ed. by David Atlas. (Illus.). 824p. 1990. 101.00 (*0-933876-86-6*) Am Meteorological.

Radar in World War II. Henry E. Guerlac. LC 85-28752. (History of Modern Physics & Astronomy Ser.). (Illus.). 1216p. 1987. text ed. 110.00 (*0-88318-486-9*) Am Inst Physics.

Radar Meteorology. Henri Sauvageot. (Radar Library). 315p. 1992. text ed. 48.00 (*0-89006-318-4*) Artech Hse.

Radar Observation of the Atmosphere. rev. ed. Louis J. Battan. (Illus.). 334p. (C). 1991. reprint ed. 59.00 (*1-878907-27-1*) TechBooks.

Radar Observer Manual. 5th ed. (Illus.). 141p. 1983. pap. text ed. 14.55 (*0-934114-42-0*, BK-112) Marine Educ.

Radar Observer's Handbook. 7th ed. William Burger. (C). 1987. 125.00 (*0-85174-443-5*, Pub. by Brwn Son Ferg) St Mut.

Radar Polarimetry for Geoscience Applications. Ed. by E. Elachi & Fawaaz T. Ulaby. (Remote Sensing Library). 350p. 1990. text ed. 48.00 (*0-89006-406-7*) Artech Hse.

Radar Principles. Nadav Levanon. LC 87-29832. 308p. 1988. text ed. 89.95 (*0-471-85881-1*) Wiley.

Radar Principles with Applications to Tracking Systems. Philip L. Bogler. LC 89-34215. 319p. 1990. text ed. 99.95 (*0-471-50192-1*) Wiley.

***Radar Processing, Technology, & Applications II.** William J. Miceli. 32p. 1997. pap. 69.00 (*0-8194-2583-4*) SPIE.

Radar Propagation at Low Altitudes. M. Littleton Meeks. (Artech Radar Library). (Illus.). 105p. (C). 1982. write for info. (*0-89006-118-1*) Artech Hse.

Radar Propagation at Low Altitudes. Marion L. Meeks. LC 82-72894. 116p. 1982. reprint ed. pap. 33.10 (*0-608-00558-4*, 2061441) Bks Demand.

Radar Range-Performance Analysis. Lamont V. Blake. LC 91-90362. (Illus.). 443p. 1991. reprint ed. 45.00 (*0-9629720-0-2*) Munro Pub Co.

Radar Reflectivity Measurement: Techniques & Applications. Ed. by Nicholas C. Currie. (Radar Library). (Illus.). 753p. 1989. text ed. 55.00 (*0-89006-324-9*) Artech Hse.

Radar Reflectivity of Land & Sea. 2nd ed. Maurice W. Long. LC 75-13435. (Illus.). 421p. reprint ed. pap. 120.00 (*0-8357-3937-6*, 2036672) Bks Demand.

Radar Remote Sensing, Vol. 1. Ed. by G. P. De Loor. (Remote Sensing Reviews Ser.: Vol. 1, No. 1). 186p. 1983. pap. text ed. 161.00 (*3-7186-0132-X*) Gordon & Breach.

Radar Resolution & Complex-Image Analysis. August W. Rihaczek. LC 96-11029. 524p. 1996. 99.00 (*0-89006-868-2*) Artech Hse.

Radar Resolution & Multipath Effects. David K. Barton. LC 74-82597. (Radars Ser.: Vol. 4). 376p. reprint ed. pap. 107.20 (*0-317-27647-6*, 2025061) Bks Demand.

***Radar Rooster: Egg-Sploring Safety Activity Book.** Mary Larson. Ed. & Illus. by Brian A. Altman. 68p. (J). (ps up). 1997. pap. 8.95 (*1-887050-26-4*) Meridian Creative.

Radar Scattering from Modulated Wind Waves. Ed. by G. J. Komen & W. A. Oost. (C). 1989. lib. bdg. 123.50 (*0-7923-0146-3*) Kluwer Ac.

***Radar Sensor Technology II.** Ed. by Robert Trebits & James L. Kurtz. 22p. 1997. pap. 59.00 (*0-8194-2481-1*) SPIE.

Radar Signal Simulation. Richard L. Mitchell. LC 75-31380. (Artech Radar Library). 224p. reprint ed. pap. 63.90 (*0-317-27681-6*, 2025054) Bks Demand.

Radar Signal Simulation. Richard L. Mitchell. LC 75-31380. 200p. 1985. reprint ed. 46.95 (*0-9615109-0-0*) Peninsula CA.

Radar Signals: An Introduction to Theory & Application. Charles E. Cook & Marvin Bernfeld. 531p. 1993. 75.00 (*0-89006-733-3*) Artech Hse.

Radar System Analysis. David K. Barton. LC 76-45811. (Artech Radar Library). (Illus.). 620p. reprint ed. pap. 176.70 (*0-318-39755-2*, 2033129) Bks Demand.

Radar System Design & Analysis. Shahen A. Hovanessian. 386p. (C). 1984. text ed. write for info. (*0-89006-147-5*) Artech Hse.

***Radar System Design & Analysis.** Shahen A. Hovanessian. LC 84-70897. (Artech House Radar Library). (Illus.). 394p. 1984. reprint ed. pap. 112.30 (*0-608-02496-1*, 2063140) Bks Demand.

Radar Systems. Paul A. Lynn. (Illus.). 144p. 1987. text ed. 17.98 (*0-442-23684-0*) Chapman & Hall.

Radar Systems Principles. Harlod R. Raemer. LC 96-8565. (Illus.). 512p. 1996. 79.95 (*0-8493-9481-3*) CRC Pr.

Radar Target Detection: Handbook of Theory & Practice. Daniel P. Meyer & Herbert A. Mayer. (Electrical Science Ser.). 1973. text ed. 155.00 (*0-12-492850-1*) Acad Pr.

***Radar Technology Encyclopedia.** David K. Barton et al. LC 96-52026. (Radar Technology Ser.). 536p. 1997. 99.00 (*0-89006-893-3*) Artech Hse.

Radar Vulnerabilty to Jamming. Robert N. Lothes et al. (Artech House Radar Library). 130p. 1990. text ed. 49.00 (*0-89006-388-5*) Artech Hse.

Radargrammetric Image Processing. Franz W. Leberl. (Remote Sensing Library). (Illus.). 595p. 1989. text ed. 88.00 (*0-89006-273-0*) Artech Hse.

***Radargrammetric Image Processing.** Franz W. Leberl. LC 89-7033. (Artech House Remote Sensing Library). (Illus.). 621p. 1990. reprint ed. pap. 177.00 (*0-608-02495-3*, 2063139) Bks Demand.

Rada's Guide to Health & Fitness Getaways in the Southwest. Georgene Rada. LC 91-60053. 192p. (Orig.). 1991. pap. 12.95 (*0-9628203-0-X*) Rada Pubns.

Radcliff & Ogden's Calculation of Drug Dosages: An Interactive Workbook. 5th ed. Sheila J. Ogden. LC 94-32094. 496p. (C). (gr. 13). 1994. wbk. ed., pap. text ed. 28.00 (*0-8151-7002-5*) Mosby Yr Bk.

Radcliffe on Trent, 1710-1837. R. Priestland. (C). 1985. text ed. 50.00 (*0-685-22173-3*, Pub. by Univ Nottingham UK) St Mut.

Radcure '84: Conference Proceedings, September 10-13, 1984, Atlanta, GA. Radcure '84 (Atlanta, Ga.) Staff. LC 84-51496. (Illus.). 681p. reprint ed. pap. 180.00 (*0-8357-6500-8*, 2035871) Bks Demand.

Radeau Land Tortoise: North America's Oldest Intact Warship. D. K. Abbass & Joseph W. Zarzynski. (Illus.). 32p. (YA). (gr. 7-12). 1994. pap. 4.95 (*0-937559-02-4*) M-Z Info.

Radecs 1993. IEEE, Nuclear & Plasma Sciences Society Staff. Ed. by Institute of Electrical & Electronics Engineers, Inc. Staff. 600p. 1993. pap. write for info. (*0-7803-1793-9*, 93TH0616-3); fiche write for info. (*0-7803-1794-7*) Inst Electrical.

Rademacher Legacy to Mathematics: Proceedings of the Centenary Conference in Honor of Hans Rademacher, July 1992, the Pennsylvania State University. Ed. by George E. Andrews et al. LC 94-12052. (Contemporary Mathematics Ser.: Vol. 166). 1994. 60.00 (*0-8218-5173-X*, CONM/166) Am Math.

Radetzky March. Joseph Roth. 1996. 18.00 (*0-679-45100-5*) McKay.

Radetzky March. Joseph Roth. Tr. by Eva Tucker & Geoffrey Dunlop from GER. LC 72-97581. 324p. 1983. 22.50 (*0-87951-198-2*); Tusk. pap. 12.95 (*0-87951-189-3*) Overlook Pr.

Radetzky March. Joseph Roth. Tr. by Joachim Neugroschel from GER. 352p. 1995. 25.00 (*0-87951-548-1*); pap. 14.95 (*0-87951-558-9*) Overlook Pr.

***Radetzky March.** Joseph Roth. pap. write for info. (*0-679-44361-4*) Random.

***Radford's Artistic Bungalows: The Complete 1908 Catalog.** Radford Architectural Co. Staff. LC 96-53259. (Illus.). 222p. 1997. reprint ed. pap. text ed. 12.95 (*0-486-29678-4*) Dover.

Radha: Diary of a Woman's Search. 2nd ed. Sivananda Radha. Ed. by Rita Foran. LC 90-32272. (Illus.). 242p. (Orig.). 1990. pap. 13.95 (*0-931454-19-0*) Timeless Bks.

Radha Sings - Gopis Speak. Kamal Kapur. (Illus.). 117p. (Orig.). 1987. pap. 10.00 (*0-932139-16-7*) Dark Child Pr.

Radhakrishna: Profile of a Universalist. Ishwar C. Harris. 1982. 17.50 (*0-8364-0778-4*) S Asia.

Radhakrishna on Hindu Moral Life & Action. Aloysius Michael. 1979. 17.50 (*0-8364-0334-7*) S Asia.

Radhakrishnan. K. Satchidananda Murty & Ashok Vohra. (His Life & Ideas Ser.). (C). 1989. 44.00 (*81-202-0253-8*, Pub. by Ajanta II) S Asia.

Radhakrishnan: A Biography. Sarvepalli Gopal. 420p. 1989. 39.95 (*0-04-440449-2*) Routledge Chapman & Hall.

Radhakrishnan: A Religious Biography. Robert N. Minor. LC 86-30191. 189p. 1987. text ed. 64.50 (*0-88706-554-6*); pap. text ed. 21.95 (*0-88706-555-4*) State U NY Pr.

Radhakrishnan: His Life & Ideas. K. Satchidananda Murty & Ashok Vohra. LC 89-39718. 239p. 1990. text ed. 57.50 (*0-7914-0343-2*); pap. text ed. 18.95 (*0-7914-0344-0*) State U NY Pr.

Radhasoami Reality: The Logic of a Modern Faith. Mark Juergensmeyer. (Illus.). 258p. 1991. text ed. 42.50 (*0-691-07378-3*) Princeton U Pr.

Radhasoami Reality: The Logic of a Modern Faith. Mark Juergensmeyer. 294p. (C). 1991. pap. text ed. 17.95 (*0-691-01092-7*) Princeton U Pr.

Radial & Astigmatic Keratotomy: A Complete Handbook for the Sucessful Practice of Incisional Keratotomy Using the Combined Technique. Kerry Assil & David J. Schanzlin. 234p. 1994. 125.00 (*0-9639097-0-3*, 69999) SLACK Inc.

Radial & Astigmatic Keratotomy: The American System for Precise, Predictable Refractive Surgery. Spencer P. Thornton. LC 94-4186. 204p. 1994. 110.00 (*1-55642-238-5*) SLACK Inc.

Radial Arm Saw Basics. Cliffe. 1991. pap. 12.95 (*0-8273-5385-5*) Delmar.

Radial Arm Saw Basics. Roger W. Cliffe. LC 91-20004. (Basics Ser.). (Illus.). 128p. 1991. pap. 10.95 (*0-8069-7218-1*) Sterling.

Radial Arm Saw Techniques. Roger W. Cliffe. LC 86-898. (Illus.). 352p. (Orig.). 1986. pap. 17.95 (*0-8069-6280-1*) Sterling.

Radial Foraminifera: Morphometrics & Evolution. C. W. Drooger. 250p. 1994. pap. 61.25 (*0-444-85768-0*, North Holland) Elsevier.

Radial Freeways & the Growth of Office Space in Central Cities. Armin K. Ludwig et al. 417p. (Orig.). 1977. pap. 25.00 (*1-55719-008-9*) U NE CPAR.

Radial Tire Conditions Analysis Guide: A Comprehensive Review of Tread Wear & Tire Conditions. (Illus.). 139p. 1994. pap. text ed., spiral bd. 95.00 (*0-88711-238-2*) Am Trucking Assns.

Radiance. large type ed. Anne Maybury. 467p. 1981. 25.99 (*0-7089-0648-6*) Ulverscroft.

Radiance & Virtue: The R. Norris Shreve Collection of Chinese Jade & Other Oriental Works of Art. Katherine R. Tsiang. LC 82-84074. (Illus.). 88p. 1983. 15.00 (*0-936260-15-7*); pap. 7.00 (*0-936260-16-5*) Ind Mus Art.

***Radiance Descending.** Paula Fox. (J). (gr. 5-7). 1997. 14.95 (*0-7894-2467-3*) DK Pub Inc.

Radiance from the Waters: Ideals of Feminine Beauty in Mende Art. Sylvia A. Boone. 303p. (C). 1990. reprint ed. pap. 20.00 (*0-300-04861-0*) Yale U Pr.

Radiance in Stone: Sculptures in Colored Marble from the Museo Nazionale Romano. Ed. by Maxwell L. Anderson & Leila Nista. (EMILOP Ser.: No. 3). (Illus.). 115p. 1995. pap. text ed. 24.95 (*0-9638169-4-2*) M C Carlos Mus.

Radiance in the Gulag. Nijole Sadunaite. 150p. (Orig.). 1992. 7.95 (*0-940535-49-1*, UP149) Franciscan U Pr.

Radiance Like Wind or Water. Richard Ronan. LC 83-72376. 73p. 1984. 14.00 (*0-937872-14-8*); pap. 6.00 (*0-937872-15-6*) Dragon Gate.

Radiance of Ancient Macedonia. Michael A. Dimitri. 66p. 1993. pap. 15.00 (*1-884191-00-2*) Alexandra Pub.

Radiance of Being: Complexity, Chaos & the Evolution of Consciousness Introduced by Herbert Guenther. Allan Combs. LC 96-41972. 350p. 1996. pap. 18.95 (*1-55778-755-7*) Paragon Hse.

Radiance of Jade & the Clarity of Water: Korean Ceramics from the Ataka Collection. Ikutaro Itoh et al. LC 91-58632. (Illus.). 160p. 1991. 50.00 (*1-55595-065-5*) Hudson Hills.

Radiance of Shabbos. Simcha Cohen-Bunim. (ArtScroll Halachah Ser.). (Illus.). 200p. 1986. 18.99 (*0-89906-212-1*); pap. 15.99 (*0-89906-213-X*) Mesorah Pubns.

Radiant. Diane Scharper. 112p. (Orig.). 1996. pap. 12.95 (*1-885938-23-3*) Cathdrl Fndtn Pr.

Radiant Child. Thomas Armstrong. LC 85-40409. 220p. (Orig.). 1985. pap. 8.95 (*0-8356-0600-7*, Quest) Theos Pub Hse.

Radiant Daughters: Fictional American Women. Thelma J. Shinn. LC 85-27196. (Contributions in Women's Studies: No. 66). 230p. 1986. text ed. 55.00 (*0-313-25197-5*, SRD/, Greenwood Pr) Greenwood.

Radiant Days: Writings by Enos Mills. Ed. by John Dotson. (Illus.). 272p. (Orig.). 1994. pap. 15.95 (*0-87480-463-9*); text ed. 35.00 (*0-87480-462-0*) U of Utah Pr.

Radiant Energy Cure Systems. 104p. 1992. 2,450.00 (*0-89336-867-9*, C-026N) BCC.

Radiant Energy in Relation to Forests. William E. Reifsynder & Howard W. Lull. LC 77-10239. (U. S. Department of Agriculture. Technical Bulletin Ser.: 1344). reprint ed. 39.50 (*0-404-16217-7*) AMS Pr.

Radiant Eternity: Reflections on Sri Ramakrishna. M. Sivaramkrishna. (C). 1995. 20.00 (*81-207-1800-3*, Pub. by Sterling Plns Pvt II) S Asia.

Radiant Faith. Rudolph F. Norden. Ed. by Oscar E. Feucht. 1968. student ed., pap. 3.50 (*0-570-03527-9*, 14-1330); teacher ed., pap. 3.50 (*0-570-03528-7*, 14-1331) Concordia.

An Asterisk (*) at the beginning of an entry indicates that the title is appearing in BIP for the first time.

R

Radiant Floor Heating: The Best Systems for Home, Farm or Workplace. Alan Saunders. (Illus.). 260p. 1993. Professional ed. 67.00 (*1-881917-02-9*); Consumer ed. pap. 35.00 (*1-881917-03-7*) Daedalus & Sons.
Radiant Health. Kevin Hunter. 33p. 1993. pap. write for info. (*1-884068-22-7*) Amethyst Pub.
Radiant Identities. Jock Sturges. (Illus.). 80p. 1994. 40.00 (*0-89381-595-0*) Aperture.
Radiant Identities. Jock Sturges. (Illus.). 80p. 1994. pap. 24.95 (*0-89381-649-3*) Aperture.
Radiant Kingdom: An Allegorical Study of Meditation. Ian Macwhinnie. LC 95-47990. 96p. 1996. pap. 8.95 (*0-89087-789-0*) Celestial Arts.
Radiant Life. Truman G. Madsen. 1994. 10.95 (*0-88494-938-9*) Bookcraft Inc.
*__Radiant Life.__ Zaleski. 25.00 (*0-06-069701-6*) HarpC.
*__Radiant Life.__ Zaleski. pap. 15.00 (*0-06-069702-4*) HarpC.
Radiant Living: The Challenge of Change. Juanita O. Keith. LC 90-85331. 126p. (Orig.). 1991. pap. 8.95 (*0-9628351-0-2*) Archer Creat Pr.
Radiant Past: Ideology & Reality in Hungary's Road to Capitalism. Michael Burawoy & Janos Lukacs. 232p. 1992. 28.95 (*0-226-08041-2*) U Ch Pr.
Radiant Past: Ideology & Reality in Hungary's Road to Capitalism. Michael Burawoy & Janos Lukacs. xvi, 232p. 1994. pap. text ed. 13.95 (*0-226-08042-0*) U Ch Pr.
Radiant Performer: The Spiral Path to Performing Power. H. Wesley Balk. (Illus.). 352p. (C). 1990. pap. 18.95 (*0-8166-1868-2*) U of Minn Pr.
Radiant Science, Dark Politics: A Memoir of the Nuclear Age. Martin D. Kamen. LC 83-13510. 350p. 1985. 40.00 (*0-520-04929-2*); pap. 11.95 (*0-520-05897-6*) U CA Pr.
Radiant Shock of Death. Richard Hughes. LC 94-25330. (American University Studies, Series VII: Vol. 183). 280p. (C). 1995. pap. text ed. 29.95 (*0-8204-2610-5*) P Lang Pubng.
Radiant Silhouette: New & Selected Work 1974-1988. John Yau. LC 89-17498. 232p. (Orig.). 1989. 20.00 (*0-87685-773-X*) Black Sparrow.
Radiant Silhouette: New & Selected Work 1974-1988. John Yau. LC 89-17498. 232p. (Orig.). 1989. pap. 13.00 (*0-87685-772-1*) Black Sparrow.
Radiant Silhouette: New & Selected Work 1974-1988, signed ed. deluxe ed. John Yau. LC 89-17498. 232p. (Orig.). 1989. 30.00 (*0-87685-774-8*) Black Sparrow.
Radiant Star Quilt. Eleanor Burns. (Illus.). 64p. 1990. 8.95 (*0-922705-20-8*) Quilt Day.
Radiant Tree. Sylvia Spencer. 1988. 9.95 (*0-913152-17-X*) Folder Edns.
Radiant Tree, & Other Stories. Temple Bailey. LC 73-116932. (Short Story Index Reprint Ser.). 1977. 21.95 (*0-8369-3434-2*) Ayer.
Radiant Way. Margaret Drabble. 384p. 1989. reprint ed. mass mkt. 5.99 (*0-8041-0365-8*) Ivy Books.
Radiant Woman. Joy Haney. 1993. pap. write for info. (*1-880969-08-4*) Schl Prophet.
Radiating Atmosphere: Proceedings of the Summer Advanced Study Institute, Queen's University, Kingston, Ontario, August 3-14, 1970. Summer Advanced Study Institute Staff. Ed. by B. M. McCormac. LC 70-154742. (Astrophysics & Space Science Library: No.24). 455p. 1971. lib. bdg. 146.00 (*90-277-0184-9*) Kluwer Ac.
Radiation. Davidson. 110p. 1986. pap. 8.50 (*0-85207-180-9*) Natl Bk Netwk.
Radiation: Cells & People. Ernest C. Pollard. (Illus.). 133p. (Orig.). (C). 1991. pap. 12.00 (*0-9612798-3-4*) Woodburn Pr.
Radiation: Doses, Effects, Risks. UNEP Staff. 96p. 1992. pap. text ed. 21.95 (*0-631-18317-5*) Blackwell Pubs.
Radiation: One Story of the M. I. T. Radiation Laboratory. Ernest C. Pollard. (Illus.). 197p. (Orig.). 1982. pap. 12.95 (*0-9612798-1-8*) Woodburn Pr.
Radiation: Risks & Realities. 1994. lib. bdg. 250.00 (*0-8490-5780-9*) Gordon Pr.
Radiation: The Hidden Enemy. Rita H. Awana. 1994. pap. text ed. 12.95 (*1-881116-22-0*) Black Forest Pr.
Radiation: What It Is, How It Affects Us & What We Can Do about It. John Davidson. 96p. (Orig.). pap. 12.95 (*0-8464-4279-5*) Beekman Pubs.
Radiation Alarms & Access Control Systems. LC 86-28486. (Report Ser.: No. 88). 81p. 1986. pap. text ed. 35.00 (*0-913392-84-7*) NCRP Pubns.
Radiation & Cancer Risk. Ed. by Tor Brustad et al. (Cancer Ser.). 300p. 1989. 94.95 (*0-89116-978-4*) Hemisp Pub.
Radiation & Cloud Processes in the Atmosphere: Theory, Observation & Modeling. Kuo-Nan Liou. (Oxford Monographs on Geology & Geophysics: No. 21). (Illus.). 512p. 1992. 105.00 (*0-19-504910-1*) OUP.
Radiation & Combined Heat Transfer in Channels. M. Tamonis. Ed. by A. A. Zukauskas. (Experimental & Applied Heat Transfer Equipment Ser.). 239p. 1987. 120.00 (*0-89116-570-3*) Hemisp Pub.
Radiation & Gut. Ed. by C. S. Potten & J. H. Hendry. 328p. 1995. 288.50 (*0-444-89053-X*) Elsevier.
Radiation & Human Health: A Comprehensive Investigation of the Evidence Relating Low-Level Radiation to Cancer & Other Diseases. John W. Gofman. LC 80-26484. (Illus.). 928p. 1982. 29.95 (*0-87156-275-8*) Sierra.
Radiation & Human Health Proposal from Nagasaki: Proceedings of the Nagasaki Symposium '95, 50th Anniversary Meeting of the Atomic Bombing in Nagasaki, Nagasaki, Japan, 19 September 1995. Ed. by Shigenobu Nagataki & Shunichi Yamashita. (International Congress Ser.: No. 1103). 306p. 1996. text ed. 176.00 (*0-444-82287-9*, Excerpta Medica) Elsevier.
Radiation & Life. 2nd ed. Eric J. Hall. 1984. 42.00 (*0-08-028819-7*, Pergamon Pr) Elsevier.
Radiation & Medicine. Lentle. (Radiation Physics & Chemistry Ser.). 1985. pap. 61.00 (*0-08-032402-9*, Pergamon Pr) Elsevier.
Radiation & Mixed Waste Incineration. U. S. Environmental Protection Agency, Office of Wetlands, Oceans, & Watersheds Staff. (EPA Research Ser.). 352p. (Orig.). 1994. pap. text ed. 89.00 (*0-86587-386-0*) Gov Insts.
Radiation & Public Perception: Benefits & Risks. Ed. by Jack P. Young & Rosalyn S. Yalow. LC 94-35190. (Advances in Chemistry Ser.: No. 243). (Illus.). 346p. 1994. 69.95 (*0-8412-2932-5*); pap. 29.95 (*0-8412-3037-4*) Am Chemical.
Radiation & Radioactivity on Earth & Beyond. Ed. by Ivan G. Draganic et al. 329p. 1989. 44.00 (*0-8493-0158-0*, QC795) CRC Pr.
Radiation & Radioactivity on Earth & Beyond. 2nd ed. Ivan G. Draganic et al. 368p. 1993. 65.00 (*0-8493-8675-6*, QC795) CRC Pr.
Radiation & Scattering from Cylindrically Conformal Printed Antennas. fac. ed. Leo C. Kempel & John L. Volakis. (University of Michigan Report: No. 031173-2-T). 177p. 1994. pap. 50.50 (*0-7837-7698-5*, 2047455) Bks Demand.
Radiation & Scattering from Printed Antennas on Cylindrically Conformal Platforms. fac. ed. Leo C. Kempel et al. (University of Michigan Report: No. 030601-3-T). 116p. 1994. pap. 33.10 (*0-7837-7692-6*, 2047448) Bks Demand.
Radiation & Scattering of Waves. Leopold B. Felsen & Nathan Marcuvitz. LC 94-15497. (Electromagnetic Waves Ser.). 928p. 1994. 79.95 (*0-7803-1088-8*, PC4424) Inst Electrical.
Radiation & Scattering of Waves. Leopold B. Felsen & Nathan Marcuvitz. (IEEE/OUP Series on Electromagnetic Wave Theory). 928p. (C). 1996. 90.00 (*0-19-859219-1*) OUP.
Radiation & Skin. C. S. Potten. 226p. 1984. 77.00 (*0-85066-257-5*) Taylor & Francis.
Radiation & Society Vol. 1: Comprehending Radiation Risk: Report to the IAEA. International Atomic Energy Agency Staff. 196p. 1994. pap. 70.00 (*92-0-102194-1*, STI/PUB/959, Pub. by IAEA AU) Bernan Associates.
*__Radiation & Society Vol. 2: Comprehending Radiation Risk.__ International Atomic Energy Agency Staff. 455p. 1996. pap. 155.00 (*92-0-103096-7*, STI/PUB/959/2, Pub. by IAEA AU) Bernan Associates.
Radiation & the Gastrointestinal Tract. Andre Dubois et al. LC 94-27144. 304p. 1994. 169.95 (*0-8493-7667-X*, 7667) CRC Pr.
Radiation & the Lymphatic System: Proceedings. Ed. by John E. Ballou. LC 75-38685. (ERDA Symposium Ser.). 265p. 1976. pap. 14.50 (*0-87079-030-7*, CONF-740930); fiche 9.00 (*0-87079-317-9*, CONF-740930) DOE.
*__Radiation & Water in the Climate System: Remote Measurements.__ Ehrhard Raschke. LC 96-27902. (NATO ASI Series H: Cell Biology). 616p. 1996. 109.50 (*3-540-61470-2*) Spr-Verlag.
Radiation & Waves in Plasmas: Proceedings of the Lockheed Symposium on Magnetohydrodynamics, 5th, Palo Alto, Calif, 1960. Lockheed Symposium on Magnetohydrodynamics Staff. Ed. by Morton Mitchner. LC 61-14651. 167p. reprint ed. pap. 47.60 (*0-317-07864-X*, 2000319) Bks Demand.
*__Radiation Belts: Models & Standards.__ J. Lemaire et al. LC 96-48740. (Geophysical Monographs). 1996. write for info. (*0-87590-079-8*) Am Geophysical.
Radiation Bioeffects & Management Test & Syllabus, Vol. 32. Louis K. Wagner et al. (Professional Self-Evaluation & Continuing Education Program Ser.). (Illus.). 500p. 1991. 190.00 (*1-55903-032-1*) Am Coll Radiology.
Radiation Biology. (Advanced Health Physics Training Ser.). (Illus.). 255p. 1983. ring bd. 110.00 (*0-87683-203-6*) GP Courseware.
Radiation Biology. Cember. 1994. write for info. (*0-8493-8856-2*, CRC Reprint) Franklin.
Radiation Biology. Ed. by Donald J. Pizzarello. 312p. 1982. 139.95 (*0-8493-6011-0*, QP82, CRC Reprint) Franklin.
Radiation Biology, 2 Pts, Pt. 1. Ed. by A. Zuppinger. (Handbook of Medical Radiology Ser.: Vol. 2, Pts. 1 & 2). (Illus.). 1966. 304.00 (*0-387-03544-3*) Spr-Verlag.
Radiation Biology, 2 Pts, Pt. 2. Ed. by A. Zuppinger. (Handbook of Medical Radiology Ser.: Vol. 2, Pts. 1 & 2). (Illus.). 1966. 304.00 (*0-387-03545-1*) Spr-Verlag.
Radiation Biology - Endothelial Cells. Rubin. 1996. write for info. (*0-8493-4840-4*) CRC Pr.
Radiation Biology of the Fetal & Juvenile Mammal: Proceedings. Ed. by Melvin R. Sikov & D. Dennis Mahlum. LC 74-603748. (AEC Symposium Ser.). 1026p. 1969. pap. 33.75 (*0-87079-318-7*, CONF-690501); fiche 9.00 (*0-87079-319-5*, CONF-690501) DOE.
*__Radiation Biophysics.__ 2nd ed. Alpen. 1997. text ed. write for info. (*0-12-053085-6*) Acad Pr.
Radiation Budget at Plateau Station, Antarctica: Paper 5 in Meteorological Studies at Plateau Station, Antarctica. M. Kuhn et al. Ed. by Joost A. Businger. (Antarctic Research Ser.: Vol. 25). (Illus.). 1977. pap. 16.90 (*0-87590-139-5*) Am Geophysical.
Radiation Carcinogenesis: Epidemiology & Biological Significance. Ed. by John D. Boice & Joseph F. Fraumeni. LC 83-21247. (Progress in Cancer Research & Therapy Ser.: No. 26). (Illus.). 509p. reprint ed. pap. 145.10 (*0-7837-7127-4*, 2046956) Bks Demand.
Radiation Carcinogenesis & DNA Alterations. Ed. by Frederic J. Burns et al. LC 87-2224. (NATO ASI Series A, Life Sciences: Vol. 124). 630p. 1987. 125.00 (*0-306-42495-9*, Plenum Pr) Plenum.
Radiation-Chemical Processes in Solid Phase: Theory & Application. Evgeniy I. Grigoriev & Leonid I. Trakhtenberg. LC 96-13918. 1996. 94.95 (*0-8493-9436-8*, 9436) CRC Pr.
Radiation Chemistry. 1981. 11.50 (*0-910362-15-7*) Chem Educ.
Radiation Chemistry: Principles & Applications. Farhataziz & M. A. Rodgers. LC 86-19061. 641p. 1987. 145.00 (*0-89573-127-4*, VCH) Wiley.
Radiation Chemistry & Its Applications. (Technical Reports: No. 84). (Illus.). 182p. 1968. pap. 25.00 (*92-0-045068-7*, IDC84, Pub. by IAEA AU) Bernan Associates.
Radiation Chemistry in Nuclear Reactor Technology. Ed. by A. W. Boyd. 70p. 1983. pap. 25.00 (*0-08-029156-2*, Pergamon Pr) Elsevier.
Radiation Chemistry of Aqueous Solutions: A Portion of Proceedings of the First All-Union Conference on Radiation Chemistry, 1st: 1957: Moscow. All-Union Conference on Radiation Chemistry Staff. 80p. reprint ed. pap. 25.00 (*0-317-27217-9*, 2024708) Bks Demand.
Radiation Chemistry of Monomers, Polymers & Plastics. Joseph E. Wilson. 684p. 1974. 225.00 (*0-8247-6095-6*) Dekker.
Radiation Chemistry of Polymers. V. S. Ivanov. (New Concepts in Polymer Science Ser.). 336p. 1991. 290.00 (*90-6764-137-5*) Coronet Bks.
Radiation, Continuous, to Stellar Luminosity see Encyclopaedic Dictionary of Physics
Radiation Curing: A Discussion of Advantages, Features & Applications. Jim Lacey & Allen H. Keough. LC 80-52815. 97p. pap. 27.70 (*0-317-10943-X*, 2019120) Bks Demand.
Radiation Curing: A Discussion of Advantages, Features & Applications. Jim Lacey & Allen H. Keough. (Illus.). 98p. 1983. 38.00 (*0-938648-15-2*, 2004) T-C Pr CA.
Radiation Curing: An Introduction to Coatings, Varnishes, Adhesives, & Inks. 2nd ed. Society of Manufacturing Engineers Staff. LC 86-71562. (Illus.). 128p. reprint ed. pap. 36.50 (*0-8357-3627-X*, 2036355) Bks Demand.
Radiation Curing: An Introduction to Coatings, Varnishes, Adhesives, & Inks. Society of Manufacturing Engineers Staff. LC 84-51595. 115p. reprint ed. pap. 32.80 (*0-685-15532-3*, 2026701) Bks Demand.
Radiation Curing Buyer's Guide, Vol. 5. Technology Marketing Corporation Staff Editors. 40p. 1983. pap. text ed. 22.00 (*0-318-01981-7*) Tech Marketing.
Radiation Curing Buyer's Guide, Vol. 6. Technology Marketing Corporation Staff Editors. 40p. 1984. pap. text ed. 22.00 (*0-318-01982-5*) Tech Marketing.
Radiation Curing Buyer's Guide Nineteen Eighty-Five. Technology Marketing Corporation Editors. 1980. pap. 22.00 (*0-686-26255-7*) Tech Marketing.
Radiation Curing Buyer's Guide, 1981, Vol. 3. Ed. by Technology Marketing Corporation Staff Editors. 48p. 1981. pap. text ed. 22.00 (*0-936840-05-6*) Tech Marketing.
Radiation Curing Buyer's Guide, 1982, Vol. 4. Technology Marketing Corporation Staff Editors. 50p. 1982. pap. text ed. 22.00 (*0-936840-06-4*) Tech Marketing.
Radiation Curing of Polymeric Materials. Ed. by Charles E. Hoyle & James F. Kinstle. LC 89-29972. (Symposium Ser.: No. 417). (Illus.). 552p. 1989. 109.95 (*0-8412-1730-0*) Am Chemical.
Radiation Curing VI: Conference Proceedings, September 20-23, 1982, Chicago, IL. International Conference on Radiation Curing (6th: 1982: Chicago, IL) Staff. LC 82-60954. 428p. reprint ed. pap. 122.00 (*0-318-35022-X*, 2030900) Bks Demand.
Radiation Curing/Polymers, II, No. 89. Roscoe Randell. 1991. 128.00 (*0-85186-377-9*) CRC Pr.
Radiation Damage in DNA: Structure/Function Relationships at Early Times. Ed. by Alfred F. Fuciarelli & John D. Zimbrick. LC 95-7178. 450p. 1995. text ed. 54.95 (*0-935470-90-5*) Battelle.
Radiation Damage in Materials. 3rd ed. F. L. Bouquet. (Illus.). 170p. 1990. 70.00 (*0-937041-74-2*); pap. 40.00 (*0-937041-75-0*) Systems Co.
Radiation Damage in Materials. 4th ed. Frank L. Bouquet. (Illus.). 180p. 1994. 99.00 (*1-56216-155-5*); pap. 69.00 (*1-56216-156-3*) Systems Co.
Radiation Damage in Metals: Papers Presented at a Seminar of the American Society for Metals, Nov. 9-10, 197. Ed. by N. L. Peterson & S. D. Harkness. LC 76-25094. (Illus.). 415p. reprint ed. pap. 118.30 (*0-317-08178-0*, 2019485) Bks Demand.
Radiation Damage in Solids. Ed. by F. L. Vook & G. W. Arnold. 49p. 6.00 (*0-917853-81-4*, IOM-11) Am Assn Physics.
*__Radiation Damage of Nuclear Power Plant Pressure Vessel Steels.__ N. N. Alekseenko. LC 97-26106. (Russian Materials Monographs). 1997. write for info. (*0-89448-564-4*) Am Nuclear Soc.
Radiation Damage of Structural Materials. Jaroslav Koutsky & Jan Kocik. LC 93-489. (Materials Science Monographs: No. 79). 362p. 1994. 256.25 (*0-444-98708-8*) Elsevier.
Radiation Detection, Course 11. Center for Occupational Research & Development Staff. (Nuclear Technology Ser.). (Illus.). 358p. (C). 1984. pap. text ed. 32.00 (*1-55502-100-X*) CORD Commns.
Radiation Detection & Measurement. 2nd ed. Glenn F. Knoll. LC 88-26142. 754p. 1989. Net. text ed. 57.50 (*0-471-81504-7*) Wiley.
Radiation Detectors. Richard K. Miller & Terri C. Walker. LC 88-84052. (Survey on Technology & Markets Ser.: No. 31). 50p. 1989. pap. text ed. 200.00 (*1-55865-104-7*) Future Tech Surveys.
Radiation Detectors: Physical Principles & Applications. C. F. Delaney & E. C. Finch. 360p. 1992. 105.00 (*0-19-853923-1*) OUP.
Radiation-Dose Reconstruction for Epidemiologic Uses. National Research Council Staff. 140p. (C). 1995. text ed. 34.95 (*0-309-05099-5*) Natl Acad Pr.
Radiation Dose to Patients from Radiopharmaceuticals. International Commission on Radiological Protection Staff. (International Commission of Radiological Protection Ser.: No. 53). (Illus.). 388p. 1988. 129.25 (*0-08-035591-9*, Pergamon Pr) Elsevier.
Radiation Doses, Effects, Risks. 64p. 1986. 12.00 (*92-807-1104-0*, E.86.III.D.4) UN.
Radiation Dosimetry: Physical & Biological Aspects. Ed. by Colin G. Orton. 340p. 1986. 89.50 (*0-306-42056-2*, Plenum Pr) Plenum.
Radiation Dosimetry: X Rays Generated at Potentials of 5 to 150 kV, No. 17. International Commission on Radiation Units & Measurements. LC 74-126755. 1970. 35.00 (*0-913394-10-6*) Intl Comm Rad Meas.
Radiation Dosimetry Instrument & Methods. Shani. 272p. 1991. 127.00 (*0-8493-0170-X*, QC795) CRC Pr.
Radiation Effects. Ed. by W. F. Sheely. LC 67-26579. (Metallurgical Society Conference Ser.: Vol. 37). 864p. reprint ed. pap. 180.00 (*0-317-11268-6*, 2001526) Bks Demand.
Radiation Effects in Breeder Reactor Structural Materials: International Conference, June 19-23, 1977, Camelback Inn, Scottsdale, AZ. International Conference Radiation Effects in Breeder Reactor Structural Materials Staff. Ed. by M. L. Bleiberg & J. W. Bennett. LC 77-90917. 931p. reprint ed. pap. 180.00 (*0-8357-2518-9*, 2052398) Bks Demand.
Radiation Effects in Electronics. American Society for Testing & Materials Staff. LC 65-18216. (American Society for Testing & Materials: No. 384). 243p. reprint ed. pap. 69.30 (*0-317-08042-3*, 2000743) Bks Demand.
Radiation Effects in MOS Devices & Circuits. T. P. Ma & Paul V. Dressendorfer. LC 88-29180. 587p. 1989. text ed. 142.00 (*0-471-84893-X*) Wiley.
*__Radiation Effects in Optoelectronic Devices.__ (Fiber Optics User's Manual & Design Ser.: Vol. XI). 342p. 1984. 75.00 (*0-614-18467-3*, 152U11) Info Gatekeepers.
Radiation Effects Information Generated on the ASTM Reference Correlation-Monitor Steels - DS 54. 84p. 1974. pap. 9.75 (*0-8031-0544-4*, 05-054000-35) ASTM.
Radiation Effects on & Dose Enhancement of Electronic Materials. J. R. Srour et al. LC 84-14770. (Illus.). 128p. 1985. 32.00 (*0-8155-1007-1*) Noyes.
Radiation Effects on Electronics. 3rd ed. F. L. Bouquet. (Illus.). 70p. 1989. 55.00 (*0-937041-76-9*); pap. 35.00 (*0-937041-77-7*) Systems Co.
Radiation Effects on Electronics. 4th ed. Frank L. Bouquet. (Illus.). 85p. 1994. text ed. 75.00 (*1-56216-055-9*); pap. text ed. 45.00 (*1-56216-056-7*) Systems Co.
Radiation Effects on Fiber Optics & Opto Electronics. rev. ed. IGIC, Inc. Staff. (Fiber Optics Reprint Ser.: Vol. 26). (Illus.). 213p. 1994. pap. 75.00 (*1-56851-075-6*) Info Gatekeepers.
Radiation Effects on Kapton. 2nd ed. Frank L. Bouquet. (Illus.). 100p. 1993. 90.00 (*1-56216-162-8*); pap. 60.00 (*1-56216-163-6*) Systems Co.
Radiation Effects on KaptonR. Frank L. Bouquet. (Illus.). 90p. (Orig.). (C). 1990. text ed. 75.00 (*0-937041-86-6*); pap. text ed. 45.00 (*0-937041-87-4*) Systems Co.
Radiation Effects on Nonelectronic Materials. Frank L. Bouquet. (Illus.). 361p. (Orig.). 1994. 110.00 (*1-56216-201-2*); pap. 80.00 (*1-56216-202-0*) Systems Co.
Radiation Effects on Teflon. Frank L. Bouquet. (Illus.). 190p. (Orig.). 1989. text ed. 79.00 (*0-937041-60-2*); pap. text ed. 49.00 (*0-937041-61-0*) Systems Co.
Radiation Effects on Teflon. 2nd ed. Frank L. Bouquet. (Illus.). 180p. (Orig.). 1993. 89.00 (*1-56216-151-2*); pap. 59.00 (*1-56216-152-0*) Systems Co.
Radiation Electrochemical Processes: A Portion of Proceedings of the First All-Union Conference on Radiation Chemistry ,1st: 1957: Moscow) All-Union Conference on Radiation Chemistry Staff. 54p. reprint ed. pap. 25.00 (*0-317-27216-0*, 2024709) Bks Demand.
Radiation Embrittlement & Surveillance of Nuclear Reactor Pressure Vessels: An International Study - STP 819. Ed. by Lendell E. Steele. LC 83-70258. 218p. 1983. text ed. 34.00 (*0-8031-0263-1*, 04-819000-35) ASTM.
Radiation Embrittlement of Nuclear Reactor Pressure Vessel Steels: An International Review, Vol. 2. Lendell E. Steele. LC 86-10811. (Special Technical Publication Ser.: No. 909). (Illus.). viii, 201p. 1986. text ed. 59.00 (*0-8031-0473-1*, 04-909000-35) ASTM.
Radiation Embrittlement of Nuclear Reactor Pressure Vessel Steels: An International Review, Vol. 4. Ed. by Lendell E. Steele. (Special Technical Publication Ser.). (Illus.). 425p. 1993. text ed. 94.00 (*0-8031-1478-8*, 04-011700-35) ASTM.
Radiation Embrittlement of Nuclear Reactor Pressure Vessel Steels, Vol. 3: An International Review. Ed. by Lendell E. Steele. (Special Technical Publication Ser.: No. STP 1011). (Illus.). 280p. 1989. text ed. 64.00 (*0-8031-1187-8*, 04-010110-35) ASTM.
Radiation Energy Treatment of Water, Wastewater, & Sludge: A State-of-the-Art Report. American Society of Civil Engineers, Environmental Engineering Division Staff. LC 92-20609. 64p. 1992. pap. text ed. 12.00 (*0-87262-901-5*) Am Soc Civil Eng.
Radiation Exchange: An Introduction. Jack H. Taylor. 127p. 1990. text ed. 49.00 (*0-12-684560-3*) Acad Pr.
Radiation Exposure & High Altitude Flight. Intro. by Charles B. Meinhold. LC 95-21369. (NCRP Commentaries Ser.: No. 12). 25p. (Orig.). 1995. pap. 20.00 (*0-929600-44-4*) NCRP Pubns.
Radiation Exposure & Occupational Risks. Ed. by E. Scherer et al. (Medical Radiology, Diagnostic Imaging & Radiation Oncology Ser.). (Illus.). 200p. 1990. 139.00 (*0-387-51174-1*) Spr-Verlag.
Radiation Exposure Monitoring & Information Transmittal, Remit, System: User's Manual. 1994. lib. bdg. 250.00 (*0-8490-5719-1*) Gordon Pr.

An Asterisk (*) at the beginning of an entry indicates that the title is appearing in BIP for the first time.

Radiation Exposure of the U. S. Population from Consumer Products & Miscellaneous Sources. LC 87-24720. (Report Ser.: No. 95). 101p. (Orig.). 1987. pap. text ed. 40.00 (*0-913392-94-4*) NCRP Pubns.

Radiation for a Clean Environment: Proceedings. (Proceedings Ser.). (Illus.). 672p. 1975. pap. 120.00 (*92-0-060075-1*, ISP402, Pub. by IAEA AU) Bernan Associates.

Radiation from Apertures in Convex Bodies: Flush-Mounted Antennas. L. N. Zakharyev et al. Tr. by Petr Beckmann from RUS. LC 76-114987. (Electromagnetics Ser.: Vol. 4). 1970. 25.00 (*0-911762-06-X*) Golem.

***Radiation from Black Holes, Future Missions to Primitive Bodies & Middle Atmospheric Fine Structures: Proceedings of the E1.1, B.5 & C2.4 Symposia of COSPAR Scientific Commissions E, B & C Held During the Thirtieth COSPAR Scientific Assembly, Hamburg, Germany, 11-21 July 1994.** Ed. by C. Day et al. (Advances in Space Research Ser.: No. 19). 196p. 1995. pap. text ed. write for info. (*0-08-043097-X*, Pergamon Pr) Elsevier.

Radiation from Charged Particles in Solids. M. A. Kumakhov & F. F. Komarov. Ed. by E. P. Welikhov. Tr. by G. Kurizki. (AIP Translation Ser.). (Illus.). 326p. 1989. 79.00 (*0-88318-600-4*) Am Inst Physics.

Radiation from Relativistic Electrons. A. A. Sokolov & I. M. Ternov. Ed. by C. W. Kilmister. Tr. by S. Chomet from RUS. LC 86-26618. (Translation Ser.). (Illus.). 328p. 1986. text ed. 75.00 (*0-88318-507-5*) Am Inst Physics.

***Radiation Hazards in Perspective.** (Technical Report Ser.: No. 248). 37p. 1962. pap. text ed. 3.00 (*92-4-120248-3*) World Health.

Radiation Heat Transfer. E. M. Sparrow & Cess. 366p. 1978. pap. 79.95 (*0-89116-923-7*) Hemisp Pub.

Radiation Heat Transfer in Disperse Systems. L. A. Dombrovsky. 256p. 1996. 112.50 (*1-56700-057-6*) Begell Hse.

Radiation Heat Transfer in Disperse Systems. L. A. Dombrovsky. LC 96-5544. 1996. write for info. (*0-614-13959-7*) Begell Hse.

Radiation Heat Transfer Notes. Don K. Edwards. LC 81-4539. (Engineering Paperback Ser.). (Illus.). 370p. (Orig.). (C). 1981. pap. text ed. 52.95 (*0-89116-231-3*) Hemisp Pub.

Radiation Histopathology, 2 vols., Vol. 1. George W. Casarett. 160p. 1981. 90.00 (*0-8493-5357-2*, RA1231) CRC Pr.

Radiation Histopathology, 2 vols., Vol. 2. George W. Casarett. 176p. 1981. 89.00 (*0-8493-5358-0*, RA1231) CRC Pr.

Radiation Hormesis. T. D. Luckey. (Illus.). 336p. 1991. 192.00 (*0-8493-6159-1*, QC) CRC Pr.

Radiation Hydrodynamics in Stars & Compact Objects. Ed. by Karl-Heinz A. Winkler & Dimitri Mihalas. (Lecture Notes in Physics Ser.: Vol. 255). vi, 454p. 1986. 59.00 (*0-387-16764-1*) Spr-Verlag.

Radiation in a Cloudy Atmosphere. Ed. by E. M. Feigelson. 1984. lib. bdg. 182.00 (*90-277-1803-2*) Kluwer Ac.

Radiation in Astrophysical Plasmas. V. V. Zheleznyakov. (Astrophysics & Space Science Library). 472p. (C). 1996. lib. bdg. 231.00 (*0-7923-3907-X*) Kluwer Ac.

Radiation in Medicine. 2nd ed. Robert C. Reno. LC 94-73544. (Illus.). 104p. (C). 1994. pap. text ed. 27.95 (*0-916615-05-7*) Bks of Sci.

Radiation in Medicine: A Need for Regulatory Reform. Institute of Medicine Staff. Ed. by Kate-Louise D. Gottfried & Gary Penn. 328p. 1996. text ed. 49.95 (*0-309-05386-2*) Natl Acad Pr.

Radiation in Our Environment. Walter Lee. 170p. 1995. 24.95 (*1-887409-04-1*); pap. 14.95 (*1-887409-03-3*) Faun Pub Co.

***Radiation in Perspective: Applications, Risks, & Protection.** NEA Staff. (Nuclear Energy & Information Ser.). 96p. 1997. pap. 27.00 (*92-64-15483-3*, 66-97-04-1, Pub. by Org for Econ FR) OECD.

Radiation in Plasmas: Proceedings of the Topical Conference on Radiation in Plasmas, Trieste, Italy, 1983, 2 vols., 1. Ed. by B. McNamara. 1000p. 1984. write for info. (*9971-966-37-9*) World Scientific Pub.

Radiation-Induced Cancer. (Proceedings Ser.). (Illus.). 498p. 1969. pap. 65.00 (*92-0-010269-7*, ISP228, Pub. by IAEA AU) Bernan Associates.

Radiation-Induced Cancer from Low-Dose Exposure: An Independent Analysis. John W. Gofman. LC 89-62431. 480p. (Orig.). (C). 1990. pap. 29.95 (*0-932682-89-8*) Comm Nuclear Respon.

Radiation Induced Changes in Microstructure: Thirteenth International Symposium, Part I. Ed. by F. A. Garner et al. LC 87-24104. (Special Technical Publication Ser.: No. 955). (Illus.). 940p. 1987. text ed. 121.00 (*0-8031-0962-8*, 04-955000-35) ASTM.

Radiation Induced F1 Sterility in Lepidoptera for Area-Wide Control. IAEA Staff. 162p. 1993. pap. 55.00 (*92-0-101793-6*, STI/PUB/929, Pub. by IAEA AU) Bernan Associates.

Radiation-Induced Voids in Metals: Proceedings. Ed. by James W. Corbett & Louis C. Ianniello. LC 72-600048. (AEC Symposium Ser.). 878p. 1972. pap. 30.00 (*0-87079-320-9*, CONF-710601); fiche 9.00 (*0-87079-321-7*, CONF-710601) DOE.

Radiation Injury: Effects, Principles, & Perspectives. Arthur C. Upton. LC 69-17672. 136p. reprint ed. pap. 38.80 (*0-317-07735-X*, 2019988) Bks Demand.

Radiation Injury to the Nervous System. Ed. by Philip H. Gutin. 496p. 1991. text ed. 143.50 (*0-88167-760-4*) Lppncott-Raven.

Radiation Measurement in Photobiology. Ed. by B. L. Diffey. 230p. 1989. text ed. 83.00 (*0-12-215840-7*) Acad Pr.

Radiation Monitoring: A Programmed Instruction Book. AEC Technical Information Center Staff et al. 287p. 1967. pap. 36.50 (*0-87079-322-5*, EDM-123) DOE.

Radiation Monitoring Techniques (Radiochemical), Course 20. Center for Occupational Research & Development Staff. (Nuclear Technology Ser.). (Illus.). 310p. (C). 1984. pap. text ed. 30.00 (*1-55502-109-3*) CORD Commns.

Radiation of Atoms in a Resonant Environment. V. P. Bykov. (Optics & Photonics Ser.). 224p. 1994. text ed. 48.00 (*981-02-1092-2*) World Scientific Pub.

Radiation of Relativistic Electrons in Periodic Structures: Proceedings of Second International Symposium (RREPS-95) Ed. by Ju L. Pivovarov & A. P. Potylitsin. (Illus.). 210p. (Orig.). 1996. pap. text ed. 148.00 (*1-898326-38-X*, Pub. by Cambdge Intl UK) Am Educ Systs.

Radiation Oncology. Stewart M. Jackson et al. (Illus.). 264p. 1985. 37.50 (*0-87527-334-3*) Green.

***Radiation Oncology: Management Decisions.** Carlos A. Perez et al. 512p. 1998. spiral bd. write for info. (*0-397-58468-7*) Lppncott-Raven.

Radiation Oncology: Principles. Leibel. 1998. text ed. write for info. (*0-7216-5336-7*) Saunders.

Radiation Oncology: Technology & Biology. Ed. by Peter Mauch & Jay Loeffler. LC 93-31650. 1994. text ed. 119.00 (*0-7216-6724-4*) Saunders.

Radiation Oncology - Radiobiological & Physiological Perspectives: The Boundary-Zone Between Clinical Radiotherapy & Fundamental Radiobiology & Physiology. Hassan K. Awwad. (Developments in Oncology Ser.). (C). 1990. lib. bdg. 257.00 (*0-7923-0783-6*) Kluwer Ac.

Radiation Oncology Annual, 1983. Ed. by David A. Pistenmaa & Theodore L. Phillips. LC 84-644857. (Illus.). 287p. 1984. reprint ed. pap. 81.80 (*0-7837-9534-3*, 2060283) Bks Demand.

***Radiation Oncology of Gynecological Cancers.** Helmut Vahrson. LC 96-29741. (Medical Radiology Ser.). 1997. write for info. (*3-540-56768-2*) Spr-Verlag.

Radiation Oncology Physics - 1986: Proceedings of the AAPM 1986 Summer School Held at Miami University, Oxford, Ohio, July 27-August 1, 1986. Ed. by James G. Kereiakes et al. (American Association of Physicists in Medicine Symposium Ser.: No. 15). 820p. 1987. 75.00 (*0-88318-533-4*) Am Inst Physics.

Radiation Oncology, 1987. Ed. by Theodore L. Phillips & William Wara. LC 87-654098. 183p. 1987. reprint ed. pap. 52.20 (*0-608-00405-7*, 2061119) Bks Demand.

Radiation Phenomena in Plasmas. Toshiro Ohnuma. 326p. 1994. text ed. 74.00 (*981-02-1840-0*) World Scientific Pub.

Radiation Physics, Course 1. Center for Occupational Research & Development Staff. (Nuclear Technology Ser.). (Illus.). 256p. (C). 1984. reprint ed. pap. text ed. 28.00 (*1-55502-065-8*) CORD Commns.

Radiation Physics, Lessons 1-7. Hendee. 200p. (C). (gr. 13). 1985. student ed., spiral bd. 27.95 (*0-8016-4552-2*) Mosby Yr Bk.

Radiation Physics & Chemistry: Magat Memorial Issue, Vols. 2 & 3. Ed. by F. Kieffer. 300p. 1980. pap. 51.00 (*0-08-025069-6*, Pergamon Pr) Elsevier.

Radiation Physics Series, Lessons 4-7. Hendee. (gr. 13). 1985. 525.00 (*0-8016-4603-0*) Mosby Yr Bk.

Radiation Preservation of Food. (Proceedings Ser.). (Illus.). 774p. (Orig.). 1973. pap. 130.00 (*92-0-010373-1*, ISP317, Pub. by IAEA AU) Bernan Associates.

Radiation Preservation of Foods: A Symposium. Edward S. Josephson. LC 67-25568. (Advances in Chemistry Ser.: No. 65). (Illus.). 192p. reprint ed. pap. 54.80 (*0-685-20420-0*, 2052229) Bks Demand.

Radiation Processing: Fourth International Meeting on Radiation Processing, Dubrovnik, Yugoslavia, October 1982, 2 vols. Ed. by V. Markovic. 980p. 1984. Set. pap. 155.00 (*0-08-029162-7*, Pergamon Pr) Elsevier.

Radiation Processing for Environmental Conservation. Ed. by S. Machi. 202p. 1985. pap. 30.00 (*0-08-031435-X*, Pergamon Pr) Elsevier.

Radiation Processing of Polymers. Ajit Singh & Joseph Silverman. 377p. (C). 1992. text ed. 84.50 (*1-56990-096-5*) Hanser-Gardner.

Radiation Protection. William H. Hallenbeck. 288p. 1994. 59.95 (*0-87371-996-4*, L996) Lewis Pubs.

Radiation Protection. Ronald L. Kathren. (Medical Physics Handbooks Ser.: No. 16). (Illus.). 212p. 1985. 84.00 (*0-85274-554-0*) IOP Pub.

Radiation Protection. Euclid Seeram. LC 96-25440. 256p. 1996. pap. text ed. 30.95 (*0-397-55032-4*) Lppncott-Raven.

Radiation Protection. rev. ed. (Illus.). 184p. 1981. text ed. 79.50 (*0-87683-173-0*) GP Courseware.

Radiation Protection: A Guide for Scientists & Physicians. 3rd ed. Jacob Shapiro. (Illus.). 494p. 1990. 47.00 (*0-674-74586-8*) HUP.

Radiation Protection: A Systematic Approach to Safety: Proceedings of the 5th Congress of the International Radiation Protection Society, March 1980, Jerusalem, 2 vols. Ed. by Ronald L. Eisenberg. (Illus.). 1055p. 1980. Set. 560.00 (*0-08-025912-X*, Pub. by Pergamon Repr UK) Franklin.

Radiation Protection - In the Health Sciences. G. Q. Macguire & Marilyn E. Noz. 300p. 1995. text ed. 66.00 (*981-02-2406-0*) World Scientific Pub.

Radiation Protection - In the Health Sciences. Gerald Q. Maguire, Jr. & Marilyn E. Noz. LC 95-49066. 300p. 1995. pap. text ed. 32.00 (*981-02-2407-9*) World Scientific Pub.

Radiation Protection - Recommendations of the ICRP. 2nd ed. International Commission on Radiological Protection. (International Commission of Radiological Protection Ser.: No. 26). 1977. pap. 17.25 (*0-08-021511-4*, Pergamon Pr) Elsevier.

Radiation Protection & Biology. Ritenour. 128p. (C). (gr. 13). 1985. student ed., wbk. ed., spiral bd. 17.95 (*0-8016-4013-X*) Mosby Yr Bk.

Radiation Protection & Biology, Lesson 1 - What Is... Ritenour. (C). (gr. 13). 1985. 150.00 incl. sl. (*0-8016-4001-6*) Mosby Yr Bk.

Radiation Protection & Biology, Lesson 2 - Radiation. Ritenour. (C). (gr. 13). 1985. 150.00 incl. sl. (*0-8016-4002-4*) Mosby Yr Bk.

Radiation Protection & Biology, Lesson 3 - Principle. Ritenour. (C). (gr. 13). 1985. 150.00 incl. sl. (*0-8016-4003-2*) Mosby Yr Bk.

Radiation Protection & Biology, Lesson 4 - Rad Prote... Ritenour. (C). (gr. 13). 1985. 150.00 incl. sl. (*0-8016-4004-0*) Mosby Yr Bk.

Radiation Protection & Biology, Lesson 5 - Protection. Ritenour. (C). (gr. 13). 1985. 150.00 incl. sl. (*0-8016-4005-9*) Mosby Yr Bk.

Radiation Protection & Measurement for Low-Voltage Neutron Generators. Intro. by Warren K. Sinclair. LC 83-62802. (Report Ser.: No. 72). 82p. 1983. pap. text ed. 30.00 (*0-913392-61-8*) NCRP Pubns.

Radiation Protection & New Medical Diagnostic Approaches, Proceedings of the Eighteenth Annual Meeting, Held on April 6-7, 1982. (Annual Meeting Proceedings Ser.: No. 4). 1983. pap. 30.00 (*0-685-16977-4*) NCRP Pubns.

Radiation Protection & the Internal Emitter Saga. J. Newell Stonnard. LC 90-13334. (Taylor Lectures: No. 14). (Orig.). 1990. pap. text ed. 25.00 (*0-929600-13-4*) NCRP Pubns.

***Radiation Protection & the Safety of Radiation Sources.** (Safety Ser.: No. 120). 24p. 1996. pap. 19.00 (*92-0-105295-2*, STI/PUB/1000, Pub. by IAEA AU) Bernan Associates.

Radiation Protection at Nuclear Reactors: 1995 Health Physics Society Summer School. Ed. by Constantine J. Maletskos. LC 95-76188. 616p. 1995. 69.95 (*0-944838-55-3*) Med Physics Pub.

Radiation Protection Concepts & Trade Offs. Hymer L. Friedell. LC 79-90466. (Taylor Lectures: No. 3). 1979. 20.00 (*0-913392-50-2*) NCRP Pubns.

Radiation Protection Dose Limit Standards & Regulations. (Advanced Health Physics Training Ser.). (Illus.). 70p. 1983. 59.50 (*0-87683-353-9*) GP Courseware.

Radiation Protection for Medical & Allied Health Personnel. LC 89-23872. (Report Ser.: No. 105). 129p. 1989. pap. text ed. 40.00 (*0-929600-09-6*) NCRP Pubns.

Radiation Protection for Radiologic Technologists. Robert Frankel. (Illus.). 1976. text ed. 36.95 (*0-07-021875-7*) McGraw.

Radiation Protection for Student Radiographers. Mary A. Statkiewicz. (Orig.). 1985. 18.95 (*0-8016-4738-X*) Mosby Yr Bk.

Radiation Protection for the Transport of Radioactive Substances. European Communities Staff. (Radiation Protection: No. 68). 163p. 1994. pap. 55.00 (*92-826-7531-9*, CR-80-93-129ENC, Pub. by Europ Com UK) Bernan Associates.

Radiation Protection Glossary. 76p. 1976. ring bd. 25.00 (*0-87683-213-3*) GP Courseware.

Radiation Protection Handbook for Laboratory Workers: Handbook, No. 14. K. J. Connor & I. S. McLintock. (Handbook Ser.). 202p. 1994. pap. 125.00 (*0-948237-21-X*, Pub. by H&H Sci Cnslts UK) St Mut.

Radiation Protection I, Course 2. Center for Occupational Research & Development Staff. (Nuclear Technology Ser.). (Illus.). 198p. (C). 1984. pap. text ed. 22.00 (*1-55502-066-6*) CORD Commns.

Radiation Protection II, Course 17. Center for Occupational Research & Development Staff. (Nuclear Technology Ser.). (Illus.). 208p. (C). 1984. pap. text ed. 25.00 (*1-55502-106-9*) CORD Commns.

Radiation Protection in Educational Institutions. LC 66-25710. (Report Ser.: No. 32). 56p. 1996. pap. text ed. 25.00 (*0-913392-14-6*) NCRP Pubns.

Radiation Protection in Hospitals. Richard F. Mould. (Medical Science Ser.). (Illus.). 224p. 1985. 92.00 (*0-85274-802-7*) IOP Pub.

Radiation Protection in Medical Radiography. 2nd ed. Scherer et al. 336p. (gr. 13). 1993. pap. text ed. 35.00 (*0-8016-5750-4*) Mosby Yr Bk.

Radiation Protection in Medical Radiography. 3rd ed. Sherer & Visconti. 352p. (gr. 13). 1997. pap. text ed. 35.00 (*0-8151-2896-7*) Mosby Yr Bk.

Radiation Protection in Medicine: Proceeding of the 28th Annual Meeting. Ed. by Andrew K. Poznanski. LC 92-48318. (Annual Meeting Proceedings Ser.: No. 14). 250p. (Orig.). 1993. pap. text ed. 40.00 (*0-929600-29-0*) NCRP Pubns.

Radiation Protection in Pediatric Radiology. LC 81-80187. (Report Ser.: No. 68). 143p. 1978. pap. text ed. 40.00 (*0-913392-54-5*) NCRP Pubns.

Radiation Protection in the Mineral Extraction Industry. Intro. by Charles B. Meinhold. LC 93-33554. (Report Ser.: No. 118). 1993. pap. text ed. 30.00 (*0-929600-33-9*) NCRP Pubns.

Radiation Protection in the X-Ray Department. Simone R. Plaut. LC 92-49239. 192p. 1993. pap. 27.50 (*0-7506-0606-1*) Buttrwrth-Heinemann.

Radiation Protection in Veterinary Medicine. LC 77-121706. (Report Ser.: No. 36). 60p. 1970. pap. text ed. 20.00 (*0-913392-18-9*) NCRP Pubns.

Radiation Protection Instrumentation & Its Application, No. 20. International Commission on Radiation Units & Measurements. LC 70-177297. (Illus.). v, 60p. 1971. 30.00 (*0-913394-13-0*) Intl Comm Rad Meas.

Radiation Protection Manual. 3rd rev. ed. Lita Lee. (Illus.). 150p. 1991. pap. 6.95 (*1-880358-00-X*) Lita Lee.

Radiation Protection of Patients. Ed. by R. J. Wootton. LC 92-49743. (Postgraduate Medical Science Ser.: No. 1). (Illus.). 192p. (C). 1993. pap. 29.95 (*0-521-42669-3*) Cambridge U Pr.

Radiation Protection of Workers - Ionising Radiations: An ILO Code of Practice. x, 71p. (Orig.). 1987. pap. 13.50 (*92-2-105996-0*) Intl Labour Office.

Radiation Protection of Workers in Mines. Ed. by M. C. Thorne. (International Commission of Radiological Protection Ser.: No. 47). 28p. 1986. pap. 32.75 (*0-08-034020-2*, Pub. by PPL UK) Elsevier.

Radiation Protection on the Threshold of the 21st Century. OECD Staff. 324p. (Orig.). 1993. pap. 56.00 (*92-64-03971-6*) OECD.

Radiation Protection Optimization 'Achievements & Opportunities' Proceedings of 4th European Scientific Seminar, Luxembourg, 20-22 April 1993. European Communities Staff. 465p. 1994. pap. 75.00 (*92-826-4529-0*, CR-NA-15234-ENC, Pub. by Europ Com UK) Bernan Associates.

Radiation Protection Principles for the Disposal of Solid Radioactive Waste. Ed. by M. C. Thorne. (International Commission of Radiological Protection Ser.: No. 46). 35p. 1986. pap. 32.75 (*0-08-033666-3*, Pub. by PPL UK) Elsevier.

Radiation Protection Programmes in the Soviet Union, Poland & Czechoslovakia. (Study Tour Reports). (Illus.). 100p. 1971. pap. 17.00 (*92-0-127071-2*, ISTR2, Pub. by IAEA AU) Bernan Associates.

Radiation Protection Progress Reports, 1978. (Commission of the European Communities Ser.). 854p. 1979. text ed. 396.00 (*3-7186-0011-0*) Gordon & Breach.

Radiation Protection Progress Reports, 1979. (Commission of the European Communities Ser.). 910p. 1980. text ed. 568.00 (*3-7186-0047-1*) Gordon & Breach.

Radiation Protection Progress Reports, 1980. (Commission of the European Communities Ser.). 1342p. 1981. text ed. 714.00 (*3-7186-0062-5*) Gordon & Breach.

Radiation Protection Quantities for External Exposure, Vol. 9. G. Burger et al. (Commission of the European Communities Ser.). 260p. 1981. text ed. 228.00 (*3-7186-0063-3*) Gordon & Breach.

***Radiation Protection Research & Training Programme Synopsis of Research Results, EUR 16800.** 182p. 1996. pap. 40.00 (*92-827-6579-2*, CGNA-16800-ENC, Pub. by Europ Com UK) Bernan Associates.

Radiation Protection Standards. Lauriston S. Taylor. (Monotopic Reprint Ser.). 112p. 1971. 29.00 (*0-8493-0111-4*, CRC Reprint) Franklin.

Radiation Protection Theory & Practice: Proceedings of the Fourth International Symposium of the Society for Radiation Protection, Malvern, 4-9 June 1989. Ed. by E. P. Goldfinch. (Illus.). 512p. 1989. 210.00 (*0-85498-052-0*) IOP Pub.

Radiation Protection Today the NCRP at Sixty Years. Ed. by Warren K. Sinclair. LC 89-13588. (Annual Meeting Proceedings Ser.: No. 11). 368p. (Orig.). 1989. pap. text ed. 40.00 (*0-929600-10-X*) NCRP Pubns.

Radiation-Protective Drugs & Their Reaction Mechanisms. J. C. Livesey et al. LC 85-15451. (Illus.). 146p. 1986. 32.00 (*0-8155-1051-9*) Noyes.

Radiation Quantities & Units, No. 33. International Commission on Radiation Units & Measurements. LC 80-812758. 1980. 40.00 (*0-913394-27-0*, SC 33) Intl Comm Rad Meas.

Radiation Regime & Architecture of Plant Stands. Juhan Ross. (Tasks for Vegetation Science Ser.: No. 3). 480p. 1981. lib. bdg. 269.50 (*90-6193-607-1*) Kluwer Ac.

Radiation Research: Proceedings of the Eighth International Congress of Radiation Research, Edingburgh, July 1987, 2 vols., Set. Ed. by E. M. Fielden et al. 1988. Two Vol. set. 450.00 (*0-85066-428-4*) Taylor & Francis.

Radiation Research: Proceedings of the Eighth International Congress of Radiation Research, Edingburgh, July 1987, 2 vols., Vol. 1. Ed. by E. M. Fielden et al. 450p. 1988. 145.00 (*0-85066-399-7*) Taylor & Francis.

Radiation Research: Proceedings of the Eighth International Congress of Radiation Research, Edingburgh, July 1987, 2 vols., Vol. 2. Ed. by E. M. Fielden et al. 1000p. 1988. 385.00 (*0-85066-385-7*) Taylor & Francis.

Radiation Risks to the Developing Nervous System. Dietrich Schmahl et al. LC 86-7703. 435p. 1986. pap. 80.00 (*0-89574-225-X*) G F Verlag.

Radiation Safety for Laboratory Technicians. Charles A. Kelsey. Ed. by Alvin F. Gardner. (Allied Health Professions Monograph). 42p. (C). 1983. 5.00 (*0-87527-319-X*) Green.

Radiation Safety in Hot Facilities. (Proceedings Ser.: No. 238). (Illus.). 754p. (Orig.). 1970. pap. 95.00 (*92-0-020070-2*, ISP238, Pub. by IAEA AU) Bernan Associates.

Radiation Safety of Gamma & Electron Irradiation Facilities. (Safety Ser.: No. 107). 64p. 1992. pap. 30.00 (*92-0-101692-1*, STI/PUB/896, Pub. by IAEA AU) Bernan Associates.

Radiation Safety Training Criteria for Industrial Radiography. LC 78-61401. (Report Ser.: No. 61). 38p. 1978. pap. text ed. 25.00 (*0-913392-45-6*) NCRP Pubns.

Radiation Science & Societal Decision Making. Ed. by Leonard A. Sagan. LC 94-3423. (NCRP Annual Meeting Proceedings Ser.: No. 15). 329p. (Orig.). 1994. pap. text ed. 45.00 (*0-929600-37-1*) NCRP Pubns.

R

An Asterisk (*) at the beginning of an entry indicates that the title is appearing in BIP for the first time.

R

Radiation Shielding. Kenneth Shultis. LC 95-52376. 544p. (C). 1996. text ed. 90.00 (*0-13-125691-2*) P-H.

Radiation Shielding, Course 19. Center for Occupational Research & Development Staff. (Nuclear Technology Ser.). (Illus.). 228p. (C). 1984. pap. text ed. 25.00 (*1-55502-108-5*) CORD Commns.

Radiation Shielding: Proceedings of the 8th International Conference, Arlington, TX, 1994, 2 vols., Set. 1400p. 1994. pap. 110.00 (*0-89448-191-6*, 700201) Am Nuclear Soc.

Radiation Shielding & Dosimetry. A. Edward Profio. LC 78-15649. (Illus.). 557p. reprint ed. pap. 159.40 (*0-685-23828-8*, 2056609) Bks Demand.

***Radiation Source Book.** (Pathways Through Science Ser.). 1993. pap. text ed. write for info. (*0-582-09426-7*, Pub. by Longman UK) Longman.

Radiation Sterilization of Plastic Medical Devices: Seminar under the Auspices of the University of Lowell, Mass., March 1979. H. K. Mann. 128p. 1980. pap. 25.00 (*0-08-025067-X*, Pergamon Pr) Elsevier.

Radiation Technician. Jack Rudman. (Career Examination Ser.: C-681). 1994. pap. 29.95 (*0-8373-0681-7*) Nat Learn.

Radiation Techniques for Water-Use Efficiency Studies. (Technical Reports: No. 168). (Illus.). 127p. 1975. pap. 30.00 (*92-0-115075-X*, IDC168, Pub. by IAEA AU) Bernan Associates.

***Radiation Technology Clinical Manual.** Robert J. Parelli. (Illus.). 300p. (Orig.). 1997. pap. text ed. 39.95 (*1-57444-147-7*, GR-St Lucie Pr) St Lucie Pr.

Radiation Theory & the Quantum Revolution. Joseph Agassi. LC 93-13904. 1993. 70.00 (*0-8176-2905-X*) Birkhauser.

Radiation Therapy & Thanatology. Richard J. Torpie et al. (Illus.). 194p. (C). 1984. 34.95 (*0-398-04885-1*) C C Thomas.

Radiation Therapy & You: A Guide to Self-Help During Treatment. (Illus.). 52p. (Orig.). 1992. pap. text ed. 20.00 (*1-56806-113-7*) DIANE Pub.

Radiation Therapy for Head & Neck Neoplasms. 3rd ed. C. C. Wang. LC 96-16482. 1996. text ed. 99.00 (*0-471-14971-3*) Wiley.

Radiation Therapy in Pediatric Oncology. K. Kian Ang et al. Ed. by J. Robert Cassady. LC 94-2790. (Medical Radiology Ser.). 1995. 115.00 (*0-387-54105-5*) Spr-Verlag.

Radiation Therapy of Benign Diseases. S. E. Order & S. Donaldson. (Medical Radiology, Diagnostic Imaging & Radiation Oncology Ser.). viii, 213p. 1991. 104.00 (*0-387-50901-1*) Spr-Verlag.

***Radiation Therapy of Benign Diseases.** 2nd ed. E. Order & S. Donaldson. (Medical Radiology Ser.). 250p. 1996. 125.00 (*3-540-58865-5*) Spr-Verlag.

Radiation Therapy of Brain Tumors, Pt. I. rev. ed. 1989. write for info. (*0-944093-06-X*) Am Brain Tumor.

Radiation Therapy of Brain Tumors, Pt. II. 1990. write for info. (*0-944093-07-8*) Am Brain Tumor.

Radiation Therapy of Brain Tumors, Pt. I: A Basic Guide. 1994. write for info. (*0-944093-28-0*) Am Brain Tumor.

Radiation Therapy of Head & Neck Cancer. (Medical Radiology Ser.). (Illus.). 320p. 1989. 198.00 (*0-387-19360-X*) Spr-Verlag.

Radiation Therapy of Tumors & Diseases of the Nervous System. Jean J. Bouchard. LC 66-23233. (Illus.). 244p. reprint ed. pap. 69.60 (*0-317-07855-0*, 2014527) Bks Demand.

Radiation Therapy Physics. Ed. by MD Altschuler et al. LC 94-25784. 1994. write for info. (*3-540-55430-0*) Spr-Verlag.

Radiation Therapy Physics. Ed. by A. R. Smith et al. 474p. 1996. 136.00 (*0-387-55430-0*) Spr-Verlag.

Radiation Therapy Physics. 2nd ed. William R. Hendee & Geoffrey S. Ibbott. 000576p. (C). (gr. 13). 1996. pap. text ed. 74.95 (*0-8016-8099-9*) Mosby Yr Bk.

Radiation Therapy Physics. William R. Hendee. LC 81-7496. (Illus.). 205p. reprint ed. pap. 58.50 (*0-8357-7594-1*, 2056915) Bks Demand.

Radiation Therapy Physics, Simulation, & Treatment Planning. 2nd ed. Washington & Dennis T. Leaver. 320p. (C). (gr. 13). 1996. text ed. 52.95 (*0-8151-9136-7*) Mosby Yr Bk.

Radiation Therapy Planning. 2nd ed. Gunilla C. Bentel. 592p. 1995. pap. text ed. 68.00 (*0-07-005115-1*) McGraw-Hill HPD.

***Radiation Therapy Planning.** Ed. by Norman M. Bleehen et al. LC 82-22017. (Fundamentals of Cancer Management Ser.: Vol. 1). 734p. 1983. reprint ed. pap. 180.00 (*0-608-03815-6*, 2064665) Bks Demand.

Radiation Toxicology. L. G. Cockerham. 76p. 1988. text ed. 88.00 (*2-88124-413-0*) Gordon & Breach.

Radiation Toxicology: Bone Marrow & Leukaemia. Jolyon H. Hendry & Brian I. Lord. 360p. 1995. 95.00 (*0-7484-0338-8*, Pub. by Tay Francis Ltd UK) Taylor & Francis.

***Radiation Transfer: Statistical & Wave Aspects.** L. A. Apresyan & Yu A. Kravtsov. 448p. 1996. text ed. 140.00 (*2-88124-920-5*) Gordon & Breach.

Radiation Transport in Spectral Lines. R. G. Athay. LC 72-188002. (Geophysics & Astrophysics Monographs: No. 1). 266p. 1972. pap. text ed. 61.00 (*90-277-0241-1*); lib. bdg. 104.50 (*90-277-0228-4*) Kluwer Ac.

Radiationless Transitions in Polyatomic Molecules. E. S. Medvedev & V. I. Osherov. LC 94-19897. (Series in Chemical Physics: Vol. 57). 1994. 141.95 (*0-387-57769-6*) Spr-Verlag.

Radiative & Collisional Characteristics of Ions in Hot Plasmas. Ed. by I. I. Sobel'man. (Proceedings of the Lebedev Physics Institute Ser.: Vol. 218). (Illus.). 345p. (C). 1993. lib. bdg. 125.00 (*1-56072-139-1*) Nova Sci Pubs.

Radiative Corrections: Results & Perspectives. Ed. by N. Dombey & F. Boudjema. LC 90-7921. (NATO ASI Series B, Physics: Vol. 233). (Illus.). 610p. 1990. 145.00 (*0-306-43670-1*, Plenum Pr) Plenum.

Radiative Corrections - Status & Outlook: Proceedings of the Tennessee International Symposium. B. F. Ward. 500p. 1995. text ed. 124.00 (*981-02-1785-4*) World Scientific Pub.

Radiative Corrections for E-E Collisions. Ed. by J. H. Kuhn. (Illus.). viii, 349p. 1989. 86.95 (*0-387-51399-X*) Spr-Verlag.

Radiative Corrections in SU (2) L X U (1) Proceedings of the Workshop on Radiative Corrections in SU (2) O X U (1), Miramore, Trieste, Italy, June 6-8. Ed. by B. W. Lynn & J. F. Wheater. 340p. 1984. 55.00 (*9971-966-26-3*); pap. 33.00 (*9971-966-28-X*) World Scientific Pub.

Radiative Energy Transfer. Goulard. (Quantitative Spectroscopy & Radiative Treatment Ser.). Date not set. pap. write for info. (*0-08-028986-X*, Pergamon Pr) Elsevier.

Radiative Heat Transfer. Michael F. Modest. LC 92-24671. (Mechanical Engineering Ser.). 1992. text ed. write for info. (*0-07-042675-9*) McGraw.

Radiative Heat Transfer: Current Research. (HTD Ser.: Vol. 276). 228p. 1994. 50.00 (*0-7918-1275-8*, H00907) ASME.

Radiative Heat Transfer: Proceedings of the First International Symposia on Radiative Heat Transfer. Ed. by M. Pinar Menguc. 400p. 1996. 127.50 (*1-56700-060-6*) Begell Hse.

Radiative Heat Transfer: Theory & Applications. Ed. by A. M. Smith & S. H. Chan. (HTD Ser.: Vol. 244). 124p. 1993. 37.50 (*0-7918-1157-3*, G00801) ASME.

Radiative Heat Transfer in Two-Phase Media. K. S. Adzerikho et al. 208p. (ENG & RUS.). 1992. 101.95 (*0-8493-9304-3*, TJ960) CRC Pr.

Radiative Processes in Astrophysics. George B. Rybicki & Alan P. Lightman. 382p. 1985. pap. text ed. 54.95 (*0-471-82759-2*) Wiley.

***Radiative Processes in Atomic Physics.** Vladimir P. Krainov et al. LC 96-47468. text ed. write for info. (*0-471-12533-4*) Wiley.

Radiative Processes in Discharge Plasmas. Ed. by Joseph M. Proud & Lawrence H. Luessen. (NATO ASI Series B, Physical Sciences: Vol. 149). 600p. 1987. 135.00 (*0-306-42550-5*, Plenum Pr) Plenum.

Radiative Properties of Hot Dense Matter. Ed. by J. Davis et al. 620p. 1985. 104.00 (*9971-978-37-7*) World Scientific Pub.

Radiative Properties of Hot Dense Matter. Ed. by W. Goldstein et al. 400p. (C). 1991. text ed. 115.00 (*981-02-0665-8*) World Scientific Pub.

Radiative Properties of Hot Dense Matter III: Proceedings of the Third International Conference, Williamsburg, Virginia, October 14-18, 1985. Ed. by C. Hooper, Jr. et al. 576p. 1987. text ed. 137.00 (*9971-5-0235-6*) World Scientific Pub.

Radiative Transfer. Subrahmanyan Chandrasekhar. (Illus.). (C). 1960. pap. 11.95 (*0-486-60590-6*) Dover.

Radiative Transfer-I: Proceedings of the First International Symposium on Radiation Transfer, Kusadasi, Turkey, August 13-18, 1995. Ed. by M. Pinar Menguc. LC 96-17763. 1996. write for info. (*1-56700-068-1*) Begell Hse.

Radiative Transfer in Curved Media. Ed. by K. K. Sen & S. J. Wilson. 360p. (C). 1990. text ed. 58.00 (*981-02-0184-2*); pap. text ed. 36.00 (*981-02-0185-0*) World Scientific Pub.

Radiative Transfer in Nontransparent, Dispersed Media. H. Reiss. (Tracts in Modern Physics Ser.: Vol. 113). (Illus.). 200p. 1988. 80.95 (*0-387-18608-5*) Spr-Verlag.

Radiative Transfer in Scattering & Absorbing Atmospheres: Standard Computational Procedures. Ed. by Jacqueline Lenoble. LC 85-31116. 300p. 1985. 71.00 (*0-937194-05-0*) A Deepak Pub.

Radiative Transfer on Discrete Spaces. Ian N. Sneddon. LC 64-12663. (International Series of Monographs on Pure & Applied Mathematics: Vol. 74). 1965. 207.00 (*0-08-010592-0*, Pub. by Pergamon Repr UK) Franklin.

Radiators & Other Heat Emitters. S. Whittome. 1990. 1,280.00 (*0-86022-269-1*, Pub. by Build Servs Info Assn UK) St Mut.

Radiators & Other Heat Emitters-3. BSRIA Staff. (C). 1988. 1,750.00 (*0-685-33891-6*, Pub. by Build Servs Info Assn UK) St Mut.

Radical. reprint ed. Set. 775.00 (*0-404-19545-8*) AMS Pr.

Radical Abolitionism: Anarchy & the Government of God in Antislavery Thought. Lewis Perry. LC 95-4355. 362p. (C). 1995. pap. text ed. 18.00 (*0-87049-899-1*) U of Tenn Pr.

Radical Adult Education: A Political & Philosophical Critique. Brendan Evans. LC 87-13572. (Radical Forum on Adult Education Ser.). 256p. 1987. 45.00 (*0-7099-0942-X*, Pub. by Croom Helm UK) Routledge Chapman & Hall.

Radical Adult Education: Theory & Practice. J. E. Thomas. 73p. (C). 1982. text ed. 60.00 (*0-685-22158-X*, Pub. by Univ Nottingham UK) St Mut.

Radical Adult Education: Theory & Practice. Ed. by J. E. Thomas. (C). 1982. 39.00 (*0-902031-87-2*, Pub. by Univ Nottingham UK) St Mut.

Radical Advice from the Ultimate Wiseguy. Lorraine Peterson. 240p. (Orig.). (YA). (gr. 8-12). 1990. pap. 7.99 (*1-55661-141-2*) Bethany Hse.

Radical Aesthetics & Music Criticism in America, 1930-1950. Alan H. Levy. LC 91-35626. 80p. 1991. lib. bdg. 49.95 (*0-7734-9621-1*) E Mellen.

Radical Analysis of Special Education: Focus on Historical Development & Learning Disabilities. Scott B. Sigmon. 136p. 1987. pap. 24.00 (*1-85000-231-2*, Falmer Pr) Taylor & Francis.

***Radical Approach to Prostate Cancer: The Most Comprehensive Prostate Cancer Book on the Market & Survivors Tell Their Story.** (Illus.). 289p. Date not set. pap. 18.95 (*1-56315-086-7*) Sterling Hse.

Radical Approach to Real Analysis. David Bressoud. (Classroom Resource Materials Ser.). 336p. 1994. pap. text ed. 32.95 (*0-88385-701-4*, RAN) Math Assn.

Radical Aristocrats: London Busworkers from the 1880s to the 1980s. Ken Fuller. (Illus.). 256p. (C). 1985. pap. 19.95 (*0-85315-649-2*, Pub. by Lawrence & Wishart UK) NYU Pr.

Radical Artifice: Writing Poetry in the Age of Media. Marjorie Perloff. (Illus.). 264p. 1992. 32.50 (*0-226-65733-7*) U Ch Pr.

Radical Artifice: Writing Poetry in the Age of Media. Marjorie Perloff. xvi, 264p. 1994. pap. text ed. 13.95 (*0-226-65734-5*) U Ch Pr.

***Radical Artisans in England & France, 1830-1870.** Iorwerth Prothero. 450p. (C). 1997. text ed. 74.95 (*0-521-58299-7*) Cambridge U Pr.

Radical Assimilation in English Jewish History, 1656-1945. Todd M. Endelman. LC 89-45475. (Modern Jewish Experience Ser.). (Illus.). 256p. 1990. 12.95 (*0-253-31952-8*) Ind U Pr.

Radical Assimilation in English Jewish History, 1656-1945. Todd M. Endelman. LC 89-45475. (Modern Jewish Experience Ser.). (Illus.). 254p. 1990. reprint ed. pap. 72.40 (*0-608-01059-6*, 2059367) Bks Demand.

Radical Beginnings: Richard Hofstadter & the 1930s. Susan S. Baker. LC 84-27930. (Contributions in American History Ser.: No. 112). xxi, 268p. 1985. text ed. 59.95 (*0-313-24713-7*, BHO/, Greenwood Pr) Greenwood.

Radical Behaviorism: The Philosophy & the Science. Mecca Chiesa. LC 93-73792. xiii, 241p. (Orig.). (C). 1994. pap. text ed. 16.95 (*0-9623311-4-7*) Authors Coop.

Radical Behaviorism: Willard Day on Psychology & Philosophy. Ed. by Sam Leigland. 208p. (Orig.). (C). 1992. text ed. 49.95 (*1-878978-08-X*); pap. text ed. 29.95 (*1-878978-02-0*) Context Pr.

Radical Bibliographies. Leon Kramer. 1979. lib. bdg. 59.95 (*0-87700-307-6*) Revisionist Pr.

Radical Biology Enlightenment. Roe. 1993. pap. text ed. 14.95 (*0-226-72365-8*) U Ch Pr.

Radical Brethren: Anabaptism & the English Reformation to 1558. Irvin B. Horst. 211p. 1972. 63.50 (*90-6004-292-1*, Pub. by B De Graaf NE) Coronet Bks.

Radical Business Ethics. Richard L. Lippke. 240p. (C). 1995. pap. text ed. 22.95 (*0-8476-8070-3*); lib. bdg. 58.50 (*0-8476-8069-X*) Rowman.

Radical Casework: A Theory of Practice. Jan Fook. 160p. 1993. pap. text ed. 19.95 (*1-86373-281-0*, Pub. by Allen Unwin AT) Paul & Co Pubs.

Radical Center. Alan Baron & William Schneider. write for info. (*0-671-46951-7*) S&S Trade.

Radical Challenge: The Response of Social Democracy. Alastair Kilmarnock. (Illus.). 228p. 1988. pap. 15.95 (*0-233-98179-9*, Pub. by A Deutsch UK) Trafalgar.

***Radical Challenge for Priesthood Today.** William D. Perri. LC 96-60952. 144p. (Orig.). 1996. pap. 14.95 (*0-89622-710-3*) Twenty-Third.

Radical Change Through Communication in Mao's China. Godwin C. Chu. LC 77-3874. 352p. reprint ed. pap. 100.40 (*0-7837-0994-3*, 2041300) Bks Demand.

Radical Chemistry. M. John Perkins. 182p. 1995. pap. text ed. 46.67 (*0-13-320920-2*) P-H.

Radical Chic & Mau-Mauing the Flak Catchers. Tom Wolfe. 153p. 1987. 16.95 (*0-374-24600-9*); pap. 11.00 (*0-374-52072-0*) FS&G.

Radical Choice & Moral Theory: Through Communicative Argumentation to Phenomenological Subjectivity. Zhenming Zhai. LC 94-16408. (Analecta Husserliana Ser.). 201p. (C). 1994. lib. bdg. 98.50 (*0-7923-2891-4*, Pub. by Klwr Acad Pubs NE) Kluwer Ac.

Radical Christian. Arthur Wallis. 189p. 1987. reprint ed. pap. 5.95 (*0-939159-05-8*) Cityhill Pub.

Radical Christian & Exemplary Lawyer: Honoring William Stringfellow. Ed. by Andrew W. McThenia, Jr. LC 95-1892. 161p. (Orig.). 1995. pap. 15.00 (*0-8028-0133-1*) Eerdmans.

Radical Christian Communities. Thomas P. Rausch. (Illus.). 216p. 1990. pap. 14.95 (*0-8146-5008-2*) Liturgical Pr.

Radical Christian Living. Richard Booker. 126p. 1990. 8.99 (*1-56043-018-4*) Destiny Image.

***Radical Christianity.** Norvel Hayes. Date not set. mass mkt. 2.99 (*0-89274-708-0*) Harrison Hse.

Radical Christianity: A Reading of Recovery. Christopher Rowland. LC 88-12402. 207p. 1988. reprint ed. pap. 59.00 (*0-7837-9824-5*, 2060553) Bks Demand.

Radical Christianity & the Flesh of Jesus. Arthur A. Vogel. LC 95-38860. 149p. 1995. pap. 17.00 (*0-8028-0881-6*) Eerdmans.

Radical Constructionism: Rethinking the Dynamics of Development. Melvin Feffer. 240p. (C). 1988. text ed. 36.00 (*0-8147-2590-2*) NYU Pr.

Radical Constructionism: Rethinking the Dynamics of Development. Melvin Feffer. 240p. (C). 1990. pap. text ed. 13.20 (*0-8147-2599-6*) NYU Pr.

***Radical Constructivism.** Ernest Von Glasersfeld. (Studies in Mathematics Education Ser.). 230p. 1996. pap. 24.95 (*0-7507-0572-8*, Falmer Pr) Taylor & Francis.

Radical Constructivism: A Way of Knowing & Learning. Ernst von Glaserfeld. LC 94-36874. 210p. 1995. 65.00 (*0-7507-0387-3*, Falmer Pr) Taylor & Francis.

Radical Constructivism in Mathematics Education. Ed. by Ernest Von Glasersfeld. 272p. (C). 1991. lib. bdg. 121.50 (*0-7923-1257-0*, Pub. by Klwr Acad Pubs NE) Kluwer Ac.

Radical Criminology. Ed. by Michael J. Lynch. (International Library of Criminology, Criminal Justice & Penology). 500p. 1997. text ed. 142.95 (*1-85521-858-5*, Pub. by Dartmth Pub UK) Ashgate Pub Co.

Radical Criminology: The Coming Crises. Ed. by James A. Inciardi. LC 80-14408. (Sage Focus Editions Ser.: No. 23). 320p. reprint ed. pap. 91.20 (*0-8357-4810-3*, 2037747) Bks Demand.

***Radical Critiques of the Law.** International Association for Philosophy of Law & Social Philosophy Staff. Ed. by Stephen M. Griffin & Robert C. Moffat. LC 97-11001. 360p. 1997. 45.00 (*0-7006-0845-1*); pap. 25.00 (*0-7006-0846-X*) U Pr of KS.

Radical Culture: Discourse, Resistance, & Surveillance, 1790-1829. David Worrall. LC 92-64371. 246p. (C). 1992. text ed. 29.95 (*0-8143-2452-5*) Wayne St U Pr.

Radical Currents in Contemporary Philosophy. David H. DeGrood. LC 73-110806. 286p. 1971. 12.75 (*0-87527-029-8*) Green.

Radical Curriculum Theory Reconsidered: A Historical Perspective. Peter S. Hlebowitsh. LC 93-8615. 160p. (C). 1993. text ed. 40.00 (*0-8077-3276-1*); pap. text ed. 16.95 (*0-8077-3275-3*) Tchrs Coll.

Radical Democracy. C. Douglas Lummis. 224p. 1996. 24.95 (*0-8014-3169-7*) Cornell U Pr.

***Radical Democracy.** C. Douglas Lummis. 200p. 1997. pap. 13.95 (*0-8014-8451-0*) Cornell U Pr.

Radical Democracy. Ed. by David Trend. 190p. 1994. pap. 9.00 (*0-8223-6419-0*) Duke.

Radical Democracy: Identity, Citizenship, & the State. Ed. by David Trend. LC 95-8488. 239p. (C). (gr. 13). 1995. pap. 17.95 (*0-415-91247-4*, Routledge NY); text ed. 65.00 (*0-415-91246-6*, Routledge NY) Routledge.

Radical Democracy: Progress Through Disunity. Edward Speyer. 384p. (Orig.). 1984. pap. 9.75 (*0-9613359-0-4*) E Speyer.

Radical Democratic Critique of Capitalist Education. Richard A. Brosio. LC 93-24033. (Counterpoints Studies in the Postmodern Theory of Education Ser.: Vol. 3). 635p. (Orig.). (C). 1994. text ed. 39.95 (*0-8204-2189-8*) P Lang Pubng.

Radical Departures: Desperate Detours to Growing Up. Saul V. Levine. LC 83-26491. 216p. 1986. pap. 4.95 (*0-15-675799-0*, Harvest Bks) HarBrace.

Radical Discontinuities: American Romanticism & Christian Consciousness. Harold P. Simonson. LC 81-72051. 180p. 1983. 32.50 (*0-8386-3159-2*) Fairleigh Dickinson.

Radical Dissonance Theory. R. V. Joule & Jean-Leon Beauvois. (European Monographs in Social Psycholgy Ser.). 250p. 1996. 79.95 (*0-7484-0472-4*); 26.95 (*0-7484-0473-2*) Taylor & Francis.

Radical Durkheim. Frank Pearce. 216p. 1989. text ed. 49.95 (*0-04-445269-1*) Routledge Chapman & Hall.

Radical Durkheim. Frank Pearce. LC 88-31366. 216p. (C). 1989. pap. text ed. 18.95 (*0-04-445270-5*) Routledge Chapman & Hall.

Radical Ecological Theory: A Bibliography. Ed. by Joan Nordquist. (Social Theory: A Bibliographic Ser.: No. 30). 64p. (Orig.). 1993. pap. 15.00 (*0-937855-59-6*) Ref Rsch Serv.

Radical Ecology: The Search for a Livable World. Carolyn Merchant. LC 92-12542. (Revolutionary Thought - Radical Movements Ser.). (Illus.). 288p. (gr. 13). 1992. pap. 16.95 (*0-415-90650-4*, A7618, Routledge NY) Routledge.

Radical Economics. Ed. by Bruce Roberts & Susan Feiner. (Recent Economic Thought Ser.). 272p. (C). 1991. lib. bdg. 78.00 (*0-7923-9178-0*) Kluwer Ac.

Radical Edge. Gordon Ferguson. 1996. pap. 21.99 incl. audio (*1-57782-017-7*) Discipleshp.

Radical Edge: The Message of the Minor Prophets. Gordon Ferguson. 60p. 1994. wbk. ed., pap. 5.99 (*1-884553-28-1*) Discipleshp.

Radical Empiricism of William James. John D. Wild. LC 80-17547. xiv, 430p. 1980. reprint ed. text ed. 41.50 (*0-313-22641-5*, WIRW, Greenwood Pr) Greenwood.

Radical Enlightenment: Pantheists, Freemasons & Republicans. Margaret C. Jacob. (Early Modern Europe Today Ser.). (Illus.). 352p. (C). 1981. text ed. 27.95 (*0-04-901029-8*) Routledge Chapman & Hall.

***Radical Enlightenments of Benjamin Franklin.** Douglas Anderson. LC 96-33236. (New Studies in American Intellectual & Cultural History). (Illus.). 288p. 1997. text ed. 39.95 (*0-8018-5445-8*) Johns Hopkins.

Radical Environmentalism: Philosophy & Tactics. Peter C. List. 276p. (C). 1993. pap. 26.95 (*0-534-17790-5*) Wadsworth Pub.

Radical Evil. Ed. by Joan Copjec. 288p. (C). (gr. 13 up). 1995. text ed. 60.00 (*1-85984-911-3*, Pub. by Vrso UK) Norton.

Radical Evil. Joan Copjec. 288p. (C). 1995. pap. text ed. 20.00 (*1-85984-006-X*, Pub. by Vrso UK) Norton.

Radical Evil on Trial. Carlos S. Nino. LC 95-53689. 224p. (C). 1996. 27.50 (*0-300-06749-6*) Yale U Pr.

Radical Expression: Political Language, Ritual, Symbol in England, 1790-1850. James A. Epstein. (Illus.). 224p. 1994. 48.00 (*0-19-506550-6*) OUP.

***Radical Eye: The Photography of Miron Zownir.** Miron Zownir. 1997. pap. text ed. 25.00 (*3-931126-13-7*, Pub. by Die Gestalten GW) Consort Bk Sales.

Radical Faces of Godard & Bertolucci. Yosefa Loshitzky. LC 94-30602. (Contemporary Film & Television Ser.). (Illus.). 288p. 1994. text ed. 44.95 (*0-8143-2446-0*) Wayne St U Pr.

Radical Faces of Godard & Bertolucci. Yosefa Loshitzky. LC 94-30602. (Contemporary Film & Television Ser.). (Illus.). 288p. 1995. pap. text ed. 18.95 (*0-8143-2447-9*) Wayne St U Pr.

***Radical Feminism.** Crow. 1997. 65.00 (*0-8147-1554-0*); pap. 22.95 (*0-8147-1555-9*) NYU Pr.

An Asterisk (*) at the beginning of an entry indicates that the title is appearing in BIP for the first time.

Radical Feminist Therapy: Working in the Context of Violence. Bonnie Burstow. (Illus.). 344p. (C). 1992. 55.00 (*0-8039-4787-9*); pap. 26.00 (*0-8039-4788-7*) Sage.

Radical Feminists of Heterodoxy: Greenwich Village, 1912-1940. 2nd rev. ed. Judith Schwarz. LC 86-62342. (Illus.). 180p. 1986. pap. 8.95 (*0-934678-08-1*) New Victoria Pubs.

Radical Fictions & the Novels of Norman Mailer. Nigel Leigh. LC 89-4564. 280p. 1990. text ed. 39.95 (*0-312-03464-4*) St Martin.

Radical Fragments. James L. Marsh. LC 91-27578. (New Studies in Aesthetics: Vol. 9). 313p. (C). 1992. text ed. 55.95 (*0-8204-1589-8*) P Lang Pubng.

Radical Future of Liberal Feminism. rev. ed. Zillah R. Eisenstein. LC 92-36248. (Northeastern Series in Feminist Theory). 288p. (C). 1993. text ed. 42.50 (*1-55553-154-7*); pap. text ed. 15.95 (*1-55553-155-5*) NE U Pr.

Radical Golf. Michael Laughlin. 192p. 1996. pap. 12.00 (*0-517-88626-X*) Crown Pub Group.

Radical Grace: Daily Meditations. Richard Rohr. Ed. by John B. Feister. 410p. 1993. 22.95 (*0-86716-151-5*) St Anthony Mess Pr.

Radical Grace: Daily Meditations by Richard Rohr. Ed. by John B. Feister. 410p. 1995. pap. 13.95 (*0-86716-257-0*) St Anthony Mess Pr.

Radical Guide for Catholics: Rooted in the Essentials of Our Faith. Bill Huebsch. LC 92-81719. 224p. (Orig.). 1992. pap. 9.95 (*0-89622-525-9*) Twenty-Third.

Radical Guide to Macbeth & Hamlet. Fintan O'Toole. 78p. 1994. pap. 5.95 (*1-874597-19-7*, Pub. by New Island Bks IE) Irish Bks Media.

Radical Hegelian: The Political & Social Philosophy of Henry Jones. David Boucher & Andrew Vincent. LC 93-39173. 1994. text ed. 49.95 (*0-312-12079-6*) St Martin.

Radical Heritage: Labor, Socialism & Reform in Washington & British Columbia, 1885-1917. Carlos A. Schwantes. 308p. 1994. reprint ed. pap. 19.95 (*0-89301-175-4*) U of Idaho Pr.

Radical Hermeneutics: Repetition, Deconstruction & the Hermeneutic Project. John D. Caputo. LC 86-46143. (Studies in Phenomenology & Existential Philosophy). 332p. 1988. 39.95 (*0-253-34785-8*); pap. 18.95 (*0-253-20442-9*, MB-442) Ind U Pr.

Radical History Review Vol. 65: Anthropology & History. Ed. by RHR Collective Staff. 200p. (C). 1996. pap. text ed. 19.95 (*0-521-57690-3*) Cambridge U Pr.

Radical Home Owner: Housing Tenure & Social Change. Ian Winter. 1995p. 1995. text ed. 45.00 (*2-88449-028-0*) Gordon & Breach.

Radical Honesty: How to Transform Your Life by Telling the Truth. Brad Blanton. 304p. 1996. pap. 12.95 (*0-440-50754-5*, Dell Trade Pbks) Dell.

Radical Hospitality. David Rupprecht & Ruth Rupprecht. LC 83-3259. 110p. 1983. pap. 4.99 (*0-87552-420-6*, Pub. by Evangelical Pr) Presby & Reformed.

Radical Hospitality: Leader's Guide. David Rupprecht et al. 1985. pap. 2.99 (*0-87552-419-2*, Pub. by Evangelical Pr) Presby & Reformed.

Radical Humanism: Selected Essays. Jean Amery. Ed. & Tr. by Sidney Rosenfeld from FRE. Tr. by Stella P. Rosenfeld from FRE. LC 83-49525. 160p. 1985. 27.50 (*0-253-34770-X*) Ind U Pr.

Radical Innocence: A Critical Study of the Hollywood Ten. Bernard F. Dick. LC 88-17366. 280p. 1989. 30.00 (*0-8131-1660-0*) U Pr of Ky.

Radical Institutionalism: Contemporary Voices. Ed. by William M. Dugger. LC 88-32791. (Contributions in Economics & Economic History Ser.: No. 90). 162p. 1989. text ed. 45.00 (*0-313-26595-X*, DRL, Greenwood Pr) Greenwood.

Radical Intercourse: How Dreams Unite Us in Love, Conflict & Other Inevitable Relationships. Joseph Goodbread. 180p. (Orig.). 1997. pap. 14.00 (*1-887078-02-9*) Lao Tse Pr.

***Radical In(ter)ventions: Identity, Politics, & Difference/s in Educational Praxis.** Ed. by Suzanne De Castell & Mary Bryson. LC 97-4953. (SUNY Series, Identities in the Classroom). 288p. (C). 1997. pap. text ed. 19.95 (*0-7914-3562-8*) State U NY Pr.

***Radical In(ter)ventions: Identity, Politics, & Difference/s in Educational Praxis.** Ed. by Suzanne De Castell & Mary Bryson. LC 97-4953. (Identities in the Classroom Ser.). 288p. (C). 1997. text ed. 59.50 (*0-7914-3561-X*) State U NY Pr.

Radical Ionic Systems Properties in Condensed Physics. A. Lund & M. Shiotani. (Topics in Molecular Organization & Engineering Ser.). 488p. 1991. lib. bdg. 206.00 (*0-7923-0988-X*) Kluwer Ac.

Radical Islam: Medieval Theology & Modern Politics. enl. ed. Emmanuel Sivan. x, 256p. (C). 1990. pap. 15.00 (*0-300-04915-3*); text ed. 35.00 (*0-300-04914-5*) Yale U Pr.

Radical Islamic Fundamentalism: The Ideological & Political Discourse of Sayyid Qutb. Ahmad S. Moussalli. 326p. (C). 1993. pap. text ed. 20.00 (*0-8156-6089-8*) Syracuse U Pr.

Radical Issues in Criminology. Ed. by Pat Carlen & Mike Collison. 212p. 1980. 44.00 (*0-389-20083-2*, 06856) B&N Imports.

Radical Jew: Paul & the Politics of Identity. Daniel Boyarin. LC 93-36269. (Contraversions Ser.: No. 1). (C). 1994. 35.00 (*0-520-08592-2*) U CA Pr.

***Radical Jew: Paul & the Politics of Identity.** Daniel Boyarin. 1997. pap. text ed. 18.95 (*0-520-21214-2*) U CA Pr.

Radical Joe: A Life of Joseph Chamberlain. Denis Judd. 330p. (C). 1993. pap. 25.00 (*0-7083-1195-4*) Paul & Co Pubs.

***Radical Journey.** Kiernan. Date not set. text ed. write for info. (*0-312-16570-6*) St Martin.

Radical Juxtaposition: The Films of Yvonne Rainer. Shelley Green. LC 94-5213. (Filmmakers Ser.: No. 41). (Illus.). 174p. 1994. 25.00 (*0-8108-2863-4*) Scarecrow.

Radical Knowledge: A Philosophical Inquiry into the Nature & Limits of Science. Gonzalo Munevar. LC 81-4258. 135p. (C). 1981. 27.95 (*0-915145-17-0*); pap. 14.95 (*0-915145-16-2*) Hackett Pub.

Radical Lawyer in Victorian England: W. P. Roberts & the Struggle for Workers' Rights. Raymond Challinor. 256p. 1990. text ed. 59.50 (*1-85043-150-7*, Pub. by I B Tauris UK) St Martin.

Radical Left & American Foreign Policy. Robert W. Tucker. LC 73-156476. (Washington Center of Foreign Policy Research. Studies in International Affairs: No. 15). 168p. reprint ed. pap. 47.90 (*0-317-55519-7*, 2029236) Bks Demand.

Radical Left in Britain, 1931-1941. James Jupp. 270p. 1982. 30.00 (*0-7146-3123-X*, Pub. by F Cass Pubs UK) Intl Spec Bk.

Radical Left in the Hungarian Revolution of 1848. Laszlo Deme. (East European Monographs: No. 19). 162p. 1976. text ed. 55.50 (*0-914710-12-5*) East Eur Monographs.

Radical Libertarianism: A Right Wing Alternative. Jerome Tucille. LC 71-106636. 1970. 5.00 (*0-672-51232-7*, Bobbs) Macmillan.

Radical Life: The Autobiography of a Woman Radical. Intro. by Vera B. Weisbord et al. 330p. 1977. 12.00 (*0-88286-101-8*) C H Kerr.

Radical Literary Education: A Classroom Experiment with Wordsworth's "Ode" Jeffrey C. Robinson. LC 86-23366. 224p. 1986. pap. text ed. 14.95 (*0-299-11064-8*) U of Wis Pr.

Radical Literary Education: A Classroom Experiment with Wordsworth's "Ode" Jeffrey C. Robinson. LC 86-23366. 224p. (C). 1987. text ed. 30.00 (*0-299-11060-5*) U of Wis Pr.

Radical Look at Changing America. Linda T. 1994. pap. text ed. 7.95 (*0-533-10864-0*) Vantage.

Radical Lord Radnor: The Public Life of Viscount Folkestone, Third Earl of Radnor, 1779-1869. Ronald K. Huch. LC 76-55172. (Minnesota Monographs in the Humanities: No. 10). 213p. reprint ed. pap. 60.80 (*0-7837-2945-6*, 2057509) Bks Demand.

Radical Love: An Approach to Sexual Spirituality. Dody H. Donnelly. 136p. 1992. reprint ed. pap. 8.00 (*0-9623086-2-5*) Dharma Cloud Pubs.

***Radical Love-Discovering Fire.** Eugene Fitzgerald. 1997. pap. 14.95 (*0-9631314-3-5*) J M S Civil War.

***Radical Man: The Process of Psycho-Social Development.** Charles Hampden-Turner. LC 79-118574. (Illus.). 446p. reprint ed. pap. 127.20 (*0-608-05348-1*, 2065053) Bks Demand.

Radical Management: Power-Politics & the Pursuit of Trust. Samuel A. Culbert & John J. McDonough. 240p. (C). 1985. 35.00 (*0-02-905940-2*, Free Press) Free Pr.

Radical Mandarin: The Memoirs of Escott Reid. Escott Reid. 35.00 (*0-8020-5811-6*) U of Toronto Pr.

Radical Mandarin: The Memoirs of Escott Reid. Escott Reid. 432p. 1992. pap. 19.95 (*0-8020-7365-4*) U of Toronto Pr.

***Radical Mansfield.** Dunbar. LC 97-7010. 1997. text ed. 55.00 (*0-312-17467-5*) St Martin.

Radical Monotheism & Western Culture: With Supplementary Essays. H. Richard Niebuhr. (Library of Theological Ethics). 112p. 1993. pap. 10.00 (*0-664-25326-1*) Westminster John Knox.

Radical Motherhood: Namibian Women's Independence Struggle. Iina Soiri. (Nordiska Afrikainstitutet Research Report Ser.: No. 99). 115p. (Orig.). 1996. pap. 33.00 (*91-7106-380-3*, Pub. by Nordisk Afrikainstitutet SW) Coronet Bks.

Radical Movement of the Nineteen Sixties. Roger G. Betsworth. LC 80-12534. (American Theological Library Association Monograph: No. 14). viii, 363p. 1980. 25.00 (*0-8108-1307-6*) Scarecrow.

Radical Moves. Franklin W. Dixon. Ed. by Ellen Winkler. (Hardy Boys Ser.: No. 113). 160p. (Orig.). (J). (gr. 3-6). 1992. pap. 3.99 (*0-671-73060-6*) PB.

Radical Nationalist in Japan: Kita Ikki, 1883-1937. George M. Wilson. LC 69-12740. (Harvard East Asian Ser.: No. 37). 246p. reprint ed. pap. 70.20 (*0-7837-3854-4*, 2043676) Bks Demand.

Radical Nature of Christianity: Church Growth Eyes Look at the Supernatural Mission of the Christian & the Church. Waldo J. Werning. LC 76-8359. 220p. 1976. pap. 6.95 (*0-87808-730-3*, Mandate) William Carey Lib.

Radical New Road to Wealth: How to Raise Venture Capital for a New Business. 8th ed. A. David Silver. 150p. 1996. pap. 15.00 (*1-56150-164-6*) Intl Wealth.

***Radical New Road to Wealth: How to Raise Venture Capital for a New Business.** 9th ed. A. David Silver. 150p. 1998. pap. 15.00 (*1-56150-214-6*) Intl Wealth.

Radical Novel in the U. S., 1900-1954: Some Interrelations of Literature & Society. Walter B. Rideout. 360p. 1992. pap. 15.50 (*0-231-08077-8*, Mrngside); text ed. 39.50 (*0-231-08076-X*, Mrngside) Col U Pr.

Radical Optimism: Rooting Ourselves in Reality. Beatrice Bruteau. 112p. (Orig.). 1993. pap. 11.95 (*0-8245-1264-2*) Crossroad NY.

Radical Papers. Ed. by Dimitrios I. Roussopoulos. 168p. 1987. 29.95 (*0-920057-87-X*, Pub. by Black Rose Bks CN); pap. 12.95 (*0-920057-86-1*, Pub. by Black Rose Bks CN) Consort Bk Sales.

Radical Papers, No. 2. Ed. by Dimitrios I. Roussopoulos. 168p. 1987. 29.95 (*0-921689-13-6*, Pub. by Black Rose Bks CN); pap. 12.95 (*0-921689-12-8*, Pub. by Black Rose Bks CN) Consort Bk Sales.

Radical Paradoxes: Dilemmas of the American Left, 1945-1970. Peter Clecak. LC 73-4072. 1973. 29.50 (*0-06-010819-3*) Irvington.

Radical Parody: American Culture & Critical Agency after Foucault. Daniel T. O'Hara. 264p. 1992. text ed. 49.50 (*0-231-07692-4*) Col U Pr.

Radical People's Theatre. Eugene Van Erven. LC 87-46368. (Illus.). 254p. 1988. 12.95 (*0-253-34788-2*) Ind U Pr.

Radical Perspectives on Social Problems: Readings in Critical Sociology. 3rd ed. Ed. by Frank Lindenfeld. 414p. (Orig.). 1987. lib. bdg. 39.95 (*0-930390-74-1*) Gen Hall.

Radical Perspectives on the Rise of Fascism in Germany, 1919 to 1945. Ed. by Michael N. Dobkowski & Isidor Wallimann. 320p. (C). 1988. 30.00 (*0-85345-757-3*); pap. 18.00 (*0-85345-758-1*) Monthly Rev.

***Radical Perversions: Black Friday?/Claposis.** Audrey Butler. (Illus.). 120p. pap. 9.95 (*0-88961-156-4*, Pub. by Wmns Pr CN) LPC InBook.

Radical Philosophy: Tradition, Counter-Tradition, Politics. Ed. by Roger S. Gottlieb. 288p. 1993. 49.95 (*1-56639-046-X*) Temple U Pr.

Radical Philosophy: Tradition, Counter-Tradition, Politics. Ed. by Roger S. Gottlieb. 304p. (C). 1993. pap. 19.95 (*1-56639-047-8*) Temple U Pr.

Radical Philosophy of Law: Contemporary Challenges to Mainstream Legal Theory & Practice. Ed. by David S. Caudill & Steven J. Gold. LC 94-18238. 386p. (C). 1995. pap. 18.50 (*0-391-03862-1*) Humanities.

Radical Philosophy of Law: Contemporary Challenges to Mainstream Legal Theory & Practice. Ed. by David S. Caudill & Steven J. Gold. LC 94-18238. 386p. (C). 1995. text ed. 49.95 (*0-391-03861-3*) Humanities.

Radical Philosophy Reader. Ed. by R. Edgley & R. Osborne. 410p. 1985. text ed. 60.00 (*0-86091-101-2*, Pub. by Verso UK); pap. text ed. 17.95 (*0-86091-809-2*, Pub. by Verso UK) Routledge Chapman & Hall.

Radical Pietists. Delburn Carpenter. LC 72-13586. (Illus.). 42.50 (*0-404-11008-8*) AMS Pr.

Radical Planning: New Directions for Urban Planning in the 1990s. Andy Thornley & John Montgomery. (Illus.). 350p. 1990. text ed. 68.95 (*0-566-05778-6*, Pub. by Avebury Pub UK) Ashgate Pub Co.

Radical Political Economy, 2 vols. Ed. by Samuel Bowles & Richard Edwards. (Schools of Thought in Economics Ser.: No. 8). (Illus.). 848p. 1990. Set. text ed. 285.00 (*1-85278-122-X*) E Elgar.

Radical Political Economy: A Critique. Andrew Sayer. (Illus.). 288p. 1995. 61.95 (*0-631-19374-X*); pap. 23.95 (*0-631-19375-8*) Blackwell Pubs.

Radical Political Economy: An Introduction to the Alternative Economics. Brian Burkitt. 208p. (C). 1984. text ed. 36.00 (*0-8147-1057-3*); pap. text ed. 14.80 (*0-8147-1058-1*) NYU Pr.

Radical Political Economy: Explorations in Alternative Economic Analysis. Ed. by Victor D. Lippit. LC 95-16934. 402p. (C). (gr. 13). 1995. pap. text ed. 28.95 (*0-87332-607-5*) M E Sharpe.

Radical Political Economy: Explorations in Alternative Economic Analysis. Ed. by Victor D. Lippit. LC 95-16934. 402p. (C). (gr. 13). 1995. text ed. 74.95 (*0-87332-606-7*) M E Sharpe.

Radical Politicians & Poets in Early Victorian Britain: The Voices of Six Chartist Leaders. Stephen Roberts. LC 93-50810. (Studies in British History: Vol. 27). 160p. 1994. text ed. 69.95 (*0-7734-9126-0*) E Mellen.

Radical Politics of Thomas Jefferson. Richard K. Matthews. LC 84-5240. xii, 172p. 1984. reprint ed. pap. 7.95 (*0-7006-0293-3*) U Pr of KS.

Radical Pragmatics. Ed. by Peter Cole. 1981. text ed. 67.00 (*0-12-179660-4*) Acad Pr.

Radical Preacher's Sermon Book. Ed. by Kathleen Schultz et al. (Illus.). 96p. 1983. pap. 4.00 (*0-9612114-0-7*) Inst Peoples Church.

Radical Priest in Mayo: The Rise & Fall of an Irish Nationalist 1825-86. Gerard Moran. (Illus.). 240p. 1994. 39.50 (*1-85182-163-5*, Pub. by Four Cts Pr IE) Intl Spec Bk.

Radical Priest in Mayo: The Rise & Fall of an Irish Nationalist 1825-86. Gerard Moran. (Illus.). 240p. 1994. pap. 19.95 (*1-85182-173-2*, Pub. by Four Cts Pr IE) Intl Spec Bk.

Radical Priorities. rev. ed. Noam Chomsky. Ed. by Carlos P. Otero. 307p. 1981. pap. 16.95 (*0-920057-17-9*, Pub. by Black Rose Bks CN) Consort Bk Sales.

Radical Priorities. 2nd rev. ed. Noam Chomsky. Ed. by Carlos P. Otero. 307p. 1981. 36.95 (*0-920057-16-0*, Pub. by Black Rose Bks CN) Consort Bk Sales.

Radical Protest & Social Structure: The Southern Farmers' Alliance Cotton Tenancy, 1880-1890. Michael Schwartz. 314p. 1988. pap. text ed. 16.00 (*0-226-74235-0*) U Ch Pr.

Radical Puritans in England 1550-1660. Acheson. (C). 1990. pap. text ed. 13.50 (*0-582-35515-X*) Addison-Wesley.

Radical Rags: Fashions of the Sixties. Joel Lobenthal. (Illus.). 256p. 1990. pap. 14.98 (*0-89659-930-2*) Abbeville Pr.

***Radical Reaction Rates in Liquids Vol. D2: Peroxyl & Related Radicals.** J. A. Howard. Ed. by H. Fischer. (Landolt-Bornstein Ser.: Vol. II, 13). xii, 432p. 1997. 1,871.00 (*3-540-60357-3*) Spr-Verlag.

Radical Reaction Rates in Liquids, Subvol. A, Carbon-Centered Radicals I see Atomic & Molecular Physics: Group II

Radical Reaction Rates in Liquids, Subvol. B, Carbon-Centered Radicals II see Atomic & Molecular Physics: Group II

Radical Reactions of Thioamides, Thioureas, & Related Compounds, Vol.3. I. I. Kandror et al. 32p. 1984. pap. text ed. 32.00 (*3-7186-0197-4*) Gordon & Breach.

Radical Reactivity & DNA Damage Pt. 1: Third Biennial Meeting of the Society for Free Radical Research, West Germany, 1986. Helmut Sies. 1987. pap. text ed. 376.00 (*3-7186-0389-6*) Gordon & Breach.

Radical Realism: Direct Knowing in Science & Philosophy. Edward Pols. LC 91-55531. 240p. 1992. 35.00 (*0-8014-2710-X*) Cornell U Pr.

***Radical Reconstruction.** Lebbeus Woods. (Illus.). 212p. 1997. 45.00 (*1-56898-090-6*) Princeton Arch.

Radical Records: Personal Perspectives on Lesbian & Gay History, 1957-87. Bob Cant & Susan Hemmings. 304p. 1988. pap. text ed. 14.95 (*0-415-00201-X*) Routledge.

Radical Red. James Duffy. LC 93-12568. 160p. (J). (gr. 5-8). 1993. lib. bdg. 15.00 (*0-684-19533-X*, C Scribner Sons Young) S&S Childrens.

Radical Reflection & the Origin of the Human Sciences. Calvin O. Schrag. LC 79-91085. 146p. 1980. pap. 8.95 (*0-911198-58-X*) Purdue U Pr.

Radical Reform in Soviet Defense Policy: Selected Papers from the Fourth World Congress for Soviet & East European Studies, Harrogate, 1990. Ed. by Roy Allison. LC 91-36102. 256p. 1992. text ed. 69.95 (*0-312-07545-6*) St Martin.

Radical Reform in the Automotive Industry: Policies in Emerging Markets. Peter O'Brien & Yannis Karmokolias. LC 94-8112. (IFC Discussion Paper Ser.: No. 21). 58p. 1994. 6.95 (*0-8213-2806-9*, 12806) World Bank.

Radical Reform in Yeltsin's Russia: Political, Economic, & Social Dimensions. Lynn D. Nelson & Irina Y. Kuzes. LC 94-41114. (Illus.). 256p. (C). (gr. 13). 1995. text ed. 69.95 (*1-56324-479-9*); pap. text ed. 26.95 (*1-56324-480-2*) M E Sharpe.

Radical Reform of Christianity: A Focus on Catholicism. Edward Brennan. LC 94-71182. (Church & the World Ser.: Vol. 7). 275p. (Orig.). 1995. pap. 19.95 (*0-940121-27-1*, P208, Cross Roads Bks) Cross Cultural Pubns.

Radical Reformation. Ed. by Michael G. Baylor. (Cambridge Texts in the History of Political Thought Ser.). 312p. (C). 1991. text ed. 59.95 (*0-521-37073-6*) Cambridge U Pr.

Radical Reformation. Ed. by Michael G. Baylor. (Cambridge Texts in the History of Political Thought Ser.). 312p. (C). 1991. pap. text ed. 19.95 (*0-521-37948-2*) Cambridge U Pr.

Radical Reformation. 3rd ed. George H. Williams. (Sixteenth Century Essays & Studies). (Illus.). 1500p. 1992. 125.00 (*0-940474-15-8*) Sixteenth Cent.

Radical Reign: Parables of Jesus. Gary Wilde. (Generation Why Ser.: Vol. 1:3). 40p. (YA). (gr. 9-12). 1995. pap. 14.95 (*0-87303-259-4*) Faith & Life.

***Radical Rejuvenation: The Revolutionary New System for the Effects of Ageing.** Roxy Dillon. (Illus.). 256p. 1997. pap. 13.95 (*0-7472-5194-0*, Pub. by Headline UK) Trafalgar.

Radical Religion in America: Millenarian Movements from the Far Right to the Children of Noah. Jeffrey Kaplan. LC 96-25627. (Religion & Politics Ser.). 364p. 1997. text ed. 39.95 (*0-8156-2687-8*, KARR); pap. text ed. 16.95 (*0-8156-0396-7*, KARRP) Syracuse U Pr.

***Radical Renfrew.** Ed. by Tom Leonard. 1990. 24.00 (*0-7486-6028-3*, Pub. by Polygon UK) Subterranean Co.

Radical Representations: Politics & Form in U. S. Proletarian Fiction, 1929-1941. Barbara Foley. LC 93-18687. (Post-Contemporary Interventions Ser.). 484p. 1993. text ed. 55.00 (*0-8223-1361-8*); pap. text ed. 19.95 (*0-8223-1394-4*) Duke.

Radical Republicans & Reconstruction: 1861-1870. Ed. by Harold M. Hyman. LC 66-16751. 1967. pap. 8.05 (*0-672-60070-6*, AHS47, Bobbs) Macmillan.

Radical Republicans & Reconstruction, 1861-1870. Ed. by Harold M. Hyman. LC 66-16751. 538p. 1967. 49.50 (*0-8290-0202-2*) Irvington.

Radical Republicans in the North: State Politics During Reconstruction. Ed. by James C. Mohr. LC 75-36939. 219p. reprint ed. pap. 62.50 (*0-7837-3389-5*, 2043347) Bks Demand.

***Radical Responses to Radical Regimes: Evaluating Preemptive Counter-Proliferation.** 1997. lib. bdg. 252.99 (*0-8490-6150-4*) Gordon Pr.

***Radical Responses to Radical Regimes: Evaluating Preemptive Counter-Proliferation.** Barry R. Schneider. 55p. (Orig.). (C). 1996. pap. 25.00 (*0-7881-3426-4*) DIANE Pub.

Radical Revisions: Rereading 1930s Culture. Ed. by Sherry Linkon & Bill Mullen. (Illus.). 280p. 1996. 14.95 (*0-252-06505-0*); text ed. 39.95 (*0-252-02206-8*) U of Ill Pr.

***Radical Rhetoric of the English Deists: The Discourse of Skepticism, 1680-1750.** James A. Herrick. LC 97-4864. (Studies in Rhetoric/Communication). 248p. 1997. 29.95 (*1-57003-166-5*) U of SC Pr.

Radical Right: A Problem for American Democracy. Seymour M. Lipset. (Reprint Series in Social Sciences). (C). 1993. reprint ed. pap. text ed. 2.90 (*0-8290-2661-4*, S-445) Irvington.

Radical Right: An International Dictionary. Ciaran O. Maolain. 500p. 1980. lib. bdg. 50.00 (*0-87436-514-7*) ABC-CLIO.

Radical Right: The New American Right. enl. rev. ed. Ed. by Daniel Bell. LC 78-167309. (Essay Index Reprint Ser.). 1977. reprint ed. 25.95 (*0-8369-2447-9*) Ayer.

Radical Right & the Welfare State. Ed. by James Midgley & Howard Glennerster. 208p. (C). 1991. text ed. 59.00 (*0-389-20976-7*) B&N Imports.

Radical Right in Western Europe: A Comparative Analysis. Herbert Kitschelt & Anthony J. McGann. LC 95-41373. (C). 1996. 49.50 (*0-472-10663-5*) U of Mich Pr.

R

***Radical Right in Western Europe: A Comparative Analysis.** Herbert Kitschelt & Anthony J. McGann. (C). 1997. pap. 24.95 (*0-472-08441-0*) U of Mich Pr.

Radical Right-Wing Populism in Western Europe. Hans-Georg Betz. LC 94-6696. 1994. text ed. 55.00 (*0-312-08390-4*) St Martin.

Radical Right-Wing Populism in Western Europe Vol. 1. Hans-Georg Betz. 1994. text ed. 18.95 (*0-312-12195-4*) St Martin.

Radical Rules: Fast, Fun & Easy Approach to World-Class Status. Stuart C. Wittrock. LC 95-90246. 64p. 1995. pap. 19.95 (*0-87718-001-6*) Willis Music Co.

Radical Satire & Print Culture, 1790-1822. Marcus Wood. LC 93-46675. (English Monographs). (Illus.). 336p. 1994. 70.00 (*0-19-811278-5*, Old Oregon Bk Store) OUP.

Radical Sects of Revolutionary New England. Stephen A. Marini. LC 81-6913. 220p. 1982. 32.00 (*0-674-74625-2*) HUP.

Radical Self: Metamorphosis to Animal Form in Modern Latin American Narrative. Nancy G. Diaz. LC 88-10000. 136p. 1989. text ed. 23.00 (*0-8262-0692-1*) U of Mo Pr.

Radical Sensibility: Literature & Ideas in the 1790s. Chris Jones. LC 92-5389. 224p. (C). (gr. 13). 1993. text ed. 62.95 (*0-415-07685-4*, A9662) Routledge.

Radical Social Work Today. Ed. by Mary Langan & Phil Lee. 276p. 1989. text ed. 65.00 (*0-04-445368-X*) Routledge Chapman & Hall.

Radical Socialism in Czechoslovakia: Bohumir Smeral, the Czech Road to Socialism, & the Origins of the Czechoslovak Communist Party. Bernard Wheaton. (East European Monographs: No. 213). 204p. 1986. text ed. 49.50 (*0-88033-110-0*) East Eur Monographs.

Radical Sociologists & the Movement: Experiences, Lessons, & Legacies. Ed. by Martin Oppenheimer et al. 256p. 1991. 29.95 (*0-87722-745-4*) Temple U Pr.

Radical Sociology of Durkheim & Mauss. Ed. by Mike Gane. LC 91-40125. 256p. (C). (gr. 13). 1992. text ed. 69.95 (*0-415-06422-8*, A7493) Routledge.

Radical Sociology of Durkheim & Mauss. Ed. by Mike Gane. LC 91-40125. 240p. (C). 1992. pap. text ed. 17.95 (*0-415-06423-6*, Routledge NY) Routledge.

Radical Soldier's Tale: John Pearman 1819-1908. Carolyn Steedman. 320p. 1988. pap. text ed. 18.95 (*0-415-00207-9*) Routledge.

Radical Son: A Journey Through Our Times. David Horowitz. 1996. 23.00 (*0-02-915085-X*, Free Press) Free Pr.

Radical Son: A Journey Through Our Times. David Horowitz. (Illus.). 468p. 1997. 27.50 (*0-684-82793-X*) Free Pr.

Radical Spinoza. Paul Wienpahl. LC 78-65448. (C). 1979. text ed. 40.00 (*0-8147-9186-7*) NYU Pr.

Radical Spirits: Spiritualism & Women's Rights in Nineteenth Century America. Ann Braude. LC 89-42599. (Illus.). 288p. 1991. pap. 16.00 (*0-8070-7501-9*) Beacon Pr.

Radical Spirituality. Dick Sutphen. 216p. 1995. pap. 12.00 (*0-87554-583-1*, B938) Valley Sun.

Radical Stage: Theater in Germany in the 1970s & 1980s. Ed. by W. G. Sebald. LC 88-14793. 200p. 1989. 19.95 (*0-85496-038-4*) Berg Pubs.

Radical Stages: Alternative History in Modern British Drama. D. Keith Peacock. LC 91-17119. (Contributions in Drama & Theatre Studies: No. 43). 208p. 1991. text ed. 55.00 (*0-313-27888-1*, PRP, Greenwood Pr) Greenwood.

Radical Surgery: What's Next for America's Health Care. Joseph A. Califano. 1994. 25.00 (*0-8129-2413-4*, Times Bks) Random.

Radical Systems Development: An Introduction to Rapid Application Development. J. Russell Robinson. 152p. 1995. pap. 34.95 (*1-57087-105-1*) Prof Pr NC.

Radical Take-Offs. Glyn Parry. (Illus.). 144p. (Orig.). (YA). (gr. 6-12). 1996. pap. 6.95 (*1-86373-692-1*, Pub. by Allen & Unwin Aust Pty AT) IPG Chicago.

Radical Theories: Paths Between Marxism & Social Democracy. Darrow Schechter. LC 93-50584. 1994. text ed. 75.00 (*0-7190-3618-6*, Pub. by Manchester Univ Pr UK); text ed. 24.95 (*0-7190-4385-9*, Pub. by Manchester Univ Pr UK) St Martin.

Radical Thought in Italy: A Potential Politics. Ed. by Paolo Virno & Michael Hardt. LC 96-11842. (Theory Out of Bounds Ser.: Vol. 7). 288p. (C). 1996. text ed. 57.95 (*0-8166-2552-2*); pap. text ed. 22.95 (*0-8166-2553-0*) U of Minn Pr.

Radical Tories: The Conservative Tradition in Canada. Charles Taylor. 229p. 1982. 9.95 (*0-88784-096-5*, Pub. by Hse of Anansi Pr CN) Genl Dist Srvs.

Radical Tory: Garfield Barwick's Reflections & Recollections. 330p. 1995. 54.00 (*1-86287-160-4*, Pub. by Federation Pr AU) Gaunt.

Radical Tragedy: Religion, Ideology, & Power in the Drama of Shakespeare & His Contemporaries. 2nd ed. Jonathan Dollimore. LC 93-9775. 380p. (C). 1993. pap. text ed. 17.95 (*0-8223-1398-7*) Duke.

Radical Underworld: Prophets, Revolutionaries & Pornographers in London, 1795-1840. Iain McCalman. (Illus.). 352p. 1988. 69.95 (*0-521-30755-4*) Cambridge U Pr.

Radical Urban Solutions: Urban Renaissance for City Schools & Communities. Dick Atkinson. (Education Ser.). (Illus.). 192p. 1994. 65.00 (*0-304-32828-6*); pap. 24.95 (*0-304-32830-8*) Cassell.

Radical Vegetable Gardening. Craig C. Dremann. 19p. (Orig.). 1993. pap. 3.75 (*0-933421-37-0*) Redwood Seed.

Radical Vegetarianism: A Dialectic of Diet & Ethic. 2nd rev. ed. Mark M. Braunstein. LC 81-4724. 160p. (Orig.). 1993. pap. 9.95 (*0-9635663-1-8*) Panacea Pr CT.

***Radical Vision: Paul Durcan.** Kathleen McCracken. 1996. 49.95 (*1-85224-345-7*, Pub. by Bloodaxe Bks UK) Dufour.

***Radical Vision: Paul Durcan.** Kathleen McCracken. 1997. pap. 49.95 (*1-85224-346-5*, Pub. by Bloodaxe Bks UK) Dufour.

Radical Visions: American Film Renaissance, 1967-1976. Glenn Man. LC 94-3049. (Contributions in the Study of Popular Culture Ser.: No. 41). 232p. 1994. text ed. 55.00 (*0-313-29306-6*, Greenwood Pr) Greenwood.

Radical Visions: Poetry by Vietnam Veterans. Vince Gotera. LC 92-27595. 384p. 1994. 45.00 (*0-8203-1510-9*) U of Ga Pr.

Radical Visions & American Dreams: Culture & Social Thought in the Depression Years. Richard H. Pells. LC 84-10420. 445p. 1984. reprint ed. pap. 126.90 (*0-608-02318-3*, 2062959) Bks Demand.

Radical Voices: A Decade of Feminist Resistance from Women's Studies International Forum. Renate D. Klein & Deborah L. Steinberg. (Athene Ser.). 272p. 1989. text ed. 37.50 (*0-08-036484-5*, Pergamon Pr) Elsevier.

Radical Voices: A Decade of Feminist Resistance from Women's Studies International Forum. Ed. by Renate D. Klein & Deborah L. Steinberg. (Athene Ser.). 244p. (C). 1989. text ed. 37.50 (*0-8077-6207-5*); pap. text ed. 16.95 (*0-8077-6206-7*) Tchrs Coll.

***Radical Wesley & Patterns for Church Renewal.** Howard Snyder. 203p. 1996. pap. 16.00 (*1-57910-001-5*) Wipf & Stock.

Radical Whigs, John Trenchard & Thomas Gordon: Libertarian Loyalists to the New House of Hanover. Marie P. McMahon. LC 89-22642. 226p. (C). 1990. lib. bdg. 41.00 (*0-8191-7627-3*) U Pr of Amer.

Radical Words of the Mohawk Language, with Their Derivatives. Jacques Bruyas. LC 10-30198. (Library of American Linguistics: Vol. 10). reprint ed. 42.75 (*0-404-50990-8*) AMS Pr.

Radical Worker in Tsarist Russia: The Autobiography of Semen Ivanovich Kanatchikov. Ed. & Tr. by Reginald E. Zelnik. LC 85-27681. 512p. (Orig.). 1986. 57.50 (*0-8047-1323-5*); pap. 19.95 (*0-8047-1331-6*) Stanford U Pr.

Radicalism & Education Reform in 20th-Century China: The Search for an Ideal Development Model. Suzanne Pepper. (Illus.). 550p. (C). 1996. text ed. 59.95 (*0-521-49669-1*) Cambridge U Pr.

Radicalism & Freethought in Nineteenth-Century Britain: The Life of Richard Carlile. Joel H. Wiener. LC 82-6168. (Contributions in Labor History Ser.: No. 13). x, 285p. 1983. text ed. 59.95 (*0-313-23532-5*, WRD/, Greenwood Pr) Greenwood.

Radicalism & Reverence: The Political Thought of Gerrard Winstanley. George Shulman. 1989. 45.00 (*0-520-06587-5*) U CA Pr.

Radicalism & Social Change in Jamaica, 1960-1972. Obika Gray. LC 90-35009. 304p. 1991. 42.50 (*0-87049-660-3*); pap. text ed. 19.95 (*0-87049-661-1*) U of Tenn Pr.

Radicalism & the Origins of the Vietnamese Revolution. Hue-Tam Ho Tai. 336p. 1996. pap. 17.95 (*0-674-74613-9*) HUP.

Radicalism & the Origins of the Vietnamese Revolution. Hue-Tam H. Tai. 325p. (C). 1992. 39.95 (*0-674-74612-0*) HUP.

Radicalism, Anti-Racism, & Representation. Alastair Bonnett. LC 93-7402. (Critical Studies in Racism & Migration). 224p. (C). (gr. 13). 1993. text ed. 74.95 (*0-415-07203-4*) Routledge.

Radicalism, Feminism & Social Work in the Nineties. Brian Trainor. LC 96-33160. 164p. 1997. 68.95 (*1-85972-290-3*, Pub. by Avebury Pub UK) Ashgate Pub Co.

Radicalism Handbook. John Button. (Global Issues Ser.). 480p. Date not set. pap. write for info. (*0-304-32711-5*) Cassell.

Radicalism Handbook: Radical Activists, Groups & Movements of the Twentieth Century. Compiled by John Button. LC 95-15213. 460p. (YA). (gr. 9 up). 1995. 49.50 (*0-87436-838-3*) ABC-CLIO.

Radicalism in Mediterranean France: Its Rise & Decline, 1848-1914. Leo A. Loubere. LC 73-171180. 258p. 1974. text ed. 32.50 (*0-87395-094-1*) State U NY Pr.

Radicalism in Minnesota, 1900-1960: A Survey of Selected Sources. Twentieth-Century Radicalism in Minnesota Project Staff. LC 94-20239. (Illus.). xiv, 109p. 1994. pap. 17.95 (*0-87351-307-X*) Minn Hist.

Radicalism in Religion, Philosophy, & Social Life: Four Papers from the Boston Courier for 1858. LC 72-1804. (Black Heritage Library Collection). 1977. reprint ed. 13.95 (*0-8369-9052-8*) Ayer.

Radicalism in the States: The Minnesota Farmer-Labor Party & the American Political Economy. Richard M. Valelly. LC 88-36843. (American Politics & Political Economy Ser.). (Illus.). 264p. 1989. 35.95 (*0-226-84535-4*) U Ch Pr.

Radicalism of Shelley & Its Sources. Daniel MacDonald. LC 76-90369. 143p. (C). 1970. reprint ed. 40.00 (*0-87753-029-7*) Phaeton.

Radicalism of the American Revolution. Gordon S. Wood. LC 92-56347. 1993. pap. 15.00 (*0-679-73688-3*, Vin) Random.

Radicalism, Racism, & Party Realignment: The Border States During Reconstruction. Ed. by Richard O. Curry. LC 72-90743. 360p. reprint ed. pap. 102.60 (*0-317-42321-5*, 2025811) Bks Demand.

Radicalizinag the World Through Social Engineering: The New World Order. D. Y. Nee. 272p. (Orig.). (C). 1993. pap. 38.00 (*0-9639876-0-7*) Inst For Systs.

Radically Elementary Probability Theory. Edward Nelson. (Annals of Mathematics Studies: No. 117). (Illus.). 86p. 1987. pap. text ed. 18.95 (*0-691-08474-2*) Princeton U Pr.

***Radically Gay: Gay Liberation in the Words of Its Founder.** Harry Hay. 1997. pap. text ed. 16.00 (*0-8070-7081-5*) Beacon Pr.

Radically Gay: Gay Liberation in the Words of Its Founder Harry Hay. Harry Hay. Ed. by Will Roscoe. LC 95-39290. 352p. 1996. 27.00 (*0-8070-7080-7*) Beacon Pr.

Radicals & Squares: Statistical Methods for the Behavioral Sciences. Richard B. Darlington. 1975. teacher ed. 30.00 (*0-918610-01-X*) Logan Hill.

Radicals & the Republic: Socialist Republicanism in the Irish Free State 1925-1937. Richard English. 420p. 1995. 65.00 (*0-19-820289-X*) OUP.

Radical's Book: The Library Catalogue of Samuel Jeake of Rye (1623-90) Ed. by Michael Hunter et al. LC 95-33656. (Illus.). 376p. (C). 1997. 108.00 (*0-85991-471-2*) Boydell & Brewer.

Radicals in Biochemistry. Ed. by M. J. Dewar et al. (Topics in Current Chemistry Ser.: Vol. 108). (Illus.). 140p. 1982. 61.95 (*0-387-11864-0*) Spr-Verlag.

Radicals in Clinical Medicine: Radical Reactivity & DNA Damage: (Third Biennial Meeting of the Society for Free Radical Research, West Germany, 1986), 2 vol. Helmut Sies. (Free Radical Research Communications Ser.: Vol. 2). 330p. 1987. pap. text ed. 340.00 (*3-7186-0395-0*) Gordon & Breach.

Radicals in Organic Synthesis. Bernd Giese. (Organic Chemistry Ser.: Vol. 5). (Illus.). 350p. 1986. text ed. 140.00 (*0-08-032493-2*, CRC Reprint) Franklin.

***Radicals in Organic Synthesis 2: Formation C-Hyd & C-Het.** Giese. (Tetrahedron Organic Chemistry Ser.). 1995. write for info. (*0-08-037052-7*, Pergamon Pr) Elsevier.

Radicals in Urban Politics: The Alinsky Approach. Robert Bailey, Jr. LC 73-90938. xii, 200p. 1974. lib. bdg. 19.50 (*0-226-03452-6*) U Ch Pr.

***Radicals, Ion Radicals, & Triplets: The Spin-Bearing Intermediates of Organic Chemistry.** Nathan L. Bauld. LC 96-37072. 1997. write for info. (*1-56081-962-6*, VCH) Wiley.

Radicals, Ions & Tissue Damage. B. Matkovics et al. (Illus.). 323p. (C). 1990. 39.00 (*963-05-5879-3*, Pub. by A K HU) Intl Spec Bk.

Radicals of the Worst Sort: Laboring Women in Lawrence, Massachusetts, 1860-1912. Ardis Cameron. LC 92-39119. (Working Class in American History - Women in American History Ser.). 240p. 1993. 36.95 (*0-252-02013-8*) U of Ill Pr.

Radicals of the Worst Sort: Laboring Women in Lawrence, Massachusetts, 1860-1912. Ardis Cameron. (Illus.). 260p. (C). 1995. pap. text ed. 14.95 (*0-252-06318-X*) U of Ill Pr.

Radicals on Surfaces. Ed. by Anders Lund & Christopher Rhodes. LC 94-31444. (Topics in Molecular Organization & Engineering Ser.: 13). 260p. (C). 1995. lib. bdg. 154.00 (*0-7923-3108-7*) Kluwer Ac.

Radicals, Reformers, & Reactionaries: The Prisoner's Dilemma & the Collapse of Democracy in Latin America. Youssef Cohen. LC 93-43274. 196p. 1994. pap. text ed. 14.95 (*0-226-11272-1*); lib. bdg. 34.95 (*0-226-11271-3*) U Ch Pr.

Radical's Response. Raymond Crotty. 170p. 8800. pap. 10.95 (*0-905169-98-0*, Pub. by Poolbeg Pr IE) Dufour.

Radie Britain: A Bio-Bibliography. Walter B. Bailey & Nancy G. Bailey. LC 89-78117. (Bio-Bibliographies in Music Ser.: No. 25). 173p. 1990. text ed. 47.95 (*0-313-26277-2*, BYR/, Greenwood Pr) Greenwood.

Radiesthetic Analysis. C. L. Cooper-Hunt. 40p. 1969. reprint ed. spiral bd. 5.50 (*0-7873-0199-X*) Hlth Research.

Radigan. Louis L'Amour. 160p. 1984. pap. 3.99 (*0-553-28082-1*) Bantam.

***Radigan.** large type ed. Louis L'Amour. LC 96-41324. 1997. 22.95 (*0-7862-0867-8*) Thorndike Pr.

Radiguet: Le Diable au corps. Radiguet. Ed. by Griffiths. (Bristol French Texts Ser.). 158p. (FRE.). 1992. pap. 17.95 (*1-85399-325-5*, Pub. by Brstl Class Pr UK) Focus Pub-R Pullins.

***Radiiological Accident at the Irradiation Facility in Nesvizh (Belarus)** International Atomic Energy Agency Staff. 76p. 1996. pap. 35.00 (*92-0-101396-5*, STI/PUB/1010, Pub. by IAEA AU) Bernan Associates.

***Radio.** (Illus.). 80p. (YA). (gr. 6-12). 1996. pap. 2.40 (*0-8395-3361-6*, 33361) BSA.

Radio. B. Balcziak. (Communication: Today & Tomorrow Ser.). (Illus.). 48p. (J). (gr. 4-8). 1989. 12.95 (*0-685-58625-1*); lib. bdg. 17.27 (*0-86592-057-5*) Rourke Corp.

Radio. Debbie Chrisfield. LC 93-26393. (Now Hiring Ser.). (J). 1994. pap. 5.95 (*0-382-24749-3*, Crstwood Hse) Silver Burdett Pr.

Radio. George Coulter & Shirley Coulter. LC 96-3906. (You Make It Work Ser.). (Illus.). (J). 1996. write for info. (*0-86625-584-2*) Rourke Pubns.

Radio. Susan J. Douglas. 1997. write for info. (*0-8129-2546-7*, Times Bks) Random.

Radio. Rudolf Arnheim. LC 73-161151. (History of Broadcasting: Radio to Television Ser.). (Illus.). 1976. reprint ed. 28.95 (*0-405-03570-5*) Ayer.

Radio: A Blast from the Past. Howard Wolff & Irwin Jacobson. (Illus.). 321p. (Orig.). 1988. pap. write for info. (*0-9620285-0-9*) Sound Music Pub.

Radio: A Reference Guide. Thomas A. Greenfield. LC 88-24647. (American Popular Culture Ser.). 185p. 1989. text ed. 49.95 (*0-313-22276-2*, SRR, Greenwood Pr) Greenwood.

Radio: The Psychology of an Art of Sound. Intro. by Rudolf Arnheim. LC 73-164504. (Cinema Ser.). 1972. reprint ed. lib. bdg. 39.50 (*0-306-70291-6*) Da Capo.

Radio - The Book: A Fun Practical Programming Manual & Idea Book for Program Directors & Operations Managers. Steve Warren. (Illus.). 208p. 1992. pap. text ed. 39.95 (*0-9644635-0-4*) MOR Media.

Radio - TV Finder: An Index to Nearly 7000 Pictures of Collectable Radios & TVs in 24 Popular Books. John Okolowicz. 100p. (Orig.). 1992. pap. 13.95 (*0-9632440-0-0*) Antique Elect.

Radio Advertising: The Authoritative Guide. Bob Schulberg. 274p. 1994. 27.95 (*0-8442-3130-4*, NTC Busn Bks) NTC Pub Grp.

Radio Advertising: The Authoritative Handbook. 2nd ed. Pete Schulberg. 208p. 1995. 29.95 (*0-8442-3118-5*, NTC Busn Bks) NTC Pub Grp.

Radio Advertising Sales Success--The Game Plan. William M. Pacelli. 176p. 1988. 19.95 (*0-945664-00-1*) Cambridge Hse Assocs.

Radio Advertising's Missing Ingredient! The Optimum Effective Scheduling System. 2nd ed. National Association of Broadcasters Staff. 118p. (Orig.). 1993. pap. 50.00 (*0-89324-206-3*) Natl Assn Broadcasters.

Radio Amateur & Listener's Data Handbook. Steve Money. (Illus.). 240p. 1995. pap. 28.95 (*0-7506-2094-3*) Buttrwrth-Heinemann.

Radio Amateur Antenna Handbook. William I. Orr & Stuart D. Cowan. LC 78-53340. (Illus.). 191p. 1978. 11.95 (*0-933616-07-4*) Radio Pubns.

Radio Amateur Antenna Handbook. William I. Orr & Stuart D. Cowan. (Illus.). 192p. 1991. pap. 13.95 (*0-8230-8706-9*, RAC Bks) Watsn-Guptill.

***Radio Amateur Callbook Vol. 1: North American Listings.** 1600p. 1996. 35.00 (*0-8230-5891-3*) Watsn-Guptill.

***Radio Amateur Callbook Vol. 2: International Listings.** 1600p. 1996. 35.00 (*0-8230-5890-5*) Watsn-Guptill.

Radio Amateur Callbook 1996: International Listings. 74th anniversary ed. Watson. 1720p. 1995. pap. 35.00 (*0-8230-5887-5*, RAC Bks) Watsn-Guptill.

Radio Amateur Callbook 1996: North American Listings. 74th anniversary ed. Watson. 1592p. 1995. pap. 35.00 (*0-8230-5888-3*, RAC Bks) Watsn-Guptill.

Radio Amateur's Digital Communications Handbook. Jonathan L. Mayo. 1992. pap. text ed. 14.95 (*0-07-156007-6*) McGraw.

Radio Amateur's Digital Communications Handbook. Jonathan L. Mayo. (Illus.). 224p. 1992. 22.95 (*0-8306-8362-3*, 3362); pap. 14.95 (*0-8306-3362-6*) McGraw-Hill Prof.

Radio Amateurs Guide to the Ionosphere. Leo F. McNamara. LC 92-32988. 176p. (Orig.). (C). 1994. pap. 39.50 (*0-89464-804-7*) Krieger.

Radio & Electric Power Supply Equipment for Schools. Edward C. Blom. LC 77-176571. (Columbia University. Teachers College. Contributions to Education Ser.: No. 409). reprint ed. 37.50 (*0-404-55409-1*) AMS Pr.

Radio & Its Future. Ed. by Martin Codel. LC 73-161135. (History of Broadcasting: Radio to Television Ser.). 1977. reprint ed. 31.95 (*0-405-03559-4*) Ayer.

Radio & Radar Reference Data. 1991. lib. bdg. 79.00 (*0-8490-4208-9*) Gordon Pr.

Radio & Radar Reference Data. 1995. lib. bdg. 258.95 (*0-8490-6662-X*) Gordon Pr.

Radio & Radio Waves: Medical Research Index with Reference Bibliography. John C. Bartone, II. LC 85-47571. 150p. 1985. 37.50 (*0-88164-316-5*); pap. 34.50 (*0-88164-317-3*) ABBE Pubs Assn.

Radio & Telegraph Operator. Jack Rudman. (Career Examination Ser.: C-1443). 1994. pap. 27.95 (*0-8373-1443-7*) Nat Learn.

Radio & Television. Peter Lafferty. LC 96-9199. (Worldwise Ser.). (J). 1997. write for info. (*0-531-14440-2*) Watts.

Radio & Television. Peter Lafferty. LC 96-9199. (Worldwise Ser.). (J). 1998. pap. write for info. (*0-531-15317-7*) Watts.

Radio & Television: A Selected, Annotated Bibliography Supplement One: 1977-1981. William E. McCavitt. LC 82-5743. 167p. 1982. 20.00 (*0-8108-1556-7*) Scarecrow.

Radio & Television: A Selected, Annotated Bibliography; Supplement Two: 1982-1986. Peter K. Pringle & Helen E. Clinton. LC 88-23968. 249p. 1989. 27.50 (*0-8108-2158-3*) Scarecrow.

Radio & Television Acting: Criticism, Theory & Practice. Edwin Duerr. LC 78-138223. 417p. 1972. reprint ed. text ed. 75.00 (*0-8371-5580-0*, DURT, Greenwood Pr) Greenwood.

Radio & Television Broadcasting in Eastern Europe. Burton Paulu. LC 74-79505. 604p. reprint ed. pap. 172.20 (*0-318-39685-8*, 2033280) Bks Demand.

Radio & Television Broadcasting on the European Continent. Paulu Burton. LC 67-27097. 302p. reprint ed. pap. 86.10 (*0-317-41749-5*, 2055897) Bks Demand.

Radio & Television Career Directory: A Practical One-Stop Guide to Getting a Job in Public Relations. 2nd ed. Ed. by Bradley J. Morgan. (Career Advisor Ser.). 300p. 1993. 39.00 (*0-8103-5612-0*, 101584) Gale.

Radio & Television Commercial. Albert C. Book et al. 232p. 1994. pap. 19.95 (*0-8442-3097-9*) NTC Pub Grp.

Radio & Television Commercial. 3rd rev. ed. Albert C. Book et al. 232p. 1995. pap. 19.95 (*0-8442-3013-8*, NTC Busn Bks) NTC Pub Grp.

Radio & Television Dictionary. A. M. Abd-El-Wahed. 320p. (ARA, ENG, FRE & GER.). 1980. 75.00 (*0-8288-0185-1*, M9762) Fr & Eur.

Radio & Television Engineer. Jack Rudman. (Career Examination Ser.: C-1444). 1994. pap. 29.95 (*0-8373-1444-5*) Nat Learn.

Radio & Television in Cuba: The Pre-Castro Era. Michael B. Salwen. LC 94-17023. 242p. 1994. text ed. 42.95 (*0-8138-2180-0*) Iowa St U Pr.

Radio & Television Mechanic. Jack Rudman. (Career Examination Ser.: C-1445). 1994. pap. 27.95 (*0-8373-1445-3*) Nat Learn.

An Asterisk (*) at the beginning of an entry indicates that the title is appearing in BIP for the first time.

Radio & Television Pioneers: A Patent Bibliography. David W. Kraeuter. LC 92-8879. 329p. 1992. 39.50 (0-8108-2556-2) Scarecrow.

Radio & Television Price Guide: 1920-1990. 2nd ed. Harry Poster. (Illus.). 264p. 1994. pap. 17.95 (0-87069-687-4, Wallace-Hmestead) Chilton.

Radio & Television Technician. Jack Rudman. (Career Examination Ser.: C-1446). 1994. pap. 27.95 (0-8373-1446-1) Nat Learn.

Radio & Television Towers: Maintaining, Modifying & Leasing. 2nd ed. Jane P. Frock. 54p. 1990. 30.00 (0-89324-079-6) Natl Assn Broadcasters.

Radio & the Printed Page: An Introduction to the Study of Radio & Its Role in the Communication of Ideas. Paul F. Lazarsfeld. LC 70-161161. (History of Broadcasting: Radio to Television Ser.). 1976. reprint ed. 28.95 (0-405-03575-6) Ayer.

Radio & TV Journalism. K. M. Shrivastava. 290p. 1990. text ed. 35.00 (81-207-0439-8, Pub. by Sterling Pubs II) Apt Bks.

***Radio & TV Premiums: Value & History from Tom Mix to Space Patrol.** Jim Harmon. (Illus.). 288p. (Orig.). 1997. pap. 24.95 (0-87341-518-3, RATV) Krause Pubns.

Radio & Wireless Telecommunications Equipment & Services - U. S. Markets & Opportunities: 1992-1997 Analysis. Ely S. Lurin. (Illus.). 237p. 1993. pap. text ed. 1,900.00 (1-878218-36-0) World Info Tech.

Radio As the Forgotten Medium. Ed. by Everette E. Dennis & Edward Pease. 204p. (C). 1994. pap. 21.95 (1-56000-798-2) Transaction Pubs.

Radio Astronomy. Alan E. Nourse. LC 89-32405. (Venture Bks.). (Illus.). 112p. (YA). (gr. 6 up). 1989. lib. bdg. 22.00 (0-531-10811-2) Watts.

Radio Astronomy. 2nd ed. J. D. Kraus. 710p. (C). 1986. pap. text ed. write for info. (1-882484-00-2) CYGNUS-QUASAR Bks.

Radio Astronomy & Cosmology. Ed. by D. L. Jauncey. (Symposia of the International Astronomical Union Ser.: No. 74). 1977. lib. bdg. 129.50 (90-277-0838-X) Kluwer Ac.

Radio Astronomy & Cosmology. Ed. by D. L. Jauncey. (Symposia of the International Astronomical Union Ser.: No. 74). 1977. pap. text ed. 70.50 (90-277-0839-8) Kluwer Ac.

***Radio Astronomy Projects.** William Lonc. (Illus.). 224p. (Orig.). 1996. pap. 20.00 (1-889076-00-7) Radio-Sky.

Radio Baha'i, Ecuador: A Baha'i Development Project. Kurt J. Hein. (Global Transformation Ser.). 215p. 1988. pap. 17.75 (0-85398-273-2) G Ronald Pub.

Radio Beasts. Ralph M. Farley. 1976. lib. bdg. 10.95 (0-89968-030-5, Lghtyr Pr) Buccaneer Bks.

Radio Book, 3 vols. Radio Ink Magazine Staff Writers. Incl. Bk. 1. Programming & Promotion. LC 95-67239. 1995. pap. 19.99 (1-886745-00-5); Bk. 2. Management. LC 95-67240. 784p. 1995. pap. 19.99 (1-886745-01-3); Bk. 3. Sales & Marketing. LC 95-67241. 784p. 1995. pap. 19.99 (1-886745-02-1); 1995. Set pap. 49.00 (1-886745-03-X) Streamline Pr.

Radio Boy. Sharon P. Denslow. LC 93-36281. (J). (ps-2). 1995. text ed. 15.00 (0-689-80295-1, S&S Bks Young Read) S&S Childrens.

Radio Broadcast Technician. Jack Rudman. (Career Examination Ser.: C-682). 1994. pap. 27.95 (0-8373-0682-5) Nat Learn.

Radio Broadcaster's Big Book, Set, Vols. I, II, III, IV. rev. ed. Ed. by McDonald. (The Broadcaster's Big Book Ser.). (Illus.). 140p. (C). 1995. 349.00 (0-938023-07-1) Wind River Inst Pr.

Radio Broadcaster's Big Book Vol. II: FCC Rules & Dictionary. Compiled by Jim McDonald. (The Broadcaster's Big Book Ser.). (Illus.). 1500p. (C). 1994. student ed. 99.00 (0-938023-10-1) Wind River Inst Pr.

Radio Broadcaster's Big Book Vol. III: Public File. Jim McDonald et al. (The Broadcaster's Big Book Ser.). 100p. (C). 1995. student ed. 99.00 (0-938023-15-2) Wind River Inst Pr.

Radio Broadcaster's Big Book Vol. IV: Encyclopedia. Jim McDonald et al. (The Broadcaster's Big Book Ser.). (Illus.). (C). 1994. student ed. 99.00 (0-938023-11-X) Wind River Inst Pr.

Radio Broadcaster's Big Book - 1995 Revision Vol. I: Operations & FCC Compliance. Ed. & Intro. by Jim McDonald. (The Broadcaster's Big Book Ser.). (Illus.). 100p. (C). 1995. student ed. 99.00 (0-938023-14-4) Wind River Inst Pr.

Radio Broadcasting Sales: Making an Intangible Tangible. Marvin R. Urlacher. LC 89-92408. 185p. (Orig.). (C). 1989. pap. 33.95 (0-9624869-9-X) MW Pub.

Radio Broadcasts of Will Rogers. Will Rogers. Ed. by Steven K. Gragert. LC 82-61001. (Writings of Will Rogers Ser.: Ser. VI, Vol. I). (Illus.). 211p. 1983. pap. 15.00 (0-914956-24-8) Okla State Univ Pr.

Radio Buyer's Sourcebook. 1991. pap. 15.00 (0-87259-345-2) Am Radio.

Radio Buyer's Sourcebook, Vol. 2. 1993. pap. 15.00 (0-87259-421-1) Am Radio.

Radio Canada International: Voice of a Middle Power. James L. Hall. LC 96-6094. (Canadian Ser.: Vol. 7). (Illus.). 300p. 1996. pap. 24.95 (0-87013-420-5, 0-87013-420-5) Mich St U Pr.

Radio Censorship. Ed. by Harrison B. Summers. LC 72-161175. (History of Broadcasting: Radio to Television Ser.). 1977. reprint ed. 25.95 (0-405-03582-9) Ayer.

Radio City & Other Memories: Echoes & Reflections. Elizabeth Schoen. LC 88-51236. 120p. (Orig.). 1991. pap. 9.95 (0-938999-04-4) Yuganta Pr.

Radio Collector's Directory & Price Guide: 1921-1965. 2nd expanded rev. ed. Robert E. Grinder. 533p. (Orig.). 1995. pap. 26.95 (1-886606-06-4) Sonoran Pub.

Radio Communication. John Foss. Ed. by Walter Salm. (CCS Security Source Library: Vol. V). (Illus.). 800p. 1997. 300.00 (1-884674-05-4) CCS Security.

Radio Communications Concepts: Analog. Ralph S. Carson. LC 89-34210. 470p. 1990. text ed. 116.00 (0-471-62169-2) Wiley.

Radio Continua During Solar Flares: Selected Contributions to the Workshop Held at Duino, Italy, May 1985. Ed. by Arnold O. Benz. 1986. lib. bdg. 152.00 (90-277-2291-9) Kluwer Ac.

Radio Contrast Agents, 2 vols. P. R. Knoefel. 1971. 351.00 (0-08-016144-8, Pub. by Pergamon Repr UK) Franklin.

Radio Control Aerobatics for Everyone. Dave Patrick. Ed. by Tom Atwood. (Illus.). 74p. (Orig.). 1994. pap. 12.95 (0-911295-31-3) Air Age.

Radio Control Airplane How-To's, Vol. 2. Model Airplane News Staff. Ed. by Frank R. Masi. (Illus.). 96p. (Orig.). 1995. pap. 14.95 (0-911295-33-X) Air Age.

Radio Control Airplane How To's: Tips from the Experts. Intro. by Tom Atwood. (Illus.). 138p. (Orig.). 1992. pap. 14.95 (0-911295-24-0) Air Age.

Radio Control Car How To's, Vol. 2. Radio Control Car Action Editors. Ed. by John Howell. (Illus.). 98p. (Orig.). 1994. pap. 14.95 (0-911295-32-1) Air Age.

Radio Control Car How To's: Hot Tech from the Pros. Intro. by Frank R. Masi. (Illus.). 136p. (Orig.). 1993. pap. 14.95 (0-911295-25-9) Air Age.

Radio Control Model Manual. D. Boddington. (Illus.). 192p. 1995. 32.95 (1-85260-480-8, Pub. by J H Haynes & Co UK) Motorbooks Intl.

Radio Control Models. Michael E. Goodman. LC 91-47750. (Hobby Guides Ser.). (Illus.). 48p. (J). (gr. 5-6). 1993. lib. bdg. 12.95 (0-89686-622-X, Crstwood Hse) Silver Burdett Pr.

Radio Control Powerboat Racing. John Finch. Ed. by Gerry Yarrish. (Illus.). 65p. (Orig.). 1996. pap. 12.95 (0-911295-29-1) Air Age.

Radio-Controlled Action Cars. Fred Murphy. (Photo-Fact Book). (Illus.). 24p. (Orig.). (J). 1990. pap. 2.50 (0-942025-87-3) Kidsbks.

Radio Corpse: Imagism & the Cryptaesthetic of Ezra Pound. Daniel Tiffany. LC 95-10353. 304p. (C). 1995. text ed. 45.00 (0-674-74662-7) HUP.

Radio Correspondence Education Planning in Thailand. Boonlert Supadhiloke. (Institute of Culture & Communication Case Studies: No. 9). xii, 107p. (Orig.). 1983. pap. text ed. 5.00 (0-86638-040-X) EW Ctr HI.

***Radio Diagram Sourcebook: With Tube Complement Guide.** Richard Gray. (Illus.). 290p. 1996. pap. 18.95 (1-886606-09-9) Sonoran Pub.

Radio Dial. Alicia S. O'Drago. LC 88-70857. 133p. (Orig.). 1988. pap. 9.95 (0-929273-00-1) AMP Publishing.

Radio Diary. Sarah Vowell. LC 96-23288. 256p. 1996. 22.95 (0-312-14712-0) St Martin.

Radio Diplomacy & Propaganda: The BBC & VOA in International Politics, 1956-64. Gary D. Rawnsley. (Studies in Diplomacy). 256p. 1996. text ed. 59.95 (0-312-12972-6) St Martin.

Radio Dispatcher. Jack Rudman. (Career Examination Ser.: C-540). 1994. pap. 23.95 (0-8373-0540-3) Nat Learn.

Radio-Electronics: From "Drawing Board" to Finished Project. Radio-Electronics Editors. (Illus.). 160p. 1989. 15.95 (0-8306-9133-2, 3133); pap. 9.95 (0-8306-3133-X, 3133) McGraw-Hill Prof.

Radio-Electronics' Guide to Computer Circuits. Radio-Electronics Editors. (Illus.). 170p. 1988. 14.95 (0-8306-0333-6); pap. 9.95 (0-8306-9333-5, 3033P) McGraw-Hill Prof.

Radio Emission from the Stars & the Sun. Ed. by A. R. Taylor & J. M. Paredes. (ASP Conference Series Proceedings: Vol. 93). 466p. 1996. 44.00 (1-886733-14-7) Astron Soc Pacific.

Radio Employee Compensation '90. National Association of Broadcasters Staff. 82p. (Orig.). 1990. pap. 100.00 (0-89324-093-1) Natl Assn Broadcasters.

Radio Equipment of the Third Reich: 1933-1945. Charles J. Barger. (Illus.). 112p. 1991. 25.00 (0-87364-592-8) Paladin Pr.

Radio Financial Report 1993. National Association of Broadcasters Staff. 225p. (Orig.). 1993. pap. 225.00 (0-89324-200-4) Natl Assn Broadcasters.

Radio Financing: A Guide to Lenders & Investors. Robin B. Martin & Erwin G. Krasnow. 51p. (Orig.). 1990. pap. 40.00 (0-89324-090-7) Natl Assn Broadcasters.

Radio France. E. A. Macaro. 1985. pap. text ed. 9.63 (0-582-35400-5, 72218); audio 16.96 (0-582-37684-X, 72581) Longman.

Radio Free Albemuth. Philip K. Dick. 224p. 1987. mass mkt. 4.99 (0-380-70288-6) Avon.

Radio Free Albemuth. Philip K. Dick. LC 85-11171. 214p. 1985. 25.00 (0-89366-172-4) Ultramarine Pub.

Radio Free Buddha. Dean Sluyter. 1996. pap. 14.00 (0-517-88662-6, Crown) Crown Pub Group.

Radio Free Europe. Robert T. Holt. LC 58-7621. 263p. reprint ed. pap. 75.00 (0-317-41747-9, 2055879) Bks Demand.

***Radio Free Europe & the Pursuit of Democracy: My War Within the Cold War.** George R. Urban. LC 97-20926. 1997. 30.00 (0-300-06921-9) Yale U Pr.

Radio-Free Queens. Susan Montez. LC 93-39304. 80p. 1994. pap. 10.95 (0-8076-1345-2) Braziller.

***Radio Free Turtle Island: A Collection of Poetry, No. 1.** Jamison C. Mahto. (Illus.). 140p. (Orig.). 1996. pap. 12.00 (1-889401-01-3) Spirit Bear.

Radio Frequency: Microwave Robust Design Techniques Applied to a Transistor Amplifier Test Fixture. Loren F. Root. LC 92-26383. (Six Sigma Research Institute Ser.). 1992. pap. write for info. (0-201-63428-7) Addison-Wesley.

Radio Frequency & E.L.F Electromagnetic Energies: The Health Professional's Handbook. Timothy Hitchcock & Robert M. Patterson. 600p. 1995. text ed. 84.95 (0-442-00945-3) Van Nos Reinhold.

Radio Frequency & Microwave Power Measurement. Ed. by A. E. Fantom et al. (Electrical Measurement Ser.: No. 7). 290p. 1990. 99.00 (0-86341-120-7) Inst Elect Eng.

Radio-Frequency & Microwave Radiation. 2nd ed. Ed. by AIHA Nonionizing Radiation Committee. (Nonionizing Radiation Guide Ser.). (Illus.). 33p. (C). 1994. pap. text ed. 20.00 (0-932627-59-5, 187-EA-94) Am Indus Hygiene.

Radio-Frequency Capacitive Discharges. Ed. by Yuri P. Raizer et al. 320p. 1995. 115.00 (0-8493-8644-6, 8644) CRC Pr.

Radio Frequency Electronics: Circuits & Applications. Jon B. Hagen. (Illus.). 368p. (C). 1996. text ed. 49.95 (0-521-55356-3) Cambridge U Pr.

Radio Frequency Interference. 1992. pap. 15.00 (0-87259-375-4) Am Radio.

Radio Frequency Power in Plasmas. Ed. by Donald B. Batchelor. LC 91-77853. (AIP Conference Proceedings Ser.: No. 244). (Illus.). 416p. 1992. lib. bdg. 99.00 (0-88318-937-2) Am Inst Physics.

Radio-Frequency Power in Plasmas. Ed. by Roger McWilliams. LC 89-45805. (AIP Conference Proceedings Ser.: No. 190). 520p. 1989. lib. bdg. 70.00 (0-88318-397-8) Am Inst Physics.

Radio Frequency Power in Plasmas. Ed. by Miklos Porkolab. (AIP Conference Proceedings Ser.: No. 289). (Illus.). 464p. 1993. text ed. 135.00 (1-56396-264-0, AIP) Am Inst Physics.

Radio Frequency Radiation: Issues & Standards. William Hammett. LC 96-49556. (Illus.). 320p. 1997. text ed. 55.00 (0-07-025929-1) McGraw.

Radio Frequency Transistors: Principles & Practical Applications. Norman E. Dye & Helge O. Granberg. (EDN Ser.). (Illus.). 235p. 1993. 47.95 (0-7506-9059-3) Buttrwrth-Heinemann.

Radio-Frequency Transmission Systems: Design & Operation. Jerry Whitaker. 512p. 1991. text ed. 55.00 (0-07-069620-9) McGraw.

Radio Handbook. Pete Wilby & Andy Conroy. LC 93-44370. (Media Practice Ser.). (Illus.). 320p. (C). 1994. pap. 24.95 (0-415-09467-4, B3799, Routledge NY); text ed. 69.95 (0-415-09466-6, B3795, Routledge NY) Routledge.

Radio Handbook. 23th ed. William I. Orr. 672p. 1986. 39.95 (0-672-22424-0) Buttrwrth-Heinemann.

***Radio Handbook.** 23th ed. William J. Orr. 1986. 39.95 (0-7506-9947-7) Buttrwrth-Heinemann.

Radio Hobbyist's Handbook. Joseph J. Carr. (Illus.). 392p. 1982. 19.95 (0-8306-1346-3, 1346) McGraw-Hill Prof.

Radio Hole-in-the-Head - Radio Liberty: An Insider's Story of Cold War Broadcasting. James Critchlow. LC 95-32855. 210p. (C). 1995. pap. text ed. 21.95 (1-879383-48-9) Am Univ Pr.

Radio Hole-in-the-Head - Radio Liberty: An Insider's Story of Cold War Broadcasting. James Critchlow. LC 95-32855. 210p. (C). 1995. lib. bdg. 47.50 (1-879383-47-0) Am Univ Pr.

Radio in Australia. John Potts. (Illus.). 189p. 1989. pap. 27.95 (0-86840-331-8, Pub. by New South Wales Univ Pr AT) Intl Spec Bk.

Radio in Rural Guatemala: Three Case Studies. Wilson H. Lowrey. (Illus.). 150p. (Orig.). (C). 1990. pap. text ed. 5.95 (0-943089-01-8) U GA CFIMCTR.

Radio in the Television Age. Pete Fornatale. LC 79-67675. 240p. 1980. 22.50 (0-87951-106-0) Overlook Pr.

Radio in the Television Age. Pete Fornatale. LC 79-67675. 240p. 1983. pap. 9.95 (0-87951-172-9) Overlook Pr.

Radio Industry: The Story of Its Development. Ed. by Christopher H. Sterling. LC 74-4687. (Telecommunications Ser.). (Illus.). 344p. 1974. reprint ed. 25.95 (0-405-06055-6) Ayer.

Radio Intercept Service of the German Air Force, 2 vols., 1. (USAF Historical Studies: No. 191). 620p. 1955. pap. text ed. 44.95 (0-89126-162-1) MA-AH Pub.

Radio Intercept Service of the German Air Force, 2 vols., 2. (USAF Historical Studies: No. 191). 620p. 1955. pap. text ed. 44.00 (0-89126-163-X) MA-AH Pub.

Radio Interferometry: Theory, Techniques & Observations. Ed. by T. Cornwell & R. Perley. (ASP Conference Series Proceedings: Vol. 19). 463p. 1991. 28.00 (0-937707-38-4) Astron Soc Pacific.

Radio Jamming Techniques. 1991. lib. bdg. 66.96 (0-8490-4636-X) Gordon Pr.

Radio Listening in America: The People Look at Radio-Again. Paul F. Lazarsfeld & Patricia L. Kendall. Ed. by Lewis A. Coser & Walter W. Powell. LC 79-7002. (Perennial Works in Sociology). (Illus.). 1980. reprint ed. lib. bdg. 18.95 (0-405-12100-8) Ayer.

***Radio Man: Don Radio: A Story in English & Spanish.** Arthur Dorros. Tr. by Sandra Dorros. (ENG & SPA.). (J). (gr. 4). 1995. 7.92 (0-395-73244-1) HM.

***Radio Man: Don Radio: A Story in English & Spanish.** large type ed. Arthur Dorros. Tr. by Sandra Dorros. 62p. (ENG & SPA.). (J). (gr. 4). 15.50 (0-615-10993-4, L-38181-00 APHB) Am Printing Hse.

Radio Man: Miles Cabot on Venus. Farley. 5.00 (0-686-00476-0); pap. 2.00 (0-686-00477-9) Fantasy Pub Co.

***Radio Man/Don Radio.** Arthur Dorros. LC 92-28369. (Trophy Book Ser.). (Illus.). 40p. (J). (gr. 1-5). 1997. pap. 5.95 (0-06-443482-6, Trophy) HarpC Child Bks.

Radio Man/Don Radio: A Story in English & Spanish. Arthur Dorros. Tr. by Sandra M. Dorros. LC 92-28369. (Illus.). 40p. (J). (gr. 1-5). 1993. 16.00 (0-06-021547-X, L-38181-00); lib. bdg. 15.89 (0-06-021548-8) HarpC Child Bks.

***Radio Man/Don Radio: A Story in English & Spanish.** large type ed. Arthur Dorros & Sandra Dorros. 62p. (ENG & SPA.). 1996. 15.50 (0-614-20614-6, L-38181-00 APHB) Am Printing Hse.

Radio Manufacturers of the 1920's, 3 vols., Set. Alan Douglas. (Illus.). 1988. pap. 84.85 (1-886606-05-6) Sonoran Pub.

Radio Manufacturers of the 1920's, Vol. 2. Alan Douglas. 266p. 1994. pap. 29.95 (1-886606-00-5) Sonoran Pub.

Radio Manufacturers of the 1920's Vol. 1: A-C Dayton to J. B. Ferguson, Inc. Alan Douglas. (Illus.). 225p. 1988. pap. 24.95 (1-886606-02-1) Sonoran Pub.

Radio Mechanic. Jack Rudman. (Career Examination Ser.: C-660). 1994. pap. 27.95 (0-8373-0660-4) Nat Learn.

Radio Monitoring: The How-To Guide. T. J. Arey. LC 95-81300. (Illus.). 336p. (Orig.). 1997. pap. 19.95 (1-56866-101-0) Index Pub Grp.

Radio Music Directing. Donna L. Halper. (Illus.). 112p. 1991. pap. 19.95 (0-240-80081-8, Focal) Buttrwrth-Heinemann.

Radio Mystery & Adventure & Its Appearances in Film, Television & Other Media. Jim Harmon. LC 92-54086. 302p. 1992. lib. bdg. 49.95 (0-89950-663-1) McFarland & Co.

Radio Networks & the Federal Government. Thomas P. Robinson. Ed. by Christopher H. Sterling. LC 78-21735. (Dissertations in Broadcasting Ser.). 1980. reprint ed. lib. bdg. 23.95 (0-405-11772-8) Ayer.

Radio Noise Spectrum. Ed. by Donald H. Menzel. LC 60-7997. (Illus.). 191p. 1960. 25.50 (0-674-74675-9) HUP.

***Radio Nutrician Service Provider's Kit: A Nutrition Education Program for the Hispanic Community.** (SPA.). 1996. write for info. incl. audio (1-886567-08-5) Assn Farmwrker.

Radio on the Road: The Traveler's Companion. William Hutchings. Ed. by Hazel Dawkins. 288p. 1996. reprint ed. pap. 12.95 (0-9648563-0-1) Arrowhead CA.

Radio on Wheels: Eastern Edition. Paul Rocheleau. 1991. pap. 8.95 (0-425-12860-1, Berkley Trade) Berkley Pub.

Radio on Wheels: Western Edition. Paul Rocheleau. 1991. pap. 8.95 (0-425-12861-X, Berkley Trade) Berkley Pub.

Radio Onederland. Keith Skues. (C). 1988. pap. 35.00 (0-900963-00-X, Pub. by T Dalton UK) St Mut.

Radio Operator. Jack Rudman. (Career Examination Ser.: C-683). 1994. pap. 27.95 (0-8373-0683-3) Nat Learn.

Radio Papers: From KRAB to KCHU-Essays on the Art & Practice of Radio Transmission. Lorenzo W. Milam. (Twenty-Five Years of Community Broadcasting Ser.). (Illus.). 224p. 1986. pap. 9.95 (0-917320-19-0) Mho & Mho.

Radio Personality Basics. Michael W. May. (Illus.). 170p. 1992. pap. text ed. 14.95 (0-9612074-1-8) M May Ent.

Radio Physics of the Sun: Proceedings of the IUA Symposium, College Park, Maryland, Aug. 7-10, 1979. International Astronomical Union Staff. Ed. by T. E. Gergely & Mukul R. Kundu. (International Astronomical Union Symposia Ser.: No. 86). 472p. 1980. pap. text ed. 78.00 (90-277-1121-6); lib. bdg. 152.00 (90-277-1120-8) Kluwer Ac.

Radio Priest: Charles Coughlin, the Father of Hate Radio. David Warren. (Illus.). 376p. 1996. 27.50 (0-684-82403-5) Free Pr.

Radio Production: A Manual for Broadcasters. 3rd ed. Robert McLeish. LC 94-1103. 272p. 1994. pap. 42.95 (0-240-51366-5, Focal) Buttrwrth-Heinemann.

Radio Production Worktext: Studio & Equipment. 2nd rev. ed. Lynne S. Gross & David E. Reese. 192p. 1993. pap. 29.95 (0-240-80179-2, Focal) Buttrwrth-Heinemann.

Radio Programming: Tactics & Strategy. Eric G. Norberg. 216p. 1996. pap. 26.95 (0-240-80234-9, Focal) Buttrwrth-Heinemann.

***Radio Programming Roles: FEBC Perspectives.** Frank Gray & Ross James. (Illus.). 84p. (Orig.). (C). 1997. pap. text ed. write for info. (0-9657870-0-1) Far East Broadcast.

Radio-Reactive Apples: Stories. Charles C. Wehrenberg. 298p. (Orig.). 1995. pap. 13.00 (1-886163-00-6) SoloZone.

Radio Receiver--Chance or Choice. Rainer Lichte. Ed. by Jeanne C. Ferrell. LC 85-80383. 224p. (Orig.). 1985. pap. 18.50 (0-914542-16-8) Gilfer.

Radio Receiver Projects You Can Build. Homer L. Davidson. 1993. pap. text ed. 21.95 (0-07-015641-7) McGraw.

Radio Receiver Projects You Can Build. Homer L. Davidson. 1993. 28.95 (0-8306-4189-0); pap. 18.95 (0-8306-4190-4) McGraw-Hill Prof.

Radio Receivers. Ed. by W. Gosling. 456p. 1986. 119.00 (0-86341-056-1, TE015) Inst Elect Eng.

Radio Recombination Lines: Proceedings of a Workshop Held in Ottawa, Canada, August 22-24, 1979. Ed. by Peter A. Shaver. (Astrophysics & Space Science Library: No. 80). 294p. 1980. lib. bdg. 100.50 (90-277-1103-8) Kluwer Ac.

Radio Recombination Lines: Twenty Five Years of Investigation. Ed. by M. A. Gordon & R. L. Sorochenko. (C). 1990. lib. bdg. 137.50 (0-7923-0804-2) Kluwer Ac.

***Radio Red Killer.** Richard A. Lupoff. LC 97-16904. (A Marvia Plum Mystery Ser.). 1997. write for info. (0-312-17181-1) St Martin.

Radio Refractivity & Meteorological Data Plots from Radiosonde Launches Trade Winds: March 1969. L. G. Rowlandson & J. S. Schwarz. LC 77-135079. 224p. 1970. 29.00 (0-403-04534-7) Scholarly.

Radio Regulation Vols. 1 & 2: Consolidated Digest. Pike & Fischer. LC 70-5088. 1969. 130.00 (0-614-10386-X, 200980) W S Hein.

Radio Regulation First Series: 1948-1963. Pike & Fischer. LC 48-2103. 1980. reprint ed. lib. bdg. 1,325.00 (0-89941-207-6, 200920) W S Hein.

Radio Regulation First Series: 1948-1963, Vol. 1, Pt. 3 & Vol. 3-25. Pike & Fischer. LC 48-2103. 1980. reprint ed. lib. bdg. 65.00 (0-685-73574-5) W S Hein.

Radio Regulation Second Series: 1963-1993, 73 vols. Pike & Fischer. LC 70-24229. 1963. lib. bdg. 5,032.00 (0-89941-208-4, 200930) W S Hein.

Radio-Relay Systems. Anton A. Huurdeman. LC 94-28033. 1994. 77.00 (0-89006-768-6) Artech Hse.

Radio Replies, 3 vols. Leslie Rumble & Charles M. Carty. LC 79-51938. 1979. reprint ed. pap. 36.00 (0-89555-159-4) TAN Bks Pubs.

Radio Replies, 3 vols., 1. Leslie Rumble & Charles M. Carty. LC 79-51938. 1979. reprint ed. pap. write for info. (0-89555-089-X) TAN Bks Pubs.

Radio Replies, 3 vols., 2. Leslie Rumble & Charles M. Carty. LC 79-51938. 1979. reprint ed. pap. write for info. (0-89555-090-3) TAN Bks Pubs.

Radio Replies, 3 vols., 3. Leslie Rumble & Charles M. Carty. LC 79-51938. 1979. reprint ed. pap. write for info. (0-89555-091-1) TAN Bks Pubs.

Radio Research: An Annotated Bibliography 1975-1988. Josephine Langham & Janine Chrichley. 368p. 1990. text ed. 69.95 (0-566-07130-4, Pub. by Avebury Pub UK) Ashgate Pub Co.

Radio Research, Nineteen Hundred Forty-One. Ed. by Paul F. Lazarsfeld et al. LC 79-7003. (Perennial Works in Sociology Ser.). (Illus.). 1980. reprint ed. lib. bdg. 29. 95 (0-405-12101-6) Ayer.

Radio Research, Nineteen Hundred Forty-Two to Nineteen Hundred Forty-Three. Ed. by Paul F. Lazarsfeld et al. LC 79-7004. (Perennial Works in Sociology). (Illus.). 1980. reprint ed. lib. bdg. 49.95 (0-405-12102-4) Ayer.

***Radio Road Guide: Your Source for Nearly 10,000 AM & FM Stations Across the U. S. A.** Briant Baker. 160p. 1997. pap. 7.99 (0-89896-326-5) Larksdale.

Radio Servicing. Jack Rudman. (Dantes Subject Standardized Tests Ser.: DANTES-35). 1994. pap. 23.95 (0-8373-6635-6) Nat Learn.

Radio Sky. Norman Dubie. 64p. 1992. pap. 8.95 (0-393-30852-9) Norton.

Radio Sound Effects: Who Did It, & How, in the Era of Live Broadcasting. Robert L. Mott. LC 92-50313. (Illus.). 303p. 1993. lib. bdg. 39.95 (0-89950-747-6) McFarland & Co.

Radio Soundtracks: A Reference Guide. 2nd ed. Michael R. Pitts. LC 85-30409. 349p. 1986. 32.50 (0-8108-1875-2) Scarecrow.

Radio Speeches of Charles A. Lindbergh: 1939-1940. Charles A. Lindbergh. 1982. lib. bdg. 250.00 (0-87700-455-2) Revisionist Pr.

Radio Stars. Ed. by Robert M. Hjellming & David M. Gibson. 1985. lib. bdg. 168.50 (90-277-2063-0) Kluwer Ac.

Radio Stars: An Illustrated Biographical Dictionary of over 953 Performers, 1920 Through 1960. Thomas A. DeLong. LC 96-24424. (Illus.). 316p. 1996. lib. bdg. 59. 50 (0-7864-0149-4) McFarland & Co.

Radio Station. 3rd ed. Michael C. Keith & Joseph M. Krause. LC 92-43593. (Illus.). 320p. (Orig.). 1993. 39.95 (0-240-80159-8, Focal) Buttrwrth-Heinemann.

Radio Station. 4th ed. Michael C. Keith. (Illus.). 322p. 1996. pap. 39.95 (0-240-80261-6, Focal) Buttrwrth-Heinemann.

Radio Station Manager. Jack Rudman. (Career Examination Ser.: C-2935). 1994. pap. 34.95 (0-8373-2935-3) Nat Learn.

Radio Station Operations: Management & Employee Perspectives. Lewis B. O'Donnell et al. 409p. (C). 1989. pap. 40.95 (0-534-09540-2) Wadsworth Pub.

Radio Station Treasury (Nineteen Hundred to Nineteen Forty-Six) Tom Kneitel. (Illus.). 176p. (Orig.). 1986. pap. 12.95 (0-939780-04-6) CRB Res.

***Radio System Design for Telecommunications & Signal Processing.** 2nd ed. Roger L. Freeman. LC 96-44722. (Telecommunications & Signal Processing Ser.). 1997. text ed. write for info. (0-471-16260-4) Wiley.

Radio System Design for Telecommunications (1-100 GHz) Roger L. Freeman. 592p. 1987. text ed. 108.00 (0-471-81236-6) Wiley.

Radio Systems for Technicians. 2nd ed. D. C. Green. (Illus.). 176p. 1995. pap. 42.50 (0-582-24516-8, Pub. by Longman Group UK) Trans-Atl Phila.

Radio Systems Technology. Derek C. Green. (C). 1996. pap. text ed. 43.95 (0-582-02697-0) Longman.

***Radio Talk.** Catherine Sadow. Date not set. pap. text ed. write for info. (0-312-15405-4) St Martin.

Radio-Tech Modifications 7A. William V. Smith. 1995. pap. 19.95 (0-917963-10-5) Artsci Inc.

Radio-Tech Modifications 7B. William V. Smith. 1995. pap. 19.95 (0-917963-11-3) Artsci Inc.

Radio Techniques for Probing the Terrestrial Ionosphere. R. D. Hunsucker. (Physics & Chemistry in Space, Planetology Ser.: Vol. 22). (Illus.). 308p. 1991. 219.95 (0-387-53406-7) Spr-Verlag.

Radio Technologies. Fraidoon Mazda. (Telecommunication Ser.). (Illus.). 350p. 1996. pap. 28.95 (0-240-51457-2, Focal) Buttrwrth-Heinemann.

Radio Technologist. Jack Rudman. (Career Examination Ser.: C-1957). 1994. pap. 27.95 (0-8373-1957-9) Nat Learn.

Radio Telephone Operator. Jack Rudman. (Career Examination Ser.: C-2883). 1994. pap. 27.95 (0-8373-2883-7) Nat Learn.

***Radio-Television-Cable Management.** 3rd ed. James A. Brown & Ward L. Quaal. 640p. (C). 1997. text ed. write for info. (0-697-13237-4) Wm C Brown Pubs.

Radio Television Career Directory: A Practical One-Stop Guide to Getting a Job. 2nd ed. Bradley J. Morgan. Ed. by Diane Dupuis. (Career Advisor Ser.). 1993. 17.95 (0-8103-9441-3, 089144) Visible Ink Pr.

Radio Times Brainbox Puzzle Book, No. 3. Clive Doig. 112p. 1994. pap. 4.95 (0-563-36933-7, Pub. by BBC UK) Parkwest Pubns.

Radio Today: The Present State of Broadcasting. Arno Huth. LC 77-161179. (History of Broadcasting: Radio to Television Ser.). 1976. reprint ed. 17.95 (0-405-03585-3) Ayer.

***Radio Tooth.** Paul Jenkins. LC 96-86558. (Award Ser.). 80p. 1997. pap. 12.95 (1-884800-11-4) Four Way Bks.

Radio Transcript, Dr. Kurt Oster Interview, Tiny Markle Show. 20p. pap. 1.00 (0-318-00545-X) Park City Pr.

Radio Transmitter Design. Vagan Shakhgildyan. 488p. (C). 1987. 90.00 (0-685-36907-2, Pub. by Collets) St Mut.

Radio, TV, & Cable Programming. 2nd ed. Herbert H. Howard et al. LC 93-45685. (Illus.). 466p. 1994. text ed. 34.95 (0-8138-0343-8) Iowa St U Pr.

Radio, TV & Modern Life: A Phenomenology of Broadcasting. Paddy Scannell. 256p. Date not set. 54. 95 (0-631-19874-1) Blackwell Pubs.

Radio, TV & Modern Life: A Phenomenology of Broadcasting. Paddy Scannell. 256p. Date not set. pap. 21.95 (0-631-19875-X) Blackwell Pubs.

Radio-T.V. Interference: Sources & Solutions. Frank P. Hughes. 41p. (Orig.). 1990. pap. 6.95 (0-936653-21-3) Tiare Pubns.

Radio-TV News Writing: A Workbook. K. Tim Wulfemeyer. 144p. 1995. pap. text ed. 24.95 (0-8138-0747-6) Iowa St U Pr.

Radio U. S. A. Betsy Errichiello. 108p. 1991. 4.95 (0-9631247-0-6) Betsy Pub.

Radio und Fernsehen Woerterbuch: Dictionary of Radio & Television. Hans N. Zahn. (ARA, ENG, FRE & GER.). 1980. 14.95 (0-8288-2320-0, M 7105) Fr & Eur.

Radio Universe. 3rd ed. J. S. Hey. LC 82-18982. (Illus.). 260p. 1983. pap. 39.95 (0-08-029151-1, Prgamon Press) Buttrwrth-Heinemann.

***Radio Voices: American Broadcasting, 1922-1952.** Michele Hilmes. (Illus.). 320p. (C). 1997. pap. 19.95 (0-8166-2621-9); text ed. 49.95 (0-8166-2620-0) U of Minn Pr.

Radio Wars: Truth, Propaganda & the Struggle for Radio Australia. Errol Hodge. (Illus.). 296p. (C). 1995. text ed. 59.95 (0-521-47380-2) Cambridge U Pr.

Radio Wave Propagation & the Ionosphere. I. L. Al'pert. LC 61-17727. 404p. reprint ed. pap. 115.20 (0-317-09200-6, 2020656) Bks Demand.

Radio Wave Scattering in the Interstellar Medium. Ed. by J. M. Cordes et al. LC 88-72092. (AIP Conference Proceedings Ser.: No. 174). 245p. 1988. lib. bdg. 60.00 (0-88318-374-9) Am Inst Physics.

Radio Waves: Life & Revolution on the FM Dial. Jim Ladd. (Illus.). 320p. 1992. pap. 12.95 (0-312-07786-6) St Martin.

Radio Waves in the Ionosphere: The Mathematical Theory of the Reflection of Radio Waves from Stratified Ionized Layers. K. G. Budden. 566p. reprint ed. pap. 161.40 (0-317-27909-2, 2055781) Bks Demand.

Radio Years: A History of Broadcasting in New Zealand, Vol. 1. Patrick Day. (Auckland University Press Bk.). (Illus.). 352p. 45.00 (1-86940-094-1, Pub. by Auckland Univ NZ) Paul & Co Pubs.

Radioactive Aerosols. A. C. Chamberlain. (Cambridge Environmental Chemistry Ser.). (Illus.). 256p. (C). 1991. text ed. 95.00 (0-521-40121-6) Cambridge U Pr.

Radioactive & Mixed Waste - Risk As a Basis for Waste Classification. Ed. by Dade W. Moeller. LC 95-22246. (Symposium Proceedings Ser.: No. 2). 201p. (Orig.). 1995. pap. text ed. 30.00 (0-929600-43-6) NCRP Pubns.

***Radioactive & Stable Isotope Geology.** H. Attendorn & Bowen. 320p. 1996. text ed. 126.95 (0-412-75280-8, Chap & Hall NY) Chapman & Hall.

Radioactive & Stable Isotope Tracers in Biomedicine: Principles & Practice of Kinetic Analysis. Robert R. Wolfe. 480p. 1992. text ed. 129.95 (0-471-56131-2, Wiley-L) Wiley.

Radioactive Decay Data Tables. DOE Technical Information Center Staff & David C. Kocher. LC 81-607800. 228p. 1981. pap. 36.50 (0-87079-124-9, DOE/TIC-11026); fiche 9.00 (0-87079-496-5, DOE/TIC-11026) DOE.

Radioactive Fallout from Nuclear Weapons Tests: Proceedings. Ed. by Alfred W. Klement, Jr. LC 65-62945. (AEC Symposium Ser.). 953p. 1965. pap. 32.25 (0-87079-323-3, CONF-765); fiche 9.00 (0-87079-324-1, CONF-765) DOE.

***Radioactive Fallout in Soils, Crops & Food.** 84p. 1989. 12. 00 (92-5-102877-X, F877X, Pub. by FAO IT) Bernan Associates.

***Radioactive Heaven & Earth: The Health & Environmental Effects of Nuclear Weapons Testing in, on, & above the Earth.** 208p. 1991. pap. 15.00 (1-85649-021-1) Intl Phys PONW.

Radioactive Heaven & Earth: The Health & Environmental Effects of Nuclear Weapons Testing in, on & above the Earth. International Physicians for the Prevention of Nuclear War Staff. LC 90-25747. (Illus.). 208p. (Orig.). 1991. pap. 15.00 (0-945257-34-1) Apex Pr.

Radioactive Isotopes in Clinical Medicine & Research. Ed. by H. Bergmann et al. LC 94-42695. (Advances in Pharmacological Sciences Ser.). 480p. 1995. 109.00 (0-8176-5082-2) Birkhauser.

Radioactive Isotopes in Clinical Medicine & Research. Ed. by Helmet F. Sinzinger & H. Bergmann. LC 94-42695. (Advances in Pharmacological Sciences Ser.). 1995. write for info. (3-7643-5082-2) Birkhauser.

***Radioactive Isotopes in Clinical Medicine & Research: Proceedings of the 22nd Badgastein Symposium.** H. Bergmann & A. Kroiss. LC 96-39717. (Advances in Pharmacological Sciences Ser.). 1997. write for info. (0-8176-5645-6) Birkhauser.

***Radioactive Isotopes in Clinical Medicine & Research: Proceedings of the 22nd Badgastein Symposium.** Ed. by H. Bergmann et al. LC 96-39717. (Advances in Pharmacological Sciences Ser.: Vol. XXIV). 528p. 1997. 155.00 (3-7643-5645-6) Spr-Verlag.

Radioactive Material Handling Techniques, Course 25. Center for Occupational Research & Development Staff. (Nuclear Technology Ser.). (Illus.). 304p. (C). 1984. pap. text ed. 30.00 (1-55502-114-X) CORD Commns.

Radioactive Materials Disposal & Management, Course 21. Center for Occupational Research & Development Staff. (Nuclear Technology Ser.). (Illus.). 268p. (C). 1984. pap. text ed. 28.00 (1-55502-110-7) CORD Commns.

Radioactive Materials Released from Nuclear Power Plants, 2 vols. 1994. lib. bdg. 395.00 (0-8490-8599-3) Gordon Pr.

Radioactive Materials Released from Nuclear Power Plants. 1990. lib. bdg. 250.00 (0-87700-883-3) Revisionist Pr.

Radioactive Nuclear Beam. W. D. Myers et al. 644p. (C). 1990. text ed. 144.00 (981-02-0101-X) World Scientific Pub.

Radioactive Nuclear Beams, 1991: Proceedings of the 2nd International Conference on Radioactive Nuclear Beams, Louvain-la-Neuve, Belgium, August 19-21, 1991. Ed. by T. Delbar. (Illus.). 464p. 1992. 190.00 (0-7503-0207-0) IOP Pub.

Radioactive Nuclides in Medicine & Biology. 3rd ed. Edith H. Quimby. LC 68-18868. 402p. reprint ed. pap. 114.60 (0-317-26277-7, 2055701) Bks Demand.

Radioactive Pharmaceuticals: Proceedings. Ed. by Gould A. Andrews et al. LC 66-60068. (AEC Symposium Ser.). 702p. 1966. pap. 25.50 (0-87079-325-X, CONF-651111); fiche 9.00 (0-87079-326-8, CONF-651111) DOE.

Radioactive Pollution: Ocean Environments. 1992. lib. bdg. 250.00 (0-8490-5593-8) Gordon Pr.

Radioactive Waste: Advanced Management Methods for Medium-Active Liquid Waste, Vol. 1. Ed. by K. W. Carley-Macauly. (Radioactive Waste Management Ser.). 328p. 1981. text ed. 307.00 (3-7186-0060-9) Gordon & Breach.

Radioactive Waste: Politics & Technology. Frans Berkhout. 256p. (C). (gr. 13). 1991. text ed. 89.95 (0-415-05492-3, A5128) Routledge.

Radioactive Waste As a Social & Political Issue: A Bibliography. Frederick Frankena & Joann Koelln Frankena. LC 89-45879. (Studies in Modern Society: No. 21). 1990. 67.50 (0-404-61628-3) AMS Pr.

***Radioactive Waste Control & Controversy: The History of Radioactive Waste Regulation in the U. K.** Steven D. Chandler. (Environmental Technology Ser.: Vol. 3). 220p. 1997. text ed. 75.00 (90-5699-065-9) Gordon & Breach.

***Radioactive Waste Control & Controversy: The History of Radioactive Waste Regulation in the U. K.** Steven D. Chandler. (Environmental Technology Ser.: Vol. 3). 220p. 1997. pap. text ed. 27.00 (90-5699-066-7) Gordon & Breach.

Radioactive Waste Disposal & Geology. Konrad B. Krauskopf et al. LC 87-33801. 150p. (gr. 13). 1991. pap. text ed. 36.95 (0-412-28640-8) Chapman & Hall.

Radioactive Waste Disposal into a Plastic Clay Formation: A Site-Specific Exercise of Probabilistic Assessment of Geological Containment. M. D'Allessandro & A. Bonne. (Radioactive Waste Management Ser.). 150p. 1981. text ed. 101.00 (3-7186-0084-6) Gordon & Breach.

Radioactive Waste Forms for the Future. Ed. by W. Lutze & R. C. Ewing. 778p. 1988. 398.25 (0-444-87104-7, North Holland) Elsevier.

Radioactive Waste from Nuclear Power Plants. Thomas B. Johansson & Peter Steen. LC 80-6052. (Illus.). 1981. 40. 00 (0-520-04199-2) U CA Pr.

Radioactive Waste in Geologic Storage. Ed. by Sherman Fried. LC 79-9754. (ACS Symposium Ser.: No. 100). 1979. 43.95 (0-8412-0498-5) Am Chemical.

***Radioactive Waste in Geologic Storage.** Sherman Fried. LC 79-9754. (ACS Symposium Ser.: Vol. 100). 351p. 1979. reprint ed. pap. 100.10 (0-608-03095-3, 2063548) Bks Demand.

Radioactive Waste Management. Robert E. Berlin. LC 88-17359. 444p. 1989. text ed. 154.00 (0-471-85792-0) Wiley.

Radioactive Waste Management. Y. S. Tang & James H. Saling. 470p. 1990. 104.00 (0-89116-666-1) Hemisp Pub.

Radioactive Waste Management: Airborne Radioactive Effluents: Releases & Processing: A Bibliography. DOE Technical Information Center Staff. 245p. 1982. pap. 16.00 (0-87079-479-5, DOE/TIC-3397); fiche 9.00 (0-87079-480-9, DOE/TIC-3397) DOE.

Radioactive Waste Management: Decontamination & Decommissioning, A Bibliography, Supplement 1. DOE Technical Information Center Staff. 84p. 1985. pap. 10. 25 (0-87079-568-6, DOE/TIC-3391 SUPPLEMENT 1); fiche 9.00 (0-87079-569-4, DOE/TIC-3391 SUPPLEMENT 1) DOE.

Radioactive Waste Management: Decontamination & Decommissioning: Bibliography. DOE Technical Information Center Staff. 124p. 1982. pap. 13.00 (0-87079-484-1, DOE/TIC-3391); fiche 9.00 (0-87079-485-X, DOE/TIC-3391) DOE.

Radioactive Waste Management: Formerly Utilized Sites-Remedial Action: A Bibliography. DOE Technical Information Center Staff. 47p. 1982. pap. 8.50 (0-87079-486-8, DOE/TIC-3392); fiche 9.00 (0-87079-487-6, DOE/TIC-3392) DOE.

Radioactive Waste Management: Formerly Utilized Sites-Remedial Action, Supplement 1. DOE Technical Information Center Staff. 53p. 1985. pap. 8.50 (0-87079-570-8, DOE/TIC-3392 SUPPLEMENT 1); fiche 9.00 (0-317-38276-4, DOE/TIC-3392 SUPPLEMENT 1) DOE.

Radioactive Waste Management: High-Level Radioactive Wastes: A Bibliography. DOE Technical Information Center Staff. 247p. 1982. pap. 16.25 (0-87079-475-2, DOE/TIC-3389, DE82012272); fiche 9.00 (0-87079-476-0, DOE/TIC-3389, DE82012272) DOE.

Radioactive Waste Management: High-Level Radioactive Wastes: A Bibliography, Supplement 1. DOE Technical Information Center Staff. Ed. by Lynda H. McLaren. 393p. 1984. pap. 44.50 (0-87079-528-7, DOE/TIC-3389 SUPPLEMENT 1, DE84013656); fiche 9.00 (0-87079-529-5, DOE/TIC-3389 SUPPLEMENT 1, DE84013656) DOE.

Radioactive Waste Management: Low-Level Radioactive Waste: A Bibliography. DOE Technical Information Center Staff. 184p. 1984. pap. 12.50 (0-87079-524-4, DOE-TIC-3387 SUPPL. 2, DE84005533); fiche 9.00 (0-87079-525-2, DOE-TIC-3387 SUPPL. 2, DE84005533) DOE.

Radioactive Waste Management: Low-Level Radioactive Waste: A Bibliography Covering January Through December 1982. DOE Technical Information Center Staff. 144p. 1983. pap. 14.50 (0-87079-502-3, DOE/TIC-3387 (SUPPL. 1), DE83007212); fiche 9.00 (0-87079-503-1, DOE/TIC-3387 (SUPPL. 1), DE83007212) DOE.

Radioactive Waste Management: Nuclear Fuel Cycle: A Bibliography, Supplement 1. DOE Technical Information Center Staff. Ed. by Lynda H. McLaren. 138p. 1984. pap. 27.50 (0-87079-532-5, DOE/TIC-3396 SUPPLEMENT 1, DE84013561); fiche 9.00 (0-87079-533-3, DOE/TIC-3396 SUPPLEMENT 1, DE84013561) DOE.

Radioactive Waste Management: Nuclear Fuel Cycle Reprocessing: A Bibliography. DOE Technical Information Center Staff. 248p. 1982. pap. 16.25 (0-87079-506-6, DOE/TIC-3396, DE82012265); fiche 9.00 (0-87079-507-4, DOE/TIC-3396, DE82012265) DOE.

Radioactive Waste Management: Radioactive Waste Inventories & Projections: A Bibliography. DOE Technical Information Center Staff. 18p. 1982. pap. 7.00 (0-87079-490-6, DOE/TIC-3394, DE82012267); fiche 9.00 (0-87079-491-4, DOE/TIC-3394, DE82012267) DOE.

Radioactive Waste Management: Spent Fuel Storage: A Bibliography. DOE Technical Information Center Staff. 154p. 1982. pap. 12.00 (0-87079-477-9, DOE/TIC-3395); fiche 6.50 (0-87079-478-7, DOE/TIC-3395) DOE.

Radioactive Waste Management: Spent Fuel Storage: A Bibliography, Supplement 1. DOE Technical Information Center Staff. Ed. by Lynda H. McLaren. 156p. 1984. pap. 11.75 (0-87079-534-1, DOE/TIC-3395-S1, DE84005534); fiche 9.00 (0-87079-535-X, DOE/TIC-3395-S1, DE84005534) DOE.

Radioactive Waste Management: Transuranic Wastes: A Bibliography. DOE Technical Information Center Staff. 147p. 1982. pap. 14.50 (0-87079-481-7, DOE/TIC-3390, DE82012271); fiche 9.00 (0-87079-482-5, DOE/TIC-3390, DE82012271) DOE.

Radioactive Waste Management: Transuranic Wastes-A Bibliography, Supplement 1. DOE Technical Information Center Staff. 132p. 1985. pap. 11.25 (0-87079-572-4, DOE/TIC-3390, SUPPLEMENT 1, DE85006324); fiche 9.00 (0-317-38277-2, DOE/TIC-3390, SUPPLEMENT 1, DE85006324) DOE.

Radioactive Waste Management: Uranium Mill Tailings - A Bibliography, Supplement 1. DOE Office of Scientific & Technical Information Staff. 75p. 1985. pap. 9.75 (0-87079-574-0, DOE/TIC-3393, SUPPLEMENT 1, DE85006278); fiche 9.00 (0-87079-575-9, DOE/TIC-3393, SUPPLEMENT 1, DE85006278) DOE.

Radioactive Waste Management: Uranium Mill Tailings: A Bibliography. DOE Technical Information Center Staff. 106p. 1982. pap. 13.00 (0-87079-492-2, DOE/TIC-3393, DE85003092); fiche 9.00 (0-87079-493-0, DOE/TIC-3393, DE85003092) DOE.

Radioactive Waste Management: Waste Isolation - A Bibliography, Supplement 1. DOE Technical Information Center Staff. 93p. 1985. pap. 12.75 (0-87079-576-7, DOE/TIC-3388, SUPPLEMENT 1); fiche 6.50 (0-87079-577-5, DOE/TIC-3388, SUPPLEMENT 1) DOE.

Radioactive Waste Management: Waste Isolation: A Bibliography. DOE Technical Information Center Staff. 297p. 1982. pap. 17.50 (0-87079-504-X, DOE/TIC-3388, DE82012273); fiche 9.00 (0-87079-505-8, DOE/TIC-3388, DE82012273) DOE.

Radioactive Waste Management & Disposal. R. Simon. 734p. 1986. text ed. 105.00 (0-521-32580-3) Cambridge U Pr.

Radioactive Waste Management & Disposal, Vol. 10. Ed. by R. Simon & S. Orlowski. (Commission of the European Communities Ser.). 692p. 1980. text ed. 364. 00 (3-7186-0056-0) Gordon & Breach.

Radioactive Waste Management in Perspective: Nuclear Energy & Information. Contrib. by OECD (Nuclear Energy Agency) Staff. 142p. (Orig.). (ENG & FRE.). 1996. pap. 63.00 (92-64-14692-X, Pub. by Org for Econ FR) OECD.

Radioactive Waste, Proceedings of the Twenty-First Annual Meeting Held on April 3-4, 1985. LC 86-5245. (Annual Meeting Proceedings Ser.: No. 7). 1986. pap. 30.00 (0-913392-81-2) NCRP Pubns.

An Asterisk (*) at the beginning of an entry indicates that the title is appearing in BIP for the first time.

R

Radioactive Waste Processing & Disposal: A Bibliography Covering January Through December 1983, Supplement 13, Pts. 1 & 2. 572p. 1985. pap. 41.00 (*0-87079-566-X*, DOE/TIC-3311-S13, PTS. 1 & 2); fiche 9.50 (*0-87079-567-8*, DOE/TIC-3311-S1) DOE.

Radioactive Waste Processing & Disposal: A Bibliography Covering January 1981 through December 1981, Supplement 11. DOE Technical Information Center Staff. 866p. 1982. pap. 91.00 (*0-87079-395-0*, DOE/TIC-3311-S11, DE82012480); fiche 20.50 (*0-87079-460-4*, DOE/TIC-3311-S11) DOE.

Radioactive Waste Processing & Disposal: A Bibliography Covering January 1982 through December 1982, Supplement 12. DOE Technical Information Center Staff. 1122p. 1983. pap. 40.00 (*0-87079-508-2*, DOE/TIC-311-S12, DE84013531); fiche 9.00 (*0-87079-509-0*, DOE/TIC-3311-S12, DE84013531) DOE.

Radioactive Waste Repository Licensing: Synopsis of a Symposium. National Research Council, Commission on Geosciences, Environment, & Resources Staff. 112p. (C). 1992. pap. text ed. 19.00 (*0-309-04691-2*) Natl Acad Pr.

Radioactive World: The Dangers. 1991. lib. bdg. 79.95 (*0-8490-4709-9*) Gordon Pr.

Radioactivity. Conrad L. Stanitski. (Modular Laboratory Program in Chemistry Ser.). 8p. (C). 1995. pap. text ed. 1.35 (*0-87540-468-5*, MISC 468-5) Chem Educ Res.

Radioactivity: A Science in Its Historical & Social Context. Edgar N. Jenkins. (Wykeham Science Ser.: No. 48). 200p. 1979. pap. 18.00 (*0-85109-730-8*) Taylor & Francis.

Radioactivity: A Science in Its Historical & Social Context. Edgar N. Jenkins & I. Lewis. LC 78-11959. (Wykeham Science Ser.: No. 52). 197p. (C). 1979. pap. 18.00 (*0-8448-1371-0*, Crane Russak) Taylor & Francis.

Radioactivity Alert: A Guide to Radiation Effects. Ed. by Y. Liritzis. (Illus.). 129p. 1992. pap. 9.95 (*960-220-069-3*) Paul & Co Pubs.

Radioactivity & Atomic Theory. Ed. by Thaddeus J. Trenn. 536p. 1975. 55.00 (*0-85066-077-7*) Taylor & Francis.

Radioactivity & Health: A History, 3 vols. J. Newell Stannard. LC 88-600371. 2010p. 1989. 97.50 (*0-87079-590-2*) Battelle.

Radioactivity & Its Measurement. 2nd ed. Ed. by W. B. Mann et al. LC 79-40881. (Illus.). 1980. text ed. 135.00 (*0-08-025028-9*, Pub. by Aberdeen U Pr) Macmillan.

Radioactivity in the Environment: Sources, Distribution & Surveillance. Ronald L. Kathren. 398p. pap. text ed. 53.00 (*3-7186-0532-5*) Gordon & Breach.

Radioactivity in the Environment, Sources, Distribution & Surveillance. Ronald L. Kathren. 398p. 1984. text ed. 141.00 (*3-7186-0203-2*) Gordon & Breach.

Radioactivity Measurements: Principles & Practice. Ed. by W. B. Mann et al. (International Journal of Applied Radiation & Isotopes Ser.: No. ARI 228 JARI 39). Orig. Title: Applied Radiation & Isotopes, Vol 39, No. 8. 212p. 1991. pap. 57.95 (*0-08-037037-3*, Prgamon Press) Buttrwrth-Heinemann.

Radioactivity Measurements: Principles & Practice. Ed. by W. B. Mann et al. (International Journal of Applied Radiation & Isotopes Ser.: No. ARI 228 JARI 39). Orig. Title: Applied Radiation & Isotopes, Vol 39, No. 8. 220p. 1991. pap. text ed. 30.00 (*0-08-037239-2*, Pergamon Pr) Elsevier.

Radioanalysis in Geochemistry. H. A. Das et al. (Developments in Geochemistry Ser.: Vol. 5). 482p. 1989. 157.00 (*0-444-87493-3*) Elsevier.

***Radioanalytical Technology: Literature Review.** 1997. lib. bdg. 250.95 (*0-8490-7709-5*) Gordon Pr.

Radioassay Systems in Clinical Endocrinology. Ed. by Guy E. Abraham. LC 81-862. (Basic & Clinical Endocrinology Ser.: No. 1). (Illus.). 687p. reprint ed. pap. 180.00 (*0-7837-0852-1*, 2041161) Bks Demand.

Radioassays & Non-Isotopic Ligand Assays Product Guide, Vol. 29, No. 5. 96p. 1983. 10.00 (*0-915274-42-6*) Am Assn Clinical Chem.

Radiobioassays, 2 vols., I. Fuad S. Ashkar. 1983. 132.00 (*0-8493-6029-3*, RB42) CRC Pr.

Radiobioassays, 2 vols., II. Fuad S. Ashkar. 240p. 1983. 132.00 (*0-8493-6030-7*, RB42) CRC Pr.

Radiobiological Disasters: Consequences of Accidents at Nuclear Power Stations. Ed. by E. B. Burlakova. 257p. (C). 1994. lib. bdg. 89.00 (*1-56072-195-2*) Nova Sci Pubs.

Radiobiology & Radiation Protection: The Past Century & Prospects for the Future. Arthur C. Upton. LC 89-12964. (Taylor Lectures: No. 13). 51p. (Orig.). 1989. pap. text ed. 25.00 (*0-929600-08-8*) NCRP Pubns.

Radiobiology for the Radiologist. 3rd ed. Donald Hall. LC 65-10127. 1987. text ed. 69.50 (*0-397-50848-4*, Lippncott) Lppncott-Raven.

Radiobiology for the Radiologist. 4th ed. Eric J. Hall. LC 93-22626. 478p. (C). 1993. text ed. 82.50 (*0-397-51248-1*) Lppncott-Raven.

Radiocaesium in Pilzen. Anette Reisinger. (Bibliotheca Mycologica Ser.: 155). (Illus.). 342p. (GER.). 1994. pap. 97.50 (*3-443-59057-8*) Lubrecht & Cramer.

Radiocarbon after Four Decades: An Interdisciplinary Perspective. Kpmg Peat Marwick Staff. (Illus.). 616p. 1992. 107.95 (*0-387-97714-7*) Spr-Verlag.

Radiocarbon Dating. Sheridan Bowman. 1990. pap. 12.00 (*0-520-07037-2*) U CA Pr.

Radiocarbon Dating. 2nd ed. Willard F Libby. LC 55-10246. 187p. reprint ed. pap. 53.30 (*0-317-08415-1*, 2005396) Bks Demand.

Radiocarbon Dating No. 1: Recent Applications & Future Potential, 1991. J. J. Lowe. 96p. Date not set. pap. text ed. 36.95 (*0-471-95699-6*) Wiley.

***Radiocarbon Dating & Italian Prehistory.** Ed. by Robin Skeates & Ruth Whitehouse. (British School at Rome Archaeological Monographs: No. 8). (Illus.). 288p. 1994. pap. 57.50 (*1-873415-11-7*, Pub. by British Schl Rome UK) David Brown.

Radiocarbon Dating Literature: The First 21 Years, 1947-1968 - An Annotated Bibliography. Ed. by Dilette Polach. 370p. 1988. text ed. 89.00 (*0-12-559290-6*) Acad Pr.

Radiocarbon User's Handbook. 2nd rev. ed. Richard Gillespie. (Illus.). 44p. 1986. 4.95 (*0-947816-03-8*, Pub. by Oxford Univ Comm Arch UK) David Brown.

Radiocehmistry & Nuclear Chemistry: Theory & Applications. Choppin et al. 1994. text ed. write for info. (*0-08-037955-9*, Pergamon Pr) Elsevier.

Radiochemical Methods. Bill Geary. Ed. by Arthur M. James. LC 86-9153. (Analytical Chemistry by Open Learning Ser.). 229p. 1986. pap. text ed. 52.95 (*0-471-91118-6*) Wiley.

Radiochemisches Lexikon der Elemente und Ihrer Isotope: Radiochemical Lexicon of Elements & Their Isotopes. M. Haissinsky. (GER.). 1968. pap. 45.00 (*0-8288-6659-7*, M-7596) Fr & Eur.

Radiochemistry: Theory & Experiment. T. A. Peacocke. (Wykeham Science Ser.: No. 50). 274p. 1978. pap. 18.00 (*0-85109-690-5*) Taylor & Francis.

Radiochemistry: Theory & Experiment. T. A. Peacocke. LC 78-57666. (Wykeham Science Ser.: No. 50). 274p. (C). 1979. pap. 18.00 (*0-8448-1360-5*, Crane Russak) Taylor & Francis.

Radiochemistry see International Congress of Pure & Applied Chemistry, 24th, Hamburg, 1973: Proceedings

Radiochemistry & Nuclear Chemistry: Nuclear Chemistry, Theory & Applications. 2nd ed. Gregory R. Choppin et al. LC 94-40183. (Illus.). 722p. 1995. pap. 47.95 (*0-7506-2300-4*, Prgamon Press) Buttrwrth-Heinemann.

Radiochemistry & Nuclear Chemistry: Theory & Applications. Choppin et al. 1994. pap. text ed. write for info. (*0-08-037954-0*) Elsevier.

Radiochemistry & Nuclear Methods of Analysis. William D. Ehman & Diane E. Vance. (Chemical Analysis Ser.). 560p. 1993. pap. text ed. 52.95 (*0-471-30628-2*) Wiley.

Radiochemistry & Nuclear Methods of Analysis. William D. Ehmann & Diane E. Vance. LC 90-26336. (Chemical Analysis: A Series of Monographs on Analytical Chemistry & Its Applications). 560p. 1991. text ed. 145.00 (*0-471-60076-8*) Wiley.

***Radiochemistry of Light Water Reactor Nuclear Power Plants.** Karl-Heinz Neeb. 720p. (C). 1997. lib. bdg. 368.90 (*3-11-013242-7*) De Gruyter.

Radiodetermination Satellite Services & Standards. Martin A. Rothblatt. LC 87-9141. (Artech House Telecommunications Library). 201p. 1987. reprint ed. pap. 57.30 (*0-608-02367-1*, 2063009) Bks Demand.

Radiodiagnosis of Endophytic Gastric Cancer. L. M. Portnoi & M. P. Dibirov. LC 95-12084. 1995. write for info. (*1-56700-028-2*) Begell Hse.

Radiodiagnosis of the Skull. J. L. Dietmann. Tr. by M. T. Wackenheim from FRE. (Exercises in Radiological Diagnosis Ser.). (Illus.). 200p. 1985. 35.95 (*0-387-13266-X*) Spr-Verlag.

Radiodiffusion Puissance Mondiale. Arno Huth. LC 72-4661. (International Propaganda & Communications Ser.). (Illus.). 511p. 1972. reprint ed. 30.95 (*0-405-04749-5*) Ayer.

Radioecological Techniques. Vincent Schultz & F. Ward Whicker. LC 81-22706. 310p. 1982. 75.00 (*0-306-40797-3*, Plenum Pr) Plenum.

Radioecology. E. Holm. 364p. 1994. text ed. 99.00 (*981-02-1778-1*) World Scientific Pub.

Radioecology: Nuclear Energy & the Environment, Vol. I. F. Ward Whicker. 224p. 1982. 89.00 (*0-8493-5353-X*, QH543) CRC Pr.

Radioecology: Nuclear Energy & the Environment, Vol. II. F. Ward Whicker. 240p. 1982. 137.00 (*0-8493-5354-8*) CRC Pr.

Radioecology after Chernobyl: Biogeochemical Pathways of Artificial Radionuclides. Ed. by Frederick Warner & Roy M. Harrison. LC 92-26475. (Scientific Committee on Problems of the Environment Ser.). 367p. 1993. text ed. 295.00 (*0-471-93168-3*) Wiley.

Radioecology & the Restoration of Radioactive Contaminated Sites: Proceedings of the NATO Advanced Study Institute on Radio-Active Contaminated Site Restoration, Zarechny, Sverdlivsk, Russia, June 19-28, 1995. M. J. Frissel. Ed. by Felix F. Luykx. LC 96-9395. (NATO Advanced Science Institutes Ser.). 304p. (C). 1996. lib. bdg. 163.00 (*0-7923-4136-8*) Kluwer Ac.

***Radiofrequency & Microwaves.** (Environmental Health Criteria Ser.: No. 16). 134p. 1981. pap. text ed. 15.00 (*92-4-154076-1*, 1160016) World Health.

Radiofrequency Catheter Ablation of Cardiac Arrhythmias: Basic Concepts & Clinical Applications. Ed. by Shoei K. Huang. LC 94-16813. (Illus.). 640p. 1994. 98.00 (*0-87993-595-2*) Futura Pub.

Radiofrequency Electromagnetic Fields: Properties, Quantities & Units, Biophysical Interaction, & Measurements. LC 80-982007. (Report Ser.: No. 67). 140p. 1981. pap. text ed. 50.00 (*0-913392-52-9*) NCRP Pubns.

Radiofrequency Hyperthermia Systems: Experimental & Clinical Assessment of the Feasibility of Radiofrenquency Hyperthermia Systems for Loco-Regional Deep Heating. G. C. Van Rhoon. 190p. (Orig.). 1994. pap. 52.50 (*90-6275-978-5*, Pub. by Delft U Pr NE) Coronet Bks.

Radiofrequency Radiation Standards: Biological Effects, Dosimetry, Epidemiology, & Public Health Policy. Ed. by B. Jon Klauenberg et al. LC 95-11437. (NATO ASI Ser.: Ser. A, Vol. 274). 455p. 1995. 120.00 (*0-306-44919-6*) Plenum.

***Radiogenic Isotope Geology.** 468p. 1997. pap. text ed. 44.95 (*0-521-59891-5*) Cambridge U Pr.

Radiogenic Isotope Geology. Alan P. Dickin. (Illus.). 400p. (C). 1995. text ed. 95.00 (*0-521-43151-4*) Cambridge U Pr.

Radioglaciology. V. V. Bogorodsky et al. 1985. lib. bdg. 158.50 (*90-277-1893-8*) Kluwer Ac.

Radiografia de un Sitio Arqueologico. Luis Barba. 138p. 1990. pap. 5.70 (*968-36-1378-0*, UN001) UPLAAP.

Radiograhic Critique. Kathy McQuillen-Martensen. (Illus.). 320p. 1996. text ed. 50.00 (*0-7216-4978-5*) Saunders.

Radiographers: Laboratory Manual for Students. 2nd rev. ed. Andrea Harvey & Linda Geisler. 288p. (Orig.). (C). 1995. lab manual ed., pap. text ed. 29.95 (*0-916973-08-5*) Burnell Co.

***Radiographer's Handbook of Hospital Practice.** D. Noreen Chesney & M. O. Chesney. 142p. 1986. pap. write for info. (*0-632-01487-3*) Blackwell Sci.

***Radiographer's Pocket Companion.** Bown. 1997. pap. text ed. write for info. (*0-7020-2166-0*, Bailliere-Tindall) Saunders.

Radiographic Anatomy. (National Medical Ser.). 1990. 26.00 (*0-685-75187-2*) Williams & Wilkins.

Radiographic Anatomy. Frank J. Slaby & E. Jacobs. (National Medical Ser.). (Illus.). 311p. 1990. 26.00 (*0-683-06266-2*) Williams & Wilkins.

Radiographic Anatomy: A Working Atlas. Harry W. Fischer. (Illus.). 205p. (C). 1988. pap. text ed. 39.00 (*0-07-021089-6*) McGraw-Hill HPD.

Radiographic Anatomy & Positioning. Alan B. Evantash et al. (C). 1991. 700.00 incl. disk (*1-56815-004-0*) Mosby Yr Bk.

Radiographic Anatomy & Positioning. Hayes. 571p. (gr. 13). 1995. wbk. ed., pap. text ed. 62.95 (*0-8016-7980-X*) Mosby Yr Bk.

Radiographic Anatomy & Positioning, Vol. 1. Hayes. 360p. (gr. 13). 1995. suppl. ed., pap. text ed. 34.95 (*0-8016-7981-8*) Mosby Yr Bk.

***Radiographic Anatomy & Positioning: An Integrated Approach.** Andrea G. Cornvelle & Dinae H. Gronefeld. LC 96-46591. 1997. text ed. 70.00 (*0-8385-8238-9*) Appleton & Lange.

Radiographic Anatomy & Positioning: To Accompany Merrill's Atlas, Vol. 2. Hayes. 304p. (gr. 13). 1995. wbk. ed., pap. text ed. 34.95 (*0-8016-7982-6*) Mosby Yr Bk.

Radiographic Anatomy & Positioning Instructor's Ma... Bontrager. 1985. spiral bd. 29.95 (*0-8016-4505-0*) Mosby Yr Bk.

Radiographic Anatomy & Positioning Instructor's Ma... Bontrager. 1985. spiral bd. 60.00 (*0-8016-4494-1*) Mosby Yr Bk.

Radiographic Anatomy & Positioning Instructor's Manual. Bontrager. 1985. spiral bd. 24.95 (*0-8016-4524-7*) Mosby Yr Bk.

Radiographic Anatomy & Positioning Series, Units 1. Bontrager. (C). (gr. 13). 1985. 950.00 incl. sl. (*0-8016-4433-X*); 975.00 incl. sl. (*0-8016-4431-3*) Mosby Yr Bk.

Radiographic Anatomy & Positioning Series, Units 9. Bontrager. (C). (gr. 13). 1985. 975.00 incl. sl. (*0-8016-4432-1*) Mosby Yr Bk.

Radiographic Anatomy & Positioning, Unit 1 - Termino... Bontrager. (C). (gr. 13). 1985. 104.65 incl. sl. (*0-8016-4434-8*) Mosby Yr Bk.

Radiographic Anatomy & Positioning, Unit 10 - Craniu... Bontrager. (C). (gr. 13). 1985. 124.65 incl. sl. (*0-8016-4443-7*) Mosby Yr Bk.

Radiographic Anatomy & Positioning, Unit 11 - Facial. Bontrager. (C). (gr. 13). 1985. 124.65 incl. sl. (*0-8016-4444-5*) Mosby Yr Bk.

Radiographic Anatomy & Positioning, Unit 12 - Mandib... Bontrager. (C). (gr. 13). 1985. 124.65 incl. sl. (*0-8016-4445-3*) Mosby Yr Bk.

Radiographic Anatomy & Positioning, Unit 13 - Coccyx. Bontrager. (C). (gr. 13). 1985. 124.65 incl. sl. (*0-8016-4446-1*) Mosby Yr Bk.

Radiographic Anatomy & Positioning, Unit 14 - T &... Bontrager. (C). (gr. 13). 1985. 124.65 incl. sl. (*0-8016-4449-6*) Mosby Yr Bk.

Radiographic Anatomy & Positioning, Unit 15 - Bony T... Bontrager. (C). (gr. 13). 1985. 129.00 incl. sl. (*0-8016-4450-X*) Mosby Yr Bk.

Radiographic Anatomy & Positioning, Unit 16 - Cerebr... Bontrager. (C). (gr. 13). 1985. 138.80 incl. sl. (*0-8016-4495-X*) Mosby Yr Bk.

Radiographic Anatomy & Positioning, Unit 17 - Cerebr... Bontrager. (C). (gr. 13). 1985. 228.80 incl. sl. (*0-8016-4496-8*) Mosby Yr Bk.

Radiographic Anatomy & Positioning, Unit 18 - Crania. Bontrager. (C). (gr. 13). 1985. 299.00 incl. sl. (*0-8016-4497-6*) Mosby Yr Bk.

Radiographic Anatomy & Positioning, Unit 19 - Upper. Bontrager. (C). (gr. 13). 1985. 195.00 incl. sl. (*0-8016-4506-9*) Mosby Yr Bk.

Radiographic Anatomy & Positioning, Unit 2 - Chest. Bontrager. 791p. (C). (gr. 13). 1985. 104.65 incl. sl. (*0-8016-4435-6*) Mosby Yr Bk.

Radiographic Anatomy & Positioning, Unit 21 - Gallbl... Bontrager. (C). (gr. 13). 1985. 199.00 incl. sl. (*0-8016-4508-5*) Mosby Yr Bk.

Radiographic Anatomy & Positioning, Unit 3 - Abdomen. Bontrager. (C). (gr. 13). 1985. 104.65 incl. sl. (*0-8016-4436-4*) Mosby Yr Bk.

Radiographic Anatomy & Positioning, Unit 4 - Fingers. Bontrager. (C). (gr. 13). 1985. 104.65 incl. sl. (*0-8016-4437-2*); 104.65 incl. sl. (*0-8016-4438-0*) Mosby Yr Bk.

Radiographic Anatomy & Positioning, Unit 6 - Shoulder. Bontrager. (C). (gr. 13). 1985. 104.65 incl. sl. (*0-8016-4439-9*) Mosby Yr Bk.

Radiographic Anatomy & Positioning, Unit 7 - Toes, F... Bontrager. (C). (gr. 13). 1985. 104.65 incl. sl. (*0-8016-4440-2*) Mosby Yr Bk.

Radiographic Anatomy & Positioning, Unit 8 - Leg, Kn... Bontrager. (C). (gr. 13). 1985. 104.65 incl. sl. (*0-8016-4441-0*) Mosby Yr Bk.

Radiographic Anatomy & Positioning, Unit 9 - Hips &... Bontrager. (C). (gr. 13). 1985. 104.65 incl. sl. (*0-8016-4442-9*) Mosby Yr Bk.

Radiographic Atlas of Child Abuse: A Case Studies Approach. Harris et al. 1995. 89.50 (*0-89640-258-4*) Igaku-Shoin.

Radiographic Atlas of Colon Disease. Ed. by Edward I. Greenbaum. LC 79-19979. (Illus.). 679p. reprint ed. pap. 180.00 (*0-8357-7618-2*, 2056941) Bks Demand.

***Radiographic Atlas of Musculoskeletal Anatomy: A Practical Approach.** Thomas L. Pope et al. (Illus.). 200p. 1997. 45.00 (*0-86577-695-4*) Thieme Med Pubs.

Radiographic Atlas of Skeletal Development of the Hand & Wrist. 2nd ed. William W. Greulich & S. Idell Pyle. (Illus.). xvi, 256p. 1959. 110.00 (*0-8047-0398-1*) Stanford U Pr.

Radiographic Cephalometry: From Basics to Videoimaging. Ed. by Alexander Jacobson. LC 95-19432. (Illus.). 336p. 1995. text ed. 88.00 (*0-86715-294-X*) Quint Pub Co.

Radiographic Evaluation of the Spine. Post. (gr. 13). 1980. 169.00 (*0-89352-050-0*) Mosby Yr Bk.

Radiographic Exposure: Principles & Practice. Jerry E. Wallace. LC 95-741. (Illus.). 574p. (C). 1995. pap. text ed. 46.95 (*0-8036-0051-8*) Davis Co.

Radiographic Exposure & Technique. Kathleen D. Euganeo & Alan B. Evantash. (C). 1992. 700.00 incl. disk (*1-56815-003-2*) Mosby Yr Bk.

***Radiographic Imaging.** Burns. 1992. lab manual ed., pap. text ed. 15.95 (*0-7216-3245-9*) Saunders.

Radiographic Imaging. 6th rev. ed. John Ball. Ed. by Tony Price. LC 95-5293. 1995. 39.95 (*0-632-03901-9*) Blackwell Sci.

Radiographic Imaging: A Guide for Producing Quality Radiographs. Evelyn F. Burns. LC 92-19465. (Illus.). 223p. 1992. text ed. 37.50 (*0-7216-3246-7*) Saunders.

***Radiographic Imaging: A Guide for Producing Quality Radiographs.** Evelyn F. Burns. (Illus.). 223p. 1992. teacher ed. write for info. (*0-7216-3247-5*) Saunders.

Radiographic Imaging: A Practical Approach. Derrick P. Roberts & Nigel L. Smith. (Illus.). 368p. (Orig.). 1988. pap. write for info. (*0-443-03061-8*) Churchill.

Radiographic Imaging: A Practical Approach. Derrick P. Roberts & Nigel L. Smith. LC 94-4029. (Orig.). 1994. 52.00 (*0-443-04397-3*) Churchill.

Radiographic Imaging for Dental Auxiliaries. 2nd ed. Dale A. Miles et al. LC 92-17230. (Illus.). 336p. 1993. pap. text ed. 41.00 (*0-7216-6729-5*) Saunders.

Radiographic Index. 8th ed. Myer Goldman & David Cope. (Illus.). 128p. 1987. pap. 27.50 (*0-7506-1807-8*) Buttrwrth-Heinemann.

Radiographic Interpretation for the Dental Hygienist. Joen I. Haring & Laura J. Lind. (Illus.). 208p. 1993. pap. text ed. 37.50 (*0-7216-3704-3*) Saunders.

Radiographic Interpretation in Orofacial Disease. Ed. by Stephen R. Porter & Crispian Scully. (Illus.). 128p. 1991. pap. 41.95 (*0-19-261585-8*) OUP.

Radiographic Neuroanatomy: A Working Atlas. Harry W. Fischer & Leena Ketonen. 224p. 1990. pap. text ed. 39.00 (*0-07-021101-9*) McGraw-Hill HPD.

Radiographic Pathology. TerriAnn Linn-Watson. LC 95-13455. (Illus.). 256p. 1995. text ed. 42.00 (*0-7216-4129-6*) Saunders.

***Radiographic Pathology.** TerriAnn Linn-Watson. (Illus.). 315p. 1996. teacher ed. write for info. (*0-7216-4134-2*) Saunders.

Radiographic Pathology Exams. Linn. 1996. 195.00 (*0-7216-4172-5*) Saunders.

Radiographic Pathology for Technologists. 2nd ed. Nina Kowalczyk. 400p. (gr. 13). 1993. pap. text ed. 38.00 (*0-8016-7059-4*) Mosby Yr Bk.

Radiographic Pathology Workbook. Linn. 1995. wbk. ed., pap. text ed. 21.00 (*0-7216-4169-5*) Saunders.

***Radiographic Planning & Assessment of Endosseous Oral Implants.** Reinhilde Jacobs & D. Van Steenberghe. LC 97-21358. 1997. write for info. (*3-540-63087-2*) Springer Pub.

Radiographic Positioning. Dowd. 1997. pap. text ed. write for info. (*0-7216-5566-1*) Saunders.

Radiographic Positioning. 2nd ed. Ronald L. Eisenberg et al. LC 94-24133. 432p. 1995. text ed. 69.95 (*0-316-22499-5*) Lppncott-Raven.

Radiographic Positioning, Vol. 1. Greathouse. (Raciographic Technology Ser.). 1998. text ed. 110.00 (*0-8273-6782-1*) Delmar.

Radiographic Positioning, Vol. 1. Greathouse. (Radiographic Technology Ser.). 1998. teacher ed. 16.00 (*0-8273-6783-X*) Delmar.

Radiographic Positioning, Vol. 1. Greathouse. (Radiographic Technology Ser.). 1998. lab manual ed. 34.95 (*0-8273-6784-8*) Delmar.

Radiographic Positioning, Vol. II. Cowling. (Radiographic Technology Ser.). 1998. text ed. 89.95 (*0-8273-6317-6*) Delmar.

Radiographic Positioning, Vol. II. Cowling. (Radiographic Technology Ser.). 1998. wbk. ed. 29.95 (*0-8273-6993-X*) Delmar.

An Asterisk (*) at the beginning of an entry indicates that the title is appearing in BIP for the first time.

Radiographic Positioning, Vol. II. Cowling. (Radiographic Technology Ser.). 1998. teacher ed. 14.00 (*0-8273-6994-8*) Delmar.

Radiographic Positioning & Related Anatomy Workbook. Bontrager. 624p. (C). (gr. 13). 1993. spiral bd. 66.95 (*0-8016-8056-5*) Mosby Yr Bk.

Radiographic Positioning & Techniques: Pocket Handbook. 2nd ed. Kenneth L. Bontrager. 290p. 1995. pap. text ed. write for info. (*0-9641723-1-3*) Bontrager Pub.

Radiographic Positioning Competency: Based Applications. James Barba & William Leonard. 340p. 1992. student ed., pap. 30.95 (*0-8273-4456-2*) Delmar.

Radiographic Positioning Competency-Based Applications: Instructor's Guide. James Barba & William Leonard. 48p. 1992. pap. 14.00 (*0-8273-4457-0*) Delmar.

Radiographic Positioning CTB, Vol. II. Cowling. (Radiographic Technology Ser.). 1998. 49.95 (*0-8273-6996-4*) Delmar.

Radiographic Positioning of Small Animals. Gerald D. Ryan. LC 80-26069. 159p. reprint ed. pap. 45.40 (*0-7837-1476-9*, 2057171) Bks Demand.

Radiographic Positioning Pocket Manual. Cynthia A. Dennis et al. LC 95-10054. 288p. 1995. spiral bd. 26.95 (*0-316-18096-3*) Lppncott-Raven.

***Radiographic Processing.** William McKinney. 359p. 1995. spiral bd. 115.00 (*1-879575-63-9*) Acad Med Sys.

Radiographic Technique: Laboratory Manual. Robert J. Parelli. 79p. (C). 1990. text ed. 18.95 (*1-880359-01-4*) Par Rad.

Radiographic Technique & Image Evaluation. E. Unett & A. Royle. (Orig.). 240p. (Orig.). 1996. pap. text ed. 45.00 (*1-56593-442-3*, 1112) Singular Publishing.

Radiographic Testing: (Classroom Training Handbook) 225p. 1983. 18.50 (*0-318-17239-9*, 1612) Am Soc Nondestructive.

Radiographic Testing Programmed Instruction Book, 5 Vols. (Self-Study Instruction Handbook Ser.). 1363p. 1983. 92.50 (*0-318-17233-X*, 1506) Am Soc Nondestructive.

***Radiography.** Bruce Bond. 1997. pap. 12.50 (*1-880238-51-9*) BOA Edns.

Radiography: Technology, Environment, Professionalism. Frances Campeau. 350p. 1997. pap. text ed. 29.95 (*0-397-55196-7*) Lppncott-Raven.

Radiography Assess Test. 2nd ed. William L. Leonard. 1995. 19.95 (*0-9644624-1-9*) JLW Pub.

Radiography Examination & Course Review by Appleton & Lange: Prep. Dorothy A. Saia. 1995. pap. text ed. 32.95 (*0-8385-8244-3*, Medical Exam) Appleton & Lange.

Radiography Examination Review. 8th ed. William L. Leonard. (Illus.). 174p. (C). 29.95 (*0-9644624-0-0*) JLW Pub.

***Radiography Examination Review.** 9th ed. William L. Leonard. (Illus.). 174p. (C). 1997. 29.95 (*0-614-30271-4*) JLW Pub.

***Radiography Examination Review.** 9th rev. ed. William L. Leonard. (Illus.). 180p. (C). 1997. pap. text ed. 29.95 (*0-9644624-2-7*) JLW Pub.

Radiography in Veterinary Technology. Lisa M. Lavin. LC 93-26133. 1994. text ed. 41.00 (*0-7216-6686-8*) Saunders.

Radiography of Cultural Material. Lang. LC 97-14630. 1997. 66.95 (*0-7506-2621-6*) Buttrwrth-Heinemann.

Radiography of Spine Injury. Phyllis Kornguth et al. (C). 1991. 400.00 incl. disk (*1-56815-007-5*) Mosby Yr Bk.

Radiography Workbook. Robert DeAngelis. (Illus.). 167p. (C). student ed. 18.95 (*0-943589-00-2*) Health & Allied.

Radiography Workbook. 5th rev. ed. Robert DeAngelis. (Illus.). 31.95 (*0-943589-18-5*) Health & Allied.

Radiography Workbook, No. I. 3rd ed. Robert DeAngelis. (Illus.). (C). 1989. 23.95 (*0-943589-11-8*) Health & Allied.

Radiography Workbook, No. II. 2nd ed. Robert DeAngelis & Michelle Edgar. (Illus.). 180p. (C). 24.95 (*0-943589-12-6*) Health & Allied.

Radiography Workbook II. 3rd ed. Robert DeAngelis & Michelle Edgar. 1992. 28.95 (*0-943589-14-2*) Health & Allied.

Radiography Workbook Two. Robert DeAngelis & Michelle Edgar. (Illus.). 178p. (C). 1988. pap. text ed. 24.95 (*0-943589-01-0*) Health & Allied.

Radiography Workbook 1. 4th ed. Robert W. DeAngelis. (Illus.). 196p. 1993. 27.95 (*0-943589-15-0*) Health & Allied.

***Radiohead.** Nick Johnstone. 64p. pap. 12.95 (*0-7119-6581-1*) Omnibus NY.

***Radiohead: Green Plastic Watering Can.** William Stone. 1996. pap. 16.99 (*1-886894-54-X*, MBS Paperbk) Mus Bk Servs.

Radioimmunoassay & Reproductive Endocrinology see **Molecular Aspects of Medicine**

Radioimmunoassay in Clinical Biochemistry. Ed. by Charles A. Pasternak. LC 76-675546. 317p. reprint ed. pap. 90.40 (*0-317-29335-4*, 2024025) Bks Demand.

Radioimmunoassay of Antibody & Its Clinical Applications. David Parratt. LC 81-12939. 174p. reprint ed. pap. 49.60 (*0-318-34726-1*, 2031940) Bks Demand.

Radioimmunoassay of Hormones for Clinical Trials of Fertility Regulating Agents in Developing Countries: Report. (Technical Report Ser.: No. 578). 1975. pap. text ed. 5.00 (*92-4-120578-4*, 1100578) World Health.

Radioiodination: Theory Practice & Biomedical Application. Mrinal K. Dewanjee. (Developments in Nuclear Medicine Ser.). 658p. (C). 1992. lib. bdg. 219.00 (*0-7923-1491-3*) Kluwer Ac.

Radioisotope Engineering. Ed. by Geoffrey G. Eichholz. LC 77-142891. (Illus.). 432p. reprint ed. pap. 123.20 (*0-317-07974-3*, 2055012) Bks Demand.

Radioisotope Studies in Cardiology. Ed. by Hans J. Biersack & Peter H. Cox. (Developments in Nuclear Medicine Ser.). 1985. lib. bdg. 193.00 (*0-89838-733-7*) Kluwer Ac.

Radioisotope Study of Salivary Glands. Ed. by Giuseppe De Rossi. 198p. 1987. 114.00 (*0-8493-6072-2*, RC815, CRC Reprint) Franklin.

Radioisotope X-Ray Fluorescence Spectrometry. (Technical Reports: No. 115). (Illus.). 102p. (Orig.). 1970. pap. 25.00 (*92-0-165170-8*, IDC115, Pub. by IAEA AU) Bernan Associates.

Radioisotopes. D. Billington et al. (Introduction to Biotechniques Ser.). 168p. (Orig.). 1992. pap. 47.50 (*1-872748-85-6*, Pub. by Bios Scientific UK) Coronet Bks.

Radioisotopes & Ionizing Radiations in Entomology: 1964-1965. (Bibliographical Ser.: No. 24). 454p. 1967. pap. 50.00 (*92-0-014067-X*, ISP21 24, Pub. by IAEA AU) Bernan Associates.

Radioisotopes & Radiation: Recent Advances in Medicine, Agriculture, & Industry. J. H. Lawrence et al. (Illus.). 1990. 12.50 (*0-8446-0765-7*) Peter Smith.

Radioisotopes in Biology: A Practical Approach. Ed. by R. J. Slater. (Practical Approach Ser.). (Illus.). 328p. 1990. pap. 45.00 (*0-19-963081-X*, IRL Pr) OUP.

Radioisotopes in Medicine-In Vitro Studies: Proceedings. Ed. by Raymond L. Hayes et al. LC 68-60071. (AEC Symposium Ser.). 753p. 1968. pap. 26.75 (*0-87079-327-6*, CONF-671111); fiche 9.00 (*0-87079-328-4*, CONF-671111) DOE.

Radioisotopic Methods for Biological & Medical Research. Herman W. Knoche. (Illus.). 448p. (C). 1991. text ed. 49.00 (*0-19-505806-2*) OUP.

Radiolabeled Blood Elements: Recent Advances in Techniques & Applications. Ed. by J. Martin-Comin et al. (NATO ASI, Series A, Life Sciences: Vol. 262). (Illus.). 382p. 1994. 115.00 (*0-306-44700-2*, Plenum Pr) Plenum.

Radiolabeled Monoclonal Antibodies for Imaging & Therapy. Ed. by S. C. Srivastava. LC 88-19623. (NATO ASI Series A, Life Sciences: Vol. 152). (Illus.). 890p. 1988. 175.00 (*0-306-42982-9*, Plenum Pr) Plenum.

Radiolaria. O. Roger Anderson. (Illus.). 350p. 1983. 186.95 (*0-387-90832-3*) Spr-Verlag.

Radiolaria: Flux, Ecology, & Taxonomy in the Pacific & Atlantic. Kozo Takahashi. Ed. by Susumu Honjo. (Ocean Biocoenosis Ser.: No. 3). (Illus.). 300p. 1991. pap. text ed. 35.00 (*1-880224-02-X*) Woods Hole Ocean.

Radiolarian Zonation & Stratigraphy of the Upper Cretaceous Portion of the Great Valley Sequence, California Coast Ranges. E. A. Pessagno, Jr. (Micropaleontology Special Publications: No. 2). 95p. 1976. 20.00 (*0-686-84250-2*) Am Mus Natl Hist.

Radiologic A & P: A Self-Paced Multimedia Learning S. Bontrager. 1995. write for info. (*0-8016-6851-4*); write for info. (*0-8016-6852-2*) Mosby Yr Bk.

Radiologic Anatomy of the Brain. G. Salamon & Y. P. Huang. LC 75-45294. (Illus.). 1976. 199.00 (*3-540-07528-3*) Spr-Verlag.

Radiologic Anatomy of the Jaws. Harrison M. Berry, Jr. LC 82-60263. (Illus.). 144p. (Orig.). 1982. pap. text ed. 22.95 (*0-8122-1130-8*) U of Pa Pr.

Radiologic & Histologic Pathology of Nontumorous Diseases of Bones & Joints, 2 vols. James W. Milgram. Ed. by John G. Gruhn. (Illus.). 1382p. 1990. 199.00 (*0-9614018-1-8*) Northbrook Pub.

Radiologic Approach to Diseases of the Chest. Irwin M. Freundlich & David G. Bragg. (Illus.). 572p. 1991. 99.00 (*0-683-03373-5*) Williams & Wilkins.

Radiologic Approach to Diseases of the Chest. 2nd ed. Irwin M. Freundlich & David G. Bragg. LC 96-13796. 866p. 1996. 139.00 (*0-683-03372-7*) Williams & Wilkins.

Radiologic Atlas of Bone Tumors. H. M. Kroon et al. LC 92-49602. 762p. 1993. 381.00 (*0-444-81293-8*) Elsevier.

Radiologic Atlas of Brain Tumors. Glenn S. Forbes. (C). 1991. 700.00 incl. disk (*1-56815-005-9*) Mosby Yr Bk.

Radiologic Atlas of Pulmonary Abnormalities in Children. 2nd ed. David B. Singleton et al. (Illus.). 368p. 1988. text ed. 120.00 (*0-7216-2062-0*) Saunders.

Radiologic Diagnosis of Chest Disease. Miriam Sperber. (Illus.). 600p. 1990. 265.00 (*0-387-97099-1*) Spr-Verlag.

***Radiologic Differential Diagnosis in Pediatrics.** K. D. Ebel & H. Blickmann. (Illus.). 880p. 1997. 189.00 (*0-86577-713-6*) Thieme Med Pubs.

Radiologic Oral Examination: Questions & Guide. Richard B. Rafal. LC 93-26566. 464p. 1994. pap. 59.50 (*0-89640-246-0*) Igaku-Shoin.

Radiologic Physics, Equipment, & Quality Control. William R. Hendee et al. LC 77-204. 301p. reprint ed. pap. 85.80 (*0-317-26174-6*, 2024265) Bks Demand.

Radiologic Science: Workbook & Laboratory Manual. 5th ed. Bushong. 400p. 1992. pap. 22.95 (*0-8016-6437-3*) Mosby Yr Bk.

Radiologic Science for Technologists. 6th ed. Bushong. LC 96-29488. 640p. (gr. 13). 1997. text ed. 58.00 (*0-8151-1579-2*) Mosby Yr Bk.

Radiologic Technologist. Jack Rudman. (Career Examination Ser.: C-1544). 1994. pap. 29.95 (*0-8373-1544-1*) Nat Learn.

Radiologic Technology. 1986. lib. bdg. 155.00 (*0-8490-3805-7*) Gordon Pr.

Radiologic Technology Clinical Manual. Robert J. Parelli. 282p. (C). 1991. text ed. 38.00 (*1-880359-04-9*) Par Rad.

Radiologic Technology Examination Review. Richard R. Carlton. (Illus.). 352p. 1993. pap. text ed. 29.95 (*0-397-54899-0*) Lppncott-Raven.

Radiologic Technology Registry Preparation: RT. Steven B. Dowd. 267p. (C). 1995. wbk. ed., pap. text ed., spiral bd. 29.95 (*0-925016-94-2*) Educ Sftware.

Radiologic Tumor Localizer. John C. Rathe & Paul Elliott. 71p. (C). 1982. 6.00 (*0-87527-249-5*) Green.

Radiological Accident in Soreq. IAEA Staff. 78p. 1993. pap. 35.00 (*92-0-101693-X*, STI/PUB/925, Pub. by IAEA AU) Bernan Associates.

Radiological Anatomy of the Cranial Nerves. C. Zacchi et al. 154p. 1981. text ed. 48.00 (*1-57235-063-6*) Piccin NY.

Radiological Aspects of Renal Transplantation: Proceedings of the Microsymposium, Nymegen, 1977. Microsymposium Staff. Ed. by William Penn. (Radiologia Clinica et Biologica Ser.: Vol. 47, No. 1). (Illus.). 1977. 15.75 (*3-8055-2844-2*) S Karger.

Radiological Assessment: Predicting the Transport, Bioaccumulation, & Uptake by Man of Radionuclides Released to the Environment. National Council on Radiation Protection & Measurements Staff. LC 84-4773. (Report Ser.: No. 76). 304p. 1984. pap. text ed. 55.00 (*0-913392-66-9*) NCRP Pubns.

Radiological Assessments for the Resettlement of Rongelap in the Republic of the Marshall Islands. National Research Council Staff. 124p. (Orig.). (C). 1994. pap. text ed. 37.00 (*0-309-05049-9*) Natl Acad Pr.

Radiological Atlas of Bone Tumours, 2 vols. Netherlands Committee on Bone Tumours. Incl. Vol. II. . 1972. 261.55 (*3-10-800119-1*); (Illus.). write for info. (*0-318-54405-9*) Mouton.

Radiological Atlas of Common Diseases of the Small Bowel. J. L. Sellink. 1976. pap. text ed. 234.00 (*90-207-0476-1*) Kluwer Ac.

Radiological, Clinical & Biomechanical Aspects of Chest Trauma. S. A. Groskin. (Illus.). 208p. 1991. 158.00 (*0-387-53712-0*) Spr-Verlag.

***Radiological Contamination & Public Health.** (Hazardous, Nuclear & Solid Waste Environmental Management Ser.: No. 3). 1996. pap. 10.00 (*1-55516-513-3*, 4660) Natl Conf State Legis.

Radiological Diagnosis in Canine & Feline Emergencies: An Atlas of Thoracic & Abdominal Changes. Sten E. Olsson. LC 71-146031. reprint ed. pap. 58.00 (*0-685-20938-5*, 2056522) Bks Demand.

Radiological Diagnosis of Breast Diseases. Edward A. Sickels. LC 96-80070. (Medical Radiology Ser.). (Illus.). 400p. 1996. 236.00 (*3-540-58863-9*) Spr-Verlag.

Radiological Emergencies, Course 18. Center for Occupational Research & Development Staff. (Nuclear Technology Ser.). (Illus.). 386p. (C). 1984. pap. text ed. 32.00 (*1-55502-107-7*) CORD Commns.

Radiological Emergencies: A Handbook for Emergency Responders. Nicholas A. Klimenko & James F. Redington. (Illus.). 200p. (Orig.). (C). 1988. teacher ed. 19.95 (*0-913019-01-1*); pap. text ed. 18.95 (*0-913019-00-3*) Bradford Commun.

Radiological Evaluation of the Spinal Cord, 2 vols., Vol. 1. Milosh Perovitch. 256p. 1981. 145.00 (*0-8493-5041-7*, RC402, CRC Reprint) Franklin.

Radiological Evaluation of the Spinal Cord, 2 vols., Vol. 2. Milosh Perovitch. 192p. 1981. 108.00 (*0-8493-5043-3*, CRC Reprint) Franklin.

Radiological Examination of the Colon. R. E. Miller & Jovitas Skucas. 1983. lib. bdg. 314.50 (*90-247-2666-2*) Kluwer Ac.

Radiological Factors Affecting Decision-Making in a Nuclear Attack. LC 74-20064. (Report Ser.: No. 42). 66p. 1974. pap. text ed. 20.00 (*0-913392-24-3*) NCRP Pubns.

Radiological Health Specialist. Jack Rudman. (Career Examination Ser.: C-3118). 1994. pap. 34.95 (*0-8373-3118-8*) Nat Learn.

Radiological Imaging: The Theory of Formation & Detection & Processing, Vol. 2. H. H. Barrett & William Swindell. LC 80-69416. (Biophysics & Bioengineering Ser.). 1981. text ed. 128.00 (*0-12-079602-3*) Acad Pr.

Radiological Imaging: The Theory of Image Formation, Detection, & Processing. Ed. by Harry Barrett & William Swindell. (Illus.). 706p. 1996. reprint ed. pap. 69.95 (*0-12-079603-1*) Acad Pr.

***Radiological Imaging of Sports Injuries.** C. Masciocchi & A. Barile. LC 97-12401. (Medical Radiology Ser.). 1997. write for info. (*3-540-60870-2*) Spr-Verlag.

Radiological Methods & Equipment. James R. Critser, Jr. (Ten R-94 Ser.). (C). 1995. pap. 105.00 (*0-88178-094-4*) Lexington Data.

Radiological Methods & Equipment, No. 10R-79. James R. Critser, Jr. (Ser. 10R-79). 1980. pap. 70.00 (*0-914428-68-3*) Lexington Data.

Radiological Methods & Equipment, No. 10R-80. James R. Critser, Jr. (Ser. 10R-80). 1981. pap. 80.00 (*0-914428-86-1*) Lexington Data.

Radiological Methods & Equipment, No. 10R-81. James R. Critser, Jr. (Ser. 10R-81). 115p. 1982. pap. 80.00 (*0-914428-97-7*) Lexington Data.

Radiological Methods & Equipment, No. 10R-82. James R. Critser, Jr. (Ser. 10R-82). 1983. pap. 80.00 (*0-88178-007-3*) Lexington Data.

Radiological Methods & Equipment, No. 10R-83. James R. Critser, Jr. (Ser. 10R-83). 88p. 1984. pap. 80.00 (*0-88178-018-9*) Lexington Data.

Radiological Methods & Equipment, No. 10R-84. James R. Critser, Jr. (Ser. 10R-84). 124p. 1985. pap. 90.00 (*0-88178-055-3*) Lexington Data.

Radiological Methods & Equipment, No. 10R-85. James R. Critser, Jr. 1986. pap. 90.00 (*0-88178-039-1*) Lexington Data.

Radiological Methods & Equipment, No. 10R-86. James R. Critser, Jr. (Ser. 10R-86). 242p. 1987. pap. 93.00 (*0-88178-049-9*) Lexington Data.

Radiological Methods & Equipment, No. 10R-87. James R. Critser, Jr. (Ser. 10R-87). 1988. pap. 95.00 (*0-88178-066-9*) Lexington Data.

Radiological Methods & Equipment, No. 10R-88. James R. Critser, Jr. (Illus.). (C). 1989. pap. 95.00 (*0-88178-071-5*) Lexington Data.

Radiological Methods & Equipment, No. 10R-89. James R. Critser, Jr. (Illus.). (C). 1990. pap. 105.00 (*0-88178-076-6*) Lexington Data.

Radiological Methods & Equipment, No. 10R-90. James R. Critser, Jr. (Illus.). (C). 1991. pap. 105.00 (*0-88178-080-4*) Lexington Data.

Radiological Methods & Equipment, No. 10R-91. James R. Critser, Jr. (Illus.). (C). 1992. pap. 105.00 (*0-88178-083-9*) Lexington Data.

Radiological Methods & Equipment, No. 10R-92. James R. Critser, Jr. (Illus.). (C). 1993. pap. 105.00 (*0-88178-086-3*) Lexington Data.

Radiological Methods & Equipment, No. 10R-93. James R. Critser, Jr. (Illus.). (C). 1994. pap. 105.00 (*0-88178-089-8*) Lexington Data.

Radiological Methods & Equipment, No. 10R-95. James R. Critser. (Radiological Methods & Equipment Ser.: No. 10R-95). (Illus.). 1996. pap. 110.00 (*0-88178-096-0*) Lexington Data.

Radiological Officer. Jack Rudman. (Career Examination Ser.: C-3406). 1994. pap. 34.95 (*0-8373-3406-3*) Nat Learn.

Radiological-Pathological Conferences of the Massachusetts General Hospital. Daniel Rosenthal et al. (C). 1991. 500.00 incl. disk (*1-56815-008-3*) Mosby Yr Bk.

Radiological Physicists. Juan A. Del Regato. 188p. 1985. 25.00 (*0-88318-469-9*) Am Inst Physics.

***Radiological Protection in Biomedical Research.** ICRP Staff. (International Commission on Radiological Protection Ser.: Vol. 62). 72p. 1993. 65.00 (*0-08-042203-9*, Pergamon Pr) Elsevier.

***Radiological Protection of the Worker in Medicine & Dentistry.** ICRP Staff. (International Commission on Radiological Protection Ser.: Vol. 57). 116p. 1990. 45.00 (*0-08-040769-2*, Pergamon Pr) Elsevier.

Radiological Safety Aspects of the Operation of Neutron Generators. R. F. Boggs. (Safety Ser.: No. 42). (Illus.). 42p. 1976. pap. 15.00 (*92-0-123076-1*, ISP427, Pub. by IAEA AU) Bernan Associates.

Radiologist. Jack Rudman. (Career Examination Ser.: C-1447). 1994. pap. 39.95 (*0-8373-1447-X*) Nat Learn.

Radiology. Taveras. (C). 1993. ring bd. write for info. (*0-318-70302-5*) Lppncott-Raven.

Radiology. Kathy Winkler. (Inventors & Inventions Ser.). 64p. (J). (gr. 3-5). 1996. lib. bdg. 17.95 (*0-7614-0075-3*, Benchmark NY) Marshall Cavendish.

Radiology: A Commemorative Edition. Eisenberg. 620p. (C). (gr. 13). 1994. 158.00 (*0-8151-3052-X*) Mosby Yr Bk.

Radiology: A Practical Guide. Robert F. Bury. (Practical Guides for General Practice Ser.: No. 3). (Illus.). 112p. 1988. pap. 10.95 (*0-19-261681-1*) OUP.

Radiology: An Illustrated History. Ronald L. Eisenberg. 608p. (C). (gr. 13). 1991. text ed. 115.00 (*0-8016-1526-7*) Mosby Yr Bk.

Radiology: MGH Clinical Review. Felix S. M. Chew et al. Ed. by Daniel I. Rosenthal et al. LC 93-20747. (Illus.). 464p. 1994. pap. text ed. 55.00 (*0-7216-4609-3*) Saunders.

Radiology: Pre-Test Self-Assessment & Review. Ed. by David M. Hovsepian. LC 92-48942. (Pretest Specialty Level Ser.). (Illus.). 256p. 1993. pap. text ed. 39.95 (*0-07-052007-0*) McGraw-Hill HPD.

***Radiology: The Essentials.** Richard B. Gunderman. (Illus.). 352p. 1997. pap. text ed. 45.00 (*0-86577-684-9*) Thieme Med Pubs.

Radiology Administration Forms, Checklists & Guidelines. Aspen Reference Group Staff. Ed. by Kenneth E. Lawrence & Dwayne E. Eutsey. LC 93-35879. ring bd. 200.00 (*0-8342-0546-7*) Aspen Pub.

Radiology an Illustrated History. Ronald L. Eisenberg. 1995. 99.00 (*0-8151-1526-1*) Mosby Yr Bk.

***Radiology & CPT 1997, Professional Edition, 2 vols.** American Medical Association Staff. 1996. spiral bd. 59.95 (*0-614-19620-5*, EP054397WE); ring bd. 64.95 (*0-614-19621-3*, LP054397WE) AMA.

***Radiology & CPT 1997, Standard Edition, 2 vols.** American Medical Association Staff. 1996. pap. 47.95 (*0-614-19623-X*, OP054397WE); spiral bd. 47.95 (*0-614-19622-1*, SP054397WE) AMA.

Radiology & Imaging for Medical Students. 6th ed. David Sutton. LC 93-19864. 1994. pap. 34.95 (*0-443-04883-5*) Churchill.

Radiology & the Kidney: Some Present Concepts. Ed. by C. J. Hodson. (Contributions to Nephrology Ser.: Vol. 5). (Illus.). 1977. 39.25 (*3-8055-2385-8*) S Karger.

***Radiology & the Law.** Albert L. Bundy. LC 87-14510. 238p. 1994. reprint ed. pap. 67.90 (*0-608-03393-6*, 2064090) Bks Demand.

Radiology & Ultrasound of Urogenital Diseases in Dogs & Cats. Norman Ackerman. (Venture Series in Veterinary Medicine). (Illus.). 192p. (C). 1991. pap. text ed. 44.95 (*0-8138-1527-4*) Iowa St U Pr.

Radiology Dictionary: Radiologisches Woerterbuch. Kurt Freye & Wayne P. Lammers. 556p. (GER.). 1982. 125.00 (*0-8288-1837-1*, M15426) Fr & Eur.

Radiology for Anaesthetists. Conrad Wittram & Graham H. Whitehouse. (Illus.). 128p. 1996. 36.00 (*0-340-55790-7*, Pub. by Ed Arnold UK) OUP.

Radiology for Anesthesia & Critical Care. Ed. by Michael Murphy & Christine H. Murphy. (Illus.). 273p. 1988. 64.00 (*0-443-08306-1*) Churchill.

Radiology for Dental Auxiliaries. 6th ed. Frommer. 416p. (C). (gr. 13). 1995. pap. text ed. 43.00 (*0-8151-3229-8*) Mosby Yr Bk.

***Radiology for the MRCP.** Nicola Strickland. (Illus.). 260p. 1997. write for info. (*0-7020-2220-9*, Pub. by W B Saunders UK) Saunders.

An Asterisk (*) at the beginning of an entry indicates that the title is appearing in BIP for the first time.

***Radiology for the MRCP.** Zezulka. (Illus.). 304p. (Orig.). 1997. pap. text ed. write for info. (0-412-58120-5, Chap & Hall NY) Chapman & Hall.

***Radiology Imaging Words & Phrases.** (Orig.). 1997. pap. write for info. (0-934385-68-8) Hlth Prof Inst.

Radiology in Inflammatory Bowel Disease. Clive I. Bartram et al. LC 83-7518. (Diagnostic Radiology Ser.: No. 2). (Illus.). 327p. reprint ed. pap. 93.20 (0-7837-4302-5, 2043993) Bks Demand.

Radiology in Intensive Care. Hillman. 177p. Date not set. write for info. (0-407-00321-5) Buttrwrth-Heinemann.

Radiology in Medical Diagnostics: Evolution of X-Ray Applications 1895-1995. Gerd Rosenbusch et al. 570p. 1995. 110.00 (0-86542-899-9) Blackwell Sci.

Radiology in Oto-Rhino-Laryngology. Ed. by S. Brunner. (Advances in Oto-Rhino-Laryngology Ser.: Vol. 21). (Illus.). 162p. 1974. 73.75 (3-8055-1632-0) S Karger.

Radiology in Practice. Intro. by Veterninary Learning Systems Staff. 286p. 1994. pap. text ed. 53.00 (1-884254-16-0) Vet Lrn Syst.

Radiology in the Management of Cancer. Ed. by R. J. Johnson et al. (Illus.). 484p. 1990. text ed. 125.00 (0-443-03732-9) Churchill.

Radiology in Veterinary Orthopedics. Joe P. Morgan. LC 71-175464. 415p. reprint ed. pap. 118.30 (0-685-15883-7, 2056191) Bks Demand.

Radiology Management: A Guide for Administrators, Supervisors, & Students, 2 vols. Eric Bouchard. (Orig.). (C). 1993. pap. text ed. 49.95 (1-881795-06-3) Eastwind Pub.

Radiology Management: A Guide for Administrators, Supervisors, & Students, 2 vols., Vol. 1. Eric Bouchard. 269p. (Orig.). (C). 1993. pap. text ed. 27.95 (1-881795-04-7) Eastwind Pub.

Radiology Medical Transcription: MDT 130. S. Turley. 120p. (C). 1993. student ed. write for info. (0-933915-51-9) CA College Health Sci.

Radiology of Acute Cervical Spine Trauma. 2nd ed. John H. Harris, Jr. et al. (Illus.). 296p. 1986. 68.00 (0-683-03928-8) Williams & Wilkins.

Radiology of Acute Cervical Spine Trauma. 3rd ed. John H. Harris, Jr. & Stuart E. Mirvis. LC 95-17806. 512p. 1995. 89.00 (0-683-03929-6) Williams & Wilkins.

Radiology of Bone Diseases. 5th ed. Greenfield. (Illus.). 962p. 1990. text ed. 149.00 (0-397-50979-0) Lppncott-Raven.

Radiology of Carpal Instability: A Practical Approach. W. R. Obermann. 200p. 1994. 233.50 (0-444-82080-9) Elsevier.

Radiology of Chest Diseases. Sebastian Lange. (Illus.). 300p. 1989. text ed. 69.00 (0-86577-313-0) Thieme Med Pubs.

***Radiology of Chest Diseases.** 2nd rev. ed. Ed. by Sebastian Lange. (Illus.). 370p. 1997. 79.00 (0-86577-637-7) Thieme Med Pubs.

Radiology of Childhood Leukemia & Its Therapy. Nancy S. Rosenfield. (Illus.). 126p. (C). 1981. pap. text ed. 22.50 (0-87527-173-1) Green.

Radiology of Congenital Heart Disease. Kurt Amplatz et al. LC 92-49972. 1992. write for info. (0-8016-0329-3) Mosby Yr Bk.

Radiology of Diabetes. B. Eyes & I. A. MacFarlane. 1986. lib. bdg. 49.00 (0-85200-936-4) Kluwer Ac.

Radiology of Emergency Medicine. 3rd ed. John H. Harris, Jr. et al. LC 92-16759. (Illus.). 1120p. 1992. 155.00 (0-683-03884-2) Williams & Wilkins.

Radiology of Facial Injury. 2nd ed. Kenneth D. Dolan. 1988. text ed. 62.95 (0-07-105263-1) McGraw.

Radiology of Haemophilic. Jeno Forrai. 1979. lib. bdg. 70. 50 (90-247-2130-X) Kluwer Ac.

Radiology of Joint Disease, Vol. 2. 3rd ed. D. M. Forrester & J. C. Brown. (Monographs in Clinical Radiology). (Illus.). 608p. 1987. text ed. 99.00 (0-7216-3827-9) Saunders.

Radiology of Liver Circulation. C. L'Hermine. LC 85-8905. (Radiology Ser.). 1985. lib. bdg. 178.50 (0-89838-715-9) Kluwer Ac.

Radiology of Occupational Chest Disease. Ed. by A. Solomon & L. Kreel. (Illus.). 220p. 1989. 147.00 (0-387-96877-6) Spr-Verlag.

Radiology of Orthopedic Procedures. Martin I. Gelman. (Monographs in Clinical Radiology: Vol. 24). (Illus.). 300p. 1984. text ed. 93.00 (0-7216-4079-6) Saunders.

Radiology of Renal Failure. 2nd ed. Griffiths. (Illus.). 272p. 1990. text ed. 72.00 (0-7216-4289-6) Saunders.

Radiology of Skeletal Disorders, 4 vols. 3rd ed. Ronald O. Murray et al. (Illus.). 2368p. 1990. text ed. 495.00 (0-443-01980-0) Churchill.

Radiology of Skeletal Trauma, 2 vols. 2nd ed. Lee F. Rogers. LC 92-9204. (Illus.). 1619p. 1992. text ed. 375. 00 (0-443-08550-1) Churchill.

Radiology of Skeletal Trauma, Vol. 1. Lee F. Rogers. LC 82-4181. (Illus.). 467p. reprint ed. pap. 121.50 (0-8357-6563-6, 2035936) Bks Demand.

Radiology of Skeletal Trauma, Vol. 2. Lee F. Rogers. LC 82-4181. (Illus.). 519p. reprint ed. pap. 148.00 (0-8357-6564-4) Bks Demand.

Radiology of Small Animal Fracture Management. Joe P. Morgan & Robert L. Leighton. LC 94-13109. (Illus.). 400p. 1994. text ed. 79.00 (0-7216-5455-X) Saunders.

Radiology of Syndromes, Metabolic Disorders, & Skeletal Dysplasias. 4th ed. Hooshang Tabyi & Ralph S. Lachman. LC 95-40103. 1152p. (C). (gr. 13). 1995. text ed. 210.00 (0-8151-8709-2) Mosby Yr Bk.

Radiology of the Acute Abdomen. Jovitas Skucas & Robert F. Spataro. (Illus.). 727p. 1986. text ed. 142.00 (0-443-08245-6) Churchill.

Radiology of the Acute Abdomen. fac. ed. Jovitas Skucas & Robert F. Spataro. LC 86-20759. (Illus.). 731p. 1986. reprint ed. pap. 180.00 (0-7837-7891-0, 2047647) Bks Demand.

Radiology of the Cat. Farrow. 480p. 1993. 80.00 (0-8016-8062-X) Mosby Yr Bk.

Radiology of the Cat. Farrow. (Illus.). 280p. (C). 1993. text ed. 95.95 (1-55664-129-X) Mosby Yr Bk.

Radiology of the Ear, Nose & Throat. Galdino E. Valvassori et al. (Illus.). 352p. 1982. text ed. 157.00 (0-7216-8952-3) Saunders.

Radiology of the Esophagus. Levine. 1989. text ed. 147.00 (0-7216-2906-7) Saunders.

Radiology of the Eye & Orbit. Thomas H. Newton & Larissa T. Bilaniuk. (Modern Neuroradiology Ser.: Vol. 4). 320p. 1990. text ed. 127.50 (0-88167-662-4, 2129) Lppncott-Raven.

Radiology of the Foot & Ankle. Ed. by Thomas H. Berquist. (Illus.). 528p. 1989. text ed. 165.50 (0-88167-445-1) Lppncott-Raven.

Radiology of the Hand. P. Bourjat. (Exercises in Radiological Diagnosis Ser.). (Illus.). 230p. 1987. 35.00 (0-387-16537-1) Spr-Verlag.

Radiology of the Hand. C. J. Thijn. (Illus.). 308p. 1986. 216.00 (0-387-15345-4) Spr-Verlag.

Radiology of the Heart. H. Spindola-Franco & B. G. Fish. (Illus.). xvii, 702p. 1985. 476.00 (0-387-90742-4) Spr-Verlag.

Radiology of the Kidney. 3rd ed. Davidson. Date not set. text ed. write for info. (0-7216-7144-6) HarBrace.

Radiology of the Kidney & Urinary Tract. 2nd ed. Ed. by Alan J. Davidson & David S. Hartman. (Illus.). 864p. 1993. text ed. 152.00 (0-7216-3552-0) Saunders.

Radiology of the Liver, Biliary Tract, & Pancreas. Ed. by Arnold C. Friedman & Abraham H. Dachman. LC 93-41167. 000957p. (gr. 13). 1993. text ed. 189.00 (1-55664-218-0) Mosby Yr Bk.

Radiology of the Lower Urinary Tract. Ed. by Erich K. Lang. LC 93-49790. (Medical Radiology: Diagnostic Imaging & Radiation). 1994. 306.00 (0-387-53720-1) Spr-Verlag.

Radiology of the Normal Skull. Robert Shapiro. LC 80-23680. (Illus.). 377p. reprint ed. pap. 107.50 (0-8357-7602-6, 2056924) Bks Demand.

Radiology of the Pancreas. Ed. by A. L. Baert & G. Delorme. LC 94-6222. (Medical Radiology, Diagnostic Imaging & Radiation Oncology Ser.). (Illus.). 296p. 1994. 249.00 (0-387-56514-0) Spr-Verlag.

Radiology of the Pediatric Chest. Ed. by Alvin H. Felman. (Illus.). 496p. 1986. text ed. 85.00 (0-07-020405-5) McGraw-Hill HPD.

Radiology of the Sella Turcica. J. F. Bonneville et al. (Illus.). 262p. 1980. 181.00 (0-387-10319-8) Spr-Verlag.

Radiology of the Small Intestine. P. Bret et al. (Illus.). 400p. 1989. 350.00 (0-387-59508-2) Spr-Verlag.

Radiology of the Stomach. Richard H. Marshak et al. (Illus.). 656p. 1983. text ed. 172.00 (0-7216-6124-6) Saunders.

Radiology of the Trachea. Paul Stark. (Illus.). 109p. 1991. text ed. 69.00 (0-86577-390-4) Thieme Med Pubs.

Radiology of the Upper Urinary Tract. Ed. by E. K. Lang et al. (Medical Radiology, Diagnostic Imaging & Radiation Oncology Ser.). (Illus.). 384p. 1991. 316.00 (0-387-52546-7) Spr-Verlag.

Radiology of the Urinary System, 1. Ed. by Milton Elkin. 1980. 135.00 (0-316-23275-0) Little.

Radiology of the Urinary System, 2. Ed. by Milton Elkin. 1980. 135.00 (0-316-23276-9) Little.

Radiology of Thoracic Diseases: A Teaching File. Stephen J. Swensen. (Illus.). 243p. (C). (gr. 13). 1992. text ed. 95. 00 (0-8151-8634-7, Yr Bk Med Pubs) Mosby Yr Bk.

Radiology of Trauma. Ed. by M. Heller & A. Fink. LC 95-46532. (Medical Radiology Ser.). (Illus.). 400p. 1996. 236.00 (3-540-59324-1) Spr-Verlag.

Radiology of Vertebral Trauma. John A. Gehweiler et al. LC 78-65376. (Monographs in Clinical Radiology: No. 16). (Illus.). 496p. 1980. text ed. 127.00 (0-7216-4065-6) Saunders.

Radiology on Call: A Survival Handbook. O'Kane & Kranis. 320p. (C). (gr. 13). 1998. pap. text ed. 39.00 (0-8151-4487-3) Mosby Yr Bk.

***Radiology On-Call Survival Guide.** Brian Funaki & Martin J. Lipton. LC 96-45213. 208p. 1996. pap. text ed. 32.95 (0-316-28237-5) Lppncott-Raven.

Radiology Physics - Electronics: Student Workbook. Robert J. Parelli. 101p. (C). 1992. pap. text ed. 15.95 (1-880359-06-5) Par Rad.

Radiology Pocket Reference: What to Order When. Ed. by Ronald L. Eisenberg & Alexander R. Margulis. LC 95-11509. 480p. 1995. pap. text ed. 39.95 (0-397-51503-0) Lppncott-Raven.

Radiology Review Manual. 2nd ed. Wolfgang F. Dahnert. LC 92-49039. (Illus.). 742p. 1993. 76.00 (0-683-02340-3) Williams & Wilkins.

Radiology Review Manual. 3rd ed. Wolfgang Dahnert. LC 95-21072. 871p. 1995. 85.00 (0-683-02338-1) Williams & Wilkins.

Radiology Secrets. Ed. by Kevin R. Math et al. (Secrets Ser.). (Illus.). 400p. (Orig.). 1996. pap. text ed. 37.95 (1-56053-158-4) Hanley & Belfus.

Radiology Word Book. Theresa Indovina & Wilburta Q. Lindh. LC 89-25983. (Illus.). 504p. (Orig.). (C). 1990. pap. text ed. 27.95 (0-8036-4856-1) Davis Co.

***Radiomap: California-Nevada Edition.** (Illus.). 72p. 1997. mass mkt. 2.95 (1-890844-01-2) Radiomap.

***Radiomap: Northwest Edition.** (Illus.). 1997. mass mkt. 2.95 (1-890844-02-0) Radiomap.

***Radiomap: Rocky Mountain Edition.** (Illus.). 1997. mass mkt. 2.95 (1-890844-03-9) Radiomap.

***Radiomap: Texas Edition.** (Illus.). 1997. mass mkt. 2.95 (1-890844-04-7) Radiomap.

Radiometric Apparatus for Use in Psychological Optics see Two Studies in Mental Tests

Radiometric Dating. Robert Whitelaw. pap. 1.49 (0-87377-113-3) GAM Pubns.

Radiometric Dating for Geologists. Ed. by E. I. Hamilton & R. M. Farquhar. LC 68-22087. 514p. reprint ed. pap. 146.50 (0-317-29875-5, 2016153) Bks Demand.

Radiometric Reporting Methods & Calibration in Uranium Exploration. (Technical Reports: No. 174). (Illus.). 57p. 1976. pap. 17.00 (92-0-145076-1, IDC174, Pub. by IAEA AU) Bernan Associates.

Radiometry & the Detection of Optical Radiation. Robert W. Boyd. LC 82-20222. (Pure & Applied Optics Ser.). 254p. 1983. text ed. 97.95 (0-471-86188-X) Wiley.

***Radionic/Homeopathic Manual: Radionic Instruction.** unabridged ed. Don Mattiuda. 230p. 1997. ring bd. 95. 00 (1-57179-072-1) Intern Guild ASRS.

Radionics - Psionics Phenomena: The Prill Method of Monitoring. Clarence E. Prill. Ed. by Thor Templar. 75p. (Orig.). spiral bd. 18.00 (1-57179-047-0) Intern Guild ASRS.

Radionics & Radiesthesia: A Handbook for Radionic Researchers. 1991. lib. bdg. 300.00 (0-8490-4920-2) Gordon Pr.

Radionics & the Subtle Anatomy of Man. David V. Tansley. (C). pap. 12.95 (0-8464-1044-3) Beekman Pubs.

Radionics & the Subtle Anatomy of Man. David V. Tansley. 110p. 1972. pap. 7.95 (0-85032-089-5, Pub. by C W Daniel UK) Natl Bk Netwk.

Radionics Manual. Clifford Williams. (Illus.). 40p. (Orig.). 1996. pap. 29.00 (0-934274-22-3) Consumertronics.

Radionuclide Bone Imaging & Densitometry. Ed. by Fred A. Mettler. (Contemporary Issues in Nuclear Imaging Ser.: Vol. 4). (Illus.). 344p. 1988. text ed. 79.00 (0-443-08546-3) Churchill.

Radionuclide Carcinogenesis: Proceedings. Ed. by C. L. Sanders & R. H. Bush. LC 73-600127. (AEC Symposium Ser.). 500p. 1973. pap. 20.75 (0-87079-329-2, CONF-720505); fiche 9.00 (0-87079-330-6, CONF-720505) DOE.

***Radionuclide Distribution & Transport in Terrestrial & Aquatic Ecosystems, 6 vols.** P. J. Doughtrey et al. 2544p. 1983. 855.00 (90-6191-277-6, Pub. by A A Balkema NE) Ashgate Pub Co.

Radionuclide Generators: New Systems for Nuclear Medicine Applications. Ed. by Fern F. Knapp & Thomas A. Butler. LC 83-25875. (ACS Symposium Ser.: No. 241). 238p. 1984. lib. bdg. 87.95 (0-8412-0822-0) Am Chemical.

***Radionuclide Generators: New Systems for Nuclear Medicine Applications.** Ed. by Furn F. Knapp, Jr. & Thomas A. Butler. LC 83-25875. (ACS Symposium Ser.: Vol. 241). 248p. 1984. reprint ed. pap. 70.70 (0-608-03122-4, 2063575) Bks Demand.

Radionuclide Imaging Artifacts. L. David Wells & Donald R. Bernier. LC 79-25910. (Illus.). 144p. reprint ed. pap. 41.10 (0-8357-3511-7, 2034267) Bks Demand.

Radionuclide Imaging of the Brain. Ed. by Bruce L. Holman. LC 84-29259. (Contemporary Issues in Nuclear Imaging Ser.: Vol. 1). (Illus.). 260p. reprint ed. pap. 74. 10 (0-7837-1614-1, 2041906) Bks Demand.

Radionuclide Imaging of the GI Tract. Ed. by Fred A. Mettler, Jr. (Contemporary Issues in Nuclear Imaging Ser.: Vol. 2). (Illus.). 363p. 1986. text ed. 57.00 (0-443-08391-6) Churchill.

Radionuclide Imaging of the GI Tract. Fred A. Mettler. LC 85-21344. (Contemporary Issues in Nuclear Imaging Ser.: No. 2). (Illus.). 373p. 1986. reprint ed. pap. 106.40 (0-7837-6811-7, 2046643) Bks Demand.

Radionuclide Imaging Techniques. Peter F. Sharp et al. (Medical Physics Ser.). 1985. text ed. 139.00 (0-12-639020-7); pap. text ed. 79.00 (0-12-639021-5) Acad Pr.

Radionuclide Release into the Environment: Assessment of Doses to Man. Ed. by F. D. Sowby. (International Commission on Radiological Protection Ser.: No 29). (Illus.). 1979. pap. 29.00 (0-08-022635-3, Pergamon Pr) Elsevier.

Radionuclide Techniques in Clinical Investigation. P. W. Horton. LC 82-9874. (Medical Physics Handbks.: No. 12). (Illus.). 184p. 1982. reprint ed. pap. 52.80 (0-7837-4505-2, 2044282) Bks Demand.

Radionuclide Techniques in Medicine. Joan M. McAlister. LC 78-68348. (Techniques of Measurement in Medicine Ser.: No. 3). 239p. reprint ed. pap. 68.20 (0-685-15640-0, 2026349) Bks Demand.

Radionuclide Tracers. Michael F. L'Annunziata. 485p. 1987. text ed. 206.00 (0-12-436252-4) Acad Pr.

Radionuclide Transformation: Energy & Intensity of Emissions: ICRP Publication. International Commission on Radiological Protection. Ed. by F. D. Sowby. (Illus.). 1200p. 1983. pap. 102.50 (0-08-030761-2, Pergamon Pr) Elsevier.

Radionuclide Ventricular Function Studies: Correlation with ECG, Echo & X-ray Data. P. J. Ell et al. 1982. lib. bdg. 266.50 (90-247-2639-5) Kluwer Ac.

Radionuclide X-Ray Fluorescence Analysis with Environmental Application. Ed. by Gyula I. Svehla et al. (Comprehensive Analytical Chemistry Ser.: Vol. 26). 282p. 1990. 172.00 (0-444-98837-8) Elsevier.

Radionuclides in Nephro-Urology. Ed. by M. D. Blaufox. (Contributions to Nephrology Ser.: Vol. 79). (Illus.). xii, 232p. 1990. 168.00 (3-8055-5073-1) S Karger.

Radionuclides in Nephrology. Ed. by A. Bischof-Delaloye & M. D. Blaufox. (Contributions to Nephrology Ser.: Vol. 56). (Illus.). x, 278p. 1987. 179.25 (3-8055-4445-6) S Karger.

Radionuclides in Therapy. Spencer. 216p. 1987. 123.00 (0-8493-5843-4) CRC Pr.

Radionuclides Production, 2 Vols., Vol. I. Ed. by Frank Helus. 176p. 1983. 94.00 (0-8493-6003-X, QD601, CRC Reprint) Franklin.

Radionuclides Production, 2 Vols., Vol. 2. Frank Helus. LC 83-2827. (Series in Radiotracers in Biology & Medicine). 184p. 1983. Vol. II, 184. 110.00 (0-8493-6004-8, CRC Reprint) Franklin.

Radiopaque Polymers to Safety see Encyclopedia of Polymer Science & Engineering

Radiopharmaceuticals: Chemistry & Pharmacology. Ed. by Adrian D. Nunn. LC 92-18394. (Drugs & the Pharmaceutical Sciences Ser.: Vol. 55). 460p. 1992. 199. 00 (0-8247-8624-6) Dekker.

Radiopharmaceuticals: Progress & Clinical Perspectives, Vol. I. Ed. by Alan R. Fritzberg. 208p. 1986. 102.00 (0-8493-6335-7, RM852, CRC Reprint) Franklin.

Radiopharmaceuticals: Progress & Clinical Perspectives, Vol. II. Ed. by Alan R. Fritzberg. 176p. 1986. 95.00 (0-8493-6336-5, CRC Reprint) Franklin.

Radiopharmaceuticals & Brain Path Studied with Pet & Spect. Diksic & Reba. 464p. 1990. 249.95 (0-8493-4863-3, RC386) CRC Pr.

Radiopharmaceuticals & Labelled Compounds, 2 vols., 1. (Proceedings Ser.). (Illus.). 847p. (Orig.). 1973. pap. 60. 00 (92-0-040073-6, ISP344-1, Pub. by IAEA AU) Bernan Associates.

Radiopharmaceuticals & Labelled Compounds, 2 vols., 2. (Proceedings Ser.). (Illus.). 847p. (Orig.). 1973. pap. 85. 00 (92-0-040173-2, ISP344-2, Pub. by IAEA AU) Bernan Associates.

Radiopharmaceuticals & Other Compounds Labelled with Short-Lived Radionuclides. Ed. by Michael J. Welch. LC 76-26764. 1977. pap. 48.00 (0-08-021344-8, Pergamon Pr) Elsevier.

Radiopharmaceuticals & Radiopharmacy Practice. Ed. by A. E. Theobald. LC 85-12559. 250p. 1985. 65.00 (0-85066-318-0) Taylor & Francis.

Radiopharmaceuticals from Generator-Produced Radionuclides. (Panel Proceedings Ser.). 205p. 1971. pap. 35.00 (92-0-111471-0, ISP294, Pub. by IAEA AU) Bernan Associates.

Radiopharmacy & Radiopharmacology: Yearbook 1. Peter H. Cox & Christine M. King. 376p. 1985. text ed. 129. 00 (2-88124-114-X); pap. text ed. 47.00 (2-88124-113-1) Gordon & Breach.

Radiopharmacy & Radiopharmacology: Yearbook 2. Ed. by Peter H. Cox. 434p. (C). 1987. text ed. 156.00 (2-88124-167-0); pap. text ed. 61.00 (2-88124-168-9) Gordon & Breach.

Radiopharmacy & Radiopharmacology: Yearbook 3. P. Cox. 348p. 1988. kivar 233.00 (2-88124-670-2) Gordon & Breach.

***Radioprotectors: Chemical, Biological, & Clincial Perspectives.** Edward A. Bump & Kamal Malaker. LC 97-22136. 1997. write for info. (0-8493-4756-4) CRC Pr.

Radiorequency Plasma Heating, Sixth Topical Conference, Callaway Gardens, GA, 1985. Ed. by D. G. Swanson. LC 85-48027. (AIP Conference Proceedings Ser.: No. 129). 256p. 1985. lib. bdg. 41.00 (0-88318-328-5) Am Inst Physics.

***Radios: Short Takes on Life & Culture.** Jerome Stern. LC 96-40078. (Illus.). 112p. 1997. 20.00 (0-393-04119-0) Norton.

Radios: The Golden Age. Philip Collins. (Illus.). 128p. 1987. 29.95 (0-87701-477-9); pap. 17.95 (0-87701-419-1) Chronicle Bks.

***Radios: The Golden Age.** Philip Collins. LC 96-37591. (Illus.). 120p. 1997. reprint ed. 12.98 (1-884822-66-5) Blck Dog & Leventhal.

Radio's Beautiful Day: Memoirs of Everett Mitchell, Pioneer Radio Announcer. A. Richard Crabb. LC 82-73438. (Illus.). 1984. 8.95 (0-916445-06-2) Crossroads Comm.

Radios by Hallicrafters. Chuck Dachis. LC 95-45247. (Illus.). 225p. (YA). (gr. 10-13). 1995. pap. 29.95 (0-88740-929-6) Schiffer.

Radio's Conquest of Space: The Experimental Rise in Radio Communication. Donald McNicol. LC 74-4689. (Telecommunications Ser.). (Illus.). 388p. 1974. reprint ed. 31.95 (0-405-06052-1) Ayer.

Radio's First Broadcaster. Elton M. Plant. (Illus.). 105p. 1989. pap. 9.95 (0-913611-03-4) W E C Plant.

Radio's 'Kentucky Mountain Boy' Bradley Kincaid. rev. ed. Loyal Jones. LC 80-26235. 193p. 1988. pap. 7.50 (0-935680-03-9) Berea College Pr.

Radio's Morning Show Personalities: Early Hour Broadcasters & Deejays from the 1920's to the 1990's. Philip A. Lieberman. LC 95-45032. (Illus.). 213p. 1996. lib. bdg. 29.95 (0-7864-0037-4) McFarland & Co.

Radio's One Hundred Men of Science. Orrin E. Dunlap, Jr. LC 70-128235. (Essay Index Reprint Ser.). 1977. 27.95 (0-8369-1916-5) Ayer.

Radios Redux: Listening in Style. Philip Collins. (Illus.). 120p. 1992. 29.95 (0-8118-0099-7); pap. 17.95 (0-8118-0086-5) Chronicle Bks.

Radiosity: A Programmer's Perspective. Ian Ashdown. 497p. 1994. pap. text ed. 44.95 (0-471-30444-1) Wiley.

Radiosity: A Programmer's Perspective. Ian Ashdown. 1995. disk 15.00 (0-471-30443-3) Wiley.

Radiosity & Global Illumination. Francois X. Sillion & Claude Puech. LC 94-26772. 251p. 1994. 49.95 (1-55860-277-1) Morgan Kaufmann.

Radiosity & Realistic Image Synthesis. John R. Wallace. (Illus.). 381p. 1993. text ed. 53.00 (0-12-178270-0, AP Prof) Acad Pr.

Radiosonde Intercomparison SONDEX: Spring 1981, Payerne. Ed. by Hans Richner & Peter Phillips. (Contributions to Current Research in Geophysics Ser.: Vol. 11). 352p. 1984. text ed. 79.95 (3-7643-1614-4) Birkhauser.

Radiostrontium Movement in Soils & Uptake in Plants. C. W. Francis. LC 78-19051. (DOE Critical Review Ser.). 142p. 1978. pap. 11.50 (0-87079-110-9, TID-27564); fiche 9.00 (0-87079-332-2, TID-27564) DOE.

Radiosurgery: Baseline & Trends. Ed. by Ladislau Steiner et al. 320p. 1991. text ed. 110.50 (*0-88167-847-3*, 2335) Lppncott-Raven.

Radiosurgery: Enhancement of Clinical Excellence. Ed. by E. Alexander, III et al. (Illus.). 112p. 1992. pap. 69.75 (*3-8055-5546-6*) S Karger.

Radiosurgery 1995. Ed. by D. Kondziolka. (Radiosurgery Ser.: Vol. 1). xii, 350p. 1996. 295.00 (*3-8055-6236-5*) S Karger.

Radio/Tech Modifications, Vol. 8A. Michael V. Smith. (Illus.). 224p. 1996. pap. 19.95 (*0-917963-17-2*) Artsci Inc.

Radio/Tech Modifications, Vol. 8B. Michael V. Smith. (Illus.). 208p. 1996. pap. 19.95 (*0-917963-18-0*) Artsci Inc.

Radiotelephone Logbook. 120p. (Orig.). 1980. pap. 5.00 (*0-934114-12-9*, BK-128) Marine Educ.

Radiotelephone Operator. rev. ed. Ed. by Richard A. Block. 68p. 1993. pap. text ed. 7.60 (*1-879778-11-4*, BK-111) Marine Educ.

RadioTeletype Monitoring: The Complete Guide. Dallas W. Williams. 57p. (Orig.). 1987. pap. 12.95 (*0-936653-08-6*) Tiare Pubns.

Radiotext(e) Ed. by Neil Strauss & Dave Mandl. 360p. Date not set. 12.00 (*0-936756-94-2*, Semiotexte) Autonomedia.

Radiotherapy: Directory of Authors of New Medical & Scientific Reviews with Subject Index. Science & Life Consultants Association Staff. 160p. 1995. 47.50 (*0-7883-0606-5*); pap. 44.50 (*0-7883-0607-3*) ABBE Pubs Assn.

Radiotherapy & Cancer Immunology. Ed. by Naresh Prasad. 216p. 1981. 98.95 (*0-8493-5901-5*, RC268) CRC Pr.

Radiotherapy for Head & Neck Cancers: Indications & Techniques. K. Kian Ang et al. LC 93-6754. (Illus.). 300p. 1993. 80.00 (*0-8121-1678-X*) Williams & Wilkins.

Radiotherapy of Intracular & Orbital Tumors. Ed. by W. E. Alberti & Robert H. Sagerman. LC 92-48365. (Medical Radiology Ser.). 1993. write for info. (*3-540-17686-1*); 299.00 (*0-387-17686-1*) Spr-Verlag.

Radiotherapy of Malignant Disease. Ed. by E. C. Easson & R. C. Pointon. (Illus.). 500p. 1985. 166.00 (*0-387-13104-3*) Spr-Verlag.

Radiotherapy of Malignant Disease: Founded by Easson. 2nd ed. Ed. by R. C. Pointon. (Illus.). 496p. 1991. 198.00 (*0-387-19622-6*) Spr-Verlag.

***Radiotherapy of Ocular Diseases: 1st International Symposium on Special Aspects of Radiotherapy, Berlin, May 1996.** Ed. by W. Hinkelbein et al. LC 97-3528. (Frontiers of Radiation Therapy & Oncology Ser.: Vol. 30, 1997). (Illus.). x, 302p. 1997. 191.50 (*3-8055-6392-2*) S Karger.

***Radiotherapy Physics & Equipment Manual.** Ed. by Pamela Cherry & Angela Duxbury. (Illus.). 224p. 1997. pap. 49.50 (*1-900151-06-5*) OUP.

Radiotherapy Physics in Practice. Ed. by J. R. Williams & D. I. Thwaites. LC 92-45160. 296p. (C). 1993. 72.00 (*0-19-963316-9*); pap. 38.00 (*0-19-963315-0*) OUP.

Radiotherapy Safety: Proceedings of a Short Course Held at the University of Wisconsin, Madison, Wisconsin, March 25-26, 1982. Ed. by Bruce Thomadsen. (American Association of Physicists in Medicine Symposium Ser.: No. 4). 175p. 1984. 45.00 (*0-88318-443-5*) Am Inst Physics.

Radiothermoluminescence & Transitions in Polymers. L. Zlatkevich. (Polymers Ser.: Vol. 12). (Illus.). 260p. 1987. 210.95 (*0-387-96407-X*) Spr-Verlag.

Radiotracer Studies of Chemical Residues in Food & Agriculture. (Panel Proceedings Ser.). (Illus.). 167p. (Orig.). 1972. pap. 30.00 (*92-0-111272-6*, ISP332, Pub. by IAEA AU) Bernan Associates.

Radiotracer Techniques & Applications, Vol. 1. Ed. by E. Anthony Evans & Mitsuo Muramatsu. LC 76-20000. (Illus.). 703p. reprint ed. pap. 180.00 (*0-7837-4211-8*, 2041280) Bks Demand.

Radiotracer Techniques & Applications, 1977, Vol. 2. Ed. by E. Anthony Evans & Mitsuo Muramatsu. LC 76-20000. (Illus.). 540p. reprint ed. pap. 153.90 (*0-7837-0974-9*, 2041280) Bks Demand.

Radiotracers for Medical Applications, Vol. I. Ed. by Garimella V. Rayudu. 320p. 1983. 155.00 (*0-8493-6015-3*, R895) CRC Pr.

Radiotracers for Medical Applications, Vol. II. Ed. by Garimella V. Rayudu. 304p. 1983. 154.00 (*0-8493-6016-1*, R895, CRC Reprint) Franklin.

RadiOutlook II: New Forces Shaping the Industry. Ed. by Austin McLean. 143p. 1991. 40.00 (*0-89324-112-1*) Natl Assn Broadcasters.

Radiowave Propagation & Antennas for Personal Communications. Kazimierz Siwiak. LC 95-15107. 320p. 1995. 89.00 (*0-89006-755-4*) Artech Hse.

Radiowave Propagation over Ground. T. S. Maclean & Z. Wu. LC 92-36063. 320p. (gr. 13). 1993. text ed. 104.95 (*0-412-42730-3*) Chapman & Hall.

Radiowaves: Music. Wholey. (College ESL Ser.). 1995. suppl. ed., wbk. ed., pap. 32.95 incl. audio (*0-8384-5796-7*) Heinle & Heinle.

Radiowaves: The Business Edition. Ed. by Mary L. Wholey & Judith Ritter. LC 94-25854. 1995. 32.95 (*0-8384-5792-4*) Heinle & Heinle.

Radiowaves: The Entertainment Edition. Ed. by Mary L. Wholey & Judith Ritter. LC 94-20843. 1995. 32.95 (*0-8384-5793-2*) Heinle & Heinle.

Radiowaves: The Environmental Edition. Ed. by Mary L. Wholey & Judith Ritter. LC 94-25848. 1995. 32.95 (*0-8384-5794-0*) Heinle & Heinle.

Radiowaves: The Health Edition. Ed. by Mary L. Wholey & Judith Ritter. LC 94-25852. 1995. 32.95 (*0-8384-5795-9*) Heinle & Heinle.

Radishchev Art Museum: Saratov. Albina Simonova. (Illus.). 176p. (C). 1985. text ed. 100.00 (*0-685-40288-6*, Pub. by Collets) St Mut.

Raditzer. Peter Matthiessen. LC 86-40557. 1987. 5.95 (*0-394-75343-7*, Vin) Random.

Radium. 1976. 94.00 (*0-387-93268-2*) Spr-Verlag.

Radium & Isotopes. 1977. suppl. ed. 255.00 (*0-387-93333-6*) Spr-Verlag.

***Radium Girls: Women & Industrial Health Reform, 1910-1935.** Claudia Clark. LC 96-27358. 384p. (C). (gr. 13). 1997. 49.95 (*0-8078-2331-7*); pap. 19.95 (*0-8078-4640-6*) U of NC Pr.

Radium Pool. Repp. 5.00 (*0-686-00478-7*); pap. 2.00 (*0-686-00479-5*) Fantasy Pub Co.

***Radius: Image Understanding for Imagery Intelligence.** Ed. by DARPA Staff. 526p. 1997. pap. 54.95 (*1-55860-450-2*) Morgan Kaufmann.

Radius and Ulna. Jesse Jupiter & Margaret McQueen. (Musculoskeletal Trauma Ser.). 208p. 1996. write for info. (*0-7506-0835-8*) Buttrwrth-Heinemann.

Radius of Doubt. Charles Ingrid. (Patterns of Chaos Ser.: No. 1). 352p. (Orig.). 1991. mass mkt. 4.99 (*0-88677-491-8*) DAW Bks.

***Radix.** Bryan Modders. 54p. (Orig.). 1997. mass mkt. 5.99 (*1-55237-205-7*, Pub. by Comnwlth Pub CN) Partners Pubs Grp.

Radix: The Original Radical Poem. Scott T. Eastham. LC 91-4152. (Revisioning Philosophy Ser.: Vol. 8). 278p. (C). 1992. text ed. 49.95 (*0-8204-1644-4*) P Lang Pubng.

Radix-Matrix: Daniel Libeskind. Daniel Libeskind. (Illus.). 192p. 1997. 65.00 (*3-7913-1727-X*, Pub. by Prestel GW) te Neues.

Radleigh's Choice. Bartle Bull. 1999. pap. 19.95 (*0-670-85368-2*); pap. 11.95 (*0-14-023458-6*) Viking Penguin.

Radman Guide to the Ionising Radiations Regulations, 1985. Radman Assoc. Staff. (Handbook Ser.: No. 1). (C). 1986. 54.00 (*0-948237-00-7*, Pub. by H&H Sci Cnslts UK) St Mut.

Radnor Lake: Nashville's Walden Pond. Photos by John Netherton. LC 84-51576. (Illus.). 72p. 1994. reprint ed. 18.95 (*0-934395-17-9*) Rutledge Hill Pr.

Radnorshire Words see English Dialect Society Publications, No. 32: Original Glossaries XXIII-XXVII

***Radographic Pathology for Technologists.** 3rd ed. Mace. LC 97-23176. 448p. (C). (gr. 13). 1997. pap. text ed. 39.00 (*0-8151-4568-3*, 30347) Mosby Yr Bk.

Radom, Nicolaus de: Collected Works. Ed. by Adam Sutkowski. (Gesamtausgaben - Collected Works Ser.: Vol. V). 80p. (ENG & GER.). lib. bdg. 4.00 (*0-912024-65-8*) Inst Mediaeval Mus.

Radome Engineering Handbook: Design & Principles. Ed. by J. D. Walton, Jr. LC 74-131300. (Ceramics & Glass: Science & Technology Ser.). (Illus.). 611p. reprint ed. pap. 174.20 (*0-317-07833-X*, 2055030) Bks Demand.

Radon. Richard K. Miller & Marcia E. Rupnow. LC 90-83851. (Survey on Technology & Markets Ser.: No. 146). 50p. 1991. pap. text ed. 200.00 (*1-55865-171-3*) Future Tech Surveys.

Radon: A Homeowner's Guide to Detection & Control. Bernard Cohen. 1989. pap. 3.95 (*0-380-70782-9*) Avon.

Radon: An Invisible Threat. Barbara Foster. (State Legislative Reports: Vol. 18, No. 8). 14p. 1993. 5.00 (*1-55516-336-X*, 7302-1808) Natl Conf State Legis.

Radon: An Ounce of Prevention. Barbara Foster. (State Legislative Reports: Vol. 19, No. 5). 14p. 1994. 5.00 (*1-55516-346-7*, 7302-1905) Natl Conf State Legis.

Radon: Index of Modern Information. Lee B. Neiderhaus. LC 88-47619. 150p. 1988. 44.50 (*0-88164-766-7*); pap. 39.50 (*0-88164-767-5*) ABBE Pubs Assn.

Radon: Prevalence, Measurements, Health Risks, & Control. Ed. by Niren L. Nagda. LC 94-11665. (ASTM Manual Ser.: MNL 15). (Illus.). 170p. 1994. text ed. 59.00 (*0-8031-2057-5*, 28-015094-17) ASTM.

Radon: Proceedings of the Twenty-Fourth Annual Meeting of the National Council on Radiation Protection & Measurements. LC 88-36232. (Annual Meeting Proceedings Ser.: No. 10). 380p. (Orig.). 1989. pap. text ed. 40.00 (*0-929600-02-9*) NCRP Pubns.

***Radon Abatement.** Richard K. Miller et al. (Market Research Survey Ser.: No. 262). 50p. 1996. 200.00 (*1-55865-287-6*) Future Tech Surveys.

Radon & Its Decay Products: Occurrence, Properties & Health Effects. Ed. by Philip K. Hopke. LC 86-32042. (ACS Symposium Ser.: No. 331). (Illus.). xi, 586p. 1987. 89.95 (*0-8412-1015-2*) Am Chemical.

***Radon & Its Decay Products: Occurrence, Properties, & Health Effects.** Ed. by Philip K. Hopke. LC 86-32042. (ACS Symposium Ser.: Vol. 331). 624p. 1987. reprint ed. pap. 177.90 (*0-608-03543-2*, 2064262) Bks Demand.

Radon & Its Decay Products in Indoor Air. Ed. by William W. Nazaroff & Anthony V. Nero. LC 87-8915. (Environmental Science & Technology Ser.). 518p. 1988. text ed. 149.00 (*0-471-62810-7*) Wiley.

Radon & Projection Transform-Based Computer Vision. J. L. Sanz et al. (Information Sciences Ser.). (Illus.). 132p. 1988. 53.95 (*0-387-18396-5*) Spr-Verlag.

Radon & the Environment. Ed. by William J. Makofske & Michael R. Edelstein. LC 87-35242. (Illus.). 465p. 1988. 39.00 (*0-8155-1161-2*) Noyes.

Radon Exposure of the U. S. Population - Status of the Problem. Intro. by Warren K. Sinclair. (Commentary Ser.: No. 6). 27p. (Orig.). 1991. pap. text ed. 20.00 (*0-929600-17-7*) NCRP Pubns.

***Radon-Hazard Potential Areas in Sandy, Salt Lake County & Provo, Utah County, Utah.** Daniel L. Nielson et al. (Special Study of the Utah Geological Survey Ser.: Vol. 85). (Illus.). 49p. (Orig.). 1994. pap. 6.00 (*1-55791-204-1*, SS85) Utah Geological Survey.

***Radon-Hazard Potential of the Central Sevier Valley, Sevier County, Utah.** Barry J. Solomon. (Special Study of the Utah Geological Survey Ser.: Vol. 89). (Illus.). 48p. (Orig.). 1996. pap. 5.50 (*1-55791-374-9*, SS89) Utah Geological Survey.

***Radon-Hazard Potential of the Lower Weber River Area, Tooele Valley & Southeastern Cache Valley, Cache, Davis, Tooele & Weber Counties, Utah.** Bill D. Black & Barry J. Solomon. (Special Study of the Utah Geological Survey Ser.: Vol. 90). (Illus.). 56p. 1996. pap. 6.00 (*1-55791-379-X*, SS90) Utah Geological Survey.

Radon-Hazard Potential of the Southern St. George Basin, Washington County & Ogden Valley, Weber County, Utah. Barry J. Solomon. (Special Study of the Utah Geological Survey Ser.: No. 87). (Illus.). 42p. (Orig.). 1995. pap. 5.95 (*1-55791-369-2*, SS-87) Utah Geological Survey.

Radon in Ground Water: Hydrogeologic Impact & Application to Indoor Airborne Contamination. Ed. by National Water Well Association Staff. (Illus.). 550p. 1987. 84.00 (*0-87371-117-3*, L117) Lewis Pubs.

Radon in the Environment. M. Wilkening. (Studies in Environmental Science: No. 40). 138p. 1990. pap. 106.25 (*0-444-88163-8*) Elsevier.

Radon in the Home: Reducing the Risks. Ed. by D. J. Scherer. (Illus.). 32p. (Orig.). 1987. pap. 3.95 (*0-918734-33-9*) Reymont.

Radon Integrals: An Abstract Approach to Integration & Riesz Representation Through Function Cones. B. Anger & C. Portenier. (Progress in Mathematics Ser.: Vol. 103). x, 326p. 1991. 84.00 (*0-8176-3630-7*) Spr-Verlag.

Radon Measurement in Schools. 1994. lib. bdg. 250.00 (*0-8490-5781-7*) Gordon Pr.

***Radon Measurements by Etched Track Detectors, Applications in Radiation Protection, Earth Sciences.** 320p. 1997. lib. bdg. 40.00 (*981-02-2666-7*) World Scientific Pub.

Radon Monitoring in Radioprotection, Environmental Radioactivity & Earth Science. L. Tommasino et al. 632p. (C). 1990. text ed. 151.00 (*981-02-0187-7*) World Scientific Pub.

Radon, Radium, & Uranium in Drinking Water. Ed. by C. Richard Cothern & Paul A. Rebers. (Illus.). 296p. 1990. 93.00 (*0-87371-207-2*, L207) Lewis Pubs.

Radon Reduction Methods: A Homeowner's Guide. 1990. lib. bdg. 79.95 (*0-87700-884-1*) Revisionist Pr.

Radon-Resistant Construction Techniques for New Residential Construction: Technical Guidance. Mike Clarkin & Terry Brennan. (Illus.). 52p. (Orig.). (C). 1993. pap. text ed. 20.00 (*1-56806-184-6*) DIANE Pub.

Radon Transform & Local Tomography. Alexander G. Ramm & Alexander I. Katsevich. LC 96-2194. (Illus.). 485p. 1996. 79.95 (*0-8493-9492-9*) CRC Pr.

Radon Transform & Some of Its Applications. rev. ed. Stanley R. Deans. LC 92-1004. 308p. (C). 1993. reprint ed. lib. bdg. 58.50 (*0-89464-718-0*) Krieger.

***Radon's Deadly Daughters: Science, Environmental Policy & the Politics of Risk.** Michael R. Edelstein & William J. Makofske. LC 96-35148. 320p. 1996. 62.50 (*0-8476-8333-8*); pap. 21.95 (*0-8476-8334-6*) Rowman.

Radozda-Vevcani Dialect of Macedonia: Structure, Text, Lexicon. P. Hendriks. viii, 309p. 1976. pap. 38.00 (*90-316-0089-X*, Pub. by Gruner NE) Benjamins North Am.

RadReview: Diagnostic Radiological Physics Examination & Study Guide. Compiled by Perry Sprawls. 82p. (Orig.). 1995. student ed., wbk. ed. 23.95 (*0-944838-56-1*) Med Physics Pub.

***Radsport und Gesellschaft.** Rudiger Rabenstein. vi, 333p. (GER.). 1995. 39.80 (*3-615-00066-8*, Pub. by Weidmann GW) Lubrecht & Cramer.

RadTech North America Conference & Exposition Conference Proceedings, 1992, Vol. II. 242p. (Orig.). 1992. pap. write for info. (*1-878664-07-7*) RadTech Intl North Amer.

RadTech North America Conference & Exposition Conference Proceedings, 1992, 2 vols., Vol. I & II. (Orig.). 1992. pap. 55.00 (*1-878664-08-5*) RadTech Intl North Amer.

RadTech '90: North America Conference Papers, 2 vols., I. 1990. 55.00 (*1-878664-00-X*) RadTech Intl North Amer.

RadTech '90: North America Conference Papers, 2 vols., II. 1990. 55.00 (*1-878664-01-8*) RadTech Intl North Amer.

RadTech '94 North America International UV - EB Processing Conference & Exhibition, Vols. I & II: Proceedings. 810p. 1994. pap. 105.00 (*1-878664-12-3*) RadTech Intl North Amer.

Radulfus Niger "De Re Militari et Triplici Via Peregrinationis Ierosolimitane" (1187-88) Ed. by Ludwig Schmugge. (Beitraege zur Geschichte und Quellenkunde des Mittelalters Ser.: Vol. 6). (C). 1976. 138.50 (*3-11-006827-3*) De Gruyter.

Radulphi de Coggeshall Chronicon Anglicanum. Ed. by Joseph Stevenson. (Rolls Ser.: No. 66). 1974. reprint ed. 70.00 (*0-8115-1134-0*) Periodicals Srv.

Radulphi de Diceto Decani Londoniensis Opera Historica: The Historical Works of Master Ralph de Diceto, Dean of London to 1202, 2 vols. Ed. by William Stubbs. (Rolls Ser.: No. 68). 1974. reprint ed. 140.00 (*0-8115-1136-7*) Periodicals Srv.

***Radulphi de Hengham Summae.** William H. Dunham. (Cambridge Studies in English Legal History). 1986. reprint ed. 42.00 (*0-614-25187-7*) Gaunt.

Radurization of Scampi, Shrimp & Cod. (Technical Reports: No. 124). (Illus.). 93p. (Orig.). 1971. pap. 25.00 (*92-0-115171-3*, IDC124, Pub. by IAEA AU) Bernan Associates.

Radu's Simply Fit: Get the Workout of Your Life with America's Leading Fitness Coach. Radu Theodorescu. 152p. 1996. pap. 18.95 (*0-8362-1504-4*) Andrews & McMeel.

Rae Katherine's Victorian Recipe Secrets. Rae K. Eighmey. (Illus.). 96p. 1996. 12.95 (*1-57427-045-1*) Howell Pr VA.

Rae of Hope: A Story of Courage & Cancer Survival. Howard S. Irons. (Illus.). 320p. 1994. pap. 12.95 (*1-881539-01-6*) Tabby Hse Bks.

RAE Table of Earth Satellites, 1957-1980 Compiled at the Royal Aircraft Establishment, Farnborough, Hants, England. Desmond King-Hele. LC 81-204567. 665p. reprint ed. pap. 180.00 (*0-685-15561-7*, 2027219) Bks Demand.

Rael: Into the Shadow of the Sun. Wilson. (Illus.). 1990. pap. 7.95 (*0-913035-84-X*) Eclipse Bks.

Raeside's Canada. Adrian Raeside. 1994. pap. 16.95 (*0-385-25476-8*) Doubleday.

Raeumliche Umwelt: Die Phaenomenologie des raeumlichen Verhaltens als Beitrag zu einer psychologischen Umwelttheorie. Lenelis Kruse. LC 73-88301. (Phaenomenologisch-Psychologische Forschungen Ser.: Vol. 15). 192p. (C). 1974. 80.00 (*3-11-004406-4*) De Gruyter.

Raewyn's Got the Writing Bug Again. Raewyn Caisley. LC 93-24529. (Voyages Ser.). (J). 1994. 4.25 (*0-383-03734-4*) SRA McGraw.

***RAF Bomber Command: In Fact, Film & Fiction.** Jonathan Falconer. (Illus.). 224p. 1996. 19.99 (*0-7509-1294-4*, Pub. by Sutton Pubng UK) Bks Intl VA.

RAF Bomber Command 1936-1968. Chris Ashworth. (Illus.). 256p. 1995. 44.95 (*1-85260-308-9*, Pub. by J H Haynes & Co UK) Motorbooks Intl.

RAF in Camera: 1939-1945. Roy C. Nesbit. (Illus.). 192p. 1996. 33.95 (*0-7509-1055-0*, Pub. by Sutton Pubng UK) Bks Intl VA.

RAF in Camera 1903-1939. Roy C. Nesbit. (Illus.). 1996. 34.95 (*0-7509-1054-2*, Pub. by Sutton Pubng UK) Bks Intl VA.

***RAF in Camera 1903-1939: Archive Photographs from the Public Record Office & the Ministry of Defence.** Roy C. Nesbit. (Illus.). 192p. (Orig.). 1997. pap. 17.95 (*0-7509-1514-5*, Pub. by Sutton Pubng UK) Bks Intl VA.

***RAF in Camera 1939-1945 Vol. 2: Archive Photographs from the Public Record Office & the Ministry of Defence.** Roy C. Nesbit. (Illus.). 192p. (Orig.). 1997. pap. 17.95 (*0-7509-1521-8*, Pub. by Sutton Pubng UK) Bks Intl VA.

***RAF in Camera, 1946-1995.** Roy C. Nesbit. (Illus.). 192p. 1996. 33.95 (*0-7509-1056-9*, Pub. by Sutton Pubng UK) Bks Intl VA.

***RAF in Camera 1946-1995 Vol. 3: Archive Photographs from the Public Record Office & the Ministry of Defence.** Roy C. Nesbit. (Illus.). 192p. (Orig.). 1997. pap. 17.95 (*0-7509-1522-6*, Pub. by Sutton Pubng UK) Bks Intl VA.

RAF Lyneham: Hercules. Wilf Perira. (Super Station in Action Ser.). (Illus.). 192p. 1991. 31.95 (*0-85429-767-7*, Pub. by G T Foulis Ltd) Haynes Pubns.

***RAF Nuclear Deterrent Forces.** Humphrey Wynn. (Illus.). 666p. 1997. pap. 39.95 (*0-11-772833-0*, Pub. by Statnry Ofc UK) Seven Hills Bk.

RAF Quiz Book. Eunice Wilson. 80p. 1993. pap. 8.95 (*0-948817-69-0*, Pub. by Grub St Pubns UK) Seven Hills Bk.

Rafael Carrera & the Emergence of the Republic of Guatemala, 1821-1871. Ralph L. Woodward, Jr. LC 91-41812. (Illus.). 672p. 1993. 65.00 (*0-8203-1448-X*) U of Ga Pr.

Rafael Ferrer: Recent Work & an Installation. Rafael Ferrer. (Illus.). 1978. pap. 3.00 (*0-910663-14-9*) ICA Inc.

***Rafael Moneo: Doucmentos de Arquitectura.** Rafael Moneo. 1997. pap. text ed. 30.00 (*0-8230-1351-0*) Watsn-Guptill.

***Rafael Palmeiro.** Barbara Marvis. LC 97-21985. (Real Life Reader Biographies Ser.). (Illus.). 32p. (J). (gr. k-4). 1997. lib. bdg. 15.95 (*1-883845-49-1*) M Lane Pubs.

***Rafael Palmeiro: At Home with the Baltimore Orioles.** Ed Brandt. LC 97-8668. (Illus.). 112p. 1997. lib. bdg. 21.95 (*1-883845-37-8*) M Lane Pubs.

***Rafael Palmeiro: At Home with the Baltimore Orioles.** Ed Brandt. LC 97-8668. (Illus.). 112p. 1997. pap. 12.95 (*1-883845-38-6*) M Lane Pubs.

***Rafael Palmeiro: Living the American Dream.** Ed Brandt & Barbara Marvis. 1997. 21.95 (*0-614-28037-0*) M Lane Pubs.

***Rafael Palmeiro: Living the American Dream.** Ed Brandt & Barbara Marvis. 1997. pap. 12.95 (*0-614-28038-9*) M Lane Pubs.

Rafaga: The Life Story of a Nicaraguan Miskito Comandante. Reynaldo Reyes & J. K. Wilson. Ed. by Tod S. Sloan. LC 92-54141. (Illus.). 232p. 1992. 27.95 (*0-8061-2453-9*) U of Okla Pr.

***Rafal Olbinski "Posters"** Rafal Olbinski. LC 96-69653. (Illus.). 76p. (Orig.). 1996. pap. 28.95 (*1-878768-00-X*) Nahan Editions.

Rafe's Island. Gina F. Wilkins. (Temptation Ser.). 1993. mass mkt. 2.99 (*0-373-25558-6*, 1-25558-7) Harlequin Bks.

Rafferty's Angel. Caroline Cross. (Desire Ser.). 1994. mass mkt. 2.99 (*0-373-05851-9*, 5-05851-6) Silhouette.

***Rafferty's Choice, Bk. 6.** Dallas Schulze. (Born in the U. S. A. Ser.). 1997. 4.50 (*0-373-47156-4*, 1-47156-4) Harlequin Bks.

Raffi: Children's Favorites. (Illus.). 172p. 1993. pap. 15.95 (*0-8256-1356-6*) Music Sales.

Raffi: Children's Favorites. (Illus.). 172p. pap. 19.95 (*0-8256-1362-0*, AM90163) Omnibus NY.

Raffi: Evergreen, Everblue. (Illus.). 56p. 1992. pap. 14.95 (*0-8256-1340-X*, AM90036) Music Sales.

An Asterisk (*) at the beginning of an entry indicates that the title is appearing in BIP for the first time.

Raffineries de Sucre des Ports en France: XIX Debut de XX Siecles. Jacques Fierain. Ed. by Stuart Bruchey. LC 77-77169. (Dissertations in European Economic History Ser.). (FRE.). 1978. lib. bdg. 60.95 (0-405-10783-8) Ayer.

Raffi's Christmas Treasury: 14 Illustrated Songs & Musical Arrangements. Raffi. (Illus.). (J). (ps up). 1988. 17.95 (0-517-56806-3) Crown Bks Yng Read.

*Raffi's Rise & Shine. Illus. by Eugenie Fernandes. (Raffi Songs to Read Ser.). (J). (ps-2). 16.00 (0-614-19292-7) Crown Pub Group.

Raffi's Top 10 Songs to Read. Raffi. LC 95-196. (Illus.). 45p. (J). (ps-2). 1995. 15.00 (0-517-70907-4, Crown) Crown Pub Group.

Raffles. W. Hornung. 302p. 1980. lib. bdg. 14.50 (0-89968-186-7, Lghtyr Pr) Buccaneer Bks.

Raffles: A Thief in the Night. E. W. Hornung. 184p. 1976. 14.95 (0-241-89358-5) Boulevard.

Raffles: The Amateur Cracksman. E. W. Hornung. 154p. 1975. 14.95 (0-241-89168-X) Boulevard.

Raffles: The Amateur Cracksman. E. W. Hornung. 204p. 1991. 20.95 (1-85089-468-X, Pub. by ISIS UK) Transaction Pubs.

Raffles & Other Singing Stories. Hoagy Carmichael. Ed. by Helen M. Stearns. (Illus.). 44p. (J). (ps up). 1989. 14.95 (0-9614281-5-5, 1477, Cricketfld Pr) Picton Pr.

*Raffles, the Amateur Cracksman. Ernest W. Hornung. LC 75-38587. (Illus.). 268p. 1976. reprint ed. pap. 76.40 (0-608-02671-9, 2063324) Bks Demand.

Raffles, the Amateur Cracksman: The Complete Stories of E W Hornung. Ernest W. Hornung. (Spies & Intrigues Ser.: No. 7). 478p. reprint ed. pap. 8.95 (0-918172-20-9) Leetes Isl.

Rafi Ahmad Kidwai: The True Nationalist. S. R. Bakshi. (Indian Freedom Fighters Ser.: No. 42). 1993. 34.00 (81-7041-606-X, Pub. by Anmol II) S Asia.

Rafinesque: Autobiography & Lives, 3 Vols. Ed. by Keir B. Sterling. LC 77-83130. (Biologists & Their World Ser.). (Illus.). 1978. lib. bdg. 57.95 (0-405-10723-4) Ayer.

*Rafols-Casamada. Victoria C. Dexeus. (Illus.). 128p. 1989. 65.00 (84-343-0563-1) A Wofsy Fine Arts.

Rafols-Casamada: El Passeig Del Poeta. limited ed. Albert Rafols-Casamada. (Ediciones Especiales y de Bibliofilo Ser.). (Illus.). 88p. (CAT.). 1993. 600.00 (0-614-00138-2) Elliots Bks.

Rafols-Casamada: El Passeig Del Poeta. limited ed. Albert Rafols-Casamada. (Ediciones Especiales y de Bibliofilo Ser.). (Illus.). 88p. (CAT.). 1993. 2,750.00 (0-614-00242-7) Elliots Bks.

Rafols-Casamada: El Passeig Del Poeta. limited ed. Albert Rafols-Casamada. (Ediciones Especiales y de Bibliofilo Ser.). (Illus.). 88p. (CAT.). 1993. 600.00 (0-614-00243-5) Elliots Bks.

Raft. Bess C. Haskell. (Wind, Waves & Away! Ser.). (Illus.). (J). (gr. 5 up). 1988. write for info. (0-933858-26-4) Kennebec River.

*Raft. Jim Lamarche. Date not set. write for info. (0-688-13977-9) Lothrop.

*Raft. Jim Lamarche. Date not set. lib. bdg. write for info. (0-688-13978-7) Lothrop.

Raft. Robert Trumbull. LC 91-25085. (Illus.). 224p. 1992. reprint ed. pap. 16.95 (1-55750-827-5) Naval Inst Pr.

*Raft & a Half: Fisher Price Great Adventure. (Great Adventure Ser.). (Orig.). 1997. pap. 2.99 (0-88743-462-2, Bison Books) U of Nebr Pr.

*Raft from Flotsam: Versifications 1948-1974. John Jordan. 56p. 7500. pap. 7.95 (0-902996-32-0) Dufour.

Raft of Medusa: Five Voices on Colonies, Nations, & Histories. Ed. by Jocelyne Doray & Julian Samuel. 200p. 1994. 38.95 (1-895431-77-8, Pub. by Black Rose Bks CN); pap. 19.95 (1-895431-76-X, Pub. by Black Rose Bks CN) Consort Bk Sales.

Raft of Sea Otters: An Affectionate Portrait. rev. ed. Ed. by Vicki Leon. LC 94-31826. (Close up Ser.). (Illus.). 48p. (YA). (gr. 5 up). 1994. pap. 7.95 (0-382-24886-4); lib. bdg. 14.95 (0-382-24885-6) Silver Burdett Pr.

Raft of the Medusa. Joe Pintauro. 1992. pap. 5.25 (0-8222-1314-1) Dramatists Play.

Rafter Book: A Modern Handbook for Roof Framers. David M. McIntire. LC 95-79996. (Illus.). 134p. 1995. 15.95 (0-9647784-0-8) Joseph Pubng.

Rafter Layout with the Framing Square. rev. ed. W. Forrest Bear & Thomas A. Hoerner. (Illus.). 48p. 1982. pap. text ed. 5.70 (0-913163-02-3, 166) Hobar Pubns.

Rafter Length Manual. Benjamin Williams. (Illus.). 1979. pap. 15.75 (0-910460-67-1) Craftsman.

Rafter Master. Nix Jacobsen. (Illus.). 68p. 1992. reprint ed. ring bd. 20.00 (0-9634888-0-5) N Jacobsen.

Rafter Tables - Layout Tables. Nix Jacobsen. (Illus.). 4p. 1991. ring bd. 10.00 (0-9634888-2-1) N Jacobsen.

*Rafters. Anette Nilsson-Hennelly. Date not set. pap. 4.95 (1-56565-616-4) Contemp Bks.

Rafting in British Columbia. D. Van Dine. Ed. by B. Fandrich. 72p. 1984. pap. 6.95 (0-88839-985-5) Hancock House.

Rafting Nepal: A Consumer's Guide. P. Knowles. 1994. pap. 42.00 (0-7855-0421-4, Pub. by Ratna Pustak Bhandar) St Mut.

Rafting the Brazos. Walter McDonald. LC 88-28073. (Texas Poets Ser.: No. 1). 120p. 1988. pap. 6.95 (0-929398-04-1) UNTX Pr.

Rafting Whitewater Rivers: The Complete Guide to Whitewater Rafting Equipment & Techniques. Jeff Bennett. (Illus.). 256p. (Orig.). 1993. pap. 15.95 (0-9629843-4-5) Swiftwater Pub.

Rafts & Dreams Outside the Whale. Robert Holman. (Methuen New Theatrescripts Ser.). 184p. (Orig.). (C). 1992. pap. 11.95 (0-413-65570-9, A0617, Pub. by Methuen UK) Heinemann.

Rag & Bone Shop of the Heart: A Poetry Anthology. Ed. by Robert Bly et al. LC 91-50460. 560p. 1993. reprint ed. pap. 16.00 (0-06-092420-9, PL) HarpC.

Rag Baby. Amy Littlesugar. LC 96-8583. (J). 1997. 16.00 (0-689-80183-1, S&S Bks Young Read) S&S Childrens.

Rag Bone Man. Charlotte Lawrence. LC 94-26188. 336p. 1994. pap. 4.99 (1-56718-412-X) Llewellyn Pubns.

Rag Chandranandan. George Ruckert. Ed. by Ali Akbar Khan. (Classical Music of North India Ser.: Vol. II, No. 2). 53p. 1996. pap. 14.95 (0-930997-05-0) East Bay Bks.

Rag Coat. Lauren Mills. (Illus.). (J). (ps-3). 1991. 16.95 (0-316-57407-4) Little.

Rag Darbari Kanra. George Ruckert. Ed. by Ali Akbar Khan. (Classical Music of North India Ser.: Vol. II, No. 1). 95p. 1996. pap. 29.95 (0-930997-04-2) East Bay Bks.

*Rag Doll: A Journey of Healing & Integration. Alayna. LC 97-72778. 107p. (Orig.). 1997. pap. 11.00 (0-9658490-0-7) Mystic Moon.

Rag Doll: From Plain to Fancy. Elinor P. Bailey. 92p. 1994. pap. 19.95 (1-881588-09-2) EZ Quilting.

Rag Doll Book: 15 Delightful Dolls to Make. Petra Boase. (Illus.). 96p. 1996. 22.95 (0-09-180819-7, Pub. by Ebury Pr UK) Trafalgar.

Rag Doll Plagues. Alejandro Morales. LC 91-2381. 200p. (Orig.). 1992. 17.95 (1-55885-036-8) Arte Publico.

Rag Doll Plagues. Alejandro Morales. LC 91-2381. 200p. (Orig.). 1993. pap. 9.95 (1-55885-104-6) Arte Publico.

Rag Doll Press. E. J. Taylor. LC 91-58808. (J). (ps up). 1992. 12.95 (1-56402-150-5) Candlewick Pr.

Rag Dolls. R. Eugene Jackson. 36p. 1981. pap. 3.50 (0-88680-158-3) I E Clark.

Rag Dolls. Bernadette Theulet-Luzie. (Crafty Hands Collection). 48p. 1995. pap. 9.99 (1-85410-329-6, Pub. by Aurum Pr UK) London Brdge.

Rag Kirwani. George Ruckert & Ali Akbar Khan. (Classical Music of North India Ser.: Vol. II, No. 3). 43p. 1996. pap. 14.95 (0-930997-06-9) East Bay Bks.

Rag Mop the Doxie Poo. Marilou Gari. LC 96-60620. (Illus.). 44p. (J). (gr. k-4). 1997. 7.95 (1-55523-802-5) Winston-Derek.

Rag Nymph. Catherine Cookson. 432p. 1992. mass mkt. 7.99 (0-552-13683-2) Bantam.

Rag Nymph: A Novel. large type ed. Catherine Cookson. LC 93-48606. 1994. write for info. (0-7862-2016-3, Thorndike Lrg Prnt); lib. bdg. 24.95 (0-7862-0167-3) Thorndike Pr.

Rag Rug Handbook. 3rd ed. Janet Meany & Paula Plaff. 1992. pap. 19.95 (0-932394-21-3) Dos Tejedoras.

Rag Rug Handbook. Janet Meany & Paula Pfaff. (Illus.). 128p. 1996. reprint ed. pap. 19.95 (1-883010-28-4) Interweave.

Rag Rug Inspirations: New Designs for Traditional Techniques. Juliet Bawden. (Illus.). 160p. 1996. 29.95 (0-304-34768-X, Pub. by Cassell UK) Sterling.

*Rag Rugs. Juju Vail. 1997. 12.98 (0-7858-0658-X) Bk Sales Inc.

Rag Rugs: Ancient & Modern Rug-Making Tech. Ann Davies. (Illus.). 96p. 1994. pap. 15.95 (0-8050-2812-9) H Holt & Co.

Rag Street Journal: The Ultimate Guide to Shopping Thrift & Consignment Stores Throughout the U. S. & Canada. Elizabeth Mason. 384p. (Orig.). 1995. pap. 14.95 (0-8050-3728-4, Owl) H Holt & Co.

Rag Theater: The Twenty-Four Hundred Block of Telegraph Avenue 1969-1973. Nacio J. Brown. LC 75-15320. (Illus.). 74p. 1979. pap. 10.95 (0-915572-42-7) Panjandrum.

Rag Time. David A. Jasen. 1998. 32.50 (0-02-864743-2) Mac Lib Ref.

Rag(a) S. Bill Costley. 1978. write for info. (0-686-08921-9) Ghost Dance.

Ragamuffin Gospel: Embracing the Unconditional Love of God. Brennan Manning. 238p. (Orig.). 1990. pap. 9.99 (0-88070-631-7, Multnomah Bks) Multnomah Pubs.

*Ragamuffin Reader. Manning. pap. 13.00 (0-06-065457-0) HarpC.

Ragas in Indian Classical Music. Anupam Mahajan. 150p. 1989. write for info. incl. audio (81-212-0269-8, Pub. by Gian Publng Hse II) S Asia.

Ragas of Early Indian Music: Modes, Melodies, & Musical Notations from the Gupta Period to c. 1250. Richard Widdess. (Monographs on Music). (Illus.). 448p. 1996. 80.00 (0-19-315464-1) OUP.

Ragas of North India. Walter Kaufmann. (C). 1993. text ed. 58.00 (81-204-0810-1, Pub. by Oxford IBH II) S Asia.

Ragas of Northern Indian Music. Alain Danielou. 1981. 32.00 (0-8364-0774-1, Pub. by Munshiram Manoharial II) S Asia.

Ragas of South India: A Catalogue of Scalar Material. Walter Kaufmann. (C). 1991. 60.00 (81-204-0607-9, Pub. by Oxford IBH II) S Asia.

Ragbag of Legal Quotations. Ed. by M. Frances McNamara. LC 92-74141. 334p. 1992. reprint ed. 50.00 (0-9630106-3-8, 307730) Lawbk Exchange.

*Ragdale: A History & Guide. Alice Hayes & Susan Moon. (Illus.). 100p. (Orig.). 1990. pap. 10.00 (0-931416-07-8) Open Books.

Ragdoll. Mark Dunster. 12p. (Orig.). 1986. pap. 4.00 (0-89642-142-2) Linden Pubs.

Ragdoll. Kelly R. Stevens. 1995. mass mkt. 4.95 (1-55748-661-1) Barbour & Co.

Ragdoll & My Clothes. (Sandseed Collection). (J). 1991. 19.95 (2-921198-73-8, Pub. by Edits Chouette CN) Orca Bk Pubs.

Ragdoll & My Food. (Sandseed Collection). (J). 1991. 19.95 (2-921198-53-3, Pub. by Edits Chouette CN) Orca Bk Pubs.

Ragdoll & My House. (Sandseed Collection). (J). 1991. 19.95 (2-921198-72-X, Pub. by Edits Chouette CN) Orca Bk Pubs.

Ragdoll & My Toys. (Sandseed Collection). (J). 1991. 19.95 (2-921198-71-1, Pub. by Edits Chouette CN) Orca Bk Pubs.

Rage. Rene C. Du Gard. (Illus.). 144p. (Orig.). (FRE.). 1990. pap. 15.00 (0-939586-17-7) Edns des Deux Mondes.

Rage. Rene C. Du Gard. Tr. by Mildred Van Sice from FRE. (Illus.). 350p. (Orig.). 1995. pap. 20.00 (0-939586-18-5) Edns des Deux Mondes.

Rage. Elizabeth Ergas. 352p. 1993. mass mkt. 4.50 (1-55817-678-0, Pinncle Kensgtn) Kensgtn Pub Corp.

Rage. Gilbert Moor. (Illus.). 304p. 1993. pap. 10.95 (0-88184-973-1) Carroll & Graf.

Rage. J. D. Rage. 58p. 1989. per., pap. 4.00 (1-886206-02-3) Venom Pr.

Rage. Clay Reynolds. 432p. 1994. 4.99 (0-451-40350-9, Sig) NAL-Dutton.

Rage. Wilbur Smith. 1989. mass mkt. 5.99 (0-449-21613-6, Crest) Fawcett.

Rage. Wilbur Smith. 640p. 1987. 19.95 (0-316-80179-8) Little.

*Rage: With Fang & Claw. Mike Tinney & Justin Achilli. (Werewolf Ser.). (Illus.). 72p. (Orig.). 1996. pap. 7.95 (1-56504-354-5, 3930) White Wolf.

Rage Across Appalachia. Jackie Cassada. (Werewolf Ser.). 1995. 18.00 (1-56504-313-8, 3107) White Wolf.

Rage Across the World, Vol. 1. Bill Bridges. (Werewolf Ser.). (Illus.). 288p. (Orig.). 1996. pap. 20.00 (1-56504-319-7, 3069) White Wolf.

Rage Across the World, Vol. 2. Bill Bridges. (Werewolf Ser.). (Illus.). 272p. (Orig.). 1996. pap. 20.00 (1-56504-320-0, 3070) White Wolf.

Rage & Fire. Francine du Plessix Gray. 1995. pap. 14.00 (0-684-80453-0, Touchstone Bks) S&S Trade.

Rage & Roll: Bill Graham & the Selling of Rock. John Glatt. LC 93-5138. (Illus.). 288p. 1993. 19.95 (1-55972-205-3, Birch Ln Pr) Carol Pub Group.

*Rage de Flic. large type ed. Gilbert Schlogel. 247p. 1996. pap. 25.99 (2-84011-156-X) Ulverscroft.

Rage de l'Expression. Francis Ponge. (FRE.). 1976. pap. 14.95 (0-7859-2780-8) Fr & Eur.

Rage de l'Expression. Francis Ponge. (Poesie Ser.). 214p. (FRE.). 1976. pap. 11.95 (2-07-032167-3) Schoenhof.

Rage for Falcons. Stephen Bodio. LC 92-8003. (Illus.). 135p. 1992. pap. 12.95 (0-87108-826-6) Pruett.

*Rage for Fame: The Ascent of Clare Boothe Luce. Sylvia J. Morris. LC 96-43084. (Illus.). 561p. 1997. 30.00 (0-394-57555-5) Random.

Rage for Justice: The Passion & Politics of Phillip Burton. John Jacobs. LC 94-36185. (Illus.). 624p. 1995. 34.95 (0-520-20076-4) U CA Pr.

*Rage for Justice: The Passion & Politics of Phillip Burton. John Jacobs. 1997. pap. text ed. 19.95 (0-520-20411-5) U CA Pr.

Rage for Order: Black-White Relations in the American South since Emancipation. Joel Williamson. 326p. 1986. pap. 12.95 (0-19-504025-2) OUP.

Rage in Chupadera. Norman Zollinger. 1996. mass mkt. 5.99 (0-8125-4843-4) Forge NYC.

Rage in Harlem. Chester Himes. (Vintage Crime Ser.). Orig. Title: For Love of Imabelle. (Orig.). 1989. pap. 10.00 (0-679-72040-5, Vin) Random.

*Rage in Paradise. Ralph Arnote. LC 96-52690. 1997. 23.95 (0-312-86198-2) St Martin.

Rage in the Hearts: A Historical Novel. Jose P. Leveriza. 167p. (Orig.). (C). 1989. pap. 12.50 (971-10-0382-1, Pub. by New Day Pub PH) Cellar.

Rage in the Streets: Mob Violence in America. Jules Archer. LC 93-5710. 272p. (J). (gr. 5-9). 1994. 16.95 (0-15-277691-5, Browndeer Pr) HarBrace.

Rage in Utopia. Jack Warren. 245p. 1992. pap. write for info. (1-880719-00-2) Grafco Prods.

*Rage of a Demon King. Raymond E. Feist. LC 96-30715. (The Serpentwar Saga Ser.: Vol. 3). 1997. 24.00 (0-380-97473-8) Avon.

Rage of a Privileged Class. Ellis Cose. 208p. 1995. pap. 12.00 (0-06-092594-9, Harp T) HarpC.

Rage of a Privileged Class: Why Do Prosperous Blacks Still Have the Blues? Ellis Cose. 176p. 1994. 20.00 (0-06-018239-3, A Asher Bks) HarpC.

*Rage of Angels. Alan Fisher. LC 96-53910. 224p. 1997. 21.00 (0-7867-0409-8) Carroll & Graf.

Rage of Angels. Sidney Sheldon. (Sheldon Continuity Ser.). 300p. 1994. 12.95 (1-56865-091-4, GuildAmerica) Dbldy Direct.

Rage of Angels. Sidney Sheldon. 504p. 1988. mass mkt. 6.99 (0-446-35661-1) Warner Bks.

Rage of Angels. Sidney Sheldon. 1991. 5.95 (0-446-77483-9) Warner Bks.

Rage of Angels. Sidney Sheldon. LC 80-13328. 504p. 1980. 18.45 (0-688-03687-2) Morrow.

Rage of Battle. Ian Slater. 352p. 1991. mass mkt. 5.99 (0-449-21988-7, Crest) Fawcett.

*Rage of Innocence. Latres Orr. LC 96-90835. (Orig.). 1997. pap. 11.95 (0-533-12186-8) Vantage.

Rage of Innocence. William D. Pease. 464p. 1994. pap. 5.99 (0-451-18031-3, Sig) NAL-Dutton.

Rage of Love. Alda Merini. Tr. by Pasquale Verdicchio from ITA. (Prose Ser.: No. 30). 80p. 1995. 12.00 (1-55071-013-3) Guernica Editions.

Rage of Maidens: Sixth Caitlin Reece Mystery. Lauren W. Douglas. 224p. 1994. pap. 10.95 (1-56280-068-X) Naiad Pr.

Rage of Regents. Nigel Tranter. 320p. 1996. 27.00 (0-340-65996-3, Pub. by H & S UK); pap. 10.95 (0-340-65997-1, Pub. by H & S UK) Trafalgar.

*Rage of Spirits. Noel Hynd. 336p. 1997. 21.95 (1-57566-127-6, Knsington) Kensgtn Pub Corp.

*Rage of Spirits. Noel Hynd. 416p. 1998. mass mkt. 5.99 (0-7860-0470-3, Pinncle Kensgtn) Kensgtn Pub Corp.

Rage of the Aquarius. Carol Ellis. (Zodiac Chillers Srs.). 169p. (J). (gr. 6-10). 1995. pap. 3.99 (0-679-87304-X) McKay.

Rage of the Bear. Bert Byfield. LC 95-70527. (Russalka Trilogy Ser.: Vol. 1). 253p. (Orig.). 1996. per. 9.00 (1-887121-01-3) Caravela Bks.

*Rage of the Innocent. large type ed. Frederick E. Smith. (Charnwood Large Print Ser.). 496p. 1997. 29.50 (0-7089-8935-7, Charnwood) Ulverscroft.

Rage of the Mountain Man. William W. Johnstone. 288p. 1994. mass mkt. 3.99 (0-8217-4567-0, Zebra Kensgtn) Kensgtn Pub Corp.

Rage of the Mountain Man. William W. Johnstone. 1996. mass mkt. 4.99 (0-8217-5361-4, Zebra Kensgtn) Kensgtn Pub Corp.

Rage of the Vulture. Barry Unsworth. 443p. 1995. pap. 12.00 (0-393-31308-5, Norton Paperbks) Norton.

Rage, Power, & Aggression. Ed. by Robert A. Glick & Steven T. Roose. LC 92-49297. (Role of Affect in Development, Motivation, & Adoption Ser.: No. 2). 288p. (C). 1993. text ed. 42.50 (0-300-05271-5) Yale U Pr.

*Rage, Power & Fulfillment: The Japanese Male Journey. Roger S. Keyes & M. H. De Young Memorial Museum Staff. LC 87-36437. 1988. 40.00 (0-8076-1197-2); pap. 22.50 (0-8076-1198-0) Braziller.

*Rage to Live. John O'Hara. LC 97-2092. 1997. 20.00 (0-679-60266-6, Modern Lib) Random.

Rage to Live. John O'Hara. 542p. 1986. reprint ed. pap. 4.95 (0-88184-216-8) Carroll & Graf.

Rage to Punish: The Unintended Consequences of Mandatory Sentencing. Lois G. Forer. LC 93-37329. 1994. 23.00 (0-393-03641-3) Norton.

*Rage to Survive: The Etta James Story. Etta James & David Ritz. LC 97-14049. 1997. write for info. (0-306-80784-X) Plenum.

Rage to Survive: The Etta James Story. Etta James & David Ritz. LC 94-23759. 1995. 20.00 (0-679-42328-1, Villard Bks) Random.

Rages of Excess: The Life & Poetry of William Everson. David A. Carpenter. LC 87-50525. 480p. (Orig.). (C). 1987. pap. text ed. 39.95 (1-55605-008-9) Wyndham Hall.

*Ragga & the Royal. Monica Grant. 197p. 1996. pap. 9.95 (1-874509-08-5) LPC InBook.

*Ragged Bear. Brigitte Weninger. (Illus.). (J). Date not set. 15.95 (1-55858-662-8); lib. bdg. 15.88 (1-55858-663-6) North-South Bks NYC.

*Ragged Borders. Fernando E. Flores. 48p. 1996. pap. 10.00 (0-9654223-0-5) Hijo Del Sol.

Ragged Dick. Horatio Alger, Jr. (YA). 1990. mass mkt. 5.95 (0-451-52480-2, Sig Classics) NAL-Dutton.

Ragged Dick. Horatio Alger, Jr. (Works of Horatio Alger Jr.). 1989. reprint ed. lib. bdg. 79.00 (0-7812-1707-5) Rprt Serv.

Ragged Dick & Mark the Matchboy. Horatio Alger, Jr. LC 62-21187. 382p. (Orig.). 1962. pap. 6.00 (0-02-041390-4) Macmillan.

Ragged Dick & Struggling Upward. Horatio Alger, Jr. (American Library). 304p. 1985. pap. 9.95 (0-14-039033-2, Penguin Classics) Viking Penguin.

Ragged Edge: The Disability Experience from the Pages of the First Fifteen Years of The Disability Rag. Ed. by Barrett Shaw. LC 94-79440. 245p. 1994. pap. 18.95 (0-9627064-5-0) Advocado Pr.

Ragged Edge of Science. L. Sprague De Camp. LC 79-92640. (Illus.). 254p. 1980. 16.00 (0-913896-06-3) Owlswick Pr.

Ragged Heart. Ed. by Norita Dittberner-Jax. (Illus.). 164p. (Orig.). (J). 1989. pap. 8.00 (0-927663-14-7) COMPAS.

Ragged Irregulars: The 91st Bomb Group in World War II. Marion Havelaar & William Hess. LC 95-67618. (Illus.). 320p. 1995. 45.00 (0-88740-810-9) Schiffer.

Ragged Lady. William Dean Howells. (Notable American Authors Ser.). 1992. reprint ed. lib. bdg. 75.00 (0-7812-3252-X) Rprt Serv.

Ragged Mountain Portable Wilderness Anthology. Ed. by Jan Adkins. LC 93-8397. (Illus.). 144p. 1993. pap. 12.95 (0-87742-370-9, Ragged Mntn) Intl Marine.

Ragged Mountain Portable Wilderness Anthology. Ed. by Jan E. Adkins. 1993. pap. text ed. 12.95 (0-07-000311-4) McGraw-Hill Prof.

*Ragged Mountain Press Guide to Outdoor Sports: Skills & Knowledge for the Whole Outdoors. Jonathan Hanson & Roseann Hanson. LC 96-54239. (Illus.). 352p. 1997. pap. text ed. 22.95 (0-07-052114-X) McGraw.

*Ragged Mountain Press Pocket Guide to Wilderness Medicine & First Aid. Paul G. Gill, Jr. (Illus.). 208p. 1997. pap. text ed. 14.95 (0-07-024552-5) McGraw.

Ragged Peddler. large type ed. Flavia M. Weedn. LC 94-15053. (Dream Maker Stories Ser.). (Illus.). 48p. (J). (ps-3). 1995. 10.95 (0-7868-0046-1) Hyprn Child.

*Ragged Prison Blues. Joyce Carbone. 50p. (Orig.). 1996. pap. 5.95 (1-878116-58-4) JVC Bks.

Ragged Rainbows. Linda Lael Miller. 1994. mass mkt. 4.50 (0-373-48300-7, 5-48300-3, Mira Bks) Harlequin Bks.

Ragged Rebel: A Common Soldier in W. H. Parsons' Texas Cavalry, 1861-1865. B. P. Gallaway. (Illus.). 202p. 1988. pap. 10.95 (0-292-77047-2) U of Tex Pr.

*Ragged Schooling. Roberts. Date not set. pap. 15.95 (1-901341-01-1) St Martin.

Ragged Schooling. R. Roberts. 1988. text ed. 13.95 (0-7190-2453-6, Pub. by Manchester Univ Pr UK) St Martin.

Ragged Shadows: Poems of Halloween Night. Lee B. Hopkins. (J). (ps-3). 1993. 15.95 (0-316-37276-5) Little.

Ragged Shaw. John B. Shaw. 112p. 1987. 12.95 (0-938501-05-4) Wessex.

Ragged Vertical. Harry E. Northup. 264p. (Orig.). 1996. pap. 15.00 (0-9649240-0-5) Cahuenga Pr.

R

Ragged War: The Story of Unconventional & Counter-Revolutionary Warfare. Leroy Thompson. (Illus.). 224p. 1996. pap. 14.95 (*1-85409-369-X*, Pub. by Arms & Armour UK) Sterling.

Ragged Way People Fall Out of Love. Elizabeth Cox. 224p. 1991. 18.95 (*0-86547-446-X*, North Pt Pr) FS&G.

Raggedy Andy Stories. Johnny Gruelle. (Illus.). (J). 1976. 26.95 (*0-8488-1353-7*) Amereon Ltd.

Raggedy Andy Stories. Johnny Gruelle. 1996. 8.99 (*0-517-14686-X*) Random Hse Value.

Raggedy Andy Stories. Johnny Gruelle. (Illus.). 96p. (J). (ps up). 1987. reprint ed. lib. bdg. 25.95 (*0-89966-618-3*) Buccaneer Bks.

Raggedy Andy Stories: Introducing the Little Rag Brother of Raggedy Ann. Johnny Gruelle. LC 93-21967. (Illus.). 96p. (J). (gr. k up). 1993. lib. bdg. 15.95 (*0-02-737586-2*, Mac Bks Young Read) S&S Childrens.

Raggedy Ann, Vol. 1. Gruelle. LC 96-26352. (J). 1997. 13.00 (*0-689-81119-5*) S&S Childrens.

Raggedy Ann, Vol. 2. Gruelle. LC 97-2. (J). 1997. 13.00 (*0-689-81120-9*) S&S Childrens.

Raggedy Ann & Andy. Adapted by Patricia Thackray. 1981. 5.25 (*0-87129-463-X*, R32) Dramatic Pub.

***Raggedy Ann & Andy & the Camel with the Wrinkled Knees.** Gruelle. (J). Date not set. mass mkt. 4.99 (*0-689-80888-7*) S&S Childrens.

Raggedy Ann & Andy Collectibles: A Handbook & Price Guide. Jan Lindenberger. LC 95-19703. (Illus.). 160p. (Orig.). 1995. pap. 19.95 (*0-88740-782-X*) Schiffer.

Raggedy Ann & Andy Family Album. Susan A. Garrison. LC 89-84172. (Illus.). 144p. 1989. pap. 19.95 (*0-88740-178-3*) Schiffer.

Raggedy Ann & Andy Giant Treasury: Four Adventures Plus 12 Short Stories. Johnny Gruelle. (Illus.). 96p. (J). (ps-1). 1985. 5.99 (*0-517-45594-3*) Random Hse Value.

Raggedy Ann & Andy Second Giant Treasury. Illus. by Johnny Gruelle. 80p. (J). 1989. 5.99 (*0-517-66719-3*) Random Hse Value.

***Raggedy Ann & More: A Bibliography & Collecting Guide to Johnny Gruelle.** LC 96-40034. 1997. write for info. (*1-56554-102-2*); write for info. (*1-56554-123-5*) Pelican.

***Raggedy Ann Christmas.** Willard. (J). Date not set. pap. 17.00 (*0-689-81893-9*) S&S Childrens.

Raggedy Ann Stories. Johnny Gruelle. LC 93-630. (Illus.). 96p. (J). (gr. k up). 1993. lib. bdg. 16.00 (*0-02-737585-4*, Mac Bks Young Read) S&S Childrens.

Raggedy Ann Stories. Johnny Gruelle. LC 93-8698. (J). 1994. 8.99 (*0-517-10037-1*) Random Hse Value.

Raggedy Man. Lillian O'Donnell. 1997. mass mkt. 5.99 (*0-449-22428-7*) Fawcett.

Raggedy Man. large type ed. Lillian O'Donnell. LC 95-21831. (Cloak & Dagger Ser.). 381p. 1995. 22.95 (*0-7862-0521-0*) Thorndike Pr.

Raggin' A Story about Scott Joplin. Barbara Mitchell. (Creative Minds Ser.). (Illus.). 64p. (J). (gr. 3-6). 1987. lib. bdg. 14.21 (*0-87614-310-9*, Carolrhoda) Lerner Group.

Raggin' A Story about Scott Joplin. Barbara Mitchell. (J). (gr. 3-6). 1992. pap. 5.95 (*0-87614-589-6*, Carolrhoda) Lerner Group.

Ragging: Unquiet Campus. S. K. Ghosh. xii, 170p. 1993. 20.00 (*81-7024-519-2*, Pub. by Ashish Pub Hse II) Nataraj Bks.

Raggly, Scraggly, No-Soap, No-Scrub Girl. David F. Birchman. LC 92-40339. (Illus.). 32p. (J). (gr. k up). 1995. 16.00 (*0-688-11060-6*); lib. bdg. 15.93 (*0-688-11061-4*) Lothrop.

Raggylug a True Story. Ernest T. Seton. (Illus.). 48p. (Orig.). (J). (gr. 3-8). 1989. pap. 10.95 (*1-880812-14-2*) S Ink WA.

Raghuvamsa of Kalidasa: With the Commentary Sanjivani of Mallinatha, Cantos I-V. M. R. Kale. (C). 1991. reprint ed. pap. text ed. 7.00 (*81-208-0861-4*, Pub. by Motilal Banarsidass II) S Asia.

Raging Beauty: Selected Poems. James Scully. LC 94-70863. 224p. (Orig.). (C). 1994. pap. 13.95 (*0-9632363-7-7*) Azul Edits.

***Raging Bull: My Story.** Jake La Motta et al. (Illus.). 247p. 1997. reprint ed. pap. 13.95 (*0-306-80808-0*) Da Capo.

Raging Bull II. Chris Anderson et al. 288p. 16.95 (*0-8184-0407-8*) Carol Pub Group.

Raging Bulls: NBA's Chicago Bulls. 1996. pap. 6.99 (*0-451-82335-4*); pap. 9.99 (*0-451-82336-2*) NAL-Dutton.

***Raging Dragon.** Date not set. 35.00 (*1-55878-102-1*) Game Designers.

Raging Forces: Earth in Upheaval. National Geographic Society Book Division Staff. LC 95-36295. 200p. 1996. 16.00 (*0-7922-2736-0*) Natl Geog.

Raging Forces: Earth in Upheaval. deluxe ed. National Geographic Society, Book Division Staff. LC 95-36295. 1995. write for info. (*0-7922-2965-7*) Natl Geog.

Raging Grannies Songbook. Ed. by Jean McLaren & Heide Brown. 1993. lib. bdg. 39.95 (*0-86571-254-9*); spiral bd. 14.95 (*0-86571-255-7*) New Soc Pubs.

Raging Heart. Sheila Weller. 1995. pap. 6.99 (*0-671-52146-2*) PB.

Raging Heart: The Intimate Story of the Tragic Marriage O. J. Simpson Nicole Simpson-Export. Sheila Weller. 1995. pap. 6.50 (*0-671-53709-1*) PB.

Raging Heart: The Intimate Story of the Tragic Marriage of O. J. & Nicole Brown Simpson. Sheila Weller. (Illus.). 1995. 18.00 (*0-671-52145-4*) PB.

***Raging Hearts.** Patricia Hagan. 1997. mass mkt. 5.50 (*0-06-108477-8*, Harp PBks) HarpC.

Raging Hormones: Do They Rule Our Lives? Gail Vines. LC 93-44921. (C). 1994. 25.00 (*0-520-08776-3*); pap. 13.00 (*0-520-08777-1*) U CA Pr.

Raging Hormones: What to Do When You Suspect Your Teen Might Be Sexually Active. Judith Balswick & Jack Balswick. 192p. 1994. pap. 10.99 (*0-310-59591-6*) Zondervan.

Raging into Apocalypse Vol. IV: Essays in Apocalypse IV. Dave Breese & William T. James. (Essays in Apocalypse Ser.). 320p. 1996. pap. text ed. 11.95 (*0-89221-320-5*) New Leaf.

Raging Moon. Chitra Pershad. 6.75 (*0-89253-716-7*); text ed. 4.80 (*0-89253-717-5*) Ind-US Inc.

Raging Passion. John Nemec. 160p. (Orig.). 1991. pap. 3.49 (*0-9618998-7-5*) Nemec Pub.

Raging Peace. Artemis OakGrove. 256p. (Orig.). 1991. reprint ed. pap. 8.95 (*1-55583-307-1*) Alyson Pubns.

Raging Red: The 1950 Red River Valley Flood. Douglas L. Ramsey & Larry E. Skroch. 300p. 1995. pap. 119.95 (*0-9635253-0-1*) Skroch & Ramsey.

Raging River. Bill Wundram. 96p. (Orig.). 1993. pap. 14.95 (*0-9627618-4-2*) Billings Gazette.

Raging Robots & Unruly Uncles. Margaret Mahy. (Illus.). 94p. (J). (gr. 3-7). 1993. 13.95 (*0-87951-469-8*) Overlook Pr.

Raging Sea, Searing Sky. Christopher Nicole. 1988. 19.00 (*0-7278-1613-6*) Severn Hse.

Raging Tide. Edward Gorey. LC 87-1843. (Illus.). 64p. 1987. 11.95 (*0-926637-08-8*) P Weed Bks.

Raging Turke, or Baiazet the Second, 2 vols., Set. Thomas Goff. Bd. with Courageous Turke, or Amvrath the Third. (Malone Society Reprint Ser.: No. 128). 80.00 (*0-404-63128-2*) AMS Pr.

Raging Waters. Brian Brown & Andrew Melrose. (Storykeepers Ser.: Vol. 2). (Illus.). 64p. (J). (gr. 2-5). 1996. pap. 3.99 (*0-310-20327-9*) Zondervan.

Raging Waters. Brian Brown & Andrew Melrose. (Storykeepers Ser.: Vol. 2). (Illus.). 64p. (J). (ps-3). 1996. pap. 3.99 (*0-310-20329-5*) Zondervan.

Raging Wet Lesbians: Bonus Words & Phrases. large type ed. Mark Stevens & Jim Preleit. LC 95-72895. 80p. (Orig.). 1996. pap. 9.95 (*0-943629-21-7*) Swan Pub.

Raging Winds of Heaven. June L. Shiplett. (Orig.). 1978. pap. 3.95 (*0-451-13135-5*, AE3135, Sig) NAL-Dutton.

Raglagger. Towana J. Brown. LC 89-90647. (Illus.). 168p. (Orig.). (J). (gr. 5-7). 1989. pap. 3.50 (*0-9622060-2-4*) T J Brown.

Ragman: And Other Cries of Faith. Walter Wangerin, Jr. LC 83-48980. 160p. 1994. pap. 11.00 (*0-06-069229-4*) Harper SF.

***Ragman's Memory.** Archer Mayor. 368p. 1997. 6.50 (*0-446-40524-8*) Mysterious Pr.

Ragman's Memory. Archer Mayor. LC 96-23331. 336p. 1996. 22.00 (*0-89296-636-X*) Warner Bks.

Ragman's Son. Kirk Douglas. Ed. by Bill Grose. 1990. mass mkt. 5.99 (*0-671-73789-9*) PB.

Ragnar Frisch: Economic Planning Studies. Ed. by Frank Long. LC 75-44219. (International Studies in Economics & Econometrics: No. 8). 1975. lib. bdg. 88.00 (*90-277-0245-4*) Kluwer Ac.

Ragnarok. Nathan Archer. (Star Trek Ser.: No. 3). 1995. mass mkt. 5.99 (*0-671-52044-X*) PB.

Ragnarok: The Age of Fire & Gravel. Ignatius Donnelly. (Notable American Authors Ser.). 1992. reprint ed. lib. bdg. 75.00 (*0-7812-2668-6*) Rprt Serv.

***Ragnar's Action Encyclopedia, Vol. 2.** Ragnar Benson. (Illus.). 256p. 1997. pap. 40.00 (*0-87364-926-5*) Paladin Pr.

Ragnar's Action Encyclopedia of Practical Knowledge & Proven Techniques: A Do-It-Yourself Guide. Ragnar Benson. (Illus.). 456p. 1995. pap. 45.00 (*0-87364-801-3*) Paladin Pr.

Ragnar's Big Book of Homemade Weapons: Building & Keeping Your Arsenal Secure. Ragnar Benson. (Illus.). 288p. 1992. pap. 25.00 (*0-87364-660-6*) Paladin Pr.

Ragnar's Guide to Home & Recreational Use of High Explosives. Ragnar Benson. (Illus.). 120p. 1988. pap. 12.00 (*0-87364-478-6*) Paladin Pr.

Ragnar's Homemade Detonators: How to Make Em, How to Salvage Em, How to Detonate Em. Ragnar Benson. (Illus.). 72p. 1993. pap. 10.00 (*0-87364-737-8*) Paladin Pr.

Ragnar's Ten Best Traps & a Few Others That Are Damn Good, Too. Ragnar Benson. (Illus.). 136p. 1985. pap. 10.00 (*0-87364-328-3*) Paladin Pr.

Ragopedia, Vol. 1: Exotic Scales of North India, 2 vols. Shiv D. Batish & Ashwin Batish. 1989. spiral bd. 35.00 (*1-882319-00-1*) Batish Pubns.

Ragotte see Oeuvres

***Rags: Broadway Selections.** Ed. by Carol Cuellar. 76p. (Orig.). (C). 1992. pap. text ed. 14.95 (*0-7692-0483-X*, TSF0071) Warner Brothers.

Rags & Ragtime: A Musical History. David A. Jasen & Trebor J. Tichenor. (Illus.). 368p. 1989. pap. 11.95 (*0-486-25922-6*) Dover.

Rags for Guitar. S. Joplin. 28p. 1986. pap. 4.95 (*0-7935-5236-2*, 50333690) H Leonard.

***Rags' New Friend.** (Four Little Friends Ser.). (Illus.). 24p. (J). (gr. 1-4). 1995. write for info. (*1-56144-729-3*, Honey Bear Bks) Modern Pub NYC.

Rags of North Indian Music: Their Structure & Evolution. N. A. Jairazbhoy. (C). 1995. reprint ed. 32.00 (*81-7154-395-2*, Pub. by Popular Prakashan II) S Asia.

***Rags of Time.** Peter Levi. 90p. 1994. pap. 17.95 (*0-85646-258-6*, Pub. by Anvil Press UK) Dufour.

***Rags to Riches.** William Jackson. 50p. (Orig.). 1996. pap. 19.95 (*1-878406-07-8*) Parker Dstb.

Rags to Riches. Francine Pascal. (Sweet Valley High Ser.: No. 16). 160p. (Orig.). (J). (gr. 5 up). 1985. pap. 3.50 (*0-553-27431-7*) Bantam.

Rags to Riches. Alice Vosper. 222p. (YA). (gr. 7 up). 1983. pap. 2.25 (*0-380-83873-7*, Flare) Avon.

Rags to Riches: Musical. Aurand Harris. (J). 1966. 5.00 (*0-87602-185-2*) Anchorage.

Rags to Riches: The Story of the Companions of Emmaus. Henri Le Boursicaud. 144p. 1989. pap. 22.00 (*1-85390-053-2*, Pub. by Veritas IE) St Mut.

Rags to Riches to Rags to Riches: The John Ross Story. John Ross. 107p. 1990. pap. 10.00 (*1-879868-00-8*) Mentor Group.

Ragsale. Artie A. Bates. LC 94-17366. (Illus.). 32p. (J). (gr. k-3). 1995. 14.95 (*0-395-70030-2*) HM.

Ragtime. E. L. Doctorow. 288p. 1996. pap. 9.95 (*0-452-27570-9*, Plume) NAL-Dutton.

Ragtime. E. L. Doctorow. LC 75-9613. 288p. 1975. 21.95 (*0-394-46901-1*) Random.

Ragtime. E. L. Doctorow. 336p. 1994. 15.50 (*0-679-60088-4*) Random.

***Ragtime.** E. L. Doctorow. 1997. pap. 10.95 (*0-452-27907-0*) NAL-Dutton.

Ragtime: A Musical & Cultural History. Edward A. Berlin. LC 78-51759. 1980. pap. 12.95 (*0-520-05219-6*) U CA Pr.

***Ragtime - Vocal Selections.** Ed. by Sy Feldman. (Illus.). 104p. (Orig.). 1997. pap. text ed. 19.95 (*1-57623-955-1*, 5206A) Warner Brothers.

Ragtime, Blues & Jazz for Banjo. Fred Sokolow. 1993. 6.95 (*1-56222-412-3*, 93936); audio 9.98 (*1-56222-609-6*, 93936C) Mel Bay.

***Ragtime, Blues & Jazz for Banjo.** Fred Sokolow. 1993. 15.95 incl. audio (*0-7866-0950-8*, 93936P) Mel Bay.

Ragtime Blues Guitar. Stefan Grossman. (Illus.). 112p. pap. 17.95 (*0-8256-0299-8*, OK64691, Oak) Music Sales.

Ragtime for Violin & Piano: Great Performers Edition. S. Joplin. 44p. 1986. pap. 11.95 (*0-7935-5467-5*, 50333320) H Leonard.

Ragtime Rarities. Trebor J. Tichenor. LC 74-28941. (Illus.). 320p. (Orig.). 1975. pap. 12.95 (*0-486-23157-7*) Dover.

Ragtime Rediscoveries: Sixty-Five Works from the Golden Age of Rag. Trebor J. Tichenor. LC 78-73573. 1979. pap. 11.95 (*0-486-23776-1*) Dover.

Ragtime Song & Dance. Compiled by Jerry Silverman. (Traditional Black Music Ser.). (Illus.). 80p. (YA). (gr. 5 up). 1995. lib. bdg. 18.95 (*0-7910-1836-9*) Chelsea Hse.

Ragtime Tumpie. Alan Schroeder. (Illus.). (J). (gr. k-4). 1989. 16.95 (*0-316-77497-9*, Joy St Bks) Little.

Ragtime Tumpie. Alan Schroeder. (J). (ps-3). 1993. mass mkt. 5.95 (*0-316-77504-5*) Little.

Ragusa & the Spanish Armada of 1588. Veselin Kostic. 50p. 1987. pap. 5.00 (*0-918660-68-8*) Ragusan Pr.

Ragusa Theme. large type ed. Ann Quinton. (Romance Suspense Ser.). 416p. 1988. 25.99 (*0-7089-1777-1*) Ulverscroft.

Ragusan Bride: Dubrovnik to San Francisco. Mary K. Ericsson. LC 80-51686. 141p. 1981. per. 10.00 (*0-918660-16-5*) Ragusan Pr.

Ragweed Cowboy Joe. I. E. Clark. (Illus.). 24p. 1974. pap. 3.50 (*0-88680-159-1*); pap. 10.00 (*0-88680-160-5*) I E Clark.

Ragweed, the Horse Who Lost Her Cool. large type ed. William O. Beazley. (Illus.). 45p. (J). (gr. k-5). 1993. reprint ed. spiral bd., pap. 7.95 (*1-884758-02-9*) W O Beazley.

Ragwitch. Garth Nix. 320p. (J). 1995. 3.99 (*0-8125-3506-5*) Tor Bks.

Ragwork. Lizzie Reakes. 96p. 1996. 14.95 (*1-85967-238-8*, Lorenz Bks) Anness Pub.

***Rahel Varnhagen: The Life of a Jewess.** Hannah Arendt & Liliane Weissberg. LC 97-6484. 1997. write for info. (*0-8018-5587-X*) Johns Hopkins.

Rahm. Tom Bacchus. (Orig.). 1995. mass mkt. 5.95 (*1-56333-315-5*, Badboy) Masquerade.

Rahner & Metz: Transcendental Theology As Political Theology. Titus F. Guenther. LC 92-44976. 1993. 62.50 (*0-8191-9033-0*) U Pr of Amer.

Rahner, Heidegger, & Truth: Karl Rahner's Notion of Christian Truth, The Influence of Heidegger. Jack A. Bonsor & Francis S. Fiorenza. 226p. (Orig.). (C). 1987. lib. bdg. 44.50 (*0-8191-6159-4*) U Pr of Amer.

***Rai 'n' Bo Heart Meet Sunny, the Funny Weather Bunny.** Victoria J. Malyurek. (Illus.). 12p. (J). (gr. 1-7). 1997. pap. 3.95 (*1-889294-09-8*) Victorias Pub.

Rai of Eastern Nepal: Ethics & Linguistic Grouping Findings of the Linguistic Survey of Nepal. W. Winter. (C). 1991. text ed. 60.00 (*0-7855-0153-3*, Pub. by Ratna Pustak Bhandar) St Mut.

Raices de la Tierra. Maria Cadilla De Martinez. LC 78-67694. (Folktale Ser.). reprint ed. 37.50 (*0-404-16065-4*) AMS Pr.

***Raices del Alma Cubana.** Florinda Alzaga. (SPA.). pap. 15.00 (*0-89729-051-8*) Ediciones.

***Raices en el Corazon.** Enrique J. Ventura. (SPA.). pap. 6.00 (*0-89729-058-5*) Ediciones.

***Raices Teologicas del Pentecostalismo.** Donald W. Dayton. Ed. by C. Rene Padilla. (Nueva Creacion Ser.). (SPA.). pap. 13.00 (*0-8028-0921-9*, Neuva Creacion) Eerdmans.

Raices y Alas (Poesias Para Ninos y Jovenes) Nieves Del Rosario Marquez. LC 81-65415. (Coleccion Espejo de Paciencia). (Illus.). (Orig.). (J). (gr. 6). 1981. pap. 5.00 (*0-89729-289-8*) Ediciones.

***Raid.** Eickhoff. LC 96-44308. 1997. 22.95 (*0-312-86238-5*) St Martin.

Raid. Eric Helm. (Super Vietnam: Ground Zero Ser.: No. 1). 352p. 1988. pap. 3.95 (*0-373-60501-3*) Harlequin Bks.

Raid. Benjamin F. Schemmer. 360p. 1986. mass mkt. 4.95 (*0-380-69942-7*) Avon.

Raid. G. Clifton Wisler. 128p. (J). (gr. 5 up). 1994. pap. 3.99 (*0-14-036937-6*) Puffin Bks.

Raid see Heinemann Guided Readers

Ra'id Al Tabbakin: Art of Cooking. Salim S. Hamzah. (Illus.). 191p. (ARA.). 1978. 15.00 (*0-86685-291-3*, LDL2913, Pub. by Librairie du Liban FR) Intl Bk Ctr.

Raid & Other Stories. Leo Tolstoy. Ed. by Aylmer Maude & Louise Maude. (World's Classics Paperback Ser.). 416p. 1982. pap. 7.95 (*0-19-281584-9*) OUP.

Raid & Other Stories. Leo Tolstoy. 23.95 (*0-8488-0647-6*) Amereon Ltd.

RAID Book: A Handbook of Storage Systems Technology. 6th ed. Raid Advisory Board Staff. Ed. by Paul Massiglia. 300p. 1996. pap. 39.95 (*1-57398-028-5*) Peer-to-Peer Communications.

Raid of the Confederate Cavalry Through Central Tennessee in October, 1863, Commanded by General Joseph Wheeler: A Paper Read Before the Ohio Commandery of the Loyal Legion. William L. Curry. Ed. by George R. Stewart. LC 87-37511. (Eyewitness Accounts of the Civil War Ser.). (Illus.). 24p. (C). 1987. reprint ed. pap. 10.00 (*0-942301-03-X*) Birm Pub Lib.

Raid of the Guerrilla, & Other Stories. Mary N. Murfree. LC 71-150556. (Short Story Index Reprint Ser.). (Illus.). 1977. reprint ed. 23.95 (*0-8369-3853-4*) Ayer.

Raid on Cabanatuan. Forrest B. Johnson. Ed. by Chiaki Takeuchi. (Illus.). 330p. (Orig.). 1988. 24.95 (*1-882032-01-2*) Thousand Autumns Pr.

Raid on Cabanatuan. Forrest B. Johnson. 314p. 1988. 24.95 (*0-929032-01-2*) Thousand Autumns Pr.

Raid on Dolores: Sweet Memories of a Mining Time Long Gone. Antonio Flores. (Illus.). 128p. 1995. pap. 14.95 (*1-880047-29-2*) Creative Des.

Raid on Qaddafi: The Untold Story of History's Longest Fighter Mission by the Pilot Who Directed It. Robert E. Venkus. 1993. mass mkt. 4.99 (*0-312-92998-6*) St Martin.

Raid on Truman. John T. Campbell. 336p. 1992. mass mkt. 4.99 (*0-380-71816-2*) Avon.

Raider. Jude Deveraux. 1991. mass mkt. 6.99 (*0-671-74381-3*) PB.

Raider Recipes. David Fleming & Dawn Fleming. 202p. (Orig.). 1991. reprint ed. 10.95 (*0-9628191-0-7*) D Fleming Pub.

Raider Sixteen. Edwin P. Hoyt. 216p. 1988. pap. 3.95 (*0-380-75449-5*) Avon.

Raiders. Harold Robbins. 1995. 23.00 (*0-671-87289-3*) S&S Trade.

Raiders. Harold Robbins. 1995. pap. 6.99 (*0-671-87293-1*, PB Trade Paper) PB.

Raiders. large type ed. Harold Robbins. 1995. 24.95 (*1-56895-262-7*, Compass) Wheeler Pub.

Raider's Bride. Kimberly Cates. Ed. by Linda Marrow. 320p. (Orig.). 1994. mass mkt. 5.50 (*0-671-75508-0*) PB.

Raider's Daughter. Kimberly Cates. Ed. by Linda Marrow. 320p. (Orig.). 1994. mass mkt. 5.50 (*0-671-75509-9*) PB.

Raiders from the Frontier. A. Brooke Lindsay, III. Ed. by Terry K. Amthor. (Space Master Ser.). (Illus.). 64p. (Orig.). (C). 1989. pap. 9.00 (*1-55806-026-X*, 9800) Iron Crown Ent Inc.

Raiders from the Sea. John Lodwick. (Illus.). 256p. 1990. 24.95 (*1-55750-525-X*) Naval Inst Pr.

Raiders of Cardolan. Jeffrey McKeage. Ed. by Coleman Charlton. (Middle-Earth Ready-to-Run Adventure Ser.). (Illus.). 32p. (Orig.). (YA). (gr. 10-12). 1988. pap. 6.00 (*1-55806-005-7*, 8108) Iron Crown Ent Inc.

***Raiders of Gor.** John Norman. 1997. mass mkt. 6.95 (*1-56333-558-1*, Masquerade SF) Masquerade.

Raiders of the Deep. Lowell Thomas. 26.95 (*0-8488-0642-5*) Amereon Ltd.

Raiders of the Deep. Lowell Thomas. (Classics of Naval Literature Ser.). (Illus.). 402p. 1994. 32.95 (*1-55750-722-8*) Naval Inst Pr.

***Raiders of the Lost Ark.** (Indiana Jones Roleplaying Game Ser.). 25.00 (*0-87431-428-3*, 45003) West End Games.

Raiders of the Lost Ark. Campbell Clark. 192p. 1987. mass mkt. 4.99 (*0-345-35375-7*) Ballantine.

Raiders of the Lost Bark: A Collection of Canine Cartoons. Shoebox Greetings Staff. (Illus.). 96p. (Orig.). 1993. pap. 6.95 (*0-8362-1731-4*) Andrews & McMeel.

Raiders of the Lost Bark: A Collection of Canine Cartoons. Shoebox Greetings Staff. (Illus.). 72p. (Orig.). 1991. pap. 5.95 (*0-87529-642-4*) Hallmark.

***Raiders of the Reich.** Martin Bowman & Theo Bolten. LC 97-3953. (Illus.). 256p. 1997. 29.95 (*0-7603-0391-6*) Motorbooks Intl.

Raiders of the Rimrock. large type ed. Luke Short. LC 95-24422. 239p. 1996. 21.95 (*0-7838-1467-4*, GK Hall) Thorndike Pr.

Raiders of White Pine. large type ed. Lew Smith. (Linford Western Library). 1991. pap. 15.99 (*0-7089-7019-2*) Ulverscroft.

Raiders of 1862. James D. Brewer. LC 96-24333. 224p. 1997. text ed. 39.95 (*0-275-95404-8*, Praeger Pubs) Greenwood.

Raiders or Elite Infantry? The Changing Role of the U. S. Army Rangers from Dieppe to Grenada. David W. Hogan, Jr. LC 92-5422. (Contributions in Military Studies: No. 128). 296p. 1992. text ed. 49.95 (*0-313-26803-7*, HHA, Greenwood Pr) Greenwood.

Raiding the Borders. Marion Lomax. 66p. 1996. pap. 15.95 (*1-85224-352-X*, Pub. by Bloodaxe Bks UK) Dufour.

Raiding the Icebox: Reflections on Twentieth-Century Culture. Peter Wollen. LC 92-44592. 230p. 1993. 35.00 (*0-253-36587-2*); pap. 15.95 (*0-253-20770-3*) Ind U Pr.

***Raiding the Reich: The Allied Strategic Bombing Offensive in Europe.** Roger A. Freeman. (Illus.). 160p. 1997. 29.95 (*1-85409-387-8*, Pub. by Arms & Armour UK) Sterling.

***Raiding the Southwest Conference: The Collective History of Red Raider Sports in the Southwest Conference.** Ed. by Gina Augustini et al. (Illus.). 176p. 1996. 39.95 (*0-9653513-0-0*) Tex Tech Univ Pr.

Raids. (Illus.). 230p. 1991. 18.00 (*0-939235-04-8*) Spec Trning Unit.

An Asterisk (*) at the beginning of an entry indicates that the title is appearing in BIP for the first time.

Raids on the Unspeakable. Thomas Merton. LC 66-17823. 1966. pap. 9.95 (0-8112-0101-5, NDP213) New Directions.

Raids on the Unspeakable. Thomas Merton. 142p. 1994. pap. 21.00 (0-86012-046-5, Pub. by Srch Pr UK) St Mut.

***Railway Revolution, 8 vols.** Ed. by Mark Casson. (Origins of Business Economics Ser.). 2000p. (C). 1997. text ed. 735.00 (0-415-15088-4) Routledge.

Raik. Ray DiPalma. LC 89-62801. (Roof Bks.). 108p. (Orig.). 1989. pap. 9.95 (0-937804-37-1) Segue NYC.

Raikes Bear & Doll Story. 2nd rev. ed. Linda Mullins. (Illus.). 120p. 1993. 22.95 (0-87588-412-1) Hobby Hse.

***Rail.** Mark Sumner. 1997. mass mkt. write for info. (0-614-20506-9, Del Rey) Ballantine.

Rail & Road in East Africa: Transport Coordination in Undeveloped Countries. Arthur Hazelwood. LC 65-6406. (Illus.). xiii, 247p. 1964. 37.50 (0-678-06271-4) Kelley.

Rail Book Bibliography: A Comprehensive Guide & Index. LC 72-96485. (Illus.). 1972. 7.50 (0-913556-01-7); pap. 5.00 (0-913556-00-9) Spec Pr NJ.

Rail Fence Quilt, for Kids of All Ages. Luann Stout. (Illus.). 48p. 1993. 8.95 (0-922705-44-5) Quilt Day.

Rail Fences & Apple Butter Days. Raymond J. Libert. 160p. 1996. 13.00 (0-8059-3839-7) Dorrance.

Rail Fences, Rolling Pins & Rainbows. Lois Costomiris. 254p. 1994. 20.00 (1-878208-25-X) Guild Pr IN.

Rail Kings. Jim Walker. (Wells Fargo Trail Ser.: Bk. 3). 304p. 1995. pap. 8.99 (1-55661-430-6) Bethany Hse.

***Rail Lines of Northern New England.** Robert M. Lindsell. (New England Rail Heritage Ser.: Vol. 3). (Illus.). 375p. (Orig.). 1997. pap. write for info. (0-942147-06-5) Branch Line Pr.

Rail Lines of Southern New England: A Handbook of Railroad History. Ronald D. Karr. LC 93-90147. (New England Rail Heritage Ser.: No. 2). (Illus.). 384p. (Orig.). 1995. pap. 22.95 (0-942147-02-2) Branch Line Pr.

Rail Mass Transit for Developing Countries. 393p. 1990. text ed. 105.00 (0-7277-1560-7, Pub. by T Telford UK) Am Soc Civil Eng.

Rail Quality & Maintenance for Modern Railway Operation. Ed. by J. J. Kalker et al. LC 93-893. 464p. (C). 1993. lib. bdg. 166.50 (0-7923-2263-0) Kluwer Ac.

Rail Steels: Developments Processing & Use, STP 644. Ed. by D. H. Stone & G. G. Knupp. 488p. 1978. 45.00 (0-8031-0545-2) ASTM.

Rail-Trail Guide to California: Recreation Trails on Railroad Grades. Fred Wert. (Illus.). 192p. (Orig.). 1995. pap. 12.95 (1-883195-02-0) Infinity WA.

***Rail Trail Handbook.** Bruce Blair. 1996. pap. 13.95 (0-931714-71-0) Nodin Pr.

Rail Trails along the Greenbrier River. Jim Hudson. (Illus.). 124p. (Orig.). 1996. pap. 8.95 (0-9646197-3-3) Quarrier Pr.

Rail Transit Philadelphia: The PTC Years, 1940-1968. Henry Elsner & Richard Viable. (Illus.). 72p. (Orig.). 1992. pap. 32.95 (0-934088-28-4) NJ Intl Inc.

Rail Transit Station Area Development: Small Area Modeling in Washington, DC. Rodney D. Green & David M. James. LC 91-12343. 352p. (gr. 13). 1992. text ed. 79.95 (0-87332-696-2) M E Sharpe.

Rail Transport of Solid Wastes. (Special Reports: No. 40). 150p. 1970. 10.00 (0-917084-10-1) Am Public Works.

***Rail Transportation: Proceedings, ASME International Mechanical Engineering Congress & Exposition, Atlanta, GA, 1996.** Ed. by Daniel H. Stone. LC 96-78678. (RTD Ser.: Vol. 12). 131p. 1996. pap. 72.00 (0-7918-1536-6, TF5) ASME.

Rail Transportation: 1994 International Mechanical Engineering Congress & Exposition, Chicago, Illinois - November 6-11, 1994. (RTD Ser.: Vol. 8). 200p. 1994. 74.00 (0-7918-1452-1, G00947) ASME.

Rail Transportation - 1995 Vol. 10: Rail Transportation - 1995. Ed. by R. R. Newman. (1995 ASME International Mechanical Engineering Congress & Exposition Ser.: RTD-Vol. 10). 164p. 1995. 56.00 (0-7918-1744-X, H01024) ASME.

Rail Transportation Proceedings, 1973: Papers & Discussions from Joint ASME-IEEE Railroad Conference, St. Louis, Missouri, April 11-12, 1973, Winter Annual Meeting of the ASME, New York, NY, November 26-30, 1972. American Society of Mechanical Engineers Staff. LC 72-139216. 277p. reprint ed. pap. 79.00 (0-8357-8754-0, 2033625) Bks Demand.

Rail Transportation 1992. LC 93-102639. (RTD Ser.: Vol. 5). 183p. 1992. pap. 52.50 (0-7918-1123-9, G00767) ASME.

Rail Transportation, 1993: Proceedings, Vol. 6. LC 89-46368. 237p. 1993. pap. 55.00 (0-7918-0696-0) ASME Pr.

Rail-Truck Intermodal Transportation Research, 1983. (Bibliography Ser.: No. 60). 41p. 1983. 7.00 (0-309-03616-X) Transport Res Bd.

Rail Ventures: The Comprehensive Guide to Train Travel in North America. 7th ed. Jack Swanson. (Illus.). 400p. (Orig.). 1996. pap. 18.95 (0-614-10988-4) Travis Ilse.

Rail Ventures: The Comprehensive Guide to Train Travel in North America. 7th ed. Jack Swanson. 420p. 1996. pap. text ed. 18.95 (1-882092-18-X) Travis Ilse.

Railbike: Cycling on Abandoned Railroads. Bob Mellin. LC 95-94676. (Illus.). 144p. (Orig.). 1996. pap. 16.95 (0-935902-29-5) Balboa Pub.

Railbird. Rex Jones. (Illus.). 157p. 1984. pap. 6.95 (0-89746-028-6) Gambling Times.

Railfan's Guide to Kansas Attractions. Robert Collins. (Illus.). (Orig.). 1996. pap. 7.95 (0-942035-37-2) South Platte.

Railing Against the Rush of Years: A Personal Journey Through Aging Via Art Therapy, Poems, Paintings, & Prose. Claire Ridker & Patricia Savage. LC 96-24802. 1996. pap. 15.95 (1-884206-02-6) Unfinish Monumnt.

Railroad & the Canyon. Rudy J. Gerber. LC 93-50208. 128p. 1994. pap. 9.95 (0-88289-986-4) Pelican.

Railroad & the City: A Technological & Urbanistic History of Cincinnati. Carl W. Condit. LC 76-55346. (Illus.). 347p. 1977. 47.50 (0-8142-0265-9) Ohio St U Pr.

Railroad Book. E. Boyd Smith. (Illus.). 56p. (J). (gr. 3-5). 1983. 18.95 (0-395-34832-3) HM.

***Railroad Bridges in the Heartland.** Stanley A. Changnon. (Illus.). 217p. (Orig.). 1997. pap. text ed. 30.00 (0-9631811-1-4) S A Changnon.

Railroad Caboose. William F. Knapke & Freeman Hubbard. LC 67-28316. (Illus.). (J). (gr. 10 up). 1968. 34.95 (0-87095-011-8) Gldn West Bks.

Railroad Capitalization. James C. Bonbright. LC 70-78003. (Columbia University. Studies in the Social Sciences: No. 215). reprint ed. 47.50 (0-404-51215-1) AMS Pr.

Railroad Caretaker. Jack Rudman. (Career Examination Ser.: C-684). 1994. pap. 23.95 (0-8373-0684-1) Nat Learn.

Railroad Clerk. Jack Rudman. (Career Examination Ser.: C-661). 1994. pap. 23.95 (0-8373-0661-2) Nat Learn.

Railroad Clerk. 3rd ed. Ed. by Hy Hammer. LC 82-18431. 176p. (Orig.). 1984. pap. 9.00 (0-668-05643-6, Arco) Macmillan Gen Ref.

Railroad Collectibles. 4th ed. Stanley Baker. 1996. pap. 14.95 (0-89145-410-1) Collector Bks.

Railroad Competition & the Oil Trade: 1855-1873. Rolland H. Maybee. LC 73-16234. (Perspectives in American History Ser.: No. 16). (Illus.). x, 451p. 1974. reprint ed. lib. bdg. 49.50 (0-87991-341-X) Porcupine Pr.

***Railroad Conference: Proceedings ASME/IEEE Joint Railroad Conference, Oakbrook, IL, 1996.** Ed. by Anthony R. Hiatt & Norman Vutz. LC 90-644036. 254p. 1996. pap. 90.00 (0-7918-1229-4, 71461) ASME Pr.

Railroad Consolidation under the Transportation Act of 1920. William N. Leonard. LC 68-58602. (Columbia University. Studies in the Social Sciences: No. 522). reprint ed. 29.50 (0-404-51522-3) AMS Pr.

Railroad Consolidation West of the Mississippi River. Stuart Daggett. Ed. by Stuart Bruchey. LC 80-1302. (Railroads Ser.). (Illus.). 1981. reprint ed. lib. bdg. 15.95 (0-405-13771-0) Ayer.

Railroad Crossing: Californians & the Railroad. William Deverell. LC 92-40128. (Illus.). 278p. (C). 1996. pap. 13.95 (0-520-20505-7) U CA Pr.

Railroad Crossing: Californians & the Railroad, 1850-1910. William Deverell. LC 92-40128. 1994. 30.00 (0-520-08214-1) U CA Pr.

Railroad Engineering, Vol. 1. 2nd ed. William W. Hay. LC 81-23117. 758p. 1982. text ed. 145.00 (0-471-36400-2, Wiley-Interscience) Wiley.

Railroad Equipment Inspector. Jack Rudman. (Career Examination Ser.: C-210). 1994. pap. 27.95 (0-8373-0210-2) Nat Learn.

Railroad Era: Business Competition & the Public Interest. G. Dale Greenawald. (Public Issues Ser.). (Illus.). 68p. (Orig.). (YA). (gr. 9-12). 1991. pap. 3.00 (0-89994-360-8); teacher ed., pap. 2.00 (0-89994-361-6) Soc Sci Ed.

Railroad Ferries of the Hudson & the Stories of a Deckhand. Raymond J. Baxter. Ed. by Arthur G. Adams. (Illus.). 264p. 29.95 (0-317-62578-0) Lind Pubns.

***Railroad for Lima: New York State's Unique Shortline - the Lima & Honeoye Falls Railroad.** Paul S. Worboys. (Illus.). 80p. 1992. pap. 8.50 (0-614-26401-4) Purple Mnt Pr.

Railroad Freight Transportation Research Needs (CP 2) Ed. by Luanne Crayton. (Conference Proceedings Ser.). (Illus.). 160p. 1994. pap. text ed. 29.00 (0-309-05503-2) Transport Res Bd.

Railroad General. Patricia T. Davis. 238p. 1994. text ed. write for info. (0-9640329-0-2) Metro Printing.

Railroad History: Essays on Entrepreneurial & Managerial Ability & Performance. Charles J. Kennedy et al. 200p. 1988. 45.50 (0-935662-02-2); write for info. (0-935662-03-0) EBHA Pr.

Railroad History Index, Nineteen Twenty-One to Nineteen Eighty-Four. Ed. by Thomas T. Taber, III. (Illus.). 176p. (Orig.). 1985. pap. 12.50 (0-9616102-0-4) Railway Loco Hist.

Railroad in American Art. Ed. by Susan Danly & Leo Marx. (Illus.). 1988. 45.00 (0-262-23126-3) MIT Pr.

Railroad Inspector. Jack Rudman. (Career Examination Ser.: C-685). 1994. pap. 27.95 (0-8373-0685-X) Nat Learn.

Railroad Issues: A Peer-Reviewed Publication of the Transportation Research Board. LC 92-25493. (Transportation Research Record Ser.: No. 1341). 82p. 1992. 21.00 (0-309-05207-6) Transport Res Bd.

Railroad Labor Board: Its History, Activities & Organization. Joshua Bernhardt. LC 72-3037. (Brookings Institution. Institute for Government Research. Service Monographs of the U. S. Government: No. 19). reprint ed. 21.50 (0-404-57119-0) AMS Pr.

Railroad Land Grants. American Bar Association, Natural Resources Law Staff. LC 87-70130. 121p. 1987. pap. 29.95 (0-89707-284-7, 535-0011) Amer Bar Assn.

Railroad Law a Decade after Deregulation. Frank J. Dooley & William E. Thoms. LC 94-8539. 208p. 1994. text ed. 55.00 (0-89930-631-4, Quorum Bks) Greenwood.

Railroad Law Digest. 2nd ed. R. V. Laverty. Ed. by J. R. Laverty. lib. bdg. 47.00 (0-318-04011-5) J R Laverty.

Railroad Maps of North America: The First Hundred Years. Andrew M. Modelski. LC 82-675134. 186p. 1984. 28.00 (0-8444-0396-2, 030-004-00021-3) Lib Congress.

Railroad Maps of North America: The First 100 Years. (Americana Ser.). 1986. lib. bdg. 85.00 (0-8490-3798-0) Gordon Pr.

Railroad Mergers & Abandonments. Michael Conant. LC 82-15834. (Publications of the Institute of Business & Economic Research, University of California). xiii, 212p. 1982. reprint ed. text ed. 55.00 (0-313-23694-1, CORAM, Greenwood Pr) Greenwood.

Railroad Mergers & the Coming of Conrail. Richard Saunders. LC 77-91095. (Contributions in Economics & Economic History Ser.: No. 19). (Illus.). 389p. 1978. text ed. 29.95 (0-313-20049-1, SRM/, Greenwood Pr) Greenwood.

***Railroad Mergers & the Language of Unification.** James B. Burns. LC 97-21854. 1998. text ed. write for info. (1-56720-166-0, Quorum Bks) Greenwood.

Railroad Night Scene. Preston Cook. (Illus.). 128p. 1991. 44.00 (1-879314-06-1) Old Line Graph.

Railroad Passenger Car: An Illustrated History of the First Hundred Years, with Accounts by Contemporary Passengers. August Mencken. LC 57-13290. 223p. reprint ed. pap. 63.60 (0-317-11162-0, 2002915) Bks Demand.

Railroad Photographs of Alfred A. Hart, Artist. Mead Kibbey. Ed. by Peter Palmquist. (Illus.). 1995. 55.00 (0-929722-85-X) CA State Library Fndtn.

Railroad Photography: How to Shoot Like the Pros. Mike Blaszak & Mike Schafer. (Illus.). 64p. (Orig.). 1993. pap. text ed. 24.95 (0-944119-10-7) Andover Junction.

Railroad Porter. Jack Rudman. (Career Examination Ser.: C-662). 1994. pap. 23.95 (0-8373-0662-0) Nat Learn.

Railroad Postcards in the Age of Steam. H. Roger Grant. LC 94-14552. (Illus.). 217p. 1994. 29.95 (0-87745-465-5) U of Iowa Pr.

Railroad Promotion & Capitalization in the United States. Frederick A. Cleveland & Fred W. Powell. Ed. by Stuart Bruchey. LC 80-1698. (Railroads Ser.). 1981. reprint ed. lib. bdg. 38.95 (0-405-13770-2) Ayer.

Railroad Protective Liability. Ed. by Diana Kowatch. 40p. 1996. 10.00 (1-56461-166-3) Rough Notes.

Railroad Question. William Larrabee. LC 76-150190. (Select Bibliographies Reprint Ser.). 1977. 25.95 (0-8369-5703-2) Ayer.

Railroad Radio: Hearing & Understanding Railroad Radio Communications & Systems. Vincent Reh. LC 96-96107. (Illus.). 208p. (Orig.). 1996. pap. 19.95 (0-9651599-0-6) Byron Hill.

Railroad Regulation Issues, Rail Passenger Services, Railroad Bridges, & Track Maintenance Management. (Transportation Research Record Ser.: No. 1177). 123p. 1988. 18.50 (0-309-04721-8) Transport Res Bd.

Railroad Reorganization. Stuart Daggett. LC 67-18576. (Library of Early American Business & Industry: No. 9). x, 404p. 1967. reprint ed. 49.50 (0-678-00239-8) Kelley.

***Railroad Safety: Continued Emphasis Needed for an Effective Track Safety Inspection Program.** (Illus.). 60p. 1994. pap. text ed. 35.00 (1-57979-087-9) BPI Info Servs.

Railroad Safety: Continued Emphasis Needed for an Effective Track Safety Inspection Program. Kenneth M. Mead. (Illus.). 60p. (Orig.). (C). 1994. pap. text ed. 25.00 (0-7881-1466-2) DIANE Pub.

Railroad Safety: Status of Efforts to Improve Railroad Crossing Safety. 58p. (Orig.). (C). 1996. pap. text ed. 20.00 (0-7881-2939-2) DIANE Pub.

***Railroad Schemes.** Holland. LC 97-19555. 1997. 23.95 (0-312-86405-1) St Martin.

Railroad Signal Specialist. Jack Rudman. (Career Examination Ser.: C-663). 1994. pap. 27.95 (0-8373-0663-9) Nat Learn.

Railroad Signatures Across the Pacific Northwest. Carlos A. Schwantes. LC 93-6505. (Illus.). 360p. 1993. 70.00 (0-295-97210-6) U of Wash Pr.

Railroad Signatures Across the Pacific Northwest. Carlos A. Schwantes. LC 93-6505. (Illus.). 360p. 1996. pap. 35.00 (0-295-97535-0) U of Wash Pr.

Railroad Sirens. Allan N. Campbell. 1979. 8.95 (0-533-03906-1) C I L Inc.

Railroad Spikes: A Collectors Guide. James M. Joyce. LC 85-2805. (Illus.). 64p. (Orig.). 1985. pap. 6.95 (0-915010-33-X) Sutter House.

Railroad Station: An Architectural History. Carroll L. Meeks. LC 95-2517. (Illus.). 320p. 1995. pap. text ed. 12.95 (0-486-28627-4) Dover.

Railroad Stations of Oregon. Lewis L. Mcarthur & Cynthia B. Gardiner. LC 96-21275. 137p. 1996. 20.00 (0-87595-261-5) Oregon Hist.

Railroad Stations of Pennsylvania, Vol. 1. James D. Van Trump. (Illus.). 48p. 1992. pap. 9.95 (0-9631050-0-0) Safe Harbour.

Railroad Stock Assistant. Jack Rudman. (Career Examination Ser.: C-1448). 1994. pap. 23.95 (0-8373-1448-8) Nat Learn.

Railroad Stockman. Jack Rudman. (Career Examination Ser.: C-664). 1994. pap. 23.95 (0-8373-0664-7) Nat Learn.

Railroad Street. Bruce Hunsberger. 1970. 5.95 (0-8184-0116-8) Carol Pub Group.

***Railroad Telegrapher's Handbook.** Tom French. 60p. 1991. pap. 9.95 (1-890024-02-3, RTH) Artifax Bks.

Railroad That Came out at Night. Frank Kyper. (Hobby Bks.: No. C-65). (Illus.). 76p. 1990. pap. 12.95 (0-911868-65-8) Carstens Pubns.

Railroad That Died at Sea: The Florida East Coast's Key West Extension. Pat Parks. LC 68-54448. (Illus.). 48p. 1986. reprint ed. pap. 6.95 (0-911607-05-6) Langley Pr Inc.

***Railroad Through the Back of Beyond: The Murphy Branch Also Known As the Great Smoky Mountains Railroad.** Mead Parce. Ed. by Alice Lawson. (Illus.). 128p. (Orig.). 1997. pap. 8.95 (0-9657461-1-9) Harmon Den.

Railroad Ties: Industry & Culture in Hagerstown, Maryland. Ed. by Susan Levitas. LC 94-33071. (Illus.). 64p. 1994. pap. 14.00 (1-878399-64-0, MD Hist Trust) Div Hist Cult Progs.

Railroad Timetables, Travel Brochures & Posters: A History & Guide for Collectors. Brad S. Lomazzi. (Illus.). 194p. 1995. 49.95 (0-9614876-8-2) Golden Hl Pr NY.

Railroad to the Pacific. Edwin Johnson. 186p. 1982. 19.95 (0-87770-264-0) Ye Galleon.

Railroad Toad. Susan Schade & Jon Buller. LC 92-23303. (Step into Reading Bks.: Step 1). (Illus.). 32p. (J). (ps-1). 1993. pap. 3.99 (0-679-83934-8) Random Bks Yng Read.

Railroad Track & Structure Inspector. Jack Rudman. (Career Examination Ser.: C-209). 1994. pap. 27.95 (0-8373-0209-9) Nat Learn.

Railroad Track Mechanics & Technology: Proceedings of Symposium Princeton University 4-75. A. Kerr. LC 77-548. 1978. 192.00 (0-08-021923-3, Pub. by Pergamon Repr UK) Franklin.

Railroad Transportation in Texas. Charles Potts. 1993. reprint ed. lib. bdg. 75.00 (0-7812-5895-2) Rprt Serv.

Railroad Transportation Issues. (Research Record Ser.: No. 1241). 52p. 1989. 9.00 (0-309-04965-2) Transport Res Bd.

Railroad Travel & the State of Business. Thor Hultgren. (Occasional Papers: No. 13). 40p. 1943. reprint ed. 20.00 (0-685-61245-7); reprint ed. mic. film 20.00 (0-685-61246-5) Natl Bur Econ Res.

Railroad War: N. B. Forrest's 1864 Raid Through Northern Alabama & Middle Tennessee. Robert Dunnavant, Jr. Ed. by Roland Langley. LC 94-61417. (Illus.). 180p. (Orig.). 1994. pap. 16.95 (0-9642084-0-7) Pea Ridge Pr.

Railroad Watches Identification & Price Guide - 95. Roy Ehrhardt. (Illus.). 180p. 1995. spiral bd. 35.00 (0-913902-88-8) Heart Am Pr.

Railroad Welding Specification (D15.1-93) (Illus.). 318p. 1993. pap. text ed. 105.00 (0-87171-403-5) Am Welding.

Railroad Wrecks. Edgar A. Haine. LC 92-53956. 1994. 29.50 (0-8453-4844-2, Cornwall Bks) Assoc Univ Prs.

Railroaded to Resurrection. Donald De Simone. 204p. 1982. 19.95 (0-88280-099-X) ETC Pubns.

Railroader. Fred W. Cottrell. (Russell Sage Foundation Reprint Ser.). 1971. reprint ed. lib. bdg. 19.00 (0-697-00210-1) Irvington.

Railroaders. L. Matthews. (Wild West in American History Ser.). (Illus.). 32p. (J). (gr. 3-8). 1989. 13.50 (0-685-67677-3); lib. bdg. 18.00 (0-86625-366-1) Rourke Corp.

Railroading. (Illus.). 48p. (J). (gr. 6-12). 1978. pap. 2.40 (0-8395-3292-X, 33292) BSA.

Railroading at Its Wildest. R. J. Fitch. (Illus.). 176p. 1993. 32.50 (0-86417-496-9, Pub. by Kangaroo Pr AT) Seven Hills Bk.

Railroading in Southern Oregon & the Founding of Medford. Bert Webber. 256p. 1985. pap. 14.95 (0-87770-352-3) Ye Galleon.

Railroading in Texas: One Man's Memories. Fred W. Picker. (Illus.). 152p. 1996. 16.00 (0-8059-3908-3) Dorrance.

Railroading in the Carolina Sandhills: The 19th Century (1825-1900), Vol. 1. S. David Carriker. (Illus.). 224p. 1985. 40.00 (0-936013-01-X) Herit Pub NC.

Railroading in the Carolina Sandhills: The 20th Century (1900-1985), 5 vols. S. David Carriker. (Illus.). 812p. 1996. pap. 140.00 (0-936013-00-1) Herit Pub NC.

Railroading in the Carolina Sandhills: The 20th Century (1900-1985), Vol. 2. S. David Carriker. (Illus.). 272p. 1987. 40.00 (0-936013-02-8) Herit Pub NC.

Railroading in the Carolina Sandhills Vol. 5: Sandhill Maps for Hiking & Study for South Carolina. Ed. by S. David Carriker. (Illus.). 84p. (Orig.). 1996. pap. text ed. 20.00 (0-936013-05-2) Herit Pub NC.

Railroading in the Carolina Sandhills, Vol. 3: The Hoffman & Troy Railroad. S. David Carriker. (Illus.). 104p. 1992. pap. text ed. 20.00 (0-936013-03-6) Herit Pub NC.

Railroading in the Carolina Sandhills, Vol. 4: Sandhill Maps for Hiking & Study for North Carolina. Ed. by S. David Carriker. (Illus.). 128p. 1992. pap. text ed. 20.00 (0-936013-04-4) Herit Pub NC.

Railroading in the Rockies a Half Century Ago. Ted Wurm et al. LC 70-102682. (Colorado Rail Annual Ser.: No. 18). (Illus.). 220p. 1990. 39.95 (0-918654-18-1) CO RR Mus.

Railroading with American Flyer. 1989. pap. 3.95 (0-911581-10-3) Heimburger Hse Pub.

Railroads. Don Ball, Jr. (Illus.). 1985. 37.50 (0-393-02236-6) Norton.

Railroads. Rose Griffiths. (First Step Math Ser.). (Illus.). 32p. (J). (gr. 1 up). 1995. lib. bdg. 18.60 (0-8368-1182-8) Gareth Stevens Inc.

Railroads. T. Harvey. LC 79-5062. (Question & Answer Bks.). (Illus.). 36p. (J). (gr. 3-6). 1980. pap. 4.95 (0-8225-9539-7, Lerner Publctns) Lerner Group.

Railroads: Bridging the Continents. Lois Warburton. LC 91-23857. (Encyclopedia of Discovery & Invention Ser.). (Illus.). 96p. (J). (gr. 5-8). 1991. lib. bdg. 18.96 (1-56006-216-9) Lucent Bks.

Railroads: Finance & Organization. William Z. Ripley. Ed. by Stuart Bruchey. LC 80-1699. (Railroads Ser.). (Illus.). 1981. reprint ed. lib. bdg. 60.95 (0-405-13823-7) Ayer.

Railroads: Pioneers in Modern Management, an Original Anthology. Ed. by Alfred D. Chandler, Jr. LC 79-7528. (History of Management Thought & Practice Ser.). 1980. lib. bdg. 27.95 (0-405-12312-4) Ayer.

R

Railroads: Rates & Regulation. William Z. Ripley. LC 73-2532. (Big Business; Economic Power in a Free Society Ser.). 1973. reprint ed. 42.95 (*0-405-05110-7*) Ayer.

Railroads: The Free Enterprise Alternative. Daniel L. Overbey. LC 82-7503. (Illus.). 296p. 1982. text ed. 49.95 (*0-89930-031-6*, OVR/, Quorum Bks) Greenwood.

Railroads: The Nation's First Big Business Sources & Readings. Ed. by Alfred D. Chandler, Jr. & Stuart Bruchey. LC 80-1298. (Railroads Ser.). 1981. reprint ed. lib. bdg. 23.95 (*0-405-13768-0*) Ayer.

Railroads: Their Origin & Problems. Charles F. Adams, Jr. Ed. by Stuart Bruchey. LC 80-1294. (Railroads Ser.). 1981. reprint ed. lib. bdg. 23.95 (*0-405-13764-8*) Ayer.

Railroads: Their Origin & Problems. Charles F. Adams, Jr. (Works of Charles Francis Adams Jr. (1835-1915)). 1989. reprint ed. lib. bdg. 79.00 (*0-7812-1406-8*) Rprt Serv.

Railroads: Their Rise & Fall. Herbert E. Bixler. 115p. (Orig.). 1982. pap. 7.95 (*0-9610066-0-9*) H E Bixler.

Railroads & American Economic Growth: Essays in Econometric History. Robert W. Fogel. LC 64-25069. (Illus.). 315p. reprint ed. pap. 89.80 (*0-8357-7663-8*, 2056990) Bks Demand.

Railroads & Clearcuts: Legacy of Congress's 1864 Northern Pacific Railroad Land Grant. Derrick Jensen & George Draffan. (Illus.). 248p. (Orig.). 1995. pap. 15.00 (*1-879628-08-2*) Keokee ID.

Railroads & Clearcuts: Legacy of Congress's 1864 Northern Pacific Railroad Land Grant: A Photographic Essay. Derrick Jensen & George Draffan. (Illus.). 40p. (Orig.). 1995. pap. 5.00 (*1-879628-09-0*) Keokee ID.

Railroads & Railroad Towns in New Mexico. William Clark & Ree Sheck. (Illus.). 48p. 1989. pap. 7.95 (*0-937206-12-1*) New Mexico Mag.

Railroads & the Granger Laws. George H. Miller. LC 75-138059. 308p. reprint ed. pap. 87.80 (*0-8357-4752-2*, 2037674) Bks Demand.

Railroads for Rent: The Local Rail Service Assistance Program. William R. Black. LC 84-48546. 351p. reprint ed. pap. 100.10 (*0-7837-3692-4*, 2057870) Bks Demand.

Railroads, Freight, & Public Policy. Theodore E. Keeler. LC 82-45985. (Studies in the Regulation of Economic Activity). 180p. 1983. 26.95 (*0-8157-4856-6*) Brookings.

Railroads in Early Postcards Vol. 1: Upstate New York. Richard F. Palmer & Harvey N. Roehl. LC 89-70721. (Illus.). 112p. (Orig.). 1990. pap. 11.95 (*0-911572-87-2*) Madison Bks UPA.

Railroads in Early Postcards, Vol. 2: Northern New England. Stephen Boothroyd & Peter Barney. LC 89-70721. (Illus.). 112p. (Orig.). 1992. pap. 11.95 (*1-879511-04-5*) Madison Bks UPA.

***Railroads in New Jersey: The Formative Years.** John T. Cunningham. (Illus.). 328p. 1997. 44.95 (*0-89359-015-0*) Afton Pub.

Railroads in the Age of Regulation, 1900-1980. Ed. by Keith L. Bryant. (Encyclopedia of American Business History & Biography Ser.). (Illus.). 560p. 1988. lib. bdg. 85.00 (*0-8160-1371-3*) Facts on File.

***Railroads in the Heartland: Steam & Traction in the Golden Age of Postcards.** H. Roger Grant. LC 97-16470. (Illus.). 184p. 1997. 29.95 (*0-87745-600-3*) U of Iowa Pr.

Railroads in the Nineteenth Century. Ed. by Robert L. Frey. (Encyclopedia of American Business History & Biography Ser.). (Illus.). 528p. 1989. lib. bdg. 85.00 (*0-8160-2012-4*) Facts on File.

Railroads in the West. Ed. by Don L. Hofsommer. (Illus.). 120p. 1978. pap. text ed. 15.00 (*0-89745-002-7*) Sunflower U Pr.

Railroads in the Woods. John T. Labbe & Vernon Goe. LC 95-52314. 258p. 1995. 39.95 (*0-9647521-0-7*) OSO Pubng.

Railroads of Coors Field. Kenton H. Forrest. LC 95-67794. (Illus.). 48p. 1995. pap. 9.95 (*0-918654-50-5*) CO RR Mus.

***Railroads of Indiana.** Richard S. Simons & Francis H. Parker. LC 97-21579. 1997. write for info. (*0-253-33351-2*) Ind U Pr.

Railroads of Lawrence, Kansas: 1854-1900. I. E. Quastler. (Illus.). pap. 25.00 (*0-87291-094-6*) Coronado Pr.

Railroads of the Adirondacks: A History. Michael Kudish. LC 96-16049. (Illus.). 496p. 1996. lib. bdg. 55.00 (*0-935796-75-4*) Purple Mnt Pr.

Railroads of the Ohio Valley, 4 vols., Set. William A. Harvey. (Illus.). 96p. (Orig.). 1995. write for info. (*0-9640251-7-5*) Silver Brook Junct.

Railroads of the Ohio Valley, 1947-1960 Bk. I: Pittsburgh, PA to Gallipolis, Ohio. Ed. by Dale W. Woodland. (Illus.). 96p. (Orig.). 1996. pap. 21.95 (*0-9640425-1-7*) Silver Brook Junct.

Railroads of the United States. Henry M. Flint. LC 75-22818. (America in Two Centuries Ser.). 1976. reprint ed. 34.95 (*0-405-07690-8*) Ayer.

Railroads of the Yosemite Valley. Hank Johnston & James Law. (Illus.). 206p. 1995. pap. 19.95 (*0-939666-80-4*) Yosemite Assn.

Railroads of Vermont, Vol. I. Robert C. Jones. LC 93-12841. (Illus.). 368p. 1993. 50.00 (*1-881535-01-0*) New Eng Pr VT.

Railroads of Vermont, Vol. II. Robert C. Jones. LC 93-12841. (Illus.). 368p. 1993. 50.00 (*1-881535-02-9*) New Eng Pr VT.

Railroads of Vermont: A Pictorial. Robert C. Jones. LC 94-32181. (Illus.). 368p. 1994. 60.00 (*1-881535-13-4*) New Eng Pr VT.

Railroads One Hundred Years Ago. Abbott & Anon. (Historical Ser.). (Illus.). 1980. pap. 3.50 (*0-89540-048-0*, SB-048) Sun Pub.

Railroads, Reconstruction & the Gospel of Prosperity. Mark W. Summers. LC 83-43094. (Illus.). 376p. 1984. text ed. 60.00 (*0-691-04695-6*) Princeton U Pr.

Railroads Recycled: How Local Initiative & Federal Support Launched the Rails-to-Trails Movement, 1965-1990. Bonnie Nevel & Peter Harnik. 104p. (Orig.). 1990. 12.95 (*0-925794-03-1*) Rails Trails.

Railroads Series, 65 Vols. Ed. by Stuart Bruchey. 1981. lib. bdg.,1,781.00 (*0-405-13750-8*) Ayer.

***Railroads Through the Coeur D'Alenes.** John V. Wood. LC 82-4168. (Illus.). 219p. pap. 62.50 (*0-608-05051-2*, 2059712) Bks Demand.

Railroads Triumphant: The Growth, Rejection, & Rebirth of a Vital American Force. Albro Martin. (Illus.). 448p. 1992. 35.00 (*0-19-503853-3*) OUP.

Rails. Don Ball, Jr. (Illus.). 1981. 24.95 (*0-393-01480-0*) Norton.

Rails Across America: The History of American Railroads. Ed. by Bill Withuhn. (Illus.). 192p. 1993. 24.98 (*0-8317-6482-1*) Smithmark.

Rails Across the Land. Ken J. Charlton. LC 91-71585. (Illus.). 240p. 1991. 41.95 (*0-91581-22-7*) Heimburger Hse Pub.

Rails across the Ranchos: Centennial Edition of the Southern Pacific Coastal Line Railroad Centennial Years. 2nd ed. Loren Nicholson. (California Heritage Ser.). (Illus.). 208p. (Orig.). reprint ed. pap. 18.95 (*0-9623233-6-5*) CA HPA.

Rails Across the Tundra: A Historical Album of the Alaska Railroad. Stan B. Cohen. LC 84-60465. (Illus.). 152p. 1984. pap. 9.95 (*0-933126-43-3*) Pictorial Hist.

Rails along the Schuylkill. G. M. Heathcliff & Alvin K. Traz. (Illus.). 72p. 1989. reprint ed. pap. 12.95 (*1-878343-00-9*) E Crist.

Rails Beyond the Rutland. Phil Jordan. (Hobby Bks.: No. C54). (Illus.). 76p. 1988. pap. 12.95 (*0-911868-54-2*, C54) Carstens Pubns.

Rails of the World. S. Dillon Ripley. LC 75-619273. (Illus.). 406p. 1977. 400.00 (*0-87923-199-8*) Godine.

Rails of the World: A Compilation of New Information, 1975-1983 (Aves Hallidae) Sidney Ripley & Bruce M. Beenler. LC 84-600393. (Smithsonian Contribution to Zoology Ser.: No. 417). 32p. reprint ed. pap. 25.00 (*0-317-41853-X*, 2026178) Bks Demand.

Rails, Rivalry, & Romance. Don Banwart. (Illus.). 577p. 39.95 (*0-9601568-7-9*) Historic Pres Bourbon.

Rails That Climb: The Moffat Road. Edward T. Bollinger. Ed. by William C. Jones. LC 79-14634. (Illus.). 344p. 1979. 44.95 (*0-918654-29-7*) CO RR Mus.

Rails to San Francisco Bay. Harre Demoro & Vernon Sappers. 1992. pap. 15.95 (*0-915276-51-8*) Quadrant Pr.

Rails to the Rim: Milepost Guide to the Grand Canyon Railway. rev. ed. Al Richmond. LC 94-75686. (Illus.). 136p. 1996. reprint ed. pap. 6.95 (*0-933269-32-3*) Gd Canyon Railway.

Rails West No. 4: Sierra Passage. Franklin Carter. 272p. (Orig.). 1995. pap. text ed. 4.99 (*0-515-11527-4*) Jove Pubns.

Railway Adventure. L. T. Rolt. (Illus.). 192p. 1992. 30.00 (*0-86299-367-9*, Pub. by Sutton Pubng UK) Bks Intl VA.

Railway Adventures: A Guide to European Steam & Mountain Railways. Bernard C. Winn. LC 89-83464. (Illus.). 120p. (Orig.). 1989. pap. 9.25 (*0-9615161-3-5*) Incline Pr.

Railway Age's Comprehensive Railroad Dictionary. abr. ed. Simmons-Boardman Publishing Corp. Staff. LC 83-51791. 162p. 1984. 17.95 (*0-911382-00-3*) Simmons Boardman.

Railway Ancestors: A Guide to the Staff Records of the Railway Companies of England & Wales 1822-1947. David T. Hawkings. (Illus.). 384p. 1996. 44.95 (*0-7509-0883-1*, Pub. by Sutton Pubng UK) Bks Intl VA.

Railway Annual 96. (Illus.). 62p. 1996. 9.95 (*1-899107-05-3*) Howell Pr VA.

***Railway Antiques.** Date not set. 25.95 (*0-8464-4415-1*) Beekman Pubs.

Railway Architecture. F. G. Cockman. 1989. pap. 25.00 (*0-85263-917-1*, Pub. by Shire UK) St Mut.

Railway Art of Kenneth Bowen. Boolarong Publications Staff. 128p. (C). 1990. 120.00 (*0-86439-021-1*, Pub. by Boolarong Pubns AT) St Mut.

Railway Carriers. Edward Paget-Tomlinson. 192p. (C). 1989. 60.00 (*0-86138-082-7*, Pub. by T Dalton UK) St Mut.

***Railway Children.** E. Nesbit. (Illus.). (J). 19.95 (*0-590-74000-8*) Scholastic Inc.

Railway Children. Edith Nesbit. (J). 1993. 12.95 (*0-679-42534-9*, Everymans Lib) Knopf.

Railway Children. Edith Nesbit. 256p. 1992. 2.95 (*0-451-52561-2*, Sig Classics) NAL-Dutton.

Railway Children. Edith Nesbit. (World's Classics Ser.). 224p. (J). 1991. pap. 4.95 (*0-19-282659-X*, 11912) OUP.

Railway Children. Edith Nesbit. (Classics Ser.). 240p. (J). (gr. 3-7). 1983. pap. 2.95 (*0-14-035005-5*, Puffin) Puffin Bks.

Railway Children. Edith Nesbit. (Classics Ser.). 240p. (J). (gr. 5 up). 1994. pap. 3.99 (*0-14-036671-7*) Puffin Bks.

Railway Children. Edith Nesbit. (J). 1997. pap. 2.95 (*0-8167-0469-4*) Troll Communs.

***Railway Children.** Edith Nesbit. 1997. pap. 2.99 (*0-7214-5708-8*, Ladybrd) Penguin.

Railway Conductors. Edwin C. Robbins. LC 76-127435. (Columbia University. Studies in the Social Sciences: No. 148). reprint ed. 32.50 (*0-404-51148-1*) AMS Pr.

Railway Dictionary. Alan A. Jackson. (Illus.). 320p. 1992. 34.00 (*0-7509-0038-5*, Pub. by Sutton Pubng UK) Bks Intl VA.

Railway Dictionary: An A-Z of Railway Terminology. 2nd rev. ed. Alan A. Jackson. (Illus.). 336p. 1996. 33.95 (*0-7509-1137-9*, Pub. by Sutton Pubng UK) Bks Intl VA.

Railway Dictionary: English-German-French-Russian. A. Dannehl. 399p. (ENG, FRE, GER & RUS.). 1983. 96.00 (*3-87097-119-3*) IBD Ltd.

Railway Disasters of the World. Peter W. Semmens. (Illus.). 264p. 1994. 32.95 (*1-85260-323-2*, Pub. by J H Haynes & Co UK) Motorbooks Intl.

Railway Economy: A Treatise on the New Art of Transport. Dionysius Lardner. LC 67-29509. (Reprints of Economic Classics Ser.). xxiii, 442p. 1968. reprint ed. 49.50 (*0-678-00361-0*) Kelley.

Railway Empire. Anthony Burton. (Illus.). 272p. 1995. 45.00 (*0-7195-5170-6*, Pub. by John Murray UK) Trafalgar.

***Railway Engineering.** 300p. 1996. 29.00 (*1-86094-012-9*) World Scientific Pub.

Railway Engineering. Vassilios Profillidis. 287p. 1995. pap. text ed. 94.95 (*0-291-39828-6*, TF145, Pub. by Avebury Technical UK) Avebury Technical UK.

Railway Expenditures: Their Extent, Object & Economy, 2 Vols. Marshall M. Kirkman, Jr. Ed. by Alfred D. Chandler. LC 79-7547. (History of Management Thought & Practice Ser.). 1980. reprint ed. lib. bdg. 66.95 (*0-405-12331-0*) Ayer.

Railway Freight Traffic in Prosperity & Depression. Thor Hultgren. (Occasional Papers: No. 5). 51p. 1942. reprint ed. 20.00 (*0-87014-320-4*); reprint ed. mic. film 20.00 (*0-685-61232-5*) Natl Bur Econ Res.

Railway Ghosts. (Ghost Ser.). (Illus.). 144p. 1993. pap. 7.95 (*0-7117-0285-3*) Seven Hills Bk.

Railway Ghosts & Railway Horrors. Daniel Cohen. 112p. (J). (gr. 3-7). 1993. pap. 2.95 (*0-590-45423-4*, Apple Paperbacks) Scholastic Inc.

Railway History Monograph, Vol. 4. LC 73-75503. 1976. lib. bdg. 10.00 (*0-916170-08-X*) J-B Pub.

Railway History Via Post Cards: How We Got There. William F. Rapp. 52p. (Orig.). 1992. pap. 14.00 (*0-916170-40-3*) J-B Pub.

Railway Imperialism. Ed. by Clarence B. Davis et al. LC 89-26025. (Contributions in Comparative Colonial Studies: No. 26). 232p. 1991. text ed. 55.00 (*0-313-25966-6*, DRY/, Greenwood Pr) Greenwood.

Railway Journey: The Industrialization & Perception of Time & Space. Wolfgang Schivelbusch. 1986. pap. 13.00 (*0-520-05929-8*) U CA Pr.

Railway King. large type ed. Margaret Mayhew. 423p. 1980. 25.99 (*0-7089-0558-7*) Ulverscroft.

Railway King of Canada: Sir William MacKenzie, 1849-1923. R. B. Fleming. (Illus.). 339p. 1991. pap. 19.95 (*0-7748-0486-6*) U of Wash Pr.

***Railway Labor Act: 1996 Supplement.** 122p. 1997. pap. 65.00 (*1-57018-039-3*, 1039-PR6) BNA Books.

Railway Labor Act, with 1996 Supplement, Incl. 1996 supplement. Ed. by Douglas L. Leslie et al. 642p. 1997. 265.00 (*0-87179-815-8*, 9039-PR6) BNA Books.

Railway Law & the National Transportation Act. Lande. 240p. 1989. 100.00 (*0-409-80661-7*) MICHIE.

Railway Legislation in the United States. Balthasar H. Meyer. LC 73-2523. (Big Business; Economic Power in a Free Society Ser.). 1973. reprint ed. 23.95 (*0-405-05102-6*) Ayer.

Railway Man: A True Story of War, Brutality & Forgiveness. Eric Lomax. (Illus.). 224p. 1995. 22.00 (*0-393-03910-2*) Norton.

Railway Man: A True Story of War, Remembrance & Forgiveness. Eric Lomax. 288p. 1996. pap. 12.00 (*0-345-40668-0*) Ballantine.

Railway Monopoly & Rate Regulation. Robert J. McFall. LC 79-76704. (Columbia University. Studies in the Social Sciences: No. 164). reprint ed. 20.00 (*0-404-51164-3*) AMS Pr.

***Railway Murders: Ten Classic True Crime Stories.** Jonathan Goodman. 1990. pap. text ed. 9.95 (*0-85031-599-9*, Pub. by A & B UK) London Brdge.

Railway Nationalization in Canada: The Problem of the Canadian National Railways. Leslie T. Fournier. Ed. by Stuart Bruchey. LC 80-1308. (Railroads Ser.). 1981. reprint ed. lib. bdg. 33.95 (*0-405-13776-1*) Ayer.

***Railway of the World on Stamps.** Howard J. Buckhalter et al. (Illus.). 266p. (Orig.). Date not set. pap. text ed. 20.00 (*0-935991-27-1*) Am Topical Assn.

***Railway Pathfinders.** Pierre Berton. (Canada Moves West Ser.). 88p. (J). (gr. 6-9). pap. 4.99 (*0-7710-1437-6*) McCland & Stewart.

Railway Practice. Samuel C. Brees. (Industrial Antiquities Ser.). (Illus.). 296p. (C). 1989. reprint ed. 420.00 (*1-85297-013-8*, Pub. by Archival Facs UK) St Mut.

Railway Printed Ephemera. William N. Fenton. (Illus.). 208p. 1992. 59.50 (*1-85149-137-6*) Antique Collect.

Railway Problems in China. Mongton C. Hsu. LC 70-76707. (Columbia University. Studies in the Social Sciences: No. 159). 1969. reprint ed. 34.50 (*0-404-51159-7*) AMS Pr.

Railway Property (Unlawful Possession) Act, 1966. Askari Hasan. 471p. 1983. 180.00 (*0-317-54690-2*) St Mut.

Railway Property (Unlawful Possession) Act, 1966. Askari Hasan. (C). 1991. text ed. 90.00 (*0-89771-477-6*) St Mut.

Railway Property, Unlawful Possession Act, 1966: Together with R. P. F. Act & Rules. 2nd ed. Ed. by Vijay Malik. (C). 1991. 90.00 (*0-89771-687-6*) St Mut.

***Railway Reading.** Kevin J. Hayes. (Illus.). 25p. 1997. pap. write for info. (*0-944026-77-X*) Am Antiquarian.

Railway Revenue: A Treatise on the Organization of Railroads & the Collection of Railway Receipts. Marshall M. Kirkman, Jr. Ed. by Alfred D. Chandler. LC 79-7548. (History of Management Thought & Practice Ser.). 1980. reprint ed. lib. bdg. 47.95 (*0-405-12332-9*) Ayer.

Railway Revolution in Mexico. Bernard Moses. 1976. lib. bdg. 59.95 (*0-8490-2499-4*) Gordon Pr.

***Railway Roundabout: A Guide to the Classic Television Series.** Rex Christiansen. (Illus.). 112p. 1997. 40.95 (*0-7110-2456-1*, Pub. by Ian Allan UK) Motorbooks Intl.

Railway Station: A Social History. Jeffrey Richards & John M. MacKenzie. (Illus.). 480p. 1986. teacher ed. write for info. (*0-318-60820-0*) OUP.

***Railway Stations.** Charles Sheppard. (Architectural Masterpieces Ser.). 1996. 10.98 (*0-7651-9941-6*) Smithmark.

Railway Stations of Britain: Just a Glimpse. J. A. Coltas. (Illus.). 1979. 9.00 (*0-916170-09-8*) J-B Pub.

Railway Steamships of Ontario. Dana Ashdown. Ed. by Noel Hudson. (Illus.). 288p. 32.50 (*0-919783-80-5*, Pub. by Boston Mills Pr CN) Genl Dist Srvs.

Railway Systems & Management see Computers in Railways V

Railway Technology & Environment see Computers in Railways V

Railway Through Talerddig. Gwyn Briwnant-Jones. 144p. 1990. pap. 23.00 (*0-86383-813-8*, Pub. by Gomer Pr UK) St Mut.

Railway Through Talerddig. Gwyn Briwnant-Jones. 144p. (C). 1990. 36.00 (*0-86383-662-3*, Pub. by Gomer Pr UK) St Mut.

Railway Traction: The Principles of Mechanical & Electrical Railway Traction. H. I. Andrews. (Studies in Mechanical Engineering: No. 5). 412p. 1986. 232.00 (*0-444-42489-X*) Elsevier.

Railway Traffic Expansion & Use of Resources in World War II. Thor Hultgren. (Occasional Papers: No. 15). 36p. 1944. reprint ed. 20.00 (*0-87014-330-1*); reprint ed. mic. film 20.00 (*0-685-61251-1*) Natl Bur Econ Res.

Railway Trivia. Alan M. Drewett. (C). 1992. text ed. 30.00 (*0-9514591-0-4*, Pub. by A M Drewett UK) St Mut.

Railways, Vol. I. Ed. by Terry Gourvish. LC 96-9261. (Studies in Transport History). 192p. 1996. 59.95 (*1-85928-299-7*, Pub. by Scolar Pr UK) Ashgate Pub Co.

Railways, Vol. II. Ed. by Terry Gourvish. (Studies in Transport History). 216p. 1996. 59.95 (*1-85928-300-4*, Pub. by Scolar Pr UK) Ashgate Pub Co.

***Railways & the Formation of the Italian State in the Nineteenth Century.** Albert Schram. (Studies in Italian History & Culture). (Illus.). 212p. (C). 1997. text ed. 54.95 (*0-521-57159-6*) Cambridge U Pr.

Railways & Trains. C. Young. (Beginner's Knowledge Ser.). (Illus.). 48p. (J). (gr. 2 up). 1992. pap. 7.95 (*0-7460-0467-2*, Usborne); lib. bdg. 15.95 (*0-88110-441-8*, Usborne) EDC.

Railways in Camera 1860-1913: Archive Photographs of the Great Age of Steam from the Public Record Office. Robin Linsley. (Illus.). 256p. Date not set. 44.95 (*0-7509-1060-7*, Pub. by Sutton Pubng UK) Bks Intl VA.

***Railways in Camera 1860-1913: Archive Photographs of the Great Age of Steam from the Public Record Office.** Robin Linsley. (Illus.). 256p. (Orig.). 1997. pap. 22.95 (*0-7509-1515-3*, Pub. by Sutton Pubng UK) Bks Intl VA.

Railways of Canada. Jim Lotz. 1988. 14.99 (*0-517-68235-4*) Random Hse Value.

Railways of Fife. William S. Bruce. 250p. (C). 1988. 52.00 (*0-906664-03-9*, Pub. by Mercat Pr Bks UK) St Mut.

Railways of Southern Quebec. Derek Booth. (Illus.). 12.00 (*0-919130-37-2*, Pub. by Boston Mills Pr CN) Genl Dist Srvs.

Railways of Southern Quebec, Vol. 2. Derek Booth. (Illus.). 168p. 18.00 (*1-919130-39-X*, Pub. by Boston Mills Pr CN) Genl Dist Srvs.

Railways of the Raj. Michael Satow & Ray Desmond. (Illus.). 120p. (C). 1980. text ed. 35.00 (*0-8147-7816-X*) NYU Pr.

Railways or No Railways. Robert Fairlie. 147p. 1984. pap. 8.95 (*0-912113-07-3*) Railhead Pubns.

Railways Revisited: A Guide to Little-Known Railways of Austria & Germany. Bernard C. Winn. LC 87-83256. (Illus.). 87p. 1988. pap. 11.95 (*0-9615161-2-7*); pap. 9.00 (*0-9615161-1-9*) Incline Pr.

Railways to Cambridge Actual & Proposed. Reginald B. Fellows. (Cambridge Town, Gown & County Ser.: Vol. 2). (Illus.). 32p. 1976. reprint ed. pap. 4.95 (*0-902675-62-1*) Oleander Pr.

***Raimond (Le Cathare)** Dominique Baudis. 435p. (FRE.). 1997. pap. 25.99 (*2-84011-198-5*) Ulverscroft.

Rain. Susan Afterman. 66p. (Orig.). 1988. pap. text ed. 9.95 (*0-7022-1617-8*, Pub. by Univ Queensland Pr AT) Intl Spec Bk.

Rain. Guillermo Bosch. (Orig.). 1995. pap. 12.95 (*1-56333-232-9*, R Kasak Bks) Masquerade.

Rain. Henry Carlile. LC 93-73476. (Poetry Ser.). 88p. (Orig.). 1994. pap. 11.95 (*0-88748-167-1*) Carnegie-Mellon.

Rain. Kay Davies & Wendy Oldfield. LC 95-6005. (See for Yourself Ser.). (Illus.). 30p. (J). (gr. k-3). 1995. lib. bdg. 19.97 (*0-8172-4043-8*) Raintree Steck-V.

Rain. Robert Kalan. LC 77-25312. (Illus.). 24p. (J). (gr. k-3). 1978. lib. bdg. 15.93 (*0-688-84139-2*) Greenwillow.

Rain. Robert Kalan. LC 77-25312. (Illus.). 24p. (J). (ps up). 1991. pap. 5.95 (*0-688-10479-7*, Mulberry) Morrow.

Rain. Andrew Kelly. LC 93-9287. (J). 1994. pap. write for info. (*0-383-03711-5*) SRA McGraw.

Rain. Michael Laser. LC 96-34179. (J). 1997. 16.00 (*0-689-80506-3*, S&S Bks Young Read) S&S Childrens.

Rain. Joy A. Palmer. LC 92-38554. (What About...? Ser.). (Illus.). 32p. (J). (gr. 2-3). 1992. lib. bdg. 21.40 (*0-8114-3413-3*) Raintree Steck-V.

Rain. Joy A. Palmer. (J). (ps-3). 1994. 4.95 (*0-8114-7774-6*) Raintree Steck-V.

Rain. Illus. by Pat Robson. (Butterfly Bks.). 32p. (J). (gr. 3-5). 1985. 8.95 (*0-86685-451-7*) Intl Bk Ctr.

Rain. Andres L. Ruiz. LC 96-25866. (Sequences of Earth & Space Ser.). (Illus.). 32p. (J). 1996. 12.95 (*0-8069-9333-2*) Sterling.

Rain. Rozanne L. Williams. (Emergent Reader Bks.). 8p. 1994. 1.59 (*0-916119-53-X*) Creat Teach Pr.

An Asterisk (*) at the beginning of an entry indicates that the title is appearing in BIP for the first time.

Rain. Rozanne L. Williams. (Emergent Reader Big Bks.). (Illus.). 8p. (Orig.). 1995. pap. 7.98 (*1-57471-065-6*) Creat Teach Pr.

Rain. Alana Willoughby. Ed. by Alton Jordan. (I Can Read Ser.). (Illus.). (J). (gr. k-3). 1984. 7.95 (*0-89868-003-4*, Read Res); pap. 3.95 (*0-89868-036-0*, Read Res) ARO Pub.

Rain. Kirsty Gunn. 104p. 1996. reprint ed. pap. 10.00 (*0-8021-3447-5*, Grove) Grove-Atltic.

Rain: A Great Day for Ducks. Jane B. Moncure. LC 89-24010. (Discovery World Ser.). (Illus.). 32p. (J). (ps-2). 1990. lib. bdg. 21.36 (*0-89565-553-5*) Childs World.

Rain: Causes & Effects. Philip Steele. LC 90-41429. (Weather Watch Ser.). (Illus.). 32p. (J). (gr. 5-8). 1991. lib. bdg. 20.00 (*0-531-10989-5*) Watts.

***Rain: Reading Group Guide.** Kirsty Gunn. 1997. pap. 10.00 (*0-8021-3469-6*) Grove-Atltic.

Rain & Hail. Franklyn M. Branley. LC 83-45058. (Let's-Read-&-Find-Out Science Bk.). (Illus.). 40p. (J). (gr. k-3). 1983. lib. bdg. 14.89 (*0-690-04353-8*, Crowell Jr Bks) HarpC Child Bks.

Rain & Other Fictions. Maurice Kenny. 1990. pap. 8.00 (*0-934834-98-9*) White Pine.

***Rain & Shine.** S. A. Lynn. (J). (ps-3). 1997. pap. 4.95 (*0-7166-4805-9*, 706609Q) World Bk.

***Rain & Shine.** Sara Lynn & Diane James. LC 96-51091. (Play & Discover Ser.). 1997. write for info. (*0-7166-4804-0*) World Bk.

Rain & Snow: The Umbrella in Japanese Art. Julia Meeck. (Illus.). 143p. 1993. pap. text ed. 32.00 (*0-913304-36-0*) Japan Soc.

Rain & Stormwater Harvesting in Rural Areas: A Report of the United Nations Environment Programme. (Water Resources Ser.: Vol. 5). (Illus.). 235p. 1983. 85.00 (*0-907567-38-X*, Tycooly Pub) Weidner & Sons.

Rain Barrel & Other Stories. George Bowering. 1994. pap. 15.95 (*0-88922-345-9*) Genl Dist Srvs.

Rain Before Seven. large type ed. Roma Grover. 1996. pap. 17.99 (*1-85389-579-2*, Dales) Ulverscroft.

Rain Came Last & Other Stories. Niccolo Tucci. LC 89-13344. (New Directions Classics Ser.). 224p. 1990. 22.95 (*0-8112-1124-X*); pap. 10.95 (*0-8112-1125-8*, NDP688) New Directions.

Rain Catchers. Jean Thesman. 192p. (J). 1992. mass mkt. 4.50 (*0-380-71711-5*, Flare) Avon.

Rain Catchers. Jean Thesman. LC 90-39343. 192p. (YA). (gr. 7 up). 1991. 14.95 (*0-395-55333-4*) HM.

Rain-Charm for the Duchy & Other Laureate Poems. Ted Hughes. 96p. 1992. 19.95 (*0-571-16605-9*); pap. 8.95 (*0-571-16713-6*) Faber & Faber.

Rain City Review No. 5: A Literary Magazine. Ed. by Brian C. Hamilton. 192p. 1994. pap. 8.00 (*1-882550-07-2*) Quiet Lion Pr.

Rain City Review No. 6: A Literary Magazine. Ed. by Brian C. Hamilton. 192p. 1995. pap. 8.00 (*1-882550-11-0*) Quiet Lion Pr.

Rain Dancing: Sanctions in Canadian & Australian Foreign Policy. Kim R. Nossal. 324p. 1994. 60.00 (*0-8020-0472-5*); pap. 21.95 (*0-8020-7571-1*) U of Toronto Pr.

Rain Decided to Help Us: Participatory Watershed Management in the State of Maharashtra, India. Crispino Lobo & Gudrun K. Orfer-Lucius. LC 95-31209. (EDI Learning Resources Ser.). 80p. 1996. 7.95 (*0-8213-3414-X*, 13414) World Bank.

***Rain Drops.** Udaya M. Kabadi. (Orig.). 1997. pap. 6.95 (*0-533-12303-8*) Vantage.

Rain Duck: A First Poem for Preschoolers & Kindergarten. Kayla Jea et al. Ed. & Illus. by Joan Abell. 50p. (J). (ps). 1994. 32.00 (*1-56611-050-5*); pap. 28.00 (*1-56611-051-3*) Jones.

Rain Feet. Angela Johnson. LC 93-49391. (Illus.). 12p. (J). (ps). 1994. bds. 4.95 (*0-531-06849-8*) Orchard Bks Watts.

Rain, Fire, & the Will of God. Donald Wetzel. 208p. 1985. reprint ed. 22.00 (*0-933256-58-2*) Second Chance.

Rain Following: Poems. Susan J. Lenier. (Modern Poets Ser.: Vol. 13). 64p. 1984. 15.00 (*0-906672-19-8*); pap. 8.95 (*0-906672-20-1*) Oleander Pr.

Rain Follows the Plow: Homesteading in Haynes County, Nebraska. Robert D. Clark. LC 96-3388. (Illus.). 352p. (Orig.). 1996. per. 17.95 (*0-934988-36-6*) Foun Bks.

Rain for the Roots: A Guide to Building Loving Relationships. Fred Herron. 84p. (Orig.). (C). 1995. pap. text ed. 14.00 (*0-8191-9834-X*) U Pr of Amer.

***Rain Forest.** R. Bernard. (J). 1997. pap. 12.95 (*0-590-59919-4*) Scholastic Inc.

Rain Forest. Penny Clarke. LC 95-49026. (Worldwise Ser.). (Illus.). (J). 1996. lib. bdg. 22.70 (*0-531-14404-6*) Watts.

***Rain Forest.** Penny Clarke. (Worldwise Ser.). 40p. (J). 1997. pap. 7.95 (*0-531-15296-0*) Watts.

Rain Forest. Helen Cowcher. (Illus.). 32p. (J). (ps up). 1988. 15.00 (*0-374-36167-3*) FS&G.

Rain Forest. Michael George. (Images Ser.). (J). 1992. lib. bdg. 16.95 (*0-88682-483-4*) Creative Ed.

Rain Forest. Billy Goodman. (Planet Earth Ser.). (Illus.). 96p. (J). (gr. 3-7). 1992. 17.95 (*0-316-32019-6*) Little.

Rain Forest. Fiona Macdonald. LC 93-24449. (New View Ser.). (J). 1994. lib. bdg. 21.40 (*0-8114-9243-5*) Raintree Steck-V.

Rain Forest. Fiona MacDonald. (New View Ser.). (J). 1995. pap. text ed. 6.95 (*0-8114-6447-4*) Raintree Steck-V.

Rain Forest. Ting Morris & Neil Morris. LC 93-26686. (Sticky Fingers Ser.). (Illus.). 32p. (J). (gr. 2-4). 1994. lib. bdg. 20.00 (*0-531-14281-7*) Watts.

Rain Forest. Paul Starry & Andrew Cleave. LC 92-60796. (Nature Search Ser.). (Illus.). 32p. (J). (gr. 4-7). 1992. 14.00 (*0-89577-448-8*, Random) RD Assn.

Rain Forest. Barbara Taylor. LC 91-58197. (Look Closer Ser.). (Illus.). 32p. (J). (gr. 1-4). 1992. 9.95 (*1-879431-91-2*) DK Pub Inc.

Rain Forest: Linking Environmental Studies with Everyday Life. Shirley Cook. Ed. by Leslie Britt. (Illus.). 64p. (Orig.). 1993. teacher ed. 8.95 (*0-86530-275-8*) Incentive Pubns.

Rain Forest: Superdoodles. LC 92-74101. (J). (gr. 1-6). 1993. pap. 4.95 (*0-88160-218-3*, LW302) Learning Wks.

Rain Forest Amerindians. Anna Lewington. LC 92-10560. (Threatened Cultures Ser.). (Illus.). 48p. (J). (gr. 5-6). 1992. lib. bdg. 24.26 (*0-8114-2302-6*) Raintree Steck-V.

Rain Forest at Night. Lynn M. Stone. LC 94-20907. (Discovering the Rain Forest Ser.). (J). 1994. write for info. (*0-86593-396-0*) Rourke Corp.

Rain Forest Babies. Kathy Darling. LC 95-37738. (Illus.). 32p. (J). (ps-3). 1996. 15.95 (*0-8027-8411-9*); lib. bdg. 16.85 (*0-8027-8412-7*) Walker & Co.

***Rain Forest Babies.** Kathy Darling. (Illus.). 32p. (J). (ps-3). 1997. pap. 5.95 (*0-8027-7503-9*) Walker & Co.

Rain Forest Birds: An Educational Coloring Book. pap. 1.99 (*0-86545-211-3*) Spizzirri.

Rain Forest in Your Kitchen: The Hidden Connection Between Extinction & Your Supermarket. Martin Teitel. LC 91-41036. 112p. (Orig.). 1992. pap. 10.95 (*1-55963-153-8*) Island Pr.

Rain Forest Mystery, Vol. 4. D'Ann Steere. (Choice Adventures Ser.: Vol. 4). (J). (gr. 3-7). 1991. pap. 4.99 (*0-8423-5028-4*) Tyndale.

***Rain Forest Organizations: A Worldwide Directory of Private & Governmental Entities.** Steve Shipp. 136p. 1997. lib. bdg. 38.50 (*0-7864-0381-0*) McFarland & Co.

Rain Forest Pop-Up: Poster & Story. Maria M. Ruth. (Illus.). (J). 1995. 16.95 (*0-671-51080-0*, Litl Simon S&S) S&S Childrens.

Rain Forest Preservation kit. Merryl Lambert. (Friends of the Forest Ser.). 1991. 19.95 (*0-9641742-6-X*) Pequot Pubng.

Rain-Forest Remedies: One-Hundred Healing Herbs of Belize. Rosita Arvigo & Michael J. Balick. LC 93-80280. 255p. (Orig.). 1994. pap. 9.95 (*0-914955-13-6*) Lotus Pr WI.

Rain Forest River Life: An Educational Coloring Book. pap. 1.99 (*0-86545-212-1*) Spizzirri.

Rain Forest Storybook. Rosalind Kerven. (Illus.). 80p. (J). 1994. text ed. 18.95 (*0-521-43502-1*); pap. text ed. 11.95 (*0-521-43533-1*) Cambridge U Pr.

Rain Forest Tree Life: An Educational Coloring Book. pap. 1.99 (*0-86545-210-5*) Spizzirri.

Rain Forest Wildlife. Jinny Johnson. (Up-Close Ser.). (Illus.). 24p. (J). (gr. 2-7). 1993. 9.95 (*0-89577-537-9*) RD Assn.

Rain Forests. (Discover Ser.). (Illus.). 48p. (J). 1993. 9.98 (*1-56173-426-8*) Pubns Intl Ltd.

Rain Forests. Sara Oldfield. LC 95-39685. (Endangered People & Places Ser.). (J). 1996. lib. bdg. 21.50 (*0-8225-2778-2*, Lerner Publctns) Lerner Group.

Rain Forests. Anna O'Mara. (Read & Discover Bks.). 24p. (J). (ps-4). 1996. lib. bdg. 13.35 (*1-56065-336-1*) Capstone Pr.

***Rain Forests.** Anna O'Mara. (Read-&-Discover Bks.). (Illus.). 24p. (J). (gr. k-3). 1996. 13.25 (*0-516-20128-X*) Childrens.

Rain Forests. Joy A. Palmer. LC 92-10634. (What About...? Ser.). (Illus.). 32p. (J). (gr. 2-3). 1992. lib. bdg. 21.40 (*0-8114-3400-1*) Raintree Steck-V.

Rain Forests. Joy A. Palmer. (J). (ps-3). 1993. pap. 4.95 (*0-8114-4911-4*) Raintree Steck-V.

***Rain Forests.** Rose Pipes. LC 97-9070. (World Habitats Ser.). (J). 1998. write for info. (*0-8172-5003-4*) Raintree Steck-V.

Rain Forests. Philip Sauvain. LC 96-10915. (Geography Detective Ser.). (J). 1997. lib. bdg. 14.96 (*1-57505-041-2*, Carolrhoda) Lerner Group.

Rain Forests. L. Stone. (Ecozones Ser.). (Illus.). 48p. (J). (gr. 4-8). 1989. 11.95 (*0-685-67720-6*); lib. bdg. 15.94 (*0-86592-437-6*) Rourke Corp.

Rain Forests. Art Wolfe. 1997. write for info. (*0-517-70381-5*) Random Hse Value.

Rain Forests: Habitats of the World. Sheri Amsel. (J). (gr. 4-7). 1993. pap. 4.95 (*0-8114-4920-3*) Raintree Steck-V.

Rain Forests: Lush Tropical Paradise. Jenny Wood. (Wonderworks of Nature Ser.). (Illus.). 32p. (J). (gr. 3-4). 1991. lib. bdg. 19.93 (*0-8368-0632-8*) Gareth Stevens Inc.

***Rain Forests: Tropical Treasures.** (Ranger Rick's Naturescope Ser.). (Illus.). 96p. (J). (gr. 1-7). 1997. text ed. 19.95 (*0-7910-4836-5*) Chelsea Hse.

Rain Forests: Tropical Treasures. National Wildlife Federation Staff. (J). (gr. k-8). 1991. pap. 7.95 (*0-945051-41-7*, 75044) Natl Wildlife.

Rain Forests & Reefs: A Kid's-Eye View of the Tropics. Caitlin Maynard et al. LC 96-33974. (Cincinnati Zoo Bks.). (Illus.). 64p. (J). (gr. 3-8). 1996. lib. bdg. 22.70 (*0-531-11281-0*) Watts.

***Rain Forests & Reefs: A Kid's-Eye View of the Tropics.** Caitlin Maynard & Thane Maynard. (Cincinnati Zoo Bks.). 64p. (J). 1997. pap. 9.95 (*0-531-15806-3*) Watts.

Rain Forests of Home: Profile of a North American Bioregion. Ed. by Peter K. Schoonmaker et al. (Illus.). 480p. 1996. pap. text ed. 27.00 (*1-55963-480-4*) Island Pr.

Rain Forests of Home: Profile of a North American Bioregion. Ed. by Peter K. Schoonmaker et al. (Illus.). 480p. (C). 1996. 50.00 (*1-55963-479-0*) Island Pr.

Rain Forests of Tasmania. Forestry Comm. of Tasmania Staff. 128p. (C). 1989. text ed. 80.00 (*0-89771-029-0*, Pub. by Bob Mossel AT) St Mut.

Rain Forests of the World. Kathlyn Gay. LC 93-39619. (Contemporary World Issues Ser.). 219p. 1993. lib. bdg. 39.50 (*0-87436-712-3*) ABC-CLIO.

Rain Forests Tropical Treasures. 2nd ed. National Wildlife Federation Staff. LC 97-10376. (Ranger Rick's NatureScope Ser.). (Illus.). 96p. (J). (gr. k-8). 1997. pap. text ed. 12.95 (*0-07-046510-X*) McGraw.

Rain Frog. Larue W. Selman. (Buppet Bks.). (Illus.). (J). (gr. 1-4). 1980. 9.95 (*0-89868-091-3*, Read Res); pap. 3.95 (*0-89868-102-2*, Read Res) ARO Pub.

Rain from a Clear Blue Sky. Mercer Simpson. 79p. 1994. pap. 21.00 (*1-85902-192-1*) St Mut.

***Rain from God.** Mark Ammerman. (The Cross & the Tomahawk Ser.: Vol. I). 1997. pap. text ed. 11.99 (*0-88965-134-5*) Chr Pubns.

Rain God. Arturo Islas. 192p. 1991. pap. 12.00 (*0-380-76393-1*) Avon.

Rain God: A Desert Tale. Arturo Islas. 180p. (Orig.). 1984. pap. 6.95 (*0-916485-01-3*) Alexand Press.

Rain, Hail, & Baked Beans: A New England Seasonal Cookbook see Old-Time New England Cookbook

Rain in Her Voice. Lawrence Fitzgerald. 24p. 1978. pap. 3.50 (*0-913719-04-8*) High-Coo Pr.

Rain in Most Places: Moments of England, Scotland, & Wales. William Greenway. 33p. (Orig.). 1992. pap. 6.00 (*0-9624453-8-X*) March Street Pr.

Rain in the Forest, Light in the Trees: Contemporary Poetry from the Northwest. Ed. by Rich Ives. 448p. (Orig.). 1983. pap. 8.00 (*0-937669-08-3*) Owl Creek Pr.

Rain in the Trees. W. S. Merwin. LC 87-46081. 96p. 1988. pap. 15.00 (*0-394-75858-7*) Knopf.

Rain in the Wind: Four Stories. Saiichi Maruya. Tr. by Dennis Keene from JPN. 240p. (YA). 1990. 18.95 (*0-87011-940-0*) Kodansha.

Rain in the Wind: Four Stories. Saiichi Maruya. Tr. by Dennis Keene from JPN. 240p. 1992. pap. 8.00 (*4-7700-1558-5*) Kodansha.

***Rain Is Liquid Silver & There Are Diamonds in the Mud.** Tanya Hallgren. 184p. (Orig.). 1997. mass mkt. 4.99 (*1-55197-885-7*, Pub. by Comnwlth Pub CN) Partners Pubs Grp.

Rain Is Not the Same: Selected Poetry, 1978-1994. 2nd ed. George Gilcrease. (Illus.). 134p. (Orig.). 1994. pap. text ed. 12.50 (*0-9641780-0-1*) G Gilcrease.

Rain Lily. Candace Camp. 352p. 1993. mass mkt. 5.50 (*0-06-108028-4*, Harp PBks) HarpC.

Rain Maiden. Jill M. Phillips. 570p. 1987. 16.95 (*0-8065-1008-0*, Citadel Pr) Carol Pub Group.

Rain-Makers: Indians of Arizona & New Mexico. Mary E. Coolidge. LC 76-43681. (Illus.). 376p. reprint ed. 49.50 (*0-404-15514-6*) AMS Pr.

Rain Makes Applesauce. Julian Scheer. (Illus.). 36p. (J). (ps-3). 1964. 16.95 (*0-8234-0091-3*) Holiday.

Rain Making: The Professional's Guide to Attracting New Clients. Ford Harding. LC 94-32884. 1994. pap. 12.95 (*1-55850-420-6*) Adams Media.

Rain Making & Other Weather Vagaries. William J. Humphreys. LC 77-10228. reprint ed. 32.00 (*0-404-16208-8*) AMS Pr.

Rain Melody: Poems by Nguyen Hien Duc. Nguyen Hien Duc. Ed. by Ronald Goforth. (Illus.). 111p. (Orig.). 1988. pap. 25.00 (*0-9622682-0-8*) H D Nguyen.

Rain of Dollars: U. S. Economic Intervention in Central America. Tom Barry. 38p. 1986. 5.95 (*0-911213-08-2*) Interhemisp Res Ctr.

Rain of Fire: B-29s Over Japan, 1945. Charles L Phillips. LC 95-78454. (Illus.). 208p. (Orig.). 1995. pap. 19.95 (*0-9647577-0-2*) B-Nijuku Pubng.

Rain of Gold. Victor Villasenor. LC 91-7587. 1991. 19.95 (*1-55885-030-9*) Arte Publico.

Rain of Gold. Victor Villasenor. 562p. 1992. reprint ed. pap. 13.95 (*0-385-31177-X*, Delta) Dell.

Rain of Iron & Ice: The Very Real Threat of Comet & Asteroid Bombardment. John S. Lewis. 208p. (C). 1996. 25.00 (*0-201-48950-3*) Addison-Wesley.

***Rain of Iron & Ice: The Very Real Threat of Comet & Asteroid Bombardment.** John S. Lewis. (C). 1997. pap. 13.00 (*0-201-15494-3*) Addison-Wesley.

Rain of Ruin: A Photographic History of Hiroshima & Nagasaki. Donald M. Goldstein et al. (World War II Commemorative Ser.). (Illus.). 192p. 1995. 31.95 (*1-57488-033-0*) Brasseys Inc.

Rain of Scorpions & Other Stories. Estela P. Trambley. LC 92-25450. (Clasicos Chicanos - Chicano Classics Ser.: No. 9). 208p. 1993. 25.00 (*0-927534-28-2*); pap. 15.00 (*0-927534-29-0*) Biling Rev-Pr.

Rain on Macy's Parade: How Greed, Ambition & Folly Ruined America's Greatest Store. Jeffrey A. Trachtenberg. LC 96-16082. 352p. 1996. 27.50 (*0-8129-2155-0*, Times Bks) Random.

Rain on the Just: A Novel. Kathleen M. Morehouse. LC 79-18762. (Lost American Fiction Ser.). 333p. 1980. reprint ed. 19.95 (*0-8093-0945-9*) S Ill U Pr.

Rain on the Wind. Walter Macken. 288p. 1994. reprint ed. pap. 11.95 (*0-86322-185-8*, Pub. by Brandon Bk Pubs IE) Irish Bks Media.

***Rain on Waterless Mountain.** Barbara LaMorticella. 26p. 1995. reprint ed. 5.00 (*0-614-30119-X*) Skydog OR.

Rain One Step Away. Melih C. Anday. Tr. by Talat S. Halman & Brian Swann. LC 80-68880. 1980. 7.50 (*0-910350-00-0*) Charioteer.

Rain or Shine. Ronald Heuninck. (Illus.). 12p. (J). (ps). 1990. bds. 5.95 (*0-86315-089-6*, 1361, Pub. by Floris Books UK) Anthroposophic.

***Rain or Shine Activity Book.** Joanna Cole & Stephanie Calmenson. (Illus.). (J). 1997. write for info. (*0-614-29271-9*, Beech Tree Bks) Morrow.

Rain Player. David Wisieniewski. (Illus.). 32p. (J). (gr. k-4). 1991. 16.95 (*0-395-55112-9*, Clarion Bks) HM.

Rain Player. David Wisniewski. (Illus.). 32p. (J). 1996. pap. 8.95 (*0-395-72084-2*, Clarion Bks) HM.

Rain Player. David Wisniewski. 1995. pap. 5.95 (*0-395-72083-4*, Clarion Bks) HM.

Rain Psalm. Victoria Ford. 28p. (Orig.). 1996. pap. 5.95 (*0-9651210-0-3*) Rose Alley Pr.

***Rain! Rain!** Carol Greene. LC 82-9509. (Rookie Reader Ser.). (Illus.). (J). (ps-2). 1982. pap. 3.50 (*0-516-42034-8*); lib. bdg. 15.00 (*0-516-02034-X*) Childrens.

Rain Rain! Peter Mills. (Window Bks.). 16p. (J). 1995. pap. text ed. 1.99 (*0-88070-791-7*) Multnomah Pubs.

***Rain, Rain Go Away.** Annalisa McMorrow. (Illus.). 80p. (Orig.). (J). (ps-k). 1997. pap. 9.95 (*1-57612-010-4*, MM2038) Monday Morning Bks.

Rain Rain Go Away. Reed. (Gullah Gullah Island Ser.). 1996. pap. 3.25 (*0-689-80395-8*, S&S Bks Young Read) S&S Childrens.

Rain Rain Rivers. Uri Shulevitz. LC 73-85370. (Illus.). 32p. (J). (ps-3). 1969. 16.00 (*0-374-36171-1*) FS&G.

Rain Rain Rivers. Uri Shulevitz. (Sunburst Ser.). (Illus.). 32p. (J). 1988. pap. 3.95 (*0-374-46195-3*) FS&G.

Rain Shadow. Cheryl St. John. (Intrigue Ser.). 1994. mass mkt. 3.99 (*0-373-28812-3*, 1-28812-5) Harlequin Bks.

***Rain, Shine or Snow.** (Four Little Friends Ser.). (Illus.). 24p. (J). (gr. 1-4). 1995. write for info. (*1-56144-730-7*, Honey Bear Bks) Modern Pub NYC.

Rain, Snow, & Ice. Ann Merk & Jim Merk. LC 94-13325. (Weather Report Ser.). (J). (gr. 3 up). 1994. write for info. (*0-86593-390-1*) Rourke Corp.

Rain. Some Fish. No Elephants. Y. York. 1989. pap. 5.95 (*0-88145-075-8*) Broadway Play.

Rain Song. Lezlie Evans. LC 94-17368. (Illus.). 32p. (J). (gr. k-3). 1995. 14.95 (*0-395-69865-0*) HM.

***Rain Song.** Lezlie Evans. 1997. pap. 5.95 (*0-395-85077-0*) HM.

***Rain Stops in Texas: One Woman's Struggle from Oppression to Freedom.** Ellie K. Belfiglio. LC 97-14519. (Illus.). 200p. 1997. pap. 18.95 (*1-57168-191-4*, Eakin Pr) Sunbelt Media.

Rain Talk. Mary Serfozo. LC 89-12178. (Illus.). 32p. (J). (ps-3). 1990. lib. bdg. 15.00 (*0-689-50496-9*, McElderry) S&S Childrens.

Rain Talk. Mary Serfozo. LC 92-29562. (Illus.). 32p. (J). (gr. k-3). 1993. reprint ed. pap. 4.95 (*0-689-71699-0*, Aladdin Paperbacks) S&S Childrens.

Rain That Falls This Far. Dennis Hinrichsen. 55p. (Orig.). 1991. pap. 9.95 (*0-913123-32-3*) Galileo.

Rain Through the Night. Buddladeva Bose. Tr. by Clinton B. Seely from BEN. (Orient Paperbacks Ser.). 139p. 1974. pap. 1.80 (*0-88253-285-5*) Ind-US Inc.

Rain Tree. large type ed. Date not set. 20.00 (*0-7838-1676-6*, GK Hall) Thorndike Pr.

Rain Tree: A Western Story. Will Cook. LC 96-5872. 1996. 20.00 (*0-7862-0665-9*, Five Star) Mac Lib Ref.

***Rain, Where Do You Come From? Where do You Come From.** Francesca Grazzini. Tr. by Talia Wise from ITA. (I Want to Know Ser.). (Illus.). 32p. (J). 1996. 11.95 (*0-916291-68-5*) Kane-Miller Bk.

***Rain, Wind, & Storm.** Nicola Baxter. LC 97-8063. (Living with the Weather Ser.). (J). 1998. write for info. (*0-8172-5050-6*) Raintree Steck-V.

Rain Without Thunder: The Ideology of the Animal Rights Movement. Gary L. Francione. LC 95-49676. (C). 1996. pap. 22.95 (*1-56639-461-9*); text ed. 59.95 (*1-56639-460-0*) Temple U Pr.

***Rainbabies.** Laura Melmed. Date not set. pap. write for info. (*0-688-15113-2*) Morrow.

Rainbabies. Laura K. Melmed. LC 91-16877. (Illus.). 32p. (J). (gr. 1 up). 1992. 16.00 (*0-688-10755-9*); lib. bdg. 15.93 (*0-688-10756-7*) Lothrop.

***Rainbird: A Central African Journey.** Jan Brokken. Tr. by Sam Garrett from DUT. (Illus.). 300p. 1997. pap. 10.95 (*0-86442-469-8*) Lonely Planet.

Rainbird's Revenge. large type ed. Marion Chesney. (Nightingale Ser.). 248p. 1990. pap. 14.95 (*0-8161-4705-1*, GK Hall) Thorndike Pr.

***Rainborough Inheritance.** large type ed. Helen Dickson. (Mills & Boon Large Print Ser.). 350p. 1997. 22.50 (*0-263-15017-8*) Ulverscroft.

Rainbow. Caroline Beecham. (J). (gr. 2 up). 1996. pap. 3.99 (*0-614-15723-4*) Random.

Rainbow. Herbert A. Gold. 232p. 1995. mass mkt. 4.99 (*1-896329-34-9*, Pub. by Comnwlth Pub CN) Partners Pubs Grp.

Rainbow. D. H. Lawrence. LC 93-1860. 1993. 20.00 (*0-679-42305-2*, Everymans Lib) Knopf.

Rainbow. D. H. Lawrence. Ed. by Mark Kinkead-Weekes. (Cambridge Edition of the Works of D. H. Lawrence). (Illus.). 752p. (C). 1989. text ed. 120.00 (*0-521-22869-7*) Cambridge U Pr.

Rainbow. D. H. Lawrence. 544p. 1991. pap. 4.95 (*0-451-52529-9*, Sig Classics) NAL-Dutton.

Rainbow. D. H. Lawrence. 1989. mass mkt. 7.95 (*0-14-018218-7*, 461, Penguin Classics) Viking Penguin.

Rainbow. D. H. Lawrence. (Twentieth Century Classics Ser.). 528p. 1995. pap. 8.95 (*0-14-018813-4*, Penguin Classics) Viking Penguin.

Rainbow. D. H. Lawrence. 1995. pap. 23.95 (*0-14-086103-3*) Viking Penguin.

***Rainbow.** D. H. Lawrence. Ed. & Intro. by Kate Flint. (The World's Classics Ser.). 544p. 1997. pap. 7.95 (*0-19-283080-5*) OUP.

Rainbow. Mao Dun. Tr. by Madeleine Zelin from CHI. LC 91-31273. (Voices from Asia Ser.: No. 4). 255p. 1992. 38.00 (*0-520-07327-4*); pap. 13.00 (*0-520-07328-2*) U CA Pr.

Rainbow. large type ed. D. H. Lawrence. (Large Print Ser.). 705p. 1993. reprint ed. lib. bdg. 25.00 (*0-939495-44-9*) North Bks.

Rainbow. D. H. Lawrence. 576p. 1989. reprint ed. lib. bdg. 35.95 (*0-89966-644-2*) Buccaneer Bks.

Rainbow: A History of the Honolulu Japanese Chamber of Commerce. 246p. 10.40 (*0-318-14327-5*) Honolulu Japanese.

An Asterisk (*) at the beginning of an entry indicates that the title is appearing in BIP for the first time.

R

Rainbow: A Search for New Life. Duane Edwards. (Twayne's Masterwork Studies: No. 51). 1990. pap. 13.95 (0-8057-8129-3, 705, Twayne) Scribnrs Ref.

Rainbow: A Search for New Life. Duane Edwards. (Twayne's Masterwork Studies: No. 51). 144p. (C). 1990. 23.95 (0-8057-9401-8, Twayne) Scribnrs Ref.

Rainbow: From Myth to Mathematics. Carl B. Boyer. (Illus.). 376p. 1987. pap. text ed. 24.95 (0-691-02405-7) Princeton U Pr.

***Rainbow & The Rose.** Nevil Shute. lib. bdg. 24.95 (0-8488-2029-0) Amereon Ltd.

Rainbow & the Worm: The Physics of Organisms. Mae-Wan Ho. 220p. 1993. pap. text ed. 21.00 (981-02-1487-1) World Scientific Pub.

Rainbow & the Worm: The Physics of Organisms. Mae-Wan Ho. 220p. 1993. text ed. 40.00 (981-02-1486-3) World Scientific Pub.

***Rainbow & You.** Edwin C. Krupp. (Illus.). (J). Date not set. write for info. (0-688-15601-0, Morrow Junior); lib. bdg. write for info. (0-688-15602-9, Morrow Junior) Morrow.

Rainbow Anthology of Spiritual Experiences: Mountain-Top Turning Points. Kay B. Weston. LC 91-92879. (Illus.). 150p. (Orig.). 1991. pap. 9.95 (0-9630068-0-0) K B Weston.

Rainbow at Midnight: Labor & Culture in the 1940s. George Lipsitz. LC 93-36425. 376p. (C). 1994. 15.95 (0-252-06394-5); text ed. 49.95 (0-252-02094-4) U of Ill Pr.

Rainbow at Night: Words & Pictures by Navajo Children. Bruce Hucko. LC 96-6861. (Illus.). 48p. (J). (gr. 1-7). 1997. 14.95 (0-8118-1294-4) Chronicle Bks.

Rainbow Bags: Instructions for Making Six Colorful Bags of Soft Toys for a Young Child in Church. 2nd ed. Lois Brokering. (Illus.). 48p. 1990. reprint ed. pap. 7.00 (0-8066-2256-3) Brokering Pr.

***Rainbow Bay.** Stephen E. Hume. (Illus.). 32p. (J). (gr. k up). 1997. 15.95 (1-895714-75-3, Pub. by Raincoast Bks CN) Orca Bk Pubs.

Rainbow Bird. Eric Maddern. (J). (gr. 4-8). 1993. 15.95 (0-316-54314-4) Little.

***Rainbow Bird.** Eric Maddern. (Illus.). 26p. (J). 4.98 (0-8317-7133-X) Smithmark.

Rainbow Book of Adventures. Ed. by Susan Remini. (Illus.). 114p. (Orig.). 1983. pap. 7.95 (0-932471-01-3) Falsoft.

Rainbow Book of Birds: A Color-by-Number Book. Querida L. Pearce. 1989. pap. 1.95 (0-8125-9442-8) Tor Bks.

Rainbow Book of Simulations. Ed. by Charles L. Springer. (Illus.). 202p. (Orig.). 1984. pap. 9.95 (0-932471-02-1) Falsoft.

Rainbow Book of Snakes, Turtles, Lizards & More: A Color-by-Number Book. Querida L. Pearce. 1989. pap. 1.95 (0-8125-9444-4) Tor Bks.

Rainbow Book of Song: Key of "C" 2nd ed. Beverly M. Hale. LC 93-73630. (Illus.). 57p. (J). (ps up). 1993. Blue spine bdg. pap. text ed. 13.95 (0-9634305-1-3) E-Z Keys Method.

Rainbow Books, 6 vol., Set. National Geographic Staff. 1993. boxed 6.50 (0-7922-1831-0) Natl Geog.

***Rainbow Bride.** Elizabeth Sites. 1997. pap. 3.25 (0-373-19244-4, 1-19244-2) Silhouette.

Rainbow Bridge. Rajneesh Osho Staff. Ed. by Krishna Prabhu. LC 85-42535. (Initiation Talks Ser.). 368p. (Orig.). (C). 1985. pap. 4.95 (0-88050-618-0) Osho America.

Rainbow Bridge. Audrey Wood. LC 92-17661. (Illus.). 32p. (J). (gr. k-5). 1995. 16.00 (0-15-265475-5, HB Juv Bks) HarBrace.

Rainbow Bridge. Audrey Wood. 32p. 1996. 19.95 (0-385-25530-6) Doubleday.

Rainbow Bridge. Mary W. Cushing. Ed. by Andrew Farkas. LC 76-29932. (Opera Biographies Ser.). (Illus.). (J). (gr. k-5). 1977. reprint ed. lib. bdg. 33.95 (0-405-09674-7) Ayer.

Rainbow Bridge. Reginald Farrer. LC 76-47496. (Illus.). 1976. reprint ed. 15.00 (0-913728-15-2) Theophrastus.

Rainbow Bridge. Reginald Farrer. (Plant Hunter Ser.). 416p. 1987. reprint ed. pap. 11.95 (0-946313-48-2) Timber.

Rainbow Bridge: A Chumash Legend. Illus. & Adapted by Kerry Nechodom. 32p. (Orig.). (J). (gr. k-3). 1992. pap. 6.95 (0-944627-36-6) Sand River Pr.

Rainbow Bridge I: The Link with the Soul. Two Disciples Staff. (Rainbow Bridge Ser.). 110p. 1988. pap. 6.95 (0-9638698-1-7) Rainbow Bdge.

Rainbow Bridge II: Link with the Soul - Purification. Two Disciples Staff. (Rainbow Bridge Ser.). 244p. 1994. reprint ed. pap. text ed. 10.95 (0-9638698-0-9) Rainbow Bdge.

Rainbow Bridge to the Inner Worlds. Ruth E. Norman. (Illus.). 391p. (C). 1985. 18.00 (0-932642-87-X) Unarius Acad Sci.

Rainbow Bridge Visualization. Two Disciples Staff. (Rainbow Bridge Ser.). 56p. 1989. pap. 7.95 (0-9638698-2-5) Rainbow Bdge.

Rainbow Cafe. limited ed. David Ossman. (Illus.). 20p. 1982. 20.00 (0-918824-37-0) Turkey Pr.

Rainbow Candles: A Chanukah Counting Book. Myra Shostak. LC 86-81718. (Illus.). 12p. (J). (ps). 1986. bds. 4.95 (0-930494-59-8) Kar-Ben.

Rainbow Challenge: The Jackson Campaign & the Future of U. S. Politics. Sheila D. Collins. LC 86-21778. 384p. 1986. reprint ed. pap. 109.50 (0-7837-9604-8, 2060361) Bks Demand.

Rainbow Chameleon. Jerome Braudet. Date not set. pap. 11.95 (0-8037-1620-6) Dial Bks Young.

Rainbow Children. Pamela Lovejoy. (Illus.). 7p. (Orig.). (J). 1994. pap. text ed. write for info. (1-880038-19-6) Learn-Abouts.

Rainbow Children: A Racial Justice & Diversity Program for Ages 5-8. Norma Poinsett & Vivian Burns. 1995. pap. 25.00 (1-55896-292-1) Unitarian Univ.

Rainbow Collection: Quilt Patterns for Rainbow Colors. Judy Martin. 44p. (Orig.). 1987. pap. 10.95 (0-9602970-2-2) Leman Pubns.

Rainbow Collection, 1985: Stories & Poetry by Young People. Ed. by Kathie Janger & Joan Korenblit. (Anthology Ser.). 160p. (J). (gr. 1-8). 1985. pap. 6.00 (0-929889-00-2) Young Writers Contest Found.

Rainbow Collection, 1986: Stories & Poetry by Young People. Ed. by Kathie Janger & Joan Korenblit. (Anthology Ser.). 160p. (J). (gr. 1-8). 1986. pap. 6.00 (0-929889-01-0) Young Writers Contest Found.

Rainbow Collection, 1987: Stories & Poetry by Young People. Ed. by Kathie Janger. (Anthology Ser.). (Illus.). 160p. (J). (gr. 1-8). 1987. pap. text ed. 6.00 (0-929889-02-9) Young Writers Contest Found.

Rainbow Collection, 1988: Stories & Poetry by Young People. Ed. by Kathie Janger. (Anthology Ser.). (Illus.). 160p. (J). (gr. 1-8). 1988. pap. 6.00 (0-929889-03-7) Young Writers Contest Found.

Rainbow Collection, 1989: Stories & Poetry by Young People. Ed. by Kathie Janger. (Illus.). 176p. (J). (gr. 1-8). 1989. pap. 6.00 (0-929889-04-5) Young Writers Contest Found.

Rainbow Collection, 1990: Stories & Poetry by Young People. Ed. by Kathie Janger. (Illus.). 176p. (J). 1990. pap. 6.00 (0-929889-06-1) Young Writers Contest Found.

Rainbow Collection, 1990-91: Stories & Poetry by Young People. Ed. by Kathie Janger. (Illus.). 160p. (Orig.). (J). (gr. 1-8). 1991. pap. 6.00 (0-929889-07-X) Young Writers Contest Found.

Rainbow Color Book of Song: A Key of "C" Book - Featuring E-Z Keys. rev. ed. Beverly M. Hale. 1985. pap. 9.95 (0-9634305-0-5) E-Z Keys Method.

Rainbow Colors in the Word: An Activity Book with Puzzles & Pictures to Color. Louise Woofenden. Ed. by Betty Hill. (Illus.). 32p. (Orig.). (J). 1992. pap. text ed. 2.50 (0-917426-08-8) Am New Church Sunday.

Rainbow Connection. Williams. (Piano-Vocal-Guitar Ser.). 6p. 1986. pap. 3.95 (0-7935-0531-3, 00351905) H Leonard.

Rainbow Cottage, Vol. 16. (Grace Livingston Hill Ser.: Vol. 16). 1990. pap. 4.95 (0-8423-5731-9) Tyndale.

Rainbow Countries of Central America. Wallace Thompson. 1978. lib. bdg. 59.95 (0-8490-2500-1) Gordon Pr.

***Rainbow County & Other Stories: Third Collection.** Jack Fritscher. 175p. (Orig.). 1997. pap. 14.95 (1-881684-12-1) L T Pubns CA.

Rainbow Crow. Nancy Van Laan. LC 88-12967. (Illus.). 40p. (J). (ps-3). 1989. lib. bdg. 15.99 (0-394-99577-5) Knopf Bks Yng Read.

Rainbow Dance Studio. Richard Retecki. Ed. by Edward Mycue. (Took Modern Poetry in English Ser.: No. 8). (Illus.). 28p. (Orig.). 1993. pap. 3.00 (1-879457-02-4) Norton Coker Pr.

Rainbow Dancer: Positive Thought, Imagery & Exercise for Self-Esteem, Inner Peace & Caring for the Earth. Melinda J. Miller & Jane Rachfalski. Ed. by Johanna Van Wert. LC 92-80720. (Illus.). 119p. (Orig.). 1991. pap. 19.95 (0-9631046-0-8) Rainbow Dancer.

Rainbow Division in the Great War, 1917-1919. James J. Cooke. LC 93-37024. 304p. 1994. text ed. 59.95 (0-275-94768-8, Praeger Pubs) Greenwood.

Rainbow Dragon: Lessons in Basic Values. Carole G. Sells. (Illus.). 34p. (Orig.). (J). (ps-6). 1988. pap. 3.95 (0-926739-00-X) Sells Pub.

Rainbow Fairies. Gypsy D. Boston. (Illus.). (J). 1991. pap. 4.95 (0-9631503-1-6); boxed 12.95 (0-9631503-0-8) Gypsy Damaris.

Rainbow Fairy Book. Andrew Lang. LC 92-33449. (Books of Wonder). (Illus.). 288p. (J). 1993. 20.00 (0-688-10878-4, Morrow Junior) Morrow.

Rainbow Family Values. Michael S. Piazza. 240p. (Orig.). 1996. pap. 14.95 (1-887129-02-2) Sources of Hope.

Rainbow Fields. Susan G. Rubin. LC 92-46875. (Illus.). 40p. (J). (gr. k-4). 1993. 14.95 (1-56844-004-9) Enchante Pub.

Rainbow Fields. 2nd rev. ed. Susan G. Rubin. Ed. by Gudrun Hoy & Bobi Martin. (Emotional Literacy Ser.). (Illus.). 40p. (J). (gr. k-5). 1995. 14.95 (1-56844-104-5) Enchante Pub.

Rainbow Fish. Marcus Pfister. LC 91-42158. (Illus.). 32p. (J). (gr. k-3). Date not set. 18.95 (1-55858-009-3) North-South Bks NYC.

Rainbow Fish. Marcus Pfister. Tr. by J. Alison James from GER. LC 91-42158. (Illus.). 32p. (J). (gr. k-3). Date not set. lib. bdg. 18.88 (1-55858-010-7) North-South Bks NYC.

Rainbow Fish. Marcus Pfister. (Illus.). 24p. (CHI & ENG.). (J). (gr. 2-4). 1995. 18.95 (1-57227-027-6); 18.95 (1-57227-028-4); 18.95 (1-57227-029-2); 18.95 (1-57227-030-6); 18.95 (1-57227-031-4); 18.95 (1-57227-032-2) Pan Asian Pubns.

Rainbow Fish. Marcus Pfister. (Illus.). 12p. (J). Date not set. bds. 9.95 (1-55858-536-2) North-South Bks NYC.

Rainbow Fish Big Book. Marcus Pfister. (Illus.). (J). (gr. k-3). Date not set. pap. 25.00 (1-55858-441-2) North-South Bks NYC.

Rainbow Fish to the Rescue! Marcus Pfister. LC 95-20322. (Illus.). 32p. (J). (gr. k-3). Date not set. 18.95 (1-55858-486-2) North-South Bks NYC.

Rainbow Fish to the Rescue! Marcus Pfister. Tr. by J. Alison James. LC 95-20322. (Illus.). 32p. (J). (gr. k-3). Date not set. lib. bdg. 18.88 (1-55858-487-0) North-South Bks NYC.

***Rainbow Fish to the Rescue.** Marcus Pfister. 1997. pap. text ed. 25.00 (1-55858-816-7) North-South Bks NYC.

***Rainbow Fish to the Rescue.** Marcus Pfister. (Illus.). 24p. (CHI & ENG.). (J). (gr. 2-4). 1996. 18.95 (1-57227-037-3); 18.95 (1-57227-038-1); 18.95 (1-57227-041-1); 18.95 (1-57227-042-X) Pan Asian Pubns.

***Rainbow Fish to the Rescue: English/Hmong.** Marcus Pfister. (Illus.). 24p. (J). (gr. 2-4). 1996. 18.95 (1-57227-039-X) Pan Asian Pubns.

***Rainbow Fish to the Rescue: English/Khmer.** Marcus Pfister. (Illus.). 24p. (J). (gr. 2-4). 1996. 18.95 (1-57227-040-3) Pan Asian Pubns.

***Rainbow Fish Treasury.** Marcus Pfister. 1997. 49.90 (1-55858-817-5) North-South Bks NYC.

***Rainbow Food Plan.** 28p. 1993. write for info. (1-56476-113-4, Victor Bks) Chariot Victor.

***Rainbow Food Plan Pocket Guide.** 1995. write for info. (1-56476-447-8, Victor Bks) Chariot Victor.

Rainbow for Patti. Carol West. (Illus.). 46p. (Orig.). 1992. pap. 9.95 (0-938837-11-7) Behav Sci Ctr Pubs.

Rainbow for Rima: Stories. Edilberto K. Tiempo. 170p. (Orig.). (C). 1988. pap. 12.50 (971-10-0332-5, Pub. by New Day Pub PH) Cellar.

Rainbow for Suzanne. George Pavloff. (Illus.). 72p. (J). (gr. 1 up). 1991. 14.95 (0-931474-40-X) TBW Bks.

Rainbow Freeware. Bruce Jackson. 170p. (Orig.). 1986. pap. 20.00 (0-939731-00-2) South Moulton Pr.

Rainbow Fun: Rainbows to Keep, Share & Give Away. Imogene Forte. LC 86-82873. (Tabletop Learning Ser.). 80p. (J). (gr. k-6). 1987. pap. text ed. 4.95 (0-86530-161-1, IP-94-5) Incentive Pubns.

Rainbow Garden. Patricia M. St. John. (Patricia St. John Bks.). 255p. (Orig.). (J). (gr. 2-5). 1980. mass mkt. 5.99 (0-8024-0028-0) Moody.

Rainbow Glass. large type ed. Alice Dwyer-Joyce. 304p. 1995. 25.99 (0-7089-3327-0) Ulverscroft.

Rainbow Goblins. Ul De Rico. LC 78-55431. (Illus.). 36p. 1994. reprint ed. 19.95 (0-500-27759-1) Thames Hudson.

Rainbow Gold. large type ed. Juliet Gray. (Linford Romance Library). 272p. 1994. pap. 15.99 (0-7089-7541-0) Ulverscroft.

Rainbow Guide to Introductory Statistics. Michael Plog & Norman Stenzel. Ed. by Belinda Kirby. 150p. (Orig.). 1987. 6.95 (0-932471-05-6) Falsoft.

***Rainbow High.** Evelin Sanders. (YA). (gr. 9 up). 1997. pap. 7.99 (0-88092-345-8) Royal Fireworks.

Rainbow Hill. large type ed. Agnes Short. (Dales Large Print Ser.). 576p. 1995. pap. 17.99 (1-85389-531-8, Dales) Ulverscroft.

***Rainbow in My Hand.** large type ed. Audrie Manley-Tucker. (Dales Large Print Ser.). 350p. 1997. pap. 18.99 (1-85389-691-8) Ulverscroft.

Rainbow in the Glen. Irene Hannon. 1993. 17.95 (0-8034-9012-7) Bouregy.

Rainbow in the Glen. large type ed. Irene Hannon. LC 95-20762. 250p. 1995. 17.95 (0-7838-1440-2, GK Hall) Thorndike Pr.

Rainbow in the Mist. Phyllis A. Whitney. 352p. 1990. mass mkt. 5.95 (0-449-21742-6, Crest) Fawcett.

Rainbow in the Mist. large type ed. Phyllis A. Whitney. 478p. 1990. reprint ed. pap. 17.95 (0-89621-939-9) Thorndike Pr.

Rainbow in the Morning. Ed. by J. Frank Dobie. LC 74-32243. (Texas Folklore Society Publications: No. 5). 203p. 1975. reprint ed. 12.95 (0-87074-150-0) UNTX Pr.

Rainbow in the Sky. May S. Hilburn. 54p. 1966. pap. 1.00 (0-88053-315-3, S-260) Macoy Pub.

Rainbow in Your Eyes: Yes You Can Find Your Colors & for Others, Too. Bernice Kentner. (Illus.). 146p. 1981. 14.95 (0-941522-01-6) Ken Kra Pubs.

Rainbow in Your Hands. 7th ed. Albert R. Davis & Walter C. Rawls, Jr. (Illus.). 101p. 1988. reprint ed. pap. 10.00 (0-911311-16-5) Acres USA.

Rainbow in Your Life: A Complete Guide & Workbook on How Color Empowers Your Life & Dreams. 2nd ed. Maryanne E. Hoffman. (Illus.). 124p. 1993. reprint ed. pap. 11.95 (0-943299-16-0) Star Visions.

Rainbow Is Not Enough. Leydel J. Willis. 72p. 1982. pap. 8.95 (0-930416-07-4) Clodele.

Rainbow Is Our Face. Laura Pegram. (J). (ps). 1994. 5.95 (0-86316-217-7) Writers & Readers.

***Rainbow Is Round.** Mamie H. Scott. 80p. 1997. write for info. (0-8233-0513-9) Golden Quill.

Rainbow Jordan. Alice Childress. 128p. 1982. mass mkt. 3.99 (0-380-58974-5, Flare) Avon.

Rainbow Kid. Jeanne Betancourt. 112p. (Orig.). (J). (gr. 3-7). 1983. pap. 2.50 (0-380-84665-9, Camelot) Avon.

***Rainbow Kids.** Mayra Fernandez. (Illus.). 20p. (Orig.). (J). (gr. 3-5). 1995. pap. 3.95 (1-57089-152-4) SpanPr.

Rainbow Kids. Eric M. St. John, 2nd. LC 94-92279. (Illus.). 20p. (J). (ps-4). 1994. pap. text ed. 9.95 (0-9643453-0-7) RKUP Pubng.

Rainbow Lightning & the Santa Fe Trail. Elizardo Brujo. 256p. 1993. pap. write for info. (0-9639582-0-8) ELMAC Press.

Rainbow Like an Emerald: Stained Glass in Lorraine in the Thirteenth & Early Fourteenth Centuries. Meredith P. Lillich. (Illus.). 256p. 1991. 49.50 (0-271-00702-8) Pa St U Pr.

Rainbow Love. Joan W. Anglund. LC 82-70028. (Illus.). 1982. 5.95 (0-915696-51-7) Determined Prods.

***Rainbow Maker.** Bonnie Eagleheart. 1997. 18.95 (1-889972-88-6) New Wrld Lib.

Rainbow Makers: The Origins of the Synthetic Dyestuffs Industry in Western Europe. Anthony S. Travis. LC 91-60412. (Illus.). 336p. 1993. 49.50 (0-934223-18-1) Lehigh Univ Pr.

Rainbow Man. M. J. Engh. LC 93-12455. 256p. 1994. pap. 10.95 (0-312-89014-1) Orb NYC.

Rainbow Man. Richard G. Rockman, Jr. Ed. by Dean C. Ouellette. (Illus.). 200p. (Orig.). 1991. pap. 9.95 (0-9630916-0-3) R G Rockman.

Rainbow Man. rev. ed. Richard G. Rockman, Jr. Ed. by Dean C. Ouellette. (Illus.). 201p. (Orig.). 1992. pap. 9.95 (0-9630916-1-1) R G Rockman.

Rainbow Masters. Masters Staff. (Phoenix Journals). 224p. 1993. pap. 6.00 (1-56935-017-5) Phoenix Source.

Rainbow Medicine: A Visionary Guide to Native American Shamanism. Wolf Moondance. LC 93-39600. (Illus.). 192p. 1994. pap. 12.95 (0-8069-0364-3) Sterling.

Rainbow Monster. Sandra G. Garrett & Philip C. Williams. LC 93-38342. (J). 1994. write for info. (0-86625-504-4) Rourke Pubns.

Rainbow Movie Tie-In. Sidaway. 1996. pap. 3.99 (0-679-87673-1) Random.

***Rainbow Nation.** R. D. Riccoboni. (Illus.). 64p. 1996. 29.95 (0-85449-240-2, Pub. by Gay Mens Pr UK) LPC InBook.

Rainbow Obsidian. Phillips Kloss. LC 85-2628. 128p. 1985. 10.95 (0-86534-070-6) Sunstone Pr.

***Rainbow of Blessings.** (Illus.). 32p. 1997. 4.99 (0-8007-7169-9) Revell.

Rainbow of Desire: The Boal Method of Theatre & Therapy. Augusto Boal. Tr. by Adrian Jackson. LC 94-13955. 200p. (gr. 13). 1995. pap. 16.95 (0-415-10349-5, B3152) Routledge.

Rainbow of Friends. P. K. Hallinan. LC 93-39257. (Illus.). 24p. (Orig.). (J). (ps-3). 1994. per., pap. 4.95 (0-8249-8653-9, Ideals Child); lib. bdg. 11.00 (0-8249-8657-1, Ideals Child) Hambleton-Hill.

***Rainbow of Friends.** rev. ed. P. K. Hallinan. LC 93-39257. (Illus.). 24p. (Orig.). (J). (ps-3). 1997. pap. 3.25 (1-57102-104-3, Ideals Child) Hambleton-Hill.

***Rainbow of Hope.** Linda Murdock. 86p. (Orig.). 1995. pap. 7.95 (1-885904-07-X) Focus Pubng.

Rainbow of Hope: 777 Inspirational Quotes Plus Selected Scriptures. 3rd ed. Billy Hughey et al. (Illus.). 336p. 1994. 19.95 (0-933657-26-9) Rainbow Studies.

Rainbow of My Own. Don Freeman. (Illus.). (J). (gr. k-3). 1982. 22.95 incl. audio (0-941078-20-5); pap. 15.95 incl. audio (0-941078-18-3) Live Oak Media.

Rainbow of My Own. Don Freeman. 32p. (J). (ps-2). 1978. pap. 4.99 (0-14-050328-5, Puffin) Puffin Bks.

Rainbow of My Own. Don Freeman. (Illus.). (J). (gr. k-3). 1966. pap. 15.99 (0-670-58928-4) Viking Child Bks.

Rainbow of My Own, 4 bks., Set. Don Freeman. (Illus.). (J). (gr. k-3). 1982. student ed., pap. 31.95 incl. audio (0-941078-19-1) Live Oak Media.

Rainbow of Readiness: Parental Guide for Better Beginnings. Ruth D. Summerlin. (Illus.). 128p. (Orig.). 1987. pap. 9.95 (0-9618841-1-8) Readiness Pubns.

Rainbow of Reflections. Karen Styons. LC 85-61902. 96p. 1985. 6.95 (0-938232-80-0) Winston-Derek.

***Rainbow of Religious Studies.** Gary D. Comstock et al. LC 96-34155. (Gay Men's Issues in Religious Studies). 1996. write for info. (0-930383-48-6) Monument Pr.

Rainbow of Rhinestone Jewelry. Sandy Fichtner & Lynn A. Russell. LC 95-37216. (Schiffer Book for Collectors). 160p. (gr. 10). 1996. pap. 19.95 (0-88740-895-8) Schiffer.

Rainbow of Saris. Ed. by Janice K. Brauer. (Illus.). 156p. (Orig.). 1996. pap. 6.00 (0-9614955-5-3, 22960) Lutheran Womens.

Rainbow of Traction. Ed. by George Krambles & Norman Carlson. LC 88-70492. (B-126 Ser.). (Illus.). 144p. 1988. 45.00 (0-915348-26-8); pap. text ed. 28.00 (0-915348-09-8) Central Electric.

***Rainbow Painting.** Tulku U. Rinpoche. 192p. 1996. pap. 20.00 (962-7341-22-3, Pub. by Rang Jung Yshe HK) Bookpeople.

Rainbow People. Claudette E. Sims. (Illus.). (Orig.). (J). (ps-5). 1992. pap. 6.95 (0-9616121-1-8) Impressions TX.

Rainbow People. Laurence Yep. LC 89-21203. (Trophy Bk.). (Illus.). 208p. (J). (gr. 3-7). 1992. pap. 4.50 (0-06-440441-2, Trophy) HarpC Child Bks.

Rainbow People of God: The Making of a Peaceful Revolution. Desmond Tutu. Ed. by John Allen. LC 94-16011. 304p. 1994. 22.95 (0-385-47546-2) Doubleday.

Rainbow People of God: The Making of a Peaceful Revolution. Desmond Tutu. 320p. 1996. pap. 12.95 (0-385-48374-0, Image Bks) Doubleday.

Rainbow Pony. Anne E. Crompton. (J). (gr. 3-6). 1995. pap. 3.50 (0-671-51121-1, Minstrel Bks) PB.

Rainbow Princess & the Land of Black & White. T. G. Ponte. LC 94-61590. (Illus.). 44p. (J). (gr. k-5). 1996. 14.95 (1-55523-730-4) Winston-Derek.

Rainbow Promise. Mary M. Landis. 195p. 1992. 7.10 (0-317-05260-8) Rod & Staff.

***Rainbow Quest: Anuenue in the Race for the Trans Pac Cup.** Stu Milligan. (Illus.). 184p. (Orig.). 1997. pap. 18.95 (0-913611-09-3) W E C Plant.

Rainbow Quest of Thomas Pynchon. rev. ed. Douglas A. Mackey. LC 80-11219. (Milford Series: Popular Writers of Today: Popular Writers of Today: Vol. 28). 68p. 1989. pap. 13.00 (0-89370-242-0); lib. bdg. 23.00 (0-89370-142-4) Borgo Pr.

Rainbow Readers, 8 vols., Set 1. Resi J. Ditzel. (Illus.). (Orig.). 1992. pap. 9.95 (1-880188-17-1) Bess Pr.

Rainbow Readers, 8 vols., Set 2. Resi J. Ditzel. (Illus.). (Orig.). 1993. pap. 9.95 (1-880188-41-4) Bess Pr.

***Rainbow Reiki: Expanding the Reiki System with Powerful Spiritual Abilities.** Walter Luebeck. (Illus.). 192p. (Orig.). 1997. pap. 14.95 (0-914955-28-4) Lotus Light.

Rainbow Remnants in Rock Bottom Ghetto Sky: Poems. Thylias Moss. LC 90-23770. (National Poetry Ser.: 1990). 72p. (Orig.). 1991. pap. 9.95 (0-89255-157-7) Persea Bks.

Rainbow Rescue. M. Hencher. 2.99 (1-871676-58-4, Pub. by Christian Focus UK) Spring Arbor Dist.

Rainbow Rhapsody. Rick Borsten. LC 88-22294. 224p. 1989. 17.95 (*0-932576-68-0*) Breitenbush Bks.

Rainbow Rhino. Peter Sis. LC 87-2679. (Illus.). 40p. (J). (ps-2). 1993. pap. 5.99 (*0-679-85005-8*) Knopf Bks Yng Read.

Rainbow Ribbon. William H. Hooks & Betty D. Boegehold. LC 93-27706. 32p. (J). Date not set. pap. 3.99 (*0-14-054092-X*) Puffin Bks.

Rainbow Rider. Dahk Knox & Josette Rice. 150p. (C). 1993. pap. text ed. 13.95 (*1-881116-16-6*, 015) Black Forest Pr.

Rainbow, River & Tree. Myron S. Hoyt. LC 85-80095. 104p. (Orig.). 1985. pap. 3.95 (*0-9614817-0-6*) Green Meadow Bks.

Rainbow Roun Mah Shoulder. Linda B. Brown. (Black History Titles Ser.). 1989. mass mkt. 4.99 (*0-345-35876-7*) Ballantine.

Rainbow Round-a-Bout. Ernest Nister. LC 91-77799. 10p. (J). 1993. 7.95 (*1-56397-088-0*) Boyds Mills Pr.

Rainbow Route: An Illustrated History of the Silverton Railroad, the Silverton Northern Railroad & the Silverton, Gladstone & Northerly Railroad. Robert E. Sloan & Carl A. Skowronski. Ed. by Jackson C. Thode et al. (Illus.). 416p. 1975. 62.00 (*0-913582-12-3*) Sundance.

Rainbow Runner. John Cunningham. 288p. 1993. mass mkt. 4.99 (*0-8125-1359-2*) Tor Bks.

Rainbow Serpent. Robert Gardner. 1995. pap. 15.00 (*0-919123-46-5*, Pub. by Inner City CN) BookWorld Dist.

Rainbow Serpent. Dick Roughsey. (J). (ps-3). 1994. pap. 7.00 (*0-207-17433-4*, Pub. by Angus & Robertson AT) HarpC.

Rainbow Serpent: A Chromatic Piece. Ed. by Ira R. Buchler & Kenneth Maddock. (World Anthropology Ser.). (Illus.). x, 228p. 1978. 43.10 (*90-279-7680-5*) Mouton.

Rainbow Slide: Kowanda Kids. S. K. Paulsen. (Illus.). 20p. (J). (ps-2). 1994. pap. 3.95 (*0-9638163-2-2*) Hisel Bk Ends.

Rainbow Sticker Book. Anna Pomaska. (Illus.). (J). (gr. k-3). 1989. pap. 1.00 (*0-486-25910-2*) Dover.

Rainbow Stories. William T. Vollmann. (Contemporary American Fiction Ser.). 544p. 1992. pap. 14.95 (*0-14-017154-1*, Penguin Bks) Viking Penguin.

Rainbow Stress Reduction: Play Your Stress Away with Colorful Healing Art & Stress Reducing Games. Newcastle Publishing Co., Staff. 1991. pap. 19.95 (*0-87877-167-0*) Red Rose Pr.

Rainbow Summer. Cynthia Harrod-Eagles. 1994. lib. bdg. 19.00 (*0-7278-4611-6*) Severn Hse.

Rainbow Summer. large type ed. Cynthia Harrod-Eagles. (Dales Large Print Ser.). 290p. 1996. pap. 17.99 (*1-85389-445-1*, Dales) Ulverscroft.

Rainbow Sword. Adrienne Martine-Barnes. 224p. 1988. pap. 3.50 (*0-380-75455-X*) Avon.

***Rainbow Through the Rain: A Tale of a Japanese Prisoner of War.** Geoffry S. Mowatt. (Illus.). 155p. 1996. pap. 14.95 (*0-9517695-9-6*, Pub. by New Cherwell UK) Intl Spec Bk.

Rainbow Trail. Zane Grey. 1976. 26.95 (*0-8488-1350-2*) Amereon Ltd.

Rainbow Trail. Zane Grey. Ed. by Doug Grad. 1984. mass mkt. 3.99 (*0-671-50523-8*) PB.

Rainbow Trail. Zane Grey. 1994. pap. 4.99 (*0-8125-4818-3*) Tor Bks.

Rainbow Trail. Zane Grey. 1995. mass mkt. 4.99 (*0-671-52666-9*) PB.

Rainbow Trail: The Authorized Edition. Zane Grey. LC 94-41451. xii, 378p. 1995. pap. 10.95 (*0-8032-7049-6*, Bison Books) U of Nebr Pr.

Rainbow Trail - The Vanishing American. Zane Grey. 640p. 1995. mass mkt. 4.99 (*0-06-100920-2*, Harp PBks) HarpC.

Rainbow Trails: Adventures in Rainbow Bridge Country. Ed. by James E. Babbitt. 120p. (Orig.). (YA). 1989. pap. 5.95 (*0-317-93359-0*) Glen Canyon Nat Hist Assn.

Rainbow Tree. Sue A. Clark. Ed. by Gary B. Clark. (Illus.). 18p. (J). (gr. 4-7). 1990. write for info. (*0-318-65868-2*) Point View Pr.

Rainbow Tribe: Ordinary People Journeying on the Red Road. Ed McGaa & Eagle Man. LC 91-55325. 1992. pap. 16.00 (*0-06-250611-0*) Harper SF.

Rainbow Trout. Ed. by G. A. Gall. LC 91-45543. 340p. 1992. 160.50 (*0-444-89127-7*) Elsevier.

***Rainbow Tulip.** Pat Mora. 1998. pap. 13.99 (*0-670-87291-1*) Viking Penguin.

Rainbow Valley. Lucy Maud Montgomery. (Anne of Green Gables). (J). 1976. 21.95 (*0-8488-0591-7*) Amereon Ltd.

Rainbow Valley. Lucy Maud Montgomery. (Anne of Green Gables Ser.). 240p. (J). 1985. mass mkt. 3.99 (*0-553-26921-6*) Bantam.

Rainbow Valley. Lucy Maud Montgomery. (Anne of Green Gables Ser.: 7). 240p. (J). 1987. mass mkt. 3.95 (*0-7704-2268-3*) Bantam.

***Rainbow Valley.** Lucy Maud Montgomery. (Illus.). 282p. (J). 6.98 (*0-7710-6182-X*) McCland & Stewart.

Rainbow Village. Stephen H. Lemberg. (Illus.). (J). (ps-1). 1993. Incl. cass. 9.95 incl. audio (*1-882500-01-6*) SmartSong.

Rainbow Warriors Awake! An Invitation to Remember. Aleia N. O'Reilly & St. Germain. 240p. 1995. pap. 15.95 (*0-9642096-0-8*) Little Hummingbird.

***Rainbow Watchers.** Diana Henery. Date not set. lib. bdg. write for info. (*0-688-10287-5*) Lothrop.

Rainbow Workshop: Building Self-Esteem Through Creative Imagination & Self-Expression! Sue A. Clark. Ed. by Gary B. Clark. (Illus.). 125p. (Orig.). 1990. pap. write for info. (*0-318-65869-0*) Point View Pr.

Rainbow World: Japan in Essays & Translations. Burton Watson. LC 89-81099. 152p. (Orig.). 1990. pap. text ed. 10.00 (*0-913089-06-0*) Broken Moon.

Rainbow Writing: A Journal with Activities for Budding Young Writers. Mary Euretig & Darlene Kreisberg. (Illus.). 100p. (Orig.). (J). (gr. 1-5). 1990. pap. 11.95 (*0-9628216-0-8*) Dream Tree Pr.

Rainbowfishes: In Nature & in the Aquarium. Gerald R. Allen. (Illus.). 182p. 28.95 (*1-56465-149-5*, 16468) Tetra Pr.

Rainbows. Katherine Stone. 512p. 1996. mass mkt. 6.99 (*0-8217-5249-9*, Zebra Kensgtn) Kensgtn Pub Corp.

Rainbows: Selected Poetry of Horiguchi (Surname) Daigaku. Horiguchi Daigaku. Tr. & Intro. by Robert Epp. 358p. (C). 1994. 30.00 (*1-880276-50-X*) Yakusha.

Rainbows: Stories & Customs from Around the World. Created by Naseem Ahmed. 80p. 1996. teacher ed. 10.99 (*1-56417-855-2*, GA1561) Good Apple.

Rainbows ... & Roses. Delia M. McGrath. (Illus.). 200p. (Orig.). 1986. pap. 10.00 (*0-9617794-0-3*) Laurel Pub TX.

Rainbows & Butterflies: Welcome to My World. Vernelle B. Allen. 1994. pap. write for info. (*1-885984-13-8*) Wings of Healing.

Rainbows & Candles: Recognition Services for StudiAct & Missions Adventures. Jan Sutton et al. Ed. by Becky Nelson. 27p. (Orig.). (YA). (gr. 7-12). 1992. pap. 3.95 (*1-56309-049-X*) Womans Mission Union.

Rainbows & Rapture. Rebecca Paisley. 400p. (Orig.). 1992. mass mkt. 4.50 (*0-380-76565-9*) Avon.

Rainbows & Reality: Selected Writings of the Author. Charles S. Rooks. Ed. by John C. Diamond. (Black Church Scholars Ser.: Vol. 1). 158p. (C). 1985. pap. 10.95 (*0-614-08303-6*) Jrnl Interdenom.

Rainbows & Rollercoasters. Glenn Hass. LC 92-56933. 58p. 1993. pap. 7.95 (*1-55523-577-8*) Winston-Derek.

***Rainbows & Shimmering Bridges: Contemporary Japanese Lacquerware.** Masami Shiraishi. (Illus.). 79p. 1996. pap. 30.00 (*0-913304-42-5*) Japan Soc.

Rainbows & Unicorns: And Other Such Realities. Ann Wilmer-Lasky. (Illus.). 28p. (Orig.). 1988. pap. 4.95 (*0-945152-02-7*) Skye Isle Ent.

***Rainbows & Wellies: The Taigh Na Mara Cookbook.** Jackie Redding & Tony Weston. (Illus.). 100p. 1995. 24.95 (*1-899171-70-3*, Pub. by Findhorn Pr UK) Words Distrib.

Rainbows Are Made: Poems by Carl Sandburg. Carl Sandburg. Ed. by Lee B. Hopkins. LC 82-47934. (Illus.). 96p. (J). (gr. 3-7). 1982. 18.00 (*0-15-265480-1*, HB Juv Bks) HarBrace.

***Rainbows Are Made: Poems by Carl Sandburg.** Carl Sandburg. Ed. by Lee B. Hopkins. (Illus.). 96p. 1984. pap. 11.00 (*0-15-265481-X*, Voyager Bks) HarBrace.

Rainbow's End. Genaro Gonzalez. LC 87-18664. 200p. (Orig.). 1988. pap. 9.50 (*0-934770-81-6*) Arte Publico.

Rainbow's End. Martha Grimes. 416p. 1995. 23.00 (*0-679-44188-3*) Knopf.

Rainbow's End. Martha Grimes. 1996. mass mkt. 6.99 (*0-345-39426-7*) Ballantine.

Rainbow's End. Luanne Tovey & Louise DeFelice. 175p. 1985. pap. 3.00 (*0-9613765-1-1*) Rainbow Pubns.

Rainbows End. Ed. by Diana Zeiger. 1996. 69.95 (*1-57553-005-8*) Watermrk Pr.

***Rainbow's End, Vol. 6.** Robert Funderburk. (Innocent Years Ser.). 1997. pap. 8.99 (*1-55661-465-9*) Bethany Hse.

Rainbow's End: A Recovery Workbook for Children & Adults Who Have Suffered Abuse. Laura C. Summer. 1995. pap. 18.95 (*0-533-11245-1*) Vantage.

Rainbow's End: Irish-Americans & the Dilemmas of Urban Machine Politics, 1840-1985. Stephen P. Erie. 359p. 1988. pap. 15.95 (*0-520-07183-2*) U CA Pr.

Rainbow's End: The Judy Garland Show. Coyne S. Sanders. 1992. mass mkt. 5.99 (*0-8217-3708-2*, Zebra Kensgtn) Kensgtn Pub Corp.

Rainbows Falling on My Head: The Magic of the Great God Pan. Al G. Manning. LC 82-90133. (Illus.). 1982. 12.95 (*0-941698-02-5*); pap. 6.95 (*0-941698-03-3*) Pan Ishtar.

Rainbows for Teachers. Janet S. Teitsort. 112p. 1992. 11.99 (*0-8010-8905-0*) Baker Bks.

Rainbows from Revelation: How to Understand the Apocalypse. Jim Combs. 252p. (Orig.). (C). 1994. pap. 19.95 (*1-884764-02-9*) Baptist Bible.

Rainbows, Halos, & Glories. R. Greenler. (Illus.). 195p. (C). 1990. pap. text ed. 31.95 (*0-521-38865-1*) Cambridge U Pr.

Rainbows in the Night. Robyn M. Davis. LC 88-92496. (Illus.). 25p. (Orig.). 1988. pap. 8.95 (*0-9621030-0-4*) Pyramid Indps.

***Rainbows Notes.** Running Press Staff. 1996. pap. text ed. 3.95 (*1-56138-693-6*) Running Pr.

Rainbows of Love. Concetta M. Rossetti. (Illus.). 72p. (Orig.). 1988. pap. 9.99 (*0-925037-03-6*) Great Lks Poetry.

Rainbows of Moon. Deane L. Romano. LC 92-82544. 240p. 1993. pap. 12.00 (*1-56002-204-3*, Univ Edtns) Aegina Pr.

Rainbows of the Moon. Tom McCaughren. 160p. (YA). (gr. 9-12). 1989. 13.95 (*0-947962-45-X*, Pub. by Childrens Pr IE); pap. 7.95 (*0-947962-51-4*, Pub. by Childrens Pr IE) Irish Bks Media.

Rainbow's Promise. Marcy Gray. (Romance Ser.). 1993. mass mkt. 2.75 (*0-373-08967-8*, 5-08967-7) Silhouette.

Rainbows, Snowflakes, & Quarks: Physics & the World Around Us. Hans C. Von Baeyer. LC 92-56852. 192p. 1993. pap. 12.00 (*0-679-73976-9*) Random.

Rainbows Through Tears. Eva H. Groce. (Illus.). 1979. pap. 2.00 (*0-9602440-2-6*) Jesus-First.

Rainbows under the Sea. unabridged ed. Bruce Johnson & Odette Johnson. (Illus.). 32p. (J). (ps up). Date not set. pap. 5.95 (*0-19-540923-X*, Pub. by Stoddart Kids CN) Genl Dist Srvs.

Rainclouds Study the Ten Commandments: A Bibly Study Drama. Sylvia L. Paull. (Illus.). 29p. (Orig.). 1993. pap. 3.25 (*0-88680-393-4*) I E Clark.

Raincoast Macabre. Philip Teece. (Illus.). 160p. (Orig.). 1991. pap. 7.95 (*0-920501-57-5*) Orca Bk Pubs.

Raindrop Children, Vol. 1. Aunt Charley, pseud. (Children of the Elements Ser.). (Illus.). 24p. (J). (gr. 1-2). 1991. pap. 5.95 (*1-880945-00-2*) Animated Elements.

Raindrops & Rainbows. Rose Wyler. Ed. by Jane Steltenpohl. (Outdoor Science Ser.). (Illus.). 32p. (J). (gr. k-2). 1989. pap. 4.95 (*0-671-66350-X*, Julian Messner) Silver Burdett Pr.

Raindrops Keep Falling on My Tent. Joy Mackay. 20p. 1981. pap. 4.95 (*0-87603-060-6*) Am Camping.

Rained Out BBQ. Sherry De Vries & Wayne De Vries. 32p. 1993. pap. 4.95 (*1-883849-01-2*) Nine Hund Forty Six Pr.

Rainer Maria Rilke. Patricia P. Brodsky. (Twayne's World Authors Ser.: Vol. 796). 192p. (C). 1988. 26.95 (*0-8057-8226-5*, Twayne) Scribnrs Ref.

Rainer Maria Rilke: Aspects of His Mind & Poetry. Rainer M. Rilke. Ed. by William Rose & G. Craig Houston. LC 73-114098. (Illus.). 189p. 1970. reprint ed. 45.00 (*0-87752-092-5*) Gordian.

Rainer Maria Rilke: Contemporary Feminist Fairy Tales in North America & England. Albert E. Flemming. 224p. 1986. pap. 11.95 (*0-415-90405-6*, Routledge NY) Routledge.

Rainer Maria Rilke: Creative Anguish of a Modern Poet. Willem L. Graff. LC 56-8381. 363p. reprint ed. pap. 103.50 (*0-317-26667-5*, 2055991) Bks Demand.

Rainer Maria Rilke: Masks & the Man. H. F. Peters. LC 77-24731. 240p. 1977. reprint ed. 45.00 (*0-87752-198-0*) Gordian.

***Rainer Maria Rilke: New Poems/Neue Gedichte.** Tr. & Text by Stephen Cohn. 296p. (ENG & GER.). 1997. pap. 18.95 (*1-85754-323-8*, Pub. by Carcanet Pr UK) Paul & Co Pubs.

Rainer Maria Rilke: Selected Poems. Tr. by Albert E. Flemming from GER. (Illus.). 224p. (Orig.). 1985. pap. 11.95 (*0-416-01191-8*) Routledge Chapman & Hall.

***Rainer Werner Fassbinder.** Ed. by Laurence Kardish & Juliane Lorenz. (Illus.). 112p. 1997. pap. 16.95 (*0-87070-109-6*, 0-8109-6170-9) Mus of Modern Art.

Rainer Werner Fassbinder: Plays. Rainer W. Fassbinder. Ed. by Denis M. Calandra. (PAJ Bks.). 192p. 1992. reprint ed. pap. 14.95 (*0-933826-82-6*) PAJ Pubns.

Rainey of Illinois: A Political Biography, 1903-34. Robert A. Walker. LC 77-23859. (Illinois Studies in the Social Sciences: No. 60). 272p. reprint ed. pap. 77.60 (*0-317-29012-6*, 2020246) Bks Demand.

Rainfall As the Basis for Urban Run-off Design & Analysis: Proceedings of a Specialised Seminar Held in Copenhagen, Denmark, 24-26 August, 1983. Ed. by Harremoes. (Illus.). 370p. 1984. pap. 88.00 (*0-08-031506-2*, Pergamon Pr) Elsevier.

Rainfall-Runoff Relationship. Ed. by Vijay P. Singh. LC 81-71290. 1982. 42.00 (*0-918334-45-4*) WRP.

Rainfed Rice Production in the Philippines: A Combined Agronomic Economic Study. Kenneth M. Menz. 90p. (C). 1989. text ed. 120.00 (*0-949511-73-0*, Pub. by ACIAR) St Mut.

Rainforest. Linda Abbott & John R. Smith. (Illus.). 52p. 1994. 11.95 (*0-936459-24-7*) Stained Glass.

Rainforest. Keith Fualkner. (Illus.). 17p. (J). (ps). 1994. 11.45 (*1-881445-36-4*) Sandvik Pub.

Rainforest. Edward R. Ricciuti. (Biomes of the World Ser.). 64p. (J). (gr. 4-6). 1995. lib. bdg. 17.95 (*0-7614-0081-8*, Benchmark NY) Marshall Cavendish.

Rainforest. Laura Tangley. (Earth at Risk Ser.). (Illus.). (YA). (gr. 5 up). 1992. lib. bdg. 19.95 (*0-7910-1579-3*) Chelsea Hse.

***Rainforest.** Selina Wood. LC 97-8237. (Closer Look at... Ser.). (J). 1997. lib. bdg. 14.90 (*0-7613-0546-7*, Copper Beech Bks) Millbrook Pr.

Rainforest Action Network Wood Users Guide. Pamela Wellner & Eugene Dickey. 64p. (Orig.). 1991. pap. write for info. (*0-9628033-1-6*) Rainforest Act.

Rainforest Animals. Michael Chinery. LC 91-53143. (Tell Me about Bks.). (Illus.). 40p. (Orig.). (J). (gr. 2-5). 1992. pap. 4.99 (*0-679-82047-7*) Random Bks Yng Read.

Rainforest Animals Dot-to-Dot. Susan Baumgart. (Illus.). 64p. (J). 1995. pap. 5.95 (*0-8069-0896-3*) Sterling.

***Rainforest Birds.** Bobbie Kalman. (Birds up Close Ser.). (Illus.). 32p. (J). 1997. pap. 5.95 (*0-86505-767-2*); lib. bdg. 18.64 (*0-86505-753-2*) Crabtree Pub Co.

Rainforest Book. Scott Lewis. LC 90-70820. 112p. 1990. pap. 7.95 (*0-9626072-1-5*) Living Planet Pr.

Rainforest Buffer Zones: Guidelines for Protected Area Management. Jeffrey A. Sayer. (Illus.). 110p. 1990. pap. 17.00 (*2-8317-0072-8*, Pub. by IUCN SZ) Island Pr.

***Rainforest Cities: The Urban Transformation of Amazonia.** John O. Browder & Brian J. Godfrey. LC 96-33481. 1997. write for info. (*0-231-10654-8*); pap. write for info. (*0-231-10655-6*) Col U Pr.

***Rainforest Counts.** Lisa McCourt. (Illus.). (J). 1997. write for info. (*0-614-29315-4*) BrdgeWater.

***Rainforest Counts.** Lisa McCourt. (Illus.). 32p. (J). (ps-3). 1997. 14.95 (*0-8167-4388-6*) BrdgeWater.

***Rainforest Counts.** Lisa McCourt. (Illus.). 32p. (J). (ps-3). 1997. pap. 4.95 (*0-8167-4458-0*) BrdgeWater.

Rainforest Edge: Plant & Soil Ecology of Maraca Island, Brazil. Ed. by John Hemming. LC 93-10964. 1994. text ed. 79.95 (*0-7190-3477-9*, Pub. by Manchester Univ Pr UK) St Martin.

Rainforest for Beginners. Naomi Rosenblatt. (Illus.). 96p. (Orig.). 1992. pap. 7.95 (*0-86316-005-0*) Writers & Readers.

Rainforest Honey. Teresa Hart. Date not set. pap. 14.99 (*0-525-45388-1*) NAL-Dutton.

Rainforest Indians. Ruth Thompson. LC 95-25250. (Footsteps in Time Ser.). (Illus.). 24p. (J). (gr. k-3). 1996. lib. bdg. 15.00 (*0-516-08074-1*) Childrens.

Rainforest into Desert: Adventures in Australia's Tropical North. Ellen E. Wohl. (Illus.). 192p. (C). 1994. 29.95 (*0-87081-334-X*) Univ Pr Colo.

Rainforest Politics: Ecological Destruction in Southeast Asia. Philip Hurst. LC 89-35865. (Illus.). 320p. (C). 1990. pap. 19.95 (*0-86232-839-X*, Pub. by Zed Bks Ltd UK) Humanities.

Rainforest Relations: Gender & Resource Use among the Mende of Gola, Sierra Leone. Melissa Leach. (Illus.). 296p. (C). 1994. text ed. 49.00 (*1-56098-500-3*) Smithsonian.

Rainforest Secrets. Arthur Dorros. 40p. (J). 1990. 15.95 (*0-590-43369-5*, Scholastic Hardcover) Scholastic Inc.

Rainforest Wildlife. Antonia Cunningham. (World Wildlife Ser.). (Illus.). 32p. (J). (gr. 3-8). 1993. pap. text ed. 6.95 (*0-7460-0940-2*, Usborne); lib. bdg. 14.95 (*0-88110-640-2*, Usborne) EDC.

Rainforests. (Conservation 2000 Ser.). (YA). (gr. 7-12). 1992. 24.95 (*0-7134-6573-5*, Pub. by Batsford UK) Trafalgar.

***Rainforests.** (At Issue Ser.). (YA). (gr. 5-12). 1997. pap. 8.96 (*1-56510-694-6*) Greenhaven.

***Rainforests.** (At Issue Ser.). (YA). (gr. 5-12). 1997. lib. bdg. 13.96 (*1-56510-695-4*) Greenhaven.

Rainforests. Rodney Aldis. LC 91-20595. (Ecology Watch Ser.). (Illus.). 48p. (J). (gr. 4-6). 1991. lib. bdg. 13.95 (*0-87518-495-2*, Dillon Silver Burdett) Silver Burdett Pr.

Rainforests. Nicola Barber. (Illus.). 45p. (J). (gr. 5-8). 1996. 19.95 (*0-237-51324-2*, Pub. by Evans Bros Ltd UK) Trafalgar.

***Rainforests.** Ladybird Staff. (J). 1997. pap. 9.99 (*0-7214-5719-3*, Ladybrd) Penguin.

Rainforests. Peter Murray. (Biomes of Nature Ser.). 32p. (J). (gr. 2-6). 1996. lib. bdg. 22.79 (*1-56766-278-1*) Childs World.

Rainforests. Kate Petty. (Around & About Ser.). (Illus.). 32p. (J). (gr. 2-4). 1993. pap. 5.95 (*0-8120-1760-9*) Barron.

***Rainforests.** Kathy Ross. (Crafts for Kids Who Are Wild about... Ser.). (J). 1997. pap. text ed. 7.95 (*0-7613-0227-1*) Millbrook Pr.

Rainforests. Lois Warburton. LC 90-46278. (Overview Ser.). (Illus.). 96p. (J). (gr. 5-8). 1991. lib. bdg. 17.96 (*1-56006-150-2*) Lucent Bks.

Rainforests. Darcy Richardson. (Bertinetti Ser.). (Illus.). 128p. 1992. reprint ed. 14.98 (*0-8317-7342-1*) Smithmark.

Rainforests: A Celebration. Compiled by Living Earth Foundation Staff. (Illus.). 224p. 1992. 35.00 (*0-87701-790-5*); pap. 22.95 (*0-8118-0155-1*) Chronicle Bks.

Rainforests: A Guide to Research & Tourist Facilities at Selected Tropical Forest Sites in Central & South America. James L. Castner. LC 89-81847. (Illus.). 416p. (Orig.). 1990. pap. 21.95 (*0-9625150-2-7*) Feline Pr.

***Rainforests of the World: Gardens of the Gods.** Art Wolfe. LC 97-4087. 1997. write for info. (*0-517-88643-X*, Crown) Crown Pub Group.

***Rainforests to Flowers - Gardens on Java.** Greg Asbury & Elvin McDonald. Ed. by Judy Smith. (Illus.). 112p. 1996. 24.95 (*0-9654003-0-1*) Mitra Publns.

***Rainhouse & Ocean: Speeches for the Papago Year.** Ruth M. Underhill et al. LC 96-52169. 160p. 1997. reprint ed. pap. 16.95 (*0-8165-1774-6*) U of Ariz Pr.

Rainier & Grace. Jeffrey Robinson. 1990. mass mkt. 4.95 (*0-380-71310-1*) Avon.

Rainier Ice Caves & Other Northwest Stories. Jeffrey H. Silver. (Illus.). 32p. (J). (gr. 5 up). 1983. pap. 4.00 (*0-910867-01-1*) Silver Seal Bks.

Rainin' Recipes Cookbook. Telephone Pioneers of America, Charles B. Hopkins Chapter Staff. LC 92-23275. 1992. 10.00 (*0-87197-347-2*) Favorite Recipes.

Raining Backwards. Roberto Fernandez. LC 87-35118. 224p. (Orig.). 1988. pap. 9.50 (*0-934770-79-4*) Arte Publico.

***Raining Cats & Dogs.** Todd Mallet. 72p. 1994. pap. 9.50 (*1-56770-304-6*) S Scheewe Pubns.

Raining Justice: Freewill Is but an Illusion. Stephan Forbes. LC 92-91103. 72p. 1993. pap. 8.00 (*1-56002-277-9*, Univ Edtns) Aegina Pr.

Raining Ruins & Rockstones. Odimumba Kwamdela, pseud. LC 81-84012. 76p. 1981. pap. 3.00 (*0-941266-00-1*) Kibo Bks.

Rainmaker. Kathryn Buchen. 153p. (Orig.). (J). 1995. pap. 7.50 (*0-9645405-0-9*) K Beson.

Rainmaker. John Grisham. 448p. 1995. 25.95 (*0-385-42473-6*) Doubleday.

Rainmaker. John Grisham. 272p. 1996. mass mkt. 7.99 (*0-440-22165-X*) Dell.

Rainmaker. limited ed. John Grisham. 1995. 250.00 (*0-385-47513-6*) Doubleday.

Rainmaker: A Passion for Politics. Keith Davey. (Illus.). 356p. 1986. 24.95 (*0-7737-2090-1*) Genl Dist Srvs.

Rainmaker: A Passion for Politics. Keith Davey. (Illus.). 416p. 1988. pap. 14.95 (*0-7737-5138-6*) Genl Dist Srvs.

Rainmaker: Saga of J. Beck. Anthony Bianco. 1993. pap. write for info. (*0-449-22135-0*) Fawcett.

Rainmaker: The Saga of Jeff Beck, Wall Street's Mad Dog. Anthony Bianco. LC 88-42821. 320p. 1991. 24.50 (*0-394-57023-5*) Random.

Rainmaker: The Story of Venerable Ngagpa Yeshe Dorje Rinpoche. Marsha Woolf & Karen Blank. 1991. 27.50 (*0-938434-18-7*); pap. 16.95 (*0-938434-15-2*) Sigo Pr.

R

Rainmaker of Cullmans Bluff: Short Vowel II Sequence. Ellis Richardson. (Read Aloud Ser.: Bk. 8). 32p. (Orig.). 1990. pap. text ed. 4.00 (*1-56775-025-7*, SVIIS8-3) ISM Teach Systs.

Rainmaker of Deadman. large type ed. Lloyd Madison. (Linford Western Library). 304p. 1987. pap. 15.99 (*0-7089-6353-6*, Linford) Ulverscroft.

Rainmakers. E. J. Bird. LC 92-29789. (J). (gr. 4 up). 1993. lib. bdg. 14.96 (*0-87614-748-1*, Carolrhoda) Lerner Group.

***Rainmakers.** Francis Harvey. 54p. 1988. pap. 11.95 (*1-85235-024-5*) Dufour.

Rainmakers: American "Pluviculture" to World War II. Clark C. Spence. LC 79-26022. (Illus.). 191p. reprint ed. pap. 54.50 (*0-7837-4645-8*, 2044369) Bks Demand.

Rainmaker's Dog. Cynthia Dresser. 1994. teacher ed., pap. text ed. 5.00 (*0-312-06742-9*) St Martin.

Rainmaker's Dog: International Folktales to Build Communicative Skills. Cynthia Dresser. 336p. 1994. pap. text ed. 14.50 (*0-312-06741-0*) St Martin.

Rainmaker's Dream. Sherry Garland. LC 96-33288. (J). 1997. pap. 6.00 (*0-15-200652-4*) HarBrace.

Rainmaking: The Intelligent Guide to Selling a Professional Service. Stuart Hoffman. 208p. (Orig.). 1990. pap. 19.95 (*0-9626828-8-8*) Propeller Head.

Rainrituals. Aneb Kgositsile. 1990. 7.00 (*0-940713-05-5*) Broadside Pr.

***Rains All the Time: A Connoisseur's History of Weather in the Pacific Northwest.** David Laskin. LC 97-16051. 224p. (Orig.). 1997. pap. 16.95 (*1-57061-063-0*) Sasquatch Bks.

***Rains-Asia: An Assessment Model for Acid Deposition in Asia.** Robert J. Downing et al. LC 97-10470. (Directions in Development Ser.). 1997. write for info. (*0-8213-3919-2*) World Bank.

Rains Came. Louis Bromfield. 1993. reprint ed. lib. bdg. 37.95 (*1-56849-190-5*) Buccaneer Bks.

RAINS Model of Acidification: Science & Strategies in Europe. Joseph Alcamo. (C). 1990. lib. bdg. 171.00 (*0-7923-0781-X*) Kluwer Ac.

Rains of the Late Season: The Holy Spirit at the Birth of a New Community. Brother Ephraim. 136p. (C). 1990. 49.00 (*0-85439-417-6*, Pub. by St Paul Pubns UK) St Mut.

Rainshadow. Mike O'Connor. 100p. 1989. ring bd. 6.95 (*0-912887-03-6*) Empty Bowl.

Rainshadow: Poems. Albert Garcia. LC 95-19725. 64p. 1996. pap. 9.95 (*0-914278-68-1*) Copper Beech.

Rainshine & Sundrops: Language Fun for Young Children. Billie W. Lee. (Illus.). 40p. (Orig.). 1987. 6.95 (*0-9619675-0-1*) P&M Bear Pubns.

Rainsinger. Ruth Wind. 1996. mass mkt. 3.99 (*0-373-24031-7*, 1-24031-6) Silhouette.

Rainsong. Phyllis A. Whitney. 1984. mass mkt. 5.99 (*0-449-20510-X*, Crest) Fawcett.

***Rainsong/Snowsong.** Philemon Sturges & Shari Halpern. (Illus.). 32p. (J). (ps-1). Date not set. lib. bdg. 15.88 (*1-55858-472-2*) North-South Bks NYC.

Rainsong/Snowsong. Philemon Sturges. LC 95-954. (Illus.). (J). (ps-1). Date not set. 15.95 (*1-55858-471-4*) North-South Bks NYC.

Rainstick: A Fable. Sandra C. Robinson & Peter Grosshauser. LC 94-21587. (Illus.). 40p. (Orig.). (J). (gr. 2 up). 1994. pap. text ed. 9.95 (*1-56044-284-0*) Falcon Pr MT.

Raintree County. Ross Lockridge, Jr. 1066p. 1991. reprint ed. lib. bdg. 49.95 (*0-89966-865-8*) Buccaneer Bks.

Raintree County: A Great American Novel about Love, Tragedy, & the American Dream. Ross Lockridge, Jr. 1088p. 1994. pap. 18.95 (*0-14-023666-X*, Penguin Bks) Viking Penguin.

Raintree Steck-Vaughn Illustrated Science Encyclopedia, 24 vols., Set. LC 96-11078. (Illus.). (J). 1996. lib. bdg. 379.00 (*0-8172-3943-X*) Raintree Steck-V.

Raintree Steck-Vaughn Science Encyclopedia: Macintosh Version, 24 vols., Set. Raintree Staff. (Illus.). (J). 1996. 429.00 incl. cd-rom (*0-8172-3917-0*) Raintree Steck-V.

Raintree Steck-Vaughn Science Encyclopedia: Windows Version. Raintree Staff. (J). 1996. 429.00 incl. cd-rom (*0-8172-3918-9*) Raintree Steck-V.

Rainwater Penetration of Modern Buildings: Investigating Water Related Defects. K. F. Endean. 160p. 1995. 84.95 (*0-566-07575-X*, Pub. by Gower UK) Ashgate Pub Co.

Rainwater Reservoirs above Ground Structures for Roof Catchment: Most Common Rainwater Tanks in Comparison & Construction Manual. Rolf Hasse. Ed. by Deutsches Zentrum fur Entwicklungs-technologien-GATE. (GATE Ser.). (Illus.). 202p. 1989. pap. 22.00 (*3-528-02049-0*, Pub. by Vieweg & Sohn GW) Informatica.

***Rainy City.** Earl Emerson. 1997. mass mkt. 5.99 (*0-345-41405-5*) Ballantine.

Rainy City. Earl W. Emerson. (Thomas Black Ser. No. 1). 240p. 1985. mass mkt. 4.99 (*0-380-89517-X*) Avon.

Rainy City Rainbow. Anne Sibley. (Whole-Language Big Bks.). (Illus.). 16p. (Orig.). (J). (ps-2). 1994. pap. 14.95 (*1-56784-060-4*) Newbridge Comms.

Rainy Day. Sandra Markle. LC 91-17059. (Illus.). 32p. (J). (ps-2). 1993. 15.95 (*0-531-05976-6*); lib. bdg. 16.99 (*0-531-08576-7*) Orchard Bks Watts.

Rainy Day: Magic for Wonderful Wet Weather. Imogene Forte. LC 83-82332. (Tabletop Learning Ser.). (Illus.). 80p. (J). (gr. k-6). 1983. pap. text ed. 4.95 (*0-86530-094-1*, IP94-1) Incentive Pubns.

Rainy Day: Stories & Poems. Ed. by Caroline Feller Bauer. LC 85-45170. (Illus.). 96p. (J). (gr. 2-5). 1986. lib. bdg. 14.89 (*0-397-32105-8*, Lipp Jr Bks) HarpC Child Bks.

Rainy Day Activities for the Commodore 64. Nancy K. Mayer. write for info. (*0-318-58231-7*) P-H.

Rainy Day Activity Book: How to Make Play Dough, Bubbles, Monster Repellent & More. Jennifer Rader. (Illus.). 112p. (J). 1995. pap. 8.95 (*0-385-48127-6*, Main St Bks) Doubleday.

Rainy Day Activity Book: How to Make Play Dough, Bubbles, Monster Spray & More. Jennifer Rader. LC 94-27587. 112p. (J). 1995. pap. 12.00 (*0-385-47544-6*) Doubleday.

Rainy Day Blues & Greens. John Stoudenmire. LC 81-90126. 105p. (Orig.). 1981. pap. 6.95 (*0-686-32117-0*) Singing River.

Rainy Day Book. Anne Ingram & Peggy O'Donnell. (Illus.). 48p. (J). (gr. 3 up). 1992. pap. 6.95 (*0-920775-44-6*, Pub. by Greey dePencier CN) Firefly Bks Ltd.

Rainy Day Book. A. Smith. (Rainy Day Bk.). (Illus.). 96p. (J). (gr. 1 up). 1995. pap. 13.95 (*0-7460-1713-8*, Usborne) EDC.

Rainy Day Book. A. Smith. (Rainy Day Bk.). (Illus.). 96p. (J). (gr. 1 up). 1995. lib. bdg. 21.95 (*0-88110-718-2*, Usborne) EDC.

Rainy Day Dream. Michael D. Chesworth. (J). (ps-3). 1992. 14.00 (*0-374-36177-0*) FS&G.

Rainy Day Fun. Karan Gleason. (Illus.). 112p. (J). (gr. k-4). 1987. pap. 10.99 (*0-86653-408-3*, GA1002) Good Apple.

Rainy Day Fun. Janet Palazzo. LC 87-10842. (Illus.). 32p. (J). (gr. k-2). 1988. lib. bdg. 12.95 (*0-8167-1095-3*) Troll Communs.

Rainy Day Kate. Lenore Blegvad. LC 87-16805. (Illus.). 32p. (J). (gr. k-4). 1988. lib. bdg. 13.95 (*0-689-50442-X*, McElderry) S&S Childrens.

Rainy Day Kisses. Debbie Macomber. (Romance Ser.: No. 3076). 1990. pap. 2.50 (*0-373-03076-2*) Harlequin Bks.

Rainy Day Play! Explore, Create, Discover, Pretend. Nancy F. Castaldo. Ed. by Susan Williamson. LC 95-50477. (Little Hands Book Ser.: No. 6). (Illus.). 144p. (Orig.). (J). (ps up). 1996. pap. 12.95 (*1-885593-00-7*) Williamson Pub Co.

Rainy Day Projects. Petra Boase. (Step by Step Ser.). 96p. 1994. 9.98 (*0-8317-8056-8*) Smithmark.

Rainy Day Projects for Children. Gerri Jenny & Sherrie Gould. (Projects for Parents Ser.). (Illus.). 128p. (Orig.). 1990. pap. 10.95 (*1-878767-61-5*) Murdoch Bks.

***Rainy Day Projects for Kids.** Petra Boase. (Illus.). 96p. (J). (gr. 2-7). 1997. pap. 9.95 (*1-85967-544-1*, Lorenz Bks) Anness Pub.

Rainy Day Projects for Kids: Activity Kits. (J). (gr. 1-5). 1996. 19.98 (*0-8317-3563-5*) Smithmark.

Rainy Day Recess: Action-Packed Ideas for the Great Indoors! Pam Schiller & Mike Artell. 64p. (J). (ps-4). 1996. 8.99 (*0-86653-864-X*, FE3864) Fearon Teach Aids.

***Rainy Day Rescue.** 24p. (J). 1997. pap. write for info. (*0-7814-3023-2*, Chariot Bks) Chariot Victor.

Rainy Day Rescue. Barbara Davoll. (Illus.). 24p. (J). 1988. audio 11.99 (*0-89693-619-8*, 3-1619, Victor Bks) Chariot Victor.

Rainy Day Rescue. Barbara Davoll. (Christopher Churchmouse Classics Ser.). (Illus.). 24p. (J). 1988. 8.99 (*0-89693-408-X*, 6-1408, Victor Bks) Chariot Victor.

Rainy Day Rhymes. Illus. by Ellen Kandoian. 48p. (J). (gr. 2-5). 1992. 13.95 (*0-395-59967-9*) HM.

Rainy Day Rhymes: A Collection of Chants, Forecasts & Tales. Ed. by Michele Palmer. LC 84-60412. (Illus.). 24p. (Orig.). (J). (gr. k up). 1984. pap. 2.95 (*0-932306-02-0*) Rocking Horse.

Rainy Day Sunny Day Any Day Activity Book No. 1. Concordia Publishing Staff. 48p. 1994. pap. 4.99 (*0-570-04759-5*, 56-1778) Concordia.

Rainy Day Sunny Day Any Day Activity Book No. 2. Concordia Publishing Staff. 48p. 1994. pap. 4.99 (*0-570-04760-9*, 56-1779) Concordia.

Rainy Day Sunny Day Any Day Activity Book No. 3. Concordia Publishing Staff. 48p. 1994. pap. 4.99 (*0-570-04761-7*, 56-1780) Concordia.

Rainy Day Surprises You Can Make. Robyn Supraner. LC 80-19858. (Illus.). 48p. (J). (gr. 1-5). 1981. lib. bdg. 12.50 (*0-89375-428-5*) Troll Communs.

Rainy Days. June M. Milam. Ed. by Chris Gilmer & Laura L. Peaster. (Drugless Douglass Tales Ser.). (Illus.). 20p. (J). (ps). 1994. student ed. 4.95 (*1-884307-12-4*); pap. 42.95 (*1-884307-11-6*) Dev Res Educ.

***Rainy Days.** June M. Milam. Ed. by Charlotte C. Daley. Tr. by Carmen Miranda. (Drugless Douglass Tales Ser.). (Illus.). 24p. (Orig.). (SPA.). (J). (ps). 1997. pap. 32.95 (*1-884307-30-2*) Dev Res Educ.

***Rainy Days.** June M. Milam. Ed. by Charlotte C. Daley. Tr. by Carmen Miranda. (Drugless Douglass Tales Ser.). (Illus.). 24p. (Orig.). (SPA.). (J). (ps). 1997. pap. 6.95 (*1-884307-31-0*) Dev Res Educ.

***Rainy Days: Dias de Lluvia: An Anthology of Spanish Women Writers.** Ed. by Montserrat Lunati. (Hispanic Classics Ser.). (Illus.). 250p. 1997. 49.95 (*0-85668-635-2*, Pub. by Aris & Phillips UK) David Brown.

***Rainy Days: Dias de Lluvia: An Anthology of Spanish Women Writers.** Ed. by Montserrat Lunati. (Hispanic Classics Ser.). (Illus.). 250p. 1997. pap. 24.95 (*0-85668-636-0*, Pub. by Aris & Phillips UK) David Brown.

Rainy Days & Sardine Tins. Marie D. Winfree. 40p. 1994. pap. 7.00 (*1-884778-01-1*) Old Mountain.

Rainy Days & Saturdays. Linda Hetzer. LC 95-967. (Illus.). 240p. (J). (gr. 1-7). 1996. pap. 9.95 (*1-56305-513-9*, 3513) Workman Pub.

Rainy Days Are for Baking: Les Recettes Preferee de Penelope P'Nutt. Nancy Palumbo. (Illus.). 32p. (J). (gr. k-6). 1989. student ed. 5.95 (*0-927024-01-2*) Crayons Pubns.

Rainy Days Are for Baking: Penelope P'Nutt los Dias Lluviosos Son Para Cocinar. Nancy Palumbo. (Illus.). 1988. 5.95 (*0-927024-00-4*) Crayons Pubns.

Rainy Days Are for Pulling Weeds. Virginia Mackay. (Illus.). 176p. 1996. pap. 10.00 (*1-885781-01-6*) Soapstone Pr.

Rainy Days in Texas Funbook. Wallace O. Chariton. (Regional Juvenile Ser.). 160p. (Orig.). (J). (gr. k-6). 1990. pap. 7.95 (*1-55622-130-4*, Rep of TX Pr) Wordware Pub.

Rainy Lake. Mary F. Rockcastle. 278p. 1994. 22.50 (*1-55597-218-7*) Graywolf.

Rainy Lake. Mary F. Rockcastle. LC 94-29928. 278p. 1996. pap. 12.95 (*1-55597-242-X*) Graywolf.

***Rainy, Rainy Saturday.** HarBrace Staff. (J). 1995. pap. 11.00 (*0-15-305581-2*) HarBrace.

Rainy, Rainy Saturday. Jack Prelutsky. LC 79-22217. (Greenwillow Read-Alone Bks.). (Illus.). 48p. (J). (gr. 1-3). 1980. lib. bdg. 15.93 (*0-688-84252-6*) Greenwillow.

Rainy River Country: A Brief History of the Region Bordering Minnesota & Ontario. Grace L. Nute. LC 71-96385. (Publications of the Minnesota Historical Society). 193p. reprint ed. pap. 55.10 (*0-8357-3314-9*, 2039538) Bks Demand.

Rainy Season. Adele Griffin. (Illus.). 208p. (J). (gr. 5-9). 1996. 14.95 (*0-395-81181-3*) HM.

Rainy Season: Haiti Since Duvalier. Amy Wilentz. 304p. 1990. pap. 9.95 (*0-671-70628-4*) S&S Trade.

***Rainy Spell & Other Korean Stories.** expanded rev. ed. Ed. & Tr. by Suh Ji-Moon from KOR. 288p. (C). (gr. 13). 1997. 62.95 (*0-7656-0138-9*, East Gate Bk) M E Sharpe.

***Rainy Spell & Other Korean Stories.** expanded rev. ed. Ed. & Tr. by Ji-moon Suh. 288p. (gr. 13). 1997. pap. 21.95 (*0-7656-0139-7*) M E Sharpe.

Rainy Sunday. Malcolm Arnold. Ed. by Linda S. Krentz. 157p. 1991. 37.50 (*0-9628256-0-3*) Swegal & Son.

Rainy Sunday. rev. ed. Franz B. Swegal & Malcolm Arnold. 157p. 1991. 19.95 (*0-9628256-1-1*) Swegal & Son.

Rainy, Windy, Snowy, Sunny Days: Linking Fiction to Nonfiction. Phyllis J. Perry. (Literature Bridges to Science Ser.). xviii, 145p. 1996. pap. text ed. 22.00 (*1-56308-392-2*) Teacher Ideas Pr.

***Rairarubia.** W. Royce Adams. 114p. (Orig.). 1997. mass mkt. 4.99 (*1-55237-203-0*, Pub. by Comnwlth Pub CN) Partners Pubs Grp.

Raisa Gorbachev. Jill Wheeler. LC 92-16678. (Leading Ladies Ser.). (J). 1992. lib. bdg. 13.98 (*1-56239-118-6*) Abdo & Dghtrs.

Raise a Banner to the Lord: 60 Dynamic Banner Designs for Worship Settings. Dale A. Bargmann. LC 93-31200. (Illus.). 96p. (Orig.). 1994. pap. 9.99 (*0-570-04626-2*, 12-3207) Concordia.

***Raise & Release: Rearing Live Butterflies for All Reasons & Seasons.** Kaela Easton. 66p. (Orig.). 1996. pap. 20.00 (*0-9655248-0-9*) Butterfly Exprs.

Raise Heaven & Earth: The Story of Martin Marietta People & Their Pioneering Achievements. William B. Harwood. LC 93-30509. 1993. 35.00 (*0-671-74998-6*) S&S Trade.

Raise Hell & Sell Newspapers: Alden J. Blethen & The Seattle Times. Sharon Boswell & Lorraine McConaghy. (Illus.). 304p. 1996. pap. 14.95 (*0-87422-127-7*) Wash St U Pr.

Raise High the Roof Beam, Carpenters & Seymour: An Introduction. J. D. Salinger. 224p. (YA). 1991. mass mkt. 4.99 (*0-316-76951-7*) Little.

Raise High the Roof Beam, Carpenters & Seymour: An Introduction. J. D. Salinger. Bd. with Seymour - An Introduction. 248p. (YA). 1963. 22.95 (*0-316-76957-6*) Little.

Raise Method Manual. Raise Language Group Staff. 480p. 1995. pap. text ed. 50.00 (*0-13-752700-4*) P-H.

Raise More Money for Your Nonprofit Organization: A Guide to Evaluating & Improving Your Fundraising. Anne L. New. (Orig.). 1991. pap. text ed. 14.95 (*0-87954-388-4*) Foundation Ctr.

Raise the Issues: An Integrated Approach to Critical Thinking. Carol Numrich. LC 93-33842. 1994. pap. text ed. 20.53 (*0-8013-1014-8*) Longman.

Raise the Issues: An Integrated Approach to Critical Thinking. Carol Numrich. LC 93-33842. 1994. audio 37.95 (*0-8013-1015-6*) Longman.

Raise the Red Dawn. Bart Davis. 352p. 1991. mass mkt. 4.95 (*0-671-69663-7*, Pocket Star Bks) PB.

Raise the Red Lantern. Su Tong. 272p. 1996. pap. 11.95 (*0-14-026030-7*) Viking Penguin.

Raise the Sail. Paul Johnson & Nicole Johnson. 48p. 1993. pap. 10.00 (*0-9635484-0-9*); write for info. (*0-9635484-9-2*); vhs 15.00 (*0-9635484-1-7*) P&N Johnson.

Raise the Speed, Reduce the Errors. B. W. Canning. (Pitman Secretarial Science Ser.). 96p. 1975. pap. 14.95 (*0-8464-0782-5*) Beekman Pubs.

Raise the Titanic! Clive Cussler. Ed. by Paul McCarthy. 352p. 1990. mass mkt. 6.99 (*0-671-72519-X*) PB.

Raise the Titanic! Clive Cussler. 1994. reprint ed. lib. bdg. 32.95 (*1-56849-269-3*) Buccaneer Bks.

Raise the White Flag: A Life in Occupied Jersey. Donald P. Journeaux. 190p. 1995. pap. 12.95 (*1-85253-321-8*) Cimino Pub Grp.

Raise the World & Other Rhymes. Alex Gerber. LC 95-95344. 56p. (Orig.). 1995. pap. 12.00 (*0-9635367-0-2*) Gerber Educ.

Raise up off Me: A Portrait of Hampton Hawes. Hampton Hawes & Don Asher. LC 79-15345. (Quality Paperbacks Ser.). 180p. 1979. reprint ed. pap. 10.95 (*0-306-80101-9*) Da Capo.

Raise Your Child's Creative IQ. Simone Bibeau. (Illus.). 128p. (Orig.). 1986. pap. text ed. 65.00 (*0-940406-14-4*); audio (*0-318-60221-0*) Perception Pubns.

Raise Your Kids to Be Winners: Secrets of Parenting with Horse-Sense. Martha N. Vogt & Christina Vogt. 136p. (Orig.). 1985. pap. 6.95 (*0-931515-02-5*) Triumph Pr.

Raise Your Productivity with an IBM PC. Andrew J. Vazsonyi. (Illus.). 240p. 1985. 30.95 (*0-13-752783-7*) P-H.

Raise Your Vibration with Nutrition & Fasting. Nogah Lord. LC 91-27781. (Illus.). 80p. (Orig.). 1991. pap. 8.95 (*0-931892-68-6*) B Dolphin Pub.

Raised by the Government: An Inside Look into America's Child Welfare System. Ira M. Schwartz et al. 248p. 1994. text ed. 22.95 (*0-669-27951-X*) Free Pr.

Raised by Wolves. Jim Goldberg. (Illus.). 320p. 1995. pap. 45.00 (*1-881616-50-9*) Dist Art Pubs.

Raised Catholic (Can You Tell?) Ed Stivender. 196p. 1992. 19.95 (*0-87483-277-2*) August Hse.

Raised Catholic (Can You Tell?) Ed Stivender. 192p. 1993. pap. 11.95 (*0-87483-336-1*) August Hse.

Raised Curtain: Report of the Twentieth Century Fund Task Force on Soviet-American Scholarly & Cultural Exchanges. 1977. pap. 3.00 (*0-87078-143-X*) TCFP-PPP.

Raised from the Dead: True Stories of 400 Resurrection Miracles. Albert J. Herbert. LC 84-51817. (Illus.). 335p. 1986. pap. 16.50 (*0-89555-251-5*) TAN Bks Pubs.

Raised in Captivity. Nicky Silver. 1995. pap. 5.25 (*0-8222-1478-4*) Dramatists Play.

Raised in Captivity. Nicky Silver. 112p. 1995. pap. 10.95 (*1-55936-113-1*) Theatre Comm.

***Raised in Captivity: Why Does America Fail It's Children?** Lucia Hodgson. 1997. 23.95 (*1-55597-261-6*) Graywolf.

Raised in Clay: The Southern Pottery Tradition. Nancy Sweezy. LC 94-6655. (Chapel Hill Bks.). (Illus.). 290p. (C). 1994. 24.95 (*0-8078-4481-0*) U of NC Pr.

Raised in East Urban: Child Care Changes in a Working Class Community. Caroline Zinsser. (Early Childhood Education Ser.). 200p. (C). 1991. text ed. 36.95 (*0-8077-3140-4*); pap. text ed. 19.95 (*0-8077-3139-0*) Tchrs Coll.

Raised in Paradise: A Saga of Little Italy. Anthony Halterlein. 72p. 1995. pap. 8.00 (*0-8059-3646-7*) Dorrance.

Raised Intracranial Pressure. North & Reilly. 109p. 1990. 65.00 (*0-433-00102-X*) Buttrwrth-Heinemann.

Raised Underground. Renate Wood. 56p. (Orig.). (C). 1991. pap. 11.95 (*0-88748-110-8*) Carnegie-Mellon.

Raisin-in-Milk Syndrome: Ten Survival Tips for Black Students at Predominantly White Colleges & Universities. Eugene Williams, Sr. (Illus.). 46p. (Orig.). (C). 1994. write for info. (*0-911849-03-3*) Comptex Assocs Inc.

Raisin in the Sun. Lorraine Hansberry. 1987. pap. 10.00 (*0-452-26485-5*, Plume) NAL-Dutton.

Raisin in the Sun. Lorraine Hansberry. 160p. 1994. pap. 5.50 (*0-679-75533-0*, Vin) Random.

Raisin in the Sun. Lorraine Hansberry. LC 95-16074. 168p. 1995. 12.50 (*0-679-60172-4*, Modern Lib) Random.

Raisin in the Sun. 25th anniversary ed. Lorraine Hansberry. Bd. with Sign in Sidney Brustein's Window. LC 87-5748. LC 87-5748. 324p. 1987. Set pap. 8.95 (*0-452-25942-8*, Plume) NAL-Dutton.

Raisin in the Sun: And, The Sign in Sidney Brustein's Window. Lorraine Hansberry. Ed. & Frwd. by Robert Nemiroff. LC 94-40843. 1995. pap. 13.00 (*0-679-75531-4*, Vin) Random.

Raisin in the Sun: The Unfilmed Original Screenplay. Lorraine Hansberry. 128p. 1992. pap. 11.95 (*0-452-26776-5*, Plume) NAL-Dutton.

Raisin in the Sun: The Unfilmed Original Screenplay. Lorraine Hansberry. 256p. 1995. mass mkt., pap. 3.99 (*0-451-18388-6*) NAL-Dutton.

Raisin in the Sun see Four Contemporary American Plays

Raisin in the Sun - Study Guide. Linda Sussman. Ed. by Joyce Friedland & Rikki Kessler. (Novel-Ties Ser.). (YA). (gr. 8-12). 1993. pap. text ed. 15.95 (*0-88122-124-4*) Lrn Links.

Raisin in the Sun Notes. Rosetta James. 1992. pap. 3.95 (*0-8220-1108-5*) Cliffs.

Raising a Calf for Beef. Phyllis Hobson. LC 76-20637. (Illus.). 128p. 1976. pap. 9.95 (*0-88266-095-0*, Garden Way Pub) Storey Comm Inc.

***Raising a Celestial Family.** Z. Reed Millar. (Orig.). 1996. pap. write for info. (*0-88290-585-6*) Horizon Utah.

Raising a Child Who Has a Physical Disability. Donna G. Albrecht. LC 94-41908. 228p. 1995. pap. text ed. 12.95 (*0-471-04240-4*) Wiley.

Raising a Child with Diabetes: A Guide for Parents. Linda M. Siminerio. (Illus.). 144p. 1996. pap. 14.95 (*0-945448-48-1*) Am Diabetes.

Raising a College-Bound Child. Joanne May & Susan McLean. 50p. (Orig.). 1995. pap. 19.95 (*0-9648740-0-8*) Sage Prods.

Raising a Creative Child: Challenging Activities for Growing Young Minds. Cynthia MacGregor. 160p. 1995. pap. 9.95 (*0-8065-1741-7*, Citadel Pr) Carol Pub Group.

Raising a Daughter: Parents & the Awakening of a Healthy Woman. Jeanne Elium & Don Elium. LC 94-6462. 256p. 1995. 19.95 (*0-89087-718-1*); pap. 12.95 (*0-89087-708-4*) Celestial Arts.

Raising a Fallen Treasure: Otto Kahn. Robert B. King. 1976. 24.95 (*0-8488-0287-X*) Amereon Ltd.

***Raising a Fallen Treasure: The Otto H. Kahn Home.** Robert B. King. Date not set. lib. bdg. 18.95 (*0-8488-1814-8*) Amereon Ltd.

***Raising a Family: Living on Planet Parenthood.** Jeanne Elium & Don Elium. 224p. 1997. 19.95 (*0-89087-819-6*); pap. 12.95 (*0-89087-818-8*) Celestial Arts.

***Raising a Happy, Confident & Successful Child: 52 Principles to Help Parents Grow.** Patricia Magee. 120p. (Orig.). 1996. pap. 9.95 (*1-889793-02-7*) Spencer Bks.

Raising a Happy Unspoiled Child. Burton L. White. 256p. 1994. 21.00 (*0-671-79661-5*) S&S Trade.

An Asterisk (*) at the beginning of an entry indicates that the title is appearing in BIP for the first time.

Raising a Happy, Unspoiled Child. Burton L. White. 1995. pap. 11.00 (*0-684-80134-5*, Fireside) S&S Trade.

Raising a Healthy Athlete. Theresa F. Digeronimo & Douglas A. Avella. 200p. 1990. 18.95 (*0-945167-36-9*); write for info. (*0-945167-37-7*); pap. 8.95 (*0-945167-32-6*) British Amer Pub.

***Raising a Healthy Guinea Pig.** Wanda L. Curran. LC 97-10460. 1997. write for info. (*0-88266-999-0*, Storey Pub) Storey Comm Inc.

Raising a Large Family. Katherine Schlaerth. 256p. 1991. pap. 12.95 (*0-02-081911-0*) Macmillan.

***Raising a Modern-Day Knight: A Father's Role in Guiding His Son to Authentic Manhood.** Robert Lewis. LC 96-52752. 1997. 16.99 (*1-56179-534-8*) Focus Family.

Raising a Reader: Make Your Child a Reader for Life. Paul Kropp. LC 95-13174. 224p. 1996. pap. 12.00 (*0-385-47913-1*, Main St Bks) Doubleday.

Raising a Responsible Child. Don Dinkmeyer. 1996. pap. 11.00 (*0-684-81516-8*) S&S Trade.

***Raising a Responsible Child: How Parents Can Avoid Indulging Too Much & Rescuing Too Often.** Elizabeth Ellis. 1996. pap. text ed. 14.95 (*0-8065-1824-3*, Citadel Pr) Carol Pub Group.

Raising a Responsible Child: How Parents Can Avoid Overindulgent Behavior & Nurture Healthy Children. Elizabeth M. Ellis. 288p. 1995. 18.95 (*1-55972-301-7*, Birch Ln Pr) Carol Pub Group.

Raising a Responsible Child: Practical Steps to a Successful Family Relationships. Don Dinkmeyer, Sr. & Gary D. McKay. 256p. 1982. pap. 11.00 (*0-671-44749-1*, Fireside) S&S Trade.

Raising a Son: Parents & the Making of a Healthy Man. Don Elium. 1992. pap. text ed. 12.95 (*0-89087-800-5*) Celestial Arts.

Raising a Son: Parents & the Making of a Healthy Man. Don Elium. 1992. 18.95 (*0-89087-801-3*) Celestial Arts.

Raising a Son: Parents & the Making of a Healthy Man. rev. ed. Don Elium & Jeanne Elium. 256p. 1996. pap. 12.95 (*0-89087-811-0*) Celestial Arts.

***Raising a Son: Parents & the Making of a Healthy Man.** rev. ed. Don Elium & Jeanne Elium. 256p. 1997. 21.95 (*0-89087-844-7*) Celestial Arts.

Raising a Thinking Child. Myrna B. Shure. (Illus.). 192p. (J). 1996. wbk. ed., pap. 14.95 (*0-8050-4383-7*, Owl) H Holt & Co.

Raising a Thinking Child: Help Your Young Child to Resolve Everyday Conflicts & Get Along with Others. Myrna B. Shure. LC 94-5166. 1994. 22.50 (*0-8050-2758-0*) H Holt & Co.

Raising a Thinking Child: Help Your Young Child to Resolve Everyday Conflicts & Get Along with Others. Myrna B. Shure et al. Ed. by Amelia Sheldon. LC 95-40331. 224p. 1996. reprint ed. pap. 12.00 (*0-671-53463-7*, PB Trade Paper) PB.

***Raising a Thinking Child Value.** Shure. 1996. 15.95 (*0-8050-4912-6*) St Martin.

Raising a Thoughtful Teenager: A Book of Answers and Values for Parents. Ben Kamin. 224p. 1996. pap. 20.95 (*0-525-93984-9*) NAL-Dutton.

***Raising a Thoughtful Teenager: A Book of Answers & Values for Parents.** Ben Kamin. 1997. pap. 10.95 (*0-452-27420-6*, Plume) NAL-Dutton.

Raising Abel: The Recovery of the Eschatological Imagination. James Alison. 228p. (Orig.). 1996. pap. text ed. 18.95 (*0-8245-1565-X*) Crossroad NY.

Raising Academic Standards: A Guide to Learning Improvement. Ruth T. Keimig. Ed. & Frwd. by Jonathan D. Fife. LC 84-117233. (ASHE-ERIC Higher Education Reports: No. 83-4). (Illus.). 100p. (Orig.). 1983. pap. 18.75 (*0-913317-03-9*) GWU Grad Schl E&HD.

Raising Achievers: A Parent's Plan for Motivating Children to Excel. Nita Weis. LC 94-30984. 264p. 1995. 17.99 (*0-8054-6160-4*, 4261-60) Broadman.

Raising Adopted Children. Lois R. Melina. LC 85-45648. 1986. pap. 12.50 (*0-06-096039-6*, PL) HarpC.

Raising America's Children. Harms. 1994. student ed. 16.95 (*0-8273-6561-6*) Delmar.

Raising America's Children Instructor's Guide. Thelma Harms & Debby Cryer. 1991. teacher ed. 8.00 (*0-8273-4851-7*) Delmar.

Raising America's Children Study Guide. Thelma Harms & Debby Cryer. 1991. student ed., pap. 16.95 (*0-8273-4783-9*) Delmar.

***Raising & Educating a Deaf Child.** Mark Marschark. (Illus.). 256p. 1997. 25.00 (*0-19-509467-0*) OUP.

Raising Arizona. Joel Coen & Ethan Coen. (Original Screenplay Ser.). (Illus.). 112p. 1989. pap. 9.95 (*0-312-02270-0*) St Martin.

Raising Arizona's Dams: Daily Life, Danger, & Discrimination in the Dam Construction Camps of Central Arizona, 1890s-1940s. A. E. Rogge et al. LC 94-21368. (Illus.). 212p. 1995. lib. bdg. 46.00 (*0-8165-1491-7*) U of Ariz Pr.

Raising Arizona's Dams: Daily Life, Danger, & Discrimination in the Dam Construction Camps of Central Arizona, 1890s-1940s. A. E. Rogge et al. LC 94-21368. (Illus.). 212p. 1995. pap. 22.95 (*0-8165-1492-5*, 20016) U of Ariz Pr.

Raising Awesome Kids in Troubled Times. Sam Laing & Geri Laing. 224p. 1994. pap. 10.99 (*1-884553-23-0*) Discipleshp.

***Raising Awesome Kids in Troubled Times: Criando Ninos Ejemplares.** Sam Laing & Geri Laing. 218p. (Orig.). (SPA.). 1997. pap. 10.99 (*1-884553-97-4*) Discipleshp.

Raising Big Bucks Through Pledge-Based Special Events. Cindy R. Kaitcer. LC 96-27805. 250p. 1996. 40.00 (*1-56625-059-5*) Bonus Books.

Raising Black Children: Questions & Answers for Parents & Teachers. James P. Comer & Alvin F. Poussaint. LC 92-53563. 400p. (Orig.). 1992. pap. 13.95 (*0-452-26839-7*, Plume) NAL-Dutton.

Raising Bookworms: A Parents Guide to Reading Success. Anthony D. Fredericks. LC 84-60980. 125p. (Orig.). (C). 1985. pap. text ed. 6.95 (*0-88247-733-1*) R & E Pubs.

Raising Brighter Children. Sidney Ledson. (Illus.). 256p. 1987. 17.95 (*0-8027-0924-9*); pap. 9.95 (*0-8027-7299-4*) Walker & Co.

Raising Brighter Children: A Program for Busy Parents. Sidney Ledson. 1994. pap. text ed. 16.95 (*0-7737-5490-3*) Genl Dist Srvs.

Raising Cain. Herbert S. Strean. 1989. mass mkt. 4.95 (*0-312-91601-9*) St Martin.

Raising Cain. Gallatin Warfield. 352p. 1996. 23.95 (*0-446-51850-6*) Warner Bks.

***Raising Cain.** Gallatin Warfield. 400p. 1998. mass mkt. 6.99 (*0-446-60513-1*) Warner Bks.

***Raising Cain: How to Help Your Children Achieve a Happy Sibling Relationship.** Herbert S. Strean & Lucy Freeman. LC 87-8921. 185p. 1988. reprint ed. pap. 52.80 (*0-608-02824-X*, 2063891) Bks Demand.

Raising Cain: How to Help Your Children Achieve a Happy Sibling Reltionship. Herbert S. Stream & Lucy Freeman. 192p. 1988. 22.95 (*0-8160-1413-2*) Facts on File.

Raising Cane: The World of Plantation Hawaii. Ronald Takaki. LC 93-5307. (Asian American Experience Ser.). (Illus.). 125p. (YA). (gr. 5 up). 1993. lib. bdg. 19.95 (*0-7910-2178-5*) Chelsea Hse.

Raising Capital: Grant Thornton's Guide for Entrepreneurs. Michael C. Bernstein & Lester Wolosoff. 171p. 1995. text ed. 50.00 (*0-7863-0150-3*) Irwin Prof Pubng.

Raising Capital: How to Write a Financing Proposal to Raise Venture Capital. Lawrence Flanagan. LC 94-5608. (Successful Business Library). (Illus.). 242p. (Orig.). 1994. pap. 19.95 (*1-55571-305-X*); ring bd. 39.95 (*1-55571-306-8*) Oasis Pr OR.

Raising Capital: Private Placement Forms & Techniques. annuals Robert L. Frome & Herbert B. Max. 723p. 1981. Annual supplements avail. suppl. ed. 85.00 (*0-15-003987-5*, H39875) HarBrace.

Raising Capital: Private Placement Forms & Techniques. 2nd ed. Robert L. Frome & Herbert B. Max. 1989. write for info. (*0-318-65482-2*, H43899) P-H.

***Raising Capital: Private Placements of Public Offerings.** (Illus.). 30p. (Orig.). 1998. pap. 19.95 (*0-9643563-1-7*) Securities Pr.

***Raising Capital: The Grant Thornton Guide for Entrepreneurs.** Michael Bernstein & Lester Wolosoff. 1996. per. 15.12 (*0-7863-1195-9*) Irwin.

Raising Capital in the 1990s: Options for the Extractive Industry: Proceedings of a Seminar Sponsored by the Economic & Finance Subsection of the New York Section of AIME & the Society of Mining Engineers, November 17-18, 1988, New York. Ed. by Simon D. Handelsman et al. LC 90-83270. 141p. 1990. reprint ed. pap. 40.20 (*0-7837-9178-X*, 2049877) Bks Demand.

Raising Career Aspirations of Hispanic Girls. Josefina V. Tinajero et al. LC 91-60199. (Fastback Ser.: No. 320). (Orig.). 1991. pap. 3.00 (*0-87367-320-4*) Phi Delta Kappa.

Raising Catholic Children. Mary A. Kuharski. LC 91-60010. (Orig.). 1991. pap. 8.95 (*0-87973-462-0*, 462) Our Sunday Visitor.

Raising Chickens & Ducks. Harlan H. D. Attfield. (Illus.). 140p. 1990. 12.95 (*0-86619-309-X*) Vols Tech Asst.

Raising Children As Peacemakers. Peggy Goding. (Orig.). 1989. pap. 13.95 (*0-933770-53-7*) Kalimat.

Raising Children Bilingually: The Pre-School Years. Lenore Arnberg. 1987. 59.00 (*0-905028-71-6*, Pub. by Multilingual Matters UK); pap. 29.50 (*0-905028-70-8*, Pub. by Multilingual Matters UK) Taylor & Francis.

Raising Children in a Socially Toxic Environment. James Garbarino. (Education Ser.). 215p. 25.00 (*0-7879-0116-4*) Jossey-Bass.

Raising Children in the Electronic Age. Steve Bennett. 1997. pap. 15.00 (*0-8129-6378-4*) Random.

Raising Children in the Electronic Age: A Guide to Balancing Technology with Tradition. Steve Bennett & Ruth Bennett. 304p. 1996. 16.00 (*0-679-77002-X*, Random Ref) Random.

Raising Children to Achieve: A Guide for Motivating Success in School & in Life. Eric W. Johnson. LC 83-40410. 208p. 1985. 14.95 (*0-8027-0765-3*); pap. 9.95 (*0-8027-7285-4*) Walker & Co.

***Raising Children to Be Gifted.** Suzanne Michaels. LC 96-70797. (Illus.). xx, 212p. (Orig.). 1997. pap. 12.95 (*0-9654779-0-8*) A-Parent Love.

Raising Children to Care: A Jewish Guide to Childrearing. Miriam Adahan. 1988. 22.95 (*0-87306-456-9*) Feldheim.

Raising Children Toxic Free: How to Keep Your Child Safe from Lead, Asbestos, Pesticides... Herbert L. Needleman & Philip J. Landrigan. 272p. 1995. pap. 12.00 (*0-380-72577-0*) Avon.

Raising Children with Love & Limits. Psyche Cattell. LC 77-187810. 240p. 1972. 26.95 (*0-911012-20-6*) Nelson-Hall.

Raising Children You Can Live With: A Guide for Frustrated Parents. Jamie B. Raser. LC 95-79577. (Illus.). 152p. (Orig.). 1995. pap. 10.95 (*1-886298-08-4*) Bayou Pubng.

Raising Compassionate, Courageous Children in a Violent World. Janice Cohn. 1996. pap. 15.95 (*1-56352-276-4*) Longstreet Pr Inc.

Raising Confident Kids. Robert G. Barnes, Jr. 176p. 1992. pap. 10.99 (*0-310-54511-0*) Zondervan.

Raising Curious Kids: Over 100 Simple Activities to Develop Your Child's Imagination. Nancy S. Green. LC 94-1195. 1995. pap. 12.00 (*0-517-88219-1*, Crown) Crown Pub Group.

Raising Curtains on Education: Drama As a Site for Critical Pedagogy. Clar Doyle. LC 92-32180. (Critical Studies in Education & Culture). 176p. 1993. text ed. 49.95 (*0-89789-273-9*, H273, Bergin & Garvey) Greenwood.

Raising Curtains on Education: Drama As a Site for Critical Pedagogy. Clar Doyle. LC 92-32180. (Critical Studies in Education & Culture). 176p. 1993. pap. text ed. 16.95 (*0-89789-274-7*, G274, Bergin & Garvey) Greenwood.

Raising Demons. Shirley Jackson. 189p. 1994. pap. 11.95 (*0-89733-413-2*) Academy Chi Pubs.

Raising Demons. Shirley Jackson. 1995. reprint ed. lib. bdg. 21.95 (*1-56849-653-2*) Buccaneer Bks.

Raising Dragons. Jerdine Nolen. LC 95-43307. (Illus.). (J). 1998. write for info. (*0-15-201288-5*) HarBrace.

***Raising Ducks Vol. 1: How to Begin.** 73p. (ENG, FRE & SPA.). 1991. 5.00 (*92-5-102939-3*, F9393, Pub. by FAO IT) Bernan Associates.

Raising Each Other: A Book for Parents & Teens. Jeanne Brondino et al. LC 89-7094. 160p. (C). 1989. lib. bdg. 27.00 (*0-89370-524-1*) Borgo Pr.

Raising Each Other: A Book for Teens & Parents. Jeanne Brondino et al. LC 87-21354. (Illus.). 160p. (Orig.). (gr. 8-12). 1988. pap. 8.95 (*0-89793-044-4*) Hunter Hse.

Raising Earthworms for Profit. Earl B. Shields. (Illus.). 128p. 1994. pap. 9.00 (*0-914116-21-5*) Shields.

Raising Educational Standards in the Inner Cities: Practical Initiatives in Action. Ed. by Michael Barber & Ruth Dann. (School Development Ser.). (Illus.). 208p. 1996. 90.00 (*0-304-33136-8*); pap. 21.00 (*0-304-33138-4*) Cassell.

Raising Emotionally Healthy Kids. H. Norman Wright & Gary J. Oliver. LC 94-41430. 240p. 1995. pap. 10.99 (*1-56476-451-6*, 6-3451, Victor Bks) Chariot Victor.

Raising Emotionally Healthy Kids - Leader's Guide. Norman Wright & Gary J. Oliver. 112p. 1995. teacher ed., pap. 7.99 (*1-56476-483-4*, 6-3483, Victor Bks) Chariot Victor.

Raising Faithful Kids in a Fast-Paced World. Paul Faulkner. 354p. 1995. pap. 11.99 (*1-878990-52-7*); audio 14.99 (*1-878990-53-5*) Howard Pub LA.

Raising Fishworms with Rabbits. rev. ed. Howard L. Mays. 1981. pap. 7.00 (*0-914116-10-X*) Shields.

Raising Funds for Charity. Elizabeth Cairns. 200p. (C). 1994. 175.00 (*0-85459-760-3*, Pub. by Tolley Pubng UK) St Mut.

Raising Funds for Your Child's School: Over Sixty Great Ideas for Parents & Teachers. Cynthia F. Gensheimer. LC 93-1709. 224p. (Orig.). 1993. 26.95 (*0-8027-1281-9*); pap. 14.95 (*0-8027-7411-3*) Walker & Co.

Raising Game Birds. 1984. 2.95 (*0-88266-336-4*) Storey Comm Inc.

Raising Game Birds. 1995. 11.95 (*0-944079-20-2*) Lessiter Pubns.

Raising Good Children. Thomas Lickona. 464p. (Orig.). 1994. pap. 13.95 (*0-553-37429-X*) Bantam.

Raising Good Kids. Louise B. Ames. 144p. 1993. pap. 9.95 (*0-440-50706-5*) Dell.

Raising Good Kids: A Developmental Approach to Discipline. Louise B. Ames. (Orig.). 1991. pap. text ed. 12.95 (*0-935493-46-8*) Modern Learn Pr.

Raising Happy Kids on a Reasonable Budget. Patricia Gallagher. 144p. (Orig.). 1993. pap. 10.95 (*1-55870-271-7*, Betterway Bks) F & W Pubns Inc.

Raising Healthy Beef Cattle. 2nd rev. ed. James B. Carlson. (Raising Healthy Animals under Primitive Conditions Ser.). (Illus.). 125p. 1990. pap. 9.00 (*1-886532-06-0*) Christian Vet.

***Raising Healthy Children in a Sexually Sick World: Leader's Guide.** Richard D. Dobbins. (Illus.). 77p. (Orig.). 1987. pap. 12.50 (*1-890329-06-1*) Totally Alive.

***Raising Healthy Children in a Sexually Sick World: Parents' Guide.** Richard D. Dobbins. (Illus.). 67p. 1987. reprint ed. pap. 2.95 (*1-890329-07-X*) Totally Alive.

Raising Healthy Children in an Alcoholic Home. Barbara L. Wood. 192p. (Orig.). 1992. pap. 11.95 (*0-8245-1205-7*) Crossroad NY.

Raising Healthy Dairy Cattle under Primitive Conditions. William T. Testerman. (Raising Healthy Animals under Primitive Conditions Ser.). (Illus.). 184p. (Orig.). 1995. pap. 9.00 (*1-886532-03-6*) Christian Vet.

Raising Healthy Fish under Primitive Conditions. 2nd unabridged ed. Lora Hanson. (Raising Healthy Animals under Primitive Conditions Ser.). (Illus.). 100p. 1987. pap. 9.00 (*1-886532-05-2*) Christian Vet.

Raising Healthy Goats under Primitive Conditions. 2nd unabridged ed. Robert A. Venderhoof. (Raising Healthy Animals under Primitive Conditions Ser.). (Illus.). 160p. 1994. pap. 9.00 (*1-886532-04-4*) Christian Vet.

Raising Healthy Kids: A Book of Child Care & Natural Family Health. Michio Kushi et al. LC 93-46170. 288p. pap. 14.95 (*0-89529-578-4*) Avery Pub.

Raising Healthy Pets: Insights of a Holistic Veterinarian. Norman Ralston & Gale Jack. 112p. (Orig.). 1996. pap. 10.95 (*1-882984-22-6*) One Peaceful World.

Raising Healthy Pigs under Primitive Conditions. 2nd rev. ed. Earl Goodman. 144p. 1994. pap. text ed. 7.50 (*1-886532-00-1*) Christian Vet.

Raising Healthy Poultry under Primitive Conditions. rev. ed. Gene Pestis. 1994. pap. text ed. 7.50 (*1-886532-02-8*) Christian Vet.

Raising Healthy Rabbits under Primitive Conditions. Sheldon Bivens. 108p. 1994. pap. text ed. 7.50 (*1-886532-01-X*) Christian Vet.

Raising Hell: A Concise History of the Black Arts & Those Who Dared Practice Them. Robert Masello. LC 96-11323. 288p. 1996. pap. 12.00 (*0-399-52238-7*, Perigee Bks) Berkley Pub.

Raising Hell: An Encyclopedia of Devil Worship & Satanic Crime. Michael Newton. 432p. (Orig.). 1993. mass mkt. 5.99 (*0-380-76837-2*) Avon.

***Raising Hell: Straight Talk from Today's Top Investigative Journalists.** Ron Chepesiuk et al. LC 97-18934. 180p. 1997. 25.00 (*0-7864-0356-X*) McFarland & Co.

Raising Her Voice. Rodger Streitmatter. LC 93-35932. 216p. 1994. pap. 14.95 (*0-8131-0830-6*) U Pr of Ky.

Raising Her Voice: African-American Women Journalists Who Changed History. Rodger Streitmatter. LC 93-35932. 216p. 1994. 30.00 (*0-8131-1861-1*) U Pr of Ky.

Raising Holy Hell. Bruce Olds. LC 95-9707. 335p. 1995. 22.50 (*0-8050-3856-6*) H Holt & Co.

Raising Holy Hell. Bruce Olds. 1997. pap. 11.95 (*0-14-025908-2*) Viking Penguin.

Raising Irish Walls. Brendan Galvin. 27p. 1989. pap. 3.50 (*0-935331-07-7*) Ampersand RI.

Raising Jewish Children in a Contemporary World: The Modern Parent's Guide to Creating a Jewish Home. Steven C. Reuben. (Illus.). 244p. 1991. 18.95 (*1-55958-150-6*) Prima Pub.

Raising Jewish Children in a Contemporary World: The Modern Parent's Guide to Creating a Jewish Home. Steven C. Reuben. 240p. 1993. pap. 12.95 (*1-55958-319-3*) Prima Pub.

***Raising Joshua: One Mother's Story of the Challenges of Parenting a Child with Tourette Syndrome.** Sheryl J. Hamer. 150p. (Orig.). 1997. pap. 12.95 (*0-9657501-6-7*) H J Rholsson.

Raising Kids. (Dialog Ser.). 123p. 1993. pap. 5.95 (*0-8341-1451-8*) Beacon Hill.

Raising Kids. James Dobson et al. 46p. 1993. teacher ed., pap. 4.95 (*0-8341-1450-X*) Beacon Hill.

Raising Kids: It Ain't Easy, But It Can Be Fun. Stanley K. Kary. 1992. 12.95 (*0-533-09576-X*) Vantage.

Raising Kids God's Way: A Biblical Guide for Christian Parents. Kathi Hudson. LC 95-15379. 256p. 1995. 16.99 (*0-89107-846-0*) Crossway Bks.

Raising Kids Right in a World Gone Wrong: Helping Your Children Discover & Develop Their Full Potential. Duane Rawlins & LeeAnn Rawlins. 148p. (Orig.). 1995. pap. 7.99 (*1-883002-30-3*) Emerald WA.

Raising Kids Who Can: Use Good Judgement, Assume Responsibility, Communicate Effectively, Respect Self & Others, Cooperate, Develop Self-Esteem & Enjoy Life. 2nd rev. ed. Betty L. Bettner & Amy Lew. LC 89-82477. (Illus.). 120p. 1990. pap. 9.50 (*0-9624841-7-2*) Connex Pr.

Raising Kids Who Can Leader's Guide. Betty L. Bettner & Amy Lew. 67p. 1996. pap. 15.00 (*0-9624841-6-4*) Connex Pr.

***Raising Kids Who Care: About Themselves, about Their World, about Each Other.** Kathleen O. Chesto. 112p. (Orig.). 1996. pap. 14.95 (*1-55612-921-1*, LL1921-1) Sheed & Ward MO.

Raising Kids Who Hunger for God. Benny Phillips & Sheree Phillips. LC 91-7367. 252p. (Orig.). (gr. 10). 1990. pap. 8.99 (*0-8007-9181-9*) Chosen Bks.

Raising Kids Who Turn Out Right. Tim Kimmel. 297p. pap. 9.99 (*0-88070-533-7*, Multnomah Bks) Multnomah Pubs.

Raising Kids with Just a Little Cash. Lisa Reid. LC 96-96469. (Illus.). 1740p. (Orig.). 1996. pap. 12.95 (*0-9651651-0-8*) Ferguson-Carol Pubs.

***Raising Lambs among Wolves: How to Protect Your Children from Evil.** Mark I. Bubeck. 256p. (Orig.). 1997. pap. 11.99 (*0-8024-7194-3*) Moody.

Raising Lazarus: A Memoir. Dwight Williams & Robert J. Pensack. 336p. 1996. pap. text ed. 12.00 (*1-57322-500-2*, Riverhd Trade) Berkley Pub.

Raising Less Corn & More Hell: Midwestern Farmers Speak Out. Jim Schwab. LC 88-1173. (Illus.). 328p. 1988. text ed. 24.95 (*0-252-01398-0*) U of Ill Pr.

***Raising Low-Fat Kids in a High-Fat World.** Joseph C. Piscatella. LC 97-9065. 1997. pap. text ed. 10.95 (*1-56305-150-8*) Workman Pub.

Raising Low-Fat Kids in a High-Fat World. Judith Shaw. LC 96-5717. (Illus.). 256p. 1997. pap. 14.95 (*0-8118-1441-6*) Chronicle Bks.

Raising Milk Goats Successfully. Gail Luttmann. Ed. by Roger Griffith. LC 86-26694. (Illus.). 176p. (Orig.). 1986. pap. 9.95 (*0-913589-24-1*) Williamson Pub Co.

Raising Milk Goats the Modern Way. rev. ed. Jerry Belanger. LC 89-45737. (Illus.). 208p. 1990. pap. 12.95 (*0-88266-576-6*, Garden Way Pub) Storey Comm Inc.

Raising Money & Cultivating Donors Through Special Events. April L. Harris. 57p. 1991. 32.00 (*0-89964-283-7*, 24602) Coun Adv & Supp Ed.

Raising Money & Having Fun (Sort of) A "How-to" Book for Small Non-Profit Groups. May Dugan Center Staff & Charlene Horton. LC 91-66345. (Illus.). 132p. 1991. pap. text ed. 18.95 (*0-9630760-0-0*) M Dugan Ctr.

Raising Money by Mail: Strategies for Growth & Financial Stability. Mal Warwick. 128p. 1996. pap. 19.95 (*0-9624891-6-6*) Strathmoor Pr.

Raising Money for Academic & Research Libraries: A How-to-Do-It Manual for Librarians. Ed. by Barbara I. Dewey. (How-to-Do-It Ser.). 160p. 1991. 39.95 (*1-55570-082-9*) Neal-Schuman.

***Raising Money for Education: A Guide to the Property Tax.** David H. Monk & Brian O. Brent. LC 97-4885. (Illus.). 144p. 1997. pap. 21.95 (*0-8039-6407-2*); text ed. 49.95 (*0-8039-6406-4*) Corwin Pr.

Raising Money for Your Church. George Barna. 99p. (Orig.). 1994. spiral bd. 28.00 (*1-882297-05-9*) Barna Res Grp.

Raising Money from Grants & Other Sources Kit. 8th ed. Tyler G. Hicks. 496p. 1996. pap. 99.50 (*1-56150-158-1*) Intl Wealth.

R

***Raising Money from Grants & Other Sources Kit.** 9th ed. Tyler G. Hicks. 496p. 1998. pap. 99.50 (*1-56150-208-1*) Intl Wealth.

Raising Money-Smart Kids. Ron Blue & Judy Blue. 256p. 1992. pap. 10.99 (*0-8407-3195-7*) Nelson.

Raising Money Through an Institutionally Related Foundation. Ed. by Timothy A. Reilley. 83p. 1985. 26.50 (*0-89964-225-X*, 23501) Coun Adv & Supp Ed.

Raising Money Wise Kids. Judith Briles. 1996. wbk. ed., pap. 12.99 (*1-881273-59-8*) Moody.

Raising Musical Kids: Great Ideas to Help Your Child Develop a Love for Music. Patrick Kavanaugh. 230p. 1995. pap. 10.99 (*0-89283-903-1*, Vine Bks) Servant.

Raising My Titanic. Mary Sheldon. 240p. 1996. pap. 17.95 (*0-7871-1039-6*, Dove Bks) Dove Audio.

Raising Nonviolent/Nonvictim Children: A Sexual Abuse Prevention Guide. Linda Nelson. (Illus.). 72p. (Orig.). 1996. teacher ed., spiral bd. 18.00 (*0-9640662-2-X*) R Lewis Pub.

Raising of Intelligence: A Selected History of Attempts to Raise Retarded Intelligence. Herman H. Spitz. 288p. 1986. text ed. 59.95 (*0-89859-836-2*) L Erlbaum Assocs.

Raising of Lazarus. John Cornish. 1979. pap. 3.50 (*0-916786-36-6*, Saint George Pubns) R Steiner Col Pubns.

Raising of Money: Thirty-Five Essentials (Accompanied by a Guide for the Professional) James G. Lord. LC 84-50377. 128p. 1984. 34.50 (*0-939120-02-X*) Third Sector.

***Raising of Predicates: Predicative Noun Phrases & the Theory of Clause Structure.** Andrea Moro. (Cambridge Studies in Linguistics: No. 80). 318p. 1997. text ed. 64.95 (*0-521-56233-3*) Cambridge U Pr.

Raising Other People's Kids: A Guide for Houseparents, Foster Parents & Direct Care Staff. M. C. Camerer & Emerson Capps. LC 94-48371. 186p. (C). 1995. text ed. 36.95 (*0-398-05985-3*); pap. text ed. 22.95 (*0-398-05986-1*) C C Thomas.

Raising Our Children's Children. Deborah Doucette-Dudman & Jeffrey R. Lacure. 240p. 1996. 19.95 (*0-925190-91-8*) Fairview Press.

***Raising Our Children's Children.** Deborah Doucette-Dudman & Jeffrey R. LaCure. 256p. 1997. reprint ed. pap. 12.95 (*1-57749-026-6*) Fairview Press.

Raising Our Future: Schools & Communities Joining Together: A Handbook of Family Support & Education Programs for Parents, Educators, Community Leaders, & Policy Makers. Harvard Family Research Project Staff. LC 91-73676. 560p. 1995. student ed., pap. 25.95 (*0-9630627-0-0*) Harvard Fam.

Raising Our Sights: Improving U. S. Mathematics & Science Achievement. John O'Neil. LC 91-32235. 40p. 1991. pap. 7.50 (*0-87120-187-9*, 611-91170) Assn Supervision.

Raising Partner. Brian Senior. 160p. (Orig.). 1994. pap. 10.95 (*0-571-16901-5*) Faber & Faber.

Raising Partner. Brian Senior. (Illus.). 144p. (Orig.). 1996. pap. 16.95 (*0-7134-7918-3*, Pub. by Batsford UK) Trafalgar.

Raising Peaceful Children in a Violent World. Nancy L. Cecil & Patricia L. Roberts. LC 95-32351. 256p. (Orig.). 1995. pap. 16.95 (*1-880913-16-X*) Innisfree Pr.

Raising Pigs Successfully. Kathy Kellogg & Bob Kellogg. LC 85-6542. (Illus.). 192p. 1985. pap. 9.95 (*0-913589-15-2*) Williamson Pub Co.

Raising Positive Kids in a Negative World. Zig Ziglar. 1989. mass mkt. 5.99 (*0-345-36188-1*) Ballantine.

***Raising Positive Kids in a Negative World.** Zig Ziglar. 1996. pap. 12.00 (*0-345-41022-X*) Ballantine.

Raising Positive Kids in a Negative World. Zig Ziglar. 288p. 1985. 15.95 (*0-8407-9039-2*) Nelson.

Raising Poultry Successfully. Will Graves. LC 85-6541. (Illus.). 192p. (Orig.). 1985. pap. 9.95 (*0-913589-09-8*) Williamson Pub Co.

Raising Poultry the Modern Way. rev. ed. Leonard S. Mercia. Ed. by Kimberly Foster. LC 89-45738. (Illus.). 240p. 1990. pap. 12.95 (*0-88266-577-4*, Garden Way Pub) Storey Comm Inc.

***Raising Preschoolers: Parenting for Today.** Sylvia Rimm. LC 97-17764. 1997. pap. write for info. (*0-609-80163-5*) Crown Pub Group.

Raising Queen Honey Bees. 2nd rev. ed. Roger A. Morse. (Illus.). 128p. 1994. pap. text ed. 12.95 (*1-878075-05-5*) Wicwas Pr.

Raising Rabbits. Harlan H. D. Attfield. 81p. (FRE.). 1977. French, 81p. pap. 9.50 (*0-86619-061-9*, 19040-BK); per. 9.50 (*0-86619-060-0*, 11040-BK) Vols Tech Asst.

Raising Rabbits. Ann Kanable. LC 77-23926. 208p. 1977. 11.95 (*0-87857-314-3*, 13-552-1) Rodale Pr Inc.

***Raising Rabbits Vol. 1: Learning about Rabbits, Building the Pens, Choosing Rabbits.** (Economic & Social Development Papers: No. 3). 56p. (ENG, FRE & SPA.). 1988. 5.00 (*92-5-102583-5*, F5835, Pub. by FAO IT) Bernan Associates.

***Raising Rabbits Vol. 2: Feeding Rabbits, Raising Baby Rabbits, Further Improvement.** (Economic & Social Development Ser.: No. 3). 49p. (ENG, FRE & SPA.). 1988. 5.00 (*92-5-102584-3*, F5843, Pub. by FAO IT) Bernan Associates.

Raising Rabbits Successfully. Bob Bennett. LC 83-27334. (Illus.). 192p. (Orig.). 1984. pap. 9.95 (*0-913589-03-9*) Williamson Pub Co.

Raising Rabbits the Modern Way. rev. ed. Bob Bennett. Ed. by Constance Oxley. LC 87-45579. (Illus.). 192p. 1988. pap. 12.95 (*0-88266-479-4*, Garden Way Pub) Storey Comm Inc.

***Raising Readers: Appealing Approaches & Successful Strategies.** Ruth Toor & Hilda K. Weisburg. 142p. (Orig.). 1997. pap. text ed. 20.00 (*0-931315-09-3*) Lib Learn Res.

Raising Readers: Helping Your Child to Literacy. Steve Bialostok. Ed. by Judy Norget. 176p. (Orig.). 1992. pap. 14.00 (*1-895411-37-8*) Peguis Pubs Ltd.

Raising Responsible Kids. Jay Kesler. 160p. 1993. mass mkt. 4.99 (*0-380-71976-2*) Avon.

***Raising Responsible Teenagers.** Bob Myers. LC 96-3424. 256p. 1996. pap. 24.95 (*1-85302-429-5*, Pub. by J Kingsley Pubs UK) Taylor & Francis.

***Raising Responsible Teenagers.** Bob Myers. 264p. 1997. pap. 16.95 (*0-86431-202-4*, Pub. by Aust Coun Educ Res AT) Paul & Co Pubs.

***Raising Rover.** Halliburton. Date not set. pap. 13.95 (*0-312-16974-4*) St Martin.

Raising Rover: Breed-by-Breed Training from Afghans to Yorkies. Judi Halliburton. 336p. 1996. 23.95 (*0-312-14399-0*) St Martin.

Raising Safe Kids in an Unsafe World: 30 Simple Ways to Prevent Your Child from Becoming Lost, Abducted, or Abused. rev. ed. Jan Wagner. LC 96-15767. Orig. Title: Not My Child. 208p. (Orig.). 1996. pap. 11.00 (*0-380-78695-8*) Avon.

Raising Self-Reliant Children in a Self-Indulgent World: Seven Building Blocks for Developing Capable Young People. H. Stephen Glenn & Jane Nelsen. 256p. 1988. pap. 10.95 (*0-914629-92-1*) Prima Pub.

Raising Sensitive Children When the World Seems So Crazy. rev. ed. Kathy Levinson. LC 94-92111. (Illus.). 96p. 1996. pap. 7.95 (*1-885843-03-8*) Saturn Press.

Raising Sexually Healthy Children. Lynn Leight. 304p. 1990. pap. 10.00 (*0-380-70857-4*) Avon.

Raising Sheep the Modern Way. rev. ed. Paula Simmons. Ed. by Deborah Burns. LC 88-45488. (Illus.). 288p. 1989. reprint ed. pap. 12.95 (*0-88266-529-4*, Garden Way Pub) Storey Comm Inc.

Raising Silent Voices. Henry T. Trueba. 1988. pap. 28.95 (*0-8384-2709-X*) Heinle & Heinle.

Raising Small Animals. E. Grant Moody. 330p. 1990. text ed. 32.95 (*0-85236-228-5*, Pub. by Farming Pr UK) Diamond Farm Bk.

Raising Small Church Esteem. Steven E. Burt & Hazel A. Roper. LC 91-78153. 116p. (Orig.). 1992. pap. 10.95 (*1-56699-053-X*, AL132) Alban Inst.

Raising Small Meat Animals. Victor M. Giammattei. LC 75-21050. 1976. 26.60 (*0-8134-1741-4*) Interstate.

Raising Sons Without Fathers: A Woman's Guide to Parenting Strong, Successful Boys. Leif G. Terdal. 288p. 1996. 19.95 (*1-55972-342-4*, Birch Ln Pr) Carol Pub Group.

***Raising Spiritual Children in a Material World: Introducing Spirituality into Family Life.** Phil Catalfo. 1997. pap. 12.00 (*0-614-27489-3*) Berkley Pub.

***Raising Spiritual Children in Material World: Introducing Spirituality into Family Life.** Phil Catalfo. 272p. 1997. pap. 12.00 (*0-425-14954-4*, Berkley Trade) Berkley Pub.

Raising Standards for American Education. 144p. (Orig.). (C). 1993. pap. text ed. 35.00 (*1-56806-683-X*) DIANE Pub.

Raising Strong Daughters. Jeanette Gadeberg. LC 95-3893. 1995. 19.95 (*0-925190-41-1*) Fairview Press.

Raising Strong Daughters. Jeanette Gadeberg. 264p. 1996. pap. 12.95 (*0-925190-98-5*) Fairview Press.

***Raising Super Kids.** Joe Siamon. LC 96-70033. 176p. 1996. 21.95 (*1-56167-331-5*) Noble Hse MD.

Raising Teenagers Right. James Dobson. 96p. 1988. pap. 3.99 (*0-8423-5139-6*) Tyndale.

Raising the Safety Net: Risk-Based Capital for Life Insurance Companies. 346p. (C). 1994. 145.00 (*0-89382-305-8*, RSN-LB) Nat Assn Insurance.

Raising the African Nightcrawler. Charlie Morgan. 1978. pap. 6.00 (*0-9600102-9-7*) Shields.

Raising the Bar. Alan Weiss. 1995. pap. 6.95 (*1-886158-04-5*) Macalester.

***Raising the Bar: Using Competencies to Enhance Employee Performance.** Hay Group Staff et al. 72p. (Orig.). 1996. pap. 125.00 (*1-57963-041-3*, A0057) Am Compensation.

Raising the Curtain on Raising Children. Florence Littauer. 305p. 1988. pap. 10.99 (*0-8499-3133-9*) Word Pub.

***Raising the Dead.** Daniel Cohen. LC 97-3135. 1997. pap. 14.99 (*0-525-65255-8*) NAL-Dutton.

Raising the Dead. Samuel J. Keyser. 42p. (Orig.). 1993. pap. 10.00 (*1-882329-03-1*) Garden St Pr.

Raising the Dead: A Doctor's Encounter with His Own Mortality. Richard Selzer. 128p. 1995. pap. 9.95 (*0-14-023489-6*, Penguin Bks) Viking Penguin.

Raising the Home Duck Flock. Dave Holderread. LC 80-10992. (Illus.). 192p. 1980. pap. 12.95 (*0-88266-169-8*, Garden Way Pub) Storey Comm Inc.

Raising the Pentagon: Three Ancient Sorcerers Caught in a Time Warp Find Themselves in 20th Century Boston. Robin L. Stratton. 240p. (Orig.). 1990. pap. 9.95 (*0-9626541-1-6*) Mockngbrd Square.

Raising the Productivity of Women Farmers in Sub-Saharan Africa. Daphne Spurling et al. (Discussion Paper Ser.: Vol. 230). 126p. 1994. 8.95 (*0-8213-2749-6*) World Bank.

Raising the Profile: Marketing the HR Function. David Clutterbuck & Desmond Dearlove. 160p. 1993. 45.00 (*0-85292-526-3*, Pub. by IPM Hse UK) St Mut.

Raising the Rafters: How to Assemble Your Team of Architects, Contractors, Interior Designers, Subcontractors, Suppliers, Engineers & Bankers to Get Your Dream House Built. Stephen F. Collier. 160p. 1994. reprint ed. pap. 12.95 (*0-87951-557-0*) Overlook Pr.

Raising the Rafters: How to Work with Architects, Contractors, Interior Designers...to Get Your Dream House Built. Stephen F. Collier. 160p. 1993. 19.95 (*0-87951-490-6*) Overlook Pr.

Raising the Rainbow Generation: Teaching Your Children to Be Successful in a Multicultural Society. Darlene P. Hopson & Derek S. Hopson. 1993. pap. 10.00 (*0-671-79806-5*, Fireside) S&S Trade.

Raising the Roof. Roland Kidd. (J). 1995. 14.95 (*1-887921-02-8*) Hab Human Intl.

Raising the Roof: A Sampler of Community Partnerships for Affordable Housing. Ed. by Alice Shabecoff. 122p. (Orig.). 1988. pap. 10.00 (*0-317-93020-6*, UC10583) United Way Amer.

Raising the Roof: Children's Stories & Activities on Houses. Jan Irving & Robin Currie. 250p. 1991. pap. text ed. 21.00 (*0-87287-786-8*) Teacher Ideas Pr.

Raising the Stakes, 3 vols. Edward G. Doyle & Samuel L. Lipsman. Ed. by Boston Publishing Company Editors & Robert Manning. (Illus.). 1982. write for info. (*0-318-50145-7*) Addison-Wesley.

Raising the Stakes, 3 vols., Vol. I. Edward G. Doyle & Samuel L. Lipsman. Ed. by Boston Publishing Company Editors & Robert Manning. (Illus.). 192p. 1982. 16.30 (*0-201-11260-4*) Addison-Wesley.

Raising the Stakes, 3 vols., Vol. II. Edward G. Doyle & Samuel L. Lipsman. Ed. by Boston Publishing Company Editors & Robert Manning. (Illus.). 208p. 1982. 16.30 (*0-201-11261-2*) Addison-Wesley.

Raising the Stakes, 3 vols., Vol. III. Edward G. Doyle & Samuel L. Lipsman. Ed. by Boston Publishing Company Editors & Robert Manning. (Illus.). 192p. 1982. 16.30 (*0-201-11262-0*) Addison-Wesley.

Raising the Standard of Morality. Mona Johnian. Ed. by David L. Young. 148p. (Orig.). 1991. pap. 4.95 (*0-929685-32-6*) Superior Bks.

Raising the Tents. Frances P. Adler. 96p. 1993. 19.95 (*0-934971-34-X*); pap. 9.95 (*0-934971-33-1*) Calyx Bks.

Raising the Tone of Philosophy: Late Essays by Immanuel Kant, Transformative Critique by Jacques Derrida. Immanuel Kant & Jacques Derrida. Ed. by Peter D. Fenves. LC 92-16600. 208p. 1993. text ed. 35.00 (*0-8018-4456-8*) Johns Hopkins.

Raising the Torch of Good News: Catholic Authority & Dialogue with the World. Ed. by Bernard P. Prusak. LC 87-31695. (College Theology Society Annual Publications: Vol. 32). 342p. (Orig.). (C). 1988. pap. text ed. 27.00 (*0-8191-6700-2*); lib. bdg. 51.00 (*0-8191-6699-5*) U Pr of Amer.

Raising the Wind: The Legend of Lapland & Finland Wizards in Literature. Ernest J. Moyne. Ed. by Wayne R. Kime. (Illus.). 224p. 1981. 34.50 (*0-87413-146-4*) U Delaware Pr.

Raising the Young Blind Child: A Guide for Parents & Educators. Shulamith Kastein et al. LC 79-17820. 208p. 1980. 35.95 (*0-87705-422-3*); pap. 20.95 (*0-89885-288-9*) Human Sci Pr.

Raising Their Voices: British Women Writers, 1650-1750. Marilyn L. Williamson. LC 89-36296. 340p. (C). 1990. text ed. 39.95 (*0-8143-2209-3*) Wayne St U Pr.

Raising Them Chaste. Richard Durfield & Renee Durfield. 192p. (Orig.). 1991. pap. 8.99 (*1-55661-171-4*) Bethany Hse.

Raising Them Right. Ed. by Mike Yorkey. 1994. 14.99 (*1-56179-277-2*) Focus Family.

Raising Them Right: A Saint's Advice on Raising Children. rev. ed. Saint Theophan the Recluse. Tr. by Hieromonk S. Rose from RUS. LC 89-61280. 76p. (C). 1989. reprint ed. pap. 5.95 (*0-9622713-0-6*) Conciliar Pr.

Raising Them Right: Three Hundred & One Ways to Be a Loving Parent. Roger Pierangelo. 1994. pap. 5.99 (*1-56171-323-6*, S P I Bks) Sure Seller.

Raising Toxic Free Children: Protecting Your Child from Common Environmental Health Threats. Herbert L. Needleman & Philip J. Landrigan. LC 93-38108. 1994. 20.00 (*0-374-24643-2*) FS&G.

Raising Turkeys, Ducks, Geese, Pigeon, & Guineas. Cynthia Haynes. (Illus.). 368p. (Orig.). 1987. 24.95 (*0-8306-0803-6*) McGraw-Hill Prof.

Raising up a Faithful Priest: Community & Priesthood in Biblical Theology. Richard D. Nelson. LC 93-10361. 1993. pap. 20.00 (*0-664-25437-3*) Westminster John Knox.

Raising up a Family to the Lord. Gene R. Cook. LC 93-8928. xxvii, 340p. 1993. 16.95 (*0-87579-713-X*) Deseret Bk.

***Raising Ursa.** Carol A. Amato. (Young Reader Ser.). (Illus.). 48p. (J). (gr. 3-6). 1996. lib. bdg. 12.95 (*1-56674-187-4*) Forest Hse.

Raising Ursa. Nicole S. Amato. LC 95-36475. (Illus.). 48p. (J). 1996. pap. 4.95 (*0-8120-9310-0*) Barron.

Raising Voices - Ensuring Quality in Residential Care. P. J. Youll & C. McCourt-Perring. 244p. 1994. pap. 35.00 (*0-11-321630-0*, HM16300, Pub. by Stationery Ofc UK) Bernan Associates.

Raising with the Moon: The Complete Guide to Gardening & Living. Jack Pyle & Taylor Reese. Ed. by Dot Jackson. LC 93-70246. (Illus.). 147p. (Orig.). 1993. pap. 13.95 (*1-878086-18-9*) Down Home NC.

Raising World-Wise but Innocent Kids: Wisdom from the Book of Proverbs. David B. Wyrtzen. 232p. (Orig.). 1995. pap. 10.99 (*1-57293-002-0*) Discovery Hse Pubs.

***Raising Yoder's Barn.** Jane Yolen. LC 97-13101. (Illus.). (J). 1998. write for info. (*0-316-96887-0*) Little.

Raising Your Child in Washington: A Guide for the Growing Years. Roberta Gottesman. 420p. (Orig.). 1995. pap. 15.95 (*0-9631756-2-9*) Piccolo Pr.

Raising Your Child, Not by Force but by Love. Sidney D. Craig. LC 72-10436. 192p. 1982. pap. 9.00 (*0-664-24413-0*, Westminster) Westminster John Knox.

Raising Your Child, Not Your Voice. Duane Cuthbertson. 168p. 1986. pap. 9.99 (*0-89693-342-3*, 6-2342, Victor Bks) Chariot Victor.

Raising Your Child to Be Gifted: Successful Parents Speak. James R. Campbell. 196p. 1995. pap. 15.95 (*1-57129-000-1*) Brookline Bks.

Raising Your Child Without Milk: Reassuring Advice & Recipes for Parents of Lactose-Intolerant & Milk-Allergic Children. Jane Zukin. 384p. 1995. pap. 16.95 (*0-7615-0131-2*) Prima Pub.

Raising Your Children. Carol Robinson et al. Ed. by Angelus Press Editors. (Integrity Magazine Anthology Ser.: No. 2). 75p. 1995. pap. 13.50 (*0-935952-27-6*) Angelus Pr.

Raising Your Child's Inner Self-Esteem: The Authoritative Guide from Infancy Through the Teen Years. Karen B. Owens. (Illus.). 371p. (C). 1995. 24.95 (*0-306-45084-4*, Plenum Pr) Plenum.

Raising Your Dreams from the Dead: What God Has in Mind When Your Hopes in Life Have Died. O. S. Hawkins. LC 95-789. 1997. 17.99 (*0-8054-5403-9*, 4254-03) Broadman.

Raising Your Family Naturally. Joy Gross. 224p. 1988. reprint ed. 12.95 (*0-8184-0459-0*) Carol Pub Group.

Raising Your Hearing-Impaired Child: Guideline for Parents. Shirley H. McArthur. 256p. 1982. pap. 12.95 (*0-88200-150-7*) Alexander Graham.

Raising Your Jewish - Christian Child: How Interfaith Parents Can Give Children the Best of Both Heritages. Lee E. Gruzen. LC 89-13818. 288p. 1991. pap. 12.95 (*1-55704-059-1*) Newmarket.

Raising Your Own Livestock. Claudia Weisburd. (Illus.). 1980. 15.95 (*0-13-752758-6*, Spectrum IN) Macmillan Gen Ref.

Raising Your Own Turkeys. Leonard S. Mercia. LC 81-6353. (Illus.). 144p. (Orig.). 1981. pap. 12.95 (*0-88266-253-8*, Garden Way Pub) Storey Comm Inc.

Raising Your Sexual Self-Esteem: How to Feel Better about Your Sexuality & Yourself. Beverly Engel. LC 94-19505. 1995. 12.00 (*0-449-90674-4*) Fawcett.

***Raising Your Spirited Child.** Mary S. Kurcinka. 208p. Date not set. wbk. ed., pap. 14.00 (*0-06-095240-7*, PL) HarpC.

Raising Your Spirited Child: A Guide for Parents Whose Child Is More Intense, Sensitive, Perceptive, Persistent, Energetic. Mary S. Kurcinka. LC 90-56376. 320p. 1992. pap. 12.00 (*0-06-092328-8*, PL) HarpC.

Raisins & Almonds. 3rd ed. Marie Einspruch & Henry Einspruch. 88p. 1967. pap. 3.95 (*1-880226-10-3*) M J Pubs.

Raissa Maritain: Pilgrim, Poet, Exile. Judith Suther. LC 89-83998. (Illus.). x, 216p. 1990. 35.00 (*0-8232-1231-9*) Fordham.

Raissa's Journal. Raissa Maritain. LC 72-95648. 425p. 1974. 16.00 (*0-87343-041-7*) Magi Bks.

Raized on the Rez. Betty Ankrum. (Illus.). 144p. (Orig.). 1996. pap. write for info. (*1-57579-008-4*) Pine Hill Pr.

Raj. Gita Mehta. 1991. pap. 12.50 (*0-449-90566-7*) Fawcett.

Raj: India & the British, 1600-1947. C. A. Bayly. (Illus.). 432p. 1994. 75.00 (*1-55859-848-0*) Abbeville Pr.

Raj & Literature: Banned Bengali Books. Hiranmoy Bhattacharya. (C). 1989. 21.50 (*0-9514244-0-8*, Pub. by Firma KLM II) S Asia.

Raj at Table: A Culinary History of the British in India. David Burton. (Illus.). 256p. 1994. pap. 12.95 (*0-571-14390-3*) Faber & Faber.

Raj Kapoor: Fabulous Showman: An Intimate Biography. Bunny Reuben. (C). 1995. pap. 21.00 (*81-7223-196-2*, Pub. by Indus Pub II) S Asia.

Raj Marwar During the British Paramountcy. P. R. Shah. 265p. 1982. 95.00 (*0-317-62306-0*, Pub. by Scientific UK) St Mut.

Raj, the Indian Mutiny, & the Kingdom of Oudh, 1801-1859. John Pemble. LC 76-55892. 303p. 1977. 39.50 (*0-8386-2092-2*) Fairleigh Dickinson.

Raja Rammohun Roy. Ed. by Verinder Grover. (Political Thinkers of Modern India Ser.: No. 1). (C). 1992. 60.00 (*81-7100-243-9*, Pub. by Deep II) S Asia.

Raja Rammohun Roy. Mini Thakur. 1987. 22.50 (*0-8364-2020-9*, Pub. by Deep II) S Asia.

Raja Rammohun Roy: Letters & Documents. Ram P. Chanda & Jatindra K. Majumdar. 1987. reprint ed. 72.50 (*81-7041-067-3*, Pub. by Anmol II) S Asia.

Raja Rammohun Roy & the Indian Renissance. Shashi Ahluwalia. (C). 1991. 28.00 (*81-7099-239-7*, Pub. by Mittal II) S Asia.

Raja Rammohun Roy & the New Learning. Ed. by B. P. Barua. 134p. 1988. text ed. 22.50 (*0-86131-886-2*, Pub. by Orient Longman Ltd II) Apt Bks.

Raja Rao. C. D. Narasimaiah. (Indian Writers Ser.). 8.50 (*0-89253-511-3*) Ind-US Inc.

Raja Rao: Man & His Works. Shyamala A. Narayan. viii, 143p. 1989. text ed. 22.50 (*81-207-0963-2*, Pub. by Sterling Pubs II) Apt Bks.

Raja Rao & Cultural Tradition. Paul Sharrad. 180p. 1988. text ed. 25.00 (*0-318-32708-2*, Pub. by Sterling Pubs II) Apt Bks.

Raja Rao, Novelist As Sadhaka. Shiva Niranjan. 154p. 1986. 13.50 (*0-8364-1664-3*, Pub. by Popular Prakashan II) S Asia.

Raja Yoga. Yogi Ramacharaka. 13.50 (*0-911662-03-0*) Yoga.

Raja-Yoga. Swami Vivekananda. LC 55-12231. 327p. (C). 1955. 12.50 (*0-911206-06-X*) Ramakrishna.

Raja-Yoga. Swami Vivekananda. LC 55-12231. 327p. (C). 1982. pap. 12.50 (*0-911206-23-X*) Ramakrishna.

Raja Yoga: A Simplified & Practical Course. Wallace Slater. LC 71-3051. 1969. pap. 5.95 (*0-8356-0131-5*, Quest) Theos Pub Hse.

Raja-Yoga: The Yoga Aphorisms of Patanjali. Tr. by Swami Vivekananda. (C). 1982. pap. 4.95 (*0-87481-160-0*, Pub. by Advaita Ashrama II) Vedanta Pr.

An Asterisk (*) at the beginning of an entry indicates that the title is appearing in BIP for the first time.

R

Raja Yoga Sutras. Tr. by Jyotinmayananda from SAN. (Illus.). 1978. pap. 6.99 (*0-934664-38-2*) Yoga Res Foun.

Raja Yoga (The Study of the Mind) Swami Jyotinmayananda. (Illus.). 1970. 14.95 (*0-934664-09-9*) Yoga Res Foun.

Rajagopalachari: A Biography. C. R. Narasimhan. 260p. 1992. 35.00 (*81-7027-156-8*, Pub. by Radiant Pubs II) S Asia.

Rajagriha: A Tale of Gautama Buddha. Kaku C. Noguchi. (C). 1992. 15.00 (*81-7023-359-3*, Pub. by Allied II) S Asia.

Rajah's Rice: A Mathematical Folktale from India. David Barry. LC 94-16087. (Illus.). 32p. (J). (ps-3). 1995. text ed. 15.95 (*0-7167-6568-3*, Sci Am Yng Rdrs) W H Freeman.

Rajah's Sapphire. M. P. Shiel. (Nautilus Ser.). (Illus.). 163p. 1981. pap. 6.00 (*0-686-92118-6*) Highflyer Pr.

Rajah's Sapphire. M. P. Shiel. 139p. reprint ed. pap. 6.00 (*0-317-14710-2*) Reynolds Morse.

Rajah's Servant. Arthur B. Ward. LC 67-63869. (Cornell University, Southeast Asia Program, Data Paper Ser.: No. 61). (Illus.). 230p. reprint ed. pap. 65.60 (*0-8357-3669-5*, 2036395) Bks Demand.

Rajani Palme Dutt: A Study in British Stalinism. John Callaghan. 256p. (C). 1993. pap. 35.00 (*0-85315-779-0*, Pub. by Lawrence & Wishart UK) NYU Pr.

Rajarsi Janakananda: A Great Western Yogi. (Illus.). 96p. 1994. pap. 5.50 (*0-87612-182-2*) Self Realization.

***Rajarsi Janakananda: A Great Western Yogi.** 191p. 1996. pap. 7.50 (*0-87612-019-2*) Self Realization.

Raja's New Clothes: Toward a Recovery of Religious Things. Joanne P. Waghorne. LC 93-20133. (Hermeneutics, Studies in the History of Religions). 1994. 49.50 (*0-271-01066-5*) Pa St U Pr.

Rajasthan. (Insight Guides Ser.). 1993. pap. 22.95 (*0-395-66288-5*) HM.

Rajasthan. Michelle Coxall & Sarina Singh. (Illus.). 352p. 1997. pap. 15.95 (*0-86442-470-1*) Lonely Planet.

Rajasthan: A Bibliographic Index of Social Science. S. N. Sahai. Ed. by D. V. Kothari. 418p. (C). 1985. 155.00 (*81-85046-23-9*, Pub. by Scientific UK) St Mut.

***Rajasthan: Polity, Economy & Society.** B. L. Panagariya & N. C. Pahariya. 1996. 36.00 (*0-614-25279-2*, Pub. by Rawat II) S Asia.

Rajasthan: Splendour in the Wilderness. Dom Moraes. (Illus.). 144p. (C). 1988. 595.00 (*81-7002-027-1*, Pub. by Himalayan Bks II) St Mut.

Rajasthan Local Laws, Nineteen Forty-Nine to Nineteen Eighty-One. Shivlal Gupta. (C). 1981. 85.00 (*0-685-36485-2*) St Mut.

Rajavaliya or Historical Narrative of Sinhalese Kings. B. Gunasekara. (C). 1995. reprint ed. 12.00 (*81-206-1029-6*, Pub. by Asian Educ Servs II) S Asia.

Rajendra Prasad: A True Gandhian. S. R. Bakshi. (C). 1990. 40.00 (*81-7041-255-2*, Pub. by Anmol II) S Asia.

Rajendra Prasad & the Indian Freedom Struggle. Nirmal Kumar. (C). 1991. 17.50 (*81-7050-128-8*, Pub. by Patriot II) S Asia.

Rajgonds. S. K. Tiwari. 1993. 36.00 (*81-7320-000-9*, Pub. by Agam II) S Asia.

Rajinder Singh Bedi: Selected Short Stories. Gopi C. Narang. (C). 1989. 12.50 (*0-8364-2620-7*, Pub. by Sahitya Akademi II) S Asia.

Rajiv. Sonia Gandhi. (Illus.). 224p. 1994. pap. 50.00 (*0-670-84607-4*, Viking) Viking Penguin.

Rajiv Gandhi: A Political Study. Bhabani S. Gupta. ix, 220p. 1989. text ed. 25.00 (*81-220-0120-3*, Pub. by Konark Pubs Pvt Ltd II) Advent Bks Div.

Rajiv Gandhi: Breaking New Grounds. B. K. Ahluwalia & S. Alhuwalia. 202p. 1985. 34.95 (*0-318-36607-X*) Asia Bk Corp.

Rajiv Gandhi: Challenges & Choices. V. K. Murthi & G. Sharma. 1985. 22.95 (*81-7027-089-8*) Asia Bk Corp.

Rajiv Gandhi: Future of India. Jagdish C. Tokas. 134p. 1987. 32.95 (*0-318-36608-8*) Asia Bk Corp.

Rajiv Gandhi: His Mind & Ideology. Attar Chand. (C). 1991. 34.00 (*81-212-0397-X*, Pub. by Gian Publng Hse II) S Asia.

Rajiv Gandhi: Life & Message. Arun Bhattacharjee. xiv, 267p. 1992. 25.00 (*81-7024-484-6*, Pub. by Ashish Pub Hse II) Nataraj Bks.

Rajiv Gandhi: The Years of Power. Kathleen Healy. 1989. text ed. 37.50 (*0-7069-4435-6*, Pub. by Vikas II) S Asia.

Rajiv Gandhi & Morality in Public Affairs. Umeshwar P. Varma. (C). 1988. 24.00 (*81-7099-045-9*, Pub. by Mittal II) S Asia.

Rajiv Gandhi & Rama's Kingdom. Ved Mehta. 224p. 1994. 25.00 (*0-300-06038-6*) Yale U Pr.

Rajiv Gandhi & Rama's Kingdom. Ved Mehta. (Illus.). 1996. pap. 14.00 (*0-300-06858-1*) Yale U Pr.

Rajiv's World. Photos by Rajiv Gandhi. (Illus.). 208p. 1995. pap. 65.00 (*0-670-85917-6*, Viking) Viking Penguin.

Rajneesh: The Mystic of Feeling. Ram C. Prasad. 239p. 1978. 16.95 (*0-318-36385-2*) Asia Bk Corp.

Rajneesh & the U. S. Postal Service. Bert Webber. LC 88-20740. (Illus.). 78p. (Orig.). 1988. pap. 9.95 (*0-936738-29-4*) Webb Research.

Rajneesh Bible, Vol. II. Rajneesh Osho Staff. Ed. by Rajneesh Academy Staff. LC 85-42539. (Talks in America Ser.). 839p. (Orig.). 1985. pap. 9.95 (*0-88050-201-0*) Osho America.

Rajneesh Bible, Vol. III. Rajneesh Osho Staff. Ed. by Rajneesh Academy Staff. LC 85-42539. (Talks in America Ser.). 1072p. (Orig.). 1985. pap. 9.95 (*0-88050-202-9*) Osho America.

Rajneesh Papers: Studies in a New Religious Movement. Susan J. Palmer. (C). 1993. text ed. 24.00 (*81-208-1080-5*, Pub. by Motilal Banarsidass II) S Asia.

Rajneeshpuram; Who Were Its People? (An Oregon Documentary) Bert Webber. LC 88-27845. (Illus.). 132p. (Orig.). 1990. 24.95 (*0-936738-44-8*); pap. 12.95 (*0-936738-30-8*) Webb Research.

Rajput Painting, 2 vols. in 1. Ananda K. Coomaraswamy. LC 72-87768. 1975. reprint ed. lib. bdg. 85.00 (*0-87817-118-5*) Hacker.

Rajput Palace Architecture. G. H. Tillotson. LC 86-24544. 245p. 1987. 50.00 (*0-300-03738-4*) Yale U Pr.

Rajput Polity: A Study of Politics & Administration of the State of Marwar, 1638-1749. G. D. Sharma. 1977. 14.00 (*0-88386-887-3*) S Asia.

Rajputs of Saurashtra. Virbhadra Singhji. (C). 1994. text ed. 44.00 (*81-7154-546-7*, Pub. by Popular Prakashan II) S Asia.

Rake & the Redhead. Emily Hendrickson. 224p. 1994. 3.99 (*0-451-17855-6*, Sig) NAL-Dutton.

Rakes & Rascals. 1995. mass mkt. 4.99 (*0-373-31219-9*, 1-31219-8) Harlequin Bks.

Rakes & Rogues. Mary Balogh et al. 352p. (Orig.). 1993. pap. 4.99 (*0-451-17639-1*, Sig) NAL-Dutton.

Rakes & Rogues. Neil King. (Drama Ser.). 128p. 1985. pap. 12.95 (*0-7175-1234-7*) Dufour.

Rakes & Rogues. Neil King. 128p. (C). 1984. 49.00 (*0-685-33825-8*, Pub. by S Thornes Pubs UK) St Mut.

Rake's Folly. Claudette Williams. 1995. pap. 3.99 (*0-8217-5007-0*) NAL-Dutton.

***Rake's Gambit.** Meg-Lynn Roberts. 224p. 1997. mass mkt. 4.99 (*0-8217-5687-7*, Zebra Kensgtn) Kensgtn Pub Corp.

Rake's Journey. Violet Hamilton. 352p. 1995. mass mkt. 4.50 (*0-8217-5049-6*, Zebra Kensgtn) Kensgtn Pub Corp.

Rake's Protegee. Barbara Hazard. 224p. 1990. pap. 3.50 (*0-451-16578-0*, Sig) NAL-Dutton.

Rake's Rainbow. Allison Lane. 224p. (Orig.). 1996. mass mkt., pap. 4.50 (*0-451-18666-4*, Sig) NAL-Dutton.

Rake's Ransom. Barbara Metzger. 224p. 1986. 15.95 (*0-8027-0911-7*) Walker & Co.

Rakes Reform. Anne Barbour. 1996. pap. 5.50 (*0-451-19048-3*, Sig) NAL-Dutton.

Rake's Reform. Cindy Holbrook. 256p. 1995. mass mkt. 3.99 (*0-8217-4876-9*, Zebra Kensgtn) Kensgtn Pub Corp.

***Rake's Revenge.** large type ed. Claire Tremaine. (Ulverscroft Large Print Ser.). 320p. 1997. 27.50 (*0-7089-3747-0*) Ulverscroft.

Rakeshells Reform. Elisabeth Fairchild. 1997. pap. 5.50 (*0-451-19122-6*, Sig) NAL-Dutton.

***Raki.** B. Wongar. LC 97-3945. 256p. 1997. 24.95 (*0-7145-3031-X*) M Boyars Pubs.

Raking the Gravel. Ben Bohnhorst. 32p. (Orig.). 1992. pap. text ed. 5.00 (*1-56439-024-1*) Ridgeway.

***Raking the Rocks.** Phil Cisneros. 100p. (J). (gr. 4-8). 1996. pap. 8.00 (*0-9651804-2-5*, 103) New Horizons Unlimited.

Raking the Snow. Elisavietta Ritchie. LC 81-86642. 55p. 1982. pap. 7.00 (*0-931846-21-8*) Wash Writers Pub.

Rakkasan! The 187th Regimental Combat Team. Arch E. Roberts. (Airborne Ser.: No. 8). (Illus.). 1981. 29.95 (*0-89839-008-7*) Battery Pr.

Rakkasans: One Hundred Eighty-Seventh Airborne "The Steel Berets" Turner Publishing Company Staff. LC 91-75250. 260p. 1991. 48.00 (*1-56311-047-4*) Turner Pub KY.

***Rakkasans: The Combat History of the 187th Airborne Infantry.** Edward M. Flanagan, Jr. LC 96-49009. 416p. 1997. 27.95 (*0-89141-604-8*) Presidio Pr.

Rakke Nokuse (Big Bear) John M. Carter, Sr. (Illus.). 112p. 1993. pap. 9.00 (*0-934188-37-8*) Evans Pubns.

Rakontoj Prapatraj Pri Nia Lando Antau Multaj Jarcentoj Kiam Okazemis Aferoj Mirindaj. David K. Jordan. 77p. (ESP.). 1996. pap. text ed. 5.15 (*1-882251-13-X*) Eldonejo Bero.

Raku: A Practical Approach. Steve Branfman. LC 90-55875. (Illus.). 176p. 1991. pap. 26.95 (*0-8019-8023-2*) Chilton.

Raku: A Review of Contemporary Work. Tim Andrews. 160p. 1994. 34.95 (*0-8019-8633-8*) Chilton.

Raku: A Review of Contemporary Work. Tim Andrews. 176p. 1994. text ed. 60.00 (*976-8097-99-X*, Pub. by Craftsman Hse VB) Gordon & Breach.

Raku: The Complete Potter. Ian Byers. Ed. by Emmanuel Cooper. (Complete Potter Ser.). (Illus.). 96p. 1996. reprint ed. pap. 19.95 (*0-7134-6131-4*, Pub. by Batsford UK) Trafalgar.

Raku & Smoke North America. (Illus.). 28p. 1984. 6.30 (*0-88321-056-8*) Am Craft.

Raku Pottery. rev. ed. Robert Piepenburg. (Illus.). 160p. 1994. pap. 26.95 (*0-9628481-1-5*) Pebble Pr.

Rakugo: The Popular Narrative Art of Japan. Heinz Morioka & Miyoko Sasaki. (East Asian Monographs: No. 138). 470p. 1990. 38.00 (*0-674-74725-9*) HUP.

Ralational Database Theory: A Comprehensive Introduction. Paolo Atzeni et al. Ed. by Sally Elliott. 350p. (C). 1993. text ed. 53.75 (*0-8053-0249-2*) Addison-Wesley.

Ralationship vs. Religion. Chester M. Wright. 200p. (Orig.). 1991. pap. 8.95 (*0-932345-07-7*) Antioch Publishes.

Ralegh. Mark Dunster. (James Ser.: Pt. 1). 21p. (Orig.). 1989. pap. 4.00 (*0-89642-169-4*) Linden Pubs.

Ralegh's Country: The South West of England in the Reign of Queen Elizabeth I. Joyce Youings. (America's 400th Anniversary Ser.). (Illus.). xiv, 74p. (Orig.). 1986. pap. 5.00 (*0-86526-207-1*) NC Archives.

Raleigh. Gousha, H. M., Editors. 1995. 2.95 (*0-671-55114-0*, H M Gousha) P-H Gen Ref & Trav.

Raleigh: A Quirky, Unorthodox History of North Carolina's Capital. Marshall Lancaster. Ed. by Dot Jackson. LC 92-72660. 266p. 1992. 19.95 (*1-878086-15-4*) Down Home NC.

Raleigh: City of Oaks. James Vickers. 1983. 22.95 (*0-89781-050-3*) Am Historical Pr.

Raleigh - Wake County, NC. (Streetfinder Ser.). (Illus.). 1994. pap. 14.95 (*0-528-91319-0*) Rand McNally.

Raleigh & Related Families. Carl J. Marsh. LC 88-70909. (Illus.). 1988. 20.00 (*0-9619972-0-6*) C & L Pubns.

Raleigh & the Rancher. Laura Anthony. (Romance Ser.). 1995. mass mkt. 2.99 (*0-373-19092-1*, 1-19092-5) Silhouette.

Raleigh, Capital of North Carolina. Writers Program, North Carolina Staff. LC 73-3648. (American Guide Ser.). reprint ed. 49.50 (*0-404-57947-7*) AMS Pr.

Raleigh Dine-a-Mate. 256p. 1994. pap. 25.00 (*1-57393-019-9*) Dine-A-Mate.

Raleigh-Durham Jobs. Steve Hines & Adam Bertolett. 300p. 1994. pap. 15.95 (*0-929255-16-X*) CareerSource.

Raleigh House Cookbook. Martha R. Johnson. (Illus.). 1991. 19.95 (*0-9631037-0-9*) M R Johnson.

Raleigh House Cookbook II. Martha R. Johnson. 288p. 1995. 19.95 (*0-9631037-1-7*) M R Johnson.

Raleigh in Guiana: Three Plays. Barrett Wendell. LC 79-50034. (One Act Plays in Reprint Ser.). 1980. reprint ed. 20.00 (*0-8486-2058-5*) Roth Pub Inc.

***Raleigh, NC.** Anderson & Fowler. (Images of America Ser.). pap. 16.99 (*0-7524-0495-4*, Arcdia) Chalford.

Raleigh Street Saga: Shattering the Legend. Claire W. Schumacher. Ed. by Gene LeRoy & Clarice LeRoy. LC 90-71810. (Duluth History Ser.). (Illus.). 178p. (Orig.). 1991. pap. 12.00 (*0-917378-07-5*) Zenith City.

Raleigh's Birthplace: The Story of East Budleigh. Lilian Sheppard. (C). 1988. 30.00 (*0-86236-019-6*, Pub. by Granary UK) St Mut.

Raleigh's Eden. Inglis Fletcher. (Albemarle Ser.). 1976. reprint ed. lib. bdg. 34.95 (*0-89244-006-6*, Queens House) Amereon Ltd.

Ralestone Luck. Andre Norton. 256p. 1988. pap. 2.95 (*0-8125-4754-3*) Tor Bks.

Ralliement in French Politics, Eighteen Ninety to Eighteen Ninety-Eight. Alexander C. Sedgwick. LC 65-12828. (Historical Studies: No. 74). 194p. 1965. 17.50 (*0-674-74751-8*) HUP.

Ralls County, Missouri, Settlement Records, 1832-1853. Sherida K. Eddlemon. iv, 120p. (Orig.). 1993. pap. 15.00 (*1-55613-821-0*) Heritage Bk.

Rally! Susan Lurie. 80p. (J). (gr. 7-10). 1993. pap. 3.50 (*0-553-48092-8*) Bantam.

Rally Car. (Things That Go Shaped Board Bks.). (Illus.). 10p. (J). 1996. 3.95 (*0-7894-1135-0*) DK Pub Inc.

Rally Cry. William R. Forstchen. (Lost Regiment Ser.: No. 1). 400p. 1990. pap. 5.99 (*0-451-45007-8*, ROC) NAL-Dutton.

***Rally Navigation.** Martin Holmes. 176p. 1997. 27.95 (*1-85260-577-4*) Haynes Pubns.

***Rally Navigation.** Martin Holmes. 1997. pap. text ed. 27.95 (*1-85960-400-5*, Pub. by J H Haynes & Co UK) Motorbooks Intl.

Rally Once Again: Battle Tactics of the American Civil War. Paddy Griffith. (C). 1989. 27.50 (*0-300-04247-7*) Yale U Pr.

Rally 'Round the Flag. Theodore Karamanski. 1993. 29.95 (*0-8304-1295-6*) Nelson-Hall.

Rally Round the Flag, Boys! Max Shulman. 1993. reprint ed. lib. bdg. 21.95 (*1-56849-139-5*) Buccaneer Bks.

Rally to Kill. large type ed. Bill Knox. 1977. 25.99 (*0-7089-0075-5*) Ulverscroft.

***Rallying.** S. Turner & T. Mason. (Illus.). 114p. Date not set. 27.95 (*0-85429-887-8*, Pub. by G T Foulis Ltd) Haynes Pubns.

Rallying - the 4 Wheel Drive Revolution. Graham Robson. LC 86-82147. (Foulis Motoring Bk.). (Illus.). 192p. 34.95 (*0-85429-547-X*, F723, Pub. by G T Foulis Ltd) Haynes Pubns.

Rallying Cries: Three Plays. Eric Bentley. 235p. 1987. reprint ed. pap. 12.95 (*0-8101-0743-0*) Northwestern U Pr.

Rallying Point. Melvin Charles. Ed. by Hazel Lockett. LC 93-74944. (Illus.). 206p. (Orig.). (YA). 1994. pap. 14.95 (*0-9638672-1-0*) Bryant & Dillon.

Rallying the Whole Village: The Comer Process for Reforming Education. James P. Comer. Ed. by Norris Haynes et al. LC 96-2130. 208p. (C). 1996. pap. 21.95 (*0-8077-3539-6*); text ed. 45.00 (*0-8077-3540-X*) Tchrs Coll.

Rallying to Win. Jean Calvin. (Illus.). 1974. 8.95 (*0-393-60002-5*) Norton.

Ralph Adams Cram, American Medievalist. Douglass S. Tucci. (Illus.). 1975. 10.00 (*0-89073-038-5*) Boston Public Lib.

Ralph Albert Blakelock. Abraham A. Davidson. 1996. 65.00 (*0-271-01504-7*) Pa St U Pr.

Ralph & Deno in Vermont. Kenneth R. Beittel & Joan N. Beittel. LC 90-86028. (Illus.). 32p. (Orig.). (J). (gr. 5 up). 1990. pap. 6.00 (*0-9628511-0-8*) HVHA.

Ralph & Kacoo, a Taste of Louisiana. 2nd ed. Ed. by Ralph Olinde & Kacoo Olinde. (Illus.). 348p. 1988. reprint ed. 13.95 (*0-9613196-0-7*) Cajun Bayou.

***Ralph Arthur Roberts - Lebensbild Eines Groben Schauspielers.** Hansjoachim Schonherr. (Studien Zur Filmgeschichte Ser.: Vol. 7). 185p. (GER.). 1992. write for info. (*3-487-09567-X*) G Olms Pubs.

Ralph Bunche: An American Life. Brian Urquhart. LC 92-46564. 480p. 1993. 27.50 (*0-393-03527-1*) Norton.

Ralph Bunche: The Man & His Times. Ed. by Benjamin Rivlin. LC 89-24666. (Illus.). 279p. (C). 1989. 39.50 (*0-8419-1145-2*) Holmes & Meier.

Ralph Connor & His Works. John Lennox. (Canadian Author Studies). 60p. (C). 1988. pap. text ed. 9.95 (*0-920763-78-2*, Pub. by ECW Press CN) Genl Dist Srvs.

Ralph Cudworth: A Treatise Concerning Eternal & Immutable Morality: With A Treatise of Freewill. Ralph Cudworth. Ed. by Sarah Hutton. (Texts in the History of Philosophy Ser.). 240p. (C). 1996. text ed. 59.95 (*0-521-47362-4*); pap. text ed. 19.95 (*0-521-47918-5*) Cambridge U Pr.

Ralph Dacre. large type ed. Anne Stevenson. 1977. 12.00 (*0-85456-510-8*) Ulverscroft.

Ralph Darnell. Meadows Taylor. 1990. reprint ed. 17.50 (*81-206-0333-8*, Pub. by Asian Educ Servs II) S Asia.

Ralph David Abernathy. Catherine Reef. LC 94-28623. (People in Focus Ser.). (Illus.). (YA). (gr. 10 up). 1995. 13.95 (*0-87518-653-X*, Dillon Silver Burdett) Silver Burdett Pr.

Ralph David Abernathy. Catherine Reef. LC 94-28623. (People in Focus Ser.). (Illus.). (YA). (gr. 5 up). 1995. pap. 7.95 (*0-382-24965-8*, Dillon Silver Burdett) Silver Burdett Pr.

Ralph Earl: The Face of the Young Republic. Richard L. Bushman et al. (Illus.). 272p. (C). 1991. text ed. 65.00 (*0-300-05041-0*) Yale U Pr.

Ralph Earl, Recorder for an Era. Laurence B. Goodrich. LC 66-64728. (Illus.). 108p. reprint ed. pap. 30.80 (*0-317-10010-6*, 2010108) Bks Demand.

Ralph Edwards. Ed Gould. (Illus.). 295p. pap. 12.95 (*0-88839-100-5*) Hancock House.

***Ralph Edwards of Lonesome Lake.** large type ed. Ed Gould. (Ulverscroft Large Print Ser.). 496p. 1997. 27.50 (*0-7089-3721-7*) Ulverscroft.

Ralph Ellison. Mark Busby. (Twayne's United States Authors Ser.: No. 582). 200p. (C). 1991. 21.95 (*0-8057-7626-5*, Twayne) Scribnrs Ref.

Ralph Ellison: A Collection of Critical Essays. Ed. by John Hersey. LC 73-16224. (Twentieth Century Views Ser.). 192p. 1973. 12.95 (*0-13-274357-4*, Spectrum IN); pap. 1.95 (*0-13-274340-X*, Spectrum IN) Macmillan Gen Ref.

Ralph Ellison: Author. Jack Bishop. Ed. by Nathan I. Huggins. (Black Americans of Achievement Ser.). (Illus.). 112p. (YA). (gr. 5 up). 1988. pap. 8.95 (*0-7910-0202-0*); lib. bdg. 19.95 (*1-55546-585-4*) Chelsea Hse.

Ralph Ellison: Critical Perspectives Past & Present. Ed. by Henry Louis Gates, Jr. & K. A. Appiah. (Literary Ser.). 1994. 24.95 (*1-56743-052-X*); pap. 14.95 (*1-56743-058-9*) Amistad Pr.

Ralph Ellison see Modern Critical Views Series

Ralph Ellison's Invisible Man see Bloom's Notes

Ralph, First Duke of Montagu, 1638-1709. Edward C. Metzger. LC 86-23797. (Studies in British History: Vol. 2). 450p. 1986. 109.95 (*0-88946-452-9*) E Mellen.

Ralph Gets a Prize. Roxanne Vallet. (Illus.). 12p. (J). (gr. k-3). 1993. pap. text ed. 12.95 (*1-56606-017-6*) Bradley Mann.

Ralph Gustafson & His Works. Dermot McCarthy. (Canadian Author Studies). 86p. (C). 1989. pap. text ed. 9.95 (*1-55022-009-8*, Pub. by ECW Press CN) Genl Dist Srvs.

Ralph Is Right Brained: A Primer for Parents & Teachers. Jack Fadely & Virginia Hosler. (Illus.). 44p. (Orig.). 1985. pap. text ed. 3.50 (*0-934293-00-7*) Huber-Copeland Pub.

Ralph J. Bunche: Peacemaker. Patricia McKissack & Fredrick McKissack. LC 90-49947. (Great African Americans Ser.). (Illus.). 32p. (J). (gr. 1-4). 1991. lib. bdg. 12.95 (*0-89490-300-4*) Enslow Pubs.

Ralph J. Bunche: Selected Speeches & Writings. Ed. by Charles P. Henry. LC 95-38748. (C). 1996. 37.50 (*0-472-10589-2*) U of Mich Pr.

Ralph Johnson of Perkins & Will: Buildings & Projects. Intro. by Robert Bruegmann. LC 95-4983. (Illus.). 224p. 1995. 60.00 (*0-8478-1862-4*); pap. 40.00 (*0-8478-1863-2*) Rizzoli Intl.

Ralph Lauren: Master of Fashion. Anne Canadeo. Ed. by Richard G. Young. LC 91-32777. (Wizards of Business Ser.). (Illus.). 64p. (J). (gr. 4-8). 1992. lib. bdg. 17.26 (*1-56074-021-3*) Garrett Ed Corp.

Ralph Lauren - Image Maker: The Man Behind the Mystique. Jeffrey A. Trachtenberg. 320p. 1988. 19.95 (*0-316-85214-7*) Little.

Ralph Morrill's Museum Quality Fish Taxidermy: A Guide to Molding with Plaster, Casting with Resin, Painting with an Airbrush. Ruth S. Billard. LC 84-70664. (Illus.). 275p. 1984. lib. bdg. 32.50 (*0-9611112-0-8*) BillArt.

Ralph Nader. Houghton Mifflin Company Staff. 1992. pap. 6.56 (*0-395-63565-9*) HM.

Ralph Nader: Crusader for Safe Consumer Products. Kelli Peduzzi. LC 90-9924. (People Who Made a Difference Ser.). (Illus.). 64p. (J). (gr. 3-4). 1991. lib. bdg. 23.93 (*0-8368-0455-4*) Gareth Stevens Inc.

Ralph Nader: Crusader for Safe Consumer Products & Lawyer for Public Interest. Kelli Peduzzi. LC 89-4282. (People Who Have Helped the World Ser.). (Illus.). 68p. (J). (gr. 5-6). 1990. lib. bdg. 23.93 (*0-8368-0098-2*) Gareth Stevens Inc.

Ralph Nader: The Consumer Revolution. Teresa Celsi. (New Directions Ser.). (Illus.). 104p. (YA). (gr. 7 up). 1991. pap. 5.95 (*1-56294-834-2*); lib. bdg. 16.40 (*1-56294-044-9*) Millbrook Pr.

Ralph Nader Presents: Practicing Democracy: A Guide to Student Action. Catherine Isaac. 112p. (C). 1994. pap. text ed. 7.00 (*0-312-10789-7*) St Martin.

Ralph One Hundred Twenty Four C, Forty One Plus. Hugo Gernsback. 142p. 1992. reprint ed. lib. bdg. 13.95 (*0-89966-911-5*) Buccaneer Bks.

Ralph Rashleigh: A Chronicle of a Migrant Experience. James Tucker. 304p. (Orig.). 1993. pap. 12.00 (*0-207-17615-9*, Pub. by Angus & Robertson AT) HarpC.

Ralph Raymonds Heir. Horatio Alger, Jr. (Works of Horatio Alger Jr.). 1989. reprint ed. lib. bdg. 79.00 (*0-685-44742-1*) Rprt Serv.

An Asterisk (*) at the beginning of an entry indicates that the title is appearing in BIP for the first time.

***Ralph Richardson: The Authorized Biography.** John Miller. (Illus.). 392p. (Orig.). 1997. pap. 9.95 (0-330-34780-2) Trafalgar.

Ralph Richardson: The Authorized Biography. John Miller. (Illus.). 399p. (Orig.). 1995. 42.50 (0-283-06237-1, Pub. by Sidgwick & Jackson UK) Trans-Atl Phila.

Ralph Roister Doister: One-Act Adaptation. Adapted by I. E. Clark. (Director's Production Script Ser.). (Illus.). 22p. 1965. pap. 10.00 (0-88680-162-1); pap. 3.25 (0-88680-161-3) I E Clark.

Ralph Roister Doister, with Introduction by Clarence Griffin Child. Nicholas Udall. (BCL1-PR English Literature Ser.). 175p. 1992. reprint ed. lib. bdg. 69.00 (0-7812-7313-7) Rprt Serv.

Ralph S. Mouse. (J). 1983. pap. 3.25 (0-440-77582-5) Dell.

Ralph S. Mouse. Beverly Cleary. 160p. (J). (gr. 5). 1993. pap. 4.50 (0-380-70957-0, Camelot) Avon.

Ralph S. Mouse. Beverly Cleary. LC 82-3516. (Illus.). 160p. (J). (gr. 4-6). 1982. 16.00 (0-688-01452-6, Morrow Junior); lib. bdg. 15.93 (0-688-01455-0, Morrow Junior) Morrow.

***Ralph Sexton Story: From the Mountains Came the Light.** Bob Terrell. (Illus.). 230p. 1997. reprint ed. pap. 14.95 (1-57090-071-X) Alexander Bks.

Ralph Steiner: Filmmaker & Still Photographer. J. S. Zuker. LC 77-22910. 1978. lib. bdg. 31.95 (0-405-10758-7) Ayer.

***Ralph Stover State Park.** Paul Nick. (Classic Rock Climbs Ser.: No. 12). (Illus.). 60p. (Orig.). 1997. pap. 9.95 (1-57540-037-5) Chockstone Pr.

Ralph Takes a Train Ride. Kosta Kontoyiannaki. (Illus.). 18p. (J). (gr. k-3). 1992. pap. 13.95 (1-895583-24-1) MAYA Pubs.

Ralph the Bunny. Hans Wilhelm. (J). 1996. pap. 15.99 (0-590-67908-2) Scholastic Inc.

Ralph the Heir. Anthony Trollope. (Illus.). 1978. pap. 7.95 (0-486-23642-0) Dover.

Ralph the Heir. Anthony Trollope. Ed. by John Sutherland. (World's Classics Ser.). 428p. 1990. pap. 9.95 (0-19-281805-8) OUP.

Ralph the Rhino. Illus. by Bob Storms. (World of Animals Ser.). 24p. (Orig.). (J). (gr. k-3). 1994. pap. 4.95 (0-89346-793-6) Heian Intl.

Ralph the Wanderer. Margaret Edwards. (Illus.). 240p. (C). 1989. text ed. 39.00 (1-872795-95-1, Pub. by Pentland Pr UK) St Mut.

***Ralph Vaughan Williams.** Michael Jameson. (Classic FM Lifelines Ser.). 112p. 1997. pap. 9.95 (1-86205-021-X, Pub. by Pavilion UK) Trafalgar.

Ralph Vaughan Williams: A Study. Hubert Foss. LC 74-9042. (Illus.). 219p. 1974. reprint ed. text ed. 38.50 (0-8371-7610-7, FORW, Greenwood Pr) Greenwood.

Ralph Waldo Emerson. Amos B. Alcott. 1978. lib. bdg. 200.00 (0-8490-7766-4) Gordon Pr.

Ralph Waldo Emerson. Ralph Waldo Emerson. Ed. by Richard Poirier. (Oxford Authors Ser.). 656p. 1990. pap. 19.95 (0-19-281437-0) OUP.

Ralph Waldo Emerson. Donald Yannella. (United States Authors Ser.: No. 414). 160p. (C). 1982. 21.95 (0-8057-7344-4, Twayne) Scribnrs Ref.

Ralph Waldo Emerson. Amos B. Alcott. LC 68-24930. (American Biography Ser.: No. 32). 1969. reprint ed. lib. bdg. 75.00 (0-8383-0908-9) M S G Haskell Hse.

Ralph Waldo Emerson. Amos B. Alcott. (Works of Amos Bronson Alcott). 1989. reprint ed. lib. bdg. 79.00 (0-685-27413-6) Rprt Serv.

Ralph Waldo Emerson. Bronson Alcott. (Illus.). 81p. 1983. reprint ed. pap. 15.00 (0-87556-553-0) Saifer.

Ralph Waldo Emerson. Oscar W. Firkins. LC 80-2532. reprint ed. 44.50 (0-404-19258-0) AMS Pr.

Ralph Waldo Emerson. Oliver W. Holmes. (BCL1-PS American Literature Ser.). 441p. 1992. reprint ed. lib. bdg. 99.00 (0-7812-6708-0) Rprt Serv.

Ralph Waldo Emerson. Oliver W. Holmes. (Notable American Authors Ser.). 1992. reprint ed. lib. bdg. 75.00 (0-7812-3170-1) Rprt Serv.

Ralph Waldo Emerson. George E. Woodberry. LC 68-24947. (American Biography Ser.: No. 32). 1969. reprint ed. lib. bdg. 75.00 (0-8383-0262-9) M S G Haskell Hse.

Ralph Waldo Emerson. George E. Woodberry. (BCL1-PS American Literature Ser.). 205p. 1992. reprint ed. lib. bdg. 79.00 (0-7812-6710-2) Rprt Serv.

Ralph Waldo Emerson: A Collection of Critical Essays. Ed. by Lawrence Buell. LC 92-17658. (New Century Views Ser.). 240p. 1992. pap. 12.95 (0-13-276783-X) P-H.

Ralph Waldo Emerson: A Descriptive Bibliography. Joel Myerson. LC 81-11502. (Series in Bibliography). (Illus.). 830p. 1982. 110.00 (0-8229-3452-3) U of Pittsburgh Pr.

Ralph Waldo Emerson: An Annotated Bibliography of Criticism, 1980-1991. Contrib. by Robert E. Burkholder & Joel Myerson. LC 93-45954. (Bibliographies & Indexes in American Literature Ser.). 248p. 1994. text ed. 75.00 (0-313-29150-0) Greenwood.

Ralph Waldo Emerson: An Estimate of His Character & Genius, in Prose & Verse. Amos B. Alcott. (BCL1-PS American Literature Ser.). 81p. 1992. reprint ed. lib. bdg. 59.00 (0-7812-6705-6) Rprt Serv.

Ralph Waldo Emerson: An Intellectual Portrait. Nikita E. Pokrovsky. 320p. 1994. write for info. (0-9642968-0-2); pap. text ed. write for info. (0-9642968-1-0) Ctr Am Studies Concord.

Ralph Waldo Emerson: Preacher & Lecturer. Lloyd Rohler. LC 95-2105. (Great American Orators Ser.: Vol. 21). 216p. 1995. text ed. 59.95 (0-313-26328-0, Greenwood Pr) Greenwood.

Ralph Waldo Emerson: Selected Essays, Lectures & Poems. Ralph Waldo Emerson. 400p. 1990. mass mkt. 5.95 (0-553-21388-1, Bantam Classics) Bantam.

Ralph Waldo Emerson: Selected Essays, Lectures & Poems. Ralph Waldo Emerson. Ed. by William H. Gilman. 1965. pap. 4.50 (0-451-52047-5, CE1832, Sig Classics) NAL-Dutton.

Ralph Waldo Emerson see Modern Critical Views Series

***Ralph Waldo Emerson & Scholarly Reception.** Sarah A. Wider. (LCENG Ser.). Date not set. 54.95 (1-57113-177-9) Camden Hse.

Ralph Waldo Emerson & the Critics: A Checklist of Criticism, 1900-1977. Jeanetta Boswell. LC 79-4670. (Author Bibliographies Ser.: No. 39). 1979. 25.00 (0-8108-1211-8) Scarecrow.

Ralph Waldo Emerson, Sa Vie et Son Oeuvre. Marie Dugard. (BCL1-PS American Literature Ser.). 418p. 1992. reprint ed. lib. bdg. 99.00 (0-7812-6707-2) Rprt Serv.

Ralph Waldo Emerson's Reading. Kenneth W. Cameron. LC 72-10872. (American Biography Ser.: No. 32). 1969. reprint ed. lib. bdg. 49.95 (0-8383-0518-0) M S G Haskell Hse.

Ralph Waldo Emerson's Reading: Guide for Source-Hunters & Scholars. Kenneth Cameron. (BCL1-PS American Literature Ser.). 144p. 1993. reprint ed. lib. bdg. 69.00 (0-7812-6961-X) Rprt Serv.

***Ralph Wollstonecraft Hedge Meets Cthu - Who?** Meade Frierson, III. (Illus.). 128p. (Orig.). 1997. pap. 10.00 (0-9639544-7-4) A F A B.

***Ralph's Complete Guide to Pill.** Ralphs. 1996. mass mkt. 6.99 (0-345-41201-X) Ballantine.

Ralph's Favorite Christmas Present. Vicki Manzo. LC 93-95025. (Illus.). 64p. (Orig.). (J). 1995. pap. 8.00 (1-56002-409-7, Univ Edtns) Aegina Pr.

Ralph's Funtime. Matthew V. Smith. (Illus.). 17p. (J). (gr. k-3). 1992. pap. 19.95 (1-895583-08-X) MAYA Pubs.

Ralph's Ready Reference DOS CD-ROM. Ed. by Rita Runchock-Droste. 1995. 350.00 incl. cd-rom (0-7876-0257-4, 109075) Gale.

Ralph's Secret Weapon. Steven Kellogg. LC 82-22115. (Pied Piper Bks.). (Illus.). (J). (ps-3). 1983. pap. 3.95 (0-8037-0307-4) Dial Bks Young.

Ralston Crawford: Painting & Visual Experience. Willaim C. Agee. (Illus.). 177p. 1983. 45.00 (0-942642-08-2) Twelvetrees Pr.

Ralston Purina Co. A Report on the Company's Environmental Policies & Practices. (Illus.). 34p. (C). 1994. reprint ed. pap. text ed. 250.00 (0-7881-0946-4, Coun on Econ) DIANE Pub.

Ralston Purina Company & Protein Technologies International's Work with Soybeans & Soybean Products - Bibliography & Sourcebook, 1934 to 1993: Detailed Information on 293 Published Documents (Extensively Annotated Bibliography), 44 Commerical Soy Products, 42 Original Interviews (Many Full Text) & Overviews, 16 Unpublished Archival Documents. Ed. by Akiko Aoyagi. (Bibliographies & Sourcebooks on Soya Ser.). 147p. (Orig.). 1994. spiral bd. 47.00 (0-933332-84-X) Soyfoods Center.

Ralston's Ring: California Plunders the Comstock Lode. George D. Lyman. 1992. reprint ed. lib. bdg. 75.00 (0-7812-5062-5) Rprt Serv.

Ram. Kwok Man-Ho. LC 93-48006. (Chinese Horoscopes Library). (Illus.). 48p. 1994. pap. 8.95 (1-56458-607-3) DK Pub Inc.

Ram Alley. Lording Barry. LC 75-133639. (Tudor Facsimile Texts. Old English Plays Ser.: No. 129). reprint ed. 59.50 (0-404-53429-5) AMS Pr.

Ram & the Black Sheep. C. C. York. LC 82-84423. 176p. 1982. 15.95 (0-8187-0050-5) Harlo Press.

Ram in the Thicket: The Story of a Roaming Homesteader Family on the Mormon Frontier. Frank C. Robertson. (Idaho Yesterdays Ser.). 350p. (C). 1995. reprint ed. pap. 15.95 (0-89301-173-8) U of Idaho Pr.

Ram Lam. Louisa V. Kyle. (Illus.). 76p. (J). (gr. 3). 1985. 5.95 (0-927044-02-1) Four OClock Farms.

Ram Mohan Ray: The Father of Modern India. Bruce C. Robertson. (Illus.). 200p. 1995. 17.95 (0-19-563417-9) OUP.

Ram Mohan Roy, the Apostle of Indian Awakening: Some Contemporary Estimates. B. M. Sankhdher. (C). 1989. 44.00 (81-7013-051-4, Pub. by Navrang) S Asia.

Ram of God. John B. Keane. 336p. 1996. 24.95 (1-57098-068-3) R Rinehart.

***Ram of Manana.** Susan Pickford. (Illus.). 8p. (Orig.). (J). (ps-6). 1996. pap. 5.50 (1-889664-02-2) SBP.

Ram Pumps How & Where They Work. Don R. Wilson. 40p. 1994. pap. 8.95 (0-9631526-2-9) Atlas Pubns.

Ram Rajya: In Search of Democracy. Marilyn Turkovich & Julian C. Hollick. (Passages to India Ser.). (C). 1989. teacher ed., spiral bd. 20.00 (1-56709-022-2) Indep Broadcast.

Ram with Red Horns. Rhys Davies. 180p. 1997. pap. 16.95 (1-85411-165-5, Pub. by Seren Bks UK) Dufour.

***Rama: The Official Strategy Guide.** Rick Barba. 288p. 1996. per., pap. 19.99 (0-7615-0879-1) Prima Pub.

Rama & Moses: The Aryan Cycle & the Mission of Israel. Edouard Schure. Tr. by F. Rothwell. 150p. 1995. pap. 16.95 (1-56459-510-2) Kessinger Pub.

Rama & the Bards: Epic Memory in the Ramayana. Robert Antoine. (Greybird Ser.). 114p. 1975. 12.00 (0-88253-821-7); pap. 6.75 (0-88253-822-5) Ind-US Inc.

***Rama & the Demon King: An Ancient Tale from India.** Jessica Souhami. (Illus.). 32p. (J). (ps-3). 1997. 14.95 (0-7894-2450-9) DK Pub Inc.

Rama Darshan: The Valmiki - Rama Dialogue. Anantanand Rambachan. (Ramayana Ser.). 94p. (Orig.). 1995. pap. write for info. (0-9634164-5-6) Vijnana Pubns.

Rama Gita: The Dialogues of Rama. Anantanand Rambachan. 100p. 1994. pap. 5.00 (0-9634164-4-8) Vijnana Pubns.

Rama II. Arthur C. Clarke & Gentry Lee. 512p. 1990. mass mkt. 6.99 (0-553-28658-7, Spectra) Bantam.

***Rama Jataka in Laos: A Study in the Phra Lak Phra Lam, 2 vols.** Sachchidanand Sahai. 1996. 105.00 (81-7018-839-3, Pub. by BR Pub II) S Asia.

Rama-Katha in Tribal & Folk Traditions of India: Proceedings of a Seminar. Ed. by K. S. Singh & Birendranath Datta. (C). 1993. pap. 16.00 (0-614-04142-2, Pub. by Seagull Bks II) S Asia.

Rama-Legends & Rama-Reliefs in Indonesia. Willem Stutterheim. Tr. by C. D. Paliwal & R. P. Jain. (C). 1989. 64.00 (81-7017-251-9, Pub. by Abhinav II) S Asia.

Rama Revealed. Arthur C. Clarke. 624p. 1995. mass mkt. 6.99 (0-553-56947-3) Bantam.

Rama Tirtha - Scientist & Mahatma: An Account of His Life & Translation of His Writings. Hari P. Shastri. (Illus.). 141p. 1997. pap. 11.00 (0-89540-294-7, SB-294) Sun Pub.

Ramachandra in India. Alain Chenneviere. Tr. by Lisa Davidson. LC 95-30981. (My Future Ser.). 1996. lib. bdg. 21.50 (0-8225-2825-8, Lerner Publctns) Lerner Group.

Ramachandra Temple at Vijayanagara. Anna L. Dallapiccola. (C). 1992. text ed. 58.00 (81-85425-27-2, Pub. by Manohar II) S Asia.

Ramadan. Suhaib H. Ghazi. LC 96-5154. (Illus.). 32p. (J). (ps-3). 1996. 15.95 (0-8234-1254-7); pap. 6.95 (0-8234-1275-X) Holiday.

Ramadan: Motivating Believers to Action. Ed. by Laleh Bakhtiar. 320p. (Orig.). 1994. pap. 19.95 (0-934905-25-8) Kazi Pubns.

Ramadan Adventures of Fasfoose Mouse. Ediba Kezzeiz. (Illus.). 36p. (Orig.). (J). (gr. 1-6). 1991. pap. 3.00 (0-89259-117-X) Am Trust Pubns.

Ramadan & Id al-Fitr. Dianne M. MacMillan. LC 93-46185. (Best Holiday Bks.). (Illus.). 48p. (J). (gr. 1-4). 1994. lib. bdg. 17.95 (0-89490-502-3) Enslow Pubs.

Ramadan Fasting & Medical Science. M. Ghulam Muazzam. (C). 1991. 35.00 (0-685-54755-8, Pub. by A H S Ltd UK); 40.00 (0-7223-2545-2, Pub. by A H S Ltd UK) St Mut.

***Ramadan Sonnets.** Daniel Moore. (Orig.). 1996. pap. 10.95 (0-9652031-0-7) City Lights.

Ramadan War: The Egyptian View. Badri et al. 1979. pap. 6.95 (0-88294-600-5) NOVA Pubns.

Ramage. Dudley Pope. 350p. 1991. reprint ed. lib. bdg. 26.95 (0-89966-840-2) Buccaneer Bks.

Ramage in South Italy. Craufurd T. Ramage. Ed. by Edith Clay. (Illus.). 232p. 1986. reprint ed. pap. 10.00 (0-89733-216-4) Academy Chi Pubs.

Ramage in South Italy. Craufurd T. Ramage. Ed. by Edith Clay. (Illus.). 232p. 1987. reprint ed. 20.00 (0-89733-217-2) Academy Chi Pubs.

Ramah Experience: Community & Commitment. Ed. by Sylvia C. Ettenberg & Geraldine Rosenfield. 1989. 15.95 (0-87334-051-5) Ktav.

***Ramakatha Rasavahini (Writings on the Story of Rama), Pt. 1.** Sai B. Sathya. Date not set. pap. 5.00 (0-614-19041-X, BA-310) Sathya Sai Bk Ctr.

***Ramakatha Rasavahini (Writings on the Story of Rama), Pt. 2.** Sai B. Sathya. Date not set. pap. 3.75 (0-614-19042-8, BA-311) Sathya Sai Bk Ctr.

Ramakrishna: A Biography in Pictures. Ed. by Advaita Ashrama Staff. (Illus.). 1976. 14.95 (0-87481-167-8, Pub. by Advaita Ashrama II) Vedanta Pr.

Ramakrishna: The Great Master, Pt. 2. rev. ed. Swami Saradananda. Tr. by Swami Jagadananda. (Illus.). 578p. 1980. pap. 9.95 (0-87481-496-0) Vedanta Pr.

Ramakrishna: The Power & the Glory. 303p. (Orig.). 1987. pap. 3.50 (0-87481-544-4, Pub. by Ramakrishna Math II) Vedanta Pr.

Ramakrishna: The Unique Phenomenon. M. Sivaramakrishna. ix, 142p. 1992. 22.50 (81-207-1138-6, Pub. by Sterling Pubs II) Apt Bks.

Ramakrishna Vol. 2: The Great Master, Pt. 1. rev. ed. Swami Saradananda. Tr. by Swami Jagadananda. (Illus.). 516p. 1980. pap. 9.95 (0-87481-495-2) Vedanta Pr.

Ramakrishna & His Disciples. Christopher Isherwood. LC 65-17100. 368p. (C). 1980. reprint ed. pap. 12.95 (0-87481-037-X) Vedanta Pr.

Ramakrishna & His Message. Swami Vivekananda. (Orig.). 1971. pap. 2.00 (0-87481-126-0) Vedanta Pr.

Ramakrishna & the Vitality of Hinduism. Solange Lemaitre. Tr. by Charles L. Markmann from FRE. LC 68-54059. (Spiritual Masters Ser.). (Illus.). 224p. 1984. 18.95 (0-87951-194-X) Overlook Pr.

Ramakrishna & the Vitality of Hinduism. Solange Lemaitre. Tr. by Charles L. Markmann from FRE. LC 68-54059. (Spiritual Masters Ser.). (Illus.). 224p. 1986. pap. 9.95 (0-87951-241-5) Overlook Pr.

Ramakrishna & Vivekananda: New Essays. Arvind Sharma. 192p. 1989. text ed. 18.95 (0-685-22941-6, Pub. by Sterling Pubs II) Apt Bks.

Ramakrishna As Sw. Avivekananda Saw Him. Swami Vivekananda. (Orig.). 1970. pap. 1.95 (0-87481-452-9) Vedanta Pr.

Ramakrishna As We Saw Him. Ed. & Tr. by Swami Chetanananda. LC 90-32015. (Illus.). 495p. 1990. 22.95 (0-916356-64-7); pap. 14.95 (0-916356-65-5) Vedanta Soc St Louis.

Ramakrishna for Children. Swami Vishwashrayananda. Tr. by Santosh Bagchi from BEN. (Illus.). 40p. (J). (gr. 3-6). 1975. pap. 4.95 (0-87481-164-3, Pub. by Advaita Ashrama II) Vedanta Pr.

Ramakrishna, His Life & Sayings. Friedrich M. Mueller. LC 73-18812. reprint ed. 32.50 (0-404-11452-0) AMS Pr.

Ramakrishna Kathamrita: Memoirs of Ramakrishna. Swami Abhedananda. Orig. Title: Gospel of Ramakrishna. 266p. 1988. 7.95 (0-87481-654-8, Pub. by Rama Ved Math II) Vedanta Pr.

Ramakrishna Math & Mission: Its Ideals & Activities. Swami Ranganathananda. (Illus.). 1954. pap. 1.00 (0-87481-448-0) Vedanta Pr.

Ramakrishna Movement: Its Ideal & Activities. Swami Tejasananda. (Illus.). 1954. pap. 2.95 (0-87481-117-1, Pub. by Advaita Ashrama II) Vedanta Pr.

Ramakrishna, Sri: Sahasra-Nama-Stotram. T. A. Bhandarkar. (Illus.). 200p. (Orig.). 1988. pap. 6.95 (0-87481-509-6, Pub. by Ramakrishna Math II) Vedanta Pr.

Ramakrishna the Spiritual Glow. pap. 5.95 (0-87481-650-5) Vedanta Pr.

Ramakrishna Upanishad. 1.95 (81-7120-038-9) Vedanta Pr.

Ramakrishna Upanishad. Chakravarti Rajagopalachari. 1953. pap. 1.95 (0-87481-430-8, Pub. by Ramakrishna Math II) Vedanta Pr.

Ramakrishna's Thoughts in a Vedantic Perspective. 3.95 (81-7120-636-0) Vedanta Pr.

Ramakrsna Paramahamsa: A Psychological Profile. Narasingha P. Sil. LC 91-28729. (Brill's Indological Library: Vol. 4). xvi, 182p. 1991. 78.75 (90-04-09478-4) E J Brill.

Ramamurti's Orthopaedics in Primary Care. 2nd ed. Gerald Steinberg et al. 408p. 1992. 68.00 (0-683-07928-X) Williams & Wilkins.

Raman Effect, Vol. 1. Ed. by Anthony Anderson. LC 77-134788. 416p. reprint ed. pap. 118.60 (0-317-08513-1, 2055067) Bks Demand.

Raman Effect, Vol. 2: Applications. Ed. by Anthony Anderson. LC 77-134788. (Illus.). 642p. reprint ed. pap. 180.00 (0-7837-0922-6, 2041227) Bks Demand.

Raman-IR Atlas of Organic Compounds. 2nd ed. B. Schrader. LC 89-5565. 1118p. 1989. 595.00 (3-527-26969-X, VCH) Wiley.

Raman Microscopy: Developments & Applications. Ed. by J. Corset & George Turrell. (Illus.). 528p. 1996. text ed. 99.95 (0-12-189690-0) Acad Pr.

Raman Spectra of Polymers. P. J. Hendra & J. Agbenyega. LC 92-39220. 240p. 1994. ring bd. 159.00 (0-471-93837-8) Wiley.

Raman Spectroscopy. D. A. Long. 1977. text ed. write for info. (0-07-038675-7) McGraw.

Raman Spectroscopy: Linear & Nonlinear, 8th International Conference, Bordeaux, 1982. International Conference on Raman Spectroscopy Staff et al. Ed. by Jean Lascombe & Pham V. Huong. 868p. reprint ed. pap. 180.00 (0-317-08718-5, 2022542) Bks Demand.

Raman Spectroscopy: Proceedings of the 6th International Conference on Raman Spectroscopy, Bangalore, India, 4-9 September 1978, 2 vols., Vol. 1: Invited Lectures. International Conference on Raman Spectroscopy Staff. Ed. by E. D. Schmid & R. S. Krishnan. LC 83-131239. reprint ed. Vol. 1 - Invited Lectures. pap. 112.30 (0-317-29336-2, 2024026) Bks Demand.

Raman Spectroscopy: Proceedings of the 6th International Conference on Raman Spectroscopy, Bangalore, India, 4-9 September 1978, 2 vols., Vol. 2: Contributed Papers. International Conference on Raman Spectroscopy Staff. Ed. by E. D. Schmid & R. S. Krishnan. LC 83-131239. reprint ed. Vol. 2 - Contributed Papers. pap. 135.50 (0-317-29337-0) Bks Demand.

Raman Spectroscopy for Catalysts. John M. Stencel. 240p. (gr. 13). 1989. text ed. 89.95 (0-442-20514-7) Chapman & Hall.

Raman Spectroscopy in Biology: Principles & Applications. Anthony T. Tu. LC 82-6901. 464p. reprint ed. pap. 132.30 (0-7837-2803-4, 2057670) Bks Demand.

Raman Spectroscopy of Gases & Liquids. Ed. by A. Weber. (Topics in Current Physics Ser.: Vol. 11). (Illus.). 1979. 40.00 (0-387-09036-3) Spr-Verlag.

Ramana Maharshi. K. Swaminathan. (National Biography Ser.). 1979. pap. 2.00 (0-89744-197-4) Auromere.

Ramana Maharshi & the Path of Self-Knowledge. Ed. by Arthur Osborne. LC 76-18194. (Illus.). 208p. 1970. pap. 12.95 (0-87728-071-1) Weiser.

Raman's One Hundred Ten Year Ephemeris of Planetary Positions (1891-2000 AD) Bangalore V. Raman. (BVR Astrology Ser.). (C). 1992. pap. 6.00 (81-85273-92-8, Pub. by UBS Pubs Dist II) S Asia.

Ramanujan: Letters & Commentary. Bruce C. Berndt et al. LC 95-5254. (History of Mathematics Ser.: No. 9). 1995. 49.00 (0-8218-0287-9, HMATH/9) Am Math.

Ramanujan's Notebooks, Pt. 1. Bruce C. Berndt. (Illus.). 430p. 1985. 107.95 (0-387-96110-0) Spr-Verlag.

Ramanujan's Notebooks, Pt. 2. Bruce C. Berndt. (Illus.). xi, 359p. 1988. 98.95 (0-387-96794-X) Spr-Verlag.

Ramanujan's Notebooks, Pt. 3. Bruce C. Berndt. (Illus.). xiii, 510p. 1997. 98.95 (0-387-97503-9) Spr-Verlag.

Ramanujan's Notebooks, Pt. IV. B. C. Berndt. 432p. 1993. 107.95 (0-387-94109-6) Spr-Verlag.

***Ramanujan's Notebooks, Pt. V.** Bruce C. Berndt. 600p. 1997. 97.95 (0-387-94941-0) Spr-Verlag.

***Ramapo College of New Jersey: The First Quarter Century, 1971-1996.** unabridged ed. Henry Bischoff. (Illus.). 150p. (Orig.). 1997. pap. write for info. (0-927351-02-1) Ramapo College.

Ramapo Mountain People. David S. Cohen. (Illus.). 285p. 1986. pap. 15.95 (0-8135-1195-X) Rutgers U Pr.

Ramar: The Rabbit with Rainbow Wings. Darrel T. Hare. 144p. 1996. 16.95 (0-312-14031-2) St Martin.

***Ramar Rabbit with Rainbow Wing.** Hare. Date not set. pap. write for info. (0-312-18162-0) St Martin.

Ramaria of Western Washington. C. D. Marr & Daniel E. Stuntz. 1973. 40.00 (3-7682-0902-4) Lubrecht & Cramer.

Ramaria, Subgenus Lentoramaria, with Emphasis on North American Taxa. R. H. Petersen. (Bibliotheca Mycologica Ser.: No. 43). 1975. text ed. 40.00 (3-7682-0961-X) Lubrecht & Cramer.

An Asterisk (*) at the beginning of an entry indicates that the title is appearing in BIP for the first time.

RAMAS - Age User Manual: Modeling Fluctuations in Age-Structured Populations. Scott Ferson & H. Resit Akcakaya. 156p. 1988. 295.00 (*1-884977-00-6*); teacher ed. 495.00 (*1-884977-01-4*) Applied Biomath.

RAMAS - Space: Spatially Structured Population Models for Conservation Biology. H. Resit Akcakaya & Scott Ferson. 114p. 1990. teacher ed. 495.00 (*1-884977-05-7*); disk 295.00 (*1-884977-04-9*) Applied Biomath.

RAMAS - Stage: Generalized Stage-Based Modeling for Population Dynamics. Scott Ferson. 107p. 1990. 295.00 (*1-884977-02-2*); teacher ed. 495.00 (*1-884977-03-0*) Applied Biomath.

***RAMAS Ecotoxicology: Ecological Risk Assessment for Food Webs & Structured Populations.** Matthew Spencer & Scott Ferson. (Illus.). 150p. (Orig.). 1997. pap. 395.00 incl. disk (*1-884977-24-3*) Applied Biomath.

Ramas/GIS: Linking GIS with Metapopulation Dynamics. H. Resit Akgakaya. (Illus.). 230p. (C). 1993. text ed. 995.00 (*1-884977-16-2*); text ed. 1,495.00 incl. disk (*1-884977-17-0*) Applied Biomath.

Ramas/Metapop: Metapopulation Viability Analysis. H. Resit Akgakaya. (Illus.). 185p. (C). 1994. text ed. 395.00 (*1-884977-14-6*); text ed. 595.00 incl. disk (*1-884977-15-4*) Applied Biomath.

Ramas/Time: Ecological Time Series Analysis. Peter Turchin & Jeffrey A. Millstein. (Illus.). 123p. (Orig.). (C). 1994. pap. text ed. 295.00 (*1-884977-18-9*); pap. text ed. 595.00 incl. disk (*1-884977-19-7*) Applied Biomath.

Ramayan. pap. text ed. 4.95 (*1-878099-14-0*) Vidya Bks.

Ramayana. William Buck. 1978. mass mkt. 5.95 (*0-452-00935-9*, Mer) NAL-Dutton.

Ramayana. William Buck. LC 78-153549. (Illus.). 1976. pap. 15.00 (*0-520-04394-4*) U CA Pr.

Ramayana. Lakskshmi Lal. 179p. 1992. pap. 7.95 (*0-86311-283-8*, Pub. by Orient Longman Ltd II) Apt Bks.

Ramayana. Shudha Mazumdar. 542p. 1974. 12.95 (*0-318-37159-6*) Asia Bk Corp.

Ramayana. R. K. Narayan. (Illus.). 1977. pap. 7.00 (*0-14-004428-0*, Penguin Bks) Viking Penguin.

Ramayana. R. K. Narayan. 190p. 1993. pap. 9.95 (*0-14-018700-6*, Penguin Classics) Viking Penguin.

Ramayana. Chakravarti Rajagopalachari. 320p. 1979. pap. 6.95 (*0-89744-930-4*) Auromere.

Ramayana. Tr. by Kamala Subramaniam. 611p. 1988. 21.95 (*0-318-37164-2*) Asia Bk Corp.

Ramayana. 3rd ed. Shri Valmiki. 320p. (Orig.). 1980. pap. 7.50 (*0-934676-17-8*) Greenlf Bks.

Ramayana: As Told by Audrey Menen. Audrey Menen. LC 72-598. 276p. 1972. reprint ed. text ed. 49.50 (*0-8371-6181-9*, VARA, Greenwood Pr) Greenwood.

***Ramayana: Global View.** Ed. by Lallan P. Vyas. 1995. 26.00 (*81-241-0244-9*, Pub. by Har-Anand Pubns II) S Asia.

Ramayana: The Story of Rama. Shri Valmiki. LC 74-77601. (Illus.). 72p. (J). (gr. 5-12). 1975. 8.50 (*0-88253-292-8*); pap. 3.50 (*0-88253-291-X*) Ind-US Inc.

Ramayana As Told by Valmiki & Kamban. K. S. Srinivasan. (C). 1994. text ed. 32.00 (*81-7017-307-8*, Pub. by Abhinav II) S Asia.

Ramayana at a Glance. Sadguru S. Keshavadas. (Orig.). (C). 1989. pap. 12.50 (*81-208-0545-3*, Pub. by Motilal Banarsidass II) S Asia.

Ramayana at a Glance. Satguru S. Keshavadas. (Illus.). 211p. (Orig.). 1978. pap. 10.00 (*0-942508-11-4*) Vishwa.

Ramayana for Children. 44p. pap. 3.95 (*81-7120-102-4*) Vedanta Ctr.

Ramayana of Tulasidasa. Tulasidas. Tr. by F. S. Growse. 1979. 26.00 (*0-8364-0363-0*) S Asia.

Ramayana of Tulasidasa. Ed. by R. C. Prasad. Tr. by F. S. Growse. lx, 719p. (C). 1995. reprint ed. 28.00 (*81-208-0205-5*, Pub. by Motilal Banarsidass II) S Asia.

Ramayana of Valmiki. Tr. by Makhanlal Sen. (C). 1994. text ed. 24.00 (*81-215-0093-1*, Pub. by Munshiram Manoharial II) S Asia.

Ramayana of Valmiki, 3 vols. Shri Valmiki. Tr. by Hari P. Shastri. 1985. pap. 60.00 (*0-7103-0136-7*) Routledge Chapman & Hall.

***Ramayana of Valmiki: An Epic of Ancient India.** Tr. by R. P. Goldman & S. S. Goldman. (Princeton Library of Asian Translations Ser.). 576p. 1996. text ed. 89.50 (*0-691-06662-0*) Princeton U Pr.

Ramayana of Valmiki: An Epic of Ancient India, Vol. IV. Ed. by Robert P. Goldman. Tr. by Rosalind Lefeber. LC 93-37044. (Library of Asian Translations). 416p. 1994. text ed. 67.50 (*0-691-06661-2*) Princeton U Pr.

Ramayana of Valmiki: An Epic of Ancient India, Vol II. Ed. by Robert P. Goldman. Tr. by Sheldon I. Pollock from SAN. LC 85-61364. (Library of Asian Translations). (Illus.). 525p. 1986. text ed. 87.50 (*0-691-06654-X*) Princeton U Pr.

Ramayana of Valmiki Vol. 1: An Epic of Ancient India: Balakanda. Tr. & Intro. by Robert P. Goldman. 287p. (Orig.). 1990. text ed. 18.95 (*0-691-01485-X*) Princeton U Pr.

Ramayana of Valmiki Balakanda, Vol. I. Tr. by Robert P. Goldman. LC 82-61364. (Library of Asian Translations: Vol. I). 450p. 1985. text ed. 75.00 (*0-691-06561-6*) Princeton U Pr.

Ramayana Pahari Paintings. Ed. by Roy C. Craven, Jr. 106p. (C). 1993. 125.00 (*81-85026-11-4*, Pub. by Marg Pubns II) St Mut.

Ramayana Tradition in Asia. Ed. by V. Raghavan. 1982. 18.00 (*0-8364-0899-3*, Pub. by National Sahitya Akademi II) S Asia.

Ramayana Traditions in Eastern India: Assam, Bengal, Orissa. W. L. Smith. (C). 1995. reprint ed. 27.50 (*81-215-0668-9*, Pub. by Munshiram Manohariai II) S Asia.

Ramaz: School, Community, Scholarship & Orthodoxy. Ed. by Jeffrey Gurock. 1989. 20.00 (*0-88125-323-5*) Ktav.

***Ramba, Bk. 1.** Delizia et al. (Eros Graphic Novel Ser.: No. 15). 120p. 1995. pap. 14.95 (*1-56097-213-0*) Fantagraph Bks.

***Ramba, Bk. 2.** Rossi et al. (Eros Graphic Novel Ser.: No. 22). 128p. 1996. pap. 14.95 (*1-56097-253-X*) Fantagraph Bks.

***Rambam.** expanded ed. (Orig.). write for info. (*0-8266-0434-X*, Merkos LInyonei Chinuch) Kehot Pubn Soc.

Rambam. 64p. (Orig.). 1985. reprint ed. 5.00 (*0-8266-0433-1*, Merkos LInyonei Chinuch) Kehot Pubn Soc.

Rambam: The Story of Rabbi Moshe Ben Maimon. Rochel Yaffe. (Illus.). 220p. (YA). (gr. 8 up). 1992. 10.95 (*0-922613-14-7*); pap. 8.95 (*0-922613-15-X*) Hachai Pubns.

Rambam, Readings in the Philosophy of Moses Maimonides. Ed. & Comment by Lenn E. Goodman. LC 75-14476. 460p. 1985. 24.00 (*0-917232-19-4*) Gee Tee Bee.

***Ramban: Philosopher & Kabbalist.** Chayim J. Henoch. 1998. write for info. (*0-7657-9958-8*) Aronson.

Ramban (Nachmanides) Commentary on the Torah, 5 vols. Charles B. Chavel. 2575p. 1971. 99.75 (*0-686-86743-2*) Shilo Pub Hse.

Ramban (Nachmanides) Commentary on the Torah, Vol. I: Book of Genesis. Charles B. Chavel. 640p. 1971. Vol. I, Book Of Genesis. 19.95 (*0-88328-006-X*) Shilo Pub Hse.

Ramban (Nachmanides) Commentary on the Torah, 5 vols., Vol. II: Book of Exodus. Charles B. Chavel. 656p. 1971. Vol. II, Book Of Exodus. 19.95 (*0-88328-007-8*) Shilo Pub Hse.

Ramban (Nachmanides) Commentary on the Torah, 5 vols., Vol. III: Book of Leviticus. Charles B. Chavel. 512p. 1972. Vol. III, Book Of Leviticus. 19.95 (*0-88328-008-6*) Shilo Pub Hse.

Ramban (Nachmanides) Commentary on the Torah, 5 vols., Vol. IV: Book of Numbers. Charles B. Chavel. 416p. 1974. Vol. IV, Book Of Numbers. 19.95 (*0-88328-009-4*) Shilo Pub Hse.

Ramban (Nachmanides) Commentary on the Torah, 5 vols., Vol. V: Book of Deuteronomy. Charles B. Chavel. 448p. 1975. Vol. V, Book Of Deuteronomy. 19.95 (*0-88328-010-8*) Shilo Pub Hse.

Ramban (Nachmanides) Writings & Discourses, 2 vols., Set. Charles B. Chavel. 768p. 1978. boxed 42.00 (*0-88328-013-2*) Shilo Pub Hse.

Rambana: The Story of Rabbi Moshe ben Maimon. Yaacor D. Shulman. LC 94-70694. 246p. (J). (gr. 5-9). Date not set. 15.95 (*1-56062-253-9*) CIS Comm.

Rambana: The Story of Rabbi Moshe ben Maimon. Yaakov D. Shulman. LC 94-70694. 248p. 1994. pap. write for info. (*1-56062-254-7*) CIS Comm.

Ramble, after Action: A Rite of Passage, a Poetic Exploration of Things Thought Known. Garvin McCurdy. 200p. pap. 15.00 (*0-9641979-1-X*) Info Age Handyman.

Ramble among the Musicians of Germany. 2nd ed. Edward Holmes. LC 68-16239. 1969. reprint ed. lib. bdg. 39.50 (*0-306-71086-2*) Da Capo.

Rambledon. Edward G. Sims. 12.95 (*0-9635917-0-3*) E G Sims.

Rambler, 3 Vols, Set. Samuel Johnson. Ed. by Walter Jackson Bate & Albrecht Strauss. (Works of Samuel Johnson Ser.: Nos. 3, 4 & 5). 1969. 130.00 (*0-300-01157-1*) Yale U Pr.

Rambler in Georgia: Travellers' Accounts of Frontier Georgia. Ed. by Mills Lane. (Illus.). 233p. 1990. 30.00 (*0-88322-003-2*) Beehive GA.

Rambler's Guide to the Trails of the East Bay Hills: Central Section Including Redwood, Chabot, Las Trampas, Sibley & Joaquin Miller Parks & Lands of East Bay MUD. Gerald W. Olmsted. (Illus.). 1987. 5.95 (*0-941969-00-2*) Olmsted Bros Map.

Ramblers Yearbook & Accommodation Guide 1996. Rambler's Assn. Staff. 219p. 1996. pap. text ed. 19.95 (*0-900613-79-3*, Pub. by W Foulsham UK) Trans-Atl Phila.

Rambles about Portsmouth. Ray Brighton. LC 93-7851. (Portsmouth Marine Society Ser.: No. 20). (Illus.). 288p. 1993. 25.00 (*0-915819-18-X*) Portsmouth Marine Soc.

Rambles about Portsmouth, 2 vols., Vol. 1. Charles Brewster. LC 70-181350. 1971. reprint ed. write for info. (*0-912274-12-3*) Picton Pr.

Rambles & Recollections of an Indian Official. W. H. Sleeman. (C). 1995. reprint ed. 64.00 (*81-206-1013-X*, Pub. by Asian Educ Servs II); reprint ed. pap. 64.00 (*81-206-1015-6*, Pub. by Asian Educ Servs II) S Asia.

Rambles & Refreshments on the Welsh Borders. H. Hurley. (C). 1988. pap. 29.00 (*0-946328-21-8*, Pub. by Thornhill Pr UK) St Mut.

Rambles & Studies in Greece. John P. Mahaffy. Date not set. write for info. (*0-8434-0137-0*, Pub. by McGrath NH) Ayer.

Rambles in Dickens' Land. R. Allbut. LC 76-52947. (Studies in Dickens: No. 52). 1977. lib. bdg. 48.95 (*0-8383-2139-9*) M S G Haskell Hse.

Rambles in Eirinn. William Bulfin. 456p. (Orig.). 1995. reprint ed. pap. 15.95 (*1-86079-010-0*, Pub. by R Wholesale Bks IE) Irish Bks Media.

Rambles in Old Norwich. Ed. by George A. Plunkett. 136p. 1990. pap. 30.00 (*0-86138-078-9*) St Mut.

Rambles in the Mammoth Cave During the Year 1844 by a Visiter. Alexander C. Bullitt. LC 85-6698. (Illus.). 134p. 1985. pap. text ed. 3.95 (*0-939748-16-9*) Cave Bks MO.

Rambles in the Pee Dee Basin, South Carolina. Harvey T. Cook. (Illus.). 512p. 1991. reprint ed. 37.50 (*0-89308-447-6*, SC 90) Southern Hist Pr.

Rambles of a Botanist among the Plants & Climates of California. John Muir. (Illus.). 43p. 1974. 10.00 (*0-87093-301-9*) Dawsons.

Ramblin' & Gamblin's on the Mississippi Coast: The Most Complete Travel & Casino Guide to the Mississippi Gulf Coast. Lynn G. Fullman & Lynn Edge. 149p. (Orig.). 1994. pap. 8.50 (*1-878561-29-4*) Seacoast AL.

Ramblin' Robots: Building a Breed of Mechanical Beasts. Ingrid Wickelgren. LC 95-48767. (Venture Bks.). 144p. (J). 1996. lib. bdg. 22.00 (*0-531-11301-9*) Watts.

***Ramblin' Robots: Building a Breed of Mechanical Beasts.** Ingrid Wickelgren. (Venture Bks.). 144p. (J). 1997. pap. 9.95 (*0-531-15829-2*) Watts.

Ramblin' Rose: The Life & Career of Rose Maddox. Jonny Whiteside. (Illus.). 256p. 1996. 27.95 (*0-915608-17-0*) Country Music Found.

Ramblin' Rose: The Life & Career of Rose Maddox. Jonny Whiteside. LC 96-34377. (Illus.). 256p. 1996. 27.95 (*0-8265-1269-0*) Vanderbilt U Pr.

Rambling in the Cotswolds. Harry Hargreaves & D. Drinkwater. (C). 1988. 29.00 (*0-685-45094-5*, Pub. by Thornhill Pr UK) St Mut.

Rambling Raft. Lynne N. Lockhart & Barbara M. Lockhart. LC 89-50761. (Illus.). 30p. (J). (gr. k-5). 1989. bds. 7.95 (*0-87033-392-5*, Tidewtr Pubs) Cornell Maritime.

Rambling Recollections of Flying & Flyers, Vol. 1. Edmund F. Ball. 240p. (Orig.). 1993. pap. write for info. (*0-9623291-7-7*) Minnetrista.

Rambling Recollections of Flying & Flyers, Vol. 2. Edmund E. Ball. 208p. (Orig.). 1993. pap. write for info. (*0-9623291-9-3*) Minnetrista.

Rambling Rose. Calder Willingham. 272p. 1991. mass mkt. 4.50 (*0-380-76683-3*) Avon.

Rambling Sketches from the Old Churches in the Diocese of Llandaff. Chas B. Fowler. (C). 1989. 59.00 (*0-905928-65-2*, Pub. by D Brown & Sons Ltd UK) St Mut.

Rambling Through Life. Charles Renfrew. (C). 1988. 39.00 (*0-85439-236-X*, Pub. by St Paul Pubns UK) St Mut.

Rambling Through Science. Adolph L. De Leevw. LC 72-315. (Essay Index Reprint Ser.). 1977. reprint ed. 23.95 (*0-8369-2788-5*) Ayer.

***Rambling Willie: The Horse That God Loved.** 4th ed. Donald Evans & Philip Pilenky. 209p. Date not set. pap. 13.95 (*0-910119-42-2*) SOCO Pubns.

Rambling with Mindy. Mildred Gaasland. (Illus.). 130p. (Orig.). 1995. pap. 9.95 (*0-9639777-2-5*) Pekin Pubns.

Ramblings from the Heart & Soul of Me, Madeenah. Madeenah A. Qayyum. 51p. 1995. pap. 9.98 (*1-888139-06-4*) Y Morris Carib.

Ramblings of an Ascetic. Yuacharya Shri Mahaprajna. xvi, 127p. 1979. 9.00 (*0-88065-212-8*, Messers Today & Tomorrow) Scholarly Pubns.

Rambo Heritage. Simmeon B. Rambo & Mary E. Rambo. (Illus.). 188p. 1983. 25.00 (*0-89308-385-2*, BFH 17) Southern Hist Pr.

Rambo Reagan: Over 1,400 Mind-Bending Trivia Questions about the 80s. David Arenson & Marilyn Werden. (Illus.). 1400p. 1996. pap. 11.95 (*0-8092-3225-1*) Contemp Bks.

***Rambo's Nursing Skills for Clinical Practice.** 4th ed. Ed. by Susan C. DeWit. (Illus.). 1994. teacher ed., pap. write for info. (*0-7216-4178-4*) Saunders.

***Rambo's Nursing Skills for Clinical Practice.** 4th ed. Ed. by Susan C. DeWit. (Illus.). 1994. student ed., pap. write for info. (*0-7216-4324-8*) Saunders.

Rambo's Nursing Skills for Clinical Practice. 4th rev. ed. Susan C. DeWit. LC 93-36409. Orig. Title: Nursing Skills for Clinical Practice. (Illus.). 1200p. 1994. pap. text ed. 34.95 (*0-7216-3642-X*) Saunders.

Rambunctious Lady Royston. Kasey Michaels. 224p. 1982. pap. 2.95 (*0-380-81448-X*) Avon.

Rambutan Cultivation. H. D. Tindall et al. (Plant Production & Protection Papers: No. 121). (Illus.). 183p. 1995. pap. 30.00 (*92-5-103325-0*, F33250, Pub. by FAO IT) Bernan Associates.

Ramcharan Caribbean Law. 1989. lib. bdg. 191.00 (*0-7923-0408-X*) Kluwer Ac.

Ramdas & the Ramdasis. Wilbur S. Deming. 1990. reprint ed. 24.00 (*81-85326-22-3*, Pub. by Vintage II) S Asia.

RAMDIL Bibliographies, Set. write for info. (*1-883215-01-3*) Ramdil.

RAMDIL Social Science Resource Guides, Set. write for info. (*1-883215-00-5*) Ramdil.

Rameau & Musical Thought in the Enlightenment. Thomas Christensen. LC 92-39886. (Cambridge Studies in Music Theory & Analysis: No. 4). (Illus.). 400p. (C). 1994. text ed. 69.95 (*0-521-42040-7*) Cambridge U Pr.

Rameau's Nephew & D'Alembert's Dream. Denis Diderot. Tr. by Leonard W. Tancock. (Classics Ser.). 240p. 1976. pap. 11.95 (*0-14-044173-5*, Penguin Classics) Viking Penguin.

Rameau's Nephew & Other Works. Denis Diderot. Tr. by Jacques Barzun & Ralph H. Brown from FRE. LC 55-9755. 1964. 29.50 (*0-672-51089-8*) Irvington.

Rameau's Niece. Cathleen Schine. LC 93-36528. 1994. pap. 10.95 (*0-452-27161-4*, Plume) NAL-Dutton.

Ramendrasundar Trivedi: A Study of His Social & Political Ideas. Dipika Majumdar. (C). 1988. 40.00 (*81-85195-13-7*, Pub. by Minerva II) S Asia.

Rames Two. Mark A. Simpkins. (J). (gr. 4-7). 1986. pap. 5.95 (*0-916095-10-X*) Pubs Pr UT.

Rameses Treasure Tomb: Find of the Century! Carole Marsh. (Wildly Educational Titles Ser.). (J). (gr. 2-9). 29.95 (*0-7933-7821-4*, C Marsh); pap. 19.95 (*0-7933-7822-2*, C Marsh) Gallopade Pub Group.

Ramesses II: A Chronological Structure of His Reign. John D. Schmidt. LC 72-6558. (Near Eastern Studies). 224p. reprint ed. 63.90 (*0-8357-9282-X*, 2011503) Bks Demand.

Ramesseum Papyri Plates. Gardiner. 1955. 29.00 (*0-900416-37-8*, Pub. by Aris & Phillips UK) David Brown.

Ramesside Administrative Documents. A. H. Gardiner. 125p. 1995. reprint ed. 62.00 (*0-900416-40-8*, Pub. by Aris & Phillips UK) David Brown.

Ramesside Inscriptions. Tr. & Anno. by Kenneth A. Kitchen. LC 92-45617. 1993. 166.95 (*0-631-18426-0*) Blackwell Pubs.

Ramesside Inscriptions. Tr. & Anno. by Kenneth A. Kitchen. LC 92-45617. 1993. 166.95 (*0-631-18434-1*) Blackwell Pubs.

Ramesside Inscriptions, Notes & Comments, Vol. II. K. A. Kitchen. 1996. 150.00 (*0-631-18435-X*) Blackwell Pubs.

Ramesside, Inscriptions, Translations Vol. II: Ramesses II, Royal Inscriptions. K. A. Kitchen. 1996. 166.95 (*0-631-18427-9*) Blackwell Pubs.

***Ramification Theoretic Methods in Algebric Geometry.** S. Abhyankar. (Annals of Mathematics Studies: No. 43). 112p. 1994. pap. text ed. 26.50 (*0-691-08023-2*) Princeton U Pr.

Ramified Integrals, Singularities, & Lacunas. A. A. Vassiliev. LC 94-35631. (Mathematics & Its Applications Ser.: Vol. 315). 1994. lib. bdg. 148.00 (*0-7923-3193-1*) Kluwer Ac.

Ramillete de Recuerdos: Poesias. Maria M. De Aguilar. LC 92-73336. (Coleccion Espejo de Paciencia). (Illus.). 96p. (Orig.). (SPA.). 1992. pap. 12.00 (*0-89729-651-6*) Ediciones.

Ramillies. large type ed. Barbara Whitehead. 1994. 25.99 (*0-7089-3213-4*) Ulverscroft.

Ramiluk Stories: Adventures of an Eskimo Family in the Prehistoric Arctic. Eugene L. Vickery. (Illus.). 124p. (Orig.). (J). (gr. 5 up). 1989. 16.00 (*0-937775-11-8*); pap. 10.95 (*0-937775-10-X*) Stonehaven Pubs.

Rami's Book: The Inner Life of a Child. Rami Vissell. LC 88-91345. (Illus.). 159p. (J). 1990. 13.95 (*0-9612720-4-X*, 104) Ramira Pub.

Ramism in William Perkins' Theology. Donald K. McKim. (American University Studies: Theology & Religion: Ser. VII, Vol. 15). 249p. (C). 1987. text ed. 38.90 (*0-8204-0285-0*) P Lang Pubng.

Ramlila in Ballet. Rajendra Jain. (C). 1994. 98.00 (*81-7018-793-1*) S Asia.

Ramlin Rose: The Boatwoman's Story. Sheila Stewart. LC 92-39869. 1993. write for info. (*0-19-212326-2*) OUP.

Rammed Earth House: Rediscovering the Most Ancient Building Material. Copernicus. 1996. pap. text ed. 30.00 (*0-930031-79-2*) Chelsea Green Pub.

Rammed Earth Structures: A Code of Practice. Julian Keable. 120p. (Orig.). 1996. pap. 24.95 (*1-85339-350-9*, Pub. by Intermed Tech UK) Women Ink.

***Ramo Song Book.** Phyllis U. Hiller. (Illus.). (Orig.). (J). 1971. pap. 6.95 (*1-884877-00-1*) Creat Mats Lib.

***Ramo Song Story Reading Book.** Phyllis U. Hiller. (SPA.). 1995. pap. 6.95 incl. audio (*1-884877-04-4*) Creat Mats Lib.

***Ramo Song Story Reading Book.** Phyllis U. Hiller. Tr. by John Crispin. (Illus.). 16p. (SPA.). (J). 1995. pap. 6.95 (*1-884877-05-2*) Creat Mats Lib.

***Ramo Song Story Reading Book.** 2nd ed. Phyllis U. Hiller. (Illus.). 16p. (J). (gr. k-4). 1970. pap. 5.95 (*1-884877-02-8*) Creat Mats Lib.

Ramon de la Cruz. John Moore. LC 70-153997. (Twayne's World Authors Ser.). 181p. (C). 1972. lib. bdg. 17.95 (*0-8290-1746-1*) Irvington.

Ramon de la Sagra: A Chronology. V. Munoz. Tr. by W. Scott Johnson. (Libertarian & Anarchist Chronology Ser.). 1979. lib. bdg. 59.95 (*0-8490-3042-0*) Gordon Pr.

Ramon de Mesonero Romanos. Richard A. Curry. LC 76-25. (Twayne's World Authors Ser.). (C). 1976. lib. bdg. 17.95 (*0-8057-6226-4*) Irvington.

Ramon Del Valle-Inclan. Robert Lima. LC 72-186643. (Columbia Essays on Modern Writers Ser.: No. 59). 1972. pap. text ed. 10.00 (*0-231-03499-7*) Col U Pr.

Ramon, el Lanzador (Paul the Pitcher) Paul Sharp. LC 84-7071. (Rookie Reader Ser.). (Illus.). 32p. (SPA.). (J). (ps-2). 1990. pap. 3.50 (*0-516-52064-4*); lib. bdg. 14.70 (*0-516-32064-5*) Childrens.

Ramon Guthrie's Maximum Security Ward: An American Classic. Sally M. Gall. LC 83-16836. 104p. 1984. pap. 12.95 (*0-8262-0430-9*) U of Mo Pr.

Ramon J. Sender. Charles L. King. LC 73-19612. (Twayne's World Authors Ser.). 196p. (C). 1974. lib. bdg. 17.95 (*0-8057-2815-5*) Irvington.

Ramon J. Sender: An Annotated Bibliography, 1928-1974. Charles L. King. LC 76-9020. 301p. 1976. 27.50 (*0-8108-0933-8*) Scarecrow.

Ramon Llull's New Rhetoric: Text & Translation of Llull's Rethorica Nova. Ed. & Tr. by Mark D. Johnston from LAT. 115p. (Orig.). (C). 1994. pap. 12.95 (*1-880393-03-4*, Hermagoras) L Erlbaum Assocs.

Ramon Lull: A Biography. Edgar A. Peers. 1980. lib. bdg. 75.00 (*0-8490-3186-9*) Gordon Pr.

Ramon Maria del Valle-Inclan: Questions of Gender. Ed. by Carol Maier & Roberta L. Salper. LC 93-42561. 1994. 42.50 (*0-8387-5261-6*) Bucknell U Pr.

***Ramon Martinez.** LC 96-40434. (Grolier All-Pro Biographies Ser.). (J). 1997. write for info. (*0-516-20699-0*) Childrens.

Ramon Perez de Ayala. Marguerite C. Rand. (Twayne's World Authors Ser.). 175p. (C). 1971. lib. bdg. 17.95 (*0-8290-1734-8*) Irvington.

Ramona. Houghton Mifflin Company Staff. (Literature Experience 1991 Ser.). (J). (gr. 3). 1990. pap. 8.48 (*0-395-55154-4*) HM.

Ramona. Helen H. Jackson. 1976. mass mkt. 4.99 (*0-380-00383-X*) Avon.

Ramona. Helen H. Jackson. 1976. lib. bdg. 20.10 (*0-89968-051-8*, Lghtyr Pr) Buccaneer Bks.

R

Ramona. Helen H. Jackson. 384p. 1988. reprint ed. pap. 4.95 (*0-451-52208-7*, Sig Classics) NAL-Dutton.

Ramona. Helen H. Jackson. (Notable American Authors Ser.). 1992. reprint ed. lib. bdg. 75.00 (*0-7812-3356-9*) Rprt Serv.

Ramona: Behind the Scenes of a Television Show. Elaine Scott. LC 87-33313. (Reading Rainbow Review Book). (Illus.). 96p. (J). (gr. 3-7). 1988. 16.00 (*0-688-06818-9*, Morrow Junior) Morrow.

Ramona & Her Family see Meet Ramona Quimby

Ramona & Her Father. Beverly Cleary. 192p. (J). (gr. 5-6). 1990. pap. 4.50 (*0-380-70916-3*, Camelot) Avon.

Ramona & Her Father. Beverly Cleary. LC 77-1614. (Illus.). 192p. (J). (gr. 3-7). 1977. 16.00 (*0-688-22114-9*, Morrow Junior); lib. bdg. 15.93 (*0-688-32114-3*, Morrow Junior) Morrow.

Ramona & Her Father see Meet Ramona Quimby

Ramona & Her Mother. Beverly Cleary. LC 79-10323. (Illus.). 208p. (J). (gr. 4-6). 1979. 17.00 (*0-688-22195-5*, Morrow Junior); lib. bdg. 16.93 (*0-688-32195-X*, Morrow Junior) Morrow.

***Ramona & Her Mother.** Beverly Cleary. (SPA.). 1999. 14.00 (*0-688-15466-2*, Morrow Junior) Morrow.

Ramona & Her Mother. Beverly Cleary. 208p. (J). 1990. reprint ed. pap. 4.50 (*0-380-70952-X*, Camelot) Avon.

Ramona & Her Mother see Meet Ramona Quimby

Ramona & Round About: A History of San Diego County's Little Known Back Country. Charles R. LeMenager. (Illus.). 252p. 1995. reprint ed. pap. 12.95 (*0-9611102-2-8*) Eagle Peak Pub.

***Ramona Book & Doll.** Beverly Cleary. (J). Date not set. write for info. (*0-688-13620-6*, Tupelo Bks) Morrow.

***Ramona Empieza El Curso/Ramona Quimby, Age 8.** Beverly Cleary. 1997. pap. 5.95 (*0-688-15487-5*, Beech Tree Bks) Morrow.

***Ramona Empieza el Curso/Ramona Quimby, Age 8.** Beverly Cleary. 1997. 14.00 (*0-688-15467-0*) Greenwillow.

Ramona, Forever. Beverly Cleary. 192p. (J). (gr. k-6). 1985. mass mkt. 4.50 (*0-440-47210-5*, YB BDD) BDD Bks Young Read.

Ramona, Forever. Beverly Cleary. LC 84-704. (Illus.). 192p. (J). (gr. 3-7). 1984. 16.00 (*0-688-03785-2*, Morrow Junior); lib. bdg. 15.93 (*0-688-03786-0*, Morrow Junior) Morrow.

Ramona Forever. Beverly Cleary. 192p. (J). (gr. 4-7). 1994. pap. 1.99 (*0-440-21937-X*) Dell.

Ramona Forever. Beverly Cleary. (J). 1996. mass mkt. 4.50 (*0-380-72801-X*) Avon.

Ramona Forever. Beverly Cleary. 192p. (J). (gr. 4-5). 1995. reprint ed. pap. 4.50 (*0-380-70960-0*, Camelot) Avon.

Ramona Forever see Meet Ramona Quimby

Ramona Gardens Investigation: Hearings by the California Senate Judiciary Subcommittee on Peace Officer Conduct. 109p. (Orig.). (C). 1993. pap. text ed. 25.00 (*1-56806-204-4*) DIANE Pub.

Ramona la Chince/Ramona the Pest. Beverly Cleary. (J). (gr. 4-7). 1996. pap. 5.95 (*0-688-14888-3*) Morrow.

Ramona La Chinche (Romona The Pest) Beverly Cleary. Tr. by Argentina Palacios. (Illus.). 208p. (SPA.). (J). (gr. 3-7). 1984. 16.00 (*0-688-02783-0*, Morrow Junior) Morrow.

Ramona, Mouse, 4 vols., Set. Beverly Cleary. (J). (gr. 4-7). 1990. boxed 16.47 (*0-380-71483-3*, Camelot) Avon.

Ramona Quimby. Beverly Cleary. 1994. pap. 5.25 (*0-87129-330-7*, R54) Dramatic Pub.

***Ramona Quimby.** Beverly Cleary. 1996. boxed, mass mkt. 15.96 (*0-380-72654-8*) Avon.

Ramona Quimby. 95th ed. HB Staff. (J). (gr. 3). 1995. text ed., lib. bdg., pap. text ed. 12.50 (*0-15-305205-8*) HB Coll Pubs.

Ramona Quimby, 4 vols., Set. Beverly Cleary. 1993. boxed, pap. 15.96 (*0-380-72123-6*, Camelot) Avon.

Ramona Quimby, Age Eight. Beverly Cleary. 192p. (J). 1992. pap. 4.50 (*0-380-70956-2*, Camelot) Avon.

Ramona Quimby, Age Eight. Beverly Cleary. LC 80-28425. (Illus.). 192p. (J). (gr. 4-6). 1981. 16.00 (*0-688-00477-6*, Morrow Junior); lib. bdg. 15.93 (*0-688-00478-4*, Morrow Junior) Morrow.

Ramona Quimby, Age Eight see Meet Ramona Quimby

Ramona Quimby Age Eight see Meet Ramona Quimby

Ramona Quimby, Age 8. Elaine Kule. Ed. by J. Friedland & R. Kessler. (Novel-Ties Ser.). 1993. pap. text ed. 15.95 (*0-88122-908-3*) Lrn Links.

Ramona Quimby Diary. Beverly Cleary. (Illus.). 160p. (J). (gr. 2 up). 1984. pap. 10.95 (*0-688-03883-2*) Morrow.

Ramona the Brave. Beverly Cleary. 192p. (J). (gr. 3-6). 1995. pap. 4.50 (*0-380-70959-7*, Camelot) Avon.

Ramona the Brave. Beverly Cleary. LC 74-16494. (Illus.). 192p. (J). (gr. 3-7). 1975. 16.00 (*0-688-22015-0*, Morrow Junior); lib. bdg. 15.93 (*0-688-32015-5*, Morrow Junior) Morrow.

Ramona the Brave: A Study Guide. Alice Sheff. (Novel-Ties Ser.). 1989. student ed., teacher ed., pap. text ed. 15.95 (*0-88122-046-9*) Lrn Links.

Ramona the Pest. Beverly Cleary. 192p. (J). 1992. pap. 4.50 (*0-380-70954-6*, Camelot) Avon.

Ramona the Pest. Beverly Cleary. LC 68-12981. (Illus.). (J). (gr. 3-7). 1968. 16.00 (*0-688-21721-4*, Morrow Junior); lib. bdg. 15.93 (*0-688-31721-9*, Morrow Junior) Morrow.

Ramona the Pest see Meet Ramona Quimby

***Ramona Y Su Madre/Ramona & Her Mother.** Beverly Cleary. 1997. pap. 5.95 (*0-688-15486-7*, Beech Tree Bks) Morrow.

Ramones: An American Band. Jim Bessman. LC 93-16437. (Illus.). 224p. (Orig.). 1993. pap. 14.95 (*0-312-09369-1*) St Martin.

Ramp Creek Rhythms: A Book of Poems. Helena Ashby. LC 85-90773. 54p. 1985. 8.00 (*0-9614781-0-1*); pap. 4.00 (*0-9614781-1-X*) H Ashby Bks.

Rampage. (Super Bolan Ser.). 1993. mass mkt. 4.99 (*0-373-61433-0*, 1-61433-8) Harlequin Bks.

Rampage. Danny Fingeroth & Eric Fein. (Spider-Man & the Incredible Hulk Ser.). 288p. (YA). 1996. mass mkt. 5.99 (*1-57297-164-9*) Blvd Books.

Rampage. William P. Wood. 1987. mass mkt. 4.50 (*0-312-90983-7*) St Martin.

Rampage. large type ed. Justin Scott. 688p. 1987. 27.99 (*0-7089-8436-3*, Charnwood) Ulverscroft.

Rampage: America's Largest Family Murder. Jim Moore. (Illus.). 216p. (C). 1991. 19.95 (*1-56530-002-5*) Summit TX.

Rampage of the Roarin' Twenties: The Illustrated History of the 312th Bombardment Group During WWII. Michael J. Claringbould & Lawrence J. Hickey. LC 89-84159. (Eagles over the Pacific Ser.: Vol. 4). (Illus.). 352p. 1997. 70.00 (*0-913511-03-X*) Intl Res & Pub.

Rampaging Frontier. Thomas D. Clark. LC 75-17477. 350p. 1976. reprint ed. text ed. 59.75 (*0-8371-8313-8*, CLRF, Greenwood Pr) Greenwood.

Rampaging Lovers. B. B. Dandekar. 312p. 1988. 14.95 (*0-942387-04-X*) AB Lit Hse.

***Rampant Women: Suffragists & the Right of Assembly.** Linda J. Lumsden. LC 97-4627. 1997. text ed. 42.00 (*0-87049-986-6*) U of Tenn Pr.

Rampart Range - Deckers, CO. rev. ed. Ed. by Trails Illustrated Staff. 1994. 8.99 (*0-925873-55-1*) Trails Illustrated.

Ramparts: Fortification from the Renaissance to West Point. Marguerita Z. Herman. (Illus.). 216p. 50.00 (*0-89529-511-3*) Avery Pub.

***Ramparts of Heaven.** Gilbert Morris. LC 96-32142. (The Wakefield Dynasty Ser.: No. 5). 1997. pap. 10.99 (*0-8423-6233-9*) Tyndale.

Rampolli. George MacDonald. (George MacDonald Original Works: Series V). 330p. 1995. reprint ed. 18.00 (*1-881084-34-5*) Johannesen.

Ramps & Wedges. LC 96-17486. (Simple Machines Ser.). (J). 1997. lib. bdg. write for info. (*1-57572-083-3*) Rigby Interact Libr.

Ramrod Revenge. Jake Foster. 1992. mass mkt. 3.50 (*0-8217-3636-1*, Zebra Kensgtn) Kensgtn Pub Corp.

Ramsar Convention on the Conservation of Wetlands: A Legal Analysis of the Adoption & Implementation of the Convention in Denmark. Veir Koester. (IUCN Environmental Policy & Law Occasional Paper: No. 23). (Illus.). 120p. (Orig.). 1989. pap. 15.00 (*2-88032-999-X*, Pub. by IUCN SZ) Island Pr.

Ramsay: Hawaii Landmark Collection. Ramsay. LC 88-83768. (Illus.). 64p. (Orig.). 1989. pap. 25.00 (*0-317-93360-4*) In Black Inc.

Ramsay McCulloch (1978-1864), Nassau Senior (1790-1864), Robert Torrens (1780-1864) Ed. by Mark Blaug. (Pioneers in Economics Ser.: No. 17). 320p. 1991. text ed. 110.00 (*1-85278-479-2*) E Elgar.

Ramsay Scallop. Frances Temple. (Trophy Bk.). 320p. (YA). (gr. 7 up). 1995. pap. 4.95 (*0-06-440601-6*, Trophy) HarpC Child Bks.

Ramsay Scallop. Frances Temple. LC 93-29697. 320p. (J). (gr. 6-9). 1994. 18.95 (*0-531-06836-6*); lib. bdg. 19.99 (*0-531-08686-0*) Orchard Bks Watts.

Ramsdell Family: William Ramsdell Genealogy. William Ramsdell. 60p. 1994. reprint ed. pap. 12.00 (*0-8328-4184-6*) Higginson Bk Co.

***Ramses Vol. I: The Son of Light.** Christian Jacq. LC 97-12882. 272p. 1997. pap. 14.99 (*0-446-67356-0*) Warner Bks.

***Ramses Vol. II: The Eternal Temple.** Christian Jacq. 384p. 1998. pap. 14.99 (*0-446-67357-9*) Warner Bks.

***Ramses Vol. III: The Battle of Kadesh.** Christian Jacq. 1998. pap. 14.99 (*0-446-67358-7*) Warner Bks.

***Ramses Vol. IV: The Lady of Abu Simbel.** Christian Jacq. 1998. pap. 14.99 (*0-446-67359-5*) Warner Bks.

***Ramses Vol. V: Under the Western Acacia.** Christian Jacq. Date not set. pap. 14.99 (*0-446-67360-9*) Warner Bks.

Ramses II: Magnificence on the Nile. Ed. by Dale Brown. LC 93-26270. (Lost Civilizations Ser.). (Illus.). 168p. 1993. 19.95 (*0-8094-9012-9*) Time-Life.

Ramses II & Thebes. Oliver Tiano. (W5 Who, What, When, Where, Why Ser.). 96p. (YA). (gr. 6 up). 1995. pap. 19.95 (*0-8050-4659-3*) TFC Bks NY.

Ramses II & Thebes. Olivier Tiano. (YA). (gr. 6 up). 1996. 19.95 (*0-614-15660-2*) H Holt & Co.

Ramses II, the Pharaoh & His Time: Exhibition Catalog, Jacksonville Art Museum, 17 November 1986 - 15 March 1987. Lisa K. Sabbahy. Ed. by C. Wilfred Griggs. write for info. (*0-8425-2257-3*) Jacksonville Art.

Ramses the Great. Bellerophon Staff. (J). (gr. 1-9). 1992. pap. 2.50 (*0-88388-148-9*) Bellerophon Bks.

Ramsey - Sleeper Architectural Graphic Standards. 9th ed. Ed. by John R. Hoke, Jr. 918p. 1994. text ed. 195.00 (*0-471-53369-6*) Wiley.

Ramsey Campbell. Gary W. Crawford. Ed. by Roger C. Schlobin. LC 87-16030. (Starmont Reader's Guide Ser.: Vol. 48). vi, 74p. 1988. pap. 15.00 (*1-55742-036-X*); lib. bdg. 25.00 (*1-55742-037-8*) Borgo Pr.

Ramsey Campbell. Joshi. 1997. 22.95 (*0-8057-4506-8*) Macmillan.

Ramsey Theory. 2nd ed. Ronald L. Graham et al. LC 89-22670. (Wiley-Interscience Series in Discrete Mathematics & Optimization). 196p. 1990. text ed. 98.00 (*0-471-50046-1*) Wiley.

***Ramseys & Related Families (with Genealogical Charts)** LC 93-84731. (Illus.). 262p. 1993. 22.00 (*0-9609192-5-2*) R H Stone.

Ramshackle Inn. George Batson. 1944. pap. 5.25 (*0-8222-0929-2*) Dramatists Play.

Ramtha. Ramtha. Ed. by Steven L. Weinberg. 224p. (Orig.). 1994. pap. 12.50 (*0-932201-03-2*) Sovereignty.

Ramtha, Vol. 1. Ed. by Steven L. Weinberg. Tr. by Antonio Campesino. vi, 227p. (Orig.). (SPA.). pap. 17.00 (*0-9632573-0-7*) Sin Limites.

Ramtha: The New Kingdom of God. Ronald G. Kaufmann. LC 89-38219. (Illus.). 208p. (Orig.). 1996. reprint ed. pap. 17.95 (*0-940539-09-8*) Heridonius.

***Ramtha - Die Alten Schulen der Weisheit.** Compiled by Diane Munoz-Smith. Orig. Title: The Ancient Schools of Wisdom - A Selection of Teachings from Ramtha. 220p. (Orig.). (GER.). 1997. pap. write for info. (*0-9652621-0-3*) Horus Pubng.

Ramtha: An Introduction see Ensenanzas Selectas

Ramtha: or an Introduction. Ramtha. Ed. by Steve L. Weinberg. LC 87-60651. 208p. (Orig.). 1988. pap. 9.95 (*0-932201-76-8*) Sovereignty.

Ramu of Lemuria Speaks. Ruth E. Norman. (Illus.). 431p. 1988. 18.00 (*0-935097-08-2*) Unarius Acad Sci.

Ramuntcho. Pierre P. Loti-Viaud. (Folio Ser.: No. 2120). (FRE.). pap. 9.95 (*2-07-038214-1*) Schoenhof.

Ramus, Method, & the Decay of Dialogue: From the Art of Discourse to the Art of Reason. Walter J. Ong. 432p. 1983. pap. 14.95 (*0-674-74802-6*) HUP.

Ramus (Pierre de la Ramee) Sa Vie, Ses Ecrits et Ses Opinions. Charles Waddington. (Medieval Studies Reprint Ser.). reprint ed. lib. bdg. 44.00 (*0-697-00020-6*) Irvington.

"Ramusio" Map of 1534: A Facsimile Edition with Commentary. fac. ed. Arthur Holzheimer & David Buisseret. (Illus.). 48p. 1992. pap. 10.00 (*0-911028-51-X*) Newberry.

Ramza. Out el Kouloub. Tr. by Nayra Atiya from FRE. (Contemporary Issues in the Middle East Ser.). (Illus.). 128p. 1994. pap. 14.50 (*0-8156-0280-4*); text ed. 30.00 (*0-8156-2618-5*) Syracuse U Pr.

Rana Juana - Jeanie the Frog. Joe Rosenberg. (Bilingual Plays for Children Ser.). (Orig.). (J). (gr. k-6). 1996. pap. 2.50 (*1-57514-162-0*, 3045) Encore Perform Pub.

Rana Mozelle: Surrealist Texts. Paul Garon. (Illus.). 16p. 1978. pap. 7.00 (*0-941194-05-1*) Black Swan Pr.

Ranaissance Magic & Hermeticism in the Shakespeare Sonnets: Like Prayers Divine. Thomas O. Jones. LC 94-22861. 188p. 1995. text ed. 79.95 (*0-7734-9027-2*) E Mellen.

Ranald Bannerman's Boyhood. George MacDonald. (George MacDonald Original Works: Series III). (Illus.). 335p. (YA). (gr. 5 up). 1993. reprint ed. 20.00 (*1-881084-13-2*) Johannesen.

***Ranald MacDonald: Pacific Rim Adventurer.** Jo A. Roe. LC 97-2019. (Illus.). 250p. 1997. 35.00 (*0-87422-147-1*); pap. 18.95 (*0-87422-146-3*) Wash St U Pr.

Ranald MacDonald: The Narrative of His Life, 1824-1894. 2nd ed. Ranald MacDonald. Ed. by William S. Lewis & Naojiro Murakami. (North Pacific Studies: No. 16). Orig. Title: Ranald MacDonald 1824-1894. (Illus.). 384p. 1990. reprint ed. 30.00 (*0-87595-229-1*) Oregon Hist.

Ranald MacDonald 1824-1894 see Ranald MacDonald: The Narrative of His Life, 1824-1894

Ranald S. Mackenzie on the Texas Frontier. Ernest Wallace. LC 92-29063. (Illus.). 256p. 1993. reprint ed. pap. 14.95 (*0-89096-487-4*) Tex A&M Univ Pr.

Ranald S. Mackenzie's Official Correspondence Relating to Texas, 1871-1873. Ed. by Ernest Wallace. 202p. 1967. 10.00 (*0-911618-04-X*) West Tex Mus.

Ranald S. Mackenzie's Official Correspondence Relating to Texas, 1873-1879. Ed. by Ernest Wallace. 241p. 1968. 10.00 (*0-911618-03-1*) West Tex Mus.

Ranald Slidell Mackenzie: Brave Cavalry Colonel. J'Nell L. Pate. LC 93-21952. (J). (gr. 4-8). 1994. 14.95 (*0-89015-901-7*) Sunbelt Media.

Ranas, Sapos y Renacuajos! Frogs & Toads, & Tadpoles, Too. Allan Fowler. LC 91-42178. (Spanish Rookie Read-About Science Ser.). (Illus.). 32p. (SPA.). (J). (ps-2). 1992. pap. 3.95 (*0-516-54925-1*); lib. bdg. 15.30 (*0-516-34925-2*) Childrens.

Ranayne's Handbook of Freemasonry. enl. rev. ed. Edmond Ronayne. reprint ed. spiral bd. 27.50 (*0-7873-0736-X*) Hlth Research.

Rance & the Trappist Legacy. Alban J. Krailsheimer. 1985. 17.95 (*0-87907-886-3*); pap. 7.95 (*0-87907-986-X*) Cistercian Pubns.

Ranch. Michael Light. (Illus.). 96p. 1993. 45.00 (*0-944092-25-X*) Twin Palms Pub.

***Ranch.** Danielle Steel. LC 96-38244. 416p. 1997. 25.95 (*0-385-31634-8*) Delacorte.

***Ranch.** Danielle Steel. 1997. 25.95 (*0-553-47835-4*) Bantam.

***Ranch.** large type ed. Danielle Steel. 1997. 29.95 (*0-385-31865-0*) Delacorte.

Ranch: A Modern History of the North American Cattle Industry. Sherm Ewing. Ed. by Daniel Greer. (Illus.). 288p. 1995. 25.00 (*0-87842-309-5*); pap. 14.00 (*0-87842-310-9*) Mountain Pr.

Ranch, a Ring & Everything. Val Daniels. (Harlequin Romance Ser.: No. 3418). 1996. mass mkt. 3.25 (*0-373-03418-0*, 1-03418-0) Harlequin Bks.

Ranch & Farm Dogs: Herders & Guards. Elizabeth Ring. LC 93-41529. (Good Dogs! Ser.). (Illus.). 32p. (J). (gr. 2-4). 1994. lib. bdg. 14.90 (*1-56294-295-6*) Millbrook Pr.

***Ranch Cook Rule Book: Questionable Rules Recipes & Rhymes.** Ham Hamilton. 18p. 1997. lib. bdg. 4.00 (*0-9643426-2-6*) A Wide Line.

Ranch Dressing: The Story of Western Wear. M. Jean Greenlaw. (Illus.). 64p. (J). (gr. 3-7). 1993. pap. 15.99 (*0-525-67432-2*, Lodestar Bks) Dutton Child Bks.

***Ranch for Sara.** Sherryl Woods. 1997. pap. 3.99 (*0-373-24083-X*, 1-24083-7) Silhouette.

Ranch Hands. Bonnie Bryant. (Saddle Club Ser.: No. 29). 144p. (J). (gr. 4-6). 1993. pap. 3.50 (*0-553-48076-6*) Bantam.

***Ranch Life.** Phoebe Cranor. (Illus.). 173p. (Orig.). 1996. pap. 10.00 (*0-9655322-0-8*) Davidson Pub.

Ranch Life & the Hunting Trail. Theodore Roosevelt, Jr. LC 76-125761. (American Environmental Studies). 1971. reprint ed. 18.95 (*0-405-02688-9*) Ayer.

Ranch Life & the Hunting-Trail. Theodore Roosevelt. LC 82-20091. (Illus.). x, 210p. 1983. reprint ed. pap. 13.95 (*0-8032-8913-8*, Bison Books) U of Nebr Pr.

Ranch Life in Southern Kansas & the Indian Territory, As Told by a Novice: How a Fortune Was Made in Cattle. Benjamin S. Miller. LC 75-111. (Mid-American Frontier Ser.). 1975. reprint ed. 19.95 (*0-405-06878-6*) Ayer.

Ranch Life in the Far West. Theodore Roosevelt. (Illus.). 1978. reprint ed. pap. 8.95 (*0-89646-034-7*) Vistabooks.

***Ranch of Dreams.** Cleveland Amory. 1997. pap. 22.95 (*0-670-87762-X*) Viking Penguin.

***Ranch on the Beaver.** Andy Adams. (Illus.). 328p. 1997. pap. 12.95 (*0-8032-5930-1*, Bison Books) U of Nebr Pr.

***Ranch on the Pecos: Microcosm U. S. A.** Sue Littleton. (Illus.). 104p. pap. 13.95 (*0-911051-88-0*) Plain View.

Ranch Papers: A California Memoir. Jane H. Wheelwright. LC 87-80275. (Illus.). 164p. 1987. pap. 19.95 (*0-932499-19-8*) Lapis Pr.

Ranch, Portrait of a Surviving Dream, Favor the Bold, A Soldier's Story. Moira Johnston. 1989. 19.98 (*0-88394-078-7*) Promntory Pr.

Ranch Rodeos in West Texas. Lawrence R. Clayton. (Illus.). (Orig.). 1989. pap. text ed. 10.00 (*0-910075-08-5*) Hardin-Simmons.

Ranch Stud. Cathy G. Thacker. (American Romance Ser.). 1996. mass mkt. 3.75 (*0-373-16629-X*, 1-16629-7) Harlequin Bks.

Ranch Trails & Short Tales. Claire C. Cordes. Ed. by Bruce M. Wilson et al. LC 91-71942. (Illus.). 112p. 1991. pap. 10.95 (*0-9627573-1-4*) Crown King Pr.

Ranch Wife. Jo Jeffers. LC 93-23764. (Illus.). 277p. 1993. reprint ed. pap. 15.95 (*0-8165-1386-4*) U of Ariz Pr.

Rancher & His Unexpected Daughter (& Baby Makes Three) Sherryl Woods. 1996. mass mkt. 3.99 (*0-373-24016-3*, 1-24016-7) Silhouette.

Rancher & the Baby. Elizabeth August. 1996. mass mkt. 3.25 (*0-373-19187-1*, 1-19187-3) Silhouette.

Rancher & the Lost Bride. Carol Grace. (Romance Ser.). 1996. mass mkt. 3.25 (*0-373-19153-7*, 1-19153-5) Silhouette.

Rancher & the Redhead. Suzannah Davis. (Desire Ser.). 1995. mass mkt. 3.25 (*0-373-05947-7*, 1-05947-6) Silhouette.

Rancher & the Redhead: Back to the Ranch. Rebecca Winters. (Romance Ser.). 1993. mass mkt. 2.99 (*0-373-03280-3*, 1-03280-4) Harlequin Bks.

***Rancher & the Runaway Bride.** Mallery. (Thirty-Six Hours Ser.). 1998. mass mkt. 4.50 (*0-373-65012-4*) Harlequin Bks.

***Rancher Takes a Wife.** Richmond P. Hobson. 1978. pap. text ed. 10.99 (*0-7710-4171-3*) McCland & Stewart.

Rancher Takes a Wife. Jackie Merritt. (Montana Mavericks Ser.). 1994. mass mkt. 3.99 (*0-373-50169-2*, 1-50169-1) Harlequin Bks.

Ranchero Revolt: The Mexican Revolution in Guerrero. Ian Jacobs. (Texas Pan American Ser.). (Illus.). 256p. 1983. text ed. 25.00 (*0-292-77026-X*) U of Tex Pr.

***Ranchers & Cowboys.** Charles L. Convis. (True Tales of the Old West Ser.: Vol. 6). (Illus.). 62p. 1997. pap. 7.95 (*0-9651954-6-5*) Pioneer Pr NV.

Rancher's Baby. Anne M. Winston. (Desire Ser.). 1996. mass mkt. 3.50 (*0-373-76031-0*, 1-76031-3) Silhouette.

Rancher's Bride. Jeanne Allan. (Romance Ser.: No. 175). 1992. pap. 2.79 (*0-373-03175-0*, 1-03175-6) Harlequin Bks.

***Rancher's Bride.** Stella Bagwell. (Twins on the Doorstep Ser.). 1997. mass mkt. 3.25 (*0-373-19224-X*, 1-19224-4) Silhouette.

Rancher's Choice. Kylie Brant. (Intimate Moments Ser.). 1994. mass mkt. 3.50 (*0-373-07552-9*, 5-07552-8) Silhouette.

***Rancher's Mistress.** Thorpe. 1997. mass mkt. 3.50 (*0-373-11924-0*) Harlequin Bks.

Ranchers, Ramblers, & Renegades: True Tales of Territorial New Mexico. Marc Simmons. LC 83-73398. (Illus.). 128p. (C). 1984. pap. text ed. 10.95 (*0-941270-17-3*) Ancient City Pr.

***Rancher's Runaway Bride.** Judith Bowen. (Men of Glory Ser.). 1997. mass mkt. 3.99 (*0-373-70739-8*, 1-70739-7) Harlequin Bks.

Rancher's Wife. Anne M. Winston. (Desire Ser.). 1995. mass mkt. 3.25 (*0-373-05936-1*, 1-05936-9) Silhouette.

***Rancher's Wife.** Anne M. Winston. (Silhouette Ser.). 1997. 20.95 (*0-373-59771-1*, Pub. by Mills & Boon UK) Thorndike Pr.

Ranches & Ranching in Spanish Texas. Lyle W. Williams. (Texas History Ser.). (Illus.). 35p. 1982. pap. text ed. 8.95 (*0-89641-121-4*) American Pr.

Ranchin' A Little Chronicle of West Texas. Jeff Streeby. (Illus.). 48p. 1990. 19.95 (*0-944551-03-3*, SunDance Press) Rainbow Tree Pubns.

Ranching, Mining, & the Human Impact of Natural Resources Development. Raymond L. Gold. (Illus.). 200p. (C). 1984. 39.95 (*0-88738-025-5*) Transaction Pubs.

Ranching Saga: The Lives of William Electious Halsell & Ewing Halsell, 2 vols., 1. William C. Holden. LC 75-9300. reprint ed. pap. 75.50 (*0-317-28178-X*, 2022567) Bks Demand.

Ranching Saga: The Lives of William Electious Halsell & Ewing Halsell, 2 vols., 2. William C. Holden. LC 75-9300. reprint ed. pap. 71.50 (*0-685-10860-0*) Bks Demand.

Ranching Traditions. (Illus.). 30p. 1995. pap. 7.95 (*1-55859-908-8*) Abbeville Pr.

An Asterisk (*) at the beginning of an entry indicates that the title is appearing in BIP for the first time.

R

Ranching Traditions: Legacy of the American West. Kathleen J. Ryan et al. (Illus.). 296p. 1993. 22.98 (*0-89660-032-7*, Artabras) Abbeville Pr.

Ranching with Lords & Commons: Or, Twenty Years on the Range. John R. Craig. LC 79-132387. reprint ed. 45.00 (*0-404-01798-3*) AMS Pr.

Ranchland Poems. rev. ed. Don I. Smith. (Illus.). 26p. 1990. pap. 3.99 (*0-932773-03-6*) High Country Bks.

Ranchman's Recollections. Frank S. Hastings. (Fred H. & Ella Mae Moore Texas History Reprint Ser.: Vol. 5). (Illus.). x, 251p. 1990. reprint ed. pap. 9.95 (*0-87611-078-2*) Tex St Hist Assn.

***Rancho Days in Southern California: An Anthology with New Perspectives.** Ed. by Kenneth Pauley. (Westerners - Los Angeles Corral Ser.: Vol. 20). (Illus.). 400p. 1997. text ed. 45.00 (*1-890125-00-8*) Wsternrs LA Corral.

Rancho de Chimayo Cookbook: The Traditional Cooking of New Mexico. Cheryl A. Jamison & Bill Jamison. Ed. by Dan Rosenberg. LC 91-24777. (Illus.). 144p. (Orig.). 1991. pap. 10.95 (*1-55832-035-0*) Harvard Common Pr.

Rancho Diablo. Anne Stuart. (Western Lovers Ser.). 1996. mass mkt. 3.99 (*0-373-88543-1*, 1-88543-3) Harlequin Bks.

Rancho Gumbo: Five Thousand Days in Montana's Piegan County. limited ed. Abner M. Wagner. (Illus.). 1983. 20.00 (*0-930704-15-0*) Sagebrush Pr.

Rancho Hollywood. Carlos Morton. LC 90-53687. 50p. (Orig.). 1991. pap. 6.00 (*0-88734-233-7*) Players Pr.

Rancho in South Texas: Continuity & Change from 1750. Joe S. Graham. LC 93-32211. 152p. (Orig.). 1993. pap. 10.00 (*0-929398-58-0*) UNTX Pr.

Rancho La Brea: A Record of Pleistocene Life in California. Chester Stock. (Science Ser.: No. 37). (Illus.). 127p. 1992. 25.00 (*0-938644-30-0*); pap. 14.00 (*0-938644-31-9*) Nat Hist Mus.

Rancho La Brea: Treasures of the Tar Pits. Ed. by John M. Harris & George Jefferson. (Science Ser.: No. 31). (Illus.). 96p. (Orig.). 1985. pap. 10.95 (*0-938644-19-X*) Nat Hist Mus.

Rancho La Puerta: A Half Century of Favorite Recipes. Deborah Szekely. (Illus.). 80p. (Orig.). 1989. pap. text ed. 12.95 (*0-685-30011-0*) Rancho La Puerta.

Rancho los Alamitos. George Salzer. (Illus.). 1975. pap. 4.50 (*0-916552-04-7*) Acoma Bks.

Rancho los Cerritos. Loretta Berner. (Illus.). 1975. pap. 4.50 (*0-916552-01-2*) Acoma Bks.

Rancho Mirage: An American Tragedy of Manners, Madness, & Murder. Aram Saroyan. LC 93-15903. 384p. 1993. 18.99 (*0-942637-95-X*) Barricade Bks.

***Rancho Punta de Agua.** Randall H. McGuire. (Archaeological Ser.: Vol. 57). (Illus.). 113p. 1977. 6.95 (*1-889747-24-6*) Ariz St Mus.

Rancho Rio. Mignon G. Eberhart. 1976. 21.95 (*0-8488-0798-7*) Amereon Ltd.

Rancho San Julian: The Story of a California Ranch & Its People. 2nd ed. A. Dibblee Poett. (Illus.). 240p. 1993. reprint ed. pap. 14.95 (*1-56474-080-3*) Fithian Pr.

Rancho Santa Fe: A California Village. Ed. by Meriam Ames et al. (Illus.). 150p. (C). 1993. 45.00 (*0-938711-20-2*) Tecolote Pubns.

Rancho Santa Margarita Remembered. 2nd rev. ed. Jerome W. Baumgartner. (Illus.). 192p. (Orig.). 1996. pap. 12.95 (*1-56474-182-6*) Fithian Pr.

Rancho Santa Margarita Remembered: An Oral History. Jerome W. Baumgartner. LC 88-32782. (Illus.). 160p. 1989. 17.95 (*0-931832-23-3*) Fithian Pr.

Ranchos De Taos: San Francisco De Asis Church. Wolfgang Pogzeba & Joy Overbeck. LC 81-82257. (Illus.). 68p. (Orig.). 1981. pap. 7.95 (*0-913504-66-1*) Lowell Pr.

Ranchos of California: A List of Spanish Concessions 1775-1822, & Mexican Grants 1822-1846. Robert G. Cowan. LC 85-21289. 151p. 1985. reprint ed. lib. bdg. 29.00 (*0-89370-863-1*) Borgo Pr.

Rancidity in Foods. Ed. by J. C. Allen & R. J. Hamilton. 290p. 1994. 119.95 (*0-7514-0219-2*, Pub. by Blackie Acad & Prof UK) Routledge Chapman & Hall.

Rancon Du Silence. Marie Balka. 192p. (FRE.). 1975. pap. 10.95 (*0-7859-1797-7*, 2070366502) Fr & Eur.

Rand - Stillwater Pass, CO. rev. ed. Ed. by Trails Illustrated Staff. 1994. 8.99 (*0-925873-36-5*) Trails Illustrated.

RAND Advanced Simulation Language Project's Declarative Modeling Formalism (DMOD) Jeff Rothenberg & Sanjai Narain. LC 94-20774. 1994. pap. text ed. 13.00 (*0-8330-1555-9*, MR-376-ARPA) Rand Corp.

Rand at War, 1899-1902: The Witwatersrand & Anglo-Boer War. Diane Cammack. 1990. 50.00 (*0-520-06852-1*) U CA Pr.

Rand at War 1899-1902: The Witwatersrand & the Angelo-Boer War. Diana Cammack. (Illus.). 240p. 1990. pap. 28.00 (*0-86980-729-3*, Pub. by Univ Natal Pr SA) Intl Spec Bk.

Rand Corporation: Case Study of a Non-Profit Advisory Corporation. Bruce L. Smith. LC 66-14454. (Harvard Political Studies). 350p. reprint ed. pap. 99.80 (*0-317-09149-2*, 2011025) Bks Demand.

Rand McNally Animal Sticker Atlas. Rand McNally Staff. (Illus.). (J). (ps-3). 1993. pap. 4.95 (*0-528-83586-6*) Rand McNally.

Rand McNally Bankers Directory, 3 vols. 2nd ed. American Banker Bond Buyer Staff. 1990. 245.00 (*1-56310-002-9*) Amer Bank Bond Buyer.

Rand McNally Bankers Directory, 3 vols., 3. American Banker Bond Buyer Staff. 1990. write for info. (*1-56310-001-0*) Amer Bank Bond Buyer.

Rand McNally Bankers Directory, 3 vols., Vols. 1 & 2. American Banker Bond Buyer Staff. 1990. write for info. (*1-56310-000-2*) Amer Bank Bond Buyer.

***Rand McNally Business Traveler's Road Atlas.** Rand McNally Staff. (Rand McNally Ser.). 1997. pap. text ed. 9.95 (*0-528-83909-8*) Rand McNally.

Rand McNally Children's Atlas of Earth Through Time see **Discovery Atlas of Dinosaurs & Prehistoric Creatures**

Rand McNally Children's Atlas of the Environment. (Illus.). 80p. (J). (gr. 2-6). 1994. lib. bdg. 18.95 (*1-878363-74-3*) Forest Hse.

Rand McNally Children's Atlas of the United States. Rand McNally Staff. (Illus.). 112p. (J). (gr. 3-6). 1991. reprint ed. lib. bdg. 18.95 (*1-878363-37-9*) Forest Hse.

Rand McNally Children's Atlas of the World. rev. ed. Rand McNally Staff. LC 92-24028. (Illus.). (J). (gr. 4-7). 1992. pap. 7.95 (*0-528-83541-6*) Rand McNally.

Rand McNally Children's Atlas of World Wildlife. Elizabeth G. Fagan. LC 93-503. (Illus.). 96p. (J). (gr. 3-7). 1993. 14.95 (*0-528-83409-6*) Rand McNally.

***Rand McNally Classroom Atlas.** rev. ed. 100p. (J). (gr. 5-8). 1996. pap. text ed. 4.95 (*0-528-17729-X*) Rand McNally.

***Rand McNally Commerical Atlas & Marketing Guide.** Rand McNally Staff. (Rand McNally Ser.). 1997. 395.00 (*0-528-83903-9*) Rand McNally.

***Rand McNally Compact Road Atlas.** Rand McNally Staff. (Rand McNally Ser.). 1997. pap. text ed. 6.95 (*0-528-83923-3*) Rand McNally.

Rand McNally Compact Road Atlas: United States-Canada-Mexico. (Illus.). 224p. 1994. pap. 5.95 (*0-528-81428-1*) Rand McNally.

Rand McNally Credit Union Directory. American Banker Bond Buyer Staff. 1990. 115.00 (*1-56310-004-5*) Amer Bank Bond Buyer.

Rand McNally Dinosaur Sticker Atlas. Rand McNally Staff. (Illus.). (J). (ps-3). 1993. pap. 4.95 (*0-528-83585-8*) Rand McNally.

Rand McNally Encyclopedia of Military Aircraft. 1991. 29.99 (*0-517-05655-0*) Random Hse Value.

Rand McNally Encyclopedia of War World II. Ed. by John Keegan. 1985. 12.98 (*0-517-43897-6*) Random Hse Value.

Rand McNally Fold-Out Airplanes. Illus. by Martin Woodward. LC 94-24423. (J). 1995. 12.95 (*0-528-83723-0*) Rand McNally.

Rand McNally Fold-Out Dinosaurs. Illus. by Steve Kirk. LC 95-16314. (Fold-Out Bk.). (J). 1995. write for info. (*0-528-83753-2*) Rand McNally.

Rand McNally Fold-Out Skyscrapers. Illus. by Stephen Conlin. LC 94-24428. (J). 1995. 12.95 (*0-528-83724-9*) Rand McNally.

Rand McNally Great National Park Vacations, 1988. 224p. (Orig.). 1988. pap. 12.95 (*0-528-88256-2*) S&S Trade.

Rand McNally Human Body. Debra Woodward. LC 95-9065. (Fold-Out Bk.). (Illus.). (J). 1995. write for info. (*0-528-83752-4*) Rand McNally.

***Rand McNally Motor Carriers' Road Atlas.** Rand McNally Staff. (Rand McNally Ser.). 1997. pap. text ed. 19.95 (*0-528-83911-X*); pap. text ed. 79.95 (*0-528-83914-4*) Rand McNally.

Rand McNally New Universal World Atlas. Rand McNally Staff. LC 94-3532. 1994. 49.95 (*0-528-83717-6*) Rand McNally.

Rand McNally Picture Atlas of Prehistoric Life. Robert M. Wood. LC 92-5761. (Illus.). 1992. 19.95 (*0-528-83525-4*) Rand McNally.

Rand McNally Picture Atlas of the World, 1995. rev. ed. Illus. by Brian Delf. LC 95-19966. (J). 1995. text ed. write for info. (*0-528-83756-7*) Rand McNally.

***Rand McNally Pocket Road Atlas.** Rand McNally Staff. (Rand McNally Ser.). 1997. pap. text ed. 2.95 (*0-528-83925-X*) Rand McNally.

Rand McNally Rainforest Fold-Out Book. Rand McNally Staff & Nicholas Harris. LC QL112.H385 1996. (J). 1996. 14.95 (*0-528-83834-2*) Rand McNally.

***Rand Mcnally Road Atlas.** Mcnally Rand. 1997. pap. text ed. 9.95 (*0-528-81587-3*) Rand McNally.

Rand McNally Road Atlas. Rand McNally Staff. 1995. pap. 9.95 (*0-395-78327-5*) HM.

***Rand McNally Road Atlas.** Rand McNally Staff. (Rand McNally Ser.). 1997. pap. text ed. 13.95 (*0-528-83918-7*) Rand McNally.

Rand McNally Road Atlas: U. S., Canada & Mexico. Rand McNally Staff. 1991. 8.95 (*0-685-83176-0*) Wehman.

***Rand McNally Road Atlas & Travel Guide.** Rand McNally Staff. (Rand McNally Ser.). 1997. pap. text ed. 7.95 (*0-528-83915-2*) Rand McNally.

***Rand McNally Road Atlas & Trip Planner.** Rand McNally Staff. (Rand McNally Ser.). 1997. pap. text ed. 5.95 (*0-528-83929-2*) Rand McNally.

Rand McNally RV Park & Campground Directory, 3 vols., Eastern. rev. ed. 582p. (Orig.). 1988. pap. 9.95 (*0-528-88224-4*) S&S Trade.

Rand McNally RV Park & Campground Directory, 3 vols., National. rev. ed. 934p. (Orig.). 1988. pap. 13.95 (*0-528-88222-8*) S&S Trade.

Rand McNally RV Park & Campground Directory, 3 vols., Western. rev. ed. 472p. (Orig.). 1988. pap. 9.95 (*0-528-88226-0*) S&S Trade.

***Rand McNally Streetfinder: Albuquerque & Vicinity, NM.** (Illus.). 1996. pap. 14.95 (*0-528-96934-X*) Rand McNally.

Rand McNally StreetFinder: Atlanta & Vicinity, GA. Rand McNally Staff. (Streetfinder Ser.). 1996. pap. text ed. 15.95 (*0-528-96918-8*) Rand McNally.

Rand McNally StreetFinder: Austin & Vicinity, TX. (Illus.). 1995. pap. 17.95 (*0-528-91338-7*) Rand McNally.

Rand McNally Streetfinder: Boston & Vicinity, MA. (Illus.). 1994. pap. 12.95 (*0-528-91102-3*) Rand McNally.

Rand McNally StreetFinder: Broward County, FL. Rand McNally Staff. (Streetfinder Ser.). 1996. pap. text ed. 15.95 (*0-528-96908-0*) Rand McNally.

***Rand McNally Streetfinder: Chicago 6-County, IL.** (Illus.). 1996. 25.95 (*0-528-96943-9*) Rand McNally.

***Rand McNally Streetfinder: Columbus & Vicinity, OH.** (Illus.). 1996. pap. 14.95 (*0-528-96907-2*) Rand McNally.

***Rand McNally Streetfinder: Dade County, FL.** (Illus.). 1996. pap. 15.95 (*0-528-96911-0*) Rand McNally.

***Rand McNally Streetfinder: Dallas & Vicinity.** Rand McNally Staff. 1996. pap. text ed. 15.95 (*0-528-96919-6*) Rand McNally.

Rand McNally Streetfinder: Daytona Beach & Vicinity, FL. (Illus.). 1993. pap. 12.95 (*0-528-95266-8*) Rand McNally.

***Rand McNally Streetfinder: Denver Regional & Vicinity.** Rand McNally Staff. 1996. pap. text ed. 34.95 (*0-528-96932-3*) Rand McNally.

Rand McNally Streetfinder: Detroit & Vicinity, MI. (Illus.). 1995. pap. 17.95 (*0-528-91261-5*) Rand McNally.

***Rand McNally Streetfinder: Ft. Worth & Vicinity, TX.** Rand McNally Staff. 1996. pap. text ed. 15.95 (*0-528-96920-X*) Rand McNally.

Rand McNally Streetfinder: Hartford, CT. (Illus.). 1994. pap. 14.95 (*0-528-91263-1*) Rand McNally.

Rand McNally Streetfinder: Jacksonville, FL. (Illus.). 1994. pap. 15.95 (*0-528-91266-6*) Rand McNally.

Rand McNally StreetFinder: Kansas City & Vicinity, MO. (Illus.). 1995. pap. 12.95 (*0-528-91366-2*) Rand McNally.

***Rand McNally Streetfinder: Lake & McHenry Counties, IL.** (Illus.). 1995. pap. 15.95 (*0-528-96940-4*) Rand McNally.

***Rand McNally Streetfinder: Las Vegas & Vicinity, NV.** (Illus.). 1996. pap. 14.95 (*0-528-96898-X*) Rand McNally.

Rand McNally Streetfinder: Los Angeles. Rand McNally Staff. 1994. pap. 17.95 (*0-528-91323-9*) Rand McNally.

***Rand McNally Streetfinder: Minneapolis/St. Paul.** Rand McNally Staff. 1996. pap. text ed. 15.95 (*0-528-96935-8*) Rand McNally.

Rand McNally Streetfinder: Nashville. Rand McNally Staff. 1994. pap. 14.95 (*0-528-91321-2*) Rand McNally.

***Rand McNally Streetfinder: New Orleans.** Rand McNally Staff. 1996. pap. text ed. 14.95 (*0-528-96933-1*) Rand McNally.

Rand McNally Streetfinder: New Orleans & Vicinity, LA. (Illus.). 1996. pap. 15.95 (*0-528-90890-1*) Rand McNally.

Rand McNally Streetfinder: Northeast Connecticut. (Illus.). 1994. pap. 14.95 (*0-528-91301-8*) Rand McNally.

Rand McNally Streetfinder: Northern Virginia, VA. (Illus.). 1992. pap. 8.95 (*0-528-91110-4*) Rand McNally.

Rand McNally Streetfinder: Orlando, Gl. Rand McNally Staff. (Streetfinder Ser.). 1996. pap. text ed. 19.95 (*0-528-96906-4*) Rand McNally.

***Rand McNally Streetfinder: Pinellas County, FL.** (Illus.). 1996. pap. 15.95 (*0-528-96912-9*) Rand McNally.

***Rand McNally Streetfinder: Pittsburgh & Vicinity, PA.** (Illus.). 1996. pap. 14.95 (*0-528-96896-3*) Rand McNally.

Rand McNally Streetfinder: San Antonio & Vicinity. (Streetfinder Ser.). (Illus.). 1995. pap. 17.95 (*0-528-91350-6*) Rand McNally.

Rand McNally StreetFinder: San Diego, CA. Rand McNally Staff. (Streetfinder Ser.). 1996. pap. text ed. 12.95 (*0-528-96930-7*) Rand McNally.

Rand McNally Streetfinder: St. Louis & Vicinity, MO. (Illus.). 1994. pap. 12.95 (*0-528-91295-X*) Rand McNally.

Rand McNally Streetfinder: Washington D. C. (Illus.). 1994. pap. 15.95 (*0-528-91117-1*) Rand McNally.

Rand McNally Streetfinder: West Palm Beach, FL. Rand McNally Staff. (Streetfinder Ser.). 1996. pap. text ed. 15.95 (*0-528-96910-2*) Rand McNally.

Rand McNally Texas Mapbook. 1991. pap. 3.95 (*0-528-91681-5*) Rand McNally.

Rand McNally, the City Maps of Europe: 16th Century Town Plans from Braun & Hogenberg. John Goss. LC 92-12722. 1992. 50.00 (*0-528-83524-6*) Rand McNally.

Rand McNally U. S.-Canada-Mexico Sticker Atlas. (Illus.). 1994. pap. 4.95 (*0-614-07162-3*) Rand McNally.

***Rand McNally Ultimate Road Atlas & Vacation Guide.** Rand McNally Staff. 1997. pap. text ed. 19.95 (*0-528-81578-4*) Rand McNally.

Rand McNally World Atlas. (Illus.). 256p. 1995. 22.95 (*0-528-83698-6*); pap. 15.95 (*0-528-83697-8*) Rand McNally.

Rand McNally World Atlas. Rand McNally Staff. LC 91-46946. 1992. write for info. (*0-8407-4253-3*) Nelson.

Rand McNally World Sticker Atlas. 1992. pap. 4.95 (*0-528-83490-8*) Rand McNally.

***Rand McNally Zip Code Finder.** Rand McNally Staff. (Rand McNally Ser.). 1997. pap. text ed. 7.95 (*0-528-83904-7*) Rand McNally.

Rand McNally Zip Finder. Rand McNally Staff. 1995. pap. 7.95 (*0-395-78328-3*) HM.

RAND Metadata Management System (RMMS) A Metadata Storage Facility to Support Data Interoperability, Reuse & Sharing. Stephanie Cammarata et al. LC 94-6663. 52p. 1995. pap. text ed. 7.50 (*0-8330-1515-X*, MR-163-OSD/A/AF) Rand Corp.

Rand R. Gar Rey. LC 92-61994. 200p. 1993. pap. 9.00 (*1-56002-206-X*, Univ Edtns) Aegina Pr.

Randall & Allied Families: William Randall, 1609-1693 of Scituate & His Descendants with Ancestral Families. F. A. Randall. (Illus.). 596p. 1993. reprint ed. pap. 89.00 (*0-8328-3733-4*); reprint ed. lib. bdg. 99.00 (*0-8328-3732-6*) Higginson Bk Co.

Randall House Bible Commentary: Galatians, Ephesians, Philippians, & Colossians. Thomas Marberry. Ed. by Robert E. Picirilli et al. (Bible Commentary Ser.). 400p. 1988. 24.95 (*0-89265-134-2*) Randall Hse.

Randall House Bible Commentary: I Thessalonians Through Philemon. Robert E. Picirilli et al. Ed. by H. D. Harrison. 1990. 24.95 (*0-89265-143-1*) Randall Hse.

Randall House Bible Commentary: Romans. F. Leroy Forlines. (Bible Commentary Ser.). 381p. 1987. 24.95 (*0-89265-116-4*) Randall Hse.

Randall House Bible Commentary: The Gospel of John. Jack Stallings. Ed. by Robert E. Picirilli & H. D. Harrison. 1989. 24.95 (*0-89265-137-7*) Randall Hse.

Randall House Bible Commentary: 1, 2 Corinthians. Robert E. Picirilli. Ed. by H. D. Harrison. 434p. 1987. 24.95 (*0-89265-118-0*) Randall Hse.

Randall House Bible Commentary - James, I & II Peter, Jude. Paul Harrison & Robert E. Picirilli. Ed. by H. D. Harrison. 359p. 1992. 24.95 (*0-89265-145-8*) Randall Hse.

Randall House Bible Commentary Series, 6 vols., 4 vols. Ed. by Robert E. Picirilli & H. D. Harrison. 1989. write for info. (*0-89265-115-6*) Randall Hse.

Randall Jarrell: A Descriptive Bibliography: 1929-1983. Stuart T. Wright. LC 85-3132. (Illus.). 389p. reprint ed. pap. 110.90 (*0-7837-4354-8*, 2044064) Bks Demand.

Randall Jarrell: A Literary Life. William H. Pritchard. 1990. 25.00 (*0-374-24677-7*) FS&G.

Randall Jarrell: A Literary Life. William H. Pritchard. 1992. pap. 14.95 (*0-374-52277-4*, Noonday) FS&G.

Randall Jarrell & the Lost World of Childhood. Richard Flynn. LC 90-30033. 176p. 1990. 30.00 (*0-8203-1243-6*) U of Ga Pr.

Randall Made Knives: The History of the Man & the Blades. Robert L. Gaddis. (Illus.). 304p. 1993. text ed. 50.00 (*0-87364-711-4*) Paladin Pr.

Randall McDaniel. Mark Stewart. LC 96-15143. (Grolier All-Pro Biographies Ser.). 48p. (J). 1996. lib. bdg. 20.00 (*0-516-20180-8*) Childrens.

Randall McDaniel. Mark Stewart. (Grolier All-Pro Biographies Ser.). (J). 1996. pap. 3.95 (*0-516-26028-6*) Childrens.

Randall Thompson: A Bio-Bibliography. Caroline C. Benser & David F. Urrows. LC 90-29279. (Bio-Bibliographies in Music Ser.: No. 38). 248p. 1991. text ed. 52.95 (*0-313-25521-0*, BRO, Greenwood Pr) Greenwood.

Randall Thompson: A Choral Legacy. Alfred Mann. 1983. pap. 10.00 (*0-911318-12-7*) E C Schirmer.

Randalls Cookbook: Dynamic - Daring - Delicious. Lori Valencic. pap. text ed. 9.95 (*0-9639196-0-1*) L Valencic & Assocs.

Randall's Practical Guide to ISO 9000: Implementation, Registration, & Beyond. Richard C. Randall. (Engineering Process Improvement Ser.). 400p. (C). 1995. pap. text ed. 34.95 (*0-201-63379-5*) Addison-Wesley.

***Randall's Wall.** Carol Fenner. 96p. 1996. pap. 3.99 (*0-440-41393-1*) Dell.

Randall's Wall. Carol Fenner. LC 90-46490. 96p. (J). (gr. 4-7). 1991. lib. bdg. 15.00 (*0-689-50518-3*, McElderry) S&S Childrens.

***Randax Education Guide to College Seeking Students: 1998 Edition.** 27th rev. ed. Ed. by Stephen E. Marshall. 128p. (YA). 1998. pap. 19.95 (*0-914880-28-4*, 28R) Educ Guide.

Randax Education Guide to Colleges Seeking Students, 1990 Edition. 19th ed. Stephen E. Marshall. (Illus.). 128p. (Orig.). 1990. pap. 12.95 (*0-914880-20-9*) Educ Guide.

Randax Education Guide to Colleges Seeking Students, 1992. 21th ed. Stephen E. Marshall. (Illus.). 128p. (Orig.). 1992. pap. 14.95 (*0-914880-22-5*) Educ Guide.

Randax Education Guide to Colleges Seeking Students, 1993 Edition. 22th ed. Stephen E. Marshall. (Illus.). 128p. 1993. pap. 15.95 (*0-914880-23-3*) Educ Guide.

Randax Education Guide to Colleges Seeking Students, 1994. 23th ed. Stephen E. Marshall. (Illus.). 128p. 1994. pap. 16.95 (*0-914880-24-1*) Educ Guide.

Randax Graduate School Directory. Ed. by Robert A. Pastman. LC 75-41652. 303p. 1976. lib. bdg. 21.50 (*0-914880-06-3*) Educ Guide.

Randazzo Hoard Nineteen Eighty & Sicilian Chronology in the Early Fifth Century B.C. Carmen Arnold-Biucchi. (ANSNS Ser.: No. 18). (Illus.). 77p. 1989. 50.00 (*0-89722-227-X*) Am Numismatic.

***Randazzo Hoard 1980 & Sicilian Chronology in the Early Fifth Century B. C.** Carmen Arnold-Biucchi. LC 92-193886. (Numismatic Studies: Vol. 18). 100p. 1990. reprint ed. pap. 28.50 (*0-608-03364-2*, 2064076) Bks Demand.

R&D Collaboration on Trial. David V. Gibson & Everett M. Rogers. 1994. text ed. 39.95 (*0-07-103429-3*) McGraw.

R&D Decisions: Strategy, Policy, & Disclosure. Ed. by Alice Belcher et al. LC 95-50137. (Research in Organizational Behaviour & Strategy Ser.). 304p. (C). 1996. text ed. 75.00 (*0-415-13777-2*) Routledge.

***R&D Management & Corporate Financial Policy.** John B. Guerard et al. LC 97-12831. 320p. 1997. 69.95 (*0-471-61837-3*) Wiley.

R&D Management Systems in Japanese Industry. Ed. by Hajime Eto & K. Matsui. 332p. 1984. 140.75 (*0-444-86808-9*, North Holland) Elsevier.

R&D Ratios & Budgets. 200p. 1994. pap. text ed. 325.00 (*1-878339-31-1*) Schonfeld & Assocs.

R

R&D Strategies in Japan: The National, Regional, & Corporate Approach. Ed. by Hajime Eto. LC 93-25938. (Advances in Industrial Engineering Ser.: Vol. 18). 324p. 1993. 170.50 (0-444-89924-3, North Holland) Elsevier.

***Randi.** Herb Oakley. 274p. (Orig.). 1997. mass mkt. 4.99 (1-55197-957-8, Pub. by Comnwlth Pub CN) Partners Pubs Grp.

***Randi's Missing Skates.** (Silver Blades Figure Eights Ser.: No. 6). 80p. (J). 1997. pap. 3.50 (0-553-48506-7, Skylark BDD) BDD Bks Young Read.

***Randi's Pet Surprise.** Effin Older. (Silver Blades Figure Eights Ser.: No. 8). (Illus.). 80p. (Orig.). (J). (gr. 1-4). 1997. pap. 3.50 (0-553-48514-8) BDD Bks Young Read.

***Randle Report: UFOs in the '90s.** Kevin Randle. (Illus.). 256p. 1997. 19.95 (0-87131-820-2) M Evans.

Randlords. P. H. Emden. 1972. 59.95 (0-8490-0927-8) Gordon Pr.

Randolph: The Biography of Winston Churchill's Son. Anita Leslie. 1985. 16.95 (0-8253-0284-6) Beaufort Bks NY.

Randolph Bourne. Sherman Paul. LC 66-64593. (University of Minnesota Pamphlets on American Writers Ser.: No. 60). 48p. (Orig.). reprint ed. pap. 25.00 (0-7837-2869-7, 2057586) Bks Demand.

Randolph Bourne: The Radical Will: Selected Writings 1911-1918. Randolph Bourne. (C). 1992. pap. 17.00 (0-520-07715-6) U CA Pr.

***Randolph Bourne & the Politics of Cultural Radicalism.** Leslie J. Vaughan. LC 96-48218. (American Political Thought Ser.). 272p. 1997. 35.00 (0-7006-0821-4) U Pr of KS.

Randolph Caldecott: The Children's Illustrator. Marguerite Lewis. (Illus.). 48p. (J). (gr. 2-7). 1992. pap. 10.95 (0-913853-22-4, 32533, Alleyside) Highsmith Pr.

Randolph County, Arkansas, Marriages, 1821-1893. Burton R. Knotts. 170p. (Orig.). 1996. pap. 24.00 (1-56546-073-1) Arkansas Res.

Randolph County, Arkansas, Marriages, 1893-1923. Ed. by Burton R. Knotts. 170p. (Orig.). 1996. pap. 24.00 (1-56546-077-4) Arkansas Res.

Randolph County, IL. Turner Publishing Company Staff. LC 95-60494. 368p. 1995. write for info. (1-56311-202-7) Turner Pub KY.

Randolph County, Indiana 1818-1990. Historical & Genealogical Society of Randolph County Staff. LC 90-71687. 320p. 1990. 49.00 (1-56311-001-6) Turner Pub KY.

Randolph County, North Carolina Marriage Bonds & Certificates, 1785-1868. Francis T. Ingmire. 200p. 1994. pap. 23.00 (0-8095-8673-8); lib. bdg. 53.00 (0-8095-8076-4) Borgo Pr.

Randolph Field: History & Guide for Texans. Work Projects Administration Staff. (Illus.). 1942. 25.00 (0-8159-6700-4) Devin.

***Randolph Lagacy.** Charbonneau. Date not set. 24.95 (0-312-86332-2) St Martin.

Randolph Lineages Vol. II: The Northerners. (Illus.). 612p. 1995. reprint ed. lib. bdg. 95.00 (0-8328-6574-5) Higginson Bk Co.

Randolph Lineages Vol. II: The Northerners. (Illus.). 612p. 1995. reprint ed. pap. 85.00 (0-8328-6575-3) Higginson Bk Co.

Randolph Lineages Vol. III: Pedigrees. 506p. 1995. reprint ed. lib. bdg. 86.00 (0-8328-4937-5) Higginson Bk Co.

Randolph Lineages Vol. III: Pedigrees. 506p. 1995. reprint ed. pap. 76.00 (0-8328-4938-3) Higginson Bk Co.

Randolph Lineages, Being the Ancestry of Iris Patricia Follows from the Time of the Saxon Invasion of England Vol. I: The Southerners. Howard H. Metcalfe. (Illus.). 500p. 1995. reprint ed. pap. 75.00 (0-8328-4936-7); reprint ed. lib. bdg. 85.00 (0-8328-4935-9) Higginson Bk Co.

Randolph-Macon Academy: A Proud Heritage: A Promising Future. Eunice K. Knight. LC 94-90488. (Illus.). 432p. 1995. text ed. 29.92 (1-56002-498-4) Aegina Pr.

Randolph Scott: A Film Biography. Jefferson B. Crow, III. LC 94-61281. (Illus.). 306p. 1994. text ed. 30.00 (0-944019-17-X) Empire NC.

Randolph Scott: The Gentleman from Virginia. rev. ed. Jefferson B. Crow, III. (Illus.). 336p. 1994. reprint ed. pap. 14.95 (0-940375-11-7) WindRiver Pub.

Randolph Scott: The Gentleman from Virginia. Jefferson B Crow, III. (Illus.). 336p. 1994. reprint ed. 29.95 (0-940375-00-1) WindRiver Pub.

Randolph Stowe. Ed. by Anthony J. Hassall. 1991. pap. 16.95 (0-7022-2284-4, Pub. by Univ Queensland Pr AT) Intl Spec Bk.

Randolph the Six Gun Cowboy. Donald L. Ferguson. LC 94-94393. (Orig.). 1995. pap. 6.95 (0-9641760-0-9) A B F Prods.

Randolph Wardell Johnston: Feel Intensely, Imagine Vividly, Control Precisely. Emily Dahlgren & Joseph A. Maggio. LC 93-93605. (Illus.). 100p. 1993. pap. 45.00 (0-9638244-1-4) Mag St Pr.

Randolph Wardell Johnston: Feel Intensely, Imagine Vividly, Control Precisely. deluxe limited ed. Emily Dahlgren & Joseph A. Maggio. LC 93-93605. (Illus.). 100p. 1993. Numbered & signed. 125.00 (0-9638244-0-6) Mag St Pr.

Random Access Files. Roy Miki. 96p. 1995. pap. 8.95 (0-88995-130-6, Pub. by Red Deer CN) Orca Bk Pubs.

Random Access Murder. Linda Grant. 192p. 1988. pap. 2.95 (0-380-75534-3) Avon.

Random Acts: A Kindness Journal. Ed. by Conari Press. 160p. (Orig.). 1995. pap. 7.95 (1-57071-034-1) Sourcebks.

Random Acts of Kindness. Conari Press Editors. LC 92-38017. (Practice of Kindness Ser.). 150p. (Orig.). 1993. pap. 8.95 (0-943233-43-7) Conari Press.

***Random Acts of Kindness.** Conari Press Editors. (Orig.). 1997. 6.98 (1-56731-197-0, MJF Bks) Fine Comms.

Random Acts of Kindness. Conari Press Editors. 150p. (Orig.). (C). 1993. reprint ed. lib. bdg. 27.00 (0-8095-5872-6) Borgo Pr.

Random Acts of Senseless Violence. Jack Womack. LC 95-38204. 256p. 1995. pap. 12.00 (0-8021-3424-6, Grove) Grove-Atltic.

Random & Rainbow Feelings. deluxe ed. Sally Lockhart. (Illus.). 16p. (Orig.). 1986. pap. 4.00 (0-9616899-0-0) Anapauo Farm.

Random & Restricted Walks: Theory & Applications, Vol. 10. M. N. Barber & B. W. Ninham. (Mathematics & Its Applications Ser.). xiv, 176p. 1970. text ed. 143.00 (0-677-02620-X) Gordon & Breach.

***Random Character of Corporate Earnings.** unabridged ed. Joseph E. Murphy. 386p. (Orig.). 1997. pap. 19.95 (0-9646292-4-0) Crossgar Pr.

Random Coefficient Models. Nicholas T. Longford. LC 93-35629. (Oxford Statistical Science Ser.: No. 11). (Illus.). 288p. (C). 1994. 70.00 (0-19-852264-9, Clarendon Pr) OUP.

Random Data: Analysis & Measurement Procedures. 2nd exp. rev. ed. Julius S. Bendat & Allan G. Piersol. LC 85-17996. 592p. 1986. text ed. 89.95 (0-471-04000-2) Wiley.

Random Discrete Structures. David Aldous & Robin Pemantle. LC 95-44886. (IMA Volumes in Mathematics & Its Applications Ser.: Vol. 76). 248p. 1995. 53.95 (0-387-94623-3) Spr-Verlag.

Random Dot Stereograms. A. A. Kinsman. (Illus.). 136p. (Orig.). 1992. pap. 13.95 (0-9630142-1-8) Kinsman Physics.

Random Dots. 1994. write for info. (1-886316-01-5, Sunny Pubns USA) Oregon Vocations.

Random Essays. James Laughlin. 302p. 1992. pap. 9.95 (0-918825-87-3) Moyer Bell.

***Random Evolutions & Their Applications.** LC 97-8244. 1997. lib. bdg. 120.00 (0-7923-4533-9) Kluwer Ac.

Random Factors in Anova. Sally E. Jackson & Dale E. Brashers. (Quantitative Applications in the Social Sciences Ser.: Vol. 97). (C). pap. text ed. 9.95 (0-8039-5090-X) Sage.

Random Fatigue: From Data to Theory. Kazimierz Sobczyk & B. F. Spencer. (Illus.). 288p. 1992. text ed. 73.00 (0-12-654225-2) Acad Pr.

Random Fatigue Life Prediction. Ed. by Y. S. Shin & M. K. Au-Yang. (PVP Ser.: Vol. 72). 148p. 1983. pap. 8.00 (0-317-02643-7, H00258) ASME.

Random Field Models in Earth Sciences. George Christakos. (Illus.). 512p. 1992. text ed. 110.00 (0-12-174230-X) Acad Pr.

Random Fields: Analysis & Synthesis. Erik Vanmarcke. (Illus.). 416p. 1983. 70.00 (0-262-22026-1) MIT Pr.

***Random Fields Estimation Theory.** Alexander G. Ramm. LC 89-33272. (Pitman Monographs & Surveys in Pure & Applied Mathematics: No. 48). 282p. pap. 80.40 (0-608-05239-6, 2065776) Bks Demand.

Random Fields on a Network: Modelling, Statistics & Applications. Xavier Guyon. LC 94-41485. (Probability & Its Applications Ser.). 1995. 54.95 (0-387-94428-1) Spr-Verlag.

Random Fluctuations & Pattern Growth: Experiments & Models. Ed. by H. Eugene Stanley & Nicole Ostrowsky. (C). 1988. pap. text ed. 73.00 (0-7923-0073-4) Kluwer Ac.

Random Fluctuations & Pattern Growth: Experiments & Models. Ed. by H. Eugene Stanley & Nicole Ostrowsky. (C). 1988. lib. bdg. 162.50 (0-7923-0072-6) Kluwer Ac.

Random Functions: A Laplacian Random Function Depending on a Point of Hilbert Space. Paul Levy. LC 56-8639. (University of California Publications in Social Welfare: Vol. 2, No. 10). 14p. reprint ed. pap. 25.00 (0-317-11008-X, 2021182) Bks Demand.

Random Functions & Hydrology. Rafael L. Bras & Ignacio Rodriguez-Iturbe. LC 93-29005. (Illus.). 559p. 1993. reprint ed. pap. 14.95 (0-486-67626-9) Dover.

Random Generation of Trees: Random Generators in Computer Science. Laurent Alonso & Rene Schott. LC 94-39286. 208p. (C). 1994. lib. bdg. 110.50 (0-7923-9528-X) Kluwer Ac.

Random Gentleman. Elizabeth Chater. 224p. 1981. pap. 1.50 (0-449-50210-4, Coventry) Fawcett.

Random Graphs, Vol. 2. Alan Frieze. LC 91-42412. 304p. 1992. text ed. 232.00 (0-471-57292-6) Wiley.

Random Graphs Eighty Seven: Proceedings of the Third International Seminar on Random Graphs & Probabilistic Methods in Combinatorics: Roznan, Poland. Ed. by Michal Karonski et al. 368p. 1991. text ed. 169.00 (0-471-92749-X) Wiley.

***Random Harvest.** James T. Flexner. 350p. 1997. 35.00 (0-8232-1730-2) Fordham.

Random Harvest. James Hilton. 327p. 1985. pap. 4.50 (0-88184-125-0) Carroll & Graf.

Random Harvest. James Hilton. 1982. reprint ed. lib. bdg. 29.95 (0-89966-414-8) Buccaneer Bks.

Random House Acrostic Puzzles, Vol. 2. Michael Ashley. 1997. pap. 9.00 (0-8129-2670-6, Times Bks) Random.

Random House Atlas of Bird Migration: Tracing the Great Journeys of the World's Birds. Ed. by Jonathan Elphick. LC 94-29378. (Illus.). 180p. 1995. 35.00 (0-679-43827-0) Random.

Random House Barbecue & Summer Foods Cookbook: Over 175 Recipes for Outdoor Cooking & Entertaining. Margaret Fraser. 1995. pap. 17.00 (0-679-75938-7) Random.

Random House Basic Dictionary: French. Ed. by Francesca L. Langbaum. (ENG & FRE.). 1986. mass mkt. 3.99 (0-345-33712-3) Ballantine.

Random House Basic Dictionary: German. Ed. by Jenni K. Moulton. 1987. mass mkt. 3.50 (0-345-34600-9) Ballantine.

Random House Basic Dictionary: Italian. Robert A. Hall, Jr. 1986. mass mkt. 3.50 (0-345-34603-3) Ballantine.

Random House Basic Dictionary: Spanish. Ed. by Donald F. Sola. (SPA.). 1986. mass mkt. 3.99 (0-345-33711-5) Ballantine.

Random House Basic Dictionary: Synonyms & Antonyms. Ed. by Laurence Urdang. 1981. mass mkt. 3.50 (0-345-29712-1) Ballantine.

Random House Basic Speller-Divider. Jess Stein. 1981. mass mkt. 4.99 (0-345-29255-3) Ballantine.

Random House Biographical Dictionary. Random House Staff. 1992. 6.00 (0-679-41580-7, Random Ref) Random.

Random House Book of Bedtime Stories. Illus. by Jane Dyer. LC 94-2631. 160p. (J). (gr. 1 up). 1994. 19.00 (0-679-80832-9) Random.

Random House Book of Bulbs. Roger Phillips & Martyn E. Rix. LC 89-10361. 256p. 1989. pap. 27.50 (0-679-72756-6) McKay.

Random House Book of Contemporary Business Letters. Strategic Communications Staff. 1989. 19.95 (0-394-58170-9) Random.

***Random House Book of Dance Stories.** Robinson Publishing Staff. 1997. pap. 9.99 (0-679-88529-3) Random.

Random House Book of Easy-to-Read Stories. LC 92-40179. (Illus.). 256p. (J). (ps-3). 1993. 18.00 (0-679-83438-9) Random Bks Yng Read.

***Random House Book of Fantasy Stories.** (YA). (gr. 5 up). 1997. 9.99 (0-614-28926-2) Random Bks Yng Read.

Random House Book of Ghost Stories. Ed. by Susan Hill. LC 87-3818. (Illus.). 224p. (J). (gr. 3-7). 1991. 21.95 (0-679-81234-2); lib. bdg. 23.99 (0-679-91234-7) Random Bks Yng Read.

Random House Book of Herbs. Roger Phillips & Nicky Foy. (Illus.). 1990. pap. 27.50 (0-679-73213-6) Random.

***Random House Book of Horse Stories.** (YA). (gr. 5 up). 1997. 9.99 (0-614-28927-0) Random Bks Yng Read.

Random House Book of Horses & Horsemanship. Paula Rodenas. LC 86-42934. (Illus.). 192p. (J). (gr. 3-7). 1991. 24.99 (0-394-88705-0) Random Bks Yng Read.

Random House Book of How Things Work. Steve Parker. LC 90-9137. (Illus.). 160p. (Orig.). (J). (gr. 3-7). 1991. pap. 18.00 (0-679-80908-2); lib. bdg. 19.99 (0-679-90908-7) Random Bks Yng Read.

Random House Book of Humor for Children. Illus. by Paul O. Zelinsky. LC 86-31478. 320p. (J). (gr. 2-6). 1988. lib. bdg. 16.99 (0-394-98049-2) Random Bks Yng Read.

Random House Book of Jokes & Anecdotes. Joe Claro. 232p. 1990. pap. 6.95 (0-679-72820-1) Random.

Random House Book of Jokes & Anecdotes. large type ed. Joe Ciaro. 1994. 20.00 (0-679-75693-0) Random Hse Lrg Prnt.

Random House Book of Mortgage & Tax Savings Tables. Eric Kaplan. 1990. pap. 8.00 (0-679-73210-1) Random.

Random House Book of Mother Goose: A Treasury of 306 Timeless Nursery Rhymes. Illus. & Selected by Arnold Lobel. LC 86-47532. 176p. (J). (gr. 2-6). 1986. lib. bdg. 16.99 (0-394-96799-2) Random Bks Yng Read.

Random House Book of Mythology. Joan D. Vinge. 1998. 18.00 (0-679-82377-8); lib. bdg. 19.99 (0-679-92377-2) Random.

Random House Book of One Thousand One Questions & Answers about Animals. Michele Staple & Linda Gamlin. LC 90-30716. (Illus.). 160p. (Orig.). (J). (gr. 3-7). 1990. lib. bdg. 12.99 (0-679-90731-9) Random Bks Yng Read.

Random House Book of One Thousand One Questions & Answers about the Human Body. Trevor Day. LC 93-6386. 160p. (J). (gr. 4-7). 1994. pap. 15.00 (0-679-85432-0) Random Bks Yng Read.

Random House Book of One Thousand-One Wonders of Science. Brenda Williams & Brian Williams. LC 89-3954. (Illus.). 160p. (J). 1990. lib. bdg. 11.99 (0-679-90080-2) Random Bks Yng Read.

Random House Book of One Thousand-One Wonders of Science. Brenda Williams & Brian Williams. LC 89-3954. (Illus.). 160p. (J). 1990. pap. 13.00 (0-679-80080-8) Random Bks Yng Read.

Random House Book of Perennials, 2 vols. Roger Phillips & Martyn E. Rix. 1991. 25.00 (0-685-74390-X) Random.

Random House Book of Perennials Vol. 1: Early Perennials, 2 vols. Martyn E. Rix & Roger Phillips. 1992. Vol. I, Early Perennials. pap. 27.50 (0-679-73797-9) Random.

Random House Book of Perennials Vol. 2: Late Perennials. Roger Phillips & Martyn Rix. 1992. pap. 27.50 (0-679-73798-7) Random.

Random House Book of Poetry for Children. Jack Prelutsky. LC 81-85940. (Illus.). 248p. (J). (gr. 1-5). 1983. 19.00 (0-394-85010-6); lib. bdg. 19.99 (0-394-95010-0) Random Bks Yng Read.

***Random House Book of Science Fiction Stories.** (YA). (gr. 5 up). 1997. 9.99 (0-614-28928-9) Random Bks Yng Read.

Random House Book of Sports Stories. Ed. by L. M. Schulman. LC 89-12834. (Illus.). 256p. (J). (gr. 5 up). 1990. lib. bdg. 16.99 (0-394-92874-1) Random Bks Yng Read.

Random House Book of Stories from the Ballet. Illus. by Angela Barrett. LC 94-22640. 112p. (J). (gr. 3-7). 1995. 20.00 (0-679-87125-X); lib. bdg. 19.99 (0-679-97125-4) Random.

Random House Book of Twentieth Century French Poetry. Ed. by Paul Auster. LC 82-17342. 688p. 1984. pap. 26.00 (0-394-71748-1, Vin) Random.

Random House Book of Vegetables. Roger Phillips & Martyn E. Rix. LC 93-13857. 1994. pap. 25.00 (0-679-75024-X) Random.

Random House Book of 1001 Questions & Answers. Bridget Ardley & Neil Ardley. LC 88-23200. (Illus.). 176p. (Orig.). (J). (gr. 3-7). 1989. lib. bdg. 12.99 (0-394-99992-4) Random Bks Yng Read.

***Random House Club Crosswords, Vol. 2.** Mel Rosen. 1997. pap. 12.50 (0-8129-2892-X, Times Bks) Random.

***Random House Club Crosswords: 120 Crosswords Never Before in Book Form, Vol. 3.** Wordsquare Publishing Staff. 1998. pap. write for info. (0-8129-2969-1, Times Bks) Random.

Random House Club Crosswords Vol. 1: Sunday-Size Puzzles from America's Exclusive Clubs, Vol. 1. Ed. by Mel Rosen & Stanley Newman. 176p. 1996. pap. 12.50 (0-8129-2638-2, Times Bks) Random.

Random House College Dictionary. Ed. by Stuart B. Flexner. (Illus.). 1979. 21.27 (0-394-05433-4); 22.60 (0-394-05434-2) Random.

Random House College Dictionary. rev. ed. Random House College Dictionary Staff. 1975. 16.45 (0-394-43500-1); Thumb-indexed ed. 17.45 (0-394-43600-8); 16.95 (0-394-51192-1) Random.

Random House College Dictionary. rev. ed. Random House College Dictionary Staff. 1982. 14.95 (0-394-52762-3) Random.

Random House College Dictionary: Leather Edition. deluxe ed. (Illus.). 1600p. 1989. 50.00 (0-394-57350-1) Random.

Random House College Dictionary & the Random House Thesaurus, Set. 1985. Boxed set. boxed 34.90 (0-394-54210-X) Random.

Random House College Thesaurus. 812p. 1989. pap. 12.95 (0-679-72710-8) Random.

Random House College Thesaurus. Random House Thesaurus Staff. LC 84-4914. 812p. (C). 1992. 17.00 (0-679-41780-X) Random.

Random House Compact Unabridged Dictionary. 2256p. 1996. 50.00 (0-679-45026-2) Fodors Travel.

Random House Compact Unabridged Dictionary: Special Edition, with CD-ROM, Version 2.0 for Windows 95. LC 95-26318. 2256p. 1996. 64.95 incl. cd-rom (0-679-44991-4) Random.

Random House Compact World Atlas. John Bartholomew. 208p. 1992. pap. 12.00 (0-679-74330-8) Random.

***Random House Compact World Atlas.** 2nd ed. Random House Staff. 1997. pap. 15.95 (0-679-77712-1) Random.

Random House Concise Encyclopedia. 768p. 1995. pap. 18.00 (0-679-76454-2) Random.

***Random House Concise Encyclopedia.** Random House Staff. Date not set. pap. 5.99 (0-517-19233-0) Random Hse Value.

Random House Concise World Atlas. John Bartholomew. 1985. 9.95 (0-394-74007-6) Random.

Random House Crossword Puzzle Dictionary. 1988. 19.95 (0-394-53513-8) Random.

Random House Crossword Puzzle Dictionary. 1995. mass mkt. 5.99 (0-8041-1349-1) Ivy Books.

Random House Crossword Puzzle Dictionary. 1996. 12.99 (0-517-15008-5) Random Hse Value.

***Random House Crossword Puzzle Dictionary.** S. Elliott. 1997. write for info. (0-679-45856-5, Random Ref) Random.

Random House Crossword Puzzle Dictionary. 2nd ed. 1104p. 1994. 23.00 (0-679-43376-7) Knopf.

Random House Crostics, Vol. 1. Michael Ashley. 80p. 1996. pap. 8.50 (0-8129-2768-0, Times Bks) Random.

Random House Cryptic Crosswords, Vol. 1. Stanley Newman. 1994. pap. 11.00 (0-8129-6371-7, Times Bks) Random.

Random House Cryptic Crossword, Vol. 2. Stanley Newman. 1995. pap. 11.00 (0-8129-2562-9, Times Bks) Random.

Random House Cryptic Crosswords, Vol. 3. Stanley Newman. 80p. 1996. pap. 11.00 (0-8129-2770-2, Times Bks) Random.

***Random House Cryptic Crosswords, Vol. 4.** Stanley Newman. 1997. pap. 12.00 (0-8129-2784-2, Times Bks) Random.

***Random House Cryptic Crosswords, Vol. 5.** Stanley Newman. 1998. pap. write for info. (0-8129-2974-8, Times Bks) Random.

Random House Dictionary. 1088p. 1983. Red, with gold stamp. 12.95 (0-394-53440-9); Blue, with silver stamp. 12.95 (0-394-53441-7); Brown, with gold stamp. 12.95 (0-394-53442-5) Random.

Random House Dictionary. 2nd unabridged ed. Random House Staff. 1993. 100.00 (0-679-42441-5, Random Ref) Random.

Random House Dictionary: Concise Edition. Random House Staff. 1980. 2.38 (0-394-51200-6) Random.

Random House Dictionary for Writers & Readers. David Grambs. 1990. 11.00 (0-679-72860-0) Random.

Random House Dictionary of Abbreviations. 1995. pap. 5.99 (0-679-76434-8, Vin) Random.

Random House Dictionary of Business Terms. Jay N. Nisberg. 1992. 6.00 (0-679-41369-3, Random Ref) Random.

Random House Dictionary of Health & Medicine: The Random House Pocket Dictionaries & Guides. Random House Staff. 1992. 6.99 (0-679-41590-4, Random Ref) Random.

Random House Dictionary of Popular Proverbs & Sayings. Gregory Y. Titelman. 468p. 1996. 30.00 (0-679-44554-4) Random.

Random House Dictionary of the English Language. 1966. 59.95 (0-394-47176-8) Random.

Random House Dictionary of the English Language. unabridged ed. 2500p. 1987. 99.95 (0-394-56500-2) Random.

***Random House Editors Choice Crosswords.** Mel Rosen. 1997. pap. 9.00 (0-8129-2895-4, Times Bks) Random.

__Random House Encyclopedia.__ rev. ed. Ed. by James Mitchell. LC 83-9596. (Illus.). 2920p. 1983. 99.95 (0-394-52883-2) Random.

__Random House Encyclopedia.__ rev. ed. Random House Staff. (Illus.). 2912p. 1990. 129.95 (0-394-58450-3) Random.

__Random House Encyclopedia of World War II.__ Norman Polmar & Thomas B. Allen. 960p. 1996. pap. 20.00 (0-679-77039-9) Random.

*__Random House Encyclopedic Dictionary of Classical Music.__ Helicon. 1997. 45.00 (0-679-45851-4, Random Ref) Random.

__Random House English Language Desk Reference.__ Random House Reference Staff. 624p. (YA). 1995. 18.00 (0-679-43898-X) Random.

__Random House ESL Library: Interactions I - a Speaking Activities Book, Vol. 5.__ Deborah P. Keller & Emily A. Thrush. 1986. pap. text ed. write for info. (0-07-553805-9) McGraw.

*__Random House Essential French Dictionary.__ Ed. by Francesca L. Langbaum & Susan Husserl-Kapit. 1997. mass mkt. 3.99 (0-345-41079-3) Ballantine.

*__Random House Essential German Dictionary.__ Jenni K. Moulton. LC 96-35119. (ENG & GER.). 1997. write for info. (0-345-40809-8) Ballantine.

*__Random House Essential Italian Dictionary.__ Ed. by Robert A. Hall & Vieri Samek-Lodovici. 1997. mass mkt. 3.99 (0-345-41077-7) Ballantine.

*__Random House Essential Italian Dictionary.__ Robert A. Hall. LC 96-35118. (ITA.). 1997. pap. write for info. (0-345-40806-3) Ballantine.

*__Random House Essential Spanish Dictionary.__ Donald F. Sola. LC 96-35117. (SPA.). 1997. pap. write for info. (0-345-40807-1) Ballantine.

*__Random House Essential Spanish Dictionary.__ 2nd ed. Ed. by Donald F. Sola & David L. Gold. 1997. mass mkt. 3.99 (0-345-41078-5) Ballantine.

*__Random House French-English English-French Dictionary.__ Helene Gutman. 1997. mass mkt. 5.99 (0-345-41438-1) Ballantine.

__Random House Geographical Dictionary.__ Random House Staff. 1992. 7.00 (0-679-41570-X, Random Ref) Random.

__Random House German Dictionary: Vest Pocket Edition.__ 2nd ed. Jennifer Hornor. 368p. (GER.). 1996. pap. 6.99 (0-679-77195-6, Random Ref) Random.

__Random House German-English English-German Dictionary.__ 1996. 20.00 (0-679-44808-X) Random.

*__Random House German-English English-German Dictionary.__ Anne Dahl. 1997. mass mkt. 5.99 (0-345-41439-X) Ballantine.

*__Random House German-English, English-German Dictionary.__ Anne Dahl. 1998. pap. write for info. (0-375-70085-4, Random Ref) Random.

__Random House Guide to Business Writing.__ J. Forman. 1990. pap. text ed. 14.95 (0-07-037601-8) McGraw.

__Random House Guide to Good Writing.__ Random House & Mitchell Ivers. 1996. mass mkt. 4.99 (0-345-90992-5) Ballantine.

__Random House Guide to Good Writing.__ Mitchell Ivers. 256p. 1993. mass mkt. 4.99 (0-345-37996-9) Ballantine.

__Random House Guide to Grammar Usage & Punctuation.__ Laurie Rozakis. 1991. 6.99 (0-394-58920-3) Random.

__Random House Guide to Writing.__ 3rd ed. Sandra Schor & Judith Fishman. 464p. (C). 1986. pap. text ed. write for info. (0-07-554588-8) McGraw.

__Random House Handbook.__ 4th ed. Frederick Crews. 1992. text ed. write for info. (0-07-013636-X) McGraw.

__Random House Handbook.__ 4th ed. Hennessey. 1992. wbk. ed., pap. text ed. write for info. (0-07-013637-8) McGraw.

__Random House Handbook: Diagnostic Tests.__ 4th ed. Frederick Crews. Date not set. pap. text ed. write for info. (0-07-013643-2) McGraw.

__Random House Handbook of Business Terms.__ Jay N. Nisber. 352p. 1988. 14.95 (0-394-53047-0) Random.

__Random House Handy Crossword Book, No. 1.__ Ed. by Stanley Newman. 1995. mass mkt. 4.99 (0-8041-1322-X) Ivy Books.

__Random House Handy Crossword Book, Vol. 6.__ Stanley Newman. 1996. mass mkt. 4.99 (0-8041-1446-3) Ivy Books.

__Random House Handy Crossword Book No. 4.__ Ed. by Stanley Newman. 1995. mass mkt. 4.99 (0-8041-1394-7) Ivy Books.

__Random House Handy Crossword Book No. 5.__ Ed. by Stanley Newman. 1995. mass mkt. 4.99 (0-8041-1395-5) Ivy Books.

*__Random House Health & Medicine Dictionary.__ Random House Staff. 1997. pap. 7.99 (0-679-77709-1, Random Ref) Random.

*__Random House Historical Dictionary of American Slang, Vol. II, H-O.__ Jonathan E. Lighter. 1997. 75.00 (0-614-28230-6, Random Ref) Random.

__Random House International Encyclopedia of Golf.__ Malcolm Campbell. LC 91-52661. (Illus.). 336p. 1991. 60.00 (0-394-58893-2) Random.

__Random House Italian Dictionary: Vest Pocket Edition.__ 2nd ed. Vieri Samek-Lodavici. 336p. (ITA.). 1996. pap. 6.99 (0-679-77194-8, Random Ref) Random.

*__Random House Japanese Dictionary.__ Seigo Nakao. 1996. pap. write for info. (0-679-74668-4, Random Ref) Random.

__Random House Japanese Dictionary.__ Random House Staff. 1996. pap. 7.99 (0-679-77373-8) Random.

__Random House Japanese-English English-Japanese Dictionary.__ Seigo Nakao. 600p. (JPN.). 1995. 22.00 (0-679-44149-2, Random Ref) Random.

*__Random House Japanese-English English-Japanese Dictionary.__ Seigo Nakao. 1997. pap. 12.00 (0-679-78001-7, Random Ref) Random.

__Random House Japanese-English English-Japanese Dictionary.__ Seigo Nakao. (Orig.). 1996. mass mkt. 6.99 (0-345-40548-X) Ballantine.

__Random House Kid's Encyclopedia.__ rev. ed. Knowledge Adventure Staff. 1995. 35.00 (1-56997-215-X) Random.

__Random House Latin American Spanish Dictionary.__ David L. Gold. (Orig.). 1996. mass mkt. 5.99 (0-345-40546-3) Ballantine.

*__Random House Latin-American Spanish Dictionary.__ David L. Gold. 1998. pap. write for info. (0-375-70084-6, Random Ref) Random.

*__Random House Latin-American Spanish Dictionary: Spanish-English, English-Spanish.__ David L. Gold. LC 96-27274. (ENG & SPA.). 1997. 22.00 (0-679-45294-X) Random.

__Random House Legal Dictionary.__ James E. Clapp. 320p. 1996. pap. 6.99 (0-679-76435-6, Random Ref) Random.

__Random House Lexercise, Vol. 2.__ Stanley Newman. 64p. 1997. pap. 8.50 (0-8129-2765-6, Times Bks) Random.

__Random House Lexercise Vol. 1: Word Games to Build Your Mental Fitness.__ Stanley Newman. 64p. 1996. pap. 8.50 (0-8129-2702-8, Times Bks) Random.

__Random House Masterpiece, Vol. 3.__ Stanley Newman. 1996. pap. write for info. (0-8129-2802-4, Times Bks) Random.

*__Random House Masterpiece Crosswords.__ Stanley Newman. 1996. pap. 16.00 (0-8129-2785-0, Times Bks) Random.

__Random House Masterpiece Crosswords, Vol. 1.__ 1994. pap. 16.00 (0-8129-6373-3, Times Bks) Random.

__Random House Masterpiece Crosswords, Vol. 2.__ Stanley Newman. 1995. pap. 16.00 (0-8129-2619-6, Times Bks) Random.

__Random House New Spanish-English, English-Spanish Dictionary.__ Ed. by Margaret H. Raventos & David L. Gold. 650p. (ENG & SPA.). 1995. 18.00 (0-679-43897-1) Random.

__Random House Parent & Child Puzzles, Vol. 2.__ Helen Hovanec. 112p. 1996. pap. 12.00 (0-8129-2703-6, Times Bks) Random.

__Random House Parent & Child Puzzles Vol. 1.__ Helene Hovanec. 1995. pap. 12.00 (0-8129-2543-2, Times Bks) Random.

__Random House Parent & Child Trivia Book.__ Helene Hovanec. 1997. pap. 12.50 (0-8129-2778-8, Times Bks) Random.

__Random House Personal Computer Dictionary.__ Philip E. Margolis. 1991. pap. 10.00 (0-679-73480-5) Random.

*__Random House Personal Computer Dictionary.__ Philip E. Margolis. 1996. write for info. (0-679-77181-6) Random.

__Random House Personal Computer Dictionary.__ 2nd ed. Philip E. Margolis. 592p. 1996. pap. 15.00 (0-679-76424-0) Random.

__Random House Personal Computer Dictionary.__ 2nd ed. Philip E. Margolis. 560p. 1996. pap. 24.95 incl. disk (0-679-77036-4) Random.

__Random House Personal Investment Calculator.__ Fred Dahl. 396p. 1990. pap. 9.95 (0-679-72800-7) Random.

__Random House Power Vocabulary Builder.__ Random House. 1996. mass mkt. 5.99 (0-345-40545-5) Ballantine.

__Random House Pro Baseball Dictionary.__ Stephen Weinstein. 1994. pap. 7.00 (0-679-75074-6, Random Ref) Random.

__Random House Russian-English Dictionary.__ C. Butlar. (RUS.). 1997. 25.00 (0-679-44964-7, Random Ref) Random.

__Random House Russian-English Dictionary.__ S. Lubensky. (ENG & RUS.). 1997. pap. write for info. (0-679-77374-6, Random Ref) Random.

__Random House Russian-English Dictionary of Idioms.__ Sophia Lubensky. 1044p. 1995. 75.00 (0-679-40580-1) Random.

__Random House School Dictionary.__ Ed. by Stuart B. Flexner. (Illus.). 966p. 1983. 23.96 (0-676-39289-X) Random.

__Random House Spanish Dictionary.__ 2nd ed. Donald F. Sola. (Vest Pocket Ser.). (SPA.). 1995. pap. 5.99 (0-679-76431-3) Random.

__Random House Spanish-English English-Spanish Dictionary.__ Margaret H. Raventos & David L. Gold. 1996. mass mkt. 5.99 (0-345-40547-1) Ballantine.

*__Random House Spanish-English English-Spanish Dictionary.__ Margaret H. Raventos. LC 97-244. 1997. pap. 12.00 (0-679-78002-5, Random Ref) Random.

__Random House Spell Checker.__ Enid Pearsons. 1992. 6.99 (0-679-40520-8) Random.

__Random House Sunday Crossword Puzzles Vol. 1.__ Stanley Newman. 1995. pap. 8.50 (0-8129-2554-8, Times Bks) Random.

__Random House Sunday Crosswords, Vol. 2.__ Stanley Newman. 64p. 1996. pap. 8.50 (0-8129-2766-4, Times Bks) Random.

*__Random House Sunday Crosswords, Vol. 3.__ Stanley Newman. 1997. pap. 9.00 (0-8129-2914-4, Times Bks) Random.

__Random House Sunday MegaOmnibus, Vol. 1.__ Ed. by Will Weng. 368p. 1996. pap. 12.50 (0-8129-2708-7, Times Bks) Random.

*__Random House Sunday Megaomnibus, Vol. 2.__ Associated Press Staff. 1997. pap. 13.50 (0-8129-2908-X, Times Bks) Random.

__Random House Thesaurus.__ 2nd ed. Costello. 1995. pap. 5.99 (0-679-76429-1) Random.

__Random House Thesaurus of Slang.__ Esther Lewin. 446p. 1989. pap. 12.00 (0-679-72700-0) Random.

__Random House Timetables of History.__ Ed. by Random House Staff. 1991. pap. 6.00 (0-679-40293-4) Random.

__Random House Timetables of History.__ rev. ed. Random House Staff. 1993. 6.00 (0-679-42395-8, Random Ref) Random.

__Random House Timetables of History.__ 2nd rev. ed. R. Castello. 320p. 1996. pap. 6.99 (0-679-76960-9, Random Ref) Random.

__Random House Treasury of Best-Loved Poem.__ Louis Phillips. 1996. pap. write for info. (0-679-77703-2, Random Ref) Random.

__Random House Treasury of Best Loved Poems.__ Ed. by Louis Phillips. 1990. 10.00 (0-394-58688-3) Random.

__Random House Treasury of Best Loved Poems.__ 2nd ed. Louis Phillips. LC 95-14513. 352p. 1995. pap. 10.00 (0-679-76315-5, Random Ref) Random.

__Random House Treasury of Humorous Quotations.__ Ed. by Louis Phillips & William Cole. 1996. pap. 14.00 (0-679-77041-0) Random.

__Random House Treasury of Light Verse.__ Louis Phillips. 1995. pap. 10.00 (0-679-76316-3, Random Ref) Random.

__Random House Treasury of Light Verse.__ Louis Phillips. 1996. pap. write for info. (0-679-77704-0, Random Ref) Random.

__Random House Ultrahard Crosswords, Vol. 1.__ Stanley Newman. 1994. pap. 8.50 (0-8129-6372-5, Times Bks) Random.

__Random House Ultrahard Crosswords, Vol. 2.__ Stanley Newman. 1995. pap. 8.50 (0-8129-2482-7, Times Bks) Random.

__Random House Ultrahard Crosswords, Vol. 3.__ Ed. by Stanley Newman. 64p. 1996. pap. 8.50 (0-8129-2701-X, Times Bks) Random.

*__Random House Ultrahard Crosswords, Vol. 4.__ Stanley Newman. 1997. pap. 9.00 (0-8129-2783-4, Times Bks) Random.

__Random House Unabridged Dictionary.__ 2nd ed. 1995. 79.00 incl. cd-rom (0-679-44046-1) Random.

__Random House Unabridged Dictionary: Print & Electronic Versions.__ 2nd rev. ed. Random House Editorial Staff. (Illus.). 2550p. 1994. 100.00 (0-679-42917-4, Random Ref) Random.

__Random House Unabridged Dictionary: Print & Electronic Versions.__ 2nd rev. ed. Random House Editorial Staff. (Illus.). 2550p. 1994. CD-ROM version. pap. 79.00 (0-679-74979-9, Random Ref) Random.

__Random House Unabridged Dictionary Book.__ 2nd ed. Random House Staff. 1994. 100.00 incl. cd-rom (0-679-75748-1) Random.

__Random House Unabridged Dictionary ROM Update.__ write for info. (0-679-76174-8) Random.

*__Random House Webster's American Dictionary.__ Random House Staff. 1997. pap. 6.99 (0-375-70058-7, Random Ref) Random.

__Random House Webster's American Sign Dictionary, Concise Edition.__ Elaine Costello. 1102p. 1994. 50.00 (0-394-58580-1) Random.

*__Random House Webster's American Sign Dictionary, Concise Edition.__ Elaine Costello. LC 97-21538. 1997. pap. 20.00 (0-679-78011-4, Random Ref) Random.

*__Random House Webster's Biographical Dictionary of Scientists.__ Random House Publishing Staff. 1997. pap. 18.00 (0-375-70057-9, Random Ref) Random.

__Random House Webster's College Dictionary.__ 1992. 20.00 (0-685-56462-2) Random.

__Random House Webster's College Dictionary.__ LC 94-29143. 1616p. 1995. 23.95 (0-679-43886-6) Random.

__Random House Webster's College Dictionary.__ Random House Editors. 1993. 30.00 (0-679-42915-8, Random Ref) Random.

__Random House Webster's College Dictionary.__ Random House Staff. 1995. 23.95 (0-676-50207-5, Random Ref) Random.

__Random House Webster's College Dictionary.__ deluxe ed. Random House Staff. 1991. 25.00 (0-679-40130-X) Random.

__Random House Webster's College Dictionary.__ rev. ed. Random House Editorial Staff. 1995. 23.95 (0-676-50205-9, Random Ref) Random.

*__Random House Webster's College Dictionary.__ 2nd deluxe ed. Random House Staff. LC 97-903. 1997. 30.00 (0-679-45858-1) Random.

*__Random House Websters College Dictionary, No. 12.__ 2nd ed. Dictionary Staff. 1997. write for info. (0-676-52705-1, Random Ref) Random.

__Random House Webster's College Dictionary & Random House College Thesaurus Desk Set.__ Random House Staff. 1992. 37.00 (0-679-41700-1, Random Ref) Random.

*__Random House Webster's College Dictionary & Thesaurus Set.__ 1996. 40.00 (0-679-45617-1, Random Ref) Random.

__Random House Webster's College GBD.__ Random House Staff. 1995. 23.95 (0-676-50483-3, Random Ref) Random.

__Random House Webster's College Thesaurus.__ 1996. 18.00 (0-679-45280-X); pap. 12.95 (0-679-77375-4) Random.

*__Random House Webster's College Thesaurus.__ Random House Staff. 1997. 20.00 (0-375-40066-4, Random Ref) Random.

__Random House Webster's Collegiate Dictionary.__ 96th ed. 1996. 22.95 (0-679-44993-0) Fodors Travel.

*__Random House Webster's Compact Dictionary.__ Random House Staff. LC 96-47193. 1997. 40.00 (0-679-45810-7, Random Ref) Random.

*__Random House Webster's Concise Dictionary.__ 1997. 9.95 (0-679-45811-5, Random Ref) Random.

*__Random House Webster's Concise Dictionary.__ 1997. write for info. (0-679-45855-7, Random Ref) Random.

*__Random House Webster's Concise Dictionary.__ Random House Staff. 1996. text ed. write for info. (0-07-052199-9) McGraw.

__Random House Webster's Concise Dictionary: For Windows.__ Electronic Publishing Staff. 1995. 4.95 (0-679-76003-2) Random.

__Random House Webster's Dictionary.__ Ed. by Sol Steinmetz. 1993. mass mkt. 5.99 (0-345-38337-0) Ballantine.

*__Random House Webster's Dictionary.__ large type ed. Random House Staff. 1997. pap. 26.00 (0-679-77710-5) Random.

*__Random House Webster's Dictionary.__ 2nd unabridged ed. Random House, Incorporated Staff. LC 97-17702. 1997. 75.00 incl. cd-rom (0-679-45853-0, Random Ref); 50.00 (0-679-45854-9, Random Ref) Random.

__Random House Webster's Dictionary of American English.__ 800p. 1996. pap. 16.95 (0-679-76425-9) Random.

__Random House Webster's Dictionary, Random House Thesaurus, Random House Basic Dictionary.__ Ballantine Staff. 1994. pap. 299.40 (0-345-38988-3) Ballantine.

*__Random House Webster's Dictionary/Roget's Thesaurus/Word Menu/Spell Checker & Abbreviations.__ Random House Staff. 1997. mass mkt. 269.52 (0-345-41486-1) Ballantine.

*__Random House Webster's English Language Desk Reference.__ Random House Staff. 1997. pap. 14.95 (0-679-78000-9, Random Ref) Random.

*__Random House Webster's French-English, English-French Dictionary.__ Random House Staff. LC 97-245. 1997. 22.00 (0-679-44851-9, Random Ref) Random.

*__Random House Webster's Medical Dictionary.__ 1997. mass mkt. write for info. (0-345-41442-X) Ballantine.

*__Random House Webster's Pocket Business Dictionary.__ 2nd ed. Random House, Incorporated Staff. 1997. pap. 6.99 (0-375-70059-5, Random Ref) Random.

*__Random House Webster's School & Office Dictionary.__ Random House, Incorporated Staff. 1998. pap. 11.95 (0-679-78008-4, Random Ref) Random.

*__Random House Webster's School & Office Dictionary.__ Random House Staff. 1996. pap. text ed. write for info. (0-07-052547-1) McGraw.

__Random House Webster's School & Office Dictionary.__ Random House Staff. 1993. pap. 8.00 (0-679-74420-7, Random Ref) Random.

__Random House Webster's School & Office Dictionary.__ rev. ed. Random House Editorial Staff. 576p. 1995. pap. 10.95 (0-679-76158-6, Random Ref) Random.

__Random House Webster's School & Office Thesaurus.__ Random House Editorial Staff. 624p. 1995. pap. 10.95 (0-679-76157-8, Random Ref) Random.

*__Random House Webster's School & Office Thesaurus.__ Random House, Incorporated. 1998. pap. 11.95 (0-679-78009-2, Random Ref) Random.

*__Random House Webster's Spell Checker & Abbreviations Dictionary.__ Dictionary Staff. 1997. mass mkt. 4.99 (0-345-41440-3) Ballantine.

*__Random House Webster's Word Menu.__ 1997. mass mkt. 5.99 (0-345-41441-1) Ballantine.

__Random House Word Menu.__ 2nd ed. Stephen Glazier. 1040p. 1996. 35.00 (0-679-44963-9) Random.

__Random House 10,000 Dollar Crossword Challenge.__ Stanley Newman. 1996. pap. 14.00 (0-8129-2772-9, Times Bks) Random.

__Random House's Jokes & Anecdotes.__ 2nd ed. Joe Claro. 272p. 1996. pap. 8.00 (0-679-76971-4) Random.

__Random Island.__ large type ed. Alex Stuart. 384p. 1985. 25.99 (0-7089-1317-2) Ulverscroft.

*__Random Iteractive Models.__ M. Duflo. LC 96-45470. (Applications of Mathematics Ser.: Vol. 34). (Illus.). 386p. 1997. 89.00 (3-540-57100-0) Spr-Verlag.

__Random Kindness & Senseless Acts of Beauty.__ Anne Herbert & Margaret M. Pavel. LC 93-21606. (Illus.). 36p. 1993. 14.95 (0-912078-89-8, Kazan Bks) Volcano Pr.

__Random Knotting & Linking.__ K. C. Millett. (Series on Knots & Everything). 208p. 1994. text ed. 48.00 (981-02-2005-7) World Scientific Pub.

__Random Lengths Buyers' & Sellers' Guide, 1987: A Directory of the Forest Products Industry.__ Ed. by David R. Bartel. 655p. 1987. 130.00 (0-9614042-1-3) Random Lgths Pubns.

__Random Lengths Buyers' & Sellers' Guide, 1988: A Directory of the Forest Products Industry.__ Ed. by David R. Bartel. 767p. 1988. 130.00 (0-9614042-2-1) Random Lgths Pubns.

__Random Lengths Buyers' & Sellers' Guide, 1989: A Directory of the Forest Products Industry.__ Ed. by David R. Bartel. 880p. 1989. 130.00 (0-9614042-3-X) Random Lgths Pubns.

__Random Lengths Buyers' & Sellers' Guide, 1990: A Directory of the Forest Products Industry.__ 928p. 1990. 140.00 (0-9614042-4-8) Random Lgths Pubns.

__Random Lengths Buyers' & Sellers' Guide, 1991: A Directory of the Forest Products Industry.__ 940p. 1991. 145.00 (0-9614042-5-6) Random Lgths Pubns.

__Random Lengths Buyers' & Sellers' Guide, 1992: A Directory of the Forest Products Industry.__ Ed. by Jon P. Anderson. 972p. 1992. 145.00 (0-9614042-6-4) Random Lgths Pubns.

__Random Lengths Buyers' & Sellers' Guide, 1993: A Directory of the Forest Products Industry.__ Ed. by Jon P. Anderson. 992p. 1993. 150.00 (0-9614042-7-2) Random Lgths Pubns.

__Random Lengths Buyers' & Sellers' Guide, 1994: A Directory of the Forest Products Industry.__ Ed. by Jon P. Anderson. 1036p. 1994. 160.00 (0-9614042-9-9) Random Lgths Pubns.

__Random Linear Operators.__ A. V. Skorohod. 1983. lib. bdg. 135.00 (90-277-1669-2) Kluwer Ac.

__Random Magnetism, High TC Superconductivity.__ W. Beyermann. 276p. 1994. text ed. 86.00 (981-02-1786-2) World Scientific Pub.

__Random Mappings.__ V. F. Kolchin. Ed. by A. V. Balakrishnan. LC 86-9316. (Translations Series in Mathematics & Engineering). 224p. 1986. text ed. 88.00 (0-911575-16-2) Optimization Soft.

Random Mappings. V. F. Kolchin. xiv, 207p. 1986. 159.95 (*0-387-96154-2*) Spr-Verlag.

Random Matrices. 2nd enl. rev. ed. Madan L. Mehta. 562p. 1990. text ed. 105.00 (*0-12-488051-7*) Acad Pr.

Random Matrices & Their Applications. Ed. by J. Cohen et al. LC 85-30842. (Contemporary Mathematics Ser.: Vol. 50). 358p. 1986. reprint ed. pap. text ed. 43.00 (*0-8218-5044-X*, CONM/50) Am Math.

Random Measures. McConnell. (Quantum Leap Ser.). 1995. mass mkt. 5.99 (*1-57297-095-2*) Blvd Books.

Random Media & Boundaries: Unified Theory, Two-Scale Method, & Applications. Koichi Furutsu. LC 92-23248. (Wave Phenomena Ser.: Vol. 13). 1993. write for info. (*3-540-55688-5*); 108.95 (*0-387-55688-5*) Spr-Verlag.

Random Noise Techniques in Nuclear Reactor Systems. Robert E. Uhrig. LC 71-110558. (Illus.). 502p. reprint ed. pap. 143.10 (*0-317-08879-3*, 2012436) Bks Demand.

Random, Non-Random, & Periodic Faulting in Crystals. M. T. Sebastian & P. Krishna. LC 93-27315. 426p. 1994. text ed. 130.00 (*2-88124-925-6*) Gordon & Breach.

Random Notes of Early Settlers of Brunswick-Topsham (ME) 24p. 1986. reprint ed. pap. 3.50 (*0-935207-31-7*) Danbury Hse Bks.

Random Notes on Red China, Nineteen Thirty-Six to Nineteen Forty-Five. Edgar R. Snow. LC 58-146. (East Asian Monographs: No. 5). 154p. (C). 1957. pap. 11.00 (*0-674-74900-6*) HUP.

Random Number Generation & Quasi-Monte Carlo Methods. Harald Niederreiter. LC 92-12567. (CBMS-NSF Regional Conference Ser.: No. 63). vi, 241p. 1992. pap. 39.75 (*0-89871-295-5*) Soc Indus-Appl Math.

***Random Packings & Packed Towers: Design & Applications.** Ralph F. Strigle. (Illus.). 296p. pap. 84.40 (*0-608-04974-3*, 2065554) Bks Demand.

Random Partial Differential Equations: Proceedings of the Conference Held at the Mathematical Research Institute at Oberwolfach, Black Forest, November 19-25, 1989. Ed. by U. Hornung et al. (International Series of Numerical Mathematics: Vol. 102). 168p. 1991. 73.00 (*0-8176-2688-3*) Birkhauser.

Random Permanents. Y. V. Borovskikh & Vladimir S. Korolyuk. 202p. 1994. 147.50 (*90-6764-184-7*, Pub. by VSP NE) Coronet Bks.

Random Perturbations of Dynamical Systems. M. I. Freidlin & Alexander D. Wentzell. (Grundlehren der Mathematischen Wissenschaften Ser.: Bd. 260). (Illus.). 340p. 1983. 144.95 (*0-387-90858-7*) Spr-Verlag.

Random Perturbations of Hamiltonian Systems. Mark I. Friedlin & Alexander D. Wentzell. LC 94-4147. (Memoirs of the American Mathematical Society Ser.: Vol. 523). 1994. pap. 31.00 (*0-8218-2586-0*, MEMO/109/523) Am Math.

Random Pieces: Vignettes from the Thirties. Elizabeth Larrabee. 96p. 1993. pap. 8.95 (*0-9636690-0-1*) Withee Pub.

Random Point Processes in Time & Space. 2nd ed. D. L. Snyder & M. I. Miller. (Texts in Electrical Engineering Ser.). (Illus.). 496p. 1995. 65.95 (*0-387-97577-2*) Spr-Verlag.

Random Processes. Murray Rosenblatt. LC 74-10956. (Graduate Texts in Mathematics Ser.: Vol. 17). (Illus.). 225p. 1974. 49.00 (*0-387-90085-3*) Spr-Verlag.

Random Processes: Measurement Analysis & Simulation. J. Cacko. (Fundamental Studies in Engineering: Vol. 8). 1987. 152.50 (*0-444-98942-0*) Elsevier.

Random Processes for Classical Equations of Mathematical Physics. S. M. Ermakov et al. (C). 1989. lib. bdg. 171.50 (*0-7923-0036-X*) Kluwer Ac.

Random Processes in Mechanical Sciences. CISM (International Center for Mechanical Sciences), Department of Automation & Inforamation Staff. Ed. by H. Parkus. (CISM Publications: No. 9). (Illus.). vi, 169p. 1973. 35.95 (*0-387-81086-2*) Spr-Verlag.

Random Processes with Independent Increments. A. V. Skorohod. (C). 1991. lib. bdg. 153.50 (*0-7923-0340-7*) Kluwer Ac.

Random Pulse Streams & Their Applications. Andrzej Dziech. Tr. by Andrzej Pach & Ireneusz Smolewski from POL. LC 92-33014. (Studies in Electrical & Electronic Engineering: Vol. 44). 1993. 137.50 (*0-444-98661-8*) Elsevier.

Random Ransom. Stephen R. Sulik & Lillian M. Mack. 246p. 1991. pap. 5.99 (*0-9630703-0-4*) D H White.

Random Recollections of an Anachronism. Keyes D. Metcalf. 401p. 1980. 35.00 (*0-918414-02-4*) Readex Bks.

Random Recollections of Early Days in Mississippi. H. S. Fulkerson. 1972. 15.00 (*0-87511-597-7*) Claitors.

Random Reminiscences of Men & Events. John D. Rockefeller. (Illus.). 124p. 1984. 12.95 (*0-912882-58-1*) Sleepy Hollow.

Random Reminiscences of Men & Events. John D. Rockefeller. LC 73-2533. (Big Business; Economic Power in a Free Society Ser.). 1979. reprint ed. 22.95 (*0-405-05111-5*) Ayer.

Random Search Algorithms: Their Development & Application in the U. S. S. R. George Tarasenko. Ed. by Rebecca Kraft. (Illus.). 159p. (Orig.). 1986. pap. text ed. 75.00 (*1-55831-049-5*) Delphic Associates.

Random Seas & Design of Maritime Structures. Yoshimi Goda. LC 85-174535. 333p. 1985. reprint ed. pap. 95.00 (*0-608-01203-3*, 2061892) Bks Demand.

Random Series & Stochastic Integrals: Single & Multiple. S. Kwapie & Wojbor Woyczyski. (Probability & Its Applications Ser.). xvi, 630p. 1992. 86.50 (*0-8176-3572-6*) Birkhauser.

Random Shots. Charles H. Clark. LC 70-164557. (American Fiction Reprint Ser.). 1977. reprint ed. 26.95 (*0-8369-7033-0*) Ayer.

Random Shots: Episodes in the Life of a Weapons Developer. Roy E. Rayle. (Military History Monograph). 136p. 1995. pap. 10.00 (*1-57638-039-4*) Merriam Pr.

Random Signal Analysis: Self Study Course Package. Carl Looney. (Illus.). 1989. student ed. 498.00 incl. disk (*0-87942-460-5*, HL0401-0) Inst Electrical.

Random Signal Analysis in Engineering Systems. John J. Komo. 302p. 1987. text ed. 78.00 (*0-12-418660-2*) Acad Pr.

Random Signal Processing. Dwight F. Mix. LC 94-15146. 608p. (C). 1995. text ed. 86.67 (*0-02-381852-2*, Macmillan Coll) P-H.

Random Signals: Detection Estimation & Data Analysis. Sam K. Shanmugan & Arthur M. Breipohl. LC 87-37273. 664p. 1988. Net. text ed. 61.00 (*0-471-81555-1*) Wiley.

Random Signals & Systems. Richard E. Mortensen. LC 86-19007. (Illus.). 246p. reprint ed. pap. 70.40 (*0-7837-3528-6*, 2057864) Bks Demand.

Random Signals Estimation & Identification: Analysis & Applications. Nirode C. Mohanty. 640p. 1986. text ed. 89.95 (*0-442-26396-1*) Van Nos Reinhold.

Random Stories. James Laughlin. 220p. 1990. pap. 9.95 (*1-55921-021-4*) Moyer Bell.

Random Summation: Limit Theorems & Applications. Boris V. Gnedenko & Victor Y. Korolev. LC 96-33765. 288p. 1996. 79.95 (*0-8493-2875-6*) CRC Pr.

Random Sums & Branching Stochastic Processes. Ibrahim Rahimov. LC 95-2595. (Lecture Notes in Statistics Ser.: Vol. 96). 1995. 43.95 (*0-387-94446-X*) Spr-Verlag.

Random Surfaces & Quantum Gravity. Ed. by O. Alvarez et al. (NATO ASI Series B, Physics: Vol. 262). (Illus.). 406p. 1991. 120.00 (*0-306-43939-5*, Plenum Pr) Plenum.

Random Talks with the Living Christ. Francis L. L'Estrange. 107p. 1988. 30.00 (*0-7223-2038-8*, Pub. by A H S Ltd UK) St Mut.

Random Test Generator for Anatomy & Physiology: Circulatory System. William C. Kleinelp, Jr. Ed. by Mary Collins. (C). 1990. 5.75 (*0-929941-07-1*) Wood River Pubns.

Random Test Generator for Anatomy & Physiology: Endocrine System. William C. Kleinelp, Jr. Ed. by Mary Collins. (C). 1990. 5.75 (*0-929941-08-X*) Wood River Pubns.

Random Test Generator for Anatomy & Physiology: Nervous System. William C. Kleinelp, Jr. Ed. by Mary Collins. (C). 1990. 5.75 (*0-929941-06-3*) Wood River Pubns.

Random Test Generator for Anatomy & Physiology: Skeletal System. William C. Kleinelp, Jr. Ed. by Mary Collins. (C). 1990. 5.75 (*0-929941-04-7*) Wood River Pubns.

Random Test Generator for Anatomy & Physiology: The Cell. William C. Kleinelp, Jr. Ed. by Mary Collins. (C). 1990. 5.75 (*0-929941-05-5*) Wood River Pubns.

Random Thoughts. Muriel R. Kulwin. 50p. 1996. pap. 10.00 (*1-889080-08-X*) Doublem Bks.

Random Thoughts: The Humanity of Teaching. Louis Schmier. 268p. 1995. 27.95 (*0-912150-43-2*) Magna Pubns.

***Random Thoughts No. II: Teaching from the Heart.** Louis Schmier. LC 96-49830. 200p. (Orig.). 1996. pap. text ed. 27.95 (*0-912150-45-9*) Magna Pubns.

Random Thoughts from the Cosmos. Klint of Denmark. Ed. & Intro. by Clinton E. Slauer. 512p. 1996. spiral bd. 13.95 (*0-9649749-3-2*); per. 11.95 (*0-9649749-4-0*) Cosmic Cnnection.

***Random Thoughts on Business & Life & Lots of Stuff.** Peter Horst. (Illus.). x, 335p. 1996. pap. write for info. (*0-9653427-0-0*) Acosta-Biggs.

Random Vibration -- Status & Recent Developments: The Stephen Harry Crandall Festschrift. Ed. by I. Elishakoff & R. H. Lyon. (Studies in Applied Mechanics: No. 14). 564p. 1986. 403.25 (*0-444-42665-5*) Elsevier.

Random Vibration & Reliability of Composite Structures. Jacob Aboudi et al. LC 91-67572. 200p. 1992. pap. text ed. 59.95 (*0-87762-865-3*) Technomic.

Random Vibration & Spectral Analysis. Andre Preumont. (Solid Mechanics & Its Applications Ser.). 288p. (C). 1994. lib. bdg. 137.50 (*0-7923-3036-6*) Kluwer Ac.

***Random Vibration & Statistical Linearization.** John B. Roberts & P. D. Spanos. LC 89-24807. (Illus.). 421p. reprint ed. pap. 120.00 (*0-608-05305-8*, 2065843) Bks Demand.

Random Vibration in Perspective. Wayne Tustin et al. LC 84-80801. (Illus.). 208p. 1984. text ed. 100.00 (*0-918247-00-4*) Tustin Tech.

Random Vibration of Structures. C. Y. Yang. 295p. 1986. text ed. 80.95 (*0-471-80262-X*) Wiley.

Random Vibrations: Theory & Practice. Paul H. Wirsching et al. LC 95-32229. 480p. 1995. text ed. 74.95 (*0-471-58579-3*) Wiley.

Random Vibrations & Reliability. K. Henning. 368p. (C). 1983. 220.00 (*0-685-46644-2*, Pub. by Collets) St Mut.

Random Walk. 6th ed. Burton G. Malkiel. 528p. 1996. pap. 15.95 (*0-393-31529-0*) Norton.

Random Walk & Beyond: An Inside Guide to the Stock Market. Mark A. Johnson. 245p. 1988. text ed. 22.95 (*0-471-63223-6*) Wiley.

Random Walk down Wall Street: Including a Life-Cycle Guide to Personal Investing. 6th ed. Burton G. Malkiel. LC 95-8148. 1995. 27.50 (*0-393-03888-2*) Norton.

Random Walk down Wall Street: Updated for the 1990s Investor. 5th ed. Burton G. Malkiel. 409p. (C). 1991. pap. 14.95 (*0-393-95961-9*) Norton.

Random Walk in Random & Non-Random Environments. P. Revesz. 348p. (C). 1990. text ed. 48.00 (*981-02-0237-7*) World Scientific Pub.

Random Walk in Science. R. L. Weber. (Illus.). 206p. 1973. 36.00 (*0-85498-027-X*) IOP Pub.

Random Walk Through Fractal Dimensions. 2nd ed. Brian H. Kaye. LC 94-13337. 1994. pap. 45.00 (*1-56081-818-2*, VCH) Wiley.

Random Walks & Electric Networks. Peter G. Doyle & J. Laurie Snell. LC 84-61495. 159p. 1984. 28.95 (*0-88385-024-9*, CAM-22) Math Assn.

Random Walks & Random Environments Vol. 1: Random Walks. B. D. Hughes. (Illus.). 656p. 1995. 95.00 (*0-19-853788-3*) OUP.

Random Walks & Random Environments Vol. 2: Random Environments. Barry D. Hughes. (Illus.). 552p. 1996. 115.00 (*0-19-853789-1*) OUP.

Random Walks & Their Applications in the Physical & Biological Sciences: NBS-La Jolla Institute - 1982. Ed. by Michael F. Shlesinger & Bruce J. West. LC 84-7028. (AIP Conference Proceedings Ser.: No. 109). 243p. 1984. lib. bdg. 38.75 (*0-88318-308-0*) Am Inst Physics.

Random Walks, Brownian Motion & Interacting Particle Systems. Ed. by R. Durrett & Harry Kesten. (Progress in Probability Ser.: Vol. 28). xii, 472p. 1991. 80.50 (*0-8176-3509-2*) Birkhauser.

Random Walks, Critical Phenomena, & Triviality in Quantum Field Theory. R. Fernandez et al. Ed. by W. Beiglbock et al. (Texts & Monographs in Physics). (Illus.). xvii, 444p. (C). 1992. 91.95 (*0-387-54358-9*) Spr-Verlag.

Random Walks in Biology. rev. ed. Howard C. Berg. LC 93-12708. 190p. (C). 1983. pap. text ed. 16.95 (*0-691-00064-6*) Princeton U Pr.

Random Walks of Infinitely Many Particles. Pal Revesz. 220p. 1994. text ed. 58.00 (*981-02-1784-6*) World Scientific Pub.

Random Walks on Boundary for Solving PDE's. N. A. Simonov & K. K. Sabelfeld. 146p. 1994. 129.50 (*90-6764-183-9*, Pub. by VSP NE) Coronet Bks.

Random Waves in Nonlinear Dispersive Media. F. K. Abdullaev. 250p. 1998. text ed. 48.00 (*981-02-2347-1*) World Scientific Pub.

Random Winds. Belva Plain. 528p. 1987. mass mkt. 6.99 (*0-440-17562-3*) Dell.

Random Winds. large type ed. Belva Plain. LC 92-38593. (General Ser.). 816p. 1993. 20.95 (*0-8161-5684-0*) G K Hall.

***Randomised Controlled Clinical Trials.** 2nd ed. Christopher J. Bulpitt. LC 96-41439. 448p. (C). 1996. lib. bdg. 170.00 (*0-7923-4257-7*) Kluwer Ac.

***Randomization Bootstrap & Monte Carlo Methods in Biology.** 2nd ed. B. Manly. 356p. 1997. 64.95 (*0-412-72130-9*) Chapman & Hall.

Randomization, Bootstrap & Monte Carlo Methods in Biology. 2nd rev. ed. Bryan Manly. (Texts in Statistical Science Ser.). 356p. (C). (gr. 13). 1997. 64.95 (*0-412-36710-6*, A5017) Chapman & Hall.

Randomization Tests. 3rd ed. Eugene S. Edgington. LC 95-21003. (Statistics: Textbooks & Monographs: Vol. 147). 440p. 1995. 69.75 (*0-8247-9669-1*) Dekker.

Randomization Tests. Eugene S. Edgington. LC 79-28105. (Statistics, Textbooks & Monographs: No. 31). 305p. reprint ed. pap. 87.00 (*0-8357-3512-5*, 2034528) Bks Demand.

Randomized Algorithms. Rajeev Motwani & Prabhakar Raghavan. 500p. (C). 1995. text ed. 44.95 (*0-521-47465-5*) Cambridge U Pr.

Randomized Clinical Trial & Therapeutic Decisions. Niels Tygstrup et al. (Statistics: Textbooks & Monographs: Vol. 43). 320p. 1982. 125.00 (*0-8247-1856-9*) Dekker.

***Randomized Experiments for Planning & Evaluation: A Practical Guide.** Robert F. Boruch. LC 96-25315. (Applied Social Research Methods Ser.: Vol. 44). 248p. 1996. 46.00 (*0-8039-3509-9*); pap. 21.95 (*0-8039-3510-2*) Sage.

Randomized Response. James A. Fox. (Quantitative Applications in the Social Sciences Ser.: Vol. 58). 96p. (Orig.). (C). 1986. pap. text ed. 9.95 (*0-8039-2309-0*) Sage.

Randomized Response: Theory & Techniques. Chaudhuri & Mukerjee. (Statistics: Textbooks & Monographs: Vol. 85). 192p. 1987. 115.00 (*0-8247-7785-9*) Dekker.

Randomized Signal Processing. Ivars Bilinskis & Arnolds Mikelsons. 300p. 1992. text ed. 36.00 (*0-13-751074-8*) P-H.

Randomized Trials in Cancer: A Critical Review by Sites. fac. ed. Ed. by Maurice J. Staquet. LC 77-17753. (Monograph Series of the European Organization for Research on Treatment of Cancer: No. 41). 208p. pap. 59.30 (*0-7837-7443-5*, 2046977) Bks Demand.

***Randomized Trials in Cancer: A Critical Review by Sites.** Ed. by Maurice L. Slevin & Maurice J. Staquet. LC 86-15607. (Monograph Series of the European Organization for Research on Treatment of Cancer: Vol. 15). 715p. 1986. reprint ed. pap. 180.00 (*0-608-03451-7*, 2064152) Bks Demand.

Randomn Perturbations of Dynamical Systems. Yuri Kifer. (Progress in Probability & Statistics Ser.: No. 16). 304p. 1988. 64.00 (*0-8176-3384-7*) Birkhauser.

Randomness & Undecidability in Physics. Karl Svozil. LC 92-19665. 250p. (C). 1993. text ed. 48.00 (*981-02-0809-X*) World Scientific Pub.

Randox Education Guide to Colleges Seeking Students, 1997 Edition. 26th rev. ed. Stephen E. Marshall. 128p. (Orig.). 1997. pap. 19.95 (*0-914880-27-6*, 27R) Educ Guide.

Randstaad, Holland. Jan Van Wessep et al. (World Cities Ser.). 224p. 1996. text ed. 65.00 (*0-471-94992-2*) Wiley.

Randstad. Gejl & Dieleman. 1992. lib. bdg. 106.00 (*0-7923-1649-5*) Kluwer Ac.

Randstad Holland. Jan Van Wessep et al. (World Cities Ser.). 224p. 1995. text ed. 49.95 (*0-470-22026-0*) Halsted Pr.

Randy. John LaCrosse. 224p. 1980. 10.95 (*0-932282-47-4*) Caledonia Pr.

Randy Bachman Collection. 112p. 1995. otabind 22.95 (*0-7935-3288-4*, 00694918) H Leonard.

Randy Brecker. 72p. 1994. otabind 14.95 (*0-7935-2795-3*, 00673234) H Leonard.

Randy Coven - Funk Me Tender: Play-It-Like-It-Is-Bass. pap. 14.95 (*0-89524-619-8*) Cherry Lane.

Randy Hayes: Women & Men, August 13-September 13, 1987. Charles M. Lovell. (Illus.). 11p. (Orig.). 1987. pap. 1.00 (*0-924335-03-3*) Tacoma Art Mus.

***Randy Johnson.** Mark Stewart. LC 96-40433. (Grolier All-Pro Biographies Ser.). (J). 1997. write for info. (*0-516-20490-4*) Childrens.

Randy of the River. Horatio Alger, Jr. (Works of Horatio Alger Jr.). 1989. reprint ed. lib. bdg. 79.00 (*0-685-27571-X*) Rprt Serv.

Randy Rhoads: Guitar - Vocal. (Illus.). 95p. (Orig.). 1990. pap. text ed. 19.95 (*0-89524-337-7*) Cherry Lane.

Randy Roy Persnazznur. David B. Creps. LC 80-51270. (Orig.). 1980. pap. 4.95 (*0-930830-32-6*) Great Basin.

Randy Travis. Don Cusic. 1990. pap. 8.95 (*0-312-04412-7*) St Martin.

***Randy Travis - An Old Time Christmas.** Ed. by Carol Cuellar. 44p. (Orig.). (C). 1990. pap. text ed. 14.95 (*0-7692-0858-4*, VF1659) Warner Brothers.

***Randy Travis - Anthology.** Ed. by Carol Cuellar. 212p. (Orig.). (C). 1994. pap. text ed. 19.95 (*0-89724-308-0*, VF2140) Warner Brothers.

***Randy Travis - Full Circle.** Ed. by Sy Feldman. 60p. (Orig.). (C). 1996. pap. text ed. 16.95 (*1-57623-617-X*, PF9639) Warner Brothers.

***Randy Travis - Greatest Hits.** Ed. by Carol Cuellar. 56p. (Orig.). (C). 1992. pap. text ed. 16.95 (*0-7692-0881-9*, VF1893) Warner Brothers.

***Randy Travis - Greatest Hits, Vol. 2.** Ed. by Carol Cuellar. 60p. (Orig.). (C). 1992. pap. text ed. 16.95 (*0-7692-0871-1*, VF1894) Warner Brothers.

***Randy Travis - Heroes & Friends.** Ed. by Carol Cuellar. 62p. (Orig.). (C). 1991. pap. text ed. 14.95 (*0-7692-0876-2*, VF1689) Warner Brothers.

***Randy Travis - This Is Me.** Ed. by Carol Cuellar. 52p. (Orig.). (C). 1994. pap. text ed. 16.95 (*0-89724-331-5*, VF2148) Warner Brothers.

Randy Travis' Favorite Recipes. Ed. by Hatcher Corporation Staff. 136p. 1989. write for info. (*0-934474-52-4*) Cookbook Pubs.

Randy Wakeman Presents. Randal P. Wakeman. (Illus.). 153p. (C). 1990. 35.00 (*0-9625587-0-2*) R P Wakeman.

Randy's Dandy Lions. Bill Peet. (Illus.). (J). (gr. k-3). 1979. pap. 5.95 (*0-395-27498-2*) HM.

Randy's Dandy Lions. Bill Peet. (Illus.). (J). (gr. k-3). 1980. 14.95 (*0-395-18507-6*) HM.

Randy's Raiders. Francess Lantz. LC 93-44345. (Boys' School Girls Ser.). (Illus.). 176p. (J). (gr. 3-6). 1994. pap. 3.95 (*0-8167-3474-7*) Troll Communs.

Raneslough. large type ed. Monica Heath. (Large Print Ser.). 400p. 1994. 25.99 (*0-7089-3008-5*) Ulverscroft.

Raney. Clyde Edgerton. 240p. 1985. 15.95 (*0-912697-17-2*) Algonquin Bks.

Raney. Clyde Edgerton. 256p. 1986. mass mkt. 5.99 (*0-345-32982-1*) Ballantine.

***Raney.** Clyde Edgerton. 1997. pap. 11.95 (*0-345-41905-7*) Ballantine.

Range. Sherm Ewing. (Illus.). 280p. 1990. 25.00 (*0-87842-274-9*); pap. 14.00 (*0-87842-267-6*) Mountain Pr.

Range. Mark Sumner. 1996. mass mkt. 5.99 (*0-345-40209-X*) Ballantine.

Range Conservationist. Jack Rudman. (Career Examination Ser.: C-686). 1994. pap. 29.95 (*0-8373-0686-8*) Nat Learn.

Range Development & Improvements. 3rd ed. John F. Vallentine. 528p. 1989. text ed. 63.00 (*0-12-710003-2*) Acad Pr.

Range Ecology. Robert R. Humphrey. LC 62-20671. 240p. reprint ed. pap. 68.40 (*0-685-10834-1*, 2015179) Bks Demand.

***Range Management.** 3rd ed. Holechek & Pieper. LC 97-21991. 1997. text ed. 87.00 (*0-13-626988-5*) P-H.

Range Management: Principles & Practices. 2nd ed. Jerry L. Holechek et al. LC 94-42186. (C). 1995. text ed. 88.00 (*0-13-174484-4*) P-H.

Range Management in Arid Zones: Proceedings of the Second International Conference on Range Management in the Arabian Gulf. Ed. by Samira A. Omar et al. LC 93-37668. (Illus.). 325p. 1996. 161.50 (*0-7103-0472-2*, Pub. by Kegan Paul Intl UK) Col U Pr.

Range of Choice in Water Management: A Study of Dissolved Oxygen in the Potomac Estuary. Robert K. Davis et al. LC 68-27737. 214p. reprint ed. pap. 61.00 (*0-7837-3134-5*, 2019821) Bks Demand.

Range of Glaciers: The Exploration & Survey of the Northern Cascade Range. Fred Beckey. (Illus.). 750p. 1996. 45.00 (*0-87595-243-7*) Oregon Hist.

***Range of Motion.** Elizabeth Berg. 1996. mass mkt. 6.50 (*0-515-11978-4*) Jove Pubns.

Range of Motion. Elizabeth Berg. LC 95-3299. 1995. 21.00 (*0-679-43745-2*) Random.

Range of Motion. large type ed. Elizabeth Berg. (Americana Ser.). 1996. lib. bdg. 22.95 (*0-7862-0613-6*) Thorndike Pr.

Range of Motion: An Anthology Featuring the Creative Works of Women & Men with Disabilities. Intro. by Cheryl M. Wade. (Anthology Ser.). (Illus.). (Orig.). 1990. pap. 10.00 (*1-878458-53-1*) Squeaky Wheels Pr.

Range of Religion: An Introductory Reader. Denise L. Carmody & John T. Carmody. (Illus.). 448p. (Orig.). (C). 1991. pap. text ed. 39.40 (*0-02-319391-3*, Macmillan Coll) P-H.

An Asterisk (*) at the beginning of an entry indicates that the title is appearing in BIP for the first time.

***Range Pirate.** large type ed. Matt Stuart & L. P. Holmes. LC 96-48189. (Nightingale Ser.). 254p. 1997. pap. 18.95 (*0-7838-2047-X*, GK Hall) Thorndike Pr.

***Range Plant Handbook.** U. S. Department of Agriculture Staff. pap. 21.95 (*0-486-25783-5*) Dover.

***Range Rats at Sea.** Dan Kovalchik. 1996. mass mkt. 4.99 (*1-55197-128-3*, Pub. by Comnwlth Pub CN) Partners Pubs Grp.

Range Research: Basic Problems & Techniques. James L. Stubbendieck. LC 85-63270. 317p. 30.00 (*0-9603692-3-6*) Soc Range Mgmt.

Range Rover: Collector's Guide. 2nd ed. James Taylor. (Collector's Guide Ser.). (Illus.). 128p. 1993. 27.95 (*0-947981-75-6*, Pub. by Motor Racing UK) Motorbooks Intl.

Range Rover: Purchase & Restoration Guide. Dave Pollard. (Illus.). 192p. 1996. 29.95 (*0-85429-968-8*, Pub. by G T Foulis Ltd) Haynes Pubns.

Range Rover: The Complete Story. James Taylor. (Illus.). 200p. 1995. 35.95 (*1-85223-910-7*, Pub. by Crowood UK) Motorbooks Intl.

Range Science: A Guide to Information Sources. Ed. by John F. Vallentine & Phillip L. Sims. (Natural World Information Guide Ser.: Vol. 2). 248p. 1980. 68.00 (*0-8103-1420-7*) Gale.

Range Service (Gas, Electric, Microwave) Ed. by A. Ross Sabin. (Illus.). 254p. (gr. 11). 1980. 20.00 (*0-938336-06-1*) Whirlpool.

***Range War.** David K. Sayer. 120p. (Orig.). 1997. mass mkt. 4.99 (*1-55237-310-X*, Pub. by Comnwlth Pub CN) Partners Pubs Grp.

***Range Wars, Vol. 1.** Vaughan. 1997. mass mkt. write for info. (*0-312-96334-3*) St Martin.

Range Wars: Heated Debates, Sober Reflections, & Other Assessments of Texas Writing. Ed. by Craig Clifford & Tom Pilkington. LC 88-42632. (Southwest Life & Letters Ser.). 208p. 1989. pap. 10.95 (*0-87074-273-6*) SMU Press.

Range Wars: Heated Debates, Sober Reflections, & Other Assessments of Texas Writing. Ed. by Craig E. Clifford & Tom Pilkington. LC 88-42632. (Southwest Life & Letters Ser.). 208p. 1989. 22.50 (*0-87074-282-5*) SMU Press.

Rangeland Ecology & Management. Harold F. Heady. (C). 1994. text ed. 59.85 (*0-8133-2052-6*) Westview.

Rangeland Entomology. 2nd ed. Ed. by J. Gordon Watts. (Range Science Ser.: No. 2). 1990. 19.95 (*0-9603692-9-5*) Soc Range Mgmt.

Rangeland Health: New Methods to Classify, Inventory, & Monitor Rangelands. Board on Agriculture Staff & National Research Council Staff. 200p. (Orig.). (C). 1993. pap. text ed. 26.00 (*0-309-04879-6*) Natl Acad Pr.

Rangeland Through Time: A Photographic Study of Vegetation Change in Wyoming 187-1985. Kendall L. Johnson. (Illus.). 196p. (Orig.). 1987. pap. 18.00 (*0-941570-05-3*) U of Wyoming.

Rangeland Wildlife. 1000p. (C). 1995. pap. text ed. write for info. (*1-884930-05-0*) Soc Range Mgmt.

Rangelands: A Resource under Siege. Ed. by P. J. Joss et al. 750p. 1987. text ed. 150.00 (*0-521-30936-0*) Cambridge U Pr.

Rangelands in a Sustainable Biosphere Proceedings of the Fifth International Rangelands Congress: Contributed Presentations, Vol. 1. 1000p. 1995. write for info. (*1-884930-03-4*) Soc Range Mgmt.

Ranger. David Nilsen. (Twenty-Three Hundred AD Ser.). (Illus.). 64p. (Orig.). (YA). 1989. pap. 8.00 (*1-55878-016-5*) Game Designers.

Ranger, Vol. I. 2nd rev. ed. Theodore Enslin. 432p. 1980. 30.00 (*0-913028-79-7*); pap. 12.95 (*0-913028-78-9*) North Atlantic.

Ranger & Other Stories. Zane Grey. 272p. 1993. mass mkt. 3.99 (*0-06-100587-8*, Harp PBks) HarpC.

***Ranger & the Schoolmarm.** Penny Richards. 1997. mass mkt. 3.99 (*0-373-24136-4*, 1-24136-3) Silhouette.

Ranger Handbook, 1992. U. S. Army Staff. (Illus.). 448p. 1993. reprint ed. pap. 24.95 (*0-87364-044-6*) Paladin Pr.

Ranger Man. Sheryl Danson. (Temptation Ser.). 1994. mass mkt. 2.99 (*0-373-25603-5*, 1-25603-1) Harlequin Bks.

Ranger Mike's Animal ABCs: A Sticker Book from A to (Almost) Z. (J). 1996. 4.99 (*0-689-80422-9*, Litl Simon S&S) S&S Childrens.

Ranger Mosby. Virgil C. Jones. LC 87-5059. 368p. 1987. reprint ed. pap. 14.95 (*0-939009-01-3*) EPM Pubns.

Ranger Ray's Campfire Story: Protecting the Wild Animals. Patty Knapp. Ed. by Patty Furbush. LC 93-79770. (Illus.). 32p. (Orig.). (J). (ps-2). 1994. pap. text ed. 2.95 (*0-9616395-4-7*, Childrens Outdoor) MI Adventure Pubns.

Ranger Rick Big Book Collection, 25 bks., Set. Ed. by Donna Schaffer. (Ranger Rick Science Spectacular Ser.). (Illus.). 16p. (J). (gr. 2-5). 1996. pap. write for info. (*1-56784-290-9*) Newbridge Comms.

Ranger Rick Big Books, 12 units, Set. Melvin Berger. Ed. by Natalie Lunis & Donna Schaffer. (J). (gr. 2-4). 1995. pap. 178.00 (*1-56784-831-1*) Newbridge Comms.

Ranger Rick Big Books, 6 units, Set, Version II. Melvin Berger. Ed. by Natalie Lunis & Donna Schaffer. (J). (gr. 2-4). 1995. pap. 89.00 (*1-56784-830-3*) Newbridge Comms.

Ranger Rick Complete Program, 25 bks., Set. Ed. by Donna Schaffer. (Ranger Rick Science Spectacular Ser.). (Illus.). 16p. (J). (gr. 2-5). 1996. pap. write for info. (*1-56784-289-5*) Newbridge Comms.

Ranger Rick Science Spectacular, 4 vols., Set. Melvin Berger. (Illus.). (J). (gr. 2-4). 1995. pap. write for info. (*1-56784-646-7*) Newbridge Comms.

Ranger Rick Student Book Classroom Library, 150 bks., Set. Ed. by Donna Schaffer. (Ranger Rick Science Spectacular Ser.). (Illus.). 16p. (J). (gr. 2-5). 1996. pap. write for info. (*1-56784-291-7*) Newbridge Comms.

Ranger Rick Student Book Starter Set, 25 bks., Set. (Ranger Rick Science Spectacular Ser.). (Illus.). 16p. (J). (gr. 2-5). 1996. pap. write for info. (*1-56784-292-5*) Newbridge Comms.

Ranger Rides to Town. Louis L'Amour. 1990. audio 9.99 (*0-553-45219-3*) Bantam.

Ranger Smokes Too Much. Pierre Coran. (Child's World Library). (Illus.). 32p. (J). (gr. k-5). 1991. lib. bdg. 18.50 (*0-89565-748-1*) Childs World.

Ranger Training & Operations. Department of the Army. 1982. lib. bdg. 250.00 (*0-87700-376-9*) Revisionist Pr.

Ranger, U. S. Park Service. Jack Rudman. (Career Examination Ser.: C-665). 1994. pap. 27.95 (*0-8373-0665-5*) Nat Learn.

Ranger Volume II. Theodore Enslin. 256p. (Orig.). 1980. 30.00 (*0-913028-75-4*); pap. 9.95 (*0-913028-74-6*) North Atlantic.

***Rangers.** Brian McFarlane. (Brian McFarlane's Original Six Ser.). (Illus.). 240p. 1997. 19.95 (*0-7737-3047-8*, Pub. by Stoddart Pubng CN) Genl Dist Srvs.

Rangers. Turner Publishing Company Staff. LC 95-60318. 144p. 1995. 48.00 (*1-56311-182-9*) Turner Pub KY.

Rangers at War. Shelby L. Stanton. 1993. mass mkt. 5.99 (*0-8041-0875-7*) Ivy Books.

Rangers at War: Combat Recon in Vietnam. Shelby L. Stanton. 1992. 25.00 (*0-517-58590-1*, Orion Bks) Crown Pub Group.

Ranger's Impartial List of the Ladies of Pleasure in Edinburgh. (Illus.). 1979. reprint ed. 16.95 (*0-8464-0783-3*) Beekman Pubs.

Rangers in World War Two. Robert W. Black. (Orig.). 1992. mass mkt. 4.99 (*0-8041-0565-0*) Ivy Books.

Rangers of Texas. Dorman H. Winfrey et al. (Illus.). 160p. 1991. 20.00 (*0-87244-006-0*) Texian.

***Rangers of the Lone Star.** Zane Gray. 1997. 17.95 (*0-614-27915-1*, Five Star) Mac Lib Ref.

Rangers of the North. John D. Ruemmler. (Illus.). 56p. (YA). (gr. 10-12). 1985. pap. 12.00 (*0-915795-22-1*, 3000) Iron Crown Ent Inc.

Rangers Wit: Reflections, Retorts & Reminiscences from the Stanley Cup Champs. Andrew K. Mekz. Ed. by Anne E. Broussard. (Orig.). 1994. pap. 6.95 (*0-9640033-6-8*) Wit Press.

Ranges of Romanticism: Five for Ten Studies. Thomas M. Harwell. LC 90-20190. 1991. 35.00 (*0-89341-604-5*, Longwood Academic) Hollowbrook.

***Ranging & Arranging.** John Fandel. 1997. pap. 12.00 (*0-87957-017-2*) Brookville Bks.

***Ranier Panorama.** Will Landon. (Illus.). 148p. 1996. pap. 60.00 (*1-56044-517-3*) Falcon Pr MT.

Ranjit Singh: A Secular Sikh Sovereign. K. S. Duggal. (Illus.). 143p. 1993. lib. bdg. 35.00 (*0-948725-07-9*, Pub. by Tricolour Bks UK) Asia Pub Hse.

Ranjit Singh: A Secular Sikh Sovereign. K. S. Duggal. (C). 1989. 44.00 (*81-7017-244-6*, Pub. by Abhinav II) S Asia.

Rank & File: Personal Histories by Working-Class Organizers. Ed. by Alice Lynd & Staughton Lynd. 320p. (YA). (gr. 9-12). 1988. reprint ed. pap. 12.00 (*0-85345-752-2*) Monthly Rev.

Rank & File Rebellion: Teamsters for a Democratic Union. Dan La Botz. (Haymarket Ser.). 360p. (C). 1991. pap. text ed. 20.00 (*0-86091-505-0*, A4502, Pub. by Vrso UK) Norton.

Rank & Privilege: The Military & Society in Latin America. Ed. by Linda A. Rodriguez. LC 94-14393. (Jaguar Books on Latin America: No. 8). 239p. 1994. 40.00 (*0-8420-2432-8*) Scholarly Res Inc.

Rank & Rivalry: The Politics of Inequality in Rural West Bengal. Marvin Davis. LC 82-9747. (Cambridge Studies in Cultural Systems: No. 7). 249p. reprint ed. pap. 71.00 (*0-318-34777-6*, 2031638) Bks Demand.

Rank & Warfare among the Plains Indians. Bernard Mishkin. LC 84-45510. (American Ethnological Society Monographs: No. 3). 1988. reprint ed. 20.00 (*0-404-62903-2*) AMS Pr.

Rank & Warfare among the Plains Indians. Bernard Mishkin. LC 92-15035. xix, 65p. 1992. reprint ed. pap. 6.95 (*0-8032-8185-4*, Bison Books) U of Nebr Pr.

***Rank Correlation Methods.** 5th ed. write for info. (*0-85264-305-5*) Lubrecht & Cramer.

Rank Correlation Methods. 5th ed. Maurice Kendall & Jean D. Gibbons. (Charles Griffin Book). (Illus.). 272p. 1990. 60.00 (*0-19-520837-4*) OUP.

Rank-It: A Risk Assessment Tool. Jerry FitzGerald. (Illus.). 64p. 1988. pap. 99.95 incl. disk (*0-932410-39-1*) FitzGerald & Assocs.

Ranka Yearbook, 1991: The Bulletin of the International Go Federation. Ed. by Yusuke Oedo. Tr. by John Power from JPN. (Illus.). 96p. (Orig.). 1991. pap. text ed. 4.00 (*0-685-50760-2*, RY91) Ishi Pr Intl.

***Rankin Family Album.** Ed. by Michael Lefferts. 88p. (Orig.). (C). 1996. pap. text ed. 19.95 (*0-7692-0472-4*, CCC112) Warner Brothers.

Ranking & Resistance: A Precolonial Cameroonian Polity in Regional Perspective. Richard G. Dillon. 328p. 1990. 45.00 (*0-8047-1571-8*) Stanford U Pr.

Ranking & Spicer: Company Law. 13th ed. J. M. Gullick. 1987. pap. 30.00 (*0-406-67890-1*, U.K.) MICHIE.

***Ranking Hazardous-Waste Sites for Remedial Action.** National Research Council, Remedial Action Priorities for Hazardous Waste Sites Committee. LC 94-66574. (Illus.). 312p. 1994. reprint ed. pap. 89.00 (*0-608-04258-7*, 2065013) Bks Demand.

***Ranking of World Stock Markets.** annuals unabridged ed. 125p. (Orig.). 1996. spiral bd., pap. 75.00 (*0-9648930-3-7*) Meridian Securities.

Ranking-Selberg Convolutions for SO21 Plus 1 times GLn: Local Theory. David Soudry. LC 93-2235. (Memoirs of the American Mathematical Society Ser.: No. 500). 1993. pap. 29.00 (*0-8218-2568-2*, MEMO/105/500) Am Math.

Ranking, Spicer & Pegler: Executorship Law & Accounts. 23th ed. K. S. Carmichael. 1988. 120.00 (*0-406-67901-0*, U.K.) MICHIE.

Ranking the Municipalities: Incomes & House Values. Joseph J. Seneca. LC 94-11398. 421p. (C). 1994. pap. text ed. 39.95 (*0-88285-150-0*) Ctr Urban Pol Res.

***Ranking Wishes.** Carl Dennis. LC 96-44352. 1997. pap. 14.95 (*0-14-058779-9*) Viking Penguin.

Ranks & Columns: Armed Forces Newspapers in American Wars. Alfred E. Cornebise. LC 92-36605. (Contributions to the Study of Mass Media & Communications Ser.: No. 38). 232p. 1993. text ed. 52.95 (*0-313-26628-X*, CFO, Greenwood Pr) Greenwood.

Ranks of Death: A Medical History of the Conquest of America. Percy M. Ashburn. Ed. by Frank D. Ashburn. LC 80-24672. (Perspectives in Latin American History Ser.: No. 2). xix, 298p. 1980. reprint ed. lib. bdg. 45.00 (*0-87991-599-4*) Porcupine Pr.

Ranks of the Black Order. Pierre Christin. (Illus.). 1989. pap. 13.95 (*0-87416-052-9*) Catalan Communs.

Ranleigh Court. large type ed. Marjorie Shoebridge. 1991. 25.99 (*0-7089-2525-1*) Ulverscroft.

Ranma One-Half, Vol. 1. Rumiko Takahashi. Ed. by Seiji Horibuchi. Tr. by Satoru Fujii from JPN. (Illus.). 304p. (Orig.). 1993. pap. 16.95 (*0-929279-93-X*) Viz Commns Inc.

Ranma One-Half, Vol. 4. Rumiko Takahashi. (Illus.). 212p. 1995. pap. 15.95 (*1-56931-085-8*) Viz Commns Inc.

Ranma One-Half, Vol. 5. Rumiko Takahashi. (Illus.). 212p. 1995. pap. 15.95 (*1-56931-084-X*) Viz Commns Inc.

Ranma 1-2, Vol. 2. Rumiko Takahashi. 1995. pap. text ed. 15.95 (*1-56931-016-5*) Viz Commns Inc.

Ranma 1-2, Vol. 3. Rumiko Takahashi. 1995. pap. text ed. 15.95 (*1-56931-020-3*) Viz Commns Inc.

Ranma 1-2, Vol. 6. Rumiko Takahashi. 1996. pap. text ed. 15.95 (*1-56931-137-4*, Viz Comics) Viz Commns Inc.

***Ranma 1-2, Vol. 8.** Rumiko Takahashi. 1997. pap. text ed. 15.95 (*1-56931-202-8*, Viz Comics) Viz Commns Inc.

***Ranma 1-2, Vol. 9.** Rumiko Takahashi. 1997. pap. text ed. 15.95 (*1-56931-203-6*, Viz Comics) Viz Commns Inc.

***Ranma 1/2, Vol. 7.** Rumiko Takahashi. 1996. pap. text ed. 15.95 (*1-56931-128-5*) Viz Commns Inc.

Ranniaia Proza, Tom One. Mikhail Bulgakov. Tr. by Tom I. Ranniaia. (Sobranie Sochinenii Ser.: Vol. 1). 421p. (RUS.). 1982. 25.00 (*0-88233-506-5*) Ardis Pubs.

Rannie Voda i Zemlya: The Early Water & Earth. Dmitri Strizhov. (Illus.). 112p. (Orig.). (RUS.). 1992. pap. 7.00 (*1-881910-00-8*) Adventure NY.

Ransack. 2nd ed. Michael Henson. 92p. 1987. pap. 5.95 (*0-931122-44-9*) West End.

Ransacked. Nancy Holt. LC 79-92752. 1980. pap. 7.50 (*0-930378-11-3*) Printed Matter.

Ransacking the Closet. Yvonne Zipter. 200p. (Orig.). 1995. pap. 9.95 (*1-883523-06-0*) Spinsters Ink.

***Ransom.** Auerbach. 1996. 25.00 (*0-8050-4078-1*) St Martin.

Ransom. Mark Dunster. 15p. (Orig.). 1986. pap. 4.00 (*0-89642-132-5*) Linden Pubs.

Ransom. Grace L. Hill. 1995. pap. 4.99 (*0-8423-5143-4*) Tyndale.

Ransom. Jay McInerney. 280p. 1985. pap. 12.00 (*0-394-74118-8*, Vin) Random.

Ransom. Gloria D. Skinner. 1996. mass mkt. 5.99 (*0-671-56059-X*) PB.

Ransom. Lois Duncan. 144p. (J). (gr. 7-12). 1990. reprint ed. mass mkt. 4.50 (*0-440-97292-2*, LLL BDD) BDD Bks Young Read.

Ransom. Grace L. Hill. reprint ed. lib. bdg. 24.95 (*0-89190-045-4*, Rivercity Pr) Amereon Ltd.

***Ransom for a Holiday: A Jeremy Ransom Emily Charters Mystery.** Fred Hunter. LC 97-25226. 1997. write for info. (*0-312-16976-0*) St Martin.

Ransom for a River Dolphin. Sarita H. Kendall. LC 93-19929. (J). (gr. 3-6). 1993. lib. bdg. 19.95 (*0-8225-0735-8*, Lerner Publctns) Lerner Group.

Ransom for an Angel. Fred W. Hunter. 1997. mass mkt. 4.99 (*0-373-26224-8*, 1-26224-5, Wrldwide Lib) Harlequin Bks.

Ransom for an Angel. Fred W. Hunter. 246p. 1995. 19.95 (*0-8027-3253-4*) Walker & Co.

Ransom for Many: A Life of Maggie Lena Walker. Gertrude W. Marlowe. 225p. 1996. 50.00 (*0-926019-83-X*) Carlson Pub.

***Ransom for Our Sins.** Fred W. Hunter. 1997. mass mkt. 4.99 (*0-373-26249-3*, 1-26249-2, Wrldwide Lib) Harlequin Bks.

Ransom for Our Sins: A Jeremy Ransom/Emily Charters Mystery. Fred W. Hunter. LC 96-3503. 238p. 1996. 22.95 (*0-8027-3284-4*) Walker & Co.

Ransom from a Poet. Jerry W. Elkins. LC 81-50913. 116p. 1981. pap. 5.95 (*0-938232-02-9*) Winston-Derek.

Ransom Game. large type ed. Howard Engel. 1989. 25.99 (*0-7089-2052-7*) Ulverscroft.

Ransom Historical Outline of the Ransom Family of America, & Genealogical Records of the Colchester, Ct., Branch. Wyllys C. Ransom. (Illus.). 408p. 1995. lib. bdg. 72.00 (*0-8328-4454-3*) Higginson Bk Co.

Ransom Historical Outline of the Ransom Family of America, & Genealogical Records of the Colchester, Ct., Branch. Wyllys C. Ransom. (Illus.). 408p. 1995. reprint ed. pap. 62.00 (*0-8328-4455-1*) Higginson Bk Co.

Ransom of Black Stealth One. Dean Ing. 480p. 1995. mass mkt. 5.99 (*0-8125-0857-2*) Tor Bks.

Ransom of Red Chief. O. Henry. 1964. 3.75 (*0-87129-400-1*, R11) Dramatic Pub.

Ransom of Red Chief. O. Henry. (One-Buck Bks.). 36p. (J). (gr. 5-8). 1995. pap. 1.00 (*0-87406-797-9*) Willowisp Pr.

Ransom of Red Chief. Brian Kral. (Orig.). (J). (gr. 3 up). 1980. 5.00 (*0-87602-227-1*) Anchorage.

Ransom of Red Chief. O. Henry. (Creative's Classic Short Stories Ser.). (Illus.). 40p. (J). (gr. 4 up). 1980. lib. bdg. 13.95 (*0-87191-776-9*) Creative Ed.

Ransom of Red Chief. O. Henry. Ed. by Walter Pauk & Raymond Harris. (Classics Ser.). (Illus.). 40p. (YA). (gr. 6-12). 1980. teacher ed. 7.32 (*0-89061-191-2*, 407); pap. text ed. 5.99 (*0-89061-189-0*, 405); audio 17.96 (*0-89061-190-4*, 406) Jamestown Pubs.

Ransom of Russian Art. John McPhee. LC 94-14723. 1994. 20.00 (*0-374-24682-3*) FS&G.

Ransom of Russian Art. John McPhee. 192p. 1996. pap. 10.00 (*0-374-52450-5*) FS&G.

Ransom of the Golden Bridge. Proctor Jones. LC 83-80825. 176p. 1983. pap. 3.95 (*0-9608860-2-8*) Proctor Jones.

Ransom of the Heart. Kate Kingsley. (Historical Ser.: No. 72). 1991. mass mkt. 3.95 (*0-373-28672-4*) Harlequin Bks.

Ransom Run. (Executioner Ser.). 1993. mass mkt. 3.50 (*0-373-61176-5*, 1-61176-3) Harlequin Bks.

Ransom Street Quartet: Poems. Juanita Tobin. LC 95-32563. 1995. pap. 14.95 (*0-9635752-8-7*) Pkway Pubs.

Ransome Inheritance. large type ed. Rachelle Edwards. (Linford Romance Library). 1996. pap. 15.99 (*0-7089-7835-5*, Linford) Ulverscroft.

Ransomed Bride. Jane Peart. (Brides of Montclair Ser.: Vol. 2). 192p. 1989. pap. 8.99 (*0-310-66961-8*) Zondervan.

***Ransomed Brides.** 1998. pap. 5.99 (*0-373-20150-8*, 1-20150-8) Harlequin Bks.

***Ransomed Heart.** large type ed. Ann Charlton. (Magna Large Print Ser.). 267p. 1996. 25.99 (*0-7505-1054-4*, Pub. by Magna Print Bks UK) Ulverscroft.

Ransomed Phoenix: Overcoming the Dream. Patrick R. Penland. 1994. pap. 12.95 (*1-884333-43-5*) Passage Communs.

Ransomed Wait. May Miller. LC 82-83856. 77p. (YA). (gr. 9-12). 1983. per. 4.50 (*0-916418-40-5*) Lotus.

Ransoming the Mind: An Integration of Yoga & Modern Therapy. Charles Bates. LC 86-50084. (Illus.). 329p. (Orig.). 1986. pap. 11.95 (*0-936663-00-6*) Yes Intl.

Ransoming the Time. Jacques Maritain. Tr. by Harry L. Binsse. LC 70-165665. 322p. 1972. reprint ed. 50.00 (*0-87752-153-0*) Gordian.

Ransoms to Time: Selected Poems. Adonis Decavalles. LC 82-49314. 144p. 1984. 26.50 (*0-8386-3180-0*) Fairleigh Dickinson.

Ranson's Folly. Richard H. Davis. LC 79-152938. (Short Story Index Reprint Ser.). (Illus.). 1977. reprint ed. 23.95 (*0-8369-3797-X*) Ayer.

Ranson's Folly & Other Stories. Richard H. Davis. (Airmont Classics Ser.). (J). (gr. 9 up). 1968. mass mkt. 1.95 (*0-8049-0192-9*, CL-192) Airmont.

Rants. Dennis Miller. 224p. 1996. 21.95 (*0-385-47804-6*) Doubleday.

***Rants.** Dennis Miller. 240p. 1997. pap. 11.95 (*0-385-47802-X*, Main St Bks) Doubleday.

Ranulphbye's Bucks County. Ranulph Bye. LC 88-63902. 120p. 1989. text ed. 50.00 (*0-317-93487-2*) Bargeron Pub.

Ranuzzi Manuscripts: An Exhibit. Maria X. Wells. 1980. 15.00 (*0-87959-094-7*) U of Tex H Ransom Ctr.

***Ranvan: A Worthy Opponent.** Diana Wieler. 1997. 16.95 (*0-88899-271-8*, Pub. by Groundwood-Douglas & McIntyre CN) Firefly Bks Ltd.

***Ranvan the Defender.** Diana Wieler. 1997. 16.95 (*0-88899-270-X*, Pub. by Groundwood-Douglas & McIntyre CN) Firefly Bks Ltd.

Ranxerox in New York. 2nd ed. Stefano Tamburini. (Ranxerox Ser.). (Illus.). 60p. 1986. pap. 10.95 (*0-87416-027-8*) Catalan Communs.

Ranxerox, No. Two: Happy Birthday, Lubna. 2nd ed. Stefano Tamburini. Ed. by Bernd Metz. (Illus.). 64p. 1987. pap. 10.95 (*0-87416-038-3*) Catalan Communs.

***Rao's Cookbook.** Frank W. Pellegrin. 1998. write for info. (*0-679-45749-6*) Random.

Raoul Bott: Collected Papers. Ed. by R. D. MacPherson. 485p. 1994. 104.50 (*0-8176-3647-1*) Spr-Verlag.

Raoul Bott: Collected Papers. Ed. by R. D. MacPherson. (Contemporary Mathematicians Ser.: Vol. 4). 484p. 1994. 104.50 (*0-8176-3648-X*) Spr-Verlag.

Raoul Bott Vol. 2: Collected Papers: Differential Operators (the 1960s) R. D. MacPherson. (Contemporary Mathematicians Ser.). (Illus.). xxxiii, 802p. 1996. 104.50 (*0-8176-3646-3*) Birkhauser.

Raoul Hausmann & Berlin Dada. Timothy O. Benson. LC 86-28049. (Studies in the Fine Arts: The Avant-Garde: No. 55). 298p. reprint ed. pap. 85.00 (*0-8357-2050-0*, 2070692) Bks Demand.

Raoul Wallenberg. LC 91-19712. (People Who Made a Difference Ser.). (Illus.). 68p. (J). (gr. 3-8). 1990. lib. bdg. 23.93 (*0-8368-0629-8*) Gareth Stevens Inc.

Raoul Wallenberg. Michael Nicholson & David Winner. LC 88-2078. (People Who Have Helped the World Ser.). (Illus.). 68p. (J). (gr. 5-6). 1990. pap. 7.95 (*0-8192-1525-2*) Morehouse Pub.

Raoul Wallenberg: Angel of Rescue. rev. ed. Harvey Rosenfeld. (Illus.). 290p. 1995. pap. 19.95 (*0-8419-1359-5*) Holmes & Meier.

Raoul Wallenberg: Hero of the Holocaust. Thelma I. Pangburn. Ed. by John G. Buchanan. (Outstanding Personalities Ser.: No. 97). (YA). (gr. 7-12). 1987. lib. bdg. 7.25 (*0-87157-597-3*) SamHar Pr.

Raoul Wallenberg: The Man Who Stopped Death. Sharon Linnea. (Illus.). 168p. 1993. 17.95 (*0-8276-0440-8*); pap. 9.95 (*0-8276-0448-3*) JPS Phila.

Raoul Wallenberg: The Swedish Diplomat Who Saved 100,000 Jews from the Nazi Holocaust Before Mysteriously Disappearing. Michael Nicholson & David Winner. Ed. by Rhoda Sherwood. LC 88-2078. (People Who Have Helped the World Ser.). (Illus.). 68p. (J). (gr. 5-6). 1989. lib. bdg. 23.93 (*1-55532-820-2*) Gareth Stevens Inc.

An Asterisk (*) at the beginning of an entry indicates that the title is appearing in BIP for the first time.

Raoul Wallenberg Compilation of Human Rights Instruments. Ed. by Goran Melander et al. LC 95-45769. 1996. text ed. 198.00 (*0-7923-3646-1*, Pub. by M Nijhoff NE) Kluwer Ac.

Rap. Mark Dunster. 17p. (Orig.). 1987. pap. 4.00 (*0-89642-146-5*) Linden Pubs.

Rap: Portraits & Lyrics of a Generation of Black Rockers. B. Adler. 1991. pap. 13.95 (*0-312-05501-3*) St Martin.

RAP: This Game of Exposure: Promoting Your Rap Record - Artist. Walt Goodridge. LC 92-97083. (This Game of Exposure Ser.). (Illus.). 250p. 1992. pap. 69.95 (*0-9629202-1-5*) Co Called W.

Rap - the Lyrics: The Words to Rap's 175 Greatest Hits. Ed. by Lawrence A. Stanley. 256p. (Orig.). 1992. pap. 15.95 (*0-14-014788-8*, Penguin Bks) Viking Penguin.

***Rap-a-Matics: Math Rap Multiplication Through Song.** Jeannette Conroy-Teri. (Illus.). 32p. (J). (gr. 2-4). 1993. wbk. ed. 11.95 (*0-933243-01-4*) Laurel Pubns New York.

RAP Attack, No. 2: African Rap to Global Hip Hop. David Toop. (Illus.). 224p. (Orig.). 1992. pap. 16.99 (*1-85242-243-2*) Serpents Tail.

Rap Beats on the Drum. Chuck Kerrigan. 76p. 1991. pap. text ed. 16.95 incl. audio (*0-931759-55-2*) Centerstream Pub.

Rap Factor: Novel. Delacorta. Tr. by Catherine Texier from FRE. LC 92-35562. 200p. 1993. pap. 11.00 (*0-87113-617-1*, Atlntc Mnthly) Grove-Atltic.

***Rap Lyrics for My Beloved Black People.** M. C. Melody. (Illus.). 56p. (Orig.). Date not set. 6.00 (*0-9655918-3-2*) Rap Lyrics.

***Rap Lyrics for My Beloved Black People.** M. C. Melody. (Illus.). 56p. (Orig.). 1996. pap. 6.00 (*0-9655918-0-8*); pap. 10.00 incl. audio (*0-9655918-2-4*) Rap Lyrics.

Rap Master Ronnie. Trudeau & Elizabeth Swados. 1985. pap. 5.95 (*0-88145-033-2*) Broadway Play.

Rap Music in the Nineteen Eighties: A Reference Guide. Judy McCoy. 275p. 1992. 32.50 (*0-8108-2649-6*) Scarecrow.

Rap on Gangsta Rap. Bakarl Kitwana. 1994. 5.00 (*0-88378-175-1*) Third World.

Rap on Race. James Baldwin & Margaret Mead. 240p. (YA). (gr. 9 up). 1974. mass mkt. 5.99 (*0-440-21176-X*) Dell.

Rap, Rock, & Role into Conflict Resolution: Conflict Resolution Presented Through Lessons & Music for Middle, Junior High, & High School Students. JoAnn Cooper & Arden Martenz. LC 93-79190. 32p. 1993. 14.95 (*1-884063-05-5*) Mar Co Prods.

Rap to Live By. Don Roberts. 128p. 1993. pap. 8.95 (*1-878901-55-9*) Hampton Roads Pub Co.

Rap with the Facts Twinset: Addition. Kim M. Thompson & Karen M. Hilderbrand. (Illus.). 48p. (J). (gr. 1-4). 1993. wbk. ed. 14.99 incl. audio (*1-882331-04-4*, TWIN 302) Twin Sisters.

Rap with the Facts Twinset: Division. Kim M. Thompson & Karen M. Hilderbrand. (Illus.). 48p. (J). (gr. 3-6). 1993. wbk. ed. 14.99 incl. audio (*1-882331-06-0*, TWIN 304) Twin Sisters.

Rap with the Facts Twinset: Multiplication. Kim M. Thompson & Karen M. Hilderbrand. (Illus.). 64p. (J). (gr. 2-6). 1993. wbk. ed., pap. 14.99 incl. audio (*1-882331-03-6*, TWIN 301) Twin Sisters.

Rap with the Facts Twinset: Subtraction. Kim M. Thompson & Karen M. Hilderbrand. (Illus.). 48p. (J). (gr. 1-4). 1993. wbk. ed. 14.99 incl. audio (*1-882331-05-2*, TWIN 303) Twin Sisters.

Rapala Fishing Guide: Secrets from Pros. LC 76-15852. (Illus.). 1976. pap. 2.95 (*0-686-17472-0*) Normark Corp.

Rapanui: A Descriptive Grammar. Veronica Du Feu. LC 94-19109. (Descriptive Grammars Ser.). 352p. (C). (gr. 13). 1995. text ed. 125.00 (*0-415-00011-4*, B2258) Routledge.

Raparapa. Ed. by Paul Marshall. 290p. (C). 1990. 90.00 (*0-7316-3328-8*, Pub. by Pascoe Pub AT) St Mut.

Rape: A Bibliography. Ed. by Joan Nordquist. (Contemporary Social Issues: A Bibliographic Ser.: No. 19). 64p. (Orig.). (C). 1990. pap. 15.00 (*0-937855-36-7*) Ref Rsch Serv.

Rape: A Philosophical Investigation. Keith Burgess-Jackson. (Applied Legal Philosophy Ser.). (Illus.). 256p. 1996. text ed. 67.95 (*1-85521-485-7*, Pub. by Dartmth Pub UK) Ashgate Pub Co.

Rape: Controversial Issues: Criminal Profiles, Date Rape, False Reports & False Memories. John M. Macdonald. 218p. (C). 1995. pap. text ed. 39.95 (*0-398-06546-2*) C C Thomas.

Rape: Controversial Issues: Criminal Profiles, Date Rape, False Reports & False Memories. John M. Macdonald. 218p. (C). 1995. text ed. 56.95 (*0-398-06545-4*) C C Thomas.

Rape: Crisis & Recovery. Ann W. Burgess & Lynda L. Holmstrom. LC 79-51507. (Illus.). 350p. (C). 1979. pap. 18.95 (*0-87619-433-1*) P-H.

Rape: How to Fight, Prevent, Use Protective Psychology or Later Identify Rapists. 3rd rev. ed. Patricia L. Miketta. LC 90-56286. 230p. 1995. 44.50 (*0-7883-0454-2*); pap. 39.50 (*0-7883-0455-0*) ABBE Pubs Assn.

Rape: Social Facts from England & America. Donna I. Qureshi. 293p. 1979. pap. text ed. 8.60 (*0-87563-178-9*) Stipes.

Rape: The Misunderstood Crime. Julie A. Allison & Lawrence S. Wrightman. LC 93-14800. 307p. (C). 1993. text ed. 52.00 (*0-8039-3706-7*); pap. text ed. 25.00 (*0-8039-3707-5*) Sage.

Rape: What Would You Do If? rev. ed. Dianna D. Booher. 160p. (J). (gr. 7 up). 1991. pap. 6.95 (*0-671-74546-8*, Julian Messner); lib. bdg. 13.95 (*0-671-74538-7*, Julian Messner) Silver Burdett Pr.

Rape: You Can Beat It. Benjamin Ayodele. 1994. pap. 8.95 (*0-533-11006-8*) Vantage.

Rape - A Hazard to Health. Solveig Dahl. (Scandinavian University Press Publication). (Illus.). 154p. (C). 1993. 35.00 (*82-00-21809-0*, 14448) Scandnvan Univ Pr.

Rape - Sexual Assault: How & Where to Find Facts & Get Help. Robert D. Reed & Danek S. Kaus. Ed. by Diane Parker. LC 92-53762. (Abuse Ser.). 48p. 1993. pap. 4.50 (*0-88247-943-1*) R & E Pubs.

Rape-! By Gov't Decree-1: (Winning Wars Without Heros) Tom Adams. LC 92-71324. 216p. 1992. 14.95 (*0-8187-0159-5*) Harlo Press.

Rape & Alcoholism: A Bibliography. Rama K. Rao. (RAMDIL Bibliographies Ser.: No. 7). 6p. 3.50 (*1-883215-07-2*) Ramdil.

Rape & Representation. Ed. by Lynn A. Higgins et al. (Gender & Culture Ser.). 326p. (C). 1993. pap. 17.00 (*0-231-07267-8*); text ed. 39.50 (*0-231-07266-X*) Col U Pr.

Rape & Revelation: The Descent to the Underworld in Modernism. Evans L. Smith. 170p. (C). 1990. lib. bdg. 38.00 (*0-8191-7644-3*) U Pr of Amer.

Rape & Ritual. Te Paske. 1995. pap. 16.00 (*0-919123-09-0*, Pub. by Inner City CN) BookWorld Dist.

Rape & Sexual Assault. Ed. by Ann W. Burgess. LC 87-23624. 354p. 1988. text ed. 20.00 (*0-8240-8528-0*, SS361) Garland.

Rape & Sexual Assault. Ed. by Ann W. Burgess. LC 91-14696. 339p. 1991. text ed. 60.00 (*0-8240-7181-6*, SS672) Garland.

Rape & Sexual Assault I: A Research Handbook. Ann W. Burgess. LC 83-48217. (Reference Library of Social Science). 452p. 1984. text ed. 25.00 (*0-8240-9049-7*) Garland.

Rape & Society: Readings on the Problem of Sexual Assault. Ed. by Patricia Searles & Ron Berger. (Crime & Society Ser.). (C). 1995. pap. text ed. 24.00 (*0-8133-8824-4*) Westview.

Rape & the Criminal Justice System. Ed. by Jennifer Temkin. 448p. 1995. text ed. 119.95 (*1-85521-670-1*, Pub. by Dartmth Pub UK) Ashgate Pub Co.

Rape & the Limits of Law Reform. Jeanne C. Marsh et al. LC 81-20621. 171p. 1982. text ed. 45.00 (*0-86569-083-9*, Auburn Hse) Greenwood.

Rape & Victims of Rape. Vimala Veeraraghavan. 126p. 1987. 16.95 (*81-85119-19-8*) Asia Bk Corp.

Rape & Violence: Index of New Information with Authors, Subjects, Research Categories & References. Richard B. Zarkado. 160p. (Orig.). 1995. 47.50 (*0-7883-0730-4*); pap. 44.50 (*0-7883-0731-2*) ABBE Pubs Assn.

Rape & Writing in the "Heptameron" of Marguerite de Navarre. Patricia F. Cholakian. LC 90-19799. (Ad Feminam Ser.). 288p. (C). 1991. 34.95 (*0-8093-1708-7*) S Ill U Pr.

Rape Bibliography for 1965-1975. LC 77-89641. 1977. 15.00 (*0-87875-120-3*) Whitston Pub.

Rape Controversy. Melissa Benn et al. (C). 1988. 25.00 (*0-946088-23-3*, Pub. by NCCL UK) St Mut.

Rape Crisis Intervention Handbook: A Guide to Victim Care. Ed. by Sharon L. McCombie. LC 80-14191. (Illus.). 250p. 1980. 45.00 (*0-306-40401-X*, Plenum Pr) Plenum.

Rape Defense Handbook for Women. Sebastian B. Ventimiglia & Salina Pesiri. (Illus.). 100p. (Orig.). 1990. pap. 9.95 (*0-9625681-0-4*) Jaz Pubns.

***Rape Hurts.** Nadine. (Orig.). Date not set. pap. write for info. (*0-9656427-1-2*) Nadines.

Rape in America: A Reference Handbook. Sandra E. Lamb. LC 95-12102. (Contemporary World Issues Ser.). 210p. 1995. lib. bdg. 39.50 (*0-87436-730-1*) ABC-CLIO.

***Rape in Antiquity: Sexual Violence in the Greek & Roman Worlds.** Ed. by Susan Deacy & Karen Pierce. (Illus.). 288p. 1997. 74.95 (*0-7156-2754-6*, Pub. by Duckworth UK) Focus Pub-R Pullins.

Rape in Intimate Relationships: Guidelines for Helping the Victims. Susan C. Elias. (Illus.). 120p. (Orig.). 1989. pap. text ed. 15.95 (*0-317-93903-3*) Womansource.

Rape in Kashmir: A Crime of War. Asia Watch Staff. 18p. 1993. pap. 2.50 (*0-614-14423-X*) Phy Human Rights.

Rape in Marriage. enl. rev. ed. Diana E. Russell. LC 89-24650. (Illus.). 462p. 1990. 39.95 (*0-253-35055-7*); pap. 16.95 (*0-253-20563-8*, MB-563) Ind U Pr.

Rape in Paradise. Theon Wright. 300p. (Orig.). 1990. reprint ed. mass mkt. 4.95 (*0-935180-88-5*) Mutual Pub HI.

Rape, Incest & Child Sexual Abuse: Consequences & Recovery. Pat Gilmartin. LC 93-33582. (Library of Sociology: Vol. 27). 392p. 1994. text ed. 63.00 (*0-8153-1326-8*, SS904) Garland.

Rape, Incest, & Sexual Harassment: A Guide for Helping Survivors. Kathryn Quina & Nancy Carlson. LC 89-16160. 275p. 1989. text ed. 55.00 (*0-275-92533-1*, C2533, Praeger Pubs) Greenwood.

Rape Investigation Manual. James R. Powers. (Illus.). 320p. 1996. pap. 50.00 (*0-87364-890-0*) Paladin Pr.

Rape Law Reform: A Grassroots Revolution & Its Impact. Cassia Spohn. (Crime & Justice Ser.). (Illus.). 190p. (C). 1992. 34.50 (*0-306-44284-1*, Plenum Pr) Plenum.

Rape of a Nation. Jimmy Swaggart. 1985. 12.95 (*0-935113-00-2*) Swaggart Ministries.

Rape of Britannia. Jack Obdam. 92p. (C). 1989. text ed. 39.00 (*1-872795-80-3*, Pub. by Pentland Pr UK) St Mut.

Rape of Childhood: No Time to Be a Kid. June E. Gilmore & Rosemarie Huber. (Illus.). 160p. (Orig.). 1990. pap. 12.95 (*0-9618561-1-4*) J&J Pub Co.

Rape of Clarissa: Writing, Sexuality & Class-Struggle in Richardson. Terry Eagleton. 113p. 1982. pap. text ed. 12.95 (*0-8166-1209-9*) U of Minn Pr.

Rape of Emergency Medicine. Phoenix Staff. 288p. (Orig.). 1992. pap. 19.95 (*0-9632237-1-2*) Phoenix.

Rape of Europa: The Fate of Europe's Treasures in the Third Reich & the Second World War. Lynn H. Nicholas. LC 93-11317. 1994. 27.50 (*0-679-40069-9*) Knopf.

Rape of Europa: The Fate of Europe's Treasures in the Third Reich & the Second World War. Lynn H. Nicholas. 1995. pap. 15.00 (*0-679-75686-8*, Vin) Random.

Rape of Europa by Jupiter, a Masque - As It Is Sung at the Queens Theatre, in Dorset-Garden: And the Masque of Acis & Galatea...in a New Opera Call'd the Mad Lover. Peter A. Motteux & John Eccles. LC 92-24905. (Augustan Reprints Ser.: No. 208). 1981. reprint ed. 14.50 (*0-404-70208-2*, M52.E27R3) AMS Pr.

Rape of Fatherhood Pt. I: Nemesis. Russell Tarrant. 72p. 1996. pap. 12.00 (*0-8059-3895-8*) Dorrance.

Rape of Florida. Albery A. Whitman. LC 75-83895. (Black Heritage Library Collection). 1977. 16.95 (*0-8369-8689-X*) Ayer.

Rape of Florida. Albery A. Whitman. LC 71-104595. reprint ed. lib. bdg. 8.00 (*0-8398-2166-2*) Irvington.

***Rape of Ganymede.** John P. Cooke. 1998. 24.00 (*0-89296-611-4*) Mysterious Pr.

Rape of God. George H. Ochsner. Ed. by Virginia Ochsner. LC 90-84940. 396p. (Orig.). 1990. pap. 12.95 (*0-945201-16-8*) Gannam-Kubat.

Rape of Justice: MacArthur & the New Guinea Hangings. Walter A. Luszki. 196p. (C). 1991. 24.95 (*0-8191-8348-2*) Madison Bks UPA.

Rape of Ma Bell: Anarchy in Communications. Constantine R. Kraus & Alfred W. Duerig. 386p. 1988. 19.95 (*0-8184-0468-X*) Carol Pub Group.

Rape of Man & Nature: An Enquiry into the Origins & Consequences of Modern Science. Philip Sherrard. 124p. 1995. 20.00 (*955-9028-00-6*) Paul & Co Pubs.

***Rape of Nanjing.** Iris Chang. 208p. 1997. 24.00 (*0-465-06835-9*) Basic.

***Rape of Nanjing.** Iris Chang. 208p. 1998. pap. write for info. (*0-465-06836-7*) Basic.

Rape of Nanking: An Undeniable History in Photographs. James Yin & Shi Young. Ed. by Ron Dorfman. (Illus.). 336p. (MAN.). 1997. 50.00 (*0-9632231-8-6*) Innovat Pub & Graph.

***Rape of Nanking: An Undeniable History in Photographs.** James Yin & Shi Young. Ed. by Ron Dorfman. (Illus.). 336p. 1997. lib. bdg. 75.00 (*0-9632231-9-4*) Innovat Pub & Graph.

Rape of Nations: A Study in Societal Economics. C. Pensare. LC 73-88364. (C). 1969. 52.75 (*0-912010-01-0*); spiral bd. 35.00 (*0-912010-00-2*) Goss.

Rape of Paradise: Columbus & the Origin of Western Racism. Jan Carew. LC 94-16194. 232p. 1994. pap. text ed. 14.95 (*1-881316-79-3*) A&B Bks.

Rape of Poland. Stanislaw Mikolajczyk. LC 73-141282. (Illus.). 309p. 1972. reprint ed. text ed. 65.00 (*0-8371-5879-6*, MIRP, Greenwood Pr) Greenwood.

Rape of Shavi. Buchi Emecheta. LC 84-27424. 178p. 1985. pap. 8.95 (*0-8076-1118-2*) Braziller.

Rape of Sita. Lindsey Collen. (African Writers Ser.). 256p. 1995. pap. 10.95 (*0-435-90958-4*, 90958) Heinemann.

Rape of the A. P. E. Allen Sherman. 375p. 1991. reprint ed. lib. bdg. 35.95 (*0-89966-796-1*) Buccaneer Bks.

Rape of the American Constitution. Chuck Shiver. LC 95-76192. 384p. (Orig.). (C). 1995. pap. 18.95 (*1-55950-127-8*, 58090) Loompanics.

Rape of the Earth: Deforestification & Desertification. Marilyn Turkovich. 1989. spiral bd. 30.00 (*1-56709-029-X*) Indep Broadcast.

Rape of the Indian Lands: An Original Anthology. Ed. by Paul W. Gates & Stuart Bruchey. LC 78-56698. (Management of Public Lands in the U. S. Ser.). 1979. lib. bdg. 25.95 (*0-405-11358-7*) Ayer.

Rape of the Innocent: Understanding & Preventing Child Sexual Abuse. Juliann Whetsell-Mitchell. 370p. 1995. 59.95 (*1-56032-408-2*) Taylor & Francis.

***Rape of the Innocent: Understanding & Preventing Child Sexual Abuse.** Juliann Whetsell-Mitchell. 315p. 1995. pap. 29.95 (*1-56032-394-9*) Taylor & Francis.

Rape of the Lock. Aubrey Beardsley & Alexander Pope. pap. 4.95 (*0-486-21963-1*) Dover.

***Rape of the Lock.** Pope. Date not set. pap. text ed. write for info. (*0-312-11569-5*) St Martin.

Rape of the Lock. 3rd ed. Alexander Pope. Ed. by G. Tillotson. 128p. (C). 1971. pap. 8.50 (*0-415-03999-1*, NO. 2389) Routledge.

Rape of the Lock. Flaubert's Mythic Realism. Robert Griffin. LC 87-81916. (French Forum Monographs: No. 70). 352p. (Orig.). 1988. pap. 24.95 (*0-917058-71-2*) French Forum.

Rape of the Masses: The Psychology of Totalitarian Political Propaganda. Serge Chakotin. LC 77-157553. (Studies in Philosophy: No. 40). 1971. lib. bdg. 75.00 (*0-8383-1264-0*) M S G Haskell Hse.

Rape of the Nicollet Mall Mannequin. Steve Hall. LC 78-64893. 1978. pap. 2.50 (*0-9602068-0-9*) Con Brio.

Rape of the Nile: Tomb Robbers, Tourists, & Archaeologists in Egypt. Brian M. Fagan. (Illus.). 416p. 1992. reprint ed. pap. 14.95 (*1-55921-066-4*) Moyer Bell.

Rape of the Powerless. Ed. by William Osborne. vi, 208p. 1971. text ed. 157.00 (*0-677-14720-1*) Gordon & Breach.

Rape of the Rose: A Novel. Glyn Hughes. 320p. 1993. 21.00 (*0-671-72516-5*) S&S Trade.

Rape of the Sleeping Woman: And the Practice of Hypnagogic Sex. D. K. Toteras. LC 94-43091. 320p. (Orig.). 1995. pap. 14.95 (*0-9644122-0-9*) Nine Muses Pr.

Rape of the Text: Reading & Misreading Pope's Essay on Man. Harry M. Solomon. LC 92-38675. 256p. (C). 1993. text ed. 34.95 (*0-8173-0696-X*) U of Ala Pr.

Rape of the Wild: Man's Violence Against Animals & the Earth. Andree Collard & Joyce Contrucci. LC 88-32042. 208p. 1989. 27.50 (*0-253-31514-X*); pap. 10.95 (*0-253-20519-0*, MB-519) Ind U Pr.

Rape of Tutankhamun. John Romer & Elizabeth Romer. (Illus.). 160p. 1993. 44.50 (*1-85479-169-9*, Pub. by M OMara Books UK) Trans-Atl Phila.

Rape on Campus. Ed. by Katie De Koster. (At Issue Ser.). 120p. (C). 1995. pap. text ed. 8.96 (*1-56510-263-0*) Greenhaven.

Rape on Campus. Ed. by Bruno Leone & Katie De Koster. LC 94-42400. (At Issue Ser.). 1995. lib. bdg. 14.96 (*1-56510-296-7*) Greenhaven.

Rape on Trial. Zsuzsanna Adler. LC 86-15586. 224p. 1987. 49.95 (*0-7102-0804-9*, 08049, RKP) Routledge.

Rape on Trial: How the Mass Media Construct Legal Reform & Social Change. Lisa M. Cuklanz. 160p. 1995. text ed. 28.95 (*0-8122-3321-2*); pap. text ed. 12.95 (*0-8122-1559-1*) U of Pa Pr.

***Rape Poems.** Frances Driscoll. LC 96-72150. 88p. (Orig.). 1997. pap. 12.95 (*0-9651413-1-4*, SAN 299-0075) Pleasure Boat.

Rape Prevention War: Rape Prevention vs. Rape Crisis: Criminologist vs. County D. A.; State A. G.; State Legislature; Federal Legislature & State Dept. of Health. Joseph E. Spott. (Illus.). 100p. (Orig.). (C). 1994. pap. text ed. 20.00 (*0-913050-50-4*) J E Spott.

Rape Reference: A Resource for People at Risk. Ed. by Maureen Harrison & Steve Gilbert. LC 95-61243. 352p. (Orig.). 1996. pap. 16.95 (*1-880780-07-0*) Excellent Bks.

***Rape Seed.** rev. ed. G. S. Weiner. Ed. by Annette Francis. 288p. 1996. pap. 10.95 (*0-9657804-0-6*) Adagio Press.

Rape, the Crime I Did Not Commit... Today Is the Day of Your Miracle. Roberto Arroyo. 100p. (Orig.). 1995. pap. text ed. 5.99 (*0-9630423-6-X*) R A Aviles.

Rape Victim: A Project of the Committee on Women of the American Psychiatric Association. Elaine H. Carmen. LC 76-5627. 110p. reprint ed. pap. 31.40 (*0-8357-7799-5*, 2036164) Bks Demand.

Rape Victim: Clinical & Community Interventions. 2nd ed. Mary P. Koss & Mary R. Harvey. (Library of Social Research: Vol. 185). (Illus.). 288p. 1991. 54.00 (*0-8039-3894-2*); pap. 24.95 (*0-8039-3895-0*) Sage.

Rape Victims, Offenders, Treatment & Jurisprudence: Medical Subject Analysis & Research Guide. American Health Research Institute Staff. Ed. by John C. Bartone. LC 83-45537. 140p. 1984. 37.50 (*0-88164-122-7*); pap. 34.50 (*0-88164-123-5*) ABBE Pubs Assn.

Rape Warfare: The Hidden Genocide in Bosnia-Herzegovina & Croatia. Beverly Allen. 208p. 1996. 19.95 (*0-8166-2818-1*) U of Minn Pr.

Rape Within Marriage: A Moral Analysis Delayed. Edward J. Bayer. LC 85-5289. 160p. (Orig.). 1985. lib. bdg. 47.50 (*0-8191-4613-7*) U Pr of Amer.

Rape 101: Sexual Assault Prevention for College Athletes. Andrea Parrot et al. 1994. pap. 21.95 (*1-55691-099-1*, 991) Learning Pubns.

Rapeseed: Chemistry & Technology. H. Niewiadomski. (Developments in Food Science Ser.: No. 23). 448p. 1990. 253.25 (*0-444-98799-1*) Elsevier.

Raphael. James H. Beck. LC 93-39102. 1994. 22.95 (*0-8109-3777-8*) Abrams.

Raphael. Roger Jones & Nicholas Penny. LC 83-1390. 240p. 1987. pap. 27.50 (*0-300-04052-0*) Yale U Pr.

Raphael. Nello Ponente. (Qui Etait Ser.). (Illus.). 150p. (FRE.). 1990. 65.00 (*0-7859-5024-9*) Fr & Eur.

Raphael. Bruno Santi. Tr. by Paul Blanchard from ITA. (Library of Great Masters). (Illus.). 80p. (Orig.). 1992. pap. 12.99 (*1-878351-15-X*) Riverside NY.

Raphael. Roger Jones & Nicholas Penny. LC 83-1390. (Illus.). 264p. reprint ed. pap. 75.30 (*0-7837-3322-4*, 2057727) Bks Demand.

Raphael: Tables of Houses. Raphael. 9.95 (*0-685-38474-8*) Wehman.

Raphael: The Stanza della Segnatura, Rome. James Beck. LC 93-13059. (Great Fresco Cycles of the Renaissance Ser.). (Illus.). 96p. 1992. 25.00 (*0-8076-1314-2*) Braziller.

***Raphael - The Apartments of Pope Julius II & Pope Leo X.** Guido Cornini. (Illus.). 351p. 250.00 (*0-00-507512-2*, Pub. by Musei Vaticani IT) Treasures Inc.

Raphael Affair. large type ed. Iain Pears. (Linford Mystery Library). 1991. pap. 15.99 (*0-7089-7155-5*) Ulverscroft.

Raphael & France: The Artist As Paradigm & Symbol. Martin Rosenberg. (Illus.). 265p. (C). 1995. 49.50 (*0-271-01300-1*) Pa St U Pr.

Raphael at the Vatican. Jacqueline Guillaud. 1990. 100.00 (*0-517-57370-9*, C P Pubs) Crown Pub Group.

Raphael Has Wings. Shannon Dugan. 1997. pap. text ed. 14.95 (*1-57532-098-3*) Press-Tige Pub.

Raphael, His Life & Works. Joseph A. Crowe. LC 72-2584. (Select Bibliographies Reprint Ser.). 1977. reprint ed. 52.95 (*0-8369-6852-2*) Ayer.

Raphael Holinshed & English Chronicle History. Taufer. Date not set. 22.95 (*0-8057-4581-5*, Twayne) Scribnrs Ref.

Raphael Lemkin's Thoughts on Nazi Genocide: Not Guilty? Ed. by Steven L. Jacobs. LC 92-276. 408p. 1992. lib. bdg. 109.95 (*0-7734-9480-4*) E Mellen.

Raphael Pumpelly: Gentleman Geologist of the Gilded Age. Peggy Champlin. LC 93-4778. (History of American Science & Technology Ser.). 288p. 1994. text ed. 49.95 (*0-8173-0691-9*) U of Ala Pr.

***Raphael Semmes: The Philosophical Mariner.** Warren F. Spencer. LC 96-9580. 352p. 1997. text ed. 37.95 (*0-8173-0844-X*) U of Ala Pr.

Raphael Semmes & the Alabama. Spencer C. Tucker. LC 95-51434. (Civil War Campaign & Commanders Ser.). (Illus.). 132p. 1996. pap. 11.95 (*1-886661-11-1*, 61111) Ryan Place Pub.

An Asterisk (*) at the beginning of an entry indicates that the title is appearing in BIP for the first time.

Raphael Semmes, Rear Admiral, Confederate States Navy, Brigadier General, Confederate States Army. Ed. & Intro. by Caldwell Delaney. (Illus.). 1978. 25.00 (*0-914334-05-0*); pap. 10.00 (*0-914334-06-9*) Museum Mobile.

Raphael Soyer: Fifty Years of Printmaking, 1917-1967. Sylvan Cole, Jr. LC 67-29917. (Graphic Art Ser.). 1983. 39.50 (*0-306-70986-4*) Da Capo.

Raphael Soyer: The Shape of Human Dignity. Howard E. Wooden. LC 88-51255. (Illus.). 19p. 1988. pap. 5.00 (*0-939324-38-5*) Wichita Art Mus.

Raphael Soyer Life Drawings & Portraits: 42 Plates. Raphael Soyer. (Art Library). 48p. (Orig.). 1986. pap. 3.95 (*0-486-25100-4*) Dover.

***Raphael Tapestry Cartoons.** Sharon Fermor. (Illus.). 96p. 1996. 35.00 (*1-85759-055-4*) Scala Books.

***Raphael, Two Angels.** Paul Brownlow. 1994. 6.99 (*1-877719-92-7*) Brownlow Pub Co.

Raphaelle Peale: Still Lifes. Nicolai Cikovsky, Jr. et al. (Illus.). 132p. 1988. pap. 6.99 (*0-89468-121-4*) Natl Gallery Art.

Raphaelle Peale Still Lifes. Nicolai Cikovsky, Jr. (Illus.). 132p. 1989. 30.00 (*0-8109-1474-3*) Abrams.

Raphael's Astro Ephemeris (Any Year) Raphael. pap. 9.95 (*0-685-22085-0*) Wehman.

Raphael's Astrological Almanac. Foulsham Editors. 1995. pap. 59.90 (*0-572-02047-3*, Pub. by Foulsham UK) Assoc Pubs Grp.

Raphael's Astrological Almanac 1994. Foulsham Editors. 1993. pap. 5.95 (*0-572-01881-9*, Pub. by Foulsham UK) Assoc Pubs Grp.

***Raphael's Astrological & Predictive Almanac.** W. Foulsham & Co. Staff. 1997. pap. text ed. 5.95 (*0-572-02325-1*, Pub. by W Foulsham UK) Trans-Atl Phila.

Raphael's Astronomical Ephemeris see Raphael's Daily Planetary Guide 1997: The Complete Aspectarian

***Raphael's Astronomical Ephemeris of the Planets for 1998.** W. Foulsham & Co. Staff. 1997. pap. text ed. 5.95 (*0-572-02260-3*, Pub. by W Foulsham UK) Trans-Atl Phila.

Raphael's Astronomical Ephemeris of the Planets' Places for 1994. Foulsham Editors. 48p. 1993. pap. 5.95 (*0-572-01851-7*, Pub. by Foulsham UK) Assoc Pubs Grp.

Raphael's Astronomical Ephemeris of the Planets' Places for 1995. Ed. by Foulsham, W., & Company Staff. 1994. pap. 9.95 (*0-572-01968-8*, Pub. by W Foulsham UK) Trans-Atl Phila.

Raphael's Astronomical Ephemeris of the Planets' Places for 1996. 73p. 1995. pap. text ed. 9.95 (*0-572-02095-3*, Pub. by W Foulsham UK) Trans-Atl Phila.

***Raphael's Astronomical Ephemeris of the Planets' Places for 1997.** 1996. pap. 9.95 (*0-572-02115-1*, Pub. by W Foulsham UK) Trans-Atl Phila.

Raphael's Bible: A Study of the Vatican Logge. Bernice F. Davidson. LC 84-43088. (College Art Association Monographs: Vol. 39). (Illus.). 198p. 1985. 35.00 (*0-271-00388-X*) Pa St U Pr.

***Raphael's Daily Planetary Guide: The Complete Aspectarian.** W. Foulsham & Co. Staff. 1997. pap. text ed. 11.95 (*0-572-02370-7*, Pub. by W Foulsham UK) Trans-Atl Phila.

***Raphael's Daily Planetary Guide 1997: The Complete Aspectarian.** Ed. by Foulsham, W., & Company Staff. Orig. Title: Raphael's Astronomical Ephemeris. 75p. (Orig.). 1996. pap. 9.95 (*0-572-02292-1*, Pub. by W Foulsham UK) Trans-Atl Phila.

Raphael's Guide to Astrology - Containing a Complete System of Genethliacal Astrology. Raphael. 132p. 1991. pap. 15.00 (*0-89540-189-4*, SB-189, Sun Bks) Sun Pub.

Raphael's Horary Astrology: By Which Every Question Relating to the Future May be Answered. 4th ed. Raphael. reprint ed. spiral bd. 5.50 (*0-7873-0703-3*) Hlth Research.

Raphael's Key to Astrology. Raphael. 118p. 1991. pap. 12.00 (*0-89540-142-8*, SB-142, Sun Bks) Sun Pub.

Raphael's Medical Astrology. Raphael. 88p. 1991. reprint ed. pap. 8.00 (*0-89540-180-0*, SB-180, Sun Bks) Sun Pub.

Raphael's Mundane Astrology. Raphael. 80p. 1996. pap. 7.00 (*0-89540-231-9*, SB-231, Sun Bks) Sun Pub.

***Raphael's School of Athens.** Ed. by Marcia B. Hall. (Masterpieces of Western Painting Ser.). (Illus.). 224p. 1997. pap. text ed. 15.95 (*0-521-44899-9*) Cambridge U Pr.

***Raphael's School of Athens.** Ed. by Marica Hall. (Masterpieces of Western Painting Ser.). (Illus.). 224p. 1997. text ed. 54.95 (*0-521-44447-0*) Cambridge U Pr.

Rapha's Twelve Step Program for Overcoming Chemical Dependency. Robert S. McGee et al. 302p. 1990. pap. 14.99 (*0-945276-10-9*) Rapha Pub.

Rapha's Twelve Step Program for Overcoming Codependency. Pat Springle. 267p. 1990. pap. 15.99 (*0-945276-14-1*) Rapha Pub.

Rapha's Twelve-Step Program for Overcoming Eating Disorders. Robert S. McGee & William D. Mountcastle. 1990. pap. 15.99 (*0-945276-19-2*) Rapha Pub.

Rapid Access Guide to Internal Medicine: Companion to Kelley's Textbook of Internal Medicine. 3rd ed. Patrick O'Kane. LC 96-15026. 416p. 1996. pap. text ed. 24.95 (*0-397-51255-4*) Lppncott-Raven.

Rapid Access Guide to Physical Examination. Novey. 548p. (C). (gr. 13). 1988. pap. text ed. 31.95 (*0-8151-6434-3*, Yr Bk Med Pubs) Mosby Yr Bk.

Rapid Analysis Methods in Food Microbiology. P. Patel. 1994. 119.00 (*0-7514-0030-0*, Pub. by Blackie Acad & Prof UK) Routledge Chapman & Hall.

Rapid Analysis of Arrhythmias: A Self-Study Program. 2nd ed. Emanuel Stein. (Illus.). 226p. 1992. pap. text ed. 24.95 (*0-8121-1499-X*) Williams & Wilkins.

Rapid Analysis of Electrocardiograms: A Self-Study Course. 2nd ed. Emanuel Stein. (Illus.). 404p. 1992. pap. 19.95 (*0-8121-1441-8*) Williams & Wilkins.

Rapid & Reliable Analysis. Reinhold Ebertin. 68p. 1970. 11.00 (*0-86690-093-4*, E1099-014) Am Fed Astrologers.

Rapid Application Development with Oracle Designer/2000. Chris Billings et al. LC 96-32379. 458p. (C). 1997. pap. text ed. 36.95 (*0-201-63444-9*) Addison-Wesley.

Rapid Application Generation of Business & Finance Software. Ed. by Sukhdev Khebbal & Chris Sharpington. LC 96-1799. 228p. (C). 1996. lib. bdg. 99.50 (*0-7923-9707-X*) Kluwer Ac.

Rapid Application Prototyping: The Storyboard Approach to User Requirements Analysis. Stephen J. Androile. 280p. 1993. pap. text ed. 49.95 (*0-471-55630-0*, GD4035) Wiley.

Rapid Appraisal & Health Policy. Bie N. Ong. (Illus.). 152p. (Orig.). 1996. pap. 49.95 (*1-56593-736-8*, 1432) Singular Publishing.

Rapid Appraisal Methods. Krishna Kumar. LC 93-21584. (Regional & Sectoral Study Ser.). 240p. 1993. 20.00 (*0-8213-2523-X*, 12523) World Bank.

Rapid Assessment. Springhouse Publishing Co. Editors. LC 90-10450. (Clinical Skillbuilders Ser.). (Illus.). 185p. 1992. spiral bd. 26.95 (*0-87434-364-X*) Springhouse Pub.

***Rapid Assessment of Sources of Air, Water & Land Pollution.** WHO Staff. (WHO Offset Publications). 113p. 1982. 12.00 (*92-4-170062-9*) World Health.

***Rapid Assessment of the Humid Forests of South Central Chuquisaca, Bolivia.** T. Schulenberg. Ed. by K. Awbrey & E. Ortiz. (RAP Working Papers). 60p. (Orig.). (C). 1997. pap. text ed. 10.00 (*1-881173-19-4*) Conser Intl.

Rapid Assessment Procedures for Nutrition & Primary Health Care. Susan C. Scrimshaw & Elena Hurtado. LC 87-3193. (Reference Ser.). 69p. (Orig.). 1987. pap. 10.95 (*0-87903-111-5*) UCLA Lat Am Ctr.

Rapid Change in the Quaternary. 1990. 10.00 (*0-317-05510-0*) Am Quaternary Assn.

Rapid Concrete & Bridge Deck Protection, Repair & Rehabilitation. Michael M. Sprinkel et al. 109p. (Orig.). (C). 1993. pap. text ed. 15.00 (*0-309-05604-7*, SHRP-S-344) SHRP.

***Rapid Course.** Longman Publishing Staff. 1983. pap. text ed. write for info. (*0-85896-027-3*) Addison-Wesley.

Rapid Course in English Literature. C. J. Daswani & T. C. Daswani. 156p. 1990. pap. text ed. 7.95 (*81-207-1271-4*, Pub. by Sterling Pubs II) Apt Bks.

***Rapid Data Warehousing with the SAS System.** 140p. (C). 1997. pap. 29.95 (*1-55544-916-6*) SAS Inst.

Rapid Debt-Reduction Strategies. John F. Avanzini. 306p. 1990. pap. 12.95 (*1-878605-01-1*) HIS Pub Co.

Rapid Deployment Force & U. S. Military Intervention in the Persian Gulf. 2nd ed. Jeffrey Record. LC 83-81086. (Special Report Ser.). 83p. 1983. 11.95 (*0-89549-053-6*) Inst Foreign Policy Anal.

Rapid Deployment Logistics. 1990. lib. bdg. 79.95 (*0-8490-4057-4*) Gordon Pr.

Rapid Deployment Underwater Search & Rescue: Organizing, Training & Equipping an Emergency Service Dive Team. Laser Tech Staff. Ed. by Eric Tackett & Ruth A. Hunsinger. (Illus.). 150p. (Orig.). 1987. teacher ed. 15.95 (*0-943155-06-1*, 1021); pap. 16.95 (*0-318-22568-9*) Laser Tech.

Rapid Descent. Barbara Sturken Peterson. 1994. 25.00 (*0-671-76069-6*) S&S Trade.

Rapid Development: Taming Wild Software Schedules. Steve M. McConnell. LC 96-21517. (Code Ser.). 648p. 1996. pap. text ed. 35.00 (*1-55615-900-5*) Microsoft.

Rapid Development Training for Small Businesses. Gary Ward. (Illus.). 200p. 1990. 42.50 (*0-9623424-0-8*) Boswell Pub.

Rapid Development with Oracle CASE: A Workshop Approach. Chris Billings & Maria Billings. LC 93-8205. 1993. 31.95 (*0-201-63344-2*) Addison-Wesley.

Rapid Diagnosis in Infectious Diseases. Michael J. Rytel. 224p. 1979. pap. 129.00 (*0-8493-5535-4*, RC112, CRC Reprint) Franklin.

Rapid Diagnosis of Mycoplasmas. Ed. by I. Kahane & A. Adoni. (FEMS Symposium Ser.: No. 62). (Illus.). 234p. 1994. 85.00 (*0-306-44621-9*, Plenum Pr) Plenum.

***Rapid ECG Interpretation.** Khan. 1997. pap. text ed. 19.95 (*0-7216-7468-2*) Saunders.

Rapid ECG Interpretation. Ann E. Norman. 1989. pap. text ed. 24.00 (*0-07-105302-6*) McGraw-Hill HPD.

Rapid Ecological Assessment of the Bladen Nature Reserve, Belize. Susan Iremonger & Roger Sayre. Ed. by Douglas S. Baker. 80p. pap. write for info. (*0-9624590-7-0*) Nature VA.

Rapid Ecological Assessment of the Blue & John Crow Mountains National Park, Jamaica. Douglas M. Muchoney et al. Ed. by Douglas S. Baker. (Illus.). 80p. pap. write for info. (*0-9624590-9-7*) Nature VA.

Rapid Ecological Assessment of the Montego Bay Marine Park, Jamaica. Kathleen M. Sullivan & Mark Chiappone. Ed. by Douglas S. Baker. (Illus.). 80p. (Orig.). pap. write for info. (*0-9624590-8-9*) Nature VA.

Rapid Electrical Estimating & Pricing: A Handy, Quick Method of Directly Determining the Selling Prices of Electrical Construction Work. 5th ed. C. Kenneth Kolstad & Gerald V. Kohnert. LC 92-34066. 1993. text ed. 65.00 (*0-07-035523-1*) McGraw.

Rapid Evaluation of Potential Fields in Particle Systems. Leslie F. Greengard. (ACM Distinguished Dissertation Ser.). 110p. 1988. 25.00 (*0-262-07110-X*) MIT Pr.

Rapid Evolutionary Development: Requirements, Prototyping & Software Creation. Lowell J. Arthur. LC 91-16670. (Series in Software Engineering Practice). 240p. 1991. text ed. 52.00 (*0-471-53633-4*) Wiley.

Rapid Excavation: Proceedings of the Tunnel & Shaft Conference on Problems & Progress, Minneapolis, 1968. Tunnel & Shaft Conference Staff. Ed. by Donald H. Yardley. LC 78-98023. (Illus.). 420p. reprint ed. pap. 119.70 (*0-317-10974-X*, 2002907) Bks Demand.

Rapid Excavation & Tunneling Conference, Proceeding: Chicago, Illinois, June 12-16, 1983, 2 vols. Rapid Excavation & Tunneling Conference Staff. LC 83-70933. (Illus.). 74p. reprint ed. Index, 74p. pap. 25.00 (*0-7837-1101-8*, 2041631) Bks Demand.

Rapid Excavation & Tunneling Conference, Proceeding: Chicago, Illinois, June 12-16, 1983, 2 vols., Vol. 1. Rapid Excavation & Tunneling Conference Staff. LC 83-70933. (Illus.). 673p. reprint ed. pap. 180.00 (*0-7837-1099-2*, 2041631) Bks Demand.

Rapid Excavation & Tunneling Conference, Proceeding: Chicago, Illinois, June 12-16, 1983, 2 vols., Vol. 2. Rapid Excavation & Tunneling Conference Staff. LC 83-70933. (Illus.). 611p. reprint ed. pap. 174.20 (*0-7837-1100-X*, 2041631) Bks Demand.

Rapid Eye, No. 1. rev. ed. Ed. by Simon Dwyer. (Illus.). 256p. 1996. pap. 19.95 (*1-871592-22-4*) Creation Bks.

Rapid Eye, No. 2. rev. ed. Ed. by Simon Dwyer. (Illus.). 256p. 1996. pap. 19.95 (*1-871592-23-2*) Creation Bks.

Rapid Eye, No. 3. rev. ed. Ed. by Simon Dwyer. (Illus.). 256p. 1995. pap. 19.95 (*1-871592-24-0*) Creation Bks.

***Rapid Eye Technology: Discovering the Perfect Self Within You.** Ranae Johnson. 205p. 1996. pap. 12.95 (*0-9631506-2-6*) Raintree.

Rapid Falcons. large type ed. Margery Forester. 496p. 1994. 25.99 (*0-7089-3109-X*) Ulverscroft.

Rapid Fire. Jack Slade. 176p. (Orig.). 1993. mass mkt., pap. text ed. 3.99 (*0-8439-3488-3*) Dorchester Pub Co.

***Rapid Force Projection: Exploring New Technology Concepts for Light Airborne Forces.** Randall Steeb et al. 80p. (Orig.). 1996. pap. text ed. 6.00 (*0-8330-2428-0*, DB-168-A/OSD) Rand Corp.

***Rapid Force Projection Technologies: A Quick-Look Analysis of Advanced Light Indirect Fire Systems.** Randall Steeb et al. 79p. 1996. pap. text ed. 6.00 (*0-8330-2427-2*, DB-169-A/OSD) Rand Corp.

Rapid Freezing, Freeze Structure & Deep Etching. Ed. by Nicholas J. Severs & David M. Shotton. LC 95-9125. 372p. 1995. text ed. 135.95 (*0-471-01433-8*) Wiley.

***Rapid Growth & Relative Decline: Modelling Macroeconomic Dynamics with Hysteresis.** LC 96-46322. 1997. text ed. 69.95 (*0-312-17268-0*) St Martin.

***Rapid Guide Hazardous Air Pollutants.** Beiml. (References Ser.). 1998. pap. 29.95 (*0-442-02515-7*) Van Nos Reinhold.

Rapid Guide to Chemical Incompatibility. Richard P. Pohanish. LC 96-37063. (Miscellaneous/Catalogs Ser.). 1997. pap. 29.95 (*0-442-02394-4*) Van Nos Reinhold.

***Rapid Guide to Hazardous Chemicals in the Environment.** Richard P. Pohanish. LC 97-14013. 1996. pap. 29.95 (*0-442-02527-0*) Van Nos Reinhold.

Rapid Guide to Hazardous Chemicals in the Workplace. 3rd ed. Richard J. Lewis. 1994. pap. 29.95 (*0-442-01759-6*) Van Nos Reinhold.

***Rapid Guide to Trade Names & Synonyms.** Pohanish. (References Ser.). (C). 1997. pap. 29.95 (*0-442-02594-7*) Van Nos Reinhold.

Rapid Healing Foods. Ben Davis. 1989. 7.95 (*0-13-753179-6*) P-H.

Rapid Interpretation of EKG's. 5th ed. Dale Dubin. LC 88-72108. (Illus.). 342p. 1996. pap. text ed. 29.99 (*0-912912-02-2*) Cover Pub.

Rapid Interpretation of Heart Sounds & Murmurs. 3rd ed. Emanuel Stein & Abner J. Delman. (Illus.). 88p. 1990. pap. text ed. 28.00 incl. audio (*0-8121-1247-4*) Williams & Wilkins.

***Rapid Interpretation of Heart Sounds & Murmurs.** 4th ed. Emanuel Stein & Abner J. Delman. 168p. 1996. pap. 37.95 incl. audio (*0-683-30084-9*) Williams & Wilkins.

***Rapid Interpretation of Heart Sounds & Murmurs.** 4th ed. Emanuel Stein & Abner J. Delman. 168p. 1996. 37.95 incl. audio compact disk (*0-683-30131-4*) Williams & Wilkins.

Rapid Interpretation of Heart Sounds, Murmurs & Arrhythmias: A Guide to Cardiac Auscultation in Dogs & Cats. Larry P. Tilley & Frances W. Smith, Jr. 70p. 1992. pap. text ed. 29.50 incl. audio (*0-8121-1568-6*) Williams & Wilkins.

Rapid Italian for Students & Tourists. Michael Cagno & Ben D'Arlon. (C). 1979. pap. 7.95 (*0-913298-05-0*) S F Vanni.

Rapid Load Fracture Testing. Ed. by Ravinder Chona & William R. Corwin. LC 91-45387. (Special Technical Publication Ser.: No. 1130). (Illus.). 192p. 1992. text ed. 63.00 (*0-8031-1429-X*, 04-011300-30) ASTM.

Rapid Mastery of Spanish. Antonia V. Scrivner. LC 95-70255. 80p. (SPA.). 1995. pap. 25.00 incl. audio (*1-887116-08-7*) Saxon West Pubns.

Rapid Math in Ten Days: The Quick-N-Easy Guide to Mastering Numbers. Edward H. Julius. 224p. (Orig.). 1994. pap. 10.95 (*0-399-52129-1*, Perigee Bks) Berkley Pub.

Rapid Math Tricks & Tips: Thirty Days to Number Power. Edward H. Julius. LC 92-10638. 240p. 1992. pap. text ed. 15.95 (*0-471-57563-1*) Wiley.

Rapid Math Without a Calculator. A. Frederick Collins. 120p. (YA). 1987. reprint ed. pap. 5.95 (*0-8065-1058-7*, Citadel Pr) Carol Pub Group.

Rapid Memory in Seven Days: The Quick & Easy Guide to Better Remembering. Joan Minninger. Ed. by Eleanor Dugan. LC 94-6937. 208p. (Orig.). 1994. pap. 10.95 (*0-399-52130-5*, Perigee Bks) Berkley Pub.

Rapid Methods & Automation in Microbiology & Immunology. Ed. by A. Vaheri et al. (Illus.). 600p. 1991. 129.95 (*0-387-53983-2*) Spr-Verlag.

Rapid Methods for Analysis of Food & Food Raw Material. Ed. by Werner Baltes. LC 90-71262. 320p. 1990. 69.95 (*0-87762-794-0*) Technomic.

Rapid Methods for Chemical Analysis of Hydraulic Cement, STP 985. Ed. by Ronald F. Gebhardt. LC 88-6302. (Special Technical Publication (STP) Ser.). (Illus.). 162p. 1988. pap. text ed. 27.00 (*0-8031-0989-X*, 04-985000-07) ASTM.

Rapid Methods in Clinical Microbiology: Present Status & Future Trends. Ed. by B. Kleger et al. LC 80-6776. (Advances in Experimental Medicine & Biology Ser.: Vol. 263). (Illus.). 158p. 1989. 69.50 (*0-306-43507-1*, Plenum Pr) Plenum.

Rapid Methods in Food Microbiology. M. R. Adams & C. F. Hope. (Progress in Industrial Microbiology Ser.: No. 26). 330p. 1989. 169.25 (*0-444-87420-8*) Elsevier.

Rapid Nursing Interventions: Neurologic. B. M. R. Staff & Deborah K. Wright. LC 95-20814. (Rapid Nursing Interventions Ser.). 224p. 1996. pap. 19.95 (*0-8273-7093-8*) Delmar.

Rapid Perspective. Geoffrey Wickham. (YA). (gr. 10 up). 9.95 (*0-85458-050-6*); pap. 7.95 (*0-85458-051-4*) Transatl Arts.

Rapid Population Change in China, 1952-1982. Ansley J. Coale. LC 84-61188. (Committee on Population & Demography Report Ser.: Vol. 27). 103p. reprint ed. pap. 29.40 (*0-7837-2415-2*, 2042552) Bks Demand.

Rapid Problem Solving with Post-It Notes. David Straker. LC 96-28070. 184p. 1996. 39.95 (*0-566-07836-8*, Pub. by Gower UK) Ashgate Pub Co.

***Rapid Problem Solving with Post-It Notes.** David Straker. LC 97-20721. (Illus.). 160p. (Orig.). 1997. pap. 14.95 (*1-55561-142-7*) Fisher Bks.

Rapid Propagation of Fast-Growing Woody Species. Ed. by F. W. Baker. 144p. 1992. 70.00 (*0-85198-742-7*) CAB Intl.

***Rapid Prototyping.** 118p. pap. text ed. 35.00 (*0-614-24701-2*, 403) Laser Inst.

Rapid Prototyping: Moving to Business - Centric Development. John P. Reilly. 300p. 1995. pap. 43.95 (*1-85032-193-0*) ITCP.

***Rapid Prototyping: Principles & Applictions in Manufacturing.** Chee Kai Chua & Kah Fai Leong. LC 96-36533. 1996. pap. text ed. 65.95 (*0-471-19004-7*) Wiley.

Rapid Prototyping & Manufacturing: Fundamentals of Stereolithography. Paul F. Jacobs. Ed. by David T. Reid. (Illus.). 420p. 1992. 80.00 (*0-87263-425-6*) SME.

Rapid Prototyping & Manufacturing: Fundamentals of StereoLithography. Paul F. Jacobs. 1992. text ed. 65.00 (*0-07-032433-6*) McGraw.

Rapid Prototyping for Computer Aided Design. Charles Thomas. 122p. (C). 1995. pap. text ed. write for info. (*1-887503-23-4*) Schroff Dev Corp.

Rapid Prototyping for Object. Mark Mullin. 1990. pap. 22.95 (*0-201-55024-5*) Addison-Wesley.

***Rapid Prototyping in Europe & Japan Vol. II: Site Reports.** unabridged ed. Friedrich B. Prinz. (JTEC Panel Reports). (Illus.). 127p. (Orig.). 1996. pap. write for info. (*1-883712-43-2*) Intl Tech Res.

***Rapid Prototyping of Application Specific Signal Processors.** Ed. by Mark A. Richards et al. 204p. (C). 1997. lib. bdg. 110.00 (*0-7923-9871-8*) Kluwer Ac.

Rapid Prototyping Systems: Fast Track to Product Realization. LC 94-67186. (Illus.). 250p. 1994. 55.00 (*0-87263-454-X*) SME.

***Rapid Prototyping '95.** (Illus.). 34p. pap. text ed. 29.00 (*0-614-24697-0*, 580D) Laser Inst.

Rapid Rail Vehicles & Systems: Technical Assistance Manual. (Illus.). 31p. (Orig.). (C). 1995. pap. text ed. 20.00 (*0-7881-1903-6*) DIANE Pub.

Rapid Reactions in Solution. Hans Strehlow. (Illus.). 341p. 1992. 115.00 (*3-527-28260-2*, VCH) Wiley.

Rapid Reading: A Home Study Course. 3rd ed. Stephen F. Holbrook. (Home Study Ser.). 1989. reprint ed. 30.00 (*0-939926-43-1*); reprint ed. audio (*0-318-64397-9*) Fruition Pubns.

Rapid Reading for Busy People. Stephen F. Holbrook. 1991. pap. text ed. 14.95 (*0-941562-12-3*) Princeton Mgmt Assocs.

Rapid Reference Guide to Adobe Illustrator. Michael Fraase. 100p. 1992. 10.00 (*1-55623-742-1*) Irwin Prof Pubng.

Rapid Reference Guide to Canvas. Michael Fraase. 112p. 1992. 10.00 (*1-55623-749-9*) Irwin Prof Pubng.

Rapid Reference Guide to Freehand. Michael Fraase. 112p. 1993. per. 10.00 (*1-55623-744-8*) Irwin Prof Pubng.

Rapid Reference Guide to HyperCard for the Macintosh. Michael Fraase. LC 92-17595. (Rapid Reference Ser.). 112p. 1992. 10.00 (*1-55623-743-X*) Irwin Prof Pubng.

Rapid Reference Guide to MacDraw Pro. Michael Fraase. (Rapid Reference Ser.). 112p. 1992. pap. 10.00 (*1-55623-741-3*) Irwin Prof Pubng.

Rapid Reference Guide to Microsoft Word 5.0. Michael Fraase. 100p. 1992. 10.00 (*1-55623-746-4*) Irwin Prof Pubng.

Rapid Reference Guide to PageMaker. Michael Fraase. LC 92-24065. (Rapid Reference Ser.). 112p. 1993. per. 10.00 (*1-55623-748-0*) Irwin Prof Pubng.

Rapid Reference Guide to QuarkXPress. Michael Fraase. LC 92-27700. (Rapid Reference Ser.). 112p. 1992. pap. 10.00 (*1-55623-740-5*) Irwin Prof Pubng.

Rapid Reference Guide to System 7. Michael Fraase. 100p. 1992. per. 10.00 (*1-55623-745-6*) Irwin Prof Pubng.

Rapid Reference Guide to System 7, the LaserWriter Family, & HyperCard. Michael Fraase. LC 92-27690. (Rapid Reference Ser.). 304p. 1993. per. 25.00 (*1-55623-902-5*) Irwin Prof Pubng.

Rapid Reference Guide to System 7, the LaserWriter Family, & PageMaker. Michael Fraase. LC 92-27691. (Rapid Reference Ser.). 304p. 1993. per. 25.00 (*1-55623-767-7*) Irwin Prof Pubng.

Rapid Reference Guide to System 7, the Lazerwriter Family, & Microsoft Word 5.0. Michael Fraase. 300p. 1992. text ed. 25.00 (*1-55623-766-9*) Irwin Prof Pubng.

Rapid Reference Guide to the Lazerwriter Family. Michael Fraase. 100p. 1992. 10.00 (*1-55623-747-2*) Irwin Prof Pubng.

Rapid Reference Guide to WordPerfect. Michael Fraase. LC 92-37425. (Rapid Reference Ser.). 125p. 1993. per. 10.00 (*1-55623-739-1*) Irwin Prof Pubng.

Rapid Reliability Assessment of VLSICs. A. P. Dorey et al. LC 89-72202. (Illus.). 212p. 1990. 75.00 (*0-306-43492-X*, Plenum Pr) Plenum.

Rapid Relief from Emotional Distress. Gary Emery & James Campbell. 1987. pap. 10.00 (*0-449-90249-8*, Columbine) Fawcett.

***Rapid Response Manufacturing.** Dong. 384p. 1997. text ed. write for info. (*0-412-78010-0*, Chap & Hall NY) Chapman & Hall.

Rapid Response Reports: FA 1993. Michael Squires et al. 112p. 1993. pap. text ed. 110.00 (*0-406-02648-3*, UK) MICHIE.

***Rapid Review: Anatomy Reference Guide.** Marcelo Oliver. Ed. by Nancy Liskar. (Illus.). 77p. (YA). (gr. 9 up). 1996. pap. 29.95 (*0-9603730-9-8*) Anatomical Chart.

***Rapid Rural Appraisal, Participatory Rural Appraisal & Aquaculture.** Food & Agriculture Organization Staff. (Fisheries Technical Paper Ser.: No. 358). 109p. 1997. pap. 12.00 (*92-5-103871-6*, F38716, Pub. by FAO IT) Bernan Associates.

***Rapid-Sequence Review of Anesthesiology: With Time-Limited Pressure.** Won K. Chee. LC 96-50977. 176p. 1997. pap. 40.00 (*0-7506-9933-7*) Buttrwrth-Heinemann.

Rapid Software Deployment. Baharami. (DC - Introduction to Computing Ser.). 1996. pap. 43.95 (*0-7895-0583-5*) Course Tech.

Rapid Software Deployment. Bahrami. (DC - Introduction to Computing Ser.). 1996. pap. 47.95 (*0-534-24186-7*) S-W Pub.

Rapid Software Development with Smalltalk. Mark Lorenz. (Advances in Object Technology Ser.: Vol. 7). (Illus.). 200p. (Orig.). 1995. pap. 29.00 (*1-884842-12-7*) SIGS Bks & Multimedia.

Rapid Software Development with SmallTalk. Mark Lorenz. 1995. pap. text ed. 29.00 (*0-13-449737-6*) P-H.

Rapid Solidification of Metals & Alloys. H. Jones. 92p. 1993. pap. text ed. 16.80 (*0-901462-18-7*, Pub. by Inst Materials UK) Ashgate Pub Co.

Rapid Solidification Technology. Ed. by T. S. Sudarsham & T. S. Srivatsan. LC 92-61491. 730p. 1992. text ed. 199.95 (*0-87762-926-9*) Technomic.

Rapid Solidification Technology. American Society for Metals Staff & R. L. Ashbrook. LC 82-74298. (Source Book Ser.). (Illus.). 448p. reprint ed. pap. 127.70 (*0-7837-1861-6*, 2042062) Bks Demand.

Rapid Solidification Technology. R. L. Ashbrook. LC 82-74298. (American Society for Metals - Source Book Ser.). (Illus.). 448p. reprint ed. pap. 127.70 (*0-8357-4092-7*, 2036858) Bks Demand.

Rapid Solidification Technology for Reduced Consumption of Strategic Materials. J. E. Flinn. LC 85-4769. (Illus.). 215p. 1985. 32.00 (*0-8155-1032-2*) Noyes.

Rapid Statistical Calculations: A Collection of Distributions-Free & Easy Methods of Estimation & Testing. 2nd ed. M. H. Quenouille. 1972. 12.50 (*0-85264-214-8*) Lubrecht & Cramer.

Rapid System Prototyping, 5th International Conference (RSP '94) LC 10-746005. 216p. 1994. pap. text ed. 40.00 (*0-8186-5885-1*, 5885) IEEE Comp Soc.

Rapid System Prototyping, 6th International Conference (RSP '95) LC 10-746005. 248p. 1995. pap. 50.00 (*0-8186-7100-9*, PR07100) IEEE Comp Soc.

Rapid System Prototyping, 7th International Workshop (RSP '96) 200p. 1996. pap. text ed. 50.00 (*0-8186-7603-5*) IEEE Comp Soc.

***Rapid System Prototyping, 8th International Workshop (RSP '97)** 200p. 1997. pap. 60.00 (*0-8186-8064-4*) IEEE Comp Soc.

Rapid Team Deployment. Sandy Pokras. Ed. by Kay Keppler. LC 95-67039. (Fifty-Minute Ser.). (Illus.). 128p. (Orig.). 1995. pap. 10.95 (*1-56052-321-2*) Crisp Pubns.

Rapid Thermal & Integrated Processing Vol. 224: Materials Research Society Symposium Proceedings. Ed. by M. L. Green et al. 503p. 1991. text ed. 74.00 (*1-55899-118-2*) Materials Res.

Rapid Thermal & Integrated Processing II. Ed. by J. C. Gelpey et al. (Symposium Proceedings Ser.: Vol. 303). 423p. 1993. text ed. 65.00 (*1-55899-199-9*) Materials Res.

Rapid Thermal & Integrated Processing III Vol. 342: Materials Research Society Symposium Proceedings. Ed. by J. C. Gelpey et al. 449p. 1994. text ed. 51.00 (*1-55899-242-1*) Materials Res.

Rapid Thermal & Integrated Processing IV. Ed. by J. C. Gelpey et al. (Symposium Proceedings Ser.: Vol. 387). 455p. 1995. text ed. 68.00 (*1-55899-290-1*) Materials Res.

Rapid Thermal & Integrated Processing V. Ed. by A. Fiory et al. (MRS Symposium Proceedings Ser.: Vol. 429). 389p. 1996. 70.00 (*1-55899-332-0*, 429) Materials Res.

***Rapid Thermal & Integrated Processing VI: Materials Research Society Symposium Proceedings, Vol. 470.** Ed. by T. J. Riley et al. 1997. text ed. 71.00 (*1-55899-374-6*) Materials Res.

Rapid Thermal Annealing/Chemical Vapor Deposition & Integrated Processing Vol. 146: Materials Research Society Symposium Proceedings, Vol. 146. T. E. Seidel. 494p. 1989. text ed. 30.00 (*1-55899-019-4*) Materials Res.

Rapid Thermal Processing, Vol. 52. Ed. by T. O. Sedgwick et al. (Materials Research Society Symposium Proceedings Ser.). 1986. text ed. 17.50 (*0-931837-17-0*) Materials Res.

***Rapid Thermal Processing: Operating Principles, Technology & Applications.** 500p. 1997. lib. bdg. 46.00 (*981-02-2833-3*) World Scientific Pub.

Rapid Thermal Processing: Science & Technology. Ed. by Richard B. Fair. LC 93-6882. (Illus.). 430p. 1993. text ed. 67.00 (*0-12-247690-5*) Acad Pr.

Rapid Thermal Processing of Electronic Materials. Ed. by Syd R. Wilson et al. (MRS Symposium Proceedings Ser.: Vol. 92). 1987. text ed. 17.50 (*0-931837-59-6*) Materials Res.

***Rapid Thermal Processing of Semiconductors.** Victor E. Borisenko & Peter J. Hesketh. LC 97-3783. (Microdevices Ser.). (Illus.). 353p. (C). 95.00 (*0-306-45054-2*, Plenum Pr) Plenum.

Rapid Transit. Edison Dupree. (Poetry Chapbook Ser.). (Illus.). 27p. (Orig.). 1988. pap. write for info. (*0-9624274-3-8*) NC Writers Network.

Rapid Transits & Other Stories: And Other Stories. Holley Rubinsky. 192p. (Orig.). 1990. pap. 10.95 (*0-919591-56-6*, Pub. by Polestar Bk Pubs CN) Orca Bk Pubs.

Rapid Turbo Pascal Graphics Tutor. J. Abas. (Illus.). 156p. 1992. pap. 38.00 (*0-7503-0206-2*); disk 270.00 (*0-7503-0280-1*) IOP Pub.

Rapid Urban Environmental Assessment Vol. 1: Lessons from Cities in the Developing World, Methodology & Preliminary Findings. Josef Leitmann. LC 94-10848. (Urban Management & the Environment Ser.: Vol. 14). 78p. 1994. 7.95 (*0-8213-2790-9*, 12790) World Bank.

Rapid Urban Environmental Assessment Vol. 2: Lessons from Cities in the Developing World, Tools & Outputs. Josef Leitmann. LC 94-9395. (Urban Management Programme Ser.: No. 15). 156p. 1994. 9.95 (*0-8213-2791-7*, 12791) World Bank.

Rapid Visual Screening of Buildings for Potential Seismic Hazards: A Handbook. (Illus.). 185p. (Orig.). (C). 1993. pap. text ed. 40.00 (*1-56806-575-2*) DIANE Pub.

Rapid Visual Screening of Buildings for Potential Seismic Hazards: Supporting Documentation. (Illus.). 137p. (Orig.). (C). 1993. pap. text ed. 40.00 (*1-56806-576-0*) DIANE Pub.

Rapid Viz: A New Method for the Rapid Visualization of Ideas. Kurt Hanks & Larry Belliston. Ed. by Phil Gerould. LC 90-21967. (Illus.). 149p. (C). 1990. reprint ed. pap. 15.95 (*1-56052-055-8*) Crisp Pubns.

Rapid Writing in Six Days: The Quick & Easy Program to Master Faster Writing. Ben E. Johnson. 256p. 1994. pap. 9.95 (*0-399-52132-1*, Perigee Bks) Berkley Pub.

Rapides Parish: An Illustrated History. Sue Eakin. LC 87-10639. 200p. 1987. 24.95 (*0-89781-201-8*) Am Historical Pr.

Rapidly Assembled Structures: Proceedings of the Conference on Mobile & Rapidly Assembled Structures (MARAS), Held in Southampton, England, in April 1991. Ed. by P. S. Bulson. LC 91-70382. (Topics in Engineering Ser.: Vol. 8). 314p. 1991. 115.00 (*1-56252-063-6*) Computational Mech MA.

***Rapidly Progressive Glomerulonephritis.** Ed. by Charles Pusey & Andrew Rees. (Oxford Clinical Nephrology Ser.). (Illus.). 192p. 1998. text ed. 115.00 (*0-19-262636-1*) OUP.

Rapidly Solidified Alloys: Processes-Structures-Properties-Applications. Liebermann. (Materials Engineering Ser.: Vol. 3). 808p. 1993. 235.00 (*0-8247-8951-2*) Dekker.

Rapidly Solidified Alloys & Their Mechanical & Magnetic Properties, Vol. 58. Ed. by Bill C. Giessen et al. (Materials Research Society Symposium Proceedings Ser.). 1986. text ed. 17.50 (*0-931837-23-5*) Materials Res.

Rapidly-Solidified Amorphous Materials Update. Business Communications Co., Inc. Staff. 269p. 1989. 2,450.00 (*0-89336-667-6*, GB-079R) BCC.

Rapidly Solidified Crystalline Alloys: Proceedings of a TMS-AIME Northeast Regional Meeting. Metallurgical Society of AIME Staff et al. Ed. by S. K. Das et al. LC 85-28833. (Illus.). 331p. reprint ed. pap. 94.40 (*0-8357-5544-4*, 2035159) Bks Demand.

Rapidly Solidified Materials: Proceedings of an International Conference, San Diego, CA, U. S. A., 3-5 February 1985 i.e. 1986. Ed. by Peter W. Lee & Robert S. Corbonars. LC 85-73692. (Illus.). 446p. reprint ed. pap. 127.20 (*0-318-39722-6*, 2033078) Bks Demand.

Rapidly Solidified Powder Aluminum Alloys STP 890. Ed. by Morris E. Fine & Edgar A. Starke, Jr. LC 86-7887. (Special Technical Publication Ser.). (Illus.). 544p. 1986. text ed. 64.00 (*0-8031-0442-1*, 04-890000-04) ASTM.

Rapidreader! Manual. Dorris M. Lee. (Illus.). 160p. (Orig.). 1988. 99.95 incl. vhs (*0-317-89789-6*) Norman Leslie.

Rapids. Alan P. Sullivan. LC 74-163830. (Social History of Canada Ser.). 283p. reprint ed. pap. 80.70 (*0-8357-6368-4*, 2035722) Bks Demand.

Rapidzap. Graves & Austin. 1989. pap. 15.00 (*0-89303-813-X*) P-H.

***Rapier & Small-Sword, 1460-1820.** A. V. Norman. (Illus.). 464p. 1980. 46.95 (*0-405-13089-9*) Ayer.

Rapier Family Record: Genealogy Maryland-Kentucky. 1973. 20.00 (*0-614-13544-3*) R C Rapier.

Rapier Looms: Assessment of Four Modern Machines. Ed. by Wira Staff. 1985. 40.00 (*0-317-43594-9*) St Mut.

Rapist. Walter E. Adams. 180p. (Orig.). 1994. pap. 6.95 (*0-937408-87-5*) GMI Pubns Inc.

Rapist. Walter E. Adams. 100p. 1996. 10.00 (*0-937408-82-4*) GMI Pubns Inc.

Rapist, Vol. III. Walter E. Adams. 220p. (Orig.). 1995. pap. 6.95 (*0-937408-84-0*) GMI Pubns Inc.

Rapists Beware. James Smith. (Illus.). 200p. 1979. 12.75 (*0-87527-301-7*) Green.

Rapist's Wife. Kathryn Casey. 376p. (Orig.). 1995. mass mkt. 5.50 (*0-380-77456-9*) Avon.

RAPmetic, the Arithmetic Rap. Gloria J. Musson & Cyril D. Musson. (Illus.). 48p. (Orig.). (J). (gr. 3 up). 1988. pap. text ed. 3.50 (*0-9619321-0-4*); audio 6.50 (*0-9619321-1-2*) Sq One Pubns.

***Raport z Podziemia -- 1942.** Marek Celt. (Illus.). 409p. (Orig.). (POL.). 1997. pap. 11.95 (*0-9635004-2-2*) Flying Heart.

Rapp on the New Market. Stan Rapp. 1996. pap. text ed. 14.95 (*0-07-052151-4*) McGraw.

Rapp on the New Market. Stan Rapp. 1997. text ed. 22.95 (*0-07-052156-5*) McGraw.

Rappaccini's Children: American Writers in a Calvinist World. William H. Shurr. LC 79-57573. 173p. reprint ed. pap. 49.40 (*0-7837-5804-9*, 2045470) Bks Demand.

Rappaccini's Daughter. Nathaniel Hawthorne. 1995. 3.00 (*0-87129-508-3*, R55) Dramatic Pub.

Rappacini's Daughter: A Play. Octavio Paz. Tr. by Sebastian Doggart from SPA. 80p. (C). 1996. 24.00 (*1-56886-034-X*); pap. 14.95 (*1-56886-035-8*) Marsilio Pubs.

Rappahannock County Marriages, 1833-1850. John Vogt & T. William Kethley, Jr. (Virginia Historic Marriage Register Ser.). (Illus.). viii, 75p. (Orig.). 1984. pap. 5.00 (*0-935931-14-7*) Borgo Pr.

Rappahannock County Marriages, 1833-1850. John Vogt & T. William Kethley, Jr. (Virginia Historic Marriage Register Ser.). viii, 75p. (Orig.). (C). 1984. reprint ed. lib. bdg. 25.00 (*0-8095-8228-7*) Borgo Pr.

Rappahannock River. Walter Nicklin. (Virginia Heritage Publications). 48p. 1994. pap. 5.95 (*1-885937-00-8*) Casco Commns.

Rappelling. 2nd rev. ed. Tom Martin. LC 91-90423. (Illus.). 304p. 1995. 16.95 (*0-930871-03-0*) Search.

Rappin' & Rhymin' Raps, Songs, Cheers, & SmartRope Jingles for Active Learning, Grades K-8. Rosella R. Wallace. (Illus.). 80p. (Orig.). 1992. teacher ed., pap. 19.95 (*0-913705-72-1*) Zephyr Pr AZ.

Rappin' Mother Goose: Nursery Rhymes. Gene Sicard et al. (Rappin' Mother Goose Fun-Rap Ser.). 24p. (J). (ps-3). 1991. 11.45 incl. audio (*1-879755-00-9*) Recorded Pubns.

***Rappin' up Careers: A Career Awareness Program.** Ken Smith & Arden Martenz. (Illus.). 48p. (Orig.). (J). (gr. 4-9). 1991. pap. 19.95 (*1-57543-005-3*) Mar Co Prods.

Rapping with Ten Thousand Carabao in the Dark. Al Robles. Ed. by Russell Leong. (Illus.). 140p. (Orig.). 1995. pap. 10.00 (*0-934052-25-5*) UCLA Asian Am Studies Ctr.

Rapport de Brodie. Jorge Luis Borges. 160p. (FRE.). 1984. pap. 10.95 (*0-7859-1999-6*, 2070375889) Fr & Eur.

Rapport Sur Les Fouilles de Koptos (Janvier-Fevrier 1910) Adolph J. Reinach. (Illus.). 58p. (FRE.). reprint ed. pap. 25.00 (*0-933175-21-3*) Van Siclen Bks.

***Rapport Sur l'Instruction Publique, Fait au Nom du Comite de Constitution a l'Assemblee Nationale: 1791 Edition.** Charles M. De Talleyrand-Perigord. Ed. & Intro. by Jeffrey Stern. (Classics in Education Ser.). 216p. 1996. reprint ed. write for info. (*1-85506-311-5*) Bks Intl VA.

***Rapports.** 4th annot. ed. Joel Walz & Jean-Pierre Piriou. (FRE.). (C). 1997. teacher ed., text ed. 56.76 (*0-669-41646-0*) HM College Div.

***Rapports.** 4th ed. Joel Walz & Jean-Pierre Piriou. 544p. (FRE.). (C). 1997. text ed. 55.56 (*0-669-41645-2*) HM College Div.

***Rapports.** 4th ed. Joel Walz & Jean-Pierre Piriou. (FRE.). (C). 1997. lab manual ed., wbk. ed., text ed. 35.96 (*0-669-41647-9*) HM College Div.

Rapports: Language, Culture, Communication. 3rd annot. ed. Joel Walz & Jean-Pierre Piriou. 544p. (ENG & FRE.). (C). 1993. Instr.'s annotated ed. teacher ed., text ed. 55.56 (*0-669-27711-8*) HM College Div.

Rapports: Language, Culture, Communication. 3rd ed. Joel Walz & Jean-Pierre Piriou. 544p. (ENG & FRE.). (C). 1993. text ed. 55.56 (*0-669-27710-X*); Instr.'s resource kit. teacher ed. 6.76 (*0-669-27723-1*); Chapter vocabulary list/Wkbk./Lab. manual answer key. student ed. 35.96 (*0-669-27712-6*); Tapescript. 2.66 (*0-669-27716-9*); Testing program. 2.66 (*0-669-27718-5*); Cassette program. audio 31.16 (*0-669-27713-4*); Overhead transparencies kit. trans. 56.36 (*0-669-27725-8*); Videocassette kit. vhs 105.16 (*0-669-33294-1*) HM College Div.

Rapports des Grecs avec l'Egypte. M. Dominique Mallet. 218p. 1980. 30.00 (*0-89005-299-9*) Ares.

Rapports entre Juifs, Cretiens et Musulmans: Eine Sammlung von Forschungsbeitragen. Ed. by Johannes Irmscher. 244p. (ENG, FRE, GER, ITA & SPA.). 1995. pap. 80.00 (*90-256-1021-8*, Pub. by A M Hakkert NE) Benjamins North Am.

Rapports pour la Preparation du XVe Plan, 65 tomes. 250.00 (*0-685-36715-0*) Fr & Eur.

Rapprochement du Droit Judiciaire de l'Union Europeenne: Approximation of Judiciary Law in the European Union. Ed. by Marcel Storme. 244p. 1994. pap. text ed. 86.50 (*0-7923-2874-4*) Kluwer Ac.

Rapprochment: The Critical Subphase of Separation-Individuation. Ed. by Ruth F. Lax et al. LC 80-66351. 528p. 1994. pap. 45.00 (*1-56821-103-1*) Aronson.

***Rapro Ultimate Success System.** Velather Weaver. LC 97-90431. (Illus.). 190p. (Orig.). (YA). (gr. 7-12). 1997. wbk. ed., pap. 20.00 (*0-9658223-3-8*) Vals Designs.

RAPS: Reading Activities Project for Older Students. Caroline R. Musselwhite. (Illus.). 188p. (YA). 1993. 29.00 (*1-884135-50-1*) Mayer-Johnson.

Raps & Rhymes. Ed. by Heather Kelly. (Illus.). 80p. 1990. teacher ed. 14.00 (*1-875327-03-7*, Pub. by E Curtain AT) Peguis Pubs Ltd.

Raps & Rhymes in Maths. Ann Baker & Johnny Baker. LC 91-16343. (Illus.). 90p. 1991. pap. 16.50 (*0-435-08325-2*, 08325) Heinemann.

Raps Clack Callspar. Michael Helsem. (Orig.). 1990. pap. 4.50 (*0-941720-82-9*) Slough Pr TX.

Rapstone Chronicles: Paradise Postponed & Titmuss Regained. John Mortimer. LC 92-39686. 704p. 1993. pap. 14.00 (*0-14-017595-4*, Penguin Bks) Viking Penguin.

Raptor. Judith Van Gleson. Ed. by Dana Isaacson. 256p. 1991. reprint ed. mass mkt. 4.99 (*0-671-73243-9*) PB.

***Raptor & the Lamb: Predators & Prey in the Living World.** Christopher McGowan. 1997. 25.00 (*0-8050-4298-9*) H Holt & Co.

***Raptor Attack: I Love Dinosaurs.** Michael Berenstain. (J). 1997. 3.95 (*1-57719-110-2*) GT Pubng Corp.

Raptor Biomedicine. Ed. by Patrick T. Redig et al. 288p. (C). 1993. text ed. 49.95 (*0-8166-2219-1*) U of Minn Pr.

Raptor Red. Robert T. Bakker. 256p. 1996. mass mkt. 6.50 (*0-553-57561-9*) Bantam.

Raptor Red. large type ed. Robert T. Bakker. (Basic Ser.). 393p. 1996. lib. bdg. 24.95 (*0-7862-0634-9*) Thorndike Pr.

Raptor Rescue! An Eagle Flies Free. Photos by Ron Winch. LC 94-41483. (Illus.). 32p. (J). 1995. pap. 15.99 (*0-525-45301-6*) Dutton Child Bks.

Raptor Zone. large type ed. Gwen Moffat. (General Ser.). 416p. 1993. 25.99 (*0-7089-2881-1*) Ulverscroft.

***Raptors.** (Birds up Close Ser.). (Illus.). 32p. (J). 1997. lib. bdg. 18.64 (*0-86505-751-6*) Crabtree Pub Co.

***Raptors.** (Birds up Close Ser.). (Illus.). 32p. (J). 1997. pap. 5.95 (*0-86505-765-6*) Crabtree Pub Co.

***Raptors: North American Birds of Prey.** Noel F. Snyder & Helen Snyder. LC 96-48508. Orig. Title: Birds of Prey: Natural History & Conservation of North American Raptors. (Illus.). 224p. 1997. pap. 24.95 (*0-89658-349-X*) Voyageur Pr.

Raptors: The Birds of Prey. Scott Weidensaul. (Illus.). 392p. 1996. 40.00 (*1-55821-275-2*) Lyons & Burford.

Raptors! The Nastiest Dinosaurs. Don Lessem. LC 95-7110. (Illus.). 32p. (J). (gr. 1-5). 1996. 14.95 (*0-316-52119-1*) Little.

Raptors, Birds of Prey. John Hendrickson. LC 92-9808. (Illus.). 96p. 1992. pap. 18.95 (*0-8118-0004-0*) Chronicle Bks.

Raptor's Claw. B. B. Calhoun, pseud. LC 95-11467. (Dinosaur Detective Ser.: Vol. 8). (Illus.). 112p. (J). 1995. pap. 4.95 (*0-7167-6607-8*, Sci Am Yng Rdrs) W H Freeman.

Raptor's Claw. B. B. Calhoun, pseud. LC 95-11467. (Dinosaur Detective Ser.: Vol. 8). (Illus.). 112p. (J). 1996. 12.95 (*0-7167-6606-X*, Sci Am Yng Rdrs) W H Freeman.

Raptors, Fossils, Fins & Fangs: A Prehistoric Creature Feature. Ray Troll & Bradford Matsen. LC 96-1823. (Illus.). 32p. (J). (gr. 2 up). 1996. 14.95 (*1-883672-41-4*) Tricycle Pr.

Raptors in Human Landscapes: Adaptations to Built & Cultivated Environments. Ed. by David Bird et al. (Illus.). 416p. 1996. text ed. 72.00 (*0-12-100130-X*) Acad Pr.

***Raptors of Arizona.** Richard L. Glinski. LC 97-21055. 1998. write for info. (*0-8165-1322-8*) U of Ariz Pr.

***Raptors of Europe & the Middle East: A Handbook of Field Identification.** Dick Forsman. (Birds Ser.). 1997. text ed. write for info. (*0-85661-098-4*) Acad Pr.

Rapture. Gordon Lindsay. 1969. 2.95 (*0-89985-063-4*) Christ for the Nations.

Rapture. Silhouette Staff. 1981. pap. 1.75 (*0-373-30762-4*) Silhouette.

Rapture. David Sosnowski. 320p. 1996. 23.00 (*0-679-45174-9*) Random.

***Rapture.** David Sosnowski. 1997. pap. 11.95 (*0-553-37896-1*) Bantam.

Rapture: A Question of Timing. William R. Kimball. LC 85-71275. 194p. (Orig.). 1985. pap. 5.99 (*0-89900-205-6*) College Pr Pub.

Rapture: Poems. Susan Mitchell. LC 91-50517. 96p. 1992. pap. 11.00 (*0-06-096906-7*, PL) HarpC.

Rapture: Pre-, Mid-, or Post-Tribulation? Gleason L. Archer, Jr. et al. LC 83-126250. 256p. (Orig.). 1984. 14.99 (*0-310-44741-0*, 12625P) Zondervan.

Rapture: The Second Coming. William Spencer-Hale et al. (Illus.). (Orig.). 1995. pap. 25.00 (*0-9648726-0-9*) Quintessential Mercy.

Rapture - but When? Before or After the Tribulation? Jim Brown. 80p. 1992. pap. 4.95 (*0-9620659-1-9*) J Brown FL.

Rapture - Get Right or Get Left. Hilton Sutton. 96p. (Orig.). 1991. pap. 5.99 (*0-89274-877-X*, HH877) Harrison Hse.

Rapture & Resurrection. Noah W. Hutchings. 150p. (Orig.). 1992. pap. 6.95 (*1-879366-27-4*) Hearthstone OK.

Rapture & the Second Coming. Wendy Borgstrom. 187p. (Orig.). 1990. pap. 7.95 (*1-55583-166-4*) Alyson Pubns.

Rapture & the Second Coming. Finis J. Dake, Sr. 119p. 1987. 8.95 (*1-55829-028-1*) Dake Bible.

Rapture & the Second Coming of Christ. Gordon Lindsay. (Revelation Ser.: Vol. 8). 1965. 1.95 (*0-89985-041-3*) Christ for the Nations.

Rapture Before the Russian Invasion of Israel, Vol. 1. Emil Gaverluk. LC 88-51429. 300p. (Orig.). 1988. pap. 9.95 (*0-317-92550-4*) WPT Pubns.

Rapture Book. Doug Chatam. 96p. 1974. mass mkt. 3.99 (*0-88368-046-7*) Whitaker Hse.

An Asterisk (*) at the beginning of an entry indicates that the title is appearing in BIP for the first time.

Rapture Book. James McKeever. 240p. (Orig.). (C). pap. text ed. 9.99 (*0-86694-106-1*) Omega Pubns OR.

Rapture Encaged: The Suppression of the Feminine in Western Culture. Ruth A. El Saffar. LC 93-47680. 192p. (C). (gr. 13). 1994. 45.00 (*0-415-11083-1*, B7075) Routledge.

Rapture Fever: Why Dispensationalism is Paralyzed. Gary North. LC 93-444. 1993. student ed. 25.00 (*0-930464-67-2*); pap. 12.95 (*0-930464-65-6*) Inst Christian.

***Rapture in Death.** J. D. Robb. 1996. mass mkt. 5.99 (*0-425-15518-8*) Berkley Pub.

Rapture in His Arms. Lynette Vinet. 352p. 1993. mass mkt. 4.25 (*0-8217-4275-2*, Zebra Kensgtn) Kensgtn Pub Corp.

***Rapture of Canaan.** Sheri Reynolds. 1997. pap. 12.00 (*0-425-16244-3*) Berkley Pub.

***Rapture of Canaan.** Sheri Reynolds. LC 97-25364. (YA). 1997. write for info. (*0-7838-8270-X*) G K Hall.

Rapture of Canaan. Sheri Reynolds. 336p. 1996. 22.95 (*0-399-14112-X*, Putnam) Putnam Pub Group.

***Rapture of Canaan.** Sheri Reynolds. 1997. 22.95 (*0-399-14352-1*) Putnam Pub Group.

Rapture of Canaan. Sheri Reynolds. 336p. 1996. reprint ed. mass mkt. 6.99 (*0-425-15543-9*) Berkley Pub.

Rapture of Matter. Frankie Paino. (Cleveland Poets Ser.: No. 47). 61p. (Orig.). 1991. pap. 8.00 (*0-914946-91-9*) Cleveland St Univ Poetry Ctr.

Rapture of Politics: The Christian Right As the United States Approaches the Year 2000. Ed. by Steve Bruce et al. LC 94-28321. 196p. (C). 1994. pap. 21.95 (*1-56000-802-4*) Transaction Pubs.

Rapture of the Flat. Peter Quinones. LC 92-91113. 80p. 1993. pap. 8.00 (*1-56002-268-X*, Univ Edtns) Aegina Pr.

Rapture Plot. David Macpherson. 256p. (Orig.). 1995. pap. 12.95 (*0-9625220-2-3*) Millennium Three Pubs.

Rapture Question. enl. rev. ed. John F. Walvoord. 304p. 1979. pap. 12.99 (*0-310-34151-5*, 10978P) Zondervan.

***Rapture Question Answered: Plain & Simple.** Robert D. Van Kampen. LC 97-1677. (Illus.). 224p. (Orig.). 1997. pap. 10.99 (*0-8007-5631-2*) Revell.

Rapture Untold Vol. 20: Gender, Mysticism & the 'Moment of Recognition' in Works by Gertrude Stein. Linda Watts. (Writing about Women Ser.). 192p. (C). 1996. text ed. 42.95 (*0-8204-2812-4*) P Lang Pubng.

Rapture...& Then What? large type ed. Eleanor B. Schultz. (Illus.). v, 48p. (Orig.). 1996. pap. 4.95 (*0-9652688-0-2*) Lanore Wrds.

Raptured. 50th ed. Ernest W. Angley. 224p. 1950. pap. 3.50 (*0-9636772-0-9*) Winston Pr OH.

***Raptured.** 51th ed. Ernest W. Angley. 224p. 1997. pap. 3.50 (*0-9636772-2-5*) Winston Pr OH.

Rapture's Angel. Sylvie F. Sommerfield. 1982. mass mkt. 2.75 (*0-89083-750-3*, Zebra Kensgtn) Kensgtn Pub Corp.

Rapture's Gold. F. Rosanne Bittner. 496p. 1986. mass mkt. 3.95 (*0-8217-1889-4*, Zebra Kensgtn) Kensgtn Pub Corp.

Rapture's Mist. Cinnamon Burke. 448p. (Orig.). 1993. mass mkt., pap. text ed. 4.99 (*0-8439-3470-0*) Dorchester Pub Co.

Rapture's Rage. Bobbi Smith. 1983. mass mkt. 3.50 (*0-8217-1121-0*, Zebra Kensgtn) Kensgtn Pub Corp.

***Rapture's Rage.** Bobbi Smith. 480p. 1997. reprint ed. mass mkt. 5.99 (*0-505-52238-1*, Love Spell) Dorchester Pub Co.

Rapture's Rendezvous. Cassie Edwards. (Orig.). 1982. mass mkt. 3.50 (*0-8217-1049-4*, Zebra Kensgtn) Kensgtn Pub Corp.

Rapture's Voyage. Sandra Lawrence. (Bedroom Adventures Ser.). 1993. write for info. (*1-884057-00-4*) Trivial Development Corp.

Rapu Nui: The Illustrated Story of the Epic Film. Kevin Reynolds & Tim R. Price. (Illus.). 160p. 1994. pap. 16.95 (*1-55704-184-9*) Newmarket.

Rapunzel. (Timeless Tales from Hallmark Fairy Tale Classics Ser.). 24p. (J). Date not set. text ed. 4.95 (*1-56987-216-3*) Landoll.

Rapunzel. Nicola Baxter. (Favorite Tales Ser.). (Illus.). 28p. (J). 1994. 2.99 (*0-7214-5451-8*, Ladybrd) Penguin.

Rapunzel. Illus. & Retold by Alix Berenzy. 32p. (J). (ps-2). 1995. 15.95 (*0-8050-1283-4*) H Holt & Co.

Rapunzel. Sidney Berger. (Illus.). 32p. (Orig.). (J). (ps up). 1991. pap. 3.50 (*0-88680-359-4*) I E Clark.

Rapunzel. Bernice Chardiet. 32p. (J). 1990. pap. 2.99 (*0-590-42281-2*) Scholastic Inc.

Rapunzel. Fred Crump, Jr. (Guilford Substance Abuse Ser.). (Illus.). 272p. (J). (gr. k-2). 1991. pap. 6.95 (*1-55523-408-9*) Winston-Derek.

Rapunzel. Fred Crump, Jr. LC 91-67499. (Illus.). 44p. (J). (gr. k-3). 1992. pap. 8.95 incl. audio (*1-55523-482-8*) Winston-Derek.

Rapunzel. Jill Downie. (Illus.). 32p. (J). 1995. bds. 13.95 (*0-86264-509-3*, Pub. by Anderson Pr UK) London Brdge.

Rapunzel. Jacob W. Grimm & Wilhelm K. Grimm. LC 92-14259. (Illus.). 32p. (J). 1992. 6.95 (*0-8362-4924-0*) Andrews & McMeel.

Rapunzel. Jacob W. Grimm & Wilhelm K. Grimm. (Creative's Collection of Fairy Tales). (Illus.). 32p. (YA). (gr. 6 up). 1986. lib. bdg. 13.95 (*0-87191-936-2*) Creative Ed.

Rapunzel. Jacob W. Grimm & Wilhelm K. Grimm. LC 92-6712. (Illus.). 32p. (J). (gr. k-3). 1992. 14.95 (*0-8249-8558-3*, Ideals Child); lib. bdg. 15.00 (*0-8249-8585-0*, Ideals Child) Hambleton-Hill.

Rapunzel. Jacob W. Grimm & Wilhelm K. Grimm. LC 92-14259. (Illus.). 32p. (J). (gr. k-3). 1995. per., pap. 5.95 (*1-57102-034-9*, Ideals Child) Hambleton-Hill.

Rapunzel. Jacob W. Grimm & Wilhelm K. Grimm. LC 81-6419. (Illus.). 32p. (J). (ps-3). 1982. lib. bdg. 15.95 (*0-8234-0454-4*) Holiday.

Rapunzel. Jacob W. Grimm & Wilhelm K. Grimm. LC 81-6419. (Illus.). 32p. (J). (ps-3). 1987. pap. 5.95 (*0-8234-0652-0*) Holiday.

Rapunzel. Jacob W. Grimm et al. LC 96-50260. (J). (ps-3). 1997. pap. 16.99 (*0-525-45607-4*) NAL-Dutton.

***Rapunzel.** Jacob W. Grimm. 1997. pap. 2.50 (*0-7214-5709-6*, Ladybrd) Penguin.

Rapunzel. Jacob W. Grimm & Wilhelm K. Grimm. LC 78-18066. (Illus.). 32p. (J). (gr. k-3). 1979. lib. bdg. 11.89 (*0-89375-135-9*) Troll Communs.

Rapunzel. Jacob W. Grimm & Wilhelm K. Grimm. LC 78-18066. (Illus.). 32p. (J). (gr. k-3). 1997. pap. 3.95 (*0-89375-113-8*) Troll Communs.

***Rapunzel.** Illus. by Jim Harris. 32p. (J). 1995. 10.95 (*0-939251-93-0*) Accord CO.

Rapunzel, Incl. Night Light. Illus. by Jim Harris. (J). 1995. 15.95 (*0-939251-50-0*) Accord CO.

***Rapunzel: A Fairy Tale.** Jacob W. Grimm et al. LC 96-44816. (Illus.). 32p. (J). (gr. k-3). 1997. 15.95 (*1-55858-684-9*); lib. bdg. 15.88 (*1-55858-685-7*) North-South Bks NYC.

***Rapunzel: A Nursery Rap.** David Vozar. LC 96-35361. (Illus.). (J). 1998. write for info. (*0-385-32314-X*) BDD Bks Young Read.

Rapunzel: Full-Color Sturdy Book. Marty Noble. LC 96-2948. (Little Activity Bks.). (J). 1996. pap. 1.50 (*0-486-29390-4*) Dover.

Rapunzel: Hidden Picture Fairy Tales. Illus. & Retold by Kit Wray. LC 90-85901. 32p. (J). (gr. k-5). 1991. 7.95 (*1-878093-25-8*) Boyds Mills Pr.

Rapunzel, & The Seven Ravens. Jacob W. Grimm & Wilhelm K. Grimm. (Original Fairy Tales from the Brothers Grimm Ser.). (Illus.). 24p. (J). 1990. 1.00 (*0-517-05386-1*) Random Hse Value.

Rapunzel & the Witch. Jack Melanos. (J). 1950. 5.00 (*0-87602-186-0*) Anchorage.

Rapunzel in Arabic. (Illus.). 52p. (J). (gr. 4-6). 1987. 4.50 (*0-86685-264-6*) Intl Bk Ctr.

Rapunzel 'N the Witch. rev. ed. William-Alan Landes. LC 89-43682. (Wondrawhopper Ser.). (J). (gr. 3-12). 1985. pap. 6.00 (*0-88734-107-1*) Players Pr.

Rapunzel 'n the Witch: Director's Guide Book. rev. ed. William-Alan Landes. LC 89-43682. (Wondrawhopper Ser.). (J). (gr. 3-12). 1985. teacher ed., pap. 30.00 (*0-88734-007-5*) Players Pr.

Rapunzel 'N the Witch: Music & Lyrics. rev. ed. William-Alan Landes. (Wondrawhopper Ser.). (J). (gr. 3-12). 1985. pap. 15.00 (*0-88734-006-7*) Players Pr.

Raquel. Garcia De La Huerta. 169p. (SPA.). 1970. 9.95 (*0-8288-7097-7*, S20233) Fr & Eur.

***Raquel Rabinovich: The Dark Is the Source of the Light.** George Quasha. 1996. pap. text ed. 15.00 (*1-886449-38-4*) Barrytown Ltd.

Raquel's Main Guide to New England Seafoods. Raquel D. Boehmer. (Illus.). (Orig.). 1988. pap. 4.95 (*0-685-22580-1*) Seafood Soundings Pr.

Raquets Unlimited. Levitt. (KM - Office Procedures Ser.). 1982. wbk. ed., pap. 13.95 (*0-538-23501-2*) S-W Pub.

Raquette Lake. Ruth Timm. (Illus.). 400p. 1989. 24.95 (*0-932052-81-9*) North Country.

Rara Arithmetica & Arithmetical Books, 2 vols. in 1. 4th ed. David E. Smith & Augustus De Morgan. LC 74-113148. (Illus.). (ENG.). 1970. text ed. 45.00 (*0-8284-0192-6*) Chelsea Pub.

Rara Mathematica: or A Collection of Treatises on the Mathematics & Subject Connected with Them, from Ancient Inedited Manuscripts. James O. Halliwell. x, 120p. 1977. reprint ed. 23.27 (*3-487-06469-3*) G Olms Pubs.

Raramuri Souls: Knowledge & Social Process in Northern Mexico. William L. Merrill. LC 87-62623. (Series in Ethnographic Inquiry). (Illus.). 248p. 1995. pap. text ed. 14.95 (*1-56098-653-0*) Smithsonian.

***Rare & Endangered Biota of Florida, Vol. 6 - 1982.** Peter C. Pritchard. LC 78-12121. (Illus.). 153p. reprint ed. pap. 43.70 (*0-608-04478-4*, 2065223) Bks Demand.

Rare & Endangered Biota of Florida No. IV: Invertebrates. Ed. by Mark Deyrup & Richard Franz. (Illus.). 828p. 1995. pap. 39.95 (*0-8130-1323-2*); lib. bdg. 75.00 (*0-8130-1322-4*) U Press Fla.

Rare & Endangered Biota of Florida Vol. 1: Mammals. Ed. by Stephen R. Humphrey. (Illus.). 480p. (C). 1992. lib. bdg. 59.95 (*0-8130-1127-2*) U Press Fla.

Rare & Endangered Biota of Florida Vol. 1: Mammals. Stephen R. Humphrey. 1992. pap. 29.95 (*0-8130-1128-0*) U Press Fla.

Rare & Endangered Biota of Florida Vol. 3: Amphibians & Reptiles. Ed. by Paul E. Moler & Ray E. Ashton, Jr. (Illus.). 272p. 1992. lib. bdg. 49.95 (*0-8130-1141-8*) U Press Fla.

Rare & Endangered Biota of Florida Vol. 3: Amphibians & Reptiles, Vol. 3. Ed. by Paul E. Moler & Ray E. Ashton, Jr. (Illus.). 272p. 1992. pap. 29.95 (*0-8130-1142-6*) U Press Fla.

Rare & Endangered Biota of Florida Vol. V: Birds. Ed. by James A. Rodgers, Jr. et al. (Illus.). 736p. 1997. lib. bdg. 65.00 (*0-8130-1448-4*) U Press Fla.

***Rare & Endangered Biota of Florida Vol. V: Birds.** Ed. by James A. Rodgers, Jr. et al. (Illus.). 736p. 1997. pap. 29.95 (*0-8130-1449-2*) U Press Fla.

Rare & Endangered Biota of Florida, Vol. 2: Fishes. Ed. by Carter R. Gilbert. (Illus.). 336p. (C). 1992. pap. 29.95 (*0-8130-1122-1*); lib. bdg. 54.95 (*0-8130-1121-3*) U Press Fla.

Rare & Endangered Plants of San Mateo & Santa Clara County. Toni Corelli & Zoe Chandik. (Illus.). 150p. 1996. pap. 25.00 (*0-9646994-0-0*) T Corelli.

Rare & Most Wonderfull Things Whiche Webbe Hath Seene: Newly Enlarged. Edward Webbe. LC 72-6038. (English Experience Ser.: No. 564). (Illus.). 33p. 1973. reprint ed. 15.00 (*90-221-0564-4*) Walter J Johnson.

Rare & Precious Love. (Rainbow Romances Ser.: No. 903). 160p. 1994. 14.95 (*0-7090-4983-8*, Hale-Parkwest) Parkwest Pubns.

***Rare & Precious Wild Flowers of China.** Feng Kuo-mei. (CHI & LAT.). 1995. 156.00 (*0-7855-0516-4*, Pub. by Wanhai Books CH) St Mut.

***Rare & Precious Wild Flowers of China.** Feng Kuo-mei. (ENG & LAT.). 1995. 175.00 (*0-7855-0517-2*, Pub. by Wanhai Books CH) St Mut.

Rare & Unlisted Toothpick Holders. William Heacock. (Illus.). 96p. (Orig.). 1984. pap. 6.48 (*0-915410-18-4*) Antique Pubns.

Rare & Unusual Animals. Nina Leen. (Illus.). 80p. (J). (gr. 3-7). 1981. 8.95 (*0-03-057478-1*, Bks Young Read) H Holt & Co.

Rare & Unusual Artifacts of the First Americans. Ray Parman, Jr. & Donald N. Brown. (Illus.). 296p. (Orig.). 1989. pap. 24.95 (*0-9623868-0-4*) F Pruett.

Rare & Unusual Fly Tying Materials: A Natural History. Paul Schmookler & Ingrid V. Sils. 304p. 1994. 89.95 (*1-886961-01-8*) Comp Sportsman.

RARE (Association of European Networking Organizations) "State of the Union" Report. Compiled by Josefien Bersee. 51p. (Orig.). (C). 1993. pap. text ed. 25.00 (*0-7881-0038-6*) DIANE Pub.

Rare Benedictine. Ellis Peters. 1989. 19.95 (*0-89296-397-2*) Mysterious Pr.

Rare Benedictine. Ellis Peters. 1991. mass mkt. 5.99 (*0-446-40088-2*, Mysterious Paperbk) Warner Bks.

***Rare Birds Day by Day.** Steve Dudley et al. (Illus.). 392p. 1996. boxed 37.50 (*0-85661-102-6*, Pub. by Poyser UK) Acad Pr.

Rare Birds in Britain & Ireland. J. N. Dymond et al. (Illus.). 480p. 1990. text ed. 37.00 (*0-85661-053-4*, Pub. by Poyser UK) Acad Pr.

Rare Birds of Southern Africa. P. A. Clancey. (Illus.). 1984. 65.00 (*0-87556-735-5*) Saifer.

Rare Birds of the West Coast of North America. Don Roberson. LC 80-51054. (Illus.). 548p. 1980. 24.95 (*0-9605352-0-9*) Woodcock.

Rare Book & Manuscript Library of Columbia University: Collections & Treasures. Ed. by Kenneth A. Lohf & Rudolph Ellenbogen. 138p. 1985. pap. 25.00 (*0-9607862-1-X*) Columbia U Libs.

Rare Book Collections: Some Theoretical & Practical Suggestions for Use by Librarians & Students. Ed. by Horace R. Archer. LC 81-13311. (ACRL Monograph: No. 27). viii, 128p. 1982. reprint ed. text ed. 49.75 (*0-313-23226-1*, ARRB) Greenwood.

Rare Book Librarianship. 2nd fac. rev. ed. Roderick Cave. LC 82-220919. 178p. 1982. reprint ed. pap. 50.80 (*0-7837-8202-0*, 2047960) Bks Demand.

Rare Book Lore: Selections from the Letters of Ernest J. Wessen. Ernest J. Wessen. Ed. by Jack Matthews. LC 91-27021. 325p. 1991. text ed. 34.95 (*0-8214-1003-2*) Ohio U Pr.

Rare Books & Special Collections in the Smithsonian Institution Libraries. Smithsonian Institution Staff et al. LC 95-6791. (Illus.). 108p. 1995. pap. 19.95 (*1-56098-625-5*) Smithsonian.

Rare Books of Freemasonry. Lionel Vibert. 1987. reprint ed. pap. 7.95 (*0-916411-73-7*, Sure Fire) Holmes Pub.

Rare Breed. Mary T. Engels. (Lucky in Love Ser.: No. 10). 320p. 1992. mass mkt. 3.99 (*0-8217-3866-6*, Zebra Kensgtn) Kensgtn Pub Corp.

Rare Breed Handbook. 2nd ed. Dee Gannon. (Illus.). 346p. 1990. 32.95 (*0-944242-01-4*) Doral Pub.

Rare Breeds. Lawrence Alderson. 1989. pap. 25.00 (*0-7478-0002-2*, Pub. by Shire UK) St Mut.

Rare Breeds Vol. 1: Endangered Farm Animals in Photographs. Photos by Robert Dowling. (Illus.). 144p. 1994. 29.95 (*0-8212-2125-6*) Bulfinch Pr.

Rare Chance. Carla Neggers. 1996. mass mkt. 5.99 (*0-671-88321-6*) PB.

Rare Coin Score. Richard Stark. 160p. 1987. 13.95 (*0-8052-8182-7*, Pub. by Allison & Busby) Schocken.

Rare Collection: Superb Recipes. Junior League of Galveston County, Inc. Staff & Paula Roberts. LC 84-81639. (Illus.). 320p. 1985. 15.95 (*0-9613779-0-9*) Jr League Galveston.

Rare Decay: Symposium. D. Bryman et al. 520p. (C). 1989. text ed. 151.00 (*9971-5-0838-9*) World Scientific Pub.

Rare Earth. Cecil Dawkins. 1995. mass mkt. 5.99 (*0-8041-1262-2*) Ivy Books.

Rare-Earth-Doped Fiber Laser Sources & Amplifiers. Ed. by Michel J. Digonnet. (Milestone Ser.: Vol. MS37). 720p. 1991. pap. 45.00 (*0-8194-0735-6*) SPIE.

Rare-Earth-Doped Fiber Laser Sources & Amplifiers. Ed. by Michel J. Digonnet. (Milestone Ser.: Vol. MS37/HC). 720p. 1991. 55.00 (*0-8194-0734-8*) SPIE.

Rare Earth Doped Fiber Lasers & Amplifiers. Digonnet. (Optical Engineering Ser.: Vol. 37). 680p. 1993. 199.00 (*0-8247-8785-4*) Dekker.

Rare-Earth Doped Semiconductors. Ed. by G. S. Pomrenke et al. (Symposium Proceedings Ser.: Vol. 301). 417p. 1993. text ed. 65.00 (*1-55899-197-2*) Materials Res.

Rare-Earth Doped Semiconductors II. Ed. by S. Coffa et al. LC 96-9886. (MRS Symposium Proceedings Ser.: Vol. 422). 366p. 1996. 70.00 (*1-55899-325-8*, 422) Materials Res.

Rare Earth Element Geochemistry. Ed. by P. Henderson. (Developments in Geochemistry Ser.: Vol. 2). 510p. 1983. 207.00 (*0-444-42148-3*) Elsevier.

Rare-Earth Iron Permanent Magnets. Ed. by J. M. Coey. LC 95-47856. (Monographs on the Physics & Chemistry of Materials: No. 54). (Illus.). 542p. 1996. 135.00 (*0-19-851792-0*) OUP.

Rare Earth Magnetism: Structures & Excitations. Jens Jensen & Allan Makintosh. (International Series of Monographs on Physics: No. 81). (Illus.). 416p. 1991. 85.00 (*0-19-852027-1*) OUP.

***Rare-Earth Magnets & Their Applications: Magnetic Anisotropy & Coercivity in Rare-Earth Transition.** 1228p. 1996. lib. bdg. 152.00 (*981-02-2762-0*) World Scientific Pub.

***Rare-Earth Magnets & Their Applications: Magnetic Anisotropy & Coercivity in Rare-Earth Transition.** 1228p. 1996. lib. bdg. write for info. (*981-02-2948-8*) World Scientific Pub.

***Rare Earth Minerals: Chemistry, Origin & Ore Deposits.** Jones et al. (Illus.). 384p. (Orig.). 1995. pap. text ed. 55.00 (*0-412-61030-2*, Chap & Hall NY) Chapman & Hall.

Rare-Earth Pegmatites of the South Platte District, Colorado. William B. Simmons. (Resource Ser.: No. 11). (Illus.). 131p. (Orig.). 1980. pap. 4.00 (*1-884216-31-5*) Colo Geol Survey.

Rare Earth Research, Vol. 1. Ed. by Joseph F. Nachman & C. E. Lundin. 354p. 1962. text ed. 426.00 (*0-677-10490-1*) Gordon & Breach.

Rare Earths. 298p. 1994. 2,650.00 (*0-89336-699-4*, GB-118R) BCC.

Rare Earths. E. Nieboehr et al. LC 67-11280. (Structure & Bonding Ser.: Vol. 22). iv, 1p. 1975. 56.95 (*0-387-07268-3*) Spr-Verlag.

Rare Earths: Extraction, Preparation & Applications, Proceedings of a Symposium on Rare Earths, Extraction, Preparation & Applications Sponsored by the TMS Reactive Metals Committee, Held at the TMS Annual Meeting in Las Vegas, Nevada, February 27-March 2, 1989. Minerals, Metals & Materials Society Staff. Ed. by Renato G. Bautista & Morton M. Wong. LC 88-42986. 415p. reprint ed. pap. 118.30 (*0-7837-5894-4*, 2052503) Bks Demand.

Rare Earths: Resources, Science, Technology & Applications. Ed. by Renato G. Bautista & N. Jackson. (Illus.). 463p. 1992. 20.00 (*0-87339-148-9*, 1489) Minerals Metals.

Rare Earths: The Lanthanides, Yttrium & Scandium. (Metals & Minerals Ser.). 1993. lib. bdg. 250.95 (*0-8490-8973-5*) Gordon Pr.

***Rare Earths - Science, Technology, & Applications III.** Ed. by R. G. Bautista et al. (Illus.). 288p. 1997. 60.00 (*0-87339-363-5*, 3635) Minerals Metals.

***Rare Earths: Resources, Science, Technology & Applications: Proceedings of an International Symposium Held Jointly by TMS & AusIMM During the TMS Annual Meeting, San Diego, CA, March 1-5-1992.** Ed. by Renato G. Bautista & Norton Jackson. LC 91-51131. (Illus.). 480p. pap. 136.80 (*0-608-04893-3*, 2065585) Bks Demand.

Rare Earths Spectroscopy. Su Qiang. 388p. (C). 1990. text ed. 101.00 (*981-02-0078-1*) World Scientific Pub.

Rare Earths Spectroscopy: Proceedings of the International Symposium on Rare Earth Spectroscopy. Ed. by B. Jezowska-Trzebiatowska et al. 692p. 1985. 125.00 (*9971-978-38-5*) World Scientific Pub.

***Rare Elegance: The Paintings of Charles Sprague Pearce.** Mary Lublin. LC 93-61440. (Illus.). 95p. 1993. 35.00 (*0-614-29363-4*) Jordan-Volpe Gall.

Rare Elements: Occurrence & Technology. B. Jezowska-Trzebiatowska et al. (Topics in Inorganic & General Chemistry Ser.: No. 23). 540p. 1990. 288.75 (*0-444-98877-7*) Elsevier.

Rare Events, Mass Extinction & Evolution. Ed. by Eric Buffetaut. (Historical Biology Ser.). 104p. 1989. text ed. 117.00 (*3-7186-4895-4*) Gordon & Breach.

Rare Halos, Mirages, Anomalous Rainbows, & Related Electromagnetic Phenomena. William R. Corliss. (Catalog of Geophysical Anomalies Ser.). (Illus.). 244p. 1984. 14.95 (*0-915554-12-7*) Sourcebook.

Rare Integrity: The Biography of L. W. Payne, Jr., A Noble Texan. Hansen Alexander. 50p. 1986. 35.00 (*0-932119-02-6*) Wind River Pr.

Rare Jewel of Christian Contentment. Jeremiah Burroughs. 1979. pap. 8.50 (*0-85151-091-4*) Banner of Truth.

Rare Masterpieces of Arab & Islamic Art. Prisse D'Avenes. 1840. 150.00 (*0-86685-373-1*) Intl Bk Ctr.

Rare Masterpieces of Arab & Islamic Designs. Said Salah. 204p. 1989. 137.85 (*1-887584-01-3*) Intl Prom Art.

Rare Masterpieces of Russian Piano Music. Ed. by Dmitry Feofanov. (Music Scores & Music to Play Ser.). 144p. 1984. pap. 7.95 (*0-486-24659-0*) Dover.

Rare Metals Handbook. 2nd ed. Ed. by Clifford A. Hampel. LC 61-10449. 732p. 1971. reprint ed. 83.50 (*0-88275-024-0*) Krieger.

Rare Nuclear Processes. Ed. by P. Povinec. 350p. (C). 1992. text ed. 98.00 (*981-02-0802-2*) World Scientific Pub.

Rare People & Rare Books. 2nd ed. E. Millicent Sowerby. (Illus.). xxii, 248p. 1987. reprint ed. 22.50 (*0-916271-04-8*) BkPr Ltd.

Rare Pig, Vol. 1: Pasitos English Language Development Books. Darlyne F. Schott. (Pasitos Hacia la Lectura Ser.). 15p. (J). (gr. k-1). 1990. pap. text ed. 11.00 (*1-56537-060-0*) D F Schott Educ.

Rare Plant Conservation: Geographic Data Organization. Ed. by L. E. Morse & M. S. Henifin. LC 80-19361. 377p. 1981. pap. 25.00 (*0-89327-223-X*) NY Botanical.

Rare Plants & Animals of Haleakala National Park. Arthur C. Medeiros & Lloyd L. Loope. (Illus.). 58p. (Orig.). 1995. pap. text ed. 7.95 (*0-940295-13-X*) HI Natural Hist.

***Rare Plants of Colorado.** 2nd ed. Colorado Native Plant Society Staff. LC 96-51430. (Illus.). 124p. 1997. pap. 16.95 (*1-56044-529-7*) Falcon Pr MT.

Rare Plants of the World. L. S. Belousova & L. V. Denisova. Tr. by B. R. Sharma from RUS. (Illus.). 354p. (C). 1992. text ed. 85.00 (*90-6191-482-5*, Pub. by A A Balkema NE) Ashgate Pub Co.

Rare Recipes & Budget Savers, Vol. I. Frank Good. (Illus.). 112p. 1993. reprint ed. pap. 4.95 (*1-880652-21-8*) Wichita Eagle.

R

Rare Recipes & Budget Savers, Vol. II. Frank Good. (Illus.). 112p. 1993. reprint ed. pap. 4.95 (*1-880652-22-6*) Wichita Eagle.

Rare Recipes & Budget Savers, Vol. III. Frank Good. (Illus.). 112p. 1993. reprint ed. pap. 4.95 (*1-880652-23-4*) Wichita Eagle.

Rare Sculptures-Selections from Some Indian Museums. Contrib. by Laxmi P. Sihare. (Illus.). 48p. 1984. 15.00 (*0-318-36251-1*) Asia Bk Corp.

Rare Sir William Davenant: Poet Laureate, Playwright, Civil War General, Restoration Theatre Manager. Mary Edmond. LC 86-33913. 1987. text ed. 35.00 (*0-312-00783-3*) St Martin.

Rare Wild Flowers of North America. 2nd limited rev. ed. Leonard Wiley. LC 73-80863. 1969. 15.00 (*0-911742-00-X*) L Wiley.

Rare Wild Flowers of North America. 2nd rev. ed. Leonard Wiley. LC 73-80863. 1969. 15.00 (*0-911742-02-6*) L Wiley.

Rarefied Gas Dynamics. Ed. by O. M. Belotserkovskii et al. 1418p. 1985. 225.00 (*0-306-41932-7*, Plenum Pr) Plenum.

Rarefied Gas Dynamics: Proceedings of the 17th International Symposium, July 8-14, 1990, Aachen, Germany. Alfred E. Beylich. 1603p. 1991. 100.00 (*3-527-28250-5*, VCH) Wiley.

Rarefied Gas Dynamics: Proceedings of the 19th International Symposium. Ed. by John Harvey & Gordon Lord. (Illus.). 1600p. 1995. 165.00 (*0-19-856505-4*) OUP.

Rarefield Gas Dynamics: Proceedings of the 14th International Symposium on Rarefield Gas Dynamics, July 16-20, 1984, Tsukuba, Japan, Vol. 1. International Symposium on Rarefield Gas Dynamics Staff. Ed. by Hakuro Oguchi. LC 85-212637. 566p. 1984. reprint ed. pap. 161.40 (*0-608-01258-0*, 2061946) Bks Demand.

***Rarer Climes of Joy: Collected Works by Kathleen Gilbert.** Kathleen Gilbert. (Illus.). 32p. (Orig.). 1997. pap. 5.00 (*0-915913-15-1*) Violetta Bks.

Rarest of the Rare: Vanishing Animals, Timeless World. Diane Ackerman. LC 95-8499. 184p. 1995. 23.00 (*0-679-40346-9*) Random.

Rarest of the Rare: Vanishing Animals, Timeless Worlds. Diane Ackerman. 1997. pap. 12.00 (*0-679-77623-0*, Vin) Random.

Raritan Reading. Ed. by Richard Poirier. LC 89-36068. 400p. (Orig.). (C). 1990. pap. 14.95 (*0-8135-1505-X*); text ed. 45.00 (*0-8135-1504-1*) Rutgers U Pr.

***Rarity.** K. Gaston. (Population & Community Biology Ser.). (Illus.). 224p. (C). (gr. 13 up). 1994. text ed. 81.95 (*0-412-47500-6*, Chap & Hall NY) Chapman & Hall.

Rarity. Kevin J. Gaston. (Population & Community Biology Ser.: 13). 205p. 1994. 34.00 (*0-412-47510-3*, Blackie & Son-Chapman NY) Routledge Chapman & Hall.

Rarotonga & the Cook Islands: Travel Survival Kit. 3rd ed. Tony Wheeler & Nancy Keller. (Illus.). 192p. 1994. pap. 11.95 (*0-86442-232-6*) Lonely Planet.

Ras Alula & the Scramble for Africa: A Political Biography: Ethiopia & Eritrea 1875-1897. rev. ed. Haggai Erlich. LC 96-11511. Orig. Title: Ethiopia & Eritrea During the Scramble for Africa. 1996. write for info. (*1-56902-028-0*); pap. 18.95 (*1-56902-029-9*) Red Sea Pr.

Ras Cardo Speaks on Reggae Issues, Vol 1, No. 1: Reggae Spectrum. Ricardo A. Scott. 200p. (Orig.). (YA). 1994. write for info. (*1-883427-20-7*) Crnerstone GA.

Ras Cardo, the Man, the Legend & Reggae Music: Where Reggae Legends Trod. Ricardo A. Scott. (Illus.). 150p. (Orig.). write for info. (*1-883427-23-1*) Crnerstone GA.

Ras Oncogenes. Ed. by D. A. Spandidos. (NATO ASI Series A, Life Sciences: Vol. 170). (Illus.). 332p. 1989. 95.00 (*0-306-43228-5*, Plenum Pr) Plenum.

Ras Shamra Mythological Texts. James A. Montgomery & Zellig S. Harris. LC 36-2726. (American Philosophical Society, Philadelphia. Memoirs Ser.: Vol. 4). 139p. reprint ed. pap. 39.70 (*0-317-09878-0*, 2000354) Bks Demand.

Ras Superfamily of GTPases. Lacal. 544p. 1993. 222.95 (*0-8493-5214-2*, RC268) CRC Pr.

RASA: Love Relationships in Transcendence. B. V. Tripurari. 120p. 1994. pap. 10.95 (*1-886069-10-7*) Clarion Call.

Rasa Mana Ke Pada of Kevalarama: A Medieval Text of the Eighth Gaddi of the Vallabha Sect. Ed. by Alan W. Entwistle. (Groningen Oriental Studies (GOS): Vol. VII). x, 398p. 1993. pap. 65.00 (*90-6980-037-3*, Pub. by Egbert Forsten NE) Benjamins North Am.

Rasa, or Knowledge of the Self. Rene Daumal. Tr. by Louise L. Levi from FRE. LC 81-22389. 128p. 1982. 12.95 (*0-8112-0824-9*); pap. 5.95 (*0-8112-0825-7*, NDP530) New Directions.

Rascacielos (Skyscrapers) J. Cooper. (Maravillas de la Humanidad (Man-Made Wonders) Ser.: Set VI). (SPA.). (J). 1991. 8.95 (*0-86592-935-1*) Rourke Enter.

Rascal. Sterling North. (J). (gr. 5 up). 1976. pap. 2.75 (*0-380-01518-8*, Flare) Avon.

***Rascal.** Sterling North. (Illus.). (J). (gr. 5). 1995. 9.00 (*0-395-73253-0*) HM.

Rascal. Sterling North. (Illus.). 192p. (J). (ps up). 1990. pap. 3.99 (*0-14-034445-4*, Puffin) Puffin Bks.

***Rascal.** large type ed. Sterling North. (Illus.). 214p. (J). (gr. 5). 53.50 (*0-614-20615-4*, L-38196-00 APHB) Am Printing Hse.

Rascal: A Memoir of a Better Era. Sterling North. LC 63-13882. (Illus.). (J). (gr. 4 up). 1984. pap. 14.99 (*0-525-18839-8*) Dutton Child Bks.

Rascal: A Study Guide. Brenda H. McGee. Ed. by Joyce Friedland & Rikki Kessler. (Novel-Ties Ser.). 26p. (YA). (gr. 9-12). 1990. pap. text ed. 15.95 (*0-88122-416-2*) Lrn Links.

Rascal King: The Life & Times of James Michael Curley. Jack Beatty. (Illus.). 592p. 1993. pap. 15.00 (*0-201-62617-9*) Addison-Wesley.

Rascal King: The Life & Times of James Michael Curley, 1874-1958. Jack Beatty. (Illus.). 608p. 1992. 25.00 (*0-201-17599-1*) Addison-Wesley.

Rascal, Mi Tremendo Mapache - Rascal. Sterling North. 1996. pap. text ed. 9.75 (*84-279-3109-3*) Lectorum Pubns.

Rascals Heaven. F. Van Wyck Mason. 1976. reprint ed. lib. bdg. 31.95 (*0-89190-351-8*, Rivercity Pr) Amereon Ltd.

Rascals in Paradise. James A. Michener. 384p. 1987. mass mkt. 6.99 (*0-449-21459-1*, Crest) Fawcett.

Rascals in Paradise. Jim Silke. (Illus.). 104p. 1995. pap. 16.95 (*1-56971-075-9*) Dark Horse Comics.

Rascal's Surprise Prize: A Book about Kindness. Paula Bussard. 24p. (J). 1991. pap. text ed. 3.99 (*1-55513-942-6*) Cook.

***Rascals, Varmints & Critters.** Shane L. Hensley. (Illus.). 128p. (Orig.). 1997. pap. 25.00 (*1-889546-06-2*) Pinnacle Ent.

Rasch Measurement Transactions, Pt. 1. Ed. by John M. Linacre. (Illus.). 208p. (Orig.). (C). 1995. pap. 25.00 (*0-941938-06-9*) Mesa Pr.

***Rasch Measurement Transactions, Pt. 2.** Ed. by John M. Linacre. LC 95-80148. (Illus.). 240p. (Orig.). (C). 1996. pap. 25.00 (*0-941938-07-7*) Mesa Pr.

Rasch Models: Foundations, Recent Developments, & Applications. Ed. by Gerhard H. Fischer & Ivo W. Molenaar. LC 95-3740. (Illus.). viii, 436p. 1995. 59.95 (*0-387-94499-0*) Spr-Verlag.

Rasch Models for Measurement. David Andrich. (Quantitative Applications in the Social Sciences Ser.: Vol. 68). 88p. 1988. pap. 9.95 (*0-8039-2741-X*) Sage.

Rasco & the Rats of NIMH. Jane L. Conly. LC 85-42634. (Illus.). 288p. (J). (gr. 4-7). 1986. 15.00 (*0-06-021361-2*); lib. bdg. 14.89 (*0-06-021362-0*) HarpC Child Bks.

Rasero. Francisco Rebolledo. 576p. 1996. pap. 12.95 (*0-14-026053-6*) Viking Penguin.

Rasero: A Novel. Francisco Rebolledo. Tr. by Helen R. Lane from SPA. LC 95-22424. (Illus.). 552p. (C). 1995. 24.95 (*0-8071-2004-9*) La State U Pr.

Rash Acts: Eighteen Snapshots for the Stage. Conrad Bishop & Elizabeth Fuller. LC 89-51731. 208p. (Orig.). (C). 1989. pap. 9.95 (*0-9624511-3-4*) WordWorkers.

Rashaayda Bedouin: Arab Pastoralists of Eastern Sudan. George D. Spindler. (Spindler Ser.). (Illus.). 176p. (C). 1995. pap. text ed. 16.00 (*0-15-501513-3*) HB Coll Pubs.

***Rashbam's Commentary on Exodus: An Annotated Translation.** Martin I. Lockshin. LC 96-52640. (Brown University Brown Judiac Studies Ser.). 452p. 1997. 39.95 (*0-7885-0225-5*, 140310) Scholars Pr GA.

***Rasherhouse.** Paul A. Roberts. 1997. pap. 14.95 (*1-898256-21-7*) Dufour.

Rashi: Commentary on the Torah: Shemos - Exodus. Yisrael I. Herczeg & A. Gold. (Sapirstein Ed. Ser.). 1994. 24.99 (*0-89906-027-7*) Mesorah Pubns.

Rashi: Commentary on the Torah: Vayikra - Leviticus. (Sapirstein Ed. Ser.). 1994. 24.99 (*0-89906-028-5*) Mesorah Pubns.

Rashi: The Man & His World. Esra Shereshevsky. LC 96-4365. 288p. 1996. pap. 25.00 (*1-56821-892-3*) Aronson.

Rashi: The Story of Rabbi Shlomo Yitzchaki. David Shulman. LC 93-72589. 200p. 1993. 14.95 (*1-56062-215-6*); pap. 11.95 (*1-56062-216-4*) CIS Comm.

Rashid Ali-Al-Gailani: Political & Military Study of the British Campaign in Iraq. W. Hamdi. 290p. 1987. 150.00 (*1-85077-164-2*, Pub. by Darf Pubs Ltd UK) St Mut.

Rashie Coat. Joan Hassall. 1985. 25.00 (*0-85411-040-2*, Pub. by Saltire Soc) St Mut.

Rashi's Commentary on Ezekiel 40-48. Abraham J. Levy. v, 122p. 1931. text ed. 15.00 (*0-685-65026-X*, Ctr Judaic Studies) Eisenbrauns.

Rashomon. Ed. by Donald Richie. (Films in Print Ser.). 226p. (C). 1987. text ed. 35.00 (*0-8135-1179-8*); pap. text ed. 18.95 (*0-8135-1180-1*) Rutgers U Pr.

Rashomon & Other Stories. Ryunosuke Akutagawa. Tr. by Takashi Kojima from JPN. LC 83-50837. (Illus.). 102p. 1952. pap. 9.95 (*0-8048-1457-0*) C E Tuttle.

Rashomon & Other Stories. Ryunosuke Akutagawa. Tr. by Kojima Takashi. LC 52-9665. (Illus.). 1970. pap. 7.95 (*0-87140-214-9*) Liveright.

Rashtriya Swayam Sewak Sangh. D. R. Goyal. 232p. 1979. 14.95 (*0-318-36601-0*) Asia Bk Corp.

***Rashunel Reasoner: A Program to Change Negative Thinking into Positive Thinking.** Stephanie Braucht. (Illus.). 30p. (Orig.). (J). (ps-5). 1993. pap. 6.95 (*1-884063-56-X*) Mar Co Prods.

Rasmala: Hindoo Annals of the Province of Goozerat in Western India, 2 vols., Set. Alexander K. Forbes. 1993. reprint ed. 57.00 (*81-85326-69-X*, Pub. by Vintage II) S Asia.

Rasmus Bjorn Anderson. Lloyd Hustvedt. Ed. by Franklyn D. Scott. LC 78-15189. (Scandinavians in America Ser.). (Illus.). 1979. reprint ed. lib. bdg. 33.95 (*0-405-11642-X*) Ayer.

***Rasmus Skov: Biographical Essays & Critical Studies.** Ebbe R. Skov. (Illus.). 350p. 1997. 200.00 (*0-9656702-0-1*) Hetagon.

***Rasmus Skov: Biographical Essays & Critical Studies.** Ebbe R. Skov. (Illus.). 350p. 1997. pap. 150.00 (*0-9656702-1-X*) Hetagon.

Rasp. Philip MacDonald. 280p. 1984. pap. 3.50 (*0-88184-094-7*) Carroll & Graf.

Rasp. Philip MacDonald. 1979. reprint ed. pap. 5.95 (*0-486-23864-4*) Dover.

Raspberries & Blackberries: Their Breeding, Diseases & Growth. D. L. Jennings. (Applied Botany & Crop Science Ser.). 230p. 1988. text ed. 69.00 (*0-12-384240-9*) Acad Pr.

***Raspberry Island.** Willa Hix. 336p. 1997. mass mkt. 5.99 (*0-515-12160-6*) Jove Pubns.

Raspberry One. Charles Ferry. LC 82-25476. 224p. (J). (gr. 7 up). 1983. 13.95 (*0-395-34069-1*) HM.

***Raspoutine.** Henri Troyat. 319p. (FRE.). 1997. pap. 25.99 (*2-84011-190-X*) Ulverscroft.

***Rasputin.** Manuel Martin, Jr. 66p. (Orig.). 1997. pap. 4.95 (*1-885901-22-4*) Presbyters Peartree.

***Rasputin.** Harry Shukman. (Get a Life...Pocket Biographies Ser.). (Illus.). 128p. Date not set. pap. 10.95 (*0-7509-1529-3*, Pub. by Sutton Pubng UK) Bks Intl VA.

Rasputin: A Life. Joseph T. Fuhrmann. LC 89-3651. 286p. 1989. text ed. 39.95 (*0-275-93215-X*, C3215, Praeger Pubs) Greenwood.

Rasputin: The Holy Devil. Rene Fulop-Miller. 396p. 1996. pap. 29.95 (*1-56459-599-4*) Kessinger Pub.

***Rasputin: The Saint Who Sinned.** Brian Moynaham. LC 97-5025. 1997. 30.00 (*0-679-41930-6*) Random.

***Rassegna Vol. 37: Barcelona.** 1996. pap. 39.95 (*88-85322-33-6*) Birkhauser.

***Rassegna Vol. 38: Neues Bauen in der Welt.** 1996. pap. 39.95 (*88-85322-34-4*) Birkhauser.

***Rassegna Vol. 39: Unconventional Transport.** 1996. pap. 39.95 (*88-85322-30-1*) Birkhauser.

***Rassegna Vol. 40: Breslau.** 1996. pap. 39.95 (*88-85322-31-X*) Birkhauser.

***Rassegna Vol. 41: The Senses of Ornament.** 1996. pap. 39.95 (*88-85322-32-8*) Birkhauser.

***Rassegna Vol. 42: The Abandoned Arts.** 1996. pap. 39.95 (*88-85322-00-X*) Birkhauser.

***Rassegna Vol. 43: Reklame & Architektur.** 1996. pap. 39.95 (*88-85322-01-8*) Birkhauser.

***Rassegna Vol. 44: Ocean Liners.** 1996. pap. 39.95 (*88-85322-02-6*) Birkhauser.

***Rassegna Vol. 47: Mart Stam 1899-1986.** 1996. pap. 39.95 (*88-85322-05-0*) Birkhauser.

***Rassegna Vol. 48: Inhabited Bridges.** 1996. pap. 39.95 (*88-85322-06-9*) Birkhauser.

***Rassegna Vol. 50: Indexes 1-50.** 1996. pap. 39.95 (*88-85322-08-5*) Birkhauser.

***Rassegna Vol. 51: Architecture in the Italian.** 1996. pap. 39.95 (*88-85322-09-3*) Birkhauser.

***Rassegna Vol. 52: The Last CIAMS.** 1996. pap. 39.95 (*88-85322-10-7*) Birkhauser.

***Rassegna Vol. 53: Karel Teige.** 1996. pap. 39.95 (*88-85322-11-5*) Birkhauser.

***Rassegna Vol. 54: Reconstruction of Europe.** 1996. pap. 39.95 (*88-85322-12-3*) Birkhauser.

***Rassegna Vol. 55: Archaeology of Architecture.** 1996. pap. 39.95 (*88-85322-13-1*) Birkhauser.

***Rassegna Vol. 58: Statement of the Interior.** 1996. pap. 39.95 (*88-85322-15-8*) Birkhauser.

***Rassegna Vol. 59: Lisbon.** 1996. pap. 39.95 (*88-85322-17-4*) Birkhauser.

***Rassegna Vol. 60: Norman Bel Geddes.** 1996. pap. 39.95 (*88-85322-18-2*) Birkhauser.

***Rassegna Vol. 61: Architecture Comp.** 1996. pap. 39.95 (*88-85322-19-0*) Birkhauser.

***Rassegna Vol. 62: The Form of the Useful.** 1996. pap. 39.95 (*88-85322-20-4*) Birkhauser.

***Rassegna Vol. 63: Electricity.** Gubler. 106p. 1996. pap. 39.95 (*88-85322-21-2*) Birkhauser.

***Rassegna Vol. 64: Edinburgh.** Travernor. 94p. 1996. pap. 39.95 (*88-85322-22-0*) Birkhauser.

***Rassegna Vol. 65: Polish Avant Garde Architecture.** Milobedzki. 1996. pap. 39.95 (*88-85322-23-9*) Birkhauser.

***Rassegna Vol. 66: London Underground.** Brandolini. 1996. pap. 39.95 (*88-85322-24-7*) Birkhauser.

***Rassegna Vol. 67: Airships.** Brandolini. 1996. pap. 39.95 (*88-85322-25-5*) Birkhauser.

***Rassegna Vol. 68: Anatole de Baudot.** Ed. by Marie-Jeanne Dumont. 1997. pap. 39.95 (*88-85322-26-3*) Birkhauser.

***Rassegna Vol. 69: Great Machines.** Ed. by Franz A. Engler. 1997. pap. 39.95 (*88-85322-27-1*) Birkhauser.

Rasselas. Samuel Johnsonn. 1977. pap. 5.95 (*0-8120-0153-2*) Barron.

Rasselas & Dinarbus. Samuel Johnson & Ellis C. Knight. Ed. by Lynne Melocarro. 256p. 1994. pap. 8.50 (*0-460-87308-3*, Everyman's Classic Lib) C E Tuttle.

Rasselas & Other Tales. Samuel Johnson. Ed. by Gwin J. Kolb. (Yale Edition of the Works of Samuel Johnson Ser.: Vol. XVI). 368p. (C). 1991. text ed. 45.00 (*0-300-04451-8*) Yale U Pr.

Rasselas, Poems, & Selected Prose. 3rd ed. Johnson. Ed. by Bertrand H. Bronson. 709p. (C). 1971. pap. text ed. 30.00 (*0-03-082785-X*) HB Coll Pubs.

Rasskazy: Stories. Fedor Sologub. Ed. by Evelyn Bristol. LC 79-25535. (RUS.). 1979. pap. 12.50 (*0-933884-10-9*) Berkeley Slavic.

Rasskazy Nazara Il'icha, Gospodina Sinebriukhova. Mikhail Zoshchenko. 89p. (RUS.). (C). 1982. reprint ed. pap. 4.00 (*0-933884-33-8*) Berkeley Slavic.

Rasstavanie S Idolom (Farewell to an Idol) Vladimir Soloukhin. LC 91-62205. 112p. (Orig.). (RUS.). (C). 1991. pap. 12.00 (*0-911971-70-X*) Effect Pub.

Rasta & Resistance: From Marcus Garvey to Walter Rodney. Horace Campbell. LC 85-73332. 240p. (Orig.). 1987. 32.95 (*0-86543-034-9*); pap. 14.95 (*0-86543-035-7*) Africa World.

Rasta Cookbook: Vegetarian Cuisine - Eaten with the Salt of the Earth. Compiled by Laura Osborne. LC 92-17760. (Illus.). 132p. (C). 1992. reprint ed. pap. 12.95 (*0-86543-133-7*) Africa World.

***Rastafari: For the Healing of the Nation.** Dennis Forsythe. xi, 268p. (Orig.). 1996. pap. 18.95 (*1-890358-00-2*) One Drop Bks.

Rastafari: Roots & Ideology. Barry Chevannes. LC 94-18608. (Utopianism & Communitarianism Ser.). 416p. 1994. pap. 17.95 (*0-8156-0296-0*); text ed. 39.95 (*0-8156-2638-X*) Syracuse U Pr.

Rastafari: The Pan-Afrikan Dimension of the Rastafari Movement. Afrikadzata Deku. LC 91-72680. (D. E. S. S. M. Phil Thesis Ser.). 98p. 1997. write for info. (*1-56454-024-3*) Cont Afrikan.

***Rastafari & Other African-Caribbean Worldviews.** Ed. by Barry Chevannes. LC 97-464. 304p. (C). 1997. text ed. 48.00 (*0-8135-2411-3*); pap. text ed. 17.95 (*0-8135-2412-1*) Rutgers U Pr.

Rastafari & Reggae: A Dictionary & Sourcebook. Rebekah M. Mulvaney & Carlos I. Nelson. LC 90-3591. 272p. 1990. text ed. 55.00 (*0-313-26071-0*, MVR/, Greenwood Pr) Greenwood.

***Rastafari Bible.** Hill. pap. 20.00 (*0-06-251332-X*) HarpC.

***Rastafarians.** rev. ed. Leonard E. Barrett, Sr. LC 97-10974. 328p. 1997. pap. 15.00 (*0-8070-1039-1*) Beacon Pr.

Rastaman Tales. Theresa Jackson & Leo Sullivan. Ed. by Lyn Stewart. (Illus.). 64p. (Orig.). 14.95 (*1-881368-11-4*); pap. 10.95 (*1-881368-13-0*) Vignette.

Rastaman Tie In. Jill Taylor. 1999. pap. 3.99 (*0-451-17676-6*, Sig) NAL-Dutton.

Raster Graphics: A Tutorial & Implementation Guide. Frankie E. Spielman & Louis H. Sharpe, II. (Illus.). 275p. (Orig.). (C). 1994. pap. text ed. 75.00 (*0-7881-0526-4*) DIANE Pub.

Raster Graphics Handbook. 2nd ed. Conrac Corporation Staff. (Illus.). 360p. 1985. text ed. 69.95 (*0-442-21608-4*) Van Nos Reinhold.

Raster Imagery in Geographic Information Systems. Stan Morain. 600p. 1996. pap. text ed. 59.95 incl. cd-rom (*1-56690-097-2*, 4110, OnWord Pr) High Mtn.

Raster Imaging & Digital Typography: Proceedings of the International Workshop, Lausanne, 1989. Ed. by J. Amdre & Roger D. Hersch. (Cambridge Series on Electronic Publishing). (Illus.). 304p. (C). 1990. text ed. 74.95 (*0-521-37490-1*) Cambridge U Pr.

Raster Imaging & Digital Typography II. Ed. by R. A. Morris & J. Andre. (Cambridge Series on Electronic Publishing). (Illus.). 250p. (C). 1991. text ed. 69.95 (*0-521-41764-3*) Cambridge U Pr.

Rat. Gunter Grass. Tr. by Ralph Manheim. LC 86-31817. 1987. 17.95 (*0-15-175920-0*) HarBrace.

Rat. Gunter Grass. Tr. by Ralph Manheim. 1989. pap. 9.95 (*0-685-31026-4*, Harvest Bks) HarBrace.

Rat. Gunter Grass. 1989. pap. 13.00 (*0-15-675830-X*) HarBrace.

Rat. Kwok Man-Ho. LC 93-48006. (Chinese Horoscopes Library). (Illus.). 48p. 1994. 8.95 (*1-56458-608-1*) DK Pub Inc.

Rat: A Novel. Andrzej Zaniewski. Tr. by Ewa Hryniewicz-Yarbrough from POL. LC 94-9937. 176p. 1994. 19.95 (*1-55970-262-1*) Arcade Pub Inc.

***Rat: A Perverse Miscellany.** Barbara Hodgeman. LC 97-6940. (Orig.). 1997. pap. 15.95 (*0-89815-926-1*) Ten Speed Pr.

Rat a Tat Tat. Sian Tucker. (J). 1994. 4.50 (*0-671-89115-4*, Litl Simon S&S) S&S Childrens.

Rat & the Devil: Journal Letters of F. O. Matthiessen & Russell Cheney. Ed. by Louis K. Hyde. LC 77-27468. (Illus.). 408p. (C). 1978. lib. bdg. 39.50 (*0-208-01655-4*, Archon Bks) Shoe String.

Rat & the Rose. unabridged ed. Arnold Rabin. 175p. (Orig.). 1996. pap. 12.95 (*0-930773-43-8*); lib. bdg. 20.95 (*0-930773-42-X*) Black Heron Pr.

Rat & the Tiger. Keiko Kasza. (Illus.). 32p. (Orig.). (J). (ps-3). 1993. lib. bdg. 14.95 (*0-399-22404-1*, Putnam) Putnam Pub Group.

***Rat & the Tiger.** Keiko Kasza. (Illus.). 32p. (Orig.). (J). (ps-3). 1997. pap. 5.95 (*0-698-11604-6*, Paperstar) Putnam Pub Group.

Rat As an Animal Model in Breast Cancer Research. Matthew J. Van Zwieten. (Developments in Oncology Ser.). 300p. 1984. lib. bdg. 149.00 (*0-89838-624-1*) Kluwer Ac.

Rat Bohemia. Sarah Schulman. LC 95-15475. 176p. 1995. pap. 19.95 (*0-525-93790-0*, Dutton) NAL-Dutton.

Rat Bohemia. Sarah Schulman. 240p. 1996. pap. 10.95 (*0-452-27182-7*, Plume) NAL-Dutton.

Rat Brain. 2nd ed. George T. Paxinos & Charles Watson. 264p. 1986. text ed. 89.00 (*0-12-547621-3*) Acad Pr.

***Rat Brain in Stereotaxic Coordinates.** 3rd ed. Ed. by George T. Paxinos & Charles Watson. (Illus.). 96p. 1996. text ed. 69.95 (*0-12-547623-X*, AP Prof) Acad Pr.

Rat Catching: Studies in the Art of Rat Catching. 2nd ed. Crispin H. Glover. (Illus.). 80p. 1990. 25.00 (*0-9622997-0-7*) Volcanic Eruptions.

Rat Dissection Manual. Bruce D. Wingerd. (Laboratory Dissection Ser.). (Illus.). 80p. (Orig.). (C). 1988. pap. text ed. 9.95 (*0-8018-3690-5*) Johns Hopkins.

Rat Histopathology: A Glossary for Use in Toxicity & Carcinogenicity Studies. 2nd rev. ed. P. Greaves & J. M. Faccini. LC 92-41672. 302p. 1992. 201.25 (*0-444-88361-4*) Elsevier.

Rat Hybrodimas & Rat Monoclonal Antibodies. Ed. by Herve Bazin. 480p. 1990. 298.95 (*0-8493-5438-2*, QR185) CRC Pr.

Rat in the Skull. Ron Hutchinson. 1996. pap. 11.95 (*0-413-70350-9*, Pub. by Methuen UK) Heinemann.

Rat Lady at the Company Dump. William Studebaker. (Illus.). (Orig.). 1990. pap. 9.95 (*0-931659-08-6*) Limberlost Pr.

Rat Man. Stuart Schneiderman. LC 86-16172. 200p. (C). 1987. text ed. 24.00 (*0-8147-7858-5*) NYU Pr.

Rat Man. Stuart Schneiderman. LC 86-16172. 200p. (C). 1988. pap. text ed. 13.20 (*0-8147-7872-0*) NYU Pr.

Rat Man of Paris. Paul West. 180p. 1993. pap. 10.95 (*0-87951-502-3*) Overlook Pr.

An Asterisk (*) at the beginning of an entry indicates that the title is appearing in BIP for the first time.

R

Rat Nervous System. 2nd ed. Ed. by George T. Paxinos. (Illus.). 1136p. 1994. text ed. 179.00 (*0-12-547635-3*) Acad Pr.

***Rat Nervous System: An Introduction to Preparatory Techniques.** J. P. Cassella et al. LC 96-30347. 1996. pap. text ed. write for info. (*0-471-96967-2*) Wiley.

***Rat of Few Words.** Koos Meinderts. LC 97-23383. (Illus.). (J). 1997. Not sold separately (*1-57379-072-9*) High-Scope.

Rat on Fire. George V. Higgins. 1990. mass mkt. 4.50 (*0-8217-3215-3*, Zebra Kensgtn) Kensgtn Pub Corp.

Rat Pack Steve. Mei-Mei Berssenbrugge. (Chapbook Ser.). 24p. (Orig.). (C). 1983. pap. 3.00 (*0-936556-09-9*) Contact Two.

Rat Palms: A Novel. David Homel. 276p. (Orig.). 1993. pap. 12.00 (*0-00-647405-5*, Pub. by HarpC CN) HarpC.

Rat Race. Dick Francis. 1993. mass mkt. 5.99 (*0-449-22112-1*) Fawcett.

Rat Race. Franklin. 5.00 (*0-686-00480-9*); pap. 2.00 (*0-686-00481-7*) Fantasy Pub Co.

Rat Race. Garson Kanin. 1976. 20.95 (*0-8488-0549-6*) Amereon Ltd.

Rat Snakes. Sherie Bargar & Johnson. (Snake Discovery Library: Set II). (Illus.). 24p. (J). (gr. 1-4). 1987. lib. bdg. 11.94 (*0-86592-247-0*) Rourke Corp.

Rat Snakes. R. Staszlo & J. Walls. (Illus.). 208p. 1994. 39.95 (*0-86622-635-4*, TS144) TFH Pubns.

Rat Snakes. J. Walls. (Illus.). 64p. 1995. pap. text ed. 9.95 (*0-7938-0256-3*, RE110) TFH Pubns.

Rat Teeth. Patricia R. Giff. 144p. (J). (gr. k-6). 1990. pap. 3.25 (*0-440-47457-4*, YB BDD) BDD Bks Young Read.

Rat Trap. Kevin Randle. (Galactic MI Ser.: No. 2). 1993. pap. 4.50 (*0-441-27243-6*) Ace Bks.

Rat Trap. Craig Thomas. 288p. 1996. mass mkt. 3.99 (*0-06-101055-3*, Harp PBks) HarpC.

***Rat Trap.** abr. large type ed. Kambriz-Azordegan. (Tootee's Magical Stories Ser.: Vol. 15). (Illus.). 34p. (J). (gr. 1-3). 1997. write for info. (*1-890571-39-3*) Parrot Prod.

Rat War. Elsie McCutcheon. LC 85-4593. 111p. (J). (gr. 4 up). 1986. 10.95 (*0-374-36182-7*) FS&G.

Rata-Pata-Scata-Fata: A Caribbean Story. Phyllis Gershator. LC 92-40695. (J). 1994. 15.95 (*0-316-30470-0*, Joy St Bks) Little.

***Ratana Pasada the Western Monasteries of Anuradhapura Excavations in the Citadel the So Called Tomb of King Dutthagamani Privy Stone, Remarks on Double Platforms.** Ed. by A. M. Hocart. 1996. reprint ed. 62.00 (*81-206-1093-8*, Pub. by Asian Educ Servs II) S Asia.

Ratas Suben a la Ciudad. Verde Doncella O el Marido para Despues. Emilio Romero. (Nueva Austral Ser.: Vol. 76). (SPA.). 1991. pap. text ed. 24.95 (*84-239-1876-9*) Elliots Bks.

Ratboy, Etc. Michael Hathaway. Ed. by Ruth M. Kempher. (Illus.). 58p. (Orig.). 1994. pap. 11.95 (*0-9637483-4-3*) Kings Estate.

Ratcatcher's Child: History of the Pest Control Industry. Robert Snetsinger et al. LC 83-82090. (Illus.). 294p. 1983. 12.00 (*0-942588-02-9*) Franzak & Foster.

Ratchet Hood. Tony Marino. LC 92-12841. (Widgets Ser.). (YA). 1992. lib. bdg. 13.99 (*1-56239-152-6*) Abdo & Dghtrs.

Rate Adaptive Cardiac Pacing. Ed. by E. U. Alt et al. LC 92-48249. (Illus.). 352p. 1993. 114.00 (*0-387-54051-2*) Spr-Verlag.

Rate Adaptive Cardiac Pacing: Single & Dual Chamber. Chu-Pak Lau. (Illus.). 448p. 1992. 80.00 (*0-87993-544-8*) Futura Pub.

Rate-Adaptive Pacing. Ed. by David G. Benditt. LC 93-36347. (Illus.). 456p. 1993. 99.95 (*0-86542-242-7*) Blackwell Sci.

Rate & Date Book, 1996. Financial Publishing Co. Staff. 128p. 1997. pap. 8.00 (*0-87600-500-8*) Finan Pub.

Rate & Direction of Inventive Activity: Economic & Social Factors. Universities-National Bureau Staff. (Conference Ser.: No. 13). 646p. 1962. reprint ed. 160.00 (*0-87014-304-2*) Natl Bur Econ Res.

Rate & Direction of Inventive Activity: Economic & Social Factors: Proceedings. Conference of the Universities. LC 75-19703. (National Bureau of Economic Research Ser.). (Illus.). 1975. reprint ed. 51.95 (*0-405-07583-9*) Ayer.

Rate Coefficients in Astrochemistry. Ed. by T. J. Millar & David A. Williams. (C). 1988. lib. bdg. 162.50 (*90-277-2752-X*) Kluwer Ac.

Rate-Controlled Drug Administraton & Action. Harry A. Struyker-Boudier. 296p. 1986. 168.00 (*0-8493-6151-6*, RS201, CRC Reprint) Franklin.

***Rate-Distortion Based Video Compression: Optimal Video Frame Compression & Object Boundary Encoding.** Guido M. Schuster. 312p. (C). 1996. lib. bdg. 120.00 (*0-7923-9850-5*) Kluwer Ac.

Rate Equations in Semiconductor Electronics. J. E. Carroll. 192p. 1986. text ed. 95.00 (*0-521-26533-9*) Cambridge U Pr.

Rate Equations in Semiconductor Electronics. J. E. Carroll. (Illus.). 177p. (C). 1990. pap. text ed. 35.95 (*0-521-38866-X*) Cambridge U Pr.

Rate Equations of Solid-Catalyzed Reactions. Ed. by R. Mezaki & H. Inoue. 420p. 1991. text ed. 140.00 (*0-86008-481-7*, Pub. by U of Tokyo JA) Col U Pr.

Rate IV: Teaching Teachers: Facts & Figures, 1991. 1991. 15.00 (*0-89333-077-9*) AACTE.

***Rate of Chemical Reaction.** Roberts. Date not set. 1.20 (*0-7167-9198-6*) W H Freeman.

Rate Processes in Plastic Deformation of Materials: The John E. Dorn Symposium Proceedings, Cleveland, 1972. International Symposium on Rate Processes in Plastic Deformation Staff. Ed. by J. C. Li & A. K. Mukherjee. LC 73-86454. (Materials-Metalworking Technology Ser.: No. 4). 768p. reprint ed. pap. 180.00 (*0-317-09740-7*, 2050984) Bks Demand.

Rate Processes of Extractive Metallurgy. Hong Y. Sohn. LC 78-15941. (Illus.). 484p. 1978. 115.00 (*0-306-31102-X*, Plenum Pr) Plenum.

Rate Reference Guide to the U. S. Treasury Market. 2nd ed. Steven R. Ricchiuto & Barclays De Zoete Wedd. 400p. 1996. per. 55.00 (*1-55738-790-7*) Irwin Prof Pubng.

***Rate Regulation of Workers' Compensation Insurance.** Patricia M. Danzon & Scott Harrington. LC 97-25288. 150p. 1997. 29.95 (*0-8447-3932-4*) Am Enterprise.

Rate Six - Teaching Teachers: Facts & Figures. 1994. 15.00 (*0-89333-110-4*) AACTE.

Rate Suppression & Its Consequences: The Private Passenger Auto & Workers Compensation Experience. Orin Kramer. 160p. 1991. 95.00 (*0-932387-33-0*) Insur Info.

Rate V: Teaching Teachers: Facts & Figures, 1991. 1991. 15.00 (*0-89333-088-4*) AACTE.

Rate VII. 1994. 15.00 (*0-89333-124-4*) AACTE.

Rate VIII. 1995. 15.00 (*0-89333-125-2*) AACTE.

Rate Your Endgame. Edmar Mednis & Colin Crouch. (Chess Library). 200p. 1991. pap. 19.95 (*0-08-037803-X*, Pub. by CHES UK) Macmillan.

Rate Your Endgame. Edmar Mednis & Colin Crouch. 244p. 1992. pap. 19.95 (*1-85744-020-X*, Pub. by Cadogan Books UK) Macmillan.

***Rate Your Endgame.** rev. ed. Mednis. 1997. pap. 19.95 (*1-85744-174-5*) Macmillan.

***Rate Your Skills As a Manager.** (Better Management Skills Ser.). 1994. pap. 12.95 (*0-7494-1341-7*) Kogan Page Ltd.

Rate Your Skills As a Manager: A Crisp Assessment Profile. Elwood N. Chapman. Ed. by Michael G. Crisp. LC 90-85866. (Fifty-Minute Ser.). (Illus.). 104p. (Orig.). 1991. pap. 10.95 (*1-56052-101-5*) Crisp Pubns.

Raten Sie Mal. N. Caro. 118p. (GER.). (C). 1984. pap. text ed. 24.75 (*3-12-550800-2*, Pub. by Klett Edition GW) Intl Bk Import.

***Rates & Equilbria of Organic Reactions.** Leffler & Grunwald. pap. 11.95 (*0-486-66068-0*) Dover.

Rates & Ratios Used in the Income Capitalization Approach. Clifford E. Fisher, Jr. 1995. 19.50 (*0-922154-23-6*) Appraisal Inst.

***Rates & Ratios Used in the Income Capitalization Approach.** Clifford E. Fisher. 1995. pap. 57.00 (*0-614-19445-8*, Pub. by R-I-C-S Bks UK) St Mut.

Rates of Chemical Weathering of Rocks & Minerals. Ed. by Steven M. Colman & David P. Dethier. LC 85-13328. 1986. text ed. 165.00 (*0-12-181490-4*) Acad Pr.

Rates of Evolution. Ed. by K. S. Campbell & M. F. Day. (Illus.). 384p. (C). 1987. text ed. 85.00 (*0-04-575030-0*) Routledge Chapman & Hall.

Rates of Exchange. Malcolm Bradbury. 320p. 1985. pap. 10.00 (*0-14-007631-X*, Penguin Bks) Viking Penguin.

Rates of Marchandizes, As They Are Set Down in the Booke of Rates. LC 72-227. (English Experience Ser.: No. 165). 1969. reprint ed. 20.00 (*90-221-0165-7*) Walter J Johnson.

Rates of Phase Transformations. R. H. Doremus. (C). 1985. text ed. 65.00 (*0-12-220530-8*) Acad Pr.

Rates of Protein Synthesis During Aging. Ed. by James R. Florini et al. 253p. 1974. text ed. 34.50 (*0-8422-7221-6*) Irvington.

Rates of Return on Investment in Technical Education in the Ante-Bellum American Economy. Terry M. Aldrich. LC 75-2573. (Dissertations in American Economic History Ser.). (Illus.). 1975. 37.95 (*0-405-07254-6*) Ayer.

Ratface. Garry Disher. LC 93-48131. 185p. (J). (gr. 5 up). 1994. 14.95 (*0-395-69451-5*) Ticknor & Flds Bks Yng Read.

Ratha's Challenge. Clare Bell. (J). 1994. 16.95 (*0-689-50586-8*, McElderry) S&S Childrens.

Rathbone Genealogy: A Complete History of the Rathbone Family, from 1574 to Date. J. C. Coaley. (Illus.). 827p. 1989. reprint ed. pap. 124.00 (*0-8328-1003-7*); reprint ed. lib. bdg. 132.00 (*0-8328-1002-9*) Higginson Bk Co.

Rather a Small Press. limited ed. Lois Rather. (Illus.). 1976. 17.50 (*0-686-20625-8*) Rather Pr.

Rather Be Audited Than Speech. David Brown. 176p. 1995. per., pap. text ed. 19.95 (*0-7872-0314-9*) Kendall-Hunt.

Rather Rude & Insensitive Handbook of Psychology & Psycho-Silly Issues for the Bubba in All of Us. Raymond H. Stem, II. LC 95-62129. (Illus.). 195p. 1996. pap. 10.95 (*1-55523-778-9*) Winston-Derek.

Rathkopf's Law of Zoning & Planning, 5 vols. 4th ed. Charles A. Rathkopf et al. LC 56-2013. (Real Property - Zoning Ser.). 1975. ring bd. 550.00 (*0-87632-020-5*) Clark Boardman Callaghan.

Rathnam's Cost & Management Accounting: Problems & Solutions. 3rd rev. ed. P. V. Rathnam. 780p. 1989. text ed. 45.00 (*0-685-21871-6*, Pub. by Sterling Pubs II) Apt Bks.

Rathsel und Gesellschaftsspiele der Alten Griechen. Konrad Ohlert. vii, 252p. 1979. reprint ed. write for info. (*3-487-06850-8*) G Olms Pubs.

Ratichon Baigneur. Boris Vian. (FRE.). 1983. pap. 14.95 (*0-7859-3184-8*, 2264004932) Fr & Eur.

Ratification of Maritime Convention: Lloyd's Shipping Law Library. Contrib. by University of Southhampton, Institute of Maritime Law Staff & International Maritime Organization Staff. 3000p. 1990. pap. text ed. 710.00 (*1-85044-301-7*) LLP.

Ratification of the Federal Constitution in North Carolina. Louise Trenholme. LC 32-19030. (Columbia University. Studies in the Social Sciences: No. 363). reprint ed. 31.50 (*0-404-51363-8*) AMS Pr.

Ratification of the Fourteenth Amendment. Joseph B. James. LC 83-26481. viii, 331p. 1984. 21.95 (*0-86554-098-5*, MUP/H090) Mercer Univ Pr.

Ratification of the Single European Act, Vol. 4. European Communities Staff. 593p. 1993. pap. 95.00 (*92-829-0232-3*, DY-04-92-0049AC, Pub. by Europ Com UK) Bernan Associates.

Ratification of the Twenty-First Amendment to the Constitution of the United States. Everett S. Brown. LC 78-114757. (American Constitutional & Legal History Ser). 1970. reprint ed. 85.00 (*0-306-71928-2*) Da Capo.

Ratifying, Amending, & Interpreting the Constitution. Intro. by Peter S. Onuf. LC 91-3502. (New American Nation, 1775-1820 Ser.: Vol. 6). 536p. 1991. text ed. 25.00 (*0-8153-0441-2*) Garland.

Ratifying the Chemical Weapons Convention. Ed. by Brad Roberts. LC 94-17403. (Significant Issues Ser.). 138p. (Orig.). (C). 1994. pap. 13.50 (*0-89206-264-9*) CSI Studies.

Ratifying the Constitution. Ed. by Michael A. Gillespie & Michael Lienesch. LC 89-30118. xiv, 418p. 1989. 29.95 (*0-7006-0402-2*); pap. 14.95 (*0-7006-0566-5*) U Pr of KS.

Rating America's Corporate Conscience. Sean O. Strub et al. LC 86-8064. 499p. 1987. 21.95 (*0-201-15886-8*); pap. 14.95 (*0-201-15879-5*) Addison-Wesley.

***Rating & Application of Single & Multiple Reduction Double-Enveloping Worm & Helical Worm Speed Reducers.** 5th rev. ed. AGMA Technical Committee. (ANSI/AGMA Standard Ser.: Vol. 6017-E86). (Illus.). (Orig.). Date not set. pap. text ed. 45.00 incl. audio compact disk (*1-55589-013-X*) AGMA.

Rating Game: Report of the Twentieth Century Fund Task Force on Municipal Bond Credit Ratings : Background Paper. Twentieth Century Fund, Task Force on Municipal Bond Credit Ratings Staff & John E. Petersen. LC 77-4987. 1977. reprint ed. pap. 12.00 (*0-87078-131-6*) TCFP-PPP.

Rating Game in American Politics: An Interdisciplinary Approach. Ed. by William O. Pederson & Ann M. McLaurin. LC 87-4145. 425p. (C). 1987. text ed. 39.50 (*0-8290-1812-3*); pap. text ed. 19.95 (*0-685-16492-6*) Irvington.

***Rating Guide to Franchises.** rev. ed. Dennis L. Foster. LC 88-3740. 240p. 1991. reprint ed. pap. 68.40 (*0-608-02865-7*, 2063929) Bks Demand.

Rating Guide to Franchises. rev. ed. Dennis L. Foster. 320p. 1991. 40.00 (*0-8160-2517-7*) Facts on File.

Rating Guide to Life in America's Fifty States. G. Scott Thomas. 575p. (C). 1994. 39.95 (*0-87975-938-0*) Prometheus Bks.

Rating Guide to Life in America's Fifty States. G. Scott Thomas. 575p. (C). 1994. pap. 19.95 (*0-87975-939-9*) Prometheus Bks.

Rating Guide to Life in America's Small Cities. G. Scott Thomas. 538p. (C). 1990. 41.95 (*0-87975-599-7*); pap. 20.95 (*0-87975-600-4*) Prometheus Bks.

Rating Maintenance Phase: Program Document. 85p. (Orig.). (C). 1994. pap. text ed. 40.00 (*0-7881-0555-8*) DIANE Pub.

Rating Maintenance Phase Version 2: Program Document. Timothy J. Begendahl et al. 55p. (Orig.). (C). 1995. pap. text ed. 20.00 (*0-7881-1905-2*) DIANE Pub.

***Rating of Electric Power Cables: Ampacity Computations for Transmission, Distribution & Industrial Applications.** George J. Anders. LC 96-43345. (IEEE Press Power Systems Engineering Ser.). 464p. 1997. 129.95 (*0-7803-1177-9*, PC5647) Inst Electrical.

Rating of Experience & Training No. 1: A Review of the Literature & Recommendations on the Use of Alternative E & T Procedures. (Assessment Ser.: Vol. 3). 1994. pap. 10.00 (*0-614-01929-X*) Intl Personnel Mgmt.

***Rating of Industrial Metal Spur Gears Research Report.** AGMA Technical Committee. (AGMA Technical Papers: Vol. P101.01). 1944. pap. text ed. 30.00 (*1-55589-128-4*) AGMA.

Rating Places: A Geographer's View on Quality of Life. Susan L. Cutter. LC 85-13469. (Resource Publications in Geography). 76p. (Orig.). 1985. pap. 15.00 (*0-89291-191-3*) Assn Am Geographers.

Rating Relief for Charitable Organizations. Shaw & Sons Ltd. Staff. (Shaway Guides Ser.). (C). 1988. 25.00 (*0-317-92365-X*, Pub. by Scientific UK) St Mut.

Rating Scale Analysis. Benjamin D. Wright & Geofferey N. Masters. LC 81-84992. (Illus.). 1982. pap. 25.00 (*0-941938-01-8*) Mesa Pr.

Rating Scale to Be Used As a Guide in Grade Determination for Clinical Practice in the Medical & Surgical Nursing Course of a Specific Basic Collegiate Program. Mary E. Palmer. LC 60-12193. 99p. reprint ed. pap. 28.30 (*0-317-30004-0*, 2051860) Bks Demand.

Rating Scales & Assessment Instruments for Use in Pediatric Psychopharmacology Research. Ed. by C. Keith Conners et al. 415p. (Orig.). (C). 1995. pap. text ed. 60.00 (*0-7881-2518-4*) DIANE Pub.

Rating Scales & Checklists: Evaluating Behavior, Personality, & Attitudes. Lewis A. Aiken. LC 95-39106. 304p. 1996. 47.50 incl. disk (*0-471-12787-6*) Wiley.

Rating Scales for Psychopathology, Health Status, & Quality of Life: A Compendium on Documentation in Accordance with the DSM-III-R & WHO Systems. Per Bech. LC 92-49556. 1993. 159.00 (*0-387-55903-5*) Spr-Verlag.

Rating the Economic Policymakers: The Bush Administration Versus the Congress. write for info. (*0-318-69881-1*, ER-239) Manu All Prod & Innov.

Rating the Movies. rev. ed. 1990. 7.99 (*0-517-05654-2*) Random Hse Value.

Rating the Movies. rev. ed. Consumer Guide Editors. 1989. pap. 6.99 (*0-517-69681-9*) Random Hse Value.

Rating the Pitting Resistance & Bending Strength of Generated Straight Bevel, ZEROL Bevel, & Spiral Bevel Gear Teeth. (Illus.). 68p. 1988. reprint ed. pap. 100.00 (*1-55589-000-8*, 2003-A86) AGMA.

Rating the Presidents: A Ranking of the Most Influential Presidents in U. S. History. William J. Ridings, Jr. & Stuart B. McIver. LC 95-50073. 1996. write for info. (*0-614-11712-7*) Carol Pub Group.

Rating the Presidents: Every Chief Executive Ranked in Order of Influence. William J. Ridings, Jr. & Stuart B. McIver. (Illus.). 304p. 1996. 22.95 (*0-8065-1799-9*, Citadel Pr) Carol Pub Group.

Rating the Risks-Assessing the Solvency Threat in the Financial Services Industry. 128p. 1991. pap. 95.00 (*0-932387-24-1*) Insur Info.

***Rating Trend Differences Between AGMA & ISO Vehicle Gears.** Octave A. LaBath. (Technical Papers: Vol. 209.12). 24p. 1981. pap. text ed. 30.00 (*1-55589-138-1*) AGMA.

Ratings Analysis: Theory & Practice. James G. Webster & Lawrence W. Lichty. 304p. 1991. pap. 24.95 (*0-8058-0949-X*); text ed. 59.95 (*0-8058-0239-8*) L Erlbaum Assocs.

Ratio Analysis Workbook. Sheryl S. Mott. Ed. by James J. Andover. LC 84-18977. 256p. 1984. student ed. 22.95 (*0-934914-57-5*) NACM.

Ratio & Invention: A Study of Medieval Lyric & Narrative. Robert R. Edwards. LC 88-26077. 215p. 1989. 24.95 (*0-8265-1231-3*) Vanderbilt U Pr.

Ratio & Percent. (TAI Mathematics Ser.). (J). 1995. 5.50 (*0-88106-164-6*, M012) Charlesbridge Pub.

***Ratio & Proportion.** Marion Smoothey. (Let's Investigate Ser.). (Illus.). 64p. (J). (gr. 4 up). 1996. lib. bdg. 17.95 (*1-85435-776-X*) Marshall Cavendish.

Ratio Correlation: A Manual for Students of Petrology & Geochemistry. Felix Chayes. LC 71-146110. 108p. 1971. pap. text ed. 5.50 (*0-226-10220-3*) U Ch Pr.

Ratio Disciplinae Fratrum Novanglorum: A Faithful Account of the Discipline Professed & Practised, in the Churches of New-England. Cotton Mather. LC 71-141114. (Research Library of Colonial Americana). 1972. reprint ed. 25.95 (*0-405-03327-3*) Ayer.

***Ratio, Fractions, Decimals & Percentages Review Book.** 32p. 1995. pap. text ed. 16.95 (*0-521-43911-6*) Cambridge U Pr.

Ration Scaling of Psychological Magnitude: In Honor of the Memory of S. S. Stevens. Ed. by S. J. Bolanowski & George A. Gescheider. 336p. (C). 1990. text ed. 69.95 (*0-8058-0710-1*) L Erlbaum Assocs.

Rational Acceptance & Purpose: An Outline of Pragmatist Epistemology. D. S. Clarke, Jr. LC 87-37680. 158p. (Orig.). (C). 1989. 55.00 (*0-8476-7599-8*); pap. 23.00 (*0-8476-7600-5*) Rowman.

Rational Analysis for a Problematic World: Problems Structuring Methods for Complexity, Uncertainty & Conflict. Ed. by Jonathan Rosenhead. 370p. 1989. text ed. 60.50 (*0-471-92285-4*) Wiley.

Rational Anarchy & What It Can Do for You. CWL. LC 88-50190. 54p. (Orig.). 1988. pap. 15.00 (*0-939856-84-0*) Tech Group.

***Rational & Social Practice.** 164p. 1997. pap. text ed. 5.00 (*1-879771-20-9*) World Scientific Pub.

Rational & the Moral Order: The Social Roots of Reason & Morality. Kurt Baier. (Paul Carus Lectures: Ser. 18). 465p. 1995. 44.95 (*0-8126-9263-2*); pap. 21.95 (*0-8126-9264-0*) Open Court.

Rational & the Social. James R. Brown. (Philosophical Issues in Science Ser.). 176p. (C). 1989. text ed. 45.00 (*0-415-02905-8*) Routledge.

***Rational Approach to Determine Case Depth Requirements in Carburized & Hardened Gears.** V. K. Sharma & Dale H. Breen. (Technical Papers). 1976. pap. text ed. 30.00 (*1-55589-253-1*) AGMA.

***Rational Approach to Radiodiagnostic Investigations.** (Technical Report Ser.: No. 689). 52p. 1983. pap. text ed. 5.00 (*92-4-120689-6*) World Health.

Rational Approaches to Structure, Activity & Ecotox Agrochem. Draber & Fujita. 608p. 1992. 224.95 (*0-8493-5859-0*, SB951) CRC Pr.

Rational Approximation & Interpolation, Vol. 1105. Ed. by P. R. Graves-Morris et al. (Lecture Notes in Mathematics Ser.). xii, 528p. 1984. 64.95 (*0-387-13899-4*) Spr-Verlag.

Rational Approximation & Its Applications in Mathematics & Physics: Proceedings, Lancut 1985. Ed. by J. Gilewicz et al. (Lecture Notes in Mathematics Ser.: Vol. 1237). xii, 350p. 1987. 51.95 (*0-387-17212-2*) Spr-Verlag.

Rational Approximation of Real Functions: Rational Approximation of Real Functions. P. P. Petrushev & V. A. Popov. (Encyclopedia of Mathematics & Its Applications Ser.: No. 28). (Illus.). 300p. 1988. text ed. 99.95 (*0-521-33107-2*) Cambridge U Pr.

Rational Approximations & Orthogonality. Nikishin et al. LC 91-18793. (Translations of Mathematical Monographs: Vol. 92). 221p. 1991. 90.00 (*0-8218-4545-4*, MMONO/92) Am Math.

Rational as Reasonable: A Treatise on Legal Justification. Aulis Aarnio. (Law & Philosophy Library: No. 4). 288p. 1986. lib. bdg. 118.50 (*90-277-2276-5*) Kluwer Ac.

Rational Association. Fred M. Frohock. 190p. 1987. text ed. 39.95 (*0-8156-2390-9*) Syracuse U Pr.

Rational Basis for Anesthesiology. G. Dal Santo. 934p. 1990. text ed. 80.00 (*1-57235-010-5*) Piccin NY.

Rational Basis of Legal Institutions. Intro. by Oliver W. Holmes et al. (Modern Legal Philosophy Ser.: Vol. 14). xxxii, 603p. 1969. reprint ed. 37.50 (0-8377-2525-9) Rothman.

Rational Behavior & Bargaining Equilibrium in Games & Social Situations. John C. Harsanyi. (Illus.). 352p. 1986. pap. text ed. 26.95 (0-521-31183-7) Cambridge U Pr.

Rational Behavior & Bargaining Equilibrium in Games & Social Situations. John C. Harsanyi. LC 75-38370. 326p. reprint ed. pap. 93.00 (0-317-29369-9, 2024474) Bks Demand.

Rational Behavior Therapy. Maxie C. Maultsby, Jr. (Illus.). 288p. (C). 1984. pap. 28.95 (0-13-752907-4) P-H.

Rational Behavior Therapy: The Self-Help Psychotherapy. Maxie C. Maultsby, Jr. (Illus.). 1990. reprint ed. pap. 16.95 (0-932838-08-1) Tangrm Bks.

***Rational Bubbles Vol. 451: Theoretical Basis, Economic Relevance, & Empirical Evidence with a Special Emphasis on the German Stock Market.** Matthias Salge. LC 97-2983. (Lecture Notes in Economics & Mathematical Systems Ser.). 1997. pap. write for info. (3-540-62629-8) Spr-Verlag.

Rational Changes in Science. Ed. by Joseph C. Pitt & Marcello Pera. 240p. (C). 1987. lib. bdg. 126.00 (90-277-2417-2, D Reidel) Kluwer Ac.

Rational Choice. Ed. by Jon Elster. LC 86-5329. (Readings in Social & Political Theory Ser.). 256p. 1986. pap. 17.50 (0-8147-2169-9) NYU Pr.

Rational Choice. Ed. by Jon Elster. LC 86-5329. (Readings in Social & Political Theory Ser.). 256p. (C). 1986. text ed. 36.00 (0-8147-2168-0) NYU Pr.

Rational Choice: The Contrast Between Economics & Psychology. Robin M. Hogarth & Melvin W. Reder. 344p. 1987. pap. text ed. 15.95 (0-226-34859-8) U Ch Pr.

Rational Choice Analysis of Union Militancy with Application to the Cases of British Coal & Fiat. Miriam Golden. (Cornell University's Western Societies Papers: Vol. 27). 65p. (Orig.). 1990. pap. 11.95 (0-8014-9651-9) Cornell U Pr.

Rational Choice & Moral Agency. David Schmidtz. LC 94-19059. 296p. 1994. text ed. 39.50 (0-691-03401-X) Princeton U Pr.

***Rational Choice & Moral Agency.** David Schmidtz. 296p. 1995. pap. text ed. 18.95 (0-691-02918-0) Princeton U Pr.

Rational Choice & Political Power. Keith M. Dowding. 208p. 1991. text ed. 80.00 (1-85278-335-4) E Elgar.

***Rational Choice & Situational Crime Prevention: Theoretical Foundations.** Ed. by Graeme Newman et al. LC 97-7934. 300p. 1997. text ed. 68.95 (1-85521-947-6, Pub. by Ashgate UK) Ashgate Pub Co.

Rational Choice, Collective Decisions & Social Welfare. K. Suzumura. LC 82-22110. 320p. 1983. 75.00 (0-521-23862-5) Cambridge U Pr.

Rational Choice in an Uncertain World. Robyn M. Dawes. 346p. (C). 1988. pap. text ed. 16.00 (0-15-575215-4) HB Coll Pubs.

Rational Choice Marxism. Ed. by Terrell Carver & Paul Thomas. LC 94-41149. 350p. 1995. 45.00 (0-271-01463-6); pap. 16.95 (0-271-01464-4) Pa St U Pr.

***Rational Choice Theories of Religion.** Lawrence A. Young. LC 96-25169. (C). 1996. pap. 17.95 (0-415-91192-3) Routledge.

***Rational Choice Theories of Religion.** Lawrence A. Young. LC 96-25169. (C). 1997. text ed. 59.95 (0-415-91191-5) Routledge.

Rational Choice Theory. Ed. by Peter Abell. (Schools of Thought in Sociology Ser.: No. 8). 432p. 1991. text ed. 150.00 (1-85278-321-4) E Elgar.

Rational Choice Theory: Advocacy & Critique. James S. Coleman. (Key Issues in Sociological Theory Ser.: Vol. 7). 240p. (C). 1992. text ed. 52.00 (0-8039-4761-5); pap. text ed. 24.00 (0-8039-4762-3) Sage.

Rational Choice Theory: Economic Models of Politics Reconsidered. Jeffrey Friedman. 1996. pap. 17.00 (0-300-06821-2) Yale U Pr.

***Rational Choice Theory & Large Scale Data Analysis.** Gerald Prein. Ed. by Hans-Peter Blossfeld. (Social Inequality Ser.). (C). 1997. text ed. 60.00 (0-8133-9027-3) Westview.

Rational Commitment: A Foundation for Macroeconomics. Brendan O'Flaherty. LC 85-13161. (Duke Press Policy Studies). (Illus.). x, 230p. 1985. text ed. 46.95 (0-8223-0454-6) Duke.

Rational Consensus in Science & Society: A Philosophical & Mathematical Study. K. Kehrer & C. Wagner. (Philosophical Studies: No. 24). 174p. 1981. pap. text ed. 49.00 (90-277-1307-3) Kluwer Ac.

Rational Consensus in Science & Society: A Philosophical & Mathematical Study. Keith Lehrer & Carl Wagner. 174p. 1981. lib. bdg. 70.50 (90-277-1306-5, D Reidel) Kluwer Ac.

Rational Constructions of Modules for Simple Lie Algebras. George B. Seligman. LC 81-12781. (Contemporary Mathematics Ser.: Vol. 5). 185p. 1981. pap. 21.00 (0-8218-5008-3, CONM/5) Am Math.

Rational Consumer: Theory & Evidence. Robert Hall. 200p. 1991. 27.50 (0-262-08197-0) MIT Pr.

Rational Counseling Primer. Howard S. Young. (Illus.). (J). (gr. 6-12). 1974. pap. 2.50 (0-917476-01-8) A Ellis Institute.

Rational Counseling with School Aged Populations: A Practical Guide. Jerry Wilde. LC 92-53190. xvi, 200p. 1992. pap. text ed. 17.95 (1-55959-040-8) Accel Devel.

Rational Curves & Surfaces: Applications to CAD. J. C. Fiorot & P. Jeannin. Tr. by M. C. Harrison. LC 92-14741. 319p. 1992. text ed. 115.00 (0-471-93092-X) Wiley.

Rational Curves on Algebraic Varieties, Vol. XII. Janos Kollar. Ed. by P. L. Lions et al. (Ergebnisse der Mathematik und Ihrer Greuzgebiete: Vol. 32). 289p. 1995. 135.95 (3-540-60168-6) Spr-Verlag.

Rational Decision & Causality. Ellery T. Eells. LC 81-18001. (Cambridge Studies in Philosophy). (Illus.). 240p. 1982. text ed. 65.00 (0-521-24213-4) Cambridge U Pr.

Rational Decision-Making: Israel's Security Choices, 1967. Janice G. Stein & Raymond Tanter. LC 80-13589. (Illus.). 415p. 1980. 50.00 (0-8142-0312-4) Ohio St U Pr.

Rational Descriptions Decisions & Designs. M. Tribus. LC 69-17175. 1969. 220.00 (0-08-006393-4, Pub. by Pergamon Repr UK) Franklin.

Rational Design. David D. Red. 148p. 1990. pap. 10.95 (0-533-08511-X) Vantage.

Rational Diet. O. Carque. 1991. lib. bdg. 75.00 (0-87700-972-4) Revisionist Pr.

Rational Diet: An Advanced Treatise on the Food Question. Otto Carque. 540p. 1971. reprint ed. spiral bd. 19.00 (0-7873-0150-7) Hlth Research.

Rational Discourse & Poetic Communication: Methods of Linguistic, Literary, & Philosophical Analysis. Roland Posner. LC 82-3502. (Janua Linguarum, Series Major: No. 103). xvi, 258p. 1982. 60.00 (90-279-3419-3) Mouton.

Rational Economic Decisions & the Current Account in Kenya. Jadish Handa & Geoffrey Mwan. (Making of Modern Africa Ser.). 160p. 1995. 59.95 (1-85972-236-9, Pub. by Avebury Pub UK) Ashgate Pub Co.

Rational Effectiveness Training: Increasing Personal Productivity at Work. Dominic Dimattia. Ed. by Stacey Mennen. (Illus.). 32p. (Orig.). 1990. pap. 3.95 (0-917476-20-4) A Ellis Institute.

Rational-Emotive Approaches to the Problems of Childhood. Ed. by Albert Ellis & Michael E. Bernard. 536p. 1983. 95.00 (0-306-41331-0, Plenum Pr) Plenum.

Rational Emotive Behavior Therapy: A Client's Guide. John Traverse & Windy Dryden. 100p. 1995. pap. 24.95 (1-56593-594-2, 1216) Singular Publishing.

Rational Emotive Behavior Therapy: A Reader. Windy Dryden. 304p. 1995. text ed. 65.00 (0-8039-7858-8); pap. text ed. 26.95 (0-8039-7859-6) Sage.

***Rational Emotive Behavior Therapy: Learning from Demonstration Sessions.** Windy Dryden. (Illus.). 250p. (Orig.). 1996. pap. 34.95 (1-56593-784-8, 1530) Singular Publishing.

Rational Emotive Consultation in Applied Settings. Ed. by Michael Bernard & Raymond DiGuiseppe. (School Psychology Ser.). 224p. 1993. text ed. 49.95 (0-8058-0578-8) L Erlbaum Assocs.

Rational-Emotive Counselling in Action. Windy Dryden. (Counselling in Action Ser.: Vol. 9). 112p. (C). 1990. text ed. 49.95 (0-8039-8269-0); pap. text ed. 21.50 (0-8039-8270-4) Sage.

Rational-Emotive Couple Counseling: A Special Issue of Journal of Rational Emotive Therapy. Russell M. Grieger. 109p. 1986. pap. 16.95 (0-89885-300-1) Human Sci Pr.

***Rational-Emotive Education Manual for Elementary Teachers.** William J. Knaus. 9.95 (0-917476-03-4, B054) Inst Rational-Emotive.

Rational-Emotive Family Therapy: A Systems Perspective. Charles H. Huber & Leroy G. Baruth. 208p. 1989. 27.95 (0-8261-6100-6) Springer Pub.

Rational-Emotive Therapy. Albert Ellis. (Practitioner Guidebook Ser.). (C). 1992. pap. text ed. 31.50 (0-205-14434-9, H4434, Longwood Div) Allyn.

Rational-Emotive Therapy Companion: A Clear, Concise, & Complete Guide to Being an RET Client. Russell M. Grieger & Paul J. Woods. (Illus.). 116p. (Orig.). 1993. 15.95 (0-914044-02-8) Scholars Pr Ltd.

Rational-Emotive Therapy with Children & Adolescents. 2nd ed. M. E. Bernard. 1994. text ed. 45.00 (0-471-57670-0) Wiley.

Rational Enterprise: Logos in Plato's Theaetetus. Rosemary Desjardins. LC 88-20001. (SUNY Series in Ancient Greek Philosophy). 275p. 1990. pap. text ed. 19.95 (0-88706-838-3) State U NY Pr.

Rational Enterprise: Logos in Plato's Theaetetus. Rosemary Desjardins. LC 88-20001. (SUNY Series in Ancient Greek Philosophy). 275p. 1990. text ed. 59.50 (0-88706-837-5) State U NY Pr.

Rational Expectations. Steven M. Shefrin. LC 82-19747. (Cambridge Surveys of Economic Literature Ser.). 215p. 1983. pap. text ed. 19.95 (0-521-28595-X) Cambridge U Pr.

Rational Expectations. 2nd ed. Steven M. Sheffrin. (Surveys of Economic Literature Ser.). (Illus.). 184p. (C). 1996. text ed. 54.95 (0-521-47400-0); pap. text ed. 18.95 (0-521-47939-8) Cambridge U Pr.

Rational Expectations: An Elementary Exposition. G. K. Shaw. LC 83-40180. 200p. 1984. text ed. 29.95 (0-312-66402-8) St Martin.

Rational Expectations: An Elementary Exposition. G. K. Shaw. LC 83-19252. 131p. 1985. pap. 9.95 (0-312-66403-6) St Martin.

Rational Expectations & Econometric Practice, 2 vols., 1. Ed. by Robert E. Lucas, Jr. & Thomas J. Sargent. LC 80-24602. 776p. (C). 1981. pap. text ed. 17.95 (0-8166-0917-9) U of Minn Pr.

Rational Expectations & Economic Policy. Ed. by Stanley Fischer. LC 79-22661. x, 304p. (C). 1982. pap. text ed. 13.50 (0-226-25134-9) U Ch Pr.

Rational Expectations & Efficiency in Futures Markets. Ed. by Barry A. Goss. (Illus.). 224p. (C). (gr. 13). 1991. text ed. 74.95 (0-415-02343-2, A6304) Routledge.

Rational Expectations & Monetary Policies. Jac J. Sijben. LC 79-56565. 144p. 1980. lib. bdg. 97.00 (90-286-0030-2) Kluwer Ac.

Rational Expectations Approach to Macroeconomics: Testing Policy Ineffectiveness & Efficient-Markets Models. Frederic S. Mishkin. LC 82-20049. (National Bureau of Economic Research Monographs). 184p. (C). 1984. pap. text ed. 10.95 (0-226-53187-2) U Ch Pr.

Rational Expectations Equilibrium Inventory Model. Ed. by T. Kollintzas. (Lecture Notes in Economics & Mathematical Systems Ser.: Vol. 322). x, 270p. 1989. 44.95 (0-387-96940-3) Spr-Verlag.

Rational Expectations Macroeconomics: An Introductory Handbook. 2nd ed. Patrick Minford. (Illus.). 240p. (C). 1992. pap. 27.95 (0-631-17788-4) Blackwell Pubs.

Rational Expectations Revolution: Readings from the Front Line. Ed. by Preston J. Miller. LC 93-5815. 292p. 1994. 47.50 (0-262-13297-4); pap. 24.00 (0-262-63155-5) MIT Pr.

Rational Expectations Revolution in Macroeconomics: Theories & Evidence. David K. Begg. LC 82-47785. 304p. (Orig.). 1982. pap. 16.95 (0-8018-2882-1) Johns Hopkins.

Rational Exultation. John D. Seelye. 1985. pap. 3.50 (0-912296-70-4) Am Antiquarian.

Rational Fabrication Specifications for the Offshore Industry. Welding Institute Staff. Ed. by N. J. Prescott & J. W. Harrison. (Illus.). 76p. (Orig.). (C). 1988. pap. 75.00 (0-85300-223-1, Pub. by Woodhead Pubng UK) Am Educ Systs.

Rational Factory: Architecture, Technology, & Work in America's Age of Mass Production. Lindy Biggs. LC 96-10947. (Johns Hopkins Studies in Industry & Society: No. 11). (Illus.). 224p. 1996. text ed. 39.95 (0-8018-5261-7) Johns Hopkins.

Rational Faith: Catholic Responses to Reformed Epistemology. Linda T. Zagzebski. LC 92-53742. (Library of Religious Philosophy: Vol. 10). (C). 1993. text ed. 38.00 (0-268-01643-7) U of Notre Dame Pr.

Rational Faith: Catholic Responses to Reformed Epistemology. Ed. by Linda T. Zagzebski. (Library of Religious Philosophy: Vol. 10). (C). 1994. pap. text ed. 17.50 (0-268-01644-5) U of Notre Dame Pr.

Rational Fasting: Regeneration Diet & Natural Cure for All Diseases. Arnold Ehret. 15p. 1994. reprint ed. spiral bd. 4.50 (0-7873-1029-8) Hlth Research.

Rational Fasting for Health & Regeneration. Arnold Ehret. 168p. 1971. pap. 3.95 (0-87904-005-X) Lust.

Rational Fears. Mark Jancovich. 224p. 1996. text ed. 19.95 (0-7190-3624-0) St Martin.

Rational Foundations of Economic Behaviour: Proceedings of the IEA Conference Held in Turin, Italy. Ed. by Kenneth J. Arrow et al. LC 95-7828. 1996. text ed. 79.95 (0-312-12708-1) St Martin.

Rational Geomancy: The Kids of the Book-Machine. Ed. by Steve McCaffery. 320p. 1991. pap. 19.95 (0-88922-300-9) LPC InBook.

Rational Geomancy, the Kids of the Book Machine: The Collected Research Reports of the Toronto Research Group, 1973-1982. Steve McCaffery & B. P. Nichol. (Illus.). 320p. (Orig.). 1993. pap. 16.95 (0-317-05589-5) Genl Dist Srvs.

Rational Hill: The Cosmic Reason. Dibinga W. Said. LC 95-92495. (Unity of Thought in Kaffric, Kushanic, Ani & Kemetic Civilizations Ser.: No. 003, Pt. I). 50p. (C). 1995. pap. text ed. 5.00 (0-943324-68-8) Omenana.

Rational Homotopy Theory & Differential Forms. P. A. Griffiths & J. Morgan. (Progress in Mathematics Ser.: Vol. 16). 256p. 1981. 45.00 (0-8176-3041-4) Birkhauser.

Rational Homotopy Type. W. T. Wu. (Lecture Notes in Mathematics Ser.: Vol. 1264). viii, 219p. 1987. 38.95 (0-387-13611-8) Spr-Verlag.

Rational Infant: Learning in Infancy. T. G. Bower. LC 88-31082. (Psychology Ser.). 210p. (C). 1995. text ed. write for info. (0-7167-2005-1); pap. text ed. write for info. (0-7167-2007-8) W H Freeman.

Rational Infidels: The American Deists. Kerry S. Walters. LC 91-15217. 300p. (C). 1992. text ed. 37.50 (0-89341-641-X, Longwood Academic) Hollowbrook.

Rational Interaction: Essays in Honor of John C. Harsanyi. Ed. by Reinhard Selten. (Illus.). ix, 438p. 1992. 143.95 (0-387-55067-4) Spr-Verlag.

Rational Investment Behavior in the Face of Floods. C. B. McGuire. LC 79-135090. 151p. 1969. 29.00 (0-403-04517-7) Scholarly.

Rational Iteration: Complex Analytic Dynamical Systems. Norbert Steinmetz. LC 93-16400. (Studies in Mathematics: Vol. 16). x, 189p. (C). 1993. lib. bdg. 59.95 (3-11-013765-8) De Gruyter.

Rational Kinematics. Ed. by J. Angeles. (Tracts in Natural Philosophy Ser.: Vol. 34). xii, 121p. 1989. 58.95 (0-387-96813-X) Spr-Verlag.

Rational Landscapes & Humanistic Geography. Edward Relph. LC 81-10782. 232p. 1981. 58.50 (0-389-20237-1, N7033) B&N Imports.

Rational Legitimacy: A Theory of Political Support. Ronald Rogowski. LC 74-2975. (Illus.). 324p. 1974. reprint ed. pap. 92.40 (0-7837-9434-7, 2060176) Bks Demand.

Rational Love. Warren Shibles. LC 77-93187. (C). 1978. pap. 7.00 (0-912386-13-4) Language Pr.

Rational Madness: The Paradox of Addiction. Ray Hoskins. 1989. text ed. 19.95 (0-07-156892-1) McGraw.

Rational Madness: The Paradox of Addiction. Ray Hoskins. 1989. 19.95 (0-8306-8001-2); pap. 14.95 (0-8306-9201-0) McGraw-Hill Prof.

***Rational Man.** Teresa Benison. 378p. 1997. 26.00 (0-09-179209-6, Pub. by Hutchnson UK) Trafalgar.

Rational Man: A Modern Interpretation of Aristotelian Ethics. Henry B. Veatch. LC 62-16161. 224p. 1962. reprint ed. pap. 63.90 (0-7837-9669-2, 2059303) Bks Demand.

***Rational Man & Irrational Society? An Introduction & Sourcebook.** Ed. by Brian Barry & Russell Hardin. LC 81-21508. 413p. 1982. reprint ed. pap. 117.80 (0-608-02989-0, 2059629) Bks Demand.

***Rational Management of Children.** Paul A. Hauck. 17.95 (0-614-23938-9, B081) Inst Rational-Emotive.

Rational Management of Children. 2nd rev. ed. Paul A. Hauck. 1972. 17.95 (0-87212-018-X) Libra.

Rational Manual Therapies. John V. Basmajian & Richard Nyberg. (Illus.). 512p. 1992. 49.00 (0-683-00420-4) Williams & Wilkins.

Rational Meaning: A New Foundation for the Definition of Words & Supplementary Essays. Laura R. Jackson & Schuyler B. Jackson. Ed. by William Harmon. LC 96-18722. 640p. 1997. text ed. 50.00 (0-8139-1682-8) U Pr of Va.

***Rational Method of Selecting Anti-Friction Bearings.** AGMA Technical Committee. (Technical Papers: Vol. 246). 5p. 1941. pap. text ed. 30.00 (1-55589-144-6) AGMA.

Rational Methods in Lie Algebras. George B. Seligman. (Lecture Notes in Pure & Applied Mathematics Ser.: Vol. 17). 360p. 1976. 160.00 (0-8247-6480-3) Dekker.

Rational Minority Business Council Directory of Minority & Women Owned Business. NMBC Staff. 144p. 1996. pap. text ed. 125.00 (0-7872-2101-5) Kendall-Hunt.

***Rational Number Project: Fraction Lessons for the Middle Grades, Level 1.** Kathleen Cramer et al. 228p. (C). 1997. pap. text ed., spiral bd. 26.95 (0-7872-3464-8) Kendall-Hunt.

***Rational Number Project: Fraction Lessons for the Middle Grades, Level 2.** Kathleen Cramer et al. 230p. (C). 1997. pap. text ed., spiral bd. 26.95 (0-7872-3470-2) Kendall-Hunt.

Rational Numbers: An Interaction of Research. Ed. by Thomas P. Carpenter et al. (Studies in Mathematical Thinking & Learning). 392p. 1993. text ed. 79.95 (0-8058-1135-4) L Erlbaum Assocs.

Rational Numbers, Algebra & Solving Equations. rev. ed. Mervin L. Keedy & Marvin L. Bittinger. (Algebra, a Modern Introduction Ser.). (gr. 7-9). 1981. pap. text ed. write for info. (0-201-03983-4) Addison-Wesley.

Rational Numbers, Bk. 5 see Key to Algebra Series

Rational Numbers Study Aid. Richard C. Davis et al. (J). 1976. pap. 3.00 (0-87738-039-2) Youth Ed.

Rational Option for a National Health Program. John Canham-Clyne et al. 112p. 1995. 17.95 (0-9630587-2-X); pap. 9.95 (0-9630587-1-1) Pamphleteers.

Rational Peasant: The Political Economy of Rural Society in Vietnam. Samuel L. Popkin. LC 77-83105. 1979. pap. 16.00 (0-520-03954-8) U CA Pr.

Rational Pesticide Use. Ed. by E. J. Brent & E. K. Atkin. (Illus.). 358p. 1987. text ed. 80.00 (0-521-32068-2) Cambridge U Pr.

Rational Plypharmacy. Ed. by Ilo E. Leppik. LC 96-43598. (Epilepsy Research Supplements Ser.: No. 11). 274p. 1997. text ed. 172.00 (0-444-82455-3) Elsevier.

Rational Points: Seminar Bonn-Wuppetal, 1983-84. A Publication of the Max-Planck-Institut fur Mathematik, Bonn. 3rd ed. Gerd Faltings et al. (Aspects of Mathematics Ser.: Vol. 6). viii, 268p. 1991. pap. 56.00 (3-528-28593-1, Pub. by Vieweg & Sohn GW) Informatica.

Rational Points on Elliptic Curves. J. H. Silverman. (Undergraduate Texts in Mathematics Ser.). (Illus.). x, 281p. 1996. 29.95 (0-387-97825-9) Spr-Verlag.

Rational Praise & Natural Lamentation: Johnson, Lycidas, & Principles of Criticism. James L. Battersby. LC 77-89774. 288p. 1980. 38.50 (0-8386-2148-1) Fairleigh Dickinson.

Rational Price Expectations & Inflation. 2nd ed. Sargent. (C). 1992. text ed. 24.00 (0-06-500280-6) Addson-Wesley Educ.

Rational Principles of Pianoforte Technique. Alfred Cortot. 102p. 1990. reprint ed. lib. bdg. 59.00 (0-7812-9174-7) Rprt Serv.

***Rational Procedure for the Preliminary Design of Minimum Volume Gears.** AGMA Technical Committee Staff. (Information Sheet Ser.). 1992. pap. text ed. 30.00 (1-55589-579-4) AGMA.

Rational Psychology. L. P. Hickok. LC 72-13798. (History of Psychology Ser.). 756p. 1973. reprint ed. lib. bdg. 90.00 (0-8201-1117-1) Schol Facsimiles.

Rational Public: Fifty Years of Trends in Americans' Policy Preferences. Benjamin I. Page & Robert Y. Shapiro. (Illus.). 506p. 1992. pap. text ed. 22.00 (0-226-64478-2) U Ch Pr.

***Rational Rabbis: Science & Talmudic Culture.** Menachem Fisch. LC 97-7349. (Jewish Literature & Culture Ser.). 1997. write for info. (0-253-33316-4) Ind U Pr.

Rational Readings on Environmental Concerns. Ed. by Jay Lehr. (Environmental Engineering Ser.). (Illus.). 900p. 1992. text ed. 77.95 (0-442-01146-6) Van Nos Reinhold.

Rational Recovery: The New Cure for Substance Addiction. Jack Trimpey. 1996. pap. 12.00 (0-671-52858-0) PB.

***Rational Recovery Quick Start Primer.** William J. Knaus. 6.00 (0-614-23923-0, B143) Inst Rational-Emotive.

Rational Representation of Algebraic Groups. S. Donkin. (Lecture Notes in Mathematics Ser.: Vol. 1140). vii, 254p. 1985. 42.95 (0-387-15668-2) Spr-Verlag.

Rational Rose Essentials: Using the Booch Method. Iseult White. LC 94-16210. 240p. (YA). 1994. Diskette. 49.50 (0-8053-0616-1) Addison-Wesley.

Rational Rose Essentials: Using the Booch Method. Iseult White. LC 94-16210. 1994. write for info. (0-201-96229-2) Benjamin-Cummings.

Rational Series & Their Languages. J. Berstel & C. Reutenauer. (EATCS Monographs on Theoretical Computer Science: Vol. 12). 150p. 1988. 53.95 (0-387-18626-3) Spr-Verlag.

An Asterisk (*) at the beginning of an entry indicates that the title is appearing in BIP for the first time.

Rational Sex Ethics. Ben N. Ard, Jr. (American University Studies: Philosophy: Ser. V, Vol. 73). 219p. (C). 1989. text ed. 35.50 (*0-8204-0857-3*) P Lang Pubng.

Rational Society: A Critical Study of Santayana's Social Thought. Beth J. Singer. LC 77-99237. 155p. reprint ed. pap. 44.20 (*0-317-08959-5*, 2003261) Bks Demand.

Rational Stories for Children. Virginia Waters. (Illus.). (J). (ps-6). 1980. pap. 6.50 (*0-917476-18-2*) A Ellis Institute.

Rational Strength of English Law. F. H. Lawson. viii, 147p. 1988. reprint ed. lib. bdg. 27.50 (*0-8377-2410-4*) Rothman.

Rational Suicide? Implications for Mental Health Professionals. James L. Werth, Jr. LC 95-38733. (Series in Death Education, Aging, & Health Care). 200p. 1996. 59.95 (*1-56032-424-4*); pap. 22.95 (*1-56032-450-3*) Hemisp Pub.

Rational System: Eighteen Thirty-Seven to Eighteen Forty-One. LC 72-2537. (British Labour Struggles Before 1850 Ser.). 1974. 23.95 (*0-405-04430-5*) Ayer.

Rational Techniques in Policy Analysis. Michael Carley. 1980. pap. text ed. 19.95 (*0-566-05491-4*, Pub. by Dartmth Pub UK) Ashgate Pub Co.

Rational Theology & Christian Philosophy in England in the 17th Century, 2 vols. John Tulloch. 1966. reprint ed. 154.70 (*0-685-66525-9*, 05101404) G Olms Pubs.

***Rational Theology & Christian Theology: In England in the 17th Century (1874 Edition), 2 vols., Set.** John Tulloch. 1023p. 1996. reprint ed. write for info. (*1-85506-210-0*) Bks Intl VA.

Rational Theory of Sexuality. Harvey Jackins. 1977. pap. 2.00 (*0-913937-11-8*) Rational Isl.

Rational Therapeutics: A Clinical Pharmacologic Guide for the Health Professional. Williams et al. (Clinical Pharmacology Ser.: Vol. 16). 808p. 1989. 210.00 (*0-8247-7946-0*) Dekker.

Rational Thermodynamics. 2nd ed. Clifford A. Truesdell. 560p. 1984. reprint ed. 175.95 (*0-387-90874-9*) Spr-Verlag.

Rational Thinking: A Study in Basic Logic. John B. Bennett. 1980. 33.95 (*0-88229-285-4*) Nelson-Hall.

Rational Transmitting Boundaries for Time-Domain Analysis of Dam-Reservoir Interaction. Benedikt Weber. LC 94-36643. (IBK Bericht Ser.). 1994. write for info. (*0-8176-5123-3*) Birkhauser.

Rational Use of Advanced Medical Technology with the Elderly. Ed. by Freddie Homburger. LC 94-1496. 296p. (C). 1994. text ed. 44.95 (*0-8261-8410-3*) Springer Pub.

***Rational Use of Diagnostic Imaging in Paediatrics: Report of a WHO Study Group, 1987.** WHO Staff. (Technical Report Ser.: No. 757). 102p. 1987. 14.00 (*92-4-120757-4*) World Health.

***Rational Use of Drugs: Report of the Conference of Experts, Nairobi.** WHO Staff. 329p. 1987. 52.00 (*92-4-156105-X*) World Health.

Rational Use of Drugs in the Management of Acute Diarrhoea in Children. iv, 71p. (ENG, FRE, RUS & SPA.). 1990. pap. text ed. 14.00 (*92-4-156142-4*, 1150355) World Health.

Rational Use of Drugs Report of the Conference of Experts, Nairobi (25-29 November 1985) 329p. 1987. pap. text ed. 29.00 (*92-4-156104-1*, 1150271) World Health.

Rational Use of Magnetic Resonance Imaging. Peter A. Rinck. (Illus.). 300p. 1996. 125.00 (*0-86542-823-9*) Blackwell Sci.

Rational Use of Water & Its Treatment in the Chemical Industry. 146p. 1991. 38.00 (*92-1-116500-8*, E.91.II. E.3) UN.

Rational Weight Control: A Revolutionary Approach to Training Your Appetite. Lois Trimpey & Jack Trimpey. LC 94-7943. 1995. write for info. (*0-385-30559-1*) Delacorte.

Rational Zen: The Mind of Dogen Zenji. Tr. by Thomas Cleary from JPN. LC 92-50126. 256p. 1993. 20.00 (*0-87773-689-8*) Shambhala Pubns.

Rational Zen: The Mind of Dogen Zenji. Thomas Cleary. 1995. pap. 14.00 (*0-87773-973-0*) Shambhala Pubns.

Rationale for Black Christian Literature. 2nd ed. Walter A. McCray. LC 92-72557. 56p. (C). 1992. reprint ed. pap. 4.95 (*0-933176-14-7*) Black Light Fellow.

Rationale for Nonviolence. Chandler Smith. (Illus.). 241p. (Orig.). 1992. pap. 15.00 (*0-9632068-1-8*) C Smith.

Rationale for Sampling & Interpretation of Ecological Data in the Assessment of Freshwater Ecosystems, STP 894. Ed. by Billy G. Isom. LC 86-3323. (Special Technical Publication Ser.). (Illus.). 194p. 1986. text ed. 39.00 (*0-8031-0455-3*, 04-894000-16) ASTM.

Rationale for Selecting Access Control List Features for the UNIX System. 72p. (Orig.). (C). 1994. pap. text ed. 25. 00 (*0-7881-0554-X*) DIANE Pub.

Rationale for Teachers Critical Pedagogy: A Handbook. W. John Smyth. (C). 1987. 60.00 (*0-7300-0673-5*, Pub. by Deakin Univ AT) St Mut.

Rationale for Teachers Critical Pedagogy: A Handbook. W. John Smyth. 1995. pap. 35.00 (*0-7300-0450-3*, Pub. by Deakin Univ AT) St Mut.

Rationale for the ANSI C Programming Language. 130p. 1990. 19.95 (*0-929306-07-4*) Silicon Pr.

Rationale for the Design of the ADA Programming Language. 390p. 1989. pap. 31.95 (*0-9615336-5-X*) Silicon Pr.

Rationale for the Design of the Ada Programming Language. J. Ichbiah et al. 450p. (C). 1991. text ed. 80. 00 (*0-521-39267-5*) Cambridge U Pr.

Rationale of Beings: Recent Developments in Particle, Nuclear & General Physics, Festschrift in Honor of Gyo Takeda, Japan, October 13, 1984. Ed. by K. Ishikawa et al. 430p. 1986. text ed. 129.00 (*9971-5-0117-1*) World Scientific Pub.

Rationale of Central Banking: And the Free Banking Alternative. Vera C. Smith. LC 90-30937. 248p. (C). 1990. reprint ed. pap. 7.00 (*0-86597-087-4*); reprint ed. text ed. 15.00 (*0-86597-086-6*) Liberty Fund.

Rationale of Crime & Its Appropriate Treatment: Being a Treatise on Criminal Jurisprudence Considered in Relation to Cerebral Organization. 2nd ed. Marmaduke B. Sampson. (Criminology, Law Enforcement, & Social Problems Ser.: No. 174). (Illus.). 1973. reprint ed. 24.00 (*0-87585-174-6*) Patterson Smith.

***Rationale of Estrogen Dose Reduction: The Justification for 20 (Micrograms) Ethinylestradiol.** Mary Short & European Society of Contraception Staff. LC 97-20954. 1997. write for info. (*1-85070-785-5*) Prthnon Pub.

***Rationale of Halakhic Man: Joseph B. Soloveitchik's Conception of Jewish Thought.** Reinier Munk. (Amsterdam Studies in Jewish Thought: Vol. 3). x, 144p. 1997. lib. bdg. 54.00 (*90-5063-607-1*, Pub. by Gieben NE) Benjamins North Am.

Rationale of Judicial Evidence: Specially Applied to English Practice, 5 vols. Jeremy Bentham. Ed. by John S. Mill. 1995. lib. bdg. 295.00 (*0-8377-1979-8*) Rothman.

Rationale of Operative Fracture Care. Joseph Schatzker. (Illus.). 545p. 1993. 266.00 (*0-387-10675-8*) Spr-Verlag.

Rationale of Operative Fracture Care. 2nd enl. rev. ed. Joseph Schatzker & Marvin Tile. LC 95-39615. 544p. 1996. 249.00 (*3-540-59388-8*) Spr-Verlag.

Rationale of Punishment: With Intro. & Index Added. Heinrich Oppenheimer. LC 72-172579. (Criminology, Law Enforcement, & Social Problems Ser.: No. 167). 1975. 24.00 (*0-87585-167-3*) Patterson Smith.

Rationale of Textual Criticism. G. Thomas Tanselle. LC 88-27990. 104p. (C). 1989. pap. 12.95 (*0-8122-1409-9*) U of Pa Pr.

Rationale of the China Question. Gideon Nye. LC 72-79834. (China Library). 1972. reprint ed. lib. bdg. 14.00 (*0-8420-1374-1*) Scholarly Res Inc.

Rationalism & Anti-Rationalism in the Origins of Economics: The Philosophical Roots of 18th Century Economic Thought. William O. Coleman. 192p. 1995. 70.00 (*1-85278-995-6*) E Elgar.

Rationalism, Empiricism, & Idealism. Anthony Kenny. (British Academy Lectures on the History of Philosophy). 192p. 1986. 65.00 (*0-19-824669-2*) OUP.

Rationalism, Empiricism & Pragmaticism: An Introduction. Bruce A. Aune. 1970. pap. text ed. write for info. (*0-07-553543-2*) McGraw.

Rationalism in Greek Philosophy. George Boas. LC 61-15638. 514p. reprint ed. pap. 146.50 (*0-317-08864-5*, 2013173) Bks Demand.

Rationalism in Politics & Other Essays. Michael Oakeshott. LC 91-6951. 584p. (Orig.). 1991. pap. 7.50 (*0-86597-095-5*); text ed. 21.00 (*0-86597-094-7*) Liberty Fund.

Rationalism, Realism, & Relativism: Perspectives in Contemporary Moral Epistemology. Robert L. Arrington. LC 89-42874. 344p. 1989. pap. 17.95 (*0-8014-9563-6*) Cornell U Pr.

Rationalism, Religion, & Domination: A Weberian Perspective. Wolfgang Schluchter. Tr. by Neil Solomon. 1989. 75.00 (*0-520-05659-0*) U CA Pr.

Rationalisme Applique. Gaston Bachelard. 224p. (FRE.). 1986. pap. 20.95 (*0-7859-3007-8*) Fr & Eur.

Rationalists. John G. Cottingham. (History of Western Philosophy Ser.: No. 4). 256p. (C). 1988. pap. text ed. 17.95 (*0-19-289190-1*) OUP.

Rationalists: Five Basic Works on Rationalism. Incl. Discourse on Method. Rene Descartes. (Orig.). (*0-318-51733-7*); Meditations. Rene Descartes. 1960. (*0-318-51734-5*); Ethics. Benedict Spinoza. (*0-318-51735-3*); Monadology. Gottfried W. Liebniz. 1960. (*0-318-51736-1*); Discourse on Metaphysics. Gottfried W. Liebniz. 1960. (*0-318-51737-X*); 480p. 1960. pap. 11.00 (*0-385-09540-6*, Anchor NY) Doubleday.

Rationalitaet der Metapher: Eine Sprachphilosophische und Kommunikations - Theoretische Untersuchung. Bernhard Debatin. (Grundlagen der Kommunikation und Kognition - Foundations of Communication & Cognition Ser.). xii, 381p. (GER.). (C). 1995. 180.00 (*3-11-014708-4*) De Gruyter.

***Rationalitat und Mentale Modelle Vol. XVII: Standortkonflikte um Abfallentsorgungsanlagen aus Okonomischer Sicht.** Jan Karpe. (Duropaische Hochschulschriften: Reihe 5: Bd. 2009). 317p. (GER.). 1997. pap. 57.95 (*3-631-31086-2*) P Lang Pubng.

***Rationalities, Historicities.** Dominique Janicaud. Tr. by Nina Belmonte. LC 96-45340. (Contemporary Studies in Philosophy & the Human Sciences). 192p. (C). 1997. text ed. 49.95 (*0-391-04037-5*) Humanities.

Rationality. Harold I. Brown. 256p. (C). 1990. pap. 18.95 (*0-415-05517-2*, A5160) Routledge.

Rationality: A Study in Behaviour. Barnett. (Australian National University Press Ser.). 1996. text ed. write for info. (*0-08-032826-1*, Pergamon Pr) Elsevier.

Rationality: An Essay Towards an Analysis. Jonathan Bennett. LC 88-30267. 134p. (C). 1989. reprint ed. pap. 6.95 (*0-87220-066-3*); reprint ed. lib. bdg. 24.95 (*0-87220-067-1*) Hackett Pub.

Rationality: Problems of Philosophy. Harold I. Brown. 224p. 1988. text ed. 35.00 (*0-415-00181-1*) Routledge.

Rationality: Psychological & Philosophical Perspectives. Ed. by K. I. Manktelow & D. E. Over. LC 92-47072. (International Library of Psychology). (Illus.). 320p. (C). 1993. text ed. 89.95 (*0-415-06955-6*, A7779, Routledge NY) Routledge.

Rationality: The Critical View. Ed. by J. Agassi & I. C. Jarvie. 490p. (C). 1987. pap. text ed. 72.50 (*90-247-3455-X*, Pub. by M Nijhoff NE); lib. bdg. 180. 50 (*90-247-3275-1*, Pub. by M Nijhoff NE) Kluwer Ac.

Rationality, Allocation & Reproduction. Vivian C. Walsh. LC 95-46908. (Illus.). 312p. (C). 1996. 65.00 (*0-19-828772-0*, Clarendon Pr) OUP.

Rationality & Collective Belief. Anthony Harris. Ed. by Gerald Platt. LC 85-20152. (Modern Sociology Ser.). 264p. 1986. text ed. 73.25 (*0-89391-044-9*) Ablex Pub.

Rationality & Coordination. Cristina Bicchieri. (Studies in Probability, Induction & Decision Theory). (Illus.). 304p. (C). 1994. text ed. 64.95 (*0-521-38123-1*) Cambridge U Pr.

***Rationality & Coordination.** Cristina Bicchieri. (Cambridge Studies in Probability, Induction & Decision Theory). 288p. 1997. pap. text ed. 14.95 (*0-521-57444-7*) Cambridge U Pr.

Rationality & Dynamic Choice: Foundational Explorations. Edward F. McClennen. 320p. (C). 1990. text ed. 64.95 (*0-521-36047-1*) Cambridge U Pr.

Rationality & Ethics in Agriculture. Hugh Lehman. 1995. pap. text ed. 24.95 (*0-89301-179-7*) U of Idaho Pr.

Rationality & Institutions: Essays in Honour of Knut Midgaard, Vol. 1. Ed. by Raino Malnes & Arild Underdal. (Studies in Politics & Government). 302p. 1992. pap. 32.50 (*82-00-21623-3*) Scandnvan Univ Pr.

Rationality & Irrationality in Economics. Maurice Godelier. Tr. by Brian Pearce from FRE. LC 72-92033. 336p. (ENG.). 1975. pap. 10.00 (*0-85345-349-7*) Monthly Rev.

Rationality & Mind in Early Buddhism. Frank J. Hoffman. 138p. 1992. 16.95 (*81-208-0211-X*) Asia Bk Corp.

Rationality & Modernity: Essays in Philosophical Pragmatics. Gunnar Skirbekk. (Scandinavian University Press Publication). 307p. 1993. 39.50 (*82-00-21718-3*) Scandnvan Univ Pr.

Rationality & Nature: A Sociological Inquiry into a Changing Relationship. Raymond Murphy. LC 94-25665. (C). 1994. pap. text ed. 23.50 (*0-8133-2169-7*) Westview.

***Rationality & Power.** Flyvbjerg. 1996. pap. text ed. 16.95 (*0-226-25451-8*); lib. bdg. 43.00 (*0-226-25449-6*) U Ch Pr.

***Rationality & Reasoning.** Evans & Over. 1996. 29.95 (*0-86377-437-7*) L Erlbaum Assocs.

Rationality & Relativism. Ed. by Martin Hollis & Steven Lukes. 320p. (C). 1982. pap. 16.95 (*0-262-58061-6*) MIT Pr.

Rationality & Relativity: The Quest for Objective Knowledge. F. P. O'Gorman. (Avebury Series in Philosophy). 160p. 1989. text ed. 68.95 (*0-566-07035-9*, Pub. by Avebury Pub UK) Ashgate Pub Co.

Rationality & Religious Belief. Cornelius F. Dalaney. LC 79-63359. (University of Notre Dame Studies in the Philosophy of Religion: No. 1). 176p. 1979. reprint ed. pap. 50.20 (*0-608-00881-8*, 2061675) Bks Demand.

Rationality & Revelation in Rahner: The Contemplative Dimension. Christopher F. Schiavone. LC 93-37304. (American Univ. Studies, VII: Vol. 169). 316p. (C). 1994. text ed. 47.95 (*0-8204-2342-4*) P Lang Pubng.

Rationality & Revolution. Ed. by Michael Taylor. (Studies in Marxism & Social Theory). 275p. 1988. 69.95 (*0-521-34419-0*) Cambridge U Pr.

Rationality & Science: Can Science Explain Everything? Roger Trigg. 256p. 1993. pap. 22.95 (*0-631-19037-6*) Blackwell Pubs.

***Rationality & Structure: The Bavli's Anomalous Juxtapositions.** Jacob Neusner. LC 97-3557. (University of South Florida Studies in the History of Judaism). 231p. 1997. 69.95 (*0-7885-0340-5*, 240144) Scholars Pr GA.

Rationality & the Analysis of International Conflict. Michael Nicholson. (Studies in International Relations). (Illus.). 288p. (C). 1992. pap. text ed. 19.95 (*0-521-39810-X*) Cambridge U Pr.

Rationality & Theistic Belief: An Essay on Reformed Epistemology. Mark S. McLeod. LC 93-7544. (Cornell Studies in the Philosophy of Religion). 288p. 1993. 39. 95 (*0-8014-2863-7*) Cornell U Pr.

Rationality in Action: Contemporary Approaches. Ed. by Paul K. Moser. 450p. (C). 1990. text ed. 85.00 (*0-521-38572-5*); pap. text ed. 32.95 (*0-521-38598-9*) Cambridge U Pr.

Rationality in Epistemology: Proceedings of a Conference Sponsored by Sociedad Filosofica Ibero-Americana 1992. Ed. by Enrique Villanueva. (Philosophical Issues Ser.: No. 2, 1992). viii, 280p. (Orig.). 1992. pap. text ed. 25.00 (*0-924922-09-5*); lib. bdg. 42.00 (*0-924922-59-1*) Ridgeview.

Rationality in Greek Thought. Ed. by Michael Frede & Gisela Striker. LC 96-1644. 368p. 1996. 60.00 (*0-19-824044-9*, Clarendon Pr) OUP.

Rationality in Question: On Eastern & Western Views of Rationality. Ed. by Shlomo Biderman & Ben-Ami Scharfstein. (Studies in the History of Religions: Vol. LII). xix, 256p. 1989. text ed. 78.50 (*90-04-09212-9*) E J Brill.

Rationality in Science & Politics. Ed. by G. Andersson. (Boston Studies in the Philosophy of Science Ser.: No. 79). 320p. 1985. pap. text ed. 65.50 (*90-277-1953-5*) Kluwer Ac.

Rationality in Science & Politics. Ed. by Gunnar Andersson. (Boston Studies in the Philosophy of Science: 79). 312p. 1984. lib. bdg. 139.50 (*90-277-1575-0*) Kluwer Ac.

Rationality in Science, Religion, & Everyday Life: A Critical Evaluation of Four Models of Rationality. Mikael Stenmark. LC 94-41140. (C). 1995. text ed. 32. 95 (*0-268-01651-8*) U of Notre Dame Pr.

Rationality in Thought & Action. Ed. by Martin Tamny & K. D. Irani. LC 85-21868. (Contributions in Philosophy Ser.: No. 29). (Illus.). 306p. 1986. text ed. 59.95 (*0-313-25017-0*, TRA/, Greenwood Pr) Greenwood.

Rationality, Institutions, & Economic Methodology. Ed. by Uskali Maki et al. LC 93-6926. (Economics As Social Theory Ser.). 272p. (C). 1993. pap. 19.95 (*0-415-09208-6*, B0145) Routledge.

Rationality, Institutions, & Economic Methodology. Ed. by Uskali Maki et al. LC 93-6926. (Economics As Social Theory Ser.). 272p. (C). (gr. 13). 1993. text ed. 79.95 (*0-415-07571-8*, B0141) Routledge.

Rationality, Justice & the Social Contract: Themes from Morals by Agreement. Ed. by David Gauthier & Robert Sugden. LC 93-16233. 192p. (C). 1993. text ed. 47.50 (*0-472-10394-6*) U of Mich Pr.

Rationality of Belief & the Plurality of Faith. Ed. by Thomas D. Senor. (Illus.). 296p. 1996. 39.95 (*0-8014-3127-1*) Cornell U Pr.

Rationality of Emotion. Ronald De Sousa. 448p. 1987. 35. 00 (*0-262-04092-1*, Bradford Bks) MIT Pr.

Rationality of Emotion. Ronald De Sousa. 400p. 1990. reprint ed. pap. 17.95 (*0-262-54057-6*) MIT Pr.

Rationality of Feeling: Understanding the Arts in Education. David Best. LC 92-37353. (Falmer Press Library on Aesthetic Education). 224p. 1993. 95.00 (*0-7507-0056-4*, Falmer Pr); pap. 34.00 (*0-7507-0057-2*, Falmer Pr) Taylor & Francis.

Rationality of Indecisive Choice Functions. Tony E. Smith. (Discussion Paper Ser.: No. 62). 1971. pap. 10.00 (*1-55869-103-0*) Regional Sci Res Inst.

Rationality of Islam. rev. ed. Murtaza Mutahhery et al. Tr. by Islamic Seminary Staff & M. A. Ansari from PER. 182p. (C). 1990. reprint ed. pap. 7.00 (*0-941724-17-4*) Islamic Seminary.

Rationality of Rural Life: Economic & Cultural Change in Tuscany, Vol. 17. Jeff Pratt. (Studies in Anthropology & History). 232p. 1995. text ed. 48.00 (*3-7186-5627-2*, Harwood Acad Pubs) Gordon & Breach.

Rationality of Science. W. H. Newton-Smith. (International Library of Philosophy). 300p. 1981. pap. 14.95 (*0-7100-0913-5*, RKP) Routledge.

***Rationality of Science.** W. H. Newton-Smith. (International Library of Philosophy Ser.). 312p. (C). 1981. pap. 17.95 (*0-415-05877-5*) Routledge.

***Rationality of the Welfare State.** Ed. by Erik O. Eriksen & Jorn Loftager. 248p. (C). 1996. lib. bdg. 36.00 (*82-00-42991-1*) Scandnvan Univ Pr.

Rationality Redeemed? Siegel. 256p. (C). 1996. text ed. 59. 95 (*0-415-91764-6*, Routledge NY) Routledge.

Rationality Redeemed? Harvey Siegel. 256p. (C). 1996. pap. 17.95 (*0-415-91765-4*, Routledge NY) Routledge.

***Rationality, Relativism & Incommensurability.** Howard Sankey. (Avebury Series in Philosophy). 200p. 1997. text ed. 59.95 (*1-85972-381-0*, Pub. by Ashgate UK) Ashgate Pub Co.

Rationality, Relativism & the Human Sciences. Ed. by James M. Margolis et al. 252p. 1986. lib. bdg. 118.50 (*90-247-3271-9*, Pub. by M Nijhoff NE) Kluwer Ac.

Rationality, Religious Belief, & Moral Commitment: New Essays in the Philosophy of Religion. Ed. by Robert Audi & William J. Wainwright. LC 85-48200. 352p. 1986. 39.95 (*0-8014-1856-9*) Cornell U Pr.

Rationality, Rules, & Utility: New Essays on the Moral Philosophy of Richard Brandt. Brad Hooker. 261p. (C). 1993. text ed. 75.00 (*0-8133-1568-9*) Westview.

Rationality, Social Action & Moral Judgement. Stuart Toddington. (Edinburgh Law & Society Ser.). 240p. 1994. 49.00 (*0-7486-0432-4*, Pub. by Edinburgh U Pr UK) Col U Pr.

Rationalization of Terrorism. Ed. by David C. Rapoport & Yonah Alexander. LC 81-70296. 210p. 1982. text ed. 39. 95 (*0-313-27098-8*, U7098, Greenwood Pr) Greenwood.

Rationalizations for Women Who Do Too Much: While Running with the Wolves. Allison McCune & Tomye B. Spears. 1994. pap. 5.95 (*1-55850-380-3*) Adams Media.

***Rationalize.** Sparky Chance. 1996. pap. 8.95 (*0-533-12046-2*) Vantage.

Rationalized Epistemology: Taking Solipsism Seriously. Albert A. Johnstone. LC 90-49126. (SUNY Series in Logic & Language). 361p. 1991. pap. text ed. 24.95 (*0-7914-0788-8*) State U NY Pr.

Rationalized Epistemology: Taking Solipsism Seriously. Albert A. Johnstone. LC 90-49126. (SUNY Series in Logic & Language). 361p. 1991. text ed. 67.50 (*0-7914-0787-X*) State U NY Pr.

***Rationalizing Acute Care Services.** Pauline Mistry. LC 96-33576. 1996. write for info. (*1-85775-125-6*, Radcliffe Med Pr) Scovill Paterson.

Rationalizing Culture: IRCAM, Boulez, & the Institutionalisation of the Avant-Garde. Georgina Born. LC 93-39386. 392p. 1995. pap. 18.00 (*0-520-20216-3*) U CA Pr.

Rationalizing Genius: Ideological Strategies in the Classic American Science Fiction Short Story. John Huntington. LC 88-36991. 248p. (C). 1989. text ed. 40. 00 (*0-8135-1429-0*); pap. text ed. 15.00 (*0-8135-1430-4*) Rutgers U Pr.

Rationalizing Justice: The Political Economy of Federal District Courts. Wolf Heydebrand & Carroll Seron. LC 89-19676. (SUNY Series in the Sociology of Work). 308p. 1990. text ed. 74.50 (*0-7914-0295-9*); pap. text ed. 24.95 (*0-7914-0296-7*) State U NY Pr.

***Rationalizing Medical Work: Decision-Support Techniques & Medical Practices.** Marc Berg. LC 96-2928. (Inside Technology Ser.). 250p. 1997. 30.00 (*0-262-02417-9*) MIT Pr.

Rationalizing Parliament: Legislative Institutions & Party Politics in France. John D. Huber. (Political Economy of Institutions & Decisions Ser.). (Illus.). 192p. 1996. text ed. 54.95 (*0-521-56291-0*) Cambridge U Pr.

Rationed Years. Alida Harvie. (Illus.). 160p. (C). 1984. 35. 00 (*0-7212-0602-6*, Pub. by Regency Press UK) St Mut.

R

Rationing America's Medical Care: The Oregon Plan & Beyond. Ed. by Martin A. Strosberg et al. (Dialogues on Public Policy Ser.). 240p. (C). 1992. pap. 12.95 (*0-8157-8197-0*) Brookings.

Rationing Beef Cattle. David Allen. (Illus.). 80p. 1992. pap. text ed. 18.50 (*0-948617-27-6*, Pub. by Chalcombe Pubns UK) Scholium Intl.

Rationing Health Care in America: Perceptions & Principles of Justice. Larry R. Churchill. LC 86-40582. (C). 1987. pap. text ed. 13.00 (*0-268-01631-3*) U of Notre Dame Pr.

Rationing Justice on Appeal: The Problems of the U. S. Courts of Appeals. Ed. by Thomas E. Baker. 426p. 1994. text ed. write for info. (*0-314-03494-3*) West Pub.

Rationing Medical Care for the Critically Ill. Ed. by Martin A. Strosberg et al. (Dialogues on Public Policy Ser.). 98p. 1989. pap. 11.95 (*0-8157-8199-7*) Brookings.

Rationing Medicine. Robert H. Blank. (Illus.). 288p. 1988. text ed. 45.00 (*0-231-06536-1*) Col U Pr.

Rationing Medicine. Robert H. Blank. 290p. 1989. pap. text ed. 17.00 (*0-231-06537-X*) Col U Pr.

Rationing of American Higher Education. Don M. Flournoy. 186p. 1982. pap. text ed. 11.95 (*0-87073-989-1*) Schenkman Bks Inc.

Ratios for Success. LERN Staff. 42p. 39.95 (*0-914951-69-6*) LERN.

Ratios in Investment Real Estate. Edric Cane. 125p. (Orig.). 1993. pap. 27.50 (*0-916785-14-9*) E Cane Sem.

Ratis Raving, & Other Moral & Religious Pieces. Joseph R. Lumby. (EETS, OS Ser.: No. 43). 1974. reprint ed. 40.00 (*0-527-00038-8*) Periodicals Srv.

Ratite Encyclopedia: Ostrich-Emu-Rhea. Ed. by Claire Drenowatz & Charlie Elrod. (Illus.). 488p. 1995. 84.95 (*0-9642940-2-8*) Ratite Records. THE RATITE ENCYCLOPEDIA is the only comprehensive guide for the ratite farmer. Each chapter is a stand-alone article on a single subject, written by the top experts from four continents especially for this indispensable reference tool. Except on subjects such as tax considerations, each species is treated separately; for instance, there are separate chapters on ostrich, emu & rhea chick rearing. Subjects include the history & geography of ratites, record keeping, breeder management, reproduction, the egg, candling, incubation & hatching, chick rearing, genetics, diseases, biosecurity, anatomy, nutrition, meat studies, leather, emu & rhea oil, working with veterinarians, farm design & layout, microchips, hauling & transportation, legal aspects, insurance & tax considerations, equipment, products, services & a glossary of agricultural & medical terminology. The book also includes lists of national & state organizations, colleges & universities currently researching ratites, trade publications & other reference material. It is profusely illustrated with charts, graphs, diagrams & color photographs. The publisher's first book on record keeping set the standard for the industry. Ratite Records, P.O. Box 790365, San Antonio, TX 78279-0365, 800-926-4695. *Publisher Provided Annotation.*

Ratite Management, Medicine, & Surgery. Ed. by Thomas N. Tully, Jr. & Simon M. Shane. LC 95-48173. (Illus.). 214p. (C). 1996. 59.00 (*0-89464-874-8*) Krieger.

Ratking. Michael Dibdin. LC 96-45600. 1997. pap. 12.00 (*0-679-76854-8*, Vin) Random.

Ratna Povijest Hrvatske (Military History of Croatia), 4 vols. Ivo Omrcanin. (CRO.). 1993. pap. 5.00 (*1-878716-08-5*) Ivor Pr.

Ratna Trekker's Pal: Nepali Phrase Book. 1991. 20.00 (*0-7855-0284-X*, Pub. by Ratna Pustak Bhandar) St Mut.

Ratna Trekker's Pocket-Pal: Nepali Word & Phrase Guide. Ed. by Ratna Pustak Bhandar Staff. (C). 1986. 22.00 (*0-89771-081-9*, Pub. by Ratna Pustak Bhandar) St Mut.

Ratner's Star. Don DeLillo. (Vintage Contemporaries Ser.). 1989. pap. 15.00 (*0-679-72292-0*) Random.

Raton en Casa - A Mouse in the House. Henrietta. Ed. by Maria Puncel & Juan J. Vasquez. (Illus.). 29p. (SPA.). (J). (gr. k-1). 1992. write for info. (*84-372-6619-X*) Santillana.

Raton Mickey - One Mickey Mouse: Un Libro Disney de Numeros - A Disney Book of Numbers. Tr. by Daniel M. Santacruz. (Libros Buena Vista Ser.). (Illus.). 12p. (SPA.). (J). 1993. bds. 5.95 (*1-56282-460-0*) Disney Pr.

Ratooning of Sugarcane. R. L. Yadav. (C). 1992. 147.50 (*81-7136-036-X*, Pub. by Periodical Expert II) St Mut.

***Ratramnus, De Corpore et Sanguine Domini.** Ed. by J. N. Bakhuizen. (Verhandelingen der Koninklijke Nederlandse Akademie van Wetenschappen, Afd. Letterkunde, Nieuwe Reeks Ser.: No. 87). 156p. 1974. pap. 40.75 (*0-7204-8288-7*) Elsevier.

***Rats.** Ginger Cardinal. 1997. 12.95 (*0-87605-428-9*) Howell Bk.

RATS. Walter Enders. (Econometric Time Ser.). 204p. 1996. 28.95 incl. cd-rom (*0-471-14894-6*) Wiley.

Rats. Susan Fox. (Illus.). 96p. 1984. 9.95 (*0-87666-933-X*, KW-128) TFH Pubns.

Rats. Israel Horovitz. 1968. pap. 3.25 (*0-8222-0930-6*) Dramatists Play.

Rats. James E. Luczak. (Orig.). 1992. pap. 3.00 (*0-87129-169-X*, R52) Dramatic Pub.

Rats. Page McBrier. (Treehouse Times Ser.: No. 7). 128p. (J). 1990. pap. 2.95 (*0-380-75901-2*, Camelot) Avon.

Rats. E. Sandy Powell. LC 93-40925. (Early Bird Nature Bks.). 48p. (J). (gr. 2-3). 1994. lib. bdg. 18.95 (*0-8225-3003-1*, Lerner Publctns) Lerner Group.

Rats. James P. Wohl. 320p. 1994. pap. 4.99 (*0-7860-0056-2*, Pinncle Kensgtn) Kensgtn Pub Corp.

Rats! abr. ed. Jane Cutler. LC 95-22953. (Illus.). 114p. (J). (gr. 2-5). 1996. 14.00 (*0-374-36181-9*) FS&G.

RATS: (Rapid Assessment & Treatment Strategies for Human Resource Personnel) Thomas McDonnell. (Orig.). 1989. pap. 9.95 (*0-931821-97-5*) Info Res Cons.

***Rats: A Complete Introduction.** Daniel R. Schwartz. (Illus.). 64p. 1997. 12.95 (*0-7938-0204-0*, WW-038) TFH Pubns.

Rats: A Complete Pet Owners Manual. Carol Himsel. (Barron's Pet Owner's Manuals Ser.). (Illus.). 64p. 1991. pap. 6.95 (*0-8120-4535-1*) Barron.

Rats Alley. John H. Irsfeld. LC 86-14655. 208p. 1987. 19.00 (*0-87417-117-2*) U of Nev Pr.

Rats & Gargoyles. Mary Gentle. 480p. 1992. pap. 5.99 (*0-451-45173-2*, ROC) NAL-Dutton.

Rats Came Back. Ross Seidel. (Illus.). 32p. (J). (ps). 1995. pap. 5.95 (*1-55037-402-8*, Pub. by Annick CN); lib. bdg. 16.95 (*1-55037-403-6*, Pub. by Annick CN) Firefly Bks Ltd.

Rat's Daughter: From an Old Tale. Joel Cook. LC 92-71871. 32p. (J). (ps-3). 1993. 14.95 (*1-56397-140-2*) Boyds Mills Pr.

Rats for Those Who Care. Dennis Kelsey-Wood. (Illus.). 32p. 1995. pap. 4.95 (*0-7938-1392-1*, B114) TFH Pubns.

Rats in the Attic & Other Stories to Make Your Skin Crawl. G. E. Stanley. 128p. (Orig.). (YA). 1995. mass mkt. 3.99 (*0-380-77389-9*, Flare) Avon.

Rats in the Sacristy. Llewelyn Powys. LC 67-30226. (Essay Index Reprint Ser.). 1977. 19.95 (*0-8369-0798-1*) Ayer.

Rats in the Trees: Stories. Jess Mowry. LC 89-27909. 160p. (Orig.). (J). 1990. pap. 8.95 (*0-936784-81-4*) J Daniel.

Rats, Lice & History: Being a Study in Biography, Which, after Twelve Preliminary Chapters Indispensable for the Preparation of the Lay Reader, Deals with the Life History of Typhus Fever... Hans Zinsser. 320p. 1996. 9.98 (*1-884822-47-9*) Blck Dog & Leventhal.

Rats' Nests: The Collected Poetry of Hagiwara (Surname) Sakutaro. Hagiwara Sakutaro. Tr. & Intro. by Robert Epp. (Translations of Modern Japanese Poetry Ser.). 252p. (C). 1993. text ed. 30.00 (*1-880276-40-2*) Yakusha.

***Rats on the Range.** James Marshall. 1997. pap. 3.99 (*0-14-038645-9*) Viking Penguin.

Rats on the Range & Other Stories. James Marshall. LC 92-28918. (J). (gr. 1-5). 1993. pap. 12.99 (*0-8037-1384-3*); lib. bdg. 12.89 (*0-8037-1385-1*) Dial Bks Young.

***Rats on the Roof.** James Marshall. (J). 1997. pap. 3.99 (*0-14-038646-7*) Viking Penguin.

Rats on the Roof: And Other Stories. James Marshall. LC 90-44084. (Illus.). 80p. (J). (gr. 1-5). 1991. pap. 13.00 (*0-8037-0834-3*); pap. 12.89 (*0-8037-0835-1*) Dial Bks Young.

Rats Saw God. Rob Thomas. (Illus.). 192p. (YA). (gr. 7 up). 1996. pap. 3.99 (*0-689-80777-5*, Aladdin Paperbacks) S&S Childrens.

Rats Saw God: A Comic Emotionally Charged Tale. Rob Thomas. LC 95-43548. (Illus.). 192p. (YA). (gr. 7 up). 1996. 17.00 (*0-689-80207-2*, Aladdin Paperbacks) S&S Childrens.

Rats, Spiders & Love. Bonnie Pryor. LC 85-25831. (Illus.). 128p. (J). (gr. 4-6). 1986. 16.00 (*0-688-05867-1*, Morrow Junior) Morrow.

***Rat's Tail.** Lucy Moreland. (Illus.). 100p. (Orig.). (J). (gr. 3-7). 1998. mass mkt. 6.99 (*1-58006-014-5*, Blue Jean) Sovereign.

Rats Tale. Tor Seidler. 187p. 1990. pap. 6.95 (*0-374-46204-6*, Sunburst Bks) FS&G.

Rat's Tale. Tor Seidler. (Illus.). 187p. (J). (gr. 1-8). 1986. 16.00 (*0-374-36185-1*) FS&G.

***Rat's Tale: Alzheimer's Mystery Story.** LC 97-93263. 193p. (Orig.). 1997. pap. 18.95 (*0-9657319-0-1*) Longleaf Pr NC.

Rats' Tales: The Staffordshire Regiment at War in the Gulf. Nicholas Benson. (Illus.). 164p. 1993. 30.00 (*1-85753-060-8*, Pub. by Brasseys UK) Brasseys Inc.

***Ratselcharakter der Kunst: Untersuchungen zu einem Topos der Philosophischen Asthetik.** Bernd Kleimann. (Europaische Hochschulschriften, Reihe 20: Bd. 514). 302p. (GER.). 1996. 57.95 (*3-631-30693-8*) P Lang Pubng.

Ratselheft. Susanne Ehrlich. (Illus.). 72p. (GER.). (J). (gr. 5 up). 1984. pap. 6.60 (*0-8442-2227-5*, Natl Textbk) NTC Pub Grp.

Ratt-Out of the Cellar: Recorded Versions. Ed. by Wolf Marshall. (Fretted Ser.). 120p. 1987. pap. 19.95 (*0-88188-764-1*, HL 00693911) H Leonard.

***Rattans.** Ed. by J. Dransfield & N. Manokaran. (PROSEA Ser.: No. 6). (Illus.). 137p. 1993. 100.00 (*90-220-1057-0*, Pub. by Backhuys Pubs NE) Balogh.

***Rattans.** Ed. by J. Dransfield & N. Manokaran. (PROSEA Ser.: No. 6). (Illus.). 137p. 1993. pap. 59.00 (*979-8316-20-7*, Pub. by Backhuys Pubs NE) Balogh.

***Rattenfanger von Hameln.** Ed. by Hanna Hutchinson. Tr. by Bettina Proffitt. (Illus.). 20p. (Orig.). (GER.). (J). (gr. 1-2). 1992. pap. 2.95 (*0-922852-12-X*, E015) Another Lang Pr.

***Rattle No. 6: Poetry for the 21st Century, Vol. 2, No. 2.** Ed. by Alan Fox. 128p. 1991. pap. 6.00 (*0-941017-51-6*) Bombshelter Pr.

***Rattle No. 7: Poetry for the 21st Century, Vol. 3, No. 1.** Ed. by Alan Fox. 162p. 1997. pap. 6.00 (*0-941017-52-4*) Bombshelter Pr.

Rattle & the Drum: Native American Rituals & Celebrations. Lisa Sita. LC 93-27209. (Illus.). 80p. (J). (gr. 3-6). 1994. lib. bdg. 19.40 (*1-56294-420-7*) Millbrook Pr.

Rattle Bag: An Anthology of Poetry. Ed. by Seamus Heaney & Ted Hughes. 498p. (J). (gr. 3 up). 1985. pap. 15.95 (*0-571-11976-X*) Faber & Faber.

***Rattle of the North: An Anthology of Ulster Prose.** Patricia Craig. 464p. 9500. pap. 24.95 (*0-85640-464-0*, Pub. by Blackstaff Pr IE) Dufour.

***Rattle-Rat.** Janwillem Van De Wetering. LC 97-20267. 1997. write for info. (*1-56947-103-7*) Soho Press.

Rattlebang: The Picture Book. Mark McCord. (Illus.). 32p. (J). (gr. k-3). 1996. 15.99 (*0-7814-0290-5*) Chariot Victor.

***Rattlebang Helps: A Book about Helpfulness.** Mark McCord. (Illus.). 8p. (J). 1996. 7.99 (*0-7814-0293-X*) Chariot Victor.

Rattlebang Picnic. Margaret Mahy. LC 93-36294. (Illus.). (J). (gr. 3 up). 1994. pap. 14.99 (*0-8037-1318-5*); pap. 14.89 (*0-8037-1319-3*) Dial Bks Young.

Rattlebang Picnic. Margaret Mahy. 1999. pap. write for info. (*0-241-13477-3*, Sig) NAL-Dutton.

Rattlebone. Maxine Clair. LC 93-50114. 1994. 19.00 (*0-374-24716-1*) FS&G.

Rattlebone. Maxine Clair. 224p. 1995. pap. 9.95 (*0-14-024825-0*, Penguin Bks) Viking Penguin.

Rattlebone Rock. Sylvia Andrews. LC 93-4426. (Illus.). 32p. (J). (ps-2). 1995. 13.95 (*0-06-023451-2*); lib. bdg. 13.89 (*0-06-023452-0*) HarpC Child Bks.

***Rattlebone Rock.** Sylvia Andrews. LC 93-4426. (Trophy Book Ser.). (Illus.). 32p. (J). (gr. k-3). 1997. pap. 4.95 (*0-06-443484-2*, Trophy) HarpC Child Bks.

Rattler. Mel Cebulash. (Author's Signature Collection). (J). (gr. 3-8). 1992. lib. bdg. 12.79 (*0-89565-880-1*) Childs World.

Rattler! Cap Iversen. (Dakota Ser.: No. 3). 222p. (Orig.). 1995. pap. 8.95 (*1-55583-228-8*) Alyson Pubns.

Rattler. Roger Rapoport. (Dare to Love Us Ser.). (J). 1995. 12.95 (*1-57143-050-4*) RDR Bks.

Rattler! A Natural History of Rattlesnakes. Chris Mattison. (Illus.). 144p. 1996. 27.95 (*0-7137-2534-6*, Pub. by Blandford Pr UK) Sterling.

***Rattler Creek.** large type ed. Ben Bridges. (Dales Large Print Ser.). (Illus.). 246p. 1996. pap. 17.99 (*1-85389-643-8*) Ulverscroft.

Rattler Tales from Northcentral Pennsylvania. C. E. Brennan. (Pitt Series in Nature & Natural History). (Illus.). 176p. (C). 1994. 29.95 (*0-8229-3856-1*) U of Pittsburgh Pr.

Rattler Tales from Northcentral Pennsylvania. C. E. Brennan. (Pitt Series in Nature & Natural History). (Illus.). 176p. (C). 1994. pap. 15.95 (*0-8229-5539-3*) U of Pittsburgh Pr.

Rattlers Roost. Robert Kammen. 224p. 1993. mass mkt. 3.50 (*0-8217-4033-4*, Zebra Kensgtn) Kensgtn Pub Corp.

Rattlesnake, Reading Level 2. Sherie Barger & Johnson. (Snake Discovery Library: Set I). (Illus.). 24p. (J). (gr. k-5). 1986. lib. bdg. 11.94 (*0-86592-956-4*) Rourke Corp.

***Rattlesnake Dance.** Jennifer Dewey. LC 96-84170. (Illus.). 48p. (J). (gr. 1 up). 1997. 17.95 (*1-56397-247-6*) Boyds Mills Pr.

Rattlesnake Grass. John O. Simon. 1978. pap. 5.00 (*0-914610-12-0*) Hanging Loose.

Rattlesnake Mesa. Dawson. 1997. 20.00 (*0-7862-0753-1*) Thorndike Pr.

Rattlesnake Mesa. large type ed. Dawson. Date not set. 20.00 (*0-7862-0776-0*, Thorndike Lrg Prnt) Thorndike Pr.

***Rattlesnake Pete.** Jeffrey W. Roberts. 50p. (Orig.). 1996. mass mkt. 2.99 (*0-9654318-0-0*) Atomic Wstrn.

Rattlesnake Railroad. large type ed. Mark Donovan. (Linford Western Library). 256p. 1993. pap. 15.99 (*0-7089-7307-8*) Ulverscroft.

***Rattlesnake Story.** Gail Jackson. Date not set. 15.95 (*0-399-23038-6*) Putnam Pub Group.

***Rattlesnake Tales: Fact & Fiction about Texas Diamondback Rattlers.** William F. Brown. (Illus.). 72p. 1997. pap. 12.95 (*1-881936-22-8*) WFB Ent.

Rattlesnake Venoms, Their Actions & Treatment. fac. ed. Ed. by Anthony T. Tu. LC 82-1376. (Illus.). 400p. 1982. pap. 114.00 (*0-7837-7716-7*, 2047478) Bks Demand.

Rattlesnakes. Beth W. Brust. (Zoobooks Ser.). (J). 1991. lib. bdg. 14.95 (*0-88682-426-5*) Creative Ed.

Rattlesnakes. J. Frank Dobie. 207p. 1982. pap. 11.95 (*0-292-77023-5*) U of Tex Pr.

Rattlesnakes. Eric Ethan. (Fangs! An Imagination Library Ser.). (J). 1995. lib. bdg. 17.27 (*0-8368-1431-2*) Gareth Stevens Inc.

Rattlesnakes. Sandra Lee. (Nature Bks.). 32p. (J). (gr. 2-6). 1992. lib. bdg. 22.79 (*0-89565-842-9*) Childs World.

Rattlesnakes. Mary A. McDonald. (Snakes Ser.). (Illus.). 48p. (J). (gr. 3-9). 1995. lib. bdg. 17.80 (*1-56065-294-2*) Capstone Pr.

Rattlesnakes. Mary A. McDonald. (Illus.). 48p. (J). (gr. 3-7). 1995. 13.35 (*0-516-35294-6*) Childrens.

Rattlesnakes. Wildlife Education, Ltd. Staff. (Zoobooks Ser.). (Illus.). 24p. (J). 1992. 13.95 (*0-937934-86-0*); pap. 2.75 (*0-937934-56-9*) Wildlife Educ.

***Rattlesnakes: Their Habits, Life Histories, & Influence on Mankind.** Laurence M. Klauber. (Illus.). 1997. 125.00 (*0-520-21056-5*) U CA Pr.

Rattlesnakes: Their Habits, Life Histories, & Influence on Mankind. abr. ed. Laurence M. Klauber. LC 80-16660. (Illus.). 400p. 1982. 40.00 (*0-520-04038-4*); pap. 16.95 (*0-520-04039-2*) U CA Pr.

Rattlesnakes & Roses. Joan Oppenheimer. LC 86-63269. 161p. (Orig.). 1987. pap. 8.95 (*0-9602676-5-4*) Persevrnce Pr.

Rattlesnakes & Scientists. David C. Ipsen. (Illus.). 111p. 1970. 12.95 (*0-8464-1179-2*) Beekman Pubs.

Rattlesnakes, Their Natural History & Care in Captivity: Their Natural History & Care in Captivity. Jerry G. Walls. (Illus.). 64p. 1996. pap. 9.95 (*0-7938-2064-2*, RE144) TFH Pubns.

Rattling Spurs & Broad-Brimmed Hats: The Civil War in Cynthiana & Harrison County, Kentucky. William A. Penn. 240p. 1995. lib. bdg. 26.00 (*0-9646989-1-9*) Battle Grove.

Rattling the Cup on Chicago Crime. Edward D. Sullivan. LC 76-150202. (Select Bibliographies Reprint Ser.). 1977. reprint ed. 18.95 (*0-8369-5715-6*) Ayer.

Rattling Those Dry Bones: Women Changing the Church. Ed. by June S. Hagen. LC 94-40380. 224p. 1995. pap. 16.95 (*0-931055-99-7*) Innisfree Pr.

Ratzinger Report. Joseph C. Ratzinger & Vittorio Messori. Tr. by Salvator Attanasio & Graham Harrison. LC 85-81218. 197p. (Orig.). (GER & ITA.). 1985. pap. 10.95 (*0-89870-080-9*) Ignatius Pr.

Rauber. Wilhelm Tell. Kabale und Liebe. unabridged ed. Schiller. (World Classic Literature Ser.). (GER.). pap. 7.95 (*3-89507-030-0*, Pub. by Bookking Intl FR) Distribks Inc.

Rauch Guide to the U. S. Ink Industry. Ed. by Carl Verbanic. (Illus.). 200p. 1998. spiral bd. 389.00 (*0-932157-02-5*) Impact Mrkting.

Rauch Guide to the U. S. Packaging Industry. Ed. by Carl Verbanic & Donald Dykes. (Illus.). 400p. 1997. spiral bd. 495.00 (*0-932157-03-3*) Impact Mrkting.

Rauch Guide to the U. S. Paint Industry. Ed. by Carl Verbanic & Donald Dykes. (Illus.). 250p. 1997. spiral bd. 398.00 (*0-932157-00-9*) Impact Mrkting.

***Rauch Guide to the U. S. Paper Industry.** (Illus.). 350p. 1998. pap. write for info. (*0-614-30127-0*) Impact Mrkting.

Rauch Guide to the U. S. Plastics Industry. Ed. by Carl Verbanic & Donald Dykes. (Illus.). 498p. 1997. spiral bd. 495.00 (*0-932157-04-1*) Impact Mrkting.

Rauch Guide to U. S. Adhesives & Sealants Industry. James A. Rauch. Ed. by Donald Dykes & Fred Keimel. (Illus.). 350p. 1996. spiral bd. 445.00 (*0-932157-05-X*) Impact Mrkting.

Rauch on Roosevelt. Harry E. Barnes. 1971. 59.95 (*0-87700-283-5*) Revisionist Pr.

***Rauf Denktash at the United Nations: Speeches on Cyprus.** Intro. by Michael Moran. 378p. 1997. 65.00 (*0-906719-50-X*, Pub. by Eothen UK) Paul & Co Pubs.

***Rauf Denktash at the United Nations: Speeches on Cyprus.** Intro. by Michael Moran. 378p. 1997. pap. 39.95 (*0-906719-55-0*, Pub. by Eothen UK) Paul & Co Pubs.

Raul: Una Historia Veridica. Raul Gonzalez. (SPA.). 1990. pap. 4.99 (*1-56063-059-0*, 498470) Editorial Unilit.

Raul - A True Story. Raul Gonzales. 240p. (Orig.). 1993. pap. 6.95 (*1-56043-777-4*) Destiny Image.

Raul Julia. Frank Perez & Ann Weil. (Contemporary Hispanic Americans Ser.). (J). (gr. 3-6). 1995. write for info. (*0-8172-3984-7*) Raintree Steck-V.

***Raul Julia.** Frank Perez & Ann Weil. (J). 1996. pap. text ed. 5.95 (*0-8114-9786-0*) Raintree Steck-V.

***Raul Julia.** large type ed. Frank Perez & Ann Weil. 54p. Date not set. write for info. (*0-614-24688-1*, L-86308-00 APHB) Am Printing Hse.

***Raul Julia.** large type ed. Frank Perez & Ann Weil. 54p. 1996. pap. 13.50 (*0-614-20574-3*, L-86308-00 APHB) Am Printing Hse.

Raul Julia: Puerto Rican Actor. Rebecca Stefoff. LC 93-42532. (Hispanics of Achievement Ser.). (Illus.). (YA). (gr. 5 up). 1994. lib. bdg. 19.95 (*0-7910-1556-4*) Chelsea Hse.

Raul Prebisch at ECLA: Years of Creative Intellectual Effort. Leopoldo Solis. 28p. 1988. English ed. pap. 6.95 (*1-55815-017-X*); Spanish ed. pap. 3.95 (*1-55815-105-2*) ICS Pr.

Raul Ruiz - Works for & about French TV. Jordi Torrent et al. (Illus.). 32p. (Orig.). 1987. pap. write for info. (*0-913263-19-2*) Exit Art.

***Raul's Revenge.** Jacqueline Baird. 1997. mass mkt. 3.50 (*0-373-11876-7*, 1-11876-9) Harlequin Bks.

Raum und Zeit im Homerischen Epos. Brigitte Hellwig. (Spudasmata Ser.: Bd. 2). ix, 153p. (GER.). 1964. write for info. (*3-487-05243-1*) G Olms Pubs.

***Raumliche Ansiedlungsdisparitaten: Empirische Analyse von Bestimmungsfaktoren im Rahmen Theoretischer Standortentscheidungsuberlegungen.** Peter Gehrung. (Illus.). xiv, 227p. (GER.). 1996. 44.95 (*3-631-30831-0*) P Lang Pubng.

Raunchy Riddles. Jackie Martling. 192p. 1993. mass mkt. 3.50 (*1-55817-771-X*, Pinncle Kensgtn) Kensgtn Pub Corp.

Raunchy Riddles. Jackie Martling. 1988. pap. 2.95 (*1-55817-072-3*) Kensgtn Pub Corp.

Raunculaceae & Rosaceae see Forest Flora of the Bombay Presidency & Sind

Rauschenberg - Art & Life. Mary L. Kotz. (Illus.). 320p. 1990. 75.00 (*0-8109-3752-2*) Abrams.

Rauschenberg Sculpture. Ed. & Contrib. by Julia B. Turrell. LC 95-80359. (Illus.). 131p. (Orig.). 1995. pap. write for info. (*0-929865-13-8*) Mod Art Mus Ft Worth.

Rausforderungen. 1995. 91.00 (*0-387-00790-3*) Spr-Verlag.

Rauvolfia Serpentina, 2 vols., 1. B. N. Sahu. (C). 1988. 80.00 (*0-685-22366-3*, Pub. by Scientific UK) St Mut.

Rauvolfia Serpentina, 2 vols., 2. B. N. Sahu. (C). 1988. 120.00 (*0-685-22367-1*, Pub. by Scientific UK) St Mut.

Rauvolfia Serpentina: Sarpagandha. B. N. Sahu. (Chemistry & Pharmacology Ser.: Vol. 2). xvi, 595p. 1983. 79.00 (*1-55528-047-1*, Pub. by Today & Tomorrows P & P II) Scholarly Pubns.

Rauvolfia Serpentina (Sarpagandha) Vol. I: Botany, Ecology & Agronomy. B. N. Sahu. 359p. 1979. 40.00 (*0-88065-186-5*, Messers Today & Tomorrow) Scholarly Pubns.

An Asterisk (*) at the beginning of an entry indicates that the title is appearing in BIP for the first time.

Rav. Chadukov. 258p. (YID.). 1985. 10.00 (*0-8266-0437-4*) Kehot Pubn Soc.

Rav. Naftali H. Ehrmann. Tr. by Karen Paritzky from GER. (Illus.). 1978. 9.95 (*0-87306-137-3*); pap. 7.95 (*0-87306-353-8*) Feldheim.

Rav Avraham Itzhak Hacohen Kook: Between Rationalism & Mysticism. Benjamin Ish-Shalom. LC 92-8087. (SUNY Series in Judaica: Hermeneutics, Mysticism, & Religion). 357p. 1993. text ed. 67.50 (*0-7914-1369-1*); pap. text ed. 24.95 (*0-7914-1370-5*) State U NY Pr.

Ravage. Rene Barjavel. 320p. (FRE.). 1972. pap. 11.95 (*0-7859-1713-6*, 2070362388) Fr & Eur.

Ravaged & Reborn: The Iranian Army 1982. William F. Hickman. LC 82-73900. 33p. 1983. pap. 6.95 (*0-8157-3611-8*) Brookings.

Ravaged Bridegroom. Marion Woodman. 214p. 1995. pap. 18.00 (*0-919123-42-2*, Pub. by Inner City CN) BookWorld Dist.

Ravaged by the New Age: Satan's Plan to Destroy Our Kids. Texe Marrs. LC 88-83897. (Illus.). 272p. (Orig.). 1989. pap. 10.95 (*0-9620086-1-3*) Living Truth Pubs.

Ravaged Temperate Forests. Terence Tompkins. LC 93-13048. (Environment Alert! Ser.). (J). 1993. lib. bdg. 18.60 (*0-8368-0728-6*) Gareth Stevens Inc.

Ravaged with Joy: A Record of the Poetry Reading at UC Davis on May 16, 1975. William Everson. Ed. by Sidney Berger et al. (Illus.). 56p. 1997. write for info. (*0-924433-06-X*) R Price.

***Ravagons.** (Torg Ser.). 15.00 (*0-87431-339-2*, 20577) West End Games.

Ravalette: The Rosicrucian's Story. Paschal B. Randolph. 283p. 1939. 7.95 (*0-932785-40-9*) Philos Pub.

Ravalette the Rosicrucian's Story. Paschal B. Randolph. reprint ed. spiral bd. 10.00 (*0-7873-0698-3*) Hlth Research.

Ravana King of Lanka. M. S. Pillai. (C). 1993. reprint ed. 10.00 (*81-206-0547-0*, Pub. by Asian Educ Servs II) S Asia.

Rave. Alan Davies. 1994. pap. 7.95 (*0-937804-55-X*) Segue NYC.

Rave Off: Politics & Deviance in Contemporary Youth Culture. Ed. by Steve Redhead. (Popular Culture in the City Ser.). 202p. 1993. 54.95 (*1-85628-463-8*, Pub. by Avebury Pub UK); pap. 21.95 (*1-85628-465-4*, Pub. by Avebury Pub UK) Ashgate Pub Co.

Rave On: Classic Texas Music Quotes. Alan Burton. LC 96-18220. (Classic Texas Quotes Ser.: Vol. 3). (Illus.). 200p. (Orig.). 1996. pap. 12.95 (*0-89672-370-4*) Tex Tech Univ Pr.

Rave On: The Biography of Buddy Holly. Philip Norman. LC 96-24543. 320p. 1996. 24.00 (*0-684-80082-9*) S&S Trade.

***Rave On: The Biography of Buddy Holly.** Philip Norman. 1997. pap. 12.00 (*0-684-83560-6*, Fireside) S&S Trade.

Rave or Rage: The Critics & John D. MacDonald. Walter Shine & Jean Shine. LC 93-19930. 1993. 20.00 (*0-929595-02-5*) Univ Florida Lib.

Ravel. David Burnett-James. (Illustrated Lives of the Great Composers Ser.). (Illus.). 144p. 1987. pap. 14.95 (*0-7119-0987-3*, OP44015) Omnibus NY.

Ravel. Tutti Staff. (TuTTi Ser.: No. 6). 176p. 1995. pap. 16.95 incl. disk (*1-57301-020-0*) TuTTi USA.

Ravel: His Life & Works. Rollo H. Myers. LC 73-2340. (Illus.). 239p. 1973. reprint ed. text ed. 59.75 (*0-8371-6841-4*, MYRA, Greenwood Pr) Greenwood.

Ravel: Man & Musician. Arbie Orenstein. 1991. pap. 9.95 (*0-486-26633-8*) Dover.

Ravel: Music Book Index. Norman Demuth. 214p. 1993. reprint ed. lib. bdg. 79.00 (*0-7812-9615-3*) Rprt Serv.

Ravel According to Ravel. Vlado Perlemuter & Helene Jourdan-Morhange. Ed. by Harold Taylor. Tr. by Frances Tanner. 92p. 1988. 16.50 (*0-912483-19-9*) Pro-Am Music.

Ravel of Waters. large type ed. Geoffrey Jenkins. 427p. 1982. 25.99 (*0-7089-0836-5*) Ulverscroft.

***Ravel Orchestral Music.** Laurence Davies. (BBC Music Guides Ser.). 64p. 1996. 4.95 (*0-563-01370-2*, BB 11148, BBC-Parkwest) Parkwest Pubns.

Ravel Very Best for Piano. Ed. by John L. Haag. (Illus.). 144p. (Orig.). 1996. pap. 14.95 (*1-56922-084-0*, 07-2035) Creat Cncpts.

Raveling of the Novel: Studies in Romantic Fiction from Walpole to Scott. rev. ed. Stephen Sandy. Ed. by Devendra P. Varma. LC 79-8476. (Gothic Studies & Dissertations). 1980. lib. bdg. 31.95 (*0-405-12660-3*) Ayer.

Ravelston Affair. large type ed. Elizabeth Harrison. 304p. 1982. 25.99 (*0-7089-0749-0*) Ulverscroft.

Raven. Charles Grant. 256p. 1995. 4.99 (*0-8125-2080-7*) Tor Bks.

Raven. Peter Landesman. 356p. 1995. 23.00 (*1-880909-37-5*) Baskerville.

***Raven.** Peter Landesman. 1997. pap. 11.95 (*0-14-026345-4*) Viking Penguin.

Raven. Mike Lundy. 224p. 1985. 15.95 (*0-8184-0377-2*) Carol Pub Group.

Raven. Thomas Strittmatter. 256p. 1993. 18.95 (*0-7011-4793-8*, Pub. by Chatto & Windus UK) Trafalgar.

Raven. 4th ed. Edgar Allan Poe. (Illus.). 48p. 1996. reprint ed. pap. 7.95 (*0-9631135-3-4*) MCE Publ Co.

Raven. Gustave Dore & Edgar Allan Poe. LC 95-45989. (Illus.). 64p. reprint ed. pap. 6.95 (*0-486-29072-7*) Dover.

Raven. Tr. by Stephane Mallarme from FRE. (Illustrated Book Reprints Ser.: Raven Bks.). (Illus.). reprint ed. boxed 75.00 (*0-932256-00-7*) Pilgrim Pr Corp NY.

Raven: A Biography of Sam Houston. Marquis James. LC 90-27766. (Illus.). 532p. 1991. reprint ed. 34.95 (*0-87797-226-5*) Cherokee.

Raven: A Biography of Sam Houston. Marquis James. (BCL1 - United States Local History Ser.). 489p. 1991. reprint ed. lib. bdg. 99.00 (*0-7812-6309-3*) Rprt Serv.

Raven: A Biography of Sam Houston. Marquis James. (Illus.). 527p. (YA). (gr. 10-12). 1988. reprint ed. pap. 14.95 (*0-292-77040-5*) U of Tex Pr.

Raven: A Biography of Sam Houston. Marquis James. 1993. reprint ed. lib. bdg. 75.00 (*0-7812-5939-8*) Rprt Serv.

***Raven: A Natural History in Britain & Ireland.** Derek A. Ratcliffe. (Poyser Birds Ser.). (Illus.). 352p. 1997. boxed 39.95 (*0-85661-090-9*, AP Prof) Acad Pr.

Raven: A Trickster Tale from the Pacific Northwest. Gerald McDermott. LC 91-14563. (Illus.). 32p. (J). (ps-3). 1993. 15.00 (*0-15-265661-8*, HB Juv Bks) HarBrace.

Raven: With the Philosophy of Composition. Edgar Allan Poe. LC 96-16144. (Illus.). 40p. 1996. pap. 7.95 (*1-55921-178-4*) Moyer Bell.

Raven - Johnson: Understanding Biology Test Bank. Van Norman. 512p. 1991. pap. 100.00 (*0-8016-4692-8*) Mosby Yr Bk.

Raven & Other Favorite Poems. Edgar Allan Poe. 1991. pap. 1.00 (*0-486-26685-0*) Dover.

Raven & Other Poems. Edgar Allan Poe & Gahan Wilson. (Classics Illustrated Ser.). (Illus.). 52p. (YA). pap. 4.95 (*1-57209-000-6*) Classics Int Ent.

Raven & Other Poems. Edgar Allan Poe. 80p. (YA). (gr. 7-9). 1992. pap. 2.95 (*0-590-45260-6*, Apple Classics) Scholastic Inc.

Raven & River. Nancy W. Carlstrom. LC 95-14773. (Illus.). (J). 1997. 15.95 (*0-316-12894-5*) Little.

Raven & the Cowboy. Sandra Chastain. 304p. 1996. mass mkt. 5.99 (*0-553-56864-7*, Fanfare) Bantam.

Raven & the Lark: Lost Children in Literature of the English Renaissance. Barbara L. Estrin. LC 83-46155. (Illus.). 232p. 1985. 38.50 (*0-8387-5075-3*) Bucknell U Pr.

Raven & the Redbird: A Play in Three Acts: Sam Houston & His Cherokee Wife. Raven Hail. 103p. 1993. reprint ed. pap. 5.00 (*0-9617696-5-3*) Raven Hail Bks.

Raven & the Rose. Virginia Henley. 400p. (Orig.). 1987. mass mkt. 5.50 (*0-440-17161-X*) Dell.

Raven & the Rose. Susan Wiggs. 512p. 1992. reprint ed. lib. bdg. 22.00 (*0-7278-4342-7*) Severn Hse.

Raven & the Swan. Laurie Grant. (Historical Ser.). 1994. mass mkt. 3.99 (*0-373-28805-0*, 1-28805-9) Harlequin Bks.

Raven & the Totem: Traditional Alaska Native Myths & Tales. John E. Smelcer. 161p. 1992. pap. 14.95 (*0-9634000-0-2*) Salmon Run.

***Raven & the Whale: Poe, Melville, & the New York Literary Scene.** Perry Miller. LC 97-12345. 1997. write for info. (*0-8018-5750-3*) Johns Hopkins.

Raven & the Whale: The War of Words & Wits in the Era of Poe & Melville. Perry Miller. LC 72-11741. 370p. 1973. reprint ed. text ed. 45.50 (*0-8371-6707-8*, MIRW, Greenwood Pr) Greenwood.

Raven & Water Monster. S. Harold Collins. (Sign Language Literature Ser.). (Illus.). 32p. (Orig.). (J). (gr. 2 up). 1996. pap. text ed. 4.95 (*0-931993-82-2*, GP-082) Garlic Pr OR.

***Raven Book.** Sylvia Peck. (J). Date not set. lib. bdg. write for info. (*0-688-09584-4*, Morrow Junior) Morrow.

***Raven Brings to the People Another Gift: A Story Based on Native American Legend.** M. Ann Reed. (American Heritage Ser.: Vol. 5). (Illus.). 18p. (Orig.). (J). (gr. 3 up). 1997. 3.95 (*1-877976-19-9*) Tipi Pr.

Raven Cloud's Poems to Her Father: A Healing Journey. Paula Parkel. Ed. by Thea Rhiannon. 26p. (Orig.). 1991. pap. text ed. 5.95 (*0-9629349-0-9*) Raven Cloud.

Raven Crown: The Origins of Buddhist Monarchy in Bhutan. Michael Aris. (Illus.). 160p. 1995. 29.95 (*0-906026-32-6*, Pub. by Serindia UK) Weatherhill.

Raven Days. Cynthia Nelson. 1994. pap. 6.00 (*1-887128-08-5*) Soft Skull Pr.

Raven Feathers His Nest. large type ed. Donald Mackenzie. 317p. 1982. 25.99 (*0-7089-0787-3*) Ulverscroft.

***Raven in a Dove House.** Pinkney. (J). 1998. write for info. (*0-15-201461-6*, HB Juv Bks) HarBrace.

***Raven in the Foregate.** Ellis Peters. 240p. 1997. mass mkt. 5.99 (*0-446-40534-5*, Mysterious Paperbk) Warner Bks.

Raven MRI Teaching File, 10 vols. Ed. by Robert B. Lufkin et al. 1991. text ed. 495.00 (*0-7817-0204-6*, RA004) Lppncott-Raven.

Raven of Zurich: The Memoirs of Felix Somary. Tr. by A. J. Sherman from GER. 320p. 1986. 19.95 (*0-317-42640-0*) St Martin.

Raven Ring. Patricia C. Wrede. 384p. mass mkt. 5.99 (*0-8125-1432-7*) Tor Bks.

Raven Rocks: A Specialized Late Woodland Rockshelter Occupation in Belmont County, Ohio. Olaf H. Prufer. LC 80-28085. (Kent State Research Papers in Archaeology: No. 1). 103p. reprint ed. pap. 29.40 (*0-7837-1343-6*, 2041491) Bks Demand.

Raven Seek Thy Brother. large type ed. Gavin Maxwell. 1970. 25.99 (*0-85456-001-7*) Ulverscroft.

Raven Speaks. Raven Hail. LC 87-62089. (Illus.). 200p. 1987. pap. 5.95 (*0-9617696-3-7*) Raven Hail Bks.

Raven Steals the Light. limited ed. Bill Reid & Robert Bringhurst. LC 84-47978. (Illus.). 94p. 1984. 200.00 (*0-295-96194-5*) U of Wash Pr.

Raven Steals the Light. 2nd ed. Illus. & Text by Bill Reid. LC 95-48942. 109p. (C). 1996. pap. 12.95 (*0-295-97524-5*) U of Wash Pr.

Raven Steals the Light: Native American Tales. Bill Reid & Robert Bringhurst. LC 95-30968. (Centaur Editions Ser.). (Illus.). 176p. 1996. pap. 10.00 (*1-57062-173-X*) Shambhala Pubns.

Raven Tells Stories: An Anthology of Alaska Native Writing. Ed. by Joseph Bruchac. LC 90-85173. 232p. (Orig.). (C). 1991. pap. 12.95 (*0-912678-80-1*) Greenfld Rev Lit.

Raven Wakes Me Up. Stephan Torre. (Orig.). 1991. pap. 8.00 (*0-912449-39-X*) Floating Island.

Raven, with Literary & Historical Commentary. John H. Ingram. LC 74-185022. (Studies in Poe: No. 23). 122p. 1972. reprint ed. lib. bdg. 75.00 (*0-8383-1382-5*) M S G Haskell Hse.

Ravenel Records: History & Genealogy of the Huguenot Family of Ravenel, of South Carolina, with Some Incidental Account of the Parish of St. Johns, Berkeley, Which Was Their Principal Location. Henry E. Ravenel. (Illus.). 279p. 1995. reprint ed. pap. 43.00 (*0-8328-4824-7*); reprint ed. lib. bdg. 53.00 (*0-8328-4823-9*) Higginson Bk Co.

Ravengers. Stephen Billias. (Cyberpunk 2.0 Ser.: Bk. 1). 288p. 1995. mass mkt. 5.50 (*0-446-60232-9*, Aspect) Warner Bks.

Ravenloft: Carnival of Fear. J. Robert King. 320p. (Orig.). 1993. pap. 4.95 (*1-56076-628-X*) TSR Inc.

Ravenloft: Dance of the Dead. Christie Golden. 320p. (Orig.). 1992. pap. 4.95 (*1-56076-352-3*) TSR Inc.

Ravenloft: Heart of Midnight. J. Robert King. 320p. (Orig.). 1992. pap. 4.95 (*1-56076-355-8*) TSR Inc.

Ravenloft: Knight of the Black Rose. James Lowder. LC 90-71507. 320p. (Orig.). 1991. pap. 5.99 (*1-56076-156-3*) TSR Inc.

Ravenloft: Tapestry of Dark Souls. Elaine Bergstrom. 320p. (Orig.). 1993. pap. 4.95 (*1-56076-571-2*) TSR Inc.

Ravenloft: Vampire of the Mists. Christie Golden. LC 90-71506. (Ravenloft Ser.). 320p. (Orig.). 1991. pap. 4.95 (*1-56076-155-5*) TSR Inc.

Ravenloft Monstrous Compendium, 1 & 2. TSR Inc. Staff. 1996. 20.00 (*0-7869-0392-9*) TSR Inc.

Ravenmocker. Jean Hager. 272p. 1992. 17.95 (*0-89296-493-6*) Mysterious Pr.

Ravenmocker. Jean Hager. 256p. 1994. mass mkt. 5.99 (*0-446-40107-2*) Mysterious Pr.

Ravenna, Biblioteca Comunale Classense, MS Classense 545. Ed. by Alexander Silbiger. (Seventeenth-Century Keyboard Music Ser.: Vol. 12). 250p. 1988. text ed. 30.00 (*0-8240-8011-4*) Garland.

Ravennetus. J. David Dean. LC 95-74738. 384p. 1996. 21.95 (*0-9646604-4-X*) Pandea Pubns.

Ravenous Hyenas & the Wounded Sun: Myth & Ritual in Ancient India. Stephanie W. Jamison. LC 90-55723. (Myth & Poetics Ser.). 360p. 1991. 57.50 (*0-8014-2433-X*) Cornell U Pr.

Ravenous Muse: A Table of Dark & Comic Contents, A Bacchanal of Books. Karen E. Gordon. 224p. 1996. 20.00 (*0-679-41861-X*) Pantheon.

Raven's Blood. Hillary Wolfe. 1996. pap. 3.99 (*0-8217-5152-2*) NAL-Dutton.

Raven's Bride. Lynn Kerstan. 416p. 1996. mass mkt. 4.99 (*0-06-108422-0*, Harp PBks) HarpC.

Raven's Bride. Elizabeth Crook. LC 92-35183. (Southwest Life & Letters Ser.). 432p. 1993. reprint ed. pap. 12.95 (*0-87074-348-1*) SMU Press.

Raven's Brood. E. F. Benson. 1993. reprint ed. pap. 14.95 (*1-873741-09-X*, Pub. by Millvres Bks UK) LPC InBook.

Raven's Cry. Christie Harris. LC 92-23934. (Illus.). 196p. 1992. pap. 14.95 (*0-295-97221-1*) U of Wash Pr.

Raven's Exile: A Season on the Green River. Ellen Meloy. (Illus.). 272p. 1995. pap. 12.95 (*0-8050-3807-8*, Owl) H Holt & Co.

Ravens in Winter. Bernd Heinrich. LC 91-50007. (Illus.). 400p. 1991. pap. 15.00 (*0-679-73236-5*, Vin) Random.

Raven's Longest Night. large type ed. Donald Mackenzie. 336p. 1985. 25.99 (*0-7089-1381-4*) Ulverscroft.

Ravens Moon. Susan King. 1997. pap. 5.99 (*0-451-18868-3*, Sig) NAL-Dutton.

Ravens of Blackwater. Edward Marston. 1996. mass mkt. 5.99 (*0-449-22410-4*) Fawcett.

Ravens of Odin: The Press in the Nordic Nations. Robert G. Picard. LC 87-22750. (Illus.). 171p. 1988. reprint ed. pap. 48.80 (*0-608-00047-7*, 2060813) Bks Demand.

Ravens Prey. Jayne Ann Krentz. 1983. pap. 2.25 (*0-373-47529-2*) Harlequin Bks.

Raven's Return: The Influence of Psychological Trauma on Individuals & Culture. Emmett Early. LC 93-22345. 152p. 1993. pap. 4.95 (*0-933029-70-5*) Chiron Pubns.

Raven's Roost. Bob Reese. (Grand Canyon Ser.). (Illus.). (J). (gr. k-6). 1987. 9.95 (*0-89868-195-2*); pap. 3.95 (*0-89868-196-0*) ARO Pub.

Raven's Song. Lyn Hughes-McDaniel. 248p. 1995. mass mkt. 4.99 (*1-896329-05-5*, Pub. by Comnwlth Pub CN) Partners Pubs Grp.

Raven's Tail. Cheryl Samuel. (Illus.). 168p. 1987. pap. 25.95 (*0-7748-0224-3*, Pub. by U BC Pr) U of Wash Pr.

***Raven's Tale.** Will Huddleston. 21p. (Orig.). (YA). (gr. 6-12). 1992. pap. 3.00 (*1-57514-193-0*, 1172) Encore Perform Pub.

***Raven's Tales.** Raven Hail. Ed. by Gregg Howard & Rick Eby. (Illus.). 75p. (Orig.). (YA). 1997. pap. text ed. 11.95 (*1-884655-24-6*) VIP Pubng.

Raven's Village: The Myths, Arts, & Traditions of Native People from the Pacific Northwest Coast. Nancy Ruddell. (Illus.). 64p. 1996. pap. 8.95 (*0-660-14035-7*, Pub. by Can Mus Civil CN) U of Wash Pr.

Raven's Vow. Gayle Wilson. 1997. mass mkt. 4.99 (*0-373-28949-9*, 1-28949-5) Silhouette.

Ravens Widows. Kohler. LC 96-25576. 256p. 1997. 22.95 (*0-312-14714-7*) St Martin.

Raven's Wing. Michael W. Eliseuson. Ed. by Edy L. Benjamin. LC 93-80517. 96p. pap. 5.95 (*1-883821-03-7*) Mother Bird.

Raven's Wing. large type ed. Geoffrey Moxon. (General Ser.). 416p. 1993. 25.99 (*0-7089-2883-8*) Ulverscroft.

Raven's Wish. Susan King. 384p. (Orig.). 1995. mass mkt. 4.99 (*0-451-40545-5*, Topaz) NAL-Dutton.

Ravensbruch Chronicles 1940-45. Stan Proper. (Illus.). 36p. (Orig.). (C). 1995. pap. 2.00 (*0-9619992-3-3*) Walden Sudbury.

Ravenscarne: And Other Ghost Stories. large type ed. Mary Williams. (Dales General Fiction Ser.). 367p. 1993. pap. 17.99 (*1-85389-403-6*, Medcom-Trainex) Ulverscroft.

***Ravensdene's Bride.** large type ed. Julia Byrne. (Mills & Boon Large Print Ser.). 350p. 1997. 22.50 (*0-263-14898-X*) Ulverscroft.

Ravenshoe. Henry Kingsley. (BCL1-PR English Literature Ser.). 535p. 1992. reprint ed. lib. bdg. 99.00 (*0-7812-7579-2*) Rprt Serv.

Ravensloch: Gothic Mystery. Genie Makinster. LC 83-26303. (Illus.). 141p. (Orig.). 1982. pap. 1.95 (*0-9608742-0-8*) Gemak Pub.

Ravensmount. large type ed. Janis Coles. 1994. 25.99 (*0-7089-3199-5*) Ulverscroft.

Ravensong. Lee Maracle. 1993. pap. 14.95 (*0-88974-044-5*, Pub. by Press Gang CN) LPC InBook.

Ravensong: Cherokee Indian Poetry. Raven Hail. 49p. (Orig.). 1995. pap. 5.00 (*0-9617696-6-1*) Raven Hail Bks.

Ravenswood: Into a Golden Light. John K. Winn. 64p. (C). 1990. 69.00 (*0-908175-86-8*, Pub. by Boolarong Pubns AT) St Mut.

Ravilious & Wedgwood: The Complete Wedgwood Designs of Eric Ravilious. (Illus.). 54p. 1995. 40.00 (*0-903685-38-8*, Pub. by R Dennis UK) Antique Collect.

***Ravine & Other Stories.** Yoshikichi Furui. Tr. by Meredith McKinney from JPN. LC 97-5234. (Rock Spring Collection of Japanese Literature). 144p. (Orig.). 1997. pap. 12.95 (*1-880656-29-9*) Stone Bridge Pr.

Ravine House Mystery. Esther Reich. 1995. 14.95 (*0-533-11086-6*) Vantage.

Raving Autumn & Other Stories. Victoria White. 223p. 1990. pap. 12.95 (*1-85371-077-6*, Pub. by Poolbeg Pr IE) Dufour.

Raving Fans. Kenneth H. Blanchard & Sheldon Bowles. LC 92-30255. 1993. 20.00 (*0-688-12316-3*) Morrow.

Ravinia - Stikhi, Pesni, Romansy. Valerii Skorov. 157p. (RUS.). 1991. pap. 14.00 (*0-911971-64-5*) Effect Pub.

Ravished. Amanda Quick. 416p. 1992. pap. 6.50 (*0-553-29316-8*) Bantam.

Ravished. large type ed. Amanda Quick. LC 92-27922. 538p. 1993. reprint ed. lib. bdg. 20.95 (*1-56054-429-5*) Thorndike Pr.

Ravished: Sexual Violence in Victorian Australia. Jill Bavin-Mizzi. 1995. pap. 25.95 (*0-86840-111-0*, Pub. by New South Wales Univ Pr AT) Intl Spec Bk.

***Ravished Armenia & the Story of Aurora Mardiganian.** Anthony Slide. LC 97-17244. (Filmmakers Ser.). 1997. write for info. (*0-8108-3311-5*) Scarecrow.

Ravished by the Spirit: Religious Revivals, Baptists, & Henry Alline. George A. Rawlyk. 190p. 1984. 44.95 (*0-7735-0439-7*, Pub. by McGill CN); pap. 17.95 (*0-7735-0440-0*, Pub. by McGill CN) U of Toronto Pr.

Ravished Heart. Iverna M. Tompkins. 144p. (Orig.). 1984. pap. 5.00 (*0-9611260-2-7*) I Tompkins.

Ravishers. Gerald A. Browne. 272p. 1990. mass mkt. 4.50 (*0-380-70418-8*) Avon.

Ravishers. Elizabeth Richards. 1992. write for info. (*0-9633891-0-6*) B S Richards.

Ravishing Doctor. large type ed. Heinz G. Konsalik. 365p. 1981. 25.99 (*0-7089-0691-5*) Ulverscroft.

Ravishing Images: Ekphrasis in the Poetry & Prose of William Wordsworth, W. H. Auden, & Philip Larkin. Katy Aisenberg. (American University Studies: Vol. 158). 216p. (C). 1995. text ed. 41.95 (*0-8204-2031-X*) P Lang Pubng.

Ravishing Maidens: Writing Rape in Medieval French Literature & Law. Kathryn Gravdal. LC 90-26337. (New Cultural Studies). 192p. (C). 1991. text ed. 34.95 (*0-8122-8247-7*) U of Pa Pr.

Ravishing of Lol Stein. Marguerite Duras. Tr. by Richard Seever. 1986. pap. 11.00 (*0-394-74304-0*) Pantheon.

Ravishing the Women of Conquered Europe. Austin J. App. 1984. lib. bdg. 79.95 (*0-87700-522-2*) Revisionist Pr.

Ravishing Tradition: Cultural Forces & Literary History. Daniel Cottom. 240p. 1996. 37.50 (*0-8014-3245-6*); pap. 15.95 (*0-8014-8324-7*) Cornell U Pr.

Ravissement de Lol V. Stein. Marguerite Duras. (Folio Ser.: No. 810). 190p. (FRE.). 1976. pap. 6.95 (*2-07-036810-6*) Schoenhof.

Ravissement de Lol V. Stein. Marguerite Duras. (FRE.). 1976. pap. 10.95 (*0-8288-3641-8*, F99841) Fr & Eur.

Raw & the Cooked: Introduction to a Science of Mythology, Vol. 1. Claude Levi-Strauss. Tr. by John Weightman & Doreen Weightman. LC 82-15895. (Illus.). 406p. 1983. pap. text ed. 24.95 (*0-226-47487-9*) U Ch Pr.

Raw & the Cooked: New Wokkin Clay in Britain. Contrib. by Alison Britton & Martina Margetts. 96p. 1993. pap. 60.00 (*0-905836-79-0*, Pub. by Museum Modern Art UK) St Mut.

Raw Courage. Dave Sargent. LC 96-33903. 204p. (J). (gr. 4 up). 1993. pap. 4.95 (*1-56763-015-4*) Ozark Pub.

Raw Courage. Dave Sargent. 204p. (YA). (gr. 4 up). 1993. lib. bdg. 18.95 (*1-56763-003-0*) Ozark Pub.

Raw Creation: Outsider Art & Beyond. John Maizels. (Illus.). 240p. 1996. 69.95 (*0-7148-3149-2*, Pub. by Phaidon Press UK) Chronicle Bks.

Raw Deal. Les Standiford. 384p. 1995. mass mkt. 5.50 (*0-06-109144-8*, Harp PBks) HarpC.

Raw Deal: New & Selected Poems, 1980-94. Jerome Sala. LC 93-36542. 158p. 1995. pap. 10.95 (*0-929968-47-6*) Another Chicago Pr.

***Raw Dog.** Eric Priestly. pap. 5.99 (*0-87067-887-6*) Holloway.

R

*__Raw Feeling: A Philosophical Account of the Essence of Consciousness.__ Robert Kirk. 264p. 1996. reprint ed. pap. 22.00 (0-19-823679-4) OUP.

Raw Food & Health. A. Estes. 445p. 1963. reprint ed. spiral bd. 25.00 (0-7873-0317-8) Hlth Research.

*__Raw Food Ideas: For Your Creative Dishes.__ Millie I. Thornton. 54p. (Orig.). 1997. pap. 7.95 (0-9655957-0-6) Thornton.

Raw Food Menus & Recipe Book. E. L. Estes. 42p. 1972. reprint ed. spiral bd. 5.00 (0-7873-0316-X) Hlth Research.

Raw Food Treatment of Cancer. Kristine Holfi. LC 95-61547. 50p. 1995. 3.95 (1-57258-057-7) Teach Servs.

Raw Food Treatment of Cancer & Other Diseases. Kristine Nolfi. 8p. 1994. reprint ed. spiral bd. 5.00 (0-7873-1028-X) Hlth Research.

Raw Fruit & Vegetable Juices & Drinks. William Lee. LC 82-82323. 32p. (Orig.). 1982. pap. 4.95 (0-87983-306-8) Keats.

Raw Garden. Helen Dunmore. LC 88-51310. 64p. 8800. pap. 10.95 (1-85224-074-1, Pub. by Bloodaxe Bks UK) Dufour.

Raw Hands & Bagging. Coco Gordon. (Illus.). 1978. pap. 10.00 (0-931956-00-5) Water Mark.

Raw Head, Bloody Bones. Mary E. Lyons. (Illus.). (J). 1995. pap. 3.95 (0-689-80306-0, Aladdin Paperbacks) S&S Childrens.

Raw Head, Bloody Bones: African-American Tales of the Supernatural. Selected by Mary E. Lyons. LC 91-10690. (Illus.). 96p. (YA). (gr. 5 up). 1991. lib. bdg. 15.00 (0-684-19333-7, C Scribner Sons Young) S&S Childrens.

Raw Honey. Marie Harris. LC 75-21787. 72p. 1975. pap. 3.95 (0-914086-09-X) Alicejamesbooks.

Raw Judicial Power? The Supreme Court & American Society. Robert J. McKeever. LC 92-21097. 1993. text ed. 79.95 (0-7190-3424-8, Pub. by Manchester Univ Pr UK) St Martin.

Raw Judicial Power? The Supreme Court & American Society. Robert J. McKeever. LC 95-30875. 256p. (C). 1996. text ed. 24.95 (0-7190-4873-7, Pub. by Manchester Univ Pr UK) St Martin.

Raw Juice Therapy. John B. Lust. 1982. 5.95 (0-87904-026-2) Lust.

Raw Material. Farrant. 1993. per. 11.95 (0-88978-262-8, Pub. by Arsenal Pulp CN) LPC InBook.

Raw Materials & Processing of Paper Making. H. F. Rance. (Handbook of Paper Science Ser.: Vol. 1). 298p. 1980. 188.25 (0-444-41778-8) Elsevier.

Raw Materials Economics. Charles Walters, Jr. LC 91-76287. 164p. 1991. pap. 14.00 (0-911311-32-7) Acres USA.

Raw Materials Economics: A Norm Primer. Charles Walters, Jr. 1993. pap. 14.95 (0-9632571-4-5) Inst Am Democracy.

Raw Materials for Industrial Polymers. Henri Ulrich. 223p. (C). 1988. text ed. 49.95 (1-56990-103-1) Hanser-Gardner.

Raw Materials for New Technologies. Proceedings of the 5th Symposium Held in Hannover (Germany) 1988. Ed. by M. Kuersten. (Illus.). 158p. 1990. pap. text ed. 40.95 (3-510-65143-X, Pub. by Schweitzerbartsche GW) Lubrecht & Cramer.

Raw Materials for Pigments Fillers & Extenders. Ed. by J. B. Griffiths. 178p. 1988. pap. text ed. 107.00 (0-947671-19-6) Metal Bulletin.

Raw Materials for the Glass & Ceramics Industries. Ed. by G. M. Clarke & J. B. Griffiths. 210p. 1987. pap. text ed. 84.00 (0-947671-13-7) Metal Bulletin.

Raw Materials for the Refractory Industry. 3rd ed. Ed. by E. M. Dickson. pap. text ed. write for info. (0-318-69936-2) Metal Bulletin.

Raw Materials in Peace & War. Eugene Staley. Ed. by Stuart Bruchey & Eleanor Bruchey. LC 76-5034. (American Business Abroad Ser.). 1976. reprint ed. 31.95 (0-405-09300-4) Ayer.

Raw Materials in the Capacitor & Resistor Industries: World Markets, Technologies & Opportunities: a 1994-1999 Technical-Economic Analysis. Dennis M. Zogbi. 90p. (Orig.). 1995. pap. 2,400.00 (0-929717-34-1) Paumanok Pubns.

Raw Materials in the Glass Industry: Minor Ingredients, 2 pts. Ed. by Alexis G. Pincus & David H. Davies. LC 83-70137. (Processing in the Glass Industry Ser.). (Illus.). 454p. 1983. text ed. 59.90 (0-911993-02-9) Ashlee Pub Co.

Raw Materials in the Glass Industry, Pt. I: Major Ingredients. Ed. by Alexis G. Pincus & David H. Davies. LC 83-70137. (Processing in the Glass Industry Ser.). (Illus.). 254p. 1983. text ed. 29.95 (0-911993-00-2) Ashlee Pub Co.

Raw Materials of Perfumery, Vol. 1. 9th ed. A. J. Jouhar. 400p. (gr. 13). 1991. text ed. 121.95 (0-412-27340-3) Chapman & Hall.

Raw Materials of the Arabian Gulf & Their Utilisation: Proceedings of the First Conference on Indigenous Raw Materials & Their Utilisation in the Gulf Region. Ed. by D. C. Almond et al. 288p. 1990. 135.00 (0-7103-0333-5, A4531) Routledge Chapman & Hall.

Raw, Medium & Well Done: A Critical Review of Editorial & Quasi-Editorial Work on Pre-European Sources for Sub-Saharan Africa, 1960-1986. Adam Jones. LC 87-11436. (Studies in African Sources: No. 1). 153p. (Orig.). 1987. pap. 30.00 (0-942615-00-X) U Wis African Stud.

Raw North. Charles Gillham. (American Autobiography Ser.). 275p. 1995. reprint ed. lib. bdg. 79.00 (0-7812-8529-1) Rprt Serv.

Raw Pork & Hard Tack: Civil War Memoir from Manassas to Appomattox. Walbrook D. Swank. LC 96-48774. (Civil War Heritage Ser.: Vol. X). 88p. (Orig.). 1996. pap. 12.00 (1-57249-031-4, Burd St Pr) White Mane Pub.

Raw Recruits. Alexander Wolff & Armen Keteyian. Ed. by Leslie Wells. 344p. 1991. reprint ed. 18.95 (0-685-37878-0); reprint ed. mass mkt. 5.95 (0-671-70428-1) PB.

Raw-Robed Few & Other Poems. Guy R. Beining. 1979. pap. 4.95 (0-930090-11-X) Applezaba.

Raw Silk. large type ed. Anne Mather. (Harlequin Romance Ser.). 1995. 20.95 (0-263-14214-0) Thorndike Pr.

Raw Silk: (Too Hot to Handle) Anne Mather. (Presents Ser.). 1995. mass mkt. 3.25 (0-373-11731-0, 1-11731-6) Harlequin Bks.

Raw Spiritual: Selected Poems, Nineteen Eighty to Nineteen Eighty-Five. Jay Ramsay. (C). 1986. pap. 38.00 (0-947612-20-3, Pub. by Rivelin Grapheme Pr) St Mut.

Raw Talent: The Adult Film Industry As Seen by Its Most Popular Male Star. Jerry Butler. Ed. by Robert H. Rimmer & Catherine Tavel. (Illus.). 323p. (Orig.). (C). 1990. 26.95 (0-87975-642-X); pap. 17.95 (0-87975-625-X) Prometheus Bks.

Raw Youth: A Play. Neal Bell. 53p. 1986. pap. 5.25 (0-8222-0931-4) Dramatists Play.

Rawa Dolu: The Story of a Mountain Village. Joanne Stephenson. (Illus.). 136p. 1996. pap. 16.00 (0-8059-3926-1) Dorrance.

Rawhead Rex. Clive Barker et al. 1993. 22.95 (1-56060-181-7); pap. 8.95 (1-56060-182-5) Eclipse Bks.

Rawhide: A Western Quintet. T. T. Flynn. LC 96-6298. 1996. 20.00 (0-7862-0660-8, Five Star) Mac Lib Ref.

Rawhide: A Western Quintet. large type ed. Flynn. Date not set. 20.00 (0-7838-1671-5, GK Hall) Thorndike Pr.

Rawhide & Lace. Margaret Brownley. 384p. (Orig.). 1994. pap. 4.99 (0-451-40461-0, Topaz) NAL-Dutton.

Rawhide & Roses. Sue Rich. Ed. by Carolyn Tolley. 272p. (Orig.). 1993. mass mkt. 4.99 (0-671-75914-0) PB.

*__Rawhide Guns.__ large type ed. Frank Bonham. LC 96-34380. (Nightingale Ser.). 1997. pap. 17.95 (0-7838-1977-3, GK Hall) Thorndike Pr.

Rawhide Knot & Other Stories. Conrad Richter. LC 84-20799. xii, 207p. 1985. reprint ed. pap. 6.50 (0-8032-8916-2, Bison Books) U of Nebr Pr.

Rawhide Laureate: John G. Neihardt, a Selected Annotated Bibliography. John T. Richards. LC 83-10117. (Author Bibliographies Ser.: No. 65). 189p. 1983. 20.00 (0-8108-1640-7) Scarecrow.

Rawhide Man. Diana Palmer. 1994. pap. 4.99 (1-55166-009-1, 1-66009-1, Mira Bks) Harlequin Bks.

Rawhide Man. Diana Palmer. 1994. mass mkt. 4.50 (0-373-48315-5, 5-48315-1) Silhouette.

Rawhide Men. large type ed. Lee Floren. (Linford Western Library). 1991. pap. 15.99 (0-7089-7035-4) Ulverscroft.

Rawhide Ransom. Doyle Trent. 224p. 1992. mass mkt. 3.50 (0-8217-3997-2, Zebra Kensgtn) Kensgtn Pub Corp.

Rawhide Rider. Peter Field. 176p. 1989. pap. 2.95 (0-380-70712-8) Avon.

Rawhide Storm. large type ed. Mark Donovan. (Linford Western Library). 304p. 1995. pap. 15.99 (0-7089-7762-6, Linford) Ulverscroft.

Rawhide Years. large type ed. Norman A. Fox. LC 90-16530. 277p. 1991. reprint ed. lib. bdg. 15.95 (1-56054-140-7) Thorndike Pr.

Rawhider. Doyle Trent. 1989. mass mkt. 2.95 (0-8217-2739-7, Zebra Kensgtn) Kensgtn Pub Corp.

Rawhiders. Jim Walker. LC 95-476. (Wells Fargo Trail Ser.: Bk. 4). 336p. 1995. pap. 8.99 (1-55661-431-4) Bethany Hse.

Rawhiders. large type ed. Lauran Paine. LC 96-19309. (Sagebrush Large Print Westerns Ser.). 272p. 1996. lib. bdg. 18.95 (1-57490-021-8) T T Beeler.

Rawleigh Man Told Me. LC 93-80990. 296p. 1994. 21.95 (1-878044-34-6) Mayhaven Pub.

Rawleigh Man Told Me. Ruth S. Thomas. LC 93-80990. 296p. (Orig.). 1994. pap. 12.95 (1-878044-21-4) Mayhaven Pub.

Rawlinson, The Recorder & China's Revolution: A Topical Biography of Frank Joseph Rawlinson, 1871-1937, 2 vols., Vol. 1. John L. Rawlinson. LC 90-82198. (Church & the World Ser.: Vol. V., Vol. VI). (Illus.). 450p. 1990. 39.50 (0-940121-12-3, H107) Cross Cultural Pubns.

Rawlinson, The Recorder & China's Revolution: A Topical Biography of Frank Joseph Rawlinson, 1871-1937, 2 vols., Vol. 2. John L. Rawlinson. LC 90-82198. (Church & the World Ser.: Vol. 5., Vol. 6). (Illus.). 520p. 1990. 39.50 (0-940121-13-1, H108) Cross Cultural Pubns.

Rawls: A Theory of Justice & Its Critics. Chandran Kukathas & Philip Pettit. LC 89-51591. (Key Contemporary Thinkers Ser.). 181p. 1990. 29.50 (0-8047-1768-0); pap. 10.95 (0-8047-1769-9) Stanford U Pr.

Rawson Family: A Revised Memoir of Edward Rawson, Secretary of the Colony of Mass. Bay, from 1650 to 1686. E. B. Crane. (Illus.). 350p. 1989. reprint ed. pap. 52.00 (0-8328-1005-3); reprint ed. lib. bdg. 60.00 (0-8328-1004-5) Higginson Bk Co.

Rawson's Dictionary of Euphemisms & Other Doubletalk: Being a Compilation of Linguistic Fig Leaves & Verbal Flourishes for Artful Users of the English Language. Hugh Rawson. LC 95-30759. 1995. 25.00 (0-517-70201-0) Crown Pub Group.

Ray. Barry Hannah. LC 93-42708. 128p. 1994. pap. 10.00 (0-8021-3387-8, Grove) Grove-Atltic.

Ray. Barry Hannah. 1981. mass mkt. 4.95 (0-14-005945-8, Penguin Bks) Viking Penguin.

Ray: In a Blaze of Power. C. Harris. Ed. by Bob Kahan. (Illus.). 144p. 1994. pap. 9.95 (1-56389-090-9) DC Comics.

Ray: Partnership Taxation. 4th ed. Nigel Davey & Maurice P. Wingfield. 400p. 1991. pap. 130.00 (0-406-00180-4) MICHIE.

Ray - Partnership Taxation Supplement: The New Rules for Simplified Assessing. Nigel Davey & Maurice Parry-Wingfield. (Orig.). 1994. pap. 35.00 (0-406-04527-5) MICHIE.

Ray & Wave Theory of Lenses. A. Walther. (Studies in Modern Optics: No. 15). (Illus.). 416p. (C). 1995. text ed. 64.95 (0-521-45144-2) Cambridge U Pr.

Ray Bradbury. David Mogen. (Twayne's United States Authors Ser.: No. 504). 184p. 1986. 21.95 (0-8057-7464-5, Twayne) Scribnrs Ref.

Ray Bradbury: Dramatist. 2nd ed. Ben P. Indick. LC 88-34666. (Essays on Fantastic Literature Ser.: No. 3). 48p. 1989. pap. 13.00 (0-89370-559-4); lib. bdg. 23.00 (0-89370-540-3) Borgo Pr.

Ray Bradbury & the Poetics of Reverie: Fantasy, Science Fiction, & the Reader. William F. Touponce. LC 84-2553. (Studies in Speculative Fiction: No. 2). 155p. reprint ed. pap. 44.20 (0-8357-1569-8, 2070523) Bks Demand.

*__Ray Bradbury & the Poetics of Reverie: Gaston Bachelard, Wolfgang Iser, & the Reader's Response to Fantastic Literature.__ 2nd ed. LC 96-37225. (I. O. Evans Studies in the Philosophy & Criticism of Literature). 1996. write for info. (0-8095-2005-2) Borgo Pr.

*__Ray Bradbury & the Poetics of Reverie: Gaston Bachelard, Wolfgang Iser, & the Reader's Response to Fantastic Literature.__ 2nd ed. LC 96-37225. (I. O. Evans Studies in the Philosophy & Criticism of Literature). 1996. pap. write for info. (0-8095-3005-8) Borgo Pr.

Ray Bradbury Chronicles, Vol. 1. deluxe limited ed. Ray Bradbury. Ed. by Byron Preiss. 80p. 1993. 45.00 (1-56163-072-1) NBM.

Ray Bradbury Chronicles, Vol. 2. deluxe limited ed. Ray Bradbury. Ed. by Byron Preiss. 80p. 1993. 45.00 (1-56163-074-8) NBM.

Ray Bradbury Chronicles, Vol. 3. deluxe limited ed. Ray Bradbury. Ed. by Byron Preiss. 80p. 1993. 45.00 (1-56163-076-4) NBM.

Ray Bradbury Chronicles, Vol. 4. Ray Bradbury. 1993. pap. 9.95 (0-685-63494-9, Spectra) Bantam.

Ray Bradbury Chronicles, Vol. 4. deluxe limited ed. Ray Bradbury. Ed. by Byron Preiss. 64p. 1993. 45.00 (1-56163-078-0) NBM.

Ray Bradbury Chronicles, Vol. 5. deluxe limited ed. Ray Bradbury. Ed. by Byron Preiss. 64p. 1993. 45.00 (1-56163-081-0) NBM.

Ray Bradbury Chronicles, Vol. 6. Ray Bradbury et al. 80p. 1994. 19.95 (1-56163-102-7) NBM.

Ray Bradbury Chronicles, Vol. 6. deluxe ed. Ray Bradbury et al. 80p. 1994. 45.00 (1-56163-103-5) NBM.

Ray Bradbury Chronicles, Vol. 7. Ray Bradbury et al. 80p. 1994. 19.95 (1-56163-112-4) NBM.

Ray Bradbury Chronicles, Vol. 7. deluxe ed. Ray Bradbury et al. 80p. 1994. 45.00 (1-56163-113-2) NBM.

Ray Bradbury Presents: Dinosaur Conquest. Stephen Leigh. 272p. (Orig.). 1995. mass mkt. 4.99 (0-380-76283-8, AvoNova) Avon.

Ray Bradbury Presents: Dinosaur Empire. Stephen Leigh & John J. Miller. (Ray Bradbury Presents Ser.). 256p. (Orig.). 1995. mass mkt. 4.99 (0-380-76282-X, AvoNova) Avon.

Ray Bradbury Presents: Dinosaur Samurai. Stephen Leigh & John J. Miller. 256p. (Orig.). 1993. mass mkt. 4.99 (0-380-76279-X, AvoNova) Avon.

Ray Bradbury Presents: Dinosaur Warriors. Stephen Leigh. 327p. (Orig.). 1994. mass mkt. 4.99 (0-380-76280-3, AvoNova) Avon.

Ray Bradbury Presents Dinosaur Planet. Stephen Leigh. 304p. (Orig.). 1993. mass mkt. 4.99 (0-380-76278-1, AvoNova) Avon.

Ray Bradbury Review. Ray Bradbury. Ed. by William F. Nolan. (Illus.). 75p. 1988. reprint ed. 45.00 (0-940941-05-8) Blood & Guts Pr.

Ray Buckland's Magic Cauldron: A Potpourri of Matters Metaphysical. Ray Buckland. LC 95-12527. (Illus.). 212p. 1995. pap. 12.95 (1-880090-13-9) Galde Pr.

Ray-Centered Astrology. Ruth Mierswa & Richard Mierswa. LC 84-90414. 1986. 16.00 (0-87212-185-2) Libra.

Ray Charles: Genius of Soul. Ruth Turk. (YA). (gr. 5 up). 1996. lib. bdg. 17.96 (0-8225-4928-X) Lerner Group.

Ray Charles: Singer & Musician. Norman Winski. (Black American Ser.). (Illus.). 192p. (Orig.). (YA). (gr. 6-12). 1994. mass mkt. 3.95 (0-87067-790-X, BH-790-X, Melrose Sq) Holloway.

Ray Charles: The Musician Who Lost Sight at Age Seven. David Ritz. LC 93-30224. (Great Achievers). (Illus.). (YA). (gr. 5 up). 1994. lib. bdg. 19.95 (0-7910-2080-0) Chelsea Hse.

Ray Charles LPs, Vol. 5. CPP Belwin Staff. 1993. pap. text ed. 13.95 (0-89724-518-0, TPF0144) Warner Brothers.

Ray Charles: The Musician Who Lost Sight at Age Seven see Great Achievers: Lives of the Physically Challenged

Ray Crowe Story: A Legend in High School Basketball. Kerry Marshall. 185p. 1992. 20.00 (0-9636873-0-1) Good Morn Pub.

Ray Dream Handbook. Craig Patchett & John Sledd. (Illus.). 400p. (Orig.). 1996. pap. 39.95 (1-886801-09-6) Chrles River Media.

*__Ray Dream Handbook.__ 2nd ed. John Sledd. (Illus.). 400p. 1997. pap. 44.95 (1-886801-36-3) Chrles River Media.

*__Ray Dream 3D Design Solutions.__ John B. Crane. 1997. 45.00 (1-56205-763-4) New Riders Pub.

Ray Eliot: The Spirit & Legend of Mr. Illini. Doug Cartland. LC 95-69133. (Illus.). 255p. 1995. 19.95 (1-57167-015-7) Sagamore Pub.

*__Ray Gun: Out of Control.__ Dean Kuipers. LC 96-50937. 1997. 45.00 (0-684-83980-6) S&S Trade.

Ray Had an Idea about Love. Eddie Lewis. 1995. 21.00 (0-671-88762-9) S&S Trade.

Ray House. August Klapp. 32p. (Orig.). 1992. reprint ed. pap. 1.75 (1-881366-00-6) Wilsons Creek NBF.

Ray Kroc, Reading Level 2. Mascola. (Reaching Your Goal Bks.: Set II). (Illus.). 24p. (J). (gr. 1-4). 1989. 10.95 (0-685-58802-5); lib. bdg. 14.60 (0-86592-433-3) Rourke Corp.

Ray Leight & Shanghai Cartoonists' Views of Columbus. Alfonz Lengyel & Hongying Liu-Lengyel. (Museum Study Ser.: No. 3). (Illus.). 17p. (Orig.). (C). 1992. pap. 8.00 (0-9626500-2-1) Fudan Mus Fndtn.

Ray Manley's Collecting Southwestern Indian Arts & Crafts. 3rd rev. ed. Clara L. Tanner et al. (Illus.). 1979. reprint ed. pap. 6.00 (0-931418-03-8) R Manley.

Ray Manley's Hopi Kachina. Clara L. Tanner. (Illus.). 1980. 6.00 (0-931418-06-2) R Manley.

Ray Manley's Indian Lands. Clara L. Tanner. (Illus.). (ENG, GER & JPN.). 1979. pap. 7.95 (0-931418-05-4) R Manley.

Ray Manley's "The Fine Art of Navajo Weaving" Steve Getzwiller. (Illus.). 1984. 19.95 (0-931418-09-7); pap. 9.95 (0-931418-08-9) R Manley.

Ray Manley's "The Vanishing Indian" Clara L. Tanner. (Illus.). 1983. pap. 6.00 (0-931418-07-0) R Manley.

Ray McLain & the National Guard. Betty M. Belvin. (Illus.). 214p. 1994. pap. 22.95 (0-89745-173-2) Sunflower U Pr.

*__Ray Methods.__ Babich. 1996. write for info. (0-582-20902-1, Pub. by Longman UK) Longman.

*__Ray Methods for Nonlinear Waves in Fluid & Plasmas.__ A. M. Anile. 1993. 125.55 (0-582-02343-2, Pub. by Longman UK) Longman.

Ray Methods of Healing. Zachary F. Lansdowne. LC 92-45541. (Illus.). 194p. (Orig.). 1993. pap. 10.95 (0-87728-745-7) Weiser.

Ray Miller's Galveston. 2nd ed. Ray Miller. LC 92-36295. 304p. 1993. 29.95 (0-88415-092-5); pap. 18.95 (0-88415-091-7) Gulf Pub.

Ray of Darkness: Sermons & Reflections. Rowan Williams. 288p. 1995. pap. 12.95 (1-56101-112-6) Cowley Pubns.

Ray of Hope: Sermons for the Christian Year. Hugh Farquhar. 120p. 1993. pap. 7.95 (1-55673-580-4) CSS OH.

Ray of Hope & Other Poems. K. V. Subrahmanyam. 1990. text ed. 7.95 (81-207-1123-8, Pub. by Sterling Pubs II) Apt Bks.

Ray of Light: Instructions in Piety & the State of the World at the End of Time. Tr. by Michael Hilko from RUS. (Illus.). 96p. 1991. pap. 6.00 (0-88465-047-2) Holy Trinity.

Ray of Sunshine. Hilda McKenzie. 384p. 1996. pap. 10.95 (0-7472-4917-2, Pub. by Headline UK) Trafalgar.

*__Ray of Sunshine.__ large type ed. Hilda McKenzie. (Large Print Ser.). 560p. 1996. 25.99 (0-7089-3636-9) Ulverscroft.

Ray Shooting, Depth Orders & Hidden Surface Removal. M. De Berg. (Lecture Notes in Computer Science Ser.: Vol. 703). x, 201p. 1993. pap. write for info. (3-540-57020-9) Spr-Verlag.

Ray Shooting, Depth Orders & Hidden Surface Removal. M. De Berg. (Lecture Notes in Computer Science Ser.). x, 201p. 1993. 39.95 (0-387-57020-9) Spr-Verlag.

Ray Smallman Symposium: Towards the Millennium: A Materials Perspective. 406p. 1996. 90.00 (0-901716-83-9, Pub. by Inst Materials UK) Ashgate Pub Co.

Ray Tracing & Radiosity Algorithms for Photorealistic Image Synthesis. A. J. Kok. 140p. 1994. pap. 57.50 (90-6275-981-5, Pub. by Delft U Pr NE) Coronet Bks.

Ray Troll's Shocking Fish Tales: Fish, Romance, & Death in Pictures. Ray Troll & Bradford Matsen. LC 93-2995. 128p. (Orig.). 1993. pap. 15.95 (0-89815-548-7) Ten Speed Pr.

Rayburn: A Biography. D. B. Hardeman & Donald C. Bacon. LC 89-7985. (Illus.). 600p. 1989. reprint ed. pap. 14.95 (0-8191-7294-4) Madison Bks UPA.

Raychem International Safety Rating System Reference Manual. 519p. Date not set. ring bd. write for info. (0-88061-169-3) Intl Loss Cntrl.

Raychem International Safety Rating System Working Copy. Date not set. spiral bd. write for info. (0-88061-170-7) Intl Loss Cntrl.

Rayden & Jackson on Divorce & Family Matters, 2 vols. 16th ed. Margaret Booth. 4600p. 1991. boxed 889.00 (0-406-35130-9, U.K.) MICHIE.

Rayford W. Logan & the Dilemma of the African-American Intellectual. Kenneth R. Janken. LC 92-43282. 336p. 1993. lib. bdg. 35.00 (0-87023-858-2) U of Mass Pr.

*__Rayford W. Logan & the Dilemma of the African American Intellectual.__ Kenneth R. Janken. LC 92-43282. 336p. 1997. pap. 16.95 (1-55849-069-8) U of Mass Pr.

*__Rayleigh-Benard Convection: Structures & Dynamics.__ 250p. 1998. lib. bdg. 33.00 (981-02-2657-8) World Scientific Pub.

*__Rayleigh-Ritz Approach to Determine Compliance & Root Stresses in Spiral Bevel Gears Using Shell Theory.__ Donald R. Houser. (1993 Fall Technical Meeting). 1993. pap. text ed. 30.00 (1-55589-596-4) AGMA.

Rayleigh Wave Theory & Application. E. A. Ash & E. G. Paige. (Wave Phenomena Ser.: Vol. 2). (Illus.). x, 360p. 1985. 89.95 (0-387-15933-9) Spr-Verlag.

Raymold Military Uniforms & Equipments Catalogue: 1895. 1989. reprint ed. 5.00 (0-913150-96-7) Pioneer Pr.

An Asterisk (*) at the beginning of an entry indicates that the title is appearing in BIP for the first time.

R

Raymond A. Bidwell Collection of Chinese Bronzes & Ceramics. (Illus.). 85p. 1965. 3.50 (*0-916746-44-5*) Springfield Lib & Mus.

Raymond A. Bidwell Collection of Prints by Utagawa Kuniyoshi. (Illus.). 167p. 1968. 7.50 (*0-916746-45-3*) Springfield Lib & Mus.

Raymond Berry Years. Skipper Steely. (Illus.). 269p. 1982. 25.00 (*0-915263-04-1*) Wright Pr.

Raymond Burr: A Film, Radio, & Television Biography. Ona L. Hill. LC 93-39505. (Illus.). 320p. 1994. lib. bdg. 39.95 (*0-89950-871-5*) McFarland & Co.

Raymond Carver: A Study of the Short Fiction. Ewing Campbell. (Twayne's Studies in Short Fiction: No. 31). 200p. (C). 1992. 23.95 (*0-8057-8300-8*, Twayne) Scribnrs Ref.

Raymond Carver: An Oral Biography. Sam Halpert. LC 94-46555. 206p. 1995. 32.95 (*0-87745-502-3*); pap. 15.95 (*0-87745-503-1*) U of Iowa Pr.

***Raymond Chandler: A Biography.** Tom Hiney. LC 97-264. 356p. 1997. 25.00 (*0-87113-690-2*, Atlntc Mnthly) Grove-Atltic.

Raymond Chandler: A Checklist. Matthew J. Bruccoli. LC 68-16892. (Serif Ser.: No. 2). 45p. reprint ed. pap. 25.00 (*0-8357-9373-7*, 2015383) Bks Demand.

Raymond Chandler: A Descriptive Bibliography. Matthew J. Bruccoli. LC 78-4280. (Series in Bibliography). 168p. 1979. 100.00 (*0-8229-3382-9*) U of Pittsburgh Pr.

Raymond Chandler & Film. 2nd ed. William Luhr. 224p. (C). 1991. reprint ed. pap. 16.95 (*0-8130-1091-8*) U Press Fla.

Raymond Chandler in Hollywood. Al Clark. (Illus.). 229p. (Orig.). 1996. pap. 19.95 (*1-879505-29-0*) Silman James Pr.

Raymond Chandler Omnibus. Raymond Chandler. LC 79-92498. 625p. 1980. 20.00 (*0-394-60492-X*, Modern Lib) Random.

***Raymond Chandler Speaking.** Raymond Chandler. Ed. by Dorothy Gardiner & Kathrine Sorley Walker. LC 96-34571. (Illus.). 1997. 15.95 (*0-520-20835-8*) U CA Pr.

Raymond Chandler Speaking. Raymond Chandler. Ed. by Dorothy Gardiner & Kathrine Sorley. LC 76-146855. (Select Bibliographies Reprint Ser.). 1977. reprint ed. 23.95 (*0-8369-5622-2*) Ayer.

Raymond Chandler's Los Angeles. Elizabeth Ward & Alain Silver. LC 86-18007. (Illus.). 1987. 35.00 (*0-87951-266-0*) Overlook Pr.

Raymond Chandler's Los Angeles: A Photographic Odyssey Accompanied by Passages from Chandler's Greatest Work. Elizabeth Ward & Alain Silver. (Illus.). 234p. 1997. reprint ed. pap. 19.95 (*0-87951-351-9*) Overlook Pr.

***Raymond Chandler's Philip Marlowe.** Michael Lark. LC 96-42005. 1997. pap. 15.00 (*0-684-82933-9*) S&S Trade.

Raymond Federman, the Supreme Indecision of the Writer: The 1994 Federman Lectures in Turkey. Raymond Federman. 136p. (Orig.). 1995. pap. 12.95 (*0-922668-14-0*) SUNYB Poetry Rare Bks.

Raymond Floyd Goes to Africa: or There Are No Bears in Africa. Mrs. Moose. (Illus.). 32p. (J). (gr. 1-4). 1993. 14.95 (*0-86543-375-5*); pap. 6.95 (*0-86543-376-3*) Africa World.

Raymond Garlick. Don Dale-Jones. 112p. 1996. pap. 9.95 (*0-7083-1322-1*, Pub. by Univ Wales Pr UK) Paul & Co Pubs.

Raymond Hood, Architect of Ideas. Walter H. Kilham, Jr. (Illus.). 1974. 14.95 (*0-8038-0218-8*) Archit CT.

Raymond III of Tripolis & the Fall of Jerusalem: 1140-1187. Marshall W. Baldwin. LC 76-29830. reprint ed. 45.00 (*0-404-15411-5*) AMS Pr.

Raymond IV, Count of Toulouse. John H. Hill & Laurita L. Hill. LC 80-11116. (Illus.). viii, 177p. 1980. reprint ed. text ed. 65.00 (*0-313-22362-9*, HIRA, Greenwood Pr) Greenwood.

Raymond Jonson: Late Abstractions. Intro. by Joseph Traugott. LC 92-81216. (Illus.). 26p. 1992. pap. 8.00 (*0-935037-46-2*) G Peters Gallery.

Raymond Knister: An Annotated Bibliography. Anne Burke. 322p. (C). 1981. pap. text ed. 9.00 (*0-920763-54-5*, Pub. by ECW Press CN) Genl Dist Srvs.

Raymond Knister & His Works (Fiction) Joy Kuropatwa. (Canadian Author Studies). 65p. (C). 1991. pap. text ed. 9.95 (*1-55022-090-X*, Pub. by ECW Press CN) Genl Dist Srvs.

Raymond Knister & His Works (Poetry) Joy Kuropatwa. (Canadian Author Studies). 40p. (C). 1987. pap. text ed. 9.95 (*0-920763-21-9*, Pub. by ECW Press CN) Genl Dist Srvs.

Raymond Leppard on Music: An Anthology of Critical & Personal Writings. Raymond Leppard. Ed. by Thomas P. Lewis. (Illus.). 760p. 1993. 45.00 (*0-912483-96-2*) Pro-Am Music.

Raymond Loewy. Paul Jodard. (Design Heroes Ser.). (Illus.). 192p. 1992. 24.95 (*0-8008-6642-8*) Taplinger.

Raymond Lully: Illuminated Doctor, Alchemist & Christian Mystic. A. E. Waite. 1993. 23.50 (*1-55818-220-9*, First Impress) Holmes Pub.

Raymond Mason. Michael Edwards. LC 94-61847. (Illus.). 252p. 1995. 50.00 (*0-500-09245-1*) Thames Hudson.

Raymond Mason, Sculptures & Drawings. Ed. by Jane Farrington. (Illus.). 120p. (C). 1989. pap. 29.50 (*0-85331-554-X*, Pub. by Lund Humphries UK) Antique Collect.

Raymond: or Life & Death: With Examples of the Evidence for Survival of Memory & Affection after Death. Oliver Lodge. 415p. 1996. pap. 29.95 (*1-56459-632-X*) Kessinger Pub.

Raymond Pettibon. 80p. 1995. pap. 32.50 (*3-85780-095-X*) Dist Art Pubs.

Raymond Pettibon. Hans R. Reust & Dennis Cooper. 352p. Date not set. pap. 50.00 (*3-85780-106-9*) Dist Art Pubs.

***Raymond Poincare.** J. F. Keiger. 396p. 1997. text ed. 64.95 (*0-521-57387-4*) Cambridge U Pr.

Raymond Queneau. Bergens. 34.50 (*0-685-37074-7*) Fr & Eur.

***Raymond Queneau/Carole Maso.** Ed. by John O'Brien. (Review of Contemporary Fiction Ser.). 220p. 1997. pap. 8.00 (*1-56478-177-1*) Dalkey Arch.

Raymond Queneau's Chene et Chien: A Translation with Commentary. Raymond Queneau. Tr. by Madeleine Velguth. LC 93-32269. 104p. (C). 1995. text ed. 33.95 (*0-8204-2311-4*) P Lang Pubng.

Raymond Radiguet. Noakes. (Coll. Poetes d'aujourd'hui). pap. 14.95 (*0-685-37076-3*) Fr & Eur.

Raymond Robins' Own Story. William Hard. LC 72-150950. (Russia Observed Ser.). (Illus.). 1971. reprint ed. 19.95 (*0-405-03080-0*) Ayer.

Raymond Roussel. Michel Foucault. (FRE.). 1992. pap. 12.95 (*0-7859-2831-6*) Fr & Eur.

Raymond Roussel. Rayner Heppenstall. 1990. 15.95 (*0-7145-0047-X*) Riverrun NY.

Raymond Roussel: Life, Death & Works. Roussel. Ed. by Alastair Brotchie. 1987. pap. 13.00 (*0-947757-14-7*, Pub. by Atlas Pr UK) Serpents Tail.

Raymond Souster & His Works. Bruce Whiteman. (Canadian Author Studies). 40p. (C). 1985. pap. text ed. 9.95 (*0-920802-85-0*, Pub. by ECW Press CN) Genl Dist Srvs.

Raymond Unwin: Architect & Planner - A Biography. Mervyn Miller. (Illus.). 240p. 1992. text ed. 59.00 (*0-7185-1363-0*) St Martin.

Raymond Williams. Tony Pinkney. 144p. 1991. 35.00 (*1-85411-047-0*, Pub. by Seren Bks UK); pap. 15.95 (*1-85411-048-9*, Pub. by Seren Bks UK) Dufour.

Raymond Williams: A Critical Reader. Ed. by Terry Eagleton. 240p. 1989. text ed. 47.50 (*1-55553-060-5*) NE U Pr.

Raymond Williams: His Life & Times. Fred Inglis. LC 95-19338. 352p. (C). (gr. 13). 1995. 24.95 (*0-415-08960-3*) Routledge.

Raymond Williams: Making Connections. John Eldridge & Lizzie Eldridge. LC 93-23297. 288p. (C). 1994. pap. 17.95 (*0-415-04088-4*, Routledge NY) Routledge.

Raymond Williams: Making Connections. John Eldridge & Lizzie Eldridge. LC 93-23297. 288p. (C). (gr. 13). 1994. text ed. 69.95 (*0-415-04087-6*, Routledge NY) Routledge.

Raymond Williams: Politics, Education, Letters. Ed. by W. John Morgan & Peter Preston. LC 92-34122. 232p. 1993. text ed. 45.00 (*0-312-08357-2*) St Martin.

***Raymond Williams Now.** Wallace. LC 96-37774. 1997. text ed. 45.00 (*0-312-17333-4*) St Martin.

Raymond Williams on Television: The Culture of Television. Raymond Williams. Ed. by Alan O'Connor. 256p. (C). 1989. pap. text ed. 14.95 (*0-415-02627-X*) Routledge.

Raymond's Run. Toni Cade Bambara. (J). (gr. 4-9). 1989. 13.95 (*0-88682-351-X*, 97222-098) Creative Ed.

Raymond's Two Crowns. David R. Previtali. (Illus.). 48p. (YA). (gr. 6-12). 1994. pap. text ed. 3.95 (*0-9625953-3-0*) Immaculata Pr.

Raymund Lully: Christian Mystic. Arthur E. Waite. 1973. 250.00 (*0-87968-100-4*) Gordon Pr.

Raymund Lully: Illuminated Doctor, Alchemist & Christian Mystic. Arthur E. Waite. 75p. 1992. pap. 12.95 (*1-56459-164-6*) Kessinger Pub.

***Raynah Files.** Laura T. Corrie. 1997. pap. write for info. (*1-57532-120-3*) Press-Tige Pub.

Raynaud Update: Pathophysiology & Treatment. Ed. by E. Davis. (Advances in Microcirculation Ser.: Vol. 12). (Illus.). vi, 162p. 1985. 110.50 (*3-8055-3992-4*) S Karger.

Raynaud's: A Guide for Health Professionals. Ed. by Stuart Roath. (Illus.). 160p. 1990. pap. 22.95 (*0-412-33680-4*, A4442) Chapman & Hall.

Raynaud's Disease: Index of New Information & Bibliography. Steven Y. Garrison. 150p. 1996. 47.50 (*0-7883-0982-X*); pap. 44.50 (*0-7883-0983-8*) ABBE Pubs Assn.

Raynaud's Phenomenon. Jay D. Coffman. (Illus.). 200p. 1989. 39.95 (*0-19-505756-2*) OUP.

Raynors of Ketchaponack: A Genealogy of the Descendants of Jonathan Raynor, Grandson of Thurston Raynor of Southampton, Long Island, NY. Stuart P. Howell. 190p. (Orig.). 1994. pap. text ed. 17.00 (*0-7884-0065-7*) Heritage Bk.

Rayo Que No Cesa. Miguel Hernandez. Ed. by Juan Cano Ballesta. (Nueva Austral Ser.: Vol. 52). (SPA.). 1991. pap. text ed. 24.95 (*84-239-1852-1*) Elliots Bks.

Rayon Spinners: The Strategic Management of Industrial Relations. A. E. Ramaswamy. 196p. 1995. 27.00 (*0-19-563537-X*) OUP.

Rayon Vert. Jules Verne. 8.95 (*0-686-55944-4*) Fr & Eur.

***Rayonier.** James Spencer. (Illus.). 152p. Date not set. write for info. (*0-933506-07-4*) Heringer Hse Pub.

Rays. Kismet D. Stam. 148p. pap. 5.95 (*90-70104-22-9*, Pub. by East-West NE) Omega Pubns NY.

***Rays: Animals with an Electric Charge.** Andreu Llamas. LC 97-8490. (Secrets of the Animal World Ser.). (Illus.). (J). 1997. lib. bdg. write for info. (*0-8368-1642-0*) Gareth Stevens Inc.

Ray's a Laugh. Richard Billingham. 112p. 1996. pap. 39.95 (*3-931141-18-7*, Pub. by Scalo Pubs) Dist Art Pubs.

Ray's Adventures with New Neighbors. Edith Witmer. (J). (gr. 3 up). 1981. 6.85 (*0-686-30774-7*) Rod & Staff.

Rays & Esoteric Psychology. Zachary F. Lansdowne. LC 89-5547. 194p. (Orig.). 1989. pap. 8.95 (*0-87728-682-5*) Weiser.

Rays & Radiation Phenomena. Oscar Brunler. 45p. reprint ed. spiral bd. 8.50 (*0-7873-1177-4*) Hlth Research.

Rays & the Initiations see Treatise on the Seven Rays

Ray's Arithmetic Set, 8 vols. 1985. teacher ed. 99.99 (*0-88062-050-1*) Mott Media.

Rays First Spaceship Ride. 60p. (J). (gr. 3-4). pap. write for info. (*0-318-62236-X*) RAPCOM Enter.

Ray's Light, Too. Charles R. Dietz. (Illus.). 168p. (Orig.). pap. 6.95 (*0-9618284-0-4*) Spirited Comns.

Rays of Hope. Denis Hayes. 1977. pap. 4.95 (*0-393-06422-0*) Norton.

Rays of Hope. D. O. Teasley. 95p. pap. 0.75 (*0-686-29137-9*) Faith Pub Hse.

Rays of Positive Electricity & Their Application to Chemical Analysis. J. J. Thompson. 1991. lib. bdg. 79.75 (*0-8490-4925-3*) Gordon Pr.

Rays of the Same Light: Parallel Passages, with Commentary, from the Bible & the Bhagavad Gita, 3 vols. J. Donald Walters. LC 88-154781. (Illus.). 558p. (Orig.). pap. 26.95 (*0-916124-50-X*) Crystal Clarity.

Rays of the Same Light: Parallel Passages, with Commentary, from the Bible & the Bhagavad Gita, 3 vols., Vol. I. J. Donald Walters. LC 88-154781. (Illus.). 160p. (Orig.). 1987. pap. 9.95 (*0-916124-38-X*, CCP1) Crystal Clarity.

Rays of the Same Light: Parallel Passages, with Commentary, from the Bible & the Bhagavad Gita, 3 vols., Vol. II. J. Donald Walters. LC 88-154781. (Illus.). 196p. (Orig.). 1988. pap. 9.95 (*0-916124-48-7*, CCP6) Crystal Clarity.

Rays of the Same Light: Parallel Passages, with Commentary, from the Bible & the Bhagavad Gita, 3 vols., Vol. III. J. Donald Walters. LC 88-154781. (Illus.). 202p. (Orig.). 1989. pap. 9.95 (*0-916124-49-5*, CCP12) Crystal Clarity.

Rays, Romance & Rivalry, vol. 5. Katherine Applegate. (Summer Ser.). (YA). (gr. 7 up). 1996. mass mkt. 3.99 (*0-671-51039-8*) PB.

Ray's Way French Blue Edition Work & Write Music Manuscript Book, No. 1. (Twelve Stave Bks.). 64p. 1990. 2.50 (*0-685-32060-X*, G047) Hansen Ed Mus.

Raystede Handbook of Homeopathic Remedies for Animals. Raymonde-Hawkins & Macleod. 129p. 1985. pap. 7.50 (*0-85207-167-1*, Pub. by C W Daniel UK) Natl Bk Netwk.

Raystede Handbook of Homoeopathic Remedies for Animals. M. Raymonde Hawkins & George Macleod. 72p. (Orig.). 11.95 (*0-8464-4281-7*) Beekman Pubs.

Raytheon Company: A Report on the Company's Environmental Policies & Practices. (Illus.). 40p. (C). 1994. reprint ed. pap. text ed. 250.00 (*0-7881-0908-1*, Coun on Econ) DIANE Pub.

Rayuela. Julio Cortazar. (SPA.). 14.95 (*0-8288-3904-2*, S1108) Fr & Eur.

Rayuela y la Creatividad Artistica. Myron I. Lichtblau. LC 88-81377. (Coleccion Polymita). 92p. (Orig.). (SPA.). 1989. pap. 12.00 (*0-89729-491-2*) Ediciones.

Raz De Sein to Benodet. Imray, Laurie, Norie & Wilson Ltd. Staff. (Illus.). (C). 1987. text ed. 60.00 (*0-685-40219-3*, Pub. by Imray Laurie Norie & Wilson UK) St Mut.

Raz-Ma-Taz. Stephen Cosgrove. (Serendipity Bks.). (Illus.). 32p. (Orig.). (J). (gr. 1-4). 1982. pap. 3.95 (*0-8431-0588-7*) Price Stern Sloan.

Razing the Bastions. Hans U. Von Balthasar. Tr. by Brian McNeil. LC 92-75071. (Communio Bk.). 103p. (Orig.). 1993. pap. 9.95 (*0-89870-428-6*) Ignatius Pr.

Razing the Ded! The Biblical Administrations for Resurrection. Bill Panko & Margaret Panko. 300p. (Orig.). 1996. pap. 19.95 (*1-885342-04-7*) Creative Ways.

Razon de Algunos Refranes. Ed. by B. Russell Thompson. (Textos B Ser.: Vol. XII). 178p. (SPA.). (C). 1975. 45.00 (*0-7293-0007-2*, Pub. by Tamesis Bks Ltd UK) Boydell & Brewer.

Razon de Ser Cristiano. Yandall Woodfin. Tr. by Francisco Almanza from ENG. (Biblioteca de Doctrina Cristiana Ser.). 144p. (Orig.). (SPA.). 1990. pap. text ed. 7.99 (*0-311-09126-1*) Casa Bautista.

Razon para Vivir. Melody Beattie. 173p. (SPA.). 1991. pap. 5.99 (*1-56063-210-0*, 498500) Editorial Unilit.

Razon por Que. Robert A. Laidlaw. 36p. (SPA.). 1989. pap. 1.79 (*1-56063-004-3*, 498100) Editorial Unilit.

Razon y el Sueno: Del Cubismo Al Surrealismo. Esther Boix. (Del Arte Moderno Ser.: Vol. II). (Illus.). 128p. (SPA.). 1993. 100.00 (*84-343-0545-3*) Elliots Bks.

Razon y Pasion: Veinticinco Anos de Estudios Cubanos. Instituto de Estudios Cubanos Staff. Ed. by Leonel A. De la Cuesta & Maria C. Herrera. LC 96-84791. (Coleccion Cuba y Sus Jueces). 311p. (Orig.). (SPA.). 1996. pap. 19.00 (*0-89729-808-X*) Ediciones.

***Razor Anthology.** Knife World Pubns. Staff. (Illus.). 248p. 1995. pap. 14.95 (*0-940362-17-1*) Knife World.

Razor Edge Book of Sharpening. John Juranitch. (Orig.). 1985. pap. 12.50 (*0-446-38002-4*) Warner Bks.

Razor Edge of Balance: A Study of Virginia Woolf. Jane Novak. LC 72-85111. 192p. 1973. 9.95 (*0-87024-247-4*) U of Miami Pr.

***Razor Edged Path.** Robert Powell. 200p. (Orig.). 1997. pap. 14.00 (*1-884997-21-X*) Blue Dove Pr.

Razor for a Goat: A Discussion of Certain Problems in the History of Witchcraft & Diabolism. Elliot Rose. 265p. 1989. pap. 15.95 (*0-8020-6768-9*) U of Toronto Pr.

Razor Jacques. large type ed. Alan Sewart. (Linford Mystery Library). 304p. 1992. pap. 15.99 (*0-7089-7264-0*, Trailtree Bookshop) Ulverscroft.

Razor Moon. Christine Monhollen. 72p. 1993. pap. 7.95 (*1-884118-00-3*) Triage Pr.

Razor Ramon. Edward R. Ricciuti. Ed. by Bruce Glassman. (Face to Face Ser.). 25p. (Orig.). (YA). (gr. 5 up). 1994. pap. text ed. 6.95 (*1-56711-071-1*, Topdog) Blackbirch.

Razor Sharp Mathematics, 4 vols. Candace Smothers. Incl. Bk. 1. Razor Sharp Mathematics. , 2 bks. (Illus.). 256p. (J). 1996. teacher ed., spiral bd., pap. 30.00 (*1-888630-01-9*); Bk. 1. Razor Sharp Mathematics. , 2 bks. (Illus.). 192p. (J). (gr. 4-6). 1996. wbk. ed., spiral bd. 22.00 (*1-888630-02-7*); Bk. 1. Razor Sharp Mathematics. , 2 bks. (Illus.). 233p. (J). (gr. 4-6). 1996. student ed., spiral bd. 18.00 (*1-888630-03-5*); Bk. 1. Razor Sharp Mathematics. , 2 bks. (Illus.). 21p. (J). (gr. 4-6). 1996. suppl. ed., pap. 5.00 (*1-888630-04-3*); (Cutting Edge Ser.). 75.00 (*1-888630-00-0*) United Smothers.

Razor Sharp Mathematics see Razor Sharp Mathematics

Razorback. Dick Stivers. (Gold Eagle Heroes Ser.: No. 404). 1992. mass mkt. 5.99 (*0-373-62404-2*) Harlequin Bks.

Razorbacks: A Story of Arkansas Football. Orville Henry & Jim Bailey. LC 96-8602. 1996. 40.00 (*1-55728-429-6*); pap. 22.00 (*1-55728-430-X*) U of Ark Pr.

***Razorbacks Handbook: Stories, Stats & Stuff about Arkansas Basketball.** Dudley E. Dawson. (Illus.). 160p. (Orig.). 1996. pap. 9.95 (*1-880652-72-2*) Wichita Eagle.

Razor's Edge. W. Somerset Maugham. 1978. mass mkt. 5.95 (*0-14-001860-3*, Penguin Bks) Viking Penguin.

Razor's Edge. W. Somerset Maugham. (Twentieth-Century Classics Ser.). 320p. 1992. pap. 10.95 (*0-14-018523-2*, Penguin Classics) Viking Penguin.

***Razors Edge.** Lisanne Norman. 1997. pap. 6.99 (*0-88677-766-6*) DAW Bks.

Razor's Edge. Osho Rajneesh. Ed. by Bodhisattva Ma Deva Barkha. (Mystery School Ser.). 374p. 1987. 21.95 (*3-89338-015-9*, Pub. by Rebel Hse GW) Osho America.

Razor's Song. Joe Monninger. 256p. 1993. mass mkt. 4.99 (*0-380-71874-X*) Avon.

Razzamatazz. Sandra Scoppettone. 392p. 1995. mass mkt. 4.95 (*0-7867-0230-3*) Carroll & Graf.

***Razzle Dazzle.** Hank Messick. Date not set. lib. bdg. 29.95 (*0-8488-1812-1*) Amereon Ltd.

Razzle Dazzle. Hank Messick. (Illus.). 215p. 1995. 29.95 (*0-9650243-1-8*) For The Love Bks.

Razzle Dazzle: The Life & Work of Bob Fosse. Kevin B. Grubb. 1991. pap. 16.95 (*0-312-05502-1*) St Martin.

Razzle Dazzle: 27 Pupil/Teacher Duets. L. Evans. 28p. 1985. pap. 4.95 (*0-7935-4315-0*, 00009069) H Leonard.

Razzle Dazzle Christmas: Five Finger Solos with Accompaniment. 16p. 1990. pap. 4.95 (*0-7935-1881-4*, 00009640) H Leonard.

Razzle Dazzle! Magic Tricks for You. Larry White & Ray Broekel. Ed. by Ann Fay. LC 87-6114. (Illus.). 48p. (J). (gr. 3-8). 1987. lib. bdg. 13.95 (*0-8075-6857-0*) A Whitman.

Razzleberry Rescue. Misty Taggart. LC 94-27158. (Angel Academy Ser.: Vol. 3). (Illus.). (J). 1994. pap. 3.99 (*0-8499-5018-X*) Word Pub.

Razzmatazz. Christopher Middleton. 1976. 17.50 (*0-935072-02-0*) W T Taylor.

RB-169 - Navigation Rules for International & Inland Waters Including the Great Lakes & Western Rivers: Revised Edition "D" Ed. by Richard A. Block. (Illus.). 294p. 1995. pap. text ed. 30.00 (*1-879778-35-1*, BK-234) Marine Educ.

RB 1980. Ed. by Timothy Fry et al. 96p. (Orig.). pap. 2.95 (*0-8146-1272-5*) Liturgical Pr.

RB 1980: The Rule of St. Benedict. unabridged ed. Ed. by Timothy Fry et al. LC 81-1013. 644p. 1981. pap. 19.95 (*0-8146-1220-2*) Liturgical Pr.

RB-36 Days at Rapid City: Rapid City Free Style. John F. Welch. (Illus.). (Orig.). 1994. pap. 20.00 (*0-9637909-1-9*) Silv Wings.

***RBAAB: The Red-Blooded, All-American Boy.** (Illus.). 249p. (Orig.). 1997. pap. 15.00 (*0-9657189-0-5*) EROSONIC.

RBE for Deterministic Effects, ICRP Publication: A Report of a Task Group of Committee 1 of the International Commission on Radiological Protection. ICRP Staff. (International Commission on Radiological Protection Ser.: Vol. 20, No. 58). (Illus.). 64p. 1990. pap. 41.50 (*0-08-040173-2*, Pergamon Pr) Elsevier.

RBOC Strategies in Data Communications. Market Intelligence Staff. 180p. 1993. 2,400.00 (*1-56753-547-X*) Frost & Sullivan.

RBOC Strategies in Information Services. Market Intelligence Staff. 180p. 1993. 2,400.00 (*1-56753-548-8*) Frost & Sullivan.

RBP Pattern Resource Book. Ed. by Valerie Wilson. (Illus.). 88p. 1986. spiral bd. 4.95 (*0-87227-016-5*) Reg Baptist.

RBRVS: Untangling the Web. Paul L. Grimaldi. 50p. 1992. 20.00 (*0-930228-92-8*) Hlthcare Fin Mgmt.

***RBRVS As a Model for Workers Compensation Medical Fee Schedules: Pros & Cons.** Ed. by Philip L. Burstein. LC 96-28615. 1996. pap. 50.00 (*0-935149-59-7*, WC-96-5) Workers Comp Res Inst.

RBRVS Clinical Coder for Cardiology, 1992. Ed. by Tricia Goroum. 250p. 1992. ring bd. 197.00 (*1-56329-094-4*, RCD) St Anthony Pub.

RBRVS Clinical Coder for Family Practice, 1992. Ed. by Tricia Goroum. 250p. 1992. ring bd. 138.00 (*1-56329-095-2*, RFP) St Anthony Pub.

RBRVS Clinical Coder for General Surgery, 1992. Ed. by Tricia Goroum. 250p. 1992. ring bd. 118.00 (*1-56329-097-9*, RGS) St Anthony Pub.

RBRVS Clinical Coder for Ophthalmalogy, 1992. Ed. by Tricia Goroum. 250p. 1992. ring bd. 158.00 (*1-56329-096-0*, REY) St Anthony Pub.

RBRVS Clinical Coder for Orthopaedics, 1992. 1992. 138.00 (*1-56329-081-2*) St Anthony Pub.

***RBRVS Converter, 1997: Calulate RBRVS Fees for Your Area (All Codes)** 349.95 (*0-614-26988-1*) Medicode Inc.

R

R.C. Gorman: The Graphic Works. Ben Q. Adams & Richard Newlin. LC 87-51653. (Illus.). 256p. (JPN & SPA.). 1988. 125.00 (*0-9619950-0-9*) Tads Editions Ltd.
R/C Pilot's Handbook. (Illus.). 191p. 1995. pap. text ed. 14.95 (*0-911295-38-0*) Air Age.
RCA & the VideoDisc: The Business of Research. Margaret B. Graham. (Studies in Economic History & Policy: The United States in the Twentieth Century). (Illus.). 256p. 1986. text ed. 54.95 (*0-521-32282-0*) Cambridge U Pr.
RCA Electro-Optics Handbook. RCA Staff. (Illus.). 1974. 4.95 (*0-913970-11-5*, EOH-11) RCA Solid State.
RCA Victor Model CE-29, 1932: Service Notes & Schematic. rev. ed. Ed. by Frank Adams. (Illus.). 8p. reprint ed. spiral bd. 12.50 (*1-56642-004-0*, R-5) A M C Corp.
RCC Pilotage Foundation: Atlantic Spain & Portugal. Imray, Laurie, Norie & Wilson Ltd. Staff. 196p. (C). 1988. 150.00 (*0-85288-110-X*, Pub. by Imray Laurie Norie & Wilson UK) St Mut.
RCIA: Renewing the Church As an Initiating Assembly. Lawrence E. Mick. 102p. 1989. pap. 4.95 (*0-8146-1787-5*) Liturgical Pr.
RCIA: Transforming the Church: A Resource for Pastoral Implementation. Thomas H. Morris. 1989. pap. 10.95 (*0-8091-3047-5*) Paulist Pr.
RCIA Spirituality: An Adventure into Mayhem & Mystery. rev. ed. Barbara Hixon. LC 89-38309. 176p. (C). 1997. pap. text ed. 17.95 (*0-89390-272-1*) Resource Pubns.
***RCIA Spirituality: Formation for the Catechumenate Team.** Barbara Hixon & Gael Gensler. LC 96-29997. 1997. pap. 17.95 (*0-89390-399-X*) Resource Pubns.
RCIA Team Manual: How to Implement the Rite of Christian Initiation of Adults in Your Parish. Patricia Barbernitz. 88p. 1986. pap. 8.95 (*0-8091-2814-4*) Paulist Pr.
***RCRA & CERCLA - Changing Requirements for Hazardous Substances in the Natural Resources Industries.** (Mineral Law Ser.). 500p. 1997. text ed. 125.00 (*0-929047-69-9*) Rocky Mtn Mineral Law Found.
RCRA Compliance & Enforcement Manual. 2nd ed. Robert E. Steinberg et al. LC 94-33461. (Environmental Law Ser.). 1994. write for info. (*0-07-172689-6*) Shepards.
RCRA Compliance Handbook. rev. ed. Charlotte L. Neitzel. (Environmental Compliance Handbook Ser.). 152p. 1994. pap. text ed. 54.95 (*0-471-11266-6*) Wiley.
RCRA Compliance Handbook. 2nd ed. Charlotte L. Neitzel. (Environmental Compliance Handbook Ser.: Vol. 3). 1992. pap. 49.95 (*0-7816-0071-5*) Exec Ent Pubns.
RCRA Corrective Action & Facility Permitting: Environmental Protection Agency's Public Involvement Manual. U. S. Environmental Protection Agency, Office of Wetlands, Oceans, & Watersheds Staff. 238p. (Orig.). 1994. pap. text ed. 72.00 (*0-86587-401-8*) Gov Insts.
RCRA Corrective Action Inspection Guidance Manual. EPA Staff. 138p. (Orig.). 1996. pap. text ed. 69.00 (*0-86587-444-1*) Gov Insts.
RCRA Deskbook. 758p. 1991. pap. 85.00 (*0-911937-40-4*) Environ Law Inst.
RCRA Generator's Compliance Manual. Jim Newton. 400p. 1994. ring bd. 70.00 (*1-888555-01-7*) MGR Pr.
RCRA Ground Water Monitoring: Draft Technical Guidance. U. S. Environmental Protection Agency, Office of Wetlands, Oceans, & Watersheds Staff. 246p. (Orig.). 1994. pap. text ed. 79.00 (*0-86587-376-3*) Gov Insts.
RCRA Hazardous Wastes Handbook. 11th ed. Ridgway M. Hall, Jr. 616p. 1995. pap. text ed. 115.00 (*0-86587-503-0*) Gov Insts.
RCRA Land Disposal Restrictions, 1995: A Guide to Compliance. 392p. 1994. pap. 85.00 (*0-615-00769-4*) Elsevier.
RCRA Regulations & Keyword Index, 1995. 1224p. pap. 125.00 (*0-615-00770-8*) Elsevier.
RCRA Regulatory Compliance Guide. Mark S. Dennison. LC 92-32509. (Illus.). 354p. 1993. 64.00 (*0-8155-1321-6*) Noyes.
RCT Mathematics Workbook. 2nd rev. ed. John Allasio et al. 182p. (YA). (gr. 8-12). 1995. pap. 9.50 (*0-937820-71-7*) WestSea Pub.
RCT Mathematics Workbook Answer Key. 2nd rev. ed. John Allasio et al. 20p. (YA). (gr. 8-12). 1995. teacher ed., pap. 3.25 (*0-937820-72-5*) WestSea Pub.
RCT Reading. rev. ed. Marie Lackner & Cynthia Paterno. 198p. 1989. pap. 7.95 (*0-937820-58-X*) WestSea Pub.
RCT Reading Answer Key. rev. ed. Marie Lackner & Cynthia Paterno. 20p. 1989. teacher ed., pap. 3.25 (*0-937820-59-8*) WestSea Pub.
***R.D. Laing: A Divided Self.** John Clay. (Illus.). 308p. 1997. 29.95 (*0-340-59049-1*, Pub. by H & S UK); pap. 13.95 (*0-340-68451-8*, Pub. by H & S UK) Trafalgar.
***R.D. Laing & the Paths of Anti-Psychiatry.** Zbigniew Kotowicz. LC 96-3254. (Makers of Modern Psychotherapy Ser.). 160p. (C). 1997. text ed. write for info. (*0-415-11610-4*) Routledge.
***R.D. Laing & the Paths of Anti-Psychiatry.** Zbigniew Kotowicz. LC 96-3254. (Makers of Modern Psychotherapy Ser.). 160p. (C). 1997. pap. write for info. (*0-415-11611-2*) Routledge.
RDA: Rats, Drugs & Assumptions. Majid Ali. (Illus.). 670p. 1995. pap. 21.00 (*1-879131-07-2*) Inst of Prev Med.
RDB: A Comprehensive Guide. 2nd ed. Lilian Hobbs & Ken England. 450p. 1995. pap. 41.95 (*1-55558-124-2*, Digital DEC) Buttrwrth-Heinemann.
Rdb - VMS: Developing a Data Warehouse. William H. Inmon & Chuck Kelley. 264p. 1993. pap. text ed. 49.95 (*0-471-56920-8*, GD4299) Wiley.
RDF Accelerated Training Program. Gary Reed. Ed. by Alex Marciniszyn & Randi Cartier. (Robotech RPG Adventures Ser.). (Illus.). 56p. (Orig.). (YA). (gr. 8 up). 1988. pap. 7.95 (*0-916211-32-0*, 555) Palladium Bks.
RDF Manual. Kevin Siembieda. Ed. by Florence Siembieda. (Robotech RPG Ser.: Bk. 2). (Illus.). 48p. (YA). (gr. 8 up). 1987. pap. 7.95 (*0-916211-23-1*, 551) Palladium Bks.
RDG Color Guide to Freight & Passenger Equipment. C. T. Bossler. (Illus.). 128p. 1994. 49.95 (*1-878887-29-7*) Morning NJ.
RDI Evaluates the Sony ICF-2010 Receiver. Lawrence Magne. (Radio Database International White Paper Ser.). (Illus.). 22p. (Orig.). 1988. pap. 6.95 (*0-914941-06-2*) IBS PA.
***RDNA Manual.** R. E. Farrell & G. Leppert. (Springer Lab Manual Ser.). (Illus.). 300p. 1996. 67.00 (*0-387-57139-6*) Spr-Verlag.
***RDO & ODBC: Client Server Database Programming with Visual BASIC.** Rob Macdonald & Steve Wilent. LC 96-32364. (Special Reports). 1996. pap. write for info. (*1-880935-50-3*) Pinnacle WA.
Re: American Dream: Six Urban Housing Prototypes for Los Angeles. Roger Sherman et al. LC 94-17461. (Illus.). 112p. (Orig.). 1995. pap. 17.95 (*1-56898-027-2*) Princeton Arch.
Re: Photography: Three Exhibitions. Alison D. Nordstrom. 12p. 1994. pap. text ed. 7.00 (*1-887040-08-0*) SE Mus Photo.
Re: Thinking. Jeanne Hoffman & Elaine Prizzi. (J). (gr. 5 up). 1989. pap. 12.99 (*0-8224-5789-X*) Fearon Teach Aids.
Re: Writing: Strategies for Student Writing. Frances Kurilich & Helen Whitaker. 464p. (C). 1988. pap. text ed. 20.75 (*0-03-004632-7*) HB Coll Pubs.
Re Vol. 4: Selected Papers from the Fourth Annual Conference on Virginia Woolf. Ed. by Eileen Barrett & Patricia Cramer. (Illus.). 320p. (Orig.). (C). 1995. pap. 37.50 (*0-944473-23-7*) Pace Univ Pr.
***Re-Aligning African Heads: Yoruba Curatives for Maafa-Related Ailments.** Adetokunbo F. Borishade. (Illus.). xxi, 101p. (Orig.). 1996. pap. text ed. 10.00 (*0-9654009-0-5*) Sankofa Prods.
Re & Amun: The Crisis of Polytheism in New Kingdom Egypt. Jan Assmann. Tr. by Anthony Alcock from GER. LC 94-10620. 256p. 1995. 76.50 (*0-7103-0465-X*) Routledge Chapman & Hall.
Re-Animator: Tales of Herbert West. H. P. Lovecraft. Ed. by Steven Jones. (Illus.). 48p. 1991. pap. 4.95 (*1-56398-027-4*) Malibu Comics Ent.
Re-Appraisal of Kierkegaard. Howard A. Slaatte. LC 95-6233. 166p. (C). 1995. lib. bdg. 37.50 (*0-8191-9933-8*) U Pr of Amer.
***Re-Appraisal of Patanjali's Yoga-Sutras in the Light of the Buddha's Teaching.** S. N. Tandon. 142p. 1996. pap. 6.95 (*81-7414-024-7*) Vipassana Res.
***Re-Arranging Your Mental Furniture.** Ken Gaub. 198p. (Orig.). 1997. pap. 9.95 (*1-57502-480-2*, P01435) Morris Pubng.
Re-Assessing Anglo-Saxon England. Eric John. LC 96-2687. 1997. text ed. 59.95 (*0-7190-4867-2*, Pub. by Manchester Univ Pr UK) St Martin.
Re-Assessment of the Telmatobiine Leptodactylid Frogs of Patagonia. John D. Lynch. (Occasional Papers: No. 72). 57p. 1978. pap. 1.00 (*0-686-80373-6*) U KS Nat Hist Mus.
***Re-Belle et Infidele/The Body Bilingual: Translation As a Re-Writing in the Feminine.** Susanne De Lotbiniere-Harwood. 176p. (ENG & FRE.). pap. 12.95 (*0-88961-166-1*, Pub. by Wmns Pr CN) LPC InBook.
Re-Biographing & Deviance: Psychotherapeutic Narrativism & the Midrash. Mordechai Rotenberg. LC 87-2451. 256p. 1987. text ed. 59.95 (*0-275-92391-6*, C2391, Praeger Pubs) Greenwood.
***Re-Bonding: Preventing & Restoring Damaged Relationships.** 2nd rev. ed. Donald M. Joy. 144p. 1996. pap. 12.95 (*0-916035-70-0*) Evangel Indiana.
Re-Careering in Turbulent Times: Skills & Strategies for Success in Today's Job Market. Ronald L. Krannich. LC 82-82720. 295p. 1983. pap. 7.95 (*0-942710-02-9*) Impact VA.
Re-Charting America's Future: Responses to Arguments Against Stabilizing U. S. Population & Limiting Immigration. Roy Beck. (Illus.). 217p. (Orig.). 1994. pap. 9.95 (*1-881780-06-6*) Social Contract.
Re-Claiming Wasted Lands for Our Future: Man's Proven Ability to Green Out the Wasteland Areas of Our Planet. J. T. Mensah & Larry Soule. (Illus.). 176p. 1993. pap. 14.95 (*0-8059-3342-5*) Dorrance.
Re-Conciliation: The Hidden Hyphen. Mary C. Morrison. LC 74-24007. 24p. (Orig.). 1974. pap. 3.00 (*0-87574-198-3*) Pendle Hill.
Re-Counting Plato: A Computer Analysis of Plato's Style. G. R. Ledger. (Illus.). 272p. 1990. 85.00 (*0-19-814681-7*) OUP.
***Re-Create Your Life: Transforming Yourself & Your World with the Decision Maker Process.** Morty Lefkoe. LC 96-43406. 256p. 1997. 22.95 (*0-8362-2167-2*) Andrews & McMeel.
***Re-Creating America: The Ethics of U. S. Immigration & Refugee Policy in a Christian Perspective.** Dana W. Wilbanks. LC 96-28840. 240p. 1996. pap. 18.95 (*0-687-00444-6*) Abingdon.
Re-Creating Ourselves: African Women & Critical Transformations. Molara Ogundipe-Leslie. LC 93-43967. 250p. 1994. 45.95 (*0-86543-411-5*); pap. 16.95 (*0-86543-412-3*) Africa World.
Re-Creating Teams During Transitions: A Practical Guide to Optimizing Team Performance During Changing Times. Paul J. Jerome. (Management Skills Ser.). (Illus.). 120p. 1994. pap. 12.95 (*1-883553-58-X*) R Chang Assocs.
***Re-Creating Your Self.** Christopher Stone. 1997. pap. text ed. 11.00 (*1-56170-378-8*) Hay House.
Re-Creating Your Self. Christopher Stone. LC 86-31125. 176p. 1988. 10.00 (*0-943920-29-9*) Metamorphous Pr.
Re-Creating Your Self. Christopher Stone. LC 90-80050. 176p. 1990. reprint ed. pap. 10.00 (*0-937611-92-1*, 124) Hay House.
Re-Creation of Eve. Rosemary Haughton. 148p. 1985. pap. 8.95 (*0-87243-135-5*) Templegate.
Re-creation of Landscape: A Study of Wordsworth, Coleridge, Constable, & Turner. James A. Heffernan. LC 84-40302. (Illus.). 278p. 1984. text ed. 40.00 (*0-87451-312-X*) U Pr of New Eng.
Re-Creations. Busch. 1995. 24.95 (*0-8212-2002-0*) Bulfinch Pr.
Re-Creations. Grace L. Hill. reprint ed. lib. bdg. 26.95 (*0-89190-046-2*, Rivercity Pr) Amereon Ltd.
Re-Creations, No. 89. Grace L. Hill. (Grace Livingston Hill Ser.: Vol. 89). 312p. 1990. pap. 5.99 (*0-8423-5334-8*) Tyndale.
Re-Descubrimiento y Re-Conquista de America en la Illustracion Espanola. Bernardita Llanos. LC 93-2313. (Sociocritism Ser.: Vol. 6). 217p. (C). 1994. text ed. 47.95 (*0-8204-2269-X*) P Lang Pubng.
Re-Discoveries of America: The Meeting of Cultures. Ed. by Johan Callens. (Illus.). 144p. 1994. pap. 19.95 (*90-5487-050-8*) Paul & Co Pubs.
Re-Discovering Colonial Writing: 1492-1992. Ed. by Rene Jara & Nicholas Spadaccini. (Hispanic Issues Ser.: Vol. 4). 1991. pap. text ed. 14.95 (*0-8166-2011-3*) U of Minn Pr.
Re-Discovering the Sacred: Spirituality in America. Phillis Tickle. 176p. 1995. 19.95 (*0-8245-1460-2*) Crossroad NY.
Re-Discovery of the Old Testament. Harold H. Rowley. LC 75-76912. (Essay Index Reprint Ser.). 1977. 21.95 (*0-8369-1154-7*) Ayer.
***Re-Dressing the Canon: Essays on Theatre & Gender.** Alisa Solomon. LC 97-2805. 1998. write for info. (*0-415-15720-X*); pap. write for info. (*0-415-15721-8*) Routledge.
Re-Echo Club. Carolyn Wells. 1987. pap. 8.95 (*0-89979-046-1*) British Am Bks.
Re-Educating Myself: An Introduction to a New Civilization. Bob Gebelein. LC 85-60221. 288p. (Orig.). 1985. pap. 9.95 (*0-9614611-0-1*) Omdega Pr.
Re-Educating the Corporation: Foundations for the Learning Organization. Daniel R. Tobin. LC 93-60677. 289p. 1994. 25.00 (*0-939246-48-1*) Wiley.
Re-Educating the Corporation: Foundations for the Learning Organization. Daniel R. Tobin. 320p. 1995. text ed. 29.95 (*0-471-13189-X*) Wiley.
Re-Educating the Imagination: Toward a Poetics, Politics, & Pedagogy of Literary Engagement. Deanne Bogdan. LC 91-46519. 408p. 1992. pap. text ed. 36.00 (*0-86709-305-6*, 0305) Boynton Cook Pubs.
Re-Educating Troubled Youth: Environments for Teaching & Treatment. Larry K. Brendtro & Arlin E. Ness. LC 83-11787. (Modern Applications of Social Work Ser.). 300p. (C). 1983. pap. text ed. 27.95 (*0-202-36034-2*); lib. bdg. 49.95 (*0-202-36033-4*) Aldine de Gruyter.
Re-Education in a Nursery Group: A Study in Clinical Psychology. Ruth W. Washburn. (SRCD Ser.: Vol. 9, No. 2). 1944. 25.00 (*0-527-01531-8*) Periodicals Srv.
Re-Education of the American Working Class. Ed. by Steven H. London et al. LC 90-36778. (Contributions in Labor Studies: No. 31). 312p. 1990. text ed. 59.95 (*0-313-26785-5*, LRB, Greenwood Pr) Greenwood.
Re-elect Nutty. Dean Hughes. LC 94-12776. 122p. (J). 1995. 14.00 (*0-689-31862-6*, Atheneum S&S) S&S Trade.
Re-Emergence of Correctional Intervention: Developments Through the 1980s & Prospects for the Future. Ted Palmer. 200p. (C). 1992. 46.00 (*0-8039-4537-X*); pap. 19.95 (*0-8039-4538-8*) Sage.
Re-Emergence of Indira Gandhi. P. Sood & P. V. Rao. 208p. 1981. 14.95 (*0-686-81394-4*, Pub. by S Chand II) Asia Bk Corp.
Re-Emergence of Small Enterprises: Industrial Restructuring in Industrialised Countries. Tr. by W. Sengenberger et al. vi, 308p. (Orig.). 1991. pap. 31.50 (*92-9014-465-3*) Intl Labour Office.
Re-Emergence of the Chinese Peasantry. Ed. by Ashwani Saith. 288p. (C). 1987. text ed. 62.50 (*0-7099-4409-8*, Pub. by Croom Helm UK) Routledge Chapman & Hall.
Re-Emergence of the Muslim Brothers in Egypt. Zohurul Bari. (C). 1995. 18.50 (*81-7095-052-X*, Pub. by Lancers Bks II) S Asia.
Re-Emerging Securities Market in China. Mei Xia et al. LC 92-9824. 200p. 1992. text ed. 49.95 (*0-89930-755-8*, GEF, Quorum Bks) Greenwood.
Re Encarnacion, los Muertos Estan Vivos. Frank Calderon. 96p. (Orig.). (SPA.). 1987. pap. 2.95 (*0-939193-15-9*) Edit Concepts.
Re-Enchanting Humanity: A Defense of the Human Spirit Against Antihumanism, Misanthropy, Mysticism & Primitivism. Murray Bookchin. (Global Issues Ser.). 288p. Date not set. pap. 17.95 (*0-304-32839-1*) Cassell.
Re-Enchantment of Everyday Life. Thomas Moore. 320p. 1996. 25.00 (*0-06-017209-6*) HarpC.
***Re-Enchantment of Everyday Life.** Thomas Moore. 416p. 1997. pap. 13.50 (*0-06-092824-7*, PL) HarpC.
***Re-Enchantment of Everyday Life.** Thomas Moore. 1997. pap. 23.95 (*0-7838-1969-2*, GK Hall) Thorndike Pr.
Re-Enchantment of Everyday Life. large type ed. Thomas Moore. LC 96-5877. 1996. reprint ed. 25.95 (*0-7838-1819-X*, GK Hall) Thorndike Pr.
Re-engineering at Work. Michael Loh. 192p. 1995. 59.95 (*0-566-07642-X*, Pub. by Gower UK) Ashgate Pub Co.
Re-Engineering Business Solutions with Object-Oriented Development. Sid Decker & Sigs Books Staff. (C). 1996. pap. text ed. 21.00 (*0-13-443003-4*) P-H.
***Re-engineering Design: An A/E/C Professional's Guide to Strategic Technology Planning.** Kristine K. Fallon. LC 96-53271. 1997. pap. 39.95 (*0-471-16807-6*) Wiley.
***Re-Engineering Female Friendly Science.** Sue V. Rosser. LC 97-5935. (Athene Ser.). (Illus.). 320p. 1997. text ed. 54.00 (*0-8077-6287-3*); pap. text ed. 24.95 (*0-8077-6286-5*) Tchrs Coll.
Re-Engineering for Time-Based Competition: Benchmarks & Best Practices for Production, R & D, & Purchasing. Robert B. Handfield. LC 95-3277. 240p. 1995. text ed. 59.95 (*0-89930-917-8*, Quorum Bks) Greenwood.
Re-Engineering the Environment. Susumu Sato & Hiromitsu Kumamoto. 1995. pap. 14.95 (*0-533-11569-8*) Vantage.
Re-Engineering the Manufacturing System. Stein. LC 96-18120. (Manufacturing Engineering & Materials Processing Ser.: Vol. 47). 328p. 1996. 59.75 (*0-8247-9747-7*) Dekker.
Re-Engineering the Performance Management Process. Franklin Hartle. 250p. 1995. 45.00 (*0-7494-1640-8*, Pub. by Kogan Pg UK) Cassell.
Re-Engineering Work: A Manifesto for Business Revolution. Michael Hammer. LC 91-5117. 1999. 22.95 (*0-446-51692-9*) Warner Bks.
Re-Engineering Your Business. Daniel C. Morris. 1994. pap. text ed. 14.95 (*0-07-043179-5*) McGraw.
Re-Engineering's Missing Ingredient: The Human Factor. Michael Oram & Richard S. Wellins. 256p. 1995. pap. 54.00 (*0-85292-621-9*, Pub. by IPM UK) St Mut.
Re-Enter Laughing. Judith Hanson. (Illus.). 36p. (Orig.). 1977. pap. 7.50 (*0-940592-00-2*) Heyeck Pr.
***Re-Enter the SAS: The Special Air Service & the Malayan Emergency.** Alan Hoe. 1997. 29.95 (*0-85052-383-4*, Pub. by L Cooper Bks UK) Trans-Atl Phila.
Re-Entering the America Zone. Spencer Tunick. 1995. pap. 6.00 (*1-887128-13-1*) Soft Skull Pr.
Re-Entering the Sign: Articulating New Russian Culture. Ed. by Ellen E. Berry & Anesa Miller-Pogacar. LC 94-41428. 1995. pap. 19.95 (*0-472-08277-9*); text ed. 47.50 (*0-472-10301-6*) U of Mich Pr.
Re-Entering the Work World: Tools & Techniques for a Successful Job Search. Denise Bissonnette et al. 70p. (Orig.). student ed., spiral bd. 15.50 (*0-942071-11-5*) M Wright & Assocs.
Re-Entering the Work World: Tools & Techniques for a Successful Job Search. Denise Bissonnette et al. 103p. (Orig.). 1989. teacher ed., pap. text ed. 28.50 (*0-942071-10-7*) M Wright & Assocs.
Re-Entry: How to Turn Your Military Experience into Civilian Success. 2nd rev. ed. Keith O. Nyman. LC 89-28850. (Illus.). 192p. 1990. pap. 13.95 (*0-8117-2317-8*) Stackpole.
Re-Entry: Making the Transition from Missions to Life at Home. Peter Jordan. 150p. 1992. pap. 7.99 (*0-927545-40-3*) YWAM Pub.
***Re-Entry Vol. 1: Surviving Your Job Search in Higher Education If You're Not Related to a Trustee.** Janet L. Meyer. LC 97-72831. (Illus.). 64p. (Orig.). (C). 1997. pap. 10.00 (*1-890852-00-7*) Inst SW Pub.
Re-Entry into the Single Life. Jim Keelan. 1977. 6.00 (*0-9606554-1-7*) Comm Unltd.
Re-Entry Programs for Female Scientists. Alma E. Lantz et al. LC 79-25364. 220p. 1980. text ed. 49.95 (*0-275-90510-1*, C0510, Praeger Pubs) Greenwood.
Re-entry Technology & the Soviet Space Program (Some Personal Observations) Victor Yevsikov. Ed. by Barbara Dash. 112p. (Orig.). 1982. pap. text ed. 75.00 (*1-55831-001-0*) Delphic Associates.
***Re-Envisioning Medicare.** League of Women Voters Education Fund Staff. 15p. 1995. 3.99 (*0-89959-398-4*, 1037) LWVUS.
Re-Envisioning Past Musical Cultures: Ethnomusicology in the Study of Gregorian Chant. Peter Jeffery. x, 222p. 1995. pap. text ed. 13.95 (*0-226-39580-4*) U Ch Pr.
Re-Establish Your Focus. rev. ed. R. A. Jackson-Woods. (Illus.). 105p. 1993. pap. 9.95 (*1-883491-01-0*) Mature Minist.
Re-Establishing Agriculture As a Priority for Development Policy in Sub-Saharan Africa. Ed. by Awudu Abdulai & Christopher L. Delgado. 1995. write for info. (*0-89629-333-5*) Intl Food Policy.
Re-Establishing Justice: Legal Terms, Concepts & Procedures in the Hebrew Bible. Pietro Bovati. (Journal for the Study of the Old Testament Supplement Ser.: Vol. 105). 478p. 75.00 (*1-85075-290-7*, Pub. by Sheffield Acad UK) CUP Services.
***Re-Evaluating Residential Care.** Sheila M. Peace et al. LC 96-46517. (Rethinking Aging Ser.). 1997. write for info. (*0-335-19393-5*, Open Univ Pr); pap. write for info. (*0-335-19392-7*, Open Univ Pr) Taylor & Francis.
Re-Evaluation Counseling: A Component in Higher Education. Barbara Love. 1987. pap. 2.00 (*0-913937-28-2*) Rational Isl.
Re-Evaluation Counseling: A "Culturally Competent" Model for Social Liberation. Eduardo Aguilar. 1995. pap. 2.00 (*1-885357-14-1*) Rational Isl.
Re-Evaluation Counseling: Social Implications. Thomas J. Scheff. 1972. pap. 2.00 (*0-911214-48-8*) Rational Isl.
Re-Evaluation Counseling Community. Carol Carrig. 1972. pap. 2.00 (*0-911214-19-4*) Rational Isl.
Re-Evaluation of the Archaeological Sequences of Preclassic Chaipas see Studies in Middle American Anthropology
Re-Evaluation of the Eldership. Dayton Keese. 1967. pap. 3.95 (*0-89137-552-X*) Quality Pubns.
Re-Evaluation Therapy: Theoretical Framework. Bernard Somers. 1972. pap. 2.00 (*0-911214-49-6*) Rational Isl.
Re-Figuring Theology: The Rhetoric of Karl Barth. Stephen H. Webb. LC 90-34275. (SUNY Series in Rhetoric & Theology). 214p. (C). 1991. text ed. 64.50 (*0-7914-0570-2*); pap. text ed. 21.95 (*0-7914-0571-0*) State U NY Pr.

An Asterisk (*) at the beginning of an entry indicates that the title is appearing in BIP for the first time.

Re-Formed Jesuits, Vol. 1: A History of Changes in Jesuit Formation. Joseph M. Becker. LC 91-76517. 422p. 1992. pap. 19.95 (*0-89870-402-2*) Ignatius Pr.

***Re-Forming the Body: Religion, Community, & Modernity.** Philip A. Mellor & Chris Shilling. Ed. by Mike Featherstone. (Theory, Culture & Society Ser.). 256p. 1997. 75.00 (*0-8039-7722-0*) Sage.

***Re-Forming the Body: Religion, Community, & Modernity.** Philip A. Mellor & Chris Shilling. Ed. by Mike Featherstone. (Theory, Culture & Society Ser.). 256p. 1997. pap. 26.95 (*0-8039-7723-9*) Sage.

Re-forming the Narrative: Toward a Mechanics of Modernist Fiction. David Hayman. LC 87-47546. (Illus.). 240p. (C). 1987. 37.50 (*0-8014-2005-9*) Cornell U Pr.

Re-Forming Tradition: Presbyterians & Mainstream Protestantism. Milton J. Coalter et al. (Presbyterian Presence Ser.). 256p. (Orig.). 1992. pap. 20.00 (*0-664-25299-0*) Westminster John Knox.

Re-Forming Tradition Study Guide: Presbyterians & Mainstream Protestantism. Ed. by Milton J. Coalter et al. LC 92-12543. (Presbyterian Presence Ser.). (Orig.). 1992. pap. 3.00 (*0-664-25411-X*) Westminster John Knox.

Re-Framing the Pre-Raphaelites: Historical & Theoretical Essays. Ellen Harding. (Illus.). 301p. 1996. text ed. 76. 95 (*1-85928-314-4*, Pub. by Scolar Pr UK) Ashgate Pub Co.

***Re-Ignite Your Business: The Secret of Leading with Confidence, Ease & Certainty.** (Illus.). 126p. (Orig.). 1997. pap. 15.95 (*1-890331-00-7*) Confident Leader.

Re-Imagined Text: Shakespeare, Adaptation, & Eighteenth-Century Literary Theory. Jean I. Marsden. LC 94-3399. 208p. 1995. text ed. 30.00 (*0-8131-1901-4*) U Pr of Ky.

Re-Imaging Japanese Women. Ed. & Intro. by Anne E. Imamura. LC 95-21416. (Illus.). 397p. (C). 1996. 50.00 (*0-520-20262-7*) U CA Pr.

Re-Imaging Japanese Women. Ed. & Intro. by Anne E. Imamura. LC 95-21416. (Illus.). 397p. 1996. pap. 18.00 (*0-520-20263-5*) U CA Pr.

Re-Imagining Evangelization: Vision, Conversion, & Contagion. Patrick J. Brennan. 176p. (Orig.). 1994. pap. 13.95 (*0-8245-1433-5*) Crossroad NY.

Re-Imagining the Parish. Patrick J. Brennan. 161p. 1991. reprint ed. pap. 11.95 (*0-8245-1074-7*) Crossroad NY.

***Re-Imagining Therapy: Living Conversations & Relational Knowing.** Eero Riikonen & Gregory M. Smith. (Inquiries in Social Construction Ser.). 133p. (C). 1997. 65.00 (*0-8039-7653-4*, 76534); pap. 21.95 (*0-8039-7654-2*, 76542) Sage.

Re-Incarnation, the Only Mode of Propagation & a Romance of Fifteen Thousand Years. G. E. Bartholomew. 140p. 1993. spiral bd. 7.00 (*0-7873-0076-4*) Hlth Research.

Re-Interpretations: Etudes Sur le Seizieme Siecle. Ed. by John O'Brien. (Michigan Romance Studies: Vol. 15). (Illus.). 278p. (Orig.). (ENG & FRE.). 1995. pap. 15.00 (*0-939730-14-6*) Mich Romance.

Re-Interpretations: Seven Studies in Nineteenth-Century German Literature. Joseph P. Stern. LC 80-49684. 380p. reprint ed. pap. 108.30 (*0-318-34667-2*, 2031729) Bks Demand.

Re-Interpreting Brecht: His Influence on Contemporary Drama & Film. Ed. by Pia Kleber & Colin Visser. (Illus.). 234p. (C). 1992. pap. 19.95 (*0-521-42900-5*) Cambridge U Pr.

Re-Interpreting Curriculum Research: Images & Arguments. Ed. by Geoffrey Milburn et al. 200p. 1989. 70.00 (*1-85000-504-4*, Falmer Pr); pap. 33.00 (*1-85000-505-2*, Falmer Pr) Taylor & Francis.

Re-Inventing Anarchy, Again. Ed. by Howard J. Ehrlich. 400p. (Orig.). 1996. pap. 19.95 (*1-873176-88-0*, AK Pr San Fran) AK Pr Dist.

Re-Inventing Influence: How to Get Things Done in a World Without Authority. Mary Bragg. (Illus.). 225p. (Orig.). 1997. pap. 17.95 (*0-273-62313-3*) Pitman Publng.

***Re-Inventing Japan: Nation, Culture, Identity.** Tessa Morris-Suzuki. (Japan in the Modern World Ser.). 250p. (C). (gr. 13). 1997. text ed. 34.95 (*0-7656-0081-1*); pap. text ed. 19.95 (*0-7656-0082-X*) M E Sharpe.

Re-Inventing Marriage: A Re-View & Re-Vision. Christopher L. Webber. LC 94-10246. 288p. (Orig.). 1994. pap. 19.95 (*0-8192-1616-X*) Morehouse Pub.

Re-inventing the Jewish Past: European Jewish Intellectuals & the Zionist Return to History. David N. Myers. (Studies in Jewish History). 288p. 1995. 49.95 (*0-19-509842-0*) OUP.

Re-Inventing Theology. Ian Fraser. (C). 1990. text ed. 30. 00 (*0-947988-29-7*, Pub. by Wild Goose Pubns UK) St Mut.

Re: Joyce 'n Beckett. Ed. by Phyllis Carey & Ed Jewinski. LC 91-31853. xviii, 199p. 1992. 25.00 (*0-8232-1340-4*); pap. 19.95 (*0-8232-1341-2*) Fordham.

Re-Learning. James Humphrey. Ed. by John Silbersack. LC 76-8704. (Illus.). (Orig.). 1976. pap. 2.50 (*0-916912-01-9*) Hellcoal Pr.

Re-Made in Japan: Everyday Life & Consumer Taste in a Changing Society. Ed. by Joseph J. Tobin. (Illus.). 272p. 1994. pap. 18.00 (*0-300-06082-3*) Yale U Pr.

Re-Making It New: Contemporary American Poetry & the Modernist Tradition. Lynn Keller. (Cambridge Studies in American Literature & Culture: No. 26). 368p. 1988. text ed. 69.95 (*0-521-33283-4*) Cambridge U Pr.

Re-Making Love: The Feminization of Sex. Barbara Ehrenreich et al. LC 86-2074. 240p. 1987. pap. 10.00 (*0-385-18499-9*, Anchor NY) Doubleday.

Re-Making Poetry: Ted Hughes & a New Critical Psychology. Nick Bishop. LC 91-31179. 286p. 1991. text ed. 49.95 (*0-312-07200-7*) St Martin.

Re-Manufacturing the American Dream. D. J. Ogden. 1994. 18.95 (*0-533-10945-0*) Vantage.

Re-Membering: Meditations & Sermons for the Table of Jesus Christ. Joseph R. Jeter, Jr. 200p. (Orig.). 1996. pap. 18.99 (*0-8272-3215-2*) Chalice Pr.

Re-Membering: The Ministry of Welcoming Alienated & Inactive Catholics. Sarah Harmony. 80p. (Orig.). 1991. pap. 4.95 (*0-8146-1997-5*) Liturgical Pr.

Re-Membering & Re-Imagining. Ed. by Nancy J. Berneking & Pamela C. Joern. LC 95-16811. (Illus.). 264p. (Orig.). 1995. pap. 15.95 (*0-8298-1074-9*) Pilgrim OH.

Re-Nacer del Alma: Desarrollo de Su Potencial Cosmico. rev. ed. Robert E. Detzler. Ed. by Mariela Loreto-Perez. Tr. by Lolimar Gimenez. (Illus.). 150p. (SPA.). 1997. pap. 15.95 (*0-9640041-3-5*) S R C Pubng.

Re-Naming the Landscape. Ed. by Jurgen Kleist & Bruce A. Butterfield. LC 94-488. (Plattsburgh Studies in the Humanities: Vol. 3). 290p. (C). 1994. text ed. 53.95 (*0-8204-2465-X*) P Lang Pubng.

Re-Nurturing: Parenting Your Child As You Reparent Your Child Within. Janice G. Tracht. LC 94-29506. 175p. (Orig.). 1994. pap. 12.95 (*0-938179-39-X*) Mills Sanderson.

Re-Ordering the Universe: Picasso & Anarchism, 1897-1914. Patricia Leighten. (Illus.). 216p. (C). 1989. pap. text ed. 24.95 (*0-691-00284-3*) Princeton U Pr.

Re-Parenting the Adult Child. 1991. teacher ed. 12.00 (*0-9622150-2-3*); student ed. 14.95 incl. audio (*0-9622150-1-5*) Aurora VA.

***Re-Pitching the Tent: Re-Ordering the Church Building for Worship & Mission in the Now.** Richard Giles. (Illus.). 256p. (Orig.). 1996. pap. 19.95 (*1-85311-119-8*, Pub. by Canterbury Press Norwich UK) Morehouse Pub.

Re-Placing Women Psychology. Janis Bohan. 160p. (C). 1995. pap. text ed. 28.08 (*0-7872-1036-6*) Kendall-Hunt.

Re-Presenting the City: Ethnicity, Capital, & Culture in the Twenty-First Century Metropolis. Ed. by Anthony D. King. (Illus.). 272p. (C). 1996. 50.00 (*0-8147-4678-0*); pap. 18.95 (*0-8147-4679-9*) NYU Pr.

RE-presenting the Object. Terri M. Hopkins. (Illus.). 28p. (Orig.). 1994. pap. text ed. 5.00 (*0-914435-22-1*) Marylhurst Art.

Re-Reading Leavis: Culture & Literary Criticism. Gary Day. LC 96-24143. 1996. text ed. 49.95 (*0-312-16419-X*) St Martin.

Re-Reading Levinas. Ed. by Robert Bernasconi & Simon Critchley. LC 90-41833. (Studies in Continental Thought). 270p. 1991. 39.95 (*0-253-31179-9*); pap. 15.95 (*0-253-20624-3*) Ind U Pr.

Re-Reading Literature: New Critical Approaches to the Study of English. Sue Hackman & Barbara Marshall. (Illus.). 177p. 1992. pap. 22.50 (*0-340-51233-4*, Pub. by Hodder & Stoughton Ltd UK) Lubrecht & Cramer.

Re: Reading, Re: Writing, Re: Teaching Virginia Woolf Vol. 4: Selected Papers from the Fourth Annual Conference on Virginia Woolf. Ed. by Eileen Barrett & Patricia Cramer. (Illus.). 320p. (Orig.). (C). 1995. 69.50 (*0-944473-22-9*) Pace Univ Pr.

Re-Reading Sappho: Reception & Transmission. Ed. by Ellen Greene. (Classics & Contemporary Thought Ser.: Vol. 3). 224p. 1997. 40.00 (*0-520-20602-9*) U CA Pr.

Re-Reading Saussure: The Dynamics of Signs in Social Life. Paul J. Thibault. LC 96-2570. 384p. (C). 1996. pap. 19. 95 (*0-415-10411-4*); text ed. 74.95 (*0-415-10410-6*) Routledge.

Re-Reading the Constitution: New Narratives in the Political History of England's Long Nineteenth Century. Ed. by James Vernon. 280p. (C). 1996. text ed. 59.95 (*0-521-46474-9*); pap. text ed. 22.95 (*0-521-58941-X*) Cambridge U Pr.

Re-Reading the Postwar Period: An Intellectual Itinerary. Samir Amin. Tr. by Michael Wolfers from FRE. 192p. 1994. 26.00 (*0-85345-893-6*); pap. 17.00 (*0-85345-894-4*) Monthly Rev.

Re-Reading Wagner. Ed. by Reinhold Grimm & Jost Hermand. LC 92-35895. (Monatshefte Occasional Ser.: Vol. 13). (Illus.). 168p. (C). 1993. lib. bdg. 25.00 (*0-299-97076-0*) U of Wis Pr.

Re Rhenium Organorhenium Compounds. Gmelin Institute for Inorganic Chemistry of the Max-Planck-Society Staff. (Gmelin Handbook of Inorganic & Organometallic Chemistry Ser.; Binuclear Compounds 1 Ser.: Pt. 5). xii, 542p. 1994. text ed. 2,162.00 (*0-387-93695-5*) Spr-Verlag.

Re-Riding History: Horseback over the Santa Fe Trail. Curtiss Frank. LC 96-45607. (Illus.). 320p. (Orig.). 1997. 30.00 (*0-86534-254-7*) Sunstone Pr.

Re-Searching Black Music. Jon M. Spencer. LC 95-41760. 168p. (C). 1996. text ed. 25.00 (*0-87049-929-7*) U of Tenn Pr.

***Re-Situating Identities: The Politics of Race, Ethnicity & Culture.** Ed. by Vered Amit-Talai & Caroline Knowles. 320p. 1996. pap. 21.95 (*1-55111-071-7*) Broadview Pr.

Re-Souled: Spiritual Awakenings of a Psychiatrist & His Patient in Alcohol Recovery. William Goodson & Dale J. LC 93-25392. 160p. (Orig.). 1993. pap. 13.95 (*0-931055-95-4*) Innisfree Pr.

Re-Stating Social & Political Change. Colin Hay. LC 95-24919. 192p. 1996. 79.00 (*0-335-19387-0*, Open Univ Pr); pap. 24.95 (*0-335-19386-2*, Open Univ Pr) Taylor & Francis.

Re-Structuring the Government of New York City: Report of the Scott Commission Task Force on Jurisdiction & Structure. Edward N Costikyan & Maxwell Lehman. LC 72-86838. (Special Studies in U. S. Economic, Social & Political Issues). 1972. 24.50 (*0-275-06320-8*) Irvington.

***Re-Thinking Abortion: Psychology, Gender, Power & the Law.** Mary Boyle. LC 97-14933. (Women & Psychology Ser.). 176p. (C). 1997. pap. write for info. (*0-415-16365-X*); text ed. write for info. (*0-415-16364-1*) Routledge.

Re-Thinking Biblical Story & Myth: Selected Lectures at the Theodor Herzl Institute 1986-1995. Arnold M. Rothstein. 104p. (Orig.). pap. text ed. write for info. (*0-9639999-1-5*) Jay St Pubs.

Re-Thinking Educational Administration: T. B. Greenfield & His Critics. Ed. by Peter C. Gronn. 166p. (C). 1983. 45.00 (*0-7300-0003-6*, Pub. by Deakin Univ AT) St Mut.

Re-Thinking Management Education. Ed. by Robert French & Christopher Grey. 224p. (C). 1996. 65.00 (*0-8039-7782-4*); pap. 26.95 (*0-8039-7783-2*) Sage.

Re-Thinking Reason: New Perspectives in Critical Thinking. Ed. by Kerry S. Walters. LC 93-42902. (SUNY Series, Teacher Empowerment & School Reform). 265p. (C). 1994. text ed. 59.50 (*0-7914-2095-7*); pap. text ed. 19.95 (*0-7914-2096-5*) State U NY Pr.

Re-Thinking Social Research: Anti-Discrimination Approaches in Research Methodology. Ed. by Beth Humphries & Carole Truman. 226p. 1994. 55.95 (*1-85628-442-5*, Pub. by Avebury Pub UK) Ashgate Pub Co.

Re-Thinking Social Research: Anti-Discriminatory Approaches in Research Methodology. Ed. by Beth Humphries & Carole Truman. 224p. 1996. pap. 28.95 (*1-85972-463-9*, Pub. by Avebury Pub UK) Ashgate Pub Co.

Re-Thinking Theory: A Critique of Contemporary Literary Theory & An Alternative Account. Richard Freadman & Seumas Miller. 278p. (C). 1992. text ed. 69.95 (*0-521-38035-9*) Cambridge U Pr.

Re-Thinking University Teaching: A Framework for the Effective Use of Educational Technology. Diana Laurillard. LC 93-20258. 272p. (C). 1993. pap. 18.95 (*0-415-09289-2*, B2545, Routledge NY) Routledge.

Re Torrismondo. Torquato Tasso. Tr. by Maria P. Passaro. LC 96-47133. xx, 200p. (ENG & ITA.). 1996. 35.00 (*0-8232-1633-0*); pap. 19.95 (*0-8232-1634-9*) Fordham.

Re-Tracing the Old Spanish Trail North Branch. Ronald E. Kessler. (Illus.). 148p. (Orig.). 1995. pap. 12.95 (*0-9644056-1-X*) Adobe Village.

Re-Upholstery Techniques. 1995. 5.98 (*0-7858-0408-0*) Bk Sales Inc.

Re-Upholstery Techniques. Derek Balfour. 1986. 9.95 (*0-316-07932-4*) Little.

Re-Use of Contaminated Land: A Handbook of Risk Assessement. Tom Cairney. 228p. 1995. text ed. 105.00 (*0-471-94893-4*) Wiley.

Re-Use of the Muse Theater: A Study of Consumer Preferences. R. K. Piper. 20p. (Orig.). 1986. pap. 2.00 (*1-55719-089-5*) U NE CPAR.

Re-Uses: 2133 Ways to Recycle & Reuse the Things You Ordinarily Throw Away. Carolyn Jobs. (Illus.). 192p. 1982. pap. 9.95 (*0-517-54363-X*, Crown) Crown Pub Group.

Re-Valuing Cummings: Further Essays on the Poet. Norman Friedman. LC 95-46724. 200p. (C). 1996. lib. bdg. 34.95 (*0-8130-1443-3*) U Press Fla.

Re-Viewing British Cinema, 1900-1992: Essays & Interviews. Ed. by Wheeler W. Dixon. LC 93-1548. 288p. 1994. pap. 19.95 (*0-7914-1862-6*); text ed. 59.50 (*0-7914-1861-8*) State U NY Pr.

Re-Viewing Classics of Joyce Criticism. Ed. by Janet E. Dunleavy. 240p. 1991. text ed. 39.95 (*0-252-01774-9*); pap. text ed. 14.95 (*0-252-06166-7*) U of Ill Pr.

Re-Viewing Reception: Television, Gender, & Postmodern Culture. Lynne Joyrich. LC 96-6931. (Theories of Contemporary Culture Ser.: No. 18). (Illus.). 288p. 1996. pap. 18.95 (*0-253-21078-X*); text ed. 39.95 (*0-253-33076-9*) Ind U Pr.

Re Views. Frank M. Re. 80p. 1975. pap. 2.95 (*0-686-14654-9*) F M Re.

Re: Views: Re: Sponses. J. W. Curry. 42p. (Orig.). 1991. pap. 10.00 (*0-926935-49-6*) Runaway Spoon.

***Re-Visioning Design & Technology: Feminist Perspectives.** Joan Rothschild. 1997. pap. text ed. 18.95 (*0-941920-46-1*) Bay Pr.

Re-Visioning Feminism Around the World. LC 95-5135. 1995. pap. 50.00 (*1-55861-114-2*) Feminist Pr.

Re-Visioning Mission: The Catholic Church & Culture in Postmodern America. Richard G. Cote. (Isaac Hecker Studies in Religion & American Culture). 224p. 1996. pap. 14.95 (*0-8091-3645-7*, 3645-7) Paulist Pr.

***Re-Visioning Our Sources: Women's Spirituality in European Perspectives.** Ed. by Annette Esser et al. 200p. 1997. pap. 24.25 (*90-390-0224-X*, Pub. by KOK Pharos NE) Eisenbrauns.

Re-Visioning Psychology. James Hillman. LC 91-50502. 320p. 1992. pap. 14.50 (*0-06-090563-8*, CN563, PL) HarpC.

Re-Visioning Romanticism: British Women Writers, 1776-1837. Ed. by Carol S. Wilson & Joel Haefner. 344p. (Orig.). (C). 1994. text ed. 41.95 (*0-8122-3231-3*); pap. text ed. 17.95 (*0-8122-1421-8*) U of Pa Pr.

Re-Visioning Secondary Art Education. Frances L. Henry & Phyllis Luckenbach-Sawyers. (Illus.). 209p. (C). 1985. pap. text ed. 19.95 (*0-89641-152-4*) American Pr.

Re-Visioning the Earth: Guide to Opening the Healing Channels Mind & Body. Paul Devereux. 288p. 1996. pap. 12.00 (*0-684-80063-2*) S&S Trade.

***Re-Wiring Business: Uniting Management & the Web.** Tim McEachern & Bob O'Keefe. LC 97-17565. 288p. 1997. 29.95 (*0-471-17556-0*) Wiley.

Re: Working Eisenman. Peter Eisenman. (Illus.). 170p. 1993. 70.00 (*1-85490-112-5*) Academy Ed UK.

Re-Writing America: Vietnam Authors in Their Generation. Philip D. Beidler. LC 90-37804. 352p. 1991. 35.00 (*0-8203-1264-9*) U of Ga Pr.

Re-Zoom. Istvan Banyai. LC 95-14265. (Illus.). 64p. (J). 1995. pap. 13.99 (*0-670-86392-0*, Viking) Viking Penguin.

***REA: Write-Realtime Computerized Shorthand Writing System.** Robert McCormick. LC 97-5143. 1997. pap. text ed. 33.33 (*0-13-490004-9*) P-H.

R

Reach. Dan Bajema. (Illus.). (Orig.). 1996. pap. 11.00 (*1-880985-19-5*) Two Thirteen Sixty-one.

Reach & Grasp of Policy Analysis: Comparative Views of the Craft. Richard I. Hofferbert. LC 89-4899. (Institute for Social Science Research Monographs). 192p. 1990. pap. text ed. 24.95 (*0-8173-0464-9*) U of Ala Pr.

Reach Around the World. Bob Friesen & Sandy Friesen. 144p. (Orig.). 1994. pap. 12.99 (*1-56476-280-7*, 6-3280, Victor Bks) Chariot Victor.

Reach for a Star Activity Book, Unit 8. (Networks Ser.). 1991. 3.90 (*0-88106-763-6*, N244) Charlesbridge Pub.

Reach for a Star Activity Book (EV) EV, Unit 8. (Networks Ser.). 1991. 3.90 (*0-88106-762-8*) Charlesbridge Pub.

Reach for a Star Anthology, Unit 8. (Networks Ser.). 1991. 7.45 (*0-88106-761-X*, N241) Charlesbridge Pub.

Reach for Charisma: A Personal Guide for Body Language Use. Sidney Vernon. Ed. by Thomas Salter. (Illus.). 50p. (Orig.). 1983. 11.95 (*0-943150-08-6*); pap. 6.95 (*0-943150-03-5*); spiral bd. 6.95 (*0-943150-07-8*) Rovern Pr.

Reach for It: A Handbook of Health, Exercise & Dance Activities for Older Adults. 2nd ed. David Corbin & Josie Metal-Corbin. 324p. 1990. pap. 32.95 (*0-945483-00-7*) E Bowers Pub.

Reach for Joy: How to Find the Right Therapist & Therapy for You. Lynne D. Finney. 1995. pap. 16.95 (*0-89594-745-5*) Crossing Pr.

Reach for the Dream! Developing Individual Service Plans for Persons with Disabilities. 2nd ed. Dale DiLeo. 50p. 1994. pap. 20.00 (*1-883302-01-3*) Trning Res.

Reach for the Ground: The Downhill Struggle of Jeffrey Bernard. J. Bernard. 192p. 1996. pap. 16.95 (*0-7156-2726-0*, Pub. by Duckworth UK) Focus Pub-R Pullins.

Reach for the Heart. Maureen O'Connell. 1995. 17.95 (*0-8034-9093-3*, 094621) Bouregy.

Reach for the Moon: What Once was White. Samantha Abeel. LC 93-46417. (Illus.). 48p. (YA). 1994. 17.95 (*1-57025-013-8*) Pfeifer-Hamilton.

Reach for the Rainbow: Advanced Healing for Survivors of Sexual Abuse. Lynne D. Finney. 336p. 1992. pap. 14.00 (*0-399-51745-6*, Body Pr-Perigree) Berkley Pub.

Reach for the Sky. Paul Brickhill. (Illus.). 346p. 1992. reprint ed. lib. bdg. 23.95 (*0-89966-910-7*) Buccaneer Bks.

Reach for the Stars. Nancy Knight. 512p. 1994. mass mkt. 4.99 (*0-8217-4691-X*, Zebra Kensgtn) Kensgtn Pub Corp.

***Reach for the Stars: Pursuing Success Through Excellence.** Charles S. Lauer. LC 96-85313. 224p. (Orig.). 1996. pap. 13.95 (*1-881802-33-7*) CCI Bks WA.

Reach for the Stars: Write Your Own Horoscope. Nancy Shavick. 382p. (Orig.). 1994. pap. 12.00 (*0-380-77233-7*) Avon.

Reach for the Top: Women & the Changing Facts of Work Life. Nancy Nichols. 1994. text ed. 24.95 (*0-07-103580-X*) McGraw.

Reach for the Top: Women & the Changing Facts of Work Life. Intro. by Nancy A. Nichols. LC 93-34718. (Harvard Business Review Book Ser.). 208p. 1994. 24.95 (*0-87584-507-X*) Harvard Busn.

Reach for the Top: Women & the Changing Facts of Work Life. Ed. & Intro. by Nancy A. Nichols. 208p. 1996. pap. 13.95 (*0-87584-739-0*) Harvard Busn.

***Reach for the Top: Women & the Changing Facts of Work Life.** Nancy A. Nichols & Harvard Business School Press Staff. 1996. pap. text ed. 13.95 (*0-07-103853-1*) McGraw.

Reach for Tomorrow. Arthur C. Clarke. (Science Fiction Ser.). (Orig.). 1987. mass mkt. 4.95 (*0-345-35376-5*, Del Rey) Ballantine.

Reach for Tomorrow. Georgette Livingston. 1995. 17.95 (*0-8034-9105-0*, 095124) Bouregy.

Reach for Us. Dorothy Roeder. 168p. (Orig.). 1995. reprint ed. pap. 13.00 (*0-929385-69-1*) Light Tech Comns Servs.

Reach for Your Dreams in 5-D Stereograms. Stephen Schutz. LC 94-20653. 1994. 17.95 (*0-88396-388-4*) Blue Mtn Pr CO.

Reach for Your Spiritual Potential. Doris Black. 1986. pap. 6.50 (*0-89137-438-8*) Quality Pubns.

***Reach Higher.** Scottie Pippen & Greg Brown. (Illus.). 40p. (J). (gr. 2-6). 1997. 14.95 (*0-87833-981-7*) Taylor Pub.

***Reach Inside.** Grant E. Henson. Ed. by Ginny Ballor & Carrie Neumann. 40p. (Orig.). (C). 1996. pap. 3.00 (*1-882294-20-3*) Green Gate.

Reach of Art: A Study in the Prosody of Pope. Jacob H. Adler. LC 64-63900. (University of Florida Humanities Monographs: No. 16). 112p. reprint ed. pap. 32.00 (*0-7837-5030-7*, 2044699) Bks Demand.

Reach of Dialogue: Confirmation, Voice & Community. Rob Anderson et al. Ed. by Brenda Dervin. LC 94-29161. (Communication Series: Communication Alternatives). 336p. (C). 1994. text ed. 69.50 (*1-881303-00-4*); pap. text ed. 27.50 (*1-881303-01-2*) Hampton Pr NJ.

Reach of Poetry. Albert Cook. LC 94-44602. 349p. 1995. 29.95 (*1-55753-068-8*); pap. 17.95 (*1-55753-069-6*) Purdue U Pr.

***Reach of Rome.** Williams. LC 97-8191. 1997. 29.95 (*0-312-15631-6*) St Martin.

Reach of Song. Tom DeTitta. LC 90-14996. 96p. 1990. pap. 6.95 (*0-87797-199-4*) Cherokee.

An Asterisk (*) at the beginning of an entry indicates that the title is appearing in BIP for the first time.

R

Reach of Song: An Appalachian Drama. Tom DeTitta. (Illus.). 96p. (Orig.). 1990. pap. 6.95 (*0-685-45899-7*) Larlin Corp.

Reach of Song, 1989-1990. Ed. by Jo A. Adkins. 224p. 1991. per. 9.00 (*0-918279-16-X*) GA State Poetry.

***Reach of the Mind.** Joseph B. Rhine. Date not set. write for info. (*0-688-05399-8*) Morrow.

Reach of the State: Sketches of the Chinese Body Politic. Vivienne Shue. LC 87-27447. 192p. 1988. 32.50 (*0-8047-1458-4*); pap. 11.95 (*0-8047-1804-0*) Stanford U Pr.

Reach of Tide, Ring of History: A Coulmbia River Voyage. Sam McKinney. (Illus.). 176p. 1987. 19.95 (*0-87595-196-1*) Oregon Hist.

Reach Out & Sell Someone: Phone Your Way to Success Through the Goodman System of Telemarketing. Gary S. Goodman. 141p. 1983. 12.95 (*0-13-753632-1*) P-H.

Reach out & Teach: Meeting the Training Needs of Parents of Visually & Multiply Handicapped Young Children. (Illus.). 1985. 40.00 (*0-89128-128-2*) Am Foun Blind.

Reach Out & Teach Someone: ESL Games & Activities Using Your Local Telephone Directory. Sharon Elwell. 52p. (Orig.). 1991. pap. text ed. 8.95 (*0-9626210-1-3*) Rattle Ok Pubns.

Reach Out & Touch Someone. Jeannie Griffin. 32p. (Orig.). 1989. pap. 2.95 (*0-685-44896-7*) Jeannie Griffin.

Reach Out for New Life. Robert H. Schuller. 240p. 1991. 12.95 (*1-879989-02-6*) New Hope Pub.

Reach Out for Your Dreams. Ed. by Susan P. Schutz. LC 80-65752. (Illus.). 64p. (Orig.). 1980. pap. 7.95 (*0-88396-078-8*) Blue Mtn Pr CO.

Reach Out to Touch. Geraldine G. Harder. 64p. 1995. pap. 12.95 (*0-9646678-0-0*) M & G Harder Pubs.

***Reach the Internet!** David B. Hecht & David Diskin. (Orig.). Date not set. pap. 12.95 (*0-9656606-0-5*) InReach Internet.

Reach Their Goal! Tristan Howard. (Leftovers Ser.: No. 4). (J). (gr. 4-7). 1996. pap. text ed. 2.99 (*0-590-92133-9*) Scholastic Inc.

Reach Your Career Dreams: CareerTrack's Handbook for Professional Women. 216p. 1986. 15.95 (*0-943066-19-0*) CareerTrack Pubns.

Reach Your Goal Math: Grades 1-2. Avaril Wedemeyer & Joyce Cejka. 1988. 5.95 (*0-89108-188-7*, 8815) Love Pub Co.

Reach Your Goals in Spite of the Old Boy Network: A Guide for African American Employees. Mike Duncan. Ed. by Nancy G. Reid & Delores Goode. LC 90-93039. 190p. 1990. 16.95 (*1-878647-00-8*) Duncan & Duncan.

Reaches of Empire. Suvendrini Perera. 224p. 1991. text ed. 39.50 (*0-231-07578-2*) Col U Pr.

Reaches of the Heart: A Biography of Charles White. Frances B. White & Anne Scott. 272p. 1994. 22.95 (*1-56980-016-2*) Barricade Bks.

Reaching. Connie Hunt. LC 82-18588. (Illus.). 96p. 1982. pap. 6.95 (*0-9609442-0-6*) Pulsar Pub.

Reaching. Julie McDonald. LC 88-61287. 202p. (Orig.). 1988. pap. 7.95 (*0-930942-12-4*) Sutherland MA.

Reaching: Poems by George P. Elliott. limited ed. George P. Elliot. (Santa Susana Press Ser.). 1979. 35.00 (*0-937048-21-6*) Santa Susana.

Reaching: The Journey to Fulfillment. Morton Kelsey. LC 94-16618. 224p. 1994. pap. 14.99 (*0-8066-2728-X*, Augsburg) Augsburg Fortress.

***Reaching a Critical Mass: A Critical Analysis of Popular Television.** Robert Abelman. LC 97-22936. (Communication Ser.). 250p. 1997. write for info. (*0-8058-2199-6*) L Erlbaum Assocs.

***Reaching a Critical Mass: A Critical Analysis of Popular Television.** Robert Abelman. LC 97-22936. (Communication Ser.). 250p. 1997. pap. write for info. (*0-8058-2200-3*) L Erlbaum Assocs.

***Reaching a Generation for Christ: A Comprehensive Guide to Youth Ministry.** Ed. by Richard R. Dunn & Mark H. Senter, III. 704p. 1997. 35.99 (*0-8024-9348-3*) Moody.

Reaching a Multicultural Student Community: A Handbook for Academic Librarians. Karen E. Downing et al. LC 93-548. (The Greenwood Library Management Collection). 240p. 1993. text ed. 55.00 (*0-313-27912-8*, DRD) Greenwood.

Reaching a New Generation: Strategies for Tomorrow's Church. Alan J. Roxburgh. LC 92-34569. (Illus.). 140p. (Orig.). 1993. pap. 9.99 (*0-8308-1340-3*, 1340) InterVarsity.

Reaching Across Boundaries of Culture & Class: Widening the Scope of Psychotherapy. Ed. by RoseMarie P. Foster et al. LC 95-52039. 296p. 1996. 35.00 (*1-56821-487-1*) Aronson.

Reaching Adolescents. Arthea J. Reed. LC 84-12905. 490p. (C). 1985. pap. text ed. 32.75 (*0-03-069342-X*) HB Coll Pubs.

Reaching Adolescents: Interdating, Intermarriage, & Jewish Identity. UAHC - CCAR Commission on Jewish Outreach Staff. 138p. 1990. pap. 10.00 (*0-8074-0442-X*, 280055) UAHC.

Reaching Adolescents: The Young Adult Book & the School. Arthea J. Reed. (Illus.). 502p. (Orig.). (C). 1993. text ed. 61.00 (*0-02-398861-4*, Macmillan Coll) P-H.

Reaching Adult Learners with Whole Language Strategies. Tirza Kroeker & Margaret Henrichs. LC 92-24379. 231p. 1993. pap. text ed. 21.95 (*1-878450-33-6*) R Owen Pubs.

Reaching Agreement with the IMF: The Nigerian Negotiations, 1983-1986. Thomas J. Biersteker. (Pew Case Studies in International Affairs). 54p. (C). 1989. pap. text ed. 3.50 (*1-56927-205-0*) Geo U Inst Dplmcy.

Reaching All Students with Mathematics. Ed. by Gilbert Cuevas & Mark Driscoll. LC 92-44679. (Illus.). 244p. (Orig.). 1993. pap. 15.00 (*0-87353-357-7*) NCTM.

***Reaching & Teaching All Children: Grassroots Efforts That Work.** Ed. by Robert L. Sinclair & Ward J. Ghory. LC 97-4787. 168p. 1997. 49.95 (*0-8039-6528-1*); pap. 21.95 (*0-8039-6529-X*) Sage.

Reaching & Teaching Diverse Library User Groups. Ed. by Teresa B. Mensching. (Library Orientation Ser.: No. 19). 169p. 1989. pap. 35.00 (*0-87650-258-3*) Pierian.

***Reaching & Teaching the Kids Today.** Carol Hoffman. 288p. (Orig.). 1996. pap. 15.95 (*1-56762-063-9*) Modern Learn Pr.

Reaching Audiences: A Guide to Better Media Writing. Katherine C. McAdams & Jan J. Elliott. LC 95-40774. 1996. pap. text ed. 33.00 (*0-02-378351-6*, Macmillan Coll) P-H.

***Reaching Back.** Alice Z. Chapin. LC 96-32033. 160p. 1997. pap. 14.99 (*1-55870-454-X*, Betrwy Bks) F & W Pubns Inc.

Reaching Back for the Neverendings. Mario R. Padilla. 100p. 1993. 8.95 (*1-881168-32-8*) Red Danceflr.

***Reaching Beyond Race.** Paul M. Sniderman. LC 97-14658. 1997. 22.95 (*0-674-14578-X*) HUP.

Reaching Children in War: Sudan, Uganda & Mozambique. Cole P. Dodge & Magne Raundelen. 160p. 1992. pap. 23.00 (*82-90373-61-9*) Taylor & Francis.

***Reaching Children Through Play Therapy: An Experential Approach.** Carol C. Norton & Byron E. Norton. (Illus.). 378p. (Orig.). 1997. pap. text ed. 19.95 (*0-9644849-4-3*) Pendleton Clay.

Reaching Decisions. Howard H. Brinton. (C). 1952. pap. 3.00 (*0-87574-065-0*) Pendle Hill.

Reaching Exercises: The IWWG Workshop Book. D. H. Melhem. LC 81-67876. 1981. reprint ed. 10.95 (*0-935468-04-8*) Dovetail.

Reaching for a Better Standard: English School Inspection & the Dilemma of Accountability for American Public Schools. Thomas Wilson. (School Reform Ser.: Vol. 8). 288p. (C). 1995. text ed. 61.00 (*0-8077-3497-7*); pap. text ed. 27.95 (*0-8077-3496-9*) Tchrs Coll.

Reaching for a Feeling. Bruce Johnson. 1976. pap. 2.00 (*0-686-14931-9*) Goranson Pr.

Reaching for a Star: The Final Campaign for Alaska Statehood. Gerald E. Bowkett. Ed. by Sue Mattson. LC 89-1563. (Illus.). 162p. (Orig.). (YA). (gr. 9-12). 1989. 22.95 (*0-945397-04-6*); pap. 14.95 (*0-945397-05-4*) Epicenter Pr.

Reaching for Answers: Bill Belton's Story. Joseph M. Lubow. (Illus.). 240p. (Orig.). 1998. pap. 10.95 (*0-89407-093-2*) Strawberry Hill.

Reaching for Art. Guy Eglinton. (Essay Index Reprint Ser.). 1977. 15.95 (*0-8369-0408-7*) Ayer.

***Reaching for College: Directory & Case Studies of College-School Partnerships, 2 vols., Set.** Gregory Henschel & Maureen McLaughlin. (Illus.). 275p. (C). 1996. pap. 50.00 (*0-614-18670-6*) DIANE Pub.

Reaching for God's Highest. Clyde T. Bryant. 240p. (Orig.). 1987. pap. write for info. (*0-9618387-0-1*) Clyde T Bryant.

Reaching for Heaven on Earth: The Theological Meaning of Economics. Robert H. Nelson. 320p. 1993. pap. 16.95 (*0-8226-3024-9*) Littlefield.

Reaching For Infinity Further: Further Puzzles, Paradoxes & Brain Teasers. Stan Gibilisco. (Illus.). 140p. 1990. 16.95 (*0-8306-8327-5*, 3327); pap. 9.95 (*0-8306-3327-8*) McGraw-Hill Prof.

Reaching for Rainbows: Resources for Creative Worship. Ann Weems. LC 80-19330. 156p. 1980. pap. 13.00 (*0-664-24355-X*, Westminster) Westminster John Knox.

Reaching for the Crescent Moon. H. Rogers. 8.50 (*1-85792-123-2*, Pub. by Christian Focus UK) Spring Arbor Dist.

***Reaching for the Dream: Monologues on Black Life.** 1995. pap. write for info. (*0-435-08148-9*, 08148) Heinemann.

Reaching for the Gold. Everett Beich. 125p. 1992. pap. 9.95 (*0-9631098-0-4*) Beich Pubng.

Reaching for the High Frontier: The American Pro-Space Movement, 1972-84. Michael A. Michaud. LC 86-91456. 462p. 1986. text ed. 59.95 (*0-275-92151-4*, C2151, Praeger Pubs) Greenwood.

Reaching for the Light: A Guide for Ritual Abuse Survivors & Their Therapists. Emilie P. Rose. LC 95-52521. 264p. (Orig.). 1996. pap. 14.95 (*0-8298-1079-X*) Pilgrim OH.

Reaching for the Mainland & Selected New Poems: 9531050. Judith O. Cofer. LC 95-31050. 88p. (Orig.). (C). 1995. pap. 9.00 (*0-927534-55-X*) Biling Rev-Pr.

Reaching for the Moon. Gerald Bauldock. LC 88-92848. 303p. (Orig.). (YA). (gr. 7-12). 1989. pap. text ed. 14.95 (*0-9621728-0-4*) B-Dock Pr.

Reaching for the Moon: On Asian Religious Paths. Kenneth W. Morgan. LC 90-751. 207p. 1990. 17.50 (*0-89012-059-5*) Col U Pr.

Reaching for the Olive Branch: UNRWA & Peace in the Middle East. Milton Viorst. LC 89-13487. (Illus.). 128p. 1989. 10.95 (*0-253-36256-3*); pap. 4.95 (*0-253-20580-8*, MB-580) Ind U Pr.

Reaching for the Oversoul. Eugene G. Jussek. LC 94-17740. 160p. (Orig.). 1994. pap. 11.00 (*0-89254-027-3*) Nicolas-Hays.

Reaching For the Skies. 1995. pap. 26.95 (*1-85490-250-4*) Academy Ed UK.

Reaching for the Stars. Troy Aikman et al. LC 93-34386. 1993. 150.00 (*0-87833-075-5*) Taylor Pub.

Reaching for the Stars. large type ed. Lucy Walker. 1981. 12.00 (*0-7089-0636-2*) Ulverscroft.

Reaching for the Stars. Nora Waln. (American Biography Ser.). 380p. 1991. reprint ed. lib. bdg. 79.00 (*0-7812-8400-7*) Rprt Serv.

***Reaching for the Stars: If It Is to Be, It Is up to Me!** Leslee A. Michaels. LC 96-80052. (Illus.). 64p. (Orig.). 1997. pap. 12.95 (*1-890059-66-8*) Happy Hrt Pr.

***Reaching for the Stars: The Illustrated History of Manned Spaceflight.** Peter Bond. 1997. pap. text ed. 19.95 (*0-304-34953-4*) Cassell.

Reaching for the Stars: The Story of Astronaut Training & the Lunar Landing. Stanley H. Goldstein. LC 87-6937. 208p. 1987. text ed. 55.00 (*0-275-92601-X*, C2601, Praeger Pubs) Greenwood.

Reaching for the Stars: Tom Hanks. Rosemary Wallner. LC 94-22191. (Reaching for the Stars Ser.). (J). (gr. 1-8). 1994. 13.98 (*1-56239-338-3*) Abdo & Dghtrs.

Reaching for the Stars Series: A Minicourse for Education of Gifted Students, 10 vols., Set. Incl. Bk. 1. Characteristics of the Gifted/Talented Students. Jackie Mallis & Alison Hartman. 106p. 1979. per., pap. 17.95 (*0-86617-001-4*); Bk. 2. Needs of the Gifted/Talented Students. Jackie Mallis & Elizabeth Duke. 70p. 1979. per., pap. 17.95 (*0-86617-002-2*); Bk. 3. Underachievers among the Gifted/Talented Students. Jackie Mallis & Alison Hartman. 50p. 1979. per., pap. 17.95 (*0-86617-003-0*); Bk. 4. Searching for the Handicapped among Gifted/Talented Students. Nancy Alexander. 62p. 1979. per., pap. 17.95 (*0-86617-004-9*); Bk. 5. Searching for the Disadvantaged among Gifted/Talented Students. Jackie Mallis & Elizabeth Duke. 56p. 1979. per., pap. 17.95 (*0-86617-005-7*); Bk. 6. Using Knowledge about Intelligence. Jackie Mallis & Alison Hartman. 70p. 1979. per., pap. 17.95 (*0-86617-006-5*); Bk. 7. Using Knowledge about Creativity. Jackie Mallis & Alison Hartman. 57p. 1979. per., pap. 17.95 (*0-86617-007-3*); Bk. 8. Providing Enrichment Activities for the Gifted/Talented Students. Jackie Mallis. 125p. 1979. per., pap. 17.95 (*0-86617-008-1*); Bk. 9. Providing Programs for the Gifted/Talented Students. Jackie Mallis & Alison Hartman. 169p. 1979. per., pap. 17.95 (*0-86617-009-X*); Bk. 10. Providing Guidance & Counseling for the Gifted/Talented Students. , Set. Jackie Mallis & Alison Hartman. 167p. 1979. per., pap. 17.95 (*0-86617-010-3*); 1979. Set per., pap. 145.54 (*0-86617-000-6*) Multi Media TX.

***Reaching for the Sun: How Plants Work.** John King. 256p. 1997. text ed. 54.95 (*0-521-55148-X*); pap. text ed. 16.95 (*0-521-58738-7*) Cambridge U Pr.

Reaching for Wisdom. Jude LaClaire. (Life Weaving Ser.: Vol. 4). (Illus.). 64p. 1995. spiral bd. write for info. (*0-9629385-4-8*) Heartlnd Personal.

Reaching Health for All. Ed. by Jon E. Rohde et al. (Illus.). 500p. 1993. 12.95 (*0-19-563236-2*) OUP.

Reaching High: The Psychology of Spiritual Living. Marvin Gawryn. LC 80-24306. 200p. 1981. pap. 7.95 (*0-938380-01-X*) Highreach WA.

Reaching High-Risk Families: Intensive Family Preservation in Human Services. Ed. by Jill Kinney et al. (Modern Applications of Social Work Ser.). 224p. (Orig.). (C). 1990. pap. text ed. 22.95 (*0-202-36058-X*); lib. bdg. 39.95 (*0-202-36057-1*) Aldine de Gruyter.

Reaching Home: Pacific Salmon, Pacific People. Tom Jay & Bradford Matsen. LC 94-25182. (Illus.). 144p. 1994. 37.95 (*0-88240-449-0*) Alaska Northwest.

Reaching Home: Pacific Salmon, Pacific People. Tom Jay & Bradford Matsen. LC 94-25182. (Illus.). 144p. 1995. pap. 26.95 (*0-88240-465-2*) Alaska Northwest.

Reaching in Silence. Kay Closson. (Contemporary Poets Ser.: No. 2). 56p. (Orig.). 1983. pap. 3.95 (*0-916982-27-0*, RL227) CCR Pubns.

Reaching India's Poor: Non-Governmental Approaches to Community Health. Ed. by Saroj Pachauri. LC 94-4731. 420p. 1994. 29.95 (*0-8039-9172-X*) Sage.

Reaching into Thought: The Minds of the Great Apes. Ed. by Anne E. Russon et al. (Illus.). 500p. (C). 1996. text ed. 84.95 (*0-521-47168-0*) Cambridge U Pr.

Reaching Just Settlements: Land Claims in British Columbia. Frank Cassidy. 153p. 1991. pap. text ed. 15.95 (*0-88645-122-1*, Pub. by Inst Res Pub CN) Ashgate Pub Co.

Reaching Kids Before HS. David R. Veerman. 204p. 1995. pap. 9.99 (*1-56476-495-8*, 6-3495, Victor Bks) Chariot Victor.

Reaching Learners Through Telecommunications: Management & Leadership Strategies for Higher Education. Becky Duning et al. LC 92-30051. (Higher & Adult Education Ser.). 325p. text ed. 36.95 (*1-55542-501-1*) Jossey-Bass.

Reaching Marginal Students: A Primary Concern for School Renewal. Robert L. Sinclair & Ward J. Ghory. LC 86-63773. (NSSE Series on Contemporary Educational Issues). 165p. (C). 1987. 30.70 (*0-8211-1860-9*) McCutchan.

***Reaching Maturity, What Are My Options?** large type ed. Jean Davis. LC 97-93390. 134p. (Orig.). 1997. pap. 12.95 (*0-9658233-2-6*) Angel Wrks LA.

Reaching Muslims for Christ. William Saal. 223p. 1993. pap. 10.99 (*0-8024-7322-9*) Moody.

***Reaching New Highs: Alternative Therapies for Drug Addicts.** H. K. Heggenhougen. 224p. 1997. 39.95 (*0-7657-0036-0*) Aronson.

Reaching Out. 6th ed. Johnson. 400p. 1996. pap. 34.00 (*0-205-19767-1*) Allyn.

Reaching Out: A Directory of National Organizations Related to Maternal & Child Health. 208p. 1994. pap. text ed. write for info. (*1-57285-001-9*) Nat Ctr Educ.

Reaching Out: A Guide to EAP Casefinding. 92p. (Orig.). 1983. pap. text ed. 9.95 (*0-9610026-0-3*) Perf Resource Pr.

Reaching Out: A History of the Rotary Club of Marquette, Michigan 1916-1981. Richard F. O'Dell. Ed. by Pryse H. Duerfeldt. LC 82-60037. (Illus.). 254p. 1982. 13.00 (*0-9609764-0-X*) Rotary Club.

Reaching Out: A Story of the General Federation of Women's Clubs. Mary J. Houde. Ed. by Vicki Montville. (Illus.). 450p. 1989. text ed. 34.95 (*0-916371-08-5*) Mobium Pr.

Reaching Out: Caring Altruism, & Prosocial Behavior, Vol. 7. Ed. & Intro. by Bill Puka. LC 94-462. 360p. 1994. Vol.7. text ed. 65.00 (*0-8153-1554-6*) Garland.

***Reaching Out: How Campus Leaders Can Communicate More Effectively with Their Constituencies.** Linda L. Weimer et al. LC 97-1218. (Orig.). 1996. pap. 37.95 (*0-912150-38-6*) Magna Pubns.

Reaching Out: Preventing Youth Suicide. Girl Scouts of the U. S. A. Staff. (Contemporary Issues Ser.). 16p. 1987. pap. 1.75 (*0-88441-464-7*, 26-824) Girl Scouts USA.

Reaching Out: The Prevention of Drug Abuse Through Increased Human Interaction. Gerald D. Edwards. 217p. 1985. reprint ed. pap. 12.00 (*0-88268-029-3*, Pulse Bks) Station Hill Pr.

Reaching Out: The Three Movements of the Spiritual Life. Henri J. Nouwen. LC 86-2901. (Illus.). 172p. 1986. pap. 9.95 (*0-385-23682-4*, Image Bks) Doubleday.

Reaching Out: Utilization of Mental Resources in El Paso & Mexico. Guido A. Barrientos. 1997. pap. text ed. 15.00 (*0-87404-240-2*) Tex Western.

Reaching Out Vol. 1: Ross Bible Church History. unabridged ed. Alfred C. Miller. (Illus.). 36p. (Orig.). 1992. pap. 7.00 (*0-9624215-4-5*) A C Miller.

***Reaching Out for Love.** large type ed. Peggy Gaddis. (Large Print Ser.). 304p. 1996. 25.99 (*0-7089-3552-4*) Ulverscroft.

***Reaching Out in Word & Deed.** Joel D. Kline. LC 90-21875. (Evangelism Study Ser.: No. 1). 94p. 1991. reprint ed. pap. 26.80 (*0-608-04178-5*, 2064912) Bks Demand.

Reaching out Just a Little Farther. rev. ed. Meta J. Mereday. (Illus.). 64p. 1995. pap. 15.00 (*0-9647131-9-5*) Emmae.

Reaching Out to Children with FAS - FAE: A Handbook for Teachers, Counselors, & Parents Who Live & Work with Children Affected by Fetal Alcohol Syndrome & Fetal Alcohol Effects. Diane Davis. LC 94-11953. 1994. pap. 27.95 (*0-87628-857-3*) Ctr Appl Res.

Reaching Out to Lonely Kids: A Guide to Surviving & Loving the Children in Your Neighborhood. Valerie Bell. 176p. 1994. pap. 8.99 (*0-310-40541-6*) Zondervan.

Reaching Out to Moscow: From Confrontation to Cooperation. Marshall Brement. LC 91-18920. 208p. 1991. text ed. 49.95 (*0-275-94073-X*, C4073, Praeger Pubs) Greenwood.

Reaching Out to Others. (Pocket Power Ser.). 16p. (Orig.). 1985. pap. 1.25 (*0-89486-311-8*, 5400B) Hazelden.

***Reaching Out to Troubled Kids: 15 Helpful Ways to Bridge the Gap Between Parents, Teachers, & Kids.** 2nd ed. Kathleen S. Fad. (Illus.). 72p. 1996. pap. 9.50 (*1-57035-075-2*, 57REACH) Sopris.

Reaching Out to Troubled Youth. rev. ed. Dwight Spotts & David R. Veerman. 240p. 1994. pap. 9.99 (*1-56476-279-3*, 6-3279, Victor Bks) Chariot Victor.

Reaching Out Without Dumbing Down: A Theology of Worship for the Turn-of-the-Century Culture. Marva J. Dawn. 327p. (Orig.). 1995. pap. 18.00 (*0-8028-4102-3*) Eerdmans.

Reaching People: The Structure of Neighborhood Services. Ed. by Daniel Thursz & Joseph L. Vigilante. LC 78-107121. (Social Service Delivery Systems Ser.: No. 3). (Illus.). 277p. reprint ed. pap. 79.00 (*0-8357-8400-2*, 2034674) Bks Demand.

Reaching Potentials: Appropriate Curriculum & Assessment for Young Children, Vol. 1. Ed. by Sue Bredekamp & Teresa Rosegrant. LC 92-85332. (Illus.). 169p. 1992. pap. text ed. 7.00 (*0-935989-53-6*, 225) Natl Assn Child Ed.

Reaching Russia. C. Philip Slate & S. E. Granberg. 71p. 1994. pap. 2.95 (*0-89112-156-0*) Abilene Christ U.

Reaching Students: Teachers' Ways of Knowing. Vivienne Collison. LC 95-50186. (Illus.). 136p. 1996. 42.95 (*0-8039-6227-4*); pap. 18.95 (*0-8039-6228-2*) Corwin Pr.

Reaching Tender Hearts, 3 vols. Lynn Groth. Ed. by R. Grunze. (Devotional Readings Ser.). (Illus.). (J). (ps). 1988. pap. text ed. write for info. (*0-938272-45-4*) WELS Board.

Reaching Tender Hearts, Vol. 1. Lynn Groth. Ed. by Richard Grunze. (Devotional Readings Ser.). 157p. (J). (ps). 1987. pap. 9.99 (*0-938272-42-X*, 06N2261) WELS Board.

Reaching Tender Hearts, Vol. 2. Lynn Groth. Ed. by Richard Grunze. (Devotional Readings Ser.). (Illus.). 176p. (J). (ps). 1988. pap. 9.99 (*0-938272-43-8*, 06N2262) WELS Board.

Reaching Tender Hearts, Vol. 3. Lynn Groth. Ed. by R. Grunze. Tr. by Lawrence May & Lawrence Steele. (Devotional Readings Ser.). (Illus.). 163p. (J). (gr. k). 1988. pap. text ed. 9.99 (*0-938272-44-6*, 06N2260) WELS Board.

Reaching That Peak: Seventy-Five Years of the Dartmouth Outing Club. David O. Hooke. LC 86-30468. (Illus.). 512p. 1987. 45.00 (*0-914659-24-3*) Phoenix Pub.

Reaching the Affect: Style in the Psychodynamic Therapies. Emanuel F. Hammer. LC 89-38897. 232p. 1990. 30.00 (*0-87668-818-0*) Aronson.

Reaching the Aged: Social Services in Forty-Four Countries. Ed. by Morton I. Teicher et al. LC 79-18525. (Social Service Delivery Systems Ser.: No. 4). 256p. reprint ed. pap. 73.00 (*0-8357-8396-0*, 2034670) Bks Demand.

Reaching the Assetless Poor: Projects & Strategies for Their Self-Reliant Development. Cheryl A. Lassen. (Special Series on Landlessness & Near-Landlessness: No. 6). 68p. (Orig.). (C). 1980. pap. text ed. 6.75 (*0-86731-073-1*) Cornell CIS RDC.

Reaching the Autistic Child: A Parent Training Program. Martin A. Kozloff. LC 83-25228. 245p. 1983. reprint ed. pap. text ed. 14.95 (*0-914797-02-6*) Brookline Bks.

Reaching the Campus Changing the World: "College Ministry That Connects" 65p. 1995. ring bd. 16.00 (*1-885702-56-6*, 7201e) WSN Pr.

An Asterisk (*) at the beginning of an entry indicates that the title is appearing in BIP for the first time.

*__Reaching the Child with Autism Through Art.__ Toni. (Illus.). 100p. (Orig.). 1996. pap. 19.95 (*1-885477-23-6*) Fut Horizons.

__Reaching the Disadvantaged Learner.__ 6th ed. Work Conference on Urban Education Staff. Ed. by Harry A. Passow. LC 69-11364. 374p. reprint ed. pap. 106.60 (*0-317-41868-8*, 2026054) Bks Demand.

__Reaching the Full Cost of Quality in Early Childhood Programs.__ Ed. by Barbara Willer. 109p. 1990. pap. text ed. 6.00 (*0-935989-42-0*, NAEYC #137) Natl Assn Child Ed.

__Reaching the Gifted Underachiever: Program Strategy & Design.__ Patricia L. Supplee. (Education & Psychology of the Gifted Ser.). 272p. (C). 1990. text ed. 43.00 (*0-8077-3020-3*); pap. text ed. 22.95 (*0-8077-3019-X*) Tchrs Coll.

__Reaching the Global Market Through Free Zones.__ Ed. by Richard L. Bolin. 142p. 1991. pap. 40.00 (*0-945951-06-X*) Flagstaff Inst.

__Reaching the Goals: Goal Six, Adult Literacy & Lifelong Learning.__ 1994. lib. bdg. 250.00 (*0-8490-5741-8*) Gordon Pr.

__Reaching the Hard to Teach: Strategy Booklet.__ Judy W. Wood. 44p. 1994. pap. text ed. 6.95 (*1-886021-00-7*) J W Wood.

__Reaching the Hard to Teach: Strategy Booklet & VHS Videocassette Packet.__ Judy W. Wood. 1994. 49.95 incl. vhs (*1-886021-02-3*) J W Wood.

*__Reaching the Heart of God: The Key to Revival.__ Mac Owen & J. Arthur Lagoe. LC 96-85872. 192p. (Orig.). 1996. pap. 8.00 (*0-9641761-1-4*) Aletheia WA.

*__Reaching the Heart of Your Teen: Basic Communication Between Teen & Parent.__ Gary Ezzo & Anne M. Ezzo. LC 96-46703. 206p. (Orig.). 1997. pap. 9.99 (*1-57673-022-0*, Multnomah Bks) Multnomah Pubs.

__Reaching the Hidden Majority: A Leader's Guide to Career Preparation for Disabled Women & Girls.__ Mary Hopkins-Best et al. LC 88-1303. 224p. 1988. 26.95 (*0-910328-42-0*) Sulzburger & Graham Pub.

__Reaching the Peak Performance Zone: How to Motivate Yourself & Others to Excel.__ Gerald Kushel. LC 94-21825. 176p. 1994. 21.95 (*0-8144-0222-4*) AMACOM.

__Reaching the Stars.__ Ruchoma Shain. 1990. 16.95 (*0-87306-513-1*) Feldheim.

*__Reaching the Top: Using the Art of Persuasion to Develop Excellence in Yourself & Others.__ Zig Ziglar. 1997. 12.99 (*0-88365-988-3*) Galahad Bks.

__Reaching the Unchurched.__ Walt Kallestad & Tim Wright. 96p. Date not set. pap. 99.95 (*0-8066-2760-3*) Augsburg Fortress.

__Reaching the Underserved: Mental Health Needs of Neglected Populations.__ Ed. by Lonnie R. Snowden. LC 82-10722. (Sage Annual Reviews of Community Mental Health Ser.: No. 3). 303p. 1982. reprint ed. pap. 86.40 (*0-608-01466-4*, 2059510) Bks Demand.

__Reaching the World Next Door: How to Spread the Gospel in the Midst of Many Cultures.__ rev. ed. Thom Hopler & Marcia Hopler. LC 93-38955. 240p. 1993. pap. 11.99 (*0-8308-1661-5*, 1661) InterVarsity.

__Reaching Their Minds: A Trainers Manual to Rational Effectiveness Training.__ Dominic J. DiMattia & Theo Ijzermans. LC 95-82381. 112p. (Orig.). (C). 1996. student ed., pap. 13.95 (*0-917476-25-5*) A Ellis Institute.

__Reaching Tomorrow's Consumers Today.__ 64p. 1991. pap. 20.00 (*0-89867-557-X*, 20258) Am Water Wks Assn.

__Reaching Toward God.__ Michael Marsh. LC 81-81683. 27p. 1981. pap. 3.00 (*0-87574-237-8*) Pendle Hill.

__Reaching Toward the Heights.__ Richard Wurmbrand. LC 77-4488. 1979. pap. 8.00 (*0-310-35470-6*); pap. write for info. (*0-310-35471-4*) Living Sacrifice Bks.

*__Reaching up for Manhood.__ Geoffrey Canada. LC 97-19919. 1998. write for info. (*0-8070-2316-7*) Beacon Pr.

__Reaching Up, Reaching Out.__ Leland E. Pulley. LC 85-90071. (Orig.). 1985. pap. 6.95 (*0-9611282-1-6*) Stewardship Enters.

__Reaching Women Who Need Prenatal Care: Strategies for Improving State Perinatal Programs.__ Ian T. Hill. Ed. by Gerry R. Feinstein. 126p. (Orig.). 1988. pap. text ed. 15.00 (*1-55877-008-9*) Natl Governor.

__Reaching Your Goal, 8 bks.__ Martin. (Illus.). 192p. (J). (gr. 1-4). 1987. lib. bdg. 116.80 (*0-86592-166-0*) Rourke Corp.

__Reaching Your Goal, 8 bks.__ Mascola et al. (Illus.). 192p. (J). (gr. 1-4). 1989. lib. bdg. 116.80 (*0-86592-425-2*) Rourke Corp.

__Reaching Your Goal, 8 bks., Set I, Reading Level 2.__ Martin. (Illus.). 192p. (J). (gr. 1-4). 1987. 87.60 (*0-685-58796-7*) Rourke Corp.

__Reaching Your Goal, 8 bks., Set II, Reading Level 2.__ Mascola et al. (Illus.). 192p. (J). (gr. 1-4). 1989. 87.60 (*0-685-58797-5*) Rourke Corp.

__Reaching Your Potential.__ Norman Vincent Peale. 1997. 6.99 (*0-517-18542-3*) Random Hse Value.

__Reaching Your Potential: Personal & Professional Development.__ Robert K. Throop. LC 92-28112. 414p. 1993. pap. 31.25 (*0-8273-5070-8*) Delmar.

__Reaching Your Potential Instructor's Guide.__ Robert K. Throop. 111p. 1993. teacher ed., pap. 16.00 (*0-8273-5071-6*) Delmar.

__React Interact.__ 2nd enl. rev. ed. Donald R. Byrd & Isis C. Cabetas. 160p. (C). 1991. pap. text ed. 15.00 (*0-13-753716-6*, 640201) P-H.

__React Interact: Situations for Communication.__ Donald R. Byrd & Isis C. Cabetas. (Illus.). 100p. (YA). (gr. 10-12). 1987. pap. text ed. 12.00 (*0-13-753377-2*, 18674) Prentice ESL.

__Reacting.__ Multimedia Development Services Staff. (Plant Fundamentals Ser.: Vol. VII, Module I). (Illus.). 1995. teacher ed. 65.00 (*1-57431-061-5*); student ed. 30.00 (*1-57431-021-6*) Tech Trng Systs.

__Reacting Flows: Combustion & Chemical Reactors, 2 pts.__ Ed. by G. Ludford. LC 86-1088. (Lectures in Applied Mathematics: Vol. 24). 1048p. 1986. 107.00 (*0-8218-1124-X*, LAM/24) Am Math.

__Reacting Flows: Combustion & Chemical Reactors, 2 pts., Pt. I.__ Ed. by G. Ludford. LC 86-1088. (Lectures in Applied Mathematics: Vol. 24). 512p. 1986. 64.00 (*0-8218-1127-4*, LAM/24.1) Am Math.

__Reacting Flows: Combustion & Chemical Reactors, 2 pts., Pt. II.__ Ed. by G. Ludford. LC 86-1088. (Lectures in Applied Mathematics: Vol. 24). 536p. 1986. 64.00 (*0-8218-1128-2*, LAM/24.2) Am Math.

*__Reacting Vinegar with Baking Soda.__ Henry D. Schreiber. Ed. by C. L. Stanitski. (Modular Laboratory Program in Chemistry Ser.). 12p. (C). 1997. pap. text ed. 1.35 (*0-87540-497-9*) Chem Educ Res.

__Reaction Against Tennyson.__ Andrew C. Bradley. 1974. 250.00 (*0-87968-139-X*) Gordon Pr.

__Reaction Against Tennyson.__ Andrew C. Bradley. (BCL1-PR English Literature Ser.). 19p. 1992. reprint ed. lib. bdg. 59.00 (*0-7812-7695-0*) Rprt Serv.

__Reaction & Counterrevolution in the Contemporary Arab World.__ Samih Farsoun et al. (Information Papers: No. 21). 55p. 1978. pap. 4.00 (*0-937694-37-1*) Assn Arab-Amer U Grads.

__Reaction & Reconstruction in English Politics, 1832 to 1852.__ Norman Gash. LC 81-1813. 227p. 1981. reprint ed. text ed. 38.50 (*0-313-22927-9*, GARR, Greenwood Pr) Greenwood.

__Reaction & Reform: The Politics of the Conservative Party under R.B. Bennett, 1928-1938.__ Larry A. Glassford. 320p. (Orig.). 1992. 45.00 (*0-8020-2798-9*); pap. 19.95 (*0-8020-7673-4*) U of Toronto Pr.

__Reaction & Renewal in South Africa.__ Paul B. Rich. 320p. 1996. text ed. 59.95 (*0-312-16149-2*) St Martin.

__Reaction & Responses to High Serum Cholesterol Results (DINROO)__ Val Calre et al. (Research Monographs: No. 6). 90p. 1992. pap. 45.00 (*0-7300-2010-X*, Pub. by Deakin Univ AT) St Mut.

__Reaction Center of Photosynthetic Bacteria: Structure & Dynamics.__ Ed. by M. E. Michel-Beyerle. LC 96-15841. (Illus.). 438p. 1996. 119.00 (*3-540-61075-8*) Spr-Verlag.

__Reaction Centers of Photosynthetic Bacteria: Feldafing-II-Meeting.__ Ed. by M. E. Michel-Beyerle. (Biophysics Ser.: Vol. 6). (Illus.). xiv, 469p. 1991. 135.95 (*0-387-53420-2*) Spr-Verlag.

__Reaction Detection in Liquid Chromatography.__ Jerry R. Krull. (Chromatographic Science Ser.: Vol. 34). 392p. 1986. 175.00 (*0-8247-7579-1*) Dekker.

__Reaction-Diffusion Equations.__ Ed. by K. J. Brown & A. A. Lacey. (Illus.). 240p. 1990. 69.00 (*0-19-853378-0*) OUP.

*__Reaction-Diffusion Equations & Their Applications & Computation Aspects: Proceedings of the China-Japan Symposium.__ 300p. 1997. lib. bdg. 53.00 (*981-02-2667-5*) World Scientific Pub.

__Reaction-Diffusion Equations & Their Applications to Biology.__ N. F. Britton. 1986. text ed. 121.00 (*0-12-135140-8*) Acad Pr.

__Reaction Dynamics: Recent Advances.__ Ed. by N. Sathyamurthy. 220p. 1991. 103.95 (*0-387-53360-5*) Spr-Verlag.

__Reaction Dynamics in Clusters & Condensed Phases: Proceedings of the Twenty-Sixth Jerusalem Symposium on Quantum Chemistry & Biochemistry Held in Jerusalem, Israel, May 17-20, 1993.__ Ed. by J. Jortner. LC 93-33794. (Jerusalem Symposia on Quantum Chemistry & Biochemistry Ser.). 592p. (C). 1994. lib. bdg. 266.50 (*0-7923-2582-6*) Kluwer Ac.

__Reaction Engineering of Step Growth Polymerization.__ Santosh K. Gupta & Anil Kumar. (Chemical Engineering Ser.). 425p. 1987. 105.00 (*0-306-42339-1*, Plenum Pr) Plenum.

__Reaction Guide for Organic Chemistry.__ Michael J. Millam. 204p. (C). 1989. pap. text ed. 16.76 (*0-669-13248-9*) HM College Div.

*__Reaction Guide for Organic Chemistry.__ Nelson. 3.50 (*0-7637-0287-0*) Jones & Bartlett.

__Reaction Guide for the Brief Organic Chemistry Course.__ Michael J. Millam. 185p. (C). 1989. pap. text ed. 15.96 (*0-669-13247-0*) HM College Div.

__Reaction Injection Molding.__ Ed. by Walter E. Becker. (Illus.). 336p. 1979. 49.00 (*0-938648-31-4*) T-C Pr CA.

__Reaction Injection Molding: Polymer Chemistry & Engineering.__ Ed. by Jiri E. Kresta. LC 84-24560. (ACS Symposium Ser.: No. 270). 291p. 1985. lib. bdg. 65.95 (*0-8412-0888-3*) Am Chemical.

*__Reaction Injection Molding: Polymer Chemistry & Engineering.__ Ed. by Jiri E. Kresta. LC 84-24560. (ACS Symposium Ser.: No. 270). (Illus.). 312p. 1985. reprint ed. pap. 89.00 (*0-608-04338-9*, 2065118) Bks Demand.

__Reaction Injection Molding Machinery & Processes.__ Sweeney. (Plastics Engineering Ser.: Vol. 13). 352p. 1987. 160.00 (*0-8247-7595-3*) Dekker.

__Reaction Kinetic & Reactor Design.__ John B. Butt. 1980. text ed. 75.00 (*0-13-753335-7*) P-H.

__Reaction Kinetics.__ 2nd ed. Michael J. Pilling & Paul W. Seakins. (Illus.). 320p. (C). 1996. pap. text ed. 32.00 (*0-19-855527-X*) OUP.

__Reaction Kinetics.__ 2nd ed. Michael J. Pilling & Paul W. Seakins. (Illus.). 320p. (C). 1996. text ed. 69.95 (*0-19-855528-8*) OUP.

__Reaction Kinetics, 2 vols., 1.__ Keith J. Laidler. LC 62-22037. 1963. pap. 100.00 (*0-08-009833-9*, Pub. by Pergamon Repr UK) Franklin.

__Reaction Kinetics, Vol. I.__ Royal Society of Chemistry Staff. 1988. 51.00 (*0-85186-756-1*) CRC Pr.

__Reaction Kinetics & Reactor Design.__ 2nd ed. John B. Butt. 1993. text ed. write for info. (*0-13-034323-4*) P-H.

__Reaction Kinetics Progress, Vol. 10, No. 4.__ K. R. Jennings. (Illus.). 98p. 1980. pap. 25.00 (*0-08-027135-9*, Pergamon Pr) Elsevier.

__Reaction Mechanisms see Pentacoordinated Phosphorus__

__Reaction Mechanisms in Environmental Organic Chemistry.__ Richard A. Larson & Eric J. Weber. 448p. 1994. 69.95 (*0-87371-258-7*, L258) Lewis Pubs.

__Reaction Mechanisms in Organic Chemistry.__ F. Badea. (Abacus Bks.). 702p. 1977. text ed. 70.00 (*0-85626-002-9*) Gordon & Breach.

__Reaction Mechanisms of Inorganic & Organometallic Systems.__ Robert B. Jordan. (Illus.). 304p. (C). 1991. text ed. 47.00 (*0-19-506945-5*) OUP.

__Reaction Mechanisms of Metal Complexes.__ R. W. Hay. 200p. 1995. text ed. 79.95 (*0-13-766106-1*) P-H.

__Reaction Modes & Products see Singlet 02 Series__

__Reaction of Sulphur Dichloride with Olefins As a Pathway to the Synthesis of Thiacyclanes, Vol. 3.__ G. A. Tolstikov. 40p. 1983. pap. text ed. 106.00 (*3-7186-0077-3*) Gordon & Breach.

__Reaction Path in Chemistry: Current Approaches & Perspectives.__ Ed. by Dietmar Heidrich. (Understanding Chemical Reactivity Ser.). 308p. (C). 1995. lib. bdg. 145.00 (*0-7923-3589-9*) Kluwer Ac.

__Reaction Patterns in Human Teeth.__ Ivar A. Mjor. 248p. 1983. 143.00 (*0-8493-6645-3*, RK280) CRC Pr.

__Reaction Patterns of the Lymph Node, Pt. 2: Reactions Associated with Neoplasia & Immune Deficient States.__ Ed. by Ekkehard Grundmann & E. Vollmer. (Current Topics in Pathology Ser.: Vol. 84/2). (Illus.). ix, 225p. 1991. 135.00 (*0-387-52288-3*) Spr-Verlag.

__Reaction Patterns of the Lymph Node, Vol. 1: Cell Types & Functions.__ Ed. by Ekkehard Grundmann et al. (Current Topics in Pathology Ser.). (Illus.). 304p. 1990. 214.00 (*0-387-52287-5*) Spr-Verlag.

__Reaction Polymers: Chemistry, Technology, Applications, Markets.__ Wilson F. Gum et al. 868p. (C). 1992. text ed. 149.00 (*1-56990-034-5*) Hanser-Gardner.

__Reaction Rates of Isotopic Molecules.__ Lars Melander & William H. Saunders, Jr. LC 85-23200. 348p. 1986. reprint ed. 49.50 (*0-89874-940-9*) Krieger.

__Reaction to the Chinese in the Pacific North West & British Columbia, 1850-1910.__ Robert E. Wynne. Ed. by Roger Daniels. LC 78-54847. (Asian Experience in North America Ser.). 1979. lib. bdg. 42.95 (*0-405-11298-X*) Ayer.

__Reaction to the Kennedy Assassination among Political Leaders.__ Samuel C. Patterson. 1967. 1.00 (*1-55614-101-7*) U of SD Gov Res Bur.

__Reactionary Essays on Poetry & Ideas.__ Allen Tate. LC 68-24856. (Essay Index Reprint Ser.). 1977. reprint ed. 20.95 (*0-8369-0924-0*) Ayer.

__Reactionary Imperative: Essays Literary & Political.__ M. E. Bradford. 236p. 1990. 25.95 (*0-89385-032-2*); pap. 12.95 (*0-89385-031-4*) Sugden.

__Reactionary Modernism: Technology, Culture & Politics in Weimar & the Third Reich.__ Jeffery Herf. 288p. 1986. pap. text ed. 19.95 (*0-521-33833-6*) Cambridge U Pr.

__Reactions: Multi-Cultural Reading Based Writing Modules.__ Robin C. Scarcella. 384p. 1992. pap. text ed. 19.80 (*0-13-756214-4*) P-H.

__Reactions & Movement of Organic Chemicals in Soils.__ Ed. by B. L. Sawhney & K. Brown. 496p. 1989. 42.00 (*0-89118-788-X*) Soil Sci Soc Am.

__Reactions & Processes.__ Ed. by O. Hutzinger. (Handbook of Environmental Chemistry Ser.: Vol. 2 Pt. B). (Illus.). 232p. 1982. 120.95 (*0-387-11107-7*) Spr-Verlag.

__Reactions & Processes.__ Ed. by O. Hutzinger. (Handbook of Environmental Chemistry Ser.: Vol. 2, Pt. C). 180p. 1984. 125.95 (*0-387-13819-6*) Spr-Verlag.

__Reactions & Processes.__ Ed. by O. Hutzinger. (Handbook of Environmental Chemistry Ser.: Vol. 2, Pt. D). (Illus.). 210p. 1988. 192.95 (*0-387-15547-3*) Spr-Verlag.

__Reactions & Processes.__ Ed. by O. Hutzinger et al. (Handbook of Environmental Chemistry Ser.: Vol. 2, Pt. F). (Illus.). xi, 255p. 1991. 158.95 (*0-387-54139-X*) Spr-Verlag.

__Reactions & Syntheses in the Organic Chemistry Lab.__ Lutz F. Tietze. 1986. pap. text ed. 58.00 (*0-935702-50-4*) Univ Sci Bks.

__Reactions & Syntheses in the Organic Laboratory.__ Theophil Eicher & Lutz F. Tietze. Tr. by Dagmar Ringe. (Illus.). 592p. (Orig.). (GER.). 1989. text ed. 58.00 (*0-935702-24-5*) Univ Sci Bks.

__Reactions Between Dogma & Philosophy Illustrated from the Works of St. Thomas Aquinas.__ Philip H. Wicksteed. LC 77-27153. (Hibbert Lectures: 1916). reprint ed. 72.50 (*0-404-60418-8*) AMS Pr.

*__Reactions Catalyzed by Inorganics Compounds, Vol. 16.__ J. J. Zuckerman. (Inorganic Reactions & Methods Ser.). 656p. 1993. 250.00 (*0-471-18666-X*) Wiley.

__Reactions in Compartmentalized Liquids.__ Ed. by W. Knoche & R. Schomacker. (Illus.). 248p. 1989. 69.95 (*0-387-51188-1*) Spr-Verlag.

__Reactions Macrochimiques chez les Champignons Suives d'Indications sur la Morphologie des Spores.__ F. Bataille. 1969. reprint ed. 32.00 (*3-7682-0654-8*) Lubrecht & Cramer.

__Reactions of Aluminum & Magnesium with Certain Chlorinated Hydrocarbons, Technical Report, No. 34.__ (C). 1993. pap. text ed. 40.00 (*1-55989-473-3*) Underwrtrs Labs.

__Reactions of Aromatic Compounds see Comprehensive Chemical Kinetics__

__Reactions of Carbon with Carbon Dioxide & with Steam.__ C. G. Von Fredersdorff. (Research Bulletin Ser.: No. 19). iv, 75p. 1955. pap. 7.50 (*0-685-43363-3*) Inst Gas Tech.

__Reactions of Coordinated Ligands, Vol. 1.__ Ed. by Paul S. Braterman. 1020p. 1987. 175.00 (*0-306-42201-8*, Plenum Pr) Plenum.

__Reactions of Coordinated Ligands, Vol. 2.__ Ed. by Paul S. Braterman. (Illus.). 422p. 1989. 125.00 (*0-306-43094-0*, Plenum Pr) Plenum.

__Reactions of Coordinated Ligands & Homogeneous Catalysis: A Symposium Sponsored by the American Chemical Society, Washington, D.C., March 22-24, 1962.__ Daryl H. Busch. LC 63-13314. (American Chemical Society Advances in Chemistry Ser.: No. 37). 263p. reprint ed. pap. 75.00 (*0-317-09028-3*, 2051256) Bks Demand.

__Reactions of Metallic Salts & Complexes & Organometallic Compounds see Comprehensive Chemical Kinetics__

__Reactions of Molecules at Electrodes.__ Ed. by N. S. Hush. LC 70-149570. 512p. reprint ed. pap. 146.00 (*0-317-29338-9*, 2024029) Bks Demand.

__Reactions of Non-Metallic Inorganic Compounds see Comprehensive Chemical Kinetics__

__Reactions of Organic Sulfur Compounds at Electrodes.__ O. Hammerich & V. D. Parker. 82p. 1981. pap. text ed. 152.00 (*3-7186-0083-8*) Gordon & Breach.

__Reactions of Ozone & Hydroxyl Radicals with Amino Acids.__ (Illus.). 156p. 1995. pap. 47.00 (*0-89867-800-5*, 90673) Am Water Wks Assn.

__Reactions of Solids with Gases.__ C. H. Bamford & C. F. Tipper. (Comprehensive Chemical Kinetics Ser.: Vol. 21). 238p. 1984. 213.00 (*0-444-42288-9*, I-450-84) Elsevier.

__Reactions of Sulphur with Organic Compounds.__ Mikhail G. Voronkov et al. LC 84-4989. 440p. 1987. 125.00 (*0-306-10978-6*, Consultants) Plenum.

__Reactions on Polymers: Proceedings of the NATO Advanced Study Institute, No. C-4, Troy, N. Y., July, 1973.__ NATO Advanced Study Institute Staff. Ed. by James A. Moore. LC 73-91207. 1973. lib. bdg. 141.50 (*90-277-0416-3*) Kluwer Ac.

__Reactions to Crime: The Public, the Police, Courts, & Prisons.__ Ed. by David P. Farrington & John Gunn. LC 84-17369. (Current Research in Forensic Psychiatry & Psychology Ser.). 201p. reprint ed. pap. 57.30 (*0-7837-4730-6*, 2044515) Bks Demand.

__Reactions to Crime & Violence.__ Ed. by Wesley G. Skogan. LC 94-68311. (Annals of the American Academy of Political & Social Science Ser.: Vol. 539). 1995. 28.00 (*0-8039-7122-2*); pap. 18.00 (*0-8039-7123-0*) Am Acad Pol Soc Sci.

__Reactions to Critical Life Events: A Social Psychological Analysis.__ Marita Inglehart. LC 90-27790. 240p. 1991. text ed. 55.00 (*0-275-93875-1*, C3875, Praeger Pubs) Greenwood.

__Reactions to Irish Nationalism, 1865-1914.__ Alan O'Day. 422p. 1987. text ed. 55.00 (*0-907628-85-0*) Hambledon Press.

__Reactions to Motherhood: The Role of Post-Natal Care.__ Jean A. Ball. (Illus.). 168p. 1987. 37.50 (*0-521-30331-1*) Cambridge U Pr.

__Reactions to Motherhood: The Role of Postnatal Care.__ 2nd ed. Jean A. Ball. (Illus.). 140p. 1994. pap. 20.00 (*1-898507-08-2*) Buttrwrth-Heinemann.

__Reactions to Psychotropic Medication.__ Frank L. Tornatore et al. LC 87-30056. (Illus.). 184p. 1987. 42.50 (*0-306-42718-4*, Plenum Med Bk) Plenum.

__Reactions to the Persian Gulf War: Editorials in the Conflict Zone.__ Carrie Chrisco. 140p. (C). 1995. lib. bdg. 29.00 (*0-7618-0082-4*) U Pr of Amer.

__Reactions under Plasma Conditions, 1.__ Ed. by M. Venugopalan. LC 78-132857. reprint ed. pap. 153.30 (*0-317-10852-2*, 22006313) Bks Demand.

__Reactions under Plasma Conditions, 2.__ Ed. by M. Venugopalan. LC 78-132857. reprint ed. pap. 155.50 (*0-317-10853-0*) Bks Demand.

__Reactions with Variable-Change Soils.__ N. J. Barrow. (Developments in Plant & Soil Sciences Ser.). (C). 1987. lib. bdg. 101.50 (*90-247-3589-0*) Kluwer Ac.

__Reactivated Man.__ Curtis Zahn. (Illus.). 48p. 1984. pap. 5.95 (*0-88145-014-6*) Broadway Play.

__Reactivation: Returning to the OT Workforce.__ American Occupational Therapy Association, Inc., Staff. 136p. (C). 1991. pap. text ed. 15.00 (*0-910317-66-6*) Am Occup Therapy.

__Reactive Aggression: Understanding & Helping Children Who Respond to Others with Aggressive Behavior.__ Thomas P. Dowd. (Boys Town National Family Home Program Informational Ser.). 13p. (Orig.). 1996. spiral bd., pap. 1.95 (*0-938510-92-4*, 19-205) Boys Town Pr.

__Reactive & Flexible Molecules in Liquids.__ Ed. by T. Dorfmuller. (C). 1989. lib. bdg. 203.00 (*0-7923-0469-1*) Kluwer Ac.

__Reactive Arthritis.__ Ed. by Auli Toivanen & Paavo Toivanen. LC 87-27648. 192p. 1988. 115.00 (*0-8493-6118-4*, RC933, CRC Reprint) Franklin.

__Reactive Data Structures for Geographic Information Systems.__ Petrus-Johannes-Maria Van Oosterom. LC 93-28964. (Spatial Information Systems). (Illus.). 216p. 1994. 45.00 (*0-19-823320-5*) OUP.

__Reactive Dyes in Biology & Medicine.__ V. B. Ivanov. 270p. 1987. text ed. 161.00 (*3-7186-0235-0*) Gordon & Breach.

__Reactive Extrusion: Principles & Practice.__ Marino Xanthos. 336p. (C). 1992. text ed. 79.95 (*1-56990-113-9*) Hanser-Gardner.

__Reactive Intermediates.__ Christopher J. Moody & Gordon H. Whitham. (Oxford Chemistry Primers Ser.: No. 8). (Illus.). 96p. (C). 1992. pap. text ed. 11.95 (*0-19-855672-1*) OUP.

__Reactive Intermediates, Vol. 2.__ Ed. by R. A. Abramovitch. LC 79-344. 614p. (C). 1982. 125.00 (*0-306-40594-6*, Plenum Pr) Plenum.

__Reactive Intermediates, Vol. 3.__ Ed. by R. A. Abramovitch. LC 82-15139. 644p. 1983. 125.00 (*0-306-40970-4*, Plenum Pr) Plenum.

__Reactive Intermediates in Organic Chemistry.__ Neil S. Isaacs. LC 73-8194. 564p. reprint ed. pap. 160.80 (*0-685-20590-8*, 2030523) Bks Demand.

Reactive Keyboard. John J. Darragh & Ian H. Witten. (Cambridge Series in Human-Computer Interaction: No. 5). (Illus.). 176p. (C). 1992. text ed. 52.95 (*0-521-40375-8*) Cambridge U Pr.

Reactive Metals: Proceedings of the 3rd Reactive Metals Conference, Buffalo, 1958. Ed. by W. R. Clough. LC 59-14889. (Metallurgical Society Conference Ser.: Vol. 2). 625p. reprint ed. pap. 178.20 (*0-317-10823-9*, 2000665) Bks Demand.

*__Reactive Modifiers for Polymers.__ Ed. by Al-Malaika. (Illus.). 320p. 1997. text ed. 129.50 (*0-7514-0265-6*, Pub. by Blackie Acad & Prof UK) Routledge Chapman & Hall.

Reactive Oligomers. S. G. Entelis et al. Tr. by V. M. David & Y. U. Rajabov from RUS. (New Concepts in Polymer Science Ser.). 320p. 1988. 187.50 (*90-6764-107-3*, Pub. by VSP NE) Coronet Bks.

Reactive Oligomers. Frank W. Harris & Harry J. Spinelli. LC 85-9215. (ACS Symposium Ser.: No. 282). 259p. 1985. lib. bdg. 65.95 (*0-8412-0922-7*) Am Chemical.

Reactive Oligonucleotide Derivatives as Tools for Site Specific Modification of Biopolymers, Vol. 12. D. G. Knorre et al. (Soviet Scientific Reviews Ser.: Vol. 12, Pt. 5). 78p. 1989. pap. text ed. 67.00 (*3-7186-4901-2*) Gordon & Breach.

Reactive Oxygen Species in Chemistry, Biology, & Medicine. Ed. by A. Quintanilha. LC 87-38498. (Illus.). 240p. 1988. 75.00 (*0-306-42808-3*, Plenum Pr) Plenum.

Reactive Power Control in Electric Systems. Ed. by Timothy J. Miller. LC 82-10838. 381p. 1982. text ed. 145.95 (*0-471-86933-3*, Wiley-Interscience) Wiley.

Reactive Processing of Polymers: Proceedings of the 2nd International Conference, November 2-4, 1982. Society of Plastics Engineers Staff. Ed. by J. T. Lindt. (Illus.). 444p. reprint ed. pap. 126.60 (*0-317-09322-3*, 2021697) Bks Demand.

Reactive Risk & Rational Action: Managing Moral Hazard in Insurance Contracts. Carol A. Heimer. (California Series on Social Choice & Political Economy: Vol. 6). 1985. pap. 14.00 (*0-520-06756-8*) U CA Pr.

*__Reactive Transport in Porous Media.__ Ed. by P. C. Lichtner et al. (Reviews in Mineralogy Ser.: Vol. 34). (Illus.). xiii, 438p. (Orig.). (C). 1996. pap. text ed. 28.00 (*0-939950-42-1*) Mineralogical Soc.

Reactive Voting in Danish General Elections 1971-1979: A Revisionist Interpretation. Peter Nannestad. (Illus.). 207p. (Orig.). (C). 1989. pap. 23.00 (*87-7288-243-3*, Pub. by Aarhus Univ Pr DK) David Brown.

Reactivite des Hypobromites. P. Brun & B. Waegell. 1976. pap. 12.75 (*0-08-021014-7*, Pergamon Pr) Elsevier.

Reactivity Accidents. IAEA Staff. (Technical Reports: No. 354). 52p. 1993. pap. 25.00 (*92-0-101493-7*, STI/DOC/354, Pub. by IAEA AU) Bernan Associates.

Reactivity & Transport of Heavy Metals in Soils. H. M. Selim & M. C. Amacher. 240p. 1996. 59.95 (*0-87371-473-3*, L473) Lewis Pubs.

Reactivity Coefficients in Large Fast Power Reactors. Hummel Okrent. LC 73-119000. (ANS Monographs). 386p. 1970. 18.40 (*0-89448-006-5*, 300002) Am Nuclear Soc.

Reactivity in Molecular Crystals. Ed. by Yuji Ohashi. LC 93-42020. 1993. 130.00 (*3-527-29098-2*, VCH) Wiley.

Reactivity in Solids: Past, Present, & Future. V. V. Boldyrev. (Chemistry for the 21st Century Monograph Ser.). (Illus.). 320p. 1996. text ed. 79.50 (*0-86542-687-2*) Blackwell Sci.

Reactivity Indices for Biomolecules. Chen-An Chin & Pill-Soon Song. (Graduate Studies: No. 24). (Illus.). 176p. 1981. 33.00 (*0-89672-093-4*); pap. 20.00 (*0-89672-092-6*) Tex Tech Univ Pr.

Reactivity, Mechanism, & Structure in Polymer Chemistry. Ed. by A. D. Jenkins & A. Ledwith. LC 73-2786. 631p. reprint ed. pap. 179.90 (*0-317-29339-7*, 2024030) Bks Demand.

Reactivity of Inorganic Substances Handbook. rev. ed. Ed. by Rostislav A. Lidin. 938p. 1996. 165.00 (*1-56700-050-9*) Begell Hse.

Reactivity of Metal-Metal Bonds. Ed. by Malcolm Chisholm. LC 81-361. (ACS Symposium Ser.: No. 155). 1981. 46.95 (*0-8412-0624-4*) Am Chemical.

*__Reactivity of Metal-Metal Bonds: Based on a Symposium.__ Ed. by Malcolm H. Chisholm. LC 81-361. (ACS Symposium Ser.: Vol. 155). 334p. 1981. reprint ed. pap. 95.20 (*0-608-03042-2*, 2063495) Bks Demand.

Reactor Auxiliary Systems, Course 9. Center for Occupational Research & Development Staff. (Nuclear Technology Ser.). (Illus.). 108p. (C). 1984. pap. text ed. 22.00 (*1-55502-073-9*) CORD Commns.

Reactor Burn-up Physics. (Panel Proceedings Ser.). (Illus.). 296p. (Orig.). 1973. pap. 40.00 (*92-0-051073-6*, ISP336, Pub. by IAEA AU) Bernan Associates.

*__Reactor Design for Chemical Engineers.__ Ed. by King & Winterbottom. (Illus.). 288p. (Orig.). 1997. pap. text ed. 36.50 (*0-7514-0254-0*, Pub. by Blackie Acad & Prof UK) Routledge Chapman & Hall.

Reactor Dosimetry. Ed. by Harry Farrar. LC 94-42668. (STP Ser.: No. 1228). 1994. write for info. (*0-8031-1899-6*) ASTM.

Reactor Dosimetry, 2 vols. J. P. Genthon & Heinz Rottger. 1985. lib. bdg. 324.50 (*90-277-2013-4*) Kluwer Ac.

Reactor Dosimetry, 2 vols., I. J. P. Genthon & Heinz Rottger. 1987. lib. bdg. 124.50 (*90-277-2011-8*) Kluwer Ac.

Reactor Dosimetry, 2 vols., II. J. P. Genthon & Heinz Rottger. 1987. lib. bdg. 124.50 (*90-277-2012-6*) Kluwer Ac.

Reactor Dosimetry: Methods, Applications, & Standardization. Ed. by Harry Farrar, IV & E. P. Lippincott. LC 88-36726. (Special Technical Publication Ser.: No. STP 1001). (Illus.). 820p. 1989. text ed. 142.00 (*0-8031-1184-3*) ASTM.

Reactor Kinetics & Control: Proceedings. Ed. by Lynn E. Weaver. (AEC Symposium Ser.). 593p. 1964. pap. 22.75 (*0-87079-333-0*, TID-7662); fiche 9.00 (*0-87079-334-9*, TID-7662) DOE.

Reactor Noise: An International Symposium: Special Multi Issue of Journal of Annals of Nuclear Energy. Ed. by M. M. Williams. 400p. 1975. pap. 67.00 (*0-08-019895-3*) Elsevier.

Reactor Noise - SMORN II: Proceedings of the 2nd Specialists' Meeting on Reactor Noise 1977. Ed. by M. M. Williams. 1978. pap. 220.00 (*0-08-022157-2*, Pergamon Pr) Elsevier.

Reactor Noise - SMORN III: Proceedings of the 3rd Specialists Meeting on Reactor Noise at Tokyo, Japan, October 26-30, 1981. Ed. by M. M. Williams. (Illus.). 620p. 1982. 170.00 (*0-08-027619-9*, Pergamon Pr) Elsevier.

Reactor Noise - SMORN IV. Ed. by M. M. Williams & Norman J. McCormick. (Illus.). 1024p. 1985. 150.00 (*0-08-031648-4*, Pub. by PPL UK) Elsevier.

Reactor-Noise Analysis in the Time Domain. Nicola Pacilio. LC 79-600321. (AEC Critical Review Ser.). 102p. 1969. pap. 10.50 (*0-87079-335-7*, TID-24512); fiche 9.00 (*0-87079-336-5*, TID-24512) DOE.

Reactor Operations, Course 7. Center for Occupational Research & Development Staff. (Nuclear Technology Ser.). (Illus.). 218p. (C). 1984. pap. text ed. 25.00 (*1-55502-071-2*) CORD Commns.

Reactor Physics, Course 12. Center for Occupational Research & Development Staff. (Nuclear Technology Ser.). (Illus.). 304p. (C). 1984. pap. text ed. 30.00 (*1-55502-101-8*) CORD Commns.

Reactor Physics Calculations for Applications in Nuclear Technology, Workshop on. D. E. Cullen et al. 756p. 1991. text ed. 147.00 (*981-02-0517-1*) World Scientific Pub.

Reactor Physics Constants. 2nd ed. Argonne National Laboratory & AEC Technical Information Center Staff. 859p. 1963. pap. 91.00 (*0-87079-337-3*, ANL-5800); fiche 9.00 (*0-87079-497-3*, ANL-5800) DOE.

Reactor Physics for Developing Countries & Nuclear Spectroscopy Research: Proceedings of the Conference on Reactor Physics for Developing Countries & Nuclear Spectroscopy Research. Ed. by G. Medrano & K. Lieb. 770p. 1986. text ed. 144.00 (*9971-5-0203-8*) World Scientific Pub.

Reactor Physics International Conference, Jackson Hole, WY, Sept. 18-22, 1988, 2 vols. 2020p. 1988. 175.00 (*0-89448-141-X*, 700141) Am Nuclear Soc.

Reactor Plant Materials. (Illus.). 298p. 1982. teacher ed., ring bd. 595.00 (*0-87683-294-X*); ring bd. 95.00 (*0-87683-293-1*) GP Courseware.

Reactor Safety, Course 8. Center for Occupational Research & Development Staff. (Nuclear Technology Ser.). (Illus.). 188p. (C). 1984. pap. text ed. 22.00 (*1-55502-072-0*) CORD Commns.

Reactor Shielding. (Technical Reports: No. 34). (Illus.). 164p. 1964. pap. 30.00 (*92-0-155064-2*, IDC34, Pub. by IAEA AU) Bernan Associates.

Reactor Shielding Design Manual. AEC Technical Information Center Staff. Ed. by Theodore Rockwell, 3rd. 467p. 1956. 52.00 (*0-87079-338-1*, TID-7004) DOE.

Reactor Shielding for Nuclear Engineers. AEC Technical Information Center Staff & N. M. Schaeffer. LC 73-600001. 801p. 1973. pap. 28.00 (*0-87079-004-8*, TID-25951); fiche 9.00 (*0-87079-339-X*, TID-25951) DOE.

Reactor Theory Course. (Illus.). 1979. teacher ed., ring bd. 79.50 (*0-87683-248-6*); teacher ed., ring bd. 95.00 (*0-87683-249-4*) GP Courseware.

Reactors & Reactions. Ed. by A. Fiechter. (Advances in Biochemical Engineering Ser.: Vol. 19). (Illus.). 250p. 1981. 103.95 (*0-387-10464-X*) Spr-Verlag.

Read. Becky Daniel. (Preschool Basic Skills Ser.). (Illus.). 64p. 1992. 8.99 (*0-86653-671-X*, GA1401) Good Apple.

Read. C. Reade. (Illus.). 148p. 1991. reprint ed. pap. 23.50 (*0-8328-2162-4*) Higginson Bk Co.

Read: Allied Families of Read, Corbin, Luttrell, & Bywaters of Culpepper Co., Va. A. M. Prichard. (Illus.). 292p. 1991. reprint ed. pap. 46.00 (*0-8328-1876-3*); reprint ed. lib. bdg. 56.00 (*0-8328-1875-5*) Higginson Bk Co.

*__Read: Dare to Dream.__ 2nd ed. Suzanne Hitt. 224p. (C). 1997. per. 27.95 (*0-7872-2165-1*) Kendall-Hunt.

Read: The Reads & Their Relatives, Being an Account of Col. Clemens & Madam Read of Bushy Forest, Lunenburg County, Virginia, Their Eight Children, Their Descendants, & Allied Families. Alice Read. (Illus.). 688p. 1993. reprint ed. pap. 99.50 (*0-8328-3389-4*); reprint ed. lib. bdg. 109.50 (*0-8328-3388-6*) Higginson Bk Co.

Read a Lot & Write Even More. rev. ed. Socorro De Jesus & David Blot. 90p. (C). 1987. pap. text ed. 5.00 (*0-317-93603-4*) D Blot Pubns.

Read about China. Pao-Chen Lee. 1953. 9.95 (*0-88710-061-9*); audio write for info. (*0-88710-062-7*) Yale Far Eastern Pubns.

Read about It: Beginning Readers. Imogene Forte. LC 82-81720. (Illus.). 80p. (J). (gr. k-1). 1982. pap. text ed. 9.95 (*0-86530-005-4*, IP 05-4) Incentive Pubns.

Read about It: Middle Grades. Imogene Forte. LC 82-80502. (Read about It Ser.). (Illus.). 80p. (J). (gr. 4-6). 1982. pap. text ed. 9.95 (*0-86530-007-0*, IP 070) Incentive Pubns.

Read about It: Primary. Imogene Forte. LC 82-80499. (Illus.). 80p. (J). (gr. 2-4). 1982. pap. text ed. 9.95 (*0-86530-006-2*, IP-062) Incentive Pubns.

Read about Rye: 1660-1960. Arlene D. Hawkins. LC 85-19679. 1985. pap. 4.95 (*0-9615327-0-X*) Rye Hist Soc.

Read Across America: Exploring 7 U. S. Regions Through Popular Children's Literature. Gloria L. Rothstein. 1996. pap. text ed. 14.95 (*0-590-60341-8*) Scholastic Inc.

Read All about It. Jim Trelease. Date not set. pap. 22.00 (*0-670-83693-1*) Viking Penguin.

Read All About It! Great Stories, Poems, & Newspaper Pieces for Reading Aloud for Preteens & Teens. Ed. by Jim Trelease. LC 93-21781. 416p. (Orig.). (YA). 1993. pap. 11.95 (*0-14-014655-5*, Penguin Bks) Viking Penguin.

Read All about It - Tutor Adults with Daily Newspaper: Leader Handbook. Margaret Williams et al. Ed. by V. K. Lawson. 1989. pap. text ed. 4.00 (*0-930713-32-X*) Lit Vol Am.

Read All About It - Tutor Adults with Daily Newspaper: Tutor Handbook. V. K. Lawson et al. 95p. 1984. pap. text ed. 4.00 (*0-930713-31-1*) Lit Vol Am.

Read All Your Life: A Subject Guide to Fiction. Barbara K. Davis. LC 89-42709. 296p. 1989. lib. bdg. 39.95 (*0-89950-370-5*) McFarland & Co.

*__Read Alone All about Me.__ (J). 1997. pap. write for info. (*0-395-88084-X*) HM.

Read along with Fat Cat-Small Book. (Phonics Readers Ser.). 8p. 1988. 2.95 (*0-88679-596-6*) Educ Insights.

Read along with Fat Cat-Tall Book. (Phonics Readers Ser.). 8p. 1988. 17.95 (*0-88679-591-5*) Educ Insights.

Read along with Freddy Frog-Small Book. (Phonics Readers Ser.). 8p. 1989. 2.95 (*0-88679-568-0*) Educ Insights.

Read along with Freddy Frog-Tall Book. (Phonics Readers Ser.). 8p. 1989. 17.95 (*0-88679-594-X*) Educ Insights.

Read along with Ginger Giraffe-Small Book. (Phonics Readers Ser.). 8p. 1989. 2.95 (*0-88679-648-2*) Educ Insights.

Read along with Ginger Giraffe-Tall Book. (Phonics Readers Ser.). 8p. 1989. 17.95 (*0-88679-595-8*) Educ Insights.

Read along with Pandy Duck-Small Book. (Phonics Readers Ser.). 8p. 1989. 2.95 (*0-88679-597-4*) Educ Insights.

Read along with Pandy Duck-Tall Book. (Phonics Readers Ser.). 8p. 1989. 17.95 (*0-88679-592-3*) Educ Insights.

Read along with Sweet Bee-Small Book. (Phonics Readers Ser.). 8p. 1989. 2.95 (*0-88679-567-2*) Educ Insights.

Read along with Sweet Bee-Tall Book. (Phonics Readers Ser.). 8p. 1989. 17.95 (*0-88679-593-1*) Educ Insights.

Read Aloud Level K-1: I Like Me. Houghton Mifflin Company Staff. (Literature Experience 1991 Ser.). (J). (gr. 1). 1990. pap. 5.44 (*0-395-53398-8*) HM.

Read-Aloud Adirondack Fairy Tales. Lettie A. Petrie. LC 96-8038. (J). 1996. write for info. (*0-925168-53-X*) North Country.

Read Aloud Anthology. (J). 1993. pap. 12.95 (*0-590-49023-0*) Scholastic Inc.

Read Aloud Baby & the Basket. Ella K. Lindvall. (J). 1996. pap. text ed. 4.99 (*0-8024-7149-8*) Moody.

Read Aloud Baby Jesus. Ella K. Lindvall. (J). 1996. pap. text ed. 4.99 (*0-8024-7123-4*) Moody.

Read-Aloud Bible Stories, Vol. 1. Ella K. Lindvall. 160p. (J). (ps-2). 1982. text ed. 18.99 (*0-8024-7163-3*) Moody.

Read-Aloud Bible Stories, Vol. 2. Ella K. Lindvall. (Illus.). (J). (ps up). 1985. 18.99 (*0-8024-7164-1*) Moody.

Read Aloud Bible Stories, Vol. 3. Ella K. Lindvall. (J). (ps-2). 1990. 18.99 (*0-8024-7165-X*) Moody.

Read-Aloud Bible Stories, Vol. 4. Ella K. Lindvall. (J). (ps up). 1995. 18.99 (*0-8024-7166-8*) Moody.

Read Aloud Daniel & the Lions. Ella K. Lindvall. (J). 1996. pap. text ed. 4.99 (*0-8024-7122-6*) Moody.

Read-Aloud Handbook. rev. ed. Jim Trelease. (Handbook Ser.). (Illus.). 272p. 1985. pap. 8.95 (*0-14-046727-0*, Penguin Bks) Viking Penguin.

Read-Aloud Handbook. 4th ed. Jim Trelease. LC 95-2269. (Illus.). 368p. (Orig.). 1995. pap. 12.95 (*0-14-046971-0*, Penguin Bks) Viking Penguin.

Read Aloud How God Made the World. Ella K. Lindvall. (J). 1996. pap. text ed. 4.99 (*0-8024-7124-2*) Moody.

Read Aloud Jonah & the Whale. Ella K. Lindvall. (J). 1996. pap. text ed. 4.99 (*0-8024-7148-X*) Moody.

Read Aloud Noahs Big Boat. Ella K. Lindvall. (J). 1996. pap. text ed. 4.99 (*0-8024-7121-8*) Moody.

*__Read-Aloud Poems for Young People: Readings from the World's Best Loved Verses.__ Glorya Hale. (YA). 1997. 12.98 (*1-884822-99-1*) Blck Dog & Leventhal.

Read Aloud Rhymes for the Very Young. Ed. by Jack Prelutsky. LC 86-7147. (Illus.). 112p. (J). (ps-3). 1986. 20.00 (*0-394-87218-5*); lib. bdg. 21.99 (*0-394-97218-X*) Knopf Bks Yng Read.

Read-Aloud Stories: Stories Exclusively for Reading Aloud. Ed. by Edward J. Kelly. 420p. (Orig.). 1989. pap. text ed. write for info. (*0-318-65496-2*) RAS Pubns.

Read Aloud the Man Who Couldn't See. Ella K. Lindvall. (J). 1996. pap. text ed. 4.99 (*0-8024-7146-3*) Moody.

Read Aloud the Man Who Said Thank You. Ella K. Lindvall. (J). 1996. pap. text ed. 4.99 (*0-8024-7147-1*) Moody.

Read-Aloud Treasury: Favorite Nursery Rhymes, Poems, Stories & More for the Very Young. Illus. by Ann Schweninger. 256p. (J). 1988. 19.95 (*0-385-18560-X*) Doubleday.

Read America First. Robert Littell. LC 68-16947. (Essay Index Reprint Ser.). 1977. reprint ed. 23.95 (*0-8369-0620-9*) Ayer.

Read & Color Book Series. (Illus.). (J). (ps-5). Date not set. pap. write for info. (*0-86545-223-7*) Spizzirri.

Read & Discover Library. (YA). 6600. pap. 25.00 (*0-7175-0284-8*) Dufour.

Read & Draw. J. M. Baggiani & V. M. Tewell. (Illus.). 12p. (J). (gr. 1-3). 1966. pap. 2.00 (*0-934329-06-0*) Baggiani-Tewell.

*__Read & Play with Peter Rabbit.__ Beatrix Potter. (Illus.). (J). 1997. write for info. (*0-614-29326-X*) Warne.

*__Read & Play with Tom Kitten.__ Beatrix Potter. (Illus.). (J). 1997. write for info. (*0-614-29327-8*) Warne.

*__Read & Pray with Me.__ 80p. (J). 1996. write for info. (*0-7814-0285-9*, Chariot Bks) Chariot Victor.

*__Read & Pray with Me.__ 80p. (J). 1997. write for info. (*0-7814-0286-7*, Chariot Bks) Chariot Victor.

Read & Remember - Book A see Gates-Peardon-LaClair Reading Exercises: Grades 1-9

Read & Remember - Book B see Gates-Peardon-LaClair Reading Exercises: Grades 1-9

Read & Remember - Book C see Gates-Peardon-LaClair Reading Exercises: Grades 1-9

Read & Respond: A Reading Improvement Text (with Readings) 3rd rev. ed. Janet Swinton & William Agopsowicz. LC 94-42934. (Illus.). 330p. (C). 1996. pap. text ed. write for info. (*0-935732-63-2*) Roxbury Pub Co.

Read & Respond: Ancient Egypt Literature. Holly Engel & Karen Brown. Ed. by Linda Milliken. (Illus.). 64p. (J). (gr. 3-6). 1994. student ed., pap. 6.95 (*1-56472-026-8*) Edupress.

Read & Respond: Colonial American Literature. Karen Brown & Holly Engel. Ed. by Linda Milliken. (Illus.). 64p. (J). (gr. 3-6). 1994. student ed., pap. 6.95 (*1-56472-028-4*) Edupress.

Read & Respond: Frontier American Literature. Karen Brown & Holly Engel. Ed. by Linda Milliken. (Illus.). 64p. (J). (gr. 3-6). 1994. student ed., pap. 6.95 (*1-56472-027-6*) Edupress.

Read & Respond: Native American Literature. Karen Brown & Holly Engel. Ed. by Linda Milliken. (Illus.). 64p. (J). (gr. 3-6). 1994. student ed., pap. 6.95 (*1-56472-029-2*) Edupress.

Read & Respond Medieval Times Literature. Holly Engel & Karen Brown. Ed. by Deneen Celecia. (Illus.). 64p. 1995. student ed., pap. 6.95 (*1-56472-046-2*) Edupress.

Read & Retell: A Strategy for the Whole Language/Natural Learning Classroom. Hazel Brown & Brian Cambourne. 144p. 1990. pap. text ed. 19.50 (*0-435-08506-9*, 08506) Heinemann.

*__Read & Rhyme Bear Country.__ (Berenstain Bears Family Time Coloring & Activity Bks.). (J). (ps-2). 1996. pap. 1.95 (*0-614-20246-9*, GT Publng) GT Pubng Corp.

*__Read & Spell.__ Jo E. Moore. (Reading & Writing Ser.). (Illus.). 32p. (J). (gr. 3-4). 1997. teacher ed., pap. 2.95 (*1-55799-412-9*, 4014) Evan-Moor Corp.

Read & Spell by Sound: A Multisensory Workbook to Help Children & Adults Develop Independent Reading-Spelling Skills. Lorna S. Werner. (Illus.). 114p. (Orig.). 1992. spiral bd. 19.95 (*1-882183-12-6*) Computer Pr.

Read & Succeed. Caroline Banks et al. 345p. (C). 1993. pap. 35.95 (*0-534-12816-5*) Wadsworth Pub.

*__Read & Think (Language)__ Phyllis Edwards. (Reading & Writing Ser.). (Illus.). 32p. (J). (gr. 3-4). 1996. teacher ed., pap. 2.95 (*1-55799-414-5*, 4016) Evan-Moor Corp.

Read & Write. (Key Words Readers Ser.: C Series, No. 641-1c). (Illus.). (J). (ps-5). 3.50 (*0-7214-0025-6*, Ladybrd); Ser. S705, No. 1. student ed. 1.95 (*0-317-04017-0*, Ladybrd) Penguin.

*__Read & Write.__ Ladybird Staff. 1997. pap. 3.50 (*0-7214-5761-4*) Dutton Child Bks.

Read & Write: A Guide to Effective Composition. James F. Dorrill & Charles W. Harwell. (C). 1987. pap. text ed. 18.75 (*0-15-575510-2*) HB Coll Pubs.

Read & Write: Fun Literature & Writing Connections for Kids. Michelle O'Brien-Palmer. (Illus.). 160p. (J). (ps-7). 1994. pap. 16.95 (*1-879235-04-8*) MicNik Pubns.

Read & Write Chinese: A Simplified Guide to the Chinese Characters. Rita M. Choy. 1983. pap. 11.95 (*0-941340-09-0*) China West.

Read & Write Chinese: A Simplified Guide to the Chinese Characters. 5th ed. Rita M. Choy. 350p. (CHI.). (C). 1990. pap. 13.95 (*0-941340-11-2*); audio write for info. (*0-318-51351-X*) China West.

Read Any Good Books? Sinclair B. Ferguson. 22p. 1992. pap. 1.95 (*0-85151-633-5*) Banner of Truth.

Read Any Good Math Lately? Children's Books for Mathematical Learning, K-6. David J. Whitin & Sandra Wilde. LC 92-2643. (Illus.). 206p. (J). 1992. pap. text ed. 21.00 (*0-435-08334-1*, 08334) Heinemann.

*__Read Around Alphabet Town Teacher's Guide.__ (Illus.). 32p. (J). (gr. k-1). 1992. teacher ed. 17.50 (*0-516-05447-3*) Childrens.

Read at Home, Grow Rich. James E. Shaw. Ed. by Sylvia J. Shaw. (Illus.). 100p. reprint ed. student ed., teacher ed., pap. 15.00 (*0-933415-02-8*) Mark Excell Pub.

Read Beyond the Lines - Book A see Gates-Peardon-LaClair Reading Exercises: Grades 1-9

Read Beyond the Lines - Book B see Gates-Peardon-LaClair Reading Exercises: Grades 1-9

Read Beyond the Lines - Book C see Gates-Peardon-LaClair Reading Exercises: Grades 1-9

Read Chinese, Bk. 1. enl. ed. Fred Wang. 1982. 14.95 (*0-88710-064-3*) Yale Far Eastern Pubns.

Read Chinese, Bk. 1. expanded ed. Fred Wang. 1982. audio write for info. (*0-88710-065-1*) Yale Far Eastern Pubns.

Read Chinese, Bk. 2. enl. ed. Richard Chang. 1983. audio write for info. (*0-88710-067-8*) Yale Far Eastern Pubns.

Read Chinese, Bk. 2. expanded ed. Richard Chang. 1983. 15.95 (*0-88710-066-X*) Yale Far Eastern Pubns.

Read Chinese, Bk. 3. Fred Wang & Richard Chang. 1963. 12.95 (*0-88710-068-6*); audio write for info. (*0-88710-069-4*) Yale Far Eastern Pubns.

*__Read Chinese Signs.__ Cornelius C. Kubler & Hsiaojung S. Chi. 1993. 39.95 (*0-88727-183-9*) Cheng & Tsui.

*__Read Chinese Signs: Institutional Edition.__ Cornelius C. Kubler & Hsiaojung S. Chi. 1993. 99.95 (*0-88727-182-0*) Cheng & Tsui.

Read Chinese Today: Understanding Chinese Characters by Their Ancestral Forms. Ping-gam Go. (Illus.). 1992. pap. 5.95 (*0-9623113-3-2*) Simplex Pubns.

Read, Dare to Dream. Suzanne Hitt. 196p. (C). 1996. per., pap. text ed. 27.24 (*0-8403-9591-4*) Kendall-Hunt.

An Asterisk (*) at the beginning of an entry indicates that the title is appearing in BIP for the first time.

R

Read Easy: Large Print Libraries for Older Adults. Anne M. Ring. 84p. (Orig.). 1991. ring bd. 19.95 (*1-878866-13-3*) CAREsource Prog.

Read 'Em & Eat: Favorite Recipes from Favorite Authors. Intro. by Bernadine Smith. 179p. (Orig.). 1991. spiral bd. 8.95 (*0-940696-29-0*) Monroe County Lib.

Read English!, Bk. 3. Demnitz. (Speak English Ser.). (Illus.). 72p. (Orig.). (C). 1991. pap. text ed. 7.95 (*0-8325-0512-9*, Natl Textbk) NTC Pub Grp.

Read English, Bk 1. Sherry Royce & Doris Zook. (Speak English Ser.). (Illus.). 80p. (Orig.). 1993. pap. text ed. 7.95 (*0-8325-0504-8*, Natl Textbk) NTC Pub Grp.

Read English, Bk. 2. Joseph Coyle. (Speak English Ser.). (Illus.). 80p. (Orig.). 1991. pap. 7.95 (*0-8325-0508-0*, Natl Textbk) NTC Pub Grp.

***Read for Me, Mama.** Vashanti Rahaman. LC 95-77784. (Illus.). 32p. (J). (gr. 1-5). 1997. 14.95 (*1-56397-313-8*) Boyds Mills Pr.

Read for the Fun of It. Caroline Feller Bauer. 372p. 1991. 45.00 (*0-8242-0824-2*) Wilson.

Read for Your Life: Turning Teens into Readers. Gladys Hunt & Barbara Hampton. 240p. 1992. pap. 9.99 (*0-310-54871-3*) Zondervan.

Read for Your Life: Two Successful Efforts to Help People Read & an Annotated List of Books That Made Them Want To. Julia R. Palmer. LC 73-14695. 508p. 1974. 37.50 (*0-8108-0654-1*) Scarecrow.

Read from the Start: Early Literacy Activities & Resources for Librarians & Educators. Jane A. Roeber. 152p. 1995. pap. text ed. 21.00 (*1-57337-019-3*) WI Dept Pub Instruct.

***Read If You Dare: Twelve Twisted Tales.** Ed. by Catherine Gourley. LC 96-44221. 160p. (YA). (gr. 5 up). 1997. lib. bdg. 16.90 (*0-7613-0046-5*) Millbrook Pr.

Read in Focus - Placement Test. 3rd ed. Defossard. (PS - Communication/English Ser.). 1990. 3.95 (*0-538-70058-0*) S-W Pub.

Read It Again! A Guide for Teaching Reading Through Literature, K-2, Bk. 1. Liz C. Rothlein & Terri Christman. (Illus.). 116p. (Orig.). 1988. pap. 9.95 (*0-673-38199-4*, GoodYrBooks) Addson-Wesley Educ.

Read It Again! Books to Prepare Children for Inclusion, Gr. 1-3. Sharon Vaughn & Liz C. Rothlein. (Illus.). 144p. (Orig.). 1994. pap. 9.95 (*0-673-36082-2*, GoodYrBooks) Addson-Wesley Educ.

Read It Again! Introducing Literature to Young Children, Preschool - Kindergarten, Bk. 1. Liz C. Rothlein & Libby Miller. (Illus.). 112p. (Orig.). (J). (ps). 1991. pap. 9.95 (*0-673-36008-3*, GoodYrBooks) Addson-Wesley Educ.

Read It Again! Multicultural Books for the Intermediate Grades. Liz C. Rothlein & Terri C. Wild. (Illus.). 144p. (Orig.). (J). (gr. 3-5). 1993. pap. 9.95 (*0-673-36081-4*, GoodYrBooks) Addson-Wesley Educ.

Read It Again! Multicultural Books for the Primary Grades, Bk. 1. Liz C. Rothlein & Terri C. Wild. (Illus.). 144p. (Orig.). (J). 1993. pap. 9.95 (*0-673-36064-4*, GoodYrBooks) Addson-Wesley Educ.

Read It Again, Bk 2, Grades 3-5: Grades 3-5. Liz C. Rothlein & Terri Christmas. 1990. pap. 9.95 (*0-673-46290-0*, GoodYrBooks) Addson-Wesley Educ.

Read It Again, More: Grades K-2, Bk. 1. Liz C. Rothlein & Terri Christman. 1990. pap. 9.95 (*0-673-46373-7*, GoodYrBooks) Addson-Wesley Educ.

Read It Again, More: Grades 3-5, Bk. 2. Liz C. Rothlein & Terri Christman. 1991. pap. 9.95 (*0-673-36007-5*, GoodYrBooks) Addson-Wesley Educ.

Read It Again! Preschool - Kindergarten, Bk. 2. Liz C. Rothlein & Libby Miller. (Illus.). 144p. (Orig.). (J). (ps). 1993. pap. 9.95 (*0-673-36042-3*, GoodYrBooks) Addson-Wesley Educ.

***Read It! Draw It! Solve It!** Elizabeth D. Miller. (J). (gr. 3). 1997. pap. text ed. 15.95 (*1-57232-436-8*) Seymour Pubns.

***Read It! Draw It! Solve It! - Grade 1: Problem Solving for Primary Grades.** Elizabeth D. Miller. Ed. by Catherine Anderson et al. 180p. (Orig.). 1996. teacher ed., pap. 16.95 (*1-57232-434-1*, 33800) Seymour Pubns.

***Read It! Draw It! Solve It! - Grade 2: Problem Solving for Primary Grades.** Elizabeth D. Miller. Ed. by Catherine Anderson et al. 180p. (Orig.). 1996. teacher ed., pap. 16.95 (*1-57232-435-X*, 33801) Seymour Pubns.

***Read It! Draw It! Solve It!, Animal Book.** Elizaebth D. Miller. (J). 1997. pap. text ed. 15.95 (*1-57232-437-6*) Seymour Pubns.

Read It in French. A. Asher & W. Webb. (C). 1989. 75.00 (*0-09-160721-3*, Pub. by S Thornes Pubs UK) St Mut.

Read It in the Classroom! Organizing an Interactive Language Arts Program, Grades 4-9. Linda Hart-Hewins & Jan Wells. 126p. 1992. pap. text ed. 16.50 (*0-435-08733-9*, 08733) Heinemann.

***Read It to Me Now! Learning at Home & at School.** 2nd ed. LC 96-47865. 1997. pap. write for info. (*0-335-19761-2*, Open Univ Pr) Taylor & Francis.

***Read It to Me Now! Learning at Home & at School.** 2nd ed. LC 96-47865. 1997. write for info. (*0-335-19762-0*, Open Univ Pr) Taylor & Francis.

Read It with Bookmarks. Barbara L. Goldenhersh. (Illus.). 128p. 1992. pap. 10.00 (*1-882429-07-9*) Classrm Catalyst.

Read It Yourself Stories. Harriet Castor et al. (Reading for Beginners Ser.). (Illus.). 96p. (J). (ps-3). 1995. 14.95 (*0-7460-2313-8*, Usborne) EDC.

Read Japanese Today. Len Walsh. LC 69-12078. 160p. 1969. pap. 8.95 (*0-8048-0496-6*) C E Tuttle.

Read Mark Learn. John Blanchard. 1987. pap. 2.99 (*0-85234-234-9*, Pub. by Evangelical Pr) Presby & Reformed.

Read Me. Duffy. (Management Information Systems Ser.). 1996. pap. 30.95 (*0-7895-0556-8*) S-W Pub.

Read Me a Fairy Tale: A Child's Book of Classic Fairy Tales. Illus. by Ian Beck. LC 92-41949. 128p. (J). (gr. k up). 1993. 16.95 (*0-590-49431-7*) Scholastic Inc.

Read Me Beraiskis. Chavie Freund. LC 90-83948. 44p. (J). 10.95 (*1-56062-042-0*) CIS Comm.

Read Me Berashis. Chanie Feund. LC 90-83948. (Read Me Ser.). (Illus.). 32p. (J). (ps-2). 1990. 9.95 (*0-685-46905-0*) CIS Comm.

Read Me First. Moore Educational Publishers Staff. Ed. by Nina Palmer et al. (Illus.). (Orig.). (C). 1996. pap. text ed. write for info. (*1-56588-002-1*) Moore Educ.

Read Me First: SGML for Writers & Editors. Ronald C. Turner. 1995. 50.00 (*0-13-432717-9*) P-H.

Read Me or Rue It. Paul O'Sullivan. LC 92-61256. 48p. 1992. pap. 1.50 (*0-89555-458-5*) TAN Bks Pubs.

Read Me the Haggadah. Chavie Freund. (Read Me Ser.). (Illus.). (J). (ps-2). 1990. 10.95 (*1-56062-021-8*) CIS Comm.

Read More about It: An Encyclopedia of Information Sources on Historical Figures & Events, Vol. 3. Ed. by C. Edward Wall. 1989. 98.00 (*0-87650-260-5*) Pierian.

Read My Desire: Lacan Against the Historicists. Joan Copjec. LC 94-383. (October Bk.). (Illus.). 288p. 1994. 30.00 (*0-262-03219-8*) MIT Pr.

Read My Desire: Lacan Against the Historicists. Joan Copjec. (Illus.). 288p. 1996. reprint ed. pap. 14.00 (*0-262-53140-2*, October Bk) MIT Pr.

***Read My Lips: A Treasury of Things Politicians Wish They Hadn't Said.** Matthew Parris & Phil Mason. 230p. 1997. 25.95 (*1-86105-043-7*, Pub. by Robson UK) Parkwest Pubns.

Read My Lips: Classic Texas Political Quotes. Kirk Dooley & Ben Price. (Classic Texas Quotes: the Ser.). (Illus.). 256p. (Orig.). 1995. pap. 12.95 (*0-89672-350-X*) Tex Tech Univ Pr.

Read My Lips: No New Pets. Linda G. Salisbury. LC 90-71430. (Illus.). 144p. (Orig.). 1990. pap. 8.95 (*0-9627974-0-5*) Tabby Hse Bks.

***Read My Lips: Sexual Subversion & the End of Gender Bashing.** Riki A. Wilchins. (Illus.). 288p. 1997. pap. 16.95 (*1-56341-090-7*); lib. bdg. 28.95 (*1-56341-091-5*) Firebrand Bks.

Read My Lips: The Unofficial Cartoon Biography of George Bush. Matt Tolbert. (Illus.). 1992. pap. 6.95 (*1-56398-041-X*) Malibu Comics Ent.

Read My Lips, Make My Day, Eat Quiche & Die! A Doonesbury Collection. Garry B. Trudeau. (Illus.). 96p. (Orig.). 1989. pap. 7.95 (*0-8362-1845-0*) Andrews & McMeel.

***Read My Mind: Young Children, Poetry & Learning.** Fred Sedgwick. LC 96-35403. 208p. (C). 1997. pap. write for info. (*0-415-14343-8*) Routledge.

Read 'n Draw: Following Directions, Bk. 1. Randy L. Womack & Christina Lew. (Illus.). 48p. (J). (gr. 4-6). 1992. student ed. 6.95 (*1-56500-032-3*) Gldn Educ.

Read-N-Grow Picture Bible. James E. Padgett. 1994. 16.99 (*0-8499-1163-X*) Word Pub.

Read 'n' Roll Train. Liane B. Onish. (J). (ps). 1997. pap. 14.99 (*0-7214-5638-3*, Ladybrd) Penguin.

Read 'n' Roll Truck. Liane B. Onish. (J). (ps). 1997. pap. 14.99 (*0-7214-5637-5*, Ladybrd) Penguin.

***Read 'n' Rolls: Baby Tweety's Flying Machine.** (J). 1996. 16.99 (*0-8289-0980-6*) Penguin.

***Read Newspapers & Magazines.** Martha Cheney. (Real-Life Reading Activities Ser.). (Illus.). 64p. (J). (gr. 4-6). 1996. teacher ed., pap. 7.95 (*1-55799-594-X*, 571) Evan-Moor Corp.

Read-O-Mat: Syllabus. Alyce E. Faber. 1976. pap. text ed. 6.95 (*0-89420-006-2*, 114008); audio 35.85 (*0-89420-179-4*, 114000) Natl Book.

Read On: A Conference Approach to Reading. David Hornsby et al. LC 87-22938. 193p. (Orig.). 1988. pap. text ed. 20.00 (*0-435-08459-3*, 08459) Heinemann.

Read On: Using Fiction in School. 152p. 1995. pap. text ed. 24.95 (*1-85396-286-4*, Pub. by Paul Chapman UK) Taylor & Francis.

Read on Rita. Stephen Cosgrove. (Illus.). 32p. (J). 1993. lib. bdg. 12.95 (*1-56674-042-8*, HTS Bks) Forest Hse.

Read On! Two. Ed. by V. K. Lawson. 60p. 1987. pap. text ed. 10.00 (*0-930713-01-X*); teacher ed., pap. text ed. 5.50 (*0-930713-20-6*); teacher ed., pap. text ed. 2.00 (*0-930713-21-4*) Lit Vol Am.

Read On! Two, Bk. 1. Artis Lee et al. Ed. by V. K. Lawson. 68p. 1987. pap. 3.75 (*0-930713-02-8*); audio 8.00 (*0-930713-08-7*) Lit Vol Am.

Read On! Two, Bk. 2. Artis Lee & Judy D. Simmons. Ed. by V. K. Lawson. 1987. audio 8.00 (*0-930713-09-5*) Lit Vol Am.

Read On! Two, Bk. 2. Judy D. Simmons & Artis Lee. Ed. by V. K. Lawson. 1987. pap. text ed. 3.75 (*0-930713-03-6*) Lit Vol Am.

Read On! Two, Bk. 3. Artis Lee & Fred Elmore. Ed. by V. K. Lawson. (Illus.). 48p. 1987. pap. text ed. 3.75 (*0-930713-04-4*); audio 8.00 (*0-930713-17-6*) Lit Vol Am.

Read On! Two, Bk. 4. Bruce Coville & Artis Lee. Ed. by V. K. Lawson. (Illus.). 1987. pap. text ed. 3.75 (*0-930713-05-2*); audio 8.00 (*0-930713-18-4*) Lit Vol Am.

Read On! Two, Bk. 5. Artis Lee. Ed. by V. K. Lawson. (Illus.). 78p. 1987. pap. text ed. 3.75 (*0-930713-06-0*); audio 10.00 (*0-318-41218-7*) Lit Vol Am.

Read On! Two, Bk. 6. Bruce Coville & Artis Lee. Ed. by V. K. Lawson. (Illus.). 48p. 1987. pap. text ed. 3.75 (*0-930713-07-9*); audio 10.00 (*0-930713-34-6*) Lit Vol Am.

Read On! Two, Set. Ed. by V. K. Lawson. 60p. 1987. pap. text ed. 45.00 (*0-930713-00-1*); 50.00 (*0-930713-46-X*) Lit Vol Am.

Read On! Two, Wkbk. 1. Artis Lee et al. Ed. by V. K. Lawson. 68p. 1987. Workbook 1, 68p. 2.75 (*0-930713-11-7*) Lit Vol Am.

Read On! Two, Wkbk. 2. Judy D. Simmons & Artis Lee. Ed. by V. K. Lawson. 56p. 1987. Workbook 2, 56p. pap. text ed. 2.75 (*0-930713-12-5*) Lit Vol Am.

Read On! Two, Wkbk. 3. Artis Lee & Fred Elmore. Ed. by V. K. Lawson. (Illus.). 48p. 1987. Workbook 3, 48p. pap. text ed. 2.75 (*0-930713-13-3*) Lit Vol Am.

Read On! Two, Wkbk. 4. Bruce Coville & Artis Lee. Ed. by V. K. Lawson. (Illus.). 56p. 1987. Workbook 4, 56p. pap. text ed. 2.75 (*0-930713-14-1*) Lit Vol Am.

Read On! Two, Wkbk. 5. Artis Lee. Ed. by V. K. Lawson. (Illus.). 84p. 1987. Workbook 5, 84p. pap. text ed. 2.75 (*0-930713-15-X*) Lit Vol Am.

Read On! Two, Wkbk. 6. Bruce Coville & Artis Lee. Ed. by V. K. Lawson. (Illus.). 48p. 1987. Workbook 6, 48p. pap. text ed. 2.75 (*0-930713-16-8*) Lit Vol Am.

R.E.A.D. Reading Enhancement & Development. 5th ed. Rhonda H. Atkinson & Debbie G. Longman. LC 94-31084. 622p. (C). 1995. pap. text ed. 32.75 (*0-314-04440-X*) West Pub.

Read Real Japanese. Janet Ashby. Ed. by Brase Suzuki. (Power Japanese Ser.). 128p. 1994. pap. 10.00 (*4-7700-1754-5*) Kodansha.

Read, Reason, Write. 4th ed. Dorothy U. Seyler. LC 94-11280. 1994. pap. text ed. write for info. (*0-07-057009-4*) McGraw.

Read Right! Comprehension Power. J. E. Sparks & Carl E. Johnson. 296p. (C). 1990. reprint ed. pap. text ed. 23.50 (*0-8191-7662-1*) U Pr of Amer.

Read Test: Reading Evaluation Adult Diagnosis Test. rev. ed. Ed. by Ruth J. Colvin & Jane H. Root. 55p. 1982. pap. text ed. 6.00 (*0-930713-23-0*) Lit Vol Am.

Read the Fine Print Before You Say "I Do" Jack Leipert. LC 94-5156. 96p. (Orig.). 1994. pap. 5.95 (*0-8091-3464-0*) Paulist Pr.

Read the Label Carefully: Separating New Age & Christianity. James Browning. Ed. by Becky Nelson. 22p. (Orig.). (YA). (gr. 7-12). 1992. pap. text ed. 1.95 (*1-56309-062-7*, Wrld Changers Res) Womans Mission Union.

Read the New Testament in Spanish. D. W. Coop & M. R. Gonzalez. (IQ Book Ser.). (Illus.). 256p. (SPA.). (YA). (gr. 9-12). 1996. wbk. ed. 14.95 (*1-883316-52-9*) K K & G.

Read the Tarot Within Seven Days. Keith Morgan. (Orig.). 1994. pap. 7.95 (*1-872189-90-3*, Pub. by Mandrake Pr UK) Holmes Pub.

Read, Think, Cut & Paste. Joy Evans & Jo E. Moore. (Learning to Read Ser.). (Illus.). 20p. (J). (gr. 1-3). 1979. teacher ed., pap. 4.95 (*1-55799-028-X*, EMC 139) Evan-Moor Corp.

Read This & Tell Me What It Says. A. Manette Ansay. LC 95-11039. 160p. (C). 1996. 22.95 (*0-87023-988-0*) U of Mass Pr.

Read This Before You Go Out in the Yard. Derek Little. (Illus.). 88p. (Orig.). 1996. pap. 12.95 (*1-888321-04-0*) Semco Bks.

Read This Book Before Your Child Starts School. Miriam W. Lukken. (Illus.). 240p. 1994. pap. 18.95 (*0-398-06093-2*) C C Thomas.

Read This Book Before Your Child Starts School. Miriam W. Lukken. (Illus.). 240p. (C). 1994. text ed. 31.95 (*0-398-05916-0*) C C Thomas.

Read This First: An Owner's Guide to the New Model Statement of Objectives for Academic Bibliographic Instruction. Ed. by Carolyn Dusenbury. 72p. 1991. pap. 19.95 (*0-8389-7548-8*) ALA.

Read This Only to Yourself: The Private Writings of Midwestern Women, 1880-1910. Elizabeth Hampsten. LC 81-47008. 255p. reprint ed. pap. 72.70 (*0-7837-1753-9*, 2057288) Bks Demand.

Read Through the Bible in a Year. John R. Kohlenberger, III. (Orig.). 1986. pap. 4.99 (*0-8024-7168-4*) Moody.

***Read to Bunny.** Rosemary Wells. LC 97-17704. (J). 1990. write for info. (*0-590-30284-1*) Scholastic Inc.

Read to Me! Kathy M. Littlefield & Robert S. Littlefield. (Illus.). 28p. (Orig.). (J). (gr. 3-6). 1990. pap. text ed. 8.95 (*1-879340-04-6*, K0105) Kidspeak.

Read to Me: Raising Kids Who Love to Read. Bernice E. Cullinan. (Illus.). 160p. 1992. pap. 4.50 (*0-590-45206-1*) Scholastic Inc.

Read to Me: Recommended Literature for Children Ages Two Through Seven. California Department of Education Staff. (Illus.). 144p. 1992. pap. 9.00 (*0-8011-1048-3*) Calif Education.

Read-to-Me: Recommended Literature for Children Ages Two Through Seven. Illus. by Jerry Pinkney. 144p. (Orig.). (C). 1996. pap. 30.00 (*0-7881-2723-3*) DIANE Pub.

Read to Me - Just One More Book. Pamela A. Kopen. LC 91-60425. (Illus.). 32p. (J). (gr. k-3). 1991. 14.95 (*0-9628914-0-1*) Padakami Pr.

Read to Me, Grandma. Gail Harvey. (J). 1993. 8.99 (*0-517-09348-0*) Random Hse Value.

Read-to-Me Storybook. Child Study Association of America Staff. LC 47-31488. (Illus.). (J). (ps-1). 1947. 16.95i (*0-690-68832-6*, Crowell Jr Bks) HarpC Child Bks.

Read to Me...& I'll Read to You: Reading Involvement with Your Child from Birth. rev. ed. Barbara A. Kohli & Carolyn N. Troutwine. LC 94-94488. 109p. (J). 1994. pap. 12.95 (*0-9624195-1-6*) Cleary Connection.

Read to Study. Silverman. (YA). (gr. 7 up). 1988. pap. 9.99 (*0-89824-172-3*) Trillium Pr.

Read to Succeed. 2nd ed. Jane Bracy & Marian McClintock. 1980. teacher ed., pap. text ed. write for info. (*0-07-007036-9*) McGraw.

***Read to Succeed: Tutor's Guide.** Lois A. Bader. LC 97-23364. 1998. write for info. (*0-13-690561-7*, Merrill Coll) P-H.

Read to Write. 3rd ed. Donald M. Murray. (Illus.). 608p. 1993. pap. text ed. 21.50 (*0-15-500190-6*); Instructor's edition. teacher ed. write for info. (*0-15-500191-4*) HarBrace.

Read to Write: A Writing Process Reader. 2nd rev. ed. Donald M. Murray. 457p. (C). 1990. pap. text ed. 19.75 (*0-03-030797-X*) HB Coll Pubs.

***Read to Write: An Integrated Course for Nonnative Speakers of English.** 7th ed. Jeri W. Gillie et al. LC 96-46646. 1997. pap. text ed. write for info. (*0-07-044398-X*) McGraw.

Read to Write: Using Children's Literature As a Springboard for Teaching Writing. 3rd ed. John W. Stewig. 296p. (Orig.). (C). 1990. pap. text ed. 17.95 (*0-913461-16-4*) R Owen Pubs.

Read Today! Read Today Big Book, N110. (Networks Ser.). (J). (gr. 1). 1991. 19.50 (*0-88106-700-8*, N110) Charlesbridge Pub.

READ Trainer's Kit. Ed. by V. K. Lawson. 1982. Cassette tape, script & guide. 20.00 incl. audio (*0-930713-40-0*) Lit Vol Am.

***Read Well in 24 Hours.** H. L. Maxwell. (Illus.). 278p. (Orig.). (J). (gr. 3-12). 1994. student ed., teacher ed. 99.95 (*0-9657797-5-0*) Read Well.

***Read Well in 24 Hours, Vol. 2.** H. L. Maxwell et al. 278p. (Orig.). (J). (gr. 3-12). 1994. student ed. 49.95 (*0-9657797-6-9*) Read Well.

Read-with-Me Stories for Grown-Ups & Others, 3 vol. set. David P. Williams & Helen C. Williams. (Illus.). (Orig.). (J). 1993. pap. 12.00 (*1-886058-00-8*) D P Williams.

***Read! With Phonics.** (Illus.). 108p. (Orig.). (J). (ps-3). 1997. pap. 8.99 (*1-56293-985-8*) McClanahan Bk.

Read with Your Child: Make a Difference. Barbara Keller & Ray Keller. (Illus.). 25p. (Orig.). 1997. pap. 2.95 (*1-881966-15-1*, 29 26-A02) Eagles MT.

Read, Write, & Research Study Guide. 2nd ed. FCCJ Foundation Staff. 232p. (C). 1996. per., pap. text ed. 28.29 (*0-7872-2519-3*) Kendall-Hunt.

Read, Write, Now! Keith Polette. (Illus.). 44p. (J). (gr. 5-9). 1993. pap. text ed. 5.95 (*1-879287-20-X*) Pieces of Lrning.

Read, Write, React: An Integrated Approach to Reading & Writing. Lonna Smith & Robert Ramonda. 1996. pap. text ed. write for info. (*0-07-059252-7*) McGraw.

Read, Write, Relate. Kathleen Malia & Sharon Warycka. 220p. (C). 1990. pap. text ed. 18.75 (*0-15-575483-1*) HB Coll Pubs.

Readability: Its Past, Present, & Future. Ed. by Beverley L. Zakaluk & S. Jay Samuels. LC 87-30549. 156p. reprint ed. pap. 44.50 (*0-8357-2638-X*, 2040126) Bks Demand.

Readability in the Classroom. Colin Harrison. LC 79-41794. (Illus.). 160p. 1980. 22.50 (*0-521-22712-7*) Cambridge U Pr.

Readability Machine: Radio Shack, TRS-80 Model 4 (Software & Documentation) Brian Pasch & Jacqueline K. Polk. 48p. 1986. 84.95 (*0-13-753609-7*) P-H.

Readability Machine: The Readability Machine for Apple II; Apple IIe, Apple IIc, & Apple-Compatible Microcomputers. Brian Pasch & Jacqueline K. Polk. 48p. 1986. 84.95 (*0-13-753617-8*) P-H.

***Readability Master 2000.** Ezra L. Stieglitz. 1997. pap. 29.95 incl. disk (*1-57129-031-1*); pap. 29.95 incl. mac ld (*1-57129-038-9*) Brookline Bks.

Readability of Literature & Popular Titles, Vol. 1. 112p. (Orig.). 1988. pap. 30.00 (*1-56497-002-7*, RR-L1) TASA.

Readability of Literature & Popular Titles, Vol. 2. 99p. (Orig.). 1991. pap. 30.00 (*1-56497-003-5*, RR-L2) TASA.

Readability of Literature & Popular Titles, Vol. 3. 100p. (Orig.). 1995. pap. 30.00 (*1-56497-020-5*, RR-L3) TASA.

***Readability of Literature & Popular Titles, Vol. 4.** 138p. (Orig.). 1997. pap. 30.00 (*1-56497-028-0*, RR-L4) TASA.

Readability of Textbooks. 10th ed. 215p. 1996. pap. 40.00 (*1-56497-025-6*, RR-P10) TASA.

Readability of Textbooks in Series. 9th ed. 121p. 1994. pap. 25.00 (*1-56497-019-1*, RR-S9) TASA.

Readability Revisited: The New Dale-Chall Readability Formula. Jeanne Chall & Edgar Dale. LC 95-16034. 176p. 1995. pap. text ed. 29.95 (*1-57129-008-7*) Brookline Bks.

Readable "Beowulf" The Old English Epic Newly Translated. Tr. by Stanley B. Greenfield. LC 81-16933. (Illus.). 173p. (C). 1982. pap. 15.95 (*0-8093-1060-0*) S Ill U Pr.

Read'em & Weep: The Songs You Forgot to Remember. Sigmund G. Spaeth. LC 79-11319. (Music Reprint Ser.). 1979. reprint ed. lib. bdg. 35.00 (*0-306-79564-7*) Da Capo.

Reader. Robert Gluck. 59p. (Orig.). (C). 1989. pap. 12.95 (*0-932499-66-X*) Lapis Pr.

***Reader.** Bernhard Schlink. LC 97-1511. 160p. 1997. 21.00 (*0-679-44279-0*) Pantheon.

***Reader.** Bernhard Schlink. 1998. pap. write for info. (*0-679-78130-7*, Vin) Random.

Reader, Bk. A. Jon George. Ed. by Louise Goss. (Frances Clark Library for Piano Students). 16p. 1969. pap. text ed. 3.50 (*0-87487-674-5*) Summy-Birchard.

Reader, Pt. C. Frances Clark. 16p. 1970. pap. text ed. 3.50 (*0-87487-676-1*) Summy-Birchard.

Reader, Pt. D. Frances Clark. 16p. 1970. pap. text ed. 3.50 (*0-87487-677-X*) Summy-Birchard.

Reader, Pt. B. Frances Clark. 16p. 1969. pap. text ed. 3.50 (*0-87487-675-3*) Summy-Birchard.

An Asterisk (*) at the beginning of an entry indicates that the title is appearing in BIP for the first time.

***Reader: Art/Dance/Music/Theatre Arts 357.** Yasuhara. 160p. (C). 1996. per., pap. text ed. 28.29 (*0-7872-2663-7*) Kendall-Hunt.

Reader: Modern Hebrew Prose & Poetry. Ed. by Ora Band. 1996. pap. 14.95 (*0-87441-480-6*) Behrman.

Reader Vol. 1: Theory. Beverly L. Ritter et al. (Realtime Machine Shorthand Ser.). 114p. (C). 1992. pap. text ed. 15.00 (*0-938643-31-2*) Stenotype Educ.

Reader & Spectator: Problems in the Interpretation of Greek Tragedy. A. Maria Van Erp Taalman Kip. 143p. (Orig.). 1990. pap. 30.00 (*90-5063-055-3*, Pub. by Gieben NE) Benjamins North Am.

***Reader & the Detective Story.** George N. Dove. LC 96-47340. 210p. 1997. 39.95 (*0-87972-731-4*); pap. 18.95 (*0-87972-732-2*) Bowling Green Univ Popular Press.

Reader & the Text: Interpretative Strategies for Latin American Literatures. Diana S. Goodrich. LC 85-30697. (Purdue University Monographs in Romance Languages: No. 18). xi, 150p. (Orig.). 1986. pap. 38.00 (*0-915027-60-7*) Benjamins North Am.

Reader Development Bibliography: Of the Free Library of Philadelphia. 1993. 14.95 (*0-88336-559-6*) New Readers.

Reader Entrapment in Eighteenth-Century Literature. Ed. by C. Kropf. LC 89-45872. (Georgia State Literary Studies: No. 8). 1992. 55.00 (*0-404-63208-4*) AMS Pr.

Reader for College Writers. 2nd ed. Ralph E. Loewe. (Illus.). 368p. (C). 1985. pap. text ed. write for info. (*0-13-753641-0*) P-H.

Reader for Developing Writers. Santi V. Buscemi. 1990. teacher ed., pap. text ed. 19.95 (*0-07-009326-1*) McGraw.

Reader for Developing Writers. 3rd ed. Santi V. Buscemi. LC 95-43248. (C). 1996. pap. text ed. write for info. (*0-07-009484-5*) McGraw.

***Reader for World History Vol. I: To 1800.** 2nd ed. Duiker. (History Ser.). 1998. pap. 23.95 (*0-534-53122-9*) Wadsworth Pub.

***Reader for World History Vol. II: Since 1500.** 2nd ed. Duiker. (History Ser.). 1998. pap. 23.95 (*0-534-53123-7*) Wadsworth Pub.

***Reader, I Murdered Him: Original Crime Stories.** Ed. by Jen Green. 234p. 1997. pap. 11.95 (*0-7043-4159-X*, Pub. by Womens Press UK) Trafalgar.

***Reader, I Murdered Him, Too: Crime Stories.** Ed. by Helen WIndrath. 214p. 1997. pap. 11.95 (*0-7043-4363-0*, Pub. by Womens Press UK) Trafalgar.

Reader in American Library History. Ed. by Michael H. Harris. LC 71-165293. 242p. 1983. text ed. 59.95 (*0-313-24040-X*, ZHR/, Greenwood Pr) Greenwood.

Reader in Children's Librarianship. Joan Foster. LC 78-26669. 450p. 1983. text ed. 55.00 (*0-313-24039-6*, ZRG/, Greenwood Pr) Greenwood.

Reader in Classification & Descriptive Cataloging. Ed. by Ann F. Painter. LC 72-78204. 320p. 1983. text ed. 55.00 (*0-313-24035-3*, ZRC/, Praeger Pubs) Greenwood.

Reader in Comparative Librarianship. Ed. by D. J. Foskett. LC 76-10124. 333p. 1983. text ed. 55.00 (*0-313-24037-X*, ZRE/, Greenwood Pr) Greenwood.

Reader in Comparative Religion: An Anthropological Approach. 4th ed. William A. Lessa & Evon Z. Vogt. (C). 1979. pap. text ed. 53.50 (*0-06-043991-2*) Addison-Wesley Educ.

Reader in Czech Sociolinguistics. Ed. by Jan Chloupek et al. LC 86-17024. (Linguistic & Literary Studies in Eastern Europe: No. 23). 344p. 1987. 94.00 (*90-272-1528-6*) Benjamins North Am.

Reader in Documents of International Organizations. Ed. by Robert D. Stevens & Helen C. Stevens. LC 73-93966. 410p. 1983. text ed. 65.00 (*0-313-24036-1*, ZRD/) Greenwood.

Reader in Electronics & Telecomunications, English-Italian. M. G. Calasso & M. L. Mirak. 470p. 1978. pap. 49.95 (*0-7859-0911-7*, M9194) Fr & Eur.

***Reader in European Integration.** David De Giustino. LC 96-45451. (C). 1997. pap. text ed. 17.95 (*0-582-29200-X*) Addison-Wesley.

Reader in Feminist Knowledge. Ed. by Sneja Gunew. LC 89-10959. 432p. (C). 1991. pap. 19.95 (*0-415-04699-8*, A4171) Routledge.

Reader in French Sociolinguistics. Ed. by Malcolm H. Offord. LC 96-3294. (Applications in French Linguistics Ser.: Vol. 1). 213p. 1996. 99.00 (*1-85359-343-5*, Pub. by Multilingual Matters UK); pap. 24.95 (*1-85359-342-7*, Pub. by Multilingual Matters UK) Taylor & Francis.

Reader in Hasidic Thought. Norman Lamm. 1995. write for info. (*0-614-07636-6*); pap. write for info. (*0-614-07637-4*) Ktav.

***Reader in International Relations & Political Theory.** Ed. by Howard Williams et al. 352p. 1992. pap. 15.99 (*0-335-15667-3*, Open Univ Pr) Taylor & Francis.

Reader in Law Librarianship. Bernard D. Reams, Jr. LC 87-82949. xv, 375p. 1987. reprint ed. lib. bdg. 45.00 (*0-89941-589-X*, 305430) W S Hein.

Reader in Library Administration. Ed. by Paul Wasserman & Mary Lee Bundy. LC 68-28324. 403p. 1983. text ed. 35.00 (*0-313-24033-7*, ZRA/, Greenwood Pr) Greenwood.

Reader in Library Services & the Computer. Ed. by Louis Kaplan. LC 70-149298. 239p. 1983. text ed. 55.00 (*0-313-24041-8*, ZRI/, Greenwood Pr) Greenwood.

Reader in Library Technology. Shirley Gray Adamovich. LC 75-8051. 236p. 1983. text ed. 55.00 (*0-313-24042-6*, ZRJ/, Greenwood Pr) Greenwood.

Reader in Marxist Philosophy. Ed. by Howard Selsam & Harry Martel. LC 63-14262. 384p. (Orig.). 1963. pap. text ed. 6.95 (*0-7178-0167-5*) Intl Pubs Co.

Reader in Medical Librarianship. Ed. by Winifred Sewell. LC 72-86634. 340p. 1983. text ed. 75.00 (*0-313-24043-4*, ZRK/, Greenwood Pr) Greenwood.

Reader in Modern Literary Arabic. Farhat J. Ziadeh. 1993. 19.95 (*0-86685-556-4*) Intl Bk Ctr.

Reader in Music Librarianship. Carol J. Bradley. LC 73-82994. 340p. 1983. text ed. 55.00 (*0-313-24044-2*, ZRL/, Greenwood Pr) Greenwood.

Reader in Peace Studies. Ed. by Paul Smoker et al. 245p. 1990. text ed. 29.95 (*0-08-036287-7*, Prgamon Press); pap. text ed. 15.00 (*0-08-036286-9*, Prgamon Press) Buttrwrth-Heinemann.

Reader in Planning Theory. Ed. by Andreas Faludi. LC 72-11536. 416p. (C). 1973. pap. text ed. 37.95 (*0-08-017067-6*, Prgamon Press) Buttrwrth-Heinemann.

Reader in Research Methods for Librarianship. Mary Lee Bundy. Ed. by Paul Wasserman & Gayle Araghi. LC 70-86858. 363p. 1983. text ed. 65.00 (*0-313-24045-0*, ZRM/, Greenwood Pr) Greenwood.

Reader in Science Information. Ed. by John Sherrod & Alfred Hodina. LC 72-97713. 403p. 1983. text ed. 65.00 (*0-313-24046-9*, ZRN/, Greenwood Pr) Greenwood.

Reader in Scientific Fraud: A Sociology of Science. A. C. Higgins. 271p. (Orig.). (C). 1995. pap. text ed. 26.50 (*1-885343-09-4*) Exams Unltd.

Reader in Social Science Documentation. Ed. by Christopher D. Needham. LC 75-8049. 538p. 1983. text ed. 65.00 (*0-313-24047-7*, ZRO/, Greenwood Pr) Greenwood.

Reader in Technical Services. Ed. by Edward L. Applebaum. LC 72-87717. 284p. 1983. text ed. 55.00 (*0-313-24048-5*, ZRP/, Greenwood Pr) Greenwood.

Reader in the Academic Library. Ed. by Michael M. Reynolds. LC 71-112300. 378p. 1983. text ed. 65.00 (*0-313-24034-5*, ZRB/, Greenwood Pr) Greenwood.

Reader in the Dickensian Mirrors: Some New Language. S. J. Schad. 236p. 1992. text ed. 49.95 (*0-312-06880-8*) St Martin.

Reader in the History of Aphasia: From Franz Gall to Norman Geschwind. Ed. by Paul Eling. (Classics in Psycholinguistics Ser.: No. 4). xvi, 392p. 1995. 110.00 (*90-272-1893-5*) Benjamins North Am.

Reader in the History of Books & Printing. Ed. by Paul A. Winckler. LC 78-17260. 406p. 1983. text ed. 59.95 (*0-313-24038-8*, ZRF/, Greenwood Pr) Greenwood.

Reader in the History of the Eastern Slavic Languages: Russian, Belorussian & Ukrainian. Ed. by George Y. Shevelov & Fred Holling. LC 58-9238. (Columbia Slavic Studies). 89p. reprint ed. pap. 25.40 (*0-317-09819-5*, 2015390) Bks Demand.

Reader in the Language of Shakespearean Drama. Vivian Salmon & Edwina Burness. LC 86-30991. (Studies in the History of Language Sciences: No. 35). xx, 523p. (C). 1987. 113.00 (*90-272-4516-9*); pap. 29.95 (*0-915027-99-2*) Benjamins North Am.

Reader in the Picaresque Novel. Helen H. Reed. (Monagrafias A Ser.: Vol. CXIV). 120p. (C). 1984. 27.00 (*0-7293-0204-0*, Pub. by Tamesis Bks Ltd UK) Boydell & Brewer.

Reader in Urban Sociology. Ed. by M. S. Rao et al. 425p. (C). 1991. 40.00 (*0-86311-151-3*, Pub. by Orient Longman Ltd II) Apt Bks.

***Reader in World Religion, Vol. 1.** Peters. Date not set. pap. text ed. write for info. (*0-312-07137-X*) St Martin.

Reader is Warned. Carter Dickson. LC 89-85728. 192p. 1989. pap. 5.95 (*1-55882-019-1*, Lib Crime Classics) Intl Polygonics.

Reader Meets Author - Bridging the Gap: A Psycholinguistic & Sociolinguistic Perspective. Ed. by Judith A. Langer & M. Trika Smith-Burke. LC 81-20769. (Illus.). 250p. reprint ed. pap. 71.30 (*0-8357-4310-1*, 2037108) Bks Demand.

Reader of Modern Arabic Short Stories. Ed. by Sabry Hafez & Catherine Cobham. 220p. 1990. 25.00 (*0-86356-191-8*, Pub. by Saqi Books UK); pap. 15.00 (*0-86356-087-3*, Pub. by Saqi Bks UK) Interlink Pub.

Reader of Modern Urdu Poetry. Muhammad A. Barker et al. LC 78-396470. 334p. (ENG & URD.). reprint ed. pap. 95.20 (*0-7837-6894-X*, 2046724) Bks Demand.

Reader on Administrative Law. Denis J. Galligan. (Oxford Readings in Socio-Legal Studies). 512p. 1996. 70.00 (*0-19-876408-1*) OUP.

Reader on Administrative Law. Denis J. Galligan. (Oxford Readings in Socio-Legal Studies). 512p. 1996. pap. 22.00 (*0-19-876409-X*) OUP.

***Reader on Classical Islam.** F. E. Peters. 430p. 1996. pap. 19.95 (*0-614-21069-0*, 1060) Kazi Pubns.

Reader on Classical Islam. F. E. Peters. 440p. 1994. text ed. 65.00 (*0-691-03394-3*); pap. text ed. 19.95 (*0-691-00040-9*) Princeton U Pr.

Reader on Criminal Justice. Ed. by Nicola Lacey. (Oxford Readings in Socio-Legal Studies). 288p. 1995. pap. 19.95 (*0-19-876361-1*) OUP.

Reader on Criminal Justice. Ed. by Nicola Lacey. (Oxford Readings in Socio-Legal Studies). 288p. 1995. 65.00 (*0-19-876362-X*) OUP.

Reader on Family Law. Ed. by John Eekelaar & Mavis Maclean. (Oxford Readings in Socio-Legal Studies). 416p. 1995. pap. 24.95 (*0-19-876363-8*) OUP.

Reader on Islam. Ed. by Arthur Jeffery. LC 79-52557. (Islam Ser.). 1980. reprint ed. lib. bdg. 63.95 (*0-8369-9264-4*) Ayer.

Reader on Punishment. Ed. by Anthony Duff & David Garland. (Oxford Readings in Socio-Legal Studies). 360p. 1995. 65.00 (*0-19-876352-2*) OUP.

Reader on Punishment. Ed. by Anthony Duff & David Garland. (Oxford Readings in Socio-Legal Studies). 360p. 1995. pap. 17.95 (*0-19-876353-0*) OUP.

***Reader on Resourcing Civil Justice.** Ed. by Alan A. Paterson & Tamara Goriely. (Oxford Readings in Socio-Legal Studies). 356p. 1997. 75.00 (*0-19-876462-6*) OUP.

***Reader on Resourcing Civil Justice.** Ed. by Alan A. Paterson & Tamara Goriely. (Oxford Readings in Socio-Legal Studies). 356p. 1997. pap. 35.00 (*0-19-876461-8*) OUP.

Reader on the Library Building. Ed. by Hal B. Schell. LC 73-93967. 359p. 1983. text ed. 65.00 (*0-313-24049-3*, ZRQ, Greenwood Pr) Greenwood.

Reader on the Sociology of the Academic Profession. Ed. by Walter P. Metzger. LC 76-55212. (Academic Profession Ser.). 1979. reprint ed. lib. bdg. 56.95 (*0-405-10039-6*) Ayer.

Reader-Printers: ANSI-AIIM MS36-1990. Association for Information & Image Management Staff. 1990. pap. 33.00 (*0-89258-110-7*, MS36) Assn Inform & Image Mgmt.

Reader Resource Series. (Orig.). Date not set. pap. write for info. (*1-883667-09-7*) Christian Meth.

***Reader Response.** Hunsberger & Labercane. 1997. pap. text ed. 24.00 (*0-205-26760-2*) P-H.

Reader Response Analysis of the Epistle of James. Randall C. Webber. 126p. 1996. 69.95 (*1-57309-087-5*); pap. 49.95 (*1-57309-086-7*) Intl Scholars.

Reader-Response Criticism: A Test of Its Usefulness in a First-Year College Course in Writing about Literature. Marian Price. LC 89-2444. (American University Studies: English Language & Literature: Ser. IV, Vol. 109). 161p. 1990. text ed. 34.95 (*0-8204-1115-9*) P Lang Pubng.

Reader-Response Criticism: From Formalism to Post-Structuralism. Ed. by Jane P. Tompkins. LC 80-7966. 320p. (C). 1981. pap. text ed. 14.95 (*0-8018-2401-X*) Johns Hopkins.

Reader Response in Elementary Classrooms: Quest & Discovery. Ed. by Nicholas J. Karolides. LC 96-20669. 384p. 1996. pap. text ed. 24.95 (*0-8058-2260-7*) L Erlbaum Assocs.

Reader Response in the Classroom. Ed. by Charles R. Chew et al. 119p. 1986. pap. text ed. 7.00 (*0-930348-13-3*) NY St Eng Coun.

Reader Response in the Classroom: Evoking & Interpreting Meaning in Literature. Ed. by Nicholas J. Karolides. 251p. (Orig.). (C). 1992. pap. text ed. 32.95 (*0-8013-0792-9*, 78846) Longman.

Reader Response to Literature: The Empirical Dimension. Ed. by Elaine F. Nardocchio. LC 92-35778. (Approaches to Semiotics Ser.: No. 108). xiv, 313p. (C). 1993. lib. bdg. 129.25 (*3-11-012764-4*) Mouton.

Reader Services in Libraries: A Day in Honor of Margaret E. Monroe. Ed. by John J. Boll. 64p. 1982. pap. 4.00 (*0-936442-09-3*) U Wis Sch Lib.

Reader Services in Polytechnic Libraries. Ed. by John Fletcher. 200p. 1985. text ed. 58.95 (*0-566-03528-6*, Pub. by Gower UK) Ashgate Pub Co.

Reader Stance & Literary Understanding: Exploring the Theories, Research, & Practice. Ed. by Joyce Many & Carole Cox. LC 92-17318. 288p. 1992. pap. 39.50 (*0-89391-916-0*); text ed. 73.25 (*0-89391-874-1*) Ablex Pub.

Reader, the Text, the Poem: The Transactional Theory of the Literary Work. Louise M. Rosenblatt. LC 78-16335. 214p. 1978. 22.50 (*0-8093-0883-5*) S Ill U Pr.

Reader, the Text, the Poem: The Transactional Theory of the Literary Work. Louise M. Rosenblatt. LC 94-1302. 232p. (C). 1994. pap. 14.95 (*0-8093-1805-9*) S Ill U Pr.

Reader 1 see Hablemos en Espanol

Reader 1 see Orientation in American English

Reader 1 see SR Italian: Lo Dica in Italiano

Reader 1: Level 2 see Gateways to Science

Reader 1: Level 2 see McGraw-Hill Mathematics

Reader 1: Level 2 see Gateways to Science

Reader 1: Level 2 see Basic Goals in Spelling

Reader 2 see Hablemos en Espanol

Reader 2 see Orientation in American English

Reader 3 see Orientation in American English

Reader 4 see Orientation in American English

Reader 5 see Orientation in American English

Reader 6 see Orientation in American English

Reader's Adviser, 6 vols. 14th ed. Ed. by Marion Sader. 1994. 500.00 (*0-8352-3320-0*) Bowker. "Heartily recommended...Since not even a reference librarian par excellence can come close to knowing the best in any given discipline, no library should be without access to this set for its patrons."--BOOKLIST "...impressively meets a quite formidable task - providing basic material on many subjects for the nonspecialist, student, librarian."--CHOICE. From age-old classics to the writings of today, THE READER'S ADVISER, 14TH EDITION helps you & your patrons select & appreciate the world's greatest books. This monumental work features: * hundreds of authors & thousands of works new to this edition, plus updated entries & revised material in every chapter * updated critical & biographical profiles reflecting the latest understanding & scholarship * more women writers, & more culturally diverse writers from around the world * title, name, & subject indexes in every volume. Order the complete 6-volume set for only $500.00 -- a savings of $160.00 if you purchased each volume separately! ***Publisher Provided Annotation.***

Reader's Adviser, 6 vols., Vol. 1. Ed. by Marion Sader. 1512p. 1994. 110.00 (*0-8352-3321-9*) Bowker.

Reader's Adviser, 6 vols., Vol. 2. 14th ed. Ed. by Marion Sader. 1162p. 1994. 110.00 (*0-8352-3322-7*) Bowker.

Reader's Adviser, 6 vols., Vol. 3. 14th ed. Ed. by Marion Sader. 1168p. 1994. 110.00 (*0-8352-3323-5*) Bowker.

Reader's Adviser, 6 vols., Vol. 4. 14th ed. Ed. by Marion Sader. 1088p. 1994. 110.00 (*0-8352-3324-3*) Bowker.

Reader's Adviser, 6 vols., Vol. 5. 14th ed. Ed. by Marion Sader. 976p. 1994. 110.00 (*0-8352-3325-1*) Bowker.

Reader's Adviser, 6 vols., Vol. 6. 14th ed. Ed. by Marion Sader. 840p. 1994. 110.00 (*0-8352-3326-X*) Bowker.

***Readers' Advisory Service in the Public Library.** 2nd ed. Joyce G. Saricks & Nancy Brown. LC 97-14211. 1997. write for info. (*0-8389-0711-3*) ALA.

Reader's Almanac. Nancy Polette. (Illus.). 148p. (J). (gr. 4-8). 1985. pap. 14.95 (*0-913839-44-2*) Pieces of Lrning.

Readers & Doers of the Word...The Fun Way: Three Hundred Sixty-Five Days of Bible-Related Activities for Children. Fern A. Richey. (Illus.). 320p. (Orig.). 1994. pap. 15.95 (*1-884898-02-5*) Eden Pubng NV.

Readers & Labyrinths: The Detective Fiction in Borges, Bustos, Domecq, & Eco. Jorge Hernandez Martin. LC 94-38652. (Latin American Studies: Vol. 4). 248p. 1995. text ed. 42.00 (*0-8153-1515-5*) Garland.

Readers & Mythic Signs: The Oedipus Myth in Twentieth-Century Fiction. Debra A. Moddelmog. LC 92-34304. (Illus.). 208p. (C). 1993. 24.95 (*0-8093-1846-6*) S Ill U Pr.

Readers & Reading. Ed. by Andrew Bennett. (Critical Readers Ser.). 288p. (C). 1996. pap. text ed. 26.50 (*0-582-21290-1*, 77027, Pub. by Longman UK) Longman.

Readers & Reading in America: Historical & Critical Perspective. David D. Hall. 21p. 1994. pap. 6.50 (*0-944026-50-8*) Am Antiquarian.

Readers & Texts in the Primary Years. Tony Martin & Bob Leather. LC 94-12241. (Rethinking Reading Ser.). 1994. write for info. (*0-335-19228-9*, Open Univ Pr); pap. write for info. (*0-335-19227-0*, Open Univ Pr) Taylor & Francis.

Readers & Their Fictions in the Novels & Novellas of Gottfried Keller. Gail Hart. LC 88-27918. (Germanic Languages & Literatures Ser.: No. 109). xiv, 144p. (C). 1989. pap. 27.50 (*0-8078-8109-0*) U of NC Pr.

Readers & Writers. Alfred R. Orage. LC 72-99714. (Essay Index Reprint Ser.). 1977. 19.95 (*0-8369-1367-1*) Ayer.

***Readers & Writers in Cuba: A Social History of Print Culture, 1830s-1990s.** Pamela M. Smorkaloff. Ed. by David W. Foster. LC 96-39152. (Latin American Studies: Vol. 10). (Illus.). 226p. 1997. text ed. 42.00 (*0-8153-2099-X*, H1935) Garland.

Reader's & Writer's Thesaurus. John P. Schumake. 556p. (Orig.). 1986. pap. 15.00 (*0-9616789-0-9*, 1B) Earnest Pubns.

Reader's & Writer's Thesaurus. rev. ed. John P. Schumake. 565p. (C). 1994. pap. text ed. 14.95 (*0-9616789-9-2*) Earnest Pubns.

Readers & Writers with a Difference: A Holistic Approach to Teaching Learning Disabled & Remedial Students. Lynn K. Rhodes & Curt Dudley-Marling. LC 87-23819. 344p. (Orig.). 1988. pap. text ed. 28.00 (*0-435-08453-4*, 08453) Heinemann.

Readers & Writers with a Difference: A Holistic Approach to Teaching Struggling Readers & Writers. 2nd ed. Lynn K. Rhodes & Curt Dudley-Marling. LC 96-5894. 1996. pap. text ed. 32.50 (*0-435-07215-3*) Heinemann.

Readers' Art: Virginia Woolf As Literary Critic. Mark Goldman. (De Proprietatibus Litterarum Ser.: No. 19). 1976. pap. text ed. 33.85 (*90-279-3275-1*) Mouton.

Readers As Writers: A Basic Rhetoric. Kathleen E. Kiefer. 352p. (C). 1986. pap. text ed. 22.00 (*0-03-070409-X*) HB Coll Pubs.

Reader's Block. David Markson. LC 96-2323. 193p. (Orig.). 1996. 12.95 (*1-56478-132-1*) Dalkey Arch.

Reader's Break, Vol. I. 250p. 1995. 18.95 (*0-9648622-6-3*) Pine Grve Pr.

Reader's Catalog. 2nd rev. ed. Ed. by Geoffrey O'Brien. LC 96-42428. (Illus.). 1500p. (Orig.). 1996. pap. 34.95 (*0-924322-01-2*) Readers Catalog.

Reader's Catalog: An Annotated Selection of More Than 40,000 of the Best Books in Print in 208 Categories. Ed. by Geoffrey O'Brien et al. (Illus.). 1380p. 1989. pap. 24.95 (*0-924322-00-4*) Readers Catalog.

Reader's Choice. 1989. teacher ed., pap. 6.90 (*0-8092-4247-8*) Contemp Bks.

***Readers Choice.** Posey. Date not set. pap. text ed. write for info. (*0-312-16693-1*) St Martin.

Reader's Choice: A Decade of Issues & Observations. Ed. by Wilfred H. Drath. (Technical Reports: No. 314G). 165p. 1990. pap. 15.00 (*0-912879-63-7*) Ctr Creat Leader.

Reader's Choice: Connections. Ed. by Griffin. 106p. 1989. pap. 9.20 (*0-8092-4426-8*) Contemp Bks.

Reader's Choice: Connections Pre & Post Tests. Contemporary Book Editors. 1992. pap. 14.85 (*0-8092-3866-7*) Contemp Bks.

Reader's Choice: Discoveries. Knapp. 106p. 1989. pap. 9.20 (*0-8092-4424-1*) Contemp Bks.

Reader's Choice: Discoveries Pre & Post Tests. Contemporary Book Editors. 1992. pap. 14.85 (*0-8092-3865-9*) Contemp Bks.

Reader's Choice: Insights. Ed. by Echaore-Yoon. 106p. 1989. pap. 9.20 (*0-8092-4427-6*) Contemp Bks.

Reader's Choice: Insights Pre & Post Tests. Contemporary Book Editors. 1992. pap. 14.85 (*0-8092-3867-5*) Contemp Bks.

Reader's Choice: Ready-to-Use Literature Activities for Grades 4-8. Ann Simpson & Teddy Meister. 256p. 1991. pap. 24.95 (*0-87628-790-9*) P-H.

Readers' Clubhouse: Organized Reading Programs with a Purpose. Jan G. Philpot. Ed. by Margaret Binkley. (Illus.). 80p. (Orig.). 1991. pap. text ed. 9.95 (*0-86530-204-9*, IP 192-7) Incentive Pubns.

An Asterisk (*) at the beginning of an entry indicates that the title is appearing in BIP for the first time.

Readers' Comments on Recommendations for Estimating Prestress Losses. (PCI Journal Reprints Ser.). 20p. 1976. pap. 12.00 (*0-318-19753-7*, JR171) P-PCI.

Readers' Comments on Shear & Torsion of Prestressed & Nonprestressed Concrete Beams. (PCI Journal Reprints Ser.). 24p. 1981. pap. 12.00 (*0-318-19760-X*, JR228A) P-PCI.

Reader's Companion: A Book Lover's Guide to the Most Important Books in Every Field of Knowledge As Chosen by the Experts. Fred Bratman & Scott Lewis. 288p. 1994. 17.95 (*0-7868-6009-X*) Hyperion.

Reader's Companion: A Book Lover's Guide to the Most Important Books in Every Field of Knowledge As Chosen by the Experts. Fred Bratman & Scott Lewis. 288p. 1995. pap. 9.95 (*0-7868-8095-3*) Hyperion.

***Reader's Companion to Alaska.** Ed. by Alan Ryan. LC 96-47184. 352p. 1997. pap. 15.00 (*0-15-600368-6*, Harvest Bks) HarBrace.

Reader's Companion to American History. Ed. by Eric Foner & John A. Garraty. (Illus.). 1000p. 1991. 35.00 (*0-395-51372-3*) HM.

***Reader's Companion to Crossing the Threshold of Hope: Sixteen Writers on the Pastoral Writings of Phyllis Tickle.** Phyllis Tickle. 1997. pap. text ed. 12.95 (*1-55725-195-9*) Paraclete MA.

Reader's Companion to Crossing the Threshold of Hope: Sixteen Writers on the Pastoral Writings of Pope John Paul II. Ed. by Charla H. Honea. 304p. 1996. 20.00 (*1-55725-170-3*) Paraclete MA.

Reader's Companion to Cuba. Ed. by Alan Ryan. LC 96-47363. 1997. pap. 15.00 (*0-15-600367-8*) HarBrace.

Reader's Companion to F. Scott Fitzgerald's Tender Is the Night. Matthew J. Bruccoli & Judith S. Baughman. LC 95-4408. (Illus.). 274p. 1996. 29.95 (*1-57003-078-2*) U of SC Pr.

***Reader's Companion to F. Scott Fitzgerald's Tender Is the Night.** Matthew J. Bruccoli & Judith S. Baughman. LC 95-4408. (Illus.). 274p. 1997. pap. 14.95 (*1-57003-223-8*) U of SC Pr.

Reader's Companion to Mexico. Ed. by Alan Ryan. LC 92-39391. 1993. write for info. (*0-15-175962-6*) HarBrace.

Reader's Companion to Military History. Robert Cowley et al. LC 96-8577. 1996. 45.00 (*0-395-66969-3*) HM.

Reader's Companion to the Fiction of Willa Cather. Ed. by Marylyn Arnold et al. LC 92-42434. 880p. 1993. text ed. 105.00 (*0-313-28767-8*, GR8767, Greenwood Pr) Greenwood.

***Readers Companion to the History of American Women.** Mankiller. 1998. 45.00 (*0-395-67173-6*) HM.

Reader's Companion to the Novels & Short Stories of Evelyn Waugh. Paul A. Doyle. (Illus.). 233p. 1989. 39.95 (*0-937664-78-2*) Pilgrim Bks OK.

Reader's Companion to the Twentieth-Century Novel. write for info. (*1-85702-209-2*) OUP.

Reader's Companion to Twentieth-Century Writers. 736p. Date not set. write for info. (*1-85702-332-3*) OUP.

Reader's Companion to World Literature. Ed. by Lillian H. Hornstein et al. 1956. mass mkt. 7.95 (*0-451-62816-0*) NAL-Dutton.

Reader's Companion to World Literature. rev. ed. Ed. by Lillian H. Hornstein et al. 1956. pap. 5.95 (*0-451-62441-6*, ME2177, Ment) NAL-Dutton.

Reader's Companion, with Black Cover. John W. McIntosh & Margaret S. McIntosh. 68p. 1994. ring bd. 19.95 (*0-9644092-0-8*) Creekside CO.

Reader's Companion, with Burgundy Cover. John W. McIntosh & Margaret S. McIntosh. 68p. 1994. ring bd. 19.95 (*0-9644092-1-6*) Creekside CO.

Reader's Delight. Noel Perrin. LC 87-40507. 220p. 1988. pap. 12.95 (*0-87451-432-0*) U Pr of New Eng.

Reader's Digest ABC's of the Human Mind: A Captivating Look at Our New Understanding of How the Mind Works. Reader's Digest Editors. LC 89-36711. (Illus.). 336p. 1990. 28.00 (*0-89577-345-7*) RD Assn.

Reader's Digest Atlas of the World. Reader's Digest Editors. LC 87-675016. (Illus.). 240p. 1987. 34.96 (*0-89577-264-7*) RD Assn.

Reader's Digest Bible for Children: Timeless Stories from the Old & New Testaments. Marie-Helene Delval. LC 95-7993. (Illus.). 168p. (J). (gr. 3-7). 1995. 19.99 (*0-89577-815-7*) RD Assn.

Reader's Digest Book of Facts. Reader's Digest Editors. LC 86-29744. (Illus.). 416p. 1987. 29.00 (*0-89577-256-6*, Random) RD Assn.

Reader's Digest Children's Atlas of World History. Reader's Digest Editors. LC 93-4320. (Illus.). 128p. (J). (gr. 4-7). 1993. 20.00 (*0-89577-526-3*) RD Assn.

Reader's Digest Children's Songbook. (J). 1986. 29.95 (*0-7935-2884-4*, 00360885) H Leonard.

Reader's Digest Children's Songbook. Reader's Digest Editors. (Illus.). 252p. (J). (ps up). 1985. 29.95 (*0-89577-214-0*, Random) RD Assn.

Reader's Digest Children's World Atlas. Reader's Digest Editors. LC 90-28667. (Illus.). 128p. (J). (gr. 3-7). 1995. 20.00 (*0-89577-816-5*) RD Assn.

Reader's Digest Complete Book of Embroidery. Melinda Coss. LC 96-7413. (Illus.). 192p. 1996. write for info. (*0-89577-874-2*) RD Assn.

Reader's Digest Country & Western Songbook. Reader's Digest Editors. (Illus.). 252p. 1983. spiral bd. 29.95 (*0-89577-147-0*, Random) RD Assn.

Reader's Digest Fun Factory: Games & Toys from Recycled Stuff. Ed. by Janet Ravenscroft & Catriona Woodburn. (Illus.). 136p. (J). (gr. 1-5). 1996. 14.99 (*1-57584-031-6*, Rdrs Dig Kids) Rdrs Dgst Yng Fam.

Reader's Digest Great Illustrated Dictionary. Reader's Digest Editors. 1987. 44.00 (*0-395-44896-4*) HM.

Reader's Digest Guide to Creative Gardening. Reader's Digest Editors. LC 87-128856. (Illus.). 384p. 1987. 32.95 (*0-276-35223-8*) RD Assn.

Reader's Digest Home Do-It-Yourself Projects: Furniture to Build Home Improvements to Make. LC 96-15812. 1996. pap. 19.95 (*0-89577-893-9*) RD Assn.

Reader's Digest Household Hints & Handy Tips: The Most Comprehensive, Best Organized, Hardest Working Collection of How-to Facts & Shortcuts. 1988. 25.95 (*0-318-36079-9*) Readrs Digest Pr.

***Reader's Digest Ideas for Your Garden.** Reader's Digest Editors. LC 96-34354. 1996. write for info. (*0-89577-919-6*) RD Assn.

***Reader's Digest Illustrated Atlas of the World.** 3rd rev. ed. Reader's Digest Editors. (Illus.). 1997. 24.00 (*0-89577-937-4*) RD Assn.

***Reader's Digest Illustrated Children's Atlas.** (Illus.). 128p. (YA). (gr. 4-9). 1997. 22.95 (*1-57584-156-8*) Rdrs Dgst Yng Fam.

Reader's Digest Illustrated Encyclopedic Dictionary, 2 vols. Reader's Digest Editors. LC 87-9650. (Illus.). 1920p. 1987. 59.96 (*0-89577-269-8*) RD Assn.

***Readers Digest Illustrated Great World Atlas.** Readers Digest Staff. 1997. 40.00 (*0-89577-988-9*) RD Assn.

Reader's Digest Illustrated Guide. Reader's Digest Editors. 1989. 30.00 (*0-394-21707-1*) Random.

Reader's Digest Kids Big Book of Space. William Edmonds. LC 94-28252. (Illus.). 48p. (J). (gr. 2-7). 1995. 15.95 (*0-89577-648-0*) RD Assn.

Reader's Digest Legal Question & Answer Book. Reader's Digest Editors. LC 87-25963. 704p. 1988. 31.00 (*0-89577-291-4*, Random) RD Assn.

Reader's Digest Merry Christmas Songbook. Reader's Digest Editors. LC 81-51285. (Illus.). 252p. 1981. 29.95 (*0-89577-105-5*, Random) RD Assn.

***Readers Digest Mysteries of the Bible: The Unanswered Questions of the Scriptures.** Reader's Digest Editors. 1997. pap. text ed. 18.95 (*0-89577-938-2*) RD Assn.

Reader's Digest Oxford Complete Wordfinder. Reader's Digest Editors. LC 96-12309. 1996. write for info. (*0-89577-894-7*) RD Assn.

***Reader's Digest Practical Guide to Home Landscaping: Planning, Planting & Building.** Reader's Digest Editors. 1996. 27.95 (*0-89577-896-3*) RD Assn.

***Reader's Digest Quotable Quotes: Wit & Wisdom for All Occasions from America's Most Popular Magazine.** Reader's Digest Editors. LC 96-3456. 1997. write for info. (*0-89577-925-0*) RD Assn.

Reader's Digest Treasury of Great Show Tunes. 1993. 32.00 (*0-7935-3046-6*, 00311644) H Leonard.

Reader's Digest Visitors' Guide to the Great Barrier Reef. Reader's Digest Editors. (Illus.). 168p. 1989. pap. 19.95 (*0-86438-073-9*, Random) RD Assn.

Reader's Digest Winner's Circle. LC 96-14823. 1996. pap. write for info. (*0-89577-887-4*) RD Assn.

Reader's Digest Word Power Quiz Book: 1,000 Word Challenges from America's Most Popular Magazine. Reader's Digest Editors. LC 96-2161. 1996. write for info. (*0-89577-901-3*) RD Assn.

Readers Digest Word Power 1. Peter Funk. 1996. pap. 12.95 (*0-7871-0661-5*, Dove Bks) Dove Audio.

Readers Digest Word Power 2. Peter Funk. 1996. pap. 12.95 (*0-7871-0662-3*, Dove Bks) Dove Audio.

Readers Digest Word Power 3. Peter Funk. 1996. pap. 12.95 (*0-7871-0663-1*, Dove Bks) Dove Audio.

Readers Digest Word Power 4. Peter Funk. 1996. pap. 12.95 (*0-7871-0664-X*, Dove Bks) Dove Audio.

Readers Digest Word Power 5. Peter Funk. 1996. pap. 12.95 (*0-7871-0665-8*, Dove Bks) Dove Audio.

Readers Digest Word Power 6. Peter Funk. 1996. pap. 12.95 (*0-7871-0666-6*, Dove Bks) Dove Audio.

***Reader's Encyclopedia of Spiritual Literature.** Willis Barnstone & Harry Ge. 800p. 1997. 40.00 (*0-06-270118-5*) HarpC.

Reader's Encyclopedia of the American West. 2nd ed. Ed. by H. Lamar. 50.00 (*0-06-270048-0*, Harper Ref) HarpC.

***Reader's Encyclopedia of Women's Literature.** Katherine A. MacGillivray. 800p. 1997. 40.00 (*0-06-270119-3*) HarpC.

Reader's Encyclopedia to Shakespeare. Ed. by J. Andrews. 1997. 45.00 (*0-06-270008-1*, Harper Ref) HarpC.

Reader's Eye: Visual Imaging as Reader Response. Ellen J. Esrock. LC 93-25075. 264p. (C). 1993. text ed. 36.50 (*0-8018-4669-2*) Johns Hopkins.

Readers for Transparent Microforms - Methods for Measuring 2 Performance Characteristics: ANSI-AIIM MS12-1990. Association for Information & Image Management Staff. 1990. pap. 33.00 (*0-89258-206-5*, MS12) Assn Inform & Image Mgmt.

Readers for Transparent Microforms - Performance Characteristics: ANSI-AIIM MS20-1990. (Illus.). 6p. 1990. pap. text ed. 33.00 (*0-89258-204-9*, MS20) Assn Inform & Image Mgmt.

Reader's Greek-English Lexicon of the New Testament: And a Beginner's Guide for the Translation of New Testament Greek. Sakae Kubo. (Andrews University Monographs). 338p. (C). 1975. text ed. 24.99 (*0-943872-04-9*) Andrews Univ Pr.

Reader's Greek-English Lexicon of the New Testament: And a Beginner's Guide for the Translation of New Testament Greek. Sakae Kubo. 327p. (C). 1975. 24.99 (*0-310-26920-2*, 6269) Zondervan.

Reader's Guide: The Development of Baha'i Literature in English. Eunice Braun. 176p. 1986. 17.95 (*0-85398-228-7*); pap. 9.50 (*0-85398-229-5*) G Ronald Pub.

Reader's Guide for Geology. Discover Staff. (C). 1994. pap. text ed. 7.00 (*0-03-010246-4*) HB Coll Pubs.

Reader's Guide MO7 Teamwork. CUNA (Ewing) Staff. 226p. 1994. 25.00 (*0-7872-0255-X*) Kendall-Hunt.

Reader's Guide to American History. Ed. by Peter J. Parish. 1997. lib. bdg. 125.00 (*1-884964-22-2*) Fitzroy Dearborn.

Reader's Guide to Astronomy. Discover Staff. (C). 1994. pap. text ed. 12.00 (*0-03-008928-X*) HB Coll Pubs.

Reader's Guide to Australian Fiction. Laurie Clancy. 416p. 1993. pap. 35.00 (*0-19-554620-2*) OUP.

Reader's Guide to Canadian History, No. 1: Beginnings to Confederation. Ed. by D. A. Muise. 256p. 1982. pap. 14.95 (*0-8020-6442-6*) U of Toronto Pr.

Readers' Guide to China's Literary Gazette, 1949-1966. Ed. by Phyllis Wang & Donald A. Gibbs. LC 92-70316. 526p. (Orig.). 1991. pap. 20.00 (*1-55729-026-1*) IEAS.

Readers Guide to Classic British Mysteries. Susan P. Oleksiw. 1989. 19.95 (*0-89296-968-7*) Mysterious Pr.

Reader's Guide to Contemporary Literary Theory. 3rd ed. Raman Selden & Peter Widdowson. LC 92-47056. 288p. (C). 1993. pap. text ed. 14.95 (*0-8131-0816-0*) U Pr of Ky.

***Reader's Guide to Contemporary Literary Theory.** 4th ed. Raman Selden et al. LC 96-41310. 1997. 25.20 (*0-13-491952-1*) P-H.

***Reader's Guide to Dorothy Richardson's Pilgrimage.** George H. Thomson. 169p. 1996. 30.00 (*0-944318-10-X*, 70133) ELT Pr.

Reader's Guide to Dylan Thomas. William Y. Tindall. LC 96-25794. 305p. 1996. reprint ed. pap. 16.95 (*0-8156-0401-7*, TIDTP) Syracuse U Pr.

Reader's Guide to Fifty European Novels. Martin Seymour-Smith. (Reader's Guide Ser.). 528p. 1980. 48.50 (*0-389-20138-3*, N6908) B&N Imports.

Reader's Guide to Finnegans Wake. William Y. Tindall. 354p. (C). 1996. pap. 16.95 (*0-8156-0385-1*, TIFWP) Syracuse U Pr.

Reader's Guide to Gerard Manley Hopkins. Norman H. MacKenzie. LC 80-69275. 256p. (C). 1981. pap. 17.95 (*0-8014-9221-1*) Cornell U Pr.

Reader's Guide to Hart Crane's White Buildings. John Norton-Smith. LC 93-18842. 164p. 1993. 79.95 (*0-7734-9257-7*) E Mellen.

Reader's Guide to James Joyce. William Y. Tindall. (Irish Studies). 304p. 1995. pap. 16.95 (*0-8156-0320-7*) Syracuse U Pr.

Reader's Guide to James Merrill's the Changing Light at Sandover. Robert Polito. 324p. 1994. pap. text ed. 14.95 (*0-472-06524-6*) U of Mich Pr.

Reader's Guide to Japanese Literature. J. Thomas Rimer. 212p. (Orig.). 1991. reprint ed. pap. 10.00 (*4-7700-1477-5*) Kodansha.

Reader's Guide to John Barth. Zack Bowen. LC 93-10378. 150p. 1993. text ed. 57.95 (*0-313-27978-0*, BJR/, Greenwood Pr) Greenwood.

***Reader's Guide to Joseph Conrad.** Frederick R. Karl. LC 97-21260. 324p. 1997. pap. 17.95 (*0-8156-0489-0*) Syracuse U Pr.

Reader's Guide to Literature in English. Ed. by Mark Hawkins-Dady. 1000p. 1996. lib. bdg. 125.00 (*1-884964-20-6*) Fitzroy Dearborn.

Reader's Guide to Mexico. Ed. by Alan Ryan. 368p. 1995. pap. 15.00 (*0-15-676021-5*) HarBrace.

Reader's Guide to Microcomputer Books. Michael Nicita & Ronald Petrusha. LC 84-15451. (Professional Librarian Ser.). 500p. 1984. 35.00 (*0-86729-122-2*, Hall Reference) Macmillan.

Reader's Guide to Murder. Jeffers. LC 96-5211. 256p. 1996. 21.95 (*0-312-14400-8*) St Martin.

Readers' Guide to Periodical Literature, Vols. 1990-94. 210.00 (*0-685-73473-0*) Wilson.

Reader's Guide to Proclamation: For Sundays & Major Feasts in Cycle A. Jerome J. DuCharme. 139p. 1974. pap. 1.50 (*0-8199-0577-1*, Frncscn Herld) Franciscan Pr.

Reader's Guide to Rational Expectations: A Survey & Comprehensive Annotated Bibliography. Deborah A. Redman. 208p. 1992. text ed. 85.00 (*1-85278-567-5*) E Elgar.

Reader's Guide to Samuel Beckett. Hugh Kenner. 220p. (C). 1996. pap. 16.95 (*0-8156-0386-X*, KESBP) Syracuse U Pr.

Reader's Guide to Short Stories of Eudora Welty. Diane R. Pingatore. LC 95-31368. 1996. 50.00 (*0-8161-7371-0*) G K Hall.

Readers Guide to Short Stories of Henry James. Albers. LC 97-6444. 1995. 50.00 (*0-8161-9099-2*) G K Hall.

Reader's Guide to the Alexander Technique: A Selected Annotated Bibliography. Phyllis Sanfilippo. 96p. (Orig.). 1987. pap. 12.50 (*0-913111-17-1*) Centerline.

Reader's Guide to the American Novel of Detection. Marvin Lachman. (G. K. Hall Reference Ser.). 200p. 1993. 50.00 (*0-8161-1803-5*, Hall Reference) Macmillan.

Reader's Guide to the Appraisal Journal, 1970-1980. 99p. 1981. pap. 9.50 (*0-911780-55-6*) Appraisal Inst.

Readers' Guide to the Appraisal Journal, 1980-1987. 80p. 1989. pap. 9.50 (*0-911780-99-8*) Appraisal Inst.

Readers' Guide to the Appraisal Journal, 1988-1993. LC 94-38185. 1994. 13.50 (*0-922154-17-1*) Appraisal Inst.

Reader's Guide to the Chopin Preludes. Jeffrey Kresky. LC 93-42788. 152p. 1994. text ed. 55.00 (*0-313-29253-1*, Greenwood Pr) Greenwood.

Reader's Guide to the Classic British Mystery. Susan P. Oleksiw. 300p. 1988. 40.00 (*0-8161-8787-8*, Hall Reference) Macmillan.

Reader's Guide to the History of Science. Ed. by Arne Hassenbruch. 1997. lib. bdg. 125.00 (*1-884964-29-X*) Fitzroy Dearborn.

Reader's Guide to the Mahatma Letters to A. P. Sinnett. George Linton & V. Hanson. 1988. 19.95 (*81-7059-113-9*) Theos Pub Hse.

Reader's Guide to the Poetry of Richard Wilbur. Rodney S. Edgecombe. LC 94-37229. 224p. (C). 1995. pap. text ed. 29.95 (*0-8173-0715-X*) U of Ala Pr.

Reader's Guide to the Police Procedural Novel. Jo A. Vicarel. LC 94-33650. (Reader's Guides to Mystery Novels Ser.). 1995. 50.00 (*0-8161-1801-9*) G K Hall.

Reader's Guide to the Private Eye Novel. Gary W. Niebuhr. LC 93-22212. (Reader's Guides to Mystery Novels Ser.). 323p. 1993. 50.00 (*0-8161-1802-7*) G K Hall.

Reader's Guide to the Roman de la Rose. Maxwell Luria. LC 81-22767. xii, 282p. (C). 1982. lib. bdg. 39.50 (*0-208-01838-7*, Archon Bks) Shoe String.

Reader's Guide to the Short Stories of Ernest Hemingway. Paul Smith. 1989. 65.00 (*0-8161-8794-0*, Hall Reference) Macmillan.

Reader's Guide to the Short Stories of Herman Melville. Lea B. Newman. (Reference Bks.). 344p. 1986. 50.00 (*0-8161-8653-7*, Hall Reference) Macmillan.

Reader's Guide to the Short Stories of Mark Twain. James D. Wilson. 248p. 1987. 45.00 (*0-8161-8721-5*, Hall Reference) Macmillan.

Reader's Guide to the Short Stories of Sherwood Anderson. Judy L. Small. LC 93-7883. 464p. 1994. 65.00 (*0-8161-8968-4*) G K Hall.

Reader's Guide to the Short Stories of Stephen Crane. Michael W. Schaefer. LC 96-10593. (Reference Publication in Literature Ser.). 468p. 1995. 50.00 (*0-8161-7285-4*, Twayne) Scribnrs Ref.

Reader's Guide to the Short Stories of Willa Cather. Sheryl L. Meyering. LC 93-10381. (Reference Ser.). 304p. 1993. 65.00 (*0-8161-1834-5*, Hall Reference) Macmillan.

Reader's Guide to the Short Stories of William Faulkner: Tales from The Country; The Village; The Wilderness; & The Middle Ground, in the Collected Stories. Diane B. Jones. LC 93-36283. (Reference Publications in Literature). 576p. 1994. 65.00 (*0-8161-7272-2*) G K Hall.

Readers Guide to the Suspense Novel. Jarvis. LC 96-40455. 1997. 45.00 (*0-8161-1804-3*, Hall Library) G K Hall.

Reader's Guide to the Twentieth-Century Novel. Peter Parker & Frank Kermode. 784p. (YA). 1995. 40.00 (*0-19-521153-7*) OUP.

Reader's Guide to the Twentieth-Century Novel in Britain. Randall Stevenson. LC 93-12702. 184p. (C). 1993. 25.00 (*0-8131-1857-3*); pap. 13.00 (*0-8131-0823-3*) U Pr of Ky.

Reader's Guide to Twentieth-Century Science Fiction. Marilyn Fletcher. LC 88-7815. 786p. 1989. text ed. 30.00 (*0-8389-0504-8*) ALA.

Reader's Guide to Twentieth-Century Writers. Ed. by Peter Parker & Frank Kermode. 825p. (C). 1996. 40.00 (*0-19-521215-0*) OUP.

Reader's Guide to Unavailable Literature & Other Omitted Media. Ed. by Bonnie Raillery. LC 94-76412. 96p. (Orig.). 1994. per. 6.50 (*0-9641544-0-4*, RGB-1) Monitor Pubns.

***Reader's Guide to Walt Whitman.** Gay W. Allen. 248p. 1997. pap. 16.95 (*0-8156-0488-2*) Syracuse U Pr.

Reader's Guide to William Butler Yeats. John Unterecker. 326p. (C). 1996. pap. 16.95 (*0-8156-0340-1*, UNRGP) Syracuse U Pr.

***Reader's Guide to Women's Studies.** Ed. by Eleanor Amico. 1997. lib. bdg. 125.00 (*1-884964-77-X*) Fitzroy Dearborn.

***Reader's Guide to Writers' Britain: An Enchanting Tour of Literary Landscapes & Shrines.** Sally Varlow. (Illus.). 280p. 1997. pap. 24.95 (*1-85375-201-0*, Pub. by Orion Bks UK) Trafalgar.

***Reader's Handbook, Vols. 1 & 2.** 1980. 85.00 (*0-8103-3001-6*, 00004176, Gale Res Intl) Gale.

Reader's Handbook: Famous Names in Fiction, Allusions, References, Proverbs, Plots, Stories, & Poems, 3 vols. E. Cobham Brewer. 1998. reprint ed. 85.00 (*1-55888-217-0*) Omnigraphics Inc.

Reader's Handbook of Famous Names in Fiction. E. Brewer. 1972. 69.95 (*0-8490-0928-6*) Gordon Pr.

Reader's Hebrew-English Lexicon of the Old Testament. Douglas L. Busby et al. 720p. 1989. 44.99 (*0-310-36980-0*) Zondervan.

Reader's History of American Literature. Thomas W. Higginson. (Notable American Authors Ser.). 1992. reprint ed. lib. bdg. 75.00 (*0-7812-3115-9*) Rprt Serv.

Readers in History: Nineteenth-Century American Literature & the Contexts of Response. Ed. by James L. Machor. LC 92-14471. 304p. 1993. text ed. 45.00 (*0-8018-4436-3*) Johns Hopkins.

Readers in History: Nineteenth-Century American Literature & the Contexts of Response. Ed. by James L. Machor. LC 92-14471. 304p. 1993. pap. text ed. 15.95 (*0-8018-4437-1*) Johns Hopkins.

Readers in Psychology & Education. Stephen N. Elliott & Thomas R. Kratochwill. 700p. (C). 1994. pap. text ed. write for info. (*0-697-23931-4*) Brown & Benchmark.

Reader's Journal: Authentic Reading for Writers. Mark D. Rentz. 208p. (C). 1992. pap. text ed. 17.70 (*0-13-755273-4*) P-H.

***Reader's Journal: Personal Impressions, Quotations, & Reflections.** (Illus.). 96p. 14.95 (*0-00-225139-6*) Collins SF.

Reader's Quotation Book. Ed. by Steve Gilbar. 1991. 15.95 (*0-916366-64-2*) Pushcart Pr.

Reader's Repentance: Women Preachers, Women Writers, & Nineteenth-Century Social Discourse. Christine L. Krueger. LC 92-5418. 362p. (C). 1992. 32.50 (*0-226-45488-6*) U Ch Pr.

Reader's Repertoire: Aims & Perspectives. Gwendolyn Gong & Sam Dragga. 544p. (C). 1996. text ed. 28.50 (*0-673-99188-1*) Addson-Wesley Educ.

Reader's Repertoire: Purpose & Focus. 1996. teacher ed. write for info. (*0-673-99189-X*) Addson-Wesley Educ.

Readers, Teachers, Learners: Expanding Literacy in the Secondary Schools. 2nd ed. William G. Brozo & Michele L. Simpson. LC 94-16927. 416p. (C). 1994. pap. text ed. 62.00 (*0-02-315661-9*, Macmillan Coll) P-H.

R

An Asterisk (*) at the beginning of an entry indicates that the title is appearing in BIP for the first time.

Readers, Texts, Teachers. Ed. by Bill Corcoran & Emrys Evans. LC 86-17556. 264p. (Orig.). 1987. pap. text ed. 23.50 (*0-86709-187-8*, 0187) Boynton Cook Pubs.

Readers' Theater Vol. 3: Entrepeneurs, Vol. 3. 2nd ed. Lois F. Roets. 100p. (Orig.). (YA). (gr. 4-12). 1995. pap. text ed. 16.00 (*0-911943-43-9*) Leadership Pub.

Readers Theater Booktalks. Nancy Polette. 128p. (Orig.). (J). (gr. 4-8). 1994. pap. 12.95 (*1-879287-18-8*) Pieces of Lrning.

Readers' Theater, Vol. 1: General Interest. Lois F. Roets. 106p. (Orig.). (YA). (gr. 5-12). 1992. pap. text ed. 16.00 (*0-911943-29-3*) Leadership Pub.

Readers' Theater, Vol. 2: Famous People. Lois F. Roets. 108p. (Orig.). (YA). (gr. 5-12). 1992. pap. text ed. 16.00 (*0-911943-30-7*) Leadership Pub.

Readers Theatre. Nancy Polette & Keith Polette. (Illus.). 48p. (J). (gr. 4-8). 1986. pap. 5.95 (*0-913839-56-6*) Pieces of Lrning.

***Readers' Theatre.** David Trembley & Lo-Ann Trembley. 18p. 1994. pap. 5.50 (*1-877871-73-7*, 3701) Ed Ministries.

Readers Theatre: Performing the Text. Susan Hill. (Illus.). 88p. 1990. teacher ed. 15.00 (*1-875327-01-0*, Pub. by E Curtain AT) Peguis Pubs Ltd.

Readers Theatre for Beginning Readers. Suzanne I. Barchers. LC 92-45813. (Illus.). vii, 97p. 1993. pap. text ed. 19.00 (*1-56308-136-9*) Teacher Ideas Pr.

Readers Theatre for Children: Scripts & Script Development. Mildred K. Laughlin & Kathy H. Latrobe. xi, 131p. 1990. pap. text ed. 17.50 (*0-87287-753-1*) Teacher Ideas Pr.

Readers Theatre for Young Adults: Scripts & Script Development. Kathy H. Latrobe & Mildred K. Laughlin. xi, 130p. 1989. pap. text ed. 20.00 (*0-87287-743-4*) Teacher Ideas Pr.

Readers Theatre Fundamentals. 2nd ed. Fran A. Tanner. (Illus.). 280p. (YA). (gr. 10-12). 1993. pap. text ed. 20.67 (*0-931054-30-3*) Clark Pub.

***Readers Theatre in the Middle School & Junior High Classroom.** Lois Walker. Ed. by Arthur L. Zapel. LC 96-43535. (Illus.). 80p. 1996. pap. 12.95 (*1-56608-027-4*, B203) Meriwether Pub.

Reader's Workshop. 1993. pap. 8.95 (*0-590-73077-0*) Scholastic Inc.

Readers, Writers & Parents Learning Together. Vince Dundas & George Strong. (Illus.). 140p. (C). 1991. ring bd. 295.00 (*1-878450-10-7*) R Owen Pubs.

Readers, Writers & Parents Learning Together: Parent Handbook, 5 vols., Set Only. Vince Dundas & George Strong. 113p. (C). 1991. pap. 59.00 (*1-878450-11-5*) R Owen Pubs.

Readers 1-5 Phonetic Reader Ser. see Dr. Wise Learn to Read Series, Vols. 1-4

Readers 11-15 in Phonetic Reader Ser. see Dr. Wise Learn to Read Series, Vols. 1-4

Readers 16-20 in Phonetic Learn to Read Ser. see Dr. Wise Learn to Read Series, Vols. 1-4

Readers 6-10 in Phonetic Reader Ser. see Dr. Wise Learn to Read Series, Vols. 1-4

Readership Research. Guy Consterdine. 200p. 1987. text ed. 65.00 (*0-566-05071-4*, Pub. by Gower UK) Ashgate Pub Co.

Readin' Country Music: Steel Guitars, Opry Stars, & Honky Tonk Bars. Ed. by Cecelia Tichi. (Special Issue of SAQ Ser.: Vol. 94, No. 1). (Illus.). 362p. 1995. pap. 10.00 (*0-8223-6425-5*) Duke.

Readin Writin & Computin. Chris Bigum. (C). 1988. 27.00 (*0-7300-0606-9*, Pub. by Deakin Univ AT) St Mut.

Readiness & Change in Couple Therapy. Barry Dym. LC 95-1750. 256p. 1995. 36.00 (*0-465-01503-4*) Basic.

Readiness Enhancement Model: A Personnel Inventory Projection Model of the Army's Reserve Components. Herbert J. Shukiar & Arroy Center Staff. LC 96-2898. 112p. 1996. pap. text ed. 9.00 (*0-8330-2400-0*, MR-659/1-A) Rand Corp.

***Readiness Factor: Preparing Yourself for the Ultimate Relationship.** Elaine Stevens. LC 97-93418. 145p. (Orig.). 1997. pap. 12.95 (*0-9657901-0-X*) Matters of the Heart.

Readiness for Kindergarten: A Coloring Book for Parents. James O. Massey. 16p. 1975. pap. 5.25 (*0-89106-014-6*, 1281) Consulting Psychol.

Readiness for Reconciliation. rev. ed. Lynn R. Buzzard et al. 32p. (Orig.). 1988. pap. text ed. 4.00 (*0-944561-18-7*) Chr Legal.

Readiness for Religion. Harold Loukes. LC 63-11818. (Orig.). 1963. pap. 3.00 (*0-87574-126-6*) Pendle Hill.

Readiness/Enough/Depends/On. Larry Eigner. (Classics Ser.: No. 138). 140p. (Orig.). 1997. pap. 12.95 (*1-55713-351-4*) Sun & Moon CA.

Reading. (Illus.). 32p. (YA). (gr. 6-12). 1983. pap. 2.40 (*0-8395-3393-4*, 33378) BSA.

Reading. 1992. 14.50 (*0-19-437130-1*) OUP.

Reading. (Regents Competency Test Ser.). Date not set. pap. 23.95 (*0-8373-6403-5*, RCT-3) Nat Learn.

Reading. Richard L. Allington & Kathleen Krull. LC 80-16547. (Beginning to Learn about Ser.). (Illus.). 32p. (J). (ps-2). 1985. pap. 3.95 (*0-8114-8235-9*) Raintree Steck-V.

Reading. Beverly Dahlen. 101p. (Orig.). (YA). (gr. 6-12). 1989. pap. 8.50 (*0-937013-33-1*) Potes Poets.

Reading. Judith Gallagher. LC 92-39395. (Foundations Ser.). 1993. pap. 11.26 (*0-8092-3833-0*) Contemp Bks.

Reading! 3rd ed. Barbara Outland. 288p. (C). 1995. per., pap. text ed. 37.74 (*0-7872-0409-9*) Kendall-Hunt.

Reading: A Research Retrospective, 1881-1941. William S. Gray. Ed. by John T. Guthrie. LC 83-26677. 101p. reprint ed. pap. 28.80 (*0-8357-4307-1*, 2037104) Bks Demand.

Reading: From 5-11 Years. L. John Chapman. (Rethinking Reading Ser.). 160p. 1988. 80.00 (*0-335-15557-X*, Open Univ Pr); pap. 27.00 (*0-335-15556-1*, Open Univ Pr) Taylor & Francis.

Reading: Grade One, Bk. 1. Schaffer, Frank, Publications Staff. (Reproducible Workbooks Ser.). (Illus.). 48p. (J). (gr. 1). 1983. student ed. 4.98 (*0-86734-029-0*, FS-2658) Schaffer Pubns.

Reading: Grade One, Bk. 2. Schaffer, Frank, Publications Staff. (Reproducible Workbooks Ser.). (Illus.). 48p. (J). (gr. 1). 1983. student ed. 4.98 (*0-86734-030-4*, FS-2659) Schaffer Pubns.

Reading: Grade One, Bk. 3. Schaffer, Frank, Publications Staff. (Reproducible Workbooks Ser.). (Illus.). 48p. (J). (gr. 1). 1983. student ed. 4.98 (*0-86734-031-2*, FS-2660) Schaffer Pubns.

Reading: Grade Three, Bk. 1. Schaffer, Frank, Publications Staff. (Reproducible Workbooks Ser.). (Illus.). 48p. (J). (gr. 3). 1983. student ed. 4.98 (*0-86734-035-5*, FS-2664) Schaffer Pubns.

Reading: Grade Two, Bk. 1. Schaffer, Frank, Publications Staff. (Reproducible Workbooks Ser.). (Illus.). 48p. (J). (gr. 2). 1983. student ed. 4.98 (*0-86734-032-0*, FS-2661) Schaffer Pubns.

Reading: Grade Two, Bk. 2. Schaffer, Frank, Publications Staff. (Reproducible Workbooks Ser.). (Illus.). 48p. (J). (gr. 2). 1983. student ed. 4.98 (*0-86734-033-9*, FS-2662) Schaffer Pubns.

Reading: Grade Two, Bk. 3. Schaffer, Frank, Publications Staff. (Reproducible Workbooks Ser.). (Illus.). 48p. (J). (gr. 2). 1983. student ed. 4.98 (*0-86734-034-7*, FS-2663) Schaffer Pubns.

Reading: Kentucky Educational Television Study Guide. rev. ed. Ed. by Cambridge Staff. (GED Program Ser.). 206p. 1988. pap. text ed. write for info. (*0-8428-9370-9*, 893-709) Cambridge Bk.

Reading: Skill Enhancement. Rosemarie Park et al. 200p. 1994. teacher ed. 8.00 (*0-318-70382-3*); pap. text ed. 10.95 (*1-56118-204-4*) Paradigm MN.

Reading: Student's Book. Don McGovern et al. LC 94-19762. (Series Emglish for Academic Study). 1994. 9.75 (*0-01-397872-1*) P-H Intl.

Reading: The Process of Creating Meaning for Sensed Stimuli. Ed. by Malcolm P. Douglass. (Claremont Reading Conference Yearbook Ser.). 234p. 1987. pap. 20.00 (*0-941742-05-9*) Claremont Grad.

Reading: The Quest for Meaning. Ed. by Malcolm P. Douglass. (Claremont Reading Conference Yearbook Ser.). 379p. 1986. pap. 20.00 (*0-941742-04-0*) Claremont Grad.

***Reading: The 1950s.** Stuart Hylton. (Illus.). 128p. 1997. pap. 17.95 (*0-7509-1463-7*, Pub. by Sutton Pubng UK) Bks Intl VA.

Reading: What Can Be Measured. 2nd ed. Roger Farr & Robert F. Carey. LC 85-28078. (IRA - Elva Knight Research Fund Monograph Ser.). 227p. reprint ed. pap. 64.70 (*0-7837-4736-5*, 2044544) Bks Demand.

Reading: What Can Be Measured. Roger C. Farr. LC 70-12333. 308p. reprint ed. pap. 87.80 (*0-317-42109-3*, 2026223) Bks Demand.

Reading - A Novel Approach. Janice Szabos. (Illus.). 112p. (J). (gr. 4-8). 1984. student ed. 12.99 (*0-86653-186-6*, GA 529) Good Apple.

Reading - Learning - Enjoying: A College Reader. Harold Newman. LC 88-19495. 94p. (C). 1988. pap. text ed. 15.00 (*0-9613577-2-X*) Prestige Educ.

Reading - Learning Disability: An Ecological Approach. Jill Bartoli & Morton Botel. 280p. (C). 1988. pap. text ed. 19.95 (*0-8077-2904-3*) Tchrs Coll.

Reading - Writing Text for ESL - EFL Global Issues. Brenda Bushell. 160p. 1995. pap. text ed. 15.60 (*0-13-150096-1*) P-H.

Reading a Ruler. Bert A. Siebold. 14p. (YA). 1989. student ed. 7.00 (*0-8064-0370-5*, F10) Bergwall.

Reading a Ruler, Vol. F10. Bert A. Siebold. Ed. by Lynn Rice. (YA). 1989. vhs 189.00 (*0-8064-0369-1*, F10) Bergwall.

Reading Abbey Cartularies, Vol. 1. Ed. by B. Kemp. (Camden Fourth Ser.). 196p. 27.00 (*0-86193-108-4*) David Brown.

Reading Abbey Cartularies, Vol. 2. B. Kemp. (Camden Fourth Ser.: No. 33). 35.00 (*0-86193-112-2*) David Brown.

Reading Ability. Charles A. Perfetti. (Illus.). 320p. 1985. 55.00 (*0-19-503501-1*) OUP.

Reading about the Environment: An Introductory Guide. Pamela E. Jansma. LC 92-12976. viii, 252p. 1993. lib. bdg. 27.50 (*0-87287-985-2*) Libs Unl.

Reading about the Grizzly Bear. Carol Greene. LC 92-26803. (Illus.). 32p. (J). (gr. k-3). 1993. lib. bdg. 16.95 (*0-89490-423-X*) Enslow Pubs.

Reading about the Manatee. Carol Greene. LC 92-26811. (Illus.). 32p. (J). (gr. k-3). 1993. lib. bdg. 16.95 (*0-89490-424-8*) Enslow Pubs.

Reading about the River Otter. Carol Greene. LC 92-26801. (Illus.). 32p. (J). (gr. k-3). 1993. lib. bdg. 16.95 (*0-89490-425-6*) Enslow Pubs.

Reading Acquisition. Ed. by Philip Gough et al. 384p. 1992. text ed. 79.95 (*0-8058-0113-8*) L Erlbaum Assocs.

Reading Acquisition Processes. Ed. by G. B. Thompson et al. LC 93-16104. (Language & Education Library: Vol. 4). 1993. 73.00 (*1-85359-194-7*, Pub. by Multilingual Matters UK); pap. 24.00 (*1-85359-193-9*, Pub. by Multilingual Matters UK) Taylor & Francis.

***Reading Across Cultures: Teaching Literature in a Diverse Society.** Ed. by Theresa Rogers & Anna O. Soter. LC 96-32594. (Language & Literacy Ser.: Vol. 28). 256p. (C). 1996. text ed. 45.00 (*0-8077-3552-3*) Tchrs Coll.

***Reading Across Cultures: Teaching Literature in a Diverse Society.** Anna O. Soter. LC 96-32594. (Language & Literacy Ser.: Vol. 28). 256p. (C). 1996. pap. text ed. 21.95 (*0-8077-3551-5*) Tchrs Coll.

Reading Across the Curriculum: A Research Report for Teachers. Ed. by Mary M. Dupuis & Linda K. Merchant. LC 92-10123. 1992. 21.95 (*0-927516-33-0*) ERIC-REC.

Reading Across the Life Span. Ed. by Steven R. Yussen & M. Cecil Smith. LC 92-40972. 1993. 65.95 (*0-387-97978-6*) Spr-Verlag.

***Reading Activities & Resources That Work.** Phyllis J. Perry. LC 97-9859. 1997. pap. 30.00 (*0-917846-94-X*) Highsmith Pr.

Reading Activities for Every Month of the School Year. Sue J. Erlenbusch. 288p. 1988. spiral bd. 27.95 (*0-87628-722-4*) Ctr Appl Res.

Reading Activities for Middle & Secondary Schools: A Handbook for Teachers. 2nd ed. Carl B. Smith & Peggy G. Elliott. LC 86-23015. (Illus.). 264p. 1986. reprint ed. teacher ed., pap. 75.30 (*0-608-00854-0*, 2061645) Bks Demand.

Reading Activities for Middle & Secondary Schools: A Handbook for Teachers. 2nd ed. Carl B. Smith & Peggy G. Elliott. 264p. (C). 1986. pap. 19.95 (*0-8077-2826-8*) Tchrs Coll.

Reading Activities for Today's Elementary Schools. Paul C. Burns & Betty D. Roe. 218p. (C). 1991. reprint ed. pap. text ed. 27.00 (*0-8191-8055-6*) U Pr of Amer.

Reading Activities in Content Areas: An Ideabook for Middle & Secondary Schools. 2nd ed. Dorothy Piercey. 590p. (C). 1981. pap. text ed. 33.95 (*0-205-07372-7*, H73729) Allyn.

***Reading Acts: A Literary & Theological Commentary on the Acts of the Apostles.** Charles H. Talbert. LC 97-10324. (Reading the New Testament Ser.). 300p. 1997. pap. 19.95 (*0-8245-1669-9*, Crossrd Herd) Crossroad NY.

Reading Adrienne Rich: Reviews & Re-Visions, 1951-81. Ed. by Jane R. Cooper. 1984. 42.50 (*0-472-09350-9*) U of Mich Pr.

Reading Ads, Legal Documents & Reference Materials. Carolyn M. Starkey & Norgina W. Penn. (Essential Life Skills Ser.). 60p. 1991. pap. 6.60 (*0-8442-5315-4*, Natl Textbk) NTC Pub Grp.

Reading Ads, Reference Materials, & Legal Documents. Carolyn M. Starkey. 64p. 1995. pap. 6.95 (*0-8442-5170-4*) NTC Pub Grp.

Reading Ads Socially. Robert Goldman. LC 92-8840. (Illus.). 256p. (C). (gr. 13). 1992. text ed. 52.95 (*0-415-05399-4*, A7061) Routledge.

Reading Advanced. 1992. 6.95 (*0-19-453403-0*) OUP.

Reading after Foucault: Institutions, Disciplines, & Technologies of the Self in Germany, 1750-1830. Ed. by Robert S. Leventhal. LC 94-16730. (Kritik: German Literary Theory & Cultural Studies). (Illus.). 278p. 1995. text ed. 38.95 (*0-8143-2510-6*) Wayne St U Pr.

Reading after Freud: Essays on Goethe, Holderlin, Habermas, Nietzsche, Brecht, Celan, & Freud. Rainer Nagele. LC 86-20730. 216p. 1987. text ed. 49.50 (*0-231-06286-9*) Col U Pr.

Reading against Culture: Ideology & Narrative in the Japanese Novel. David Pollack. LC 92-52769. 272p. 1992. 42.50 (*0-8014-2752-5*); pap. 15.95 (*0-8014-8035-3*) Cornell U Pr.

Reading Against Racism. Ed. by Emrys Evans. LC 92-16901. 1992. pap. 27.00 (*0-335-09544-5*, Open Univ Pr) Taylor & Francis.

Reading Aids Through the Grades: A Guide to Materials & 501 Activities for Individualizing Reading Instruction. 4th rev. ed. David Russell et al. Ed. by Anne M. Mueser. LC 75-15639. 320p. 1981. pap. text ed. 19.95 (*0-8077-2609-5*) Tchrs Coll.

***Reading Aids Through the Grades: A Guide to Materials & 501 Activities for Individualizing Reading Instruction.** David H. Russell et al. LC 80-23048. (Illus.). 327p. 1981. reprint ed. pap. 93.20 (*0-608-04166-1*, 2064899) Bks Demand.

Reading All Types of Writing. Alison B. Littlefair. (Rethinking Reading Ser.). 128p. 1990. 80.00 (*0-335-09278-0*, Open Univ Pr); pap. 27.00 (*0-335-09277-2*, Open Univ Pr) Taylor & Francis.

***Reading Alone, Reading Together.** Gerald Keen. (C). 1997. teacher ed., pap. text ed. 22.50 (*0-15-502921-5*) HarBrace.

Reading Aloud to Your Child. Elizabeth L. Fontaine. LC 84-60976. 125p. (Orig.). (C). 1985. pap. text ed. 6.50 (*0-88247-732-3*) R & E Pubs.

Reading Althusser: An Essay on Structural Marxism. Steven B. Smith. LC 83-45943. 240p. 1984. 35.00 (*0-8014-1672-8*) Cornell U Pr.

Reading America: Essays on American Literature. Denis Donoghue. 1987. 22.95 (*0-394-55939-8*) Knopf.

Reading America: Essays on American Literature. Denis Donoghue. 320p. (C). 1988. pap. 14.00 (*0-520-06424-0*) U CA Pr.

Reading American Photographs: Images As History from Matthew Brady to Walker Evans. Alan Trachtenberg. (Illus.). 336p. 1990. pap. 16.00 (*0-374-52249-9*, Noonday) FS&G.

Reading an Erased Code: Romantic Religion & Literary Aesthetics in France. Michel Despland. (Romance Ser.). 223p. 1994. 45.00 (*0-8020-0578-0*) U of Toronto Pr.

Reading Ancient Greek: A Reasonable Approach, 2 Pt. J. D. Ellsworth. 498p. (C). 1982. 45.00 (*0-87291-162-4*) Coronado Pr.

Reading Ancient Greek: The Second Year. J. D. Ellsworth. 358p. 1990. pap. 45.00 (*0-87291-202-7*) Coronado Pr.

Reading & Believing. Jacob Neusner. LC 86-30399. (Brown Judaic Studies). 129p. (C). 1986. 27.50 (*0-89130-976-4*, 14-01-13); pap. 21.50 (*0-89130-977-2*, 14 01 13) Scholars Pr GA.

***Reading & Berks County: A History, 3 vols. in 2.** Ed. by Cyrus T. Fox. (Illus.). 1035p. 1997. reprint ed. lib. bdg. 112.00 (*0-8328-6442-0*) Higginson Bk Co.

Reading & Cases in Information Systems: A Management Approach. Steven R. Gordon & Judith R. Gordon. 264p. (C). 1996. suppl. ed., pap. text ed. 26.50 (*0-03-016317-X*) Dryden Pr.

Reading & Cases in Marketing Management. Alvin C. Burns & David W. Cravens. 448p. (C). 1987. pap. text ed. 31.95 (*0-256-03161-4*) Irwin.

Reading & Computers. Henney. 1985. 13.95 (*0-13-754797-8*) P-H.

***Reading & Computers: Issues for Theory & Practice.** Ed. by David Reinking. LC 87-10053. (Computers & Education Ser.). 219p. 1987. reprint ed. pap. 62.50 (*0-608-02759-6*, 2063822) Bks Demand.

Reading & Critical Thinking in the Content Areas. Ed. by Barnes. 1988. pap. 10.26 (*0-8092-4478-0*) Contemp Bks.

Reading & Dating Roman Imperial Coins. Zander Klawans. (Illus.). 1982. reprint ed. pap. 10.00 (*0-686-79427-3*) S J Durst.

Reading & Deafness. C. M. King & Stephen P. Quigley. 326p. 1985. write for info. (*0-85066-585-X*) Taylor & Francis.

Reading & Deafness. Cynthia M. King & Stephen P. Quigley. LC 85-5694. 422p. (C). 1985. text ed. 39.00 (*0-88744-107-6*, 1718) PRO-ED.

Reading & Evaluating Financial Reports. 1977. 49.95 (*0-935268-00-6*) Learn Int.

Reading & Fiction in Golden Age Spain: A Platonist Critique & Some Picaresque Replies. B. W. Ife. (Cambridge Iberian & Latin American Studies). 270p. 1985. 59.95 (*0-521-30375-3*) Cambridge U Pr.

Reading & Interpreting Strong Motion Accelerograms. D. E. Hudson. LC 79-53973. 112p. 1979. 25.00 (*0-685-14388-0*) Earthquake Eng.

Reading & Its Difficulties: A Psychological Study. Magdalen D. Vernon. 219p. reprint ed. pap. 62.50 (*0-685-16238-9*, 2027270) Bks Demand.

***Reading & Language Arts for All Students: A Practical Guide for Content Area Teachers.** Evelyn Miller. 504p. (C). 1996. per. 52.44 (*0-7872-2093-0*) Kendall-Hunt.

Reading & Language Arts Programs: A Guide to Evaluation. Mary W. Olson & Samuel D. Miller. (Essential Tools for Educators Ser.). 120p. 1993. pap. 19.95 (*0-8039-6042-5*) Corwin Pr.

Reading & Language Processing. Ed. by John M. Henderson et al. 360p. 1995. pap. 34.50 (*0-8058-1903-7*) L Erlbaum Assocs.

Reading & Learning Across the Disciplines. Mary-Jane McCarthy et al. 424p. (C). 1993. pap. 25.75 (*0-534-12817-3*) Wadsworth Pub.

Reading & Learning Across the Disciplines. 2nd ed. Mary-Jane McCarthy et al. 1996. pap. 37.95 (*0-534-25722-4*) Wadsworth Pub.

Reading & Learning Disabilities: Research & Practice. Joyce N. French et al. LC 94-44990. (Garland Reference Library of Social Science: Vols. 512 & 45). 442p. 1995. text ed. 65.00 (*0-8240-4790-7*, SS512) Garland.

***Reading & Learning Disability: A Neuropsychological Approach to Evaluation & Instruction.** Estelle L. Fryburg. LC 97-4163. (Illus.). 398p. 1997. text ed. 79.95 (*0-398-06744-9*); pap. text ed. 64.95 (*0-398-06745-7*) C C Thomas.

Reading & Learning from Text. 2nd ed. Harry Singer & Dan Donlan. 696p. 1988. text ed. 45.00 (*0-89859-789-7*) L Erlbaum Assocs.

Reading & Learning in the Content Areas. Randy Ryder & Michael Graves. 416p. (C). 1993. pap. text ed. 44.00 (*0-02-404945-X*, Macmillan Coll) P-H.

Reading & Learning Power. 3rd ed. Dorothy Rubin. 360p. 1990. pap. 21.00 (*0-536-57654-8*) Ginn Pr.

Reading & Learning to Read. 3rd ed. Joanne L. Vacca et al. LC 94-26317. (C). 1995. text ed. 58.50 (*0-673-99089-3*) Addson-Wesley Educ.

Reading & Libraries: Proceedings of Library History Seminar VIII, 9-11 May 1990, Bloomington, Indiana. Ed. by Donald G. Davis, Jr. 492p. 1991. 15.00 (*0-938729-01-2*) UTX SLIS.

Reading & Loving. Leila Berg. 1976. 19.95 (*0-7100-8475-7*, RKP); pap. 11.95 (*0-7100-8476-5*, RKP) Routledge.

Reading & More: Grade 1. ECS Learning Systems Staff. (ECS Home Study Bk.). (Illus.). 64p. (Orig.). (J). 1995. wbk. ed., pap. 4.95 (*1-57022-021-2*) ECS Lrn Systs.

Reading & More: Grade 2. ECS Learning Systems Staff. (ECS Home Study Bk.). (Illus.). 64p. (Orig.). (J). 1995. wbk. ed., pap. 4.95 (*1-57022-022-0*) ECS Lrn Systs.

Reading & More: Grade 3. ECS Learning Systems Staff. (ECS Home Study Bk.). (Illus.). 64p. (Orig.). (J). 1995. wbk. ed., pap. 4.95 (*1-57022-023-9*) ECS Lrn Systs.

Reading & More: Grade 4. ECS Learning Systems Staff. (ECS Home Study Bk.). (Illus.). 64p. (Orig.). (J). 1995. wbk. ed., pap. 4.95 (*1-57022-024-7*) ECS Lrn Systs.

Reading & More: Grade 5. ECS Learning Systems Staff. (ECS Home Study Bk.). (Illus.). 64p. (Orig.). (J). 1995. wbk. ed., pap. 4.95 (*1-57022-025-5*) ECS Lrn Systs.

Reading & More: Grade 6. ECS Learning Systems Staff. (ECS Home Study Bk.). (Illus.). 64p. (Orig.). (J). 1995. wbk. ed., pap. 4.95 (*1-57022-026-3*) ECS Lrn Systs.

Reading & Ninth Grade Achievement. Eva Wagner. LC 71-176792. (Columbia University. Teachers College. Contributions to Education Ser.: No. 756). reprint ed. 37.50 (*0-404-55756-2*) AMS Pr.

Reading & Praying the New Testament: A Book-by-Book Guide for Catholics. Peter Kreeft. 172p. 1992. pap. 9.99 (*0-89283-755-1*, Charis) Servant.

Reading & Readers. Kenneth S. Goodman. 24p. (Orig.). (C). 1981. pap. 2.50 (*0-918374-20-0*) City Coll Wk.

Reading & Reasoning. Resnick & Benjamin I. Page. 352p. (C). 1984. pap. text ed. 53.00 (*0-02-399320-0*, Macmillan Coll) P-H.

Reading & Responding to Literature. SuzAnne C. Cole & Jeff W. Lindemann. 328p. (C). 1989. pap. text ed. 17.50 (*0-15-575501-3*) HB Coll Pubs.

Reading & Responding to Mircea Eliade's History of Religious Ideas. John R. Mason. LC 93-15344. 136p. 1993. text ed. 69.95 (*0-7734-9283-6*) E Mellen.

Reading & Responding to Poetry: Patterns in the Process. Patrick Dias. LC 95-43115. 124p. 1995. pap. text ed. 22.00 (*0-86709-372-2*, 0372) Boynton Cook Pubs.

Reading & Speaking about Russian Newspapers. 3rd ed. F. J. Miller et al. (Focus Texts Ser.). 246p. (RUS.). (C). 1995. pap. 28.95 (*0-941051-11-0*) Focus Pub-R Pullins.

Reading & Speaking about Russian Newspapers. 3rd ed. F. J. Miller et al. (Focus Texts Ser.). 98p. (RUS.). (C). 1995. wbk. ed., pap. 12.95 (*0-941051-12-9*) Focus Pub-R Pullins.

***Reading & Spelling: Development & Disorders.** Ed. by R. Malatesha Joshi & Charles Hulme. LC 97-18656. 450p. 1997. write for info. (*0-8058-2773-0*) L Erlbaum Assocs.

***Reading & Spelling: Development & Disorders.** Ed. by R. Malatesha Joshi & Charles Hulme. LC 97-18656. 450p. 1997. pap. write for info. (*0-8058-2774-9*) L Erlbaum Assocs.

Reading & Study Skills. Wong. (C). 1995. pap. 15.96 (*0-395-74774-0*) HM.

Reading & Study Skills, Bk. II. 3rd ed. Ronald V. Schmelzer & William L. Christen. 672p. 1996. per. 32.49 (*0-8403-7016-4*) Kendall-Hunt.

***Reading & Study Skills: A Rhetorical Approach.** Joan Kimmelman et al. 352p. (C). 1996. per., pap. text ed. 29.34 (*0-7872-2498-7*) Kendall-Hunt.

Reading & Study Skills: A Workbook for Writers, Form A. 5th ed. John Langan. 1992. text ed. write for info. (*0-07-036383-8*) McGraw.

Reading & Study Skills: A Workbook for Writers, Form B. 5th ed. John Langan. LC 93-36861. 1994. pap. text ed. write for info. (*0-07-036413-3*) McGraw.

Reading & Study Skills: Book 1. 3rd ed. Ronald V. Schmelzer & William L. Christen. 320p. 1992. per. 28.29 (*0-8403-7014-8*) Kendall-Hunt.

Reading & Study Skills Text. Smilkstein. (C). pap. text ed. 18.75 (*0-15-501171-5*) HB Coll Pubs.

Reading & Studying Skills. Patricia Grant. 384p. (C). 1988. pap. text ed. 43.00 (*0-13-762238-4*) P-H.

Reading & the Adult Learner. Ed. by Laura S. Johnson. LC 79-16085. (Illus.). 84p. (Orig.). reprint ed. pap. 25.00 (*0-8357-8296-4*, 2034159) Bks Demand.

Reading & the Art of Librarianship: Selected Essays of John B. Nicholson, Jr. John B. Nicholson, Jr. Ed. by Paul Z. Du Bois & Dean H. Keller. LC 86-18442. (Collection Management: Vol. 8, Nos. 3-4). 271p. 1986. 49.95 (*0-86656-585-X*) Haworth Pr.

Reading & the Black English-Speaking Child: An Annotated Bibliography. Jean R. Harber & Jane N. Beatty. LC 78-101733. (IRA Annotated Bibliography Ser.). 47p. reprint ed. pap. 25.00 (*0-685-23636-6*, 2027949) Bks Demand.

Reading & the Law. Ed. by Robert J. Harper & Gary Kilarr. LC 78-6213. 156p. reprint ed. pap. 44.50 (*0-685-15970-1*, 2026815) Bks Demand.

Reading & the Middle School: Strategies to Enhance Literacy. Judith L. Irvin. 256p. 1989. text ed. 54.50 (*0-205-11958-1*, H1958-1) Allyn.

***Reading & the Middle School Student: Strategies to Enhance Literacy.** 2nd ed. Judith L. Irvin. LC 97-1535. 1997. 45.00 (*0-205-16379-3*) Allyn.

Reading & the Psychology of Perception. Hunter Diack. LC 77-138220. (Illus.). 155p. 1971. reprint ed. text ed. 65.00 (*0-8371-5577-0*, DIRP, Greenwood Pr) Greenwood.

Reading & the Special Learner. Ed. by Carolyn N. Hedley & John S. Hicks. LC 88-4118. 272p. 1988. text ed. 45.00 (*0-89391-495-9*); pap. text ed. 22.50 (*0-89391-517-3*) Ablex Pub.

Reading & the Writing Process. 2nd ed. Susan Day et al. LC 93-10711. 640p. (C). 1993. pap. text ed. 36.00 (*0-02-327901-X*, Macmillan Coll) P-H.

Reading & Thinking. A. J. Evans. 1979. teacher ed., pap. text ed. 1.95 (*0-8077-2565-X*) Tchrs Coll.

Reading & Thinking, Bk. 1. A. J. Evans. (gr. 2-3). 1979. pap. text ed. 4.95 (*0-8077-2563-3*) Tchrs Coll.

Reading & Thinking, Bk. 2. A. J. Evans. (J). (gr. 3-4). 1979. student ed., pap. text ed. 4.95 (*0-8077-2564-1*) Tchrs Coll.

***Reading & Thinking, Bk. 2.** Arthur J. Evans. (Illus.). 65p. pap. 25.00 (*0-608-05096-2*, 2065652) Bks Demand.

Reading & Thinking: A Process Approach. James E. Twining. 352p. (C). 1985. pap. text ed. 20.75 (*0-03-063196-3*) HB Coll Pubs.

Reading & Translating Contemporary Russian. Horace W. Dewey. 208p. 1995. pap. 16.95 (*0-8442-4243-8*, Natl Textbk) NTC Pub Grp.

Reading & Understanding. Joseph H. Danks & Kathy Pezdek. Ed. by Frank B. Murray. LC 80-11688. (IRA Series on the Development of the Reading Process). 81p. (Orig.). reprint ed. pap. 25.00 (*0-8357-8659-5*, 2035106) Bks Demand.

Reading & Understanding: An Introduction to the Psychology of Reading. Geoffrey Underwood & Vivienne Batt. (Illus.). 288p. (C). 1996. 54.95 (*0-631-17949-6*); pap. 24.95 (*0-631-17951-8*) Blackwell Pubs.

Reading & Understanding: Teaching from the Perspective of Artificial Intelligence. Roger C. Schank. (Illus.). 208p. 1982. pap. 22.50 (*0-89859-208-9*); text ed. 39.95 (*0-89859-169-4*) L Erlbaum Assocs.

Reading & Understanding Multivariate Statistics. Ed. by Laurence G. Grimm & Paul R. Yarnold. 373p. (Orig.). 1994. pap. text ed. 24.95 (*1-55798-273-2*) Am Psychol.

Reading & Understanding Nonfiction: Level One. 372p. (YA). (gr. 9-10). 1990. 21.21 (*0-89061-690-6*); teacher ed. 5.99 (*0-89061-495-4*); pap. 17.22 (*0-89061-487-3*) Jamestown Pubs.

Reading & Understanding Nonfiction: Level Two. 388p. (YA). (gr. 11-12). 1990. 22.54 (*0-89061-694-9*); teacher ed. 5.99 (*0-89061-499-7*); pap. 18.55 (*0-89061-491-1*) Jamestown Pubs.

Reading & Understanding Plays: Level One. 404p. (YA). (gr. 9-10). 1990. 25.20 (*0-89061-691-4*); teacher ed. 5.99 (*0-89061-496-2*); pap. 21.61 (*0-89061-488-1*) Jamestown Pubs.

Reading & Understanding Plays: Level Two. 356p. (YA). (gr. 11-12). 1990. 26.53 (*0-89061-695-7*); teacher ed. 5.99 (*0-89061-525-X*); pap. 22.54 (*0-89061-492-X*) Jamestown Pubs.

Reading & Understanding Poems: Level One. 274p. (YA). (gr. 9-10). 1990. 17.22 (*0-89061-692-2*); teacher ed. 5.99 (*0-89061-497-0*); pap. 13.23 (*0-89061-489-X*) Jamestown Pubs.

Reading & Understanding Poems: Level Two. 242p. (YA). (gr. 11-12). 1990. 18.55 (*0-89061-696-5*); teacher ed. 5.99 (*0-89061-526-8*); pap. 14.56 (*0-89061-493-8*) Jamestown Pubs.

Reading & Understanding Short Stories: Level One. 356p. (YA). (gr. 9-10). 1990. 21.21 (*0-89061-689-2*); teacher ed. 5.99 (*0-89061-494-6*); pap. 17.22 (*0-89061-486-5*) Jamestown Pubs.

Reading & Understanding Short Stories: Level Two. 340p. (YA). (gr. 11-12). 1990. 22.54 (*0-89061-693-0*); teacher ed. 5.99 (*0-89061-498-9*); pap. 18.55 (*0-89061-490-3*) Jamestown Pubs.

Reading & Understanding Technical Information. Richard S. Marsh. (Illus.). (J). (gr. 5). 1986. student ed. 5.25 (*0-89525-758-0*) Ed Activities.

Reading & Understanding the Bible. Vic Lockman. (Illus.). 56p. (J). (gr. 6). 1992. 6.00 (*0-936175-18-4*) V Lockman.

***Reading & Understanding the Variations Between the Critical Apparatuses of Nestle's 25th & 26th Editions of Novum Testamentum-Graece.** 2nd ed. Samuel C. Gipp. 68p. 1992. reprint ed. pap. 10.00 (*1-890120-06-5*) Frnd To Churches.

Reading & Variant in Petronius: Studies in the French Humanists & Their Manuscript Sources. Wade Richardson. 187p. 1993. 60.00 (*0-8020-2866-7*) U of Toronto Pr.

Reading & Vocabulary Strategies for the ESL Student. Orsini Gonzalez. 128p. (C). 1991. pap. text ed. 28.29 (*0-8403-6793-7*) Kendall-Hunt.

Reading & Wisdom: The De Doctrina Christiana of Augustine in the Middle Ages. Ed. by Edward D. English. LC 94-15467. (Notre Dame Conferences in Medieval Studies: Vol. 6). (C). 1995. text ed. 34.50 (*0-268-01650-X*) U of Notre Dame Pr.

Reading & Word Study: For Students of English As a Second Language. Kenneth Croft. (Illus.). 1969. pap. text ed. write for info. (*0-13-756742-1*) P-H.

***Reading & Writing.** (Fisher-Price First Grade Workbooks Ser.). (Illus.). 72p. (J). (gr. 1). 1997. pap. write for info. (*1-56144-930-X*, Honey Bear Bks) Modern Pub NYC.

Reading & Writing. Robertson Davies. LC 92-40787. 80p. (C). 1993. 12.95 (*0-87480-426-4*) U of Utah Pr.

***Reading & Writing.** Martha A. Lane. (Passport to the World of English Ser.: Bk. 3). (Illus.). 240p. 1997. teacher ed., ring bd. 23.00 incl. audio (*1-877596-29-9*) Literacy & Evangelism.

***Reading & Writing.** Martha A. Lane. (Passport to the World of English Ser.: Bk. 3). (Illus.). 200p. 1997. student ed., ring bd. 20.00 incl. audio (*1-877596-30-2*) Literacy & Evangelism.

Reading & Writing: Teaching for Connection. 2nd ed. Bill Harp. 600p. (C). 1995. 59.75 (*0-15-500958-3*) HB Coll Pubs.

Reading & Writing: Teaching for the Connections. Bill Harp & Joann Brewer. 500p. (C). 1990. text ed. 40.00 (*0-15-575491-2*) HB Coll Pubs.

Reading & Writing: Teaching for the Connections. 2nd ed. Harp. (C). 1995. teacher ed., pap. text ed. 32.00 (*0-15-503300-X*) HB Coll Pubs.

Reading & Writing about Computer Careers. Ethel M. Howard & Ralph Cappell. (Career Ser.). 81p. 1985. student ed. 4.25 (*0-910307-03-2*) Comp Pr.

Reading & Writing about Health Careers. Ralph Cappell & Ethel M. Howard. (Career Ser.). 79p. 1984. student ed. 4.25 (*0-910307-02-4*) Comp Pr.

Reading & Writing about Literature: Fiction, Poetry, Drama, & the Essay. Edward Proffitt. 1030p. (C). 1990. pap. text ed. 28.00 (*0-15-575526-9*); pap. text ed. 3.00 (*0-15-575527-7*) HB Coll Pubs.

Reading & Writing about Office Careers. Ralph Cappell & Ethel M. Howard. (Career Ser.). 79p. 1986. student ed. 4.50 (*0-910307-06-7*) Comp Pr.

Reading & Writing about Short Fiction. Edward Proffitt. 605p. (C). 1988. pap. text ed. 18.75 (*0-15-575520-X*) HB Coll Pubs.

Reading & Writing Acquisition: A Developmental Neuro Psychological Perspective. Virginia W. Berninger. LC 96-1280. (Developmental Psychology Ser.). (C). 1996. pap. text ed. 18.95 (*0-8133-3000-9*) Westview.

Reading & Writing Acquisition: A Developmental Neuropsychological Perspective. Virginia W. Berninger. 240p. (C). 1993. pap. write for info. (*0-697-14558-1*) Brown & Benchmark.

Reading & Writing Across the Curriculum. Delores Liscomb. 125p. (YA). (gr. 5-12). 1988. wbk. ed. 15.65 (*0-941484-06-8*) Urban Res Pr.

Reading & Writing Across the Curriculum: A Generic, Hands-on Program Easily Integrated into Any Teaching Style at Any Grade Level (PreK-6) Dinah Zike. (Illus.). 130p. 1994. pap. 19.95 (*1-882796-02-0*, CCC 97) Dinah-Might Act.

***Reading & Writing American History: An Introduction to the Historian's Craft.** Peter C. Hoffer & William Stueck. (C). 1994. teacher ed., text ed. 2.66 (*0-669-24904-1*) HM College Div.

Reading & Writing American History: An Introduction to the Historian's Craft, 2 vols., Vol. 1. Peter C. Hoffer & William Stueck. 149p. (C). 1994. pap. text ed. 20.36 (*0-669-24902-5*) HM College Div.

Reading & Writing American History: An Introduction to the Historian's Craft, 2 vols., Vol. 2. Peter C. Hoffer & William Stueck. 168p. (C). 1994. pap. text ed. 20.36 (*0-669-24903-3*) HM College Div.

Reading & Writing Chinese: A Guide to the Chinese Writing System. William McNaughton. LC 77-77699. (Illus.). 368p. 1989. reprint ed. pap. 16.95 (*0-8048-1583-6*) C E Tuttle.

Reading & Writing Communities: Co-Operative Literacy Learning in the Classroom. Susan Hill & Joelie Hancock. (Illus.). 144p. (Orig.). 1993. teacher ed., pap. 16.00 (*1-875327-12-6*, Pub. by E Curtain AT) Peguis Pubs Ltd.

Reading & Writing Connection. Jeri W. Gillie & Susan Ingle. LC 96-46646. 1997. pap. text ed. write for info. (*0-07-023721-2*) McGraw.

Reading & Writing Essays: The Imaginative Task. Pat C. Hoy. 1992. pap. text ed. write for info. (*0-07-030607-9*) McGraw.

***Reading & Writing from Literature.** John Schwiebert. 1152p. (C). 1997. pap. text ed. 33.56 (*0-395-74125-4*) HM.

***Reading & Writing in English Bk. 1: An Interactive Text for Intermediate ESL Students.** Kristan Cavina. LC 96-92732. 175p. (Orig.). 1996. pap. text ed. write for info. (*1-889850-00-4*) De Anza Pr.

***Reading & Writing in English Bk. 1: An Interactive Text for Intermediate ESL Students.** Kristan Cavina. 44p. (Orig.). 1996. teacher ed. write for info. (*1-889850-01-2*) De Anza Pr.

***Reading & Writing in English Bk. 2: An Interactive Text for Intermediate ESL Students.** Kristan Cavina. LC 97-91561. 170p. (Orig.). 1997. pap. text ed. write for info. (*1-889850-02-0*) De Anza Pr.

Reading & Writing in Shakespeare. Ed. by David M. Bergeron. LC 95-24193. (Illus.). 288p. 1996. 42.50 (*0-87413-557-5*) U Delaware Pr.

Reading & Writing in the Academic Community. Mary L. Kennedy & Hadley M. Smith. LC 92-46764. 473p. (C). 1993. pap. text ed. 34.60 (*0-13-007972-3*) P-H.

Reading & Writing in the Arts: A Handbook. rev. ed. Bernard Goldman. LC 77-27856. 172p. 1978. text ed. 26.00 (*0-8143-1604-2*); pap. text ed. 15.95 (*0-8143-1605-0*) Wayne St U Pr.

Reading & Writing in the Elementary Classrooms: Strategies & Observations. 3rd rev. ed. Patricia M. Cunningham et al. LC 94-29678. 537p. (C). 1995. text ed. 55.50 (*0-8013-1264-7*) Longman.

Reading & Writing in the Middle Grades: A Whole-Language View. Maryann M. Manning et al. 1990. pap. 8.95 (*0-8106-3071-0*) NEA.

Reading & Writing in the Primary Grades. Maryann M. Manning et al. 80p. 1987. pap. 9.95 (*0-8106-1697-1*) NEA.

Reading & Writing Intervals: A Self-Instruction Book. Gerald Lefkoff. 130p. 1980. pap. text ed. 21.95 (*0-935964-01-0*) Glyphic Pr.

Reading & Writing Music: Fifty Ready-to-Use Activities for Grades 3-9. Audrey J. Adair. (Music Curriculum Activities Library). 112p. 1987. pap. 12.95 (*0-13-762196-5*) P-H.

Reading & Writing Nature: The Poetry of Robert Frost, Wallace Stevens, Marianne Moore, & Elizabeth Bishop. Guy Rotella. 253p. 1990. text ed. 45.00 (*1-55553-086-9*) NE U Pr.

Reading & Writing Non-Fiction. Ed. & Intro. by Philip M. Anderson. (Illus.). 109p. (C). 1994. pap. text ed. 10.00 (*0-930348-19-2*) NY St Eng Coun.

Reading & Writing Poetry: A Guide for Teachers. Judith W. Steinbergh. 176p. 1992. pap. 19.95 (*0-590-49168-7*) Scholastic Inc.

Reading & Writing, Pt. II see Tamil for Beginners

***Reading & Writing Remediation Kit: Ready-to-Use Strategies & Activities to Build Content Reading & Writing Skills.** Wilma H. Miller. 448p. 1996. spiral bd. 29.95 (*0-87628-753-4*) Ctr Appl Res.

Reading & Writing Short Arguments. William Vesterman. LC 93-25549. 335p. (Orig.). (C). 1994. pap. text ed. 24.95 (*1-55934-222-6*, 1222) Mayfield Pub.

Reading & Writing Short Arguments. 2nd rev. ed. William Vesterman. LC 96-15054. (Illus.). 356p. (C). 1996. pap. text ed. 24.95 (*1-55934-642-6*, 1642) Mayfield Pub.

***Reading & Writing Short Arguments - Instructor's Manual.** 2nd rev. ed. William Vesterman. 105p. 1996. pap. text ed. write for info. (*0-614-24421-8*, 1634) Mayfield Pub.

Reading & Writing Short Arguments, Instructor's Manual. William Vesterman. LC 93-25549. (Orig.). (C). 1994. teacher ed., pap. text ed. write for info. (*1-55934-223-4*, 1223) Mayfield Pub.

Reading & Writing Short Essays. 3rd ed. Morton A. Miller. 416p. (C). 1986. pap. text ed. write for info. (*0-07-554763-5*) McGraw.

Reading & Writing Short Essays. 3rd ed. Morton A. Miller. 405p. 1986. pap. text ed. write for info. (*0-318-55406-2*) Random.

Reading & Writing Skills in Primary Education: A Report of the Educational Research Workshop Held in Tilburg. M. Young et al. vi, 218p. 1988. 41.00 (*90-265-0880-8*) Swets.

Reading & Writing Story Starters. Frank Finney. 36p. 1985. 2.50 (*0-910307-05-9*) Comp Pr.

Reading & Writing Task Hierarchy. Deborah Ross & Sara H. Spencer. (Illus.). 350p. (C). 1981. spiral bd., pap. 49.95 (*0-398-04642-5*) C C Thomas.

Reading & Writing Termcap Entries see Termcap & Terminfo

Reading & Writing the Self: Autobiography in Education & the Curriculum. Robert Graham. (Critical Issues in Curriculum Ser.: No. 1). 192p. (C). 1991. text ed. 40.00 (*0-8077-3126-9*); pap. text ed. 17.95 (*0-8077-3125-0*) Tchrs Coll.

Reading & Writing Through Cloze: A First Book. Frank Finney. 54p. 1987. student ed. 3.25 (*0-910307-15-6*) Comp Pr.

Reading & Writing Workshop: Getting Started. Scholastic Books Staff. 136p. 1996. pap. 16.95 (*0-590-49167-9*) Scholastic Inc.

Reading Andreas Gryphius: Critical Trends 1664-1993. Erika Metzger & Mic Metzger. (LCGERM Ser.). xii, 156p. 1994. 55.95 (*1-57113-005-5*) Camden Hse.

Reading Arabic: Al Kira al-Mouhawaka. (Illus.). 68p. (ARA.). (J). 1979. student ed., pap. 9.95 (*0-86685-406-1*, LDL4061, Pub. by Librairie du Liban FR) Intl Bk Ctr.

Reading Arabic: Al Kira al-Mouhawaka, exercise bk. (Illus.). (ARA.). (J). 1979. pap. 9.95 (*0-86685-706-0*, LDL4153E, Pub. by Librairie du Liban FR) Intl Bk Ctr.

Reading Arabic for Muslims, Vol. I. Mahmoud Sieny. 1992. 14.95 (*0-86685-565-3*) Intl Bk Ctr.

Reading Architectural Plans for Residential & Commercial Construction. 3rd ed. Ernest R. Weidhaas. (Illus.). 328p. 1989. teacher ed. write for info. (*0-318-63884-3*, H18914); pap. text ed. 66.67 (*0-205-11890-9*, H18906) P-H.

Reading Architectural Working Drawings: Commercial Construction, Vol. II. 3rd ed. Edward J. Muller & Robert L. Myatt, Jr. (Illus.). 1988. pap. text ed. 66.67 (*0-13-755794-9*) P-H.

Reading Architectural Working Drawings Vol. 1: Basics, Residential & Light Construction. 4th ed. Edward J. Muller. LC 95-16326. (Illus.). 300p. (C). 1995. pap. text ed. 68.00 (*0-13-440108-5*) P-H.

Reading Aristotle's Ethics: Virtue, Rhetoric, & Political Philosophy. Aristide Tessitore. LC 96-12731. 155p. (C). 1996. text ed. 54.50 (*0-7914-3047-2*); pap. text ed. 17.95 (*0-7914-3048-0*) State U NY Pr.

***Reading Around the School.** Jo E. Moore. (Real-Life Reading Activities Ser.). (Illus.). 64p. (J). (gr. k-1). 1996. teacher ed., pap. 7.95 (*1-55799-585-0*, 562) Evan-Moor Corp.

Reading Around the World. Elaine Prizzi & Jeanne Hoffman. (J). (gr. 4-6). 1985. pap. 7.99 (*0-8224-3182-3*) Fearon Teach Aids.

Reading Around Town. Elaine Prizzi & Jeanne Hoffman. (J). (gr. 4-6). 1985. pap. 7.99 (*0-8224-3181-5*) Fearon Teach Aids.

***Reading As Communication.** 5th ed. May. 1997. text ed. 60.00 (*0-13-494683-9*) P-H.

Reading as Communication: An Interactive Approach. 4th ed. Frank B. May. 640p. (C). 1993. text ed. 70.00 (*0-02-378242-0*, Macmillan Coll) P-H.

Reading Asian American Literature: From Necessity to Extravagance. Sau-Ling C. Wong. LC 92-42251. 272p. 1993. text ed. 42.50 (*0-691-06875-5*); pap. text ed. 15.95 (*0-691-01541-4*) Princeton U Pr.

Reading Assessment: An Instructional Decision Making Perspective. James F. Baumann. 416p. (C). 1990. pap. text ed. 39.00 (*0-675-20840-8*, Merrill Coll) P-H.

***Reading Assessment & Instruction: A Qualitative Approach to Diagnosis.** Rona F. Flippo. 384p. (C). 1996. pap. text ed. write for info. (*0-03-079564-8*) HB Coll Pubs.

Reading at Berkeley. Charles Olson. 1966. 15.00 (*0-685-80372-4*) SPD-Small Pr Dist.

Reading at Mass: Guidelines for the Lector. Frank Mulligan. 140p. 1989. pap. 7.95 (*0-8146-1907-X*) Liturgical Pr.

Reading at the Social Limit: Affect, Mass Culture, & Edgar Allan Poe. Jonathan Elmer. LC 95-2254. 236p. 1995. 35.00 (*0-8047-2541-1*) Stanford U Pr.

***Reading at the Supermarket.** Jill Norris. (Real-Life Reading Activities Ser.). (Illus.). 64p. (J). (gr. 2-3). 1996. teacher ed., pap. 7.95 (*1-55799-592-3*, 569) Evan-Moor Corp.

Reading at the University. Linda H. Hillman. (C). 1990. pap. 26.95 (*0-8384-2100-8*) Heinle & Heinle.

Reading Auden: The Returns of Caliban. John R. Boly. LC 91-6948. 256p. 1991. 37.50 (*0-8014-2565-4*) Cornell U Pr.

Reading Audiences: Young People & the Media. Ed. by David Buckingham. LC 93-13598. 1993. text ed. 74.95 (*0-7190-3869-3*, Pub. by Manchester Univ Pr UK); text ed. 27.95 (*0-7190-3870-7*, Pub. by Manchester Univ Pr UK) St Martin.

Reading Australian Poetry. Andrew Taylor. LC 86-27246. 218p. (C). 1988. pap. 29.95 (*0-7022-2062-0*, Pub. by Univ Queensland Pr AT) Intl Spec Bk.

Reading Baseball. Barbara Gregorich & Christopher Jennison. 128p. (J). (gr. 4-8). 1996. pap. 9.95 (*0-673-36307-4*, GoodYrBooks) Addson-Wesley Educ.

Reading-Based Writing. Stephen McDonald & William Salomone. LC 95-33217. (C). 1996. pap. 33.95 (*0-534-20094-X*) Wadsworth Pub.

Reading Becomes a Necessity of Life: Material & Cultural Life in Rural New England, 1780-1835. William J. Gilmore. LC 88-10692. (Illus.). 568p. 1989. text ed. 49.95 (*0-87049-586-0*); pap. text ed. 24.00 (*0-87049-768-5*) U of Tenn Pr.

Reading Begins at Home: Preparing Children for Reading Before They Go to School. 2nd rev. ed. Dorothy Butler & Marie Clay. LC 87-326. (Illus.). 48p. 1987. pap. 8.95 (*0-435-08443-7*, 08443) Heinemann.

Reading "Beowulf" An Introduction to the Poem, Its Background, & Its Style. J. D. Ogilvy & Donald C. Baker. LC 83-47835. (Illus.). 240p. 1986. reprint ed. pap. 17.95 (*0-8061-2019-3*) U of Okla Pr.

Reading Berlin 1900. Peter Fritzsche. LC 95-37608. (Illus.). 320p. 1996. 39.95 (*0-674-74881-6*) HUP.

***Reading Between the Bones: The Pioneers of Dinosaur Paleontology.** Susan Clinton. LC 96-36132. (Lives in Science Ser.). (J). 1997. lib. bdg. 22.00 (*0-531-11324-8*) Watts.

Reading Between the Lines. 1990. 12.00 (*0-89333-068-X*) AACTE.

Reading Between the Lines. Lucille H. Blum. LC 79-182040. 183p. 1972. 28.50 (*0-8236-5770-1*); pap. 24.95 (*0-8236-8268-4*, 25770) Intl Univs Pr.

Reading Between the Lines, 2 cass. John McRae & Roy Boardman. 120p. 1984. pap. 32.95 (*0-521-25992-4*); pap. text ed. 13.95 (*0-521-27789-2*); pap. text ed. 14.95 (*0-521-27790-6*) Cambridge U Pr.

Reading Between the Lines. Annabel Patterson. LC 92-50257. 350p. (Orig.). (C). 1993. pap. 17.95 (*0-299-13544-6*); lib. bdg. 48.50 (*0-299-13540-3*) U of Wis Pr.

Reading Between the Lines: A Christian Approach to Literature. Gene E. Veith. LC 90-80623. (Turning Point Christian Worldview Ser.). 256p. (Orig.). (C). 1990. pap. 12.99 (*0-89107-582-8*) Crossway Bks.

Reading Between the Lines: An Introduction to Bar Code Technology. 4th ed. Russ Adams & Craig Harmon. 298p. 1989. 34.00 (*0-911261-02-8*); pap. 23.95 (*0-685-34515-7*) Helmers Pub.

Reading Between the Lines: Discovering the One Purpose Behind the Twenty-Seven Books of the New Testament. Alger Fitch. 1995. 9.99 (*0-89900-733-3*) College Pr Pub.

Reading Between the Lines: Handwriting Analysis. Roger Weeks. LC 92-90813. (Illus.). 75p. (Orig.). 1992. pap. 10.00 (*0-9632952-0-9*) R Weeks.

Reading Between the Lines: The Basics of Handwriting Analysis. P. Scott Hollander. LC 91-26619. (Llewellyn's Self-Help Ser.). 272p. (Orig.). 1991. pap. 14.95 (*0-87542-309-4*) Llewellyn Pubns.

Reading Between the Lips: A Totally Deaf Man Makes It in the Mainstream. Lew Golan. 363p. 1995. text ed. 22.95 (*1-56625-021-8*) Bonus Books.

Reading Between the Texts: Intertextuality & the Hebrew Bible. Ed. by Danna N. Fewell. (Literary Currents in Biblical Interpretation Ser.). 240p. (Orig.). 1992. pap. 23.00 (*0-664-25393-8*) Westminster John Knox.

Reading Beyond. 5th ed. Adams. (C). 1994. teacher ed., pap. text ed. 33.75 (*0-15-501786-1*) HB Coll Pubs.

Reading Beyond Words. 4th ed. W. Royce Adams & Jane Brody. (Illus.). 382p. (C). 1991. pap. text ed. 22.00 (*0-03-052769-4*) HB Coll Pubs.

Reading Beyond Words. 5th ed. Royce Adams & Jane Brody. (Illus.). 370p. (C). 1994. pap. text ed. 34.25 (*0-15-501629-6*) HarBrace.

Reading Beyond Words: Native History in Context. Ed. by Jennifer S. Brown & Elizabeth Vibert. 472p. 1996. pap. 26.95 (*1-55111-070-9*) Broadview Pr.

Reading Bibles, Writing Bodies: Identity & the Book. Ed. by Timothy K. Beal & David M. Gunn. LC 96-1112. (Biblical Limits Ser.). 336p. (C). 1996. pap. 18.95 (*0-415-12665-7*); text ed. 69.95 (*0-415-12664-9*) Routledge.

Reading Big Books. Melinda Willens. Ed. by J. Friedland & R. Kessler. (Novel-Ties Ser.). 1994. student ed., pap. text ed. 20.95 (*1-56982-155-0*) Lrn Links.

Reading Billy Budd. Hershel Parker. 190p. (Orig.). 1990. 29.95 (*0-8101-0961-1*); pap. 14.95 (*0-8101-0962-X*) Northwestern U Pr.

Reading Black, Reading Feminist: A Critical Anthology. Henry Louis Gates, Jr. 544p. 1990. 14.95 (*0-685-38914-6*, NAL Bks) NAL-Dutton.

Reading Black, Reading Feminist: A Literary Critical Anthology. Ed. by Henry Louis Gates, Jr. 480p. 1990. pap. 15.95 (*0-452-01045-4*, Mer) NAL-Dutton.

Reading Blake's Designs. Christopher Heppner. (Illus.). 290p. (C). 1995. text ed. 69.95 (*0-521-47381-0*) Cambridge U Pr.

***Reading Boileau: An Integrative Study of the Early "Satires"** Robert T. Corum, Jr. LC 97-16246. (Studies in Romance Literatures: Vol. 15). 176p. 1997. 36.95 (*1-55753-110-2*) Purdue U Pr.

Reading Book: By the Staff of the Centre for Language in Primary Education. CLPE Staff. Ed. by Myra Barrs & Anne Thomas. LC 93-22324. 116p. (C). 1993. pap. text ed. 19.50 (*0-435-08789-4*, 08789) Heinemann.

Reading Book for Human Relations Training. 7th ed. Ed. by Lawerence M. Porter & Bernard Mohr. 91p. 1984. per. 11.95 (*0-9610392-2-1*) NTL Inst.

Reading Books: Essays on the Material Text & Literature in America. Ed. by Michele Moylan & Lane Stiles. LC 96-8322. (Studies in Print Culture & the History of the Book). (Illus.). 304p. (C). 1997. 50.00 (*1-55849-062-0*); pap. 16.95 (*1-55849-063-9*) U of Mass Pr.

***Reading Books: Grade 1.** Frank Schaffer Publications, Incorporated Staff. 1997. pap. text ed. 3.95 (*0-7647-0215-7*) Schaffer Pubns.

***Reading Books: Grade 2.** Frank Schaffer Publications, Incorporated Staff. (J). 1997. pap. text ed. 3.95 (*0-7647-0216-5*) Schaffer Pubns.

***Reading Books: Grade 3.** Frank Schaffer Publications, Incorporated Staff. (J). 1997. pap. text ed. 3.95 (*0-7647-0217-3*) Schaffer Pubns.

Reading Books for Math. Gloria Armstrong & Katherine Jillson. Ed. by J. Friedland & R. Kessler. (Novel-Ties Ser.). 1993. student ed., pap. text ed. 20.95 (*1-56982-027-9*) Lrn Links.

Reading Books for Science: A Study Guide. Carol Klitzner. Ed. by Joyce Friedland & Rikki Kessler. (Primary Ser.). (J). (gr. 1-3). 1991. pap. text ed. 20.95 (*0-88122-691-2*) Lrn Links.

Reading Books for Social Studies: A Study Guide. Arlene Pilar. Ed. by Joyce Friedland & Rikki Kessler. (Primary Ser.). (J). (gr. 1-3). 1991. pap. text ed. 20.95 (*0-88122-692-0*) Lrn Links.

Reading Box: Multicultural Workshop. Linda L. Blanton & Linda Lee. 200p. 1996. pap. 291.95 (*0-8384-5021-0*) Heinle & Heinle.

Reading Brain: The Biological Basis of Dyslexia. Ed. by Drake D. Duane & David B. Gray. LC 91-65273. (Illus.). 192p. (C). 1991. pap. text ed. 30.50 (*0-912752-25-4*) York Pr.

Reading Brainstorms. Becky Daniel. 80p. (J). (gr. 1-4). 1990. 10.99 (*0-86653-560-8*, GA1171) Good Apple.

Reading Brooke Shields: The Garden of Failure. Eldon Garnet. 1995. pap. 8.00 (*1-57027-052-X*) Autonomedia.

***Reading Building Plans.** Leonard Koel. (Construction/Building Trades Ser.). (C). 1997. pap. 22.95 (*0-314-20488-1*) West Pub.

Reading Bulgarian II. 1991. student ed., pap. 21.00 (*0-87415-232-1*, 96); teacher ed., pap. 15.50 (*0-87415-233-X*, 96A) OSU Foreign Lang.

Reading Bulgarian III No. 120: OSU Foreign Language Publications. Ernest A. Scatton. (Bulgarian Individualized Instruction Ser.). (Illus.). 350p. (Orig.). (BUL.). (C). 1994. student ed., pap. 25.00 (*0-87415-276-3*, 120) OSU Foreign Lang.

Reading Bulgarian III No. 120A: OSU Foreign Language Publications. Ernest A. Scatton. (Bulgarian Individualized Instruction Ser.). 126p. (Orig.). (BUL.). (C). 1994. teacher ed., pap. 13.50 (*0-87415-277-1*, 120A) OSU Foreign Lang.

Reading Bulgarian Through Russian. Charles E. Gribble. 181p. (Orig.). (C). 1987. pap. text ed. 16.95 (*0-89357-106-7*) Slavica.

Reading Bulgarian 1. Lyubomira P. Gribble & Charles E. Gribble. (Illus.). 135p. (Orig.). (BUL.). (C). 1990. teacher ed., pap. 14.00 (*0-87415-171-6*, 70A); student ed., pap. text ed. 24.00 (*0-87415-170-8*, 70) OSU Foreign Lang.

Reading Bulletin Boards. Imogene Forte. (Easy-To-Make-&-Use Ser.). (Illus.). 64p. (J). (gr. k-6). 1986. pap. text ed. 7.95 (*0-86530-134-4*, IP-112-3) Incentive Pubns.

Reading Bulletin Boards & Displays Kit. Jerry J. Mallett. 288p. 1987. pap. 19.95 (*0-318-32867-4*, Busn) P-H.

***Reading Business Park: A Bronze Age Landscape.** J. Moore & D. Jennings. (Kennet Valley Ser.: Vol. 1). (Illus.). 130p. 1992. pap. 28.00 (*0-947816-81-X*, Pub. by Oxford Univ Comm Arch UK) David Brown.

Reading by All Means. Fraida Dubin & Elite Olshtain. (Illus.). (C). 1981. pap. text ed. write for info. (*0-201-10077-0*) Addison-Wesley.

Reading by All Means. 2nd ed. Fraida Dubin. (Illus.). 208p. (C). 1990. pap. text ed. 25.27 (*0-201-50352-2*) Addison-Wesley.

Reading by Starlight: Postmodern Science Fiction. LC 94-9505. (Popular Fiction Ser.). 224p. (Orig.). (C). 1994. pap. 16.95 (*0-415-09789-4*, B4755) Routledge.

Reading by Starlight: Postmodern Science Fiction. Damien Broderick. LC 94-9505. (Popular Fiction Ser.). 224p. (Orig.). (C). (gr. 13). 1994. text ed. 59.95 (*0-415-09788-6*, B4751) Routledge.

Reading by the Colors: Overcoming Dyslexia & Other Reading Disabilities Through the Irlen Method. Helen Irlen. LC 91-17212. (Illus.). 216p. (Orig.). pap. 9.95 (*0-89529-482-6*) Avery Pub.

Reading by the Colors: Overcoming Dyslexia & Other Reading Disabilities Through the Irlen Method. Helen Irlen. LC 91-17212. (Illus.). 216p. (Orig.). 1991. pap. 9.95 (*0-89529-476-1*) Avery Pub.

***Reading by Touch.** Susanna Miller. 224p. (C). 1997. pap. 24.95 (*0-415-06838-X*); text ed. 69.95 (*0-415-06837-1*) Routledge.

Reading Can Be Child's Play: An Aid for Teachers. James H. Humphrey & Joy N. Humphrey. 174p. 1990. pap. 22.95 (*0-398-06172-6*) C C Thomas.

Reading Can Be Child's Play: An Aid for Teachers. James H. Humphrey & Joy N. Humphrey. 174p. (C). 1990. text ed. 37.95 (*0-398-05657-9*) C C Thomas.

***Reading Capital.** Louis Althusser. Date not set. pap. 20.00 (*1-85984-164-3*, Pub. by Verso UK) Routledge Chapman & Hall.

Reading Capital. Louis Althusser & Etienne Balibar. Tr. by Ben Brewster from FRE. 340p. (C). 1985. pap. text ed. 20.00 (*0-902308-56-4*, Pub. by Vrso UK) Norton.

Reading Castaneda: A Prologue to the Social Sciences. David Silverman. 1975. pap. 12.95 (*0-7100-8146-4*, RKP) Routledge.

Reading Chekhov's Text. Intro. by Robert L. Jackson. (Studies in Russian Literature & Theory). 300p. 1993. 49.95 (*0-8101-1080-6*) Northwestern U Pr.

Reading Children's Writing: A Linguistic View. John Harris & Jeff Wilkinson. Ed. by John Sinclair. (Aspects of English Ser.). 220p. (C). 1985. text ed. 49.95 (*0-04-407021-7*); pap. text ed. 18.95 (*0-04-407022-5*) Routledge Chapman & Hall.

Reading Chinese for Proficiency: An Introduction to Signs. Ted T. Yao. (Illus.). (Orig.). (YA). 1994. 12.95 (*0-88710-183-6*) Yale Far Eastern Pubns.

***Reading Chinese Newspaper Tactics & Skills Students Workbook.** Stanley L. Mickel. 95p. (Orig.). (C). 1996. pap. 15.95 (*0-88710-185-2*) Yale Far Eastern Pubns.

Reading Chinese Newspapers: Tactics & Skills. Stanley Mickel. 250p. (CHI.). 1991. pap. text ed. 24.95 (*0-88710-165-8*) Yale Far Eastern Pubns.

Reading Chinua Achebe: Language & Ideology in Fiction. Simon Gikandi. LC 90-26560. (Studies in African Literature). 165p. (Orig.). (C). 1991. pap. 17.50 (*0-435-08057-1*) Heinemann.

Reading "Clarissa" The Struggles of Interpretation. William B. Warner. 273p. 1979. 42.00 (*0-300-02321-9*) Yale U Pr.

Reading Classical Latin: The Second Year. Robert J. Ball. 510p. 1990. pap. 45.00 (*0-87291-203-5*) Coronado Pr.

Reading Colossians, Ephesians, & 2 Thessalonians: A Literary & Theoological Commentary. Bonnie Thurston. LC 94-48659. (Reading the New Testament Ser.). 260p. (Orig.). 1995. pap. 14.95 (*0-8245-1475-0*) Crossroad NY.

Reading Columbus. Margarita Zamora. LC 92-39234. 1993. 45.00 (*0-520-08052-1*); pap. 18.00 (*0-520-08297-4*) U CA Pr.

Reading Commitment. 2nd ed. Michael E. Adelstein & Jean G. Pival. 390p. (C). 1982. teacher ed. write for info. (*0-318-52975-0*) HB Coll Pubs.

Reading Company Frieght Cars Vol. I: Covered Hopper Cars. Bobb Losse. 56p. (Orig.). 1995. pap. 24.95 (*1-882559-01-0*) D Carol Pubns.

Reading Comprehension. 1996. pap. 10.95 (*0-590-49136-9*) Scholastic Inc.

Reading Comprehension. Carson & Dellosa. (Home Workbooks Ser.). (Illus.). 64p. (Orig.). (J). (gr. 1-2). 1995. wbk. ed., pap. 2.49 (*0-88724-325-8*, CD6822) Carson-Dellos.

Reading Comprehension. Carson & Dellosa. (Home Workbooks Ser.). (Illus.). 64p. (Orig.). (J). (gr. 2-3). 1995. wbk. ed., pap. 2.49 (*0-88724-326-6*, CD6823) Carson-Dellos.

Reading Comprehension. Carson & Dellosa. (Home Workbooks Ser.). (Illus.). 64p. (Orig.). (J). (gr. 3-4). 1995. wbk. ed., pap. 2.49 (*0-88724-327-4*, CD6824) Carson-Dellos.

Reading Comprehension. Carson & Dellosa. (Home Workbooks Ser.). (Illus.). 64p. (Orig.). (J). (gr. 4-6). 1995. wbk. ed., pap. 2.49 (*0-88724-328-2*, CD6825) Carson-Dellos.

Reading Comprehension. Frank Schaffer Publications, Inc. Staff. (Back-to-Basics Ser.). 32p. (J). (gr. 1). 1996. wbk. ed. 3.95 (*0-86734-969-7*, FS-30020) Schaffer Pubns.

Reading Comprehension. Frank Schaffer Publications, Inc. Staff. (Back-to-Basics Ser.). 32p. (J). (gr. 2). 1996. wbk. ed. 3.95 (*0-86734-970-0*, FS-30021) Schaffer Pubns.

Reading Comprehension. Frank Schaffer Publications, Inc. Staff. (Back-to-Basics Ser.). 32p. (J). (gr. 3). 1996. wbk. ed. 3.95 (*0-86734-971-9*, FS-30022) Schaffer Pubns.

Reading Comprehension. Frank Schaffer Publications, Inc. Staff. (Back-to-Basics Ser.). 32p. (J). (gr. 4). 1996. wbk. ed. 3.95 (*0-86734-972-7*, FS-30023) Schaffer Pubns.

Reading Comprehension. Frank Schaffer Publications, Inc. Staff. (Back-to-Basics Ser.). 32p. (J). (gr. 5). 1996. wbk. ed. 3.95 (*0-86734-973-5*, FS-30024) Schaffer Pubns.

Reading Comprehension. Frank Schaffer Publications, Inc. Staff. (Back-to-Basics Ser.). 32p. (J). (gr. 6). 1996. wbk. ed. 3.95 (*0-86734-974-3*, FS-30025) Schaffer Pubns.

Reading Comprehension. Frank Schaffer Publications, Inc. Staff. (Back-to-Basics Ser.). 32p. (J). (gr. 7). 1996. wbk. ed. 3.95 (*0-86734-975-1*, FS-30026) Schaffer Pubns.

Reading Comprehension. Frank Schaffer Publications, Inc. Staff. (Back-to-Basics Ser.). 32p. (J). (gr. 8). 1996. wbk. ed. 3.95 (*0-86734-976-X*, FS-30027) Schaffer Pubns.

Reading Comprehension: From Research to Practice. Ed. by Judith M. Orasanu. 408p. (C). 1985. pap. 36.00 (*0-89859-798-6*); text ed. 79.95 (*0-89859-528-2*) L Erlbaum Assocs.

Reading Comprehension: Grade 2. School Zone Publishing Company Staff. (I Know It! Bks.). (Illus.). 32p. (Orig.). 1996. wbk. ed., pap. write for info. (*0-88743-134-8*, 02025) Sch Zone Pub Co.

Reading Comprehension: New Directions for Classroom Practice. McNeil. (C). 1991. text ed. 26.00 (*0-673-46425-3*) Addson-Wesley Educ.

Reading Comprehension: Reasoned Understanding. Barbara Travis. 64p. (C). 1993. pap. text ed. 18.84 (*0-8403-6670-1*) Kendall-Hunt.

Reading Comprehension: Successful Conversation. 2nd ed. Barbara Travis. 96p. (C). 1993. per. 15.22 (*0-8403-7817-3*) Kendall-Hunt.

Reading Comprehension Activities Kit. Wilma H. Miller. 1990. pap. text ed. 27.95 (*0-87628-789-5*) P-H.

Reading Comprehension & Language Proficiency among Eskimo Children. Virginia Streiff. Ed. by Francesco Cordasco. LC 77-90559. (Bilingual-Bicultural Education in the U. S. Ser.). 1978. lib. bdg. 33.95 (*0-405-11097-9*) Ayer.

Reading Comprehension Assessment: A Cognitive Basis. Peter H. Johnston. LC 82-12640. 102p. reprint ed. pap. 29.10 (*0-8357-2631-2*, 2040119) Bks Demand.

Reading Comprehension Builder. Research & Education Association Staff. 608p. 1996. pap. 14.95 (*0-87891-793-4*) Res & Educ.

Reading Comprehension Difficulties: Processes & Intervention. Ed. by Cesare Cornoldi & Jane Oakhill. 350p. 1996. text ed. 74.95 (*0-8058-1845-6*) L Erlbaum Assocs.

Reading Comprehension Grade 1. Elizabeth Strauss. 1996. pap. text ed. 2.25 (*0-88743-136-4*) Sch Zone Pub Co.

Reading Comprehension in 20 Minutes a Day. LC 96-17816. 1996. pap. 16.00 (*1-57685-039-0*) LrningExprss.

Reading Comprehension Instruction: Issues & Strategies. Katherine Maria. LC 90-70057. 306p. (C). 1990. pap. text ed. 29.50 (*0-912752-20-3*) York Pr.

***Reading Comprehension Instruction, 1783-1987: A Review of Trends & Research.** H. Alan Robinson et al. Ed. by Jill Fitzgerald. LC 89-38010. 212p. 1990. reprint ed. pap. 60.50 (*0-608-03473-8*, 2064183) Bks Demand.

***Reading Comprehension Passages Bk. 4: Text.** John. 1991. pap. text ed. write for info. (*0-00-370104-2*) Addison-Wesley.

Reading Comprehension Workbook for the GRE-GMAT-LSAT-MCAT. Stewart. 1995. pap. 10.00 (*0-671-52001-6*) S&S Trade.

Reading Connection. Salvatore J. Iacone. 288p. (C). 1983. pap. write for info. (*0-02-359380-6*, Macmillan Coll) P-H.

***Reading Connection: Bringing Parents, Teachers, & Librarians Together.** Elizabeth Knowles & Martha Smith. 135p. 1997. lib. bdg. 20.00 (*1-56308-436-8*) Teacher Ideas Pr.

***Reading Connections.** Mary Bannister et al. (Illus.). 336p. (Orig.). (J). (ps-1). 1996. pap. 24.95 (*1-878279-97-1*, MM2026) Monday Morning Bks.

Reading Connections. Marianne C. Reynolds. LC 94-31933. 222p. (C). 1995. pap. 32.95 (*0-534-24456-4*) Wadsworth Pub.

Reading Construction Drawings. Paul I. Wallach & Donald E. Hepler. (Illus.). 1979. pap. text ed. 32.95 (*0-07-067935-5*) McGraw.

Reading Construction Drawings. 2nd ed. Paul I. Wallach & Donald E. Hepler. 512p. 1989. text ed. write for info. (*0-07-909317-5*) McGraw.

Reading Context. Dorothy U. Seyler. 1996. pap. text ed. 33.00 (*0-205-18545-2*) Allyn.

Reading Corinthians: A Literary & Theological Commentary on I & II Corinthians. Charles H. Talbert. 1989. pap. 16.95 (*0-8245-0968-4*) Crossroad NY.

Reading Course Supplement. 2nd ed. Frank C. Hoeppel. 72p. (C). 1995. spiral bd. 12.54 (*0-8403-7749-5*) Kendall-Hunt.

Reading Crisis: Why Poor Children Fall Behind. Jeanne S. Chall et al. 256p. (C). 1991. pap. 14.95 (*0-674-74885-9*) HUP.

***Reading Critically: Text, Charts & Graphs.** 2nd ed. Olson. (C). 1996. pap. text ed. 9.95 (*0-673-97365-4*) Addison-Wesley.

Reading Critically & Writing Well. 4th ed. Axelrod. 1996. pap. text ed. 23.00 (*0-312-11525-3*); teacher ed., pap. text ed. 0.98 (*0-312-11526-1*) St Martin.

Reading Critically & Writing Well. 4th ed. Axelrod. 1996. teacher ed., pap. text ed. 2.70 (*0-312-11527-X*) St Martin.

Reading Critically & Writing Well: Pocket Style Manual. Axelrod. 1996. pap. text ed. 27.90 (*0-312-11709-4*) St Martin.

Reading Critically, Writing Well: A Reader & Guide. 3rd ed. Rise B. Axelrod & Charles R. Cooper. LC 92-50039. 608p. (C). 1993. pap. text ed. 19.50 (*0-312-05809-8*) St Martin.

Reading, Criticism, & Culture: Theory & Teaching in the United States & England, 1820-1950. David Bartine. Ed. by Thomas W. Benson. LC 91-27244. (Studies in Rhetoric & Communication). 177p. 1992. text ed. 34.95 (*0-87249-791-7*) U of SC Pr.

Reading Culture: Contexts for Critical Reading & Writing. 2nd ed. Diana George. Ed. by John Trimbur. LC 94-26627. (C). 1995. 18.75 (*0-673-99024-9*) HarpC.

***Reading Culture, Reading Books.** Robert A. Gross. 19p. 1997. reprint ed. pap. 4.00 (*0-944026-71-0*) Am Antiquarian.

***Reading Cultures: The Construction of Readers in the Twentieth Century.** Molly A. Travis. LC 97-10063. 1997. write for info. (*0-8093-2146-7*); pap. write for info. (*0-8093-2147-5*) S Ill U Pr.

Reading Curriculum (ECT412) Deakin University Press Staff. 153p. (C). 1985. 70.00 (*0-7300-0319-1*, Pub. by Deakin Univ AT) St Mut.

Reading Curriculum Theory: The Development of a New Hermeneutic. William M. Reynolds. (American University Studies: Language: Ser. XIV, Vol. 19). 238p. (C). 1989. text ed. 30.95 (*0-8204-1001-2*) P Lang Pubng.

Reading Czech 1. Charles E. Townsend & Daniela T. Kliment. 120p. (Orig.). (CZE.). (C). 1987. teacher ed., pap. 13.00 (*0-87415-145-7*, 58A); student ed., pap. text ed. 15.00 (*0-87415-144-9*, 58) OSU Foreign Lang.

Reading Czech 2. Charles E. Townsend & Daniela T. Kliment. 117p. (Orig.). (CZE.). (C). 1987. teacher ed. 12.50 (*0-87415-147-3*, 59A); student ed., pap. text ed. 16.00 (*0-87415-146-5*, 59) OSU Foreign Lang.

Reading Czech 3. Charles E. Townsend & Daniela T. Kliment. 120p. (Orig.). (CZE.). (C). 1989. teacher ed., pap. 13.00 (*0-87415-158-9*, 65A); student ed., pap. text ed. 11.00 (*0-87415-157-0*, 65) OSU Foreign Lang.

Reading Dancing: Bodies & Subjects in Contemporary Dance. Susan L. Foster. (Illus.). 224p. 1986. pap. 21.95 (*0-520-06333-3*) U CA Pr.

Reading Daughters' Fictions, 1709-1834: Novels & Society from Manley to Edgeworth. Caroline Gonda. (Studies in Romanticism: No. 19). (Illus.). 269p. (C). 1996. text ed. 54.95 (*0-521-55395-4*) Cambridge U Pr.

Reading De Man Reading. Ed. by Lindsay Waters. LC 88-4580. (Theory & History of Literature Ser.: Vol. 59). 319p. (Orig.). 1989. pap. text ed. 14.95 (*0-8166-1661-2*) U of Minn Pr.

Reading Deconstruction-Deconstructive Reading. G. Douglas Atkins. LC 83-10308. 168p. 1983. pap. 10.95 (*0-8131-0165-4*) U Pr of Ky.

Reading Development & Dyslexia. Charles Hulme & Margaret Snowling. (Illus.). 252p. (Orig.). (C). 1994. pap. text ed. 42.50 (*1-56593-368-0*, 0745) Singular Publishing.

An Asterisk (*) at the beginning of an entry indicates that the title is appearing in BIP for the first time.

Reading Development in a Second Language: Theoretical, Empirical & Classroom Perspectives. Elizabeth B. Bernhardt. Ed. by Robert J. DiPietro. (Second Language Learning Ser.: Vol. 1). 272p. (C). 1991. pap. 39.50 (*0-89391-734-6*); text ed. 73.25 (*0-89391-675-7*) Ablex Pub.

Reading Development of Non-native Speakers of English. John G. Barnitz. (Language in Education Ser.). 114p. 1986. pap. text ed. 10.00 (*0-13-754805-2*) P-H.

Reading Diagnosis & Remediation. 3rd ed. William H. Rupley & Timothy R. Blair. 480p. (C). 1989. write for info. (*0-675-20932-3*, Merrill Coll) P-H.

Reading Diagnosis & Remediation of Reading & Writing Diabilities. Tom Gunning. (C). 1997. text ed. write for info. (*0-8013-1393-7*) Addison-Wesley.

Reading Diagnosis for Teachers: An Instructional Approach. 3rd rev. ed. Rebecca Barr et al. LC 94-27768. 350p. (C). 1995. pap. text ed. 40.95 (*0-8013-0842-9*) Longman.

Reading Diagnosis Kit. 3rd ed. Wilma H. Miller. 1986. spiral bd. 24.95 (*0-87628-720-8*) Ctr Appl Res.

Reading Diagnosis Kit. 3rd ed. Wilma H. Miller. 376p. 1986. pap. 27.95 (*0-317-66024-1*, Ctr Appl Res) P-H.

Reading Dialogics. Lynne Pearce. (Interrogating Texts Ser.). 192p. 1995. text ed. 16.95 (*0-340-55052-X*, B2527, Pub. by E Arnld UK) St Martin.

Reading Dick & Jane with Me. Clarissa Sligh. (Illus.). 24p. (Orig.). 1989. pap. 10.00 (*0-89822-059-9*) Visual Studies.

Reading Dido: Gender, Textuality, & Medieval Aeneid. Marilynn Desmond. LC 94-6447. (Medieval Cultures Ser.: Vol. 8). 1994. text ed. 44.95 (*0-8166-2246-9*); pap. text ed. 17.95 (*0-8166-2247-7*) U of Minn Pr.

Reading Diesels Vol. 2: Second Generation. Dale W. Woodland. (Illus.). xii, 188p. 1996. 60.00 (*0-9620844-7-6*) Garrigues Hse.

Reading Diesels, Vol. 1: The First Generation. Dale W. Woodland. LC 90-86079. (Illus.). 168p. 1990. 55.00 (*0-9620844-2-5*) Garrigues Hse.

Reading Difficulties. 7th ed. Bond & Tinker. 1993. text ed. 59.00 (*0-205-15091-8*) Allyn.

Reading Disabilities: A Developmental Language Perspective. Ed. by Alan G. Kamhi & Hugh W. Catts. 384p. (Orig.). (C). 1991. pap. text ed. 56.00 (*0-205-13543-9*) Allyn.

Reading Disabilities - Diagnosis & Component Processes: Proceedings of the NATO Advanced Study Institute on Differential Diagnosis & Treatments of Reading & Writing Disorders, Chateau de Bonas, France September 30-October 11, 1991. Ed. by R. Malatesha Joshi & Che K. Leong. LC 93-15556. (NATO Advanced Science Institutes Series C: Mathematical & Physical Sciences: No. 74). 352p. (C). 1993. lib. bdg. 170.50 (*0-7923-2302-5*) Kluwer Ac.

Reading Disabilities in College & High School: Diagnosis & Management. P. G. Aaron & Catherine Baker. LC 90-72124. (Illus.). 207p. 1991. pap. text ed. 21.50 (*0-912752-23-8*) York Pr.

Reading Disability: Progress & Research Needs in Dyslexia. Johns Hopkins Conference on Research Needs & Prospects in Dyslexia & Related Aphasic Disorders Staff. Ed. by John Money. LC 62-14360. (Illus.). 232p. reprint ed. pap. 66.20 (*0-8357-8295-6*, 2034143) Bks Demand.

Reading Douglas Dunn. Ed. by Robert Crawford & David Kinloch. (Modern Scottish Writers Ser.). 256p. 1993. pap. text ed. 27.50 (*0-7486-0369-7*, Pub. by Edinburgh U Pr UK) Col U Pr.

Reading Drama. David Scanlan. LC 87-31293. 181p. 1988. pap. text ed. 22.95 (*0-87484-735-4*, 735) Mayfield Pub.

Reading Drama: A Method of Analysis with Selections for Study. Fred B. Millett. LC 71-111110. (Play Anthology Reprint Ser.). 1977. reprint ed. 20.95 (*0-8369-8203-7*) Ayer.

Reading Drawing Building. Michael Silver. (Pamphlet Architecture Ser.: Vol. 19). (Illus.). 40p. (Orig.). 1996. pap. 11.95 (*1-56898-079-5*) Princeton Arch.

Reading Drawings. Multimedia Development Services Staff. (Plant Fundamentals Ser.: Vol. IX, Module I). (Illus.). 1995. teacher ed. 65.00 (*1-57431-068-2*); student ed. 30.00 (*1-57431-028-3*) Tech Trng Systs.

Reading Drills: Advanced Level. Jamestown Publishers Staff. (J). 1995. student ed., pap. 13.97 (*0-89061-533-0*) Jamestown Pubs.

Reading Drills: Intermediate Level. Jamestown Publishers Staff. (J). 1995. student ed., pap. 13.23 (*0-89061-532-2*) Jamestown Pubs.

Reading Drills: Introductory Level. Jamestown Publishers Staff. (J). 1995. student ed., pap. 12.64 (*0-89061-531-4*) Jamestown Pubs.

Reading Dubliners Again: A Lacanian Perspective. Garry M. Leonard. (Irish Studies). 260p. 1993. text ed. 49.95 (*0-8156-2574-X*) Syracuse U Pr.

Reading Dubliners Again: A Lacanian Perspective. Garry M. Leonard. LC 92-33860. (Irish Studies). 384p. (C). 1993. pap. text ed. 18.95 (*0-8156-2600-2*) Syracuse U Pr.

Reading Dutch. William Z. Shetter. (C). 1985. text ed. 110.00 (*90-6890-021-8*, Pub. by S Thornes Pubs UK) St Mut.

Reading Dworkin Critically. Ed. by Alan Hunt. LC 91-19642. (Social & Legal Studies). 301p. 1992. 49.95 (*0-85496-761-3*) Berg Pubs.

***Reading Eco: An Anthology.** Rocco Capozzi. LC 96-48021. (Advances in Semiotics Ser.). 1997. write for info. (*0-253-33275-3*) Ind U Pr.

***Reading Eco: An Anthology.** Eco Umberto. LC 96-48021. (Advances in Semiotics Ser.). 1997. pap. write for info. (*0-253-21116-6*) Ind U Pr.

***Reading Edge: Thirteen Ways to Build Reading Comprehension.** 2nd ed. Ben E. Johnson. (C). 1994. teacher ed., text ed. 33.56 (*0-669-29765-8*) HM College Div.

Reading Edge: Thirteen ways to Build Reading Comprehension. 2nd ed. Ben E. Johnson. 486p. (C). 1994. pap. text ed. 34.36 (*0-669-29763-1*) HM College Div.

Reading Educational Research. 2nd ed. Andrea Vierra & Judith Pollock. 408p. (C). 1992. pap. text ed. 39.95 (*0-89787-532-X*) Gorsuch Scarisbrick.

***Reading Educational Research.** 3rd ed. Andrea Vierra et al. LC 97-5516. 1997. write for info. (*0-89787-542-7*) Gorsuch Scarisbrick.

***Reading Educational Research.** 3rd ed. Andrea Vierra & Judith Pollock. (C). 1997. pap. text ed. 33.00 (*0-13-680034-3*) P-H.

Reading Egyptian Art. Richard H. Wilkinson. LC 91-67312. (Illus.). 224p. 1994. pap. 16.95 (*0-500-27751-6*) Thames Hudson.

Reading Empirical Research Studies: The Rhetoric of Research. Ed. by John Hayes et al. 584p. (C). 1992. pap. 39.95 (*0-8058-1031-5*); text ed. 99.95 (*0-8058-1030-7*) L Erlbaum Assocs.

***Reading Engagement: Motivating Readers Through Integrated Instruction.** Ed. by John T. Guthrie & Allan Wigfield. LC 96-47428. 260p. (Orig.). 1997. pap. 28.95 (*0-87207-148-0*, 148) Intl Reading.

***Reading Engelhardt: Essays on the Thought of H. Tristram Engelhardt, Jr.** Brendan Minogue et al. LC 97-16317. 1997. lib. bdg. write for info. (*0-7923-4572-X*) Kluwer Ac.

Reading Engineering Drawings Through Conceptual Sketching. Jay D. Helsel. (Illus.). 1979. text ed. 29.95 (*0-07-028031-2*) McGraw.

***Reading English.** Joan Barrie. (Illus.). 132p. (Orig.). (J). (gr. k-3). 1995. ring bd. 18.95 (*0-614-29815-6*) Evrst Cultural.

Reading Enrichment Center: Lab Manual. 2nd ed. Tobias & Bosco. 64p. 1996. spiral bd. 9.66 (*0-8403-8897-7*) Kendall-Hunt.

Reading Environment: How Adults Help Children Enjoy Books. Aidan Chambers. 96p. 1996. pap. text ed. 10.00 (*1-57110-029-6*) Stenhse Pubs.

Reading Epic: An Introduction to the Ancient Narratives. Peter Toohey. LC 92-7032. 240p. (C). 1992. pap. 16.95 (*0-415-04228-3*, A9618) Routledge.

Reading Epic: An Introduction to the Ancient Narratives. Peter Toohey. LC 92-7032. 272p. (C). (gr. 13). 1992. text ed. 59.95 (*0-415-04227-5*, A9614) Routledge.

Reading Esther: A Case for the Literary Carnivalesque. Kenneth Craig. (Literary Currents in Biblical Interpretation Ser.). 144p. (Orig.). 1995. pap. 17.00 (*0-664-25518-3*) Westminster John Knox.

Reading Etc. An Integrated Skills Text. Robert Roseberry & Rachel Weinstock. 304p. (C). 1991. pap. text ed. 21.45 (*0-13-763467-6*, 640806) P-H.

Reading Ethnographic Research. Martyn Hammersley. (Aspects of Modern Sociology Ser.). 224p. (C). 1991. pap. text ed. 27.50 (*0-582-05310-2*) Longman.

Reading Ethnography. David C. Jacobson. LC 90-35230. 138p. (C). 1991. text ed. 64.50 (*0-7914-0546-X*); pap. text ed. 21.95 (*0-7914-0547-8*) State U NY Pr.

Reading Everyday Stuff. Elaine Prizzi & Jeanne Hoffman. (J). (gr. 4-6). 1985. pap. 7.99 (*0-8224-3180-7*) Fearon Teach Aids.

Reading Exercises Bk. C: Follow Directions, Step by Step. 2nd ed. Arthur I. Gates & Celeste C. Peardon. 55p. 1982. reprint ed. pap. 25.00 (*0-608-02429-5*, 2063072) Bks Demand.

Reading Experiences in Science: Apes; Bats; Bees; Beavers; Dinosaurs; Frogs; Spiders; Whales, 8 bks. Ed. by Orin Cochrane. (Illus.). 128p. (Orig.). 1980. pap. 16.00 (*1-895411-12-2*) Peguis Pubs Ltd.

Reading Fabliaux. Norris J. Lacy. LC 93-8245. 192p. 1993. Alk. paper. text ed. 35.00 (*0-8153-1510-4*, H1805) Garland.

Reading Faces. Leopold Bellak & Samm S. Baker. 1981. 12.45 (*0-03-057869-8*) CPS Inc.

***Reading Faces: Window to the Soul?** LC 96-52663. (New Directions in Social Psychology Ser.). 1997. text ed. 65.00 (*0-8133-2746-6*) Westview.

***Reading Faces: Window to the Soul?** Leslie A. Zebrowitz. LC 96-52663. (New Directions in Social Psychology Ser.). (C). 1997. pap. text ed. 19.00 (*0-8133-2747-4*) Westview.

Reading Faster & Understanding More, Bk. 1. 4th ed. Miller & Sharon D. Steeber. (Illus.). 400p. (C). 1995. text ed. 31.95 (*0-673-52385-3*) Addson-Wesley Educ.

Reading Faster & Understanding More, Bk. II. 3rd ed. Wanda M. Miller & Sharon Steeber de Orozco. (C). 1990. text ed. 31.50 (*0-673-39939-7*) Addson-Wesley Educ.

Reading Faster & Understanding More, Bk. 2. 4th ed. Miller & Sharon D. Steeber. (Illus.). 432p. (C). 1996. pap. text ed. 31.95 (*0-673-52387-X*) Addson-Wesley Educ.

Reading Faster & Understanding More, Bk. 2. 4th ed. Miller & Sharon D. Steeber. Date not set. teacher ed., pap. write for info. (*0-673-52386-1*) Addson-Wesley Educ.

Reading Faster & Understanding More, Bk. 2. 4th ed. Miller & Sharon D. Steeber. Date not set. teacher ed., pap. write for info. (*0-673-52388-8*) Addson-Wesley Educ.

Reading Faster & Understanding More, Bk. III. Wanda M. Miller & Sharon Steeber. (C). 1987. pap. text ed. 33.50 (*0-673-39286-4*) Addson-Wesley Educ.

Reading Faster for Ideas. Elaine L. Cohen & Mary A. Poppino. LC 83-18586. 336p. (C). 1984. text ed. 19.75 (*0-03-061959-9*) HB Coll Pubs.

Reading Faulkner. Wesley Morris & Barbara A. Morris. LC 89-40806. (Wisconsin Project on American Writers Ser.). 304p. (C). 1989. text ed. 24.95 (*0-299-12220-4*) U of Wis Pr.

Reading Faulkner: Light in August: Glossary & Commentary. James Hinkle & Robert McCoy. LC 94-17077. (Reading Faulkner Ser.). 200p. 1995. text ed. 45.00 (*0-87805-731-5*); pap. text ed. 17.50 (*0-87805-732-3*) U Pr of Miss.

Reading Faulkner: Sanctuary. Edwin T. Arnold & Dawn Trouard. (Reading Faulkner Ser.). 256p. (C). 1996. 45.00 (*0-87805-873-7*); pap. 17.50 (*0-87805-874-5*) U Pr of Miss.

Reading Faulkner: The Sound & the Fury. Stephen Ross & Noel Polk. (Illus.). 176p. (C). 1996. text ed. 45.00 (*0-87805-935-0*) U Pr of Miss.

Reading Faulkner: The Sound & the Fury. Stephen M. Ross & Noel Polk. (Illus.). 176p. (C). 1996. pap. text ed. 17.50 (*0-87805-936-9*) U Pr of Miss.

Reading Faulkner: The Unvanquished: Glossary & Commentary. Compiled by James C. Hinkle & Robert McCoy. LC 94-43863. (Reading Faulkner Ser.). 1995. 45.00 (*0-87805-784-6*); pap. 17.50 (*0-87805-785-4*) U Pr of Miss.

Reading Faulknerian Tragedy. Warwick Wadlington. LC 86-29166. 272p. (C). 1987. 35.00 (*0-8014-2011-3*) Cornell U Pr.

Reading Fin de Siecle Fictions. Lyn Pykett. (Critical Readers Ser.). 256p. (C). 1996. pap. text ed. 21.50 (*0-582-23390-9*) Longman.

Reading Fin de Siecle Fictions. 21th ed. Lyn Pykett. (Critical Readers Ser.). 256p. (C). 1996. text ed. 54.50 (*0-582-23392-5*) Longman.

Reading First. 2nd ed. Suzanne D. Robertshaw et al. 1990. pap. 26.95 (*0-8384-3384-7*) Heinle & Heinle.

Reading Football: How the Popular Press Created an American Spectacle. Michael Oriard. LC 92-42840. (Cultural Studies of the United States). xxviii, 320p. (C). 1993. 16.95 (*0-8078-2083-0*) U of NC Pr.

Reading for a Living: How to Be a Professional Story Analyst for Film & Television. T. L. Katahn. LC 90-81591. 192p. (Orig.). 1990. pap. text ed. 12.95 (*0-9625803-9-2*) Blue Arrow Bks.

Reading for a Purpose. Parry. .p. 1992. teacher ed., pap. text ed. 20.50 (*0-312-07229-5*) St Martin.

Reading for a Purpose. Kate Parry. LC 91-68108. 400p. (Orig.). (C). 1992. pap. text ed. 21.50 (*0-312-03627-2*); pap. text ed. 5.00 (*0-312-03628-0*) St Martin.

Reading for a Reason. Dobbs. 1989. pap. text ed. 18.30 (*0-13-761123-4*) P-H.

Reading for Boys & Girls: Illinios: a Subject Index & Annotated Bibliography. Dorothy Hinman & Ruth Zimmerman. LC 75-118853. 134p. reprint ed. pap. 38.20 (*0-317-26830-9*, 2024215) Bks Demand.

Reading for Comprehension Skills. Mary Carter. (Illus.). (J). (gr. 2-7). 1982. student ed. 4.50 (*0-89525-177-9*) Ed Activities.

Reading for Concepts: Bks. A-H, Bk. C. 2nd ed. William Liddle. (Illus.). (gr. 3-9). 1977. pap. text ed. 7.40 (*0-07-037663-8*) McGraw.

Reading for Concepts: Bks. A-H, Bk. D. 2nd ed. William Liddle. (Illus.). (gr. 3-9). 1977. pap. text ed. 7.40 (*0-07-037664-6*) McGraw.

Reading for Concepts: Bks. A-H, Bk. A. 2nd ed. William Liddle. (Illus.). (gr. 3-9). 1977. pap. text ed. 7.40 (*0-07-037661-1*) McGraw.

Reading for Concepts: Bks. A-H, Bk. B. 2nd ed. William Liddle. (Illus.). (gr. 3-9). 1977. pap. text ed. 7.40 (*0-07-037662-X*) McGraw.

Reading for Concepts: Bks. A-H, Bk. E. 2nd ed. William Liddle. (Illus.). (gr. 3-9). 1977. pap. text ed. 7.40 (*0-07-037665-4*) McGraw.

Reading for Concepts: Bks. A-H, Bk. F. 2nd ed. William Liddle. (Illus.). (gr. 3-9). 1977. pap. text ed. 7.96 (*0-07-037666-2*) McGraw.

Reading for Concepts: Bks. A-H, BK. G. 2nd ed. William Liddle. (Illus.). (gr. 3-9). 1977. Bk. G. pap. text ed. 7.96 (*0-07-037667-0*) McGraw.

Reading for Concepts: Bks. A-H, Bk. H. 2nd ed. William Liddle. (Illus.). (gr. 3-9). 1977. pap. text ed. 7.96 (*0-07-037668-9*) McGraw.

Reading for Daily Living. McGowan. (YA - Adult Education Ser.). 1993. pap. 5.95 (*0-538-70771-2*) S-W Pub.

Reading for Difference: Texts on Gender, Race & Class. Melissa E. Barth et al. 608p. (Orig.). (C). 1993. pap. text ed. 23.00 (*0-15-500216-3*); Instructor's manual. teacher ed. write for info. (*0-15-500151-5*) HB Coll Pubs.

Reading for Employment. McGowan. (YA - Adult Education Ser.). 1993. pap. 5.95 (*0-538-70770-4*) S-W Pub.

Reading for Excellence, 2 Vols. Laraine M. Flemming. (C). 1996. pap. 32.36 (*0-395-78290-2*); pap. text ed. 33.56 (*0-395-78291-0*) HM.

Reading for Executives. Donna Litherland. (Illus.). 100p. (Orig.). (C). 1982. pap. text ed. 12.50 (*0-9607888-0-8*) Barney Pr.

***Reading for Good: Narrative Theology & Ethics in the Joseph Story from the Perspective of Ricoeur's Hermeneutics.** Theo L. Hettema. 380p. 1996. pap. 42.00 (*90-390-0252-5*, Pub. by KOK Pharos NE) Eisenbrauns.

***Reading for Information.** Jo E. Moore. (Real-Life Reading Activities Ser.). (Illus.). 64p. (J). (gr. 2-3). 1996. teacher ed., pap. 7.95 (*1-55799-589-3*, 566) Evan-Moor Corp.

Reading for Job & Personal Use. McGowan. (YA - Adult Education Ser.). 1992. pap. 9.95 (*0-538-70477-2*) S-W Pub.

Reading for Life: A First Book for Adults & Their Tutors. Virginia F. Allen. 288p. (Orig.). 1987. pap. text ed. 18.50 (*0-940723-00-X*) SIIS.

***Reading for Life: Beauty, Pluralism & Responsibility.** Margaret R. Miles. LC 96-40925. 228p. 1997. 29.95 (*0-8264-1009-X*) Continuum.

Reading for Meaning. A. Ediger et al. 1989. pap. text ed. 14.67 (*0-8013-0052-5*, 75716) Longman.

Reading for Meaning. Swaffar & Arens. 1990. text ed. 31.50 (*0-13-753765-4*) P-H.

***Reading for Meaning.** Tina Thoburn et al. Ed. by Stephanie Pliakas. (Thinking Skills Library). (Illus.). 110p. (Orig.). (J). (gr. 2-5). 1997. teacher ed., pap. 9.95 (*1-56784-703-X*) Newbridge Comms.

Reading for Meaning see Language Learning: The Intermediate Phase

***Reading for Moral Progress: 19th Century Institutions Promoting Social Change.** J. Mark Tucleer et al. (Occasional Papers: No. 207). (Orig.). 1996. pap. 10.00 (*0-614-24097-2*) U of Ill Grad Sch.

Reading for Ourselves. Sarah Crowley. 24p. (C). 1993. pap. 5.00 (*0-85598-201-2*, Pub. by Oxfam UK) Humanities.

Reading for Pleasure: Guidelines. Dixie L. Spiegel. LC 81-8395. (Reading Aids Ser.). 78p. (Orig.). reprint ed. pap. 25.00 (*0-8357-2633-9*, 2040121) Bks Demand.

Reading for Real. Swinscoe. 1992. pap. 22.95 (*0-8384-3429-0*) Heinle & Heinle.

Reading for Real. Ed. by Barrie Wade. (English, Language & Education Ser.). 176p. 1990. pap. 27.00 (*0-335-09554-2*, Open Univ Pr) Taylor & Francis.

Reading for Real Annotated Bibliography: The Literature Project, Grades 4-8. Developmental Studies Center Staff. (Reading for Real Ser.). 80p. (Orig.). 1995. pap. 11.00 (*1-885603-56-8*) Develop Studies.

Reading for Real Handbook. Ed. by Colin Harrison & Martin Coles. LC 92-7609. 240p. (C). 1992. pap. 18.95 (*0-415-08047-9*, A7711) Routledge.

Reading for Real Handbook. Ed. by Colin Harrison & Martin Coles. LC 92-7609. 240p. (C). (gr. 13). 1992. text ed. 79.95 (*0-415-08046-0*, A7707) Routledge.

Reading for Real Program Manual: The Literature Project, Grades 4-8. Developmental Studies Center Staff. 80p. (Orig.). 1995. pap. 19.00 (*1-885603-66-5*) Develop Studies.

Reading for Real Teacher's Guide to "A Day No Pigs Would Die" Partner Unit, Grade 7. Developmental Studies Center Staff. (Reading for Real Ser.). 24p. (Orig.). 1996. teacher ed., pap. 13.95 (*1-57621-091-X*) Develop Studies.

Reading for Real Teacher's Guide to "A Gathering of Days" Partner Unit, Grade 8. Developmental Studies Center Staff. (Reading for Real Ser.). 24p. (Orig.). 1996. teacher ed., pap. 13.95 (*1-57621-134-7*) Develop Studies.

Reading for Real Teacher's Guide to "A Gathering of Flowers" Read Aloud Unit, Grade 8. Developmental Studies Center Staff. (Reading for Real Ser.). 24p. (Orig.). 1996. teacher ed., pap. 13.95 (*1-57621-092-8*) Develop Studies.

Reading for Real Teacher's Guide to "A Gift for Mama" Partner Unit, Grade 4. Developmental Studies Center Staff. (Reading for Real Ser.). 24p. (Orig.). 1996. teacher ed., pap. 13.95 (*1-57621-052-9*) Develop Studies.

Reading for Real Teacher's Guide to "A Raisin in the Sun" Partner Unit, Grade 8. Developmental Studies Center Staff. (Reading for Real Ser.). 24p. (Orig.). 1996. teacher ed., pap. 13.95 (*1-57621-093-6*) Develop Studies.

Reading for Real Teacher's Guide to "A Thief in the Village" Combined Units, Grade 7: Paartner & Read Aloud. Developmental Studies Center Staff. (Reading for Real Ser.). 24p. (Orig.). 1996. teacher ed., pap. 13.95 (*1-57621-094-4*) Develop Studies.

Reading for Real Teacher's Guide to "A Thief in the Village" Combined Units, Grade 7: Partner & Read Aloud. Developmental Studies Center Staff. (Reading for Real Ser.). 24p. (Orig.). 1996. teacher ed., pap. 13.95 (*1-57621-095-2*) Develop Studies.

Reading for Real Teacher's Guide to "Adam & Eve & Pinch-Me" Partner Unit, Grade 8. Developmental Studies Center Staff. (Reading for Real Ser.). 24p. (Orig.). 1996. teacher ed., pap. 13.95 (*1-57621-068-5*) Develop Studies.

Reading for Real Teacher's Guide to "Alien's in the Family" Partner Unit, Grade 7. Developmental Studies Center Staff. (Reading for Real Ser.). 24p. (Orig.). 1996. teacher ed., pap. 13.95 (*1-57621-067-7*) Develop Studies.

Reading for Real Teacher's Guide to "All Joseph Wanted" Read Aloud Unit, Grade 6. Developmental Studies Center Staff. (Reading for Real Ser.). 24p. (Orig.). 1996. pap. 13.95 (*1-885603-44-4*) Develop Studies.

Reading for Real Teacher's Guide to "America Street" Partner Unit, Grade 6. Developmental Studies Center Staff. (Reading for Real Ser.). 24p. (Orig.). 1996. pap. 13.95 (*1-885603-54-1*) Develop Studies.

Reading for Real Teacher's Guide to "& Now Miguel" Read Aloud Unit, Grade 6. Developmental Studies Center Staff. (Reading for Real Ser.). 24p. (Orig.). 1996. teacher ed., pap. 13.95 (*1-885603-08-8*) Develop Studies.

Reading for Real Teacher's Guide to "Annie John" Read Aloud Unit, Grade 8. Developmental Studies Center Staff. (Reading for Real Ser.). 24p. (Orig.). 1996. teacher ed., pap. 13.95 (*1-57621-096-0*) Develop Studies.

Reading for Real Teacher's Guide to "Baseball in April (La Bamba)" Read Aloud Unit, Grade 6. Developmental Studies Center Staff. (Reading for Real Ser.). 24p. (Orig.). 1996. teacher ed., pap. 13.95 (*1-885603-09-6*) Develop Studies.

Reading for Real Teacher's Guide to "Baseball in April (Seventh Grade)" Read Aloud Unit, Grade 6. Developmental Studies Center Staff. (Reading for Real Ser.). 24p. (Orig.). 1996. teacher ed., pap. 13.95 (*1-885603-10-X*) Develop Studies.

Reading for Real Teacher's Guide to "Bridge to Terabithia" Read Aloud Unit, Grade 5. Developmental Studies Center Staff. (Reading for Real Ser.). 24p. (Orig.). 1996. teacher ed., pap. 13.95 (*1-57621-079-0*) Develop Studies.

R

R

Reading for Real Teacher's Guide to "Bunkhouse Journal" Read Aloud Unit, Grade 7. Developmental Studies Center Staff. (Reading for Real Ser.). 24p. (Orig.). 1996. teacher ed., pap. 13.95 (*1-57621-097-9*) Develop Studies.

Reading for Real Teacher's Guide to "C. O. L. A. R." Read Aloud Unit, Grade 5. Developmental Studies Center Staff. (Reading for Real Ser.). 24p. (Orig.). 1996. teacher ed., pap. 13.95 (*1-57621-080-4*) Develop Studies.

Reading for Real Teacher's Guide to "Cat Running" Read Aloud Unit, Grade 5. Development Studies Center Staff. (Reading for Real Ser.). 24p. (Orig.). 1996. teacher ed., pap. 13.95 (*1-57621-129-0*) Develop Studies.

Reading for Real Teacher's Guide to "Child of the Owl" Partner Unit, Grade 6. Developmental Studies Center Staff. (Reading for Real Ser.). 24p. (Orig.). 1996. pap. 13.95 (*1-885603-17-7*) Develop Studies.

Reading for Real Teacher's Guide to "Child of the Silent Night" Read Aloud Unit, Grade 4. Developmental Studies Center Staff. (Reading for Real Ser.). 24p. (Orig.). 1996. teacher ed., pap. 13.95 (*1-57621-070-7*) Develop Studies.

Reading for Real Teacher's Guide to "Children of the Dust Bowl" Read Aloud Unit, Grade 5. Developmental Studies Center Staff. (Reading for Real Ser.). 24p. (Orig.). 1996. pap. 13.95 (*1-885603-42-8*) Develop Studies.

Reading for Real Teacher's Guide to "Come Sing, Jimmy Jo" Read Aloud Unit, Grade 6. Developmental Studies Center Staff. (Reading for Real Ser.). 24p. (Orig.). 1996. teacher ed., pap. 13.95 (*1-885603-11-8*) Develop Studies.

Reading for Real Teacher's Guide to "Cousins" Read Aloud Unit, Grade 6. Developmental Studies Center Staff. (Reading for Real Ser.). 24p. (Orig.). 1996. teacher ed., pap. 13.95 (*1-885603-12-6*) Develop Studies.

Reading for Real Teacher's Guide to "Crazy Lady!" Read Aloud, Grade 7. Developmental Studies Center Staff. (Reading for Real Ser.). 24p. (Orig.). 1996. pap. 13.95 (*1-885603-47-9*) Develop Studies.

Reading for Real Teacher's Guide to "Crow Boy" Read Aloud Unit, Grade 6. Developmental Studies Center Staff. (Reading for Real Ser.). 24p. (Orig.). 1996. teacher ed., pap. 13.95 (*1-885603-13-4*) Develop Studies.

Reading for Real Teacher's Guide to "Dear Mr. Henshaw" Partner Unit, Grade 4. Developmental Studies Center Staff. (Reading for Real Ser.). 24p. (Orig.). 1996. teacher ed., pap. 13.95 (*1-57621-050-2*) Develop Studies.

Reading for Real Teacher's Guide to "Fallen Angels" Partner Unit, Grade 8. Developmental Studies Center Staff. (Reading for Real Ser.). 24p. (Orig.). 1996. teacher ed., pap. 13.95 (*1-57621-098-7*) Develop Studies.

Reading for Real Teacher's Guide to "Farewell to Manzanar" Partner Unit, Grade 8. Developmental Studies Center Staff. (Reading for Real Ser.). 24p. (Orig.). 1996. teacher ed., pap. 13.95 (*1-57621-099-5*) Develop Studies.

Reading for Real Teacher's Guide to "Fast Sam, Cool Clyde & Stuff" Partner Unit, Grade 7. Developmental Studies Center Staff. (Reading for Real Ser.). 24p. (Orig.). 1996. teacher ed., pap. 13.95 (*1-57621-100-2*) Develop Studies.

Reading for Real Teacher's Guide to "Felita" Partner Unit, Grade 4. Developmental Studies Center Staff. (Reading for Real Ser.). 24p. (Orig.). 1996. pap. 13.95 (*1-885603-40-1*) Develop Studies.

Reading for Real Teacher's Guide to "Freedom Train, The Story of Harriet Tubman" Read Aloud Unit, Grade 4. Developmental Studies Center Staff. (Reading for Real Ser.). 24p. (Orig.). 1996. teacher ed., pap. 13.95 (*1-57621-072-3*) Develop Studies.

Reading for Real Teacher's Guide to "Grab Hands & Run" Read Aloud, Grade 7. Developmental Studies Center Staff. (Reading for Real Ser.). 24p. (Orig.). 1996. pap. 13.95 (*1-885603-49-5*) Develop Studies.

Reading for Real Teacher's Guide to "Grandfather's Journey" Read Aloud Unit, Grade 8. Developmental Studies Center Staff. (Reading for Real Ser.). 24p. (Orig.). 1996. teacher ed., pap. 13.95 (*1-57621-089-8*) Develop Studies.

Reading for Real Teacher's Guide to "Heartbeats & Other Stories" Read Aloud Unit, Grade 8. Developmental Studies Center Staff. (Reading for Real Ser.). 24p. (Orig.). 1996. teacher ed., pap. 13.95 (*1-57621-101-0*) Develop Studies.

Reading for Real Teacher's Guide to "Homecoming" Read Aloud Unit, Grade 6. Developmental Studies Center Staff. (Reading for Real Ser.). 24p. (Orig.). 1996. teacher ed., pap. 13.95 (*1-885603-14-2*) Develop Studies.

Reading for Real Teacher's Guide to "I Heard the Owl Call My Name" Read Aloud Unit, Grade 8. Developmental Studies Center Staff. (Reading for Real Ser.). 24p. (Orig.). 1996. teacher ed., pap. 13.95 (*1-57621-102-9*) Develop Studies.

Reading for Real Teacher's Guide to "In the Year of the Boar & Jackie Robinson" Read Aloud Unit, Grade 5. Developmental Studies Center Staff. (Reading for Real Ser.). 24p. (Orig.). 1996. teacher ed., pap. 13.95 (*1-57621-081-2*) Develop Studies.

Reading for Real Teacher's Guide to "Is That You, Miss Blue?" Partner Unit, Grade 7. Developmental Studies Center Staff. (Reading for Real Ser.). 24p. (Orig.). 1996. teacher ed., pap. 13.95 (*1-57621-103-7*) Develop Studies.

Reading for Real Teacher's Guide to "Island of the Blue Dolphins" Partner Unit, Grade 6. Developmental Studies Center Staff. (Reading for Real Ser.). 24p. (Orig.). 1996. pap. 13.95 (*1-885603-18-5*) Develop Studies.

Reading for Real Teacher's Guide to "J. T." Partner Unit, Grade 4. Developmental Studies Center Staff. (Reading for Real Ser.). 24p. (Orig.). 1996. teacher ed., pap. 13.95 (*1-57621-053-7*) Develop Studies.

Reading for Real Teacher's Guide to "Journey to Jo'Burg" Partner Unit, Grade 7. Developmental Studies Center Staff. (Reading for Real Ser.). 24p. (Orig.). 1996. teacher ed., pap. 13.95 (*1-57621-104-5*) Develop Studies.

Reading for Real Teacher's Guide to "Justin & the Best Biscuits in the World" Partner Unit, Grade 4. Developmental Studies Center Staff. (Reading for Real Ser.). 24p. (Orig.). 1996. teacher ed., pap. 13.95 (*1-57621-054-5*) Develop Studies.

Reading for Real Teacher's Guide to "Lincoln: A Photobiography" Read Aloud Unit, Grade 8. Developmental Studies Center Staff. (Reading for Real Ser.). 24p. (Orig.). 1996. teacher ed., pap. 13.95 (*1-57621-105-3*) Develop Studies.

Reading for Real Teacher's Guide to "Little Brother" Partner Unit, Grade 6. Developmental Studies Center Staff. (Reading for Real Ser.). 24p. (Orig.). 1996. teacher ed., pap. 13.95 (*1-57621-066-9*) Develop Studies.

Reading for Real Teacher's Guide to "Lyddie" Read Aloud, Grade 8. Developmental Studies Center Staff. (Reading for Real Ser.). 24p. (Orig.). 1996. pap. 13.95 (*1-885603-52-5*) Develop Studies.

Reading for Real Teacher's Guide to "Maizon at Blue Hill" Read Aloud Unit, Grade 7. Developmental Studies Center Staff. (Reading for Real Ser.). 24p. (Orig.). 1996. pap. 13.95 (*1-885603-50-9*) Develop Studies.

Reading for Real Teacher's Guide to "Make Lemonade" Read Aloud, Grade 8. Developmental Studies Center Staff. (Reading for Real Ser.). 24p. (Orig.). 1996. pap. 13.95 (*1-885603-53-3*) Develop Studies.

Reading for Real Teacher's Guide to "Missing May" Partner Unit, Grade 8. Developmental Studies Center Staff. (Reading for Real Ser.). 24p. (Orig.). 1996. teacher ed., pap. 13.95 (*1-57621-069-3*) Develop Studies.

Reading for Real Teacher's Guide to "Morning Girl" Read Aloud Unit, Grade 6. Developmental Studies Center Staff. (Reading for Real Ser.). 24p. (Orig.). 1996. pap. 13.95 (*1-885603-45-2*) Develop Studies.

Reading for Real Teacher's Guide to "Mrs. Fish, Ape & Me, the Dump Queen" Partner Unit, Grade 4. Developmental Studies Center Staff. (Reading for Real Ser.). 24p. (Orig.). 1996. teacher ed., pap. 13.95 (*1-885603-05-3*) Develop Studies.

Reading for Real Teacher's Guide to "Mrs. Frisby & the Rats of NIMH" Partner Unit, Grade 5. Developmental Studies Center Staff. (Reading for Real Ser.). 24p. (Orig.). 1996. teacher ed., pap. 13.95 (*1-57621-060-X*) Develop Studies.

Reading for Real Teacher's Guide to "My Brother Sam Is Dead" Partner Unit, Grade 5. Developmental Studies Center Staff. (Reading for Real Ser.). 24p. (Orig.). 1996. teacher ed., pap. 13.95 (*1-57621-061-8*) Develop Studies.

Reading for Real Teacher's Guide to "Number the Stars" Read Aloud Unit, Grade 6. Developmental Studies Center Staff. (Reading for Real Ser.). 24p. (Orig.). 1996. pap. 13.95 (*1-885603-15-0*) Develop Studies.

Reading for Real Teacher's Guide to "One-Eyed Cat" Partner Unit, Grade 6. Developmental Studies Center Staff. (Reading for Real Ser.). 24p. (Orig.). 1996. pap. 13.95 (*1-885603-19-3*) Develop Studies.

Reading for Real Teacher's Guide to "Out of Nowhere" Read Aloud Unit, Grade 7. Developmental Studies Center Staff. (Reading for Real Ser.). 24p. (Orig.). 1996. teacher ed., pap. 13.95 (*1-57621-087-1*) Develop Studies.

Reading for Real Teacher's Guide to "Queenie Peavy" Partner Unit, Grade 5. Developmental Studies Center Staff. (Reading for Real Ser.). 24p. (Orig.). 1996. teacher ed., pap. 13.95 (*1-57621-062-6*) Develop Studies.

Reading for Real Teacher's Guide to "Rasmus & the Vagabond" Partner Unit, Grade 4. Developmental Studies Center Staff. (Reading for Real Ser.). 24p. (Orig.). 1996. pap. 13.95 (*1-57621-135-5*) Develop Studies.

Reading for Real Teacher's Guide to "Roll of Thunder, Hear My Cry" Read Aloud Unit, Grade 7. Developmental Studies Center Staff. (Reading for Real Ser.). 24p. (Orig.). 1996. teacher ed., pap. 13.95 (*1-57621-106-1*) Develop Studies.

Reading for Real Teacher's Guide to "Sadako & the Thousand Paper Cranes" Read Aloud Unit, Grade 4. Developmental Studies Center Staff. (Reading for Real Ser.). 24p. (Orig.). 1996. teacher ed., pap. 13.95 (*1-57621-077-4*) Develop Studies.

Reading for Real Teacher's Guide to "Sami & the Time of the Troubles" Read Aloud Unit, Grade 5. Developmental Studies Center Staff. (Reading for Real Ser.). 24p. (Orig.). 1996. pap. 13.95 (*1-885603-41-X*) Develop Studies.

Reading for Real Teacher's Guide to "Sarah, Plain & Tall" Read Aloud Unit, Grade 5. Developmental Studies Center Staff. (Reading for Real Ser.). 24p. (Orig.). 1996. teacher ed., pap. 13.95 (*1-57621-083-9*) Develop Studies.

Reading for Real Teacher's Guide to "Scorpions" Partner Unit, Grade 7. Developmental Studies Center Staff. (Reading for Real Ser.). 24p. (Orig.). 1996. teacher ed., pap. 13.95 (*1-57621-107-X*) Develop Studies.

Reading for Real Teacher's Guide to "See Ya, Simon" Read Aloud Unit, Grade 7. Developmental Studies Center Staff. (Reading for Real Ser.). 24p. (Orig.). 1996. teacher ed., pap. 13.95 (*1-57621-088-X*) Develop Studies.

Reading for Real Teacher's Guide to "Shadow of a Bull" Partner Unit, Grade 6. Developmental Studies Center Staff. (Reading for Real Ser.). 24p. (Orig.). 1996. pap. 13.95 (*1-885603-21-5*) Develop Studies.

Reading for Real Teacher's Guide to "Sixth Grade Can Really Kill You" Partner Unit, Grade 6. Developmental Studies Center Staff. (Reading for Real Ser.). 24p. (Orig.). 1996. pap. 13.95 (*1-885603-22-3*) Develop Studies.

Reading for Real Teacher's Guide to "Slake's Limbo" Partner Unit, Grade 6. Developmental Studies Center Staff. (Reading for Real Ser.). 24p. (Orig.). 1996. pap. 13.95 (*1-885603-23-1*) Develop Studies.

Reading for Real Teacher's Guide to "Somehow Tenderness Survives" Read Aloud Unit, Grade 8. Developmental Studies Center Staff. (Reading for Real Ser.). 24p. (Orig.). 1996. teacher ed., pap. 13.95 (*1-57621-108-8*) Develop Studies.

Reading for Real Teacher's Guide to "Taking Care of Yoki" Partner Unit, Grade 4. Developmental Studies Center Staff. (Reading for Real Ser.). 24p. (Orig.). 1996. teacher ed., pap. 13.95 (*1-57621-055-3*) Develop Studies.

Reading for Real Teacher's Guide to "Talk about a Family" Read Aloud Unit, Grade 5. Developmental Studies Center Staff. (Reading for Real Ser.). 24p. (Orig.). 1996. teacher ed., pap. 13.95 (*1-57621-084-7*) Develop Studies.

Reading for Real Teacher's Guide to "Ten Top Stories" Partner Unit, Grade 8. Developmental Studies Center Staff. (Reading for Real Ser.). 24p. 1996. teacher ed., pap. 13.95 (*1-57621-109-6*) Develop Studies.

Reading for Real Teacher's Guide to "The Best Bad Thing" Partner Unit, Grade 5. Developmental Studies Center Staff. (Reading for Real Ser.). 24p. (Orig.). 1996. pap. 13.95 (*1-885603-43-6*) Develop Studies.

Reading for Real Teacher's Guide to "The Book of Three" Read Aloud Unit, Grade 5. Developmental Studies Center Staff. (Reading for Real Ser.). 24p. (Orig.). 1996. teacher ed., pap. 13.95 (*1-57621-078-2*) Develop Studies.

Reading for Real Teacher's Guide to "The Bridge Dancers" Read Aloud Unit, Grade 4. Developmental Studies Center Staff. (Reading for Real Ser.). 24p. (Orig.). 1996. pap. 13.95 (*1-885603-39-8*) Develop Studies.

Reading for Real Teacher's Guide to "The Bully of Barkham Street" Partner Unit, Grade 5. Developmental Studies Center Staff. (Reading for Real Ser.). 24p. (Orig.). 1996. teacher ed., pap. 13.95 (*1-57621-057-X*) Develop Studies.

Reading for Real Teacher's Guide to "The Captive" Partner Unit, Grade 6. Developmental Studies Center Staff. (Reading for Real Ser.). 24p. (Orig.). 1996. teacher ed., pap. 13.95 (*1-57621-065-0*) Develop Studies.

Reading for Real Teacher's Guide to "The Clay Marble" Partner Unit, Grade 7. Developmental Studies Center Staff. (Reading for Real Ser.). 24p. (Orig.). 1996. pap. 13.95 (*1-885603-51-7*) Develop Studies.

Reading for Real Teacher's Guide to "The Endless Steppe" Read Aloud Unit, Grade 7. Developmental Studies Center Staff. (Reading for Real Ser.). 24p. (Orig.). 1996. teacher ed., pap. 13.95 (*1-57621-110-X*) Develop Studies.

Reading for Real Teacher's Guide to "The First Strawberries" Read Aloud Unit, Grade 4. Developmental Studies Center Staff. (Reading for Real Ser.). 24p. (Orig.). 1996. pap. 13.95 (*1-885603-38-X*) Develop Studies.

Reading for Real Teacher's Guide to "The Flunking of Joshua T. Bates" Read Aloud Unit, Grade 4. Developmental Studies Center Staff. (Reading for Real Ser.). 24p. (Orig.). 1996. teacher ed., pap. 13.95 (*1-57621-071-5*) Develop Studies.

Reading for Real Teacher's Guide to "The Friends" Partner Unit, Grade 8. Developmental Studies Center Staff. (Reading for Real Ser.). 24p. (Orig.). 1996. teacher ed., pap. 13.95 (*1-57621-111-8*) Develop Studies.

Reading for Real Teacher's Guide to "The Friendship/The Gold Cadillac" Partner Unit, Grade 7. Developmental Studies Center Staff. (Reading for Real Ser.). 24p. (Orig.). 1996. pap. 13.95 (*1-885603-58-4*) Develop Studies.

Reading for Real Teacher's Guide to "The Gift-Giver" Partner Unit, Grade 5. Developmental Studies Center Staff. (Reading for Real Ser.). 24p. (Orig.). 1996. teacher ed., pap. 13.95 (*1-57621-058-8*) Develop Studies.

Reading for Real Teacher's Guide to "The Giver" Partner, Grade 7. Developmental Studies Center Staff. (Reading for Real Ser.). 24p. (Orig.). 1996. pap. 13.95 (*1-885603-48-7*) Develop Studies.

Reading for Real Teacher's Guide to "The Goats" Partner Unit, Grade 7. Developmental Studies Center Staff. (Reading for Real Ser.). 24p. (Orig.). 1996. teacher ed., pap. 13.95 (*1-57621-112-6*) Develop Studies.

Reading for Real Teacher's Guide to "The Great Brain" Read Aloud Unit, Grade 4. Developmental Studies Center Staff. (Reading for Real Ser.). 24p. (Orig.). 1996. teacher ed., pap. 13.95 (*1-57621-073-1*) Develop Studies.

Reading for Real Teacher's Guide to "The Great Gilly Hopkins" Partner Unit, Grade 5. Developmental Studies Center Staff. (Reading for Real Ser.). 24p. (Orig.). 1996. teacher ed., pap. 13.95 (*1-57621-059-6*) Develop Studies.

Reading for Real Teacher's Guide to "The Green Book" Read Aloud Unit, Grade 4. Developmental Studies Center Staff. (Reading for Real Ser.). 24p. (Orig.). 1996. teacher ed., pap. 13.95 (*1-57621-074-X*) Develop Studies.

Reading for Real Teacher's Guide to "The Hundred Dresses" Read Aloud Unit, Grade 4. Developmental Studies Center Staff. (Reading for Real Ser.). 24p. (Orig.). 1996. teacher ed., pap. 13.95 (*1-57621-075-8*) Develop Studies.

Reading for Real Teacher's Guide to "The Lion, the Witch & the Wardrobe" Read Aloud Unit, Grade 4. Developmental Studies Center Staff. (Reading for Real Ser.). 24p. (Orig.). 1996. teacher ed., pap. 13.95 (*1-57621-076-6*) Develop Studies.

Reading for Real Teacher's Guide to "The Miracle Worker" Partner Unit, Grade 8. Developmental Studies Center Staff. (Reading for Real Ser.). 24p. (Orig.). 1996. teacher ed., pap. 13.95 (*1-885603-07-X*) Develop Studies.

Reading for Real Teacher's Guide to "The Outsiders" Partner Unit, Grade 7. Developmental Studies Center Staff. (Reading for Real Ser.). 24p. (Orig.). 1996. teacher ed., pap. 13.95 (*1-57621-113-4*) Develop Studies.

Reading for Real Teacher's Guide to "The Pearl" Partner Unit, Grade 8. Developmental Studies Center Staff. (Reading for Real Ser.). 24p. (Orig.). 1996. teacher ed., pap. 13.95 (*1-57621-114-2*) Develop Studies.

Reading for Real Teacher's Guide to "The Pinballs" Partner Unit, Grade 6. Developmental Studies Center Staff. (Reading for Real Ser.). 24p. (Orig.). 1996. pap. 13.95 (*1-885603-20-7*) Develop Studies.

Reading for Real Teacher's Guide to "The Real Thief" Read Aloud Unit, Grade 5. Developmental Studies Center Staff. (Reading for Real Ser.). 24p. (Orig.). 1996. teacher ed., pap. 13.95 (*1-57621-082-0*) Develop Studies.

Reading for Real Teacher's Guide to "The Red Comb" Partner Unit, Grade 4. Developmental Studies Center Staff. (Reading for Real Ser.). 24p. (Orig.). 1996. teacher ed., pap. 13.95 (*1-57621-132-0*) Develop Studies.

Reading for Real Teacher's Guide to "The Sign of the Beaver" Partner Unit, Grade 5. Developmental Studies Center Staff. (Reading for Real Ser.). 24p. (Orig.). 1996. teacher ed., pap. 13.95 (*1-57621-063-4*) Develop Studies.

Reading for Real Teachers Guide to "The Sign of the Chrysanthemum" Partner Unit, Grade 8. Developmental Studies Center Staff. (Reading for Real Ser.). 24p. (Orig.). 1996. pap. 13.95 (*1-885603-55-X*) Develop Studies.

Reading for Real Teacher's Guide to "The Whipping Boy" Read Aloud Unit, Grade 5. Developmental Studies Center Staff. (Reading for Real Ser.). 24p. (Orig.). 1996. teacher ed., pap. 13.95 (*1-57621-085-5*) Develop Studies.

Reading for Real Teacher's Guide to "The Winter Camp" Read Aloud Unit, Grade 5. Developmental Studies Center Staff. (Reading for Real Ser.). 24p. (Orig.). 1996. teacher ed., pap. 13.95 (*1-57621-133-9*) Develop Studies.

Reading for Real Teacher's Guide to "The Winter Room" Read Aloud Unit, Grade 7. Developmental Studies Center Staff. (Reading for Real Ser.). 24p. (Orig.). 1996. teacher ed., pap. 13.95 (*1-57621-115-0*) Develop Studies.

Reading for Real Teacher's Guide to "Throwing Shadows" Read Aloud Unit, At the Home, Grade 7. Developmental Studies Center Staff. (Reading for Real Ser.). 24p. (Orig.). 1996. teacher ed., pap. 13.95 (*1-57621-116-9*) Develop Studies.

Reading for Real Teacher's Guide to "Throwing Shadows" Read Aloud Unit, In the Village of the Weavers, Grade 7. Developmental Studies Center Staff. (Reading for Real Ser.). 24p. (Orig.). 1996. teacher ed., pap. 13.95 (*1-57621-117-7*) Develop Studies.

Reading for Real Teacher's Guide to "Throwing Shadows" Read Aloud Unit, On Shark's Tooth Beach, Grade 7. Developmental Studies Center Staff. (Reading for Real Ser.). 24p. (Orig.). 1996. pap. 13.95 (*1-57621-118-5*) Develop Studies.

Reading for Real Teacher's Guide to "To Hell with Dying" Read Aloud Unit, Grade 7. Developmental Studies Center Staff. (Reading for Real Ser.). 24p. (Orig.). 1996. teacher ed., pap. 13.95 (*1-57621-119-3*) Develop Studies.

Reading for Real Teacher's Guide to "Tuck Everlasting" Read Aloud Unit, Grade 6. Developmental Studies Center Staff. (Reading for Real Ser.). 24p. (Orig.). 1996. pap. 13.95 (*1-885603-16-9*) Develop Studies.

Reading for Real Teacher's Guide to "Twenty & Ten" Partner Unit, Grade 5. Developmental Studies Center Staff. (Reading for Real Ser.). 24p. (Orig.). 1996. teacher ed., pap. 13.95 (*1-57621-064-2*) Develop Studies.

Reading for Real Teacher's Guide to "Uncle James" Read Aloud Unit, Grade 6. Developmental Studies Center Staff. (Reading for Real Ser.). 24p. (Orig.). 1996. teacher ed., pap. 13.95 (*1-57621-086-3*) Develop Studies.

Reading for Real Teacher's Guide to "War Comes to Willy Freeman" Partner Unit, Grade 5. Developmental Studies Center Staff. (Reading for Real Ser.). 24p. (Orig.). 1996. teacher ed., pap. 13.95 (*1-885603-06-1*) Develop Studies.

Reading for Real Teacher's Guide to "Westmark" Partner Unit, Grade 8. Developmental Studies Center Staff. (Reading for Real Ser.). 24p. (Orig.). 1996. teacher ed., pap. 13.95 (*1-57621-120-7*) Develop Studies.

Reading for Real Teacher's Guide to "When the Monkeys Came Back" Read Aloud Unit, Grade 4. Developmental Studies Center Staff. (Reading for Real Ser.). 24p. (Orig.). 1996. teacher ed., pap. 13.95 (*1-57621-128-2*) Develop Studies.

Reading for Real Teacher's Guide to "Where the Lilies Bloom" Partner Unit, Grade 6. Developmental Studies Center Staff. (Reading for Real Ser.). 24p. (Orig.). 1996. pap. 13.95 (*1-885603-24-X*) Develop Studies.

Reading for Real Teacher's Guide to "Words of Stone" Partner Unit, Grade 6. Developmental Studies Center Staff. (Reading for Real Ser.). 24p. (Orig.). 1996. pap. 13.95 (*1-885603-46-0*) Develop Studies.

Reading for Real Teacher's Guide to "Zeely" Partner Unit, Grade 4. Developmental Studies Center Staff. (Reading, Thinking & Caring Ser.). 24p. (Orig.). 1996. teacher ed., pap. 13.95 (*1-57621-056-1*) Develop Studies.

Reading for Realism: The History of a U. S. Literary Institution, 1850-1910. Nancy Glazener. LC 96-14207. (New Americanists Ser.). 392p. 1997. pap. text ed. 18.95 (*0-8223-1870-9*); lib. bdg. 54.95 (*0-8223-1880-6*) Duke.

Reading for Results. 3rd ed. Laraine M. Flemming. LC 86-81106. 1987. pap. text ed. 22.36 (*0-318-36891-9*) HM.

***Reading for Results, 6 Vols.** 6th annot. ed. Laraine M. Flemming. (C). 1995. teacher ed., text ed. 31.96 (*0-395-74775-9*) HM College Div.

***Reading for Results, 6 Vols.** 6th ed. Laraine M. Flemming. 544p. (C). 1995. pap. text ed. 33.16 (*0-395-71965-8*) HM College Div.

An Asterisk (*) at the beginning of an entry indicates that the title is appearing in BIP for the first time.

***Reading for Results, 6 Vols.** 6th ed. Laraine M. Flemming. (C). 1995. teacher ed., text ed. 11.96 (*0-395-74890-9*) HM College Div.

Reading for Students with Special Needs. Frank J. Guszak. 216p. (C). 1994. pap. text ed. 20.95 (*0-8403-9168-4*) Kendall-Hunt.

Reading for Success, 3 Vols. Fleming. (Orig.). (C). 1995. suppl. ed., teacher ed., pap. 11.96 (*0-395-68481-1*) HM.

Reading for Success. Laraine M. Flemming. (C). 1995. pap. 33.16 (*0-395-67299-6*); pap. 31.96 (*0-395-67298-8*) HM.

Reading for Success: A School-to-Work Approach. Raymond F. Morgan et al. LC 95-24414. 1996. pap. 22.95 (*0-538-63717-X*) S-W Pub.

Reading For Success I. Laraine M. Flemming. (C). 1995. pap. text ed. 11.96 (*0-395-67300-3*) HM.

Reading for Success in Elementary School. Earl H. Cheek, Jr. et al. 512p. (C). 1996. per. write for info. (*0-697-27926-X*) Brown & Benchmark.

Reading for Success in Elementary Schools. Earl H. Cheek et al. (Illus.). 544p. (C). 1989. text ed. 40.00 (*0-03-012608-8*) HB Coll Pubs.

Reading for Survival in Today's Society, Bk. 1. 2nd ed. Elsa Woods & Beverly Lancaster. (Illus.). 224p. (J). (gr. 7-9). 1993. pap. 14.95 (*0-673-36077-6*, GoodYrBooks) Addson-Wesley Educ.

Reading for Survival in Today's Society, Bk. 2. 2nd ed. Elsa Woods & Beverly Lancaster. (Illus.). 224p. (YA). (gr. 8 up). 1993. pap. 14.95 (*0-673-36078-4*, GoodYrBooks) Addson-Wesley Educ.

Reading for the Funeral Mass. Brian Magee. 72p. 1989. pap. 22.00 (*0-86217-222-5*, Pub. by Veritas IE) St Mut.

Reading for the Plot. Peter Brooks. 363p. 1992. pap. 14.95 (*0-674-74892-1*) HUP.

Reading for the Point. William J. Kerrigan. 141p. (C). 1979. pap. text ed. 16.00 (*0-15-575640-0*) HB Coll Pubs.

Reading for Thinking. Laraine M. Flemming. (C). 1992. pap. 32.36 (*0-395-43406-8*) HM.

Reading for Thinking. Lariane M. Flemming. (C). 1992. teacher ed., pap. 2.76 (*0-395-65540-4*) HM.

Reading for TOEFL. 2nd ed. Educational Testing Service Staff. 1991. pap. 14.00 incl. audio (*0-446-39228-6*) Warner Bks.

Reading for Understanding. Marianne C. Reynolds. 451p. (C). 1992. pap. 25.95 (*0-534-17064-1*) Wadsworth Pub.

Reading for Understanding. 2nd ed. Marianne C. Reynolds. LC 94-31932. 466p. (C). 1995. pap. 37.95 (*0-534-23274-4*) Wadsworth Pub.

***Reading for Understanding: Grade 1.** Barbara Allen. (Illus.). (J). 1997. pap. text ed. 2.29 (*0-7647-0094-4*) Schaffer Pubns.

***Reading for Understanding: Grade 2.** Bill Linderman. (Illus.). (J). 1997. pap. text ed. 2.29 (*0-7647-0095-2*) Schaffer Pubns.

***Reading for Understanding: Grade 3.** Sally Fisk. (Illus.). (J). 1997. pap. text ed. 2.29 (*0-7647-0096-0*) Schaffer Pubns.

Reading for Understanding & Stimulation: A College Reader. Harold Newman. (Orig.). (C). 1990. pap. text ed. write for info. (*0-9613577-3-8*) Prestige Educ.

Reading for Workplace Success. Rosemarie Park et al. 351p. (C). 1991. pap. text ed. 17.95 (*1-56118-200-1*); teacher ed., pap. text ed. 8.00 (*1-56118-201-X*) Paradigm MN.

Reading Frames in Modern Fiction. Mary A. Caws. LC 84-16092. 327p. reprint ed. pap. 93.20 (*0-7837-0243-4*, 2040552) Bks Demand.

Reading French in the Arts & Sciences, 4 Vols. 4th ed. Edward M. Stack. LC 86-80905. (C). 1986. pap. 32.76 (*0-395-35968-6*) HM.

Reading Freud: Explorations & Entertainments. Peter Gay. LC 89-28615. 240p. (C). 1990. 35.00 (*0-300-04681-2*) Yale U Pr.

Reading Freud: Explorations & Entertainments. Peter Gay. 220p. (C). 1991. reprint ed. pap. 18.00 (*0-300-05127-1*) Yale U Pr.

Reading Freud: Psychology, Neurosis, & Religion. Volney P. Gay. LC 83-2917. (American Academy of Religion, Studies in Religion). 142p. (C). 1983. pap. 14.95 (*0-89130-613-7*, 01 00 32) Scholars Pr GA.

Reading Freud's Reading. Ed. by Sander L. Gilman et al. LC 93-11102. (Literature & Psychoanalysis Ser.: Vol. 5). 320p. (C). 1993. 45.00 (*0-8147-3051-5*) NYU Pr.

Reading Freud's Reading. Ed. by Sander L. Gilman et al. 320p. (C). 1995. pap. 18.50 (*0-8147-3078-7*) NYU Pr.

Reading from Left to Right: One Man's Political History. H. S. Ferns. 384p. 1983. 14.95 (*0-8020-6655-0*) U of Toronto Pr.

Reading from Left to Right: One Man's Political History. Henry S. Ferns. LC 83-227884. 384p. reprint ed. pap. 109.50 (*0-8357-6397-8*, 2035753) Bks Demand.

Reading from Modern Mexican Authors. Frederick Starr. 1976. lib. bdg. 50.00 (*0-8490-0929-4*) Gordon Pr.

Reading from the Heart: Women, Literature, & the Search for True Love. Suzanne Juhasz. 304p. 1995. pap. 10.95 (*0-14-016855-9*, Penguin Bks) Viking Penguin.

***Reading from the Margins: Textual Studies, Chaucer, & Medieval Literature.** Seth Lerer. LC 96-31096. 1996. 12.00 (*0-87328-163-2*) Huntington Lib.

***Reading from the Margins: Textual Studies Chaucer & Medieval Literature.** Ed. by Seth Lerer. LC 96-31096. (Huntington Library Quarterly: Vol. 58, No. 1). 168p. 1996. reprint ed. pap. 47.90 (*0-608-03465-7*, 2064172) Bks Demand.

Reading from This Place: Social Location & Biblical Interpretation in the United States. Ed. by Fernando F. Segovia & Mary A. Tolbert. LC 94-33208. 304p. 1995. pap. 19.00 (*0-8006-2812-8*, Fortress Pr) Augsburg Fortress.

Reading from This Place Vol. 2: Social Location & Biblical Interpretation in Global Perspective. Ed. by Fernando F. Segovia & Mary A. Tolbert. 1995. pap. 24.00 (*0-8006-2949-3*, 1-2949, Fortress Pr) Augsburg Fortress.

***Reading Fun: Quick & Easy Activities for the School Library Media Center.** Mona Kerby. LC 97-21445. (School Library Media Ser.). 1997. pap. write for info. (*0-8108-3361-1*) Scarecrow.

Reading Games. R. Gibson. (You & Your Child Ser.). (Illus.). 32p. (J). (ps-9). 1993. pap. 5.95 (*0-7460-1292-6*, Usborne); lib. bdg. 14.95 (*0-88110-645-3*, Usborne) EDC.

***Reading Games.** Hadfield. 1995. pap. text ed. write for info. (*0-17-556891-X*) Addison-Wesley.

Reading Games Make Reading Fun. Joseph Bielawsky. 163p. 1975. pap. 19.95 (*0-914138-00-6*) Technomic.

Reading Gaol by Reading Town. Peter Southerton. LC 92-42383. 1993. 16.00 (*0-7509-0296-5*, Pub. by Sutton Pubng UK) Bks Intl VA.

Reading George Steiner. Ed. by Nathan A. Scott & Ronald A. Sharp. 312p. (C). 1994. text ed. 48.50 (*0-8018-4832-6*); pap. text ed. 14.95 (*0-8018-4888-1*) Johns Hopkins.

***Reading German: A Course Book & Reference Grammar.** Waltraud Coles & Bill Dodd. 392p. 1997. pap. 29.95 (*0-19-870020-2*) OUP.

***Reading German: A Course Book & Reference Grammar.** Waltraud Coles & Bill Dodd. 392p. 1997. 95.00 (*0-19-870004-0*) OUP.

Reading Gertrude Stein: Body, Text, Gnosis. Lisa Ruddick. LC 89-46133. (Reading Women Writing Ser.). 288p. 1990. 39.95 (*0-8014-2364-3*) Cornell U Pr.

Reading Gertrude Stein: Body, Text, Gnosis. Lisa Ruddick. LC 89-46133. (Reading Women Writing Ser.). 288p. 1991. reprint ed. pap. 15.95 (*0-8014-9957-7*) Cornell U Pr.

Reading God: Lectio Divina. Garcia M. Colombas. Ed. by Alphonse M. Lauer. Tr. by Gregory J. Roettger from SPA. (Schuyler Spiritual Ser.: No. 9). 144p. (Orig.). (C). 1993. pap. 5.50 (*1-56788-010-X*, 10-009) BMH Pubns.

***Reading Goethe.** Martin Swales. (GERM Ser.). 200p. Date not set. 55.00 (*1-57113-252-X*) Camden Hse.

Reading Gothic Fiction: A Bakhtinian Approach. Jacqueline Howard. 320p. 1994. 60.00 (*0-19-811992-5*) OUP.

Reading Grade 1. Carson & Dellosa. (Home Workbooks Ser.). (Illus.). 64p. (Orig.). (J). (gr. 1). 1995. wbk. ed., pap. 2.49 (*0-88724-322-3*, CD6819) Carson-Dellos.

Reading Grade 2. Carson & Dellosa. (Home Workbooks Ser.). (Illus.). 64p. (Orig.). (J). (gr. 2). 1995. wbk. ed., pap. 2.49 (*0-88724-323-1*, CD6820) Carson-Dellos.

Reading Grade 3. Carson & Dellosa. (Home Workbooks Ser.). (Illus.). 64p. (Orig.). (J). (gr. 3). 1995. pap. 2.49 (*0-88724-324-X*, CD6821) Carson-Dellos.

Reading Greek: An Independent Study Guide. Joint Association of Classical Teachers Staff. 320p. (C). 1995. suppl. ed., pap. text ed. 22.95 (*0-521-47863-4*) Cambridge U Pr.

Reading Greek: Grammar, Vocabulary & Exercises. Joint Association of Classical Teachers Staff. LC 77-91090. 384p. 1978. pap. text ed. 22.95 (*0-521-21977-9*) Cambridge U Pr.

Reading Greek: Morphology Charts. Joint Association of Classical Teachers Staff. LC 77-91090. 16p. 1979. suppl. ed., pap. text ed. 12.95 (*0-521-22052-1*) Cambridge U Pr.

Reading Greek: Teacher's Notes. Joint Association of Classical Teachers Staff. 240p. 1986. teacher ed., pap. text ed. 24.95 (*0-521-31872-6*) Cambridge U Pr.

Reading Greek: Text. Joint Association of Classical Teachers Staff. 204p. 1978. pap. text ed. 17.95 (*0-521-21976-0*) Cambridge U Pr.

Reading Greek Culture: Texts & Images, Rituals & Myths. Christiane Sourvinou-Inwood. (Illus.). 336p. 1991. 89.00 (*0-19-814750-3*) OUP.

"Reading" Greek Death: To the End of the Classical Period. Christiane Sourvinou-Inwood. (Illus.). 512p. 1996. reprint ed. pap. 29.95 (*0-19-815069-5*) OUP.

Reading Greek Tragedy. Simon Goldhill. 336p. 1986. pap. text ed. 21.95 (*0-521-31579-4*) Cambridge U Pr.

Reading Group Choices, 1996: Selections for Lively Book Discussions. Ed. by Mark Kaufman & Donna Paz. 94p. (Orig.). 1996. pap. 2.50 (*0-9644876-1-6*) Paz & Assoc.

***Reading Group Choices 1997: Selections for Lively Discussions.** Ed. by Mark Kaufman. 96p. (Orig.). 1997. pap. 2.50 (*0-9644876-2-4*) Paz & Assoc.

Reading Group Companion: Starting & Sustaining a Book Discussion Group. David Laskin & Holly Hughes. LC 94-30200. 1995. write for info. (*0-452-27201-7*) Macmillan.

***Reading Group Guide.** Ambrose. 1997. pap. write for info. (*0-684-00454-2*, Touchstone Bks) S&S Trade.

***Reading Group Guide.** Denby. 1997. pap. write for info. (*0-684-00381-3*, Touchstone Bks) S&S Trade.

***Reading Group Guide.** Ladd. 1997. pap. write for info. (*0-684-00545-X*, Scribners PB Fict) S&S Trade.

***Reading Group Guide.** Proulx. 1997. pap. write for info. (*0-684-00349-X*, Scribners PB Fict) S&S Trade.

Reading Group Handbook: Everything You Need to Know, from Choosing Members to Leading Discussions. Rachel Jacobsohn. 240p. (Orig.). 1994. pap. 10.95 (*0-7868-8002-3*) Hyperion.

Reading Guidance in a Media Age. Nancy Polette & Marjorie Hamlin. LC 75-26833. (Illus.). 275p. 1975. 27.50 (*0-8108-0873-0*) Scarecrow.

Reading Guide to the Old Testament. David H. Mulholland. iv, 261p. 1989. pap. 9.95 (*0-87579-283-9*) Deseret Bk.

Reading Habermas. David M. Rasmussen. 256p. 1990. pap. 24.95 (*0-631-15274-1*) Blackwell Pubs.

Reading Handbook: With This Book, You Can Teach Someone to Read. Maryjane Cable. 1986. teacher ed., ring bd. 30.00 (*0-9619050-0-X*, 2 027-282) M Cable.

Reading Hebrew: A Programmed Instruction Book. Clifford Yudell & Lillian W. Adler. 1995. teacher ed., pap. 14.95 (*0-87441-215-3*) Behrman.

Reading Hebrew: Sefardic. Lillian W. Adler & C. Castberg. 1972. pap. 7.95 (*0-87441-042-8*) Behrman.

Reading Heidegger: Commemorations. Ed. by John Sallis. LC 91-27080. (Studies in Continental Thought). (Illus.). 448p. 1993. text ed. 45.00 (*0-253-35053-0*); pap. text ed. 19.95 (*0-253-20712-6*, MB-712) Ind U Pr.

Reading Heidegger from the Start: Essays in His Early Thought. Ed. by Theodore J. Kisiel & John Van Buren. LC 93-38957. (SUNY Series in Contemporary Continental Philosophy). 480p. (C). 1994. pap. text ed. 24.95 (*0-7914-2068-X*) State U NY Pr.

Reading Heidegger from the Start: Essays in His Early Thought. Ed. by Theodore J. Kisiel & John Van Buren. LC 93-38957. (SUNY Series in Contemporary Continental Philosophy). 480p. (C). 1994. text ed. 74.50 (*0-7914-2067-1*) State U NY Pr.

Reading Hemingway: The Facts in the Fictions. Miriam Mandel. LC 94-14481. 609p. 1995. 72.50 (*0-8108-2870-7*) Scarecrow.

Reading Henry James. Louis Auchincloss. LC 74-25934. (Illus.). 189p. reprint ed. pap. 53.90 (*0-8357-7001-X*, 2033200) Bks Demand.

Reading Henry James in French Cultural Contexts. Pierre A. Walker. LC 94-21528. (Illus.). 240p. 1995. lib. bdg. 28.50 (*0-87580-192-7*) N Ill U Pr.

Reading Holinshed's Chronicles. Annabel Patterson. LC 93-47629. 359p. (C). 1994. pap. text ed. 16.95 (*0-226-64912-1*); lib. bdg. 43.00 (*0-226-64911-3*) U Ch Pr.

Reading Houses & Building Books: Andrew Jackson Downing & the Architecture of Popular Antebellum Literature, 1835-1855. Adam Sweeting. LC 95-39747. (Illus.). 242p. 1996. 35.00 (*0-87451-750-8*) U Pr of New Eng.

***Reading Human Geography.** pap. write for info. (*0-340-63208-9*, Pub. by E Arnold UK) Routledge Chapman & Hall.

Reading Human Geography: The Poetics & Politics of Inquiry. Ed. by Trevor Barnes & Derek Gregory. Date not set. text ed. 54.95 (*0-470-23538-1*); pap. text ed. 29.95 (*0-470-23537-3*) Halsted Pr.

Reading Hungarian 1. Martha Pereszlenyi-Pinter & Julianna N. Ludanyi. (Illus.). 119p. (Orig.). (HUN.). (C). 1987. teacher ed., pap. 12.50 (*0-87415-149-X*, 60A); student ed., pap. text ed. 26.00 (*0-87415-148-1*, 60) OSU Foreign Lang.

Reading Hungarian 1, 2 cass., Set. Martha Pereszlenyi-Pinter & Julianna N. Ludanyi. (Orig.). (HUN.). (C). 1987. audio 10.00 (*0-87415-159-7*, 60B) OSU Foreign Lang.

Reading Ideas. 1981. pap. 12.95 (*0-590-49009-5*, Scholastic Hardcover) Scholastic Inc.

Reading Ideas Ready to Use! Barbara Gruber. (Instant Idea Bks.). (Illus.). 64p. 1983. 7.95 (*0-86734-049-5*, FS-8303) Schaffer Pubns.

Reading Images. Gunther Kress & Teho Van Leeuwen. 135p. (C). 1995. pap. 56.00 (*0-7300-1257-3*, ECS816, Pub. by Deakin Univ AT) St Mut.

Reading Images. Gunther Kress & Theo Van Leeuwen. 135p. 1993. 75.00 (*0-614-04018-3*, ECS806, Pub. by Deakin Univ AT) St Mut.

Reading Images: Grammar of Visual Design. Gunther Kress & Theo Van Leeuwen, pseud. (Illus.). 320p. (C). 1996. pap. 22.95 (*0-415-10600-1*, Routledge NY) Routledge.

Reading Images: Narrative Discourse & Reception in the Thirteenth-Century Illuminated Apocalypse. Suzanne Lewis. (Illus.). 448p. (C). 1995. text ed. 85.00 (*0-521-47920-7*) Cambridge U Pr.

Reading Images: The Grammar of Visual Design. Gunther Kress & Theo Van Leeuwen. LC 95-9798. 1995. pap. write for info. (*0-415-51060-0*) Routledge.

Reading Images: The Grammar of Visual Design. Gunther Kress & Theo Van Leeuwen. LC 95-9798. 320p. (C). (gr. 13). 1996. text ed. 74.95 (*0-415-10599-4*) Routledge.

***Reading Images Viewing Texts.** McQuade. Date not set. pap. text ed. write for info. (*0-312-18016-0*) St Martin.

Reading Improvement: A Complete Course for Increasing Speed and Comprehension. Barbara M. Klaeser. LC 76-49042. 306p. 1977. 35.95 (*0-88229-232-3*) Nelson-Hall.

Reading Improvement: Exercises for Students of English As a Second Language. David P. Harris. (Orig.). 1966. pap. text ed. write for info. (*0-13-755058-8*) P-H.

Reading in a Foreign Language. Ed. by J. Charles Alderson & A. H. Urquhart. (Applied Linguistics & Language Ser.). 324p. (Orig.). 1984. pap. text ed. 33.09 (*0-582-55372-5*, 74390) Longman.

Reading in Agricultural Geography. L. Sukhla. 408p. (C). 1991. 375.00 (*81-85046-98-0*, Pub. by Scientific Pubs II) St Mut.

Reading in America: A Progress Report. James Flood & Diane K. Lapp. (University Research Lectures: No. 6). 43p. 1992. 10.00 (*1-879691-09-4*) SDSU Press.

Reading in America: Literature & Social History. Ed. by Cathy N. Davidson. LC 88-35821. 320p. 1989. pap. text ed. 15.95 (*0-8018-3800-2*) Johns Hopkins.

Reading in American Schools: A Guide to Information Sources. Ed. by Maria E. Schantz & Joseph F. Brynner. LC 79-23770. (Education Information Guide Ser.: Vol. 5). 280p. 1980. 68.00 (*0-8103-1456-8*) Gale.

Reading in an Age of Mass Communication: Report of the Committee on Reading at the Secondary School & College Levels. National Council of Teachers of English Staff. Ed. by William S. Gray. LC 70-167390. (Essay Index Reprint Ser.). 1977. reprint ed. 13.95 (*0-8369-2811-3*) Ayer.

***Reading in an Age of Theory.** Ed. by Bridget G. Lyons. LC 96-45633. 256p. (C). 1997. text ed. 45.00 (*0-8135-2430-X*) Rutgers U Pr.

Reading in & Out of School: Factors Influencing the Literary Achievement of American Students in Grades 4, 8, & 12, in 1988 & 1990. Mary A. Foertsch. (Nation's Report Card Ser.). (Illus.). 64p. (Orig.). (C). 1993. pap. text ed. 20.00 (*1-56806-183-8*) DIANE Pub.

Reading in Art History, Vol. I: Ancient Egypt Through the Middle Ages. 3rd ed. Ed. by Harold Spencer. LC 76-7404. (Illus.). 502p. (C). 1982. pap. text ed. 45.33 (*0-02-414380-4*, Macmillan Coll) P-H.

Reading in Attitude Theory & Measurement. Martin Fishbein. LC 67-22410. (Illus.). 509p. reprint ed. pap. 145.10 (*0-317-08010-5*, 2055145) Bks Demand.

Reading in Bed: Personal Essays on the Glories of Reading. Ed. by Steven Gilbar. 160p. 1996. pap. 18.95 (*1-56792-035-7*) Godine.

Reading in Community: Exploring Individual, Social, & Global Issues. Dennis Keen. 504p. (C). 1996. pap. text ed. 31.75 (*0-15-502920-7*) HB Coll Pubs.

Reading in Community Work. Ed. by Paul Henderson & David Thomas. 1981. 50.00 (*0-317-54598-1*, Pub. by Natl Inst Soc Work) St Mut.

Reading in Detail: Aesthetics & the Feminine. Naomi Schor. 1987. 27.50 (*0-416-01511-5*, 1179) Routledge Chapman & Hall.

Reading in Exile: The Libraries of John Ramridge, Thomas Harding & Henry Joliffe, Recusants in Louvain. Ed. by Christian Coppens. (Title Libri Pertinentes Ser.: Vol. 2). 250p. 1993. pap. text ed. 26.00 (*0-9518811-1-6*, MRLP2, Pub. by Libri Pertinentes UK) MRTS.

Reading in Focus: Learning to Get the Message Module A, Module B & Module C, Module C. 3rd ed. Esta De Fossard. 352p. (C). 1990. pap. 28.95 (*0-538-70050-5*, EG40CB2) S-W Pub.

Reading in Focus: Learning to Get the Message Module A, Module B & Module C, Module A. 3rd ed. Esta De Fossard. 352p. (C). 1990. pap. 28.95 (*0-538-70048-3*, EG40CB) S-W Pub.

Reading in Focus: Learning to Get the Message Module A, Module B & Module C, Module B. 3rd ed. Esta De Fossard. 352p. (C). 1990. pap. 28.95 (*0-538-70049-1*, EG40CB1) S-W Pub.

Reading in International Political Economy. Ed. by David N. Balaam & Michael Veseth. LC 95-34434. 1995. pap. text ed. 30.60 (*0-13-149600-X*) P-H.

Reading in Junior Classes. Department of Education New Zealand Staff. 160p. (Orig.). (C). 1985. pap. text ed. 27.00 (*0-913461-77-6*) R Owen Pubs.

Reading in Memoriam. Timothy Peltason. LC 85-42698. (Princeton Essays in Literature Ser.). 193p. 1985. reprint ed. pap. 55.10 (*0-7837-9418-5*, 2060159) Bks Demand.

Reading in Multilingual Classrooms. 1995. student ed. 179.00 (*0-7049-0768-2*, Pub. by Multilingual Matters UK); teacher ed., pap. 45.95 (*0-7049-0769-0*, Pub. by Multilingual Matters UK) Taylor & Francis.

Reading in Mythology: An Original Anthology. Ed. by Kees W. Bolle. LC 77-139. (Mythology Ser.). (FRE & GER.). 1978. lib. bdg. 17.95 (*0-405-10573-8*) Ayer.

Reading in Public Sector Economics. Baker. (Fe - Public Finance Ser.). 1997. text ed. 29.95 (*0-538-86524-5*) S-W Pub.

Reading in Ritual Studies. Ed. by Ronald L. Grimes. LC 95-25288. 1995. pap. text ed. 44.00 (*0-02-347253-7*, Macmillan Coll) P-H.

Reading in the Age of the Computer. Ed. by Malcolm P. Douglass. (Clarement Reading Conference Yearbook Ser.). 255p. 1984. pap. 7.00 (*0-941742-02-4*) Claremont Grad.

Reading in the Composition Classroom: Second Language Perspectives. Ed. by Joan Carson & Ilona Leki. LC 92-31766. 1993. pap. 26.95 (*0-8384-3972-1*) Heinle & Heinle.

Reading in the Content Areas: An Interactive Approach for Advanced Students. Patricia A. Richard-Amato. (YA). 1990. pap. text ed. 22.59 (*0-8013-0247-1*, 75902) Longman.

Reading in the Content Areas: Improving Classroom Instruction. 3rd ed. Ernest K. Dishner. 480p. 1991. per. 41.94 (*0-8403-6408-3*) Kendall-Hunt.

Reading in the Content Areas: Research for Teachers. Ed. by Mary M. Dupuis. LC 83-8577. 87p. reprint ed. pap. 25.00 (*0-8357-4311-X*, 2037109) Bks Demand.

***Reading in the Dark.** Seamus Deane. LC 96-49635. 246p. 1997. 23.00 (*0-394-57440-0*) Knopf.

***Reading in the Dark.** Seamus Deane. 1998. pap. write for info. (*0-375-70023-4*, Vin) Random.

Reading in the Disciplines: An Anthology for College Writers. Harvey S. Wiener. 1990. pap. text ed. write for info. (*0-07-070174-1*) McGraw.

Reading in the Early Years Handbook. Robin Campbell. LC 94-40594. 1995. 37.50 (*0-335-19310-2*, Open Univ Pr); pap. 12.99 (*0-335-19309-9*, Open Univ Pr) Taylor & Francis.

***Reading in the Loft Vol. 1: Sound Chart Letters & Sounds.** large type ed. Sylvia Seymour & Sandra Cusack. (Illus.). 48p. (Orig.). (J). (gr. 1-6). 1997. pap. 9.95 (*0-9651396-0-3*) StoryLoft.

Reading in the Mathematics Classroom. Cyrus F. Smith & Henry S. Kepner. 64p. 1981. pap. 8.95 (*0-8106-3203-9*) NEA.

Reading in the Middle School. 2nd ed. Gerald G. Duffy. 246p. 1990. pap. 14.95 (*0-87207-121-9*) Intl Reading.

Reading in the Middle School. Ed. by Gerald G. Duffy. LC 74-23428. (Perspectives in Reading Ser.: No. 18). 220p. reprint ed. 62.70 (*0-317-55487-5*, 2029594) Bks Demand.

***Reading in the Middle School: An Integrated Approach.** Susan Blair-Larson. 80p. (C). 1997. per. 25.95 (*0-7872-3783-3*) Kendall-Hunt.

R

Reading in the Science Classroom. Judith Bechtel & Bettie Franzblau. 64p. 1980. pap. 8.95 (*0-8106-3201-2*) NEA.

Reading in the Social Studies Classroom. Terry L. Bullock & Karl D. Hesse. 64p. 1981. pap. 8.95 (*0-8106-3202-0*) NEA.

Reading in Tudor England. Eugene R. Kintgen. LC 95-53193. (Series in Composition, Literacy, & Culture). 256p. (C). 1996. text ed. 40.00 (*0-8229-3939-8*) U of Pittsburgh Pr.

Reading Instruction: Application. Jack Rudman. (ACT Proficiency Examination Program Ser.: PEP-25). 1994. pap. 23.95 (*0-8373-5525-7*) Nat Learn.

Reading Instruction: Diagnostic Teaching in the Classroom. 4th ed. Larry A. Harris & Carl B. Smith. ix, 769p. (C). 1986. text ed. write for info. (*0-02-350580-X*, Macmillan Coll) P-H.

Reading Instruction: Instruction & Assessment. 2nd ed. Barbara Taylor et al. 1994. text ed. write for info. (*0-07-063182-4*) McGraw.

Reading Instruction: Theoretical Foundations. Jack Rudman. (ACT Proficiency Examination Program Ser.: PEP-26). 1994. pap. 23.95 (*0-8373-5526-5*) Nat Learn.

***Reading Instruction Essentials.** Anita Davis. (Illus.). 249p. (C). 1966. pap. text ed. 22.95 (*0-89641-296-2*) American Pr.

Reading Instruction for the Gifted. Donald C. Cushenbery. 182p. 1987. 41.95 (*0-398-05332-4*) C C Thomas.

Reading Instruction for the Gifted. Donald C. Cushenbery. 182p. 1987. pap. 29.95 (*0-398-06084-3*) C C Thomas.

Reading Instruction for Today. 2nd ed. Jana M. Mason & Kathryn H. Au. (C). 1990. text ed. 60.95 (*0-673-38774-7*) Addson-Wesley Educ.

Reading Instruction for Today's Children. 2nd ed. H. Robinson & Nila B. Smith. 1980. write for info. (*0-13-755157-6*) P-H.

Reading Instruction in the Elementary School. Jack Rudman. (Regents College Proficiency Examination Ser.: CPEP-25). 1994. pap. 23.95 (*0-8373-5425-0*) Nat Learn.

Reading Instruction in the Elementary School. Jack Rudman. (ACT Proficiency Examination Program (PEP) Ser.: Vol. PEP-31). 1994. pap. 23.95 (*0-8373-5531-1*) Nat Learn.

Reading Intermediate. 1992. 6.95 (*0-19-453401-4*) OUP.

Reading Interpretation in Social Studies, Natural Sciences, & Literature (G. E. D.) Jack Rudman. (General Aptitude & Abilities Ser.: CS-34). 1994. pap. 17.95 (*0-8373-6734-4*) Nat Learn.

Reading into Cultural Studies. Ed. by Martin Barker & Anne Beezer. LC 92-33391. 240p. (C). 1992. pap. 17.95 (*0-415-06377-9*, A7916) Routledge.

Reading into Cultural Studies. Ed. by Martin Barker & Anne Beezer. LC 92-33391. 240p. (C). (gr. 13). 1992. text ed. 69.95 (*0-415-06376-0*) Routledge.

Reading into Racism: Bias in Children's Literature & Learning Materials. Gillian Klein. (Education Bks.). 192p. (Orig.). (C). 1986. pap. text ed. 13.95 (*0-7102-0160-5*, RKP) Routledge.

Reading Inventory for the Classroom. 2nd ed. E. Sutton Flynt & Robert B. Cooter, Jr. 232p. (C). 1995. ring bd., pap. 28.50 (*0-89787-538-9*) Gorsuch Scarisbrick.

Reading Inventory for the Classroom. 3rd ed. E. Sutton Flynt & Robert B. Cooter, Jr. 240p. (C). 1997. pap. text ed. write for info. (*0-614-16056-1*) Gorsuch Scarisbrick.

***Reading Is Fun.** (Preschool Concepts Ser.). (Illus.). 32p. (J). (ps). 1996. pap. write for info. (*1-56144-826-5*, Honey Bear Bks) Modern Pub NYC.

Reading Is Not a Spectator Sport. Mary H. Pelton. (Illus.). xix, 264p. 1993. pap. text ed. 23.00 (*1-56308-118-0*) Teacher Ideas Pr.

Reading Is Only the Tiger's Tail. 12th rev. ed. Marlene J. McCracken & Robert A. McCracken. 248p. (J). (gr. k-4). 1987. reprint ed. teacher ed., pap. 15.00 (*0-920541-13-5*) Peguis Pubs Ltd.

Reading Isaiah. Edgar W. Conrad. LC 91-18768. (Overtures to Biblical Theology Ser.). 208p. (Orig.). 1991. pap. 15.00 (*0-8006-1560-3*, 1-1560, Fortress Pr) Augsburg Fortress.

Reading Japanese. Eleanor H. Jorden & Hamako I. Chaplin. LC 75-18176. (Linguistic Ser.). (C). 1976. 70.00 (*0-300-01912-2*); pap. text ed. 28.50 (*0-300-01913-0*) Yale U Pr.

Reading Japanese Around You. Robert P. Magee. 160p. (Orig.). 1994. pap. 11.95 (*4-89684-240-5*, Pub. by Yohan Pubns JA) Weatherhill.

Reading Japanese Financial Newspapers. Association for Japanese-Language Staff. 160p. 1991. pap. 35.00 (*0-87011-956-7*) Kodansha.

Reading Japanese Signs: Deciphering Daily Life in Japan. Ian McArthur. Ed. by Kuromachi-san & Megumi Ikeda. (Illus.). 138p. 1994. pap. 10.00 (*4-7700-1671-9*) Kodansha.

Reading Jazz. Ed. by David Meltzer. LC 92-44561. 304p. (Orig.). 1997. reprint ed. pap. 14.95 (*1-56279-038-2*) Mercury Hse Inc.

Reading Jazz: A Gathering of Autobiography, Reportage & Criticism from 1919 to Now. Ed. by Robert Gottlieb. 1088p. 1996. 37.50 (*0-679-44251-0*) Pantheon.

Reading Jeremiah As Sacred Scripture Today. Steven J. Scherrer. LC 93-84750. 167p. (Orig.). 1993. pap. write for info. (*1-883411-01-7*) St Jerome Pubns.

Reading Job Ads. Larry Mikulecky. 1990. 12.50 (*0-13-852211-1*) P-H.

Reading John: A Literary & Theological Commentary on the Fourth Gospel & Johannine Epistles. Charles H. Talbert. 300p. 1994. reprint ed. pap. 14.95 (*0-8245-1414-9*) Crossroad NY.

***Reading Joyce Politically.** Trevor L. Williams. LC 97-7555. (Florida James Joyce Ser.). 272p. 1997. 49.95 (*0-8130-1513-8*) U Press Fla.

Reading Joyce's "Ulysses" Daniel R. Schwarz. LC 86-6680. 240p. 1987. text ed. 14.95 (*0-312-00086-3*) St Martin.

Reading Jung: Science, Psychology, & Religion. Volney P. Gay. LC 84-1322. (American Academy of Religion, Studies in Religion). 166p. (C). 1984. pap. 15.95 (*0-89130-731-1*, 01 00 34) Scholars Pr GA.

***Reading Keyboard Music.** 1996. teacher ed. 35.00 (*1-881986-21-7*) Demibach Eds.

Reading Keyboard Music, 3 vols. Martha Miner et al. pap. text ed. 24.00 (*1-881986-16-0*) Demibach Eds.

Reading Keyboard Music, Vol. 1. Martha Miner et al. 44p. 1994. pap. text ed. 9.00 (*1-881986-13-6*) Demibach Eds.

Reading Keyboard Music, Vol. 2. Martha Miner et al. 45p. 1994. pap. text ed. 7.50 (*1-881986-14-4*) Demibach Eds.

Reading Keyboard Music, Vol. 3. Martha Miner et al. 45p. 1994. pap. text ed. 7.50 (*1-881986-15-2*) Demibach Eds.

***Reading Knowledge: An Introduction to Foucault, Barthes & Althusser.** Michael Payne. LC 96-46163. 200p. 1997. 52.95 (*0-631-19566-1*) Blackwell Pubs.

***Reading Knowledge: An Introduction to Foucault, Barthes & Althusser.** Michael Payne. LC 96-46163. 200p. 1997. pap. 21.95 (*0-631-19567-X*) Blackwell Pubs.

Reading Knowledge in German. Mary L. Apelt. 152p. (ENG & GER.). 1984. pap. 34.95 (*0-7859-7457-1*, 3503022872) Fr & Eur.

Reading Knowledge in German for Art Historians & Archaeologists: An English-German Course in Art History & Archaeology. 2nd ed. H. P. Apelt. 152p. 1991. pap. 35.95 (*3-503-03025-5*) Adlers Foreign Bks.

Reading Kristeva: Unraveling the Double-Bind. Kelly Oliver. LC 92-9543. 240p. (C). 1993. 35.00 (*0-253-34173-6*); pap. 15.95 (*0-253-20761-4*, MB-761) Ind U Pr.

Reading 'La Regenta' Duplicitious Discourse & the Entropy of Structure. Stephanie A. Sieburth. LC 89-17735. (Purdue University Monographs in Romance Languages: No. 29). viii, 127p. 1990. 41.00 (*1-55619-069-7*); pap. 21.95 (*1-55619-070-0*) Benjamins North Am.

Reading Lab Kit. Caleb Gattegno. 1973. 32.50 (*0-87825-009-3*) Ed Solutions.

Reading Lab Manual. Kreta Trammel. 80p. (C). 1992. pap. text ed. 11.49 (*0-8403-8301-0*) Kendall-Hunt.

Reading Labels, Directions & Newspaper: Essential Life Skills. Carolyn M. Starkey. 64p. 1994. pap. 6.95 (*0-8442-5169-0*) NTC Pub Grp.

Reading Lacan. Jane Gallop. LC 85-7892. 200p. 1985. 35.00 (*0-8014-1585-3*); pap. 13.95 (*0-8014-9443-5*) Cornell U Pr.

Reading, Language, & Literacy: Reading Instruction for the Twenty-First Century. Ed. by Fran Lehr & Jean Osborn. 312p. 1994. text ed. 59.95 (*0-8058-1166-4*) L Erlbaum Assocs.

Reading Latin. Peter Jones & Keith Sidwell. (Illus.). 176p. 1986. Text, 176pgs. pap. text ed. 17.95 (*0-521-28623-9*); Grammar, Vocabulary & Exercises, 550pgs. pap. text ed. 28.95 (*0-521-28622-0*) Cambridge U Pr.

Reading Learning Centers for the Primary Grades. Shirleen Wait. 240p. 1991. pap. 24.95 (*0-87628-794-1*) Ctr Appl Res.

Reading Level 5 see Snapshots: A Collection of Readings for Adults

Reading Level 6 see Snapshots: A Collection of Readings for Adults

Reading Level 7 see Snapshots: A Collection of Readings for Adults

Reading Leviticus: Responses to Mary Douglas. Ed. by John F. Sawyer. (JSOTS Ser.: No. 227). 263p. 1996. 52.00 (*1-85075-628-7*, Pub. by Sheffield Acad UK) CUP Services.

Reading Light. Adams. (C). 1995. pap. text ed. 31.00 (*0-15-502398-5*) HB Coll Pubs.

Reading Like Kings & Queens: Introductory Sequence. Ellis Richardson. (Read Aloud Ser.: Bk. 2). 36p. (Orig.). 1988. pap. text ed. 4.00 (*1-56775-013-3*, INS2-3) ISM Teach Systs.

Reading List for Students in Conservation of Historic & Artistic Works on Paper & Photographs. Anne Clapp & Roy Perkinson. 1980. 3.75 (*0-933098-09-X*) Am Inst Conser Hist.

Reading Lists for College-Bound Students. 2nd ed. Doug Estell et al. 272p. 1993. pap. 10.00 (*0-671-84712-0*, Arco) Macmillan Gen Ref.

Reading Lists in Radical Social Science. Union for Radical Political Economics (URPE) Staff. 330p. (C). 1982. pap. text ed. 12.00 (*0-85345-616-X*) Monthly Rev.

Reading Lives & the Lives of Reading. Galbraith. LC 97-11631. 1997. text ed. write for info. (*0-312-12143-1*) St Martin.

Reading Luke: A Literary & Theological Commentary on the Third Gospel. Charles H. Talbert. 256p. 1984. pap. 14.95 (*0-8245-0668-5*) Crossroad NY.

Reading Luke-Acts: Dynamics of Biblical Narrative. William S. Kurz. LC 93-18125. 288p. (Orig.). 1993. pap. 17.00 (*0-664-25441-1*) Westminster John Knox.

Reading Made Easy: A First Book for Deaf & Dumb Children. W. R. Scott. 1973. 59.95 (*0-8490-0930-8*) Gordon Pr.

Reading Maps. Paul Riffel. LC 79-13628. (Illus.). (YA). (gr. 7 up). 1973. spiral bd. 9.95 (*0-8331-1300-3*, 440) Hubbard Sci.

Reading Maps, Globes, Charts, Graphs. Ann Edson & Eunice Insel. (J). (gr. 4-6). 1982. student ed. 2.69 (*0-89525-175-2*) Ed Activities.

***Reading Mark.** Van Iersel. pap. 27.95 (*0-567-29159-6*, Pub. by T & T Clark UK) Bks Intl VA.

Reading Mark from the Outside: Eco & Iser Leave Their Mark. W. Randolph Tate. LC 94-28295. 1994. 54.95 (*1-883255-83-X*); pap. 34.95 (*1-883255-82-1*) Intl Scholars.

Reading Marx Writing: Melodrama, the Market, & the "Grundrisse" Thomas M. Kemple. LC 94-42468. (Illus.). 286p. 1995. 35.00 (*0-8047-2408-3*) Stanford U Pr.

Reading Mary Wroth: Representing Alternatives in Early Modern England. Ed. by Naomi J. Miller & Gary Waller. LC 91-390. 256p. (C). 1991. 42.00 (*0-87049-709-X*); pap. text ed. 20.00 (*0-87049-710-3*) U of Tenn Pr.

Reading Matter: Multidisciplinary Perspectives on Material Culture. Arthur A. Berger. 145p. (C). 1991. text ed. 32.95 (*0-88738-435-8*) Transaction Pubs.

Reading Matters: A Practical Philosophy. J. Webster. 208p. 1983. text ed. 11.00 (*0-07-084134-9*) McGraw.

***Reading Matters: Narrative in the New Media Ecology.** Ed. by Joseph Tabbi & Michael Wutz. (Illus.). 328p. 1996. 42.50 (*0-8014-3366-5*); pap. 16.95 (*0-8014-8403-0*) Cornell U Pr.

Reading Matthew: A Literary & Theological Commentary. David E. Garland. 300p. 1995. pap. 14.95 (*0-8245-1496-3*) Crossroad NY.

Reading Medieval European Coins. Ralph S. Walker. (Illus.). 1979. 7.50 (*0-915018-41-1*) Attic Bks.

Reading Medieval Latin. Keith Sidwell. 362p. (C). 1995. 74.95 (*0-521-44239-7*); pap. text ed. 24.95 (*0-521-44747-X*) Cambridge U Pr.

***Reading Methods: From Process to Practice.** Suzanne I. Barchers. (C). 1998. text ed. 54.95 (*0-534-53856-8*) Wadsworth Pub.

***Reading Methods in Contemporary Elementary Classrooms.** Arne Sippola. 140p. (C). 1997. per. 25.95 (*0-7872-3675-6*) Kendall-Hunt.

Reading Middlemarch: Reclaiming the Middle Distance. Jeanie Thomas. LC 87-5874. (Nineteenth-Century Studies). 123p. reprint ed. pap. 35.10 (*0-8357-1797-6*, 2070643) Bks Demand.

Reading Miscue Inventory: Alternative Procedures. Yetta M. Goodman et al. LC 86-28604. 240p. (Orig.). (C). 1987. pap. text ed. 21.95 (*0-913461-80-6*) R Owen Pubs.

Reading Moby-Dick & Other Essays. William Hamilton. (American University Studies: English Language & Literature: Ser. IV, Vol. 69). 252p. (C). 1989. text ed. 39.50 (*0-8204-0613-9*) P Lang Pubng.

Reading Modern Poetry. Michael Schmidt. 128p. (C). 1989. pap. text ed. 12.95 (*0-415-01569-3*, A3846) Routledge.

Reading Modern Russian. Jules F. Levin et al. (Illus.). vi, 321p. 1979. pap. text ed. 18.95 (*0-89357-059-1*) Slavica.

Reading Montaigne. Ed. by Dikka Berven. LC 94-41683. (Montaigne Ser.: Vol. 5). 400p. 1995. text ed. 70.00 (*0-8153-1843-X*) Garland.

Reading Motivation. 2nd ed. Ed. by Linworth Publishing, Inc. Staff. (Professional Growth Ser.). (Illus.). 120p. 1993. pap. text ed. 19.95 (*0-938865-26-9*) Linworth Pub.

***Reading Mystical Lyric: The Case of Jalal al-Din Rumi.** Fatemeh Keshavarz. 180p. 1997. 29.95 (*1-57003-180-0*) U of SC Pr.

***Reading Myth: Classical Mythology & Its Interpretations in Medieval French Literature.** Renate Blumenfeld-Kosinski. LC 97-718. (Figurae Ser.). 1997. write for info. (*0-8047-2810-0*) Stanford U Pr.

Reading Narrative: Form, Ethics, Ideology. Ed. by James Phelan. (Illus.). 336p. (C). 1989. text ed. 47.50 (*0-8142-0458-9*) Ohio St U Pr.

Reading Narrative as Literature: Signs of Life. Andrew Stibbs. (English, Language & Education Ser.). 176p. 1991. pap. 29.00 (*0-335-09419-8*, Open Univ Pr) Taylor & Francis.

Reading Narrative Discourse: Studies in the Novel from Cervantes to Beckett. Andrew Gibson. LC 89-36453. 220p. 1990. text ed. 45.00 (*0-312-03609-4*) St Martin.

Reading Narrative Fiction. Seymour B. Chatman. 720p. (Orig.). (C). 1992. pap. text ed. 31.33 (*0-02-322111-9*, Macmillan Coll) P-H.

Reading Nasta'liq: Persian & Urdu Hands from 1500 to the Present. William L. Hanaway, Jr. & Brian Spooner. LC 94-35249. (Bibliotheca Iranica Ser.: No. 3). (Illus.). 287p. 1995. lib. bdg. 24.95 (*1-56859-033-4*) Mazda Pubs.

Reading National Geographic. Catherine A. Lutz & Jane L. Collins. LC 92-40698. (Illus.). 328p. (C). 1993. pap. text ed. 19.95 (*0-226-49724-0*) U Ch Pr.

Reading Nature's Clues: A Guide to the Wild. Doug Sadler. (Illus.). 248p. 1988. pap. 16.95 (*0-921149-15-8*) Broadview Pr.

Reading New Testament Greek: Complete Word Lists & Reader's Guide. Bernard B. Scott et al. LC 93-39436. 208p. 1993. pap. 14.95 (*1-56563-014-9*) Hendrickson MA.

Reading Nietzsche. Ed. by Robert C. Solomon & Kathleen M. Higgins. 272p. 1990. reprint ed. pap. 19.95 (*0-19-506673-1*) OUP.

Reading North by South: On Latin American Literature, Culture & Politics. Neil Larsen. LC 94-43194. 1995. text ed. 18.95 (*0-8166-2584-0*) U of Minn Pr.

Reading North by South: On Latin American Literature, Culture & Politics. Neil Larsen. LC 94-43194. 1995. text ed. 44.95 (*0-8166-2583-2*) U of Minn Pr.

Reading Norwegian. Einar Haugen. LC 75-24258. 208p. (C). 1977. pap. 12.00 (*0-87950-172-3*) Spoken Lang Serv.

***Reading Nursing Texts.** Faulkner. (C). Date not set. pap. write for info. (*0-395-77036-X*); pap. write for info. (*0-395-77037-8*) HM.

Reading of Dante's Inferno. Wallace Fowlie. LC 80-19025. 248p. 1981. pap. text ed. 8.95 (*0-226-25888-2*) U Ch Pr.

Reading of E. M. Forster. Glen Cavaliero. 187p. 1979. 38.00 (*0-8476-6191-1*) Rowman.

Reading of Edward Taylor. Thomas M. Davis. LC 90-50935. 240p. 1992. 40.00 (*0-87413-428-5*) U Delaware Pr.

Reading of George Herbert. Rosemond Tuve. LC 82-158013. (Midway Reprint Ser.). (Illus.). 218p. reprint ed. pap. 62.20 (*0-685-23855-5*, 2056640) Bks Demand.

Reading of "Gulliver's Travels" Kathleen M. Swaim. 1972. text ed. 49.25 (*90-279-2304-3*) Mouton.

Reading of Hegel's Phenomenology of Spirit. rev. ed. Quentin Lauer. LC 92-9891. (Illus.). 344p. 1993. 30.00 (*0-8232-1354-4*); pap. 17.50 (*0-8232-1355-2*) Fordham.

Reading of Henry Green. A. Kingsley Weatherhead. LC 61-8767. 180p. 1961. 25.00 (*0-295-73902-9*) U of Wash Pr.

Reading of Imagery in the Chinese Poetic Tradition. Pauline Yu. 242p. 1986. text ed. 42.50 (*0-691-06682-5*) Princeton U Pr.

***Reading of International Relations.** 2nd ed. Williams. (C). 1998. pap. text ed. 25.25 (*0-15-505543-7*) HB Coll Pubs.

***Reading of James Joyce's Finnegans Wake.** Patrick Healy. Date not set. pap. 39.95 (*1-874675-62-7*) Dufour.

Reading of Life. Sidney R. Lysaght. LC 70-142659. (Essay Index Reprint Ser.). 1977. 20.95 (*0-8369-2060-0*) Ayer.

Reading of "Mansfield Park" An Essay in Critical Synthesis. Avrom Fleishman. 109p. 1970. reprint ed. pap. 12.95 (*0-8018-1149-X*) Johns Hopkins.

Reading of Modern Art. Dore Ashton. LC 68-19064. (Illus.). 255p. reprint ed. pap. 72.70 (*0-317-10195-1*, 2002261) Bks Demand.

***Reading of Proust.** David R. Ellison. LC 83-48057. 229p. 1984. reprint ed. pap. 65.30 (*0-608-03683-8*, 2064509) Bks Demand.

Reading of Sacred Scripture & How a Christian Should Pray. St. Symeon the New Theologian. 1993. pap. 0.35 (*0-89981-150-7*) Eastern Orthodox.

Reading of Silence: Virginia Woolf in the English Tradition. Patricia O. Laurence. LC 90-23636. 253p. 1991. 39.50 (*0-8047-1831-8*) Stanford U Pr.

Reading of Silence: Virginia Woolf in the English Tradition. Patricia O. Laurence. 253p. (C). 1993. pap. 13.95 (*0-8047-2179-3*) Stanford U Pr.

Reading of the Canterbury Tales. Bernard F. Huppe. LC 64-17577. 256p. (C). 1964. text ed. 39.50 (*0-87395-011-9*, PSU2) Pegasus Pr.

Reading of the Canterbury Tales. Ed. by Bernard F. Huppe. LC 64-17577. 245p. (C). 1964. pap. text ed. 12.95 (*0-87395-022-4*) State U NY Pr.

Reading of the Iliad. R. M. Frazer. LC 93-4812. 286p. (Orig.). (C). 1993. pap. text ed. 29.50 (*0-8191-9202-3*) U Pr of Amer.

Reading of Time: A Semantic-Semiotic Approach. Julio C. Pinto. (Approaches to Semiotics Ser.: No. 82). x, 162p. (C). 1989. lib. bdg. 79.25 (*0-89925-354-7*) Mouton.

Reading of Verbal Material in Ninth Grade Algebra. Margaret G. McKim. LC 71-177032. (Columbia University. Teachers College. Contributions to Education Ser.: No. 850). reprint ed. 37.50 (*0-404-55850-X*) AMS Pr.

Reading of Villon's Testament. David A. Fein. LC 84-50322. 112p. 1984. pap. 10.95 (*0-917786-04-1*) Summa Pubns.

Reading Old & New. Daphne Phillips. 96p. 1987. pap. 30.00 (*0-905392-73-6*) St Mut.

***Reading Old English Texts.** Ed. by Katherine O. O'Keeffe. LC 96-47374. 256p. (C). 1997. text ed. 59.95 (*0-521-46575-3*); pap. text ed. 18.95 (*0-521-46970-8*) Cambridge U Pr.

Reading Old Friends: Essays, Reviews, & Poems on Poetics 1975-1990. John Matthias. LC 90-28980. (SUNY Series, The Margins of Literature). 348p. (C). 1992. text ed. 64.50 (*0-7914-0879-5*); pap. text ed. 21.95 (*0-7914-0880-9*) State U NY Pr.

Reading on Development of Children. Miller & Gauvain. 1995. write for info. (*0-7167-2582-7*) W H Freeman.

Reading on Indian Music. Gowri Kuppuswamy & M. Hariharan. (Illus.). 239p. 1979. 16.95 (*0-318-36331-3*) Asia Bk Corp.

Reading on Purpose: Cognitive Skills for Intermediate Learners. Fraida Dubin & Elite Olshtain. (Illus.). (C). 1987. spiral bd. 22.60 (*0-201-11671-5*) Addison-Wesley.

Reading on Your Own. Kearney. 1992. pap. 26.95 (*0-8384-2274-8*) Heinle & Heinle.

Reading Opera. Ed. by Arthur Groos & Roger Parker. 381p. 1988. text ed. 65.00 (*0-691-09132-3*); pap. text ed. 19.95 (*0-691-02709-9*) Princeton U Pr.

Reading Ourselves to Sleep. Donald Finkel et al. 24p. 1985. pap. 15.00 (*0-931757-23-1*) Pterodactyl Pr.

Reading Pacifics, No. 10. Bert Pennypacker. (Classic Power Ser.: No. 10). (Illus.). 80p. 1997. pap. write for info. (*0-934088-36-5*) NJ Intl Inc.

Reading Papyri, Writing Ancient History. Roger S. Bagnall. LC 95-4136. (Approaching the Ancient World Ser.). 168p. (C). 1995. pap. 15.95 (*0-415-09377-5*) Routledge.

Reading Papyri, Writing Ancient History. Roger S. Bagnall. LC 95-4136. (Approaching the Ancient World Ser.). 168p. (C). (gr. 13). 1995. text ed. 59.95 (*0-415-09376-7*) Routledge.

***Reading Parfit.** Ed. by Jonathan Dancy. (Illus.). 352p. 1997. pap. text ed. 54.95 (*0-631-16871-0*) Blackwell Pubs.

***Reading Parfit.** Ed. by Jonathan Dancy. (Illus.). 352p. (C). 1997. pap. text ed. 24.95 (*0-631-19726-5*) Blackwell Pubs.

***Reading Passages.** Carolyn H. Fitzpatrick & Marybeth B. Ruscica. 450p. (C). 1997. pap. text ed. 27.56 (*0-669-20168-5*) HM College Div.

***Reading Passages.** Carolyn H. Fitzpatrick & Marybeth B. Ruscica. (C). 1997. teacher ed., text ed. 28.76 (*0-669-41848-X*) HM College Div.

Reading Pathways. Carolyn H. Fitzpatrick & Marybeth B. Ruscica. 479p. (C). 1991. pap. text ed. 34.76 (*0-669-20170-7*) HM College Div.

Reading Pathways. 2nd ed. Carolyn H. Fitzpatrick & Marybeth B. Ruscica. 550p. (C). 1995. pap. text ed. 34.76 (*0-669-35144-X*) HM College Div.

***Reading Pathways.** 2nd ed. Carolyn H. Fitzpatrick & Marybeth B. Ruscica. (C). 1995. teacher ed., text ed. 2.66 (*0-669-35146-6*) HM College Div.

An Asterisk (*) at the beginning of an entry indicates that the title is appearing in BIP for the first time.

Reading Paulo Freire: His Life & Work. Moacir Gadotti. Tr. by John Milton. LC 93-26751. (SUNY Series, Teacher Empowerment & School Reform). (Illus.). 204p. (C). 1994. text ed. 49.50 (*0-7914-1923-1*); pap. text ed. 16.95 (*0-7914-1924-X*) State U NY Pr.

***Reading Peirce Reading.** Richard A. Smyth. LC 97-3365. 336p. 1997. 67.50 (*0-8476-8432-6*); pap. 24.95 (*0-8476-8433-4*) Rowman.

Reading Petronius. Niall W. Slater. LC 89-43484. 264p. 1990. text ed. 42.00 (*0-8018-3984-X*) Johns Hopkins.

Reading Philip Roth. Ed. by Asher Z. Milbauer & Donald G. Watson. 225p. 1988. text ed. 32.50 (*0-312-00934-8*) St Martin.

Reading Philosophy for the Twenty-First Century. Ed. by George F. McLean. LC 89-30882. (Cultural Heritage & Contemporary Life Series I. Culture & Values: Vol. 3). 336p. (Orig.). 1989. 45.00 (*0-8191-7414-9*); pap. 17.50 (*0-8191-7415-7*) Coun Res Values.

Reading Pictures, Viewing Texts. Claude Gandelman. LC 90-42147. (Illus.). 192p. 1991. 29.95 (*0-253-32532-3*) Ind U Pr.

Reading "Piers Plowman" & "The Pilgrim's Progress" Reception & the Protestant Reader. Barbara A. Johnson. 272p. (C). 1992. 29.95 (*0-8093-1653-6*) S Ill U Pr.

Reading Plays: Interpretation & Reception. Ed. by Hanna Scolnicov & Peter R. Holland. (Illus.). 256p. (C). 1991. text ed. 49.95 (*0-521-39411-2*) Cambridge U Pr.

Reading Poetry: An Introduction to Skills, Theories, & Histories. Tom Furnace & Michael Bath. 1996. pap. 27.40 (*0-13-355298-5*) P-H.

Reading Points-in-Time Coloring Book. Vicki Rhodier. (Illus.). 32p. (J). 1994. pap. text ed. 5.00 (*1-887762-03-5*) His Soc Brks Cnty.

Reading Polish 1. Jerzy R. Krzyzanowski et al. (OSU Foreign Language Publications: No. 11). (Illus.). 155p. (POL.). (C). 1984. teacher ed. 14.50 (*0-87415-011-6*, 11A); student ed., pap. text ed. 35.00 (*0-87415-010-8*) OSU Foreign Lang.

Reading Polish 1, 5 cass., Set. Jerzy R. Krzyzanowski et al. (OSU Foreign Language Publications: No. 11). (POL.). (C). 1984. audio 25.00 (*0-87415-012-4*, 11B) OSU Foreign Lang.

Reading Polish 2. Jerzy R. Krzyzanowski & Deborah W. Roney. (Illus.). 116p. (Orig.). (POL.). (C). 1986. teacher ed. 12.00 (*0-87415-108-2*, 45A); student ed., pap. text ed. 29.00 (*0-87415-107-4*, 45) OSU Foreign Lang.

Reading Polish 3. Jerzy R. Krzyzanowski & Deborah W. Roney. (Illus.). 119p. (Orig.). (POL.). (C). 1987. teacher ed. 12.50 (*0-87415-143-0*, 57A); student ed., pap. text ed. 35.00 (*0-87415-142-2*, 57) OSU Foreign Lang.

Reading Political Stories: Representations of Politics in Novels & Pictures. Ed. by Maureen Whitebrook. 224p. (C). 1991. text ed. 59.50 (*0-8476-7722-2*) Rowman.

Reading Pope's Imitations of Horace. Jacob Fuchs. LC 87-46437. 168p. 1989. 32.50 (*0-8387-5148-2*) Bucknell U Pr.

***Reading Popular Narrative: A Source Book.** Ed. by Bob Ashley. 250p. (C). 1997. pap. 24.95 (*0-7185-0083-0*, Pub. by Leicester Univ Pr); text ed. 69.95 (*0-7185-0082-2*, Pub. by Leicester Univ Pr) Bks Intl VA.

***Reading Power.** Lois Hassan. (C). 1995. teacher ed., text ed. 2.66 (*0-669-34072-3*) HM College Div.

***Reading Power.** 2nd ed. Bea Mickulecky. 1997. pap. text ed. write for info. (*0-201-84674-8*) Addison-Wesley.

Reading Power. 3rd ed. James I. Brown. LC 86-80504. 361p. (C). 1987. pap. text ed. 17.00 (*0-318-40039-1*) HM College Div.

Reading Power. 5th ed. James I. Brown & Vivian V. Fishco. 448p. (C). 1995. pap. text ed. 33.96 (*0-669-34071-5*) HM College Div.

Reading Power: Book 1. Angelica W. Cass. 128p. (Orig.). 1985. pap. 8.00 (*0-668-05968-0*, Arco) Macmillan Gen Ref.

Reading Power: Book 2. Angelica W. Cass. 176p. (Orig.). 1985. pap. 8.00 (*0-668-05969-9*, Arco) Macmillan Gen Ref.

Reading Power: Book 3. Angelica W. Cass. 160p. (Orig.). 1983. pap. 8.00 (*0-668-05970-2*, Arco) Macmillan Gen Ref.

Reading Power: Book 4. Angelica W. Cass. 192p. (Orig.). 1985. pap. 8.00 (*0-668-05971-0*, Arco) Macmillan Gen Ref.

Reading Power & Study Skills for College Work. 2nd ed. Carl A. Lefevre & Helen E. Lefevre. 356p. (C). 1984. pap. text ed. 18.75 (*0-15-575759-8*) HB Coll Pubs.

***Reading Power with "Newsweek"** 5th ed. James I. Brown & Vivian V. Fishco. (C). 1995. text ed. 40.76 (*0-669-39519-6*) HM College Div.

Reading Prints: A Selection of Sixteenth to Early Nineteenth Century Prints from the Menil Collections. Elizabeth Glassman. LC 81-83964. (Illus.). 122p. (C). 1985. pap. 12.50 (*0-939594-14-5*) Menil Found.

Reading Problems. 3rd ed. Caldwell & Margaret A. Richek. 1995. text ed. 53.00 (*0-205-16388-2*) Allyn.

Reading Problems: Consultation & Remediation. P. G. Aaron & R. Malatesha Joshi. LC 92-3124. (Guilford School Practitioner Ser.). 285p. 1992. lib. bdg. 27.95 (*0-89862-365-0*) Guilford Pr.

Reading Process: The Teacher & the Learner. 6th ed. Miles V. Zintz. 720p. (C). 1992. per. write for info. (*0-697-12581-5*) Brown & Benchmark.

Reading Process & Practice: From Socio-Psycholinguistics to Whole Language. 2nd ed. Constance Weaver. LC 93-19844. (Illus.). 707p. (C). 1994. pap. text ed. 35.00 (*0-435-08799-1*, 08799) Heinemann.

Reading Program: Critical Reading, Bk. G. 2nd ed. Amy Awtrey & Carol Markos. 72p. 1982. pap. 4.50 (*0-88069-006-2*) L A Meyer.

Reading Program: Essay Structure, Bk. F. 2nd ed. Amy Awtrey & Carol Markos. 72p. 1982. pap. 4.50 (*0-88069-005-4*) L A Meyer.

Reading Program: Relationships, Bk. E. 3rd ed. Amy Awtrey & Carol Markos. 58p. 1982. pap. 4.50 (*0-88069-004-6*) L A Meyer.

Reading Program: Sentence Structure, Bk. C. 2nd ed. Amy Awtrey & Carol Markos. 48p. 1982. pap. 4.50 (*0-88069-002-X*) L A Meyer.

Reading Program: Signals, Bk. D. 2nd ed. Amy Awtrey & Carol Markos. 62p. 1982. pap. 4.50 (*0-88069-003-8*) L A Meyer.

Reading Program: Vocabulary, Bk. B. 2nd ed. Amy Awtrey & Carol Markos. 48p. 1982. pap. 4.50 (*0-88069-001-1*) L A Meyer.

Reading Program: Word Patterns, Bk. A. 3rd ed. Amy Awtrey & Carol Markos. 48p. 1982. pap. 4.50 (*0-88069-000-3*) L A Meyer.

***Reading Programs for Young Adults: Complete Plans for 50 Theme-Related Units for Public, Middle School or High School Libraries.** Martha S. Simpson. LC 97-1499. 320p. 1997. pap. 38.50 (*0-7864-0357-8*) McFarland & Co.

Reading Progress Feedback System (RFFS) Ellis Richardson & Harold Freeman, Jr. 86p. (Orig.). 1981. pap. 15.00 (*0-939632-32-2*) ILM.

***Reading Prophetic Narratives.** Uriel Simon. LC 96-40267. (Indiana Studies in Biblical Literature). 1997. write for info. (*0-253-33227-3*); pap. write for info. (*0-253-21093-3*) Ind U Pr.

Reading Proust: In Search of the Wolf-Fish. Maria Paganini. Tr. by Caren Litherland from FRE. LC 93-27830. (Theory & History of Literature Ser.: Vol. 84). 1994. pap. 19.95 (*0-8166-2040-7*); text ed. 49.95 (*0-8166-2039-3*) U of Minn Pr.

Reading Proust Now. Ed. by Mary A. Caws & Eugene Nicole. LC 90-6063. (Reading Plus Ser.: Vol. 8). 316p. (C). 1990. text ed. 89.00 (*0-8204-1239-2*) P Lang Pubng.

Reading Putnam. Ed. by Peter Clark & Bob Hale. (Illus.). 310p. 1994. 55.95 (*0-631-17907-0*) Blackwell Pubs.

Reading Putnam. Ed. by Peter Clarke & Bob Hale. 302p. 1995. pap. 24.95 (*0-631-19995-0*) Blackwell Pubs.

Reading Quilts. Joan Martin. Ed. by J. Friedland & R. Kessler. (Novel-Ties Ser.). 1992. student ed., pap. text ed. 20.95 (*0-88122-856-7*) Lrn Links.

Reading Race: White American Poets & Racial Discourse in the Twentieth Century. Aldon L. Nielsen. LC 88-3942. (South Atlantic Modern Language Association Award Study). 192p. 1990. pap. 15.00 (*0-8203-1273-8*) U of Ga Pr.

Reading Railroad: History of a Coal Age Empire, the 20th Century, Vol. 2. James L. Holton. LC 89-85292. xii, 440p. 1992. 68.00 (*0-9620844-3-3*) Garrigues Hse.

Reading Railroad Vol. 1: History of a Coal-Age Empire: The Nineteenth Century. James L. Holton. LC 89-85292. (Illus.). xiv, 356p. 1989. 65.00 (*0-9620844-1-7*) Garrigues Hse.

"Reading Rainbow" Guide to Children's Books. rev. ed. Twila C. Liggett & Cynthia M. Benfield. (Illus.). 288p. 1996. pap. 14.95 (*0-8065-1796-4*, Citadel Pr) Carol Pub Group.

Reading Rainbow Guide to Children's Books: The 101 Best Titles. Twila C. Liggett & Cynthia Mayer. LC 93-46695. 1994. 19.95 (*1-55972-222-3*, Birch Ln Pr); pap. 12.95 (*0-8065-1493-0*, Birch Ln Pr) Carol Pub Group.

Reading Rawls: Critical Studies on Rawls' "A Theory of Justice" Ed. by Norman Daniels. LC 88-60487. (Series in Philosophy). 408p. 1989. reprint ed. pap. 17.95 (*0-8047-1503-3*) Stanford U Pr.

Reading Raymond Carver. Randolph P. Runyon. LC 91-36790. 246p. 1992. 34.95 (*0-8156-2563-4*) Syracuse U Pr.

Reading Raymond Carver. Randolph P. Runyon. LC 91-36790. 246p. (C). 1993. reprint ed. pap. text ed. 16.95 (*0-8156-2631-2*) Syracuse U Pr.

Reading Readiness, Bk. 1. Joan Hoffman. (I Know It! Bks.). (Illus.). 32p. (J). (ps-1). 1980. student ed. 1.99 (*0-938256-04-1*) Sch Zone Pub Co.

Reading Readiness, Bk. 2. Joan Hoffman. (I Know It! Bks.). (Illus.). 32p. (J). (ps-1). 1980. student ed. 1.99 (*0-938256-05-X*) Sch Zone Pub Co.

Reading Readiness Book: For the New Hebrew & Heritage Siddur Program. Carol Levy. (Illus.). (J). 1995. pap. 4.95 (*0-87441-518-7*) Behrman.

Reading Readiness Program, 2 kits. Sullivan Associates Staff. Incl. Kit No. 1. Letters of the Alphabet. 1972. 328.20 (*0-07-079581-9*); Kit No. 2. Sounds & Letters. 1972. 328.00 (*0-07-079582-7*); write for info. (*0-318-54195-5*) McGraw.

Reading Reading. 3rd ed. Peter L. Spencer. LC 78-128391. (C). 1978. pap. 5.00 (*0-914522-02-7*) Alpha Iota.

Reading Reading: Fiftieth Anniversary Perspectives. Ed. by Malcolm P. Douglass. (Claremont Reading Conference Yearbook Ser.). 241p. 1983. pap. 6.00 (*0-941742-01-6*) Claremont Grad.

***Reading Readings: Essays on Shakespeare Editing in the Eighteenth Century.** Joanna Gondris. LC 97-9794. 1997. write for info. (*0-8386-3712-4*) Fairleigh Dickinson.

Reading Real Books. Robin Campbell. (Rethinking Reading Ser.). 112p. 1992. 24.00 (*0-335-15793-9*, Open Univ Pr); pap. 75.00 (*0-335-15794-7*, Open Univ Pr) Taylor & Francis.

Reading Real Russian, Bk. I. Irene Thompson & Emily Urevich. 320p. (C). 1990. pap. text ed. 39.60 (*0-13-761156-0*) P-H.

Reading Real Russian, Bk. II. Irene Thompson & Emily Urevich. 384p. (C). 1991. pap. text ed. 36.00 (*0-13-761834-4*) P-H.

Reading Realism in Stendhal. Ann Jefferson. (Cambridge Studies in French: No. 22). 288p. 1988. 69.95 (*0-521-26274-7*) Cambridge U Pr.

Reading Recovery: A Guidebook for Teachers in Training. Marie Clay. LC 93-24028. 112p. 1993. pap. text ed. 17.50 (*0-435-08764-9*, 08764) Heinemann.

***Reading Reference Materials.** Martha Cheney. (Real-Life Reading Activities Ser.). (Illus.). 64p. (J). (gr. 4-6). 1996. teacher ed., pap. 7.95 (*1-55799-593-1*, 570) Evan-Moor Corp.

Reading Reinforcers: For the Primary Grades. Imogene Forte. Ed. by Leslie Britt. (Illus.). 96p. (Orig.). 1994. pap. text ed. 9.95 (*0-86530-278-2*) Incentive Pubns.

***Reading Relationships.** Brown. (C). Date not set. pap. write for info. (*0-395-88977-4*) HM.

Reading Rembrandt: Beyond the Word Image Opposition. Mieke Bal. (Studies in New Art History & Criticism). (Illus.). 512p. (C). 1994. pap. text ed. 34.95 (*0-521-46664-4*) Cambridge U Pr.

Reading Renaissance Drama: A Process Approach. Lila Geller & Catherine Gannon. LC 90-24424. (American University Studies: English Language & Literature: Ser. IV, Vol. 115). 254p. (C). 1991. text ed. 43.95 (*0-8204-1261-9*) P Lang Pubng.

Reading Report Card. 72p. 1988. 9.00 (*0-317-67885-X*) Educ Testing Serv.

Reading Rescue. Susan Gillet & Michael Bernard. (C). 1990. 65.00 (*0-86431-054-4*, Pub. by Aust Council Educ Res AT) St Mut.

Reading Research & Librarianship: A History & Anaylsis. Stephen Karetzky. LC 80-1715. (Contributions in Librarianship & Information Science Ser.: No. 36). (Illus.). xxi, 385p. 1982. text ed. 65.00 (*0-313-22226-6*, KRR/, Greenwood Pr) Greenwood.

Reading Research into the Year 2000. Ed. by Anne P. Sweet & Judith I. Anderson. 184p. 1993. text ed. 36.00 (*0-8058-1305-5*) L Erlbaum Assocs.

Reading Resource Book. Mary Jett-Simpson. LC 83-81433. 224p. (Orig.). (J). (ps-3). 1986. pap. 16.95 (*0-89334-095-2*) Humanics Ltd.

Reading Resource Book: Parents & Beginning Reading. Mary Jett-Simpson. LC 83-81433. (Illus.). 224p. 1986. lib. bdg. 26.95 (*0-89334-178-9*, 178-9) Humanics Ltd.

Reading Resource Book: Tried & True Reading Activities for Elementary Students. Virginia N. Fulk. LC 83-83317. 224p. (Orig.). 1984. pap. text ed. 19.95 (*0-918452-68-6*, 686) Learning Pubns.

***Reading Resource Handbook for School Leaders.** Del Patty et al. 425p. (J). (gr. k-6). 1996. pap. 44.95 (*0-926842-50-1*) CG Pubs Inc.

Reading, Responding, & Writing. 2nd ed. Caruso. 1992. teacher ed., pap. text ed. 18.50 (*0-312-03606-X*) St Martin.

Reading, Responding, Writing. 2nd ed. Domenick Caruso & Stephen Weidenborner. LC 91-67515. 256p. (C). 1992. pap. text ed. 19.50 (*0-312-03604-3*) St Martin.

Reading, Responding, Writing. 2nd ed. Domenick Caruso & Stephen Weidenborner. LC 91-67515. 256p. (C). 1992. pap. text ed. 5.00 (*0-312-07219-8*) St Martin.

Reading Response. Ed. by Mike Hayhoe & Stephen Parker. (English, Language & Education Ser.). 192p. 1990. 32.00 (*0-335-09439-2*, Open Univ Pr) Taylor & Francis.

Reading Response Logs. Kooy & Wells. 127p. 1996. pap. text ed. 14.50 (*0-435-07208-0*) Heinemann.

Reading, Rhymes & Recipes: Stories & Recipes Just for Kids. Creative Colleagues Staff. (Illus.). 72p. (J). (gr. 2-6). 1994. pap. 9.00 (*0-9647181-0-3*) Sunshine Herit Pr.

Reading Riddles. Rick Detorie. 1989. 1.95 (*0-8125-7313-7*) Tor Bks.

Reading Rochester. Ed. by Edward Burns. LC 95-15317. 1996. text ed. 39.95 (*0-312-12788-X*) St Martin.

Reading Rodney King - Reading Urban Uprising. Ed. by Robert Gooding-Williams. 256p. (gr. 13). 1993. pap. 16.95 (*0-415-90735-7*, A9972, Routledge NY) Routledge.

Reading Rodney King - Reading Urban Uprising. Ed. by Robert Gooding-Williams. 256p. (C). (gr. 13). 1993. text ed. 59.95 (*0-415-90734-9*, A9968, Routledge NY) Routledge.

***Reading Romans: A Literary & Theological Commentary.** Luke T. Johnson. (Reading the New Testament Ser.). 240p. (Orig.). 1997. pap. 19.95 (*0-8245-1624-9*, Crossrd Herd) Crossroad NY.

Reading Romantics: Texts & Contexts. Peter J. Manning. 336p. 1990. 52.00 (*0-19-505787-2*) OUP.

Reading (Rooks) 1. Rooks. (College ESL Ser.). 1994. pap. 21.95 (*0-8384-4824-0*) Heinle & Heinle.

Reading Rooms: America's Foremost Writers Celebrate Our Public Libraries with Stories, Memoirs, Essays, & Poems. Susan A. Toth & John Coughlan. 512p. 1992. pap. 12.00 (*0-671-74764-9*, WSP) PB.

Reading Rorty: Critical Response to Philosophy & the Mirror of Nature. Ed. by Alan Malachowski. 288p. 1990. pap. 24.95 (*0-631-16149-X*) Blackwell Pubs.

Reading Rousseau in the Nuclear Age. Grace G. Roosevelt. 288p. 1990. 44.95 (*0-87722-679-2*) Temple U Pr.

Reading Russian 1. Anelya Rugaleva. (OSU Foreign Language Publications: No. 7). (Illus.). 249p. (Orig.). (RUS.). (C). 1984. teacher ed., pap. 12.50 (*0-87415-001-9*, 7A); student ed., pap. text ed. 20.50 (*0-87415-000-0*) OSU Foreign Lang.

Reading Russian 2. Anelya Rugaleva et al. (OSU Foreign Language Publications: No. 8). (Illus.). 308p. (Orig.). (RUS.). (C). 1984. teacher ed., pap. 8.50 (*0-87415-003-5*, 8A); student ed., pap. text ed. 25.00 (*0-87415-002-7*) OSU Foreign Lang.

Reading Russian 3. Anelya Rugaleva. (Illus.). 101p. (Orig.). (RUS.). (C). 1986. teacher ed., pap. 11.50 (*0-87415-110-4*, 46A); student ed., pap. text ed. 17.50 (*0-87415-109-0*, 46) OSU Foreign Lang.

Reading Ruth: Contemporary Women Reclaim a Sacred Story. Ed. by Judith A. Kates & Gail T. Reimer. LC 94-9913. 416p. 1996. pap. 12.50 (*0-345-38032-0*) Ballantine.

Reading Sacred Texts Through American Eyes: Biblical Interpretation as Cultural Critique. Charles Mabee. LC 91-14356. (Studies in American Biblical Hermeneutics). 128p. (C). 1991. 24.95 (*0-86554-385-2*, H313); pap. text ed. 16.95 (*0-86554-403-4*, MUP/P095) Mercer Univ Pr.

Reading Saint Benedict: Reflections on the Rule. Adalbert De Vogue. Tr. by Colette Friedlander. LC 93-27072. (Cistercian Studies: No. 151). 1994. 36.95 (*0-87907-651-8*); pap. 24.95 (*0-87907-751-4*) Cistercian Pubns.

Reading Sappho: Contemporary Approaches. Ed. by Ellen Greene. LC 96-13702. (Classics & Contemporary Thought Ser.: Vol. 2). (C). 1996. pap. write for info. (*0-520-20601-0*) U CA Pr.

Reading Sappho: Contemporary Approaches. Ed. by Ellen Greene. LC 96-13702. (Classics & Contemporary Thought Ser.: Vol. 2). 256p. (C). 1997. 40.00 (*0-520-20195-7*) U CA Pr.

Reading Saussure. Roy Harris. 265p. 1987. 29.95 (*0-8126-9049-4*); pap. 18.95 (*0-8126-9050-8*) Open Court.

Reading Science: A Literary, Political & Sociological Analysis. Ben Agger. LC 89-80379. (Illus.). 272p. 1989. text ed. 39.95 (*0-930390-93-8*) Gen Hall.

***Reading Science: Critical & Functional Perspectives on Discourses of Science.** J. R. Martin & Robert Veel. LC 97-21777. 1998. write for info. (*0-415-16789-2*); pap. write for info. (*0-415-16790-6*) Routledge.

Reading Scripture As the Word of God: Practical Approaches & Attitudes. 3rd ed. George Martin. 180p. 1993. pap. 10.99 (*0-89283-152-9*, Charis) Servant.

Reading Seed: Twelve Simple Steps for Preparing Your Infant to Become an Early Reader. Celeste Heiter. 48p. pap. 3.50 (*0-9642658-4-2*) Small Wonder.

Reading Seminar XI: Lacan's Four Fundamental Concepts of Psychoanalysis: The Paris Seminars in English. Ed. by Richard Feldstein et al. LC 93-50120. (SUNY Series in Psychoanalysis & Culture). 291p. 1994. pap. text ed. 19.95 (*0-7914-2148-1*) State U NY Pr.

Reading Seminar XI: Lacan's Four Fundamental Concepts of Psychoanalysis: The Paris Seminars in English. Ed. by Richard Feldstein et al. LC 93-50120. (SUNY Series in Psychoanalysis & Culture). 291p. 1995. text ed. 59.50 (*0-7914-2147-3*) State U NY Pr.

Reading Seminars I & II: Lacan's Return to Freud. Ed. by Richard Feldstein et al. LC 94-12517. (Psychoanalysis & Culture Ser.). 444p. 1996. pap. text ed. 21.95 (*0-7914-2780-3*) State U NY Pr.

Reading Seminars I & II: Lacan's Return to Freud. Ed. by Richard Feldstein et al. LC 94-12517. (SUNY Series in Psychoanalysis & Culture). 444p. 1996. text ed. 64.50 (*0-7914-2779-X*) State U NY Pr.

Reading Serbo-Croatian 1. Biljana Sljivic-Simsic & Robert F. Price. 74p. (Orig.). (CRO & SER.). (C). 1988. teacher ed., pap. 9.50 (*0-87415-153-8*, 62A); student ed., pap. text ed. 55.00 (*0-87415-152-X*, 62) OSU Foreign Lang.

Reading Serbo-Croatian 2. Biljana Sljivic-Simsic & Robert F. Price. (Illus.). 73p. (Orig.). (CRO & SER.). (C). 1988. teacher ed., pap. 9.50 (*0-87415-155-4*, 63A); student ed., pap. text ed. 60.00 (*0-87415-154-6*, 63) OSU Foreign Lang.

Reading Series Four, Quarter Four. Rudy Moore & Betty Moore. (J). (gr. 4). 1994. 8.99 (*0-88062-215-6*) Mott Media.

Reading Series Four, Quarter One. Rudy Moore & Betty Moore. (J). (gr. 4). 1988. pap. 8.99 (*0-88062-212-1*) Mott Media.

Reading Series Four, Quarter Three. Rudy Moore & Betty Moore. (J). (gr. 4). 1988. pap. 8.99 (*0-88062-214-8*) Mott Media.

Reading Series Four, Quarter Two. Rudy Moore & Betty Moore. (J). (gr. 4). 1988. pap. 8.99 (*0-88062-213-X*) Mott Media.

Reading Series One, Quarter Four. Rudy Moore & Betty Moore. (J). (gr. 1). 1991. 8.99 (*0-88062-203-2*) Mott Media.

Reading Series One, Quarter One. Rudy Moore & Betty Moore. (J). (gr. 1). 1988. pap. 8.99 (*0-88062-200-8*) Mott Media.

Reading Series One, Quarter Three. Rudy Moore & Betty Moore. (J). (gr. 1). 1994. pap. 8.99 (*0-88062-202-4*) Mott Media.

Reading Series One, Quarter Two. Rudy Moore & Betty Moore. (J). (gr. 1). 1995. pap. 8.99 (*0-88062-201-6*) Mott Media.

Reading Series Three, Quarter Four. Rudy Moore & Betty Moore. (J). (gr. 3). 1994. 8.99 (*0-88062-211-3*) Mott Media.

Reading Series Three, Quarter One. Rudy Moore & Betty Moore. (J). (gr. 3). 1988. pap. 8.99 (*0-88062-208-3*) Mott Media.

Reading Series Three, Quarter Three. Rudy Moore & Betty Moore. (J). (gr. 3). 1989. pap. 8.99 (*0-88062-210-5*) Mott Media.

Reading Series Three, Quarter Two. Rudy Moore & Betty Moore. (J). (gr. 3). 1988. pap. 8.99 (*0-88062-209-1*) Mott Media.

Reading Series Two, Quarter Four. Rudy Moore & Betty Moore. (J). (gr. 2). 1991. 8.99 (*0-88062-207-5*) Mott Media.

Reading Series Two, Quarter One. Rudy Moore & Betty Moore. (J). (gr. 2). 1988. pap. 8.99 (*0-88062-204-0*) Mott Media.

Reading Series Two, Quarter Three. Rudy Moore & Betty Moore. (J). (gr. 2). 1989. pap. 8.99 (*0-88062-206-7*) Mott Media.

R

R

Reading Series Two, Quarter Two. Rudy Moore & Betty Moore. (J). (gr. 2). 1988. pap. 8.99 (*0-88062-205-9*) Mott Media.

Reading Shakespeare Historically. Lisa Jardine. LC 95-35506. 240p. (C). 1996. pap. 17.95 (*0-415-13490-0*); text ed. 55.00 (*0-415-13489-7*) Routledge.

Reading Shakespeare in Performance: King Lear. James P. Lusardi & June Schlueter. LC 89-46412. (Illus.). 248p. 1991. 37.50 (*0-8386-3394-3*) Fairleigh Dickinson.

Reading Shakespeare on Stage. H. R. Coursen. LC 94-39270. (Illus.). 304p. 1995. 45.00 (*0-87413-538-9*) U Delaware Pr.

Reading Shakespeare's Characters: Rhetoric, Ethics, & Identity. Christy Desmet. LC 92-14742. (Massachusetts Studies in Early Modern Culture). 232p. 1992. 30.00 (*0-87023-807-8*) U of Mass Pr.

***Reading Sight Words.** Jo E. Moore. (Reading & Writing Ser.). (Illus.). 32p. (J). (gr. 1-2). 1997. teacher ed., pap. 2.95 (*1-55799-408-0*, 4010) Evan-Moor Corp.

Reading Signs, Directories, Schedules, Maps, Charts & Graphs: Essential Life Skills. 3rd ed. Carolyn M. Starkey. 64p. 1995. pap. 6.95 (*0-8442-5172-0*) NTC Pub Grp.

Reading Skills. School Zone Publishing Company Staff. (I Know It! Bks.). (Illus.). 32p. (Orig.). 1996. wbk. ed., pap. write for info. (*0-88743-133-X*, 02024) Sch Zone Pub Co.

Reading Skills. 2nd ed. Lynda G. Vern. (C). 1997. pap. text ed. 17.00 (*0-15-502334-9*) HB Coll Pubs.

Reading Skills: Preparing for the TASP Test. Lynda G. Vern. 256p. (C). 1992. pap. text ed. 13.50 (*0-03-073144-5*); pap. text ed. 5.50 (*0-03-073146-1*) HB Coll Pubs.

Reading Skills for College Students. 3rd ed. Ophelia H. Hancock. LC 94-33522. 400p. (C). 1994. pap. text ed. 33.60 (*0-13-225632-0*) P-H.

***Reading Skills for College Students.** 4th ed. Hancock. LC 97-2940. 1997. pap. text ed. 30.67 (*0-13-628371-3*) P-H.

Reading Skills for Law Students. Craig K. Mayfield. 170p. 1980. pap. 14.00 (*0-87215-313-4*) MICHIE.

Reading Skills for Social Science. 1989. 11.95 (*0-19-451230-4*) OUP.

Reading Skills for Successful Living. 3rd ed. Irwin L. Joffe. 360p. (C). 1987. pap. 33.95 (*0-534-07236-4*) Wadsworth Pub.

Reading Skills Grade 1. Elizabeth Strauss. 1996. pap. text ed. 2.25 (*0-88743-135-6*) Sch Zone Pub Co.

Reading Skills Handbook, 6 Vols. Wiener. (C). 1993. pap. 30.76 (*0-395-66146-3*) HM.

Reading Skills Handbook, 6 Vols. alternate ed. Wiener. (C). 1993. pap. 34.36 (*0-395-66145-5*) HM.

***Reading Skills Handbook, 7 Vols.** 7th ed. Harvey S. Wiener & Charles Bazerman. (C). 1996. teacher ed., text ed. 35.43 (*0-395-79796-9*) HM.

Reading Skills Handbook: Testbank, 7 Vols. Wiener. (C). Date not set. suppl. ed., pap. 11.96 (*0-395-79797-7*) HM.

Reading Skills Songbook, Vol. 1: Read, Rapp, & Rock to the Skills of Reading. James Bryer. (Illus.). 48p. (Orig.). (J). (gr. 2-6). 1989. pap. 14.95 incl. audio (*0-9622499-0-4*) Soundbox Pubns.

Reading Smart: A Practical Guide to Fast Effective Reading Skills. Nicholas R. Schaffzin. (Princeton Review Ser.). 1994. pap. 12.00 (*0-679-75361-3*, Villard Bks) Random.

Reading Smarter! More Than 200 Reproducible Activities to Build Reading Proficiency in Grades 7-12. Patricia Osborn. LC 94-34552. 1995. spiral bd. 29.95 (*0-87628-850-6*) Ctr Appl Res.

Reading Southeast Asia. Intro. by Takashi Shiraishi. (Translation Ser.: No. 1). 188p. (Orig.). (C). 1990. pap. text ed. 14.00 (*0-87727-400-2*) Cornell SE Asia.

Reading Specialist. Jack Rudman. (National Teacher Examination Ser.: NT-30). 1994. pap. 23.95 (*0-8373-8440-0*) Nat Learn.

Reading Stanley Elkin. Peter J. Bailey. LC 84-8735. 242p. 1985. text ed. 24.95 (*0-252-01172-4*) U of Ill Pr.

Reading Statistics & Research. 2nd ed. Huck & Cormier. (Illus.). 672p. (C). 1996. text ed. 43.50 (*0-06-500606-2*) Addson-Wesley Educ.

Reading Step-by-Step: A Winning Formula. Charlotte Lenzen. (Illus.). 286p. 1989. ring bd. 89.95 (*0-9623658-3-1*) Chalen Edu Systs.

Reading Stories. 1982. 1.00 (*0-939418-43-6*) Ferguson-Florissant.

***Reading Stories for Comprehension Success: Intermediate Level (Grades 4-6): 45 High-Interest Lessons with Reproducible Selections & Questions That Make Kids Think.** Katherine L. Hall. 340p. 1996. spiral bd. 28.95 (*0-87628-890-5*) Ctr Appl Res.

***Reading Stories for Comprehension Success: Intermediate Level (Grades 4-6): 45 High-Interest Lessons with Reproducible Selections & Questions That Make Kids Think.** Katherine L. Hall. 340p. 1996. pap. 28.50 (*0-87628-889-1*) Ctr Appl Res.

***Reading Stories for Comprehension Success: 45 High-Interest Lessons with Reproducible Selections & Questions That Make Kids Think.** Katherine L. Hall. LC 96-32585. 1996. pap. write for info. (*0-87628-755-0*); pap. write for info. (*0-87628-888-3*) Ctr Appl Res.

Reading Strategies. Laura Robb. 1996. pap. 12.95 (*0-590-25111-2*) Scholastic Inc.

Reading Strategies: Focus on Comprehension. 2nd rev. ed. Yetta M. Goodman et al. LC 95-49164. 256p. (Orig.). 1996. pap. text ed. 24.95 (*1-878450-86-7*) R Owen Pubs.

Reading Strategies & Practices. 4th ed. Tierney & John E. Readence. 1994. pap. text ed. 52.00 (*0-205-16285-1*) Allyn.

Reading Strategies for the Primary Grades. Kim Katz & Claudia Katz. Ed. by Warren W. Lewis. LC 91-3238. (Teaching Resources in the ERIC Database (TRIED) Ser.). (Illus.). 102p. (Orig.). 1991. pap. 14.95 (*0-927516-23-3*) ERIC-REC.

Reading Success: A Specialized Literacy Program for Learners with Challenging Reading Needs. Lorna Idol. (Orig.). 1996. pap. text ed. write for info. (*0-89079-700-5*, 7953) PRO-ED.

Reading Success for Children: What Every Parent Should Know. Joyce Corbin. 93p. (Orig.). (J). 1992. pap. 8.95 (*0-9630773-0-9*) Learn Strat.

Reading Success for Each Child Every Day. Janet L. Prange & David L. Zufelt. (Illus.). 184p. 1980. pap. text ed. 14.95 (*0-89641-037-4*) American Pr.

Reading Survival Skills: For the Middle Grades. Imogene Forte. Ed. by Leslie Britt. (Illus.). 80p. (Orig.). 1994. pap. text ed. 9.95 (*0-86530-279-0*) Incentive Pubns.

***Reading Tasks Text.** Benitez. Date not set. pap. text ed. write for info. (*0-582-00512-4*, Pub. by Longman UK) Longman.

Reading Tea Leaves. Highland Seer. LC 94-31884. 1995. 12.00 (*0-517-70034-4*, C P Pubs) Crown Pub Group.

Reading Teacher's Almanack: Hundreds of Practical Ideas, Games, Activities, Bulletin Boards, & Reproducibles for Every Month of the Year. Patricia T. Muncy. 272p. 1991. 27.95 (*0-87628-791-7*) P-H.

Reading Teacher's Book of Lists. Edward B. Fry et al. 195p. 1984. 17.50 (*0-13-762112-4*, Busn) P-H.

***Reading Teacher's Book of Lists.** 3rd ed. Edward B. Fry et al. 320p. 1996. pap. 29.50 (*0-13-034893-7*) P-H.

Reading Teacher's Book of Lists. 3rd ed. Edward Bernard Fry et al. LC 93-9256. 1993. 29.95 (*0-13-762014-4*) P-H.

Reading Teacher's Complete Diagnosis & Correction Manual. Wilma H. Miller. 256p. 1988. spiral bd. 29.95 (*0-87628-772-0*) Ctr Appl Res.

Reading Teacher's Complete Diagnosis & Correction Manual. Wilma H. Miller. 296p. 1988. pap. 24.95 (*0-318-35308-3*) P-H.

Reading Technical Books. 2nd ed. Anne Eisenberg. 260p. (C). 1989. pap. text ed. 24.00 (*0-13-753435-3*) P-H.

Reading Television. John Fiske & John Hartley. (New Accents Ser.). 224p. (C). 1978. pap. 13.95 (*0-415-04291-7*, NO. 2781) Routledge Chapman & Hall.

Reading Terminal & Market: Philadelphia's Historic Gateway & Grand Convention Center. Carol M. Highsmith & James L. Holton. (Illus.). 96p. (Orig.). 1994. 29.95 (*0-9620877-1-8*); pap. 19.95 (*0-685-71568-X*) Chls Pub Inc.

***Reading Terminal Market Cookbook.** Ann Hazan & Irina M. Smith. LC 96-47964. (Illus.). 240p. (Orig.). 1997. pap. 14.95 (*0-940159-33-3*) Camino Bks.

***Reading Test: Georgia Regents'** 2nd ed. Linda Arthur. 230p. (C). 1996. pap. text ed. 29.34 (*0-7872-2187-2*) Kendall-Hunt.

Reading Tests & Reviews II: A Monograph Consisting of the Reading Sections of the Seventh Mental Measurements Yearbook (1972) & Tests in Print II (1974) Ed. by Oscar K. Buros. LC 70-13495. 285p. reprint ed. pap. 81.30 (*0-685-15587-0*, 2026563) Bks Demand.

Reading Tests & Teachers: A Practical Guide. Ed. by Robert Schreiner. LC 79-17271. (Illus.). 89p. (Orig.). reprint ed. pap. 25.40 (*0-8357-8653-6*, 2035098) Bks Demand.

Reading Tests-Reinhart Reader. Jean Wyrick. (C). 1993. pap. text ed. 3.00 (*0-03-098260-X*) HB Coll Pubs.

Reading Textbooks. Wiener. (C). Date not set. pap. 31.16 (*0-395-71868-6*) HM.

***Reading Textbooks.** annot. ed. Harvey S. Wiener & Charles Bazerman. (C). 1997. teacher ed., text ed. 32.36 (*0-395-83867-3*) HM.

Reading Texts: An Introduction to Strategies of Interpretation. Danuta Fjellestad & Eleanor Wikborg. 190p. 1995. 33.00 (*82-00-22696-4*) Scandnvan Univ Pr.

Reading Texts: Reading, Responding, Writing. Kathleen A. McCormick et al. LC 86-82150. 320p. (C). 1987. pap. text ed. 31.96 (*0-669-09564-8*) HM College Div.

Reading Texts: Teaching Suggestions. Danuta Fjellestad & Eleanor Wikborg. 110p. 1995. 25.00 (*82-00-22695-6*) Scandnvan Univ Pr.

Reading Texts for Students of German: Twenty Years of the AATG National Examination. K. Eckhard Kuhn-Osius. 142p. (Orig.). (GER.). 1990. pap. text ed. 10.95 (*0-942017-06-4*) Amer Assn Teach German.

Reading Thackeray. Michael Lund. LC 88-1295. 176p. 1988. 24.95 (*0-8143-1987-4*) Wayne St U Pr.

Reading Thackeray. Michael Lund. LC 88-1295. 176p. (C). 1992. pap. text ed. 15.95 (*0-8143-1988-2*) Wayne St U Pr.

Reading the African Novel. Simon Gikandi. LC 86-14998. (African Writers Ser.). 172p. (Orig.). (C). 1987. pap. 17.50 (*0-435-08018-0*, 08018) Heinemann.

Reading the Apostolic Fathers: An Introduction. Clayton Jefford & Lewis Amezaga, Jr. 160p. 1996. pap. 16.95 (*1-56563-154-4*) Hendrickson MA.

Reading the Archive: On Texts & Institutions, Yale French Studies, Vol. 77. E. S. Burt. 1990. pap. text ed. 17.00 (*0-300-04540-9*) Yale U Pr.

Reading, the Arts & the Creation of Meaning. Ed. by Elliot W. Eisner. (Illus.). 159p. (C). 1978. 15.00 (*0-937652-21-0*) Natl Art Ed.

Reading the Bible. Geoffrey Thomas. 1991. reprint ed. pap. 1.95 (*0-85151-318-2*) Banner of Truth.

***Reading the Bible: An Introduction.** Richard Walsh. 350p. (C). 1998. 25.00 (*0-940121-43-3*, H313, Cross Roads Bks) Cross Cultural Pubns.

Reading the Bible: Intention, Text, Interpretation. Robert D. Lane. 222p. (Orig.). (C). 1993. pap. text ed. 24.50 (*0-8191-9114-0*) U Pr of Amer.

Reading the Bible As History. Theodore Plantinga. 110p. (Orig.). 1980. pap. 4.25 (*0-919532-58-6*) Dordt Coll Pr.

Reading the Bible Book by Book: An Introductory Study Guide to the Separate Books of the Bible with Apocrypha. Richard H. Hiers. LC 87-45893. 256p. 1988. pap. 18.00 (*0-8006-2074-7*, 1-2074, Fortress Pr) Augsburg Fortress.

Reading the Bible for Yourself. David Tavendor. 32p. (Orig.). 1995. pap. 3.00 (*1-880573-24-5*) Grace WI.

Reading the Bible Together. Publications Staff Veritas. 1989. pap. 30.00 (*1-85390-088-5*, Pub. by Veritas IE) St Mut.

Reading the Body: Ohashi's Book of Oriental Diagnosis. Watari Ohashi & Tom Monte. 156p. (Orig.). 1991. pap. 18.95 (*0-14-019362-6*, Arkana) Viking Penguin.

Reading the Body Politic: Feminist Criticism & Latin American Women Writers. Amy Kaminsky. LC 92-16023. 192p. (C). 1992. pap. 13.95 (*0-8166-1948-4*) U of Minn Pr.

Reading the Book: Making the Bible a Timeless Text. Burton L. Visotzky. 264p. 1996. pap. 13.00 (*0-8052-1072-5*) Random Hse Value.

Reading the Book of Himself: Narrative Strategies in the Works of James Joyce. Michael P. Gillespie. 300p. 1989. text ed. 47.50 (*0-8142-0488-0*) Ohio St U Pr.

Reading the Book of Nature: A Phenomenological Study of Creative Expression in Science & Painting. Edwin Jones. LC 88-13092. (Series in Continental Thought: Vol. 14). 190p. 1988. 29.95 (*0-8214-0908-5*) Ohio U Pr.

Reading the Book of Nature: An Introduction to the Philosophy of Science. Peter Kosso. 224p. (C). 1992. text ed. 49.95 (*0-521-41675-2*); pap. text ed. 14.95 (*0-521-42682-0*) Cambridge U Pr.

Reading the Building Code: A Short Hermeneutic. Joseph P. McEvoy. 89p. (C). 1991. pap. text ed. 20.00 (*0-89801-020-9*) NE Univ Pub.

Reading the Changes. Eleanor Anderson. (Rethinking Reading Ser.). 128p. 1992. 80.00 (*0-335-15643-6*, Open Univ Pr); pap. 27.00 (*0-335-15642-8*, Open Univ Pr) Taylor & Francis.

Reading the Chest Radiograph: A Physiologic Approach. Milne & Pistolesi. (Illus.). 383p. (C). (gr. 13). 1992. text ed. 125.00 (*0-8016-3303-6*) Mosby Yr Bk.

Reading the Classics & Paradise Lost. William Porter. LC 92-24241. xx, 222p. 1993. text ed. 35.00 (*0-8032-3706-5*) U of Nebr Pr.

Reading the Corinthian Correspondence: An Introduction. Kevin Quast. LC 94-15074. 288p. 1994. pap. 14.95 (*0-8091-3481-0*) Paulist Pr.

Reading the Difference: Gender & Reading in Elementary Classrooms. Ed. by Myra Barrs & Sue Pidgeon. (Illus.). 144p. (Orig.). (C). 1994. pap. text ed. 17.00 (*1-57110-005-9*) Stenhse Pubs.

Reading the Easter Gospels. Lionel Swain. 140p. (Orig.). 1993. pap. 9.95 (*0-8146-5699-4*) Liturgical Pr.

***Reading the Environment.** LC 97-8894. 1997. pap. text ed. write for info. (*0-435-08383-X*) Heinemann.

Reading the Environment. Ed. by Melissa Walker. (C). 1994. pap. text ed. 27.95 (*0-393-96509-0*) Norton.

Reading the Environment. Ed. by Melissa Walker. (C). 1994. pap. text ed. write for info. (*0-393-96510-4*) Norton.

Reading the Eye, Pulse & Tongue for the Indicated Remedy. Eli G. Jones. Ed. by Wade Boyle. 99p. (Orig.). 1990. pap. 10.00 (*0-9623518-2-2*) BNP.

Reading the Fights. Ed. by Joyce Carol Oates & Daniel Halpen. 1988. 17.95 (*0-8050-0510-2*) H Holt & Co.

Reading the Fights. Joyce Carol Oates. (Spectator Ser.). 1990. pap. 9.95 (*0-685-46179-3*) P-H.

Reading the Financial Pages. Jeffrey B. Little. (Basic Investor's Library). (Illus.). 48p. 1988. lib. bdg. 12.95 (*1-55546-623-0*) Chelsea Hse.

Reading the Financial Pages. Jeffrey B. Little & Lucien Rhodes. 1977. pap. 2.95 (*0-8306-3004-X*, 30004, Liberty Hse) TAB Bks.

***Reading the Fire: Essays in the Traditional Indian Literatures of the Far West.** Jarold Ramsey. LC 82-21775. 272p. 1983. reprint ed. pap. 77.60 (*0-608-03476-2*, 2064186) Bks Demand.

Reading the Forested Landscape: A Natural History of New England. Tom Wessels. LC 96-48144. (Illus.). 200p. 1997. 24.95 (*0-88150-378-9*) Countryman.

Reading the Fractures of Genesis: Historical & Literary Approaches. David M. Carr. LC 95-46693. 424p. 1996. 39.00 (*0-664-22071-1*) Westminster John Knox.

Reading the French Gardens: Story & History. Denise Le Dantec & Jean-Pierre Le Dantec. Tr. by Jessica Levine. (Illus.). 288p. (C). 1993. pap. 14.95 (*0-262-62087-1*) MIT Pr.

Reading the French Gardens: Story & History. Denise Le Dentec & Jean-Pierre Le Dantec. Tr. by Jessica Levine from FRE. (Illus.). 296p. 1990. 27.50 (*0-262-12144-1*) MIT Pr.

Reading the Gospel of John: An Introduction. Kevin Quast. LC 91-32111. 176p. 1992. pap. 11.95 (*0-8091-3297-4*) Paulist Pr.

Reading the Gospels with the Church: From Christmas Through Easter. Raymond E. Brown. (Orig.). 1996. pap. 7.95 (*0-86716-268-6*, B2686) St Anthony Mess Pr.

Reading the Ground: The Poetry of Thomas Kinsella. Brian John. LC 95-17095. 275p. 1996. 44.95 (*0-8132-0837-8*) Cath U Pr.

Reading the Ground: The Poetry of Thomas Kinsella. Brian John. LC 95-17095. 275p. 1997. pap. 27.95 (*0-8132-0838-6*) Cath U Pr.

***Reading the Irish Landscape.** Frank Mitchell & Michael Ryan. (Illus.). 380p. 1997. pap. 29.95 (*0-946172-54-4*) R Rinehart.

***Reading The Irish Landscape.** 3rd ed. Frank Mitchell. 1997. pap. text ed. 29.95 (*1-86059-055-1*) R Rinehart.

Reading the Japanese Mind: The Realities Behind Their Thoughts & Actions. Robert M. March. 208p. 1996. 25.00 (*4-7700-2044-9*) Kodansha.

Reading the Landscape. Valenti. (C). 1995. teacher ed., pap. text ed. 28.00 (*0-15-502175-3*) HB Coll Pubs.

Reading the Landscape. Valenti. (C). 1995. pap. text ed. 28.75 (*0-15-501432-3*) HB Coll Pubs.

Reading the Letters of Edith Wharton. Arthur Zilversmit. 114p. 1991. pap. text ed. 24.00 (*2-88124-515-3*) Gordon & Breach.

Reading the Literatures of Asian America. Ed. by Shirley Geok-Lin Lim & Amy Ling. LC 92-16844. (Asian American History & Culture Ser.). 384p. (C). 1992. 54.95 (*0-87722-935-X*); pap. 19.95 (*0-87722-936-8*) Temple U Pr.

Reading the Lives of Others. David Bartholomae. 1994. pap. text ed. 17.50 (*0-312-11511-3*); teacher ed., pap. text ed. 5.00 (*0-312-11728-0*) St Martin.

Reading the Lives of Others. David Bartholomae & Anthony Petrosky. 288p. 1995. pap. 10.64 (*0-615-00213-7*) St Martin.

Reading the Medical Record. Mary D. Litchford & Laura Yordy. 1995. 139.00 (*1-880989-40-9*); 139.00 (*1-880989-41-7*); 139.00 (*1-880989-42-5*); 139.00 (*1-880989-43-3*) Case Sftware.

Reading the Medical Record. rev. ed. Mary D. Litchford & Laura Yordy. 1995. pap. 6.00 (*1-880989-45-X*) Case Sftware.

***Reading the Mind.** Sally Shaywirtz. 1998. pap. write for info. (*0-679-78159-5*, Vin) Random.

Reading the Mind of God: In Search of the Principle of Universality. James S. Trefil. (Illus.). 240p. 1990. pap. 9.95 (*0-385-41566-4*) Doubleday.

Reading the Modern Chinese Short Story. Ed. by Theodore Huters. LC 90-8088. (Studies on Modern China). 218p. (C). (gr. 13). 1990. 59.95 (*0-87332-572-9*, East Gate Bk); pap. 27.95 (*0-87332-710-1*, East Gate Bk) M E Sharpe.

Reading the Morte Darthur see Introduction to Malory

Reading the Movies: Twelve Great Films on Video & How to Teach Them. William V. Costanzo. (Illus.). 201p. (C). 1992. pap. 14.95 (*0-8141-3910-8*) NCTE.

Reading the Muslim Mind. Hassan Hathout. LC 94-46150. 1994. write for info. (*0-89259-156-0*); pap. write for info. (*0-89259-157-9*) Am Trust Pubns.

***Reading the New Testament.** John M. Court. LC 96-33159. (New Testament Readings Ser.). 192p. (C). 1997. pap. write for info. (*0-415-10368-1*); text ed. write for info. (*0-415-10367-3*) Routledge.

Reading the New Testament. Patrick Grant. LC 91-1051. 171p. reprint ed. pap. 48.80 (*0-7837-0515-8*, 2040839) Bks Demand.

Reading the New Testament: An Introduction. 2nd rev. ed. Pheme Perkins. 368p. 1988. pap. 10.95 (*0-8091-2939-6*) Paulist Pr.

Reading the New Testament: Methods of Interpretation. Christopher Tuckett. LC 86-46429. 200p. 1987. pap. text ed. 15.00 (*0-8006-2058-5*, Fortress Pr) Augsburg Fortress.

Reading the New Testament for Understanding. Robert G. Hoerber. 192p. 1986. pap. 8.99 (*0-570-03988-6*, 12-3016) Concordia.

Reading the News. Ed. by Robert K. Manoff & Michael Schudson. LC 86-72639. 256p. 1987. pap. 11.16 (*0-394-74649-X*) Pantheon.

Reading the Newspaper. Ed. by Jamestown Publishers Staff. 1987. pap. 15.93 (*0-8092-0057-0*) Jamestown Pubs.

Reading the Newspaper: Advanced Level. Karen K. Allen & Margery S. Miller. 190p. (Orig.). (YA). (gr. 9-12). 1989. pap. text ed. 14.96 (*0-89061-500-4*) Jamestown Pubs.

Reading the Newspaper: Middle Level. Margery S. Miller & Karen K. Allan. (Illus.). (Orig.). 1987. pap. text ed. 14.56 (*0-89061-480-6*) Jamestown Pubs.

***Reading the Night Sky.** Margo Stever. 36p. 1996. 5.00 (*1-890044-06-7*) Riverstone PA.

Reading the Odyssey: Selected Interpretive Essays. Ed. & Intro. by Seth L. Schein. LC 95-10938. 288p. 1996. text ed. 49.50 (*0-691-04440-6*) Princeton U Pr.

Reading the Odyssey: Selected Interpretive Essays. Seth L. Schein. 288p. (C). 1996. pap. text ed. 17.95 (*0-691-04439-2*) Princeton U Pr.

Reading the Old Testament: An Introduction. Lawrence E. Boadt. LC 84-60723. 416p. (Orig.). (C). 1984. pap. 14.95 (*0-8091-2631-1*) Paulist Pr.

Reading the Old Testament: An Introduction to the Hebrew Bible. Barry L. Bandstra. LC 94-13210. 576p. 1995. pap. 53.95 (*0-534-21354-5*) Wadsworth Pub.

Reading the Old Testament: Method in Biblical Study. John Barton. LC 84-3640. 272p. (C). 1984. pap. 18.00 (*0-664-24555-2*, Westminster) Westminster John Knox.

***Reading the Old Testament: Method in Biblical Study.** enl. rev. ed. John Barton. 312p. 1997. pap. 25.00 (*0-664-25724-0*) Westminster John Knox.

Reading the Other: Novels & the Problem of Other Minds. Carol D. Rifelj. 250p. (C). 1992. text ed. 44.50 (*0-472-10340-7*) U of Mich Pr.

Reading the Outdoors at Night. Vinson Brown. LC 82-1949. (Illus.). 192p. 1982. reprint ed. pap. 12.95 (*0-8117-2187-6*) Stackpole.

Reading the Past: Current Approaches to Interpretation in Archaeology. 2nd ed. Ian Hodder. (Illus.). 226p. (C). 1991. pap. text ed. 15.95 (*0-521-40957-8*) Cambridge U Pr.

Reading the Past: Current Approaches to Interpretation in Archaeology. 2nd ed. Ian Hodder. (Illus.). 226p. (C). 1991. text ed. 44.95 (*0-521-40142-9*) Cambridge U Pr.

Reading the Past: Essays on Medieval Literature & Society. John Scattergood. 310p. 1995. 55.00 (*1-85182-189-9*, Pub. by Four Cts Pr IE) Intl Spec Bk.

An Asterisk (*) at the beginning of an entry indicates that the title is appearing in BIP for the first time.

Reading the Past in Late Antiquity. Ed. by Graeme Clarke. 370p. 1990. 39.00 (*0-08-034407-0*, Pergamon Pr) Elsevier.

Reading the Popular. John Fiske. (Illus.). 220p. 1989. pap. 15.95 (*0-415-07875-X*, Routledge NY) Routledge.

Reading the Popular. John Fiske. 224p. 1989. text ed. 44.95 (*0-04-445436-8*); pap. text ed. 14.95 (*0-04-445437-6*) Routledge Chapman & Hall.

Reading the Portraits of Queen Elizabeth I. Elizabeth W. Pomeroy. LC 88-34623. (Illus.). 98p. (C). 1989. lib. bdg. 27.50 (*0-208-02189-2*, Archon Bks) Shoe String.

Reading the Postmodern Polity: Political Theory As Textual Practice. Michael J. Shapiro. 288p. (C). 1991. text ed. 39.95 (*0-8166-1964-6*); pap. text ed. 16.95 (*0-8166-1965-4*) U of Minn Pr.

*__Reading "The Prostitute" Appearance, Place, & Time in British & Irish Press Stories of Prostitution.__ Lorna Ryan. (Illus.). 286p. 1997. text ed. 59.95 (*1-85972-539-2*, Pub. by Ashgate UK) Ashgate Pub Co.

Reading the Psalms As a Book. Norman Whybray. (JSOTS Ser.: No. 222). 250p. 1996. 49.00 (*1-85075-622-8*, Pub. by Sheffield Acad UK) CUP Services.

Reading the Rabbis: The Talmud as Literature. David Kraemer. 192p. 1996. 29.95 (*0-19-509623-1*) OUP.

Reading the Ranaissance: Culture, Poetics, & Drama. Ed. by Jonathan Hart. LC 95-25955. (Studies in the Renaissance: No. 4). 304p. 1996. text ed. 55.00 (*0-8153-2355-7*, H1986) Garland.

*__Reading the Red Island: Travel Writing & Maps of Madagascar.__ Karen A. Korn. (Winner Graduate Term Paper Competitions Ser.). 40p. 1994. pap. 2.00 (*0-941934-71-3*) Indiana Africa.

Reading the Riot Act: The Magistracy, the Police & the Army in Civil Disorder. Richard Vogler. (New Directions in Criminology Ser.). 192p. 1991. 95.00 (*0-335-15185-X*, Open Univ Pr); pap. 39.00 (*0-335-15184-1*, Open Univ Pr) Taylor & Francis.

*__Reading the River: A Voyage down the Yukon.__ John Hildebrand. LC 96-49088. (Illus.). 260p. 1997. reprint ed. 17.95 (*0-299-15494-7*) U of Wis Pr.

Reading the Road: U. S. 40 & the American Landscape. rev. ed. Thomas J. Schlereth. LC 96-4486. (Illus.). 160p. 1997. pap. text ed. 24.95 (*0-87049-945-9*) U of Tenn Pr.

Reading the Romance: Women, Patriarchy & Popular Literature. 2nd ed. Janice A. Radway. LC 91-50284. x, 296p. (C). 1991. reprint ed. pap. 12.95 (*0-8078-4349-0*) U of NC Pr.

Reading the Romantic Heroine: Text, History, Ideology. Leslie W. Rabine. LC 85-13955. (Women & Culture Ser.). 238p. 1985. reprint ed. pap. 67.90 (*0-7837-5653-4*, 2059078) Bks Demand.

Reading the Russian Language: A Guide for Librarians & Other Professionals. Rosalind Kent. LC 74-81799. (Books in Library & Information Science: No. 9). 245p. reprint ed. pap. 69.90 (*0-7837-0764-9*, 2041078) Bks Demand.

Reading the Shape of Nature: Comparative Zoology at the Agassiz Museum. Mary P. Winsor. LC 91-8742. (Science & Its Conceptual Foundations Ser.). (Illus.). 342p. 1991. pap. text ed. 26.95 (*0-226-90215-3*); lib. bdg. 60.00 (*0-226-90214-5*) U Ch Pr.

Reading the Shape of the World: Toward an International Cultural Studies. Richard Dienst. Ed. by Henry Schwarz. (C). 1996. pap. text ed. 24.00 (*0-8133-2877-2*) Westview.

*__Reading the Signs: A Sensible Approach to Revelation & Other Apocalyptic Writings.__ T. C. Smith. LC 97-7919. 1997. write for info. (*1-57312-156-8*) Smyth & Helwys.

Reading the Signs of the Times: Resources for Social & Cultural Analysis. Ed. by T. Howland Sanks & John A. Coleman. LC 92-42017. 240p. 1993. pap. 14.95 (*0-8091-3377-6*) Paulist Pr.

Reading the Sky. Sarah Litsey. LC 89-84745. 80p. 1989. 9.00 (*0-8233-0458-2*) Golden Quill.

Reading the Social Body. Ed. by Catherine B. Burroughs & Jeffrey D. Ehrenreich. LC 92-40753. (Illus.). 285p. 1993. pap. 14.95 (*0-87745-402-7*); text ed. 35.00 (*0-87745-401-9*) U of Iowa Pr.

*__Reading the Splendid Body: Gender & Consumerism in Eighteenth-Century British Writing on India.__ Nandini Bhattacharya. LC 97-5222. 1997. write for info. (*0-87413-612-1*) U Delaware Pr.

Reading the Sports Page: A Guide to Understanding Sports Statistics. Jeremy R. Feinberg. LC 92-18972. (Illus.). 80p. (YA). (gr. 6 up). 1992. lib. bdg. 12.95 (*0-02-734420-7*, Mac Bks Young Read) S&S Childrens.

*__Reading "The Sun Also Rises" Hemingway's Political Unconscious.__ Marc D. Baldwin. (Modern American Literature Ser.: Vol. 4). 168p. (C). 1997. 39.95 (*0-8204-3033-1*) P Lang Pubng.

*__Reading the Talmud: A Woman's Approach.__ Judith Hauptman. (Radical Traditions Ser.). 1997. text ed. 24.00 (*0-8133-3400-4*) Westview.

Reading the Tarot: Understanding the Cards of Destiny. Leo L. Martello. LC 89-494121. (Illus.). 208p. (Orig.). pap. 8.95 (*0-89529-441-9*) Avery Pub.

Reading the Vampire. Ken Gelder. LC 93-44485. (Popular Fictions Ser.). 176p. (C). (gr. 13). 1994. pap. 16.95 (*0-415-08013-4*, B4327); text ed. 59.95 (*0-415-08012-6*, B4323) Routledge.

Reading the Voice: Native American Oral Poetry on the Written Page. Paul Zolbrod. LC 94-42708. 160p. (C). 1995. 25.00 (*0-87480-457-4*) U of Utah Pr.

Reading "The Waste Land" Modernism & the Limits of Interpretation. Jewel S. Brooker & Joseph Bentley. LC 89-36484. 256p. (C). 1990. pap. 16.95 (*0-87023-803-5*) U of Mass Pr.

*__Reading the Water.__ Charles H. Webb. 96p. 1997. pap. 10.95 (*1-55553-325-6*) NE U Pr.

Reading the Water: A Fly Fisher's Handbook for Finding Trout in All Types of Water. Dave Hughes. LC 88-2195. (Illus.). 224p. (Orig.). 1988. pap. 14.95 (*0-8117-2263-5*) Stackpole.

Reading the Water: Stories & Essays of Flyfishing & Life. Mallory Burton. LC 88-21851. 256p. (Orig.). 1995. pap. 13.95 (*1-879628-10-4*) Keokee ID.

Reading the West. Brown. 1997. text ed. 35.00 (*0-312-16373-8*) St Martin.

*__Reading the West.__ Brown. 1997. pap. text ed. 8.50 (*0-312-13761-3*) St Martin.

Reading the West: New Essays on the Literature of the American West. Ed. by Michael Kowalewski. (Studies in American Literature & Culture: No. 98). (Illus.). 225p. (C). 1996. text ed. 64.95 (*0-521-45061-6*); pap. text ed. 22.95 (*0-521-56559-6*) Cambridge U Pr.

Reading the West - Writing the East: Studies in Comparative Literature & Culture. E. San Juan, Jr. LC 91-45196. (American University Studies: Comparative Literature: Ser. III, Vol. 44). 254p. (Orig.). (C). 1992. text ed. 29.95 (*0-8204-1841-2*) P Lang Pubng.

Reading the Wind: The Literature of the Vietnam War. Timothy J. Lomperis. LC 86-23982. xii, 174p. 1986. 36.95 (*0-8223-0705-7*); pap. text ed. 17.95 (*0-8223-0749-9*) Duke.

Reading the Wisconsin Landscape: A Traveler's Guide. Dean W. Proctor. (Illus.). 180p. 1998. pap. 14.95 (*1-879483-30-0*) Prairie Oak Pr.

Reading the Wood: Projects from a Master Woodworker. Michael Elkan. LC 95-44149. 128p. 1996. pap. 19.95 (*0-8069-4274-6*) Sterling.

Reading the World: Selected Writings, 1935-1976, Vol. 1. Northrop Frye. Ed. by Robert D. Denham. LC 90-45974. 416p. (C). 1990. text ed. 72.00 (*0-8204-1214-7*) P Lang Pubng.

Reading the World with Folktales. Nancy Polette. (Illus.). 124p. (Orig.). (J). (gr. 2-4). 1993. pap. 12.95 (*1-879287-19-6*) Pieces of Lrning.

Reading the Written Image: Verbal Play, Interpretation, & the Roots of Iconophobia. Christopher Collins. 224p. 1991. 30.00 (*0-271-00763-X*) Pa St U Pr.

Reading Their World: The Young Adult Novel in the Classroom. Ed. by Virginia R. Monseau & Gary M. Salvner. LC 92-22108. (Young Adult Literature Ser.). 200p. (YA). (gr. 6 up). 1992. pap. text ed. 21.50 (*0-86709-306-4*, 0306) Boynton Cook Pubs.

Reading, Then Writing: From Source to Essay. Thayle Anderson & Kent Forrester. 1992. pap. text ed. write for info. (*0-07-001957-6*) McGraw.

Reading Theory: An Introduction to Lacan, Derrida & Kristeva. Michael Payne. (Illus.). 250p. (C). 1993. pap. 22.95 (*0-631-18289-6*) Blackwell Pubs.

*__Reading Therapy.__ Ed. by Jean M. Clarke & Eileen Bostle. LC 88-19750. 230p. 1988. reprint ed. pap. 65.60 (*0-608-02482-1*, 2063125) Bks Demand.

Reading Thinker Sheets. Becky Daniel. 64p. (J). (gr. 4-8). 1989. 8.99 (*0-86653-501-2*, GA1097) Good Apple.

Reading, Thinking & Caring Annotated Bibliography: The Literature Project, Grades K-3. Developmental Studies Center Staff. (Reading, Thinking & Caring Ser.). 48p. (Orig.). 1995. pap. 11.00 (*1-885603-57-6*) Develop Studies.

Reading, Thinking & Caring Program Manual: The Literature Project, Grades K-3. Developmental Studies Center Staff. (Reading, Thinking & Caring Ser.). 80p. (Orig.). 1995. pap. 19.00 (*1-885603-65-7*) Develop Studies.

Reading, Thinking & Caring Teacher's Guide to "A Bargain for Frances" Partner Unit, Grade 2. Developmental Studies Center Staff. (Reading, Thinking & Caring Ser.). 24p. (Orig.). 1996. pap. 13.95 (*1-885603-95-9*) Develop Studies.

Reading, Thinking & Caring Teacher's Guide to "A Boy, A Dog & A Frog" Partner Unit, Grade K. Developmental Studies Center Staff. (Reading, Thinking & Caring Ser.). 24p. (Orig.). 1996. pap. 13.95 (*1-885603-84-3*) Develop Studies.

Reading, Thinking & Caring Teacher's Guide to "A Chair for My Mother" Partner Unit, Grade 2. Developmental Studies Center Staff. (Reading, Thinking & Caring Ser.). 24p. (Orig.). 1996. pap. 13.95 (*1-885603-96-7*) Develop Studies.

Reading, Thinking & Caring Teacher's Guide to "A Fruit & Vegetable Man" Read Aloud Unit, Grade 2. Developmental Studies Center Staff. (Reading, Thinking & Caring Ser.). 24p. (Orig.). 1996. teacher ed., pap. 13.95 (*1-57621-127-4*) Develop Studies.

Reading, Thinking & Caring Teacher's Guide to "A Place for Grace" Read Aloud Unit, Grade 3. Developmental Studies Center Staff. (Reading, Thinking & Caring Ser.). 24p. (Orig.). 1996. teacher ed., pap. 13.95 (*1-57621-130-4*) Develop Studies.

Reading, Thinking & Caring Teacher's Guide to "Alfie Gives a Hand" Read Aloud Unit, Grade K. Developmental Studies Center Staff. (Reading, Thinking & Caring Ser.). 24p. (Orig.). 1996. teacher ed., pap. 13.95 (*1-57621-012-X*) Develop Studies.

Reading, Thinking & Caring Teacher's Guide to "Amos & Boris" Read Aloud Unit, Grade 2. Developmental Studies Center Staff. (Reading, Thinking & Caring Ser.). 24p. (Orig.). 1996. teacher ed., pap. 13.95 (*1-57621-030-8*) Develop Studies.

Reading, Thinking & Caring Teacher's Guide to "Amy's Goose" Read Aloud Unit, Grade 1. Developmental Studies Center Staff. (Reading, Thinking & Caring Ser.). 24p. (Orig.). 1996. teacher ed., pap. 13.95 (*1-57621-020-0*) Develop Studies.

Reading, Thinking & Caring Teacher's Guide to "Arthur's Funny Money" Partner Unit, Grade 2. Developmental Studies Center Staff. (Reading, Thinking & Caring Ser.). 24p. (Orig.). 1996. pap. 13.95 (*1-885603-94-0*) Develop Studies.

Reading, Thinking & Caring Teacher's Guide to "Best Friends for Frances" Read Aloud Unit, Grade K. Developmental Studies Center Staff. (Reading, Thinking & Caring Ser.). 24p. (Orig.). 1996. teacher ed., pap. 13.95 (*1-57621-013-8*) Develop Studies.

Reading, Thinking & Caring Teacher's Guide to "Bigmama's" Read Aloud Unit, Grade K. Developmental Studies Center Staff. (Reading, Thinking & Caring Ser.). 24p. (Orig.). 1996. teacher ed., pap. 13.95 (*1-885603-01-0*) Develop Studies.

Reading, Thinking & Caring Teacher's Guide to "Born in the Gravy" Read Aloud Unit, Grade K. Developmental Studies Center Staff. (Reading, Thinking & Caring Ser.). 24p. (Orig.). 1996. pap. 13.95 (*1-885603-25-8*) Develop Studies.

Reading, Thinking & Caring Teacher's Guide to "Brave Irene" Read Aloud Unit, Grade 2. Developmental Studies Center Staff. (Reading, Thinking & Caring Ser.). 24p. (Orig.). 1996. teacher ed., pap. 13.95 (*1-57621-031-6*) Develop Studies.

Reading, Thinking & Caring Teacher's Guide to "Bread & Jam for Frances" Read Aloud Unit, Grade K. Developmental Studies Center Staff. (Reading, Thinking & Caring Ser.). 24p. (Orig.). 1996. teacher ed., pap. 13.95 (*1-57621-014-6*) Develop Studies.

Reading, Thinking & Caring Teacher's Guide to "Charlotte's Web" Read Aloud Unit, Grade 3. Developmental Studies Center Staff. (Reading, Thinking & Caring Ser.). 24p. (Orig.). 1996. teacher ed., pap. 13.95 (*1-57621-042-1*) Develop Studies.

Reading, Thinking & Caring Teacher's Guide to "Chicken Sunday" Read Aloud Unit, Grade 2. Developmental Studies Center Staff. (Reading, Thinking & Caring Ser.). 24p. (Orig.). 1996. teacher ed., pap. 13.95 (*1-885603-02-9*) Develop Studies.

Reading, Thinking & Caring Teacher's Guide to "Crow Boy" Partner Unit, Grade 2. Developmental Studies Center Staff. (Reading, Thinking & Caring Ser.). 24p. (Orig.). 1996. teacher ed., pap. 13.95 (*1-885603-03-7*) Develop Studies.

Reading, Thinking & Caring Teacher's Guide to "Daniel's Duck" Partner Unit, Grade 2. Developmental Studies Center Staff. (Reading, Thinking & Caring Ser.). 24p. (Orig.). 1996. pap. 13.95 (*1-885603-97-5*) Develop Studies.

Reading, Thinking & Caring Teacher's Guide to "Evan's Corner" Read Aloud Unit, Grade 2. Developmental Studies Center Staff. (Reading, Thinking & Caring Ser.). 24p. (Orig.). 1996. teacher ed., pap. 13.95 (*1-57621-032-4*) Develop Studies.

Reading, Thinking & Caring Teacher's Guide to "Family Pictures" Partner Unit, Grade 3. Developmental Studies Center Staff. (Reading, Thinking & Caring Ser.). 24p. (Orig.). 1996. teacher ed., pap. 13.95 (*1-57621-006-5*) Develop Studies.

Reading, Thinking & Caring Teacher's Guide to "Farmer Schulz's Ducks" Read Aloud Unit, Grade 2. Developmental Studies Center Staff. (Reading, Thinking & Caring Ser.). 24p. (Orig.). 1996. teacher ed., pap. 13.95 (*1-57621-033-2*) Develop Studies.

Reading, Thinking & Caring Teacher's Guide to "First Grade Takes a Test" Read Aloud Unit, Grade 1. Developmental Studies Center Staff. (Reading, Thinking & Caring Ser.). 24p. (Orig.). 1996. teacher ed., pap. 13.95 (*1-57621-021-9*) Develop Studies.

Reading, Thinking & Caring Teacher's Guide to "Follow the Drinking Gourd" Partner Unit, Grade 3. Developmental Studies Center Staff. (Reading, Thinking & Caring Ser.). 24p. (Orig.). 1996. pap. 13.95 (*1-885603-83-5*) Develop Studies.

Reading, Thinking & Caring Teacher's Guide to "Frog & Toad Are Friends" Partner Unit, Grade 1. Developmental Studies Center Staff. (Reading, Thinking & Caring Ser.). 24p. (Orig.). 1996. pap. 13.95 (*1-885603-88-6*) Develop Studies.

Reading, Thinking & Caring Teacher's Guide to "Go Fish" Partner Unit, Grade 3. Developmental Studies Center Staff. (Reading, Thinking & Caring Ser.). 24p. (Orig.). 1996. pap. 13.95 (*1-885603-37-1*) Develop Studies.

Reading, Thinking & Caring Teacher's Guide to "Gregory Cool" Read Aloud Unit, Grade 3. Developmental Studies Center Staff. (Reading, Thinking & Caring Ser.). 24p. (Orig.). 1996. teacher ed., pap. 13.95 (*1-57621-131-2*) Develop Studies.

Reading, Thinking & Caring Teacher's Guide to "How My Parents Learned to Eat" Read Aloud Unit, Grade 2. Developmental Studies Center Staff. (Reading, Thinking & Caring Ser.). 24p. (Orig.). 1996. teacher ed., pap. 13.95 (*1-57621-036-7*) Develop Studies.

Reading, Thinking & Caring Teacher's Guide to "I Know a Lady" Partner Unit, Grade 1. Developmental Studies Center Staff. (Reading, Thinking & Caring Ser.). 24p. (Orig.). 1996. pap. 13.95 (*1-885603-89-4*) Develop Studies.

Reading, Thinking & Caring Teacher's Guide to "I Want a Dog" Read Aloud Unit, Grade 3. Developmental Studies Center Staff. (Reading, Thinking & Caring Ser.). 24p. (Orig.). 1996. pap. 13.95 (*1-885603-32-0*) Develop Studies.

Reading, Thinking & Caring Teacher's Guide to "If You Give a Mouse a Cookie" Partner Unit, Grade 1. Developmental Studies Center Staff. (Reading, Thinking & Caring Ser.). 24p. (Orig.). 1996. teacher ed., pap. 13.95 (*1-57621-002-2*) Develop Studies.

Reading, Thinking & Caring Teacher's Guide to "Ira Sleeps Over" Partner Unit, Grade 1. Developmental Studies Center Staff. (Reading, Thinking & Caring Ser.). 24p. (Orig.). 1996. pap. 13.95 (*1-885603-90-8*) Develop Studies.

Reading, Thinking & Caring Teacher's Guide to "Jamaica's Find" Read Aloud Unit, Grade 1. Developmental Studies Center Staff. (Reading, Thinking & Caring Ser.). 24p. (Orig.). 1996. teacher ed., pap. 13.95 (*1-57621-023-5*) Develop Studies.

Reading, Thinking & Caring Teacher's Guide to "Jim's Dog Muffins" Partner Unit, Grade 1. Developmental Studies Center Staff. (Reading, Thinking & Caring Ser.). 24p. (Orig.). 1996. pap. 13.95 (*1-885603-91-6*) Develop Studies.

Reading, Thinking & Caring Teacher's Guide to "Keep the Lights Burning, Abbie" Partner Unit, Grade 2. Developmental Studies Center Staff. (Reading, Thinking & Caring Ser.). 24p. (Orig.). 1996. pap. 13.95 (*1-885603-99-1*) Develop Studies.

Reading, Thinking & Caring Teacher's Guide to "Little Bear" Partner Unit, Grade 1. Developmental Studies Center Staff. (Reading, Thinking & Caring Ser.). 24p. (Orig.). 1996. pap. 13.95 (*1-885603-92-4*) Develop Studies.

Reading, Thinking & Caring Teacher's Guide to "Luka's Quilt" Read Aloud Unit, Grade 1. Developmental Studies Center Staff. (Reading, Thinking & Caring Ser.). 24p. (Orig.). 1996. teacher ed., pap. 13.95 (*1-57621-125-8*) Develop Studies.

Reading, Thinking & Caring Teacher's Guide to "Maebelle's Suitcase" Read Aloud Unit, Grade 1. Developmental Studies Center Staff. (Reading, Thinking & Caring Ser.). 24p. (Orig.). 1996. teacher ed., pap. 13.95 (*1-57621-024-3*) Develop Studies.

Reading, Thinking & Caring Teacher's Guide to "Mike Mulligan & His Steam Shovel" Read Aloud Unit, Grade 1. Developmental Studies Center Staff. (Reading, Thinking & Caring Ser.). 24p. (Orig.). 1996. teacher ed., pap. 13.95 (*1-57621-025-1*) Develop Studies.

Reading, Thinking & Caring Teacher's Guide to "Miss Maggie" Read Aloud Unit, Grade 3. Developmental Studies Center Staff. (Reading, Thinking & Caring Ser.). 24p. (Orig.). 1996. teacher ed., pap. 13.95 (*1-57621-043-X*) Develop Studies.

Reading, Thinking & Caring Teacher's Guide to "Moonlight" Partner Unit, Grade K. Developmental Studies Center Staff. (Reading, Thinking & Caring Ser.). 24p. (Orig.). 1996. teacher ed., pap. 13.95 (*1-57621-001-4*) Develop Studies.

Reading, Thinking & Caring Teacher's Guide to "Mrs. Tibbles & the Special Someone" Read Aloud Unit, Grade 1. Developmental Studies Center Staff. (Reading, Thinking & Caring Ser.). 24p. (Orig.). 1996. teacher ed., pap. 13.95 (*1-57621-026-X*) Develop Studies.

Reading, Thinking & Caring Teacher's Guide to "Mufaro's Beautiful Daughters" Read Aloud Unit, Grade 2. Developmental Studies Center Staff. (Reading, Thinking & Caring Ser.). 24p. (Orig.). 1996. teacher ed., pap. 13.95 (*1-57621-037-5*) Develop Studies.

Reading, Thinking & Caring Teacher's Guide to "Nadia the Willful" Read Aloud Unit, Grade 2. Developmental Studies Center Staff. (Reading, Thinking & Caring Ser.). 24p. (Orig.). 1996. teacher ed., pap. 13.95 (*1-57621-038-3*) Develop Studies.

Reading, Thinking & Caring Teacher's Guide to "Nathaniel Talking" Read Aloud Unit, Grade 3. Developmental Studies Center Staff. (Reading, Thinking & Caring Ser.). 24p. (Orig.). 1996. teacher ed., pap. 13.95 (*1-57621-044-8*) Develop Studies.

Reading, Thinking & Caring Teacher's Guide to "Niki's Little Donkey" Read Aloud Unit, Grade 1. Developmental Studies Center Staff. (Reading, Thinking & Caring Ser.). 24p. (Orig.). 1996. teacher ed., pap. 13.95 (*1-57621-027-8*) Develop Studies.

Reading, Thinking & Caring Teacher's Guide to "No Good in Art" Read Aloud Unit, Grade K. Developmental Studies Center Staff. (Reading, Thinking & Caring Ser.). 24p. (Orig.). 1996. teacher ed., pap. 13.95 (*1-57621-016-2*) Develop Studies.

Reading, Thinking & Caring Teacher's Guide to "Old Mother Witch" Partner Unit, Grade 3. Developmental Studies Center Staff. (Reading, Thinking & Caring Ser.). 24p. (Orig.). 1996. teacher ed., pap. 13.95 (*1-57621-007-3*) Develop Studies.

Reading, Thinking & Caring Teacher's Guide to "One Frog Too Many" Partner Unit, Grade K. Developmental Studies Center Staff. (Reading, Thinking & Caring Ser.). 24p. (Orig.). 1996. pap. 13.95 (*1-885603-85-1*) Develop Studies.

Reading, Thinking & Caring Teacher's Guide to "Owen" Read Aloud Unit, Grade K. Developmental Studies Center Staff. (Reading, Thinking & Caring Ser.). 24p. (Orig.). 1996. teacher ed., pap. 13.95 (*1-57621-124-X*) Develop Studies.

Reading, Thinking & Caring Teacher's Guide to "Petunia" Read Aloud Unit, Grade 1. Developemental Studies Center Staff. (Reading, Thinking & Caring Ser.). 24p. (Orig.). 1996. teacher ed., pap. 13.95 (*1-57621-028-6*) Develop Studies.

Reading, Thinking & Caring Teacher's Guide to "Peter's Chair" Read Aloud Unit, Grade K. Developmental Studies Center Staff. (Reading, Thinking & Caring Ser.). 24p. (Orig.). 1996. teacher ed., pap. 13.95 (*1-57621-017-0*) Develop Studies.

Reading, Thinking & Caring Teacher's Guide to "Ramona Forever" Partner Unit, Grade 3. Developmental Studies Center Staff. (Reading, Thinking & Caring Ser.). 24p. (Orig.). 1996. teacher ed., pap. 13.95 (*1-57621-008-1*) Develop Studies.

R

Reading, Thinking & Caring Teacher's Guide to "Ramona the Pest" Partner Unit, Grade 3. Developmental Studies Center Staff. (Reading, Thinking & Caring Ser.). 24p. (Orig.). 1996. teacher ed., pap. 13.95 (*1-57621-009-X*) Develop Studies.

Reading, Thinking & Caring Teacher's Guide to "Rosalie" Read Aloud Unit, Grade 1. Developmental Studies Center Staff. (Reading, Thinking & Caring Ser.). 24p. (Orig.). 1996. teacher ed., pap. 13.95 (*1-57621-029-4*) Develop Studies.

Reading, Thinking & Caring Teacher's Guide to "Ruby the Copycat" Real Aloud Unit, Grade K. Developmental Studies Center Staff. (Reading, Thinking & Caring Ser.). 24p. (Orig.). 1996. pap. 13.95 (*1-885603-27-4*) Develop Studies.

Reading, Thinking & Caring Teacher's Guide to "Sam" Read Aloud Unit, Grade K. Developmental Studies Center Staff. (Reading, Thinking & Caring Ser.). 24p. (Orig.). 1996. teacher ed., pap. 13.95 (*1-57621-018-9*) Develop Studies.

Reading, Thinking & Caring Teacher's Guide to "Sam, Bangs & Moonshine" Read Aloud Unit, Grade 3. Developmental Studies Center Staff. (Reading, Thinking & Caring Ser.). 24p. (Orig.). 1996. teacher ed., pap. 13. 95 (*1-57621-045-6*) Develop Studies.

Reading, Thinking & Caring Teacher's Guide to "School" Partner Unit, Grade K. Developmental Studies Center Staff. (Reading, Thinking & Caring Ser.). 24p. (Orig.). 1996. teacher ed., pap. 13.95 (*1-57621-121-5*) Develop Studies.

Reading, Thinking & Caring Teacher's Guide to "Shoeshine Girl" Partner Unit, Grade 3. Developmental Studies Center Staff. (Reading, Thinking & Caring Ser.). 24p. (Orig.). 1996. teacher ed., pap. 13.95 (*1-57621-010-3*) Develop Studies.

Reading, Thinking & Caring Teacher's Guide to "Six-Dinner Sid" Partner Unit, Grade 3. Developmental Studies Center Staff. (Reading, Thinking & Caring Ser.). 24p. (Orig.). 1996. teacher ed., pap. 13.95 (*1-57621-123-1*) Develop Studies.

Reading, Thinking & Caring Teacher's Guide to "Song & Dance Man" Read Aloud Unit, Grade 3. Developmental Studies Center Staff. (Reading, Thinking & Caring Ser.). 24p. (Orig.). 1996. teacher ed., pap. 13. 95 (*1-57621-046-4*) Develop Studies.

Reading, Thinking & Caring Teacher's Guide to "Sophie & Lou" Partner Unit, Grade 3. Developmental Studies Center Staff. (Reading, Thinking & Caring Ser.). 24p. (Orig.). 1996. pap. 13.95 (*1-885603-36-3*) Develop Studies.

Reading, Thinking & Caring Teacher's Guide to "Storm in the Night" Read Aloud Unit, Grade 3. Developmental Studies Center Staff. (Reading, Thinking & Caring Ser.). 24p. (Orig.). 1996. teacher ed., pap. 13.95 (*1-57621-047-2*) Develop Studies.

Reading, Thinking & Caring Teacher's Guide to "Story of Ferdinand" Partner Unit, Grade 1. Developmental Studies Center Staff. (Reading, Thinking & Caring Ser.). 24p. (Orig.). 1996. pap. 13.95 (*1-885603-93-2*) Develop Studies.

Reading, Thinking & Caring Teacher's Guide to "Sunshine" Partner Unit, Grade K. Developmental Studies Center Staff. (Reading, Thinking & Caring Ser.). 24p. (Orig.). 1996. pap. 13.95 (*1-885603-86-X*) Develop Studies.

Reading, Thinking & Caring Teacher's Guide to "The Angel & the Soldier Boy" Partner Unit, Grade K. Developmental Studies Center Staff. (Reading, Thinking & Caring Ser.). 24p. (Orig.). 1996. teacher ed., pap. 13. 95 (*1-57621-000-6*) Develop Studies.

Reading, Thinking & Caring Teacher's Guide to "The Carp in the Bathtub" Read Aloud Unit, Grade 3. Developmental Studies Center Staff. (Reading, Thinking & Caring Ser.). 24p. (Orig.). 1996. teacher ed., pap. 13. 95 (*1-57621-041-3*) Develop Studies.

Reading, Thinking & Caring Teacher's Guide to "The Crying Christmas Tree" Read Aloud Unit, Grade 1. Developmental Studies Center Staff. (Reading, Thinking & Caring Ser.). 24p. (Orig.). 1996. pap. 13.95 (*1-885603-28-2*) Develop Studies.

Reading, Thinking & Caring Teacher's Guide to "The Day of Ahmed's Secret" Read Aloud Unit, Grade 1. Developmental Studies Center Staff. (Reading, Thinking & Caring Ser.). 24p. (Orig.). 1996. pap. 13.95 (*1-885603-29-0*) Develop Studies.

Reading, Thinking & Caring Teacher's Guide to "Theodor & Mr. Balbini" Read Aloud Unit, Grade 3. Developmental Studies Center Staff. (Reading, Thinking & Caring Ser.). 24p. (Orig.). 1996. teacher ed., pap. 13. 95 (*1-57621-048-0*) Develop Studies.

Reading, Thinking & Caring Teacher's Guide to "The Goat in the Rug" Read Aloud Unit, Grade 2. Developmental Studies Center Staff. (Reading, Thinking & Caring Ser.). 24p. (Orig.). 1996. teacher ed., pap. 13.95 (*1-57621-034-0*) Develop Studies.

Reading, Thinking & Caring Teacher's Guide to "The Gold Coin" Read Aloud Unit, Grade 2. Developmental Studies Center Staff. (Reading, Thinking & Caring Ser.). 24p. (Orig.). 1996. teacher ed., pap. 13.95 (*1-57621-035-9*) Develop Studies.

Reading, Thinking & Caring Teacher's Guide to "The Half-Birthday Party" Read Aloud Unit, Grade 1. Developmental Studies Center Staff. (Reading, Thinking & Caring Ser.). 24p. (Orig.). 1996. teacher ed., pap. 13. 95 (*1-57621-022-7*) Develop Studies.

Reading, Thinking & Caring Teacher's Guide to "The Josefina Story Quilt" Partner Unit, Grade 2. Developmental Studies Center Staff. (Reading, Thinking & Caring Ser.). 24p. (Orig.). 1996. pap. 13.95 (*1-885603-98-3*) Develop Studies.

Reading, Thinking & Caring Teacher's Guide to "The Little Painter of Sabana Grande" Read Aloud Unit, Grade 3. Developmental Studies Center Staff. (Reading, Thinking & Caring Ser.). 24p. (Orig.). 1996. pap. 13.95 (*1-885603-33-9*) Develop Studies.

Reading, Thinking & Caring Teacher's Guide to "The Lost Lake" Partner Unit, Grade 3. Developmental Studies Center Staff. (Reading, Thinking & Caring Ser.). 24p. (Orig.). 1996. pap. 13.95 (*1-885603-35-5*) Develop Studies.

Reading, Thinking & Caring Teacher's Guide to "The Mice Who Lived in a Shoe" Partner Unit, Grade 2. Developmental Studies Center Staff. (Reading, Thinking & Caring Ser.). 24p. (Orig.). 1996. teacher ed., pap. 13. 95 (*1-57621-003-0*) Develop Studies.

Reading, Thinking & Caring Teacher's Guide to "The Mother's Day Mice" Read Aloud Unit, Grade K. Developmental Studies Center Staff. (Reading, Thinking & Caring Ser.). 24p. (Orig.). 1996. teacher ed., pap. 13. 95 (*1-57621-015-4*) Develop Studies.

Reading, Thinking & Caring Teacher's Guide to "The Outside Dog" Partner Unit, Grade 1. Developmental Studies Center Staff. (Reading, Thinking & Caring Ser.). 24p. (Orig.). 1996. teacher ed., pap. 13.95 (*1-57621-122-3*) Develop Studies.

Reading, Thinking & Caring Teacher's Guide to "The Patchwork Quilt" Read Aloud Unit, Grade 2. Developmental Studies Center Staff. (Reading, Thinking & Caring Ser.). 24p. (Orig.). 1996. teacher ed., pap. 13. 95 (*1-57621-039-1*) Develop Studies.

Reading, Thinking & Caring Teacher's Guide to "The Quarreling Book" Partner Unit, Grade 1. Developmental Studies Center Staff. (Reading, Thinking & Caring Ser.). 24p. (Orig.). 1996. pap. 13.95 (*1-885603-31-2*) Develop Studies.

Reading, Thinking & Caring Teacher's Guide to "The Signmaker's Assistant" Read Aloud Unit, Grade 1. Developmental Studies Center Staff. (Reading, Thinking & Caring Ser.). 24p. (Orig.). 1996. pap. 13.95 (*1-885603-30-4*) Develop Studies.

Reading, Thinking & Caring Teacher's Guide to "The Stories Julian Tells" Partner Unit, Grade 3. Developmental Studies Center Staff. (Reading, Thinking & Caring Ser.). 24p. (Orig.). 1996. teacher ed., pap. 13.95 (*1-57621-011-1*) Develop Studies.

Reading, Thinking & Caring Teacher's Guide to "Thy Friend, Obadiah" Partner Unit, Grade 2. Developmental Studies Center Staff. 24p. (Orig.). 1996. teacher ed., pap. 13.95 (*1-885603-04-5*) Develop Studies.

Reading, Thinking & Caring Teacher's Guide to "Uncle Jed's Barbershop" Read Aloud Unit, Grade 3. Developmental Studies Center Staff. (Reading, Thinking & Caring Ser.). 24p. (Orig.). 1996. pap. 13.95 (*1-885603-34-7*) Develop Studies.

Reading, Thinking & Caring Teacher's Guide to "Very Last First Time" Read Aloud Unit, Grade 2. Developmental Studies Center Staff. (Reading, Thinking & Caring Ser.). 24p. (Orig.). 1996. teacher ed., pap. 13.95 (*1-57621-040-5*) Develop Studies.

Reading, Thinking & Caring Teacher's Guide to "Wagon Wheels" Partner Unit, Grade 2. Developmental Studies Center Staff. (Reading, Thinking & Caring Ser.). 24p. (Orig.). 1996. teacher ed., pap. 13.95 (*1-57621-004-9*) Develop Studies.

Reading, Thinking & Caring Teacher's Guide to "Wednesday Surprise" Partner Unit, Grade 2. Developmental Studies Center Staff. (Reading, Thinking & Caring Ser.). 24p. (Orig.). 1996. teacher ed., pap. 13.95 (*1-57621-005-7*) Develop Studies.

Reading, Thinking & Caring Teacher's Guide to "When Will I Read?" Read Aloud Unit, Grade K. Developmental Studies Center Staff. (Reading, Thinking & Caring Ser.). 24p. (Orig.). 1996. teacher ed., pap. 13.95 (*1-57621-019-7*) Develop Studies.

Reading, Thinking & Caring Teacher's Guide to "Where's Al?" Partner Unit, Grade K. Developmental Studies Center Staff. (Reading, Thinking & Caring Ser.). 24p. (Orig.). 1996. pap. 13.95 (*1-885603-87-8*) Develop Studies.

Reading, Thinking & Caring Teacher's Guide to "Will Gets a Haircut" Read Aloud Unit, Grade 1. Developmental Studies Center Staff. (Reading, Thinking & Caring Ser.). 24p. (Orig.). 1996. teacher ed., pap. 13.95 (*1-57621-126-6*) Develop Studies.

Reading, Thinking & Caring Teacher's Guide to "Yang the Youngest & His Terrible Ear" Read Aloud Unit, Grade 3. Developmental Studies Center Staff. (Reading, Thinking & Caring Ser.). 24p. (Orig.). 1996. teacher ed., pap. 13.95 (*1-57621-049-9*) Develop Studies.

Reading, Thinking & Caring Teacher's Guide to "Zinnia & Dot" Read Aloud Unit, Grade K. Developmental Studies Center Staff. (Reading, Thinking & Caring Ser.). 24p. (Orig.). 1996. pap. 13.95 (*1-885603-26-6*) Develop Studies.

Reading, Thinking, & Concept Development: A Guide. Films Humanities Staff. (C). 1993. ring bd. write for info. (*0-697-21548-2*) Brown & Benchmark.

Reading, Thinking, & Writing about Multicultural Literature. Carol B. Olson. 704p. (Orig.). 1995. pap. 29. 95 (*0-673-36296-5*, GoodYrBooks) Addson-Wesley Educ.

Reading, Thinking, & Writing with Sources. Patrick J. Slattery & Susan R. Carlton. (Illus.). 432p. (Orig.). (C). 1992. teacher ed. write for info. (*0-318-69278-3*) Macmillan.

Reading, Thinking, & Writing with Sources. Patrick J. Slattery & Susan R. Carlton. (Illus.). 432p. (Orig.). (C). 1992. pap. text ed. 36.00 (*0-02-411561-4*, Macmillan Coll) P-H.

Reading, Thinking, Writing: A Text for Students of English As a Second Language. Mary S. Lawrence. (C). 1975. 17.95 (*0-472-08548-4*); teacher ed. 2.00 (*0-472-08549-2*) U of Mich Pr.

Reading Thresholds. Carolyn H. Fitzpatrick & Marybeth B. Ruscica. 320p. (C). 1993. pap. text ed. 34.76 (*0-669-20166-9*); Instr.'s ed. teacher ed. 33.96 (*0-669-29707-0*) HM College Div.

*__Reading Thresholds with "Newsweek"__ Carolyn H. Fitzpatrick & Marybeth B. Ruscica. (C). 1993. text ed. 40.76 (*0-669-33272-0*) HM College Div.

*__Reading Through Hebrews.__ C. R. Hume. 144p. (Orig.). 1997. pap. 14.00 (*0-334-02689-X*, SCM Pr) TPI PA.

Reading Through Imagery: Grades K-5. Edward Lavin. 1989. pap. 15.00 (*0-89824-095-6*) Trillium Pr.

*__Reading Through Writing about Literature.__ Ed. by Bishop. (C). 1998. text ed. write for info. (*0-321-01027-2*) Addson-Wesley Educ.

Reading Time: A Comprehensive Reading Program Using Real Books. Debbie Strayer. (Reading Skills Discovery Ser.). (Illus.). 60p. (J). (gr. 4-6). 1993. student ed., pap. 10.00 (*1-880892-52-9*); teacher ed., spiral bd. 16.00 (*1-880892-51-0*) Com Sense FL.

Reading Tips for Reports on Research. 32p. 1986. pap. 6.00 (*0-912452-63-3*, R-6) Am Phys Therapy Assn.

*__Reading to Follow Instructions.__ Jo E. Moore. (Real-Life Reading Activities Ser.). (Illus.). 64p. (J). (gr. 2-3). 1996. teacher ed., pap. 7.95 (*1-55799-590-7*, 567) Evan-Moor Corp.

Reading to Learn in Content Areas. 3rd ed. Richardson. (Education Ser.). 1997. student ed., pap. 17.95 (*0-534-50739-5*) Wadsworth Pub.

Reading to Learn in the Content Areas. Judy S. Richardson & Raymond F. Morgan. 544p. (C). 1990. text ed. 45.95 (*0-534-11748-1*) Wadsworth Pub.

Reading to Learn in the Content Areas. 2nd ed. Judy S. Richardson & Raymond F. Morgan. 558p. 1994. text ed. 42.75 (*0-534-20328-0*) Wadsworth Pub.

Reading to Learn in the Content Areas. 3rd ed. Judy S. Richardson & Raymond F. Morgan. (Education Ser.). (C). 1997. text ed. 58.95 (*0-534-50737-9*) Wadsworth Pub.

Reading to Matthew. Jackie Vivelo. LC 93-84912. (Illus.). 40p. (J). (gr. 3-8). 1993. 15.95 (*1-879373-60-2*) R Rinehart.

Reading to, with, & by Children. Margaret E. Mooney. LC 90-30678. 104p. (Orig.). (C). 1990. pap. text ed. 12.95 (*0-913461-18-0*) R Owen Pubs.

Reading to Write: A Practical Rhetoric. Kathleen A. Kelly. LC 88-63042. 340p. (Orig.). (C). 1990. pap. text ed. 24. 50 (*0-312-01143-1*) St Martin.

Reading to Write: A Practical Rhetoric. Kathleen A. Kelly. LC 88-63042. 340p. (Orig.). (C). 1990. pap. text ed. 5.00 (*0-312-01144-X*) St Martin.

Reading-to-Write: Exploring a Cognitive & Social Process. Linda J. Flower et al. (Social & Cognitive Studies in Writing & Literacy). (Illus.). 280p. 1990. 45.00 (*0-19-506190-X*) OUP.

Reading to Writing. O'Keefe. (C). 1991. teacher ed., pap. 3.00 (*0-15-575785-7*) HB Coll Pubs.

Reading to Writing: Form & Meaning. Jack O'Keefe. 352p. (C). 1990. pap. text ed. 20.00 (*0-15-575784-9*) HB Coll Pubs.

Reading to You. Siri Hustvedt. 32p. (Orig.). 1983. pap. 3.95 (*0-940170-12-4*) Open Bk Pubns.

Reading Today & Tomorrow: Kingdoms, Level 15. Beck. (J). (gr. 4). 1989. wbk. ed., pap. 21.50 (*0-15-718037-9*) HB Schl Dept.

Reading Today & Tomorrow: Level 1 Sundrops. 89th ed. Beck. 1989. student ed. 14.50 (*0-15-718000-X*) HB Schl Dept.

Reading Today & Tomorrow Level 1: Sundrops. 1,989th ed. Beck. (J). (gr. 1). 1989. teacher ed., pap. 61.75 (*0-15-718001-8*) HB Schl Dept.

Reading Today & Tomorrow Level 4: End of Book Test. Beck. (Reading Ser.). (J). 1989. teacher ed., pap. 17.00 (*0-15-718335-1*) HB Schl Dept.

Reading Today & Tomorrow Level 4: Kingdoms. Beck. (Reading Ser.). (J). (gr. 4). 1989. teacher ed., pap. 45.00 (*0-15-718031-X*) HB Schl Dept.

Reading Today & Tomorrow Level 5: End of Book Test. Beck. (Reading Ser.). (J). 1989. teacher ed., pap. 17.00 (*0-15-718345-9*) HB Schl Dept.

Reading Today & Tomorrow Level 5: End of Unit Test A. Beck. (Reading Ser.). (J). (gr. 5). 1989. teacher ed., pap. 17.00 (*0-15-718049-2*) HB Schl Dept.

Reading Today & Tomorrow Level 6: End of Book Test. Beck. (Reading Ser.). (J). 1989. teacher ed., pap. 17.00 (*0-15-718355-6*) HB Schl Dept.

Reading Today & Tomorrow Level 6: End Unit Test A. Beck. (Reading Ser.). (J). (gr. 6). 1989. teacher ed., pap. 17.00 (*0-15-718059-X*) HB Schl Dept.

Reading Today & Tomorrow Level 7: End of Book Test. Beck. (Reading Ser.). (J). 1989. teacher ed., pap. 17.00 (*0-15-718365-3*) HB Schl Dept.

Reading Today & Tomorrow Level 7: End of Unit Test A. Beck. (Reading Ser.). (J). (gr. 7). 1989. teacher ed., pap. 17.00 (*0-15-718069-7*) HB Schl Dept.

Reading Today & Tomorrow Level 8: End of Book Test. Beck. (Reading Ser.). (J). 1989. teacher ed., pap. 17.00 (*0-15-718375-0*) HB Schl Dept.

Reading Today & Tomorrow Level 8: End Unit Test A. Beck. (Reading Ser.). (J). (gr. 8). 1989. teacher ed., pap. 17.00 (*0-15-718079-4*) HB Schl Dept.

Reading Today & Tomorrow Level 9: End of Book Test. Beck. (Reading Ser.). (J). 1989. teacher ed., pap. 17.00 (*0-15-718385-8*) HB Schl Dept.

Reading Today & Tomorrow Level 9: End of Unit Test A. Beck. (Reading Ser.). (YA). (gr. 9). 1989. teacher ed., pap. 17.00 (*0-15-718089-1*) HB Schl Dept.

Reading Today & Tomorrow Level 11: End of Unit Test. Beck. (Reading Ser.). (YA). (gr. 11). 1989. teacher ed., pap. 17.00 (*0-15-718109-X*) HB Schl Dept.

Reading Today & Tomorrow Level 12: End of Unit Test A. Beck. (Reading Ser.). (YA). (gr. 12). 1989. teacher ed., pap. 17.00 (*0-15-718119-7*) HB Schl Dept.

Reading Today & Tomorrow Level 13: End of Unit Test A. Beck. (Reading Ser.). (J). 1989. teacher ed., pap. 17.00 (*0-15-718129-4*) HB Schl Dept.

Reading Today & Tomorrow Level 14: End of Unit Test A. Beck. (Reading Ser.). (J). 1989. teacher ed., pap. 17.00 (*0-15-718139-1*) HB Schl Dept.

Reading Today & Tomorrow Level 14: End Unit Test B. Beck. (Reading Ser.). (J). 1989. teacher ed., pap. 17.00 (*0-15-718262-2*) HB Schl Dept.

Reading Today & Tomorrow Level 15: End Unit Test B. Beck. (Reading Ser.). (J). 1989. teacher ed., pap. 17.00 (*0-15-718272-X*) HB Schl Dept.

Reading Today & Tomorrow Level Kindergarten. Beck. (Reading Ser.). (J). 1989. teacher ed., pap. 78.75 (*0-15-718371-8*) HB Schl Dept.

Reading Today & Tomorrow Levels 9-15: Placement Tests. Beck. (Reading Ser.). (J). 1989. teacher ed., pap. 18.50 (*0-15-718233-9*) HB Schl Dept.

Reading Today & Tomorrow Skill Master Level 1: End of Book Test. Beck. (J). (gr. 1). 1989. teacher ed., pap. 17. 00 (*0-15-718007-7*) HB Schl Dept.

*__Reading TOEFL.__ 1988. 13.00 (*0-446-38839-4*) Warner Bks.

Reading TOEFL. 1994. 14.00 (*0-446-77733-1*) Warner Bks.

Reading TOEFL. Educational Testing Service Staff. 1987. pap. 13.00 (*0-446-38522-0*) Warner Bks.

*__Reading Toes.__ Date not set. 19.95 (*0-8464-4570-0*) Beekman Pubs.

Reading Together. Robin Campbell. (Rethinking Reading Ser.). 100p. 1990. 75.00 (*0-335-09450-3*, Open Univ Pr); pap. 24.00 (*0-335-09449-X*, Open Univ Pr) Taylor & Francis.

Reading Together. Feagin. 1990. pap. 6.06 (*0-8092-4138-2*) Contemp Bks.

Reading Together. Karl Krahnke. 1995. pap. text ed. 16.50 (*0-312-11601-2*) St Martin.

Reading Together. 2nd ed. Karl Krahnke. 1995. teacher ed., pap. text ed. 0.50 (*0-312-11603-9*) St Martin.

*__Reading Together, Vol. 1.__ 2nd ed. Krahnke. Date not set. pap. text ed. write for info. (*0-312-11602-0*) St Martin.

Reading Too Soon: How to Understand & Help the Hyperlexic Child. Susan M. Miller. 128p. (Orig.). 1993. pap. 14.95 (*0-9637921-0-5*) Ctr for Speech.

*__Reading Treasure Map Signs & Symbols.__ large type ed. Mitchell Waite. (Illus.). 70p. (Orig.). 1997. pap. 7.95 (*1-881260-16-X*) Southwest Pubns.

Reading Trout Streams: An Orvis Guide. Tom Rosenbauer. (Illus.). 160p. 1988. pap. 17.95 (*0-941130-78-9*) Lyons & Burford.

Reading Tudor-Stuart Texts Through Cultural Historicism. Albert H. Tricomi. LC 95-45465. 216p. 1996. lib. bdg. 39.95 (*0-8130-1435-2*) U Press Fla.

Reading Ukrainian I. Assya Humesky et al. Ed. by Otterbein College Staff. (OSU Foreign Language Publications: No. 109). (Illus.). 206p. (Orig.). (UKR.). (C). 1994. student ed., pap. text ed. 17.50 (*0-87415-255-0*) OSU Foreign Lang.

Reading Ukrainian I, Instructor Manual. Assya Humesky et al. Ed. by Otterbein College Staff. (OSU Foreign Language Publications: No. 109A). (Illus.). 55p. (Orig.). (UKR.). (C). 1994. pap. 8.50 (*0-87415-256-9*) OSU Foreign Lang.

Reading Ukrainian III, Student Manual. Assya Humesky & Ruth Shamraj. Ed. by Ohio Otterbein College Staff. (OSU Foreign Language Publications, Ukrainian Individualized Instruction). (Illus.). 255p. (Orig.). (UKR.). (C). 1994. pap. text ed. 20.50 (*0-87415-259-3*, 111) OSU Foreign Lang.

Reading Ukrainian III, Student Manual. Assya Humesky & Ruth Shamraj. Ed. by Ohio Otterbein College Staff. (OSU Foreign Language Publications, Ukrainian Individualized Instruction: No. 111A). (Illus.). 67p. (Orig.). (UKR.). (C). 1994. pap. 9.00 (*0-87415-260-7*, 111A) OSU Foreign Lang.

*__Reading under the Covers.__ Claudette C. Mitchell et al. (Visions: African-American Experiences: Vol. 14). (Illus.). 8p. (Orig.). (J). (gr. k-1). 1996. pap. text ed. 3.00 (*1-57518-056-1*) Arborlake.

Reading Visual Poetry after Futurism Vol. 4: Marinetti, Apollinaire, Schwitters, Cummings. Michael P. Webster. LC 90-42247. (Literature & the Visual Arts Ser.: Vol. 4). 256p. (C). 1995. text ed. 49.95 (*0-8204-1292-9*) P Lang Pubng.

Reading Vocabulary Development: Grades 1-6 Multigraded. Frank D. Taylor. 1989. pap. 5.95 (*0-89108-210-7*, 8906) Love Pub Co.

Reading Voices: Literature & the Phonotext. Garrett Stewart. LC 89-20518. 348p. 1990. 50.00 (*0-520-06877-7*); pap. 17.00 (*0-520-07039-9*) U CA Pr.

*__Reading Voices, Dan Dha Ts'edenintth'e: Oral & Written Interpretations of the Yukon's Past.__ Julie Cruikshank. (Illus.). 158p. 1997. 24.95 (*0-88894-728-3*) U of Wash Pr.

Reading Voltaire's "Contes" A Semiotics of Philosophical Narration. Carol Sherman. LC 84-3553. (Studies in the Romance Languages & Literatures: No. 223). 304p. 1984. pap. text ed. 27.50 (*0-8078-9227-0*) U of NC Pr.

Reading Wagner: A Study in the History of Ideas. L. J. Rather. LC 89-37814. 368p. 1990. text ed. 45.00 (*0-8071-1557-6*) La State U Pr.

*__Reading What's In the Mailbox.__ Jill Norris. (Real-Life Reading Activities Ser.). (Illus.). 64p. (J). (gr. k-1). 1996. teacher ed., pap. 7.95 (*1-55799-587-7*, 564) Evan-Moor Corp.

An Asterisk (*) at the beginning of an entry indicates that the title is appearing in BIP for the first time.

R

*Reading While You Shop. Jill Norris. (Real-Life Reading Activities Ser.). (Illus.). 64p. (J). (gr. k-1). 1996. teacher ed., pap. 7.95 (1-55799-588-5, 565) Evan-Moor Corp.

Reading Wilde: Querying Spaces. Ed. by Marvin J. Taylor & Carolyn Dever. 92p. (C). 1995. pap. 9.50 (0-8147-2601-1) NYU Pr.

Reading Will Be Easy. Michael A. Williams. (Illus.). 50p. 1988. student ed. write for info. (1-878527-00-2) Black Phoenix Pr.

Reading William Blake. Stephen C. Behrendt. 1992. text ed. 49.95 (0-312-06835-2) St Martin.

Reading with a Difference: Gender, Race, & Cultural Identity: A Criticism Book. Ed. by Arthur F. Marotti et al. LC 93-28532. 400p. 1993. pap. 16.95 (0-8143-2493-2) Wayne St U Pr.

Reading with a Passion: Rhetoric, Autobiography & the American West in the Gospel of John. Jeffrey L. Staley. LC 95-20812. (Illus.). 256p. 1995. 29.50 (0-8264-0859-1) Continuum.

Reading with Clarice Lispector. Helene Cixous. Tr. & Intro. by Verena A. Conley. (Theory & History of Literature Ser.: Vol. 73). (Illus.). 187p. (C). 1990. pap. text ed. 14.95 (0-8166-1829-1) U of Minn Pr.

Reading with Feeling: The Aesthetics of Appreciation. Susan L. Feagin. 280p. 1996. 35.00 (0-8014-3200-6) Cornell U Pr.

Reading with Meaning: Strategies for College Reading. 3rd ed. Dorothy G. Hennings. LC 95-8759. 416p. (C). 1995. pap. text ed. 33.60 (0-13-205873-1) P-H.

Reading with Music. Nancy Polette. (Illus.). 48p. (J). (gr. 4-7). 1992. pap. 5.95 (1-879287-04-8) Pieces of Lrning.

Reading with Sounds. (Key Words Readers Ser.: C Series, No. 641-6c). (Illus.). (J). (ps-5). 3.50 (0-7214-0549-5, Ladybrd) Penguin.

Reading with Sounds, Ser. S705, No. 6. (Key Words Readers Ser.: C Series, No. 641-6c). (Illus.). (J). (ps-5). student ed. 1.95 (0-317-04021-9, Ladybrd) Penguin.

*Reading with the Saints: The Love of Literature & the Life of Faith. William H. Willimon. LC 97-26043. 1998. write for info. (0-8358-0847-5) Upper Room Bks.

Reading with the Troubled Reader. Margaret Y. Phinney. LC 88-11211. (Illus.). 138p. (Orig.). (C). 1988. pap. text ed. 18.50 (0-435-08480-1, 08480) Heinemann.

*Reading with the Troubled Reader. Margaret Y. Phinney. (Orig.). pap. 16.95 (0-590-71881-9) Scholastic Inc.

*Reading with Understanding. Marilyn Evans. (Reading & Writing Ser.). (Illus.). 32p. (J). (gr. 4-6). 1997. teacher ed., pap. 2.95 (1-55799-415-3, 4017) Evan-Moor Corp.

Reading with Young Children. Nancy E. Jackson & Cathy M. Roller. (Illus.). 79p. (Orig.). (C). 1994. pap. text ed. 20.00 (0-7881-1341-0) DIANE Pub.

Reading Within & Beyond the Classroom. D. Taverner. 1990. pap. 27.00 (0-335-09579-8, Open Univ Pr) Taylor & Francis.

Reading Without Books. Julie Burns & Dorothy Swan. LC 78-72078. (J). (gr. 4-6). 1979. pap. 9.99 (0-8224-5830-6) Fearon Teach Aids.

*Reading Without Nonsense. 3rd rev. ed. Frank Smith. LC 96-3467. 176p. (C). 1996. pap. text ed. 15.95 (0-8077-3472-1) Tchrs Coll.

Reading Woman: A Journal. Intro. by Maxine R. Schur. (Illus.). 128p. 1991. 17.95 (0-87654-816-8, A590) Pomegranate Calif.

Reading Women's Magazines: An Analysis of Everyday Media Use. Joke Hermes. 200p. 1995. text ed. 52.95 (0-7456-1270-9); pap. text ed. 20.95 (0-7456-1271-7) Blackwell Pubs.

Reading Workbook Grade 2. (Early Learner Ser.: No. IV). (Illus.). 192p. (J). (gr. 1-3). 1995. pap. 4.95 (1-56144-648-3) Modern Pub NYC.

Reading Workout. Dennis Graham. Ed. by Livian Perez. (Reading Safari Ser.: Vol. 4). (Illus.). 12p. (Orig.). (J). (gr. 2-3). 1996. pap. 19.95 (1-56767-157-8) Educ Insights.

Reading Workout. Jann Huizenga. 1994. pap. 22.95 (0-8384-3980-2) Heinle & Heinle.

Reading Workout. Shirley S. Levine. (Illus.). (Orig.). 1995. pap. 10.00 (0-9648436-0-9) Readsmart.

*Reading Workshop Survival Kit: Management Techniques, Reproducible Worksheets, & 100 Mini-Lessons Covering Topics & Skills in Reading. Gary R. Muschla. LC 97-17265. 1997. write for info. (0-87628-592-2) Ctr Appl Res.

Reading World Literature: Theory, History, Practice. Ed. & Intro. by Sarah Lawall. LC 94-4041. (Illus.). 376p. (C). 1994. text ed. 50.00 (0-292-74679-2) U of Tex Pr.

Reading, Writing: A Tutorial Guide in the Language Arts. 2nd ed. Earl S. Zehr. LC 90-48414. vi, 86p. (C). 1990. pap. text ed. 12.00 (0-926487-08-6) Rowan Mtn Pr.

Reading, Writing & Computers: Planning for Integration. Sherry H. Howie. 250p. 1989. text ed. 54.50 (0-205-11965-4, H19656) Allyn.

Reading, Writing & Creativity. Raymond E. Laurita. LC 72-75225. 253p. (Orig.). 1973. pap. text ed. 9.95 (0-914051-15-6) Leonardo Pr.

Reading, Writing & Interpreting Literature: Pedagogy, Positions & Research. Intro. by Robert W. Blake. 273p. (C). 1989. pap. text ed. 10.00 (0-930348-15-X) NY St Eng Coun.

*Reading, Writing, & Justice: School Reform As If Democracy Mattered. James W. Fraser. LC 96-41493. (SUNY Series, Interruptions). 320p. 1997. pap. text ed. 19.95 (0-7914-3406-0) State U NY Pr.

*Reading, Writing, & Justice: School Reform As If Democracy Mattered. James W. Fraser. LC 96-41493. (SUNY Series, Interruptions). 320p. 1997. text ed. 59.50 (0-7914-3405-2) State U NY Pr.

Reading, Writing & Language: A Practical Guide for Primary Teachers. 2nd ed. Robert A. McCracken & Marlene J. McCracken. (Illus.). 296p. (J). (gr. k-3). 1995. teacher ed. 17.00 (1-895411-70-X) Peguis Pubs Ltd.

Reading, Writing, & Learning in ESL: A Resource Book for K-12 Teachers. 2nd ed. Suzanne F. Peregoy & Owen F. Boyle. (C). 1997. teacher ed., pap. text ed. write for info. (0-8013-1548-4) Longman.

Reading, Writing, & Learning in ESL: A Resource Book for K-8 Teachers. Suzanne Peregoy & Owen F. Boyle. LC 92-32444. 240p. (C). 1993. pap. text ed. 29.50 (0-8013-0844-5) Longman.

Reading, Writing, & Learning in Esl: A Resource Book for K-8 Teachers. 2nd ed. Suzanne Peregoy. (C). 1997. pap. text ed. 30.50 (0-8013-1628-6) Addison-Wesley.

Reading, Writing & Library Research. Vanessa Shannon & Harriet Stettiner. 272p. (C). 1994. per., pap. text ed. 20.94 (0-8403-9741-0) Kendall-Hunt.

Reading, Writing, & Race: The Desegregation of the Charlotte Schools. Davison M. Douglas. LC 94-39347. 1995. pap. text ed. 15.95 (0-8078-4529-9); lib. bdg. 39.95 (0-8078-2216-7) U of NC Pr.

Reading, Writing & Rage: The Terrible Price Paid by Victims of School Failure. 2nd rev. ed. Dorothy F. Ungerleider. LC 84-15514. 240p. 1996. pap. 16.95 (0-9650252-0-9) RWR Pr.

Reading, Writing & Reasoning. 2nd ed. Marilyn S. Sternglass. 368p. (C). 1991. pap. text ed. 37.00 (0-02-417211-1, Macmillan Coll) P-H.

Reading, Writing & Reasoning: A Guide for Students. Gavin J. Fairbairn & Christopher Winch. 160p. 1991. 75.00 (0-335-09596-8, Open Univ Pr); pap. 22.00 (0-335-09595-X, Open Univ Pr) Taylor & Francis.

Reading, Writing & Reasoning: A Guide for Students. 2nd ed. Gavin Fairbairn & Christopher Winch. LC 96-19902. 224p. 1996. 59.95 (0-335-19741-8, Open Univ Pr); pap. 17.95 (0-335-19740-X, Open Univ Pr) Taylor & Francis.

Reading, Writing & Remembering: A Literary Record. Edward V. Lucas. (Illus.). 1971. reprint ed. 24.00 (0-403-01076-4) Scholarly.

Reading, Writing & Resistance: Adolescence & Labor in a Junior High School. Robert B. Everhart. (Critical Social Thought Ser.). 288p. 1983. 24.50 (0-7100-9450-7, RKP) Routledge.

Reading, Writing, & Rewriting the Prostitute Body. Shannon Bell. LC 93-5447. (Illus.). 240p. 1994. 35.00 (0-253-31166-7); pap. 13.95 (0-253-20859-9) Ind U Pr.

*Reading, Writing & Rhythm-Atick: An Anthology of the Poetry of Members of the Wallace Stevens Chapter of PPS, Inc. Ed. by Ann Gasser. 80p. (Orig.). 1997. pap. 2.50 (1-884257-20-8) AGEE Keyboard.

*Reading, Writing & Ritualizing. Ronald Grimes. 312p. 1993. pap. 19.95 (1-56929-007-5) Pastoral Pr.

Reading, Writing, & Spelling in Spanish One: A Complete Guide to Teaching Your Child Beginning Written Spanish. Heidi A. Spietz. LC 93-14955. 218p. 1993. pap. 12.95 (0-929487-77-X) Am Montessori Consult.

Reading, Writing, & Studying Strategies: An Integrated Curriculum. Pearl I. Seidenberg. 592p. 1991. 139.00 (0-8342-0229-8) Aspen Pub.

Reading, Writing, & the Humanities. Jo R. McCuen & Anthony C. Winkler. 750p. (C). 1991. pap. text ed. 21.50 (0-15-575512-9) HB Coll Pubs.

Reading, Writing, & the Study of Literature. Ed. by Arthur W. Biddle & Toby Fulwiler. 160p. (C). 1989. pap. text ed. write for info. (0-07-553538-6) McGraw.

Reading, Writing & Thinking. Gloria Haney & Richard Alden. 230p. (C). 1990. pap. text ed. 30.82 (0-929655-94-X) CT Pub.

Reading, Writing & TV: A Video Handbook for Teachers. Betsy Newman & Joseph Mara. 190p. 1995. pap. 25.00 (0-917846-33-8, 95583) Highsmith Pr.

Reading, Writing & Understanding Numerals 0-10. Donna Burk et al. (Box It or Bag It Mathematics Ser.). (Illus.). 60p. (C). 1988. teacher ed., ring bd. 7.25 (1-886131-05-8, BB4) Math Lrning.

Reading-Writing Connections: From Theory to Practice. Mary F. Heller. 320p. (Orig.). (C). 1991. pap. text ed. 30.50 (0-8013-0139-4, 75803) Longman.

Reading-Writing Connections: From Theory to Practice. 2nd ed. Mary F. Heller. LC 93-50861. 416p. (C). 1995. pap. text ed. 39.95 (0-8013-1244-2, 79854) Longman.

Reading Writing Connections: Learning from Research. Ed. by Judith W. Irwin & Mary A. Doyle. LC 91-41538. 310p. 1992. reprint ed. pap. 88.40 (0-608-00501-0, 2061321) Bks Demand.

Reading, Writing, Recipes: A Collection of Dishes from Literacy Students & Volunteers from America & Around the World. 222p. 1994. 14.95 (0-9642471-0-0) Lit Volunteers.

Reading Yellow Pages for Students & Teachers. LC 87-83365. (Yellow Pages Ser.). 64p. (J). (gr. k-6). 1988. pap. text ed. 8.95 (0-86530-029-1, IP 89-1) Incentive Pubns.

Reading Your Future in the Cards. Louise Woods. 1989. pap. 3.95 (0-942272-20-X) Original Pubns.

Reading Your Students: Their Writing & Their Selves. Anne Martin. 64p. 1983. pap. 5.95 (0-915924-32-3) Tchrs & Writers Coll.

Reading Zukofsky's "80 Flowers" Michele J. Leggott. LC 88-6769. 464p. 1989. text ed. 60.00 (0-8018-3368-X) Johns Hopkins.

Reading 4QMMT: New Perspectives on Qumran Law & History. Ed. by John Kampen & Moshe J. Bernstein. LC 95-51505. (Society of Biblical Literature Symposium Ser.: No. 2). 169p. 1996. 39.95 (0-7885-0222-0, 060702); pap. 24.95 (0-7885-0223-9, 06 07 02) Scholars Pr GA.

Reading 8-10. Beverly Dahlen. 158p. (Orig.). 1992. pap. 12.00 (0-925904-08-2) Chax Pr.

Readings. 2nd ed. M. D. McIroy. (Unix Programmer's Ser.: Vol. II). 630p. (C). 1990. pap. text ed. 44.25 (0-03-047529-5) SCP.

Readings: "John at Patmos" & "A Book of Hours" Catherine De Vinck. LC 78-55341. 68p. 1978. 5.75 (0-911726-32-2, CODE REC); per. 3.75 (0-911726-33-0, CODE REB) Alleluia Pr.

Readings: Child Psychology. Ed. by George R. Smrtic & Victor P. Garlock. LC 73-4447. 145p. 1973. pap. text ed. 12.00 (0-8422-5094-8) Irvington.

Readings: Crime. Ed. by Robert D. Crutchfield et al. LC 95-43519. (Crime & Society Ser.: No. 1). 1996. pap. 30.95 (0-8039-9078-2) Pine Forge.

Readings: The Poetics of Blanchot, Joyce, Kafka, Kleist, Lispector, & Tsvetayeva. Helene Cixous. Tr. & Intro. by Verena A. Conley. (Theory & History of Literature Ser.: Vol. 77). 192p. (C). 1991. text ed. 39.95 (0-8166-1940-9) U of Minn Pr.

Readings: The Poetics of Blanchot, Joyce, Kafka, Kleist, Lispector, & Tsvetayeva. Helene Cixous. Tr. & Intro. by Verena A. Conley. (Theory & History of Literature Ser.: Vol. 77). 192p. (C). 1991. pap. 15.95 (0-8166-1941-7) U of Minn Pr.

Readings - California Civilization. 3rd ed. Howard DeWitt. 240p. (C). 1994. per., pap. text ed. 24.67 (0-8403-8967-1) Kendall-Hunt.

Readings about the Social Animal. 7th ed. Elliot Aronson. LC 87-25270. (Series of Books in Psychology). 536p. 1995. 24.95 (0-7167-2625-4) W H Freeman.

Readings Across American Cultures. Helen Gillotte & Jan Gregory. 336p. (C). 1996. per., pap. text ed. 45.87 (0-8403-9773-9) Kendall-Hunt.

Readings Activities Human Geography. Lucy Jarosz & Katharyn Mitchell. 256p. (C). 1995. pap. text ed. 30.39 (0-7872-1119-2) Kendall-Hunt.

Readings & Applications in Ethics for Field Managers. American College Staff. LC 94-74178. 75p. (Orig.). 1995. pap. text ed. 9.95 (0-943590-65-5) Amer College.

Readings & Applications in Financial Accounting. 2nd ed. Graeme Rankine & Earl K. Stice. LC 92-36014. 1992. pap. text ed. 29.20 (0-13-156803-5) P-H.

Readings & Cases in Auditing. 6th ed. Thomas D. Hubbard et al. LC 83-70549. (Orig.). 1989. pap. 22.95 (0-87393-084-3) Dame Pubns.

Readings & Cases in Business Communications. Steven P. Golen et al. LC 83-17066. (Business Communications Ser.: 1-573). 260p. (C). 1984. pap. text ed. 22.95 (0-471-86953-8) P-H.

Readings & Cases in Business Communications. Steven P. Golen & Ross F. Figgins. 1989. pap. text ed. 34.40 (0-13-761164-1) P-H.

Readings & Cases in Direct Marketing. Herbert Brown & Bruce Buskirk. 352p. 1994. pap. 24.95 (0-8442-3183-5, NTC Busn Bks) NTC Pub Grp.

Readings & Cases in Educational Psychology. Anita E. Woolfolk. LC 92-37249. 1992. pap. text ed. 21.00 (0-205-13821-7) Allyn.

Readings & Cases in Governmental & Nonprofit Accounting. rev. ed. Richard J. Vargo & Paul A. Dierks. LC 82-70506. 272p. (C). 1983. pap. text ed. 25.95 (0-931920-37-X) Dame Pubns.

Readings & Cases in International Human Resources Management. 2nd ed. Ed. by Mark Mendenhall & Gary Oddou. LC 94-37700. 1995. pap. 37.95 (0-538-84737-9) S-W Pub.

Readings & Cases in Labor Relations & Collective Bargaining. James Martin & Timothy J. Keaveny. Ed. by Robert Allen. LC 84-14484. 512p. 1985. teacher ed. write for info. (0-201-12354-1); pap. text ed. 22.36 (0-201-12353-3) Addison-Wesley.

Readings & Cases on an Introduction to the Anglo-American Legal System: Introduction, Readings & Cases. 2nd ed. Edgar Bodenheimer et al. (American Casebook Ser.). 166p. (C). 1988. reprint ed. pap. 21.00 (0-314-36662-8) West Pub.

Readings & Conversations: About the United States, Its People, Its History & Its Customs, 2 vols., 1. rev. ed. English Language Services Staff. 1976. text ed. 4.95 (0-87789-195-8) ELS Educ Servs.

Readings & Conversations: About the United States, Its People, Its History & Its Customs, 2 vols., 2. rev. ed. English Language Services Staff. 1976. text ed. 4.95 (0-87789-196-6) ELS Educ Servs.

Readings & Conversations: About the United States, Its People, Its History & Its Customs, 2 vols., No. 1. rev. ed. English Language Services Staff. 1976. Cassettes 1. audio 95.00 (0-87789-201-6) ELS Educ Servs.

Readings & Conversations: About the United States, Its People, Its History & Its Customs, 2 vols., No. 2. rev. ed. English Language Services Staff. 1976. Cassettes 2. audio 95.00 (0-87789-202-4) ELS Educ Servs.

Readings & Exercises in Organizational Behavior. Jane W. Gibson & Richard M. Hodgetts. 262p. (C). 1985. pap. text ed. 23.50 (0-15-575808-X, OBR) Dryden Pr.

Readings & Information Systems: A Managerial Perspective. James C. Wetherbe et al. 486p. (C). 1988. pap. text ed. 41.00 (0-314-65767-3) West Pub.

Readings & Interpreting Diagrams in Air Conditioning & Refrigeration. Edward F. Mahoney. (C). 1983. teacher ed. write for info. (0-8359-6484-1, Reston) P-H.

Readings & Issues in Cost Management. Ed. by James M. Reeve. LC 94-11412. 1995. text ed. 26.95 (0-538-84248-2) S-W Pub.

Readings & Materials for Managerial Communication. Donald Leonard et al. 315p. 1991. pap. 25.00 (0-536-57984-9) Ginn Pr.

*Readings & Materials on Tax Policy. Philip D. Oliver & Fred W. Peel, Jr. (University Casebook Ser.). 803p. 1996. text ed. write for info. (1-56662-427-4) Foundation Pr.

Readings & Notes on Financial Accounting: Issues & Controversies. 4th ed. Ed. by Stephen A. Zeff & Bala G. Dharan. LC 93-36033. 1993. pap. text ed. write for info. (0-07-016726-5) McGraw.

*Readings & Notes on Financial Accounting: Issues & Controversies. 5th ed. Stephen A. Ziff & Bala G. Dharan. LC 96-35211. 1996. pap. text ed. write for info. (0-07-073006-7) McGraw.

Readings & Writings: Semiotic Counter-Strategies. Peter Wollen. 228p. (C). 1985. pap. text ed. 19.00 (0-86091-755-X, Pub. by Vrso UK) Norton.

Readings Are Writings: A Guide to Reading & Writing Well. Jan Youga et al. LC 95-15721. 512p. (C). 1995. pap. text ed. 31.60 (0-13-097882-5) P-H.

Readings, Cases, Materials in Canon Law: A Textbook for Ministerial Students. rev. ed. Dan Ward & Jordan F. Hite. LC 79-24977. 512p. (Orig.). (C). 1980. pap. text ed. 24.95 (0-8146-1081-1) Liturgical Pr.

Readings for a Basic Writing Program. Murray. 1992. pap. text ed. write for info. (0-07-044258-4) McGraw.

Readings for a New Public Health. Ed. by Claudia J. Martin & David V. McQueen. 250p. 1988. 55.00 (0-85224-598-X, Pub. by Edinburgh U Pr UK) Col U Pr.

Readings for a New Public Health. Ed. by Claudia J. Martin & David V. McQueen. 336p. 1991. pap. text ed. 29.00 (0-85224-616-1, Pub. by Edinburgh U Pr UK) Col U Pr.

Readings for Anthropology & Education. Ed. by Charles Harrington. 1971. pap. text ed. 7.95 (0-8290-1178-1) Irvington.

Readings for Astronomy. Pine & Hartman. (Adaptable Courseware Ser.). 1994. pap. 33.95 (0-534-32035-X) Wadsworth Pub.

Readings for Calculus. Ed. by Underwood Dudley. LC 92-62283. (Notes Ser.: Vol. 31). 1993. pap. 34.95 (0-88385-087-7, NTE-31) Math Assn.

Readings for College English. Ronald A. Horton. 420p. (Orig.). (C). 1990. pap. text ed. 20.33 (0-89084-534-4, 048272) Bob Jones Univ Pr.

Readings for Composition: A Writer's Anthology. Steven Robins & Adrienne Robins. LC 91-67516. 432p. (Orig.). (C). 1992. pap. text ed. 8.00 (0-312-04005-9) St Martin.

Readings for Composition: A Writer's Anthology. Steven Robins & Adrienne Robins. LC 91-67516. 432p. (Orig.). (C). 1992. pap. text ed. 5.00 (0-312-04007-5) St Martin.

*Readings for Cultural Geography Pak. Robert Hoffpauir. 312p. (C). 1996. 52.44 (0-7872-2620-3) Kendall-Hunt.

*Readings for Educators. 178p. 1991. pap. 13.00 (0-614-29488-6) Orton Dyslexia.

Readings for Enrichment in Secondary School Mathematics. Ed. by Max A. Sobel. LC 87-34855. (Illus.). 258p. (Orig.). 1988. pap. 12.50 (0-87353-252-X) NCTM.

*Readings for Environmental Literacy 1998. 2nd ed. McKinney. (Biology Ser.). (C). 1998. pap. 12.95 (0-534-54198-4) Wadsworth Pub.

Readings for History of the Military Art. USMA (Salter) Staff. 304p. (C). 1996. per., pap. text ed. 21.50 (0-7872-1874-X) Kendall-Hunt.

Readings for Holy Week. 128p. 1996. 6.00 (1-878422-23-5) Moravian Ch in Amer.

Readings for Holy Week. large type ed. 128p. 1996. 8.00 (1-878422-24-3) Moravian Ch in Amer.

*Readings for Holy Week with Music. 160p. 1996. 10.00 (1-878422-26-X) Moravian Ch in Amer.

Readings for Lent & Easter: From the Upper Room. LC 92-61444. 144p. 1993. pap. 8.95 (0-8358-0681-2) Upper Room Bks.

*Readings for Logical Analysis. 2nd ed. Stephen R. Hicks & David Kelley. LC 97-25812. 1998. pap. write for info. (0-393-97214-3) Norton.

Readings for Logical Analysis to Accompany the Art of Reasoning with Symbolic Logic. enl. ed. David Kelley & Stephen Hicks. (Orig.). (C). 1994. pap. text ed. 3.95 (0-393-96555-4) Norton.

Readings for Logical Analysis to Accompany the Art of Reasoning with Symbolic Logic. 2nd enl. ed. David Kelley & Stephen Hicks. (Orig.). (C). 1994. pap. text ed. 13.95 (0-393-96500-7) Norton.

*Readings for Marriage & Family Experience. 3rd ed. Strong. (Sociology-Upper Level Ser.). (C). 1998. pap. 49.95 (0-534-53763-4) Wadsworth Pub.

Readings for Older Women. 2nd ed. Ed. by Meg Bowman & Diane Haywood. 1997. 11.95 (0-940483-04-1) Hot Flash Pr.

*Readings for Reflective Teaching in the Primary School. Ed. by Andrew Pollard. (Education Ser.). (Illus.). 256p. 1996. pap. 24.95 (0-304-33799-4); text ed. 70.00 (0-304-33798-6) Cassell.

Readings for Social Psychology. Ed. by Martin F. Kaplan. LC 72-86188. 146p. 1972. 26.50 (0-8422-5043-3); pap. text ed. 12.50 (0-8422-0228-5) Irvington.

Readings for Social Work Practice, Vol. 1. Everett Busby et al. LC 72-8103. 174p. 1972. pap. text ed. 14.95 (0-686-76955-4) Irvington.

*Readings for Teaching Science in Elementary & Middle Schools Pak. Richard Rezba. 538p. (C). 1996. 50.50 (0-7872-2654-8) Kendall-Hunt.

Readings for Technical Writers. fac. ed. Debra Journet & Julie L. Kling. LC 83-16482. 239p. 1984. reprint ed. pap. 68.20 (0-7837-8340-X, 2049128) Bks Demand.

Readings for the Daily Office from the Early Church. Ed. by J. Robert Wright. 608p. 1991. 39.95 (0-89869-201-6) Church Pub Inc.

Readings for the History of the English Language. Ed. by Charles T. Scott & Jon L. Erickson. LC 68-20532. 1968. 64.50 (0-89197-370-2) Irvington.

Readings for the 21st Century. 3rd ed. William Vesterman & Josh Ozersky. LC 96-15116. 444p. 1996. pap. text ed. 29.00 (0-205-19803-1) Allyn.

An Asterisk (*) at the beginning of an entry indicates that the title is appearing in BIP for the first time.

Readings for the 21st Century: Tomorrow's Issues for Today's Students. 2nd ed. Ed. by Josh Ozersky. LC 93-33503. 1993. write for info. (*0-205-15874-9*) Allyn.

***Readings for the 21st Century: Tomorrow's Issues for Today's Students.** 3rd ed. 1997. suppl. ed., teacher ed. write for info. (*0-205-26182-5*) Allyn.

Readings for Women's Programs. expanded rev. ed. Ed. by Meg Bowman & Connie Springer. 125p. (Orig.). 1996. pap. 8.95 (*0-940483-00-9*) Hot Flash Pr.

Readings for Writers. 6th ed. Jo R. McCuen & Anthony C. Winkler. 1008p. (C). 1989. pap. text ed. 21.50 (*0-15-575835-7*) HB Coll Pubs.

Readings for Writers. 7th ed. Jo R. McCuen & Anthony C. Winkler. 850p. (C). 1992. pap. text ed. 22.75 (*0-15-575837-3*) HB Coll Pubs.

Readings for Writers. 8th ed. Jo R. McCuen. (C). 1994. pap. text ed. 31.00 (*0-15-501267-3*) HB Coll Pubs.

Readings for Writers. 8th ed. Jo R. McCuen. (C). 1994. teacher ed., pap. text ed. 33.75 (*0-15-502170-2*) HB Coll Pubs.

***Readings for Writers.** 9th ed. Jo R. McCuen. (C). 1997. pap. text ed. 29.75 (*0-15-503844-3*) HB Coll Pubs.

Readings for Your Wedding. Brian Magee. 88p. 1989. pap. 22.00 (*0-86217-211-X*, Pub. by Veritas IE) St Mut.

Readings from AI Magazine: Nineteen Eighty to Nineteen Eighty-Four. Ed. by Robert Engelmore. (Illus.). 664p. (C). 1988. pap. text ed. 74.95 (*0-929280-01-6*) AAAI Pr.

***Readings from Bhagabata.** G. N. Das. 1996. 14.00 (*81-7017-337-X*, Pub. by Abhinav II) S Asia.

Readings from Childhood Education, Vol. II. Ed. by James D. Quisenberry et al. LC 91-23454. (Illus.). 390p. 1991. 24.50 (*0-87173-121-5*) ACEI.

Readings from Classical Rhetoric. Ed. by Patricia P. Matsen et al. LC 89-36897. 400p. (C). 1990. 34.95 (*0-8093-1592-0*); pap. 19.95 (*0-8093-1593-9*) S Ill U Pr.

Readings from Conservation Biology: Genes, Populations & Species. Ed. by David Ehrenfeld. LC 94-46719. (Readings from Conservation Biology Ser.). 1995. pap. 24.95 (*0-86542-452-7*) Blackwell Sci.

***Readings from Disciplines.** Christine Hult. 220p. 1997. pap. text ed. 16.00 (*0-205-26916-8*) P-H.

Readings from Durkheim. Selected by Kenneth Thompson. (Key Texts Ser.). 150p. 1985. pap. 9.95 (*0-85312-901-0*, 9585, Pub. by Tavistock-E Horwood UK) Routledge Chapman & Hall.

Readings from Educational Leadership: Coaching & Staff Development. Ed. by Ronald S. Brandt. LC 89-6543. 216p. 1989. pap. 25.95 (*0-87120-158-5*, 611-89123) Assn Supervision.

Readings from Educational Leadership: Effective Schools & School Improvement. Ed. by Ronald S. Brandt. LC 89-6523. 180p. 1989. pap. 25.95 (*0-87120-159-3*, 611-89124) Assn Supervision.

Readings from Educational Leadership: Performance Assessment. Ed. by Ronald S. Brandt. LC 92-27747. 1992. pap. 25.95 (*0-87120-195-X*) Assn Supervision.

Readings from Educational Leadership: Restructuring Schools. Ed. by Ronald S. Brandt. LC 92-47443. 1993. 29.95 (*0-87120-206-9*) Assn Supervision.

Readings from Educational Leadership: Students at Risk. Ed. by Ronald S. Brandt. LC 90-36145. 171p. 1990. pap. 25.95 (*0-87120-172-0*, 611-90092) Assn Supervision.

Readings from Educational Leadership: Teaching Thinking. Ed. by Ronald S. Brandt. LC 89-6544. 215p. 1989. pap. 25.95 (*0-87120-160-7*, 611-89125) Assn Supervision.

***Readings from Emile Durkheim.** Ed. by Kenneth Thompson. 150p. (C). 1985. pap. 12.95 (*0-415-04320-4*) Routledge.

Readings from Karl Marx. Ed. by Derek Sayer. 256p. 1989. pap. 7.95 (*0-415-01810-2*) Routledge.

Readings from Mennonite Writings New & Old. J. Craig Haas. LC 92-38440. 436p. 1992. pap. 14.95 (*1-56148-064-9*) Good Bks PA.

Readings from Progressive Education, Vol. I: A Movement & Its Professional Journal. Ed. by Stephen I. Brown et al. LC 88-5713. 366p. (Orig.). (C). 1988. pap. text ed. 29.50 (*0-8191-6917-X*); lib. bdg. 50.00 (*0-8191-6916-1*) U Pr of Amer.

Readings from Talcott Parsons. Selected by Peter Hamilton. (Key Texts Ser.). 150p. 1985. pap. 9.95 (*0-85312-854-5*, 9586, Pub. by Tavistock-E Horwood UK) Routledge Chapman & Hall.

Readings from the American Mercury. American Mercury Staff. Ed. by G. C. Knight. LC 68-16902. (Essay Index Reprint Ser.). 1977. 20.95 (*0-8369-0150-9*) Ayer.

***Readings from the First-Century World: Primary Sources for New Testament Study.** Ed. by Walter A. Elwell & Robert W. Yarbrough. (Encountering Biblical Studies). 432p. Date not set. pap. 19.99 (*0-8010-2157-X*) Baker Bks.

Readings from the History of the Episcopal Church. Ed. by Robert W. Prichard. LC 86-12741. 192p. (Orig.). 1986. pap. 14.95 (*0-8192-1383-7*) Morehouse Pub.

Readings from the New Book on Nature: Physics & Metaphysics in the Modern Novel. Robert L. Nadeau. LC 81-2625. 224p. 1981. lib. bdg. 30.00 (*0-87023-331-9*) U of Mass Pr.

Readings from the People's Daily. Vivian L. Hsu. 1974. 10.95 (*0-88710-070-8*) Yale Far Eastern Pubns.

Readings in Abnormal Psychology. Jill M. Giiket et al. LC 88-26796. 612p. 1989. Net. pap. text ed. 18.00 (*0-471-63107-8*) Wiley.

***Readings in Accident Prevention.** 3rd ed. Insurance Institute of America Staff & Albert C. Wagner, III. LC 95-79643. 100p. (Orig.). 1995. pap. 18.00 (*0-89462-086-X*, ALCM74) IIA.

Readings in Accounting for Management Control. Clive R. Emmanuel et al. 256p. 1991. pap. 39.95 (*0-412-41490-2*, A6305) Chapman & Hall.

***Readings in Accounting for Management Control.** 3rd ed. C. Emmanuel & David T. Otley. 704p. 1995. pap. 29.95 (*0-412-62590-3*) Chapman & Hall.

Readings in Accounting Theory. Mohamed Ibrahim. 384p. (C). 1994. per., pap. text ed. 39.84 (*0-8403-9768-2*) Kendall-Hunt.

Readings in African Law, 2 vols. Ed. by N. N. Rubin & E. Cotran. 351p. 1970. 95.00 (*0-7146-2602-3*, Pub. by F Cass Pubs UK) Intl Spec Bk.

Readings in African Philosophy: An Akan Collection. Ed. by Safro Kwame. 318p. (Orig.). (C). 1995. lib. bdg. 56.00 (*0-8191-9910-9*) U Pr of Amer.

Readings in African Philosophy: An Akan Collection. Ed. by Safro Kwame. 318p. (Orig.). (C). 1995. pap. text ed. 34.50 (*0-8191-9911-7*) U Pr of Amer.

***Readings in African Popular Culture.** Karin Barber. LC 97-11211. 1997. write for info. (*0-253-33294-X*) Ind U Pr.

***Readings in Agents.** Michael Huhns & Munindar Singh. 500p. (C). 1997. pap. 49.95 (*1-55860-495-2*) Morgan Kaufmann.

Readings in American Educational History. Ed. by Edgar W. Knight & Clifton L. Hall. LC 70-97347. 799p. 1970. reprint ed. text ed. 67.50 (*0-8371-2835-8*, KNAE, Greenwood Pr) Greenwood.

Readings in American Folklore. Jan H. Brunvand. (Illus.). (C). 1979. pap. text ed. 19.95 (*0-393-95029-8*) Norton.

Readings in American Government: The State of the Union. David C. Saffell. 300p. (C). 1990. pap. write for info. (*0-318-68286-9*) P-H.

Readings in American Health Care: Current Issues in Socio-Historical Perspective. Ed. by William G. Rothstein. LC 95-12317. 426p. 1995. 49.95 (*0-299-14530-1*); pap. 17.95 (*0-299-14534-4*) U of Wis Pr.

Readings in American History. 1996. pap. text ed. 22.25 (*0-03-095052-X*) HR&W Schl Div.

Readings in American History. Ed. by Jerry R. Baydo. 128p. 1992. 12.00 (*0-911541-21-7*) Gregory Pub.

Readings in American History, Bk. 2. Jack Abramowitz. (J). (gr. 4-5). 1987. pap. text ed. 5.25 (*0-89525-862-5*) Ed Activities.

Readings in American History, Vol. II. Kant et al. 384p. (C). 1992. pap. text ed. 32.49 (*0-8403-7456-9*) Kendall-Hunt.

Readings in American History: The Age of Exploration to Reconstruction, Vol. 1. Thom Armstrong. 240p. (C). 1993. per. 32.49 (*0-8403-8486-6*) Kendall-Hunt.

Readings in American History, Vol. II: Reconstruction to Watergate. Thom Armstrong. 288p. (C). 1990. per. 28.29 (*0-8403-5894-6*) Kendall-Hunt.

Readings in American Legal History. Ed. by Mark A. Howe. LC 70-155924. (American Constitutional & Legal History Ser). 1971. reprint ed. lib. bdg. 59.50 (*0-306-70159-6*) Da Capo.

Readings in Ancient Greek Philosophy: From Thales to Aristotle. Ed. by S. M. Cohen et al. LC 94-44162. 800p. (C). 1995. text ed. 45.00 (*0-87220-313-1*); pap. text ed. 27.95 (*0-87220-312-3*) Hackett Pub.

***Readings in Ancient History.** 5th ed. Nels M. Bailkey. 527p. (C). 1996. pap. text ed. 24.76 (*0-669-39766-0*) HM College Div.

Readings in Ancient History: Thought & Experience from Gilgamesh to St. Augustine. 4th ed. Nels M. Bailkey. 507p. (C). 1992. pap. text ed. 25.56 (*0-669-27744-4*) HM College Div.

Readings in Anglican Spirituality. Ed. by David Hein. 72p. (Orig.). 1991. pap. 1.95 (*0-88028-125-1*, 1137) Forward Movement.

Readings in Animal Cognition. Ed. by Marc Bekoff & Dale Jamieson. (Illus.). 496p. 1995. pap. 30.00 (*0-262-52208-X*, Bradford Bks) MIT Pr.

Readings in Anthropology. Eugene Cooper & Andrei Simic. 240p. (C). 1994. per., pap. text ed. 45.09 (*0-8403-9193-5*) Kendall-Hunt.

Readings in Anthropology: People of the Bering Sea. Ed. by Ted Bank. 1971. pap. text ed. 6.95 (*0-8422-0137-8*) Irvington.

***Readings in Anthropology of Human Movement Vol. 1: The Study of Dances.** Drid Williams. LC 96-33151. 1997. 38.00 (*0-8108-3236-4*) Scarecrow.

Readings in Aphasia. Ed. by Ruben H. Douglas & Nancy R. Macciomei. (Special Education Ser.). 110p. (C). 1986. 24.95 (*0-582-28631-X*); pap. text ed. 16.95 (*0-582-28617-4*) Longman.

***Readings in Applied Anthropology.** Ferraro. (Anthropology Ser.). (C). 1998. pap. 12.95 (*0-534-53324-8*) Wadsworth Pub.

Readings in Arab Middle Eastern Societies & Cultures. Abdulla H. Lutfiyya. Ed. by Charles W. Churchill. LC 69-19116. (Orig.). 1970. pap. text ed. 38.50 (*90-279-1062-6*) Mouton.

Readings in Argumentation. Ed. by William L. Benoit et al. LC 92-9887. (Studies in Argumentation in Pragmatics & Discourse Analysis: Vol. 11). xii, 813p. 1992. lib. bdg. 244.65 (*3-11-013576-0*) Mouton.

Readings in Art History: The Renaissance to the Present, Vol. 2. 3rd ed. Harold Spencer. LC 76-7404. 520p. (C). 1982. pap. text ed. 45.33 (*0-02-414390-1*, Macmillan Coll) P-H.

Readings in Art History Ancient Egypt. Harold Spencer. 1985. pap. 12.95 (*0-684-17619-X*) S&S Trade.

Readings in Artificial Intelligence. Ed. by Bonnie L. Webber & Nils J. Nilsson. LC 85-24203. (Illus.). 557p. (Orig.). (C). 1981. pap. text ed. 29.95 (*0-934613-03-6*) Morgan Kaufmann.

Readings in Artificial Intelligence & Databases. Ed. by John Mylopoulos & Michael Brodie. 650p. (C). 1988. pap. text ed. 44.95 (*0-934613-53-2*) Morgan Kaufmann.

Readings in Artificial Intelligence & Software Engineering. Ed. by Charles Rich & Richard C. Waters. LC 86-18627. (Illus.). 624p. (Orig.). 1986. pap. text ed. 29.95 (*0-934613-12-5*) Morgan Kaufmann.

Readings in Behavior. Ed. by William G. Van der Kloot et al. LC 73-15700. (Illus.). 1974. pap. text ed. 19.50 (*0-03-084077-5*) Irvington.

Readings in Behavior Modification. Marilyn T. Erickson et al. LC 73-8528. 1973. 29.75 (*0-8422-5106-5*); pap. 14.95 (*0-8422-0312-5*) Irvington.

Readings in Behavior Modification Research with Children. Marilyn T. Erickson et al. LC 73-8536. 1973. pap. text ed. 24.95 (*0-8422-0313-3*) Irvington.

Readings in Behavioral Issues in Safety. Ed. by Daniel C. Petersen. 106p. 1985. 10.00 (*0-939874-63-6*) ASSE.

Readings in Biblical Hebrew: An Intermediate Textbook. Ed. by Maxine Hancock & Richard Beinert. LC 93-18751. (Language Ser.). 256p. (C). 1993. text ed. 37.50 (*0-300-05573-0*) Yale U Pr.

Readings in Biological Science. 3rd ed. Ed. by Irving W. Knobloch. LC 72-93743. (C). 1973. pap. text ed. 14.95 (*0-89197-371-0*) Irvington.

Readings in Black Aged. Ed. by Peter Chang. 212p. 1977. 29.50 (*0-8422-0556-X*) Irvington.

Readings in Black American Music. Eileen Southern. (C). 1983. pap. text ed. 10.95 (*0-393-95280-0*) Norton.

Readings in Business & Society. 2nd ed. Sethi & Steidemeier. 576p. (C). 1996. pap. text ed. 44.00 (*0-13-490145-2*) P-H.

Readings in Business Communication. Ed. by Robert D. Gieselman. 1986. pap. 11.60 (*0-87563-287-4*) Stipes.

Readings in Business Cycle Theory. Compiled by American Economic Association Staff. LC 76-29403. (BCL Ser.). 736p. reprint ed. 41.50 (*0-404-15330-5*) AMS Pr.

Readings in Business Cycles & National Income. Ed. by Alvin H. Hansen & Richard V. Clemence. (Modern Revivals in Economics Ser.). 585p. (C). 1994. text ed. 93.95 (*0-7512-0247-9*, Pub. by Gregg Revivals UK) Ashgate Pub Co.

Readings in Business Ethics & Social Responsibility. William A. Wines & Steven C. Anderson. 264p. (C). 1994. per. 52.44 (*0-8403-9144-7*) Kendall-Hunt.

Readings in Business Law & the Legal Environment of Business. Douglas Whitman & John W. Gergacz. 1991. pap. text ed. write for info. (*0-07-069994-1*) McGraw.

Readings in Business Law & the Legal Environment of Business. 2nd ed. Ed. by Douglas Whitman. LC 93-28556. 1993. pap. text ed. write for info. (*0-07-070004-4*) McGraw.

Readings in Business Today. Barbara Pletcher. (C). 1980. 12.50 (*0-256-02376-X*) Irwin.

Readings in California Catholic History. Francis J. Weber. 22.00 (*0-87026-000-6*) Westernlore.

Readings in Caribbean History & Economics: An Introduction to the Region. Roberta M. Delson. (Caribbean Studies). 336, xxiip. 1981. text ed. 207.00 (*0-677-05280-4*) Gordon & Breach.

Readings in Child Development. Nancy Lauter-Klatell. LC 90-46200. 178p. (C). 1991. pap. text ed. 22.95 (*0-87484-942-X*, 942) Mayfield Pub.

Readings in Child Development. 2nd ed. A. Lynn Scoresby & Alvin H. Price. 1992. pap. text ed. write for info. (*0-07-055963-5*) McGraw.

Readings in Chinese Communist Ideology: A Manual for Students of the Chinese Language. Wen-Shun Chi. LC 67-11201. 452p. reprint ed. pap. 128.90 (*0-685-20500-2*, 2029949) Bks Demand.

Readings in Chinese Geography, 2 vols., Vol. 1: Chinese Text. Jack F. Williams & Yung Teng Chia-yee. 61p. reprint ed. Vol. 1, Chinese Text. pap. 20.00 (*0-8357-8534-3*, 2034837) Bks Demand.

Readings in Chinese Geography, 2 vols., Vol.: Note, Glossary & Translation. Jack F. Williams & Yung Teng Chia-yee. 61p. reprint ed. Vol. 2, Note, Glossary & Translation. pap. 50.80 (*0-8357-3592-3*) Bks Demand.

Readings in Chinese Literary Thought. Stephen Owen. (Harvard-Yenching Institute Monograph Ser.: No. 30). 600p. 1992. 55.00 (*0-674-74920-0*) Harvard E Asian.

Readings in Chinese Literary Thought. Stephen Owen. (Harvard-Yenching Institute Monographs: No. 30). 674p. 1996. pap. 25.00 (*0-674-74921-9*) HUP.

Readings in Christian Ethics: A Historical Sourcebook. Ed. by J. Philip Wogaman & Douglas M. Strong. 352p. (Orig.). 1996. pap. 23.00 (*0-664-25574-4*) Westminster John Knox.

***Readings in Christian Ethics: Theory & Method.** Ed. by David K. Clark & Robert V. Rakestraw. LC 93-30274. 1919. pap. 39.99 (*0-8010-2094-8*) Baker Bks.

Readings in Christian Ethics Vol. 1: Theory & Method. Ed. by David K. Clark & Robert V. Rakestraw. LC 93-30274. 328p. (Orig.). (C). 1994. pap. 17.99 (*0-8010-2581-8*) Baker Bks.

Readings in Christian Ethics Vol. 2: Issues & Applications. Ed. by David K. Clark & Robert V. Rakestraw. LC 93-30274. 552p. (Orig.). (C). 1995. pap. 27.99 (*0-8010-2056-5*) Baker Bks.

Readings in Christian Theology. Ed. by Peter C. Hodgson & Robert H. King. LC 84-48721. 432p. 1985. pap. 25.00 (*0-8006-1849-1*, 1-1849, Fortress Pr) Augsburg Fortress.

Readings in Christian Thought. Ed. by Hugh T. Kerr. LC 66-14992. 1990. pap. 25.95 (*0-687-35547-8*) Abingdon.

Readings in Christianity: A Reader. Robert E. Van Voorst. (Religion Ser.). (Illus.). 384p. (C). 1997. pap. text ed. 30.95 (*0-534-25392-X*) Wadsworth Pub.

Readings in Church & State: Selections from Journal of Church & State, 1959-1988. Intro. by James E. Wood, Jr. 438p. (Orig.). 1989. pap. text ed. 9.95 (*0-929182-01-4*) Baylor U J M Dawson.

Readings in Classical Rhetoric. Ed. by Thomas W. Benson & Michael H. Prosser. xii, 341p. (C). 1988. reprint ed. pap. text ed. 19.95 (*0-9611800-3-X*, Hermagoras) L Erlbaum Assocs.

Readings in Clinical Spectrography in Speech. Ed. by Ronald J. Baken & Raymond G. Daniloff. (Illus.). 576p. (Orig.). (C). 1990. pap. text ed. 49.95 (*1-879105-04-7*, 0005) Singular Publishing.

***Readings in Cognitive Psychology.** Sternberg. (C). 1998. pap. text ed. 25.50 (*0-15-504105-3*) HB Coll Pubs.

***Readings in Community Health Nursing.** 5th ed. Barbara W. Spradley & Judith A. Allender. LC 96-31654. 672p. 1996. pap. text ed. 29.95 (*0-397-55436-2*) Lppncott-Raven.

Readings in Community Work. Ed. by Paul Henderson & David Thomas. 1981. 40.00 (*0-317-05809-6*, Pub. by Natl Inst Soc Work) St Mut.

Readings in Companion Animal Behavior. Victoria L. Voith & Peter L. Borchelt. 1996. pap. text ed. 59.00 (*1-884254-23-3*) Vet Lrn Syst.

Readings in Computational Auditory Scene Analysis: Proceedings of the IJCAI-95 Workshop. Ed. by David F. Rosenthal & Hirishi G. Okuno. LC 97-5936. 408p. 1997. pap. 25.00 (*0-8058-2284-4*) L Erlbaum Assocs.

Readings in Computational Auditory Scene Analysis: Proceedings of the IJCAI-95 Workshop. Ed. by David F. Rosenthal & Hiroshi G. Okuno. LC 97-5936. 408p. 1997. text ed. 50.00 (*0-8058-2283-6*) L Erlbaum Assocs.

Readings in Computer-Generated Music. Denis Baggi. LC 92-15303. 232p. 1992. 45.00 (*0-8186-2747-6*, 2747) IEEE Comp Soc.

Readings in Computer Vision: Issues, Problems, Principles & Paradigms. Ed. by Martin Fischler & Oscar Firschein. LC 86-27692. (Illus.). 802p. (Orig.). 1987. pap. 44.95 (*0-934613-33-8*) Morgan Kaufmann.

Readings in Contemporary Criminological Theory. Larry J. Siegel. LC 96-19387. (Illus.). 432p. 1996. text ed. 60.00 (*1-55553-223-3*); pap. text ed. 22.50 (*1-55553-224-1*) NE U Pr.

Readings in Contemporary Culture. Alice S. Horning. 1979. text ed. 6.00 (*0-07-030352-5*) McGraw.

Readings in Contemporary Sociological Theory: From Modernity to Post-Modernity. Ed. by Donald Mcquarie & R. Serge Denisoff. LC 94-3991. 440p. 1994. pap. text ed. 33.33 (*0-13-104266-1*) P-H.

Readings in Contrastive Spanish Linguistics, Vol II. Ed. by Rose Nash & Domitila Belaval. LC 73-85939. 265p. 1980. pap. 7.95 (*0-913480-41-X*) Inter Am U Pr.

Readings in Controversial Issues in Education of the Mentally Retarded. Ed. by Frank Warner & Robert Thrapp. 1972. 29.50 (*0-8422-5007-7*) Irvington.

Readings in Cost & Management Accounting. Abdelkhalik. (AB - Accounting Principles Ser.). 1995. text ed. 24.95 (*0-538-84477-9*) S-W Pub.

Readings in Cost Benefit-Cost Control. Ed. by Foster C. Rinefort. 88p. 1985. 10.00 (*0-939874-68-7*) ASSE.

Readings in Cost Engineering. Compiled by American Society of Civil Engineers Staff. 730p. 1979. pap. 54.00 (*0-87262-147-2*) Am Soc Civil Eng.

Readings in Criminal Justice. Richter H. Moore, Jr. et al. LC 75-38727. 1976. pap. 10.95 (*0-672-61371-9*, Bobbs) Macmillan.

Readings in Cross-Cultural Methodology. Ed. by Frank W. Moore. LC 66-28127. (Comparative Studies). 350p. 1966. reprint ed. 15.00 (*0-87536-101-3*); reprint ed. pap. 10.00 (*0-87536-102-1*) HRAFP.

Readings in Cross-Cultural Psychology: Proceedings of the Inaugural Meeting of the International Association for Cross-Cultural Psychology Held in Hong Kong, August 1972. International Association for Cross-Cultural Psychology. Ed. by John L. Dawson & Walter J. Lonner. LC 75-324540. 413p. reprint ed. pap. 117.80 (*0-685-17124-8*, 2027834) Bks Demand.

***Readings in Cultural Anthropology.** Peoples. Date not set. pap. write for info. (*0-314-02820-X*) West Pub.

Readings in Current Economics. Reuben Slesinger. 340p. (C). 1990. pap. text ed. 26.32 (*0-929655-46-X*) CT Pub.

Readings in Curriculum: A Process Approach. C. H. Edwards. (C). 1977. pap. 7.80 (*0-87563-068-5*) Stipes.

Readings in Curriculum & Supervision. Ed. by V. Eugene Yarbrough et al. 250p. 1974. 29.00 (*0-8422-5203-7*) Irvington.

Readings in Czech. Michael Heim et al. (UCLA Slavic Studies: Vol. 13). 147p. (Orig.). 1985. pap. text ed. 16.95 (*0-89357-154-7*) Slavica.

Readings in Database Systems. 2nd ed. Ed. by Michael Stonebraker. 970p. (C). 1993. pap. 49.95 (*1-55860-252-6*) Morgan Kaufmann.

Readings in Decision Analysis. Ed. by Simon French. 244p. 1989. 59.95 (*0-412-31120-8*) Chapman & Hall.

Readings in Decision Analysis. Ed. by Simon French. 244p. (gr. 13). 1989. pap. text ed. 38.95 (*0-412-32170-X*) Chapman & Hall.

Readings in Delaware History. Ed. by Carol E. Hoffecker. LC 74-160876. 220p. 12.50 (*0-87413-107-3*) U Delaware Pr.

Readings in Descriptive Bibliography. Ed. by John B. Jones. LC 74-76529. 218p. reprint ed. pap. 62.20 (*0-7837-1347-9*, 2041495) Bks Demand.

Readings in Deviant Behavior. Ed. by Alex Thio & Thomas C. Calhoun. (C). 1995. text ed. 31.95 (*0-673-99261-6*) Addson-Wesley Educ.

Readings in Distributed Artificial Intelligence. Ed. by Alan Bond & Les Gasser. 650p. 1988. pap. text ed. 49.95 (*0-934613-63-X*) Morgan Kaufmann.

Readings in Early Childhood Music Education. Barbara L. Andress & Linda M. Walker. 112p. (Orig.). (C). 1992. teacher ed., pap. 21.00 (*1-56545-015-9*, 1043) Music Ed Natl.

An Asterisk (*) at the beginning of an entry indicates that the title is appearing in BIP for the first time.

R

Readings in Earth Science & Physical Science. Ed. by Marjorie P. Weiser. 128p. 1988. pap. text ed. 7.00 (*0-8428-3007-3*) Cambridge Bk.

Readings in Eastern Religions. Ed. by Ronald W. Neufeldt et al. (C). 1988. pap. 24.95 (*0-88920-955-3*) Wilfrid Laurier.

Readings in Ecology. Ed. by Polley A. Randolph & James C. Randolph. (Illus.). (C). 1973. text ed. 39.50 (*0-8422-5085-9*) Irvington.

Readings in Ecology & Feminist Theology. Mary H. MacKinnon & Moni McIntyre. 360p. (Orig.). 1995. pap. 19.95 (*1-55612-762-6*) Sheed & Ward MO.

Readings in Econometric Theory. Ed. by J. Malcolm Dowling & Fred R. Glahe. LC 79-128867. 586p. reprint ed. pap. 167.10 (*0-8357-5523-1*, 2035139) Bks Demand.

Readings in Econometric Theory & Practice: A Volume in Honor of George Judge. Ed. by W. E. Griffiths et al. LC 92-15019. (Contributions to Economic Analysis Ser.: Vol. 209). 378p. 1992. 125.50 (*0-444-89574-4*, North Holland) Elsevier.

Readings in Economic Geography. Ed. by Howard G. Roepke. LC 67-19451. 678p. reprint ed. pap. 180.00 (*0-317-10035-1*, 2012580) Bks Demand.

Readings in Educational Management. Ed. by John M. Good. LC 73-80183. 190p. reprint ed. pap. 54.20 (*0-317-07957-3*, 2004503) Bks Demand.

***Readings in Educational Psychology.** Woolfolk. 1997. pap. text ed. 17.00 (*0-205-27889-2*) P-H.

Readings in Emotional Disturbance. Phyllis L. Newcomer. LC 93-5040. 245p. 1993. pap. text ed. 19.00 (*0-89079-588-6*, 6666) PRO-ED.

Readings in English, Bk. 1: Leisure. Andrew Jenkins-Murphy. (Readings in English Ser.). (YA). (gr. 9-12). 1987. pap. text ed. write for info. (*0-13-756016-8*, 18882) Prentice ESL.

Readings in English, Bk. 2: Travel. Thoedore Gross. (Readings in English Ser.). (gr. 9-12). 1987. pap. text ed. write for info. (*0-13-756024-9*, 18883) Prentice ESL.

Readings in English, Bk. 3: Careers. Marianthy McCarthy. (Readings in English Ser.). 105p. (gr. 9-12). 1987. pap. text ed. write for info. (*0-13-756032-X*, 18884) Prentice ESL.

Readings in English, Bk. 4: The Arts. Lee Paradise. (Readings in English Ser.). 118p. (gr. 9-12). 1987. pap. text ed. write for info. (*0-13-756040-0*, 18885) Prentice ESL.

Readings in Environmental Economics. Dodds. (C). 1996. pap. text ed. write for info. (*0-03-002269-X*) HB Coll Pubs.

Readings in Environmental Impact. Ed. by Peter E. Black. LC 74-13079. 345p. 1974. text ed. 39.50 (*0-8422-5201-0*) Irvington.

Readings in Environmental Literacy. Michael L. McKinney. (C). 1996. pap. text ed. write for info. (*0-314-07569-0*) West Pub.

Readings in Environmental Psychology. Ed. by Daniel Stokols. (C). 1974. pap. text ed. 14.95 (*0-8422-0458-X*) Irvington.

Readings in Environmental Psychology Series. David Canter. 1995. pap. text ed. 106.24 (*0-12-158810-6*) Acad Pr.

Readings in Environmental Studies. Olszewski & Schiavo. 416p. (C). 1992. pap. text ed. 27.24 (*0-8403-7324-4*) Kendall-Hunt.

***Readings in Epidemiology & Preventive Medicine Pak.** Daniel Hoffman. 312p. (C). 1996. 99.64 (*0-7872-2636-X*) Kendall-Hunt.

Readings in Epistemology. Ed. by Reginald F. O'Neill. LC 61-18427. 1979. reprint ed. pap. text ed. 14.95 (*0-89197-604-3*) Irvington.

Readings in Epistemology: From Aquinas, Bacon, Galileo, Descartes, Locke, Hume, Kant. 2nd ed. Vincent G. Potter et al. LC 92-45079. xvi, 235p. (C). 1993. 27.50 (*0-8232-1493-1*); pap. 14.50 (*0-8232-1492-3*) Fordham.

Readings in Ethical Issues. William Smith. 304p. (C). 1994. per., pap. text ed. 38.79 (*0-8403-8426-2*) Kendall-Hunt.

Readings in Ethics. John Moore. 175p. 1989. 20.00 (*0-614-13741-1*) Haven Pubns.

***Readings in Ethics.** 3rd rev. ed. Gordon H. Clark et al. (Trinity Papers: Vol. 51). 450p. 1997. reprint ed. pap. text ed. 21.95 (*0-940931-51-6*) Trinity Found.

Readings in European History 1789-Present: A Collection of Primary Sources. 2nd ed. John L. Heineman. 478p. (C). 1996. student ed., spiral bd. write for info. (*0-8403-9125-0*) Kendall-Hunt.

Readings in Evaluation Research. 2nd ed. Ed. by Francis G. Caro. LC 76-12706. 436p. 1977. 50.00 (*0-87154-201-3*) Russell Sage.

Readings in Existential Psychology & Psychiatry. Ed. by Keith Hoeller. LC 93-24311. (Studies in Existential Psychology & Psychiatry). 362p. (Orig.). (C). 1992. pap. 22.50 (*0-391-03781-1*) Humanities.

***Readings in Family & Child Development.** Mize. 1997. pap. text ed. write for info. (*0-07-047108-8*) McGraw.

Readings in Family Law: Divorce & Its Consequences. Frederica K. Lombard. 182p. 1989. pap. text ed. 10.50 (*0-88277-787-4*) Foundation Pr.

Readings in Family Nursing. Wegner & Alexander. 440p. 1993. pap. text ed. 27.95 (*0-397-55033-2*) Lppncott-Raven.

Readings in Federal Taxation. 2nd ed. Michael J. McIntyre et al. LC 83-16356. 625p. 1983. pap. text ed. 24.50 (*0-88277-145-0*) Foundation Pr.

Readings in Finance & Accounting. L. Chadwick. (C). 1990. 170.00 (*0-7487-0402-7*, Pub. by Stanley Thornes UK) Trans-Atl Phila.

***Readings in Financial Planning.** 2nd ed. Ed. by David M. Cordell. LC 96-79583. 350p. (C). 1997. pap. text ed. 23.00 (*0-943590-88-4*) Amer College.

Readings in First Kings: An Interpretation Arranged for Personal & Group Bible Study with Questions & Notes. Ronald S. Wallace. LC 95-40216. 190p. (Orig.). 1996. pap. 15.00 (*0-8028-4200-3*) Eerdmans.

Readings in Forest Hydrology. Ed. by Arthur R. Eschner & Peter E. Black. (Illus.). 293p. (C). 1975. text ed. 29.50 (*0-8422-5228-2*) Irvington.

Readings in Fuzzy Sets for Intelligent Systems. Ed. by Didier Dubois et al. LC 93-35702. 916p. (Orig.). (C). 1993. pap. 54.95 (*1-55860-257-7*) Morgan Kaufmann.

Readings in General Anthropology. Ed. by Lowell D. Holmes. LC 70-146457. (Illus.). 614p. reprint ed. pap. 175.00 (*0-317-09978-7*, 2012547) Bks Demand.

***Readings in General Economics.** 3rd ed. Frank Kahl. 224p. (C). 1997. per. 42.95 (*0-7872-3657-8*) Kendall-Hunt.

Readings in General Psychology. Michael Kubovy. 112p. 1995. pap. text ed. 27.24 (*0-7872-1686-0*) Kendall-Hunt.

Readings in General Psychology. Ed. by Wayne Dennis. LC 71-167334. (Essay Index Reprint Ser.). 1977. reprint ed. 34.95 (*0-8369-2493-2*) Ayer.

Readings in Geography. Ed. by R. W. Sreniawski. LC 72-86201. 320p. (C). 1972. text ed. 39.50 (*0-8422-5031-X*); pap. text ed. 16.95 (*0-8422-0226-9*) Irvington.

***Readings in Gerontological Nursing.** Judith Allender & Cherie Rector. 688p. 1998. pap. text ed. write for info. (*0-7817-9201-0*) Lppncott-Raven.

Readings in Global History, Vol. II. Anthony Snyder & Sherri West. 400p. (C). 1995. per. 31.43 (*0-8403-9009-2*) Kendall-Hunt.

Readings in Goethean Science. Ed. by H. H. Koepf & L. Jolly. 62p. 1980. pap. 4.20 (*0-938250-02-7*) Bio-Dynamic Farm.

Readings in Groupware & Computer-Supported Cooperative Work: Assisting Human-Human Collaboration. Ed. by Ronald M. Baecker. LC 92-43986. 882p. 1992. pap. 59.95 (*1-55860-241-0*) Morgan Kaufmann.

Readings in Her Story: Women in Christian Tradition. Ed. by Barbara J. MacHaffie. LC 92-3693. 144p. (Orig.). 1992. pap. 15.00 (*0-8006-2575-7*, 1-2575, Fortress Pr) Augsburg Fortress.

Readings in Historical Phonology: Chapters in the Theory of Sound Change. Ed. by Philip Baldi & Ronald N. Werth. LC 77-13895. (C). 1978. pap. 18.95 (*0-271-00539-4*) Pa St U Pr.

Readings in Human-Computer Interaction: Toward the Year 2000. 2nd ed. Ronald Baecker et al. 900p. 1995. pap. 64.95 (*1-55860-246-1*) Morgan Kaufmann.

Readings in Human Resource Development. T. V. Rao. (C). 1991. text ed. 29.50 (*81-204-0585-4*, Pub. by Oxford IBH II) S Asia.

Readings in Human Resource Management. Compiled by Raymond A. Noe et al. LC 93-42315. (C). 1994. text ed. 46.25 (*0-256-14852-X*) Irwin.

Readings in Human Resource Management. Bert A. Spector. LC 84-25977. 752p. 1985. pap. 24.95 (*0-02-902370-X*, Free Press) Free Pr.

***Readings in Human Resource Management.** 2nd ed. Raymond A. Noe. LC 96-39077. (C). 1996. 113.65 (*0-256-25542-3*) Irwin.

***Readings in Human Resource Management.** 2nd ed. Raymond A. Noe et al. LC 96-39077. 704p. (C). 1996. text ed. 46.25 (*0-256-25865-1*) Irwin.

Readings in Human Sexuality. Davis. (C). Date not set. pap. text ed. write for info. (*0-15-504117-7*) HarBrace.

Readings in Humanist Sociology: Social Criticism & Social Change. Walda K. Fishman & C. George Benello. LC 85-80417. 232p. 1986. lib. bdg. 36.95 (*0-930390-62-8*) Gen Hall.

Readings in Humanities I. Joe DiMassa. (C). pap. text ed. write for info. (*1-884155-08-1*) Day & Nite Pub.

***Readings in Income Taxation.** 14th ed. Ed. by James F. Ivers, III. LC 89-640071. 170p. (C). 1997. pap. text ed. 20.00 (*0-943590-86-8*) Amer College.

Readings in Indian Agricultural Development. Ed. by Pramit Chaudhuri. LC 72-191003. 192p. reprint ed. pap. 54.80 (*0-317-41744-4*, 2023324) Bks Demand.

Readings in Indian Public Finance. Ed. by D. Dwivedi. 1981. 17.00 (*0-8364-0805-5*, Pub. by Chanakya II) S Asia.

Readings in Indian Zoogeography, Vol. I. S. K. Tiwari. (Illus.). 525p. (C). 1983. 55.00 (*0-88065-221-7*, Pub. by Today & Tomorrows P & P II) Scholarly Pubns.

Readings in Indian Zoogeography: An Atlas of Indian Wild Life, Vol. 2. S. K. Tiwari. (Illus.). viii, 110p. 1985. 45.00 (*1-55528-166-4*, Pub. by Today & Tomorrows P & P II) Scholarly Pubns.

Readings in Indiana History. Gayle Thornbrough. 625p. 1991. pap. 21.95 (*1-885323-14-X*) IN Hist Bureau.

Readings in Inflation Accounting. Ed. by P. T. Wanless & D. A. Forrester. LC 79-40741. (Illus.). 592p. reprint ed. pap. 168.80 (*0-8357-4606-2*, 2037539) Bks Demand.

***Readings in Information Retrieval.** Ed. by Peter Willett & Karen Sparck-Jones. LC 97-18612. 600p. 1997. pap. 59.95 (*1-55860-454-5*) Morgan Kaufmann.

Readings in Innovation. Ed. by Stanley S. Gryskiewicz & David A. Hills. 257p. 1992. pap. 25.00 (*0-912879-69-6*) Ctr Creat Leader.

Readings in Input-Output Analysis: Theory and Applications. Ed. by Ira Sohn. LC 85-15351. (Illus.). 416p. 1986. text ed. 55.00 (*0-19-503674-3*) OUP.

Readings in Insect-Plant Disease Relationships. J. W. Brewer et al. LC 72-10029. (Illus.). (C). 1973. pap. text ed. 13.25 (*0-8422-0264-1*) Irvington.

Readings in Integrated Rural Development. S. R. Subramanian et al. (C). 1987. 12.50 (*81-204-0163-8*, Pub. by Oxford IBH II) S Asia.

***Readings in Intelligent User Interfaces.** Ed. by Mark T. Maybury & Wolfgang Wahlster. 736p. 1997. pap. 59.95 (*1-55860-444-8*) Morgan Kaufmann.

***Readings in International Accounting.** Ed. by John Blake & Mahmud Hossein. 304p. 1996. 75.00 (*0-415-13685-7*); pap. 22.95 (*0-415-13686-5*) Chapman & Hall.

***Readings in International Business.** Ed. by Michael Czinkota & Masaaki Kotabe. 352p. (C). Date not set. text ed. 64.95 (*0-631-20799-6*) Blackwell Pubs.

***Readings in International Business.** Ed. by Michael Czinkota & Masaaki Kotabe. 352p. (C). Date not set. pap. text ed. 34.95 (*1-57718-127-1*) Blackwell Pubs.

***Readings in International Business.** Ed. by Seung H. Kim et al. LC 96-3422. 300p. 1997. pap. text ed. 47.00 (*0-7618-0498-6*) U Pr of Amer.

Readings in International Business: A Decision Approach. Ed. by Robert Z. Aliber & Reid W. Click. LC 92-21502. (Illus.). 347p. 1993. 40.00 (*0-262-01132-8*); pap. 24.50 (*0-262-51066-9*) MIT Pr.

Readings in International Finance: Fifty Cases & Problems. Gunter Dufey & Ian H. Giddy. LC 86-3424. 416p. (C). 1987. pap. text ed. 37.75 (*0-201-05127-3*) Addison-Wesley.

Readings in International Law from the Naval War College Review 1978-1994. Ed. by John N. Moore & Robert F. Turner. (International Law Studies: Vol. 68). 1995. write for info. (*0-614-09348-1*) Naval War Coll.

Readings in Interpretation: Holderlin, Hegel, Heidegger. Andrzej Warminski. LC 86-1310. (Theory & History of Literature Ser.: Vol. 26). 286p. (Orig.). 1987. pap. text ed. 12.95 (*0-8166-1240-4*) U of Minn Pr.

Readings in Investments. Ed. by Stephen Lofthouse. 448p. text ed. 70.00 (*0-471-95209-5*) Wiley.

Readings in Investments. Ed. by Stephen Lofthouse. LC 93-29957. 448p. 1995. pap. text ed. 60.00 (*0-471-95208-7*) Wiley.

***Readings in Italian Mannerism.** Ed. by Lianna D. Cheney. (American University Studies XX: Vol. 24). 384p. (C). 1997. text ed. 55.95 (*0-8204-2483-8*) P Lang Pubng.

Readings in Japanese Social Anthropology & Sociology, 2 Vol., 1. Ed. by Joseph K. Yamagiwa. LC 66-3553. reprint ed. pap. 58.00 (*0-317-26711-6*, 2056010) Bks Demand.

Readings in Japanese Social Anthropology & Sociology, 2 Vol., 2. Ed. by Joseph K. Yamagiwa. LC 66-3553. reprint ed. pap. 115.00 (*0-685-10711-6*) Bks Demand.

***Readings in Judaism, Christianity & Islam.** Corrigan & Fred Denny. (C). 1997. pap. text ed. 25.33 (*0-02-325098-4*) P-H.

Readings in Knowledge Acquisition & Learning: Automating the Construction & Improvement of Expert Systems. Ed. by Bruce G. Buchanan & David C. Wilkins. 906p. 1992. pap. 49.95 (*1-55860-163-5*) Morgan Kaufmann.

Readings in Knowledge Representation. Ed. by Ronald J. Brachman & Hector J. Levesque. LC 85-16400. 571p. (Orig.). (C). 1985. pap. text ed. 39.95 (*0-934613-01-X*) Morgan Kaufmann.

Readings in Latin American History: The Formative Centuries, Vol. 1. Ed. by Peter Bakewell et al. LC 85-4347. vii, 428p. (C). 1985. pap. 21.95 (*0-8223-0637-9*) Duke.

Readings in Latin American History, Vol. 2: The Modern Experience. Ed. by John J. Johnson et al. LC 85-4347. (Illus.). vi, 484p. (C). 1985. 41.95 (*0-8223-0646-8*); pap. 18.95 (*0-8223-0638-7*) Duke.

Readings in Law & Psychiatry. Ed. by Richard C. Allen et al. LC 74-24384. 848p. reprint ed. pap. 180.00 (*0-317-09569-2*, 2004407) Bks Demand.

Readings in Life Science. rev. ed. Ed. by Marjorie P. Weiser. 128p. 1988. pap. text ed. 7.00 (*0-8428-3006-5*) Cambridge Bk.

Readings in Life Science - Exercise Book. Rebecca Motil. (C). 1990. pap. text ed. write for info. (*0-13-753674-7*) P-H.

Readings in Linguistics I & II, 1925-1957. abr. ed. Eric P. Hamp et al. xiv, 302p. 1995. pap. text ed. 19.95 (*0-226-41027-7*) U Ch Pr.

Readings in Linguistics One: The Development of Descriptive Linguistics in America, 1925-1956. 4th ed. Ed. by Martin Joos. LC 58-13036. 430p. 1966. lib. bdg. 37.50 (*0-226-41026-9*) U Ch Pr.

***Readings in Local Government Management & Development: A Southern African Perspective.** P. S. Reddy. 333p. 1996. pap. 36.00 (*0-7021-3612-3*, Pub. by Juta SA) Gaunt.

Readings in Louisiana. 2nd ed. 1988. pap. 14.00 (*0-87511-835-6*) Claitors.

Readings in Machine Learning. Jude W. Shavlik. (Machine Learning Ser.). (Illus.). 853p. 1990. pap. 49.95 (*1-55860-143-0*) Morgan Kaufmann.

Readings in Macroeconomics. Ed. by Tim Jenkinson. 272p. (C). 1996. 75.00 (*0-19-829065-9*); pap. 29.95 (*0-19-829064-0*) OUP.

***Readings in Managed Health Care.** Peter Kongstvedt. 1997. 35.00 (*0-8342-0963-2*, 20963) Aspen Pub.

Readings in Management. Philip B. DuBose. (Illus.). 400p. (C). 1987. pap. text ed. 31.40 (*0-13-755166-5*) P-H.

Readings in Management Accounting. Ibrahim Aly. 432p. (C). 1995. per., pap. text ed. 44.56 (*0-7872-0315-7*) Kendall-Hunt.

***Readings in Management Accounting.** 2nd ed. Mark S. Young. 364p. (C). 1996. pap. text ed. 30.80 (*0-13-491911-4*) P-H.

Readings in Managerial Accounting: From "The Wall Street Journal" Jonathan B. Schiff. 7.95 (*0-405-12623-9*) Ayer.

Readings in Managerial Economics. 4th ed. Coyne. (C). 1984. pap. text ed. 25.95 (*0-256-03056-1*) Irwin.

Readings in Managerial Economics. 5th ed. Thomas J. Coyne. 465p. (C). 1992. pap. text ed. 34.50 (*0-9633192-0-5*) Coyne Pub.

Readings in Managerial Psychology. Harold J. Leavitt et al. (Illus.). 784p. 1988. pap. text ed. 28.00 (*0-226-46992-1*) U Ch Pr.

Readings in Managerial Psychology. 4th ed. Harold J. Leavitt et al. (Illus.). 784p. 1988. lib. bdg. 72.00 (*0-226-46991-3*) U Ch Pr.

Readings in Managing the Marketing Research Function. Lee Adler & Charles S. Mayer. LC 80-11092. 199p. reprint ed. pap. 56.80 (*0-7837-2491-8*, 2042656) Bks Demand.

Readings in Market Research for Real Estate. Ed. by James D. Vernor. 324p. 1985. pap. 14.50 (*0-911780-76-9*) Appraisal Inst.

Readings in Market Segmentation. Donald W. Scotton & Ronald L. Zellocco. LC 80-478. 208p. reprint ed. pap. 59.30 (*0-685-15389-4*, 2026672) Bks Demand.

Readings in Market Value. 231p. 1981. pap. 14.50 (*0-911780-57-2*) Appraisal Inst.

Readings in Marketing: The Qualitative & Quantitative Areas. Ed. by Philip R. Cateora & Lee Richardson. LC 67-10928. (Illus.). (Orig.). 1967. pap. text ed. 9.95 (*0-89197-373-7*) Irvington.

Readings in Marketing Strategy. 2nd ed. Victor J. Cook & Jean-Claude Larreche. 320p. (C). 1990. pap. 31.75 (*0-89426-139-8*) Course Tech.

Readings in Medical Artificial Intelligence: The First Decade. Clancey. 1984. 33.29 (*0-201-10854-2*) Addison-Wesley.

***Readings in Medical Sociology.** Cockerham. LC 97-15095. 1997. pap. write for info. (*0-13-617937-1*) P-H.

Readings in Medical Sociology. Ed. by Sarah Cunningham-Burley & Neil P. Mckeganey. 232p. (C). 1990. pap. text ed. 24.95 (*0-415-00833-6*, A3774) Routledge.

Readings in Medieval English Romance. Ed. by Carol M. Meale. LC 93-47652. 246p. (C). 1994. 53.00 (*0-85991-404-6*, DS Brewer) Boydell & Brewer.

Readings in Medieval History. Patrick J. Geary. 848p. (C). 1989. pap. text ed. 22.95 (*0-921149-38-7*) Broadview Pr.

Readings in Medieval History, Vol. 1. Ed. by Patrick J. Geary. 400p. 1992. pap. text ed. 15.95 (*0-921149-95-6*) Broadview Pr.

Readings in Medieval History, Vol. 2. Ed. by Patrick J. Geary. 1992. pap. text ed. 15.95 (*0-921149-97-2*) Broadview Pr.

Readings in Medieval Philosophy. Ed. by Andrew B. Schoedinger. 864p. (C). 1996. pap. text ed. 31.95 (*0-19-509293-7*) OUP.

Readings in Medieval Philosophy. Ed. by Andrew B. Schoedinger. 864p. (C). 1996. text ed. 68.00 (*0-19-509292-9*) OUP.

Readings in Medieval Poetry. A. C. Spearing. 288p. (C). 1989. pap. text ed. 23.95 (*0-521-31133-0*) Cambridge U Pr.

Readings in Medieval Rhetoric. Ed. by Joseph M. Miller et al. LC 73-77857. 319p. reprint ed. pap. 91.00 (*0-8357-6690-X*, 2056870) Bks Demand.

Readings in Mergers & Acquisitions. Ed. by Patrick A. Gaughan. LC 94-6135. 352p. (C). 1994. text ed. 66.95 (*1-55786-408-X*); pap. text ed. 36.95 (*1-55786-409-8*) Blackwell Pubs.

Readings in Microeconomics. Ed. by Tim Jenkinson. 264p. (C). 1996. 75.00 (*0-19-877493-1*); pap. 29.95 (*0-19-877492-3*) OUP.

Readings in Middle School Curriculum: A Continuing Conversation. Ed. by Tom Dickinson. 232p. (C). 1993. pap. text ed. 25.00 (*1-56090-078-4*) Natl Middle Schl.

Readings in Mind & Language. Ed. by Heimir Geirsson & Michael Losonsky. (Illus.). 600p. (C). 1996. 59.95 (*1-55786-670-8*) Blackwell Pubs.

Readings in Model-Based Diagnosis. Ed. by Walter Hamscher et al. LC 92-25701. 1992. 49.95 (*1-55860-249-6*) Morgan Kaufmann.

Readings in Modern Chinese. Ed. by Liu Wei-ping et al. 162p. 1990. pap. text ed. 25.00 (*0-9590735-4-X*, Pub. by Wild Peony Pty AT) UH Pr.

Readings in Modern Chinese Literature, 2 vols. Ed. by Tien-Yi Li & Liu Wu-Chi. Incl. Vol. 1. Plays & Poems with Notes. 3rd ed. 1953. 11.95 (*0-88710-071-6*); Vol. 2 Stories. rev. ed. (C). 1953. pap. text ed. 13.95 (*0-88710-072-4*); Set audio write for info. (*0-88710-074-0*) Yale Far Eastern Pubns.

Readings in Modern Dance, Vol. 1. Ed. by Jane Edelson. 82p. audio 15.00 (*0-685-18019-0*) Dance Notation.

Readings in Modern Dance, Vol. I. Jane Edelson et al. (Illus.). 82p. 1974. pap. text ed. 21.95 (*0-932582-13-3*, Pub. by Dance Bks UK) Princeton Bk Co.

Readings in Modern Dance, Vol. 2. Ed. by Michele J. Varon. LC 76-359498. (Illus.). v, 86p. (C). 1977. audio 15.00 (*0-685-08571-6*) Dance Notation.

Readings in Modern Dance, Vol. II. Ed. by Michelle Varon. LC 76-359498. (Illus.). 86p. (C). 1974. pap. text ed. 21.95 (*0-932582-23-0*, Pub. by Dance Bks UK) Princeton Bk Co.

Readings in Modern Linguistics: An Anthology. Ed. by Bertil Malmberg. 384p. (Orig.). 1972. pap. text ed. 70.80 (*90-279-2100-8*) Mouton.

Readings in Modern Theology: Britain & America. Ed. by Robin Gill. LC 95-7774. 1995. 26.95 (*0-687-01461-1*) Abingdon.

Readings in Moral Theology, No. 6: Dissent in the Church. Richard A. McCormick & Charles E. Curran. 560p. 1988. pap. 14.95 (*0-8091-2930-2*) Paulist Pr.

Readings in Moral Theology, No. 7: Natural Law & Theology. Ed. by Charles E. Curran & Richard S. McCormick. 1991. pap. 14.95 (*0-8091-3179-X*) Paulist Pr.

Readings in Motor Learning. Ed. by Robert N. Singer. LC 79-146033. 490p. reprint ed. 139.70 (*0-8357-9418-0*, 2014583) Bks Demand.

Readings in Multiple Criteria Decision Aid. Ed. by C. A. Bana e Costa. (Illus.). xii, 660p. 1990. 129.95 (*0-387-52950-0*) Spr-Verlag.

R

Readings in Music Learning Theory. Darrel L. Walters & Cynthia C. Taggart. LC 89-84093. 386p. (C). 1989. 28.95 (*0-941050-17-3*, G3302) GIA Pubns.

Readings in Natural Language Processing. Bonnie L. Webber. LC 86-18488. (Illus.). 664p. (Orig.). 1986. pap. text ed. 44.95 (*0-934613-11-7*) Morgan Kaufmann.

Readings in Natural Resource Economics. John E. Reynolds. 199p. (C). 1974. text ed. 29.00 (*0-685-50581-2*) Irvington.

Readings in Object-Oriented Database Systems. Stanley B. Zdonik. 640p. (C). 1990. pap. text ed. 49.95 (*1-55860-000-0*) Morgan Kaufmann.

Readings in Occupational Health & Hygiene. 2nd ed. Ed. by George L. Head. LC 91-71644. 248p. 1991. pap. 18.00 (*0-89462-065-7*, ALCM76) IIA.

Readings in Oncology. Stacey B. Day et al. LC 80-80708. (Foundation Publication Ser.). (Illus.). 227p. (Orig.). (C). 1980. pap. 15.00 (*0-934314-01-2*) Intl Found Biosocial Dev.

Readings in Organizational Communication. Kevin L. Hutchinson. 496p. (C). 1991. per. write for info. (*0-697-12770-2*) Brown & Benchmark.

Readings in Organizational Communication. Miller. (Speech & Theater Ser.). Date not set. pap. 29.95 (*0-534-52083-9*) Wadsworth Pub.

Readings in Pediatric Psychology. Ed. by Michael Roberts et al. LC 93-7736. (Illus.). 388p. (C). 1993. pap. 34.50 (*0-306-44423-2*, Plenum Pr) Plenum.

Readings in Personality Assessment. Ed. by Leonard D. Goodstein & Richard I. Lanyon. LC 77-149770. 808p. (C). reprint ed. 180.00 (*0-8357-9972-7*, 2012426) Bks Demand.

Readings in Personnel & Human Resource Management. 3rd ed. Randall S. Schuler. 600p. 1987. pap. text ed. 37.00 (*0-314-33750-4*) West Pub.

Readings in Pharmacology. fac. ed. Ed. by B. Holmstedt & G. Liljestrand. LC 81-10872. (Illus.). 409p. pap. 116.60 (*0-7837-7289-0*, 2047017) Bks Demand.

Readings in Philosophy & Cognitive Science. Ed. by Alvin I. Goldman. LC 93-1739. 700p. 1993. 60.00 (*0-262-07153-3*, Bradford Bks); pap. 32.50 (*0-262-57100-5*, Bradford Bks) MIT Pr.

Readings in Philosophy of Psychology, Vol. I. Ed. by Ned Block. (Language & Thought Ser.). 318p. 1983. pap. 16.50 (*0-674-74876-X*) HUP.

Readings in Philosophy of Psychology, Vol. 2. Ed. by Ned Block. (Language & Thought Ser.). 372p. 1985. pap. 16.95 (*0-674-74878-6*) HUP.

Readings in Physical Science - Exercise Book. Rebecca Motil. (C). 1990. pap. text ed. write for info. (*0-13-753682-8*) P-H.

Readings in Planning. Ed. by James Allen et al. 1990. 49.95 (*1-55860-130-9*) Morgan Kaufmann.

Readings in Planning Theory. Ed. by Scott Campbell & Susan Fainstein. 380p. 1996. 74.95 (*1-55786-612-0*) Blackwell Pubs.

Readings in Planning Theory. Ed. by Scott Campbell & Susan Fainstein. LC 95-36047. 380p. (C). 1996. pap. 27.95 (*1-55786-613-9*) Blackwell Pubs.

***Readings in Politics: Issues & Polemics.** Robert Hazan. 320p. (C). 1997. per., pap. text ed. write for info. (*0-7872-3398-6*) Kendall-Hunt.

Readings in Popular Culture: Trivial Pursuits? Ed. by Gary Day. LC 89-34357. (Insights Ser.). 290p. 1990. text ed. 45.00 (*0-312-03550-0*) St Martin.

Readings in Population Research: Policy, Methodology & Perspectives. Ed. by P. Krishnan. (C). 1992. 45.00 (*81-7018-732-X*, Pub. by BR Pub II) S Asia.

Readings in Primary School Development. Ed. by Geoff Southworth. LC 94-28781. 230p. 1994. 75.00 (*0-7507-0355-5*, Falmer Pr); pap. 29.00 (*0-7507-0356-3*, Falmer Pr) Taylor & Francis.

Readings in Primary School Management. Ed. by Geoff Southworth. 260p. 1987. 60.00 (*1-85000-245-2*, Falmer Pr); pap. 30.00 (*1-85000-246-0*, Falmer Pr) Taylor & Francis.

Readings in Principles & Curriculum of Secondary Education. D. Quist et al. 1971. pap. text ed. 4.75 (*0-8422-0178-5*) Irvington.

Readings in Property Protection. 2nd ed. Insurance Institute of America Staff. Ed. by George L. Head. LC 90-83979. 345p. (Orig.). 1990. pap. 18.00 (*0-89462-054-1*, ALCM75) IIA.

Readings in Prose. Agnes B. Werner et al. LC 80-17845. 103p. (C). 1980. pap. 5.50 (*0-8477-3327-0*) U of PR Pr.

Readings in Psychiatric Rehabilitation. Ed. by William A. Anthony & LeRoy Spaniol. LC 94-72719. 552p. (C). 1994. pap. text ed. 34.95 (*1-878512-02-1*) Boston Univ Ctr Psy Rehab.

Readings in Psychology & Culture. Ed. by Walter J. Lonner & Roy S. Malpass. LC 93-14050. 1993. pap. text ed. 26.00 (*0-205-14899-9*) Allyn.

***Readings in Public Administration.** Jay M. Shafritz. (C). 1998. pap. text ed. write for info. (*0-321-00501-5*) Addison-Wesley Educ.

Readings in Public Policy. Ed. by J. M. Pogodzinski. LC 94-26134. (Illus.). 350p. (C). 1995. pap. text ed. 31.95 (*1-55786-521-3*) Blackwell Pubs.

Readings in Public Sector Economics. Ed. by Samuel H. Baker & Catherine S. Elliott. LC 89-84052. 603p. (C). 1990. pap. text ed. 28.36 (*0-669-18027-0*) HM College Div.

Readings in Qualitative Reasoning about Physical Systems. Ed. by Daniel S. Weld & Johan De Kleer. (Representation & Reasoning Ser.). 600p. (Orig.). (C). 1989. pap. text ed. 49.95 (*1-55860-095-7*) Morgan Kaufmann.

Readings in Real Property Valuation Principles, Vol. 1. 322p. 1977. pap. 14.50 (*0-911780-41-6*) Appraisal Inst.

Readings in Real Property Valuation Principles, Vol. II. 160p. 1985. 14.50 (*0-911780-83-1*) Appraisal Inst.

Readings in Rehabilitation Counseling. C. H. Patterson & H. Moses. 1971. pap. 8.60 (*0-87563-034-0*) Stipes.

Readings in Religious Studies. Joe DiMassa. (C). pap. text ed. write for info. (*1-884155-09-X*) Day & Nite Pub.

Readings in Remote Sensing Applications. T. S. Chouhan & K. N. Joshi. (C). 1992. text ed. 460.00 (*81-7233-040-5*, Pub. by Scientific Pubs II) St Mut.

Readings in Rhetorical Criticism. Ed. by Carl R. Burgchardt. LC 94-69190. 656p. (C). 1995. pap. text ed. write for info. (*0-9634489-2-7*) Strata Pub Co.

Readings in Risk. Ed. by Theodore S. Glickman & Michael Gough. LC 90-35402. 262p. 1990. pap. 24.95 (*0-915707-55-1*) Resources Future.

Readings in Romance Linguistics. James M. Anderson & JoAnn Creore. (Illus.). 472p. (Orig.). 1972. pap. text ed. 50.00 (*90-279-2303-5*) Mouton.

Readings in Russian Civilization, 3 vols. rev. ed. Ed. by Thomas Riha. Incl. Vol. 1. Russia Before Peter the Great, 900-1700. LC 69-14825. 1969. pap. text ed. 15.95 (*0-226-71853-0*); Vol. 2. Imperial Russia, 1700-1917. LC 69-14825. 1969. pap. text ed. 10.95 (*0-226-71855-7*); Vol. 3. Soviet Russia, 1917-Present. LC 69-14825. 1969. pap. text ed. 17.95 (*0-226-71857-3*); LC 69-14825. 1969. write for info. (*0-318-56069-0*) U Ch Pr.

Readings in Russian History, Vol. II. Watson & Nicholas V. Riasanovsky. 192p. (C). 1996. pap. text ed. 23.04 (*0-8403-7160-8*) Kendall-Hunt.

Readings in Russian History: From Alexander II to the Soviet Period, Vol. 2. 4th ed. Warren B. Walsh. 1963. pap. 12.95 (*0-8156-2082-9*) Syracuse U Pr.

Readings in Russian History: From Ancient Times to Nicholas I, Vol. 1. 4th ed. Ed. by Warren B. Walsh. 1963. pap. 12.95 (*0-8156-2081-0*) Syracuse U Pr.

Readings in Russian History: From the Reign of Paul to Alexander III, Vol. II. Ed. by Warren B. Walsh. 1963. pap. 9.95 (*0-8156-2051-9*) Syracuse U Pr.

Readings in Russian Philosophical Thought. Ed. by Louis J. Shein. LC 68-15528. 1968. pap. text ed. 21.35 (*0-686-22454-X*) Mouton.

Readings in Russian Philosophical Thought: Logic & Aesthetics. Ed. by Louis J. Shein. LC 73-83931. 337p. 1973. pap. text ed. 24.65 (*90-279-2511-9*) Mouton.

Readings in Sales Force Management. Ed. by Kenneth R. Davis & Frederick E. Webster, Jr. LC 68-20550. (Illus.). 475p. reprint ed. pap. 135.40 (*0-317-10053-X*, 2012394) Bks Demand.

Readings in Sayable Chinese, 3 vols., 1. Yuen Ren Chao. (Spoken Language Ser.). 1985. 15.00 (*0-87950-325-4*) Spoken Lang Serv.

Readings in Sayable Chinese, 3 vols., Set. Yuen Ren Chao. (Spoken Language Ser.). 1985. 45.00 (*0-87950-328-9*); audio 230.00 (*0-87950-336-X*) Spoken Lang Serv.

Readings in Sayable Chinese, 3 vols., Vol. 1. Yuen Ren Chao. (Spoken Language Ser.). 1985. audio 85.00 (*0-87950-333-5*) Spoken Lang Serv.

Readings in Sayable Chinese, 3 vols., Vol. 2. Yuen Ren Chao. (Spoken Language Ser.). 296p. 1985. 15.00 (*0-87950-326-2*); audio 65.00 (*0-87950-334-3*) Spoken Lang Serv.

Readings in Sayable Chinese, 3 vols., Vol. 3. Yuen Ren Chao. (Spoken Language Ser.). 370p. 1985. 15.00 (*0-87950-327-0*); audio 80.00 (*0-87950-335-1*) Spoken Lang Serv.

Readings in Semantics. Ed. by Farhang Zabeeh et al. LC 74-639. 861p. reprint ed. pap. 180.00 (*0-317-08056-3*, 2022270) Bks Demand.

Readings in Service Marketing: Quality & Financial Impact Reader. Roland T. Rust et al. LC 95-47028. 384p. (C). 1996. text ed. 26.50 (*0-673-98308-0*) Addson-Wesley Educ.

Readings in Social & Political Philosophy. 2nd ed. Robert M. Stewart. 472p. (C). 1996. pap. text ed. 31.95 (*0-19-509518-9*) OUP.

Readings in Social Evolution & Development. Ed. by S. N. Eisenstadt. LC 78-96463. 1970. 209.00 (*0-08-006813-8*, Pub. by Pergamon Repr UK) Franklin.

Readings in Social Psychology. 2nd rev. ed. Taylor et al. 384p. (C). 1988. pap. text ed. 30.60 (*0-13-761081-5*) P-H.

Readings in Social Psychology: Perspective & Method. Ed. by Bryan Byers. LC 92-26106. 1992. pap. text ed. 35.00 (*0-205-13856-X*) Allyn.

***Readings in Social Sciences, 1996-97.** James Sheets. 1996. pap. text ed. write for info. (*0-07-057869-9*) McGraw.

Readings in Social Theory: The Classic Tradition to Post-Modernism. 2nd ed. Ed. by James Farganis & George Ritzer. LC 95-30405. 1996. pap. text ed. write for info. (*0-07-020574-4*) McGraw.

Readings in Social Theory: The Classic Tradition to Postmodernism. Intro. by James Farganis. LC 92-30637. 1993. pap. text ed. write for info. (*0-07-019946-9*) McGraw.

Readings in Sociocultural Studies in Education. Roumaniere. 1993. pap. text ed. write for info. (*0-07-054099-3*) McGraw.

Readings in Soviet Semiotics: Russian Texts. Ed. by Ladislav Matejka et al. (Michigan Slavic Materials Ser.: No. 15). 1977. pap. 10.00 (*0-930042-08-5*) Mich Slavic Pubns.

Readings in Spanish-English Contrastive Linguistics, Vol. I. Ed. by Rose Nash. LC 73-85939. 249p. 1973. pap. 4.50 (*0-913480-20-7*) Inter Am U Pr.

Readings in Spanish-English Contrastive Linguistics, Vol. III. Ed. by Rose Nash & Domitila Belaval. LC 73-85939. 270p. (C). 1982. pap. text ed. 9.95 (*0-913480-42-8*) Inter Am U Pr.

Readings in Speech Recognition. Ed. by Alex Waibel & Kai-Fu Lee. 680p. 1990. pap. 49.95 (*1-55860-124-4*) Morgan Kaufmann.

Readings in St. John's Gospel. William Temple. LC 84-62374. 391p. 1985. pap. 8.95 (*0-8192-1360-8*) Morehouse Pub.

Readings in State & Local Government: Problems & Prospects. Ed. by David C. Saffell & Harry Basehart. LC 93-37331. 1993. pap. text ed. write for info. (*0-07-054479-4*) McGraw.

Readings in State & Local Public Finance. Matthew P. Drennan. Ed. by Dick Netzer. 500p. (C). 1997. pap. text ed. 39.95 (*1-55786-713-5*) Blackwell Pubs.

Readings in Strategic Management. 4th ed. Arthur A. Thompson, Jr. et al. 416p. (C). 1992. per. 37.75 (*0-256-09720-8*) Irwin.

Readings in Strategic Management. 5th ed. Ed. by Arthur A. Thompson, Jr. et al. LC 94-22556. 624p. (C). 1994. 39.25 (*0-256-15026-5*) Irwin.

Readings in Strategic Marketing. 2nd ed. Weitz. (C). 1996. pap. text ed. 39.00 (*0-03-032764-4*) HB Coll Pubs.

Readings in Strategic Marketing: Analysis, Planning & Implementation. Bart Weitz & Robin Wensley. (Illus.). 538p. (C). 1988. pap. text ed. 43.75 (*0-03-020864-5*) Dryden Pr.

Readings in Strategies & Tactics in Behavioral Research: Text. 2nd ed. James M. Johnston & Henry S. Pennypacker. 408p. 1993. text ed. 45.00 (*0-8058-0905-8*) L Erlbaum Assocs.

Readings in Stratificational Linguistics. Ed. by Adam Makkai & David G. Lockwood. viii, 331p. 1973. 48.00 (*0-933104-24-3*) Jupiter Pr.

Readings in Survey Research. Ed. by Robert Ferber. LC 78-14428. 614p. reprint ed. pap. 175.00 (*0-685-15379-7*, 2026669) Bks Demand.

Readings in Sustainable Forest Management. FAO Staff. (Forestry Papers: No. 122). 274p. 1995. pap. 25.00 (*92-5-103401-X*, F3401X, Pub. by FAO IT) Bernan Associates.

Readings in Technology. Ed. by Nancy M. Viggiano. LC 84-193516. (Illus.). 201p. reprint ed. pap. 57.30 (*0-7837-1185-9*, 2041714) Bks Demand.

Readings in Technology Education. Thomas Erekson. 1993. pap. 53.95 (*0-8273-5091-0*) Delmar.

Readings in Texas History. Ed. by Robert J. Rosenbaum. (Illus.). 216p. (C). 1982. pap. text ed. 17.95 (*0-89641-136-2*) American Pr.

Readings in Texas History. Ed. by Cary D. Wintz. (Texas History Ser.). (Illus.). 344p. (Orig.). 1983. pap. text ed. 24.95 (*0-89641-134-6*) American Pr.

***Readings in Thanatology.** Ed. by John D. Morgan. LC 96-36868. (Death, Value & Meaning Ser.). 584p. 1997. text ed. 59.95 (*0-89503-149-3*) Baywood Pub.

Readings in the Appraisal of Special Purpose Properties. 285p. 1981. pap. 14.50 (*0-911780-52-1*) Appraisal Inst.

Readings in the Canon of Scripture: Written for Our Learning. David Jasper. LC 95-5576. 1995. text ed. 55.00 (*0-312-12687-5*) St Martin.

Readings in the Christian Initiation of Children. Ed. by Victoria M. Tufano. LC 94-22214. 150p. (Orig.). 1994. pap. 9.95 (*1-56854-026-4*, RDG-IC) Liturgy Tr Pubns.

Readings in the Concept & Measurement of Income. Ed. by Robert H. Parker & G. C. Harcourt. LC 75-87137. 410p. reprint ed. pap. 116.90 (*0-317-27570-4*, 2024513) Bks Demand.

Readings in the Development of Moral Thought. 2nd ed. George & Henberg. 288p. (C). 1992. pap. text ed. 26.19 (*0-8403-8046-1*) Kendall-Hunt.

Readings in the Development of Settlement Work. Ed. by Lorene M. Pacey. LC 79-142688. (Essay Index Reprint Ser.). 1977. 23.95 (*0-8369-2198-4*) Ayer.

Readings in the Economics of Contract Law. Ed. by Victor P. Goldberg. (Illus.). 272p. (C). 1989. 69.95 (*0-521-34120-5*); pap. text ed. 20.95 (*0-521-34920-6*) Cambridge U Pr.

Readings in the History & Systems of Psychology. James Brennan. 332p. 1994. pap. text ed. 29.40 (*0-13-103763-3*) P-H.

***Readings in the History & Systems of Psychology.** 2nd ed. James F. Brennan. LC 97-7923. 1997. write for info. (*0-13-626797-1*) P-H.

Readings in the History of Christian Theology Vol. I: From Its Beginnings to the Eve of the Reformation, Vol. 1. William C. Placher. LC 87-29540. 204p. (Orig.). 1988. pap. 20.00 (*0-664-24057-7*, Westminster) Westminster John Knox.

Readings in the History of Christian Theology Vol. II: From the Reformation to the Present, Vol. 2. William C. Placher. LC 87-29540. 216p. (Orig.). 1988. pap. 20.00 (*0-664-24058-5*, Westminster) Westminster John Knox.

Readings in the History of Education: Mediaeval Universities. Arthur O. Norton. LC 78-173801. reprint ed. 34.50 (*0-404-04797-1*) AMS Pr.

Readings in the History of Mathematics Education. Ed. by James K. Bidwell & Robert G. Clason. LC 74-113172. 706p. 1970. 25.00 (*0-87353-087-X*) NCTM.

Readings in the History of Music in Performance. Ed. & Tr. by Carol MacClintock. LC 78-8511. (Illus.). 448p. 1994. text ed. 35.00 (*0-253-14495-7*) Ind U Pr.

Readings in the History of Music in Performance. Ed. & Tr. by Carol MacClintock. LC 78-8511. (Illus.). 448p. 1994. pap. 18.95 (*0-253-20285-X*) Ind U Pr.

Readings in the History of the American Indian. Ed. by Melvin W. Roe. 1971. pap. 6.95 (*0-8422-0134-3*) Irvington.

Readings in the Income Approach to Real Property Valuation, Vol. 1. 226p. 1977. pap. 14.50 (*0-911780-43-2*) Appraisal Inst.

Readings in the Income Capitalization Approach to Real Property Valuation, Vol. II. 136p. 1985. 14.50 (*0-911780-84-X*) Appraisal Inst.

Readings in the Latin American Policy of the United States. Ed. by Thomas L. Karnes. LC 70-182882. 316p. reprint ed. pap. 90.10 (*0-317-41737-1*, 2022757) Bks Demand.

Readings in the Management of Innovation. 2nd ed. Ed. by Michael L. Tushman & William L. Moore. 656p. 1988. pap. text ed. 30.00 (*0-88730-244-0*) Harper Busn.

Readings in the Modern Essay. Ed. by Edward S. Noyes. LC 70-121494. (Essay Index Reprint Ser.). 1977. 36.95 (*0-8369-2008-2*) Ayer.

Readings in the Philosophical Problems of Parapsychology. Antony G. Flew. LC 86-25342. 376p. 34.95 (*0-87975-382-X*); pap. 24.95 (*0-87975-385-4*) Prometheus Bks.

***Readings in the Philosophy of Language.** Peter Ludlow. LC 96-39198. 1997. 70.00 (*0-262-12205-7*); pap. 35.00 (*0-262-62114-2*) MIT Pr.

Readings in the Philosophy of Law. 2nd ed. John Arthur & William H. Shaw. 640p. 1993. pap. text ed. 52.33 (*0-13-753849-9*) P-H.

Readings in the Philosophy of Psychology, 2 vols., Vol. 2. Ed. by Ned Block. LC 79-25593. (Language & Thought Ser.). 372p. 1981. 37.00 (*0-674-74877-8*) HUP.

Readings in the Philosophy of Religion: An Analytic Approach. 2nd ed. Baruch A. Brody. 672p. (C). 1991. text ed. 36.80 (*0-13-756206-3*, 660801) P-H.

Readings in the Philosophy of Social Science. Ed. by Michael Martin & Lee C. McIntyre. 800p. 1994. 60.00 (*0-262-13296-6*, Bradford Bks); pap. 35.00 (*0-262-63151-2*, Bradford Bks) MIT Pr.

Readings in the Political Economy of Aging. Ed. by Meredith Minkler & Carroll L. Estes. (Policy, Politics, Health & Medicine Ser.: Vol. 6). 278p. (Orig.). 1984. pap. 28.00 (*0-89503-042-X*) Baywood Pub.

Readings in the Psychology of Parent-Child Relations. Ed. by Gene R. Medinnus. LC 67-12565. 384p. reprint ed. 109.50 (*0-8357-9973-5*, 2055146) Bks Demand.

Readings in the Psychology of Perception. Ed. by Thomas L. Bennett. 179p. (C). 1971. pap. text ed. 8.95 (*0-8422-0160-2*) Irvington.

Readings in the Psychology of Perception. 2nd ed. Ed. by Thomas L. Bennett. 1973. pap. text ed. 9.95 (*0-685-48425-4*, 0-8422-0325) Irvington.

Readings in the Qur'an. Kenneth Cragg. LC 87-24981. 392p. 1996. reprint ed. pap. 18.00 (*0-00-627959-7*, Pub. by Fount UK) Harper SF.

Readings in the Social Control of Industry. Ed. by American Economic Association Staff. LC 72-14175. (Essay Index Reprint Ser.). 1977. reprint ed. 30.95 (*0-518-10001-4*) Ayer.

Readings in the Swedish Class Structure. Ed. by Richard Scase. 1976. 139.00 (*0-08-016663-6*, Pub. by Pergamon Repr UK) Franklin.

***Readings in the Text of African Popular Culture.** Karin Barber. LC 97-11211. 1997. pap. text ed. 18.95 (*0-253-21140-9*) Ind U Pr.

Readings in the Theory of Action. Ed. by Norman S. Care et al. LC 68-27339. 446p. reprint ed. pap. 127.20 (*0-317-08105-5*, 2050050) Bks Demand.

Readings in the Theory of Income Distribution. Compiled by American Economic Association Staff. LC 76-29414. (BCL Ser. II). reprint ed. 52.50 (*0-404-15332-1*) AMS Pr.

***Readings in the Western Humanities.** 3rd ed. Roy T. Matthews et al. LC 96-52519. 1997. write for info. (*1-55934-577-2*); write for info. (*1-55934-578-0*) Mayfield Pub.

Readings in the Western Humanities, Vol. I. rev. ed. Ed. by Julie Wildhaber et al. LC 94-35337. 244p. (C). 1994. text ed. 14.95 (*1-55934-456-3*, 1456) Mayfield Pub.

Readings in the Western Humanities, Vol. II. rev. ed. Ed. by Julie Wildhaber et al. LC 94-35337. 255p. (C). 1994. pap. text ed. 14.95 (*1-55934-457-1*, 1457) Mayfield Pub.

Readings in Total Quality Management. Harry Costin. LC 93-72495. 626p. (C). 1994. pap. text ed. 40.75 (*0-03-097301-5*) Dryden Pr.

Readings in Trade Unionism. Ed. by David J. Saposs. LC 70-89762. (American Labor, from Conspiracy to Collective Bargaining Ser., No. 1). 415p. 1978. reprint ed. 25.95 (*0-405-02147-X*) Ayer.

Readings in Transition. Gallagher. (Illus.). 512p. (C). (gr. 13). 1991. pap. text ed. 29.95 (*0-8016-1952-1*) Mosby Yr Bk.

Readings in Trial Advocacy & the Social Sciences, 4 vol. Ed. by Robert M. Krivoshey. LC 93-32631. 1994. 278.00 (*0-8153-1418-3*) Garland.

Readings in True & Fair. Ed. by R. H. Parker et al. LC 95-52020. (New Works in Accounting History). 344p. 1996. reprint ed. text ed. 70.00 (*0-8153-2273-9*) Garland.

Readings in United States History with Topics, Vol. II. Contrib. by Jerry R. Baydo et al. (Illus.). 553p. 1995. 25.00 (*0-911541-37-3*) Gregory Pub.

Readings in Urban Dynamics, Vol. 1. Ed. by Nathaniel J. Mass. LC 73-89545. (Illus.). 303p. (C). 1974. text ed. 45.00 (*0-262-13140-4*) Prod Press.

Readings in Urban Dynamics, Vol. 2. Ed. by Walter W. Schroeder, III et al. LC 73-89545. (Illus.). 305p. (C). 1975. text ed. 55.00 (*0-262-19170-9*) Prod Press.

Readings in Urban Geography. Ed. by Harold M. Mayer & Clyde F. Kohn. LC 59-11973. (Illus.). 625p. reprint ed. pap. 180.00 (*0-8357-7002-8*, 2056776) Bks Demand.

Readings in Urban Studies: An Introduction. Roger W. Caves. 1994. 59.95 (*0-8039-5637-1*); pap. 28.00 (*0-8039-5638-X*) Sage.

Readings in Urban Theory. Ed. by Susan Fainstein & Scott Campbell. LC 95-35754. 340p. (C). 1996. pap. 27.95 (*1-55786-609-0*) Blackwell Pubs.

Readings in Urban Theory. Ed. by Susan S. Fainstein & Scott Campbell. LC 95-35754. 340p. (C). 1996. 74.95 (*1-55786-608-2*) Blackwell Pubs.

An Asterisk (*) at the beginning of an entry indicates that the title is appearing in BIP for the first time.

Readings in Urban Transportation. Ed. by George Smerk. LC 68-14613. 348p. reprint ed. pap. 99.20 (*0-685-16312-1*, 2056238) Bks Demand.

Readings in Vedic Literature. Satsvarupa Das Gosvami. 243p. 1985. pap. 7.95 (*0-912776-88-9*) Bhaktivedanta.

***Readings in Wealth Accumulation Planning.** 9th ed. Ed. by American College Faculty. LC 97-12146. 475p. 1997. pap. text ed. 38.00 (*0-943590-97-3*) Amer College.

Readings in Western Religious Thought: The Ancient World. Ed. by Patrick Reid. 304p. (Orig.). 1987. pap. 22.95 (*0-8091-2850-0*) Paulist Pr.

Readings in Western Religious Thought II: The Middle Ages Through the Reformation. Ed. by Patrick V. Reid. 400p. (Orig.). (C). 1995. pap. 24.95 (*0-8091-3533-7*) Paulist Pr.

Readings in Wildlife Conservation. Ed. by James A. Bailey et al. LC 74-28405. (Illus.). 722p. (Orig.). (C). 1974. pap. 12.00 (*0-933564-02-3*) Wildlife Soc.

Readings in World Civilization, 2 vols., Vol. 1. 3rd ed. Kevin Reilly. 352p. 1995. pap. text ed. 19.00 (*0-312-09647-X*) St Martin.

Readings in World Civilization, 2 vols., Vol. 2. 3rd ed. Kevin Reilly. 368p. 1995. pap. text ed. 19.00 (*0-312-09648-8*) St Martin.

Readings in World History. Created by Harcourt Brace Staff. 1990. pap. text ed. 24.00 (*0-15-373498-1*) HR&W Schl Div.

Readings in World History. Created by Harcourt Brace Staff. 1990. teacher ed., pap. 3.50 (*0-15-373557-0*) HR&W Schl Div.

Readings in World Politics. Ed. by Thomas O. Schlesinger. 84p. (C). 1969. pap. text ed. 9.95 (*0-8290-1090-4*) Irvington.

Readings in World Religions. Gisela Webb. 300p. 1995. per. 31.44 (*0-8403-8747-4*) Kendall-Hunt.

Readings in Wyoming History: Issues in the History of the Equality State. Ed. by Phil Roberts. (Wyoming History Ser.). 120p. (Orig.). 1994. pap. 6.95 (*0-914767-22-4*) Skyline West Pr.

Readings in Nineteenth Century Art. Janis A. Tomlinson. LC 95-10581. 1995. pap. text ed. 31.33 (*0-13-104142-8*) P-H.

Readings in 20th Century Crisis. Ed. by Silvano A. Wueschner. 132p. (Orig.). (C). 1994. pap. text ed. 10.40 (*0-9636151-2-2*) St Andrews IA.

Readings, Issues, & Questions in Public Finance. Eleanor Brown. (C). 1988. pap. text ed. 26.95 (*0-256-06316-8*) Irwin.

***Reading's Movie Memories.** (Illus.). viii, 130p. (Orig.). 1997. pap. 18.95 (*0-9658505-0-1*) B A Wade.

Readings of Biological Concern. Ed. by Robert H. Catlett. LC 72-6695. 84p. 1972. pap. text ed. 4.75 (*0-8422-0239-0*) Irvington.

Readings of the Wreck. Ed. by Peter S. Milward & Raymond S. Schoder. 1976. 2.00 (*0-8294-0249-7*) Loyola Pr.

Readings on Accounting Development: Original Anthology. Ed. by Paul S. Garner et al. LC 77-87313. (Development of Contemporary Accounting Thought Ser.). 1978. lib. bdg. 37.95 (*0-405-10926-1*) Ayer.

Readings on American Subnational Government: Diversity, Innovation, & Rejuvenation. Ed. by John R. Baker. LC 92-21755. (C). 1993. text ed. 28.50 (*0-06-500722-0*) Addson-Wesley Educ.

***Readings on Charles Dickens.** Ed. by Clarice Swisher. LC 97-10493. (Literary Companion Ser.). (YA). (gr. 9-12). 1997. pap. 12.96 (*1-56510-589-3*); lib. bdg. 20.96 (*1-56510-590-7*) Greenhaven.

Readings on Cognitive Ergonomics: Mind & Computers. Ed. by G. C. Van Der Veer et al. (Lecture Notes in Computer Science Ser.: Vol. 178). vi, 269p. 1984. 33.00 (*0-387-13394-1*) Spr-Verlag.

***Readings on Color Vol. 1: The Philosophy of Color.** Ed. by Alexander Byrne & David R. Hilbert. LC 96-44539. (Illus.). 368p. 1997. 50.00 (*0-262-02424-1*, Bradford Bks); pap. 30.00 (*0-262-52230-6*, Bradford Bks) MIT Pr.

***Readings on Color Vol. 2: The Science of Color.** Ed. by Alexander Byrne & David R. Hilbert. LC 96-44539. (Illus.). 368p. 1997. 50.00 (*0-262-02425-X*, Bradford Bks); pap. 30.00 (*0-262-52231-4*, Bradford Bks) MIT Pr.

Readings on Communicating with Strangers. william B. Gudykunst & Young un Kim. 1992. text ed. write for info. (*0-07-025140-1*) McGraw.

Readings on Compensation. (Readings Collection: No. 5). 272p. 1991. pap. 20.00 (*0-914945-07-6*) Intl Personnel Mgmt.

Readings on Conversation to Judaism. Ed. by Lawrence J. Epstein. LC 94-40779. 216p. 1995. pap. 22.50 (*1-56821-417-0*) Aronson.

Readings on Diarrhoea. vii, 147p. (ENG & FRE.). 1992. student ed., pap. text ed. 20.00 (*92-4-154444-9*, 1150386) World Health.

***Readings on Edgar Allan Poe.** Ed. by Bonnie Szumski & Carol Prime. LC 97-12902. (Literary Companion Ser.). (YA). (gr. 9-12). 1997. pap. 12.96 (*1-56510-632-6*); lib. bdg. 20.96 (*1-56510-633-4*) Greenhaven.

Readings on Edmund Husserl's Logical Investigations. Ed. by Jitendra N. Mohanty. 219p. 1977. pap. text ed. 84.00 (*90-247-1928-3*, Pub. by M Nijhoff NE) Kluwer Ac.

Readings on Electronic Commerce. Ravi Kalakota & Andrew Whinston. LC 96-27588. 352p. (Orig.). (C). 1997. pap. text ed. 36.95 (*0-201-88060-1*) Addison-Wesley.

***Readings on Emergency Contraception from Family Planning Perspectives & International Family Planning Perspectives 1992-1996.** 64p. 1996. pap. 15.00 (*0-939253-42-9*) Guttmacher Inst.

Readings on Equal Education: Forty Years after the Brown Decision: Implications of School Desegregation for U. S. Education, Vol. 13. Ed. by Kofi Lomotey & Charles Teddlie. 229p. 1996. 62.50 (*0-404-10113-5*) AMS Pr.

Readings on Equal Education: Qualitative Investigations into Schools & Schooling, Vol. II. Ed. by Michele Foster. LC 77-83137. 1991. 62.50 (*0-404-10111-9*) AMS Pr.

Readings on Equal Education Vol. 12: Civil Rights in Schools. Ed. by Steven S. Goldberg & Kathleen K. Lynch. 1995. 62.50 (*0-404-10112-7*) AMS Pr.

Readings on Equal Education, Vol. 10: Critical Issues for a New Administration and Congress. Incl. Vol. 1. School Year 1968-1969. Ed. by Allan C. Ornstein. LC 77-83137. 67.50 (*0-404-10101-1*); Vol. 2. School Year 1969-1970. Ed. by Allan C. Ornstein et al. LC 77-83137. 67.50 (*0-404-10102-X*); Vol. 3. School Year 1970-1971. Maxine Hawkins. Ed. by Russell C. Doll. LC 77-83137. 47.50 (*0-404-10103-8*); Vol. 4. School Year 1971-72. Ed. by Erwin Flaxman. LC 77-83137. 47.50 (*0-404-10104-6*); Vol. 5. School Year 1972-1975. Ed. by Steven S. Goldberg. LC 77-83137. 47.50 (*0-404-10105-4*); Vol. 7. School Year 1977-1979. Ed. by Marguerite R. Barnett. LC 77-83137. 47.50 (*0-404-10107-0*); Vol. 8. Race, Sex & National Origin: Public Attitudes of Desegregation. Ed. by Steven S. Goldberg. LC 77-83137. 1985. 47.50 (*0-404-10108-9*); Vol. 9. Education Policy in an Era of Conservative Reform. Ed. by Marguerite R. Barnett et al. LC 77-83137. 47.50 (*0-404-10109-7*); Vol. 11. Qualitative Investigations into Schools & Schooling. Ed. by Michele Foster. LC 77-83137. 47.50 (*0-685-67473-8*); LC 77-83137. Orig. Title: Educating the Disadvantaged. write for info. (*0-318-50695-5*) AMS Pr.

***Readings on F. Scott Fitzgerald.** Ed. by Katie DeKoster. LC 96-44977. (Literary Companion Ser.). (YA). (gr. 9-12). 1997. pap. 12.96 (*1-56510-460-9*); lib. bdg. 20.96 (*1-56510-461-7*) Greenhaven.

Readings on Fascism & National Socialism. University of Colorado, Department of Philosophy Staff. LC 83-24173. 112p. (Orig.). 1952. pap. 9.95 (*0-8040-0259-2*) Swallow.

Readings on Financial Institutions & Makets. 6th ed. Ed. by Peter S. Rose. LC 93-29612. (Series in Finance). 432p. (C). 1993. per. 21.95 (*0-256-14515-6*) Irwin.

Readings on Financial Institutions & Markets. 4th ed. Donald R. Fraser & Peter S. Rose. 448p. (C). 1989. pap. text ed. 21.95 (*0-256-08339-8*) Irwin.

Readings on Financial Institutions & Markets. 5th ed. Ed. by Peter S. Rose. LC 92-32270. 448p. (C). 1992. pap. text ed. 21.95 (*0-256-09454-3*) Irwin.

Readings on Financial Institutions & Markets: 1995-1996 Edition. 8th ed. Peter S. Rose. 304p. (C). 1995. per. 22.85 (*0-256-14530-X*) Irwin.

Readings on Historical Method. E. Lacy. 1969. pap. text ed. 7.95 (*0-8290-1180-3*) Irvington.

***Readings on Homer.** Ed. by Don Nardo. LC 97-9458. (Literary Companion Ser.). (YA). (gr. 9-12). 1997. pap. 12.96 (*1-56510-638-5*); lib. bdg. 20.96 (*1-56510-639-3*) Greenhaven.

***Readings on Language & Literacy: Essays in Honor of Jeanne S. Chall.** Ed. by Lillian R. Putnam. LC 97-11360. (Orig.). 1997. pap. text ed. 19.95 (*1-57129-039-7*) Brookline Bks.

Readings on Language, Schools & Classrooms. Ed. by Michael Stubbs & Hilary Hillier. (Contemporary Sociology of the School Ser.). 140p. 1983. pap. 14.95 (*0-416-35180-8*, NO. 3958) Routledge Chapman & Hall.

Readings on Men from Family Planning Perspectives, 1987-1995. 332p. 1996. pap. 30.00 (*0-939253-41-0*) Guttmacher Inst.

Readings on Microsoft Windows & WOSA. Microsoft Corporation Staff. (Professional Editions Ser.). 512p. 1995. pap. 39.95 (*1-55615-836-X*) Microsoft.

***Readings on Modern American Social Issues.** Mike Beery. 128p. (C). 1996. per., pap. text ed. 19.95 (*0-7872-2696-3*) Kendall-Hunt.

***Readings on Of Mice & Men.** Ed. by Jill Karson. LC 97-10484. (Literary Companion Ser.). (YA). (gr. 9-12). 1997. pap. 12.96 (*1-56510-652-0*); lib. bdg. 20.96 (*1-56510-653-9*) Greenhaven.

Readings on Parties & Elections in the United States. Chester L. Jones. LC 70-129946. 354p. 1970. reprint ed. text ed. 52.50 (*0-8371-4994-0*, JPE&, Greenwood Pr) Greenwood.

Readings on Police Use of Deadly Force. James J. Fyfe. LC 81-86057. 1982. write for info. (*0-318-57053-X*) Police Found.

Readings on Research in Stuttering. Ed. by E. Charles Healey. 256p. (Orig.). (C). 1991. pap. text ed. 32.95 (*0-8013-0410-5*, 78220) Longman.

***Readings on Romeo & Juliet.** Ed. by Don Nardo. LC 97-10491. (Literary Companion Ser.). (YA). (gr. 9-12). 1997. pap. 12.96 (*1-56510-646-6*); lib. bdg. 20.96 (*1-56510-647-4*) Greenhaven.

Readings on Second Language Acquisition. Ed. by H. Douglas Brown & Susan Gonzo. LC 93-42222. 500p. 1994. pap. text ed. 21.95 (*0-13-102260-1*) P-H.

***Readings on Teenage Pregnancy from Family Planning Perspectives 1985-1989.** 386p. 1989. pap. 15.00 (*0-939253-16-X*) Guttmacher Inst.

Readings on the Development of Children. Ed. by Mary Gauvain & Michael Cole. LC 93-10142. (C). 1995. text ed. write for info. (*0-7167-2480-4*); pap. text ed. write for info. (*0-7167-2492-8*) W H Freeman.

***Readings on the Development of Children.** 2nd ed. Mary Gauvain & Michael Cole. LC 96-31308. 284p. 1996. 22.95 (*0-7167-2860-5*) W H Freeman.

***Readings on the Great Gatsby.** Ed. by Katie DeKoster. LC 97-12901. (Literary Companion Ser.). (YA). (gr. 9-12). 1997. pap. 12.96 (*1-56510-644-X*); lib. bdg. 20.96 (*1-56510-645-8*) Greenhaven.

Readings on the History & System of the Common Law. 3rd ed. Ed. by Roscoe Pound & Theodore F. Plucknett. LC 93-78456. 756p. 1993. reprint ed. 110.00 (*1-56169-043-0*) Gaunt.

Readings on the Israeli Political System: Structures & Processes. Ed. by Gregory S. Mahler. LC 81-40031. 450p. (Orig.). 1982. pap. text ed. 37.00 (*0-8191-2118-5*) U Pr of Amer.

Readings on the Management of Working Capital. 3rd ed. Keith V. Smith & George W. Gallinger. 717p. (C). 1988. pap. text ed. 41.00 (*0-314-85300-6*) West Pub.

Readings on the Paradiso of Dante: Chiefly Based on the Commentary of Benvenuto da Imola; with an Introduction by the Bishop of Ripon, 2 vols. William W. Vernon. LC 74-38372. (Select Bibliographies Reprint Ser.). 1977. reprint ed. 68.95 (*0-8369-6789-5*) Ayer.

Readings on the Principles & Applications of Decision Analysis, 2 vols. 3rd ed. Ronald A. Howard et al. (Illus.). 955p. (C). 1989. reprint ed. 75.00 (*0-9623074-0-8*) Strategic Decisions.

Readings on the Relation of Government to Property & Industry. Ed. by Samuel P. Orth. LC 73-2527. (Big Business; Economic Power in a Free Society Ser.). 1973. reprint ed. 44.95 (*0-405-05106-9*) Ayer.

***Readings on the Six Yogas of Naropa.** Glenn H. Mullin. 175p. 1997. pap. 16.95 (*1-55939-074-3*) Snow Lion Pubns.

Readings on the Vertical File. Ed. by Michael D. Spencer. xv, 174p. 1993. lib. bdg. 27.50 (*0-87287-993-3*) Libs Unl.

Readings on Wildfires. Ed. by Michael P. Jones. (Illus.). 96p. (Orig.). 1985. text ed. 12.20 (*0-89904-118-3*); pap. text ed. 9.70 (*0-89904-119-1*) Crumb Elbow Pub.

***Readings on William Faulkner.** Ed. by Clarice Swisher. LC 97-12900. (Literary Companion Ser.). (YA). (gr. 9-12). 1997. pap. 12.96 (*1-56510-640-7*); lib. bdg. 20.96 (*1-56510-641-5*) Greenhaven.

***Readings Plus with Weblinks: Issues in Womens Health & Wellness - '97/'98.** Ed. by Amanda Rittenhouse. 210p. (Orig.). (C). 1997. pap. text ed. 13.95 (*0-89582-348-9*) Morton Pub.

Readings Skills, 7 Vols. Wiener. (C). 1996. wbk. ed., pap. 34.36 (*0-395-77641-4*) HM.

Readings/Lessons Harper's Grammar French. Rosenberg. (College French Ser.). 1983. pap. 30.95 (*0-8384-3747-8*) Heinle & Heinle.

Reading/Writing Remedies: How to Book of Materials & Activities, Resource Lists & Sample Materials for Language Arts Skills Development. Nancy E. Walentas. (Illus.). 214p. 1996. teacher ed., pap. text ed. 39.95 (*0-9650329-3-0*); teacher ed., lib. bdg. 39.95 (*0-9650329-0-6*); teacher ed., ring bd. 39.95 (*0-9650329-2-2*) Reading Manipulatives.

Readjuster Movement in Virginia. C. C. Pearson. 1990. 14.50 (*0-8446-1344-4*) Peter Smith.

***Readjustment Counseling Service: Vet Centers Address Multiple Client Problems, but Improvement Is Needed.** (Illus.). 42p. (Orig.). (C). 1996. pap. 25.00 (*0-7881-3461-2*) DIANE Pub.

Readjustment of Indian Affairs: Hearings. U. S. Congress, House Committee on Indian Affairs. LC 74-15123. reprint ed. 49.50 (*0-404-11983-2*) AMS Pr.

Read...Set...Read & Laugh: A Funny Treasury for Beginning Readers. Illus. by Margot Apple et al. LC 9432535. 144p. (J). (ps-3). 1995. 17.95 (*0-385-32119-8*) BDD Bks Young Read.

***Readville Massachusetts & Camp Meigs.** N. M. Hannan & M. E. Pitts. 100p. (Orig.). 1990. pap. 15.00 (*0-913553-09-3*) Albert Hse Pub.

***Readville Massachusetts...James Read in Readville & the Training Camps at Meigs Field 1861-1865.** N. H. Hannan. (Illus.). 50p. (Orig.). 1990. pap. 9.00 (*0-614-28424-4*) Albert Hse Pub.

Ready! A Step by Step Guide to Training the Search & Rescue Dog. Susan Bulanda. Ed. by Luana Luther. LC 93-74002. (Illus.). 170p. 1994. pap. 26.50 (*0-944875-41-6*) Doral Pub.

Ready About. Mike Peyton. 96p. (C). 1990. text ed. 59.00 (*0-906754-95-X*, Pub. by Fernhurst Bks UK) St Mut.

Ready, Aim, Change: A Toolbook for Managing Personal Change. Bob Marsenich. 218p. (Orig.). 1989. pap. 11.95 (*0-9622988-3-2*) Seaglass Pubns.

***Ready, Aim, Fire!** Adapted by Brian Brown & Andrew Melrose. (Storykeepers Easy Reader Ser.: Bk. 4). (J). (ps-3). 1997. mass mkt. 3.99 (*0-310-20336-8*); mass mkt. 3.99 (*0-310-20334-1*) Zondervan.

Ready, Aim, Hire: Developing Your Brand Name Resume. Allan Karson. 160p. 1990. pap. 15.00 (*1-55623-368-X*) Irwin Prof Pubng.

Ready, Aim, Hire! How to Master the Hiring Process. Ed. by Miles B. Canning. 224p. (Orig.). 1992. pap. 19.95 (*0-9632704-0-0*) PerSysCo.

Ready-Aim-Hire: Win the Work Search Game & Get the Job You Really Want. Carolyn E. Graves. (Illus.). 49p. 1992. Wkbk. student ed., pap. text ed. 4.75 (*1-882716-02-7*); student ed., pap. text ed. 19.95 incl. digital audio (*1-882716-00-0*) PAVE.

Ready, Aim...Retire! William C. Brown, Jr. & Amy Abraham. 50p. (Orig.). 1993. pap. 19.95 (*0-9638898-0-X*) C Brown.

Ready Always. Stanley M. Horton. LC 74-76802. (Radiant Life Ser.). 127p. 1974. pap. 3.95 (*0-88243-575-2*, 02-0575) Gospel Pub.

***Ready & Waiting.** Rick Rodgers. 1998. pap. write for info. (*0-688-15803-X*) Morrow.

Ready & Waiting: One Hundred Sixty All-New Recipes for the Slow Cooker. Ed. by Rick Rodgers. LC 92-9862. 1992. 22.00 (*0-688-11023-1*) Hearst Bks.

***Ready Answers to Religious Questions.** A. C. Williams & Harvey Dykes. 200p. (Orig.). 1986. pap. 1.95 (*0-933672-99-3*, C-2056) Star Bible.

Ready-Art Portfolio: Motivation & Achievement Headings & Illustrations. 1987. 42.95 (*0-87280-903-X*, 663, Asher-Gallant) Caddylak Systs.

Ready-Art Portfolio - Humor in the Workplace. 1987. 42.95 (*0-87280-905-6*, 665, Asher-Gallant) Caddylak Systs.

Ready Brigade of the 82nd Airborne in Desert Storm: A Combat Memoir by a Headquarters Company Commander. Dominic J. Caraccilo. LC 92-50945. (Illus.). 223p. (YA). (gr. 8-12). 1993. pap. 19.95 (*0-89950-829-4*) McFarland & Co.

Ready Defense: The Best of Josh McDowell. Josh McDowell. LC 92-41360. 496p. 1992. reprint ed. pap. 18.99 (*0-8407-4419-6*) Nelson.

Ready, Fire, Aim: Avoiding Management by Impulse. Harry Levinson. LC 86-10593. 304p. 1986. pap. 12.95 (*0-916516-07-5*) Levinson Inst.

Ready for Any Challenge: An Advanced Training Guide for Getting a Good Systemic Handle on Change. Lutz H. Schlicke & Heinz M. Schlicke. LC 94-15997. (Illus.). 384p. 1994. pap. 19.95 (*0-942963-43-1*) Distinctive Pub.

Ready for Battle: Thirty One Studies on Christian Discipleship. R. Arthur Mathews. LC 93-35784. 144p. 1993. pap. 7.99 (*0-87788-727-6*, OMF Books) Shaw Pubs.

Ready for Bed. Ronnie W. Shipman. (Illus.). 24p. (J). 1995. 6.95 (*0-307-17560-X*) Western Pub.

Ready for Business. Andrew Vaughan & Neil Heyen. (Business English Ser.). 80p. 1990. audio 24.95 (*0-582-05145-2*, 78667) Longman.

Ready for Business. Andrew Vaughan & Neil Heyen. (Business English Ser.). 80p. 1990. pap. text ed. 16.52 (*0-582-05142-8*, 78665) Longman.

Ready for Kindergarden: An Award Winning Teacher's Plan to Prepare Your Child for School. Sharon Wilkins. 160p. 1996. pap. 9.99 (*0-88070-918-9*, Gold & Honey) Multnomah Pubs.

Ready for Life, 6 vols. 72p. (Orig.). (YA). 1994. pap. 29.99 (*1-56476-397-8*, 6-3397, Victor Bks) Chariot Victor.

Ready for Marriage. Debbie Macomber. (Romance Ser.). 1994. mass mkt. 2.99 (*0-373-03307-9*, 1-03307-5) Harlequin Bks.

Ready for Marriage. Debbie Macomber. 1994. pap. 2.99 (*0-373-15553-0*) Harlequin Bks.

Ready for Marriage. large type ed. Debbie Macomber. 1995. pap. 19.95 (*0-7838-1176-4*, GK Hall) Thorndike Pr.

Ready for Reading. J. Tyler & G. Round. (First Learning Ser.). (Illus.). 24p. (J). (ps up). 1989. pap. 3.95 (*0-7460-0267-X*, Usborne) EDC.

Ready for Reading: Classroom Games for Reading Readiness. Markanne Gantt. 149p. 1980. pap. 9.95 (*0-87762-285-X*) Technomic.

***Ready for Responsibility: How to Equip your Children for Work & Marriage.** Robert Barnes. LC 96-35876. 240p. (Orig.). 1997. pap. 10.99 (*0-310-20135-7*) Zondervan.

Ready for Romance. Wayne Loveless. 200p. 1995. pap. 11.00 (*0-8059-3793-5*) Dorrance.

Ready for Romance. Debbie Macomber. (Romance Ser.). 1993. mass mkt. 2.99 (*0-373-03288-9*, 1-03288-7) Harlequin Bks.

Ready for Romance. Debbie Macomber. 1993. pap. 2.99 (*0-373-15534-4*) Harlequin Bks.

Ready for School. (Golden Step Ahead Workbooks Ser.). (Illus.). 32p. (J). (ps). 1985. pap. 2.19 (*0-307-03585-9*, Golden Pr) Western Pub.

***Ready for School.** (Fisher-Price Preschool Workbooks Ser.). (Illus.). 72p. (J). (ps). 1996. pap. write for info. (*1-56144-768-4*, Honey Bear Bks) Modern Pub NYC.

Ready For School. Michael Berenstain. (J). (ps). 1990. pap. write for info. (*0-307-11642-5*) Western Pub.

Ready for School? Jim Grant. 40p. (Orig.). 1992. pap. text ed. 6.00 (*0-935493-85-9*) Programs Educ.

Ready for School: How Parents Can Prepare Children for School Success. Geraldine Chapey. (Illus.). 164p. (Orig.). 1986. pap. text ed. 9.25 (*0-8191-5317-6*) U Pr of Amer.

Ready for Sea: The Bicentennial History of the U. S. Navy Supply Corps. Frank J. Allston. LC 95-13662. (Illus.). 668p. 1995. 49.95 (*1-55750-033-9*) Naval Inst Pr.

Ready for Something New. Mikal Keefer. (Really Reading! Bks). (Illus.). 48p. (Orig.). (J). (gr. 1-3). 1993. pap. 4.49 (*0-7847-0097-4*, 03947) Standard Pub.

Ready for the Defense. Martin Garbus. 300p. 1987. reprint ed. pap. 4.95 (*0-88184-373-3*) Carroll & Graf.

Ready for the Ha Ha. Jane Mayhall. LC 66-23198. 102p. 1966. 30.00 (*0-87130-014-1*) Eakins.

Ready for the Real World. William C. Hartel et al. 360p. 1994. pap. 26.95 (*0-534-17712-3*) Wadsworth Pub.

Ready for the River. Neal Bell. 1991. pap. 5.25 (*0-8222-0932-2*) Dramatists Play.

Ready for What? Constructing Meanings of Readiness for Kindergarten. M. Elizabeth Graue. LC 91-38885. (SUNY Series, Early Childhood Education). 313p. (C). 1992. text ed. 59.50 (*0-7914-1203-2*); pap. text ed. 19.95 (*0-7914-1204-0*) State U NY Pr.

Ready for Writing. J. Tyler & G. Round. (First Learning Ser.). (Illus.). 24p. (J). (ps up). 1989. pap. 3.95 (*0-7460-0218-1*, Usborne) EDC.

Ready from Within: A First Person Narrative: Septima Clark & the Civil Rights Movement. Ed. by Cynthia S. Brown. LC 90-80668. (Illus.). 145p. (C). 1990. reprint ed. 29.95 (*0-86543-173-6*); reprint ed. pap. 9.95 (*0-86543-174-4*) Africa World.

Ready, Get Set, Go! Sharon Peters. (Illus.). 32p. (J). (gr. k-2). 1997. pap. 2.50 (*0-89375-285-1*) Troll Communs.

Ready! Get Set! Grow! Jim Plueddemann. (Bible Discovery Guide for Junior Campers Ser.). (Illus.). 48p. (J). 1987. Camper Ed. pap. text ed. 1.50 (*0-87788-715-2*); Counselor Ed. pap. text ed. 3.50 (*0-87788-716-0*) Shaw Pubs.

R

An Asterisk (*) at the beginning of an entry indicates that the title is appearing in BIP for the first time.

Ready-Go-Begin-To-Learn. Eunice Insel & Ann Edson. (Illus.). (J). (ps-1). 1980. student ed. 4.25 (*0-89525-098-5*) Ed Activities.

Ready made Access Applications. Ed Jones. LC 93-1968. 1993. 36.95 (*0-8306-4603-5*); pap. write for info. (*0-8306-4604-3*) TAB Bks.

Ready Made Access Applications. Ed Jones. 1993. pap. text ed. 36.95 incl. disk (*0-07-032772-6*) McGraw.

Ready Made Access Applications. Ed Jones. 1994. pap. text ed. 36.95 (*0-07-032774-2*) McGraw.

Ready-Made Activities for Customer Care Skills. Simon Johnson. (Secrets of Excellent Customer Service Ser.). 224p. (Orig.). 1994. pap. 52.50 (*0-273-60684-0*, Pub. by Pitman Pub Ltd UK) Trans-Atl Phila.

Ready Made Activities for Customer Care Skills. Simon Johnson. 224p. 1994. pap. 60.00 (*0-614-04094-9*, Pub. by Pitman Pubng UK) St Mut.

Ready Made Activities for Developing Your Staff. David Taylor & Sue Bishop. (Institute of Management Ser.). 192p. (Orig.). 1994. pap. 52.50 (*0-273-60560-7*, Pub. by Pitman Pub Ltd UK) Trans-Atl Phila.

Ready Made Activities for Financial Skills. Derrick Fellows. (Institute of Management Ser.). 224p. (Orig.). 1994. pap. 52.50 (*0-273-60730-8*, Pub. by Pitman Pub Ltd UK) Trans-Atl Phila.

Ready-Made Activities for Negotiation Skills. Sheila Cane. 224p. 1994. pap. 49.50 (*0-273-60764-2*, Pub. by Pitman Pub Ltd UK) Trans-Atl Phila.

Ready-Made Activities for Presentation Skills. Patrick Forsyth. (Institute of Management Ser.). 224p. 1994. pap. 52.50 (*0-273-60731-6*, Pub. by Pitman Pub Ltd UK) Trans-Atl Phila.

Ready-Made Activities for Selling Skills. Patrick Forsyth. 224p. 1994. pap. 65.00 (*0-614-04096-5*, Pub. by Pitman Pubng UK) St Mut.

Ready-Made Activities for Selling Skills: Developing a Skilled & Successful Sales Team. Patrick Forsyth. (Institute of Management Ser.). 224p. (Orig.). 1994. pap. 52.50 (*0-273-60592-5*, Pub. by Pitman Pub Ltd UK) Trans-Atl Phila.

***Ready-Made Family.** Laurie Paige. 1997. pap. 3.99 (*0-373-24114-3*, 1-24114-0) Silhouette.

Ready-Made Paradox. Patricia A. Hartman. (Illus.). 368p. 1993. pap. 29.95 (*0-8306-4388-5*, Windcrest) TAB Bks.

Ready Made Power Builder Applications. Ed Jones. 1995. pap. text ed. 39.95 (*0-07-912062-8*) McGraw.

Ready-Made PowerBuilder Applications. Jones. 1996. pap. 39.95 (*0-07-032777-7*) McGraw.

Ready-Made PowerBuilder 4 Applications. Ed Jones. LC 95-15906. 1995. pap. write for info. (*0-07-012062-5*) McGraw.

***Ready Mapbook of East Hawaii Island, Vol. 1.** Carol L. Anderson. (Illus.). 75p. (Orig.). 1997. pap. 9.95 (*0-9654158-0-5*) Rec Copy Serv.

Ready-Mixed Concrete Industry. (Illus.). 160p. 1993. 995.00 (*0-318-00504-2*) Busn Trend.

Ready Notes: Macroeconomics-Principles of Economics. Gottheil. (Economics Ser.). 1996. 12.95 (*0-538-86013-8*) S-W Pub.

Ready Notes: Microeconomic Principles of Economics. Gottheil. (Economics Ser.). 1996. 12.95 (*0-538-86014-6*) S-W Pub.

Ready or Not: A Poetry Collection. Maureen Becker. 1995. 8.95 (*0-533-11151-X*) Vantage.

Ready or Not: Retirement Planning Review. 20th ed. Suzanne Arnold et al. 94p. (Orig.). 1993. pap. 7.95 (*1-882548-00-0*) Manpower Ed Inst.

***Ready or Not Vol. 24: Your Retirement Guide.** 24th ed. Suzanne Arnold et al. (Illus.). 114p. (Orig.). 1997. pap. 10.95 (*1-882548-03-5*) Manpower Ed Inst.

Ready..., Or Not..., I Told You So! George C. Wilson. 70p. (Orig.). 1991. pap. text ed. 15.00 (*0-9630320-0-3*) Dated Visions.

Ready Or Not It's Barndoor Bones. Andy McDonnell. (Illus.). 64p. 1995. pap. 3.95 (*0-8059-3576-2*) Dorrance.

Ready or Not Retirement Guide. Suzanne Arnold & Jeanne Brock. 112p. 1996. pap. text ed. 10.95 (*1-882548-02-7*) Manpower Ed Inst.

***Ready or Not-You're a Grandparent.** 224p. 1997. write for info. (*0-7814-0244-1*, Victor Bks) Chariot Victor.

Ready Reading. Faye Crow. (Illus.). 135p. (Orig.). (J). (ps-2). 1987. pap. 10.95 (*0-9617529-0-4*) Ready Work.

Ready Reference, American Indians, 3 Vols. Ed. by Salem Press Staff & Harvey Markowitz. LC 94-47633. 953p. (YA). (gr. 9-12). 1995. lib. bdg. 270.00 (*0-89356-757-4*) Salem Pr.

Ready Reference, American Justice, 3 vols., Set. Salem Press Editors. Ed. by Harvey Markowitz. LC 95-51529. (Illus.). 960p. 1996. lib. bdg. 270.00 (*0-89356-761-2*) Salem Pr.

***Ready Reference, Censorship, 3 vols., Vol. 1.** Ed. by Carl Jensen et al. LC 97-14245. (Illus.). 1056p. 1997. lib. bdg. 280.00 (*0-89356-444-3*) Salem Pr.

Ready Reference Ethics, 3 vols., Set. Salem Press Editors. Ed. by John K. Roth. LC 94-3995. (Illus.). 952p. 1994. lib. bdg. 270.00 (*0-89356-395-1*) Salem Pr.

Ready Reference for Critical Care. Rhonda M. Strawn & Bonnie P. Stewart. (Nursing-Health Science Ser.). 200p. (C). 1992. spiral bd. 32.50 (*0-86720-327-7*) Jones & Bartlett.

Ready Reference for Critical Care Drugs with Nursing Care Plans. 2nd ed. Bonnie P. Stewart & Rhonda M. Strawn. 1997. 33.75 (*0-86720-455-9*) Jones & Bartlett.

***Ready Reference Guide for Critical Care Nursing.** 2nd ed. Rhonda M. Strawn. LC 96-37503. 1997. 27.00 (*0-7637-0251-X*) Jones & Bartlett.

***Ready Reference Handbook.** Jack Dodds. LC 96-27260. 412p. 1997. spiral bd. 25.00 (*0-205-15906-0*) Allyn.

Ready Reference Pocket Manual. LC 92-43896. 1993. pap. 12.95 (*0-7931-0519-6*, 5606-4701, R & R Newkirk) Dearborn Finan.

Ready Reference to Philosophy East & West. Eugene F. Bales. 314p. (C). 1988. lib. bdg. 44.00 (*0-8191-6640-5*) U Pr of Amer.

***Ready Reference, Women's Issues.** Ed. by Margaret McFadden. LC 96-48989. (Illus.). 960p. 1997. lib. bdg. 270.00 (*0-89356-765-5*) Salem Pr.

Ready Reply: Answering Challenging Questions about the Gospel. Michael T. Griffith. 128p. 1994. 12.98 (*0-88290-506-6*, 1046) Horizon Utah.

Ready Reserve Force: Ship Readiness Has Improved, but Other Concerns Remain. (Illus.). 63p. (Orig.). (C). 1995. pap. text ed. 25.00 (*0-7881-1712-2*) DIANE Pub.

Ready Sell Aim: Get Ready to Sell, Sell the Modern Way, Aim for Repeat Customers. Robert H. Bloch. Ed. by Marilyn A. Bloch. (Illus.). 136p. (Orig.). 1995. pap. 16.95 (*0-9650771-0-1*) Swiss Alp.

Ready, Set - Regina! Lynn Cullen. 96p. (Orig.). (J). 1996. pap. 3.99 (*0-380-78427-0*, Camelot) Avon.

Ready... Set... Build: A Consumer's Guide to Home Improvement Planning & Contracts. Steve Gonzalez. Ed. by Joseph Pappas. LC 93-17327. (Illus.). 112p. (Orig.). 1993. pap. 9.95 (*0-9628336-7-3*, Womens Pubns) Consumer Press.

Ready, Set, Cooperate. Marlene Barron & Karen R. Young. LC 95-36111. (Ready, Set, Learn Ser.). 160p. 1996. pap. text ed. 12.95 (*0-471-10275-X*) Wiley.

Ready, Set, Count. Marlene Barron. LC 95-1306. (Ready, Set, Learn Ser.). 160p. (J). 1995. pap. text ed. 12.95 (*0-471-10282-2*) Wiley.

Ready, Set, Draw! Fun with Art. Laurie Steding. (Great Beginnings Ser.: Level 1). (J). 1997. pap. 1.95 (*0-8167-3390-2*) Troll Communs.

Ready, Set, Explore. Marlene Barron. (Ready, Set, Learn Ser.). 176p. 1996. pap. text ed. 12.95 (*0-471-10273-3*) Wiley.

Ready, Set, Go! John Stadler. LC 95-26452. (I Can Read Bk.). (Illus.). 32p. (J). (ps-3). 1996. 14.95 (*0-06-024944-7*) HarpC Child Bks.

Ready, Set, Go! John Stadler. LC 95-26452. (I Can Read Bk.). (Illus.). 32p. (J). (ps-3). 1996. lib. bdg. 14.89 (*0-06-024947-1*) HarpC Child Bks.

Ready, Set, Go! A Counting Book. (Little Golden Bks.). (Illus.). 24p. (J). (ps-2). 1995. pap. 1.49 (*0-307-30261-X*, Golden Pr) Western Pub.

***Ready, Set, Go! A Student Guide to SPSS for Windows.** Thomas W. Pavkov & Kent A. Pierce. LC 96-37292. (Illus.). 121p. (Orig.). (C). 1996. pap. text ed. 12.95 (*1-55934-841-0*, 1841) Mayfield Pub.

Ready, Set, Go: An Agency Guide to Independent Living. Helen D. Stone. 57p. 1987. 7.50 (*0-87868-304-6*) Child Welfare.

Ready, Set, Go! Children's Programming for Bookmobiles & Other Small Spaces. Dolores Chupela. LC 94-744. (Illus.). 250p. (J). (ps-3). 1994. spiral bd. 19.95 (*0-913853-34-8*, 32528, Alleyside) Highsmith Pr.

***Ready Set Go: Retirement Planning Strategies.** Robert R. Julian. 144p. 13.95 (*0-614-25563-5*, 00HR19043) Print Indus Am.

***Ready! Set!! Goals!!!** unabridged ed. James R. Allen & Carol L. Allen. (Illus.). 250p. 1997. wbk. ed. write for info. (*0-9657365-0-4*, Life Goals) Goals Pub.

Ready, Set, Grammar! A Beginning Grammar Program for Non-Readers. Mark Barrett et al. 1988. student ed., spiral bd. 31.95 (*1-55999-067-8*) LinguiSystems.

Ready Set Grow. Debora Pearson. 1996. 9.95 (*0-590-62986-7*) Scholastic Inc.

Ready, Set, Grow: A Guide to Gardening with Children. Suzanne F. Bales. 144p. 1996. 17.95 (*0-02-860399-0*) Macmillan.

Ready, Set, Grow! A Kid's Guide to Gardening. Rebecca Hershey. 104p. (Orig.). (J). (ps-6). 1995. spiral bd., pap. 9.95 (*0-673-36139-X*, GoodYrBooks) Addson-Wesley Educ.

Ready, Set, Grow! Devotions for Spiritual Growth. Gordon Thiessen. 178p. (Orig.). (YA). (gr. 6 up). 1994. pap. 8.95 (*1-887002-04-9*) Cross Trng.

Ready, Set, Hop! Stuart J. Murphy. LC 95-4729. (MathStart Ser.). (Illus.). 40p. (J). (gr. 1-3). 1996. 14.95 (*0-06-025877-2*) HarpC Child Bks.

Ready, Set, Hop! Stuart J. Murphy. LC 95-4729. (Trophy MathStart Tool Ser.). (Illus.). 40p. (J). (gr. 2 up). 1996. pap. 4.95 (*0-06-446702-3*, Trophy); lib. bdg. 14.89 (*0-06-025878-0*) HarpC Child Bks.

Ready, Set, Listen! A Beginning Listening Program for Non-Readers. Claire Morency et al. (Illus.). 200p. 1991. spiral bd. 31.95 (*1-55999-182-8*) LinguiSystems.

Ready, Set, Organize! Get Your Stuff Together. Pipi C. Peterson. LC 95-35702. (Illus.). 152p. (Orig.). 1995. pap. 12.95 (*1-57112-072-6*, P0726) Park Ave Prods.

Ready, Set, Play: Ideas for Creating Educational Games for Children. Kathy Strawn et al. Ed. by Jennifer Law. 44p. 1995. pap. text ed. 6.95 (*1-56309-129-1*, New Hope) Womans Mission Union.

Ready, Set, Practice: Fundamentals of Landscape Architecture Professional Practice. Bruce G. Sharky. 280p. 1994. text ed. 59.95 (*0-471-55512-6*) Wiley.

Ready Set Read, 12 titles. (J). 1992. 179.76 (*0-8172-3587-6*) Raintree Steck-V.

Ready! Set! Read! Joanna Cole. 144p. (J). 1990. 17.95 (*0-385-41416-1*) Doubleday.

Ready, Set, Read: Best Books to Prepare Preschoolers. Ellen V. Mahoney & Leah Wilcox. LC 83-27087. 1985. 32.50 (*0-8108-1684-9*) Scarecrow.

Ready, Set, Read! Reading Readiness. Laurie Steding. (Great Beginnings Ser.: Level 1). (J). 1997. pap. 1.95 (*0-8167-3248-5*) Troll Communs.

Ready, Set, Read & Write. Marlene Barron. 160p. (J). 1995. pap. text ed. 12.95 (*0-471-10283-0*) Wiley.

Ready, Set, Recycle! Richard Chevat. (J). (ps-3). 1993. pap. 1.95 (*0-307-10554-7*, Golden Pr) Western Pub.

Ready, Set, Retire! How Much Money You Need & the Tax-Smart Way to Get It & Keep It. J. William Brimacombe. LC 94-66841. 210p. 1994. 24.99 (*0-9641532-3-8*) Financial Freedom.

Ready, Set, Retire! How Much Money You Need & the Tax-Smart Way to Get It & Keep It. J. William Brimacombe. LC 94-66841. 210p. 1995. pap. 12.95 (*0-9641532-4-6*) Financial Freedom.

Ready, Set, Sequence: A Beginning Sequencing Program Geared for Non Readers. Laura E. Cherf et al. 1993. student ed., spiral bd. 31.95 (*1-55999-261-1*) LinguiSystems.

Ready, Set, Study! Building Study Skills. Echaore-Yoon. 1990. pap. 9.86 (*0-8092-4268-0*) Contemp Bks.

Ready, Set, Study! Improving Study Skills. Stein. 1990. pap. 9.86 (*0-8092-4267-2*) Contemp Bks.

Ready, Set, Write! Creative Ideas to Get Kids Writing. Debra Kuzbik. (Orig.). (J). (gr. k-5). 1996. teacher ed., pap. 12.00 (*1-895411-84-X*) Peguis Pubs Ltd.

Ready, Set...Sing! (Songs for Sunday & Everyday) Ed. by Mary M. Nicol & Pamela K. Roth. 96p. (Orig.). (J). 1989. pap. 10.00 (*0-8170-1155-2*) Judson.

Ready, Set...Wait! Help for Life on Hold. Karen Barber. LC 96-10264. 208p. (YA). (gr. 10). 1996. pap. 12.99 (*0-8010-5712-4*) Baker Bks.

Ready Steady Go. Sandra Redmond. (Orig.). (J). (gr. k-6). 1995. pap. 5.00 (*0-87602-333-2*) Anchorage.

Ready Steady Grow! Angela Macnamara. 1989. pap. 22.00 (*0-86217-166-0*, Pub. by Veritas IE) St Mut.

***Ready to Answer All Bells: A Blueprint for Successful Naval Engineering.** David D. Bruhn et al. LC 97-11970. (Illus.). 216p. 1997. 22.95 (*1-55750-227-7*) Naval Inst Pr.

***Ready to Be Revealed.** Steve Rush. 152p. (Orig.). 1996. pap. 8.99 (*1-57502-369-5*, PO1178) Morris Pubng.

Ready-To-Build Telephone Enhancements. Delton T. Horn. LC 93-12883. 1993. pap. 17.60 (*0-8306-4359-1*) McGraw-Hill Prof.

Ready-to-Build Telephone Enhancements. Delton T. Horn. 1993. pap. text ed. 17.95 (*0-07-030412-2*) McGraw.

Ready to Catch Him Should He Fall. Neil Bartlett. LC 92-53570. 320p. 1992. pap. 11.95 (*0-452-26873-7*, Plume) NAL-Dutton.

Ready to Communicate: Help Your Child Develop the Skills Necessary for School Success. Elizabeth McKinnon. LC 96-60425. (Getting Ready for School Ser.). (Illus.). 96p. (Orig.). (J). (ps-k). 1997. pap. 6.95 (*1-57029-114-4*, 3204, Totline Bks) Warren Pub Hse.

***Ready-to-Do Children's Message Kit.** Ed. by Jan Kershner. LC 97-16130. 64p. (Orig.). (J). 1997. pap. 19.99 (*0-7644-2029-1*) Group Pub.

Ready-To-frame Storybook Illustrations: A Biography. Jessie W. Smith. 1989. pap. 3.95 (*0-486-26063-1*) Dover.

Ready to Go. Tom Mandel. LC 81-4904. 69p. (Orig.). 1981. pap. 4.00 (*0-87886-113-0*, Greenfld Rev Pr) Greenfld Rev Lit.

Ready to Go. Ronnie W. Shipman. (Illus.). 24p. (J). 1995. 6.95 (*0-307-17561-8*) Western Pub.

Ready to Go! Travel Fun for All Ages. William S. Halsey. (Travel Activities & Games Ser.). 80p. 1993. pap. 6.95 (*1-883643-00-7*) Stilling Pub.

***Ready-to-Go Book Report Projects.** Scholastic Professional Books Staff. (J). 1997. pap. text ed. 12.95 (*0-590-31444-0*) Scholastic Inc.

Ready-to-Go Resumes. Yana Parker. LC 95-1099. 128p. 1995. pap. 29.95 incl. disk (*0-89815-733-1*) Ten Speed Pr.

Ready to Hazard: A Biography of Commodore William Bainbridge, 1774-1833. David F. Long. LC 80-29146. 359p. reprint ed. pap. 102.40 (*0-317-30023-7*, 2025021) Bks Demand.

Ready to Learn: A Mandate for the Nation. Ernest L. Boyer. LC 91-46817. (Illus.). 193p. (Orig.). 1991. pap. 8.00 (*0-931050-44-8*) Carnegie Fnd Advan Teach.

Ready to Learn: A Mandate to the Nation. Ernest L. Boyer. 1994. 14.00 (*0-89333-119-8*) AACTE.

Ready to Learn: How Schools Can Help Kids Be Healthier & Safer. Ed. by Edward Miller. (Reprint Ser.: Vol. 2). 124p. (Orig.). (C). 1995. pap. 15.00 (*1-883433-01-0*) Harv Educ Letter.

Ready to Learn Colors, Shapes & Numbers: Help Your Child Develop the Skills Necessary for School Success. Elizabeth S. McKinnon. LC 96-60121. (Getting Ready for School Ser.). (Illus.). 96p. (Orig.). (J). (ps-k). 1997. pap. 6.95 (*1-57029-107-1*, 3201, Totline Bks) Warren Pub Hse.

Ready to Listen & Explore the Senses: Help Your Child Develop the Skills Necessary for School Success. Gayle Bittinger. LC 96-60426. (Getting Ready for School Ser.). (Illus.). 96p. (Orig.). (J). (ps-k). 1997. pap. 6.95 (*1-57029-115-2*, 3205, Totline Bks) Warren Pub Hse.

Ready to Live, Prepared to Die: A Provocative Guide to the Rest of Your Life. Amy Harwell. LC 94-12462. 160p. 1995. pap. 10.99 (*0-87788-704-7*) Shaw Pubs.

***Ready to Practice? Social Workers & Probation Officers: Their Training in the First Year of Work.** Peter Marsh & John Triseliotis. 250p. 1996. text ed. 59.95 (*1-85972-478-7*, Pub. by Avebury Pub UK) Ashgate Pub Co.

Ready to Read. 1989. 11.95 (*0-19-434368-5*) OUP.

Ready to Read. Kelly Sedon. 1983. text ed. 11.81 (*0-201-05600-3*) Addison-Wesley.

Ready to Read: Help Your Child Develop the Skills Necessary for School Success. Theodosia Spewock. Ed. by Kathleen Cubley. LC 96-60122. (Getting Ready for School Ser.). (Illus.). 96p. (Orig.). (J). (ps-k). 1997. pap. 6.95 (*1-57029-106-3*, 3203, Totline Bks) Warren Pub Hse.

Ready-to-Read, Ready-to-Count Handbook. Teresa Savage. LC 91-12286. 272p. 1991. pap. 11.95 (*1-55704-093-1*) Newmarket.

Ready to Read! Student Workbook. 2nd rev. ed. Janet S. Fenholt. LC 96-96009. (Illus.). iv, 113p. (Orig.). 1996. pap. text ed. 22.00 (*1-888706-06-6*) Fenholt Pubng.

Ready to Read! Teaching Set. 2nd rev. ed. Janet S. Fenholt. LC 96-96008. (Illus.). xii, 120p. (Orig.). 1996. pap. text ed. 26.00 (*1-888706-07-4*) Fenholt Pubng.

Ready to Rebuild: The Imminent Plan to Build the Last Days Temple. Thomas Ice & Randall Price. 160p. (Orig.). 1992. pap. 11.99 (*0-89081-956-4*); vhs 19.99 (*1-56507-032-1*) Harvest Hse.

Ready to Restore. Jay E. Adams. (Orig.). 1981. pap. 7.99 (*0-87552-070-7*, Pub. by Evangelical Pr) Presby & Reformed.

Ready to Survive. Jacqueline Lapidus. LC 75-9593. 24p. 1975. pap. 4.00 (*0-914610-04-X*) Hanging Loose.

Ready-to-Tell Tales: Surefire Stories from America's Favorite Storytellers. Ed. by David Holt & Bill Mooney. LC 94-27184. (Illus.). (J). 1994. pap. 19.95 (*0-87483-381-7*) August Hse.

Ready-to-Use Accents & Attention-Getters. Carol B. Grafton. 64p. 1984. pap. 4.50 (*0-486-24692-2*) Dover.

Ready-to-Use Activities for Before & After School Programs. Marian J. Wirch et al. 256p. 1989. spiral bd. 29.95 (*0-87628-691-0*) Ctr Appl Res.

***Ready-to-Use Activities for Teaching A Midsummer Night's Dream.** John W. Swope. LC 96-32577. (Shakespeare Teacher's Activiies Library). 1996. write for info. (*0-87628-915-4*) Ctr Appl Res.

Ready-to-Use Activities for Teaching Hamlet. John W. Swope. (Shakespeare Teacher's Activities Library). 27.95 (*0-87628-116-1*) Ctr Appl Res.

Ready-to-Use Activities for Teaching Julius Caesar. John W. Swope. LC 93-5221. (Shakespeare Teacher's Activities Library). 1993. text ed. 27.95 (*0-87628-117-X*) Ctr Appl Res.

Ready-to-Use Activities for Teaching Macbeth. John W. Swope. (Shakespeare Teacher's Activities Library). text ed. 27.95 (*0-87628-115-3*) Ctr Appl Res.

Ready-to-Use Activities for Teaching Romeo & Juliet. John W. Swope. LC 93-13964. (Shakespeare Teacher's Activities Library). 1993. text ed. write for info. (*0-87628-114-5*) Ctr Appl Res.

Ready-to-Use Activities Through the Year. Sue J. Erlenbusch. 240p. 1991. spiral bd. 27.95 (*0-87628-793-3*) Ctr Appl Res.

Ready-to-Use American History Activities. James F. Silver. 283p. 1996. pap. 28.95 (*0-87628-756-9*) P-H.

Ready-to-Use American History Activities for Grades 5-12: Lessons & Skill Sheets from Pre-Columbus to the Space Age. James F. Silver. LC 95-13220. 1995. write for info. (*0-87628-142-0*) Ctr Appl Res.

Ready-to-Use Animal Silhouettes. Ellen Sandbeck. (Illus.). 64p. 1989. pap. 4.50 (*0-486-26058-5*) Dover.

***Ready-to-Use Antique Cuts.** Carol B. Grafton. (Illus.). pap. 4.95 (*0-486-28004-7*) Dover.

Ready-to-Use Arrows. Ed. by Theodore Menten. (Clip Art Ser.). (Illus.). 1979. pap. 4.50 (*0-486-23783-4*) Dover.

Ready-to-Use Art Deco Borders. Theodore Menten. 64p. (Orig.). 1985. pap. 4.50 (*0-486-24967-0*) Dover.

Ready-to-Use Art Deco Letters. Ed. by Carol B. Grafton. (Clip Art Ser.). (Illus.). 64p. (Orig.). 1991. pap. 4.50 (*0-486-26733-4*) Dover.

Ready-to-Use Art Nouveau Alphabets. Dan X. Solo. 1986. pap. 4.50 (*0-486-25140-3*) Dover.

Ready-to-Use Art Nouveau Borders. Theodore Menten. (Illus.). 64p. (Orig.). 1983. pap. 4.50 (*0-486-24431-8*) Dover.

Ready-to-Use Art Nouveau Small Frames & Borders. Theodore Menten. 64p. (Orig.). 1985. pap. 4.50 (*0-486-24975-1*) Dover.

Ready-to-Use Authentic Civil War Illustrations. Carol B. Grafton. (Illus.). 64p. Date not set. pap. 5.95 (*0-486-28511-1*) Dover.

Ready-to-Use Banners. Theodore Menten. (Clip Art Ser.). (Illus.). 1979. pap. 4.50 (*0-486-23899-7*) Dover.

***Ready-to-Use Baseball Illustrations.** Bob Giuliani. (Illus.). pap. 5.95 (*0-486-26060-7*) Dover.

Ready-to-Use Bible Activity Sheets. Nellie De Vries. (REPRObooks Ser.). (Illus.). 128p. (J). (gr. 2-7). 1992. pap. 10.99 (*0-8010-3008-0*) Baker Bks.

Ready-to-Use Borders. Ed. by Theodore Menten. (Clip Art Ser.). (Illus.). 1979. pap. 4.50 (*0-486-23782-6*) Dover.

Ready-to-Use Borders on Layout Grids. Carol B. Grafton. (Clip Art Ser.). 48p. 1985. pap. 4.50 (*0-486-24812-7*) Dover.

Ready-to-Use Business Forms: A Complete Package for the Small Business. 3rd ed. (Business Ser.). (Illus.). 128p. 1992. otabind, pap. 12.95 (*1-55180-110-8*) Self-Counsel Pr.

***Ready-to-Use Celtic Borders on Layout Grids.** Mallory Pearce. (Illus.). pap. 5.95 (*0-486-27041-6*) Dover.

Ready-to-Use Christmas Designs. Ed Sibbett, Jr. (Clip Art Ser.). (Illus.). 1979. pap. 3.95 (*0-486-23900-4*) Dover.

Ready-to-Use Christmas Silhouettes. Bob Censoni. 64p. (Orig.). 1985. pap. 4.95 (*0-486-24954-9*) Dover.

Ready-to-Use Computer Literacy Activities Kits, Level I. Dwight E. Mostoller et al. 64p. (J). (gr. 4-6). 1987. student ed. 5.95 (*0-317-66399-2*); teacher ed. 24.95 (*0-13-762022-5*) P-H.

Ready-to-Use Computer Literacy Activities Kits Level II. Dwight E. Mostoller et al. 64p. (J). (gr. 7-10). 1987. student ed. 5.95 (*0-317-66401-8*); teacher ed. 24.95 (*0-13-762048-9*) P-H.

An Asterisk (*) at the beginning of an entry indicates that the title is appearing in BIP for the first time.

Ready-to-Use Conflict Resolution Activities for Secondary Students: Strategies for Dealing with Conflict in Real-Life Situations, Plus Guidelines for Creating a Peer Mediation Program. Ruth Perlstein & Gloria Thrall. LC 95-23617. 368p. 1996. spiral bd. 29.95 (*0-87628-195-1*) Ctr Appl Res.

Ready-to-Use Discovery Center Activities for Preschool Children. Lorraine Clancy. 256p. 1993. pap. 27.95 (*0-87628-810-7*) Ctr Appl Res.

***Ready-to-Use Dollhouse Floor Coverings.** Hendler. (Illus.). pap. 4.95 (*0-486-23666-8*) Dover.

***Ready-to-Use Dollhouse Stained Glass Windows.** Ed Sibbett. (Illus.). pap. 3.95 (*0-486-23740-0*) Dover.

Ready-to-Use Dollhouse Wallpaper: Six Full-Color Patterns to Decorate Six Rooms. Katzenbach & Warren, Inc. Staff. LC 77-70052. (Illus.). 1978. pap. 5.95 (*0-486-23495-9*) Dover.

***Ready-to-Use Endangered Animals Illustrations.** Bob Giuliani. (Illus.). 64p. 1997. pap. 5.95 (*0-486-29599-0*) Dover.

Ready-to-Use ESL Activities for Every Month of the School Year. Carol A. Josel. LC 93-45738. (Illus.). 1994. spiral bd. 27.95 (*0-87628-848-4*) Ctr Appl Res.

Ready-to-Use Fitness & Exercise Illustrations. Bob Giuliani. (Clip Art Ser.). (Illus.). 64p. (Orig.). 1991. pap. 4.50 (*0-486-26699-0*) Dover.

Ready-to-Use Flannel Board Stories, Figures & Activities for ESL Children. Elizabeth Krepelin & Bonnie M. Smith. LC 94-34637. 1994. spiral bd. 29.95 (*0-87628-853-0*) Ctr Appl Res.

Ready-to-Use Floral Designs. Ed Sibbett, Jr. (Illus.). 64p. pap. 4.95 (*0-486-23976-4*) Dover.

Ready-to-Use Food & Drink Spot Illustrations. Susan Gaber. (Clip Art Ser.). 1981. pap. 4.50 (*0-486-24139-4*) Dover.

Ready-to-Use Geography Activities for the American Continents: Lessons & Skillsheets Featuring North & South America. James F. Silver. 1996. pap. write for info. (*0-87628-356-3*); spiral bd. write for info. (*0-87628-355-5*) Ctr Appl Res.

***Ready-to-Use Golf & Tennis Illustrations.** Bob Giuliani. (Illus.). pap. 4.95 (*0-486-27985-5*) Dover.

Ready-to-Use Gourmet Food Illustrations. Ryuji Otani. (Clip Art Ser.). (Illus.). 64p. (Orig.). 1991. pap. 4.50 (*0-486-26652-4*) Dover.

Ready-to-Use Graphic Attention-Getters. Dan X. Solo. 64p. 1988. pap. 4.50 (*0-486-25744-4*) Dover.

***Ready-to-Use Group Activities: What Am I Going to Do for the Next 20 Minutes.** Randy L. Womack & James L. Shoemaker. (Illus.). 48p. (Orig.). (J). (gr. k-6). 1997. pap. text ed. 7.95 (*1-56500-042-0*) Gldn Educ.

Ready-to-Use Headlines. Ed. by Theodore Menten. (Clip Art Ser.). 1979. pap. 4.50 (*0-486-23454-1*) Dover.

***Ready to Use Holiday Small Frames.** 1997. pap. 5.95 (*0-486-29623-7*) Dover.

***Ready to Use Holiday Spot Illustrations.** Fleming. 1996. pap. 5.95 (*0-486-29236-3*) Dover.

Ready-to-Use Humorous Four Seasons Illustrations. Bob Censoni. (Clip Art Ser.). (Illus.). 64p. (Orig.). 1991. pap. 4.50 (*0-486-26656-7*) Dover.

Ready-to-Use Humorous Sports Illustrations. Bob Censoni. (Illus.). 64p. 1989. pap. 4.95 (*0-486-25955-2*) Dover.

Ready-To-Use Humorous Spot Illustrations. Illus. by Bob Censoni. (Clip Art Ser.). 64p. 1984. pap. 4.50 (*0-486-24644-2*) Dover.

Ready to Use Humourous Mortise. Bob Censoni. 1986. pap. 3.95 (*0-486-25041-5*) Dover.

***Ready-to-Use Hunting & Fishing Illustrations.** Bob Giuliani. (Illus.). pap. 5.95 (*0-486-28713-0*) Dover.

Ready-to-Use Illustrations for Holidays & Special Occasions. Ed. by Ed Sibbett, Jr. (Illus.). 64p. (Orig.). 1983. pap. 4.50 (*0-486-24440-7*) Dover.

Ready-to-Use Illustrations of Children (Clip Art) Tom Tierney. (Pictorial Archive Ser.). (Illus.). 64p. (Orig.). 1983. reprint ed. pap. 4.50 (*0-486-24405-9*) Dover.

Ready-to-Use Illustrations of Hands. Illus. by Tom Tierney. (Clip Art Ser.). (Orig.). 1983. pap. 4.50 (*0-486-24570-5*) Dover.

Ready-to-Use Illustrations of Men's Heads. Tom Tierney. (Pictorial Archive Ser.). (Illus.). 64p. (Orig.). 1982. pap. 4.50 (*0-486-24413-X*) Dover.

***Ready-to-Use Illustrations of Plants, Shrubs & Trees.** Barry Sherman. pap. 5.95 (*0-486-28734-3*) Dover.

Ready-to-Use Illustrations of Toys, Dolls & Games. Carol Pate. (Clip Art Ser.). (Illus.). 64p. (Orig.). 1991. pap. 4.95 (*0-486-26671-0*) Dover.

***Ready-to-Use Illustrations of Water Sports.** Bob Giuliani. (Illus.). pap. 4.95 (*0-486-27033-5*) Dover.

Ready-to-Use Illustrations of Women's Heads (Clip Art) Tom Tierney. (Pictorial Archive Ser.). (Illus.). 64p. (Orig.). 1982. pap. 4.50 (*0-486-24341-9*) Dover.

Ready-to-Use Jewish Motifs & Illustrations. Virginia Hanlon. (Clip Art Ser.). (Illus.). 64p. (Orig.). 1991. pap. 4.50 (*0-486-26725-3*) Dover.

Ready-to-Use Language Articulation & Development Activities for Special Children. Anita McMillan. 244p. 1992. spiral bd. 24.95 (*0-87628-807-7*) Ctr Appl Res.

Ready-to-Use Learning Disabilities Activities Kit. Joan M. Harwell. 288p. 1993. spiral bd. 29.95 (*0-87628-846-8*) Ctr Appl Res.

***Ready-to-Use Lessons & Activities for the Inclusive Primary Classroom.** LC 96-50116. 1997. spiral bd. write for info. (*0-87628-754-2*) Ctr Appl Res.

***Ready-to-Use Lessons & Activities for the Inclusive Primary Classroom.** Eileen Kennedy. LC 96-50116. 1997. write for info. (*0-87628-506-X*) Ctr Appl Res.

Ready-to-Use Library Skills Games: Reproducible Activities for Building Location & Literature Skills. Ruth Snoddon. 256p. 1987. pap. 22.95 (*0-87628-721-6*) P-H.

Ready-to-Use Literature Activities: With Techniques & Ideas for Using Video in the Classroom. Patricia Altmann & Lisa Luciano. 156p. 1988. pap. text ed. 27.95 (*0-87628-779-8*) Ctr Appl Res.

Ready to Use Literature Activities for Grades 7-12 with Techniques & Ideas for Using Video in the Classroom. Patricia Altmann & Lisa Luciano. 264p. 1988. pap. 24.95 (*0-685-22934-3*) P-H.

Ready-to-Use Marbelized Papers. Judith Saurman & Judith Pierce. 28p. 1979. pap. 4.95 (*0-486-23901-2*) Dover.

Ready-to-Use Math Activities for Primary Children. Sonia F. Helton. 288p. 1993. pap. 24.95 (*0-87628-852-2*) Ctr Appl Res.

***Ready-to-Use Math Games Activities Kit: Games for Meeting Math Curriculum Grades 3-8.** Sandra J. Cameron. LC 97-16632. 1997. pap. text ed. 27.95 (*0-87628-717-8*) Ctr Appl Res.

***Ready-to-Use Math Games Activities Kit: Games for Meeting Math Curriculum Standards in Grades 3-8.** Sandra J. Cameron. LC 97-16632. 1997. pap. text ed. 27.50 (*0-87628-552-3*) Ctr Appl Res.

***Ready to Use Medieval Herb Pla.** 1997. pap. 5.95 (*0-486-29610-5*) Dover.

***Ready-to-Use Menu Illustrations.** Leslie E. Cabarga. (Illus.). pap. 4.95 (*0-486-26417-3*) Dover.

Ready-to-Use Mirror-Image Ornaments & Decorations. Ed. by Carol B. Grafton. (Clip Art Ser.). (Illus.). 64p. (Orig.). 1991. pap. 4.50 (*0-486-26720-2*) Dover.

Ready-to-Use Multicultural Activities for Primary Children. Saundrah C. Grevious. LC 93-16912. (Illus.). 1993. spiral bd. 27.95 (*0-87628-849-2*) Ctr Appl Res.

Ready-to-Use Multicultural Activities for the American History Classroom: Four Centuries. Hallie A. Wannamaker. 384p. 1995. spiral bd. 28.95 (*0-87628-858-1*) Ctr Appl Res.

Ready-to-Use Music Activities Kit. Audrey J. Adair. LC 83-17480. 291p. 1983. pap. text ed. 29.95 (*0-13-762295-3*, Parker Publishing Co) P-H.

Ready to Use Music Reading Activities Kit. Loretta Mitchell. 256p. 1991. pap. text ed. 26.95 (*0-13-756164-4*) P-H.

Ready-to-Use News Announcements. Jean Larcher. 1981. pap. 4.50 (*0-486-24173-4*) Dover.

***Ready to Use North American Indian.** 1996. pap. 5.95 (*0-486-29262-2*) Dover.

***Ready-to-Use Old-Fashioned Auto Illustrations.** Carol B. Grafton. (Illus.). pap. 4.95 (*0-486-28028-4*) Dover.

***Ready-to-Use Old-Fashioned Eating & Drinking Illustrations.** Carol B. Grafton. (Illus.). pap. 5.95 (*0-486-25781-9*) Dover.

***Ready-to-Use Old-Fashioned Patriotic Cuts.** Carol B. Grafton. (Illus.). pap. 5.95 (*0-486-25595-6*) Dover.

Ready-to-Use Old-Fashioned Sports Illustrations. Carol B. Grafton. 64p. 1988. pap. 4.95 (*0-486-25776-2*) Dover.

***Ready-to-Use Old West Cuts.** Carol B. Grafton. (Illus.). pap. 5.95 (*0-486-28752-1*) Dover.

Ready-to-Use Outdoor Recreations Spot Illustrations. David Carlson. (Clip Art Ser.). 64p. 1985. pap. 4.50 (*0-486-24784-8*) Dover.

Ready-to-Use P.E. Activities, Vol. 1. Maxwell J. Landy & Joanne Landy. LC 92-21049. 1992. write for info. (*0-13-673054-X*, Parker Publishing Co) P-H.

Ready to Use Physical Education Activities. Joanne Landy. (J). (gr. 5-9). 1993. pap. 27.95 (*0-685-63549-X*) P-H.

Ready-To-Use Physical Education Activities for Grades 3-4, Vol. 2. Maxwell J. Landy. 1993. pap. 27.95 (*0-13-673088-4*) P-H.

Ready-to-Use Physical Education Activities for Grades 5-6. Joanne Landy. 1993. pap. 27.95 (*0-13-673070-1*) P-H.

Ready to Use Physical Education Activities for Grades 7-9. 1993. pap. 27.95 (*0-13-673062-0*) P-H.

***Ready-to-Use Reading & Study Skills Mastery Activities: Secondary Level.** Henriette L. Allen et al. LC 96-26401. 1996. write for info. (*0-87628-593-0*) Ctr Appl Res.

Ready-to-Use Sale Announcements. David Gatti. (Clip Art - Pictorial Archive Ser.). (Illus.). 64p. (Orig.). 1980. pap. 4.50 (*0-486-24012-6*) Dover.

Ready-to-Use Science Activities for the Elementary Classroom. Debra L. Seabury & Susan L. Peeples. 256p. 1987. pap. 24.95 (*0-87628-743-7*) Ctr Appl Res.

Ready-to-Use Science Activities for the Elementary Classroom. Debra L. Seabury & Susan L. Peeples. 224p. 1987. pap. 17.95 (*0-317-66406-9*) P-H.

Ready-to-Use Secondary P.E. Activities Program: Lessons, Tournaments & Assessments. Ken Lumsden. 288p. 1996. pap. 29.95 (*0-13-470007-4*) P-H.

Ready-to-Use Self-Esteem Activities for Secondary Students with Special Needs. Darlene Mannix. 1996. pap. write for info. (*0-87628-887-5*); spiral bd. write for info. (*0-87628-758-5*) Ctr Appl Res.

***Ready to Use Self-Esteem Activities for Young Children.** Jean R. Feldman. 256p. 1996. pap. 27.95 (*0-87628-886-7*) Ctr Appl Res.

Ready-to-Use Self Esteem & Conflict Solving Activities. Beth Teolis. 336p. (J). (gr. 4-8). 1995. spiral bd. 27.95 (*0-87628-611-2*) Ctr Appl Res.

Ready-to-Use Signboard Mortised Cuts. Leslie Franz. (Clip Art Ser.). (Illus.). 64p. (Orig.). 1991. pap. 4.95 (*0-486-26644-3*) Dover.

Ready-to-Use Silhouette Spot Illustrations. Bob Censoni. 64p. 1984. pap. 4.95 (*0-486-24711-2*) Dover.

Ready-to-Use Small Frames & Borders (Clip Art) Ed. by Carol B. Grafton. (Pictorial Archive Ser.). (Illus.). 64p. (Orig.). 1982. pap. 3.95 (*0-486-24375-3*) Dover.

Ready-to-Use Social Skills Lessons & Activities. Ruth W. Begun. 240p. 1996. spiral bd. 27.95 (*0-87628-865-4*) Ctr Appl Res.

Ready-to-Use Social Skills Lessons & Activities. Ruth W. Begun. 240p. 1995. spiral bd. 27.95 (*0-87628-866-2*) Ctr Appl Res.

Ready-to-Use Social Skills Lessons & Activities for Grades PreK-K. Ruth W. Begun. 240p. 1995. spiral bd. 27.95 (*0-87628-863-8*) Ctr Appl Res.

Ready-to-Use Social Skills Lessons & Activities for Grades 1-3. Ruth W. Begun. 240p. 1995. spiral bd. 27.95 (*0-87628-864-6*) Ctr Appl Res.

Ready-to-Use Social Studies Activities for the Elementary Classroom. Debra L. Seabury & Susan L. Peeples. 192p. 1990. pap. 27.95 (*0-87628-788-7*) Ctr Appl Res.

Ready-to-Use Sports Illustrations (Clip Art) David Carlson. (Pictorial Archive Ser.). (Illus.). 64p. (Orig.). 1982. pap. 4.50 (*0-486-24344-3*) Dover.

Ready-to-Use Teddy Bear Illustrations. Theodore Menten. 64p. (Orig.). 1985. pap. 4.50 (*0-486-24943-3*) Dover.

Ready to Use Thematic Activities for Grades 4-8: Includes Twelve Integrated Thematic Teaching Units with over 200 Illustrated Reproductibles Featuring Inventions, Mysteries, Government, the Future & More! Barbara F. Bannister & Janice B. Carlile. LC 94-17660. (Illus.). 1994. spiral bd. 27.95 (*0-87628-855-7*) Ctr Appl Res.

Ready-to-Use Thematic Borders. Ed Sibbett, Jr. (Illus.). 64p. 1982. pap. 4.50 (*0-486-24254-4*) Dover.

Ready-To-Use Thinking Skills Activities for Grades 4-8. Fred B. Chernow & Carol Chernow. LC 85-21732. 227p. 1986. pap. 18.95 (*0-13-762303-8*, Parker Publishing Co) P-H.

Ready-to-Use Victorian Alphabets. Dan X. Solo. 1986. pap. 4.50 (*0-486-25053-9*) Dover.

Ready-to-Use Victorian Borders on Layout Grids. Ed. by Carol B. Grafton. (Clip Art Ser.). (Illus.). 64p. (Orig.). 1991. pap. 4.50 (*0-486-26589-7*) Dover.

Ready to Use Victorian Color. Carol B. Grafton. 1983. pap. 3.50 (*0-486-24551-9*) Dover.

***Ready-to-Use Victorian Women's Fashion Cuts.** Carol B. Grafton. (Illus.). pap. 5.95 (*0-486-27825-5*) Dover.

Ready-to-Use Vocabulary, Word Analysis & Comprehension Activities. Henriette L. Allen et al. LC 96-18332. (Reading Skills Activities Library). 1996. write for info. (*0-87628-932-4*); write for info. (*0-87628-934-0*) Ctr Appl Res.

Ready-To-Use Vocabulary, Word Analysis & Comprehension Activities. Henriette L. Allen et al. LC 96-18332. (Reading Skills Activities Library). 1996. write for info. (*0-87628-933-2*) Ctr Appl Res.

***Ready-to-Use Wining & Dining Illustrations.** Tom Tierney. (Illus.). pap. 5.95 (*0-486-25944-7*) Dover.

***Ready-to-Use Winter Sport Illustrations.** Bob Giuliani. pap. 4.95 (*0-486-27312-1*) Dover.

Ready-to-Use World Geography Activities for Grades 5-12. James F. Silver. LC 92-17883. (Illus.). 1992. spiral bd. 29.95 (*0-87628-945-6*) Ctr Appl Res.

Ready to Wear - Pret-a-Porter. Robert Altman. (Illus.). 190p. 1995. pap. 19.95 (*0-7868-8103-8*) Hyperion.

Ready-to-Wear & Ready-to-Work: A Century of Industry & Immigrants in Paris & New York. Nancy L. Green. LC 96-24659. (Comparative & International Working-Class History Ser.). (Illus.). 448p. 1997. pap. text ed. 19.95 (*0-8223-1874-1*) Duke.

Ready-to-Wear & Ready-to-Work: A Century of Industry & Immigrants in Paris & New York. Nancy L. Green. LC 96-24659. (Comparative & International Working-Class History Ser.). (Illus.). 448p. 1997. lib. bdg. 59.95 (*0-8223-1884-9*) Duke.

Ready to Wear Apparel Analysis. Patty Brown. (Illus.). 490p. (C). 1991. text ed. 48.00 (*0-02-315611-2*, Macmillan Coll) P-H.

***Ready-to-Wear Apparel Analysis.** 2nd ed. Patty Brown & Janett Rice. LC 97-8726. 1997. 50.00 (*0-13-606591-0*, Merrill Coll) P-H.

Ready to Work: Win the Job Game. Visual Education Center Staff. 1990. pap. 9.86 (*0-8092-4099-8*) Contemp Bks.

Ready to Write. Karen L. Blanchard. 1984. pap. text ed. 15.34 (*0-582-79830-2*) Addison-Wesley.

Ready to Write, 2 vols. Ed. by World Book Editors. LC 93-60512. (Illus.). 120p. (J). (gr. 4-7). 1993. lib. bdg. 17.95 (*0-7166-2993-3*) World Bk.

Ready to Write & Develop Motor Skills: Help Your Child Develop the Skills Necessary for School Success. Ed. by Susan Hodges. LC 96-60424. (Getting Ready for School Ser.). (Illus.). 96p. (Orig.). (J). (ps-k). 1997. pap. 6.95 (*1-57029-113-6*, 3202, Totline Bks) Warren Pub Hse.

***Ready-to-Write Resource Book & Journal.** (J). (gr. 3-6). 1996. 11.95 (*0-7166-2393-5*, 257) World Bk.

***Ready, Willing & Enabled: Easy Guidelines for Living Your Dreams.** R. Scott Cooper. LC 96-94692. (Illus.). 235p. (Orig.). 1997. pap. 14.95 (*0-9654444-0-6*) Life Guides.

Ready, Willing & Terrified: A Coward's Guide to Risk-Taking. Casey Chaney. Ed. by Berdell Moffett & Thea Rhiannon. 144p. (Orig.). (YA). 1991. pap. 10.95 (*0-9626403-1-X*) Mocha Pub.

***Ready with an Answer: For the Tough Questions about God.** John Ankerberg & John Weldon. LC 96-51535. 400p. (Orig.). 1997. pap. 10.99 (*1-56507-618-4*) Harvest Hse.

Ready...Aim...Fire! Small Arms Ammunition in the Battle of Gettysburg. rev. ed. Dean S. Thomas. (Illus.). 76p. (Orig.). 1981. pap. 7.50 (*0-939631-00-8*) Thomas Publications.

Readymade Business Letters. Jim Dening. 173p. 1993. pap. 14.95 (*0-87243-192-4*) Templegate.

***Readymade Business Letters That Get Results.** 2nd ed. Jim Douglas. (Daily Express Guides Ser.). 1994. pap. 14.95 (*0-7494-1186-4*) Kogan Page Ltd.

***Readymade Business Opportunities.** Greg Clarke. (Small Business Ser.). 1994. pap. 14.95 (*0-7494-1264-X*) Kogan Page Ltd.

***Readymade CVS.** Lynn Williams. (Careers & Testing Ser.). 1996. pap. 15.95 (*0-7494-1947-4*) Kogan Page Ltd.

***Readymade Interview Questions.** 2nd ed. Malcolm Peel. (Human Resource Management Ser.). 1996. pap. 14.95 (*0-7494-1942-3*) Kogan Page Ltd.

Ready...Set...Read! rev. ed. Ed. by Joanna Cole & Stephanie Calemenson. (Illus.). 144p. (J). 1993. 14.50 (*1-56865-008-6*, GuildAmerica) Dblday Direct.

Ready...Set...Ready & Laugh! Ed. by Joanna Cole & Stephanie Calmenson. (Illus.). 160p. 1995. 15.00 (*1-56865-118-X*, GuildAmerica) Dblday Direct.

***Ready...Set...R.E.L.A.X. A Research Base Program of Relaxation, Learning & Self Esteem for Children.** Jeffrey S. Allen & Roger J. Klein. LC 93-90702. (Illus.). 205p. (Orig.). (J). (ps-8). 1996. pap. 23.95 (*0-9636027-0-5*) Allen & Klein.

Reaeration Research. Compiled by American Society of Civil Engineers Staff. 376p. 1979. pap. 28.00 (*0-87262-142-1*) Am Soc Civil Eng.

Reaffirm the Status Quo! Patrick Oliphant. (Illus.). 160p. (Orig.). 1996. pap. 10.95 (*0-8362-2135-4*) Andrews & McMeel.

Reaffirmation & Redemption. Robert A. Hessling. 775p. 1994. 105.00 (*1-55834-154-4*) MICHIE.

Reaffirmation of Republicanism: Eisenhower & the Eighty-third Congress. Gary W. Reichard. LC 75-1017. (Twentieth-Century America Ser.). 330p. reprint ed. pap. 94.10 (*0-8357-8607-2*, 2035004) Bks Demand.

Reaffirming Life in a Culture of Death: A Catholic Response to Critical Issues. Mark Neilsen. LC 95-80149. 112p. (Orig.). 1995. pap. 6.95 (*0-89243-871-1*) Liguori Pubns.

***Reagan.** Strober. 1998. 35.00 (*0-395-77193-5*) HM.

Reagan: American Icon. Robert P. Metzger. LC 89-60966. (Illus.). 144p. 1989. pap. 34.95 (*0-8122-1302-5*) U of Pa Pr.

Reagan: The Man from Main Street. deluxe ed. Vance H. Trimble. (Illus.). 64p. 1982. 24.00 (*0-88014-025-9*) Mosaic Pr OH.

Reagan Administration: A Reconstruction of American Strength? Ed. by Helga Haftendorn & Jakob Schissler. (Studies on North America: No. 1). xii, 306p. (C). 1989. lib. bdg. 64.65 (*3-11-011372-4*) De Gruyter.

Reagan Administration & Human Rights. Tinsley E. Yarbrough. LC 85-16699. 288p. 1985. text ed. 49.95 (*0-275-90239-0*, C0239, Praeger Pubs) Greenwood.

Reagan Administration & Lebanon. David M. Kennedy. (Pew Case Studies in International Affairs). 50p. (C). 1994. pap. text ed. 3.50 (*1-56927-340-5*) Geo U Inst Dplmcy.

Reagan Administration, the Auto Producers, & the 1981 Agreement with Japan. Simon Reich. (Pew Case Studies in International Affairs). 50p. (C). 1992. pap. text ed. 3.50 (*1-56927-119-4*) Geo U Inst Dplmcy.

Reagan & Public Discourse in America. Ed. by Michael Weiler & W. Barnett Pearce. LC 92-1349. (Speech & Rhetoric Communication Ser.). 368p. (C). 1992. text ed. 39.95 (*0-8173-0585-8*) U of Ala Pr.

Reagan & the Cities. Ed. by George E. Peterson & Carol W. Lewis. (Changing Domestic Priorities Ser.). (Illus.). 251p. (Orig.). 1986. pap. text ed. 23.00 (*0-87766-385-8*) Urban Inst.

Reagan & the Economy: Nine Intimate Perspectives. Murray L. Weidenbaum et al. Ed. by Kenneth W. Thompson. LC 94-22991. (Miller Center: Reagan Oral History Ser.: Vol. 4). 1995. 56.00 (*0-8191-9711-4*); pap. 24.50 (*0-8191-9712-2*) U Pr of Amer.

Reagan & the Middle East. N. Aruri et al. (Monographs: No. 17). 95p. (Orig.). 1983. pap. text ed. 5.50 (*0-937694-59-2*) Assn Arab-Amer U Grads.

Reagan & the States. Richard P. Nathan et al. LC 87-45529. 392p. 1987. reprint ed. pap. 111.80 (*0-7837-9400-2*, 2060145) Bks Demand.

Reagan & the World. Ed. by David E. Kyvig. LC 89-25883. (Contributions in American History Ser.: No. 141). 208p. 1990. text ed. 49.95 (*0-313-27341-3*, KRB/, Greenwood Pr); pap. text ed. 16.95 (*0-275-93565-5*, B3565, Greenwood Pr) Greenwood.

Reagan & the World: Imperial Policy in the New Cold War. Jeff McMahan. 320p. 1985. pap. 12.00 (*0-85345-678-X*) Monthly Rev.

Reagan & Woman. Arthur F. Ide. LC 84-8503. (Woman in History Ser.: Vol. 100). (Illus.). 120p. 1988. pap. 6.00 (*0-918827-00-0*) Texas Ind Pr.

Reagan As President: Contemporary Views of the Man, His Politics, & His Policies. Ed. by Paul Boyer. 288p. 1990. pap. text ed. 8.95 (*0-929587-28-6*); lib. bdg. 25.00 (*0-929587-27-8*) I R Dee.

Reagan Block Grants: What We Have Learned? George E. Peterson et al. (Illus.). 134p. (Orig.). 1986. pap. text ed. 23.50 (*0-87766-400-5*) Urban Inst.

Reagan, Bush, & Clinton. Eileen Lucas. LC 95-26666. (Complete History of Our Presidents Ser.: Vol. 12). (J). 1996. write for info. (*0-86593-414-2*) Rourke Corp.

Reagan Defense Program: An Interim Assessment. Ed. by Stephen J. Cimbala. LC 86-962. 215p. (C). 1986. 40.00 (*0-8420-2243-0*); pap. 14.95 (*0-8420-2262-7*) Scholarly Res Inc.

Reagan Doctrine: Sources of American Conduct in the Cold War's Last Chapter. Mark P. Lagon. LC 93-23676. 208p. 1994. text ed. 52.95 (*0-275-94798-X*, Praeger Pubs) Greenwood.

Reagan Electionomics: How Reagan Ambushed the Pollsters, 1976-1984. Donald J. Devine. LC 84-108682. 105p. 1984. 14.95 (*0-89803-130-3*) Jameson Bks.

Reagan Experiment: An Examination of Economic & Social Policies under the Reagan Administration. Ed. by John L. Palmer & Isabel V. Sawhill. (Illus.). 530p. (Orig.). 1982. pap. text ed. 24.00 (*0-87766-316-5*); lib. bdg. 71.00 (*0-87766-315-7*) Urban Inst.

Reagan for Beginners. David Smith & Melinda Gebbie. (Illus.). 160p. 1984. pap. 4.95 (*0-86316-065-4*) Writers & Readers.

An Asterisk (*) at the beginning of an entry indicates that the title is appearing in BIP for the first time.

R

Reagan in the Workplace: Unraveling the Health & Safety Net. Philip J. Simon. 103p. 1983. pap. 10.00 (*0-936758-12-0*) Ctr Responsive Law.

Reagan Legacy: Promise & Performance. Charles O. Jones. LC 88-18137. 324p. reprint ed. pap. 92.40 (*0-7837-4491-9*, 2044268) Bks Demand.

Reagan on Cuba: Selected Statements by the President. Ronald Reagan. 1986. 4.00 (*0-317-90497-3*) Cuban Amer Natl Fndtn.

***Reagan Paradox: American Foreign Policy in the 1980s.** Coral Bell. 192p. 1989. 70.00 (*1-85278-203-X*) E Elgar.

Reagan Paradox: U. S. Foreign Policy in the 1980s. Coral Bell. 224p. (Orig.). 1989. pap. 14.95 (*0-8135-1474-6*) Rutgers U Pr.

Reagan Phenomenon & Other Speeches on Foreign Policy. Jeane J. Kirkpatrick. LC 82-16434. 230p. 1983. 28.50 (*0-8447-1361-9*) Am Enterprise.

Reagan Poems. Allen Cohen. 31p. (Orig.). 1984. pap. text ed. 3.50 (*1-879594-11-0*) Androgyne Bks.

Reagan Presidency: An Actor's Finest Performance. Wilbur Edel. 360p. 1993. pap. 11.95 (*0-7818-0127-3*) Hippocrene Bks.

Reagan Presidency: An Early Assessment. Ed. by Fred I. Greenstein. LC 83-48056. 208p. 1983. pap. 14.95 (*0-8018-3057-5*) Johns Hopkins.

Reagan Presidency: An Incomplete Revolution? Ed. by Dilys M. Hill et al. LC 89-36458. 284p. 1990. text ed. 35.00 (*0-312-03646-9*) St Martin.

***Reagan Presidency: Ten Intimate Perspectives of Ronald Reagan.** Ed. by Kenneth W. Thompson. LC 97-1747. (Portraits of American Presidents Ser.: Vol. IX). 184p. 1997. 44.50 (*0-7618-0722-5*); pap. 24.50 (*0-7618-0723-3*) U Pr of Amer.

Reagan Presidency & the Governing of America. Ed. by Lester M. Salamon & Michael S. Lund. LC 84-27065. (Changing Domestic Priorities Ser.). 500p. (Orig.). (C). 1984. pap. text ed. 28.00 (*0-87766-347-5*); lib. bdg. 62.00 (*0-87766-370-X*) Urban Inst.

Reagan Range: The Nostalgic Myth in American Politics. James Combs. LC 92-73977. 151p. 1993. 29.95 (*0-87972-565-6*); pap. 11.95 (*0-87972-566-4*) Bowling Green Univ Popular Press.

Reagan Regulatory Strategy: An Assessment. Ed. by George C. Eads & Michael Fix. (Changing Domestic Priorities Ser.). 227p. (Orig.). 1984. pap. text ed. 22.50 (*0-87766-346-7*) Urban Inst.

***Reagan Reversal: Foreign Policy & the End of the Cold War.** Beth A. Fischer. 1997. 27.50 (*0-8262-1138-0*) U of Mo Pr.

Reagan Speaks: The Making of an American Myth. Paul D. Erickson. 192p. (C). 1985. text ed. 20.00 (*0-8147-2167-2*) NYU Pr.

Reagan Speaks: The Making of an American Myth. Paul D. Erickson. 192p. (C). 1991. pap. text ed. 10.36 (*0-8147-2184-2*) NYU Pr.

Reagan-Suzuki Comminque. Thomas Drohan. (Pew Case Studies in International Affairs). 50p. (C). 1993. pap. text ed. 3.50 (*1-56927-152-6*) Geo U Inst Dplmcy.

Reagan, Thatcher, & the Politics of Decline. Joel Krieger. (Europe & the International Order Ser.). 247p. 1986. pap. 19.95 (*0-19-520529-4*) OUP.

Reagan, Trilateralism & the Neoliberals: Containment & Intervention in the 1980s. Holly Sklar. LC 86-6763. (Institute for New Communications Pamphlet Ser.). (Illus.). 80p. (Orig.). 1986. per. 4.75 (*0-89608-213-X*) South End Pr.

Reagan Way. Jeffrey B. Morris. LC 94-24644. (Great Presidential Decisions Ser.). (Illus.). 124p. (J). (gr. 6-9). 1995. lib. bdg. 22.95 (*0-8225-2931-9*, Lerner Publctns) Lerner Group.

Reagan Wit. Bill Adler. LC 81-38509. 120p. 1981. 6.95 (*0-89803-090-0*) Jameson Bks.

***Reagan Wit.** Bill Adler. Date not set. write for info. (*0-688-15514-6*) Morrow.

Reagan Years A to Z. Kenneth F. Kurz. 240p. 1996. 30.00 (*1-56565-462-5*) Lowell Hse.

***Reagan Years A to Z.** Kenneth F. Kurz. 1996. 26.00 (*0-614-19828-3*) Little.

***Reagan Years A to Z.** 2nd ed. Kenneth Kurz. 312p. 1997. reprint ed. pap. 16.00 (*1-56565-815-9*, Extension Pr) Lowell Hse.

Reagan Years 1981-88, 8 yearbooks, Set 7. 570.00 (*0-8160-2751-X*) Facts on File.

Reaganomics: An Insider's Account. William A. Niskanen. (Illus.). 363p. 1988. 30.00 (*0-19-505394-X*) OUP.

Reaganomics: Rhetoric vs. Reality. Frank Ackerman. LC 82-80689. 166p. 1982. 35.00 (*0-89608-142-7*); pap. 7.50 (*0-89608-141-9*) South End Pr.

Reaganomics: Successes & Failures. Khalid R. Mehtabdin. LC 86-21674. 1986. pap. 59.95 (*0-88946-204-6*) E Mellen.

Reagan's America. Lloyd DeMause. LC 82-73581. 200p. 1984. 23.95 (*0-940508-02-8*) Creative Roots.

Reagan's Federalism: His Efforts to Decentralize Government. Richard S. Williamson. LC 89-35578. 250p. (C). 1990. lib. bdg. 53.00 (*0-8191-7534-X*) U Pr of Amer.

Reagan's Nuclear Terrorism. Udai Narain. 1985. 18.50 (*0-8364-1312-1*, Pub. by Deep II) S Asia.

Reagan's Ruling Class: Portraits of the President's Top 100 Officials. Ronald Brownstein. Ed. by Nina Easton. LC 82-60917. (Illus.). 759p. 1983. 24.50 (*0-936486-03-1*) Presidential Acct.

Reagan's Secret Wars. Jay Peterzell. LC 83-226461. 100p. 1984. pap. 3.95 (*0-86566-033-6*) Ctr Natl Security.

Reagan's Squeeze on Small Business: How the Administration Plan Will Increase Economic Concentration, Vol. 1. Nina Easton. Ed. by Ronald Brownstein. (Presidential Examiner Ser.: Vol. 1, No. 1). 83p. (Orig.). 1981. pap. text ed. 7.00 (*0-936486-02-3*) Presidential Acct.

Reagan's Terrible Swift Sword. Donald Devine. 228p. 1992. 19.95 (*0-89803-163-X*) Jameson Bks.

Reagent Chemicals. 7th ed. LC 86-20569. (Illus.). xiii, 675p. 1986. 98.95 (*0-8412-0991-X*) Am Chemical.

Reagent Chemicals: American Chemical Society Specifications, Official from April 1, 1993. 8th ed. American Chemical Society Staff. LC 92-44959. (Illus.). 806p. 1992. 149.95 (*0-8412-2502-8*) Am Chemical.

Reagents for Better Metallurgy. Ed. by D. Malhotra & B. A. Hancock. LC 93-86997. (Illus.). 365p. (Orig.). 1994. pap. 68.00 (*0-87335-128-2*) SMM&E Inc.

Reagents for Better Metallurgy. fac. ed. Ed. by P. S. Mulukutla. LC 93-86997. (Illus.). 373p. 1994. reprint ed. pap. 107.80 (*0-7837-8205-5*, 2047963) Bks Demand.

Reagents for Biotechnology. 179p. 1992. 2,850.00 (*0-89336-953-5*, C-144) BCC.

Reagents for Food Testing: Impact of New Regulations & Biotechnology. Business Communications Co., Inc. Staff. 217p. 1992. 2,850.00 (*0-89336-773-7*, C121) BCC.

Reagents for Organic Synthesis, 17 vols. Louis E. Feiser & Mary Fieser. (Fieser's Reagents for Organic Synthesis Ser.: Vol. 1). 1457p. 1967. text ed. 114.00 (*0-471-25875-X*) Wiley.

Reagents for Organic Synthesis, 17 vols., Vol. 2. Louis E. Feiser & Mary Fieser. LC 66-27894. (Fieser's Reagents for Organic Synthesis Ser.: Vol. 2). 552p. 1969. text ed. 82.95 (*0-471-25876-8*) Wiley.

Reagents for Organic Synthesis, 17 vols., Vol. 3. Louis E. Feiser & Mary Fieser. (Fieser's Reagents for Organic Synthesis Ser.: Vol. 3). 416p. 1972. text ed. 78.95 (*0-471-25879-2*) Wiley.

Reagents for Organic Synthesis, 17 vols., Vol. 4. Louis E. Feiser & Mary Fieser. (Fieser's Reagents for Organic Synthesis Ser.: Vol. 4). 672p. 1974. text ed. 82.95 (*0-471-25881-4*) Wiley.

Reagents for Organic Synthesis, 17 vols., Vol. 5. Louis E. Feiser & Mary Fieser. (Fieser's Reagents for Organic Synthesis Ser.). 880p. 1975. text ed. 87.95 (*0-471-25882-2*) Wiley.

Reagents for Organic Synthesis, 17 vols., Vol. 6. Louis E. Feiser & Mary Fieser. (Fieser's Reagents for Organic Synthesis Ser.: Vol. 6). 765p. 1977. text ed. 87.95 (*0-471-25873-3*) Wiley.

Reagents for Organic Synthesis, 17 vols., Vol. 7. Louis E. Feiser & Mary Fieser. LC 66-27894. (Fieser's Reagents for Organic Synthesis Ser.: Vol. 8). 487p. 1979. text ed. 77.95 (*0-471-02918-1*) Wiley.

Reagents for Organic Synthesis, 17 vols., Vol. 8. Louis E. Feiser & Mary Fieser. LC 66-27894. (Fieser's Reagents for Organic Synthesis Ser.: Vol. 8). 616p. 1980. text ed. 87.95 (*0-471-04834-8*) Wiley.

Reagents for Organic Synthesis, 17 vols., Vol. 9. Fieser & Fieser's Staff. (Fieser's Reagents for Organic Synthesis Ser.: Vol. 9). 608p. 1981. text ed. 87.95 (*0-471-05631-6*) Wiley.

Reagents for Organic Synthesis, 17 vols., Vol. 10. Fieser & Fieser's Staff. (Fieser's Reagents for Organic Synthesis Ser.: Vol. 10). 536p. 1982. text ed. 82.95 (*0-471-86636-9*) Wiley.

Reagents for Organic Synthesis, 17 vols., Vol. 11. Fieser & Fieser's. (Fieser's Reagents for Organic Synthesis Ser.: Vol. 11). 688p. 1984. text ed. 82.95 (*0-471-88628-9*) Wiley.

Reagents for Organic Synthesis, 17 vols., Vol. 12. Fieser & Fieser's Staff. (Fieser's Reagents for Organic Synthesis Ser.: Vol. 12). 656p. 1986. text ed. 82.95 (*0-471-83469-6*) Wiley.

Reagents for Organic Synthesis, 17 vols., Vol. 15. Mary Fieser & Janice G. Smith. (Fieser's Reagents for Organic Synthesis Ser.: Vol. 15). 432p. 1990. text ed. 78.95 (*0-471-52113-2*) Wiley.

Reagents for Transition Metal Complex & Organometallic Syntheses: Inorganic Synthesis, Vol. 28. Ed. by Robert J. Angelici. (Inorganic Syntheses Ser.). 463p. 1990. text ed. 99.95 (*0-471-52619-3*) Wiley.

Reagents in Mineral Technology. P. Somasundaran. (Surfactant Science Ser.: Vol. 27). 776p. 1987. 275.00 (*0-8247-7715-8*) Dekker.

Real. Holman. LC 96-47457. 1997. 16.00 (*0-689-80772-4*, S&S Bks Young Read) S&S Childrens.

Real: The Letters of Mina Harker & Sam D'Allesandro. Dodie Bellamy & Sam D'Allesandro. LC 94-22918. 218p. 1994. pap. 10.95 (*1-883689-16-3*); lib. bdg. 30.95 (*1-883689-17-1*) Talisman Hse.

REAL: The Yearbook of Research in English & American Literature, Vol. 5. Ed. by Herbert Grabes et al. 329p. (C). 1988. lib. bdg. 142.35 (*3-11-011498-4*) De Gruyter.

***Real AA: Beyond the Myth of 12-Step Recovery.** rev. ed. Ken Ragge. 256p. 1997. pap. 12.95 (*1-884365-14-0*) See Sharp Pr.

Real Adjustment Processes under Floating Exchange Rates. Ed. by F. Gehrels et al. (Studies in International Economics & Institutions). vi, 302p. 1990. 71.95 (*0-387-52591-2*) Spr-Verlag.

Real Alaskans. Lew Freesman. 224p. 1990. pap. 16.95 (*0-88839-254-0*) Hancock House.

***Real Ale Almanac.** 4th ed. Roger Protz. 320p. 1996. pap. 14.95 (*1-897784-34-1*, Pub. by N Wilson UK) Interlink Pub.

Real Ale Drinkers Almanac. 3rd ed. Roger Protz. (Illus.). 320p. 1993. per. 14.99 (*1-897784-17-1*, Pub. by Camra Bks UK) Info Devels.

Real Algebraic Geometry: Proceedings of the Conference Held in Rennes, France, June 24-28, 1991. Ed. by M. Coste et al. LC 92-27019. 1992. 79.95 (*0-387-55992-2*) Spr-Verlag.

Real Algebraic Geometry & Topology: A Conference on Real Algebraic Geometry & Topology, December 17-21, 1993, Michigan State University. Conference on Real Algebraic Geometry & Toplogy Staff. Ed. by Selman Akbulut. LC 94-44468. (Contemporary Mathematics Ser.: Vol. 182). 1995. pap. 39.00 (*0-8218-0292-5*, CONM/182) Am Math.

Real Algebraic Surfaces. R. Silhol. (Lecture Notes in Mathematics Ser.: Vol. 1392). x, 215p. 1989. 36.95 (*0-387-51563-1*) Spr-Verlag.

Real All about Her! Texas Women's History: a Working Bibliography. Elizabeth Snapp & Harry F. Snapp. xiv, 1070p. (C). 1995. lib. bdg. 125.00 (*0-9607488-3-0*) TX Womans U Pr.

Real America. Elijah Brown. LC 73-13124. (Foreign Travelers in America, 1810-1935 Ser.). 308p. 1974. reprint ed. 26.95 (*0-405-05447-5*) Ayer.

Real American Cowboy. Jack Weston. LC 87-35005. 267p. (C). 1988. reprint ed. pap. 14.95 (*0-941533-27-1*) New Amsterdam Bks.

Real American Politics: Changing Perspectives on American Government. Ralph P. Hummel & Robert A. Isaak. (Illus.). 336p. 1986. 27.00 (*0-13-762360-7*); pap. text ed. write for info. (*0-13-762352-6*) P-H.

Real American Quarter Horse: Versatile Athletes Who Proved Supreme. Paul R. Mattson. LC 91-90201. (Illus.). 160p. 1991. pap. 26.00 (*1-879984-77-6*) Premier KS.

Real Analysis. J. A. Anderson. x, 346p. 1969. text ed. 410.00 (*0-677-61460-8*) Gordon & Breach.

Real Analysis. Nicolas Artemiadis. LC 75-29189. 594p. 1976. 24.95 (*0-8093-0727-8*) S Ill U Pr.

Real Analysis. Andrew Bruckner & Judith Bruckner. LC 96-22123. (C). 1996. 73.00 (*0-13-458886-X*) P-H.

Real Analysis. Patrick M. Fitzpatrick. (Mathematics Ser.). 1996. text ed. 77.95 (*0-534-92611-8*) PWS Pubs.

Real Analysis. Norman B. Haaser. 1990. pap. 8.95 (*0-486-66509-7*) Dover.

***Real Analysis.** Sally. Date not set. text ed. 74.95 (*0-534-35181-6*) Brooks-Cole.

Real Analysis. 2nd ed. Serge A. Lang. (C). 1983. 45.95 (*0-201-14179-5*, Adv Bk Prog) Addison-Wesley.

Real Analysis. 3rd ed. Serge A. Lang. LC 92-21208. 600p. 1993. 54.95 (*0-387-94001-4*) Spr-Verlag.

Real Analysis. 3rd ed. H. L. Royden. 505p. (C). 1988. text ed. 73.00 (*0-02-404151-3*, Macmillan Coll) P-H.

Real Analysis: A First Course. Russell Gordon. 256p. (C). 1997. text ed. 58.50 (*0-201-83210-0*) Addison-Wesley.

Real Analysis: A First Course with Foundations. Malcolm W. Pownall. 496p. (C). 1993. text ed. write for info. (*0-697-12908-X*) Wm C Brown Pubs.

Real Analysis: Modern Techniques & Their Applications. Gerald B. Folland. LC 84-10435. (Pure & Applied Mathematics Ser.: No. 1-237). 368p. 1984. text ed. 84.95 (*0-471-80958-6*) Wiley.

Real Analysis & Foundations. Steven G. Krantz. 336p. 1991. 61.95 (*0-8493-7156-2*, QA) CRC Pr.

Real Analysis & Probability. Robert B. Ash. (Probability & Mathematical Statistics Ser.). 476p. 1972. text ed. 70.00 (*0-12-065201-3*) Acad Pr.

***Real Analysis & Probability.** Dudley. (C). (gr. 13 up). 1989. text ed. 69.50 (*0-412-05161-3*) Chapman & Hall.

Real Analysis & Probability. Richard M. Dudley. LC 88-25936. (Wadsworth & Brooks-Cole Mathematics Ser.). 436p. (C). 1989. 63.00 (*0-534-10050-3*) Chapman & Hall.

Real Analytic & Algebraic Geometry: Proceedings of the Conference Held in Trento, Italy, October 3-7, 1988. Ed. by M. Galbiati et al. (Lecture Notes in Mathematics Ser.: Vol. 1420). iv, 366p. 1990. 48.90 (*0-387-52313-8*) Spr-Verlag.

Real Analytic & Algebraic Geometry: Proceedings of the International Conference on Real Analytic & Algebraic Geometry (1992: Trento, Italy) Ed. by Fabrizio Broglia et al. LC 94-42179. 294p. (C). 1995. 128.95 (*3-11-013778-X*) De Gruyter.

Real Analytic Theory of Teichmueller Space. W. Abikoff. (Lecture Notes in Mathematics Ser.: Vol. 820). (Illus.). 144p. 1989. 34.95 (*0-387-10237-X*) Spr-Verlag.

Real & Artificial Intelligence: Can Machines Think? Ravi V. Gomatam. (Illus.). 39p. 1988. pap. text ed. 3.00 (*0-941525-12-0*) Bhaktvdnta Institute.

Real & Complex Analysis. 3rd ed. Walter Rudin. (Higher Mathematics Ser.). 480p. (C). 1987. text ed. write for info. (*0-07-054234-1*) McGraw.

***Real & Complex Singularities.** W. L. Marar. 1993. pap. 38.95 (*0-582-27780-9*, Pub. by Longman UK) Longman.

Real & Demonstrative Evidence: Applications & Theory. Ronald J. Rychlak. 577p. 1995. 95.00 (*0-614-05953-4*) MICHIE.

***Real & Demonstrative Evidence: Applications & Theory.** Ronald J. Rychlak. 577p. 1995. 95.00 (*1-55834-220-6*, 66800) MICHIE.

***Real & Demonstrative Evidence: Applications & Theory.** Ronald J. Rychlak. 1996. suppl. ed. write for info. (*0-614-25247-4*, 66801) MICHIE.

Real & Etale Cohomology. Claus Scheiderer. LC 94-34404. (Lecture Notes in Mathematics Ser.: Vol. 1588). 1994. 43.00 (*0-387-58436-6*) Spr-Verlag.

Real & Etale Cohomology. Claus Scheiderer. LC 94-34404. (Lecture Notes in Mathematics Ser.: Vol. 1588). 1994. 52.95 (*3-540-58436-6*) Spr-Verlag.

Real & False Alarms. David A. Evans. LC 84-73284. 64p. 1985. pap. 5.25 (*0-933532-45-8*) BkMk.

Real & Functional Analysis, Part A: Real Analysis. 2nd ed. A. Mukherjea & K. Pothoven. (Mathematical Concepts & Methods in Science & Engineering Ser.: Vol. 27). 352p. 1984. 95.00 (*0-306-41557-7*, Plenum Pr) Plenum.

Real & Functional Analysis, Pt B: Functional Analysis. 2nd ed. A. Mukherjea & K. Pothoven. (Mathematical Concepts & Methods in Science & Engineering Ser.: Vol. 28). 276p. 1985. 85.00 (*0-306-41558-5*, Plenum Pr) Plenum.

Real & Imaginary Beings: The Netsuke Collection of Joseph & Edith Kurstin. Barbara T. Okada & Mary G. Neill. LC 79-67298. (Illus.). 135p. 1980. 30.00 (*0-89467-012-3*) Yale Art Gallery.

Real & Imagined Women: Gender, Culture, & Postcolonialism. Rajeswari S. Rajan. LC 93-6923. (Illus.). 176p. (C). 1993. pap. 17.95 (*0-415-08504-7*, B2281) Routledge.

Real & Imagined Women: Gender, Culture, & Postcolonialism. Rajeswari S. Rajan. LC 93-6923. (Illus.). 176p. (C). (gr. 13). 1993. text ed. 62.95 (*0-415-08503-9*, B2277) Routledge.

Real & Imagined Worlds: The Novel & Social Science. Morroe Berger. 320p. 1977. 32.00 (*0-674-74941-3*) HUP.

Real & Personal Securities. W. D. Duncan & Lindy Willmott. 294p. 1990. pap. 53.00 (*1-86287-035-7*, Pub. by Federation Pr AU) Gaunt.

Real and Precious Thing. Bancroft. (Heartsong ser.). 176p. 1994. pap. text ed. 4.95 (*1-55748-464-3*) Barbour & Co.

***Real & Stochastic Analysis: Recent Advances.** M. M. Rao. LC 97-143. (Probability & Stochastics Ser.). 1997. write for info. (*0-8493-8078-2*) CRC Pr.

Real & the Spiritual: Nineteenth-Century French Drawings from the Musee des Beaux-Arts de Lyon. Dominique Brachlianoff. Ed. by DeCourcy E. McIntosh. Tr. by Anne Bertrand from FRE. LC 92-71570. (Illus.). 188p. (Orig.). (C). 1992. pap. 39.95 (*1-881403-00-9*) Frick Art Mus.

***Real Angel.** Cassie Miles. 1997. mass mkt. 3.75 (*0-373-22443-5*, 1-22443-5) Harlequin Bks.

Real Animal Heroes: Trues Stories of Courage, Devotion & Sacrifice. P. T. Stevens. 1997. pap. 5.99 (*0-451-19155-2*, Sig) NAL-Dutton.

Real Anita Hill: The Untold Story. David Brock. 456p. 1994. pap. 12.95 (*0-02-904656-4*, Free Press) Free Pr.

Real Baby Animals, 4 bks., Set. Gisela Buck & Siegfried Buck. (Illus.). 96p. (J). (gr. 1 up). lib. bdg. 69.08 (*0-8368-1500-9*) Gareth Stevens Inc.

***Real Balti Cookbook: Over 100 Quick & Authentic Recipes.** Mridula Baljekar. (Illus.). 128p. 1997. 24.95 (*0-09-180975-4*, Pub. by Ebury Pr UK) Trafalgar.

Real Baptism. Charles F. Baker. 80p. 1994. 4.25 (*0-89814-045-5*) Grace Publns.

Real Barry Humphries. Peter Coleman. (Illus.). 191p. 1995. 24.95 (*0-86051-678-4*, Robson-Parkwest) Parkwest Pubns.

Real Barry Humphries. Peter Coleman. (Illus.). 191p. 1992. pap. 8.95 (*0-340-55907-1*, Pub. by H & S UK) Trafalgar.

Real Barry Humphries. Peter Coleman. 246p. 1991. 21.95 (*1-85089-541-4*, Pub. by ISIS UK); pap. 13.95 (*1-85089-337-3*, Pub. by ISIS UK) Transaction Pubs.

Real Beauty. Eddy M. Zemach. LC 96-23182. 1997. 45.00 (*0-271-01638-8*); pap. 18.95 (*0-271-01639-6*) Pa St U Pr.

Real Beauty ... Real Women: A Workbook for Making the Best of Your Own Good Looks. Kathleen Walas. (Illus.). 1992. 19.50 (*0-942361-45-8*) MasterMedia Pub.

Real Beer & Good Eats. B. Aidells & D. Kelly. 368p. 1996. pap. 18.00 (*0-679-76579-4*) Random.

Real Beer & Good Eats: The Rebirth of America's Beer & Food Traditions. Bruce Aidells. 1992. 27.50 (*0-394-58267-5*) Knopf.

Real Beneficiaries of Federal Dredging: A Legal, Political & Economic Assessment of the Fifty-Foot Channel for the Port of Baltimore. pap. 4.00 (*0-943676-00-2*) MD Sea Grant Col.

Real Benjamin Franklin. Andrew M. Allison et al. LC 82-70110. (American Classic Ser.). (Illus.). xx, 504p. (Orig.). 1982. 16.95 (*0-88080-000-3*); pap. 13.95 (*0-88080-001-1*) Natl Ctr Constitutional.

***Real Bettie Page: The Truth about the Queen of the Pinups.** Richard Foster. 1997. 21.95 (*1-55972-432-3*, Birch Ln Pr) Carol Pub Group.

Real Blake. Edwin J. Ellis. LC 75-117994. (Studies in Blake: No. 3). 1970. reprint ed. lib. bdg. 75.00 (*0-8383-1049-4*) M S G Haskell Hse.

***Real Blues for Keyboard.** Jeff Hammer. 64p. pap. 9.95 incl. cd-rom (*0-7119-4514-4*) Omnibus NY.

***Real Blues Guitar.** Ed. by Aaron Stang. 84p. (Orig.). (C). 1993. pap. text ed. 17.95 (*0-7604-0070-9*, F3267GTXAT) Warner Brothers.

Real Books for Reading: Learning to Read with Children's Literature. Linda Hart-Hewins & Jan Wells. LC 90-43145. 112p. 1990. pap. 10.95 (*0-435-08547-6*, 08547) Heinemann.

Real Bread: A Fearless Guide to Making It. 2nd ed. Maggie Baylis & Coralie Castle. LC 92-30790. (One Hundred One Productions Ser.). (Illus.). 240p. 1993. reprint ed. pap. 10.95 (*1-56426-554-4*, One Hund One Prods) Cole Group.

Real Business: It Starts & It Ends Here. Frank Kubic. LC 93-83813. 256p. (Orig.). 1993. pap. 13.00 (*0-9636320-0-0*) Nuggets Wisdom.

Real Cajun School of Cooking Cookbook. Tim Edler. (Illus.). 64p. (Orig.). 1990. pap. 5.95 (*0-931108-15-2*) Little Cajun Bks.

***Real Ceylon.** C. Brooke Elliott. (C). 1995. 27.00 (*81-206-1135-7*, Pub. by Asian Educ Servs II) S Asia.

Real Change Leaders: How You Can Be Part of Revolution Transforming Your Company. RCL Team & Jon R. Katzenbach. 288p. 1995. 27.50 (*0-8129-2626-9*, Times Bks) Random.

***Real Change Leaders: How You Can Create Growth & High Performance at Your Company.** Jon R. Katzenbach. 1997. pap. 16.00 (*0-8129-2923-3*, Times Bks) Random.

An Asterisk (*) at the beginning of an entry indicates that the title is appearing in BIP for the first time.

Real Change Leader's Handbook for Action. RCL Team Staff et al. LC 95-26113. 1996. write for info. (*0-8129-2799-0*, Times Business) Random.

Real Characters. Michael T. Darkow. 155p. (Orig.). 1996. mass mkt. 4.99 (*1-55197-107-0*, Pub. by Comnwlth Pub CN) Partners Pubs Grp.

Real Characters. J. Vernon McGee. LC 94-48154. 256p. 1995. 14.99 (*0-7852-7732-3*) Nelson.

Real Character's in the Making. Lorraine Peterson. LC 85-7373. 224p. (YA). (gr. 8-12). 1985. pap. 7.99 (*0-87123-824-1*) Bethany Hse.

Real Charlotte. Edith O. Somerville & Martin Ross. Ed. by Virginia Beards. 350p. (Orig.). 1986. text ed. 35.00 (*0-8135-1133-X*); pap. text ed. 14.00 (*0-8135-1134-8*) Rutgers U Pr.

Real Charlotte. large type ed. Edith O. Somerville. 500p. 1996. lib. bdg. 24.00 (*0-939495-91-0*) North Bks.

Real Charlotte. Edith O. Somerville. LC 85-14248. 326p. 1986. reprint ed. pap. 93.00 (*0-608-02327-2*, 2062968) Bks Demand.

Real Chief. Meda C. Ryan. 1986. pap. 13.95 (*0-85342-764-X*) Dufour.

***Real Chili Cookbook.** P. Quarto. 1996. pap. text ed. 12.98 (*0-7858-0624-5*) Bk Sales Inc.

***Real Choices: Listening to Women, Looking for Alternatives to Abortion.** Frederica Mathewes-Green. LC 97-24460. 1997. write for info. (*1-888212-07-1*) Conciliar Pr.

Real Choices - New Voices: The Case for Proportional Representation Elections in the United States. Douglas J. Amy. LC 92-46631. (C). 1993. 39.50 (*0-231-08154-5*) Col U Pr.

Real Choices/New Voices: The Case for Proportional Representation Elections in the United States. Douglas J. Amy. 278p. 1995. pap. 16.50 (*0-231-08155-3*) Col U Pr.

Real Chord Changes & Substitutions: U. K. Edition. 248p. per. 19.95 (*0-7935-1925-X*, 00240010) H Leonard.

Real Chord Changes & Substitutions - Christmas Favorites. Champ Champagne. 120p. 1992. spiral bd. 14.95 (*0-7935-1666-8*, 00240005) H Leonard.

***Real Christianity: Discerning True & False Faith.** William Wilberforce. (Classics of Faith & Devotion Ser.). 1997. pap. text ed. 9.99 (*1-55661-832-8*) Bethany Hse.

Real Christians Don't Dance. John Fischer. LC 88-458. 192p. (Orig.). 1988. 12.99 (*1-55661-010-6*) Bethany Hse.

Real Christians Don't Dance! Sorting the Truth from the Trappings in a Born-Again Culture. John Fischer. 192p. 1994. pap. 8.99 (*1-55661-496-9*) Bethany Hse.

Real Christmas Story. Paul R. Pontis. 1994. pap. 7.95 (*1-55673-857-9*) CSS OH.

Real Christmas This Year. Karen L. Williams. LC 94-43096. (J). 1995. 13.95 (*0-395-70115-5*, Clarion Bks) HM.

Real Christmas This Year. Karen L. Williams. (J). 1995. 14.95 (*0-395-70117-1*) HM.

Real Christmas Tree. Ardith Dorrough. 48p. (Orig.). 1983. pap. 2.50 (*0-88144-020-5*, CPS/020) Christian Pub.

Real Cinderella Rap. Alan Trussell-Cullen. LC 93-24528. (Voyages Ser.). (Illus.). (J). 1994. 4.25 (*0-383-03771-9*) SRA McGraw.

***Real City Kid.** Bird & Falk. (New Trend Fiction C Ser). (J). 1993. pap. text ed. write for info. (*0-582-80036-6*, Pub. by Longman UK) Longman.

Real Colonel House. A. D. Smith. 1972. lib. bdg. 59.95 (*0-8490-0931-6*) Gordon Pr.

Real Conflict Between China & Japan: An Analysis of Opposing Ideologies. Harley F. MacNair. (Double-Page Reprint Ser.). 116p. reprint ed. pap. 33.10 (*0-317-29846-1*, 2020114) Bks Demand.

Real Contexts. Anderson. (College ESL Ser.). 1995. pap. 21.95 (*0-8384-4706-6*) Heinle & Heinle.

Real Contexts. Anderson. (College ESL Ser.). 1995. teacher ed., pap. 9.95 (*0-8384-4707-4*) Heinle & Heinle.

Real Conversations, No. 1. Cathcart & Vaughn. 1992. pap. 15.95 (*0-8384-2247-0*) Heinle & Heinle.

Real Conversations, No. 1. Cathcart & Vaughn. 1992. teacher ed., pap. 12.95 (*0-8384-2337-X*); audio 51.95 (*0-8384-2250-0*) Heinle & Heinle.

Real Conversations, No. 2. Cathcart & Vaughn. 1992. pap. 15.95 (*0-8384-2248-9*) Heinle & Heinle.

Real Conversations, No. 2. Cathcart & Vaughn. 1992. teacher ed., pap. 12.95 (*0-8384-2347-7*); audio 51.95 (*0-8384-2251-9*) Heinle & Heinle.

Real Cool Killers. Chester Himes. (Crime Ser.). 159p. (Orig.). 1988. pap. 10.00 (*0-679-72039-1*, Vin) Pantheon.

Real Copies. Reynolds Price. LC 88-62140. (Orig.). 1988. pap. 10.00 (*0-933598-08-4*) NC Wesleyan Pr.

Real Corvette: An Illustrated History of Chevrolet's Sports Car. Ray Miller & Glenn Embree. LC 75-8100. (Chevy Chase Ser.: Vol. 3). (Illus.). 320p. 1975. 24.98 (*0-913056-06-5*) Evergreen Pr.

***Real Counties of Britain.** Russell Grant. (Illus.). 256p. 1996. 24.95 (*1-85227-479-4*, Pub. by Virgin Pub UK) London Brdge.

Real County, Texas History. Marjorie Kellner. (Illus.). 755p. 1996. 80.00 (*0-88107-255-9*) Curtis Media.

Real Cowboys. Joe E. Troutt. LC 90-55247. 87p. (Orig.). 1991. pap. 6.95 (*1-56002-056-3*) Aegina Pr.

Real Crime, Virtual Justice: The Flawed Prosecution of Crime in America. H. Richard Uviller. 312p. 1996. 30.00 (*0-300-06483-7*) Yale U Pr.

Real Dakota! Dale Gorder et al. (Real States Ser.). (Orig.). 1989. pap. 11.95 (*0-933025-07-6*) Blue Bird Pub.

***Real Data: A Statistics Workbook Based on Empirical Data.** Zealure C. Holcomb. (Illus.). 144p. (C). 1996. wbk. ed. 19.95 (*1-884585-04-3*) Pyrczak Pub.

Real Data: Student Package. Kolb. (C). student ed., pap. text ed. 32.00 (*1-55786-796-8*) Blackwell Pubs.

***Real Davvening: Jewish Prayer As a Spiritual Practice & a Form of Meditation for Beginning & Experienced Davveners.** Yitzlak Buxbaum. (Jewish Booklet Ser.: No. 1). 50p. (Orig.). 1996. pap. 7.95 (*0-9657112-1-8*) Jewish Spirit.

***Real Deal: How to Get Signed to a Record Label from A to Z.** Daylle D. Schwarz. LC 96-49874. 1997. write for info. (*0-8230-7611-3*) Watsn-Guptill.

Real Diary of a Real Boy. Henry A. Shute. 200p. 1990. reprint ed. lib. bdg. 21.95 (*0-89966-687-6*) Buccaneer Bks.

Real Difficulties. (YouthTalk Ser.). 32p. (YA). 1994. teacher ed., pap. 4.95 (*0-8066-0262-7*) Augsburg Fortress.

Real Difficulties. (YouthTalk Ser.). 48p. (YA). 1994. pap. 5.25 (*0-8066-0261-9*, 15-5216) Augsburg Fortress.

Real Disaster Is above Ground: A Mine Fire & Social Conflict. J. Stephen Kroll-Smith & Stephen R. Couch. LC 89-39905. 216p. 1990. 24.00 (*0-8131-1667-8*) U Pr of Ky.

Real Discovery of America: Mexico, November 8, 1519. Hugh Thomas. (C). 1992. 14.95 (*1-55921-069-9*) Moyer Bell.

Real Discovery of America: Mexico, November 8, 1519. Hugh Thomas. (Anshen Transdisciplinary Lectureships in Art, Science, & the Philosophy of Culture Ser.: Monograph 2). 64p. 1994. pap. 9.95 (*1-55921-072-9*) Moyer Bell.

Real Dogs Don't Eat Leftovers: A Guide to All That Is Truly Canine. Lee Lorenz. (Illus.). 1983. write for info. (*0-671-47757-9*) S&S Trade.

Real Dream Teams: Seven Practices Used by World-Class Team Leaders to Achieve Extraordinary... Bob Fisher & Bo Thomas. 190p. 1995. 24.95 (*1-57444-006-3*) St Lucie Pr.

Real Economy of Zaire: The Contribution of Smuggling & Other Unofficial Activities to National Wealth. Janet MacGaffey et al. LC 91-3844. 192p. (Orig.). (C). 1991. text ed. 31.95 (*0-8122-3140-6*); pap. text ed. 20.95 (*0-8122-1365-3*) U of Pa Pr.

Real Eichmann Trial. Paul Rassinier. 170p. 1980. pap. 7.50 (*0-911038-48-5*) Legion Survival.

Real Elizabeth Hollister. Trisha Alexander. (Special Edition Ser.). 1995. pap. 3.75 (*0-373-09940-1*, 1-09940-7) Silhouette.

Real English: The Grammar of English Dialects in the British Isles. Ed. by James Milroy & Lesley Milroy. LC 92-42775. (Real Language Ser.). 1993. pap. text ed. write for info. (*0-582-08176-9*) Longman.

Real English: The Grammar of English Dialects in the British Isles. Ed. by James Milroy & Lesley Milroy. LC 92-42775. (Real Language Ser.). 1993. write for info. (*0-582-08177-7*) Longman.

Real Estate. Rodney Davis. LC 79-155. (Career Competencies in Marketing Ser.). (Illus.). (gr. 11-12). 1979. text ed. 12.04 (*0-07-015672-7*) McGraw.

Real Estate. Mariwyn Evans. (VGM Career Planner Ser.). 128p. 1993. pap. 7.95 (*0-8442-8676-1*, VGM Career Bks) NTC Pub Grp.

Real Estate. James B. Kau & C. F. Sirmans, Jr. 816p. 1985. text ed. write for info. (*0-07-033306-8*) McGraw.

Real Estate. George Milko. (Random House Practical Law Manual Ser.). 165p. 1990. pap. write for info. (*0-679-72980-1*) HALT DC.

Real Estate. Charles P. Nemeth. (Paralegal Workbook Ser.). 104p. (C). 1995. pap. 9.95 (*0-87084-584-5*) Anderson Pub Co.

Real Estate. Louise Page. (Methuen New Theatrescripts Ser.). 39p. (Orig.). (C). 1988. pap. 7.95 (*0-413-57950-6*, A0233, Pub. by Methuen UK) Heinemann.

***Real Estate.** Wendy Sacket & Christine L. Hainsworth-Straus. LC 97-6818. (Money & Me Ser.). (J). 1997. write for info. (*0-86625-612-1*) Rourke Corp.

Real Estate. Robert Sohns. 96p. pap. 9.00 (*0-685-23168-2*, 41,575R) NCLS Inc.

Real Estate. 2nd ed. Jerome Dasso. 638p. 1995. text ed. 79.00 (*0-13-766239-4*) P-H.

Real Estate. 2nd ed. Guttery & Dasso. 1995. student ed., pap. text ed. 17.80 (*0-13-766247-5*) P-H.

Real Estate. 3rd ed. Larry E. Wofford & Terrance M. Clauretie. LC 91-41571. 688p. (C). 1992. Net. text ed. 44.50 (*0-471-54848-0*) Wiley.

Real Estate: A Bibliography of the Monographic Literature. Ed. by Peter D. Haikalis & Jean K. Freeman. LC 82-23071. xii, 317p. 1983. text ed. 59.95 (*0-313-23680-1*, HAK/, Greenwood Pr) Greenwood.

Real Estate: Adventures, Principles & Practices. Joseph W. DeCarlo. (Orig.). (C). 1993. pap. 14.95 (*0-937841-09-9*) JD Pub & Seminars.

Real Estate: An Introduction to the Profession. 4th ed. Bruce M. Harwood. (C). 1986. teacher ed. write for info. (*0-318-59129-4*, Reston) P-H.

Real Estate: An Introduction to the Profession. 7th ed. Bruce M. Harwood. 1986. pap. 11.90 (*0-13-762451-4*) P-H.

Real Estate: An Introduction to the Profession. 7th ed. Charles J. Jacobus & Bruce M. Harwood. LC 96-1241. 1996. pap. text ed. 39.20 (*0-13-452103-X*) P-H.

Real Estate: An Introduction to the Profession: Polley Associates Edition. 6th ed. Jacobus. 592p. 1997. pap. text ed. 14.10 (*0-13-125410-3*) P-H.

Real Estate: Analysis & Appraisal. Achour. 400p. 1987. pap. 50.00 (*0-409-80108-9*) MICHIE.

Real Estate: Case Study Approach. William J. Poorvu. 464p. 1992. pap. text ed. 49.00 (*0-13-763483-8*) P-H.

Real Estate: Exam PREP Guide-Texas. Leslie K. Purvis. Ed. by Lynn Purvis. (Illus.). 320p. (Orig.). 1996. pap. text ed. 29.95 (*0-9638207-9-6*) Purvis Real Est.

***Real Estate: Learning the Practices of the Profession.** Randal S. Van Reken & Sandra E. Byrd. LC 97-22039. 1998. 22.67 (*0-13-780172-6*) P-H.

Real Estate: Questions & Answers on California Real Estate Laws, Rules & Regulations. John R. Johnsich. 1985. pap. write for info. (*0-914256-05-X*) Real Estate Pub.

Real Estate: The Best Game in Town. Wade B. Cook. 143p. (Orig.). pap. 11.95 (*0-910019-10-X*) Lghthse Pub Gp.

Real Estate: The Most Successful Real Estate Listing & Selling Techniques. Intro. by John R. Johnsich. 1979. pap. 11.95 (*0-914256-09-2*) Real Estate Pub.

Real Estate Accounting & Mathematics Handbook. 2nd ed. Robert J. Wiley. 380p. 1986. text ed. 90.00 (*0-471-81681-7*) Wiley.

Real Estate Accounting & Mathematics Handbook. 3rd ed. Robert J. Wiley. 368p. 1993. text ed. 135.00 incl. disk (*0-471-57231-4*) Wiley.

Real Estate Accounting & Reporting: A Guide for Developers, Investors, & Lenders. 3rd ed. Nicholas Cammarano & James J. Klink. LC 94-48266. 330p. 1995. text ed. 120.00 (*0-471-51069-6*) Wiley.

***Real Estate Accounting & Reporting: A Guide for Developers, Investors, & Lenders, 1996.** 3rd ed. Nicholas Cammarano & James J. Klink. 96p. 1996. suppl. ed., pap. 50.00 (*0-471-14021-X*) Wiley.

Real Estate Accounting & Reporting Manual, No. 2731. annuals rev. ed. Benedetto Buongiorno & Robert R. Garland. 976p. 1989. Supplemented annually. suppl. ed., boxed 155.00 (*0-7913-0395-0*) Warren Gorham & Lamont.

Real Estate Accounting & Reporting Manual, No. 2731. rev. ed. Benedetto Buongiorno & Robert R. Garland. 976p. 1991. Supplement, 1991. suppl. ed., text ed. 57.00 (*0-7913-0792-1*) Warren Gorham & Lamont.

Real Estate Advertising Handbook. Donald R. Brown & Wendell G. Mathews. Ed. by Helene Berlin. LC 81-51380. (Illus.). 96p. 1981. reprint ed. 10.00 (*0-686-73397-5*, 340) Realtors Natl.

Real Estate Advertising That Works! Linda Lipman. (Illus.). 298p. 1992. reprint ed. pap. 19.95 (*1-887145-01-X*) Argyle Pr NV.

Real Estate Agency Law in Queensland. 2nd ed. W. D. Duncan. xxx, 348p. 1990. pap. 49.00 (*0-455-21009-8*, Pub. by Law Bk Co AT) Gaunt.

Real Estate Agent. Jack Rudman. (Career Examination Ser.: C-2179). 1994. pap. 23.95 (*0-8373-2179-4*) Nat Learn.

Real Estate Agent & Appraiser Liability: In Plain Language. Clarance E. Hagglund et al. 261p. 1993. 49.50 (*0-9631290-1-5*) Common Law.

Real Estate Agent's Action Guide to Listing & Sales Success. Bob Deutsch. 209p. (Orig.). 1993. pap. 22.95 (*0-7931-0714-8*, 19070701, Real Estate Ed) Dearborn Finan.

Real Estate Agents & Special Studies Zones Disclosure: The Response of California Home Buyers to Earthquake Hazards Information. Risa I. Palm. (Program on Environment & Behavior Monograph Ser.: No. 32). 147p. (Orig.). (C). 1981. pap. 8.00 (*0-685-28106-X*) Natural Hazards.

Real Estate Agent's Business Planning Guide. Carla Cross. 256p. 1994. pap. 24.95 (*0-7931-0955-8*, 19071101) Dearborn Finan.

Real Estate Aide. Jack Rudman. (Career Examination Ser.: C-687). 1994. pap. 23.95 (*0-8373-0687-6*) Nat Learn.

Real Estate Almanac. Ed. by Robert D. Allen & Thomas E. Wolfe. LC 80-12417. (Real Estate For Professional Practitioners Ser.). 468p. reprint ed. pap. 133.40 (*0-317-10964-2*, 2055413) Bks Demand.

Real Estate Analysis: An Introduction. 2nd ed. Jerry T. Ferguson. 384p. 1993. per. 38.79 (*0-8403-8491-2*) Kendall-Hunt.

Real Estate Analysis Workbook. Jerry T. Ferguson. 100p. (C). 1994. pap. text ed., spiral bd. 13.59 (*0-8403-9796-8*) Kendall-Hunt.

Real Estate & Construction Lending: A Special Collection from the Journal of Commercial Bank Lending, Vol. 2. Ed. by Joan H. Behr. LC 86-8567. (Illus.). 128p. 1990. pap. text ed. 45.00 (*0-936742-76-3*, 36042) Robt Morris Assocs.

Real Estate & Construction Lending, Vol. 1: A Special Collection from the Journal of Commercial Bank Lending. Ed. by Charlotte Weisman. LC 86-8567. (Illus.). 116p. 1986. pap. text ed. 45.00 (*0-936742-31-3*) Robt Morris Assocs.

Real Estate & Finance. 2nd ed. Sherman J. Maisel. 570p. (C). 1992. text ed. 56.00 (*0-15-575852-7*) Dryden Pr.

Real Estate & Property Management. George Allen. Ed. by Nancy Bowman. (Monograph Ser.: No. 1). 30p. (C). 1993. 25.00 (*1-878350-01-3*) PMN Pub.

Real Estate & the Money Markets. James Gibbons. 47p. 1989. 6.50 (*0-685-45282-4*) Couns Real Estate.

Real Estate & the RTC. Ed. by Leonard A. Zax. LC 90-71544. 1990. 42.95 (*0-87420-711-8*) Urban Land.

Real Estate Appraisal. Scott Failing. 450p. (C). 1991. pap. text ed. 69.95 (*1-878025-19-8*) Western Schls.

Real Estate Appraisal. Jack P. Friedman et al. (C). 1985. teacher ed. write for info. (*0-8359-6509-0*, Reston); text ed. 24.33 (*0-8359-6508-2*, Reston) P-H.

Real Estate Appraisal. William M. Shenkel. (C). 1992. text ed. 64.95 (*0-538-81375-X*, FL60AA) S-W Pub.

Real Estate Appraisal. William M. Shenkel. (UW - Real Estate Ser.). 1992. wbk. ed., pap. 26.95 (*0-538-81376-8*) S-W Pub.

Real Estate Appraisal. 3rd ed. Halbert C. Smith et al. LC 94-30924. 345p. 1994. per. 29.95 (*0-89787-937-6*) Gorsuch Scarisbrick.

Real Estate Appraisal Bibliography, 1945-1972. 436p. 1973. pap. 7.00 (*0-911780-33-5*) Appraisal Inst.

Real Estate Appraisal Bibliography, 1973-1980. 146p. 1981. pap. 12.50 (*0-911780-53-X*) Appraisal Inst.

Real Estate Appraisal in a Nutshell: A Restatement & Simplification of Theory & Practice. 2nd ed. James I. Stewart. LC 79-186283. 263p. reprint ed. pap. 75.00 (*0-8357-8297-2*, 2034023) Bks Demand.

Real Estate Appraisal Terminology. N. B. Boyce. 367p. 59.95 (*0-318-42554-8*, M8555); 59.95 (*0-8288-7624-X*, M8555) Fr & Eur.

Real Estate Appraiser. Jack Rudman. (Career Examination Ser.: C-1640). 1994. reprint ed. pap. 23.95 (*0-8373-1640-5*) Nat Learn.

Real Estate Appraiser's Liability. Mark L. Levine. 1997. write for info. (*0-317-01846-9*) Prof Pubns & Educ.

Real Estate Appraisers' Liability. annuals rev. ed. Mark L. Levine. LC 91-60906. (Real Property-Zoning Ser.). 1991. Revised annually with supplement. suppl. ed. 135.00 (*0-685-59814-4*) Clark Boardman Callaghan.

Real Estate Appraising from A to Z: The Real Facts Other Books Don't Tell You! 3rd rev. ed. Guy Cozzi. (Home Inspection from A to Z Ser.). (Illus.). 200p. 1995. write for info. (*1-887450-01-7*); pap. write for info. (*1-887450-02-5*) NeMMaR.

Real Estate Appraising from A to Z: The Real Facts Other Books Don't Tell You!, Set. 3rd rev. ed. Guy Cozzi. (Home Inspection from A to Z Ser.). (Illus.). 200p. 1995. pap. write for info. incl. audio (*1-887450-05-X*) NeMMaR.

Real Estate Appraising (Step-by-Step) 2nd ed. Paul G. Creteau. LC 73-90006. 1974. 18.00 (*0-9603372-1-0*) Castle Pub Co.

Real Estate Assistant. Jack Rudman. (Career Examination Ser.: C-688). 1994. pap. 23.95 (*0-8373-0688-4*) Nat Learn.

Real Estate Bargains! Peter Martin. 52p. (Orig.). 1990. pap. 7.95 (*1-882066-01-4*) Peters Pr.

Real Estate Book Forms, Letters, & Clauses: The Ultimate Paper Trail. Oliver E. Frascona & Katherine E. Reece. Ed. by Joseph L. Frascona & Jean E. Frascona. LC 94-25141. (Real Estate Law Ser.). (Orig.). 1995. pap. text ed. 49.95 (*0-941937-02-X*) Real Law Bks.

Real Estate Books & Periodicals in Print: A Guide to Real Estate Publications, Their Authors, Prices, Publishers' Addresses & Other Bibliographic Data. John R. Johnsich. 1977. 19.95 (*0-914256-07-6*); pap. 15.95 (*0-914256-08-4*) Real Estate Pub.

Real Estate Books & Periodicals in Print: A Guide to Real Estate Publications, Their Authors, Prices, Publishers' Addresses & Other Bibliographic Data. John R. Johnsich. 1982. pap. 19.95 (*0-914256-15-7*) Real Estate Pub.

Real Estate Books & Periodicals in Print: A Guide to Real Estate Publications, Their Authors, Prices, Publishers' Addresses & Other Bibliographic Data. John R. Johnsich. 168p. 1988. pap. 29.95 (*0-914256-19-X*) Real Estate Pub.

Real Estate Books & Periodicals in Print: 1990-95 Supplement. John R. Johnsich. (Orig.). 1995. pap. 29.95 (*0-914256-27-0*) Real Estate Pub.

Real Estate Books & Periodicals in Print, 1990-93 Supplement. John R. Johnsich. (Orig.). 1993. pap. 15.95 (*0-914256-25-4*) Real Estate Pub.

Real Estate Broker. Jack Rudman. (Career Examination Ser.: C-666). 1994. pap. 23.95 (*0-8373-0666-3*) Nat Learn.

Real Estate Broker (REB) Jack Rudman. (Admission Test Ser.: ATS-3). 1994. pap. 23.95 (*0-8373-5003-4*) Nat Learn.

Real Estate Brokerage. Bruce J. Lindeman. 450p. (C). 1981. text ed. 27.00 (*0-8359-6517-1*, Reston) P-H.

Real Estate Brokerage. 4th ed. John E. Cyr et al. 470p. 1995. pap. 37.95 (*0-7931-1065-3*, 1965-0104, Real Estate Ed) Dearborn Finan.

Real Estate Brokerage: Law & Practice, 1 vol. Patrick J. Rohan. (Real Estate Transactions Ser.). 1985. Looseleaf updates avail. write for info. (*0-8205-1486-1*) Bender.

Real Estate Brokerage Law. Arthur R. Gaudio. 564p. 1986. text ed. write for info. (*0-314-31298-6*) West Pub.

Real Estate Brokerage Management. 3rd ed. Bruce J. Lindeman. 323p. (C). 1993. text ed. 56.00 (*0-13-763459-5*, 160801) P-H.

***Real Estate Brokerage Management.** 4th ed. Lindemann. (C). 1997. text ed. 34.67 (*0-13-639634-8*) P-H.

Real Estate Buy-Sell Manual: For Buyers, Sellers, Brokers, Lawyers. 4th ed. James R. Deal. 200p. 1994. pap. 19.95 (*1-884949-02-9*) Great Ideas.

Real Estate Buying-Selling Guide for British Columbia: Canadian Edition. 11th ed. E. Syberg-Olsen. (Legal Ser.). 248p. 1994. pap. 10.95 (*0-88908-498-X*) Self-Counsel Pr.

Real Estate Buying-Selling Guide for Florida. Richard Badgley. (Legal Ser.). 176p. 1992. pap. 9.95 (*0-88908-778-4*) Self-Counsel Pr.

Real Estate Buying-Selling Guide for Oregon. 2nd ed. Fred A. Granata. (Legal Ser.). 128p. 1990. pap. 8.95 (*0-88908-828-4*) Self-Counsel Pr.

Real Estate Buying-Selling Guide for Washington. 4th ed. Charles J. Covello. (Legal Ser.). (Illus.). 96p. 1991. pap. 8.95 (*0-88908-747-4*) Self-Counsel Pr.

Real Estate by Yourself. J. James Hasenau. LC 80-85022. (Illus.). 1985. pap. 17.95 (*0-913042-12-9*) Holland Hse Pr.

Real Estate Careers: Twenty-Five Growing Opportunities for Good Times & Bad. Carolyn Janik & Ruth Rejnis. 214p. 1994. pap. text ed. 19.95 (*0-471-59203-X*) Wiley.

Real Estate Challenge: Capitalizing on Change. William J. Poorvu. LC 95-26522. 1995. pap. text ed. 48.00 (*0-13-452137-4*) P-H.

***Real Estate Closing Deskbook.** K. F. Boackle. LC 97-18900. 1997. pap. write for info. (*1-57073-449-6*) Amer Bar Assn.

R

Real Estate Closing Procedures (1992) Christine Li et al. LC 84-153773. 147p. 1992. 35.00 (*0-685-10481-8*) NJ Inst CLE.

Real Estate Closings. 2nd ed. Robert E. Schreiner & Robert E. Schreiner, Jr. LC 83-161974. (Illus.). 344p. (C). 1983. text ed. 25.00 (*0-9618320-1-0*) R E Schreiner.

Real Estate Contracts. Robert E. Schreiner & Robert E. Schreiner, Jr. LC 87-90696. (Illus.). 200p. (Orig.). 1987. pap. text ed. 15.95 (*0-9618320-0-2*) R E Schreiner.

Real Estate Counseling. American Society of Real Estate Counselors Staff. Ed. by James H. Boykin. 316p. 1988. 15.00 (*0-13-762444-1*) Couns Real Estate.

Real Estate Counseling in a Plain Brown Wrapper. Jared Shlaes. 1992. 19.00 (*0-939653-00-1*) Couns Real Estate.

Real Estate Crisis & How to Invest in It for Profit. 1993. lib. bdg. 255.95 (*0-8490-8930-1*) Gordon Pr.

***Real Estate Development: Principles & Process.** 2nd ed. Mike E. Miles et al. LC 95-61581. 554p. 1996. 59.95 (*0-87420-773-8*, R32) Urban Land.

Real Estate Development: Strategies for Changing Markets. Stuart M. Saft. LC 90-35304. (Real Estate Practice Library). 734p. 1990. text ed. 125.00 (*0-471-51938-3*) Wiley.

Real Estate Development Manual. Ed. by Jerome B. Alenick. LC 90-70402. (Illus.). 585p. 1990. text ed. 150.00 (*0-7913-0550-3*) Warren Gorham & Lamont.

Real Estate Development Syndication. Joseph T. Howell. LC 83-17764. 254p. 1983. text ed. 49.95 (*0-275-91010-5*, C1010, Praeger Pubs) Greenwood.

Real Estate Development Workbook. Howard A. Zuckerman. 1991. 89.95 (*0-13-763491-9*) P-H.

Real Estate Dictionary. Michael C. Thomsett. LC 87-43196. (Illus.). 232p. 1988. lib. bdg. 32.50 (*0-89950-321-7*) McFarland & Co.

Real Estate Dictionary. 6th ed. John Talamo. 192p. 1991. pap. 8.40 (*0-87600-510-5*) Finan Pub.

Real Estate Dictionary of Terms & Definitions. John R. Johnsich. (Orig.). 1973. 11.95 (*0-914256-00-9*) Real Estate Pub.

Real Estate Dictionary of Terms & Definitions. 3rd ed. John R. Johnsich. (Real Estate Dictionary Ser.). 272p. 1991. pap. 11.95 (*0-914256-22-X*) Real Estate Pub.

Real Estate Economics. Hugh J. Smith. 450p. (C). 1991. pap. text ed. 69.95 (*1-878025-20-1*) Western Schls.

Real Estate Encyclopedia of Home Design, Construction, & Architecture. Leonard Kleeman. LC 80-17891. 330p. 1981. 29.95 (*0-13-762542-1*, Parker Publishing Co) P-H.

Real Estate Ethics Good Ethics = Good Business. 3rd ed. William H. Pivar & Donald L. Harian. 192p. 1995. pap. 16.95 (*0-7931-1236-2*, 1966-0103, Pub. by R-I-C-S Bks UK) St Mut.

Real Estate Exam Guide for ASI. 1995. 3.5 hd 35.00 (*0-7931-1424-1*, 1516-2401, Real Estate Ed); 5.25 ld 35.00 (*0-7931-1423-3*, 1516-2301, Real Estate Ed) Dearborn Finan.

Real Estate Exam Guide for ASI. 4th ed. William H. Pivar. LC 94-24988. 1995. pap. text ed. 22.95 (*0-7931-1107-2*, 1970-0604, Real Estate Ed) Dearborn Finan.

***Real Estate Exam Guide for ASI.** 5th ed. William H. Pivar. LC 97-10587. 271p. 1997. pap. text ed. 24.95 (*0-7931-2527-8*, 1970-0605, Real Estate Ed) Dearborn Finan.

Real Estate Exchange: Using Tax-Deferred Exchange in Real Estate Investment Management. Ed. by Howard A. Zuckerman & Rochelle Stone. 325p. 1992. 65.00 (*1-55738-415-0*) Irwin Prof Pubng.

Real Estate Exchanges, Taxation & Investment: A Systems Approach. Harley J. Smith. (Illus.). 1977. per. 29.95 (*0-685-64690-4*) Harley Smith Invest.

Real Estate Finance. Stephen L. Barter. 1988. 116.00 (*0-406-11500-1*, U.K.) MICHIE.

Real Estate Finance. William Brogan. 288p. 1995. per. 32.50 (*0-89787-940-6*) Gorsuch Scarisbrick.

Real Estate Finance. Scott Failing. 450p. (C). 1991. pap. text ed. 69.95 (*1-878025-18-X*) Western Schls.

Real Estate Finance. Robert de Heer. 1995. pap. text ed. write for info. (*0-7931-1249-4*, 1520-3201, Real Estate Ed) Dearborn Finan.

Real Estate Finance. Ross H. Johnson & Thomas P. Henderson. 464p. (C). 1985. write for info. (*0-675-20195-0*, Merrill Coll) P-H.

Real Estate Finance. Madison. 1991. 57.00 (*0-316-54363-2*) Little.

Real Estate Finance. Sherman J. Maisel. (Illus.). 448p. (C). 1987. text ed. 46.75 (*0-15-575847-0*) HB Coll Pubs.

Real Estate Finance. Stanley S. Reyburn. 582p. (C). 1994. pap. text ed. 29.95 (*1-884811-00-0*) Felde Pubng.

Real Estate Finance. William M. Shenkel. 608p. (C). 1988. text ed. 62.95 (*0-256-02206-2*); disk 15.95 (*0-256-06505-5*) Irwin.

Real Estate Finance. Arthur Warner et al. (C). 1985. teacher ed. write for info. (*0-8359-6566-X*, Reston); text ed. 25.95 (*0-8359-6565-1*, Reston) P-H.

***Real Estate Finance.** Lynne A. Weinman. 250p. (C). 1996. pap. text ed. 74.95 (*1-878025-97-X*) Western Schls.

Real Estate Finance. Arefaine G. Yohannes. 413p. (C). 1994. pap. text ed. 25.00 (*1-57074-111-5*) Greyden Pr.

Real Estate Finance. 2nd ed. Michael R. Buchanan & Ronald D. Johnson. (Illus.). 522p. (C). 1988. text ed. 49.00 (*0-89982-351-3*, 050020) Am Bankers.

Real Estate Finance. 2nd ed. C. F. Sirmans, Jr. (Illus.). 560p. 1989. text ed. write for info. (*0-07-057698-X*) McGraw.

Real Estate Finance. 7th ed. John P. Wiedemer. LC 94-33890. 352p. 1994. text ed. 47.00 (*0-13-185570-0*) P-H.

Real Estate Finance: Theory & Practice. 2nd ed. Terrence M. Clauretie & G. Stacy Sirmans. LC 95-40427. 1995. 70.00 (*0-13-433475-2*) P-H.

***Real Estate Finance & Investment Manual.** Jack Cummings. LC 96-29527. 1997. write for info. (*0-13-493396-6*); pap. write for info. (*0-13-493388-5*) P-H.

Real Estate Finance & Investments. 9th ed. William B. Brueggeman et al. 832p. (C). 1992. text ed. 68.25 (*0-256-08290-1*) Irwin.

Real Estate Finance & Investments. 10th ed. William B. Brueggeman & Jeffrey Fisher. LC 96-23787. 880p. (C). 1996. text ed. 68.25 (*0-256-15254-3*) Irwin.

Real Estate Finance in a Nutshell. 3rd ed. Jon W. Bruce. (Nutshell Ser.). 287p. 1991. reprint ed. pap. text ed. 15.50 (*0-314-87477-1*) West Pub.

***Real Estate Finance in a Nutshell: In a Nutshell.** 4th ed. Jon W. Bruce. LC 97-9347. (Nutshell Ser.). 264p. 1997. pap. text ed. write for info. (*0-314-21161-6*) West Pub.

Real Estate Finance Journal. Ed. by William Zucker. 140.00 (*0-685-70158-1*, JREF) Warren Gorham & Lamont.

Real Estate Finance Law. 3rd ed. Grant S. Nelson & Dale A. Whitman. LC 93-43024. (Hornbook Ser.). 1091p. 1994. text ed. 39.00 (*0-314-03453-6*) West Pub.

Real Estate Finance Law. Grant S. Nelson & Dale A. Whitman. LC 85-13660. (Hornbook Ser.). 1052p. 1991. reprint ed. student ed., text ed. 36.50 (*0-314-91412-9*) West Pub.

Real Estate Finance Law, 2 vols., Vol. 1. 3rd ed. Grant S. Nelson & Dale A. Whitman. (Practitioner's Treatise Ser.). 842p. 1993. text ed. 62.50 (*0-314-02296-1*) West Pub.

Real Estate Finance Law, 2 vols., Vol. 2. Grant S. Nelson & Dale A. Whitman. (Practitioner Treatise Ser.). 825p. 1993. text ed. 62.50 (*0-314-02434-4*) West Pub.

Real Estate Financial Management. 2nd ed. David Doeleman & Ronald C. Rogers. LC 86-62851. 152p. 1987. 22.00 (*0-913652-61-X*) Realtors Natl.

Real Estate Financing: Text, Forms, Tax Analysis, 7 vols. Patrick J. Rohan. (Real Estate Transactions Ser.). 1973. Updates. ring bd. write for info. (*0-8205-1592-2*) Bender.

Real Estate Financing Manual: A Guide to Money Making Strategies. Jack Cummings. (Illus.). 458p. 1988. 18.95 (*0-13-762535-9*, Busn) P-H.

Real Estate Financing Manual: A Guide to Money-Making Strategies: Complete Guide to Real Estate Financing. Jack Cummings. 530p. 1987. text ed. 54.95 (*0-13-763418-8*) P-H.

Real Estate for Pennies! Investing in Tax Liens for Profit & Property. Ed C. Tomlinson. 1993. pap. 11.95 (*0-9626776-4-7*) Diamond Pubns.

***Real Estate for Real People.** Wade Cook. 1996. 22.95 (*0-910019-92-4*) Lghthse Pub Gp.

***Real Estate Foreclosure.** Charles P. Nemeth. 400p. text ed. 48.95 (*0-929563-34-4*) Pearson Pubns.

Real Estate Foreclosure: Paralegal Practice & Procedure. Charles P. Nemeth & Grayson P. VanHorn. 508p. 1994. text ed. 98.00 (*0-471-30722-X*, Pub. by Wiley Law Pubns) Wiley.

Real Estate Form Packet for Buying & Selling Your Home on Your Own. Scotch Christian. (Orig.). 1996. pap. 10.95 (*0-533-11635-X*) Vantage.

Real Estate Forms Approved for Colorado. Robert E. Schreiner & Robert E. Schreiner, Jr. LC 86-190261. (Illus.). 344p. (C). 1986. text ed. 12.00 (*0-9618320-2-9*) R E Schreiner.

Real Estate Forms from ALI-ABA Course Materials. 2nd ed. Frwd. by Paul A. Wolkin. LC 91-71726. 638p. 1991. suppl. ed., ring bd. 425.00 (*0-8318-0670-2*, B730) Am Law Inst.

Real Estate Fundamentals. 4th rev. ed. Wade E. Gaddy, Jr. & Robert E. Hart. LC 95-39704. (Orig.). 1995. 22.95 (*0-7931-1730-5*, 1513-014A, Real Estate Ed) Dearborn Finan.

Real Estate Fundamentals. Mark L. Levine. LC 76-3508. 440p. reprint ed. pap. 125.40 (*0-317-20531-5*, 2022843) Bks Demand.

Real Estate Gamble: Lessons From Fifty Years of Boom & Bust. Alan Rabinowitz. LC 80-65706. 320p. reprint ed. pap. 91.20 (*0-317-26698-5*, 2023508) Bks Demand.

Real Estate Guide. Prentice Hall Editorial Staff. 1966. 131.50 (*0-13-762740-8*) P-H.

Real Estate Handbook. 2nd rev. ed. Financial Publishing Co. Staff. 336p. 1992. pap. 9.45 (*0-87600-412-5*) Finan Pub.

Real Estate Handbook. 3rd ed. Jack P. Friedman & Jack C. Harris. 700p. 1993. 29.95 (*0-8120-6330-9*) Barron.

Real Estate Handbook: Land Laws of Alabama. 5th ed. Robert L. McCurley, Jr. & Penny A. Davis. 685p. 1990. suppl. ed. 80.00 (*0-87473-508-4*) MICHIE.

Real Estate Helpful Tips. J. A. Alexander. 180p. 1992. write for info. (*0-9632254-0-5*) J A Alexander.

Real Estate Home Inspection: A Comprehensive Study. 2nd rev. ed. Russel W. Burgess. LC 93-50826. 454p. (C). 1994. pap. 74.95 (*0-7931-0867-5*, 1531-0102, Real Estate Ed) Dearborn Finan.

Real Estate Ideas from Ray Foster. Ray Foster. 1980. 9.95 (*0-8359-6524-4*, Reston) P-H.

Real Estate in Greece: How to Buy, Sell or Build. George Voryas. LC 95-60965. (Orig.). (GRE.). 1995. 48.00 (*0-9647344-7-8*) Typoma Pubng.

Real Estate in Probate & As a Nonprobate Asset. John G. Grimsley. 1986. ring bd. write for info. (*0-318-61953-9*) Am Coll Trust & Est.

Real Estate in the Nineties: A Whole New World Ahead. Thomas W. Dooley & Charles M. Dahlheimer. 304p. 1989. pap. text ed. 19.95 (*0-9623018-0-9*) NAC Group Inc.

Real Estate Index, 2 vols. National Association of Realtors Staff. 1987. 169.00 (*0-938785-00-1*) Natl Assoc Realtors.

Real Estate Index, 2 vols., Vol. I: Author-Title. National Association of Realtors Staff. 1987. 99.00 (*0-938785-01-X*) Natl Assoc Realtors.

Real Estate Index, 2 vols., Vol. II: Subject. National Association of Realtors Staff. 1987. 99.00 (*0-938785-02-8*) Natl Assoc Realtors.

Real Estate Index - Supplement, Vol. 3. National Association of Realtors Staff. LC 86-23878. 1800p. 1988. 49.50 (*0-938785-04-4*) Natl Assoc Realtors.

Real Estate Index, 1991. National Association of Realtors Staff. 1992. 15.00 (*0-685-63292-X*) Natl Assoc Realtors.

Real Estate Information Sources. Ed. by Janice B. Babb & B. F. Dordick. LC 63-16246. (Management Information Guide Ser.: No. 1). 318p. 1972. 68.00 (*0-8103-0801-0*) Gale.

Real Estate Inspection Book: A Guide to Self Home Inspection. Lisa E. Mammone & Jack Moore. (Illus.). 49p. (Orig.). 1995. pap. 6.95 (*0-9648713-0-0*) Kooba.

Real Estate Interest Reporting: A Compliance Guide to IRS Reporting Requirements. Price Waterhouse Staff. 1994. pap. text ed. 75.00 (*1-55738-703-6*) Irwin Prof Pubng.

Real Estate Investing: A Complete Guide to Wealth-Building Secrets. Charles Klotsche. 340p. 1982. 29.95 (*0-13-762948-6*) P-H.

***Real Estate Investing from A to Z.** 2nd ed. LC 96-48061. 264p. 1997. text ed. 19.95 (*0-7863-1214-9*) Irwin Prof Pubng.

Real Estate Investing in New York City: A Handbook for the Small Investor. Robert L. Lewis. 128p. (Orig.). 1995. pap. 7.95 (*0-9647940-9-8*) Adventura Pubng.

Real Estate Investing in the 1990's. Ed. by Susan Hudson-Wilson. 145p. (Orig.). 1995. pap. text ed. 30.00 (*1-879087-46-4*) ICFARF.

Real Estate Investment. Clinloy. 1988. lib. bdg. 124.00 (*0-89838-233-5*) Kluwer Ac.

***Real Estate Investment.** Sindt. 1997. pap. text ed. 32.00 (*0-13-449687-6*) P-H.

Real Estate Investment. 3rd ed. John P. Wiedemer. (C). 1985. teacher ed. write for info. (*0-8359-6494-9*, Reston) P-H.

Real Estate Investment. 5th ed. John P. Wiedemer. LC 93-16922. 334p. (C). 1993. text ed. 48.00 (*0-13-763558-3*) P-H.

Real Estate Investment: Analysis & Management. Robert H. Plattner. 464p. (C). 1988. write for info. (*0-675-20524-7*, Merrill Coll) P-H.

Real Estate Investment: Analysis & Strategy. Robert J. Wiley. LC 75-14950. (Illus.). 384p. 1977. reprint ed. pap. 109.50 (*0-7837-3481-6*, 2057814) Bks Demand.

Real Estate Investment: Strategy, Analysis, Decision - Problems & Casebook. James R. Cooper & Stephen A. Phyrr. 45p. (Orig.). 1983. pap. 19.95 (*0-88406-169-8*) GA St U Busn Pr.

Real Estate Investment: Strategy, Analysis, Decisions. 2nd ed. Stephen A. Pyhrr et al. LC 88-27961. 962p. 1989. Net. text ed. 49.50 (*0-471-87953-3*) Wiley.

Real Estate Investment Analysis. Jerry T. Ferguson & Jay Helzer. 500p. 1990. trans. write for info. (*0-318-66335-X*, H23096) P-H.

Real Estate Investment Analysis: How to Spot the Top Performers for High Return Real Estate Investing. Robert W. Hall. LC 82-9239. 232p. 1982. text ed. 49.95 (*0-87624-487-8*, Inst Busn Plan) P-H.

Real Estate Investment & Acquisition Workbook. Howard A. Zuckerman. 576p. 1989. text ed. 49.95 (*0-13-762584-7*) P-H.

Real Estate Investment & Taxation. 4th ed. Stephen D. Messner et al. 464p. 1990. text ed. 73.00 (*0-13-763053-0*) P-H.

Real Estate Investment Strategy: Selected Articles from the National Newsletter. John T. Reed. 290p. 1991. pap. 39.95 (*0-939224-23-2*) John T Reed.

Real Estate Investment Trust. Theodore S. Lynn & Micah Bloomfield. 1088p. 145.00 (*0-7913-1932-6*) Warren Gorham & Lamont.

Real Estate Investment Trusts. New York Institute of Finance Staff. 320p. 1988. 17.95 (*0-13-763228-2*) NY Inst Finance.

***Real Estate Investment Trusts: Structure, Analysis, & Strategy.** Richard T. Garrigan. LC 97-25325. 1997. 70.00 (*0-7863-0002-7*) Irwin Prof Pubng.

Real Estate Investment Trusts Handbook. William A. Kelley, Jr. LC 89-82449. 131p. 1991. Supplement 1991. suppl. ed., text ed. 55.00 (*0-8318-0643-5*, B655); suppl. ed., text ed. 55.00 (*0-8318-0655-9*) Am Law Inst.

Real Estate Investment Trusts Handbook, Suppl. 1992. William A. Kelley, Jr. LC 89-82449. 131p. 1990. pap. text ed. 20.00 (*0-8318-0678-8*, B678) Am Law Inst.

***Real Estate Investment Trusts Handbook, 1996.** Peter M. Fass et al. (Securities Law Ser.). 1995. pap. write for info. (*0-87632-414-6*) Clark Boardman Callaghan.

Real Estate Investments. Fowler. 1996. pap. text ed. 49.00 (*0-15-601939-6*) Profess Pubns.

Real Estate Investments: A Step-by-Step Guide. Charles W. McMullen. LC 80-20704. (Real Estate For Professional Practitioners Ser.). 192p. reprint ed. pap. 54.80 (*0-317-41743-6*, 2023143) Bks Demand.

***Real Estate Investments & How to Make Them.** Milt Tanzer. 1997. pap. 19.95 incl. disk (*0-614-27615-2*) P-H.

Real Estate Investments & How to Make Them. 2nd ed. Milt Tanzer. 352p. 1988. pap. 12.95 (*0-13-762519-7*) P-H.

Real Estate Investments & How to Make Them. 3rd ed. Milt Tanzer. LC 95-25935. 1996. write for info. (*0-13-459777-X*) P-H.

Real Estate Investments & How to Make Them. 3rd ed. Milt Tanzer. 352p. 1996. 24.95 (*0-13-463381-4*) P-H.

Real Estate Investments & How to Make Them: The Only Guide You'll Ever Need. Milt Tanzer. LC 80-15706. (Illus.). 355p. 1981. 34.95 (*0-87624-482-7*, Inst Busn Plan); pap. 10.95 (*0-87624-481-9*, Inst Busn Plan) P-H.

Real Estate Investor & the Federal Income Tax. 2nd ed. Gaylon E. Greer. LC 81-14793. 283p. pap. 80.70 (*0-317-26098-7*, 2025175) Bks Demand.

Real Estate Investor's Answer Book. Jack Cummings. 1994. pap. text ed. 19.95 (*0-07-015052-4*) McGraw.

Real Estate Investor's Answer Book. Jack Cummings. 1994. pap. text ed. 17.95 (*0-07-015152-0*) McGraw.

Real Estate Investor's Complete Handbook. Martin J. Miles. LC 82-351. 572p. 1982. 49.95 (*0-13-763086-7*, Busn) P-H.

Real Estate Investor's Deskbook. annuals 2nd rev. ed. Alvin L. Arnold. LC 87-50237. 825p. (C). 1987. Supplemented annually. suppl. ed. 145.00 (*0-88712-825-4*) Warren Gorham & Lamont.

Real Estate Investor's Deskbook. 2nd rev. ed. Alvin L. Arnold. LC 87-50237. 825p. (C). 1992. suppl. ed. 50.00 (*0-685-55894-0*) Warren Gorham & Lamont.

Real Estate Investor's Deskbook. 2nd rev. ed. Alvin L. Arnold. 1994. text ed. 138.00 (*0-685-69664-2*, REID) Warren Gorham & Lamont.

Real Estate Investor's Master Guide to Real Estate Wealth & Success. Jeff Rickerson. Ed. by Robert B. Rickerson. LC 84-62753. 285p. 1985. 30.00 (*0-933001-00-2*); pap. 25.00 (*0-317-17995-0*) Intl Inst Fin Res.

Real Estate Investor's Tax Guide. 2nd ed. Vernon Hoven. 289p. 1995. pap. 27.95 (*0-7931-1477-2*, 5608-7102, Real Estate Ed) Dearborn Finan.

Real Estate Is the Gold in Your Future. Dempsey J. Travis. LC 87-37177. 216p. 1988. 18.95 (*0-941484-07-6*) Urban Res Pr.

Real Estate Issues. American Society of Real Estate Counselors. 56p. 33.00 (*0-318-13259-1*) Couns Real Estate.

Real Estate Issues in the Health Care Industry: Proceedings of the First Annual Conference of the Health Care Real Estate Institute. Ed. by Ronald S. Barak. (Current Topics in Real Estate Finance & Economics Ser.). 184p. (C). 1996. lib. bdg. 65.00 (*0-7923-9696-0*) Kluwer Ac.

***Real Estate Law.** Michael R. Diamond. LC 97-21662. 1998. write for info. (*0-314-12615-5*) West Pub.

Real Estate Law. Carol K. Irvin & James D. Irvin. 440p. (Orig.). (C). 1990. pap. text ed. 34.00 (*0-89787-917-1*) Gorsuch Scarisbrick.

Real Estate Law. Charles J. Jacobus. (C). 1986. teacher ed. write for info. (*0-8359-6602-X*, Reston) P-H.

***Real Estate Law.** Lawchek Limited, Staff. (Lawchek Personal Legal Sourcebooks). 1997. pap. text ed. 24.95 (*0-02-861763-0*) Macmillan.

Real Estate Law. Nelson. Date not set. teacher ed., pap. text ed. write for info. (*0-314-03376-9*) West Pub.

Real Estate Law. 2nd ed. Benjamin N. Henszey & Ronald M. Friedman. 383p. 1984. Net. text ed. 51.00 (*0-471-88857-5*) Wiley.

***Real Estate Law.** 2nd ed. Jacobus. 1997. text ed. 38.67 (*0-13-631813-4*) P-H.

Real Estate Law. 2nd ed. Charles J. Jacobus. (C). 1985. text ed. 50.00 (*0-8359-6601-1*, Reston) P-H.

Real Estate Law. 3rd ed. Marianne M. Jennings. 775p. 1992. text ed. 55.95 (*0-534-93029-8*) S-W Pub.

Real Estate Law. 3rd ed. George J. Siedel, III. Ed. by Hannan. LC 92-39549. 550p. (C). 1993. text ed. 61.50 (*0-314-01217-6*) West Pub.

Real Estate Law. 4th ed. Marianne M. Jennings. LC 94-28480. 1995. pap. 72.95 (*0-538-84604-6*) S-W Pub.

Real Estate Law. 4th ed. James P. Karp & Elliot I. Klayman. 1997. 39.95 (*0-7931-2260-0*, 15600104, Real Estate Ed) Dearborn Finan.

***Real Estate Law.** 5th ed. Jennings. Date not set. text ed. 65.95 (*0-538-87173-3*) S-W Pub.

Real Estate Law. 8th ed. Robert Kratovil & Raymond J. Werner. 640p. 1983. Student ed. student ed., text ed. 36.33 (*0-686-82022-3*) P-H.

Real Estate Law. 10th ed. Raymond J. Werner & Robert Kratovil. LC 92-13579. 688p. 1992. text ed. 63.00 (*0-13-763475-7*) P-H.

Real Estate Law, Set. 2nd ed. Burke. 1993. 145.00 (*0-316-11781-1*) Little.

Real Estate Law: Concepts & Applications. Theron R. Nelson & Thomas A. Potter. Ed. by Burvikovs. LC 93-36562. 600p. (C). 1994. text ed. 53.25 (*0-314-02824-2*) West Pub.

Real Estate Law & Practice Series, 1992-1993, 11 vols., Set. 1993. pap. 450.00 (*0-685-69482-8*) PLI.

Real Estate Law Digest, 2 vols. 3rd ed. James Douglas et al. 1991. 135.00 (*0-7913-0749-2*); suppl. ed. 51.00 (*0-7913-1193-7*); suppl. ed. 52.50 (*0-685-56393-6*); Supplemented semi-annually. suppl. ed. write for info. (*0-318-68839-5*) Warren Gorham & Lamont.

Real Estate Law for Homeowner & Broker. Margaret C. Jasper. (Legal Almanac Ser.). 98p. 1995. lib. bdg. 22.50 (*0-379-11226-4*) Oceana.

Real Estate Law in California. 9th ed. Arthur G. Bowman & Denny Milligan. 1995. text ed. 56.00 (*0-13-437617-X*) P-H.

Real Estate Law Journal. Ed. by Robert J. Aalberts. 140.00 (*0-685-69650-2*, RELJ) Warren Gorham & Lamont.

Real Estate Law Journal: 1972-1995/96, 25 vols., Set. Bound set. 2,125.00 (*0-8377-9134-0*) Rothman.

Real Estate Law of Texas. Harold F. Thurow. 1991. pap. 35.00 (*0-409-25582-3*) MICHIE.

Real Estate Law of Texas. 11th rev. ed. Harold F. Thurow. 1985. 17.95 (*0-914696-15-7*, KFT1312. T48); pap. 16.95 (*0-914696-17-3*) Hemphill.

Real Estate Law of Texas. 12th ed. Harold F. Thurow. 460p. 1994. ring bd. 115.00 (*0-409-25581-5*); suppl. ed., ring bd. 65.00 (*0-685-74603-8*) MICHIE.

Real Estate Law Report. Alvin L. Arnold. 130.00 (*0-685-69651-0*, RELR) Warren Gorham & Lamont.

Real Estate Law Revision Manual. Dunn. 350p. 1997. pap. text ed. write for info. (*0-314-09848-8*) West Pub.

An Asterisk (*) at the beginning of an entry indicates that the title is appearing in BIP for the first time.

Real Estate Law, with Forms: 85 Pocket Parts, 2 vols. 2nd ed. Maurice E. Park & Dorcas D. Park. LC 80-54847. (Massachusetts Practice Ser.). 1981. 106.00 (0-685-42577-0) West Pub.

Real Estate Leasing in Massachusetts. Ed. by Edward Bloom. LC 94-73529. 1995. ring bd. write for info. (0-944490-81-6) Mass CLE.

Real Estate Leasing Practice Manual. 1116p. 1992. Supplement, 1992. suppl. ed. 50.00 (0-685-55631-X) Warren Gorham & Lamont.

Real Estate Leasing Practice Manual. annuals 1116p. 1992. Supplemented annually. suppl. ed. 185.00 (0-7913-1220-8) Warren Gorham & Lamont.

Real Estate License Examination Review Program for the ASI Exam. Susan Olenick. 62p. 1990. pap. text ed. 59.00 (0-13-291733-5) P-H.

Real Estate License Examinations: Salesperson & Broker. 4th ed. Joseph H. Martin & Eve P. Steinberg. LC 93-4597. 1993. pap. 15.00 (0-671-84835-6) P-H Gen Ref & Trav.

Real Estate License Supercourse. 2nd ed. Garton-Good. 1995. 25.00 (0-02-860024-X) Macmillan.

Real Estate Liens Encumbrances & Secured Transactions. 2nd ed. Stuart J. Faber. 1979. pap. 27.50 (0-89074-065-8) Lega Bks.

Real Estate Limited Partnerships. 3rd ed. Theodore S. Lynn et al. LC 90-28277. (Real Estate Practice Library). 522p. 1991. text ed. 140.00 (0-471-52022-5) Wiley.

Real Estate Listing Magic. Gael Himmah. LC 88-91317. 390p. 1989. 33.00 (0-9600488-3-9) Gael Himmah Pub.

***Real-Estate Loan Getters Kit.** 9th ed. Tyler G. Hicks. 160p. 1998. pap. 100.00 (1-56150-243-X) Intl Wealth.

Real-Estate Loan Getters Kit, 2 bks., Set. 8th ed. Tyler G. Hicks. 160p. 1996. pap. 100.00 (1-56150-193-X) Intl Wealth.

Real Estate Loans. 2nd ed. Clifford W. Marshall et al. (Financial Tables for Better Money Management Ser.). 352p. 1993. pap. 7.95 (0-8120-1618-1) Barron.

Real Estate Management Forms & Letters for Rental Properties. Allen N. Elgart & Cathy S. Kelly. LC 92-2567. 240p. 1993. text ed. 90.00 incl. disk (0-471-57788-X) Wiley.

Real Estate Management Office: Income, Expenses, & Profits. 1,992th ed. 50p. 1992. pap. 30.00 (0-944298-82-6) Inst Real Estate.

Real Estate Management Trainee. Jack Rudman. (Career Examination Ser.: C-667). 1994. pap. 23.95 (0-8373-0667-1) Nat Learn.

Real Estate Manager. Jack Rudman. (Career Examination Ser.: C-689). 1994. pap. 29.95 (0-8373-0689-2) Nat Learn.

Real Estate Market Analysis: Methods & Applications. Ed. by John M. Clapp & Stephen D. Messner. LC 87-15832. 368p. 1988. text ed. 69.50 (0-275-92414-9, C2414, Praeger Pubs) Greenwood.

Real Estate Market Analysis: Supply & Demand Factors. Appraisal Institute Staff. 1993. 25.00 (0-922154-14-7) Appraisal Inst.

Real Estate Market Analysis: Techniques & Applications. Neil G. Carn et al. (Illus.). 368p. (C). 1988. text ed. 51.00 (0-13-763368-8) P-H.

Real Estate Market Analysis & Appraisal. (AIREA Research Ser.: No. 3). 127p. 1988. pap. 14.00 (0-911780-94-7) Appraisal Inst.

Real Estate Marketing. Tom J. Morton & Dean Stout. (C). 1985. teacher ed. write for info. (0-8359-6491-4, Reston) P-H.

Real Estate Math. J. Barry Patchett. Ed. by Rebecca C. Hedrick. 110p. (C). 1989. reprint ed. pap. text ed. 18.95 (0-317-93337-X) PDIL.

Real Estate Math: Explanation, Problems, Solutions. George Gaines, Jr. et al. LC 96-283. (Illus.). 1996. pap. 18.95 (0-7931-1634-1, 1610-0705, Real Estate Ed) Dearborn Finan.

Real Estate Math Made Easy. Dennis S. Tosh, Jr. & Nicholas O. Ordway. (C). 1981. text ed. 20.33 (0-8359-6556-2, Reston) P-H.

Real Estate Math Made Easy: A Step-by-Step Instructional Approach. 2nd ed. Nicholas O. Ordway. 1985. pap. text ed. 42.00 (0-8359-6485-X) P-H.

Real Estate Mathematics: Study Manual & Reference Book. John R. Johnsich. (Illus.). 130p. (Orig.). 1975. pap. text ed. 11.95 (0-914256-03-3) Real Estate Pub.

Real Estate Mathematics: Study Manual & Reference Book. rev. ed. John R. Johnsich. (Illus.). 131p. (Orig.). (C). 1980. pap. 11.95 (0-914256-13-0) Real Estate Pub.

Real Estate Mathematics - Fundamentals & Applications. 2nd ed. Kenneth M. Lusht. 1986. text ed. write for info. (0-538-19680-7, S68) S-W Pub.

Real Estate Money Machine. 4th rev. ed. Wade B. Cook. (Illus.). 210p. 1996. reprint ed. text ed. 24.95 (0-910019-43-6) Lghthse Pub Gp.

Real Estate Office Management. Anthony Schools Corporation Staff. (Real Estate College-Level Ser.). (Illus.). 339p. (C). 1987. pap. text ed. 39.95 (0-941833-04-6) Anthony Schools.

Real Estate Office Management. Real Estate Brokerage Council Staff. 1996. pap. 24.95 (0-7931-1530-2, 19071503, Real Estate Ed) Dearborn Finan.

Real Estate Office Management: People, Functions Systems. 2nd ed. Albert J. Mayer, III. LC 88-31636. (Illus.). 350p. 1988. reprint ed. pap. 23.00 (0-913652-64-4, 113) Realtors Natl.

Real Estate on the Brink: Making Money in Distressed Properties. Skip Lombardo. 225p. 1993. per. 24.95 (1-55738-469-X) Irwin Prof Pubng.

Real Estate Operation Education Designation: Business License Real Estate. Vallie J. Whitfield. LC 77-7338. 37p. 1977. 7.95 (0-930920-05-8) Whitfield Bks.

Real Estate Operation Education Designation: Business License Real Estate. Vallie J. Whitfield. LC 77-7338. 37p. 1977. pap. 3.00 (0-930920-06-6) Whitfield Bks.

***Real Estate Opinion Letter Practice: 1995 Cumulative Supplement.** Robert A. Thompson. 1995. suppl. ed., pap. text ed. 65.00 (0-471-11853-2) Wiley.

Real Estate Periodicals Index, 1981, Vol. 1. Robert A. Munro. Ed. by Munro, John A., Associates, Inc. Staff et al. 118p. (Orig.). 1982. pap. text ed. 60.00 (0-911553-00-2) Munro Assocs.

Real Estate Periodicals Index, 1982, Vol. 2. Robert A. Munro. Ed. by Munro, John A., Associates, Inc. Staff. 135p. (Orig.). 1983. pap. 60.00 (0-911553-01-0) Munro Assocs.

Real Estate Perspectives: An Introduction to Real Estate. 2nd ed. John B. Corgel & Halbert C. Smith. 747p. (C). 1991. text ed. 69.25 (0-256-07914-5) Irwin.

Real Estate Perspectives: An Introduction to Real Estate. 3rd ed. John Corgel & Halbert C. Smith. 768p. (C). 1997. per. 69.25 (0-256-15245-4) Irwin.

Real Estate Perspectives & the Life Insurance Contract: Insurance & Real Estate Perspectives. 2nd ed. Halbert C. Smith. (C). 1994. 34.50 (0-256-17633-7) Irwin.

Real Estate Planning. 3rd ed. Norton L. Steuben. 1989. text ed. 43.75 (0-88277-713-0) Foundation Pr.

Real Estate Planning: Revised Problem & Statutory Supplement. 3rd rev. ed. Norton L. Steuben. (University Casebook Ser.). 211p. 1990. pap. text ed. 13.00 (0-88277-850-1) Foundation Pr.

Real Estate Planning: Teacher's Manual to Accompany Case Study Materials, Problems, Questions & Commentary on the Planning of Real Estate Transactions. 3rd ed. Norton L. Steuben. (University Casebook Ser.). 363p. 1989. pap. text ed. write for info. (0-88277-777-7) Foundation Pr.

Real Estate Poetry to Duplicate & Use, Bk. 1. Alpha Pyramis. 20p. 1985. ring bd. 41.95 (0-913597-82-1) Prosperity & Profits.

Real Estate, Polley Associates: An Introduction to the Profession. 5th ed. Bruce M. Harwood. LC 89-36930. 1990. pap. 14.00 (0-13-763061-1) P-H.

Real Estate Portfolios: Acquision, Management & Disposition. Mark W. Patterson. (Real Estate Practice Library). 392p. 1995. text ed. 130.00 (0-471-58702-8, Pub. by Wiley Law Pubns) Wiley.

Real Estate Practice. Scott Failing. 450p. (C). 1991. pap. text ed. 69.95 (1-878025-17-1) Western Schls.

Real Estate Practice: New Perspectives. Harris Ominsky. 480p. (Orig.). 1996. pap. 29.00 (1-57804-000-0, PBI Pr) PA Bar Inst.

Real Estate Practice in Ontario: Professional Edition. 4th ed. Donahue & Quinn. 336p. 1990. boxed 81.00 (0-409-80571-8) MICHIE.

Real Estate Practice in Ontario: Student Edition. 4th ed. Donahue & Quinn. 328p. 1991. pap. 46.95 (0-409-90620-4) Buttrwrth-Heinemann.

Real Estate Practitioner's Tax Guide. annuals Mark A. Segal. 450p. 1990. ring bd. 135.00 (1-878337-26-2) Knowles Law.

Real Estate Primer see California Real Estate Primer

***Real Estate Principals & Practices.** 5th ed. Arlyne Geschwender. 1997. pap. 20.21 (0-13-778028-1) P-H.

Real Estate Principles. Scott Failing. 450p. (Orig.). (C). 1991. pap. text ed. 69.95 (1-878025-24-4) Western Schls.

***Real Estate Principles.** McIntosh. 1997. text ed. write for info. (0-256-12777-8); student ed., pap. text ed. write for info. (0-256-12778-6) McGraw.

Real Estate Principles. Robert H. Plattner. 607p. (C). 1984. text ed. 48.75 (0-15-575844-6) HB Coll Pubs.

Real Estate Principles. 4th ed. Charles F. Floyd. LC 93-21090. 473p. 1994. 59.95 (0-7931-0520-X, 1515-0104) Dearborn Finan.

Real Estate Principles. 4th ed. Bruce M. Harwood. (C). 1986. teacher ed. write for info. (0-8359-6604-6, Reston) P-H.

Real Estate Principles. 5th ed. Charles F. Floyd & Marcus T. Allen. 544p. 1996. 66.95 (0-7931-1680-5, 15150105, Real Estate Ed) Dearborn Finan.

Real Estate Principles. 7th ed. Bruce M. Harwood & Charles J. Jacobus. LC 95-22860. 1996. text ed. 44.00 (0-13-452111-0) P-H.

Real Estate Principles & Practices. James E. Larsen. Ed. by Bruckner. LC 93-44421. 600p. (C). 1994. text ed. 60.25 (0-314-02823-4) West Pub.

***Real Estate Principles & Practices.** Randall S. Van Reken. 175p. (C). wbk. ed., pap. text ed. write for info. (0-614-24134-0) Gorsuch Scarisbrick.

***Real Estate Principles & Practices.** 4th ed. Palmer. 1997. pap. 29.95 (0-13-777335-8) P-H.

Real Estate Principles & Practices. 4th ed. Ralph A. Palmer. LC 96-28062. 464p. (C). 1996. pap. text ed. 29.95 (0-89787-949-X) Gorsuch Scarisbrick.

Real Estate Principles & Practices. 5th ed. Arlyne Geschwender. (Illus.). 360p. (Orig.). (C). 1996. pap. text ed. 25.50 (0-89787-957-0) Gorsuch Scarisbrick.

Real Estate Principles & Practices. 6th ed. Edmund F. Ficek et al. LC 93-2939. 598p. (C). 1993. text ed. 84.00 (0-02-337151-X, Macmillan Coll) P-H.

Real Estate Principles & Practices. 9th ed. Alfred A. Ring & Jerome Dasso. (Illus.). 752p. 1981. student ed. 29.95 (0-685-03905-6) P-H.

Real Estate Principles & Practices. 10th ed. Alfred A. Ring & Jerome Dasso. 768p. (C). 1985. 45.95 (0-13-765983-0) P-H.

Real Estate Principles & Practices Plus: Harrison's Illustrated. Henry S. Harrison & Barbara L. Drisko. (Illus.). (C). 1994. pap. text ed. 34.95 (0-927054-20-5) H Sq Co.

Real Estate Principles for License Preparation (ASI Version) 4th ed. Dennis S. Tosh, Jr. & Nicholas O. Ordway. 412p. 1990. pap. text ed. 43.00 (0-13-765777-3) P-H.

Real Estate Principles for License Preparation in Mississippi. 2nd ed. Dennis S. Tosh, Jr. & Nicholas O. Ordway. 432p. 1990. pap. text ed. 46.00 (0-13-762899-4) P-H.

Real Estate Problem Loans: Workout Strategies & Procedures. Thomas A. Myers. 500p. 1989. text ed. 80.00 (1-55623-148-2) Irwin Prof Pubng.

Real Estate Professional's Signage Advertising Guidebook. O. M. Allred. LC 89-91590. (Illus.). 85p. (Orig.). 1989. pap. 26.00 (0-936035-06-4) O M Allred.

Real Estate Professionals Tax Guide. Alvin Arnold & Myron Kove. 500p. 1996. 140.00 (0-7913-2647-0) Warren Gorham & Lamont.

Real Estate Property Management. William M. Shenkel. 1995. 46.25 (0-13-501297-X) P-H.

Real Estate Psychology: The Dynamics of Successful Selling. James E. Lumley. LC 81-10473. (Real Estate For Professional Practitioners Ser.). 245p. reprint ed. pap. 69.90 (0-7837-3454-9, 2057780) Bks Demand.

Real Estate Quick & Easy. 10th ed. Roy T. Maloney. (Illus.). 384p. 1990. pap. 18.95 (0-913257-03-6) Dropzone Pr.

Real Estate Reader. Jaffe. (C). pap. text ed. 34.95 (1-878975-45-5) Blackwell Pubs.

Real Estate Recording Guide, 6 vols., Set. Carl R. Ernst. Ed. & Illus. by C. Alexander Ernst. 1996. ring bd. write for info. (0-9649140-0-X) Real Est Guide.

Real Estate Recording Guide, Vol. 1. Carl R. Ernst. (Illus.). 1995. ring bd. write for info. (0-9649140-1-8) Real Est Guide.

Real Estate Recording Guide, Vol. 2. Carl R. Ernst. (Illus.). 1995. ring bd. write for info. (0-9649140-2-6) Real Est Guide.

Real Estate Recording Guide, Vol. 3. Carl R. Ernst. (Illus.). 1995. ring bd. write for info. (0-9649140-3-4) Real Est Guide.

Real Estate Recording Guide, Vol. 4. Carl R. Ernst. (Illus.). 1995. ring bd. write for info. (0-9649140-4-2) Real Est Guide.

Real Estate Recording Guide: A Comprehensive Guide to the Recording of Real Estate Documents, Vol. V. Carl R. Ernst. Ed. & Illus. by C. Alexander Ernst. 400p. 1996. ring bd. write for info. (0-9649140-5-0) Real Est Guide.

Real Estate Recording Guide: A Comprehensive Guide to the Recording of Real Estate Documents, Vol. VI. Carl R. Ernst. Ed. & Illus. by C. Alexander Ernst. 400p. 1996. ring bd. write for info. (0-9649140-6-9) Real Est Guide.

Real Estate Repair & Remodel Cost Guide 1994. 4th ed. Marshall & Swift. 224p. per. 59.95 (1-56842-018-8) Marshall & Swift.

Real Estate Repair & Remodel Guide: Accurate Estimates, Not Guesses - Current Home Improvement Costs. Fred Atkinson. 165p. 1993. write for info. (1-56842-005-6) Marshall & Swift.

Real Estate Resource Book 4-3. Bruce M. Harwood. (C). 1986. student ed. 12.95 (0-317-47529-0) P-H.

Real Estate Review. Ed. by Norman Weinberg. 105.00 (0-685-69665-0, RER) Warren Gorham & Lamont.

Real Estate Review: 1971-1996/97, 26 vols., Set. Bound set. 1,690.00 (0-8377-9135-9) Rothman.

Real Estate Riches Success Kit. 8th ed. Tyler G. Hicks. 466p. 1996. pap. 99.50 (1-56150-156-5) Intl Wealth.

***Real Estate Riches Success Kit.** 9th ed. Tyler G. Hicks. 466p. 1998. pap. 99.50 (1-56150-206-5) Intl Wealth.

Real Estate Sale-Leaseback. Society of Industrial Realtors Staff. 1993. pap. text ed. 25.00 (0-939623-29-3) Soc Industrial Realtors.

Real Estate Sales: Is It the Career for You? Barry Braun. 160p. 1990. pap. 16.95 (0-7737-5353-2) Genl Dist Srvs.

Real Estate Sales Contracts. 2nd ed. Robert E. Schreiner & Robert E. Schreiner, Jr. LC 89-92019. (Illus.). 147p. (Orig.). (C). 1989. pap. text ed. 14.95 (0-9618320-3-7) R E Schreiner.

Real Estate Sales Handbook. 9th ed. LC 73-85708. 210p. (C). 1985. pap. 13.50 (0-913652-01-6) Realtors Natl.

Real Estate Sales Handbook. 10th ed. Ed. by Gail G. Lyons. 273p. 1994. pap. 19.95 (0-7931-0947-7, 1913-2310) Dearborn Finan.

***Real Estate Sales Handbook: Como Superer a La Competencia.** Ed. by Gail G. Lyons. 273p. (SPA.). 1996. pap. 19.95 (0-7931-2151-5, 1913-4401) Dearborn Finan.

Real Estate Sales Manager's Desk Book. Larry L. Sandifar. LC 82-7696. 280p. 1982. 29.95 (0-13-766352-8, Busn) P-H.

Real Estate Salesman. Jack Rudman. (Career Examination Ser.: C-668). 1994. pap. 23.95 (0-8373-0668-X) Nat Learn.

Real Estate Salesman (RES) Jack Rudman. (Admission Test Ser.: ATS-4). 1994. pap. 23.95 (0-8373-5004-2) Nat Learn.

Real Estate, Securities & Syndication Picture Dictionary. Edward Hooper & Darlene Hooper. LC 84-90432. (Illus.). 350p. (Orig.). 1984. pap. 18.95 (0-9613648-0-7) Hooper Pub Co.

Real Estate Securities & Title Insurance Terminology. Intro. by John R. Johnsich. (Orig.). 1980. pap. 6.95 (0-914256-12-2) Real Estate Pub.

Real Estate Software Directory. Mark Baumann & Ted Jones. Ed. by Shirley Bovey & Kammy Senter. 275p. pap. 30.00 (1-56248-009-X) TX A&M Univ Real Estate Ctr.

Real Estate Software Guidelines: Property Management. LC 83-83110. (Real Estate Software Guidelines Ser.). (Illus.). 145p. 1984. ring bd. 39.95 (0-912104-75-9) Inst Real Estate.

Real Estate Super Course. 2nd ed. Garton Good. 1995. pap. 25.00 (0-671-89922-8) PB.

Real Estate Syndication Manual: Investment, Tax & Marketing Strategies. Alvin L. Arnold. 580p. (C). 1992. Supplemented annually. 135.00 (0-88712-176-4) Warren Gorham & Lamont.

Real Estate Syndicator's Handbook. Charles Klotsche. LC 85-8319. 360p. 1985. text ed. 39.95 (0-13-766452-4) P-H.

Real Estate Tax Abatement Practice & Procedure. John M. Lynch. LC 92-81121. 162p. 1992. pap. text ed. 45.00 (0-944490-45-X) Mass CLE.

Real Estate Tax Appeals: Law, Practice & Forms, 3 vols. Patrick J. Rohan. (Real Estate Transactions Ser.). 1984. write for info. (0-8205-1575-2) Bender.

Real Estate Tax Delinquency: Private Disinvestment & Public Response. Robert W. Lake & Thomas E. Fitzgerald, Jr. LC 79-12207. 268p. 1979. 1.00 (0-88285-046-6) Ctr Urban Pol Res.

Real Estate Tax Digest: Federal Income, Estate & Gift Taxes. rev. ed. James A. Douglas et al. LC 83-51782. 464p. 1984. Supplemented semi-annually. suppl. ed. 130.00 (0-7913-0641-0) Warren Gorham & Lamont.

Real Estate Tax Digest: Federal Income, Estate & Gift Taxes, No. 1. rev. ed. James A. Douglas et al. LC 83-51782. 464p. 1991. Supplement, 1991-1. suppl. ed. 42.00 (0-7913-0884-7) Warren Gorham & Lamont.

Real Estate Tax Digest: Federal Income, Estate & Gift Taxes, No. 2. rev. ed. James A. Douglas et al. LC 83-51782. 464p. 1991. Supplement, 1991-2. suppl. ed. 45.00 (0-7913-1027-2) Warren Gorham & Lamont.

Real Estate Tax Exemption for Continuing Education. Alexander N. Charters. LC 76-189508. (Occasional Papers: No. 26). 1972. pap. 2.00 (0-87060-049-4, OCP 26) Syracuse U Cont Ed.

Real Estate Tax Forms. J. Scott Morris. LC 80-84025. 1981. 65.00 (0-316-58382-0) Little.

Real Estate Tax Ideas. 120.00 (0-685-69565-4, RETI) Warren Gorham & Lamont.

Real Estate Tax Law after 1986: Unscrambling the Tax Reform Act of 1986. George M. Yeiter. Ed. by Marie-Louise Crozat. (Illus.). 145p. (Orig.). (C). 1987. pap. 24.95 (0-942037-16-2) M A Enter.

Real Estate Tax Planning. J. Scott Morris. 1977. 65.00 (0-316-58390-1) Little.

Real Estate Tax Sale Manual: How to Research, Bid & Profit at County Tax Sales. Thomas Hendricks. (Illus.). 156p. (Orig.). 1989. pap. 29.95 (0-9623141-7-X) Tax Property.

Real Estate Tax Update Outline (1987) Mark L. Levine. 1997. write for info. (0-318-58317-8) Prof Pubns & Educ.

Real Estate Taxation. Windish. 720p. 1992. 60.00 (0-685-67025-2, 4973) Commerce.

Real Estate Taxes & Abatements Handbook. Robert L. Marzelli. 301p. 1980. 34.00 (0-318-03671-1) Lawyers Weekly.

***Real Estate TaxPak (TM) USA, 6 vols.** Paul M. Marzell. Incl. Residential. (Illus.). 115p. 1996. ring bd. 39.00 (1-889646-00-8); Residential Condominium. (Illus.). 114p. 1996. ring bd. 39.00 (1-889646-01-6); Hotel/Motel/Inn/Bed & Breakfast. (Illus.). 102p. 1996. ring bd. 79.00 (1-889646-02-4); Industrial Building. (Illus.). 112p. 1996. ring bd. 99.00 (1-889646-03-2); Office/Professional Building. (Illus.). 109p. 1996. ring bd. 99.00 (1-889646-04-0); Retail/Commercial Building. (Illus.). 113p. 1996. ring bd. 99.00 (1-889646-05-9); write for info. (1-889646-06-7) Marzell Pub.

Real Estate Terms & Definitions Wordbook. Anthony Schools Corporation Staff. (Real Estate License Course Ser.). 48p. (Orig.). 1994. pap. text ed. 8.00 (0-941833-47-X) Anthony Schools.

Real Estate Timesharing & the Property Tax. Real Estate Timesharing & the Property Staff. Ed. by Stuart M. Bloch. (Lincoln Institute Monograph Ser.: No. 85-4). 115p. reprint ed. pap. 32.80 (0-7837-2159-5, 2042462) Bks Demand.

Real Estate Titles. 2nd ed. New York State Bar Association Staff. Ed. & Pref. by James M. Pedowitz. LC 93-86812. (Illus.). 1216p. 1994. text ed. 95.00 (0-942954-66-1) NYS Bar.

Real Estate Titles. 2nd ed. Ed. by James M. Pedowitz. 65p. 1994. reprint ed. pap. text ed. 25.00 (0-942954-58-0) NYS Bar.

***Real Estate Titles: 1996 Supplement.** 2nd ed. 696p. 1996. ring bd. 50.00 (0-614-26708-0, 52105) NYS Bar.

Real Estate to a Better Future & Financial Independence. Thomas J. Pluskat. 275p. (Orig.). (C). pap. text ed. write for info. (0-9618963-1-0) Innovat Dynamics.

Real Estate Transactions. Burke. 1993. 25.95 (0-316-11773-0) Little.

Real Estate Transactions: Adaptable to Courses Utilizing Goldstein & Korngold's Casebook on Real Estate Transactions. Casenotes Publishing Co., Inc. Staff et al. (Legal Briefs Ser.). (Orig.). 1994. pap. text ed. write for info. (0-87457-207-X, 1621) Casenotes Pub.

Real Estate Transactions: Cases & Materials on Land Transfer, Development & Finance; Statute, Form & Problem Supplement. 3rd ed. Paul Goldstein & Gerald Korngold. LC 93-14767. (University Casebook Ser.). 975p. 1993. text ed. 46.95 (1-56662-064-3) Foundation Pr.

Real Estate Transactions: Structure & Analysis with Forms. Alvin L. Arnold. 1990. ring bd. 140.00 (0-685-69652-9, REIS) Warren Gorham & Lamont.

R

An Asterisk (*) at the beginning of an entry indicates that the title is appearing in BIP for the first time.

R

Real Estate Transactions & Environmental Risks: A Practical Guide. 2nd ed. Donald C. Nanney. 429p. 1992. 79.95 (*0-7816-0255-6*, P7420) Exec Ent Pubns.

***Real Estate Transactions, Cases & Materials on Land Transfer, Development & Finance: Cases & Materials on Land Transfer, Development & Finance.** 3rd rev. ed. Paul Goldstein & Gerald Korngold. LC 97-10268. (University Casebook Ser.). 1002p. 1997. text ed. write for info. (*1-56662-535-1*) Foundation Pr.

Real Estate Transactions, Cases & Materials on Land Transfer, Development & Finance Statute: Form & Problem Supplement To. 3rd ed. Paul Goldstein & Gerald Korngold. (University Casebook Ser.). 200p. 1993. pap. text ed. 11.95 (*1-56662-079-1*) Foundation Pr.

Real Estate Transactions, Cases & Materials on Land Transfer, Development & Finance, Teacher's Guide. 3rd ed. Paul Goldstein & Gerald Korngold. (University Casebook Ser.). 191p. 1993. pap. text ed. write for info. (*1-56662-122-4*) Foundation Pr.

Real Estate Transactions from Kish. Henry F. Lutz. LC 32-813. (University of California Publications in Social Welfare: Vol. 10, No. 3). 32p. reprint ed. pap. 25.00 (*0-317-10207-9*, 2021474) Bks Demand.

Real Estate Transactions System. 2nd ed. John L. Horwich et al. LC 94-9126. 700p. 1995. 1,115.00 (*0-945574-60-6*) State Bar WI CLE Bk Div.

Real Estate Transactions, Tax Planning. Mark L. Levine. 1998. write for info. (*0-317-01848-5*) Prof Pubns & Educ.

***Real Estate Transactions, Tax Planning & Consequences.** Mark L. Levine. 1375p. (C). Date not set. pap. text ed. write for info. (*0-314-21623-5*) West Pub.

Real Estate Transactions, Tax Planning & Consequences. Mark L. Levine. 1390p. (C). 1993. pap. text ed. write for info. (*0-314-02383-6*) West Pub.

Real Estate Transactions, Tax Planning & Consequences: 1995 Edition. Mark L. Levine. 1450p. (C). 1995. pap. text ed. write for info. (*0-314-06362-5*) West Pub.

Real Estate Transfer & Finance Adaptable to Courses Utilizing Nelson & Whitman's Casebook on Real Estate Transfer, Finance, & Development. Casenotes Publishing Co., Inc. Staff. Ed. by Norman S. Goldenberg & Peter Tenen. (Legal Briefs Ser.). (Orig.). (C). 1992. pap. text ed. write for info. (*0-87457-157-X*, 1620) Casenotes Pub.

Real Estate Tycoon's Handbook! Secrets & Essentials of Today's Sharpest Property Magnates. Laurence Leichman. 1995. pap. 14.95 (*0-9636867-1-2*) Leichman Assocs.

Real Estate Valuation: Guide to Investment Strategies. Terry V. Grissom & Julian Diaz. LC 91-10657. (Real Estate Practice Library). 480p. 1991. text ed. 135.00 (*0-471-60087-3*) Wiley.

Real Estate Valuation Colloquium, 1984: A Redefinition of Real Estate Appraisal Precepts & Processes. Real Estate Valuation Colloquium Staff. Ed. by William N. Kinnard, Jr. LC 86-1388. (Lincoln Institute of Land Policy Book Ser.). 415p. reprint ed. pap. 118.30 (*0-7837-3268-6*, 2043287) Bks Demand.

Real Estate Valuation in Litigation. 2nd ed. James D. Eaton. 489p. 1995. 41.25 (*0-911780-65-3*) Appraisal Inst.

Real Estate Valuing, Counseling, Forecasting: Selected Writings of John Robert White. John R. White. 275p. 1984. 17.50 (*0-911780-72-6*) Appraisal Inst.

Real Estate Wealth Building Opportunities. 1987. lib. bdg. 79.95 (*0-8490-3879-0*) Gordon Pr.

Real Estate Wealth Building Opportunities. Russ Von Hoelscher. 357p. 1984. pap. 14.95 (*0-940398-09-5*) Profit Ideas.

Real Estate Workouts & Bankruptcies - 1992. (Real Estate Law & Practice Course Handbook Ser.). 808p. 1992. pap. 70.00 (*0-685-69483-6*) PLI.

Real Estate Workouts & Bankruptcies, 1991. 282p. 1991. pap. text ed. 17.50 (*0-685-49959-6*, N4-4551) PLI.

Real Estate Workouts & Bankruptcies 1993. (Real Estate Law & Practice Course Handbook Ser.: Vols. 389 & 390). 1272p. 1993. 80.00 (*0-685-69754-1*, N4-4574) PLI.

***Real Estates Confronts Reality.** Stefan Swanepoel et al. 160p. 1998. 24.95 (*0-7931-2709-2*, 1907-2301, Real Estate Ed) Dearborn Finan.

Real-Exchange-Rate Variability from 1920-1926 & 1973-1982. Paul De Grauwe et al. LC 85-14308. (Studies in International Finance: No. 56). 50p. 1985. pap. text ed. 11.00 (*0-88165-228-8*) Princeton U Int Finan Econ.

Real Exchange Rates, Devaluation, & Adjustments: Exchange Rate Policy in Developing Countries. Sebastian Edwards. 392p. 1989. 44.00 (*0-262-05039-0*) MIT Pr.

Real Exercise for Real People. Peter Francis. 1996. pap. 14.95 (*0-7615-0331-5*) Prima Pub.

Real Facts about Ethiopia. J. A. Rogers. (Illus.). 34p. 1982. reprint ed. pap. 3.00 (*0-933121-07-5*) Black Classic.

Real Facts of Life: Feminism & the Struggle for Female Sexual Autonomy 1850-1940. Margaret Jackson. Ed. by June Purvis. (Gender & society Series: Feminist Perspectives on the Past & Present). 224p. 1994. 75.00 (*0-7484-0099-0*, Pub. by Tay Francis Ltd UK); pap. 25.00 (*0-7484-0100-8*, Pub. by Tay Francis Ltd UK) Taylor & Francis.

Real Faith. Kenneth E. Hagin. 1970. pap. 1.95 (*0-89276-017-6*) Hagin Ministries.

Real Faith: One of the Classic Faith-Builders. Charles S. Price. 125p. 1972. pap. 8.95 (*0-88270-000-6*) Bridge-Logos.

***Real Faith Never Fails: Correcting (& Detecting) Four Common Faith Mistakes.** Mac Hammond. 1996. pap. 1.00 (*1-57399-031-0*) Mac Hammond.

Real Faith Never Fails: Detecting (& Correcting) Four Common Faith Mistakes. Mac Hammond. 22p. 1993. pap. 1.00 (*1-57399-003-5*) Mac Hammond.

Real Families: From Patriarchs to Prime Time. Curtis W. Dubble. LC 94-41676. (Covenant Bible Study Ser.). 86p. 1995. pap. 5.95 (*0-87178-735-0*) Brethren.

Real Family Stories. Anne Turyn. (Illus.). 24p. (Orig.). 1982. pap. 3.00 (*0-917061-13-6*) Top Stories.

Real Family Values: Keeping the Faith in an Age of Cultural Chaos. Robert Lewis. 1995. 17.99 (*1-885305-22-2*) Multnomah Pubs.

Real Family Values: The Ten Steps to Incorporating Meaningful Ethics into Everyday Life. Mel Krantzler & Patricia B. Krantzler. LC 96-8170. 256p. 1996. 22.95 (*0-8092-3165-4*) Contemp Bks.

***Real Fantasies: Edward Steichen's Advertising Photography.** Patricia A. Johnston. LC 97-3747. 1998. write for info. (*0-520-07020-8*) U CA Pr.

***Real Fantasy.** large type ed. Caroline Anderson. (Mills & Boon Large Print Ser.). 288p. 1997. 22.50 (*0-263-14997-8*) Ulverscroft.

Real Farm. Patricia T. Westfall. 176p. 1991. pap. 7.95 (*0-380-71221-0*) Avon.

Real Farm: Encounters with Perception. Patricia T. Westfall. (Illus.). 192p. (Orig.). 1989. 14.95 (*0-942257-17-0*) New Chapter Pr.

***Real Fast Desserts.** Nigel Slater. LC 96-29312. 224p. 1997. 23.95 (*0-87951-755-7*) Overlook Pr.

Real Fast Food: 350 Recipes Ready-to-Eat in 30 Minutes. Nigel Slater. LC 95-34602. (Illus.). 320p. 1996. 23.95 (*0-87951-642-9*) Overlook Pr.

Real Feelings: Heaven on Earth. Brother Bob. LC 95-71962. (Illus.). 126p. (Orig.). 1996. pap. 10.95 (*0-9644021-3-0*) Peaceful Express.

Real Fighting: Adrenaline Stress Conditioning Through Scenario-Based Training. Peyton Quinn. (Illus.). 192p. 1996. pap. 19.95 (*0-87364-893-5*) Paladin Pr.

Real-Financial Linkages among Open Economies. Ed. by Sven W. Arndt & J. David Richardson. 216p. 1987. 27.50 (*0-262-01096-8*) MIT Pr.

Real Fishermen Are Never Thin. John Davis. (Illus.). 123p. (Orig.). 1993. pap. 7.95 (*0-9635865-0-5*) Pinegrove Pubns.

Real Fishermen Never Lie. John Davis. (Illus.). 123p. (Orig.). 1993. pap. 7.95 (*0-9635865-1-3*) Pinegrove Pubns.

***Real Fishermen Never Wear Suits.** John Davis. (Illus.). 120p. (Orig.). 1996. pap. 7.95 (*0-9635865-3-X*) Pinegrove Pubns.

Real Florida: Key Lime Pies, Worm Fiddlers, a Man Called Frog & Other Endangered Species. Jeff Klinkenberg. Ed. by Jerry Bledsoe. LC 93-71406. (Illus.). 288p. (Orig.). 1993. pap. 14.95 (*1-878086-22-7*) Down Home NC.

Real Food. Joann Grohman. (Illus.). 179p. (Orig.). 1992. pap. 18.95 (*0-9631814-0-8*) Coburn Pr.

Real Food: A Spirituality of the Eucharist. Robert Fabing. LC 93-26902. 144p. (Orig.). 1994. pap. 7.95 (*0-8091-3435-7*) Paulist Pr.

Real Food: Regain Good Health with Natural Fibers the Safe Way! Eat Generously-Lose Weight with Real Food (tm). A Simple, Natural Unrefined Diet...Fat-, Sugar-Free. 4th ed. Myrtle B. Findley. (Illus.). 94p. 1983. reprint ed. pap. 1.00 (*0-9611550-0-0*) Real Food.

Real Food Cookbook (Digest Size) 2nd ed. Ethel H. Renwick. LC 83-48080. 272p. 1983. reprint ed. pap. 10.00 (*0-87983-346-7*) Keats.

***Real Food for People with Diabetes.** Doris Cross & Alice Williams. 304p. 1997. per. 15.00 (*0-7615-1103-2*) Prima Pub.

***Real Food Real Fast: A New & Easy System for Preparing Delicious Nutritious Meals in 12 Minutes or Less.** large type ed. Rico Cavegua. (Illus.). 150p. (Orig.). 1997. pap. 12.95 (*1-890904-00-7*) Ageless Living.

Real Fossils. Carol Benanti. Ed. by Michael Frank. (Real Collections). (Illus.). 32p. (Orig.). (J). (gr. 3-8). pap. 6.95 (*1-880592-06-1*) Pace Prods.

Real Frank Zappa Book. Frank Zappa. 1990. pap. 10.95 (*0-671-70572-5*) S&S Trade.

Real Freedom for All: What (If Anything) Can Justify Capitalism. Philippe Van Parijs. (Oxford Political Theory Ser.). 320p. 1995. 38.00 (*0-19-827905-1*) OUP.

***Real Freedom for All: What (If Anything) Can Justify Capitalism?** Philippe Van Parijs. (Oxford Political Theory Ser.). 344p. 1997. reprint ed. pap. 19.95 (*0-19-829357-7*) OUP.

Real Friends. Ed. by Mac Anderson. (Illus.). 78p. (Orig.). 1989. pap. 7.95 (*0-931089-26-3*) Great Quotations.

Real Friends. Dorothy Hole. 144p. (Orig.). (J). (gr. 5-8). 1994. pap. 2.99 (*0-87406-678-6*) Willowisp Pr.

Real Friends. Susan Sharpe. (J). 1994. lib. bdg. 14.95 (*0-02-782352-0*) S&S Childrens.

Real Function Algebras. Ed. by Kulkarni & Limaye. (Pure & Applied Mathematics Ser.: Vol. 168). 208p. 1992. 125.00 (*0-8247-8653-X*) Dekker.

Real Functions. B. S. Thomson. (Lecture Notes in Mathematics Ser.: Vol. 1170). vii, 229p. 1985. 37.95 (*0-387-16058-2*) Spr-Verlag.

Real Functions: Contemporary Aspects. Vasile Ene. 1995. write for info. (*0-387-60008-6*) Spr-Verlag.

Real Functions - Current Topics. V. Ene. Ed. by A. Dold & F. Takens. (Lecture Notes in Mathematics Ser.: Vol. 1603). 310p. 1995. pap. 57.00 (*3-540-60008-6*) Spr-Verlag.

Real Functions, Abstract Spaces & Orthogonal Series. M. Mikolas. 400p. 1994. 69.00 (*963-05-6652-4*, Pub. by A K HU) Intl Spec Bk.

Real Gardeners' True Confessions. Pat Stone. (Illus.). 176p. (Orig.). 1997. pap. 12.95 (*0-88266-946-X*) Storey Comm Inc.

Real George Washington. Jay A. Parry & Andrew M. Allison. LC 90-5607. (American Classic Ser.). (Illus.). 928p. 1990. 24.95 (*0-88080-013-5*); pap. 19.95 (*0-88080-014-3*) Natl Ctr Constitutional.

Real Ghosts. Daniel Cohen. Ed. by Pat MacDonald. 128p. (J). (gr. 3-6). pap. 2.99 (*0-671-78622-9*, Minstrel Bks) PB.

Real Ghosts Don't Wear Sheets. Don W. Farrant. (Illus.). 80p. (Orig.). (J). 1985. pap. 7.00 (*0-935604-02-2*) Ivystone.

Real Girls Don't Do Maths: Gender & the Construction of Privilege. Ed. by Sue Willis. (C). 1995. pap. 40.00 (*0-7300-0631-X*, ECS807, Pub. by Deakin Univ AT) St Mut.

Real Glasgow Archipelago. Jack Withers. (Illus.). (C). 1993. write for info. (*1-874640-85-8*, Pub. by Argyll Pubng UK) St Mut.

Real Glasgow Archipelago. Jack Withers. (Illus.). 96p. (C). 1993. pap. write for info. (*1-874640-25-4*, Pub. by Argyll Pubng UK) St Mut.

Real God: A Response to Anthony Freeman's God in Us. Richard Harries & Bishop of Oxford. 96p. 1995. pap. 10.95 (*0-264-67384-0*, Pub. by Mowbray-Cassell UK) Morehouse Pub.

Real Gold in the Golden Years. Charles Garrett. LC 94-67196. (Illus.). 150p. 1994. pap. 9.95 (*0-915920-78-6*) Ram Pub.

Real Golfers Don't Take Mulligans. Robert E. Zorn. 1994. pap. 8.95 (*0-9637510-0-X*) Marksmen Pub.

Real Gone. Jim Lewis. (Illus.). 56p. 1994. 15.00 (*0-9631095-2-9*) Artspace Bks.

***Real Good Food.** Nigel Slater. (Illus.). 228p. 1997. pap. 19.95 (*1-85702-370-6*, Pub. by Fourth Estate UK) Trafalgar.

Real Gorgeous: The Truth about Body & Beauty. Kaz Cooke. 288p. (Orig.). 1995. pap. 13.00 (*0-393-31355-7*, Norton Paperbks) Norton.

Real Grandmas Don't Bake Cookies Anymore. Therese McGee. Ed. by Carmelita J. Conn. LC 88-23949. (Illus.). 96p. (Orig.). 1988. pap. text ed. 8.00 (*0-943663-00-8*) San Joaquin Eagle.

Real Grass, Real Heroes. Dom DiMaggio. 320p. 1991. mass mkt. 4.95 (*0-8217-3409-1*, Zebra Kensgtn) Kensgtn Pub Corp.

***Real Guide to Grad School: What You Better Know Before You Choose.** Franca Lingua. 1997. pap. text ed. 19.95 (*0-9630238-0-2*) Lingua Franca.

Real Happily Ever after Book: The Kids' Stuff People. LC 80-80256. (Illus.). (J). (gr. k-3). 1980. pap. 9.95 (*0-913916-66-8*, IP 66-8) Incentive Pubns.

Real Hawaii: Its History & Present Conditions Including the True Story of the Revolution. Lucien Young. LC 77-111760. (American Imperialism: Viewpoints of United States Foreign Policy, 1898-1941 Ser.). 1970. reprint ed. 25.95 (*0-405-02054-6*) Ayer.

***Real Heat: Gender & Race in the Urban Fire Service.** Carol Chetkovich. 304p. (C). 1997. text ed. 50.00 (*0-8135-2409-1*); pap. text ed. 18.95 (*0-8135-2410-5*) Rutgers U Pr.

***Real Hero.** Bird & Falk. (New Trend Fiction C Ser.). (J). 1993. pap. text ed. write for info. (*0-582-80038-2*, Pub. by Longman UK) Longman.

Real Heroes. Marilyn Kaye. 160p. (J). (gr. 4). 1994. reprint ed. pap. 3.50 (*0-380-72283-6*, Camelot) Avon.

Real Heroes Eat Pizza. Tim Hansel. LC 94-35154. (Illus.). 128p. (Orig.). (J). (gr. 5-7). 1995. pap. 6.99 (*0-7814-0197-6*, Chariot Bks) Chariot Victor.

Real Heroes of Business - & Not a CEO among Them. Schlesinger Fromm. 320p. 1994. 24.95 (*0-385-42555-4*) Doubleday.

***Real High School Handbook.** Lieberman. 1997. pap. 9.95 (*0-395-79760-8*) HM.

***Real History: Reflections on Historical Practice.** Martin Bunzl. LC 97-9101. (Philosophical Issues in Science Ser.). (C). 1998. pap. write for info. (*0-415-15962-8*); text ed. write for info. (*0-415-15961-X*) Routledge.

Real History of the Rosicrucians. Edward Wait. 311p. 1960. reprint ed. spiral bd. 17.50 (*0-7873-0917-6*) Hlth Research.

Real History of the Rosicrucians, Vol. 20. Arthur E. Waite. LC 76-53632. (Illus.). 456p. 1982. reprint ed. lib. bdg. 23.95 (*0-89345-018-9*, Spir Sci Lib) Garber Comm.

Real Hole. Beverly Cleary. LC 85-18815. (J). 1996. pap. 4.95 (*0-688-14741-0*, Mulberry) Morrow.

Real Hole. rev. ed. Beverly Cleary. LC 85-18815. (Illus.). 32p. (J). (ps-1). 1986. 11.95 (*0-688-05850-7*, Morrow Junior); lib. bdg. 11.88 (*0-688-05851-5*, Morrow Junior) Morrow.

Real Horror. Franklin W. Dixon. Ed. by Anne Greenberg. (Hardy Boys Casefiles Ser.: No. 71). 160p. (Orig.). (J). (gr. 6 up). 1993. mass mkt. 3.99 (*0-671-73107-6*, Archway) PB.

Real Ideal: Poems. Joel Lipman. (Illus.). 23p. (Orig.). 1996. pap. 6.00 (*0-935350-59-4*) Luna Bisonte.

Real Illusions. Russell Haley. LC 84-14866. 132p. 1985. pap. 7.95 (*0-8112-0929-6*, NDP586) New Directions.

Real Image: Poems. Manuel S. De Bustamante. LC 91-11822. 64p. (Orig.). 1991. pap. 7.50 (*0-931832-84-5*) Fithian Pr.

***Real Indian Cookery Course.** Veena Chopra. 1997. pap. text ed. 14.95 (*0-572-02270-0*, Pub. by W Foulsham UK) Trans-Atl Phila.

Real Inspector Hound: And Other Entertainments. Tom Stoppard. 256p. 1993. pap. 11.95 (*0-571-16571-0*) Faber & Faber.

Real Inspector Hound & after Magritte. Tom Stoppard. LC 75-995. 106p. 1970. pap. 8.95 (*0-8021-5205-8*, Grove) Grove-Atltic.

Real Inspector Hound & Other Entertainments. Tom Stoppard. 256p. (Orig.). 1993. 19.95 (*0-571-16569-9*) Faber & Faber.

Real Interest Parity, Dynamic Convergence & the European Monetary System. fac. ed. Andrew G. Haldane & Mahmood Pradhan. LC 93-61984. (Bank of England, Work Paper Ser.: No. 1). (Illus.). 22p. 1992. pap. 25.00 (*0-7837-7649-7*, 2047402) Bks Demand.

Real Interest Rates & Investment & Borrowing Strategy. Peter S. Spiro. LC 89-3864. 238p. 1989. text ed. 59.95 (*0-89930-453-2*, SIJ, Quorum Bks) Greenwood.

Real Intimacy. Mike Devine & David Routh. 1991. pap. 5.95 (*0-9625096-0-4*) Starside Pub.

Real Intimacy: Extended Lovemaking in the Committed Relationship. Mike Devine & David Routh. (Illus.). 74p. 1989. reprint ed. pap. 5.95 (*0-685-29990-2*) Starside Pub.

Real Ireland: People & Landscape. Brendan Kennelly. (Illus.). 110p. 1984. 11.95 (*0-86281-053-1*, Pub. by Appletree Pr IE) Irish Bks Media.

Real Is Not the Rational. Joan Stambaugh. LC 85-14673. (SUNY Series in Buddhist Studies). 130p. (Orig.). (C). 1986. text ed. 49.50 (*0-88706-166-4*); pap. text ed. 16.95 (*0-88706-167-2*) State U NY Pr.

Real Issue. William A. White. LC 72-98603. (Short Story Index Reprint Ser.). 1977. 19.95 (*0-8369-3177-7*) Ayer.

Real Italians: A Study of European Psychology. Carlo Sforza. LC 42-14340. reprint ed. 20.00 (*0-404-05758-6*) AMS Pr.

Real Japanese Question. Kiyoshi K. Kawakami. Ed. by Roger Daniels. LC 78-54819. (Asian Experience in North America Ser.). 1979. reprint ed. lib. bdg. 23.95 (*0-405-11275-0*) Ayer.

Real Jazz. Hughes Panassie. LC 73-13328. 284p. 1973. reprint ed. text ed. 59.75 (*0-8371-7123-7*, PARJ, Greenwood Pr) Greenwood.

Real Jesus Is the Christ of Faith. Luke T. Johnson. LC 95-19885. 192p. 1996. 22.00 (*0-06-064177-0*) Harper SF.

Real Jesus Is the Christ of Faith. Luke T. Johnson. 1997. pap. 12.00 (*0-06-064166-5*) Harper SF.

Real Johnny Appleseed. Julie Lawlor. LC 94-22010. (Illus.). 63p. (J). (gr. 4-8). 1994. lib. bdg. 13.95 (*0-8075-6909-7*) A Whitman.

***Real Justice: 101 Family Group Conferences.** Ted Wachtel. LC 96-92917. 200p. (Orig.). 1997. pap. text ed. 25.00 (*0-9633887-3-8*) Pipers Pr.

Real Justice Training Manual: Coordinating Family Group Conferences. John McDonald et al. LC 96-116467. (Illus.). 128p. (Orig.). (C). 1995. pap. text ed. 25.00 (*0-9633887-2-X*) Pipers Pr.

Real Kids - Real Science Books: Entomology, Marine Biology, Invertebrate Zoology, Entomology. Ellen Doris. (Real Kids/Real Science Ser.). 1993. 16.95 (*0-500-19004-6*) Thames Hudson.

Real Kids - Real Science Books: Entomology, Marine Biology, Invertebrate Zoology, Invertebrate Zoology. Ellen Doris. (Real Kids/Real Science Ser.). 1993. 16.95 (*0-500-19005-4*) Thames Hudson.

Real Kids - Real Science Books: Entomology, Marine Biology, Invertebrate Zoology, Marine Biology. Ellen Doris. (Real Kids/Real Science Ser.). 1993. 16.95 (*0-500-19007-0*) Thames Hudson.

***Real Kids, Real Adventures.** Deborah Morris. LC 97-5391. 112p. (J). 1997. mass mkt. 3.99 (*0-425-15975-2*) Berkley Pub.

***Real Kids, Real Adventures.** Deborah Morris. LC 97-5391. 112p. (J). 1997. mass mkt. 3.99 (*0-425-16043-2*) Berkley Pub.

***Real Kids Real Adventures No. 1: Shark Attack.** Deborah Morris. (Real Kids, Real Adventures Ser.). 112p. (J). 1997. mass mkt. 3.99 (*0-425-15938-8*) Berkley Pub.

Real King Arthur: A History of Post-Roman Britannia, A.D. 410-A.D. 593. P. F. Turner. 480p. 1993. pap. 29.95 (*0-9637434-2-2*) SKS Publishing.

***Real Knockouts: The Physical Feminism of Women's Self-Defense.** Martha McCaughey. LC 97-4774. 280p. 1997. 45.00 (*0-8147-5512-7*) NYU Pr.

***Real Knockouts: The Physical Feminism of Women's Self-Defense.** Martha McCaughey. LC 97-4774. 280p. 1997. pap. 18.95 (*0-8147-5577-1*) NYU Pr.

***Real Knockouts: The Physical Feminism of Women's Self-Defense.** Martha McCaughey. 1997. pap. 18.95 (*0-614-27683-7*) NYU Pr.

Real Knowing: New Versions of the Coherence Theory. Linda M. Alcoff. 272p. 1996. 35.00 (*0-8014-3047-X*) Cornell U Pr.

***Real Lace.** Stephen Birmingham. 336p. 1997. pap. 17.95 (*0-8156-0509-9*) Syracuse U Pr.

***Real Learning, Real Work.** Adria Steinberg. LC 97-14659. (Transforming Teaching Ser.). 192p. (C). 1997. pap. write for info. (*0-415-91793-X*); text ed. write for info. (*0-415-91792-1*) Routledge.

Real Lies. Craig McGregor. LC 87-10770. 126p. (Orig.). 1987. pap. 14.95 (*0-7022-2088-4*, Pub. by Univ Queensland Pr AT) Intl Spec Bk.

Real Life. Valerie Freireich. Date not set. pap. 5.99 (*0-451-45549-5*, ROC) NAL-Dutton.

***Real Life.** Contrib. by Christopher P. Nichols et al. 29p. (J). (gr. 10-12). 1996. pap. 3.00 (*0-87129-663-2*, R59) Dramatic Pub.

Real Life. Karl Tate. (Illus.). 118p. (Orig.). 1983. pap. 2.95 (*0-9609796-1-1*) K R Holmes.

Real Life: A Novel. France Daigle. 160p. Date not set. pap. text ed. 10.95 (*0-88784-561-4*, Pub. by Hse of Anansi Pr CN) Genl Dist Srvs.

Real Life: My Best Friend Died. Alan Gelb. Ed. by Lisa Clancy. (Real Life, Real Answers Ser.). 209p. (Orig.). (J). (gr. 6 up). 1995. pap. 3.50 (*0-671-87273-7*, Archway) PB.

An Asterisk (*) at the beginning of an entry indicates that the title is appearing in BIP for the first time.

R

Real Life: Ten Stories of Aging. Ed. by Patrick L. McKee & Jon Thiem. 192p. 1994. 29.95 (0-87081-354-4); pap. 17.50 (0-87081-355-2) Univ Pr Colo.

Real Life Citizens. (YA). (gr. 9-12). Date not set. pap. 6.75 (0-590-35496-5) Scholastic Inc.

Real-Life Construction Set. Gary Bryant. 50p. 1993. pap. 4.95 (1-881442-03-9) New Legends Pub.

Real Life Decisions. (YA). (gr. 9-12). Date not set. pap. 6.75 (0-590-35491-4) Scholastic Inc.

Real Life Dictionary of the Law: Taking the Mystery Out of Legal Language. Gerald Hill et al. LC 95-12249. 480p. 1995. 19.95 (1-881649-74-1) Genl Pub Grp.

***Real Life Dictionary of the Law: Taking the Mystery Out of Legal Language.** Gerald Hill & Kathleen Hill. 480p. 1997. pap. 12.95 (1-57544-054-7) Genl Pub Grp.

Real Life Drama. Wendy Smith. LC 91-44170. 482p. 1992. pap. 14.95 (0-8021-3300-2, Grove) Grove-Atltic.

***Real-Life Drama for Real, Live Students: A Collection of Monologues, Duet Acting Scenes, & a Full-Length Play.** Judy T. Mecca. Ed. by Jan Keeling. (Illus.). 112p. 1997. pap. text ed. 10.95 (0-86530-352-5) Incentive Pubns.

Real Life Economics: Understanding Wealth Creation. Ed. by Paul Ekins & Manfred Max-Neef. LC 92-8827. 432p. (C). 1992. pap. 24.95 (0-415-07977-2, A9696) Routledge.

Real Life Employment. (J). (gr. 6-9). Date not set. pap. 6.75 (0-590-35486-8) Scholastic Inc.

Real Life Employment. (YA). (gr. 9-12). Date not set. pap. 8.75 (0-590-35489-2) Scholastic Inc.

Real Life English ESL. (J). Date not set. pap. 6.75 (0-590-35481-7) Scholastic Inc.

Real-Life Ghost Stories. Karla Dougherty. 128p. (J). (gr. 5-8). 1994. pap. 2.99 (0-87406-661-1) Willowisp Pr.

Real Life Guide for the Second Time Bride. Anita T. Williams. (Illus.). 172p. 1988. pap. 11.95 (0-945633-00-9) Bounty Pr Inc.

***Real Life Guide to Graduate School.** Pam Richardson. (Real Life Ser.). 320p. (Orig.). 1997. 29.95 (1-890586-05-6) Pipeline Pr.

***Real Life Guide to Internet Resources for Graduates.** (Real Life Ser.). 1997. 24.95 (1-890586-04-8) Pipeline Pr.

***Real Life Guide to Life after College.** Michael Hoffman et al. Ed. by Pam Richardson. (Real Life Ser.). 230p. (Orig.). 1997. 24.95 (1-890586-00-5) Pipeline Pr.

Real-Life Guide to Organizational Change. George Blair & Sandy Meadows. LC 96-8723. 200p. 1996. text ed. 59.95 (0-566-07711-6, Pub. by Gower UK) Ashgate Pub Co.

***Real Life Guide to Personal Finance after College.** Ed. by Pam Richardson. (Real Life Ser.). 272p. (Orig.). 1997. 21.95 (1-890586-01-3) Pipeline Pr.

***Real Life Guide to Starting Your Career.** Michael Hoffman. Ed. by Pam Richardson. (Real Life Ser.). 288p. (Orig.). 1997. pap. 21.95 (1-890586-02-1) Pipeline Pr.

***Real-Life Handicapping: An Eclectic Horseplayers Year at the Track.** Dave Litfin. (Illus.). 190p. (Orig.). 1997. per., pap. 25.00 (0-933944-18-7) City Miner Bks.

***Real Life Investing Guide: How to Buy Whatever You Want, Save for Retirement, & Take the Vacation of Your Dreams--While You're Still Young.** Kenan Pollack & Eric Heighberger. 1997. pap. text ed. 12.95 (0-07-050319-2) McGraw.

Real-Life Learning & Sunday School. 40p. (Orig.). pap. 4.95 (0-87510-304-9) Christian Sci.

Real Life Macintosh Adventures. Lorilee Sadler & Alan Eliason. 464p. (C). 1993. pr. 33.35 (0-697-20716-1) Bus & Educ Tech.

Real Life Marriage. Lucy Guernsey & Dennis Guernsey. LC 87-25319. 202p. 1987. pap. 12.95 (0-8499-3095-2) Hope Pub Hse.

Real Life Math. (J). (gr. 6-9). Date not set. pap. 6.75 (0-590-35476-0) Scholastic Inc.

Real Life Math. (J). Date not set. teacher ed., pap. 8.75 (0-590-35479-5) Scholastic Inc.

***Real Life Math Investigations: 30 Activities That Apply Mathematical Thinking to Real-Life Situa.** Martin Lee. (J). 1997. pap. text ed. 10.95 (0-590-96384-8) Scholastic Inc.

Real Life Math Mysteries. Mary F. Washington. 106p. 1995. pap. 19.95 (1-882664-14-0) Prufrock Pr.

Real-Life Math Problems. Mark Lllingworth. 1996. pap. 15.95 (0-590-48804-X) Scholastic Inc.

Real-Life Monsters. Walt Disney Productions Staff. (Walt Disney's Fun-to-Learn Library Ser.: Vol. 6). (Illus.). 44p. (J). (gr. 1-6). 1983. reprint ed. 3.49 (0-9619525-7-1) Advance Pubs.

Real Life of Alejandro Mayta. Mario Vargas Llosa. Tr. by Alfred Mac Adam. 310p. 1986. 16.95 (0-374-24776-5) FS&G.

Real Life of Mary Ann Evans: George Eliot, Her Letters & Fiction. Rosemarie Bodenheimer. (Illus.). 320p. 1994. 37.50 (0-8014-2988-9) Cornell U Pr.

Real Life of Mary Ann Evans: George Eliot, Her Letters & Fiction. Rosemarie Bodenheimer. (Illus.). 320p. 1996. pap. 15.95 (0-8014-8184-8) Cornell U Pr.

Real Life of Sebastian Knight. Vladimir Nabokov. LC 59-9489. 1959. 16.00 (0-8112-0327-1) New Directions.

Real Life of Sebastian Knight. Vladimir Nabokov. LC 59-9489. 1977. pap. 9.95 (0-8112-0644-0, NDP432) New Directions.

Real Life of Sebastian Knight. Vladimir Nabokov. 1992. pap. 12.00 (0-679-72726-4, Vin) Random.

Real Life One Hundred One: The Graduates Survival Guide. Susan Kleinman. 1992. pap. 9.95 (0-942361-44-X) MasterMedia Pub.

***Real-Life Problem Solving: A Collaborative Approach to Interdisciplinary Learning.** Beau F. Jones et al. LC 96-39391. (APA Psychology in the Classroom Ser.). 1997. pap. 17.95 (1-55798-294-5) Am Psychol.

Real Life Reading. (J). pap. 3.93 (0-590-34160-X) Scholastic Inc.

Real Life Reading. (YA). (gr. 9-12). Date not set. pap. 6.75 (0-590-35466-3) Scholastic Inc.

Real Life, Real Faith: Being Christian in Today's World. Bill Thomason. 176p. 1994. pap. 15.00 (0-8170-1218-4) Judson.

Real Life, Real People. (Word in Life Priorities for Living Ser.). 192p. 1995. pap. 9.99 (0-8407-2099-8) Nelson.

***Real Life, Real Spirituality: For Busy People Who Want to Pray.** Judy Esway. LC 96-60697. 120p. (Orig.). 1997. pap. 9.95 (0-89622-706-5) Twenty-Third.

Real-Life Resumes That Work! On Line Resources & Job-Winning Resumes. Bob Stirling & Pat Morton. (Career Works). 176p. 1995. pap. 11.00 (1-880030-43-8) DBM Pub.

Real-Life Scenic Techniques for Model Railroaders. Carl Caiati. (Illus.). 144p. 1987. pap. 14.95 (0-8306-2765-0, NO. 2765) McGraw-Hill Prof.

Real-Life Science: Classroom Experiments. Frank Schaffer Publications, Inc. Staff. (Middle School Bks.). (Illus.). 1996. wbk. ed. 10.95 (0-7647-0022-7, FS-10198) Schaffer Pubns.

Real-Life Science: Outdoor Experiments. Frank Schaffer Publications, Inc. Staff. (Middle School Bks.). (Illus.). 1996. wbk. ed. 10.95 (0-7647-0051-0, FS-10203) Schaffer Pubns.

Real-Life Science: Take-Home Experiments. Frank Schaffer Publications, Inc. Staff. (Middle School Bks.). (Illus.). 1996. wbk. ed. 10.95 (0-7647-0019-7, FS-10195) Schaffer Pubns.

Real Life Selection Chinese Version - Simplified Characters: Excerpts From What is Heard in American Daily Life. Dee G. Davis. 96p. (CHI.). 1989. reprint ed. pap. 5.00 (0-929350-39-1) Am Spoken English.

Real Life Selections 1-14 Japanese Version: Excerpts from What Is Heard in American Daily Life. Dee G. Davis. 89p. (JPN.). 1989. reprint ed. pap. 5.00 (0-929350-41-3) Am Spoken English.

Real Life Selections 1-14 Spanish Version: Ingles Hablado - Selecciones de la Vida Real 1-41 Excerpts from What Is Heard in American Daily Life. Dee G. Davis. 73p. (SPA.). 1989. reprint ed. pap. 5.00 (0-929350-42-1) Am Spoken English.

Real Life Selections 1-41 Chinese Version in Traditional Characters: Excerpts From What Is Heard in American Daily Life. Dee G. Davis. 96p. (CHI.). 1989. reprint ed. pap. 5.00 (0-929350-40-5) Am Spoken English.

Real Life System Administration with Solaris. Mary Morris. 1994. pap. text ed. 27.75 (0-13-125543-6) P-H.

Real Life, True Love. Mark Sungar. LC 91-75208. 128p. 1991. pap. 5.95 (0-9630185-1-5) Starboard Pr.

Real Life Windows 95. Dan Gookin. 600p. 1995. pap. 24.99 (1-56884-483-2) IDG Bks.

Real Life Windows 95 Bundle with Mousepad. 1995. pap. 24.99 (1-56884-849-8) IDG Bks.

Real Life Writing. (J). (gr. 6-9). Date not set. pap. 6.75 (0-590-35471-X) Scholastic Inc.

Real Life 101: Almost Surviving Your First Year Out of College. rev. ed. Susan Kleinman. 288p. 1989. 19.95 (0-942361-11-3); pap. 9.95 (0-942361-13-X) MasterMedia Pub.

Real Linear Algebra. Fekete. (Pure & Applied Mathematics Ser.: Vol. 91). 456p. 1985. 145.00 (0-8247-7238-5) Dekker.

Real Little Bunny: A Sequel to The Velveteen Rabbit. Jennifer Greenway. LC 92-37149. (Illus.). 40p. (J). 1993. 14.95 (0-8362-4936-4) Andrews & McMeel.

Real Live Dinosaur & Other Stories. Kenneth Lillington. (Children's Paperbacks Ser.). (Illus.). 144p. (J). (gr. 3-7). 1992. pap. 4.95 (0-571-16318-1) Faber & Faber.

***Real Live Missionary.** 48p. 1984. 2.99 (0-8341-0882-8) Nazarene.

Real Live Monsters! Ellen Schecter. LC 94-23276. (Ready-to-Read Ser.). (Illus.). 48p. (J). (gr. 1-3). 1995. pap. 3.99 (0-553-37574-1, Bank St) BDD Bks Young Read.

Real Live Monsters! Ellen Schecter. LC 96-6345. (Bank Street Ready-to-Read Ser.). (Illus.). (J). 1996. lib. bdg. 17.27 (0-8368-1620-X) Gareth Stevens Inc.

***Real Live Nude Girl: Chronicles of Sex-Positive Culture.** Carol Queen. LC 96-50998. 200p. (Orig.). 1997. pap. 14.95 (1-57344-073-6) Cleis Pr.

Real Live Science: Top Scientists Present Amazing Activities Any Kid Can Do. Jay Ingram. (Illus.). 48p. (J). (gr. 4 up). 1992. pap. 9.95 (0-920775-87-X, Pub. by Greey dePencier CN); text ed. 16.95 (1-895688-00-0, Pub. by Greey dePencier CN) Firefly Bks Ltd.

***Real Live Science: Top Scientists Present Amazing Activities Any Kid Can Do.** Jay Ingram. (YA). (gr. 4 up). 1997. reprint ed. pap. 9.95 (0-614-28745-6) FS&G.

Real Lives: Eleven Teenagers Who Don't Go to School. Ed. & Intro. by Grace Llewellyn. (Illus.). 320p. (Orig.). (YA). (gr. 7-12). 1993. pap. 17.00 (0-9629591-3-8, LC32.R) Lowry Hse.

Real Log Cabin. Harry Drabik. (Illus.). 167p. 1994. pap. 14.95 (0-931714-51-6) Nodin Pr.

***Real Love.** Beatles. 3.95 (0-7935-6654-1) H Leonard.

Real Love: The Best of the Simon & Kirby Romance Comics. Simon & Schuster Staff. (Illus.). 1990. pap. 12.95 (0-913035-63-7) Eclipse Bks.

Real Love: The Ultimate Dating, Marriage & Sex Question Book. Mary B. Bonacci. 322p. 1996. pap. text ed. 12.95 (0-89870-613-0) Ignatius Pr.

Real Love by Appointment. Marie L. Jordan. LC 84-24207. 1986. 13.95 (0-87949-247-3) Ashley Bks.

Real Magic. Wayne W. Dyer. 368p. 1993. mass mkt. 5.99 (0-06-109150-2, Harp PBks) HarpC.

Real Magic: An Introductory Treatise on the Basic Principles of Yellow Magic. Isaac Bonewits. LC 88-13099. 186p. 1989. pap. 12.95 (0-87728-688-4) Weiser.

Real Magnet Book. Mae Freeman. (J). (gr. k-3). 1970. pap. 1.75 (0-590-01660-1) Scholastic Inc.

Real Majority. Ben Wattenberg. 1992. pap. 12.95 (1-55611-297-1, Primus Lib Contemp) D I Fine.

Real Majority: Nineteen Seventy-Six. Richard M. Scammon. 1976. 1.00 (1-55614-102-5) U of SD Gov Res Bur.

Real Majority: Nineteen Seventy-Two. Richard M. Scammon. 1972. 1.00 (1-55614-103-3) U of SD Gov Res Bur.

Real Majority, Media Minority: The Costs of Sidelining Women in Reporting. Laura Flanders. LC 96-52246. 275p. (Orig.). 1997. pap. 16.95 (1-56751-090-6); lib. bdg. 29.95 (1-56751-091-4) Common Courage.

Real Man. Edwin Cole. 1993. pap. 10.99 (0-8407-6974-1) Nelson.

Real Man & Other Stories. Shylah Boyd. Ed. by Margaret Mirabelli. 152p. 1990. 17.95 (0-945167-27-X) British Amer Pub.

***Real Management for Real People.** Lloyd M. Smigel. LC 97-26167. 264p. 1997. pap. 15.00 (1-56565-814-0, Extension Pr) Lowell Hse.

Real Marijuana Danger. Malcolm E. Smith. 256p. 1981. 9.95 (0-936066-02-4) Suffolk Hse.

Real Markets: Social & Political Issues of Food Reform. Ed. by Cynthia Hewitt de Alcantara. LC 92-41261. 1993. 37.50 (0-7146-4094-8, Pub. by F Cass Pubs UK) Intl Spec Bk.

***Real Marriage Material.** Jodi O'Donnell. (Romance Ser.). 1997. mass mkt. 3.25 (0-373-19213-4, 1-192137) Silhouette.

***Real Matter.** David Robertson. LC 96-50029. 182p. 1997. 39.95 (0-87480-533-3); pap. 15.95 (0-87480-534-1) U of Utah Pr.

Real McCoy. Patricia Knoll. (Romance Ser.). 1993. pap. 2.89 (0-373-03264-1, 1-03264-8) Harlequin Bks.

Real McCoy, I. (Illus.). 5.95 (0-9600678-3-3) P Coates.

Real McCoy, II. (Illus.). 7.95 (0-685-77478-3) P Coates.

Real McCoy: African-American Invention & Innovation, 1619-1930. Portia James. LC 89-42810. (Illus.). 100p. (C). 1990. pap. 19.95 (0-87474-557-8) Smithsonian.

Real McCoy: The Bi-Centennial Price Guide. (Illus.). 1976. 5.95 (0-9600678-6-8) P Coates.

Real McCoy: The Life of an African-American Inventor. Wendy Towle. 32p. (J). (ps-3). 1995. pap. 4.95 (0-590-48102-9) Scholastic Inc.

Real Me. Betty Miles. 124p. (J). (gr. 4-7). 1978. pap. 2.75 (0-380-00347-3, Camelot) Avon.

Real Me, Real God: One Hundred Short Stories of Faith, Life & Reality. Wynne Gillis. LC 94-96527. 100p. 1994. pap. 7.95 (0-9643670-0-9) W Gillis.

Real Meat Cookbook. Frances Bissell. (Illus.). 384p. 1994. 34.95 (0-7011-3645-6, Pub. by Chatto & Windus UK) Trafalgar.

***Real Men: Daily Nuggets to Inspire Your Walk As a Real Man in a World of Males.** Robert E. Mills. LC 96-92760. 175p. (Orig.). 1997. pap. 7.99 (0-9655593-0-0) R E M Mktg.

Real Men Belch Downwind: Modern Etiquette for the Primitive Man. Mike Nichols. Ed. by Mike Towle. (Illus.). 142p. 1993. pap. 6.95 (1-56530-054-8) Summit TX.

Real Men Don't Bond: How to Be a Real Man in an Age of Whiners. Bruce Feirstein. 112p. (Orig.). 1992. mass mkt. 6.99 (0-446-39463-7) Warner Bks.

***Real Men Don't Get Lost & Other Oddities of Life.** Tim Swavely. (Illus.). 120p. (Orig.). 1996. pap. 10.50 (0-9655346-0-X) Off Wall Pub Co.

***Real Men Don't Get Lost & Other Oddities of Life.** Tim Swavely. (Illus.). 120p. 1996. pap. 12.50 (0-614-26654-8) Off Wall Pub Co.

Real Men Don't Vacuum: And Other Misguided Stereotypes That Cause Conflict in Relationships. J. S. Gelb. 77p. (Orig.). 1991. pap. 9.95 (1-55852-055-4) Natl Pr Pubns.

***Real Men Have Feelings, Too.** Gary J. Oliver. (Men of Integrity Ser.). 288p. 1997. pap. 11.99 (0-8024-7133-1) Moody.

Real Men Have Feelings Too: Regaining a Male Passion for Life. Gary J. Oliver. (Men of Integrity Ser.). 1993. text ed. 18.99 (0-8024-7125-0) Moody.

Real Men Pray Vol. 28, No. 2: Prayer Thoughts for Husbands & Fathers. Thomas Couser. 304p. 1996. pap. 12.99 (0-570-04849-4) Concordia.

Real Men Wear Boxer Shorts. Dewey Friedel. 182p. 1995. pap. 8.99 (1-56043-847-9) Destiny Image.

Real Men Worship. LaMar Boschman. 200p. (Orig.). 1996. pap. 10.99 (0-89283-936-8, Vine Bks) Servant.

Real Menstrual Cycle. Doreen Asso. 214p. 1983. pap. text ed. 35.00 (0-471-90175-X) Wiley.

Real Menstrual Cycle. Doreen Asso. LC 83-5890. (Illus.). 230p. reprint ed. pap. 65.60 (0-8357-4559-7, 2037461) Bks Demand.

Real Mexico. E. Fyfe. 1976. lib. bdg. 59.95 (0-8490-2501-X) Gordon Pr.

Real Moments. Barbara De Angelis. LC 94-11593. 272p. 1994. 21.95 (0-385-31068-4) Delacorte.

Real Moments. Barbara De Angelis. 288p. 1995. reprint ed. pap. 10.95 (0-440-50729-4, Dial Pr) Dell.

Real Moments for Lovers. Barbara De Angelis. 112p. 1995. 14.95 (0-385-31429-9) Delacorte.

***Real Moments for Lovers.** Barbara De Angelis. 112p. 1997. pap. 8.95 (0-440-50778-2) Dell.

Real Moments for Lovers. Barbara De Angelis. 1997. pap. 8.95 (0-614-17748-0) Delacorte.

Real Money: The Case for the Gold Standard. Lewis E. Lehrman. 13.50 (0-394-51904-3) Random.

Real Monster Goose. (Mother Goose Monsters Big Bks.). 48p. (J). (ps up). 1995. 7.95 (1-56293-587-9) McClanahan Bk.

Real Monsters. Wigand. LC 96-25018. (Ready-to-Read Ser.: No. 3). (J). 1997. 3.99 (0-689-81256-6) S&S Childrens.

Real Monsters. Wigand. LC 96-24131. (Ready-to-Read Ser.: No. 4). (J). 1997. 3.99 (0-689-81257-4) S&S Childrens.

Real Monsters: Rosh - O - Monsters. Babbie Mason. 1997. 3.99 (0-689-81155-1) S&S Childrens.

Real Monsters: Spontaneously Combustible. Gilmour. 1997. 3.99 (0-689-81154-3) S&S Childrens.

Real Mormonism. Robert C. Webb. LC 72-2971. reprint ed. 55.00 (0-404-10736-2) AMS Pr.

Real Mother Goose. Illus. by Blanche F. Wright. 128p. (J). (ps-3). 1994. 8.95 (0-590-22517-0, Cartwheel) Scholastic Inc.

Real Mother Goose. 75th anniversary ed. (J). (ps). 1991. 19.95 (1-56288-144-2) Checkerboard.

Real Mother Goose. Illus. by Blanche F. Wright. 128p. (J). (ps-1). 1991. reprint ed. 12.95 (1-56288-041-1) Checkerboard.

Real Mother Goose, 4 bks., Set. Illus. by Blanche F. Wright. 96p. (J). (ps-2). pap. 16.98 incl. audio (1-55886-018-5) Smarty Pants.

Real Mother Goose, Vol. I. Illus. by Blanche F. Wright. 24p. (J). (ps-2). Incl. cassettes. pap. 5.98 incl. audio (1-55886-012-6) Smarty Pants.

Real Mother Goose, Vol. II. Illus. by Blanche F. Wright. 24p. (J). (ps-2). Incl. cassettes. pap. 5.98 incl. audio (1-55886-013-4) Smarty Pants.

Real Mother Goose, Vol. III. Illus. by Blanche F. Wright. 24p. (J). (ps-2). Incl. cassettes. pap. 5.98 incl. audio (1-55886-014-2) Smarty Pants.

Real Mother Goose, Vol. IV. Illus. by Blanche F. Wright. 24p. (J). (ps-2). Incl. cassettes. pap. 5.98 incl. audio (1-55886-015-0) Smarty Pants.

Real Mother Goose: Book of American Rhymes. Ed. by Debby Slier. (Illus.). 128p. (J). (ps-5). 1993. 12.95 (1-56288-399-2) Checkerboard.

***Real Mother Goose: Gift Set.** (J). (ps up). 1996. pap. 10.95 (0-614-18983-7) Scholastic Inc.

Real Mother Goose: Husky Book Yellow. (J). (ps). 1991. 4.95 (1-56288-066-7) Checkerboard.

Real Mother Goose - Husky Book Blue. (J). (ps). 1991. 4.95 (1-56288-068-3) Checkerboard.

Real Mother Goose - Husky Book Green. (J). (ps). 1991. 4.95 (1-56288-067-5) Checkerboard.

Real Mother Goose - Husky Book Red. (J). (ps). 1991. 4.95 (1-56288-065-9) Checkerboard.

Real Mother Goose Book of American Rhymes. Illus. by Patty McCloskey-Padgett et al. LC 94-48663. 128p. (J). 1995. 8.95 (0-590-50955-1) Scholastic Inc.

Real Mother Goose Book of Christmas Carols. Laurence Schorsch. 64p. (J). (ps-3). 1994. 7.95 (0-590-22518-9) Scholastic Inc.

Real Mother Goose Book of Christmas Carols. Compiled by Lawrence Schorsch. (J). 1993. 9.95 (1-56288-405-0) Checkerboard.

Real Mother Goose Clock Book. Jane Chambless-Rigie. 22p. (J). (ps-3). 1994. 6.95 (0-590-22519-7) Scholastic Inc.

Real Mother Goose Clock Book. Illus. by Blanche F. Wright. 22p. (J). (ps-2). 6.95 (1-56288-095-0) Checkerboard.

***Real Mother Goose Gift Set: Book, Soap, & Terry Cloth Puppet.** (Illus.). (J). 1996. bds. 10.95 (0-590-92174-6) Scholastic Inc.

Real Mother Goose 80th Anniversary Deluxe Edition. annot. ed. (J). 1996. pap. 14.95 (0-590-99527-8) Scholastic Inc.

Real Mothers. Thomas. 1994. pap. 12.95 (0-88922-191-X) Genl Dist Srvs.

Real Mummies Don't Bleed: Friendly Tales for October Nights. Susan Whitcher. (J). (gr. 4-7). 1993. 15.00 (0-374-36213-0) FS&G.

Real Mummies Don't Bleed: Friendly Tales for October Nights. Susan Whitcher. (Illus.). 128p. (J). (gr. 2-7). 1994. pap. 4.95 (0-374-46209-7, Sunburst Bks) FS&G.

Real Munchhausen: Baron of Bodenwerder. Illus. by Harry Carter. 224p. (J). (gr. 6 up). 1960. 10.00 (0-8159-6701-2) Devin.

Real New Mexico Chile: An Insider's Guide to Cooking with Chile. Sandy Szwarc. LC 96-1767. 112p. (Orig.). 1996. pap. 6.95 (1-885590-15-6) Golden West Pub.

Real Numbers: Algebra Basics. Suter. 1991. pap. 8.86 (0-8092-4209-5) Contemp Bks.

Real Numbers: Analyzing Income Properties for a Profitable Investment. Joseph T. Sinclair. 396p. 1993. text ed. 65.00 (1-55623-817-7) Irwin Prof Pubng.

Real Numbers: Arithmetic. Layman E. Allen. 1966. 3.00 (0-911624-04-X) Wffn Proof.

Real Numbers: Fraction & Percent. Suter. 1990. pap. 8.86 (0-8092-4212-5) Contemp Bks.

Real Numbers: Geometry Basics. Suter. 1990. pap. 8.86 (0-8092-4210-9) Contemp Bks.

Real Numbers: Measurement. Suter. 1991. pap. 8.86 (0-8092-4208-7) Contemp Bks.

Real Numbers: Tables, Graphs, & Data. Suter. 1990. pap. 8.86 (0-8092-4217-6) Contemp Bks.

Real Numbers: Whole Numbers & Decimals. Suter. 1990. pap. 8.86 (0-8092-4214-1) Contemp Bks.

Real Numbers, Generalizations of the Reals, & Theories of Continua. Ed. by Philip Ehrlich. LC 93-47519. (Synthese Library: Vol. 235). 320p. (C). 1994. lib. bdg. 137.50 (0-7923-2689-X, Pub. by Klwr Acad Pubs NE) Kluwer Ac.

Real Objects & Models. J. Steven Soulier. Ed. by James E. Duane. LC 80-21450. (Instructional Media Library: Vol. 12). (Illus.). 96p. 1981. 27.95 (0-87778-172-9) Educ Tech Pubns.

R

Real Ones: Four Generations of the First Family of Coca-Cola. Elizabeth C. Graham & Ralph Roberts. LC 92-18778. 1992. 21.95 (*0-942637-62-3*) Barricade Bks.

Real Ones: Four Generations of the First Family of Coca-Cola. Elizabeth C. Graham & Ralph Roberts. 344p. 1995. reprint ed. 21.95 (*1-57102-503-0*) Hambleton-Hill.

Real Options: Managerial Flexibility & Strategy in Resource Allocation. Lenos Trigeorgis. LC 95-17410. (Illus.). 400p. 1996. 45.00 (*0-262-20102-X*) MIT Pr.

Real Options in Capital Investment: Models, Strategies & Applications. Ed. by Lenos Trigeorgis. LC 94-13735. 384p. 1995. text ed. 69.50 (*0-275-94616-9*, Praeger Pubs) Greenwood.

Real Paradise. Ann M. Davi. (C). 1989. text ed. 59.00 (*1-85821-044-5*, Pub. by Pentland Pr UK) St Mut.

Real Paradise: Flora & Fauna of the Gold Coast & Hinterland. Neil MacLeod. 112p. (C). 1990. 60.00 (*0-86439-049-1*, Pub. by Boolarong Pubns AT) St Mut.

Real Parents, Real Children: Parenting the Adopted Child. Holly Van Gulden & Lisa M. Bartels-Rabb. 228p. 1995. pap. 14.95 (*0-8245-1514-5*) Crossroad NY.

Real Patriots of the American Revolution. Robert Young. (Both Sides Ser.). (J). 1996. pap. 5.95 (*0-382-39171-3*, Dillon Silver Burdett); lib. bdg. 13.95 (*0-87518-612-2*, Dillon Silver Burdett) Silver Burdett Pr.

Real Peace - No More Vietnams. Richard M. Nixon. (Richard Nixon Library). 1990. pap. 12.95 (*0-671-70620-9*, Touchstone Bks) S&S Trade.

***Real People.** Lurie. 1997. pap. 12.95 (*0-8050-5181-3*) H Holt & Co.

Real People: Amish & Mennonites in Lancaster County, Pennsylvania. 4th ed. A. Martha Denlinger. LC 92-26887. (Illus.). 96p. 1993. pap. 4.99 (*0-8361-3616-0*) Herald Pr.

Real People: Personal Identity Without Thought Experiments. Kathleen V. Wilkes. (Illus.). 264p. 1994. reprint ed. pap. 18.95 (*0-19-824080-5*) OUP.

Real People & the Children of Thunder: The Yup'ik Eskimo Encounter with Moravian Missionaries John & Edith Kilbuck. Ann Fienup-Riordan. LC 90-50687. (Illus.). 432p. 1991. 39.95 (*0-8061-2329-X*) U of Okla Pr.

Real People, Real Jobs: Reflecting Your Interests in the World of Work: 40 People Tell Their Stories. Christopher J. Shinkman et al. LC 95-8818. 272p. (Orig.). 1995. pap. 15.95 (*0-89106-077-4*, 7115) Davies-Black.

***Real People. Real Needs. Real Victories.** 230p. Date not set. 8.95 (*1-57562-112-6*) K Copeland Pubns.

Real People. Real Needs. Real Victories. Copeland, Kenneth, Publications Staff. (Illus.). 225p. 1996. pap. write for info. (*1-57562-095-2*) K Copeland Pubns.

Real People, Real Problems: An Evaluation of the Long-Term Care Ombudsman Programs of the Older Americans Act. Ed. by Jo Harris-Wehling et al. LC 94-42711. 1995. write for info. (*0-614-03362-4*) Inst of Med.

Real People, Real Work: Parables on Leadership in the Nineties. 2nd ed. Lee Cheaney & Maury Cotter. (Illus.). 178p. 1991. pap. 15.00 (*0-945320-11-6*) SPC Pr.

Real People Working in Communications. Blythe Camenson & Jan Goldberg. LC 96-28072. (On the Job Ser.). 192p. 1996. 17.95 (*0-8442-4730-8*); pap. 12.95 (*0-8442-4731-6*) NTC Pub Grp.

***Real People Working in Education.** Blyth Camenson. LC 96-45455. (On the Job Ser.). 1997. write for info. (*0-8442-4734-0*) NTC Pub Grp.

***Real People Working in Education.** Blythe Camenson. LC 96-45455. (On the Job Ser.). 1997. pap. write for info. (*0-8442-4735-9*) NTC Pub Grp.

***Real People Working in Engineering.** Blythe Camenson. LC 97-21515. (On the Job Ser.). 1997. write for info. (*0-8442-4741-3*); pap. write for info. (*0-8442-4742-1*) NTC Pub Grp.

Real People Working in Health Care. Blythe Camenson & Jan Goldberg. LC 96-26671. (On the Job Ser.). 192p. 1996. 17.95 (*0-8442-4725-1*); pap. 12.95 (*0-8442-4727-8*) NTC Pub Grp.

***Real People Working in Helping Professions.** Blythe Camenson. LC 97-23005. (On the Job Ser.). 1997. write for info. (*0-8442-4721-9*) NTC Pub Grp.

***Real People Working in Helping Professions.** Camenson, Blythe Camenson. LC 97-23005. (On the Job Ser.). 1997. pap. write for info. (*0-8442-4722-7*, VGM Career Bks) NTC Pub Grp.

***Real People Working in Law.** LC 96-45454. (On the Job Ser.). 1997. write for info. (*0-8442-4738-3*) NTC Pub Grp.

***Real People Working in Law.** LC 96-45454. (On the Job Ser.). 1997. pap. write for info. (*0-8442-4739-1*) NTC Pub Grp.

Real People Working in Sales & Marketing. Blythe Camenson & Jan Goldberg. LC 96-28073. (On the Job Ser.). 192p. 1996. 17.95 (*0-8442-4728-6*); pap. 12.95 (*0-8442-4729-4*) NTC Pub Grp.

Real People Working in Service Businesses. Blythe Camenson & Jan Goldberg. LC 96-27790. (On the Job Ser.). 192p. 1996. 17.95 (*0-8442-4732-4*); pap. 12.95 (*0-8442-4733-2*) NTC Pub Grp.

***Real, Personal, & Intellectual Property Law in the NAFTA Region.** Ed. by Boris Kozolchyk. (Towards Seamless Borders Ser.: Vol. 2). 1997. 95.00 (*0-935328-85-8*) Intl Law Inst.

Real Philosophy: An Anthology of the Universal Search for Meaning. Ed. by Jacob Needleman & David Appelbaum. 352p. 1991. pap. 12.95 (*0-14-019256-5*, Arkana) Viking Penguin.

Real Photo Postcards: The "Life-Size" Edition. Robert Ward. (Illus.). 240p. 1994. spiral bd. 31.95 (*0-9640451-0-9*) Antique Paper.

Real Places: An Unconventional Guide to America's Generic Landscape. Grady Clay. (Illus.). 328p. 1994. 35.00 (*0-226-10946-1*) U Ch Pr.

Real Plato Jones. Nina Bawden. LC 92-43873. (J). 1993. 13.95 (*0-395-66972-3*, Clarion Bks) HM.

Real Plato Jones. Nina Bawden. 176p. (J). 1996. pap. 4.99 (*0-14-037947-9*) Puffin Bks.

***Real Police: Stories from the Crescent City.** James S. Prine. LC 96-92574. 142p. (Orig.). 1996. pap. 12.95 (*0-9653752-0-X*) J S Prine.

***Real Politics: Politics & Everyday Life.** Jean B. Elshtain. LC 97-2054. 1997. write for info. (*0-8018-5599-3*) Johns Hopkins.

Real Ponies Don't Go Oink! Patrick F. McManus. 224p. 1991. 16.95 (*0-8050-1651-1*) H Holt & Co.

Real Ponies Don't Go Oink! Patrick F. McManus. 208p. 1992. pap. 8.95 (*0-8050-2107-8*, Owl) H Holt & Co.

Real Positive Definite Completion Problem: Cycle Completability, No. 584. Wayne W. Barrett et al. (Memoirs of the American Mathematical Society Ser.). 1996. pap. 32.00 (*0-8218-0473-1*, MEMO/122/584) Am Math.

Real Power: Stages of Personal Power in Organizations. rev. ed. Janet Hagberg. 269p. (C). 1994. pap. text ed. 14.50 (*1-879215-17-9*) Sheffield WI.

Real Power of Brands: Putting Brands to Work in a Changing World. Stuart Crainer. 240p. 1995. 29.95 (*0-273-61379-0*) Pitman Publng.

Real Preacher. Magdalena. 1986. 20.00 (*0-946270-23-6*, Pub. by Pentland Pr UK) St Mut.

Real Presence: Lawrence Writers. write for info. (*0-614-10736-9*) Fairleigh Dickinson.

Real Presence: The Glory of Christ with Us & Within Us. Leanne Payne. LC 94-46185. 192p. (YA). (gr. 10). 1995. pap. 12.99 (*0-8010-5172-X*, Hamewith MI) Baker Bks.

Real Presence Through the Ages: Jesus Adored in the Sacrament of the Altar. Compiled by Michael L. Gaudoin-Parker. LC 92-42274. 272p. 1993. pap. 14.95 (*0-8189-0662-6*) Alba.

Real Presences. George Steiner. LC 89-4897. x, 248p. 1991. pap. 12.95 (*0-226-77234-9*) U Ch Pr.

Real Presences: Is There Anything in What We Say? George Steiner. 246p. 1989. 23.95 (*0-226-77233-0*) U Ch Pr.

Real Pretend. Joan Donaldson. (Illus.). 32p. (J). (ps-3). 1992. 12.95 (*1-56288-158-2*) Checkerboard.

***Real Process: How Logic & Chemistry Combine in Hegel's Philosophy of Nature.** John W. Burbidge. (Toronto Studies in Philosophy). 304p. 1996. 75.00 (*0-8020-0897-6*) U of Toronto Pr.

Real Professional Teacher's Role & the Instructional Excellence Support Team. Don Stewart. (Chance for Instructional Excellence Ser.: Bk. 2). (Illus.). 459p. (Orig.). 1989. 22.95 (*0-913448-18-4*); pap. 16.95 (*0-913448-19-2*) SLATE Servs.

Real Projective Plane. 2nd ed. Harold Coxeter & Scott Macdonald. LC 60-3540. 238p. reprint ed. pap. 67.90 (*0-317-09189-1*, 2050796) Bks Demand.

Real Projective Plane: With an Appendix for Mathematics by George Beck. 3rd ed. H. S. Coxeter. LC 92-22637. (Illus.). 232p. 1992. reprint ed. 64.95 incl. disk (*0-387-97890-9*); reprint ed. 64.95 incl. disk (*0-387-97889-5*) Spr-Verlag.

Real Property. (Essential Principles Ser.). 1982. 12.95 (*0-940366-37-1*) Sum & Substance.

Real Property. Paul Goldstein. LC 84-5919. (University Casebook Ser.). 1362p. 1984. text ed. 43.00 (*0-88277-170-1*) Foundation Pr.

***Real Property.** Kate Squires. (LawPrep Essentials Ser.). 267p. (Orig.). (C). 1996. pap. 12.95 (*1-878844-07-5*) Lawprep.

Real Property. 2nd ed. Kimm Walton. (Law in a Flash Ser.). 644p. 1994. 16.95 (*1-56542-565-0*) E Pub Corp.

Real Property: Commentary & Materials. 3rd ed. C. M. Sappideen et al. xxxix, 676p. 1990. 109.00 (*0-455-20960-X*, Pub. by Law Bk Co AT); pap. 85.00 (*0-455-20961-8*, Pub. by Law Bk Co AT) Gaunt.

Real Property Vol. 1: Shanghai. 330.00 (*962-7708-36-4*, Pub. by Euromoney UK) Am Educ Systs.

Real Property Vol. 2: Guangdong. 330.00 (*962-7708-37-2*, Pub. by Euromoney UK) Am Educ Systs.

Real Property Vol. 3: Beijing & Northern China. 330.00 (*962-7708-38-0*, Pub. by Euromoney UK) Am Educ Systs.

Real Property Vol. 4: Shenzhen & Other Sez's. 330.00 (*0-614-17842-8*, Pub. by Euromoney UK) Am Educ Systs.

Real Property Vol. 5: PRC National Property Law. 1995. 330.00 (*962-7708-40-2*, Pub. by Euromoney UK) Am Educ Systs.

Real Property - Landlord Tenant. Ed. by Will G. Barber. (Texas Court's Charge Ser.: Vol. 6). 450p. 1992. spiral bd. 85.00 (*0-409-25662-X*) MICHIE.

Real Property & Commercial Transactions Deadlines, Pt. 6: Summer 1992, Action Guide. Thomas M. Murray & David M. Hymer. Ed. by Carolyn J. Stein. (Meeting Statutory Deadlines Ser.). 78p. 1992. pap. text ed. 47.00 (*0-88124-557-7*, RE-11412) Cont Ed Bar-CA.

Real Property & Conveyancing. Ed. by Ross Caotes. (C). 1991. text ed. 22.00 (*1-85431-127-1*, Pub. by Blackstone Pr UK) Gaunt.

Real Property & Conveyancing. R. M. Coates. (C). 1990. 110.00 (*1-85431-089-5*, Pub. by Blackstone Pr UK) St Mut.

Real Property & Land Use Litigation, Pt. 2: Summer 1992. Douglas L. Hendricks et al. Ed. by Ellen C. Lester. (Meeting Statutory Deadlines Ser.). 86p. 1992. pap. 47.00 (*0-88124-528-3*, CP-11372) Cont Ed Bar-CA.

Real Property Appraisal Technician. Jack Rudman. (Career Examination Ser.: C-2185). 1994. pap. 23.95 (*0-8373-2185-9*) Nat Learn.

Real Property Appraiser. Jack Rudman. (Career Examination Ser.: C-841). 1994. pap. 23.95 (*0-8373-0841-0*) Nat Learn.

Real Property Appraiser - Arbitrator Supervisor. Jack Rudman. (Career Examination Ser.: C-3276). 1994. pap. 39.95 (*0-8373-3276-1*) Nat Learn.

Real Property Appraiser-Arbitrator. (Career Examination Ser.: C-3275). 1994. pap. 34.95 (*0-8373-3275-3*) Nat Learn.

Real Property Appraiser I. Jack Rudman. (Career Examination Ser.: C-842). 1994. pap. 23.95 (*0-8373-0842-9*) Nat Learn.

Real Property Appraiser II. Jack Rudman. (Career Examination Ser.: C-843). 1994. pap. 27.95 (*0-8373-0843-7*) Nat Learn.

Real Property Appraiser III. Jack Rudman. (Career Examination Ser.: C-844). 1994. pap. 29.95 (*0-8373-0844-5*) Nat Learn.

Real Property Appraiser IV. Jack Rudman. (Career Examination Ser.: C-845). 1994. pap. 29.95 (*0-8373-0845-3*) Nat Learn.

Real Property Assessor. Jack Rudman. (Career Examination Ser.: C-2199). 1994. pap. 23.95 (*0-8373-2199-9*) Nat Learn.

Real Property Assistant. Jack Rudman. (Career Examination Ser.: C-699). 1994. pap. 23.95 (*0-8373-0699-X*) Nat Learn.

Real Property Basics. Renny J. Avey. 1986. per. 12.00 (*0-88252-132-2*) Paladin Hse.

Real Property Cases. Marsh. 1992. 23.00 (*0-316-54716-6*) Little.

Real Property Examiner. Jack Rudman. (Career Examination Ser.: C-3345). 1994. pap. 27.95 (*0-8373-3345-8*) Nat Learn.

Real Property Financing in Singapore. Hairani Saban. 390p. 1988. boxed 176.00 (*9971-70-062-X*) MICHIE.

Real Property in a Nutshell. 3rd ed. Roger Bernhardt. LC 93-24677. (Nutshell Ser.). 475p. 1993. pap. 17.00 (*0-314-02436-0*) West Pub.

Real Property Information System Specialist. Jack Rudman. (Career Examination Ser.: C-3138). 1994. pap. 29.95 (*0-8373-3138-2*) Nat Learn.

Real Property Issues in Bankruptcy. Thomas G. Kelch & Michael K. Slattery. (Real Property - Zoning Ser.). 1995. ring bd. write for info. (*0-614-06272-1*) Clark Boardman Callaghan.

Real Property Issues in Bankruptcy. Thomas G. Kelch & Michael K. Slattery. LC 95-35196. 1995. ring bd. write for info. (*0-87632-391-3*) Clark Boardman Callaghan.

Real Property Law, a Comprehensive Manual for N.Y.S. 800p. 1997. ring bd. 24.95 (*0-930137-83-3*) Looseleaf Law.

Real Property Management: Reforms in Four Countries Promote Competition. (Illus.). 48p. (Orig.). (C). 1995. pap. text ed. 20.00 (*0-7881-1733-5*) DIANE Pub.

Real Property Manager. Jack Rudman. (Career Examination Ser.: C-698). 1994. pap. 29.95 (*0-8373-0698-1*) Nat Learn.

Real Property Manual, 1992. Wake Forest University School of Law - CLE Staff. 830p. 1992. pap. text ed. 90.00 (*0-685-63240-7*) Wake Forest Law.

Real Property Probate & Trust Journal: 1966-1995/96, 27 vols. mic. film write for info. (*0-318-57455-1*) Rothman.

Real Property Probate & Trust Journal: 1966-1995/96, 30 vols., Set. Bound set. 1,426.00 (*0-8377-9010-7*) Rothman.

Real Property Receivership: Real Property Receivership. Andrew Besser et al. 216p. 1994. pap. text ed. 80.00 (*0-406-02292-5*, UK) MICHIE.

Real Property Recorder. Jack Rudman. (Career Examination Ser.: C-3102). 1994. pap. 27.95 (*0-8373-3102-1*) Nat Learn.

Real Property Tax, Differential Assessment, & the Loss of Farmland on the Rural-Urban Fringe. Thomas Plaut. (Discussion Paper Ser.: No. 97). 1977. pap. 10.00 (*1-55869-104-9*) Regional Sci Res Inst.

Real Property Tax Examiner. Jack Rudman. (Career Examination Ser.: C-1835). 1994. pap. 27.95 (*0-8373-1835-1*) Nat Learn.

Real Property Tax Specialist. Jack Rudman. (Career Examination Ser.: C-2227). 1994. pap. 29.95 (*0-8373-2227-8*) Nat Learn.

Real Property Tax Supervisor. Jack Rudman. (Career Examination Ser.: C-3604). 1994. pap. 34.95 (*0-8373-3604-X*) Nat Learn.

Real Property, Teacher's Guide. Paul Goldstein. (University Casebook Ser.). 415p. 1984. pap. text ed. write for info. (*0-88277-218-X*) Foundation Pr.

Real Property Time Shares: An Appraisal Guide & Bibliography. Robert M. Clatanoff. (Bibliographic Ser.). 9p. 1982. pap. 5.00 (*0-88329-116-9*) IAAO.

Real Property Valuation: Principles & Applications. Kenneth M. Lusht. 608p. (C). 1996. 55.00 (*0-256-19059-3*) Irwin.

Real Property, 1988 Supplement. Paul Goldstein. (University Casebook Ser.). 83p. 1988. pap. text ed. 5.95 (*0-88277-681-9*) Foundation Pr.

***Real Rain Man.** Fran Peek. Ed. by Stevens Anderson. Date not set. pap. 11.95 (*0-9651163-0-1*) Harkness Pubng.

Real Rainman: Kim Peek. Francis Peek. Ed. by Stevens W. Anderson. (Illus.). 180p. (Orig.). 1996. pap. 12.00 (*0-614-14631-3*) Harkness Publishing Co.

Real Rape. Susan R. Estrich. 176p. 1988. reprint ed. pap. text ed. 12.00 (*0-674-74944-8*) HUP.

Real Reading, 36 vols. (J). (gr. 1-4). 1990. 539.28 (*0-8172-3545-0*) Raintree Steck-V.

Real Real World. Hillary Johnson & Nancy Rommelman. 1995. pap. 16.00 (*0-671-54525-6*) PB.

Real Reason for Christmas: Letters to Children for the Twelve Nights of Christmas. Margaret Taliaferro. (Illus.). 118p. (J). (gr. 1-7). reprint ed. pap. 6.95 (*0-9618730-0-0*) FEA Pub.

Real Recipes for Casual Cooks: A Comic Book Cookbook. Lynn Gordon. 128p. 1996. pap. 10.95 (*0-385-48208-6*) Doubleday.

Real Reciprocity: Balancing U. S. Economic & Security Policies in the Pacific Basin. David B. Denoon. LC 93-12622. 100p. 1993. 14.95 (*0-87609-144-3*) Coun Foreign.

Real Reductive Groups, I. Ed. by Nolan R. Wallach. (Pure & Applied Mathematics Ser.). 412p. 1988. text ed. 102.00 (*0-12-732960-9*) Acad Pr.

Real Rights. Carl Wellman. 288p. 1995. text ed. 52.00 (*0-19-509500-6*) OUP.

Real Ritual Magick: For People Ready to Enjoy Life Now. Al G. Manning. LC 86-63701. 180p. (Orig.). 1987. pap. 7.95 (*0-941698-15-7*) Pan Ishtar.

Real Rock Radio. (Stereo Boom Box Ser.: Vol. 4). 160p. (J). (gr. 1-6). 1994. ring bd. 149.95 (*1-57405-051-6*) CharismaLife Pub.

Real Romantic Marketplace: (Know Good Women?) Andrew S. Ryan, Jr. 1991. 14.95 (*0-533-09317-1*) Vantage.

***Real Roswell Crashed Saucer Coverup.** Philip J. Klass. 1997. 24.95 (*1-57392-164-5*) Prometheus Bks.

***Real Rules.** Barbara De Angelis. 1997. mass mkt. 4.99 (*0-440-22448-9*, Island Bks) Dell.

Real Runabouts, Book II. Robert G. Speltz. 230p. 1978. 27.95 (*0-89279-017-2*) Graphic Pub.

Real Runabouts, Book III. Robert G. Speltz. 330p. 1980. 33.95 (*0-89279-018-0*) Graphic Pub.

Real Runabouts, Book IV. Robert G. Speltz. 573p. 1983. 39.95 (*0-89279-048-2*) Graphic Pub.

Real Runabouts, Vol. II. Robert G. Speltz. 230p. 1978. reprint ed. 27.95 (*0-932299-01-6*) R G Speltz.

Real Runabouts, Vol. 6. Robert G. Speltz. 354p. 1987. 59.95 (*0-932299-06-7*) R G Speltz.

Real Runabouts Review of Canoes. Robert T. Speltz. 72p. (Orig.). (YA). 1991. pap. 12.95 (*0-932299-08-3*) R G Speltz.

Real Runabouts Review of Outboard Motors. Robert G. Speltz. 144p. (Orig.). 1991. pap. 16.95 (*0-932299-09-1*) R G Speltz.

Real Runabouts V: History of Inboard-Powered Pleasure Boats, Nomenclature & Descriptions. Robert G. Speltz. 289p. 1984. 38.95 (*0-932299-04-0*) R G Speltz.

Real Russians. L. Wesley Jones. LC 95-13083. 1995. write for info. (*0-929540-20-4*) Pub Designs.

Real Sailor-Songs. Ed. by John Ashton. LC 78-160612. (Illus.). 1972. reprint ed. 30.95 (*0-405-08224-X*, Pub. by Blom Pubns UK) Ayer.

Real Salesmen Drive Company Cars. Jim Keil. LC 87-92192. (Illus.). 50p. (Orig.). 1987. pap. 4.95 (*0-9619809-0-7*) Smilin Ed Pr.

Real SATs. College Board Staff. 352p. pap. 14.00 (*0-87447-511-2*) College Bd.

Real Science, Real Decisions: A Collection of Thinking Activities from "The Science Teacher" (Illus.). 32p. 1990. pap. text ed. 8.50 (*0-87355-097-8*) Natl Sci Tchrs.

Real Secrets of Beauty: Every Woman's Guide to Style & Glamour. Diane Irons. (Illus.). 1993. pap. 17.95 (*0-9639394-0-8*) Intl Image.

Real Security: Converting the Defense Economy & Building Peace. Ed. by Kevin J. Cassidy & Gregory A. Bischak. LC 93-32011. (SUNY Series, Global Conflict & Peace Education). 308p. (C). 1993. pap. 21.95 (*0-7914-1608-9*) State U NY Pr.

Real Security: Converting the Defense Economy & Building Peace. Ed. by Kevin J. Cassidy & Gregory A. Bischak. LC 93-32011. (SUNY Series, Global Conflict & Peace Education). 308p. (C). 1993. text ed. 64.50 (*0-7914-1607-0*) State U NY Pr.

Real Self: A Developmental, Self, & Object Relations Approach. James F. Masterson. LC 85-12824. 192p. 1985. text ed. 34.95 (*0-87630-400-5*) Brunner-Mazel.

Real Self: The Inner Journey of Courage. Sandra J. Merwin. 104p. (Orig.). 1991. pap. text ed. 7.95 (*0-9628522-0-1*) TigerLily Pr.

Real Sex Education: Let's Not Weave a Tangled Web. Cuyler Poor. 16p. 1996. pap. 6.00 (*0-8059-3833-8*) Dorrance.

***Real Shakespeare: Retrieving the Early Years, 1564-1594.** Eric Sams. 1997. pap. text ed. 17.00 (*0-300-07282-1*) Yale U Pr.

Real Shakespeare: Retrieving the Early Years (1564-94) Eric Sams. 304p. 1995. 32.50 (*0-300-06129-3*) Yale U Pr.

Real Sisters. Susan Wright. (Illus.). 24p. (J). (ps-3). 1995. pap. 5.95 (*0-921556-42-X*) LPC InBook.

Real-Skin Rubber Monster Mask. Miriam Cohen. LC 89-34620. (Illus.). 32p. (J). (gr. k up). 1990. lib. bdg. 12.88 (*0-688-09123-7*) Greenwillow.

Real-Skin Rubber Monster Mask. Miriam Cohen. (Illus.). 32p. (J). (gr. k-3). 1995. pap. 4.99 (*0-440-40949-7*, Picture Yearling) BDD Bks Young Read.

Real Sleeper. Theodore R. Gardner, II. LC 95-36080. 229p. 1995. 14.95 (*0-9627297-8-7*) A A Knoll Pubs.

Real Solids & Radiation. A. E. Hughes & D. Pooley. (Wykeham Science Ser.: No. 35). 208p. 1975. pap. 18.00 (*0-85109-011-7*) Taylor & Francis.

Real Solids & Radiation. A. E. Hughes et al. LC 74-32348. (Wykeham Science Ser.: No. 35). 208p. (C). 1975. 18.00 (*0-8448-1162-9*, Crane Russak) Taylor & Francis.

Real Soul Food & Other Poetic Recipes. Stacey L. Evans. (Black Words Ser.: No. 2). 112p. 1995. 17.95 (*1-888018-02-X*); pap. 9.95 (*1-888018-01-1*) Alexndr Pub.

An Asterisk (*) at the beginning of an entry indicates that the title is appearing in BIP for the first time.

***Real South Cooking: Authentic, Traditional Southern Food.** Patricia B. Mitchell. 1997. pap. 4.00 (*0-925117-85-4*) Mitchells.

Real Space: Martorell - Bohigas - Mackay - Puigdomnech. Philip Drew. (Illus.). 240p. 1993. 85.00 (*3-8030-2803-5*, Pub. by Ernst Wasmuth GW) Dist Art Pubs.

***Real Spin on Tennis: Grasping the Mind, Body, & Soul of the Game.** Jack W. Broudy. LC 96-39534. (Illus.). 200p. (Orig.). 1997. pap. 14.00 (*0-9654872-0-2*) J&B Pub.

Real Sports, Vol. 95, No. 2. Ed. by James T. Fisher. 320p. 1996. pap. text ed. 12.00 (*0-8223-6435-2*) Duke.

Real Story: The Gap into Conflict. Stephen R. Donaldson. (Gap Ser.: No. 1). 272p. 1992. mass mkt. 5.99 (*0-553-29509-8*) Bantam.

Real Story of the Bonobos Who Wore Spectacles. Adela Turin & Nella Bosnia. (Feminist Fables for Children Ser.). Orig. Title: La Vera Storia Dei Bonobo Con Gli Occhiali. (Illus.). 32p. (J). (gr. 3-6). 1980. 6.95 (*0-904613-18-6*) Writers & Readers.

Real Story of the Pirate. A. Hyatt Verrill. (Illus.). 374p. 1989. reprint ed. pap. 15.00 (*0-87380-167-9*) Rio Grande.

Real Structure of High-Tc Superconductors. Ed. by V. S. Shekhtman. (Materials Science Ser.: Vol. 23). (Illus.). 210p. 1993. write for info. (*3-540-56559-0*) Spr-Verlag.

Real Structure of High-Tc Superconductors. Veniamin S. Shenkhtman. LC 93-13429. (Materials Science Ser.: Vol. 23). 1993. 97.95 (*0-387-56559-0*) Spr-Verlag.

Real Stuck, Way Up. Benette W. Tiffault. LC 94-44593. (Illus.). 32p. (J). 1995. pap. 4.95 (*0-8120-9166-3*) Barron.

Real Stuff: A History of NASA's Astronaut Recruitment Policy. Joseph D. Atkinson, Jr. & Jay M. Shafritz. LC 85-9460. 192p. 1985. text ed. 49.95 (*0-275-90195-5*, C0195, Praeger Pubs); pap. text ed. 15.95 (*0-275-91808-4*, B1808, Praeger Pubs) Greenwood.

Real Taste of Jamaica. Enid Donaldson. (Illus.). 160p. (Orig.). 1996. pap. 18.95 (*1-895629-64-0*, Pub. by Warwick Pub CN) Firefly Bks Ltd.

Real Taste of Jamaica. Enid Donaldson. (Illus.). 160p. (Orig.). pap. 15.95 (*976-8100-46-X*, Pub. by Ian Randle JM) Paul & Co Pubs.

Real Taste of the Pacific. Susan Parkinson et al. (Illus.). 112p. (Orig.). 1996. pap. 17.95 (*1-895629-66-7*, Pub. by Warwick Pub CN) Firefly Bks Ltd.

Real Terror Network: Terrorism in Fact & Progaganda. Edward S. Herman. LC 82-80687. 250p. 1982. 35.00 (*0-89608-135-4*); pap. 16.00 (*0-89608-134-6*) South End Pr.

Real Terror Network: Terrorism in Fact & Propaganda. Edward S. Herman. LC 85-90013. 270p. 1985. reprint ed. pap. 77.00 (*0-608-00450-2*, 2061269) Bks Demand.

Real Texans: Don't Drink Scotch in Their Dr. Pepper. Bill Walraven. 96p. 4.95 (*0-89015-701-4*) Sunbelt Media.

Real Texans Don't Drink Scotch in Their Dr. Pepper. Bill Walraven. (Illus.). 96p. (Orig.). 1991. pap. 4.95 (*0-9609870-1-0*) Sandcrab.

Real Texas Coloring Book: (For "Real" Texans) Pamela J. Roberts. (Buzz E. Fiddlefeathers Edition Ser.). (Illus.). 38p. (J). (ps-3). 1992. pap. 3.95 (*1-881345-00-9*) Penzance Co.

Real Thai: The Best of Thailand's Regional Cooking. Nancie McDermott. 208p. 1992. pap. 9.95 (*0-8118-0017-2*) Chronicle Bks.

Real Thief. William Steig. LC 73-77910. (Sunburst Ser.). (Illus.). 64p. (J). (ps up). 1976. 12.95 (*0-374-36217-3*) FS&G.

Real Thief. William Steig. LC 73-77910. (Sunburst Ser.). (Illus.). 64p. (J). (ps up). 1984. pap. 3.95 (*0-374-46208-9*, Sunburst Bks) FS&G.

Real Thing. William Carney. 1995. pap. 10.95 (*1-56333-280-9*, R Kasak Bks) Masquerade.

Real Thing. Barbara Delinsky. 1994. mass mkt. 4.50 (*0-373-83277-X*, 1-83277-3) Harlequin Bks.

Real Thing. Henry James. 1996. pap. 1.99 (*0-679-77197-2*) Random.

Real Thing. Ray & Patricia Nardiello. 1986. teacher ed., pap. 9.95 (*0-8384-3366-9*) Heinle & Heinle.

***Real Thing.** Shi. 1996. pap. text ed. 7.00 (*0-312-15355-4*) St Martin.

Real Thing? Philip Tait. 1993. pap. 1.75 (*0-946462-30-5*, Pub. by Evangelical Pr) Presby & Reformed.

Real Thing: A Skill-Building Book & Video That Prepares Students for College Success. Martha E. Kendall. LC 93-91394. 114p. 1993. pap. 16.95 (*0-945783-05-1*) Highland Pub Group.

Real Thing: Imitation & Authenticity in American Culture, 1880-1940. Miles Orvell. LC 88-20886. (Cultural Studies of the United States). (Illus.). xxvi, 382p. (C). 1989. 49.95 (*0-8078-1837-2*); pap. 17.95 (*0-8078-4246-X*) U of NC Pr.

Real Thing: Stories & Sketches. Doris Lessing. LC 91-59932. 224p. 1993. pap. 12.00 (*0-06-092417-9*, PL) HarpC.

Real Thing: Testimonial Discourse & Latin America. Ed. by George M. Gugelberger. LC 96-41261. 328p. 1996. text ed. 49.95 (*0-8223-1851-2*); pap. text ed. 17.95 (*0-8223-1844-X*) Duke.

Real Thing & Other Tales. Henry James. LC 70-167453. (Short Story Index Reprint Ser.). 1977. reprint ed. 20.95 (*0-8369-3979-4*) Ayer.

Real Thomas Jefferson. 2nd ed. Andrew M. Allison et al. LC 83-17404. (American Classic Ser.). (Illus.). 709p. 1983. 17.95 (*0-88080-005-4*); pap. 14.95 (*0-88080-006-2*) Natl Ctr Constitutional.

***Real Time: Preparing for the Age of the Never Satisfied Customer.** Harvard Business School Press Staff. 1997. text ed. 24.95 (*0-07-105056-6*) McGraw.

***Real Time: Preparing for the Eventuality of Everything.** Regis McKenna. LC 97-12475. 1997. write for info. (*0-87584-794-3*) Harvard Busn.

Real-Time: Theory in Practice: REX Workshop, Mook, The Netherlands, June 3-7, 1991: Proceedings. Ed. by J. W. De Bakker et al. LC 92-14687. (Lecture Notes in Computer Science Ser.: Vol. 600). viii, 723p. 1992. 106.95 (*0-387-55564-1*) Spr-Verlag.

Real-Time Advantage: An Introduction to Computerized Accounting. Phyllis S. Yasuda & John W. Wanlass. 144p. (C). 1992. 28.75 incl. 3.5 hd (*0-15-571231-4*); 28.75 incl. 5.25 hd (*0-15-571230-6*) Dryden Pr.

Real-Time Animation Toolkit in C++ Rex E. Bradford. LC 95-18613. 800p. 1995. pap. 49.95 (*0-471-12147-9*) Wiley.

Real-Time Applications: Proceedings of the Second IEEE Workshop on Real-Time Applications, 1994, Washington, D. C. IEEE Workshop on Real-Time Applications Staff. LC 94-76634. 184p. 1994. pap. 40.00 (*0-8186-6475-5*) IEEE Comp Soc.

Real Time Approximation of a Function by a Sum of Complex Exponentials. Tapan K. Sarkar et al. 300p. 1997. text ed. 92.00 (*981-02-1819-2*) World Scientific Pub.

Real-Time Computer Control: An Introduction. 2nd ed. Stuart Bennett. LC 93-28154. (International Systems Control Engineering Ser.). 432p. 1994. pap. text ed. 82.00 (*0-13-764176-1*) P-H.

Real-Time Computer Vision. Ed. by Christopher M. Brown & Demetri Terzopoulos. (Publications of the Newton Institute: No. 3). (Illus.). 256p. (C). 1995. text ed. 52.95 (*0-521-47278-4*) Cambridge U Pr.

Real Time Computing. Ed. by Wolfgang A. Halang & Alexander D. Stoyenko. LC 93-46646. (NATO ASI Series F: Computer & Systems Science: Vol. 127). 1994. 165.00 (*0-387-57558-8*) Spr-Verlag.

Real-Time Computing in Patient Management: A Symposium Held in June, 1975. Ed. by James P. Payne & D. W. Hill. LC 76-367573. (Chartridge Symposium Ser.). 215p. reprint ed. pap. 61.30 (*0-8357-7003-6*, 2033459) Bks Demand.

Real-Time Computing Systems & Applications: Proceedings of the 3rd International Workshop on Real-Time Computing Systems & Applications, Seoul, Korea, 1996. LC 96-76639. 328p. 1996. pap. 80.00 (*0-8186-7626-4*) IEEE Comp Soc.

Real-Time Computing Systems & Applications, 2nd International Workshop. LC 95-76442. 280p. 1995. pap. 60.00 (*0-8186-7106-8*, PR07106) IEEE Comp Soc.

***Real-Time Computing Systems & Applications, 4th International Workshop (Rtcsa '97)** 350p. 1997. pap. 80.00 (*0-8186-8073-3*) IEEE Comp Soc.

Real-Time Control Networks. Daniel T. Miklovic. LC 93-13670. (Resources for Measurement & Control Ser.). 277p. 1993. 68.00 (*1-55617-231-1*) ISA.

Real Time Control of Large Scale Systems. Ed. by Spyros G. Tzafestas et al. (Lecture Notes in Control & Information Sciences Ser.: Vol. 67). xi, 650p. 1985. 70.95 (*0-387-15033-1*) Spr-Verlag.

Real-Time Control of Walking. Marc Donner. (Progress in Computer Science Ser.: No. 7). 192p. 1986. 48.50 (*0-8176-3332-4*) Birkhauser.

***Real-Time Database Systems: Issues & Applications.** Azer Bestavros et al. LC 97-9510. (International Series in Engineering & Computer Science, Real-Time Systems). 1997. lib. bdg. 138.50 (*0-7923-9897-1*) Kluwer Ac.

Real Time Digital Signals. Elsharkawy. 1990. pap. text ed. 68.00 (*0-13-767138-5*) P-H.

***Real Time English.** Michael Rost. 1994. wbk. ed., pap. text ed. 7.00 (*0-582-25975-4*, Pub. by Longman UK) Longman.

Real Time English. Michael A. Rost. (YA). 1994. teacher ed. 18.95 (*0-582-09223-X*); pap. text ed. 12.67 (*0-582-09221-3*); pap. text ed. 38.00 (*0-582-22927-8*) Longman.

Real-Time Expert Systems Computer Architecture. Robert F. Hodson & Abraham Kandel. 288p. 1991. 77.00 (*0-8493-4215-5*, QA76) CRC Pr.

Real Time Fault Monitoring of Industrial Processes. A. D. Pouliezos & G. S. Stavrakakis. LC 94-2137. (International Series on Microprocessor-Based & Intelligent Systems Engineering: Vol. 12). 576p. (C). 1994. lib. bdg. 278.50 (*0-7923-2737-3*) Kluwer Ac.

Real-Time Forecasting of Hydroclimatic Variables. J.B. Valdes & T. Sastri. Date not set. write for info. (*0-614-17902-5*) Elsevier.

Real-Time Futures Trading: How to Use Price, Volume & Volatility to Master the Markets. Al Gietzen. 210p. 1992. text ed. 45.00 (*1-55738-402-9*) Irwin Prof Pubng.

Real-Time Imaging: Theory, Techniques, & Application. Ed. by Phillip A. Laplante & Alexander D. Stoyenko. 328p. 1996. 79.95 (*0-7803-1068-3*, PC4242) Inst Electrical.

Real-Time Integration Methods for Mechanical System Simulation. Ed. by Edward J. Haug & R. C. Deyo. (NATO ASI Series F: Computer & Systems Sciences, Special Programme AET: Vol. 69). viii, 352p. 1991. 91.95 (*0-387-53280-3*) Spr-Verlag.

Real Time Method of Radar Plotting. Max H. Carpenter & Wayne M. Waldo. LC 89-156916. (Illus.). 48p. 1975. reprint ed. pap. text ed. 20.00 (*0-87033-204-X*) Cornell Maritime.

Real Time Microcomputer Control of Industrial Processes. Ed. by Spyros G. Tzafestas & J. K. Pal. (C). 1990. lib. bdg. 206.00 (*0-7923-0779-8*) Kluwer Ac.

Real-Time Microcomputer System Design: An Introduction. P. Lawrence & K. Mauch. (Electrical Engineering Ser.). 592p. 1987. text ed. write for info. (*0-07-036731-0*) McGraw.

***Real Time Network Management.** J. Filipiak. 446p. 1991. 166.25 (*0-444-88881-0*, North Holland) Elsevier.

Real-Time Object Measurement & Classification. Ed. by A. K. Jain. (NATO Asi Series F: Vol. 42). 407p. 1988. 100.95 (*0-387-18766-9*) Spr-Verlag.

Real Time Object-Oriented Modeling. Brian Selic et al. 525p. 1994. text ed. 49.95 (*0-471-59917-4*) Wiley.

Real-Time Operating Systems & Software, 11th IEEE Workshop. LC 93-81372. 128p. 1994. pap. 30.00 (*0-8186-5710-3*, 5710) IEEE Comp Soc.

Real-Time Optical Information Processing. Ed. by Bahram Javidi & Joseph L. Horner. (Illus.). 536p. 1994. text ed. 104.00 (*0-12-381180-5*) Acad Pr.

Real-Time Profit Management: Making Your Bottom Line a Sure Thing. Ernst & Young LLP Staff & Bob Dragoo. LC 95-14612. 244p. 1995. text ed. 34.95 (*0-471-12617-9*) Wiley.

***Real Time Programming: Languages, Specification & Verification.** 600p. 1998. 60.00 (*981-02-2566-0*) World Scientific Pub.

Real-Time Programming (WRTP '92) Preprints of the IFAC Workshop, Bruges, Belgium, 23-26 June 1992. Ed. by L. Boullart & J. A. De La Puente. LC 92-40442. 290p. 1992. pap. text ed. 102.50 (*0-08-041894-5*, Pergamon Pr) Elsevier.

Real-Time Programming 1988. Crespo & De La Puente. (IFAC Proceedings Ser.). 97p. 1989. 47.00 (*0-08-036236-2*, Pergamon Pr) Elsevier.

Real Time Programming 1994: IFAC Workshop, Isle of Reichenau, Lake Constance, Germany, 22-24 June, 1994. IFAC-IFIP Worship on Real-Time Programming Staff. Ed. by W. A. Halang. LC 94-34488. 202p. 1994. pap. 78.00 (*0-08-042372-8*, Pergamon Pr) Elsevier.

Real-Time Programming 1995. Laplante. (IFAC Postprint Ser.). 220p. Date not set. pap. 69.25 (*0-08-042590-9*, Pergamon Pr) Elsevier.

Real-Time Programming 1996. Ed. by Carlos E. Pereira & W. Halang. (IFAC Postprint Ser.). 1997. pap. text ed. write for info. (*0-08-042614-X*, Pergamon Pr) Elsevier.

Real-Time Proven Commodity Spreads. George Angell. 1985. 72.00 (*0-930233-02-6*) Windsor.

Real-Time Radiologic Imaging: Medical & Industrial - STP 716. Ed. by D. A. Garrett & D. A. Bracher. 352p. 1980. 36.50 (*0-8031-0546-0*, 04-716000-22) ASTM.

Real Time Scheduling Problems in a General Flexible Manufacturing System. Narayan Raman. LC 93-49427. (Studies on Industrial Productivity). 136p. 1994. text ed. 44.00 (*0-8153-1672-0*) Garland.

***Real-Time Search for Learning Autonomous Agents.** LC 97-15500. 1997. text ed. 195.00 (*0-7923-9944-7*) Kluwer Ac.

Real Time Software Control. Auslander & Tham. 1990. text ed. 83.00 (*0-13-762824-2*) P-H.

Real Time Software Design: A Guide for Microprocessor Systems. Philip Heller. 116p. 1986. 32.00 (*0-8176-3201-8*) Birkhauser.

Real-Time Statistical Process Control. Paul C. Badavas. 320p. 1992. text ed. 52.60 (*0-13-763574-5*) P-H.

Real Time Strategic Change: How to Involve an Entire Organization in Fast & Far-Reaching Change. Robert W. Jacobs. LC 94-13444. (Illus.). 260p. 1994. 27.95 (*1-881052-45-1*) Berrett-Koehler.

***Real Time Strategic Change: How to Involve an Entire Organization in Fast & Far-Reaching Change.** Robert W. Jacobs. LC 94-13444. 354p. 1997. reprint ed. pap. 24.95 (*1-57675-030-2*) Berrett-Koehler.

Real-Time Strategy: Improvised Team-Based Planning for a Fast Changing World. Lee T. Perry et al. LC 92-34982. 272p. 1993. text ed. 34.95 (*0-471-58564-5*) Wiley.

Real-Time Structured Methods: Structured Design. Keith Edwards. (Software Engineering Ser.). 450p. 1996. text ed. 60.00 (*0-471-95077-7*) Wiley.

Real-Time Structured Methods: Systems Analysis. Keith Edwards. LC 93-8775. (Series in Industrial Software Engineering Practice). 554p. 1993. text ed. 80.00 (*0-471-93415-1*) Wiley.

Real-Time Systems. Kang G. Shin & C. M. Krishna. LC 96-39004. (Illus.). 448p. 1996. text ed. 50.00 (*0-07-057043-4*) McGraw.

***Real-Time Systems: Design Principles for Distributed Embedded Applications.** Hermann Kopetz. LC 97-9124. (International Series in Engineering & Computer Science, Real-Time Systems). 1997. lib. bdg. 72.50 (*0-7923-9894-7*) Kluwer Ac.

Real-Time Systems: Implementation of Industrial Computerized Process Automation. Wolfgang A. Halang & K. M. Sacha. 380p. 1992. text ed. 86.00 (*981-02-1063-9*); pap. text ed. 36.00 (*981-02-1064-7*) World Scientific Pub.

Real Time Systems: Investigating Industrial Practice. Ian C. Pyle et al. LC 93-12285. (Software-Based Systems Ser.). 329p. 1993. text ed. 82.00 (*0-471-93553-0*) Wiley.

Real-Time Systems: Specification, Verification, & Analysis. Ed. by Mathai Joseph. (Prentice Hall International Series in Computer Science). 400p. (C). 1995. pap. text ed. 63.00 (*0-13-455297-0*) P-H.

Real Time Systems: Theory & Applications. H. Zedan. 1990. 145.00 (*0-444-88625-7*) Elsevier.

Real-Time Systems & Their Programming. 2nd ed. Alan Burns. (C). 1997. pap. text ed. 41.95 (*0-201-40365-X*) Addison-Wesley.

Real-Time Systems & Their Programming Languages. Alan Burns. (C). 1990. text ed. 38.95 (*0-201-17529-0*) Addison-Wesley.

***Real-Time Systems Design & Analysis.** Philip Laplante. Ed. by James Waight & Ronald Wasley. 80p. 1994. student ed. 219.00 incl. disk, vdisk (*0-7803-2262-2*, HL4705) Inst Electrical.

***Real-Time Systems Design & Analysis: An Engineer's Handbook.** 2nd ed. Phillip A. Laplante. LC 96-29044. 384p. 1996. 59.95 (*0-7803-3400-0*, PC5383) Inst Electrical.

Real-Time Systems Education Workshop, 1996. LC 96-77020. 200p. 1996. pap. 50.00 (*0-8186-7649-3*) IEEE Comp Soc.

Real-Time Systems Engineering & Applications. Ed. by Michael Schiebe. (International Series in Engineering & Computer Science, VLSI, Computer Architecture, & Digital Screen Processing). 464p. (C). 1992. lib. bdg. 132.00 (*0-7923-9196-9*) Kluwer Ac.

Real-Time Systems Programming for PCs: Using the IRMX for Windows Operating System. Christopher Vickery. 1993. pap. text ed. 29.95 (*0-07-067466-3*) McGraw.

Real-Time Systems Symposium: Proceedings (16th: 1995: Pisa, Italy) LC 95-79851. 368p. 1995. pap. 70.00 (*0-8186-7337-0*, QA76.54) IEEE Comp Soc.

Real-Time Systems with Transputers. Ed. by H. Zedan. (Transputer & Occam Engineering Ser.). 250p. (gr. 12). 1990. pap. 69.00 (*90-5199-041-3*, Pub. by IOS Pr NE) IOS Press.

Real-Time Systems, 6th Euromicro Workshop On. LC 10-683070. 256p. 1994. pap. 56.00 (*0-8186-6340-5*, 6340) IEEE Comp Soc.

Real-Time Systems, 7th Euromicro Workshop On. LC 10-683070. 376p. 1995. pap. 80.00 (*0-8186-7112-2*, PR07112) IEEE Comp Soc.

***Real-Time Systems, 9th Euromicro Workshop.** 320p. 1997. pap. 90.00 (*0-8186-8034-2*) IEEE Comp Soc.

Real-Time Technology & Applications: Proceedings of the Real-Time Technology & Applications Symposium (1995: Chicago, IL) LC 10-801812. 272p. 1995. pap. 50.00 (*0-8186-6980-2*, PR06980) IEEE Comp Soc.

***Real-Time Technology & Applications Symposium.** 3rd ed. 250p. 1997. pap. 60.00 (*0-8186-8016-4*) IEEE Comp Soc.

Real-Time Technology & Applications Symposium, 1996 IEEE. LC 10-801812. 200p. 1996. pap. 50.00 (*0-8186-7448-2*, PRO7448) IEEE Comp Soc.

Real-Time Ultrasonography. Ed. by Fred Winsberg & Peter L. Cooperberg. LC 82-4479. (Clinics in Diagnostic Ultrasound Ser.: No. 10). (Illus.). 333p. reprint ed. pap. 95.00 (*0-8357-6571-7*, 2035945) Bks Demand.

Real-Time Ultrasound: A Manual for Physician & Technical Personnel. 2nd ed. Royal J. Bartrum, Jr. & Harte C. Crow. LC 77-72802. (Illus.). 1983. text ed. 62.00 (*0-7216-1552-X*) Saunders.

Real-Time Ultrasound Imaging in the Abdomen. M. Leon Skolnick. (Illus.). xi, 241p. 1981. 109.00 (*0-387-90570-7*) Spr-Verlag.

Real Time Ultrasound in Perinatal Medicine. Ed. by R. Chef. (Contributions to Gynecology & Obstetrics Ser.: Vol. 6). (Illus.). 1979. pap. 63.25 (*3-8055-2976-7*) S Karger.

***Real-Time Video Compression: Techniques & Algorithms.** Raymond Westwater & Borivoje Furht. LC 96-38469. (Kluwer International Series in Engineering & Computer Science: Multimedia Systems & Applications). 176p. (C). 1996. lib. bdg. 87.50 (*0-7923-9787-8*) Kluwer Ac.

***Real Time Web Broadcasting.** Que Development Group Staff. 400p. 1997. pap. text ed. 39.99 incl. cd-rom (*0-7897-0948-1*) Que.

Real Toads in Imaginary Gardens: Narrative Accounts of Liberalism. Maureen Whitebrook. LC 94-20511. 160p. reprint ed. pap. 21.95 (*0-8476-7984-5*) Rowman.

Real Toads in Imaginary Gardens: Narrative Accounts of Liberalism. Maureen Whitebrook. LC 94-20511. 160p. 1994. reprint ed. 49.50 (*0-8476-7983-7*) Rowman.

Real Toads in Imaginary Gardens: Suggestions & Starting Points for Young Creative Writers. Stephen P. Policoff & Jeffrey Skinner. LC 91-26524. 200p. (Orig.). (YA). (gr. 5 up). 1991. pap. 11.95 (*1-55652-137-5*) Chicago Review.

Real Tooth Fairy. Marilyn Kaye. (Illus.). 32p. (J). (ps-3). 1990. 14.00 (*0-15-265780-0*) HarBrace.

Real Tooth Fairy. Marilyn Kaye. LC 88-6205. (Illus.). 32p. (J). (ps-3). 1994. pap. 6.00 (*0-15-200120-4*) HarBrace.

Real Treasure: A Real Treasure. Mouse Works Staff. (J). 1995. 5.98 (*1-57082-276-X*) Mouse Works.

Real, True Angel, Vol. 1. unabridged ed. Robin Lippincott. (Fleur-de-lis Ser.). 150p. 1996. pap. 12.00 (*0-9652520-0-0*) Fleur-de-lis Pr.

Real Truth about Baptism in Jesus' Name. John Paterson. 32p. 1995. reprint ed. pap. 2.00 (*1-56722-035-5*) Word Aflame.

Real Truth about Mutual Funds: And How to Make Money on Your Investments. Herbert Ringold. 224p. 1996. 22.95 (*0-8144-0314-X*) AMACOM.

Real Truth Concerning Apostolos Makrakis. Themistocles Livadeas & Minas Charitos. Ed. by Orthodox Christian Educational Society Staff. Tr. by Denver Cummings. 230p. (Orig.). 1952. pap. 5.95 (*0-938366-30-0*) Orthodox Chr.

***Real Twelve Days of Christmas.** Helen Haidle. (Illus.). 32p. (J). 1997. 14.99 (*1-57673-201-0*, Gold & Honey) Multnomah Pubs.

Real Vampires. Daniel Cohen. LC 94-22028. (J). 1995. pap. 13.99 (*0-525-65189-6*, Cobblehill Bks) Dutton Child Bks.

Real Vampires. Daniel Cohen. (J). 1996. pap. text ed. 3.50 (*0-590-64542-0*) Scholastic Inc.

Real Variable & Integration. John J. Benedetto. (Illus.). 1976. pap. 49.95 (*3-519-02209-5*) Adlers Foreign Bks.

Real Variable Method for the Cauchy Transform, & Analytic Capacity. T. Mural. (Lecture Notes in Mathematics Ser.: Vol. 1307). viii, 133p. 1988. 31.95 (*0-387-19091-0*) Spr-Verlag.

Real Variables. Alberto Torchinsky. (C). 1994. pap. 49.95 (*0-201-48327-0*) Addison-Wesley.

Real Variables: With Basic Metric Space Topology. Robert Ash. LC 92-53187. (Illus.). 232p. (C). 1993. text ed. 49.95 (*0-7803-0408-X*, PC0304-6) Inst Electrical.

***Real Vegetarian Thai.** Nancie McDermott. LC 96-37096. 1997. pap. 11.95 (*0-8118-1151-4*) Chronicle Bks.

Real Vermonters Address Book. Frank Bryan & Bill Mares. (Illus.). 112p. spiral bd. 6.95 (*0-933050-24-0*) New Eng Pr VT.

Real Vermonters Don't Milk Goats. Frank Bryan & Bill Mares. LC 83-61500. (Illus.). 96p. (Orig.). 1983. pap. 6.95 (0-933050-16-X) New Eng Pr VT.

Real Virginian: The Saga of Edwin Burnham Trafton, Last of the Stagecoach Robbers. John Watson. (Great West & Indian Ser.: Vol. 53). (Illus.). 1989. 26.95 (0-87026-071-5) Westernlore.

Real Vitamin & Mineral Book: Going Beyond the RDA for Optimum Health. Shari Lieberman & Nancy P. Bruning. LC 90-40460. 326p. (Orig.). 1990. pap. 9.95 (0-89529-449-4) Avery Pub.

Real Vitamin & Mineral Book: Using Supplements for Optimum Health. 2nd ed. Shari Lieberman & Nancy P. Bruning. 368p. Date not set. mass mkt. 6.95 (0-89529-690-X) Avery Pub.

Real Vitamin & Mineral Book: Using Supplements for Optimum Health. 2nd ed. Shari Lieberman & Nancy P. Bruning. 336p. 1996. pap. 12.95 (0-89529-769-8) Avery Pub.

Real Voices. Davis. LC 96-9726. 1997. text ed. 35.00 (0-312-16475-0) St Martin.

Real Wages & Employment: Keynes, Monetarism & the Labour Market. Andres Drobny. 240p. (C). 1988. text ed. 67.50 (0-415-00386-5) Routledge.

Real Wages in Manufacturing: 1890-1914. Albert E. Rees. LC 75-19735. (National Bureau of Economic Research Ser.). (Illus.). 1975. reprint ed. 20.95 (0-405-07612-6) Ayer.

Real Wages in Manufacturing, 1890-1914. Albert E. Rees. (General Ser.: No. 70). 179p. 1961. reprint ed. 46.60 (0-87014-069-8) Natl Bur Econ Res.

Real Wages in Nineteenth & Twentieth Century Europe: Historical & Comparative Perspectives. Peter Scholliers. LC 88-35074. 267p. 1990. 19.95 (0-85496-273-5) Berg Pubs.

Real War. Richard M. Nixon. (Richard Nixon Library). 1990. pap. 12.95 (0-671-70617-9, Touchstone Bks) S&S Trade.

Real War: How the Persian Gulf War Was Actually Fought. Michael Gordon. 1993. 23.00 (0-671-75563-3) S&S Trade.

Real War, Nineteen Fourteen to Nineteen Eighteen. Basil H. Liddell-Hart. 1963. pap. 16.95 (0-316-52505-7) Little.

Real War on Crime: The Report of the National Criminal Justice Commission. Ed. by Steven R. Donziger. 1996. 40.00 (0-06-055365-0) HarpC.

Real War on Crime: The Report of the National Criminal Justice Commission. Steven R. Donziger. (Illus.). 320p. 1996. pap. 15.00 (0-06-095165-6) HarpC.

Real War on Inflation Has Not Begun. Robert S. Morrison. LC 82-5057. (Illus.). 1982. 15.00 (0-912400-25-0); pap. 9.50 (0-912400-26-9) Western Res Pr.

Real War Will Never Get in the Book: Selections from Writers During the Civil War. Ed. by Louis P. Masur. (Illus.). 320p. 1995. pap. 13.95 (0-19-509837-4) OUP.

Real Wealth. Wade Cook. 1985. 16.95 (0-910019-12-6) Lghthse Pub Gp.

Real Weather. Kathleen Aguero. 1987. 15.00 (0-914610-46-5) Hanging Loose.

Real Weather. Kathleen Aguero. 1987. pap. 7.00 (0-914610-42-2) Hanging Loose.

***Real West.** (Illus.). 96p. 1996. 12.95 (0-942576-36-5) CO Hist Soc.

Real West Marginal Way: A Poet's Autobiography. Richard Hugo. (Illus.). 288p. 1992. pap. 10.95 (0-393-30860-X) Norton.

Real Winners. Shaun Gayle. (Illus.). 144p. (J). 1995. 13.99 (1-56476-493-1, 6-3493, Victor Bks) Chariot Victor.

Real Women: Advice, Commentary & Encouragement for Today's Woman. Ed. by Concetta Belleggia. LC 93-80663. 244p. pap. 12.95 (0-89870-462-6) Ignatius Pr.

Real Women Don't Diet. Ken Mayer. 224p. 1995. pap. 4.99 (0-7860-0247-6, Pinncle Kensgtn) Kensgtn Pub Corp.

Real Women Don't Diet! One Man's Praise of Large Women & His Outrage at the Society That Rejects Them. Ken Mayer. LC 93-36312. (Illus.). 1993. 18.95 (0-910155-27-5) Bartleby Pr.

***Real Women Have Curves.** Josefina Lopez. 80p. 1996. pap. 5.25 (0-87129-725-6, R60) Dramatic Pub.

Real Women Only Want One Thing! Peter Devine. 140p. 1995. pap. write for info. (0-9645804-1-1) Devine Prod.

Real Work: Interviews & Talks. Gary Snyder. Ed. by Scott McLean. LC 79-27319. 224p. 1980. 10.00 (0-8112-0760-9); pap. 10.95 (0-8112-0761-7, NDP499) New Directions.

Real World? Michel Tremblay. Tr. by John Van Burek. 1994. pap. 10.95 (0-88922-260-6) Genl Dist Srvs.

Real World. Robert Herrick. (Collected Works of Robert Herrick). 1988. reprint ed. lib. bdg. 59.00 (0-7812-1265-0) Rprt Serv.

Real World: 1861-1968. Tom C. Schleck. 90p. (Orig.). 1995. pap. 5.95 (1-57502-053-X) Morris Pubng.

Real World see Collected Works of Robert Herrick

***Real World after Effects.** Sherry London. 536p. 1997. pap. text ed. 44.95 incl. cd-rom (0-201-68839-5) Peachpit Pr.

***Real World: An Insider's Guide.** Carter. 1997. pap. 16.00 (0-671-01534-6, PB Trade Paper) PB.

Real World & Mathematics. Hugh Burkhardt. 188p. (C). 1981. pap. text ed. 14.95 (0-216-91084-6) Birkhauser.

Real World Answers to Cattle Management Problems. D. Porter Price. (Illus.). 250p. (Orig.). 1991. pap. 37.50 (0-685-50311-9) SWI.

Real World Apple Guide. Jesse Feiler. LC 95-1878. 1995. 39.95 incl. cd-rom (1-55851-429-5, M&T Books) H Holt & Co.

Real World Banking: A Money & Banking Reader. 2nd ed. Dollars & Sense Staff et al. (Illus.). 44p. (C). 1993. pap. text ed. 4.95 (1-878585-56-8) Dollars & Sense.

***Real World Bryce 2.** Susan A. Kitchens. 752p. 1997. 49.95 incl. cd-rom (0-201-69419-0) Peachpit Pr.

***Real World Calculations.** Messler. 1998. pap. text ed. write for info. (0-7216-7556-5) Saunders.

Real World Client-Server: Learn How to Successfully Migrate to Client Server Computing from Someone Who's Actually Done It. Steve Krantz. Ed. by Jim Hoskins. LC 94-29380. (Orig.). 1995. pap. 29.95 (0-9633214-7-1) Maximum Pr.

Real World Computers Graphics Real Lime. 1998. 49.99 (0-672-30750-2) Sams.

Real-World Customer Service: What to Really Say When the Customer Complains. Bernice B. Johnston. LC 95-36909. (Small Business Sourcebooks Ser.). 144p. 1995. pap. 9.95 (1-57071-062-7) Sourcebks.

Real World Diaries. MTV Staff. 1996. pap. 18.00 (0-671-00373-9, MTV Bks) PB.

Real World Economic Applications: The Wall Street Journal. 2nd ed. Michael B. Lehmann. 276p. (C). 1991. text ed. 33.95 (0-256-09102-1) Irwin.

***Real World Economic Applications: The Wall Street Journal.** 6th ed. Lehmann. 1997. wbk. ed., text ed. 29.20 (0-256-14024-3) McGraw.

Real World Economic Applications: The Wall Street Journal Workbook. 4th ed. Michael B. Lehmann. 272p. (C). 1995. per. 36.50 (0-256-13729-3) Irwin.

Real World Electrology: The Blend Method: The Illustrated Manual of the Blend Method of Electrolysis. Michael Bono. (Illus.). 368p. (Orig.). (C). 1994. pap. text ed. 45.00 (0-9642682-0-5) Tortoise Press.

Real-World Engineering: A Guide to Career Success. Lawrence J. Kamm. LC 91-2043. 256p. 1991. reprint ed. 29.95 (0-87942-279-3, PP02733) Inst Electrical.

"Real World" Ethics: Frameworks for Educators & Human Service Professionals. Robert J. Nash. LC 96-21591. (Professional Ethics in Education Ser.: Vol. 8). 192p. (C). 1996. text ed. 46.00 (0-8077-3557-4); pap. text ed. 21.95 (0-8077-3556-6) Tchrs Coll.

Real World FreeHand 4. Olav M. Kvern. (Illus.). 632p. (C). 1994. pap. text ed. 29.95 (1-56609-103-9) Peachpit Pr.

Real World FreeHand 5.0 - 5.5. Olav M. Kvern. (Illus.). 732p. (C). 1996. pap. text ed. 29.95 (0-201-88360-0) Peachpit Pr.

***Real World Illustrator 7.** Deke McClelland. (Illus.). 816p. (C). 1997. pap. text ed. 29.95 (0-201-69612-6) Peachpit Pr.

Real-World Intelligence: Organized Information for Executives. Herbert E. Meyer. 102p. 1991. 19.95 (0-935166-05-X) Storm King Pr.

Real-World Interfacing with Your PC: A Hands-On Guide to Parallel Port Projects. James J. Barbarello. LC 96-67583. (Illus.). 119p. (Orig.). (C). 1996. pap. 16.95 (0-7906-1078-7) Prompt Publns.

Real World International. 2nd ed. Dollars & Sense Staff et al. Ed. by Marc Breslow & David Levy. (Illus.). (C). 1994. pap. text ed. 6.50 (1-878585-06-1) Dollars & Sense.

Real World International. 3rd rev. ed. Ed. by Marc Breslow et al. (Illus.). 84p. (C). 1996. pap. text ed. 6.50 (1-878585-10-X) Dollars & Sense.

Real-World Linguist: Linguistic Applications in the 1980's. Ed. by Peter C. Bjarkman & Victor Raskin. LC 85-46067. 384p. 1986. text ed. 73.25 (0-89391-357-X) Ablex Pub.

Real World Look at Windows Help Authoring Tools. Cheryl L. Zubak. (Illus.). 450p. (Orig.). 1995. pap. text ed. 45.00 (0-9645293-0-0) WorkWrite.

Real World Macro. 12th ed. Dollars & Sense Staff et al. Ed. by Marc Breslow et al. (Illus.). 1995. pap. text ed. 12.95 (1-878585-07-X) Dollars & Sense.

Real World Macro. 13th rev. ed. Ed. by Marc Breslow et al. (Illus.). 128p. (Orig.). (C). 1996. pap. text ed. 12.95 (1-878585-09-6) Dollars & Sense.

***Real World Macro.** 14th rev. ed. Ed. by Marc Breslow et al. (Orig.). 1997. pap. text ed. 14.50 (1-878585-11-8) Dollars & Sense.

Real World Math. Karen Brown. Ed. by Deneen Celecia. (Illus.). 80p. 1994. student ed., pap. 8.95 (1-56472-172-8) Edupress.

Real World Measurement. Robert Rohm & John W. Shaw. LC 79-730249. (Illus.). 1979. student ed. 89.00 incl. audio (0-89290-097-0, A513-SATC) Soc for Visual.

Real World Micro. 5th ed. Dollars & Sense Staff. Ed. by Marc Breslow et al. (C). 1994. pap. text ed. 12.95 (1-878585-33-9) Dollars & Sense.

Real World Micro. 6th rev. ed. Ed. by Randy Albelda et al. (Illus.). 128p. (Orig.). (C). 1996. pap. text ed. 12.95 (1-878585-34-7) Dollars & Sense.

***Real-World Networking with NT4.** William Holderby. 1996. pap. text ed. 39.99 (1-57610-055-3) Coriolis Grp.

Real World of Alternate ID Acquisition. D. P. Rochelle. 28p. 1987. pap. 8.00 (0-87364-440-9) Paladin Pr.

Real World of Buying & Selling Your Home. Bob Dean. Ed. by William W. Denlinger & R. Annabel Rathman. LC 84-23045. (Real Estate Ser.). 208p. 1985. pap. 6.95 (0-87714-119-3) Denlingers.

Real World of Chemistry. 2nd ed. Lois Fruen. 320p. 1996. pap. text ed., spiral bd. 34.95 (0-7872-1987-8) Kendall-Hunt.

Real World of Child Interrogations. Ralph C. Underwager & Hollida C. Wakefield. 376p. 1989. pap. 43.95 (0-398-06469-5) C C Thomas.

Real World of Child Interrogations. Ralph C. Underwager & Hollida C. Wakefield. 376p. (C). 1989. text ed. 73.95 (0-398-05620-X) C C Thomas.

Real World of Democracy. C. B. Macpherson. 78p. 1972. pap. 9.95 (0-19-501534-7) OUP.

Real World of Democracy Revisited: And Other Essays on Democracy & Socialism. Frank Cunningham. LC 93-14234. 176p. (C). 1994. text ed. 45.00 (0-391-03837-0) Humanities.

Real World of Democracy Revisited: And Other Essays on Democracy & Socialism. Frank Cunningham. LC 93-14234. 176p. (C). 1994. pap. 15.00 (0-391-03838-9) Humanities.

Real World of Engineering: Case Histories 1-40. 65.00 (0-614-05207-6, RWE04903.5M) ASFE.

Real World of Engineering: Case Histories 41-65. 50.00 (0-614-05208-4) ASFE.

Real World of Engineering No. 41: Case History. 3.50 (0-614-05209-2, CHN04205913.5M) ASFE.

Real World of Engineering No. 42: Case History. 3.50 (0-614-05210-6, CHN04205913.5M) ASFE.

Real World of Engineering No. 43: Case History. 3.50 (0-614-05211-4, CHN04305913.5M) ASFE.

Real World of Engineering No. 44: Case History. 3.50 (0-614-05212-2, CHN04305913.5M) ASFE.

Real World of Engineering No. 44: Case History. 3.50 (0-614-05213-0, CHN04459913.5M) ASFE.

Real World of Engineering No. 45: Case History. 3.50 (0-614-05214-9, CHN04505913.5M) ASFE.

Real World of Engineering No. 46: Case History. 3.50 (0-614-05215-7, CHN04605913.5M) ASFE.

Real World of Engineering No. 47: Case History. 3.50 (0-614-05216-5, CHN04705913.5M) ASFE.

Real World of Engineering No. 48: Case History. 3.50 (0-614-05217-3, CHN04805913.5M) ASFE.

Real World of Engineering No. 49: Case History. 3.50 (0-614-05218-1, CHN04905913.5M) ASFE.

Real World of Engineering No. 50: Case History. 3.50 (0-614-05219-X, CHN05005913.5M) ASFE.

Real World of Engineering No. 51: Case History. 3.50 (0-614-05220-3, CHN05105913.5M) ASFE.

Real World of Engineering No. 52: Case History. 3.50 (0-614-05221-1, CHN05205913.5M) ASFE.

Real World of Engineering No. 53: Case History. 3.50 (0-614-05222-X, CHN05305913.5M) ASFE.

Real World of Engineering No. 54: Case History. 3.50 (0-614-05223-8, CHN05405913.5M) ASFE.

Real World of Engineering No. 55: Case History. 3.50 (0-614-05224-6, CHN05505913.5M) ASFE.

Real World of Engineering No. 56: Case History. 3.50 (0-614-05225-4, CHN05605923.5M) ASFE.

Real World of Engineering No. 57: Case History. 3.50 (0-614-05226-2, CHN05705923.5M) ASFE.

Real World of Engineering No. 58: Case History. 3.50 (0-614-05227-0, CHN05805923.5M) ASFE.

Real World of Engineering No. 59: Case History. 3.50 (0-614-05228-9, CHN05905913.5M) ASFE.

Real World of Engineering No. 60: Case History. 3.50 (0-614-05229-7, CHN06005923.5M) ASFE.

Real World of Engineering No. 61: Case History. 3.50 (0-614-05230-0, CHN06103943.5M) ASFE.

Real World of Engineering No. 62: Case History. 3.50 (0-614-05231-9, CHN06203943.5M) ASFE.

Real World of Engineering No. 63: Case History. 3.50 (0-614-05232-7, CHN06303943.5M) ASFE.

Real World of Engineering No. 64: Case History. 3.50 (0-614-05233-5, CHN06403943.5M) ASFE.

Real World of Engineering No. 65: Case History. 3.50 (0-614-05234-3, CHN06503943.5M) ASFE.

Real World of Fairies. Dora Van Gelder. LC 77-5250. (Illus.). (Orig.). 1977. pap. 10.00 (0-8356-0497-7, Quest) Theos Pub Hse.

Real World of Manuel Cordova. W. S. Merwin. 47p. 1995. 450.00 (0-9614597-9-4) Ninja Pr.

Real World of Sherlock Holmes: The True Crime Casebooks of Arthur Conan Doyle. Peter Costello. 240p. 1991. 19.95 (0-88184-738-0) Carroll & Graf.

Real World of Sherlock Holmes: The True Crimes Investigated by Arthur Conan Doyle. Peter Costello. (Illus.). 256p. 1993. pap. 10.95 (0-7867-0020-3) Carroll & Graf.

Real World of the Small Business Owner. Richard Scase & Robert Goffee. 166p. 1987. pap. 19.95 (0-7099-5416-6, Pub. by Croom Helm UK) Routledge Chapman & Hall.

Real World Order: Zones of Peace, Zones of Turmoil. rev. ed. Max Singer & Aaron Wildavsky. LC 95-33627. (Illus.). (C). 1996. pap. text ed. 19.95 (1-56643-031-3) Chatham Hse Pubs.

Real World PageMaker 4 Mac. Olav M. Kvern. 1990. pap. 27.95 (0-679-79022-5) Random.

Real World Photoshop 3. David Blatner & Bruce Fraser. 600p. (C). 1995. pap. text ed. 39.95 (1-56609-169-1) Peachpit Pr.

***Real World Photoshop 4.** 2nd ed. (C). 1997. pap. text ed. 39.95 (0-201-68888-3) Peachpit Pr.

Real World PostScript: Techniques from PostScript. Ed. by Stephen F. Roth. 400p. 1988. pap. 22.95 (0-201-06663-7) Addison-Wesley.

Real-World Programming with Visual Basic 4. 2nd ed. Anthony T. Mann. (Illus.). 1184p. 1995. 45.00 (0-672-30779-0) Sams.

Real-World Programming with Visual C++ 1998. 45.00 (0-672-30836-3) Sams.

***Real-World Project Management: New Approaches for Adapting to Change & Uncertainty.** Gilles et al. LC 96-53330. 230p. 1997. 42.50 (0-527-76321-7) Qual Resc.

***Real World QuarkImmedia.** David Blatner. 464p. 1997. 39.95 incl. cd-rom (0-201-88679-0) Peachpit Pr.

Real World Reading. Karen Brown & Holly Engel. Ed. by Deneen Celecia. (Illus.). 80p. 1994. student ed., pap. 8.95 (1-56472-044-6) Edupress.

***Real-World Research.** Peterson. (C). Date not set. pap. write for info. (0-395-74124-6) HM.

Real World Research: A Resource for Social Scientists & Practitioner-Researchers. Colin Robson. LC 92-21782. 512p. 1993. pap. 29.95 (0-631-17689-6) Blackwell Pubs.

Real World Scanning & Halftones. David Blatner & Stephen F. Roth. (Illus.). 296p. (C). 1993. pap. text ed. 24.95 (1-56609-093-8) Peachpit Pr.

Real World Science. Holly Engel. Ed. by Deneen Celecia. (Illus.). 80p. 1994. student ed., pap. 8.95 (1-56472-174-4) Edupress.

***Real-World Science & Technology.** Zondra Knapp. Ed. by Joel Kupperstein. (Investigations in Science Ser.). (Illus.). 144p. (Orig.). 1997. pap. 15.98 (1-57471-221-7, 2810) Creat Teach Pr.

***Real World Whitetail Behavior.** Jim Roy. Ed. by Craig Boddington. (Whitetail Secrets Ser.: No. 9). (Illus.). 190p. (YA). (gr. 10 up). 1996. 17.95 (1-56416-159-5) Derrydale Pr.

Real Worlds of Canadian Politics. 3rd ed. Robert Campbell. 300p. 1994. pap. 12.95 (1-55111-029-6) Broadview Pr.

***Real Worship.** Wiersbe. Date not set. pap. 10.99 (0-8407-9585-8) Nelson.

***Real Writing.** Anker. Date not set. teacher ed., pap. text ed. write for info. (0-312-13293-X); teacher ed., pap. text ed. write for info. (0-312-13344-8) St Martin.

Real Writing: Argumentation, Reflection, Information. Walter H. Beale. LC 85-14512. 398p. reprint ed. pap. 113.50 (0-7837-5208-3, 2044936) Bks Demand.

Real Writing: Essential Effective Writing. Schwartz. 1989. pap. 10.26 (0-8092-4241-9) Contemp Bks.

***Real Writing with Readings.** Anker. Date not set. pap. text ed. write for info. (0-312-13342-1) St Martin.

***Real You.** Kennie Anderson. 96p. (Orig.). 1997. pap. 5.00 (1-57502-401-2, P01245) Morris Pubng.

Real You: Discovering Your Identity in Christ. Bill Hybels. (Interactions: Small Group Ser.). 96p. 1996. student ed., pap. 5.99 (0-310-20682-0) Zondervan.

Realencyclopaedie der Classischen Altertumswissenschaft, 68 vols & 15 suppl. vols. A. F. Pauly & G. Wissowa. write for info. (3-476-00826-6) Adlers Foreign Bks.

***Realidad Aparte.** Carlos Castaneda. 1992. pap. text ed. 11.99 (968-16-0218-8) Fondo de Cultura Economica.

Realidad Como Resultado. Enrique T. Galvan. 106p. (C). 1966. pap. 1.50 (0-8477-2802-1) U of PR Pr.

Realidad Invisible (Nineteen Seventeen-Nineteen Twenty, Nineteen Twenty-Four) Antonio S. Romeralo. Ed. by Juan R. Jimenez. (Textos B Ser.: Vol. XXI). 383p. (SPA.). (C). 1983. 63.00 (0-7293-0070-6, Pub. by Tamesis Bks Ltd UK) Boydell & Brewer.

Realidad y Mito de la I Republica. Jose M. Jover Zamora. (Nueva Austral Ser.: Vol. 194). (SPA.). 1991. pap. text ed. 24.95 (84-239-1994-3) Elliots Bks.

Realife, 4 bks., Set. Heather K. Bohr. Ed. by Thomas Unterseher. 127p. (Orig.). (JPN.). 1993. pap. text ed. 89.99 incl. audio (1-57237-045-9); pap. text ed. 89.99 incl. audio (1-57237-044-0); pap. text ed. 89.99 incl. audio (1-57237-046-7); pap. text ed. 89.99 incl. audio (1-57237-047-5) Cultural Designs.

Realife: Business. Heather K. Bohr. Ed. by Thomas Unterseher. 32p. (Orig.). (SPA.). 1993. pap. text ed. 22.99 incl. audio (1-57237-026-2); pap. text ed. 22.99 incl. audio (1-57237-030-0); pap. text ed. 22.99 incl. audio (1-57237-034-3); pap. text ed. 22.99 incl. audio (1-57237-038-6); pap. text ed. 22.99 incl. audio (1-57237-042-4); audio compact disk 29.99 (1-57237-001-7); audio compact disk 29.99 (1-57237-005-X); audio compact disk 29.99 (1-57237-009-2); audio compact disk 29.99 (1-57237-013-0); audio compact disk 29.99 (1-57237-021-1) Cultural Designs.

Realife: Entertainment. Heather K. Bohr. Ed. by Thomas Unterseher. 32p. (Orig.). (SPA.). 1993. pap. text ed. 22.99 incl. audio (1-57237-025-4); pap. text ed. 22.99 incl. audio (1-57237-029-7); pap. text ed. 22.99 incl. audio (1-57237-033-5); pap. text ed. 22.99 incl. audio (1-57237-037-8); pap. text ed. 22.99 incl. audio (1-57237-041-6); pap. text ed. 29.99 incl. audio compact disk (1-57237-004-1); pap. text ed. 29.99 incl. audio compact disk (1-57237-000-9); audio compact disk 29.99 (1-57237-008-4); audio compact disk 29.99 (1-57237-012-2); audio compact disk 29.99 (1-57237-020-3) Cultural Designs.

Realife: Etiquette. Heather K. Bohr. Ed. by Thomas Unterseher. 31p. (Orig.). (SPA.). 1993. pap. text ed. 22.99 incl. audio (1-57237-027-0); pap. text ed. 22.99 incl. audio (1-57237-031-9); pap. text ed. 22.99 incl. audio (1-57237-035-1); pap. text ed. 22.99 incl. audio (1-57237-039-4); pap. text ed. 22.99 incl. audio (1-57237-048-3); audio compact disk 29.99 (1-57237-022-X); audio compact disk 29.99 (1-57237-002-5); audio compact disk 29.99 (1-57237-006-8); audio compact disk 29.99 (1-57237-010-6); audio compact disk 29.99 (1-57237-014-9) Cultural Designs.

Realife: Relationships. Heather K. Bohr. Ed. by Thomas Unterseher. 32p. (Orig.). (SPA.). 1993. pap. text ed. 22.99 incl. audio (1-57237-028-9); pap. text ed. 22.99 incl. audio (1-57237-032-7); pap. text ed. 22.99 incl. audio (1-57237-036-X); pap. text ed. 22.99 incl. audio (1-57237-040-8); pap. text ed. 22.99 incl. audio (1-57237-049-1); audio compact disk 29.99 (1-57237-023-8); audio compact disk 29.99 (1-57237-003-3); audio compact disk 29.99 (1-57237-007-6); audio compact disk 29.99 (1-57237-011-4); audio compact disk 29.99 (1-57237-015-7) Cultural Designs.

Realignment of World Power, 1. Oton Ambroz. LC 73-149631. 744p. 1972. 13.95 (0-8315-0114-6) Speller.

Realignment of World Power, 2. Oton Ambroz. LC 73-149631. 744p. 1972. 13.95 (0-8315-0115-4) Speller.

Realignments in the Welfare State: Health Policy in the United States, Britain, & Canada. Mary Ruggie. LC 96-10966. (Illus.). 336p. 1996. 40.00 (0-231-10484-7); pap. 18.50 (0-231-10485-5) Col U Pr.

An Asterisk (*) at the beginning of an entry indicates that the title is appearing in BIP for the first time.

Realisation d'Une Etude de Faisabilite: Activites de Formation Pour Creer Ou Faire le Bilan d'Une Petite Entreprise. Ed. by Suzanne Kindervatter. LC 87-63406. (Formation Commerciale Appropriee pour la Femme du Tiers Monde Ser.). (Illus.). 170p. (Orig.). (FRE.). 1987. pap. 17.00 (*0-912917-16-4*) UNIFEM.

Realising CIM's Industrial Potential: Proceedings of CIM Europe Ninth Annual Conference, 12-14 May, 1993, Amsterdam, Netherlands. Ed. by J. Bastos et al. LC 93-78139. (Design & Manufacturing Ser.: Vol. 2). 397p. (gr. 12). 1993. 117.00 (*90-5199-130-4*, Pub. by IOS Pr NE) IOS Press.

Realism. Ed. by Daniel O. Dahlstrom. (Proceedings of the American Catholic Philosophical Association Ser.: Vol. 59). 250p. 1985. 20.00 (*0-918090-19-9*) Am Cath Philo.

Realism. Lilian Furst. 350p. (C). 1993. pap. text ed. 29.50 (*0-582-08531-4*, 79353) Longman.

Realism. Tom Mandel. (Burning Deck Poetry Ser.). 80p. (Orig.). 1991. pap. 8.00 (*0-930901-70-3*) Burning Deck.

Realism. Linda Nochlin. (Style & Civilization Ser.). (Orig.). 1972. pap. 10.95 (*0-14-021305-8*, Penguin Bks) Viking Penguin.

Realism. Linda Nochlin. 1972. pap. 12.95 (*0-14-013222-8*) Viking Penguin.

Realism. limited ed. Tom Mandel. (Burning Deck Poetry Ser.). 80p. (Orig.). 1991. Signed. pap. 15.00 (*0-930901-71-1*) Burning Deck.

Realism: A Critique of Brentano & Meinong. Gustav Bergmann. 468p. (Orig.). 1967. 25.00 (*0-299-04330-4*) U of Wis Pr.

Realism: An Attempt to Trace Its Origin & Development in Its Chief Representatives. Saiyid Zafar al-Hasan. LC 74-173110. 1972. reprint ed. 23.95 (*0-405-09111-7*) Ayer.

Realism: Restatements & Renewal. Ed. by Benjamin Frankel. (Cass Series on Security). 300p. (Orig.). (C). 1996. pap. 20.00 (*0-7146-4146-4*, Pub. by F Cass Pubs UK); text ed. 45.00 (*0-7146-4608-3*, Pub. by F Cass Pubs UK) Intl Spec Bk.

Realism: The Foundation of Perestroika. Yakovlev. Date not set. write for info. (*0-08-040807-9*, Pergamon Pr) Elsevier.

Realism & Allegory in the Early Fiction of Mao Tun. Yu-shih Chen. LC 84-48486. (Studies in Chinese Literature & Society). 272p. 1986. 25.95 (*0-253-34950-8*) Ind U Pr.

Realism & Anti-Realism in the Philosophy of Science: Beijing International Conference, 1992. Ed. by Robert S. Cohen. LC 94-39752. (Boston Studies in the Philosophy of Science: Vol. 169). 510p. (C). 1996. lib. bdg. 199.00 (*0-7923-3233-4*, Pub. by Klwr Acad Pubs NE) Kluwer Ac.

*__Realism & Explanatory Priority.__ John Wright. LC 97-2850. (Philosophical Studies). 1997. lib. bdg. 149.00 (*0-7923-4484-7*) Kluwer Ac.

Realism & Hope. Ronald H. Stone. (C). 1977. pap. text ed. 22.50 (*0-8191-0128-1*) U Pr of Amer.

Realism & Imagination. Joseph Chiari. LC 74-131248. 218p. (C). 1970. reprint ed. 50.00 (*0-87752-019-4*) Gordian.

Realism & Invention in the Prints of Albrecht Durer. David R. Smith & Liz Guenther. LC 95-81131. (Illus.). 84p. 1996. pap. 15.95 (*0-9648953-0-7*) U NH Art Gallery.

Realism & Naturalism in Nineteenth-Century American Literature. rev. ed. Donald Pizer. LC 83-20406. 176p. 1984. 19.95 (*0-8093-1125-9*) S Ill U Pr.

Realism & Naturalism in Puerto Rico. Julia M. Guzman. (Puerto Rico Ser.). 1979. lib. bdg. 59.95 (*0-8490-2993-7*) Gordon Pr.

Realism & Nominalism Revisited. Henry B. Veatch. (Aquinas Lectures). 1954. 15.00 (*0-87462-119-4*) Marquette.

Realism & Politics in Victorian Art of the Crimean War. Matthew P. Lalumia. LC 83-24284. (Studies in the Fine Arts: Iconography: No. 9). (Illus.). 304p. reprint ed. pap. 86.70 (*0-8357-1499-3*, 2070502) Bks Demand.

Realism & Power: Postmodern British Fiction. Alison Lee. 176p. (C). 1990. pap. text ed. 16.95 (*0-415-04103-1*, A4026) Routledge.

Realism & Relativism: A Perspective on Kenneth Burke. Robert L. Heath. LC 86-12825. 320p. (C). 1986. 36.95 (*0-86554-231-7*, MUP-H204) Mercer Univ Pr.

Realism & Representation: Essays on the Problem of Realism in Relation to Science, Literature & Culture. Ed. by George Levine. LC 92-26774. (Science & Literature Ser.). 348p. (Orig.). (C). 1993. 50.00 (*0-299-13630-2*); pap. 23.50 (*0-299-13634-5*) U of Wis Pr.

Realism & Revolution: Balzac, Stendahl, Zola & the Performances of History. Sandy Petrey. LC 88-18117. 224p. 1989. 35.00 (*0-8014-2216-7*) Cornell U Pr.

*__Realism & Social Vision in Courbet & Proudhon.__ James H. Rubin. LC 80-17559. (Princeton Essays on the Arts Ser.: No. 10). (Illus.). 230p. 1980. reprint ed. pap. 65.60 (*0-608-02742-1*, 2063407) Bks Demand.

Realism & the Aim of Science: From the Postscript to the Logic of Scientific Discovery. Karl R. Popper. Ed. by W. W. Bartley, III. LC 91-45665. 463p. (C). 1992. pap. 22.95 (*0-415-08400-8*, Routledge NY) Routledge.

Realism & the American Dramatic Tradition. Ed. by William W. Demastes. 312p. (Orig.). (C). 1996. pap. text ed. 29.95 (*0-8173-0837-7*) U of Ala Pr.

Realism & the Background of Phenomenology. Ed. by Roderick M. Chisholm. vii, 308p. 1981. reprint ed. pap. text ed. 15.00 (*0-917930-14-2*); reprint ed. lib. bdg. 30.00 (*0-917930-34-7*) Ridgeview.

Realism & the Birth of the Modern United States: Literature, Cinema, & Culture. Stanley Corkin. LC 94-23968. 1995. 40.00 (*0-8203-1730-6*) U of Ga Pr.

Realism & the Cinema: A Reader. Ed. by Christopher Williams. (BFI Readers in Film Ser.). 320p. 1980. 29.50 (*0-7100-0477-X*, RKP); pap. 13.95 (*0-7100-0478-8*, RKP) Routledge.

Realism & the Drama of Reference: Strategies of Representation in Balzac, Flaubert, & James. Meili Steele. LC 87-22467. 160p. 1988. lib. bdg. 30.00 (*0-271-00618-8*) Pa St U Pr.

Realism & the Progress of Science. Peter Smith. LC 81-6151. (Cambridge Studies in Philosophy). 160p. 1982. text ed. 27.95 (*0-521-23937-0*) Cambridge U Pr.

Realism & Tinsel: Cinema & Society in Britain, 1989-48. Robert Murphy. (Cinema & Society Ser.). 288p. 1989. 49.50 (*0-415-02982-1*, A3176) Routledge.

*__Realism & Truth.__ 2nd ed. Michael Devitt. LC 96-28286. 340p. 1997. pap. text ed. 18.95 (*0-691-01187-7*) Princeton U Pr.

Realism, Character, & Bias: The Fiction of Mendele Mocher Sefarim. David Aberbach. (Littman Library of Jewish Civilization). 144p. 1993. 29.95 (*1-874774-07-2*); pap. 14.95 (*1-874774-08-0*) Bnai Brith Bk.

Realism, Idealism, & International Politics. Martin Griffiths. 240p. (C). 1995. pap. 16.95 (*0-415-12472-7*, C0558) Routledge.

Realism, Idealism & International Politics: A Reinterpretation. Martin Griffiths. LC 91-47982. 208p. (C). (gr. 13). 1992. text ed. 52.95 (*0-415-06971-8*, A7558) Routledge.

Realism, Identity & Emotion: Reclaiming Social Psychology. John D. Greenwood. 256p. 1994. 49.95 (*0-8039-8926-1*); pap. 25.95 (*0-8039-8927-X*) Sage.

Realism in Alexandrian Poetry: A Literature & Its Audience. Graham Zanker. 272p. 1987. 59.95 (*0-7099-3005-4*, Pub. by Croom Helm UK) Routledge Chapman & Hall.

Realism in Environmental Testing & Control: Proceedings of the Institute of Environmental Sciences 19th Annual Meeting, Anaheim, CA. LC 62-38584. (Illus.). 1973. pap. text ed. 75.00 (*0-915414-13-9*) Inst Environ Sci.

Realism in European Theater & Drama, 1870-1920: A Bibliography. Compiled by Robert D. Boyer. LC 78-19934. 236p. 1979. text ed. 49.95 (*0-313-20607-4*, BOR/, Greenwood Pr) Greenwood.

Realism in Green Politics: Social Movements & Ecological Reform in Germany. Helmut Wiesenthal. Ed. by Timothy O'Riordan & Albert Weale. (Issues in Environmental Politics Ser.). 208p. 1993. text ed. 79.95 (*0-7190-3701-8*, Pub. by Manchester Univ Pr UK) St Martin.

Realism in Law-Making. Ed. by Adriaan Bos & Hugo Siblesz. 1986. lib. bdg. 132.00 (*90-247-3399-5*) Kluwer Ac.

Realism in Literature & Art. Clarence Darrow. 1973. 59.95 (*0-8490-0932-4*) Gordon Pr.

Realism in Mathematics. Penelope Maddy. 216p. 1992. pap. 21.00 (*0-19-824035-X*) OUP.

Realism in Nineteenth Century Music. Carl Dahlhaus. Tr. by Mary Whittall from GER. 160p. 1985. pap. 17.95 (*0-521-27841-4*) Cambridge U Pr.

Realism in Polish Politics: Warsaw Positivism & National Survival in Nineteenth Century Poland. Stanislaus A. Blejwas. LC 83-51814. (Yale Russian & East European Publications: No. 5). xii, 312p. 1984. 27.50 (*0-936586-05-2*) Yale Russian.

Realism in Retrospect: The Works of James Peter Cost. Norton, R. W., Art Gallery Staff. LC 75-164700. (Contemporary Realists Ser.). (Illus.). 1971. pap. 3.50 (*0-9600182-3-9*) Norton Art.

Realism in the Application of ACI Standard 214-65. American Concrete Institute Staff. LC 73-75845. (Publication Ser.: No. SP-37). 223p. reprint ed. pap. 63.60 (*0-7837-2181-1*, 2042519) Bks Demand.

*__Realism in the Sciences: Proceedings of the Ernan McMullin Symposium, 1995.__ Ed. by Igor Douven & Leon Horsten. (Louvain Philosophical Studies: No. 10). 216p. 1996. pap. 52.50 (*90-6186-763-0*, Pub. by Leuven Univ BE) Coronet Bks.

Realism in Wood: Carving Twenty-Two Different Birds & Animals. George Lehman & David Hunt. (Woodcarvers' Favorite Patterns Ser.: Bk. 2). 96p. 1991. spiral bd. 19.95 (*1-56523-005-1*) Fox Chapel Pub.

Realism, Meaning, & Truth. Crispin Wright. LC 92-19114. 1993. pap. 27.95 (*0-631-17118-5*) Blackwell Pubs.

Realism, Myth, & History in Defoe's Fiction. Maximillian E. Novak. LC 82-11141. 199p. reprint ed. pap. 56.80 (*0-7837-2087-4*, 2042363) Bks Demand.

Realism of the Coming. Ilija Poplasen. (Illus.). 540p. 1993. 20.00 (*0-935352-25-2*) MIR PA.

Realism of William Dean Howells, 1889-1920. George N. Bennett. LC 72-1345. 254p. 1973. 24.95 (*0-8265-1180-5*) Vanderbilt U Pr.

Realism, Rationalism, Surrealism: Art Between the Wars. David Batchelor et al. (Illus.). 371p. (C). 1993. reprint ed. pap. 27.00 (*0-300-05519-6*) Yale U Pr.

Realism Rescued: How Scientific Progress Is Possible. Jerrold L. Aronson et al. 223p. 1995. text ed. 49.95 (*0-8126-9288-8*); pap. text ed. 18.95 (*0-8126-9289-6*) Open Court.

Realism Text & Prints. (Illus.). 20p. 1992. pap. text ed. 175.00 (*0-935493-66-2*) Modern Learn Pr.

Realism Today: Aspects of the Contemporary West German Novel. Keith Bullivant. LC 86-31018. 257p. 1987. 19.95 (*0-85496-521-1*) Berg Pubs.

Realism, Utopia, & the Mushroom Cloud: Four Activist Intellectuals & Their Strategies for Peace, 1945-1989. Michael Bess. LC 93-9707. (Illus.). 344p. 1993. pap. text ed. 19.95 (*0-226-04421-1*); lib. bdg. 54.95 (*0-226-04420-3*) U Ch Pr.

Realism with a Human Face. Hilary Putnam. 424p. (C). 1992. pap. 15.95 (*0-674-74945-6*) HUP.

Realism, Writing, Disfiguration: On Thomas Eakins & Stephen Crane. Michael Fried. LC 86-16478. (Illus.). 232p. 1987. 35.00 (*0-226-26210-3*) U Ch Pr.

Realism, Writing, Disfiguration: On Thomas Eakins & Stephen Crane. Michael Fried. LC 86-16478. (Illus.). xvi, 240p. 1988. pap. text ed. 18.95 (*0-226-26211-1*) U Ch Pr.

Realism/Antirealism & Epistemology. Ed. by Christopher B. Kulp. (Studies in Epistemology & Cognitive Theory: No. 35). 240p. 1996. 57.50 (*0-8476-8335-4*); pap. 22.95 (*0-8476-8336-2*) Rowman.

*__Realismo Magico y lo Real Maravilloso en "El Reino de Este Mundo" y "El Siglo de las Luces" de Alejo Carpentier.__ Juan Varroso. (SPA.). pap. 12.00 (*0-89729-110-7*) Ediciones.

Realist at War: The Mature Years 1885-1920 of William Dean Howells. Edwin H. Cady. LC 86-3174. 311p. 1986. reprint ed. text ed. 96.00 (*0-313-25205-X*, CARE, Greenwood Pr) Greenwood.

Realist Conception of Truth. William P. Alston. 296p. 1996. 35.00 (*0-8014-3187-5*) Cornell U Pr.

*__Realist Conception of Truth.__ William P. Alston. 296p. 1996. pap. 16.95 (*0-8014-8410-3*) Cornell U Pr.

Realist Criminology: Crime Control & Policing in the 1990s. Ed. by John Lowman & Brian D. MacLean. LC 92-95006. 370p. 1992. pap. 24.95 (*0-8020-7702-1*) U of Toronto Pr.

Realist Fantasy: Fiction & Reality Since Clarissa. Paul Coates. LC 83-8637. 225p. 1984. text ed. 29.95 (*0-312-66524-5*) St Martin.

Realist Fiction & the Problem of Vision. John Rignall. LC 91-47726. 240p. (C). (gr. 13). 1992. text ed. 69.95 (*0-415-06383-3*, A7973) Routledge.

Realist Image in Social Science. Derek Layder. LC 89-34396. 256p. 1990. text ed. 49.95 (*0-312-03532-2*) St Martin.

Realist in the American Theatre: Selected Drama Criticism of William Dean Howells. Intro. by Brenda Murphy. LC 92-14195. 270p. (C). 1992. text ed. 34.95 (*0-8214-1036-9*) Ohio U Pr.

Realist Novel: An Introductory Textbook. Ed. by Dennis Walder. LC 95-25354. (Open University Set Bks./ Approaching Literature Ser.). 352p. (C). 1996. pap. 17.95 (*0-415-13572-9*); text ed. 65.00 (*0-415-13571-0*) Routledge.

Realist of Distances: Flannery O'Connor Revisited. Ed. by Karl-Heinz Westarp & Jan N. Gretlund. 240p. (Orig.). (C). 1987. pap. 25.00 (*87-7288-069-4*, Pub. by Aarhus Univ Pr DK) David Brown.

Realist Social Theory: The Morphogenetic Approach. Margaret S. Archer. (Illus.). 392p. (C). 1995. text ed. 59.95 (*0-521-48176-7*); pap. text ed. 19.95 (*0-521-48442-1*) Cambridge U Pr.

*__Realist Theory of Science.__ Roy Bhaskar. (C). Date not set. pap. text ed. 18.00 (*1-85984-103-1*) Routledge Chapman & Hall.

Realist Tradition: French Painting & Drawing 1830-1900. Gabriel P. Weisberg. LC 80-16579. (Illus.). 360p. 1981. 15.00 (*0-910386-60-9*) Cleveland Mus Art.

Realist Vision of Adolf Konrad: A Retrospective. Barbara J. Mitnick & John M. Mitnick. 63p. 1992. 9.00 (*0-9613046-7-7*) Morris Mus.

Realist Watercolors. John Arthur. (Illus.). 32p. 1990. 9.95 (*0-911209-41-7*) Palmer Mus Art.

Realistic Approach to U. S. Energy Independence. Ernest J. Oppenheimer. (Orig.). 1980. pap. 5.00 (*0-9603982-0-1*) Pen & Podium.

Realistic Compiler Generation. Peter Lee. (Foundations of Computing Ser.). 225p. 1989. 32.50 (*0-262-12141-7*) MIT Pr.

Realistic Cost Estimating for Manufacturing. 2nd ed. William O. Winchell. LC 89-61736. 150p. 1989. 27.00 (*0-87263-364-0*) SME.

Realistic Decoys: Carving, Texturing, Painting & Finishing. Keith Bridenhagen & Patrick Spielman. LC 84-8608. (Illus.). 232p. (Orig.). 1986. pap. 17.95 (*0-8069-7908-9*) Sterling.

Realistic Defense Tactics for the Unarmed Person. 1991. lib. bdg. 74.95 (*0-8490-5164-9*) Gordon Pr.

Realistic Dinosaurs Stickers. Turi Maccombie. (Illus.). (J). (gr. k-3). 1994. pap. 1.00 (*0-486-28066-7*) Dover.

*__Realistic Duck Carving: A Step-by-Step Illustrated Manual.__ Alfred M. Ponte. (Illus.). 1997. pap. text ed. 9.95 (*1-56523-086-8*) Fox Chapel Pub.

*__Realistic Evaluation.__ Ray Pawson & Nick Tilley. 256p. 1997. text ed. 69.95 (*0-7619-5008-7*) Sage.

*__Realistic Evaluation.__ Ray Pawson & Nick Tilley. 256p. 1997. pap. text ed. 21.95 (*0-7619-5009-5*) Sage.

Realistic Figure Drawing. Joseph Sheppard. (Illus.). 144p. (Orig.). 1991. pap. 19.99 (*0-89134-374-1*, 30305, North Lght Bks) F & W Pubns Inc.

Realistic Job Search. Fiona Armstrong et al. (Lifeworks Ser.). (Illus.). 1980. text ed. 13.96 (*0-07-002518-5*) McGraw.

Realistic Love: The Second Passage of Marriage. Brian Newman et al. LC 92-22986. 1993. 9.99 (*0-8407-4550-8*) Nelson.

Realistic Love Study Guide: Your Handbook for Strengthening the Bond. Frank Minirth et al. LC 92-28823. 1993. 5.99 (*0-8407-4564-8*) Nelson.

Realistic Oil Painting Techniques. Kurt Anderson. LC 94-12941. (Illus.). 144p. 1995. 27.99 (*0-89134-576-0*, North Lght Bks) F & W Pubns Inc.

Realistic Philosophy Defended in a Philosophic Series, 2 vols. James McCosh. LC 75-3265. reprint ed. 75.00 (*0-404-59251-1*) AMS Pr.

Realistic Planning for Arid Lands: Natural Resource Limitations to Agricultural Development, Vol. 2. W. G. Matlock. (Advances in Desert & Arid Land Technology & Development Ser.). 262p. 1981. text ed. 194.00 (*3-7186-0051-X*) Gordon & Breach.

*__Realistic Plastic Structures for Toy Train Layouts.__ Art Curren. (Illus.). 80p. (Orig.). 1997. pap. 14.95 (*0-89778-410-3*, 10-8050, Kalmbach Books) Kalmbach.

Realistic Railroading with Toy Trains: Building the O Gauge Hi-Rail JL/ATSF Railway. Joe Lesser & Pete Youngblood. (Illus.). 96p. (Orig.). 1995. pap. 17.95 (*0-89778-399-9*, 10-7975, Greenberg Books) Kalmbach.

Realistic Revolt in Modern Poetry. Arthur M. Clark. (Studies in Comparative Literature: No. 35). (C). 1970. reprint ed. pap. 27.95 (*0-8383-0087-1*) M S G Haskell Hse.

Realistic Scenery for Toy Train Layouts. Dave Frary. 96p. (Orig.). 1996. pap. 18.95 (*0-89778-402-2*, 10-8025, Greenberg Books) Kalmbach.

*__Realistic Socio-Legal Theory: Pragmatism & a Social Theory of Law.__ Brian Tamanaha. (Oxford Socio-Legal Studies). 296p. 1997. 75.00 (*0-19-826560-3*) OUP.

Realistic Spirit: Wittgenstein, Philosophy, & the Mind. Cora Diamond. 1995. pap. 18.95 (*0-262-54074-6*, Bradford Bks) MIT Pr.

*__Realistic Technique.__ Judy Sleight. 70p. 1995. pap. 9.50 (*1-56770-341-0*) S Scheewe Pubns.

Realistic Theory of Categories: An Essay on Ontology. Roderick M. Chisholm. 120p. (C). 1996. text ed. 49.95 (*0-521-55426-8*); pap. text ed. 14.95 (*0-521-55616-3*) Cambridge U Pr.

Realistic Theory of Science. Clifford A. Hooker. LC 86-19169. 479p. (Orig.). (C). 1987. text ed. 64.50 (*0-88706-315-2*); pap. text ed. 21.95 (*0-88706-316-0*) State U NY Pr.

Realistic Therapist: Modesty & Relativism in Therapy & Research. Robert G. Ryder. LC 86-1765. 205p. 1987. reprint ed. pap. 58.50 (*0-608-00819-2*, 2061607) Bks Demand.

*__Realistic Track Plans for O Gauge Trains.__ Martin McGuirk. (Illus.). 80p. (Orig.). 1997. pap. 16.95 (*0-89778-434-0*, 10-8215, Kalmbach Books) Kalmbach.

Realistic Utopias: The Ideal Imaginary Societies of the Renaissance 1516-1630. Miriam Eliav-Feldon. (Oxford Historical Monographs). 154p. 1982. 55.00 (*0-19-821889-3*) OUP.

Realistiche Themen in der greichischen Kunst der archaischen und klassischen Zeit. Nikolaus Himmelmann. (Jahrbuch des Deutschen Archaeologischen Instituts Ser.). 160p. (GER.). (C). 1994. lib. bdg. 113.85 (*3-11-014173-6*) De Gruyter.

Realities. David Howard. LC 76-47802. (Illus.). 1976. pap. text ed. 9.95 (*0-685-89025-2*) SF Center Vis Stud.

Realities. Regina I. Waligora. LC 95-90780. 1996. 19.95 (*0-533-11708-9*) Vantage.

Realities & Ideals: Social, Political, Literary & Artistic. Frederic Harrison. LC 78-117803. (Essay Index Reprint Ser.). 1977. 29.95 (*0-8369-1708-1*) Ayer.

Realities & Opportunities: Early Intervention with Visually Handicapped Infants & Children - Proceedings of the International Symposium on Visually Handicapped Infants & Young Children (Birth-7); Aug. 7-13, 1988, Edinburgh, Scotland. International Symposium on Visually Handicapped Infants & Young Children Staff et al. Ed. by Stuart A. Aitken. 244p. reprint ed. pap. 69.60 (*0-7837-2046-7*, 2042321) Bks Demand.

Realities & Relationships: Soundings in Social Construction. Kenneth J. Gergen. LC 94-27463. (Illus.). 368p. 1995. text ed. 39.95 (*0-674-74930-8*, GERREA) HUP.

*__Realities & Relationships: Soundings in Social Construction.__ Kenneth J. Gergen. 1997. pap. text ed. 16.95 (*0-674-74931-6*) HUP.

Realities & Rewards of Trusteeship: Board Members & Staff of Nonprofit Organizations Share Their Stories. Compiled by Trustee Renewal Project Staff. (Nonprofit Governance Ser., No. 60: Stories from the Board: Vol. I). 48p. (Orig.). (C). 1994. pap. text ed. 18.00 (*0-925299-35-9*) Natl Ctr Nonprofit.

Realities & Shams. Lawrence P. Jacks. LC 70-134099. (Essay Index Reprint Ser.). 1977. 20.95 (*0-8369-1977-7*) Ayer.

Realities Behind Diplomacy: Background Influences on British External Policy, 1865-1980. Paul M. Kennedy. 416p. (Orig.). 1983. pap. text ed. 12.95 (*0-685-42558-4*) Routledge Chapman & Hall.

Realities Behind Diplomacy: Background Influences on British Foreign Policy, 1865-1980. Paul M. Kennedy. 416p. (C). 1981. text ed. 37.95 (*0-04-902005-6*) Routledge Chapman & Hall.

Realities Contemporary Nursing. 2nd ed. Pevsis M. Hamilton. LC 95-8827. (C). 1996. pap. text ed. 26.95 (*0-8053-2020-2*) Addison-Wesley.

Realities in Childbearing. 2nd ed. Mary Lou Moore. 1160p. 1983. text ed. 75.00 (*0-7216-6498-9*) Saunders.

Realities in Contemporary Nursing. Persis M. Hamilton. 544p. (C). 1992. pap. text ed. 29.25 (*0-201-06675-0*) Addison-Wesley.

Realities in Coping with Progressive Neuromuscular Diseases. Ed. by Leon I. Charash et al. LC 87-71168. 228p. (C). 1987. text ed. 34.95 (*0-914783-20-3*) Charles.

*__Realities in Motion.__ Betty J. Fagbemi. 1996. 8.95 (*0-533-11419-5*) Vantage.

*__Realities of Adoption.__ Jerome Smith. LC 96-53055. 1997. pap. write for info. (*1-56833-090-1*) Madison Bks UPA.

Realities of Aging. 5th ed. Cary S. Kart. 576p. 1996. 55.00 (*0-205-19154-1*) Allyn.

Realities of American-Palestine Relations. Frank E. Manuel. LC 72-596. 378p. 1975. reprint ed. text ed. 69.50 (*0-8371-5999-7*, MARA, Greenwood Pr) Greenwood.

Realities of Dental Therapy: A Detailed Review of Periodontal Prosthetic Treatment. Ronald L. Moloff & Stephen D. Stein. (Illus.). 456p. 1982. text ed. 110.00 (*0-931386-42-X*) Quint Pub Co.

An Asterisk (*) at the beginning of an entry indicates that the title is appearing in BIP for the first time.

R

Realities of Fiction: A Book about Writing. Nancy Hale. LC 76-53839. 247p. 1977. reprint ed. text ed. 55.00 (*0-8371-9351-6*, HARE, Greenwood Pr) Greenwood.

Realities of Management Promotion. Marian N. Ruderman & Patricia J. Ohlott. LC 93-43611. (Technical Reports: No. 157G). 52p. 1993. pap. 20.00 (*0-912879-88-2*) Ctr Creat Leader.

Realities of Managing Development Projects. Ed. by Farhad Analoui. 306p. 1994. 63.95 (*1-85628-514-6*, Pub. by Avebury Pub UK) Ashgate Pub Co.

Realities of Naval History. Brian Tunstall. LC 76-37914. (Select Bibliographies Reprint Ser.). 1977. reprint ed. 18.95 (*0-8369-6751-8*) Ayer.

Realities of Nuclear Power: International Economic & Regulatory Experience. S. D. Thomas. (Cambridge Energy Studies). (Illus.). 304p. 1988. text ed. 95.00 (*0-521-32750-4*) Cambridge U Pr.

Realities of Nutrition. 2nd ed. Ronald M. Deutsch & Judi S. Morrill. 1993. pap. 24.95 (*0-923521-25-9*) Bull Pub.

Realities of the Dreaming Mind. Sivananda Radha. LC 94-16766. (Illus.). 384p. 1994. 29.95 (*0-931454-68-9*); pap. 18.95 (*0-931454-69-7*) Timeless Bks.

Realities of the Dreaming Mind. Sivananda Radha. 304p. 1996. pap. 15.00 (*1-57062-140-3*) Shambhala Pubns.

Realities of Transference. Arnold Goldberg. (Progress in Self Psychology Ser.: Vol. 6). 288p. 1990. text ed. 39.95 (*0-88163-114-0*) Analytic Pr.

Realities, the Miracle of God. Basilea Schlink. pap. 3.99 (*0-551-00008-2*) Zondervan.

Reality. H. J. Ariston. LC 83-80423. 60p. (Orig.). 1983. pap. 5.95 (*0-935344-03-9*) Jupiter Bks.

Reality. Paul Weiss. LC 67-11699. (Arcturus Books Paperbacks). 318p. 1967. pap. 8.95 (*0-8093-0244-6*) S Ill U Pr.

Reality. Ed. by Jonathan Westphal & Carl Levenson. LC 93-44706. (Readings in Philosophy Ser.). 192p. (C). 1994. pap. text ed. 7.95 (*0-87220-224-0*); lib. bdg. 24.95 (*0-87220-225-9*) Hackett Pub.

Reality: Drugs & Guns--No-Win Solutions. Stephen D. Allen. LC 92-64322. 126p. (J). (gr. k-8). 1992. pap. 14.95 (*0-9634084-7-X*) S D A Pub.

***Reality: How It Works & Why It Mostly Doesn't.** Rik Dent. (Orig.). 1997. pap. 29.95 (*1-86163-018-2*, Pub. by Capall Bann Pubng UK) Holmes Pub.

Reality: The Hope of Glory. Aaron Katz. 160p. 1990. reprint ed. pap. 5.95 (*1-878327-05-4*) Morning NC.

***Reality Activities: A How to Manual for Increasing Orientation.** 2nd rev. ed. Richelle N. Cunninghis. (Illus.). 50p. 1995. pap. 10.00 (*1-882883-21-7*, 189) Idyll Arbor.

Reality Activities: A How-to Manual for Use with Confused & Disoriented Elderly. Richelle N. Cunninghis. (Illus.). 26p. 1982. pap. text ed. 6.95 (*0-937663-01-8*) Idyll Arbor.

Reality & Dream: A Christmas Story. B. J. Morison. LC 85-20870. (Illus.). 63p. (Orig.). 1985. pap. 3.95 (*0-89621-096-0*) Nrth Country Pr.

***Reality & Dreams.** Muriel Spark. LC 96-52913. 160p. 1997. 22.00 (*0-395-83811-8*) HM.

Reality & Empathy: Physics, Mind, & Science in the 21st Century. Alex Comfort. LC 83-9318. 272p. 1984. text ed. 64.50 (*0-87395-762-8*); pap. text ed. 21.95 (*0-87395-763-6*) State U NY Pr.

Reality & Experience: Four Philosophical Essays. E. Kaila. Ed. by Robert S. Cohen. (Vienna Circle Collection: No. 12). 370p. 1978. pap. text ed. 75.00 (*90-277-0919-X*); lib. bdg. 152.00 (*90-277-0915-7*) Kluwer Ac.

Reality & Fiction in Modern Japanese Literature. Noriko M. Lippit. LC 79-67859. 231p. 1980. reprint ed. pap. 65.90 (*0-7837-9925-X*, 2060652) Bks Demand.

Reality & Illusion in the New Testament Scholarship: A Primer in Critical Realist Hermeneutics. Ben F. Meyer. 256p. (Orig.). 1995. pap. text ed. 16.95 (*0-8146-5771-0*, M Glazier) Liturgical Pr.

Reality & Myth: Essays in American Literature in Memory of Richmond Croom Beatty. Ed. by William E. Walker & Robert L. Welker. LC 63-14647. 322p. reprint ed. pap. 91.80 (*0-8357-3268-1*, 2039489) Bks Demand.

Reality & Representation. David Papineau. 304p. (C). 1991. pap. 27.95 (*0-631-17552-0*) Blackwell Pubs.

Reality & Research: Social Science & U. S. Urban Policy since 1960. Ed. by George C. Galster. 264p. 1995. pap. text ed. 21.50 (*0-87766-639-3*); lib. bdg. 52.50 (*0-87766-638-5*) Urban Inst.

Reality & Rhetoric. Peter T. Bauer. 192p. 1986. pap. 12.95 (*0-674-74947-2*) HUP.

Reality & Rhetoric: Studies in the Economics of Development. Peter T. Bauer. 192p. 1984. 24.50 (*0-674-74946-4*) HUP.

Reality & Scientific Truth: Discussions with Einstein, von Laue, & Planck. Ilse Rosenthal-Schneider. LC 80-13950. (Illus.). 149p. reprint ed. pap. 42.50 (*0-318-39785-4*, 2033187) Bks Demand.

Reality & the Physicist: Knowledge, Duration & the Quantum World. Bernard D'Espagnat. (Illus.). 280p. (C). 1989. text ed. 85.00 (*0-521-32940-X*); pap. text ed. 30.95 (*0-521-33846-8*) Cambridge U Pr.

Reality & the Poet in Spanish Poetry. Pedro Salinas. Tr. by Edith F. Helman from SPA. LC 80-12201. xxx, 165p. 1980. reprint ed. text ed. 42.50 (*0-313-22436-6*, SARP, Greenwood Pr) Greenwood.

Reality & Time in the Oleza Novels of Gabriel Miro. Marian G. Coope. (Monografias A Ser.: Vol. CII). (Illus.). 235p. (C). 1984. 63.00 (*0-7293-0182-6*, Pub. by Tamesis Bks Ltd UK) Boydell & Brewer.

Reality & Value Judgment in Policymaking: A Study of Expert Judgments about Alternative Energy Technologies. Robert J. Dillon. Ed. by Stuart Bruchey. LC 78-22674. (Energy in the American Economy Ser.). (Illus.). 1979. lib. bdg. 18.95 (*0-405-11977-1*) Ayer.

Reality & Virtual Reality. Michael S. Zdepski. LC 91-73081. (Illus.). 240p. 1991. pap. 50.00 (*1-880250-00-4*) Assoc Comp Aid Des.

Reality & /Or Realities. Mauricio Abadi & Susan Rogers. LC 95-5895. 1995. 30.00 (*1-56821-536-3*) Aronson.

Reality at Dawn. Ram Chandra. 50p. (RUS.). 1990. 5.00 (*0-945242-16-6*) Shri Ram Chandra.

Reality at Dawn. Ram Chandra. 120p. 1988. reprint ed. pap. 5.00 (*0-945242-02-6*) Shri Ram Chandra.

Reality at Risk: A Defence of Realism in Philosophy & the Sciences. Roger Trigg. 216p. 1980. 56.50 (*0-389-20037-9*, N6809) B&N Imports.

***Reality by Design: Rhetoric, Technology, & the Creation of Authentic Learning Environments.** Joseph Petraglia. (Rhetoric, Knowledge & Society Ser.). 250p. 1997. write for info. (*0-8058-2041-8*) L Erlbaum Assocs.

***Reality by Design: Rhetoric, Technology, & the Creation of Authentic Learning Environments.** Joseph Petraglia. (Rhetoric, Knowledge & Society Ser.). 250p. 1997. write for info. (*0-8058-2042-6*) L Erlbaum Assocs.

***Reality Bytes: Twenty-Five Truths for the Rest of Your Life.** Len Woods. (Illus.). 96p. (YA). Date not set. 9.99 (*0-8010-1158-2*) Baker Bks.

Reality Check. John Grimes. (Illus.). 128p. (Orig.). 1993. pap. 7.95 (*0-89815-544-4*) Ten Speed Pr.

***Reality Check: One Father's Opinion on World Affairs.** Mike O'Byrne. LC 96-44112. 1996. write for info. (*0-938106-22-8*) Laing Res Servs.

Reality Check: One Woman's Perspective, No. 1. Karen L. Walton. 42p. 1995. 10.95 (*0-9649785-0-4*) Walton Co.

Reality Check: Teenage Fathers Speak Out, 8 vols. Margi Trapani. LC 95-42450. (Teen Pregnancy Prevention Library). (Illus.). 64p. (YA). (gr. 7-12). 1996. lib. bdg. 16.95 (*0-8239-2255-3*) Rosen Group.

Reality Check: What's Going On Out There? Tom Clancy. 1995. 26.95 (*0-399-14008-5*) Putnam Pub Group.

Reality Check: Winning the Mind Game. Rich Miller & Neil Anderson. (Freedom in Christ for Teens Ser.: 2). 150p. (YA). 1996. pap. 7.99 (*1-56507-409-2*) Harvest Hse.

Reality Check: You've Heard the Hype, Wired Asked the Experts, Here's the Real Future. Ed. by Brad Wieners & David Pescovitz. (Illus.). 168p. 1996. pap. 16.95 (*1-888869-03-8*) HardWired.

Reality Construction in an Eastern Mystical Cult. Alan Lopez. LC 92-16320. (Cults & Nonconventional Religious Groups Ser.). 280p. 1992. text ed. 25.00 (*0-8153-0772-1*) Garland.

Reality Creation Workbook. Zera Starchild. 267p. 1994. spiral bd. 25.00 (*0-9632970-4-X*) Doorway.

Reality, Disinformation & Communication. 1991. lib. bdg. 79.95 (*0-8490-4700-5*) Gordon Pr.

***Reality Dysfunction Pt. 1: Emergence.** Peter F. Hamilton. 592p. 1997. pap. 5.99 (*0-446-60515-8*, Aspect) Warner Bks.

***Reality Dysfunction Pt. 2: Expansion.** Peter F. Hamilton. 576p. 1997. pap. 5.99 (*0-446-60516-6*, Aspect) Warner Bks.

***Reality Effect in the Writing of History: The Dynamics of Historiographical Topology.** F. R. Ankersmit. (Mededelingen der Koninklijke Nederlandse Akademie van Wetenschappen, Afd. Letterkunde Ser.: No. 52(1)). 1989. pap. text ed. 17.50 (*0-444-85704-4*) Elsevier.

***Reality Factor: Mind Control Exposes.** Teresa Wiater. LC 96-90346. 142p. (Orig.). 1996. pap. 10.00 (*0-9652994-0-6*) Global Intell.

Reality Fictions: The Films of Frederick Wiseman. Thomas W. Benson & Carolyn Anderson. LC 88-17613. 480p. (C). 1989. text ed. 44.95 (*0-8093-1364-2*) S Ill U Pr.

Reality Game: A Guide to Humanistic Counselling & Therapy. John Rowan. 160p. (C). 1992. pap. 16.95 (*0-415-04046-9*) Routledge.

Reality Gap: Global Access to Health Care & the Legislative Impact of the World Health Organization's "HEA2000" David R. Schanker. Ed. by Victoria J. Cuffel. LC 93-655022. (MacArthur Scholar Series, Occasional Paper: No. 19). 141p. (Orig.). (C). 1993. pap. 4.50 (*1-881157-16-4*) In Ctr Global.

Reality Illusion: How You Create the World You Experience. rev. ed. Ralph Strauch. (Illus.). 224p. 1989. reprint ed. pap. text ed. 10.95 (*0-88268-079-X*) Station Hill Pr.

Reality in Advertising. Rosser Reeves. 1961. 20.00 (*0-394-44228-8*) Knopf.

Reality in Three Dimensions: Reflection of the Trinity. Mary H. Kelley. 384p. (Orig.). 1992. pap. 15.00 (*0-942971-26-4*) His Way.

Reality in Transition. Michael S. Spiegel. Ed. by Ellen A. Edelen. (Illus.). 128p. (Orig.). 1985. pap. 10.00 (*0-932163-00-9*) Separate Real.

Reality in Which We Live: Occult Movements Through the Ages. F. Zeylmans. 1973. lib. bdg. 79.95 (*0-87968-569-7*) Krishna Pr.

Reality Inspector. John Caris. (Illus.). 1982. pap. 7.95 (*0-9607320-0-4*) Westgate Hse.

Reality Is What You Can Get Away With. Robert A. Wilson. LC 96-67337. (Illus.). 176p. (Orig.). 1996. pap. 14.95 (*1-56184-080-7*) New Falcon Pubns.

Reality Isn't What It Used to Be: Theatrical Politics, Ready-to-Wear Religion, Global Myths, Primitive Chic, & Other Wonders of the Post Modern World. Walter T. Anderson. LC 89-45950. 1992. reprint ed. pap. 13.00 (*0-06-250017-1*) Harper SF.

Reality Living. Jeff Adams. 94p. 1990. 5.00 (*0-9643021-0-1*) Reality Living.

Reality Living. Jeff Adams. 94p. 1990. pap. 3.50 (*0-9643021-1-X*) Reality Living.

Reality Machine. Edward Packard. (Choose Your Own Adventure Ser.: No. 142). 128p. (YA). 1993. pap. 3.50 (*0-553-56401-3*) Bantam.

Reality Maintenance 101. August Stahr. 30p. (Orig.). 1993. pap. 20.00 (*1-884686-00-1*) Celestl Guardn.

Reality of Angels. Lester Sumrall. 128p. 1993. mass mkt. 4.99 (*0-88368-292-3*) Whitaker Hse.

***Reality of Appearances: Vision & Representation in Emerson, Hawthorne & Melville.** A. Sarbu. 276p. 1996. pap. 43.00 (*963-05-7314-8*, Pub. by A K HU) Intl Spec Bk.

Reality of Christian Learning: Strategies for Faith-Discipline Integration. Ed. by Harold Heie & David L. Wolfe. LC 86-19631. 351p. reprint ed. pap. 100.10 (*0-7837-3193-0*, 2042797) Bks Demand.

Reality of Dyslexia. John Osmond. (Education Ser.). (Illus.). 160p. 1993. 60.00 (*0-304-32762-X*); pap. 22.50 (*0-304-32763-8*) Weidner & Sons.

Reality of Dyslexia. rev. ed. John Osmond. 150p. 1995. pap. text ed. 14.95 (*1-57129-017-6*) Brookline Bks.

Reality of God: Thoughts on the Death of God Controversy. Alexander Purdy. LC 67-23314. (Orig.). 1967. pap. 3.00 (*0-87574-154-1*) Pendle Hill.

Reality of God & Other Essays. Schubert M. Ogden. LC 90-52663. 238p. 1992. reprint ed. pap. text ed. 12.95 (*0-87074-318-X*) SMU Press.

Reality of Illusion: An Ecological Approach to Cognitive Film Theory. Joseph D. Anderson. LC 94-48221. 232p. (C). 1995. 29.95 (*0-8093-2000-2*) S Ill U Pr.

***Reality of International Economic Policy Coordination.** H. J. Blommestein. (Contributions to Economic Analysis Ser.: Vol. 199). 230p. 1991. 125.50 (*0-444-89040-8*, North Holland) Elsevier.

Reality of Jesus. Dermont A. Lane. LC 77-70635. (Exploration Bk.). 180p. 1977. pap. 11.95 (*0-8091-2020-8*) Paulist Pr.

Reality of Jesus. Ermot Lane. 180p. 1989. pap. 22.00 (*0-901810-85-1*, Pub. by Veritas IE) St Mut.

***Reality of Jesus Christ.** Carolyn T. Abbot. (Orig.). 1996. pap. write for info. (*1-57553-303-0*) Watermrk Pr.

***Reality of Law: Work & Talk in a Firm of Criminal Lawyers.** Max Travers. (Socio-Legal Studies). 190p. 1997. text ed. 64.95 (*1-84014-028-3*, KD474.T73, Pub. by Ashgate UK) Ashgate Pub Co.

Reality of Linguistic Rules. Gregory K. Iverson et al. LC 94-27030. (Studies in Language Companion: No. 26). xxiii, 480p. 1994. 115.00 (*1-55619-378-5*) Benjamins North Am.

Reality of Man. Baha'u'llah & Abdu'l-Baha. 93p. 1990. pap. 5.50 (*0-909991-39-1*) Bahai.

***Reality of Management.** 3rd ed. Rosemary Stewart. 1997. 39.95 (*0-7506-3287-9*) Buttrwrth-Heinemann.

Reality of Music. Rutland Boughton. LC 72-80495. 260p. 1977. reprint ed. 17.95 (*0-405-08294-0*, Pub. by Blom Pubns UK) Ayer.

Reality of National Computer Networking for Higher Education. 200p. 16.00 (*0-318-14032-2*) EDUCOM.

***Reality of Partnership.** Gibbs et al. 1991. text ed. write for info. (*0-582-08487-3*, Pub. by Longman UK) Longman.

Reality of Prayer. E. M. Bounds. (E. M. Bounds Classics on Prayer Ser.). 120p. (gr. 10). 1992. pap. 6.99 (*0-8010-1012-8*, Hour Glass) Baker Bks.

Reality of Probation: A Formal Ethnography of Process & Practice. Jason Ditton & Roslyn Ford. 116p. 1994. 51.95 (*1-85628-858-7*, Pub. by Avebury Pub UK) Ashgate Pub Co.

Reality of Psychic Phenomena. W. J. Crawford. 1991. lib. bdg. 83.00 (*0-8490-4527-4*) Gordon Pr.

Reality of Retirement: Revised & Updated by Cory Willing. Jules Z. Willing. LC 88-13821. 224p. 1989. reprint ed. pap. 9.95 (*0-9612746-0-3*) Lively Mind Bks.

Reality of Strategic HRM. Michael Armstrong & Phil Long. 224p. (C). 1994. pap. 40.00 (*0-85292-563-8*, Pub. by IPM Hse UK) St Mut.

Reality of the Cross of Christ. (Christian Library). 132p. 1988. reprint ed. 8.97 (*1-55748-013-3*) Barbour & Co.

Reality of the Historical Past. Paul Ricoeur. LC 84-60012. (Aquinas Lectures). 51p. 1984. 15.00 (*0-87462-152-6*) Marquette.

Reality of the Kingdom: Making Sense of God's Reign in a World Like Ours. Paul R. Clifford. 141p. 1996. pap. text ed. 12.00 (*0-8028-0867-0*) Eerdmans.

Reality of the Kingdom of Demons. H. Clifton Black. 96p. 1993. pap. 6.95 (*0-925591-27-0*) Covenant Hse Bks.

Reality of the Mind: Augustine's Philosophical Arguments for the Human Soul As Spiritual Substance. Ludger Holscher. (Studies in Phenomenological & Classical Realism). 304p. 1986. 57.50 (*0-7102-0777-8*, 07778, RKP) Routledge.

***Reality of the Mother Plane.** unabridged ed. Hassan Muhammad. (Illus.). 80p. (Orig.). 1996. pap. 8.00 (*1-56411-157-1*, 4BBG0158) Untd Bros & Sis.

Reality of the Path. Muhammad A. Salam & Muhammad B. Salimi. 54p. (Orig.). 1993. pap. 10.00 (*0-926606-04-2*) Pac Rsch Pubns.

Reality of the Psyche. Ed. by Joseph B. Wheelwright. LC 68-15614. (Illus.). 1968. 16.00 (*0-913430-16-1*) C G Jung Foun.

Reality of the Spiritual World. Thomas Kelly. LC 76-9644. (Orig.). 1942. pap. 3.00 (*0-87574-021-9*) Pendle Hill.

Reality of Time. Errol E. Harris. LC 88-2136. (SUNY Series in Philosophy). 204p. 1988. text ed. 64.50 (*0-88706-860-X*); pap. text ed. 21.95 (*0-88706-861-8*) State U NY Pr.

Reality of Time - a Definitive Explanation: "Including Corrected Formula for the Grand Unified (Field) Theory" Robert D. Boyd. (Illus.). 68p. (Orig.). 1996. pap. 10.00 (*0-9620197-5-5*) R D Boyd.

***Reality of Time - A Definitive Explanation: Including Corrected Formula for the Grand Unified (Field) Theory.** Robert D. Boyd. (Illus.). 68p. 1996. lib. bdg. 15.00 (*0-614-29889-X*) R D Boyd.

Reality of Time & the Existence of God: The Project of Proving God's Existence. David Braine. 400p. 1988. 95.00 (*0-19-824459-2*) OUP.

Reality of Work & Promotion. Fiona Armstrong et al. (Illus.). 208p. 1980. text ed. 13.96 (*0-07-002519-3*) McGraw.

Reality Orientation: Psychological Approaches to the 'Confused' Elderly. 2nd ed. Una P. Holden & Robert T. Woods. (Illus.). 264p. 1988. pap. text ed. write for info. (*0-443-03460-5*) Churchill.

Reality Orientation for the Elderly. 3rd ed. Sylvester Kohut, Jr. et al. 150p. (Orig.). 1987. pap. 27.95 (*0-87489-436-0*) Med Econ.

Reality, Racism, & A Racist Judge: A Personal Journey Through American Bias. Frank E. Foy. (Illus.). 128p. (Orig.). 1990. pap. 9.95 (*0-9626152-0-X*) LeHana Enterprises.

Reality-Realidad. Benito Perez Galdos. Tr. by Karen Austin from SPA. LC 92-36541. (Hispanic Literature Ser.: Vol. 15). 272p. 1992. 89.95 (*0-7734-9175-9*) E Mellen.

Reality, Representation & Projection. Ed. by John Haldane & Crispin Wright. LC 92-39896. (Mind Association Occasional Ser.). 416p. (C). 1993. 60.00 (*0-19-507878-0*) OUP.

Reality Revolution: Return to the Way. Erriel D. Roberson, pseud. LC 96-75530. 352p. (Orig.). 1996. pap. 18.50 (*0-9644932-1-7*) Kujichagulia Pr.

Reality Ribs. Roberto T. Duran. LC 93-20055. 112p. 1993. pap. 11.00 (*0-927534-35-5*) Biling Rev-Pr.

***Reality Rules: Picturing the World in Mathematics, 2 vols.** John L. Casti. pap. text ed. 59.95 (*0-471-18437-3*, Wiley-Interscience) Wiley.

Reality Rules: Picturing the World in Mathematics, 2 vols. John L. Casti. 864p. 1992. 109.00 (*0-471-57797-9*) Wiley.

***Reality Rules: Picturing the World in Mathematics, Vol. 1.** John L. Casti. 1992. pap. text ed. 16.00 (*0-471-58941-1*) Wiley.

***Reality Rules: Picturing the World in Mathematics - The Frontier, Vol. 2.** John L. Casti. pap. text ed. 34.95 (*0-471-18436-5*, Wiley-Interscience) Wiley.

***Reality Rules: Picturing the World in Mathematics - The Fundamentals, Vol. 1.** John L. Casti. pap. text ed. 34.95 (*0-471-18435-7*, Wiley-Interscience) Wiley.

Reality Rules Vol. 1: Picturing the World in Mathematics, the Fundamentals. John L. Casti. LC 92-12213. 416p. 1992. text ed. 73.95 (*0-471-57021-4*) Wiley.

Reality Rules Vol. 2: Picturing the World in Mathematics, The Frontier, Vol. 2. John L. Casti. LC 92-12213. 448p. 1992. text ed. 73.95 (*0-471-57798-7*) Wiley.

Reality Sandwiches. R. M. Host. (Dog River Review Poetry Ser.). 28p. (Orig.). 1995. pap. 4.00 (*0-916155-26-9*) Trout Creek.

Reality Sandwiches: Poems, 1953-1960. Allen Ginsberg. LC 63-12219. (Pocket Poets Ser.: No. 18). (Orig.). 1963. pap. 7.95 (*0-87286-021-3*) City Lights.

Reality Slices. John Vieira. 34p. (Orig.). 1996. pap. 5.00 (*1-57141-020-1*) Runaway Spoon.

Reality Therapy: A New Approach to Psychiatry. William Glasser. LC 89-45657. 1989. pap. 11.00 (*0-06-090414-3*, CN414, PL) HarpC.

Reality Therapy: A New Approach to Psychiatry. William Glasser. 176p. (C). 1990. reprint ed. lib. bdg. 31.00 (*0-8095-9006-9*) Borgo Pr.

Reality Therapy: A New Approach to Psychiatry. William Glasser. 1975. reprint ed. pap. 7.50 (*0-06-080348-7*, P348, PL) HarpC.

Reality Through Arts. 3rd ed. Dennis J. Sporre. 1996. student ed., pap. text ed. 16.80 (*0-13-602020-8*) P-H.

Reality Through the Arts. 3rd ed. Dennis J. Sporre. 1996. pap. text ed. 50.67 (*0-13-492943-8*) P-H.

***Reality Through the Looking-Glass: Science & Awareness in the Postmodern World.** C. J. Clarke. 1997. pap. text ed. 19.95 (*0-86315-216-3*, Pub. by Floris Books UK) Anthroposophic.

Reality vs. Romance in South Central Africa. 2nd rev. ed. James Johnston. (Illus.). 353p. 1969. 35.00 (*0-7146-1871-3*, Pub. by F Cass Pubs UK) Intl Spec Bk.

Reality's Dark Dream: Dejection in Coleridge. Beverly Fields. LC 67-64939. (Kent Studies in English: No. 5). 207p. reprint ed. 59.00 (*0-8357-9374-5*, 2011315) Bks Demand.

Reality's Dark Dream: The Narrative Fiction of Ludwig Tieck. William J. Lillyman. (C). 1979. 100.00 (*3-11-007710-8*) De Gruyter.

Reality's Mirror: Exploring the Mathematics of Symmetry. Bryan Bunch. 286p. 1989. text ed. 19.95 (*0-471-50127-1*) Wiley.

Realizability Theory for Continuous Linear Systems. unabridged ed. Armen H. Zemanian. 256p. 1995. reprint ed. pap. text ed. 8.95 (*0-486-68823-2*) Dover.

Realizable Ideals. Theodore Roosevelt, Jr. LC 77-90676. (Essay Index Reprint Ser.). 1977. 19.95 (*0-8369-1233-0*) Ayer.

Realization. Ernest Weltmore. 204p. 1961. reprint ed. spiral bd. 10.00 (*0-7873-0952-4*) Hlth Research.

Realization: The Final Report of the Knapp School Libraries Project. American Association of School Librarians Staff. Ed. by Peggy Sullivan. LC 68-29658. 410p. reprint ed. pap. 116.90 (*0-317-27855-X*, 2024216) Bks Demand.

Realization & Enlightenment. S. Adam & M. Adam. LC 96-96353. (Illus.). 157p. (Orig.). 1996. pap. 14.95 (*0-9649152-0-0*) M Smolko.

Realization & Modelling in System Theory. M. A. Kaashoek et al. (Progress in Systems & Control Theory Ser.: Vol. 3). 570p. 1990. 80.00 (*0-685-45913-6*) Birkhauser.

An Asterisk (*) at the beginning of an entry indicates that the title is appearing in BIP for the first time.

R

Realization & Suppression of the Situationist International: An Annotated Bibliography, 1972-1990. Simon Ford. LC 94-25741. 1994. 10.95 (1-873176-82-1, AK Pr San Fran) AK Pr Dist.

*__Realization Book.__ Janet McClure. 1997. pap. text ed. 11.95 (0-929385-61-6) Light Tech Comns Servs.

Realization of Anti-Racist Teaching. Godfrey L. Brandt. 220p. 1987. 60.00 (1-85000-126-X, Falmer Pr); pap. 25.00 (1-85000-127-8, Falmer Pr) Taylor & Francis.

Realization of Life Aspirations Through Vocational Careers. Edgar Krau. LC 96-20690. 280p. 1997. text ed. 65.00 (0-275-95700-4, Praeger Pubs) Greenwood.

Realization of Oneness: The Practice of Spiritual Healing. Joel S. Goldsmith. 200p. 1974. reprint ed. pap. 5.95 (0-8065-0453-6, Citadel Pr) Carol Pub Group.

Realization of the Supreme Self: The Bhagavad Gita Yogas. Trevor P. Leggett. (Illus.). 240p. 1995. 59.50 (0-7103-0433-1, Pub. by Kegan Paul Intl UK) Col U Pr.

Realization of the Verbal Composition of Speech by Preschool Children. S. Karpova. (Janua Linguarum, Ser. Major: No. 56). 1977. 96.95 (90-279-3186-0) Mouton.

*__Realization Spaces of Polytopes, Vol. 164.__ Jurgen Richter-Gebert. LC 96-51634. (Lectures Notes in Mathematics Ser.). 187p. 1996. pap. 35.00 (3-540-62084-2) Spr-Verlag.

Realization Theory. Ed. by A. Ruberti. LC 76-21964. 1977. pap. 23.00 (0-08-021276-X, Pergamon Pr) Elsevier.

Realizations: Personal Empowerment Through Self-Awareness. William A. Guillory. LC 85-60283. (Illus.). (Orig.). 1985. pap. 7.95 (0-933241-00-3) Innovations UT.

Realizations: The Art of Walter Anderson. 34p. 1985. 15.00 (0-9614558-0-2) Anderson Estate.

*__Realizations of Polylogarithms, Vol. 165.__ Jorg Wildeshaus. (Lecture Notes in Mathematics Ser.). 1997. 64.00 (3-540-62460-0) Spr-Verlag.

Realizations of the Future: An Inquiry into the Authority of Praxis. George Allan. LC 89-77404. (SUNY Series in Philosophy). 318p. 1990. text ed. 64.50 (0-7914-0441-2); pap. text ed. 21.95 (0-7914-0442-0) State U NY Pr.

Realizations of Usonia: Frank Lloyd Wright in Westchester. Priscilla Henken & David Henken. (Illus.). 36p. (Orig.). 1985. pap. 10.00 (0-943651-12-3) Hudson Riv.

Realize & Rejoice. Richard C. Hoefler. 1981. 4.00 (0-89536-468-9, 1803) CSS OH.

Realizing Eternal Selfhood. Ivan G. McDaniel. Ed. by Paul P. Ricchio. 297p. 1981. 12.95 (0-932785-41-7) Philos Pub.

Realizing Gender Equality in Higher Education: The Need to Integrate Work - Family Issues. Ed. by Nancy Hensel. LC 91-66411. (ASHE-ERIC Higher Education Reports: No. 91-2). 98p. 1991. pap. write for info. (1-878380-07-9) GWU Grad Schl E&HD.

Realizing Investment Value. William Bygrave et al. 256p. 1993. 87.50 (0-273-60336-1, Pub. by Pitman Pub Ltd UK) Trans-Atl Phila.

Realizing Mental Health. Roger C. Mills. 207p. (Orig.). (C). 1995. pap. text ed. 12.99 (0-945819-78-1) Sulzburger & Graham Pub.

*__Realizing Mental Health: Toward a New Psychology of Resilence.__ Roger C. Mills. 207p. 1995. 28.99 (0-945819-79-X) Sulzburger & Graham Pub.

Realizing Our Dream: How to Become the You You Really Want to Be. 2nd ed. Patricia Collwtte & Mark Jones. 105p. (Orig.). 1992. reprint ed. mass mkt., pap. 7.95 (0-614-13236-3) Evolvement.

Realizing Peace: An Introduction to Peace Studies. Thomas Keefe & Ron E. Roberts. LC 90-25720. 250p. (C). 1991. pap. text ed. 29.95 (0-8138-1562-2) Iowa St U Pr.

Realizing Rawls. Thomas W. Pogge. LC 89-42879. (Illus.). 320p. 1989. 42.50 (0-8014-2124-1); pap. 15.95 (0-8014-9685-3) Cornell U Pr.

Realizing Teacher Reform: A State Action Plan for Developing the Profession. 41p. 1990. 6.00 (0-317-05344-2) NASBE.

Realizing the Educational Potential of Residence Halls. Charles C. Schroeder et al. (Higher & Adult Education Ser.). 364p. text ed. 34.95 (0-7879-0018-4) Jossey-Bass.

Realizing the Information Future: The Internet & Beyond. National Research Council, Renaissance Committee Staff. 320p. (Orig.). (C). 1994. pap. 24.95 (0-309-05044-8) Natl Acad Pr.

Realizing the Object-Oriented Lifecycle. Hollowell. 1995. text ed. 47.00 (0-13-124454-X) P-H.

Realizing the Potential of Women & Minorities in Engineering: Four Perspectives from the Field. Jane Z. Daniels et al. Ed. by Karen Glass. 132p. (Orig.). 1990. pap. text ed. 20.00 (1-55877-118-2) Natl Governor.

Realizing What's Available in the World of Work. Fiona Armstrong et al. (Lifeworks Ser.). (Illus.). 1979. text ed. 13.96 (0-07-002516-9) McGraw.

Reallexikon der aegyptischen Religionsgeschichte. 2nd ed. Hans Bonnet. (Illus.). (GER.). (C). 1971. 176.95 (3-11-003365-8) De Gruyter.

Reallexikon der Deutschen Literaturgeschichte. Band 5: Sachregister - Index. Ed. by K. Kanzog & J. S. Koch. xxviii, 510p. (C). 1988. lib. bdg. 126.15 (3-11-008816-9) De Gruyter.

Reallexikon der deutschen Literaturgeschichte, 3 vols. 2nd ed. Ed. by Werner Kohlschmidt & Werner Mohr. Incl. Vol. 1 A-K. . 915p. 1958. 93.35 (3-11-000294-9); Vol. 2 L-O. . 847p. 1964. 93.35 (3-11-000295-7); Vol. 3, Pt. 1. . 1977. 118.70 (3-11-007399-4); (C). write for info. (0-318-51639-X) De Gruyter.

*__Reallexikon der Deutschen Literaturwissenschaft Bd. 1: A-G.__ Ed. by Harald Fricke et al. xxii, 754p. (GER.). (C). 1997. lib. bdg. 183.70 (3-11-010896-8) De Gruyter.

Reallexikon der Germanischen Altertumskunde, Set. 2nd enl. rev. ed. Johannes Hoops. Incl. Vol. 1. Aachen-Bajuwaren. (Illus.). xxxiv, 627p. 1976. 252.00 (3-11-004489-7); Vol. 2. Bake Billigkeit. 1976. 237.35 (3-11-006740-4); (C). 1976. 222.00 (0-685-01379-0) De Gruyter.

Really Active Christmas Book. LC 50-104. (Illus.). 32p. (J). (gr. 1-5). 1993. pap. 5.99 (0-7459-2658-4) Lion USA.

Really Amazing Animal Book. LC 97-3336. (Illus.). 24p. (J). 1997. 9.95 (0-7894-1265-9) DK Pub Inc.

Really Bad News. Glasgow University, Media Group Staff. 14.95 (0-86316-051-4); pap. 6.95 (0-906495-44-X) Writers & Readers.

*__Really Big Cats.__ Allan Fowler. LC 97-17895. (Rookie Read-About Science Ser.). 1998. write for info. (0-516-20805-5) Childrens.

*__Really Big L. D. Block Book, Vol. 1.__ William H. Bennett & Teresa A. Gonsalves. (Illus.). v, 274p. (Orig.). (YA). (gr. 7-12). 1989. pap. text ed. 47.00 (1-889510-08-4) Chmpionship Debate.

*__Really Big L. D. Block Book, Vol. 2.__ Sam A. Donaldson. (Illus.). vii, 265p. (Orig.). (YA). (gr. 7-12). 1992. pap. text ed. 47.00 (1-889510-07-6) Chmpionship Debate.

*__Really Big Theory Block Book.__ William H. Bennett. (Illus.). vi, 277p. (Orig.). (YA). (gr. 7-12). 1995. pap. text ed. 47.00 (1-889510-02-5) Chmpionship Debate.

Really Cute Corpse. Joan Hess. 1991. mass mkt. 4.99 (0-345-36158-X) Ballantine.

Really, Doctor! large type ed. Ann Jennings. (Linford Romance Library). 304p. 1996. pap. 15.99 (0-7089-7897-5, Linford) Ulverscroft.

Really "Down & Delicious" Home Cookin' Casey Smith. Ed. by Lori Smith. LC 88-2798. (Illus.). 150p. (Orig.). 1996. pap. 12.95 (0-945294-08-5) Cloud Nine Pubns.

Really Easy Broadway Songs. 8.95 (0-7935-4930-2, 00310081) H Leonard.

Really Easy Flute Book: Flute/Piano. 1988. 9.95 (0-571-50881-2, 50489985) H Leonard.

Really Easy Horn Book: Horn/Piano. Gunning. 1994. 9.95 (0-571-50996-7, 50489249) H Leonard.

Really Easy Trombone Book with Piano. Gout. 1987. 9.95 (0-571-50999-1, 50489250) H Leonard.

Really Existing Nationalism: A Post-Communist View from Marx & Engels. Erica Benner. 280p. 1996. 55.00 (0-19-827959-0) OUP.

Really Fearsome Blood-Loving Vampire Bats: And Other Creatures with Strange Eating Habits. (Really Horrible Guides Ser.). (Illus.). 24p. (J). 1996. 9.95 (0-7894-1029-X) DK Pub Inc.

*__Really Final Solution.__ Claud C. Crawford. 160p. (Orig.). 1997. pap. 9.95 (0-933697-07-4) Claud Crawford.

Really Good Game Book. Charles Tongue. 97p. 1992. pap. 7.95 (0-86051-556-7, Robson-Parkwest) Parkwest Pubns.

Really Governing: How Health System & Hospital Boards Can Make More of a Difference. Dennis D. Pointer & Charles M. Ewell. LC 94-25555. 240p. 1994. text ed. 39.95 (0-8273-5577-7) Delmar.

*__Really Great News: A Grandfather's Legacy.__ iv, 205p. (Orig.). 1996. pap. 3.50 (0-9654214-0-6) Dorilou.

Really Hairy Scary Spider: And Other Creatures with Lots of Legs. (Really Horrible Guides Ser.). (Illus.). 24p. (J). 1996. 9.95 (0-7894-1028-1) DK Pub Inc.

Really Horrible Horned Toad: And Other Cold, Clammy Creatures. (Really Horrible Guides Ser.). (Illus.). 24p. (J). 1996. 9.95 (0-7894-1117-2) DK Pub Inc.

Really Important Stuff My Kids Have Taught Me. Cynthia C. Lewis. Ed. by Sally Kovalchick. LC 94-31588. 416p. (Orig.). 1994. pap. 6.95 (1-56305-700-X, 3700) Workman Pub.

Really Managing: The Work of Effective CEOs in Large Health Organizations. Anthony R. Kovner. LC 88-2673. 200p. 1988. 37.00 (0-910701-32-6, 0871) Health Admin Pr.

Really Managing Healthcare. Valerie Iles. LC 96-17866. (Health Services Management Ser.). 224p. 1996. 89.00 (0-335-19415-X, Open Univ Pr); pap. 27.00 (0-335-19414-1, Open Univ Pr) Taylor & Francis.

Really No Big Deal. Margaret Bechard. LC 93-31065. 144p. (J). (gr. 3-7). 1994. pap. 13.99 (0-670-85444-1) Viking Child Bks.

Really No Big Deal. Margaret Bechard. 160p. (J). (gr. 3-7). 1996. pap. 3.99 (0-14-036912-0) Puffin Bks.

Really, Not Really. Lesley Frost. (Illus.). 64p. (J). (ps-3). 1966. 10.00 (0-8159-6702-4) Devin.

Really Now, Why Can't Our Johnnies Read? Illus. by Jon Eisenson. LC 88-23354. 160p. 1989. 17.95 (0-87015-258-0) Pacific Bks.

Really Practical Guide to National Curriculum 5-11. Ed. by D. Clemson & W. Clemson. (C). 1989. 54.00 (0-7487-0056-0, Pub. by S Thornes Pubs UK) St Mut.

Really Practical Guide to Primary RE. H. Smith. (C). 1990. text ed. 55.00 (1-871402-30-1, Pub. by Stanley Thornes UK) Trans-Atl Phila.

*__Really Quick & Easy Cook Book.__ Shirley M. Heston. 175p. 1996. 10.00 (0-9641411-1-6) Shirleys Ckbooks.

Really Radical Reptiles & Amphibians. Leslee Elliott. (Amazing Animals Ser.). (Illus.). 64p. (Orig.). (J). (gr. 3-6). 1995. pap. 9.95 (0-8069-1269-3) Sterling.

Really Ragged Shaw. John B. Shaw. 161p. 1993. 16.95 (0-938501-18-6) Wessex.

Really Raising Standards: Cognitive Intervention & Academic Achievement. Philip Adey & Michael Shayer. LC 93-9022. 224p. (C). 1994. pap. 19.95 (0-415-10145-X) Routledge.

*__Really Reading! 10 Simple & Effective Methods to Develop Your Child's Love for Reading!__ Janet Gardner. LC 96-54818. 1997. pap. text ed. 7.95 (1-55850-708-6) Adams Media.

*__Really, Really Bad Sports Jokes.__ Katy Hall. (Illus.). 1998. pap. write for info. (0-7636-0433-X) Candlewick Press.

*__Really Rural: Authentic French Country Interiors.__ Marie-France Boyer. LC 97-60246. 120p. 1997. 22.50 (0-500-01799-9) Thames Hudson.

Really Scared Stiff: Three Creepy Tales. Marshall Efron & Alfa-Betty Olsen. (Golden Star Readers Ser.). (Illus.). 48p. (J). (gr. 2-4). 1992. pap. write for info. (0-307-11469-4, 11469, Golden Pr) Western Pub.

Really Short Poems of A. R. Ammons. A. R. Ammons. 1991. 17.95 (0-393-02870-4) Norton.

Really Short Poems of A. R. Ammons. A. R. Ammons. 176p. 1992. pap. 9.95 (0-393-30850-2) Norton.

Really Simple, No Nonsense Nutrition Guide. Ed Blonz. 130p. (Orig.). 1993. pap. 8.95 (0-943233-45-3) Conari Press.

Really Simple, No-Nonsense Nutrition Guide. Edward R. Blonz. (Illus.). 175p. (C). 1993. reprint ed. lib. bdg. 27.00 (0-8095-5874-2) Borgo Pr.

Really Simple Party Cakes. Evelyn H. Fryatt. (Illus.). 96p. 1994. pap. 10.95 (1-895569-24-9, Pub. by Tamos Bks CN) Sterling.

Really the Blues. Mezz Mezzrow & Bernard Wolfe. 1990. pap. 14.95 (0-8065-1205-9, Citadel Pr) Carol Pub Group.

Really the Blues: A Photographic Journey. Photos by Stephen Green. LC 96-60616. (Illus.). 128p. 1996. pap. 21.95 (0-942627-31-8) Woodford Pubng.

*__Really Useful Bunny Guide.__ Carolina James. (Illus.). 48p. 1998. pap. 6.95 (1-85279-033-4, GB-020) TFH Pubns.

Really Useful Science Book: A Framework of Knowledge for Primary Teachers. Steve Farrow. 240p. 1995. pap. 19.95 (0-7507-0376-8) Taylor & Francis.

Really Weird Animals. Bobbie Kalman. (Crabapple Ser.). (Illus.). 32p. (J). (gr. 2-5). 1995. pap. 5.95 (0-86505-727-3); lib. bdg. 18.08 (0-86505-627-7) Crabtree Pub Co.

Really Weird News Stories. Dana Del Prado. LC 95-38663. (Kidbacks Ser.). (J). (gr. 3-7). 1996. pap. 5.99 (0-679-87475-5) Random.

Really Wicked Droning Wasp: And Other Things that Bite & Sting. (Really Horrible Guides Ser.). (Illus.). 24p. (J). 1996. 9.95 (0-7894-1118-0) DK Pub Inc.

Really Wild Guide to Britain: A Guide to Wildlife Activities for Children over 200 Sites Included. Compiled by Eric Rowan & David Wallace. (Illus.). 289p. 1995. pap. 9.95 (0-563-36788-1, BBC-Parkwest) Parkwest Pubns.

*__Really Wild Pets: Crocodile.__ Jill Newton. (Really Wild Pets Ser.). (Illus.). 10p. (J). (ps-k). 1997. 14.95 (0-7613-0189-5) Millbrook Pr.

*__Really Wild Pets: Elephant.__ Jill Newton. (Really Wild Pets Ser.). (Illus.). 10p. (J). (ps-k). 1997. 14.95 (0-7613-0188-7) Millbrook Pr.

*__Really Wild Pets: Giraffe.__ Jill Newton. (Really Wild Pets Ser.). (Illus.). 10p. (J). (ps-k). 1997. 14.95 (0-7613-0186-0) Millbrook Pr.

*__Really Wild Pets: Penguin.__ Jill Newton. (Really Wild Pets Ser.). (Illus.). 10p. (J). (ps-k). 1997. 14.95 (0-7613-0187-9) Millbrook Pr.

Really Writing! Ready-to-Use Writing Process Activities for the Elementary Grades. Cherlyn Sunflower. LC 93-45005. 1994. spiral bd. 27.95 (0-87628-113-7) Ctr Appl Res.

*__Realm.__ Tyson M. Reimers. 276p. (Orig.). 1997. mass mkt. 4.99 (1-55237-038-0, Pub. by Comnwlth Pub CN) Partners Pubs Grp.

Realm of a Rain-Queen: A Study of the Pattern of Lovedu Society. Eileen J. Krige & Jack D. Krige. (Illus.). 252p. 1980. reprint ed. pap. write for info. (0-7021-1060-4, Pub. by Univ Natal Pr SA) Intl Spec Bk.

Realm of a Rain-Queen, A Study of the Pattern of Louedu Society. Eileen J. Krige. LC 75-41168. reprint ed. 32.50 (0-404-14564-7) AMS Pr.

Realm of Ends: Or, Pluralism & Theism. James Ward. LC 77-27173. (Gifford Lectures: 1907-10). reprint ed. 34.50 (0-404-60464-1) AMS Pr.

Realm of Haden: A Space-Age Fantasy. Joseph P. Rogers. 183p. 1995. pap. 8.95 (0-9642331-0-X) Rogers Pubng.

Realm of Humanitas: Responses to the Writings of Hannah Arendt. Reuben Garner. LC 89-13244. (American University Studies: Philosophy: Ser. V, Vol. 83). 272p. 1990. text ed. 45.50 (0-8204-1107-8) P Lang Pubng.

Realm of Interacting Binary Stars. Ed. by J. Sahade. (Astrophysics & Space Science Library). 448p. (C). 1993. lib. bdg. 177.00 (0-7923-1675-4) Kluwer Ac.

Realm of Possibilities: Wolfgang Hildesheimer's Non-Traditional Non-Fictional Prose. Patricia H. Stanley. LC 88-19118. 198p. (C). 1988. lib. bdg. 41.50 (0-8191-7119-0) U Pr of Amer.

Realm of Prester John. Robert Silverberg. 432p. 1996. reprint ed. pap. 16.95 (0-8214-1138-1) Ohio U Pr.

Realm of Rhetoric. Chaim Perelman. Tr. by William Kluback. LC 79-66378. (C). 1982. pap. text ed. 11.50 (0-268-01605-4) U of Notre Dame Pr.

Realm of Rights. Judith J. Thomson. LC 90-31045. 383p. 1990. 42.00 (0-674-74948-0) HUP.

Realm of Rights. Judith J. Thomson. 400p. 1992. pap. 16.95 (0-674-74949-9) HUP.

*__Realm of St. Steven.__ Engel. Date not set. text ed. 69.50 (1-86064-061-3, Pub. by I B Tauris UK) St Martin.

Realm of the Dead. Kyle Garrett et al. (Illus.). 112p. 1995. 14.95 (0-941613-67-4) Stabur Pr.

Realm of the Extra-Human: Agents & Audiences. Ed. by Agehananda Bharati. (World Anthropology Ser.). (Illus.). xii, 556p. 1976. 58.50 (90-279-7749-6) Mouton.

Realm of the Extra-Human: Ideas & Actions. Ed. by Agehananda Bharait. (World Anthropology Ser.). (Illus.). xii, 522p. 1976. 51.55 (90-279-7759-3) Mouton.

Realm of the Gods. Tamora Pierce. LC 96-45006. (J). 1998. pap. 4.99 (0-679-88291-X, Bullseye Bks) Random Bks Yng Read.

Realm of the Immortals: Daoism in the Arts of China. Stephen Little. LC 87-35473. 76p. 1988. 14.95 (0-910386-92-7) Cleveland Mus Art.

Realm of the Iroquois. Time-Life Books Editors. LC 92-39727. (American Indians Ser.). 176-184p. 1993. 19.95 (0-8094-9437-X); lib. bdg. write for info. (0-8094-9438-8) Time-Life.

Realm of the Long Eyes: A Brief History of Kitt Peak National Observatory. 2nd ed. James E. Kloeppel. (Illus.). 148p. 1991. pap. 15.00 (0-912183-01-2) Univelt Inc.

Realm of the Nebulae. Edwin Hubble. (YA). 1991. pap. 6.95 (0-486-66762-6) Dover.

Realm of the Nebulae. Edwin Hubble. LC 81-16155. (Silliman Milestones in Science Ser.). 226p. 1982. reprint ed. 14.00 (0-300-02499-1) Yale U Pr.

Realm of the Sacred: Verbal Symbolism & Ritual Structures. Ed. by Sitakanta Mahapatra. (Illus.). 248p. 1993. 32.00 (0-19-562610-9) OUP.

*__Realm of the Spirit: Essays in Honor of Virginia Held.__ Ed. by Joram G. Haber & Mark S. Halfon. 256p. 1997. 62.50 (0-8476-8490-3); pap. 23.95 (0-8476-8491-1) Rowman.

Realm of the Underdark. Brian Thomsen. 1996. pap. 5.99 (0-7869-0487-9) TSR Inc.

Realm of the Universe. 5th ed. Abell. (C). 1992. teacher ed., pap. text ed. 28.00 (0-03-074924-7) HB Coll Pubs.

Realm of the Universe. 5th ed. Abell. (C). 1992. suppl. ed., teacher ed., pap. text ed. 34.00 (0-03-074926-3) HB Coll Pubs.

Realm of the Universe. 5th ed. George O. Abell et al. (Illus.). 540p. (C). 1992. pap. text ed. 41.25 (0-03-074919-0) SCP.

Realm of the Universe. 94th ed. George O. Abell et al. LC 93-34228. (C). 1993. pap. text ed. 59.00 (0-03-001664-9) SCP.

Realm of the Universe: 1994 Version with Discover Special Issue & Astronomy Now! 94th ed. Abell. (C). 1994. pap. text ed. 60.25 (0-03-006732-4) HR&W Schl Div.

*__Realm of the Wild: Life & Death of the African Savannah.__ Michel Denis-Huot. 1997. 24.98 (0-7651-9330-2) Smithmark.

*__Realm of the Wolf.__ David L. Falconer. 1996. mass mkt. 4.99 (1-55197-795-8, Pub. by Comnwlth Pub CN) Partners Pubs Grp.

Realm of the Word: Language, Gender & Christianity in a Southern African Kingdom. Paul S. Landau. LC 94-24942. (Social History of Africa Ser.). 249p. 1995. 60.00 (0-435-08963-3, 08963); pap. 24.95 (0-435-08965-X, 08965) Heinemann.

Realm of Tolerance. Ed. by P. Ivanyi. (Illus.). 300p. 1989. 46.95 (0-387-51056-7) Spr-Verlag.

Realm of Totality. Kevin R. O'Neil. 49p. (Orig.). 1984. pap. 6.00 (0-86627-011-6) Crises Res Pr.

Realm of Unknowing: Meditations on Art, Suicide, & Other Transformations. Mark Rudman. LC 94-39701. 193p. 1995. pap. 14.95 (0-8195-1224-9, Wesleyan Univ Pr); text ed. 35.00 (0-8195-2220-1, Wesleyan Univ Pr) U Pr of New Eng.

Realm Where Opposites Meet. Coyd Walker. LC 91-78094. 1993. 16.95 (0-8158-0483-0) Chris Mass.

Realms. William James. (Illus.). x, 86p. (Orig.). 1977. 8.50 (0-940578-01-8); pap. text ed. 5.95 (0-940578-02-6) Galahand Pr.

Realms. Paul Kircher. (Illus.). 80p. (Orig.). 1987. pap. 11.95 (0-87416-043-X) Catalan Communs.

Realms of Apollo: Literature & Healing in Seventeenth-Century England. Raymond A. Anselment. LC 94-46922. 1995. 47.50 (0-87413-553-2) U Delaware Pr.

Realms of Arkania: The Charlatan: A Novel. Ulrich Keisow. 1996. mass mkt. 5.99 (0-7615-0233-5) Prima Pub.

Realms of Arkania: The Lioness - A Novel. Ina Kramer. 312p. 1996. mass mkt., per. 5.99 (0-7615-0477-X) Prima Pub.

Realms of Arkania: The Sacrifice - A Novel. Ina Kramer. 320p. 1996. mass mkt., per. 5.99 (0-7615-0476-1) Prima Pub.

Realms of Beauty: A Guide to the Wilderness Areas of East Texas. rev. ed. Edward C. Fritz & Jess Alford. LC 92-35009. (Illus.). 132p. 1993. pap. 14.95 (0-292-72479-9) U of Tex Pr.

Realms of Gold. A. Scaasi. Date not set. pap. write for info. (0-8217-4116-0) NAL-Dutton.

Realms of Gold. Margaret Drabble. 384p. 1989. reprint ed. mass mkt. 5.99 (0-8041-0363-1) Ivy Books.

Realms of Gold: A Catalogue of the Map Collection in the Library of the American Philosophical Society. Murphy D. Smith. LC 91-55271. (Memoirs Ser.: Vol. 195). (Illus.). 599p. (C). 1991. 50.00 (0-87169-195-7, M195-SMM) Am Philos.

*__Realms of Gold: An Iliad of Our Time.__ Arthur N. Frangos. LC 93-85265. 470p. (Orig.). 1993. pap. text ed. 22.95 (0-918618-53-3) Pella Pub.

Realms of Gold: The Classics in Christian Perspective. Leland Ryken. (Wheaton Literary Ser.). 240p. (Orig.). (C). 1991. pap. 14.99 (0-87788-717-9) Shaw Pubs.

Realms of Infamy. James Lowder. (Forgotten Realms Ser.). 1995. pap. 4.95 (1-56076-911-4) TSR Inc.

Realms of Knowledge: Academic Departments in Secondary Schools. Leslie S. Siskin. LC 93-26449. 192p. 1994. 75.00 (0-7507-0278-8, Falmer Pr); pap. 25.00 (0-7507-0279-6, Falmer Pr) Taylor & Francis.

Realms of Magic. Ed. by Brian Thomsen. (Forgotten Realms Anthology Ser.). 352p. (Orig.). 1995. pap. 5.99 (0-7869-0303-1) TSR Inc.

Realms of Meaning: An Introduction to Semantics. T. R. Hofmann. LC 92-35281. (Learning about Language Ser.). 1993. pap. text ed. 39.02 (0-582-02886-8, 79591) Longman.

Realms of Memory: The Construction of the French Past. abr. rev. ed. Ed. by Lawrence D. Kritzman. LC 95-49349. (Illus.). 651p. (C). 1996. 39.50 (0-231-08404-8) Col U Pr.

R

*Realms of Memory: The Construction of the French Past Symbols, Vol. 3. Pierre Nora. (Realms of Memory Ser.). 1998. 39.50 (0-231-10926-1) Col U Pr.

*Realms of Memory Vol. 2: Traditions. Pierre Nora. 576p. (C). 1997. 37.50 (0-231-10634-3) Col U Pr.

*Realms of Philosophy. William S. Sahakian & Mabel L. Sahakian. LC 65-13253. (Illus.). 689p. reprint ed. pap. 180.00 (0-608-05352-X, 2065058) Bks Demand.

Realms of Ritual: Burgundian Ceremony & Civic Life in Late Medieval Ghent. Peter J. Arnade. LC 96-15632. 1996. write for info. (0-8014-3098-4, Comstock Pub) Cornell U Pr.

Realms of Silver. Compton Mackenzie. Ed. by Mira Wilkins. LC 78-3934. (International Finance Ser.). (Illus.). 1979. reprint ed. lib. bdg. 35.95 (0-405-11236-X) Ayer.

*Realms of the Arcane. (Forgotten Realms Novel Ser.). 1997. pap. 5.99 (0-7869-0647-2) TSR Inc.

Realms of the Gods. Tamora Pierce. (J). 1996. 17.00 (0-689-31990-8, S&S Bks Young Read) S&S Childrens.

Realms of the Russian Bear. John Sparks. 1992. 29.95 (0-316-80494-0) Little.

Realms of the Sea. Ed. by Leah Bendavid-Val. (Illus.). 1991. vhs 41.95 (0-87044-856-0) Natl Geog.

Realms of the Sea. Ed. by Leah Bendavid-Val. (Illus.). 1994. Incl. Seasons in the Sea Video. 35.00 (0-87044-855-2) Natl Geog.

Realms of the Self: Variations on a Theme in Modern Drama. Arthur Ganz. (Gotham Library). 256p. (C). 1981. text ed. 24.00 (0-8147-2979-7) NYU Pr.

Realms of the Unknown Player's Manual. Timothy A. Dohrer, III & Gerard J. Evenwel. 24p. 1991. pap. 8.00 (0-9630833-1-7) Walnut Grp.

Realms of the Unknown Realm Controller's Manual. Timothy A. Dohrer, III & Gerard J. Evenwel. 82p. 1991. pap. 15.00 (0-9630833-0-9) Walnut Grp.

Realms of Thought. Martin Kooken. 1995. 8.95 (0-533-11109-9) Vantage.

Realms of Tolkien: Images of Middle-Earth. LC 96-23452. 144p. 1996. pap. 27.50 (0-06-105532-8) Harper SF.

Realms of Valor: Anthology. 320p. (Orig.). 1993. pap. 4.95 (1-56076-557-7) TSR Inc.

*Realspace in Quicktimes: Architecture & Digitization. Ole Bouman. 1996. pap. text ed. 24.95 incl. cd-rom (90-5662-017-7, Pub. by NAi Uitgevers NE) Dist Art Pubs.

Realtime Ophthalmic Ultrasonography & Biometry. Richard S. Koplin et al. 134p. 1984. 41.95 (0-316-50169-7) Little.

Realtime, Shadowtime. John Peel. (J). 14.00 (0-671-79894-4, S&S Bks Young Read) S&S Childrens.

*Realtime Software Systems. (ITCP-UK Computer Science Ser.). 1997. pap. 59.95 (1-85032-274-0) ITCP.

*Realtime Systems. Nimal Nissanke. LC 96-49195. (Computer Science Ser.). 1997. 42.00 (0-13-651274-7) P-H.

Realtors' Liability. Mark L. Levine. 1979. write for info. (0-317-00910-9) Prof Pubns & Educ.

Realtors Liability. Mark L. Levine. LC 79-4133. (Real Estate For Professional Practitioners Ser.). 285p. reprint ed. pap. 81.30 (0-317-09301-0, 2022419) Bks Demand.

Realty & Reality or Why Won't Your House Sell. Robert L. Feinstein. 1995. pap. 16.95 (0-9648371-0-2) Dorsh Pubng.

Realty Bluebook. 31th ed. Robert De Heer. 672p. 1995. pap. 20.95 (0-7931-1539-6, 1965-1031, Real Estate Ed) Dearborn Finan.

*Realty Bluebook. 32th ed. Robert De Heer. 672p. 1997. pap. text ed. 2,095.00 (0-7931-2659-2, 1965-1032, Real Estate Ed) Dearborn Finan.

Realty Bluebook Financial Tables. 520p. 1994. pap. 9.95 (0-7931-1016-5, 1965-1129, Real Estate Ed) Dearborn Finan.

Realty Partnership in Default, 1991. (Real Estate Law & Practice Ser.). 1036p. 1991. pap. text ed. 17.50 (0-685-56945-4, N4-4558) PLI.

*Realworld Guide: Classic Jump Rope Rhymes. Klutz Press Staff. (J). 1997. pap. 4.95 (1-57054-068-3) Klutz Pr.

*Realworld Guide: Classic Outdoor Games. Klutz Press Staff. (J). 1997. pap. 8.95 (1-57054-071-3) Klutz Pr.

*Realworld Guide: Glove Compartment Games. Klutz Press Staff. (J). 1997. pap. 4.95 (1-57054-091-8) Klutz Pr.

Reams Family Genealogy, Sixteen Hundred & Fifty to Nineteen Hundred & Eighty-Seven. Mildred R. Kantorowicz. 264p. 1987. pap. write for info. (0-918292-13-1) Griggs Print.

Reams' Legal Citation-at-a-Glance. Bernard D. Reams, Jr. 1995. pap. 3.00 (1-57588-355-4, 303320) W S Hein.

Reanalyzing Program Evaluations. Ed. by Robert F. Boruch et al. LC 81-2841. (Jossey-Bass Social & Behavioral Science Ser.). 423p. reprint ed. pap. 120.60 (0-685-20947-4, 2056559) Bks Demand.

Reanimation in Philosophy. Palmer Talbutt, Jr. LC 86-23356. (Illus.). 220p. (Orig.). (C). 1987. pap. text ed. 22.50 (0-8191-5648-5) U Pr of Amer.

Reanimation of the Paralyzed Face. Lawrence P. Burgess & Richard L. Goode. Ed. by Charles M. Steirnberg. (American Academy of Facial Plastic & Reconstructive Surgery (AAFPRS) Ser.). (Illus.). 72p. 1994. 79.00 (0-86577-519-2) Thieme Med Pubs.

Reap the Whirlwind. Bernice M. Chappel. LC 87-50674. 408p. (Orig.). 1987. pap. 10.95 (0-9611596-8-5) Wilderness Adventure Bks.

Reap the Whirlwind. C. J. Cherryh & Mercedes Lackey. (Sword of Knowledge Ser.: Bk. 3). 288p. (Orig.). 1989. mass mkt. 4.99 (0-671-69846-X) Baen Bks.

Reap the Whirlwind, No. 9. Terry C. Johnston. 512p. 1994. 6.50 (0-553-29974-3) Bantam.

Reap the Whirlwind: Augusta & the Revolution. Anne R. Osborne. LC 89-10334. 1990. 4.95 (0-87844-087-9) Sandlapper Pub Co.

*Reap the Whirlwind: The Untold Story of 6 Group Canadas Bomber Force of World War II. Spencer Dunmore. 1997. pap. text ed. 19.99 (0-7710-2926-8) McCland & Stewart.

Reap the Wind. Iris Johansen. 544p. 1991. mass mkt. 5.99 (0-553-29244-7) Bantam.

*Reaper. Ben Mezrich. LC 97-3984. 320p. 1997. 24.00 (0-06-018751-4) HarpC.

Reaper Essays. Mark Jarman & Robert McDowell. 250p. (Orig.). 1996. pap. 12.00 (1-885266-21-9) Story Line.

Reaper Man. Terry Pratchett. 352p. (Orig.). 1992. pap. 4.99 (0-451-45168-6, ROC) NAL-Dutton.

Reapers of the Dust: A Prairie Chronicle. Lois P. Hudson. LC 84-14720. xvi, 173p. 1984. reprint ed. pap. 8.95 (0-87351-177-8, Borealis Book) Minn Hist.

Reapers of the Harvest: The Redemptorists in Great Britain & Ireland 1843-1898. John Sharp. 320p. 1989. 45.00 (1-85390-068-0, Pub. by Veritas IE) St Mut.

Reaping the Revenue Code: Why We Need Sensible Tax Reform. Justin Ward et al. 142p. 1989. 10.00 (0-317-01838-8) Natl Resources Defense Coun.

Reaping the Whirlwind: The Civil Rights Movement in Tuskegee. Robert J. Norrell. LC 85-40845. (Illus.). 272p. 1985. 19.95 (0-394-53688-6) Knopf.

Reaping the Whirlwind: The Civil Rights Movement in Tuskegee. Robert J. Norrell. LC 86-40151. 269p. 1986. pap. 10.36 (0-394-74407-1, Vin) Random.

Reappearance of Christ in the Etheric. Rudolf Steiner. 11p. (Orig.). 1969. reprint ed. spiral bd. 3.50 (0-7873-0834-X) Hlth Research.

Reappearance of the Christ. Alice A. Bailey. LC 48-11756. 1948. 21.00 (0-85330-014-3) Lucis.

Reappearance of the Christ. Alice A. Bailey. LC 48-11756. 1962. pap. 11.00 (0-85330-114-X) Lucis.

Reappearance of the Christ & the Masters of Wisdom. Benjamin Creme. LC 80-50639. 253p. (Orig.). 1980. pap. 7.00 (0-936604-00-X) Tara Ctr. In this first of six books on the subject, British artist & lecturer Benjamin Creme made the startling announcement that the Christ, as World Teacher for the coming age, is already among us -- gradually emerging into full public recognition. Known at this time as Maitreya, but expected by various religions under different names. He is here to promote cooperation among the many ideological factions, galvanize world goodwill & sharing, & inspire sweeping political, social, economic & environmental reforms. Creme puts the most profound event of the last 2,000 years into its correct historical & esoteric context & describes what effect the World Teacher's presence will have on both the world's institutions & the average person. Through his telepathic contact with a Master of Wisdom, Creme answers a myriad of questions well beyond the scope of his personal knowledge. New insights are offered on such subjects as the soul & reincarnation, telepathy, nuclear energy, ancient civilizations, problems of the developing world & a new economic order -- & he clarifies misunderstandings about the anti-Christ & the Last Judgement. Creme delivers his extraordinary message of hope through lectures & media interviews worldwide. His books are available in eight languages. Distributed by Bookpeople, DeVorss, New Leaf, Dempsey.
Publisher Provided Annotation.

Reappearance of the Dove. Helena E. Ruhnau. LC 75-27625. (Illus.). 1978. 14.95 (0-941036-03-0) Colleasius Pr.

Reappearing American. Robert M. Ricketts. 360p. 1993. text ed. 21.95 (0-9635961-0-1) Wright & Co.

Reappearing Characters in Balzac's "Comedie Humaine" Arthur G. Canfield. Ed. by Edward B. Ham. LC 77-14166. (Studies in Romance Languages & Literature: No. 37). 61p. 1977. reprint ed. text ed. 45.00 (0-8371-9836-4, CARC, Greenwood Pr) Greenwood.

Reapportionment Policy. Bernard Grofman et al. (Orig.). 1981. pap. 15.00 (0-918592-45-3) Pol Studies.

*Reappraisal of Econometrics. Ed. by Omar F. Hamouda & J. C. Rowley. (Foundations of Probability, Econometrics & Economic Games Ser.: Vol. 9). 544p. 1997. 170.00 (1-85898-441-6) E Elgar.

Reappraisal of Franco-American Relations, Eighteen Thirty to Eighteen Seventy-One. Henry Blumenthal. LC 79-25197. 255p. 1980. reprint ed. text ed. 59.75 (0-313-22138-3, BLRA, Greenwood Pr) Greenwood.

Reappraisal of the Efficiency of Financial Markets. Ed. by R. M. Guimaraes et al. (NATO Asi Series F: Vol. 54). x, 804p. 1989. 154.00 (0-387-51107-5) Spr-Verlag.

Reappraisal of Welfare Economics. S. K. Nath. LC 70-80108. vii, 247p. 1969. 35.00 (0-678-06507-1) Kelley.

Reappraisals: Shifting Alignments in Postwar Critical Theory. Peter U. Hohendahl. LC 91-10217. 256p. 1991. 39.95 (0-8014-2455-0); pap. 15.95 (0-8014-9706-X) Cornell U Pr.

Reappraisals in Renaissance Thought. Charles B. Schmitt. Ed. by Charles Webster. (Collected Studies: No. CS297). 330p. (C). 1989. lib. bdg. 94.95 (0-86078-245-X, Pub. by Variorum UK) Ashgate Pub Co.

Reappraisals of the Scientific Revolution. Ed. by David C. Lindberg & Robert S. Westman. (Illus.). 530p. (C). 1990. pap. 25.95 (0-521-34804-8); text ed. 80.00 (0-521-34262-7) Cambridge U Pr.

Reappraising an Empire: New Perspectives on Philippine-American History. Intro. by Peter W. Stanley. (Studies in American-East Asian Relations: No. 10). 300p. 1985. 20.00 (0-674-74975-8) HUP.

Reappraising Benjamin Franklin: A Bicentennial Perspective. Ed. by J. A. Lemay. LC 91-50237. (Illus.). 504p. (C). 1993. 39.50 (0-87413-448-X) U Delaware Pr.

Reappraising Gupta History for S. R. Goyal. B. C. Chhabra et al. (C). 1992. 34.00 (81-85179-78-6, Pub. by Aditya Prakashan II) S Asia.

Reappraising J. A. Hobson: Humanism & Welfare. Ed. by Michael Freeden. 272p. (C). (gr. 13). 1990. text ed. 59.95 (0-04-445106-7) Routledge Chapman & Hall.

Reappraising Political Theory. Terence Ball. 328p. 1995. pap. 19.95 (0-19-827995-7) OUP.

Reappraising Social Security: Toward an Alternative System. Jeffrey D. Dunn. 244p. 1982. pap. 5.95 (0-89940-850-8) LBJ Sch Pub Aff.

Reappraising Special Needs Education. Brahm Norwich. Ed. by Peter Mittler. (Special Needs in Ordinary Schools Ser.). 208p. 1990. pap. text ed. 22.50 (0-304-32286-5) Cassell.

Reappraising the Munich Pact: Continental Perspectives. Ed. by Maya Latynski. LC 91-45734. (Woodrow Wilson Center Press Ser.). 120p. 1992. text ed. 22.00 (0-943875-38-2); pap. text ed. 10.95 (0-943875-39-0) Johns Hopkins.

Reapropiaciones: Cultura y Nueva Escritura en Puerto Rico. Julio Ortega. 264p. 1991. pap. 10.50 (0-8477-3620-2) U of PR Pr.

Rear Admiral John Rodgers: 1812-1882. Robert E. Johnson. LC 79-6110. (Navies & Men Ser.). (Illus.). 1980. reprint ed. lib. bdg. 44.95 (0-405-13039-2) Ayer.

*Rear Axle Noise Quality Test Stand. D. E. Wente. (Technical Papers). (Illus.). (Orig.). 1972. pap. text ed. 30.00 incl. audio compact disk (1-55589-383-X) AGMA.

Rear Column & Other Plays. Simon Gray. (Methuen Modern Plays Ser.). 192p. (Orig.). (C). 1988. pap. 8.95 (0-413-39170-1, A0234, Pub. by Methuen UK) Heinemann.

*Rear View. Jean L. Henning. 1998. pap. write for info. (0-609-80184-8, Crown) Crown Pub Group.

*Rear View: A Brief & Elegant History of Bottoms Through the Ages. Jean-Luc Hennig. 1997. 21.00 (0-517-70814-0) Crown Pub Group.

Rear-View Mirrors. Paul Fleischman. LC 85-45387. (Charlotte Zolotow Bk.). 128p. (YA). (gr. 7 up). 1986. 12.95 (0-06-021866-5) HarpC Child Bks.

Rear Window. Cornell Woolrich. 20.95 (0-8488-0333-7) Amereon Ltd.

Rear Window: And Other Stories. Cornell Woolrich. 192p. 1994. pap. 5.95 (0-14-023426-8, Penguin Bks) Viking Penguin.

Rearing African Children under American Occupation. Kwame R. Vanderhorst. (Illus.). 64p. (Orig.). 1996. pap. 7.95 (0-9652104-0-5) Prep Our Youth.

Rearing (Children) unabridged ed. Eugene C. Kane. 130p. 1996. pap. 35.00 (0-9650762-1-0) Paloma Pub Grp.

Rearming the Phoenix: U. S. Military Assistance to the Federal Republic of Germany, 1950-1960. Ed. by A. J. Birtle. LC 91-19695. (Modern American History Ser.). 464p. 1991. text ed. 25.00 (0-8240-1899-0) Garland.

Rearrangements: The Courchene Papers. Thomas J. Courchene. 235p. 1995. lib. bdg. 43.00 (0-8095-4808-9) Borgo Pr.

Rearrangements: The Courchene Papers. Thomas J. Courchene. 235p. 1992. pap. 16.95 (0-88962-507-7) Mosaic.

Rearrangements & Convexity of Level Sets in PDE. B. Kawohl. (Lecture Notes in Mathematics Ser.: Vol. 1150). v, 136p. 1985. 29.95 (0-387-15693-3) Spr-Verlag.

Rearrangements of Pencillanic Acid Derivatives. R. J. Stoodley. 1976. pap. 15.50 (0-08-020477-5, Pergamon Pr) Elsevier.

Rearrangements of Series in Banach Spaces. V. Kadets. LC 91-6522. (Translations of Mathematical Monographs: Vol. 86). 123p. 1991. 75.00 (0-8218-4546-2, MMONO/86) Am Math.

*Rearranging: And Other Stories. David Gifaldi. LC 97-17348. (J). 1998. 16.00 (0-689-81750-9, Atheneum S&S) S&S Trade.

Rearview. Donald Verger. LC 95-70048. 64p. 1995. pap. 6.95 (1-887716-04-1) Designs Disc.

Rearview Mirror. Ellen Feldman. LC 95-12742. 312p. 1996. 22.95 (0-385-30913-9) Delacorte.

Rearview Mirror. Ellen Feldman. 384p. 1996. mass mkt. 5.99 (0-440-21516-1) Dell.

*Rearwin: Story of Men, Planes, & Aircraft Manufacturing During the Great Depression. William C. Wright. (Illus.). 260p. 1996. 34.95 (0-89745-208-9); pap. 26.95 (0-89745-207-0) Sunflower U Pr.

*REA's Authoritative Guide to Law Schools. Research & Education Association Staff. 1997. pap. 21.95 (0-87891-478-1) Res & Educ.

*REA's Authoritative Guide to Medical/Dental School. Research & Education Association Staff. 1997. pap. 21.95 (0-87891-479-X) Res & Educ.

*Rea's Quick & Easy Guide to Writing a Winning Thesis. Research & Education Association Staff. 1996. pap. text ed. 8.95 (0-87891-787-X) Res & Educ.

*Rea's Quick & Easy Guide to Writing Your A+ Term Paper. Research & Education Association Staff. 1996. pap. text ed. 6.95 (0-87891-785-3) Res & Educ.

*Rea's Quick & Easy Guide to Writing Your Research Paper. Research & Education Association Staff. 1996. pap. text ed. 7.95 (0-87891-786-1) Res & Educ.

Reason Aflame: Unamuno & the Heroic Will. Victor Ouimette. (Romantic Studies, Second Ser.: No. 24). 1974. 35.00 (0-300-01666-2) Yale U Pr.

Reason & Action. Bruce A. Aune. (Studies in Philosophy & Religion: No. 9). 217p. 1977. lib. bdg. 88.00 (90-277-0805-3, D Reidel) Kluwer Ac.

Reason & Analysis. 2nd ed. Brand Blanshard. LC 62-9576. (Paul Carus Lectures). 505p. 1964. pap. 18.95 (0-87548-112-4) Open Court.

Reason & Argument. Richard Feldman. LC 92-31318. 448p. (C). 1992. pap. text ed. 44.00 (0-13-767229-2) P-H.

Reason & Argument. Peter T. Geach. LC 76-19961. 1977. pap. 12.95 (0-520-03289-6, CAMPUS 182) U CA Pr.

*Reason & Authority: A Treatise on the Dynamic Paradigm of Legal Dogmatics. Aulis Aarnio. LC K230.A23R43. 330p. 1997. text ed. 72.95 (1-85521-933-6, Pub. by Ashgate UK) Ashgate Pub Co.

Reason & Being. Boris G. Kuznetsov. 464p. 1987. lib. bdg. 180.50 (90-277-2181-5, D Reidel) Kluwer Ac.

Reason & Belief: Based on Gifford Lectures at St. Andrews & Noble Lectures at Harvard. Brand Blanshard. LC 75-301090. 626p. reprint ed. pap. 178.50 (0-8357-8755-9, 2033673) Bks Demand.

*Reason & Conduct in Hume's Treatise: 1946 Edition. Rachael M. Kydd. 212p. 1996. reprint ed. write for info. (1-85506-067-1) Bks Intl VA.

Reason & Controversy in the Arts. Mortimer R. Kadish. LC 67-27796. 296p. reprint ed. pap. 84.40 (0-317-13007-2, 2001794) Bks Demand.

Reason & Culture: A Sociological & Philosophical Study of the Role of Rationality & Rationalism. Ernest Gellner. 208p. 1992. pap. 21.95 (0-631-13711-4) Blackwell Pubs.

Reason & Democracy. Thomas A. Spragens, Jr. LC 89-71474. 295p. (C). 1990. text ed. 45.95 (0-8223-1050-3); pap. text ed. 21.95 (0-8223-1068-6) Duke.

*Reason & Education: Essays in Honor of Israel Scheffler. Ed. by Harvey Siegel. LC 96-38073. 288p. (C). 1996. pap. text ed. 45.00 (0-7923-4362-X) Kluwer Ac.

Reason & Emotion. John Macmurray. LC 91-32302. 232p. (C). 1992. pap. 17.50 (0-391-03729-3) Humanities.

Reason & Emotion in Psychotherapy. rev. ed. Albert Ellis. LC 94-19042. 1994. 22.95 (1-55972-248-7, Birch Ln Pr) Carol Pub Group.

Reason & Emotion in Psychotherapy: A Comprehensive Method of Treating Human Disturbances. rev. ed. Albert Ellis. 504p. 1996. pap. 18.95 (0-8065-1790-5, Citadel Pr) Carol Pub Group.

Reason & Existenz. Karl Jaspers. LC 97-15980. (Studies in Philosophy: No. 11). (C). 1997. reprint ed. pap. 25.00 (0-87462-611-0) Marquette.

Reason & Experience. W. H. Walsh. (Modern Revivals in Philosophy Ser.). 268p. 1992. 56.95 (0-7512-0020-4, Pub. by Gregg Revivals UK) Ashgate Pub Co.

Reason & Experience: Dialogues in Modern Philosophy. John DeLucca. LC 72-91229. 448p. (C). 1973. 38.75 (0-87735-517-7) Jones & Bartlett.

Reason & Faith Revisited. Francis H. Parker. LC 79-154285. (Aquinas Lectures). 1971. 15.00 (0-87462-136-4) Marquette.

Reason & Freedom in Sociological Thought. Frank Hearn. 220p. (C). 1985. text ed. 49.95 (0-04-301194-2); pap. text ed. 16.95 (0-04-301195-0) Routledge Chapman & Hall.

Reason & Genius: Studies in Their Origin. Alfred Hock. LC 70-138150. 138p. (C). 1971. reprint ed. text ed. 59.75 (0-8371-5607-6, HORG, Greenwood Pr) Greenwood.

Reason & God: Encounters of Philosophy with Religion. John E. Smith. LC 77-13887. 274p. 1978. reprint ed. text ed. 59.75 (0-8371-9867-4, SMRG, Greenwood Pr) Greenwood.

Reason & Hope: Selections from the Jewish Writings of Hermann Cohen. Tr. & Intro. by Eva Jospe. LC 93-7895. 237p. 1993. reprint ed. pap. 14.95 (0-87820-211-0) Hebrew Union Coll Pr.

Reason & Human Good in Aristotle. John M. Cooper. LC 74-30852. 206p. reprint ed. pap. 58.80 (0-7837-3852-8, 2043674) Bks Demand.

Reason & Human Good in Aristotle. John M. Cooper. LC 86-19468. 216p. (C). 1986. reprint ed. pap. text ed. 12.95 (0-87220-022-1); reprint ed. lib. bdg. 34.95 (0-87220-115-5) Hackett Pub.

*Reason & Imagination: Reflections on Research in Organic Chemistry. 892p. 1996. 39.00 (981-02-2596-2) World Scientific Pub.

Reason & Insight: Western & Eastern Perspectives on the Pursuit of Moral Wisdom. Timothy Shanahan & Robin Wang. LC 95-16728. 483p. (C). 1996. pap. 41.95 (0-534-23167-5) Wadsworth Pub.

Reason & Intuition. A. C. Ewing. 1970. reprint ed. pap. 39.95 (0-8383-0115-0) M S G Haskell Hse.

Reason & Intuition & Other Essays. John L. Stocks. Ed. by D. Emmet. LC 77-111866. (Essay Index Reprint Ser.). 1977. 21.95 (0-8369-1777-4) Ayer.

Reason & Its Other: Rationality in Modern German Philosophy & Culture. Ed. by Dieter Freundlieb & Wayne Hudson. LC 93-18012. (European Studies Ser.). 256p. 1993. 39.95 (0-85496-372-3) Berg Pubs.

Reason & Justice. Richard D. Winfield. LC 87-17952. (SUNY Series in Systematic Philosophy). 318p. 1988. text ed. 64.50 (0-88706-710-7); pap. text ed. 24.95 (0-88706-711-5) State U NY Pr.

Reason & Life: The Introduction to Philosophy. Julian Marias Aquilera. Tr. by Kenneth S. Reid & Edward Sarmiento from SPA. LC 74-25891. 413p. 1975. reprint ed. text ed. 75.00 (0-8371-7866-5, MARLI, Greenwood Pr) Greenwood.

Reason & Light: Essays on Primo Levi. Ed. by Susan Tarrow. (Western Societies Papers: Vol. 25). 125p. (Orig.). 1990. pap. 11.95 (0-8014-9650-0) Cornell U Pr.

Reason & Morality. Alan Gewirth. LC 77-13911. 416p. 1982. pap. text ed. 19.95 (0-226-28876-5) U Ch Pr.

An Asterisk (*) at the beginning of an entry indicates that the title is appearing in BIP for the first time.

Reason & Morality. Ed. by Joanna Overing. (ASA Monographs). 240p. (C). 1985. pap. text ed. 15.95 (*0-422-79810-X*, 9605, Pub. by Tavistock UK) Routledge Chapman & Hall.

Reason & Nature. Morris R. Cohen. 1978. reprint ed. pap. 8.95 (*0-486-23633-1*) Dover.

Reason & Nature: A Taxonomy of the Abstract & Natural Sciences. Alfred H. Lotring. Ed. by Aubrey R. McKinney. (Adventures in Science Ser.). (Illus.). 208p. 1989. 24.95 (*0-914587-06-4*) Helix Pr.

Reason & Obligation: A Contemporary Approach to Law & Political Morality. R. George Wright. 210p. (Orig.). (C). 1994. pap. text ed. 25.50 (*0-8191-9340-2*); lib. bdg. 52.00 (*0-8191-9339-9*) U Pr of Amer.

***Reason & Passion: Justice Brennan's Enduring Influence.** Ed. by E. Joshua Rosenkranz & Bernard Schwartz. LC 96-43133. 320p. (C). 1997. 30.00 (*0-393-04110-7*) Norton.

Reason & Passion: Representations of Gender in a Malay Society. Michael G. Peletz. LC 94-45698. (Illus.). 371p. 1996. pap. 20.00 (*0-520-20070-5*) U CA Pr.

Reason & Passion: Representations of Gender in a Malay Society. Michael G. Peletz. LC 94-45698. (Illus.). 371p. (C). 1996. 50.00 (*0-520-20069-1*) U CA Pr.

Reason & Rationality in Natural Science: A Group of Essays. Nicholas Rescher. 228p. (Orig.). 1985. lib. bdg. 49.50 (*0-8191-4763-X*) U Pr of Amer.

Reason & Reality. Stig Jorgensen. (Acta Jutlandica Ser.: No. 62:2). 160p. (C). 1986. pap. 35.00 (*87-7288-002-3*, Pub. by Aarhus Univ Pr DK) David Brown.

Reason & Reality: The Relationship Between Science & Theology. John Polkinghorne. LC 91-23518. 128p. (C). 1991. pap. 13.95 (*1-56338-019-6*) TPI PA.

***Reason & Reality in the Methodologies of Economics: An Introduction.** Glenn Fox. LC 97-5356. (Advances in Economic Methodology Ser.). 160p. 1997. 65.00 (*1-85898-597-8*) E Elgar.

Reason & Relativism: A Sartrean Investigation. Steve Hendley. LC 90-44726. 253p. (C). 1991. text ed. 64.50 (*0-7914-0723-3*); pap. text ed. 21.95 (*0-7914-0724-1*) State U NY Pr.

***Reason & Religion in the Traditions of China & India.** D. L. Johnson. Ed. & Illus. by Davies Group Staff. LC 96-84972. 203p. 1997. pap. 10.50 (*1-888570-04-0*) Davies Grp.

Reason & Religious Belief: An Introduction to the Philosophy of Religion. Michael Peterson et al. 304p. (C). 1990. pap. text ed. 21.95 (*0-19-506155-1*) OUP.

***Reason & Religious Belief: An Introduction to the Philosophy of Religion.** 2nd ed. Michael Peterson et al. 368p. (C). 1997. 24.00 (*0-19-511347-0*) OUP.

Reason & Religious Faith. Terence Penelhum. LC 95-2902. (Focus Ser.). 174p. (C). 1995. pap. text ed. 19.95 (*0-8133-2036-4*) Westview.

***Reason & Republicanism: Thomas Jefferson's Legacy of Liberty.** Ed. by Gary L. McDowell & Sharon L. Noble. 208p. 1997. 70.00 (*0-8476-8520-9*) Rowman.

***Reason & Republicanism: Thomas Jefferson's Legacy of Liberty.** Ed. by Gary L. McDowell & Sharon L. Noble. 208p. 1997. pap. 27.95 (*0-8476-8521-7*) Rowman.

***Reason & Responsibility.** 10th ed. Feinberg. (Philosophy Ser.). (C). Date not set. text ed. 51.95 (*0-534-54351-0*) Wadsworth Pub.

Reason & Responsibility: Readings in Some Basic Problems of Philosophy. 8th ed. Joel Feinberg. 607p. (C). 1993. text ed. 36.25 (*0-534-19722-1*) Wadsworth Pub.

Reason & Responsibility: Readings in Some Basic Problems of Philosophy. 9th ed. Ed. by Joel Feinberg. LC 95-9394. 653p. (C). 1996. text ed. 53.95 (*0-534-25986-3*) Wadsworth Pub.

Reason & Revelation: From Paul to Pascal. Richard H. Akeroyd. LC 91-18226. 130p. (C). 1991. pap. 12.95 (*0-86554-405-0*, P097) Mercer Univ Pr.

Reason & Revelation: John Duns Scotus on Natural Theology. Cecil B. Currey. LC 77-9614. (Synthesis Ser.). 1977. pap. 1.00 (*0-8199-0717-0*, Frncscn Herld) Franciscan Pr.

Reason & Revolution: Hegel & the Rise of Social Theory. 2nd ed. Herbert Marcuse. LC 89-35982. (Humanities Paperback Library). 456p. (C). 1991. reprint ed. pap. 18.50 (*0-391-02999-1*) Humanities.

Reason & Revolution: The Political Thought of the Abbe Sieyes. Murray Forsyth. LC 87-10854. 264p. 1987. 49.50 (*0-8419-1143-6*) Holmes & Meier.

Reason & Rhetoric: The Intellectual Foundations of Twentieth Century Liberal Educational Policy. Walter Feinberg. LC 74-16009. 301p. (C). reprint ed. 85.80 (*0-8357-9974-3*, 2055147) Bks Demand.

***Reason & Rhetoric in the Philosophy of Hobbes.** 468p. 1997. pap. text ed. 19.95 (*0-521-59645-9*) Cambridge U Pr.

Reason & Rhetoric in the Philosophy of Hobbes. Quentin Skinner. 468p. (C). 1996. text ed. 49.95 (*0-521-55436-5*) Cambridge U Pr.

Reason & Right. Garth L. Hallett. LC 83-40595. 192p. 1984. pap. 11.50 (*0-268-01622-4*); text ed. 22.00 (*0-268-01621-6*) U of Notre Dame Pr.

Reason & Romanticism. Herbert E. Read. LC 72-6856. (English Literature Ser.: No. 33). 1974. lib. bdg. 75.00 (*0-8383-1640-9*) M S G Haskell Hse.

Reason & Spontaneity: An Essay in Moral Philosophy. A. C. Graham. LC 84-12358. 244p. (C). 1985. text ed. 42.00 (*0-389-20510-9*, BNB 08068, Pub. by Curzon Press UK) UH Pr.

Reason & Spontaneity: An Essay in Moral Philosophy. A. C. Graham. 244p. (C). 1985. text ed. 42.00 (*0-7007-0172-9*, Pub. by Curzon Press UK) UH Pr.

Reason & Teaching. Israel Scheffler. LC 72-86641. 214p. (C). 1981. pap. text ed. 9.95 (*0-87220-084-1*); lib. bdg. 27.95 (*0-87220-085-X*) Hackett Pub.

Reason & the Christian Religion: Essays in Honour of Richard Swinburne. Ed. by Alan G. Padgett. 378p. 1995. text ed. 69.00 (*0-19-824042-2*) OUP.

Reason & the Heart: A Prolegomenon to a Critique of Passional Reason. William J. Wainwright. LC 95-18022. (Studies in the Philosophy of Religion). 184p. 1995. 28.50 (*0-8014-3139-5*) Cornell U Pr.

***Reason & the Lover.** John V. Fleming. LC 83-42557. 204p. 1984. reprint ed. pap. 58.20 (*0-608-02542-9*, 2063186) Bks Demand.

Reason & the Nature of Texts. James L. Battersby. LC 96-21300. 224p. 1996. text ed. 34.95 (*0-8122-3359-X*) U of Pa Pr.

Reason & the Passions in the Comedias of Calderon. David J. Hildner. (Purdue University Monographs in Romance Languages: No. 11). xii, 119p. 1982. 35.00 (*90-272-1721-1*) Benjamins North Am.

Reason & the Radical Crisis of Faith. Shabbir Akhtar. (American University Studies: Theology & Religion: Ser. VII, Vol. 30). 217p. (C). 1987. text ed. 40.00 (*0-8204-0451-9*) P Lang Pubng.

Reason & the Search for Knowledge. Dudley Shapere. 483p. (Orig.). 1983. lib. bdg. 182.50 (*90-277-1551-3*, D Reidel) Kluwer Ac.

Reason & the World Workbook. Peter J. Vernezze. 184p. (C). 1995. per., pap. text ed. 24.09 (*0-7872-1189-3*) Kendall-Hunt.

Reason & Therapeutic Change. Dryden. 334p. 1991. pap. 48.95 (*1-56593-530-6*, 0306) Singular Publishing.

Reason & Values: New Essays in Philosophy of Education. Ed. by John P. Portelli & Sharon Bailin. 228p. (Orig.). (C). 1993. pap. text ed. 20.95 (*1-55059-066-9*) Temeron Bks.

Reason & World: Between Tradition & Another Beginning. Wesley Marx. 125p. 1971. pap. 68.00 (*90-247-5048-2*, Pub. by M Nijhoff NE) Kluwer Ac.

Reason & Write: A Step-by-Step Approach for Success on Written Exams. Stephen J. Mahoney. 160p. 1995. teacher ed. 13.99 (*1-56417-637-1*, GA1546) Good Apple.

Reason at Work. 3rd ed. Cahn. (C). 1995. 38.75 (*0-15-502096-X*) HB Coll Pubs.

Reason at Work: Introductory Readings in Philosophy. 2nd ed. Steven M. Cahn et al. 740p. (C). 1989. text ed. 28.75 (*0-15-575991-4*) HB Coll Pubs.

Reason Awake: Science for Man. Rene J. Dubos. LC 70-111327. 280p. 1970. text ed. 49.50 (*0-231-03181-5*) Col U Pr.

***Reason, Democracy, Society: A Treatise on the Basis of Legal Thinking.** Sebastian Urbina. (Law & Philosophy Library). 256p. (C). 1996. lib. bdg. 117.00 (*0-7923-4262-3*) Kluwer Ac.

***Reason Diminished: Shakespeare & the Marvelous.** Peter G. Platt. LC 96-31074. 304p. 1997. text ed. 45.00 (*0-8032-3714-6*) U of Nebr Pr.

Reason, Emotion & Habit in the Training of a Torah Personality. Nachman Bulman. (Annual Fryer Memorial Lectures). 1.50 (*0-914131-53-2*, B120) Torah Umesorah.

Reason, Ethics, & Society: Themes from Kurt Baier, with His Responses. Jerome B. Schneewind. 316p. 1996. pap. 21.95 (*0-8126-9316-7*) Open Court.

Reason, Ethics, & Society: Themes from Kurt Baier, with His Responses. Jerome B. Schneewind. 316p. 1996. 41.95 (*0-8126-9315-9*) Open Court.

Reason, Experience, & God: John E. Smith in Dialogue. Ed. by Vincent M. Colapietro. LC 97-8014. (American Philosophy Ser.: Vol. 7). 210p. (C). 1996. text ed. 28.00 (*0-8232-1706-X*); pap. text ed. 18.00 (*0-8232-1707-8*) Fordham.

Reason for a Flower. Ruth Heller. (Illus.). (J). (ps-3). 1983. 13.95 (*0-448-14495-6*, G&D) Putnam Pub Group.

***Reason for a Flower.** Ruth Heller. (FRE.). (J). pap. 6.99 (*0-590-71999-8*) Scholastic Inc.

Reason for Being. Emerson M. Clymer. 116p. 1971. 6.95 (*0-932785-42-5*) Philos Pub.

Reason for Being. S. Bradford Williams, Jr. LC 84-71446. (Illus.). (Orig.). 1984. pap. 4.00 (*0-9608522-2-0*) Copper Orchid.

Reason for Faith. John H. Gerstner. 245p. 1995. pap. 14.95 (*1-57358-021-X*) Soli Deo Gloria.

Reason for Hope: Liberation Theology Confronts a Liberal Faith. Fredric J. Muir. LC 93-86732. 160p. (Orig.). (C). 1994. pap. 10.00 (*0-931104-39-4*) Sunflower Ink.

Reason for Janey. Nancy H. Wilson. 160p. (J). 1995. pap. 3.99 (*0-380-72257-7*, Camelot) Avon.

Reason for Janey. Nancy H. Wilson. LC 93-22930. 160p. (J). (gr. 3-7). 1994. lib. bdg. 15.00 (*0-02-793127-7*, Mac Bks Young Read) S&S Childrens.

Reason for Living. George Roche. LC 89-36663. 156p. 1990. 17.95 (*0-89526-545-1*) Regnery Pub.

***Reason for My Hope: How God's Grace & Love Strengthens, Rebuilds & Restores.** Charles Stanley. 256p. 1997. 19.99 (*0-8407-7765-5*) Nelson.

Reason for Nasturtiums. Chitra Divakaruni. 72p. 1990. pap. 6.95 (*0-917658-28-0*) BPW & P.

Reason for Optimism: Treating Cancer with a Bone Marrow Transplant. Barbara J. Munson. LC 96-60273. (Illus.). 110p. (Orig.). 1996. pap. 13.95 (*0-9648754-0-3*) Two Pillars.

Reason for Science. Donald R. Strombeck. Ed. by Walter Hearn. (Illus.). 246p. (C). 1987. 15.95 (*0-9619272-0-8*) Stonegate Rancho.

***Reason for Season.** Thomas-Cochran. (What a Wonderful World Intro Ser.). 1993. pap. text ed. write for info. (*0-582-91078-1*, Pub. by Longman UK) Longman.

Reason for the Hope Within: Sermons on the Theory of Religious Belief. John H. Newman. 368p. 1985. pap. 16.95 (*0-87193-219-9*) Dimension Bks.

Reason for the Pelican. John Ciardi. LC 93-61163. (Illus.). 64p. (J). (gr. 1 up). 1994. 13.95 (*1-56397-370-7*, Wordsong) Boyds Mills Pr.

***Reason for the Season.** Marsh. 4.85 (*0-687-35622-9*) Abingdon.

Reason for Treason. Lubomir Lacho & Florence W. Biros. (Illus.). 256p. 8.95 (*0-936369-41-8*) Son-Rise Pubns.

Reason for Treason: A True Story of Intrigue & Romance. Lubomir Lacho & Florence W. Biros. (Illus.). 250p. 1994. pap. 8.95 (*0-936369-07-8*) Son-Rise Pubns.

Reason, Freedom, & Religion: Closing the Gap Between the Humanistic & Scientific Study of Religion. Lorne L. Dawson. (Toronto Studies in Religion: Vol. 6). 247p. 1988. text ed. 46.95 (*0-8204-0600-7*) P Lang Pubng.

Reason, Grace & Sentiment Vol. 1: A Study of the Language of Religion & Ethics in England, 1660-1780: Whichcote to Wesley. Isabel Rivers. (Studies in Eighteenth-Century English Literature & Thought: No. 8). 320p. (C). 1991. text ed. 59.95 (*0-521-38340-4*) Cambridge U Pr.

Reason, History, & Politics: The Communitarian Grounds of Legitimation in the Modern Age. David Ingram. LC 94-28754. (SUNY Series in Social & Political Thought). 1995. pap. text ed. 19.95 (*0-7914-2350-6*) State U NY Pr.

Reason, History, & Politics: The Communitarian Grounds of Legitimation in the Modern Age. David Ingram. LC 94-28754. (SUNY Series in Social & Political Thought). 467p. (C). 1995. text ed. 59.50 (*0-7914-2349-2*) State U NY Pr.

Reason in a Storm: A Study of the Use of Ambiguity in the Writings of T. S. Eliot. Geoffrey B. Williams. 282p. (C). 1991. pap. text ed. 29.50 (*0-8191-8271-0*); lib. bdg. 54.50 (*0-8191-8270-2*) U Pr of Amer.

Reason in Action: Essays in the Philosophy of Social Science. Martin Hollis. (Illus.). 293p. (C). 1996. text ed. 59.95 (*0-521-44263-X*); pap. text ed. 18.95 (*0-521-44779-8*) Cambridge U Pr.

Reason in Exile Vol. 13: Essays on Catalan Philosophers. Manuel Duran. LC 93-46253. (Catalan Studies: Vol. 13). 104p. (C). 1994. text ed. 27.95 (*0-8204-2361-0*) P Lang Pubng.

Reason in History. Steve Ostovich. 289p. 1990. 22.95 (*1-55540-424-3*, 01 01 71); pap. 14.95 (*1-55540-425-1*, 01 01 71) Scholars Pr GA.

Reason in History: Hegel. Robert S. Hartman. 144p. (C). 1953. pap. text ed. 9.07 (*0-02-351320-9*, Macmillan Coll) P-H.

Reason in History Vol. 68: Annual ACPA Proceedings, 1994. Ed. by Therese-Anne Druart. 1995. pap. 20.00 (*0-614-11342-3*) Am Cath Philo.

Reason in Human Affairs. Herbert A. Simon. LC 82-62448. 125p. 1983. 29.50 (*0-8047-1179-8*); pap. 10.95 (*0-8047-1848-2*) Stanford U Pr.

Reason in Law. 4th ed. Lief H. Carter. LC 93-5194. (C). 1994. text ed. 24.50 (*0-673-52269-5*) Addson-Wesley Educ.

***Reason in Law.** 5th ed. Ed. by Carter. (C). 1998. text ed. write for info. (*0-321-01111-2*) Addson-Wesley Educ.

Reason in Madness: An Existential Approach to Psychiatric Disorders. Molly D. Niv. Ed. by Joyce Declan. LC 95-60784. (Illus.). 469p. (Orig.). (C). 1996. 19.95 (*0-9634433-0-5*) EVER Pub.

Reason in Madness: Critical Essays. Allen Tate. LC 68-26479. (Essay Index Reprint Ser.). 1977. reprint ed. 24.95 (*0-8369-0925-9*) Ayer.

Reason in Religion: The Foundations of Hegel's Philosophy of Religion. Walter Jaeschke. Tr. by J. Michael Stewart & Peter C. Hodgson. LC 90-33264. 400p. 1990. 58.00 (*0-520-06518-2*) U CA Pr.

Reason in Science. George Santayana. 320p. 1983. reprint ed. pap. 6.95 (*0-486-24439-3*) Dover.

Reason in Society. George Santayana. 224p. 1980. reprint ed. pap. 5.95 (*0-486-24003-7*) Dover.

Reason in Society: Five Types of Decisions & Their Social Conditions. Paul Diesing. LC 72-11328. 262p. 1973. reprint ed. pap. 4.95 (*0-8371-8941-1*, DIRPB); reprint ed. text ed. 59.75 (*0-8371-6660-8*, DIRS) Greenwood.

Reason in the Age of Science. Hans-Georg Gadamer. Tr. by Frederick G. Lawrence from GER. (Studies in Contemporary German Social Thought). 216p. (C). 1983. reprint ed. pap. 13.95 (*0-262-57061-0*) MIT Pr.

Reason in the Balance: The Case Against Naturalism in Science, Law & Education. Phillip E. Johnson. LC 95-12620. 192p. 1995. 19.99 (*0-8308-1610-0*, 1610) InterVarsity.

Reason Informed by Faith: Foundations of Christian Morality. Richard M. Gula. 1989. pap. 14.95 (*0-8091-3066-1*) Paulist Pr.

Reason Is Powerless in the Expression of Love. Reshad Feild. (Orig.). 1990. pap. 9.00 (*0-9625412-0-6*) Chalice Guild.

Reason, Life, Culture - Part 1: Phenomenology in the Baltics. Ed. by Anna-Teresa Tymieniecka. LC 92-22158. (Analecta Husserliana Ser.: Vol. 39). 312p. 1993. lib. bdg. 137.00 (*0-7923-1902-8*, Pub. by Klwr Acad Pubs NE) Kluwer Ac.

Reason of Following: Christology & the Ecstatic I. Robert P. Scharlemann. LC 91-11615. (Religion & Postmodernism Ser.). 226p. 1991. 37.50 (*0-226-73659-8*) U Ch Pr.

Reason of Metaphor: A Study in Politics. Donald F. Miller. 268p. (C). 1992. text ed. 29.95 (*0-8039-9410-9*) Sage.

Reason of the Laws of Moses. Moses Maimonides. Ed. by James Townley. LC 78-97294. 451p. 1970. reprint ed. text ed. 35.00 (*0-8371-2618-5*, MARL, Greenwood Pr) Greenwood.

Reason over Passion: Harriet Martineau & the Novel. Valerie Sanders. LC 86-3938. 272p. 1986. text ed. 39.95 (*0-312-66533-4*) St Martin.

Reason over Precedents: Origins of American Legal Thought. Craig E. Klafter. LC 92-45071. (Contributions in Legal Studies: No. 73). 240p. 1993. text ed. 59.95 (*0-313-28675-2*, KRP, Greenwood Pr) Greenwood.

Reason Plays at War: The American Liberal Vision & Revolutionary Warfare. William Bode. 150p. (C). pap. text ed. 24.00 (*0-8191-9572-3*); lib. bdg. 45.00 (*0-8191-9571-5*) U Pr of Amer.

Reason, Reality, & Speculative Philosophy. Arthur E. Murphy. Ed. & Intro. by Marcus G. Singer. LC 96-5988. (Illus.). 330p. 1996. 45.00 (*0-299-15040-2*) U of Wis Pr.

Reason, Regulation & Realism: Toward a Regulatory Systems Theory of Reason & Evolutionary Epistemology. Clifford A. Hooker. LC 94-5769. (SUNY Series in Philosophy & Biology). 432p. 1995. text ed. 74.50 (*0-7914-2261-5*); pap. text ed. 24.95 (*0-7914-2262-3*) State U NY Pr.

Reason, Revelation, & the Foundations of Political Philosophy. James V. Schall. LC 86-27624. 264p. 1987. text ed. 35.00 (*0-8071-1303-4*) La State U Pr.

Reason Revisited: The Philosophy of Karl Jaspers. Sebastian Samay. LC 72-160423. 318p. reprint ed. pap. 90.70 (*0-317-26140-1*, 2024371) Bks Demand.

Reason, Science & Paradox. Joseph W. Smith. 320p. 1986. 65.00 (*0-7099-4430-6*, Pub. by Croom Helm UK) Routledge Chapman & Hall.

Reason, Social Myths, & Democracy. Sidney Hook. (Great Books in Philosophy). 302p. (C). 1991. reprint ed. pap. 11.95 (*0-87975-672-1*) Prometheus Bks.

Reason, the Understanding, & Time. Arthur O. Lovejoy. LC 61-8177. 224p. reprint ed. pap. 63.90 (*0-317-20645-1*, 2024135) Bks Demand.

Reason to Believe. Mario Cuomo. 182p. 1995. 21.00 (*0-684-81517-6*) S&S Trade.

Reason to Believe. Mario Cuomo. 208p. 1996. pap. 11.00 (*0-684-82533-3*) S&S Trade.

Reason to Believe. Kathleen Eagle. 384p. (Orig.). 1995. mass mkt. 5.50 (*0-380-77633-2*) Avon.

Reason to Believe. R. C. Sproul. 160p. 1982. pap. 7.99 (*0-310-44911-1*, 12370P) Zondervan.

***Reason to Believe: A Practical Guide to Psychic Phenomena.** Michael Clark. 224p. (Orig.). 1997. mass mkt. 5.99 (*0-380-78474-2*) Avon.

Reason to Believe: Pupil Text. Ann Walsh. 208p. 1994. pap. 30.00 (*1-85390-277-2*, Pub. by Veritas IE) St Mut.

Reason to Deceive. Karen West. (Rainbow Romances Ser.). 160p. 1993. 14.95 (*0-7090-4921-8*, Hale-Parkwest) Parkwest Pubns.

Reason to Hope: A Psychosocial Perspective on Violence & Youth. Ed. by Leonard D. Eron et al. 492p. 1994. text ed. 39.95 (*1-55798-272-4*, 431-6460) Am Psychol.

Reason to Hope: A Synthesis of Teilhard de Chardin's Vision & Systems Thinking. R. Wayne Kraft. (Systems Inquiry Ser.). 292p. 1983. pap. 13.95 (*0-914105-14-0*) Intersystems Pubns.

Reason to Live. Ed. by Melody Beattie. 167p. 1991. pap. 8.99 (*0-8423-0988-8*) Tyndale.

Reason to Live. Donalyn Powell. 160p. (Orig.). (YA). (gr. 8-12). 1989. pap. 6.99 (*1-55661-076-9*) Bethany Hse.

Reason to Live. John H. Robinson. (American Heroes Ser.). (Illus.). 446p. 1989. 19.95 (*0-916693-12-0*) Castle Bks.

Reason to Read Vol. 1: Thinking Strategies for Life Through Literature. Cathy C. Block & John N. Mangieri. LC 95-187327. 252p. 1995. pap. 25.49 (*0-201-49047-1*) Addison-Wesley.

Reason to Read Vol. II: Thinking Strategies for Life Through Literature. Cathy C. Block & John N. Mangieri. Ed. by Lois Fowkes & Rachel Farber. (Reason to Read Ser.). (Illus.). 282p. (Orig.). 1995. teacher ed., pap. 18.95 (*0-201-49048-X*) Supplementary Div.

Reason to Read Vol. III: Thinking Strategies for Life Through Literature, Vol. 3. Collins Block et al. (Reason to Read Ser.). (Illus.). 300p. (Orig.). (J). 1996. teacher ed., pap. 23.70 (*0-201-49049-8*) Addison-Wesley.

Reason to Tremble. Bob Mustin. 340p. (Orig.). 1996. mass mkt. 5.99 (*1-55197-216-6*, Pub. by Comnwlth Pub CN) Partners Pubs Grp.

Reason, Tolerance & Christianity: The Ingersoll Debates. Robert G. Ingersoll. (Freethought Library: Freethought Library). 154p. 1993. pap. 14.95 (*0-87975-851-1*) Prometheus Bks.

Reason, Truth & Self: The Postmodern Reconditioned. Michael Luntley. LC 95-14748. 272p. (C). 1995. pap. 16.95 (*0-415-11853-0*) Routledge.

Reason, Truth & Self: The Postmodern Reconditioned. Michael Luntley. LC 95-14748. 272p. (C). (gr. 13). 1995. text ed. 59.95 (*0-415-11852-2*) Routledge.

Reason vs. the Sword: A Treatise. John M. Washburn. LC 75-137559. (Peace Movement in America Ser.). 470p. 1972. reprint ed. lib. bdg. 48.95 (*0-89198-090-3*) Ozer.

Reason Why. Robert A. Laidlaw. (Christian Classics Ser.). 1995. pap. 2.99 (*1-56570-011-2*) Meridian MI.

***Reason Why.** Ruth Rendell. 1997. 3.99 (*0-517-17569-X*) Random Hse Value.

Reason Why. Cecil Woodham-Smith. (C). 1991. pap. 12.95 (*0-14-001278-8*, Penguin Bks) Viking Penguin.

Reason Why. Robert A. Laidlaw. LC 93-70313. 60p. 1994. reprint ed. pap. text ed. 1.50 (*0-88270-649-7*) Bridge-Logos.

Reason Why: An Anthology of the Murderous Mind. Ruth Rendell. 256p. 1996. 24.00 (*0-517-70347-5*) Random.

Reason Why in Astrology: or Philosophy & First Principles. H. S. Green. 125p. 1997. pap. 10.00 (*0-89540-319-6*, SB-319, Sun Bks) Sun Pub.

Reason, Will, & Sensation: Studies in Descartes' Metaphysics. Ed. by John Cottingham. 344p. 1994. 59.00 (*0-19-824083-X*) OUP.

Reason Within the Bounds of Religion. Nicholas Wolstertoff. 161p. 1993. reprint ed. pap. 9.95 (*1-57383-011-9*) Regent College.

Reason Wounded: An Experience of India's Emergency. P. Lewis. 207p. 1978. 16.95 (*0-318-36609-6*) Asia Bk Corp.

Reasonable Accommodation: Profitable Compliance with the Americans with Disabilities Act. Jay Spechler. 430p. 1996. 39.95 (*1-884015-94-8*) St Lucie Pr.

Reasonable Accommodation of Disabled Employees: A Comprehensive Case Law Reference. abr. ed. Brian C. Shaw. 90p. 1989. pap. 15.00 (*0-88364-200-X*) Natl Sch Boards.

Reasonable Accommodation under the Americans with Disabilities Act. Barbara A. Lee. (ADA Practice Ser.). 47p. 1994. pap. 16.00 (*0-934753-92-X*) LRP Pubns.

Reasonable Adventurer. Roy A. Heath. LC 64-12487. 192p. (C). 1994. pap. 14.95 (*0-8229-5071-5*) U of Pittsburgh Pr.

Reasonable Affliction: 1001 Love Poems to Read to Each Other. James Wakeman & Sally A. Berk. (Illus.). 804p. 1996. 14.98 (*1-884822-84-3*) Blck Dog & Leventhal.

Reasonable Care. Grant Gillett. LC 89-35926. (Mind Matters Ser.). 150p. 1990. text ed. 35.00 (*0-312-04002-4*) St Martin.

Reasonable Care: Legal Perspectives on the Doctor-Patient Relationship. Harvey Teff. 304p. 1995. 52.00 (*0-19-825578-0*) OUP.

Reasonable Children: Moral Education & Moral Learning. Michael S. Pritchard. LC 96-25633. 192p. 1996. 29.95 (*0-7006-0796-X*); pap. 12.95 (*0-7006-0797-8*) U Pr of KS.

Reasonable Christianity. John Rendle-Short. 1991. pap. 8.99 (*0-85234-289-6*, Pub. by Evangelical Pr) Presby & Reformed.

Reasonable Circulation. P. J. Barry. 1989. pap. 3.25 (*0-8222-0947-0*) Dramatists Play.

Reasonable Creatures. Katha Pollitt. 1995. pap. 11.00 (*0-679-76278-7*) Random Hse Value.

Reasonable Creatures: Feminism & Society in American Culture at the End of the Twentieth Century. Katha Pollitt. LC 93-47492. 1994. 25.00 (*0-394-57060-X*) Knopf.

Reasonable Defense. William W. Kaufmann. LC 85-73331. (Studies in Defense Policy). 113p. 1986. pap. 8.95 (*0-8157-4879-5*) Brookings.

Reasonable Democracy: Jurgen Habermas & the Politics of Discourse. Simone Chambers. 256p. 1996. pap. 16.95 (*0-8014-8330-1*) Cornell U Pr.

Reasonable Democracy: Jurgen Habermas & the Politics of Discourse. Simone Chambers. LC 95-45577. 256p. (C). 1996. 39.95 (*0-8014-2668-5*) Cornell U Pr.

Reasonable Doubt. Philip Friedman. 448p. 1990. mass mkt. 6.99 (*0-8041-0749-1*) Ivy Books.

***Reasonable Doubt.** Scott Raab. 1998. write for info. (*0-679-45772-0*, Villard Bks) Random.

Reasonable Doubt. Steve Vogel. 1992. mass mkt. 5.99 (*0-312-92908-0*) St Martin.

Reasonable Doubt. large type ed. Alan M. Dershowitz. LC 96-16211. 380p. 1996. 23.95 (*0-7862-0785-X*, Thorndike Lrg Prnt) Thorndike Pr.

***Reasonable Doubts.** Alan Dershowitz. 1997. pap. 13.00 (*0-684-83264-X*, Touchstone Bks) S&S Trade.

Reasonable Doubts. 2nd rev. ed. Scott Richards. Orig. Title: Myths the World Taught Me. 256p. 1996. pap. 9.99 (*0-936728-60-4*) Word for Today.

Reasonable Doubts: The O. J. Simpson Case & the Criminal Justice System. Alan M. Dershowitz. LC 96-1688. 238p. 1996. 20.00 (*0-684-83021-3*) S&S Trade.

Reasonable Enthusiast: John Wesley & the Rise of Methodism. Henry D. Rack. LC 93-15360. 658p. (C). 1993. pap. text ed. 29.95 (*0-687-35625-3*) Abingdon.

Reasonable Faith. Tony Campolo. 1995. pap. 10.99 (*0-8499-3634-9*) Word Pub.

Reasonable Faith: Christian Apologetics. Winfried Corduan. LC 93-12443. 304p. 1993. 24.99 (*0-8054-1549-1*, 4215-49) Broadman.

Reasonable Faith: Christian Truth & Apologetics. rev. ed. William L. Craig. LC 94-21577. 350p. (Orig.). 1994. pap. 15.99 (*0-89107-764-2*) Crossway Bks.

Reasonable Force, Pt. 1: Adapting the U. S. Army & Marine Corps to the New Era, Threat Environment & Force Size Requirement. Carl Conetta & Charles Knight. (Briefing Reports: No. 3). 82p. 1992. reprint ed. pap. 12.00 (*1-881677-01-X*) Commonwlth Inst.

Reasonable Insanity: A True Story of the Seventies. Carol L. Mithers. LC 93-30571. 1994. 23.00 (*0-201-57071-8*) Addison-Wesley.

***Reasonable Life.** 2nd ed. Mate Ferenc. Date not set. pap. 11.00 (*0-920256-36-8*) Norton.

Reasonable Life. Arnold Bennett. LC 74-16364. (Collected Works of Arnold Bennett: Vol. 69). 1977. reprint ed. 19.95 (*0-518-19150-8*) Ayer.

Reasonable Life: Toward a Simpler, Secure, More Humane Existence. Ferenc Mate. 1993. 17.95 (*0-920256-25-2*) Norton.

Reasonable Life: Toward a Simpler, Secure, More Humane Existence. Ferenc Mate. 1994. pap. 9.95 (*0-920256-30-9*) Norton.

Reasonable Madness. Fran Dorf. 1990. 18.95 (*1-55972-045-X*, Birch Ln Pr) Carol Pub Group.

Reasonable Man: Trollope's Legal Fiction. Coral Lansbury. LC 80-8560. 240p. pap. 68.40 (*0-8357-4649-6*, 2037579) Bks Demand.

Reasonable Romantic: Essays on Alessandro Manzoni. Sante Matteo & Larry H. Peer. 274p. 1987. text ed. 49.50 (*0-8204-0372-5*) P Lang Pubng.

***Reasonable Self-Esteem.** Richard Keshen. 1995. pap. 25.95 (*0-7735-1373-6*, Pub. by McGill CN) U of Toronto Pr.

***Reasonable Self-Esteem.** Richard Keshen. 1995. 39.95 (*0-7735-1372-8*, Pub. by McGill CN) U of Toronto Pr.

***Reasonable Sufficiency.** David Glueck. 1997. mass mkt. 6.99 (*1-55197-290-5*, Pub. by Comnwlth Pub CN) Partners Pubs Grp.

Reasonable World. Damon Knight. 1991. mass mkt. 3.99 (*0-8125-0978-1*) Tor Bks.

***Reasonableness of Christianity.** John Locke. LC 89-38836. 224p. 1997. pap. 12.95 (*0-89526-402-1*) Regnery Pub.

Reasonableness of Christianity, & A Discourse of Miracles. John Locke. Ed. by I. T. Ramsey. 104p. 1958. pap. 10.95 (*0-8047-0341-8*) Stanford U Pr.

Reasonableness of Reason: Explaining Rationality Naturalistically. Bruce W. Hauptli. 286p. 1995. pap. text ed. 19.95 (*0-8126-9283-7*) Open Court.

Reasonableness of Scripture-Belief. Charles Wolseley. LC 73-2618. 488p. 1973. reprint ed. lib. bdg. 75.00 (*0-8201-1113-9*) Schol Facsimiles.

Reasonably Intelligent Person's Windows Survival Guide: Step-by-Step PC Methods with Hands-On Windows 3.1 & 95. William Gulley. Ed. by Craig Froelich. (Reasonably Intelligent Person's Ser.). (Illus.). 160p. (Orig.). 1996. pap. 11.95 (*0-9650691-0-9*) Madison Tech.

Reasoned Argument in Social Science. Eugene J. Meehan. LC 80-1198. (Linking Research to Policy Ser.). (Illus.). xvi, 218p. 1981. text ed. 55.00 (*0-313-22481-1*, MRE/, Greenwood Pr) Greenwood.

Reasoned Faith. Ed. by Eleonore Stump. LC 92-33439. (Illus.). 384p. 1993. 45.00 (*0-8014-2571-9*); pap. 17.95 (*0-8014-9796-5*) Cornell U Pr.

Reasoned Freedom: John Locke & Enlightenment. Peter A. Schouls. LC 92-52771. 256p. 1992. 42.50 (*0-8014-2758-4*); pap. 15.95 (*0-8014-8037-X*) Cornell U Pr.

Reasoned Programming. Krysia Broda. LC 94-8502. 360p. 1994. pap. text ed. 40.00 (*0-13-098831-6*) P-H.

Reasoning. Michael Scriven. (C). 1977. text ed. write for info. (*0-07-055882-5*) McGraw.

Reasoning Ability of Children in the Fourth, Fifth, & Sixth School Grades. Frederick G. Bonser. LC 70-176580. (Columbia University. Teachers College. Contributions to Education Ser.: No. 37). reprint ed. 37.50 (*0-404-55037-1*) AMS Pr.

Reasoning about Actions & Plans: Proceedings of the 1986 Workshop. Ed. by Michael Georgeff & Amy Lansky. LC 86-27748. (Illus.). 425p. (Orig.). 1987. pap. 19.95 (*0-934613-30-3*) Morgan Kaufmann.

Reasoning about Change: Time & Causation from the Standpoint of Artificial Intelligence. Yoav Shoham. (Artificial Intelligence Ser.). (Illus.). 216p. 1987. 32.50 (*0-262-19269-1*) MIT Pr.

Reasoning About Knowledge. Ronald Fagin et al. 500p. 1995. 45.00 (*0-262-06162-7*) MIT Pr.

Reasoning about Luck: Probability & Its Uses in Physics. Vinay Ambegaokar. (Illus.). 256p. (C). 1996. text ed. 59.95 (*0-521-44217-6*); pap. text ed. 19.95 (*0-521-44737-2*) Cambridge U Pr.

Reasoning about Mental States Formal Theories & Applications: Papers from the 1993 Spring Symposium. Ed. by John Horty & Yoav Shoham. (Technical Reports). (Illus.). 188p. (Orig.). 1993. spiral bd. 25.00 (*0-929280-43-1*) AAAI Pr.

Reasoning about Plans. James Allen et al. Ed. by Ronald J. Brachman. (Representation & Reasoning Ser.). 500p. 1991. pap. text ed. 49.95 (*1-55860-137-6*) Morgan Kaufmann.

Reasoning & Choice: Explorations in Political Psychology. Paul M. Sniderman et al. (Illus.). 320p. (C). 1991. text ed. 69.95 (*0-521-40255-7*) Cambridge U Pr.

Reasoning & Choice: Explorations in Political Psychology. Paul M. Sniderman et al. (Illus.). 320p. (C). 1993. pap. text ed. 18.95 (*0-521-40770-2*) Cambridge U Pr.

Reasoning & Decision Making. Ed. by P. N. Johnson-Laird & Eldar Shafir. (Cognition Special Issues Ser.). Orig. Title: Cognition. 208p. 1994. reprint ed. pap. text ed. 23.95 (*1-55786-601-5*) Blackwell Pubs.

Reasoning & Decision Making in Hematology. Benjamin Djulbegovic. 253p. 1992. pap. text ed. 47.00 (*0-443-08858-6*) Churchill.

Reasoning & Discourse Processes. Ed. by Terry Myers et al. (Cognitive Science Ser.). 312p. 1986. text ed. 152.00 (*0-12-512320-5*) Acad Pr.

Reasoning & Logic. Richard B. Angell. LC 63-16209. (Century Philosophy Ser.). (Illus.). 1964. 39.50 (*0-89197-375-3*) Irvington.

Reasoning & Methods in Economics: An Introduction to Economic Methodology. Ian M. Stewart. (Modern Revivals in Economic Methodology Ser.). 248p. 1993. 54.95 (*0-7512-0202-9*, Pub. by Gregg Revivals UK) Ashgate Pub Co.

Reasoning & Problem Solving: A Handbook for Elementary School Teachers. Stephen Krulik & Jesse A. Rudnick. LC 92-34069. 352p. 1992. pap. text ed. 29.95 (*0-205-14006-8*, Longwood Div) Allyn.

Reasoning & Revision in Hybrid Representation Systems. Bernhard Nebel. Ed. by Joerg H. Siekmann. (Lecture Notes in Artificial Intelligence Ser.: Vol. 422). xii, 270p. 1990. pap. 32.70 (*0-387-52443-6*) Spr-Verlag.

Reasoning & Rhetoric in Religion. Nancey C. Murphy. LC 94-36455. 304p. (Orig.). (C). 1994. pap. 19.00 (*1-56338-098-6*) TPI PA.

Reasoning & Rhetoric in Religion: Key to the Exercises. Nancey C. Murphy. LC 94-36455. 24p. 1994. pap. 5.00 (*1-56338-099-4*) TPI PA.

Reasoning & the Logic of Things. Charles S. Peirce. 297p. 1993. pap. 22.50 (*0-674-74967-7*) HUP.

Reasoning & the Seasoning of Jewish Cooking: A Project of the University Women of the University of Judaism. Betty Kabaker. Ed. by Miriam D. Landres. LC 94-66029. (Illus.). 260p. 1994. 24.75 (*0-934710-32-5*) J Simon.

Reasoning & Writing: An Introduction to Critical Thinking. Donald L. Hatcher & L. Anne Spencer. LC 93-26452. 320p. (Orig.). (C). 1993. pap. text ed. 26.95 (*0-8476-7881-4*) Rowman.

***Reasoning & Writing Well.** Betty M. Dietsch. LC 97-11087. 1997. write for info. (*1-55934-553-5*) Mayfield Pub.

Reasoning Builder for Standardized Tests. (Illus.). 250p. 1994. pap. text ed. 12.95 (*0-87891-932-5*) Res & Educ.

Reasoning Criminal: Rational Choice Perspectives on Offending. D. B. Cornish & R. V. Clarke. LC 86-1275. (Research in Criminology Ser.). 1986. 95.95 (*0-387-96272-7*) Spr-Verlag.

Reasoning from the Scriptures with the Jehovah's Witnesses. Ron Rhodes. LC 93-3488. 1993. pap. 11.99 (*1-56507-106-9*) Harvest Hse.

Reasoning from the Scriptures with the Mormons. Ron Rhodes & Marian M. Bodine. (Orig.). 1995. pap. 11.99 (*1-56507-328-2*) Harvest Hse.

Reasoning Heart: Toward a North American Theology. Ed. by Frank M. Oppenheim. LC 86-4655. 159p. (Orig.). reprint ed. pap. 45.40 (*0-7837-6336-0*, 2046048) Bks Demand.

***Reasoning in Boolean Networks: Logic Synthesis & Verification Using Testing Techniques.** Wolfgang Kunz & Dominik Stoffel. LC 97-19833. (Frontiers in Electronic Testing Ser.). 1997. text ed. write for info. (*0-7923-9921-8*) Kluwer Ac.

Reasoning in Chemistry. Gail B. Marsella. LC 95-83552. 100p. (Orig.). (C). 1995. pap. text ed. 10.00 (*0-9646155-9-2*) Branch Text Pr.

Reasoning in Medicine: An Introduction to Clinical Inference. Daniel A. Albert et al. LC 87-3243. (Johns Hopkins Series in Contemporary Medicine & Public Health). 280p. reprint ed. pap. 79.80 (*0-7837-4261-4*, 2043953) Bks Demand.

Reasoning into Reality: A System-Cybernetics Model & Therapeutic Interpretation of Buddhist Middle Path Analysis. Peter Fenner. LC 94-9957. 288p. (Orig.). 1995. pap. 18.00 (*0-86171-060-6*) Wisdom MA.

Reasoning, Learning, & Action: Individual & Organizational. Chris Argyris. LC 81-48662. (Management Ser.). 525p. text ed. 42.95 (*0-87589-524-7*) Jossey-Bass.

Reasoning, Necessity & Logic: Developmental Perspectives. Ed. by W. F. Overton. (Jean Piaget Symposia Ser.). 344p. (C). 1990. text ed. 69.95 (*0-8058-0090-5*) L Erlbaum Assocs.

Reasoning Things Out. John Young. 72p. (C). 1982. pap. 2.50 (*0-909615-05-5*) Stella Maris Bks.

Reasoning under Incomplete Information in Articial Intelligence. Group L. Sombe. 472p. 1990. text ed. 69.95 (*0-471-52979-6*) Wiley.

Reasoning Voter. Samuel L. Popkin. 332p. (C). 1994. pap. text ed. 13.95 (*0-226-67545-9*) U Ch Pr.

Reasoning Voter: Communication & Persuasion in Presidential Campaigns. Samuel L. Popkin. LC 91-7610. (Illus.). 302p. 1991. 19.95 (*0-226-67544-0*) U Ch Pr.

Reasoning with a Computer. Daniel Solow. 512p. (C). 1986. teacher ed. write for info. (*0-318-60948-7*); pap. text ed. 34.50 (*0-201-12060-7*); teacher ed. write for info. (*0-201-12061-5*) Addison-Wesley.

Reasoning with a Computer in Pascal. Carolyn K. Cuff. 44p. 1986. teacher ed. write for info. (*0-318-60949-5*) Addison-Wesley.

***Reasoning with Complex Cases.** Friedrich Gebhardt. LC 97-3997. (International Series in Engineering & Computer Science). 1997. lib. bdg. 125.00 (*0-7923-9882-3*) Kluwer Ac.

Reasoning with Democratic Values: Ethical Problems in United States History, 2 vols. Alan L. Lockwood & David E. Harris. (gr. 9-12). 1985. teacher ed., pap. 11.95 (*0-8077-6101-X*) Tchrs Coll.

Reasoning with Democratic Values: Ethical Problems in United States History, 2 vols., Vol. I: 1607-1876. Alan L. Lockwood & David E. Harris. (gr. 9-12). 1985. pap. 9.95 (*0-8077-6094-3*) Tchrs Coll.

Reasoning with Democratic Values: Ethical Problems in United States History, 2 vols., Vol. II: 1877 to Present. Alan L. Lockwood & David E. Harris. (gr. 9-12). 1985. pap. 12.95 (*0-8077-6095-1*) Tchrs Coll.

Reasoning with Diagrammatic Representations: Papers from the 1992 Spring Symposium. Ed. by B. Chandrasekaran & Herbert Simon. (Technical Reports). (Illus.). 240p. 1994. spiral bd. 25.00 (*0-929280-63-6*) AAAI Pr.

Reasoning with Incomplete Information. David W. Etherington. 212p. (Orig.). (C). 1988. pap. text ed. 180.00 (*0-273-08785-1*, Pub. by Pitman Pubng UK) St Mut.

***Reasoning with Logic Programming, Vol. 111.** Jose J. Alferes & Luis M. Pereira. LC 96-27904. (Lecture Notes in Artificial Intelligence). 326p. 1996. pap. 44.50 (*3-540-61488-5*) Spr-Verlag.

***Reasoning with Rules: An Essay on Legal Reasoning & Its Underlying Logic.** Jaap Hage. LC 96-37517. (Law & Philosophy Library). 264p. (C). 1996. lib. bdg. 114.00 (*0-7923-4325-5*) Kluwer Ac.

Reasoning with Statistics. 4th ed. Frederick Williams. 224p. (C). 1992. pap. text ed. 21.50 (*0-03-053158-6*) HB Coll Pubs.

Reasoning with the Charter. Trakman. 288p. 1991. student ed., pap. 25.00 (*0-409-90617-4*); boxed 57.00 (*0-409-80896-2*) MICHIE.

Reasoning with Uncertainty in Robotics: Proceedings of the International Workshop, Rur 95, Amsterdam, the Netherlands, December 1995. L. Dorst et al. LC 96-22126. (Lecture Notes in Computer Science: Lecture Notes in Artificial Intelligence: Vol. 109). 387p. 1996. pap. 62.00 (*3-540-61376-5*) Spr-Verlag.

Reasoning Writer: A Guide to Argument & Critical Thinking. Richard P. Batteiger. LC 93-1714. 1993. pap. text ed. 32.00 (*0-205-14025-4*) Allyn.

***Reasoning...Poetry for the Nineties.** Gwendolyn B. Bobo. 96p. (Orig.). 1997. mass mkt. 5.99 (*1-55197-917-9*, Pub. by Comnwlth Pub CN) Partners Pubs Grp.

Reasons & Methods: Poems by Kirk Robertson, with Constellations, Typoglifs by Karl Kempton. Kirk Robertson. (Illus.). 20p. (Orig.). (C). 1981. pap. 2.50 (*0-916918-15-7*) Duck Down.

Reasons & Persons. Derek Parfit. (Illus.). 543p. 1986. pap. text ed. 28.00 (*0-19-824908-X*) OUP.

Reason's Disciples: Seventeenth-Century English Feminists. Hilda Smith. LC 81-14834. 264p. 1982. text ed. 27.50 (*0-252-00912-6*) U of Ill Pr.

Reasons for a New Edition of Shakespeare's Works. J. Payne Collier. LC 79-113586. reprint ed. 39.50 (*0-404-01616-2*) AMS Pr.

Reasons for Anger. Robert Briffault. LC 68-58774. (Essay Index Reprint Ser.). 1977. 20.95 (*0-8369-1024-9*) Ayer.

***Reasons for Duty.** John H. Gerstner. 238p. 1995. pap. 14.95 (*1-57358-019-8*) Soli Deo Gloria.

Reasons for Hope. rev. ed. W. H. Carroll et al. 254p. (C). 1982. pap. 6.95 (*0-931888-07-7*) Christendom Pr.

Reasons for Hope: Instructive Experiences in Rural Development. Ed. by Anirudh Krishna et al. LC 96-26552. (Books on International Development). (Illus.). viii, 328p. (C). 1996. 40.00 (*1-56549-064-9*); pap. 19.95 (*1-56549-063-0*) Kumarian Pr.

Reasons for Jewish Customs & Traditions. Matts & Sperling. LC 68-31711. 310p. 1989. pap. 10.95 (*0-8197-0184-X*) Bloch.

Reasons for Knocking at an Empty House: Writings 1973-1994. Bill Viola. Ed. by Robert Violette. LC 95-14426. (Illus.). 301p. 1995. pap. 19.95 (*0-262-72025-6*) MIT Pr.

Reasons for Learning: Expanding the Conversation on Student-Teacher Collaboration. Ed. by John Nicholls & Theresa Thorkildsen. 192p. (C). 1995. pap. text ed. 16.95 (*0-8077-3397-0*) Tchrs Coll.

Reasons for Learning: Expanding the Conversation on Student-Teacher Collaboration. Ed. by John Nicholls & Theresa Thorkildsen. 192p. (C). 1995. text ed. 34.00 (*0-8077-3398-9*) Tchrs Coll.

Reasons for Living: A Basic Ethics. Burton F. Porter. 747p. (C). 1988. pap. text ed. 52.67 (*0-02-396050-7*, Macmillan Coll) P-H.

Reasons for Marriage. large type ed. Stephanie Laurens. 350p. 1995. 21.50 (*0-263-14190-X*, Pub. by M & B UK) Ulverscroft.

Reasons for Moving. Mark Strand. LC 68-19151. (C). 1972. 4.95 (*0-689-10262-3*, Atheneum S&S) S&S Trade.

Reasons for Moving, Darker, And the Sargentville Notebook. Mark Strand. 1992. pap. 14.00 (*0-679-73668-9*) Knopf.

Reasons for Pardoning the Haymarket Anarchists. Intro. by Leon M. Despres. LC 86-80035. 80p. reprint ed. pap. 7.00 (*0-88286-124-7*) C H Kerr.

Reasons for Rhyming, Vol. 1. Arthur C. Ford. (Orig.). 1990. pap. 3.80 (*0-9625375-0-0*) Poet Band.

Reasons for Romans. Alexander J. Wedderburn. (Studies of the New Testament & Its World). 184p. 1995. text ed. 37.95 (*0-567-09499-5*, Pub. by T & T Clark UK) Bks Intl VA.

Reasons for Seasons. Gail Gibbons. LC 94-32904. (Illus.). (J). (ps-3). 1995. lib. bdg. 15.95 (*0-8234-1174-5*) Holiday.

Reasons for Seasons. Gail Gibbons. (Illus.). 32p. (J). (ps-3). 1996. pap. 6.95 (*0-8234-1238-5*) Holiday.

Reasons for Seasons: The Great Cosmic Megagalactic Trip Without Moving from Your Chair. Linda Allison. (Brown Paper School Bks). (Illus.). 128p. (J). (gr. 4 up). 1975. pap. 11.95 (*0-316-03440-1*) Little.

Reasons for the Sky. Jim Hanson. LC 79-10984. 15p. (Orig.). 1979. pap. 3.00 (*0-915124-26-2*, Toothpaste) Coffee Hse.

Reasons for Waking. Albert Cook. LC 95-43093. 184p. 1996. pap. 24.95 (*0-7734-2674-4*, Mellen Poetry Pr) E Mellen.

Reasons for Welfare: The Political Theory of the Welfare State. Robert E. Goodin. Ed. by Marshall Cohen. (Studies in Moral, Political, & Legal Philosophy). 392p. 1988. pap. text ed. 24.95 (*0-691-02279-8*) Princeton U Pr.

Reasons for Writing. Joan F. Gilliland & Joan T. Mead. 320p. (C). 1991. pap. text ed. 36.80 (*0-13-971037-X*) P-H.

***Reasons for Writing.** Raign. (C). 1997. teacher ed., pap. text ed. 26.75 (*0-15-508264-7*) HB Coll Pubs.

Reasons in Writing: A Commando's View of the Falklands War. Ewen Southby-Tailyour. (Illus.). 383p. 1993. 44.50 (*0-85052-310-9*, Pub. by L Cooper Bks UK) Trans-Atl Phila.

Reason's Muse: Sexual Difference & the Birth of Democracy. Genevieve Fraisse. Tr. by Jane M. Todd. LC 93-25145. (Women in Culture & Society Ser.). 226p. 1994. lib. bdg. 30.00 (*0-226-25969-2*) U Ch Pr.

Reason's Muse: Sexual Difference & the Birth of Democracy. Genevieve Fraisse. Tr. by Jane M. Todd. 226p. 1994. pap. text ed. 14.95 (*0-226-25970-6*) U Ch Pr.

Reasons of Hate. large type ed. John Welcome. (General Ser.). 352p. 1993. 25.99 (*0-7089-2796-3*) Ulverscroft.

Reasons of State. Alejo Carpentier. Tr. by Frances Partridge from SPA. 320p. 1981. pap. 4.95 (*0-904613-52-6*) Writers & Readers.

Reasons of State. Shashi Tharoor. 438p. 1982. 30.95 (*0-318-36602-9*) Asia Bk Corp.

Reasons of State: Oil Politics & the Capacities of American Government. G. John Ikenberry. LC 88-3660. (Cornell Studies in Political Economy). 232p. 1988. 39.95 (*0-8014-2155-1*); pap. 14.95 (*0-8014-9488-5*) Cornell U Pr.

An Asterisk (*) at the beginning of an entry indicates that the title is appearing in BIP for the first time.

Reasons of the Heart: A Journey into Solitude & Back Again into the Human Circle. John S. Dunne. LC 79-18513. 1979. reprint ed. pap. 11.50 (*0-268-01606-2*) U of Notre Dame Pr.

Reasons of the Heart: Recovering Christian Persuasion. William Edgar. LC 96-19575. 128p. (Orig.). (YA). (gr. 10). 1996. pap. 7.99 (*0-8010-5138-X*, Hour Glass) Baker Bks.

Reasons of the Infinite. Blay. 1994. lib. bdg. 48.00 (*0-226-05834-4*) U Ch Pr.

Reasons of the Infinite. Blay. 1996. pap. text ed. 17.95 (*0-226-05835-2*) U Ch Pr.

Reasons One: Sects & Cults with Non-Christian Roots. rev. ed. Bill Evenhouse. 120p. (Orig.). (J). 1991. 6.75 (*0-930265-97-1*); teacher ed. 6.75 (*1-56212-007-7*) CRC Pubns.

Reasons, Roles & Realities: A Hands-On Seminar in Resource Based Instruction. Ruth Toor & Hilda K. Weisburg. 190p. 1989. 27.95 (*0-931315-04-2*) Lib Learn Res.

Reasons Skeptics Should Consider Christianity. Josh McDowell & Don Stewart. (Living Bks.). 256p. 1986. mass mkt. 4.99 (*0-8423-5287-2*) Tyndale.

Reasons to Be Cheerful. Judith Martin. (Illus.). 80p. (J). (ps-4). 1985. pap. 4.50 (*0-9606662-1-4*) Paper Bag.

***Reasons to Believe Today.** John Martinetti. (Studies in Theology: Vol. 11). 216p. (Orig.). 1996. pap. 25.00 (*0-87462-635-8*) Marquette.

Reasons to Live. Amy Hempel. LC 95-22684. 144p. 1995. pap. 10.00 (*0-06-097672-1*, PL) HarpC.

***Reasons to Roast: More Than 130 Simple & Intensely Flavorful Recipes.** Georgia C. Downard & Evie Righter. Ed. by Rux Martin. LC 97-13760. (Illus.). 304p. (Orig.). 1997. pap. 14.95 (*1-57630-061-7*) Chapters Pub.

Reasons to Say WOW!!! Celebration of Life's Simple Pleasures. Barb Wingfield. 1995. pap. 9.95 (*0-9646060-3-8*) WEB Pubs.

Reasons Two: Sects & Cults with Christian Roots. Bill Evenhouse. 67p. (Orig.). (YA). (gr. 10-12). 1981. teacher ed. 6.75 (*0-933140-26-6*); text ed. 6.75 (*0-933140-25-8*) CRC Pubns.

Reasons Why. Simon Miles. (C). 1989. 24.95 (*1-871058-04-X*, Pub. by Dragonheart Pr UK) St Mut.

Reassembling Assembling. Ed. by Richard Kostelanetz et al. 2000p. lib. bdg. 2,500.00 (*0-915066-26-2*) Assembling Pr.

***Reassessing Anglo-Saxon England.** John. 1997. text ed. 24.95 (*0-7190-5053-7*, Pub. by Manchester Univ Pr UK) St Martin.

Reassessing Arms Control: Studies in Disarmament & Conflicts. Ed. by David Carlton & Carlo Schaerf. LC 84-40339. 232p. 1985. text ed. 27.50 (*0-312-66545-8*) St Martin.

Reassessing Brazil. (Industrial Development Review Ser.: No. L776). 1994. 345.00 (*0-85058-768-9*) Economist Intell.

Reassessing Community Care. Ed. by Nigel A. Malin. (C). 1987. 57.50 (*0-7099-1738-4*, Pub. by Croom Helm UK) Routledge Chapman & Hall.

Reassessing Fatherhood. Ed. by Charles Lewis & Margaret O'Brien. LC 87-60199. 288p. (C). 1987. text ed. 45.00 (*0-8039-8019-1*); pap. text ed. 24.00 (*0-8039-8020-5*) Sage.

Reassessing Foucault: Power Medicine & the Body. Ed. by Colins Jones & Roy Porter. LC 93-30858. (Studies in the Social History of Medicine). 240p. (C). 1994. text ed. 79.95 (*0-415-07542-4*) Routledge.

Reassessing Human Resource Management. Paul Blyton & Peter Turnbull. (Illus.). 272p. (C). 1992. 62.00 (*0-8039-8697-1*); pap. 22.95 (*0-8039-8698-X*) Sage.

Reassessing Language & Literacy. Ed. by Mike Hayhoe & Stephen Parker. LC 92-5708. (English, Language & Education Ser.). 1992. 30.00 (*0-335-15798-X*, Open Univ Pr) Taylor & Francis.

Reassessing Nuclear Power: The Fallout from Chernobyl. Christopher Flavin. LC 87-50070. 92p. (Orig.). 1987. pap. 5.00 (*0-916468-76-3*) Worldwatch Inst.

Reassessing Psychotherapy Research. Ed. by Robert L. Russell. LC 94-8548. 240p. 1994. lib. bdg. 31.50 (*0-89862-755-9*, C2755) Guilford Pubns.

***Reassessing Social Work Practice with Children.** Ed. by John Pardeck & Martha Markward. (Special Aspects of Education Ser.: Vol. 17). 210p. 1997. text ed. 68.00 (*90-5699-546-4*, ECU57) Gordon & Breach.

Reassessing the Role of Government in the Mixed Economy. Herbert Giersch. 296p. 1983. lib. bdg. 67.50 (*3-16-344675-2*, Pub. by J C B Mohr GW) Coronet Bks.

***Reassessing the Sixties.** Stephen Macedo. Date not set. pap. write for info. (*0-393-31700-5*) Norton.

***Reassessing the Sixties.** Stephen Macedo. (C). Date not set. pap. text ed. 15.95 (*0-393-97142-2*) Norton.

Reassessing the Sixties: Debating the Political & Cultural Legacy. Stephen Macedo. LC 96-23185. 320p. 1996. 25.00 (*0-393-03940-4*) Norton.

Reassessment in Psychology: The Interbehavioral Alternative. Ed. by Noel W. Smith et al. LC 83-1234. 550p. (Orig.). (C). 1983. pap. text ed. 36.00 (*0-8191-3082-6*); lib. bdg. 70.50 (*0-8191-3081-8*) U Pr of Amer.

Reassessment of Absolute Skepticism & Religious Faith: Standing Before the Mystery. Jay G. Williams. LC 95-35397. (Toronto Studies in Theology: Vol. 71). 124p. 1996. text ed. 59.95 (*0-7734-8842-1*) E Mellen.

Reassessment of D.H. Lawrence's "Aaron's Rod" Paul G. Baker. Ed. by A. Walton Litz. LC 83-9224. (Studies in Modern Literature: No. 31). 224p. reprint ed. pap. 63.60 (*0-8357-1470-5*, 2070492) Bks Demand.

Reassessment of Inactivated Poliomyelitis Vaccine. Ed. by W. Hennessen & Antonius L. Van Wezel. (Developments in Biological Standardization Ser.: Vol. 47). (Illus.). viii, 364p. 1981. pap. 64.00 (*3-8055-1820-X*) S Karger.

***Reassessment of Metals Criteria for Aquatic Life Protection: Priorities for Research & Implementation.** Society of Environmental Toxicology & Chemistry (SETAC) Staff. Ed. by Harold L. Bergman & Elaine J. Dorward-King. LC 97-3646. (Technical Publications Ser.). 114p. 1997. lib. bdg. 29.95 (*1-880611-04-X*, SETAC Pr) SETAC.

Reassessment of New England Agriculture in the Last Thirty Years of the Nineteenth Century: New Hampshire, a Case History. Paul G. Munyon. LC 77-14783. (Dissertations in American Economic History Ser.). 1978. 33.95 (*0-405-11051-0*) Ayer.

Reassessment of the Marine Salvage Posture of the United States. National Research Council Staff. 144p. (Orig.). (C). 1994. pap. text ed. 33.00 (*0-309-05149-5*) Natl Acad Pr.

Reassessment of Weimar Classicism. Ed. by Gerhart Hoffmeister. LC 95-47582. 224p. 1996. text ed. 89.95 (*0-7734-1348-0*) E Mellen.

Reassessments of First Wave Feminism. Ed. by E. Sarah. 187p. 1983. 19.75 (*0-08-030200-9*, Pergamon Pr) Elsevier.

Reauthorizing Joyce. Vicki Mahaffey. 280p. 1988. text ed. 54.95 (*0-521-35250-9*) Cambridge U Pr.

Reauthorizing Joyce. Vicki Mahaffey. LC 94-34181. (Florida James Joyce Ser.). 248p. (C). 1995. pap. text ed. 19.95 (*0-8130-1344-5*) U Press Fla.

Reaver Road. Dave Duncan. (Orig.). 1992. mass mkt. 4.99 (*0-345-37481-9*, Del Rey) Ballantine.

Reavivamento Como to Experimenta. Charles G. Finney. Orig. Title: How to Experience Revival. 144p. (POR.). 1987. pap. 3.95 (*0-8297-1601-7*) Life Pubs Intl.

Reawakening. Primo Levi. 1995. pap. 11.00 (*0-684-82635-6*) S&S Trade.

Reawakening of Christian Faith. Bernard E. Meland. LC 72-142670. (Essay Index Reprint Ser.). 1977. reprint ed. 18.95 (*0-8369-2663-3*) Ayer.

Reawakening the Spirit in Work: The Power of Dharmic Management. Jack Hawley. LC 93-19995. 224p. 1993. 24.95 (*1-881052-22-2*) Berrett-Koehler.

Reawakenings. Thomas Keating. 128p. 1991. 10.95 (*0-8245-1149-2*) Crossroad NY.

Reb Aharon's Treasure. Hanna Bandes. (Illus.). 104p. (J). (gr. 2-5). 1993. 8.95 (*1-56871-034-8*) Targum Pr.

Reb Aryeh: A Portrait of the Jerusalem Tzaddik Reb Aryeh Levin. Tzira Karlenstein. (Illus.). (J). (gr. 4-7). 1989. 11.95 (*0-87306-490-9*) Feldheim.

Reb Chaim Ozer: The Life & Ideals of Rabbi Chaim Ozer Grodzenski of Vilna. Shimon Finkelman. (ArtScroll History Ser.). (Illus.). 272p. 1987. 20.99 (*0-89906-486-8*); pap. 17.99 (*0-89906-487-6*) Mesorah Pubns.

Reb Chaim Volozhin: Biography. D. Eliach. 1993. 18.99 (*0-89906-100-1*); 15.99 (*0-89906-101-X*) Mesorah Pubns.

Reb Chaim's Discourses: The Shmuessen of Rabbi Chaim Shmulevitz. Chaim Shmulevitz. Ed. by Samsom R. Weiss. Tr. by E. M. Klugman & A. Scheinman from HEB. (ArtScroll Judaica Classics Ser.). 276p. 1989. 20.99 (*0-89906-943-6*); pap. 17.99 (*0-89906-944-4*) Mesorah Pubns.

Reb Elchonon: The Life & Ideals of Rabbi Elchonon Bunim Wasserman of Baranovich. Simcha Wasserman. (ArtScroll History Ser.). (Illus.). 416p. 1982. 20.99 (*0-89906-450-7*); pap. 17.99 (*0-89906-451-5*) Mesorah Pubns.

***Reb Mendel & His Wisdom: The Enduring Lessons of the Legendary Rosh Yeshivah.** Yisroel Greenwald. 18.99 (*0-89906-117-6*, RMEH); pap. 15.99 (*0-89906-118-4*, RMEP) Mesorah Pubns.

***Reb Michel's Shmuessen: The Inspiring Ethical Lectures of a Patriarch of Mussar, the Mashgiach of Mesivtha Tifereth Jerusalem.** Michel Barenbaum. 18.99 (*0-89906-638-0*, RMWH); pap. 15.99 (*0-89906-639-9*, RMWP) Mesorah Pubns.

Reb Moshe: The Life & Ideals of Rabbi Moshe Feinstein. Shimon Finkelman & Nosson Scherman. (ArtScroll History Ser.). (Illus.). 270p. 1986. 20.99 (*0-89906-480-9*); pap. 17.99 (*0-89906-481-7*) Mesorah Pubns.

***Reb Simcha Speaks: Rabbi Simcha Wasserman's Insights & Teachings on Vital Principles of Life & Faith.** Akiva Tatz & Yaakov Branfman. 17.99 (*0-89906-115-X*, RSSH); pap. 14.99 (*0-89906-116-8*, RSSP) Mesorah Pubns.

Reb Yaakov. J. Rosenblum. 1993. 20.99 (*0-89906-413-2*); pap. 17.99 (*0-89906-415-9*) Mesorah Pubns.

Reb Yitzchak's Jewel: Rashi's Father Gets a Reward. Nosson Scherman. (Artscroll Junior Classic Ser.). (Illus.). 32p. (J). (gr. k-6). 1988. 7.99 (*0-89906-525-2*) Mesorah Pubns.

Reba: Country Music's Queen. Don Cusic. (Illus.). 256p. (Orig.). 1991. pap. 10.95 (*0-312-06450-0*) St Martin.

Reba: For My Broken Heart, No. 135. 48p. 1993. pap. 6.95 (*0-7935-2486-5*, 00102285) H Leonard.

Reba: My Story. Reba McEntire & Tom Carter. LC 94-1466. 336p. 1994. 22.95 (*0-553-09607-9*) Bantam.

Reba: My Story. Reba McEntire & Tom Carter. 352p. 1995. mass mkt. 5.99 (*0-553-57238-5*) Bantam.

Reba Vol. 1: Country Music's Queen. Don Cusic. 1994. mass mkt. 4.99 (*0-312-95342-9*) St Martin.

Reba - for My Broken Heart. (Piano-Vocal-Guitar Personality Folio Ser.). 56p. (Orig.). 1992. pap. 14.95 (*0-7935-1295-6*, 00308129) H Leonard.

Reba McEntire: Read My Mind. 64p. 1994. otabind 14.95 (*0-7935-3643-X*, 00308249) H Leonard.

Rebalancing the Public & Private Sectors: Developing Country Experience. Organization for Economic Cooperation & Development Staff. 270p. (Orig.). 1991. pap. 32.00 (*92-64-13440-9*) OECD.

***Rebbe: The Biography of Rabbi Esriel Hildesheimer.** Jacob H. Sinason. LC 96-38519. 1996. 16.95 (*0-87306-772-X*) Feldheim.

Rebbe Talks to Children, Vol. 1. Menachem M. Schneerson. 329p. (YID.). (J). (gr. 4-10). 1995. 16.95 (*0-922613-96-6*) Hachai Pubns.

Rebbe Talks to Children, Vol. 2. Menachem M. Schneerson. 329p. (YID.). (J). (gr. 4-10). 1996. 16.95 (*0-922613-97-4*) Hachai Pubns.

Rebbes of Ger: Sfas emes & Imrei Emes. A. Y. Bromberg. Tr. by Uri Kaploun from HEB. (ArtScroll History Ser.). (Illus.). 302p. 1987. 20.99 (*0-89906-484-1*); pap. 17.99 (*0-89906-485-X*) Mesorah Pubns.

Rebbe's Treasure. Beth Jacob Hebrew Teachers College Staff. write for info. (*0-934390-01-0*); pap. write for info. (*0-934390-02-9*) B J Hebrew Tchrs.

***Rebbetzin Grunfeld.** Miriam Dansky. 20.99 (*0-89906-119-2*, GRUH); pap. 17.99 (*0-89906-120-6*, GOIP) Mesorah Pubns.

Rebeca Tells of a Miracle of Life: A Special Belief in the Healing Power of Love. Geraldine M. Bennett. Ed. by Tracy Rider & Audrey Shell. (Katrina Tells Ser.: Bk. 3). (Illus.). 42p. (Orig.). (J). (gr. 3-8). 1995. pap. 2.79 (*1-882786-12-2*) New Dawn NY.

Rebecca. (Fiction Ser.). (YA). 1993. pap. text ed. 6.50 (*0-582-08486-5*, 79825) Longman.

Rebecca. Mary C. Borntrager. LC 89-32328. (Ellie's People Ser.: Vol. 2). 176p. (Orig.). 1989. pap. 7.99 (*0-8361-3500-8*) Herald Pr.

Rebecca. Daphne Du Maurier. 384p. 1948. 25.00 (*0-385-04380-5*) Doubleday.

Rebecca. Daphne Du Maurier. 384p. 1994. mass mkt. 6.99 (*0-380-77855-6*) Avon.

Rebecca. Daphne Du Maurier. 1946. pap. 5.25 (*0-8222-0933-0*) Dramatists Play.

Rebecca. Daphne Du Maurier. 1997. pap. 23.95 (*0-14-086391-5*) Viking Penguin.

Rebecca. Dumaurier. 1993. pap. 24.95 (*1-55927-261-9*) St Martin.

Rebecca. large type ed. Mary C. Borntrager. (Ellie's People Ser.: Bk. 2). 176p. (Orig.). 1993. pap. 8.99 (*0-8361-3637-3*) Herald Pr.

Rebecca. Daphne Du Maurier. 384p. 1988. reprint ed. mass mkt. 5.99 (*0-380-00917-X*) Avon.

Rebecca: A Father's Journey from Grief to Gratitude. Robert A. Jonas. 168p. 1996. 16.95 (*0-8245-1552-8*) Crossroad NY.

Rebecca: A Novel for Children. Ronald F. Reed. 37p. (Orig.). (J). (ps-4). 1990. pap. 8.00 (*0-924303-00-X*) TX Wesleyan Coll.

Rebecca & Daniel Boone. Ione M. Thompson. (Illus.). 118p. (Orig.). 1993. pap. text ed. 10.95 (*0-9643687-0-6*) Cloud Nine.

***Rebecca Collection, Vols. 1-3.** Eric Wiggin & Kate D. Wiggin. (Illus.). 1996. boxed 20.99 (*0-934998-67-1*) Bethel Pub.

Rebecca Davis - Roger Asay: Touching Earth. Rebecca Davis & Roger Asay. Ed. by Joanne Stuhr. (Illus.). 31p. 1995. pap. 10.00 (*0-911611-03-7*) Tucson Mus Art.

Rebecca Finds a New Way: How Kids Learn, Play, & Live with Spinal Cord Injuries & Illnesses. Connie Panzarino & Marilyn Lash. (Illus.). 56p. (Orig.). 1995. pap. text ed. 20.00 (*0-7881-2360-2*) DIANE Pub.

Rebecca Goes Out. Selena Richards. (Grandmother Days Ser.). (Illus.). 18p. (J). (ps). 1992. 3.50 (*1-56288-269-4*) Checkerboard.

Rebecca Goes to the Country. Selena Richards. (Grandmother Days Ser.). (Illus.). 18p. (J). (ps). 1992. 3.50 (*1-56288-270-8*) Checkerboard.

Rebecca Goes to the Park. Selena Richards. (Grandmother Days Ser.). (Illus.). 18p. (J). (ps). 1992. 3.50 (*1-56288-271-6*) Checkerboard.

***Rebecca Gratz: Women's Judaism in Antebellum America.** Dianne Ashton. LC 97-24407. (Illus.). 384p. 1997. text ed. 39.95 (*0-8143-2666-8*) Wayne St U Pr.

Rebecca Harding Davis. Jane A. Rose. (Twayne's United States Authors Ser.). 216p. 1993. 22.95 (*0-8057-3958-0*, Twayne) Scribnrs Ref.

***Rebecca Harding Davis: Great American Short Stories III.** Illus. by James Balkovek. LC 95-76747. (Classic Short Stories Ser.). 80p. (YA). (gr. 6-12). 1995. pap. 5.95 (*0-7854-0597-6*, 40083) Am Guidance.

Rebecca Harding Davis & American Realism. Sharon M. Harris. LC 91-7806. 360p. (C). 1991. text ed. 45.00 (*0-8122-3080-9*); pap. text ed. 18.95 (*0-8122-1335-1*) U of Pa Pr.

Rebecca Harding Davis Reader: "Life in the Iron-Mills," Selected Fiction, & Essays. Ed. & Intro. by Jean Pfaelzer. LC 95-3296. 640p. 1995. 35.00 (*0-8229-3887-1*) U of Pittsburgh Pr.

Rebecca Harding Davis Reader: "Life in the Iron Mills," Selected Fiction, & Essays. Ed. by Jean Pfaelzer. 640p. (C). 1995. pap. 24.95 (*0-8229-5569-5*) U of Pittsburgh Pr.

Rebecca Horn. 1994. 65.00 (*0-8109-6870-3*) Abrams.

Rebecca Horn. Germano Celant. 1993. 59.95 (*0-89207-110-9*) S R Guggenheim.

***Rebecca Letters.** Laynie Browne. LC 97-9462. 1997. pap. 10.00 (*0-614-29414-2*) Kelsey St Pr.

***Rebecca Letters.** Laynie Browne. Ed. by Patricia Dienstfrey. LC 97-9462. 80p. 1997. per. 10.00 (*0-932716-43-1*) Kelsey St Pr.

Rebecca Mary. Annie H. Donnell. LC 72-4455. (Short Story Index Reprint Ser.). (Illus.). 1977. reprint ed. 23.95 (*0-8369-4173-X*) Ayer.

Rebecca of Blossom Prairie: Grandmother of a Vice President. Maurine W. Liles. Ed. by M. Roberts. (Illus.). 112p. (J). 1990. 14.95 (*0-89015-754-5*) Sunbelt Media.

Rebecca of Grand Hotel. Robin Agnew. (Illus.). 72p. (J). 1990. text ed. 15.95 (*0-9627301-0-6*) Grand Hotel.

Rebecca of Sunnybrook Farm. Kate Douglas-Wiggins. Ed. by Don Hinkle. LC 87-15475. (Illus.). 48p. (J). (gr. 3-6). 1988. pap. 5.95 (*0-8167-1218-2*); lib. bdg. 14.95 (*0-8167-1217-4*) Troll Communs.

***Rebecca of Sunnybrook Farm.** L. M. Montgomery. Ed. by Joshua Hanft. (Great Illustrated Classics Ser.: Vol. 48). (Illus.). 240p. (J). (gr. 3-6). 1995. 9.95 (*0-86611-999-X*) Playmore Inc.

Rebecca of Sunnybrook Farm. Kate D. Wiggan. (Deluxe Watermill Classic Ser.). 320p. (YA). 1992. 10.89 (*0-8167-2556-X*) Troll Communs.

Rebecca of Sunnybrook Farm. Eric Wiggin & Kate D. Wiggin. (Rebecca Ser.: No. 1). 254p. pap. 6.99 (*0-934998-51-5*) Bethel Pub.

Rebecca of Sunnybrook Farm. Kate D. Wiggin. (Airmont Classics Ser.). (J). (gr. 5 up). 1967. mass mkt. 1.50 (*0-8049-0144-9*, CL-144) Airmont.

Rebecca of Sunnybrook Farm. Kate D. Wiggin. (J). 23.95 (*0-8488-0854-1*) Amereon Ltd.

Rebecca of Sunnybrook Farm. Kate D. Wiggin. 256p. (J). (gr. k-6). 1986. pap. 3.99 (*0-440-47533-3*) Dell.

Rebecca of Sunnybrook Farm. Kate D. Wiggin. LC 94-9899. (Books of Wonder Ser.). (Illus.). 384p. (J). 1994. 20.00 (*0-688-13481-5*, Morrow Junior) Morrow.

Rebecca of Sunnybrook Farm. Kate D. Wiggin. 288p. (J). (gr. 5-8). 1993. pap. 2.99 (*0-87406-655-7*) Willowisp Pr.

Rebecca of Sunnybrook Farm. Kate D. Wiggin. (Puffin Classics Ser.). 288p. (YA). (gr. 5 up). 1995. pap. 3.99 (*0-14-036759-4*) Puffin Bks.

***Rebecca of Sunnybrook Farm.** unabridged ed. Kate D. Wiggin. 175p. 1997. reprint ed. pap. 14.95 (*1-57002-021-3*) Univ Publng Hse.

Rebecca of Sunnybrook Farm. Kate D. Wiggin. 239p. (J). 1981. reprint ed. lib. bdg. 25.95 (*0-89966-354-0*) Buccaneer Bks.

Rebecca of Sunnybrook Farm. Kate D. Wiggin. 259p. (J). 1981. reprint ed. lib. bdg. 21.95 (*0-89967-028-8*) Harmony Raine.

Rebecca of the Brick House. Eric Wiggin & Kate D. Wiggin. (Rebecca Ser.: No. 2). 250p. pap. 6.99 (*0-934998-52-3*) Bethel Pub.

Rebecca Purdum: Paintings. Dana Friis-Hansen. LC 89-64405. (Illus.). 34p. 1990. pap. 7.50 (*0-938437-29-1*) MIT List Visual Arts.

Rebecca Returns to Sunnybrook. Eric Wiggin. (Rebecca Ser.: No. 3). 239p. pap. 6.99 (*0-934998-53-1*) Bethel Pub.

***Rebecca Sitton's Spelling Sourcebook Reviews for High-Use Writing Words 1-400.** Rebecca Sitton. (Spelling Sourcebook Reviews Ser.). 168p. 1996. teacher ed., spiral bd. 38.50 (*1-886050-09-0*) Egger Pub Inc.

Rebecca Tells of a Miracle of Life: A Special Belief in the Healing Power of Love. Geraldine M. Bennett. Ed. by Tracy Rider & Audrey Sheil. LC 92-83744. (Katrina Tells Ser.: Bk. 3). (Illus.). 42p. (Orig.). (J). (gr. 3-8). 1994. pap. 7.98 (*0-9630718-4-X*) New Dawn NY.

Rebecca West: An Annotated Bibliography. Joan G. Packer. LC 91-11183. 164p. 1991. text ed. 25.00 (*0-8240-5692-2*, H1158) Garland.

Rebecca West A Saga of the Century. Carl Rollyson. LC 96-24231. 544p. 1996. 35.00 (*0-684-19430-9*) S&S Trade.

Rebecca West Revisited. Cowan. Date not set. 22.95 (*0-8057-4606-4*, Twayne) Scribnrs Ref.

***Rebeccah's Crossing.** Nina L. Schildknecht. LC 96-70018. 256p. 1996. pap. 14.95 (*1-57636-021-0*) SunRise Pbl.

Rebecca's Children: A Study of Rural Society, Crime, & Protest. David J. Jones. (Illus.). 440p. 1990. 85.00 (*0-19-820099-4*) OUP.

Rebecca's Children: Judaism & Christianity in the Roman World. Alan F. Segal. LC 85-17656. 219p. 1986. 27.50 (*0-674-75075-6*) HUP.

Rebecca's Children: Judaism & Christianity in the Roman World. Alan F. Segal. 219p. 1989. reprint ed. pap. 14.95 (*0-674-75076-4*) HUP.

Rebecca's Daughters. Dylan Thomas. LC 82-7986. (Illus.). 160p. 1983. 8.50 (*0-8112-0852-4*); pap. 5.95 (*0-8112-0884-2*, NDP564) New Directions.

Rebecca's Nap. Smithmark Staff. 3.98 (*0-8317-5474-5*) Smithmark.

Rebecca's Rainy Day. Selena Richards. (Grandmother Days Ser.). (Illus.). 18p. (J). (ps). 1992. 3.50 (*1-56288-272-4*) Checkerboard.

Rebekah: The Mother of Twins. C. Mackenzie. (BibleTime Bks.). (J). 1995. 2.99 (*0-906731-45-3*, Pub. by Christian Focus UK) Spring Arbor Dist.

Rebel. 144p. 1991. per. 18.00 (*0-87431-178-0*, 40054) West End Games.

Rebel. 4.98 (*0-8317-2997-X*) Smithmark.

Rebel. Bediako Asare. (African Writers Ser.). 156p. (C). 1969. pap. 8.95 (*0-435-90059-5*, 90059) Heinemann.

Rebel. Bernard Cornwell. LC 92-53344. 512p. 1994. mass mkt. 5.99 (*0-06-109187-1*, Harp PBks) HarpC.

Rebel. Leonor V. De Magnon. Ed. by Clara Lomas. 250p. 1994. pap. 12.00 (*1-55885-056-2*) Arte Publico.

Rebel. Heather Graham. 1997. pap. 6.99 (*0-451-40689-3*, Topaz) NAL-Dutton.

Rebel. Grace Johnson. LC 95-44519. (Illus.). 1996. pap. 10.99 (*0-8423-5301-1*) Tyndale.

Rebel. Pepe Moreno. (Illus.). 72p. (Orig.). 1986. pap. 10.95 (*0-87416-020-0*) Catalan Communs.

Rebel. Osho. Ed. by Mahasattva Swami Geet Govind. (Questions & Answers Ser.). 358p. 1989. 21.95 (*3-89338-021-3*, Pub. by Rebel Hse GW) Osho America.

An Asterisk (*) at the beginning of an entry indicates that the title is appearing in BIP for the first time.

R

Rebel. Nancy N. Rue. LC 96-8549. (Christian Heritage Ser.: Bk. 7). (J). 1996. pap. 5.99 (*1-56179-478-3*) Focus Family.

Rebel. John Schoenherr. LC 94-15568. (Illus.). 32p. (J). (ps-2). 1995. 15.95 (*0-399-22727-X*, Philomel Bks) Putnam Pub Group.

Rebel. Donald Spoto. 1996. 25.00 (*0-614-95701-X*) HarpC.

***Rebel.** Donald Spoto. 336p. 1997. mass mkt. 6.99 (*0-06-109400-5*, Harp PBks) HarpC.

Rebel. large type ed. Bernard Cornwell. LC 93-16473. (Starbuck Chronicles Ser.: Vol. 1). 1993. lib. bdg. 22.95 (*1-56054-693-X*) Thorndike Pr.

Rebel. large type ed. Bernard Cornwell. LC 93-16473. (Starbuck Chronicles Ser.: Vol. 1). 1994. lib. bdg. 14.95 (*1-56054-879-7*) Thorndike Pr.

***Rebel.** large type ed. Heather Graham. LC 97-15910. 1997. 23.95 (*1-56895-464-6*) Wheeler Pub.

Rebel: A Biography of Agnes Smedley. Ruth Price. 400p. 1994. text ed. 24.95 (*0-02-925452-3*, Free Press) Free Pr.

Rebel: An Essay on Man in Revolt. Albert Camus. LC 91-50022. (Vintage International Ser.). 320p. 1991. pap. 12.00 (*0-679-73384-1*, Vin) Random.

Rebel: The Life & Legend of James Dean. Donald Spoto. LC 96-1048. 384p. 1996. 25.00 (*0-06-017656-3*) HarpC.

Rebel: The Life & Times of John Singleton Mosby. Kevin H. Siepel. 384p. 1988. pap. 9.95 (*0-312-01507-0*, Thomas Dunne Bks) St Martin.

***Rebel: The Life & Times of John Singleton Mosby.** Kevin H. Siepel. LC 96-45721. (Illus.). 384p. 1997. reprint ed. pap. 15.95 (*0-306-80775-0*) Da Capo.

Rebel Against Injustice: The Life of Frank P. O'Hare. Peter H. Buckingham. Ed. by William E. Foley. (Missouri Biography Ser.). (Illus.). 296p. (C). 1995. 39.95 (*0-8262-1055-4*) U of Mo Pr.

Rebel Alliance: Ships of the Fleet. Bill Smith. (Illus.). 10p. (J). (ps up). 1996. 15.95 (*0-316-53509-5*) Little.

Rebel America. Lillian Symes. LC 76-172100. (Civil Liberties in American History Ser.). 408p. 1972. reprint ed. lib. bdg. 47.50 (*0-306-70226-6*) Da Capo.

Rebel & Saint: Muslim Notables, Populist Protest, & Colonial Encounters - Algeria & Tunisia, 1800-1904. Julia A. Clancy-Smith. LC 93-17223. (Comparative Studies on Muslim Societies: Vol. 18). 1994. 45.00 (*0-520-08242-7*) U CA Pr.

***Rebel & Saint: Muslim Notables, Populist Protest, Colonial Encounters.** Julia A. Clancy-Smith. 370p. 1996. 45.00 (*0-614-21169-7*, 1062) Kazi Pubns.

***Rebel & Saint: Muslim Notables, Populist Protest, Colonial Encounters (Algeria & Tunisia)** Julia A. Clancy-Smith. 1997. pap. text ed. 16.95 (*0-520-21216-9*) U CA Pr.

Rebel & the Hero. Helen R. Myers. (Desire Ser.). 1995. mass mkt. 3.25 (*0-373-05941-8*, 1-05941-9) Silhouette.

***Rebel & the Lily.** Christine Dorsey. 256p. 1997. mass mkt. 5.50 (*0-8217-5704-0*, Zebra Kensgtn) Kensgtn Pub Corp.

***Rebel & the Redcoat.** large type ed. Jan Constant. LC 97-288. (Nightingale Ser.). 250p. 1997. pap. 17.95 (*0-7838-8109-6*, GK Hall) Thorndike Pr.

Rebel & the Rose. Joan Wolf. 1986. pap. 3.95 (*0-451-14537-2*, Sig) NAL-Dutton.

Rebel Angel: or The Confessions of an Angry Nigger! Kevin D. Hicks. 111p. (Orig.). 1992. pap. 9.95 (*0-9635742-0-5*) Kadmus & Jewels.

Rebel Angels. Robertson Davies. 336p. 1983. pap. 11.95 (*0-14-006271-8*, Penguin Bks) Viking Penguin.

Rebel Angels. Laura Young. 176p. (Orig.). (J). 1996. mass mkt. 4.50 (*0-06-106437-8*, Harp PBks) HarpC.

Rebel Angels: 25 Poets of the New Formalism. Ed. by Mark Jarman & David Mason. LC 96-31967. 288p. 1996. 25.00 (*1-885266-33-2*); pap. 12.00 (*1-885266-30-8*) Story Line.

Rebel Armies Deep into Chad. Mark Lee. 1989. pap. 5.25 (*0-8222-0934-9*) Dramatists Play.

***Rebel Assault II: Official Strategy Guide.** 1996. pap. 19.99 (*0-7615-9995-9*) Prima Pub.

Rebel Assault Official Insiders Guide. Joe Hutsko. 1994. pap. 19.95 (*1-55958-789-X*) Prima Pub.

***Rebel at Heart.** Gina Wilkins. 1998. mass mkt. 4.50 (*0-373-81025-3*, 1-81025-8) Harlequin Bks.

Rebel at Heart. Gina F. Wilkins. (Temptation Ser.: No. 337). 1991. pap. 2.95 (*0-373-25437-7*) Harlequin Bks.

Rebel at Large: American Autobiography. George Creel. 384p. 1995. lib. bdg. 89.00 (*0-7812-8492-9*) Rprt Serv.

Rebel at Large: Recollections of Fifty Crowded Years. George Creel. (History - United States Ser.). 384p. 1993. reprint ed. lib. bdg. 89.00 (*0-7812-4921-X*) Rprt Serv.

Rebel at Law. P. L. Lakhanpal. (C). 1987. 125.00 (*0-685-36505-0*) St Mut.

Rebel Baseball: The Summer the Game Was Returned to the Fans. Steve Perlstein. LC 94-8634. (Illus.). 256p. 1994. 22.00 (*0-9640334-9-6*) Onion Pr.

***Rebel Bishop: Augustin Verot, Florida's Civil War Prelate.** Michael Gannon. LC 96-37488. (Florida Sand Dollar Bk.). (Illus.). 277p. 1997. reprint ed. pap. 19.95 (*0-8130-1522-7*) U Press Fla.

Rebel Boast: First at Bethel - Last at Appomattox. Manly W. Wellman. Ed. by Ralph Roberts. LC 96-17998. (Illus.). 320p. 1997. reprint ed. pap. 16.95 (*1-888295-01-5*) Elephant Books.

Rebel Brass: The Confederate Command System. Frank E. Vandiver. LC 56-9169. (Illus.). 143p. (C). 1993. pap. 9.95 (*0-8071-1862-1*) La State U Pr.

Rebel Bride. Catherine Coulter. 1979. pap. 2.50 (*0-451-13837-6*, AE1719, Sig) NAL-Dutton.

Rebel Bride. Catherine Coulter. 384p. 1994. 6.99 (*0-451-40432-7*, Topaz) NAL-Dutton.

***Rebel Bride.** Catherine Coulter. LC 96-35470. 1997. 27.95 (*0-7838-2002-X*) G K Hall.

***Rebel Bride.** large type ed. Catherine Coulter. LC 96-43098. (Star-Romance Ser.). 405p. 1997. 23.95 (*0-7862-0915-1*, Five Star) Mac Lib Ref.

Rebel Brothers: The Civil War Letters of the Truehearts. Charles W. Trueheart & Henry M. Trueheart. Ed. by Edward B. Williams. LC 95-13098. (Texas A&M University Military History Ser.: No. 44). (Illus.). 288p. (C). 1995. 35.00 (*0-89096-656-7*) Tex A&M Univ Pr.

Rebel Bureaucrat: Frederick John Shore 1799-1837 as Critic of William Bentinck's India. Peter Penner & Richard MacLean. 1982. 24.00 (*0-8364-0920-5*, Pub. by Chanakya II) S Asia.

Rebel Came Home: The Diary & Letters of Floride Clemson, 1863-1866. rev. ed. Ernest M. Lander, Jr. & Charles M. McGee, Jr. Ed. by Carol Bleser & Elizabeth Fox-Genovese. (Women's Diaries & Letters of the Nineteenth-Century South Ser.). 205p. 1989. reprint ed. text ed. 29.95 (*0-87249-642-2*) U of SC Pr.

Rebel Dad: (Fabulous Fathers) Kristin Morgan. (Romance Ser.). 1994. pap. 2.75 (*0-373-08982-1*, 5-08985-6) Silhouette.

Rebel Daughters: Women & the French Revolution. Ed. by Sara E. Melzer & Leslie W. Rabine. (University of California Humanities Research Institute Ser.). (Illus.). 288p. 1992. pap. 18.95 (*0-19-507016-X*) OUP.

Rebel Destiny: Among the Bush Negroes of Dutch Guiana. Melville J. Herskovits & Frances S. Herskovits. LC 72-154077. (Black Heritage Library Collection). 1977. 34.95 (*0-8369-8788-8*) Ayer.

Rebel for Rights: Abigail Scott Duniway. Ruth B. Moynihan. LC 83-1142. (Yale Historical Publications: No. 130). (Illus.). 320p. 1985. pap. 17.00 (*0-300-03478-4*) Yale U Pr.

***Rebel for the Hell of It: Tupac Shakur's Art Life.** Armond White. LC 96-53671. 1997. pap. text ed. 12.95 (*1-56025-122-0*) Thunders Mouth.

***Rebel Georgia.** F. N. Boney. LC 97-431. 112p. (Orig.). 1997. 24.95 (*0-86554-545-6*); pap. 15.95 (*0-86554-551-0*) Mercer Univ Pr.

Rebel Girl: An Autobiography - My First Life. Elizabeth G. Flynn. LC 72-94154. (Illus.). 368p. 1994. reprint ed. pap. 9.95 (*0-7178-0368-6*) Intl Pubs Co.

Rebel Glory. Sigmund Brouwer. (Lightning on Ice Ser.: Vol. 1). 128p. (J). (gr. 5-9). 1995. pap. 5.99 (*0-8499-3637-3*) Word Pub.

***Rebel Heart.** Padraic O'Farrell. Orig. Title: Break the Green Bough. 317p. 1996. pap. 11.95 (*0-86322-221-8*, Pub. by Brandon Bk Pubs IE) Irish Bks Media.

***Rebel Hearts.** Toolis. 1997. pap. 14.95 (*0-312-15632-4*) St Martin.

Rebel Hearts. Kevin Toolis. 384p. 1996. 25.95 (*0-312-14478-4*) St Martin.

Rebel Heat. Judith Steel. 352p. 1996. mass mkt. 4.99 (*0-8217-5195-6*, Zebra Kensgtn) Kensgtn Pub Corp.

Rebel Heiress. Jane A. Hodge. 288p. 1981. pap. 2.25 (*0-449-22960-2*, Crest) Fawcett.

Rebel in Cuba: An American's Memoir. Neill Macaulay. 199p. 1991. 19.95 (*1-879915-00-6*); pap. 11.95 (*1-879915-01-4*) Affil Writers America.

Rebel in Disguise. Lucy Gordon. (Romance Ser.). 1996. mass mkt. 3.25 (*0-373-03425-3*, 1-03425-5) Harlequin Bks.

***Rebel in Disguise.** Lucy Gordon. (Mills & Boon Large Print Ser.). 288p. 1997. 22.50 (*0-263-14968-4*) Ulverscroft.

***Rebel in the Soul: An Ancient Egyptian Dialogue Between a Man & His Destiny.** Bika Reed. LC 97-4969. (Illus.). 144p. 1997. pap. 16.95 (*0-89281-615-5*) Inner Tradit.

Rebel Invasion of Missouri & Kansas & the Campaign of the Army of the Border Against General Sterling Price in October & November 1864. Richard J. Hinton. (Illus.). 362p. (C). 1995. text ed. 40.00 (*1-878882-05-8*) KS Heritage Pr.

Rebel Lands: An Investigation into the Origins of Early Mesopotamian Mythology. J. V. Kinnier-Wilson & Herman L. Vanstiphout. LC 77-1272. (Oriental Publications: No. 29). (Illus.). 1979. 54.95 (*0-521-21469-6*) Cambridge U Pr.

Rebel Lions. Michael McClure. LC 90-48705. 128p. (Orig.). 1991. pap. 10.95 (*0-8112-1164-9*, NDP712) New Directions.

Rebel Love. Jackie Merritt. 1995. mass mkt. 3.25 (*0-373-05965-5*, 1-05965-8) Silhouette.

Rebel Males: Clift, Brando, & Dean. Graham McCann. LC 92-33768. (Illus.). 235p. (C). 1993. pap. 14.95 (*0-8135-1953-5*); text ed. 38.00 (*0-8135-1952-7*) Rutgers U Pr.

Rebel Moon. Beal & Bruce Bethke. 1996. mass mkt. 5.99 (*0-671-00236-8*) PB.

***Rebel Moon: Anarchist Rants & Poems.** Norman Nawrocki. (Illus.). 112p. 1996. pap. 9.95 (*1-873176-08-2*, AK Pr San Fran) AK Pr Dist.

***Rebel Moon Rising: The Official Strategy Guide.** Kip Ward. 240p. 1997. per. 19.99 (*0-7615-1085-0*) Prima Pub.

***Rebel on the Right: Henry Page Croft & the Crisis of British Conservatism, 1903-1914.** Larry L. Witherell. LC 97-13256. 1997. write for info. (*0-87413-622-9*) U Delaware Pr.

Rebel Passion. Betina M. Krahn. 464p. 1996. mass mkt. 5.99 (*0-8217-5526-9*, Zebra Kensgtn) Kensgtn Pub Corp.

Rebel Pen: The Writings of Mary Heaton Vorse. Ed. by Dee Garrison. (New Feminist Library). 320p. 1985. 26.50 (*0-85345-669-0*); pap. 16.00 (*0-85345-670-4*) Monthly Rev.

Rebel, Priest & Prophet: A Biography of Dr. Edward McGlynn. Stephen Bell. 303p. 1968. 5.00 (*0-911312-28-5*) Schalkenbach.

Rebel Private. W. A. Fletcher. 1997. pap. 11.95 (*0-452-01157-4*, Mer) NAL-Dutton.

Rebel Private - Front & Rear: Memoirs of a Confederate Soldier. William A. Fletcher. LC 94-45324. 1995. pap. 20.95 (*0-525-93992-X*, Dutton) NAL-Dutton.

Rebel Private, Front & Rear. William A. Fletcher. 1983. reprint ed. 25.95 (*0-89201-107-6*) Zenger Pub.

Rebel Queen. Walter Besant. LC 74-27964. (Modern Jewish Experience Ser.). 1975. reprint ed. 40.95 (*0-405-06695-3*) Ayer.

Rebel Radio: The Story of El Salvador's Radio Venceremos. Jose T. Vigil. Tr. by Mark Fried. 288p. (SPA.). 1994. 19.95 (*1-880684-21-7*) Curbstone.

Rebel Raider. Raphael Semmes. (American Autobiography Ser.). 218p. 1995. reprint ed. lib. bdg. 79.00 (*0-7812-8635-2*) Rprt Serv.

Rebel Raider: The Life of General John Hunt Morgan. James A. Ramage. 336p. 1995. pap. 18.95 (*0-8131-0839-X*) U Pr of Ky.

Rebel Rhymes & Rhapsodies. Ed. by Frank Moore. 1976. lib. bdg. 59.95 (*0-8490-2503-6*) Gordon Pr.

Rebel Rivers: A Guide to the Civil War Sites on the Potomac, Rappahannock, York, & James. Mark V. Nesbitt. LC 93-20180. (Illus.). 166p. 1993. pap. 12.95 (*0-8117-2538-3*) Stackpole.

Rebel Rose. Ishbel Ross. LC 54-8986. 245p. 1987. pap. 4.95 (*0-89176-026-1*, Mckingbird) R Bemis Pub.

Rebel Saints. Mary A. Best. LC 68-55839. (Essay Index Reprint Ser.). 1977. 20.95 (*0-8369-0205-X*) Ayer.

Rebel Scouts: The Last Ride Home. Moody K. Connell. 186p. (Orig.). 1995. pap. write for info. (*1-885591-97-7*) Morris Pubng.

Rebel Son G. P. Ed. by Eileen M. Simpson. 114p. (C). 1990. 75.00 (*0-947333-16-9*, Pub. by Pascoe Pub AT) St Mut.

Rebel Sons of Erin. Ed Gleeson. 390p. 1993. 29.95 (*1-878208-23-3*); pap. 24.95 (*1-878208-24-1*) Guild Pr IN.

***Rebel Sourcebook.** (Star Wars Ser.). 22.00 (*0-87431-209-4*, 40091) West End Games.

Rebel Sourcebook. Harry Heckel. Ed. by Lawrence R. Sims. (Illus.). 96p. (Orig.). (YA). 1996. pap. 11.95 (*1-889155-09-8*, ODS901B) Optimus Design.

Rebel Storehouse: Florida in the Confederate Economy. Robert A. Taylor. LC 94-28532. (Illus.). 232p. 1995. text ed. 29.95 (*0-8173-0776-1*) U of Ala Pr.

Rebel Temptress. Constance O'Banyon. (Orig.). 1983. mass mkt. 3.50 (*0-8217-1215-2*, Zebra Kensgtn) Kensgtn Pub Corp.

***Rebel Trail.** Dwight Bennett Newton. LC 96-52578. (Sagebrush Large Print Westerns Ser.). 1997. lib. bdg. 17.95 (*1-57490-114-1*, Beeler LP Bks) T T Beeler.

Rebel Voices: An IWW Anthology with a Short Treatise on Wobbly Cartoons. Intro. by Joyce L. Kornbluh. (Illus.). 464p. (Orig.). 1988. 60.00 (*0-88286-145-X*) C H Kerr.

Rebel War Clerk's Diary. John B. Jones. LC 93-8968. 545p. 1993. pap. 16.95 (*0-8071-1882-6*) La State U Pr.

Rebel War Clerk's Diary at the Confederate States Capital. John B. Jones. (Notable American Authors Ser.). 1992. reprint ed. lib. bdg. 75.00 (*0-7812-3524-3*) Rprt Serv.

***Rebel Watchdog: The Confederate States Army Provost Guard.** Kenneth Radley. (Illus.). 360p. 1997. pap. 16.95 (*0-8071-2173-8*) La State U Pr.

Rebel Wind. Leanne Grayson. 384p. (Orig.). 1993. pap. 4.99 (*0-451-40412-2*, Topaz) NAL-Dutton.

Rebel Wind. Stobie Piel. 416p. 1995. mass mkt. 4.99 (*0-8217-0110-X*, Zebra Kensgtn) Kensgtn Pub Corp.

Rebel with a Cause. Franklin Graham. LC 95-20501. (Illus.). 336p. 1995. 22.99 (*0-7852-7915-6*) Nelson.

Rebel with a Cause. Kim Hansen. (American Romance Ser.). 1996. mass mkt. 3.75 (*0-373-16634-6*, 1-16634-7) Harlequin Bks.

Rebel with a Cause. expanded rev. ed. Hans Eysenck. LC 96-20339. 360p. (Orig.). 1996. pap. text ed. 21.95 (*1-56000-938-1*) Transaction Pubs.

***Rebel with a Cause.** Franklin Graham. (Illus.). 335p. 1997. reprint ed. pap. 12.99 (*0-7852-7170-8*) Nelson.

Rebel with a Cause: P. D. East, Southern Liberalism & the Civil Rights Movement, 1953-71. Gary L. Huey. LC 84-23516. 232p. 1985. 40.00 (*0-8420-2228-7*) Scholarly Res Inc.

***Rebel Without a Bride.** Catherine Leigh. 1997. pap. 3.25 (*0-373-15715-0*, 1-15715-5) Harlequin Bks.

***Rebel Without a Bride.** Catherine Leigh. 1997. pap. 3.25 (*0-373-03469-5*, 1-03469-3) Harlequin Bks.

Rebel Without a Car: Surviving & Appreciating Your Child's Teen Years. Fred Mednick. 224p. (Orig.). 1996. pap. 12.95 (*1-57749-014-2*) Fairview Press.

Rebel Without a Cause. Adapted by James Fuller. 1986. pap. 5.25 (*0-87129-278-5*, R12) Dramatic Pub.

Rebel Without a Crew: Or How a 23-Year-Old Filmmaker with $7,000 Became a Hollywood Player. Robert Rodriguez. 1996. pap. 11.95 (*0-452-27187-8*, Plume) NAL-Dutton.

Rebel Without a Crew: or How a 23-Year Old Filmmaker with 7,000 Dollars Became a Hollywood Player. Robert Rodriguez. (Illus.). 256p. 1995. pap. 22.95 (*0-525-93794-3*) NAL-Dutton.

Rebel Without Applause. Jay Landesman. LC 86-62451. 286p. 1987. 22.00 (*0-932966-75-6*) Permanent Pr.

Rebel Without Applause. Lemn Sissay. 62p. 9300. pap. 13.95 (*1-85224-202-7*, Pub. by Bloodaxe Bks UK) Dufour.

Rebel Women. Thomas Babe. 1976. pap. 5.25 (*0-8222-0935-7*) Dramatists Play.

***Rebel Women: Feminism, Modernism & the Edwardian Novel.** Jane E. Miller. LC 96-38641. 1996. pap. text ed. 15.95 (*0-226-52677-1*) U Ch Pr.

***Rebel Yell.** Wes Scantlin. 264p. (Orig.). 1998. mass mkt. 7.99 (*1-58006-012-9*, Appaloosa) Sovereign.

Rebel Yell & the Yankee Hurrah: The Civil War Journal of a Maine Volunteer. John Haley. Ed. by Ruth L. Silliker. LC 84-51560. (Illus.). 320p. 1985. pap. 10.95 (*0-89272-250-9*) Down East.

Rebelion de los Negros. Jose Sanchez-Boudy. LC 79-56654. (Coleccion Teatro). 78p. (Orig.). (SPA.). 1980. pap. 5.95 (*0-89729-247-2*) Ediciones.

Rebelling, Loving & Liberation: A Metaphysics of the Concrete. Paul F. Schmidt. LC 73-152513. 208p. 1971. 14.00 (*0-912998-00-8*); pap. 7.00 (*0-912998-01-6*) Hummingbird.

Rebellion. Jerry Ahern. (Survivalist Ser.: No. 12). 1989. mass mkt. 2.95 (*0-8217-2777-X*, Zebra Kensgtn) Kensgtn Pub Corp.

Rebellion. Cynthia Blair. (Dark Moon Legacy Ser.: No. 3). 320p. (YA). 1993. mass mkt. 3.99 (*0-06-106160-3*, Harp PBks) HarpC.

***Rebellion.** Marianne Brandis. 288p. 1996. pap. 16.95 (*0-88984-175-6*, Pub. by Porcupines Quill CN) Genl Dist Srvs.

Rebellion. W. J. Scanlan. 160p. 1989. 18.95 (*0-7737-2271-8*); pap. 9.95 (*0-7737-5285-4*) Genl Dist Srvs.

Rebellion: Essays 1980-1991. Minnie B. Pratt. LC 91-35238. 248p. (Orig.). 1991. pap. 12.95 (*1-56341-006-0*); lib. bdg. 26.95 (*1-56341-007-9*) Firebrand Bks.

***Rebellion: The Official Strategy Guide.** Joe G. Bell. 240p. 1997. per. 19.99 (*0-7615-1028-1*) Prima Pub.

Rebellion Against Rome: Boudica & the Iceni Uprising in the Year A. D. 61. Peter Fry. 88p. (C). 1988. 65.00 (*0-86138-014-2*, Pub. by T Dalton UK) St Mut.

Rebellion Against Victorianism: The Impetus for Cultural Change in 1920s America. Stanley Coben. (Illus.). 256p. 1991. 25.00 (*0-19-504593-9*) OUP.

Rebellion & Democracy in Meiji Japan: A Study of Commoners in the Popular Rights Movement. Roger W. Bowen. LC 78-51755. 450p. 1980. pap. 18.00 (*0-520-05230-7*) U CA Pr.

Rebellion & Factionalism in a Chinese Province: Zhejiang, 1966-1976. Keith Forster. LC 89-49160. (Studies on Contemporary China). 352p. (gr. 13). 1990. text ed. 74.95 (*0-87332-535-4*, East Gate Bk) M E Sharpe.

Rebellion & Its Enemies in Late Imperial China: Militarization & Social Structure, 1796-1864. Philip A. Kuhn. (East Asian Ser.: No. 49). 272p. 1980. pap. 14.95 (*0-674-74954-5*) HUP.

Rebellion & Realignment: Arkansas's Road to Succession. James M. Woods. LC 85-21024. 288p. 1987. 28.00 (*0-938626-59-0*) U of Ark Pr.

Rebellion & Reconciliation: Satirical Prints on the Revolution at Williamsburg. Joan D. Dolmetsch. LC 75-41443. (Illus.). viii, 221p. 1976. 17.50 (*0-87935-032-6*) Colonial Williamsburg.

Rebellion & Repression in the Philippines. Richard J. Kessler. LC 89-30536. 256p. (C). 1989. 37.50 (*0-300-04406-2*) Yale U Pr.

Rebellion & Repression in the Philippines. Richard J. Kessler. 239p. (C). 1991. reprint ed. pap. text ed. 18.00 (*0-300-05130-1*) Yale U Pr.

Rebellion & Riot: Popular Disorder in England During the Reign of Edward VI. Barrett L. Beer. LC 81-19341. 270p. reprint ed. pap. 77.00 (*0-7837-0574-3*, 2040918) Bks Demand.

Rebellion, Death & Aesthetics in Italy: The Demons of Scapigliatura. David Del Principe. LC 95-49129. (Illus.). 184p. (C). 1996. 32.95 (*0-8386-3638-1*) Fairleigh Dickinson.

Rebellion Eighteen Fifty-Seven: A Symposium. Ed. by P. C. Joshi. 354p. 1986. reprint ed. 21.00 (*0-8364-2038-1*, Pub. by KP Bagchi IA) S Asia.

Rebellion from the Roots: Indian Uprising in Chiapas. John Ross. 250p. (Orig.). 1994. pap. 16.95 (*1-56751-042-6*) Common Courage.

Rebellion in Chiapas: Rural Reforms, Campesino Radicalism & the Limits to Salinismo. rev. ed. Neil Harvey. (Transformation of Rural Mexico Ser.: No. 5). 1995. pap. 8.00 (*1-878367-23-4*, DP-05) UCSD Ctr US-Mex.

Rebellion in India: How to Prevent Another. John B. Norton. (C). 1988. reprint ed. 35.00 (*81-7013-059-X*, Pub. by Navrang) S Asia.

Rebellion in India, 1857. F. W. Rawding. (Cambridge Introduction to World History Topic Bks.). (Illus.). 48p. (YA). (gr. 7 up). 1977. pap. text ed. 10.95 (*0-521-20683-9*) Cambridge U Pr.

Rebellion in Nineteenth-Century China. Albert Feuerwerker. (Michigan Monographs in Chinese Studies: No. 21). 101p. 1975. pap. text ed. 15.00 (*0-89264-021-9*) Ctr Chinese Studies.

Rebellion in Rhyme. Clarke. per. 9.95 (*0-86543-231-7*) Africa World.

***Rebellion in Rhyme: The Early Poetry of John Henrik Clarke.** John H. Clarke. 1996. 24.95 (*0-86543-230-9*) Africa World.

Rebellion in the Backlands. Euclides DaCunha. Tr. by Samuel Putnam. (Illus.). xxx, 562p. 1957. reprint ed. pap. text ed. 19.95 (*0-226-12444-4*, P22) U Ch Pr.

Rebellion in the Borderlands: Anarchism & the Plan of San Diego, 1904-1923. James A. Sandos. LC 91-50870. (Illus.). 240p. 1992. 24.95 (*0-8061-2433-4*) U of Okla Pr.

Rebellion in the Unions: A Handbook for Rank & File Action. George Morris. LC 74-173354. 160p. 1971. pap. 2.75 (*0-685-23466-5*) New Outlook.

Rebellion in the University. Seymour M. Lipset. LC 92-14855. (Foundations of Higher Education Ser.). 372p. (C). 1992. pap. 24.95 (*1-56000-596-3*) Transaction Pubs.

Rebellion in the Veins: Political Struggle in Bolivia 1952-1982. James Dunkerley. 385p. 1984. text ed. 44.95 (*0-86091-089-X*, Pub. by Verso UK) Routledge Chapman & Hall.

Rebellion Is the Circle of a Lover's Hand: Rebelion es el Giro de Manos del Amante. Martin Espada. Tr. by Camilo Perez-Bustillo from ENG. LC 90-52756. 120p. (Orig.). (ENG & SPA.). 1991. pap. 9.95 (*0-915306-95-6*) Curbstone.

Rebellion of Humans. David A. Anderson-Sankofa. (Illus.). 32p. (J). 1994. 18.95 (*0-9629978-6-2*) Sights Prods.

Rebellion of the Hanged. B. Traven. 252p. 1994. pap. 12.95 (*1-56663-064-9*, Elephant Paperbacks) I R Dee.

***Rebellion on the Borders: Feminist Theology Between Theory & Praxis.** Hedwig Meyer-Wilmes. Tr. by Irene Smith-Bouman. 263p. 1995. pap. 39.00 (*90-390-0046-8*, Pub. by KOK Pharos NE) Eisenbrauns.

Rebellion or Revolution? England 1640-1660. G. E. Aylmer. (Opus Ser.). 288p. 1987. pap. 16.95 (*0-19-289212-6*) OUP.

Rebellion, Racism, & Representation: The Adam Clayton Powell Case & Its Antecedents. P. Allan Dionisopoulos. LC 76-125335. 175p. 1970. 18.00 (*0-87580-018-1*); pap. 12.00 (*0-87580-504-3*) N Ill U Pr.

***Rebellion Record: A Diary of American Events.** Frank Moore. Date not set. write for info. (*0-405-10877-X*) Ayer.

Rebellion Record: A Diary of American Events, 12 Vols., Set. Ed. by Frank Moore. (Illus.). 1976. reprint ed. pap. 300.00 (*0-405-09846-4*) Ayer.

Rebellion Sourcebook. Marc W. Miller. (MegaTraveller Ser.). (Illus.). 96p. (Orig.). 1988. pap. 10.00 (*0-943580-63-3*) Game Designers.

Rebellion with Purpose: A Young Adult's Guide to the Improvement of Self & Society. Richard V. Sidy. 192p. (YA). (gr. 10 up). 1993. pap. text ed. 9.95 (*0-9633744-1-9*) SNS Pr.

Rebellions & Revolutions: China from the 1800s to the 1980s. Jack C. Gray. (Short Oxford History of the Modern World Ser.). (Illus.). 528p. 1990. pap. text ed. 22.00 (*0-19-821576-2*) OUP.

Rebellions, Perversities, & Main Events. Murray Kempton. 1995. pap. 16.00 (*0-8129-2528-9*, Times Bks) Random.

Rebellions, Resistance, & Runaways Within the Slave South. Ed. by Paul Finkelman. (Articles on American Slavery Ser.). 420p. 1990. reprint ed. text ed. 37.00 (*0-8240-6793-2*) Garland.

Rebellious Alphabet. Diaz. 1996. pap. 6.95 (*0-8050-4901-0*, Bks Young Read) H Holt & Co.

Rebellious Alphabet. Jorge Diaz. Tr. by Geoffrey Fox. LC 93-12697. (Edge Graphics Ser.). (Illus.). 32p. (YA). (gr. 7 up). 1993. 14.95 (*0-8050-2765-3*, Bks Young Read) H Holt & Co.

Rebellious Body: Reclaim Your Life from Environmental Illness or Chronic Fatigue Syndrome. Janice S. Wittenberg. (Illus.). 310p. (C). 1996. 18.95 (*0-306-45402-5*, Plenum Insight) Plenum.

Rebellious Bride. Adrienne Day. 352p. (Orig.). 1995. mass mkt. 4.99 (*0-380-77413-5*) Avon.

Rebellious Desire. Julie Garwood. Ed. by Linda Marrow. 320p. 1991. pap. 6.99 (*0-671-73784-8*, Pocket Books) PB.

Rebellious Desire. large type ed. Julie Garwood. (General Ser.). 391p. 1992. pap. 16.95 (*0-8161-5394-9*, GK Hall); lib. bdg. 20.95 (*0-8161-5393-0*, GK Hall) Thorndike Pr.

Rebellious Fraser's: Nol Yorke's Magazine in the Days of Maginn, Thackeray & Carlyle. Miriam M. Thrall. LC 35-1070. reprint ed. 29.50 (*0-404-06458-2*) AMS Pr.

***Rebellious House.** Barbara M. Dickinson. (Illus.). 280p. 1997. 24.95 (*1-55618-165-5*) Brunswick Pub.

***Rebellious Laughter: People's Humor in American Culture.** Joseph Boskin. LC 97-11092. 224p. 1997. 39.95 (*0-8156-2747-5*); pap. 17.95 (*0-8156-2748-3*) Syracuse U Pr.

Rebellious People: Basques, Protests, & Politics. Cyrus E. Zirakzadeh. LC 91-2185. (Basque Ser.). (Illus.). 272p. 1991. 39.95 (*0-87417-173-3*) U of Nev Pr.

Rebellious Puritan: Portrait of Mr. Hawthorne. Lloyd R. Morris. (BCL1-PS American Literature Ser.). 369p. 1992. reprint ed. lib. bdg. 89.00 (*0-7812-6730-7*) Rprt Serv.

Rebellious Ranger: Rip Ford & the Old Southwest. W. J. Hughes. LC 64-11323. (Illus.). 328p. 1990. pap. 14.95 (*0-8061-1084-8*) U of Okla Pr.

***Rebellious Recipes.** Tony Basile. (Illus.). 116p. 1997. pap. 6.95 (*0-9646605-1-2*) Panther Mtn.

Rebellious River. J. P. Kemper. LC 72-2848. (Use & Abuse of America's Natural Resources Ser.). 284p. 1972. reprint ed. 23.95 (*0-405-04514-X*) Ayer.

Rebellious Spirit. Rajneesh Osho Staff. Ed. by Krishna Prabhu et al. LC 87-42814. (Mystery School Ser.). 325p. (Orig.). 1987. pap. 14.95 (*3-907757-16-5*) Osho America.

Rebellious Structures: Woman Writers & the Crisis of the Novel 1880-1900. Gerd Bjorhovde. (Scandinavian University Press Publication). (Illus.). 216p. 1987. 38.50 (*82-00-02502-0*) Scandnvan Univ Pr.

Rebellious Ward. Joan Wolf. (Regency Romance Ser.). 224p. 1984. pap. 3.99 (*0-451-15401-0*, Sig) NAL-Dutton.

Rebello Transcripts: Governor Phillip's Portuguese Prelude. Kenneth G. McIntyre. 257p. (C). 1984. 24.95 (*0-285-62603-5*) Intl Spec Bk.

Rebels. large type ed. John Jakes. (Kent Family Chronicles Ser.: Vol. 2). 1993. 85.95 (*0-7838-1109-8*, GK Hall) Thorndike Pr.

Rebels: A Brotherhood of Outlaw Bikers. Daniel R. Wolf. 372p. 1992. 29.95 (*0-8020-2724-5*); pap. 19.95 (*0-8020-7363-8*) U of Toronto Pr.

Rebels: The Irish Rising of 1916. Peter De Rosa. 544p. 1992. pap. 14.00 (*0-449-90682-5*, Columbine) Fawcett.

Rebels - Rebeldes. S. E. Hinton. (SPA.). (J). 8.95 (*84-204-3919-3*) Santillana.

Rebels Against Slavery: American Slave Revolts. Patricia C. McKissack & Frederick McKissack. LC 94-41089. 176p. (J). (gr. 3-9). 1996. 14.95 (*0-590-45735-7*, Scholastic Hardcover) Scholastic Inc.

Rebels Against the Future. Kirkpatrick Sale. 336p. (YA). 1996. pap. 13.00 (*0-201-40718-3*) Addison-Wesley.

Rebels Against the Future: The Luddites & Their War on the Industrial Revolution - Lessons for the Computer Age. Kirkpatrick Sale. LC 94-41354. 320p. 1995. 24.00 (*0-201-62678-0*) Addison-Wesley.

Rebels Against War: The American Peace Movement, 1933-1983. Lawrence S. Wittner. LC 83-27523. 384p. 1984. pap. 18.95 (*0-87722-342-4*) Temple U Pr.

Rebels & Colleagues: Advertising & Social Change in French Canada. Frederick Elkin. (Illus.). 240p. 1973. 34.95 (*0-7735-0135-5*, Pub. by McGill CN) U of Toronto Pr.

Rebels & Colleagues: Advertising & Social Change in French-Canada. Frederick Elkin. LC 72-88133. 247p. reprint ed. pap. 70.40 (*0-317-41742-8*, 2023847) Bks Demand.

Rebels & Democrats. E. P. Douglass. LC 77-160853. (Era of the American Revolution Ser.). 368p. 1971. reprint ed. 45.00 (*0-306-70402-1*) Da Capo.

Rebels & Democrats: The Struggle for Equal Political Rights & Majority Rule During the American Revolution. Elisha P. Douglass. 384p. 1989. reprint ed. pap. text ed. 9.95 (*0-929587-12-X*, Elephant Paperbacks) I R Dee.

Rebels & Devils: The Psychology of Liberation. Christopher S. Hyatt et al. LC 94-69288. (Illus.). 384p. (Orig.). 1996. pap. 17.95 (*1-56184-121-8*) New Falcon Pubns.

Rebels & Gentlemen: Philadelphia in the Age of Franklin. Carl Bridenbaugh & Jessica Bridenbaugh. LC 78-657. (Illus.). 393p. 1978. reprint ed. text ed. 38.50 (*0-313-20300-8*, BRRE, Greenwood Pr) Greenwood.

Rebels & Redcoats: The American Revolution Throught the Eyes of Those Who Fought & Lived It. George F. Scheer & Hugh F. Rankin. (Quality Paperbacks Ser.). 574p. 1987. reprint ed. pap. 16.95 (*0-306-80307-0*) Da Capo.

Rebels & Reinforcements. Steven Schend. mass mkt. 2.50 (*0-7869-0292-2*) TSR Inc.

Rebels & Renegades. Max Nomad. LC 68-20326. (Essay Index Reprint Ser.). 1977. 23.95 (*0-8369-0745-0*) Ayer.

Rebels & Revolutionaries in North China, 1845-1945. Elizabeth J. Perry. LC 79-65179. xvi, 324p. 1980. 45.00 (*0-8047-1055-4*); pap. 15.95 (*0-8047-1175-5*) Stanford U Pr.

Rebels & Rivals: The Contestive Spirit in the Canterbury Tales. Ed. by Susanna G. Fein et al. (Studies in Medieval Culture: No. 29). 1991. pap. 14.95 (*0-918720-42-7*); boxed 32.95 (*0-918720-41-9*) Medieval Inst.

Rebels & Rulers, Fifteen Hundred to Sixteen-Sixty, 2 vols. Perez Zagorin. Incl. Vol. 2. Provincial Rebellion: Revolutionary Civil Wars, 1560-1660. LC 81-17039. 240p. 1982. pap. text ed. 21.95 (*0-521-28712-X*); LC 81-17039. 304p. 1982. write for info. (*0-318-56684-2*) Cambridge U Pr.

Rebels & Whips: An Analysis of Dissension, Discipline & Cohesion in British Political Parties. Robert J. Jackson. LC 68-19078. 1969. text ed. 25.00 (*0-312-66570-9*) St Martin.

Rebels & Yankees. William Davis. 1989. 24.98 (*0-8317-3264-4*) Smithmark.

Rebels & Yankees. William Davis. 1990. 24.98 (*0-8317-1505-7*) Smithmark.

Rebels & Yankees: Battlefields of the Civil War. William C. Davis. 1991. 24.98 (*0-8317-0702-X*) Smithmark.

Rebel's Bride. Christine Flynn. 1996. mass mkt. 3.99 (*0-373-24034-1*, 1-24034-0) Silhouette.

Rebel's Choice. Patricia H. Easton. 160p. (YA). (gr. 7 up). 1989. 15.00 (*0-15-200571-4*, Gulliver Bks) HarBrace.

Rebel's Dilemma. Mark I. Lichbach. (Economics, Cognition, & Society Ser.). 550p. 1994. text ed. 47.50 (*0-472-10532-9*) U of Mich Pr.

Rebels Forever! large type ed. Steven Gray. 220p. 1996. pap. 17.99 (*1-85389-572-5*, Dales) Ulverscroft.

Rebels in Bohemia: The Radicals of "The Masses", 1911-1917. Leslie Fishbein. LC 81-24105. (Illus.). xv, 270p. 1982. 37.50 (*0-8078-1519-5*) U of NC Pr.

Rebels in the Name of the Tsar. Daniel Field. LC 88-20829. 240p. (C). 1988. pap. 17.95 (*0-04-445190-3*) Routledge Chapman & Hall.

Rebels in the Rif: Abd el Krim & the Rif Rebellion. David S. Woolman. (Illus.). xiv, 257p. 1968. 42.50 (*0-8047-0664-6*) Stanford U Pr.

Rebels in the Shadows. Robert T. Reilly. LC 78-66069. 187p. (J). (gr. 3-7). 1979. pap. 8.95 (*0-8229-5304-8*) U of Pittsburgh Pr.

Rebels in White Gloves: Coming of Age with Wellesley Class of '69. Miriam Horn. 1996. write for info. (*0-8129-2501-7*, Times Bks) Random.

Rebels of Hastings. Betsy D. Boyce. (Illus.). 232p. 1992. 45.00 (*0-8020-5986-4*); pap. 16.95 (*0-8020-6920-7*) U of Toronto Pr.

Rebels of Highland Guatemala: The Quiche-Mayas of Momostenango. Robert M. Carmack. LC 95-18047. (Civilization of the American Indian Ser.: Vol. 215). (Illus.). 560p. 1996. 39.95 (*0-8061-2760-0*) U of Okla Pr.

Rebels of Sabrehill. Raymond Giles. 1981. pap. 2.95 (*0-449-13695-7*, GM) Fawcett.

Rebels of the Heavenly Kingdom. Katherine Paterson. 240p. (J). (gr. 7 up). 1984. pap. 2.95 (*0-380-68304-0*, Flare) Avon.

Rebels of the Heavenly Kingdom. Katherine Paterson. LC 83-1529. 224p. (YA). (gr. 12 up). 1983. pap. 14.99 (*0-525-66911-6*, Lodestar Bks) Dutton Child Bks.

Rebels of the Heavenly Kingdom. Katherine Paterson. 240p. (YA). (gr. 7 up). 1995. pap. 3.99 (*0-14-037610-0*) Puffin Bks.

Rebels of the New South. Walter M. Raymond. LC 72-2027. (Black Heritage Library Collection). (Illus.). 1977. reprint ed. 19.95 (*0-8369-9055-2*) Ayer.

Rebels of the Woods: The I.W.W. in the Pacific Northwest. Robert L. Tyler. LC 68-1776. 240p. 1967. pap. 14.95 (*0-87071-388-4*) Oreg St U Pr.

Rebels on the Rio Grande: The Civil War Journal of A.B. Peticolas. Ed. by Don E. Alberts. (Illus.). 187p. 1993. pap. 12.95 (*0-9636915-0-3*) Merit Pr NM.

Rebels on the Rise: An Athletic History. Kelly Anderson. Ed. by Missouri Editing Group Staff. (Illus.). 1992. write for info. (*1-56166-020-5*) Walsworth Pub.

Rebels or Reformers? Dissenting Priests in American Life. William B. Faherty. LC 88-309. 122p. 1988. 5.50 (*0-8294-0587-9*) Loyola Pr.

Rebels, Outlaws, & General Heretics. Nick Ierullo. 1990. 6.95 (*0-533-09008-3*) Vantage.

Rebel's Progress. Tom Earley. 82p. (C). 1979. pap. 20.00 (*0-85088-521-3*, Pub. by Gomer Pr UK) St Mut.

Rebel's Recollections. George C. Eggleston. LC 96-27324. 192p. 1996. pap. 10.95 (*0-8071-2125-8*) La State U Pr.

Rebels Resurgent. (Civil War Ser.). (Illus.). 176p. 1985. 18.95 (*0-8094-4748-7*); lib. bdg. 25.93 (*0-8094-4749-5*) Time-Life.

Rebel's Revenge. Tabor Evans. (Longarm Ser.: No. 179). 1993. pap. 3.99 (*0-515-11238-0*) Jove Pubns.

Rebel's Silhouette: Selected Poems. rev. ed. Faiz Ahmed Faiz. Tr. & Intro. by Agha Shahid Ali. LC 94-40502. 128p. 1995. pap. 14.95 (*0-87023-975-9*) U of Mass Pr.

Rebel's Spirit. Susan Connell. 1996. pap. 3.50 (*0-373-76044-2*, 1-76044-6) Silhouette.

Rebels United: The Enduring Reality of James Dean. 2nd ed. Joel Brean. Ed. by Elbert Jones. (Illus.). 140p. 1987. pap. 10.50 (*0-317-63846-7*) Brean-Jones Pub.

Rebels West. Jack Cummings. 1991. mass mkt. 3.50 (*1-55817-525-3*, Pinncle Kensgtn) Kensgtn Pub Corp.

Rebels West. Jack Cummings. 1987. 15.95 (*0-8027-0943-5*) Walker & Co.

Rebels with a Cause: We Ride the Harley. Gail Demarco. (Illus.). 1994. 34.95 (*0-916290-73-5*) Squarebooks.

Rebels with Causes: A Study of Revolutionary Syndicalist Culture among the French Primary School Teachers Between 1880 & 1919. Francis M. Feeley. (American University Studies: History: Ser. IX, Vol. 54). 368p. (C). 1989. text ed. 55.95 (*0-8204-1025-X*) P Lang Pubng.

***Rebels Within the Ranks: Psychologists' Critique of Scientific Authority & Democratic Realities in New Deal America.** Katherine Pandora. (Studies in the History of Psychology). 272p. (C). 1997. text ed. 59.95 (*0-521-58358-6*) Cambridge U Pr.

Rebirth. Mark Dunster. 9p. (Orig.). 1993. pap. 4.00 (*0-89642-224-0*) Linden Pubs.

Rebirth: My Transplant Experience. Nancy Cassell. 64p. (Orig.). 1993. pap. 4.95 (*0-9625402-3-4*) Altan Pub.

Rebirth: Poems. Foroogh Farrokhzaad. Tr. by David C. Martin. (Iran-e NO Literary Collection Ser.). (Illus.). 172p. 1985. pap. 9.95 (*0-939214-30-X*) Mazda Pubs.

Rebirth & Karma. Sri Aurobindo. LC 90-63095. 184p. (Orig.). 1991. pap. 9.95 (*0-941524-63-9*) Lotus Light.

Rebirth for Christianity. Alvin B. Kuhn. LC 76-104032. 1970. 9.95 (*0-8356-0015-7*, Quest) Theos Pub Hse.

Rebirth of a Nation: Wales, 1880-1890. Kenneth O. Morgan. (Oxford History of Wales Ser.: Vol. VI). (Illus.). 480p. 1987. pap. 19.95 (*0-19-821760-9*) OUP.

Rebirth of African Civilization. Chancellor Williams. (Orig.). 1993. pap. 14.95 (*1-56411-057-5*) Untd Bros & Sis.

Rebirth of African Civilization. Chancellor Williams. 342p. (C). 1993. reprint ed. pap. text ed. 16.95 (*0-88378-129-8*) Third World.

Rebirth of America. large type ed. Marianne Williamson. (Large Print Ser.). 1996. pap. write for info. (*0-679-75899-2*) Random.

Rebirth of Anthropological Theory. Stanley R. Barrett. 288p. 1988. pap. 17.95 (*0-8020-6718-2*) U of Toronto Pr.

Rebirth of Classical Political Rationalism: An Introduction to the Thought of Leo Strauss. Leo Strauss. 324p. 1989. pap. text ed. 17.95 (*0-226-77715-4*) U Ch Pr.

Rebirth of Democracy: 12 Constitutions of Central & Eastern Europe. Ed. by International Institute for Democracy Staff. 625p. (Orig.). 1995. pap. 18.00 (*92-871-2676-3*, Pub. by Council of Europe FR) Manhattan Pub Co.

***Rebirth of Democracy: 12 Constitutions of Centraland Eastern Europe.** 2nd rev. ed. Ed. by International Institute for Democracy Staff. 446p. 1996. pap. 30.00 (*92-871-3094-9*, Pub. by Council of Europe FR) Manhattan Pub Co.

Rebirth of East Europe. 2nd ed. Michael G. Roskin. LC 93-27337. 212p. (C). 1993. pap. text ed. 33.00 (*0-13-035957-2*) P-H.

***Rebirth of East Europe.** 3rd ed. Michael Roskin. 224p. (C). 1997. 28.00 (*0-13-613647-8*) P-H.

Rebirth of Eden: The Final Sexual Culture Revolution. Janus Christian. 110p. Date not set. 20.01 (*0-614-97217-5*) Powerhse Publng.

***Rebirth of England & English: The Vision of William Barnes.** Andrew Phillips. 160p. 1997. pap. 18.95 (*1-898281-17-3*, Pub. by Anglo-Saxon Bks UK) Paul & Co Pubs.

Rebirth of Europe. Michael G. Roskin. 224p. (C). 1991. pap. text ed. write for info. (*0-13-763442-0*) P-H.

Rebirth of Federalism: Slouching Toward Washington. David B. Walker. LC 94-22025. (Illus.). 384p. (Orig.). 1995. pap. text ed. 29.95 (*1-56643-005-4*) Chatham Hse Pubs.

Rebirth of History: Eastern Europe in the Age of Democracy. Misha Glenny. (Illus.). 256p. 1993. pap. 11.95 (*0-14-017286-6*, Penguin Bks) Viking Penguin.

Rebirth of Jewish Art: The Unfolding of Jewish Art in the Nineteenth Century. Hyman J. Lewbin. LC 74-76483. (Illus.). 1974. 20.00 (*0-88400-007-9*) Shengold.

***Rebirth of Liberty.** Clarence B. Carson. 350p. 1976. pap. 14.95 (*0-910614-55-5*) Foun Econ Ed.

Rebirth of Music. LaMar Boshman. 96p. (SPA.). 1988. reprint ed. pap. 7.99 (*0-914903-79-9*, Revival Pr) Destiny Image.

Rebirth of Music: English Version. LaMar Boschman. 112p. (Orig.). 1992. pap. 7.99 (*0-914903-80-2*) Destiny Image.

Rebirth of Nature: The Greening of Science & God. Rupert Sheldrake. (Illus.). 256p. 1994. pap. 12.95 (*0-89281-510-8*, Destiny Bks) Inner Tradit.

***Rebirth of New York City.** Spacemaker Press Staff. Date not set. pap. 19.95 (*0-688-15367-4*) Morrow.

***Rebirth of New York City's Bryant Park.** J. William Thompson. (Land Marks Ser.). 1997. pap. text ed. 19.95 (*1-888931-05-1*) Watsn-Guptill.

Rebirth of Norway's Peasantry: Folk Leader Hans Nielsen Hauge. Magnus Nodtuedt. 305p. 1965. 5.95 (*0-685-02327-3*) Holmes.

***Rebirth of Politics in Russia.** Michael E. Urban. 400p. 1997. text ed. 64.95 (*0-521-56248-1*); pap. text ed. 24.95 (*0-521-56611-8*) Cambridge U Pr.

Rebirth of Power: Overcoming the Effects of Sexual Abuse Through the Experiences of Others. Ed. by Pamela Portwood et al. LC 87-62737. 210p. 1988. pap. 9.95 (*0-941300-07-2*) Mother Courage.

Rebirth of Private Policing. Les Johnston. LC 91-13442. 272p. (C). (gr. 13 up). 1992. text ed. 74.95 (*0-415-05192-4*, Routledge NY) Routledge.

Rebirth of Private Policing. Les Johnston. LC 91-13442. 272p. (C). 1992. pap. 18.95 (*0-415-05193-2*, Routledge NY) Routledge.

Rebirth of Rhetoric: Essays in Language & Education. Ed. by Richard Andrews. (Illus.). 256p. (C). (gr. 13). 1992. text ed. 62.95 (*0-415-06261-6*, A9565) Routledge.

Rebirth of Robert Samuels. Wilsome Pinnock. 96p. (Orig.). 1995. pap. 9.95 (*0-571-17662-3*) Faber & Faber.

Rebirth of Russian Democracy: An Interpretation of Political Culture. Nicolai N. Petro. LC 94-45431. (Illus.). 240p. (C). 1995. text ed. 39.95 (*0-674-75001-2*) HUP.

***Rebirth of Russian Democracy: An Interpretation of Political Culture.** Nicolai N. Petro. 1997. pap. text ed. 16.95 (*0-674-75002-0*) HUP.

***Rebirth of the American School System.** Christine Villani. 179p. 1997. 39.00 (*1-56072-424-2*) Nova Sci Pubs.

***Rebirth of the Goddess.** Carol P. Christ. 1997. 24.00 (*0-201-14398-4*) Addison-Wesley.

Rebirth of the Habsburg Army: Friedrich Beck & the Rise of the General Staff. Scott A. Lackey. LC 95-7897. (Contributions in Military Studies: 161). 272p. 1995. text ed. 62.95 (*0-313-29361-9*, Greenwood Pr) Greenwood.

Rebirth of the Jupiter & 119: Building the Replica Locomotives at Golden Spike. Robert R. Dowty. Ed. by Rose Houk & T. J. Priehs. LC 94-66380. 52p. 1994. pap. 6.95 (*1-877856-43-6*) SW Pks Mnmts.

Rebirth of the Missouri Pacific, 1956-1983. H. Craig Miner. LC 83-45097. (Illus.). 258p. 1984. 29.95 (*0-89096-159-X*) Tex A&M Univ Pr.

Rebirth of the Older Child. Brita Bergland. (Poetry Ser.). 64p. (Orig.). 1993. pap. 8.00 (*0-930901-85-1*) Burning Deck.

Rebirth of the Older Child. limited ed. Brita Bergland. (Poetry Ser.). 64p. (Orig.). 1993. pap. 15.00 (*0-930901-86-X*) Burning Deck.

Rebirth of the Paraguayan Republic: The First Colorado Era, 1878-1904. Harris G. Warren. LC 84-19528. (Latin American Ser.). (Illus.). 395p. 1985. 49.95 (*0-8229-3507-4*) U of Pittsburgh Pr.

Rebirth of the Small Family Farm: A Handbook for Starting a Successful Organic Farm Based on the Concepts of Community Supported Agriculture. Bob Gregson & Bonnie Gregson. (Illus.). 64p. (Orig.). 1996. pap. 8.65 (*0-9652233-0-2*) Islnd Meadow.

Rebirth of the Trade Union Movement: 1838-1847. LC 72-2539. (British Labour Struggles Before 1850 Ser.). 1974. 23.95 (*0-405-04431-3*) Ayer.

Rebirth of the Virginia & Truckee R. R. Amazing Revival of a Steam Railroad. Ted Wurm. Ed. by Dick Murdock & Jayne Murdock. LC 92-13141. (Illus.). 80p. (Orig.). 1992. 5.95 (*0-932916-16-3*) May-Murdock.

Rebirth of the West: Culture, Politics & Society 1945-1958. Peter Duignan & L. H. Gann. (Illus.). 700p. (C). 1991. text ed. 77.95 (*1-55786-089-0*) Blackwell Pubs.

Rebirth of the West: The Americanization of the Democratic World, 1945-1958. Peter Duignan & L. H. Gann. 745p. (C). 1996. pap. text ed. 29.95 (*0-8476-8198-X*) Rowman.

Rebirth of Urban Democracy. Jeffrey M. Berry et al. 326p. 1993. 42.95 (*0-8157-0928-5*); pap. 18.95 (*0-8157-0927-7*) Brookings.

Rebirth of Value: Meditations on Beauty, Ecology, Religion, & Education. Frederick Turner. LC 90-32500. 204p. (C). 1991. pap. text ed. 19.95 (*0-7914-0474-9*) State U NY Pr.

Rebirth of Value: Meditations on Beauty, Ecology, Religion, & Education. Frederick Turner. LC 90-32500. 204p. (C). 1991. text ed. 59.50 (*0-7914-0473-0*) State U NY Pr.

Rebirth of Witchcraft. Doreen Valiente. (Illus.). 240p. 1989. pap. 12.50 (*0-919345-39-5*) Phoenix WA.

Rebirth of Wonder. Lawrence Watt-Evans. 224p. (Orig.). 1992. mass mkt. 3.99 (*0-8125-1406-8*) Tor Bks.

Rebirth, Reform, & Resilience: Universities in Transition, 1300-1700. Ed. by James M. Kittelson & Pamela J. Transue. LC 83-25095. (Illus.). 373p. 1984. 52.50 (*0-8142-0356-6*) Ohio St U Pr.

Rebirthing in the New Age. Leonard D. Orr & Sondra Ray. LC 76-53337. 240p. 1995. pap. 12.95 (*0-89087-134-5*) Celestial Arts.

An Asterisk (*) at the beginning of an entry indicates that the title is appearing in BIP for the first time.

Rebirthing in the New Age. Leonard D. Orr. pap. 9.95 (*0-318-23462-9*) L Orr.

Rebirthing: The Science of Enjoying all of Your Life see Vivation: The Science of Enjoying All of Your Life

Rebolusyon: A Generation of Struggle in the Philippines. Benjamin Pimentel. 365p. 1991. 26.00 (*0-85345-822-7*); pap. 15.00 (*0-85345-823-5*) Monthly Rev.

Rebonding with the Natural World: A Primer for Inter-Species Communication. Shinan N. Barclay. (Illus.). 200p. (Orig.). (C). 1991. pap. 11.95 (*0-685-35728-7*) Sunlight Prodns.

Reborn. F. Paul Wilson. 1990. mass mkt. 5.99 (*0-515-10343-8*) Jove Pubns.

Reborn in Canada. 2nd rev. ed. Trent Sands. LC 90-64008. 96p. 1991. reprint ed. pap. 15.00 (*1-55950-058-1*, 61114) Loompanics.

Reborn in the Light: Life after Near-Death Experiences. Cherie Sutherland. 320p. 1995. mass mkt. 5.99 (*0-553-56980-5*) Bantam.

Reborn in the U. S. A. 2nd expanded rev. ed. Trent Sands. LC 90-64007. 128p. 1991. 16.00 (*1-55950-057-3*, 61115) Loompanics.

Reborn in the West: The Reincarnation Masters. Vicki Mackenzie. LC 95-49991. (Illus.). 215p. 1996. 22.95 (*1-56924-826-5*); pap. 13.95 (*1-56924-804-4*) Marlowe & Co.

Reborn Love. Sandra L. Glenn. 1995. pap. 9.95 (*0-533-11471-3*) Vantage.

Reborn Overseas: Identity Building in Europe, Australia & New Zealand. Trent Sands. LC 90-64228. 120p. (Orig.). (C). 1991. pap. 16.00 (*1-55950-061-1*, 61127) Loompanics.

Reborn Spirit. Margoe Jane. LC 79-84678. (Illus.). 64p. 1979. 6.00 (*0-9602330-0-8*) Margoe Jane.

Reborn to Be Wild. Doug Hall. LC 93-19211. (Illus.). 104p. (Orig.). 1993. pap. 6.99 (*0-8308-1838-3*, 1838) InterVarsity.

Reborn with Credit. Trent Sands. (Illus.). 72p. (Orig.). 1992. pap. 12.00 (*1-55950-090-5*, 61131) Loompanics.

***Rebound!** Hank Herman. (Super Hoops Ser.: No. 15). 96p. (Orig.). (J). (gr. 2-5). 1998. pap. 3.50 (*0-553-48595-4*) BDD Bks Young Read.

Rebound: The Enduring Friendhsip of Dennis Rodman & Byrne Rich. Dennis Rodman et al. LC 93-14373. 1994. 22.00 (*0-517-59294-0*, Crown) Crown Pub Group.

Rebound: The Odyssey of Michael Jordan. Bob Greene. (Illus.). 256p. 1995. pap. 22.95 (*0-670-86678-4*, Viking); pap. 16.95 (*0-14-086234-X*) Viking Penguin.

Rebound: The Odyssey of Michael Jordan. Bob Greene. 1996. mass mkt. 5.99 (*0-451-19157-9*, Sig) NAL-Dutton.

Rebound with Weights. Chuck Pfeiffer. LC 83-70893. (Illus.). 136p. (Orig.). 1983. pap. 6.95 (*0-9611234-0-0*) Beaver Pubns.

Rebounder. Thomas J. Dygard. 192p. (YA). (gr. 5 up). 1996. pap. 3.99 (*0-14-037702-6*) Puffin Bks.

Rebounder. Thomas J. Dygard. LC 94-51257. 192p. (YA). (gr. 7 up). 1994. 16.00 (*0-688-12821-1*, Morrow Junior) Morrow.

Rebounding from Childbirth: Toward Emotional Recovery. Lynn Madsen. LC 93-40162. 192p. 1994. pap. text ed. 14.95 (*0-89789-348-4*, Bergin & Garvey) Greenwood.

Rebounding to Better Health: A Practical Guide to the Ultimate Exercise. Linda Brooks. 96p. (Orig.). 1995. pap. 5.95 (*0-9647265-0-5*) KE Pub.

Rebours. Joris K. Huysmans. (Folio Ser.: No. 895). (FRE.). pap. 9.95 (*2-07-036898-X*) Schoenhof.

Rebours see Against the Grain

Rebs & Yanks: Cartoons & Commentary on the Way They See the World. Gary Waltrip & Rusty Summarell. 96p. 1992. pap. 9.95 (*1-885897-03-0*) Lynx Pubng.

Rebugging Your Home & Garden: A Step-by-Step Guide to Modern Pest Control. Ruth Troetschler et al. (Illus.). 256p. 1996. pap. 19.95 (*0-9648515-0-4*) PTF Pr.

Rebuild. Ed. by R. Derricott & S. S. Chissick. LC 81-21942. (Properties of Materials Safety & Environmental Factors Ser.). (Illus.). 300p. reprint ed. pap. 85.50 (*0-685-20587-8*, 2030519) Bks Demand.

***Rebuild America's Community Partnership Handbook.** (Illus.). 110p. (Orig.). (C). 1996. pap. 30.00 (*0-7881-3629-1*) DIANE Pub.

Rebuild Your Life: How to Survive a Crisis. Dale E. Galloway. Orig. Title: Dream a New Dream. 130p. 1975. pap. 8.95 (*1-885605-03-X*) Scott-Twnty-Twnty.

Rebuilder's Guide. Bill Gothard. LC 80-80352. (Illus.). 250p. 1982. 15.00 (*0-916888-06-1*) Inst Basic Life.

Rebuilding. Daniel Solomon. (Illus.). 144p. (Orig.). 1992. pap. 24.95 (*1-878271-61-X*) Princeton Arch.

Rebuilding: When Your Relationship Ends. 2nd ed. Bruce Fisher. LC 92-17193. (Illus.). 336p. 1992. pap. 11.95 (*0-915166-95-X*) Impact Pubs CA.

***Rebuilding a House Divided.** Hans Genscher. LC 97-11772. 752p. 1997. 40.00 (*0-553-06712-5*) Broadway BDD.

Rebuilding a Lost Faith: By an American Agnostic. John L. Stoddard. LC 90-71103. 297p. 1990. reprint ed. pap. 15.00 (*0-89555-410-0*) TAN Bks Pubs.

Rebuilding a Low-Income Housing Policy. Rachel G. Bratt. LC 88-19106. 368p. 1994. pap. text ed. 24.95 (*1-56639-263-2*) Temple U Pr.

Rebuilding a Nation: Philippine Challenges & American Policy. Ed. by Carl H. Lande. LC 86-32610. (Illus.). 592p. 1987. 37.95 (*0-88702-023-2*); pap. 22.95 (*0-88702-024-0*) Washington Inst Pr.

Rebuilding America: Financing Public Works in the 1980's, 2 vols., Vol. 2. Roger J. Vaughan. LC 83-840. 1983. 16.95 (*0-934842-21-3*) CSPA.

Rebuilding America: Infrastructure Rehabilitation: Proceedings of a Conference Sponsored by the Metropolitan Association of Urban Designers & Environmental Planners. Ed. by Walter H. Kraft & Mary F. Brown. 277p. 1985. 27.00 (*0-87262-437-4*) Am Soc Civil Eng.

Rebuilding America: Planning & Managing Public Works in the 1980's, 2 vols., Vol. 1. Roger J. Vaughan & Barbara Dyer. LC 83-840. 182p. 1984. 16.95 (*0-934842-22-1*) CSPA.

Rebuilding America: The Case for Economic Regulation. Frederick C. Thayer, Jr. LC 83-17789. 190p. 1984. text ed. 42.95 (*0-275-91750-9*, C1750, Praeger Pubs) Greenwood.

***Rebuilding America - the Self-Destructing Democracy.** limited ed. 140p. 1996. pap. 60.00 (*0-9656541-0-9*) Rebuilding Amer.

Rebuilding America's Infrastructure: An Agenda for the 1980's. Ed. by Michael Barker. LC 83-16614. (Duke Press Policy Studies). xxxv, 330p. 1983. 41.95 (*0-8223-0568-2*) Duke.

Rebuilding America's Workforce: Business Strategies to Close the Competitive Gap. William H. Kolberg & Foster C. Smith. Ed. by Cinthia Zigmund. 250p. 1991. text ed. 27.00 (*1-55623-622-0*) Irwin Prof Pubng.

Rebuilding & Tuning Fords Kent Crossflow Engine. Peter Wallage & Valerie Wallage. (Illus.). 192p. 1995. 32.95 (*1-85010-938-9*, Pub. by J H Haynes & Co UK) Motorbooks Intl.

Rebuilding Capitalism: Alternative Roads after Socialism & Dirigisme. Ed. by Andres Solimano et al. LC 93-33321. 376p. 1994. text ed. 57.50 (*0-472-10520-5*) U of Mich Pr.

Rebuilding Central Park: A Management & Restoration Plan. Elizabeth B. Rogers et al. Ed. by John Berendt. (Illus.). 176p. 1987. 37.50 (*0-262-18127-4*) MIT Pr.

Rebuilding Children's Lives: A Blueprint for Treatment Foster Parents. Christena B. Baker et al. 235p. (Orig.). 1996. pap. 19.99 (*0-938510-76-2*, 63-003) Boys Town Pr.

Rebuilding Cleveland: The Cleveland Foundation & Its Evolving Urban Strategy. Diana Tittle. (Historical Perspectives on Business Enterprise Ser.). (Illus.). 360p. 1992. text ed. 40.00 (*0-8142-0560-7*) Ohio St U Pr.

Rebuilding Communities: Experiences & Experiments in Europe. Ed. by Vithal Rajan. (Illus.). 288p. (Orig.). 1996. pap. 18.95 (*1-870098-50-1*, Pub. by Green Bks UK) Coun Oak Bks.

Rebuilding Community in America: Housing for Ecological Living, Personal Empowerment, & the New Extended Family. Ken Norwood & Kathleen Smith. (Illus.). 432p. 1994. pap. 24.50 (*0-9641346-2-4*) Shared Liv Res.

***Rebuilding Coventry.** Sue Townsend. LC 96-46812. 160p. 1997. pap. 11.00 (*1-56947-090-1*) Soho Press.

Rebuilding Downtrodden Job Market & Madhouse Society. Marvin F. Burgess. LC 95-46537. 257p. 1996. 34.00 (*1-56072-283-5*); pap. 19.50 (*1-56072-269-X*) Nova Sci Pubs.

Rebuilding Europe: Western Europe, America & Postwar Reconstruction. David W. Ellwood. 288p. (C). 1992. pap. text ed. 31.95 (*0-582-02244-4*, 79351) Longman.

Rebuilding Europe's Bombed Cities. Ed. by Jeffry M. Diefendorf. LC 88-33330. (Illus.). 288p. 1990. text ed. 45.00 (*0-312-02828-8*) St Martin.

Rebuilding Facilitators Manual: When Your Relationship Ends. Bruce Fisher & Jere Bierhaus. (Illus.). 197p. (Orig.). 1994. pap. text ed. 50.00 (*0-9607250-2-4*) Fisher Pubng.

Rebuilding God's People: Strategies for Revitalizing Declining Churches. Mike McCutcheon. LC 92-74654. 200p. (Orig.). 1993. pap. text ed. 9.99 (*0-87509-505-4*) Chr Pubns.

Rebuilding Grain Reserves: Toward an International System. Philip H. Trezise. LC 76-8911. 78p. reprint ed. pap. 25.00 (*0-317-26592-X*, 2025415) Bks Demand.

Rebuilding Inner City Communities: An Emerging National Strategy Against Urban Decay. Research & Policy Committee of the Committee for Economic Development. LC 95-1695. 1995. 18.00 (*0-87186-120-8*) Comm Econ Dev.

***Rebuilding of Bosnia.** James P. Reger. LC 96-29638. (Overview Ser.). (Illus.). (YA). (gr. 4-12). 1997. lib. bdg. 17.96 (*1-56006-190-1*) Lucent Bks.

Rebuilding of Old Commonwealths. Walter H. Page. LC 79-125175. reprint ed. 34.50 (*0-404-04859-5*) AMS Pr.

Rebuilding of Old Commonwealths: And Other Documents of Social Reform in the Progressive Era South. Ed. by William A. Link. 166p. 1996. text ed. 35.00 (*0-312-12251-9*) St Martin.

Rebuilding of Old Commonwealths: Being Essays Towards the Training of the Forgotten Man in the Southern States. Walter H. Page. (BCL1 - United States Local History Ser.). 153p. 1991. reprint ed. text ed. 69.00 (*0-7812-6293-3*) Rprt Serv.

Rebuilding of Old Commonwealth: Documents of Social Reform in the Progressive Era South. William A. Link. 160p. 1996. pap. text ed. 7.50 (*0-312-10590-8*) St Martin.

Rebuilding of Psychology. Gary Collins. 212p. 1976. pap. 9.99 (*0-8423-5315-1*) Tyndale.

Rebuilding Poland: Workers & Communists, 1945-1950. Padraic Kenney. LC 96-21388. (Illus.). 360p. 1996. 39.95 (*0-8014-3287-1*) Cornell U Pr.

Rebuilding Prairies & Forests. Natalie Goldstein. (Restoring Nature: Success Stories Ser.). (Illus.). 96p. (J). (gr. 3-6). 1994. lib. bdg. 24.70 (*0-516-05542-9*) Childrens.

Rebuilding Romania: Energy, Efficiency, & Economic Transition. Walt Patterson. 144p. (C). 1994. pap. 19.95 (*1-85383-207-3*) Brookings.

Rebuilding Russia: Toward Some Formulations. Aleksandr I. Solzhenitsyn. 96p. 1991. 14.95 (*0-374-17342-7*) FS&G.

Rebuilding Shakespeare's Globe. Andrew Gurr & John Orrell. (Illus.). 200p. 1989. 25.00 (*0-685-26528-5*) Routledge Chapman & Hall.

Rebuilding Societies after Civil War: Critical Roles for International Assistance. Ed. by Krishna Kumar. LC 96-25508. 325p. 1996. pap. text ed. 24.95 (*1-55587-652-8*, 876528); lib. bdg. 45.00 (*1-55587-642-0*, 876420) Lynne Rienner.

Rebuilding the Christian Commonwealth: New England Congregationalists & Foreign Missions, 1800-1830. John A. Andrew, III. LC 75-38214. 240p. 1976. 26.00 (*0-8131-1333-4*) U Pr of Ky.

Rebuilding the City: Property-Led Urban Regeneration. Ed. by Patsy Healey et al. LC 92-20324. 1992. write for info. (*0-442-31635-6*, E & FN Spon) Routledge Chapman & Hall.

Rebuilding the Famous Ford Flathead. Ron Bishop. 1981. pap. text ed. 10.95 (*0-07-156316-4*) McGraw.

Rebuilding the Famous Ford Flathead. Ron Bishop. (Illus.). 140p. 1981. 9.95 (*0-8306-9965-1*, 2066H); pap. 9.95 (*0-8306-2066-4*, 2066P) McGraw-Hill Prof.

***Rebuilding the Financial System in Central & Eastern Europe, 1918-1994.** Philip L. Cottrell. LC 96-40378. (European Banking History Association Ser.). 200p. 1997. text ed. 67.95 (*1-85928-413-2*, Pub. by Scolar Pr UK) Ashgate Pub Co.

***Rebuilding the Garden: Healing the Spiritual Wounds of Childhood Sexual Assault.** Karla McLaren. LC 96-95404. (Illus.). 256p. 1997. pap. 11.00 (*0-9656583-0-9*) Laughing Tree Pr.

Rebuilding the Inner City: A History of Neighborhood Initiatives to Address Poverty in the United States. Robert Halpern. LC 94-27659. 272p. 1995. 49.50 (*0-231-08114-6*); pap. 17.00 (*0-231-08115-4*) Col U Pr.

Rebuilding the Land of Israel. Garson Canaan. (Illus.). 221p. 1991. 24.50 (*0-942655-05-2*) Archit CT.

Rebuilding the Nest: A New Commitment to the American Family. Ed. by David Blankenhorn et al. LC 90-44116. 280p. 1990. pap. 20.95 (*0-87304-242-5*) Families Intl.

Rebuilding the One Church. Rene Girault. 224p. (C). 1990. 49.00 (*0-85439-425-7*, Pub. by St Paul Pubns UK) St Mut.

Rebuilding the Partnership for Public Education. Larry Kilbourne et al. 112p. (Orig.). Date not set. pap. 14.95 (*0-930388-10-0*) Comm Collaborators.

Rebuilding the Pulp & Paper Workers' Union, 1933-1941. Robert H. Zieger. LC 83-10227. (Twentieth-Century America Ser.). (Illus.). 296p. 1984. 30.00 (*0-87049-407-4*) U of Tenn Pr.

Rebuilding the Schoolhouse: Views & Issues in Education. Washington Post Writers Staff. 1993. pap. text ed. 17.95 (*0-205-15417-4*) Allyn.

Rebuilding the Temple: Tradition & Change in Modern Asia. Ralph Buultjens. LC 73-85288. 256p. reprint ed. pap. 73.00 (*0-8357-7004-4*, 2033532) Bks Demand.

Rebuilding the World. John B. Robinson. 1972. 250.00 (*0-8490-0934-0*) Gordon Pr.

***Rebuilding Therapy: Incorporating the Past for a More Effective Future.** Michael Gass. LC 96-36360. 1997. text ed. write for info. (*0-275-95329-7*, Praeger Pubs) Greenwood.

Rebuilding Workbook: When Your Relationship Ends. Bruce Fisher & Jere Bierhaus. (Illus.). 116p. (Orig.). 1994. pap. text ed. 10.00 (*0-9607250-1-6*) Fisher Pubng.

Rebuilding Your Broken World. enl. ed. Gordon MacDonald. 1988. pap. 12.99 (*0-8407-9576-9*) Nelson.

Rebuilding Your Dream: Family Life with a Disabled Child. Rhonda Krahl. (Illus.). 72p. (Orig.). 1990. pap. 5.75 (*0-87414-086-2*) U IA Pubns Dept.

***Rebus Bears.** Seymour Reit. LC 97-1367. (Bank Street Ready-To-Read Ser.). (Illus.). (J). 1997. write for info. (*0-8368-1750-8*) Gareth Stevens Inc.

Rebus Bears-Bank Street. Seymour V. Reit. 32p. (J). (ps-3). 1989. pap. 3.99 (*0-553-34689-X*) Bantam.

Rebus Book: Picture Puzzles to Tax Your Mind. Martin Greif. (Illus.). 128p. 1996. pap. 5.95 (*0-8069-3826-9*) Sterling.

Rebus Escape. Ray J. Lum. LC 91-76970. 64p. (Orig.). (J). (gr. 3-5). 1992. pap. 5.95 (*0-943864-63-1*) Davenport.

Rebus Riot. Bonnie Christensen. LC 96-7470. (J). 1997. pap. 14.99 (*0-8037-1998-1*); pap. 14.89 (*0-8037-2000-9*) Dial Bks Young.

Rebus Treasure. Jean Marzollo. 1986. 6.95 (*0-416-95530-4*) Routledge Chapman & Hall.

Rebus Treasury: Forty-Four Stories Kids Can Read by Following the Pictures. Compiled by Highlights for Children Editors. LC 90-85899. (Illus.). 48p. (J). (ps-2). 1991. 9.95 (*1-878093-23-1*) Boyds Mills Pr.

Rebus Treasury 2: Forty-Four Stories Kids Can Read by Following the Pictures. Highlights for Children Editors. LC 92-75882. (Illus.). 48p. (Orig.). (J). (ps-2). 1993. pap. 4.95 (*1-56397-063-5*) Boyds Mills Pr.

Rebuses for Readers. Pat Martin et al. ix, 138p. 1992. pap. text ed. 18.00 (*0-87287-920-8*) Teacher Ideas Pr.

Rec Tiles: A Geometric Introduction to Algebra. Nicholas Branca. 48p. (J). (gr. 5-9). 1991. pap. text ed. 25.95 (*0-938587-19-6*) Cuisenaire.

Recados de Mama. Lynn Salem & Josie Stewart. Tr. by Mariana Robles. (Illus.). 16p. (J). (gr. k-1). 1994. pap. 3.50 (*1-880612-22-4*) Seedling Pubns.

Recalcitrance, Faulkner, & the Professors: A Critical Fiction. Austin M. Wright. LC 90-32909. (Illus.). 260p. (C). 1990. pap. 16.95 (*0-87745-301-2*); text ed. 29.95 (*0-87745-285-7*) U of Iowa Pr.

Recalcitrant Rich: A Comparative Analysis of the Northern Responses to the Demands for a New International Economic Order. Ed. by Helge O. Bergesen et al. LC 81-9127. 1982. text ed. 29.95 (*0-312-66573-3*) St Martin.

Recall. (Illus.). 248p. (Orig.). 1995. pap. 14.95 (*0-9652882-0-X*) A & L Walker.

Recall: Activities for Word Retrieval. Linda B. Collins. 1991. 45.00 (*0-937857-20-3*, 1591) Speech Bin.

***Recall: Tribunal of the People.** Joseph F. Zimmerman. LC 97-9179. 1997. text ed. write for info. (*0-275-96008-0*, Praeger Pubs) Greenwood.

Recall & Recognition. Ed. by John Brown. 285p. reprint ed. pap. 81.30 (*0-685-20327-1*, 2052240) Bks Demand.

Recall to Oz. Michelle Van Loon. 1984. pap. 1.75 (*0-912963-07-7*) Eldridge Pub.

Recalled by Life. Anthony J. Sattilaro & Tom Monte. 240p. 1994. mass mkt. 5.99 (*0-380-65573-X*) Avon.

Recalled to Life. Reginald Hill. 400p. 1993. mass mkt. 4.99 (*0-440-21573-0*) Dell.

Recalling August. H. R. Coursen. LC 95-2044. 56p. pap. 10.00 (*1-880664-11-9*) E M Pr.

Recalling Details. Sheldon L. Tilkin & Judith Conoway. (Horizons F Ser.). (Illus.). 24p. (J). (gr. 4-5). 1980. student ed., pap. 3.95 (*0-89403-578-9*) EDC.

Recalling Details. Sheldon L. Tilkin. (Horizons E Ser.). (Illus.). 24p. (J). (gr. 4-5). 1980. student ed., pap. 3.95 (*0-89403-568-1*) EDC.

Recalling Great Events in Sports. Don Clerkin. (Illus.). 112p. (Orig.). 1990. pap. 12.95 (*0-9627494-1-9*) D Clerkin.

Recalling Great Events in Sports. rev. ed. Don Clerkin. (Illus.). 112p. (Orig.). 1992. pap. 5.95 (*0-9627494-4-3*) D Clerkin.

***Recalling Our Own Stories: Spiritual Renewal for Religious Caregivers.** Edward P. Wimberly. 1997. pap. text ed. 14.95 (*0-7879-0363-9*) Jossey-Bass.

Recalling Past Lives. Carl R. Green & William R. Sanford. LC 93-74. (Illus.). 48p. (J). (gr. 4-10). 1993. lib. bdg. 14.95 (*0-89490-458-2*) Enslow Pubs.

Recalling the Good Fight: An Autobiography of the Spanish Civil War. John Tisa & Milton Wolff. (Illus.). 256p. 1985. text ed. 39.95 (*0-89789-078-7*, Bergin & Garvey); pap. text ed. 16.95 (*0-89789-079-5*, Bergin & Garvey) Greenwood.

Recalling the Revolution: Memoirs of a Filipino General. Santiago V. Alvarez. Tr. by Paula C. Malay. LC 92-71216. 280p. (Orig.). (C). 1992. pap. 14.95 (*1-881261-05-0*) U Wisc Ctr SE Asian.

Recalling Your Memories on Paper, Tape or Videotape: How to Preserve Valuable Memoirs for Your Family or the Public. Margaret G. Bigger. LC 96-84100. (Illus.). 160p. (Orig.). 1996. pap. 13.95 (*0-9640606-4-7*) A Borough Bks.

Recapitulation. Wallace Stegner. 1980. pap. 2.50 (*0-449-24263-3*, Crest) Fawcett.

***Recapitulation.** Wallace Stegner. 1997. pap. 11.95 (*0-14-026673-9*) Viking Penguin.

Recapitulation. Wallace Stegner. LC 85-20961. vi, 280p. 1986. reprint ed. pap. 9.95 (*0-8032-9165-5*, Bison Books) U of Nebr Pr.

Recapitulation, 1610-1700 see History of French Dramatic Literature in the Seventeenth Century

Recapitulations: Essays in Philosophy. Thomas Prufer. LC 91-44978. (Studies in Philosophy & the History of Philosophy: Vol. 26). 112p. 1993. 34.95 (*0-8132-0764-9*) Cath U Pr.

Recapture of Guam. O. R. Lodge. reprint ed. pap. 12.00 (*0-915266-16-4*) Awani Pr.

Recapture of Guam. O. R. Lodge. (Elite Unit Ser.: No. 28). (Illus.). 248p. 1991. reprint ed. 32.50 (*0-89839-160-1*) Battery Pr.

Recapturing Anthropology: Working in the Present. Ed. by Richard G. Fox. LC 91-26724. (Advanced Seminar Ser.). 248p. (Orig.). 1991. 35.00 (*0-933452-77-2*); pap. 15.95 (*0-933452-78-0*) Schol Am Res.

Recapturing Biblical Intercession: A Manual on Prayer for the Serious Intercessor. 2nd ed. Robert Finley. 159p. (C). 1985. reprint ed. pap. 10.00 (*0-9614569-0-6*) Prayer Resources.

Recapturing Competence: A System's Change for Geropsychiatric Care. Gail S. Fidler. LC 91-4998. 160p. 1991. 27.95 (*0-8261-7760-3*) Springer Pub.

Recapturing Marxism: An Appraisal of Recent Trends in Sociological Theory. Ed. by Rhonda F. Levine & Jerry Lembeke. LC 87-11589. 264p. 1987. text ed. 59.95 (*0-275-92576-5*, C2576, Praeger Pubs); pap. text ed. 14.95 (*0-275-92638-9*, B2638, Praeger Pubs) Greenwood.

Recapturing the Constitution. Stephen B. Presser. 416p. 1994. 24.95 (*0-89526-492-7*) Regnery Pub.

***Recapturing the Renaissance: New Perspectives on Humanism, Dialogue & Texts.** Ed. by Paul A. Miller & Diane S. Wood. 224p. (Orig.). 1996. pap. text ed. 22.95 (*1-886935-14-9*) New Prdigm Pr.

Recapturing the Spirit: Essays on the Bill of Rights at 200. Eric Neisser. 291p. 1991. 19.95 (*0-945612-22-2*); pap. text ed. 12.95 (*0-945612-23-0*) Madison Hse.

Recapturing the Spirit of Enterprise. George Gilder. 340p. 1992. reprint ed. pap. 19.95 (*1-55815-201-6*) ICS Pr.

Recasting: "Gone with the Wind" in American Culture. Ed. by Darden A. Pyron. LC 82-20310. 242p. 1983. pap. 34.95 (*0-8130-0747-X*) U Press Fla.

Recasting America: Culture & Politics in the Age of Cold War. Ed. by Larry May. LC 88-21618. (Illus.). 320p. 1988. pap. text ed. 17.95 (*0-226-51176-6*) U Ch Pr.

Recasting America: Culture & Politics in the Age of Cold War. Ed. by Larry May. LC 88-21618. (Illus.). 320p. 1989. lib. bdg. 60.00 (*0-226-51175-8*) U Ch Pr.

Recasting Ancient Egypt in the African Context. Clinton Crawford. 200p. 1995. pap. text ed. 18.95 (*0-86543-381-X*) Africa World.

Recasting Ancient Egypt in the African Context: Toward a Model Curriculum Using Art & Language. Clinton Crawford. LC 95-51262. 200p. 1996. 59.95 (*0-86543-380-1*) Africa World.

Recasting Autobiography: Women's Counterfictions in Contemporary German Literature & Film. Barbara Kosta. (Reading Women Writing Ser.). (Illus.). 232p. 1994. 37.50 (*0-8014-2889-0*); pap. 14.95 (*0-8014-8203-8*) Cornell U Pr.

Recasting Bourgeois Europe: Stabilization in France, Germany, & Italy in the Decade After World War One. Charles S. Maier. LC 73-2488. 700p. 1988. pap. text ed. 26.95 (*0-691-10025-X*) Princeton U Pr.

Recasting Conservatism: Michael Oakeshott, Leo Strauss, & Conservative Political Thought's Response to Postmodernism. Robert Devigne. LC 93-29941. 256p. 1994. 35.00 (*0-300-05594-3*) Yale U Pr.

Recasting Conservatism: Oakeshott, Strauss & the Response to Postmodernism. Robert Devigne. 1996. pap. 16.00 (*0-300-06868-9*) Yale U Pr.

Recasting Europe's Economies: National Strategies in the 1980s. Ed. by David P. Calleo & Claudia Morgenstern. 228p. (C). 1990. pap. text ed. 23.50 (*0-8191-7651-6*); lib. bdg. 42.00 (*0-8191-7650-8*) U Pr of Amer.

Recasting Persian Poetry: Scenarios of Poetic Modernity in Iran. Ahmad Karimi-Hakkak. 325p. 1996. text ed. 45.00 (*0-87480-492-2*) U of Utah Pr.

Recasting Social Values in the Work of Virginia Woolf. Judy S. Reese. LC 95-37374. 168p. 1996. 29.50 (*0-945636-83-0*) Susquehanna U Pr.

Recasting the European Order: Security Architectures & Economic Cooperation. James Sperling & Emil J. Kirchner. LC 96-25061. (Europe in Change Ser.). 1997. text ed. 69.95 (*0-7190-3986-X*, Pub. by Manchester Univ Pr UK); text ed. 22.95 (*0-7190-3987-8*, Pub. by Manchester Univ Pr UK) St Martin.

Recasting the Imperial Far East: Britain & America in China, 1945-1950. Lanxin Xiang. LC 94-30256. 272p. (C). (gr. 13). 1995. 69.95 (*1-56324-459-4*, East Gate Bk); pap. 26.95 (*1-56324-460-8*, East Gate Bk) M E Sharpe.

Recasting the Ruhr, 1945-1958: Manpower, Economic Recovery & Labour Relations. Mark Roseman. (Illus.). 370p. 1992. 29.95 (*0-85496-606-4*) Berg Pubs.

Recasting the Text: Inquiry-Based Activities for Comprehending & Composing. Fran Claggett et al. 192p. 1996. pap. text ed. 19.50 (*0-86709-402-8*, 0402) Boynton Cook Pubs.

Recasting the World: Writing after Colonialism. Ed. by Jonathan White. LC 93-22456. (Parallax). 304p. (C). 1993. text ed. 45.00 (*0-8018-4605-6*); pap. text ed. 15.95 (*0-8018-4606-4*) Johns Hopkins.

Recasting Women in India: Essays in Colonial History. Ed. by Kumkum Sangari & Sudesh Vaid. LC 90-30892. 372p. (C). 1990. text ed. 42.00 (*0-8135-1579-3*); pap. text ed. 19.95 (*0-8135-1580-7*) Rutgers U Pr.

Receded Tides of Empire: Aspects of the Economic & Social History of Natal & Zululand since 1910. Ed. by Bill Guest & John M. Sellers. 332p. 1994. pap. 26.95 (*0-86980-891-5*) Intl Spec Bk.

Receding Frontier: Aspects of the Internationalization of U. S.-Mexican Agriculture & Their Implications for Bilateral Relations in the 1980s. Steven E. Sanderson. (Research Reports: No. 15). 44p. (Orig.). (C). 1981. pap. 5.00 (*0-935391-14-2*, RR-15) UCSD Ctr US-Mex.

Receipts of Pastry & Cookery: For the Use of His Scholars. Edward Kidder. Ed. by David E. Schoonover. LC 92-45739. (Iowa Szathmary Culinary Arts Ser.). (Illus.). 192p. 1993. 22.95 (*0-87745-410-8*) U of Iowa Pr.

Receive All God Has to Give. Katie Fortune. (Booklet Ser.). 32p. 1971. pap. 1.25 (*0-930756-00-2*, 542001) Aglow Communs.

***Receive Miracle Healing.** T. L. Osborn & Daisy Osborn. Date not set. pap. 8.99 (*0-89274-221-6*) Harrison Hse.

***Receive Miracle Healing.** 2nd ed. T. L. Osborn. (Illus.). (Orig.). (RUS.). 1995. mass mkt. write for info. (*1-890863-08-4*) Wrld Wide Print.

***Receive the Gift.** Louise Marley. 304p. 1997. mass mkt. 5.99 (*0-441-00486-5*) Ace Bks.

Receive the Holy Spirit. Arlo F. Newell. 1984. pap. 3.95 (*0-87162-409-5*, D6431) Warner Pr.

Received Truths: Bertolt Brecht & the Problem of Gestus & Musical Meaning. Kenneth Fowler. LC 89-29125. (Studies in German Literature & Culture: No. 1). 1991. 29.50 (*0-404-64051-6*) AMS Pr.

Received Wisdom? Reviewing the Role of Tradition in Christian Ethics. Bernard Hoose. 1995. pap. 19.95 (*0-225-66739-8*, Pub. by Geoffrey Chapman UK) Morehouse Pub.

Receivers Handbook for Insurance Company Insolvencies. 435p. (C). 1992. ring bd. 250.00 (*0-89382-218-3*) Nat Assn Insurance.

Receivers Handbook for Insurance Company Insolvencies. 1996. ring bd. 75.00 (*0-89382-381-3*, REC-BU95) Nat Assn Insurance.

Receivers Handbook for Insurance Company Insolvencies. annuals 660p. (C). 1994. ring bd. 250.00 (*0-89382-307-4*) Nat Assn Insurance.

***Receivers Handbook for Insurance Company Insolvencies.** 2nd rev. ed. Michael Surguine. 744p. (C). 1996. ring bd. 275.00 (*0-89382-403-8*, REC-BM) Nat Assn Insurance.

Receiving a Gift & Giving It Back. Jude LaClaire. (Life Weaving Ser.: Vol. 5). (Illus.). 64p. 1995. spiral bd. 9.95 (*0-9629385-5-6*) Heartlnd Personal.

***Receiving a Prophet.** Kristin Plummer & Clive E. Neil. 110p. (Orig.). 1996. pap. 9.99 (*1-889389-04-8*) End-Time Wave.

Receiving Answers to Our Prayers. Gene R. Cook. LC 96-21309. 128p. 1996. 14.95 (*0-87579-803-9*) Deseret Bk.

Receiving Answers to Prayer. Blaine M. Yorgason & Brenton Yorgason. (Gospel Power Ser.). 51p. (Orig.). (C). 1989. pap. text ed. 3.95 (*0-929985-25-7*) Jackman Pubng.

Receiving-Checking-Marking-Stocking Clerk. 2nd ed. Carol G. Moffett & Rebecca Strydesky. (Illus.). 160p. (YA). (gr. 10-12). 1980. text ed. 13.32 (*0-07-042667-8*) McGraw.

Receiving Divine Revelation. Fuchsia Pickett. 180p. (Orig.). 1997. pap. 10.99 (*0-88419-441-8*) Creation House.

Receiving Gifts: Issues in Ecumenism. Margaret O'Gara. (Orig.). 1998. pap. write for info. (*0-8146-5858-X*) Liturgical Pr.

Receiving His Blessing, Giving His Love. Roy Lessin. 96p. 1993. pap. 5.95 (*1-884009-02-6*) DaySpring.

Receiving Holy Communion. Lawrence G. Lovasik. (Saint Joseph Picture Bks.). (Illus.). 1991. pap. text ed. 1.25 (*0-89942-491-0*, 491-00) Catholic Bk Pub.

***Receiving Holy Communion.** Lawrence G. Lovasik. (Saint Joseph Beginner Ser.). (Illus.). (J). 1992. 3.25 (*0-89942-221-7*, 221/22) Catholic Bk Pub.

Receiving Love. Joseph Biuso & Brian Newman. 240p. 1996. 16.99 (*1-56476-539-3*, 6-3539, Victor Bks) Chariot Victor.

***Receiving Power.** Carol Heiden. Orig. Title: Why Speak in Tongues & Prophesy. 186p. 1974. mass mkt. 4.99 (*0-88368-398-9*) Whitaker Hse.

Receiving Resurrection Power! Marilyn Hickey. (Orig.). pap. 1.00 (*1-56441-163-X*) M Hickey Min.

Receiving Righteousness from Jesus: Romans. Linda R. McGinn. (Women in the Word Ser.). 112p. (gr. 10). 1996. pap. 4.99 (*0-8010-5043-X*) Baker Bks.

Receiving Righteousness from Jesus Leaders Guide: Romans. Linda R. McGinn. (Women in the Word Ser.). 112p. (YA). (gr. 10). 1996. teacher ed., pap. 7.99 (*0-8010-5717-5*) Baker Bks.

Receiving Soren Kierkegaard: The Early Impact & Transmission of His Thought. Habib C. Malik. LC 96-23905. 439p. (C). 1997. text ed. 59.95 (*0-8132-0878-5*) Cath U Pr.

Receiving Systems Design. Stephen J. Erst. LC 84-70222. 241p. reprint ed. pap. 68.70 (*0-7837-1335-5*, 2041483) Bks Demand.

***Receiving the Anointing of the Spirit.** Larry Keefauver. 1997. pap. 5.99 (*0-88419-475-2*) Creation House.

Receiving the Power: Preparing the Way for the Holy Spirit. Zeb B. Long & Douglas McMurry. LC 96-8075. 240p. (gr. 10). 1996. pap. 13.99 (*0-8007-9246-7*) Chosen Bks.

Receiving the Vision: The Anglican-Roman Catholic Reality Today. David Bird et al. 184p. (Orig.). 1995. pap. 14.95 (*0-8146-2173-2*, Liturg Pr Bks) Liturgical Pr.

***Receiving the Word: How New Approaches to the Bible Impact Our Biblical Faith & Lifestyle.** LC 96-95095. 368p. (Orig.). 1996. pap. 10.95 (*1-890014-00-1*) Berean Bks.

Receiving Woman: Studies in the Psychology & Theology of the Feminine. Ann B. Ulanov. LC 80-26813. 186p. (C). 1981. pap. 12.00 (*0-664-24360-6*, Westminster) Westminster John Knox.

Receiving Your Healing by Faith. Leonard Farrar. 32p. 1987. pap. 0.75 (*0-88144-096-5*) Christian Pub.

***Recemos el Santo Rosario.** J. M. Lelen. (Illus.). (SPA.). 1978. pap. 0.90 (*0-89942-048-6*, 48S) Catholic Bk Pub.

Recensements de la Nouvelle-France (Quebec Censuses, 1666 & 1667) 33p. (FRE.). 1985. reprint ed. pap. 4.50 (*0-935207-20-1*) Danbury Hse Bks.

Recensions of the Naganandа by Haesadeva, Vol. 1. Ed. by Madhava C. Ghosa. (C). 1991. 17.50 (*81-85179-72-7*, Pub. by Aditya Prakashan II) S Asia.

Recent Advance in Zeolite Science: Proceedings of the Meeting of the British Zeolite Association, Cambridge, U. K., April 17-19, 1989. Ed. by Jacek Klinowski & P. J. Barrie. (Studies in Surface Science & Catalysis: No. 52). 310p. 1990. 227.00 (*0-444-88129-8*) Elsevier.

Recent Advances & Future Directions in Bone Marrow Transplantation. Ed. by S. J. Baum et al. (Experimental Hematology Today 1987 Ser.). (Illus.). xxiii, 200p. 1987. 108.00 (*0-387-96582-3*) Spr-Verlag.

Recent Advances & Historical Development of Vector Optimization. Ed. by J. Jahn & W. Krabs. (Lecture Notes in Economics & Mathematical Systems Ser.: Col. 294). vii, 405p. 1987. 54.95 (*0-387-18215-2*) Spr-Verlag.

Recent Advances & New Developments in Hemostaseology: Abstracts. Ed. by H. K. Breddin et al. (Journal: Haemostasis: Vol. 16, Suppl. 5, 1986). iv, 148p. 1986. pap. 36.00 (*3-8055-4505-3*) S Karger.

Recent Advances & New Horizons in Zeolite Science & Technology. Ed. by H. Chon et al. LC 96-22634. (Studies in Surface Science & Catalysis: Vol. 102). 484p. 1996. text ed. 262.50 (*0-444-82499-5*) Elsevier.

Recent Advances & New Syndromes. Ed. by Robert Summit & Daniel Bergsma. (Alan R. Liss, Inc. Ser.: Vol. 14, No. 6B). 1978. 55.00 (*0-686-23950-4*) March of Dimes.

Recent Advances in Adaptive & Sensory Materials & Their Applications. C. A. Rogers & R. C. Rogers. LC 92-80289. 850p. 1992. text ed. 149.95 (*0-87762-947-1*) Technomic.

Recent Advances in Aerospace Medicine: Proceedings of the International Congress of Aviation & Space Medicine, 18th, Amdersterdam, 1969. International Congress of Aviation & Space Medicine Staff. Ed. by D. E. Busby. LC 74-131264. 358p. 1970. lib. bdg. 100.50 (*90-277-0162-8*) Kluwer Ac.

***Recent Advances in Agricultural Health & Safety.** Kelly J. Donham & Risto Rautiainen. LC 97-20493. (Journal of Agromedicine Ser.: Vol. 4, Nos. 1/2/3/4). 523p. 1997. 89.95 (*0-7890-0312-0*) Haworth Pr.

Recent Advances in AIDS & Kaposi's Sarcoma. Ed. by G. Giraldo et al. (Antibiotics & Chemotherapy Ser.: Vol. 38). (Illus.). vii, 196p. 1987. 136.00 (*3-8055-4512-6*) S Karger.

Recent Advances in Anaerobic Bacteriology. Ed. by S. P. Borriello & J. M. Hardie. (New Perspectives in Clinical Microbiology Ser.). 1986. lib. bdg. 171.00 (*0-89838-847-3*) Kluwer Ac.

Recent Advances in Anaesthesia & Analgesia, Vol. 18. Ed. by R. S. Atkinson & A. P. Adams. (Illus.). 196p. 1993. pap. 53.00 (*0-443-04849-5*) Churchill.

Recent Advances in Anaesthesia & Analgesia 17. Ed. by R. S. Atkinson & A. P. Adams. (Illus.). 202p. (Orig.). 1992. pap. text ed. 49.95 (*0-443-04456-2*) Churchill.

Recent Advances in Analysis of Heat Transfer for Fintype Surfaces. Ed. by B. Sunden. (Developments in Heat Transfer Ser.). 300p. 1997. text ed. 138.00 (*1-85312-449-4*, 4494) Computational Mech MA.

Recent Advances in Animal Nutrition - 1977: Proceedings of the Nutrition Conference for Feed Manufacturers, 11th, University of Nottingham, 1977. Nutrition Conference for Feed Manufacturers Staff et al. LC 77-30256. (Studies in the Agricultural & Food Sciences). 214p. reprint ed. pap. 61.00 (*0-317-41858-0*, 2025738) Bks Demand.

Recent Advances in Animal Nutrition - 1989. Haresign. 298p. 1989. 175.00 (*0-408-04149-8*) Buttrwrth-Heinemann.

Recent Advances in Animal Nutrition 1990. W. Haresign & D. J. Cole. (Illus.). 270p. 1990. 92.95 (*0-408-04150-1*) Buttrwrth-Heinemann.

Recent Advances in Animal Nutrition, 1991. D. J. Cole & W. Haresign. 256p. 1991. 125.00 (*0-7506-1397-1*) Buttrwrth-Heinemann.

Recent Advances in Animal Nutrition, 1992: Proceedings from the 26th University of Nottingham Feed Manufacturer's Conference. Ed. by W. Haresign & D. J. Cole. (Illus.). 256p. 1992. 155.00 (*0-7506-0714-9*) Buttrwrth-Heinemann.

Recent Advances in Basic Microcirculatory Research: Proceedings, Pt. 1. Conference of the European Society for Microcirculation, 9th, Antwerp, July 5-9, 1976. Ed. by G. Wolf-Heidegger & D. H. Lewis. (Bibliotheca Anatomica Ser.: No. 15). (Illus.). 1977. 158.50 (*3-8055-2757-8*) S Karger.

Recent Advances in Basic Microcirculatory Research: Proceedings, Pt. 2. Conference of the European Society for Microcirculation, 9th, Antwerp, July 5-9, 1976. Ed. by G. Wolf-Heidegger & D. H. Lewis. (Bibliotheca Anatomica Ser.: No. 16). (Illus.). 1977. 158.50 (*3-8055-2758-6*) S Karger.

Recent Advances in Beta Blockade 1986. Ed. by Shaul G. Massry et al. (Journal, American Journal of Nephrology: Vol. 6, Suppl. 2). (Illus.). iv, 116p. 1986. pap. 33.75 (*3-8055-4442-1*) S Karger.

Recent Advances in Bile Acid Research. Ed. by Luigi Barbara et al. LC 85-25797. (Illus.). 347p. 1985. reprint ed. pap. 98.90 (*0-7837-9557-2*, 2060306) Bks Demand.

Recent Advances in Biochemistry of Fruits & Vegetables. Ed. by John Friend. (Phytochemical Society of Europe Symposia Ser.: No. 18). 1982. text ed. 99.00 (*0-12-268420-6*) Acad Pr.

Recent Advances in Biological Psychiatry. Incl. Vol. 4. Proceedings of the Annual Convention & Scientific Program of the Society of Biological Psychiatry, 16th, Atlantic City, NJ, June 9-11, 1961. LC 58-14190. pap. 99.80 (*0-317-28463-0*); Vol. 5. Proceedings of the Annual Convention & Scientific Program of the Society of Biological Psychiatry, 17th, Toronto, Ontario, May 4-6, 1962. LC 58-14190. pap. 98.50 (*0-317-28464-9*); Vol. 8. Proceedings of the Annual Convention & Scientific Program of the Society of Biological Psychiatry, 20th, New York City, April 30 - May 2, 1965. LC 58-14190. pap. 95.30 (*0-317-28465-7*); Vol. 10. Proceedings of the Annual Convention & Scientific Program of the Society of Biological Psychiatry, 22nd, Detroit, Michigan, May 5-7, 1967. LC 58-14190. pap. 86.00 (*0-317-28466-5*); LC 58-14190. reprint ed. write for info. (*0-318-59359-9*, 2020716) Bks Demand.

Recent Advances in Biological Psychiatry, 2 vols., Vol. 6. Society of Biological Psychiatry Staff. Ed. by Joseph Mortis. LC 58-14190. 1963. pap. 71.00 (*0-317-10483-7*, 2003369) Bks Demand.

Recent Advances in Biological Psychiatry, 2 vols., Vol. 7. Society of Biological Psychiatry Staff. Ed. by Joseph Mortis. LC 58-14190. 1964. pap. 78.00 (*0-317-10484-5*) Bks Demand.

Recent Advances in Biological Psychiatry, Vol. 9. Ed. by Joseph Wortis. LC 58-14190. 389p. reprint ed. pap. 110.90 (*0-685-15827-6*, 2026306) Bks Demand.

***Recent Advances in Biomedical Imaging: Proceedings of the International Workshop on Biomedical Imaging: MR & Pet Spect, Fukui, Japan, 28-30 August 1996.** Ishii, Yasushi, Workshop on Biomedical Imaging: MR & Pet/Spect Staff. LC 97-12193. (International Congress Ser.). 1997. write for info. (*0-444-82539-8*) Elsevier.

Recent Advances in Biophoton Research & Its Applications. Ed. by Fritz-Albert Popp. 300p. 1992. text ed. 98.00 (*981-02-0855-3*) World Scientific Pub.

Recent Advances in Biotechnology: Proceedings of the NATO Advanced Study Institute on Recent Advances in Industrial Applications of Biotechnology, Kusadasi, Turkey, 16-27 September. Ed. by Fazilet Vardar-Sukan. 580p. (C). 1992. lib. bdg. 220.00 (*0-7923-1632-0*) Kluwer Ac.

Recent Advances in Blood Coagulation, No. 5. Ed. by L. Poller. (Illus.). 312p. 1991. text ed. 75.00 (*0-443-04343-4*) Churchill.

Recent Advances in Blood Coagulation, No. 6. Ed. by L. Poller. (Illus.). 228p. 1993. text ed. 65.95 (*0-443-04755-3*) Churchill.

Recent Advances in Botany. P. Kachroo. 407p. 1976. 175.00 (*0-685-21840-6*, Pub. by Intl Bk Distr II) St Mut.

Recent Advances in Botany. P. Kachroo. 105p. (C). 1976. text ed. 275.00 (*0-89771-558-6*, Pub. by Intl Bk Distr II) St Mut.

Recent Advances in Brain Tumor Research. Ed. by W. G. Bingham. (Progress in Experimental Tumor Research Ser.: Vol. 17). 1972. 112.00 (*3-8055-1402-6*) S Karger.

Recent Advances in Burns & Plastic Surgery: The Chinese Experience. Ed. by Tishen Chang et al. 1985. lib. bdg. 369.00 (*0-85200-814-7*) Kluwer Ac.

Recent Advances in Calcium Channels & Calcium Antagonists. K. Yamada & S. Shibata. 1990. text ed. 42.50 (*0-07-105336-0*) McGraw.

Recent Advances in Canadian Neuropsychopharmacology. Ed. by P. Grof & B. Saxena. x, 238p. 1981. pap. 78.50 (*3-8055-1459-X*) S Karger.

***Recent Advances in Cardiac Pacing: Goals for the 21st Century.** S. Serge Barold & Jacques Mugica. (Cardiostim Monograph Ser.). (Illus.). 352p. 1997. write for info. (*0-87993-639-8*) Futura Pub.

Recent Advances in Cardiology - Eleven. Ed. by Derek J. Rowlands. (Illus.). 224p. (Orig.). 1993. pap. text ed. 79.95 (*0-443-04565-8*) Churchill.

Recent Advances in Carotid Chemotransduction. Ed. by S. J. Fidone. (Journal Ser.: Vol. 4, No. 5, 1995). (Illus.). 70p. 1996. pap. 31.50 (*3-8055-6268-3*) S Karger.

Recent Advances in Cell Biology of Acute Leukemia: Impact on Clinical Diagnosis & Therapy. Ed. by W. D. Ludwig & E. Thiel. LC 93-16157. (Recent Results in Cancer Research Ser.: Vol. 131). 1993. 150.00 (*0-387-56417-9*) Spr-Verlag.

Recent Advances in Cellular & Molecular Aspects of Angiotensin Receptors, Vol. 396. Ed. by Mohan K. Raizada et al. (Advances in Experimental Medicine & Biology Ser.: Vol. 396). (Illus.). 275p. (C). 1996. 85.00 (*0-306-45209-X*, Plenum Pr) Plenum.

Recent Advances in Cervical Pathology & Colposcopy. L. Carenza et al. (Advances in Gynecological & Obstetric Research Ser.: Vol. 3). (Illus.). 600p. 1993. 98.00 (*1-85070-375-2*) Prthnon Pub.

Recent Advances in Chemical Information 2. Ed. by H. Collier. 322p. 1989. 22.95 (*0-85186-235-7*) CRC Pr.

Recent Advances in Chemistry of B-Lactam Antibiotics, No. 38. 2nd ed. Royal Society of Chemistry Staff. 1989. 46.00 (*0-85186-815-0*) CRC Pr.

Recent Advances in Chemistry of B-Lactam Antibiotics, No. 52. 3rd ed. Brown. 1988. 122.00 (*0-85186-955-6*) CRC Pr.

Recent Advances in Chemistry of B-Lactam Technology, No. 28. Royal Society of Chemistry Staff. 1989. 65.00 (*0-85186-198-9*) CRC Pr.

Recent Advances in Chemotherapy: Proceedings of the 18th International Congress of Chemotherapy, Stockholm, Sweden, June 27-July 2, 1993. Ed. by Jerzy Einhorn et al. LC 94-6905. 1120p. 1994. 96.00 (*1-55581-074-8*) Am Soc Microbio.

Recent Advances in Chiral Separations. Ed. by D. Stevenson & I. D. Wilson. LC 90-29055. (Chromatographic Society Symposium Ser.). (Illus.). 224p. 1991. 75.00 (*0-306-43836-4*, Plenum Pr) Plenum.

Recent Advances in Clinical Neurology, No. 6. Ed. by Christopher Kennard. (Illus.). 276p. 1990. text ed. 59.00 (*0-443-04116-4*) Churchill.

Recent Advances in Clinical Neurology - 7. Christopher Kennard. (Illus.). 224p. (Orig.). 1993. text ed. 82.00 (*0-443-04570-4*) Churchill.

Recent Advances in Clinical Neurophysiology: Proceedings of the Xth International Congress of EMG & Clinical Neurophysiology, Kyoto, Japan, 15-19 October 1995. Ed. by Jun L. Kimura & Hiroshi Shibasaki. LC 96-23426. (International Congress Ser.). 1062p. 1996. 328.25 (*0-444-82297-6*) Elsevier.

Recent Advances in Clinical Psychiatry - 8. Ed. by Kenneth Granville-Grossman. (Illus.). 224p. 1993. text ed. 72.00 (*0-443-04696-4*) Churchill.

Recent Advances in Clinical Psychiatry 7. Ed. by Kenneth L. Granville-Grossman. (Illus.). 200p. 1991. text ed. 48.00 (*0-443-04499-6*) Churchill.

Recent Advances in Clinical Trial Design and Analysis. Peter F. Thall. LC 94-41111. (Cancer Treatment & Research Ser.: No. 75). 272p. (C). 1995. lib. bdg. 175.00 (*0-7923-3235-0*) Kluwer Ac.

Recent Advances in Clinical Virology. Gueh-Djen Hsiung. LC 80-25926. 128p. 1981. text ed. 45.00 (*0-275-90647-7*, C0647, Praeger Pubs) Greenwood.

Recent Advances in Coal Geochemistry. Ed. by L. L. Chyi & C. L. Chou. (Special Papers: No. 248). (Illus.). 112p. 1990. pap. 11.00 (*0-8137-2248-9*) Geol Soc.

Recent Advances in Coated Steels Used for Automobile. Koji Yamakawa & Hisao Fujikawa. LC 96-26740. (Current Japanese Materials Research Ser.). 192p. 1996. 126.75 (*0-444-82513-4*) Elsevier.

Recent Advances in Cognitive-Developmental Theory, Progress in Cognitive Developmental Research. Ed. by Charles J. Brainerd. (Cognitive Development Ser.). (Illus.). 270p. 1983. 94.95 (*0-387-90767-X*) Spr-Verlag.

Recent Advances in Combustion Modelling. Ed. by Bernard Larrouturou. (Series on Advances in Mathematics for Applied Sciences: Vol. 6). 240p. 1990. text ed. 84.00 (*981-02-0380-2*) World Scientific Pub.

Recent Advances in Communication & Control Theory. Ed. by R. E. Kalman et al. LC 97-18604. 500p. 1987. text ed. 82.00 (*0-911575-46-4*) Optimization Soft.

Recent Advances in Composites in the United States & Japan: A Symposium. American Society for Testing & Materials Staff. Ed. by Jack R. Vinson & Minoru Taya. LC 85-6119. (ASTM Special Technical Publication Ser.: No. 864). (Illus.). 739p. reprint ed. pap. 180.00 (*0-7837-4787-X*, 2044824) Bks Demand.

R

An Asterisk (*) at the beginning of an entry indicates that the title is appearing in BIP for the first time.

R

Recent Advances in Computer-Aided Control Systems Engineering. Ed. by Mohammad Jamshidi & C. J. Herget. LC 92-30695. (Studies in Automation & Control: Vol. 9). 456p. 1992. 214.25 (*0-444-89255-9*) Elsevier.

Recent Advances in Connective Tissue Research. Ed. by Peter Ghosh. (Agents & Actions Supplements Ser.: Vol. 18). 160p. 1986. 55.50 (*0-8176-1775-2*, Pub. by Birkhauser Vlg SZ) Birkhauser.

Recent Advances in Control & Optimization of Manufacturing Systems, Vol. 214. George Yin & Qing Zhang. LC 96-287. (Lecture Notes in Control & Information Sciences). 229p. 1996. pap. 54.00 (*3-540-76055-5*) Spr-Verlag.

Recent Advances in Coronary Circulation. Ed. by E. Maruyama et al. 1994. 199.00 (*0-387-70130-3*) Spr-Verlag.

Recent Advances in Corporate Finance. Ed. by Jeremy Edwards et al. 320p. 1986. text ed. 64.95 (*0-521-32964-7*) Cambridge U Pr.

***Recent Advances in Coupled-Cluster Methods.** Rodney J. Bartlett. LC 97-6030. (Recent Advances in Computational Chemistry Ser.). 1997. write for info. (*981-02-3112-1*) World Scientific Pub.

Recent Advances in Creep & Fracture of Engineering Materials & Structures. Ed. by B. Wilshire & D. R. Owen. 353p. 1982. text ed. 63.00 (*0-906674-18-2*, Pub. by Inst Materials UK) Ashgate Pub Co.

Recent Advances in Critical Microcirculatory Research: Proceedings of the European Conference on Microcirculation, 8th le Touguet, 1974. European Conference on Microcirculation Staff. Ed. by D. H. Lewis. (Bibliotheca Anatomica Ser.: No. 13). (Illus.). 380p. 1975. 113.00 (*3-8055-2277-0*) S Karger.

Recent Advances in Cryogenic Engineering 1993. Ed. by J. P. Kelley & J. Goodman. LC 93-73597. 65p. pap. 30.00 (*0-7918-1044-5*) ASME.

Recent Advances in Cryptogamic Botany, 2 vols. Ed. by Scientific Publishers Staff. (C). 1988. 24.00 (*0-685-22321-3*, Pub. by Scientific UK) St Mut.

Recent Advances in Cytochalasans. Ed. by G. S. Pendse. 202p. (gr. 13). 1987. text ed. 150.95 (*0-412-29350-1*) Chapman & Hall.

Recent Advances in Cytology. C. D. Darlington. LC 88-21258. (Genes Cells & Organisms Ser.). 696p. 1988. text ed. 10.00 (*0-8240-1376-X*) Garland.

***Recent Advances in Density Functional Methods.** 340p. 1997. text ed. 32.00 (*981-02-3160-1*) World Scientific Pub.

Recent Advances in Density Functional Methods, Pt. 1. Ed. by Delano P. Chong. LC 95-45326. (Recent Advances in Computational Chemistry Ser.: Vol. 1). 400p. 1995. 86.00 (*981-02-2442-7*) World Scientific Pub.

***Recent Advances in Density Functional Methods Part II.** 400p. 1997. text ed. 53.00 (*981-02-3150-4*) World Scientific Pub.

Recent Advances in Dermatology, No. 8. Ed. by Robert H. Champion & Richard J. Pye. (Illus.). 248p. 1990. text ed. 59.00 (*0-443-04168-7*) Churchill.

Recent Advances in Dermatology 9. Ed. by Robert H. Champion & Richard J. Pye. (Illus.). 226p. 1992. text ed. 69.95 (*0-443-04451-1*) Churchill.

Recent Advances in Descriptive Multivariate Analysis. Ed. by W. J. Krzanowski. (Royal Statistical Society Lecture Notes Ser.: No. 2). (Illus.). 432p. (C). 1995. pap. text ed. 17.95 (*0-19-289249-5*) OUP.

Recent Advances in Descriptive Multivariate Analysis. Ed. by W. J. Krzanowski. (Royal Statistical Society Lecture Notes Ser.: No. 2). (Illus.). 352p. 1995. 65.00 (*0-19-852285-1*) OUP.

Recent Advances in Developmental Morphology of Crop Plants: Proceedings of the Symposium Held at the Andhra University, India 1985. Ed. by H. Maheswari Devi et al. (Illus.). 405p. 1990. text ed. 45.00 (*81-211-0040-2*, Pub. by Mahendra Pal Singh II) Lubrecht & Cramer.

Recent Advances in Diagnosis & Treatment of Infections: Special Issue of Journal of Medicine. Ed. by Thomas R. Beam, Jr. 1983. 35.00 (*0-915340-12-7*) PJD Pubns.

Recent Advances in Diseases of the Esophagus: Selected Papers in the 5th World Congress of the International Society for Diseases of the Esophagus, Kyoto, Japan, 1992. Fifth World Congress of the International Society for Diseases of the Esophagus Staff. Ed. by K. Nabeya et al. LC 93-5883. 1993. 378.00 (*0-387-70121-4*) Spr-Verlag.

Recent Advances in Drug Delivery Systems. Ed. by James M. Anderson & Sung W. Kim. LC 84-3387. 404p. 1984. 95.00 (*0-306-41627-1*, Plenum Pr) Plenum.

Recent Advances in Dryland Agriculture. L. L. Somani. (C). 1992. text ed. 200.00 (*81-7233-035-9*, Pub. by Scientific Pubs II) St Mut.

Recent Advances in Dynamical Astronomy: Proceedings of the NATO Advanced Study Institute in Dynamical Astronomy, Cortina D'ampezzo, August, 1972. NATO Advanced Study Institute Staff. Ed. by Byron D. Tapley & Victor G. Szebehely. LC 73-83571. (Astrophysics & Space Science Library: No. 39). 490p. 1973. lib. bdg. 175.00 (*90-277-0348-5*) Kluwer Ac.

Recent Advances in Ecology & Environment. Ed. by V. B. Purohit. (Recent Researches in Ecology, Environment & Pollution Ser.: Vol. 1). 200p. 1988. 35.00 (*1-55528-157-5*, Messers Today & Tomorrow) Scholarly Pubns.

Recent Advances in Elasticity, Viscoelasticity & Inelasticity: Festschrift Volume in Honor of Professor Tse-Chien Woo on the Occasion of His 70th Birthday. Ed. by K. R. Rajagopal. LC 94-23839. (Series on Advances in Mathematics for Applied Sciences). 248p. 1995. text ed. 99.00 (*981-02-2103-7*) World Scientific Pub.

Recent Advances in Electric Vehicle Technology. 136p. 1989. 29.00 (*0-89883-784-7*, SP793) Soc Auto Engineers.

Recent Advances in Electromagnetic Theory. Ed. by D. L. Jaggard & Haralambos N. Kritikos. (Illus.). 416p. 1990. 146.95 (*0-387-97143-2*) Spr-Verlag.

Recent Advances in Endocrinology & Metabolism, No. 3. Ed. by Christopher R. Edwards & Dennis W. Lincoln. (Illus.). 324p. 1989. text ed. 80.00 (*0-443-03951-8*) Churchill.

Recent Advances in Endocrinology & Metabolism 4. Ed. by Christopher R. Edwards & Dennis W. Lincoln. (Illus.). 208p. 1992. text ed. 79.95 (*0-443-04518-6*) Churchill.

Recent Advances in Engineering Mechanics & Their Impact on Civil Engineering Practice, 2 Vols. Ed. by Wai-Fah Chen & A. D. Lewis. 1378p. 1983. pap. 116.00 (*0-87262-358-0*) Am Soc Civil Eng.

Recent Advances in Environmental Analysis, Vol. 2. Ed. by Roland W. Frei. (Current Topics In Environmental & Toxicological Chemistry Ser.: Vol.2). 3542p. 1979. text ed. 293.00 (*0-677-15950-1*) Gordon & Breach.

Recent Advances in Event-Related Brain Potential Research: Proceedings of the 11th International Conference on Event-Related Potentials (EPIC), Okinawa, Japan, 25-30 June 1995. Ed. by C. Ogura et al. LC 96-25000. (International Congress Ser.: No. 1099). 1118p. 1996. text ed. 324.25 (*0-444-82280-1*, Excerpta Medica) Elsevier.

Recent Advances in Experimental Mechanics: Proceedings of the 10th International Conference, Lisbon, Portugal, July 1994, 2 vols. J. F. Silva-Gomes et al. (Illus.). 1200p. (C). 1994. 140.00 (*90-5410-395-7*, Pub. by A A Balkema NE) Ashgate Pub Co.

Recent Advances in Experimental Nuclear Physics. 548p. (C). 1989. text ed. 159.00 (*9971-5-0848-6*) World Scientific Pub.

Recent Advances in Fast Ion Conducting Materials & Devices: Second Asian Conf on S S Ionics. B. V. Chowdari et al. 620p. 1990. text ed. 127.00 (*981-02-0294-6*) World Scientific Pub.

Recent Advances in Fertility Control: Proceedings of the 2nd International Symposium on Recent Advances in Fertility Control, Tokyo, Japan, Oct. 24, 1987, Vol. 2. Ed. by Shoichi Matsumoto. (Current Clinical Practice Ser.: No. 50). 40p. 1989. 25.75 (*90-219-1676-2*, Excerpta Medica) Elsevier.

Recent Advances in Field Theory & Statistical Mechanics: Les Houches, Vol. 39. J. B. Zuber & R. Stora. 1984. 402.00 (*0-444-86675-2*) Elsevier.

Recent Advances in Flame Retardancy of Polymeric Materials, 1991: Annual Conference Proceedings. Business Communications Company, Inc. Staff. 1992. pap. 275.00 (*0-685-62464-1*) BCC.

Recent Advances in Fourier Analysis & Its Applications. Ed. by J. S. Byrnes & Jennifer L. Byrnes. (C). 1990. lib. bdg. 257.00 (*0-7923-0875-1*) Kluwer Ac.

Recent Advances in Fractional Calculus: A Collection of Papers. Ravindra N. Kalia. (Global Research Notes in Mathematics Ser.). ix, 307p. 1993. pap. text ed. 45.00 (*0-9638155-0-4*); lib. bdg. 65.00 (*0-9638155-1-2*) Global Pubng.

***Recent Advances in Fracture.** Ed. by R. K. Mahidhara et al. (Illus.). 300p. 1997. 74.00 (*0-87339-364-3*, 3643) Minerals Metals.

Recent Advances in Gas Chromatography. Ed. by Irving I. Domsky & John A. Perry. LC 72-145881. (Illus.). 430p. reprint ed. pap. 122.60 (*0-7837-0851-3*, 2041160) Bks Demand.

Recent Advances in Gastroenterology, No. 8. Ed. by Roy Pounder. (Illus.). 280p. 1990. text ed. 75.00 (*0-443-04324-8*) Churchill.

Recent Advances in Gastroenterology - Nine. Ed. by Roy Pounder. (Illus.). 258p. 1993. text ed. 79.95 (*0-443-04674-3*) Churchill.

Recent Advances in General Relativity: Essays in Honor of Ted Newman. Ed. by A. I. Janis & J. R. Porter. (Einstein Studies: Vol. 4). xi, 266p. 1991. 127.50 (*0-8176-3541-6*) Birkhauser.

Recent Advances in Geomathematics: An International Symposium. Ed. by Daniel F. Merriam. 245p. 1978. 387.25 (*0-08-022095-9*, Pergamon Pr) Elsevier.

Recent Advances in Geosciences: Selection of Papers Presented at the 7th EUG Conference, Strasbourg, April 4-8, 1993. EUG Scientific Committee Staff. LC 93-27572. 1270p. 1993. 387.25 (*0-444-81673-9*) Elsevier.

Recent Advances in Global Optimization. Ed. by Christodoulos A. Floudas & Panos M. Pardalos. 912p. 1991. pap. text ed. 49.50 (*0-691-02527-4*) Princeton U Pr.

Recent Advances in Haematology 6. Ed. by A. Victor Hoffbrand & M. K. Brenner. (Illus.). 235p. 1992. text ed. 69.00 (*0-443-04380-9*) Churchill.

Recent Advances in Hamiltonian Systems: Proceedings of the International Conference, L'Aquila, June 10-13, 1986. Ed. by G. F. Dell'Antonio & B. D'Onofrio. 256p. 1987. text ed. 74.00 (*9971-5-0246-1*) World Scientific Pub.

Recent Advances in Hazardous Materials Transportation Research: An International Exchange. Transportation Research Board Staff. (State of the Art Reports: No. 03). 212p. (C). 1986. pap. text ed. 22.00 (*0-309-03973-8*) Transport Res Bd.

***Recent Advances in Heat Transfer.** A. A. Zukauskas. (Transport Processes in Engineering Ser.: Vol. 2). xvi, 1274p. 1992. 488.25 (*0-444-89394-6*) Elsevier.

Recent Advances in Heat Transfer & Microstructure Modelling for Metal Processing Vol. 67-4: Proceedings of the ASME International Mechanical Engineering Congress & Exposition, 1995, San Francisco, CA. Ed. by R. M. Guo & J. J. Too. LC 95-81253. (1995 ASME International Mechanical Engineering Congress & Exposition Ser.: MD-Vol. 67/MED-Vol. 4). 264p. 1995. 88.00 (*0-7918-1749-0*, H01030) ASME.

Recent Advances in Histopathology, No. 14. Ed. by Peter P. Anthony & Roderick N. MacSween. (Illus.). 308p. (Orig.). 1989. pap. text ed. 45.00 (*0-443-03998-4*) Churchill.

Recent Advances in Histopathology 15. Ed. by Peter P. Anthony & Roderick N. MacSween. (Illus.). 257p. (Orig.). 1992. pap. text ed. 59.95 (*0-443-04519-4*) Churchill.

Recent Advances in Homotopy Theory. George W. Whitehead. LC 79-145639. (CBMS Regional Conference Series in Mathematics: No. 5). 82p. 1971. pap. 17.00 (*0-8218-1654-3*, CBMS/5) Am Math.

Recent Advances in Hormonal Therapy in Cancer: Supplement 2, 1992. Ed. by P. F. Bruning & N. S. Tchekmedyian. (Journal: Oncology: Vol. 49). (Illus.). iv, 56p. 1992. pap. 17.50 (*3-8055-5710-8*) S Karger.

Recent Advances in Hydraulic Physical Modelling. Ed. by Rui Martins. (C). 1989. lib. bdg. 242.00 (*0-7923-0196-X*) Kluwer Ac.

Recent Advances in Imaging & Intervention in Cardiovascular Diseases. S. Sharma. LC 96-25733. 1996. pap. write for info. (*981-3083-02-6*) Spr-Verlag.

Recent Advances in Inborn Errors of Metabolism. Ed. by K. Tada et al. (Reprint from Journal Enzyme Ser.: Vol. 38, No. 1-4, 198). (Illus.). 332p. 1988. 78.50 (*3-8055-4772-2*) S Karger.

Recent Advances in Insect Physiology Morphology & Ecology. S. C. Pathak. (Illus.). xiii, 324p. 1986. 39.00 (*1-55528-079-X*, Pub. by Today & Tomorrows P & P II) Scholarly Pubns.

Recent Advances in Instrumentation, Data Acquisition & Testing in Soil Dynamics. Ed. by Shobha K. Batia & Geoffrey W. Blaney. LC 91-30336. 136p. 1991. pap. text ed. 19.00 (*0-87262-854-X*) Am Soc Civil Eng.

Recent Advances in Iterative Methods. Gene H. Golub et al. LC 93-50626. (IMA Volumes in Mathematics & Its Applications Ser.: Vol. 60). (Illus.). 248p. 1994. 59.95 (*0-387-94252-1*) Spr-Verlag.

Recent Advances in Japanese Brewing Technology, Vol. 2. Takashi Inoue et al. (Japanese Technology Reviews Section E: Biotechnology Ser.: Vol. 2, No. 1). 120p. 1992. pap. text ed. 48.00 (*2-88124-856-X*) Gordon & Breach.

Recent Advances in Knowledge of the Phytoseiidae. Marjorie A. Hoy. (Illus.). 92p. (Orig.). 1982. pap. 5.00 (*0-931876-62-1*, 3284) ANR Pubns CA.

Recent Advances in Labour Economics. Ed. by G. Hutchinson & J. G. Treble. LC 83-40628. 256p. 1984. text ed. 32.50 (*0-312-66575-X*) St Martin.

Recent Advances in Life-Test & Reliability Statistics. Balakrishnan. 672p. 1995. 95.00 (*0-8493-8972-0*) CRC Pr.

Recent Advances in Lifeline Earthquake Engineering. Ed. by T. Ariman et al. LC 87-72298. 245p. 1987. 49.00 (*0-931215-71-4*) Computational Mech MA.

Recent Advances in Lifeline Earthquake Engineering in Japan: Presented at the 1980 Pressure Vessels & Piping Conference, ASME Century 2 - Emerging Technology Conferences, San Francisco, California, August 12-15, 1980. Symposium on Recent Advances in Lifeline Earthquake Engineering in Japan Staff. Ed. by Heki Shibata et al. LC 80-66038. (PVP Ser.: Vol. 43). (Illus.). 166p. reprint ed. pap. 47.40 (*0-8357-2844-7*, 2039079) Bks Demand.

Recent Advances in Lower Carboniferous Geology. Ed. by P. Strogen et al. (Geological Society Special Publication: Series 107). vi, 458p. 1996. 120.00 (*1-897799-58-6*, 218, Pub. by Geol Soc Pub Hse UK) AAPG.

Recent Advances in Magnetism of Magnetic Materials: Proceedings of 5th Symposium on Magnetism & Magnetic Materials. H. L. Huang & P. C. Kuo. 364p. 1990. text ed. 130.00 (*981-02-0071-4*) World Scientific Pub.

Recent Advances in Magnetism of Transition Metal Compounds: A Festschrift in Honor of Professor K. Motizuki. A. Kotani & N. Suzuki. 392p. 1993. text ed. 109.00 (*981-02-1150-3*) World Scientific Pub.

Recent Advances in Management of Digestive Cancers: Proceedings of UICC Kyoto International Symposium on Recent Advances in Management of Digestive Cancers, March 31-April 2, 1993. Symposium on Recent Advances in Management of Digestive Cancers Staff. Ed. by T. Takahashi. LC 93-37128. 1994. 232.00 (*0-387-70131-1*) Spr-Verlag.

Recent Advances in Marine Biology. Ed. by P. S. James. (Illus.). 600p. 1985. 79.00 (*1-55528-048-X*, Pub. by Today & Tomorrows P & P II) Scholarly Pubns.

Recent Advances in Materials Research. Ed. by C. M. Srivastava. 379p. (C). 1984. text ed. 125.00 (*90-6191-411-6*, Pub. by A A Balkema NE) Ashgate Pub Co.

Recent Advances in Matrix Theory. Ed. by Hans Schneider. LC 64-20843. (U. S. Army. Mathematics Research Center Publication Ser.: No. 12). 154p. reprint ed. pap. 43.90 (*0-317-09153-0*, 2015372) Bks Demand.

Recent Advances in Mechanics of Structured Continua 1993. Ed. by M. Massoudi & K. R. Rajagopal. LC 93-71574. (AMD Series, Vol. 160; MD: Vol. 41). 159p. 1993. pap. 45.00 (*0-7918-1139-5*, G00783) ASME.

Recent Advances in Mechanistic & Synthetic Aspects of Polymerization. Ed. by M. Fontanille & A. Guyot. (C). 1987. lib. bdg. 204.50 (*90-277-2602-7*) Kluwer Ac.

Recent Advances in Medical Thermology. Ed. by Francis J. Ring & Barbara Phillips. LC 84-3366. 723p. 1984. 135.00 (*0-306-41672-7*, Plenum Pr) Plenum.

Recent Advances in Medically Assisted Conception: Report of a WHO Scientific Group. (Technical Report Ser.: No. 820). 111p. (ENG, FRE & SPA.). 1992. pap. text ed. 15.00 (*92-4-120820-1*, 1100820) World Health.

Recent Advances in Medicinal Aromatic & Spice Crops, 2 vols. S. P. Raychaudhuri. (Illus.). 1000p. 1991. Set. 150.00 (*1-55528-260-1*, Pub. by Today & Tomorrows P & P II) Scholarly Pubns.

Recent Advances in Medicinal, Aromatic & Spice Crops: International Conference Held on 28-31, January 1989, at New Delhi, India, Vol. 1. Ed. by S. P. Raychaudhuri. (Illus.). 280p. 1992. 59.00 (*1-55528-229-6*, Pub. by Today & Tomorrows P & P II) Scholarly Pubns.

Recent Advances in Medicinal, Aromatic & Spice Crops: International Conference Held on 28-31, January 1989, at New Delhi, India, Vol. 2. Ed. by S. P. Raychaudhuri. 568p. 1992. 59.00 (*1-55528-266-0*, Pub. by Today & Tomorrows P & P II) Scholarly Pubns.

Recent Advances in Medicinal, Aromatic & Spice Crops, Vol. 1: International Conference Held at New Delhi, India, Jan. 1989. Ed. by S. P. Raidchaudhuri. (Illus.). 272p. 1991. text ed. 59.00 (*81-7019-372-9*, Pub. by Today Tomorrow II) Lubrecht & Cramer.

Recent Advances in Microcirculatory Research. Ed. by P. Gaehtgens. (Bibliotheca Anatomica Ser.: No. 20). (Illus.). xvi, 740p. 1981. 236.00 (*3-8055-2272-X*) S Karger.

Recent Advances in Microwave Technology (IAP) Proceedings of the 2nd International Symposium on Recent Advances in Microwave Technology, Beijing, China, 4-8 September 1989. Ed. by B. Rawat & Zhou Siyong. (International Academic Publishers Ser.). 800p. 1990. 230.00 (*0-08-040184-8*, Pub. by IAP UK) Elsevier.

Recent Advances in Mining & Processing of Low-Grade Submarginal Mineral Deposits. LC 76-11771. 1976. 96.00 (*0-08-021051-1*, Pub. by Pergamon Repr UK) Franklin.

Recent Advances in Molecular & Biochemical Research in Proteins: Proceedings of the Iubmb Sym on Protein. Y-H Wei. 296p. 1994. text ed. 121.00 (*981-02-1520-7*) World Scientific Pub.

Recent Advances in Molecular Spectroscopy of Polyatomic Molecules & Small Clusters, Pt. 1. Ed. by Koji Kaya. 104p. 1994. pap. text ed. 222.00 (*3-7186-5517-9*, Harwood Acad Pubs) Gordon & Breach.

Recent Advances in Molecular Spectroscopy of Polyatomic Molecules & Small Clusters, Pt. 2. Ed. by Koji Kaya. 190p. 1994. pap. text ed. 498.00 (*3-7186-5518-7*, Harwood Acad Pubs) Gordon & Breach.

Recent Advances in Molecular Spectroscopy of Polyatomic Molecules & Small Clusters, Set, Pts. 1 & 2. Ed. by Koji Kaya. 1995. pap. text ed. 720.00 (*3-7186-5519-5*, Harwood Acad Pubs) Gordon & Breach.

Recent Advances in Musculoskeletal Oncology. Ed. by A. Uchida & K. Ono. LC 92-2230. (Illus.). 350p. 1992. 207.00 (*0-387-70099-4*) Spr-Verlag.

Recent Advances in Mycoplasmology: Proceedings of the 7th Congress of the International Organization for Mycoplasmology, Vol. 20. Joseph G. Tully. 962p. 1990. 280.00 (*0-89574-318-3*, VCH) Wiley.

Recent Advances in Nemertean Biology. Ed. by P. Sundberg et al. (Developments in Hydrobiology Ser.). (C). 1988. lib. bdg. 180.50 (*90-6193-647-0*) Kluwer Ac.

Recent Advances in Nervous System Toxicology. Ed. by Corraldo L. Galli et al. LC 85-25805. (NATO ASI Series A, Life Sciences: Vol. 100). 390p. 1987. 115.00 (*0-306-42209-3*, Plenum Pr) Plenum.

Recent Advances in Neuropsychopharmacology: Selected Papers from the 12th Congress of the Collegium Internationale Neuro-Psychopharmacologicum Goteborg, Sweden, 22-26 June, 1980. D. Wheatley. (Illus.). 401p. 1981. 97.00 (*0-08-026382-8*, Pergamon Pr) Elsevier.

Recent Advances in Neurotraumatology. Ed. by Norio Nakamura et al. LC 92-48234. 1993. 174.00 (*0-387-70115-X*) Spr-Verlag.

Recent Advances in Non-Newtonian Flows. Ed. by D. A. Siginer. (AMD Series, Vol. 153: FED Vol.: Vol. 141). 160p. 1992. 45.00 (*0-7918-1121-2*) ASME.

Recent Advances in Nonsmooth Optimization. Ed. by Ding-Zhu Du et al. 400p. 1995. text ed. 78.00 (*981-02-2265-3*) World Scientific Pub.

Recent Advances in Nuclear Structure. Ed. by D. Bucurescu et al. 528p. (C). 1991. text ed. 147.00 (*981-02-0533-3*) World Scientific Pub.

Recent Advances in Obesity & Diabetes Research. Ed. by N. Melchionda et al. LC 83-19133. (Serono Symposia Publications from Raven Press: No. 8). (Illus.). 442p. 1984. reprint ed. pap. 126.00 (*0-7837-9530-0*, 2060279) Bks Demand.

Recent Advances in Obesity Research, Vol. II. Ed. by G. A. Bray. 510p. 1978. 71.00 (*0-917678-07-9*) Food & Nut Pr.

Recent Advances in Obesity Research, Vol. V. Eleazar Shafrir. 416p. 1987. 74.00 (*0-917678-22-2*) Food & Nut Pr.

Recent Advances in Obstetrics & Gynaecology 17. Ed. by John Bonnar. (Illus.). 244p. (Orig.). 1992. pap. text ed. 44.95 (*0-443-04402-3*) Churchill.

Recent Advances in Obstetrics & Gynecology, No. 16. Ed. by John Bonnar. (Illus.). 278p. 1990. pap. text ed. 39.95 (*0-443-04117-2*) Churchill.

Recent Advances in Oilfield Chemistry. Ed. by P. H. Ogden. 332p. 1995. 129.95 (*0-85186-941-6*, R6941) CRC Pr.

Recent Advances in Ophthalmology 8. Ed. by S. I. Davidson & B. Jay. (Illus.). 214p. 1992. text ed. 62.95 (*0-443-04373-6*) Churchill.

An Asterisk (*) at the beginning of an entry indicates that the title is appearing in BIP for the first time.

R

***Recent Advances in Optimization: Proceedings of the 8th French-German Conference on Optimization, Trier, July 21-26, 1996, Vol. 452.** Peter Gritzmann. LC 97-19500. (Lecture Notes in Economics & Mathematical Systems Ser.). 1997. pap. write for info. (3-540-63022-8) Spr-Verlag.

Recent Advances in Optimization Techniques: Proceedings of the Symposium, Carnegie Institute of Technology, 1965. Recent Advances in Optimization Techniques Symposium Staff. Ed. by Abrahim Lavi et al. LC 66-4421. 670p. reprint ed. pap. 180.00 (0-317-08576-X, 2006349) Bks Demand.

Recent Advances in Oral Health: Report of a WHO Expert Committee. (Technical Report Ser.: No. 826). vi, 37p. (CHI, ENG, FRE & SPA.). 1992. pap. text ed. 7.00 (92-4-120826-0, 1100826) World Health.

Recent Advances in Orthopaedics 6. Ed. by A. Catterall. (Illus.). 175p. (Orig.). 1992. pap. text ed. 65.00 (0-443-04386-8) Churchill.

Recent Advances in Otitis Media. Ed. by Goro Mogi et al. LC 93-41768. (Illus.). xxxvi, 875p. 1994. text ed. 266.00 (90-6299-101-7, Pub. by Kugler NE) Kugler Pubns.

***Recent Advances in Otitis Media: Proceedings of the Sixth International Symposium.** David J. Lim. 1996. 115.00 (1-55009-028-3, Pub. by B C Decker CN) Blackwell Sci.

Recent Advances in Paediatrics, Vol. 13. Ed. by T. J. David. 233p. 1995. pap. 39.95 (0-443-05100-3) Churchill.

Recent Advances in Paediatrics - 10. Ed. by T. J. David. (Illus.). 246p. (Orig.). 1992. pap. 45.95 (0-443-04520-8) Churchill.

Recent Advances in Paediatrics - 11. Ed. by T. J. David. (Illus.). 224p. (Orig.). 1993. pap. text ed. 54.00 (0-443-04753-7) Churchill.

Recent Advances in Paediatrics - 9. Ed. by T. J. David. (Illus.). 239p. 1991. pap. text ed. 45.00 (0-443-04304-3) Churchill.

Recent Advances in Parsing Technology. Harry C. Bunt & Masaru Tomita. LC 96-25047. (Text, Speech, & Language Technology). 1996. lib. bdg. 128.00 (0-7923-4152-X) Kluwer Ac.

Recent Advances in Partial Differential Equations. Ed. by M. A. Herrero & E. Zuazua. (Applied Mathematics Ser.). 150p. 1995. pap. text ed. 54.95 (0-471-94455-6) Wiley.

Recent Advances in Pediatric Nephrology. Ed. by J. F. Pascual & P. L. Calcagno. (Contributions to Nephrology Ser.: Vol. 27). (Illus.). vi, 98p. 1981. pap. 52.00 (3-8055-1851-X) S Karger.

Recent Advances in Perinatal Medicine. Ed. by G. C. Di Renzo et al. LC 93-12026. (Ettore Majorana International Life Sciences Ser.: Vol. 10). 350p. 1994. text ed. 70.00 (3-7186-5348-6) Gordon & Breach.

Recent Advances in Periodontology, Vol. II: Proc. of the 4th Internat. Academy of Periodontology Meeting, Istanbul, 17-20 Sept., 1990. Ed. by S. I. Gold et al. (International Congress Ser.: No. 957). 332p. 1991. 220.75 (0-444-81424-8, Excerpta Medica) Elsevier.

Recent Advances in Phytochemistry, Vol. 2: Proceedings of the 7th Annual Symposium of. Phytochemical Society of North America Staff. Ed. by Margaret K. Seikel. 187p. reprint ed. pap. 53.30 (0-317-26217-3, 2055689) Bks Demand.

Recent Advances in Phytopathological Researches. A. K. Roy & K. K. Sinha. 211p. 1995. pap. 150.00 (81-85880-76-X, Pub. by Print Hse II) St Mut.

Recent Advances in Phytopathological Researches. Ed. by A. K. Roy & K. K. Sinha. 211p. 1995. pap. 130.00 (0-614-09722-3, Pub. by Print Hse II) St Mut.

Recent Advances in Plastic Surgery - 4. Ed. by Ian T. Jackson & Brian C. Sommerlad. (Illus.). 200p. 1992. text ed. 80.00 (0-443-04453-8) Churchill.

Recent Advances in Postpartum Psychiatric Disorders. Ed. by David G. Inwood. LC 85-15619. (Clinical Insights Ser.). 139p. reprint ed. pap. 39.70 (0-8357-7835-5, 2036209) Bks Demand.

Recent Advances in Prenatal Diagnosis: Proceedings of the First International Symposium on Recent Advances in Prenatal Diagnosis, Bologna, September 15-16, 1980. Ed. by Camillo Orlandi et al. LC 81-198305. (Illus.). 344p. reprint ed. pap. 98.10 (0-317-58634-3, 2029638) Bks Demand.

***Recent Advances in Prostate Cancer & BPH: Proceedings of the IV Congress on Progress & Controversies on Oncological Urology (PACIOU IV), Held in Rotterdam, The Netherlands, April 1996.** Ed. by F. H. Schroder. LC 96-44493. 1996. text ed. 101.00 (1-85070-784-7) Prthnon Pub.

Recent Advances in Psychogeriatrics 2. Ed. by Tom Arie. (Illus.). 224p. 1992. text ed. 59.00 (0-443-04468-6) Churchill.

***Recent Advances in Quantum Monte Carlo Methods.** 250p. 1997. 34.00 (981-02-3009-5) World Scientific Pub.

Recent Advances in Real Algebraic Geometry & Quadratic Forms: Proceedings of the RAGSQUD Year, Berkeley, 1990-1991. Ed. by William B. Jacob et al. LC 93-6377. (Contemporary Mathematics Ser.: Vol. 155). 420p. 1993. pap. 39.00 (0-8218-5154-3, CONM/155) Am Math.

Recent Advances in Reinforcement Learning. Ed. by Leslie P. Kaelbling. LC 96-3971. 1996. lib. bdg. 74.00 (0-7923-9705-3) Kluwer Ac.

Recent Advances in Renal Cell Carcinoma. Ed. by C. G. Bollack & J. Cinqualbre. (Progress in Surgery Ser.: Vol. 17). (Illus.). viii, 160p. 1983. ring bd. 104.00 (3-8055-3621-6) S Karger.

Recent Advances in Renal Metabolism. Ed. by Kiyoshi Kurokawa & R. Tanner. (Journal: Mineral & Electrolyte Metabolism: Vol. 9, Nos. 5-6). (Illus.). vi, 148p. 1983. 136.00 (3-8055-3652-6) S Karger.

Recent Advances in Renal Physiology: Proceedings of the International Symposium on Renal Handling of Sodium, Brestenberg, 1971. International Symposium on Renal Handling of Sodium Staff. Ed. by H. Wirz & F. Spinelli. 300p. 1972. 78.50 (3-8055-1405-0) S Karger.

Recent Advances in Renal Research: Contributions from Japan. Ed. by K. Maeda et al. (Contributions to Nephrology Ser.: Vol. 9). (Illus.). 1978. 39.25 (3-8055-2826-4) S Karger.

Recent Advances in Respiratory Medicine 5. Ed. by David Mitchell. (Illus.). 294p. 1991. text ed. 59.00 (0-443-04467-8) Churchill.

Recent Advances in Robot Kinematics. Vincenzo Parenti-Castelli. Ed. by Jadran Lenarcic. LC 96-22088. (Diverse Ser.). 468p. (C). 1996. lib. bdg. 208.00 (0-7923-4124-4) Kluwer Ac.

Recent Advances in Robot Learning, Vol. 368. Tom M. Mitchell & Sebastian Thrun. Ed. by Judy A. Franklin. LC 96-18680. (International Series in Engineering & Computer Science, Natural Language Processing & Machine Translation). 224p. (C). 1996. lib. bdg. 94.00 (0-7923-9745-2) Kluwer Ac.

Recent Advances in Robust Control. Ed. by Peter Dorato & R. K. Yedavalli. LC 90-4563. (Illus.). 512p. 1990. text ed. 79.95 (0-87942-266-1, PC02584) Inst Electrical.

Recent Advances in Schizophrenia. Ed. by A. Kales et al. (Illus.). 416p. 1989. 59.00 (0-387-97024-X) Spr-Verlag.

Recent Advances in Sensory Aids for Hearing Impairment. Ed. by Harry Levitt & Allen E. Boysen. (Illus.). 136p. (Orig.). (C). 1994. pap. text ed. 35.00 (0-7881-0355-5) DIANE Pub.

Recent Advances in Social Psychology, Vol. 1: Proceedings of the 24th International Congress of Psychology of the International Union of Psychological Science, Sydney, Australia, Aug. 28-Sept. 2, 1988. Ed. by Joseph P. Forgas & J. M. Innes. 544p. 1990. 167.50 (0-444-88519-6, North Holland) Elsevier.

Recent Advances in Solids & Structures 1995: Proceedings of the ASME International Mechanical Engineering Congress & Exposition, 1995, San Francisco, CA. Ed. by H. H. Chung & Young W. Kwon. (1995 International Mechanical Engineering Congress & Exposition Ser.: PVP-Vol. 321/NE-Vol. 18). 200p. 1995. 72.00 (0-7918-1747-4, H01026) ASME.

***Recent Advances in Solids, Structures & Applications of Metallic Materials: Proceedings, ASME International Mechanical Engineering Congress & Exposition, Atlanta, GA, 1996.** Ed. by Young W. Kwon et al. LC 96-78666. 235p. 1996. pap. 84.00 (0-7918-1522-6, TA647) ASME.

Recent Advances in Spatial Equilibrium Modeling, Methodology & Applications. Jeroen C. Van Den Bergh et al. LC 96-4809. (Advances in Spatial Science Ser.). 1996. write for info. (0-387-60708-0) Spr-Verlag.

Recent Advances in Spatial Equilibrium Modelling: Methodology & Applications. Folke Snickars. (Advances in Spatial Science Ser.). (Illus.). viii, 392p. 1996. 117.00 (3-540-60708-0) Spr-Verlag.

Recent Advances in Special Education & Rehabilitation. Ronald C. Eaves et al. LC 94-40046. 1995. 36.00 (0-89079-651-3) PRO-ED.

Recent Advances in Speech Understanding & Dialog Systems. Ed. by H. Niemann et al. (NATO Asi Series F: Vol. 46). (Illus.). x, 521p. 1988. 129.95 (0-387-19245-X) Spr-Verlag.

Recent Advances in Statistical Physics: Proceedings of the International Base Symposium on Statistical Physics. Ed. by B. Dutta & M. Dutta. 176p. (C). 1987. text ed. 81.00 (9971-5-0369-7) World Scientific Pub.

Recent Advances in Statistics & Probability. Ed. by J. P. Vilaplana & M. L. Puri. 470p. 1994. 275.00 (90-6764-170-7, Pub. by VSP NE) Coronet Bks.

Recent Advances in Steroid Biochemistry, Vol. 2. Ed. by Jorge R. Pasqualini. LC 75-4332. 312p. 1975. pap. 67.00 (0-08-019709-4, Pub. by Pergamon Repr UK) Franklin.

Recent Advances in Steroid Hormone Action. Ed. by Virinder K. Moudgil. 552p. (C). 1987. lib. bdg. 207.70 (3-11-010762-7) De Gruyter.

Recent Advances in Stochastic Calculus. Ed. by J. S. Baras & V. Mirelli. (Progress in Automation & Information Systems Ser.). ix, 217p. 1990. 64.95 (0-387-97273-0) Spr-Verlag.

Recent Advances in Structural Dynamics. Ed. by Gerald C. Pardoen. (Sessions Proceedings Ser.). 53p. 1986. 12.00 (0-87262-530-3) Am Soc Civil Eng.

Recent Advances in Structural Mechanics: 1994 International Mechanical Engineering Congress & Exposition, Chicago, Illinois - November 6-11, 1994. (PVP - NE Ser.: Vol. 295, Vol. 16). 332p. 1994. 90.00 (0-7918-1450-5, G00945) ASME.

Recent Advances in Structural Mechanics - 1992. Ed. by Young W. Kwon & H. H. Chung. (PVP Ser.: Vol. 248). 196p. 1992. 52.50 (0-7918-1131-X, G00775) ASME.

Recent Advances in Structural Mechanics 1993. Ed. by H. H. Chung & Young W. Kwon. LC 87-71096. 181p. pap. 55.00 (0-7918-1260-X) ASME.

Recent Advances in Superconductivity. S. L. Kakani & C. Hemrajani. 178p. (C). 1991. lib. bdg. 45.50 (0-89464-542-0) Krieger.

Recent Advances in Surgery, No. 16. Ed. by I. Taylor & C. D. Johnson. (Illus.). 250p. (Orig.). 1993. pap. text ed. 57.00 (0-443-04688-3) Churchill.

Recent Advances in Surgery - 14. Ed. by I. Taylor & C. D. Johnson. (Illus.). 263p. 1991. pap. text ed. 45.00 (0-443-04403-1) Churchill.

Recent Advances in Surgery - 15. Ed. by I. Taylor & C. D. Johnson. (Illus.). 272p. (Orig.). 1992. pap. text ed. 55.00 (0-443-04569-0) Churchill.

Recent Advances in Sympathetic Neurotransmission: Sixth Meeting on Adrenergic Mechanisms Held in Honour of Professor J. Garrett. Ed. by S. Guimaraes. (Journal: Blood Vessels: Vol. 24, No. 5, 1987). (Illus.). 68p. 1987. pap. 27.25 (3-8055-4659-9) S Karger.

Recent Advances in Systemic Lupus Erythematosus. Ed. by Paul H. Lambert et al. 1984. text ed. 99.00 (0-12-434620-0) Acad Pr.

Recent Advances in Temporal Databases: Proceedings of the International Workshop on Temporal Databases, Zurich, 17-18 September 1995. Ed. by James Clifford & Alexander Tuzhilin. (Workshops in Computing Ser.). 362p. 1995. 79.00 (3-540-19945-4) Spr-Verlag.

Recent Advances in the Aerospace Sciences. Ed. by Corrado Casci. 454p. 1985. 120.00 (0-306-41079-6, Plenum Pr) Plenum.

Recent Advances in the Biochemistry & Biology of Cancer. Ed. by K. M. Anderson et al. (Journal: Clinical Physiology & Biochemistry: Vol. 5, No. 3-4). (Illus.). 132p. 1987. pap. 69.75 (3-8055-4643-2) S Karger.

Recent Advances in the Biology of Alcoholism. Ed. by Charles S. Lieber. LC 82-1033. (Advances in Alcohol & Substance Abuse Ser.: Vol. 1, No. 2). 123p. 1982. text ed. 39.95 (0-86656-104-8) Haworth Pr.

Recent Advances in the Chemistry of Beta-Lactam Antibiotics: 4th International Symposium 1988. Ed. by P. H. Bentley. 368p. 1989. 109.00 (0-85186-816-9, R6816) CRC Pr.

***Recent Advances in the Chemistry of Insect Control, Vol. 2.** Crombie. (C). 1990. text ed. 132.00 (0-85186-627-1) CRC Pr.

Recent Advances in the Chemistry of Insect Control, I, No. 53. James. 1988. 65.00 (0-85186-965-3) CRC Pr.

Recent Advances in the Chemistry of Meat, No. 47. Royal Society of Chemistry Staff. 1989. 49.00 (0-85186-905-X) CRC Pr.

Recent Advances in the Development & Germination of Seeds. Ed. by R. B. Taylorson. LC 90-33668. (NATO ASI Series A, Life Sciences: Vol. 187). (Illus.). 304p. 1990. 95.00 (0-306-43521-7, Plenum Pr) Plenum.

Recent Advances in the Developmental Biology of Central Nervous System Malformations. Ed. by Ntinos C. Myrianthopoulos & Daniel Bergsma. LC 79-4947. (Alan R. Liss Ser.: Vol. 15, No. 3). 1979. 19.00 (0-685-03296-5) March of Dimes.

Recent Advances in the Epidemiology & Prevention of Gallstone Disease: Proceedings of the Second International Workshop on Epidemiology & Prevention of Gallstone Disease. Ed. by L. Capocaccia et al. (Developments in Gastroenterology Ser.). 192p. 1991. lib. bdg. 104.50 (0-7923-0994-4) Kluwer Ac.

Recent Advances in the Management of Infertility. Ed. by Christopher Chen et al. (Illus.). 368p. 1990. text ed. write for info. (0-07-099188-X) McGraw-Hill HPD.

Recent Advances in the Management of Pain. fac. ed. Ed. by Costantino Benedetti et al. LC 84-15111. (Advances in Pain Research & Therapy Ser.: No. 7). (Illus.). 712p. pap. 180.00 (0-7837-7510-5, 2046995) Bks Demand.

Recent Advances in the Management of Patients with Acute Myocardial Infarction. Ed. by J. S. Alpert. (Journal: Cardiology: Vol. 76, No. 2). (Illus.). 92p. 1989. pap. 51.25 (3-8055-5038-3) S Karger.

Recent Advances in the Modeling of Hydrologic Systems. Ed. by David S. Bowles & P. Edna O'Connell. 684p. (C). 1991. lib. bdg. 250.00 (0-7923-1398-4) Kluwer Ac.

Recent Advances in the Paleobiology & Geology of the Cnidaria, Vol. 54. (Illus.). 558p. 1984. 60.00 (0-87710-399-2) Paleo Res.

Recent Advances in the Pharmcological Control of Gonadal Function. Ed. by A. Caufriez & M. G. Forest. (Journal: Hormone Research: Vol. 28, No. 2-4, 1987). vi, 212p. 1988. pap. 99.25 (3-8055-4822-2) S Karger.

Recent Advances in the Quantum Theory of Polymers: Proceedings. Ed. by J. M. Andre et al. (Lecture Notes in Physics Ser.: Vol. 113). 306p. 1980. pap. 26.00 (3-540-09731-7) Spr-Verlag.

Recent Advances in the Reconstruction of Common Slavic (1971 to 1982) Henrik Birnbaum & Peter T. Merrill. vi, 141p. (Orig.). 1985. pap. 17.95 (0-89357-116-4) Slavica.

Recent Advances in the Representation Theory of Rings & C-Algebras by Continuous Sections. Ed. by K. H. Hofmann & J. Liukkonen. LC 74-11237. (Memoirs Ser.: No. 1/148). 182p. 1974. pap. 19.00 (0-8218-1848-1, MEMO/1/148) Am Math.

Recent Advances in the Structural Dynamic Modeling of Composite Motor Blades & Thick Composites. Ed. by P. P. Friedmann & J. B. Kosmatka. (AD Ser.: Vol. 30). 196p. 1992. 52.50 (0-7918-1105-0, G00749) ASME.

Recent Advances in the Study of Dental Calculus. J. M. Ten Cate. (Dental Research Group Workshop Proceedings Ser.). (Illus.). 284p. 1989. 80.00 (0-19-963122-0, IRL Pr) OUP.

Recent Advances in the Study of Hepatitis C Virus: Epidemiological, Clinical & Molecular Basis. Ed. by O. Hino. (Journal: Intervirology Ser.: Vol. 37, No. 2, 1994). (Illus.). 84p. 1994. pap. 72.25 (3-8055-6059-1) S Karger.

Recent Advances in the Study of Plant Viruses. K. M. Smith. 423p. 1987. pap. 175.00 (0-7855-0386-2, Pub. by Intl Bks & Periodicals II) St Mut.

Recent Advances in the Superworld: Proceedings of the International Workshop. J. L. Lopez & D. V. Nanopoulos. 396p. 1994. text ed. 106.00 (981-02-1730-7) World Scientific Pub.

Recent Advances in the Usage of Mitomycin. Ed. by I. C. Henderson. (Journal: Oncology: Vol. 50, Suppl. 1, 1993). (Illus.). 84p. 1993. pap. 46.25 (3-8055-5775-2) S Karger.

Recent Advances in Theoretical Physics: Proceedings of the Silver Jubille Workshop, IIT, Kanpur, 5-16 December, 1984. Ed. by R. Ramachandran. 464p. 1985. 78.00 (9971-5-0014-0) World Scientific Pub.

Recent Advances in Therapeutic Diets. 5th ed. LC 95-25268. 416p. 1995. text ed., ring bd. 49.95 (0-8138-1074-4) Iowa St U Pr.

Recent Advances in Thin-Layer Chromatography. Ed. by F. A. A. Dallas et al. LC 88-17880. (Illus.). 262p. 1988. 85.00 (0-306-42934-9, Plenum Pr) Plenum.

Recent Advances in Titanium Metal Matrix Composites: Proceedings: Symposium on Recent Advances in Titanium Metal Matrix Composites (1994: Rosemont, Illinois): Proceedings. Ed. by F. H. Froes & J. Storer. LC 95-74272. (Illus.). 450p. 1995. 102.00 (0-87339-285-X, 285X) Minerals Metals.

***Recent Advances in Total Least Squares Techniques & Errors-in-Variables Modeling.** Ed. by Sabine Van Huffel. (SIAM Proceedings in Applied Mathematics Ser.: Vol. PR 93). 350p. (Orig.). 1997. pap. text ed. 56.00 (0-89871-393-5) Soc Indus-Appl Math.

Recent Advances in Tourism Marketing Research. Ed. by Daniel R. Fesenmaier et al. LC 96-32039. (Journal of Travel & Tourism Marketing: Vol. 5, Nos. 1/2/3). 279p. (C). 1996. 45.00 (1-56024-836-X) Haworth Pr.

Recent Advances in Tropical Neurology. Ed. by F. Clifford Rose. LC 95-49192. (Developments in Neurology Ser.: No. 10). 438p. 1995. 285.25 (0-444-82272-0) Elsevier.

Recent Advances in Tryptophan Research: Tryptophan & Serotonin Pathways. Ed. by Graziella A. Filippini et al. LC 96-20315. (Advances in Experimental Medicine & Biology Ser.: Vol. 398). (Illus.). 680p. (C). 1996. 149.50 (0-306-45309-6, Plenum Pr) Plenum.

Recent Advances in Ultrasound in Biomedicine, Vol. 1. Ed. by D. N. White. LC 78-643268. (Ultrasound in Biomedicine Ser.). 270p. reprint ed. pap. 77.00 (0-8357-7005-2, 2033356) Bks Demand.

***Recent Advances in Upper Extremity Arthroplasty: Proceedings of the Brussels International Upper Extremity Conference.** 300p. 1997. lib. bdg. 55.00 (981-02-2699-3) World Scientific Pub.

Recent Advances in Urology - Andrology, No. 5. Ed. by W. F. Hendry. (Illus.). 236p. 1991. text ed. 66.00 (0-443-04354-X) Churchill.

Recent Advances in Urology-Andrology, Vol. 6. Ed. by W. F. Hendry & R. S. Kirby. (Illus.). 240p. 1993. 84.00 (0-443-04868-1) Churchill.

Recent Advances in Uveitis. Ed. by J. P. Dernouchamps et al. (Illus.). 632p. 1993. lib. bdg. 200.00 (90-6299-092-4) Kugler Pubns.

Recent Advances in Ventricular Conduction: Proceedings of the International Symposium, Portugal, July, 1973. Ed. by M. Cerqueira-Gomes. (Advances in Cardiology Ser.: Vol. 14). 250p. 1975. 111.25 (3-8055-2094-8) S Karger.

Recent Advances in Verocytotoxin-Producing Escherichia Coli Infections: Proceedings of the Second International Symposium & Workshop on Verocytotoxin (Shiga-Like Toxin) - Producing Escherichia Coli Infections, Bergamo, Italy, 27-30 June, 1994. Ed. by Mohamed A. Karmali & Antonio G. Goglio. LC 94-40507. (International Congress Ser.: No. 1072). 406p. 1994. 210.50 (0-444-81840-5) Elsevier.

Recent Advances in Virus Diagnosis. Ed. by M. S. McNulty & J. B. McFerran. (Current Topics in Veterinary Medicine & Animal Science Ser.). 1984. lib. bdg. 117.50 (0-89838-674-8) Kluwer Ac.

Recent Advances in Wavelet Analysis. Ed. by Larry L. Schumaker & Glenn Webb. (Wavelet Analysis & Its Applications Ser.). (Illus.). 364p. 1993. text ed. 67.00 (0-12-632370-4) Acad Pr.

Recent Advances in Wind Engineering: Proceedings of the Second Asia-Pacific Symposium on Wind Engineering, Beijing, China, 26-29 June, 1989, 2 vols. Ed. by T. F. Sun. LC 89-8562. (International Academic Publishers Ser.). (Illus.). 1223p. 1990. 360.00 (0-08-037872-2, Pergamon Pr) Elsevier.

Recent Advances in X-Ray Characterization of Materials-II, Volume 18. Ed. by P. Krishna. (Progress in Crystal Growth & Characterization Ser.: No. 18). 278p. 1989. 263.75 (0-08-037368-2, Pergamon Pr) Elsevier.

***Recent Advances in 3D Digital Imaging & Modeling, 1997.** 368p. 1997. pap. 90.00 (0-8186-7943-3) IEEE Comp Soc.

Recent Advances of Chemistry & Molecular Biology in Cancer Research: Proceedings from the International Symposium on Recent Advances of Chemistry & Molecular Biology in Cancer Research. Ed. by Q Dai et al. 1994. 157.95 (0-387-57384-4) Spr-Verlag.

Recent Advances of the Chronobiology of Allergy & Immunology: Symposium on Chronobiology in Allergy & Immunology, Israel, 1979. Michael H. Smolensky. LC 80-41028. (Illus.). 358p. 1980. 76.00 (0-08-025891-3, Pergamon Pr) Elsevier.

Recent Advances on Environmentally Compliant Manufacturing. Mohammad Jamshidi. 1993. boxed write for info. (0-13-769977-8) P-H.

Recent Advantages in the Management of Infertility. Christopher Chen. 1989. text ed. 50.00 (0-07-099144-8) McGraw.

Recent America: The United States since 1945. Dewey W. Grantham. LC 86-6321. (Illus.). 464p. 1987. pap. text ed. write for info. (0-88295-841-0) Harlan Davidson.

***Recent America: The United States since 1945.** 2nd ed. Dewey W. Grantham. (Illus.). 500p. (C). 1998. pap. text ed. 24.95 (0-88295-941-7) Harlan Davidson.

Recent American Art. Jean-Claude Lebensztejn. LC 94-42314. 184p. 1995. pap. text ed. 17.95 (0-226-46997-2); lib. bdg. 40.00 (0-226-46996-4) U Ch Pr.

Recent American Foreign Policy: Basic Documents 1941-1951. Francis O. Wilcox & Thorsten V. Kalijarvi. LC 77-141283. (Illus.). 927p. (C). 1972. reprint ed. text ed. 95.00 (0-8371-5880-X, WIAF, Greenwood Pr) Greenwood.

R

Recent American Opera: A Production Guide. Rebecca Kornick. 1991. text ed. 57.50 (*0-231-06920-0*) Col U Pr.

Recent & Ancient Nonmarine Depositional Environments: Models for Exploration: Based on a Symposium Sponsored by the Rocky Mountain Section. Ed. by Frank G. Ethridge & Romeo M. Flores. LC 81-184668. (Society of Economic Paleontologists & Mineralogists, Special Publication Ser.: No. 31). 357p. reprint ed. pap. 101.80 (*0-8357-2956-7*, 2039212) Bks Demand.

Recent & Fossil Diatoms Flora of the Golf of Dansk, Southern Baltic Sea Vol. 28. A. Witkowski. (Bibliotheca Diatomologica Ser.). (Illus.). 228p. 1994. text ed. 125.00 (*3-443-57019-4*) Lubrecht & Cramer.

Recent & Fossil Marine Molluska of Tongatabu. J. M. Ostergaard. (BMB Ser.). 1974. reprint ed. pap. 25.00 (*0-527-02237-3*) Periodicals Srv.

Recent Antarctic & Subantarctic Brachiopods. Ed. by M. W. Foster. LC 74-9234. (Antarctic Research Ser.: Vol. 21). (Illus.). 189p. 1974. 39.00 (*0-87590-121-2*) Am Geophysical.

Recent Applications in Computational Mechanics. Ed. by Dimitris L. Karabalis. (Sessions Proceedings Ser.). 208p. 1986. 25.00 (*0-87262-554-0*) Am Soc Civil Eng.

Recent Approaches to Axiology. Ed. by H. M. Joshi. (C). 1991. 34.00 (*81-217-0093-0*, Pub. by Bharat Vidya II) S Asia.

Recent Archaeological Discoveries & Biblical Research. William G. Dever. (Illus.). 200p. (C). 1993. pap. 14.95 (*0-295-97261-0*) U of Wash Pr.

Recent Aspects of Quantum Fields: Proceedings of the XXX Int. Universitatswochen fur Kernphysik, Schladming, Austria February & March 1991. Ed. by H. Mitter et al. (Lecture Notes in Physics Ser.: Vol. 396). xiii, 332p. 1992. 55.00 (*0-685-54830-9*) Spr-Verlag.

Recent Books on World War Two. Francis Neilson. (Revisionist Historiography Ser.). 1979. lib. bdg. 39.95 (*0-685-96636-4*) Revisionist Pr.

Recent Case Histories of Permanent Geosynthetic-Reinforced Soil Retaining Walls: Proceedings of Seiken Symposium No. 11, Tokyo, November 1992. F. Tatsuoka & D. Leshchisky. (Illus.). 360p. (C). 1994. 80.00 (*90-5410-358-2*, Pub. by A A Balkema NE) Ashgate Pub Co.

Recent Centralizing Tendencies in State Educational Administration. William C. Webster. LC 68-56693. (Columbia University. Studies in the Social Sciences: No. 20). reprint ed. 37.50 (*0-404-51020-5*) AMS Pr.

Recent Changes in American Constitutional Theory. John W. Burgess. LC 76-172206. (Right Wing Individualist Tradition in America Ser.). 1972. reprint ed. 19.95 (*0-405-00417-6*) Ayer.

Recent Changes in European Trade. Unece Staff. (Economic Bulletin for Europe). 1985. pap. 27.00 (*0-08-032665-X*, Pergamon Pr) Elsevier.

Recent Changes in Production. Charles A. Bliss. (NBER Bulletin Ser.: No. 51). 1934. reprint ed. 20.00 (*0-685-61164-7*) Natl Bur Econ Res.

Recent Changes in State, Local, & State-Local Tax Levels. Steven D. Gold. (Legislative Finance Papers: No. 75). 30p. 1991. 15.00 (*1-55516-075-1*, 5101-75) Natl Conf State Legis.

***Recent Changes in the Treatment of Congestive Heart Failure: Satellite Symposium at the Joint XIIth World Congress of Cardiology & XVIth of the European Society of Cardiology, Berlin, September 1994.** Ed. by Peter A. Van Zwieten. (Journal: Vol. 88, Suppl. 2, 1997). (Illus.). IV, 36p. 1997. pap. 21.75 (*3-8055-6520-8*) S Karger.

Recent Chinese Studies of the Boxer Movement. David D. Buck. LC 87-12910. 224p. (Orig.). (gr. 13). 1987. pap. text ed. 33.95 (*0-87332-441-2*) M E Sharpe.

Recent Clinical Developments in Gynecologic Oncology. Ed. by C. Paul Morrow et al. LC 83-3312. (Progress in Cancer Research & Therapy Ser.: No. 24). (Illus.). 233p. 1983. reprint ed. pap. 66.50 (*0-7837-9517-3*, 2060266) Bks Demand.

Recent Commonwealth Literature, 2 vols. Ed. by R. K. Dhawan et al. 300p. 1989. text ed. 50.00 (*81-85218-09-9*, Pub. by Prestige II) Advent Bks Div.

Recent Concepts in ORL. Ed. by K. Jahnke & C. R. Pfaltz. (Advances in Oto-Rhino-Laryngology Ser.: Vol. 39). (Illus.). xii, 152p. 1988. 119.25 (*3-8055-4725-0*) S Karger.

Recent Concepts in Sarcoma Treatment. Ed. by J. R. Ryan & L. O. Baker. (Developments in Oncology Ser.). (C). 1988. lib. bdg. 157.50 (*0-89838-376-5*) Kluwer Ac.

Recent Controversies in Political Economy. Ed. by Russell Lewis. LC 91-45321. 320p. (C). (gr. 13). 1992. text ed. 79.95 (*0-415-06163-6*, A7333) Routledge.

Recent Corporate Profits in the United States. Solomon Fabricant. (NBER Bulletin Ser.: No. 50). 1934. reprint ed. 20.00 (*0-685-61163-9*) Natl Bur Econ Res.

***Recent Demographic Development in Europe 1996.** Ed. by European Population Committee. (Illus.). 414p. 1996. pap. 18.00 (*92-871-3108-2*, Pub. by Council of Europe FR) Manhattan Pub Co.

Recent Development in Bulk Queueing Models. Jyoti P. Medhi. (C). 1986. 18.00 (*0-85226-549-2*) S Asia.

Recent Development in Flow Separation. Paul K. Chang. LC 83-72431. (Illus.). 300p. 1983. write for info. (*0-9612410-6-3*) P K Chang.

Recent Development in the Genetics of Insect Disease Vectors. Ed. by William Steiner et al. (Illus.). 665p. 1982. text ed. 26.00 (*0-87563-224-6*) Stipes.

Recent Development of Nuclear Study Using Electron & Photon Beams. Tong Cheon. 250p. 1995. text ed. 71.00 (*981-3049-04-9*) World Scientific Pub.

Recent Developments & Applications in Mathematics & Computer Science: Proceedings of the College ICTP, Trieste, Italy 7 May-1 June 1990. Ed. by R. F. Churchhouse et al. 250p. 1991. text ed. 83.00 (*981-02-0842-1*) World Scientific Pub.

Recent Developments & Applications of DFT 1. J.M. Seminario. 1996. write for info. (*0-614-17893-2*) Elsevier.

***Recent Developments & Applications of Modern Density Functional Theory.** LC 96-37345. (Theoretical & Computational Chemistry Ser.). 862p. 1996. 409.50 (*0-444-82404-9*) Elsevier.

Recent Developments in Aerosol Science. Symposium on Aerosol Science & Technology Staff. Ed. by David T. Shaw. LC 78-17487. (Wiley-Interscience Publications). 343p. 1978. reprint ed. pap. 97.80 (*0-7837-3469-7*, 2057800) Bks Demand.

Recent Developments in Alcoholism. Ed. by Marc Galanter et al. (Alcohol & Violence-Epidemiology, Neurobiology, Psychology, Family Issues Ser.: Vol. 13). (Illus.). 406p. (C). 1997. 89.50 (*0-306-45358-4*, Plenum Pr) Plenum.

Recent Developments in Alcoholism, Vol. 1. Ed. by Marc Galanter. 506p. 1983. 89.50 (*0-306-41202-0*, Plenum Pr) Plenum.

Recent Developments in Alcoholism, Vol. 2. Ed. by Marc Galanter. 452p. 1984. 89.50 (*0-306-41534-8*, Plenum Pr) Plenum.

Recent Developments in Alcoholism, Vol. 3. Ed. by Marc Galanter. 316p. 1985. 89.50 (*0-306-41852-5*, Plenum Pr) Plenum.

Recent Developments in Alcoholism, Vol. 4. Ed. by Marc Galanter. 440p. 1986. 89.50 (*0-306-42170-4*, Plenum Pr) Plenum.

Recent Developments in Alcoholism, Vol. 5. Ed. by Marc Galanter. 450p. 1987. 89.50 (*0-306-42427-4*, Plenum Pr) Plenum.

Recent Developments in Alcoholism, Vol. 6. Ed. by Marc Galanter. LC 83-643791. (Illus.). 440p. 1988. 89.50 (*0-306-42721-4*, Plenum Pr) Plenum.

Recent Developments in Alcoholism Vol. 12: Alcoholism & Women. Ed. by Marc Galanter et al. 472p. 1995. 89.50 (*0-306-44921-8*) Plenum.

Recent Developments in Alcoholism, Vol. 10: Alcohol & Cocaine: Similarities & Differences. Ed. by Marc Galanter. (Illus.). 336p. 1992. 79.50 (*0-306-44145-4*, Plenum Pr) Plenum.

Recent Developments in Alcoholism, Vol. 11: Ten Years of Progress. Ed. by Marc Galanter. LC 83-643791. (Illus.). 518p. (C). 1993. 85.00 (*0-306-44442-9*, Plenum Pr) Plenum.

Recent Developments in Alcoholism, Vol. 7: Treatment Research. Ed. by Marc Galanter. LC 83-643791. (Illus.). 404p. 1989. 89.50 (*0-306-43042-8*, Plenum Pr) Plenum.

Recent Developments in Alcoholism, Vol. 8: Combined Alcohol & Other Drug Dependence. Ed. by Marc Galanter. LC 83-643791. (Illus.). 366p. 1990. 85.00 (*0-306-43349-4*, Plenum Insight) Plenum.

Recent Developments in Alcoholism, Vol. 9: Children of Alcoholics: Genetic Predisposition, Fetal Alcohol Syndrome, Vulnerability to Disease, Social & Environmental. Ed. by Marc Galanter. (Illus.). 350p. 1991. 85.00 (*0-306-43840-2*, Plenum Pr) Plenum.

Recent Developments in Applied Demand Analysis: Alcohol, Advertising & Global Consumption. E. Antony Selvanathan. LC 95-30838. (Illus.). 396p. 1995. 117.00 (*3-540-59197-4*) Spr-Verlag.

Recent Developments in Aquaculture, No. 4. J. E. Muir & Ronald Roberts. (Illus.). 450p. 1993. 125.00 (*0-632-02898-X*) Blackwell Sci.

***Recent Developments in Bevel & Hypoid Gearing.** A. H. Candee. (Technical Papers). 1936. pap. text ed. 30.00 (*1-55589-416-X*) AGMA.

Recent Developments in Biofouling Control. Ed. by M. Fingerman et al. (Illus.). 464p. (C). 1994. text ed. 95.00 (*90-5410-251-9*, Pub. by A A Balkema NE) Ashgate Pub Co.

Recent Developments in Catalysis: Theory & Practice. Editions Technip Staff. Ed. by B. Viswanathan & C. N. Pillai. (Illus.). 815p. (C). 1991. 480.00 (*2-7108-0626-6*, Pub. by Edits Technip FR) St Mut.

Recent Developments in Catfish Aquaculture: Selected Papers from the 1992 Catfish Research Symposium Held in Orange Beach, Alaska. Ed. by Craig S. Tucker. LC 94-27. (Journal of Applied Aquaculture). (Illus.). 410p. 1994. lib. bdg. 69.95 (*1-56022-047-3*) Haworth Jrnl Co-Edits.

Recent Developments in Chemical Process & Plant Design. Ed. by Y. A. Liu et al. LC 87-17610. 509p. 1987. text ed. 190.00 (*0-471-84780-1*) Wiley.

Recent Developments in Chemotherapy of Narcotic Addiction, Vol. 311. Ed. by Benjamin Kissin et al. (Annals Ser.). 1978. pap. 42.00 (*0-89072-067-3*) NY Acad Sci.

Recent Developments in Civil Aviation in India. Shri J. Tytler. 1987. 26.00 (*81-7095-004-X*, Pub. by Lancer II) S Asia.

Recent Developments in Clinical Research. Ed. by C. E. Orfanos. (Current Problems in Dermatology Ser.: Vol. 13). (Illus.). viii, 192p. 1984. 131.25 (*3-8055-3928-2*) S Karger.

Recent Developments in Computational Mechanics. Ed. by P. K. Basu & A. Nagar. LC 93-73611. 139p. pap. 47.50 (*0-7918-1254-5*) ASME.

Recent Developments in Computer Vision: Proceedings, Second Asian Conference on Computer Vision, ACCV '95, Singapore, December 5-8, 1995. Ed. by S. Li et al. LC 96-4291. (Lecture Notes in Computer Science Ser.: Vol. 1035). 604p. 1996. pap. text ed. 94.00 (*3-540-60793-5*) Spr-Verlag.

Recent Developments in Concrete Floater Technology. Dag N. Jenssen. 1989. 150.00 (*90-6314-530-6*, Pub. by Lorne & MacLean Marine) St Mut.

Recent Developments in Concrete Floater Technology. Day N. Jenssen. (C). 1989. 125.00 (*0-89771-735-X*, Pub. by Lorne & MacLean Marine) St Mut.

Recent Developments in Conformal Field Theories: Trieste Conference. Ed. by S. Randjbar-Dacmi et al. 320p. (C). 1990. pap. 37.00 (*981-02-0280-6*); text ed. 101.00 (*981-02-0279-2*) World Scientific Pub.

Recent Developments in Decision Support Systems. Ed. by Clyde W. Holsapple & Andrew B. Whinston. LC 92-41642. (NATO ASI Series F: Computer & Systems Sciences, Special Programme AET: Vol. 101). 1993. 149.00 (*0-387-56157-9*) Spr-Verlag.

Recent Developments in Digital Imaging: Proceedings of the AAPM 1984 Summer School Held at the University of Notre Dame, South Bend, Indiana, July 22-27, 1984. Ed. by Kunio Doi et al. (American Association of Physicists in Medicine Symposium Ser.: No. 12). 580p. 1985. 70.00 (*0-88318-463-X*) Am Inst Physics.

Recent Developments in Dominion-Provincial Fiscal Relations in Canada. James A. Maxwell. (Occasional Papers: No. 25). 64p. 1948. reprint ed. 20.00 (*0-87014-340-9*); reprint ed. mic. film 20.00 (*0-685-61274-0*) Natl Bur Econ Res.

Recent Developments in Electronic Engine Control & Fuel Injection Management. 84p. 1987. 19.00 (*0-89883-974-2*, SP703) Soc Auto Engineers.

Recent Developments in European Thought. Ed. by Francis S. Marvin. LC 71-111851. (Essay Index Reprint Ser.). 1977. 21.95 (*0-8369-1619-0*) Ayer.

Recent Developments in Experimental Economics, 2 vols. Ed. by John D. Hey & Graham Loomes. (International Library of Critical Writings in Economics Ser.: No. 29). 832p. 1993. 275.00 (*1-85278-730-9*) E Elgar.

Recent Developments in External Debt Restructuring. K. Burke Dillon et al. (Occasional Paper Ser.: No. 40). vii, 68p. 1985. pap. 7.50 (*0-939934-52-3*) Intl Monetary.

Recent Developments in Finance. Ed. by Anthony Saunders. 224p. 1991. text ed. 40.00 (*1-55623-706-5*) Irwin Prof Pubng.

Recent Developments in Fish Otolith Research. Ed. by David H. Secor et al. (Illus.). 600p. (C). 1995. text ed. 65.00 (*1-57003-011-1*) U of SC Pr.

***Recent Developments in Flavor & Fragrance Chemistry: Proceedings of the 3rd International Haarmann & Reimer Symposium.** R. Hopp & K. Mori. (Illus.). xii, 304p. 1993. 105.00 (*3-527-28535-0*, VCH) Wiley.

Recent Developments in Fluvial Sedimentology. Ed. by Frank G. Ethridge et al. (Special Publications: No. 39). 398p. 1987. 55.00 (*0-918985-67-6*) SEPM.

***Recent Developments in Fluvial Sedimentology: Contributions from the Third International Fluvial Sedimentology Conference.** Ed. by Frank G. Ethridege et al. LC 87-160013. (Society of Economic Paleontologists & Mineralogists Ser.: No. 39). (Illus.). 397p. 1987. reprint ed. pap. 113.20 (*0-608-02974-2*, 2063442) Bks Demand.

***Recent Developments in Forensic Linguistics.** Ed. by Hannes Kniffka et al. LC 96-10789. 406p. 1996. pap. 63.95 (*0-8204-3153-2*, P123) P Lang Pubng.

Recent Developments in Game Theory. John Creedy et al. 240p. 1992. text ed. 85.00 (*1-85278-533-0*) E Elgar.

Recent Developments in Geometry. Ed. by S. Cheng et al. LC 89-18039. (Contemporary Mathematics Ser.: Vol. 101). 338p. 1989. pap. 46.00 (*0-8218-5107-1*, CONM/101) Am Math.

Recent Developments in Geotextile Filters & Prefabricated Drainage Geocomposites, No. 1281. Ed. by Shobha Bhatia & L. David Suits. LC 96-14901. (STP Ser.: Vol. 1281). (Illus.). 240p. 1996. text ed. 43.00 (*0-8031-2047-8*, 04-012810-38) ASTM.

Recent Developments in Germanic Linguistics. Ed. by Rosina L. Lippi-Green. LC 92-34480. (Current Issues in Linguistic Theory Ser.: No. 93). xii, 163p. 1992. 47.00 (*1-55619-154-5*) Benjamins North Am.

Recent Developments in Graphic Arts Research see Advances in Printing Science & Technology

Recent Developments in Gravitation: Proceedings of the Relativity Meeting 1989. E. Verdaguer et al. 1990. pap. 36.00 (*981-02-0269-5*); text ed. 113.00 (*981-02-0268-7*) World Scientific Pub.

Recent Developments in Gravitation: Proceedings of the Relativity Meeting 1991. A. Feinstein & J. Ibanes. 260p. 1992. text ed. 81.00 (*981-02-1110-4*) World Scientific Pub.

***Recent Developments in Gravitation & Mathematical Physics.** 408p. 1996. lib. bdg. 60.00 (*981-02-2755-8*) World Scientific Pub.

Recent Developments in Ground Improvement Techniques: Proceedings of the International Symposium Held at Asian Institute of Technology, Bangkok, 29 November - 3 December 1982. Ed. by A. S. Balasubramaniam et al. 598p. (C). 1985. text ed. 170.00 (*90-6191-568-6*, Pub. by A A Balkema NE) Ashgate Pub Co.

Recent Developments in High Energy Physics. Ed. by H. Mitter & C. B. Lang. (Acta Physica Austriaca Ser.: Suppl. 25). (Illus.). 547p. 1983. 111.95 (*0-387-81771-9*) Spr-Verlag.

***Recent Developments in High Speed Chain Drives.** G. M. Bartlett. (Technical Papers). 1926. pap. text ed. 30.00 (*1-55589-440-2*) AGMA.

***Recent Developments in High Temperature Superconductivity: Proceedings of th First Polish-U. S. Conference, Held at Wrocaw & Dusznikizdroj, Poland, 11-15 September 1995.** Ed. by Jan Klamut & B. W. Veal. LC 96-36118. (Lecture Notes in Physics Ser.: Vol. 475). 362p. 1996. 84.00 (*3-540-61631-4*) Spr-Verlag.

Recent Developments in Historical Phonology. Ed. by Jacek Fisiak. (Trends in Linguistics Ser.). 1978. pap. text ed. 152.35 (*90-279-7706-2*) Mouton.

Recent Developments in Hydrogen Technology, Vol. I. Ed. by Kenneth D. Williamson, Jr. 168p. 1985. 101.00 (*0-8493-5126-X*, TP359, CRC Reprint) Franklin.

Recent Developments in Hydrogen Technology, Vol. 2. Kenneth D. Williamson, Jr. & F. J. Edeskuty. LC 84-29360. 168p. 1986. Vol. II, 168p. 98.00 (*0-8493-5127-8*, TP359, CRC Reprint) Franklin.

***Recent Developments in Infant Nutrition.** Ed. by J. Bindels. 416p. (C). 1996. lib. bdg. 130.00 (*0-7923-8707-4*) Kluwer Ac.

Recent Developments in Insect Neurohormones. Marie Raabe. (Illus.). 484p. 1989. 120.00 (*0-306-43175-0*, Plenum Pr) Plenum.

Recent Developments in International Banking & Finance, Vol. 2. Ed. by Sarkis J. Khoury & Alo Ghosh. LC 85-46007. 448p. 1988. text ed. 59.00 (*0-669-16197-7*) Free Pr.

Recent Developments in International Banking & Finance, Vols. IV & V. Ed. by Foundation for Research in International Banking & Finance Staff & Sarkis J. Khoury. 524p. 1991. 168.75 (*0-444-88626-5*, North Holland) Elsevier.

Recent Developments in Inventory Theory. Moshe F. Friedman. 74p. 1981. pap. 46.00 (*0-08-025844-1*, Pergamon Pr) Elsevier.

***Recent Developments in Jack-Up Platforms.** Date not set. 195.00 (*0-8464-4167-5*) Beekman Pubs.

Recent Developments in Jack-up Platforms: Design, Construction, & Operation. Ed. by L. F. Boswell & C. D'Mello. LC 92-10000. (Illus.). 1992. 165.00 (*0-632-03281-2*) Blackwell Sci.

Recent Developments in Job Analysis: Proceedings of the International Symposium on Job Analysis. Ed. by Kurt Landau & Walter Rohmert. 290p. 1989. 99.00 (*0-85066-790-9*) Taylor & Francis.

Recent Developments in Laboratory & Field Tests & Analysis of Geotechnical Problems: Proceedings of International Symposium, Bangkok, 6-9 December 1983. Ed. by A. S. Balasubramaniam et al. 632p. (C). 1986. text ed. 190.00 (*90-6191-623-2*, Pub. by A A Balkema NE) Ashgate Pub Co.

Recent Developments in Lattice Theory. W. D. Ludwig. (Tracts in Modern Physics Ser.: Vol. 43). (Illus.). 1967. 86.95 (*0-387-03982-1*) Spr-Verlag.

Recent Developments in Macroeconomics, 3 vols. Ed. by Edmund S. Phelps. (International Library of Critical Writings in Economics Ser.: Vol. 13). 1432p. 1991. text ed. 445.00 (*1-85278-297-8*) E Elgar.

Recent Developments in Mathematical Programming. Ed. by H. I. Kumar. 469p. Date not set. pap. text ed. 62.00 (*2-88124-800-4*) Gordon & Breach.

Recent Developments in Mathematical Programming. Ed. by H. I. Kumar. 469p. 1991. text ed. 136.00 (*2-88124-820-9*) Gordon & Breach.

Recent Developments in Mechanical Testing - STP 608. A. Karl Schmieder. 133p. 1976. pap. 14.50 (*0-8031-0547-9*, 04-608000-23) ASTM.

Recent Developments in Medical & Physiological Imaging. Ed. by Ray Clark & Mervyn Goff. 180p. 1986. pap. text ed. 25.00 (*0-85066-955-3*) Taylor & Francis.

Recent Developments in Medical & Physiological Imaging. Ed. by Ray Clark & Mervyn Goff. 180p. 1986. 69.00 (*0-85066-939-1*) Taylor & Francis.

Recent Developments in Micromechanics: Proceedings of the Mini-Symposium on Micromechanics at the CSME Mechanical Engineering Forum 1990, University of Toronto, June 3-9, 1990. Ed. by D. R. Axelrad & W. Muschik. viii, 204p. 1991. 59.00 (*0-387-53362-1*) Spr-Verlag.

Recent Developments in Molecular Spectroscopy: Proceedings of the 10th National Conference with International Participation. P. Simova et al. 764p. 1989. text ed. 138.00 (*9971-5-0782-X*) World Scientific Pub.

Recent Developments in Mucosal Immunology, Pt. A: Cellular Interactions. Ed. by Jiri Mestecky et al. LC 87-14129. (Illus.). 1866p. 1987. Pt. A, Cellular Interactions. 135.00 (*0-306-42614-5*, Plenum Pr) Plenum.

Recent Developments in Mucosal Immunology, Pt. B: Effector Functions. Ed. by Jiri Mestecky et al. LC 87-14129. (Illus.). 1866p. 1987. Pt. B, Effector Functions. 155.00 (*0-306-42775-3*, Plenum Pr) Plenum.

***Recent Developments in NC & CNC Gear Hobbing.** W. Eggert. (AGMA Technical Paper). 1981. pap. text ed. 30.00 (*1-55589-168-3*) AGMA.

***Recent Developments in Non-Neoclassical Economics.** Stanley Bober. 490p. 1997. 76.95 (*1-85972-338-1*, Pub. by Avebury Pub UK) Ashgate Pub Co.

Recent Developments in Nonequilibrium Thermodynamics: Fluids & Related Topics. Ed. by J. Casas-Vazquez et al. (Lecture Notes in Physics Ser.: Vol. 253). x, 392p. 1986. 59.95 (*0-387-16489-8*) Spr-Verlag.

Recent Developments in Nonequilibrium Thermodynamics: Proceedings of the Meeting Held at Bellaterra School of Thermodynamics, Autonomous University of Barcelona, Spain, Sept. 26-30, 1983. Ed. by J. Casas-Vazquez et al. (Lecture Notes in Physics Ser.: Vol. 199). xiii, 485p. 1984. 47.95 (*0-387-12927-8*) Spr-Verlag.

Recent Developments in Numerical Methods & Software for ODEs - DAEs - PDEs. William E. Schiesser. 350p. (C). 1992. text ed. 108.00 (*981-02-0557-0*) World Scientific Pub.

Recent Developments in Obstetrics & Gynecology. Ed. by A. R. Genazzani et al. 750p. 1996. 98.00 (*1-85070-700-6*) Prthnon Pub.

Recent Developments in Operator Theory & Its Applications: International Conference in Winnipeg, October 2-6, 1994. I. Gohberg et al. LC 96-20165. (Operator Theory, Advances, & Applications Ser.: Vol. 87). 1996. write for info. (*0-8176-5413-5*) Birkhauser.

Recent Developments in Optimization: Seventh French-German conference on Optimization. Roland Durier & Christian Michelot. LC 95-30519. (Lecture Notes in Economics & Mathematical Systems Ser.: No. 429). 1995. write for info. (*0-387-60041-8*) Spr-Verlag.

Recent Developments in Optimization: Seventh French-German Conference on Optimization, Vol. VIII. Christian Michelot. (Lecture Notes in Economics & Mathematical Systems Ser.: Vol. 429). (Illus.). 356p. 1995. pap. 78.00 (*3-540-60041-8*) Spr-Verlag.

***Recent Developments in Optimization Theory & Nonlinear Analysis: AMS IMU Special Session on Optimization & Nonlinear Analysis, May 24-26, 1995, Jerusalem, Vol. 204.** Yair Al Censor & Simeon Reich. LC 96-29934. (Contemporary Mathematics Ser.). 1997. 49.00 (*0-8218-0515-0*, CONM/204) Am Math.

***Recent Developments in Parkinson's Disease.** Ed. by Stanley Fahn et al. LC 85-18359. 397p. 1986. reprint ed. pap. 113.20 (*0-608-03406-1*, 2064103) Bks Demand.

Recent Developments in Pesticide Toxicology & Registration. Myron A. Mehlman. (Toxicology & Industrial Health Ser.: Vol. 4, No. 3). (Illus.). 250p. 1988. 55.00 (*0-911131-34-5*) Princeton Sci Pubs.

Recent Developments in Plant Sciences: Prof. S. M. Sircar Memorial Volume. Ed. by S. P. Sen. (Illus.). 395p. 1982. 39.00 (*0-88065-241-1*, Pub. by Today & Tomorrows P & P II) Scholarly Pubns.

Recent Developments in Post Keynesian Economics. Ed. by Philip Arestis & Victoria Chick. (Post Keynesian Economics Study Group Ser.). 224p. 1992. 80.00 (*1-85278-412-1*) E Elgar.

***Recent Developments in Power Electronics: Selected Readings.** Muhammad H. Rashid. 1996. pap. text ed. 49.95 (*0-7803-2311-4*, SR102) Inst Electrical.

Recent Developments in Prophylactic Immunisation. Ed. by Arie J. Zuckerman. (Immunology & Medicine Ser.). (C). 1989. lib. bdg. 139.50 (*0-7923-8910-7*) Kluwer Ac.

Recent Developments in Psychoanalysis: A Critical Evaluation. Morris N. Eagle. LC 87-196. 272p. 1987. pap. 15.95 (*0-674-75080-2*) HUP.

Recent Developments in Psychogeriatrics: A Symposium. Ed. by David Kay & Alexander Walk. LC 70-502113. (British Journal of Psychiatry. Special Publication Ser.: No. 6). 135p. reprint ed. pap. 38.50 (*0-318-34924-8*, 2031459) Bks Demand.

Recent Developments in Public Education Law. Larry D. Bartlett & Lelia B. Helms. 47p. 1993. reprint ed. pap. 9.95 (*1-56534-086-8*) Ed Law Assn.

Recent Developments in Quantum Mechanics: Proceedings of the Brasov Conference, Poiana Brasov 1989, Romania. Ed. by Anne B. De Monvel et al. (C). 1991. lib. bdg. 157.50 (*0-7923-1148-5*) Kluwer Ac.

Recent Developments in Quantum Optics. Ed. by Ramarao Inguva. LC 92-46382. (Illus.). 588p. (C). 1993. 139.50 (*0-306-44403-8*, Plenum Pr) Plenum.

Recent Developments in Rotor Forging Steels. LC 90-80323. 136p. 1990. 20.00 (*0-932897-50-9*) Iron & Steel.

Recent Developments in Ruminant Nutrition, 2. W. Haresign & D. J. Cole. (Illus.). 387p. 1988. 74.95 (*0-407-01164-1*) Buttrwrth-Heinemann.

Recent Developments in Separation Science, 2 vols. N. Li. LC 72-88417. 1982. 243.00 (*0-8493-5031-X*) CRC Pr.

Recent Developments in Separation Science, Vol. VI. Norman N. Li. 208p. 1982. 113.00 (*0-8493-5487-0*, TP156, CRC Reprint) Franklin.

Recent Developments in Separation Science, Vol. VII. Norman N. Li. 224p. 1982. 130.00 (*0-8493-5488-9*, CRC Reprint) Franklin.

Recent Developments in Separation Science, Vol. VIII. Ed. by Norman N. Li & James D. Navratil. 344p. 1986. 204.00 (*0-8493-5489-7*, TP156) CRC Pr.

Recent Developments in Separation Science, Vol. IX. Ed. by Norman N. Li & Joseph M. Calo. 352p. 1986. 197.00 (*0-8493-5490-0*, TP156, CRC Reprint) Franklin.

Recent Developments in Shock Tube Research: Proceedings of the International Shock Tube Symposium, 9th, Stanford University, 1973. International Shock Tube Symposium Staff. Ed. by Daniel Bershader & Wayland Griffith. LC 73-80624. (Illus.). 848p. 1973. 95.00 (*0-8047-0842-8*) Stanford U Pr.

Recent Developments in Space Flight Mechanics. Ed. by P. B. Richards. (Science & Technology Ser.: Vol. 9). 1966. 25.00 (*0-87703-037-5*) Univelt Inc.

Recent Developments in Stability, Vibration, & Control of Structural Systems. Ed. by A. Guran. LC 93-71581. (AMD Ser.: Vol. 167). 264p. 1993. pap. 55.00 (*0-7918-1146-8*, G00790) ASME.

Recent Developments in Structural Optimization. Ed. by Franklin Y. Cheng. (Sessions Proceedings Ser.). 108p. 1986. 16.00 (*0-87262-557-5*) Am Soc Civil Eng.

***Recent Developments in Structured Continua, Vol. 2.** Ed. by D. De Kee & Purna N. Kaloni. LC 86-13264. (Pitman Research Notes in Mathematics Ser.: Vol. 229). 360p. 1990. reprint ed. pap. 102.60 (*0-608-03594-7*, 2064417) Bks Demand.

Recent Developments in the Chemistry of Natural Carbon Compound, Vol. 8. C. S. Szantay & L. Novac. (Synthesis of Prostaglandins Ser.). 267p. 1978. 89.00 (*0-569-08421-0*, Pub. by Collets) St Mut.

Recent Developments in the Chemistry of Natural Carbon Compounds, Vol. 6. Ed. by Collet's Holdings, Ltd. Staff. 198p. 1975. 50.00 (*0-569-08195-5*, Pub. by Collets) St Mut.

Recent Developments in the Chemistry of Natural Carbon Compounds, Vol. 9. Ed. by Collet's Holdings, Ltd. Staff. 420p. 1979. 150.00 (*0-569-08590-X*, Pub. by Collets) St Mut.

Recent Developments in the Chemistry of Natural Carbon Compounds, Vol. 10. I. Ninomiya & T. Naito. 210p. (C). 1984. 150.00 (*0-685-46655-8*, Pub. by Collets) St Mut.

Recent Developments in the Chemistry of Sulfur- & Hitrogen-Containing Heterocycles & Related Compounds, Vol. 4. Alexander Senning. (Sulfer Reports: Vol. 4, No. 8). 50p. 1986. pap. text ed. 44.00 (*3-7186-0319-5*) Gordon & Breach.

Recent Developments in the Economics of Education. Ed. by Elchanan Cohn & Geraint Johnes. (International Library of Critical Writings in Economics Ser.: Vol. 40). 680p. 1994. 200.00 (*1-85278-828-3*) E Elgar.

Recent Developments in the Field of Thrombin Inhibitors. Ed. by Jorg Struzebecher. 110p. 1995. pap. text ed. 230. 00 (*3-7186-5783-X*, Harwood Acad Pubs) Gordon & Breach.

Recent Developments in the Foundations of Utility & Risk Theory. L. Daboni et al. 1986. lib. bdg. 165.50 (*90-277-2201-3*) Kluwer Ac.

Recent Developments in the Inverse Galois Problem: A Joint Summer Research Conference on Recent Developments in the Inverse Galois Problem, July 17-23, 1993, University of Washington, Seattle. Joint Summer Research Conference on Recent Developments in the Inverse Galois Problem. Ed. by Michael D. Fried & Shreeram S. Abhyankar. LC 95-15047. (Contemporary Mathematics Ser.: Vol. 186). 1995. pap. 65.00 (*0-8218-0299-2*, CONM/186) Am Math.

Recent Developments in the Nuclear Many-Body Problem. Collet's Holdings, Ltd. Staff. 1986. 49.00 (*0-317-52961-7*, Pub. by Collets) St Mut.

Recent Developments in the Nuclear Many Body Problems. L. Munchow & R. Reif. 152p. (C). 1985. 60.00 (*0-685-36856-4*, Pub. by Collets) St Mut.

Recent Developments in the Pharmacology of Inflammatory Mediators. Ed. by I. L. Bonta. (Agents & Actions Supplements Ser.: No. 2). 178p. 1980. 50.00 (*0-8176-0914-8*) Birkhauser.

Recent Developments in the Physics of Fluids: Proceedings of the International Symposium Held 3-5 April 1991 in Oxford U. K. Ed. by W. S. Howells & A. K. Soper. 348p. 1992. 142.00 (*0-7503-0164-3*) IOP Pub.

Recent Developments in the Study of Benign Breast Disease. 4th ed. R. E. Mansel. (Illus.). 200p. 1992. 68. 00 (*1-85070-386-8*) Prthnon Pub.

Recent Developments in the Study of Benign Breast Disease: The Proceedings of the 5th International Symposium on Benign Breast Disease. 5th ed. Ed. by R. E. Mansel. LC 93-41022. (Illus.). 280p. (C). 1993. pap. text ed. 45.00 (*1-85070-532-1*) Prthnon Pub.

***Recent Developments in the Study of Benign Breast Disease: The Proceedings of the 6th International Symposium on Benign Breast Disease.** Ed. by R. E. Mansel. LC 97-3902. (Illus.). 170p. 1997. pap. text ed. 58.00 (*1-85070-775-8*) Prthnon Pub.

Recent Developments in the Synthesis & Chemistry of 2(1H)-Pyridinethiones & Related Compounds. Alexander Senning. (Sulfur Reports: Vol. 8, Pt. 3). 48p. 1988. pap. text ed. 64.00 (*3-7186-4835-0*) Gordon & Breach.

Recent Developments in the Textual Criticism of the Greek Bible. F. G. Kenyon. (British Academy, London, Schweich Lectures on Biblical Archaeology Series, 1930). 1974. reprint ed. pap. 25.00 (*0-8115-1274-6*) Periodicals Srv.

Recent Developments in the Theory of Function Spaces. Hans Triebel. 286p. (C). 1983. text ed. 73.95 (*3-7643-1381-1*) Birkhauser.

Recent Developments in the Theory of Industrial Organization. Ed. by Alfredo Del Monte. LC 91-40854. 336p. (C). 1992. text ed. 60.00 (*0-472-10337-7*) U of Mich Pr.

Recent Developments in the Theory of Involuntary Unemployment. Carl Davidson. LC 90-21175. 171p. 1990. text ed. 24.00 (*0-88099-105-4*); pap. text ed. 14.00 (*0-88099-106-2*) W E Upjohn.

Recent Developments in Theoretical Fluid Mechanics. Ed. by Giovanni P. Galdi & Jindrich Necas. LC 93-4707. (Pitman Research Notes in Mathematics Ser.). 1993. pap. 59.95 (*0-582-22684-8*) Longman.

Recent Developments in Theoretical Physics: Proceedings of the National Symposium. Ed. by E. C. Sudarshan & K. Strinivasa Rao. 352p. (C). 1988. text ed. 100.00 (*9971-5-0457-X*) World Scientific Pub.

Recent Developments in Theory & History: The Semiotic Web 1990. Ed. by Thomas A. Sebeok & Jean Umiker-Sebeok. (Approaches to Semiotics Ser.: No. 100). (Illus.). xii, 554p. (C). 1991. lib. bdg. 229.25 (*3-11-012796-2*, 150-91) Mouton.

Recent Developments in Therapeutic Drug Monitoring & Clinical Toxicology. Irving Sunshine. 824p. 1992. 235. 00 (*0-8247-8586-X*) Dekker.

Recent Developments in Thermophysical Properties Research: Presented at the Winter Annual Meeting of the ASME, Washington, D. C., Dec. 1, 1971. Ed. by A. Cezairliyan. LC 76-180675. (American Society of Mechanical Engineers, Applied Mechanics Division Ser.: Vol. 3). 20p. reprint ed. pap. 25.00 (*0-317-08191-8*, 2016902) Bks Demand.

Recent Developments in Toxicology: Trends, Methods & Problems: Proceedings of the European Society of Toxicology Meeting Held in Leipzig, September 12-14, 1990. Ed. by P. L. Chambers et al. (Archives of Toxicology Ser.: Suppl. 14). (Illus.). 320p. 1991. 158.00 (*0-387-51422-8*) Spr-Verlag.

Recent Developments in Transplantation Medicine: New Immunosuppressive Drugs. Ed. by Donna Przepiorka & Hans Sollinger. LC 94-65128. (Illus.). 208p. 1994. 42.95 (*0-614-05152-5*) Phys Sci Pub.

***Recent Developments in Transport Economics.** Nash. Ed. by De Rus. 314p. 1997. 63.95 (*1-85972-500-7*, Pub. by Ashgate UK) Ashgate Pub Co.

Recent Developments in Turbulence Management: Proceedings of the 5th Drag Reduction in Engineering Flows Meeting. Ed. by K. S. Choi. 358p. (C). 1991. lib. bdg. 153.50 (*0-7923-1477-8*) Kluwer Ac.

Recent Developments in Well-Posed Variational Problems. Ed. by Roberto Lucchetti. (Mathematics & Its Applications Ser.). 276p. (C). 1995. lib. bdg. 145.00 (*0-7923-3576-7*) Kluwer Ac.

***Recent Developments of General Topology & Its Applications: International Conference in Memory of Felix Hausdorff (1868-1942)** Ed. by W. Gahler et al. 1992. text ed. 80.00 (*3-05-501423-5*) Wiley.

***Recent Developments on Debris Flows.** A. Armanini & Masanori Michiue. LC 96-30076. (Lecture Notes in Earth Sciences Ser.). 1997. 78.00 (*3-540-62466-X*) Spr-Verlag.

***Recent Developments on Engine Emissions: Proceedings - Spring Technical Conference of the ASME Internal Combustion Engine Division 1996: Youngstown, OH, Set.** Ed. by Teoman Uzkan. 269p. Date not set. pap. 204.00 (*0-7918-1766-0*, TJ1075) ASME.

Recent Developments on Several Complex Variables. Ed. by John Fornaess. LC 80-8548. (Annals of Mathematics Studies: No. 100). 565p. 1981. pap. text ed. 35.00 (*0-691-08281-2*) Princeton U Pr.

Recent Directions in Particle Theory: From Superstrings & Black Holes to the Standard Model, Tasi-92. Jeffrey Harvey. Ed. by Joseph Polchinski. LC 93-26813. 800p. 1993. text ed. 137.00 (*981-02-1233-X*) World Scientific Pub.

***Recent Directions in Particle Theory: From Superstrings & Black Holes to the STD Model.** 800p. 1993. text ed. 49.00 (*981-02-1270-4*) World Scientific Pub.

Recent Discoveries & the Biblical World. Raymond E. Brown. 103p. 1989. pap. 24.00 (*0-86217-181-4*, Pub. by Veritas IE) St Mut.

Recent Discoveries Attributed to Early Man in America. Ales Hrdlicka. (Bureau of American Ethnology Bulletins Ser.). 67p. 1995. lib. bdg. 79.00 (*0-7812-4066-2*) Rprt Serv.

Recent Discoveries Relating to the Life & Works of William Shakspere. Arthur Field. LC 76-153318. reprint ed. 20.00 (*0-404-02379-7*) AMS Pr.

Recent Doctoral Research in Economic History: Proceedings of the Tenth International Economic History Congress, Leuven, Belgium, August 1990. Ed. by E. Aerts & H. Van der Wee. (Studies in Social & Economic History: No. 21). 204p. (Orig.). 1990. pap. 49. 50 (*90-6186-393-7*, Pub. by Leuven Univ BE) Coronet Bks.

Recent Drawings & Etchings. Lucian Freud. (Illus.). 1994. pap. 20.00 (*1-880146-09-6*) M Marks.

***Recent Durability Tests on Helical Gears.** G. P. Maurer. (Technical Papers). (Illus.). (Orig.). 1938. pap. text ed. 30.00 incl. audio compact disk (*1-55589-390-2*) AGMA.

Recent Earth Movements: An Introduction to Neotectonics. Claudio Vita-Finzi. 1986. text ed. 116.00 (*0-12-722370-3*) Acad Pr.

***Recent Economic & Legal Developments in European Environmental Policy: Generale Bank Lectures 1993-1994.** Ed. by Filip Abraham et al. (Law Ser.: Vol. 5). 272p. (Orig.). 1995. pap. 87.50 (*90-6186-703-7*, Pub. by Leuven Univ BE) Coronet Bks.

Recent Economic Changes in the United States, 2 vols., 1. Committee on Recent Economic Changes of the President's Conference on Unemployment & National Bureau Special Staff. (General Ser.: No. 13). 1929. reprint ed. mic. film 59.80 (*0-685-61144-2*) Natl Bur Econ Res.

Recent Economic Changes in the United States, 2 vols., 2. Committee on Recent Economic Changes of the President's Conference on Unemployment & National Bureau Special Staff. (General Ser.: No. 13). 1929. reprint ed. mic. film 68.80 (*0-685-66185-7*) Natl Bur Econ Res.

Recent Economic Changes in the United States, 2 vols., Vol. 1. Committee on Recent Economic Changes of the President's Conference on Unemployment & National Bureau Special Staff. (General Ser.: No. 13). 460p. 1929. reprint ed. 119.60 (*0-87014-012-4*) Natl Bur Econ Res.

Recent Economic Changes in the United States, 2 vols., Vol. 2. Committee on Recent Economic Changes of the President's Conference on Unemployment & National Bureau Special Staff. (General Ser.: No. 13). 329p. 1929. reprint ed. 137.60 (*0-685-61143-4*) Natl Bur Econ Res.

***Recent Essays (1990-1996)** Peter Halley. 64p. (Orig.). (C). 1997. pap. text ed. 10.00 (*0-9646466-1-7*) Edgewise Pr.

Recent Events. Kevin Magee. 1995. pap. 10.00 (*0-9649595-0-X*) Hypobololemaioi.

Recent Evolution & Seismicity of the Mediterranean Region: Proceedings of the NATO Advanced Research Workshop, Erice, Italy, September 17-18, 1992. Ed. by E. Boschi et al. LC 93-19532. (NATO Advanced Science Institutes Series C: Mathematical & Physical Sciences). 436p. (C). 1993. lib. bdg. 218.50 (*0-7923-2325-4*) Kluwer Ac.

Recent Evolution of Financial Systems. Jack Revell. LC 96-24400. 1997. text ed. 79.95 (*0-312-16347-9*) St Martin.

Recent Excavations in Israel: Studies in Iron Age Archaeology. Ed. by Seymour Gitin & William G. Dever. LC 89-1096. (Annual of the American Schools of Oriental Research Ser.: Vol. 49). xii, 152p. 1989. text ed. 49.50 (*0-89757-049-9*, 859106) Am Sch Orient Res.

Recent Experiences in Human Resources Development. T. V. Rao & D. F. Pereira. (C). 1986. 18.50 (*81-204-0120-4*, Pub. by Oxford IBH II) S Asia.

Recent Experiences with Surges in Capital Inflows. (Occasional Paper Ser.: No. 108). 1993. pap. 15.00 (*1-55775-350-4*) Intl Monetary.

Recent Experimental & Computational Advances in Molecular Spectroscopy: Proceedings of the NATO Advanced Study Institute on Molecular Spectroscopy. R. Fausto. LC 93-14524. (NATO Advanced Study Institutes Series C, Mathematical & Physical Sciences: Vol. 406). 480p. (C). 1993. lib. bdg. 225.50 (*0-7923-2388-2*) Kluwer Ac.

Recent Fertility Trends in the Pacific Islands. Michael J. Levin & Robert D. Retherford. LC 86-16739. (Papers of the East-West Population Institute: No. 101). (Illus.). viii, 72p. 1986. pap. 3.00 (*0-86638-083-3*) EW Ctr HI.

Recent Fiction from China 1987-1988: Selected Stories & Novellas. Ed. by Long Xu. LC 91-23443. 232p. 1991. lib. bdg. 89.95 (*0-7734-9664-5*) E Mellen.

Recent Geodetic & Gravimetric Research in Latin America. Ed. by Wolfgang Torge et al. LC 92-35108. (International Association of Geodesy Symposia Ser.: No. 111). 1993. 114.95 (*0-387-56121-8*) Spr-Verlag.

Recent Geomorphic History of the Pontchartrain Basin. Roger T. Saucier. LC 63-22267. (Coastal Studies: Vol. 9). (Illus.). 138p. reprint ed. 39.40 (*0-8357-9391-5*, 2051665) Bks Demand.

Recent Graduate Works & Programs in Environmental Education & Communications, Vol. 14. Nicholas J. Smith-Sebasto. 106p. 1996. pap. 10.00 (*1-884008-27-5*) NAAEE.

Recent Historians of Great Britain: Essays on the Post-1945 Generation. Walter L. Arnstein. LC 90-4478. 217p. 1990. reprint ed. pap. 61.90 (*0-608-00114-7*, 2060879) Bks Demand.

Recent History of an Ethiopian Delta: The Omo River & the Level of Lake Rudolf. Karl W. Butzer. LC 70-184080. (University of Chicago Department of Geography Research Paper Ser.: No. 136). 220p. 1971. reprint ed. pap. 62.70 (*0-608-02236-5*, 2062796) Bks Demand.

Recent Ideas of Divine Conflict: The Influences of Psychological & Sociological Theories of Conflict upon the Trinitarian Theology of Paul Tillich & Jurgen Moltmann. Randall B. Bush. LC 91-24962. 340p. 1991. lib. bdg. 99.95 (*0-7734-9949-0*) E Mellen.

Recent Imagining: Interviews with Harold Bloom, Geoffrey Hartman, Paul DeMan, J. Hillis Miller. Robert Moynihan. LC 86-17445. (Illus.). xvi, 168p. (C). 1986. lib. bdg. 29.50 (*0-208-02120-5*, Archon Bks) Shoe String.

Recent Immigration from Latin America: Social, Economic & Political Aspects: A Bibliography. Joan Nordquist. (Contemporary Social Issues: A Bibliographic Ser.: No. 37). 76p. (Orig.). 1995. pap. 15.00 (*0-937855-72-3*) Ref Rsch Serv.

Recent Industrialization Experience of Turkey in a Global Context. Ed. by Fikret Senses. LC 93-30983. (Contributions in Economics & Economic History Ser.: No. 155). 240p. 1994. text ed. 65.00 (*0-313-27381-2*, Greenwood Pr) Greenwood.

Recent Innovations in PCR Technology. Griffin. 384p. 1994. 52.00 (*0-8493-8674-8*, QP606) CRC Pr.

Recent Innovations in Public Sector Assessment see IPMA Assessment Council Monograph Series, Vol. II

Recent Insect Invasions in Ohio. Herbert Osborn et al. 1948. 3.00 (*0-86727-039-X*) Ohio Bio Survey.

Recent Investigations at Towosahgy State Historic Site & Its Physical Environment: Recent Investigations at Towosahgy State Historic Site & Its Physical Environment. Roger T. Saucier et al. (Missouri Archaeologist Ser.: Vol. 51). (Illus.). 91p. (Orig.). 1993. pap. 6.50 (*0-943414-74-1*) MO Arch Soc.

Recent Issues in Pattern Analysis & Recognition. Ed. by V. Cantoni et al. (Lecture Notes in Computer Science Ser.: Vol. 399). vii, 400p. 1990. 44.95 (*0-387-51815-0*) Spr-Verlag.

Recent Issues in the Analysis of Behavior. B. F. Skinner. 150p. (C). 1990. text ed. 31.60 (*0-675-20674-X*, Merrill Coll) P-H.

Recent Japanese Philosophical Thought 1862-1994: A Survey. 3rd rev. ed. Gino K. Piovesana. (Japan Library). 320p. (C). 1997. text ed. 49.00 (*1-873410-65-4*, Pub. by Curzon Press UK) UH Pr.

Recent Japanese Studies of Modern Chinese History. Ed. & Tr. by Joshua A. Fogel. LC 88-37051. 192p. (gr. 13). 1989. text ed. 59.95 (*0-87332-564-8*) M E Sharpe.

Recent Japanese Studies of Modern Chinese History. Ed. & Tr. by Joshua A. Fogel. (Chinese Studies in History: Vol. 18, No. 1-2, Fall-Winter 1984-85). 1984. reprint ed. pap. 67.60 (*0-7837-9980-2*, 2060707) Bks Demand.

Recent Jewish Progress in Palestine: American Jewish Yearbook 5676. Henrietta Szold. Ed. by Moshe Davis. LC 77-70746. (America & the Holy Land Ser.). 1977. reprint ed. lib. bdg. 19.95 (*0-405-10292-5*) Ayer.

Recent Legal Issues for American Indians, 1968 to the Present: 1968 to the Present. Ed. by John R. Wunder. LC 96-29373. (Native Americans & the Law Ser.: Vol. 4). 344p. 1996. reprint ed. text ed. 70.00 (*0-8153-2488-X*) Garland.

Recent Levels & Trends of Contraceptive Use. 123p. 1987. 12.50 (*92-1-151095-3*) UN.

Recent Lifeline Seismic Risk Studies. Ed. by Anne S. Kiremidjian. LC 90-14455. 72p. 1990. pap. text ed. 15. 00 (*0-87262-783-7*) Am Soc Civil Eng.

Recent Mammals of Arizona: Their Taxonomy & Distribution. E. Lendell Cockrum. LC 60-15914. (Illus.). 282p. reprint ed. pap. 80.40 (*0-317-58753-6*, 2029650) Bks Demand.

R

Recent Marxian Theory: Class Formation & Social Conflict in Contemporary Capitalism. John F. Sitton. LC 95-31700. (SUNY Series in Political Theory). 358p. 1996. text ed. 49.50 (*0-7914-2941-5*); pap. text ed. 17.95 (*0-7914-2942-3*) State U NY Pr.

Recent Mathematical Methods in Dynamic Programming. Ed. by I. Capuzzo Dolcetta et al. (Lecture Notes in Mathematics Ser.: Vol. 1119). vi, 202p. 1985. 37.95 (*0-387-15217-2*) Spr-Verlag.

*__Recent Mathematical Methods in Nonlinear Wave Propagation: Lectures Given at the 1st Session of the Centro Internazionale Matematico Estivo (C.I.M.E.), Held in Montecatini Terme, Italy, May 23-31, 1994.__ G. Boillat et al. LC 96-36819. (Lecture Notes in Mathematics Ser.: Vol. 1640). 142p. 1996. pap. 29.00 (*3-540-61907-0*) Spr-Verlag.

Recent Modelling Approaches in Applied Energy Economics. O. Bjerkholt et al. (International Studies in Economic Modelling). (Illus.). 352p. (gr. 13). 1990. text ed. 126.95 (*0-412-35340-7*, A5104) Chapman & Hall.

Recent Mollusks of the Gulf of Mexico & Pleistocene & Pliocene Species from the Gulf States. C. J. Maury. 282p. 1971. reprint ed. 9.00 (*0-87710-361-5*) Paleo Res.

Recent Monument Worship in Lowland Guatemala see Middle American Research Records

Recent Multilateral Debt Restructurings with Official & Bank Creditors. E. Brau et al. (Occasional Paper Ser.: No. 25). 43p. 1983. pap. 5.00 (*1-55775-080-7*) Intl Monetary.

Recent Nepal: An Analysis of Recent Democratic Upsurge & Its Aftermath. Laksman Bahadur. xxiiii, 217p. 1993. 25.00 (*81-85693-24-2*, Pub. by Nirala Pubns II) Nataraj Bks.

Recent Nepal: An Analysis of Recent Democratic Upsurge & Its Aftermath. L.B.K.C. Staff. (C). 1993. 85.00 (*0-7855-0212-2*, Pub. by Ratna Pustak Bhandar) St Mut.

Recent Past: Readings on America since World War II. Allan M. Winkler. 432p. (C). 1988. pap. text ed. 31.50 (*0-06-047142-5*) Addson-Wesley Educ.

Recent Perspectives in American Philosophy. Y. H. Krikorian. 97p. 1973. pap. text ed. 41.50 (*90-247-1518-0*, Pub. by M Nijhoff NE) Kluwer Ac.

Recent Perspectives of Early Indian History. Ed. by Romila Thapar. (C). 1995. 20.00 (*81-7154-556-4*, Pub. by Popular Prakashan II) S Asia.

Recent Perspectives on American Sign Language. Ed. by Harlan Lane & Francois Grosjean. 176p. 1989. reprint ed. pap. 34.50 (*0-8058-0560-5*) L Erlbaum Assocs.

Recent Perspectives on Prehistoric Art in India & Allied Subjects: Essays in Honour of Dr. Shyam Kumar Pandey. Ed. by R. K. Sharma & K. K. Tripathi. (Illus.). xxxvii, 336p. (C). 1996. 99.00 (*81-7305-070-8*, Pub. by Aryan Bks Intl II) Nataraj Bks.

Recent Philosophers. John Passmore. 1991. pap. 15.95 (*0-8126-9142-3*) Open Court.

*__Recent Philosophy.__ John Laird. LC 73-5955. Date not set. write for info. (*0-518-19054-4*) Ayer.

Recent Plate Movements & Deformation. Ed. by K. Kasahara. (Geodynamics Ser.: Vol. 20). (Illus.). 96p. 1988. 20.00 (*0-87590-520-X*) Am Geophysical.

Recent Poetry of Spain: A Bilingual Anthology. Tr. by Louis Hammer & Sara Schyfter from SPA. LC 83-11235. xxii, 340p. 1983. 24.00 (*0-937584-07-X*); pap. 11.95 (*0-937584-08-8*) Sachem Pr.

Recent Portuguese Immigrants to Fall River, Massachusetts: An Analysis of Relative Economic Success. Dorothy A. Gilbert. LC 87-45779. (Immigrant Communities & Ethnic Minorities in the U. S. & Canada Ser.: No. 14). 1989. 42.50 (*0-404-19424-9*) AMS Pr.

*__Recent Progress in Actinides Separation Chemistry: Proceedings of the Workshop on Actinides Solution Chemistry.__ 300p. 1997. lib. bdg. 52.00 (*981-02-2748-5*) World Scientific Pub.

Recent Progress in Analytic Number Theory, Vol. I. Ed. by H. Halberstam & C. Hooley. LC 81-66693. 1981. text ed. 168.00 (*0-12-318201-8*) Acad Pr.

Recent Progress in Analytic Number Theory, Vol. II. Ed. by H. Halberstam & C. Hooley. LC 81-66693. 1981. text ed. 168.00 (*0-12-318202-6*) Acad Pr.

Recent Progress in Antifungal Chemotherapy. Ed. by Hideyo Yamaguchi et al. 576p. 1991. 175.00 (*0-8247-8529-0*) Dekker.

Recent Progress in Atherosclerosis Research. Ed. by E. Vollmer & A. Roessner. LC 93-31211. (Current Topics in Pathology Ser.: Vol. 87). 1994. 199.00 (*0-387-54394-5*) Spr-Verlag.

Recent Progress in Blood Coagulation & Thrombosis Research. Ed. by O. N. Ulutin. (Bibliotheca Haematologica Ser.: No. 44). (Illus.). 1978. 78.50 (*3-8055-2896-5*) S Karger.

Recent Progress in Cardiovsacular Mechanics. Ed. by Saichi Hosada et al. LC 93-43890. 400p. 1994. text ed. 70.00 (*3-7186-5417-2*) Gordon & Breach.

Recent Progress in Cell Biology: Leukocytes & Platelets. Ed. by O. N. Ulutin. (Bibliotheca Haematologica Ser.: No. 45). (Illus.). 1978. pap. 75.25 (*3-8055-2897-3*) S Karger.

Recent Progress in Child & Adolescent Psychiatry. Ed. by M. Shimizu. (Illus.). 214p. 1996. pap. 89.00 (*4-431-70172-9*) Spr-Verlag.

Recent Progress in Colorectal Cancer: Biology & Management of High Risk Groups, Proceedings of the 5th International Symposium on Colorectal Cancer, Biology & Management of High Risk Groups, Torino, 24-26 September 1991. Ed. by Francesco P. Rossini et al. LC 92-10023. (International Congress Ser.: No. 990). 1992. 144.50 (*0-444-89310-5*, Excerpta Medica) Elsevier.

Recent Progress in Electropharmacology of the Heart. Ed. by Junji Toyama et al. 240p. 1995. 131.95 (*0-8493-7691-2*, 7691) CRC Pr.

Recent Progress in Failing Heart Syndrome. Ed. by S. Sasayama & Hiroyuki Suga. (Illus.). 336p. 1992. 205.00 (*0-387-70073-0*) Spr-Verlag.

Recent Progress in Hormone Research, Vol. 49. Ed. by C. Wayne Bardin. (Illus.). 400p. 1994. text ed. 89.00 (*0-12-571149-2*) Acad Pr.

Recent Progress in Hormone Research: Proceedings, Vols. 1-43. Ed. by Laurentian Hormone Conferences Staff & Gregory Pincus. Incl. Vols. 26-27. . 1971. (*0-318-50358-1*); write for info. (*0-318-50355-7*) Acad Pr.

Recent Progress in Hormone Research Vol. 50, Vol. 50. Ed. by C. Wayne Bardin. (Illus.). 497p. 1995. boxed 90.00 (*0-12-571150-6*) Acad Pr.

Recent Progress in Hormone Research Vol. 51: Proceedings of the 1995 Conference. Ed. by P. Michael Conn. (Illus.). 510p. (C). 1996. text ed. 105.00 (*1-879225-22-0*) Endocrine Soc.

*__Recent Progress in Hormone Research Vol. 52: Proceedings of the 1996 Conference.__ Ed. by P. Michael Conn. (Illus.). 512p. (C). 1997. text ed. 110.00 (*1-879225-26-3*) Endocrine Soc.

Recent Progress in Many-Body Theories, Vol. 1. Ed. by A. J. Kallio et al. LC 88-2511. (Illus.). 416p. 1988. 95.00 (*0-306-42830-X*, Plenum Pr) Plenum.

Recent Progress in Many-Body Theories, Vol. 2. Ed. by Y. Avishai. (Illus.). 330p. 1990. 105.00 (*0-306-43705-8*, Plenum Pr) Plenum.

Recent Progress in Many-Body Theories, Vol. 3. Ed. by T. L. Ainsworth et al. (Illus.). 514p. (C). 1992. 135.00 (*0-306-44246-9*, Plenum Pr) Plenum.

Recent Progress in Many-Body Theories Vol. 4: Proceedings of the Eighth International Conference Held in Liebnitz, Austria, August 22-24, 1994, Vol. 4. Ed. by E. Schachinger et al. 477p. (C). 1995. 135.00 (*0-306-45103-4*, Plenum Pr) Plenum.

*__Recent Progress in Mathematical Psychology.__ Ed. by Cornelia Dowling et al. (Scientific Psychology Ser.). 350p. 1997. write for info. (*0-8058-1975-4*) L Erlbaum Assocs.

Recent Progress in Medico-Social Problems in Juvenile Diabetics, Pt. II. Ed. by Z. Laron & A. Galatzer. (Pediatric & Adolescent Endocrinology Ser.: Vol. 11). (Illus.). x, 210p. 1983. 122.50 (*3-8055-3594-5*) S Karger.

Recent Progress in Microbial Production of Amino Acids. Hitoshi Enei et al. Ed. by Toshiaki Ikoma. (Japanese Technology Reviews Ser.: Vol. 5). 142p. 1989. pap. text ed. 158.00 (*2-88124-324-X*) Gordon & Breach.

Recent Progress in Pediatric Endocrinology. Ed. by Giuseppe Chiumello & Mark Sperling. LC 82-47695. (Illus.). 391p. reprint ed. pap. 111.50 (*0-7837-7130-4*, 2046959) Bks Demand.

Recent Progress in Posterior Pituitary Hormones 1988: Proceedings of the Satellite Symposium, Hakone, Japan, 14-16 July, 1988. Ed. by S. Yoshida & L. Share. (International Congress Ser.: No.797). 428p. 1989. 165.75 (*0-444-81045-5*, Excerpta Medica) Elsevier.

*__Recent Progress in QCD Spectral Sum Rules.__ 250p. 1998. lib. bdg. 27.00 (*981-02-2651-9*) World Scientific Pub.

Recent Progress in Random Magnets. Ed. by D. H. Ryan. LC 92-16899. 300p. 1992. text ed. 98.00 (*981-02-0885-5*) World Scientific Pub.

Recent Progress in Statistical Mechanics & Quantum Field Theory. P. Bouwknegt et al. 600p. 1995. text ed. 150.00 (*981-02-2065-0*) World Scientific Pub.

Recent Progress in Surface Physics: Proceedings of the Asia Pacific Symposium on Surface Physics (APSSP) Ed. by X-D Xie. 500p. (C). 1987. text ed. 156.00 (*9971-5-0386-7*) World Scientific Pub.

Recent Progress in the Chemical Synthesis of Antibiotics. Ed. by Gabor Lukacs & M. Ohno. 816p. 1990. 290.95 (*0-387-52444-4*) Spr-Verlag.

Recent Progress in the Chemical Synthesis of Antibiotics & Related Microbial Products, Vol. 2. Ed. by Gabor Lukacs. LC 93-2183. (Illus.). 980p. 1993. 307.95 (*0-387-56754-2*) Spr-Verlag.

Recent Progress in the Genetic Epidemiology of Cancer. Ed. by Henry T. Lynch & P. Tautu. (Illus.). 160p. 1991. 79.95 (*0-387-53022-3*) Spr-Verlag.

Recent Progress in Topology. Ed. by Miroslav Husek & Jan Van Mill. LC 92-30224. 796p. 1992. 184.00 (*0-444-89674-0*, North Holland) Elsevier.

Recent Progress of Astronomy: Especially in the United States. Elias Loomis. Ed. by I. Bernard Cohen. LC 79-7972. (Three Centuries of Science in America Ser.). 1980. reprint ed. lib. bdg. 23.95 (*0-405-12554-2*) Ayer.

Recent Progress of Diabetes Mellitus in East Asia: Proceedings of the Third Japan-China Symposium, Shanghai, China, 11-12 October 1991. Ed. by Goro Mimura & Chi Zhisheng. LC 92-49546. (International Congress Ser.: No. 997). 1992. 160.75 (*0-444-88503-X*, Excerpta Medica) Elsevier.

Recent Progress on Kinins: Proceedings of the International Conference, Kinin 91 Munich, held in Munich, September 8-14, 1991, 3 vols. LC 92-49586. 1992. 235.50 (*0-8176-2816-9*) Birkhauser.

Recent Progress on Kinins: Proceedings of the International Conference, Kinin 91 Munich, held in Munich, September 8-14, 1991, 3 vols., 38-1. LC 92-49586. 1992. 115.50 (*0-8176-2817-7*) Birkhauser.

Recent Progress on Kinins: Proceedings of the International Conference, Kinin 91 Munich, held in Munich, September 8-14, 1991, 3 vols., 38-2. LC 92-49586. 1992. 89.50 (*0-8176-2818-5*) Birkhauser.

Recent Progress on Kinins: Proceedings of the International Conference, Kinin 91 Munich, held in Munich, September 8-14, 1991, 3 vols., 38-3. LC 92-49586. 1992. 94.50 (*0-8176-2819-3*) Birkhauser.

Recent Progress on Polyamine Research. N. Seiler et al. 634p. (C). 1985. 195.00 (*963-05-4243-9*, Pub. by Akad Kiado HU) St Mut.

*__Recent Progress on the Molecular Aspects of Endocrine Tumors: Clinical Implications: 39th International Henri-Pierre Kotz Symposium on Hormone Binding Proteins, Paris, May 1996.__ Ed. by Xavier Bertagna. (Journal: Vol. 47, No. 4-6, 1997). (Illus.). 166p. 1997. pap. 120.00 (*3-8055-6504-6*) S Karger.

*__Recent Publications in Planning, Vol. 1.__ Dennis Jenks. 61p. 1993. pap. 10.00 (*0-86602-294-5*, Sage Prdcls Pr) Sage.

*__Recent Publications in Planning, Vol. 2.__ Dennis Jenks. 56p. 1993. pap. 10.00 (*0-86602-295-3*, Sage Prdcls Pr) Sage.

*__Recent Publications in Planning, Vol. 3.__ Dennis Jenks. 59p. 1993. pap. 10.00 (*0-86602-296-1*, Sage Prdcls Pr) Sage.

Recent Puerto Rican Theatre: Five Plays from New York. Ed. by John Antush. LC 90-32908. 256p. (Orig.). 1994. pap. 11.00 (*1-55885-019-8*) Arte Publico.

Recent Rades in Radiobiological Research. P. Umadavi. (C). 1992. text ed. 175.00 (*81-85046-99-9*, Pub. by Scientific Pubs II) St Mut.

Recent Recruiting Trends & Their Implications: Preliminary Analysis & Recommendations. Beth J. Asch & Bruce R. Orvis. 46p. 1995. pap. text ed. 7.50 (*0-8330-1628-8*, MR-549-A/OSD) Rand Corp.

Recent Reference Books in Religion: A Guide for Students, Scholars, Researchers, Buyers & Readers. William M. Johnston. 295p. (Orig.). 1996. 34.99 (*0-8308-1440-X*, 1440) InterVarsity.

Recent Research Advances in the Fluid Mechanics of Turbulent Jets & Plumes. NATO Advanced Research Workshop on Recent Research Advances in the Fluid Mechanics of Turbulent Jets & Plumes. Ed. by Viana Do Castelo. LC 94-684. (NATO Advanced Study Institutes Series E, Applied Sciences: Vol. 255). 1994. lib. bdg. 250.00 (*0-7923-2699-7*) Kluwer Ac.

Recent Research Along the Lower Colorado River. Joseph A. Ezzo. (Statistical Research Technical Ser.: No. 51). (Illus.). 195p. (Orig.). (C). 1994. spiral bd. 20.00 (*1-879442-44-2*) Stats Res.

Recent Research in Developmental Psychopathology. Ed. by J. E. Stevenson. (Illus.). 261p. 1984. 31.50 (*0-08-030828-7*, Pergamon Pr) Elsevier.

Recent Research in Entrepreneurship: The Third International EIASM Workshop. Leslie G. Davies & Allan A. Gibb. (Avebury Business School Library). 369p. 1991. text ed. 85.95 (*1-85628-135-3*, Pub. by Avebury Pub UK) Ashgate Pub Co.

Recent Research in Financial Modelling. Ed. by E. J. Stokking & G. Zambruno. (Contributions to Management Science Ser.). (Illus.). vi, 174p. 1993. 75.00 (*0-387-91448-X*) Spr-Verlag.

Recent Research in Heat Pump Design, Analysis, & Application. Ed. by K. E. Herold & V. Mei. (AES Ser.: Vol. 28). 152p. 1992. 45.00 (*0-7918-1113-1*, G00757) ASME.

Recent Research in Psychosomatics. Ed. by R. A. Pierloot. (Psychotherapy & Psychosomatics Journal: Vol. 18, No. 1-6). (Illus.). viii, 376p. 1970. reprint ed. 91.25 (*3-8055-1219-8*) S Karger.

Recent Research on Anglo-Irish Writers. Richard J. Finneran. LC 82-12575. (Supplement to: Anglo-Irish Literature, A Review of Research Ser.). 377p. reprint ed. pap. 107.50 (*0-8357-4077-3*, 2036767) Bks Demand.

Recent Research on European Sign Languages. Ed. by F. Loncke et al. vi, 166p. 1984. pap. 40.75 (*90-265-0465-9*) Swets.

Recent Research on Gynecological Endocrinology, 2 vols. Ed. by A. R. Genazzani et al. (Illus.). 1989. Set. 110.00 (*1-85070-209-8*) Prthnon Pub.

Recent Research on Mechanical Behavior of Solids. Ed. by Hiroshi Miyamoto. LC 80-670073. 435p. 1979. reprint ed. pap. 124.00 (*0-608-01245-9*, 2061933) Bks Demand.

Recent Research on Tucson Basin Prehistory: Proceedings of the Second Tucson Basin Conference. Ed. by William H. Doelle & Paul R. Fish. (Anthropological Papers: No. 10). (Illus.). 430p. (Orig.). 1988. pap. 10.00 (*1-886398-01-1*) Desert Archaeol.

Recent Research on Wood & Wood-Based Materials. Ed. by N. Shiraishi et al. (Current Japanese Materials Research Ser.: Vol. 11). 262p. 1994. 199.00 (*0-444-81691-7*, Pub. by Elsevier Applied Sci UK) Elsevier.

*__Recent Research Towards Advanced Man-Machine Interface Through Spoken Language.__ H. Fujisaki. LC 96-34509. 542p. 1996. 240.75 (*0-444-81607-0*) Elsevier.

Recent Researches in Coldwater Fisheries: National Workshop on Research & Development Need Coldwater Fisheries. K. L. Sehgal. 250p. 1991. 60.00 (*1-55528-265-2*, Pub. by Today & Tomorrows P & P II) Scholarly Pubns.

Recent Researches in Ecology, Environment & Pollution, Vol. 2. 1988. 35.00 (*1-55528-151-6*, Messers Today & Tomorrow) Scholarly Pubns.

Recent Researches in Ecology, Environment & Pollution, Vol. 4. 1990. 45.00 (*1-55528-210-5*, Messers Today & Tomorrow) Scholarly Pubns.

Recent Researches in Ecology, Environment & Pollution, Vol. 7. 1991. 65.00 (*0-685-59966-3*, Messers Today & Tomorrow) Scholarly Pubns.

Recent Researches in Geology, Vol. 2: Products & Processes of Rock Weathering. S. Sinha-Roy & S. K. Ghosh. 1985. 52.00 (*0-8364-2288-0*, Pub. by Hindustan IA) S Asia.

Recent Researches in Palynology: Hensferdinand Linskens Commemoration Volume. Ed. by C. P. Malik. (Illus.). 295p. 1984. 50.00 (*1-55528-071-4*, Pub. by Today & Tomorrows P & P II) Scholarly Pubns.

Recent Results & Instrumental Perspective Developments in X- & Gamma-Ray Astronomy: Proceedings of the Topical Meeting of the COSPAR Interdisciplinary Scientific Commission E (Meetings E4 & E8) of the COSPAR 28th Plenary Meeting Held in The Hague, The Netherlands, 25 June - 6 July 1990. Ed. by L. Bassani et al. (Advances in Space Research Ser.: Vol. 11, No. 8). 434p. 1991. pap. 147.00 (*0-08-041162-2*, Pergamon Pr) Elsevier.

*__Recent Results in the Theory of Graph Spectra.__ D. M. Cvetkovic et al. (Annals of Discrete Mathematics Ser.: Vol. 36). 306p. 1988. 166.25 (*0-444-70361-6*, North Holland) Elsevier.

Recent Results of Research on Arteriosclerosis. F. Gotthard Schettler. (Sitzungsberichte der Heidelberger Akademie der Wissenschaften Ser., Mathematisch-Naturwissenschaftliche Klasse, Jahrgang 1991: Suppl. 4). (Illus.). 34p. 1989. 19.95 (*0-387-50288-2*) Spr-Verlag.

Recent Results on Function Algebras. I. Glicksberg. LC 75-38927. (CBMS Regional Conference Series in Mathematics: Vol. 11). 38p. 1972. 18.00 (*0-8218-9901-5*, CBMS/11C) Am Math.

Recent Results on Function Algebras. Irving L. Glicksberg. LC 75-38927. (Regional Conference Series in Mathematics: No. 11). 44p. 1972. reprint ed. pap. 25.00 (*0-7837-8296-9*, 2049082) Bks Demand.

Recent Results on Mars & Venus: Proceedings of Symposium 3 of the COSPAR 28th Plenary Meeting Held in the Hague, the Netherlands, 25 June-6 July 1990. Ed. by R. W. Shorthill et al. (Advances in Space Research Ser.: No. 12). 292p. 1992. pap. 165.00 (*0-08-041856-2*, Pergamon Pr) Elsevier.

Recent Sediments of Southeast Texas - A Field Guide to the Brazos Alluvial & Deltaic Plains & the Galveston Barrier Island Complex. H. A. Bernard et al. (Guidebook Ser.: GB 11). 132p. 1970. reprint ed. pap. 7.00 (*0-686-29319-3*) Bur Econ Geology.

Recent Social Trends in France, 1960-1990. Michel Forse et al. (Comparative Charting of Social Change Ser.). 384p. 1993. 70.00 (*0-7735-0887-2*, Pub. by McGill CN) U of Toronto Pr.

Recent Social Trends in Quebec, 1960-1990. Simon Langlois et al. 1992. 70.00 (*0-7735-0879-1*, Pub. by McGill CN) U of Toronto Pr.

*__Recent Social Trends in Russia 1960-1995.__ Ed. by Irene A. Boutenko & Kyrill E. Razlogov. (Comparative Charting of Social Change Ser.). 360p. 1997. 65.00 (*0-7735-1610-7*, Pub. by McGill CN) U of Toronto Pr.

Recent Social Trends in the United States, 2 Vols., Set. President's Research Committee on Social Trends. Ed. by Lewis A. Coser & Walter W. Powell. LC 79-7010. (Perennial Works in Sociology). (Illus.). 1979. reprint ed. lib. bdg. 122.95 (*0-405-12107-5*) Ayer.

Recent Social Trends in the United States, 2 Vols., Vol. 1. President's Research Committee on Social Trends. Ed. by Lewis A. Coser & Walter W. Powell. LC 79-7010. (Perennial Works in Sociology Ser.). (Illus.). 1980. reprint ed. lib. bdg. 61.95 (*0-405-12108-3*) Ayer.

Recent Social Trends in the United States, 2 Vols., Vol. 2. President's Research Committee on Social Trends. Ed. by Lewis A. Coser & Walter W. Powell. LC 79-7010. (Perennial Works in Sociology). (Illus.). 1980. reprint ed. lib. bdg. 61.95 (*0-405-12109-1*) Ayer.

Recent Social Trends in the United States, 1960-1990. Theodore Caplow et al. 1991. 70.00 (*0-7735-0872-4*, Pub. by McGill CN) U of Toronto Pr.

Recent Social Trends in the United States, 1960-1990. Theodore Caplow et al. (Comparative Charting of Social Change Ser.). 604p. (C). 1994. pap. text ed. 24.95 (*0-7735-1212-8*, Pub. by McGill CN) U of Toronto Pr.

Recent Social Trends in West Germany, 1960-1990. Wolfgang Glatzer et al. 620p. 1992. 70.00 (*0-7735-0909-7*, Pub. by McGill CN) U of Toronto Pr.

Recent Soviet Psychology. Ed. by N. O'Connor. (C). 1961. text ed. 9.50 (*0-87140-864-3*) Liveright.

Recent Spanish Poetry & the Role of the Reader. Margaret H. Persin. LC 85-43247. 176p. 1987. 36.50 (*0-8387-5100-8*) Bucknell U Pr.

Recent Strategies for the Study of Invasive & Metastatic Cancer. (Journal: Invasion & Metastasis: Vol. 4, Suppl. 1, 1984). (Illus.). iv, 68p. 1985. pap. 22.50 (*3-8055-4008-6*) S Karger.

Recent Studies in Atomic & Molecular Physics. Ed. by A. E. Kingston. LC 87-7263. (Physics of Atoms & Molecules Ser.). (Illus.). 230p. 1987. 75.00 (*0-306-42687-0*, Plenum Pr) Plenum.

Recent Studies in Bioclimatology: A Group. Ed. by F. Sargent, II & R. G. Stone. (Meteorological Monograph: Vol. 2, No. 8). (Illus.). 121p. (Orig.). 1954. pap. 17.00 (*0-933876-03-3*) Am Meteorological.

Recent Studies in Geophysical Hazards. Ed. by M. I. El-Sabh et al. LC 94-21075. (Advances in Natural & Technological Hazards Research Ser.). 260p. (C). 1994. lib. bdg. 155.00 (*0-7923-2972-4*) Kluwer Ac.

Recent Studies in Modern Armenian History. Ed. by Robert Thomson. (Illus.). 153p. 1972. 12.95 (*0-935411-07-0*); pap. 7.95 (*0-935411-04-6*) Natl Assn Arm.

Recent Studies in Myths & Literature 1970-1990: An Annotated Bibliography. Compiled by Bernard Accardi et al. LC 91-18070. (Bibliographies & Indexes in World Literature Ser.: No. 29). 264p. 1991. text ed. 55.00 (*0-313-27545-9*, HSQ, Greenwood Pr) Greenwood.

Recent Studies in Sanskrit & Indology. Dharmendra K. Gupta. 1982. 28.00 (*0-8364-0913-2*, Pub. by Ajanta II) S Asia.

Recent Studies in Sanskrit & Indology. Dharmendra K. Gupta. 1983. 14.00 (*0-8364-2562-6*, Pub. by Ajanta II) S Asia.

An Asterisk (*) at the beginning of an entry indicates that the title is appearing in BIP for the first time.

Recent Studies of Hypothalamic Function: Proceedings of the Symposium, Calgary, Alberta, May 1973. Symposium, Calgary, Alberta Staff. Ed. by K. Lederis & K. E. Cooper. (Illus.). 450p. 1974. 46.50 (*3-8055-1694-0*) S Karger.

Recent Studies on the Human Thalamus: Proceedings of the Annual Meeting of the Japanese Society for Sterotactic 8, Functional Neurosurgery, 15th, Maebashi, October 1976. Annual Meeting of the Japanese Society for Stereotactic & Functional Neurosurgery Staff. Ed. by P. L. Gildenberg & Chihiro Ohye. (Applied Neurophysiology Ser.: Vol. 39, No. 3-4). (Illus.). 1977. 46.50 (*3-8055-2847-7*) S Karger.

Recent Study of Hebrew: A Survey of the Literature with Selected Bibliography. Nahum M. Waldman. (Bibliographica Judaica Ser.: No. 10). xxi, 464p. 1989. 37.50 (*0-87820-908-5*) Hebrew Union Coll Pr.

Recent Synthetic Differential Geometry. H. Busemann. LC 13-120381. (Ergebnisse der Mathematik und Ihrer Grenzgebiete Ser.: Vol. 54). 1970. 64.95 (*0-387-04810-3*) Spr-Verlag.

Recent TCM Research From China. Ed. & Tr. by Bob Flaws from CHI. Tr. by Charles Chace from CHI. LC 94-70761. 200p. (Orig.). 1994. pap. 18.95 (*0-936185-56-2*) Blue Poppy Pr.

***Recent Technical Developments in Telecommunications.** P. Levaux. viii, 402p. 1992. 167.50 (*0-444-89227-3*, North Holland) Elsevier.

Recent Technological & Economic Developments in the Petrochemical Industry. Editions Technip Staff. (Illus.). 224p. (C). 1970. pap. 185.00 (*2-7108-0148-5*, Pub. by Edits Technip FR) St Mut.

Recent Technologies of the Uses of Peat: Reports of the International Symposium. Ed. by G. W. Luettig. (Illus.). 223p. 1983. pap. text ed. 61.95 (*3-510-65115-4*) Lubrecht & Cramer.

Recent Theoretical (Computational) Developments in Atomic Collisions in Solids: Proceedings of a Conference, Strasbourg, France, July 14-16, 1981. Ed. by H. Y. Ohtsuki. 162p. 1983. 46.00 (*9971-950-33-2*) World Scientific Pub.

Recent Theories of Administration & Management. R. T. Jangham. (C). 1989. 7.50 (*81-204-0367-3*, Pub. by Oxford IBH II) S Asia.

Recent Theories of Narrative. Wallace Martin. LC 85-22401. 248p. (C). 1986. 37.50 (*0-8014-1771-6*); pap. 13.95 (*0-8014-9355-2*) Cornell U Pr.

Recent Topics in Semiconductor Physics: In Commemoration of the 60th Birthday of Yasutada Uemura, Tokyo University, Japan, March 29, 1982. Hiroshi Kamimura & Y. Toyozawa. 1983. 60.00 (*9971-950-54-5*); pap. 33.00 (*9971-950-55-3*) World Scientific Pub.

Recent Topics in Theoretical Physics. Ed. by H. Takayama. (Proceedings in Physics Ser.: Vol. 24). (Illus.). 150p. 1988. 71.95 (*0-387-18604-2*) Spr-Verlag.

Recent Trends & Contacts Between Cytogenetics Embryology & Morphology, 1976. Ed. by V. R. Dnyansagar et al. (Current Trends in Life Sciences Ser.: Vol. 5). xiv, 592p. 1977. 50.00 (*0-88065-081-8*, Messers Today & Tomorrow) Scholarly Pubns.

Recent Trends in Aerobiology, Allergy & Immunology. Ed. by S. N. Agashe. (Illus.). 332p. 1994. text ed. 90.00 (*1-886106-02-9*) Science Pubs.

***Recent Trends in Aeroelasticity, Structures, & Structural Dynamics.** University of Florida, R. L. Bisplinghoff Memorial Symposium Staff. Ed. by Prabhat Hajela. LC 87-8120. (Illus.). 427p. reprint ed. pap. 121.70 (*0-608-04461-X*, 2065205) Bks Demand.

Recent Trends in Allergen & Complement Research. Ed. by K. Ishizaka et al. (Progress in Allergy Ser.: Vol. 30). (Illus.). xiv, 234p. 1982. 106.50 (*3-8055-2580-X*) S Karger.

Recent Trends in Botanical Research. R. N. Gohil. 334p. (C). 1985. text ed. 130.00 (*81-85046-24-7*, Pub. by Scientific Pubs II); text ed. 150.00 (*0-7855-0101-0*, Pub. by Scientific Pubs II) St Mut.

Recent Trends in Chemical Reaction Engineering. Kulkarni. (C). 1988. 120.00 (*0-85226-509-3*) S Asia.

Recent Trends in Commerce & Management Education. V. V. Khanzode. 272p. 1990. text ed. 32.50 (*81-207-1183-1*, Pub. by Sterling Pubs II) Apt Bks.

Recent Trends in Data Type Specification: Eighth Workshop on Specification of Abstract Data Types, Joint with the 3rd COMPASS Workshop, Dourdan, France, August 26-30, 1991: Selected Papers. Ed. by M. Bidoit & C. Choppy. LC 92-42107. (Lecture Notes in Computer Science Ser.: Vol. 655). 1993. 55.95 (*0-387-56379-2*) Spr-Verlag.

Recent Trends in Data Type Specification: Proceedings of the 10th Workshop on Specification of Abstract Data Types, Joint with the 5th COMPASS Workshop, S. Margherita, Italy, May 3-June 3, 1994. Workshop on Specification of Abstract Data Types Staff. Ed. by Egidio Astesiano et al. LC 95-10172. (Lecture Notes in Computer Science Ser.: Vol. 906). 1995. write for info. (*0-387-59132-X*) Spr-Verlag.

Recent Trends in Data Type Specification: 10th Workshop on Specification of Abstract Data Types Joint with the 5th COMPASS Workshop, S. Margherita, Italy, May 30-June 3, 1994. Proceedings. Ed. by E. Astesiano et al. (Lecture Notes in Computer Science Ser.: Vol. 906). viii, 523p. 1995. 81.00 (*3-540-59132-X*) Spr-Verlag.

***Recent Trends in Data Type Specification: 11th Workshop on Specification of Abstract Data Types, Joint with the 8th Compass Workshop, Oslo, Norway, September 19-23, 1995 - Selected Papers.** Magne Haveraaen et al. LC 96-36459. (Lecture Notes in Computer Science Ser.: Vol. 1130). 551p. 1996. 87.00 (*3-540-61629-2*) Spr-Verlag.

Recent Trends in Data Type Specification: 7th Workshop on Specification of Abstract Data Types, Wusterhausen-Dosse, FRG, April 17-20, 1990 Proceedings. Ed. by H. Ehrig et al. (Lecture Notes in Computer Science Ser.: Vol. 534). viii, 379p. 1991. 39.95 (*0-387-54496-8*) Spr-Verlag.

Recent Trends in Data Type Specifications. Ed. by D. Sannella & Andrzej Tarlecki. (Lecture Notes in Computer Science Ser.: Vol. 332). x, 259p. 1988. 36.00 (*0-387-50325-0*) Spr-Verlag.

Recent Trends in Differential Equations. Ed. by Ravi P. Agarwal. (Series in Applicable Analysis: Vol. 1). 550p. 1992. text ed. 81.00 (*981-02-0963-0*) World Scientific Pub.

Recent Trends in Fertility & Mortality in Indonesia. National Research Council Staff et al. LC 87-11178. (Papers of the East-West Population Institute: No. 105). (Illus.). xvi, 96p. (Orig.). 1987. pap. text ed. 3.00 (*0-86638-092-2*) EW Ctr HI.

Recent Trends in Forest Utilization. R. K. Suri. 140p. 1984. pap. 100.00 (*81-7089-067-5*, Pub. by Intl Bk Distr II) St Mut.

Recent Trends in Forest Utilization. R. K. Suri. 140p. (C). 1984. 165.00 (*0-685-21821-X*, Pub. by Intl Bk Distr II) St Mut.

Recent Trends in High Pressure Research: Proceedings of the 13th Airapt International Conference. Ed. by A. K. Singh. 948p. 1992. text ed. 176.00 (*81-204-0713-X*) World Scientific Pub.

Recent Trends in High Pressure Research: XIII International AIRAPT Conference. A. K. Singh. 948p. 1993. text ed. 126.00 (*81-204-0698-2*) World Scientific Pub.

Recent Trends in Hydrogeology. Ed. by T. N. Narasimhan. LC 82-2872. (Geological Society of America, Special Paper Ser.: No. 189). (Illus.). 456p. reprint ed. pap. 130.00 (*0-7837-1850-0*, 2042050) Bks Demand.

Recent Trends in Invertebrates. H. S. Juneja. (C). 1991. text ed. 225.00 (*81-7041-473-3*, Pub. by Anmol II) S Asia.

Recent Trends in Mathematics Reinhardsbrunn, Nineteen Eighty-Two. Herbert Kurke. 336p. (C). 1986. 115.00 (*0-685-36881-5*, Pub. by Collets) St Mut.

Recent Trends in Medical Genetics: Proceedings of the Conference on Recent Trends in Medical Genetics, Madras, India, 8-10 December, 1983. Ed. by K. M. Marimuthu & P. M. Gopinath. (Illus.). 370p. 1986. 114.25 (*0-08-031993-9*, Pergamon Pr) Elsevier.

Recent Trends in Mobile Robots. Yuan F. Zheng. (Series in Robotics & Automated Systems). 400p. 1994. text ed. 121.00 (*981-02-1511-8*) World Scientific Pub.

Recent Trends in Nutrition. Ed. by C. Gopalan. (Illus.). 236p. 1994. 29.95 (*0-19-562998-1*) OUP.

Recent Trends in Occupational Mobility. Natalie Rogoff. Ed. by Lewis A. Coser & Walter W. Powell. LC 79-7016. (Perennial Works in Sociology). (Illus.). 1979. reprint ed. lib. bdg. 18.95 (*0-405-12115-6*) Ayer.

***Recent Trends in Optimization Theory & Applications.** 496p. 1995. text ed. 59.00 (*981-02-2382-X*) World Scientific Pub.

Recent Trends in Plant Disease Control: National Symposium Proceedings. Ed. by H. B. Singh. (Current Trends in Life Sciences Ser.: Vol. XIX). (Illus.). 286p. 1992. 75.00 (*1-55528-274-1*, Pub. by Today & Tomorrows P & P II) Scholarly Pubns.

Recent Trends in Radiation Polymer Chemistry. Ed. by Sandanori Okamura. (Advances in Polymer Science Ser.: Vol. 105). (Illus.). 166p. 1993. 119.95 (*0-387-55812-8*) Spr-Verlag.

Recent Trends in Raman Spectroscopy. Ed. by S. B. Banerjee & S. S. Jha. 408p. (C). 1989. pap. 40.00 (*9971-5-0794-3*); text ed. 109.00 (*9971-5-0786-2*) World Scientific Pub.

Recent Trends in Regeneration Research. Ed. by V. Kiortsis et al. (NATO ASI Series A, Life Sciences: Vol. 172). (Illus.). 514p. 1989. 135.00 (*0-306-43232-3*, Plenum Pr) Plenum.

Recent Trends in Soviet Psycho-Linguistics. James V. Wertsch. LC 77-85715. 232p. reprint ed. pap. 66.20 (*0-317-29618-3*, 2021863) Bks Demand.

Recent Trends in Systems Theory. Ed. by S. D. Bedrosian & W. A. Porter. 1976. pap. 40.00 (*0-08-020590-9*, Pergamon Pr) Elsevier.

***Recent Trends in the Fisheries & Environment in the General Fisheries Council for the Mediterranean (GFCM) Area.** 78p. 1990. 12.00 (*92-5-103033-2*, F0332, Pub. by FAO IT) Bernan Associates.

Recent Trends in Theoretical Psychology. Ed. by W. J. Baker et al. (Recent Research in Psychology Ser.). (Illus.). 380p. 1988. 61.95 (*0-387-96757-5*) Spr-Verlag.

Recent Trends in Theoretical Psychology: Proceedings of the Fourth Biennial Conference of the International Society for Theoretical Psychology, June 24-28, 1991. Ed. by J. Stam Henderikus et al. LC 92-21112. (Recent Research in Psychology Ser.: Vol. 3). 1993. 67.95 (*0-387-97963-8*) Spr-Verlag.

Recent Trends in Theoretical Psychology: Proceedings of the Third Biennial Conference of the International Society for Theoretical Psychology April 17-21, 1989, Vol. 2. S. J. Terwee. (Recent Research in Psychology Ser.). (Illus.). xix, 465p. 1990. 64.95 (*0-387-97311-7*) Spr-Verlag.

Recent Turkish Coin Hoards & Numismatic Studies. C. S. Lightfoot. (Monographs: No. 12). (Illus.). 34p. 1991. pap. 60.00 (*0-946897-27-1*, Pub. by Brit Inst Arch UK) David Brown.

Recent United States History. Gilbert C. Fite & Norman A. Graebner. LC 79-188639. (Illus.). 911p. reprint ed. pap. 180.00 (*0-7837-3439-5*, 2057762) Bks Demand.

Recent Vertebrate Carcasses & Their Paleobiological Implications. Johannes Weigelt. Tr. by Judith Schaefer. LC 89-4698. (Illus.). 296p. 1989. pap. text ed. 25.00 (*0-226-88167-9*); lib. bdg. 72.00 (*0-226-88166-0*) U Ch Pr.

Recent Vertical Poetry. Roberto Juarroz. Tr. by Mary Crow. 118p. 1991. pap. 11.00 (*1-877727-08-3*) White Pine.

Recent Views on Hypertrophic Cardiomyopathy. Ed. by Ernst E. Van der Wall & K. I. Lie. (Developments in Cardiovascular Medicine Ser.). 1985. lib. bdg. 97.00 (*0-89838-694-2*) Kluwer Ac.

Recent Vitamin Research. Ed. by M. H. Briggs. 224p. 1984. 130.00 (*0-8493-5618-0*, QP771, CRC Reprint) Franklin.

Recent Work in Critical Theory, 1989-1995: An Annotated Bibliography. William Baker & Kenneth Womack. LC 96-18346. (Bibliographies & Indexes in World Literature Ser.: Vol. 51). 608p. 1996. text ed. 99.50 (*0-313-29434-8*, Greenwood Pr) Greenwood.

Recent Work in Women's History: East & West. Ed. by Esther Katz. LC 85-30223. (Trends in History Ser.: Vol. 4, No. 1). 151p. 1986. 39.95 (*0-86656-139-0*) Haworth Pr.

Recent Work of James Stirling Michael Wilford & Associates. (Architecture & Urbanism Extra Edition Ser.). (Illus.). 268p. (Orig.). (ENG & JPN.). (C). pap. text ed. 82.50 (*4-900211-30-3*, Pub. by Japan Architect JA) Gingko Press.

Recent Work of Jurgen Habermas: Reason, Justice, & Modernity. Stephen K. White. 200p. 1988. text ed. 49.95 (*0-521-34360-7*) Cambridge U Pr.

Recent Work of Jurgen Habermas: Reason, Justice & Modernity. Stephen K. White. 201p. (C). 1989. pap. text ed. 15.95 (*0-521-38959-3*) Cambridge U Pr.

Recent Works: October 13 - November 8, 1995, Tyler Art Gallery, Suny Oswego. Kumi Korf. (Illus.). 16p. (Orig.). 1995. pap. 15.00 (*0-930845-04-8*) Mycotaxon Ltd.

Recent Works by Imi Knoebel. Fred Hoffman. (Illus.). 20p. 1989. pap. 20.00 (*0-317-93494-5*) F Hoffman Gallery.

Recent Works by Michael Hiezer. Fred Hoffman. (Illus.). 20p. 1989. pap. 20.00 (*0-317-93495-3*) F Hoffman Gallery.

Recent Works by Walter Dahn. Fred Hoffman. (Illus.). 20p. 1989. pap. 20.00 (*0-317-93496-1*) F Hoffman Gallery.

Recent Writings in British Cinema. Ed. by Andrew Higson. (Film Studies (Rethinking British Cinema)). 256p. Date not set. write for info. (*0-304-33528-2*); pap. write for info. (*0-304-33529-0*) Cassell.

Recently Discovered Tales of Life among the Indians. James W. Schultz. Ed. by Warren L. Hanna. LC 88-9241. 152p. 1988. pap. 10.00 (*0-87842-221-8*) Mountain Pr.

***Receptarea Literaturii Americane in Romania in Secolul al 19-lea Si Prima Jumatate a Sec. al 20-Lea: The Reception of American Literature in Romania.** unabridged ed. Dumitru Dorobat. 442p. (RUM.). (C). 1996. text ed. 30.00 (*0-9653217-0-3*) D Durobat.

***Reception & Poetics in Keats.** Robinson. Date not set. text ed. 55.00 (*0-312-21001-9*) St Martin.

Reception at the Mongolian Embassy. Nicholas Kolumban. 1987. pap. 4.00 (*0-89823-090-X*) New Rivers Pr.

Reception of Calvinistic Thought in England. Charles D. Cremeans. LC 83-45578. reprint ed. 41.50 (*0-404-19896-1*) AMS Pr.

Reception of Christine De Pizan from the Fifteenth Through the Nineteenth Centuries: Visitors to the City. Ed. by Glenda K. McLeod. LC 91-44257. 184p. 1992. lib. bdg. 79.95 (*0-7734-9689-0*) E Mellen.

Reception of English Literature in Germany. Lawrence M. Price. LC 68-21223. 1972. reprint ed. 36.95 (*0-405-08863-9*) Ayer.

Reception of Georg Kaiser (1915-1945) Texts & Analysis, 2 vols. Peter K. Tyson. LC 84-47844. (Canadian Studies in German Language & Literature: Vol. 32). 1054p. (Orig.). (C). 1984. pap. text ed. 51.60 (*0-8204-0145-5*) P Lang Pubng.

Reception of German Literature in U. S. German Texts, 1864-1918. John H. Tatum. (Studies in Modern German Literature). 397p. 1988. text ed. 49.45 (*0-8204-0420-9*) P Lang Pubng.

Reception of Grimms' Fairy Tales: Responses, Reactions, Revisions. Ed. by Donald Haase. LC 92-47394. (Illus.). 348p. (Orig.). 1996. pap. 16.95 (*0-8143-2208-5*) Wayne St U Pr.

Reception of Grimms' Fairy Tales: Responses, Reactions, Revisions. Ed. by Donald P. Haase. LC 92-47394. (Illus.). 348p. 1993. text ed. 35.95 (*0-8143-2207-7*) Wayne St U Pr.

Reception of Hydrodynamic Stimuli in Aquatic & Semiaquatic Animals. Horst Bleckmann. (Fortschritte der Zoologie/Progress in Zoology Ser.: No. 41). (Illus.). x, 115p. (Orig.). 1994. pap. 65.00 (*3-437-30772-X*, Pub. by G Fischer Verlag GW) Lubrecht & Cramer.

Reception of Jazz in America: A New View. James L. Collier. LC 88-80503. (I.S.A.M. Monographs: No. 27). 104p. (Orig.). 1988. pap. 12.00 (*0-914678-30-2*) Inst Am Music.

Reception of Joyce Carol Oates's & Gabriele Wohmann's Short Fiction. Sigrid Mayer & Martha Hanscomau. (COMLIT Ser.). 1998. 55.00 (*1-57113-083-7*) Camden Hse.

Reception of Myth in English Romanticism. Anthony J. Harding. 312p. 1995. text ed. 39.95 (*0-8262-1007-4*) U of Mo Pr.

***Reception of Religious Television: Social Semeiology Applied to an Empirical Case Study.** Alf Linderman. (Psychologia & Sociologia Religionum Ser.: No. 12). 229p. (Orig.). 1996. pap. 48.50 (*91-554-3809-1*) Coronet Bks.

Reception of the Church Fathers in the West: From the Carolingians to the Maurists. Irena D. Backus & Antoinina Bevan. LC 96-20106. 1996. write for info. (*90-04-10635-9*) E J Brill.

Reception of the Church Fathers in the West: From the Carolingians to the Maurists. Antoinina Bevan. Ed. by Irena D. Backus. LC 96-20106. (Illus.). 1000p. 1996. 322.75 (*90-04-09722-8*) E J Brill.

Reception of the Church Fathers in the West: From the Carolingians to the Maurists. Stuart J. Murphy. LC 96-20106. (Illus.). 1997. pap. write for info. (*90-04-10636-7*) E J Brill.

Reception of the Picaresque in the French, English, & German Traditions, Vol. 18. Ellen T. Guiterrez. LC 93-50939. (Currents in Comparative Romance Languages & Literatures Ser.: Vol. 18). 152p. (C). 1995. text ed. 40.95 (*0-8204-2161-8*) P Lang Pubng.

Reception of Vatican II. Ed. by Giuseppe Alberigo et al. Tr. by Matthew J. O'Connell from FRE. LC 87-15175. 384p. 1988. pap. 19.95 (*0-8132-0654-5*) Cath U Pr.

Reception of Vatican II. Ed. by Giuseppe Alberigo. 362p. 1994. pap. 60.00 (*0-86012-167-4*, Pub. by Srch Pr UK) St Mut.

Reception Theory. R. Holub. (C). pap. text ed. 16.38 (*0-7870-0006-X*) Digital Print.

Reception Theory: A Critical Introduction. Robert C. Holub. LC 83-13385. 189p. 1984. pap. 11.95 (*0-416-33590-X*, NO. 4041) Routledge Chapman & Hall.

Receptionist. J. W. Twing & Georgia Alpharetta. 160p. 1983. text ed. 13.56 (*0-07-065641-X*) McGraw.

Receptionist. Jack Rudman. (Career Examination Ser.: C-1636). 1994. reprint ed. pap. 19.95 (*0-8373-1636-7*) Nat Learn.

Receptionist: A Practical Course in Office Reception Techniques. Merle W. Wood & Margaret McKenna. 1966. text ed. 25.85 (*0-07-071590-4*) McGraw.

***Receptionist in Action.** Rushen. 1987. pap. text ed. write for info. (*0-85896-333-7*) Addison-Wesley.

Receptions of War: Vietnam in American Culture. Andrew Martin. LC 92-33825. (Project for Discourse & Theory Ser.: Vol. 10). 216p. 1994. pap. 12.95 (*0-8061-2540-3*) U of Okla Pr.

Receptive One-Word Picture Vocabulary Test. Morrison Gardner. (ENG & SPA.). 1985. 10.00 (*0-87879-462-X*); student ed. 17.00 (*0-685-44984-X*); student ed., vinyl bd. 75.00 (*0-87879-459-X*); 10.00 (*0-685-44983-1*) Acad Therapy.

Receptive One-Word Picture Vocabulary Test-Upper Extension. Rick Brownell. 29p. (ENG & SPA.). 1987. 10.00 (*0-87879-591-X*); 17.00 (*0-685-31204-6*); student ed., vinyl bd. 70.00 (*0-87879-588-X*); 30.00 (*0-87879-589-8*); 10.00 (*0-685-44985-8*); lp 20.00 (*0-87879-590-1*) Acad Therapy.

Receptive Oral Language Inventory. Annabelle M. Markoff. Ed. by Nancy Martin. 64p. 1995. 40.00 (*0-87879-996-6*, 996-6); pap. 17.00 (*0-87879-997-4*, 996-6) Acad Therapy.

Receptive Prayer: A Christian Approach to Meditation. Grace A. Brame. LC 84-29302. 144p. (Orig.). 1985. pap. 9.99 (*0-8272-3211-X*) Chalice Pr.

***Receptivity to Malaria & Other Parasitic Diseases: Report on a WHO Working Group.** (EURO Reports & Studies: No. 15). 103p. 1979. 10.00 (*92-9020-154-1*, 1330015) World Health.

Receptor Activation by Antigens, Cytokines, Hormones, & Growth Factors, Vol. 766. Ed. by David Naor et al. LC 95-31753. (Annals of the New York Academy of Sciences Ser.). 1995. write for info. (*0-89766-951-7*); pap. write for info. (*0-89766-952-5*) NY Acad Sci.

***Receptor Agonists & Blockers: Products, Applications, Medical Sales & New Developments.** (Report Ser.: No. B-102). 255p. 1996. 3,450.00 (*1-56965-020-9*) BCC.

Receptor Autoradiography: Principles & Practice. Ed. by John Wharton & Julia M. Polak. LC 93-6952. (Modern Methods in Pathology Ser.). 370p. 1994. 59.95 (*0-19-262209-9*) OUP.

Receptor Binding. Ed. by Alan A. Boulton et al. LC 86-7142. (Neuromethods Ser.: Vol. 4). (Illus.). 608p. 1986. 89.50 (*0-89603-078-4*) Humana.

Receptor Binding Radiotracers, Vol. I. Ed. by W. C. Eckelman. 200p. 1982. 112.00 (*0-8493-6019-6*, QP519) CRC Pr.

Receptor Binding Radiotracers, Vol. II. Ed. by W. C. Eckelman. 248p. 1982. 138.00 (*0-8493-6020-X*, QP519, CRC Reprint) Franklin.

Receptor Biochemistry: A Practical Approach. Ed. by E. C. Hulme. (Practical Approach Ser.). (Illus.). 352p. 1990. 95.00 (*0-19-963092-5*, IRL Pr) OUP.

Receptor Biochemistry: A Practical Approach. Ed. by E. C. Hulme. (Practical Approach Ser.: 65). (Illus.). 352p. 1990. pap. 55.00 (*0-19-963093-3*, IRL Pr) OUP.

Receptor Characterization & Their Regulation. Agrawal. 232p. 1992. write for info. (*0-8493-4230-9*, CRC Reprint) Franklin.

Receptor Characterization & Their Regulation. Devendra K. Agrawal. 1997. write for info. (*0-8493-7819-2*) CRC Pr.

***Receptor Classification: The Integration of Operational, Structural, & Transductional Information.** Ed. by D. G. Trist et al. 1997. 90.00 (*0-614-24851-5*) NY Acad Sci.

***Receptor Classification: The Integration of Operational, Structural, & Transductional Information.** D. G. Trist. LC 97-6552. (Annals of the New York Academy of Sciences Ser.). 1997. write for info. (*0-89766-987-8*); pap. write for info. (*0-89766-988-6*) NY Acad Sci.

Receptor Desensitization & Ca2+-Signaling: Cellular Aspects of Possible Molecular Dynamics. Ed. by M. K. Uchida. (Illus.). viii, 214p. 1996. 231.50 (*3-8055-6283-7*) S Karger.

R

Receptor Dynamics in Neural Development. Ed. by Christopher A. Shaw. LC 95-42841. (Pharmacology & Toxicology Ser.). 400p. 1996. 131.95 (*0-8493-7817-6*) CRC Pr.

Receptor-Effector Coupling: A Practical Approach. Ed. by E. C. Hulme. (Practical Approach Ser.). (Illus.). 248p. 1990. 75.00 (*0-19-963094-1*, IRL Pr) OUP.

***Receptor Localization: Laboratory Methods & Procedures.** Marjorie Ariano. (Receptor Biochemistry & Methodology Ser.). 320p. 1998. text ed. 99.95 (*0-471-16571-9*) Wiley.

***Receptor Localization: Laboratory Methods & Procedures.** Marjorie Ariano. (Receptor Biochemistry & Methodology Ser.). 320p. 1998. pap. text ed. 56.95 (*0-471-19524-3*) Wiley.

Receptor Mediated Antisteroid Action. Ed. by M. K. Agarwal. 523p. (C). 1987. lib. bdg. 229.25 (*3-11-011355-4*) De Gruyter.

Receptor-Mediated Biological Processes: Implications Forevaluating Carcinogenesis: Proceedings of the Sixth International Conference on Carcinogenesis & Risk Assessment, Held in Austin, Texas, on December 8-11, 1992. Ed. by Hugh L. Spitzer & Thomas J. Slaga. 366p. 1994. text ed. 145.00 (*0-471-02045-1*) Wiley.

Receptor Modeling for Air Quality Management. Ed. by Philip K. Hopke. (Data Handling in Science & Technology Ser.: No. 7). 330p. 1991. 211.75 (*0-444-88218-9*) Elsevier.

Receptor Modelling in Environmental Chemistry. Philip K. Hopke. LC 84-19568. (Chemical Analysis Ser.). 319p. 1985. text ed. 199.00 (*0-471-89106-1*) Wiley.

Receptor Pharmacology & Function. Williams et al. (Clinical Pharmacology Ser.: Vol. 13). 800p. 1988. 235.00 (*0-8247-7841-3*) Dekker.

Receptor Phosphorylation. Ed. by Virinder K. Moudgil. LC 88-4339. 400p. 1989. 220.00 (*0-8493-6318-7*, QP552, CRC Reprint) Franklin.

Receptor Purification Vol. 1: Receptors for CNS Agents, Growth Factors, Hormones, & Related Substances. Ed. by Gerald Litwack. LC 90-4689. (Illus.). 514p. 1990. 99.50 (*0-89603-167-5*) Humana.

Receptor Purification, Vol. 2: Receptors for Steroid Hormones, Thyroid Hormones, Water-Balancing Hormones, & Others. Ed. by Gerald Litwack. LC 90-4689. (Illus.). 432p. 1990. 99.50 (*0-89603-183-7*) Humana.

Receptor-Receptor Interactions: A New Intramembrane Integrative Mechanism. Ed. by K. Fuxe & Luigi F. Agnati. LC 87-942721. (Wenner-Gren International Symposia Ser.: Vol. 48). (Illus.). 580p. 1987. 125.00 (*0-306-42719-2*, Plenum Pr) Plenum.

Receptor Research Methods. Ben Greenstein. 352p. 1995. text ed. 115.00 (*3-7186-5670-1*, Harwood Acad Pubs); spiral bd. 48.00 (*3-7186-5671-X*, Harwood Acad Pubs) Gordon & Breach.

***Receptor Signal Transduction Protocols.** Ed. by R. A. Challiss. (Methods in Molecular Biology: Vol. 83). 296p. 1997. 99.50 (*0-89603-495-X*); spiral bd. 69.50 (*0-89603-418-6*) Humana.

Receptor Subunits & Complexes. Ed. by E. A. Barnard & Arnold S. Burgen. (Illus.). 450p. (C). 1992. text ed. 120.00 (*0-521-36612-7*) Cambridge U Pr.

Receptors. Richard M. Restak. 228p. 1995. pap. 12.95 (*0-553-37441-9*) Bantam.

Receptors, Vol. 1. Ed. by J. Jacob. LC 78-41027. (Illus.). 295p. 1979. pap. 40.00 (*0-08-023205-1*, Pub. by Pergamon Repr UK) Franklin.

Receptors: Models for Binding, Trafficking, & Signaling. Douglas A. Lauffenburger & Jennifer J. Linderman. (Illus.). 384p. (C). 1996. pap. text ed. 35.00 (*0-19-510663-6*) OUP.

Receptors: Recent Findings. Ed. by Mannfred A. Hollinger. LC 94-11607. 212p. 1995. 117.95 (*0-8493-9424-4*) CRC Pr.

Receptors & Ion Channels: Proceedings of the Symposium, Tashkent, U. S. S. R., October 2-5, 1986. Y. A. Ovchinnikov & F. Hucho. xi, 351p. 1987. lib. bdg. 169.25 (*3-11-010346-X*) De Gruyter.

Receptors & Ligands in Neurological Disorders. Ed. by Amartya K. Sen & Tyrone Lee. (Intercellular & Intracellular Communications Ser.: No. 4). (Illus.). 372p. 1988. text ed. 125.00 (*0-521-30720-1*) Cambridge U Pr.

Receptors & Ligands in Psychiatry. Ed. by Amartya K. Sen & Tyrone Lee. (Intercellular & Intracellular Communications Ser.: No. 3). (Illus.). 500p. 1988. text ed. 170.00 (*0-521-30719-8*) Cambridge U Pr.

Receptors & Mechanism of Action of Steroid Hormones, 2 pts., Pt. 1. Ed. by Jorge R. Pasqualini. LC 76-40597. (Modern Pharmacology-Toxicology Ser.: No. 8). (Illus.). 325p. reprint ed. pap. 87.80 (*0-7837-0679-0*, 2041013) Bks Demand.

Receptors & Mechanism of Action of Steroid Hormones, 2 pts., Pt. 2. Ed. by Jorge R. Pasqualini. LC 76-40597. (Modern Pharmacology-Toxicology Ser.: No. 8). (Illus.). 439p. reprint ed. pap. 125.20 (*0-7837-0680-4*) Bks Demand.

Receptors & Sensory Perception. Ragnar Granit. LC 75-14597. (Mrs. Hepsa Ely Silliman Memorial Lectures). (Illus.). 369p. 1975. reprint ed. text ed. 65.00 (*0-8371-8213-1*, GRRS, Greenwood Pr) Greenwood.

Receptors As Surramolecular Entities: Proceedings of the Biannual Capo Bio Conference, Cagliari, Italy, 7-10 June, 1981. Pier F. Spano. (Advances in the Biosciences Ser.: Vol. 44). (Illus.). 476p. 1983. 110.00 (*0-08-029804-4*, Pergamon Pr) Elsevier.

Receptors in Pharmacology. Ed. by John R. Smythies & Ronald J. Bradley. LC 76-41470. (Modern Pharmacology-Toxicology Ser.: No. 11). (Illus.). 516p. reprint ed. pap. 147.10 (*0-7837-0811-4*, 2041126) Bks Demand.

Receptors in the Cardiovascular System. Pieter A. Van Zwieten & Edward Schonbaum. (Progress in Pharmacology Ser.: Vol. 6, No. 2). 193p. 1986. pap. 85.00 (*0-89574-227-6*, Pub. by G Fischer Verlag GW) Lubrecht & Cramer.

Receptors in the Developing Nervous System, 1. Ed. by Ian S. Zagon & Patricia J. McLaughlin. LC 92-49100. 272p. (gr. 13). 1993. text ed. 123.95 (*0-412-45240-5*) Chapman & Hall.

Receptors in the Developing Nervous System, 2. Ed. by Ian S. Zagon & Patricia J. McLaughlin. LC 92-49100. 276p. (gr. 13). 1993. text ed. 92.95 (*0-412-49400-0*) Chapman & Hall.

Receptors in the Developing Nervous System, Set. Ed. by Ian S. Zagon & Patricia J. McLaughlin. LC 92-49100. 264p. (gr. 13). 1993. text ed. 174.95 (*0-412-54520-9*) Chapman & Hall.

Receptors in Tumour Biology. Ed. by C. M. Chadwick. (Intercellular & Intracellular Communications Ser.: No. 2). (Illus.). 250p. 1986. 64.95 (*0-521-32117-4*) Cambridge U Pr.

Receptors, Membrane Transport & Signal Transduction. Ed. by A. E. Evangelopoulos et al. (NATO ASI Series H: Vol. 29). (Illus.). viii, 387p. 1989. 146.95 (*0-387-50421-4*) Spr-Verlag.

Recerchari, Motetti, Canzoni, Libro Primo see Monuments of Music & Music Literature in Facsimile: Series One

Recertification: A Look at the Issues. Group for the Advancement of Psychiatry Staff. LC 77-357584. (Group for the Advancement of Psychiatry, Symposium Ser.: Vol. 9, No. 96). 63p. reprint ed. pap. 25.00 (*0-7837-2108-0*, 2042386) Bks Demand.

Recertification: New Evaluation Methods & Strategies. Ed. by Elliott L. Mancall & Philip G. Bashook. LC 94-70217. 195p. 1994. lib. bdg. 44.95 (*0-934277-19-2*) Am Bd Med Spec.

Recertification & Stress Classification Issues: Proceedings of the Pressure Vessels & Piping Conference, Minneapolis, MN, 1994. Ed. by J. N. Petrinec, Jr. LC 94-71356. (PVP Ser.: Vol. 277). 169p. 1994. pap. 50.00 (*0-7918-1350-9*) ASME.

Recertification for Medical Specialists. Ed. by Donald G. Langsley & John S. Lloyd. LC 87-72510. 276p. 1987. lib. bdg. 39.95 (*0-934277-10-9*) Am Bd Med Spec.

Recess. Bob Reese. LC 92-12184. (School Days Ser.). (Illus.). 24p. (J). (ps-2). 1992. lib. bdg. 14.00 (*0-516-05581-X*) Childrens.

Recess: Prayer Meditations for Teachers. Elspeth C. Murphy. 96p. (Orig.). (gr. 10). 1988. 7.99 (*0-8010-6244-6*) Baker Bks.

Recess Mess: First-Grade Friends. Grace Maccarone. (Hello Reader! Ser.). (Illus.). 32-48p. (J). (ps-1). 1996. 3.50 (*0-590-73878-X*, Cartwheel) Scholastic Inc.

Recess, or, a Tale of Other Times, 3 Vols., Set. Sophia Lee. LC 77-131325. (Gothic Novels Ser.). 1979. reprint ed. 54.95 (*0-405-00806-6*) Ayer.

Recession & Depressionproof Careers & Businesses. Roger A. Kessinger. 176p. (Orig.). 1989. pap. 21.00 (*0-922802-02-5*) Kessinger Pub.

Recession & Recovery of 1973-1976. Victor Zarnowitz & Geoffrey H. Moore. (Explorations in Economic Research Four Ser.: No. 4). 87p. 1977. reprint ed. 35.00 (*0-685-61415-8*) Natl Bur Econ Res.

Recession As a Policy Instrument: Israel, 1965-1969. Carol S. Greenwald. LC 73-2895. 154p. 1973. 29.50 (*0-8386-1396-9*) Fairleigh Dickinson.

Recession, Crime, & Punishment. Steven Box. LC 87-1825. 240p. 1987. 56.50 (*0-389-20724-1*, 08282) B&N Imports.

Recessional. James A. Michener. 1995. mass mkt. 6.99 (*0-449-22387-6*) Fawcett.

Recessional. James A. Michener. 1994. 125.00 (*0-679-43828-9*) Random.

Recessional. James A. Michener. 1995. mass mkt. 6.99 (*0-449-22345-0*) Fawcett.

Recessive Oncogenes & Tumor Suppression. Ed. by Webster Cavenee et al. (Current Communications in Molecular Biology Ser.). (Illus.). 234p. (C). 1989. pap. text ed. 24.00 (*0-87969-332-0*) Cold Spring Harbor.

Recetas: Biblioteca Universitaria, Salamanca MS.2262. Ed. by Maria Carmen De La Cal. (Medieval Spanish Medical Texts Ser.: No. 20). 6p. (SPA.). 1987. 10.00 incl. fiche (*0-940639-16-5*) Hispanic Seminary.

Recetas Norteamericanas en Ingles y Espanol. 168p. 1980. 5.95 (*0-686-27595-0*, 0-9607690) Lang Svcs CA.

Receuil des Cours 1980, No. IV. Academie de Droit International de la Haye Staff. 380p. 1984. lib. bdg. 129.00 (*90-247-2976-9*) Kluwer Ac.

Receyt of the Ladie Kateryne. Ed. by Gordon Kipling. (Early English Text Society Original Ser.: Vol. 296). (Illus.). 280p. 1996. 45.00 (*0-19-722298-6*) Boydell & Brewer.

Recharge Your Career & Your Life. Paul R. Timm. Ed. by Michael G. Crisp. LC 89-82097. 185p. (Orig.). 1991. pap. 13.95 (*1-56052-027-2*) Crisp Pubns.

Recharge Your Life. Judith Gelwicks. 64p. (Orig.). student ed. write for info. (*0-318-72657-2*); pap. write for info. (*0-9638015-0-3*) Cody Pubns.

Rechargeable Batteries: Advances Since 1977. Ed. by Robert W. Graham. LC 80-13152. (Energy Technology Review Series & Chemical Technology Review Ser.: Nos. 55 & 160). 452p. 1980. 54.00 (*0-8155-0802-6*) Noyes.

Rechargeable Batteries: Applications Handbook. Gates Energy Products, Technical Marketing Staff. (Electrical Engineering - EDN Ser.). 312p. 1992. 59.95 (*0-7506-9227-8*) Buttrwrth-Heinemann.

Rechargeable Lithium & Lithium Ion (RCT) Batteries. S. Megahead et al. 510p. 1995. 70.00 (*1-56677-087-4*, PV 94-28) Electrochem Soc.

***Rechargeable Zinc Batteries: Commemorating the 100th Birthday of A. N. Frumkin.** Ed. by A. J. Salkind et al. (Illus.). 262p. 1996. 43.00 (*1-56677-109-9*, PV95-14) Electrochem Soc.

Recharging Your Relationship: Finding the Fun Again. Jack Mumey & Cynthia Tinsley. 224p. 1995. pap. 10.95 (*0-925190-34-9*) Fairview Press.

***Recharting the Caribbean: Land, Law, & Citizenship in the British Virgin Islands.** Bill Maurer. LC 96-51247. (C). 1997. 44.50 (*0-472-10811-5*) U of Mich Pr.

Recharting the Thirties. Patrick J. Quinn. LC 96-3539. 304p. 1996. 43.50 (*0-945636-90-3*) Susquehanna U Pr.

Rechenka's Eggs. Patricia Polacco. (Illus.). 32p. (J). (ps-3). 1988. 15.95 (*0-399-21501-8*, Philomel Bks) Putnam Pub Group.

Rechenka's Eggs. Patricia Polacco. (Illus.). 32p. (J). (ps-3). 1996. pap. 5.95 (*0-698-11385-3*, Paperstar) Putnam Pub Group.

Recherche & Litterature Canadienne-Francaise. Paul Wyczynski et al. LC 70-470011. (Cahiers du Centre de Recherches en Litterature Canadienne-Francaise: Vol. 2). 299p. 1969. reprint ed. pap. 85.30 (*0-608-01989-5*, 2062645) Bks Demand.

Recherche de la Base et du Sommet. Rene Char. (FRE.). 1977. pap. 10.95 (*0-8288-3823-2*) Fr & Eur.

Recherche de la Base et du Sommet. Rene Char. (Poesie Ser.). 192p. (FRE.). 1977. pap. 7.95 (*2-07-031918-0*) Schoenhof.

Recherche de l'Absolu. Honore De Balzac. Bd. with Messe de l'Athee. (Folio Ser.: No. 739). (FRE.). Set pap. 9.95 (*2-07-036739-8*, 2163) Schoenhof.

Recherche De l'Absolu, la Messe De l'Athee. Honore De Balzac. (FRE.). 1976. pap. 12.95 (*0-7859-1816-7*, 2070367398) Fr & Eur.

Recherche des Bouches du Mississippi et Voyage a Travers le Continent Depuis les Cotes du Texas jusqu'a Quebec (1669-1698) see Decouvertes et Establissements des francais dans l'ouest et dans le sud de l'Amerique septentrional: 1614-1754

Recherche du Don Perdu: Points de Repere dans le Roman de Marcel Proust. Per Nykrog. LC 85-73551. (Harvard Studies in Romance Languages: No. 42). 100p. (Orig.). (FRE.). 1986. pap. 10.00 (*0-940940-42-6*) Harvard U Romance Lang & Lit.

Recherche d'une Eglise. Jules Romains. 192p. (FRE.). 1962. pap. 10.95 (*0-7859-1403-X*, 2080506226) Fr & Eur.

Recherche Recipes from Sound Food Restaurant & Bakery. Ed. by Melane Lohmann. (Illus.). 51p. (Orig.). 1984. pap. 6.95 (*0-9615672-0-1*) Sound Food Co.

Recherches Photographiques. Niepce De Saint-Victor. Ed. by Peter C. Bunnell & Robert A. Sobieszek. LC 76-23058. (Sources of Modern Photography Ser.). (FRE.). 1979. reprint ed. lib. bdg. 11.95 (*0-405-09622-4*) Ayer.

Recherches Sur Arrien: Sa Personnalite et Ses Ecrits Atticistes, 2 vols., Set. Henry Tonnet. (FRE.). 1988. pap. 210.00 (*90-256-0934-1*, Pub. by A M Hakkert NE) Benjamins North Am.

Recherches Sur Jean Grolier, Sur Sa Vie et Sa Bibliotheque. Antoine J. Le Roux de Lincy. (In Zusammenarbeit Mit Dem Verlag B. de Graaf, Nieuwkoop Ser.). lix, 491p. 1971. reprint ed. write for info. (*3-487-04035-2*) G Olms Pubs.

Recherches sur la Crete Occidentale: De l'Epoque Geometrique a la Conquete Romaine. Daphne Gondicas. (Inventaire des Sources Archeologiques et Textuelles, Position du Probleme Ser.). xii, 364p. (FRE.). 1988. pap. 104.00 (*90-256-0942-2*, Pub. by A M Hakkert NE) Benjamins North Am.

Recherches Sur la Langue et le Style d'Isee. Jean-Marc Denomme. xiii, 395p. 1974. write for info. (*3-487-05085-4*) G Olms Pubs.

Recherches sur la poesie de Dafydd ab Gwilym, barde gallois du XIVe siecle. Theodor M. Chotzen. LC 78-72622. (Celtic Language & Literature Ser.: Goidelic & Brythonic). reprint ed. 42.50 (*0-404-17546-5*) AMS Pr.

Recherches Sur le Stoicisme Aux XVIe et XVIIe Siecles. Julien E. D'Angers, pseud. (Studien und Materialien Zur Geschichte der Philosophie Ser.: Vol. XIX). xi, 532p. 1976. write for info. (*3-487-05580-5*) G Olms Pubs.

Recherches sur le Symbolisme Funeraire des Romains. Franz Cumont. LC 75-10632. (Ancient Religion & Mythology Ser.). (Illus.). (FRE.). 1976. reprint ed. 63.95 (*0-405-07007-1*) Ayer.

Recherches sur le Vocabulaire du General de Gaulle: Analyse Statistique des Allocutions Radiodiffusees (1958-1965) Cotteret & Josephine Moreau. 23.65 (*0-685-33949-1*, F101840) Fr & Eur.

Recherches Sur les Chrysophycees: Morphologie, Phylogenie, Systematique. Pierre Bourrelly. (Illus.). 1971. reprint ed. 70.00 (*3-7682-0703-X*) Lubrecht & Cramer.

Recherches Sur les Ornementations Sporales Des Discomycetes Opercules. M. Le Gal. 1970. reprint ed. 40.00 (*3-7682-0694-7*) Lubrecht & Cramer.

Recherches Sur les Sources Latines Des Contes et Romans Courtois Du Moyen Age. Edmond Faral. LC 72-178580. reprint ed. 52.50 (*0-404-56600-6*) AMS Pr.

Recherches Sur les Systemes Significants: Symposium De Varsovie, 1968. Ed. by Josette Rey-Debove. (Approaches to Semiotics Ser.: No. 18). (Illus.). 1973. 140.00 (*90-279-2379-5*) Mouton.

Recherches sur L'Histoire de L'Astronomie Ancienne. Paul Tannery. LC 75-13297. (History of Ideas in Ancient Greece Ser.). (FRE.). 1976. reprint ed. 33.95 (*0-405-07341-0*) Ayer.

Recherches Sur l'Histoire De l'Astronomie Ancienne. Paul Tannery. viii, 370p. 1976. reprint ed. write for info. (*3-487-06051-5*) G Olms Pubs.

Recherches sur l'historie de la France medievale: Des Merovingiens aux premiers Capetians. Robert-Henri Bautier. Ed. by J. Dufour. (Collected Studies: No. CS 351). 350p. 1991. text ed. 99.50 (*0-86078-300-6*, Pub. by Variorum UK) Ashgate Pub Co.

Recherches sur l'Origine, l'Esprit et la Progres des Arts de la Grece. Pierre D'Hancarville. LC 78-60885. (Myth & Romanticism Ser.: Vol. 12). 1203p. 1984. text ed. 25.00 (*0-8240-3561-5*) Garland.

***Rechnungslegung Nach der Equity-Methode im Konsolidierten Abschulb: Ein Beitrag zur Entstehung, Anwendung & Ausgestaltung des Verfahrens vor dem Hintergrund der Bestimmungen in der Europaischen Union & der Verlautbarungen Internationaler Organisationen.** Gerhard Schmidt. (Illus.). 575p. (GER.). 1996. 88.95 (*3-631-30437-4*) P Lang Pubng.

***Rechnungslegung und Kreditfinanzierung: Zum Zusammenhang von Ausschuttungsbegrenzung, Bilanzieller Gewinnermittlung und Vorsichtiger Rechnungslegung.** Christian Leuz. (Betriebswirtschaftliche Studien: Bd. 32). 250p. (GER.). 1996. pap. 54.95 (*3-631-30150-2*) P Lang Pubng.

Recht des Gottesdienstes in der Diozese Mainz zur Zeit von Bischhof Joseph Ludwig Colmar, Vol. 1. Georg May. (Kanonistische Studien und Texte Ser.: No. 36). xiv, 762p. 1987. 71.00 (*0-685-53316-6*, Pub. by B R Gruener NE) Benjamins North Am.

Recht des Gottesdienstes in der Diozese Mainz zur Zeit von Bischhof Joseph Ludwig Colmar (1802-1818), Band 2. Georg May. (Kanonistische Studien und Texte Ser.: Vol. 37). xii, 692p. (GER.). 1987. 60.00 (*90-6032-290-8*, Pub. by B R Gruener NE) Benjamins North Am.

Recht Im "Reinhart Fuchs" Sigrid Widmaier. (Quellen und Forschungen zur Sprach und Kulturgeschichte der Germanischen Voelker Ser.: NF Band 102 (226)). x, 293p. (GER.). (C). 1993. lib. bdg. 109.25 (*3-11-013730-5*) De Gruyter.

Recht in der Korrelation von Dogmatik & Ethik. Kerstin Gafgen. (Theologische Bibliothek Toepelmann Ser.: Vol. 52). xii, 339p. (GER.). (C). 1991. lib. bdg. 95.40 (*3-11-012790-3*) De Gruyter.

Recht (Materien, Fortsetzung), Vol. 14 see Aufstieg und Niedergang der Roemischen Welt: Selection 2, Principat

Recht (Methoden, Schulen, Einzelne Juristen) Vol. 15. Ed. by Hildegard Temporini & Wolfgang Haas. 1976. 233.35 (*3-11-006736-6*) De Gruyter.

Recht (Normen, Verbreitung, Materien), Vol. 13 see Aufstieg und Niedergang der Roemischen Welt: Selection 2, Principat

Rechtfertigung und zukuenftiges Heil. Untersuchungen zu Roemer 5, 1-11. Michael Wolter. (Beiheft zur Zeitschrift fuer die Neuetestamentliche Wissenschaft Ser.: No. 43). (C). 1978. 77.70 (*3-11-007579-2*) De Gruyter.

***Rechtliche Rahmenbedingungen fur den Technologietransfer von Deutschland nach der Islamischen Republik Iran Vol. XXXIX: Vertragsrecht, Staatliche Regelung und Immaterialguterrecht im Iran.** Sassan D. Khatib-Shahidi. (Studien zum Internationalen Privat-, Wirtschafts- und Steuerrecht Ser.: Bd. 4). 464p. (GER.). 1997. pap. 82.95 (*3-631-31200-8*) P Lang Pubng.

Rechtschreibungs-Woerterbuch der Medizin. Klaus P. Eschenbach. 206p. (ENG & GER.). 1985. 39.95 (*0-8288-1836-3*, M15433) Fr & Eur.

Rechtsentwicklungen in Deutschland. 3rd ed. Adolf Laufs. (Lehrbuch der Allgemeinen Geographie Ser. Vol. 12). 1984. 32.35 (*3-11-009758-3*) De Gruyter.

***Rechtsextremismus und die Presse.** Maria Busche-Baumann. (Hildesheimer Schriftenreihe Zur Sozialpadagogik und Sozialarbeit Ser.: Vol. 7). 276p. (GER.). 1994. write for info. (*3-487-09900-4*) G Olms Pubs.

Rechtshcreibung Bertelsmann. Hermann. 923p. (GER.). 1993. 45.00 (*0-614-00356-3*, 3570105067) Fr & Eur.

Rechtssaetze in gebundener Sprache und Rechtssatzreihen im israelitischen Recht: Ein Beitrag zur Gattungsforschung. Volker Wagner. (Beiheft 127 zur Zeitschrift fuer die Alttestamentliche Wissenschaft Ser.). (C). 1972. 54.65 (*3-11-003945-1*) De Gruyter.

Rechtssoziologie in der Deutschen Demokratischen Republik & in der Bundesrepublik Deutschland. Wolfgang Hoffmann-Riem et al. 336p. (GER.). 1990. pap. 81.00 (*3-7890-1902-X*, Pub. by Nomos Verlags GW) Intl Bk Import.

Rechtstreitigkeiten der Altassyrischen Handler. Renate Wernisch. (GER.). 1996. write for info. (*90-72371-65-8*, Pub. by Styx NE) Eisenbrauns.

Rechtswoerterbuch: Law Dictionary. H. Kniepkamp. 216p. (ENG & GER.). 1954. 65.00 (*0-8288-6873-5*, M-7598) Fr & Eur.

Recidivism: Habitual Criminality & Habitual Petty Delinquency. John F. Sutherland. (Criminology Ser.). 1992. lib. bdg. 88.75 (*0-8490-5310-2*) Gordon Pr.

Recidivism of Criminal Offenders Assigned to Community Correctional Programs or Released from Prison: Final Report. Stevens H. Clarke & Anita L. Harrison. 56p. (Orig.). (C). 1992. pap. text ed. 12.00 (*1-56011-204-2*, 92.02) Institute Government.

Recife - Manual Bandeira. Manual Bandeira. Tr. by Eddie Flintoff. 56p. (C). 1988. pap. 25.00 (*0-947612-04-1*, Pub. by Rivelin Grapheme Pr) St Mut.

Recipe Book. Geraldine Holt. (Illus.). 128p. 1995. 10.98 (*0-8317-7463-0*) Smithmark.

Recipe Book: Practical Ideas for the Language Classroom. Ed. by Seth Lindstromberg. (Pilgrims Resource Bks.). 91p. 1990. pap. text ed. 21.32 (*0-582-03764-6*, 78673) Longman.

An Asterisk (*) at the beginning of an entry indicates that the title is appearing in BIP for the first time.

Recipe Book - A Taste of Wales. Wales Tourist Board Staff. (Illus.). 106p. (Orig.). 1994. pap. 7.95 (*0-85013-051-4*, Pub. by Jarrold Pub UK) Seven Hills Bk.

Recipe Book for 10. Lynn E. Robbins. 416p. (C). 1994. pap. 125.00 (*1-888143-02-9*) Robbins Mgmt.

Recipe Book for 100. Lynn E. Robbins. 416p. (C). 1994. pap. 125.00 (*1-888143-05-3*) Robbins Mgmt.

Recipe Book for 200. Lynn E. Robbins. 416p. (C). 1994. pap. 125.00 (*1-888143-06-1*) Robbins Mgmt.

Recipe Book for 25. Lynn E. Robbin. 416p. (C). 1994. pap. 125.00 (*1-888143-03-7*) Robbins Mgmt.

Recipe Book for 50. Lynn E. Robbins. 416p. (C). 1994. pap. 125.00 (*1-888143-04-5*) Robbins Mgmt.

***Recipe Collector: Collect, Organize & Share Recipes with Family & Friends!** (Illus.). 224p. 1997. spiral bd. 7.95 (*0-9655073-2-7*) Lusions Pub.

***Recipe Encyclopedia.** Random House Value Publishing. LC 97-17176. 1997. 24.99 (*0-517-18442-7*) Random Hse Value.

***Recipe File for Camps.** ix, 172p. 1995. ring bd. 15.00 (*0-9655851-0-7*) J Reath.

***Recipe File for Camps.** ix, 172p. 1995. spiral bd. 15.00 (*0-9655851-1-5*) J Reath.

***Recipe File for Your Church Kitchen.** viii, 165p. 1996. ring bd. 15.00 (*0-9655851-2-3*) J Reath.

***Recipe File for Your Church Kitchen.** viii, 165p. 1996. spiral bd. 15.00 (*0-9655851-3-1*) J Reath.

Recipe Finder. Marian Carey. (Illus.). 103p. (Orig.). pap. 14.95 (*0-9620559-0-5*) M J Carey.

Recipe for a Crime. adapted ed. Alfonso Paso. 1962. pap. 5.25 (*0-8222-0936-5*) Dramatists Play.

Recipe for Death. large type ed. Janet Laurence. LC 93-20595. 1993. lib. bdg. 17.95 (*1-56054-794-4*) Thorndike Pr.

***Recipe for Grant Writing: A Simplistic Guide for Schools, Religious, & Community Agencies.** Algeania Freeman. 80p. (Orig.). 1997. pap. 15.00 (*1-57502-484-5*, PO1447) Morris Pubng.

Recipe for Happy Days. Patricia O'Grady. (Illus.). 65p. (Orig.). 1982. pap. 4.25 (*0-9601846-2-7*) PM Ent.

Recipe for Life: How I Reversed My Heart Disease. Ron Burt & Joy Burt. LC 96-96471. (Illus.). 250p. 1997. pap. 14.95 (*0-9646147-9-0*) Alfie Pub.

Recipe for Math Program: Complete Program, Set. Nina Traub. 1985. pap. text ed. 59.95 (*0-87594-250-4*) Book-Lab.

Recipe for Math Program: Instructor's Guide. Nina Traub. 1985. Set of 4. teacher ed., spiral bd. 24.95 (*0-87594-245-8*) Book-Lab.

Recipe for Math Program: Manipulatives. Nina Traub. 1985. 29.95 (*0-87594-247-4*) Book-Lab.

Recipe for Math Program: Workbook Set. Nina Traub. 1985. wbk. ed., pap. text ed. 14.95 (*0-87594-246-6*) Book-Lab.

Recipe for Romance. Faith E. Garner. 1995. 17.95 (*0-8034-9092-5*, 094612) Bouregy.

Recipe for Romance. Sybil Josty. (Rainbow Romances Ser.). 160p. 1993. 14.95 (*0-7090-4896-3*, Hale-Parkwest) Parkwest Pubns.

Recipe for Success in Network Marketing. Leonard Baker. Ed. by Linda Fuller. 128p. (Orig.). 1992. pap. text ed. 12.00 (*0-910973-04-0*) Arrowhead AZ.

Recipe Greetings - A Poetry Reference for Greeting Cards to Duplicate & Use. rev. ed. Bibliotheca Press Staff. 50p. (Orig.). 1993. ring bd. 25.95 (*0-317-01784-5*, Bibliotheca Pr) Prosperity & Profits.

Recipe Greetings for Barter. Barter Publishing Staff. 53p. 1989. ring bd. 25.95 (*0-911617-87-6*, Barter Pub) Prosperity & Profits.

Recipe Gree'ings to Duplicate & Use. A. C. Doyle. 79p. 1991. ring bd. 25.95 (*0-913597-15-5*) Prosperity & Profits.

Recipe Index, Nineteen Seventy: The Eater's Guide to Periodical Literature. Ed. by John Forsman. LC 72-884. 784p. 1972. 52.00 (*0-8103-0525-9*) Gale.

Recipe Index, Nineteen Seventy-One: The Eater's Guide to Periodical Literature. Ed. by John Forsman. LC 72-884. 774p. 1974. 52.00 (*0-8103-0526-7*) Gale.

Recipe Ingredient Substitution Cookbook. Alpha Pyramis. 60p. 1992. ring bd. 19.95 (*0-913597-23-6*) Prosperity & Profits.

Recipe Notebook. Joanna Isles. 1992. 14.99 (*1-85145-690-2*, Pavilion Bks) Viking Penguin.

Recipe of Memory: Five Generations of Mexican Cuisine. Victor M. Valle & Mary L. Valle. (Illus.). 224p. 1995. 22.00 (*1-56584-126-3*) New Press NY.

***Recipe of Memory: Five Generations of Mexican Cuisine.** Victor M. Valle & Mary L. Valle. (Illus.). 1997. pap. 14.00 (*1-56584-127-1*) New Press NY.

Recipe Rescue Cookbook. pap. 18.95 (*1-884943-01-2*) Eat Well Bks.

Recipe Rescue Cookbook: Healthy New Approaches to Traditional Favorites. Ed. by Patricia Jamieson & Cheryl Dorschner. LC 93-17814. 1993. 24.95 (*0-944475-48-5*); pap. 18.95 (*0-944475-47-7*) Camden Hse Pub.

Recipe Rescue Cookbook: Healthy New Approaches to Traditional Favorites. Ed. by Patricia Jamieson & Cheryl Dorschner. 1994. 24.95 (*1-884943-00-4*) Eat Well Bks.

Recipe Research Correspondence Course. Cookbook Consortium Educational Division Staff. 1984. ring bd. 25.95 (*0-318-04319-X*) Prosperity & Profits.

Recipe Research Correspondence Course for Pastries & Deserts. Cookbook Consortium Educational Division Staff. 1984. ring bd. 21.95 (*0-318-04320-3*, Cookbk Consort) Prosperity & Profits.

***Recipe Revelation: KJ's Passed down Recipes Forwarded.** Kay J. Mays. LC 96-80325. (Illus.). 56p. 1997. 8.95 (*0-9656248-0-3*) K J Mays.

Recipe Story Rhyme Cookbook. Story Rhyme Staff. (Illus.). 60p. (YA). (gr. 7-10). 1993. ring bd. 21.95 (*1-56820-103-6*) Story Time.

Recipe Story Rhyme Greetings to Duplicate & Use. Story Rhyme Staff. (Illus.). 60p. (YA). (gr. 7-10). 1993. ring bd. 29.95 (*1-56820-104-4*) Story Time.

Recipe Treasury. Ed. by Bonnie S. Mickelson. (Illus.). 80p. 1992. ring bd. 19.95 (*0-9622412-2-9*) Pickle Point.

***Recipe Writer's Handbook.** Barbara G. Ostmann. LC 96-48845. 256p. 1997. text ed. 34.95 (*0-471-17294-4*) Wiley.

Recipes: A Notebook for Cooks. Illus. by Binny Mathews. 142p. 1988. 14.95 (*0-948751-02-9*) Interlink Pub.

Recipes & Escapades from a Countrywoman's Journal. Gladys Manyan. LC 87-71572. (Illus.). 248p. 1987. pap. 5.95 (*0-941216-38-1*) Cay-Bel.

Recipes & People of a Northwest Neighborhood. rev. ed. Helen Anschell & Marsha Malkin. Ed. by Martin Malkin & Gertrude Lewis. (Illus.). 96p. 1988. reprint ed. pap. 8.95 (*0-926060-00-7*) Anschell Pub Co.

Recipes & Reminiscences of New Orleans. Illus. by Emery Clark. 237p. (Orig.). 1971. pap. 7.95 (*0-9604718-0-4*) Ursuline.

Recipes & Reminiscences of New Orleans, Vol. II. (Our Cultural Heritage Ser.). (Illus.). 389p. (Orig.). 1981. pap. 11.95 (*0-9604718-1-2*) Ursuline.

Recipes & Rendezvous. Gail R. Parker. (Illus.). 108p. (Orig.). 1984. pap. 5.95 (*0-910115-02-8*) PS Pubns.

Recipes for a Healthy Lifestyle: Low Fat, Low Cholesterol, Low Sodium. Virginia Defendorf. 1994. pap. 6.95 (*0-914846-95-7*) Golden West Pub.

***Recipes for a Sensual Bath.** Carmen Pagano. iv, 42p. (Orig.). 1997. pap. write for info. (*0-9657518-8-0*) Carmen.

Recipes for a Small Planet. Ellen B. Ewald. (Orig.). 1985. mass mkt. 5.95 (*0-345-32492-7*) Ballantine.

Recipes for Art & Craft Materials. rev. ed. Helen R. Sattler. LC 86-34271. (Illus.). 128p. (J). (gr. 6 up). 1987. 16.00 (*0-688-07374-3*) Lothrop.

Recipes for Art & Craft Materials. Helen R. Sattler. LC 93-26182. (Illus.). 144p. (J). (gr. 5 up). 1994. reprint ed. pap. 4.95 (*0-688-13199-9*) Morrow.

***Recipes for Change.** Lissa Deangelis. 1998. pap. write for info. (*0-452-27293-9*, Plume) NAL-Dutton.

Recipes for Change: Gourmet Wholefood Cooking for Health & Vitality at Menopause. Lissa DeAngelis & Molly Siple. LC 95-25810. 416p. 1996. pap. 27.95 (*0-525-93894-X*, Dutton) NAL-Dutton.

Recipes for Change: Wholefood Gourmet Cooking for Health & Vitality at Menopause. Lissa DeAngelis & Molly Siple. 1996. 24.95 (*0-614-96796-1*, Dutton) NAL-Dutton.

Recipes for Diabetics. Billie Little. 288p. 1991. mass mkt. 6.50 (*0-553-29378-8*) Bantam.

Recipes For Diabetics. rev. ed. Billie Little. 288p. 1990. pap. 12.00 (*0-399-51643-3*, Perigee Bks) Berkley Pub.

Recipes for Fat Free Desserts, Vol. 3. Jyl Steinback. 318p. 1995. 15.95 (*0-9636876-4-6*) Fat Free Living.

Recipes for Fat Free Living. Jyl Steinback. 193p. 1993. pap. 14.95 (*0-9636876-6-2*) Fat Free Living.

***Recipes for Fat Free Living, Breads.** Jyl Steinback. (Recipes for Fat Free Living Cookbooks). 190p. (Orig.). 1996. pap. 14.95 (*0-9636876-5-4*) Fat Free Living.

Recipes for Fat Free Living 2. Jyl Steinback. 291p. 1994. 15.95 (*0-9636876-8-9*) Fat Free Living.

Recipes for Fitness for Very Busy People. rev. ed. Eleanor A. Brown. (Illus.). 89p. 1985. pap. 6.95 (*0-9618805-1-1*) Fitness Ojai.

***Recipes for Fun! What to Do When There's Nothing to Do.** Jo Berg. 80p. (YA). 1996. 6.95 (*1-888827-16-5*) Castlemoyle Bks.

***Recipes for Happiness.** Grampa Gray. (Tree of Life Mini-Books Ser.: Vol. 5). (Illus.). 12p. (Orig.). 1996. pap. 2.50 (*1-885631-32-4*, 32-4) G F Hutchison.

Recipes for Health: Anaemia: Over 100 Recipes for Overcoming Iron-Deficiency. Jill Davies. 1995. pap. 9.00 (*0-7225-2914-7*) Thorsons SF.

Recipes for Health: Cancer: Over 100 Recipes for Coping with Cancer During & after Treatment. Clare Shaw & Maureen Hunter. 224p. 1995. pap. 10.00 (*0-7225-3138-9*) Harper SF.

***Recipes for Health: Candida Albicans: Over 100 Yeast-Free & Sugar-Free Recipes.** Shirley Trickett. 224p. 1995. pap. 9.00 (*0-7225-2967-8*) Thorsons SF.

Recipes for Health: Diabetes: Low Fat, Low Sugar, Carbohydrate Counted Recipes for the Management of Diabetes. Azmina Govindji et al. 224p. 1995. pap. 10.00 (*0-7225-3139-7*) Harper SF.

Recipes for Health: High Blood Pressure. Maggie Pannell. 1995. pap. 9.00 (*0-7225-3144-3*) Thorsons SF.

Recipes for Health: Irritable Bowel Syndrome: Over 100 Recipes for Coping with This Digestive Disorder. Ann Page-Wood & Jill Davies. 224p. 1995. pap. 9.00 (*0-7225-3141-9*) Harper SF.

Recipes for Health: Low-Fat Cooking: Over 100 Low-Fat Recipes for a Healthier Life. Sarah Bounds. 224p. 1995. pap. 9.00 (*0-7225-3172-9*) Harper SF.

Recipes for Health: Migraine: Appetizing Recipes Which Eliminate the Common Migraine Triggers. Cecilia Norman. 224p. 1995. pap. 9.00 (*0-7225-3143-5*) Harper SF.

Recipes for Health: PMS: Over 100 Recipes for Overcoming Premenstrual Syndrome. Jill Davies. 224p. 1995. pap. 9.00 (*0-7225-3140-0*) Harper SF.

Recipes for Health: Wheat, Milk & Egg-Free: Over 100 Recipes Which Avoid These Common Allergens. Rita Greer. 1996. pap. 11.00 (*0-7225-3197-4*) Harper SF.

Recipes for Health: Gluten-Free: Over 100 Recipes for Those Allergic to Gluten. Rita Greer. 1995. pap. 11.00 (*0-7225-3198-2*) Harper SF.

Recipes for Improvisation: Keyboard Games for Pianists of All Ages. Joy Yelin. Ed. by Jane Meryll. 35p. (Orig.). 1990. teacher ed. 13.00 (*0-9626150-0-5*) Musical Mosaics.

Recipes for Kids to Lower Their Fat Thermostats. Larene Gaunt & Edward A. Parent. LC 93-61785. (Illus.). 1994. pap. 15.95 (*0-912547-14-6*) Vitality Hse Int Inc.

Recipes for Life: From the Kitchens of Healthy Choice Foods. Cy DeCosse Incorporated Staff. LC 94-12932. 256p. 1994. 24.95 (*0-86573-941-2*) Cowles Creative.

Recipes for Living. Virginia M. Pribyl. (Illus.). 160p. (Orig.). 1988. pap. 9.95 (*0-9621089-0-1*) VMP Servs.

Recipes for Living - Mind, Body & Spirit: A Friendly Collection. Marilyn Beck et al. (Illus.). 54p. 1993. spiral bd. 7.95 (*1-877809-52-7*) Park Pl Pubns.

Recipes for Longer Life. Ann Wigmore. (Illus.). 208p. pap. 9.95 (*0-89529-195-9*) Avery Pub.

Recipes for Parent Survival: Revealing the Amazing Secrets of SUPERCHEF, the Great. Carl Lampner. LC 95-23140. (Illus.). 324p. 1995. pap. 19.95 (*0-942963-63-6*) Distinctive Pub.

Recipes for Quantity Service. 1986. lib. bdg. 79.95 (*0-8490-3791-3*) Gordon Pr.

***Recipes for Reading: Community Cookbooks, Stories, Histories.** Ed. by Anne L. Bower. (Illus.). 240p. 1997. pap. 15.95 (*1-55849-089-2*); text ed. 45.00 (*1-55849-088-4*) U of Mass Pr.

Recipes for Romance: Gail Greco's Little Bed & Breakfast Cookbooks. Gail Greco. LC 96-30489. 1996. 12.95 (*1-55853-455-5*) Rutledge Hill Pr.

Recipes for Romance: 50 Ways to Sweeten Your Love Life. Jimmy Caplan & Leslie Caplan. 128p. (Orig.). 1996. pap. 8.95 (*1-880032-78-3*) New Wrld Lib.

***Recipes for Success.** Illus. by Beth Eidelberg. 160p. 1997. 17.95 (*0-9656887-0-4*) Wrm Sprgs Rehab Fnd.

Recipes for Success: A Guide to Advanced Cuisine. Roland Chaton. LC 87-22380. 1988. pap. 35.95 (*0-8273-3027-8*) Delmar.

***Recipes for Success: From Leading Women & Premiere Chefs.** 128p. 1996. 18.95 (*0-9654707-0-9*) Patriots Trail.

Recipes for Success: Guide to Advanced Cuisine. Talmage. 1988. teacher ed., pap. 11.75 (*0-8273-3028-6*) Delmar.

Recipes for Surface Vol. II: New & Exciting Ideas for Decorative Paint Finishes. Mindy Drucker & Nancy Rosen. 1995. pap. 20.00 (*0-684-80179-5*, Fireside) S&S Trade.

Recipes For Surfaces. Mindy Drucker & Pierre Finkelstein. 256p. 1990. pap. 20.00 (*0-671-68249-0*) S&S Trade.

Recipes for the Loaf Pan. Rose Grant. (Illus.). 176p. (Orig.). 1996. pap. 8.95 (*1-55867-137-4*, Nitty Gritty Ckbks) Bristol Pub Ent CA.

Recipes for the Pressure Cooker. Joanna White. (Illus.). 176p. (Orig.). 1993. pap. 8.95 (*1-55867-086-6*, Nitty Gritty Ckbks) Bristol Pub Ent CA.

***Recipes for Today's Menus.** Ed. by Ken Lively & Caleb Pirtle. 100p. 1996. write for info. (*1-879234-43-2*) Herit Pub TX.

Recipes for Travellers. Janet Ash & Dulcie Robert. 224p. 1996. pap. 10.00 (*0-7225-3292-X*) Harper SF.

Recipes for Wellness. Julie Griffin et al. LC 95-62406. (Illus.). 196p. 1995. pap. 34.95 (*1-57691-000-8*) TWT Pubng.

Recipes for Writing: Motivation, Skills, & Activities. Murray Suid. 1988. pap. text ed. 22.00 (*0-201-22122-5*) Addison-Wesley.

Recipes for Yogurt Cheese. Joanna White. 160p. (Orig.). 1996. pap. 8.95 (*1-55867-158-7*, Nitty Gritty Ckbks) Bristol Pub Ent CA.

Recipes Free & Almost Free: A One Thousand & More Possibilities Workbook. Center for Self Sufficiency, Research Division Staff. 200p. 1983. ring bd. 21.95 (*0-910811-13-X*) Ctr Self Suff.

Recipes from a Caring World. Animal Rescue League Auxiliary Staff & Rosemarie Schuler. (Illus.). 236p. 1993. 15.00 (*0-9636615-0-7*) Animal Rescue.

***Recipes from a Country Kitchen: Inspiring Ideas to Evoke a Taste of Country All Year Round.** Liz Trigg. 1996. 12.98 (*0-7651-9839-8*) Smithmark.

Recipes from a Deep South Inn. Edna Holland. LC 93-39791. (Recipes from a Country Inn Ser.). (Illus.). 120p. (Orig.). 1994. pap. 12.95 (*1-56626-040-X*) Country Rds.

Recipes from a Downeast Inn. Mark Hodesh et al. LC 94-5413. (Recipes from a Country Inn Ser.). 140p. 1995. pap. 12.95 (*1-56626-114-7*) Country Rds.

Recipes from a French Country Kitchen: The Very Best of Real French Regional Cooking. Carole Clements. 1996. 12.98 (*0-8317-7308-1*) Smithmark.

Recipes from a Kentucky Blackberry Patch. Sharon Thompson. LC 92-82075. (Illus.). 64p. 1993. 9.95 (*0-9635603-0-1*) WindStone Farms.

Recipes from a Kitchen Garden. Renee Shepherd. LC 87-90646. (Illus.). 92p. (Orig.). 1987. pap. 7.95 (*0-9618856-0-2*) Shepherds Garden Pubs.

Recipes from a Kitchen Garden. Renee Shepherd. 176p. (Orig.). 1993. pap. 11.95 (*0-89815-540-1*) Ten Speed Pr.

Recipes from a Kitchen Garden, Vol. II. Renee Shepherd & Fran Raboff. (Illus.). 96p. (Orig.). 1990. pap. text ed. 8.95 (*0-9618856-1-0*) Shepherds Garden Pubs.

Recipes from a New England Inn. Trudy Cutrone. LC 92-71641. (Recipes from a Country Inn Ser.). (Illus.). 120p. (Orig.). 1992. pap. 14.95 (*1-56626-012-4*) Country Rds.

Recipes from a Pacific Northwest Inn. Pat Swanson. LC 94-38074. (Recipes from a Country Inn Ser.). (Illus.). 160p. (Orig.). 1995. pap. 12.95 (*1-56626-086-8*) Country Rds.

Recipes from a Provencal Kitchen. Michel Biehn. (Illus.). 200p. 1996. 35.00 (*2-08-013586-4*, Pub. by Flammarion FR) Abbeville Pr.

Recipes from a Wisconsin Inn. Lynn Greene. (Recipes from a Country Inn Ser.). (Illus.). 180p. (Orig.). 1996. pap. 14.95 (*1-56626-143-0*) Country Rds.

Recipes from America's Farm Kitchens. Cathy J. Perrin. 1995. 11.90 (*0-9646525-0-1*) Perrin Prod.

Recipes from an Ecological Kitchen. Lorna J. Sass. 492p. 1992. 25.00 (*0-688-10051-1*) Morrow.

Recipes from an English Master Chef. John Burton-Race. (Illus.). 256p. 1995. 39.95 (*0-7472-0901-4*, Pub. by Headline UK) Trafalgar.

Recipes from an Old New Orleans Kitchen. Suzanne Ormond. LC 88-12478. 1988. pap. 6.95 (*0-88289-699-7*) Pelican.

Recipes from Arizona with Love. Liza Golden & Ferol Golden. (Orig.). 1985. spiral bd. 13.95 (*0-913703-10-9*) Strawberry Pt.

Recipes from Around the World: For Young People 8-14. Cobblestone Publishing, Inc. Staff. (Illus.). 36p. (J). (gr. 4-8). 1987. pap. text ed. 4.95 (*0-942389-03-4*) Cobblestone Pub.

Recipes from Central Market. Phyllis P. Good & Louise Stoltzfus. LC 96-27558. 224p. (Orig.). 1996. 23.95 (*1-56148-210-2*); pap. 15.95 (*1-56148-222-6*) Good Bks PA.

Recipes from Grandma's Kitchen. Carla Capalbo. (Illus.). 64p. 1995. 5.98 (*0-8317-7458-4*) Smithmark.

Recipes from Hope, Arkansas: Birthplace of Bill Clinton. Ed. by Wanda Powell. 178p. 1992. pap. text ed. 12.95 (*0-9636174-0-0*) Legacy Pubs.

Recipes from Iowa: With Love. Peg Hein & Kathy Cramer. Ed. by Dorothy Yeglin. (Illus.). 194p. 1982. spiral bd. 13.95 (*0-913703-01-X*) Strawberry Pt.

Recipes from Ireland. Ed. by Joanne Asala. 1995. pap. 5.95 (*1-57216-017-9*) Penfield.

Recipes from La Isla: New & Traditional Puerto Rican Cuisine. Judith H. Rosado. LC 95-31564. 192p. 1995. 28.00 (*1-56565-339-4*) Lowell Hse.

Recipes from La Isla! New & Traditional Puerto Rican Cuisine. Robert Rosado & Judith H. Rosado. 368p. 1996. pap. 16.00 (*1-56565-476-5*) Lowell Hse.

Recipes from Maine: With Love. Peter Hodgkin. (Illus.). 200p. (Orig.). 1985. spiral bd. 13.95 (*0-913703-08-7*) Strawberry Pt.

Recipes from Massachusetts: With Love. Liz Anton & Beth Dooley. (Illus.). 250p. (Orig.). 1985. spiral bd. 13.95 (*0-913703-07-9*) Strawberry Pt.

Recipes from Minnesota: With Love. Betty Malisow. (Illus.). 199p. 1981. spiral bd. 13.95 (*0-913703-00-1*, MN29) Strawberry Pt.

Recipes from Miss Daisy's. Daisy King. 160p. 1985. reprint ed. spiral bd. 6.95 (*0-934395-15-2*) Rutledge Hill Pr.

Recipes from Missouri: With Love. Sandy Buege. 190p. 1986. spiral bd. 13.95 (*0-913703-13-3*) Strawberry Pt.

Recipes from My Mom's Kitchen. Myrna P. Roberts. Ed. by Myrna L. Roberts. 150p. (Orig.). 1990. pap. 12.95 (*0-9627075-0-3*) Conch Shell Pubns.

Recipes from New Perry Hotel. Bobbe Nelson. Ed. by Robin Couey. (Illus.). 264p. 1994. reprint ed. 16.95 (*0-9652529-0-6*) New Perry Hotel.

Recipes from Old Charleston. Compiled by Jane W. Fickling. LC 63-62002. (Illus.). (Orig.). Date not set. pap. write for info. (*0-614-10443-2*) Banner Pr AL.

Recipes from Old Virginia. 1946. spiral bd. 8.75 (*0-87517-000-5*) Dietz.

***Recipes from Our House.** 203p. 1996. 12.00 (*0-9656750-0-9*, R2-1413-96) Assist Leag Denver.

***Recipes from Paradise: Life & Food on the Italian Riviera.** Fred Plotkin. LC 97-1813. 1996. 29.95 (*0-316-71071-7*) Little.

Recipes from Parenting. Sandy S. McDaniel. (Orig.). 1990. pap. 12.50 (*0-9626359-0-1*) S McDaniel Enter.

Recipes from Parenting. 2nd ed. 164p. reprint ed. pap. 12.95 (*0-9626359-1-X*) S McDaniel Enter.

Recipes from Pasquale's Kitchen. Pasquale Carpino. LC 84-10251. (Illus.). 212p. 1985. pap. 14.95 (*0-385-19307-6*) Doubleday.

Recipes from Quilters: A Book of Postcards. Good Books Staff. pap. 8.95 (*1-56148-166-1*) Good Bks PA.

Recipes from South Fork Lodge: Favorites from Molly McCombe's Kitchen in Chicken, Alaska. Sharon Haney. (Illus.). (Orig.). 1992. pap. 5.00 (*0-9611326-2-0*) Windsong Pr.

Recipes from the Bottom of the Sea. Dorothy Anderson & Robert Anderson. Ed. by Eva Lampert & Erv Lampert. (Illus.). 168p. (Orig.). 1993. pap. 12.95 (*0-932855-32-6*) Winner Enter.

Recipes from the Dump. Date not set. pap. write for info. (*0-393-31433-2*) Norton.

Recipes from the Dump. Abigail Stone. 272p. 1996. pap. 10.00 (*0-380-72882-6*) Avon.

Recipes from the Dump. Abigail Stone. LC 95-6686. 224p. 1995. 18.00 (*0-393-03854-8*) Norton.

Recipes from the Feathered Pipe Ranch. Ed. by India Supera. 162p. (Orig.). 1992. pap. 15.00 (*0-9635075-0-8*) Feathered Pipe.

***Recipes from the Flying Kitchen: On Pacific Tour in an Albatross.** Joyce A. Proctor. (Illus.). 200p. (YA). 1996. 29.95 (*0-9653893-0-8*) Albatross Trvls.

Recipes from the French Wine Harvest: Vintage Feasts from the Vineyards. Rosi Hanson. 160p. 1996. 27.95 (*0-304-34540-7*, Pub. by Cassell UK) Sterling.

Recipes from the Global Kitchen: A Collection of Vegetarian Recipes. Ed. by Plenty International Staff & Charles T. Haren. LC 95-14033. 122p. (Orig.). 1995. pap. 11.95 (*1-57067-006-4*) Book Pub Co.

Recipes from the Heart. Maurice Beaudet & Tonya Erion. (Illus.). 96p. 1988. 10.95 (*0-9617850-0-4*) Spot Press.

Recipes from the Moon. Gary Beardsworth. 176p. 1995. pap. 14.95 (*0-89815-681-5*) Ten Speed Pr.

Recipes from the Old Mill: Baking with Whole Grains. Sarah E. Myers & Mary B. Lind. LC 95-35567. 252p. 1995. pap. 13.95 (*1-56148-176-9*) Good Bks PA.

R

Recipes from the Portuguese of Provincetown. Margaret H. Koehler. (Illus.). 128p. (Orig.). 1977. pap. 14.95 (*0-85699-060-4*) Chatham Pr.

Recipes from the Raleigh Tavern Bake Shop. Colonial Williamsburg Foundation Staff. (Illus.). 29p. 1984. pap. 3.95 (*0-87935-106-3*) Colonial Williamsburg.

Recipes from the Regional Cooks of Mexico see Mexican Regional Cooking

Recipes from the Russians of San Francisco. Margaret H. Koehler. LC 73-89766. (Illus.). 1974. 16.95 (*0-85699-092-2*) Chatham Pr.

Recipes from the San Juan Islands. Greg Atkinson. (Illus.). 28p. 1992. text ed. 5.95 (*0-912365-70-6*) Sasquatch Bks.

Recipes from the Vineyards of Oregon. Leslie J. Whipple. 192p. 1994. pap. 14.95 (*0-89288-247-6*) Maverick.

***Recipes from the Wineries of the Great Lakes.** Joe Borrello. Ed. by Ruth Moen. 200p. (Orig.). 1997. pap. 17.00 (*1-881892-04-2*) Spradlin & Assocs.

Recipes From...the Hearthstone Inn. enl. rev. ed. Ed. by Dot Williams & Ruth L. Williams. (Illus.). 190p. (Orig.). (C). 1992. 10.95 (*0-9616308-2-5*) Hearthstn Inn.

Recipes into Type: A Style Manual for Writers & Editors of Cookbooks. Joan Whitman & Dolores Simon. LC 89-46120. 384p. 1993. 27.50 (*0-06-270034-0*, Harper Ref) HarpC.

Recipes My Mother Gave Me. Vale F. Kelley. LC 95-94258. (Illus.). 84p. (Orig.). 1996. pap. 15.95 (*0-9647884-0-3*) Brown Dog Pubng.

Recipes of Madison County. Jane M. Hemminger & Courtney A. Work. 112p. 1995. 14.95 (*0-8487-1506-3*) Oxmoor Hse.

Recipes of Note. Rochester Civic Music Guild Staff. (Illus.). 215p. (Orig.). 1988. write for info. (*0-318-63718-9*) Rochester Civic Mus Guild.

Recipes of Note for Entertaining. Rochester Civic Music Guild Staff. 346p. (Orig.). 1994. 18.00 (*0-9621066-1-5*) Rochester Civic Mus Guild.

***Recipes of the Five Brothers.** Ed. by Leah Rosch. (Illus.). 42p. 1997. text ed. 10.00 (*0-9655889-0-4*) Van den Bergh.

Recipes of the Pacific Northwest. Carla Capalbo. (Illus.). 64p. 1995. 5.98 (*0-8317-7457-6*) Smithmark.

Recipes of the Philippines. Ed. by E. David-Parez. (Illus.). 170p. 1982. 6.50 (*0-318-36301-1*) Asia Bk Corp.

Recipes Remembered. Marcia Adams. 1995. 18.00 (*0-517-59906-6*, Crown Arts & Letters) Crown Pub Group.

Recipes Remembered: A Collection of Modernized Nostalgia. Fran Stoser. (Illus.). 336p. (Orig.). 1989. pap. 14.95 (*0-685-44855-X*) Highland KY.

Recipes Sworn to Secrecy. Constantina Linardakis & Nikos M. Linardakis. (Illus.). 64p. (Orig.). 1995. pap. 12.95 (*1-884084-08-7*) Michaelis Med.

Recipes to Lower Your Fat Thermostat. 2nd ed. LaRene Gaunt. LC 84-52705. (Fat Thermostat Program Ser.). (Illus.). 456p. 1992. pap. 15.95 (*0-912547-10-3*) Vitality Hse Int Inc.

Recipes to Warm the Heart: From the Heart of America. Cookbooks Unlimited Staff et al. 744p. 1993. pap. 12.95 (*0-9638796-0-X*) Ckbks Unltd.

***Recipes Worth Sharing.** Janet Majure. (Illus.). 192p. (Orig.). 1997. pap. 14.95 (*0-9656695-0-5*) Breadbasket Pub.

Recipes 1-2-3: Fabulous Food Using Only Three Ingredients. Rozanne Gold. 307p. 1996. pap. 22.95 (*0-670-86584-2*, Viking) Viking Penguin.

Recipients, Commonly Called the Data. Euclid. Tr. by Robert Schmidt from GRE. (Illus.). 150p. 1988. lib. bdg. 30.00 (*0-318-35240-0*) Golden Hind Pr.

Recipients of the Distinguished Conduct Medal, 1914-1920. R. W. Walker. 219p. (C). 1987. 135.00 (*0-317-90452-3*, Pub. by Picton UK) St Mut.

***Reciprocal Teaching Interactivities.** Lisbeth Ceaser. 264p. (C). 1997. per., pap. text ed. 29.95 (*0-7872-3486-9*) Kendall-Hunt.

Reciprocating Compressors: Operating & Maintenance. Heinz P. Bloch & John J. Hoefner. (Illus.). 504p. 1996. 85.00 (*0-88415-525-0*, 5525) Gulf Pub.

Reciprocating Power Pump Standard for Nomenclature, Definitions, Application & Operation, No. 6.1-6.5. (Hydraulic Institute Ser.: No. 6.1-6.5). 62p. 1994. 59.00 (*1-880952-10-6*, S114) Hydraulic Inst.

Reciprocating Pump: Theory, Design & Use. 2nd ed. John E. Miller. LC 91-2639. 484p. (C). 1994. lib. bdg. 74.50 (*0-89464-599-4*) Krieger.

Reciprocating Pump Test Standard, No. 6.6. (Hydraulic Institute Ser.: No. 6.6). 17p. 1994. 39.00 (*1-880952-11-4*, S115) Hydraulic Inst.

Reciprocity. Lawrence C. Becker. 448p. 1986. 35.00 (*0-7102-0828-6*, 08286, RKP) Routledge.

Reciprocity. Lawrence C. Becker. LC 85-19431. x, 448p. 1990. pap. text ed. 18.95 (*0-226-04106-9*) U Ch Pr.

Reciprocity: A New Approach to World Trade Policy? William R. Cline. LC 82-15678. (Policy Analyses in International Economics Ser.: No. 2). 41p. (Orig.). 1982. pap. 8.00 (*0-88132-001-3*) Inst Intl Eco.

Reciprocity Among Private Multiemployer Pension Plans. McDonald. (C). 1975. 12.95 (*0-256-01736-0*) Irwin.

Reciprocity & Retaliation in U. S. Trade Policy. Thomas O. Bayard & Kimberly A. Elliott. LC 94-22348. 503p. 1994. pap. 25.00 (*0-88132-084-6*) Inst Intl Eco.

Reciprocity & Ritual: Homer & Tragedy in the Developing City-State. Richard Seaford. 416p. 1994. 85.00 (*0-19-814949-2*) OUP.

Reciprocity & Ritual: Homer & Tragedy in the Developing City-State. Richard Seaford. 480p. 1995. pap. 29.95 (*0-19-815036-9*) OUP.

Reciprocity Guide for Private Motor Carriers. 1982. 22.00 (*0-686-31450-6*) Private Carrier.

Reciprocity, Spatial Mapping & Time Reversal in Electromagnetics. C. Altman & K. Suchy. (C). 1991. lib. bdg. 149.50 (*0-7923-1339-9*) Kluwer Ac.

Reciprocity, U. S. Trade Policy, & the GATT Regime. Carolyn Rhodes. 256p. 1993. 35.00 (*0-8014-2864-5*) Cornell U Pr.

Recirculating Electron Acclerators. Roy E. Rand. (Nuclear Physics Ser.: Vol. 3). 275p. 1984. text ed. 224.00 (*3-7186-0183-4*) Gordon & Breach.

Recirculation - Aeration: Bibliography for Aquaculture. Ed. by Peter W. Perschbacher et al. 78p. (Orig.). (C). 1995. pap. text ed. 30.00 (*0-7881-2394-7*) DIANE Pub.

Recit, Chroniques et Polemiques. Fyodor Dostoyevsky. (FRE.). 1969. 110.00 (*0-8288-3441-5*, F118460) Fr & Eur.

Recit de l'expedition en Ecosse l'an 1546. John Berteville. LC 79-39436. (Bannatyne Club, Edinburgh. Publications: No. 10). reprint ed. 37.50 (*0-404-52710-8*) AMS Pr.

Recital. Elena Gerhardt. 1988. reprint ed. lib. bdg. 75.00 (*0-7812-0206-X*) Rprt Serv.

Recital. Elena Gerhardt. LC 78-181162. 1953. reprint ed. 39.00 (*0-403-01564-2*) Scholarly.

Recital Concerning the Sweet Land of Cyprus, 2 vols., Set. Leontios Machairas. Ed. by R. M. Dawkins. LC 78-63351. (Crusades & Military Orders Ser.: Second Series). reprint ed. 92.50 (*0-404-17030-7*) AMS Pr.

Recital in a Private Home. Eve Shelnutt. LC 88-70390. (Poetry Ser.). 1989. pap. 11.95 (*0-88748-074-8*) Carnegie-Mellon.

Recitation & Interpretation of the Qur'an. Muhammad A. Quasem. 1979. 12.00 (*0-318-00410-0*) Quasem.

Recitation & Interpretation of the Qur'an: Al-Gharzali's Theory. Muhammad A. Quasem. 124p. (Orig.). 1982. pap. 14.95 (*0-7103-0035-2*) Routledge Chapman & Hall.

***Recitations for Church Occasions.** 1995. 6.99 (*0-8341-9354-X*) Lillenas.

Recited Koran: A History of the First Recorded Version. Labib Said. Tr. by Bernard Weiss et al. LC 73-20717. (Illus.). 156p. 1975. reprint ed. pap. 44.50 (*0-608-01039-1*, 2052545) Bks Demand.

Reciters Treasury of Verse: Serious & Humerous. Ernest Pertwee. LC 77-37018. (Granger Index Reprint Ser.). 1977. reprint ed. 42.95 (*0-8369-6317-2*) Ayer.

Recits, Chroniques et Polemiques. Fyodor Dostoyevsky. 1872p. 45.00 (*0-686-56506-1*) Fr & Eur.

Recits D'Aujourd'hui. Anne Gillain & Martine A. Loutfi. (Illus.). 180p. (Orig.). (FRE.). (C). 1989. pap. text ed. 19.50 (*0-03-013159-6*) HB Coll Pubs.

Recits des Temps de Guerre, 2 vols., Set. Georges Duhamel. 720p. (FRE.). 1949. pap. 28.95 (*0-7859-5428-7*) Fr & Eur.

Recits et Essais. Jean Giono. (FRE.). 1989. 140.00 (*0-8288-3484-9*, F132450) Fr & Eur.

Recits Fantastiques. unabridged ed. Gautier. (FRE.). pap. 7.95 (*2-87714-155-1*, Pub. by Bookking Intl FR) Distribks Inc.

Reckless. Nellie Bly. 1996. pap. 22.95 (*0-8217-5223-5*) NAL-Dutton.

***Reckless.** Beth Henderson. (Historical Ser.: No. 370). 1997. mass mkt. 4.99 (*0-373-28970-7*, 1-28970-1) Harlequin Bks.

Reckless. Craig Lucas. 1985. pap. 5.25 (*0-8222-0937-3*) Dramatists Play.

Reckless. Amanda Quick. 400p. 1992. mass mkt. 6.50 (*0-553-29315-X*) Bantam.

***Reckless.** Ruth Wind. (Intimate Moments Ser.: No. 796). 1997. mass mkt. 3.99 (*0-373-07796-3*, 1-07796-5) Silhouette.

Reckless. Woods. 1989. pap. 3.95 (*0-445-20819-8*) Warner Bks.

Reckless. large type ed. Amanda Quick. LC 92-42499. (Romance Ser.). 528p. 1993. reprint ed. lib. bdg. 21.95 (*1-56054-657-3*) Thorndike Pr.

Reckless. large type ed. Amanda Quick. 528p. 1993. reprint ed. pap. 13.95 (*1-56054-882-7*) Thorndike Pr.

Reckless: A Teenage Love Story. Jeanette Mines. 176p. 1983. pap. 2.95 (*0-380-83717-X*, Flare) Avon.

Reckless: The Rise & Fall of the Kennedy Dynasty. Nellie Bly. 1996. 21.00 (*0-614-15417-0*) Kensgtn Pub Corp.

Reckless & Blue Window: Two Plays. Craig Lucas. LC 89-4413. 128p. 1989. pap. 9.95 (*0-930452-95-X*) Theatre Comm.

Reckless Angel. Jane Feather. 384p. (Orig.). 1989. mass mkt. 4.99 (*0-380-75807-5*) Avon.

Reckless Angel. Susan K. Law. 368p. 1995. mass mkt. 4.99 (*0-06-108306-2*, Harp PBks) HarpC.

Reckless Angel. Maggie Shayne. (Intimate Moments Ser.). 1993. mass mkt. 3.50 (*0-373-07522-7*, 5-07522-1) Silhouette.

Reckless Appetites: A Culinary Romance. Jacqueline Deval. LC 93-22175. 1993. 22.00 (*0-88001-322-2*) Ecco Pr.

Reckless Appetites: A Culinary Romance. Jacqueline Deval. 1993. pap. 12.00 (*0-88001-412-1*) Ecco Pr.

***Reckless Breeding: A Voice on the Road Between Adoption, Choice, Family Secrets & Open Records.** Nancy Craig. 65p. (Orig.). 1997. pap. 10.95 (*0-9657876-0-5*) Super Ego.

Reckless Character, & Other Stories. Ivan S. Turgenev. Tr. by Isabel F. Hapgood from RUS. LC 78-178465. (Short Story Index Reprint Ser.). 1977. reprint ed. 23.95 (*0-8369-4066-0*) Ayer.

Reckless Conduct. Susan Napier. 1996. mass mkt. 3.50 (*0-373-11847-3*, 1-11847-0) Harlequin Bks.

***Reckless Conduct.** Susan Napier. 1997. 20.95 (*0-263-14800-9*) Thorndike Pr.

Reckless Crusade. large type ed. Patricia Wilson. 1993. 19.95 (*0-263-13322-2*) Thorndike Pr.

Reckless Decade: America in the 1890s. H. W. Brands. LC 95-31798. (Illus.). 375p. 1995. 25.95 (*0-312-13594-7*) St Martin.

Reckless Deception. Angela Wells. (Presents Ser.). 1993. mass mkt. 2.99 (*0-373-11581-4*, 1-11581-5) Harlequin Bks.

Reckless Desire. Madeline Baker. 448p. 1995. mass mkt., pap. text ed. 4.99 (*0-8439-3727-0*) Dorchester Pub Co.

Reckless Destiny. Teresa Southwick. 336p. 1995. mass mkt. 4.99 (*0-06-108370-4*, Harp PBks) HarpC.

Reckless Disregard: Corporate Greed, Government Indifference & the Kentucky School Bus Crash. James S. Kunen. (Illus.). 368p. 1994. 23.00 (*0-671-70533-4*) S&S Trade.

Reckless Driver. Lisa Vice. 288p. 1996. pap. 10.95 (*0-452-27261-0*, Plume) NAL-Dutton.

Reckless Ecstasy. Wanda Owen. mass mkt. 3.95 (*0-317-43144-7*, Zebra Kensgtn) Kensgtn Pub Corp.

Reckless Faith: When the Church Loses It's Will to Discern. John F. MacArthur, Jr. LC 94-39874. 256p. 1994. 17.99 (*0-89107-793-6*) Crossway Bks.

Reckless Heart. Madeline Baker. 430p. (Orig.). 1995. mass mkt., pap. text ed. 5.99 (*0-8439-3788-2*) Dorchester Pub Co.

Reckless Heart. Bonnie K. Winn. 320p. (Orig.). 1995. pap. text ed. 4.99 (*0-515-11609-2*) Jove Pubns.

Reckless Heart: Meleager & Atalanta. Daniel R. Butterly. LC 86-71503. 64p. (Orig.). 1986. 25.00 (*0-86516-172-0*); pap. 15.00 (*0-86516-173-9*) Bolchazy-Carducci.

***Reckless Homicide.** Genberg. Date not set. write for info. (*0-312-17974-X*) St Martin.

Reckless Homicide: Ford's Pinto Trial. Lee P. Strobel. LC 80-123374. (Illus.). 285p. 1980. 8.95 (*0-89708-022-X*) And Bks.

Reckless Hope: Understanding & Reaching Baby Busters. Todd Hahn & David Verhaagen. LC 96-33887. (Illus.). 160p. (C). 1996. pap. 11.99 (*0-8010-9018-0*) Baker Bks.

Reckless Lady. large type ed. Rae Foley. 1977. 25.99 (*0-7089-0020-8*) Ulverscroft.

Reckless Love. Madeline Baker. 480p. (Orig.). 1995. mass mkt., pap. text ed. 5.99 (*0-8439-3869-2*) Dorchester Pub Co.

Reckless Love. Elizabeth Lowell. 1995. mass mkt. 5.99 (*0-373-15308-2*, 1-15308-9) Harlequin Bks.

Reckless Love. Elizabeth Lowell. 1996. pap. 5.99 (*0-373-83328-8*, 1-83328-4) Harlequin Bks.

Reckless Lover. Carly Bishop. (Intrigue Ser.). 1996. mass mkt. 3.75 (*0-373-22357-9*, 1-22357-7) Harlequin Bks.

Reckless River. Teresa Southwick. 320p. (Orig.). 1994. mass mkt. 4.99 (*0-7865-0018-2*) Diamond.

***Reckless Seduction.** Jane Feather. 448p. 1997. mass mkt. 5.99 (*0-8217-5748-2*, Zebra Kensgtn) Kensgtn Pub Corp.

Reckless Sleeper. Norman Dukes. Ed. by Peter Kaplan. LC 75-23871. 1975. 2.00 (*0-915176-11-4*) Pourboire.

Reckless Splendor. Maria Greene. 384p. 1987. pap. 3.95 (*0-380-75441-X*) Avon.

***Reckless Surrender.** Rochelle Alers. 1997. pap. text ed. 8.95 (*1-885478-17-8*) Genesis Press.

Reckless Wedding. Maria Flook. (Classic Contemporaries Ser.). 64p. (C). 1996. reprint ed. pap. 12.95 (*0-88748-226-0*) Carnegie-Mellon.

***Recklessly Abandoned.** Michael Howard. Ed. by Rosella Heyns. 184p. (Orig.). 1996. pap. 8.00 (*1-888529-00-8*) Out of Africa Pub.

Reckmire Marsh. large type ed. Hylton. 1996. lib. bdg. 20.00 (*0-7838-1697-9*, GK Hall) Thorndike Pr.

Reckmire Marsh. large type ed. Sara Hylton. 622p. 1996. lib. bdg. 22.95 (*0-7862-0681-0*, Thorndike Lrg Prnt) Thorndike Pr.

Reckoned Expense: Edmund Campion & the Early English Jesuits: Essays in Celebration of the First Centenary of Campion Hall, Oxford, 1896-1996. Ed. by Thomas M. McCoog. 364p. 1996. 71.00 (*0-85115-590-1*) Boydell & Brewer.

Reckoners: From Relays to the Stored Program Concept, 1935-1945. Paul E. Ceruzzi. LC 82-20980. (Contributions to the Study of Computer Science Ser.: No. 1). (Illus.). 240p. 1983. text ed. 45.00 (*0-313-23382-9*, CED/, Greenwood Pr) Greenwood.

***Reckoning.** Anonymous. 1996. mass mkt. 7.95 (*1-56201-099-9*) Blue Moon Bks.

***Reckoning.** Jeanette Baker. 304p. 1997. mass mkt. 5.50 (*0-7860-0441-X*, Pinncle Kensgtn) Kensgtn Pub Corp.

Reckoning. David Halberstam. 800p. 1987. mass mkt. 6.99 (*0-380-70447-1*) Avon.

Reckoning. David Halberstam. 800p. 1994. pap. 10.00 (*0-380-72147-3*) Avon.

Reckoning. James B. Huggins. 1995. pap. 11.99 (*1-56507-367-3*) Harvest Hse.

Reckoning. Ruby J. Jensen. 352p. 1992. mass mkt. 4.99 (*0-8217-3902-6*, Zebra Kensgtn) Kensgtn Pub Corp.

Reckoning. Maria Madison. 1993. mass mkt. 5.95 (*1-56201-042-5*) Blue Moon Bks.

Reckoning. Charles Nicholl. LC 93-23694. 1994. 24.95 (*0-15-175981-2*) HarBrace.

Reckoning. Douglas T. Ward. 1970. pap. 5.25 (*0-8222-0938-1*) Dramatists Play.

Reckoning: A Novel. Sharon K. Penman. 608p. 1992. pap. 12.50 (*0-345-37888-1*, Ballantine Trade) Ballantine.

***Reckoning: A Novel.** May Sarton. 256p. 1997. reprint ed. pap. 12.00 (*0-393-31621-1*) Norton.

Reckoning: Drugs, the Cities, & the American Future. Elliott Currie. 405p. 1994. pap. 12.00 (*0-8090-1571-4*) Hill & Wang.

Reckoning: The Murder of Christopher Marlowe. Charles Nicholl. LC 95-3004. 424p. 1995. pap. 14.95 (*0-226-58024-5*) U Ch Pr.

Reckoning at Dusk. Mary Welch. pap. 3.95 (*0-910924-41-4*) Macalester.

Reckoning at Rimbow. Norman A. Fox. 192p. 1987. pap. 2.75 (*0-380-70297-5*) Avon.

Reckoning at Rimbow. large type ed. Norman A. Fox. LC 90-26970. 286p. 1991. reprint ed. lib. bdg. 15.95 (*1-56054-109-1*) Thorndike Pr.

Reckoning at Yankee Flat. Will Henry. 176p. 1989. pap. 2.75 (*0-380-70603-2*) Avon.

***Reckoning at Yankee Flat.** Will Henry. 1997. 17.50 (*0-7451-4698-8*, Gunsmoke) Chivers N Amer.

Reckoning Heart: An Anthropologist Looks at Her World. Manisha Roy. LC 96-457. (Illus.). 272p. 1996. 19.95 (*1-882265-04-1*) Tandem Alley.

***Reckoning Infinity.** John E. Stith. 1997. 23.95 (*0-312-86298-9*) St Martin.

Reckoning of Angels. Alfredo Vea, Jr. LC 96-6772. 336p. 1996. pap. 24.95 (*0-525-94077-4*, Dutton) NAL-Dutton.

Reckoning the Earth: Some Lessons from the Land. Sandra Murphy. LC 94-13180. 136p. (Orig.). 1994. pap. 12.95 (*0-87358-590-9*) Northland AZ.

***Reckoning with Aggression: Theology, Violence & Vitality.** Kathleen Greider. 1997. pap. text ed. 15.00 (*0-664-25668-6*) Westminster John Knox.

Reckoning with Apocalypse: Terminal Politics & Christian Hope. Dale Aukerman. 264p. 1993. 24.95 (*0-8245-1243-X*) Crossroad NY.

Reckoning with Reagan. Michael Schaller. (Illus.). 208p. 1994. reprint ed. pap. 11.95 (*0-19-509049-7*) OUP.

Reckoning with Reagan: America & Its President in the 1980s. Michael Schaller. (Illus.). 224p. 1992. 19.95 (*0-19-506915-3*) OUP.

Reckoning with Sally. Matthew V. Smith. (Illus.). 22p. (J). (gr. k-4). 1995. pap. 9.95 (*1-895583-73-X*) MAYA Pubs.

Reckoning with the Beast: Animals, Pain, & Humanity in the Victorian Mind. James Turner. LC 80-11559. (Johns Hopkins University Studies in Historical & Political Science: 98th Series, 2). 204p. reprint ed. pap. 58.20 (*0-7837-0046-6*, 2040293) Bks Demand.

Reckoning with the Dead: The Larsen Bay Repatriation & the Smithsonian Institution. Ed. by Tamara L. Bray & Thomas W. Killion. LC 94-2652. (Illus.). 352p. 1994. pap. text ed. 29.95 (*1-56098-365-5*) Smithsonian.

***Reckoning with the Past: Contemporary Chinese Painting.** Chang Tsong-Zung et al. (Illus.). 104p. 1997. pap. 35.00 (*0-947912-42-8*) Dist Art Pubs.

Reckoning with the Past: Historical Essays on American Evangelicalism from the Institute for the Study of American Evangelicals. Ed. by D. G. Hart. LC 94-36916. 432p. (Orig.). (C). 1994. pap. 22.99 (*0-8010-4397-2*) Baker Bks.

Reckoning with Winslow Homer: His Late Paintings & Their Influence. Bruce Robertson. LC 90-31989. 212p. 1990. 40.00 (*0-940717-02-6*); pap. 29.95 (*0-940717-03-4*) Cleveland Mus Art.

Reclaim Our Stories. Colombo. 1997. pap. text ed. 26.00 (*0-312-10334-4*) St Martin.

Reclaim Plastics: Minimize It, Utilize It; Regional Technical Conference, Ramada Inn-Airport West, Mississauga, Ontario, Canada, October 14, 1981. Society of Plastics Engineers Staff. 106p. reprint ed. pap. 30.30 (*0-317-29905-0*, 2017597) Bks Demand.

Reclaim Your Health. David Frahm & Anne Frahm. LC 94-24442. 240p. 1995. pap. 12.00 (*0-89109-869-0*) Pinon Press.

Reclaimed Powers: Men & Women in Later Life. David Gutmann. (Psychosocial Issues Ser.). 300p. 1994. reprint ed. pap. 16.95 (*0-8101-1120-9*) Northwestern U Pr.

Reclaiming a Conversation. Samuel E. Martin. LC 85-2372. 221p. 1987. pap. 14.00 (*0-300-03999-9*, Y-684) Yale U Pr.

Reclaiming a Lost Heritage: Land-Grant & Other Higher Education Initiatives for the Twenty-First Century. John R. Campbell. LC 95-30989. 288p. (C). 1995. 36.95 (*0-8138-2159-2*) Iowa St U Pr.

Reclaiming a Mission: New Direction for the Church-Related College. Arthur J. De Jong. LC 90-32554. 181p. reprint ed. pap. 51.60 (*0-7837-5556-2*, 2045331) Bks Demand.

Reclaiming a Resource: Papers from the Friends Bible Conference, 1989. Ed. by Charles Fager. 275p. (Orig.). 1990. pap. 12.95 (*0-945177-06-2*) Kimo Pr.

***Reclaiming a Scientific Anthropology.** Lawrence A. Kuznar. LC 96-35699. 292p. 1996. 42.00 (*0-7619-9113-1*); pap. 19.95 (*0-7619-9114-X*) AltaMira Pr.

Reclaiming African Heritage at Salem, Indiana. Coy D. Robbins. 234p. (Orig.). 1995. pap. 33.00 (*0-7884-0325-7*) Heritage Bk.

Reclaiming America: Restoring Nature to Culture. Richard C. Austin. LC 87-45550. (Environmental Theology Ser.: Bk. 4). (Illus.). 240p. (Orig.). 1990. pap. 14.00 (*0-9625831-0-3*) Creekside VA.

Reclaiming America's Children: Raising & Educating Morally Healthy Kids, a Resource for Parents & Teachers. M. V. Willis. LC 90-64132. 96p. 1991. pap. 8.95 (*0-9607028-2-2*) Ocean East.

Reclaiming Capital: Democratic Initiatives & Community Development. Christopher Gunn & Hazel D. Gunn. LC 90-55725. 184p. 1991. 37.50 (*0-8014-2323-6*); pap. 13.95 (*0-8014-9574-1*) Cornell U Pr.

Reclaiming Christian Piety. Thomas Murray. 1993. pap. 6.95 (*1-55673-548-0*, 7972) CSS OH.

***Reclaiming Democracy: Sixties in Politics & Memory.** Meta Mendel-Reyes. 208p. 1996. pap. 15.95 (*0-415-91135-4*, Routledge NY) Routledge.

Reclaiming Democracy: The Sixties in Politics & Memory. Meta Mendel-Reyes. LC 95-700. 210p. (C). (gr. 13). 1995. text ed. 22.95 (*0-415-91134-6*, B4901, Routledge NY) Routledge.

***Reclaiming Democracy: The Sixties in Politics & Memory.** Meta Mendel-Reyes. 244p. 1996. pap. 15.95 (*0-415-91820-0*, Routledge NY) Routledge.

Reclaiming Dietrich Bonhoeffer: The Promise of His Theology. Charles Marsh. LC 93-30806. 208p. 1994. 35.00 (*0-19-508723-2*) OUP.

An Asterisk (*) at the beginning of an entry indicates that the title is appearing in BIP for the first time.

*__Reclaiming Dietrich Bonhoeffer: The Promise of His Theology.__ Charles Marsh. 216p. 1996. reprint ed. pap. 14.95 (*0-19-511144-3*) OUP.

Reclaiming Educational Administration As a Caring Profession. Lynn G. Beck. (Critical Issues in Educational Leadership Ser.). 176p. (C). 1994. text ed. 43.00 (*0-8077-3314-8*); pap. text ed. 18.95 (*0-8077-3313-X*) Tchrs Coll.

Reclaiming English Kinship. Mary Bouquet. (Illus.). 256p. (C). 1993. text ed. 69.95 (*0-7190-3026-9*, Pub. by Manchester Univ Pr UK) St Martin.

Reclaiming Friendship: Relating to Each Other in a Frenzied World. Ajith Fernando. LC 92-37250. 160p. 1993. reprint ed. pap. 7.99 (*0-8361-3630-6*) Herald Pr.

Reclaiming Her Story: The Witness of Women in the Old Testament. Jon L. Berquist. 184p. (Orig.). 1992. pap. 14.99 (*0-8272-3212-8*) Chalice Pr.

Reclaiming Herstory: Ericksonian Solution-Focused Therapy for Sexual Abuse. Cheryl Bell-Gadsby & Anne L. Siegenberg. 288p. 1996. text ed. 31.95 (*0-87630-777-2*) Brunner-Mazel.

*__Reclaiming Higher Ground: Creating Organizations that Inspire the Soul.__ Lance H. K. Secretan. 1997. text ed. 21.95 (*0-07-057919-9*) McGraw.

Reclaiming Intimacy in Your Marriage: Plan for Facing Life's Ebb & Flow...Together. Robert Bruce & Debra Bruce. LC 96-25293. 240p. 1996. pap. 9.99 (*1-55661-807-7*) Bethany Hse.

Reclaiming Literature: A Teacher's Dilemma. William A. Glasser. LC 94-17005. 192p. 1994. text ed. 45.00 (*0-275-94959-1*, Praeger Pubs) Greenwood.

Reclaiming Male Sexuality: A Guide to Potency, Vitality, & Prowess. George Ryan. 256p. (Orig.). 1997. pap. 14.95 (*0-87131-809-1*) M Evans.

*__Reclaiming Medusa: Contemporary Short Stories by Puerto Rican Women Writers.__ rev. ed. Ed. by Diana Velez. LC 97-11836. 1997. pap. text ed. 9.95 (*1-879960-52-4*) Aunt Lute Bks.

Reclaiming Medusa: Short Stories by Contemporary Puerto Rican Women. Ed. & Tr. by Diana Velez. LC 88-11430. 169p. (Orig.). 1988. pap. 9.95 (*1-879960-28-1*); lib. bdg. 18.95 (*1-879960-29-X*) Aunt Lute Bks.

Reclaiming Mine Soils & Overburden in the Western United States: Analytic Parameters & Procedures. Ed. by R. Dean Williams & Gerald E. Schuman. LC 87-9797. 336p. 1987. text ed. 30.00 (*0-935734-14-7*) Soil & Water Conserv.

Reclaiming Morality in America. William Murchison. LC 94-11492. 1994. 16.99 (*0-7852-8168-1*) Nelson.

Reclaiming Myths of Power: Women Writers & the Victorian Spiritual Crisis. Ruth Y. Jenkins. LC 94-20113. 1995. 35.00 (*0-8387-5278-0*) Bucknell U Pr.

Reclaiming of Power. Harvey Jackins. LC 83-61106. 400p. 1983. 16.00 (*0-911214-86-0*); pap. 13.00 (*0-911214-87-9*) Rational Isl.

Reclaiming of Power. Harvey Jackins. (DUT.). 1993. 13.00 (*0-913937-80-0*) Rational Isl.

Reclaiming Offender Accountability: Intermediate Sanctions for Probation & Parole Violators. American Correctional Association Staff. 114p. (Orig.). 1993. pap. 21.00 (*0-929310-59-4*, 499) Am Correctional.

Reclaiming Our Cities & Towns: Better Living with Less Traffic. David Engwicht. 192p. 1993. pap. 12.95 (*0-86571-283-2*); lib. bdg. 39.95 (*0-86571-282-4*) New Soc Pubs.

Reclaiming Our Democracy: Healing the Break Between People & Government. Sam Harris. LC 93-2569. 240p. 1994. 22.00 (*0-940159-24-4*) Camino Bks.

Reclaiming Our Health: Exploding the Medical Myth & Embracing the Source of True Healing. John Robbins. Ed. by Nancy Carleton. LC 96-19149. 432p. 1996. 24.00 (*0-915811-69-3*) H J Kramer Inc.

Reclaiming Our Lives: Adult Survivors of Incest. Carol Poston & Karen C. Lison. 1989. 17.95 (*0-316-71472-0*) Little.

Reclaiming Our Nation at Risk: Lessons Learned - Reforming Our Public Schools. unabridged ed. Terrel H. Bell et al. (Illus.). 600p. (Orig.). 1997. pap. 20.00 (*0-9634636-2-4*) T H Bell.

*__Reclaiming Our Nation at Risk: Lessons Learned-Reforming Our Elementary Schools.__ unabridged ed. Terrel H. Bell et al. (Illus.). 300p. (Orig.). 1997. pap. 15.00 (*0-9634636-3-2*) T H Bell.

Reclaiming Our Past, Honoring Our Ancestors: New York's Eighteenth Century African American Burial Ground & the Memorial Competition. Ed. by Edward Kaufman. vi, 96p. pap. write for info. (*0-9642985-0-3*) African Burial.

Reclaiming Our Schools: Creating Classrooms That Work. Larry Martz. 320p. 1992. pap. 12.00 (*0-8129-1939-4*, Times Bks) Random.

Reclaiming Our Schools: Teaching Character, Academics, & Discipline. 2nd ed. Edward A. Wynne & Kevin Ryan. LC 96-6855. 1996. pap. text ed. 28.00 (*0-13-459041-4*, Merrill Pub Co) Macmillan.

Reclaiming Our Schools: The Struggle for Chicago School Reform. Maribeth Vander Weele. LC 93-42171. 366p. 1994. pap. 12.95 (*0-8294-0773-1*) Loyola Pr.

Reclaiming Our Schools: The Struggle for Chicago School Reform. Maribeth Vander Weele. 366p. 1994. 21.95 (*0-8294-0812-6*) Loyola Pr.

*__Reclaiming Our Youth.__ Clarence E. Alston. 80p. (Orig.). (YA). 1997. pap. 7.95 (*1-883928-20-6*) Longwood.

*__Reclaiming Paradise: American Women Photograph the Land.__ Gretchen Garner & Martha A. Sandweiss. (Illus.). 64p. (Orig.). 1987. pap. 15.00 (*1-889523-03-8*) Tweed Mus.

Reclaiming Paradise: The Global Environmental Movement. John McCormick. LC 87-46408. (Illus.). 278p. (Orig.). 1989. 35.00 (*0-253-34952-4*) Ind U Pr.

Reclaiming Paradise: The Global Environmental Movement. John McCormick. LC 87-46408. (Illus.). 278p. (Orig.). 1991. pap. 13.95 (*0-253-20660-X*, MB-660) Ind U Pr.

Reclaiming Pedagogy: The Rhetoric of the Classroom. Ed. by Patricia Donahue & Ellen Quandahl. LC 88-39324. 216p. (C). 1989. 24.95 (*0-8093-1534-3*) S Ill U Pr.

Reclaiming Personal Authority. Charles. 1998. 23.00 (*0-02-917305-1*, Free Press) Free Pr.

Reclaiming Power: How to Take Back Our Government from Career Politicians. Bill LaVere. 215p. (Orig.). 1994. pap. 14.95 (*1-886335-02-8*) Bydand.

Reclaiming Prosperity: A Blueprint for Progressive Economic Reform. Ed. by Todd Schafer & Jeff Faux. LC 95-43828. (Economic Policy Institute Ser.). 362p. (C). (gr. 13). 1996. 69.95 (*1-56324-768-2*); pap. 23.95 (*1-56324-769-0*) M E Sharpe.

Reclaiming Reality: Philosophical Underlabouring. Roy Bhaskar. 180p. 1989. 50.00 (*0-86091-237-X*, A3346) Routledge Chapman & Hall.

Reclaiming Reality: Philosophical Underlabouring. Roy Bhaskar. 180p. (C). 1989. pap. text ed. 23.00 (*0-86091-951-X*, A3350, Pub. by Vrso UK) Norton.

*__Reclaiming Realty: Healing the Scars of Addiction.__ David R. Olsen. LC 96-92387. 90p. (Orig.). 1996. pap. write for info. (*0-7880-0692-4*) CSS OH.

Reclaiming Rhetorica: Women in the Rhetorical Tradition. Ed. by Andrea A. Lunsford. LC 95-3298. (Series in Composition, Literary, & Culture). 400p. 1995. 59.95 (*0-8229-3872-3*) U of Pittsburgh Pr.

Reclaiming Rhetorica: Women in the Rhetorical Tradition. Ed. by Andrea A. Lunsford. LC 95-3298. (Pitt Series in Composition, Literacy, & Culture). 400p. 1995. pap. 22.95 (*0-8229-5553-9*) U of Pittsburgh Pr.

*__Reclaiming Social Rights: International & Comparative Politics.__ Paul Hunt. LC 96-44642. (Illus.). 326p. 1996. 62.95 (*1-85521-845-3*, Pub. by Dartmth Pub UK) Ashgate Pub Co.

Reclaiming Sodom. Ed. by Jonathan Goldberg. LC 93-43680. 288p. (C). 1994. text ed. 59.95 (*0-415-90754-3*, Routledge NY) Routledge.

Reclaiming Sodom. Ed. by Jonathan Goldberg. LC 93-43680. 288p. (C). (gr. 13). 1994. pap. 17.95 (*0-415-90755-1*, Routledge NY) Routledge.

*__Reclaiming Sovereignty.__ Laura Brace & John Hoffman. LC 97-1100. 1997. write for info. (*1-85567-456-4*, Pub. by Pntr Pubs UK) Bks Intl VA.

Reclaiming Surrendered Ground: Protecting Your Family from Spiritual Attacks. Jim Logan. 1995. pap. 10.99 (*0-8024-3948-9*) Moody.

Reclaiming the Adult Vol. 1: How to Take Responsibility for Your Life & Make Your Relationships Work. Peter Florsheim & Fran Florsheim. Ed. by Pam Butler. LC 96-92131. (Illus.). (Orig.). 1996. pap. 14.95 (*0-9651582-0-9*) Sycamore Press.

Reclaiming the American Dream: The Keys to Financial Freedom. William J. Quain. 144p. 1994. pap. 9.95 (*0-9623646-1-4*) Wales Pub.

Reclaiming the American Dream: The Role of Private Individuals & Voluntary Associations. rev. ed. Richard C. Cornuelle. LC 92-32936. (Philanthropy & Society Ser.). 258p. (C). 1993. pap. text ed. 24.95 (*1-56000-655-2*) Transaction Pubs.

Reclaiming the American Dream by Reconstructing the American Republic. Tom Rose. 44p. (Orig.). 1996. pap. 6.95 (*0-9612198-8-2*) A E P.

Reclaiming the American Library Past: Writing the Women In. Suzanne Hildenbrand. LC 95-43839. (Information Management & Policy Ser.). 324p. 1996. text ed. 73.25 (*1-56750-233-4*) Ablex Pub.

Reclaiming the American Library Past: Writing the Women In. Ed. by Suzanne Hildenbrand. LC 95-43839. (Information Management & Policy Ser.). 324p. 1996. pap. 39.50 (*1-56750-234-2*) Ablex Pub.

Reclaiming the Arid West. William D. Rowley. LC 95-34788. (American West in the Twentieth Century Ser.). 216p. 1996. 27.50 (*0-253-33002-5*) Ind U Pr.

*__Reclaiming the Authentic Self.__ Dianne Lancaster. LC 96-90739. 208p. (Orig.). 1996. pap. 14.95 (*0-9655069-4-0*) Four-Sight Pr.

Reclaiming the Authentic Self: Dynamic Psychotherapy with Gay Men. Carlton Cornett. LC 94-24827. 224p. 1995. text ed. 35.00 (*1-56821-395-6*) Aronson.

Reclaiming the Author: Figures & Fictions from Spanish America. Lucille Kerr. LC 91-36087. 247p. 1992. pap. text ed. 19.95 (*0-8223-1224-7*) Duke.

Reclaiming the Author: Figures & Fictions from Spanish America. Lucille Kerr. LC 91-36087. 247p. 1992. text ed. 38.95 (*0-8223-1227-1*) Duke.

Reclaiming the Bible: Words for the Nineties. Robert M. Brown. LC 94-8687. 160p. (Orig.). 1994. pap. 11.00 (*0-664-25553-1*) Westminster John Knox.

Reclaiming the Bible for the Church. Ed. by Carl E. Braaten & Robert W. Jenson. 152p. (Orig.). 1995. pap. 13.00 (*0-8028-0898-0*) Eerdmans.

*__Reclaiming the Church: Where the Mainline Church Went Wrong & What to Do about It.__ John B. Cobb, Jr. 120p. (Orig.). 1997. pap. 12.00 (*0-664-25720-8*) Westminster John Knox.

*__Reclaiming the City.__ Ed. by A. Coupland. (Illus.). 304p. 1997. text ed. 84.00 (*0-419-21360-0*, E & FN Spon) Routledge Chapman & Hall.

Reclaiming the Classroom: Teacher Research as an Agency for Change. Ed. by Dixie Goswami & Peter R. Stillman. LC 86-21581. 242p. (Orig.). 1986. pap. text ed. 24.00 (*0-86709-065-0*, 0065) Boynton Cook Pubs.

Reclaiming the Connections: A Contemporary Spirituality. Kathleen Fischer. LC 89-61212. 112p. (Orig.). 1989. pap. 7.95 (*1-55612-271-3*) Sheed & Ward MO.

Reclaiming the Culture. Ed. by Alan Crippen. (Orig.). 1996. pap. 12.99 (*1-56179-440-6*) Focus Family.

Reclaiming the Dark Feminine: The Price of Desire. Carolyn Baker. LC 96-68642. 160p. (Orig.). 1996. pap. 12.95 (*1-56184-088-2*) New Falcon Pubns.

Reclaiming the Dead Sea Scrolls: The History of Judaism, the Background of Christianity, the Lost Library of Qumran. Lawrence H. Schiffman. LC 95-17280. (Anchor Bible Reference Library). (Illus.). 556p. 1995. pap. 24.95 (*0-385-48121-7*, Anchor NY) Doubleday.

Reclaiming the Dead Sea Scrolls: The History of Judaism, the Background of Christianity, the Lost Library of Qumran. Lawrence H. Schiffman. LC 94-26489. 520p. 1994. 34.95 (*0-8276-0530-7*) JPS Phila.

*__Reclaiming the Early Church.__ Mike Dowgiewicz & Sue Dowgiewicz. 1996. pap. 13.95 (*1-888582-04-9*) Aslan Pubng.

Reclaiming the Federal Courts. Larry W. Yackle. LC 94-8608. 309p. 1994. text ed. 39.95 (*0-674-75007-1*, YACREC) HUP.

Reclaiming the Future: A Manual on Futures Studies for African Planners. World Futures Studies Federation for the United National Development Programme Staff. 214p. 1986. text ed. 90.00 (*1-85148-010-2*, Tycooly Pub) Weidner & Sons.

*__Reclaiming the Great Tradition: Evangelicals, Catholics & Orthodox in Dialogue.__ Ed. by James S. Cutsinger. LC 96-39119. 214p. (Orig.). 1997. pap. 18.99 (*0-8308-1889-8*, 1889) InterVarsity.

Reclaiming the Heartland: Lesbian & Gay Voices from the Midwest. Ed. by Karen L. Osborne & William J. Spurlin. LC 95-46718. 256p. (C). 1996. 18.95 (*0-8166-2754-1*) U of Minn Pr.

*__Reclaiming the History of Ethics: Essays for John Rawls.__ Ed. by Andrews Reath et al. 416p. 1997. 59.95 (*0-521-47240-7*) Cambridge U Pr.

Reclaiming the Humanities: The Roots of Self-Knowledge in the Greek & Biblical Worlds. R. Thomas Simone & Richard I. Sugarman. 226p. (Orig.). (C). 1985. pap. text ed. 23.00 (*0-8191-5094-0*) U Pr of Amer.

Reclaiming the Imagination: Philosophical Perspectives for Writers & Teachers of Writing. Ed. by Ann E. Berthoff. LC 83-15537. 286p. (Orig.). 1984. pap. text ed. 23.50 (*0-86709-059-6*, 0059) Boynton Cook Pubs.

Reclaiming the Inner Child. Ed. by Jeremiah Abrams. (New Consciousness Reader Ser.). 336p. (Orig.). 1990. pap. 14.95 (*0-87477-551-5*, Tarcher Putnam) Putnam Pub Group.

Reclaiming the Mainstream: Individualist Feminism Rediscovered. Joan K. Taylor. 271p. (C). 1992. 27.95 (*0-87975-717-5*) Prometheus Bks.

Reclaiming the Middle Ground. Donald G. Lenihan et al. 162p. 1995. pap. 16.95 (*0-88645-167-1*, Pub. by Inst Res Pub CN) Ashgate Pub Co.

Reclaiming the Muse. Ed. by Nicola LeFanu & Sophie Fuller. (Contemporary Music Review Ser.: Vol. 2). 349p. 1995. pap. text ed. 67.00 (*3-7186-5528-4*, ECU56, Harwood Acad Pubs) Gordon & Breach.

Reclaiming the Past: Landmarks of Women's History. Ed. by Page P. Miller. LC 91-46604. (Illus.). 256p. 1992. 35.00 (*0-253-33842-5*) Ind U Pr.

Reclaiming the Sacred: Lay Religion & Popular Politics in Revolutionary France. Suzanne Desan. Ed. by David Laitin. LC 90-55120. (Wilder House Series in Politics, History, & Culture). (Illus.). 272p. 1990. 37.50 (*0-8014-2404-6*) Cornell U Pr.

*__Reclaiming the Sacred: The Bible in Gay & Lesbian Culture.__ Ed. by Raymond-Jean Frontain. 305p. 1996. 49.95 (*0-7890-0026-1*); pap. 24.95 (*1-56023-097-5*) Haworth Pr.

*__Reclaiming the Shadow Self.__ Christine Breese. (Illus.). 336p. (Orig.). 1997. pap. 15.95 (*0-9657511-0-4*) Starlght Pr.

*__Reclaiming the Sociological Classics.__ Ed. by Charles Camic. 320p. (C). 1998. text ed. 59.95 (*1-57718-030-5*) Blackwell Pubs.

*__Reclaiming the Sociological Classics.__ Ed. by Charles Camic. 320p. (C). 1998. pap. text ed. 25.95 (*1-57718-031-3*) Blackwell Pubs.

Reclaiming the Soul: The Search for Meaning in a Self-Centered Culture. Jeffrey H. Boyd. LC 95-51177. 192p. (Orig.). 1996. pap. 15.95 (*0-8298-1080-3*) Pilgrim OH.

*__Reclaiming the Soul of America.__ Charles Colson. Date not set. write for info. (*0-345-40709-1*, Moorings) Ballantine.

*__Reclaiming the Spirit: Gay Men & Women Come to Terms with Religion.__ David Shallenberger. LC 97-24856. (Illus.). 304p. 1998. 26.00 (*0-8135-2488-1*) Rutgers U Pr.

Reclaiming the Tacit Dimension: Symbolic Form in the Rhetoric of Silence. George Kalamaras. LC 93-18294. (SUNY Series, Literacy, Culture, & Learning: Theory & Practice). 255p. (C). 1994. pap. text ed. 21.95 (*0-7914-1758-1*) State U NY Pr.

Reclaiming the Tacit Dimension: Symbolic Form in the Rhetoric of Silence. George Kalamaras. LC 93-18294. (SUNY Series, Literacy, Culture, & Learning: Theory & Practice). 255p. (C). 1994. text ed. 64.50 (*0-7914-1757-3*) State U NY Pr.

Reclaiming the Urban Family: How to Mobilize the Church As a Family Training Center. Willie Richardson. 192p. 1996. pap. 9.99 (*0-310-20008-3*) Zondervan.

Reclaiming the Vision: Past, Present, & Future: Native Voices for the Eighth Generation. Ed. by Lee Francis & James Bruchac. LC 95-81637. (Illus.). 120p. (Orig.). (YA). (gr. 9-12). 1996. pap. 15.95 (*0-87886-140-8*) Greenfld Rev Lit.

Reclaiming the Wasteland: TV & Gifted Children. Bob Abelman. Ed. by Mark A. Runco. (Perspectives on Creativity Ser.). 256p. (C). 1995. text ed. 52.50 (*1-57273-014-5*); pap. text ed. 19.95 (*1-57273-015-3*) Hampton Pr NJ.

Reclaiming the West: The Coal Industry & Surface Mined Lands. Daniel P. Wiener et al. Ed. by Joseph Mohbat. LC 80-81777. 466p. reprint ed. pap. 132.90 (*0-7837-0334-1*, 2040653) Bks Demand.

Reclaiming Truth: Contribution to a Critique of Cultural Relativism. Christopher Norris. LC 96-15885. (Post-Contemporary Interventions Ser.). 272p. 1996. text ed. 49.95 (*0-8223-1882-2*); pap. text ed. 17.95 (*0-8223-1872-5*) Duke.

Reclaiming Truth: Contribution to a Critique of Cultural Relativism. Christopher Norris. 244p. 1996. pap. 12.99 (*0-85315-815-0*, Pub. by Lawrence & Wishart UK) NYU Pr.

Reclaiming Wastelands: A Case Study of Amethi-Block District Sultanpur. Hridai R. Yadav. 1990. 18.50 (*81-7022-273-7*, Pub. by Concept II) S Asia.

*__Reclaiming William Morris: Englishness, Sublimity, & the Rhetoric of Dissent.__ Michelle Weinroth. 302p. 1996. 55.00 (*0-7735-1439-2*, PR5087, Pub. by McGill CN) U of Toronto Pr.

Reclaiming Your Family: Seven Ways to Gain Control of What Goes on in Your Home. Robert Bruce & Debra Bruce. LC 94-9672. 256p. 1994. pap. 11.99 (*0-8054-6150-7*, 4261-50) Broadman.

Reclaiming Your Future: Finding Your Path after Recovery. Kendall Johnson. LC 92-38002. 224p. 1992. pap. 10.95 (*0-89793-093-2*) Hunter Hse.

Reclaiming Your Future: Finding Your Path after Recovery. Kendall Johnson. 208p. 1992. reprint ed. lib. bdg. 31.00 (*0-8095-6341-X*) Borgo Pr.

Reclaiming Your Inner Child: A Self-Discovery Workbook. Ken Parker. 1993. pap. 14.99 (*0-8407-4332-7*) Nelson.

Reclaiming Your Life: A Step-by-Step Guide to Using Regression Therapy to Overcome the Effects of Childhood Abuse. Jean C. Jenson. LC 94-34390. 244p. 1995. pap. 20.95 (*0-525-93948-2*, Dutton) NAL-Dutton.

Reclaiming Your Life: A Step-by-Step Guide to Using Regression Therapy to Overcome the Effects of Childhood Abuse. Jean C. Jenson. Date not set. pap. 11.95 (*0-452-27545-8*) Viking Penguin.

Reclaiming Your Life: A Step-by-Step Guide to Using Regression Therapy to Overcome the Effects of Childhood Abuse. Jean C. Jenson. 224p. 1996. pap. 11.95 (*0-452-01169-8*, Mer) NAL-Dutton.

*__Reclaiming Your Life: The Gay Man's Guide to Love, Self-Acceptance, & Trust.__ Rik Isensee. LC 97-19054. 242p. (Orig.). 1997. reprint ed. pap. 12.95 (*1-55583-422-1*) Alyson Pubns.

Reclaiming Youth at Risk: Our Hope for the Future. Larry Brendtro et al. (Illus.). 100p. (Orig.). 1990. pap. 19.95 (*1-879639-05-X*) Natl Educ Serv.

Reclamation. Theresa A. Lucadano. Ed. by Alana Sherman. (Chapbooks Fourth Ser.). 20p. 1991. pap. 4.95 (*0-939689-13-8*) Alms Hse Pr.

Reclamation. Sarah Zettel. 464p. (Orig.). 1996. mass mkt. 5.99 (*0-446-60292-2*, Aspect) Warner Bks.

Reclamation & Rededication Through Synergistic Unity: Creating a Violent Free Community "Crime" Through Community Empowerment. Hugh F. Brockington, II. Ed. by Dorothy Lewis-Brockington. 1996. 7.95 (*0-925783-04-8*) Natl BIE Pub.

Reclamation & Reprocessing of Spent Solvents. Bernard A. Donahue et al. LC 89-22887. (Pollution Technology Review Ser.: No. 175). (Illus.). 190p. 1990. 42.00 (*0-8155-1222-8*) Noyes.

Reclamation & Transformation: Three Self-Taught Chicago Artists. Terra Museum of American Art Staff & Tom Patterson. LC 94-60034. (Illus.). 104p. (Orig.). (C). 1994. pap. 22.50 (*0-932171-07-9*) Terra Mus.

Reclamation & Use of Disturbed Land in the Southwest. Ed. by John Thames. LC 76-17133. 376p. reprint ed. 107.20 (*0-8357-9623-X*, 2055250) Bks Demand.

Reclamation & Vegetative Restoration of Problem Soils & Disturbed Lands. Darrell Brown et al. LC 86-17957. (Pollution Technology Review Ser.: No. 137). (Illus.). 560p. 1987. 48.00 (*0-8155-1102-7*) Noyes.

Reclamation of a Queen: Guinevere in Modern Fantasy. Barbara A. Gordon-Wise. LC 90-45324. (Contributions to the Study of Science Fiction & Fantasy Ser.: No. 44). 184p. 1991. text ed. 49.95 (*0-313-26323-X*, GWG, Greenwood Pr) Greenwood.

Reclamation of Black Prisoners: A Challenge to the African American Church. James H. Costen et al. Ed. by Gloria Askew & Gayraud Wilmore. (Black Church Scholars Ser.: Vol. 3). 134p. (C). 1992. pap. 8.95 (*0-614-08301-X*) Jrnl Interdenom.

Reclamation of Former Coal Mines & Steelworks. I. G. Richards et al. (Studies in Environmental Science: Vol. 56). 740p. 1993. 299.50 (*0-444-81703-4*) Elsevier.

Reclamation of Fugitives from Service. Salmon P. Chase. LC 77-138334. (Black Heritage Library Collection). 1977. 15.95 (*0-8369-8726-8*) Ayer.

Reclamation of Surface Mined Lands, 2 vols., Set. Ed. by L. R. Hossner. LC 87-896. (Soil Scientists & Enviromental Engineers Ser.). 1988. 281.00 (*0-8493-5702-0*, TD195, CRC Reprint) Franklin.

Reclamation of Surface Mined Lands, Vol. 1. L. R. Hossner. LC 87-896. 1988. 132.00 (*0-8493-5703-9*, TD195, CRC Reprint) Franklin.

Reclamation of Surface Mined Lands, Vol. 2. L. R. Hossner. LC 87-896. 1988. 149.00 (*0-8493-5704-7*, TD195, CRC Reprint) Franklin.

Reclamation Safety & Health Standards, 2 vols., Set. 1994. lib. bdg. 573.95 (*0-8490-5800-7*) Gordon Pr.

Reclamation, Treatment & Utilization of Coal Mining Wastes: Proceedings of the Third International Symposium, Glasgow, 3-7 September 1990. Ed. by A. K. Rainbow. (Illus.). 544p. (C). 1990. text ed. 130.00 (*90-6191-154-0*, Pub. by A A Balkema NE) Ashgate Pub Co.

Reclamations. Thomas Grimes. 54p. (Orig.). 1995. pap. 8.95 (*0-9644145-1-1*) Parfait de Cocoa.

Reclamo/Reclamation. 2nd rev. ed. Lisa Alvarado. (Illus.). 46p. 1994. pap. 9.00 (*0-9648506-0-5*) La Onda Negra.

Reclassification of the European Tetrastrichinae (Hymenoptera: Eulophidae) Revision of the Remaining Genera. Marcus Graham. (Memoir Ser.: No. 49). 332p. 1991. 45.00 (*1-56665-048-8*) Assoc Pubs FL.

Reclassification of the Perceval Romances. George Woods. (Studies in Comparative Literature: No. 35). (C). 1970. reprint ed. pap. 22.95 (*0-8383-0083-9*) M S G Haskell Hse.

***Reclassification of World Dyschiriini with a Revision of the Palearctic Fauna (Coleoptera, Carabidae)** D. N. Fedorenko. (Illus.). 224p. 1996. pap. 69.95 (*954-642-009-3*) Intl Scholars.

Reclining Figure. Harry Kurnitz. 1955. pap. 5.25 (*0-8222-0939-X*) Dramatists Play.

Recluse of Loyang: Shao Yung & the Moral Evolution of Early Sung Thought. Don J. Wyatt. (Illus.). 384p. 1996. text ed. 42.00 (*0-8248-1755-9*) UH Pr.

Recluse of the Heavenly House. Wang Weizheng. Tr. by Liu Shicong. 220p. 1994. pap. 10.95 (*7-5071-0223-8*) Cheng & Tsui.

Reclusion Solitaire. Tahar B. Jelloun. 1981. pap. 11.95 (*0-7859-2685-2*) Fr & Eur.

Recnik Pravnih Termina: Multilingual Law Dictionary. Jasmina Jovanovic. (ENG, FRE & SER.). 1990. lib. bdg. 350.00 (*0-8288-3923-9*, F14123) Fr & Eur.

Recnik Srpskohrvatskoga Knjizevnog Jezika: Serbocroatian Dictionary of Literary Terms, 6 vols., Set. 5732p. 1982. 250.00 (*0-8288-1997-1*, F78640) Fr & Eur.

Recobrando el Sueno Americano: Claves para Alcanzar la Libertad Financiera. Bill Quain. Tr. by Ricardo Monterrosa. (Illus.). 124p. (Orig.). (SPA.). 1995. pap. 9.95 (*0-9623646-6-5*) Wales Pub.

Recodings: Art, Spectacle, Cultural Politics. Hal Foster. LC 85-70184. (Illus.). 256p. 1985. pap. 10.95 (*0-941920-04-6*) Bay Pr.

Recognising Islam: Religion & Society in the Modern Middle East. Michael Gilsenan. 284p. 1993. text ed. 19.95 (*1-85043-743-2*, Pub. by I B Tauris UK) St Martin.

Recognition. Stan Schmidt & Randall G. Hassell. 302p. (Orig.). 1995. pap. 8.95 (*0-911921-17-6*) Focus Pubns MO.

Recognition: Advancing Ecumenical Thinking. Gerard Kelly. (American University Studies, Series VII: Vol. 186). 312p. (C). 1996. text ed. 49.95 (*0-8204-2780-2*) P Lang Pubng.

Recognition: Fichte & Hegel on the Other. Robert R. Williams. LC 90-27203. (SUNY Series in Hegelian Studies). 332p. (C). 1992. text ed. 64.50 (*0-7914-0857-4*); pap. text ed. 21.95 (*0-7914-0858-2*) State U NY Pr.

Recognition: The Quality Way. Toni LaMotta. LC 95-1339. 240p. 1995. 31.00 (*0-527-76223-7*) Qual Resc.

Recognition, A Logical & Experimental Study see Horizontal-Vertical Illusion of Brightness

Recognition & Alleviation of Pain & Distress in Laboratory Animals. National Research Council Staff. 160p. 1992. text ed. 29.95 (*0-309-04275-5*) Natl Acad Pr.

Recognition & Discrimination see Mental & Physical Measurements of Working Children

Recognition & Enforcement of Cross-Border Insolvency: A Guide to International Practice. Neil H. Cooper & Rebecca E. Jarvis. LC 96-22533. (Wiley Series in Commercial Law). 1996. pap. write for info. (*0-471-96310-0*) Wiley.

Recognition & Enforcement of Foreign Judgments in the Common Law Units of the British Commonwealth. Horace E. Read. LC 38-18887. (Harvard Studies in the Conflict of Laws: Vol. 2). xiv, 371p. 1978. reprint ed. lib. bdg. 47.50 (*0-89941-127-4*, 302790) W S Hein.

Recognition & Management of Food Allergy in Children. Ed. by A. J. Franklin. (Illus.). 168p. 1988. 58.00 (*1-85070-142-3*) Prthnon Pub.

Recognition & Management of Nursing Home Infections. (Illus.). 89p. 1992. 6.00 (*0-9614520-1-3*) NFID.

Recognition & Management of Pesticide Poisonings. 1994. lib. bdg. 260.95 (*0-8490-6442-2*) Gordon Pr.

***Recognition & Management of Pesticide Poisoning.** 4th ed. Donald P. Morgan. (Illus.). 206p. (C). 1996. pap. 30.00 (*0-7881-3176-1*) DIANE Pub.

Recognition & Regulation in Cell-Mediated Immunity. Ed. by James D. Watson & John Marbrook. LC 85-6834. (Receptors & Ligands in Intercellular Communication Ser.: No. 5). 480p. 1985. reprint ed. pap. 136.80 (*0-7837-8318-3*, 2049104) Bks Demand.

***Recognition & the United Nations.** 208p. 1993. text ed. 57.95 (*0-521-46322-X*) Cambridge U Pr.

Recognition & the United Nations. John Dugard. 208p. (C). 1987. 110.00 (*0-949009-00-8*, Pub. by Grotius Pubns UK) St Mut.

***Recognition, Gratitude, & Celebration.** Patrick Townsend. 1997. pap. text ed. 12.95 (*1-56052-432-4*) Crisp Pubns.

Recognition, Identification & Prevention of Acute Viral Infections. Donald H. McLean. 389p. 1991. 42.50 (*0-87527-480-3*) Green.

Recognition in Financial Statements: Underlying Concepts & Practical Conventions. L. Todd Johnson & Reed K. Storey. LC 82-71737. (Financial Accounting Standards Board Research Report Ser.). (Illus.). 267p. (Orig.). 1982. pap. 20.00 (*0-910065-16-0*) Finan Acct Found.

Recognition of Ancient Sedimentary Environments. Ed. by J. Keith Rigby & W. Kenneth Hamblin. LC 72-194231. (Society of Economic Paleontologists & Mineralogists, Special Publication Ser.: No. 16). 350p. reprint ed. pap. 99.80 (*0-317-27126-1*, 2024741) Bks Demand.

Recognition of Child Abuse for the Mandated Reporter. 2nd rev. ed. Ed. by James A. Monteleone. LC 96-32412. (Illus.). 275p. (C). 1996. pap. 35.00 (*1-878060-24-4*, 30961) GW Medical.

Recognition of Commercial Judgments & Awards in the Commonwealth. K. W. Patchett. 384p. 1984. boxed 136.00 (*0-406-40320-1*, U.K.) MICHIE.

Recognition of Contractual Rights & Obligations: An Exploratory Study of Conceptual Issues. Yuji Ijiri. LC 80-71000. (Financial Accounting Standards Board Research Report Ser.). (Illus.). 92p. (Orig.). 1980. pap. 9.25 (*0-910065-10-1*) Finan Acct Found.

***Recognition of Deformation, Microstructures & Mechanisms in Rocks.** T. Blenkinsop. (Illus.). 224p. 1997. text ed. 109.00 (*0-412-73480-X*, Chap & Hall NY) Chapman & Hall.

Recognition of Depreciation by Not-for-Profit Institutions. Ed. by Yamile Kahn. 159p. 1988. 11.95 (*0-915164-37-X*) NACUBO.

Recognition of Discharges: Discrimination & Classification. A. Krivda. (Illus.). 203p. (Orig.). 1995. pap. 87.50 (*90-407-1156-9*, Pub. by Delft U Pr NE) Coronet Bks.

Recognition of Facial Expression: An Original Anthology. Ed. by Martha Davis. LC 74-9160. (Body Movement Perspectives in Research Ser.). 252p. 1975. reprint ed. 35.95 (*0-405-06198-6*) Ayer.

Recognition of Fluvial Depositional Systems & Their Resource Potential. Romeo M. Flores et al. (Short Course Notes Ser.: No. 19). 290p. 1985. pap. 26.50 (*0-918985-53-6*) SEPM.

***Recognition of Fluvial Depositional Systems & Their Resource Potential.** Romeo M. Flores et al. (Lecture Notes for Short Course Ser.: No. 19). (Illus.). 296p. 1985. reprint ed. pap. 84.40 (*0-608-02978-5*, 2063446) Bks Demand.

Recognition of Foreign Enterprises As Taxable Entities. (Cahiers de Droit Fiscal International Ser.: Vol. LXXIIIa). 648p. 1988. pap. 102.00 (*90-6544-362-2*) Kluwer Law Tax Pubs.

***Recognition of Government 1850-1995.** Peterson. LC 97-16329. 1997. text ed. 59.95 (*0-312-17519-1*) St Martin.

***Recognition of Governments in International Law: With Particular Reference to Governments in Exile.** Stefan Talmon. (Oxford Monographs in International Law). 300p. 1997. 85.00 (*0-19-826573-5*) OUP.

Recognition of Health Hazards in Industry: A Review of Materials & Processes. 2nd ed. William A. Burgess. 538p. 1995. text ed. 74.95 (*0-471-57716-2*) Wiley.

Recognition of Henry David Thoreau: Selected Criticism since 1848. Wendell Glick. LC 69-15845. 402p. reprint ed. pap. 114.60 (*0-317-29154-8*, 2055608) Bks Demand.

Recognition of Israel: An End & a New Beginning. Ed. by Aaron Klieman. (American Zionism Ser.: Vol. 13). 576p. 1991. text ed. 55.00 (*0-8240-7361-4*) Garland.

Recognition of M. Leprae Antigens. Tom Ottenhoff & Rene De Vries. (Development in Hematology & Immunology Ser.). (C). 1987. lib. bdg. 101.50 (*0-89838-887-2*) Kluwer Ac.

Recognition of Merit in Superintendents' Reports to the Public. Zenas R. Clark. LC 77-176650. (Columbia University. Teachers College. Contributions to Education Ser.: No. 471). reprint ed. 37.50 (*0-404-55471-7*) AMS Pr.

Recognition of Nathaniel Hawthorne: Selected Criticism since 1828. Ed. by B. Bernard Cohen. LC 70-83454. 320p. reprint ed. pap. 91.20 (*0-317-29153-X*, 2055609) Bks Demand.

Recognition of Reality: Reflections & Prose Poems. Adam Curle. (Conflict & Peacemaking Ser.). 105p. 1987. pap. 14.95 (*1-869890-12-4*, 1292, Pub. by Hawthorn Press UK) Anthroposophic.

Recognition of Speech by Machine - A Bibliography. Ed. by A. S. House. 498p. 1988. text ed. 79.00 (*0-12-356785-8*) Acad Pr.

Recognition of Timber & Timberland Asset Values for Financial Reporting: Seminar Proceedings May 9 & 10, 1983. Ed. by William R. Sizemore & Robert E. Hoskin. 105p. reprint ed. pap. 30.00 (*0-7837-6040-X*, 2045853) Bks Demand.

Recognition Redefined: Building Self-Esteem at Work. Roger L. Hale & Rita F. Maehling. 180p. 1993. text ed. 19.95 (*1-882407-04-0*) Monochrome Pr.

Recognition Redefined: Building Self-Esteem at Work. Roger L. Hale & Rita F. Maehling. 192p. 1992. pap. text ed. 19.95 (*0-9633950-0-9*) Tennant Co.

Recognition Technology in the Information Industry. Herbert F. Schantz. Ed. by Wendy Wicks & Ann M. Cunningham. (Report Series, 1992: No. 1). 120p. (Orig.). (C). 1992. pap. text ed. 100.00 (*0-942308-34-4*) NFAIS.

Recognitions. Clare Butterfield & L. Johnston. Ed. by Johnston William et al. (Chapbook Ser.: No. 11). 18p. 1983. pap. 3.00 (*0-932884-10-5*) Red Herring.

Recognitions. William Gaddis. 1994. 24.00 (*0-8446-6740-4*) Peter Smith.

Recognitions. William Gaddis. (Twentieth Century Classics Ser.). 976p. 1993. pap. 14.95 (*0-14-018708-1*, Penguin Classics) Viking Penguin.

Recognitions: A Study in Poetics. Terence Cave. 544p. 1990. reprint ed. pap. 35.00 (*0-19-815163-2*) OUP.

Recognitions: Images of a Woman Artist. Nancy Roberts. LC 88-51097. 96p. (Orig.). 1989. 25.00 (*0-944072-02-X*); pap. 15.95 (*0-944072-03-8*) Zoland Bks.

Recognitions: Images of a Woman Artist. limited ed. Nancy Roberts. LC 88-51097. 96p. (Orig.). 1989. 50.00 (*0-944072-05-4*) Zoland Bks.

Recognize. Kevin Powell. (Illus.). 128p. 1995. pap. 11.00 (*0-86316-324-6*) Writers & Readers.

Recognize & Manage Your Allergies. Doris J. Rapp. (Self-Care Health Library). 32p. (Orig.). 1987. pap. 2.50 (*0-87983-396-3*) Keats.

***Recognized Component Directory 1996, 2 vols.** (C). 1996. pap. text ed. 55.00 (*1-55989-956-5*) Underwrtrs Labs.

***Recognized Component Directory 1997, 2 vols.** (C). 1997. pap. text ed. 60.00 (*0-7629-0098-9*) Underwrtrs Labs.

Recognizing Alcoholism & Its Effects: A Mini-Guide. H. R. St. Clair. x, 106p. 1991. pap. 21.75 (*3-8055-5395-1*) S Karger.

Recognizing & Healing the Family Scapegoat: Avoid Carrying Childhood Roles into Adulthood. Sharon A. Smith. 208p. (Orig.). 1995. pap. write for info. (*0-9650609-1-8*) Steppe Pubns.

Recognizing & Identifying Hazardous Materials. 2nd ed. 87p. 1995. student ed., teacher ed. 170.00 incl. audio, sl. (*0-614-09658-8*, AVA19203SS00CDL) Natl Tech Info.

Recognizing & Identifying Hazardous Materials, 10 bks., Set. 64p. 1995. student ed. 31.00 (*0-614-09659-6*, AVA19204BB00CDL) Natl Tech Info.

***Recognizing & Interpreting Arrhythmias.** 3rd rev. ed. Ochs. LC 96-29695. 1997. pap. text ed. 39.95 (*0-8385-4323-5*) Appleton & Lange.

Recognizing & Managing Children with Fetal Alcohol Syndrome/Effects: A Guidebook. Brenda McCreight. LC 97-9039. 1997. 16.95 (*0-87868-607-X*) Child Welfare.

***Recognizing & Recording Reform in Mathematics Education Project: Insights & Implications.** Joan Ferrini-Mundy & Thomas Schram. LC 97-8647. 1997. write for info. (*0-87353-433-6*) NCTM.

Recognizing & Resolving Racism: A Survival Guide for Humane Beings, Vol. 1. Phavia Kujichagulia. 460p. 1995. pap. text ed. write for info. (*1-886856-01-X*) Wisdom Co CA.

***Recognizing & Verbalizing Correct Grammar.** Jean G. DeGaetano. (Illus.). 80p. (Orig.). 1997. pap. text ed. 24.00 (*1-886143-39-0*, G843) Grt Ideas Tching.

Recognizing Biography. William H. Epstein. LC 87-19770. 242p. 1987. text ed. 41.95 (*0-8122-8081-4*) U of Pa Pr.

Recognizing Cause & Effect. Sheldon L. Tilkin. (Horizons E Ser.). (Illus.). 24p. (J). (gr. 3-4). 1980. pap. 3.95 (*0-89403-574-6*) EDC.

Recognizing Cause & Effect. Sheldon L. Tilkin & Judith Conoway. (Horizons F Ser.). (Illus.). 24p. (J). (gr. 4-5). 1980. student ed., pap. 3.95 (*0-89403-584-3*) EDC.

Recognizing Child Abuse: A Guide for the Concerned. Douglas J. Besharov. 270p. 1990. pap. 14.95 (*0-02-903082-X*, Free Press) Free Pr.

Recognizing Community Choices by Individuals with Profound Disabilities: An Assessment. Phillip J. Belfiore. LC 93-48120. (Innovations Ser.: No. 1). 1994. 21.95 (*0-940898-33-0*) Am Assn Mental.

Recognizing Cultural Differences in the Classroom: Training Module III. Ed. by Frank Gonzales. (Illus.). 44p. (Orig.). 1988. pap. text ed. 7.50 (*1-878550-12-8*) Inter Dev Res Assn.

Recognizing European Modernities: A Montage of the Present. Allan Pred. LC 94-46281. (Illus.). 304p. (C). 1995. pap. 21.95 (*0-415-12136-1*, C0003) Routledge.

Recognizing European Modernities: A Montage of the Present. Allan Pred. LC 94-46281. (Illus.). 304p. (C). (gr. 13). 1995. text ed. 69.95 (*0-415-11904-9*, C0002) Routledge.

***Recognizing Excellence in the Mathematical Sciences: An International Compilation of Awards, Prizes, & Recipients.** Ed. by Janice M. Jaguszewski et al. (Foundations in Library & Information Science Ser.: Vol. 41). 1997. 78.50 (*0-7623-0235-6*) Jai Pr.

Recognizing Faculty Work: Reward Systems for the Year 2000. Ed. by Robert M. Diamond & Bronwyn E. Adam. LC 85-644752. (New Directions for Higher Education Ser.: No. 81). 125p. (Orig.). 1993. pap. 19.00 (*1-55542-691-3*) Jossey-Bass.

Recognizing God. Winged Wolf & Heather Hughes-Calero. (Illus.). 256p. 1997. pap. 16.95 (*0-932927-13-0*) Higher Consciousness.

***Recognizing Islam: Religion & Society in the Modern Middle East.** Michael Gilsenan. 284p. 1996. pap. 19.95 (*0-614-21188-3*, 1063) Kazi Pubns.

Recognizing Mood, Character & Plot. Sheldon L. Tilkin & Judith Conoway. (Horizons E Ser.). (Illus.). 24p. (J). (gr. 3-4). 1980. student ed., pap. 3.95 (*0-89403-576-2*) EDC.

Recognizing Mood, Character & Plot. Sheldon L. Tilkin & Judith Conoway. (Horizons F Ser.). (Illus.). 24p. (J). (gr. 4-5). 1980. student ed., pap. 3.95 (*0-89403-586-X*) EDC.

Recognizing Non-Traditional Families. (BNA Special Report Series on Work & Family: No. 38). 32p. 1991. 35.00 (*1-55871-212-7*, BSP206) BNA Plus.

Recognizing Planar Objects Using Invariant Image Features. Thomas H. Reiss. LC 93-19397. 1993. 35.00 (*0-387-56713-5*) Spr-Verlag.

Recognizing Quality Achievement: Noncash Award Programs. Kathryn L. Troy. (Report: No. 1008). (Illus.). 54p. (Orig.). 1992. pap. text ed. 100.00 (*0-8237-0456-4*) Conference Bd.

Recognizing Reality: A Staff Report. C. D. Howe Institute Staff. LC 82-206933. (Policy Review & Outlook Ser.: No. 1982). 77p. 1982. reprint ed. pap. 25.00 (*0-608-01380-3*, 2062128) Bks Demand.

Recognizing Reality: Dharmakirti's Philosophy & Its Tibetan Interpretations. Georges B. Dreyfus. (Series in Buddhist Studies). 480p. (C). 1997. text ed. 68.50 (*0-7914-3097-9*); pap. text ed. 22.95 (*0-7914-3098-7*) State U NY Pr.

Recognizing the Angel. Mary A. Coleman. LC 91-62436. (Illus.). x, 59p. (Orig.). 1991. 30.00 (*0-912960-20-5*); pap. 12.00 (*0-912960-19-1*) Nightowl.

***Recognizing the Latino Resurge.** Ana M. Diaz-Stevens. (Explorations Ser.). (C). 1997. text ed. 80.00 (*0-8133-2509-9*); pap. text ed. 24.00 (*0-8133-2510-2*) Westview.

Recognizing Tone: Advanced Level. 2nd ed. Ed. by Kraft. (Comprehension Skills Ser.). 64p. 1993. pap. 8.45 (*0-89061-621-3*) Jamestown Pubs.

Recognizing Tone: Introductory Level. Ed. by Kraft. (Comprehension Skills Ser.). 64p. 1993. pap. 7.91 (*0-89061-661-2*) Jamestown Pubs.

Recognizing Tone: Middle Level. 2nd ed. Ed. by Kraft. (Comprehension Skills Ser.). 64p. 1993. pap. 8.31 (*0-89061-641-8*) Jamestown Pubs.

Recognizing Words. Ellen B. Church. 1996. pap. text ed. 3.95 (*0-590-97700-8*) Scholastic Inc.

Recoil. Jim Thompson. 1992. pap. 10.00 (*0-679-73308-6*, Vin) Random.

Recollected Words of Abraham Lincoln. Ed. by Don E. Fehrenbacher & Virginia Fehrenbacher. LC 95-37774. 648p. 1996. 60.00 (*0-8047-2636-1*) Stanford U Pr.

Recollecting Our Lives: Women's Experience of Childhood Sexual Abuse. Womens Research Centre Staff. 1990. pap. 14.95 (*0-88974-019-4*) Inland Pub.

Recollecting the Future: A View of Business, Technology & Innovation in the Next 30 Years. Hugh B. Stewart. 250p. 1988. text ed. 26.00 (*1-55623-143-1*) Irwin Prof Pubng.

Recollection & Experience: Plato's Theory of Learning & Its Successors. Dominic Scott. 284p. (C). 1995. text ed. 59.95 (*0-521-47455-8*) Cambridge U Pr.

Recollection & Reconstruction. Ed. by Bernard D. Fine et al. LC 74-147778. (Kris Study Group Monograph: No. 4). 1971. 27.50 (*0-8236-5785-X*) Intl Univs Pr.

Recollection of a Happy Childhood by Mary Esther Huger, Daughter of Francis Kinloch Huger of Long House Near Pendleton, South Carolina 1826-1848. Ed. & Intro. by Mary Stevenson. LC 76-4386. (Illus.). 1976. 15.00 (*0-912462-07-8*) Foun Hist Rest.

Recollection of a Journey. R. C. Hutchinson. (Twentieth Century Classics Ser.). 400p. 1995. pap. 12.95 (*0-7490-0128-3*, Pub. by A & B UK) London Brdge.

Recollection of Air Combat, Europe & the Balkans, Foggia, 1944: As Flies. . .Or Sparrows, Scripts & Scraps from under My Hat. Merle L. Perkins. LC 95-69074. 119p. (Orig.). 1996. pap. 20.75 (*0-9637220-6-9*); lib. bdg. 37.75 (*0-9637220-5-0*) SHAPE WI.

Recollection of Marcella Sembrich. H. Goddard Owen. LC 81-22197. (Music Reprint Ser.). (Illus.). 80p. 1982. reprint ed. lib. bdg. 21.50 (*0-306-76141-6*) Da Capo.

Recollection of Olden Days. Jose Palomo. (Educational Ser.: No. 13). (Illus.). 175p. (C). 1992. 9.95 (*1-878453-11-4*) Univ Guam MAR Ctr.

Recollections. Andrew J. Chambers. Bd. with Reminiscences. 1975. 14.95 (*0-87770-156-3*) Ye Galleon.

Recollections. Harry Frazier. 100p. 1938. 1.00 (*0-939487-01-2*) Ches & OH Hist.

Recollections. Helen P. Jochum. LC 88-91440. (Illus.). 160p. 1988. text ed. 15.00 (*0-9606206-1-3*) Jochum.

Recollections. Judith B. Montano. Ed. by Harold Nadel. LC 92-44544. (Illus.). 152p. 1993. 16.95 (*0-914881-59-0*, 10071) C & T Pub.

Recollections, 2 vols., Set. John Morley. LC 75-30034. reprint ed. 95.00 (*0-404-14080-7*) AMS Pr.

***Recollections: Ten Stories on Five Themes.** Adkins & Shackleton. 1990. pap. text ed. write for info. (*0-17-556199-0*) Addison-Wesley.

Recollections: The French Revolution of 1848. Alexis De Tocqueville. Ed. & Intro. by J. P. Mayer. 373p. 1986. reprint ed. pap. 21.95 (*0-88738-658-X*) Transaction Pubs.

Recollections: The People of the Blue Ridge Remember. Dorothy Noble-Smith. 96p. 1995. 12.95 (*1-57087-162-0*) Prof Pr NC.

Recollections & Experiences of an Abolitionist, from 1885-1865. Alexander M. Ross. (American Biography Ser.). 224p. 1991. reprint ed. lib. bdg. 69.00 (*0-7812-8331-0*) Rprt Serv.

Recollections & Impressions of James A. McNeill Whistler. Arthur J. Eddy. LC 71-176163. (Illus.). 296p. 1972. reprint ed. 23.95 (*0-405-08484-6*, Pub. by Blom Pubns UK) Ayer.

Recollections & Impressions, 1822-1890. Octavius B. Fronthingham. (Notable American Authors Ser.). 1992. reprint ed. lib. bdg. 75.00 (*0-7812-2911-1*) Rprt Serv.

Recollections & Letters of Robert E. Lee. Robert E. Lee. (Civil War Ser.). 471p. 1993. 12.95 (*0-914427-66-0*) W S Konecky Assocs.

Recollections & Opinions of an Old Pioneer. Peter H. Burnett. LC 76-87661. (American Scene Ser.). 1969. reprint ed. lib. bdg. 55.00 (*0-306-71765-4*) Da Capo.

Recollections & Reflections. James R. Planche. LC 78-17733. (Music Reprint Ser.). (Illus.). 1978. reprint ed. lib. bdg. 65.00 (*0-306-79501-9*) Da Capo.

Recollections & Reflections. Richard Strauss. Ed. by Willi Schuh. Tr. by L. J. Lawrence. LC 74-72. (Illus.). 173p. 1974. reprint ed. text ed. 49.75 (*0-8371-7366-3*, STRF, Greenwood Pr) Greenwood.

Recollections & Reflections. J. J. Thomson. LC 74-26297. (History, Philosophy & Sociology of Science Ser.). (Illus.). 1975. reprint ed. 40.95 (*0-405-06622-8*) Ayer.

***Recollections & Short Stories.** Judd R. Wilkins. LC 97-90221. (Orig.). 1997. pap. 10.95 (*0-533-12325-9*) Vantage.

Recollections at Play: A Life in Australian Theatre. John Sumner. (Illus.). 352p. (Orig.). 1993. pap. 29.95 (*0-522-84494-4*, Pub. by Melbourne Univ Pr AT) Paul & Co Pubs.

***Recollections from My Time in the Indian Service 1935-1942: Maria Martinez Makes Pottery.** Alfreda W. Maloof. (Illus.). 72p. (Orig.). 1997. pap. 15.00 (*0-9651377-1-6*) Liv Gold Pr.

Recollections in Verse. Leo J. Molner. 1995. 10.95 (*0-533-11291-5*) Vantage.

An Asterisk (*) at the beginning of an entry indicates that the title is appearing in BIP for the first time.

R

Recollections of a Busy Life. Horace Greeley. LC 74-83912. (Black Heritage Library Collection). 1977. 46.95 (*0-8369-8582-6*) Ayer.

Recollections of a Busy Life. James B. Forgan. LC 75-2632. (Wall Street & the Security Market Ser.). (Illus.). 1975. reprint ed. 31.95 (*0-405-06957-X*) Ayer.

Recollections of a Busy Life. Horace Greeley. LC 74-125695. (American Journalists Ser.). 1978. reprint ed. 46.95 (*0-405-01674-3*) Ayer.

Recollections of a Busy Life. Horace Greeley. (American Biography Ser.). 624p. 1991. reprint ed. lib. bdg. 109.00 (*0-7812-8155-5*) Rprt Serv.

Recollections of a Chinese Physicist. C. K. Jen. 239p. 1991. write for info. (*0-9627581-0-8*) Signition.

Recollections of a Confederate Staff Officer. G. Moxley Sorrel. 1994. 12.98 (*0-8317-2192-8*) Smithmark.

***Recollections of a Confederate Staff Officer.** Moxley Sorrell. (Civil War Library). 320p. 1996. reprint ed. 10.98 (*1-56852-029-8*) W S Konecky Assocs.

Recollections of a Fallen Sky: Velikovsky & Cultural Amnesia. Ed. by Earl R. Milton. 176p. 1992. pap. 12.00 (*0-940268-28-0*) Metron Pubns.

***Recollections of a First Chair Bassoonist: 52 Years in the Hollywood Studio Orchestras.** unabridged ed. Don Christlieb. Ed. by Anthony Christlieb & Carolyn Beck. LC 96-96415. (Illus.). ix, 152p. (Orig.). 1996. pap. 24.95 (*0-9653870-0-3*) Christlieb Prod.

Recollections of a Georgia Loyalist. Elizabeth L. Johnston. Ed. by Arthur W. Eaton. LC 76-187388. (Illus.). 224p. 1972. reprint ed. 20.00 (*0-87152-083-4*) Reprint.

Recollections of a Golden Age: An Autobiography by Rudolph Schevill 1874-1946. Rudolph Schevill. Ed. by Yvette E. Miller. LC 84-29985. (Discoveries Ser.). 224p. 1985. 25.00 (*0-935480-19-6*) Lat Am Lit Rev Pr.

Recollections of a Handcart Pioneer of 1860: A Woman's Life on the Mormon Frontier. Mary A. Hafen. LC 82-23868. (Illus.). 100p. 1983. reprint ed. pap. 6.95 (*0-8032-7219-7*, Bison Books) U of Nebr Pr.

Recollections of a Happy Life. Elizabeth C. Hobson. 1977. 17.95 (*0-8369-6978-2*, 7857) Ayer.

Recollections of a Happy Life: Being the Autobiography of Marianne North, Vol. 1. Marianne North. Ed. by Susan Morgan. LC 93-12326. 400p. 1993. reprint ed. text ed. 60.00 (*0-8139-1469-8*); reprint ed. pap. text ed. 19.50 (*0-8139-1470-1*) U Pr of Va.

Recollections of a High School District 1893-1968: An Informal History of the Kern County Union High School & Junior College District. J. S. Wallace. LC 87-83580. 289p. 1987. 15.00 (*0-9619924-0-9*) Kern HS Dist.

Recollections of a Lifetime: or Men & Things I Have Seen, 2 vols., Set. Peter Parley, pseud. (American Biography Ser.). 1991. reprint ed. lib. bdg. 148.00 (*0-7812-8149-0*) Rprt Serv.

Recollections of a Literary Life. Mary R. Mitford. LC 74-178342. reprint ed. 67.50 (*0-404-56789-4*) AMS Pr.

Recollections of a Long Life. Jeremiah B. Jeter. Ed. by Edwin S. Gaustad. LC 79-52595. (Baptist Tradition Ser.). 1980. reprint ed. lib. bdg. 27.95 (*0-405-12462-7*) Ayer.

Recollections of a Long Life: With Additional Extracts from His Private Diaries, 6 vols., Set. John C. Broughton. Ed. by Lady Dorchester. LC 09-25987. reprint ed. 459.00 (*0-404-03320-2*) AMS Pr.

Recollections of a Maryland Confederate Soldier & Staff Officer under Johnston, Jackson & Lee. McHenry Howard. Ed. by James I. Robertson. (Illus.). 483p. 1975. 30.00 (*0-89029-019-9*) Morningside Bkshop.

Recollections of a Medical Doctor in Jerusalem: From the Notebooks of Professor Julius J. Kleeberg, 1930-1988. P. Gillon. (Illus.). vi, 174p. 1992. 61.00 (*3-8055-5522-9*) S Karger.

Recollections of a Mint Director. Frank A. Leach & David Q. Bowers. (Illus.). 136p. (Orig.). 1987. pap. 9.95 (*0-943161-01-0*) Bowers & Merena.

Recollections of a Mountain Boy Plus Stories of Sudden Death. Red Fleming. Ed. by Jennifer Rose. (Illus.). 112p. (Orig.). (YA). 1992. pap. 9.95 (*0-930401-55-7*) Artex Pub.

Recollections of a Mustang: In Memory of World War Two. Robert W. Eigell. (Illus.). 213p. (Orig.). 1994. pap. text ed. 20.00 (*0-9642322-8-6*) R W Eigell.

Recollections of a Naval Officer, 1841-1865. William H. Parker. LC 84-22788. (Classics of Naval Literature Ser.). 403p. 1985. reprint ed. 32.95 (*0-87021-533-7*) Naval Inst Pr.

Recollections of a New England Educator. William A. Mowry. LC 73-89207. (American Education: Its Men, Institutions, & Ideas. Series 1). 1978. reprint ed. 21.95 (*0-405-01446-5*) Ayer.

Recollections of a New York Chief of Police with Historic Supplement of the Denver Police. George W. Walling. LC 70-129311. (Criminology, Law Enforcement, & Social Problems Ser.: No. 133). (Illus.). 682p. 1972. reprint ed. 35.00 (*0-87585-133-9*) Patterson Smith.

Recollections of a Newspaperman: (A Record Life & Events in California) Frank A. Leach. (American Biography Ser.). 146p. 1991. reprint ed. lib. bdg. 59.00 (*0-7812-8239-X*) Rprt Serv.

Recollections of a One-Room Schoolhouse: An Interview with Marian Brooks. 1975. pap. 0.75 (*0-918374-13-8*) City Coll Wk.

Recollections of a Private Soldier in the Army of the Potomac. Frank Wilkeson. LC 70-39471. (Select Bibliographies Reprint Ser.). 1977. reprint ed. 17.95 (*0-8369-9923-1*) Ayer.

Recollections of a Rambling Life. T. Archer. 358p. (C). 1990. 90.00 (*0-86439-074-2*, Pub. by Boolarong Pubns AT) St Mut.

Recollections of a Southern Matron. Caroline H. Gilman. (American Biography Ser.). 272p. 1991. reprint ed. lib. bdg. 69.00 (*0-7812-8145-8*) Rprt Serv.

Recollections of a Texas Educator. Louis H. Hubbard. 1964. 10.00 (*0-686-72458-5*) A Jones.

***Recollections of a Tour Made in Scotland.** Dorthy Wordsworth & Carol K. Walker. LC 96-52071. 1997. write for info. (*0-300-07155-8*) Yale U Pr.

Recollections of a Tour Made in Scotland, A. D. 1803. John C. Shairp. LC 70-37730. reprint ed. 41.50 (*0-404-56857-2*) AMS Pr.

Recollections of a Varied Life. George C. Eggleston. (Notable American Authors Ser.). 1992. reprint ed. lib. bdg. 75.00 (*0-7812-2784-4*) Rprt Serv.

Recollections of a Violinist. Maurice Solway. (Illus.). 160p. 1995. lib. bdg. 39.00 (*0-8095-4918-2*) Borgo Pr.

Recollections of a Violinist. Maurice Solway. (Illus.). 160p. pap. write for info. (*0-88962-233-7*) Mosaic.

Recollections of Abraham Lincoln, 1847-1865. Ward H. Lamon. Ed. by Dorothy L. Teillard. LC 94-18220. (Illus.). 1326p. 1994. reprint ed. pap. 14.95 (*0-8032-7950-7*, Bison Books) U of Nebr Pr.

Recollections of Alexis de Tocqueville. Alexis De Tocqueville. Ed. by J. P. Mayer. Tr. by Alexander T. De Mattos. LC 78-13685. 331p. 1979. reprint ed. text ed. 37.50 (*0-313-21052-7*, TRRE, Greenwood Pr) Greenwood.

Recollections of an Irish Judge: Press, Bar & Parliament. M. M'D. Bidkin. illus, 366p. 1996. reprint ed. 97.00 (*1-56169-196-8*) Gaunt.

Recollections of an Old Cartman: Old New York Street Life. Isaac Lyon. (Illus.). 114p. 1983. reprint ed. 17.50 (*0-9608788-4-X*) NY Bound.

***Recollections of an Old Dominion Dragoon.** Garland C. Hudgins & Richard B. Kleese. (Illus.). 128p. 1993. 19.95 (*0-942365-04-6*) North South Trader.

Recollections of an Old Musician. Thomas Ryan. (Music Reprint Ser.). 290p. 1979. reprint ed. lib. bdg. 37.50 (*0-306-79521-3*) Da Capo.

Recollections of Anais Nin: By Her Contemporaries. Ed. by Benjamin Franklin, 5th. 175p. 1996. pap. 14.95 (*0-8214-1165-9*); text ed. 29.95 (*0-8214-1164-0*) Ohio U Pr.

Recollections of Bar & Bench. Viscount Alverstone. xi, 331p. 1996. reprint ed. 86.00 (*1-56169-205-0*) Gaunt.

Recollections of Benjamin Franklin Bonney. Fred Lockley. 1971. reprint ed. pap. 4.95 (*0-87770-060-5*) Ye Galleon.

Recollections of British Administration in the Cameroons & Northern Nigeria, 1921-1957: "But Always As Friends" Bryan Sharwood-Smith. LC 69-20048. 480p. reprint ed. pap. 136.80 (*0-317-26089-8*, 2023768) Bks Demand.

Recollections of Caernarvon Township: A Portrait of a Lancaster County Town. Mary T. Petrofske. LC 93-33392. (Illus.). 304p. 1993. 35.00 (*0-914659-67-7*) Phoenix Pub.

Recollections of Ceylon (after a Residence of Nearly Thirteen Years; with an Account of the Church Missionary Society's Operations Is the Island: & Extracts from a Journal) James Selkirk. (C). 1993. text ed. 48.00 (*81-7013-109-X*, Pub. by Navrang) S Asia.

Recollections of Charley Russell. Harold G. Merriam. LC 63-18074. (Illus.). 196p. 1988. pap. 14.95 (*0-8061-2112-2*) U of Okla Pr.

Recollections of Country Joe. S. E. Lee. LC 75-31650. (Illus.). 104p. 1976. 11.95 (*0-88289-040-9*) Pelican.

Recollections of Dante Gabriel Rossetti & His Circle. Henry T. Dunn. Ed. by Gale Pedrick. LC 73-129379. reprint ed. 29.50 (*0-404-02222-7*) AMS Pr.

Recollections of DGB 1843: Rural Rides in South Australia. Daniel G. Brock. (C). 1981. 39.00 (*0-7855-0327-7*, Pub. by Royal Geograp Soc AT) St Mut.

Recollections of Early Texas: Memoirs of John Holland Jenkins. Ed. by John H. Jenkins, III. (Personal Narratives of the West Ser.). (Illus.). 347p. 1987. reprint ed. pap. 12.95 (*0-292-77037-5*) U of Tex Pr.

Recollections of Eminent Economists, 2 vols., 2. Ed. by J. A. Kregel. (C). 1989. text ed. 32.00 (*0-8147-4600-4*) NYU Pr.

Recollections of Eminent Economists, 2 vols., I. Ed. by J. A. Kregel. (C). 1989. text ed. 32.00 (*0-8147-4599-7*) NYU Pr.

Recollections of Eminent Economists, 2 vols., Set. Ed. by J. A. Kregel. (C). 1989. text ed. 72.00 (*0-8147-4601-2*) NYU Pr.

Recollections of Eugene P. Wigner As Told to Andrew Szanton. Andrew Szanton. LC 92-17040. (Illus.). 359p. (C). 1992. 24.50 (*0-306-44326-0*, Plenum Pr) Plenum.

Recollections of Frontier Life. Elizabeth A. Roe. Ed. by Annette K. Baxter. LC 79-8809. (Signal Lives Ser.). (Illus.). 1980. reprint ed. lib. bdg. 34.95 (*0-405-12855-X*) Ayer.

Recollections of Geoffrey Hamlyn. Henry Kinglsey. 1971. reprint ed. 24.00 (*0-403-01057-8*) Scholarly.

Recollections of Geoffry Hamlyn. Henry Kingsley. (BCL1-PR English Literature Ser.). 475p. 1992. reprint ed. lib. bdg. 99.00 (*0-7812-7580-6*) Rprt Serv.

Recollections of Great Memories. Lucille M. Asa. (Illus.). 48p. 1996. 9.00 (*0-8059-3969-5*) Dorrance.

Recollections of Grover Cleveland. George F. Parker. LC 70-165649. (Select Bibliographies Reprint Ser.). 1977. reprint ed. 36.95 (*0-8369-5958-2*) Ayer.

Recollections of James Lenox, & the Formation of His Library. Henry Stevens. (Illus.). 187p. 1951. 35.00 (*0-87104-155-3*) NY Pub Lib.

Recollections of Judy Greenwood. Ed. by Jean Nandi & Rica Anderson. (Illus.). 92p. (Orig.). 1990. pap. 10.00 (*0-9622023-3-9*) Bon Gout Pub.

***Recollections of Life in Ohio, from 1813 to 1840.** W. Cooper Howells. (Illus.). 207p. 1997. reprint ed. lib. bdg. 29.50 (*0-8328-6286-X*) Higginson Bk Co.

Recollections of Life in Ohio from 1813 to 1840. William C. Howells. LC 63-7082. 1977. reprint ed. 50.00 (*0-8201-1260-7*) Schol Facsimiles.

Recollections of Life in Ohio, 1813-1840. William C. Howells. 1993. reprint ed. lib. bdg. 89.00 (*0-7812-5378-0*) Rprt Serv.

Recollections of Literary Characters & Celebrated Places, 2 vols. in 1. Katherine Thomson. LC 70-37725. (Women of Letters Ser.). reprint ed. 90.00 (*0-404-56847-5*) AMS Pr.

Recollections of Long Life, 1829-1915. Isaac Stephenson. 1977. 18.95 (*0-8369-6991-X*, 7868) Ayer.

Recollections of Mary Lyon, with Selections from Her Instructions to the Pupils in Mt. Holyoke Female Seminary. Fidelia Fisk. 338p. 1995. reprint ed. pap. text ed. 10.00 (*0-933380-08-9*) Olive Pr Pubns.

Recollections of Mississippi & Mississippians. Davis Reuben. (American Biography Ser.). 456p. 1991. reprint ed. lib. bdg. 89.00 (*0-7812-8100-8*) Rprt Serv.

Recollections of My Era. Webb Young. (Illus.). 87p. (Orig.). 1989. pap. write for info. (*0-318-66627-8*) Pajarito Pr.

Recollections of My Life. Santiago R. Cajal. Tr. by E. Horne Craigie & Juan Cano from SPA. (Illus.). 688p. 1989. reprint ed. pap. 20.00 (*0-262-68060-2*) MIT Pr.

Recollections of Ninety-One Years. Lila Newsom. 1989. pap. 7.95 (*0-89137-116-8*) Quality Pubns.

Recollections of Ninety-Two Years 1824-1916. Elizabeth A. Meriwether. LC 94-23586. (Illus.). 256p. (Orig.). 1994. pap. 14.95 (*0-939009-84-6*) EPM Pubns.

Recollections of Persons & Places in the West. Henry M. Brachenridge. (Works of Henry Marie Brackenridge). 1989. reprint ed. lib. bdg. 79.00 (*0-7812-2030-0*) Rprt Serv.

Recollections of Phantom Ranch. Elizabeth Simpson. (Illus.). 28p. 1979. pap. 2.95 (*0-938216-08-2*) GCA.

Recollections of R J S Stevens: An Organist in Georgian London. Ed. by Mark Argent. (Music in Georgian & Victorian Society Ser.). (Illus.). 212p. (C). 1991. 34.95 (*0-8093-1790-7*) S Ill U Pr.

***Recollections of Reagan: A Portrait of Ronald Reagan.** Ed. by Peter Hannaford. LC 97-19129. (Illus.). 256p. 1997. write for info. (*0-688-14613-9*) Morrow.

Recollections of Regret. Pat'rick N. Pugh. (Illus.). (Orig.). pap. 7.95 (*1-883184-16-9*) PNP.

Recollections of Richard Dewey: Pioneer in American Psychiatry. Richard Dewey. Ed. by Ethel L. Dewey. LC 73-2395. (Mental Illness & Social Policy; the American Experience Ser.). 1973. reprint ed. 23.95 (*0-405-05203-0*) Ayer.

Recollections of Rossetti. Hall Caine. 1972. 59.95 (*0-8490-0935-9*) Gordon Pr.

Recollections of Rossetti. Hall Caine. LC 72-6285. (English Literature Ser.: No. 33). 267p. 1972. reprint ed. lib. bdg. 75.00 (*0-8383-1634-4*) M S G Haskell Hse.

Recollections of Seventy Years. Elizabeth R. Farrar. Ed. by Annette K. Baxter. LC 79-8791. (Signal Lives Ser.). 1980. reprint ed. lib. bdg. 37.95 (*0-405-12838-X*) Ayer.

Recollections of Seventy Years. Daniel A. Payne. LC 68-29015. (American Negro: His History & Literature, Ser. 1). (Illus.). 1969. reprint ed. 32.95 (*0-405-01834-7*) Ayer.

Recollections of Seventy Years, 2 vols., Set. Franklin B. Sanborn. (History - United States Ser.). 1992. reprint ed. lib. bdg. 150.00 (*0-7812-6162-7*) Rprt Serv.

Recollections of Solar Pons. Basil Copper. 1995. 25.00 (*1-878252-20-8*) Fedogan & Bremer.

Recollections of Solar Pons. limited ed. Basil Copper. 1995. 75.00 (*1-878252-21-6*) Fedogan & Bremer.

Recollections of Tartar Steppes & Their Inhabitants. Lucy Atkinson. 351p. 1972. reprint ed. 37.50 (*0-7146-1531-5*, Pub. by F Cass Pubs UK) Intl Spec Bk.

Recollections of Tartar Steppes & Their Inhabitants. Thomas W. Atkinson. LC 71-115503. (Russia Observed, Ser. 1). 1970. reprint ed. 23.95 (*0-405-03003-7*) Ayer.

Recollections of the American Congress on Surveying & Mapping. Walter S. Dix. 94p. 1991. 25.00 (*0-614-06109-1*, S294) Am Congrs Survey.

Recollections of the Catawba Valley. J. Alexander Mull & Gordon Boger. LC 82-20721. 1983. 6.50 (*0-913239-05-4*) Appalach Consortium.

Recollections of the Civil War. Charles A. Dana. LC 95-50715. xxix, 296p. 1996. pap. 12.95 (*0-8032-6601-4*, Bison Books) U of Nebr Pr.

***Recollections of the Early Republic: Selected Autobiographies.** Ed. by Joyce O. Appleby. LC 96-48086. (Illus.). 300p. 1997. text ed. 45.00 (*1-55553-302-7*); pap. text ed. 16.95 (*1-55553-301-9*) NE U Pr.

Recollections of the Early Settlement of Carroll County, Indiana. James H. Stewart. 372p. 1993. reprint ed. lib. bdg. 42.00 (*0-8328-3453-X*) Higginson Bk Co.

Recollections of the Early Settlement of the Wabash Valley. Sandford C. Cox. LC 78-117870. (Select Bibliographies Reprint Ser.). 1977. 24.95 (*0-8369-5323-1*) Ayer.

Recollections of the Golden Triangle. Alain Robbe-Grillet. Tr. by J. A. Underwood from FRE. LC 86-45233. Orig. Title: Souvenirs due triangle d'or. 160p. (C). 1986. reprint ed. pap. 11.00 (*0-8021-5200-7*, Grove) Grove-Atltic.

Recollections of the Jersey Prison Ship: From the Manuscript of Thomas Dring. Albert Greene. LC 92-6512. 148p. 1986. pap. 9.95 (*0-918222-92-3*) Applewood.

Recollections of the Last Days of Shelley & Byron. Edward J. Trelawny. LC 72-160998. (Select Bibliographies Reprint Ser.). 1977. reprint ed. 19.95 (*0-8369-5866-7*) Ayer.

Recollections of the Last Ten Years in the Valley of the Mississippi. 2nd ed. Timothy Flint. LC 68-24891. (American Scene Ser.). 1968. reprint ed. lib. bdg. 49.50 (*0-306-71136-2*) Da Capo.

Recollections of the Life of John O'Keeffe, 2 Vols. John O'Keeffe. LC 70-89711. 1972. 48.95 (*0-405-08828-0*) Ayer.

Recollections of the New Deal: When the People Mattered. Thomas H. Eliot. Ed. by John Kenneth Galbraith. 176p. 1992. text ed. 28.95 (*1-55553-134-2*) NE U Pr.

Recollections of the Old Quarter. William S. Gordon. LC 75-39084. (Black Heritage Library Collection). 1977. reprint ed. 21.95 (*0-8369-9022-6*) Ayer.

Recollections of the Peninsula. Moyle Sherer. 1996. 29.95 (*1-885119-36-4*) Sarpedon.

***Recollections of the Peninsula.** Moyle Sherer. 1996. 37.95 (*1-873376-66-9*) Sarpedon.

***Recollections of the Pioneers of Lee County, Illinois.** (Illus.). 583p. 1997. reprint ed. lib. bdg. 62.00 (*0-8328-5760-2*) Higginson Bk Co.

Recollections of the Powys Brothers. Intro. by Belinda Humfrey. 288p. 1980. 30.00 (*0-317-65921-9*, Pub. by P Owen Ltd UK) Dufour.

Recollections of the Powys Brothers. Ed. by Belinda Humfrey. 288p. 8000. 32.00 (*0-7206-0547-4*) Dufour.

Recollections of the Third Republic. Joseph Paul-Boncour. 9.95 (*0-8315-0050-6*) Speller.

Recollections of the Youkon. Francois Mercier. Ed. by Linda F. Yarborough. (Alaska Historical Commission Studies in History: No. 188). (Illus.). 1986p. (Orig.). 1986. pap. 10.00 (*0-943712-19-X*) Alaska Hist.

Recollections of Thirteen Presidents. John S. Wise. LC 68-55865. (Essay Index Reprint Ser.). 1977. 23.95 (*0-8369-1005-2*) Ayer.

***Recollections of Trauma: Scientific Evidence & Clinical Practice.** Ed. by D. Read & S. Lindsay. LC 97-17155. (NATO ASI Series A, Life Sciences: Vol. 291). (C). 1997. write for info. (*0-306-45618-4*, Plenum Pr) Plenum.

Recollections of Virginia Woolf by Her Contemporaries. Ed. by Joan R. Noble. 208p. 1994. reprint ed. pap. text ed. 16.95 (*0-8214-1105-5*) Ohio U Pr.

Recollections of West Hunan. Sehn Congwen. 196p. 1995. lib. bdg. 29.00 (*0-8095-4517-9*) Borgo Pr.

Recollections of West Hunan. Congwen Shen. Tr. by Gladys Yang from CHI. 196p. (Orig.). 1982. pap. 6.95 (*0-295-96016-7*) U of Wash Pr.

***Recollections of Yesterday.** Ed. by Melissa Mitchell. 1996. 69.95 (*1-57553-151-8*) Watermrk Pr.

Recollections, Personal & Literary. Richard H. Stoddard. LC 76-153874. reprint ed. 39.50 (*0-404-06280-6*) AMS Pr.

Recollections, Personal & Literary. Richard H. Stoddard. (American Biography Ser.). 333p. 1991. reprint ed. lib. bdg. 79.00 (*0-7812-8368-X*) Rprt Serv.

Recollections, Personal & Literary. Richard H. Stoddard. (BCL1-PS American Literature Ser.). 333p. 1992. reprint ed. lib. bdg. 89.00 (*0-7812-6868-0*) Rprt Serv.

Recollective Resolve: A Phenomenological Understanding of Time & Myth. Sanford Krolick. LC 87-1581. 160p. 1987. 24.95 (*0-86554-248-1*, MUP H-214) Mercer Univ Pr.

Recolonization & Resistance: Southern Africa in the 1990s. John S. Saul. LC 93-4675. 1993. 39.95 (*0-86543-389-5*); pap. 12.95 (*0-86543-390-9*) Africa World.

Recombinant & Synthetic Vaccines. Ed. by Gursaran P. Talwar et al. 512p. 1995. 121.00 (*0-387-57527-8*) Spr-Verlag.

Recombinant Bovine Growth Hormone: FDA Approval Should Be Withheld until the Mastitis Issue Is Resolved. 64p. (Orig.). (C). 1993. pap. text ed. 20.00 (*1-56806-394-6*) DIANE Pub.

***Recombinant Cell Surface Receptors: Focal Point for Therapeutic Intervention.** Michael J. Browne. LC 96-43707. (Biotechnology Intelligence Unit Ser.). 214p. 1996. 79.95 (*1-57059-410-4*) R G Landes.

Recombinant DNA. 2nd ed. James D. Watson. (C). 1995. pap. text ed. write for info. (*0-7167-2282-8*) W H Freeman.

Recombinant DNA & Bacterial Fermentation, Vol. 1. Ed. by Jennifer A. Thomson. 285p. 1988. 178.00 (*0-8493-6022-6*, TP248, CRC Reprint) Franklin.

***Recombinant DNA & Biotechnology: A Guide for Teachers.** Helen Kreuzer & Adrianne Massey. (Illus.). 564p. (Orig.). 1996. teacher ed., pap. text ed. 39.95 (*1-55581-101-9*); student ed., pap. text ed. 35.95 (*1-55581-110-8*) Am Soc Microbio.

Recombinant DNA & Technology: Concepts & Biomedical Applications. Mark Steinberg et al. 256p. 1993. text ed. 76.00 (*0-13-221995-6*) P-H.

Recombinant DNA Basics - a Primer: Programmed Learning. Edith Z. Helman. (Illus.). 60p. 1993. pap. 17.95 (*0-910224-15-3*) Berkeley Sci.

Recombinant DNA Biotechnology III: The Integration of Biological & Engineering Sciences. Ed. by Juan A. Asenjo & Barbara A. Andrews. LC 96-7239. (Annals of the New York Academy of Sciences: Vol. 782). 569p. 1996. 160.00 (*0-89766-961-4*); pap. write for info. (*0-89766-962-2*) NY Acad Sci.

Recombinant DNA Experiments: An Introduction. R. L. Rodriguez & R. C. Tait. 1983. pap. text ed. 29.25 (*0-201-10870-4*) Benjamin-Cummings.

Recombinant DNA Laboratory Manual. 2nd rev. ed. Judith W. Zyskind & Sanford I. Bernstein. (Illus.). 224p. 1992. pap. 32.00 (*0-12-784401-5*) Acad Pr.

Recombinant DNA Methodology. Ed. by Ray Wu & Kivie Moldave. (Selected Methods in Enzymology Ser.). 750p. 1989. spiral bd. 45.00 (*0-12-765560-3*) Acad Pr.

An Asterisk (*) at the beginning of an entry indicates that the title is appearing in BIP for the first time.

R

Recombinant DNA Methodology II. Ed. by Ray Wu et al. LC 95-18967. (Selected Methods in Enzymology Ser.). (Illus.). 904p. 1995. spiral bd. 69.95 (*0-12-765561-1*) Acad Pr.

Recombinant DNA Products: Insulin, Interferon & Growth Hormone. Arthur P. Bollon. 208p. 1985. 118.00 (*0-8493-5542-7*, QH442, CRC Reprint) Franklin.

Recombinant DNA Research & the Human Prospect. Ed. by Earl D. Hanson. (Other Technical Bks.). 129p. 1983. text ed. 21.95 (*0-8412-0750-X*); pap. text ed. 16.95 (*0-8412-0754-2*) Am Chemical.

***Recombinant DNA Research & the Human Prospect: A Sesquicentennial Symposium of Wesleyan University, Middletown, CT, March 4-6, 1982.** Ed. by Earl D. Hanson. LC 82-20613. (Illus.). 170p. 1983. reprint ed. pap. 48.50 (*0-608-04347-8*, 2065127) Bks Demand.

Recombinant DNA Research & Viruses. Ed. by Yechiel Becker. (Developments in Molecular Virology Ser.). 1984. lib. bdg. 133.00 (*0-89838-683-7*) Kluwer Ac.

Recombinant DNA Techniques. Velten. 1993. write for info. (*0-8493-8684-5*) CRC Pr.

Recombinant DNA Technologies in Neuroendocrinology. Ed. by Hirro Imura. LC 92-48664. (Current Topics in Neuroendocrinology Ser.: Vol. 11). 1992. 217.00 (*0-387-55455-6*) Spr-Verlag.

Recombinant DNA Technology I. Ed. by Ales Prokop & Rakesh K. Bajpai. LC 92-5973. (Annals Ser.: Vol. 646). 386p. 1992. pap. 115.00 (*0-89766-674-7*, TP248) NY Acad Sci.

Recombinant DNA Technology II. Ed. by Rakesh K. Bajpai & Ales Prokop. LC 94-14381. (Annals of the New York Academy of Sciences Ser.: Vol. 721). 1994. write for info. (*0-89766-821-9*); pap. 110.00 (*0-89766-822-7*) NY Acad Sci.

Recombinant DNA Vaccines: Rationale & Strategy. Ed. by Richard E. Issacson. LC 92-17708. 432p. 1992. 145.00 (*0-8247-8699-8*) Dekker.

***Recombinant Gene Expression Protocols.** Ed. by Ricky S. Tuan. (Methods in Molecular Biology Ser.: Vol. 62). 532p. 1997. 99.50 (*0-89603-480-1*) Humana.

Recombinant Gene Expression Protocols. Ed. by Rocky S. Tuan. (Methods in Molecular Biology Ser.: Vol. 62). 532p. 1997. spiral bd. 74.50 (*0-89603-333-3*) Humana.

***Recombinant Human A-Macroglobulins: Analysis of Two Functional Domains: The Internal Thiol Ester & the Bait Domain.** Luc Van Rompaey. (Acta Biomedica Lovaniensia Ser.: No. 132). (Illus.). 113p. (Orig.). 1996. pap. 39.50 (*90-6186-748-7*, Pub. by Leuven Univ BE) Coronet Bks.

Recombinant Inteferons: New Aspects in Research & Therapy. Ed. by S. Eckhardt. (Journal: Oncology: Vol. 42, Suppl. 1, 1985). iv, 46p. 1985. pap. 22.50 (*3-8055-4238-0*) S Karger.

Recombinant Lymphokines & Their Receptors. Ed. by Steven Gillis. LC 87-8856. (Immunology Ser.: No. 35). 357p. 1987. reprint ed. pap. 101.80 (*0-608-01304-8*, 2062049) Bks Demand.

Recombinant Microbes for Industrial & Agricultural Applications. Ed. by Murooka & Imanaka. (Bioprocess Technology Ser.: Vol. 19). 896p. 1993. 220.00 (*0-8247-9141-X*) Dekker.

Recombinant Molecules: Impact on Science & Society. fac. ed. Ed. by Roland F. Beers, Jr. & Edward G. Bassett. LC 76-5675. (Miles International Symposium Ser.: No. 10). (Illus.). 554p. pap. 157.90 (*0-7837-7512-1*, 2046993) Bks Demand.

Recombinant Poxviruses. Binns. 368p. 1992. 224.95 (*0-8493-6179-6*, QR412) CRC Pr.

***Recombinant Protein Production from Plants: Production & Isolation of Clinically Useful Compounds.** Ed. by Charlie Cunningham & Andy Porter. (Methods in Biotechnology Ser.: Vol. 3). (Illus.). 320p. 1997. 89.50 (*0-89603-390-2*) Humana.

Recombinant Protein Protocols: Detection & Isolation. Ed. by Rocky S. Tuan. LC 97-4023. (Methods in Molecular Biology Ser.: Vol. 63). 472p. 1997. spiral bd. 74.50 (*0-89603-400-3*) Humana.

***Recombinant Proteins Protocols: Detection & Isolation.** Ed. by Rocky S. Tuan. (Methods in Molecular Biology Ser.: Vol. 63). 472p. 1997. 99.50 (*0-89603-481-X*) Humana.

Recombinant Technology in Hemostasis & Thrombosis. Ed. by Leon W. Hoyer & W. N. Drohan. (Advances in Experimental Medicine & Biology Ser.). (Illus.). 248p. 1991. 79.50 (*0-306-43893-3*, Plenum Pr) Plenum.

Recombinant Vectors in Vaccine Development. Ed. by F. Brown. (Developments in Biological Standardization Ser.: Vol. 82). (Illus.). viii, 272p. 1994. pap. 217.50 (*3-8055-5997-6*) S Karger.

Recombination at the DNA Level. Cold Spring Harbor Symposia on Quantitative Biology Staff. LC 34-8174. (Cold Spring Harbor Symposia on Quantitative Biology Ser.: Vol. 49). (Illus.). 880p. 1984. pap. 180.00 (*0-7837-8988-2*, 2049766) Bks Demand.

Recombination in Semiconductors. Peter T. Landsberg. (Illus.). 600p. (C). 1992. text ed. 195.00 (*0-521-36122-2*) Cambridge U Pr.

Recombination in Semiconductors: Selected Proceedings of the International Conference Held at the University of Southampton, England. 30 August - 1st September 1978. Ed. by Peter T. Landsberg & A F Willoughby. 1979. pap. 63.00 (*0-08-024226-X*, Pergamon Pr) Elsevier.

Recombination of Atomic Ions. Ed. by W. G. Graham et al. LC 92-18584. (NATO ASI Series B, Physics: Vol. 296). 334p. 1992. 105.00 (*0-306-44243-4*, Plenum Pr) Plenum.

Recombination, Variability & Evolution: Algorithms of Estimation & Population Genetics. A. B. Korol. 376p. (gr. 13). 1994. text ed. 120.95 (*0-412-49410-8*) Chapman & Hall.

Recombinational Repair of Damage. Andrei Kuzminov. (Medicine Ser.). 1996. text ed. 69.95 (*0-412-10671-X*) Van Nos Reinhold.

Recombinational Repair of DNA Damage. Andrei Kuzminov. (Molecular Biology Intelligence Unit Ser.). 211p. 1996. 89.95 (*1-57059-373-6*) R G Landes.

Recomendaciones e Informes del Comite Jurico Interamericano Documetos Oficiales: Vol. 2, 1974-1977. Oas General Secretariat Staff. 675p. (C). 1981. 50.00 (*0-8270-1284-5*) OAS.

Recomendaciones e Informes, 1981, Vol. XIII. OAS, General Secretariat of Development & Codification of International Law. (Comite Juridico Interamericano Ser.). 125p. (C). 1981. pap. 8.00 (*0-8270-1441-4*) OAS.

Recommendations on Equipment for the Towing of Disabled Tankers. OCIMF Staff. 1981. 150.00 (*0-317-61454-1*, Pub. by Witherby & Co UK) St Mut.

Recommandations CIPR: (French Edition of ICRP 60, 1990 Recommendations) H. P. Jammet. 221p. (FRE.). 1993. pap. 84.75 (*0-08-042275-6*, Pergamon Pr) Elsevier.

Recommendation Concerning Fire Safety Requirements for Cargo Ships. IMO Staff. (FRE.). (C). 1976. 35.00 (*0-7855-0006-5*, IMO 849F, Pub. by Intl Maritime Org UK) St Mut.

Recommendation Concerning Fire Safety Requirements for Passenger Ships Carrying Not More Than 36 Passengers. IMO Staff. (C). 1978. English ed. 25.00 (*0-7855-0003-0*, IMO 842E, Pub. by Intl Maritime Org UK); French ed. 25.00 (*0-685-74527-9*, IMO 843F, Pub. by Intl Maritime Org UK) St Mut.

Recommendation Concerning Regulations for Machinery & Electrical Installations in Passenger & Cargo Ships. IMO Staff. (FRE.). (C). 1976. French ed. 22.00 (*0-7855-0002-2*, IMO 837F, Pub. by Intl Maritime Org UK); Spanish ed. 22.00 (*0-685-74528-7*, IMO 328S, Pub. by Intl Maritime Org UK) St Mut.

Recommendation for Manifolds Refrigerated Liquefied Natural Gas Carriers, LNG. OCIMF Staff. 1994. 70.00 (*1-85609-066-3*, Pub. by Witherby & Co UK) St Mut.

Recommendation for the Design & Construction of Refrigerated Liquified Gas Storage Tanks. EEMUA Staff. 1986. 125.00 (*0-85931-113-9*, Pub. by EEMUA UK) St Mut.

Recommendation for the Format of Bills of Lading. ICS Staff. (C). 1978. 85.00 (*0-906270-00-6*, Pub. by Witherby & Co UK) St Mut.

Recommendation on International Effluent Standards & Guidelines for Performance Tests for Sewage Treatment Plants. International Maritime Organization Staff. 1977. text ed. 55.00 (*0-89771-966-2*, Pub. by Intl Maritime Org UK) St Mut.

Recommendations & Guidelines for Linked Ship - Shore Emergency Shut-Down of Liquefied Gas Cargo Transfer. SIGTTO Staff. (C). 1987. 75.00 (*0-685-26150-6*, Pub. by Witherby & Co UK) St Mut.

Recommendations & Guidelines for Linked Ship- Shore Emergency Shut-Down of Liquified Gas Cargo Transfer. SIGTTO Staff. (C). 1987. 75.00 (*0-685-31793-5*, Pub. by Witherby & Co UK) St Mut.

Recommendations & Guidelines for Linked Ship-Shore Emergency Shut-Down of Liquefied Gas Cargo Transfer. SIGTTO Staff. (C). 1987. 120.00 (*0-948691-39-5*, Pub. by Witherby & Co UK) St Mut.

Recommendations & Guidelines for Trade Efficiency. 106p. 1994. 36.00 (*92-1-112363-1*, E.94.II.D.29) UN.

Recommendations de la Comision Internationale de Protection Radiologique. International Commission on Radiological Protection. Ed. by A. Duchene & H. Jammet. (International Commission of Radiological Protection Ser.: No. 26). 63p. (FRE.). 1980. pap. 19.75 (*0-08-025529-9*, Pergamon Pr) Elsevier.

***Recommendations for a Telecommunications-Based Delivery System (for Higher Education in Missouri)** 137p. (Orig.). (C). 1997. pap. text ed. 35.00 (*0-7881-3838-3*) DIANE Pub.

Recommendations for Child Care Centers. rev. ed. Gary T. Moore et al. (Publications in Architecture & Urban Planning: No. R79-2). (Illus.). viii, 450p. 1994. 27.50 (*0-938744-06-2*) U of Wis Ctr Arch-Urban.

Recommendations for Child Play Areas. Uriel Cohen et al. (Publications in Architecture & Urban Planning: No. R79-1). (Illus.). vi, 380p. 1992. reprint ed. 25.00 (*0-938744-07-0*) U of Wis Ctr Arch-Urban.

Recommendations for Equipment Employed in the Mooring of Ships at Single Point Moorings. OCIMF Staff. (C). 1988. 80.00 (*0-948691-56-5*, Pub. by Witherby & Co UK) St Mut.

Recommendations for Equipment Employed in the Mooring of Ships at Single Point Moorings. OCIMF Staff. (C). 1991. 170.00 (*1-85609-020-5*, Pub. by Witherby & Co UK) St Mut.

Recommendations for Estimating Prestress Losses. Prestressed Concrete Institute Staff. (PCI Journal Reprints Ser.). 36p. 1975. pap. 12.00 (*0-318-19842-8*, JR162) P-PCI.

Recommendations for Improving Trustee Selection in Public Colleges & Universities. 54p. 1980. 11.00 (*0-318-17384-0*) Assn Gov Bds.

Recommendations for Manifolds for Refrigerated Liquefied Gas Carriers for Cargoes from 0'C to Minus 104'C. OCIMF Staff. (C). 1988. 80.00 (*0-685-36228-0*, Pub. by Witherby & Co UK) St Mut.

Recommendations for Manifolds for Refrigerated Liquified Gas Carriers for Cargos from 0 C to Minus 104 C. OCIMF Staff. (C). 1987. 80.00 (*0-685-31792-7*, Pub. by Witherby & Co UK) St Mut.

Recommendations for Offshore Sailing. U. S. Sailing Staff. (Illus.). 50p. 1996. pap. 7.50 (*1-882502-35-3*) US Sail Assn.

Recommendations for Offshore Sailing 1995: Including ORC Special Regulations. 42p. 1993. pap. text ed. 7.50 (*1-882502-24-8*) US Sail Assn.

Recommendations for Oil Tanker Manifolds & Associated Equipment. OCIMF Staff. (C). 1991. 115.00 (*1-85609-017-5*, Pub. by Witherby & Co UK) St Mut.

Recommendations for Standards in Hydraulics. Task Committee on Recommendations for Standards in Hydraulics. LC 94-4063. 1994. 18.00 (*0-87262-971-6*) Am Soc Civil Eng.

Recommendations for the Avoidance of Variable Penetration in Gas Tungsten Arc Welding. J. F. Lancaster & K. C. Mills. (Illus.). 44p. 1994. pap. 98.00 (*1-85573-148-7*, Pub. by Woodhead Pubng UK) Am Educ Systs.

Recommendations for the Design Calculation. P. Habib. (Illus.). 136p. (C). 1989. text ed. 70.00 (*90-6191-737-9*, Pub. by A A Balkema NE) Ashgate Pub Co.

Recommendations for the Design Calculation. P. Habib. (Illus.). 136p. (C). 1990. pap. 46.00 (*90-6191-736-0*, Pub. by A A Balkema NE) Ashgate Pub Co.

Recommendations for the Disposal of Chemical Agents & Munitions. Commission on Engineering & Technical Systems Staff. 220p. (Orig.). (C). 1994. pap. text ed. 34.00 (*0-309-05046-4*) Natl Acad Pr.

Recommendations for the Identifying Information to Be Placed on Write-Once-Read-Many (WORM) & Rewritable Optical Disk (OD) Cartridge Label(s) & Optical Disk Cartridge Packaging (Shipping Containers) AIIM TR21-1991. (TR21 Ser.). (Orig.). (C). 1991. 39.00 (*0-89258-232-4*) Assn Inform & Image Mgmt.

Recommendations for the Nineteen Ninety Censuses... 1987. 25.00 (*92-1-116412-5*, E 87.II.E.38) UN.

Recommendations for the Protection of Diesel Engines for Use in Zone 2 Hazardous Areas. EEMUA Staff. 1992. 125.00 (*0-85931-060-4*, Pub. by EEMUA UK) St Mut.

Recommendations for the Protection of Diesel Engines Operating in Hazardous Areas. (C). 1983. 130.00 (*0-685-54764-7*, Pub. by EEMUA UK) St Mut.

Recommendations for Tube End Welding Pt. 1: Tubular Heat Ransfer Equipment, Gerrous Materials. EEMUA Staff. 1977. 125.00 (*0-85931-093-0*, Pub. by EEMUA UK) St Mut.

Recommendations of the International Commission on Radiological Protection, 1990. ICRP Staff. (International Commission on Radiological Protection Ser.: No. 60). (Illus.). 215p. 1991. pap. 157.00 (*0-08-041144-4*, Pergamon Pr) Elsevier.

Recommendations on Equipment for the Towing of Disabled Tankers. OCIMF Staff. (C). 1981. 160.00 (*0-900886-65-X*, Pub. by Witherby & Co UK) St Mut.

***Recommendations on Equipment for the Towing of Disabled Tankers.** OCIMF Staff. 1997. pap. 200.00 (*1-85609-096-5*, Pub. by Witherby & Co UK) St Mut.

***Recommendations on Lipoprotein Measurement.** (Illus.). 186p. (C). 1996. reprint ed. pap. 35.00 (*0-7881-3362-4*) DIANE Pub.

Recommendations on the Safe Transport, Handling & Storage of Dangerous Substances in Port Areas, 1981 Edition. International Maritime Organization Staff. 1983. text ed. 25.00 (*0-89771-883-6*, Pub. by Intl Maritime Org UK) St Mut.

Recommendations on the Safe Transport, Handling & Storage of Dangerous Substances in Port Areas, 1983 Edition. International Maritime Organization Staff. 1983. text ed. 50.00 (*0-89771-882-8*, Pub. by Intl Maritime Org UK) St Mut.

Recommendations on the Safe Use of Pesticides in Ships. International Maritime Organization Staff. 1981. text ed. 90.00 (*0-89771-878-X*, Pub. by Intl Maritime Org UK) St Mut.

Recommendations on the Transport of Dangerous Goods. 5th rev. ed. 504p. 1987. pap. 55.00 (*92-1-139023-0*, E. 87.VIII.1) UN.

Recommendations on the Transport of Dangerous Goods. 6th rev. ed. 505p. 55.00 (*92-1-139027-3*, E.89.VIII.1) UN.

Recommendations on the Transport of Dangerous Goods. 6th rev. ed. United Nations Economic & Social Council Staff. (Illus.). 1990. ring bd. 65.00 (*0-940394-30-8*, UN-90A) Labelmaster.

Recommendations on the Transport of Dangerous Goods. 7th rev. ed. 515p. 1992. 70.00 (*92-1-139035-4*) UN.

Recommendations on the Transport of Dangerous Goods. 8th ed. 528p. 1993. 80.00 (*92-1-139042-7*) UN.

Recommendations on the Transport of Dangerous Goods. 9th ed. 549p. 1995. pap. 95.00 (*92-1-139048-6*) UN.

Recommendations on the Transport of Dangerous Goods: Tests & Criteria. 3rd ed. 324p. 1995. 60.00 (*92-1-139049-4*) UN.

Recommendations on the Transport of Dangerous Goods - Test & Criteria, Vol.VIII. 2nd ed. 324p. 1990. 45.00 (*92-1-139033-8*, 90.VIII.1) UN.

Recommendations on Tourism Statistics. 76p. 1994. 19.95 (*92-1-161362-0*) UN.

Recommendations Regarding the Use of Advanced Telecommunications Technologies to Improve Rural Health Education & Health Care Delivery in Minnesota. (Illus.). 141p. (Orig.). (C). 1995. pap. text ed. 30.00 (*0-7881-1962-1*) DIANE Pub.

Recommendations to the U. N. Commission on Sustainable Development. 1995. pap. 20.00 (*0-89553-301-4*) Am Solar Energy.

Recommended Aids for the Partially Sighted Including: A Nontechnical Explanation of Basic Optical Principles. 2nd rev. ed. Louise L. Sloan & Stephen J. Ryan. LC 79-28059. 64p. pap. 25.00 (*0-7837-0135-7*, 2040424) Bks Demand.

Recommended Basic Sets for Endosurgery. George Cristino. 108p. (C). text ed. 95.00 (*1-886974-02-0*) Inst Knowledge.

***Recommended Bed & Breakfasts in California: A Selective Guide to More Than 400 B&B Establishments Throughout California.** 7th rev. ed. Kathy Strong. Orig. Title: Bed & Breakfast in California. (Illus.). 320p. 1997. pap. 16.95 (*0-7627-0125-0*) Globe Pequot.

***Recommended Bed & Breakfasts in New England.** Eleanor Berman. LC 97-14816. (Illus.). 320p. 1997. pap. 16.95 (*0-7627-0120-X*) Globe Pequot.

***Recommended Bed & Breakfasts in the Mid-Atlantic States.** Suzi F. Chase. (Illus.). 320p. 1997. pap. 16.95 (*0-7627-0117-X*) Globe Pequot.

***Recommended Books in Spanish for Children & Young Adults, 1991-1995.** Isabel Schon. LC 96-3244. 1996. 42.50 (*0-8108-3235-6*) Scarecrow.

***Recommended Core Curriculum Guidelines on Culturally Sensitive & Competent Health Care.** 7p. 1996. reprint ed. write for info. (*0-614-23629-0*) Soc Tchrs Fam Med.

Recommended Country Hotels of Britain 1997. (Illus.). 160p. (Orig.). 1997. pap. 7.95 (*1-55650-766-6*) Hunter NJ.

***Recommended Country Hotels of Britain '98.** 98th ed. 160p. (Orig.). 1998. pap. 9.95 (*1-55650-806-9*) Hunter NJ.

Recommended Country Inns Mid-Atlantic & Cheseapeake Region. 7th rev. ed. Brenda B. Chapin. Ed. by Suzi F. Chase. (Recommended Country Inns Ser.). (Illus.). 432p. 1996. pap. 16.95 (*0-7627-0000-9*) Globe Pequot.

Recommended Country Inns New England. 15th rev. ed. Elizabeth Squier. (Recommended Country Inns Ser.). 432p. 1996. pap. 16.95 (*0-7627-0002-5*) Globe Pequot.

Recommended Country Inns Rocky Mountain Region. 6th rev. ed. Doris Kennedy. (Recommended Country Inns Ser.). (Illus.). 400p. 1996. pap. 16.95 (*0-7627-0004-1*) Globe Pequot.

Recommended Country Inns the Midwest. 6th rev. ed. Bob Puhala. (Recommended Country Inns Ser.). (Illus.). 480p. 1996. pap. 16.95 (*0-7627-0001-7*) Globe Pequot.

Recommended Country Inns the South. 6th rev. ed. Sara Pitzer. (Recommended Country Inns Ser.). (Illus.). 384p. 1996. pap. 16.95 (*0-7627-0003-3*) Globe Pequot.

Recommended Country Inns the Southwest. 6th rev. ed. Eleanor Morris. (Recommended Country Inns Ser.). (Illus.). 416p. 1996. pap. 16.95 (*0-7627-0006-8*) Globe Pequot.

Recommended Country Inns West Coast. rev. ed. Julianne Belote. (Recommended Country Inns Ser.). (Illus.). 480p. 1996. pap. 16.95 (*0-7627-0005-X*) Globe Pequot.

Recommended Data of Selected Compounds & Binary Mixtures: Tables, Diagrams & Calculations, 2 pts. K. Stephan & H. Hildwein. (Dechema Chemistry Data Ser.: Vol. 4, Pts. 1 & 2). (Illus.). 715p. 1987. text ed. 380.00 (*3-921567-80-7*, Pub. by Dechema GW) Scholium Intl.

Recommended Diagramming Standards for Analysts & Programmers. James Martin. (Illus.). 432p. 1986. text ed. 87.00 (*0-13-767377-9*) P-H.

Recommended Dietary Allowances. 10th ed. National Research Council, Subcommittee on Metabolic Modifiers Staff. 302p. 1989. 24.95 (*0-309-04041-8*); pap. 16.95 (*0-309-04633-5*) Natl Acad Pr.

Recommended Environments for Standards Laboratories. 1975. pap. 25.00 (*0-87664-391-8*, RP52.1) ISA.

Recommended Good Practice for Community Dump. (Six Hundred Ser.). pap. 16.75 (*0-685-58208-6*, IN 601-92) Natl Fire Prot.

Recommended Guide for the Prediction of the Dispersion of Airborne Effluents. 3rd ed. Ed. by M. E. Smith & J. R. Martin. LC 90-75471. 87p. 1979. 10.00 (*0-686-62958-2*, H00037) ASME.

Recommended Guidelines for Feed Mills Subject to FDA Inspection. 94p. 1983. 15.00 (*0-318-01823-3*) Am Feed Industry.

Recommended Guidelines for Plants Subject to OSHA Inspection. 81p. 1981. 15.00 (*0-318-01825-X*) Am Feed Industry.

Recommended Guidelines for Redundancy Design & Rating of Two-Girder Steel Bridges. (National Cooperative Highway Research Program Report Ser.: No. 319). 142p. 1989. 13.00 (*0-309-04616-5*) Transport Res Bd.

***Recommended Health-Based Limits in Occupational Exposure to Heavy Metals: Report of a WHO Study Group.** (Technical Report Ser.: No. 647). 116p. 1980. 8.00 (*92-4-120647-0*, 1100647) World Health.

Recommended Health-Based Limits in Occupational Exposure to Selected Mineral Dusts (Silica, Coal) (Technical Report Ser.: No. 734). 82p. 1986. pap. text ed. 12.00 (*92-4-120734-5*, 1100734) World Health.

***Recommended Health-Based Limits in Occupational Exposure to Selected Organic Solvents.** (Technical Report Ser.: No. 664). 84p. 1981. pap. text ed. 6.00 (*92-4-120664-0*) World Health.

***Recommended Health-Based Occupational Exposure Limits for Respiratory Irritants.** (Technical Report Ser.: No. 707). 154p. 1984. pap. text ed. 14.00 (*92-4-120707-8*) World Health.

***Recommended Health-Based Occupational Exposure Limits for Selected Vegetable Dusts.** (Technical Report Ser.: No. 684). 78p. 1983. pap. text ed. 6.00 (*92-4-120684-5*) World Health.

Recommended Instrumentation for Uranium & Thorium Exploration. (Technical Reports). 104p. (Orig.). 1974. pap. 19.00 (*92-0-145074-5*, IDC158, Pub. by IAEA AU) Bernan Associates.

Recommended Law Books. 2nd ed. LC 86-71141. 168p. 1986. pap. 24.95 (*0-89707-239-1*, 507-0070-01) Amer Bar Assn.

Recommended Lighting for Walkways & Class I Bikeways. (Design Guides Ser.). (Illus.). 16p. 1994. pap. 25.00 (*0-87995-106-0*, DG-5-94) Illum Eng.

An Asterisk (*) at the beginning of an entry indicates that the title is appearing in BIP for the first time.

Recommended Literature, Grades 9-12. California Department of Education Staff. (Illus.). 118p. 1990. pap. 8.00 (*0-8011-0831-4*) Calif Education.

***Recommended Maintenance Practices Manual.** rev. ed. 1996. text ed. 150.00 (*0-88711-347-8*) Am Trucking Assns.

Recommended Nomenclature for Physical Quantities in Medical Application of Light. M. Patterson et al. (Report Ser.: No. 57). 10p. (Orig.). 1996. write for info. (*1-888340-02-9*) AAPM.

Recommended Practice, File Format for Storage & Exchange of Image, Bi-Level Image File Format. ANSI Staff. 48p. 1993. pap. 52.00 (*0-89258-257-X*, MS53) Assn Inform & Image Mgmt.

Recommended Practice for Alphanumeric Computer-Output Microforms - Operational Practices for Inspection & Quality Control: ANSI-AIIM MS1-1996. Association for Information & Image Management Staff. 15p. 1996. pap. 33.00 (*0-89258-129-8*, MS01) Assn Inform & Image Mgmt.

Recommended Practice for Backflow Prevention & Cross-Connection Control, No. M14. 2nd rev. ed. 132p. 1990. pap. 45.00 (*0-89867-527-8*, 30014) Am Water Wks Assn.

Recommended Practice for Cleanroom Product & Support Equipment: RP-015-87-T. LC 62-38584. 10p. (Orig.). 1987. pap. text ed. 50.00 (*0-317-59762-0*, IES-RP-CC-015-8) Inst Environ Sci.

Recommended Practice for Design, Manufacture, & Installation of Prestressed Concrete Piling. (PCI Journal Reprints Ser.). 32p. 1985. pap. 12.00 (*0-318-19763-4*, JR187) P-PCI.

Recommended Practice for Electrical Installations in Petroleum Processing Plants. 3rd ed. 64p. 1991. 50.00 (*0-685-57382-6*, 822-54000) Am Petroleum.

Recommended Practice for Equipment Calibration or Validation Procedures: IES RP CC. 1986. 50.00 (*0-317-52597-2*, IES-RP-CC-013-86-T) Inst Environ Sci.

Recommended Practice for Erection of Precast Concrete. 96p. 1985. 25.00 (*0-318-35225-7*, MNL-127-85) P-PCI.

Recommended Practice for Field Match Flame Test for Textiles. 7p. 1993. 16.75 (*0-685-64961-X*, 705-93) Natl Fire Prot.

Recommended Practice for Frozen Food Distribution Centers. 1987. pap. 10.00 (*0-318-32896-8*) Am Inst Baking.

Recommended Practice for Glass Fiber Reinforced Concrete Panels. 92p. 1987. 20.00 (*0-318-35226-5*, MNL-128-87) P-PCI.

Recommended Practice for Grouting of Post-Tensioned Prestressed Concrete. Prestressed Concrete Institute Staff. (PCI Journal Reprints Ser.: No. 119). 8p. 1972. pap. 10.00 (*0-318-19838-X*, JR119) P-PCI.

Recommended Practice for Identification of Microforms: ANSI-AIIM MS19-1993. Association for Information & Image Management Staff. 1993. pap. 33.00 (*0-89258-120-4*, MS19) Assn Inform & Image Mgmt.

Recommended Practice for Inspection of Stored Silver-Gelatin Microforms for Evidence of Deterioration: ANSI-AIIM MS45-1990. Association for Information & Image Management Staff. 1990. pap. 33.00 (*0-89258-203-0*, MS45) Assn Inform & Image Mgmt.

Recommended Practice for Microfilming Printed Newspapers on 35mm Roll Microfilm: ANSI-AIIM MS111-1994. Association for Information & Image Management Staff. 1994. pap. 33.00 (*0-89258-258-8*) Assn Inform & Image Mgmt.

Recommended Practice for Microfilming Public Records on Silver-Halide Film: ANSI-AIIM MS48-1990. Association for Information & Image Management Staff. 1990. pap. 33.00 (*0-89258-199-9*, MS48) Assn Inform & Image Mgmt.

Recommended Practice for Microphotography of Cartographic Materials: ANSI-AIIM MS37-1996. Association for Information & Image Management Staff. 1996. pap. 33.00 (*0-89258-141-7*, MS37) Assn Inform & Image Mgmt.

Recommended Practice for Operational Procedures - Inspection & Quality Control of Duplicate Microforms of Documents & from COM: ANSI-AIIM MS43-1988. Association for Information & Image Management Staff. 1988. pap. 39.00 (*0-89258-140-9*) Assn Inform & Image Mgmt.

Recommended Practice for Operational Procedures, Quality Control & Inspection of Graphic Computer-Output Microforms: ANSI-AIIM MS39-1987. Association for Information & Image Management Staff. 1987. pap. 33.00 (*0-89258-106-9*, MS39) Assn Inform & Image Mgmt.

Recommended Practice for Precast Post-Tensioned Segmental Construction. 52p. 1982. pap. 18.00 (*0-685-06886-2*, JR-252) P-PCI.

Recommended Practice for Precast Prestressed Concrete Circular Storage Tanks. 48p. 1987. 22.00 (*0-318-35237-0*, JR-334) P-PCI.

Recommended Practice for Producing Quality Instrument Air. rev. ed. 1984. reprint ed. pap. 25.00 (*0-87664-845-6*, RP7.7) ISA.

Recommended Practice for Quality Control of Image Scanners: ANSI-AIIM MS44-1988(R1993) Association for Information & Image Management Staff. 1988. pap. 39.00 (*0-89258-167-0*, MS44) Assn Inform & Image Mgmt.

Recommended Practice for the Expungement, Deletion, Correction or Amendment of Records on Microforms: ANSI-AIIM MS42-1989. (Illus.). 6p. 1989. pap. text ed. 33.00 (*0-89258-173-5*, MS42) Assn Inform & Image Mgmt.

Recommended Practice for the Requirements & Characteristics of Original Documents Intended for Optical Scanning. (Illus.). 6p. 1991. pap. text ed. 39.00 (*0-89258-234-0*, MS52) Assn Inform & Image Mgmt.

Recommended Practice for the Requirements & Characteristics of Original Documents That May Be Microfilmed: ANSI-AIIM MS35-1990. Association for Information & Image Management Staff. 1990. pap. 33.00 (*0-89258-211-1*, MS35) Assn Inform & Image Mgmt.

Recommended Practice for Use of High Range Water Reducing Admixtures in Precast Prestressed Concrete Operations. (PCI Journal Reprints Ser.). 24p. 1985. pap. 14.00 (*0-318-19774-X*, JR247) P-PCI.

Recommended Practice No. SNT-TC-1A. 1984. pap. 37.00 (*0-931403-52-9*, 2035) Am Soc Nondestructive.

***Recommended Practice No. SNT-TC-1A: 1996 Edition.** 118p. (C). 1996. pap. 41.60 (*1-57117-050-2*, 2055) Am Soc Nondestructive.

Recommended Practice No. SNT-TC-1A, 1988. American Society for Nondestructive Testing (ASNT) Staff. 1989. 41.60 (*0-931403-50-2*, 2045) Am Soc Nondestructive.

Recommended Practice No. SNT-TC-1A, 1992. 106p. 1993. pap. text ed. 41.60 (*0-931403-18-9*, 2050) Am Soc Nondestructive.

Recommended Practices & Procedures for Welding Low Carbon Steel Pipe (D10.12-89) (Illus.). 58p. 1989. pap. 27.00 (*0-87171-300-4*) Am Welding.

Recommended Practices for Air Carbon Arc Gouging & Cutting (C5.3-91) (Illus.). 19p. 1991. pap. 21.00 (*0-87171-351-9*) Am Welding.

Recommended Practices for Automotive Weld Quality - Resistance Spot Welding (D8.7-88) (Illus.). 16p. 1988. 27.00 (*0-87171-292-X*) Am Welding.

Recommended Practices for Design, Manufacture, & Inspection of Critical Brazed Components (C3.3-80) 14p. 1980. 21.00 (*0-87171-211-3*) Am Welding.

Recommended Practices for Design Professionals Engaged As Experts in the Resolution of Construction Industry Disputes. 5.00 (*0-614-05193-2*, RP05893.0M) ASFE.

Recommended Practices for Electrogas Welding (C5.7-89) (Illus.). 64p. 1989. 36.00 (*0-87171-312-8*) Am Welding.

Recommended Practices for Friction Welding (C6.1-89) (Illus.). 27p. 1989. 36.00 (*0-87171-309-8*) Am Welding.

Recommended Practices for Gas Metal Arc Welding (C5.6-89) 65p. 1989. 36.00 (*0-87171-301-2*) Am Welding.

Recommended Practices for Gas Shielded Arc Welding of Aluminum & Aluminum Alloy Pipe (D10.7-86) (Illus.). 41p. 1986. 21.00 (*0-87171-260-1*) Am Welding.

Recommended Practices for Gas Tungsten Arc Welding (C5.5-80) 46p. 1980. 36.00 (*0-87171-193-1*) Am Welding.

Recommended Practices for Gas Tungsten Arc Welding of Titanium Piping & Tubing (D10.6-91) (Illus.). 12p. 1991. 21.00 (*0-87171-357-8*) Am Welding.

Recommended Practices for Laying Concrete Block. 24p. 1993. 11.00 (*0-89312-168-1*, PA043M) Portland Cement.

Recommended Practices for Local Heating of Welds in Piping & Tubing (D10.10-90) (Illus.). 1990. 27.00 (*0-87171-343-8*) Am Welding.

Recommended Practices for Plasma-Arc Cutting (C5.2-83) (Illus.). 13p. 1983. pap. 21.00 (*0-87171-219-9*) Am Welding.

Recommended Practices for Plasma-Arc Welding (C5.1-73) (Illus.). 68p. 1973. pap. text ed. 21.00 (*0-87171-107-9*) Am Welding.

Recommended Practices for Resistance Welding (C1.1-66) 115p. 1966. 21.00 (*0-317-33300-3*) Am Welding.

Recommended Practices for Root Pass Welding of Pipe Without Backing (D10.11-87) 20p. 1987. pap. 21.00 (*0-87171-274-1*) Am Welding.

Recommended Practices for Shielding Gases for Welding & Plasma Arc Cutting (C5.10-94) (Illus.). 46p. 1994. pap. 39.00 (*0-87171-423-X*) Am Welding.

Recommended Practices for Stud Welding (C5.4-93) (Illus.). 26p. 1993. pap. 27.00 (*0-87171-418-3*) Am Welding.

Recommended Practices for the Welding of Rails & Related Rail Components for Use by Rail Vehicles (D15.2-94) (Illus.). 29p. 1994. pap. 39.00 (*0-87171-424-8*) Am Welding.

Recommended Practices for Ultrasonic Inspection of Brazed Joints (C3.8-90) 2p. 1990. pap. 21.00 (*0-87171-325-X*) Am Welding.

Recommended Practices for Welding Authentic Chromium-Nickel Stainless Steel Piping & Tubing (D10.4-86) Illus. by Summit Technical Associates Staff. 34p. 1986. pap. 16.00 (*0-87171-267-9*) Am Welding.

Recommended Practices in Gifted Education: A Critical Analysis. Bruce M. Shore et al. (Education & Psychology of the Gifted Ser.: No. 7). 392p. (C). 1991. text ed. 46.00 (*0-8077-3084-X*) Tchrs Coll.

***Recommended Procedure for Carburized Aerospace Gearing.** AGMA Technical Committee. (Standard Ser.: Vol. 246.02A). Date not set. pap. text ed. 45.00 (*1-55589-027-X*) AGMA.

Recommended Procedures for Disease & Serological Surveillance, As Part of the Global Rinderpest Eradication Programme. (Illus.). 51p. (Orig.). (C). 1995. pap. text ed. 25.00 (*0-7881-1950-8*) DIANE Pub.

Recommended Procedures for the Safety Performance Evaluation of Highway Appurtenances. (National Cooperative Highway Research Program Report Ser.: No. 230). 42p. 1981. 6.00 (*0-309-03155-9*) Transport Res Bd.

Recommended Publications for Legal Research, 1979. Compiled by Oscar J. Miller & Mortimer D. Schwartz. (Orig.). 1985. pap. text ed. 37.50 (*0-8377-2527-5*) Rothman.

Recommended Publications for Legal Research, 1980. Oscar J. Miller et al. LC 86-17669. 1986. 37.50 (*0-8377-2529-1*) Rothman.

Recommended Publications for Legal Research, 1981. Oscar J. Miller & Mortimer D. Schwartz. LC 87-10106. 1987. 37.50 (*0-8377-2533-X*) Rothman.

Recommended Publications for Legal Research, 1983. Oscar J. Miller & Mortimer D. Schwartz. LC 87-4837. 1987. 37.50 (*0-8377-2531-3*) Rothman.

Recommended Publications for Legal Research, 1984. Oscar J. Miller & Mortimer D. Schwartz. LC 86-3253. 1986. 37.50 (*0-8377-2528-3*) Rothman.

Recommended Publications for Legal Research, 1985. Oscar J. Miller & Mortimer D. Schwartz. LC 86-31543. 1987. 37.50 (*0-8377-2530-5*) Rothman.

Recommended Publications for Legal Research, 1986. Oscar J. Miller & Mortimer D. Schwartz. LC 87-12723. 1987. 37.50 (*0-8377-2532-1*) Rothman.

Recommended Reading: 500 Classics Reviewed. Salem Press Editors. LC 95-15947. 320p. (YA). (gr. 9-12). 1995. lib. bdg. 35.00 (*0-89356-911-9*) Salem Pr.

Recommended Reading Dossier: A Guide to English & Foreign Language Publications in Graphology & Related Areas. AHAF Research Committee Staff. 24p. 1984. pap. text ed. 9.95 (*1-877772-05-4*) AHAF.

Recommended Readings in Literature, K-8. (Illus.). 146p. (C). 1996. pap. 25.00 (*0-7881-2722-5*) DIANE Pub.

***Recommended Readings in Literature, K-8.** annot. rev. ed. California Department of Education Staff. (Illus.). 176p. 1996. 10.00 (*0-8011-1171-4*, 1171) Calif Education.

Recommended Readings in Spanish Literature, K-8. California Department of Education Staff. 64p. 1991. pap. 7.00 (*0-8011-0895-0*) Calif Education.

Recommended Reference Books for Small & Medium-Sized Libraries & Media Centers, 1992. Ed. by Bohdan S. Wynar. 300p. 1992. lib. bdg. 38.50 (*0-87287-976-3*) Libs Unl.

Recommended Reference Books for Small & Medium-Sized Libraries & Media Centers, 1993. Ed. by Bohdan S. Wynar & Anna G. Patterson. 300p. 1993. lib. bdg. 39.50 (*1-56308-155-5*) Libs Unl.

Recommended Reference Books for Small & Medium-Sized Libraries & Media Centers, 1994. Ed. by Bohdan S. Wynar. 300p. 1994. lib. bdg. 45.00 (*1-56308-283-7*) Libs Unl.

Recommended Reference Books for Small & Medium-Sized Libraries & Media Centers 1995. Ed. by Bohdan S. Wynar. 300p. 1995. lib. bdg. 45.00 (*1-56308-352-3*) Libs Unl.

Recommended Reference Books for Small & Medium-Sized Libraries & Media Centers, 1996. Ed. by S. Wynar Bohdan. 287p. 1996. lib. bdg. 45.00 (*1-56308-432-5*) Libs Unl.

***Recommended Reference Books for Small & Medium Sized Libraries & Media Centers, 1997.** Ed. by Bohdan S. Wynar. 300p. 1997. lib. bdg. 45.00 (*1-56308-555-0*) Libs Unl.

Recommended Reference Books in Paperback. 2nd ed. Ed. by Andrew L. March. LC 92-15875. 350p. 1992. lib. bdg. 47.50 (*1-56308-067-2*) Libs Unl.

Recommended Reference Materials for Realization/Physiochemical Properties. Marsh. 1991. 99.00 (*0-632-01718-X*) CRC Pr.

Recommended Research Issues for the Future Study of the State's Above-Ground Historic Resources. Maryland Historical Trust Staff. (White Papers Series on Preservation Planning: No. 4). 11p. 1987. 2.00 (*1-878399-22-5*) Div Hist Cult Progs.

Recommended Research Questions for the Study of Maryland's Archaeological Resources. (White Papers Series on Preservation Planning: No. 3). 15p. 1987. 2.00 (*1-878399-21-7*) Div Hist Cult Progs.

Recommended Romantic Inns. 3rd rev. ed. Recommended Country Inns Series Authors. (Illus.). 384p. 1996. pap. 16.95 (*0-7627-0007-6*) Globe Pequot.

Recommended Safe Practices for Electron Beam Welding & Cutting (F2.1-78) 8p. 1978. pap. 21.00 (*0-87171-158-3*) Am Welding.

Recommended Safe Practices for the Preparation for Welding & Cutting of Containers & Piping (F4.1-94) 12p. 1994. pap. 21.00 (*0-87171-439-6*) Am Welding.

Recommended SI & Other Metric Units for the Petroleum & Petrochemical Industries, Including Basic Rules of the Oil Companies Materials Association. rev. ed. Institute of Petroleum (Great Britain) Staff. LC 72-104038. 18p. reprint ed. pap. 25.00 (*0-317-26012-X*, 2023699) Bks Demand.

***Recommended Standards for a College Health Program.** Ed. by Elizabeth D. Langan et al. 80p. 1991. pap. 100.00 (*0-614-30085-1*) Am Coll Hlth.

Recommended Standards for Cataloguing-in-Publication: The CIP Data Sheet & the CIP Record in the Book. Ed. by International Federation of Library Associations & Institutions Staff. iii, 30p. reprint ed. pap. 30.00 (*3-598-10964-4*) K G Saur.

Recommended System for the Indentification of the Fire Hazards of Materials. (Seven Hundred Ser.). 1990. pap. 16.75 (*0-685-58213-2*, 704-90) Natl Fire Prot.

Recommended Tax Law Changes. American Institute of Certified Public Accountants. LC 82-165275. 105p. reprint ed. 30.00 (*0-685-16112-9*, 2027575) Bks Demand.

Recommended Videos for Schools. Ed. by Beth Blenz-Clucas & Gloria Gribble. LC 91-13091. 300p. 1991. lib. bdg. 55.00 (*0-87436-644-5*) ABC-CLIO.

Recommended Videos for Schools. 2nd ed. Ed. by Tiniki Roxton. 300p. 1992. lib. bdg. 55.00 (*0-87436-688-7*) ABC-CLIO.

***Recommended Wayside & Country Inns of Britain '98.** 98th ed. (Illus.). 160p. (Orig.). 1998. pap. 9.95 (*1-55650-807-7*) Hunter NJ.

Recommended Wayside Inns of Britain 1997. (Illus.). 160p. (Orig.). 1997. pap. 7.95 (*1-55650-765-8*) Hunter NJ.

Recommunion: A True Story. Whitey Stuart. 145p. (Orig.). 1989. pap. 8.95 (*0-685-25191-8*) Thundblt Pr NV.

Recomposition of the British State During the 1980s. Werner Bonefeld. 290p. 1993. 59.95 (*1-85521-377-X*, Pub. by Dartmth Pub UK) Ashgate Pub Co.

Reconceiving Decision-Making in Democratic Politics: Attention, Choice & Public Policy. Bryan D. Jones. 290p. 1994. lib. bdg. 42.00 (*0-226-40650-4*) U Ch Pr.

Reconceiving Decision-Making in Democratic Politics: Attention, Choice & Public Policy. Bryan D. Jones. 290p. 1995. pap. text ed. 15.95 (*0-226-40651-2*) U Ch Pr.

Reconceiving Experience: A Solution to a Problem Inherited from Descartes. John T. Kearns. (SUNY Series in Logic & Language). 474p. (C). 1996. text ed. 84.50 (*0-7914-3071-5*); pap. text ed. 28.95 (*0-7914-3072-3*) State U NY Pr.

***Reconceiving International Refugee Law.** James C. Hathaway. LC 97-16414. (Nijhoff Law Specials Ser.). 1997. pap. write for info. (*90-411-0418-6*) Kluwer Law Tax Pubs.

Reconceiving Liberalism: Dilemmas of Contemporary Liberal Public Policy. Oren M. Levin-Waldman. LC 96-25190. (Pitt Series in Political Science). 256p. 1997. 44.95 (*0-8229-3937-1*) U of Pittsburgh Pr.

Reconceiving Liberalism: Dilemmas of Contemporary Liberal Public Policy. Oren M. Levin-Waldman. LC 96-25190. (Pitt Series in Political Science). 256p. 1997. pap. 19.95 (*0-8229-5594-6*) U of Pittsburgh Pr.

Reconceiving Mathematics Instruction: A Focus on Errors. Rafaella Borasi. (Issues in Curriculum Theory, Policy, & Research Ser.). (Illus.). 321p. 1996. pap. 39.50 (*1-56750-168-0*); text ed. 73.25 (*1-56750-167-2*) Ablex Pub.

Reconceiving Texts as Speech Acts: An Analysis of 1 John. Dietmar Neufeld. LC 94-1367. (Biblical Interpretation Ser.: Vol. 7). 1994. 64.00 (*90-04-09853-4*) E J Brill.

Reconceiving Women: Separating Motherhood from Female Identity. Mardy S. Ireland. LC 92-45776. 176p. 1993. pap. text ed. 17.95 (*0-89862-016-3*); lib. bdg. 39.95 (*0-89862-123-2*) Guilford Pr.

Reconceiving Writing, Rethinking Writing Instruction. Ed. by Joseph Petraglia. 288p. (C). 1995. text ed. 59.95 (*0-8058-1691-7*) L Erlbaum Assocs.

Reconceiving Writing, Rethinking Writing Instruction. Ed. by Joseph Petraglia. 288p. (C). 1995. pap. text ed. 24.50 (*0-8058-1692-5*) L Erlbaum Assocs.

***Reconcentration of Radioactive Material Released to Sanitary Sewers.** 1997. lib. bdg. 250.95 (*0-8490-7708-7*) Gordon Pr.

Reconceptions in Philosophy & Other Arts & Sciences. Nelson Goodman & Catherine Z. Elgin. LC 87-31339. (Illus.). 192p. (C). 1990. pap. 16.95 (*0-87220-053-1*); lib. bdg. 37.95 (*0-87220-052-3*, 0-053) Hackett Pub.

***Reconceptualising the Sciences & the Humanities: An Integral Approach.** S. C. Malik. 1995. 26.00 (*81-7304-113-X*, Pub. by Manohar II) S Asia.

Reconceptualizing American Literary/Cultural Studies: Rhetoric, History, & Politics in the Humanities. William E. Cain. LC 96-14419. (Wellesley Studies in Critical Theory, Literary History & Culture: Vol. 12). 248p. 1996. text ed. 45.00 (*0-8153-2391-3*, H2000) Garland.

Reconceptualizing School-Based Curriculum Development. Colin J. Marsh. Ed. by Christopher W. Day et al. 225p. 1990. 75.00 (*1-85000-500-1*, Falmer Pr); pap. 33.00 (*1-85000-595-8*, Falmer Pr) Taylor & Francis.

Reconceptualizing the Early Childhood Curriculum: Beginning the Dialogue. Ed. by Shirley A. Kessler & Beth B. Swadener. (Early Childhood Education Ser.). 336p. (C). 1992. text ed. 49.00 (*0-8077-3199-4*); pap. text ed. 22.95 (*0-8077-3198-6*) Tchrs Coll.

***Reconceptualizing the Literacies in Adolescents' Lives.** Ed. by Donna E. Alvermann et al. 432p. 1998. write for info. (*0-8058-2559-2*) L Erlbaum Assocs.

***Reconceptualizing the Literacies in Adolescents' Lives.** Ed. by Donna E. Alvermann et al. 432p. 1998. pap. write for info. (*0-8058-2560-6*) L Erlbaum Assocs.

Reconceptualizing the Peasantry. Michael Kearney. (Critical Essays in Anthropology Ser.). 1996. text ed. 59.95 (*0-8133-0987-5*) Westview.

Reconceptualizing the Peasantry Class. Michael Kearney. (Critical Essays in Anthropology Ser.). (C). 1996. pap. text ed. 19.95 (*0-8133-0988-3*) Westview.

Reconcilable Differences? Congress, the Budget Process, & the Deficit. John Gilmour. 1990. 40.00 (*0-520-06778-9*); pap. 14.95 (*0-520-06943-9*) U CA Pr.

Reconcilable Differences: How Are Men & Women Different? Tim Downs et al. (Life Skills Ser.). (Illus.). 6p. (C). 1995. teacher ed., ring bd. 1.25 (*1-885702-17-5*, 742-009t); student ed., ring bd. 3.25 (*1-885702-16-7*, 742-009s) WSN Pr.

Reconcilable Differences: Issues in African American-Japanese Relations. Reginald Kearny. 33p. 1992. 12.00 (*0-685-70370-3*) Japan Soc.

Reconcilable Differences: Mending Broken Relationships. rev. ed. Jim Talley. LC 85-18947. 1991. pap. 10.99 (*0-8407-3196-5*) Nelson.

Reconcilable Differences? United States - Japan Economic Conflict. C. Fred Bergsten & Marcus Noland. LC 93-13689. 271p. 1993. pap. 19.95 (*0-88132-129-X*) Inst Intl Eco.

***Reconciled Life: A Critical Theory of Counseling.** R. Paul Olson. LC 97-11084. 1997. text ed. write for info. (*0-275-95630-X*, Praeger Pubs) Greenwood.

***Reconciled Through Christ: On Reconciliation & Greater Collaboration Between Hispanic American Catholics & African American Catholics.** Ruth Doyle. Ed. by Marina Herrera. (Illus.). 88p. (Orig.). (ENG & SPA.). Date not set. pap. 7.95 (*1-57455-025-X*) US Catholic.

Reconciliation: A Change of Heart. Mary C. Senger. (Illus.). 96p. 1987. pap. 6.95 (*0-8146-1563-5*) Liturgical Pr.

R

Reconciliation: A Study of Bibical Families in Conflict. Mike Moore. 185p. pap. 9.99 (*0-89900-684-1*) College Pr Pub.

Reconciliation: A Youth Ministry Handbook. Robert Grgic. 48p. (Orig.). 1992. pap. 9.95 (*1-55612-422-8*, LL1422) Sheed & Ward MO.

Reconciliation: Mission & Ministry in a Changing Social Order. Ed. by Robert J. Schreiter. LC 91-40877. (Orbis - BTI Ser.: Vol. 3). 96p. (Orig.). 1992. pap. 12.50 (*0-88344-809-2*) Orbis Bks.

***Reconciliation: Our Greatest Challenge - Our Only Hope.** Curtiss P. DeYoung. LC 96-49543. 144p. (Orig.). 1997. pap. 14.00 (*0-8170-1256-7*) Judson.

Reconciliation: Preparing for Confession in the Episcopal Church. Martin L. Smith. LC 85-21271. 121p. (Orig.). 1985. pap. 9.95 (*0-936384-30-1*) Cowley Pubns.

***Reconciliation: The Ubuntu Theology of Desmond Tutu.** Michael Battle. LC 97-8407. 280p. (Orig.). 1997. pap. 19.95 (*0-8298-1158-3*) Pilgrim OH.

Reconciliation & Justification: The Sacrament & Its Theology. Kenan B. Osborne. LC 89-48584. 320p. 1990. pap. 14.95 (*0-8091-3143-9*) Paulist Pr.

Reconciliation & Penance. 140p. 1984. pap. 7.95 (*1-55586-951-3*) US Catholic.

Reconciliation & Revival: James R. Mann & the House Republicans in the Wilson Era. Herbert F. Margulies. LC 95-36434. (Contributions in American History Ser.: No. 166). 264p. 1996. text ed. 57.95 (*0-313-29817-3*, Greenwood Pr) Greenwood.

Reconciliation of Income & Expenditure: Balanced Estimates of National Income for the United Kingdom: 1920-1990. James Sefton & Martin Weale. (Studies in the National Income & Expenditure of the United Kingdom: No. 7). 341p. (C). 1996. text ed. 69.95 (*0-521-49635-7*) Cambridge U Pr.

***Reconciliation of Peoples: Challenge to the Churches.** Ed. by Gregory Baum & Harold Wells. LC 96-45029. 200p. (Orig.). 1997. pap. 18.00 (*1-57075-107-2*) Orbis Bks.

Reconciliation of Roles: Women, Work & Family in Sri Lanka. Ed. by Sirima Kiribamune. (Sri Lanka Studies: No. 3). (C). 1993. text ed. 30.00 (*81-7013-103-0*, Pub. by Navrang) S Asia.

Reconciliation Road: A Family Odyssey. John D. Marshall. 296p. 1996. reprint ed. pap. 16.00 (*1-886913-07-2*) Hungry Mind.

Reconciliation Road: A Family Odyssey of War & Honor. John D. Marshall. (Illus.). 304p. 34.95 (*0-8156-0274-X*) Syracuse U Pr.

Reconciliation Services for Children: 18 Prayer Services to Celebrate God's Forgiveness. Gwen Costello. LC 92-60230. 72p. (Orig.). 1992. pap. 9.95 (*0-89622-516-X*) Twenty-Third.

Reconciliation Sourcebook. Ed. by Joseph Favazzaa & Kathleen Hughes. LC 97-698. 200p. (Orig.). 1997. pap. 15.00 (*1-56854-098-1*, RECON) Liturgy Tr Pubns.

Reconciling Community: The Rite of Penance. James Dallen. 446p. 1992. pap. 19.95 (*0-8146-6076-2*, Pueblo Bks) Liturgical Pr.

Reconciling Conflicts under the Endangered Species Act: The Habitat Conservation Planning Experience. Michael J. Bean et al. (Illus.). 127p. 1991. pap. 17.50 (*0-89164-130-0*) World Wildlife Fund.

***Reconciling Economy & Society: Towards a Plural Economy.** Ed. by Patrice Sauvage. 228p. (Orig.). 1996. pap. 50.00 (*92-64-14803-5*, 04-96-01-1, Pub. by Org for Econ FR) OECD.

Reconciling Man with the Environment. Eric Ashby. LC 77-91909. x, 104p. 1978. 22.50 (*0-8047-0986-6*); pap. 10.95 (*0-8047-1041-4*) Stanford U Pr.

Reconciling Physics With Reality: An Inaugural Lecture. A. B. Pippard. LC 70-187082. 40p. reprint ed. pap. 25.00 (*0-317-08599-9*, 2051384) Bks Demand.

Reconciling Rights & Responsibilities of Colleges & Students: Offensive Speech, Assembly, Drug Testing & Safety. Annette Gibbs. Ed. by Jonathan D. Fife. LC 92-63195. (ASHE-ERIC Higher Education Reports: No. 92-5). 92p. (Orig.). 1993. pap. text ed. 20.75 (*1-878380-18-4*) GWU Grad Schl E&HD.

Reconciling the Past: Two Basketry Ka'ai & the Legendary Liloa & Lonoikamakahiki. Roger G. Rose. (Bishop Museum Bulletin in Anthropology Ser.: No. 5). 1992. pap. 12.95 (*0-930897-76-5*) Bishop Mus.

Reconciling the Solitudes: Essays on Canadian Federalism & Nationalism. Charles Taylor. 192p. 1993. 49.95 (*0-7735-1105-9*, Pub. by McGill CN); pap. 19.95 (*0-7735-1110-5*, Pub. by McGill CN) U of Toronto Pr.

***Reconciling Trade, Environment, & Development Policies: The Role of Development Cooperation.** OECD Staff. 152p. (Orig.). 1996. pap. 20.00 (*92-64-15362-4*, 43-96-20-1, Pub. by Org for Econ FR) OECD.

Recondo: LRRPs in the 101st Airborne. Larry Chambers. (Orig.). 1992. mass mkt. 5.99 (*0-8041-0843-9*) Ivy Books.

***Reconfigurable Architectures: High Performance by Configware.** Ed. by Reiner Hartenstein & Viktor Prasanna. (Microsystems Engineering Ser.: No. 208). (Illus.). 224p. (Orig.). 1997. pap. 42.00 (*0-9639887-1-9*) IT Press.

Reconfigurable Processor-Array: A Bit-Sliced Parallel Computer. Andrew Rushton. (Research Monographs in Parallel & Distributed Computing). 192p. (Orig.). 1989. pap. 27.95 (*0-262-68057-2*) MIT Pr.

Reconfigurable Processor-Array: A Bit Sliced Parallel Computer. Ed. by Andrew Rushton. 192p. (C). 1989. pap. text ed. 180.00 (*0-273-08799-1*, Pub. by Pitman Pubng UK) St Mut.

Reconfigurations: Critical Theory & General Economy. Arkady Plotnitsky. LC 92-22271. 440p. 1993. 49.95 (*0-8130-1172-8*); pap. 29.95 (*0-8130-1173-6*) U Press Fla.

Reconfigured Eye: Visual Truth in the Post-Photographic Era. William J. Mitchell. (Illus.). 283p. 1994. 24.95 (*0-262-63160-1*) MIT Pr.

Reconfigured Spheres: Feminist Explorations of Literary Space. Ed. by Margaret Higonnet & Joan Templeton. LC 94-16551. (Illus.). 224p. (C). 1994. pap. 15.95 (*0-87023-938-4*) U of Mass Pr.

Reconfigured Spheres: Feminist Explorations of Literary Space. Ed. by Margaret Higonnet & Joan Templeton. LC 94-16551. (Illus.). 224p. (C). 1994. 40.00 (*0-87023-937-6*) U of Mass Pr.

Reconfiguring Boundaries - Defining Spaces. Constance W. Glenn et al. (Illus.). 23p. (Orig.). 1994. pap. 10.00 (*0-936270-32-2*) CA St U LB Art.

Reconfiguring Modernism. Schwarz. LC 97-3588. 1997. text ed. 45.00 (*0-312-12655-7*) St Martin.

Reconfiguring Modernism. Schwarz. Date not set. text ed. 18.95 (*0-312-12660-3*) St Martin.

Reconfiguring the Renaissance: Essays in Critical Materialism. Ed. by Jonathan Crewe. LC 91-55211. (Bucknell Review Ser.: Vol. 35, No. 2). (Illus.). 176p. 1992. 21.00 (*0-8387-5223-3*) Bucknell U Pr.

Reconfiguring Truth: Postmodernism, Science Studies & the Search for a New Model of Knowledge. Steven C. Ward. LC 96-17631. 184p. 1996. 52.50 (*0-8476-8259-5*); pap. 21.95 (*0-8476-8260-9*) Rowman.

Reconfort de Madame de Fresne. De La Salle. Ed. by Hill. 76p. (FRE.). Date not set. pap. text ed. 19.95 (*0-85989-185-2*, Pub. by Univ Exeter Pr UK) Northwestern U Pr.

Reconnaissance & Excavation in Southeastern New Mexico. Harry P. Mera. LC 39-14217. (AAA Memoirs: No. 51). 1938. 25.00 (*0-527-00550-9*) Periodicals Srv.

Reconnaissance Geology of the State of Baja California. R. Gordon Gastil et al. LC 74-83806. (Geological Society of America, Memoir Ser.: No. 140). 248p. reprint ed. pap. 70.70 (*0-317-29112-2*, 2023734) Bks Demand.

Reconnaissance of the Point Barrow Region, Alaska. S. Paige et al. (Shorey Historical Ser.). (Illus.). 56p. reprint ed. pap. 4.95 (*0-8466-8004-1*, G4) Shorey.

Reconnaissance Survey of Potential Carbonate Whiting Sources in Pennsylvania. Samuel W. Berkheiser, Jr. (Mineral Resource Reports: No. 83). (Illus.). 53p. (Orig.). 1983. pap. 4.45 (*0-8182-0024-3*) Commonweal PA.

Reconnaissances. Rodney Needham. LC 81-160186. 132p. reprint ed. pap. 37.70 (*0-8357-8298-0*, 2034013) Bks Demand.

Reconnaissances: Poems. John M. Steadman. LC 94-46937. 76p. 1995. pap. 12.95 (*0-7734-2752-X*, Mellen Poetry Pr) E Mellen.

Reconnecting. Susan D. Allen & Colleen A. Holloran. (Illus.). 32p. 1991. pap. text ed. 2.75 (*0-916999-11-4*) HERC Inc.

Reconnecting. Anton Harfmann & Mike Fraser. (Illus.). 232p. 1994. pap. text ed. 50.00 (*1-880250-03-9*) Assoc Comp Aid Des.

Reconnecting. Frwd. by Samuel Sachs. (Illus.). 30p. 1987. pap. 4.99 (*0-89558-129-9*) Det Inst Arts.

Reconnecting: How to Renew & Preserve the 3 Vital Elements of a Spiritual Life. Ronnie Floyd. LC 93-11191. 176p. 1993. 14.99 (*0-8054-6088-8*, 4260-88) Broadman.

Reconnecting Families: A Guide to Strengthening Family Reunification Services. Robin Warsh et al. (Orig.). 1996. pap. 18.95 (*0-87868-574-X*) Child Welfare.

***Reconnecting God's Story to Ministry: Crosscultural Storytelling at Home & Abroad.** Tom A. Steffen. (Illus.). 140p. (Orig.). (C). 1996. pap. text ed. 10.95 (*1-882757-03-3*) Ctr Organ & Minist.

Reconnecting the Love Energy: Don't Bypass Your Heart. Phyllis Krystal. LC 95-36571. 175p. (Orig.). 1995. pap. 9.95 (*0-87728-849-6*) Weiser.

***Reconnecting with Nature: Finding Wellness through Restoring Your Bond with the Earth.** 2nd ed. Michael J. Cohen. LC 96-29597. 230p. 1997. pap. 14.95 (*0-9639705-2-6*) Ecopress.

Reconnecting Youth: A Peer Group Approach to Building Life Skills. Leona L. Eggert et al. (Illus.). 584p. 1995. 139.00 (*1-879639-42-4*) Natl Educ Serv.

Reconnecting Youth: The Next Stage of Reform. 47p. 1985. 7.00 (*0-318-22536-0*, AR-85-1) Ed Comm States.

Reconnection: Dualism to Holism in Literary Study. Betty J. Craige. LC 87-16243. 176p. 1988. pap. 15.00 (*0-8203-1014-X*) U of Ga Pr.

Reconocimiento Arqueologico en la Parte Mexicana de la Presa de la Amistad. Francisco Gonzalez. 151p. 1990. pap. 6.00 (*968-6068-96-1*, IN037) UPLAAP.

Reconquest of Burma: 1943-1945. Geoffery Matthews. pap. 3.95 (*0-685-56071-6*) Beachcomber Bks.

Reconquest of Montreal: Language Policy & Social Change in a Bilingual City. Marc V. Levine. (Illus.). 320p. 1990. 44.95 (*0-87722-703-9*) Temple U Pr.

Reconquest of Montreal: Language Policy & Social Change in a Bilingual City. Marc V. Levine. (Illus.). 320p. 1991. pap. 18.95 (*0-87722-899-X*) Temple U Pr.

Reconquest of Spain. Derek W. Lomax. LC 77-3030. reprint ed. pap. 56.00 (*0-317-27796-0*, 2025242) Bks Demand.

Reconquista de Tu Cuidad. Leonard Ravenhill. (SPA.). pap. 6.99 (*0-88113-023-0*) Edit Betania.

Reconquista y Literatura Medieval: Cuatro Ensayos. Giorgio Perissinotto. 127p. 1990. 29.50 (*0-916379-48-5*) Scripta.

Reconsecrating America. George Goldberg. LC 84-13610. 163p. reprint ed. pap. 46.50 (*0-685-20789-7*, 2030064) Bks Demand.

Reconsider Baby: The Definitive Elvis Sessionography 1954-1977. rev. ed. Ernst Jorgensen et al. Ed. by Thomas Schultheiss. (Rock & Roll Reference Ser.: No. 27). (Illus.). 308p. 1986. 28.50 (*1-56075-041-3*) Popular Culture.

Reconsideration of Health Behavior Change Models, Vol. 4. Ed. by Gary L. Albrecht. (Advances in Medical Sociology Ser.). 280p. 1994. 73.25 (*1-55938-758-0*) Jai Pr.

Reconsiderations. Ernest E. Kellett. LC 75-99704. (Essay Index Reprint Ser.). 1977. 23.95 (*0-8369-1356-6*) Ayer.

Reconsiderations on the Revolutionary War: Selected Essays. Ed. by Don Higginbotham. LC 77-84752. (Contributions in Military History Ser.: No. 14). 217p. 1978. text ed. 55.00 (*0-8371-9846-1*, HIA/, Greenwood Pr) Greenwood.

Reconsidering Age-Adjustment Procedures: Workshop Proceedings. LC 92-25492. (Vital & Health Statistics Ser.: No. 29). 83p. 1992. 5.50 (*0-8406-0464-5*) Natl Ctr Health Stats.

Reconsidering Age Adjustment Procedures: Workshop Proceedings. 83p. (Orig.). (C). 1993. pap. text ed. 25.00 (*1-56806-504-3*) DIANE Pub.

Reconsidering American Liberalism: The Troubled Odyssey of the Liberal Idea. James P. Young. 448p. (C). 1995. pap. text ed. 25.00 (*0-8133-0648-5*) Westview.

Reconsidering American Politics. Nicholas L. Henry & John S. Hall. 544p. (C). 1985. per. write for info. (*0-697-06806-4*) Brown & Benchmark.

Reconsidering Aubrey Beardsley. Ed. by Robert Langenfeld & Nicholas Salerno. LC 89-34603. 526p. 1991. 50.00 (*0-8357-1979-0*) Univ Rochester Pr.

***Reconsidering Children's Early Development & Learning: Toward Common Views & Vocabulary.** 1997. lib. bdg. 250.99 (*0-8490-8239-0*) Gordon Pr.

***Reconsidering Difference: Nancy, Derrida, Levinas, & Deleuze.** Todd May. LC 96-42210. 1997. 32.50 (*0-271-01657-4*); pap. 16.95 (*0-271-01658-2*) Pa St U Pr.

Reconsidering "No Man Knows My History" Perspectives on Fawn M. Brodie & Joseph Smith Jr. Ed. by Newell G. Brighurst. 192p. 1996. 34.95 (*0-87421-205-7*); pap. 17.95 (*0-87421-214-6*) Utah St U Pr.

Reconsidering Social Constructionism: Debates in Social Problems Theory. Ed. by James A. Holstein & Gale Miller. LC 92-36344. (Social Problems & Social Issues Ser.). 576p. 1993. lib. bdg. 76.95 (*0-202-30456-6*) Aldine de Gruyter.

Reconsidering South Africa: The Prospects for U. S. Investment. Jennifer D. Kibbe. 55p. (Orig.). 1993. pap. 15.00 (*1-879775-11-5*) IRRC Inc DC.

Reconsidering the Democratic Public. Ed. by George E. Marcus & Russell L. Hanson. LC 92-33653. 464p. 1993. 55.00 (*0-271-00917-9*); pap. 17.95 (*0-271-00927-6*) Pa St U Pr.

Reconsidering the Object of Art. Ed. by Ann Goldstein & Anne Rorimer. (Illus.). 320p. (C). 1995. pap. 35.00 (*0-262-57111-0*) MIT Pr.

Reconsidering the Renaissance: Papers of the Twenty-First Annual Conference of the Center for Medieval & Early Renaissance Studies. Ed. by Mario A. Di Cesare. LC 92-17281. (Medieval & Renaissance Texts & Studies: Vol. 93). (Illus.). 528p. 1992. 40.00 (*0-86698-107-1*, MR93) MRTS.

Reconsidering Tocqueville's Democracy in America. Ed. by Abraham S. Eisenstadt. 314p. (C). 1988. pap. text ed. 18.95 (*0-8135-1299-9*) Rutgers U Pr.

Reconsidering Tu Fu: Literary Greatness & Cultural Context. Eva Shan Chou. (Studies in Chinese History, Literature & Institutions). 240p. (C). 1995. text ed. 44.95 (*0-521-44039-4*) Cambridge U Pr.

Reconsidering Vietnam. David Tucker. (Occasional Paper of the Study of Statesmanship & Political Philosophy: No. 7). 32p. (Orig.). (C). 1983. pap. text ed. 2.00 (*0-930783-13-1*) Claremont Inst.

***Reconsrtuction.** Casper. Date not set. pap. write for info. (*0-312-18164-7*) St Martin.

Reconstituted Family: A Study of Remarried Couples & Their Children. Lucile Duberman. LC 75-8840. 200p. 1975. 31.95 (*0-88229-168-8*) Nelson-Hall.

Reconstituting a Production Capability: Past Experience, Restart Criteria & Suggested Policies. John Birkler et al. LC 93-29793. 127p. 1993. pap. 15.00 (*0-8330-1445-5*, MR-273-ACQ) Rand Corp.

Reconstituting America's Defense: The New U. S. National Security Strategy. Ed. by James J. Tritten & Paul Stockton. LC 91-43442. 192p. 1992. text ed. 47.95 (*0-275-94249-X*, C4249, Praeger Pubs) Greenwood.

Reconstituting India. Pradip Sarbadhikari. 224p. 1996. text ed. 19.95 (*0-19-563700-3*) OUP.

Reconstituting Rurality: The Changing Countryside in an Urban Context. Jonathan Murdoch & Terry Marsden. (Reconstructing Rural Areas Ser.: No. 2). 192p. 1994. 59.95 (*1-85728-041-5*, Pub. by UCL Pr UK) Taylor & Francis.

Reconstituting Rurality: The Changing Countryside in an Urban Context. Jonathan Murdoch & Terry Marsden. (Reconstructing Rural Areas Ser.: No. 2). 192p. 1996. pap. 27.50 (*1-85728-645-6*, Pub. by UCL Pr UK) Taylor & Francis.

Reconstructed Corpse. Simon Brett. (WWL Mystery Ser.). 1996. mass mkt. 5.50 (*0-373-26194-2*, 1-26194-0, Wrldwide Lib) Harlequin Bks.

Reconstructed Corpse. large type ed. Simon Brett. LC 94-30492. 1994. 23.95 (*1-56895-117-5*) Wheeler Pub.

Reconstructed Corpse: A Charles Paris Mystery. Simon Brett. LC 93-50797. 192p. 1994. 20.00 (*0-684-19700-6*) S&S Trade.

Reconstructed Human Skin, Nineteen Ninety: Journal: Skin Pharmacology, Vol. 3, No. 2. Ed. by R. Schmidt. (Illus.). 88p. 1990. pap. 41.75 (*3-8055-5283-1*) S Karger.

***Reconstructed Lives: Women & Iran's Islamic Revolution.** Haleh Esfandiari. LC 97-3080. (Woodrow Wilson Center Press Ser.). 200p. 1997. text ed. 42.50 (*0-8018-5618-3*) Johns Hopkins.

***Reconstructed Lives - Women & Iran's Islamic Revolution.** Haleh Esfandiari. LC 97-3080. (Woodrow Wilson Center Press Ser.). 200p. 1997. pap. text ed. 15.95 (*0-8018-5619-1*) Johns Hopkins.

Reconstructed Marriage Records of Breathitt Co., KY, 1839-1873, Including Marriages from Breathitt Co. Marriage Book 1, 1874-1877. rev. ed. Margaret M. Hayes. 199p. 1994. pap. text ed. 19.00 (*0-7884-0016-9*) Heritage Bk.

Reconstructed Passenger Lists for 1850: Hamburg to Australia, Brazil, Canada, Chile & the United States, 4 pts., Set. Tr. by Clifford N. Smith from GER. (German & Central European Emigration Ser.: No. 1). 79p. 1981. pap. 20.00 (*0-915162-50-4*) Westland Pubns.

Reconstructed Passenger Lists for 1851 Via Hamburg: Emigrants from Germany, Austria, Bohemia, Hungary, Poland, Russia, Scandinavia & Switzerland to Australia, Brazil, Canada, Chile, the U. S. & Venezuela. Clifford N. Smith. (German & Central European Emigration Ser.: No. 2, Pt. 1). 45p. (Orig.). 1986. pap. 20.00 (*0-915162-51-2*) Westland Pubns.

Reconstructed Passengers Lists for 1851 Via Hamburg: Emigrants from Germany, Austria, Bohemia, Hungary, Poland, Russia, Scandinavia, & Switzerland to Australia, Brazil, Canada, Chile, the United States & Venezuela, Pt. 3 of 5. Clifford N. Smith. (German & Central European Emigration Ser.: No. 2). 52p. (Orig.). 1986. pap. 20.00 (*0-915162-53-9*) Westland Pubns.

Reconstructed Passengers Lists for 1851 Via Hamburg: Emigrants from Germany, Austria, Bohemia, Hungary, Poland, Russia, Scandinavia, & Switzerland to Australia, Brazil, Canada, Chile, the United States & Venezuela, Pt. 4 of 5. Clifford N. Smith. (German & Central European Emigration Ser.: No. 2). 25p. (Orig.). 1986. pap. 16.00 (*0-915162-54-7*) Westland Pubns.

Reconstructed Passengers Lists for 1851 Via Hamburg: Emigrants from Germany, Austria, Bohemia, Hungary, Poland, Russia, Scandinavia, & Switzerland to Australia, Brazil, Canada, Chile, the United States & Venezuela, Pt. 5 of 5. Clifford N. Smith. (Orig.). 1986. Pt. 5 M-Z. pap. write for info. (*0-915162-55-5*) Westland Pubns.

Reconstructed Seventeen Ninety Census of Delaware. Leone De Valinger, Jr. (Illus.). 83p. 8.50 (*0-915156-10-5*, 10) Natl Genealogical.

Reconstructed Seventeen Ninety Census of Georgia Substitutes for Georgia's Lost 1790 Census. Marie De Lamar & Elisabeth Rothstein. LC 84-73075. 235p. 1989. reprint ed. 20.00 (*0-8063-1111-8*) Genealog Pub.

***Reconstructed World: A Feminist Biography of Gertrude Richardson.** Barbara Roberts. 1996. 55.00 (*0-7735-1394-9*, Pub. by McGill CN) U of Toronto Pr.

Reconstructing a Chicano - a Literary Heritage: Hispanic Colonial Literature of the Southwest. Ed. by Maria Herrera-Sobek. LC 92-45616. 213p. 1993. 32.00 (*0-8165-1350-3*) U of Ariz Pr.

Reconstructing 'A' Level English. Patrick Scott. 160p. 1989. pap. 32.00 (*0-335-09594-1*, Open Univ Pr) Taylor & Francis.

Reconstructing a Women's Prison: The Holloway Redevelopment Project, 1968-88. Paul E. Rock. (Clarendon Studies in Criminology). (Illus.). 384p. 1996. 69.95 (*0-19-826095-4*, Clarendon Pr) OUP.

Reconstructing African Culture History. Ed. by Creighton Gabel & Norman Bennett. LC 67-25932. 1967. 12.50 (*0-8419-8704-1*, Boston Univ) Holmes & Meier.

***Reconstructing America: The Symbol of America in Modern Thought.** James W. Ceaser. LC 96-52890. 1997. write for info. (*0-300-07053-5*) Yale U Pr.

Reconstructing American Education. Michael B. Katz. 240p. 1989. pap. 15.95 (*0-674-75093-4*) HUP.

Reconstructing American Law. Bruce A. Ackerman. 128p. 1984. 29.00 (*0-674-75015-2*); pap. 13.50 (*0-674-75016-0*) HUP.

Reconstructing American Literary & Historical Studies. Ed. by Gunter H. Lenz et al. LC 90-32645. 435p. 1990. text ed. 49.95 (*0-312-04661-8*) St Martin.

Reconstructing American Literary History. Ed. by Sacvan Bercovitch. (English Studies: No. 13). 384p. 1985. 20.00 (*0-674-75085-3*) HUP.

Reconstructing American Literary History. Ed. by Sacvan Bercovitch. (English Studies: No. 13). 384p. 1986. pap. 9.95 (*0-674-75086-1*) HUP.

Reconstructing American Literature: Courses, Syllabi, Issues. Ed. by Paul Lauter. LC 83-20730. 288p. 1983. pap. 12.95 (*0-935312-14-5*) Feminist Pr.

Reconstructing Archaeology: Theory & Practice. 2nd ed. Michael Shanks & Christopher Tilley. (Illus.). 296p. (C). 1993. pap. 25.00 (*0-415-08870-4*, A9869) Routledge.

Reconstructing Architecture: Critical Discourses & Social Practices. Ed. by Thomas A. Dutton & Lisa H. Mann. (Pedagogy & Cultural Practices Ser.: Vol. 5). 336p. (C). 1996. text ed. 54.95 (*0-8166-2808-4*); pap. text ed. 21.95 (*0-8166-2809-2*) U of Minn Pr.

Reconstructing Architecture for the Twenty-First Century: An Inquiry into the Architect's World. Anthony Jackson. (Illus.). 224p. 1995. 50.00 (*0-8020-0625-6*); pap. 17.95 (*0-8020-7584-3*) U of Toronto Pr.

Reconstructing Argumentative Discourse. Frans H. Van Eemeren et al. LC 93-18082. (Studies in Rhetoric & Communication). 216p. 1993. text ed. 34.95 (*0-8173-0697-8*) U of Ala Pr.

Reconstructing Babylon: Essays on Women & Technology. Ed. by Patricia H. Hynes. LC 90-39330. 222p. 1991. 35.00 (*0-253-32881-0*); pap. 5.95 (*0-253-20622-7*, MB-622) Ind U Pr.

An Asterisk (*) at the beginning of an entry indicates that the title is appearing in BIP for the first time.

Reconstructing Beckett: Language & Being in Samuel Beckett's Fiction. P. J. Murphy. 256p. 1990. 40.00 (*0-8020-5868-X*) U of Toronto Pr.

***Reconstructing Biblical Dead Sea Scrolls: A New Method Applied to the Reconstruction of 4QSam(a)** Edward D. Herbert. LC 96-50476. (Studies on the Texts of the Desert of Judah: Vol. 22). (Illus.). 344p. 1997. text ed. 78.25 (*90-04-10684-7*) E J Brill.

Reconstructing Biology: Genetics & Ecology in the New World Order. John Vandermeer. LC 95-12076. 480p. 1996. pap. text ed. 34.95 (*0-471-10917-7*) Wiley.

Reconstructing Cambodia - Human Resources, Human Rights, & Law: Three Essays. Dolores A. Donovan et al. LC 92-38817. 1993. write for info. (*0-941700-79-8*) JH FPI SAIS.

Reconstructing Camelot: French Romantic Medievalism & the Arthurian Tradition. Michael Glencross. (Arthurian Studies). 202p. (C). 1995. 53.00 (*0-85991-463-1*) Boydell & Brewer.

Reconstructing Catholicism for a New Generation. Robert Ludwig. 192p. (Orig.). 1995. pap. 17.95 (*0-8245-1462-9*) Crossroad NY.

Reconstructing Christian Ethics: Selected Writings. Frederick D. Maurice. Ed. by Ellen K. Wondra. (Library of Theological Ethics). 208p. (Orig.). 1995. pap. 19.00 (*0-664-25601-5*) Westminster John Knox.

Reconstructing Christian Theology. Ed. by Rebecca S. Chopp & Mark L. Taylor. LC 94-2827. 1994. pap. 22.00 (*0-8006-2696-6*, 1-2696, Fortress Pr) Augsburg Fortress.

***Reconstructing City Politics: Alternative Economic Development & Urban Regimes.** David L. Imbroscio. LC 96-35645. (Cities & Planning Ser.: Vol. 1). 192p. 1997. 42.00 (*0-7619-0612-6*); pap. 18.95 (*0-7619-0613-4*) Sage.

Reconstructing Consensus: American Foreign Policy since the Vietnam War. Richard A. Melanson. LC 90-39670. 240p. (Orig.). 1990. text ed. 65.00 (*0-312-05238-3*) St Martin.

Reconstructing Criminal Law: Text & Materials. Dirk J. Meure et al. (Law in Context Ser.). 568p. (C). 1994. text ed. 70.00 (*0-297-82027-3*); pap. text ed. 39.95 (*0-297-82028-1*) Northwestern U Pr.

Reconstructing Desire: The Role of the Unconscious in Women's Reading & Writing. Jean Wyatt. LC 90-12010. xii, 272p. (C). 1990. text ed. 37.50 (*0-8078-1915-8*); pap. text ed. 15.95 (*0-8078-4285-0*) U of NC Pr.

Reconstructing Education: Towards a Pedagogy of Critical Humanism. Greta H. Nemiroff. LC 91-33944. 224p. 1992. text ed. 52.95 (*0-89789-266-6*, H266, Bergin & Garvey); pap. text ed. 18.95 (*0-89789-267-4*, G267, Bergin & Garvey) Greenwood.

Reconstructing Eliade: Making Sense of Religion. Bryan S. Rennie. LC 95-12358. 293p. 1996. text ed. 59.50 (*0-7914-2763-3*); pap. text ed. 19.95 (*0-7914-2764-1*) State U NY Pr.

Reconstructing Europe after the Great War. Dan P. Silverman. LC 81-6836. (Illus.). 359p. 1982. 39.00 (*0-674-75025-X*) HUP.

Reconstructing Gender: A Multicultural Anthology. Ed. by Estelle Disch. LC 96-17516. 593p. (Orig.). (C). 1996. pap. text ed. 27.95 (*1-55934-579-9*, 1579) Mayfield Pub.

Reconstructing Gender in the Middle East: Tradition, Identity, & Power. Ed. by Shiva Balachi. LC 94-3733. 272p. 1995. 45.00 (*0-231-10122-8*); pap. 16.50 (*0-231-10123-6*) Col U Pr.

Reconstructing Herod's Temple Mount in Jerusalem. Kathleen Ritmeyer & Leen Ritmeyer. (Illus.). 31p. (Orig.). (C). 1990. pap. text ed. 7.95 (*0-9613089-1-5*) Biblical Arch Soc.

Reconstructing Historical Communities. Alan Macfarlane et al. LC 77-24234. 1978. 13.95 (*0-521-21796-2*) Cambridge U Pr.

Reconstructing History from Ancient Inscriptions: The Lagash-Umma Border Conflict. J. S. Cooper. (Sources from the Ancient Near East Ser.: Vol. 2-1). (Illus.). 61p. (C). 1983. pap. text ed. 10.75 (*0-89003-059-6*) Undena Pubns.

Reconstructing History from Ancient Inscriptions: The Lagash-Umma Border Conflict. Jerrold S. Cooper. (Sources from the Ancient Near East Ser.: Vol. 2, Issue 1). (Illus.). 61p. 1983. 10.75 (*0-89003-003-0*) Undena Pubns.

Reconstructing Human Origins. Glenn Conroy. LC 96-25161. (C). 1997. pap. text ed. 42.95 (*0-393-97042-6*) Norton.

Reconstructing Illness: Studies in Pathography. Anne H. Hawkins. LC 92-49892. 200p. (C). 1993. 28.00 (*1-55753-030-0*); pap. 14.95 (*1-55753-038-6*) Purdue U Pr.

Reconstructing Individualism: Autonomy, Individuality, & the Self in Western Thought. Ed. by Thomas C. Heller et al. LC 85-27678. 384p. (Orig.). 1986. 47.50 (*0-8047-1292-1*); pap. 16.95 (*0-8047-1291-3*) Stanford U Pr.

Reconstructing Judaism: An Autobiography. Ira Eisenstein. 1986. 17.95 (*0-935457-37-2*) Reconstructionist Pr.

Reconstructing Justice: An Agenda for Trial Reform. Franklin D. Strier. LC 93-50068. 328p. 1994. text ed. 59.95 (*0-89930-568-7*, Quorum Bks) Greenwood.

Reconstructing Justice: An Agenda for Trial Reform. Franklin D. Strier. 328p. 1996. pap. 15.95 (*0-226-77718-9*) U Ch Pr.

Reconstructing Kemetic Culture: Papers, Perspectives, Projects. Ed. by Maulana Karanga. 240p. (Orig.). 1990. pap. 14.95 (*0-943412-13-7*) Univ Sankore Pr.

Reconstructing Keynesian Economics with Imperfect Competition: A Desk-Top Simulation. Robin Marris. 352p. 1991. text ed. 85.00 (*1-85278-541-1*) E Elgar.

Reconstructing Languages & Cultures. Ed. by Edgar C. Polome & Werner Winter. LC 91-45260. (Trends in Linguistics, Studies & Monographs: No. 58). ix, 550p. 1992. lib. bdg. 190.80 (*3-11-012671-0*) Mouton.

Reconstructing Large-Scale Climatic Patterns from Tree-Ring Data: A Diagnostic Analysis. Harold C. Fritts. LC 91-15764. (Illus.). 286p. 1991. 66.00 (*0-8165-1218-3*) U of Ariz Pr.

Reconstructing Literature in an Ideological Age: A Biblical Poetics & Literary Studies from Milton to Burke. Daniel E. Ritchie. 311p. (Orig.). 1996. pap. 27.00 (*0-8028-4140-6*) Eerdmans.

Reconstructing Lives, Recapturing Meaning. Ed. by Linda Camino. 253p. 1994. text ed. 40.00 (*2-88449-109-0*); pap. text ed. 20.00 (*2-88449-110-4*) Gordon & Breach.

Reconstructing Marxian Economics: Marx Based Upon a Sraffian Commodity Theory of Value. Spencer L. Pack. LC 84-26279. 174p. 1985. text ed. 49.95 (*0-275-90152-1*, C0152, Praeger Pubs) Greenwood.

Reconstructing Marxism: Essays on Explanation & the Theory of History. Erik O. Wright et al. LC 91-40400. 260p. (C). 1992. pap. text ed. 20.00 (*0-86091-554-9*, A6526, Pub. by Vrso UK) Norton.

Reconstructing Marxism: Essays on Explanation & the Theory of History. Erik O. Wright et al. LC 91-40400. 260p. (C). (gr. 13). 1992. text ed. 65.00 (*0-86091-342-2*, A6522, Pub. by Vrso UK) Norton.

Reconstructing Mathematics Education: Stories of Teachers Meeting the Challenge of Reform. Deborah Schifter & Cathy T. Fosnot. 256p. (C). 1992. text ed. 46.00 (*0-8077-3206-0*); pap. text ed. 18.95 (*0-8077-3205-2*) Tchrs Coll.

Reconstructing Memory: Black Literary Criticism. Fred Hord. 1991. 12.95 (*0-88378-144-1*) Third World.

Reconstructing Modernism: Art in New York, Paris & Montreal, 1945-1964. Ed. by Serge Guilbault. (Illus.). 448p. 1992. pap. 20.00 (*0-262-57092-0*) MIT Pr.

Reconstructing Nature: Alienation, Emancipation, & the Division of Labour. Peter Dickens. LC 95-26748. 240p. (C). 1996. pap. 19.95 (*0-415-08922-0*); text ed. 69.95 (*0-415-08921-2*) Routledge.

***Reconstructing Nursing: Beyond.** Diane Marks-Maran. 1996. pap. text ed. 27.00 (*0-7020-2000-1*) Saunders.

Reconstructing Political Pluralism. Avigail I. Eisenberg. LC 94-49026. (SUNY Series in Political Theory). 211p. (C). 1995. text ed. 49.50 (*0-7914-2561-4*); pap. text ed. 16.95 (*0-7914-2562-2*) State U NY Pr.

***Reconstructing Political Theory: Feminist Perspectives.** Mary L. Shanley & Uma Narayan. LC 97-7126. 1997. 45.00 (*0-271-01724-4*); pap. 17.95 (*0-271-01725-2*) Pa St U Pr.

Reconstructing Prehistorical Dialects: Initial Vowels in Slavic & Baltic. Henning Andersen. (Trends in Linguistics Ser.: Vol. 91). x, 238p. (C). 1996. lib. bdg. 141.45 (*3-11-014705-X*) Mouton.

Reconstructing Prehistory: Scientific Method in Archaeology. James A. Bell. 320p. 1994. 59.95 (*1-56639-159-8*); pap. 24.95 (*1-56639-160-1*) Temple U Pr.

Reconstructing Proto-Afroasiatic (Proto-Afrasian) Vowels, Tone, Consonants, & Vocabulary. Christopher Ehret. LC 95-13152. (Publications in Linguistics: Vol. 126). 575p. 1995. pap. 62.00 (*0-520-09799-8*) U CA Pr.

Reconstructing Public Philosophy. William M. Sullivan. LC 81-16418. 256p. 1982. pap. 15.00 (*0-520-05890-9*) U CA Pr.

***Reconstructing Quaternary Environments.** 2nd ed. Lowe. (C). 1996. pap. text ed. 49.95 (*0-582-10266-9*, Pub. by Longman UK) Longman.

Reconstructing Quaternary Environments. 2nd ed. John J. Lowe. (C). 1996. pap. text ed. 31.95 (*0-582-10166-2*) Addison-Wesley.

Reconstructing Reality in the Courtroom: Justice & Judgment in American Culture. W. Lance Bennett & Martha S. Feldman. (Crime, Law & Deviance Ser.). 213p. 1981. pap. 15.00 (*0-8135-1078-3*) Rutgers U Pr.

Reconstructing Reality in the Courtroom: Justice & Judgment in American Culture. Lance W. Bennett & Martha S. Feldman. LC 81-5125. (Crime, Law & Deviance Ser.). 213p. 1981. reprint ed. pap. 60.80 (*0-7837-9213-1*, 2049963) Bks Demand.

Reconstructing Realpolitik. Ed. by Frank W. Wayman & Paul F. Diehl. LC 94-15289. 350p. 1994. text ed. 67.50 (*0-472-10355-5*); pap. text ed. 23.95 (*0-472-08268-X*) U of Mich Pr.

Reconstructing Schizophrenia. Richard P. Bentall. LC 89-10209. 336p. (C). 1992. pap. 19.95 (*0-415-07524-6*, A7062) Routledge.

Reconstructing Science for Public Consumption: Journalism As Science Education. Sharon Dunwoody. 104p. 1993. 60.00 (*0-7300-1604-8*, ESC810, Pub. by Deakin Univ AT) St Mut.

Reconstructing Scientific Revolutions: Thomas S. Kuhn's Philosophy of Science. Paul Hoyningen-Huene. Tr. by Alexander J. Levine. LC 92-34288. 330p. (C). 1993. pap. text ed. 16.95 (*0-226-35551-9*) U Ch Pr.

***(Re)Constructing Social Work: Exploring Social Work Through Text & Talk.** Peter J. Camilleri. 200p. 1996. text ed. 59.95 (*1-85972-480-9*, Pub. by Avebury Pub UK) Ashgate Pub Co.

Reconstructing Teacher Education. Ed. by John Elliott. LC 92-30043. 1993. 90.00 (*0-7507-0127-7*, Falmer Pr); pap. 31.00 (*0-7507-0128-5*, Falmer Pr) Taylor & Francis.

Reconstructing the Academy: Women's Education & Women's Studies. Elizabeth Minnich et al. 320p. 1988. pap. text ed. 16.00 (*0-226-53014-0*); lib. bdg. 33.00 (*0-226-53013-2*) U Ch Pr.

Reconstructing the Balkans: Geography of the New South East Europe. Ed. by Derek Hall & Darrick Danta. 1996. text ed. 95.00 (*0-471-95758-5*) Wiley.

Reconstructing the Canon: Samuel Johnson & the Universal Visiter. Bonnie M. Ferrero. LC 92-28960. (Studies in European Thought: Vol. 5). 146p. (C). 1993. text ed. 42.95 (*0-8204-1986-9*) P Lang Pubng.

Reconstructing the Christ Symbol: Essays in Feminist Christology. Ed. by Maryanne Stevens. 160p. (Orig.). 1994. pap. 9.95 (*0-8091-3439-X*) Paulist Pr.

Reconstructing the Classics: Political Theory from Plato to Marx. Edward B. Portis. LC 93-27199. (Chatham House Studies in Political Thinking). 192p. (Orig.). (C). 1994. pap. text ed. 19.95 (*1-56643-003-8*) Chatham Hse Pubs.

***Reconstructing the Classics: Political Theory from Plato to Marx.** 2nd ed. Edward B. Portis. (Studies in Political Thinking). (Illus.). 224p. (Orig.). (C). 1997. pap. text ed. 19.95 (*1-56643-049-6*) Chatham Hse Pubs.

Reconstructing the Common Good: Theology & the Social Order. Gary J. Dorrien. LC 90-31698. 1992. reprint ed. pap. 20.00 (*0-88344-797-5*) Orbis Bks.

Reconstructing the Criminal: Culture, Law & Policy in England, 1830-1914. Martin J. Wiener. (Illus.). 400p. (C). 1990. text ed. 59.95 (*0-521-35045-X*) Cambridge U Pr.

Reconstructing the Criminal: Culture, Law & Policy in England, 1830-1914. Martin J. Wiener. (Illus.). 400p. (C). 1994. pap. text ed. 19.95 (*0-521-47882-0*) Cambridge U Pr.

Reconstructing the Family in Contemporary American Fiction. Desmond F. McCarthy. LC 94-38218. (Studies on Themes & Motifs in Literature: Vol. 6). 176p. (C). 1997. text ed. 39.95 (*0-8204-2306-8*) P Lang Pubng.

Reconstructing the Federal Budget: A Trillion Dollar Quandry. Ed. by Albert T. Sommers. LC 83-23801. 255p. 1984. text ed. 59.95 (*0-275-91273-6*, C1273, Praeger Pubs) Greenwood.

Reconstructing the History of Basin & Range Extension Using Sedimentology & Stratigraphy. Ed. by Kathi K. Beratan. (Special Papers: No. 303). (Illus.). 212p. 1996. 78.50 (*0-8137-2303-5*) Geol Soc.

Reconstructing the Household: Families, Sex, & the Law in the Nineteenth-Century South. Peter W. Bardaglio. LC 95-11798. (Studies in Legal History). 384p. (C). 1995. text ed. 45.00 (*0-8078-2222-1*) U of NC Pr.

Reconstructing the Mind: Replicability in Research on Human Development. Rene Van der Veer et al. 296p. (C). 1994. text ed. 78.50 (*0-89391-871-7*) Ablex Pub.

Reconstructing the Past: Blacks in Britain, c. 1780-1830. Norma Myers. LC 96-6900. (Slave & Post-Slave Societies & Cultures Ser.). 200p. 1996. 37.00 (*0-7146-4575-3*, Pub. by F Cass Pubs UK); pap. 18.00 (*0-7146-4130-8*, Pub. by F Cass Pubs UK) Intl Spec Bk.

Reconstructing the Past: The Role of Psychologists in Criminal Trials. Ed. by Arne Trankell. 400p. 1983. pap. 46.00 (*90-6544-112-3*) Kluwer Ac.

Reconstructing the Past Parsimony, Evolution, & Inference. Elliott Sober. 288p. 1991. reprint ed. pap. 15.95 (*0-262-69144-2*, Bradford Bks) MIT Pr.

Reconstructing the Rhythm of Beowulf. Robert P. Creed. LC 89-29252. (Illus.). 232p. 1990. text ed. 42.50 (*0-8262-0722-7*) U of Mo Pr.

Reconstructing the Subject: Modernist Painting in Western Germany. Yule F. Heibel. LC 94-28054. 268p. 1995. text ed. 47.50 (*0-691-03646-2*) Princeton U Pr.

Reconstructing the Tradition of Sophia in Gnostic Literature. Deirdre J. Good. LC 86-20253. (Society of Biblical Literature Monographs). 118p. 1987. 25.95 (*1-55540-058-2*, 06-00-32); pap. 16.95 (*1-55540-059-0*, 06 00 32) Scholars Pr GA.

Reconstructing the Union: Theory & Policy During the Civil War. Herman Belz. LC 78-21311. 336p. 1979. reprint ed. text ed. 75.00 (*0-313-20862-X*, BERU, Greenwood Pr) Greenwood.

Reconstructing the Welfare State: Pragmatic Responses to the Welfare Crisis. Howard J. Karger et al. 224p. (C). 1991. pap. 24.00 (*0-8476-7727-3*); lib. bdg. 59.50 (*0-8476-7679-X*) Rowman.

Reconstructing the Western Alliance: Europe & the U. S. A. J. Lucien Radel. LC 89-92795. (Illus.). 100p. (Orig.). (C). 1990. pap. 6.75 (*0-9625359-0-7*) Lakesider Pub.

Reconstructing Theory: Gadamer, Habermas, Luhmann. Ed. by David Roberts. (Interpretations Ser.). 144p. 1995. pap. 14.95 (*0-522-84570-3*, Pub. by Melbourne Univ Pr AT) Paul & Co Pubs.

Reconstructing Urban Regime Theory: Regulating Urban Politics in a Global Economy. Ed. by Mickey Lauria. LC 96-25361. 278p. 1996. 52.00 (*0-7619-0150-7*); pap. 23.95 (*0-7619-0151-5*) Sage.

Reconstructing Womanhood: The Emergence of the Afro-American Woman Novelist. Hazel V. Carby. 240p. 1989. pap. 18.95 (*0-19-506071-7*) OUP.

Reconstructing Womanhood, Reconstructing Feminism: Writings on Black Women. Ed. by Delia Jarrett-Macauley. LC 95-14756. (Women's Studies/Sociology). 224p. (C). 1995. pap. 17.95 (*0-415-11649-X*) Routledge.

Reconstructing Womanhood, Reconstructing Feminism: Writings on Black Women. Ed. by Delia Jarrett-Macauley. LC 95-14756. (Women's Studies/Sociology). 224p. (C). (gr. 13). 1995. text ed. 59.95 (*0-415-11648-1*) Routledge.

Reconstructing Women's Thoughts: The Women's International League for Peace & Freedom Before World War II. Linda Schott. LC 96-20604. (Modern America Ser.). 1997. write for info. (*0-8047-2746-5*) Stanford U Pr.

Reconstructing Yeats: "The Secret Rose" & "The Wind among the Reeds" Steven Putzel. LC 85-22986. 256p. 1986. 53.00 (*0-389-20600-8*, N8158) B&N Imports.

Reconstructing Your Personality. Norman Cawfield. 160p. 1986. mass mkt. 4.99 (*0-88368-172-2*) Whitaker Hse.

***Reconstruction.** Claudia Casper. 1996. 22.95 (*0-312-15199-3*) St Martin.

Reconstruction. David W. Felder. 52p. 1996. pap. text ed. 8.95 (*0-910959-63-3*) Wellington Pr.

Reconstruction. Isherwood. 256p. 1998. 23.00 (*0-06-118001-7*, HarpT) HarpC.

Reconstruction: A Tragic Era? Ed. by Seth M. Scheiner. LC 78-12422. (American Problem Studies). 128p. 1978. reprint ed. pap. text ed. 10.50 (*0-88275-748-2*) Krieger.

Reconstruction: America after the Civil War. Zak Mettger. (Illus.). 96p. (J). 1994. pap. 16.99 (*0-525-67490-X*, Lodestar Bks) Dutton Child Bks.

Reconstruction: America's First Effort at Racial Democracy. Hans L. Trefousse & Louis L. Snyder. LC 79-9722. (Anvil Ser.). 234p. 1979. reprint ed. pap. 12.50 (*0-88275-902-7*) Krieger.

Reconstruction: America's Unfinished Revolution, 1863-1877. Eric Foner. LC 87-45608. (New American Nation Ser.). (Illus.). 736p. 1989. reprint ed. pap. 20.00 (*0-06-091453-X*, PL 1453, PL) HarpC.

Reconstruction: An Anthology of Revisionist Writings. Ed. by Kenneth M. Stampp & Leon F. Litwack. LC 69-17626. (Illus.). xii, 532p. 1969. pap. text ed. 16.95 (*0-8071-0138-9*) La State U Pr.

Reconstruction: Binding the Wounds. Cheryl Edwards. LC 95-68766. (Perspectives on History Ser.). (Illus.). 68p. (Orig.). (YA). (gr. 5 up). 1995. pap. 5.95 (*1-878668-51-X*) Disc Enter Ltd.

Reconstruction: Opposing Viewpoints. Ed. by William Dudley. (American History Ser.). (Illus.). 310p. 1995. pap. text ed. 12.96 (*1-56510-226-6*, 2266); lib. bdg. 20.96 (*1-56510-227-4*, 2274) Greenhaven.

Reconstruction: The Battle for Democracy, 1865-1876. James S. Allen. LC 37-34604. (History of the American People Ser.). (Illus.). 256p. reprint ed. pap. 73.00 (*0-8357-3513-3*, 2034248) Bks Demand.

Reconstruction - Deconstruction. (Orig.). 1994. pap. 26.95 (*1-85490-243-1*) Academy Ed UK.

***Reconstruction after Disaster: Issues & Practices.** Adenrele Awotona. 200p. 1997. text ed. 59.95 (*1-85972-551-1*, Pub. by Avebury Pub UK) Ashgate Pub Co.

Reconstruction after the Civil War. 2nd ed. John H. Franklin. LC 94-27366. (Chicago History of American Civilization Ser.). 280p. 1994. pap. text ed. 15.95 (*0-226-26079-8*) U Ch Pr.

Reconstruction-Analysis of "Buried Child" by Playwright Sam Shepard. Frederick J. Perry. LC 92-865. 172p. 1992. lib. bdg. 79.95 (*0-7734-9810-9*) E Mellen.

Reconstruction & Re-Equipment of Kuwait: New Business Opportunities, 3 vols., Set. Robert Bailey & John Whelan. 600p. 1991. pap. text ed. 615.00 (*1-85333-585-1*) G & T Inc.

Reconstruction & Reaction: The Black Experience of Emancipation, 1861-1913. Michael Golay. (Library of African-American History). 128p. (J). 1996. 17.95 (*0-8160-3318-8*) Facts on File.

Reconstruction & Reform. Joy Hakim. (History of US Ser.: Vol. 7). (Illus.). 160p. (J). (gr. 3-10). 1994. pap. 10.95 (*0-19-507758-X*); lib. bdg. 14.95 (*0-19-507757-1*) OUP.

Reconstruction & Reform. Joy Hakim. (History of US Ser.: Vol. 7). (Illus.). 192p. (J). (gr. 3-10). 1994. 15.95 (*0-19-509512-X*) OUP.

Reconstruction & Regional Diplomacy in the Persian Gulf. Hooshang Amirahmadi & Nader Entessar. LC 92-9290. 256p. (C). (gr. 13). 1992. text ed. 69.95 (*0-415-06485-6*, A7515) Routledge.

Reconstruction & the Constitution. John W. Burgess. LC 72-457. reprint ed. 29.50 (*0-404-00010-X*) AMS Pr.

Reconstruction & Union: Eighteen Sixty-Five & Nineteen Twelve. Paul L. Haworth. LC 72-1097. reprint ed. 29.00 (*0-404-00060-6*) AMS Pr.

Reconstruction at Sewanee. Arthur B. Chitty. (Illus.). 206p. 1993. pap. 15.00 (*0-9627687-6-6*) Univ South Pr.

Reconstruction Bonds & Twentieth-Century Politics: South Dakota Versus North Carolina, 1904. Robert F. Durden. LC 62-10051. 290p. reprint ed. 82.70 (*0-8357-9116-5*, 2017901) Bks Demand.

Reconstruction-Deconstruction. (Architectural Design Profiles Ser.). (Illus.). 88p. 1990. pap. 19.95 (*0-312-03984-0*) St Martin.

Reconstruction Era: Eyewitness Accounts. Intro. by Albert B. Hart. (American History As Told By Contemporaries Ser.). (Illus.). 120p. (C). 1992. pap. text ed. 2.25 (*1-877891-29-0*) Paperbook Pr Inc.

Reconstruction for Oncology. Kroll. 1995. write for info. (*0-8493-5757-8*) CRC Pr.

Reconstruction in Georgia: Economic, Social, Political 1865-1872. C. Mildred Thompson. 1964. 14.50 (*0-8446-1447-5*) Peter Smith.

Reconstruction in Georgia: Economic, Social, Political, 1865-1872. C. Mildred Thompson. LC 76-169777. (Select Bibliographies Reprint Ser.). 1977. reprint ed. 28.95 (*0-8369-5997-3*) Ayer.

Reconstruction in North Carolina. Joseph G. Hamilton. 1964. 17.00 (*0-8446-1219-7*) Peter Smith.

Reconstruction in North Carolina. Joseph G. Hamilton. LC 73-173607. (Black Heritage Library Collection: Columbia University Studies in History, Economics, & Public Law). 1977. reprint ed. 39.95 (*0-8369-8899-X*) Ayer.

Reconstruction in North Carolina. Joseph G. Hamilton. (BCL1 - United States Local History Ser.). 683p. 1991. reprint ed. lib. bdg. 109.00 (*0-7812-6296-8*) Rprt Serv.

Reconstruction in Philosophy. John Dewey. 1957. pap. 15.00 (*0-8070-1585-7*) Beacon Pr.

Reconstruction in Postwar Germany: British Occupation & the Western Zones, 1945-55. Ed. by Ian D. Turner. LC 88-23452. 438p. 1989. 19.95 (*0-85496-096-1*) Berg Pubs.

Reconstruction in Psychoanalysis: Childhood Revisited & Recreated. Harold P. Blum. LC 93-38933. 1994. 32.00 (*0-8236-5783-3*) Intl Univs Pr.

R

Reconstruction in Texas. Cary D. Wintz. (Texas History Ser.). (Illus.). 70p. (Orig.). (C). 1983. pap. text ed. 8.95 (*0-89641-142-7*) American Pr.

Reconstruction in Texas. Charles W. Ramsdell. 1993. reprint ed. lib. bdg. 75.00 (*0-7812-5897-9*) Rprt Serv.

Reconstruction in Texas. Charles W. Ramsdell. (Texas History Paperbacks Ser.: No. 6). 324p. 1970. reprint ed. pap. 8.95 (*0-292-70031-8*) U of Tex Pr.

***Reconstruction Justice of Salmon P. Chase: In Re Turner & Texas v. White.** Harold M. Hyman. LC 96-54819. (Landmark Law Cases & American Society Ser.). 232p. 1997. 25.00 (*0-7006-0834-6*); pap. 12.95 (*0-7006-0835-4*) U Pr of KS.

Reconstruction of a Spanish Golden Age Playhouse: El Corral del Principe (1583-1744) John J. Allen. LC 83-1241. (Illus.). xii, 129p. 1984. 49.95 (*0-8130-0755-0*) U Press Fla.

Reconstruction of American History. Ed. by John Higham. LC 80-14047. 244p. 1980. reprint ed. text ed. 38.50 (*0-313-22460-9*, HIRH, Greenwood Pr) Greenwood.

Reconstruction of American Political Ideology, 1865-1917. Frank Tariello. LC 81-14734. 208p. reprint ed. pap. 59.30 (*0-8357-3141-3*, 2039404) Bks Demand.

Reconstruction of Cell Evolution: A Periodic System. Werner Schwemmler. LC 83-26280. 256p. 1984. 148.00 (*0-8493-5532-X*, QH371, CRC Reprint) Franklin.

Reconstruction of Central America: The Role of the European Community. Ed. by Joaquin Roy. 424p. (C). 1992. pap. 24.95 (*0-935501-46-0*) U Miami N-S Ctr.

Reconstruction of County Representation. Alan L. Clem. 1968. 1.00 (*1-55614-104-1*) U of SD Gov Res Bur.

Reconstruction of Demographic Profiles from Ossuary Skeletal Samples: A Case Study from the Tidewater Potomac. Douglas H. Ubelaker. LC 73-16117. (Smithsonian Contribution to Anthropology Ser.: No. 18). 91p. reprint ed. pap. 26.00 (*0-317-28477-0*, 2020309) Bks Demand.

Reconstruction of Economic Theory. Ed. by Philip Mirowski. 1986. lib. bdg. 81.50 (*0-89838-211-4*) Kluwer Ac.

Reconstruction of Economics: An Analysis of the Fundamentals of Institutional Economics. Allan G. Gruchy. LC 86-25721. (Contributions in Economics & Economic History Ser.: No. 71). 193p. 1987. text ed. 49.95 (*0-313-25679-9*, GRS/, Greenwood Pr) Greenwood.

Reconstruction of Education. William Boyd et al. (School Development Ser.). (Illus.). 208p. 1996. 65.00 (*0-304-33176-7*); pap. 24.95 (*0-304-33179-1*) Cassell.

Reconstruction of Family Policy. Ed. by Elaine A. Anderson & Richard C. Hula. LC 91-46. (Contributions in Family Studies: No. 15). 296p. 1991. text ed. 59.95 (*0-313-27899-7*, HRK, Greenwood Pr) Greenwood.

Reconstruction of Fragmented Ecosystems: Global & Regional Perspectives. Ed. by D. Saunders et al. 326p. 1993. 150.00 (*0-949324-50-7*, Pub. by Surrey Beatty & Sons AT) St Mut.

Reconstruction of Georgia. Alan Conway. LC 66-18867. 254p. reprint ed. pap. 72.40 (*0-685-15886-1*, 2056193) Bks Demand.

Reconstruction of Georgia. Edwin C. Woolley. LC 74-120211. (Columbia University. Studies in the Social Sciences: No. 36). reprint ed. 34.50 (*0-404-51036-1*) AMS Pr.

Reconstruction of Historical Materialism. Jorge A. Larrain. (Modern Revivals in Philosophy Ser.). 138p. 1992. 48.95 (*0-7512-0048-4*, Pub. by Gregg Pub UK) Ashgate Pub Co.

Reconstruction of Historical Materialism. Jorge A. Larrain. Ed. by Thomas B. Bottomore & Michael Mulkay. LC 85-18699. (Controversies in Sociology Ser.: No. 19). 120p. 1986. text ed. 44.95 (*0-04-301207-8*); pap. text ed. 17.95 (*0-04-301208-6*) Routledge Chapman & Hall.

Reconstruction of International Monetary Arrangements. Ed. by Robert Z. Aliber. LC 86-3758. 320p. 1987. text ed. 39.95 (*0-312-66590-3*) St Martin.

Reconstruction of Kuwait. Whelan. 1991. pap. text ed. 218.00 (*1-85333-590-8*) Kluwer Law Tax Pubs.

Reconstruction of Leadership. William Foster. 88p. (C). 1986. 48.00 (*0-7300-0415-5*, Pub. by Deakin Univ AT) St Mut.

Reconstruction of Life from the Skeleton. Ed. by M. Yasar Iscan & Kenneth A. Kennedy. 332p. 1989. text ed. 86.50 (*0-471-56229-7*) Wiley.

Reconstruction of Palestine: Urban & Rural Development. Ed. by A. B. Zahlan. LC 96-16434. 580p. 1996. pap. 34.00 (*0-7103-0557-5*, Pub. by Kegan Paul Intl UK) Col U Pr.

Reconstruction of Patriotism: Education for Civic Consciousness. Morris B. Janowitz. LC 83-14540. 234p. 1984. lib. bdg. 30.00 (*0-226-39304-6*) U Ch Pr.

Reconstruction of Poland, 1914-23. Ed. by Paul Latawski. LC 91-19886. 217p. 1992. text ed. 69.95 (*0-312-06536-1*) St Martin.

Reconstruction of Proto-Ainu. Alexander Vovin. LC 93-32292. (Japanese Studies Library: Vol. 4). xiv, 220p. 1993. 68.00 (*90-04-09905-0*) E J Brill.

Reconstruction of Religious Thoughts in Islam. Muhammad Iqbal. 29.00 (*0-933511-33-7*); pap. 19.95 (*1-56744-114-9*) Kazi Pubns.

Reconstruction of the Child's Hand. Peter R. Carter. LC 90-6068. (Illus.). 321p. 1990. text ed. 89.00 (*0-8121-1350-0*) Williams & Wilkins.

Reconstruction of the Church - on What Pattern? E. Stanley Jones. (Abingdon Classics Ser.). 208p. (Orig.). 1992. reprint ed. pap. 2.38 (*0-687-35731-4*) Abingdon.

Reconstruction of the International Economy, 1945-1960. Ed. by Barry Eichengreen. LC 95-36672. (Growth of the World Economy Ser.: Vol. 5). (Illus.). 672p. 1996. 210.00 (*1-85278-979-4*) E Elgar.

Reconstruction of the International Monetary System: The Attempts of 1922 & 1933. Stephen V. Clarke. LC 73-9360. (Princeton Studies in International Finance Ser.: No. 33). 52p. reprint ed. pap. 25.00 (*0-317-28836-9*, 2017823) Bks Demand.

***Reconstruction of the Knee Joint, Vol. XII.** Ed. by S. Niwa et al. (Illus.). 420p. 1997. 198.00 (*4-431-70170-2*) Spr-Verlag.

Reconstruction of the New York Democracy, 1861-1874. Jerome Mushkat. LC 78-16826. 328p. 1981. 33.50 (*0-8386-3002-2*, 3002) Fairleigh Dickinson.

Reconstruction of the Oral Cavity. 2nd rev. ed. Jonas T. Johnson et al. LC 94-31837. (Self-Instructional Package Ser.). (Illus.). 75p. (C). 1994. pap. text ed. 25.00 (*1-56772-014-5*) AAO-HNS.

Reconstruction of the Skull of Gigantopithecus Blacki. Steven N. Byers. (Illus.). viii, 87p. 1986. reprint ed. pap. text ed. 9.45 (*1-55567-033-4*) Coyote Press.

Reconstruction of the Spiritual Ideal. Felix Adler. LC 77-27148. (Hibbert Lectures: 1923). reprint ed. 35.00 (*0-404-60422-6*) AMS Pr.

Reconstruction of the West Breakwater at Port Sines, Portugal. Rubble Mound Structures Committee of the Waterway, Port, & Ocean Division of the American Society of Civil Engineers & Administracao do Porto de Sines, Sines, Portugal. LC 94-30076. 1994. 41.00 (*0-7844-0044-X*) Am Soc Civil Eng.

Reconstruction of Thinking. Robert C. Neville. LC 81-5347. 350p. 1981. text ed. 59.50 (*0-87395-494-7*); pap. text ed. 19.95 (*0-87395-495-5*) State U NY Pr.

Reconstruction of Trauma: Monograph II. Ed. by Arnold Rothstein. LC 86-10672. (Workshop Series of the American Psychoanalytic Association). 280p. (C). 1986. 40.00 (*0-8236-5786-8*) Intl Univs Pr.

Reconstruction of Trees from Their Automorphism Groups. Matatyahu Rubin. LC 93-11577. (Contemporary Mathematics Ser.: Vol. 151). 274p. 1993. pap. 56.00 (*0-8218-5187-X*, CONM/151) Am Math.

Reconstruction of Western Europe 1945-51. Alan S. Milward. LC 83-17931. 500p. 1984. pap. 18.95 (*0-520-06035-0*) U CA Pr.

Reconstruction, Political & Economic, 1865-1877. William A. Dunning. (History - United States Ser.). 378p. 1993. reprint ed. lib. bdg. 89.00 (*0-7812-4818-3*) Rprt Serv.

Reconstruction Surgery & Traumatology, Vol. 12. Ed. by G. Chapchal. 1971. 78.50 (*3-8055-1183-3*) S Karger.

Reconstruction Surgery & Traumatology, Vol. 14. G. Chapchal. (Illus.). 200p. 1974. 78.50 (*3-8055-1563-4*) S Karger.

Reconstruction Surgery & Traumatology, Vol. 15. Ed. by G. Chapchal. 1976. 39.25 (*3-8055-2250-9*) S Karger.

Reconstruction Surgery & Traumatology, Vol. 16. Ed. by G. Chapchal. (Illus.). 1977. 46.50 (*3-8055-2696-2*) S Karger.

***Reconstruction Surgery & Traumatology Vol. 13: Operative Treatment of Cerebral Palsy.** Ed. by G. Chapchal. (Illus.). 1972. 85.25 (*3-8055-1385-2*) S Karger.

Reconstruction to the Spanish-American War: Significant Events & the People Who Shaped Them see Profiles in American History

Reconstruction Trilogy: The Leopard's Spots; The Clansman; The Traitor. Thomas Dixon, Jr. xx, 550p. (C). 1994. 28.00 (*0-939482-49-5*, Noontide Pr); pap. 18.00 (*0-939482-48-7*, Noontide Pr) Legion Survival.

Reconstructionists see IVP Booklets

Reconstructions. Avant-Garde Art in Japan 1945-1965: Museum of Modern Art. David Elliott et al. 96p. 1986. pap. 44.00 (*0-905836-54-5*, Pub. by Museum Modern Art UK) St Mut.

Reconstructions of Early Christian Documents. Herbert J. Bardsley. 1977. lib. bdg. 59.95 (*0-8490-2504-4*) Gordon Pr.

Reconstructive & Esthetic Mammoplasty. Guthrie & Schwartz. 848p. 1989. text ed. 169.00 (*0-7216-2806-0*) Saunders.

Reconstructive Flaps in the Head & Neck. Hayden. 350p. (C). (gr. 13). 1998. text ed. 195.00 (*0-8151-4453-9*) Mosby Yr Bk.

Reconstructive Knee Surgery. (Illus.). 1994. sl. 450.00 (*0-7817-0252-6*) Lppncott-Raven.

Reconstructive Knee Surgery. Ed. by Douglas W. Jackson. LC 94-2265. (Master Techniques in Orthopaedic Surgery Ser.). (Illus.). 336p. 1994. text ed. 189.00 (*0-7817-0031-0*) Lppncott-Raven.

Reconstructive Microsurgery. Bernard M. O'Brien & Wayne A. Morrison. (Illus.). 540p. 1987. text ed. 275.00 (*0-443-02557-6*) Churchill.

Reconstructive Microvascular Surgery. E. Biemer & W. Duspiva. (Illus.). 151p. 1982. 144.00 (*0-387-11320-7*) Spr-Verlag.

***Reconstructive Phase Transitions: In Crystals & Quasicrystals.** Pierre Toledano & Vladimir Dmitriev. LC 96-9517. 1996. pap. write for info. (*981-02-2840-6*) World Scientific Pub.

Reconstructive Phase Transitions - Density-Wave Theory of Phase Transition in Crystal. Pierre Toledano & Vladimir Dmitriev. 350p. 1996. text ed. 78.00 (*981-02-2364-1*) World Scientific Pub.

Reconstructive Plastic Surgery: Principles & Procedures in Correction Reconstruction & Transplantation, 7 vols., 1. 2nd ed. Ed. by John M. Converse. LC 74-21010. (Illus.). 1977. text ed. 135.00 (*0-7216-2680-7*) Saunders.

Reconstructive Plastic Surgery: Principles & Procedures in Correction Reconstruction & Transplantation, 7 vols., 2. 2nd ed. Ed. by John M. Converse. LC 74-21010. (Illus.). 1977. text ed. 135.00 (*0-7216-2681-5*) Saunders.

Reconstructive Plastic Surgery: Principles & Procedures in Correction Reconstruction & Transplantation, 7 vols., 3. 2nd ed. Ed. by John M. Converse. LC 74-21010. (Illus.). 1977. text ed. 135.00 (*0-7216-2682-3*) Saunders.

Reconstructive Plastic Surgery: Principles & Procedures in Correction Reconstruction & Transplantation, 7 vols., 4. 2nd ed. Ed. by John M. Converse. LC 74-21010. (Illus.). 1977. text ed. 135.00 (*0-7216-2683-1*) Saunders.

Reconstructive Plastic Surgery: Principles & Procedures in Correction Reconstruction & Transplantation, 7 vols., 5. 2nd ed. Ed. by John M. Converse. LC 74-21010. (Illus.). 1977. text ed. 135.00 (*0-7216-2684-X*) Saunders.

Reconstructive Plastic Surgery: Principles & Procedures in Correction Reconstruction & Transplantation, 7 vols., 6. 2nd ed. Ed. by John M. Converse. LC 74-21010. (Illus.). 1977. text ed. 135.00 (*0-7216-2685-8*) Saunders.

Reconstructive Plastic Surgery: Principles & Procedures in Correction Reconstruction & Transplantation, 7 vols., 7. 2nd ed. Ed. by John M. Converse. LC 74-21010. (Illus.). 1977. text ed. 135.00 (*0-7216-2686-6*) Saunders.

Reconstructive Plastic Surgery: Principles & Procedures in Correction Reconstruction & Transplantation, 7 vols., Set. 2nd ed. Ed. by John M. Converse. LC 74-21010. (Illus.). 1977. text ed. 865.00 (*0-7216-2691-2*) Saunders.

***Reconstructive Plastic Surgery External.** Ehrlich. 1998. text ed. write for info. (*0-7216-6328-1*) Saunders.

Reconstructive Plastic Surgery for Cancer. Stephen S. Kroll. 336p. (C). (gr. 13). 1995. text ed. 105.00 (*0-8151-5264-7*) Mosby Yr Bk.

Reconstructive Preprosthetic Oral & Maxillofacial Surgery, 2 vols., Set. 2nd ed. Raymond J. Fonseca & W. Howard Davis. LC 94-31809. (Illus.). 1040p. 1995. text ed. 269.00 (*0-7216-3307-2*) Saunders.

Reconstructive Surgery: Clinical Applications. Stephen J. Mathes & Foad Nahai. (Illus.). 600p. 1997. 150.00 (*0-942219-94-5*) Quality Med Pub.

***Reconstructive Surgery: Principles, Anatomy & Technique.** Stephen J. Mathes & Foad Nahai. LC 96-29462. 1996. write for info. (*0-443-07981-1*) Churchill.

Reconstructive Surgery: Principles, Anatomy & Technique, 2 vols., Set. Stephen J. Mathes & Foad Nahai. LC 96-29462. (Illus.). 1500p. 1996. 425.00 (*0-942219-02-3*) Quality Med Pub.

Reconstructive Surgery in Gynecology. Ed. by Paul G. Knapstein et al. (Illus.). 282p. 1990. text ed. 189.00 (*0-86577-356-4*) Thieme Med Pubs.

Reconstructive Surgery of the Joints, 2 vols., Set. 2nd rev. ed. Ed. by Bernard F. Morrey. LC 95-44399. Orig. Title: Joint Replacement Arthroplasty. 1876p. 1995. 350.00 (*0-443-08982-5*) Churchill.

Reconstructive Surgery of the Long Bones with Autogenous & Homogenous Grafts. O. Verbeek et al. 1973. lib. bdg. 112.00 (*90-207-0343-9*) Kluwer Ac.

Reconstructive Surgery of the Rear Foot & Ankle. Dennis Gusman. 400p. 1994. 89.00 (*0-8016-7002-0*) Mosby Yr Bk.

Reconstructive Urology. George Webster et al. (Illus.). 1152p. 1992. 325.00 (*0-86542-229-X*) Blackwell Sci.

Recontres sur le Mississipi, 1682-1763. Gail Buzhardt & Margaret Hawthorne. (Illus.). 280p. (YA). (gr. 10-12). 1993. text ed. 28.00 (*0-87805-665-3*) U Pr of Miss.

Recopilacion de Trabajos Manuales. Cristina M. De Higuero. LC 90-71851. 50p. (Orig.). (SPA.). (J). (gr. 3-6). 1990. pap. 20.00 (*0-9605082-2-8*) Allied Ent.

Recopilacion en Metro: Edicion Facsimil (Sevilla, 1554) Diego Sanchez de Badajoz. 134p. (SPA.). 1968. 125.00 (*0-614-00131-5*) Elliots Bks.

Recopilacion en Metro: Edicion Facsimil (Sevilla, 1554) Diego Sanchez de Badajoz. 134p. (SPA.). 1968. pap. 125.00 (*0-614-00236-2*) Elliots Bks.

Record & Documentary History of Simsbury, Ct. Lucius I. Barber. 429p. 1993. reprint ed. lib. bdg. 45.00 (*0-8328-2853-X*) Higginson Bk Co.

Record & Music Publishing Forms of Agreement in Current Use. Compiled by Irwin O. Spiegel & Jay L. Cooper. LC 72-144789. 859p. 1971. ring bd. 59.00 (*0-88238-028-1*) Law Arts.

Record & Remember: Tracing Your Roots Through Oral History. Jane Lewit. 1993. pap. 10.95 (*0-8128-8550-3*, Scrbrough Hse) Madison Bks UPA.

Record & Revelation. Ed. by Henry W. Robinson. LC 76-29395. reprint ed. 35.50 (*0-404-15354-2*) AMS Pr.

Record Book, International Edition: A Guide to the World of the Phonograph. David A. Hall. LC 78-5686. 1394p. 1978. reprint ed. text ed. 95.00 (*0-313-20425-X*, HATR, Greenwood Pr) Greenwood.

Record Book of Daniel Schumacher, 1754-1773. Tr. by FRederick S. Weiser. 320p. 1994. 29.50 (*0-89725-117-2*, 1425) Picton Pr.

Record Book of the St. Louis Philosophical Society, Founded February, 1866. Ed. by Kurt F. Leidecker. LC 89-37669. (Studies in the History of Philosophy: Vol. 14). (Illus.). 136p. 1990. lib. bdg. 69.95 (*0-88946-289-5*) E Mellen.

Record Book of Trophy Animals (Africa), Vol. 1. 8th ed. Safari Club International Staff. (Illus.). 900p. 1994. pap. 60.00 (*0-940143-95-X*) Safari Pr.

Record Book of USGA Championships & International Events: 1895 Through 1980, 2 vols. 7.50 (*0-686-30840-9*) US Golf Assn.

Record Book of USGA Championships & International Events: 1895 Through 1980, 2 vols. 1981. suppl. ed. 1.00 (*0-685-05204-4*) US Golf Assn.

Record Book of USGA Championships & International Events: 1895 Through 1980, 2 vols. 1982. suppl. ed. 1.00 (*0-685-05205-2*) US Golf Assn.

Record Book of USGA Championships & International Events: 1895 Through 1980, 2 vols. 1983. suppl. ed. 1.00 (*0-685-05207-9*) US Golf Assn.

Record Book of USGA Championships & International Events: 1895 Through 1980, 2 vols. 1984. suppl. ed. 1.00 (*0-685-05206-0*) US Golf Assn.

Record Book of USGA Championships & International Events: 1895 Through 1980, 2 vols. 1985. suppl. ed. 1.00 (*0-685-05208-7*) US Golf Assn.

Record Book of USGA Championships & International Events: 1895 Through 1980, 2 vols. 1986. suppl. ed. 1.00 (*0-685-05209-5*) US Golf Assn.

Record Book Plus. Lee Canter. 158p. 1992. student ed. 6.95 (*0-939007-43-6*) Lee Canter & Assocs.

Record Breakers. LC 95-12485. (Look Inside Cross-Sections Ser.). (Illus.). 32p. (YA). (gr. 5 up). 1995. pap. 5.95 (*0-7894-0320-X*, 5-70670) DK Pub Inc.

Record Breakers. (Baseball's Best Ser.). (Illus.). 24p. (J). (gr. 1 up). 1991. pap. 3.95 (*0-671-73634-5*, Litl Simon S&S) S&S Childrens.

***Record Breakers & Other Speed Machines.** Moira Butterfield et al. (Illus.). (J). pap. 8.99 (*0-590-24653-4*) Scholastic Inc.

Record Breakers of the Air. Rupert O. Matthews. LC 89-5212. (Illus.). 32p. (J). (gr. 2-6). 1990. lib. bdg. 9.95 (*0-8167-1921-7*) Troll Communs.

Record Breakers of the Land. Rupert O. Matthews. LC 89-5202. (Illus.). 32p. (J). (gr. 2-6). 1990. lib. bdg. 9.95 (*0-8167-1923-3*) Troll Communs.

Record Breakers of the Sea. Rupert O. Matthews. LC 89-35503. (Illus.). 32p. (J). (gr. 2-6). 1990. lib. bdg. 9.95 (*0-8167-1925-X*) Troll Communs.

Record Breaking Heatwave. Jeff Friedman. LC 86-71497. 1986. 8.00 (*0-933532-59-8*) BkMk.

Record Collector's Fact Book, Vol. I. Chuck Brigermann. LC 82-73474. (Illus.). 96p. 1983. pap. 7.95 (*0-89709-037-3*) Liberty Pub.

Record Collector's Record Books. Alan Leibowitz. Ed. by Roger Adler & Andrew Adler. 1979. pap. 5.95 (*0-916844-07-2*) Turtle Pr.

Record Forms for the Uzgiris-Hunt Scales, 5 pts., Set. Ina C. Uzgiris & J. McVicker Hunt. 1982. 15.75 (*0-252-00905-3*) U of Ill Pr.

Record, Genealogical, Biographical, & Statistical of Thomas Stanton of Connecticut & His Descendants, 1635-1891. W. A. Stanton. (Illus.). 613p. 1989. reprint ed. pap. 92.00 (*0-8328-1111-4*); reprint ed. lib. bdg. 100.00 (*0-8328-1110-6*) Higginson Bk Co.

Record Guide. John Sarian. LC 79-63060. 1979. pap. 3.00 (*0-933706-05-7*) Ararat Pr.

Record Guide, 2 vols. Edward Sackville-West & Desmond Shawe-Taylor. LC 78-5028. 1978. reprint ed. Incl. supplement. suppl. ed., text ed. 95.00 (*0-313-20404-7*, SWRG, Greenwood Pr) Greenwood.

Record Guide, 2 vols., 1. Edward Sackville-West & Desmond Shawe-Taylor. LC 78-5028. 1978. reprint ed. text ed. 75.00 (*0-313-20405-5*, SWRG01, Greenwood Pr) Greenwood.

Record Guide, 2 vols., Vol. 2. Edward Sackville-West & Desmond Shawe-Taylor. LC 78-5028. 1978. reprint ed. text ed. 45.00 (*0-313-20406-3*, SWRG02, Greenwood Pr) Greenwood.

Record Industry Book, No. 1. 7th rev. ed. Walter E. Hurst. (Entertainment Industry Ser.). 1979. pap. 10.00 (*0-911370-32-3*); text ed. 15.00 (*0-911370-31-5*) Seven Arts.

Record Interpreter: A Collection of Abbreviations, Latin Words & Names Used in English Historical Manuscripts & Records. Charles T. Martin. 404p. 1910. reprint ed. lib. bdg. 132.00 (*3-487-02295-8*) G Olms Pubs.

Record Interpreter: A Collection of Abbreviations, Latin Words & Names Used in English Historical Manuscripts & Records. Charles T. Martin. xv, 464p. 1969. reprint ed. 76.70 (*0-685-66494-5*, 05102295) G Olms Pubs.

Record Keeping & Archives in West Germany. Maralyn A. Wellauer. 54p. 1987. pap. 10.00 (*0-932019-10-2*) Roots Intl.

Record Keeping Applications Using the Microcomputer. Keith Weidkamp. (BB - Record Keeping I Ser.). 1988. pap. 20.95 (*0-538-02000-8*) S-W Pub.

Record Keeping for Business: Syllabus. Marvin W. Hempel. 1977. pap. text ed. 12.95 (*0-89420-018-6*, 359090); audio 139.80 (*0-89420-180-8*, 359000) Natl Book.

***Record Keeping for Massage/Bodywork Professionals.** Jefferson C. Saunders. 1997. pap. text ed. 18.00 (*1-877738-18-2*) Superior Pub WA.

Record Keeping for Personal Finance: Syllabus. Marvin W. Hempel. 1976. pap. text ed. 11.75 (*0-89420-005-4*, 358080); audio 124.25 (*0-89420-181-6*, 358000) Natl Book.

Record Keeping for Small Rural Businesses. Eligia Murcia. (Technical Notes Ser.: No. 26). (Illus.). 25p. (Orig.). pap. text ed. 2.00 (*0-932288-75-8*) Ctr Intl Ed U of MA.

***Record Keeping Guidelines for Occupational Injuries & Illnesses.** 1996. lib. bdg. 255.75 (*0-8490-6359-0*) Gordon Pr.

Record Keeping in the Computer Age. 6th ed. Baron & Steinfeld. (BB - Record Keeping I Ser.). 1986. text ed. 48.95 (*0-538-02010-5*) S-W Pub.

Record Keeping in the Computer Age. 6th ed. Baron & Steinfeld. (Bb-Record Keeping Ser.: Vol. 1). 1986. pap. 15.95 (*0-538-02011-3*) S-W Pub.

Record Keeping in the Computer Age - Working Papers. 6th ed. Baron & Steinfeld. (BB - Record Keeping I Ser.). 1986. pap. 28.95 (*0-538-02016-4*) S-W Pub.

Record Keeping in the Computer Age - Working Papers. 6th ed. Baron & Steinfeld. (BB = Record Keeping I Ser.). 1986. pap. 16.95 (*0-538-02012-1*) S-W Pub.

Record Keeping in the Computer Age, Tests. 6th ed. Baron & Steinfeld. (BB - Record Keeping I Ser.). 1986. 2.95 (*0-538-02013-X*); 2.95 (*0-538-02014-8*) S-W Pub.

Record Label Guide for Domestic LPs. Joe Lindsay. (Illus.). 200p. (Orig.). 1986. pap. 14.95 (*0-9617347-0-1*) BIODISC.

Record Management. Jerry Belch. Ed. by Valerie Harris. (Simulating the Medical Office). 76p. 1993. Record Management, 76p. 7.98 (*0-89262-313-6*) Career Pub.

Record Management see Simulating the Medical Office

An Asterisk (*) at the beginning of an entry indicates that the title is appearing in BIP for the first time.

Record of a Life: An Autobiographical Sketch. Georg Lukacs. Tr. by Rodney Livingstone from GER. 204p. (C). 1983. pap. text ed. 20.00 (*0-86091-771-1*, Pub. by Vrso UK) Norton.

Record of a Quaker Conscience see Civil War Diary of Cyrus Pringle: Record of Quaker Conscience

Record of a School. Elizabeth P. Peabody. LC 74-89218. (American Education: Its Men, Institutions, & Ideas. Series 1). 1974. reprint ed. 20.95 (*0-405-01457-0*) Ayer.

Record of Achievement of Dr. Lawrence C. Bryant. Lawrence C. Bryant. 1966. 5.00 (*0-686-05556-X*) L C Bryant.

***Record of American Uniform & Historical Buttons, Bicentennial Edition.** Alphaeus H. Albert. LC 76-58596. (Illus.). 511p. 1977. 40.00 (*0-614-29612-9*) North South Trader.

Record of an Obscure Man. Mary T. Putnam. LC 70-82213. (Anti-Slavery Crusade in America Ser.). 1970. reprint ed. 25.95 (*0-405-00652-7*) Ayer.

Record of Auroral Phenomena. Peter Force. (Notable American Authors Ser.). 1992. lib. bdg. 75.00 (*0-7812-2870-0*) Rprt Serv.

***Record of Buddhist Monasteries in Lo-Yang.** Hsuan-chih Yang. LC 83-42586. (Princeton Library of Asian Translations). 333p. 1984. reprint ed. pap. 95.00 (*0-608-03323-5*, 2064035) Bks Demand.

Record of Buddhistic Kingdoms. Hien Fa. 1991. pap. 5.95 (*0-486-26760-1*) Dover.

Record of Buddhistic Kingdoms. Tr. by Legge. (C). 1991. 23.50 (*0-685-50018-7*, Pub. by Munshiram Manoharial II) S Asia.

Record of Conference Papers Industry Applications Society 42nd Annual Petroleum & Chemical Industry Conference. IEEE, Industry Applications Society Staff. Ed. by Institute of Electrical & Electronics Engineers, Inc. Staff. LC 73-641120. 350p. 1995. pap. text ed. 106.00 (*0-7803-2909-0*, 95CH35840); lib. bdg. 106.00 (*0-7803-2910-4*, 95CB35840); fiche 106.00 (*0-7803-2911-2*, 95CM35840) Inst Electrical.

Record of Connecticut Militia in the War of 1812. (Illus.). 180p. 1995. reprint ed. lib. bdg. 32.50 (*0-8328-4651-1*) Higginson Bk Co.

Record of Deaths - Town of Ludlow, Vermont. Rufus S. Warner & Charles D. Townsend. 109p. 1995. reprint ed. pap. 25.00 (*1-878545-06-X*) ACETO Bookmen.

Record of Deaths in Columbia South Carolina & Elsewhere As Recorded by John Glass 1859-1877. Brent H. Holcomb. 223p. (C). 1986. 20.00 (*0-913363-05-7*) SCMAR.

Record of European Armour & Arms Through Seven Centuries, 5 vols., Set. Guy F. Laking. LC 79-8365. (Illus.). reprint ed. 295.00 (*0-404-18344-1*) AMS Pr.

***Record of Events in Norfolk County, from April 19th, 1861, to May 10th, 1862, with a History of the Soldiers & Sailors of Norfolk Co., Norfolk City & Portsmouth Who Served in the Confederate Army or Navy.** John W. Porter. (Illus.). 366p. 1997. reprint ed. lib. bdg. 42.00 (*0-8328-6516-8*) Higginson Bk Co.

Record of Evidence & Statements Before the Penitentiary Investigating Committee: Appointed by the Thirty-Third Legislature of Texas. Texas, Penitentiary Investigating Committee. LC 74-3847. (Criminal Justice in America Ser.). 1974. reprint ed. 34.95 (*0-405-06171-4*) Ayer.

Record of Hawksbill Church 1788-1850, Page County, Virginia. Klaus Wust. 1979. pap. 10.00 (*0-917968-06-9*) Shenandoah Hist.

Record of Indentures (1771-1773) Of Individuals Bound Out As Apprentices, Servants, etc. & of German & Other Redemptioners in the Office of the Mayor of the City of Philadelphia, October 3, 1771, to October 5, 1773. 364p. 1995. reprint ed. pap. 30.00 (*0-614-10011-9*, 4590) Clearfield Co.

***Record of Interments at the Friends Burial Ground, Baltimore, Maryland.** E. Erick Hoopes & Christina Hoopes. 66p. 1996. reprint ed. pap. 10.00 (*0-614-23540-5*, 9143) Clearfield Co.

Record of Living Officers of the U. S. Hamersley. 1976. 27.95 (*0-8488-1036-8*) Amereon Ltd.

Record of Meetings. P. D. Ouspensky. 672p. 1993. pap. 18.95 (*0-14-019307-3*, Arkana) Viking Penguin.

Record of My Life-Work in Entomology. C. R. Osten-Sacken & K. G. Smith. 1978. 50.00 (*0-317-07172-6*) St Mut.

***Record of Officers & Men of New Jersey in the Civil War, 1861-1865, 2 vols., Set.** Compiled by Office of the Adj General Staff. 1996. reprint ed. lib. bdg. 199.00 (*0-8328-5212-0*) Higginson Bk Co.

Record of Oral Language & Biks & Gutches. Marie M. Clay et al. (Illus.). 91p. (Orig.). (C). 1983. pap. text ed. 19.50 (*0-86863-269-4*, 00571) Heinemann.

Record of Pennsylvania Marriages Prior to 1810, 2 vols. John B. Linn & William H. Egle. 1987. reprint ed. 75.00 (*0-8063-0214-3*, 3400) Genealog Pub.

Record of Service of Connecticut Men in the Army & Navy of the United States, During the War of the Rebellion. 1071p. 1996. reprint ed. lib. bdg. 105.00 (*0-8328-4979-0*) Higginson Bk Co.

Record of Singing, 2 vols. Michael Scott. LC 92-46984. 1993. reprint ed. pap. text ed. 55.00 (*1-55553-163-6*) NE U Pr.

Record of Staff Visits to Restricted Units. rev. ed. American Correctional Association Staff. 196p. 1991. pap. 24.95 (*0-929310-50-0*, 431) Am Correctional.

Record of the Bartholomew Family: Historical, Genealogical, & Biographical. George W. Bartholomew, Jr. (Illus.). 769p. 1988. reprint ed. pap. 115.00 (*0-8328-0197-6*); reprint ed. lib. bdg. 123.00 (*0-8328-0196-8*) Higginson Bk Co.

Record of the Boston Stage. William W. Clapp. LC 11-19303. 1853. 12.00 (*0-403-00473-X*) Scholarly.

Record of the Boston Stage. William W. Clapp. LC 68-58197. 1972. reprint ed. 36.95 (*0-405-08362-9*, Pub. by Blom Pubns UK) Ayer.

Record of the Buddhist Religion As Practiced in India & the Malaysia Archipelago AD 671-695. I-Tsing. 1982. 23.50 (*0-8364-2613-4*, Pub. by Munshiram Manoharial II) S Asia.

Record of the Descendants of Charles Bowler. N. P. Bowler & C. B. Malone. (Illus.). 298p. 1988. reprint ed. pap. 44.50 (*0-8328-0293-X*); reprint ed. lib. bdg. 52.50 (*0-8328-0292-1*) Higginson Bk Co.

Record of the Descendants of George Denison of Stonington, Conn. J. D. Baldwin & W. Clift. (Illus.). 424p. 1989. reprint ed. pap. 63.50 (*0-8328-0471-1*); reprint ed. lib. bdg. 71.50 (*0-8328-0470-3*) Higginson Bk Co.

Record of the Descendants of John & Elizabeth Bull, Early Settlers in Pennsylvania. James H. Bull. (Illus.). 387p. 1993. reprint ed. pap. 60.00 (*0-8328-3018-6*); reprint ed. lib. bdg. 70.00 (*0-8328-3017-8*) Higginson Bk Co.

Record of the Descendants of John Clark of Farmington, Connecticut. J. Gay. (Illus.). 94p. 1993. reprint ed. pap. 18.50 (*0-8328-1351-6*); reprint ed. lib. bdg. 28.50 (*0-8328-1350-8*) Higginson Bk Co.

Record of the IEEE 1995 International Radar Conference. IEEE, Aerospace & Electronics Systems Society Staff. Ed. by IEEE Staff. LC 90-81178. 704p. 1995. pap. text ed. write for info. (*0-7803-2120-0*, 94CH35710); lib. bdg. write for info. (*0-7803-2121-9*, 94CH35710); fiche write for info. (*0-7803-2122-7*) Inst Electrical.

Record of the Ninth COMPUMAG Conference on the Computation of Electromagnetic Fields, 1993. IEEE, Miami Section, Florida Council Staff & IEEE, Region Three Staff. LC 93-80304. 800p. 1993. pap. write for info. (*0-7803-1490-5*, 93TH0598-3); fiche write for info. (*0-7803-1491-3*, 93TH0598-3) Inst Electrical.

Record of the Opera in Philadelphia. W. G. Armstrong. LC 74-27327. reprint ed. 41.50 (*0-404-12853-X*) AMS Pr.

***Record of the Revolutionary Soldiers Buried in Lake County, with a Partial List of Those in Geauga Co.** New Connecticut Chapter D.A.R. Staff. (Illus.). 94p. 1997. reprint ed. pap. 17.00 (*0-8328-6333-5*) Higginson Bk Co.

Record of the Rust Family, Embracing the Descendants of Henry Rust, Who Came from England & Settled in Hingham, Mass., 1634-1635. A. D. Rust. (Illus.). 544p. 1989. reprint ed. pap. 81.50 (*0-8328-1043-6*); reprint ed. lib. bdg. 89.50 (*0-8328-1042-8*) Higginson Bk Co.

Record of the Service: Of the Fifty-Fifth Regiment of Massachusetts Volunteer Infantry. LC 72-168519. (Black Heritage Library Collection). 1977. reprint ed. 22.95 (*0-8369-8871-X*) Ayer.

Record of the Services: Of the Seventh Regiment. LC 79-168518. (Black Heritage Library Collection). 1977. reprint ed. 22.95 (*0-8369-8870-1*) Ayer.

***Record of the Services of Illinois Soldiers in the Black-Hawk War, 1831-32, & in the Mexican War, 1846-48, Containing a Complete Roster...** Isaac H. Elliott. (Illus.). 343p. 1997. reprint ed. lib. bdg. 39.50 (*0-8328-5709-2*) Higginson Bk Co.

Record of the Services of the Commissioned Officers & Enlisted Men of Kittery & Eliot, Maine, in the American Revolution. Oliver P. Remick. LC 86-60507. (Illus.). 235p. 1986. reprint ed. 25.00 (*0-89725-062-1*, 1217) Picton Pr.

***Record of the Services of the Commissioned Officers & Enlisted Men of Kittery & Eliot, Who Served Their Country...in the Revolution, 1775-1783.** Oliver P. Remick. (Illus.). 223p. 1997. reprint ed. pap. 25.00 (*0-8328-5864-1*) Higginson Bk Co.

Record of the 114th Regiment. N.Y.S.V. Where It Went, What It Saw, & What It Did. Harris H. Beecher. 592p. 1996. reprint ed. pap. 70.00 (*1-887530-08-8*) RSG Pub.

Record of the 114th Regiment of New York: State Volunteers of the Civil War. H. H. Beecher. 592p. 1996. reprint ed. 80.00 (*1-887530-05-3*) RSG Pub.

Record of Transmitting the Light: Zen Master Keizan's Denkoroku. Francis H. Cook. 300p. 1991. text ed. write for info. (*0-916820-19-X*); pap. text ed. write for info. (*0-916820-20-3*) Center Pubns.

Record of Tung-shan. William F. Powell. LC 86-4305. (Classics in East Asian Buddhism Ser.). 112p. 1986. pap. text ed. 9.00 (*0-8248-1070-8*) UH Pr.

Record of Walton's Creek Baptist Church, Ohio County, KY, 1814-1914. 100p. 1988. 10.00 (*0-318-23377-0*) West Cent KY Family Re Assoc.

Record Offices: How to Find Them. (C). 1987. 30.00 (*0-317-89812-4*, Pub. by Birmingham Midland Soc UK) St Mut.

Record Offices in England & Wales: How to Find Them. 5th ed. J. S. Gibson & Pamela Peskett. (Illus.). 60p. 1991. 7.50 (*0-8063-1357-9*, 2185) Genealog Pub.

Record Producer's Handbook. Don Gere & David Campbell. LC 78-69921. 1978. pap. 7.95 (*0-918226-07-4*) Acrobat.

Record-Setting Animals. Melinda Burgener. write for info. (*0-318-62787-6*) S&S Trade.

Record Shelf Guide to Classical CDs & Audiocassettes. 4th rev. ed. Jim Svejda. LC 94-21510. 1994. pap. 18.95 (*1-55958-573-0*) Prima Pub.

Record Shelf Guide to Classical CDs & Audiocassettes. 5th rev. ed. Jim Svejda. LC 96-25446. 880p. 1996. pap. text ed. 20.00 (*0-7615-0591-1*) Prima Pub.

Record Shelf Guide to the Classical Repertoire. 3rd enl. rev. ed. Jim Svejda. 528p. (Orig.). 1992. pap. 16.95 (*1-55958-223-5*) Prima Pub.

Record Statistics. Mohammad Ahsanullah. (Illus.). 227p. (C). 1994. lib. bdg. 69.00 (*1-56072-203-7*) Nova Sci Pubs.

Record 24th Michigan Infantry Civil War 1861-1865. 184p. 1995. 12.95 (*0-914905-24-4*) Detroit Bk Pr.

***Recordable CD Bible.** Mark Chambers. 1997. pap. 49.99 (*0-7645-3103-4*) IDG Bks.

Recordando Sus Vidas Pasadas. Ed. by Maria E. Alvarez del Real. (Illus.). 288p. (Orig.). (SPA.). 1991. pap. 4.95 (*1-56259-000-6*) Editorial Amer.

Recordar Es. Felix Guardiola. 148p. 1985. 10.00 (*0-917049-01-2*) Saeta.

Recordatio rei Antelatae: Zur Semantik Anaphorischer Pronomina - Untersuchungen Scholastischer & Moderner Theorien. Reinhard Hulsen. (Studien und Texte zur Geistesgeschichte des Mittelalters Ser.: No. 41). 1993. 163.00 (*90-04-09832-1*, NLG210) E J Brill.

Recorded Hits, Vol. 11. 72p. Date not set. pap. 7.95 (*0-7935-2127-0*, 00100560) H Leonard.

Recorded Performances of Gerard Souzay: A Discography. Compiled by Manuel Morris. LC 90-13978. (Discographies Ser.: No. 41). 260p. 1990. text ed. 55.00 (*0-313-27392-8*, MGG/, Greenwood Pr) Greenwood.

Recorded Sayings of Ma-Tsu. Tr. by Julian F. Pas from DUT. LC 87-18536. (Studies in Asian Thought & Religion: Vol. 6). 1987. lib. bdg. 99.95 (*0-88946-058-2*) E Mellen.

Recorder: A Guide to Writings about the Instrument for Players & Researchers. Richard Griscom & David Lasocki. LC 94-28796. (Music Research & Information Guides Ser.: No. 19). 528p. 1994. text ed. 74.00 (*0-8240-2945-3*, H1026) Garland.

Recorder & Autoharp. Dexter. 1990. 4.95 (*0-685-32170-3*, H546) Hansen Ed Mus.

Recorder Book. Kenneth Wollitz. 1982. pap. 17.00 (*0-394-74999-5*) Knopf.

Recorder Book: The Beginners Recorder Book. Carmela Mercuri. (Illus.). (Orig.). 1993. pap. 4.95 (*0-935474-23-4*) Carousel Pubns Ltd.

Recorder Book of Medieval & Renaissance Music. Franz Zeidler. 1993. 5.95 (*0-87166-673-1*, 93435) Mel Bay.

Recorder Fingering Charts: 18 Large Charts for Soprano & Tenor Recorder. Peg Hoenack et al. (Recorder & "Flute" Ser.). (Illus.). 1974. ring bd. 18.95 (*0-913500-14-3*, C-1) Peg Hoenack MusicWorks.

Recorder for Beginners Class or Individual Instruction: For Soprano Alto & Tenor. D. Bennett. 32p. 1987. pap. 3.95 (*0-7935-2589-6*, 50489258) H Leonard.

***Recorder Fun! Teach Yourself the Easy Way!** Leonard, Hal, Corporation Staff. 1997. pap. text ed. 7.95 incl. audio compact disk (*0-7935-6650-9*) H Leonard.

Recorder Fun with Disney Favorites. (J). (ps-3). 1990. pap. 14.95 (*0-7935-0295-0*, HL660210) H Leonard.

Recorder Guide. Arthur Nitka & Joanna E. Kulbach. (Illus.). 128p. pap. 15.95 (*0-8256-0020-0*, OK63743, Oak) Music Sales.

Recorder Method. R. F. Shambaugh. 1971. 4.50 (*0-87511-103-3*) Claitors.

Recorder Method Textbook. Edward J. Bostley. 260p. (C). 1994. pap. text ed., spiral bd. 32.49 (*0-8403-9685-6*) Kendall-Hunt.

Recorder Music for Children. Jerry Silverman. 1993. 6.95 (*0-87166-974-9*, 94381); audio 9.98 (*0-87166-975-7*, 94381C) Mel Bay.

***Recorder Music for Children.** Jerry Silverman. 1993. 15.95 incl. audio (*0-7866-1020-4*, 94381P) Mel Bay.

Recorder of Births & Deaths. William Joyce. 190p. 1990. pap. 9.75 (*0-922820-08-2*) Watermrk Pr.

Recorder of the Black Experience: A Biography of Monroe Nathan Work. Linda O. McMurry. LC 84-10008. (Southern Biography Ser.). (Illus.). 154p. 1985. text ed. 27.50 (*0-8071-1171-6*) La State U Pr.

Recorder Player's Companion: A Compendium of Technical Exercises for Recorder Players. Frances Blaker. (Educational Ser.: No. 3). (Illus.). i, 41p. 1993. pap. text ed. 19.00 (*1-56571-059-2*, ED003) PRB Prods.

Recorder Player's Companion: A Compendium of Technical Exercises for Recorder Players. 2nd rev. ed. Frances Blaker. (Educational Ser.: No. 3). (Illus.). i, 42p. 1994. pap. text ed. 19.00 (*1-56571-120-3*) PRB Prods.

Recorder Player's Handbook. rev. ed. Tr. by H. M. Linde from GER. 1974. pap. 29.95 (*0-930448-11-1*, ST12322) Eur-Am Music.

Recorder Pocketbook. pap. 0.95 (*0-87166-553-0*, 93705) Mel Bay.

Recorder Teaching: A Classroom Approach: A Practical Step-by-Step Guide. Mim Chapman et al. (Recorder & "Flute" "Let's Sing & Play" Ser.). (Illus.). 178p. 1987. 23.95 (*0-913500-25-9*, L-6TE) Peg Hoenack MusicWorks.

Recorder Technique. Anthony Rowland-Jones. 178p. (YA). (gr. 9 up). 1983. pap. 27.95 (*0-19-322342-2*) OUP.

Recorders on Parade, for Recorder Quintet. Martha Bishop. (Contemporary Consort Ser.: No. 26). i, 16p. 1993. pap. text ed. 12.00 (*1-56571-076-2*, CC026) PRB Prods.

Recording: Guidelines for Social Workers. Suanna J. Wilson. LC 79-7636. 1980. pap. 17.95 (*0-02-935810-8*, Free Press) Free Pr.

Recording America's Past: An Interpretation of the Development of Historical Studies in America, 1607-1884. David D. Van Tassel. LC 60-14404. reprint ed. pap. 58.80 (*0-317-28116-X*, 2024105) Bks Demand.

***Recording & Notification of Occupational Accidents & Diseases: An ILO Code of Practice.** xxii, 96p. 1996. pap. 18.00 (*92-2-109451-0*) Intl Labour Office.

***Recording & Production Techniques.** Paul White. 192p. (Orig.). pap. 14.95 (*1-86074-188-6*, SG00617, Pub. by Sanctuary Pr UK) Omnibus NY.

Recording Angel: Music in Our Time. Evan Eisenberg. 1986. pap. write for info. (*0-07-019052-6*) McGraw.

Recording Clerk. Jack Rudman. (Career Examination Ser.: C-2914). 1994. pap. 23.95 (*0-8373-2914-0*) Nat Learn.

Recording Contract. Robert A. Livingston. 1988. pap. 20.00 (*0-932303-07-2*) GLGLC Music.

Recording Historic Structures. National Park Service, U.S. Department of the Interior, Historic American Buildings Survey - Historic American Engineering Record Staff & John A. Burns. (Illus.). 270p. 1989. pap. 19.95 (*1-55835-021-7*) AIA Press.

***Recording Industry.** Hull. 1997. pap. text ed. 24.00 (*0-205-19689-6*) P-H.

Recording Industry Sourcebook 1996. Mix Books Staff. 450p. 1996. spiral bd. 79.00 (*0-918371-09-0*) Cardinal Busn Media.

***Recording Industry Sourcebook 97.** 8th ed. Cardinal Business Media Staff. 425p. 1997. spiral bd. 79.95 (*0-918371-12-0*, MixBooks) Cardinal Busn Media.

Recording Natural History Sounds. Richard Margoschis. (Illus.). 1979. 8.95 (*0-913714-24-0*); pap. 5.95 (*0-913714-25-9*) Legacy Books.

Recording Oral History: A Practical Guide for Social Scientists. Valerie R. Yow. 240p. (C). 1994. text ed. 48.00 (*0-8039-5578-2*); pap. text ed. 21.95 (*0-8039-5579-0*) Sage.

Recording Production Techniques for Musicians. Bruce Nazarian. (Illus.). 96p. 1988. pap. 17.95 (*0-8256-1177-6*, AM69402) Music Sales.

Recording Structures of Mammals: Determination of Age & Reconstruction of Life History. Galina A. Klevezal. Tr. by A. V. Oreshkin & M. V. Mina from RUS. (Illus.). 274p. (C). 1996. 125.00 (*90-5410-621-2*, Pub. by A A Balkema NE) Ashgate Pub Co.

***Recording Studio/Production Directory.** Robert A. Livingston. 1996. pap. 34.95 (*0-932303-25-0*) GLGLC Music.

Recording, Syncing & Synths. Paul Goldfield et al. Ed. by Peter L. Alexander. (Recording, Syncing & Synths for Home & Studio Recording Ser.). (Illus.). 87p. (C). 1988. pap. text ed. 17.95 (*0-939067-66-8*) Alexander Pub.

***Recording Techniques: For Small Studios.** David Mellor. (Illus.). 160p. 1996. pap. 15.95 (*1-870775-29-5*, Pub. by Electric Pencil UK) Cimino Pub Grp.

Recording the Classics: Maestros, Music, & Technology. James Badal. LC 95-35978. (Illus.). 225p. 1996. 24.00 (*0-87338-542-X*) Kent St U Pr.

***Recording the Guitar: Get a Great Sound onto Tape.** John Harris. (Illus.). 128p. 1997. pap. 15.95 (*1-870775-45-7*, Pub. by Electric Pencil UK) Cimino Pub Grp.

Recording the Performance of U. S. Undergraduates at British Institutions: Guidelines Toward Standardized Reporting for Study Abroad. Ed. by David Rex & Thomas Roberts. 9p. 1988. 12.00 (*0-912207-22-1*) NAFSA Washington.

Recording Your Family History. William Fletcher. Orig. Title: Talking Your Roots. 314p. 1989. reprint ed. pap. 14.95 (*0-89815-324-7*) Ten Speed Pr.

Recordings in the Public Library. Mary D. Pearson. LC 62-20852. 40p. reprint ed. pap. 25.00 (*0-317-09931-0*, 2011140) Bks Demand.

Recordings of Beethoven. High Fidelity Magazines Editors. LC 77-26057. 173p. 1978. reprint ed. text ed. 49.75 (*0-313-20171-4*, HFRB, Greenwood Pr) Greenwood.

Recordings of the Traditional Music of Bali & Lombok. Ed. by Andrew Toth. 243p. 1980. 15.00 (*0-318-16570-8*) Soc Ethnomusicology.

Recordkeeping Requirements: The First Practical Guide to Help You Control Your Records. Donald S. Skupsky. 245p. 1994. pap. text ed. 35.00 (*0-929316-21-5*) Info Requirements.

Records & Database Management. 4th ed. Jeffrey R. Stewart, Jr. et al. 246p. (C). 1989. text ed. 17.75 (*0-07-061474-1*) McGraw.

Records & Files of the Quarterly Courts of Essex County. Complete Record of Wills, Inventories, Vital Records, Court Cases, Fines, Depositions, Etc., Presented in Abstracted but with All "Particulars" Needed for Research. Ed. by George F. Dow. (Illus.). 1995. reprint ed. lib. bdg. 325.00 (*0-8328-4593-0*) Higginson Bk Co.

Records & Files of the Quarterly Courts of Essex County, Massachusetts, Vol. 9: September 25, 1683 - April 20, 1686. Ed. by Mary G. Thresher. LC 12-951. 1975. 30.00 (*0-88389-051-8*, Essx Institute) Peabody Essex Mus.

Records & Recollections of James Jenkins. Ed. by J. William Frost. LC 83-26537. (Texts & Studies in Religion: Vol. 18). 550p. 1984. lib. bdg. 119.95 (*0-88946-807-9*) E Mellen.

Records & Reminiscences of Bonhill Parish. John Neill. 280p. (C). 1986. 49.00 (*0-9506620-0-3*) St Mut.

Records at the Archivo General de Indias in Seville, Spain: Their Usefulness for the Genealogist. Peter E. Carr. 85p. (Orig.). 1995. pap. 18.95 (*0-9631209-9-9*) TCI Gene Res.

Records Center Operations: A Guideline. 51p. 1986. 27.00 (*0-933887-11-6*, A4540) ARMA Intl.

Records Clerk. Jack Rudman. (Career Examination Ser.: C-3612). 1994. pap. 23.95 (*0-8373-3612-0*) Nat Learn.

Records from Erech, Time of Cyrus & Cambyses. Archibald Tremayne. LC 78-63536. (Yale Oriental Series: Babylonian Texts: No. 7). (Illus.). 200p. reprint ed. 37.50 (*0-404-60257-6*) AMS Pr.

Records from Erech, Time of Nabonidus (555-538 B.C.) Raymond P. Dougherty. LC 78-63535. (Yale Oriental Series: Babylonian Texts: No. 6). (Illus.). 224p. reprint ed. 40.00 (*0-404-60256-8*) AMS Pr.

Records from Ur & Larsa Dated in the Larsa Dynasty. Ettalene M. Grice. LC 78-63534. (Yale Oriental Series: Babylonian Texts: No. 5). (Illus.). reprint ed. 42.50 (*0-404-60255-X*) AMS Pr.

Records Guide for the Family. William F. Keefe. 374p. 1987. write for info. (*0-89434-087-5*) Ferguson.

Records in Review. High Fidelity Staff. 1990. reprint ed. lib. bdg. 79.00 (*0-7812-9286-7*) Rprt Serv.

Records in Stone: Papers in Memory of Alexander Thom. Ed. by Clive Ruggles. (Illus.). 524p. 1988. text ed. 130.00 (*0-521-33381-4*) Cambridge U Pr.

Records Management. David Hyslop & Irene M. Place. (C). 1982. teacher ed. write for info. (*0-8359-6607-0*, Reston) P-H.

*****Records Management.** Kennedy. Date not set. pap. text ed. write for info. (*0-582-91178-8*, Pub. by Longman UK) Longman.

Records Management. 4th ed. Mina M. Johnson & Norman F. Kallaus. 1987. text ed. 46.95 (*0-538-11690-0*, K69) S-W Pub.

Records Management. 5th ed. Norman F. Kallaus & Mina M. Johnson. 384p. 1992. text ed. 43.95 (*0-538-70335-0*) S-W Pub.

Records Management. 5th ed. Norman F. Kallaus. (KI - P/S Record Management Ser.). 1992. wbk. ed., pap. 14. 95 (*0-538-70384-9*) S-W Pub.

Records Management. 6th ed. Smith. (KG - Filing/Records Management Ser.). 1997. text ed. 41.95 (*0-538-71438-7*) S-W Pub.

Records Management. 6th ed. Smith. (KG - Filing/Records Management Ser.). 1997. student ed., pap. 14.95 (*0-538-71439-5*) S-W Pub.

Records Management. 6th ed. Smith. (KG - Filing/Records Management Ser.). 1997. suppl. ed., pap. 28.95 (*0-538-71440-9*) S-W Pub.

Records Management: A Practical Guide. 3rd ed. Susan Z. Diamond. LC 95-4604. 272p. 1995. 29.95 (*0-8144-0295-X*) AMACOM.

Records Management: A Practical Guide. Susan Z. Diamond. LC 82-18477. 192p. reprint ed. pap. 54.80 (*0-7837-4242-8*, 2043931) Bks Demand.

Records Management: A Practical Guide for Cities & Counties. Julian L. Mims, III. (Special Report Ser.). 191p. 1996. pap. 45.00 (*0-87326-110-0*) Intl City-Cnty Mgt.

Records Management - Integrated Informations Systems. 2nd ed. Patricia E. Wallace et al. LC 86-23422. 192p. 1987. pap. text ed. 31.95 (*0-471-82160-8*); Applications manual. pap. text ed. 17.50 (*0-471-82162-4*) P-H.

Records Management & the Library: Issues & Practices. Candy Schwartz & Peter Hernon. LC 92-41735. (Information Management, Policies & Services Ser.). 328p. 1993. pap. 39.50 (*0-89391-998-5*); text ed. 73.25 (*0-89391-964-0*) Ablex Pub.

Records Management Assistant. (Career Examination Ser.: C-3647). pap. 27.95 (*0-8373-3647-3*) Nat Learn.

Records Management for an Information Age. Joseph V. Arn & Paula H. Titlow. 416p. 1991. disk 45.95 (*0-8273-3553-9*) Delmar.

Records Management for an Information Age. Joseph V. Arn & Paula H. Titlow. 416p. 1991. teacher ed. 14.95 (*0-8273-3552-0*) Delmar.

Records Management for an Information Age. Joseph V. Arn & Paula H. Titlow. 416p. 1991. pap. 58.95 (*0-8273-3551-2*) Delmar.

Records Management for Michigan Municipalities: A Suggested Retention & Disposal Schedule. (Information Bulletin Ser.: No. 108). 1984. 12.00 (*0-318-23507-2*) MI Municipal.

Records Management Handbook. 2nd ed. Ira A. Penn et al. 1994. 64.95 (*0-566-07510-5*, Pub. by Gower UK) Ashgate Pub Co.

Records Management Manual for Michigan Municipalities. Zane K. Quible et al. LC 81-620018. 71p. 1981. 7.50 (*0-941872-32-7*) MSU Dept Res Dev.

Records, Notes, Reports Connected with the Removal to Germany in the Year 1945. Hungarian Historical Research Society Staff. LC 77-95243. 120p. 1980. pap. 6.50 (*0-935484-06-X*) Universe Pub Co.

Records of a Voyage to the Western Coast of Africa in His Majesty's Ship Dryad & of Service on That Station for the Suppression of the Slave Trade in the Years 1830, 1831 & 1832. Peter Leonard. (B. E. Ser.: No. 154). 1833. 30.00 (*0-8115-3072-8*) Periodicals Srv.

*****Records of American Business.** Ed. by James M. O'Toole. LC 97-24781. 400p. 1997. 39.95 (*0-931828-45-7*) Soc Am Archivists.

*****Records of Bahrain: Primary Documents 1820-1960, 8 vols.** Ed. by P. Tuson & A. Burdett. (Arabian Regional Records Ser.). (Illus.). 6700p. 1993. reprint ed. lib. bdg. 1,595.00 (*1-85207-350-0*, Pub. by Archive Editions UK) N Ross.

*****Records of Bahrain 1961-1963, 3 vols.** (Arabian Regional Records Ser.). Date not set. reprint ed. lib. bdg. 595.00 (*0-614-25967-3*, Pub. by Archive Editions UK) N Ross.

Records of Baptism, Marriages, Burials Solemnized by G. G. Ingersoll, Minister First Congregational Society, Burlington, Vermont. George G. Ingersoll. Ed. & Pref. by Charles D. Townsend. 33p. 1995. pap. 5.00 (*1-878545-10-8*) ACETO Bookmen.

Records of Bird Skins Collected along the Oregon Coast. Range D. Bayer. LC 89-16883. (Studies in Oregon Ornithology: No. 7). 246p. 1989. pap. 20.00 (*0-939819-06-6*) Gahmken Pr.

Records of Botanical Survey of India, 11 vols. BSI Staff. (C). 1988. text ed. 800.00 (*0-685-22123-7*) St Mut.

Records of California Men in the War of the Rebellion: 1861-1867. Compiled by Richard Orton. LC 78-23517. 888p. 1979. reprint ed. 110.00 (*0-8103-3347-3*) Gale.

Records of Clinton Lutheran Church, South Buffalo Township, Armstrong County, PA. Peggy C. Cramer. 17p. 1990. pap. text ed. 5.00 (*1-55856-063-7*) Closson Pr.

Records of Coal Center Methodist Church, 1873-1938: Washington County, PA. G. D. Dixon. 75p. 1996. pap. 8.50 (*1-55856-213-3*) Closson Pr.

*****Records of Communication & Transport in the Gulf States & Saudi Arabia, 9 vols.** Ed. by A. L. Burdett. (Illus.). 5200p. 1995. reprint ed. lib. bdg. 2,195.00 (*1-85207-620-8*, Pub. by Archive Editions UK) N Ross.

Records of Conscience. Peter Brock. (Orig.). (C). 1989. pap. 21.00 (*0-685-67816-4*, Pub. by W Sessions UK) St Mut.

Records of Conscience. Ed. by Peter Brock. 72p. (Orig.). pap. 12.95 (*1-85072-117-3*, Pub. by Ebor Pr UK) Syracuse U Pr.

Records of Deaths in First Church of Rowley, Massachusetts 1696-1777. Ed. by George B. Blodgett. Orig. Title: Copy of the Records of Deaths of the First Church of Rowley, Massachusetts. 56p. 1996. reprint ed. pap. 15.00 (*1-878545-21-3*) ACETO Bookmen.

*****Records of Defence & Military Policy in the Gulf States & Saudi Arabia 1920-1960, 12 vols.** Ed. by A. L. Burdett. 8000p. Date not set. reprint ed. lib. bdg. 3,295.00 (*1-85207-500-7*, Pub. by Archive Editions UK) N Ross.

Records of Early English Drama: Herefordshire & Worcestershire. Ed. by David Klausner. 747p. 1990. 125.00 (*0-8020-2758-X*) U of Toronto Pr.

Records of Early English Drama: Somerset, 2 vols., Set. Ed. by James Stokes. 900p. 1996. 175.00 (*0-8020-0459-8*) U of Toronto Pr.

Records of Effingham County, Georgia. Silas E. Lucas, Jr. & Caroline P. Wilson. 410p. 1976. 30.00 (*0-89308-019-5*) Southern Hist Pr.

Records of Emigrants from England & Scotland to North Carolina, 1774-1775. Ed. by A. R. Newsome. 30p. 1989. pap. 3.00 (*0-86526-134-2*) NC Archives.

*****Records of English Court Music Vol. I.** Andrew Ashbee. 288p. 1992. 67.95 (*0-9507207-2-0*, Pub. by Scolar Pr UK) Ashgate Pub Co.

*****Records of English Court Music Vol. II.** Andrew Ashbee. 288p. 1992. 52.95 (*0-9507207-3-9*, Pub. by Scolar Pr UK) Ashgate Pub Co.

*****Records of English Court Music Vol. III.** Andrew Ashbee. 288p. 1992. 52.95 (*0-9507207-4-7*, Pub. by Scolar Pr UK) Ashgate Pub Co.

*****Records of English Court Music Vol. IV.** Andrew Ashbee. 288p. 1992. 52.95 (*0-9507207-5-5*, Pub. by Scolar Pr UK) Ashgate Pub Co.

*****Records of English Court Music Vol. V.** Andrew Ashbee. 288p. 1992. 52.95 (*0-85967-858-X*, Pub. by Scolar Pr UK) Ashgate Pub Co.

Records of English Court Music Vol. VIII. Ed. by Andrew Ashbee. 416p. 1995. 59.95 (*1-85928-234-2*, Pub. by Scolar Pr UK) Ashgate Pub Co.

Records of English Court Music Vol. IX: Index. Compiled by Andrew Ashbee. 256p. 1996. text ed. 68.95 (*1-85928-274-1*, Pub. by Scolar Pr UK) Ashgate Pub Co.

Records of English Court Music Vol. VI: 1558-1603. Andrew Ashbee. 288p. 1992. 49.95 (*0-85967-859-8*, Pub. by Scolar Pr UK) Ashgate Pub Co.

Records of English Court Music Vol. VII: 1485-1558. Andrew Ashbee. 492p. 1993. 59.95 (*0-85967-860-1*, Pub. by Scolar Pr UK) Ashgate Pub Co.

Records of Ethnic Fraternal Benefit Associations in the United States: Essays & Inventories. Immigration History Research Center Staff. vii, 169p. 1981. pap. text ed. 8.95 (*0-932833-03-9*) Immig His Res.

Records of Government. National Council on Public History Staff. LC 87-3384. 192p. 1987. reprint ed. lib. bdg. 22.50 (*0-89464-231-6*) Krieger.

Records of Hampstead, New Hampshire. Harriette E. Noyes. 60p. 1984. pap. 6.50 (*0-912606-23-1*) Hunterdon Hse.

Records of Harrison County, Indiana from Walter S. Beanblossom's Collection with Additional Material. Sherry Healy. 176p. 1989. pap. 22.50 (*1-889221-20-1*) Ancestral Trails.

Records of High Sanghans, Vol. I. Tripitaka Master Hua. Tr. by Buddhist Text Translation Society from CHI. 160p. (Orig.). 1983. pap. 7.00 (*0-88139-012-7*) Buddhist Text.

Records of Impeachment. Michael Honey. LC 86-16307. (Milestone Documents in the National Archives Ser.). (Illus.). 20p. (Orig.). (YA). 1987. pap. text ed. 3.50 (*0-911333-49-5*, 200109) National Archives & Recs.

Records of Indentured Servants & of Certification for Land: Northumberland County, Virginia, 1650-1795. 398p. (Orig.). 1996. pap. 33.50 (*0-7884-0425-3*, H095) Heritage Bk.

*****Records of Islam: Arabia & the Holy Places 1517-1975, 10 vols.** Ed. by A. D. Rush. 7000p. Date not set. reprint ed. lib. bdg. write for info. (*0-614-25979-7*, Pub. by Archive Editions UK) N Ross.

Records of Jasper County, Georgia, 1802-1922. Robert S. Davis, Jr. 485p. 1990. 40.00 (*0-89308-659-2*, GA 91) Southern Hist Pr.

*****Records of Jordan 1919-1965, 14 vols.** Ed. by J. Priestland. 10,000p. 1996. reprint ed. lib. bdg. 3,995.00 (*1-85207-645-3*, Pub. by Archive Editions UK) N Ross.

Records of Kuwait 1899-1961, 8 vols. Ed. by A. Rush. (Illus.). 5000p. (C). 1989. reprint ed. lib. bdg. 1,595.00 (*1-85207-200-8*, Pub. by Archive Editions UK) N Ross.

*****Records of Kuwait 1961-1963, 4 vols.** Ed. by A. Burdett. Date not set. reprint ed. lib. bdg. 595.00 (*0-614-25968-1*, Pub. by Archive Editions UK) N Ross.

Records of Living Officers of the U. S. Navy & Marine Corps: With a History of Naval Operations During the Rebellion of 1861-1865 & a List of the Ships & Officers Participating in the Great Battles. Lewis R. Hamersly. 1985. 27.95 (*0-8488-0024-9*, J M C & Co) Amereon Ltd.

Records of Louisiana Confederate Soldiers & Louisiana Confederate Commands, 3 Vols., Set. Compiled by Andrew B. Booth. LC 84-22844. 3707p. 1995. reprint ed. 250.00 (*0-87152-400-7*) Reprint.

Records of Ming Scholars. Tsung-hsi Huang. Ed. by Julia Ching & Chaoying Fang. LC 86-27257. 360p. 1987. text ed. 30.00 (*0-8248-1028-7*) UH Pr.

Records of North American Big Game. 8th deluxe limited ed. Ed. by W. H. Nesbitt & Philip L. Wright. (Records of North American Big Game Ser.). (Illus.). xii, 412p. 1981. 199.00 (*0-940864-01-0*) Boone & Crockett.

Records of North American Big Game. 9th ed. Ed. by W. H. Nesbitt & Jack Reneau. (Illus.). 512p. 1988. 49.95 (*0-940864-13-4*) Boone & Crockett.

Records of North American Big Game. Ed. by Prentiss N. Gray. 178p. 1988. reprint ed. 79.95 (*0-940864-15-0*) Boone & Crockett.

Records of North American Big Game, 1993. 10th ed. Ed. by Jack Reneau & Susan C. Reneau. (Illus.). 624p. 1993. 49.95 (*0-940864-20-7*) Boone & Crockett.

Records of North American Elk & Mule Deer, 1991. Ed. by W. H. Nesbitt & Jack Reneau. LC 91-73121. (Illus.). viii, 264p. (Orig.). 1991. pap. 16.95 (*0-940864-18-5*) Boone & Crockett.

Records of North American Elk & Mule Deer, 1996. 2nd ed. Ed. by Jack Reneau & Susan C. Reneau. (Illus.). 352p. (Orig.). 1996. per., pap. 18.95 (*0-940864-25-8*) Boone & Crockett.

*****Records of North American Elk & Mule Deer, 1996.** 2nd ed. Ed. by Jack Reneau & Susan C. Reneau. (Illus.). 352p. (Orig.). 1996. 24.95 (*0-940864-27-4*) Boone & Crockett.

Records of North American Sheep, Goats & Pronghorn. Ed. by Jack Reneau & Susan C. Reneau. (Illus.). 300p. 1996. per., pap. 18.95 (*0-940864-26-6*) Boone & Crockett.

*****Records of North American Sheep, Goats & Pronghorn.** Ed. by Jack Reneau & Susan C. Reneau. (Illus.). 300p. 1996. 24.95 (*0-940864-28-2*) Boone & Crockett.

Records of North American Whitetail Deer, 1987. Ed. by W. H. Nesbitt & Jack Reneau. (Illus.). 246p. 1987. pap. 14.95 (*0-940864-12-6*) Boone & Crockett.

Records of North American Whitetail Deer, 1991. 2nd ed. Ed. by W. H. Nesbitt & Jack Reneau. LC 91-973120. (Illus.). viii, 312p. (Orig.). 1991. pap. 16.95 (*0-940864-17-7*) Boone & Crockett.

Records of North American Whitetail Deer, 1995. 3rd ed. Ed. by Jack Reneau & Susan C. Reneau. LC 95-79533. (Illus.). 448p. 1995. pap. 18.95 (*0-940864-24-X*) Boone & Crockett.

Records of Northumberland Co., VA Abstracts from the Earliest Extant Records, 1647-1652, Index & Will Abstracts from Record Book 1710-1713 & Selected Records from Order Book 1737-1743. Carolyn H. Jett. 109p. (Orig.). 1994. pap. text ed. 17.50 (*1-55613-933-0*) Heritage Bk.

Records of Officers & Men of New Jersey in Wars 1791-1815. New Jersey Adjutant-General Office Staff. 410p. 1993. reprint ed. pap. 42.50 (*0-685-69932-3*, 4035) Clearfield Co.

*****Records of Officers & Men of New Jersey in Wars 1791-1815.** New Jersey, Adjutant-General's Office Staff. 410p. 1993. reprint ed. pap. 39.50 (*0-614-23548-0*, 4035) Clearfield Co.

Records of Oman 1867-1960, 12 vols. Ed. by Ronald W. Bailey. (Illus.). 8500p. (C). 1988. reprint ed. lib. bdg. 2, 795.00 (*1-85207-120-6*, Pub. by Archive Editions UK) N Ross.

*****Records of Oman 1961-1963, 3 vols.** Ed. by A. Burdett. Date not set. reprint ed. lib. bdg. 595.00 (*0-614-25970-3*, Pub. by Archive Editions UK) N Ross.

Records of Oxford, MA Including Chapters of Nipmuck, Huguenot & English History from the Earliest Date, 1630 with Manners & Fashions of the Time. Mary D. Freeland. (Illus.). 429p. 1992. reprint ed. lib. bdg. 45.00 (*0-8328-2064-4*) Higginson Bk Co.

Records of Oxford, Massachusetts. Mary D. Freeland. 429p. 1993. reprint ed. lib. bdg. 45.00 (*0-8328-3139-5*) Higginson Bk Co.

Records of Pastoral Acts at Emanual Lutheran Church (Known in the Eighteen Century as the Warwick Congregation, Near Brickerville, Elizabeth Township, Lancaster County) 1743-1799. Tr. by Frederick S. Weiser. (Sources & Documents Ser.: No. 8). 229p. 1983. pap. 15.00 (*0-911122-47-8*) Penn German Soc.

*****Records of Qatar: Primary Documents 1820-1960, 8 vols.** Ed. by P. Tuson. (Arabian Regional Records Ser.). (Illus.). 1991. reprint ed. lib. bdg. 1,595.00 (*1-85207-300-4*, Pub. by Archive Editions UK) N Ross.

*****Records of Qatar: Primary Documents 1961-1963, 3 vols.** Ed. by A. Burdett. (Arabian Regional Records Ser.). Date not set. reprint ed. lib. bdg. 595.00 (*0-614-25969-X*, Pub. by Archive Editions UK) N Ross.

Records of Randolph County, Missouri 1833-1964. 106p. (Orig.). 1996. pap. 16.00 (*0-7884-0411-3*, E130) Heritage Bk.

Records of Rev. Edward F. Cutter of Maine, 1833-1856. Ed. by Elizabeth M. Mosher. LC 88-63777. 96p. 1989. 20.00 (*0-929539-19-2*, 1119) Picton Pr.

Records of Salem Witchcraft, Copied from the Original Documents, 2 Vols. LC 78-75274. (Law, Politics & History Ser.). 1969. reprint ed. lib. bdg. 45.00 (*0-306-71309-8*) Da Capo.

*****Records of Saudi Arabia 1902-1960, 10 vols.** Ed. by P. Tuson & A. Burdett. 6000p. 1992. reprint ed. lib. bdg. 2, 795.00 (*1-85207-325-X*, Pub. by Archive Editions UK) N Ross.

*****Records of Saudi Arabia 1961-1963, 4 vols.** 2000p. Date not set. reprint ed. lib. bdg. 595.00 (*0-614-25971-1*, Pub. by Archive Editions UK) N Ross.

Records of Shelley, Byron & the Author, 2 Vols. Edward J. Trelawny. LC 68-20230. 1972. reprint ed. 36.95 (*0-405-09031-5*) Ayer.

Records of Shelley, Byron, & the Author, 2 vols. Edward J. Trelawny. (BCL1-PR English Literature Ser.). 1992. reprint ed. lib. bdg. 150.00 (*0-7812-7523-7*) Rprt Serv.

*****Records of Southport: Vital Records, Cemeteries, 1850 Census, Chrurch Records.** Compiled by J. J. Haskell & G. Lilly. (Illus.). 62p. 1997. reprint ed. pap. 12.50 (*0-8328-5914-1*) Higginson Bk Co.

Records of St. Matthew's Evangelical Church 1741-1831. Frederick S. Weiser. 160p. 1994. 24.50 (*0-89725-146-6*, 1463) Picton Pr.

Records of Tennyson, Ruskin & Browning. Anne T. Ritchie. LC 70-172549. 190p. 1972. reprint ed. 24.95 (*0-405-08893-0*, Pub. by Blom Pubns UK) Ayer.

Records of the American Women's Hospitals 1917-1982: An Inventory. Nancy A. Hewitt. (Illus.). 55p. (Orig.). (C). 1987. 5.00 (*0-944542-01-8*) Med Coll PA ASCWM.

Records of the Antrim Family of America. Harriet S. Antrim. (Illus.). 232p. 1988. reprint ed. lib. bdg. 43.00 (*0-8328-0132-1*) Higginson Bk Co.

Records of the Bailey Family. Descendants of William Bailey of Newport, R. I., Chiefly in the Line of His Son, Hugh Bailey of East Greenwich, R. I. H. C. Hopkins. (Illus.). 207p. 1988. reprint ed. pap. 31.00 (*0-8328-0157-7*); reprint ed. lib. bdg. 39.00 (*0-8328-0156-9*) Higginson Bk Co.

*****Records of the Boston Overseers of the Poor, 1735-1795.** Ed. by Eric G. Nellis. 550p. 1997. 49.50 (*0-9620737-4-1*) Colonial MA.

Records of the Botanical Survey of India. B. S. I. Staff. (C). 1991. text ed. 2,750.00 (*0-89771-575-6*, Pub. by Intl Bk Distr II) St Mut.

Records of the Botanical Survey of India, Set, Vols. 1-11. International Book Staff. 1989. Set. 2,750.00 (*0-685-21768-X*, Pub. by Intl Bk Distr II) St Mut.

Records of the Botanical Survey of India, Vol. 8: Flora Arabica, No. 1, Pt. 1: Rancinculaceae Moringaceae. E. Blatter. 69p. (C). 1978. 80.00 (*0-685-22305-1*, Pub. by Scientific UK) St Mut.

Records of the Bureau of Indian Affairs Central Classified Files, 1907-1939. Robert E. Lester. LC 95-18006. 1995. 3,130.00 (*1-55655-550-4*) U Pubns Amer.

Records of the Burgh of Prestwick in the Sheriffdom of Ayr. Ed. by John Fullarton. LC 76-174286. (Maitland Club, Glasgow. Publications: No. 27). reprint ed. 37.50 (*0-404-52983-6*) AMS Pr.

Records of the Church of Christ, Buxton, (ME) 88p. 1985. reprint ed. pap. 10.00 (*0-935207-16-3*) Danbury Hse Bks.

Records of the Church of Christ in Buxton, Maine, 1763-1817. rev. ed. Ed. by Lewis B. Rohrbach. LC 88-63778. 104p. 1989. reprint ed. 20.00 (*0-929539-02-8*, 1102) Picton Pr.

Records of the Colony of New Plymouth in New England, 12 Vols in 6, Set. Ed. by Nathaniel B. Shurtleff & David Pulsifer. LC 01-12098. reprint ed. 1,050.00 (*0-404-06040-4*) AMS Pr.

Records of the Colony of Rhode Island & Providence Plantations in New England, 10 vols., Set. Ed. by John R. Bartlett. reprint ed. lib. bdg. 900.00 (*0-404-00680-9*) AMS Pr.

Records of the Columbia Historical Society of Washington, D. C., Vol. 52. Ed. by J. Kirkpatrick Flack. LC 01-17677. 375p. reprint ed. pap. 106.90 (*0-7837-2431-4*, 2042579) Bks Demand.

Records of the Court of Assistants of the Colony of the Massachusetts Bay, 1630-1692, 3 vols., Set. Massachusetts Colony Court of Assistants Staff. LC 70-172853. reprint ed. 247.50 (*0-404-07350-6*) AMS Pr.

Records of the Court of Sessions of Suffolk County in the Province of New York, 1670-1688. Thomas W. Cooper. xix, 331p. (Orig.). 1993. pap. 26.50 (*1-55613-799-0*) Heritage Bk.

Records of the Courts of Sussex County, Delaware: 1677-1710, 2 vols. Intro. by Craig W. Horle. LC 91-27116. 1464p. (C). 1992. text ed. 130.00 (*0-8122-3078-7*) U of Pa Pr.

Records of the Dawn of Photography: Talbot's Notebooks P & Q. Larry J. Schaaf. 360p. (C). 1996. text ed. 150.00 (*0-521-44051-3*) Cambridge U Pr.

Records of the Department of State Relating to the Internal Affairs of China, 1910-1949: A Descriptive Guide & Subject Index to Microcopy No. 329. Ed. by Mordechai Rozanski. LC 79-13351. 61p. 1979. lib. bdg. 30.00 (*0-8420-2133-7*) Scholarly Res Inc.

Records of the Descendants of Hugh Clark of Watertown, Mass. 1640-1866. J. Clark. (Illus.). 261p. 1993. reprint ed. pap. 39.00 (*0-8328-1349-4*); reprint ed. lib. bdg. 49. 00 (*0-8328-1348-6*) Higginson Bk Co.

Records of the Descendants of Nathaniel Ely, Who Settled First in Newtown, Now Cambridge, Mass. H. Ely. (Illus.). 525p. 1989. reprint ed. pap. 77.00 (*0-8328-0517-3*); reprint ed. lib. bdg. 85.00 (*0-8328-0516-5*) Higginson Bk Co.

Records of the Dorland Family in America: Including Principal Branches Dorland, Dorlon, Dorlan, Durland, Daarling in the U. S. & Canada. J. Cremer. 320p. 1989. reprint ed. pap. 48.00 (*0-8328-0487-8*); reprint ed. lib. bdg. 56.00 (*0-8328-0486-X*) Higginson Bk Co.

Records of the Dutch Reformed Church in New Amsterdam & New York. Samuel S. Purple. 1972. 50.00 (*0-8490-0936-7*) Gordon Pr.

Records of the Early Hittite Empire (C. 1450-1380 B. C.) Philo H. Houwink Ten Cate. xvi, 87p. 1970. pap. text ed. 28.00 (*0-614-03997-5*, Pub. by Netherlands Inst NE) Eisenbrauns.

Records of the Emirates (UAE) 1820-1960, 12 vols. Ed. by P. Tuson. (Illus.). 8000p. (C). 1990. reprint ed. lib. bdg. 2,795.00 (*1-85207-230-X*, Pub. by Archive Editions UK) N Ross.

Records of the Executive Council, 1664-1734. Ed. by Robert J. Cain. (Colonial Records of North Carolina Ser.: Vol. 7). 1984. 25.00 (*0-86526-210-1*) NC Archives.

Records of the Executive Council, 1735-1754. Ed. by Robert J. Cain. (Colonial Records of North Carolina Ser.: Vol. 8). lxxxvii, 723p. 1988. 45.00 (*0-86526-251-9*) NC Archives.

An Asterisk (*) at the beginning of an entry indicates that the title is appearing in BIP for the first time.

R

Records of the Executive Council, 1755-1775. Ed. by Robert J. Cain. (Colonial Records of North Carolina Ser.: Vol. 9). lxxix, 870p. 1994. 75.00 (*0-86526-261-6*) NC Archives.

Records of the Federal Convention of 1787, 4 vols. Ed. by Max Farrand. Incl. Vol. 1. . LC 86-50311. (Illus.). 640p. 1986. 50.00 (*0-300-00447-8*); Vol. 1. . LC 86-50311. (Illus.). 640p. 1986. pap. 19.00 (*0-300-00080-4*); Vol. 2. . LC 86-50311. (Illus.). 680p. 1986. 50.00 (*0-300-00448-6*); Vol. 2. . LC 86-50311. (Illus.). 680p. 1986. pap. 19.00 (*0-300-00081-2*); Vol. 3. . LC 86-50311. 640p. 1986. pap. 19.00 (*0-300-00082-0*); Vol. 3. . LC 86-50311. 640p. 1986. pap. 19.00 (*0-685-57810-0*); LC 86-50311. 1986. 55.00 (*0-300-00449-4*) Yale U Pr.

Records of the First Church in Salem, Massachusetts, 1629-1736. Ed. by Richard D. Pierce. LC 73-93302. 1974. 30.00 (*0-88389-050-X*, Essx Institute) Peabody Essex Mus.

Records of the First Church of Christ, Biddeford (ME) 54p. 1985. reprint ed. pap. 6.50 (*0-935207-24-4*) Danbury Hse Bks.

Records of the First Church of Christ in Biddeford (Maine) William F. Goodwin. 1985. reprint ed. pap. 3.00 (*0-935207-50-3*) Danbury Hse Bks.

Records of the First Church of Wareham, Massachusetts, 1739-1891. Leonard H. Smith, Jr. & Norma H. Smith. 164p. 1993. reprint ed. pap. 24.95 (*0-685-69929-3*, 9562) Clearfield Co.

Records of the First Congregational Church in Scarborough (Me)-Baptisms. 64p. 1986. reprint ed. pap. 7.50 (*0-935207-35-X*) Danbury Hse Bks.

Records of the First Congregational Church in Scarborough (Me)-Marriages. 21p. 1986. reprint ed. pap. 3.50 (*0-935207-43-0*) Danbury Hse Bks.

Records of the First Reformed Protestant Dutch Church & First Presbyterian Church 1799-1828: Located at Manny's Corners, Town of Amsterdam First Reformed Protestant Dutch Church, 1799-1803 Reorganized as the First Presbyterian Church Feb. 1, 1803. Donald A. Keefer. 62p. 1991. pap. 13.50 (*1-56012-116-5*, 109) Kinship Rhinebeck.

Records of the First Reformed Protestant Dutch Church of the Town of Glen: Organized As the First Reformed Protestant Dutch Church of the Town of Charlestown, Montgomery County, New York on March 18, 1795. Donald A. Keefer. 106p. 1990. lib. bdg. 25.00 (*1-56012-109-2*, 102) Kinship Rhinebeck.

Records of the General Conference 27th Session, 1993 Vol. 3: Proceedings. Unesco Staff. 69p. 1995. pap. text ed. 80.00 (*92-3-003237-9*, U5634, Pub. by UNESCO FR) Bernan Associates.

Records of the General Conference 27th Session, 1993 Resolutions. UNESCO Staff. 69p. 1994. pap. 18.00 (*92-3-102955-X*, U2955, Pub. by UNESCO FR) Bernan Associates.

Records of the Governor & Company of Massachusetts Bay in New England, 1628-1686, 5 Vols in 6, Set. Ed. by Nathaniel B. Shurtleff. LC 72-1721. reprint ed. lib. bdg. 890.00 (*0-404-06020-X*) AMS Pr.

Records of the Governor & Council of the State of Vermont, 8 Vols, Set. Vermont. Ed. by Eliakim P. Walton. LC 74-177562. reprint ed. 725.00 (*0-404-07600-9*) AMS Pr.

Records of the Grand Historian: Han Dynasty & Qin Dynasty, 3 vols., Vol. I. rev. ed. Sima Qian. Tr. by Burton Watson from CHI. LC 92-34085. (Records of Civilization: Sources & Studies: No. 65). 540p. (C). 1993. text ed. 95.00 (*0-231-08164-2*) Col U Pr.

Records of the Grand Historian: Han Dynasty & Qin Dynasty, 3 vols., Vol. II. rev. ed. Sima Qian. Tr. by Burton Watson from CHI. LC 92-34085. (Records of Civilization: Sources & Studies: No. 65). 520p. (C). 1993. text ed. 95.00 (*0-231-08166-9*) Col U Pr.

Records of the Grand Historian: Han Dynasty & Qin Dynasty, 3 vols., Vol. III. rev. ed. Sima Qian. Tr. by Burton Watson from CHI. LC 92-34085. (Records of Civilization: Sources & Studies: No. 65). 210p. (C). 1993. text ed. 65.00 (*0-231-08168-5*) Col U Pr.

Records of the Grand Historian of China, 2 vols. Chien Ssu-ma. Incl. Vol. 1. Early Years of the Han Dynasty, 209 to 141 B.C. LC 60-13348. pap. 109.30 (*0-685-07741-1*); Vol. 2. Age of Emperor Wu, 140 to c. 100 B.C. LC 60-13348. pap. 120.00 (*0-685-07742-X*); LC 60-13348. (Records of Civilization Sources & Studies: No. 65). (Illus.). Set pap. write for info. (*0-318-57562-0*, 2005779) Bks Demand.

***Records of the Hajj: A Documentary History of the Pilgrimage to Mecca, 10 vols.** Ed. by A. D. Rush. (Illus.). 6000p. (ARA & ENG.). 1993. reprint ed. lib. bdg. 2,795.00 (*1-85207-430-2*, Pub. by Archive Editions UK) N Ross.

***Records of the Hashimite Dynasties, 15 vols.** Ed. by A. D. Rush. 10,000p. 1994. reprint ed. lib. bdg. 3,995.00 (*1-85207-590-2*, Pub. by Archive Editions UK) N Ross.

***Records of the Hijaz 1798-1925, 8 vols.** Ed. by A. L. Burdett. 5000p. 1996. reprint ed. lib. bdg. 2,195.00 (*1-85207-655-0*, Pub. by Archive Editions UK) N Ross.

Records of the Historian. Tr. by Burton Watson from CHI. LC 70-89860. (Translations from the Oriental Classics Ser.). Orig. Title: Chapters from the Shih Chi of Ssu-Ma Ch'ien. 1969. pap. text ed. 24.00 (*0-231-03321-4*) Col U Pr.

Records of the Judicial Conference, Common Rules of Practice & Procedure: 1989. Ed. by Congressional Information Service, Inc., Staff. 1992. write for info. (*0-88692-249-6*) Cong Info.

Records of the Life of Jesus. Henry B. Sharmans. 11.00 (*0-87574-955-0*) Pendle Hill.

Records of the Life of Jesus: Revised Standard Version. Henry B. Sharman. 264p. 1991. text ed. 12.95 (*0-917479-12-2*) Guild Psy.

Records of the Life of Tripitaka Master Hua, Vol. 1. Biography of Master Hsuan Hua Publication Committee. (Illus.). 90p. (Orig.). 1981. pap. 5.00 (*0-917512-78-2*) Buddhist Text.

Records of the Life of Tripitaka Master Hua, Vol. 2. Biography of Master Hsuan Hua Publication Committee. (Illus.). 229p. (Orig.). 1976. pap. 8.00 (*0-917512-10-3*) Buddhist Text.

Records of the Massachusetts Volunteer Militia: Called Out by the Governor of Massachusetts to Suppress a Threatened Invasion During the War of 1812-1814. Gardner W. Pearson. 448p. 1993. reprint ed. pap. 35.00 (*0-685-69925-0*, 9286) Clearfield Co.

Records of the Medieval Sword. R. Ewart Oakeshott. (Illus.). 320p. 1992. 117.00 (*0-85115-539-1*) Boydell & Brewer.

Records of the National Council of Women of the United States, Inc., 1988-ca. 1970: A Guide to the Microfiche Edition. Ed. by Laura K. O'Keefe. 41p. 1988. pap. 15.00 (*0-8357-0799-7*) Univ Microfilms.

Records of the New York Stage: Seventeen Fifty to Eighteen Sixty, 2 Vols., Set. Joseph N. Ireland. LC 65-27912. 1972. 72.95 (*0-405-08657-1*) Ayer.

Records of the New York Stage: Seventeen Fifty to Eighteen Sixty, 2 Vols., Vol. 1. Joseph N. Ireland. LC 65-27912. 1972. 36.95 (*0-405-08658-X*) Ayer.

Records of the New York Stage: Seventeen Fifty to Eighteen Sixty, 2 Vols., Vol. 2. Joseph N. Ireland. LC 65-27912. 1972. 36.95 (*0-405-08659-8*) Ayer.

Records of the New York Stage from 1750 to 1860, 2 vols. Joseph N. Ireland. (Notable American Authors Ser.). 1992. reprint ed. lib. bdg. 75.00 (*0-7812-3339-9*) Rprt Serv.

Records of the Past: Being English Translations of the Ancient Monuments of Egypt & Western Asia, 6 Vols., Set. Archibald H. Sayce. LC 72-83175. 1977. reprint ed. 78.95 (*0-405-08918-X*) Ayer.

Records of the Past: Being English Translations of the Ancient Monuments of Egypt & Western Asia, 6 Vols., Vol. 1. Archibald H. Sayce. LC 72-83175. 1977. reprint ed. 39.95 (*0-405-08919-8*) Ayer.

Records of the Past: Being English Translations of the Ancient Monuments of Egypt & Western Asia, 6 Vols., Vol. 2. Archibald H. Sayce. LC 72-83175. 1977. reprint ed. 39.95 (*0-405-08922-8*) Ayer.

***Records of the Persian Gulf Pearl Fisheries 1857-1962, 4 vols.** Ed. by A. L. Burdett. (Illus.). 2000p. 1995. reprint ed. lib. bdg. 895.00 (*1-85207-605-4*, Pub. by Archive Editions UK) N Ross.

Records of the Presbyterian Church in the United States of America, 1706-1788. Presbyterian Church in the United States of America Staff. LC 75-83434. (Religion in America Ser.: Series 1). 1975. reprint ed. 33.95 (*0-405-00259-9*) Ayer.

***Records of the Proprieters of Narraganset Township, No. 1 Now Buxton, Maine.** Ed. by William F. Goodwin. LC 96-70750. (Illus.). 416p. 1996. 49.50 (*0-89725-280-2*, 1411) Picton Pr.

***Records of the Proprietors of the Common Lands in the Town of Barnstable, Massachusetts 1703-1795.** Andrea Leonard. iv, 234p. (Orig.). 1996. pap. 21.00 (*0-7884-0572-1*, L156) Heritage Bk.

Records of the Recorder's Office of Highland County, Ohio, 1805-1850. David N. McBride & Jane N. McBride. (Vital Records of Highland County, Ohio Ser.). 570p. reprint ed. lib. bdg. 45.00 (*0-941000-03-6*) S Ohio Genealog.

***Records of the Reformed Dutch Church of New Hackensack, Dutchess County.** Ed. by Maria B. Tower. (Illus.). 333p. 1997. reprint ed. lib. bdg. 39.00 (*0-8328-6181-2*) Higginson Bk Co.

Records of the Reformed Dutch Church of New Hackensack, Dutchess County, New York: Comprising Baptismal Register, 1757-1906 Marriage Register, 1765-1906, Etc. Ed. by Maria B. Tower. 153p. 1993. reprint ed. 26.00 (*1-56012-126-2*, 122) Kinship Rhinebeck.

Records of the Reformed Dutch Church of New Paltz, N.Y. 269p. 1994. reprint ed. lib. bdg. 29.50 (*0-8328-3912-4*) Higginson Bk Co.

Records of the Reformed Protestant Dutch Church of Middletown (Now Mapletown) in the Town of Canajoharie, Montogomery County, NY, 1803-1901. Donald A. Keefer. (Palatine Transcripts Ser.). 150p. 1985. lib. bdg. 29.50 (*1-56012-073-8*, 72) Kinship Rhinebeck.

***Records of the Revolutionary War.** 3rd ed. William T. Saffell. 598p. 1996. reprint ed. pap. 45.00 (*0-614-23513-8*, 5080) Clearfield Co.

Records of the Second General Assembly. Nepal National Commission for UNESCO Staff. (UNESCO Reports). 136p. 1966. 12.50 (*0-318-17087-6*, 68) Am-Nepal Ed.

Records of the Socialist Labor Party of America, 1877-1907: Guide to a Microfilm Edition. Ed. by F. Gerald Ham. 29p. 1970. pap. 55.00 (*0-89887-184-0*) Chadwyck-Healey.

Records of the Town of Braintree, Mass., 1640-1793. Ed. by Samuel A. Bates. 939p. 1989. reprint ed. lib. bdg. 94.00 (*0-8328-0810-5*, MA0218) Higginson Bk Co.

Records of the Town of Cambridge Massachusetts 1630-1703. Ed. by J. Brandon. 397p. 1985. reprint ed. 30.00 (*0-917890-50-7*) Heritage Bk.

Records of the Town of Newark, New Jersey, from its Settlement in 1666 to its Incorporation as a City in 1836, Vol. 6. Ed. by Samuel H. Congar. 308p. 1966. reprint ed. pap. 8.50 (*0-686-81799-0*) NJ Hist Soc.

Records of the Town of Plymouth, 3 Vols. Intro. by Wm. T. Davis. 1989. reprint ed. Vol. 1, 1705-1743, 348p. write for info. (*1-55613-181-X*); reprint ed. Vol. 2, 1743-1783, 372p. write for info. (*1-55613-182-8*); reprint ed. Vol. 3, 1743-1783, 482p. write for info. (*1-55613-183-6*) Heritage Bk.

Records of the Town of Plymouth (1636-1705, 1705-1743, 1743-1783), 3 vols. in 1. Ed. by William T. Davis. 1193p. 1995. reprint ed. pap. 75.00 (*0-614-10003-8*, 9124) Clearfield Co.

***Records of the Town of Smithtown, Long Island, with Other Ancient Documents of Historic Value, with Notes & Introduction.** William S. Pelletreau. (Illus.). 503p. 1997. reprint ed. lib. bdg. 52.50 (*0-8328-6243-6*) Higginson Bk Co.

Records of the Trial of Walter Langeton. A. Beardwood. (Camden Fourth Ser.: No. 6). 27.00 (*0-901050-02-4*) David Brown.

Records of the Tuesday Club of Annapolis, 1745-56. Ed. by Elaine G. Breslaw. 640p. 1988. text ed. 49.95 (*0-252-01334-4*) U of Ill Pr.

Records of the U. S. Judicial Conference, Common Rules of Practice and Procedure: 1935-1988. Ed. by Congressional Information Service, Inc., Staff. 1991. write for info. (*0-88692-228-3*) Cong Info.

Records of the U. S. Judicial Conference, Common Rules of Practice and Procedure, 1990. Ed. by Congressional Information Service, Inc., Staff. 176p. 1995. write for info. (*0-88692-316-6*) Cong Info.

***Records of the UAE 1961-1963, 3 vols.** 2000p. Date not set. reprint ed. lib. bdg. 595.00 (*0-614-25972-X*, Pub. by Archive Editions UK) N Ross.

Records of the Virginia Company of London, 4 vols., Set. Virginia Company of London Staff. Ed. by Susan M. Kingsbury. LC 74-19621. reprint ed. 230.00 (*0-404-12457-7*) AMS Pr.

Records of the Virginia Company of London Vol. 4: Documents, II, 1623-1626. Susan M. Kingsbury. (Illus.). 637p. 1996. pap. 42.00 (*0-7884-0253-6*, K355) Heritage Bk.

Records of the Virginia County of London: Documents, I, 1607-1622, Vol. 3. Ed. by Susan M. Kingsbury. (Illus.). 769p. 1995. reprint ed. pap. text ed. 44.00 (*0-7884-0210-2*) Heritage Bk.

Records of United Bronx Parents, Inc. Ed. by Evelina L. Antonetty. (Finding Aid Ser.). (Illus.). 15p. (C). 1992. reprint ed. pap. text ed. 5.00 (*1-878483-23-4*) Hunter Coll CEP.

Records of Washington County, Georgia. Marie De Lamar & Elisabeth Rothstein. LC 84-73076. 184p. 1985. reprint ed. 18.50 (*0-8063-1110-X*) Genealog Pub.

Records of William Spooner of Plymouth, Massachusetts, & of His Descendants, Vol. 1. 694p. 1989. reprint ed. pap. 104.00 (*0-8328-1103-3*); reprint ed. lib. bdg. 112.00 (*0-8328-1102-5*) Higginson Bk Co.

***Records of Wind & Earth: A Translation of Fudoki, with Introduction & Commentaries.** Michiko Y. Aoki. LC 96-36340. 1996. write for info. (*0-924304-32-4*) Assn Asian Studies.

Records of Woman. Felicia Hemans. LC 91-31815. 344p. 1991. reprint ed. 55.00 (*1-85477-071-3*, Pub. by Woodstock Bks UK) Cassell.

Records of Ye Towne Meetings of Lynn, 7 vols. pap. 30.00 (*1-882162-10-2*) Lynn Hist Soc.

Records of Ye Towne Meetings of Lynn, 1691-1701- 2, Pt. I. 83p. 1949. pap. 5.00 (*1-882162-03-X*) Lynn Hist Soc.

Records of Ye Towne Meetings of Lynn, 1701- 1717, Vol. 2. 107p. 1956. pap. 5.00 (*1-882162-04-8*) Lynn Hist Soc.

Records of Ye Towne Meetings of Lynn, 1717- 1730, Pt. 3. 97p. 1960. pap. 5.00 (*1-882162-05-6*) Lynn Hist Soc.

Records of Ye Towne Meetings of Lynn, 1730- 1742, Pt. 4. 94p. 1964. pap. 5.00 (*1-882162-06-4*) Lynn Hist Soc.

Records of Ye Towne Meetings of Lynn, 1742- 1759, Pt. 5. 98p. 1966. pap. 5.00 (*1-882162-07-2*) Lynn Hist Soc.

Records of Ye Towne Meetings of Lynn, 1759- 1771, Pt. 6. 98p. 1970. pap. 5.00 (*1-882162-08-0*) Lynn Hist Soc.

Records of Ye Towne Meetings of Lynn, 1771- 1783, Pt. 7. 100p. 1971. pap. 5.00 (*1-882162-09-9*) Lynn Hist Soc.

***Records of Yemen 1798-1960, 16 vols.** Ed. by D. Ingrams & L. Ingrams. (Arabian Regional Records Ser.). (Illus.). 12,000p. 1993. reprint ed. lib. bdg. 3,995.00 (*1-85207-370-5*, Pub. by Archive Editions UK) N Ross.

Records on Nepalese Development Nepal District Profile. 1994. pap. 300.00 (*0-7855-0476-1*, Pub. by Ratna Pustak Bhandar) St Mut.

***Records Relating to American Prisoners of War & Missing in Action from the Vietnam War Era, 1960-1994.** Ed. by Charles E. Schamel. 127p. (Orig.). 1997. pap. text ed. 35.00 (*0-7881-4038-8*) DIANE Pub.

Records Relating to the Early History of Boston, 39 vols. Boston Registry Department Staff. LC 74-19611. reprint ed. write for info. (*0-404-12343-0*) AMS Pr.

Records Relating to the Gold Coast Settlements from 1750 to 1874. J. J. Crooks. 576p. 1973. reprint ed. 55.00 (*0-7146-1647-8*, BHA-01647, Pub. by F Cass Pubs UK) Intl Spec Bk.

Records Retention Guidelines for U. S. Based Real Estate Organizations. Janice L. Peck & Florence M. Ochsner. 60p. 1993. pap. 36.00 (*0-933887-48-5*, A4519) ARMA Intl.

Records Retention Guidelines for U. S. Based Telephone Companies. 160p. 1990. pap. 21.00 (*0-933887-35-3*, A4569) ARMA Intl.

Records Retention Procedures: Your Guide to Determine How Long to Keep Your Records & How to Safely Destroy Them! Donald S. Skupsky. 192p. 1994. pap. text ed. 39.00 (*0-929316-03-7*) Info Requirements.

Records Retention Resource Guidelines for U. S. Based Electric Utilities. Utilities Industry Action Committee. 54p. 1995. pap. 23.00 (*0-933887-52-3*, A4598) ARMA Intl.

Records Supervisor. Jack Rudman. (Career Examination Ser.: C-3613). 1994. pap. 29.95 (*0-8373-3613-9*) Nat Learn.

Recoumbinant FSH (Puregon) Preclinical & Clinical Experiences. Ed. by H. J. Out & H. J. Bennink. LC 96-20463. (Studies in Profertility Ser.: Vol. 5). 175p. 1996. 65.00 (*1-85070-746-4*) Prthnon Pub.

Recources in Technology. Itea. (Technology & Industrial Education Ser.). 1984. pap. 17.95 (*0-87192-152-9*) S-W Pub.

Recover & Heal: Meditations on the Twelve Steps. Karen Albertus. 308p. 1992. pap. 12.95 (*0-86716-153-1*) St Anthony Mess Pr.

***Recover the Dream: A Call to Mainstream Churches of Christ.** Jim Harris. 184p. (Orig.). 1996. pap. 8.95 (*1-56794-112-5*, C-2431) Star Bible.

Recovered Land. Alicia Nitecki. LC 94-41650. (Illus.). 128p. 1995. 19.95 (*0-87023-976-7*) U of Mass Pr.

***Recovered Memories & False Memories.** Ed. by Martin Conway. (Debates in Psychology Ser.). (Illus.). 320p. 1997. 75.00 (*0-19-852387-4*); pap. 29.95 (*0-19-852386-6*) OUP.

***Recovered Memories of Abuse: Assessment, Therapy, Forensics.** Kenneth S. Pope & Laura S. Brown. LC 96-33009. 1996. pap. 24.95 (*1-55798-395-X*) Am Psychol.

***Recovered Memories of Trauma: Transferring the Present to the Past.** C. Brooks Brenneis. 220p. 1997. 31.50 (*0-8236-5788-4*, BN05788) Intl Univs Pr.

Recovered Memory & Other Assaults Upon the Mysteries of Consciousness: Hypnosis, Psychotherapy, Fraud & the Mass Media. William Rogers. LC 95-15794. 152p. 1995. lib. bdg. 26.50 (*0-7864-0109-5*) McFarland & Co.

Recovered Memory/False Memory Debate. Ed. by Kathy Pezdek & William P. Banks. (Illus.). 394p. 1996. boxed 49.95 (*0-12-552975-9*) Acad Pr.

Recovered Roots: Collective Memory & the Making of Israeli National Tradition. Yael Zerubavel. LC 94-9441. (Illus.). 360p. 1995. 32.50 (*0-226-98157-6*) U Ch Pr.

***Recovered Roots: Collective Memory & the Making of Israeli National Tradition.** Yael Zerubavel. (Illus.). 360p. 1996. pap. text ed. 19.95 (*0-226-98158-4*) U Ch Pr.

Recovered Truths. Edward Dennett. 52p. pap. text ed. 2.50 (*0-9640037-6-7*) Pres Truth.

Recovered Writers/Recovered Texts: Race, Class, & Gender in Black Women's Literature. Ed. by Dolan Hubbard. LC 96-10119. (Tennessee Studies in Literature: No. 38). 200p. 1997. 30.00 (*0-87049-959-9*) U of Tenn Pr.

Recovered Yesterdays in Literature. William A. Quayle. LC 74-117829. (Essay Index Reprint Ser.). 1977. 21.95 (*0-8369-1678-6*) Ayer.

Recoveries: True Stories by People who Conquered Addictions & Compulsions. Ed. by Lindsey Hall & Leigh Cohn. 224p. (Orig.). 1987. pap. 9.95 (*0-936077-11-5*) Gurze Bks.

Recoveries & Yields from Pacific Fish & Shellfish. rev. ed. C. Crapo et al. (Marine Advisory Bulletin Ser.: No. 37). 36p. 1993. pap. 5.00 (*1-56612-012-8*) AK Sea Grant CP.

Recoveries (1975-1986) Poems. Frederic Will. LC 92-31913. 56p. 1993. pap. 12.95 (*0-7734-0041-9*, Mellen Poetry Pr) E Mellen.

Recovering: A Journal. May Sarton. 1980. 14.95 (*0-393-01402-9*) Norton.

Recovering: A Journal. May Sarton. (Illus.). 256p. 1987. reprint ed. pap. 5.95 (*0-393-30339-X*) Norton.

Recovering a Body. Helen Dunmore et al. 64p. 9500. pap. 14.95 (*1-85224-289-2*, Pub. by Bloodaxe Bks UK) Dufour.

***Recovering a Journal.** May Sarton. Date not set. pap. 12.00 (*0-393-31717-X*) Norton.

Recovering American Literature. Peter Shaw. LC 93-40507. 208p. 1994. text ed. 22.00 (*1-56663-053-3*) I R Dee.

Recovering American Literature. Peter Shaw. 204p. 1995. pap. 12.95 (*1-56663-095-9*) I R Dee.

Recovering at Home after a Stroke: A Practical Guide for Your & Your Family. Florence Weiner et al. LC 93-42637. (Howard A. Rusk Institute of Rehabilitation Medicine Ser.). 208p. 1994. pap. 11.00 (*0-399-51843-6*, Body Pr-Perigee) Berkley Pub.

Recovering at Home with a Heart Condition: A Practical Guide for You & Your Family. Florence Weiner et al. LC 93-32926. (Howard A. Rusk Institute of Rehabilitation Medicine Ser.). 208p. 1994. pap. 11.00 (*0-399-51844-4*, Body Pr-Perigee) Berkley Pub.

Recovering Berryman: Essays on a Poet. Ed. by Richard J. Kelly & Alan K. Lathrop. 300p. 1993. text ed. 44.50 (*0-472-10419-5*) U of Mich Pr.

Recovering Biblical Manhood & Womanhood. Ed. by John Piper & Wayne A. Grudem. LC 90-20258. 576p. (Orig.). 1991. pap. 19.99 (*0-89107-586-0*) Crossway Bks.

***Recovering Bodies: Illness, Disability, & Life-Writing.** G. Thomas Couser. LC 97-11952. (Wisconsin Studies in American Autobiography). 336p. 1997. 55.00 (*0-299-15560-9*); pap. 24.95 (*0-299-15564-1*) U of Wis Pr.

Recovering Catholic: Personal Journeys of Women Who Left the Church. Joanne H. Meehl. 288p. 1995. 24.95 (*0-87975-927-5*) Prometheus Bks.

Recovering Catholics: What to Do When Religion Comes Between You & God. Earnie Larsen & Janee Parnegg. LC 91-58903. 1992. pap. 12.00 (*0-06-064955-0*) Harper SF.

Recovering Catholics & the God Who Loves Them, 5 pamphlets. Earnie Larsen. 64p. 1990. pap. 5.00 (*0-936098-61-9*) Intl Marriage.

Recovering Correctional Costs Through Offender Fees. (Illus.). 65p. (Orig.). (C). 1994. pap. text ed. 25.00 (*1-56806-151-X*) DIANE Pub.

Recovering Couples Anonymous: Big Book. 2nd ed. 122p. 1992. pap. 18.00 (*0-9637495-1-X*) Recov Couples.

R

Recovering Couples Anonymous: Big Book. 3rd rev. ed. 140p. 1996. pap. 14.95 (*0-9637495-2-8*) Recov Couples.

Recovering Damages for Psychiatric Injury. Michael Napier & Kay Wheat. 208p. 1995. 19.95 (*1-85431-352-5*, Pub. by Blackstone Pr UK) Gaunt.

Recovering Ethical Life: Jurgen Habermas & the Future of Critical Theory. J. M. Bernstein. LC 94-12152. 304p. (C). (gr. 13). 1994. text ed. 69.95 (*0-415-06194-6*, B4138) Routledge.

Recovering Ethical Life: Jurgen Habermas & the Future of Critical Theory. J. M. Bernstein. LC 94-12152. 304p. (C). 1995. pap. 19.95 (*0-415-11783-6*, B4759) Routledge.

Recovering Feminine Spirituality: The Mysteries & the Mass As Symbols of Individuation. Evangeline Kane. 1994. pap. 17.95 (*1-879041-23-5*) Sigo Pr.

Recovering for Psychological Injuries. 2nd ed. William A. Barton. LC 90-30974. 417p. 80.00 (*0-941916-51-0*); pap. 65.00 (*0-685-47507-7*) ATLA Pr.

Recovering from a Disaster: How to Process Your Own Insurance Claim. Les Watrous. (Illus.). 132p. (Orig.). 1996. lib. bdg. 29.95 (*0-9654537-0-7*) TGWB. "Oh No!, What do we do now?"--If you find yourself in a situation of property damage to your home, be it natural disaster or a simple pipe break damaging floor, walls, or ceiling, RECOVERING FROM A DISASTER - HOW TO PROCESS YOUR OWN INSURANCE CLAIM, is a must read for you. "My claim was initially denied by my insurance company, but after I read RECOVERING FROM A DISASTER - HOW TO PROCESS YOUR OWN INSURANCE CLAIM, I understand how the insurance process works & with a new approach & knowledge, successfully negotiated a settlement of my claim for a very substantial amount."--Cindy R., Fullerton, California. This fully illustrated book, RECOVERING FROM A DISASTER - HOW TO PROCESS YOUR OWN INSURANCE CLAIM, guides you through the entire insurance process including the submission of your claim, negotiating your claim, dealing with troublesome adjusters, hiring the right contractor, & getting paid by the insurance company. Contributors to this book include: insurance claims managers, claims adjusters, insurance litigation specialists, attorneys, consumer groups, restoration & reconstruction contractors. RECOVERING FROM A DISASTER - HOW TO PROCESS YOUR OWN INSURANCE CLAIM, includes tips, anecdotal examples, checklists, claimant responsibility, policy interpretation, sample letters & dozens of necessary forms & logs for copying. This book will get results & save you thousands of dollars. To order: TGWB Publishing, 2232 East Wilson Ave., Orange, CA 92667. Ph. 888-766-3237.** ***Publisher Provided Annotation.

Recovering from a Heart Attack. Weiss. 1980. 12.95 (*0-02-625830-7*) Macmillan.

Recovering from Addictions: Guided Steps Through the Healing Process. J. R. Baugh. LC 90-39718. (Illus.). 310p. 1990. 22.95 (*0-306-43561-6*, Plenum Insight) Plenum.

Recovering from Affairs: A Handbook. Peggy Vaughan & James Vaughan. 53p. (Orig.). 1996. pap. 15.00 (*0-936390-06-9*, B05EX) Dialog Pr.

Recovering from Breast Surgery: Exercises to Strengthen Your Body & Relieve Pain. Diana Stumm. 128p. 1995. lib. bdg. 33.00 (*0-8095-6348-7*) Borgo Pr.

Recovering from Breast Surgery: Exercises to Strengthen Your Body & Relieve Pain. Diana Stumm. LC 95-3153. (Illus.). 128p. 1995. pap. 11.95 (*0-89793-180-7*) Hunter Hse.

Recovering from Catastrophes: Federal Disaster Relief Policy & Politics. Peter J. May. LC 84-19731. (Contributions in Political Science Ser.: No. 128). (Illus.). x, 186p. 1985. text ed. 55.00 (*0-313-24698-X*, MYR/, Greenwood Pr) Greenwood.

Recovering from Chronic Fatigue Syndrome: A Guide to Self Empowerment. William Collinge. LC 92-35606. 224p. (Orig.). 1993. pap. 13.95 (*0-399-51807-X*, Body Pr-Perigree) Berkley Pub.

Recovering from Churches that Abuse. Ronald Enroth. 176p. 1994. pap. 15.99 (*0-310-39870-3*) Zondervan.

Recovering from Divorce. Michael Warnke. 1992. 14.95 (*0-932081-29-0*) Victory Hse.

Recovering from Divorce...& the Horse You Rode in On. Bill Wear, Jr. 135p. 1992. pap. 14.95 (*0-9632411-1-7*) Insight Prods.

Recovering from Incest: Imagination & the Healing Process. Evangeline Kane. 232p. (Orig.). 1989. 27.50 (*0-938434-43-8*); pap. 16.95 (*0-938434-42-X*) Sigo Pr.

Recovering from Rape. Linda E. Ledray. LC 84-9138. 272p. 1986. pap. 9.95 (*0-03-064001-6*, Owl) H Holt & Co.

Recovering from Rape. Linda E. Ledray. LC 84-9138. 272p. 1989. pap. 9.95 (*0-8050-1253-2*, Owl) H Holt & Co.

Recovering from Rape. 2nd ed. Linda E. Ledray. 1994. pap. 12.95 (*0-8050-2928-1*) H Holt & Co.

Recovering from Sexual Abuse & Incest: A Twelve-Step Guide. Jean Gust & Patricia D. Sweeting. LC 92-17290. 192p. 1992. pap. 9.95 (*0-938179-32-2*) Mills Sanderson.

Recovering from Surgery, Illness & Injury. 1994. lib. bdg. 250.95 (*0-8490-5667-5*) Gordon Pr.

Recovering from the Loss of a Child. Katherine F. Donnelly. 304p. 1994. pap. text ed. 5.99 (*0-425-13909-3*) Berkley Pub.

Recovering from the Loss of a Loved One to AIDS. Katherine F. Donnelly. 272p. 1994. 22.95 (*0-312-11050-2*) St Martin.

Recovering from the Loss of a Loved One to AIDS: Help for Surviving Family, Friends, & Lovers Who Grieve. Katherine F. Donnelly. 272p. 1995. pap. 10.00 (*0-449-90990-5*) Fawcett.

Recovering from the Loss of a Parent. Katherine F. Donnelly. 304p. (Orig.). 1993. mass mkt. 5.99 (*0-425-13916-6*) Berkley Pub.

Recovering from the Losses of Life. H. Norman Wright. LC 91-643. 224p. (gr. 10). 1993. reprint ed. pap. 9.99 (*0-8007-5487-5*) Revell.

Recovering Literature's Lost Ground: Essays in American Autobiography. James M. Cox. LC 88-22052. 221p. 1989. text ed. 30.00 (*0-8071-1491-X*) La State U Pr.

Recovering Love: Codependency to CoRecovery. J. Richard Cookerly. 192p. 1992. pap. write for info. (*0-8306-3837-7*, 4121) McGraw-Hill Prof.

Recovering Love: Codependency to CoRecovery. J. Richard Cookerly. 192p. 1992. 17.95 (*0-8306-3838-5*, 4121, TAB-Human Servs Inst) TAB Bks.

Recovering Love: From Codependency to Corecovery. J. Richard Cookerly. 1992. text ed. 17.95 (*0-07-012699-2*); pap. text ed. 17.95 (*0-07-012700-X*) McGraw.

Recovering Love: Overcoming Standoffs & Stalemates in a Valued Relationship. Richard Driscoll. 1993. pap. 11.95 (*0-02-907755-9*, Free Press) Free Pr.

Recovering My Sanity: Poems & Short Stories. Beecher Smith. 95p. (Orig.). 1996. pap. 9.95 (*1-880964-16-3*) Zapizdat Pubns.

Recovering of the Lord's Testimony in Fullness. T. A. Sparks. 146p. 1993. pap. text ed. 6.60 (*1-883137-12-8*) Christ Stewards.

Recovering Pragmatism's Voice: The Classical Tradition, Rorty, & the Philosophy of Communication. Ed. by Lenore Langsdorf & Andrew R. Smith. LC 94-1571. (SUNY Series in the Philosophy of the Social Sciences). 336p. 1994. text ed. 59.50 (*0-7914-2213-5*); pap. text ed. 19.95 (*0-7914-2214-3*) State U NY Pr.

Recovering Prosperity Through Quality: The Midland City Story. Robert A. Schwarz. LC 93-4981. 165p. 1993. 19.95 (*0-87389-261-5*, H0817) ASQC Qual Pr.

Recovering Sarepta, a Phoenician City. James B. Pritchard. LC 77-28304. (Illus.). 180p. 1978. pap. text ed. 13.95 (*0-691-00213-4*) Princeton U Pr.

Recovering Shakespeare's Theatrical Vocabulary. Alan C. Dessen. 256p. (C). 1995. text ed. 54.95 (*0-521-47080-3*) Cambridge U Pr.

Recovering the Ancient Magic. Max F. Long. (Illus.). 125p. 1978. reprint ed. pap. 6.95 (*0-910764-01-8*) Huna Res Inc.

Recovering the Canon: Essays on Isaac Bashevis Singer. David N. Miller. (Studies in Judaism in Modern Times: Vol. 8). xxii, 154p. 1986. 44.50 (*90-04-07681-6*) E J Brill.

Recovering the Ground: Critical Exercises in Recollection. William H. Poteat. LC 93-45489. 235p. (C). 1994. pap. text ed. 16.95 (*0-7914-2132-5*) State U NY Pr.

Recovering the Ground: Critical Exercises in Recollection. William H. Poteat. LC 93-45489. 235p. (C). 1994. text ed. 49.50 (*0-7914-2131-7*) State U NY Pr.

Recovering the Human Jesus. Kenneth H. Ives. LC 90-91523. 300p. (Orig.). 1990. pap. 5.00 (*0-89670-022-4*) Progresiv Pub.

Recovering the Lost Tools of Learning: An Approach to Distinctively Christian Education. Douglas Wilson. LC 90-29904. (Turning Point Christian Worldview Ser.). 224p. (Orig.). 1991. pap. 12.99 (*0-89107-583-6*) Crossway Bks.

Recovering the Orient: Artists, Scholars, Appropriations, Vol. 11. Ed. by C. Andrew Gerstle. (Studies in Anthropology & History). 362, ixp. 1994. text ed. 54.00 (*3-7186-5341-9*, Harwood Acad Pubs) Gordon & Breach.

Recovering the Orient: Artists, Scholars, Appropriations, Vol. 11. Ed. by C. Andrew Gerstle. (Studies in Anthropology & History). 362p. 1995. pap. text ed. 26.00 (*3-7186-5687-6*, Harwood Acad Pubs) Gordon & Breach.

Recovering the Personal: Religious Language & the Post-Critical Quest of H. Richard Niebuhr. R. Melvin Keiser. LC 87-23354. (American Academy of Religion, Studies in Religion). 182p. 1988. pap. 14.95 (*1-55540-186-4*, 01-00-52) Scholars Pr GA.

Recovering the Personal Past: The Conceptual Background of Autobiographical Memory. Bruce M. Ross. 272p. 1992. 35.00 (*0-19-506894-7*) OUP.

Recovering the Role of Women: Power & Authority in Rabbinic Jewish Society. Ed. by Peter J. Haas. LC 92-31629. (USF Studies in the History of Judaism: Vol. 59). 132p. 1992. 49.95 (*1-55540-765-X*, 24 00 59) Scholars Pr GA.

Recovering the Sacred Papers from the Academy & the Sanctuary. Earl G. Hunt, Jr. 260p. 1992. 14.95 (*0-9631308-0-3*) J Creek Pr.

Recovering the Self: Morality & Social Theory. Victor J. Seidler. LC 93-49036. 256p. (C). 1994. pap. 17.95 (*0-415-11151-X*, B3905, Routledge NY) Routledge.

Recovering the Self: Morality & Social Theory. Victor J. Seidler. LC 93-49036. 240p. (C). (gr. 13). 1994. text ed. 62.95 (*0-415-11150-1*, B3901, Routledge NY) Routledge.

Recovering the Social Contract. Ron Replogle. LC 87-33024. 256p. (C). 1989. 56.50 (*0-8476-7591-2*) Rowman.

***Recovering the Soul.** 10.95 (*1-56176-152-4*) Mystic Fire.

Recovering the Soul: A Scientific & Spiritual Search. Larry Dossey. 336p. 1989. pap. 13.95 (*0-553-34790-X*) Bantam.

Recovering the Soul: A Season of Change. Erin T. Palmeter. (Illus.). 32p. (Orig.). 1995. 14.95 (*0-9650744-7-1*, RTS-101) Palmeter Grp.

Recovering the U. S. Hispanic Literary Heritage. Ed. by Ramon Gutierrez & Genaro Padilla. LC 92-45114. 268p. 1993. pap. 17.95 (*1-55885-058-9*); text ed. 34.95 (*1-55885-063-5*) Arte Publico.

Recovering the Word: Essays on Native American Literature. Ed. by Brian Swann & Arnold Krupat. LC 86-19150. 644p. reprint ed. pap. 180.00 (*0-7837-4685-7*, 2044432) Bks Demand.

Recovering Vegetarian Cookbook: 12 Easy Steps to Eating Meat Again. Ralph Roberts & Pat Roberts. (Illus.). 208p. (Orig.). Date not set. pap. 14.99 (*1-888295-03-1*) Elephant Books.

Recovering Your Business. Maria Abruzzo & Thomas Abruzzo. 188p. 1993. 19.95 (*0-9638710-0-5*) Tamp Computer.

Recovery. J. M. Dillard. Ed. by Kevin Ryan. (Star Trek Ser.: No. 73). 288p. (Orig.). 1995. mass mkt. 5.50 (*0-671-88342-9*) PB.

Recovery. Chris Woods. 63p. 9300. pap. 16.95 (*1-870612-43-4*, Pub. by Enitha Pr UK) Dufour.

Recovery. large type ed. Stanley Middleton. 1990. 25.99 (*0-7089-2242-2*) Ulverscroft.

Recovery. Steven L. Thompson. 352p. (Orig.). 1988. reprint ed. pap. 3.95 (*0-373-97079-X*) Harlequin Bks.

Recovery: A Guide for Adult Children of Alcoholics. Herbert L. Gravitz & Julia D. Bowden. 122p. 1987. pap. 10.00 (*0-671-64528-5*, Fireside) S&S Trade.

Recovery: A Lifelong Journey. Juanita Ryan & Dale Ryan. (Life Recovery Guides Ser.). 64p. (Orig.). 1993. wbk. ed., pap. 4.99 (*0-8308-1166-4*, 1166) InterVarsity.

Recovery: A Pull from the Source: The Meaning & Measurement of Recovery from Alcoholism & Addictions. Robert S. Helgoe. 96p. (Orig.). 1989. pap. 7.95 (*0-685-26967-1*) Sundown M Found.

Recovery: A Taste for Vanilla & The Step-By-Step Guide for Relational, Emotional, Spiritual & Physical Health. Allan Gates & Charlie Baker. LC 90-62929. (Illus.). 182p. (Orig.). 1991. pap. 11.95 (*0-913507-15-6*) New Forums.

Recovery: How to Survive Sexual Assault for Women, Men, Teenagers, Their Friends & Families. rev. ed. Helen Benedict. LC 94-15856. 1994. 39.50 (*0-231-09674-7*); pap. 14.95 (*0-231-09675-5*) Col U Pr.

Recovery: Loss & Return of Vision. (Illus.). 1991. 16.95 (*0-9628434-0-7*) J Grubb Taylor.

Recovery: Stories of Alcoholism & Survival. Amy Stromsten. LC 82-620025. 1982. 20.00 (*0-911290-14-1*) Rutgers Ctr Alcohol.

***Recovery - Flag Full of Stars - Traitor Winds.** (Star Trek: The Lost Years Ser.). 1996. mass mkt. 22.98 (*0-671-85154-3*) PB.

Recovery After Traumatic Brain Injury. Ed. by Barbara P. Uzzell & Henry H. Stonnington. (Institute for Research in Behavioral Neuroscience Ser.). 336p. 1996. 69.95 (*0-8058-1823-5*); pap. 34.50 (*0-8058-1824-3*) L Erlbaum Assocs.

Recovery Analysis: New Methods & a Computer Program in Well Hydraulics. Michael Kasenow. 350p. 1996. 85.00 (*0-918334-98-5*, RAN) WRP.

Recovery & Isolation of Significant Food. L. Sterneta. 1993. text ed. write for info. (*0-442-01034-6*) Van Nos Reinhold.

Recovery & Management of Neuropsychological Impairments. fac. ed. Edgar Miller. LC 83-21582. 185p. 1984. reprint ed. pap. 52.80 (*0-7837-8286-1*, 2049068) Bks Demand.

Recovery & Recrystallization of Metals: Proceedings. Ed. by L. Himmel. LC 62-18705. 399p. reprint ed. pap. 113.80 (*0-317-10276-1*, 2000680) Bks Demand.

***Recovery & Refining of Precious Metals.** (C). (gr. 13 up). 1984. text ed. 45.50 (*0-412-07901-1*) Chapman & Hall.

***Recovery & Refining of Precious Metals.** 2nd ed. LC 97-18. 1997. pap. write for info. (*0-412-72060-4*) Chapman & Hall.

Recovery & Relapse Prevention for Parents of Chemically Dependent Children. Dennis Daley & Judy Miller. 1993. pap. 4.95 (*1-56246-027-7*, P183) Johnsn Inst.

Recovery & Restoration of Damaged Ecosystems: Proceedings of the International Symposium on the Recovery of Damaged Ecosystems Held at Virginia Polytechnic Institute & State University, Blacksburg, Virginia, on March 23-25, 1975. International Symposium on the Recovery of Damaged Ecosystems Staff. Ed. by J. Cairns, Jr. et al. LC 76-49453. (Illus.). 543p. reprint ed. pap. 154.80 (*0-8357-8526-2*, 2034824) Bks Demand.

Recovery Book. Al Mooney et al. LC 92-50284. 624p. 1992. pap. 14.95 (*1-56305-084-6*, 3084) Workman Pub.

Recovery Dynamics: Client Guide Book. Joe McQuany. 104p. 1989. pap. text ed. 15.00 (*1-883094-02-X*) Kelly Fnd.

Recovery Dynamics: Counselors Manual. Joe McQuany. 400p. 1989. text ed. 60.00 (*1-883094-01-1*) Kelly Fnd.

Recovery Dynamics: Individual Evaluation Packet. Joe McQuany. 96p. 1989. pap. text ed. 14.00 (*1-883094-03-8*) Kelly Fnd.

Recovery Education: A Guide for Teaching Chemically Dependent People. Merlene Miller. 1992. pap. 4.00 (*0-8309-0565-0*) Herald Hse.

Recovery for Wrongful Death & Injury, 3 vols. 3rd ed. Stuart M. Speiser. LC 92-72190. 1992. ring bd. 345.00 (*0-685-59912-4*) Clark Boardman Callaghan.

Recovery for Wrongful Death & Injury: Economic Handbook. 3rd ed. Stuart M. Speiser. LC 87-82546. 1988. 135.00 (*0-685-59913-2*) Clark Boardman Callaghan.

Recovery from Abuse. Dale Ryan & Juanita Ryan. (Life Recovery Guides Ser.). 64p. 1990. wbk. ed., pap. 4.99 (*0-8308-1158-3*, 1158) InterVarsity.

Recovery from Abusive Groups. rev. ed. Wendy Ford. 166p. 1993. pap. 9.95 (*0-931337-04-6*) Am Family Foun.

Recovery from Addiction. John Finnegan & Daphne Gray. LC 90-1941. 192p. (Orig.). 1995. pap. 14.95 (*0-89087-599-5*) Celestial Arts.

Recovery from Addictions. Dale Ryan & Juanita Ryan. (Life Recovery Guides Ser.). 64p. (Orig.). 1990. wbk. ed., pap. 4.99 (*0-8308-1155-9*, 1155) InterVarsity.

Recovery from AIDS by Natural Methods & Restoring the Immune System. (AIDS Ser.). 1991. lib. bdg. 79.95 (*0-8490-4804-4*) Gordon Pr.

Recovery from Alcoholism. Jerome D. Levin. LC 93-74242. 296p. 1994. reprint ed. pap. 25.00 (*1-56821-186-4*) Aronson.

Recovery from Alcoholism: Beyond Your Wildest Dreams. Jerome D. Levin. LC 90-1232. 296p. 1991. 30.00 (*0-87668-625-0*) Aronson.

Recovery from Aphasia. Frwd. by Joseph M. Wepman. LC 51-687. 288p. reprint ed. pap. 82.10 (*0-317-07897-6*, 2012482) Bks Demand.

Recovery from Bereavement. Colin M. Parkes & Robert S. Weiss. LC 94-77919. 344p. 1995. pap. text ed. 40.00 (*1-56821-361-1*) Aronson.

Recovery from Bitterness. Dale Ryan & Juanita Ryan. (Life Recovery Guides Ser.). 64p. (Orig.). 1990. wbk. ed., pap. 4.99 (*0-8308-1154-0*, 1154) InterVarsity.

Recovery from Brain Damage: Reflections & Directions. F. David Rose. (Advances in Experimental Medicine & Biology Ser.: Vol. 325). (Illus.). 200p. (C). 1993. 75.00 (*0-306-44344-9*, Plenum Pr) Plenum.

Recovery from Broken Relationships. Juanita Ryan & Dale Ryan. (Life Recovery Guides Ser.). 64p. (Orig.). 1993. wbk. ed., pap. 4.99 (*0-8308-1165-6*, 1165) InterVarsity.

Recovery from Cancer: A Personal Story of Sickness & Health. Elaine Nussbaum. LC 92-3385. 192p. (Orig.). pap. 9.95 (*0-89529-504-0*) Avery Pub.

Recovery from Codependence: A Jewish 12-Step Guide to Healing Your Soul. Kerry M. Olitzky. LC 93-20051. (Illus.). 160p. (Orig.). 1993. 21.95 (*1-879045-27-3*); pap. 13.95 (*1-879045-32-X*) Jewish Lights.

Recovery from Codependency. Dale Ryan & Juanita Ryan. (Life Recovery Guides Ser.). 64p. (Orig.). 1990. wbk. ed., pap. 4.99 (*0-8308-1156-7*, 1156) InterVarsity.

Recovery from Compulsive Eating: A Complete Guide to the Twelve Step Program. LC 93-45762. 192p. 1994. 8.95 (*1-56838-017-8*, 5156A) Hazelden.

Recovery from Cults: Help for Victims of Psychological & Spiritual Abuse. Ed. by Michael D. Langone. 400p. (C). 1994. 37.00 (*0-393-70164-6*) Norton.

Recovery from Cults: Help for Victims of Psychological & Spiritual Abuse. Ed. by Michael D. Langone. 432p. 1995. pap. 17.95 (*0-393-31321-2*, Norton Paperbks) Norton.

Recovery from Depression. Dale Ryan & Juanita Ryan. (Life Recovery Guides Ser.). 64p. (Orig.). 1993. wbk. ed., pap. 4.99 (*0-8308-1161-3*, 1161) InterVarsity.

Recovery from Distorted Images of God. Dale Ryan & Juanita Ryan. (Life Recovery Guides Ser.). 64p. 1990. wbk. ed., pap. 4.99 (*0-8308-1152-4*, 1152) InterVarsity.

Recovery from Distorted Images of Self. Dale Ryan & Juanita Ryan. (Life Recovery Guides Ser.). 64p. (Orig.). 1993. wbk. ed., pap. 4.99 (*0-8308-1162-1*, 1162) InterVarsity.

Recovery from Family Dysfunctions. Dale Ryan & Juanita Ryan. (Life Recovery Guides Ser.). 64p. 1990. wbk. ed., pap. 4.99 (*0-8308-1151-6*, 1151) InterVarsity.

Recovery from Guilt. Juanita Ryan & Dale Ryan. (Life Recovery Guides Ser.). 64p. (Orig.). 1993. wbk. ed., pap. 4.99 (*0-8308-1163-X*, 1163) InterVarsity.

Recovery from Illness. Jenifer Wilson-Barnett & Morva Fordham. LC 82-2739. (Wiley Series on Developments in Nursing Research: Vol. 1). 151p. reprint ed. pap. 43.10 (*0-685-23945-4*, 2031497) Bks Demand.

Recovery from Loss. Dale Ryan & Juanita Ryan. (Life Recovery Guides Ser.). 64p. (Orig.). 1990. wbk. ed., pap. 4.99 (*0-8308-1157-5*, 1157) InterVarsity.

Recovery from Psychiatric Illness. Dennis Daley & Bennett Leslie. 1992. pap. 5.95 (*1-55691-091-6*, 916) Learning Pubns.

Recovery from Rescuing. Jacqueline Castine. 1989. pap. 7.95 (*1-55874-016-3*) Health Comm.

Recovery from Schizophrenia. 2nd rev. ed. Richard Wagner. LC 93-38556. 320p. (C). 1994. pap. 25.00 (*0-415-09261-2*, B7010); text ed. 74.95 (*0-415-09260-4*, B4325) Routledge.

Recovery from Schizophrenia: Psychiatry & Political Economy. Richard Warner. 416p. 1988. pap. text ed. 18.95 (*0-7102-1395-6*, RKP) Routledge.

Recovery from Shame. Dale Ryan & Juanita Ryan. (Life Recovery Guides Ser.). 64p. 1990. wbk. ed., pap. 4.99 (*0-8308-1153-2*, 1153) InterVarsity.

Recovery from Smoking: Quitting with the Twelve Step Process. Elizabeth H. Hoffman. 176p. 1991. pap. 9.95 (*0-89486-783-0*, 5176A) Hazelden.

Recovery from Spiritual Abuse. Juanita Ryan & Dale Ryan. (Life Recovery Guides Ser.). 64p. (Orig.). 1992. wbk. ed., pap. 4.99 (*0-8308-1159-1*, 1159) InterVarsity.

Recovery from the Depression: Australia & the World Economy in the 1930s. Ed. by R. G. Gregory & Noel G. Butlin. (Illus.). 392p. (C). 1989. text ed. 74.95 (*0-521-36245-8*) Cambridge U Pr.

Recovery from Workaholism. Juanita Ryan & Dale Ryan. (Life Recovery Guides Ser.). 64p. (Orig.). 1993. wbk. ed., pap. 4.99 (*0-8308-1164-8*, 1164) InterVarsity.

Recovery Handbook. James M. Mathers. LC 90-86083. (Orig.). 1992. pap. 15.95 (*0-9628640-0-5*) Helion Pub.

Recovery in Aphasics. Ed. by Y. Lebrun & R. Hoops. (Neurolinguistics Ser.: Vol. 4). 270p. 1976. 41.50 (*90-265-0228-1*) Swets.

***Recovery in God's Light, Vol. 5.** Upper Room Books Staff. (In God's Light Ser.). 1997. pap. text ed. 19.75 (*0-8358-0794-0*) Upper Room Bks.

***Recovery in Parallel Database Systems.** Svein-Olaf Hvasshovd. 302p. 1995. 70.00 (*3-528-05411-5*) Informatica.

Recovery in Wages & Employment. Leo Wolman. (NBER Bulletin Ser.: No. 63). 1936. reprint ed. 20.00 (*0-685-61179-5*) Natl Bur Econ Res.

Recovery of a Cancer Patient: A Personal Diary. Barbara A. Arpante. Ed. by Aaron Melenski. (Illus.). 54p. (Orig.). 1992. pap. text ed. 7.95 (*0-9625313-2-4*) Mntn Pr MA.

Recovery of American Education: Reclaiming a Vision. Stephen M. Krason. 183p. (C). 1991. pap. text ed. 21.00 (*0-8191-8125-0*); lib. bdg. 43.50 (*0-8191-8124-2*) U Pr of Amer.

Recovery of Black Presence: An Interdisciplinary Exploration. 256p. (Orig.). 1995. pap. 16.95 (*0-687-35735-7*) Abingdon.

Recovery of Damages for Bad Faith, 2 vols., Set. 5th ed. John C. McCarthy. LC 83-81290. 530p. 1992. 150.00 (*0-915544-46-6*) Lawpress CA.

Recovery of Damages for Crimes & Intentional Wrongs. Darrell McGowen. LC 92-75760. 500p. 1993. 95.00 (*0-915544-24-5*) Lawpress CA.

Recovery of Damages for Fraud. 2nd ed. Robert L. Dunn. 440p. 1995. 95.00 (*0-915544-26-1*) Lawpress CA.

Recovery of Damages for Lost Profits, 2 vols., Set. 4th ed. Robert L. Dunn. LC 87-80806. 1080p. 1992. 160.00 (*0-915544-47-4*) Lawpress CA.

Recovery of Faith. Sarvepalli Radhakrishnan. 1968. reprint ed. text ed. 65.00 (*0-8371-0197-2*, RARF, Greenwood Pr) Greenwood.

Recovery of Faith. Sarvepalli Radhakrishnan. (Orient Paperbacks Ser.). 187p. 1981. reprint ed. 9.00 (*0-86578-201-6*); reprint ed. pap. 4.25 (*0-88253-073-9*) Ind-US Inc.

Recovery of Faith. Sarvepalli Radhakrishnan. (C). 1995. reprint ed. 8.00 (*81-7223-145-8*, Pub. by Indus Pub II) S Asia.

***Recovery of Form Vol. 69: Annual ACPA Proceedings, 1995.** Ed. by Therese A. Druart. 1996. pap. 20.00 (*0-918090-29-6*) Am Cath Philo.

Recovery of Function in the Nervous System. Ed. by F. Cohadon & J. Lobo Antunes. (FIDIA Research Ser.: Vol. 13). xii, 191p. 1988. 82.00 (*0-387-96785-0*) Spr-Verlag.

Recovery of God's House & God's City. Witness Lee. 84p. per. 3.00 (*0-87083-034-1*, 08023001) Living Stream Ministry.

Recovery of Hope. Naomi Lederach & John Lederach. LC 91-74057. 169p. 1991. pap. 11.95 (*1-56148-046-0*) Good Bks PA.

Recovery of Indirect Costs: Pricing of Equitable Adjustments, Terminations for Convenience. 260p. 1989. pap. 40.00 (*0-89707-416-5*, 539-0084-01) Amer Bar Assn.

Recovery of Innocence. Pico Iyer. (Illus.). 1984. 8.75 (*0-88695-019-8*) Concord Grove.

Recovery of Interest - Practice & Precedents. Peter K. Thompson. 1985. pap. 70.00 (*0-406-26140-7*, U.K.) MICHIE.

***Recovery of Internationally Abducted Children: A Comprehensive Guide.** Maureen Dabbagh. LC 97-14081. 216p. 1997. lib. bdg. 42.50 (*0-7864-0289-X*) McFarland & Co.

Recovery of Meaning: Historical Archaeology in the Eastern United States. Ed. by Mark P. Leone & Parker B. Potter, Jr. LC 87-26499. (Anthropological Society of Washington Ser.). (Illus.). 506p. (C). 1994. pap. text ed. 19.95 (*1-56098-460-0*) Smithsonian.

Recovery of Metals from Sludges & Wastewaters. E. Radha Krishnan et al. LC 92-25243. (Pollution Technology Review Ser.: No. 207). (Illus.). 137p. 1993. 45.00 (*0-8155-1310-0*) Noyes.

***Recovery of Mission: Beyond the Pluralist Paradigm.** Vinoth Ramachandra. 307p. 1997. pap. 25.00 (*0-8028-4349-2*) Eerdmans.

***Recovery of Philosophy in America: Essays in Honor of John Edwin Smith.** Ed. by Thomas P. Kasulis & Robert C. Neville. LC 96-53656. 334p. (C). 1997. pap. text ed. 21.95 (*0-7914-3356-0*) State U NY Pr.

***Recovery of Philosophy in America: Essays in Honor of John Edwin Smith.** Ed. by Thomas P. Kasulis & Robert C. Neville. LC 96-53656. 334p. (C). 1997. text ed. 65.50 (*0-7914-3355-2*) State U NY Pr.

Recovery of Political Theory: Limits & Possibilities. fac. ed. William C. Havard. LC 83-14933. 247p. 1984. reprint ed. pap. 70.40 (*0-7837-7929-1*, 2047685) Bks Demand.

Recovery of Race in America. Aaron D. Gresson, III. LC 94-36195. 1995. text ed. 49.95 (*0-8166-2446-1*); pap. text ed. 19.95 (*0-8166-2448-8*) U of Minn Pr.

Recovery of Religious Roots. Henry F. McCreery. (Illus.). 192p. 1993. 13.50 (*0-9637435-0-3*) Sea Stack Pr.

Recovery of Rhetoric: Persuasive Discourse & Disciplinarity in the Human Sciences. Ed. by R. H. Roberts & J. M. Good. LC 92-39541. (Knowledge, Disciplinarity & Beyond Ser.). 278p. (C). 1993. text ed. 45.00 (*0-8139-1455-8*); pap. text ed. 20.00 (*0-8139-1456-6*) U Pr of Va.

Recovery of Sacred Psychology. Peter Reinhart. 1996. write for info. (*0-201-48396-3*) Addison-Wesley.

Recovery of Self: Regression & Redemption in Religious Experience. Kevin Fauteux. LC 93-37488. 256p. (Orig.). 1994. pap. 18.95 (*0-8091-3423-3*) Paulist Pr.

Recovery of the Anabaptist Vision: A Sixtieth Anniversary Tribute to Harold S. Bender. Ed. by Guy F. Hershberger. LC 57-10214. 368p. reprint ed. pap. 104.90 (*0-317-26605-5*, 2025419) Bks Demand.

Recovery of the Measure: Interpretation & Nature. Robert C. Neville. LC 89-11444. 369p. 1989. text ed. 64.50 (*0-7914-0098-0*); pap. text ed. 21.95 (*0-7914-0099-9*) State U NY Pr.

Recovery of the Modern: Architectural Review Critique 1980-1995. Michael Spens. (Illus.). 256p. 1996. 74.95 (*0-7506-2789-1*, Butterwrth Archit) Buttrwrth-Heinemann.

Recovery of the Sacred: Reforming the Reformed Liturgy. James Hitchcock. LC 94-75662. 186p. (Orig.). 1995. pap. 11.95 (*0-89870-544-4*) Ignatius Pr.

Recovery of the Soul: An Aristotelian Essay on Self-Fulfillment. Kenneth Rankin. 1991. 55.00 (*0-7735-0796-5*, Pub. by McGill CN) U of Toronto Pr.

Recovery of Unconscious Memories: Hypermnesia & Reminiscence. Matthew H. Erdelyi. (John D. & Catherine T. MacArthur Foundation Series on Mental Health & Development). (Illus.). 264p. 1996. 28.95 (*0-226-21660-8*) U Ch Pr.

Recovery of Virtue: The Relevance of Aquinas for Christian Ethics. Jean Porter. 300p. (Orig.). 1990. text ed. 25.00 (*0-664-21924-1*) Westminster John Knox.

Recovery of Your Inner Child. Lucia Capacchione. (Illus.). 304p. (Orig.). 1991. pap. 13.00 (*0-671-70135-5*, Fireside) S&S Trade.

Recovery of Your Self-Esteem: A Guide for Women. Carolyn Hillman. 304p. (Orig.). 1992. pap. 11.00 (*0-671-73813-5*, Fireside) S&S Trade.

Recovery or Relapse in the Global Economy: Comparative Perspectives on Restructuring in Central America. Ed. by Jolyne Melmed-Sanjak et al. LC 93-17117. 256p. 1993. text ed. 57.95 (*0-275-94605-3*, C4605, Praeger Pubs) Greenwood.

Recovery Problem in the United States. Harold G. Moulton et al. LC 73-176337. (FDR & the Era of the New Deal Ser.). (Illus.). 1972. reprint ed. lib. bdg. 85.00 (*0-306-70421-8*) Da Capo.

Recovery Processes for Biological Materials. Ed. by John F. Kennedy & Joaquim M. Cabral. 400p. 1993. text ed. 180.00 (*0-471-93349-X*) Wiley.

***Recovery Program: Endangered & Threatened Species, Report to Congress (1994)** (Illus.). 62p. (C). 1996. reprint ed. pap. 25.00 (*0-7881-3044-7*) DIANE Pub.

Recovery Room! A Nurse's Guide to Care of the Patient, Post Anesthesia. Jimmie R. Rankin. 150p. 1994. pap. 24.95 (*1-883938-15-5*) Dry Bones Pr.

Recovery, Sexuality & HIV see Mart Series

***Recovery Survival Guide.** L. S. Gordon. LC 96-69168. (Orig.). 1996. pap. text ed. 6.99 (*0-9653168-0-7*) RSS-Rec Surv.

Recovery Through Revolution. Ed. by Samuel D. Schmalhausen. LC 72-130994. reprint ed. 37.50 (*0-404-05607-5*) AMS Pr.

Recovery Workbook: Practical Coping & EM Powerment Strategies for People with Psychiatric Disability. LeRoy Spaniol et al. 120p. 1994. pap. text ed. 29.95 (*1-878512-01-3*) Boston Univ Ctr Psy Rehab.

***Recovery Yoga: Practical Guide for Chronically Ill.** Sam Dworkis. LC 97-6239. 1997. pap. 22.00 (*0-517-88399-6*) Crown Pub Group.

Recreacion Cristiana. Viola D. Campbell. (Illus.). 160p. (SPA.). 1986. reprint ed. pap. 9.50 (*0-311-11037-1*) Casa Bautista.

Recreating Authority in Revolutionary France. Ed. by Bryant T. Ragan, Jr. & Elizabeth A. Williams. LC 91-45492. 260p. (C). 1992. text ed. 40.00 (*0-8135-1841-5*); pap. text ed. 17.00 (*0-8135-1842-3*) Rutgers U Pr.

Recreating Butte: Men, Women, & Leisure in a Western Mining City, 1914-41. Mary Murphy. LC 96-9990. (Women in American History Ser.). (Illus.). 320p. 1996. text ed. 39.95 (*0-252-02267-X*); pap. text ed. 18.95 (*0-252-06569-7*) U of Ill Pr.

Recreating Jane. Karl Kerr. LC 86-72869. 158p. (Orig.). 1987. pap. 6.00 (*0-916383-21-0*) Aegina Pr.

Recreating Japanese Women, 1600-1945. Ed. by Gail L. Bernstein. LC 90-11194. (Illus.). 352p. 1991. pap. 16.95 (*0-520-07017-8*) U CA Pr.

***Recreating Marriage with the Same Old Spouse: A Guide for Couples - Couples Guide.** Sandra G. Bender. LC 96-52259. 184p. (Orig.). 1997. pap. 15.00 (*0-664-25726-7*) Westminster John Knox.

***Recreating Marriage with the Same Old Spouse: A Guide for Couples - Leader's Guide.** Sandra G. Bender. 144p. (Orig.). 1997. pap. write for info. (*0-664-25589-2*) Westminster John Knox.

Recreating Motherhood, Ideology & Technology in a Patriarchal Society. Barbara K. Rothman. 1990. pap. 10.95 (*0-393-30712-3*) Norton.

Recreating Our Schools for the Twenty-first Century. James Lewis, Jr. 280p. 1987. 24.95 (*0-915253-10-0*) Wilkerson Pub Co.

Recreating Recipes: Nutritious & Delicious II. Becky Plumlee. (Illus.). (Orig.). 1993. pap. 14.95 (*0-9637340-9-1*) Beckys Body.

Recreating Relationships: Collaboration & Educational Reform. Ed. by Helen Christiansen et al. LC 96-24411. (SUNY Series, Teacher Preparation & Development). 330p. (C). 1997. text ed. 65.50 (*0-7914-3303-X*); pap. text ed. 21.95 (*0-7914-3304-8*) State U NY Pr.

Recreating Sexual Politics: Men, Feminism & Politics. Victor J. Seidler. (Male Orders Ser.). 256p. (C). 1991. pap. 18.95 (*0-415-05854-6*, A5558) Routledge.

***Recreating the Academic Library: Breaking Virtual Ground.** Ed. by Cheryl M. LaGuardia. (New Library Ser.: Vol. 1). 250p. 1997. pap. 59.95 (*1-55570-293-7*) Neal-Schuman.

Recreating the Parish: A Reproducible Parish Resource. Thomas O. Sweetser et al. 170p. (Orig.). 1995. pap. 29.95 (*1-55612-808-8*) Sheed & Ward MO.

***Recreating the Web Site.** Marc Rettig. 400p. 1997. pap. text ed. 39.99 (*1-56830-332-7*) Hayden.

Recreating the Workplace: The Pathway to High Performance Work Systems. Steven R. Rayner. LC 92-85209. 281p. 1993. 27.50 (*0-939246-32-5*) Wiley.

Recreating the Workplace: The Pathway to High Performance Work Systems. Steven R. Rayner. 288p. 1995. text ed. 29.95 (*0-471-13202-0*) Wiley.

Recreating the World/Word: The Mythic Mode as Symbolic Discourse. Lynda D. McNeil. LC 91-17324. (SUNY Series, The Margins of Literature). 326p. 1992. text ed. 64.50 (*0-7914-1007-2*); pap. text ed. 21.95 (*0-7914-1008-0*) State U NY Pr.

Recreating Utopia in the Desert: A Sectarian Challenge to Modern Mormonism. Hans A. Baer. LC 87-10133. 225p. 1988. text ed. 74.50 (*0-88706-681-X*); pap. text ed. 24.95 (*0-88706-682-8*) State U NY Pr.

Recreating Your Self: Building Self-Esteem Through Imaging & Self-Hypnosis. Nancy J. Napier. pap. 10.95 (*0-393-31243-7*) Norton.

Recreating Yuletides Past: Celebrations of Yuletide in America Before 1860 Recreated at Winterthur. (Illus.). 1987. pap. 5.00 (*0-912724-18-8*) Winterthur.

***Recreation.** Julian Rowe. LC 96-33352. (Science Encounters Ser.). (J). 1997. write for info. (*1-57572-092-2*) Rigby Interact Libr.

Recreation. 5th ed. Corbin & Williams. 1996. text ed. write for info. (*0-205-18125-2*) Allyn.

***Recreation: Adrenaline Rush.** Chris Fife. (Illus.). 23p. (Orig.). 1996. pap. 4.00 (*1-890143-09-X*) Kinetic Aesthetics.

Recreation: Current Selected Research 1989-1991, Set, Vols. 1-3. Ed. by James H. Humphrey & Fred Humphrey. 1989. write for info. (*0-404-63900-3*) AMS Pr.

Recreation: What Do We Do to Have Fun? 2nd rev. ed. Ed. by Margaret Mitchell et al. (Compact Reference Ser.). (Illus.). 40p. 1996. pap. text ed. 12.95 (*1-57302-022-2*) Info Plus TX.

Recreation Activities for the Elderly. Barbara C. Wilhite et al. (Adulthood & Aging Ser.). 240p. 1988. pap. 35.95 (*0-8261-6030-1*) Springer Pub.

Recreation Aide. Jack Rudman. (Career Examination Ser.: C-1449). 1994. pap. 23.95 (*0-8373-1449-6*) Nat Learn.

Recreation & Amusement among Negroes in Washington, D. C. William H. Jones. LC 72-88440. 216p. 1970. reprint ed. text ed. 52.50 (*0-8371-1847-6*, JOA&, Greenwood Pr) Greenwood.

Recreation & Entertainment Industries: An Information Sourcebook. Norman F. Clarke. LC 89-43641. 264p. 1990. lib. bdg. 55.00 (*0-89950-464-7*) McFarland & Co.

Recreation & Leisure. 4th ed. Janet R. Maclean. 370p. (C). 1985. text ed. 88.00 (*0-02-374370-0*, Macmillan Coll) P-H.

Recreation & Leisure: Issues in an Era of Change. 3rd ed. Ed. by Thomas Goodale & Peter A. Witt. LC 90-71927. 465p. (Orig.). 1991. 22.95 (*0-910251-42-8*) Venture Pub PA.

Recreation & Leisure in Modern Society. 4th ed. Richard G. Kraus. (C). 1990. text ed. 56.95 (*0-673-46058-4*) Addson-Wesley Educ.

Recreation & Leisure Service for the Disadvantaged. Ed. by John A. Nesbitt et al. LC 76-115026. (Illus.). 612p. reprint ed. 174.50 (*0-8357-9419-9*, 2014568) Bks Demand.

Recreation & Outdoor Life Directory. 2nd ed. Steven R. Wasserman. LC 79-4594. 1040p. 1983. 160.00 (*0-8103-0316-7*) Gale.

Recreation & Park Education Curriculum Catalog, 1989-1990. Society of Park & Recreation Educators Staff. 418p. 1989. reprint ed. pap. 119.20 (*0-7837-1550-1*, 2041840) Bks Demand.

Recreation & Sports: An Activity Guide. Lynn Winston. Ed. by Betty Garee. LC 85-72420. 72p. (Orig.). (YA). (gr. 9-12). 1985. pap. 4.95 (*0-915708-18-3*, #1770) Cheever Pub.

***Recreation & the Environment.** Liddle. (Conservation Biology Ser.). (Illus.). 400p. (C). (gr. 13 up). 1997. text ed. 55.00 (*0-412-26630-X*) Chapman & Hall.

Recreation & the Law. 2nd ed. Valerie Collins. LC 93-17601. 1993. write for info. (*0-419-18240-3*, E & FN Spon) Routledge Chapman & Hall.

Recreation & the Local Church. Ed. by Frances Clemens et al. LC 57-18412. 191p. reprint ed. pap. 54.50 (*0-317-28391-X*, 2022409) Bks Demand.

Recreation & the Quality of Urban Life: Recreational Resources, Behaviors, & Evaluations of People in the Detroit Region. Robert W. Marans & J. Mark Fly. 240p. (Orig.). 1981. pap. 16.00 (*0-87944-273-5*) Inst Soc Res.

Recreation & the Quality of Urban Life: Recreational Resources, Behaviors, & Evaluations of People in the Detroit Region. Robert W. Marans & J. Mark Fly. LC 81-623446. (Institute for Social Research, Research Report Ser.). (Illus.). 240p. (Orig.). reprint ed. pap. 68.40 (*0-7837-5255-5*, 2044992) Bks Demand.

Recreation & Tourism as a Catalyst for Urban Waterfront Redevelopment: An International Survey. Ed. by Stephen J. Craig-Smith & Michael Fagence. LC 95-3329. 192p. 1995. text ed. 55.00 (*0-275-94550-2*, Praeger Pubs) Greenwood.

Recreation Areas, Their Design & Equipment. 2nd ed. George D. Butler. LC 57-11288. 192p. 1958. reprint ed. pap. 54.80 (*0-7837-3433-6*, 2057754) Bks Demand.

Recreation Assistant. Jack Rudman. (Career Examination Ser.: C-526). 1994. pap. 23.95 (*0-8373-0526-8*) Nat Learn.

Recreation Assistant (Men) Jack Rudman. (Career Examination Ser.: C-690a). 1994. pap. 23.95 (*0-8373-0690-6*) Nat Learn.

Recreation Assistant (Women) Jack Rudman. (Career Examination Ser.: C-690b). 1994. pap. 23.95 (*0-685-03531-X*) Nat Learn.

Recreation Can Be Risky. Bill Gutman. (Focus on Safety Ser.). (Illus.). 64p. (J). (gr. 5-8). 1996. lib. bdg. 15.98 (*0-8050-4143-5*) TFC Bks NY.

***Recreation Connection to Self-Esteem: A Resource Manual for the Park, Recreation & Community Services Professional.** 105p. 1994. 19.95 (*0-614-23165-5*) Venture Pub PA.

Recreation Director. Jack Rudman. (Career Examination Ser.: C-679). 1994. pap. 34.95 (*0-8373-0679-5*) Nat Learn.

Recreation Director, Handicapped Children's Recreation Program. Jack Rudman. (Career Examination Ser.: C-3095). 1994. pap. 39.95 (*0-8373-3095-5*) Nat Learn.

Recreation Economic Decisions: Comparing Benefits & Costs. Richard G. Walsh. LC 86-50932. (Illus.). 637p. 1986. pap. 27.95 (*0-910251-15-0*) Venture Pub PA.

Recreation Experiences for the Severely Impaired or Nonambulatory Child. Susan P. Levine et al. (Illus.). 96p. 1983. spiral bd., pap. 19.95 (*0-398-04783-9*) C C Thomas.

Recreation Facility Manager. Jack Rudman. (Career Examination Ser.: C-1450). 1994. pap. 27.95 (*0-8373-1450-X*) Nat Learn.

***Recreation for Design.** Simon Bell. (Illus.). 224p. 1996. 42.95 (*0-419-20350-8*, E & FN Spon) Routledge Chapman & Hall.

Recreation for the Disabled Child. Ed. by Donna B. Bernhardt. LC 84-19330. (Physical & Occupational Therapy in Pediatrics Ser.: Vol. 4, No. 3). 110p. 1985. text ed. 39.95 (*0-86656-263-X*) Haworth Pr.

Recreation Guide to Barrier-Free Facilities, Southwestern National Forests. (Illus.). 70p. (Orig.). (C). 1995. pap. text ed. 25.00 (*0-7881-1561-8*) DIANE Pub.

Recreation Guide to Washington National Forests. Wendy Walker. LC 92-54597. (Falcon Guides Ser.). (Illus.). 165p. (Orig.). 1993. pap. 9.95 (*1-56044-163-1*) Falcon Pr MT.

Recreation Handbook: 342 Games & Other Activities for Teams & Individuals. Robert L. Loeffelbein. LC 92-50310. (Illus.). 255p. (J). 1992. pap. 27.50 (*0-89950-744-1*) McFarland & Co.

Recreation in Michigan. MSU (MREC), Michigan Recreation Educators Conso Staff. 176p. (C). 1995. pap. 20.94 (*0-7872-1397-7*) Kendall-Hunt.

Recreation Instructor. Jack Rudman. (Career Examination Ser.: C-691). 1994. pap. 27.95 (*0-8373-0691-4*) Nat Learn.

Recreation Lakes of California. 11th ed. D. J. Dirksen. (Illus.). 256p. (Orig.). 1995. pap. text ed. 16.95 (*0-943798-18-3*) Recreation Sales Pub.

Recreation Leader. Jack Rudman. (Career Examination Ser.: C-669). 1994. pap. 27.95 (*0-8373-0669-8*) Nat Learn.

Recreation, Leisure, & Chronic Illness: Therapeutic Rehabilitation As Intervention in Health Care. Miriam P. Lahey et al. LC 93-16983. (Loss, Grief & Care Ser.: Vol. 6, No. 4). (Illus.). 162p. 1993. lib. bdg. 29.95 (*1-56024-418-6*) Haworth Pr.

Recreation Markets: Trends Toward the Year 2000. 2nd ed. John R. Kelly & Rodney Warnick. Orig. Title: Trends Toward the Year 2000. 200p. 1997. 25.00 (*1-57167-026-2*) Sagamore Pub.

Recreation Planning & Development, 2 Vols. 775p. 1979. pap. 62.00 (*0-87262-200-2*) Am Soc Civil Eng.

Recreation Program Coordinator. (Career Examination Ser.: C-3407). 1994. pap. 34.95 (*0-8373-3407-1*) Nat Learn.

Recreation Programming. Kraus. 240p. 1996. pap. 43.00 (*0-205-16574-5*) Allyn.

Recreation Programming: Designing Leisure Experiences. 2nd ed. J. Robert Rossman. (Illus.). 465p. 1994. 37.95 (*0-915611-95-3*) Sagamore Pub.

Recreation Programming Activities for Older Adults. Jerold E. Elliott & Judy A. Sorg-Elliott. LC 91-66104. 225p. 1991. spiral bd. 24.95 (*0-910251-46-0*) Venture Pub PA.

Recreation Programming for Visually Impaired Children & Youth. Ed. by Jerry D. Kelley. LC 81-14955. (Illus.). 184p. 1981. pap. 29.95 (*0-89128-106-1*) Am Foun Blind.

Recreation Programs That Work for at-Risk Youth: The Challenge of Shaping the Future. Ed. by Peter A. Witt & John L. Crompton. LC 96-60090. 362p. (C). 1996. text ed. 39.95 (*0-910251-80-0*, WWY84) Venture Pub PA.

Recreation, Reflection & Re-Creation: Perspectives on Rabelais's Pantagruel. Raymond C. La Charite. LC 79-53402. (French Forum Monographs: No. 19). 137p. (Orig.). 1980. pap. 10.95 (*0-917058-18-6*) French Forum.

Recreation Specialist. Jack Rudman. (Career Examination Ser.: C-692). 1994. pap. 27.95 (*0-8373-0692-2*) Nat Learn.

Recreation Supervisor. Jack Rudman. (Career Examination Ser.: C-693). 1994. pap. 29.95 (*0-8373-0693-0*) Nat Learn.

Recreation Therapist. Jack Rudman. (Career Examination Ser.: C-2698). 1994. pap. 27.95 (*0-8373-2698-2*) Nat Learn.

Recreation Trends: Toward the Year 2000. John R. Kelly. LC 87-71775. 170p. (C). 1987. pap. text ed. 14.95 (*0-915611-06-6*) Sagamore Pub.

Recreation Vehicle Park Design & Management. 52p. 1977. 10.00 (*0-318-18047-2*) RV Indus Assn.

Recreation Worker. Jack Rudman. (Career Examination Ser.: C-429). 1994. pap. 27.95 (*0-8373-0429-6*) Nat Learn.

Recreational Boating Safety: State Policies & Programs. Chris Pattarozzi. 40p. 1992. pap. text ed. 10.00 (*1-55516-989-9*, 9348) Natl Conf State Legis.

***Recreational Dance Ballroom, Cajun & Country-Western.** Jerry Duke. 110p. (C). 1996. pap. text ed. 9.95 (*0-89641-277-6*) American Pr.

Recreational Development Handbook. J. Eric Smart et al. LC 81-51294. (Community Builders Handbook Ser.). (Illus.). 257p. (C). 1981. 64.95 (*0-87420-599-9*, R13) Urban Land.

Recreational Drugs. Professor Buzz. LC 88-46125. (Illus.). 168p. (Orig.). 1989. pap. 21.95 (*0-915179-88-1*, 85102) Loompanics.

Recreational Drugs: The Complete Guide to Amphetamines, Analgesics, Hallucinogens, THC, Tranquilizers, Sedatives & Hypnotics. 1991. lib. bdg. 77.95 (*0-8490-4605-X*) Gordon Pr.

Recreational Facilities Design. 39.99 (*1-56496-195-8*) Rockport Pubs.

Recreational Fisheries: Management, Theory, & Application. William F. Sigler & John W. Sigler. LC 89-21512. (Illus.). 432p. 1990. 44.95 (*0-87417-139-3*) U of Nev Pr.

Recreational Fisheries of Coastal New England. Michael R. Ross. LC 90-49253. (Illus.). 288p. 1991. pap. 17.95 (*0-87023-743-8*); lib. bdg. 45.00 (*0-87023-742-X*) U of Mass Pr.

Recreational Jazz Dance. 2nd ed. Ann I. Czompo. Ed. by Andor Czompo. LC 79-26223. (Illus.). (C). 1979. pap. text ed. 9.95 (*0-935496-00-9*) AC Pubns.

***Recreational Lakes of Arizona.** Reinhardt. 113p. 1996. pap. 15.95 (*0-9639649-0-9*) Sunflower Sales.

Recreational Land Management. 2nd ed. W. Seabrooke & C. W. Miles. LC 92-37629. 1992. write for info. (*0-419-13500-6*, E & FN Spon) Routledge Chapman & Hall.

Recreational Mathematics, Vol. 1. T. Satyanarayana Raju. (Illus.). vi, 189p. (Orig.). (YA). (gr. 7-12). 1996. pap. 29.95 (*0-9650901-1-6*) Inst of Vedic.

Recreational Nudity & the Law: Abstracts of Cases. 2nd ed. Gordon Gill. LC 95-77903. 198p. (C). 1995. 29.99 (*1-887471-00-6*) Dr Leisure.

***Recreational Pilot & Private Pilot: Computerized Testing Supplement.** 1997. lib. bdg. 251.95 (*0-8490-7743-5*) Gordon Pr.

***Recreational Pilot & Private Pilot Knowledge Test Guide.** 1997. lib. bdg. 250.95 (*0-8490-8128-9*) Gordon Pr.

Recreational Pilot Flight Maneuvers. Irvin N. Gleim. LC 89-85119. 288p. (Orig.). 1989. pap. 11.95 (*0-917539-22-2*) Gleim Pubns.

Recreational Pilot Groundschool Guide. Don Gladney. (Orig.). (C). 1989. pap. write for info. (*0-318-65366-4*) ATDI.

***Recreational Pilot Practical Test Standards.** 1997. lib. bdg. 250.99 (*0-8490-8126-2*) Gordon Pr.

Recreational Pilot Practical Test Standards: Airplane (Single-Engine Land) FAA Staff. (Practical Test Standards Ser.). (Illus.). 1989. reprint ed. pap. text ed. 4.95 (*1-56027-040-3*, ASA-8081-3) Av Suppl & Acad.

***Recreational Railroads.** P. Quarto. 1996. 19.98 (*0-7858-0654-7*) Bk Sales Inc.

Recreational Safety: The Standard of Care. Jay S. Shivers. LC 85-47630. (Illus.). 320p. 1986. 49.50 (*0-8386-3241-6*) Fairleigh Dickinson.

***Recreational Sports Management.** 3rd ed. Richard F. Mull et al. LC 96-44985. (Illus.). 344p. 1997. text ed. 38.00 (*0-87322-808-1*, BMUL0808) Human Kinetics.

***Recreational Terror: Women & the Pleasures of Horror Film Viewing.** Isabel C. Pinedo. LC 97-8033. (SUNY Series, Interruptions). 160p. 1997. text ed. 44.50 (*0-7914-3441-9*); pap. text ed. 14.95 (*0-7914-3442-7*) State U NY Pr.

Recreational Use of Domestic Water Supply Reservoirs: Perception & Choice. Duane D. Baumann. LC 69-318025. (University of Chicago, Department of Geography, Research Paper Ser.: No. 121). 139p. reprint ed. pap. 39.70 (*0-7837-0398-8*, 2040719) Bks Demand.

Recreational Uses of Coastal Areas: A Research Project of the Commission on the Coastal Environment, International Geographical Union. Ed. by Paolo Fabbri. (C). 1990. lib. bdg. 167.50 (*0-7923-0279-6*) Kluwer Ac.

Recreational Vehicle Parks. (Five Hundred Ser.). 1993. pap. 16.75 (*0-685-58222-1*, 501D-93) Natl Fire Prot.

Recreational Vehicles. (Five Hundred Ser.). 26p. 1993. pap. 20.25 (*0-685-46038-X*, 501C-93) Natl Fire Prot.

***Recreational Vehicles: Finding the Best Buy.** 2nd ed. Bill Alderman & Eleanore Wilson. 1996. pap. text ed. 9.95 (*1-56625-070-6*) Bonus Books.

Recreational Vehicles & Travel: A Resource Guide. Bernard Mergen. LC 84-28974. (American Popular Culture Ser.). ix, 221p. 1985. text ed. 59.95 (*0-313-23672-0*, MER/, Greenwood Pr) Greenwood.

Recreational Water Quality Management. Ed. by David Kay. LC 92-21722. 225p. 1992. 45.00 (*0-13-770025-3*, Pub. by Tavistock-E Horwood UK) Routledge Chapman & Hall.

Recreational Water Quality Management: Fresh Waters, Vol. 2. David Kay & Roger Hanbury. 1993. text ed. 99.00 (*0-13-767302-7*) P-H.

Recreational Welfare. Fred Coalter et al. 220p. 1988. text ed. 63.95 (*0-566-05665-8*, Pub. by Avebury Pub UK) Ashgate Pub Co.

Recreations in Logic. D. G. Wells. LC 79-51882. (Illus.). (Orig.). 1980. pap. 2.95 (*0-486-23895-4*) Dover.

Recreations in the Theory of Numbers. Albert H. Beiler. (Orig.). 1964. pap. 7.95 (*0-486-21096-0*) Dover.

Recreations of a Southern Barrister. A. H. Sands. LC 75-152929. (Black Heritage Library Collection). 1977. 22.95 (*0-8369-8774-8*) Ayer.

Recreations of an Anthologist. Brander Matthews. LC 67-26766. (Essay Index Reprint Ser.). 1977. 19.95 (*0-8369-0699-3*) Ayer.

Recres du Petit Nicolas. Jean-Jacques Sempe & R. Goscinny. (Folio - Junior Ser.: No. 468). 181p. (FRE.). (J). (gr. 5-10). 1987. pap. 9.95 (*2-07-033468-6*) Schoenhof.

Recriminalizaing Delinquency: Violent Juvenile Crime & Juvenile Justice Reform. Simon I. Singer. (Criminology Ser.). (Illus.). 248p. (C). 1996. text ed. 54.95 (*0-521-48208-9*) Cambridge U Pr.

***Recriminalizing Delinquency: Violent Juvenile Crime & Juvenile Justice Reform.** 246p. 1997. pap. text ed. 18.95 (*0-521-62920-9*) Cambridge U Pr.

Recruiter's Almanac of Scripts, Rebuttals, & Closes. William G. Radin. Ed. by Ruth Lorber & Lou Scott. 138p. (Orig.). 1990. pap. 49.95 (*0-9626147-2-6*) Innovative Consulting.

***Recruiter's Internet Survival Guide.** John R. Sumser. 203p. (Orig.). 1996. pap. 89.50 (*1-883814-04-9*) Staff Ind Analysts.

Recruiter's Technique Book: Best of RSR. Kenneth J. Cole. Ed. by Joan S. Cole. 108p. 1983. 79.50 (*1-878451-00-6*) Recruiting & Search.

Recruiting: How to Do It. Iain Maitland. (Illus.). 224p. 1996. pap. 19.95 (*0-304-33315-8*) Cassell.

Recruiting Academic Library Director: A Companion to the Search Committee Handbook. Sharon Rogers & Ruth J. Person. 1991. pap. 18.95 (*0-8389-7484-8*) Assn Coll & Res Libs.

Recruiting & Managing Volunteers in Libraries: A-How-to-Do-It Manual. Bonnie F. McCune & Charleszine T. Nelson. (How-to-Do-It Manuals Ser.: Vol. 51). (Illus.). 174p. (Orig.). 1995. pap. 39.95 (*1-55570-204-X*) Neal-Schuman.

Recruiting & Retaining Adult Students. Ed. by Peter S. Cookson. LC 85-644750. (New Directions for Adult & Continuing Education Ser.: No. 41). 1989. 19.00 (*1-55542-860-6*) Jossey-Bass.

Recruiting & Selecting Teachers for Urban Schools. Martin Haberman. 1987. pap. 9.35 (*0-685-41079-X*) Assn Tchr Ed.

Recruiting & Selection Procedures, No. 146. (Personnel Policies Forum Surveys Ser.). 1988. 30.00 (*0-87179-986-3*) BNA.

Recruiting & Training Volunteers for Church & Synagogue Libraries. Lorraine E. Burson. LC 86-9682. (Guide Ser.: No. 14). 32p. 1986. pap. 7.25 (*0-915324-24-5*) CSLA.

Recruiting, Educating, & Training Cataloging Librarians: Solving the Problems. Ed. by Sheila S. Intner & Janet S. Hill. LC 88-33643. (New Directions in Information Management Ser.: No. 19). 448p. 1989. text ed. 59.95 (*0-313-26693-X*, IRE, Greenwood Pr) Greenwood.

Recruiting, Educating & Training Librarians for Collection Development. Ed. by Peggy Johnson & Sheila S. Intner. LC 93-35839. (New Directions in Information Management Ser.: No. 33). 264p. 1994. text ed. 55.00 (*0-313-28561-6*, Greenwood Pr) Greenwood.

Recruiting Effective Insurance Agents. Didactic Systems Staff. (Simulation Game Ser.). 1973. pap. 26.25 (*0-89401-082-4*); pap. 24.90 (*0-89401-083-2*) Didactic Syst.

Recruiting for Profit. Ed. by John Courtis. 128p. (C). 1989. pap. 60.00 (*0-85292-427-5*, Pub. by IPM Hse UK) St Mut.

Recruiting for Uncle Sam: Citizenship & Military Manpower Policy. David R. Segal. LC 88-34461. (Modern War Studies). x, 222p. 1989. 29.95 (*0-7006-0391-3*); pap. 14.95 (*0-7006-0549-5*) U Pr of KS.

Recruiting Game: Toward a New System of Intercollegiate Sports. 2nd rev. ed. John F. Rooney. LC 86-19152. 254p. reprint ed. pap. 72.40 (*0-7837-6177-5*, 2045899) Bks Demand.

Recruiting Good College Faculty: Practical Advice for a Successful Search. Baron Perlman & Lee I. McCann. 224p. 1996. 34.95 (*1-882982-11-8*) Anker Pub.

Recruiting in Sports. Hank Nuwer. LC 89-9151. (Teen Issues Ser.). (Illus.). 112p. (YA). (gr. 9 up). 1989. lib. bdg. 22.70 (*0-531-10796-5*) Watts.

Recruiting, Interviewing, Selecting, & Orienting New Employees. 2nd ed. Diane Arthur. 350p. 1991. 49.95 (*0-8144-5007-5*) AMACOM.

Recruiting Leaders for Tomorrow's Church. Roy M. Oswald. pap. 10.00 (*1-56699-162-5*) Alban Inst.

Recruiting Local Government Executives: Practical Insights for Hiring Authorities & Candidates. David N. Ammons & James J. Glass. LC 89-45575. (Public Administration Ser.). 272p. 39.95 (*1-55542-190-3*) Jossey-Bass.

Recruiting Minorities into Teaching. Rita G. Greer & William L. Husk. LC 89-61960. (Fastback Ser.: No. 290). 40p. (Orig.). (C). 1989. pap. 3.00 (*0-87367-290-9*) Phi Delta Kappa.

Recruiting Minority Classroom Teachers: A National Challenge. Denise A. Alston. 40p. (Orig.). 1988. pap. text ed. 7.50 (*1-55877-007-0*) Natl Governor.

Recruiting Minority Teachers: A Practical Guide. 1990. 20.00 (*0-89333-061-2*) AACTE.

Recruiting Nurse. large type ed. Jane Converse. (Linford Romance Library). 256p. 1993. pap. 15.99 (*0-7089-7394-9*, Linford) Ulverscroft.

Recruiting Officer. George Farquhar. Ed. & Pref. by Peter Dixon. (Illus.). 307p. (C). 1988. pap. write for info. (*0-318-59113-8*) St Martin.

Recruiting Officer. George Farquhar. Ed. by Michael Shugrue. LC 91-43822. (Regents Renaissance Drama Ser.). xxii, 138p. 1992. pap. text ed. 9.95 (*0-8032-5357-5*, Bison Books) U of Nebr Pr.

Recruiting Officer. 2nd ed. John Ross. (New Mermaid Ser.). (C). Date not set. pap. text ed. 5.95 (*0-393-90065-7*) Norton.

Recruiting Officer & Other Plays. George Farquhar. Ed. by William Myers. (The World's Classics Ser.). 400p. 1995. 74.00 (*0-19-812153-9*); pap. 11.95 (*0-19-282249-7*) OUP.

Recruiting Qualified Disabled Workers: An Employer's Directory to Placement Services in the Greater New York Area. Compiled by Lana Smart. LC 79-92836. 160p. 1980. 5.95 (*0-686-38815-1*) Human Res Ctr.

Recruiting Realities: Educating the High School Student-Athlete in the Recruiting Process. 2nd ed. Jack H. Renkens. (Illus.). 110p. (Orig.). (YA). (gr. 9-12). 1995. reprint ed. mass mkt., pap. 19.95 (*0-9647041-9-6*) Brookes & John.

Recruiting, Retaining, & Motivating the Federal Workforce. Gail C. Johnson. LC 90-45143. 176p. 1991. text ed. 49.95 (*0-89930-562-8*, JRC, Quorum Bks) Greenwood.

Recruiting Revolution in Real Estate: Finding & Keeping Top-Quality Agents. Carol Johnson. 284p. 1989. pap. 34.95 (*0-88462-826-4*, 1978-02) Dearborn Finan.

Recruiting Sales Associates. 2nd ed. Kenneth Reyhons. LC 86-63281. 153p. 1990. 22.00 (*0-913652-62-8*) Realtors Natl.

Recruiting Strategies for Christian Schools: How to Recruit & Retain Students. Dennis M. Demuth & Carol M. Demuth. 240p. 1991. pap. text ed. 22.95 (*1-880705-00-1*) Demuth Enter.

Recruiting Struggle. Lee Caryer. 273p. 1996. pap. 18.95 (*0-9652793-0-8*) Caryer Ent.

Recruiting Superior Teachers: The Interview Process. William Goldstein. LC 85-63694. (Fastback Ser.: No. 239). 50p. (Orig.). 1986. pap. 3.00 (*0-87367-239-9*) Phi Delta Kappa.

Recruiting Survival Guide: How to Be a Smart Recruit. Chuck Mooney, III. Ed. by Kelly S. Bucheit. (Illus.). 84p. (Orig.). (YA). (gr. 11-12). 1991. pap. 9.95 (*0-9630239-0-X*) C Mooney.

Recruiting, Training, & Compensating Attorney Staff. 38p. 1986. pap. 9.95 (*0-685-19016-1*, 511-0203-01) Amer Bar Assn.

Recruiting, Training & Maintaining Volunteer Firefighters: The Volunteer Firefighter: A Breed Apart Resource Manual. OnGuard Inc. Staff. 264p. 1993. student ed., ring bd. 15.95 (*1-56916-057-0*) OnGuard.

Recruiting, Training & Motivating Volunteers. rev. ed. Arthur R. Pell. LC 71-180210. 62p. 1989. pap. 4.95 (*0-87576-141-0*) Pilot Bks.

Recruiting, Training, & Retaining New Employees: Managing the Transition from College to Work. Jack J. Phillips. LC 86-46332. 346p. reprint ed. pap. 98.70 (*0-7837-6520-7*, 2045632) Bks Demand.

Recruiting Volunteers: A Guide for Non-Profits. Carl Liljenstolpe & Mary A. Burke. Ed. by Beverly Manber. LC 91-76308. (Fifty-Minute Ser.). (Illus.). 90p. (Orig.). 1992. pap. 10.95 (*1-56052-141-4*) Crisp Pubns.

Recruiting Volunteers for Difficult or Long-Term Positions. Steve McCurley. 1991. pap. 8.00 (*0-911029-30-3*) Heritage Arts.

Recruitment. Personnel Management Services, Ltd. Staff. 150p. (C). 1990. 125.00 (*0-85292-449-6*, Pub. by IPM Hse UK) St Mut.

Recruitment: Science & Practice. James A. Breaugh. 288p. 1992. pap. 31.95 (*0-534-91943-X*) S-W Pub.

Recruitment, Admissions, & Students with Disabilities. Rhona C. Hartman et al. 16p. 1994. 7.00 (*0-929851-25-0*) Am Assn Coll Registrars.

Recruitment Advertising: A Means of Communication. Ed. by Maurice Ray. 240p. (C). 1980. 85.00 (*0-85292-259-0*, Pub. by IPM Hse UK) St Mut.

Recruitment & Career Destinations of Town Planning Students in the Early 1980's. W. K. Thomas. (C). 1985. 35.00 (*0-685-30262-8*, Pub. by Oxford Polytechnic UK) St Mut.

Recruitment & Selection. Ed. by Philip Plumbley. 176p. (C). 1985. 90.00 (*0-85292-342-2*, Pub. by IPM Hse UK) St Mut.

Recruitment & Selection. Ed. by Philip Plumbley. 176p. (C). 1991. pap. text ed. 59.00 (*0-85292-459-3*, Pub. by IPM Hse UK) St Mut.

Recruitment & Training in the Solicitors' Practice. Alan Pannett. 164p. 1989. pap. 62.00 (*0-406-12750-6*, U.K.) MICHIE.

Recruitment in the Nineties. Peter Herriot. 112p. (C). 1989. 90.00 (*0-85292-420-8*, Pub. by IPM Hse UK) St Mut.

Recruitment Letters: Motivating Your Members to Faithful Service. Ed. by Cindy G. Spear & Tamara Johnson. 45p. 1994. student ed., ring bd. 44.95 (*0-941005-96-8*) Chrch Grwth VA.

Recruitment of Political Leaders: A Study of Citizen-Politicians. Kenneth Prewitt. LC 81-6344. (Urban Government Ser.). (Illus.). 234p. 1981. reprint ed. text ed. 59.75 (*0-313-22744-6*, PRRP, Greenwood Pr) Greenwood.

Recruitment, Retention, & Employee Relations: Field-Tested Strategies for the '90s. D. Keith Denton. LC 92-162. 232p. 1992. text ed. 49.95 (*0-89930-661-6*, DRB/, Quorum Bks) Greenwood.

Recruitment, Retention, & Utiliation of Federal Scientists & Engineers. National Research Council Staff. 192p. 1990. pap. text ed. 17.00 (*0-309-04330-1*) Natl Acad Pr.

***Recruitment Workbook.** Stan Crabtree. (Business Action Guides Ser.). 1991. pap. 16.95 (*0-7494-0110-9*) Kogan Page Ltd.

Recruits to Labour: The British Labour Party, 1914-1931. Catherine A. Cline. LC 63-13888. 1963. 39.95 (*0-8156-2046-2*) Syracuse U Pr.

***Recrystallization & Related Annealing Phenomena.** Humphreys. 498p. 1996. pap. 48.00 (*0-08-042685-9*, Pergamon Pr) Elsevier.

Recrystallization & Related Annealing Phenomena. F. J. Humphreys & M. Hatherly. LC 94-44667. 498p. 133.50 (*0-08-041884-8*, Pergamon Pr) Elsevier.

Recrystallization '90: International Conference on Recrystallization in Metallic Materials: Conference Proceedings. International Conference on Recrystallization in Metallic Materials (1st: 1990: Univ. Wollong) Staff. Ed. by T. Chandra. LC 90-61460. 896p. 1990. reprint ed. pap. 180.00 (*0-608-00774-9*, 2061572) Bks Demand.

Recsk - Emberek az embertelensegben (Recsk Man in Inhumanity) Zoltan Nyeste. LC 82-82973. (Tanuk Korukrol Ser.). (Illus.). 80p. 1982. pap. 6.00 (*0-910539-00-6*) Hungarian Alumni.

Rectal Bleeding, a Danger Signal? G. Fijten. 150p. 1993. pap. 23.50 (*90-5170-224-8*, Pub. by Thesis Pubs NE) IBD Ltd.

Rectal Bleeding & Colon Polyps. John M. MacKeigan & Kathleen M. Hillary. Ed. by Oliver D. Grin & Dorothy L. Bouwman. (Patient Education Ser.). (Illus.). 26p. 1990. pap. text ed. 4.00 (*0-929689-43-7*) Ludann Co.

***Rectal Cancer Surgery: Optimisation, Standardisation & Documentation.** Ed. by O. Soreide & J. Norstein. LC 96-38509. (Illus.). 470p. 1996. 139.00 (*3-540-61566-0*) Spr-Verlag.

Rectangles. Mary C. Penders. LC 91-36292. (Quilts from Simple Shapes Ser.). (Illus.). 32p. 1991. pap. 9.95 (*0-8442-2635-1*) Quilt Digest Pr.

Rectangles. David L. Stienecker. LC 96-3172. (Discovering Shapes Ser.). (Illus.). (J). (gr. 3 up). 1996. lib. bdg. 14.95 (*0-7614-0460-0*, Benchmark NY) Marshall Cavendish.

Rectangular Morning Poem. Peter Ganick. 112p. (Orig.). 1989. pap. 9.00 (*0-937013-27-7*) Potes Poets.

Rectangular Record. Lou Stevens. (Illus.). 44p. (Orig.). 1981. 8.95 (*0-9606222-2-5*); pap. 3.95 (*0-9606222-1-7*) Clone Recs NY.

Rectification: Known-Unknown Birthtimes. Henry Niemann. 1990. pap. 21.95 (*0-86690-373-9*, 3043-014) Am Fed Astrologers.

Rectification of Birth Time: An Analytical Approach. Ed. by P. S. Sastri. (C). 1992. pap. 6.00 (*0-8364-2841-2*, Pub. by Ranjan Pubs II) S Asia.

Rectification of Memory-Errors. Brian Madison. (C). 1991. pap. text ed. 9.99 (*0-913412-57-0*) Brandon Hse.

Rectification of the Birth Time. Gustav Schwickert. 176p. 1954. write for info. (*0-86690-158-2*, S1457-014) Am Fed Astrologers.

Rectifiers, Cycloconverters, & AC Controllers. Thomas H. Barton. LC 93-46642. (Monographs in Electrical & Electronic Engineering: No. 33). (Illus.). 720p. 1994. 65.00 (*0-19-856163-6*, Clarendon Pr) OUP.

Recto Verso by Margatet Honda, Vol. 1. Margaret Honda. (Focus Ser.). (Illus.). 41p. (Orig.). 1994. pap. 15.00 (*0-914357-37-9*) Los Angeles Mus Contemp.

Rector's Daughter. large type ed. F. M. Mayor. 1993. 39.95 (*0-7066-1030-X*, Pub. by Remploy Pr CN) St Mut.

Rector's Daughter in Victorian England: Memories of Childhood & Girlhood. Maud B. Booth. Ed. & Intro. by Susan F. Welty. (Illus.). 85p. 1994. 7.00 (*1-885287-01-1*) Volunteers Amer.

***Rector's Wife.** Joanna Trollope. 1996. mass mkt. 6.99 (*0-425-15529-3*) Berkley Pub.

Rector's Wife. Joanna Trollope. 288p. 1993. pap. 10.95 (*0-552-99470-7*) Bantam.

Rector's Wife. Joanna Trollope. LC 94-20625. 1994. 21.00 (*0-679-43702-9*) Random.

Rector's Wife. large type ed. Joanna Trollope. LC 95-2006. (Large Print Bks.). 1995. 22.95 (*1-56895-200-7*) Wheeler Pub.

***Rectory.** Anita I. Wisdom. 409p. (Orig.). 1997. mass mkt. 5.99 (*1-55197-986-1*, Pub. by Comnwlth Pub CN) Partners Pubs Grp.

***Rectory Murder.** Kenneth Saunders. 29.95 (*1-55028-271-9*, Pub. by J Lorimer CN) Formac Dist Ltd.

***Rectory Murder.** Kenneth Saunders. pap. 16.95 (*1-55028-273-5*, Pub. by J Lorimer CN) Formac Dist Ltd.

Recueil de Chansons Populaires, 6 tomes. Romain Rolland. 85.00 (*0-685-36691-X*) Fr & Eur.

Recueil de Contes Populaires de la Senegambie. Laurent J. Berenger-Feraud. (B. E. Ser.: No. 38). (FRE.). 1885. 30.00 (*0-8115-2989-4*) Periodicals Srv.

Recueil de contredances. fac. ed. Raoul-Auger Feuillet. (Monuments of Music & Music Literature in Facsimile Ser., Series II: Vol. 135). 1968. lib. bdg. 40.00 (*0-8450-2335-7*) Broude.

Recueil De Dissertations Sur Plusieurs Tragedies De Corneille et De Racine, 2 vols. in 1. Francois Granet. cxxvi, 787p. 1975. reprint ed. write for info. (*3-487-05604-6*) G Olms Pubs.

Recueil De Farces Francaises Inedites Du XVe Siecle. Ed. by Gustave Cohen. (Medieval Academy Bks.: No. 47). 1949. 30.00 (*0-910956-21-9*) Medieval Acad.

Recueil De Motets Francais Des Twelfth et Thirteenth Siecles. Gaston Raynaud. (Bibliotheque Francaise Du Moyen Age Ser.: No. 1-2). liv, 811p. 1972. reprint ed. write for info. (*3-487-04274-6*) G Olms Pubs.

Recueil de Plans d'Eglises Cisterciennes, 2 tomes. Dimier. 100.75 (*0-685-34012-0*, F22250) Fr & Eur.

Recueil de Terminologie Multilinque du Soudage et des Techniques Connexes, 18p. (ENG & FRE.). pap. 49.95 (*0-686-56760-9*, M-6480) Fr & Eur.

Recueil d'Emblemes Divers, 2 vols. Jean Baudoin. 1296p. 1977. reprint ed. 240.00 (*3-487-06299-2*) G Olms Pubs.

An Asterisk (*) at the beginning of an entry indicates that the title is appearing in BIP for the first time.

Recueil des Cours. Academie de Droit International de la Haye Staff. 1985. lib. bdg. 129.00 (*90-247-3231-X*) Kluwer Ac.

Recueil des Cours. Academie de Droit International de la Haye Staff. 1986. lib. bdg. 129.00 (*90-247-3323-5*) Kluwer Ac.

Recueil des Cours. Academie de Droit International de la Haye Staff. 1986. lib. bdg. 129.00 (*90-247-3336-7*) Kluwer Ac.

Recueil des Cours. Academie de Droit International de la Haye Staff. 1986. lib. bdg. 129.00 (*90-247-3373-1*) Kluwer Ac.

Recueil des Cours, Vol. 194. Ed. by Academie de Droit International de la Haye Staff. 1987. lib. bdg. 129.00 (*90-247-3636-6*) Kluwer Ac.

Recueil des Cours, Vol. 200. Ed. by Academie de Droit International de la Haye Staff. 1987. lib. bdg. 129.00 (*90-247-3644-7*) Kluwer Ac.

Recueil des Cours, Vol. 210, 1988-III. Ed. by Academie de Droit International de la Haye Staff. (C). 1989. lib. bdg. 129.00 (*0-7923-0398-9*) Kluwer Ac.

Recueil des Cours, Vol. 214. Ed. by Academie de Droit International de la Haye Staff. (C). 1990. lib. bdg. 129. 00 (*0-7923-0722-4*) Kluwer Ac.

Recueil des Cours, Vol. 215 (1989-III) Ed. by Academie de Droit International de la Haye Staff. (C). 1990. lib. bdg. 129.00 (*0-7923-0815-8*) Kluwer Ac.

Recueil des Cours, Vol. 216 (1989-IV) Ed. by Academie de Droit International de la Haye Staff. 416p. 1990. lib. bdg. 129.00 (*0-7923-1048-9*) Kluwer Ac.

Recueil des Cours, Vol. 217 (1989-V) Ed. by Academie de Droit International de la Haye Staff. 456p. 1990. 117.00 (*0-07-923104-7*) Kluwer Ac.

Recueil des Cours: 1985-IV, Vol. 193. Ed. by Academie de Droit International de la Haye Staff. 1986. lib. bdg. 129. 00 (*90-247-3424-X*) Kluwer Ac.

Recueil des Cours: 1988, Vol. 212. Academie de Droit International de La Haye Staff. 388p. (C). 1991. lib. bdg. 129.00 (*0-7923-1411-5*) Kluwer Ac.

Recueil Des Cours: 1989-VI, Vol. 218. Ed. by Academie de Droit International de la Haye Staff. 412p. (C). 1991. lib. bdg. 129.00 (*0-7923-1324-0*) Kluwer Ac.

Recueil Des Cours: 1990 - III, Vol. 222. 424p. (C). 1991. lib. bdg. 129.00 (*0-7923-1354-2*) Kluwer Ac.

Recueil des Cours - Collected Courses, Vol. 219 (1989-VII) Ed. by Academie de Droit International de la Haye Staff. 416p. (C). 1993. lib. bdg. 129.00 (*0-7923-2140-5*) Kluwer Ac.

Recueil des Cours - Collected Courses, Vol. 224 (1990-V) Ed. by Academie de Droit International de la Haye Staff. 416p. (C). 1993. lib. bdg. 129.00 (*0-7923-2317-3*) Kluwer Ac.

Recueil des Cours - Collected Courses, Vol. 225 (1990-VI) Ed. by Academie de Droit International de la Haye Staff. 484p. (C). 1993. lib. bdg. 129.00 (*0-7923-2372-6*) Kluwer Ac.

Recueil Des Cours - Collected Courses, Vol. 226. Academie de Droit International de la Haye Staff. 432p. (C). 1992. lib. bdg. 129.00 (*0-7923-1704-1*) Kluwer Ac.

Recueil des Cours - Collected Courses, Vol. 227 (1991-II) Academie de Droit International de la Haye Staff. 432p. (C). 1992. lib. bdg. 129.00 (*0-7923-1785-8*) Kluwer Ac.

Recueil des Cours - Collected Courses, Vol. 229, 1991-IV. Ed. by Academie de Droit International de la Haye Staff. (C). 1992. lib. bdg. 129.00 (*0-7923-1984-2*) Kluwer Ac.

Recueil des Cours - Collected Courses, Vol. 230 (1991-V) Ed. by Academie de Droit International de la Haye Staff. 423p. (C). 1993. lib. bdg. 129.00 (*0-7923-2472-2*) Kluwer Ac.

Recueil des Cours - Collected Courses, Vol. 233 (1992-II) Ed. by Academie de Droit International de la Haye Staff. 416p. (C). 1993. lib. bdg. 129.00 (*0-7923-2409-9*) Kluwer Ac.

Recueil des Cours - Collected Courses, Vol. 234, 1992, No. III. Ed. by Academie de Droit International de la Haye Staff. 436p. (C). 1993. lib. bdg. 129.00 (*0-7923-2260-6*) Kluwer Ac.

Recueil des Cours - Collected Courses, Vol. 235, 1992-IV. Ed. by Academie de Droit International de la Haye Staff. 416p. (C). 1993. lib. bdg. 129.00 (*0-7923-2641-5*) Kluwer Ac.

Recueil des Cours - Collected Courses, Vol. 236 (1992-V) Ed. by Academie de Droit International de la Haye Staff. 464p. (C). 1994. lib. bdg. 129.00 (*0-7923-2869-8*) Kluwer Ac.

Recueil des Cours - Collected Courses, Vol. 239 (1993-II) Ed. by Academie de Droit International de la Haye Staff. 428p. (C). 1994. lib. bdg. 129.00 (*0-7923-2870-1*) Kluwer Ac.

Recueil des Cours - Collected Courses: (1981-IV), Vol. 173. Ed. by Academie de Droit International de La Haye Staff. 444p. 1992. lib. bdg. 129.00 (*0-7923-2050-6*) Kluwer Ac.

Recueil des Cours - Collected Courses: (1985-VI), Vol. 195. Ed. by Academie de Droit International de La Haye Staff. 1992. lib. bdg. 129.00 (*0-7923-2051-4*) Kluwer Ac.

Recueil des Cours - Collected Courses Vol. 240 (1993-III) Ed. by Academie de Droit International de la Haye Staff. 500p. 1994. lib. bdg. 129.00 (*0-7923-2953-8*) Kluwer Ac.

Recueil des Cours - Collected Courses Vol. 241 (1993-IV) Ed. by Academie de Droit International de la Haye Staff. (C). 1994. lib. bdg. 129.00 (*0-7923-2954-6*) Kluwer Ac.

Recueil des Cours de l'Academie de Droit International de la Haye: Collected Courses of the Hague Academy of International Law, Vol. 152 (1976-iv) F. Durante et al. 478p. 1980. lib. bdg. 129.00 (*90-286-0590-8*) Kluwer Ac.

Recueil des Cours de l'Academie de Droit International de la Haye: Collected Courses of the Hague Academy of International Law General Index to Volumes 126 to 151. 1980. lib. bdg. 129.00 (*90-286-0630-0*) Kluwer Ac.

Recueil des Cours de l'Academie de Droit International de la Haye: Collected Courses of the Hague Academy of Int'l Law, Vol. 156 (1977-III) Tugrul Ansay et al. 482p. 1980. lib. bdg. 129.00 (*90-286-0600-9*) Kluwer Ac.

Recueil des Cours de l'Academie de Droit International de la Haye: Collected Courses of the Hague Academy of Int'l Law, Vol. 162 (1979-i) E. Vitta et al. 1980. lib. bdg. 129.00 (*90-286-0530-4*) Kluwer Ac.

Recueil des Cours, Vol. 202 (1987-II) Ed. by Academie de Droit International de la Haye Staff. (C). 1988. lib. bdg. 129.00 (*90-247-3725-7*) Kluwer Ac.

Recueil des Cours, Vol. 203 (1987-III) Ed. by Academie de Droit International de la Haye Staff. (C). 1988. lib. bdg. 129.00 (*90-247-3726-5*) Kluwer Ac.

Recueil des Cours, Vol. 204 (1987-IV) Ed. by Academie de Droit International de la Haye Staff. (C). 1988. lib. bdg. 129.00 (*90-247-3742-7*) Kluwer Ac.

Recueil des Cours, Vol. 205: (1987 - V) Ed. by Academie de Droit International de la Haye Staff. (C). 1989. lib. bdg. 129.00 (*0-7923-0322-9*) Kluwer Ac.

Recueil des Cours, Vol. 209: (1988 - II) (C). 1989. lib. bdg. 129.00 (*0-7923-0323-7*) Kluwer Ac.

Recueil des Cours, Vol. 213: 1989 - I. Ed. by Academie de Droit International de la Haye Staff. (C). 1990. lib. bdg. 129.00 (*0-7923-0647-3*) Kluwer Ac.

Recueil des Cours 1983, Vol. 183. Academie de Droit International de la Haye Staff. 1985. lib. bdg. 129.00 (*90-247-3248-4*) Kluwer Ac.

Recueil Des Cours, 1984, Vol. 189. Ed. by Academie de Droit International de la Haye Staff. (International Law Ser.). (C). 1989. lib. bdg. 129.00 (*0-7923-0057-2*) Kluwer Ac.

Recueil des Cours, 1984-85, Vol. 188. Academie de Droit International de la Haye Staff. 1986. lib. bdg. 129.00 (*90-247-3291-3*) Kluwer Ac.

Recueil des Cours 1988-I, Vol. 208. Ed. by Academie de Droit International de la Haye Staff. (C). 1988. lib. bdg. 129.00 (*0-7923-0058-0*) Kluwer Ac.

Recueil des Cours 1989-V, Vol. 217. Ed. by Academie de Droit International de la Haye Staff. (C). 1990. lib. bdg. 129.00 (*0-7923-1047-0*) Kluwer Ac.

Recueil des Cours 1990-II, Vol. 221. Ed. by Academie de Droit International de la Haye Staff. 406p. 1991. lib. bdg. 129.00 (*0-7923-1223-6*) Kluwer Ac.

Recueil des Cours 1990-1, Vol. 220. Ed. by Academie de Droit International de la Haye Staff. 404p. (C). 1991. lib. bdg. 129.00 (*0-7923-1077-2*) Kluwer Ac.

Recueil des Courts (1990-IV), Vol. 223. Academie de Droit International de la Haye Staff. 416p. 1991. lib. bdg. 129. 00 (*0-7923-1524-3*) Kluwer Ac.

Recueil des Croniques et Anchiennes Istories de la Grant: Bretaigne, a Present Nomme Engleterre par...Siegneur du Forestel; Albina-1471, 5 vols., 1. Jehan De Waurin. Ed. by William Hardy & Edward L. Hardy. (Rolls Ser.: No. 39). 1974. reprint ed. write for info. (*0-8115-1092-1*) Periodicals Srv.

Recueil des Croniques et Anchiennes Istories de la Grant: Bretaigne, a Present Nomme Engleterre par...Siegneur du Forestel; Albina-1471, 5 vols., 2. Jehan De Waurin. Ed. by William Hardy & Edward L. Hardy. (Rolls Ser.: No. 39). 1974. reprint ed. write for info. (*0-8115-1093-X*) Periodicals Srv.

Recueil des Croniques et Anchiennes Istories de la Grant: Bretaigne, a Present Nomme Engleterre par...Siegneur du Forestel; Albina-1471, 5 vols., 3. Jehan De Waurin. Ed. by William Hardy & Edward L. Hardy. (Rolls Ser.: No. 39). 1974. reprint ed. write for info. (*0-8115-1094-8*) Periodicals Srv.

Recueil des Croniques et Anchiennes Istories de la Grant: Bretaigne, a Present Nomme Engleterre par...Siegneur du Forestel; Albina-1471, 5 vols., 4. Jehan De Waurin. Ed. by William Hardy & Edward L. Hardy. (Rolls Ser.: No. 39). 1974. reprint ed. write for info. (*0-8115-1095-6*) Periodicals Srv.

Recueil des Croniques et Anchiennes Istories de la Grant: Bretaigne, a Present Nomme Engleterre par...Siegneur du Forestel; Albina-1471, 5 vols., 5. Jehan De Waurin. Ed. by William Hardy & Edward L. Hardy. (Rolls Ser.: No. 39). 1974. reprint ed. write for info. (*0-8115-1096-4*) Periodicals Srv.

Recueil des Dames: Poesies et Tombeaux. Pierre De Brantome. Ed. by Jacques Vaucheret. (FRE.). 1991. lib. bdg. 185.00 (*0-7859-3897-4*) Fr & Eur.

Recueil des Inscriptiones Grecques Chretiennes d'Asie Mineure. H. Gregoire. iv, 128p. 1985. reprint ed. 20.00 (*0-89005-291-3*) Ares.

Recueil Des Monuments Egyptiens. Heinrich K. Brugsch. 196p. 1981. reprint ed. 375.00 (*3-487-06979-2*) G Olms Pubs.

Recueil d'Inscriptions Grecques. Charles Michel. (Subsidia Epigraphica Ser.). xxvi, 1000p. (GER.). 1976. reprint ed. write for info. (*3-487-05634-8*) G Olms Pubs.

Recueil d'Inscriptions Grecques: Supplement. Charles Michel. (Subsidia Epigraphica Ser.). 106p. (GER.). 1976. reprint ed. write for info. (*3-487-06140-6*) G Olms Pubs.

Recueil D'inscriptions Grecques: Supplements, 1912-1927. C. Michel. 227p. 1976. 25.00 (*0-89005-110-0*) Ares.

Recueil d'Inscriptions Inedites Du Musee Egyptien Du Louvre. Paul Pierret. ix, 320p. 1978. reprint ed. write for info. (*3-487-06534-7*) G Olms Pubs.

Recueil Quadrilingue de Mots Usuels en Hydrologie. P. Dubreuil. 113p. 1969. pap. 9.95 (*0-8288-6613-9*, M-6176) Fr & Eur.

Recueil Terminologique Multilingue de Soudage et des Techniques Connexes: Projection a Chaud, Vol. 6. (ENG & FRE.). pap. 49.95 (*0-686-56761-7*, M-6479) Fr & Eur.

Recueil Terminologique Multilingue de Soudage et des Techniques Connexes: Soudage Electrique a l'Arc, Vol. 3. 52p. (ENG & FRE.). pap. 95.00 (*0-686-56764-1*, M-6476) Fr & Eur.

Recueil Terminologique Multilingue du Soudage et des Techniques Connexes. 52p. (CZE, FRE, POL, RUS, SLV & TUR.). pap. 49.95 (*0-686-56743-9*, M-6474) Fr & Eur.

Recueil Terminologique Multilingue du Soudage et des Techniques Connexes: Coupage Thermique, Vol. 5. (ENG & FRE.). pap. 49.95 (*0-686-56762-5*, M-6478) Fr & Eur.

Recueil Terminologique Multilingue du Soudage et des Techniques Connexes. Soudage Electrique Par Resistance, Vol. 4. 254p. (ENG & FRE.). pap. 49.95 (*0-686-56763-3*, M-6477) Fr & Eur.

Recueils des Notes Theosophiques, Vol. VII. Robert Amadou. write for info. (*0-318-71428-0*) G Olms Pubs.

Recueils Poetiques d'Avant l'Exil. Victor Hugo. 256p. (FRE.). 1971. 5.95 (*0-7859-0007-1*, F64400) Fr & Eur.

Recuerdos. Archer M. Huntington. 1949. 5.00 (*0-87535-063-1*) Hispanic Soc.

Recuerdos. Andres Rivero. LC 80-66235. (Short Stories in Spanish Ser.). 80p. 1980. pap. 9.95 (*0-933648-02-2*) ARO.

Recuerdos De La Boda: Wedding Memories. Beverly Clark. 72p. 1994. 16.95 (*0-934081-08-5*) Wlshre Pubns.

Recuerdos de los Viejitos: Tales of the Rio Puerco. Ed. by Nasario Garcia. LC 08-20283. (Historical Society of New Mexico Publications). (Illus.). 287p. 1987. pap. 11. 95 (*0-8263-1021-4*) U of NM Pr.

Recuerdos de Nuestra Boda. S. Carter. 31p. (SPA.). 1991. pap. 12.99 (*1-56063-162-7*, 497605) Editorial Unilit.

***Recuerdos Viven Eternamente: Un Libro de Recuerdos para Ninos Afligidos con una Muerta.** 3rd ed. Sharon Rugg et al. (Illus.). 35p. (Orig.). (ENG & SPA.). (J). (gr. k-9). 1997. pap. 5.00 (*0-9652410-1-7*) S Rugg.

Recuerdos 2 Pianos 4 Hands. Weins Bolcom. 48p. 1993. pap. 15.00 (*0-7935-1949-9*, 00008707) H Leonard.

Recuperacion para Toda la Familia. Harold A. Swift & Terence Williams. 16p. (Orig.). (SPA.). 1983. pap. 2.50 (*0-89486-202-2*, 1386) Hazelden.

Recuperation & Economic Utilization of By-Products of the Iron & Steel Industry. 250p. 1990. 42.00 (*92-1-116478-8*, 90.II.E.13) UN.

Recurrence: What Do I Do Now? Donald F. Kaltenbach. 24p. (Orig.). 1995. pap. 5.00 (*0-9651827-0-3*) Proste Cancer.

Recurrence in Ergodic Theory & Combinatorial Number Theory. H. Furstenberg. LC 80-7518. (Rice University, Dept. of Mathematics, M. B. Porter Lectures). 228p. 1981. text ed. 45.00 (*0-691-08269-3*) Princeton U Pr.

***Recurrence in Topological Dynamics: Furstenberg Families & Ellis Actions.** E. Akin. LC 97-24363. (University Series in Mathematics). (Illus.). 266p. (C). 1997. write for info. (*0-306-45550-1*, Plenum Pr) Plenum.

Recurrence of Fate: Theatre & Memory in Twentieth-Century Russia. Spencer Golub. LC 93-23631. (Studies in Theatre History & Culture). (Illus.). 293p. 1994. pap. 14.95 (*0-87745-458-2*); text ed. 27.95 (*0-87745-457-4*) U of Iowa Pr.

Recurrence Relations - Counting Backwards. Margaret Cozzens & Richard Porter. (Hi Map Ser.: No. 2). (Illus.). 60p. pap. text ed. 9.99 (*0-614-05323-4*, HM 5602) COMAP Inc.

Recurrence Relations, Continued Fractions & Orthogonal Polynomials. Richard Askey & Mourad Ismail. LC 84-3075. (Memoirs of the American Mathematical Society Ser.: No. 49/300). 108p. 1984. pap. 18.00 (*0-8218-2301-9*, MEMO 49/300) Am Math.

Recurrent Dislocation of the Shoulder. Herbert F. Moseley. 175p. reprint ed. pap. 49.90 (*0-317-20727-X*, 2023824) Bks Demand.

Recurrent Education, Earnings & Well-Being: A Fifty-Year Longitudinal Study of a Cohort of Swedish Men. Albert Tuijnman. (Stockholm Studies in Education & Psychology: No. 24). 284p. (Orig.). 1989. pap. 44.50 (*91-22-01317-2*, Pub. by Umea U Bibl SW) Coronet Bks.

Recurrent Maladies in Scholarly Writing. Eugene S. McCartney. LC 77-90361. 141p. (C). 1969. reprint ed. 40.00 (*0-87752-068-2*) Gordian.

Recurrent Mood Disorders: New Perspectives in Therapy. Ed. by G. F. Placidi et al. LC 92-48355. 1993. 178.00 (*3-540-54046-6*); 143.00 (*0-387-54046-6*) Spr-Verlag.

Recurring Dream of Equality: Communal Sharing & Communism Throughout History. James R. Ozinga. 313p. (Orig.). (C). 1995. pap. text ed. 32.50 (*0-7618-0188-X*) U Pr of Amer.

Recurring Issues in Auditing: Professional Debate, 1875-1900. Ed. by Roy A. Chandler & John Edwards. LC 93-29294. (New Works in Accounting History). 384p. 1994. text ed. 25.00 (*0-8153-1719-0*) Garland.

Recurring Logistic Problems As I Have Observed Them. Carter B. Magruder. 134p. (Orig.). (C). 1994. pap. text ed. 45.00 (*0-7881-1310-0*) DIANE Pub.

Recurring Silent Spring. H. Patricia Hynes. (Athene Ser.). 272p. (C). 1989. pap. text ed. 15.95 (*0-8077-6252-0*) Tchrs Coll.

Recurring Silent Spring. Patricia H. Hynes. (Athene Ser.). (Illus.). 272p. 1989. text ed. 30.00 (*0-08-037117-5*, Pergamon Pr); pap. text ed. 14.95 (*0-08-037116-7*, Pergamon Pr) Elsevier.

Recurring Themes in Education. Tina Bruce & Anne Findlay. 1995. pap. 29.95 (*1-85396-264-3*, Pub. by Paul Chapman UK) Taylor & Francis.

Recursion Method: Application to Many-Body Dynamics. V. S. Viswanath & Gerhard M. Muller. LC 94-28932. (Lecture Note in Physics, New Series M, Monographs). 1994. 59.95 (*0-387-58319-X*) Spr-Verlag.

Recursion Method: Application to Many-Body Dynamics, 23. V. S. Viswanath & Gerhard M. Muller. LC 94-28932. (Lecture Note in Physics, New Series M, Monographs). 1994. write for info. (*3-540-58319-X*) Spr-Verlag.

Recursion Method & Its Applications. Ed. by D. G. Pettifor & D. L. Weaire. (Solid-State Sciences Ser.: Vol. 58). (Illus.). 200p. 1985. 68.95 (*0-387-15173-7*) Spr-Verlag.

Recursion-Theoretic Hierarchies. P. G. Hinman. (Perspectives in Mathematical Logic Ser.). 1978. 118.95 (*0-387-07904-1*) Spr-Verlag.

Recursion Theory. Ed. by Anil Nerode & R. Shore. LC 84-18525. (Proceedings of Symposia in Pure Mathematics Ser.: Vol. 42). 528p. 1985. text ed. 82.00 (*0-8218-1447-8*, PSPUM/42) Am Math.

Recursion Theory. Joseph R. Schoenfield. LC 93-34447. (Lecture Notes in Logic Ser.: No. 1). 1995. 35.95 (*0-387-57093-4*) Spr-Verlag.

Recursion Theory for Metamathematics. Raymond M. Smullyan. LC 92-40495. (Oxford Logic Guides Ser.: No. 22). 184p. 1993. 45.00 (*0-19-508232-X*) OUP.

Recursion Theory Week. Ed. by H. D. Ebbinghaus et al. (Lecture Notes in Mathematics Ser.: Vol. 1141). ix, 418p. 1985. 54.95 (*0-387-15673-9*) Spr-Verlag.

Recursion Theory Week: Proceedings of a Conference Held in Oberwolfach, FRG March 19-29, 1989. Ed. by Klaus Ambos-Spies et al. (Lecture Notes in Mathematics Ser.: Vol. 1432). (Illus.). vi, 393p. 1990. pap. 50.00 (*0-387-52772-9*) Spr-Verlag.

Recursive Algorithm for the Best Approximate Solution of Linear Equations with Applications to System Identification & State Estimation. Manfred H. Werther. LC 70-132895. 143p. 1969. 19.00 (*0-403-04547-9*) Scholarly.

Recursive Algorithms. Richard J. Lorentz. LC 93-9056. (Computations Sciences Ser.). 200p. 1994. pap. 39.50 (*1-56750-037-4*); text ed. 78.50 (*0-89391-913-6*) Ablex Pub.

Recursive Aspects of Descriptive Set Theory. Richard Mansfield & Galen Weitkamp. (Oxford Logic Guides Ser.). 154p. 1985. 24.95 (*0-19-503602-6*) OUP.

Recursive Design. Sally Shlaer. 400p. (C). 1996. text ed. 26. 25 (*0-13-206137-6*) P-H.

***Recursive Desire: Rereading Epic Poetry.** Jeremy M. Downes. LC 96-9789. 336p. 1997. text ed. 46.95 (*0-8173-0841-5*) U of Ala Pr.

Recursive Function Theory. Pure Mathematics Symposium Staff. Ed. by J. Dekker. LC 50-1183. (Proceedings of Symposia in Pure Mathematics Ser.: Vol. 5). 247p. 1962. reprint ed. pap. 42.00 (*0-8218-1405-2*, PSPUM/5) Am Math.

Recursive Functionals. Luis E. Sanchis. LC 92-10555. (Studies in Logic & the Foundations of Mathematics: Vol. 131). 278p. 1992. 131.50 (*0-444-89447-0*, North Holland) Elsevier.

Recursive Introduction to the Theory of Computation. Carl Smith. LC 94-21785. (Graduate Texts in Computer Science Ser.). 1994. 36.95 (*0-387-94332-3*) Spr-Verlag.

Recursive Linear Mod. Thomas J. Sargent. (C). 1993. 35.00 (*0-691-04277-2*) Princeton U Pr.

Recursive Methods in Economic Dynamics. Nancy L. Stokey & Robert E. Lucas, Jr. LC 88-37681. (Illus.). 560p. 1989. 47.50 (*0-674-75096-9*) HUP.

Recursive Model of Personal Sector Expenditure & Accumulation. E. P. Davis. (Bank of England. Technical Series. Discussion Papers: No. 6). 100p. reprint ed. pap. 28.50 (*0-317-20795-4*, 2024789) Bks Demand.

Recursive Neural Networks for Associative Memory. Yves Kamp. LC 90-42923. 194p. 1990. text ed. 95.00 (*0-471-92866-6*) Wiley.

Recursive Nonlinear Estimation: A Geometric Approach, Vol. 216. Rudolf Kulhav. LC 96-21895. (Lecture Notes inControl & Information Sciences Ser.). 224p. 1996. pap. 54.00 (*3-540-76063-6*) Spr-Verlag.

Recursive Programming Techniques. William H. Burge. LC 74-28812. (IBM Systems Programming Ser.). (Illus.). 280p. 1975. text ed. write for info. (*0-201-14450-6*) Addison-Wesley.

Recursive Source Coding. G. Gabor & Z. Gyorfi. (Illus.). 120p. 1986. 67.95 (*0-387-96309-X*) Spr-Verlag.

Recursive Universe: Cosmic Complexity & the Limits of Scientific Knowledge. William Poundstone. Date not set. pap. write for info. (*0-688-07290-9*, Quill) Morrow.

Recursive Vision: Ecological Understanding & Gregory Bateson. Peter Harries-Jones. 328p. 1995. 55.00 (*0-8020-0636-1*); pap. 17.95 (*0-8020-7591-6*) U of Toronto Pr.

Recursively Enumerable Sets & Degrees: A Study of Computable Functions & Computably Generated Sets. R. I. Soare. (Perspectives in Mathematical Logic Ser.). 460p. 1987. 59.95 (*0-387-15299-7*) Spr-Verlag.

***Recursos Extraordinarios.** 2nd rev. ed. David Rive-Rivera. 460p. (SPA.). 1997. pap. text ed. 50.00 (*1-881711-03-X*) Univ Interamrcna.

***Recutting & Repairing Diamonds.** Leonard Ludel. Ed. by Michael Riggs. LC 96-95231. (Illus.). 75p. (Orig.). 1996. pap. 33.20 (*0-9617615-1-2*) L Ludel.

Recuyell of the Historyes of Troye, 2 vols. in 1. Raoul Lefevre. Tr. by William Caxton. LC 70-178542. reprint ed. 115.00 (*0-404-56624-3*) AMS Pr.

Recyclable Scrap: Locations; a Workbook. Wellthe Publishing Staff. 150p. 1983. ring bd. 28.95 (*0-317-03157-0*) Prosperity & Profits.

Recyclable Scrap Locating - a Workbook. Data Notes Publishing. 60p. 1983. ring bd. 29.95 (*0-317-00336-4*) Prosperity & Profits.

Recyclables Fun: Creative Craft Ideas. Diane Cherkerzian. LC 94-71024. (Illus.). 48p. (J). (ps-2). 1995. pap. 4.95 (*1-56397-275-1*) Boyds Mills Pr.

R

Recycle! A Handbook for Kids. Gail Gibbons. (Illus.). 32p. (J). (ps-3). 1992. 15.95 (*0-316-30971-0*) Little.

Recycle! A Handbook for Kids. Gail Gibbons. (Illus.). 32p. (J). (ps-3). 1996. pap. 4.95 (*0-316-30943-5*) Little.

Recycle & Secondary Recovery of Metals: Proceedings of the International Symposium on Recycle & Secondary Recovery of Metals & the Fall Extractive & Process Metallurgy Meeting. Metallurgical Society of AIME Staff. Ed. by Patrick R. Taylor et al. LC 85-21792. (Illus.). 874p. reprint ed. pap. 180.00 (*0-8357-7006-0*, 2052275) Bks Demand.

Recycle Stream Effects on Water Treatment. (Illus.). 178p. 1993. pap. 70.00 (*0-89867-689-4*, 90629) Am Water Wks Assn.

Recycle That! Fay Robinson. LC 94-35626. (Rookie Read-About Science Ser.). 32p. (J). (ps-2). 1995. lib. bdg. 17.30 (*0-516-06033-3*) Childrens.

Recycle That! Fay Robinson. (Rookie Read-About Science Ser.). (Illus.). 32p. (J). (ps-2). 1995. pap. 3.95 (*0-516-46033-1*) Childrens.

Recycle Your Boss: 99 Ways to Put a Bad Boss to Good Use. Pat Hucklebee. (Illus.). 104p. 1995. pap. 6.95 (*0-8362-1778-0*) Andrews & McMeel.

***Recycled.** (Paranoia Ser.). 8.00 (*0-87431-166-7*, 12011) West End Games.

Recycled Container Arts & Crafts Activities: Week-by-Week Projects Using All Kinds of Containers. Jo J. Cavalline & Jo A. O'Donnell. Ed. by Judy Mitchell. (Illus.). 112p. (Orig.). (J). (gr. k-3). 1996. teacher ed., pap. 10.95 (*1-57310-040-4*) Teachng & Lrning Co.

***Recycled Dishes for the 21st Century.** Astrid Doramajian. vi, 203p. (Orig.). 1997. pap. 14.95 (*0-9656404-0-X*) A Doramajian.

Recycled Doonesbury: Second Thoughts on a Gilded Age. Garry B. Trudeau. (Illus.). 256p. (Orig.). 1990. pap. 12.95 (*0-8362-1824-8*) Andrews & McMeel.

***Recycled High Fashion.** Florence Ayre. (Illus.). 108p. (Orig.). 1997. pap. 12.95 (*0-9658064-0-5*) F Ayre.

Recycled Metals in the U. S. 1994. lib. bdg. 250.00 (*0-8490-8425-3*) Gordon Pr.

Recycled Paper Technology: An Anthology of Published Papers. Ed. by Mahendra Doshi. 342p. (Orig.). 1994. pap. 90.00 (*0-89852-282-X*, 0101R237) TAPPI.

Recycled Papers: The Essential Guide. Claudia Thompson. (Illus.). 200p. 1992. 40.00 (*0-262-20089-9*); pap. 25.00 (*0-262-70046-8*) MIT Pr.

Recycled, Re-Seen: Folk Art from the Global Scrap Heap. Ed. by Charlene Cerny & Suzanne Seriff. LC 95-52751. (Illus.). 208p. 1996. pap. 29.95 (*0-8109-2666-0*) Abrams.

Recycled Sonnets. Ruth M. Kempher. LC 94-43770. 64p. 1995. pap. 12.95 (*0-7734-2746-5*, Mellen Poetry Pr) E Mellen.

Recycled Sonnets. Ruth M. Kempher. LC 94-43770. 1995. write for info. (*0-7734-2946-8*, Mellen Poetry Pr) E Mellen.

Recycled Teenager. Bruce Cochran. (Illus.). 10p. 1994. write for info. (*1-886386-27-7*) Trisar.

Recycled Tire Rubber in Asphalt Payments. LC 92-22590. 44p. 1992. 17.00 (*0-309-05203-3*, R1339) Transport Res Bd.

Recycled Treasures from Grandma's Attic. Eleanor Burns. (Illus.). 32p. 1993. 8.95 (*0-922705-42-9*) Quilt Day.

***Recycled Words: Collected Poems (1980-1996)** Rick K. Theis. LC 96-78656. 180p. (Orig.). 1996. pap. 12.95 (*0-9655454-1-5*) Media Wrks.

Recycler. Joanne Barkan. (Truckin' Board Bks.). (J). 1996. bds. 4.99 (*0-689-81149-7*) S&S Childrens.

Recyclers Handbook. Earth Works Group Staff. 132p. 1990. pap. 4.95 (*0-929634-08-X*) Grnleaf Pubs.

Recycler's Manual for Business, Government, & Environmentalists. David R. Powelson & Melinda A. Powelson. LC 92-10099. 1992. text ed. 74.95 (*0-442-01190-3*) Van Nos Reinhold.

Recycling. Blackbirch Graphics Staff. LC 96-23068. (J). 1996. lib. bdg. 16.98 (*0-8050-4622-4*) H Holt & Co.

Recycling. Jean F. Blashfield & Wallace B. Black. LC 90-400. (Saving Planet Earth Ser.). (Illus.). 128p. (J). (gr. 4-8). 1991. lib. bdg. 29.30 (*0-516-05502-X*) Childrens.

***Recycling.** Chandler. 1996. write for info. (*0-8050-5270-4*) H Holt & Co.

Recycling. Susan Hassol & Beth Richman. (Creating a Healthy World - 101 Practical Tips for Home & Work Ser.). (Illus.). (Orig.). 1989. pap. 3.95 (*0-9622492-3-8*) Windstar Foundation.

Recycling. Emilie U. Lepthien & Joan Kalbacken. LC 90-21275. (New True Bks.). (Illus.). 48p. (J). (gr. k-4). 1991. pap. 5.50 (*0-516-41118-7*); lib. bdg. 19.00 (*0-516-01118-9*) Childrens.

Recycling. Don Nardo. LC 92-27849. (Overview Ser.: Our Endangered Planet). (Illus.). 112p. (J). (gr. 5-8). 1992. lib. bdg. 17.96 (*1-56006-135-9*) Lucent Bks.

Recycling. Rebecca Stefoff. (Earth at Risk Ser.). (Illus.). 128p. (YA). (gr. 5 up). 1991. lib. bdg. 19.95 (*0-7910-1573-4*) Chelsea Hse.

Recycling: How to Find or Locate Information on Recycling Workbook. Center for Self-Sufficiency, Research Division Staff. 80p. 1992. student ed., ring bd. 24.95 (*0-910811-91-1*) Prosperity & Profits.

Recycling: Opportunities & Constraints: Proceedings of the Conference Co-Sponsored by the Federation of Materials Science & the U. S. Bureau of Mines, Washington, D. C., U. S. A., 17-19 July 1984. Ed. by Michael B. Bevin & M. E. Henstock. 136p. 1985. pap. 85.00 (*0-08-032635-8*, E135, D145, G13, Pub. by PPL UK) Elsevier.

Recycling: Reuse of Waste Resources: Presented At the TAPPI Empire State Section, Annual Spring Conference, June 9-10, 1972. Technical Association of the Pulp & Paper Industry Staff. LC 74-153924. (Technical Association of the Pulp & Paper Car Ser.: No. 45). 109p. reprint ed. pap. 31.10 (*0-317-29317-6*, 2022355) Bks Demand.

Recycling: Successful Strategies for Residential & Commercial Properties. 76p. 1993. pap. 29.95 (*0-685-71675-9*, 710) Inst Real Estate.

Recycling: The Alternative to Disposal: A Case Study of the Potential for Increased Recycling of Newspapers & Corrugated Containers in the Washington Metropolitan Area. Thomas H. Quimby. LC 74-6836. 144p. reprint ed. pap. 41.10 (*0-317-41739-8*, 2020949) Bks Demand.

Recycling Activities for the Primary Grades. Jean Stangl. (J). (ps-3). 1993. pap. 9.99 (*0-86653-938-7*) Fearon Teach Aids.

Recycling Alternatives for a City of 25,000. John P. Allison. 31p. (Orig.). (C). 1992. pap. 7.95 (*0-9632789-9-1*) RMC Pub Grp.

Recycling & Incineration: Evaluating the Choices. Richard Denison & John Ruston. LC 90-37971. 320p. 1990. 34.95 (*1-55963-055-8*); pap. 19.95 (*1-55963-054-X*) Island Pr.

***Recycling & Recovery of Plastics.** Johannes Brandrup. LC 96-36331. 893p. 1996. 240.00 (*1-56990-214-3*) Hanser-Gardner.

Recycling & Resource Recovery Engineering: Principles of Waste Processing. Richard I. Stessel. LC 96-18936. (Environmental Engineering Ser.). 263p. 1996. 74.95 (*3-540-61100-2*) Spr-Verlag.

Recycling & Reuse of Industrial Wastes. Jeffrey L. Means et al. LC 95-1591. 116p. 1995. pap. 34.95 (*0-935470-89-1*) Battelle.

Recycling & Reuse of Material Found on Superfund Sites. Jeffrey L. Means. (Illus.). 84p. (Orig.). (C). 1995. pap. text ed. 25.00 (*0-7881-1617-7*) DIANE Pub.

Recycling & the Politics of Urban Waste. Matthew Gandy. LC 94-7198. 1994. text ed. 49.95 (*0-312-12203-9*); text ed. 20.95 (*0-312-12204-7*) St Martin.

Recycling & Waste: An Exploration of Contemporary Environmental Policy. Matthew Gandy. (Studies in Green Research). 341p. 1993. 63.95 (*1-85628-542-1*, Pub. by Avebury Pub UK) Ashgate Pub Co.

Recycling Businesses: Suggestions for Types of Recycling Businesses. rev. ed. Center for Self-Sufficiency, Research Division Staff. 50p. 1991. 19.95 (*0-685-48413-0*) Ctr Self Suff.

Recycling Businesses: Suggestions for Types of Recycling Businesses. rev. ed. Center for Self-Sufficiency, Research Division Staff. 108p. 1992. ring bd. 32.95 (*0-910811-34-2*) Ctr Self Suff.

Recycling Commodity Exchange Encyclopaedia: World Mapping Edition. rev. ed. Barter Publishing Staff. 102p. 1991. ring bd. 95.00 (*0-911617-77-9*, Barter Pub) Prosperity & Profits.

Recycling Concepts & Procedures. Ed. by M. Neitzel. 88p. 1993. 98.00 (*1-85573-145-2*, Pub. by Woodhead Pubng UK) Am Educ Systs.

Recycling Coordinator. Jack Rudman. (Career Examination Ser.: C-3567). 1994. pap. 34.95 (*0-8373-3567-1*) Nat Learn.

Recycling Dump. 2nd ed. Andrea Butler. (Let Me Read). (Illus.). (J). (ps). 1995. bds. 2.95 (*0-673-36267-1*, GoodYrBooks) Addson-Wesley Educ.

Recycling Economic Development Through Scrap-Based Manufacturing. Michael Lewis. LC 94-5188. (Illus.). 42p. 1994. pap. text ed. 20.00 (*0-917582-97-7*) Inst Local Self Re.

Recycling Equipment & Technology for Municipal Solid Waste: Material Recovery Facilities. Joseph T. Swartzbaugh et al. LC 92-25263. (Pollution Technology Review Ser.: No. 210). (Illus.). 150p. 1993. 45.00 (*0-8155-1316-X*) Noyes.

Recycling for the Soul. Elvin McDonald. 1997. 18.95 (*0-02-861012-1*) Macmillan.

Recycling Handbook. Herbert F. Lund. LC 92-18267. 1992. text ed. 87.50 (*0-07-039096-7*) McGraw.

Recycling Handbook for Business. Robert Feinbaum. (Illus.). 130p. (Orig.). (C). 1992. pap. text ed. 35.00 (*1-878630-34-2*) CA Chamber Commerce.

Recycling Handbook for Local Governments & Organizations. 92p. 1991. student ed. 29.95 (*1-882403-01-0*) The Innovation Grps.

Recycling Household Waste: The Way Ahead. 218p. 1991. pap. text ed. 52.00 (*0-7277-1650-6*, Pub. by T Telford UK) Am Soc Civil Eng.

***Recycling in America.** 2nd ed. Debi Kimball. 256p. 1997. 39.50 (*0-87436-889-8*) ABC-CLIO.

Recycling in America: A Reference Handbook. Debi Kimball. LC 92-29984. (Contemporary World Issues Ser.). 254p. 1992. lib. bdg. 39.50 (*0-87436-663-1*) ABC-CLIO.

Recycling Is More Than Collections: Questions & Concerns from the Ground Up. League of Women Voters Education Fund Staff. 1992. 5.95 (*0-89959-421-2*, 926) LWVUS.

Recycling Lessons Learned. (Special Report Ser.). 85p. 1991. pap. 28.00 (*0-87326-801-6*) Intl City-Cnty Mgt.

Recycling Market & Resource Directory. 49p. (Orig.). (C). 1993. pap. text ed. 20.00 (*1-56806-737-2*) DIANE Pub.

Recycling Means Business in Baltimore, D.C., & Richmond. Brenda A. Platt et al. 86p. 1995. 12.00 (*0-614-18039-2*) Inst Local Self Re.

Recycling Nonferrous Metals. (Metals & Minerals Ser.). 1993. lib. bdg. 255.95 (*0-8490-9016-4*) Gordon Pr.

Recycling of Biruminous Pavements - STP 662. Ed. by L. E. Wood. 153p. 1984. pap. 24.00 (*0-8031-0776-5*, 04-662000-08) ASTM.

Recycling of Consumer Dry Cell Batteries. David J. Hurd et al. LC 92-47241. (Pollution Technology Review Ser.: No. 213). (Illus.). 276p. 1993. 48.00 (*0-8155-1325-9*) Noyes.

***Recycling of Demolished Concrete & Masonry.** Ed. by Hansen. (Rilem Report Ser.). (Illus.). 316p. text ed. 92.50 (*0-419-15820-0*, E & FN Spon) Routledge Chapman & Hall.

Recycling of Demolished Concrete & Masonry. Ed. by T. C. Hansen. (RILEM Reports: No. 6). 300p. 1991. 79.95 (*0-412-38520-1*) Chapman & Hall.

Recycling of Demolished Concrete & Masonry. Ed. by T. C. Hansen. 300p. 1992. 79.95 (*0-442-31251-2*) Chapman & Hall.

Recycling of Metals & Engineered Materials: Third International Symposium. Ed. by P. B. Queneau & R. D. Peterson. (Illus.). 800p. 1995. 170.00 (*0-87339-318-X*, 318X) Minerals Metals.

Recycling of Metals & Other Materials: Selected Papers from the Fourth Recycling World Congress, April 5-7, 1982, New Orleans, U. S. A. Ed. by M. E. Henstock. 96p. 1983. 66.01 (*0-08-030262-9*, 16(99), 15(99), 19(5), Pergamon Pr) Elsevier.

Recycling of Papermaking Fibers: Deinking by Washing. Robert G. Horacek. Ed. by Harold E. Corwin. 37p. reprint ed. pap. 25.00 (*0-317-20541-2*, 2022829) Bks Demand.

Recycling of Papermaking Fibers: Flotation Deinking. Herbert E. Ortner. Ed. by Harold E. Corwin. 38p. reprint ed. pap. 25.00 (*0-317-20560-9*, 2022814) Bks Demand.

Recycling Opportunities. 160p. 1990. 2,500.00 (*0-945235-23-2*) Lead Edge Reports.

Recycling Organizer for Business. Ed. by Robert Feinbaum. 57p. 1993. pap. text ed. 25.00 (*1-878630-36-9*) CA Chamber Commerce.

Recycling Paper: From Fiber to Finished Product, 2 vols., Vol. 1. Ed. by Matthew Coleman. LC 90-19531. 446p. reprint ed. pap. 120.50 (*0-8357-3002-6*, 2039271) Bks Demand.

Recycling Paper: From Fiber to Finished Product, 2 vols., Vol. 2. Ed. by Matthew Coleman. LC 90-19531. 391p. reprint ed. pap. 105.60 (*0-8357-3003-4*, 2039271) Bks Demand.

Recycling Plastics. Business Communications Co., Inc. Staff. 154p. 1988. pap. 2,250.00 (*0-89336-537-8*, P-084) BCC.

Recycling Projects for Creating Summer & Year Around Jobs-Possibilities. rev. ed. Center for Self-Sufficiency Staff. 78p. 1992. ring bd. 27.95 (*0-910811-42-3*) Ctr Self Suff.

Recycling Seminar-Workshop: Workbook. Center for Self-Sufficiency, Research Division Staff. 25p. 1984. student ed., ring bd. 31.95 (*0-910811-90-3*) Ctr Self Suff.

Recycling Shakespeare. Charles Marowitz. (Illus.). 256p. 1991. 32.95 (*1-55783-093-2*); pap. 14.95 (*1-55783-094-0*) Applause Theatre Bk Pubs.

Recycling Simulation Activity Sessions, Vol. 1. Alpha Pyramis Research Division Staff. 60p. 1984. ring bd. 29.95 (*0-913597-57-0*) Prosperity & Profits.

Recycling Solid Waste: The First Choice for Private & Public Sector Management. Thomas E. Duston. LC 92-31709. 224p. 1993. text ed. 55.00 (*0-89930-754-X*, DRG, Quorum Bks) Greenwood.

Recycling Sourcebook. Ed. by Thomas J. Cichonski & Karen Hill. (Environmental Library). 1992. 85.00 (*0-8103-8855-3*, 101455) Gale.

Recycling Stories That Rhyme. Story Time Stories That Rhyme Staff. (Illus.). 1996. ring bd. 19.95 (*1-56820-005-6*) Story Time.

***Recycling Story Samphlet of Stories.** Story Time Staff. (Illus.). (Orig.). 1997. teacher ed., pap. 19.95 (*1-56820-196-6*) Story Time.

Recycling Supervisor. Jack Rudman. (Career Examination Ser.: C-3568). 1994. pap. 29.95 (*0-8373-3568-X*) Nat Learn.

***Recycling Symposium, 1994: Sheraton Boston, Boston, MA, May 15-18.** Technical Association of the Pulp & Paper Industry Staff. (TAPPI Proceedings Ser.). (Illus.). 546p. reprint ed. pap. 155.70 (*0-608-05357-0*, 2082405) Bks Demand.

Recycling the Family: Remarriage after Divorce. Frank F. Furstenberg, Jr. & Graham B. Spanier. LC 87-9695. 212p. 1987. reprint ed. pap. 60.50 (*0-608-01467-2*, 2059511) Bks Demand.

Recycling Tips for Teachers & Librarians. Carol Smallwood. LC 94-43243. 183p. 1995. pap. 24.50 (*0-7864-0009-9*) McFarland & Co.

Recycling Two-Liter Containers for the Teaching of Science. Alfred Devito. (Illus.). 88p. 1995. pap. 14.95 (*0-942034-09-0*) Creat Ventures IN.

Recycling Waste. Paul I. Smith. 1976. text ed. 30.00 (*0-87936-011-9*) Scholium Intl.

Recycling Workbook: Based on Recycling for Living, Fun & Profit. Ed. by Bibliotheca Press Research Division Staff. 50p. 1983. ring bd. 24.95 (*0-939476-50-9*, Biblio Pr) Prosperity & Profits.

Recycling Works! State & Local Solutions to Solid Waste Management Problems. (Illus.). 52p. (Orig.). 1996. pap. text ed. 20.00 (*0-7881-2616-4*) DIANE Pub.

Recycling 35 mm Cannisters for the Teaching of Science. Alfred Devito. (Illus.). 40p. 1993. pap. 12.95 (*0-942034-08-2*) Creat Ventures IN.

Recyclings. Richard Kostelanetz. 1984. 6.00 (*0-918406-26-9*); pap. 5.00 (*0-918406-27-7*) Future Pr.

Recyclings. deluxe limited ed. Richard Kostelanetz. 1984. 100.00 (*0-918406-28-5*) Future Pr.

Recyclings: A Literary Autobiography. Richard Kostelanetz. (Illus.). 64p. (Orig.). 1974. pap. 3.00 (*0-915066-08-4*) Assembling Pr.

Recyclings: A Literary Autobiography. Richard Kostelanetz. (Illus.). 64p. (Orig.). 1984. write for info. (*0-915066-44-0*); pap. 8.00 (*0-685-64986-5*) Assembling Pr.

Recyclings: A Literary Autobiography. deluxe limited ed. Richard Kostelanetz. (Illus.). 64p. (Orig.). 1974. 40.00 (*0-915066-63-7*) Assembling Pr.

Recyclings: A Literary Autobiography. deluxe limited ed. Richard Kostelanetz. (Illus.). 64p. (Orig.). 1984. write for info. (*0-915066-45-9*) Assembling Pr.

Recyclopedia. Robin Simons. 1976. pap. 13.95 (*0-395-59641-6*) HM.

Red. Karen Bryant-Mole. LC 95-51092. (Images Ser.). (Illus.). (J). 1996. pap. 4.95 (*0-382-39622-7*, Silver Pr NJ) Silver Burdett Pr.

Red. Mark Dunster. (Rin Ser.: Pt. 46). 1979. pap. 5.00 (*0-89642-054-X*) Linden Pubs.

Red. Linda France. 80p. 9300. pap. 14.95 (*1-85224-178-0*, Pub. by Bloodaxe Bks UK) Dufour.

Red. Belinda Recio. LC 95-46325. (Color Ser.: Vol. 2). (Illus.). 96p. 1996. 19.95 (*0-87905-738-6*) Gibbs Smith Pub.

Red. Erica Spindler. (Mira Bks.). 1995. mass mkt. 4.99 (*1-55166-042-3*, 1-66042-2, Mira Bks) Harlequin Bks.

Red. Gabrielle Woolfitt. (J). (gr. k-3). 1992. lib. bdg. 17.50 (*0-87614-706-6*, Carolrhoda) Lerner Group.

Red. Karen Bryant-Mole. LC 95-51092. (Images Ser.). (Illus.). (J). 1996. reprint ed. lib. bdg. 10.95 (*0-382-39586-7*, Silver Pr NJ) Silver Burdett Pr.

Red: A Biography of Red Smith. Ira Berkow. LC 85-40829. (Illus.). 320p. 1986. 17.95 (*0-8129-1203-9*, Times Bks) Random.

Red Acre Farm. Burke. (J). 1996. 14.95 (*0-8050-2047-0*) H Holt & Co.

Red Actions: Selected Poems 1960-1993. Robert Kelly. LC 95-35351. 398p. (Orig.). (C). 1995. 30.00 (*0-87685-978-3*); pap. 17.50 (*0-87685-977-5*) Black Sparrow.

Red Actions: Selected Poems 1960-1993, signed ed. deluxe ed. Robert Kelly. LC 95-35351. 398p. (Orig.). (C). 1995. 35.00 (*0-87685-979-1*) Black Sparrow.

Red Adam. Mark Mirsky. (New American Fiction Ser.: No. 19). (Illus.). 168p. (Orig.). 1990. pap. 10.95 (*0-940650-92-4*) Sun & Moon CA.

***Red Address.** David Ives. pap. 5.25 (*0-8222-1606-X*) Dramatists Play.

Red Against Blue: The Liberal Party in Colombian Politics, 1863-1899. Helen Delpar. LC 79-19081. 278p. 1981. pap. 79.30 (*0-7837-8368-X*, 2059178) Bks Demand.

Red Ain't Dead: 150 More Ways to Tell if You're a Redneck. Jeff Foxworthy. LC 91-61935. (Illus.). 80p. 1991. pap. 6.95 (*1-56352-005-2*) Longstreet Pr Inc.

Red Air Fighter. Manfred F. Von Richthofen. 192p. 1991. 35.00 (*1-85367-079-0*, 5577) Stackpole.

Red Air Fighter. Manfred F. Von Richthofen. LC 78-169441. (Literature & History of Aviation Ser.). (Illus.). 192p. 1976. reprint ed. 16.95 (*0-405-03784-8*) Ayer.

***Red All Over: A Newspaper of Folktales Riddles & Words.** Shannon. (J). 1998. mass mkt. 5.99 (*0-689-81891-2*) S&S Childrens.

Red & Black: An Annotated Text with Critical Essays. Robert Stendhal. Ed. by Robert M. Adams. (Critical Editions Ser.). (C). 1969. pap. text ed. 14.95 (*0-393-09821-4*) Norton.

***Red & Blue Illusion Book: How to Create 3-D Drawings & Other Optical Tricks.** Mark Hilner. (Illus.). 60p. (J). (gr. 5-6). 1997. pap. 14.95 (*1-899618-05-8*, Pub. by Tarquin UK) Parkwest Pubns.

Red & Green Chile Book: Southwestern & Mexican Recipes. 2nd ed. Jacqueline H. McMahan. (Illus.). 210p. 1992. reprint ed. pap. 14.95 (*0-9612150-5-4*) Olive Pr.

Red & Hot: The Fate of Jazz in the Soviet Union with a New Chapter on the Final Years. rev. ed. S. Frederick Starr. LC 94-2587. (Illus.). 440p. 1994. reprint ed. pap. 18.95 (*0-87910-180-6*) Limelight Edns.

***Red & the Black.** Stendal. pap. 6.50 (*0-460-87643-0*, Everyman's Classic Lib) C E Tuttle.

Red & the Black. Stendhal. Tr. by C. K. Moncrieff. LC 84-4612. 633p. 1984. 9.95 (*0-394-60511-X*, Modern Lib) Random.

Red & the Black. Stendhal. 32.95 (*0-8488-0635-2*) Amereon Ltd.

Red & the Black. Renate Stendhal. 770p. 1995. 17.50 (*0-679-60162-7*) Random.

Red & the Black. Robert Stendhal. Tr. by Lloyd C. Parks. (Illus.). 1970. pap. 5.99 (*0-451-51793-8*, CE1793, Sig Classics) NAL-Dutton.

Red & the Black. Stendhal. 532p. 1987. reprint ed. lib. bdg. 35.95 (*0-89966-619-1*) Buccaneer Bks.

Red & the Black: A Chronicle of Nineteenth Century. Stendhal. Tr. & Notes by Catherine Slater. (World's Classics Ser.). 592p. 1991. pap. 6.95 (*0-19-281715-9*) OUP.

Red & the Black: Mimetic Desire & the Myth of Celebrity. Jefferson Humphries. (Twayne's Masterwork Studies: No. 74). 120p. 1991. 23.95 (*0-8057-8352-0*, Twayne); pap. 13.95 (*0-8057-8149-8*, Twayne) Scribnrs Ref.

Red & the Black: Studies in Greek Pottery. Brian A. Sparkes. LC 95-40622. 208p. 1996. pap. 18.95 (*0-415-12661-4*) Routledge.

Red & the Black: Studies in Greek Pottery. Brian A. Sparkes. LC 95-40622. 208p. (C). 1996. text ed. 69.95 (*0-415-12660-6*) Routledge.

Red & the Colonel: A Radio Friendship. Bob Edwards. (Illus.). 256p. 1993. 21.00 (*0-671-87013-0*) S&S Trade.

Red & the Green. Iris Murdoch. 288p. 1988. pap. 10.95 (*0-14-002756-4*, Penguin Bks) Viking Penguin.

R

*Red & the Green: The Rise & Fall of Collectivized Agriculture in Marxist Regimes. Frederic L. Pryor. LC 91-32459. 563p. reprint ed. pap. 160.50 (0-608-02568-2, 2063213) Bks Demand.

Red & the White: The History of Wine in France & Italy in the Nineteenth Century. Leo A. Loubere. LC 78-2304. (Illus.). 401p. 1978. text ed. 19.50 (0-87395-370-3) State U NY Pr.

Red & White on the New York Frontier: A Struggle for Survival, Insights from the Papers of Erastus Granger, Indian Agent, 1807-1819. Charles M. Snyder. LC 78-14239. (Illus.). 1978. 15.00 (0-916346-28-5) Purple Mnt Pr.

*Red & Yellow. Janie L. Hunt. LC 96-37228. (Through the Window Ser.). (Illus.). 24p. (J). (ps-k). 1997. 9.95 (0-7613-0279-4) Millbrook Pr.

Red & Yellow, Black & White... Deborah Brunsman. 184p. 1991. 12.99 (0-89900-385-0) College Pr Pub.

Red & Yellow Boat: Poems. Anthony Petrosky. LC 93-32204. 64p. 1994. pap. 8.95 (0-8071-1831-1); text ed. 15.95 (0-8071-1830-3) La State U Pr.

*Red & Yellow Catch. Beverly Coyle. 1998. pap. 21.95 (0-670-86398-X) Viking Penguin.

Red Angel. Roxanne Longstreet. 352p. 1994. mass mkt. 4.50 (0-8217-4532-8, Zebra Kensgtn) Kensgtn Pub Corp.

Red Angel: The Life & Times of Elaine Black Yoneda, 1906-1988. Vivian M. Raineri. LC 91-15038. (Illus.). xiv, 332p. 1991. 19.00 (0-7178-0688-X); pap. 9.95 (0-7178-0686-3) Intl Pubs Co.

Red Apocalypse: The Religious Evolution of Soviet Communism. Arthur J. Klinghoffer. 190p. (C). 1996. pap. text ed. 28.50 (0-7618-0221-5); lib. bdg. 49.50 (0-7618-0220-7) U Pr of Amer.

*Red Arctic: Polar Exploration & the Myth of the North in the Soviet Union, 1932-1939. John McCannon. (Illus.). 256p. 1997. 49.95 (0-19-511436-1) OUP.

Red Aristocrats: Michael & Catherine Karolyi. Richard Andersen. 250p. 1991. pap. 12.50 (0-915597-85-3) Amana Bks.

Red Armies in Crisis. Bruce Porter. (Significant Issues Ser.: Vol. 13, No. 10). 128p. 1992. pap. text ed. 14.95 (0-89206-175-8) CSI Studies.

Red Armor: A History. Paul Hofrichter. (Military History Monograph). 50p. 1995. pap. 6.00 (1-57638-037-8) Merriam Pr.

Red Army. Ralph Peters. Ed. by Paul McCarthy. 416p. 1990. mass mkt. 5.50 (0-671-67669-5) PB.

Red Army & Society: A Sciology of the Soviet Military. Ellen Jones. 230p. (C). 1986. pap. 17.95 (0-04-497016-1) Routledge Chapman & Hall.

Red Army & Society: A Sociology of the Soviet Military. Ellen Jones. LC 84-12336. 280p. 1985. text ed. 37.95 (0-04-322011-8) Routledge Chapman & Hall.

Red Army & the Wehrmacht: How the Soviets Militarized Germany, 1922-33, & Paved the Way for Fascism. Yuri L. Djakov & Tatjana S. Bushuyeva. (Illus.). 348p. (C). 1994. 24.95 (0-87975-937-2) Prometheus Bks.

Red Army Combat Orders: Combat Regulations for Tank & Mechanized Forces 1944. Ed. by Richard N. Armstrong. Tr. by Joseph G. Welsh. 163p. 1991. text ed. 39.50 (0-7146-3401-8, Pub. by F Cass Pubs UK) Intl Spec Bk.

Red Army Legacies: Essays on Forces, Capabilities & Personalities. Richard N. Armstrong. LC 95-67622. (Illus.). 320p. 1995. 24.95 (0-88740-805-2) Schiffer.

Red Army Tank Commanders: The Armored Guards. Richard Armstrong. LC 93-87474. (Illus.). 475p. 1994. 24.95 (0-88740-581-9) Schiffer.

Red Army Uniforms of World War II in Color Photographs. Andrew Mollo & Anton Shalito. (Europa Militaria Ser.: No. 14). (Illus.). 64p. 1994. pap. 15.95 (1-872004-59-8, Pub. by Windrow & Green UK) Motorbooks Intl.

Red Army 1941-45. Steven J. Zaloga. (Men-at-Arms Ser.: No. 216). (Illus.). 48p. pap. 11.95 (0-85045-939-7, 9149, Pub. by Osprey UK) Stackpole.

Red Arrow Men: Stories about the 32nd Division on the Villa Verde. John M. Carlisle. (Combat Arms Ser.: No. 22). 215p. 1990. reprint ed. 29.95 (0-89839-149-0) Battery Pr.

Red As in Russia & Measles & Love. Linda J. Niedfeldt. LC 92-63029. 128p. (Orig.). 1993. pap. 7.99 (0-8100-0469-0, 17N1623) Northwest Pub.

Red Azalea. Anchee Min. 320p. 1995. mass mkt. 6.99 (0-425-14776-2, Berkley Trade) Berkley Pub.

Red Azalea. Anchee Min. 1995. pap. 17.95 (0-7871-0253-9, Dove Bks) Dove Audio.

Red Azalea: Chinese Poetry Since the Cultural Revolution. Ed. & Tr. by Edward Morin from CHI. Tr. by Fang Dai et al. from CHI. LC 90-41829. 256p. 1990. pap. 15.95 (0-8248-1320-0); text ed. 37.00 (0-8248-1256-5) UH Pr.

Red Badge of Courage. 1995. pap. 5.25 (0-19-585419-5) OUP.

Red Badge of Courage. 1994. pap. 29.95 (0-7871-0062-5, Dove Bks) Dove Audio.

*Red Badge of Courage. (Classics Illustrated Study Guides Ser.). (Illus.). (Orig.). 1997. mass mkt. write for info. (1-57840-040-6) Acclaim Bks.

Red Badge of Courage. Stephen Crane. (Classics Ser.). (YA). (gr. 7 up). 1962. mass mkt. 2.50 (0-8049-0003-5, CL-3) Airmont.

Red Badge of Courage. Stephen Crane. LC 91-58649. (Literary Classics Ser.). 128p. 1992. 5.98 (1-56138-115-2) Courage Bks.

Red Badge of Courage. Stephen Crane. LC 95-77839. (Wishbone Classics Ser.: No. 10). 128p. (J). (gr. 3-7). 1996. mass mkt. 3.99 (0-06-106497-1, Harp PBks) HarpC.

*Red Badge of Courage. Stephen Crane. 1997. pap. 3.95 (0-451-52647-3, Sig Classics) NAL-Dutton.

Red Badge of Courage. Stephen Crane. (J). (gr. 4-7). 1993. pap. 4.95 (0-8114-6837-2) Raintree Steck-V.

Red Badge of Courage. Stephen Crane. (C). 1951. pap. write for info. (0-318-54362-1, T45) Random.

Red Badge of Courage. Stephen Crane. LC 42-36053. 251p. 1980. 10.95 (0-394-60493-8, Modern Lib); pap. 4.00 (0-685-03394-5, Modern Lib) Random.

Red Badge of Courage. Stephen Crane. LC 90-50273. (Vintage-Library of America Ser.). 160p. 1990. pap. 9.50 (0-679-73223-3, Vin) Random.

Red Badge of Courage. Stephen Crane. 252p. 1993. 13.50 (0-679-60044-2, Modern Lib) Random.

Red Badge of Courage. Stephen Crane. 1997. pap. 2.95 (0-89375-606-7) Troll Communs.

Red Badge of Courage. Stephen Crane. Ed. by Henry Binder. 208p. 1987. pap. 3.50 (0-380-70432-3) Avon.

Red Badge of Courage. Stephen Crane. 160p. (gr. 7-12). 1981. pap. 2.95 (0-553-21011-4, Bantam Classics) Bantam.

Red Badge of Courage. Stephen Crane. Ed. by Malcom Bradbury. 140p. 1993. pap. 1.95 (0-460-87381-4, Everyman's Classic Lib) C E Tuttle.

Red Badge of Courage. Stephen Crane. 112p. 1990. pap. 1.00 (0-486-26465-3) Dover.

Red Badge of Courage. Stephen Crane. 1951. pap. text ed. write for info. (0-07-555608-1) McGraw.

Red Badge of Courage. Stephen Crane. Ed. by Irwin Shapiro. LC 73-75464. (Now Age Illustrated Ser.). (Illus.). 64p. (J). (gr. 5-10). 1973. pap. 2.95 (0-88301-101-8) Pendulum Pr.

Red Badge of Courage. Stephen Crane. Ed. by Harry Shefter. (Enriched Classics Edition Ser.). 224p. mass mkt. 4.99 (0-671-74081-4, WSP) PB.

Red Badge of Courage. Stephen Crane. LC 81-2611. (Short Classics Ser.). (Illus.). 48p. (J). (gr. 4 up). 1983. lib. bdg. 24.26 (0-8172-1670-7) Raintree Steck-V.

Red Badge of Courage. Stephen Crane. (Portland House Illustrated Classics Ser.). (Illus.). 224p. (YA). 1991. 9.99 (0-517-66844-0) Random Hse Value.

Red Badge of Courage. Stephen Crane. (YA). 1990. pap. 2.50 (0-8125-0479-8) Tor Bks.

*Red Badge of Courage. Stephen Crane. LC 97-12339. 1997. 22.95 (1-56000-528-9) Transaction Pubs.

Red Badge of Courage. Stephen Crane. (Puffin Classics Ser.). 224p. (YA). (gr. 5 up). 1995. pap. 3.99 (0-14-036710-1) Puffin Bks.

Red Badge of Courage. Stephen Crane. 1995. pap. 16.95 (0-7871-0421-3, Dove Bks) Dove Audio.

Red Badge of Courage. Stephen Crane. 1996. mass mkt. 5.99 (0-671-00275-9) PB.

*Red Badge of Courage. Stephen Crane. (Illustrated Classics Collection 1). 64p. 1994. pap. 4.95 (0-7854-0669-7, 40352) Am Guidance.

*Red Badge of Courage. Stephen Crane. Ed. by Joshua Hanft. (Great Illustrated Classics Ser.: Vol. 27). (Illus.). 240p. (J). (gr. 3-6). 1993. 9.95 (0-86611-978-7) Playmore Inc.

Red Badge of Courage. Created by Harcourt Brace Staff. 1990. student ed., teacher ed., pap. 22.75 (0-15-348532-9, Harp PBks) HarpC.

Red Badge of Courage. Created by Harcourt Brace Staff. 1990. student ed., pap. 10.00 (0-15-348533-7) HR&W Schl Div.

Red Badge of Courage. Kathryn S. Miller. (Orig.). (YA). 1995. pap. 5.50 (0-87602-336-7) Anchorage.

Red Badge of Courage. large type ed. Stephen Crane. reprint ed. 10.00 (0-89064-053-X) NAVH.

Red Badge of Courage. rev. ed. Stephen Crane. Ed. by Robert J. Dixson. (American Classics Ser.: Bk. 10). (gr. 9 up). 1987. pap. text ed. 5.75 (0-13-024605-0, 18129); audio 65.00 (0-13-024795-2, 58235) Prentice ESL.

*Red Badge of Courage. unabridged ed. Stephen Crane. 135p. 1997. reprint ed. pap. 14.95 (1-57002-051-5) Univ Publng Hse.

Red Badge of Courage. 3rd ed. Stephen Crane. Ed. by Donald Pizer. LC 93-9918. (Critical Text Ser.). (C). 1993. pap. text ed. 9.95 (0-393-96430-2) Norton.

Red Badge of Courage. Stephen Crane. LC 67-26616. 1967. reprint ed. 40.00 (0-8201-1010-8) Schol Facsimiles.

Red Badge of Courage. Stephen Crane. 180p. (YA). (gr. 7-12). 1972. reprint ed. pap. 2.25 (0-590-02117-6) Scholastic Inc.

Red Badge of Courage. Stephen Crane. (Works of Stephen Crane Ser.). 1990. reprint ed. lib. bdg. 79.00 (0-7812-2426-8) Rprt Serv.

Red Badge of Courage: A Facsimile of the Manuscript. limited ed. Ed. by Fredson Bowers. 1972. boxed 200.00 (0-910971-28-5) Bruccoli.

Red Badge of Courage: A Study Guide. Mary Medland. (Novel-Ties Ser.). (YA). (gr. 9-12). 1990. pap. text ed. 15.95 (0-88122-414-6) Lrn Links.

Red Badge of Courage: An Episode of the American Civil War. Stephen Crane. 1993. write for info. (0-318-69700-9, Modern Lib) Random.

Red Badge of Courage: An Episode of the American Civil War. Stephen Crane. (American Library). 162p. 1983. pap. 2.95 (0-14-039021-9, Penguin Classics) Viking Penguin.

Red Badge of Courage: An Historically Annotated Edition. Stephen Crane. Ed. by Charles J. LaRocca. LC 95-22834. (Illus.). 212p. 1995. pap. 18.00 (0-935796-68-1) Purple Mnt Pr.

Red Badge of Courage: Redefining the Hero. Donald B. Gibson. (Twayne's Masterwork Studies: No. 15). 112p. (C). 1988. 23.95 (0-8057-7961-2, Twayne); pap. 13.95 (0-8057-8014-9, Twayne) Scribnrs Ref.

Red Badge of Courage: Student Activity Book. Marcia Sohl & Gerald Dackerman. (Now Age Illustrated Ser.). (Illus.). 16p. (J). (gr. 4-10). 1976. pap. 1.25 (0-88301-184-0) Pendulum Pr.

Red Badge of Courage & Other Stories. Stephen Crane & Pascal Covici. Ed. by Pascal Covici. 304p. 1991. pap. 8.95 (0-14-039081-2, Penguin Classics) Viking Penguin.

Red Badge of Courage & Other Stories. Stephen Crane. 224p. 1960. pap. 3.95 (0-451-52368-7, CW1592, Sig Classics) NAL-Dutton.

Red Badge of Courage & Other Writings. Stephen Crane. Ed. by Richard Chase. (YA). (gr. 9 up). 1972. pap. 11.56 (0-395-05143-6, RivEd) HM.

Red Badge of Courage & Selected Prose & Poetry. 3rd ed. Stephen Crane. Ed. by William M. Gibson. 652p. (C). 1968. pap. text ed. 22.50 (0-03-073360-X) HB Coll Pubs.

Red Badge of Courage & Selected Stories. Stephen Crane. 224p. 1987. reprint ed. lib. bdg. 21.95 (0-89966-620-5) Buccaneer Bks.

Red Badge of Courage (Crane) Dixler. (Book Notes Ser.). (C). 1984. pap. 3.50 (0-8120-3438-4) Barron.

Red Badge of Courage Notes. J. M. Lybyer. 1994. pap. 3.75 (0-8220-1120-4) Cliffs.

*Red Badge of Courage Readalong. Stephen Crane. (Illustrated Classics Collection 1). 64p. 1994. pap. 14.95 incl. audio (0-7854-0710-3, 40354) Am Guidance.

Red Baker. Robert Ward. Ed. by Jane Rosenman. 1986. mass mkt. 5.95 (0-671-61747-8, WSP) PB.

Red Ball. Joanna Yardley. Ed. by Jane Yolen. (Illus.). 32p. (J). (ps-3). 1991. 15.00 (0-15-200894-2, J Yolen Bks) HarBrace.

Red Balloon. Albert Lamorisse. (Classic Short Stories Ser.). 32p. (J). (gr. 6). 1990. lib. bdg. 13.95 (0-88682-304-8) Creative Ed.

Red Balloon. Albert Lamorisse. LC 57-9229. (Illus.). 45p. (J). (ps-3). 1967. 16.95 (0-385-00343-9) Doubleday.

Red Balloon. Albert Lamorisse. LC 57-9229. (Illus.). 45p. (J). (ps-3). 1978. pap. 10.95 (0-385-14297-8) Doubleday.

*Red Balloons Fly High. Cindy D. Holms. LC 96-79860. (Illus.). 24p. (Orig.). (J). 1997. pap. 8.95 (1-57543-023-1) Mar Co Prods.

Red Bandanna & Carcajou's Trail. Max Brand. (Special Double Action Western Ser.: No. 15). 1991. pap. 3.50 (0-8125-1314-2) Tor Bks.

Red Bank, NJ. Randall Gabrielan. (Images of America Ser.). 1995. pap. 16.99 (0-7524-0216-1, Arcdia) Chalford.

Red Bank, NJ, Vol. II. Randall Gabrielan. (Images of America Ser.). 1996. pap. 16.99 (0-7524-0402-4, Arcdia) Chalford.

Red Barbarian. large type ed. Margaret Gaan. 633p. 1989. 25.99 (0-7089-1958-8) Ulverscroft.

Red Baron: Manfred von Richthofen. William Haiber & Robert Haiber. LC 91-921821. (World War I Aces Ser.). (Illus.). 96p. (Orig.). 1992. per. 19.99 (0-944089-10-0) Info Devels.

*Red Baron II: The Official Strategy Guide. Prima Publishing Temp Staff. 240p. 1997. pap. 19.99 (0-7615-0948-8) Prima Pub.

*Red Baron's Last Flight: A Mystery Investigated. Norman Franks & Alan Bennett. (Illus.). 128p. 1998. 24.95 (1-898697-75-2, Pub. by Grub St Pubns UK) Seven Hills Bk.

Red Barrister: A Biography of Ted Laurie. Peter S. Cook. 1995. pap. text ed. 29.95 (1-86324-414-X, Pub. by LaTrobe Univ AT) Intl Spec Bk.

Red Barry. Will Gould. Ed. by Richard Marschall. (Illus.). 104p. 1989. pap. 9.95 (0-930193-37-7) Fantagraph Bks.

Red Beans. Victor H. Cruz. LC 91-25377. 142p. (Orig.). 1991. pap. 11.95 (0-918273-91-9) Coffee Hse.

Red Beans & Rice see Phonics Is My Way Series

*Red Beans & Rice & Other Rock 'n Roll Recipes. Johnny Otis. LC 97-17359. (Illus.). 128p. (Orig.). 1997. pap. 16.00 (0-7649-0361-6, A902) Pomegranate Calif.

Red Beret: The Story of the Parachute Regiment at War 1940-45. 19th ed. Hilary Saunders. (Airborne Ser.). 336p. 1985. 29.95 (0-89839-087-7) Battery Pr.

Red Bikini Dream. Max Martinez. LC 89-35416. 144p. (Orig.). 1990. pap. 9.50 (1-55885-001-5) Arte Publico.

Red Bird. Barbara Mitchell. LC 95-9664. (Illus.). 32p. (J). (gr. k-4). 1996. 16.00 (0-688-10859-8); lib. bdg. 15.93 (0-688-10860-1) Lothrop.

*Red Bird: A Novel. Stephanie G. Whitson. LC 97-14039. (Prairie Winds: 3). 288p. 1997. pap. 10.99 (0-7852-7484-7, J Thoma Bks) Nelson.

Red Blackboard: An American Teacher in China. Ruth Koenig. LC 93-37123. 256p. 1994. 16.95 (0-913720-88-7) Beil.

Red Bleeds the Sun. Anne Drybrough. (C). 1990. 45.00 (0-7223-2551-7, Pub. by A H S Ltd UK) St Mut.

*Red Blood. Jack Forbes. 300p. (Orig.). 1997. pap. 15.95 (0-919441-65-3, Pub. by Theytus Bks Ltd CN) Orca Bk Pubs.

Red Blood & Black Ink: The Story of Journalism in the Old West. David Dary. 1998. 30.00 (0-679-44655-9) Knopf.

Red Blood Cell Aging. Ed. by M. Magnani & A. De Flora. (Advances in Experimental Medicine & Biology Ser.). (Illus.). 380p. 1991. 120.00 (0-306-44021-0, Plenum Pr) Plenum.

Red Blood Cell Membranes: Structure, Function, Clinical Implications. Agre & Parker. (Hematology Ser.: Vol. 11). 760p. 1989. 230.00 (0-8247-8022-1) Dekker.

Red Blood Cell Substitutes. Chang & Geyer. 736p. 1988. 175.00 (0-8247-8027-2) Dekker.

*Red Blood Cell Substitutes: Basic Principles & Applications. Ed. by Rudolph et al. 496p. 1997. write for info. (0-8247-0058-9) Dekker.

Red Blood Cells As Carriers for Drugs. Ed. by DeLoach et al. (Current Studies in Hematology & Blood Transfusion: No. 51). (Illus.). viii, 162p. 1985. 83.25 (3-8055-3940-1) S Karger.

Red Blood Cells As Carriers for Drugs: Potential Therapeutic Applications. Ed. by C. Ropars et al. (Illus.). 272p. 1987. 120.00 (0-08-036137-4, Pergamon Pr) Elsevier.

Red Blue & Yellow Yarn. Miriam Kosman. LC 95-79439. (Illus.). 32p. (J). (gr. k-1). 1996. 9.95 (0-922613-78-8) Hachai Pubns.

Red, Blue, Yellow Shoe. Tana Hoban. LC 86-3095. (Illus.). 12p. (J). (ps). 1986. pap. 4.95 (0-688-06563-5) Greenwillow.

Red Bluff Review Vol. 1: A Journal of the Sense of Place on the Eastern Shore. Ed. by Robbie Wolff & Sonny Brewer. (Illus.). 72p. 1995. 29.00 (0-9648891-0-2) Wolff Pubng.

Red Book. Abbeville Press Staff. 1994. 10.95 (1-55859-915-0) Abbeville Pr.

Red Book: The Hanrahan Case Against Merck, Sharp & Dohme. Jerry O'Callaghan. (Illus.). 228p. (Orig.). 1992. pap. 15.95 (1-85371-167-5, Pub. by Poolbeg Pr IE) Dufour.

Red Book see Miquon Math Lab Series

Red Book of Appin. Ethan A. Hitchcock. 17.95 (0-89314-413-4) Philos Res.

*Red Book of Mathematical Problems. unabridged ed. Kenneth S. Williams & Kenneth Hardy. LC 96-43820. 192p. 1996. reprint ed. pap. text ed. 6.95 (0-486-69415-1) Dover.

Red Book of the Exchequer, 3 vols. Ed. by Hubert Hall. (Rolls Ser.: No. 99). 1974. reprint ed. 300.00 (0-8115-1178-2) Periodicals Srv.

Red Book of Varieties & Schemes. D. Mumford. (Lecture Notes in Mathematics Ser.: Vol. 1358). v, 309p. 1996. 52.95 (0-387-50497-4) Spr-Verlag.

Red Book on Transportation of Hazardous Materials. 2nd ed. Lawrence W. Bierlein. LC 86-32558. 800p. 1988. text ed. 135.95 (0-442-21044-2) Van Nos Reinhold.

*Red Book Update. 101th rev. ed. Date not set. pap. text ed. 99.00 (1-56363-237-3) Med Econ.

Red Book, 1994. Heidi M. Garrett. 1994. write for info. (1-56363-068-0) Med Econ.

Red Books, Green Hills: The Impact of Economic Reform on Restoration Ecology in the Midlands of Northern Vietnam. Ed. by Le T. Cuc et al. 1995. write for info. (0-86638-179-1) EW Ctr HI.

Red Books Service: (Does Not Include the International Volume) Ed. by National Register Publishing Co. Staff. 1996. 1,039.95 (0-87217-318-6) Natl Register.

*Red Boots for Christmas. Adapted by Carol Greene. 32p. (J). (ps-3). 1995. 5.99 (0-570-04787-0, 56-1807) Concordia.

Red Bows on White Lambs. Diana J. Lamoreux. (Illus.). 128p. 1994. pap. 9.95 (1-881576-40-X) Providence Hse.

Red Branch. Morgan Llywelyn. 528p. 1990. mass mkt. 5.95 (0-8041-0591-X) Ivy Books.

Red Bread: Collectivization in a Russian Village. Maurice Hindus. LC 88-45100. (Illus.). 392p. (Orig.). 1988. reprint ed. 29.95 (0-253-34953-2); reprint ed. pap. 13.95 (0-253-20485-2, MB-485) Ind U Pr.

Red Brick Three Flat. Henry Kranz. 72p. (Orig.). 1985. pap. 3.95 (0-942582-09-8) Erie St Pr.

Red Bride. Christopher Fowler. 368p. 1994. 4.99 (0-451-45293-3, ROC) NAL-Dutton.

*Red Brigades. Michael Roach. 1996. mass mkt. 4.99 (1-55197-345-6, Pub. by Comnwlth Pub CN) Partners Pubs Grp.

Red Brigades: The Story of Italian Terrorism. Robert C. Meade, Jr. 313p. 1989. text ed. 29.95 (0-312-03593-4) St Martin.

Red Brother. R. Ray Baker. (J). 1927. 12.50 (0-911586-03-2) Wahr.

Red Brotherhood at War. rev. ed. Grant Evans & Kelvin Rowley. 320p. (C). 1990. pap. text ed. 19.00 (0-86091-501-8, A4512, Pub. by Vrso UK) Norton.

Red Bud Women-Four Dramatic Episodes. Mark Odea. LC 76-40391. (One-Act Plays in Reprint Ser.). 1976. 20.00 (0-8486-2006-2) Roth Pub Inc.

Red Buffalo. large type ed. Hank Mitchum. (Nightingale Series Large Print Bks.). 300p. 1992. pap. 14.95 (0-8161-5322-1, GK Hall) Thorndike Pr.

Red Cabin Cookbook. Pat Harris. (Illus.). 128p. (Orig.). 1981. pap. 8.95 (0-939688-05-0) Directed Media.

Red Calypso. Geoffrey Wagner. 1988. pap. 12.95 (0-89526-773-X) Regnery Pub.

Red Camp. Debra Diaz. LC 96-16936. 1996. pap. 11.95 (1-55885-169-0) Arte Publico.

Red Cap. G. Clifton Wisler. 160p. (J). (gr. 5-9). 1991. pap. 15.99 (0-525-67337-7, Lodestar Bks) Dutton Child Bks.

Red Cap. G. Clifton Wisler. 176p. (J). (gr. 5 up). 1994. pap. 3.99 (0-14-036936-8) Puffin Bks.

Red Capitalism: An Analysis of the Navajo Economy. Kent Gilbreath. LC 72-12547. 167p. reprint ed. pap. 47.60 (0-317-29296-X, 2055512) Bks Demand.

*Red Capitalism in South China. George C. Lin. (Urbanization in Asia Ser.). 256p. 1997. 75.00 (0-7748-0616-8, Pub. by U BC Pr) U of Wash Pr.

Red Captain: The Life of Hugo O'Conor, Commandant Inspector of the Interior Provinces of New Spain. Mark Santiago. LC 94-29068. (Museum Monograph: No. 9). 1994. pap. 15.95 (0-910037-33-7) AZ Hist Soc.

Red Card. Richard Hoyt. 256p. 1995. 4.99 (0-8125-3096-9) Forge NYC.

Red Cat, White Cat: China & the Contradictions of "Market Socialism" Robert Weil. 288p. (C). 1996. text ed. 32.00 (0-85345-968-1); pap. text ed. 16.00 (0-85345-967-3) Monthly Rev.

*Red Caterpillar on College Street. Afua Cooper. (Illus.). 32p. (J). (ps-3). Date not set. pap. 6.95 (0-920813-87-9, Pub. by Sister Vision CN) LPC InBook.

An Asterisk (*) at the beginning of an entry indicates that the title is appearing in BIP for the first time.

R

Red Cavalry: A Critical Companion. Ed. by Charles Rougle. LC 96-8498. (Northwestern/Aatseel Critical Companions To Russian Literature Ser.). 180p. (C). 1996. pap. text ed. 14.95 (0-8101-1213-2) Northwestern U Pr.

Red Cell. Richard Marcinko & John Weisman. (Rogue Warrior Ser.). 1994. 22.00 (0-671-79956-8) PB.

Red Cell. Richard Marcinko & John Weisman. Ed. by Judith Regan & Paul McCarthy. (Rogue Warrior Ser.: No. 2). 416p. 1994. reprint ed. mass mkt. 5.99 (0-671-79957-6) PB.

Red Cell: Production, Metabolism, Destruction, Normal & Abnormal. rev. ed. John W. Harris & Robert Kellermeyer. (Commonwealth Fund Publications). 815p. 1970. pap. 24.50 (0-674-75102-7) HUP.

Red Cell Deformability & Filterability. Ed. by John A. Dormandy. (Developments in Hematology & Immunology Ser.). 1983. lib. bdg. 117.50 (0-89838-578-4) Kluwer Ac.

Red Cell Manual. 7th ed. Robert S. Hillman. (Illus.). 190p. (C). 1996. pap. text ed. 23.95 (0-8036-0145-X) Davis Co.

Red Cell Membrane: A Model for Solute Transport. Ed. by Beat U. Raess & G. Tunnicliff. LC 89-15438. (Contemporary Biomedicine Ser.: Vol. 10). (Illus.). 496p. 1990. 99.50 (0-89603-158-6) Humana.

Red Cell Membranes. Ed. by Stephen B. Shohet & Narla Mahandas. (Methods in Hematology Ser.: Vol. 19). (Illus.). 328p. 1988. text ed. 75.00 (0-443-08352-5) Churchill.

Red Cell Membranes. fac. ed. Ed. by Stephen B. Shohet & Narla Mohandas. LC 87-37512. (Methods in Hematology Ser.: No. 19). (Illus.). 338p. 1988. reprint ed. pap. 91.30 (0-7837-7895-3, 2047651) Bks Demand.

Red Cell Shape: Physiology, Pathology, Ultrastructure. Ed. by M. Bessis et al. LC 73-77351. (Illus.). 180p. 1973. 45.00 (0-387-06257-2) Spr-Verlag.

***Red Cell Transfusion: A Practical Guide.** Ed. by Marion E. Reid & Sandra J. Nance. (Contemporary Hematology Ser.). (Illus.). 232p. 1997. 99.50 (0-89603-412-7) Humana.

Red Chameleon. Stuart M. Kaminsky. 208p. 1989. mass mkt. 4.99 (0-8041-0465-4) Ivy Books.

Red Child, White Child: The Strange Disappearance of Casper Partridge. William C. Haygood. (Wisconsin Stories Ser.). (Illus.). 146p. 1979. pap. 1.75 (0-87020-185-9) State Hist Soc Wis.

***Red Chile Bible: Southwest Classic & Gourmet Recipes.** LC 97-3648. 180p. (Orig.). 1997. pap. 12.95 (0-940666-93-6) Clear Light.

Red China Blues. Jan Wong. 336p. 1996. 32.95 (0-385-25490-3) Doubleday.

Red China Blues: My Long March from Mao to Now. Jan Wong. (Illus.). 416p. 1996. 23.95 (0-385-47679-5, Anchor NY) Doubleday.

***Red China Blues: My Long March from Mao to Now.** Jan Wong. 1997. pap. 14.95 (0-385-48232-9, Anchor NY) Doubleday.

Red China in Prophecy. Gordon Lindsay. (Prophecy Ser.). 1972. per. 2.25 (0-89985-059-6) Christ for the Nations.

Red China Today: The Other Side of the River. rev. ed. Edgar R. Snow. (Illus.). 1971. 25.00 (0-394-46261-0) Random.

Red China's Fighting Hordes: A Realistic Account of the Chinese Communist Army by a U. S. Army Officer. Robert B. Rigg. LC 70-138177. (Illus.). 378p. 1971. reprint ed. text ed. 35.00 (0-8371-5634-3, RIRC, Greenwood Pr) Greenwood.

Red Christmas. Patrick Ruell. 184p. 1995. 18.50 (0-7451-8671-8, Black Dagger) Chivers N Amer.

Red Cigarette: A Book of Poetry & Visual Imagery. J. Vincent-Walters. LC 95-83121. 72p. 1996. pap. 9.95 (0-9649547-0-2) Amalgamate.

Red Circle. Michael A. Stackpole. (Illus.). 1987. 5.95 (0-940244-21-7) Flying Buffalo.

Red City, Blue Period: Social Movements in Picasso's Barcelona. Temma Kaplan. (C). 1992. 30.00 (0-520-07507-2) U CA Pr.

Red City, Blue Period: Social Movements in Picasso's Barcelona. Temma Kaplan. LC 91-4686. (C). 1993. pap. 15.00 (0-520-08440-3) U CA Pr.

Red Claw: Raising the Giant Australian Crayfish. Don R. Wilson. (Illus.). 52p. (Orig.). 1995. pap. 8.95 (0-9631526-3-7) Atlas Pubns.

Red Clay. Linda Hogan. 96p. 1991. pap. 9.95 (0-912678-83-6) Greenfld Rev Lit.

Red Clay. Myldred F. Hutchins. LC 88-17794. (Illus.). 132p. 1988. 7.95 (0-87797-075-0) Cherokee.

Red Clay, Pink Cadillacs, & White Gold: The Kaolin Chalk Wars. Charles Seabrook & Marcy Louza. 280p. 1995. 20.00 (1-56352-229-2) Longstreet Pr Inc.

***Red Clay Survey: Fifth Biennial Exhibition of Contemporary Southern Art.** (Illus.). 68p. 1996. pap. 15.00 (1-885820-03-8) Huntsville.

Red Clay Survey: Fourth Biennial Exhibition of Contemporary Southern Art. Huntsville Museum of Art Staff. 60p. 1994. pap. text ed. 15.00 (1-885820-00-3) Huntsville.

Red Cloud: Sioux Warrior. William R. Sanford. LC 93-42256. (Native American Leaders of the Wild West Ser.). (Illus.). 48p. (J). (gr. 4-10). 1994. lib. bdg. 14.95 (0-89490-513-9) Enslow Pubs.

***Red Cloud: Warrior-Statesman of the Lakota Sioux.** Robert W. Larson. LC 96-30793. (Oklahoma Western Biographies Ser.: Vol. 13). 352p. 1997. 24.95 (0-8061-2930-1) U of Okla Pr.

Red Cloud & the Sioux Problem. James C. Olson. LC 65-10048. (Illus.). xii, 401p. 1965. reprint ed. pap. 12.50 (0-8032-5817-8, Bison Books) U of Nebr Pr.

Red Cloud Revenge. Terry C. Johnston. 1991. mass mkt. 5.99 (0-312-92733-9) Tor Bks.

Red Cloud: Sioux War Chief see North American Indians of Achievement

Red Cloud: Sioux War Chief see North Americans Indians of Achievement

Red Cloud's Folk: A History of the Oglala Sioux Indians. George E. Hyde. LC 76-360988. (Civilization of the American Indian Ser.: Vol. 15). (Illus.). 352p. (Orig.). 1979. pap. 15.95 (0-8061-1520-3) U of Okla Pr.

Red Cloud's Revenge. William Hezlep. LC 94-19077. 22p. (Orig.). (J). (gr. 2 up). 1994. pap. 5.00 (0-88734-416-X) Players Pr.

Red Clover Science. N. L. Taylor & K. H. Quesenberry. LC 95-51138. 1996. lib. bdg. 107.00 (0-7923-3887-1) Kluwer Ac.

Red Coat. limited ed. Jean McGarry. (Illus.). 24p. 1990. 35.00 (0-9623585-0-9) Flockophobic Pr.

Red Coat: And Other Poems. Linda Anfuso. 16p. 1995. pap. 3.00 (1-57433-013-6) Interset Pr.

Red Cocaine: The Drugging of America. Joseph D. Douglass, Jr. (Illus.). 304p. 1990. 19.95 (0-9626646-0-X) Soundview Pubns.

***Red Colt.** Julie M. Caracci. (Illus.). 70p. (Orig.). (YA). (gr. 5-6). 1996. pap. 4.50 (1-57502-265-6, PO949) Morris Pubng.

Red Comb. Fernando Pico. Tr. by Argentina Palacios from SPA. LC 94-9832. (Illus.). 48p. (J). (gr. k-4). 1996. pap. 14.95 (0-8167-3539-5) BrdgeWater.

Red Comb. Fernando Pico. Tr. by Argentina Palacios from SPA. LC 94-9832. (Illus.). 48p. (J). (gr. k-4). 1995. pap. 4.95 (0-8167-3540-9, Troll Medallion) Troll Communs.

Red Corvette. Robert S. Reid. 256p. 1992. 18.95 (0-88184-803-4) Carroll & Graf.

Red Corvette. Robert S. Reid. 256p. 1993. pap. 4.50 (0-88184-990-1) Carroll & Graf.

Red Cottage. Dennis Finnell. 1994. pap. 9.95 (0-08-082668-7, Pergamon Pr) Elsevier.

Red Cottage. Dennis Finnell. LC 90-43308. 96p. 1991. pap. 9.95 (0-87023-668-7); lib. bdg. 20.00 (0-87023-667-9) U of Mass Pr.

Red Cover, Bk. B. (Big Christmas Coloring & Activity Ser.). (Illus.). 160p. (Orig.). (J). (gr. k-2). 1994. pap. 4.95 (1-56144-511-8, Honey Bear Bks) Modern Pub NYC.

Red Creek: A Requiem. Margaret Robison. (Illus.). (Orig.). 1992. pap. 10.00 (0-941895-08-4) Amherst Wri Art.

Red Cross - Goals & Roles: Index of Actions & Progress. Sally Z. Hollinder. LC 92-34650. 1992. 44.50 (1-55914-960-4); pap. 39.50 (1-55914-961-2) ABBE Pubs Assn.

Red Cross, A Story of The. Clara Barton. (Airmont Classics Ser.). (Illus.). (J). (gr. 4 up). 1968. mass mkt. 1.50 (0-8049-0170-8, CL-170) Airmont.

Red Cross & the Red Crescent. Michael Pollard. LC 93-26383. (Organizations That Help the World Ser.). 64p. (J). 1994. lib. bdg. 13.95 (0-02-774720-4, New Dscvry Bks) Silver Burdett Pr.

Red Cross & the Red Crescent. Michael Pollard. LC 93-26383. (Organizations That Help the World Ser.). 64p. (J). 1994. pap. 7.95 (0-382-24738-8, New Dscvry Bks) Silver Burdett Pr.

Red Cross, Black Eagle: A Biography of Albania's American School. Joan F. Kontos. (East European Monographs: No. 75). 214p. 1981. text ed. 46.00 (0-914710-69-9) East Eur Monographs.

Red Cross/Red Crescent. Leslie Burger & Debra L. Rahm. LC 96-384. (J). 1996. 21.50 (0-8225-2698-0, Lerner Publctns) Lerner Group.

Red Crown. P. T. Deutermann. Date not set. pap. write for info. (0-451-18304-5, Sig) NAL-Dutton.

Red-Crowned Crane. Edward Voeller. LC 89-11718. (Remarkable Animals Ser.). (Illus.). 60p. (J). (gr. 3 up). 1990. lib. bdg. 13.95 (0-87518-417-0, Dillon Silver Burdett) Silver Burdett Pr.

***Red Crystal.** Clare Francis. 416p. 1986. pap. 16.95 (0-330-29384-2, Pub. by Pan Books UK) Trans-Atl Phila.

***Red Crystal.** Clare Francis. Date not set. write for info. (0-688-06375-6) Morrow.

Red Cuentitos Mios. (Rimas y Risas Red Ser.). (Illus.). 65p. (Orig.). (SPA.). (J). (gr. k-3). 1990. pap. text ed. 6.00 (0-917837-58-4) Hampton-Brown.

Red Cuentitos Mios Twenty-Pack, Set. (Rimas y Risas Red Ser.). (Illus.). 65p. (Orig.). (SPA.). (J). (gr. k-3). 1990. pap. text ed. 96.00 (0-917837-65-7) Hampton-Brown.

Red Dancing Shoes. Denise L. Patrick. LC 91-32666. (Illus.). 32p. (J). (ps up). 1993. 16.00 (0-688-10392-8, Tambourine Bks); lib. bdg. 15.93 (0-688-10393-6, Tambourine Bks) Morrow.

Red Danube. Carl A. Posey. 352p. 1988. reprint ed. pap. 3.95 (0-373-97082-X) Harlequin Bks.

Red Data Birds in Britain: Action for Rare, Threatened & Important Species. L. A. Batten et al. 349p. 1991. text ed. 37.00 (0-85661-056-9, 784656, Pub. by Poyser UK) Acad Pr.

Red Dawn: Present Signs/Terminal Future? Guy Elliott. LC 95-83630. 98p. (Orig.). 1996. pap. 9.95 (0-9649721-0-7) StarCross.

Red Days. Stephen Kimball. 384p. 1993. pap. 4.99 (0-451-17683-9, Sig) NAL-Dutton.

Red Days. Stephen Kimball. Date not set. pap. write for info. (0-525-93582-7) NAL-Dutton.

Red Death. P. N. Elrod. 1993. mass mkt. 4.99 (0-441-71094-8) Ace Bks.

***Red Death.** Walter Mosley. (An Easy Rawlins Mystery Ser.). 1997. mass mkt. 3.99 (0-671-01006-9, Pocket Books) PB.

Red Death. Walter Mosley. 1991. 19.95 (0-393-02998-0) Norton.

Red Death. large type ed. Walter Mosley. LC 93-18588. 1993. lib. bdg. 21.95 (1-56054-723-5) Thorndike Pr.

Red Death. Walter Mosley. Ed. by Jane Chelius. 256p. reprint ed. mass mkt. 5.99 (0-671-74989-7) PB.

Red Decade: The Stalinist Penetration of America. Eugene Lyons. 1980. reprint ed. lib. bdg. 75.00 (0-87700-313-0) Revisionist Pr.

Red Deer. Floyce Alexander. LC 79-26383. 75p. 1982. pap. 4.95 (0-934332-21-5) LEpervier Pr.

Red Deer: An Illustrated History. Michael Dawe. (Illus.). 1989. 27.95 (0-89781-261-1) Am Historical Pr.

Red Deer: Behavior & Ecology of Two Sexes. T. H. Clutton-Brock et al. LC 81-22025. (Wildlife Behavior & Ecology Ser.). (Illus.). 400p. (C). 1982. pap. text ed. 26.00 (0-226-11057-5) U Ch Pr.

Red Detachment of Women see Supplementary Readers for Intermediate Chinese Reader

Red Devil Battery Sign. Tennessee Williams. LC 87-15212. 96p. 1988. 14.95 (0-8112-1046-4); pap. 6.95 (0-8112-1047-2, NDP650) New Directions.

Red Devil Dream Book. Zonite. 4.00 (0-685-26808-X) Wehman.

***Red Devil of the Range.** Max Brand. 320p. 1996. reprint ed. mass mkt. 4.50 (0-8439-4122-7) Dorchester Pub Co.

Red Diamond Regiment: The 17th Maine Infantry 1862-1865. William B. Jordon, Jr. LC 95-46172. (Illus.). 437p. (C). 1996. 30.00 (0-942597-72-9) White Mane Pub.

Red Diaper Baby: Three Comic Monologues. Josh Kornbluth. 192p. (Orig.). 1996. pap. 12.95 (1-56279-087-0) Mercury Hse Inc.

Red Dice. Christopher Pike. (Last Vampire Ser.: Vol. 3). (YA). (gr. 9 up). 1995. 14.00 (0-671-87260-5, Archway); pap. 3.99 (0-671-87268-0, Archway) PB.

***Red Dirt: Growing up Okie.** Roxanne Dunbar-Ortiz. LC 97-13070. 1997. 25.00 (1-85984-856-7, Pub. by Verso UK) Routledge Chapman & Hall.

Red Dirt & Isinglass: A Wartime Biography of a Confederate Soldier. Henry V. McCrea. 578p. 1992. 31.95 (0-9646766-0-5) Chipola Pr.

Red-Dirt Jessie. Anna Myers. 107p. (YA). 1992. 13.95 (0-8027-8172-1) Walker & Co.

***Red-Dirt Jessie.** Anna Myers. LC 97-15220. (J). 1997. pap. 3.99 (0-14-038734-X, Puffin) Puffin Bks.

Red-Dirt Marijuana & Other Tastes. Terry Southern. 1990. pap. 9.95 (0-8065-1167-2, Citadel Pr) Carol Pub Group.

Red Dog. Bill Wallace. LC 86-46202. 192p. (J). (gr. 3-7). 1987. 15.95 (0-8234-0650-4) Holiday.

Red Dog. Bill Wallace. 176p. (J). (gr. 5 up). pap. 3.50 (0-671-70141-X, Archway) PB.

Red Dog, Blue Fly: Football Poems. Sharon B. Mathis. (Illus.). 32p. (J). (gr. 1-5). 1995. pap. 4.99 (0-14-054337-6) Puffin Bks.

***Red Doran: The Story of a Derryman.** John Doran & Joe Connolly. 240p. 9700. pap. 14.95 (0-85640-573-6, Pub. by Blackstaff Pr IE) Dufour.

***Red Dragon.** Thomas Harris. 352p. 1997. pap. 11.95 (0-385-31967-3) Doubleday.

***Red Dragon.** Thomas Harris. Date not set. mass mkt. 11.95 (0-385-31906-1) Doubleday.

Red Dragon. large type ed. Thomas Harris. 496p. 1984. 27.99 (0-7089-8169-0) Ulverscroft.

Red Dragon. Thomas Harris. 352p. 1991. reprint ed. lib. bdg. 24.95 (0-89966-877-1) Buccaneer Bks.

Red Dragon. Thomas Harris. 368p. 1990. reprint ed. mass mkt. 6.99 (0-440-20615-4) Dell.

Red Dragon: Grand Grimofre. Robert Blanchard. Ed. by Thor Templar. (Illus.). 325p. 1995. 75.00 (1-57179-055-1) Intern Guild ASRS.

Red Dragon: Le Dragon Rouge. Simon & Schuster Staff. (Magickal Manuscript Ser.). (Illus.). 128p. 1992. lib. bdg. 18.00 (0-939708-07-8) Magickal Childe.

Red Dragon & St. George's. Nicki J. Neilsen. (Illus.). 66p. 1983. pap. 7.50 (0-9607358-2-8) Fathom Pub.

Red Dragon & the Black Shirts: How Italy Found Her Soul, the True Story of the Fascisti Movement. Percival Phillips. 1982. lib. bdg. 69.95 (0-87700-349-1) Revisionist Pr.

Red Dragonfly on My Shoulder: Haiku. Sylvia Cassedy & Kunihiro Suetake. LC 91-18443. (Illus.). 32p. (J). (gr. k-5). 1992. lib. bdg. 14.89 (0-06-022625-0) HarpC Child Bks.

Red-Dressed Zionists: Symbols of Power in a Swazi Independent Church. Anders Fogelqvist. (Uppsala Research Reports in Cultural Anthropology). 212p. (Orig.). 1986. pap. text ed. 71.50 (91-506-0505-4, Pub. by Uppsala Universitet SW) Coronet Bks.

Red Drum: Poetry of the American West. Jane C. Coleman. 72p. (Orig.). 1994. pap. 9.95 (0-931271-28-2) Hi Plains Pr.

Red Dust. Zhang Ailian. (Illus.). 60p. (Orig.). 1988. pap. text ed. 10.95 (0-9620765-2-X) Victory Press.

Red Dust. Paul J. McAuley. 400p. 1995. mass mkt. 4.99 (0-380-77528-X, AvoNova) Avon.

Red Dust One: New Writing. F. W. Willetts et al. LC 78-127954. 180p. 1971. 5.25 (0-87376-016-6); pap. 3.00 (0-87376-017-4) Red Dust.

Red Dust Three: New Writing. Thomas Fallon et al. LC 72-12794. 1979. 8.95 (0-87376-026-3) Red Dust.

Red Dust Two: New Writing. Alan Burns et al. LC 72-127954. (Orig.). 1972. 5.25 (0-87376-019-0); pap. 3.00 (0-87376-020-4) Red Dust.

Red Dwarf, 2 vols. in 1. Grant Naylor. 432p. 1993. 10.98 (1-56865-049-3, GuildAmerica) Dblday Direct.

Red Dwarf: Better Than Life. Grant Naylor. 304p. (Orig.). 1993. pap. 5.99 (0-451-45231-3, ROC) NAL-Dutton.

Red Dwarf: Infinity Welcomes Careful Drivers. Grant Naylor. 304p. 1992. pap. 5.99 (0-451-45201-1, ROC) NAL-Dutton.

***Red Dwarf Programme Guide.** Chris Howarth & Steve Lyons. (Illus.). 304p. 1996. mass mkt. 5.95 (0-86369-682-1, Pub. by Virgin Pub UK) London Brdge.

***Red Dwarf Programme Guide.** 2nd rev. ed. Chris Howarth & Steve Lyons. (Virgin Ser.). 1997. mass mkt. 6.95 (0-7535-0103-1, Pub. by Virgin Pub UK) London Brdge.

Red Dyed Hair. Kostas Mourselas. Tr. by Fred A. Reed. (Modern Greek Writers Ser.). 431p. pap. 19.95 (960-04-0577-8, Pub. by Kedros Pubs GR) Paul & Co Pubs.

***Red Dyes: Cochineal, Madder & Murex Purple.** Gosta Sandberg. Ed. by Dawn Cusick. LC 96-44273. Orig. Title: Purpur Koshenill Krapp. 216p. 1997. 29.95 (1-887374-17-5) Lark Books.

Red Eagle: The Army in Polish Politics, 1944-1988. Andrew A. Michta. (Publication Ser.: No. 386). 270p. (C). 1989. 27.95 (0-8179-8861-0); pap. 18.95 (0-8179-8862-9) Hoover Inst Pr.

Red Eagle & the Wars with the Creek Indians of Alabama. George C. Eggleston. LC 76-43695. reprint ed. 34.50 (0-404-15528-6) AMS Pr.

Red Eagles. David Downing. 256p. 1989. reprint ed. pap. 4.50 (0-373-97097-8) Harlequin Bks.

Red Eagles of the Northwest: The Story of Chief Joseph & His People. Francis Haines. LC 76-43728. (Illus.). (C). reprint ed. 52.50 (0-404-15569-3) AMS Pr.

***Red-Eared Ghosts.** Vivien Alcock. (J). (gr. 5-9). 1997. 15.95 (0-614-28825-8) HM.

Red Eared Slider Turtles. Jordan Patterson. (Illus.). 64p. 1995. pap. text ed. 9.95 (0-7938-0253-9, RE109) TFH Pubns.

***Red-Eared Sliders.** (Herpetological Library). 6.00 (0-614-29986-1) Serpents Tale.

***Red Earth.** Chandra. 1997. pap. 14.95 (0-316-13293-4) Little.

***Red Earth: A Vietnam Warrior's Journey.** Philip H. Red Eagle. 1997. pap. text ed. 12.95 (0-930100-74-3) Holy Cow.

Red Earth: A Vietnamese Memoir of Life on a Colonial Rubber Plantation. Tran Tu Binh. Tr. by John Spragens. LC 84-20616. (Monographs in International Studies, Southeast Asia Ser.: No. 66). xii, 98p. 1985. pap. text ed. 11.00 (0-89680-119-5, Ohio U Ctr Intl) Ohio U Pr.

Red Earth: Agrarian Reform in Revolutionary Nicaragua. Van K. Collinsworth. LC 88-81879. (Illus.). 200p. (Orig.). 1988. pap. 10.95 (0-929797-00-0) Earth Review Pr.

Red Earth: Revolution in a Chinese Village. Stephen Endicott. 262p. (C). 1990. 25.00 (0-941533-99-9) New Amsterdam Bks.

Red Earth & Pouring Rain. Vikram Chandra. LC 94-48841. 560p. 1995. 24.95 (0-316-13276-4) Little.

Red Earth & Pouring Rain: A Novel. Vikram Chandra. LC 94-48841. 1995. write for info. (0-316-13266-7) Little.

Red Earth, White Earth. Will Weaver. 1987. pap. 4.50 (0-317-63701-0) PB.

Red Earth, White Lies: Native Americans & the Myth of Scientific Fact. Vine Deloria, Jr. 1995. 23.00 (0-684-80700-9) S&S Trade.

***Red Earth, White Lies: Native Americans & the Myth of Scientific Fact.** Vine DeLoria, Jr. LC 97-21689. 288p. 1997. reprint ed. pap. 16.95 (1-55591-388-1) Fulcrum Pub.

Red Eggs & Dragon Boats: Celebrating Chinese Festivals. Carol Stepanchuk. LC 93-85733. 48p. (J). (gr. 3-8). 1994. 16.95 (1-881896-08-0) Pacific View Pr.

Red Electrics: Southern Pacific's Oregon Interurban. Tom Dill & Walter R. Grande. Ed. by Pacific Fast Mail Staff. (Illus.). 136p. 1994. 39.50 (0-915713-28-4) Pac Fast Mail.

Red Eminence: A Biography of Mikhail A. Suslov. Serge P. Petroff. LC 87-81055. 273p. (C). 1988. 25.00 (0-940670-13-5) Kingston Pr.

Red Emma Speaks: An Emma Goldman Reader. 3rd ed. Emma Goldman. Ed. & Compiled by Alix K. Shulman. LC 95-21456. (Contemporary Studies in Philosophy & the Human Sciences Ser.). 470p. (C). 1996. pap. 19.95 (0-391-03952-0) Humanities.

***Red Empire.** 1991. 12.00 (1-55878-058-0) Game Designers.

Red Envelope. CarolAnn Russell. LC 85-9163. (University of Central Florida Contemporary Poetry Ser.). 94p. (Orig.). 1985. pap. 10.95 (0-8130-0828-X) U Press Fla.

Red Executive: A Study of the Organization Man in Russian Industry. David Granick. Ed. by Lewis A. Coser & Walter W. Powell. LC 79-6993. (Perennial Works in Sociology). (Illus.). 1980. reprint ed. lib. bdg. 29.95 (0-405-12094-X) Ayer.

Red Exodus: Finnish-American Emigration to Russia. Mayme Sevander. 232p. (Orig.). 1993. pap. 14.95 (1-887801-45-6) Trident MN.

Red Eye of Love. Arnold Weinstein. (Classics Ser.: No. 155). 100p. (Orig.). 1997. pap. 10.95 (1-55713-305-0) Sun & Moon CA.

Red-Eyed Monster. Pam Adams. (J). (gr. 4 up). 1985. 8.99 (0-85953-196-1) Childs Play.

Red-Eyes & Other Leaf Frogs. Jerry G. Walls. (Illus.). 64p. 1996. pap. 9.95 (0-7938-2051-0, RE139) TFH Pubns.

***Red Face & Other Facial Rashes.** Marks. (Illus.). 160p. (C). 1997. text ed. write for info. (0-412-63520-8, Chap & Hall NY) Chapman & Hall.

Red Fairy Book. Andrew Lang. 1976. 17.95 (0-8488-1403-7) Amereon Ltd.

Red Fairy Book. Ed. by Andrew Lang. (Illus.). 367p. (J). (gr. 4-6). pap. 6.95 (0-486-21673-X) Dover.

Red Fairy Book. Ed. by Andrew Lang. (Illus.). (J). 1994. 8.98 (1-56731-060-5, MJF Bks) Fine Comms.

Red Fairy Book. Lancelot Speed. (Illus.). (J). (gr. 2 up). 1990. 20.00 (0-8446-0756-8) Peter Smith.

Red Fairy Book. Andrew Lang. 1987. reprint ed. lib. bdg. 16.95 (0-89966-602-7) Buccaneer Bks.

Red Fascism: Boring from Within by the Subversive Forces of Communism. Jack B. Tenney. Ed. by Gerald Grob. LC 76-46106. (Anti-Movements in America Ser.). 1977. lib. bdg. 59.95 (0-405-09977-0) Ayer.

An Asterisk (*) at the beginning of an entry indicates that the title is appearing in BIP for the first time.

Red Feather Lakes - Glendevey. rev. ed. Ed. by Trails Illustrated Staff. 1995. 8.99 (*0-925873-32-2*) Trails Illustrated.

Red Feather Lakes the First Hundred Years. Evadene B. Swanson. 88p. 1986. pap. 5.00 (*0-9600862-0-X*) E Swanson.

Red Fez: On Art & Possession in Africa. Fritz Kramer. Tr. by Malcolm R. Green. 288p. (C). (gr. 13). 1993. 18.95 (*0-86091-465-8*, B0535, Pub. by Verso UK) Routledge Chapman & Hall.

Red-Figure Pottery. Sharon Herbert. LC 77-3070. (Corinth Ser.: Vol. 7, Pt. 4). x, 88p. 1977. 35.00 (*0-87661-074-2*) Am Sch Athens.

Red Figure Vases of South Italy & Sicily. Arthur D. Trendall. LC 88-51535. (World of Art Ser.). (Illus.). 288p. 1989. pap. 14.95 (*0-500-20225-7*) Thames Hudson.

*__Red-Figured Vases of Paestum.__ Arthur D. Trendall. (Illus.). 452p. 1987. 90.00 (*0-904152-11-1*, Pub. by British Schl Rome UK) David Brown.

Red Flag. Frederick B. Austin. LC 72-37258. (Short Story Index Reprint Ser.). 1977. reprint ed. 23.95 (*0-8369-4069-5*) Ayer.

Red Flag Green Flag People. Rape & Abuse Crisis Ctr. Staff. (Illus.). 28p. (J). (gr. k up). 1985. student ed., pap. 4.00 (*0-914633-10-4*) Rape Abuse Crisis.

*__Red Flag Green Flag People II: A Sexual Abuse Prevention Program for Older Elementary Age Children.__ Beth Haseltine. 30p. Date not set. pap. 3.00 (*0-914633-20-1*) Rape Abuse Crisis.

Red Flag Green Flag People Program Guide. Carol Grimm & Becky Montgomery. (Illus.). 36p. 1985. pap. 10.95 (*0-914633-12-0*) Rape Abuse Crisis.

Red Flag in Japan: International Communism in Action, 1919-1951. A. Rodger Swearingen & Paul Langer. LC 68-54440. (Illus.). 276p. 1968. reprint ed. text ed. 59.75 (*0-8371-0242-1*, SWRF, Greenwood Pr) Greenwood.

Red Flag over Hong Kong. Bruce Bueno de Mesquita et al. LC 95-50248. 208p. (C). 1996. 25.00 (*1-56643-041-0*); pap. text ed. 17.95 (*1-56643-040-2*) Chatham Hse Pubs.

Red Flag Riots: A Study in Intolerance. Raymond Evans. LC 87-30189. (Illus.). 252p. (Orig.). 1988. text ed. 29.95 (*0-7022-2073-6*, Pub. by Univ Queensland Pr AT) Intl Spec Bk.

Red Flag Waves: A Guide to the Hung-Ch'i p'iao-p'iao Collection. Robert Rinden & Roxane Witke. LC 68-65796. (China Research Monographs: No. 3). 159p. 1968. pap. 2.00 (*0-912966-04-1*) IEAS.

Red Flags. James C. Prendergast. 1994. pap. text ed. write for info. (*0-7931-1203-6*, 1520-2901, Real Estate Ed) Dearborn Finan.

Red Flags on Forged Checks: Detection & Defense. Joe Lucas & Katherine Koppanhaver. 63p. (Orig.). (C). 1995. pap. text ed. 20.00 (*0-9632206-5-9*) Foren Pubs Joppa.

*__Red Floral.__ Courage Books Staff. 1997. 6.98 (*0-7624-0228-8*) Courage Bks.

Red Flower of China. Zhai Zhenhua. LC 92-44047. 245p. 1994. pap. 13.00 (*1-56947-009-X*) Soho Press.

Red Fog over America. William G. Carr. 1978. pap. 6.00 (*0-911038-30-2*, Noontide Pr) Legion Survival.

Red Fog over America. William G. Carr. 280p. 1996. reprint ed. pap. 8.00 (*0-913022-35-7*) CPA Bk Pub.

Red Foley's Best Baseball Book Ever. 10th ed. MBKA Staff. (J). 1996. pap. 9.95 (*0-689-80811-9*) S&S Childrens.

Red Foley's Best Baseball Book Ever, 1996 Edition. 10th ed. Red Foley. (J). 1996. pap. 9.95 (*0-689-80780-5*) S&S Childrens.

Red Foley's Cartoon History of Baseball. Red Foley. (Illus.). 96p. (J). (gr. 3 up). 1992. pap. 8.95 (*0-671-73627-2*, Litl Simon S&S) S&S Childrens.

Red Forge: The Soviet Military Industry since 1965. Peter Almquist. 272p. 1990. text ed. 37.50 (*0-231-07066-7*) Col U Pr.

Red Fox. Anthony Hyde. 1986. mass mkt. 5.99 (*0-345-32839-6*) Ballantine.

Red Fox. Karen Wallace. LC 93-32381. (Read & Wonder Bks.). (Illus.). 32p. (J). (ps up). 1994. 14.95 (*1-56402-422-9*) Candlewick Pr.

Red Fox. Karen Wallace. LC 93-32381. (Read & Wonder Bks.). (J). (ps up). 1996. pap. 5.99 (*1-56402-661-2*) Candlewick Pr.

Red Fox. large type ed. Gerald Seymour. 448p. 1984. 27.99 (*0-7089-8190-9*) Ulverscroft.

Red Fox: Symposium on Behavior & Ecology. Ed. by E. Zimen. (Biogeographica Ser.: Vol. 18). 286p. 1980. lib. bdg. 175.00 (*90-6193-219-X*) Kluwer Ac.

Red Fox: The Catlike Canine. J. David Henry. (Smithsonian Nature Bks.). (Illus.). 174p. 1996. pap. 15.95 (*1-56098-635-2*) Smithsonian.

Red Fox & His Canoe. Nathaniel Benchley. LC 64-16650. (Harper I Can Read Bk.). (Illus.). 64p. (J). (gr. k-3). 1964. lib. bdg. 14.89 (*0-06-020476-1*) HarpC Child Bks.

Red Fox & His Canoe. Nathaniel Benchley. LC 64-16650. (Trophy I Can Read Bk.). (Illus.). 64p. (J). (gr. k-3). 1985. reprint ed. pap. 3.50 (*0-06-444075-3*, Trophy) HarpC Child Bks.

Red Fox & the Baby Bunnies. Alan Baron. LC 96-83533. (Illus.). 24p. (J). (ps up). 1997. 9.99 (*0-7636-0085-7*) Candlewick Pr.

*__Red Fox & the Baby Bunnies.__ Alan Baron. (Giggle Club Ser.). (Illus.). (J). 1998. pap. text ed. 3.29 (*0-7636-0402-X*) Candlewick Pr.

Red Fox Dances. Alan Baron. (Illus.). 24p. (J). (ps). 1996. 9.99 (*0-615-00912-3*) Candlewick Pr.

Red Fox Dances. Alan Baron. LC 95-71372. (Illus.). 24p. (J). (ps). 1997. reprint ed. pap. 3.29 (*0-7636-0127-6*) Candlewick Pr.

Red Fox Monster. Alan Baron. LC 96-83536. (Illus.). 24p. (J). (ps). 1996. 9.99 (*0-7636-0018-0*) Candlewick Pr.

*__Red Fox Monster.__ Alan Baron. (Giggle Club Ser.). (Illus.). (J). 1998. pap. text ed. 3.29 (*0-7636-0280-9*) Candlewick Pr.

Red Fox Running. Eve Bunting. (J). (ps-3). 1993. 15.95 (*0-395-58919-3*, Clarion Bks) HM.

Red Fox Running. Eve Bunting. (Illus.). (J). 1996. pap. 5.95 (*0-395-79723-3*) HM.

Red Gang. G. Lehmann. 1988. pap. 4.95 (*0-87508-439-7*) Chr Lit.

Red Gardenias. Jonathan Latimer. LC 91-70601. 280p. 1991. reprint ed. pap. 8.95 (*1-55882-094-9*, Lib Crime Classics) Intl Polygonics.

Red Geranium. Janette Oke. LC 95-481. 80p. 1995. 10.99 (*1-55661-662-7*) Bethany Hse.

Red Geranium. large type ed. Janette Oke. LC 95-44011. (Large Print Bks.). 1995. 17.95 (*1-56895-269-4*) Wheeler Pub.

Red Ghost: Letterpress Edition Collector's Item. deluxe ed. Joel Chace. (Persephone Press Poetry Award Ser.: No. 1). 24p. 1992. pap. 10.00 (*1-879009-05-6*) S P-Persephone Pr.

Red Giants & White Dwarfs. 3rd ed. Robert Jastrow. 1990. pap. 11.95 (*0-393-85004-8*) Norton.

Red Gods. Christopher Nicole. 320p. 1996. 24.00 (*0-7278-4972-7*) Severn Hse.

Red Gold. M. Lloyd Bush. LC 93-87293. 262p. (Orig.). 1994. pap. 10.00 (*0-9636845-6-6*) Senior Pr.

Red Gold. Alan Furst. 1997. write for info. (*0-679-45186-2*) Random.

Red Gold of Africa: Copper in Precolonial History & Culture. Eugenia W. Herbert. LC 83-40264. (Illus.). 391p. 1984. text ed. 32.50 (*0-299-09600-9*) U of Wis Pr.

Red Grange Story: An Autobiography. Afterword & Told to Ira Morton. LC 93-11212. (Illus.). 232p. 1993. reprint ed. 9.95 (*0-252-06329-5*) U of Ill Pr.

Red, Green & Black. Charles Bernstein & Olivier Cadiot. 48p. (Orig.). 1990. pap. 8.00 (*0-937013-34-X*) Potes Poets.

*__Red Green Talks Cars: A Love Story.__ Steve Smith & Rick Green. 128p. 1997. spiral bd. 11.00 (*0-7615-1112-1*) Prima Pub.

Red, Green, Yellow see Learn-To-Read Series

*__Red Grooms.__ Eleanor Heartney. Ed. by Stephen C. Wicks. (Illus.). 16p. (Orig.). 1997. pap. 10.00 (*0-9635881-6-8*) Knoxville Mus.

*__Red Grooms: A Retrospective, 1956-1984.__ Judith E. Stein et al. (Illus.). 240p. (Orig.). 1985. pap. 35.00 (*0-943836-03-4*) Penn Acad Art.

Red Grooms - Basketball Player. Red Grooms. (Illus.). 18p. 1993. pap. text ed. 19.50 (*1-56762-049-3*) Modern Learn Pr.

Red Grooms - Charlie Chaplin. Red Grooms. (Illus.). 18p. pap. text ed. 19.50 (*1-56762-051-5*) Modern Learn Pr.

Red Grooms - Double-Decker Bus. Red Grooms. (Illus.). 18p. pap. text ed. 19.50 (*1-56762-053-1*) Modern Learn Pr.

Red Grooms - Fats Domino. Red Grooms. (Illus.). 18p. pap. text ed. 17.50 (*1-56762-052-3*) Modern Learn Pr.

Red Grooms - Taxi Cab. Red Grooms. (Illus.). 18p. 1993. pap. text ed. 17.50 (*1-56762-050-7*) Modern Learn Pr.

Red Grooms, Michael C. McMillen: A Collaboration. Marie De Alcuaz. LC 87-83038. (Illus.). 32p. (Orig.). 1987. pap. 1.00 (*0-936429-09-7*) LA Municipal Art.

Red Grooms' Philadelphia Cornucopia & Other Sculpto-Pictoramas. Janet Kardon et al. (Illus.). 48p. 1982. pap. 18.00 (*0-88454-029-4*) U of Pa Contemp Art.

Red Guards & Workers' Militias in the Russian Revolution. Rex A. Wade. LC 82-60488. (Illus.). 416p. 1984. 52.50 (*0-8047-1167-4*) Stanford U Pr.

Red Guards' Path to Violence: Political, Educational, & Psychological Factors. Jing Lin. LC 91-2272. 200p. 1991. text ed. 49.95 (*0-275-93872-7*, C3872, Praeger Pubs) Greenwood.

Red Guidebook of U. S. Coins. R. S. Yeoman. 1984p. 1991. 9.95 (*0-685-22090-7*) Wehman.

Red Hair & the Jesuit. Lyn Lifshin. (Backpocket Poets Ser.). 36p. (Orig.). 1988. pap. 2.50 (*0-916155-05-6*) Trout Creek.

Red-Haired Android. Jeremy Reed. 280p. (Orig.). 1993. pap. 12.95 (*0-87286-283-6*) City Lights.

*__Red Hand, White Walking Person.__ Joseph A. Uphoff, Jr. 40p. 1996. pap. text ed. 2.00 (*0-943123-32-1*) Arjuna Lib Pr.

Red Harvest. Dashiell Hammett. 1989. pap. 10.00 (*0-679-72261-0*, Vin) Random.

Red Harvest. Dashiell Hammett. 1992. pap. 9.00 (*0-394-23904-0*, Vin); pap. 9.00 (*0-679-74093-7*) Random.

Red Harvest. Dashiell Hammett. 209p. 1994. 35.00 (*1-883402-95-6*) S&S Trade.

Red Harvest. Dashiell Hammett. 736p. 1991. Not sold separately (*0-615-00019-3*) Random Hse Value.

Red Harvest: The Communist Party & American Farmers. Lowell K. Dyson. LC 81-8200. 271p. reprint ed. pap. 77.30 (*0-8357-5550-9*, 2035169) Bks Demand.

Red Hat LINUX Unleashed. Kamran Husain et al. 1176p. 1996. 49.99 (*0-672-30962-9*) Mac Comp Pub.

*__Red Hat Linux Unleashed.__ 2nd ed. Pappas & Rensing. 1997. 49.99 (*0-672-31173-9*) Mac Comp Pub.

Red Hawk & the Sky Sisters: A Shawnee Legend. Gloria Dominic. LC 96-9111. (Native American Lore & Legends Ser.). 1996. write for info. (*0-86593-432-0*) Rourke Corp.

Red Hawk's Account of Custer's Last Battle. Paul Goble. LC 91-23170. (Illus.). 64p. (YA). 1992. reprint ed. pap. 9.95 (*0-8032-7033-X*, Bison Books) U of Nebr Pr.

Red Head: A Chronological Survey of "Red" Nichols & His Five Pennies. Stephen M. Stroff. (Studies in Jazz: No. 21). 220p. 1996. 32.50 (*0-8108-3061-2*) Scarecrow.

Red-Headed Gooseberry Ghost. Rick Detorie. (Haunted House Storybks.). 24p. (J). (gr. k-3). 1997. pap. 2.25 (*0-8167-1458-4*) Troll Communs.

Red-Headed League. Arthur Conan Doyle. (Classic Short Stories Ser.). 64p. (Orig.). (J). (gr. 6). 1990. lib. bdg. 13.95 (*0-88682-300-5*) Creative Ed.

Red-Headed League. Arthur Conan Doyle. (Sherlock Holmes Ser.). 27p. (Orig.). 1996. pap. 2.50 (*1-57514-260-0*, 3068) Encore Perform Pub.

Red-Headed League. Arthur Conan Doyle. (Jamestown Classics Ser.). (Orig.). 1995. teacher ed., pap. 7.32 (*0-89061-061-4*) Jamestown Pubs.

Red-Headed League. Arthur Conan Doyle. (Jamestown Classics Ser.). (Orig.). (J). 1995. student ed., pap. 5.99 (*0-89061-060-6*) Jamestown Pubs.

*__Red Headed Outfield.__ Zane Grey. Date not set. write for info. (*0-688-11089-4*, Morrow Junior) Morrow.

Red-Headed Outfield. Zane Grey. 302p. reprint ed. lib. bdg. 22.95 (*0-89190-759-9*, Rivercity Pr) Amereon Ltd.

Red Headed Tree. Bettye Givens. 67p. 1985. 10.00 (*0-911051-22-8*) Plain View.

Red-Headed Woman. Katharine Brush. 1993. reprint ed. lib. bdg. 89.00 (*0-7812-5347-0*) Rprt Serv.

Red-Headed Woodpeckers. James E. Gerholdt. LC 96-312. (J). 1997. lib. bdg. 12.95 (*1-56239-588-2*) Abdo & Dghtrs.

*__Red Heart.__ Thom J. Alexander. 1997. 25.00 (*0-345-39004-0*) Ballantine.

Red Heart Afghans & Crochet Classics. Red Heart Yarn Staff. 1996. pap. text ed. 14.95 (*0-8487-1513-6*) Oxmoor Hse.

Red Heat. Don Pendleton. (Super Bolan Ser.: No. 50). 1996. mass mkt. 5.50 (*0-373-61450-0*, 1-61450-2, Wrldwide Lib) Harlequin Bks.

Red Heat. Robert Tine. 224p. 1988. pap. 3.50 (*0-380-75565-3*) Avon.

Red Heels. Robert San Souci. (Illus.). 32p. (J). (gr. k up). 1996. pap. 15.99 (*0-8037-1133-6*) Dial Bks Young.

Red Heels. Robert D. San Souci. (Illus.). 32p. (J). (gr. k up). 1996. pap. 15.89 (*0-8037-1134-4*) Dial Bks Young.

*__Red Hen.__ Cullinan. 1994. 11.00 (*0-15-302302-3*) HarBrace.

Red Hen & Sly Fox. Vivian French. (Illus.). (J). (ps-2). 1995. 15.00 (*0-689-80010-X*, S&S Bks Young Read) S&S Childrens.

Red Herring. Clarica Burns. 304p. (Orig.). 1995. pap. 4.95 (*0-9645041-0-3*) Cntryside Pub.

Red Herring. Gunther E. Hartel. 1962. 12.95 (*0-8392-1090-6*) Astor-Honor.

Red Herring Guide to the Digital Universe: The Inside Look at Technology Business - From Silicon Valley to Hollywood. Red Herring Editors. 496p. 1996. 27.95 (*0-446-52018-7*) Warner Bks.

*__Red Herring Mystery.__ Paul Adshead. (J). 1996. pap. 7.99 (*0-85953-955-5*) Childs Play.

Red Herring Mystery. Paul S. Adshead. LC 95-42317. (Illus.). (J). 1995. 13.99 (*0-85953-954-7*) Childs Play.

Red Highway. Loren D. Estleman. 212p. 1994. 3.95 (*0-7867-0178-1*) Carroll & Graf.

Red Hills. Cornelius Weygandt. 1993. reprint ed. lib. bdg. 89.00 (*0-7812-5855-3*) Rprt Serv.

Red Hills & Cotton: An Upcountry Memory. Ben Robertson. (Southern Classics Ser.). 341p. 1973. reprint ed. pap. 12.95 (*0-87249-306-7*) U of SC Pr.

*__Red Hills of Florida, 1528-1865.__ Clifton Paisley. LC 88-5767. (Illus.). 306p. pap. 87.30 (*0-608-05137-3*, 2065698) Bks Demand.

Red Hole in Time. Muriel Marshall. LC 87-21715. (Elma Dill Russell Spencer Series in the West & Southwest: No. 9). (Illus.). 312p. 1988. 29.50 (*0-89096-316-9*) Tex A&M Univ Pr.

Red Hole in Time. Muriel Marshall. LC 87-21715. (Essays on the American West Ser.: No. 9). (Illus.). 312p. 1989. pap. 15.95 (*0-89096-332-0*) Tex A&M Univ Pr.

Red Holocaust. James Axler. (Deathlands Ser.: No. 2). 256p. 1986. mass mkt. 4.99 (*0-373-63058-1*) Harlequin Bks.

Red Horizons: Chronicles of a Communist Spy Chief. Ion M. Pacepa. LC 87-26378. (Illus.). 396p. 1987. lib. bdg. 19.95 (*0-89526-570-2*) Regnery Pub.

Red Horizons: The True Story of Nicolae & Elena Ceausescus' Crimes, Lifestyle, & Corruption. Ion M. Pacepa. LC 87-26378. (Illus.). 456p. 1990. pap. 12.95 (*0-89526-746-2*) Regnery Pub.

*__Red Horse.__ 1997. mass mkt. 3.75 (*0-373-64226-1*, 1-64226-3, Wrldwide Lib) Harlequin Bks.

Red Horse & the Buffalo Robe Man. Janice Dygert. Ed. by Hap Gilliland. (Indian Culture Ser.). (Illus.). (J). (gr. 4-8). 1978. pap. 4.95 (*0-89992-074-8*) Coun India Ed.

Red Horse Haunting. Ann Wigley. 147p. (C). 1990. pap. 21.00 (*0-85131-545-3*, Pub. by J A Allen & Co UK) St Mut.

Red Horseman. Stephen Coonts. Ed. by Paul McCarthy. 416p. 1994. reprint ed. pap. 6.99 (*0-671-74888-2*) PB.

Red Horseman (Export) Stephen Coonts. 1993. pap. 6.50 (*0-671-88413-1*) PB.

Red Horses. Kathleen Lignell. LC 91-61223. 56p. 1991. pap. 7.95 (*0-9621570-1-5*) North Lights.

Red Hot & Blue. Date not set. pap. 19.95 (*0-7893-0045-1*) St Martin.

Red, Hot & Blue: A Smithsonian Salute to the American Musical. Amy Henderson & Dwight B. Bowers. LC 95-51339. (Illus.). 288p. 1996. 39.95 (*1-56098-698-0*) Smithsonian.

Red, Hot & Green: 50 Spicy Vegetarian Recipes for Cooking with Chiles, Peppercorns, Mustards, Horseradish & Ginger. Janet Hazen. LC 95-31835. (Illus.). 120p. 1996. pap. 14.95 (*0-8118-1052-6*) Chronicle Bks.

Red, Hot & Rich: An Oral History of Cole Porter. David Grafton. LC 86-42684. (Illus.). 242p. 1987. 17.95 (*0-8128-3112-8*, Scrbrough Hse) Madison Bks UPA.

*__Red Hot Bible Puzzles.__ Nancy I. Sanders. (Sizzling Bible Puzzles Ser.). 80p. (J). (gr. 3-7). 1996. 4.99 (*0-570-04790-0*, 56-1810) Concordia.

Red Hot Chili Peppers. Dave Thompson. (Illus.). 288p. (Orig.). 1993. pap. 13.95 (*0-312-09902-9*) St Martin.

Red Hot Chili Peppers: Blood - Sugar - Sex - Magick. 27.95 (*0-7935-4876-4*, 00672324) H Leonard.

Red Hot Chili Peppers: Blood - Sugar - Sex - Magik. 88p. otabind 19.95 (*0-7935-4582-X*, 00690055) H Leonard.

Red Hot Chili Peppers: Blood - Sugar - Sex - Magik. 64p. otabind 17.95 (*0-7935-4879-9*, 00690064) H Leonard.

Red Hot Chili Peppers: BloodSugarSex Magik. (Illus.). 208p. 1996. pap. 24.95 (*0-8256-1338-8*, AM 90034) Music Sales.

*__Red Hot Chili Peppers: Interview CD Book.__ (Illus.). Date not set. pap. 14.99 (*1-57899-013-0*, MBS Paperbk) Mus Bk Servs.

Red Hot Chili Peppers: Out in LA. 88p. otabind 19.95 (*0-7935-4999-X*, 00690027) H Leonard.

Red Hot Chili Peppers: Selections from the Best of What Hits? with Notes & Tablature. 136p. 1994. otabind 22.95 (*0-7935-3738-X*, 00694968) H Leonard.

Red Hot Chili Peppers: The Complete Story. Joey Lorenzo. (Illus.). 48p. (Orig.). pap. 12.95 (*0-7119-4810-0*, OP 47744) Omnibus NY.

Red Hot Chili Peppers Quilting. Patricia B. Campbell & Michelle L. Jack. (Illus.). 48p. 1994. 12.95 (*0-614-06711-1*) Tex Stars.

Red Hot Cold Call Selling: Prospecting Techniques That Pay Off. Paul S. Goldner. 160p. (Orig.). 1995. pap. 16.95 (*0-8144-7880-8*) AMACOM.

*__Red Hot Gourmet.__ Cole Group Staff. (Cooking Companion Ser.). 96p. 1995. pap. 7.95 (*1-56426-800-4*) Cole Group.

Red-Hot Hightops. Matt Christopher. (Illus.). 128p. (YA). (gr. 4-6). 1987. 15.95 (*0-316-14056-2*) Little.

Red Hot Lipstick. Jeremy Reed. 144p. 9600. 28.95 (*0-7206-0988-7*, Pub. by P Owen Ltd UK) Dufour.

Red Hot Lipstick. Jeremy Reed. 160p. 9700. pap. 27.00 (*0-7206-0943-7*, Pub. by P Owen Ltd UK) Dufour.

*__Red Hot Lipstick.__ deluxe ed. Jeremy Reed. 144p. 1996. boxed write for info. (*0-7206-0989-5*, Pub. by P Owen Ltd UK) Dufour.

Red Hot Mamas: Coming Into Our Own at Fifty. Colette Dowling. LC 95-36807. 320p. 1996. 23.95 (*0-553-09059-3*, Bantam Trade Bks) Bantam.

*__Red Hot Mamas: Coming Into Our Own at Fifty.__ Colette Dowling. 304p. 1997. pap. 13.95 (*0-553-37495-8*, Bantam Trade Bks) Bantam.

Red Hot Monogamy: In Just Sixty Seconds a Day Keeping Your Relationship Sizzling. Patrick Hunt. Ed. by Cliff Carle. 1993. pap. 6.95 (*0-918259-53-3*) CCC Pubns.

*__Red Hot Mountain.__ Bird & Falk. (nc). (J). 1993. pap. text ed. write for info. (*0-582-80037-4*, Pub. by Longman UK) Longman.

Red Hot on a Silver Note. Maketa Groves. LC 96-869. 64p. 1997. pap. 10.95 (*1-880684-22-5*) Curbstone.

Red-Hot Pepper Fiasco. Patricia Hickman. LC 95-30736. (Cactusville Kids Ser.). (Illus.). 1995. pap. 5.99 (*0-8066-2737-9*) Augsburg Fortress.

Red Hot Peppers: A Cookbook for the Not So Faint of Heart. Jean Andrews. LC 93-25604. (Illus.). 256p. 1993. 25.00 (*0-02-502251-2*) Macmillan.

Red Hot Peppers: Book, Audio, & Speed Rope. Bob Boardman. (Illus.). 64p. (J). (gr. 2 up). 1994. 18.95 incl. audio (*1-57061-002-9*) Sasquatch Bks.

Red Hot Peppers: The Skookum Book of Jump Rope Games, Rhymes, & Fancy Footwork. Bob Boardman. (Illus.). 64p. (Orig.). (J). (gr. 3 up). 1993. pap. 8.95 (*0-912365-74-9*) Sasquatch Bks.

Red-Hot Ranchman. Victoria Pade. (American Romance Ser.: No. 656). 1996. mass mkt. 3.75 (*0-373-16656-7*, 1-16656-0) Harlequin Bks.

Red Hot Rod. Bob Wright. Tr. by Phyllis Bourne & Eugenia Tusquets. (Tom & Ricky Spanish-English Readers Ser.). (Illus.). 96p. (ENG & SPA.). (J). (gr. 1-5). 1988. pap. 4.95 (*0-87879-661-4*) High Noon Bks.

Red House. Edward Hollamby. (Architecture in Detail Ser.). (Illus.). 60p. 1991. pap. 42.95 (*0-442-30821-3*) Van Nos Reinhold.

Red House. Lya Luft. Tr. by Giovanni Pontiero from POR. 182p. 1995. 27.95 (*1-85754-019-0*, Pub. by Carcanet Pr UK) Paul & Co Pubs.

*__Red House: Bexleyheath 1859 Philip Webb.__ Edward Hollamby. (Architecture in Detail Ser.). (Illus.). 60p. (Orig.). Date not set. pap. 29.95 (*0-7148-3130-1*, Pub. by Phaidon Press UK) Chronicle Bks.

Red House Mystery. Ruth Perry & A. A. Milne. 96p. 1956. pap. 5.00 (*0-87129-115-0*, R34) Dramatic Pub.

Red House Mystery. A. A. Milne. reprint ed. lib. bdg. 20.95 (*0-89190-487-5*, Rivercity Pr) Amereon Ltd.

Red Hugh, Prince of Donegal. Robert T. Reilly. Orig. Title: Ma Premiere Communion. (Illus.). 155p. (YA). (gr. 5 up). 1997. reprint ed. pap. 11.95 (*1-883937-22-1*, 22-1) Bethlehem ND.

Red Hunters & the Animal People. Charles A. Eastman. LC 74-7964. (Illus.). reprint ed. 42.50 (*0-404-11852-6*) AMS Pr.

*__Red Hunting in the Promised Land: Anti-Communism & the Making of America.__ Joel Kovel. LC 97-24272. 1997. pap. text ed. 18.95 (*0-304-70048-7*) Cassell.

*__Red Hunting in the Promised Land: Anticommunism & the Making of America.__ Joel Kovel. (Global Issues Ser.). 352p. 1997. pap. 17.95 (*0-304-37048-7*) Cassell.

Red Ice. R. Karl Largent. 448p. (Orig.). 1995. mass mkt., pap. text ed. 5.99 (*0-8439-3774-2*) Dorchester Pub Co.

R

Red Image: American Attitudes Toward Communism in the Cold War Era. Les K. Adler. LC 91-31886. (Modern American History Ser.). 545p. 1992. text ed. 35.00 (0-8240-1905-9) Garland.

Red Ink. Greg Dinallo. LC 93-49358. 1995. pap. 6.50 (0-671-73314-1, PB Trade Paper) PB.

Red Ink. large type ed. Greg Dinallo. 474p. 1995. 27.99 (0-7089-5806-0) Ulverscroft.

*Red Ink: The Budget, Deficit, & Debt of the U. S. Government. Gary Evans. (Illus.). 320p. 1997. pap. 29.95 (0-12-244080-3, AP Prof); boxed 59.95 (0-12-244079-X, AP Prof) Acad Pr.

*Red Ink Behaviors: Measure the Surprisingly High Cost of Problem Behaviors in Valuable Employees. Jean A. Hollands. 150p. (Orig.). 1997. pap. 14.95 (0-614-30129-7) Select Bks CA.

*Red Ink Behaviors: Measure the Surprisingly High Cost of Problem Behaviors in Valuable Employees. Jean A. Hollands. 140p. (Orig.). 1997. pap. 14.95 (0-9657939-0-7) Blake Madsen.

Red Ink II: A Guide to Understanding the Continuing Deficit Dilemma. Alfred J. Watkins. LC 87-36000. 120p. (Orig.). (C). 1988. 17.95 (0-8191-6838-6, Hamilton Pr Roosevelt); pap. 7.95 (0-8191-6839-4, Hamilton Pr Roosevelt) U Pr of Amer.

Red Iron Nights. Glen Cook. 272p. (Orig.). 1991. pap. 5.50 (0-451-45108-2, ROC) NAL-Dutton.

Red Is Best. Kathy Stinson. 32p. (J). (gr. k-3). 1982. pap. 5.95 (0-920236-26-X, Pub. by Annick CN); lib. bdg. 15.95 (0-920236-24-3, Pub. by Annick CN) Firefly Bks Ltd.

Red Is Best. Kathy Stinson. (Annikin Ser.: No. 12). (Illus.). (J). (ps-1). 1992. 0.99 (1-55037-252-1, Pub. by Annick CN) Firefly Bks Ltd.

Red Is the River. Theodore V. Olsen et al. 416p. (Orig.). 1995. mass mkt., pap. text ed. 4.99 (0-8439-3747-5) Dorchester Pub Co.

Red Is the Valley. Wayne D. Overholser. 160p. 1988. pap. 2.75 (0-380-70680-6) Avon.

*Red Jacket & His People: Sa-Go-Ye-Wat-Ha Seneca War Chief. J. Niles Hubbard. 351p. 1986. pap. 24.50 (0-614-26379-4) Purple Mnt Pr.

Red, Jacquard. 80p. 1990. 3.00 (0-9620519-4-2) Iris Bks.

Red Jasmine. Inglis Fletcher. 320p. reprint ed. lib. bdg. 23.95 (0-89244-012-0, Queens House) Amereon Ltd.

Red Jewel of the East. Alvin E. Moore. 300p. 1989. per. 11.95 (0-89697-310-7) Intl Univ Pr.

Red Jews: Antisemitism in an Apocalyptic Age, 1200-1600. Andrew C. Gow. LC 94-43431. (Studies in Medieval & Reformation Thought: Vol. 55). 420p. 1995. 128.50 (90-04-10255-8) E J Brill.

*Red Keep: A Story of Burgundy in the Year 1165. Allen French. (Adventure Library). (Illus.). 380p. (Orig.). (YA). (gr. 6 up). 1997. pap. 14.95 (1-883937-29-9, 29-9) Bethlehem ND.

Red King's Rebellion: Racial Politics in New England 1675-1678. Russell Bourne. (Illus.). 304p. 1991. pap. 12.95 (0-19-506976-5, 12173) OUP.

Red Kite in Wales. John Evans. (C). 1992. 40.00 (0-7154-0711-2, Pub. by C Davies Pubs) St Mut.

Red Knight. large type ed. Geoffrey Moxon. 1990. 25.99 (0-7089-2286-4) Ulverscroft.

Red Knight: A Novel. J. Madison Davis. 232p. 1992. 19.95 (0-8027-1199-5) Walker & Co.

Red Knight of Germany. Floyd P. Gibbons. (War & Warriors Ser.). 383p. 1991. 18.95 (0-939482-38-X, Noontide Pr) Legion Survival.

Red Knight of Germany: The Story of Baron Von Richthofen, Germany's Great War Bird. Floyd P. Gibbons. Ed. by James B. Gilbert. LC 79-7256. (Flight: Its First Seventy-Five Years Ser.). (Illus.). 1980. reprint ed. lib. bdg. 37.95 (0-405-12167-9) Ayer.

Red Lace, Yellow Lace. Mike Casey & Judith Herbst. LC 95-39550. (Illus.). 24p. (J). 1996. spiral bd. 9.95 (0-8120-6553-0) Barron.

Red Ladies in Waiting: Soviet Aircraft in Storage. (Aircraft Specials Ser.). (Illus.). 64p. 1994. pap. 11.95 (0-89747-325-6) Squad Sig Pubns.

Red Lake Nation: Portraits of Ojibwe Life. 2nd rev. ed. Charles Brill. (Illus.). 192p. (C). 1992. reprint ed. 24.95 (0-8166-1906-9) U of Minn Pr.

Red Lamp. Mary R. Rinehart. 336p. 1987. mass mkt. 3.50 (0-8217-2017-1, Zebra Kensgtn) Kensgtn Pub Corp.

Red Lamp. Mary R. Rinehart. 24.95 (0-8488-1139-9) Amereon Ltd.

*Red Lamp. Mary R. Rinehart. 352p. 1997. mass mkt. 5.99 (1-57566-213-2, Knsington) Kensgtn Pub Corp.

Red Lamp of Incest: An Enquiry into the Origins of Mind & Society. Robin Fox. LC 83-16686. 284p. (C). 1983. pap. text ed. 15.00 (0-268-01620-8) U of Notre Dame Pr.

Red Land, Black Land: Daily Life in Ancient Egypt. Barbara Mertz. LC 89-17875. (Illus.). 386p. 1990. pap. 15.95 (0-87226-222-7) P Bedrick Bks.

Red Laugh. Leonid Andreyev. (Dedalus European Fiction Classics Ser.). 232p. pap. 11.95 (0-946626-41-3, Pub. by Dedalus Bks UK) Hippocrene Bks.

Red Leaf Six Forty-Five. Warren M. Evans. Ed. by Michael Winn. 224p. (Orig.). 1990. pap. 5.50 (0-922510-03-2) Lucky Bks.

Red Leaf, Yellow Leaf. Lois Ehlert. (Illus.). 36p. (J). (ps-3). 1991. 16.00 (0-15-266197-2, HB Juv Bks) HarBrace.

Red Leaves. Paullina Simons. LC 96-21592. 400p. 1996. 24.95 (0-312-14715-5) St Martin.

*Red Leaves. large type ed. Paullina Simons. LC 96-44357. 1996. 24.95 (1-56895-387-9) Wheeler Pub.

*Red Leaves, Vol. 1. Simons. 1997. mass mkt. 6.99 (0-312-96225-8) St Martin.

Red Leaves in the Air. Peggy Lyles. 20p. 1979. pap. 2.00 (0-913719-37-4) High-Coo Pr.

Red Legs & Rim Rocks: A Chukar Hunter's Almanac. Lynn Levy. (Illus.). 156p. (Orig.). 1997. pap. write for info. (0-87108-882-7) Pruett.

Red Letter Alphabet Book. Ellen Gould. (Illus.). 29p. (J). (gr. k up). 1983. pap. 7.00 (0-938017-00-4) Learn Tools.

Red Letter Day. Tom Pow. 96p. 1996. pap. 16.95 (1-85224-368-6, Pub. by Bloodaxe Bks UK) Dufour.

Red Letter Day: The Mail Carrier. Patricia Lakin. LC 94-28680. (My Community Ser.). (Illus.). (J). 1995. lib. bdg. 21.40 (0-8114-8264-2) Raintree Steck-V.

Red Letter Days. Mekeel McBride. (Poetry Ser.). 1988. pap. 11.95 (0-88748-065-9) Carnegie-Mellon.

Red Letter Days. Mekeel McBride. (Poetry Ser.). 1988. 20.95 (0-88748-064-0) Carnegie-Mellon.

Red Letter Days. Peter Rogers. (Illus.). 240p. 1995. 39.95 (1-85223-783-X, Pub. by Crowood Pr UK) Trafalgar.

Red-Letter Days: A Journal to Track Life's "Periods" Mae Mary. 192p. (Orig.). 1995. pap. 9.95 (1-887679-11-1) Foxglove Found.

Red-Letter Days: A Journal to Track Life's Periods. Mae Mary. 192p. (Orig.). (JPN.). 1996. pap. 14.95 (1-887679-23-5) Foxglove Found.

Red Letter Days of Samuel Pepys. E. F. Allen. 1972. 59.95 (0-8490-0937-5) Gordon Pr.

Red Letter Edition. 1990. 29.95 (1-55568-119-0) Gospel Films.

Red Letter Nights. James Agate. LC 71-91886. 1972. reprint ed. 24.95 (0-405-08193-6, Pub. by Blom Pubns UK) Ayer.

Red-Letter Poems: By English Men & Women. LC 71-167480. (Granger Index Reprint Ser.). 1977. reprint ed. 35.95 (0-8369-6285-0) Ayer.

Red Letters. Reg Saner. (QRL Poetry Bks.: Vols. XXVIII-XXIX). 1989. 20.00 (0-614-06424-4) Quarterly Rev.

Red Licorice: Monologues for Young People. Carole Tippit. LC 94-3655. 72p. (Orig.). (J). (gr. 3-7). 1994. pap. 8.95 (0-940669-28-5, D-32) Dramaline Pubns.

Red Lies & White Lies. Barbara F. Lefcowitz. LC 93-85470. 270p. (Orig.). 1994. pap. 9.00 (0-9637290-0-4) East Coast Bks.

Red Light: Inside the Sex Industry. James Ridgeway. (Illus.). 256p. 1996. 39.95 (1-57687-000-6, pwerHse Bks) pwerHse Cultrl.

Red Light: Inside the Sex Industry. limited ed. James Ridgeway. (Illus.). 256p. 1996. boxed 135.00 (1-57687-001-4, pwerHse Bks) pwerHse Cultrl.

Red Light, Green Light. Margaret Wise Brown. 40p. (J). (ps-3). 1994. pap. 4.95 (0-590-44559-6) Scholastic Inc.

Red Light, Green Light: The Life of Garrett Morgan & His Invention of the Stop Light. 4th ed. Dovie D. Sweet. (Orig.). (J). (gr. 1-6). 1988. pap. 5.00 (0-682-49088-1) Kitwardo Pubs.

Red Light, Green Light, Mama & Me. Cari Best. LC 94-33010. (Illus.). 32p. (J). (ps-2). 1995. 15.95 (0-531-09452-9); lib. bdg. 16.99 (0-531-08752-2) Orchard Bks Watts.

*Red Light, Green Light Preventing Teen Pregnancy. Janet O. Colberg. LC 96-70009. (Illus.). 138p. (Orig.). 1997. pap. 14.50 (0-9653647-0-4) Summer Kitchen Press.

Red Light Stop, Green Light Go. Andrew Kulman. LC 92-14228. (Illus.). (J). (ps). 1993. pap. 15.00 (0-671-79493-0, S&S Bks Young Read) S&S Childrens.

*Red Light Stop Green Light Go. Andrew Kulman. (Illus.). 26p. (J). 3.98 (0-7651-0092-4) Smithmark.

Red Lights: Selected Tanka Sequences from Shakko. Mokichi Saito. Tr. by Seishi Shinoda & Sanford Goldstein. LC 87-25911. (Illus.). 400p. 1989. 32.50 (0-911198-90-3) Purdue U Pr.

Red Lights of Baja, Mexico see Baja at Night: A Guide to Baja's Adult Night Life

Red Limit: The Search for the Edge of the Universe. rev. ed. Timothy Ferris. LC 83-3068. (Illus.). 288p. 1983. reprint ed. pap. 12.95 (0-688-01836-X, Quill) Morrow.

Red Line. Betsy Sholl. LC 92-50197. (Poetry Ser.). 80p. (C). 1992. pap. 10.95 (0-8229-5482-6); text ed. 19.95 (0-8229-3722-0) U of Pittsburgh Pr.

Red Lion: The Elixir of Eternal Life. Maria Orsi. 364p. 1987. pap. 8.95 (0-9632370-0-4) Comput Composit.

Red Lion Inn Cookbook. Suzi F. Chase. 1992. 29.95 (0-936399-29-5); pap. 16.95 (0-936399-28-7) Berkshire Hse.

Red-Listed: Haunted by the Washington Witch Hunt. Selma R. Williams. (Illus.). 1993. 24.95 (0-201-55069-5) Addison-Wesley.

Red London. Stewart Home. 160p. (Orig.). 1994. pap. 12.95 (1-873176-12-0, AK Pr San Fran) AK Pr Dist.

Red Mafia. Werner Raith. Tr. by Edna McCown from GER. 192p. 1996. 22.00 (1-56858-073-8) FWEW.

Red Magician. Lisa Goldstein. 192p. 1995. 10.95 (0-312-89007-9) Tor Bks.

Red Man in the United States: An Intimate Study of the Social, Economic & Religious Life of the American Indian. Gustavus E. Lindquist. LC 68-56243. (Illus.). xxvii, 461p. 1973. reprint ed. lib. bdg. 49.50 (0-678-00798-5) Kelley.

Red Man's America: A History of Indians in the United States. rev. ed. Ruth M. Underhill. LC 79-171345. (Illus.). 408p. 1971. pap. 18.95 (0-226-84165-0, P437) U Ch Pr.

Red Man's Land/White Man's Law: The Past & Present Status of the American Indian. 2nd ed. Wilcomb E. Washburn. LC 94-38444. 320p. 1995. pap. 14.95 (0-8061-2740-6) U of Okla Pr.

Red Man's Religion: Beliefs & Practices of the Indians North of Mexico. Ruth M. Underhill. LC 65-24985. 352p. 1972. pap. text ed. 16.95 (0-226-84167-7, P481) U Ch Pr.

Red Market: Industrial Co-operation & Specialisation in Comecon. Vladimir Sobell. LC 83-16316. 265p. 1984. text ed. 56.95 (0-566-00647-2, Pub. by Dartmth Pub UK) Ashgate Pub Co.

Red Mars, No. 1. Kim S. Robinson. 592p. 1993. mass mkt. 6.50 (0-553-56073-5, Spectra) Bantam.

Red Match the Rhyme Book. (Match the Rhyme Ser.). (J). (gr. 2-6). 1991. 4.95 (1-879332-02-7) XYZ Group.

Red Means Good Fortune: A Story of San Francisco's Chinatown. Barbara D. Goldin. (Once Upon America Ser.). (Illus.). 64p. (J). (gr. 2-6). 1996. pap. 3.99 (0-14-036082-4) Puffin Bks.

*Red Meat: From the Secret Files of Max Cannon. Max Cannon. LC 96-83598. (Illus.). 106p. (Orig.). 1996. pap. 9.95 (0-9647925-2-4) Black Spring.

Red Meat: Poems by John Wright. John Wright. Ed. by Chuck Taylor. (Illus.). 52p. (Orig.). 1989. text ed. 4.00 (0-941720-67-5); lib. bdg. 8.00 (0-941720-68-3) Slough Pr TX.

*Red Mecury. Bell. Date not set. write for info. (0-312-16977-9) St Martin.

Red Meekins. William A. Fraser. LC 72-125212. (Short Story Index Reprint Ser.). 1977. 20.95 (0-8369-3579-9) Ayer.

Red Men in Red Square. Claude C. Smith. LC 94-11454. (Illus.). 344p. (Orig.). 1994. 21.95 (0-936015-47-0); pap. 16.95 (0-936015-46-2) Pocahontas Pr.

Red Men of Nigeria: Account of a Lengthy Residence among the Fulani. J. R. Wilson-Haffenden. (Illus.). 318p. 1967. reprint ed. 47.50 (0-7146-1111-5, Pub. by F Cass Pubs UK) Intl Spec Bk.

Red Men on the Brandywine. C. A. Weslager. (Illus.). 155p. pap. 9.95 (0-912608-20-X) Mid Atlantic.

Red Menace. Dick Stivers. (Able Team Gold Eagle Ser.). 1988. pap. 2.75 (0-373-61237-0) S&S Trade.

Red Menace: A Novel. Michael Anania. (Illus.). 152p. (Orig.). 1993. reprint ed. pap. 7.95 (1-55921-088-5) Moyer Bell.

*Red Mercury. Max Barclay. 1997. mass mkt. 5.99 (0-7871-1416-2, Dove Bks) Dove Audio.

Red Mercury. Max Barclay. 416p. 1996. pap. 22.95 (0-7871-0920-7, Sig) NAL-Dutton.

*Red Mercury. Craig A. Copetas. Date not set. write for info. (0-688-12547-6) Morrow.

Red Microchip: Technology Transfer, Export Control, & Economic Restructuring in the Soviet Union. Daniel L. Burghart. 272p. 1992. 59.95 (1-85521-308-7, Pub. by Dartmth Pub UK) Ashgate Pub Co.

Red Miracle. Edward Podolsky. LC 70-167402. (Essay Index Reprint Ser.). 1977. 24.95 (0-8369-2818-0) Ayer.

Red Mirror: Children of China's Cultural Revolution. Chihua Wen. Ed. by Bruce Jones. LC 94-29828. 170p. (C). 1994. pap. text ed. 18.95 (0-8133-2488-2) Westview.

Red Moon: Understanding & Using the Gifts of the Menstrual Cycle. Miranda Gray. 172p. 1994. pap. 11.95 (1-85230-496-0) Element MA.

Red Moon - Red Lake. Ascher-Straus. LC 88-23017. 128p. 1988. 16.00 (0-914232-96-7); pap. 8.00 (0-914232-97-5) McPherson & Co.

*Red Moon Anthology 1996. Ed. by Jim Kacian. 160p. (Orig.). 1997. pap. 13.95 (0-9657818-0-1) Red Moon Pr.

*Red Moon Passage. Bonnie Horrigan. 1997. pap. 14.00 (0-517-88830-0) Crown Pub Group.

Red Moon Passage: The Power & Wisdom of Menopause. Bonnie Horrigan. 288p. 1996. 24.00 (0-517-70386-6, Harmony) Crown Pub Group.

Red Moon-Red Lake. Ascher & Straus. 32p. (Orig.). 1984. pap. 3.00 (0-917061-21-7) Top Stories.

Red Mound: Celestial Light. Kathleen L. Mendel. (Illus.). 40p. (Orig.). (C). 1994. pap. 6.10 (1-878142-36-4) Telstar FL.

Red Mountain. large type ed. Will A. Comstock. (Linford Western Library). 320p. (Orig.). 1992. pap. 15.99 (0-7089-7246-2) Ulverscroft.

Red Mountain Rendezvous. Ed. by John Curbow & Evelyn Hurley. (Rendezvous Ser.: Vol. 1). (Orig.). 1993. pap. 5.00 (0-9632842-3-1) Curbow Pubns.

Red Mud Analysis & Utilization. R. S. Thakur & S. N. Das. (International Series on Environment). 1994. write for info. (81-7236-093-2, Pub. by Wiley Estrn II) Franklin.

Red Mule. 2nd ed. Jesse H. Stuart. LC 92-31439. (Jesse Stuart Foundation Juvenile Ser.). (Illus.). 96p. (J). (gr. 3-6). 1993. reprint ed. 12.00 (0-945084-34-X); reprint ed. pap. text ed. 6.00 (0-945084-33-1) J Stuart Found.

Red Multinationals or Red Herrings? The Activities of Enterprises from Socialist Countries in the West. Ed. by Geoffrey Hamilton. LC 85-25102. 200p. 1986. text ed. 39.95 (0-312-66656-X) St Martin.

Red Neck. McAlister Coleman. LC 74-22772. (Labor Movement in Fiction & Non-Fiction Ser.). reprint ed. 42.50 (0-404-58412-8) AMS Pr.

Red Network: A "Who's Who" & Handbook of Radicalism for Patriots. Elizabeth K. Dilling. LC 76-46073. (Anti-Movements in America Ser.). 1977. reprint ed. lib. bdg. 30.95 (0-405-09946-0) Ayer.

Red Nichols Story: After Intermission, 1942-1965. Stanley Hester et al. LC 95-198579. (Studies in Jazz: No. 22). 450p. 1997. 79.50 (0-8108-3096-5) Scarecrow.

Red Nights. Alexander Simmons. (J). 1998. pap. 5.99 (0-679-88205-7, Bullseye Bks) Random Bks Yng Read.

Red Notebook of Charles Darwin. Charles Darwin. Ed. by Sandra Herbert. LC 78-74215. (Illus.). 150p. 1980. 49.95 (0-8014-1226-9) Cornell U Pr.

Red November, Black November: Culture & Community in the Industrial Workers of the World. Salvatore Salerno. LC 88-39378. (SUNY Series in American Labor History). 220p. (Orig.). 1989. text ed. 64.50 (0-7914-0088-3); pap. text ed. 21.95 (0-7914-0089-1) State U NY Pr.

Red Oaks & Black Birches: The Science & Lore of Trees. Rebecca Rupp. Ed. by Jill Mason. LC 90-55043. (Illus.). 288p. 1990. pap. 12.95 (0-88266-620-7) Storey Comm Inc.

*Red Ocher Culture of the Upper Great Lakes & Adjacent Areas. Robert E. Ritzenthaler & George I. Quimby. LC 62-15263. (Chicago Natural History Museum Anthropology Ser.: Vol. 36, No. 11, March 27, 1962). (Illus.). 33p. 1962. reprint ed. pap. 25.00 (0-608-02706-5, 2063371) Bks Demand.

Red Oleanders. Rabindranath Tagore. 105p. 1985. 5.50 (0-333-90006-5) Asia Bk Corp.

Red Orchestra: Instruments of Soviet Policy in Latin America & the Caribbean. Ed. by Dennis L. Bark. (Publication Ser.: No. 308). 140p. (C). 1986. pap. 2.78 (0-8179-8082-2) Hoover Inst Pr.

Red Orchestra: The Case of Africa. Ed. by Dennis L. Bark. (Publication Ser.: No. 374). 231p. (C). 1988. pap. text ed. 5.18 (0-8179-8742-8) Hoover Inst Pr.

Red Orchestra: The Case of the Southwest Pacific. Ed. by Dennis L. Bark & Owen Harries. (Publication Ser.: No. 376). 271p. (C). 1989. pap. text ed. 5.98 (0-8179-8762-2) Hoover Inst Pr.

Red Orchestra: The Soviet Spy Network Inside Nazi Europe. V. E. Tarrant. LC 95-33276. 224p. 1996. text ed. 24.95 (0-471-13439-2) Wiley.

Red over Black: Black Slavery among the Cherokee Indians. R. Halliburton, Jr. LC 76-15329. (Illus.). 219p. 1977. text ed. 42.95 (0-8371-9034-7, HAR/, Greenwood Pr) Greenwood.

Red Overcoat & Other Stories. Frank Ananicz. 24p. 1983. pap. 3.50 (0-933292-12-0) Arts End.

Red Owl. Robert Morgan. 88p. (Orig.). (C). 1972. pap. text ed. 1.95 (0-393-04136-0) Norton.

Red Ozier: A Literacy Fine Press. Michael Peich. (Illus.). 102p. 1993. 130.00 (1-882916-00-X) Yellow Barn.

Red Panda Biology. Ed. by A. R. Glatston. (Illus.). xv, 187p. pap. 50.00 (90-5103-026-6, Pub. by SPB Acad Pub NE) Balogh.

Red Panda, Olingos, Coatis, Raccoons & Their Relatives: An Action Plan for the Conservation of Procyonids & Ailurids. Ed. by Angela R. Glatston. (C). 1994. pap. text ed. 25.00 (2-8317-0046-9, Pub. by IUCN SZ) Island Pr.

Red Patriots: The Story of the Seminoles. A Facsimile Reproduction of the 1898 Edition with an Introduction by Charlton E. Tebeau. Charles H. Coe. LC 73-5702. (Bicentennial Floridian Facsimile Ser.). 365p. reprint ed. pap. 104.10 (0-8357-6926-7, 2037985) Bks Demand.

Red Pavilion. Robert H. Van Gulik. LC 94-645. (Judge Dee Mystery Ser.). (Illus.). 176p. (C). 1994. pap. 6.95 (0-226-84873-6) U Ch Pr.

Red Pavilion. large type ed. Jean Chapman. (Magna Large Print Ser.). 540p. 1996. 25.99 (0-7505-0876-0, Pub. by Magna Print Bks UK) Ulverscroft.

Red Pawns. Leonard Wibberley. 1992. 22.50 (0-8446-6558-4) Peter Smith.

Red Pencil: Artists, Scholars, & Censors in the U. S. S. R. Marianna T. Choldin & Maurice Friedberg. 256p. 1989. text ed. 55.00 (0-04-445203-9) Routledge Chapman & Hall.

*Red Peony Night. Helen Conkling. LC 97-4919. (Pitt Poetry Ser.). 80p. 1997. text ed. 25.00 (0-8229-4042-6) U of Pittsburgh Pr.

*Red Peony Night. Helen Conkling. LC 97-4919. (Pitt Poetry Ser.). 80p. 1997. pap. 12.95 (0-8229-5647-0) U of Pittsburgh Pr.

Red Pepper Burns. Grace S. Richmond. reprint ed. lib. bdg. 21.95 (0-89190-491-3, Rivercity Pr) Amereon Ltd.

Red Pepper Fudge & Blue Ribbon Biscuits: Favorite Recipes & Cooking Stories from North Carolina State Fair Winners. Amy Rogers. (Illus.). 160p. (Orig.). 1995. pap. 13.95 (1-878086-43-X) Down Home NC.

Red Pepper's Patients. Grace S. Richmond. reprint ed. lib. bdg. 23.95 (0-89190-492-1, Rivercity Pr) Amereon Ltd.

*Red Petals. Deborah Satinwood. 352p. 1997. mass mkt. 4.99 (0-8217-5810-1, Zebra Kensgtn) Kensgtn Pub Corp.

Red Phoenix. Larry Bond. LC 88-40602. 1990. mass mkt. 6.99 (0-446-35968-8) Warner Bks.

Red Phoenix. Larry Bond. 1992. 5.95 (0-446-77584-3) Warner Bks.

Red Phoenix: The Rise of Soviet Air Power, 1941-1945. Von Hardesty. LC 82-600153. (History of Aviation Ser.). (Illus.). 288p. (C). 1991. pap. text ed. 19.95 (1-56098-071-0) Smithsonian.

Red Pine, Black Ash. Richard Aldridge. LC 80-18598. (Illus.). 143p. 1980. 10.00 (0-89621-062-6) Nrth Country Pr.

Red Planet. Robert A. Heinlein. 192p. 1986. mass mkt. 5.99 (0-345-34039-6, Del Rey) Ballantine.

Red Planet: Mars. rev. ed. Isaac Asimov et al. (Library of the Universe). (Illus.). (J). (gr. 3 up). 1994. lib. bdg. 18.60 (0-8368-1132-1) Gareth Stevens Inc.

Red Planet Rising. Andrew M. Seddon. LC 95-31030. 240p. (Orig.). 1995. pap. 9.99 (0-89107-825-8) Crossway Bks.

Red Planet Run. Dana Stabenow. 240p. (Orig.). 1995. mass mkt. 5.50 (0-441-00135-1) Ace Bks.

Red Plot Against America. Robert E Stripling. Ed. by Bob Considine & Gerald Grob. LC 76-46105. (Anti-Movements in America Ser.). 1977. reprint ed. lib. bdg. 25.95 (0-405-09976-2) Ayer.

Red Pony. John Steinbeck. 112p. 1993. pap. 5.95 (0-14-017736-1, Penguin Bks) Viking Penguin.

Red Pony. John Steinbeck. LC 94-8791. 128p. 1994. pap. 8.95 (0-14-018739-1, Penguin Classics) Viking Penguin.

*Red Pony. John Steinbeck. 10.00 (0-89064-251-6) NAVH.

Red Pony. large type ed. John Steinbeck. LC 93-34865. 1994. lib. bdg. 19.95 (0-8161-5899-1, GK Hall) Thorndike Pr.

Red Pony. large type ed. John Steinbeck. LC 93-34865. 1994. pap. 14.95 (0-8161-5900-9, GK Hall) Thorndike Pr.

An Asterisk (*) at the beginning of an entry indicates that the title is appearing in BIP for the first time.

R

Red Pony. John Steinbeck. (Illus.). (J). (gr. 7 up). 1986. reprint ed. pap. 15.95 (*0-670-59184-X*) Viking Child Bks.

Red Pony: A Literature Unit. Mari L. Robbins. (Literature Units Ser.). (Illus.). 48p. (Orig.). (J). (gr. 6-8). 1993. student ed., pap. 7.95 (*1-55734-443-4*) Tchr Create Mat.

Red Pony: A Study Guide. Joy Leavitt. (Novel-Ties Ser.). 1985. student ed., teacher ed., pap. text ed. 15.95 (*0-88122-125-2*) Lrn Links.

Red Pony, Chrysanthemums & Flight Notes. Gary K. Carey. (Orig.). 1978. pap. text ed. 3.75 (*0-8220-1135-2*) Cliffs.

Red Poppies for a Little Bird. Jonathan Sherwood. (Illus.). 40p. (J). (gr. k-4). 1993. 14.95 (*1-56844-005-7*) Enchante Pub.

Red Poppies for a Little Bird. 2nd rev. ed. Jonathan Sherwood. Ed. by Gudrun Hoy & Bobi Martin. (Emotional Literacy Ser.). (Illus.). 40p. (J). (gr. k-5). 1995. 14.95 (*1-56844-105-3*) Enchante Pub.

Red Poppy. Irmgard Lucht. Tr. by Frank Jacoby-Nelson. LC 94-15057. (Illus.). 32p. (J). (ps-3). 1997. pap. 4.95 (*0-7868-1161-7*) Hyprn Child.

Red Poppy. large type ed. Irmgard Lucht. Tr. by Frank Jacoby-Nelson. LC 94-15057. (Illus.). 32p. (J). (ps-3). 1995. 13.95 (*0-7868-0055-0*); lib. bdg. 13.89 (*0-7868-2043-8*) Hyprn Child.

Red Power: The American Indians' Fight for Freedom. Alvin M. Josephy, Jr. LC 84-20821. xviii, 247p. 1985. reprint ed. pap. 9.95 (*0-8032-7563-3*, Bison Books) U of Nebr Pr.

Red Power on the Rio Grande. Franklin Folsom. 144p. (J). (gr. 4 up). 1989. reprint ed. 12.95 (*0-89992-421-2*); reprint ed. pap. 9.95 (*0-89992-121-3*) Coun India Ed.

Red Prophet. Orson Scott Card. (Tales of Alvin Maker Ser.: Bk. II). 320p. 1992. mass mkt. 4.99 (*0-8125-2426-8*) Tor Bks.

***Red Queen.** Draulens. LC 97-8806. 1997. 20.95 (*0-312-15636-7*) St Martin.

Red Queen: Sex & the Evolution of Human Nature. Matt Ridley. 416p. 1995. pap. 13.95 (*0-14-024548-0*, Penguin Bks) Viking Penguin.

Red Racer. Audrey Wood. LC 95-44061. (J). 1996. 15.00 (*0-689-80553-5*) S&S Childrens.

Red Racer. Audrey Wood. (J). 1995. 15.00 (*0-671-88720-3*, S&S Bks Young Read) S&S Childrens.

Red Rackham's Treasure. Herge. (Illus.). 62p. (J). 19.95 (*0-8288-5057-7*) Fr & Eur.

Red Rackham's Treasure. Herge. LC 73-21253. (Adventures of Tintin Ser.). (Illus.). 64p. (J). (gr. k up). 1974. reprint ed. pap. 8.95 (*0-316-35834-7*, Joy St Bks) Little.

***Red Raider Handbook: Stories, Stats & Stuff about Texas Tech Sports.** Novvall Pollard & Doug Hensley. (Illus.). 160p. (Orig.). 1996. pap. 9.95 (*1-880652-68-4*) Wichita Eagle.

Red Rain. William H. Lovejoy. 512p. 1996. mass mkt. 5.99 (*0-7860-0230-1*, Pinncle Kensgtn) Kensgtn Pub Corp.

Red Rain Too. Michael Basinski. 17p. (Orig.). 1992. pap. 3.00 (*0-926935-64-X*) Runaway Spoon.

Red Ranger Came Calling. Berkeley Breathed. (Illus.). (J). 1994. 16.95 (*0-316-10881-2*) Little.

***Red Ranger Came Calling.** Berkeley Breathed. 1997. pap. text ed. 6.95 (*0-316-10249-0*) Little.

Red Record: The Oldest Native North American History. David McCutchen. LC 92-23247. (Illus.). 240p. pap. 14.95 (*0-89529-525-3*) Avery Pub.

Red Record of the Sioux. Willis F. Johnson. LC 76-43757. reprint ed. 64.50 (*0-404-15598-7*) AMS Pr.

Red, Red Robin. Stephen Gallagher. LC 94-42787. 1995. 18.00 (*0-345-38644-2*) Ballantine.

Red, Red Robin. Stephen Gallagher. 1996. mass mkt. 5.99 (*0-345-40649-4*) Ballantine.

***Red, Red Robin.** large type ed. Stephen Gallagher. (Charnwood Large Print Ser.). 544p. 1996. 27.99 (*0-7089-8880-6*) Ulverscroft.

Red Red Rose. Teri Kovak Shapiro. 1980. pap. 1.50 (*0-373-58048-7*) Harlequin Bks.

Red Redmaynes. Eden Phillpotts. (Illus.). 384p. (C). 1982. reprint ed. pap. 6.95 (*0-486-24255-2*) Dover.

Red Republican, 2 vols. John Saville. (C). 1966. text ed. 21.95 (*0-85036-096-X*, Pub. by Merlin Pr UK) Humanities.

Red Resurrection. Blain B. Hudson. 1995. pap. 10.95 (*0-533-11470-5*) Vantage.

Red Rhino. Alan Rogers. LC 90-9830. (Little Giants Ser.). (Illus.). 16p. (J). (ps-1). 1990. lib. bdg. 17.27 (*0-8368-0403-1*) Gareth Stevens Inc.

***Red Rhino.** Alan Rogers. (Little Giants Ser.). (J). (ps-2). 1997. 7.95 (*0-7166-4406-1*); pap. 2.95 (*0-7166-4402-9*) World Bk.

Red Ribbon. Sarah Weeks. LC 94-38309. (Laura Geringer Bk.). (Illus.). 32p. (J). (ps-3). 1995. 15.95 (*0-06-025430-0*); lib. bdg. 15.89 (*0-06-025431-9*) HarpC Child Bks.

Red Ribbon: A Story of Hope. Illus. by Greg Ramsey. 35p. (SPA.). (J). (gr. k-5). 1994. 19.95 (*0-9642815-9-7*) Natl Fmly Prtnship.

Red Ribbon: A Story of Hope. Illus. by Greg Ramsey. 35p. (J). (gr. k-5). 1994. 19.95 (*0-9642815-0-3*) Natl Fmly Prtnship.
THE RED RIBBON is the tale of a very sad kingdom whose happiness is restored when a Weaver's magical red ribbon brings people together. As citizens stand side-by-side holding up their part of the ribbon, they begin to work together. Then they discover the magic isn't in the ribbon after all, but in the "hands & hearts of those who embrace it." The beautifully illustrated storybook has won numerous awards, including a book award for outstanding contribution to children's literature from Church & Synagogue Library Association, a national Addy Award & a Benny. National Family Partnership, a nonprofit whose mission is drug prevention, published the book as a tool for parents & teachers because although it makes no mention of drugs, it is a pro-active, practical & entertaining way to instill in children the values which will safeguard them against potential abuse. The book's theme is the heart of prevention: prevention begins with families & communities joining together to make a difference. THE RED RIBBON, published in 1994, is in its third printing. Adults & children, drawn to the captivating story & appealing illustrations, find it is a "story of hope." ***Publisher Provided Annotation.***

Red Ribbon: A Story of Hope. Illus. by Greg Ramsey. (J). (ps-5). 1994. teacher ed. 2.95 (*0-9642815-1-1*) Natl Fmly Prtnship.

Red Ribbon: A Story of Hope. deluxe ed. Illus. by Greg Ramsey. 35p. (J). (gr. k-5). 1994. 100.00 (*0-9642815-2-X*) Natl Fmly Prtnship.

Red Ribbon Christmas. Pam McKee et al. 64p. 1995. pap. 7.95 (*1-56523-068-X*) Fox Chapel Pub.

Red Ribbon on a White Horse. rev. ed. Anzia Yezierska. 228p. 1988. pap. 9.95 (*0-89255-124-0*) Persea Bks.

Red Ribbon Rosie. Jean Marzollo. LC 87-29641. (Stepping Stone Bks.). (Illus.). 64p. (Orig.). (J). (gr. 2-4). 1988. lib. bdg. 5.99 (*0-394-99608-9*) Random Bks Yng Read.

Red Ribbon Rosie. Jean Marzollo. LC 87-29641. (Stepping Stone Bks.). (Illus.). 64p. (Orig.). (J). (gr. 2-4). 1988. pap. 3.99 (*0-394-89608-4*) Random Bks Yng Read.

Red Ribbons for Emma. limited ed. New Mexico People & Energy Collective Staff et al. LC 80-83883. (Illus.). 48p. (Orig.). (J). (gr. 3 up). 1981. pap. 12.00 (*0-938678-07-8*) New Seed.

Red Riding Hood. (First Fairy Tales Ser.: No. S852-10). (Illus.). (J). (ps-2). 3.95 (*0-7214-5103-9*, Ladybrd) Penguin.

Red Riding Hood. (Diamond Series Pop-Ups). (Illus.). (J). (ps-1). 1.29 (*0-517-47346-1*) Random Hse Value.

Red Riding Hood. (Derrydale Fairytale Library). (Illus.). (J). (ps-3). 1985. 2.98 (*0-517-28810-9*) Random Hse Value.

Red Riding Hood. Coady. 1995. 4.98 (*0-8317-6215-2*) Smithmark.

Red Riding Hood. Edens. (J). 1998. 14.95 (*0-671-75190-5*, S&S Bks Young Read) S&S Childrens.

***Red Riding Hood.** Ed. by Hanna Hutchinson. (Illus.). 20p. (Orig.). (J). (gr. 1-2). 1989. pap. 2.95 (*0-922852-01-4*, V003) Another Lang Pr.

Red Riding Hood. Illus. by Laszio Kubinyi. LC 90-25377. 32p. (J). (gr. k up). 1991. pap. 19.95 incl. audio (*0-88708-163-0*, Rabbit) S&S Childrens.

Red Riding Hood. James Marshall. LC 86-16722. (Illus.). 32p. (J). (ps-3). 1987. pap. 14.99 (*0-8037-0344-9*); lib. bdg. 10.89 (*0-8037-0345-7*) Dial Bks Young.

Red Riding Hood. James Marshall. (J). (ps-3). 1991. pap. 4.95 (*0-8037-1054-2*, Puff Pied Piper) Puffin Bks.

Red Riding Hood. James Marshall. (J). 1993. pap. 4.99 (*0-14-054693-6*, Puff Pied Piper) Puffin Bks.

Red Riding Hood. James Marshall. (Illus.). 32p. (J). (ps-3). 1993. pap. 17.99 (*0-14-054976-5*, Puff Pied Piper) Puffin Bks.

Red Riding Hood. Lee Mendelson et al. write for info. (*0-318-58236-8*) P-H.

Red Riding Hood. Roberts. (J). (gr. k up). 1995. 10.95 incl. audio (*0-689-80203-X*, Rabbit) S&S Childrens.

Red Riding Hood. Tom Roberts. LC 93-12152. (Illus.). (J). (ps-6). 1993. Incl. cassette. 9.95 incl. audio (*0-88708-320-X*, Rabbit) S&S Childrens.

Red Riding Hood: Retold in Verse for Boys & Girls to Read Themselves. 2nd ed. Beatrice S. De Regniers. LC 89-38024. (Illus.). 48p. (J). (gr. k-3). 1990. pap. 4.95 (*0-689-71373-8*, Aladdin Paperbacks) S&S Childrens.

Red Riding Hood. Hanna Hutchinson. Tr. by Bounta Phitsanoukanh. (Interlingo Ser.). (Illus.). 24p. (Orig.). (LAO.). (J). (gr. 1-2). 1995. pap. 2.95 (*0-922852-34-0*, A011) Another Lang Pr.

Red Ridinghood see Chapeuzinho Vermelho

Red Ridinghood see Caperucita Roja

***Red Right Hand.** Joel T. Rogers. 192p. 1997. mass mkt. 4.95 (*0-7867-0446-2*) Carroll & Graf.

Red Right Hand. Joel T. Rogers. 198p. 1983. reprint ed. pap. 3.50 (*0-88184-008-4*) Carroll & Graf.

***Red Right Returning.** Edmunds. 1997. mass mkt. 4.99 (*0-373-26258-2*) Harlequin Bks.

Red Right Returning. St Edmunds. 224p. 1996. 20.95 (*0-312-14033-9*) St Martin.

Red Rising: The Transcendent Paintings of Howard Thomas. Donald Kuspit. Ed. by Myra Engelhardt. (Illus.). 40p. (Orig.). (C). 1995. write for info. (*0-9629384-1-6*) Harn Mus Art.

Red River Bad. Allan K. Echols. 1993. 17.50 (*0-7451-4574-4*, Gunsmoke) Chivers N Amer.

Red River Blues: The Blues Tradition in the Southeast. Bruce Bastin. (Music in American Life Ser.). 432p. (C). 1995. 17.95 (*0-252-06521-2*) U of Ill Pr.

Red River Campaign: Politics & Cotton. L. H. Johnson. 31.00 (*0-8488-1063-5*) Amereon Ltd.

Red River Campaign: Politics & Cotton in the Civil War. Ludwell H. Johnson. LC 92-40019. 336p. 1993. pap. 16.00 (*0-87338-486-5*) Kent St U Pr.

Red River Campaign: Politics & Cotton in the Civil War. Ludwell H. Johnson. LC 58-59976. reprint ed. pap. 82.30 (*0-685-09006-X*, 2001834) Bks Demand.

Red River City: A 3-Dimensional Story Frieze with Punch-Out Characters. Illus. by Rosemary Woods. 16p. (J). (gr. k up). 1994. pap. 14.95 (*0-688-13709-1*, Tupelo Bks) Morrow.

***Red River Crossings: Contemporary Native American Artists Respond to Peter Rindisbacher (1806-1834)** Margaret Archuleta et al. (Illus.). 60p. (Orig.). Date not set. pap. 15.00 (*1-884692-04-4*) Swiss Inst.

Red River Haint: Musical - with Sing-a-Long Cassette. Arlie Garrett & Debby Garrett. 33p. (J). 1995. pap. 5.50 incl. audio (*0-87129-613-6*, R58) Dramatic Pub.

Red River Journal & Other Papers Relative to the Red River Resistance of 1869-1870, Vol. 34. Alexander Begg. Ed. by W. L. Morton. LC 69-14506. 636p. 1969. reprint ed. text ed. 85.00 (*0-8371-5074-4*, BERR, Greenwood Pr) Greenwood.

Red River of Life - Chinese Edition. Moody Institute of Science Staff. Tr. by CRM Staff. 15p. (CHI.). 1977. 0.40 (*1-56582-061-4*) Christ Renew Min.

Red River Prosecutor: True Cases of Oklahoma Crime. Kenneth D. Bacon. LC 95-38693. (Illus.). 320p. (Orig.). 1995. pap. 19.95 (*1-880090-14-7*) Galde Pr.

Red River Story. Alfred Silver. 576p. 1990. mass mkt. 5.95 (*0-345-36562-3*) Ballantine.

Red River Trails: Oxcart Routes Between St. Paul & the Selkirk Settlement, 1820-1870. Rhoda R. Gilman et al. LC 78-11045. (Illus.). x, 105p. 1979. pap. 11.95 (*0-87351-133-6*) Minn Hist.

Red River Valley Fighter Pilots. Turner Publishing Company Staff. LC 89-50046. 152p. 1990. 48.00 (*0-938021-38-9*) Turner Pub KY.

Red River Valley Fighter Pilots Association History Book, Vol. II. Turner Publishing Company Staff. LC 89-50046. (Illus.). 142p. 1992. 48.00 (*1-56311-032-6*) Turner Pub KY.

Red River Valley Illustrated Album of Biography of the Famous Valley of the Red River of the North & the Park Regions: Containing Biographical Sketches of Hundreds of Prominent Old Settlers & Representative Citizens. (Illus.). 844p. 1996. reprint ed. lib. bdg. 85.00 (*0-8328-5048-9*) Higginson Bk Co.

Red River Women. Sherrie S. McLeroy. (Women of the West Ser.). 250p. 1996. pap. 12.95 (*1-55622-501-6*, Rep of TX Pr) Wordware Pub.

Red Rock. Thomas N. Page. Ed. by Lucas Carpenter. 1991. 16.95 (*0-8084-0439-3*) NCUP.

Red Rock - Sacred Mountain: The Canyons & Peaks from Sedona to Flagstaff. Stewart Aitchison. LC 92-19896. (Illus.). 128p. (Orig.). 1992. pap. 5.95 (*0-89658-215-9*) Voyageur Pr.

Red Rock, a Chronicle of Reconstruction. Thomas N. Page. LC 67-29275. (Americans in Fiction Ser.). (Illus.). 599p. reprint ed. lib. bdg. 22.00 (*0-8398-1551-4*) Irvington.

Red Rock, a Chronicle of Reconstruction. Thomas N. Page. (Americans in Fiction Ser.). (Illus.). 599p. 1986. reprint ed. pap. text ed. 9.95 (*0-8290-1920-0*) Irvington.

Red Rock Recipes. Eloise Carleton. LC 93-51503. 144p. (Orig.). 1994. spiral bd. 9.95 (*0-87358-571-2*) Northland AZ.

Red Rocks Park: Geology & Flowers. L. W. LeRoy & D. O. LeRoy. LC 78-15784. 29p. 1978. pap. 3.00 (*0-918062-02-0*) Colo Sch Mines.

Red Rocks Select. 2nd ed. Todd Swain. (Illus.). 246p. 1995. pap. 25.00 (*0-934641-86-2*) Chockstone Pr.

Red Rosa. Michael Collins. 304p. 1989. reprint ed. mass mkt. 3.95 (*0-373-97099-4*) Harlequin Bks.

Red Rose for Francis: A Story of the Young Life of Francis Siedlisha. 2nd ed. Claire J. Mohan. (Illus.). (J). (gr. 4-7). 1990. lib. bdg. write for info. (*0-9621500-9-6*) Young Sparrow Pr.

Red Rose for Francis: A Story of the Young Life of Francis Siedliska. Claire J. Mohan. (Illus.). (J). (gr. 4-7). 1989. lib. bdg. 5.95 (*0-9621500-8-8*) Young Sparrow Pr.

Red Roses & Petrol. Joseph O'Connor. 1996. pap. 11.95 (*0-413-69990-0*, Pub. by Methuen UK) Heinemann.

Red Rover. James Fenimore Cooper. 1976. lib. bdg. 29.95 (*0-89968-158-1*, Lghtyr Pr) Buccaneer Bks.

Red Rover. James Fenimore Cooper. 1976. 30.95 (*0-8488-1407-X*) Amereon Ltd.

***Red Rover.** James Fenimore Cooper. Date not set. lib. bdg. 28.95 (*0-8488-1966-7*) Amereon Ltd.

Red Rover. James Fenimore Cooper. (Works of James Fenimore Cooper Ser.). 1990. reprint ed. lib. bdg. 79.00 (*0-7812-2376-8*) Rprt Serv.

Red Rover: A Tale. James Fenimore Cooper. Ed. by Thomas Philbrick & Marianne Philbrick. LC 89-31289. 676p. 1991. text ed. 59.50 (*0-7914-0188-X*); pap. text ed. 19.95 (*0-7914-0189-8*) State U NY Pr.

Red Rover, Red Rover. Edith Fowke. 1988. pap. 12.95 (*0-385-25172-6*) Doubleday.

Red Rover, Red Rover. Oliver Hailey. 1979. pap. 5.25 (*0-8222-0940-3*) Dramatists Play.

Red Rubber. Edmund D. Morel. LC 79-95442. (Studies in Russian Literature & Life: No. 100). 1970. reprint ed. lib. bdg. 75.00 (*0-8383-0995-X*) M S G Haskell Hse.

Red Rubber: The Story of the Rubber Slave Trade Flourishing on the Congo in the Year of Grace 1906. 2nd ed. Edmund D. Morel. LC 71-76859. (Illus.). 213p. 1969. reprint ed. text ed. 45.00 (*0-8371-1161-7*, MOR&, Greenwood Pr) Greenwood.

Red Rum Punch: Forging into the First Post-Communist Quagmire with My Partner Uncle Sam. Ceylon L. Barclay. LC 94-60436. (Illus.). 350p. (Orig.). 1994. pap. text ed. 14.95 (*0-940121-15-8*, P201, Cross Roads Bks) Cross Cultural Pubns.

Red Runs the Earth. 2nd ed. Joe E. Pierce. LC 70-93459. 1977. pap. 5.95 (*0-913244-06-6*) Hapi Pr.

Red Sail. Francis H. Wise & Joyce M. Wise. (Illus.). (J). (ps-1). 1978. pap. 1.50 (*0-614-08378-8*) Wise Pub.

Red Sail. Francis H. Wise. 1981. 1.50 (*0-915766-39-6*) Wise Pub.

Red Sails in the Sunset. LeRoy F. Oates. 1996. 8.95 (*0-533-11721-6*) Vantage.

Red Saint. Warwick Deeping. 1976. lib. bdg. 16.75 (*0-89968-024-0*, Lghtyr Pr) Buccaneer Bks.

***Red Sand.** R. Karl Largent. 400p. (Orig.). 1997. mass mkt. 6.99 (*0-8439-4301-7*, Leisure Bks) Dorchester Pub Co.

Red Sands. Victor Milan. 416p. (Orig.). 1993. mass mkt. 4.99 (*0-446-35840-1*) Warner Bks.

Red Sauce, Whiskey & Snow. August Kleinzahler. LC 94-24437. 1995. 19.00 (*0-374-28924-7*) FS&G.

Red Sauce, Whiskey & Snow. August Kleinzahler. 112p. 1996. pap. text ed. 10.00 (*0-374-52472-6*, Noonday) FS&G.

Red Scare: Memories of the American Inquisition. Griffin Fariello. 576p. 1996. pap. 15.00 (*0-380-72711-0*) Avon.

Red Scare: Memories of the American Inquisition: An Oral History. Griffin Fariello. 596p. 1995. 29.95 (*0-393-03732-0*) Norton.

Red Scare in Court: New York versus the International Workers Order. Arthur J. Sabin. LC 92-30645. (Illus.). 392p. (C). 1993. text ed. 36.95 (*0-8122-3189-9*) U of Pa Pr.

Red Scare or Red Menace? American Communism & Anticommunism in the Cold War Era. John E. Haynes. (American Ways Ser.). 224p. 1995. 24.95 (*1-56663-090-8*) I R Dee.

Red Scare or Red Menace? American Communism & Anticommunism in the Cold War Era. John E. Haynes. (American Ways Ser.). 1996. pap. text ed. 9.95 (*1-56663-091-6*) I R Dee.

Red Scare the Cost of Anti-Communist Hysteria. Katz. (J). 1995. 13.95 (*0-689-31609-7*, Atheneum Bks Young) S&S Childrens.

***Red Scarf Girl: A Memoir of the Cultural Revolution.** Ji-Li Jiang. LC 97-5089. (YA). 1997. write for info. (*0-06-027585-5*); lib. bdg. write for info. (*0-06-027586-3*) HarpC.

Red Scorpion: The War Patrols of the USS Rasher. Peter T. Sasgen. LC 94-48541. (Illus.). 448p. 1995. 28.95 (*1-55750-760-0*) Naval Inst Pr.

Red Scream. Mary W. Walker. 416p. 1995. mass mkt. 5.99 (*0-553-57172-9*, Crimeline) Bantam.

Red Scream. large type ed. Mary W. Walker. (Niagara Large Print Ser.). 524p. 1995. 27.99 (*0-7089-5814-1*) Ulverscroft.

Red Screen: Politics, Society, Art in Soviet Cinema. Ed. by Anna Lawton. LC 91-33268. 352p. 1992. 67.50 (*0-415-07818-0*, A8196) Routledge.

Red Screen: Politics, Society, Art in Soviet Cinema. Ed. by Anna Lawton. LC 91-33268. 352p. (C). 1992. pap. text ed. 22.95 (*0-415-07819-9*, A8197) Routledge.

Red Sea. David Doubilet & Andrea Ghisotti. (Illus.). 160p. 1995. 22.98 (*0-8317-7592-0*) Smithmark.

Red Sea. Peter Vine. 128p. (C). 1995. 81.00 (*0-907151-10-8*, Pub. by IMMEL Pubng UK) St Mut.

Red Sea. Peter Vine. 128p. 1995. pap. 66.00 (*0-614-07672-2*, Pub. by IMMEL Pubng UK) St Mut.

Red Sea: Prospects for Stability. Ed. by Abdel M. Farid. LC 84-40040. 192p. 1984. text ed. 29.95 (*0-312-66716-7*) St Martin.

Red Sea - Black Russia: Prolegomena to the History of North-Central Eurasia in Antiquity & the Middle Ages. Jacques Bacic. 396p. 1995. 56.00 (*0-88033-318-9*) East Eur Monographs.

Red Sea & Adjacent Countries at the Close of the Seventeenth Century As Described by Joseph Pitts, William Daniel & Charles Jaques. Ed. by William Foster. (Hakluyt Society Second Ser.: Vol. 100). (Illus.). 232p. 1996. 45.00 (*0-85115-987-7*, Pub. by Hakluyt Soc UK) Boydell & Brewer.

Red Sea & Indian Ocean Cruising Guide. Alan Lucas. 190p. (C). 1985. 160.00 (*0-85288-096-0*, Pub. by Imray Laurie Norie & Wilson UK) St Mut.

***Red Sea & the Arabian Gulf.** Julia Waterlow. LC 96-40997. (Seas & Oceans Ser.). (J). 1997. lib. bdg. 24.26 (*0-8172-4515-4*) Raintree Steck-V.

Red Sea Coasts of Egypt: Sinai & the Mainland. Jenny Jobbins. (Illus.). 125p. 1990. pap. text ed. 14.95 (*977-424-206-8*, Pub. by Am Univ Cairo Pr UA) Col U Pr.

Red Sea Coral Reefs. Gunnar Bemert & Rupert F. Ormond. (Illus.). 192p. 1981. 55.00 (*0-7103-0007-7*) Routledge Chapman & Hall.

Red Sea Diver's Guide. Tamara Double & Alex Double. 172p. 1995. pap. 54.00 (*1-898162-00-X*, Pub. by IMMEL Pubng UK) St Mut.

Red Sea Divers Guide, 2 vols., Vol. 1. Tamara Double & Alex Double. 192p. (C). 1995. 105.00 (*0-907151-94-9*, Pub. by IMMEL Pubng UK) St Mut.

Red Sea Divers Guide, 2 vols., Vol. 2. Tamara Double & Alex Double. 172p. (C). 1990. 125.00 (*0-907151-40-X*, Pub. by IMMEL Pubng UK) St Mut.

Red Sea Escape, Vol. 10013. Lou E. Smith. (Illus.). (J). (gr. 1-8). 1996. 8.00 (*1-888535-06-7*) Firefly Prods.

Red Sea Explorers. Peter Vine & Hagen Schmid. (Illus.). 206p. 1995. pap. 51.00 (*0-907151-30-2*, Pub. by IMMEL Pubng UK) St Mut.

Red Sea Haggadah. Moses Muses & Laurance Wieder. 96p. 1995. pap. 10.00 (*1-887478-00-0*, WiseAcre) Red Sea NY.

Red Sea Invertebrates. Peter Vine. (Illus.). 224p. 1995. 120.00 (*0-907151-11-6*, Pub. by IMMEL Pubng UK) St Mut.

Red Sea Is Your Blood. Alvin B. Kuhn. 60p. 1993. pap. 9.95 (*1-56459-328-2*) Kessinger Pub.

Red Sea (Is Your Blood) Alvin B. Kuhn. 60p. 1976. reprint ed. spiral bd. 5.00 (*0-7873-0515-4*) Hlth Research.

Red Sea Pilot: Aden to Cyprus. Elaine Morgan & Stephen Davies. (Illus.). 260p. 1995. 69.95 (*0-85288-253-X*, Pub. by Imray Laurie Norie & Wilson UK) Bluewater Bks.

An Asterisk (*) at the beginning of an entry indicates that the title is appearing in BIP for the first time.

R

Red Sea Reef Fishes. John E. Randall. (Illus.). 192p. 1995. pap. 85.00 (*0-907151-87-6*, Pub. by IMMEL Pubng UK) St Mut.

Red Sea Reef Fishes. John E. Randall. (Illus.). 192p. (C). 1995. 110.00 (*0-907151-04-3*, Pub. by IMMEL Pubng UK) St Mut.

Red Sea Region: Local Actors & the Superpowers. Roberto Aliboni. LC 84-24024. (Contemporary Issues in the Middle East Ser.). 200p. 1985. text ed. 29.95 (*0-8156-2332-1*) Syracuse U Pr.

Red Sea Safety: Guide to Dangerous Marine Animals. Peter Vine. 144p. (C). 1990. 100.00 (*0-907151-12-4*, Pub. by IMMEL Pubng UK) St Mut.

Red Sea Safety: Guide to Dangerous Marine Animals. Peter Vine. 144p. 1995. 54.00 (*0-614-07669-2*, Pub. by IMMEL Pubng UK); pap. 39.00 (*1-898162-70-0*, Pub. by IMMEL Pubng UK) St Mut.

Red Sea Sharks. Herge. (Illus.). (J). (gr. 3-8). 19.95 (*0-8288-5058-5*) Fr & Eur.

Red Sea Sharks. Herge. (Adventures of Tintin Ser.). (J). (gr. k up). 1976. pap. 8.95 (*0-316-35848-7*, Joy St Bks) Little.

Red Sea Shells. Doreen Sharabati. (Illus.). 128p. (Orig.). 1985. pap. 29.95 (*0-7103-0103-0*) Routledge Chapman & Hall.

***Red Shadow: A Physician's Memoir of the Soviet Occupation of Eastern Poland, 1944-1956.** Zygmunt Klukowski. Ed. & Tr. by Andrew G. Klukowski. Tr. by George Klukowski. LC 97-1447. (Illus.). 192p. 1997. boxed 32.50 (*0-7864-0328-4*) McFarland & Co.

Red Shadow of Steel Mills: Photos & Poems. David J. Adams et al. Ed. by Larry Smith. (Midwest Writers Ser.). (Illus.). 155p. (Orig.). 1991. pap. 8.95 (*0-933087-18-7*) Bottom Dog Pr.

Red Shadows. Larry Hancock & Michael Cherkas. (Silent Invasion Ser.: No. 2). 80p. (Orig.). 1988. pap. 8.95 (*0-918348-55-2*) NBM.

Red Shark. 2nd ed. Ruth M. Tabrah. (Illus.). 224p. (J). (gr. 5-10). 1991. reprint ed. pap. 8.95 (*0-916630-67-6*) Pr Pacifica.

Red Shift. Peter Inman. LC 87-63135. 60p. 1988. pap. 6.00 (*0-937804-28-2*) Segue NYC.

Red Shi'ism. Ali Shariati. Tr. by Habib Shirazi from PER. 1980. pap. 2.00 (*0-941722-17-1*) Book Dist Ctr.

Red Shirt. Lois Leardi. 137p. 1991. 19.00 (*1-883285-07-0*) Delphinium.

Red Shirt. Lois Leardi. 1994. pap. 9.95 (*1-883285-12-7*) Delphinium.

Red Shoes. Hans Christian Andersen. (Oxford Graded Readers Ser.). (YA). (gr. 7-12). 1983. pap. 3.50 (*0-19-421741-8*) OUP.

***Red Shoes.** Barbara Bazilian & H. C. Andersen. LC 96-29257. (J). 1997. write for info. (*1-879085-56-9*) Whsprng Coyote Pr.

***Red Shoes.** Powell. Date not set. pap. 9.95 (*0-312-15637-5*) St Martin.

Red Shoes. large type ed. Michael Powell & Emeric Pressburger. (Basic Ser.). 288p. 1996. 20.95 (*0-7862-0674-8*, Thorndike Lrg Prnt) Thorndike Pr.

Red Shoes. Hans J. Schmidt. 73p. 1956. reprint ed. pap. 3.45 (*0-87129-042-1*, R47) Dramatic Pub.

Red Shoes: A Novel. Michael Powell & Emeric Pressburger. LC 95-36147. 192p. 1995. 17.95 (*0-312-14034-7*, Wyatt Bk) St Martin.

Red Shoes & Other Tattered Tales. Karen E. Gordon. LC 95-25958. (Illus.). 192p. (Orig.). 1996. pap. 12.95 (*1-56478-092-9*) Dalkey Arch.

Red Signal. Grace L. Hill. reprint ed. lib. bdg. 23.95 (*0-89190-047-0*, Rivercity Pr) Amereon Ltd.

***Red Signature.** Mary Leader. 72p. (Orig.). 1997. pap. 12.95 (*1-55597-255-1*) Graywolf.

***Red Skies.** R. Karl Largent. 400p. (Orig.). 1996. mass mkt. 6.99 (*0-8439-4117-0*) Dorchester Pub Co.

Red Skies of Eighty-Eight: The 1988 Forest Fire Season in the Northern Rockies, the Northern Great Plains & the Greater Yellowstone Area. A. Richard Guth & Stan B. Cohen. LC 89-50399. (Illus.). 136p. (Orig.). (YA). 1989. pap. text ed. 12.95 (*0-929521-17-X*) Pictorial Hist.

Red Sky. Ron Rendleman. vi, 160p. (Orig.). 1996. pap. 9.95 (*0-9650884-0-5*) Sterling Prodns.

Red Sky & Blue Airplane. Jim Jordan. 1971. 4.00 (*0-685-67922-5*) Windless Orchard.

***Red Sky at Morning.** Andrea Wyman. 1997. pap. 3.99 (*0-380-72877-X*) Avon.

Red Sky at Morning. Andrea Wyman. LC 91-55029. 240p. (J). (gr. 3-7). 1991. 15.95 (*0-8234-0903-1*) Holiday.

Red Sky at Morning. Richard Bradford. 256p. 1991. reprint ed. lib. bdg. 33.00 (*0-8095-9095-6*) Borgo Pr.

Red Sky at Morning. Richard Bradford. LC 86-45309. 256p. 1986. reprint ed. pap. 12.50 (*0-06-091361-4*, PL/1361, PL) HarpC.

***Red Sky at Night.** Jim Hall. LC 96-45621. 1997. 23.95 (*0-385-31638-0*) Delacorte.

Red Sky at Night: Circling the Pacific in Stornoway. Marjorie Petersen. LC 94-67446. (Illus.). (Orig.). 1994. pap. 12.95 (*0-9642394-1-8*) Paxi Press.

Red Sky at Night, Lovers' Delight. Jane A. Hodge. 1978. pap. 2.75 (*0-449-23745-1*, Crest) Fawcett.

***Red Sky in Mourning.** Patricia H. Rushford. (Helen Bradley Mysteries Ser.). 1997. pap. 9.99 (*1-55661-731-3*) Bethany Hse.

Red Sky, Red Water: Powell on the Colorado. Charles Hood. (Illus.). 80p. (Orig.). 1990. 20.00 (*0-933313-12-8*); pap. 12.95 (*0-933313-13-6*) SUN Gemini Pr.

Red Sky, Red Water: Powell on the Colorado. deluxe limited ed. Charles Hood. (Illus.). 80p. (Orig.). 1990. 30.00 (*0-933313-11-X*) SUN Gemini Pr.

Red Sky Warrior. Genell Dellin. 336p. (Orig.). 1996. mass mkt. 5.50 (*0-380-77526-3*) Avon.

Red Slayer: Being the Second of the Sorrowful Mysteries of Brother Athelstan. Paul Harding. 288p. 1995. mass mkt. 4.99 (*0-380-72106-6*) Avon.

Red Snake. George McMullen. 152p. 1993. pap. 9.95 (*1-878901-58-3*) Hampton Roads Pub Co.

Red Sorghum. Mo Yan. Tr. by Howard Goldblatt. 368p. 1994. pap. 10.95 (*0-14-016854-0*, Penguin Bks) Viking Penguin.

Red Sox: A Reckoning. Dan Valenti. LC 78-68729. 72p. (Orig.). 1979. 10.95 (*0-943514-00-2*); pap. 6.95 (*0-685-19245-8*) Literations.

Red Sox Fan's Little Book of Wisdom. Curt Smith. LC 94-23541. 1994. pap. 5.95 (*0-912083-76-X*) Diamond Communications.

Red Sox Reader. enl. rev. ed. Ed. by Dan Riley. (Illus.). 304p. 1991. pap. 13.00 (*0-395-58776-X*) HM.

Red Sox Reader Thirty Years of Musings on Baseball's Most Amusing Team. Ed. by Dan Riley. LC 87-50180. (Illus.). 240p. (Orig.). 1987. pap. 9.95 (*0-941913-00-7*) Ventura Arts.

Red Spider, 2 vols. in 1. Sabine Baring-Gould. LC 79-8232. reprint ed. 44.50 (*0-404-61772-7*) AMS Pr.

Red-Spotted Newt. Doris Gove. LC 91-34497. (Illus.). 32p. (J). (gr. 2 up). 1994. text ed. 14.95 (*0-689-31697-6*, Atheneum Bks Young) S&S Childrens.

Red Square. Martin Cruz Smith. 1993. mass mkt. 5.99 (*0-345-38473-3*) Ballantine.

Red Square. large type ed. Martin C. Smith. 657p. 1993. reprint ed. pap. 15.95 (*1-56054-888-6*) Thorndike Pr.

Red Square. large type ed. Martin C. Smith. 657p. 1994. reprint ed. 23.95 (*1-56054-610-7*) Thorndike Pr.

Red Square, Black Square: Organon for Revolutionary Imagination. Vladislav Todorov. LC 93-47101. (SUNY Series, The Margins of Literature). 200p. (C). 1994. text ed. 49.50 (*0-7914-2191-0*); pap. text ed. 16.95 (*0-7914-2192-9*) State U NY Pr.

***Red Squirrels.** Tom Tew. (Illus.). 48p. (Orig.). (YA). 1997. pap. 9.95 (*1-900455-24-2*, Pub. by Colin Baxter Ltd UK) Voyageur Pr.

Red Stacks over the Horizon: The Story of the Goodrich Steamboat Line. James L. Elliott. (Illus.). 314p. 1995. reprint ed. 20.00 (*0-940473-30-5*); reprint ed. pap. 12.95 (*0-940473-31-3*) Wm Caxton.

Red Stains on Vietnam Doves. William F. Gausman. 251p. 1989. 13.95 (*0-9625721-0-1*); pap. 7.95 (*0-9625721-1-X*) Veracity Pubns.

Red Star: The First Bolshevik Utopia. Alexander Bogdanov. Ed. by Loren R. Graham & Richard Stites. Tr. by Charles Rougle from RUS. LC 83-48637. (Soviet History, Politics, Society & Thought Ser.). (Illus.). 272p. (Orig.). 1984. pap. 13.95 (*0-253-20317-1*, MB 317) Ind U Pr.

Red Star & the Lotus: The Political Dynamics of Indo-Soviet Relations. S. S. Rai. 400p. 1990. text ed. 37.50 (*81-220-0177-7*, Pub. by Konark Pubs Pvt Ltd II) Advent Bks Div.

Red Star in Orbit. James E. Oberg. (Illus.). 1981. 16.95 (*0-394-51429-7*) Random.

Red Star over China. rev. ed. Edgar R. Snow. LC 68-17724. 592p. 1989. pap. 15.95 (*0-8021-5093-4*, Grove) Grove-Atltic.

Red Star over Cuba: The Russian Assault on the Western Hemisphere. Nathaniel Weyl. 1960. 9.95 (*0-8159-6705-5*) Devin.

Red Star over Cuba: The Russian Assault on the Western Hemisphere. Nathaniel Weyl. LC 60-53203. 301p. reprint ed. pap. 85.80 (*0-317-28236-0*, 2022711) Bks Demand.

Red Star over Malaya: Resistance & Social Conflict During & after the Japanese Occupation, 1941-1946. 2nd ed. Cheah B. Kheng. 384p. (Orig.). 1987. pap. 34.00 (*9971-69-111-6*, Pub. by Sgapore Univ SI) Coronet Bks.

Red Star over Southern Africa. Morgan Norval. LC 87-51366. 220p. 1988. 18.95 (*0-944273-00-9*); pap. 5.95 (*0-944273-02-5*) Selous Found Pr.

Red Star over Tibet. 2nd ed. Dawa Norbu. LC 87-80663. 300p. 1988. text ed. 30.00 (*0-938719-19-X*, Envoy Pr) Apt Bks.

Red Star over Tibet. 2nd ed. Dawa Norbu. LC 87-80663. 300p. 1988. pap. 14.95 (*0-938719-26-2*, Envoy Pr) Apt Bks.

***Red Star Rising.** Jamie Allen. 1997. pap. text ed. 19.95 (*981-00-8083-2*) Buttrwrth-Heinemann.

Red Stars: Political Aspects of Soviet Science Fiction. Patrick L. McGuire. LC 84-28099. (Studies in Speculative Fiction: No. 7). 170p. reprint ed. pap. 48.50 (*0-8357-1579-5*, 2070509) Bks Demand.

Red Steel. Tim Beach. 1994. 30.00 (*1-56076-895-9*) TSR Inc.

Red Steel Savage Barn. 1995. 20.00 (*0-7869-0123-3*) TSR Inc.

Red Storm on the Reich: The Soviet March on Germany, 1945. Christopher Duffy. (Illus.). 415p. 1993. reprint ed. pap. 14.95 (*0-306-80505-7*) Da Capo.

Red Storm Rising. 1988. audio 17.00 (*0-394-29866-7*) Random.

Red Storm Rising. Tom Clancy. 736p. 1987. pap. 7.50 (*0-425-10107-X*) Berkley Pub.

Red Storm Rising. Tom Clancy. 480p. 1986. 24.95 (*0-399-13149-3*, Putnam) Putnam Pub Group.

Red Storm Rising. large type ed. Tom Clancy. LC 89-20219. 1289p. 1991. lib. bdg. 23.95 (*0-89621-885-6*) Thorndike Pr.

Red Strawberry. John Clementson. LC 95-80314. (Illus.). 10p. (J). (ps). 1995. pap. 4.00 (*0-15-200314-2*, Red Wagon Bks) HarBrace.

Red Streams of George Through Pages. Jefferson Hansen. 18p. (Orig.). 1993. pap. 5.00 (*0-926935-84-4*) Runaway Spoon.

Red String. Margot Blair. LC 95-39555. (Illus.). 40p. (J). (ps-8). 1996. pap. 16.95 (*0-89236-340-1*, J P Getty Museum) J P Getty Trust.

Red Student Activity Book. Debbie Strayer & Susan S. Simpson. (Learning Language Arts Through Literature Ser.). 159p. 1992. 16.00 (*1-880892-25-1*) Com Sense FL.

Red Suitcase. Naomi S. Nye. (American Poets Continuum Ser.: No. 29). 90p. 1994. 20.00 (*1-880238-14-4*); pap. 12.50 (*1-880238-15-2*) BOA Edns.

Red Sunset: The Failure of Soviet Politics. Philip G. Roeder. LC 93-4047. (Illus.). 344p. (C). 1993. pap. text ed. 17.95 (*0-691-01942-8*) Princeton U Pr.

***Red Surf.** Bird & Falk. (New Trend Fiction A Ser.). (J). 1993. pap. text ed. write for info. (*0-582-80042-0*, Pub. by Longman UK) Longman.

Red Swan: Myths & Tales of the American Indians. Ed. by John Bierhorst. LC 92-3299. (Illus.). 398p. 1992. pap. 15.95 (*0-8263-1355-8*) U of NM Pr.

Red Swastika: At the Crystal Palace. Tom O. Jones. LC 93-94249. 360p. (Orig.). 1995. pap. 10.00 (*1-56002-416-X*, Univ Edtns) Aegina Pr.

Red Tag Comes Back. Frederick B. Phleger. LC 61-11452. (Science I Can Read Bks.). (Illus.). 64p. (J). (gr. k-3). 1961. lib. bdg. 13.89 (*0-06-024706-1*) HarpC Child Bks.

Red Tag Mystery. Terese Guglielmino. Ed. by Jane Weinberger. LC 93-60462. 160p. (J). (gr. 3-6). 1993. pap. 6.95 (*0-932433-19-7*) Windswept Hse.

Red-Tail Angels: The Story of the Tuskegee Airmen of World War II. Patricia McKissack & Frederick McKissack. (Illus.). 144p. (YA). (gr. 5 up). 1995. 19.95 (*0-8027-8292-2*); lib. bdg. 20.85 (*0-8027-8293-0*) Walker & Co.

***Red-Tailed Boas.** (Herpetological Library). 7.50 (*0-614-29987-X*) Serpents Tale.

Red Tailed Boas, Their Care & Breeding. Glen Drewnowski. (Illus.). 64p. 1995. pap. 9.95 (*0-7938-0275-X*, RE123) TFH Pubns.

Red-Tailed Tropicbird on Kure Atoll. Robert R. Fleet. 64p. 1974. 5.50 (*0-943610-16-8*) Am Ornithologists.

***Red Tails, Black Wings: The Men of America's Black Airforce.** John B. Holway. LC 96-61290. (Illus.). 400p. 1997. 22.95 (*1-881325-21-0*) Yucca Tree Pr.

Red Talons Tribebook. Ben Chessell & White Wolf Staff. (Werewolf Ser.). (Illus.). 72p. (Orig.). 1996. pap. 10.00 (*1-56504-328-6*, 3057) White Wolf.

Red Tape. Bill Thomas. 1999. pap. 11.00 (*0-452-27031-6*, Plume) NAL-Dutton.

***Red Tape.** Bill Thomas & Charles Sutherland. 272p. 3.98 (*0-8317-3346-2*) Smithmark.

Red Tape: Its Origins, Uses & Abuses. Herbert Kaufman. LC 77-11083. 100p. 1977. 26.95 (*0-8157-4842-6*); pap. 9.95 (*0-8157-4841-8*) Brookings.

***Red Tape & Pigeon-Hole Generals.** Ed. by Frederick B. Arner. (Illus.). 1997. write for info. (*1-883522-15-3*) Rockbridge Pub.

Red Tape Cutter's Handbook: A Working Tool for Dealing with Bureaucracies. Carol L. Clark. LC 80-21193. 326p. reprint ed. pap. 93.00 (*0-8357-4256-3*, 2037045) Bks Demand.

Red Tape in America: Stories from the Front Line. Geoff C. Ziebart. 120p. 1995. 14.95 (*0-89195-059-1*) Heritage Found.

Red Tara Commentary: Instructions for the Concise Practice Known As Red Tara, an Open Door to Bliss & Ultimate Awareness. Jane Tromge. 85p. (Orig.). 1994. pap. 7.00 (*1-881847-04-7*) Chagdud Gonpa-Padma.

Red Tears. Giorgis. 29.95 (*0-932415-34-2*) Red Sea Pr.

Red Tempest: The Life of a Surgeon in Gulag. Isaac J. Vogelfanger. (C). 1996. 24.95 (*0-7735-1404-X*, Pub. by McGill CN) U of Toronto Pr.

***Red Tent.** Diamant. LC 97-16825. 1997. 23.95 (*0-312-16978-7*) St Martin.

Red the Fiend. Gilbert Sorrentino. LC 94-32006. 208p. 1995. 19.95 (*0-88064-163-0*) Fromm Intl Pub.

Red the Firedog's How to Plan for a Safe Escape Kid-Pak. rev. ed. Ann Lupo. Ed. by Greg Fox. (Life-Skill Builder Educational Ser.). (Illus.). 20p. (J). (ps-3). 1991. pap. text ed. 3.95 (*1-56230-137-3*); pap. text ed. 4.95 incl. audio (*1-56230-134-9*) Syndistar.

Red Thread. unabridged ed. Gitta Deutsch. (Studies in Austrian Literature, Culture & Thought; Translation Ser.). Orig. Title: Bocklinstrassenelegie. (Illus.). 145p. 1996. 16.95 (*1-57241-019-1*) Ariadne CA.

***Red Thumb Mark.** R. Austin Freeman. 3.95 (*0-7867-0240-0*) Carroll & Graf.

Red Thumb Mark. R. Austin Freeman. 305p. 1986. pap. 3.95 (*0-88184-240-0*) Carroll & Graf.

Red Thumb Mark. R. Austin Freeman. 320p. 1986. reprint ed. pap. 6.95 (*0-486-25210-8*) Dover.

Red Thunder, Tropic Lightning: The World of a Combat Division in Vietnam. Eric M. Bergerud. (Illus.). 352p. 1994. pap. 12.95 (*0-14-023545-0*, Penguin Bks) Viking Penguin.

Red Tide. R. Karl Largent. 448p. (Orig.). 1992. mass mkt., pap. text ed. 4.99 (*0-8439-3366-6*) Dorchester Pub Co.

Red Tide. Christopher Nicole. 352p. 1996. 24.00 (*0-7278-4850-X*) Severn Hse.

Red Tides: Biology, Environmental Science, & Toxicology. Ed. by T. Okaichi et al. 489p. 1988. 97.50 (*0-444-01343-1*) P-H.

Red Tiles, Blue Skies: More Tales of Santa Barbara from Adobe Days to Present Days. Ed. by Steven Gilbar. LC 96-16123. 192p. (Orig.). 1996. pap. 12.95 (*1-880284-17-0*) J Daniel.

Red Tory Blues: A Political Memoir. Heath MacQuarrie. 320p. 1992. 35.00 (*0-8020-5958-9*) U of Toronto Pr.

Red Triangle. Arthur Morrison. LC 75-116962. (Short Story Index Reprint Ser.). 1977. 21.95 (*0-8369-3466-0*) Ayer.

Red Trousseau. Carol Muske. 96p. 1993. pap. 12.00 (*0-14-058686-5*, Penguin Bks) Viking Penguin.

***Red Truck with a Green Bed.** 2nd unabridged ed. Hugh Wilder. xviii, 145p. (Orig.). 1997. pap. 19.95 incl. audio compact disk (*0-9655323-0-5*, D N T Bks) Dime Novel Triad.

Red Umbrellas. Kelvin Lindemann. LC 74-30367. 214p. 1975. reprint ed. text ed. 55.00 (*0-8371-7521-6*, LIRU, Greenwood Pr) Greenwood.

Red under the Skin. Natasha Saje. (Agnes Lynch Starret Poetry Prize, 1993 Ser.). 88p. (C). 1994. 22.95 (*0-8229-3865-0*); pap. 10.95 (*0-8229-5545-8*) U of Pittsburgh Pr.

***Red Unicorn.** Tannith Lee. LC 96-54590. 1997. 20.95 (*0-312-86265-2*) St Martin.

Red Velvet. Barbara Boswell. 400p. (Orig.). 1995. pap. text ed. 5.99 (*0-515-11743-9*) Jove Pubns.

Red Vienna & the Golden Age of Psychology, 1918-1938. Sheldon Gardner & Gwendolyn Stevens. LC 91-36401. 304p. 1992. text ed. 59.95 (*0-275-94013-6*, C4013, Praeger Pubs) Greenwood.

Red Virgin: A Poem of Simone Weil. Stephanie Strickland. LC 93-12949. (Brittingham Prize in Poetry Ser.). 96p. (Orig.). (C). 1993. 17.95 (*0-299-13990-5*); pap. 10.95 (*0-299-13994-8*) U of Wis Pr.

Red Virgin Soil: Soviet Literature in the 1920's. Robert A. Maguire. LC 86-24391. 504p. (C). 1987. reprint ed. pap. 17.95 (*0-8014-9447-8*) Cornell U Pr.

Red Wagon. Ted Berrigan. LC 76-26054. 1976. 7.95 (*0-916328-05-8*); pap. 3.00 (*0-916328-01-5*) Yellow Pr.

Red Wagon. deluxe ed. Ted Berrigan. LC 76-26054. 1976. 15.00 (*0-685-93040-8*) Yellow Pr.

Red Wagon, Vol. 3. Ilya Nabakov. (Illus.). 60p. 1993. pap. 65.00 (*0-8109-2539-7*) Abrams.

Red Wagon Year. Kathi Appelt. LC 95-37920. (Illus.). 28p. (J). (ps). 1996. 11.00 (*0-15-277991-4*, Red Wagon Bks) HarBrace.

Red Wagons & White Canvas: Mollie Bailey, Circus Queen of the Southwest. Marjorie A. Gurasich. Ed. by Melissa Roberts. (Illus.). 88p. (J). (gr. 4-7). 1988. pap. 6.95 (*0-89015-646-8*) Sunbelt Media.

Red Walls & Homesteads. Ed. by Margaret B. Hanson. (Illus.). 196p. 1987. 14.50 (*0-9605834-3-2*); pap. 10.00 (*0-318-32981-6*) Hanson.

Red Walls, Black Hats: An Amish Barnraising. Jim Weyer. LC 84-90471. (Illus.). 128p. 1988. 19.95 (*0-9613834-3-7*) Weyer Intl Bk Div.

Red, White & Black: The Peoples of Early North America. 3rd ed. Gary B. Nash. 352p. (C). 1991. pap. text ed. 30.00 (*0-13-769878-X*) P-H.

Red, White & Blue Day: Literature-Based History Activities for Children, Grades 4-8. Patricia L. Roberts. LC 95-48955. 1996. 25.95 (*0-205-14737-2*) Allyn.

Red, White, & Blue Valentine. Patricia R. Giff. (Lincoln Lions Band Ser.: No. 5). 80p. (J). (ps-3). 1993. mass mkt. 3.25 (*0-440-40768-0*) Dell.

***Red, White & Blues.** Michael D. Haldeman. (On the Great Divide Ser.: Bk. 1). 146p. (Orig.). 1996. pap. 9.95 (*0-918072-09-3*) Whitehorse Prodns.

Red, White, & Blues. Rob Kantner. 432p. 1993. mass mkt. 4.99 (*0-06-104128-9*, Harp PBks) HarpC.

Red, White & Greens. Faith Willinger. pap. 15.00 (*0-06-095044-7*) HarpC.

Red, White & Greens: The Italian Way with Vegetables. Faith Willinger. 306p. 1996. 25.00 (*0-06-018366-7*) HarpC.

Red White & Oh So Blue. Mary Kay Blakely. LC 96-18549. 192p. 1996. 20.00 (*0-684-82450-7*) S&S Trade.

***Red, White & Oh So Blue.** Mary Kay Blakely. 1996. 20.00 (*0-614-19886-0*) Scribnrs Ref.

Red, White & True Blue: The Loyalists in the Revolution. Ed. by Esmond Wright. LC 76-23976. (Studies in Social History: No. 1). 1976. lib. bdg. 34.50 (*0-404-15400-X*) AMS Pr.

Red White Blue & God Bless You: A Portrait of Northern New Mexico. Alex Harris. LC 91-45977. (Illus.). 128p. 1992. 34.95 (*0-8263-1367-1*) U of NM Pr.

Red Wind & Thunder Moon. Max Brand. LC 95-43100. vi, 166p. (C). 1996. text ed. 25.00 (*0-8032-1268-2*) U of Nebr Pr.

***Red Window: Poems by Pamela Stewart.** Pamela Stewart. LC 96-31227. (Contemporary Poetry Ser.). 1997. pap. 14.95 (*0-8203-1894-9*) U of Ga Pr.

***Red Wine.** Daniel Mayland. LC 97-65386. 180p. (Orig.). 1997. pap. 11.95 (*0-9656585-9-7*) New American.

Red Wine for Dummies. Ed McCarthy. 256p. 1996. pap. 12.99 (*0-7645-5012-8*, Dummies Tech) IDG Bks.

Red Wing. Raymond Chandler. 1995. pap. 4.99 (*0-7871-0269-5*, Dove Bks) Dove Audio.

Red Wing Art Pottery: Including Pottery Made for Rumrill. Raymond F. Reiss. LC 94-67711. 240p. 1995. 50.00 (*0-9642087-0-9*) Property IL.

Red Wing Art Pottery, 1920s-1960s: Identification & Value Guide. Brenda L. Dollen. (Illus.). 144p. 1996. pap. 19.95 (*0-89145-733-X*, 4726) Collector Bks.

***Red Wing Collectibles.** DePasquale. (Illus.). 160p. 1995. pap. 9.95 (*0-614-22571-X*, 1670) Collector Bks.

Red Wing Collectibles. Dan DePasquale & Larry Peterson. (Illus.). 160p. 1995. pap. 9.95 (*0-89145-313-X*) Collector Bks.

Red Wing Potters & Their Wares. 3rd rev. ed. Gary T. Tefft & Bonnie J. Tefft. Ed. & Illus. by Bonnie J. Tefft. 200p. 1996. pap. 18.95 (*0-9606730-6-7*) Locust Ent.

Red Wing Rocking Chair. Lucy E. Hurley. LC 90-55253. (Illus.). 54p. (Orig.). 1992. pap. 7.00 (*1-56002-062-8*) Aegina Pr.

Red Wing Stoneware. Dan DePasquale et al. (Illus.). 160p. 1995. pap. 9.95 (*0-89145-234-6*) Collector Bks.

Red-Winged Blackbird: The Biology of a Strongly Polygynous Songbird. Les D. Beletsky. (Illus.). 352p. 1996. text ed. 64.95 (*0-12-084745-0*) Acad Pr.

An Asterisk (*) at the beginning of an entry indicates that the title is appearing in BIP for the first time.

Red-Winged Blackbirds: Decision-Making & Reproductive Success. Les D. Beletsky & Gordon H. Orians. LC 96-18894. (Illus.). 288p. 1996. pap. text ed. 21.95 (*0-226-04187-5*); lib. bdg. 65.00 (*0-226-04186-7*) U Ch Pr.

Red Wings Book. Andrews Podnieks. 500p. 1996. pap. text ed. 18.95 (*1-55022-283-X*, Pub. by ECW Pr CN) LPC InBook.

Red Wings of Christmas. Wesley Eure. LC 92-5457. (Illus.). 176p. (J). (gr. 3-7). 1992. 19.95 (*0-88289-902-3*); audio 14.95 (*0-88289-998-8*) Pelican.

Red Winter. Michael Cormany. 1989. 14.95 (*0-8184-0497-3*) Carol Pub Group.

Red Wizard. Nancy Springer. LC 88-29376. 144p. (J). (gr. 4 up). 1990. lib. bdg. 13.95 (*0-689-31485-X*, Atheneum Bks Young) S&S Childrens.

Red Wolf. Virginia B. Silverstein et al. LC 93-42480. (Endangered in America Ser.). (Illus.). 64p. (J). (gr. 4-6). 1994. lib. bdg. 16.90 (*1-56294-416-9*) Millbrook Pr.

Red Wolf Country. Jonathan London. LC 95-10384. (Illus.). 32p. (J). (ps-4). 1996. pap. 15.99 (*0-525-45191-9*) Dutton Child Bks.

Red Wolf, Red Wolf. W. P. Kinsella. LC 90-52661. 192p. 1990. reprint ed. 22.50 (*0-87074-319-8*); reprint ed. pap. 10.95 (*0-87074-314-7*) SMU Press.

Red Wolves & Black Bears. Edward Hoagland. 288p. 1995. pap. 14.95 (*1-55821-371-6*) Lyons & Burford.

Red Woolen Blanket. Bob Graham. LC 95-36002. (Illus.). 32p. (J). (ps up). 1996. pap. 4.99 (*1-56402-848-8*) Candlewick Pr.

Red Work, Black Widow. Steve Richmond. LC 76-15539. (Illus.). 1976. pap. 2.00 (*0-916918-03-3*) Duck Down.

Red World & White: Memories of a Chippewa Boyhood. John Rogers. LC 96-19036. (Civilization of the American Indian Ser.: Vol. 126). 176p. 1996. pap. 11.95 (*0-8061-2891-7*) U of Okla Pr.

***Red Wyvern.** Katharine Kerr. 416p. 1997. pap. 12.95 (*0-553-37290-4*) Bantam.

Red Years-Black Years: A Political History of Spanish Anarchism, 1911-1937. Robert W. Kern. LC 77-13595. 374p. reprint ed. pap. 106.60 (*0-317-42090-9*, 2025711) Bks Demand.

Redaccion Comercial. Carmen S. Reyes. 381p. 1992. pap. text ed. 12.95 (*0-8477-3679-2*) U of PR Pr.

Redaccion Comercial Estructurada. 2nd ed. Nelson Rojas. 200p. 1982. text ed. 15.36 (*0-07-053566-3*) McGraw.

Redaccion II. Humberto L. Morales. 229p. 1990. pap. 9.25 (*0-8477-3624-5*) U of PR Pr.

Redaccion One. 3rd ed. Humberto L. Morales. 144p. (SPA.). 1990. reprint ed. pap. 7.75 (*0-8477-3617-2*) U of PR Pr.

Redaccion y Estilo. 6th ed. Matilde Albert-Robatto. Ed. by Marle, Inc. Staff. 400p. pap. 20.00 (*0-9627933-0-2*) A L Matilde.

Redaccion y Revision: Estrategies para la Composicion en Espanol. Lisa Gerrard & Sheri S. Long. 1993. pap. text ed. write for info. (*0-07-038697-8*) McGraw.

Redaction of the Babylonian Talmud: Amoraic or Saboraic? Richard Kalmin. (Monographs of the Hebrew Union College: No. 12). 210p. 1989. 30.00 (*0-87820-411-3*) Hebrew Union Coll Pr.

Redaction of the Books of Esther: On Reading Composite Texts. Michael Fox. (Society of Biblical Literature Monographs). 206p. 1991. 29.95 (*1-55540-443-X*, 060040); pap. 18.95 (*1-55540-444-8*, 060040) Scholars Pr GA.

Redactional Process in the Book of the Twelve. James Nogalski. LC 93-37633. (Beiheft zur Zeitschrift fuer die Alttestamentliche Wissenschaft Ser.: Vol. 218). xi, 300p. (C). 1993. lib. bdg. 106.15 (*3-11-013767-4*) De Gruyter.

Redactional Style in the Marcan Gospel: A Study of Syntax & Vocabulary as Guides to Redaction in Mark. E. J. Pryke. LC 76-52184. (Society for New Testament Studies, Monograph: No. 33). 206p. reprint ed. pap. 58.80 (*0-318-34839-X*, 2031714) Bks Demand.

Redactive. Dorothy T. Lusk. 64p. 1991. pap. 8.95 (*0-88922-279-7*) SPD-Small Pr Dist.

Redating Matthew, Mark & Luke: A Fresh Assault on the Synoptic Problem. John W. Wenham. LC 91-39328. 319p. (Orig.). 1992. pap. 19.99 (*0-8308-1760-3*, 1760) InterVarsity.

Redbeans & Rice, Good Ole Grits, & Other Southern Foods: A Celebration of the Dishes of Dixie. Lillie P. Gallagher. (Illus.). 128p. 1986. 6.95 (*0-9610174-4-9*) Petit Press.

Redbird. Patrick Fort. LC 87-23591. (Illus.). 18p. (J). (ps-5). 1988. 24.95 (*0-531-05746-1*) Orchard Bks Watts.

***Redbird at Rockefeller Center.** LC 96-45728. 1997. pap. 14.89 (*0-8037-2257-5*) Dial Bks Young.

Redbirds: The Centennial Celebration of Cardinal Baseball. Bob Broeg. Ed. by Missouri Editing Group Staff & Kelly Anderson. (Illus.). 1992. write for info. (*1-56166-075-2*) Walsworth Pub.

Redbird's Cry. Jean Hager. 256p. 1995. mass mkt. 5.50 (*0-446-40106-4*) Mysterious Pr.

Redbird's Cry. large type ed. Jean Hager. LC 94-11180. 357p. 1994. pap. 18.95 (*0-8161-7402-4*, GK Hall) Thorndike Pr.

Redbirds Revisited: Great Memories & Stories from St. Louis Cardinals. David Craft & Tom Owens. LC 89-81939. (Illus.). 246p. 1990. 19.95 (*0-929387-12-0*) Bonus Books.

Redbook's Guide to Buying Your First Home. Ruth F. Pomeroy. 1980. pap. 4.95 (*0-686-60934-4*, 24716, Fireside) S&S Trade.

Redburn. Herman Melville. Ed. by Harrison Hayford et al. (Northwestern-Newberry Edition of the Writings of Herman Melville: Vol. 4). 384p. 1972. 69.95 (*0-8101-0013-4*); pap. 19.95 (*0-8101-0016-9*) Northwestern U Pr.

Redburn. Herman Melville. Ed. by Harold Beaver. (English Library). 448p. 1977. pap. 12.95 (*0-14-043105-5*, Penguin Classics) Viking Penguin.

Redburn. Herman Melville. (BCL1-PS American Literature Ser.). 346p. 1993. reprint ed. lib. bdg. 89.00 (*0-7812-6990-3*) Rprt Serv.

Redburn ou Sa Premiere Croisiere. Herman Melville. (FRE.). 1980. pap. 13.95 (*0-7859-4142-8*) Fr & Eur.

Redburn, White-Jacket, Moby-Dick. Herman Melville. Ed. by G. Thomas Tanselle. LC 82-18677. 1436p. 1983. 35.00 (*0-940450-09-7*) Library of America.

***Redcaps British Military Police.** Chappel. 1997. 12.95 (*1-85532-670-1*, Pub. by Osprey UK) Stackpole.

***Redcoat.** Gregory Sass. 96p. 1985. pap. 7.95 (*0-88984-083-0*, Pub. by Porcupines Quill CN) Genl Dist Srvs.

Redcoats & Courtesans: The Birth of the British Army 1660-1690. Noel St. John-Williams. (Illus.). 240p. 1994. 30.00 (*1-85753-097-7*, Pub. by Brasseys UK) Brasseys Inc.

Redcoats & Rebels: The American Revolution Through British Eyes. Christopher Hibbert. 416p. 1991. pap. 13.50 (*0-380-71544-9*) Avon.

Reddened Water Flows Clear: Poems from Sri Lanka. Jean Arasanayagam. 143p. (Orig.). 9100. pap. 21.00 (*0-948259-96-5*, Pub. by Forest Bks UK) Dufour.

Redder Blood. William M. Ashby. LC 73-18570. reprint ed. 34.50 (*0-404-11380-X*) AMS Pr.

Rede Me & Be Nott Wrothe. Jerome Barlowe & William Roye. Ed. by Douglas H. Parker. 272p. 1992. 50.00 (*0-8020-2681-8*) U of Toronto Pr.

Rede Me & Be Nott Wrothe for I Say No Thynge but Trothe. William Roy. LC 76-38221. (English Experience Ser.: No. 485). 144p. 1972. reprint ed. 25.00 (*90-221-0485-0*) Walter J Johnson.

***Redecision Therapy: A Brief, Action-Oriented Approach.** Ed. by Carolyn E. Lennox. LC 96-41624. 336p. 1997. 40.00 (*0-7657-0043-3*) Aronson.

***Redeem the Time.** Sue Frost. 560p. 1997. pap. 17.95 (*0-09-179160-X*, Pub. by Hutchinson UK) Trafalgar.

Redeem the Time: The Puritan Sabbath in Early America. Winton U. Solberg. LC 76-26672. (Publication of the Center for the Study of the History of Liberty in America, Harvard University Ser.). 418p. 1977. reprint ed. pap. 120.30 (*0-7837-4192-8*, 2059042) Bks Demand.

Redeem Us from Virtue. Allen A. Baldwin. 157p. 1993. pap. 8.95 (*1-880365-36-7*) Prof Pr NC.

Redeemed! Eschatological Redemption & the Kingdom of God. Boyd Hunt. 1993. 24.99 (*0-8054-1046-5*, 4210-46) Broadman.

Redeemed! Readers Theatre for Building the Body. Bette D. Moore. 1995. 8.99 (*0-8341-9271-3*, MP-756) Lillenas.

Redeemed Captive. John Williams. LC 93-35966. 192p. 1987. pap. 9.95 (*1-55709-118-8*) Applewood.

Redeemed Captive Returning to Zion: Or, a Faithful History of Remarkable Occurrences in the Captivity & Deliverance of Mr. John Williams. Ed. by Stephen W. Williams. LC 78-109637. (Select Bibliographies Reprint Ser.). 1977. 21.95 (*0-8369-5246-4*) Ayer.

Redeemed Captive Returning to Zion: or A Faithful History of Remarkable Occurences in the Captivity & Deliverance. John Williams. (American Biography Ser.). 192p. 1991. reprint ed. lib. bdg. 59.00 (*0-7812-8420-1*) Rprt Serv.

Redeemed! Counsel for New Christians. James A. Stewart. 19p. (C). 1964. pap. 0.89 (*1-56632-094-1*) Revival Lit.

Redeemed from Poverty, Sickness, & Spiritual Death. 2nd ed. Kenneth E. Hagin. 1983. pap. 1.95 (*0-89276-001-X*) Hagin Ministries.

Redeemed from the Curse. Perry A. Gaspard. 64p. 1983. pap. 2.50 (*0-931867-03-7*) Abundant Life Pubns.

Redeemed People. Gilbert W. Stafford. (Eagle Bible Ser.). 1989. pap. 0.99 (*0-87162-552-0*, D9154) Warner Pr.

***Redeemed Will Walk There.** 112p. 1983. 6.99 (*0-8341-0839-9*) Nazarene.

***Redeemer, Friend & Mother: Salvation in Antiquity & in the Gospel of John.** J. Masyngbaerde Ford. LC 96-51001. 1997. pap. 29.00 (*0-8006-2778-4*, Fortress Pr) Augsburg Fortress.

Redeemer in the Womb: Jesus Living in Mary. John Saward. LC 92-74111. 190p. 1993. 12.95 (*0-89870-427-8*) Ignatius Pr.

Redeemer Nation: The Idea of America's Millenial Role. Ernest L. Tuveson. LC 68-14009. (Midway Reprint Ser.). 252p. 1980. pap. text ed. 24.00 (*0-226-81921-3*) U Ch Pr.

***Redeemer of Israel.** Ed. by Norman L. Heap. 1994. pap. 14.00 (*0-945905-07-6*) Family Hstory Pubns.

Redeemer of Man. Pope John Paul, II. 100p. (Orig.). 1979. pap. 6.95 (*1-55586-003-6*) US Catholic.

***Redeemer of Man: Redemptor Hominis.** Pope John Paul, II. 64p. pap. 1.25 (*0-8198-6433-1*) Pauline Bks.

Redeemers, Bourbons & Populists: Tennessee, 1870-1896. Roger L. Hart. LC 73-91776. 308p. 1975. reprint ed. pap. 87.80 (*0-7837-9875-X*, 2060601) Bks Demand.

Redeeming America: Evangelicals & the Road to Civil War. Curtis D. Johnson. LC 93-11242. (American Ways Ser.). 224p. 1993. 22.50 (*1-56663-031-2*); pap. text ed. 9.95 (*1-56663-032-0*) I R Dee.

Redeeming America: Piety & Politics in the New Christian Right. Michael Lienesch. LC 92-45782. xii, 332p. 1993. pap. 18.95 (*0-8078-4428-4*) U of NC Pr.

***Redeeming American Political Theory: Essays on American Political Thought.** Judith N. Shklar et al. LC 97-25. 1998. pap. text ed. 13.95 (*0-226-75348-4*); lib. bdg. 36.00 (*0-226-75347-6*) U Ch Pr.

Redeeming Creation: The Biblical Basis for Environmental Stewardship. Fred Van Dyke et al. LC 95-26751. 213p. (Orig.). 1996. pap. 14.99 (*0-8308-1872-3*, 1872) InterVarsity.

***Redeeming Culture: American Religion in an Age of Science, 1925-1962.** LC 96-47973. 1996. pap. 21.50 (*0-226-29321-1*) U Ch Pr.

***Redeeming Culture: American Religion in an Age of Science, 1925-1962.** James Gilbert. LC 96-47973. 336p. 1996. 28.95 (*0-226-29320-3*) U Ch Pr.

Redeeming Eve: Women Writers of the English Renaissance. Elaine V. Beilin. 370p. (C). 1987. pap. text ed. 17.95 (*0-691-01500-7*) Princeton U Pr.

Redeeming Fallen Brokers: Managing the Aftermath of Broker-Dealer Enforcement Proceedings. Ralph C. Ferrara & Gregory S. Crespi. 260p. 1988. boxed 95.00 (*0-88063-249-6*) MICHIE.

***Redeeming Laughter: The Comic Dimension of Human Experience.** Peter L. Berger. LC 97-12095. 240p. 1997. lib. bdg. 23.95 (*3-11-015562-1*) De Gruyter.

***Redeeming Love.** Francine Rivers. LC 97-14694. 1997. pap. text ed. 12.99 (*1-57673-186-3*, Multnomah Bks) Multnomah Pubs.

Redeeming Love. large type ed. Francine Rivers. LC 93-13563. 1993. lib. bdg. 23.95 (*0-8161-5823-1*, GK Hall) Thorndike Pr.

Redeeming Marriage. Edward S. Gleason. LC 87-29960. 158p. (Orig.). 1988. pap. 8.95 (*0-936384-55-7*) Cowley Pubns.

Redeeming Men: Religion & Masculinities. Ed. by Stephen B. Boyd et al. LC 96-21403. 304p. (Orig.). 1996. pap. 29.00 (*0-664-25544-2*) Westminster John Knox.

Redeeming Modernity: Contradictions in Media Criticism. Joli Jensen. (Communication & Human Values Ser.). 175p. (C). 1990. 52.00 (*0-8039-3476-9*); pap. 24.95 (*0-8039-3477-7*) Sage.

***Redeeming Modernity: Contradictions in Media Criticism.** Joli Jensen. LC 90-8269. (Communication & Human Values Ser.). 221p. 1990. reprint ed. pap. 63.00 (*0-608-03008-2*, 2063458) Bks Demand.

Redeeming Politics. Peter I. Kaufman. Ed. by John F. Wilson. (Studies in Church & State). 224p. (C). 1990. text ed. 45.00 (*0-691-07372-4*); pap. text ed. 17.95 (*0-691-01928-2*) Princeton U Pr.

Redeeming Television: How TV Changes Christians - How Christians Can Change TV. Quentin J. Schultze. LC 92-12474. 180p. (Orig.). 1992. pap. 10.99 (*0-8308-1383-7*, 1383) InterVarsity.

Redeeming the Republic: Federalists, Taxation, & the Origins of the Constitution. Roger H. Brown. LC 92-28958. 320p. 1993. text ed. 38.50 (*0-8018-4497-5*) Johns Hopkins.

***Redeeming the Routines: Bringing Theology to Life.** Robert Banks. LC 92-41788. 200p. (C). 1993. pap. 15.99 (*0-8010-2116-2*, Bridgept Bks) Baker Bks.

***Redeeming the South: Religious Cultures & Racial Identities among Southern Baptists, 1865-1925.** Paul Harvey. LC 96-32882. (Fred W. Morrison Series in Southern Studies). 384p. (C). (gr. 13). 1997. 49.95 (*0-8078-2324-4*); pap. 17.95 (*0-8078-4634-1*) U of NC Pr.

Redeeming the Text: Latin Poetry & the Hermeneutics of Reception. Charles Martindale. (Roman Literature & Its Contexts Ser.). (Illus.). 140p. (C). 1993. text ed. 49.95 (*0-521-41717-1*); pap. text ed. 16.95 (*0-521-42719-3*) Cambridge U Pr.

Redeeming the Time. Russell Kirk. 304p. 1996. 24.95 (*1-882926-14-5*) Intercoll Studies.

Redeeming the Time: A Christian Approach to Work & Leisure. Leland Ryken. LC 95-18568. 304p. (C). 1995. pap. 17.99 (*0-8010-5169-X*) Baker Bks.

Redeeming the Time: A Political Theology of the Environment. Stephen B. Scharper. LC 96-53591. 256p. 1997. 29.95 (*0-8264-0935-0*) Continuum.

Redeeming the Time: An Historical & Theological Study of the Church's Rule of Prayer & the Regular Services of the Church. Byron D. Stuhlman. 256p. 1992. 23.95 (*0-89869-204-0*) Church Pub Inc.

Redeeming the Time: The Christian Walk in a Hurried World. Philip D. Patterson. LC 94-44044. 1995. 8.99 (*0-89900-726-0*) College Pr Pub.

***Redeeming the Time: The Christian Walk in a Hurried World.** Philip D. Patterson. LC 94-44044. 1996. audio 14.99 (*0-89900-741-4*) College Pr Pub.

Redeeming the Wasteland: Television Documentary & Cold War Politics. Michael Curtin. LC 95-12436. (Communications, Media & Culture Ser.). (Illus.). 350p. (C). 1995. text ed. 52.00 (*0-8135-2221-8*); pap. text ed. 18.95 (*0-8135-2222-6*) Rutgers U Pr.

Redefining a Period Style: "Renaissance," "Mannerist" & "Baroque" in Literature. John M. Steadman. LC 90-2925. (Duquesne Studies: Language & Literature Ser.: Vol. 10). 240p. 1990. text ed. 48.50 (*0-8207-0221-8*) Duquesne.

Redefining a Public Health System: How the Veterans Health Administration Improve Quality Measurement. Galen L. Barbour. LC 96-16103. 196p. 1996. 39.95 (*0-7879-0282-9*) Jossey-Bass.

Redefining AIDS: The Dead & the Disposessed, 4 vols. Neal A. Dickerson. LC 93-2599. (Politics of AIDS Ser.: Vol. 4). (Illus.). xii, 159p. 1993. pap. 12.00 (*0-930383-36-2*) Monument Pr.

Redefining Airmanship. Anthony T. Kern. LC 96-41788. (Illus.). 352p. 1997. text ed. 29.95 (*0-07-034284-9*) McGraw.

Redefining American History Painting. Ed. by Patricia M. Burnham & Lucretia H. Giese. (Illus.). 448p. (C). 1995. text ed. 100.00 (*0-521-46059-X*) Cambridge U Pr.

Redefining American Literary History. Ed. by A. LaVonne Ruoff, Jr. & Jerry W. Ward, Jr. LC 90-6530. (Committee on Literatures & Languages of America Ser.). iv, 406p. 1990. pap. 19.75 (*0-87352-188-9*, B105P); lib. bdg. 45.00 (*0-87352-187-0*, B105C) Modern Lang.

Redefining Autobiography in Twentieth-Century Women's Fiction. Ed. by Janice Morgan & Colette Hall. LC 90-49120. (Gender & Genre in Literature Ser.: Vol. 3). 336p. 1991. text ed. 55.00 (*0-8240-7392-4*, H1386) Garland.

Redefining Black Film. Mark A. Reid. 1993. 35.00 (*0-520-07901-9*); pap. 15.95 (*0-520-07902-7*) U CA Pr.

Redefining California: Latino Social Engagement in a Multicultural Society. Aida Hurtado et al. LC 92-8300. 101p. 1992. 15.00 (*0-89551-093-6*) UCLA Chicano Studies.

Redefining Comparative Politics: Promise Versus Performance. Lawrence C. Mayer. (Library of Social Research). 320p. (C). 1989. text ed. 54.00 (*0-8039-3463-7*); pap. text ed. 24.95 (*0-8039-3464-5*) Sage.

***Redefining Comparative Politics: Promise vs. Performance.** Lawrence C. Mayer. LC 89-34765. (Sage Library of Social Research: No. 173). (Illus.). 303p. 1989. reprint ed. pap. 86.40 (*0-608-04318-4*, 2065097) Bks Demand.

Redefining Conservatism: An Essay on the Bias of India's Economic Reform. Narendar Pani. LC 93-48277. 1994. 28.50 (*0-8039-9164-9*) Sage.

Redefining Corporate Responsibility in a Global Economy: An Agenda for Action. Jobs for the Future Staff. 44p. (Orig.). 1996. pap. 10.00 (*1-887410-82-1*) Jobs for Future.

Redefining Corporate Soul: Linking Purpose & People. Allan Cox & Julie Liesse. 144p. 1996. text ed. 24.95 (*0-7863-0555-X*) Irwin Prof Pubng.

Redefining Designing: From Form to Experience. C. Thomas Mitchell. 1993. pap. 39.95 (*0-442-00987-9*) Van Nos Reinhold.

Redefining Diversity. R. Roosevelt Thomas, Jr. 272p. 1996. 24.95 (*0-8144-0228-3*) AMACOM.
A nationally recognized & respected authority on diversity issues & founder & president of the American Institute for Managing Diversity, Inc., in Atlanta, GA, R. Roosevelt Thomas, Jr., continues to challenge American business to expand its concept of diversity beyond affirmative action & beyond skin color, ethnicity, & sexual persuasion. REDEFINING DIVERSITY is Dr. Thomas's new breakthrough work--a book that not only broadens the definition of diversity within the workplace but awakens managers in all industries to diversity's untapped potential. Building upon the bold ideas presented in his highly acclaimed BEYOND RACE & GENDER (AMACOM), Dr. Thomas demonstrates how diversity is far more than a human resources issue--how diversity affects & enhances all areas of business, especially those most strategically demanding & complex. Through his innovative management model called the Diversity Paradigm, Dr. Thomas identifies eight options for decision making & change, equipping managers to assess where their organizations are now & where they would like them to be. The book goes far beyond theory. Through vivid & detailed case studies & corporate examples, Dr. Thomas illuminates the latent power of "diversity at work." Dr. Thomas urges managers to "talk the talk" through education & launching; to "think the talk" through strategic planning, diagnosis, implementation, & monitoring; & to "walk the talk" through application & continuous improvement. Breaking down barriers between employees & shattering entrenched misconceptions, REDEFINING DIVERSITY will change the way corporate America thinks about this vital issue. Order from AMACOM Books, 1601 Broadway, New York, NY 10019, phone 212-903-8315 or 800-262-9699. ***Publisher Provided Annotation.***

***Redefining Equality.** Ed. by Neal Devins & Davison Douglas. (Illus.). 256p. 1997. pap. 18.95 (*0-19-511665-8*) OUP.

***Redefining Equality.** Ed. by Neal Devins & Davison Douglas. (Illus.). 256p. 1997. 45.00 (*0-19-511664-X*) OUP.

Redefining Europe: New Patterns of Conflict & Cooperation. Ed. by Hugh Miall. LC 94-15091. 1994. pap. 22.00 (*1-85567-258-8*, Pub. by Pntr Pubs UK) Bks Intl VA.

Redefining Europe: New Patterns of Conflict & Cooperation. Ed. by Hugh Miall. LC 94-15091. 320p. 1994. 55.00 (*1-85567-257-X*, Pub. by Pntr Pubs UK) Bks Intl VA.

Redefining Excellence: The Financial Performance of America's "Best Run" Companies. Arabinda Ghosh. LC 89-3859. 176p. 1989. text ed. 49.95 (*0-275-93339-3*, C3339, Praeger Pubs) Greenwood.

Redefining Families: Implications for Children's Development. Ed. by A. E. Gottfried & A. W. Gottfried. (Illus.). 200p. (C). 1994. 34.50 (*0-306-44559-X*, Plenum Pr) Plenum.

Redefining Family Support: Innovations in Public-Private Partnerships. Singer et al. (Family, Community & Disability Ser.). 368p. 1995. pap. 45.00 (*1-55766-217-7*) P H Brookes.

R

R

Redefining Film Preservation. 1995. lib. bdg. 253.99 (*0-8490-6852-5*) Gordon Pr.

Redefining Film Preservation: A National Plan: Recommendations of the Librarian of Congress in Consultation with the National Film Preservation Board. Ed. by Annette Melville & Scott Simon. LC 94-29345. 1994. write for info. (*0-8444-0819-0*) Lib Congress.

Redefining General Education in the American High School. fac. ed. Arthur D. Roberts & Gordon Cawelti. LC 84-71655. (Illus.). 168p. (Orig.). 1984. reprint ed. pap. 47.90 (*0-608-01033-2*, 2082509) Bks Demand.

Redefining Genre: French & American Painting, 1850-1900. Gabriel P. Weisberg & Petra T. Chu. (Illus.). 111p. (C). 1995. pap. 25.00 (*0-295-97462-1*) U of Wash Pr.

***Redefining Mexican "Security" Society, State, & Region under NAFTA.** James F. Rochlin. LC 97-13585. 1997. write for info. (*1-55587-569-6*) Lynne Rienner.

Redefining National Security. Lester R. Brown. 1977. pap. write for info. (*0-916468-13-5*) Worldwatch Inst.

Redefining National Water Policy: New Roles & Directions. fac. ed. Ed. by Stephen M. Born. (AWRA Special Publication Ser.: No. 89-1). 99p. (Orig.). 1989. reprint ed. pap. 28.30 (*0-608-00999-7*, 2061857) Bks Demand.

Redefining Nature: Ecology, Culture & Domestication. Ed. by R. F. Ellen et al. LC 96-13812. (Explorations in Anthropology Ser.). 608p. 1996. 45.95 (*1-85973-130-9*); pap. 24.95 (*1-85973-135-X*) Berg Pubs.

Redefining Politics. Leftwich. 1986. 32.00 (*0-416-68150-6*) Routledge Chapman & Hall.

Redefining Progress: Working Toward a Sustainable Future. 225p. (Orig.). (C). 1995. pap. text ed. 40.00 (*0-7881-2589-3*) DIANE Pub.

Redefining Self-Help in the Human Services: Policy & Practice. Frank Riessman & David Carroll. LC 94-38982. (Health-Social & Behavioral Sciences Ser.). 236p. text ed. 29.95 (*0-7879-0066-4*) Jossey-Bass.

Redefining Sexual Ethics: A Sourcebook of Essays, Stories, & Poems. Ed. by Susan E. Davies & Eleanor H. Haney. LC 91-33864. 400p. (Orig.). 1991. pap. 24.95 (*0-8298-0912-0*) Pilgrim OH.

Redefining Shakespeare. LC 96-40037. 1997. write for info. (*0-87413-604-0*) U Delaware Pr.

Redefining Social Problems. Ed. by Edward Seidman & Julian Rappaport. (Perspectives in Social Psychology Ser.). 334p. 1986. 49.50 (*0-306-42052-X*, Plenum Pr) Plenum.

Redefining Student Learning: Roots of Educational Change. Hermine H. Marshall. 336p. (C). 1992. pap. 39.50 (*0-89391-917-9*); text ed. 73.25 (*0-89391-854-7*) Ablex Pub.

Redefining Success: Women's Unique Paths. Nancy C. Johnson. Ed. by Marge Columbus. (Illus.). 220p. 1995. pap. 18.95 (*0-963827-5-1*) Sibyl Pubns.

Redefining the American Dream: The Novels of Willa Cather. Sally P. Harvey. LC 93-44678. 1995. 34.50 (*0-8386-3557-1*) Fairleigh Dickinson.

Redefining the American Gothic: From "Wieland" to "Day of the Dead" Louis Gross. Ed. by Robert Scholes. LC 88-29568. (Studies in Speculative Fiction: No. 20). 120p. reprint ed. pap. 34.20 (*0-8357-1901-4*, 2070720) Bks Demand.

Redefining the Career Criminal: Priority Prosecution of High-Rate Dangerous Offenders. (Illus.). 91p. (Orig.). (C). 1993. pap. text ed. 20.00 (*1-56806-808-5*) DIANE Pub.

***Redefining the Career Criminal: Priority Prosecution of High-Rate Dangerous Offenders.** (Illus.). 102p. 1990. pap. text ed. 30.00 (*1-57979-190-5*) BPI Info Servs.

Redefining the Church: Vision & Practice. Ed. by Richard Lennan. 176p. 1995. pap. 9.95 (*0-85574-230-5*, Pub. by E J Dwyer AT) Morehouse Pub.

Redefining the CSCE: Challenges & Opportunities in the New Europe. Ed. by Ian M. Cuthbertson. LC 92-18018. 1992. 12.85 (*0-913449-33-4*) Inst EW Stud.

Redefining the Discipline of Adult Education. Ed. by Robert D. Boyd & Jerold W. Apps. LC 80-8006. (Adult Education Association Handbook Series in Adult Education). 239p. reprint ed. pap. 68.20 (*0-8357-4933-9*, 2037863) Bks Demand.

Redefining the Egyptian Nation, 1930-1945. Israel Gershoni & James P. Jankowski. (Middle East Studies: No. 2). (Illus.). 300p. (C). 1995. text ed. 57.95 (*0-521-47535-X*) Cambridge U Pr.

Redefining the First Freedom: The Supreme Court & the Consolidation of State Power, 1980-1990. Gregg Ivers. 248p. (C). 1992. 34.95 (*1-56000-054-6*) Transaction Pubs.

Redefining the Past: Essays in Diplomatic History in Honor of William Appleman Williams. Ed. by Lloyd Gardner. LC 86-8427. (Illus.). 272p. 1986. text ed. 33.95 (*0-87071-348-5*) Oreg St U Pr.

Redefining the Place to Learn. OECD Staff. (Programme on Educational Building Ser.). 172p. (Orig.). 1995. pap. 37.00 (*92-64-14563-X*, Pub. by Org for Econ FR) OECD.

Redefining the Political Novel: American Women Writers, 1797-1901. Ed. by Sharon M. Harris. LC 94-28331. 224p. (C). 1995. text ed. 32.50 (*0-87049-869-X*) U of Tenn Pr.

Redefining the Process of Retirement. Ed. by W. Schmahl. 190p. 1989. 49.00 (*0-387-50826-0*) Spr-Verlag.

Redefining the Role of Government in Agriculture for the 1990s. Odin K. Knudsen et al. (Discussion Paper Ser.: No. 105). 110p. 1990. 7.95 (*0-8213-1690-7*, 11690) World Bank.

Redefining the Self: Coming Out As Lesbian. Laura Markowe. LC 96-798. 230p. 1996. 54.95 (*0-7456-1128-1*, Pub. by Polity Pr UK); pap. 21.95 (*0-7456-1129-X*, Pub. by Polity Pr UK) Blackwell Pubs.

Redefining the State in Latin America. OECD Staff. 273p. (Orig.). 1994. pap. 42.00 (*92-64-14089-1*) OECD.

***Redefining the U. S. - Japan Alliance: Tokyo's National Defense Program.** Patrick M. Cronin & Michael J. Green. 61p. (Orig.). (C). 1996. pap. 25.00 (*0-7881-3281-4*) DIANE Pub.

***Redefining the U. S.-Japan Alliance: Tokyo's National Defense Program.** 68p. 1994. pap. text ed. 35.00 (*1-57979-169-7*) BPI Info Servs.

***Redefining the Welfare State.** Katz. Date not set. 30.00 (*0-8050-5208-9*) St Martin.

Redefining the Whole Curriculum for Pupils with Learning Difficulties. Judy Sebba et al. 128p. 1993. pap. 26.00 (*1-85346-226-8*, Pub. by D Fulton UK) Taylor & Francis.

Redefining Wealth & Progress: New Ways to Measure Economic, Social & Environmental Change. Caracas Report on Alternative Indicators Staff. LC 90-892. 112p. (Orig.). 1990. pap. 9.95 (*0-942850-24-6*) Bootstrap Pr.

Redefining What's Essential to Business Performance: Pathways to Productivity, Quality, & Service. Leonard R. Sayles. (Technical Reports: No. 142G). 52p. 1990. pap. 20.00 (*0-912879-40-8*) Ctr Creat Leader.

Redemocratization of Argentine Culture, 1983 & Beyond. David W. Foster. LC 88-36644. 63p. 1989. pap. 8.00 (*0-87918-070-6*) ASU Lat Am St.

***Redemption.** Anne Cartier. 320p. 1997. mass mkt. 4.99 (*0-614-23649-5*, Pinncle Kensgtn) Kensgtn Pub Corp.

***Redemption.** Anne Cartier. 1997. pap. 4.99 (*0-7860-0362-6*, Pinncle Kensgtn) Kensgtn Pub Corp.

Redemption. Chantal Chawaf. Tr. by Monique F. Nagem from FRE. LC 92-511. 97p. 1992. 19.95 (*1-56478-003-1*) Dalkey Arch.

***Redemption.** Denise Domning. 1998. mass mkt. 5.99 (*0-451-40771-7*, Onyx) NAL-Dutton.

***Redemption.** Golden Books Staff. (Batman Ser.). (Illus.). (J). 1997. pap. text ed. 2.29 (*0-307-08435-3*, Golden Books) Western Pub.

***Redemption.** Francis Stuart. 252p. Date not set. pap. 14.95 (*1-874597-08-1*) Dufour.

Redemption. Leon Uris. 896p. 1996. mass mkt. 7.99 (*0-06-109174-X*, Harp PBks) HarpC.

Redemption. large type ed. Leon Uris. LC 95-20823. 1152p. 1995. 26.95 (*0-7838-1453-4*, GK Hall) Thorndike Pr.

***Redemption: A Collection of Short Stories.** Grace P. Tazewell. 54p. (Orig.). 1996. pap. 10.00 (*1-57000-051-4*) W S Dawson.

Redemption: A Novel of War in Lebanon. Liston Pope, Jr. LC 93-91788. (Works Ser.: I). 294p. 1994. 24.95 (*0-9638900-0-X*) N A Gilbert.

***Redemption: A Novel of War in Lebanon.** 2nd ed. Liston Pope, Jr. 294p. 1997. reprint ed. pap. 19.95 (*0-9638900-2-6*) Mantis Press.

Redemption: Accomplished & Applied. John Murray. 1955. pap. 10.00 (*0-8028-1143-4*) Eerdmans.

Redemption: Three Sermons, 1637-1656. Thomas Hooker. LC 56-9145. 1977. reprint ed. 50.00 (*0-8201-1234-8*) Schol Facsimiles.

Redemption & Dialogue: Reading "Redemptoris Missio" & "Dialogue & Proclamation" Ed. by William R. Burrows. LC 94-11990. 300p. (Orig.). 1994. pap. 20.00 (*0-88344-935-8*) Orbis Bks.

Redemption & Madness: Three Nineteenth-Century Feminist Views on Motherhood & Childbearing. Andrea B. Frantz. LC 92-41177. (Woman in History Ser.: Vol. 61). 100p. 1992. pap. 6.00 (*0-86663-203-4*) Ide Hse.

Redemption & Utopia - Jewish Libertarian Thought in Central Europe: A Study in Elective Affinity. Michael Lowy. Tr. by Hope Heaney from FRE. LC 89-51763. 282p. (C). 1992. 37.50 (*0-8047-1776-1*) Stanford U Pr.

Redemption, Conceived & Revealed. H. P. Robinson. 3.95 (*0-911866-59-0*); pap. 2.95 (*0-911866-89-2*) LifeSprings Res.

Redemption, Hindu & Christian: The Religious Quest of India. Sydney Cave. LC 73-102230. (Select Bibliographies Reprint Ser.). 1977. 26.95 (*0-8369-5115-8*) Ayer.

Redemption Is. Edward C. Wharton. 110p. (Orig.). 1992. pap. 8.99 (*1-878990-05-5*) Howard Pub LA.

***Redemption Motifs.** Marie-Louise Von Franz. 1996. pap. 15.00 (*0-919123-01-5*, Pub. by Inner City CN) BookWorld Dist.

Redemption of Africa & Black Religion. St. Claire Drake. LC 70-171226. (Orig.). 1970. pap. 6.95 (*0-88378-017-8*) Third World.

Redemption of Corporal Nolan Giles. 2nd ed. Jeane H. Candido. LC 96-51044. 250p. (Orig.). 1996. pap. 11.95 (*1-886383-14-6*) Pride OH.

***Redemption of Deke Summers.** Gayle Wilson. (Hidden Identity Ser.). 1997. mass mkt. 3.75 (*0-373-22414-1*, 1-22414-6) Harlequin Bks.

Redemption of God: A Theology of Mutual Relation. Isabel C. Heyward. LC 81-43706. 266p. (Orig.). 1982. pap. text ed. 23.00 (*0-8191-2390-0*) U Pr of Amer.

Redemption of Howard Gray. C. W. Naylor. 72p. pap. 0.50 (*0-686-29162-X*) Faith Pub Hse.

Redemption of Jesse James. large type ed. Preston Lewis. LC 95-35732. 496p. 1995. 20.95 (*0-7838-1500-X*, GK Hall) Thorndike Pr.

Redemption of Light. Kathleen M. O'Neal. (Powers of Light Ser.: Bk. 3). 1991. mass mkt. 4.99 (*0-88677-470-5*) DAW Bks.

***Redemption of the Feminine Erotic Soul.** unabridged ed. Rachel Hillel. (Illus.). 160p. (Orig.). 1997. pap. 16.95 (*0-89254-038-9*) Nicolas-Hays.

Redemption of the "Harper's Ferry Cowards" The Story of the 111th & 126th New York Volunteer Regiments at Gettysburg. R. L. Murray. (Illus.). 178p. 1994. pap. 12.95 (*0-9646261-0-1*) R L Murray NY.

Redemption of Thinking: A Study in the Philosophy of Thomas Aquinas. Rudolf Steiner. Tr. by A. P. Shepherd & Mildred R. Nicoll from GER. Orig. Title: Die Philosophie des Thomas von Aquino. 191p. 1983. reprint ed. pap. text ed. 12.95 (*0-88010-044-3*) Anthroposophic.

Redemption of Tragedy: The Literary Vision of Simone Weil. Katherine T. Brueck. LC 94-9152. (SUNY Series, Simone Weil Studies). 185p. (C). 1994. pap. text ed. 16.95 (*0-7914-2282-8*) State U NY Pr.

Redemption of Tragedy: The Literary Vision of Simone Weil. Katherine T. Brueck. LC 94-9152. (SUNY Series, Simone Weil Studies). 185p. (C). 1995. text ed. 49.50 (*0-7914-2281-X*) State U NY Pr.

***Redemption Player's Guide.** David M. Easterling. Ed. by Rodger T. Moloney. (Illus.). 168p. (Orig.). 1996. pap. 9.95 (*1-889055-04-2*) Cactus Game.

***Redemption Realized Through Christ: A Study of the Bible's Teachings on Redemption.** Leland M. Haines. Ed. by Richard Poleyn. 256p. (Orig.). 1997. pap. 10.95 (*1-890133-03-5*) Biblical Viewpts.

***Redemption Realized Through Christ: A Study of the Bible's Teachings on Redemption.** Leland M. Haines. Ed. by Richard Poleyn. 256p. (Orig.). 1997. lib. bdg. 20.00 (*1-890133-33-7*) Biblical Viewpts.

Redemption Song, The Boot Dance, Les Femmes Noires: Three Plays. Edgar White. 192p. 1986. pap. 9.95 (*0-7145-2837-4*) M Boyars Pubs.

Redemption Songs: A Life of Te Kooti Arikirangi Te Turuki. Judith Binney. (Illus.). 676p. 1996. 55.00 (*1-86940-131-X*, Pub. by Auckland Univ NZ) Paul & Co Pubs.

***Redemption Songs: Life of Te Kooti Arikirangi Te Turuki.** Judith Binney. LC 97-7318. 1997. text ed. 34.00 (*0-8248-1975-6*) UH Pr.

Redemption: The Exodus from Egypt see Torah Anthology: Meam Lo'ez

Redemption Trail. Suzann Ledbetter. 304p. 1996. mass mkt. 5.99 (*0-451-18749-0*, Sig) NAL-Dutton.

Redemption Truths. Robert Anderson. LC 80-16161. (Sir Robert Anderson Library). Orig. Title: For Us Men. 192p. 1980. reprint ed. pap. 7.99 (*0-8254-2131-4*, Kregel Class) Kregel.

Redemptioners & Indentured Servants in the Colony & Commonwealth of Pennsylvania. Karl F. Geiser. 1901. 89.50 (*0-614-01810-2*) Elliots Bks.

Redemptions: A Costa Rican Novel. Carlos Gagini. LC 84-51946. (Illus.). 130p. (Orig.). 1985. 20.00 (*0-916304-66-3*) SDSU Press.

Redemptive Almsgiving in Early Christianity. R. Garrison. (Journey for the Study of the New Testament Supplement Ser.: No. 77). 175p. 35.00 (*1-85075-376-8*, Pub. by Sheffield Acad UK) CUP Services.

Redemptive Dancing: Prayer Dance & Congregational Dance in the Life of the Contemporary Church. Janet Skidmore. Ed. by Doug Adams. 1987. pap. 3.00 (*0-941500-46-2*) Sharing Co.

Redemptive Encounters: Three Modern Styles in the Hindu Tradition. Lawrence A. Babb. (Comparative Studies in Religion & Society: Vol. 1). 1987. 45.00 (*0-520-05645-0*) U CA Pr.

Redemptive Encounters: Three Modern Styles in the Hindu Tradition. Lawrence A. Babb. (Comparative Studies in Religion & Society: No. 1). 268p. 1991. reprint ed. pap. 16.00 (*0-520-07636-2*) U CA Pr.

Redemptive History & the New Testament Scriptures. Herman N. Ridderbos. Tr. by Richard B. Graffin & H. De Jongste, Jr. LC 87-32875. Orig. Title: The Authority of the New Testament Scriptures. 110p. (DUT.). 1988. pap. 6.99 (*0-87552-416-8*, Pub. by Evangelical Pr) Presby & Reformed.

Redemptive Intimacy: A New Perspective for the Journey to Adult Faith. Dick Westley. LC 80-54810. 180p. 1981. pap. 7.95 (*0-89622-123-7*) Twenty-Third.

***Redemptive Suffering: Understanding Suffering: Living with It, Growing Through It.** William J. O'Malley. LC 97-15540. 1997. write for info. (*0-8245-1680-X*) Crossroad NY.

Redemptive Suffering in Islam. Mahmoud Ayoub. (Religion & Society Ser.: No. 10). 1978. 70.00 (*90-279-7948-0*) Mouton.

Redemptive Theology of William Booth: War on Two Fronts. Roger J. Green. 1989. 9.95 (*0-86544-055-7*) Salv Army Suppl South.

***Redemptive Work: Railway & Nation in Ecuador 1895-1930.** A. Kim Clark. LC 97-14679. (Latin American Silhouettes Ser.). 236p. (C). 1998. text ed. write for info. (*0-8420-2674-6*, SR Bks) Scholarly Res Inc.

Redemptorist on the American Missions, 3 Vols. Joseph Wissel. 1978. 126.95 (*0-405-10867-2*) Ayer.

Reden Gehalten in Wissenschaftlichen Versammlungen und Kleinere Aufsatze Vermischten Inhalts, 3 Vols. Karl E. Von Baer. Ed. by Keir B. Sterling. LC 77-81114. (Biologists & Their World Ser.). (GER.). 1978. reprint ed. lib. bdg. 102.95 (*0-405-10700-5*) Ayer.

Reden Gehalten in Wissenschaftlichen Versammlungen und Kleinere Aufsatze Vermischten Inhalts, 3 Vols., Vol. 1. Karl E. Von Baer. Ed. by Keir B. Sterling. LC 77-81114. (Biologists & Their World Ser.). (GER.). 1978. reprint ed. lib. bdg. 51.95 (*0-405-10701-3*) Ayer.

Reden Gehalten in Wissenschaftlichen Versammlungen und Kleinere Aufsatze Vermischten Inhalts, 3 Vols., Vol. 2. Karl E. Von Baer. Ed. by Keir B. Sterling. LC 77-81114. (Biologists & Their World Ser.). (GER.). 1978. reprint ed. lib. bdg. 51.95 (*0-405-10702-1*) Ayer.

Reden, Mitreden, Dazwischenreden. 2nd ed. C. Kramsch. (Orig.). 1990. 41.95 incl. audio (*0-8384-1940-2*) Heinle & Heinle.

Reden und Aufsatze. Theodor Mommsen. vi, 479p. 1976. reprint ed. write for info. (*3-487-06043-4*) G Olms Pubs.

Reden und Schriften see Essays & Speeches on Various Subjects

Reden und Vortrage, 2 vols. in 1. Ulrich Von Wilamowitz-Moellendorff. 1967. write for info. (*3-296-16350-6*); Bd. I, viii, 384p. write for info. (*0-318-70844-2*); Bd. II, 298p. write for info. (*0-318-70845-0*) G Olms Pubs.

Redescription of Etheostoma Australe & a Key for the Identification of Mexican Etheostoma (Percidae) Lawrence M. Page. (Occasional Papers: No. 89). 10p. 1981. 1.00 (*0-317-04828-7*) U KS Nat Hist Mus.

Redescubrimiento De Dios. Michael Griffith. 176p. (SPA.). 1990. pap. 1.50 (*0-8297-0856-1*) Life Pubs Intl.

Redesign of Governance in Higher Education. Roger Benjamin et al. LC 93-5689. 1993. pap. 15.00 (*0-8330-1428-5*, MR-222-LE) Rand Corp.

Redesigning American Education. James S. Coleman. LC 97-21628. (C). 1997. text ed. 45.00 (*0-8133-2495-5*) Westview.

Redesigning an Education System: Early Observations from Kentucky. Jane L. David. 42p. (Orig.). 1993. pap. text ed. 15.00 (*1-55877-204-9*) Natl Governor.

***Redesigning City Squares & Plazas.** 1997. pap. text ed. 39.95 (*0-8230-4514-5*) Watsn-Guptill.

Redesigning Collegiate Leadership: Teams & Teamwork in Higher Education. Estela M. Bensimon & Anna Newmann. LC 92-29728. 224p. 1993. text ed. 35.00 (*0-8018-4561-0*) Johns Hopkins.

Redesigning Collegiate Leadership: Teams & Teamwork in Higher Education. Estela M. Bensimon & Anna Neumann. 200p. 1994. reprint ed. pap. text ed. 15.95 (*0-8018-4956-X*) Johns Hopkins.

***Redesigning Curricula: Models of Service Learning Syllabi.** 160p. 1994. pap. 10.00 (*0-614-30598-5*) Ed Comm States.

Redesigning Defense: Planning the Transition to the Future U. S. Defense Industrial Base. (Illus.). 118p. (Orig.). (C). 1994. pap. text ed. 30.00 (*1-56806-154-4*) DIANE Pub.

Redesigning Education. Kenneth G. Wilson & Bennett Daviss. LC 96-24412. 272p. 1996. pap. 18.95 (*0-8077-3585-X*) Tchrs Coll.

Redesigning Education: A Guide for Developing Human Greatness. Lynn Stoddard. (Illus.). 104p. (Orig.). 1992. pap. 19.00 (*0-913705-64-0*) Zephyr Pr AZ.

Redesigning English. Ed. by Goodman. LC 96-18428. 224p. (C). 1997. text ed. 65.00 (*0-415-13123-5*) Routledge.

Redesigning English. Ed. by Graddol. LC 96-18428. 224p. (C). 1997. pap. 22.95 (*0-415-13124-3*) Routledge.

Redesigning Healthcare Delivery: A Practical Guide to Reengineering, Restructuring, & Renewal. Peter Boland. (Illus.). 940p. 1996. 159.00 (*0-9652717-1-4*) Boland Hlthcare.

***Redesigning Higher Education: Producing Dramatic Gains in Student Learning.** Lion F. Gardiner. Ed. by Jonathan D. Fife. LC 96-75971. (ASHE-ERIC Higher Education Reports). (Illus.). 226p. (Orig.). 1996. pap. 21.75 (*1-878380-63-X*) GWU Grad Schl E&HD.

Redesigning Library Services: A Manifesto. Michael Buckland. LC 92-10546. 130p. (C). 1992. pap. text ed. 23.00 (*0-8389-0590-0*) ALA.

Redesigning Nursing Care Delivery: Transforming Our Future. Dominick L. Flarey. LC 94-7894. (Illus.). 304p. 1994. text ed. 47.95 (*0-397-55132-0*, Lippncott) Lppncott-Raven.

***Redesigning Print for the Web.** Mario R. Garcia. 300p. 1997. 45.99 (*1-56830-343-2*) Mac Comp Pub.

***Redesigning Public Services: A Partnership Approach.** Brendan Martin. (C). 1997. pap. 22.50 (*1-85649-502-7*, Pub. by Zed Bks Ltd UK) Humanities.

Redesigning Rural Development: A Strategic Perspective. Bruce F. Johnston & William C. Clark. LC 81-17138. 336p. 1982. text ed. 48.00 (*0-8018-2731-0*); pap. text ed. 19.95 (*0-8018-2732-9*) Johns Hopkins.

***Redesigning School: Lessons for the 21st Century.** Joseph P. MacDonald. LC 96-25339. (Education Ser.). 1997. write for info. (*0-7879-0321-3*) Jossey-Bass.

Redesigning School Health Services. Annette Lynch. LC 82-12178. (Illus.). 351p. 1983. 45.95 (*0-89885-102-5*) Human Sci Pr.

***Redesigning Teacher Education.** Alan R. Tom. LC 96-48413. (SUNY Series in Teacher Preparation & Development). 244p. (C). 1997. text ed. 59.50 (*0-7914-3469-9*); pap. text ed. 19.95 (*0-7914-3470-2*) State U NY Pr.

Redesigning Teaching: Professionalism or Bureaucracy? William A. Firestone & Beth D. Bader. LC 91-30791. (SUNY Series, Teacher Preparation & Development). 283p. (C). 1992. text ed. 67.50 (*0-7914-1123-0*); pap. text ed. 24.95 (*0-7914-1124-9*) State U NY Pr.

Redesigning the American Dream: The Future of Housing, Work, & Family Life. Dolores Hayden. LC 83-9339. (Illus.). 270p. 1986. pap. 15.95 (*0-393-30317-9*) Norton.

Redesigning the American Lawn: A Search for Environmental Harmony. F. Herbert Bormann et al. Ed. by Lisa Vernegaard. (Illus.). 256p. (C). 1993. text ed. 25.00 (*0-300-05401-7*) Yale U Pr.

Redesigning the American Lawn: A Search for Environmental Harmony. F. Herbert Bormann et al. (Illus.). 1995. pap. text ed. 13.00 (*0-300-06197-8*) Yale U Pr.

Redesigning the Communist Economy: Economic Reform in Eastern Europe. Paul M. Johnson. 281p. 1989. text ed. 56.50 (*0-88033-167-4*) East Eur Monographs.

Redesigning the Firm. Ed. by Edward Bowman & Bruce Kogut. 288p. 1995. 30.00 (*0-19-508710-4*) OUP.

Redesigning the Molecules of Life. Ed. by S. A. Benner. (Illus.). vii, 175p. 1988. 51.95 (*0-387-19166-6*) Spr-Verlag.

Redesigning the Nonprofit Organization, No. 53. Gwendolyn C. Baker. 23p. (Orig.). (C). 1993. pap. text ed. 16.00 (*0-925299-30-8*) Natl Ctr Nonprofit.

An Asterisk (*) at the beginning of an entry indicates that the title is appearing in BIP for the first time.

Redesigning the State: The Politics of Constitutional Change. Ed. by Keith Banting & Richard Simeon. 269p. 1985. pap. 17.95 (*0-8020-6569-4*) U of Toronto Pr.

Redesigning the State: The Politics of Constitutional Change. Ed. by Keith G. Banting & Richard Simeon. 269p. reprint ed. pap. 76.70 (*0-8357-3629-6*, 2036357) Bks Demand.

Redesigning the Work of Human Services. John O'Looney. LC 95-24915. 344p. 1996. text ed. 69.50 (*0-89930-941-0*, Quorum Bks) Greenwood.

Redesigning the World: William Morris, the 1880s, & the Arts & Crafts. Peter Stansky. LC 95-46531. (Illus.). 310p. 1996. pap. 17.95 (*0-930664-15-9*) SPOSS.

Redesigning Work: A Strategy for Change. Mary D. Lee & J. Richard Hackman. (Studies in Productivity: Vol. 9). 43p. 1979. pap. 55.00 (*0-08-029490-1*) Work in Amer.

Redeveloping Working Poor Communities & Neighborhoods: A General Guide. J. Muruku Waiguchu. LC 93-18918. 194p. 1993. 54.95 (*1-880921-32-4*); pap. 34.95 (*1-880921-25-1*) Austin & Winfield.

***Redevelopment & Race: Planning a Finer City in Postwar Detroit.** June M. Thomas. LC 96-29370. (Creating the North American Landscape Ser.). (Illus.). 304p. 1997. text ed. 39.95 (*0-8018-5444-X*) Johns Hopkins.

Redevelopment in California. 2nd ed. David F. Beatty et al. 464p. (Orig.). 1995. pap. 42.00 (*0-923956-33-6*) Solano Pr.

***Redevelopment in California: 1997 Supplement.** David F. Beatty et al. 1997. pap. 15.00 (*0-923956-48-4*, RS7) Solano Pr.

Redewendungen Tranzosisch - Deutsch: Thematisches Woerterbuch und Ubungsbuch. Vilmos Bardosi. 259p. (FRE & GER.). 1992. 49.95 (*0-7859-8510-7*, 3825217035) Fr & Eur.

Redewendungen und Sprichwortliche Redensarten, 12 vols., Vol. 11. (Duden Ser.). 850p. (GER.). 1996. 33.50 (*3-411-04111-0*) Langenscheidt.

Redeye: A Western. Clyde Edgarton. 256p. 1996. pap. 10.95 (*0-14-025491-9*, Penguin Bks) Viking Penguin.

Redeye: A Western. Clyde Edgerton. LC 94-43341. 252p. 1995. 17.95 (*1-56512-060-4*) Algonquin Bks.

Redeye: A Western. large type ed. Clyde Edgerton. LC 95-30939. (Americana Ser.). 319p. 1995. 22.95 (*0-7862-0536-9*) Thorndike Pr.

Redfearn: History of the Redfearn Family. rev. ed. D. H. Redfearn. (Illus.). 377p. 1992. reprint ed. pap. 56.00 (*0-8328-2711-8*); reprint ed. lib. bdg. 66.00 (*0-8328-2710-X*) Higginson Bk Co.

***Redfield Register, 1903 (Town History & Directory)** Compiled by H. E. Mitchell. (Illus.). 80p. 1997. reprint ed. pap. 16.00 (*0-8328-5902-8*) Higginson Bk Co.

Redfish Book: A Complete Angler's Guide. Frank Sargeant. LC 91-90328. (Inshore Ser.). (Illus.). 160p. (Orig.). 1991. pap. 11.95 (*0-936513-12-8*) Larsens Outdoor.

Redgauntlet. Walter Scott. Ed. by G. A. Wood & David Hewitt. LC 97-6313. 528p. 1996. 47.50 (*0-231-10720-X*) Col U Pr.

Redgauntlet. 2nd ed. Walter Scott. Ed. by Kathryn Sutherland. (WC-P Ser.). 560p. 1985. pap. 7.95 (*0-19-281668-3*) OUP.

Redgrave, Fife & Machin's: Health & Safety in Factories. 2nd ed. Ian Fife & E. Anthony Machin. 1982. reprint ed. 170.00 (*0-406-14601-2*) MICHIE.

Redhead Encyclopedia: The Complete Book on Redhead History, Facts, & Folklore. Stephen Douglas. (Illus.). 240p. (Orig.). 1996. pap. 19.95 (*0-9645216-0-1*) Redheads Intl.

Redheaded Orphan. L. Travis. LC 95-3137. (Ben & Zack Ser.: Bk. 3). 154p. (Orig.). (J). (gr. 4-8). 1995. pap. 5.99 (*0-8010-4023-X*) Baker Bks.

Redheaded Outfield & Other Baseball Stories. Zane Grey. LC 95-32410. 1995. 8.99 (*0-517-12423-8*, Pub. by Gramercy) Random Hse Value.

Redheaded Renegade: Chief Benge of the Cherokee Nation. Clara T. Fugate. (Tales of the Virginia Wilderness Ser.: No. 3). (Illus.). pap. write for info. (*0-936015-09-8*) Pocahontas Pr.

Redheaded Woman. Eustis. (J). 1998. pap. 2.95 (*0-671-75208-1*, S&S Bks Young Read) S&S Childrens.

Redheads. Joel Meyerowitz. LC 91-52798. (Illus.). 110p. 1991. 39.95 (*0-8478-1419-X*) Rizzoli Intl.

Redhot Lovenotes for Lovers: A Candid Peek at Two Hearts Dancing in the Bedroom. 240p. 1998. pap. 9.95 (*1-881558-04-5*) Career Assurance.

Redhouse English Turkish Dictionary. 17th ed. James W. Redhouse. 1152p. (ENG & TUR.). 1990. lib. bdg. 95.00 (*0-7859-0640-1*, M2050) Fr & Eur.

Redhouse Portable Turkish - English, English - Turkish Dictionary. 11th ed. Robert Avery. 503p. (ENG & TUR.). 1988. 29.95 (*0-8288-9053-6*, F65420) Fr & Eur.

Redhouse Turkish & English Lexicon. James W. Redhouse. 2224p. (ENG & TUR.). 1994. 95.00 (*0-86685-127-5*, LDL1275, Pub. by Librairie du Liban FR) Intl Bk Ctr.

Redi Fox. Dave Sargent & Pat L. Sargent. LC 96-1496. (Animal Pride Ser.). (Illus.). 43p. (J). 1996. 12.95 (*1-56763-085-5*) Ozark Pub.

Redi Fox. Dave Sargent & Pat L. Sargent. (Animal Pride Ser.: No. 3). (Illus.). 43p. (J). (gr. 2-8). 1996. pap. 2.95 (*1-56763-010-3*) Ozark Pub.

Redi-Reference. Bob Phillips. 1975. mass mkt. 2.99 (*0-89081-043-5*) Harvest Hse.

Redi-Reference Daily Bible Reading Plan. Bob Phillips. 1992. mass mkt. 2.99 (*0-89081-997-1*) Harvest Hse.

Redigging the Wells. Monroe E. Hawley. 1976. 9.95 (*0-89137-513-9*); pap. 7.50 (*0-89137-512-0*) Quality Pubns.

Redimido de la Pobreza, Enfermedad, y Muerte Espiritual. 2nd ed. Kenneth E. Hagin. (SPA.). 1982. pap. 1.95 (*0-89276-101-6*) Hagin Ministries.

Reding Resistance Value: Deconstructive Practice & the Politics of Literary Critical Encounters. Alan Kennedy. 290p. 1990. text ed. 45.00 (*0-312-04094-6*) St Martin.

Redington: John Redington of Topsfield, Mass. & Some of His Descendants, with Notes on the Wales Family. C. M. Carter. Ed. by J. G. Leach. (Illus.). 86p. 1994. reprint ed. pap. 17.00 (*0-8328-4375-X*); reprint ed. lib. bdg. 27.00 (*0-8328-4374-1*) Higginson Bk Co.

Redington Field Guides to Biological Interactions: Plants in Wetlands. Charles B. Redington. 416p. (C). 1996. ring bd. 30.39 (*0-8403-8983-3*) Kendall-Hunt.

Redirecting Boards: A New Vision of Governance for Planned Parenthood. R. James LeFevre. LC 92-46519. 134p. 1993. 11.95 (*0-934586-73-X*) Plan Parent.

***Redirecting Children's Behavior.** Kathryn J. Kvols. 1997. 19.95 (*1-884734-31-6*); pap. text ed. 14.95 (*1-884734-30-8*) Parenting Pr.

Redirecting Children's Behavior: Discipline That Builds Self-Esteem. rev. ed. Kathryn Kvols. (Illus.). 235p. 1993. pap. text ed. 11.95 (*0-9645425-0-1*) Intl Network Chldrn.

Redirecting Education, 2 vols. Ed. by Rexford G. Tugwell & Leon H. Keyserling. LC 74-128323. (Essay Index Reprint Ser.). 1977. 48.95 (*0-8369-2031-7*) Ayer.

***Redirecting Energies: Sustainable Energy Futures.** Peter Colley. 1997. 49.95 (*0-7453-1266-7*, Pub. by Pluto Pr UK); pap. text ed. 16.95 (*0-7453-1261-6*, Pub. by Pluto Pr UK) LPC InBook.

Redirecting Science: Niels Bohr, Philanthropy, & the Rise of Nuclear Physics. Finn Aaserud. (Illus.). 369p. (C). 1990. text ed. 65.00 (*0-521-35366-1*) Cambridge U Pr.

Redirecting Science Education: Reform for a Culturally Diverse Classroom. Julia V. Clark. 88p. 1996. 26.95 (*0-8039-6275-4*) Corwin Pr.

Redirecting Science Education: Reform for a Culturally Diverse Classroom. Julia V. Clark. 88p. 1996. pap. 11.95 (*0-8039-6276-2*) Corwin Pr.

Redirections in Organizational Analysis. Michael Reed. 180p. (C). 1985. pap. text ed. 18.95 (*0-422-78940-2*, 9589, Pub. by Tavistock UK) Routledge Chapman & Hall.

Rediscover America. James Piety. 155p. (C). 1986. student ed. 10.80 (*0-87563-286-6*) Stipes.

Rediscover Grammar. David Crystal. (J). 1987. pap. text ed. 15.08 (*0-582-00258-3*, 78071) Longman.

Rediscover the Evangeline Trail: A Guide to Nova Scotia from Yarmouth to Windsor. Patty Mintz. (Illus.). 156p. (Orig.). 1996. pap. 10.95 (*1-55109-158-5*, Pub. by Nimbus Publishing Ltd CN) Chelsea Green Pub.

***Rediscover the Joy of Learning.** Don A. Blackerby. 196p. (Orig.). 1996. pap. 24.95 (*1-889997-00-5*) Success Skills.

Rediscover the Lighthouse Route: A Personal Guide to the South Shore of Nova Scotia. Judith Comfort. (Illus.). 128p. 1995. pap. 10.95 (*1-55109-106-2*) Chelsea Green Pub.

***Rediscovered Bean.** Judith Choate. 1997. 14.98 (*0-7651-9432-5*) Smithmark.

Rediscovered Country. S. E. White. (Illus.). 440p. 1987. reprint ed. 25.00 (*0-935632-51-4*) Wolfe Pub Co.

Rediscovered Fiction by American Women: A Personal Selection, 18 bks. Ed. by Elizabeth Hardwick. (Illus.). 1977. lib. bdg. 496.00 (*0-405-10060-4*) Ayer.

Rediscovered Lewis Carroll Puzzles. Lewis Carroll. Ed. & Compiled by Edward Wakeling. LC 95-30151. 1995. pap. write for info. (*0-486-28861-7*) Dover.

Rediscoverers: Major Writers in the Portuguese Literature of National Regeneration. Ronald W. Sousa. LC 80-21453. (Illus.). 208p. 1981. 30.00 (*0-271-00300-6*) Pa St U Pr.

Rediscoveries: American Short Stories by Women: 1800-1916. Ed. by Barbara H. Solomon. 400p. 1994. 5.99 (*0-451-62850-0*, Ment) NAL-Dutton.

Rediscoveries: Literature & Place in Illinois. Robert C. Bray. LC 81-3353. 184p. (C). 1982. text ed. 24.95 (*0-252-00911-8*) U of Ill Pr.

Rediscoveries & Reformations: Humanistic Methodologies for International Studies. Hayward R. Alker. (Studies in International Relations: No. 41). 464p. (C). 1996. text ed. 69.95 (*0-521-46130-8*) Cambridge U Pr.

Rediscoveries & Reformations: Humanistic Methodologies for International Studies. Hayward R. Alker. (Studies in International Relations: No. 41). 464p. (C). 1996. pap. text ed. 24.95 (*0-521-46695-4*) Cambridge U Pr.

Rediscoveries in American Sculpture: Studio Works, 1893-1939. Janis Conner & Joel Rosenkrantz. (Illus.). 216p. 1989. 45.00 (*0-292-70401-1*) U of Tex Pr.

Rediscoveries in Children's Literature. Suzanne Rahn. LC 94-39594. (Studies in Children's Literature: Vol. 2). (Illus.). 208p. 1995. text ed. 40.00 (*0-8153-0930-9*, SS862) Garland.

Rediscovering Antiquity: Karl Weber & the Excavation of Herculaneum, Pompeii & Stabiae. Christopher C. Parslow. (Illus.). 416p. (C). 1995. text ed. 95.00 (*0-521-47150-8*) Cambridge U Pr.

Rediscovering Art Deco U. S. A. A Nationwide Tour of Architectural Delights. Barbara Capitman et al. (Illus.). 192p. 1994. pap. 40.00 (*0-525-93442-1*, Dutton Studio); pap. 25.00 (*0-525-48604-6*, Dutton Studio) Studio Bks.

***Rediscovering Basho.** Stephen H. Gill. 1996. pap. 24.95 (*1-86034-019-9*, Pub. by Global Bks UK) Talman.

Rediscovering Childhood Trauma: Historical Casebook & Clinical Applications. Ed. by Jean M. Goodwin. LC 92-17706. (Clinical Practice Ser.: No. 28). 215p. 1993. text ed. 33.00 (*0-88048-460-8*, 8460) Am Psychiatric.

***Rediscovering China: Dynamics & Dilemmas of Reform.** Cheng Li. LC 96-45616. (Illus.). 384p. 1996. pap. 21.95 (*0-8476-8338-9*); text ed. 64.00 (*0-8476-8337-0*) Rowman.

Rediscovering Christianity: Searching for the Roots of Modern Democracy in Our Religious Past & Present. Page Smith. 224p. 1993. 17.95 (*0-312-10531-2*) St Martin.

***Rediscovering Church: The Story & Vision of Willow Creek Community Church.** Lynne Hybels & Bill Hybels. Date not set. audio 14.99 (*0-310-59328-X*) Zondervan.

Rediscovering Church: The Story & Vision of Willow Creek Community Church. Lynne Hybels & Bill Hybels. 240p. 1995. 18.99 (*0-310-59320-4*); vhs 24.99 (*0-310-59329-8*) Zondervan.

Rediscovering Expository Preaching. Master's Seminary Faculty Staff & John F. MacArthur, Jr. Ed. by Richard L. Mayhue & Robert L. Thomas. LC 92-10804. (MacArthur Resource Library). 400p. 1992. 24.99 (*0-8499-0908-2*) Word Pub.

Rediscovering Fatima. Robert J. Fox. LC 82-60667. (Illus.). 144p. (Orig.). 1982. pap. 5.95 (*0-87973-657-7*, 657) Our Sunday Visitor.

Rediscovering Forgotten Radicals: British Women Writers, 1889-1939. Ed. by Angela Ingram & Daphne Patai. LC 92-46074. viii, 320p. 1993. pap. 18.95 (*0-8078-4414-4*); text ed. 49.95 (*0-8078-2087-3*) U of NC Pr.

Rediscovering Freedom. John Lester & Pierre Spoerri. (Illus.). 149p. (Orig.). 1992. pap. 12.95 (*1-85239-016-6*) Grosvenor USA.

Rediscovering Geography: New Relevance for Science & Society. National Research Council, Rediscovering Geography Committee. LC 97-4630. 300p. (Orig.). (C). 1997. text ed. 34.95 (*0-309-05199-1*) Natl Acad Pr.

Rediscovering God. R. T. Kendall. 10.99 (*1-85792-072-4*, Pub. by Christian Focus UK) Spring Arbor Dist.

Rediscovering Governance: A Guide to "Nonservice" Approaches to Address Neighborhood Problems. annuals 80p. 1980. 10.00 (*0-318-16231-8*, PI80900) Pub Tech Inc.

Rediscovering Hawthorne. Kenneth Dauber. LC 76-45893. 248p. reprint ed. 70.70 (*0-8357-9510-1*, 2014030) Bks Demand.

Rediscovering Herbert Horne: Poet, Architect, Typographer, Art Historian. Ian Fletcher. LC 90-81094. (British Authors, 1880-1920 Ser.: No. 3). 224p. 1990. lib. bdg. 30.00 (*0-944318-02-9*) ELT Pr.

Rediscovering History: Culture, Politics, & the Psyche. Ed. by Michael S. Roth. LC 93-33732. (Cultural Sitings Ser.). xx, 536p. 1994. 65.00 (*0-8047-2309-5*); pap. 24.95 (*0-8047-2313-3*) Stanford U Pr.

Rediscovering Holiness. J. I. Packer. 278p. 1994. pap. 12.99 (*0-89283-860-4*, Vine Bks) Servant.

***Rediscovering Holiness: The Search for the Sacred Today.** Melvyn Matthews. 112p. 1995. pap. 11.95 (*0-687-06639-5*) Abingdon.

Rediscovering Hope: Our Greatest Teaching Strategy. Richard L. Curwin. 182p. (Orig.). 1992. pap. 19.95 (*1-879639-24-6*) Natl Educ Serv.

Rediscovering India-Indian Philosophy Library, 71 vols. Prints India Staff. (C). 1988. 1,600.00 (*0-7855-0047-2*, Pub. by Print Hse II) St Mut.

Rediscovering Institutions: The Organizational Basis of Politics. James G. Marsh & Johan P. Olsen. 1989. 32.95 (*0-02-920115-2*, Free Press) Free Pr.

Rediscovering Interlanguage. Larry Selinker. (Applied Linguistics & Language Ser.). 304p. (C). 1991. pap. text ed. 28.26 (*0-582-06401-5*) Longman.

Rediscovering Japanese Space. Kisho Kurokawa. (Illus.). 150p. 1989. 29.95 (*0-8348-0224-4*) Weatherhill.

Rediscovering Jesus. Edmund Flood. 1989. pap. 3.95 (*0-8091-5204-5*) Paulist Pr.

***Rediscovering Lafcadio Hearn.** Sukehiro Hirakawa. 1996. pap. 29.95 (*1-86034-014-8*, Pub. by Global Bks UK) Talman.

***Rediscovering Machupicchu: The Lost City of the Incas.** Moises Aragon Castro. Tr. by Alfonso S. Lee. (Illus.). 180p. 1998. pap. 24.95 (*0-9630180-7-8*) Pangaea Pub.

***Rediscovering Machupicchu: The Lost City of the Incas.** Moises A. Castro. Tr. by Alfonso S. Lee. (Illus.). 180p. (ENG & SPA.). 1998. 32.95 (*0-9630180-8-6*) Pangaea Pub.

Rediscovering Mantua (Portage County, Ohio) Elmer F. Pfaff. (Illus.). 212p. (Orig.). 1985. pap. 10.00 (*0-9615749-0-9*) Mage In Nation.

Rediscovering Mary: Insights from the Gospels. Tina Beattie. LC 95-16613. 128p. (Orig.). 1995. pap. 9.95 (*0-89243-820-7*, Triumph Books) Liguori Pubns.

Rediscovering Mary: Insights from the Gospels. Tina Beattie. 128p. (Orig.). 1994. pap. 20.00 (*0-86012-247-6*, Pub. by Srch Pr UK) St Mut.

Rediscovering Masculinity: Reason, Language & Sexuality. Victor J. Seidler. 224p. (C). 1989. pap. 14.95 (*0-415-03199-0*, A3693) Routledge.

Rediscovering Mathematics. Adelbert F. Hackert. 501p. 1982. pap. text ed. 21.95 (*0-935920-41-2*, Ntl Pubs Blck) P-H.

Rediscovering Myself & Others in God: The Never-Ending Dialogue. Robert E. Lauder. LC 86-32171. 73p. (Orig.). 1987. pap. 4.95 (*0-8189-0517-4*) Alba.

Rediscovering Nancy Drew. Nancy T. Romalov. LC 95-8514. (Illus.). 297p. 1995. 24.95 (*0-87745-500-7*) U of Iowa Pr.

Rediscovering Nancy Drew. Nancy T. Romalov. LC 95-8514. (Illus.). 297p. 1995. pap. 12.95 (*0-87745-501-5*) U of Iowa Pr.

Rediscovering Northwest Denver: Its History, Its People, Its Landmarks. Ruth E. Wiberg. (Illus.). 212p. 1995. pap. 24.95 (*0-87081-372-2*) Univ Pr Colo.

Rediscovering Nursing: An-Up-date for the Returning Nurse. Martin Johnson et al. 172p. 1990. pap. 24.95 (*0-412-35440-3*, A5044) Chapman & Hall.

Rediscovering Optics. Nahum Kipnis. xii, 259p. (YA). (gr. 10-12). 1992. pap. 24.95 (*0-9636784-0-X*) BENA Pr.

Rediscovering Oscar Wilde. Ed. by C. George Sandulescu. 464p. (C). 1995. lib. bdg. 98.00 (*0-86140-376-2*) B&N Imports.

Rediscovering Our Foremothers: Nineteenth Century Canadian Women Writers. Ed. by Lorraine McMullen. 210p. 1990. pap. 21.00 (*0-7766-0197-0*, Pub. by Univ Ottawa Pr CN) Paul & Co Pubs.

***Rediscovering Our Spirit.** Bryant. 14.80 (*0-687-60971-2*) Abingdon.

Rediscovering Our Spiritual Gifts. Charles V. Bryant. LC 90-71865. 187p. (Orig.). 1991. pap. 9.95 (*0-8358-0633-2*) Upper Room Bks.

Rediscovering Our Spiritual Gifts: A Workbook. John I. Penn. 64p. 1996. wbk. ed., pap. 5.95 (*0-8358-0771-1*) Upper Room Bks.

Rediscovering Palestine: Merchants & Peasants of Jabal Nablus, 1700-1900. Beshara Doumani. LC 94-30401. (Illus.). 340p. 1995. 50.00 (*0-520-08895-6*); pap. 20.00 (*0-520-20370-4*) U CA Pr.

Rediscovering Passover: A Complete Guide for Christians. rev. ed. Joseph M. Stallings. LC 94-24330. 384p. (Orig.). (C). 1995. pap. text ed. 21.95 (*0-89390-270-5*) Resource Pubns.

Rediscovering Pastoral Ministry. John MacArthur, Jr. LC 95-6452. (MacArthur Resource Library). 400p. 1995. 24.99 (*0-8499-1092-7*) Word Pub.

Rediscovering Quality: What Healthcare Leaders & Managers Need to Know about the Total Quality Transformation. Barry S. Bader. (Illus.). 121p. (Orig.). 1992. pap. text ed. 9.50 (*0-915963-11-6*, RDQ) Capitol Publns.

Rediscovering Russia in Asia: Siberia & the Russian Far East. Ed. by Stephen Kotkin & David Wolff. LC 95-1849. (Illus.). 380p. (C). (gr. 13). 1995. 74.95 (*1-56324-546-9*) M E Sharpe.

Rediscovering Russia in Asia: Siberia & the Russian Far East. Ed. by Stephen Kotkin & David Wolff. LC 95-1849. (Illus.). 380p. (C). (gr. 13). 1995. pap. 28.95 (*1-56324-547-7*) M E Sharpe.

Rediscovering Self-Help: Its Role in Social Care. Ed. by Diane L. Pancoast et al. LC 83-3126. (Social Service Delivery Systems Ser.: No. 6). 295p. reprint ed. pap. 84.10 (*0-8357-8503-3*, 2034782) Bks Demand.

Rediscovering Some New England Artists: 1875-1900. Rolf H. Kristiansen & John J. Leahy. LC 86-60495. (Illus.). 316p. (Orig.). 1987. pap. 16.95 (*0-9616580-0-2*) Gardner-O'Brien.

Rediscovering the Angels & Natives of Eternity. 8th ed. Flower A. Newhouse. (Illus.). 156p. 1966. 16.00 (*0-910378-02-9*) Christward.

Rediscovering the Book of Mormon. John L. Sorenson & Melvin J. Thorne. LC 90-29124. xii, 274p. 1991. pap. 14.95 (*0-87579-387-8*) Deseret Bk.

***Rediscovering the Christian Feasts: A Study in the Services of the Christian Year.** Robert E. Webber. 120p. (Orig.). 1997. pap. 7.95 (*1-56563-276-1*) Hendrickson MA.

***Rediscovering the First Nations of Canada.** John W. Friesen. (Illus.). 320p. (Orig.). 1997. pap. text ed. 19.95 (*1-55059-143-6*, Pub. by Detselig CN) Temeron Bks.

Rediscovering the Forgotten Vienna Circle: Austrian Studies on Otto Neurath & the Vienna Circle. Ed. by Thomas E. Uebel. 340p. (C). 1991. lib. bdg. 141.50 (*0-7923-1276-7*, Pub. by Klwr Acad Pubs NE) Kluwer Ac.

Rediscovering the Harlem Renaissance: The Politics of Exclusion. Eloise E. Johnson. LC 96-8260. (Studies in African American History & Culture). 180p. 1996. text ed. 42.00 (*0-8153-2278-X*) Garland.

Rediscovering the I Ching. Gregory Whincup. 256p. 1995. pap. 10.95 (*0-312-14131-9*, Griffin) St Martin.

Rediscovering the Ideas of Liberty: The Foundations of America's Greatness. Ed. by W. David Stedman & LaVaughn G. Lewis. (Illus.). 84p. (Orig.). 1995. pap. 15.00 (*0-9645614-0-9*) W D Stedman.

Rediscovering the Jesus Story: A Participatory Guide. Joseph A. Grassi. LC 95-22277. 240p. (Orig.). 1995. pap. 12.95 (*0-8091-3589-2*) Paulist Pr.

***Rediscovering the Landscape of the Americas.** Photos by Dan Morse. (Illus.). 111p. (Orig.). 1996. pap. 19.95 (*0-935037-95-0*) G Peters Gallery.

Rediscovering the Lord's Supper: Communion with Israel, with Christ, & among the Guests. Markus Barth. LC 87-46294. 117p. reprint ed. pap. 33.40 (*0-7837-2635-X*, 2042985) Bks Demand.

Rediscovering the Lost Treasure of Family Worship. Jerry Marcellino. 24p. 1996. 2.95 (*0-9652883-0-7*) Audubon Pr.

Rediscovering the Missing Jewel: A Study in Worship Through the Centuries. Robert E. Webber. 120p. 1997. pap. 7.95 (*1-56563-257-5*) Hendrickson MA.

Rediscovering the Moral Life: Philosophy & Human Practice. James Gouinlock. 344p. (C). 1993. 35.95 (*0-87975-815-5*) Prometheus Bks.

Rediscovering the Muses: Women's Musical Traditions. Ed. by Kimberly Marshall. (Illus.). 352p. 1993. text ed. 42.50 (*1-55553-173-3*) NE U Pr.

Rediscovering the Muses: Women's Musical Traditions. Ed. by Kimberly Marshall. (Illus.). 352p. 1993. pap. text ed. 15.95 (*1-55553-219-5*) NE U Pr.

Rediscovering the New World: Inter-American Literature in a Comparative Context. Earl E. Fitz. LC 90-20995. 291p. (C). 1991. pap. 13.95 (*0-87745-330-6*); text ed. 34.95 (*0-87745-311-X*) U of Iowa Pr.

Rediscovering the Past at Mexico's Periphery: Essays on the History of Modern Yucatan. Gilbert M. Joseph. LC 85-1185. (Illus.). 222p. 1986. reprint ed. pap. 63.30 (*0-608-01673-X*, 2062329) Bks Demand.

Rediscovering the Power of the Gospel: Jesus' Theology of the Kingdom. J. Arthur Baird. LC 82-83623. (C). 1982. pap. 9.95 (*0-910789-00-2*) Iona Pr.

R

Rediscovering the Religious Factor in American Politics. David C. Leege & Lyman A. Kellstedt. LC 92-34293. 320p. (C). (gr. 13). 1993. text ed. 59.95 (*1-56324-133-1*); pap. text ed. 24.95 (*1-56324-134-X*) M E Sharpe.

Rediscovering the Sacred: Perspectives on Religion in Contemporary Society. Robert Wuthnow. 176p. 1992. pap. 15.00 (*0-8028-0633-3*) Eerdmans.

Rediscovering the Soul. Eugene Habecker. 240p. 1996. 15.99 (*1-56476-536-9*, 6-3536, Victor Bks) Chariot Victor.

Rediscovering the Soul of Business: A Renaissance of Values. Ed. by Bill Defoore & John Kenasch. 379p. 1995. 35.00 (*0-9630390-6-7*) New Leaders.

Rediscovering the Traditions of Israel. Douglas A. Knight. LC 75-6868. (Society of Biblical Literature. Dissertation Ser.: No. 9). 455p. reprint ed. pap. 129.70 (*0-317-07884-4*, 2017515) Bks Demand.

Rediscovering the West: An Inquiry into Nothingness & Relatedness. Stephen C. Rowe. LC 93-37857. (SUNY Series in Western Esoteric Traditions). 222p. (C). 1994. pap. 19.95 (*0-7914-1992-4*); text ed. 59.50 (*0-7914-1991-6*) State U NY Pr.

Rediscovering the Wheel: Contrary Thinking & Investment Strategy. Bradbury K. Thurlow. LC 81-68904. 1981. pap. 17.00 (*0-87034-062-X*) Fraser Pub Co.

Rediscovering the Wissahickon Through Its Science & History. Sarah West. (Illus.). 146p. (Orig.). 1993. pap. write for info. (*0-9635697-0-8*) Westford PA.

Rediscovering the Woodburning Cookstove. Robert Bobrowski. LC 76-4680. (Illus.). 98p. 1976. pap. 9.95 (*0-85699-130-9*) Chatham Pr.

***Rediscovering Values: Coming to Terms with PostModernism.** Hugh M. Curtler. LC 97-9281. 176p. (C). (gr. 13). 1997. text ed. 52.95 (*0-7656-0059-5*) M E Sharpe.

***Rediscovering Values: Coming to Terms with Postmodernism.** Hugh M. Curtler. LC 97-9281. 1997. pap. write for info. (*0-7656-0060-9*) M E Sharpe.

Rediscovery: A Novel of Darkover. Marion Zimmer Bradley & Mercedes Lackey. 368p. 1994. reprint ed. mass mkt. 4.99 (*0-88677-529-9*) DAW Bks.

Rediscovery: Ancient Pathways - New Directions, a Guidebook to Outdoor Education. 2nd rev. ed. Thom Henley. (Illus.). 288p. 1996. pap. 14.95 (*1-55105-077-3*, 1-55105) Lone Pine.

Rediscovery--Harvey Ellis: Artist, Architect. Jean R. France et al. 56p. 1991. reprint ed. pap. text ed. 15.00 (*0-918098-04-1*) Mem Art Gallery U Roch.

***Rediscovery of America: The Story of the Free Trade Agreement.** Hermann Von Bertrab. LC 96-54796. (Washington Papers: 172). 1997. text ed. write for info. (*0-275-95934-1*, Praeger Pubs); pap. text ed. write for info. (*0-275-95935-X*, Praeger Pubs) Greenwood.

Rediscovery of Ancient Egypt. Peter Clayton. 1990. 15.99 (*0-517-01510-2*) Random Hse Value.

Rediscovery of Black Nationalism. Theodore Draper. 1970. write for info. (*0-318-61740-4*) Viking Penguin.

Rediscovery of Color. Heinrich O. Proskauer. (Illus.). 180p. 1990. pap. 16.95 (*0-88010-088-5*, 1055) Anthroposophic.

Rediscovery of Creation: A Bibliographical Study of the Church's Response to the Environmental Crisis. Joseph K. Sheldon. LC 92-104. (American Theological Library Association Monograph: No. 29). 300p. 1992. 37.50 (*0-8108-2539-2*) Scarecrow.

Rediscovery of Greece: Travellers & Painters of the Romantic Era. Fani-Maria Tsigakou. (Illus.). 208p. 1981. 60.00 (*0-89241-354-9*) Caratzas.

Rediscovery of John Wesley. George C. Cell. LC 83-6505. 438p. (C). 1983. reprint ed. pap. text ed. 27.00 (*0-8191-3222-5*) U Pr of Amer.

Rediscovery of Jones, Studies in the Obvious. Simeon Strunsky. LC 67-22064. (Essay Index Reprint Ser.). 1977. 19.95 (*0-8369-0911-9*) Ayer.

Rediscovery of Man: The Complete Short Science Fiction of Cordwainer Smith. James Mann. Ed. by Cordwainer Smith. LC 93-84365. xvi, 671p. 1993. 24.95 (*0-915368-56-0*) New Eng SF Assoc.

Rediscovery of North America. Barry Lopez. LC 92-50087. 1992. pap. 8.00 (*0-679-74099-6*, Vin) Random.

Rediscovery of North America. Barry Lopez. LC 90-24487. 64p. 1991. 15.00 (*0-8131-1742-9*) U Pr of Ky.

Rediscovery of the Family & Other Lectures: Sister Marie Hilda Memorial Lectures 1954-1973. 112p. 1981. pap. text ed. 11.00 (*0-08-025754-2*, Pergamon Pr) Elsevier.

Rediscovery of the Frontier. Percy H. Boynton. LC 31-28011. (Illus.). 184p. 1969. reprint ed. text ed. 49.75 (*0-8371-0480-7*, BORE, Greenwood Pr) Greenwood.

Rediscovery of the Holy Land in the Nineteenth Century. 2nd ed. Y. Ben-Arieh. 266p. (C). 1983. text ed. 25.00 (*965-223-326-9*, Pub. by Magnes Press IS) Eisenbrauns.

Rediscovery of the Holy Land in the Nineteenth Century. Yehoshua Ben-Arieh. LC 79-67619. (Illus.). 266p. reprint ed. pap. 75.90 (*0-7837-3649-5*, 2043520) Bks Demand.

Rediscovery of the Mind. Ed. by John R. Searle. (Representation & Mind Ser.). (Illus.). 320p. 1992. 30.00 (*0-262-19321-3*, Bradford Bks) MIT Pr.

Rediscovery of the Mind. John R. Searle. (Representation & Mind Ser.). (Illus.). 288p. 1992. pap. 14.00 (*0-262-69154-X*, Bradford Bks) MIT Pr.

Rediscovery of the Old Testament. H. H. Rowley. 224p. 1946. 14.00 (*0-227-67576-2*) Attic Pr.

Redistribution of Population in Africa. John I. Clarke & Leszek A. Kosinski. 212p. (C). 1982. pap. text ed. 22.50 (*0-435-95031-2*, 95031) Heinemann.

Redistribution Through Public Choice. Harold M. Hochman & George E. Peterson. LC 73-19748. 1974. text ed. 60.00 (*0-231-03775-9*) Col U Pr.

Redistributive Effects of Government Programmes: The Chilean Case. Alejandro Foxley et al. (Illus.). 1979. 108.00 (*0-08-023130-6*, Pub. by Pergamon Repr UK) Franklin.

Redistricting. Butler. 1991. pap. text ed. 22.00 (*0-02-317585-0*, Macmillan Coll) P-H.

Redistricting in the Nineteen Eighties: A 50-State Survey. Ed. by Leroy Hardy et al. 277p. 1993. pap. text ed. 45.00 (*1-883638-00-3*) Rose Inst.

Redivision of Labor: Women & Economic Choice in Four Guatemalan Communities. Laurel H. Bossen. LC 83-426. (SUNY Series in the Anthropology of Work). (Illus.). 396p. 1984. text ed. 59.50 (*0-87395-740-7*); pap. text ed. 19.95 (*0-87395-741-5*) State U NY Pr.

Redlight Ladies of Virginia City, Nevada. George J. Williams, III. (Nevada Prostitution Ser.). (Illus.). (Orig.). 1984. 17.95 (*0-935174-13-3*); pap. 5.95 (*0-935174-12-5*) Tree by River.

Redline the Stars. Andre Norton. 304p. 1994. mass mkt. 4.99 (*0-8125-1986-8*) Tor Bks.

Redliners. David Drake. 384p. 1996. 19.00 (*0-671-87733-X*) Baen Bks.

***Redliners.** David Drake. 384p. 1997. mass mkt. 5.99 (*0-671-87789-5*) Baen Bks.

Redmagic. Crawford Killian. (The Wizards of Fantasy Promotion). 1995. mass mkt. 5.99 (*0-345-38370-2*, Del Rey) Ballantine.

Redmen of Mars. John R. Fearn. (Drew Ser.: No. 3). 1995. pap. 15.00 (*0-936071-49-4*) Gryphon Pubns.

Redmond Barry: An Anglo-Irish Australian. Ann Galbally. 184p. 1995. 44.95 (*0-522-84516-9*, Pub. by Melbourne Univ Pr AT) Paul & Co Pubs.

Redneck. Oel Futrell. LC 95-62082. 66p. (YA). (gr. 5-12). 1996. pap. 7.95 (*1-55523-775-4*) Winston-Derek.

Redneck & the High Maintenance Woman. Doyle High & Roberta High. (Illus.). (Orig.). 1994. pap. 8.95 (*0-9645563-0-8*) D High.

Redneck Bites the Big Apple. Bo Whaley. 170p. (Orig.). 1995. pap. 6.95 (*1-55853-363-X*) Rutledge Hill Pr.

***Redneck Christmas Carol: Dickens Does Dixie.** John Yow. 1997. pap. text ed. 8.95 (*1-56352-429-5*); pap. text ed. 53.70 (*1-56352-430-9*) Longstreet Pr Inc.

Redneck Classic: The Best of Jeff Foxworthy. Jeff Foxworthy. (Illus.). 144p. 1995. pap. 9.95 (*1-56352-228-4*) Longstreet Pr Inc.

***Redneck Cookbook: 134 Down Home Recipes Complete with All the Trimmin's.** Lo'Retta Love. LC 97-20705. 1997. write for info. (*1-889372-57-9*) Sweetwater Pr.

***Redneck Cookbook: 165 Mighty Fine Down Home Recipes - Complete with All the Trimmin's.** Lo'retta Love. LC 96-53240. (Illus.). 128p. 1997. pap. 7.98 (*1-884822-69-X*) Blck Dog & Leventhal.

Redneck Exercise Book. Paul Johnson & Nell Weaver. LC 84-62351. (Illus.). 50p. 1984. pap. 4.95 (*0-914546-58-9*) Rose Pub.

Redneck Heaven: Portrait of a Vanishing Culture. Bethany E. Bultman. LC 96-12719. 304p. 1996. pap. 14.95 (*0-553-37804-X*) Bantam.

Redneck Instruction Book. Scrawls. LC 96-16301. (Illus.). 96p. (Orig.). 1996. pap. 4.95 (*1-56554-176-6*) Pelican.

Redneck Liberal: Theodore G. Bilbo & the New Deal. Chester M. Morgan. LC 85-11023. 288p. 1985. pap. 82.10 (*0-7837-8516-X*, 2049325) Bks Demand.

***Redneck Manifesto.** Jim Goad. LC 97-7865. 1997. 22.00 (*0-684-83113-9*) S&S Trade.

***Redneck Night Before Christmas.** David Davis. LC 97-14421. (Illus.). (J). 1997. write for info. (*1-56554-293-2*) Pelican.

***Redneck Night Before Christmas.** E. J. Sullivan. LC 96-27294. 1996. pap. 3.95 (*1-889372-00-5*) Sweetwtr Pr AL.

Redneck Rhymer Strikes. Roy Manning. 44p. Date not set. pap. 7.95 (*0-932662-56-0*) St Andrews NC.

Redneck Way of Knowledge. Blanche M. Boyd. 1995. pap. 10.00 (*0-679-75767-8*, Vin) Random.

Redneckin' Made Easy. Bo Whaley. LC 88-18348. 95p. 1988. pap. 3.50 (*0-934395-94-2*) Rutledge Hill Pr.

Rednecks & Niggers. Vondra C. Porter. 64p. (Orig.). 1993. pap. 7.95 (*1-56167-150-9*) Am Literary Pr.

Rednecks & Other Bonafide Americans. rev. ed. Bo Whaley. LC 91-10858. (Illus.). 192p. 1991. pap. 6.95 (*1-55853-106-8*) Rutledge Hill Pr.

Redney: A Life of Sara Jeannette Duncun. Marian Fowler. 333p. 1983. 9.95 (*0-88784-099-X*, Pub. by Hse of Anansi Pr CN) Genl Dist Srvs.

Redo Compendium: Reverse Engineering for Software Maintenance ILI Special Report. Henk Van Zuylen. LC 92-40218. 405p. 1993. text ed. 300.00 (*0-471-93607-3*) Wiley.

***Redoble por Rancas.** Manuel Scorza. 1997. pap. 12.95 (*0-14-026585-6*) Viking Penguin.

Redon: Postcardbook. Michael Gibson. 1996. pap. text ed. 9.99 (*3-8228-8642-4*) Taschen Amer.

***Redoutable Marcus la Puce.** Gilles Gauthier. (Novels in the Premier Roman Ser.). 64p. (FRE.). (J). (gr. 2-5). 1996. pap. 7.95 (*2-89021-232-7*, Pub. by Les Editions CN) Firefly Bks Ltd.

Redoute: The Man Who Painted Flowers. Carolyn Croll. LC 93-42394. (Illus.). 40p. (J). (gr. 3 up). 1996. 15.95 (*0-399-22606-0*, Putnam) Putnam Pub Group.

Redoute Album: Bouquets & Lilies. Intro. by Graham Arader, III. (Illus.). 340p. 1991. 95.00 (*0-87951-439-6*) Overlook Pr.

***Redoute Rose Prints.** Pierre-Joseph Redoute. (Illus.). pap. 3.95 (*0-486-26270-7*) Dover.

Redox Chemistry & Interfacial Behavior of Biological Molecules. Ed. by G. Dryhurst & K. Niki. LC 88-29382. (Illus.). 672p. 1988. 145.00 (*0-306-43038-X*, Plenum Pr) Plenum.

Redrawing the Boundaries of Literary Study in English. Ed. by Stephen Greenblatt & Giles Gunn. LC 92-24416. 595p. 1992. pap. 19.75 (*0-87352-396-2*, T170P); lib. bdg. 45.00 (*0-87352-395-4*, T170C) Modern Lang.

Redress of Poetry. Seamus Heaney. LC 95-19556. 212p. 1995. 22.00 (*0-374-24853-2*) FS&G.

Redress of Poetry. Seamus Heaney. 240p. 1996. pap. 12.00 (*0-374-52488-2*) FS&G.

Redress of Public Grievances. M. L. Malhotra. 1993. 30.00 (*81-207-1337-0*, Pub. by Sterling Pubs II) Apt Bks.

Redressing the Balance: American Women's Literary Humor from Colonial Times to the 1980s. Ed. by Nancy Walker & Zita Dresner. LC 88-17536. 480p. (Orig.). 1988. pap. 20.00 (*0-87805-364-6*) U Pr of Miss.

Redridge & Its Steel Dam. (Copper Country Local History Ser.: Vol. 42). (Illus.). 120p. 1992. 3.00 (*0-942363-41-8*) C J Monette.

Redruff the Partridge of Don Valley. Ernest T. Seton. (Illus.). 48p. (Orig.). (YA). (gr. 4-12). 1994. pap. 9.95 (*1-880812-15-0*) S Ink WA.

Redruth Parish Church - St. Euny's. Frank Mitchell. (C). 1989. 30.00 (*1-85022-036-0*, Pub. by Dyllansow Truran UK) St Mut.

Reds Bring Reaction. W. J. Ghent. 1977. lib. bdg. 59.95 (*0-8490-2505-2*) Gordon Pr.

Reds Bring Reaction. William J. Ghent. 1977. 19.95 (*0-405-09952-5*, 10047) Ayer.

Reds or Rackets: The Making of Radical & Conservative Unions on the Waterfront. Howard Kimeldorf. 270p. 1988. 40.00 (*0-520-06308-2*) U CA Pr.

Reds or Rackets? The Making of Radical & Conservative Unions on the Waterfront. Howard Kimeldorf. 1992. pap. 14.00 (*0-520-07886-1*) U CA Pr.

Reds, Reds, Copper Reds. Robert Tichane. Tr. by Thomas Elmer. LC 84-62546. (Oriental Glaze Ser.). (Illus.). 306p. 1985. 25.00 (*0-914267-04-3*) NYS Inst Glaze.

Red's Story. Storey & Snyder. 256p. 1995. mass mkt. 7.99 (*0-7704-2711-1*) Bantam.

Redshift - Blueshift. Chris Mansell. 64p. (C). 1990. 45.00 (*0-9587972-1-8*, Pub. by Pascoe Pub AT) St Mut.

Redshift Connection: Concerning the Gravitational Interaction of Mass with Electromagnetic Radiation. Stanislaw A. Milianowicz. LC 95-81001. (Illus.). ix, 237p. (Orig.). 1995. pap. 48.00 (*0-9652987-3-6*) Arysutt AMS.
In the early years of cosmological redshift discovery choice had to be made between the phenomena of velocity-shifts & those of photon energy loss, as the cause of these redshifts. In his book "The Observational Approach to Cosmology" (Oxford University Press, 1937) Edwin Hubble gives a very lucid description of reasons for velocity-shifts being accepted as true sources of redshift. Photon energy loss was, at that time believed to be "some unknown reaction between the light & the medium through which it travels" quoting from page 45 of Hubble's book. REDSHIFT CONNECTION provides a rigorous, quantitative analysis of gravitational interaction of mass with electromagnetic radiation, where gravitational field of a photon is not regarded as being negligibly small & its inclusion in the calculations shows that gravity rather than spacetime expansion is the true cause of cosmological redshift. Other, related, paradigms are examined in the light of this finding, such as: gravitational vs. inertial mass, production of long range force, nature of dark matter & the source of cosmic background radiation. The ideas presented in REDSHIFT CONNECTION put in question many presently held theories, not only in the study of Astronomy & Cosmology, but in all of Physics. Order from: Arysutt AMS, P.O. Box 119, Trafford, PA 15085-0119; 412-327-6565. ***Publisher Provided Annotation.***

Redskin Morning, & Other Stories. Joan M. Grant & Ralph Layers. 1980. 21.95 (*0-405-11787-6*) Ayer.

Redskins. James Fenimore Cooper. (Works of James Fenimore Cooper Ser.). 1990. reprint ed. lib. bdg. 79.00 (*0-7812-2395-4*) Rprt Serv.

Redskins, Ruffleshirts & Rednecks: Indian Allotments in Alabama & Mississippi 1830-1860. Mary E. Young. LC 61-15150. (Civilization of the American Indian Ser.: No. 61). (Illus.). 233p. reprint ed. pap. 66.50 (*0-8357-9739-2*, 2016284) Bks Demand.

Reduce: Software for Algebraic Computation. Gerhard Rayna. LC 87-20535. 335p. 1987. 65.95 (*0-387-96598-X*) Spr-Verlag.

REDUCE for Physicists. N. MacDonald. (Illus.). 167p. 1994. 51.00 (*0-7503-0277-1*) IOP Pub.

Reduce, Reuse, Recycle. Rozanne L. Williams. (Emergent Reader Big Bks.). (Illus.). 8p. (Orig.). (J). (gr. k-2). 1995. pap. 7.98 (*1-57471-014-1*) Creat Teach Pr.

Reduce, Reuse, Recycle, Level 1. Rozanne L. Williams. (Emergent Reader Science Ser.). 8p. 1994. 1.59 (*0-916119-30-0*, 3507) Creat Teach Pr.

***Reduce Stress - Communicate.** David C. Rainham. (Orig.). 1996. pap. 3.00 (*1-884241-36-0*, EHO550) Energeia Pub.

Reduce Your Risks to Professional Liability Claims in Real Estate. Leland M. Kraft, Jr. LC 91-92475. 288p. 1992. pap. 29.95 (*0-9631800-0-2*) Apollo Pubns.

Reduce Your Test Anxiety! 128 Strategies to Help You Make the Grade. Robert H. Phillips. (Strategy Guidebooks Ser.). 52p. (YA). 1996. pap. 6.95 (*1-888614-01-3*) Balance Enter.

Reduced Activation Materials for Fusion Reactors. Ed. by R. L. Klueh et al. LC 89-18582. (Special Technical Publication Ser.: No. 1047). (Illus.). 260p. 1990. text ed. 55.00 (*0-8031-1267-X*, 04-010470-35) ASTM.

Reduced Constructions in Spanish. rev. ed. John C. Moore et al. Ed. by Jorge Hankamer. LC 96-36742. (Outstanding Dissertations in Linguistics Ser.). 283p. 1996. text ed. 72.00 (*0-8153-2579-7*) Garland.

Reduced Dose Mammography. Wende W. Logan & E. Phillip Muntz. LC 79-63202. (Illus.). 576p. (gr. 13). 1979. 62.00 (*0-89352-060-8*, Yr Bk Med Pubs) Mosby Yr Bk.

Reduced Emissions & Fuel Consumption in Automobile Engines. 200p. 1995. 85.00 (*1-56091-681-8*, R-157) Soc Auto Engineers.

Reduced Emissions & Fuel Consumption in Automobile Engines. Fred Schafer & Richard Van Basshuysen. LC 95-38356. 1996. 128.00 (*3-211-82718-8*) Spr-Verlag.

Reduced Enrichment for Research & Test Reactors. Ed. by Peter Von der Hardt & A. Travelli. 1986. lib. bdg. 165.50 (*90-277-2233-1*) Kluwer Ac.

Reduced Forms of Rational Expectations Models, Vol. 42. Laurence Broze. (Fundamentals of Pure & Applied Economics Ser.). 199, xp. 1991. text ed. 45.00 (*3-7186-5031-2*, Harwood Acad Pubs) Gordon & Breach.

***Reduced Fuel Consumption & Emissions Due to Better Integration of Engine & Transmission.** B. Hahn. (1992 Fall Technical Meeting). 1992. pap. text ed. 30.00 (*1-55589-583-2*) AGMA.

Reduced Kinetic Mechanisms & Asymptotic Approximations for Methane-Air Flames: A Topical Volume. Ed. by M. D. Smooke et al. (Lecture Notes in Physics Ser.: Vol. 384). v, 245p. 1991. 42.95 (*0-387-54210-8*) Spr-Verlag.

Reduced Kinetic Mechanisms for Applications in Combustion Systems. Ed. by Norbert Peters & Bernd Rogg. LC 92-42967. (Lecture Notes in Physics Ser.: Vol. M15). 1993. write for info. (*3-540-56372-5*); 69.95 (*0-387-56372-5*) Spr-Verlag.

Reduced Rank Regression: With Applications to Quantitative Structure-Activity Relationships. H. Schmidli. (Contributions to Statistics Ser.). (Illus.). 179p. 1995. 59.00 (*3-7908-0871-7*) Spr-Verlag.

***Reduced Reserve Requirements: Alternatives for the Conduct of Monetary Policy & Reserve Management.** 1996. lib. bdg. 258.75 (*0-8490-6942-4*) Gordon Pr.

Reduced Thermal Processing for ULSI. Ed. by R. A. Levy. LC 89-23011. (NATO ASI Series B, Physics: Vol. 207). (Illus.). 450p. 1989. 125.00 (*0-306-43382-6*, Plenum Pr) Plenum.

Reduced Working Hours: Cure for Unemployment Or Economic Burden? John D. Owen. LC 88-30352. 192p. 1989. text ed. 34.50 (*0-8018-3784-7*) Johns Hopkins.

Reduced Worktime & the Management of Production. Chris Nyland. (Illus.). 240p. (C). 1989. text ed. 54.95 (*0-521-34547-2*) Cambridge U Pr.

Reducing Aggression in Children: Boys Town Strategies for Dealing with Outgoing Aggressive Behavior. Thomas P. Dowd. (Boys Town National Family Home Program Informational Ser.). 12p. (Orig.). 1996. spiral bd., pap. 1.95 (*0-938510-91-6*, 19-204) Boys Town Pr.

Reducing Anger: Harnessing Passion & Fury to Work for You - Not Against Others. Dale R. Olen. (Illus.). 212p. (Orig.). 1992. pap. text ed. 5.95 (*1-56583-009-1*) JODA.

***Reducing Bar Costs: A Survival Plan for the '90s.** Robert A. Plotkin. LC 93-93670. 101p. 1993. pap. 20.00 (*0-945562-13-6*) PSD Pub.

Reducing Benzodiazepine Consumption. M. A. Cormack et al. (Recent Research in Psychology Ser.). x, 96p. 1989. 53.95 (*0-387-97035-5*) Spr-Verlag.

Reducing Breast Cancer Risk in Women. Ed. by Basil A. Stoll. LC 94-29394. 264p. 1995. lib. bdg. 100.00 (*0-7923-3064-1*) Kluwer Ac.

Reducing CO B2 S Emissions: A Comparative Input-Output Study for Germany & the U. K. John L. Proops et al. LC 92-34932. 1993. 97.00 (*0-387-55947-7*) Spr-Verlag.

Reducing Construction Conflicts Between Highway & Utilities. (National Cooperative Highway Research Program Report Ser.: No. 115). 73p. 1984. 8.80 (*0-309-04871-0*) Transport Res Bd.

Reducing Cost of Space Transportation: Proceedings of the Goddard Memorial Symposium, 7th, Washington, D.C., 1969. Ed. by George K. Chacko. (Science & Technology Ser.: Vol. 21). (Illus.). 1969. 25.00 incl. fiche (*0-87703-049-9*) Univelt Inc.

Reducing Crime & Assuring Justice. Committee for Economic Development. LC 72-81298. 86p. 1972. pap. 1.50 (*0-87186-046-5*); lib. bdg. 2.50 (*0-87186-746-X*) Comm Econ Dev.

Reducing Debt & Improving Your Credit. Gail Liberman & Alan Lavine. (ICFP Personal Wealth Building Guides Ser.). 212p. 1994. pap. text ed. 14.95 (*0-471-58374-X*) Wiley.

Reducing Delinquency. Goldstein. (Practitioner Guidebook Ser.). (C). 1992. pap. text ed. 30.95 (*0-205-14338-5*, H43383, Longwood Div) Allyn.

Reducing Delinquency. Goldstein. 1989. text ed. 47.95 (*0-205-14435-7*) P-H.

***Reducing Disproportionate Representation of Culturally Diverse Students in Special & Gifted Education.** Ed. by Alfredo J. Artiles & Grace Z. Duran. LC 97-17073. 98p. (Orig.). 1997. pap. text ed. write for info. (*0-86586-297-4*) Coun Exc Child.

Reducing Earthquake Hazards: Lessons Learned from Earthquakes. 208p. 1986. pap. 15.00 (*0-943198-27-5*) Earthquake Eng.

Reducing Earthquake Hazards: Lessons Learned from the Mexico Earthquake. Ed. by V. Bertero. 190p. 1989. pap. 15.00 (*0-943198-29-1*) Earthquake Eng.

***Reducing Earthquake Losses.** 1996. lib. bdg. 252.99 (*0-8490-6376-0*) Gordon Pr.

Reducing Educational Disadvantage. Paul Widlake. LC 86-8676. 160p. 1986. 80.00 (0-335-15241-4, Open Univ Pr); pap. 27.00 (0-335-15240-6, Open Univ Pr) Taylor & Francis.

Reducing Employee Absenteeism Through Self-Management Training: A Research-Based Analysis & Guide. Colette A. Frayne. LC 90-8407. 144p. 1991. text ed. 45.00 (0-89930-553-9, FSM/, Quorum Bks) Greenwood.

Reducing Employee Theft: A Guide to Financial & Organizational Controls. Neil H. Snyder et al. LC 90-26208. 216p. 1991. text ed. 55.00 (0-89930-588-1, SNO/, Quorum Bks) Greenwood.

Reducing Environmental Pollution: Looking Back, Thinking Ahead. OECD Staff. 48p. (Orig.). 1994. pap. 9.00 (92-64-14214-2) OECD.

Reducing Failures of Engineered Facilities: Proceedings of a Workshop Sponsored by the National Science Foundation & ASCE. 108p. 1985. 15.00 (0-87262-485-4) Am Soc Civil Eng.

Reducing Farm Injuries: Issues & Methods. Robert A. Aherin et al. LC 92-74621. 70p. 1992. pap. 19.00 (0-929355-35-0, C1692) Am Soc Ag Eng.

*__Reducing Firearm Injury & Death: A Public Health Sourcebook on Guns.__ Trudy Karlson & Stephen Hargarten. (Illus.). 224p. (C). 1997. text ed. 50.00 (0-8135-2420-2); pap. text ed. 24.95 (0-8135-2421-0) Rutgers U Pr.

Reducing Frailty & Falls in Older Persons: Categorical & Noncategorical Perspectives. Ed. by Richard Weindruch et al. (Illus.). 550p. 1991. pap. 55.95 (0-398-06481-4) C C Thomas.

Reducing Frailty & Falls in Older Persons: Categorical & Noncategorical Perspectives. Ed. by Richard Weindruch et al. (Illus.). 550p. (C). 1991. text ed. 95.95 (0-398-05752-4) C C Thomas.

Reducing Gun Violence: What Communities Can Do. Lauren Brosler & Jean O'Neil. Ed. by Judy Kirby. 42p. (Orig.). 1995. pap. 9.95 (0-934513-04-X) Natl Crime DC.

Reducing Hazardous Waste Generation: An Evaluation & a Call for Action. National Research Council Staff. 76p. 1985. pap. text ed. 9.95 (0-309-03498-1) Natl Acad Pr.

Reducing Home Building Costs with Optimum Value Engineered Design & Construction see Cost-Effective Home Building: A Design & Construction Handbook

Reducing Home Heating & Cooling Costs. W. Calvin Kilgore. (Illus.). 41p. (Orig.). 1994. pap. 20.00 (0-7881-1337-2) DIANE Pub.

Reducing Inappropriate Use of Juvenile Detention in Los Angeles County. 1987. 7.00 (0-318-23566-8) Natl Coun Crime.

*__Reducing Inflation: Motivation & Strategy.__ Christina Romer & David Romer. LC 96-44811. (National Bureau of Economic Research Project Reports). 1996. 58.00 (0-226-72484-0) U Ch Pr.

Reducing Labor Turnover in Financial Institutions. Presley T. Creery & Katherine W. Creery. LC 87-37572. (Illus.). 186p. 1988. text ed. 55.00 (0-89930-296-3, CYR/, Quorum Bks) Greenwood.

Reducing Litigation: Evidence from Wisconsin. Leslie I. Boden. 1988. 25.00 (0-935149-16-3, WC-88-7) Workers Comp Res Inst.

Reducing Litigation: Using Disability Guidelines & State Evaluators in Oregon. Leslie I. Boden et al. LC 91-33586. 1991. 25.00 (0-935149-29-5, WC-91-3) Workers Comp Res Inst.

Reducing New Home Costs As Much As 30,000 Dollars. rev. ed. Richard L. May. LC 90-70961. (Orig.). 1990. 7.95 (0-9627119-0-X) J Zachary Pub.

Reducing Nuclear Arsenals. Ed. by Carlo Schaerf & David Carlton. LC 91-11661. 256p. 1991. text ed. 69.95 (0-312-06535-3) St Martin.

Reducing Nuclear Danger: The Road Away from the Brink. McGeorge Bundy et al. 128p. 1993. 14.95 (0-87609-149-4) Coun Foreign.

Reducing Nuclear Danger: The Road Away from the Brink. McGeorge Bundy et al. 107p. 1993. pap. text ed. 12.95 (0-87609-170-2) Coun Foreign.

Reducing Personal Income Tax: A Guide to Deductions & Credits. John E. Davidian & Jacob L. Todres. 1988. ring bd. 70.00 (0-318-23689-3) NY Law Pub.

Reducing Personal Income Taxes: A Guide to Deductions & Credits. John E. Davidian & Jacob L. Todres. 700p. 1988. ring bd. 80.00 (0-317-05397-3, 00605) NY Law Pub.

Reducing Pollution from Selected Energy Transformation Sources. Chem Systems International, Ltd. Staff. 230p. 1976. lib. bdg. 73.00 (0-86010-036-7) G & T Inc.

Reducing Poverty in America: Views & Approaches. Ed. by Michael R. Darby & John E. Anderson. LC 95-35748. 360p. 1995. 52.00 (0-7619-0006-3); pap. 26.50 (0-7619-0007-1) Sage.

Reducing Premium Fraud in the Workers' Compensation System in Minnesota. Brian Zaidman. 62p. (Orig.). (C). 1994. pap. text ed. 20.00 (0-7881-0572-8) DIANE Pub.

*__Reducing Project Risk.__ Ralph Kleim & Irwin Lundin. LC 96-37780. 200p. 1997. text ed. 56.95 (0-566-07799-X, Pub. by Gower UK) Ashgate Pub Co.

Reducing Racial Tension in the Schools Through Values Clarification. L. Jalik Petty. LC 81-52146. 56p. (Orig.). (C). 1982. pap. 4.95 (0-942428-00-5) Universal Ministries.

Reducing Regulatory & Financial Impediments to Energy Conservation. 120p. 1982. 20.00 (0-318-17714-5, DG82-316) Pub Tech Inc.

Reducing Reliance on Pesticides in Great Lakes Basin Agriculture: Barriers & Opportunities. World Wildlife Fund, Agricultural Pollution Prevention Project Staff et al. LC 95-21298. (Illus.). 314p. (Orig.). (C). 1997. pap. text ed. 16.50 (0-89164-145-9) World Wildlife Fund.

Reducing, Reusing, & Recycling. Bobbie Kalman. (Environment Ser.). (Illus.). 32p. (J). (gr. 3-4). 1991. pap. text ed. 7.95 (0-86505-456-8); lib. bdg. 19.16 (0-86505-426-6) Crabtree Pub Co.

Reducing Risk: Participatory Learning Activities for Disaster Mitigation in Southern Africa. Astrid Von Kotze & Ailsa Holloway. 300p. 1996. pap. 29.95 (0-85598-347-7, Pub. by Oxfam UK) Humanities.

Reducing Risk & Liability Through Better Specifications & Inspection. Compiled by American Society of Civil Engineers Staff. LC 82-70874. 165p. 1982. pap. 21.00 (0-87262-301-7) Am Soc Civil Eng.

Reducing Risk in Paint Stripping: Proceedings of an International Conference. Ed. by Gretchen Flock. 230p. (Orig.). 1991. pap. 30.00 (0-614-14305-5) Terrene Inst.

Reducing Risks for Mental Disorders: Frontiers for Preventive Intervention. Institute of Medicine Staff. Ed. by Patricia J. Mrazek & Robert J. Haggerty. 636p. (C). 1994. text ed. 49.95 (0-309-04939-3) Natl Acad Pr.

Reducing School Violence Through Conflict Resolution. David W. Johnson & Roger T. Johnson. LC 95-32482. 1995. pap. 18.95 (0-87120-252-2, 195198) Assn Supervision.

Reducing Seismic Hazards of Existing Buildings: Workshop Proceedings. Ed. by Roger E. Scholl. (Illus.). 212p. (Orig.). (C). 1993. pap. text ed. 45.00 (1-56806-573-6) DIANE Pub.

Reducing Space Mission Cost. Ed. by James R. Wertz & Wiley J. Larson. (Space Technology Library). (Illus.). 617p. (Orig.). (C). 1996. pap. text ed. 39.95 (1-881883-05-1) Microcosm.

Reducing Space Mission Cost. James R. Wertz. LC 96-16835. (Space Technology Library). 1996. lib. bdg. 198.00 (0-7923-4021-3, D Reidel) Kluwer Ac.

Reducing Stigma Through Education, 7 vols., Set. Date not set. 1,000.00 (1-889022-00-4) Mental Hlth KY.

Reducing Stigma Through Education: Alcohol Use & Misuse. Perilou Goddard. Ed. by Peter M. Monti. Date not set. 175.00 (1-889022-07-1) Mental Hlth KY.

Reducing Stigma Through Education: Alzheimer's Disease. James H. Thomas. Ed. by Laura L. Carstensen. Date not set. 175.00 (1-889022-03-9) Mental Hlth KY.

Reducing Stigma Through Education: Anxiety Disorders. Perilou Goddard. Ed. by David H. Barlow. Date not set. 175.00 (1-889022-02-0) Mental Hlth KY.

Reducing Stigma Through Education: Attention Deficity Hyperactivity Disorder. James H. Thomas. Ed. by David L. Rabiner. Date not set. 175.00 (1-889022-04-7) Mental Hlth KY.

Reducing Stigma Through Education: Depression. Perilou Goddard. Ed. by Ian H. Gotlib. Date not set. 175.00 (1-889022-01-2) Mental Hlth KY.

Reducing Stigma Through Education: Post Traumatic Stress Disorder. Dushka Crane-Ross. Ed. by Terence M. Keane. Date not set. 175.00 (1-889022-06-3) Mental Hlth KY.

Reducing Stigma Through Education: Schizophrenia. Perilou Goddard. Ed. by Howard Berenbaum. Date not set. 175.00 (1-889022-05-5) Mental Hlth KY.

Reducing Stress in Young Children's Lives. Ed. by Janet B. McCracken. LC 86-62564. (Illus.). 170p. 1986. pap. 7.00 (0-935989-03-X, NAEYC 216) Natl Assn Child Ed.

Reducing the Carcinogenic Risks in Industry. Paul F. Deisler, Jr. (Occupational Safety & Health Ser.: Vol. 9). 272p. 1984. 145.00 (0-8247-7250-4) Dekker.

Reducing the Cost of LAN Ownership: The Business of Running a Network. Salvatore Salamone & Greg Gianforte. 175p. 1994. pap. 39.95 (0-442-01904-1) Van Nos Reinhold.

Reducing the Cost of Surveys. Seymour Sudman. LC 67-17611. (Monographs in Social Research: No. 10). 1967. 9.95 (0-202-30030-7) Natl Opinion Res.

*__Reducing the Deficit: Spending & Revenue Options, 3 vols.__ (Illus.). xxiv, 496p. 1996. pap. 105.00 (0-9656560-6-3) BPI Info Servs.

Reducing the Deficit: Spending & Revenue Options. 1995. lib. bdg. 275.99 (0-8490-6865-7) Gordon Pr.

Reducing the Deficit: Spending & Revenue Options. (Illus.). 435p. (Orig.). (C). 1995. pap. text ed. 50.00 (0-7881-2291-6) DIANE Pub.

Reducing the Energy Cost Burden on Low Income Residents. 87p. 1982. 15.00 (0-318-17347-6, DG/82-308) Pub Tech Inc.

Reducing the Estrogen Dose in Oral Contraception. Ed. by O. Ylikorkala. (Illus.). 90p. 1991. 36.00 (1-85070-369-8) Prthnon Pub.

Reducing the Health Consequences of Smoking: 25 Years of Progress: A Report of the Surgeon General. (Illus.). 703p. (Orig.). (C). 1995. pap. text ed. 50.00 (0-7881-2313-0) DIANE Pub.

Reducing the Impacts of Natural Hazards: A Strategy for the Nation. 88p. (Orig.). (YA). (gr. 12 up). 1994. pap. text ed. 30.00 (0-7881-0830-1) DIANE Pub.

Reducing the Military's Inventory: Applying Commercial Logistics Practices to Reduce Maintenance & Supply Costs. (Illus.). 98p. (Orig.). (C). 1994. pap. text ed. 35.00 (0-7881-0212-5) DIANE Pub.

Reducing the Risk. 2nd ed. Richard P. Barth. 60p. (SPA.). 1995. pap. 18.95 (1-56071-453-0) ETR Assocs.

Reducing the Risk: Building Skills to Prevent Pregnancy, STD & HIV. 2nd ed. Richard P. Barth. LC 92-39092. 1993. 34.95 (1-56071-147-7) ETR Assocs.

Reducing the Risk: Building Skills to Prevent Pregnancy, STD & HIV. 3rd ed. Richard P. Barth. LC 95-30962. 1995. write for info. (1-56071-398-4) ETR Assocs.

Reducing the Risk Vol. 2: A School Leader's Guide to AIDS Education. 2nd ed. Kathleen A. McCormick. 43p. (Orig.). 1990. pap. text ed. 5.00 (0-88364-170-4) Natl Sch Boards.

Reducing the Risk of Child Sexual Abuse in Your Church. Richard R. Hammar et al. 96p. (Orig.). (C). 1993. pap. text ed. 8.95 (1-880562-07-3) Christ Minist.

Reducing the Risks: Schools As Communities of Support. Ed. by Gary G. Wehlage. 280p. 1989. 65.00 (1-85000-530-3, Falmer Pr); pap. 29.00 (1-85000-531-1, Falmer Pr) Taylor & Francis.

Reducing the Risks of Nonstructural Earthquake Damage: A Practical Guide. Eduardo A. Fierro et al. (Illus.). 131p. (Orig.). 1995. pap. text ed. 30.00 (0-7881-2603-2) DIANE Pub.

Reducing the Size of the Federal Civilian Work Force. Amy Belasco & R. Mark Musell. (Illus.). 72p. (Orig.). (C). 1994. pap. text ed. 30.00 (0-7881-0702-X) DIANE Pub.

Reducing Toxics: A New Approach to Policy & Industrial Decisionmaking. Ed. by Robert Gottlieb. LC 94-46257. 450p. (Orig.). (C). 1995. pap. text ed. 35.00 (1-55963-336-0) Island Pr.

Reducing Undesirable Behaviors. Lewis Polsgrove. 33p. 1991. pap. text ed. 9.75 (0-86586-201-X, P342) Coun Exc Child.

Reducing Unemployment: A Case for Government Deregulation. Garry K. Ottosen & Douglas N. Thompson. LC 95-30555. 184p. 1996. text ed. 49.95 (0-275-95360-2, Praeger Pubs) Greenwood.

Reducing Vehicle Noise & Vibration. (International Pacific Conference on Automotive Engineering, 7th Ser.). 78p. 1993. pap. 30.00 (1-56091-427-0, SP-991) Soc Auto Engineers.

*__Reducing Wastes from Decommissioned Nuclear Submarines in the Russian Northwest: Political, Technical & Econo.__ Sanoma L. Kellogg & Elizabeth J. Kirk. LC 97-15940. 1997. write for info. (0-87168-606-6) AAAS.

Reducing Workweeks to Prevent Layoffs: The Economic & Social Impacts of Unemployment Insurance Supported Work Sharing. Fred Best. LC 87-10097. 228p. (C). 1988. 39.95 (0-87722-506-0) Temple U Pr.

Reducing Your Risks. 24p. 1993. pap. 24.95 (0-685-71683-X, 717) Inst Real Estate.

Reduction: Techniques & Applications in Organic Synthesis. Ed. by Robert L. Augustine. LC 68-12550. (Techniques & Applications in Organic Synthesis Ser.). (Illus.). 252p. reprint ed. pap. 71.90 (0-7837-3385-2, 2043343) Bks Demand.

Reduction see Comprehensive Organic Synthesis: Selectivity, Strategy & Efficiency in Modern Organic Chemistry

Reduction & Prediction of Natural Disasters. John Rundle. (C). 1996. pap. 31.95 (0-201-87049-5) Addison-Wesley.

Reduction & Resolution: Computation & Logic. Rene Lalement. 400p. 1993. pap. text ed. 44.00 (0-13-770009-1) P-H.

Reduction, Explanation, & Realism. Ed. by David Charles & Kethleen Lennon. (Illus.). 456p. 1992. pap. 39.95 (0-19-875131-1) OUP.

Reduction in Fleet Fuel Consumption. 76p. 1981. 15.00 (0-318-16232-6, DG81801) Pub Tech Inc.

Reduction in Force Testament. Donald L. Newcomb & George W. Rimler. LC 89-92738. 84p. (Orig.). 1989. pap. text ed. 24.95 (0-9625257-0-7) LACY Pub VA.

Reduction in Science: Structure, Examples, Philosophical Problems. Ed. by Wolfgang Balzer et al. (Synthese Library: 175). 453p. 1984. lib. bdg. 149.00 (90-277-1811-3) Kluwer Ac.

Reduction in the Abstract Sciences. Daniel A. Bonevac. vi, 180p. (C). 1982. lib. bdg. 24.00 (0-915145-14-6) Ridgeview.

Reduction Mammaplasty. Robert M. Goldwyn. 1989. 220.00 (0-316-31977-5) Little.

Reduction of Animal Usage in the Development & Control of Biological Products. Ed. by I. Davidson & W. Hennessen. (Developments in Biological Standardization Ser.: Vol. 64). (Illus.). x, 330p. 1986. pap. 96.00 (3-8055-4460-X) S Karger.

Reduction of Anticancer Drug Toxicity: Pharmacologic, Biologic, Immunologic & Molecular Genetic Approaches. W. J. Zeller. (Beitraeger Zur Onkologie - Contributions to Oncology Ser.: Vol. 48). (Illus.). viii, 210p. 1995. 174.00 (3-8055-6042-7) S Karger.

Reduction of Christianity: A Biblical Response to Dave Hunt. Gary DeMar & Peter Leithart. LC 87-73071. 403p. (Orig.). 1990. pap. 8.95 (0-930462-63-7) Inst Christian.

Reduction of Drug Related Harm. Russell Newcombe. 272p. (C). 1992. pap. text ed. 18.95 (0-415-06693-X, Routledge NY) Routledge.

Reduction of Gear Pair Transmission Error by Minimizing Mesh Stiffness Variation. W. S. Rouverol & W. J. Pearce. (Fall Technical Meeting Papers 88FTM11). (Illus.). 20p. 1988. pap. text ed. 30.00 (1-55589-516-6) AGMA.

Reduction of Gold & Silver Ore. L. K. Hodges. (Shorey Prospecting Ser.). 24p. reprint ed. pap. 2.95 (0-8466-1993-8, S134D) Shorey.

Reduction of Impediments to Alternative Energy Use. 120p. 1982. 20.00 (0-318-17718-8, DG 82-316) Pub Tech Inc.

Reduction of JFET Parameter Drift in IC Operational Amplifiers Using Statistical Process Characterization. Arvid C. Carlson & Sam L. Sundaram. LC 92-25875. (Six Sigma Research Institute Ser.). 1993. write for info. (0-201-63429-5) Addison-Wesley.

Reduction of Mayan Dates. Herbert J. Spinden. (HU PMP Ser.). 1924. 30.00 (0-527-01209-2) Periodicals Srv.

Reduction of Military Budgets. (Study Ser.: No. 15). 74p. 1986. 9.50 (92-1-142117-9, E.86.IX.2) UN.

Reduction of Nitrogen Oxide Emissions. Ed. by Umit S. Ozkan et al. LC 95-2400. (ACS Symposium Ser.: No. 587). 248p. 1995. 79.95 (0-8412-3150-8) Am Chemical.

Reduction of Peak-Power Demand for Electric Rail Transit Systems. (National Cooperative Transit Research Program Synthesis Ser.: No. 3). 142p. 1983. 10.40 (0-309-03713-1) Transport Res Bd.

Reduction of the Product of Two Irreducible Unitary Representations of the Proper Orthochronous Quantummechanical Poincare Group. M. Schaaf. LC 72-139677. (Lecture Notes in Physics Ser.: Vol. 5). 1970. 13.95 (0-387-05194-5) Spr-Verlag.

Reduction of Working Time: Scope & Implications in Industrialised Market Economies. Rolande Cuvillier. vi, 150p. (C). 1984. pap. 22.50 (92-2-102702-3); text ed. 31.50 (92-2-103817-3) Intl Labour Office.

Reduction on Vehicle Fuel Consumption. 76p. 1981. 15.00 (0-318-17351-4, DG/81-801) Pub Tech Inc.

Reduction, Symmetry & Phases in Mechanics. Montgomery et al. LC 90-1143. (Memoirs Ser.: Vol. 88/436). 110p. 1990. pap. text ed. 20.00 (0-8218-2498-8, MEMO/88/436) Am Math.

Reductionism & Cultural Being. Joseph W. Smith. 392p. 1984. lib. bdg. 159.50 (90-247-2884-3, Pub. by M Nijhoff NE) Kluwer Ac.

Reductionism & Systems Theory in the Life Sciences. Ed. by Paul Hoyningen-Huene & Franz M. Wuketits. 190p. (C). 1989. lib. bdg. 110.00 (0-7923-0375-X, Pub. by Klwr Acad Pubs NE) Kluwer Ac.

Reductionism in Academic Disciplines. Ed. by Arthur Peacocke. 1985. 46.00 (1-85059-006-0) Taylor & Francis.

Reductionism in Drama & the Theatre: The Case of Samuel Beckett. Gerhard Hauck. LC 92-11316. 1992. 59.50 (0-916379-98-1) Scripta.

*__Reductions by the Alumino- & Borohydrides in Organic Synthesis.__ 2nd ed. Jacqueline Seyden-Penne. LC 96-49776. 1997. write for info. (1-56081-939-1) Wiley.

Reductions by the Alumino- & Borohydrides in Organic Synthesis: A Tec & Doc Translation. Jacqueline Seyden-Penne. 193p. 1991. 65.00 (1-56081-099-8, VCH) Wiley.

*__Reductions by the Alumino & Borohydrides in Organic Synthesis.__ 2nd ed. Jacqueline Seyden-Penne. LC 96-49776. 1997. write for info. (0-471-19036-5) Wiley.

Reductions in Organic Chemistry, Vol. 188. 2nd ed. Milos Hudlicky. LC 96-26758. (Monograph Ser.: No. 188). (Illus.). 429p. 1996. 109.95 (0-8412-3344-6) Am Chemical.

Reductions in Organic Synthesis: Recent Advances & Practical Applications, Vol. 641. Ed. by Ahmed F. Abdel-Magid. (Symposium Ser.: No. 641). (Illus.). 240p. 1996. 89.95 (0-8412-3381-0) Am Chemical.

Reductions in U. S. Domestic Spending: How They Affect State & Local Governments. Ed. by John W. Ellwood. LC 82-10975. (Illus.). 401p. 1982. 34.95 (0-87855-472-6); pap. 24.95 (0-87855-923-X) Transaction Pubs.

Reductive Object. (Illus.). 1979. 3.00 (0-910663-22-X) ICA Inc.

Reductive Subgroups of Exceptional Algebraic Groups. Martin W. Liebeck & Gary M. Seitz. LC 96-4542. (Memoirs of the American Mathematical Society Ser.: No. 580). 1996. pap. 36.00 (0-8218-0461-8, MEMO/121/580) Am Math.

Reductons with Modernization: An Arms Control Mirage. Herbert Scoville, Jr. (CISA Working Papers: No. 52). 22p. (Orig.). 1985. pap. 15.00 (0-86682-066-3) Ctr Intl Relations.

Redundancy. Alan Fowler. 160p. (C). 1939. pap. 80.00 (0-85292-497-6, Pub. by IPM Hse UK) St Mut.

Redundancy Counselling for Managers. IPM Information Services Staff & Giles Burrow. 84p. (C). 1985. 65.00 (0-85292-352-X) St Mut.

Redundancy, Layoffs & Plant Closures: Their Nature & Social Impact. Ed. by Raymond M. Lee. 352p. 1986. 59.95 (0-7099-4129-3, Pub. by Croom Helm UK) Routledge Chapman & Hall.

Redundant Disk Arrays: Reliable, Parallel Secondary Storage. Garth A. Gibson. (ACM Distinguished Dissertation Ser.: No. 91). (Illus.). 250p. 1992. 37.50 (0-262-07142-8) MIT Pr.

Redundant Heart. large type ed. Eileen Barry. (Linford Romance Library). 320p. 1995. pap. 15.99 (0-7089-7772-3, Linford) Ulverscroft.

Reduplication in South Asian Languages: An Areal, Typological & Historical Study. Anvita Abbi. (C). 1992. 19.00 (81-7023-310-0, Pub. by Allied II) S Asia.

*__Redux: The Miracle Weight Loss Drug.__ Marilyn Larkin. (Orig.). 1997. mass mkt. 5.99 (0-614-27709-4) Avon.

*__Redux: The Revolutionary Weight Loss Drug.__ Marilynn Larkin. 224p. (Orig.). 1997. mass mkt. 5.99 (0-380-79218-4) Avon.

Redux Revolution: Everything You Need to Know about the Most Important Weight Loss Discovery of the Century. Sheldon Levine. LC 96-26000. 192p. 1996. 20.00 (0-688-15153-1) Morrow.

Redvers Come Home. Roscoe Howells. 135p. 1994. pap. 40.00 (1-85902-117-4) St Mut.

Redwall. Brian Jacques. 352p. 1990. mass mkt. 5.99 (0-380-70827-2) Avon.

Redwall. Brian Jacques. LC 86-25467. (J). (gr. k up). 1987. 19.95 (0-399-21424-0, Philomel Bks) Putnam Pub Group.

*__Redwall Anniversary Edition.__ Brian Jacques. (Illus.). 368p. (YA). (gr. 5 up). 1997. 22.95 (0-399-23160-9, Philomel Bks) Putnam Pub Group.

Redward Edward Papers. Avram Davidson. LC 74-27578. 208p. 1978. 25.00 (0-89366-265-8) Ultramarine Pub.

Redware, America's Folk Art Pottery. Kevin McConnell. LC 88-64156. (Illus.). 96p. 1989. pap. 12.95 (0-88740-159-7) Schiffer.

Redwing Blackbird. Paul Foreman. 1973. pap. 2.50 (0-914476-15-7) Thorp Springs.

R

Redwing's Flight: A Potawatomi Fable. Jack Wooldridge. (Potawatomi Fables Ser.). (Illus.). 44p. (J). (gr. k-7). 1996. pap. 7.50 (*1-887963-06-5*) Pota Pr.

*__Redwood: A Guide to Redwood National & State Parks, California, Vol. 154.__ United States Parks Service Staff. LC 96-52957. (Handbook Ser.). 1997. write for info. (*0-912627-61-1*) Natl Park Serv.

Redwood: A Tale. Catherine M. Sedgwick. 1972. reprint ed. lib. bdg. 29.50 (*0-8422-8108-8*) Irvington.

Redwood: The Story Behind the Scenery. Richard A. Rasp. LC 88-80122. (Illus.). 54p. (Orig.). 1989. pap. 7.95 (*0-88714-022-X*) KC Pubns.

Redwood Bear & the Crash Boom. Justine Korman. Date not set. write for info. incl. audio (*0-679-87995-1*) Random.

Redwood City Seed Company Catalog of Endangered Cultivated Plants 1996. Craig C. Dremann. (Illus.). 28p. 1996. pap. 1.00 (*0-933421-39-7*) Redwood Seed.

Redwood Classic. Ralph W. Andrews. LC 85-61521. (Illus.). 174p. 1985. reprint ed. pap. 12.95 (*0-88740-049-3*) Schiffer.

Redwood Coast. Jason Cooper. LC 95-12307. (Natural Wonders Ser.). (J). (gr. 2-6). 1995. write for info. (*1-57103-018-2*) Rourke Pr.

Redwood Country. Lynwood Carranco. (Illus.). 360p. (Orig.). 1986. pap. 15.95 (*0-89863-097-5*) Star Pub CA.

Redwood Curtain. Lanford Wilson. 1995. pap. 5.25 (*0-8222-1360-5*) Dramatists Play.

Redwood Empire. A. E. Maxwell. 416p. 1987. mass mkt. 3.95 (*0-373-97049-8*) Harlequin Bks.

Redwood Empire. A. E. Maxwell. (Historical Ser.). 1995. mass mkt. 4.50 (*0-373-28867-0*, 1-28867-9) Harlequin Bks.

Redwood Empire, Wildflower Jewels see Redwood Empire Wildflowers

Redwood Empire Wildflowers. 4th rev. ed. Dorothy K. Young. LC 76-12996. Orig. Title: Redwood Empire, Wildflower Jewels. (Illus.). 80p. (Orig.). 1989. pap. 7.95 (*0-87961-197-9*) Naturegraph.

Redwood Forest & Native Grasses & Their Stories. Craig C. Dremann. (Orig.). 1987. pap. 3.00 (*0-933421-19-2*) Redwood Seed.

Redwood Lumber Industry. Lynwood Carranco. LC 82-15870. (Illus.). 218p. 1982. 17.50 (*0-87095-084-3*) Gldn West Bks.

Redwood National & State Parks: Tales, Trails, & Auto Tours. Jerry Rohde & Gisela Rohde. LC 94-75098. 288p. 1994. pap. 15.95 (*0-9640261-0-4*) MtnHome Bks.

Redwood National Park, CA. rev. ed. Ed. by Trails Illustrated Staff. (Illus.). 1993. Folded topographical map. 8.99 (*0-925873-96-9*) Trails Illustrated.

Redwood Region Flower Finder. Phoebe Watts. (Illus.). 62p. 1979. pap. 3.00 (*0-912550-08-2*) Nature Study.

Redwood Seed. Kelsey Morton. (Wellspring Bks.). (Illus.). 128p. 1988. pap. 8.95 (*0-916349-45-4*) Amity Hse Inc.

Redwood Trees. John F. Prevost. LC 96-6069. (Trees Ser.). (Illus.). (J). 1996. lib. bdg. 13.98 (*1-56239-617-X*) Abdo & Dghtrs.

Redwoods. Adams. 1991. 30.00 (*0-8212-1821-2*) Bulfinch Pr.

Redwoods. Peter Murray. (Nature Bks.). 32p. (J). (gr. 2-6). 1996. lib. bdg. 22.79 (*1-56766-216-1*) Childs World.

Redwoods & Roses: The Gardening Heritage of California & the Old West. Maureen Gilmer. LC 95-24498. (Illus.). 200p. 1995. 19.95 (*0-87833-894-2*) Taylor Pub.

Redwork. Michael Bedard. 224p. (YA). 1992. pap. 3.50 (*0-380-71612-7*, Flare) Avon.

*__Redy-Refs for Critical Care Nurses.__ Deborah Borelli. (Illus.). 50p. 1996. text ed. 12.95 (*0-943202-57-4*) H & H Pub.

*__Redy-Refs for Medical - Surgical Nurses.__ Deborah Borelli. (Illus.). 40p. 1996. text ed. 12.95 (*0-943202-56-6*) H & H Pub.

Reebok: The Ultimate Guide to Fitness. Chantel Gosselin. 1995. 9.99 (*0-517-14191-4*) Random Hse Value.

Reed. W. H. Reed. (Illus.). 529p. 1991. reprint ed. pap. 81.50 (*0-8328-2052-0*); reprint ed. lib. bdg. 91.50 (*0-8328-2051-2*) Higginson Bk Co.

Reed Cutter & Captain Shigemoto's Mother. Junichiro Tanizaki. Tr. by Anthony H. Chambers from JPN. LC 93-260. 1994. 22.00 (*0-679-42010-X*) Knopf.

Reed Cutter & Captain Shigemoto's Mother. Junichiro Tanizaki. 1995. pap. 11.00 (*0-679-75791-0*, Vin) Random.

Reed, Descendants of Reade or Reed: William Reade & Mabel (Kendall), His Wife; Supply Reed & Susannah (Byam), His Wife; John Reed & Rebecca (Bearce), His Wife. F. L. Meadows & J. M. Ames. 285p. 1993. reprint ed. pap. 44.00 (*0-8328-3240-5*); reprint ed. lib. bdg. 54.00 (*0-8328-3239-1*) Higginson Bk Co.

Reed Design for Early Woodwinds. David H. Smith. LC 91-38825. (Publications of the Early Music Institute). (Illus.). 176p. 1992. pap. text ed. 9.95 (*0-253-20727-4*, MB-727) Ind U Pr.

Reed Ferris' Nineteen-Thirty to Nineteen Forty-Three Bird Banding Records & Birds Observations for Tillamook County, Oregon. Range D. Bayer & Reed W. Ferris. LC 87-81812. (Studies in Oregon Ornithology: No. 3). (Illus.). ix, 131p. (Orig.). 1987. pap. 17.00 (*0-939819-02-3*) Gahmken Pr.

Reed Genealogy, Descendants of William Reade of Weymouth, Mass., from 1635-1902. J. L. Reed. (Illus.). 786p. 1989. reprint ed. pap. 109.00 (*0-8328-1015-0*); reprint ed. lib. bdg. 117.00 (*0-8328-1014-2*) Higginson Bk Co.

Reed Maker's Manual: Step-by-Step Instructions for Making Oboe & English Horn Reeds. David B. Weber & Ferald B. Capps. Ed. & Illus. by Vendla K. Weber. 134p. (C). 1990. spiral bd. 35.00 (*0-9627910-0-8*) D B Weber & F.B Capps.

Reed-Making Diary for the Bassoonist. Harvey R. Snitkin. (Illus.). 50p. 1987. reprint ed. wbk. ed., spiral bd. 8.95 (*1-888732-02-4*) HMS Pubns CT.

Reed-Making Diary for the Oboist. Harvey R. Snitkin. (Illus.). 50p. 1987. reprint ed. wbk. ed., spiral bd. 8.95 (*1-888732-01-6*) HMS Pubns CT.

Reed-Making Diary for the Single-Reed Player. Harvey R. Snitkin. (Illus.). 50p. 1987. reprint ed. wbk. ed., spiral bd. 8.95 (*1-888732-03-2*) HMS Pubns CT.

*__Reed Music.__ Peter Levi. 80p. 1997. pap. 18.95 (*0-85646-279-9*, Pub. by Anvil Press UK) Dufour.

*__Reed of God.__ Caryll Houselander. 1996. pap. text ed. 5.95 (*0-87061-212-3*) Chr Classics.

Reed of God. Caryll Houselander. LC 78-51561. 128p. 1987. reprint ed. pap. 5.95 (*0-88479-013-4*, 6936) Chr Classics.

Reed Organ: Its Design & Construction. H. F. Milne. (Illus.). 168p. 1932. pap. 20.00 (*0-913746-02-9*) Organ Lit.

Reed-Read Lineage: Captain John Reed of Providence, Rhode Island, & Norwalk, Connecticut, & His Descendants Through His Sons, John & Thomas, 1660-1909. E. Reed-Wright. (Illus.). 796p. 1989. reprint ed. pap. 109.00 (*0-8328-1017-7*); reprint ed. lib. bdg. 117.00 (*0-8328-1016-9*) Higginson Bk Co.

Reed Shaken by the Wind: A Journey Through the Unexplored Marshlands of Iraq. large type ed. Gavin Maxwell. 283p. 1990. 19.95 (*1-85089-272-5*, Pub. by ISIS UK) Transaction Pubs.

Reed Smoot: Apostle in Politics. Milton R. Merrill. LC 89-22621. (Western Experience Ser.). 447p. 1990. reprint ed. pap. 127.40 (*0-7837-9254-9*, 2049994) Bks Demand.

Reed-Solomon Codes & Their Applications. Ed. by Stephen B. Wicker & Vijay Bhargava. LC 94-3160. 336p. 1994. 89.95 (*0-7803-1025-X*, PC03749) Inst Electrical.

Reeder & Felson's Gamuts in Bone, Joint, & Spine Radiology: Comprehensive Lists of Roentgen Differential Diagnosis. Maurice M. Reeder. xx, 501p. 1993. 35.00 (*0-387-94016-2*) Spr-Verlag.

Reeder & Felson's Gamuts in Cardiovascular Radiology: Comprehensive Lists of Radiographic & Angiographic Differential Diagnosis. Maurice M. Reeder. LC 93-46633. 1994. 28.00 (*0-387-94219-X*) Spr-Verlag.

Reeder & Felson's Gamuts in Neuroradiology: Comprehensive Lists of roentgen & MRI Differential Diagnosis. Maurice M. Reeder & William G. Bradley, Jr. LC 93-10195. 1993. Alk. paper. 34.00 (*0-387-94034-0*) Spr-Verlag.

*__Reeder & Felson's Gamuts in Radiology: Comprehensive Lists of Roentgen Differential Diagnosis.__ Maurice M. Reeder & William G. Bradley. 1996. cd-rom 185.00 (*0-387-14228-2*) Spr-Verlag.

Reeder & Felson's Gamuts in Radiology: Comprehensive Lists of Roentgen Differential Diagnosis. 3rd ed. Maurice M. Reeder & William G. Bradley, Jr. LC 92-49707. 640p. 1992. write for info. (*3-540-97891-7*) Spr-Verlag.

Reeder & Felson's Gamuts in Radiology: Comprehensive Lists of Roentgen Differential Diagnosis. 3rd ed. Maurice M. Reeder & William G. Bradley, Jr. LC 92-49707. 640p. 1993. 95.00 (*0-387-97891-7*) Spr-Verlag.

Reeds & Mud. Vicente Blasco-Ibanez. Tr. by Lester Beberfall. (Orig.). 1966. pap. 5.95 (*0-8283-1470-5*) Branden Pub Co.

*__Reed's Beach.__ Bret Lott. 342p. 4.98 (*0-8317-2824-8*) Smithmark.

Reed's Beach. Bret Lott. Ed. by Jane Rosenman. 352p. 1994. reprint ed. pap. 10.00 (*0-671-79239-3*, WSP) PB.

Reed's Channel West & Solent, 1992: Nautical Almanac for Yachtsmen. Imray, Laurie, Norie & Wilson Ltd. Staff. 172p. (C). 1989. 110.00 (*0-9517096-1-5*, Pub. by Imray Laurie Norie & Wilson UK) St Mut.

Reed's Guide to Farms & Barns in Eastern Pennsylvania, New Jersey, & Delaware. Patti Reed. (Illus.). 112p. 1993. per. 10.95 (*0-9637181-0-X*) Horse Tales.

Reed's Music Shop. Bonnie Worth. (J). 1996. bds. 4.99 (*0-689-80429-6*, Litl Simon S&S) S&S Childrens.

*__Reed's Nautical Almanac 1997 Caribbean.__ C. Degnon & B. Ellison. (Illus.). 800p. 1996. pap. 29.95 (*1-884666-16-7*) T Reed Pubns.

*__Reed's Nautical Almanac 1997 North American East Coast.__ B. Ellison. (Illus.). 1100p. 1996. pap. 29.95 (*1-884666-18-3*) T Reed Pubns.

*__Reed's Nautical Almanac 1997 North American West Coast.__ B. Ellison. (Illus.). 900p. 1996. pap. 29.95 (*1-884666-17-5*) T Reed Pubns.

*__Reed's Nautical Almanac 1998 Caribbean.__ Ed. by Ben Ellison. (Illus.). 800p. (Orig.). 1997. pap. 29.95 (*1-884666-25-6*) T Reed Pubns.

*__Reed's Nautical Almanac 1998 North American East Coast.__ Ed. by Ben Ellison. (Illus.). 1100p. (Orig.). 1997. pap. 29.95 (*1-884666-27-2*) T Reed Pubns.

*__Reed's Nautical Almanac 1998 North American West Coast.__ Ed. by Ben Ellison. (Illus.). 1000p. (Orig.). 1997. pap. 29.95 (*1-884666-26-4*) T Reed Pubns.

*__Reed's Nautical Companion.__ 2nd ed. Ed. by Ben Ellison. (Illus.). 600p. 1997. pap. 19.95 (*1-884666-24-8*) T Reed Pubns.

Reef. Romesh Guresekera. 192p. 1996. pap. 10.00 (*1-57322-533-9*, Riverhd Trade) Berkley Pub.

Reef. Edith Wharton. 384p. 1977. 20.00 (*0-684-15557-5*) S&S Trade.

Reef. Edith Wharton. 336p. 1996. 16.00 (*0-679-44724-5*) Random.

Reef. Edith Wharton. 368p. 1996. pap. 10.00 (*0-684-82444-2*) S&S Trade.

Reef. Edith Wharton. 368p. 1995. pap. 9.95 (*0-14-018731-6*, Penguin Classics) Viking Penguin.

Reef: A Novel. Romesh Gunesekera. LC 94-22577. 1995. 20.00 (*1-56584-219-7*) New Press NY.

Reef: A Safari Through the Coral World. Jeremy Stafford-Deitsch. LC 90-25432. (Illus.). 200p. 1993. reprint ed. pap. 20.00 (*0-87156-541-2*) Sierra.

Reef & Shore Fauna of Hawaii: Protozoa Through Ctenophora. Ed. by D. M. Devaney & L. G. Eldredge. LC 77-89747. (Special Publication Ser.: No. 64 (1)). (Illus.). 290p. 1977. pap. 22.50 (*0-910240-22-1*) Bishop Mus.

Reef & Shore Fauna of Hawaii: Sections 2 & 3. Ed. by D. M. Devaney & L. G. Eldredge. (Illus.). 468p. 1987. 58.50 (*0-930897-11-0*, SP64) Bishop Mus.

Reef Animals of the Pacific Northeast. Richard J. Rosenthal. (Illus.). 160p. (C). 1995. pap. 51.00 (*0-907151-54-X*, Pub. by IMMEL Pubng UK) St Mut.

Reef Aquarium: A Comprehensive Guide to the Identification & Care of Tropical Marine Invertebrates. J. Charles Delbeek & Julian Sprung. (Illus.). 560p. (C). 1994. 84.95 (*1-883693-12-8*) Ricordea Pubng.

Reef Coral Identification: Florida, Caribbean, Bahamas. Paul Humann. Ed. & Photos by Ned DeLoach. LC 92-62377. (Illus.). 252p. (Orig.). 1993. spiral bd. 32.95 (*1-878348-03-5*) New World FL.

Reef Creature Identification: Florida, Caribbean, Bahamas. Paul Humann. Ed. & Photos by Ned DeLoach. LC 91-67361. (Illus.). 344p. (Orig.). 1992. spiral bd. 37.95 (*1-878348-01-9*) New World FL.

Reef Diagenesis. Ed. by J. H. Schroeder & B. H. Purser. (Illus.). 450p. 1986. 135.00 (*0-387-16594-0*) Spr-Verlag.

Reef Fish Identification: Florida, Caribbean, Bahamas. Paul Humann. Ed. by Ned DeLoach. (Illus.). 424p. 1999. lib. bdg. 49.95 (*1-878348-14-0*) New World FL.

Reef Fish Identification: Florida, Caribbean, Bahamas. 2nd ed. Paul Humann. Ed. & Photos by Ned DeLoach. (Illus.). 426p. 1994. spiral bd. 39.95 (*1-878348-07-8*) New World FL.

Reef Fish Identification: Galapagos. Paul Humann. Ed. & Photos by Ned DeLoach. LC 93-86620. (Illus.). 200p. (Orig.). 1994. pap. text ed. 34.95 (*1-878348-06-X*) New World FL.

Reef Fishing Book. Frank Sargeant. LC 95-81614. (Illus.). 160p. (Orig.). 1996. pap. 13.95 (*0-936513-23-3*) Larsens Outdoor.

*__Reef Notes: Revisited & Revised, Vol. 2.__ rev. ed. Julian Sprung. (Illus.). 192p. pap. 19.95 (*1-883693-23-3*) Ricordea Pubng.

*__Reef Notes: Revisited & Revised, Vol. 3.__ rev. ed. Julian Sprung. (Illus.). 192p. pap. 19.95 (*1-883693-24-1*) Ricordea Pubng.

Reef Notes 1: 1988/1990. Julian Sprung. 192p. 1995. pap. text ed. 19.95 (*1-883693-22-5*) Ricordea Pubng.

*__Reef of Death.__ Paul Zindel. LC 97-21864. (J). 1998. write for info. (*0-06-024728-2*); lib. bdg. write for info. (*0-06-024733-9*) HarpC.

Reef Set: Florida-Caribbean-Bahamas, 3 bks., Set. 2nd ed. Paul Humann. Ed. & Photos by Ned DeLoach. (Illus.). 1994. 115.00 (*1-878348-08-6*) New World FL.

*__Reef Set - Traveler's Edition: Florida Caribbean Bahamas, 3 bks.__ Paul Humann. Ed. & Photos by Ned DeLoach. (Illus.). 1995. 130.00 (*1-878348-19-1*) New World FL.

Reef Sharks & Rays of the World: A Guide to Their Identification, Behavior, & Ecology. Scott W. Michael. Ed. by Ken Hashagen & Hans Bertsch. LC 92-46402. (Illus.). 112p. (Orig.). (C). 1993. pap. 24.95 (*0-930118-18-9*, 188M) Sea Chall.

Reef Tank Owners Manual. Albert J. Thiel. (Illus.). 320p. (Orig.). pap. write for info. (*0-945777-06-X*) Aardvark Pr.

*__Reef Tank Owners Manual.__ John H. Tullock. Ed. by Omer K. Dersom. (Coralife Ser.). (Illus.). 268p. 1996. 39.95 (*0-9640147-1-8*) Energy Savers.

Reefer Market. G. P. Wild (International) Ltd. Staff. (Lloyd's Business Intelligence Centre Ser.). 130p. 1994. pap. 745.00 (*1-85044-576-1*) LLP.

ReeferTrans Eighty-Nine. Ed. by Cargo Systems International Staff. (C). 1989. 150.00 (*0-907499-68-6*, Pub. by Cargo Systs UK) St Mut.

Reefs in Time & Space: Selected Examples from the Recent & Ancient. Ed. by Leo F. Laporte. LC 74-165238. (Society of Economic Paleontologists & Mineralogists, Special Publication Ser.: No. 18). 260p. reprint ed. pap. 74.10 (*0-317-27147-4*, 2024745) Bks Demand.

Reefs, Lagoons & Atolls: Let's Travel to the Maldives Together see Windows on the World Series

Reefs of Florida & the Dry Tortugas, No. T176. Ed. by Shinn. (IGC Field Trip Guidebooks Ser.). 64p. 1989. 21.00 (*0-87590-648-6*) Am Geophysical.

Reefs, Wrecks & Rigs. Tom Bailey. (Illus.). 160p. (Orig.). 1993. pap. 6.95 (*1-878561-18-9*) Seacoast AL.

*__Reekie's Architectural Drawing.__ write for info. (*0-340-57324-4*, Pub. by E Arnold UK) Routledge Chapman & Hall.

Reekie's Architectural Drawing. 4th ed. Fraser Reekie. 249p. 1995. pap. text ed. 39.95 (*0-470-23569-1*) Halsted Pr.

Reeking Havoc. Steve Ginsberg. 1989. 19.95 (*0-09-174454-7*) Warner Bks.

Reel America & World War I: A Comprehensive Filmography & History of Motion Pictures in the United States, 1914-1920. Craig Campbell. LC 83-42890. (Illus.). 347p. 1985. lib. bdg. 49.95 (*0-89950-087-0*) McFarland & Co.

Reel Art: Great Posters from the Golden Age of the Silver Screen. Stephen Rebello & Richard Allen. (Illus.). 342p. 39.98 (*0-89660-033-5*, Artabras) Abbeville Pr.

Reel Art: Great Posters from the Golden Age of the Silver Screen. Stephen Rebello & Richard Allen. (Tiny Folios Ser.). (Illus.). 271p. 1992. pap. 11.95 (*1-55859-403-5*) Abbeville Pr.

*__Reel Black Talk: A Sourcebook of 50 American Filmmakers.__ Spencer Moon. LC 96-47539. 424p. 1997. text ed. 79.50 (*0-313-29830-0*, Greenwood Pr) Greenwood.

Reel Change: A Guide to Films on Appropriate Technology. SoftAware Associates, Inc. Staff. LC 79-90198. (Illus.). 1979. pap. 3.50 (*0-913890-34-0*) Friends of Earth.

Reel Characters: Great Movie Character Actors. Jordan R. Young. LC 86-8514. (Illus.). 208p. (Orig.). 1986. 24.95 (*0-940410-80-X*, Moonstone Pr); pap. 9.95 (*0-940410-79-6*, Moonstone Pr) Past Times.

Reel Conversations: Candid Interviews with Film's Foremost Directors. George Hickenlooper. 1991. pap. 12.95 (*0-8065-1237-7*, Citadel Pr) Carol Pub Group.

Reel Conversations: Reading Film with Young Adults. Alan B. Teasley & Ann Wilder. (Orig.). 1996. pap. text ed. 22.00 (*0-86709-377-3*, 0377) Boynton Cook Pubs.

Reel Cowboy: Essays on the Myth in Movies & Literature. Buck Rainey. LC 96-3191. (Illus.). 400p. 1996. lib. bdg. 39.95 (*0-7864-0106-0*) McFarland & Co.

Reel Deep in Montana's Rivers. John Holt. LC 93-8660. (Illus.). 170p. 1993. 15.95 (*0-87108-832-0*) Pruett.

Reel Elvis! The Ultimate Trivia Guide to the King's Movies. Pauline Bartel. LC 93-48746. 192p. 1994. pap. 10.95 (*0-87833-852-7*) Taylor Pub.

Reel Exposure: How to Publicize & Promote Today's Motion Pictures. Steven J. Rubin. (Illus.). 337p. (C). 1992. pap. 19.95 (*0-911747-20-6*) Broadway Pr.

Reel Extra Money: The Background Actor's Handbook. Rod Pitman. (Orig.). pap. write for info. (*0-9642118-6-6*) Cascade Press.

Reel Families: A Social History of Amateur Film. Patricia R. Zimmermann. LC 94-22840. 192p. 1995. 29.95 (*0-253-36876-6*); pap. 14.95 (*0-253-20944-7*) Ind U Pr.

Reel Guide & Subject Index to the Microfilm Collection of Early American Orderly Books, 1748 to 1817 from the Collection of the New York Historical Society. LC 77-84856. 74p. 1977. 80.00 (*0-89235-022-9*) Primary Srce Media.

Reel Index to the Microfilm Collection of County Histories of the "Old Northwest" Series II: Ohio. 24p. 1975. 30.00 (*0-89235-043-1*) Primary Srce Media.

Reel Index to the Microfilm Collection of Illinois County & Regional Histories & Atlases: Series IV. 32p. 1976. 30.00 (*0-89235-045-8*) Primary Srce Media.

Reel Index to the Microfilm Collection of Michigan County & Regional Histories & Atlases. 31p. 1975. 30.00 (*0-89235-047-4*) Primary Srce Media.

Reel Index to the Microfilm Collection of the "Old Northwest" Series III: Indiana. 20p. 1973. 30.00 (*0-89235-046-6*) Primary Srce Media.

Reel Index to the Microfilm Collection, Pennsylvania County & Regional Histories. 31p. 1975. 30.00 (*0-89235-042-3*) Primary Srce Media.

Reel Index to the Microfilm Edition of New York County & Regional Histories & Atlases. 38p. 1977. 30.00 (*0-89235-044-X*) Primary Srce Media.

Reel Index to the Microfilm Edition of Utah & the Mormons. 12p. 1982. 25.00 (*0-89235-134-9*) Primary Srce Media.

Reel Index to the Microform Edition of California County & Regional Histories. 14p. 30.00 (*0-89235-048-2*) Primary Srce Media.

*__Reel Ism.__ Jerry Cooper. 24p. (Orig.). 1996. pap. 3.95 (*1-889419-23-0*) J Cooper.

Reel Justice: The Courtroom Goes to the Movies. Paul Bergman & Michael R. Asimow. LC 95-44217. (Illus.). 288p. (Orig.). 1996. pap. 14.95 (*0-8362-1035-2*) Andrews & McMeel.

Reel Life - Real Life: A Video Guide for Personal Discovery. Mary A. Horenstein et al. 512p. (Orig.). 1995. pap. 17.95 (*0-9643154-0-8*) Fourth Write.

Reel Life on Hollywood Movie Sets. May W. Brown. LC 95-10391. (Biography, Autobiography, Memoirs Ser.). (Illus.). 225p. 1995. pap. 19.95 (*1-57241-016-7*) Ariadne CA.

*__Reel Patriotism: The Movies & World War I.__ Leslie M. DeBauche. LC 96-45979. (Wisconsin Studies in Film). (Illus.). 224p. 1997. 50.00 (*0-299-15400-9*); pap. 15.95 (*0-299-15404-1*) U of Wis Pr.

Reel People II. Tom Hollatz. Ed. by Larry D. Names. (Illus.). 180p. (Orig.). 1989. 14.95 (*0-685-26590-0*); pap. 8.95 (*0-685-26591-9*) D C Davis & Son Pub.

Reel Power: Spiritual Growth Through Film. Marsha Sinetar. LC 92-44676. 192p. (Orig.). 1993. pap. 9.95 (*0-89243-529-1*, Triumph Books) Liguori Pubns.

Reel Power: The Struggle for Influence & Success in The New Hollywood. Mark Litwak. LC 94-2909. 336p. pap. 14.95 (*1-879505-19-3*) Silman James Pr.

*__Reel Terror.__ Ed. by Sebastian Wolfe. 9.95 (*0-7867-0821-2*) Carroll & Graf.

Reel Terror! The Stories That Inspired the Great Horror Movies. Ed. by Sebastian Wolfe. (Illus.). 288p. 1992. pap. 9.95 (*0-88184-821-2*) Carroll & Graf.

Reel Thrills. Franklin W. Dixon. (Hardy Boys Ser.: No. 127). (YA). (gr. 3-6). 1994. pap. 3.99 (*0-671-87211-7*, Minstrel Bks) PB.

*__Reel to Real: Making the Most of Movies with Youth, Vol. 2.__ Abingdon Press Staff. 1997. pap. text ed. 8.95 (*0-687-98209-X*) Abingdon.

*__Reel to Real: Making the Most of the Movies with Youth, Vol. 1.__ Abingdon Press Staff. 1997. pap. text ed. 8.95 (*0-687-98074-7*) Abingdon.

*__Reel to Real: Making the Most of the Movies with Youth, Vol. 3.__ Abingdon Press Staff. 1997. pap. text ed. 8.95 (*0-687-98239-1*) Abingdon.

*__Reel to Real: Making the Most of the Movies with Youth, Vol. 4.__ Abingdon Press Staff. 1997. pap. text ed. 8.95 (*0-687-98269-3*) Abingdon.

An Asterisk (*) at the beginning of an entry indicates that the title is appearing in BIP for the first time.

Reel to Real: Race, Sex & Class at the Movie. Bell Hooks. 256p. (C). 1997. text ed. 59.95 (*0-415-91823-5*) Routledge.

Reel to Real: Race, Sex & Class at the Movies. Bell Hooks. 235p. 1996. pap. 16.95 (*0-415-91824-3*) Routledge.

Reel Wars: A Facts Quiz Book about War Films. Monica E. Jacoby & Frederick C. Fulfer. (Illus.). 80p. (Orig.). 1986. pap. 9.00 (*0-913337-08-0*) Southfarm Pr.

***Reel Women: The World of Women Who Fish.** Lula Foggia. 1997. pap. 16.00 (*0-609-80028-0*) Random Hse Value.

Reel Women: The World of Women Who Fish. Lyla Foggia. LC 95-30814. 294p. 1995. 24.95 (*1-885223-18-8*) Beyond Words Pub.

***Reel Works: Artists Film & Video of the 1970s.** Text by Chris Chang. (Illus.). 64p. 1996. pap. 15.95 (*1-888708-00-X*, 620461) Museum of Contemp.

***Reel World Freehand 7.** 4th ed. Olav M. Kvorn. 744p. (C). 1997. pap. text ed. 34.95 (*0-201-68887-5*) Peachpit Pr.

Reel 3-D Enterprises' Guide to the Nimslo 3D Camera. 2nd rev. ed. David Starkman & Susan Pinsky. Orig. Title: The Nimslo 3D Book. (Illus.). 64p. 1988. pap. 11. 95 (*0-939617-00-5*, 1030) Reel Three-D.

***Reelecting Bill Clinton: Why America Chose a "New" Democrat.** John Hohenberg. LC 97-8381. 224p. 1997. 26.95 (*0-8156-0491-2*) Syracuse U Pr.

Reelfoot Lake. Russell H. Caldwell. (Illus.). 160p. (Orig.). 1989. pap. 9.95 (*0-317-94051-1*) Caldwells Office.

Reelfoot Lake: History - Duck Call Makers - Hunting Tales. rev. ed. Russell H. Caldwell. (Illus.). 270p. 1989. 24.95 (*0-9623039-2-5*) Caldwells Office.

Reelfoot Lake: History-Duck Call Makers-Hunting Tales. Russell H. Caldwell. LC 88-92272. (Illus.). 240p. 1988. 24.95 (*0-9623039-0-9*) Caldwells Office.

Reelfoot Lake: The Tourists' Guide. Russell H. Caldwell. (Illus.). 160p. (Orig.). 1989. pap. 9.95 (*0-9623039-1-7*) Caldwells Office.

Reelin' & Rockin' The Golden Age of American Rock & Roll, Vol. II: 1956-1959. Lee Cotten. Ed. by Thomas Schultheiss. (Rock & Roll Reference Ser.: No. 39). (Illus.). 300p. 1995. lib. bdg. 55.00 (*1-56075-039-1*) Popular Culture.

Reeling & Writhing. Candida Lawrence. LC 93-80395. 346p. 1994. 22.95 (*1-878448-60-9*) MacMurray & Beck.

Reemergence of the Purchasing Power Parity Doctrine in the 1970s. Louka T. Katseli-Papaefstratious. LC 79-25140. (Special Papers in International Economics: No. 13). (Illus.). 43p. reprint ed. pap. 25.00 (*0-8357-3181-2*, 2039449) Bks Demand.

Reemergence of World Literature: A Study of Asia & the West. A. Owen Aldridge. LC 84-40806. 232p. 1986. 35. 00 (*0-87413-277-0*) U Delaware Pr.

Reemerging Jewish Culture in Germany: Life & Literature since 1989. Ed. by Sander L. Gilman & Karen Remmler. LC 94-1286. 250p. (C). 1994. 45.00 (*0-8147-3062-0*) NYU Pr.

Reemerging Jewish Culture in Germany: Life & Literature since 1989. Ed. by Sander L. Gilman & Karen Remmler. LC 94-1286. 250p. (C). 1994. pap. 17.50 (*0-8147-3065-5*) NYU Pr.

Reemployment Assistance for Laid-Off Workers. Robert G. Wegmann. 36p. 1983. 4.25 (*0-318-22186-1*, IN258) Ctr Educ Trng Employ.

Reena & Other Stories. Paule Marshall. LC 83-16592. 224p. 1983. pap. 11.95 (*0-935312-24-2*) Feminist Pr.

Reenchanted Science: Holism in German Culture from Wilhelm II to Hitler. Anne Harrington. 368p. 1996. text ed. 39.50 (*0-691-02142-2*) Princeton U Pr.

Reenchanting Humanity: A Defense of the Human Spirit Against Antihumanism, Misanthropy & Primitivism. Murray Bookchin. 1996. 65.00 (*0-304-32843-X*, Pub. by Cassell Pubng UK) LPC InBook.

Reenchantment of Art. Suzi Gablik. LC 90-71571. (Illus.). 192p. 1992. pap. 15.95 (*0-500-27689-7*) Thames Hudson.

Reenchantment of Science: Postmodern Proposals. Ed. by David R. Griffin. LC 87-30692. (SUNY Series in Constructive Postmodern Thought). 173p. 1988. pap. text ed. 19.95 (*0-88706-785-9*) State U NY Pr.

Reenchantment of Science: Postmodern Proposals. Ed. by David R. Griffin. LC 87-30692. (SUNY Series in Constructive Postmodern Thought). 173p. 1988. text ed. 59.50 (*0-88706-784-0*) State U NY Pr.

Reenchantment of the World. Morris Berman. LC 81-67178. (Illus.). 368p. 1981. pap. 16.95 (*0-8014-9225-4*) Cornell U Pr.

Reengineering: Leveraging the Power of Integrated Product Development. V. Daniel Hunt. LC 92-85208. 282p. 1993. 75.00 (*0-939246-33-3*) Wiley.

Reengineering: Leveraging the Power of Integrated Product Development. V. Daniel Hunt. 300p. 1995. text ed. 29. 95 (*0-471-13200-4*) Wiley.

Reengineering Alternative: A Plan for Making Your Current Culture Work. William E. Schneider. LC 93-38860. 192p. 1994. text ed. 30.00 (*0-7863-0120-1*) Irwin Prof Pubng.

Reengineering & Business Process Redesign: Management Control & Audit Implications. C. M. Winters. Ed. by MASP Professional Consulting Staff. (Illus.). 150p. (Orig.). 1996. pap. text ed. 175.00 (*0-940706-34-2*) Management Advisory Pubns.

Reengineering & Reuseability. Eric G. Vesely. 280p. (C). 1996. text ed. 26.25 (*0-13-769993-X*) P-H.

Reengineering Business Processes. Harmon. 1995. 24.95 (*0-13-449265-X*) P-H.

Reengineering Business Processes & People Systems. (Illus.). 240p. 1994. pap. 59.95 (*0-9633398-2-6*, QT14) QualTeam.

Reengineering COBOL with Objects: Step by Step Tp Sustainable Legacy Systems. Robert Levey. 1995. text ed. 40.00 (*0-07-037774-X*) McGraw.

***Reengineering Corporate Training: Intellectual Capital & Transfer of Learning.** Robert E. Haskell. 1998. text ed. write for info. (*1-56720-148-2*, Quorum Bks) Greenwood.

Reengineering for Agility. Alvin Gunneson. 240p. (C). 1997. text ed. 26.95 (*0-201-63496-1*) Addison-Wesley.

Reengineering for Patient-Focused Care. Ed. by Joanne Ashton & Ruthita Fike. 198p. 1996. 34.95 (*0-9633819-3-8*) Prescott Pub.

Reengineering for Results: A Step-by-Step Guide. Robert Janson et al. LC 95-19353. 195p. 1995. pap. 24.95 (*0-527-76303-9*) Qual Resc.

Reengineering for Results: Keys to Success from Government Experience. unabridged ed. 128p. (Orig.). 1994. pap. 15.00 (*1-57744-005-6*) Nat Acad Public Admin.

Reengineering Handbook: A Step-by-Step Guide to Business Transformation. Raymond L. Manganelli & Mark M. Klein. LC 94-26609. 288p. 1994. 29.95 (*0-8144-0236-4*) AMACOM.

Reengineering Handbook: A Step-by-Step Guide to Business Transformation. Raymond L. Manganelli & Mark M. Klein. 320p. 1996. pap. 17.95 (*0-8144-7923-5*) AMACOM.

Reengineering Handbook: A Step-by-Step Guide to Business Transformation. 2nd rev. ed. Brian Leary. Ed. by Patti Carlisle. (AT&T Quality Library). 146p. (Orig.). 1992. pap. 24.95 (*0-932764-36-3*, 500-449) AT&T Customer Info.

Reengineering Health Care: Building on CQI. John R. Griffith et al. LC 94-42697. 300p. 1995. 45.00 (*1-56793-022-0*, 0952) Health Admin Pr.

Reengineering Human Resources: Achieving Radical Increases in Service Quality--with 50% to 90 % Cost & Head Count Reductions. Lyle M. Spencer. LC 95-11736. 288p. 1995. text ed. 69.95 (*0-471-01535-0*) Wiley.

Reengineering IBM Networks. Anur Guruge. LC 96-10799. 416p. 1996. pap. text ed. 39.95 (*0-471-14274-3*) Wiley.

Reengineering Information Systems. Melissa Cook. 193p. 1996. pap. 25.95 (*0-13-440256-1*) P-H.

Reengineering Information Technology: Success Through Empowerment. Stephen Baxter & David Lisburn. LC 94-7188. (BCS Practitioner Ser.). 1994. pap. text ed. 42. 00 (*0-13-123332-7*) P-H Intl.

Reengineering Management: The Mandate for New Leadership. James Champy. 256p. 1996. pap. 13.00 (*0-88730-796-5*) Harper Busn.

***Reengineering Manual for Healthcare Organizations.** Quorum Health Resources Staff. 112p. 1996. text ed. 175.00 (*0-7863-1126-6*) Irwin Prof Pubng.

Reengineering MIS: Aligning Information Technology with Business Operations. Kevin Coleman et al. 408p. (C). 1996. text ed. 59.95 (*1-878289-30-6*) Idea Group Pub.

Reengineering Nursing & Health Care Delivery: The Handbook for Organizational Transformation. Suzanne S. Blanlett & Dominick L. Flarey. 416p. 1995. 65.00 (*0-8342-0660-9*, 20660) Aspen Pub.

Reengineering of Operative & Invasive Services: Preparing for the Capitated Dollar. Mae T. Moss. LC 96-2940. 240p. 1996. spiral bd. 79.00 (*0-8342-0850-4*, 20850) Aspen Pub.

***Reengineering Performance Management: Breakthroughs in Achieving Strategy Through People.** Tracey B. Weiss & Franklin Hartle. 240p. 1997. 39.95 (*1-57444-041-1*) St Lucie Pr.

Reengineering Performance Measurement CPS-Chapter 4. Archie Lockamy, III & James F. Cox, III. (Loyola College Edition Ser.). (C). 1995. per. 5.95 (*0-7863-0470-7*) Irwin Prof Pubng.

Reengineering Revolution: A Handbook. Michael Hammer & Steven Stanton. LC 95-73. 320p. 1995. pap. 15.00 (*0-88730-736-1*) Harper Busn.

Reengineering Survival Guide: Managing in the Changing Workplace. Andrew Du Brin. 320p. 1996. text ed. 32. 95 (*0-538-84387-X*) S-W Pub.

Reengineering the A & D Industry: Proceedings of the 1994 Aerospace & Defense Symposium. (Orig.). 1994. pap. 25.00 (*1-55822-111-5*) Am Prod & Inventory.

Reengineering the Bank: A Blueprint for Survival & Success. Paul H. Allen. 1994. text ed. 40.00 (*1-55738-715-X*) Irwin Prof Pubng.

***Reengineering the Bank: A Blueprint for Survival & Success.** Paul H. Allen. LC 97-1289. 240p. 1997. per. 24.95 (*0-7863-1111-8*) Irwin Prof Pubng.

Reengineering the Corporation: A Manifesto for Business Revolution. Michael Hammer & James Champy. LC 92-54748. 240p. 1994. reprint ed. pap. 14.00 (*0-88730-687-X*) Harper Busn.

Reengineering the Credit Function. Credit Research Foundation Staff. Ed. by Teresa Donohue. 106p. 1995. pap. 26.00 (*0-934914-94-X*) NACM.

Reengineering the Factory: A Primer for World-Class Manufacturing. A. Richard Shores. LC 93-41650. 94p. 1994. pap. 19.00 (*0-87389-249-6*, H0806) ASQC Qual Pr.

Reengineering the Finance Function. Hackett Group Staff. LC 95-60289. 73p. (Orig.). 1995. pap. text ed. 35.00 (*1-885065-04-3*, 095-03) Finan Exec.

Reengineering the HR Function. HR Effectiveness, Inc. Staff. 73p. (Orig.). 1994. pap. 95.00 (*0-939900-65-3*, PB26) Soc Human Resc Mgmt.

Reengineering the Information Technology Organization. Computer Technology Research Corp. Staff. (Illus.). 172p. (Orig.). 1996. 275.00 (*1-56607-961-6*) Comput Tech Res.

Reengineering the Organization: A Step-by-Step Approach to Corporate Revitalization. Jeffrey N. Lowenthal. LC 93-44774. (Illus.). 185p. 1994. 30.00 (*0-87389-258-5*, H0813) ASQC Qual Pr.

Reengineering the Training Function: How to Align Training with the New Corporate Agenda. Donald Shandler. (Illus.). 300p. 1996. 39.95 (*1-57444-019-5*) St Lucie Pr.

Reengineering through Cycle Time Management. Wayne L. Douchkoff & Thomas E. Petroski. LC 95-26503. 174p. 1996. 29.95 (*0-945456-12-3*) PT Pubns.

Reengineering Tool Kit: Fifteen Tools & Technologies for Reengineering Your Organization. Cheryl Currid et al. LC 93-48147. 1994. 24.95 (*1-55958-504-8*) Prima Pub.

Reengineering Toolkit: 15 Tools & Technologies for Reengineering Your Organization. Cheryl Currid. 320p. 1996. per. 18.00 (*0-7615-0438-9*) Prima Pub.

Reengineering Work Simulation: Leader's Guide. Crescencio Torres. (Consensus Decision-Making Simulations Ser.). (Orig.). 1995. pap. write for info. (*0-87425-285-7*) HRD Press.

Reengineering Your Nonprofit Organization: A Guide to Strategic Transformation. Alceste T. Pappas. LC 95-400. (Nonprofit Law, Finance & Management Ser.). 288p. 1995. text ed. 34.95 (*0-471-11807-9*) Wiley.

***Reengineering Your Web Site.** Que Development Group. 600p. 1997. 39.99 (*0-7897-1216-4*) Que.

Reengineering Yourself: A Blueprint for Personal Success in the New Corporate Culture. Daniel L. Araoz & William S. Sutton. LC 94-28763. 1994. pap. 12.95 (*1-55850-405-2*) Adams Media.

Reep Family Bibliography. James W. Reep & Reynold F. Reep. LC 81-85071. (Illus.). 196p. 1985. 14.00 (*0-9614602-0-2*) James Reep.

Rees Howells: Intercessor. Norman Grubb. 264p. 1952. pap. 7.95 (*0-87508-188-6*, 188) Chr Lit.

Reese: Genealogy of the Reese Family in Wales & America from Their Arrival in America to the Present Time (1903) M. E. Reese. (Illus.). 322p. 1995. reprint ed. pap. 49.50 (*0-8328-4826-3*); reprint ed. lib. bdg. 59.50 (*0-8328-4825-5*) Higginson Bk Co.

Reese: The Untamed. Susan Connell. (Desire Ser.). 1996. mass mkt. 3.50 (*0-373-05981-7*, 1-05981-5) Silhouette.

Reese Chronological Bible. Compiled by Edward Reese. 1624p. 1980. reprint ed. 39.99 (*0-87123-115-8*) Bethany Hse.

Reestablishment of the Navy, 1787-1801: Historical Overview & Select Bibliography. Michael J. Crawford & Christine F. Hughes. (Naval History Bibliographies Ser.: No. 4). 1995. pap. text ed. 3.50 (*0-945274-32-7*) Naval Hist Ctr.

Reevaluating Eisenhower: American Foreign Policy in the Fifties. Ed. by Richard A. Melanson & David Mayer. LC 86-4363. (Illus.). 288p. 1987. text ed. 29.95 (*0-252-01340-9*); pap. text ed. 12.95 (*0-252-06067-9*) U of Ill Pr.

Reevaluating Major Naval Combatants of World War II. Ed. by James J. Sadkovich. LC 89-11910. (Contributions in Military Studies: No. 92). 225p. 1989. text ed. 55.00 (*0-313-26149-0*, SVH/, Greenwood Pr) Greenwood.

Reevaluating the Third Reich. Ed. by Thomas Childers & Jane Caplan. LC 91-37761. (Europe Past & Present Ser.). 286p. 1993. 39.95 (*0-8419-1178-9*); pap. 19.95 (*0-8419-1228-9*) Holmes & Meier.

***Reevaluation of Residential Rent Controls.** Anthony Downs. LC 96-61396. 210p. 1996. pap. text ed. 36.95 (*0-87420-801-7*, R02) Urban Land.

Reevaluation of the Bedford-Berea Sequence in Ohio & Adjacent States: Forced Regression in a Foreland Basin. Jack C. Pashin & Frank R. Ettensohn. LC 95-3060. (Special Papers: Vol. 298). 1995. pap. 30.00 (*0-8137-2298-5*) Geol Soc.

Reevaluations of Dosimetric Factors, Hiroshima & Nagasaki: Proceedings. Ed. by V. P. Bond & J. W. Thiessen. LC 82-9698. (DOE Symposium Ser.). 300p. 1982. pap. 15.75 (*0-87079-398-5*, CONF-810928, DE81026279); fiche 9.00 (*0-87079-402-7*, CONF-810928, DE81026279) DOE.

Reeves' History of the English Law from the Time of the Romans to the End of the Reign of Elizabeth, 5 vols. John Reeves. Ed. by W. F. Finlason et al. LC 80-84861. (Historical Writings in Law & Jurisprudence Ser.: No. 24, Bks.34-38). 2812p. 1981. reprint ed. lib. bdg. 240.00 (*0-89941-240-8*, 302480) W S Hein.

Reeve's Prologue & Tale. Geoffrey Chaucer. Ed. by A. C. Spearing et al. LC 78-19695. (Selected Tales from Chaucer Ser.). 136p. 1979. pap. text ed. 9.95 (*0-521-22211-7*) Cambridge U Pr.

Reexamination of Chitinozoa from the Cedar Valley Formation of Iowa with Observations on their Morphology & Distribution, No. 275 see Bulletins of American Paleontology: Vol. 63

Reexamination of Mark Twain's 'Joan of Arc' Thomas A. Maik. LC 92-5601. 168p. 1992. lib. bdg. 79.95 (*0-88946-164-3*) E Mellen.

Reexamination of Sir William Hamilton's Philosophy: Mill on Hamilton. Dallas L. Ouren. LC 91-44634. (Illus.). 216p. 1992. lib. bdg. 89.95 (*0-7734-9940-7*) E Mellen.

Reexamination of the Socio-Political History of Pakistan: Reproduction of Class Relations & Ideology. Hassan N. Gardezi. LC 91-31577. 176p. 1991. lib. bdg. 79.95 (*0-7734-9722-6*) E Mellen.

***Reexamining America's Global Role.** Public Agenda Foundation Staff. 1996. pap. text ed. write for info. (*0-07-052214-6*) McGraw.

Reexamining Democracy. Gary Marks & Larry Diamond. 352p. (C). 1992. text ed. 32.00 (*0-8039-4641-4*) Sage.

Reexamining Family Stress: New Theory & Research. Wesley R. Burr & Shirley Klein. (Library of Social Research: Vol. 193). (Illus.). 224p. (C). 1993. text ed. 54. 00 (*0-8039-4929-4*); pap. text ed. 24.95 (*0-8039-4930-8*) Sage.

Reexamining Reading Diagnosis: New Trends & Procedures. Ed. by Susan M. Glazer et al. 186p. 1988. pap. 11.95 (*0-87207-532-X*) Intl Reading.

Reexamining the Eisenhower Presidency. Ed. by Shirley A. Warshaw. LC 92-42430. (Contributions in American History Ser.: No. 149). 256p. 1993. text ed. 55.00 (*0-313-28792-9*, GM8792, Greenwood Pr) Greenwood.

Reexamining the Soviet Experience: Essays in Honor of Alexander Dallin. Ed. by David Holloway & Norman M. Naimark. 288p. (C). 1996. text ed. 56.00 (*0-8133-8954-2*) Westview.

Reexploring the Book of Mormon: A Decade of Recent Research. Ed. by John W. Welch. LC 91-47719. 314p. (Orig.). 1992. pap. text ed. 12.95 (*0-87579-600-1*) Deseret Bk.

Ref, Bk. 1. Wolfgang Hageney. (Illus.). 96p. (ENG, FRE, GER, ITA & SPA.). 1984. pap. 12.95 (*88-7070-046-1*) Belvedere USA.

Ref, Bk. 2. Wolfgang Hageney. (Illus.). 96p. (ENG, FRE, GER, ITA & SPA.). 1984. pap. 12.95 (*88-7070-047-X*) Belvedere USA.

Ref, Bk. 3. Wolfgang Hageney. (Illus.). 88p. (ENG, FRE, GER, ITA & SPA.). 1984. pap. 12.95 (*88-7070-048-8*) Belvedere USA.

Ref, Bk. 4. Wolfgang Hageney. (Illus.). 96p. (ENG, FRE, GER, ITA & SPA.). 1984. pap. 12.95 (*88-7070-049-6*) Belvedere USA.

Ref, Bk. 5. Wolfgang Hageney. (Illus.). 112p. (ENG, FRE, GER, ITA & SPA.). 1984. pap. 12.95 (*88-7070-050-X*) Belvedere USA.

Ref, Bk. 6. Wolfgang Hageney. (Illus.). 96p. (ENG, FRE, GER, ITA & SPA.). 1984. pap. 12.95 (*88-7070-051-8*) Belvedere USA.

REF Field Guide. Kevin Siembieda. Ed. by Alex Marciniszyn. (Robotech II RPG Ser.). (Illus.). 160p. (Orig.). (YA). (gr. 8 up). 1989. pap. 15.95 (*0-916211-36-3*, 558) Palladium Bks.

***Refacing Cabinets: Making an Old Kitchen New.** Herrick Kimball. LC 97-20244. (Illus.). 160p. 1997. pap. 19.95 (*1-56158-197-6*, 070307) Taunton.

Refactory Metals: Extraction, Processing & Applications: Proceedings of a Symposium Sponsored by the Reactive Metals Committee, Held at the Annual Meeting of the Minerals, Metals & Materials Society in New Orleans, February 17-21, 1991. Minerals, Metals & Materials Society, Meeting (1991: New Orleans, LA) Staff. Ed. by Nona C. Liddell et al. LC 90-63759. 374p. 1990. reprint ed. pap. 106.60 (*0-608-00780-3*, 2061578) Bks Demand.

Refal-5, Programming Guide & Reference Manual. Valentin F. Turchin. 192p. (Orig.). 1989. pap. text ed. 15.00 (*0-914265-12-1*) New Eng Pub MA.

Refashioning "Knights & Ladies Gentle Deeds" The Intertextuality of Spenser's Faerie Queene & Malory's Morte d'Arthur. Paul R. Rovang. LC 95-16880. 160p. 1996. 32.50 (*0-8386-3598-9*) Fairleigh Dickinson.

Refashioning Nature. David S. Goodman & Michael Redclift. (Illus.). 276p. (C). 1992. pap. 18.95 (*0-415-06703-0*, A6742); text ed. 69.95 (*0-415-06702-2*, A6738) Routledge.

Referecia Rapida de la Biblia. Ernest Clevenger, Jr. (Parchment Ready Reference Ser.). 1987. pap. 1.00 (*0-88428-054-3*) Parchment Pr.

Refereed & Nonrefereed Economic Journals: A Guide for Publishing Opportunities. Compiled by A. Carolyn Miller & Victoria J. Punsalan. LC 87-25158. 269p. 1988. text ed. 65.00 (*0-313-25857-0*, MPB/, Greenwood Pr) Greenwood.

Referee's Companion. Marc W. Miller. (MegaTraveller Ser.). (Illus.). 96p. (Orig.). 1988. pap. 10.00 (*0-943580-71-4*) Game Designers.

Referee's Handbook for Youth Soccer. 13th ed. James N. Gennrich. (Illus.). 63p. (Orig.). (YA). (gr. 9-12). 1996. pap. 8.00 (*0-9616953-0-7*) Soccer Ed.

Referee's Referee: Becoming the Best. Abraham Klein & Rubi Shalev. (Illus.). (Orig.). 1995. pap. 9.95 (*0-916802-26-4*) Soccer for Am.

Referee's Report Writing Handbook. Joyce J. George. LC 92-3842. 284p. 1992. 38.50 (*0-89941-787-6*, 306410) W S Hein.

Referee's Rulebook. Joe Williams & Kathleen Williams. (Legendary Lives Ser.). (Illus.). 90p. (Orig.). 1989. pap. 11.95 (*0-685-30416-7*) Marquee Pr.

Reference. Katie Yates. 16p. (Orig.). 1991. pap. 5.00 (*0-9627192-3-4*) We Pr.

Reference & Collection Development on the Internet: A How-To-Do-It Manual for Librarians. Elizabeth Thomsen. (Illus.). 240p. (Orig.). 1996. pap. 45.00 (*1-55570-243-0*) Neal-Schuman.

Reference & Computation: An Essay in Applied Philosophy of Language. Amichai Kronfeld. (Studies in Natural Language Processing). 250p. (C). 1990. 64.95 (*0-521-36636-4*); pap. text ed. 18.95 (*0-521-39982-3*) Cambridge U Pr.

Reference & Information Services: A New Reader. Compiled by Bill Katz & Anne Clifford. LC 81-16680. 432p. 1982. 39.50 (*0-8108-1483-8*) Scarecrow.

Reference & Information Services: A Reader for the Nineties. Compiled by Bill Katz. LC 91-42224. (Illus.). 423p. 1991. 45.00 (*0-8108-2486-8*) Scarecrow.

Reference & Information Services: A Reader for Today. Compiled by Bill Katz. LC 86-13122. (Illus.). 433p. 1986. text ed. 39.50 (*0-8108-1873-6*) Scarecrow.

Reference & Information Services: An Introduction. rev. ed. Ed. by Richard E. Bopp & Linda C. Smith. (Library Science Text Ser.). xxiv, 626p. 1995. pap. text ed. 35.00 (*1-56308-129-6*) Libs Unl.

Reference & Information Services: An Introduction. 2nd rev. ed. Ed. by Richard E. Bopp & Linda C. Smith. (Library Science Text Ser.). xxiv, 626p. 1995. lib. bdg. 47.50 (*1-56308-130-X*) Libs Unl.

Reference & Information Services in Health Sciences Librarianship. M. Sandra Wood. Ed. by Alison Bunting. LC 94-5665. (Current Practice in Health Sciences Librarianship Ser.: Vol. 1). 394p. 1994. 39.50 (*0-8108-2765-4*) Scarecrow.

Reference & Online Services Handbook: Guidelines, Policies & Procedures, Vol. II. Ed. by Bill Katz. LC 81-11290. 602p. 1986. lib. bdg. 39.95 (*0-918212-74-X*) Neal-Schuman.

Reference & Professional Information Business: A Study of Reference, Professional, Scientific, Technical, Directory & Database Publishing, 1990 Edition. James Moses. 218p. 1991. ring bd. 125.00 (*0-9626749-1-5*) Primary Research.

Reference & Referent Accessibility. Ed. by Thorstein Fretheim & Jeanette K. Gundel. LC 96-12697. (Pragmatics & Beyond Ser.: Vol. 38). xii, 312p. 1996. lib. bdg. 85.00 (*1-55619-331-9*) Benjamins North Am.

***Reference & Selected Procedures for the Quantitative Determination of Hemoglobin in Blood: Approved Standard (1994)** Contrib. by A. Richardson Jones. 1994. 75.00 (*1-56238-237-3*, H15-A2) Natl Comm Clin Lab Stds.

Reference Assessment Manual. American Library Association, Evaluation of Reference & Adult Services Committee Management Staff. 384p. 1995. pap. 35.00 (*0-87650-344-X*) Pierian.

Reference Book & Technology Report. James Moses. 218p. 1990. per. write for info. (*0-9626749-0-7*) Primary Research.

Reference Book for Composite Technology, Vol. 1. Stuart M. Lee. LC 89-50073. 334p. 1989. 39.95 (*0-87762-564-6*) Technomic.

Reference Book for Composite Technology, Vol. 2. Stuart M. Lee. LC 89-50073. 203p. 1989. 39.95 (*0-87762-565-4*) Technomic.

Reference Book for Gravity: Magnetic & Bathymetric Data of the Pacific Ocean & Adjacent Seas, 1963-71. Yoshibumi Tomoda. LC 75-305077. 158p. 1974. reprint ed. pap. 45.10 (*0-608-01560-1*, 2061976) Bks Demand.

Reference Book for World Traders, 1987. LC 61-10661. 1990. write for info. (*0-87514-000-9*) Croner.

***Reference Book of Corporate Managements: America's Corporate Leaders, 1996, 3 vols.** Dun & Bradstreet Staff. 1996. 795.00 (*1-56203-469-3*) Dun & Bradstreet.

Reference Book of Marine Insurance Clauses. 1993. 80.00 (*1-85609-060-4*, Pub. by Witherby & Co UK) St Mut.

***Reference Book of Marine Insurance Clauses.** 1996. pap. 75.00 (*1-85609-089-2*, Pub. by Witherby & Co UK) St Mut.

Reference Book of Marine Insurance Clauses. Witherby & Co. Ltd. Staff. 266p. (C). 1989. pap. 180.00 (*0-948691-64-6*, Pub. by Witherby & Co UK) St Mut.

Reference Book of Marine Insurance Clauses. Witherby & Co. Ltd. Staff. 250p. 1991. pap. 165.00 (*1-85609-033-7*, Pub. by Witherby & Co UK) St Mut.

Reference Book of Marine Insurance Clauses. 57th ed. 240p. 1985. pap. 160.00 (*0-900886-57-9*, Pub. by Witherby & Co UK) St Mut.

Reference Book of Marine Insurance Clauses. 58th ed. 250p. 1986. pap. 165.00 (*0-948691-18-2*, Pub. by Witherby & Co UK) St Mut.

Reference Book on Major Transnational Corporations Operating in Namibia. 1986. 19.00 (*92-1-104159-7*, E. 85.II.A.5) UN.

Reference Book Review Index: 1973-1975. Ed. by M. Balachandran & S. Balachandran. LC 79-83697. 1980. 60.00 (*0-87650-073-4*) Pierian.

Reference Book Review Index, 1970-1972. Ed. by Shirley Smith. LC 75-13992. 1975. 60.00 (*0-87650-048-3*) Pierian.

Reference Books, 4 vols. boxed 14.90 (*0-317-12482-X*) PB.

Reference Books for Children. 4th ed. Carolyn S. Peterson & Ann D. Fenton. LC 92-14234. 414p. 1992. 45.00 (*0-8108-2543-0*) Scarecrow.

Reference Books for Children's Collections. 2nd ed. Ed. by Dolores Vogliano. (Illus.). 109p. (Orig.). 1991. pap. 7.00 (*0-87104-712-8*, Branch Libraries) NY Pub Lib.

Reference Catalogue of Bright Galaxies. Gerard H. De Vaucouleurs & Antoinette De Vaucouleurs. 276p. 1964. 40.00 (*0-292-73348-8*) U of Tex Pr.

Reference Catalogue of Indian Books in Print: Title Index, Vol. 1. 1425p. 1973. 30.00 (*0-88065-000-1*, Messers Today & Tomorrow) Scholarly Pubns.

Reference Catalogue of Indian Books in Print in English: Author Index with a Directory of Publishers. 1980p. 1974. 50.00 (*0-88065-001-X*, Messers Today & Tomorrow) Scholarly Pubns.

Reference Catalogue of Indian Books in Print in English: Subject Guide, Vol. 3. 1736p. 1977. 70.00 (*0-88065-003-6*, Messers Today & Tomorrow) Scholarly Pubns.

Reference Catalogue of Indian Books in Print in English: Supplement to Vol. 1 & 2--Containing Books Published During 1973-75. 547p. 1976. 50.00 (*0-88065-002-8*, Messers Today & Tomorrow) Scholarly Pubns.

Reference Collections Shelved in the Reading Room & Acquisitions Department: Classified & Alphabetical Listings. Harvard University Library Staff. LC 77-128715. (Widener Library Shelflist: No. 33). 140p. 1971. text ed. 10.00 (*0-674-75201-5*) HUP.

***Reference Companion to Dylan Thomas.** Ed. by James A. Davies. 1998. text ed. write for info. (*0-313-28774-0*, Greenwood Pr) Greenwood.

Reference Companion to the History of Abnormal Psychology, 2 vols. John G. Howells & M. Livia Osborn. LC 80-27163. xviii, 1141p. 1984. text ed. 250.00 (*0-313-22183-9*, HOL/) Greenwood.

Reference Companion to the History of Abnormal Psychology, 2 vols., 1. John G. Howells & M. Livia Osborn. LC 80-27163. xviii, 1141p. 1984. text ed. 150.00 (*0-313-24261-5*, HOL/01) Greenwood.

Reference Companion to the History of Abnormal Psychology, 2 vols., Vol. 2. John G. Howells & M. Livia Osborn. LC 80-27163. xviii, 1141p. 1984. text ed. 150.00 (*0-313-24262-3*, HOL/02) Greenwood.

Reference Data for Engineers: Radio, Electronics, Computer, & Communications. 3rd ed. Mac Valkenburg. 1500p. 1993. 99.95 (*0-672-22753-3*) Buttrwrth-Heinemann.

Reference Data on Atoms, Molecules & Ions. A. A. Radzig & Boris M. Smirnov. (Chemical Physics Ser.: Vol. 31). (Illus.). 430p. 1985. 99.00 (*0-387-12415-2*) Spr-Verlag.

Reference Data on Multicharged Ions. V. G. Palchikov & V. P. Shevelko. LC 94-29200. (Series on Atoms & Plasmas: Vol. 16). 1994. 152.95 (*0-387-58259-2*) Spr-Verlag.

Reference Encyclopedia for the IBM Personal Computer, 2 Vols. Ed. by Gary Phillips. 1984. 69.95 (*0-317-03007-8*) P-H.

***Reference Encyclopedia of the American Indian.** 8th ed. B. Klein. 890p. 1997. pap. 95.00 (*0-915344-74-2*) Todd Pubns.

***Reference Encyclopedia of the American Indian.** 8th ed. Barry T. Klein. 890p. 1997. 125.00 (*0-915344-75-0*) Todd Pubns.

Reference Encyclopedia of the American Indian, 1995. 6th ed. 1000p. 1995. 125.00 (*0-685-59688-5*) B Klein Pubns.

Reference Flipper: A Guide to Reference Material. Sybilla Cook. 49p. (YA). (gr. 5 up). 1988. reprint ed. 6.75 (*1-878383-09-4*) C Lee Pubns.

Reference Fossils of Canada, Pt. 1: Devonian Faunas of Western Canada. Geological Association of Canada Staff et al. (Geological Association of Canada. Special Paper Ser.: No. 1). (Illus.). 73p. reprint ed. pap. 25.00 (*0-685-44030-3*, 2030314) Bks Demand.

Reference Frames. Jean Kovalevsky. (C). 1989. lib. bdg. 171.50 (*0-7923-0182-X*) Kluwer Ac.

Reference Grammar: English Grammar of Communication. Guido De Devitiis & Luciano Mariani. 312p. 75.00 (*0-7859-8865-3*) Fr & Eur.

Reference Grammar of Chinese Sentences with Exercises. Henry H. Tiee. LC 86-14679. 348p. 1986. pap. 27.95 (*0-8165-0965-4*) U of Ariz Pr.

Reference Grammar of Classical Tamil Poetry. V. S. Rajam. LC 91-76989. (Memoirs Ser.: Vol. 199). 672p. (C). 1992. 45.00 (*0-87169-199-X*, M199-RAV) Am Philos.

Reference Grammar of German. Herbert Lederer. 1981. 22.50 (*0-684-41329-9*) S&S Trade.

Reference Grammar of Japanese. Samuel E. Martin. 1198p. 1988. 69.95 (*0-8048-1550-X*) C E Tuttle.

Reference Grammar of Korean. Samuel E. Martin. 1040p. 1993. 74.95 (*0-8048-1887-8*) C E Tuttle.

Reference Grammar of Maithili. Ramawater Yadav. LC 95-24892. (Trends in Linguistics Ser.: Vol. 11). xii, 400p. (C). 1996. lib. bdg. 146.70 (*3-11-014558-8*) Mouton.

Reference Grammar of Modern French. Anne Judge & F. G. Healy. 528p. 1985. pap. 32.95 (*0-7131-6453-0*, A3040, Pub. by E Arnold UK) Routledge Chapman & Hall.

Reference Grammar of Modern French. Anne Judge & Frederick G. Healey. 528p. 1995. pap. 29.95 (*0-8442-1631-3*) NTC Pub Grp.

Reference Grammar of Punjabi. Harjit S. Gill. 170p. 1992. 19.95 (*0-8288-8444-7*) Fr & Eur.

Reference Grammar of Southeastern Tepehuan. Thomas L. Willett. LC 91-65341. (Publications in Linguistics: No. 100). xii, 282p. (Orig.). 1991. pap. 21.00 incl. fiche (*0-88312-802-0*) Summer Instit Ling.

Reference Grammar of Spoken Kannada. Harold F. Schiffman. LC 83-1170. (Publications on Asia of the School of International Studies: No. 39). 198p. 1984. text ed. 35.00 (*0-295-96031-0*) U of Wash Pr.

Reference Grammar of Syrian Arabic. Mark W. Cowell. (Richard Slade Harrell Arabic Ser.). 579p. 1964. pap. 16.95 (*0-87840-009-5*); audio 20.00 (*0-87840-019-2*) Georgetown U Pr.

Reference Grammar of Tamazight. Ernest T. Abdel-Massih. LC 72-32219. (C). 1970. pap. text ed. 20.00 (*0-932098-05-3*) UM Ctr MENAS.

Reference Grammar of the German Language. Herbert Lederer. (C). 1969. pap. text ed. write for info. (*0-13-033713-7*) P-H.

Reference Grammar of the German Language. Ed. by Herbert Lederer et al. LC 69-17352. 709p. (C). 1969. pap. text ed. 42.80 (*0-13-033705-6*) P-H.

Reference Guide for Allied Video Corporation's Video Production of The Greenhouse Effect. Charles E. Brown, IV. 24p. 1994. pap. 5.95 (*1-56913-022-1*) Allied Video.

***Reference Guide for Botany & Horticulture.** Ronald F. Simon. LC 96-78185. (Illus.). 508p. (Orig.). 1996. pap. 39.95 (*0-9653962-0-7*) Instruct Media.

Reference Guide for English Studies. Michael Marcuse. 1990. 120.00 (*0-520-05161-0*); pap. 40.00 (*0-520-07992-2*) U CA Pr.

Reference Guide for Mathematica: Version 2. Stephen Wolfram. (C). 1992. pap. text ed. 20.50 (*0-201-51012-X*) Addison-Wesley.

Reference Guide to Acronyms. Randall L. Voight. 207p. (C). pap. write for info. (*0-930318-17-X*) Intl Res Eval.

Reference Guide to Afro-American Publications & Editors, 1827-1946. Vilma Potter. LC 91-17167. 116p. 1993. text ed. 26.95 (*0-8138-0677-1*) Iowa St U Pr.

Reference Guide to American Literature. 3rd ed. Ed. by Jim Kamp. LC 94-21548. (Reference Guides Ser.). 1202p. 1994. 140.00 (*1-55862-310-8*) St James Pr.

Reference Guide to Audiovisual Information. James L. Limbacher. LC 72-1737. 107p. reprint ed. pap. 30.50 (*0-317-10299-0*, 2050190) Bks Demand.

***Reference Guide to Casino Gambling: How to Win.** 2nd ed. Henry J. Tamburin. 168p. 1996. pap. 11.95 (*0-912177-12-8*) Res Serv Unltd.

Reference Guide to Edmund Spenser. F. I. Carpenter. 1980. 14.50 (*0-8446-1102-6*) Peter Smith.

Reference Guide to English. 2nd ed. Alice Maclin. 496p. (C). 1987. pap. text ed. 15.50 (*0-03-004193-7*) HB Coll Pubs.

Reference Guide to English Literature, 3 vols. 91th ed. Ed. by Daniel L. Kirkpatrick. 2000p. 1991. 295.00 (*1-55862-080-X*, 200178) St James Pr.

Reference Guide to Environmental Management, Engineering & Pollution Control Resources. Randall L. Voight & George Franklin, Jr. 305p. 1986. pap. 95.00 (*0-930318-12-9*) Intl Res Eval.

Reference Guide to Fantastic Films: Science Fiction, Fantasy, Horror. Ed. by Walt Lee. (Illus.). 750p. 1995. lib. bdg. 279.00 (*0-913616-30-3*) Hollywd Film Arch.

Reference Guide to Fantastic Films: Science Fiction, Fantasy, Horror. Ed. by Walt Lee. (Illus.). 1995. reprint ed. lib. bdg. 149.00 (*0-913616-32-X*) Hollywd Film Arch.

Reference Guide to Fantastic Films: Science Fiction, Fantasy, Horror. Ed. by Walt Lee. (Illus.). 1995. reprint ed. lib. bdg. 179.00 (*0-913616-31-1*) Hollywd Film Arch.

Reference Guide to Fantastic Films, Science Fiction, Fantasy, & Horror. Ed. by Walt Lee. LC 72-88775. (Illus.). 742p. (Orig.). 1974. lib. bdg. 169.00 (*0-913974-04-8*) Chelsea-Lee Bks.

Reference Guide to Fantastic Films, Science Fiction, Fantasy, & Horror, Vol. 3: P-Z. Ed. by Walt Lee. LC 72-88775. (Illus.). 270p. (Orig.). 1974. pap. 29.95 (*0-913974-03-X*) Chelsea-Lee Bks.

Reference Guide to First Aid Procedures. Tel-A-Train, Inc. Staff. 1988. student ed. 3.50 (*1-56355-231-0*) Tel-A-Train.

Reference Guide to Handbooks & Annuals: 1994 Edition. J. William Pfeiffer. LC 93-87780. 304p. 1994. pap. text ed. 9.95 (*0-88390-414-4*, Pfffr & Co) Jossey-Bass.

Reference Guide to Historical Fiction for Children & Young Adults. Lynda G. Adamson. LC 87-7533. 420p. 1987. text ed. 69.50 (*0-313-25002-2*, ARH/, Greenwood Pr) Greenwood.

Reference Guide to Management Techniques & Activities. I. G. Bloor. LC 86-30266. 114p. 1987. 48.00 (*0-08-034268-X*, Pub. by Pergamon Repr UK) Franklin.

***Reference Guide to Medicinal Plants: Herbal Medicine Past & Present.** J. K. Crellin & Jane Philpott. LC 97-17089. 1997. pap. write for info. (*0-8223-2068-1*) Duke.

Reference Guide to Miniature Makers Marks. Lee S. Frank & Alice H. Frank. LC 95-90359. 554p. 1996. 65.00 (*0-9644481-0-6*) A-L Miniatrs.

Reference Guide to Modern Fantasy for Children. Pat Pflieger. LC 83-10692. 768p. 1984. text ed. 79.50 (*0-313-22886-8*, PFC/, Greenwood Pr) Greenwood.

Reference Guide to Russian Literature. Ed. by Neil Cornwell. 1000p. 1997. lib. bdg. 125.00 (*1-884964-10-9*) Fitzroy Dearborn.

Reference Guide to Science Fiction, Fantasy, & Horror. Michael Burgess. (Reference Sources in the Humanities Ser.). xvi, 404p. 1992. lib. bdg. 55.00 (*0-87287-611-X*) Libs Unl.

Reference Guide to Short Fiction. Ed. by Noelle Watson. LC 93-33650. (St. James Reference Guide Ser.). 1000p. 1993. 140.00 (*1-55862-334-5*) St James Pr.

***Reference Guide to Short Fiction.** 2nd ed. Date not set. 130.00 (*1-55862-222-5*, 00109209) St James Pr.

Reference Guide to SURVEYS. Randall L. Voight et al. (Decision Support Ser.). 448p. 1981. 125.00 (*0-930318-11-0*) Intl Res Eval.

Reference Guide to Texas Law & Legal History. Karl T. Gruben. 110p. 1987. boxed 35.00 (*0-614-05771-X*) MICHIE.

Reference Guide to Texas Law & Legal History: Sources & Documentation. 2nd ed. Ed. by Karl T. Gruben & James E. Hambleton. 110p. 1987. boxed 35.00 (*0-409-25201-8*) MICHIE.

***Reference Guide to the Bible in Emily Dickinson's Poetry.** Fordyce R. Bennett. LC 96-42431. 512p. 1996. 49.00 (*0-8108-3247-X*) Scarecrow.

Reference Guide to the Big Book of Alcoholics Anonymous. Stewart C. Crossland. Ed. by Ciaran O'Mahony. 148p. (Orig.). (C). 1986. pap. 9.95 (*0-934125-01-5*) Hazelden.

Reference Guide to the Gymnosperms of the World. Hubertus Nimsch. (Illus.). 180p. 1995. pap. 25.00 (*1-878762-52-4*) Balogh.

Reference Guide to the Iranian Oral History Project. 2nd ed. Habib Ladjevardi. LC 93-61276. (Orig.). 1993. 9.95 (*0-932885-10-1*) Harvard CMES.

Reference Guide to the U. S. Military, 1607-1815. Ed. by Charles R. Schrader. (Reference Guide to the U. S. Military Ser.). (Illus.). 288p. 1991. 50.00 (*0-8160-1836-7*) Facts on File.

Reference Guide to the U. S. Military, 1815-1865. Ed. by Charles R. Schrader. (Reference Guide to the U. S. Military Ser.). (Illus.). 320p. 1993. lib. bdg. 50.00 (*0-8160-1837-5*) Facts on File.

Reference Guide to the U. S. Military, 1865-1919. Ed. by Charles R. Schrader. (Reference Guide to the U. S. Military Ser.). (Illus.). 320p. 1993. 50.00 (*0-8160-1838-3*) Facts on File.

Reference Guide to the World's Famous Landmarks: Bridges, Tunnels, Dams, Roads, & Other Structures. Lawrence H. Berlow. (Illus.). 224p. 1997. 49.95 (*0-89774-966-9*) Oryx Pr.

Reference Guide to U. S. Military History: 1919-1945, Vol. 4. Ed. by Charles R. Shrader. (Illus.). 320p. 1993. 50.00 (*0-8160-1839-1*) Facts on File.

Reference Guide to U. S. Military History: 1945 to the Present, Vol. 5. Ed. by Charles R. Shrader. (Illus.). 366p. 1994. 50.00 (*0-8160-1840-5*) Facts on File.

Reference Guide to United States Department of State Special Files. Gerald K. Haines. LC 84-4483. (Illus.). xliv, 394p. 1985. text ed. 72.50 (*0-313-22750-0*, HUS/, Greenwood Pr) Greenwood.

Reference Guide to World Literature. 2nd ed. Lesley Henderson. LC 94-34483. 1995. 280.00 (*1-55862-195-4*) St James Pr.

Reference Guide to World Literature, Vol. 1. 2nd ed. Henderson. 1995. write for info. (*1-55862-332-9*) Gale.

Reference Guide to World Literature, Vol. 2. 2nd ed. Henderson. 1995. write for info. (*1-55862-333-7*) Gale.

Reference Handbook for Cogeneration for the Pulp & Paper Industry. Technical Association of the Pulp & Paper Industry Staff. Ed. by Donald K. Wooden et al. 167p. reprint ed. pap. 47.60 (*0-318-39736-6*, 2033108) Bks Demand.

Reference Handbook of Cosmetology & Related Fields. Violet B. Jones. LC 85-51719. (Illus.). 91p. (Orig.). 1986. pap. 10.00 (*0-933675-00-3*) Scratch & Scribble.

Reference Handbook on Insurance Company Insolvency. 3rd ed. 1128p. 1993. pap. 99.95 (*0-89707-857-8*, 519-0226) Amer Bar Assn.

Reference Handbook on the Comprehensive General Liability Policy: Coverage Provisions, Exclusions, & Other Litigation Issues. American Bar Association Staff. LC 95-77230. 297p. 1995. pap. 79.95 (*1-57073-209-4*, 519-0249) Amer Bar Assn.

Reference Handbook on the Deserts of North America. Ed. by Gordon L. Bender. LC 80-24791. (Illus.). xiii, 594p. 1982. text ed. 135.00 (*0-313-21307-0*, BRD/, Greenwood Pr) Greenwood.

Reference In Intentionality. Olav Asheim. 227p. (C). 1992. text ed. 32.00 (*82-560-0811-3*, Pub. by Solum Verlag NO) Intl Spec Bk.

***Reference in Multidisciplinary Perspective: Philosophical Object, Cognitive Subject, Intersubjective Process.** Ed. by Richard A. Geiger. x, 764p. 1995. write for info. (*3-487-09846-6*) G Olms Pubs.

***Reference Information for the Software Verification & Validation Process.** 1997. lib. bdg. 250.95 (*0-8490-6264-0*) Gordon Pr.

***Reference Information for the Software Verification & Validation Process.** 1997. lib. bdg. 250.95 (*0-8490-7735-4*) Gordon Pr.

Reference Information Skills Game. Myram F. Tunnicliff & Susan S. Soenen. xvi, 107p. 1995. pap. text ed. 24.50 (*1-56308-296-9*) Libs Unl.

***Reference Interview As a Creative Art.** 2nd ed. Elaine Z. Jennerich & Edward J. Jennerich. LC 96-54018. (Illus.). xi, 124p. 1997. 26.50 (*1-56308-466-X*) Libs Unl.

Reference Interviews, Questions, & Materials: Includes "Answer Key to the Third Edition" 3rd ed. Thomas P. Slavens. LC 93-24488. 226p. 1994. 25.00 (*0-8108-2718-2*) Scarecrow.

Reference Leukocyte Differential Count (Proportional) & Evaluation of Instrumental Methods: Approved Standard, Vol. 4. National Committee for Clinical Laboratory Standards. 1992. 85.00 (*1-56238-131-8*, H20-A) Natl Comm Clin Lab Stds.

Reference Librarian & Implications of Mediation. Ed. by M. Keith Ewing & Robert Hauptman. LC 92-19037. (Reference Librarian Ser.: No. 37). (Illus.). 196p. 1992. lib. bdg. 39.95 (*1-56024-318-X*) Haworth Pr.

Reference Library, 4 vols. 1985. boxed 13.90 (*0-345-32965-1*, Del Rey) Ballantine.

Reference Library of Black America, 5 vols. Compiled by Harry A. Ploski. (Illus.). 1600p. 1990. lib. bdg. 179.90 (*0-685-49222-2*) Afro Am Pr.

***Reference Library of Black America, 5 vols.** 94th ed. 1994. 179.00 (*0-7876-0389-9*, 00109633, Gale Res Intl) Gale.

***Reference Library of Black America 1996, 5 vols.** 1996. 179.00 (*0-7876-1534-X*, 00156805, Gale Res Intl) Gale.

Reference Library User: Problems & Solutions. Ed. by Bill Katz. (Reference Librarian Ser.: No. 31). 151p. 1990. text ed. 39.95 (*1-56024-022-9*) Haworth Pr.

Reference List of Manuscripts Relating to the History of Maine (1938) Elizabeth Ring. (Illus.). 970p. 1992. reprint ed. lib. bdg. 89.00 (*0-8328-2519-0*) Higginson Bk Co.

Reference Man. International Commission on Radiological Protection. (International Commission of Radiological Protection Ser.: No. 23). 512p. 1975. 120.50 (*0-08-017024-2*, Pergamon Pr) Elsevier.

Reference Manual. Clu. 1984. 42.95 (*0-387-91253-3*) Spr-Verlag.

Reference Manual: For the Office. 7th ed. House. (KM - Office Procedures Ser.). 1989. text ed. 21.95 (*0-538-11460-6*) S-W Pub.

Reference Manual: For the Office. 7th ed. Clifford R. House & Kathie Sigler. 368p. (C). 1989. text ed. 25.95 (*0-538-11461-4*, K46U) S-W Pub.

***Reference Manual for Citizenship Instructors.** (Illus.). 73p. 1996. reprint ed. pap. 20.00 (*0-7881-3031-5*) DIANE Pub.

Reference Manual for Communicative Sciences & Disorders: Speech & Language. Raymond D. Kent. 450p. (C). 1991. text ed. 54.00 (*0-89079-419-7*, 1578) PRO-ED.

***Reference Manual for Growth & Development.** 2nd ed. John M. Buckler. LC 96-30415. (Illus.). 128p. 1997. pap. text ed. 29.95 (*0-86542-680-5*) Blackwell Sci.

An Asterisk (*) at the beginning of an entry indicates that the title is appearing in BIP for the first time.

Reference Manual for Human Performance Measurement in the Field of Physical Education & Sports Sciences. Ed. by David A. Brodie. LC 95-47646. (Mellen Studies in Education: Vol. 26). 252p. 1996. text ed. 89.95 (*0-7734-8788-3*) E Mellen.

Reference Manual for Scientific Evidence. Federal Judicial Center Staff. 1995. pap. 45.00 (*0-87632-269-0*) Clark Boardman Callaghan.

Reference Manual for Teachers of Dance Exercise. Jill P. May. (Illus.). 128p. (Orig.). 1988. pap. 28.50 (*0-572-01472-4*, Pub. by W Foulsham UK) Trans-Atl Phila.

Reference Manual for Telecommunications Engineering. 2nd ed. Roger L. Freeman. LC 92-35910. 2308p. 1993. text ed. 225.00 (*0-471-57960-2*) Wiley.

Reference Manual for Telecommunications Engineering: 1995 Update. 2nd ed. Roger L. Freeman. LC 92-35910. 368p. 1995. pap. text ed. 75.00 (*0-471-04756-2*) Wiley.

Reference Manual for Telecommunications Engineering, 1996 Update. 2nd ed. Roger L. Freeman. 1996. text ed. 75.00 (*0-471-14119-4*) Wiley.

Reference Manual for the ADA Programming Language. (MIL STD 1815A 1983 Ser.). 344p. 1983. pap. 21.00 (*0-16-001468-9*, 008-000-00394-7) USGPO.

***Reference Manual for the ADA Programming Language, 2 vols.** 1997. lib. bdg. 605.95 (*0-8490-7733-8*) Gordon Pr.

Reference Manual for the Office. 8th ed. House. (KM - Office Procedures Ser.). 1994. student ed., pap. 10.95 (*0-538-61993-7*) S-W Pub.

Reference Manual for the Office. 8th ed. Clifford R. House & Kathie Sigler. LC 93-45740. 1994. text ed. 23.95 (*0-538-61991-0*); text ed. 23.95 (*0-538-61992-9*) S-W Pub.

Reference Manual for the Office Study Guide. 7th ed. House. (KM - Office Procedures Ser.). 1989. pap. 5.95 (*0-538-11462-2*) S-W Pub.

Reference Manual for Writing Rehabilitation Therapy Treatment Plans. Penny Hogberg & Mary Johnson. LC 94-61216. 112p. 1994. pap. 16.95 (*0-910251-67-3*) Venture Pub PA.

Reference Manual of Countermeasures for Hazardous Substance Releases. Robert W. Melvold et al. 304p. 1988. 63.95 (*0-89116-066-3*) Hemisp Pub.

Reference Manual of the Official Documents of The American Occupational Therapy Association, Inc. 5th ed. 1993. pap. text ed. 40.00 (*0-910317-93-3*) Am Occup Therapy.

Reference Manual of Woody Plant Propagation: From Seed to Tissue Culture. Michael A. Dirr & Charles W. Heuser. (Illus.). 240p. 1987. pap. 31.95 (*0-942375-00-9*) Varsity Pr.

***Reference Manual on Scientific Evidence, 2 vols.** (Law Ser.). 1997. lib. bdg. 600.99 (*0-8490-8223-4*) Gordon Pr.

***Reference Manual on Scientific Evidence.** Ed. by William W. Schwarzer. (Illus.). 637p. (Orig.). (C). 1997. pap. text ed. 75.00 (*0-7881-4006-X*) DIANE Pub.

Reference Map of Oceania: The Pacific Islands of Micronesia, Polynesia, Melanesia. James A. Bier. 1995. pap. 7.95 (*0-8248-1687-0*) UH Pr.

Reference Maps of the Island of Hawaii: Hawaii. 5th ed. James A. Bier. 1993. pap. 3.95 (*0-8248-1568-8*) UH Pr.

Reference Maps of the Islands of Hawai'i - Kaua'i. 5th ed. James A. Bier. (Illus.). 1991p. 1995. pap. 2.95 (*0-8248-1711-7*) UH Pr.

Reference Maps of the Islands of Hawai'i - Oahu. 5th ed. James A. Bier. 1996. pap. 3.95 (*0-8248-1844-X*) UH Pr.

Reference Maps of the Islands of Hawaii: Maui. 5th ed. James A. Bier. 1993. pap. 3.95 (*0-8248-1559-9*) UH Pr.

Reference Maps of the Islands of Hawaii: Molokai & Lanai. 3rd ed. James A. Bier. 1990. pap. 2.95 (*0-8248-1326-X*) UH Pr.

Reference Materials. (Basic Academics Ser.: Module 10). (Illus.). 60p. 1982. spiral bd. 19.50 (*0-87683-234-6*) GP Courseware.

Reference Materials. (Principles of Steam Generation Ser.: Module 20). 45p. 1982. spiral bd. 17.50 (*0-87683-270-2*) GP Courseware.

Reference Materials for Environmental Analysis. Ray W. Clement et al. LC 96-22062. 1996. write for info. (*1-56670-102-3*) Lewis Pubs.

Reference Materials of the European Communities: Results of Hemocompatibility Tests. Ed. by W. Lemm. LC 92-30458. 272p. (C). 1992. lib. bdg. 123.50 (*0-7923-2002-6*) Kluwer Ac.

***Reference Method for Broth Dilution Antifungal Susceptibility Testing of Yeasts: Tentative Guideline (1992)** Contrib. by John N. Galgiani. 1995. 75.00 (*1-56238-186-5*, M27-T) Natl Comm Clin Lab Stds.

Reference Methods for Marine Radioactivity Studies - 2. (Technical Reports: No. 169). (Illus.). 240p. 1975. pap. 45.00 (*92-0-125275-7*, IDC169, Pub. by IAEA AU) Bernan Associates.

Reference Model for Frameworks of Software Engineering Environments: Technical Report. 1994. lib. bdg. 250.00 (*0-8490-8581-0*) Gordon Pr.

Reference Model for Frameworks of Software Engineering Environments (SEE) 97p. (Orig.). (C). 1994. pap. text ed. 30.00 (*0-7881-0625-2*) DIANE Pub.

Reference Notebook Set, 3 bks., Set. Don Swenson & Timothy Zurick. 540p. (Orig.). 1995. 19.95 (*1-885863-01-2*) Busn News.

***Reference Point, Mesh Stiffness & Dynamic Behavior of Solid, Semi-Solid & Thin-Rimmed Spur Gears.** J. Brousseau & Claude Gosselin. (1994 Fall Technical Meeting). 1994. pap. text ed. 30.00 (*1-55589-643-X*) AGMA.

Reference Puzzles & Word Games for Grades 7-12. Carol Smallwood. LC 91-52815. 198p. 1991. pap. 24.95 (*0-89950-623-2*) McFarland & Co.

Reference Realist in Library Academia. Patricia Gebhard. LC 96-46874. 198p. 1997. lib. bdg. 34.50 (*0-7864-0237-7*) McFarland & Co.

Reference Service. 3rd rev. ed. Krishan Kumar. x, 431p. (C). 1988. text ed. 35.00 (*0-7069-3765-1*, Pub. by Vikas II) S Asia.

Reference Service. S. R. Ranganathan. 432p. 1990. reprint ed. pap. 18.95 (*81-85273-20-0*, Pub. by Sarada Ranganathan Endowment for Library Science II) Advent Bks Div.

Reference Service: A Perspective. Ed. by Sul H. Lee. LC 83-60917. (Library Management Ser.: No. 6). 140p. 1983. 30.00 (*0-87650-150-1*) Pierian.

Reference Service Expertise. Ed. by Bill Katz. LC 93-23090. (Reference Librarian Ser.: No. 40). (Illus.). 168p. 1993. lib. bdg. 29.95 (*1-56024-460-7*) Haworth Pr.

Reference Service for Publications of Intergovernmental Organizations. Ed. by Alfred Kagan. (IFLA Publication Ser.: Vol. 56). vi, 158p. 1991. 48.00 (*3-598-21785-4*) K G Saur.

Reference Service in the Small Library. Geraldine B. King. LC 85-20083. (LAMA Small Libraries Publications: No. 12). 12p. 1985. pap. 5.00 (*0-8389-3323-8*) ALA.

Reference Services Administration & Management. Ed. by Bill Katz & Ruth A. Fraley. LC 82-1085. (Reference Librarian Ser.: No. 3). 147p. 1982. text ed. 49.95 (*0-86656-164-1*) Haworth Pr.

Reference Services & Library Instruction: A Handbook for Library Management. David F. Kohl. LC 85-13431. (Handbooks for Library Management Ser.). 324p. 1985. lib. bdg. 49.00 (*0-87436-432-9*) ABC-CLIO.

Reference Services & Public Policy. Ed. by Richard D. Irving & Bill Katz. LC 87-35779. (Reference Librarian Ser.: No. 20). (Illus.). 221p. 1988. text ed. 49.95 (*0-86656-742-9*) Haworth Pr.

Reference Services & Technical Services: Interactions in Library Practice. Ed. by Gordon Stevenson & Sally Stevenson. LC 83-22790. (Reference Librarian Ser.: No. 9). 176p. 1984. text ed. 49.95 (*0-86656-174-9*) Haworth Pr.

***Reference Services for Archives & Manuscripts.** Ed. by Laura B. Cohen. LC 96-51733. (Reference Librarian Monograph Ser.: Vol. 26, No. 56). 215p. (C). 1997. 49.95 (*0-7890-0042-3*); pap. text ed. 24.95 (*0-7890-0048-2*) Haworth Pr.

Reference Services for Children & Young Adults. Ed. by Bill Katz & Ruth A. Fraley. LC 83-325. (Reference Librarian Ser.: Nos. 7 & 8). 215p. 1983. text ed. 49.95 (*0-86656-201-X*) Haworth Pr.

Reference Services for Children & Young Adults. Rosemarie Riechel. LC 91-31973. xvi, 219p. (C). 1991. lib. bdg. 36.00 (*0-208-02290-2*, Lib Prof Pubns) Shoe String.

Reference Services for the Unserved. Ed. by Fay Zipkowitz. LC 95-46713. (Reference Librarian Ser.: No. 53). 108p. 1996. text ed. 39.95 (*1-56024-797-5*) Haworth Pr.

Reference Services in Archives. Ed. by Lucille Whalen & Bill Katz. LC 85-17534. (Reference Librarian Ser.: No. 13). 210p. 1986. text ed. 49.95 (*0-86656-521-3*); pap. text ed. 24.95 (*0-86656-522-1*) Haworth Pr.

Reference Services in the Humanities. Ed. & Intro. by Judy Reynolds. LC 94-26131. (Reference Librarian Ser.: No. 47). 161p. 1994. lib. bdg. 49.95 (*1-56024-692-8*) Haworth Pr.

Reference Services in the 1980s. Ed. by Bill Katz. LC 81-20196. (Reference Librarian Ser.: Nos. 1 & 2). 188p. 1982. pap. 39.95 (*0-86656-110-2*) Haworth Pr.

Reference Services Planning in the 90s. Ed. by Gail Z. Eckwright & Lori M. Keenan. LC 93-44336. (Reference Librarian Ser.: No. 43). (Illus.). 222p. 1994. 39.95 (*1-56024-619-7*) Haworth Pr.

Reference Services Today: From Interview to Burnout. Ed. by Bill Katz & Ruth Fraley. LC 86-29481. (Reference Librarian Ser.: No. 16). 312p. 1987. 49.95 (*0-86656-572-8*) Haworth Pr.

***Reference Skills.** Jo E. Moore. (Reading & Writing Ser.). (Illus.). 32p. (J). (gr. 4-6). 1997. teacher ed., pap. 2.95 (*1-55799-418-8*, 4020) Evan-Moor Corp.

Reference Source Guide to Military Aeroplanes 1914-1918. B. E. Kelly. (C). 1992. 135.00 (*0-9519899-0-1*, Pub. by Hikoki Pubns UK) St Mut.

Reference Sourcebook of Colorado. Richard Knowles & Evelyn D. Scott. 200p. 1994. ring bd. 20.00 (*0-931510-53-8*) Hi Willow.

Reference Sources: A Brief Guide. 9th ed. Eleanor A. Swidan. 1988. pap. 7.95 (*0-910556-26-1*) Enoch Pratt.

Reference Sources: An Annotated Bibliography for Institutional Research. Ed. by William R. Fendley, Jr. & Linda T. Seeloff. 116p. (C). 1993. pap. text ed. 9.95 (*1-882393-03-1*) Assn Instl Res.

Reference Sources: 1981. S. Balachandran & M. Balachandran. LC 77-79318. 1982. 75.00 (*0-87650-134-X*) Pierian.

Reference Sources for Small & Medium-Sized Libraries. 5th ed. ALA, Reference & Adult Services Division Ad Hoc Committee. Ed. by Jovian P. Lang. LC 92-10007. 352p. (C). 1992. pap. text ed. 40.00 (*0-8389-3406-4*) ALA.

Reference Sources in English & American Literature: An Annotated Bibliography. Robert C. Schweik & Dieter Riesner. (C). 1977. pap. text ed. 10.95 (*0-393-09104-X*) Norton.

Reference Sources in History: An Introductory Guide. Ronald H. Fritze et al. LC 90-45169. 319p. 1990. lib. bdg. 55.00 (*0-87436-164-8*) ABC-CLIO.

Reference Sources in History: An Introductory Guide. Ronald H. Fritze et al. LC 90-45169. 319p. 1991. pap. text ed. 24.75 (*0-87436-679-8*) ABC-CLIO.

Reference Sources in Science, Engineering, Medicine, & Agriculture. Ed. by H. Robert Malinowsky. LC 94-16133. 368p. 1994. 49.95 (*0-89774-742-9*); pap. 39.95 (*0-89774-745-3*) Oryx Pr.

Reference Sources 1977. Ed. by Linda Mark. LC 77-79318. 1977. 75.00 (*0-87650-084-X*) Pierian.

Reference Sources 1978. Ed. by Linda Mark. LC 77-79318. 1978. 75.00 (*0-87650-096-3*) Pierian.

Reference Sources 1979. Ed. by Linda Mark. LC 77-79318. 1980. 75.00 (*0-87650-117-X*) Pierian.

Reference Sources 1980. Ed. by S. Balachandran & M. Balachandran. LC 77-79318. 1981. 75.00 (*0-87650-127-7*) Pierian.

Reference Sources, 1982. Terry Silver. LC 77-79318. 1984. 75.00 (*0-87650-165-X*) Pierian.

Reference Sources, 1983. Terry Silver. LC 77-79318. 1985. 75.00 (*0-87650-167-6*) Pierian.

Reference Spectra & Energy Levels for Neutral & Singly-Ionized Platinum. 223p. (Orig.). (C). 1992. pap. text ed. 50.00 (*0-941375-73-0*) DIANE Pub.

Reference Supplement for Shinto Bengi Oshigata. Seyssel-Hawley. 1990. pap. 7.50 (*0-910704-70-8*) Hawley.

Reference to Abstract Objects in Discourse. Nicholas Asher. LC 93-14793. (Studies in Linguistics & Philosophy: Vol. 50). 468p. 1993. Alk. paper. lib. bdg. 166.50 (*0-7923-2242-8*, Pub. by Klwr Acad Pubs NE) Kluwer Ac.

Reference to the Present. Ilija Poplasen. 241p. 1982. 20.00 (*0-935352-11-2*) MIR PA.

Reference Tools for Fine Arts Visual Resources Collections. Ed. by Christine Bunting. (Occasional Papers: 4). 56p. 1984. pap. 12.00 (*0-942740-02-5*) Art Libs Soc.

Reference Training in Academic Libraries. Association of College & Research Libraries. LC 96-20726. (CLIP Note Ser.: No. 24). 180p. 1996. 31.95 (*0-8389-7842-8*) Assn Coll & Res Libs.

Reference Update 80: Selected Recent Works in the Social Sciences. Ed. by Kathy Jursik & Grace Waibel. (CPL Bibliographies Ser.: No. 50). 69p. 1981. 10.00 (*0-86602-050-0*, Sage Prdcls Pr) Sage.

Reference Values in Human Chemistry: Proceedings of the 2nd Symposium of the Internal Colloquium on Automatisation & Prospective Biology Pont-a-Mousson, Oct, 1972. International Colloquium, Automatisation & Prospective Biology Symposium Staff. Ed. by G. Siest. 1973. 103.25 (*3-8055-1622-3*) S Karger.

Reference Values in Laboratory Medicine: The Current State of the Art. Ed. by R. Grasbeck & T. Alstrom. LC 80-42312. (Wiley-Interscience Publications). (Illus.). 427p. reprint ed. pap. 121.70 (*0-8357-8636-6*, 2035060) Bks Demand.

Reference Wales. John May. 300p. 1994. pap. 19.95 (*0-7083-1234-9*, Pub. by Univ Wales Pr UK) Paul & Co Pubs.

Reference Work in School Library Media Centers: A Book of Case Studies. Amy G. Job & MaryKay W. Schnare. LC 95-42554. 136p. 1996. pap. text ed. 18.50 (*0-8108-3098-1*) Scarecrow.

Reference Work in School Library Media Centers: A Book of Case Studies. Amy G. Job & MaryKay W. Schnare. 136p. 1996. text ed. 39.50 (*0-8108-3145-7*) Scarecrow.

Reference Work in the Humanities. Edmund F. Santa-Vicca. LC 80-18783. 173p. 1980. 20.00 (*0-8108-1342-4*) Scarecrow.

Reference Works for Theological Research: An Annotated Selective Bibliographical Guide. 3rd ed. Robert J. Kepple & John J. Muether. 264p. (C). 1992. pap. text ed. 27.50 (*0-8191-8565-5*); lib. bdg. 54.50 (*0-8191-8564-7*) U Pr of Amer.

Reference Works in British & American Literature, Vol. 1: English & American Literature. James K. Bracken. Ed. by James Rettig. (Reference Sources in the Humanities Ser.). xii, 252p. 1990. lib. bdg. 45.00 (*0-87287-699-3*) Libs Unl.

Reference Works in British & American Literature, Vol. 2: English & American Writers. James K. Bracken. Ed. by James Rettig. (Reference Sources in the Humanities Ser.). xxiv, 310p. 1991. lib. bdg. 55.00 (*0-87287-700-0*) Libs Unl.

Referenced Index Guide to the Warren Commission. Walt Brown. 304p. 1995. 30.00 (*1-887934-00-6*) Delmax.

References & Conference Proceedings Toward the Understanding of Fracture Mechanics. Ed. by Pir M. Toor & C. Michael Hudson. LC 85-26713. (ASTM Data Series Publication). (Illus.). 54p. 1985. text ed. 12.00 (*0-8031-0466-9*, 05-063000-30) ASTM.

References & Indexes, 1951-1960 see International Bibliography of Studies on Alcohol

***References en Biologie Clinique.** G. Henry Siest & F. Schiele. 680p. 1990. pap. 140.00 (*2-906077-16-X*) Elsevier.

References in Biology: A Selected Topical Bibliography. rev. ed. Illus. by Antonino DeSalvo. 287p. (YA). (gr. 9 up). 1994. reprint ed. student ed., ring bd. 25.00 (*0-916209-07-5*) Owlet Pubns.

References on Fatigue, 1965-1966 - STP 9P. 1968. 11.00 incl. fiche (*0-8031-0132-5*, 04-009160-30) ASTM.

References, Subvol. G see Crystal & Solid State Physics: Group III

References, 1901-1950 see International Bibliography of Studies on Alcohol

***Referencias Biblicas Consejero.** John G. Kruis. (SPA.). 1.50 (*0-8297-1835-4*) Life Pubs Intl.

Referendum: Direct Democracy in Switzerland. Kris W. Kobach. (Illus.). 282p. 1993. 59.95 (*1-85521-397-4*, Pub. by Dartmth Pub UK) Ashgate Pub Co.

Referendum Device: A Conference. Ed. by Austin Ranney. LC 80-25657. (AEI Symposia Ser.: No. 80G). 208p. reprint ed. pap. 59.30 (*0-7837-1085-2*, 2041617) Bks Demand.

Referendum Experience in Europe. Michael Gallagher & Pier V. Uleri. 256p. 1996. text ed. 69.95 (*0-312-16164-6*) St Martin.

Referendum Experience, Scotland 1979. Ed. by J. M. Bochel et al. (Illus.). 224p. 1981. text ed. 26.00 (*0-08-025734-8*, R120, Pergamon Pr) Elsevier.

Referendum in America. Ellis P. Oberholtzer. LC 71-119939. (Select Bibliographies Reprint Ser.). 1977. reprint ed. 20.95 (*0-8369-5382-7*) Ayer.

Referendum in America. Ellis P. Oberholtzer. LC 70-153370. (American Constitutional & Legal History Ser). 1971. reprint ed. lib. bdg. 59.50 (*0-306-70149-9*) Da Capo.

Referendum Machine: A Prescription for Democratic Government in the 21st Century. Paul Thomas. Ed. by Sunie B. Clark. (Illus.). 180p. 1993. pap. 8.95 (*0-9631345-1-5*) Regal Direct.

Referendum Voting: Social Status & Policy Preferences. Harlan Hahn & Sheldon Kamieniecki. LC 87-8419. (Contributions in Political Science Ser.: No. 190). 184p. 1987. text ed. 45.00 (*0-313-25611-X*, KRM/, Greenwood Pr) Greenwood.

Referendums Around the World: The Growing Use of Direct Democracy. Ed. by David Butler & Austin Ranney. LC 94-13296. 318p. 1994. pap. 19.95 (*0-8447-3853-0*) Am Enterprise.

Referential Communication: Barrier Activities for Speakers & Listeners, 2 pts., Pt. I. Nancy L. McKinley & Linda Schwartz. 100p. (Orig.). (J). (gr. k-8). 1985. pap. text ed. 89.00 (*0-930599-00-4*) Thinking Pubns.

Referential Communication: Barrier Activities for Speakers & Listeners, 2 pts., Pt. II. Nancy L. McKinley & Linda Schwartz. 100p. (Orig.). (YA). (gr. 5 up). 1985. 89.00 (*0-930599-01-2*) Thinking Pubns.

***Referential Communication Tasks.** George Yule. LC 96-52269. (Second Language Acquisition Research Series: Theoretical & Methodical Issues). 128p. 1997. 36.00 (*0-8058-2003-5*); pap. 17.50 (*0-8058-2004-3*) L Erlbaum Assocs.

Referential Practice: Language & Lived Space among the Maya. William F. Hanks. LC 90-32169. (Illus.). 616p. 1990. pap. text ed. 33.00 (*0-226-31546-0*) U Ch Pr.

Referential Practice: Language & Lived Space among the Maya. William F. Hanks. LC 90-32169. (Illus.). 616p. 1990. lib. bdg. 78.00 (*0-226-31545-2*) U Ch Pr.

Referentially Oriented Cerebral MRI Anatomy. J. Talairach & P. Tournoux. (Illus.). 268p. 1993. text ed. 225.00 (*0-86577-488-9*) Thieme Med Pubs.

Referral Instructor Manual. Robert A. Clark. 90p. 1991. pap. text ed. 40.00 (*0-943717-96-5*) Concept Sys.

***Referral Instructor Manual.** rev. ed. Robert Clark. 60p. 1996. pap. text ed. write for info. (*1-880229-34-X*) Concept Sys.

***Referral Instructor Seminar Outline.** 32p. 1996. pap. text ed. write for info. (*1-880229-28-5*) Concept Sys.

Referral Process in Libraries: A Characterization & an Exploration of Related Factors. George S. Hawley. LC 87-9201. 196p. 1987. 25.00 (*0-8108-2010-2*) Scarecrow.

***Referred Pain Zones of the Muscles of the Human Body.** (Illus.). 12p. 1995. wbk. ed., spiral bd. 9.95 (*0-9655679-0-7*) BodyGuide.

***Referring to Space: Studies in Austronesian & Papual Languages.** Ed. by Gunter Senft. LC 97-10037. (Oxford Studies in Anthropological Linguistics: No. 11). (Illus.). 384p. 1997. 85.00 (*0-19-823647-6*) OUP.

***Refighting the Last War.** D. Clayton James & Anne S. Wells. 282p. 4.98 (*0-8317-9101-2*) Smithmark.

Refighting the Last War: Command & Crisis in Korea, 1950-1953. D. Clayton James & Anne S. Wells. 290p. 1992. 29.95 (*0-02-916001-4*, Free Press) Free Pr.

Refiguring America: A Study of William Carlos Williams' In the American Grain. Bryce Conrad. 192p. 1990. text ed. 29.95 (*0-252-01704-8*) U of Ill Pr.

***Refiguring American Film Genres: History & Theory.** Nick Browne. 1997. pap. text ed. 19.95 (*0-520-20731-9*) U CA Pr.

Refiguring Anthropology: First Principles of Probability & Statistics. David H. Thomas. (Illus.). 532p. (C). 1986. reprint ed. text ed. 26.95 (*0-88133-223-2*) Waveland Pr.

Refiguring Authority: Reading, Writing & Rewriting in Cervantes. E. Michael Gerli. LC 95-16577. 152p. 1996. 22.95 (*0-8131-1922-7*) U Pr of Ky.

***Refiguring Chaucer in the Renaissance.** Theresa M. Krier. LC 97-8740. 1998. write for info. (*0-8130-1552-9*) U Press Fla.

Refiguring La Fontaine: Tercentenary Studies. Ed. by Anne L. Birberick. LC 95-33255. (EMF Monographs). 242p. 1996. lib. bdg. 39.95 (*1-886365-00-8*) Rookwood Pr.

Refiguring Life: Metaphors of Twentieth-Century Biology. Evelyn F. Keller. LC 94-44222. (Wellek Lectures). (Illus.). 144p. 1995. 20.00 (*0-231-10204-6*) Col U Pr.

Refiguring Life: Metaphors of Twentieth-Century Biology. Evelyn F. Keller. 160p. 1996. pap. 15.50 (*0-231-10205-4*) Col U Pr.

Refiguring Modernism. Bonnie K. Scott. LC 95-3579. 320p. 1995. 39.95 (*0-253-32936-1*); pap. 18.95 (*0-253-20995-1*) Ind U Pr.

Refiguring Modernism Vol. 2: Postmodern Feminist Readings of Woolf, West, & Barnes. Bonnie Kime & Bonnie K. Scott. 192p. 1995. pap. text ed. 15.95 (*0-253-21002-X*) Ind U Pr.

Refiguring Modernism Vol. 2: Postmodern Feminist Readings of Woolf, West, & Barnes. Bonnie Kime & Scott. LC 95-3579. 192p. 1995. 34.95 (*0-253-32937-X*) Ind U Pr.

***Refiguring Revolutions: Aesthetics & Politics from the English Revolution to the Romantic Revolution.** Kevin Sharpe & Steven N. Zwicker. LC 97-24626. 1998. write for info. (*0-520-20919-2*); pap. write for info. (*0-520-20920-6*) U CA Pr.

R

An Asterisk (*) at the beginning of an entry indicates that the title is appearing in BIP for the first time.

R

Refiguring Self & Psychology. Kenneth J. Gergen. (Benchmark Ser.). 288p. 1993. 59.95 (*1-85521-369-9*, Pub. by Dartmth Pub UK) Ashgate Pub Co.

***Refiguring Spain: Cinema/Media/Representation.** Marsha Kinder. LC 96-39967. (Illus.). 352p. 1997. pap. text ed. 16.95 (*0-8223-1938-1*); lib. bdg. 49.95 (*0-8223-1932-2*) Duke.

Refiguring the Father: New Feminist Readings of Patriarchy. Ed. by Patricia Yaeger & Beth Kowaleski-Wallace. LC 89-6118. 344p. (C). 1989. 34.95 (*0-8093-1529-7*) S Ill U Pr.

Refiguring the Hero: From Peasant to Novel in Lope De Vega & Calderon. Dian Fox. 256p. 1991. 32.50 (*0-271-00737-0*) Pa St U Pr.

Refiguring the Post Classical City: Dura Europos, Jerash, Jerusalem & Ravenna. Annabel J. Wharton. LC 94-44727. (Illus.). 400p. (C). 1996. text ed. 85.00 (*0-521-48185-6*) Cambridge U Pr.

Refiguring the Real: Picture & Modernity in Word & Image, 1400-1700. Christopher Braider. (Illus.). 312p. 1992. text ed. 47.50 (*0-691-06957-3*) Princeton U Pr.

Refiguring Woman: Perspectives on Gender & the Italian Renaissance. Ed. by Marilyn Migiel & Juliana Schiesari. LC 90-55736. 304p. 1991. 39.95 (*0-8014-2538-7*); pap. 15.95 (*0-8014-9771-X*) Cornell U Pr.

Refilling the Jars. Neil Rhodes & Noline Rhodes. 182p. 1996. pap. text ed. 9.99 (*1-884369-31-6*, EBED Pubns) McDougal Pubng.

Refinding the Object & Reclaiming the Self. David E. Scharff. LC 91-45267. 384p. 1992. 50.00 (*0-87668-458-4*) Aronson.

Refined by Fire. Gordon Ferguson. 1996. pap. 20.99 incl. audio (*1-57782-018-5*) Discipleshp.

Refined by Fire: A Study Guide to the Letters of First & Second Peter. Gordon Ferguson. 36p. 1993. wbk. ed., pap. 4.99 (*1-884553-14-1*) Discipleshp.

***Refined by Fire: The Evolution of Straight Chiropractic.** Joseph B. Strauss. (Illus.). 315p. 1994. text ed. 30.00 (*1-890419-06-0*) Fnd Chiropractic Educ.

Refined Iterative Methods for Computation of the Solution & the Eigenvalues of Self-Adjoint Boundary Value Problems. M. Engeli et al. (MIM Ser.: No. 8). (Illus.). 108p. 1980. 26.00 (*0-8176-0098-1*) Birkhauser.

***Refined Large Deviation Limit Theorems.** V. Vinogradov. 1994. pap. 46.95 (*0-582-25499-X*, Pub. by Longman UK) Longman.

Refined Large Deviation Limit Theorems. Vladimir Vinogradov. LC 94-3325. (Pitman Research Notes in Mathematics Ser.). 1994. write for info. (*0-615-00148-3*) Longman.

Refined Petroleum Solvents. 1995. lib. bdg. 252.75 (*0-8490-6683-2*) Gordon Pr.

Refinement & Reduction in Animal Testing. Steven M. Niemi. LC 93-84516. 138p. 1993. pap. 25.00 (*0-614-06559-3*) Scientists Ctr.

Refinement of America: Persons, Houses, Cities. Richard L. Bushman. LC 93-13118. 1993. reprint ed. pap. 18.00 (*0-679-74414-2*, Vin) Random.

Refinement of Character. Ali Miskawayh. Tr. by Constantine Zurayk. 1977. pap. 14.00 (*0-8156-6051-0*, Am U Beirut) Syracuse U Pr.

***Refinement of Production: Ecological Modernization Theory & the Chemical Industry.** Arthur P. Mol. 452p. (Orig.). 1996. pap. 49.00 (*90-6224-979-5*, Pub. by Uitgeverij Arkel NE) LPC InBook.

Refinement Workshop, Third: Organised by the Programming Research Group, Oxford & IBM UK Laboratories, Hursley Park, 9-11 January 1990. Ed. by Carroll Morgan & J. C. Woodcock. (Workshops in Computing Ser.). viii, 199p. 1991. pap. 40.00 (*0-387-19624-2*) Spr-Verlag.

Refiner's Fire. Mark Helprin. 1990. pap. 14.00 (*0-15-676240-4*) HarBrace.

Refiners Fire. Sigrid R. McPherson. 1995. pap. 18.00 (*0-919123-54-6*, Pub. by Inner City CN) BookWorld Dist.

Refiner's Fire: Living Holy in a World of Compromise. Rod Parsley. 78p. (Orig.). 1992. pap. 5.95 (*0-89274-903-2*) Christian Pub.

Refiner's Fire: The Making of Mormon Cosmology, 1644-1844. John L. Brooke. LC 93-37366. (Illus.). 432p. (C). 1994. text ed. 39.95 (*0-521-34545-6*) Cambridge U Pr.

Refiner's Fire: The Making of Mormon Cosmology, 1644-1844. John L. Brooke. (Illus.). 443p. 1996. pap. text ed. 16.95 (*0-521-56564-2*) Cambridge U Pr.

Refinery. Claudia Keelan. LC 94-70383. (CSU Poetry Ser.: No. XLIII). 59p. (Orig.). 1994. pap. 10.00 (*1-880834-08-1*) Cleveland St Univ Poetry Ctr.

Refinery-Petrochemical Plant Construction & Maintenance, Plant Operation & Control, Noise & Pollution Control in Refiner-Petrochemical Plants: A Workbook for Engineers: Presented at 38th Petroleum Mechanical Engineering Workshop & Conference, September 12-14, 1982, Philadelphia, Pennsylvania. Petroleum Mechanical Engineering Workshop & Conference Staff. Ed. by J. E. Reagan. LC 82-228729. (Illus.). 154p. reprint ed. pap. 43.90 (*0-8357-2845-5*, 2039080) Bks Demand.

Refinery Safety: Benefit, Not Burden. (Illus.). 141p. (Orig.). 1991. pap. 12.50 (*0-89215-166-8*) U Cal LA Indus Rel.

Refining & Reformulation: The Challenge of Green Motor Fuels. Adam Seymour. 95p. 1992. 29.95 (*0-948061-68-5*) PennWell Bks.

Refining Composition Skills. 4th ed. Smalley. (College ESL Ser.). 1995. teacher ed., pap. 7.95 (*0-8384-5211-6*) Heinle & Heinle.

Refining Composition Skills: Rhetoric & Grammar for ESL Students. 4th ed. Regina L. Smalley & Mary K. Ruetten. LC 94-41330. 500p. 1995. pap. 26.95 (*0-8384-5210-8*) Heinle & Heinle.

Refining Fire. Stephen Cheung. Tr. by Billy S. Ching. 154p. (CHI.). 1993. pap. 8.00 (*1-882840-02-X*) Comm Christian.

***Refining Fire.** W. E. Davis. LC 96-48569. (Valley of the Peacemaker Ser.: 3). 352p. (Orig.). 1997. pap. 10.99 (*0-89107-936-X*) Crossway Bks.

Refining Fire: Herakles & Other Heroes in T. S. Eliot's Works. De Abruno L. Niesen. (American University Studies: English Language & Literature: Ser. IV, Vol. 62). 188p. (C). 1988. text ed. 35.95 (*0-8204-0550-7*) P Lang Pubng.

Refining of Synthetic Crudes. Ed. by Martin L. Gorbaty & Brian M. Harney. LC 79-21098. (Advances in Chemistry Ser.: No. 179). 1979. 43.95 (*0-8412-0456-X*) Am Chemical.

***Refining of Synthetic Crudes.** Ed. by Martin L. Gorbaty & Brian M. Harney. LC 79-21098. (Advances in Chemistry Ser.: Vol. 179). 224p. 1979. reprint ed. pap. 63.90 (*0-608-03852-0*, 2064299) Bks Demand.

Refining Precious Metal Wastes. C. M. Hoke. 29.95 (*0-931913-22-5*) Met-Chem Rsch.

Refining Statistics Sourcebook. 400p. 1994. 245.00 (*0-318-72986-5*) PennWell Bks.

Refinishing & Finishing Wood. Cy DeCosse Incorporated Staff. LC 94-30079. (Black & Decker Home Improvement Library). (Illus.). 128p. 1994. 16.95 (*0-86573-739-8*); pap. 14.95 (*0-86573-740-1*) Cowles Creative.

Refinishing & Restoring Your Piano. Peg Kehret. (Illus.). 128p. 1985. 16.95 (*0-8306-0871-0*, 1871); pap. 9.95 (*0-8306-1871-6*, 1871P) McGraw-Hill Prof.

Refinishing Old Furniture. E. Wagner & George. 1991. pap. text ed. 14.95 (*0-07-157512-X*) McGraw.

Refinishing Old Furniture. E. George Wagoner. (Illus.). 208p. 1991. pap. 13.95 (*0-8306-3496-7*) McGraw-Hill Prof.

Refinishing Old Furniture. E. George Wagoner. (Illus.). 208p. 1991. 19.95 (*0-8306-7496-9*, 3496) TAB Bks.

Refirnation. Wilson & Armesto. 1996. 50.00 (*0-385-25624-8*) Doubleday.

Reflation & Austerity: Economic Policy under Mitterand. Pierre-Alain Muet & Alain Fonteneau. Tr. by Malcolm Slater. LC 89-28948. 335p. 1991. 19.95 (*0-85496-644-7*) Berg Pubs.

Reflect: Yesterday, Today, & Tomorrow. Ronald Raleigh. (Orig.). 1996. pap. write for info. (*1-57553-108-9*) Watermrk Pr.

Reflected Glory: An Account of a British Soldier in Northern Ireland. Carney Lake. 240p. 1994. 39.50 (*0-85052-366-4*, Pub. by L Cooper Bks UK) Trans-Atl Phila.

Reflected Glory: The Life of Pamela Churchill Harriman. Sally B. Smith. LC 96-28681. (Illus.). 560p. 1996. 30.00 (*0-684-80950-8*) S&S Trade.

***Reflected Glory: The Life of Pamela Churchill Harriman.** Sally B. Smith. 1997. pap. 16.00 (*0-684-83563-0*, Touchstone Bks) S&S Trade.

***Reflected in Water: A Crisis in Social Responsibility.** Colin Ward. LC 96-35189. (Global Issues Ser.). 1996. write for info. (*0-304-33567-3*); pap. write for info. (*0-304-33568-1*) Cassell.

Reflected Light: A Century of Photography in Chester County. Pamela C. Powell. (Illus.). 80p. 1988. 30.25 (*0-929706-01-3*); pap. 24.25 (*0-929706-02-1*) Chester Co Hist Soc.

Reflected Truth: Former Workers & Followers Unmask Life in a Large, Little-Known Sect. Joan F. Daniel et al. LC 96-67803. 450p. (Orig.). 1996. pap. 10.45 (*0-9639419-3-3*) Res Info Servs.

Reflecting a Prairie Town: A Year in Peterson. Drake Hokanson. LC 94-6369. (American Land & Life Ser.). (Illus.). 344p. 1994. 34.95 (*0-87745-466-3*) U of Iowa Pr.

Reflecting Black: African-American Cultural Criticism. Michael E. Dyson. (American Culture Ser.: Vol. 9). 352p. (C). 1993. pap. 19.95 (*0-8166-2143-8*) U of Minn Pr.

***Reflecting Children's Lives: A Handbook for Planning Child-Centered Curriculum.** Deb Curtis & Margie Carter. LC 96-41080. (Illus.). 192p. (Orig.). 1996. pap. 21.95 (*1-884834-27-2*, 3043) Redleaf Pr.

Reflecting Christ. Ellen G. White. Ed. by Raymond H. Woolsey. (Daily Devotional Ser.). 384p. 1985. 10.99 (*0-8280-0305-X*) Review & Herald.

Reflecting Davidson: Donald Davidson Responding to an International Forum of Philosophers. Ed. by Ralf Stoecker. LC 93-37480. (Foundations of Communication & Cognition Ser.). x, 393p. 1993. lib. bdg. 98.95 (*3-11-013180-3*) De Gruyter.

Reflecting His Image. Curt Nordhielm. LC 90-80689. 160p. (Orig.). (C). 1990. pap. 5.99 (*0-89900-357-5*) College Pr Pub.

Reflecting His Image: Discovering Your Worth in Christ from A to Z. Liz C. Higgs. 119p. 1996. pap. 12.99 (*0-8407-6335-2*) Nelson.

Reflecting His Image: Leader's Guide. Curt Nordhielm. 32p. (Orig.). 1991. pap. text ed. 2.99 (*0-89900-365-6*) College Pr Pub.

***Reflecting on a History of Developmental Research.** Ed. by Barbara Rogoff. (Journal: No. 40). (Illus.). 68p. 1997. pap. 21.75 (*3-8055-6517-8*) S Karger.

Reflecting on Anna Karenina. Mary Evans. (Heroines? Ser.). 96p. 1989. pap. 9.95 (*0-415-01719-X*) Routledge.

Reflecting on Art. John A. Fisher. LC 91-44294. 428p. (C). 1993. text ed. 51.95 (*0-87484-821-0*, 821) Mayfield Pub.

Reflecting on Jane Eyre. Pat Macpherson. (Heroines? Ser.). 96p. (C). 1989. pap. text ed. 9.95 (*0-415-01787-4*) Routledge.

Reflecting on Miss Marple. Marion Shaw & Sabine Vanacker. (Heroines? Ser.). 128p. (C). 1991. pap. 17.95 (*0-415-01794-7*, A1615) Routledge.

Reflecting on Nature: Readings in Environmental Philosophy. Lori Gruen & Dale Jamieson. 384p. (C). 1994. pap. text ed. 26.95 (*0-19-508290-7*, 569) OUP.

***Reflecting on Our Work: NSF Teacher Enhancement in K-6 Mathematics.** Susan N. Friel & George W. Bright. LC 96-39396. 286p. 1997. 54.00 (*0-7618-0633-4*); pap. write for info. (*0-7618-0634-2*) U Pr of Amer.

Reflecting on Proficiency from the Classroom Perspective. Ed. by June K. Phillips. (Reports of the Northeast Conference on the Teaching of Foreign Languages). 222p. 1993. pap. 12.95 (*0-8442-9271-0*) NE Conf Teach Foreign.

Reflecting on Research Practice: Issues in Health & Social Welfare. Ed. by Pam Shakespeare et al. LC 93-1683. 160p. (C). 1993. 90.00 (*0-335-19039-1*, Open Univ Pr); pap. 27.50 (*0-335-19038-3*, Open Univ Pr) Taylor & Francis.

Reflecting on The Bell Jar. Pat Macpherson. (Heroines? Ser.). 128p. (C). 1991. pap. text ed. 13.95 (*0-415-04393-X*, A5733) Routledge.

Reflecting on the Past, Envisioning the Future. (Conference Proceedings Ser.). 172p. 1994. 20.00 (*1-882147-24-3*) Am Art Therapy.

Reflecting on the Well of Loneliness: Stephen Gordon, A Lesbian's Heroine? Rebecca O'Rourke. (Heroines? Ser.). 96p. 1989. pap. 9.95 (*0-415-01841-2*) Routledge.

Reflecting on Things Past. Peter L. Carrington. 1989. write for info. (*0-318-64757-5*) HM.

Reflecting Pond. Liane Cordes. 1985. pap. 9.00 (*0-89486-121-2*, 1068A) Hazelden.

Reflecting Reality: Toys, Lamps & Lanterns from the New York City Fire Museum. Barbara Hayward. (Illus.). 60p. (Orig.). 1995. pap. 12.95 (*0-9647413-0-X*) NY City Fire Mus.

Reflecting Senses: Perception & Appearance in Literature, Culture & the Arts. Ed. by Walter Pape & Frederick Burwick. LC 94-37129. 375p. (C). 1995. lib. bdg. 190.00 (*3-11-014580-4*) De Gruyter.

Reflecting Team: Dialogues & Dialogues about the Dialogues. Ed. by Tom Andersen. 192p. 1991. 22.95 (*0-393-70120-4*) Norton.

Reflecting Team in Action: Collaborative Practice in Family Therapy. Ed. by Steven Friedman. LC 95-14307. (Family Therapy Ser.). 1995. lib. bdg. 36.95 (*1-57230-003-5*) Guilford Pr.

Reflecting Telescope Optics 1: Basic Design Theory & Its Historical Development, Vol. 1. R. N. Wilson. LC 96-5556. (Astronomy & Astrophysics Library). (Illus.). xiv, 573p. 1996. 98.50 (*3-540-58964-3*) Spr-Verlag.

Reflecting What Light We Can't Absorb. Laura Fargas. 32p. (Orig.). 1993. pap. 9.00 (*0-936600-08-X*) Riverstone Foothills.

Reflecting with Solomon: Selected Studies on the Book of Ecclesiastes. Ed. by Roy B. Zuck. LC 94-1703. 432p. (Orig.). (C). 1994. pap. 22.99 (*0-8010-9939-0*) Baker Bks.

Reflection. Diane Chamberlain. 384p. 1996. 24.00 (*0-06-017652-0*) HarpC.

***Reflection.** Diane Chamberlain. 368p. 1997. mass mkt. 5.99 (*0-06-109396-3*, Harp PBks) HarpC.

Reflection. Willie G. Corbett. LC 95-61088. 165p. 1996. 9.95 (*1-55523-751-7*) Winston-Derek.

Reflection. Dennis Merritt. LC 92-71914. (Illus.). 114p. (Orig.). 1993. pap. 9.95 (*1-881674-00-2*) Amziod.

Reflection. Andrew Neiderman. 384p. (Orig.). 1986. mass mkt. 3.50 (*0-373-97027-7*, Wrldwide Lib) Harlequin Bks.

Reflection. large type ed. Diane Chamberlain. 586p. 1996. lib. bdg. 24.95 (*0-7838-1836-X*, GK Hall) Thorndike Pr.

Reflection: An Exhibition of Original Paintings by Shlomo Schwartz. Aviv International Fine Art Gallery Staff. (Illus.). 40p. (Orig.). 1989. pap. 15.00 (*0-940429-07-1*) M B Glass Assocs.

Reflection & Action. Nathan Rotenstreich. (Phaenomenologica Ser.: No. 97). 222p. 1984. lib. bdg. 112.00 (*90-247-2969-6*, Pub. by M Nijhoff NE) Kluwer Ac.

Reflection & Action. Nathan Rotenstreich. (Phaenomenologica Ser.: No. 97). 222p. 1988. pap. text ed. 49.00 (*90-247-3128-3*, Pub. by M Nijhoff NE) Kluwer Ac.

Reflection & Action: Essays on the Bildungsroman. Ed. by James N. Hardin. 531p. 1991. text ed. 49.95 (*0-87249-792-5*) U of SC Pr.

Reflection & Beyond. Blass. 1993. pap. 21.95 (*0-8384-2305-1*) Heinle & Heinle.

Reflection & Beyond. Blass. 1993. teacher ed., pap. 9.95 (*0-8384-4248-X*); student ed. 22.95 incl. audio (*0-8384-4136-X*) Heinle & Heinle.

Reflection & Controversy: Essays on Social Work. Ann Hartman. 192p. 1994. lib. bdg. 20.95 (*0-87101-233-2*) Natl Assn Soc Wkrs.

Reflection & Doubt in the Thought of Paul Tillich. Robert P. Scharlemann. LC 79-81430. 240p. reprint ed. 68.40 (*0-8357-9481-4*, 2013185) Bks Demand.

***Reflection & Remembrance: An Anthology of "Notes from FEE"** Hans F. Sennholz. LC 97-67127. 264p. 1997. pap. 14.95 (*1-57246-066-0*) Foun Econ Ed.

Reflection Electron Microscopy & Spectroscopy for Surface Analysis. Zhong Lin Wang. (Illus.). 346p. 1996. text ed. 95.00 (*0-521-48266-6*) Cambridge U Pr.

Reflection Groups & Coxeter Groups. J. E. Humphreys. (Studies in Advanced Mathematics: No. 29). (Illus.). 216p. (C). 1992. pap. text ed. 28.95 (*0-521-43613-3*) Cambridge U Pr.

Reflection Guide on Human Sexuality & the Ordained Priesthood. 72p. 1983. pap. 3.95 (*1-55586-865-7*) US Catholic.

Reflection High-Energy Electron Diffraction & Reflection Electron Imaging of Surfaces. Ed. by P. K. Larsen & P. J. Dobson. LC 88-28843. (NATO ASI Series B, Physics: Vol. 188). (Illus.). 556p. 1988. 135.00 (*0-306-43035-5*, Plenum Pr) Plenum.

Reflection in a Madman's Mirror. John P. Feeney. LC 82-90264. 51p. (Orig.). 1982. 5.50 (*0-9608508-0-5*); pap. 3.25 (*0-9608508-1-3*) Gravesend Pr.

Reflection-in Action. Ed. by W. John Smyth. 118p. (C). 1986. 48.00 (*0-7300-0418-X*, Pub. by Deakin Univ AT) St Mut.

Reflection in Teacher Education. Ed. by Peter P. Grimmett & Gaalen L. Erickson. 224p. (C). 1988. text ed. 31.00 (*0-8077-2949-3*) Tchrs Coll.

***Reflection of Evil.** Brett Bartholomaus. 155p. (Orig.). 1997. mass mkt. 4.99 (*1-55197-867-9*, Pub. by Comnwlth Pub CN) Partners Pubs Grp.

Reflection of Humanity. 2nd ed. Ali Shariati. Tr. by Fathollah Marjani from PER. 37p. 1984. pap. 3.00 (*0-941722-11-2*) Book Dist Ctr.

Reflection on Courtship & Marriage. Benjamin Franklin. (Notable American Authors Ser.). 1992. reprint ed. lib. bdg. 75.00 (*0-7812-2886-7*) Rprt Serv.

***Reflection on Jewish American Writings.** D. Venkateswarlu. 160p. 1996. 35.00 (*81-85427-65-8*, Pub. by Sussex Acad Pr UK) Intl Spec Bk.

Reflection on the Holocaust. Irene G. Shur & Franklin H. Littell. Ed. by Richard D. Lambert. LC 80-66618. (Annals of the American Academy of Political & Social Science Ser.: No. 450). 272p. 1980. pap. text ed. 18.00 (*0-87761-253-6*) Am Acad Pol Soc Sci.

Reflection on the Relationship Between Seminary & Vocation Personnel. Bishops' Committee on Vocations Staff & National Conference of Catholic Bishops Staff. 78p. (Orig.). 1988. pap. 8.95 (*1-55586-248-9*) US Catholic.

Reflection on the Study of the Law. Richard W. Bridgman. xiv, 143p. 1996. reprint ed. lib. bdg. 35.00 (*0-8377-1980-1*) Rothman.

Reflection, Recollection & Change: The Nevada State Board of Medical Examiners. Anita E. Watson. 124p. 1996. lib. bdg. 32.00 (*1-56475-370-0*) U NV Oral Hist.

Reflection Seismology: A Tool for Energy Resource Exploration. 3rd ed. Kenneth H. Waters. LC 91-46427. 554p. (C). 1992. reprint ed. lib. bdg. 74.50 (*0-89464-712-1*) Krieger.

Reflection Supports Inspiration. Nancy Brady. 77p. (Orig.). 1995. pap. text ed. 9.95 (*1-887863-00-1*) To Sense Greetings.

Reflection Through Interaction: The Classroom Experience of Pupils with Learning Difficulties. Judith Watson. 200p. 1996. 69.95 (*0-7507-0562-0*, Falmer Pr); pap. 24.95 (*0-7507-0563-9*, Falmer Pr) Taylor & Francis.

Reflections. Steve Allen. LC 94-11257. 326p. (Orig.). (C). 1994. 24.95 (*0-87975-904-6*) Prometheus Bks.

Reflections. Foster Bailey. 1979. pap. 10.00 (*0-85330-134-4*) Lucis.

***Reflections.** John C. Banker, Jr. (Orig.). 1996. pap. write for info. (*1-57553-378-2*) Watermrk Pr.

Reflections. Judith A. Berges. Tr. by Hans-Martin Schreiber. (Illus.). (Orig.). (ENG & GER.). 1993. pap. 18.95 (*0-685-75403-0*) Berges Tours.

Reflections. Judith A. Berges. Tr. by Hans-Martin Schreiber from GER. (Illus.). (Orig.). 1993. pap. 18.95 (*0-9637411-0-1*) Berges Tours.

Reflections. Jeanne M. Blanchette. LC 88-83847. (Illus.). 84p. (Orig.). 1989. pap. 8.95 (*0-9620908-1-6*) Kokoro Enter.

Reflections. Ed. by Mary G. Brown. 154p. 1988. pap. 25.00 (*0-09-173185-2*) Dufour.

Reflections. Barbara R. Clark et al. Ed. by Ruby Davis et al. 72p. (Orig.). (J). (gr. 4-12). 1982. pap. 4.95 (*0-686-37922-5*) Williams SC.

***Reflections.** Eileen C. Coscia. (Orig.). 1997. pap. write for info. (*1-57553-359-6*) Watermrk Pr.

Reflections. Carol E. Doering. (Illus.). 136p. 1996. pap. 12.95 (*0-9652754-0-X*) R A D Works.

Reflections. David Dooley. (Illus.). 104p. Date not set. write for info. (*1-878044-15-X*) Mayhaven Pub.

Reflections. Dave Fisher. (Reflections in the Stocktank Ser.: Vol. 2). 24p. 1994. pap. 2.95 (*1-885766-12-2*) Brand Cross.

Reflections. Helen Frankenthaler. (Illus.). 1995. pap. 10.00 (*0-614-13070-0*) Tyler Graphics Ltd.

Reflections. Albert Glenn. 20p. (YA). (gr. 9-12). 1991. pap. text ed. 4.95 (*1-877860-08-5*) Eula Intl Pub.

Reflections. Jim Harryman, pseud. LC 91-67924. 158p. (Orig.). 1992. pap. 6.95 (*1-56002-175-6*, Univ Edtns) Aegina Pr.

Reflections. Evelyn Heinz. 120p. 1985. pap. 6.95 (*0-89697-264-X*) Intl Univ Pr.

Reflections. James N. Hilton, Jr. (Illus.). 144p. 1994. pap. 7.50 (*0-9622166-7-4*) Honoribus Pr.

Reflections. Mark Insingel. LC 72-82381. 1972. 4.95 (*0-87376-021-2*) Red Dust.

Reflections. Ann Jonas. LC 86-33545. (Illus.). 24p. (J). (gr. k-3). 1987. 16.00 (*0-688-06140-0*); lib. bdg. 15.93 (*0-688-06141-9*) Greenwillow.

***Reflections.** Eve Kiley. 1996. pap. 5.00 (*1-57502-296-6*) Morris Pubng.

Reflections. Russell Knott. LC 76-22308. 1976. 7.95 (*0-916434-19-2*) Plycon Pr.

Reflections. C. Randolph Lukens. LC 91-67926. 64p. 1993. pap. 8.00 (*1-56002-190-X*, Univ Edtns) Aegina Pr.

Reflections. Melinda Malone. 40p. 1993. pap. text ed. 13.00 (*1-885156-06-5*) Animas Quilts.

***Reflections.** Caeia March. 250p. 1997. pap. 13.95 (*0-7043-4419-X*, Pub. by Womens Press UK) Trafalgar.

Reflections. LeVonne D. Mulrooney. (Orig.). 1995. pap. write for info. (*1-57553-054-6*) Watermrk Pr.

An Asterisk (*) at the beginning of an entry indicates that the title is appearing in BIP for the first time.

Reflections. David N. Nelson. (Illus.). 45p. (Orig.). 1994. pap. text ed. 10.00 (*1-886615-03-9*) D N Nelson.

Reflections. Dorothy M. Obe. 189p. (C). 1989. text ed. 50.00 (*0-946270-55-4*, Pub. by Pentland Pr UK) St Mut.

***Reflections.** Nell Ogilvie. (Orig.). 1996. pap. write for info. (*1-57553-358-8*) Watermrk Pr.

Reflections. Charles Rich. LC 86-17732. 131p. 1986. pap. 6.95 (*0-932506-49-6*) St Bedes Pubns.

***Reflections.** Shirley Richburg. (Illus.). vii, 50p. (Orig.). 1997. pap. 9.95 (*0-9658432-0-3*) Peoples MD.

Reflections. Nora Roberts. (NR Flowers Ser.: No. 6). 1992. mass mkt. 3.59 (*0-373-51006-3*, 5-51006-0) Harlequin Bks.

Reflections. Ed. by Michael Ryan. 168p. (Orig.). 1993. pap. 5.95 (*1-56245-033-6*) Great Quotations.

Reflections. Idries Shah. 147p. 1978. 18.00 (*0-900860-07-3*, Pub. by Octagon Pr UK) ISHK.

Reflections. Jose Silva. 5.95 (*0-913343-30-7*) Inst Psych Inc.

***Reflections.** Marilyn K. Walker. (Orig.). 1996. pap. write for info. (*1-57553-321-9*) Watermrk Pr.

Reflections. Ron Wilson. 1996. 8.95 (*0-533-11591-4*) Vantage.

Reflections. 2nd ed. John Dennis & Suzanne Griffin. LC 93-47459. 1994. pap. 21.95 (*0-8384-4846-1*) Heinle & Heinle.

Reflections. 2nd ed. George B. Johnston. xvi, 32p. 1988. reprint ed. pap. 3.50 (*0-9616760-3-5*, PS 3560-0388R4) White Rhino Pr.

Reflections... A Collection of Poems for & about Children. Emory H. Jennings. (Collection of Poems for & about Children). 65p. (J). (gr. k-6). 1993. pap. 7.95 (*1-885754-02-7*) E H Jennings.

Reflections: A Collection of Poetry & Prose. Miriam Dansky. 128p. 1990. 10.95 (*0-944070-51-5*) Targum Pr.

Reflections: A Fifteenth Anniversary Collection. Cathy Guisewite. (Illus.). 288p. (Orig.). 1991. pap. 12.95 (*0-8362-1877-9*) Andrews & McMeel.

Reflections: A History of the San Diego Gas & Electric Company 1881-1991. Iris Engstrand & Kathleen Crawford. (Illus.). 294p. 1991. 29.95 (*0-918740-13-4*) San Diego Hist.

Reflections: A Journal. 60p. 1988. write for info. (*0-318-63700-6*) Evolution CA.

Reflections: A Treasury of Daily Readings. D. Martyn Lloyd-Jones. 384p. 1995. 14.99 (*0-529-10251-X*, REFL) World Publng.

Reflections: A Woman's Own Journal with Illustrations & Quotes. 96p. (Orig.). 1987. pap. 5.95 (*1-56138-700-2*) Running Pr.

Reflections: A Writer's Life, a Writer's Work. Harry M. Petrakis. 252p. (Orig.). 1983. reprint ed. 19.95 (*0-941702-04-9*); reprint ed. pap. 9.95 (*0-941702-05-7*) Lake View Pr.

Reflections: An Oral History of Detroit. Ed. by Irene Rosemond. LC 92-90956. 106p. (YA). (gr. 12 up). 1992. 10.00 (*0-940713-08-X*) Broadside Pr.

Reflections: Book. Susan C. Lothner. (Illus.). 80p. (J). 1995. pap. text ed. 11.95 (*1-887343-60-1*) Angel Works.

Reflections: Card/Book Set. Susan C. Lothner. (Illus.). 80p. (J). 1995. boxed 29.95 (*1-887343-61-X*) Angel Works.

Reflections: Essays, Aphorisms, Autobiographical Writings. Walter Benjamin. Ed. by Peter Demetz. Tr. by Edmund Jephcott. LC 85-26232. 392p. 1986. reprint ed. pap. 15.00 (*0-8052-0802-X*) Schocken.

Reflections: Essays on Place & Family. Louis J. Masson. LC 95-45267. 128p. (C). 1996. 25.00 (*0-87422-130-7*); pap. 12.95 (*0-87422-131-5*) Wash St U Pr.

Reflections: Guideposts & Images for the Journey. Marvel E. Harrison & Terry Kellogg. (Illus.). 48p. pap. 10.00 (*1-880257-06-8*) BRAT Pub.

Reflections: Inspired Wisdom on Gods & Symbols, the Human Mind, Angels & Guides, Healing Addictions, Healing the Hurt Child. Ron Scolastico. LC 93-17056. 260p. (Orig.). 1993. pap. 12.95 (*1-56170-065-7*, 153) Hay House.

Reflections: Jewish Youth Confront the Holocaust. (Reflections on the March of the Living Ser.: Vol. 4). (Illus.). (Orig.). 1997. pap. 25.00 (*0-930029-10-0*) Central Agency.

Reflections: Jewish Youth Confront the Holocaust. Ed. by Bobbi Kaufman. (Illus.). 231p. (Orig.). (YA). 1994. pap. 25.00 (*0-930029-09-7*) Central Agency.

***Reflections: Memoirs of Japanese American Women in Minnesota.** Ed. by John N. Tsuchida. 476p. (Orig.). 1994. pap. 24.95 (*1-879600-70-6*) Pac Asia Pr.

Reflections: Opus I. Joseph L. Glaude. 1995. 7.95 (*0-533-11164-1*) Vantage.

***Reflections: Performers - Audiences - Recordings.** Ed. by Jon Tolansky & Basil Tschaikov. (Musical Performance Ser.: Vol. 1, Pt. 1). 119p. 1996. text ed. 76.00 (*3-7186-5868-2*, ECU58, Harwood Acad Pubs) Gordon & Breach.

***Reflections: Performers - Audiences - Recordings.** Ed. by Jon Tolansky & Basil Tschaikov. (Musical Performance Ser.: Vol. 1, Pt. 1). 119p. 1996. pap. text ed. 23.00 (*3-7186-5858-5*, ECU16, Harwood Acad Pubs) Gordon & Breach.

Reflections: Personal Essays by Thirty-Three Distinguished Educators. 1991. 14.00 (*0-87367-450-2*) Phi Delta Kappa.

Reflections: Poems for Thought. Richard McGee. LC 95-62085. 60p. 1996. pap. 5.95 (*1-55523-772-X*) Winston-Derek.

Reflections: Psychological & Spiritual Images of the Heart. Photos by George R. Merrill. (Illus.). 1990. pap. 6.95 (*0-8091-3127-7*) Paulist Pr.

Reflections: Selected Creative Works by Jeanne Blanchet. Jeanne M. Blanchette. LC 88-83847. (Illus.). 84p. 1989. pap. 8.95 (*0-317-91258-5*) Kokoro Enter.

***Reflections: Stories of the Great Lakes.** (Great Lakes Marine History Ser.). (Illus.). 144p. pap. 17.95 (*0-614-25667-4*, Pub. by Riverbank Trade CN) Partners Pubs Grp.

Reflections: The Anthropological Muse. Ed. by J. Iain Prattis. (Special Publication). 1985. pap. 24.00 (*0-913167-10-X*) Am Anthro Assn.

Reflections: The Beal Family: As I Remember. John R. Beal. Ed. by Robert Bixby & Kathleen Bixby. (Illus.). 245p. 1990. 25.00 (*0-9624453-0-4*) March Street Pr.

Reflections: The Plateaus of Endurance. Muriel R. Kulwin. 13p. 1990. pap. 10.00 (*1-889080-00-4*) Doublem Bks.

Reflections: The White Bear Yacht Club, 1889-1989. Patricia C. Johnston. (Illus.). 144p. 1989. write for info. (*0-9621926-0-0*) White Bear Yacht Club.

Reflections: The Workers, the Gospel & the Nameless House Sect. Daurelle Chapman et al. 716p. (Orig.). 1994. pap. 10.45 (*0-9639419-1-7*) Res Info Servs.

Reflections: Verses from the Bahai Teachings. Compiled by Akwasi O. Osei. 128p. 1994. pap. 11.95 (*0-85398-386-0*) G Ronald Pub.

Reflections: Windows on the Past. Louise E. Gray. LC 94-38895. (Illus.). 1994. 23.50 (*1-55618-146-9*) Brunswick Pub.

Reflections: Woman's Self-Image in Contemporary Photography. Edna C. Southard. LC 88-61957. (Illus.). 94p. (Orig.). 1988. pap. 20.00 (*0-940784-11-4*) Miami Univ Art.

Reflections Level 14: HBJ Reading 1987. Early. (J). 1987. student ed., pap. 48.25 (*0-15-330514-2*) HB Schl Dept.

Reflections - Refractions: Reading Luisa Valenzuela. Sharon Magnarelli. (American University Studies: Romance Languages & Literature: Ser. II, Vol. 80). 243p. (C). 1988. text ed. 34.50 (*0-8204-0638-4*) P Lang Pubng.

Reflections & Comments. Edwin L. Godkin. (Notable American Authors Ser.). 1992. reprint ed. lib. bdg. 75.00 (*0-7812-2924-3*) Rprt Serv.

Reflections & Comments, Eighteen Sixty-Five to Eighteen Ninety-Five. Edwin L. Godkin. 1977. 18.95 (*0-8369-7315-1*, 8108) Ayer.

Reflections & Directions in Low Energy Heavy-Ion Physics. J. H. Hamilton et al. 430p. 1993. text ed. 114.00 (*981-02-0882-0*) World Scientific Pub.

Reflections & Inspirations. Ron Palmer. 1996. pap. write for info. (*1-57553-263-8*) Watermrk Pr.

Reflections & Ironies: Packaged in Rhyme. Pat D'Amico. LC 95-92830. (Illus.). 80p. (Orig.). 1996. pap. 8.95 (*0-9650543-0-6*) Pilot Pubns.

Reflections & Meditations on the Signs. Louise Huber. LC 83-73610. 248p. 1984. 19.00 (*0-86690-272-4*, H2527-014) Am Fed Astrologers.

Reflections & Other Poems. Albert M. Juergens, Jr. LC 92-75912. (Illus.). 94p. 1995. 19.95 (*0-9635010-0-3*) Huntersfld Mtn.

Reflections & Perspectives: Essays in Philosophy. E. D. Klemke. LC 73-81810. 109p. (Orig.). 1974. pap. text ed. 19.25 (*90-279-7316-4*) Mouton.

Reflections & Ponderings: Poetry from Beyond the Bench. Glenn Toothman, Sr. 102p. (Orig.). 1988. pap. write for info. (*0-318-62979-8*) Osage Pr.

***Reflections & Refractions: Essays on Science Fiction, Science & Other Matters.** Robert Silverberg. LC 96-50494. 496p. 1997. 50.00 (*1-887424-23-7*); pap. 19.95 (*1-887424-22-9*) Underwood Bks.

***Reflections & Refractions: Thoughts on Science-Fiction, Science & Other Matters.** Robert Silverberg. 1997. 29.95 (*1-887424-24-5*) Underwood Bks.

Reflections & Research on Ragtime. Edward A. Berlin. LC 86-81842. (I.S.A.M. Monographs: No. 24). (Illus.). 112p. 1987. pap. 10.00 (*0-914678-27-2*) Inst Am Music.

Reflections at Daybreak: Musings of God's Blessings & Life. Marcie Sell & Carolyn A. Simpson. 120p. (Orig.). 1995. pap. 5.95 (*1-57502-075-0*) Morris Pubng.

Reflections at Seventy-Five. Henry P. Gaewsky. 64p. 1993. pap. 5.95 (*1-880365-17-0*) Prof Pr NC.

Reflections Behind the Wheel of a Taxi: The Autobiography of a 30-Year Dropout. Albert Murray. 258p. (Orig.). 1990. pap. 19.95 (*1-877586-01-3*) Braimanna Pubs.

Reflections by Alee. Alee M. Soderman. (Illus.). 64p. (Orig.). 1985. pap. 7.95 (*0-9615939-0-3*) Valee Studios.

***Reflections by Kevin.** Kevin McPhee. 42p. (Orig.). 1996. pap. 14.95 (*0-9653332-0-5*) Olive or Twist.

Reflections by Teachers Who Write. Ed. by Charles R. Chew. 250p. 1987. pap. text ed. 7.00 (*0-930348-14-1*) NY St Eng Coun.

Reflections, Cader Publishing. Sharon Derderian. 132p. 1991. 45.00 (*0-8187-0148-X*) Harlo Press.

Reflections (Collective Work) 1980. write for info. (*0-938838-01-6*) Textile Bridge.

Reflections During a Monsoon. Michael Simay. LC 94-60944. (Illus.). 79p. 1996. 7.95 (*1-55523-717-7*) Winston-Derek.

Reflections for Busy Educators: 180 Affirmations to Help You Through the School Year. JoAnn Lordahl. LC 95-21433. 112p. 1995. 37.00 (*0-8039-6376-9*); pap. 15.00 (*0-8039-6320-3*) Corwin Pr.

Reflections for Each Day from the Classic Leaves of Gold: Marble Edition. deluxe ed. Ed. by Paul C. Brownlow. (Daily Reflections). 1990. spiral bd. 7.99 (*1-877719-17-X*) Brownlow Pub Co.

Reflections for Growth. Jean Kirkpatrick. 1980. 0.75 (*0-686-30133-1*) WFS.

Reflections for Living. Dale Rosenburg. 147p. (C). 1995. pap. text ed. 19.30 (*1-56226-273-4*) CT Pub.

Reflections for Managers. Bruce N. Hyland. 1994. text ed. 14.95 (*0-07-031739-9*) McGraw.

Reflections for Managers. Bruce N. Hyland. 1995. pap. text ed. 22.95 incl. disk (*0-07-912107-1*) McGraw.

Reflections for Managers: A Collection of Wisdom & Inspiration from the World's Best Managers. Bruce N. Hyland. 1995. pap. text ed. 9.95 (*0-07-031786-0*) McGraw.

Reflections for People Living with Memory Loss. Carmel Sheridan. write for info. (*0-943873-58-4*) Elder Bks.

***Reflections for the Workplace: A Collection of Wisdom & Inspiration for Working People Everywhere.** Bruce N. Hyland & Merle J. Yost. LC 96-40315. 160p. 1997. text ed. 14.95 (*0-07-031820-4*) McGraw.

Reflections for Working Parents: A Treasure Chest of Truths for Every Working Parent. Carol A. Turkington. 160p. 1996. text ed. 14.95 (*0-07-050514-4*) McGraw.

Reflections For Working Women: Common Sense, Sage Advice, & Unconventional Wisdom. Carol A. Turkington. 160p. 1996. text ed. 14.95 (*0-07-065521-9*) McGraw.

Reflections from a Cinematic Cesspool. George Kuchar & Mike Kuchar. (Illus.). 180p. (Orig.). 1997. per. 19.95 (*0-915906-34-1*) Zanja Pr-Dangerous.

***Reflections from a Garden.** Susan Hill & Rory Stuart. (Illus.). 208p. 1997. pap. 16.95 (*0-614-28623-9*, Pub. by Pavilion UK) Trafalgar.

Reflections from a Life of Prayer: Meditations & Prayers. George Appleton. 160p. 1995. pap. 10.95 (*0-687-85004-5*, Pub. by Society Promot Chrst Know UK) Abingdon.

***Reflections from a Liquid Mirror.** Erik Brinson. LC 96-90394. (Orig.). 1997. pap. 8.95 (*0-533-12025-X*) Vantage.

Reflections from a Mother's Heart. Countryman. 1995. 12.99 (*0-8499-5215-8*) Word Pub.

Reflections from a Unicorn. Richard D. Creech. 1992. pap. 12.95 (*0-9632333-0-0*) RC Pub.

***Reflections from Canoe Country: Paddling the Waters of the Adirondacks & Canada.** Christopher Angus. LC 97-4281. (Illus.). 256p. 1997. 24.95 (*0-8156-0444-0*) Syracuse U Pr.

***Reflections from Flatbush Ave. & Other Exotic Places.** Robert H. Kane. 60p. (Orig.). 1996. pap. write for info. (*1-889534-06-4*) Jay St Pubs.

Reflections from the Flo Crossroads: True Stories from a Native Son of a Country Crossroads. Mark Taylor, pseud. LC 94-60007. 294p. (Orig.). 1994. pap. 14.95 (*0-9640038-0-5*) Wheelock Creek.

Reflections from the Golden Mind. Sri Akhenaton. LC 93-86392. 92p. 1994. 12.95 (*0-9621839-6-2*) Portal MD.

Reflections from the Heart. Alicia Sirkin. (Illus.). 27p. 1995. 9.95 (*0-9651066-0-8*) HeartFelt. Inspirational poetry & wisdom with a slant toward healing the body, mind & spirit, REFLECTIONS FROM THE HEART is aimed toward self-help & gift-giving audiences. Offering the reader an opportunity for self-reflection, personal freedom & inner peace, these poems are calming, uplifting & full of hope. Simply illustrated & rich with insights from the author's personal experiences, the poems speak on themes of nature, communication, healing, forgiveness & the celebration of life: a message from the heart. This elegant, individually handcrafted gift book is distinctly personal. The rich, heavily textured soft white cover, appliqued with natural grass paper is hand-bound with carefully knotted lustrous cord. Every detail reflects love & beauty. The perfect gift for yourself or someone you love. For orders, shipping & discount information, contact: Heartfelt Publishing, 3500 South Bayhomes Drive, Miami, FL 33133. Tel. 305-665-7288, FAX: 305-665-3349. ***Publisher Provided Annotation.***

Reflections from the Heart of Educational Inquiry: Understanding Curriculum & Teaching through the Arts. Ed. by George Willis & William H. Schubert. LC 90-9906. (SUNY Series in Curriculum Issues & Inquiries). 388p. (C). 1991. pap. 21.95 (*0-7914-0557-5*) State U NY Pr.

***Reflections from the Keyboard.** 2nd ed. Dubal. LC 97-25757. 1997. 22.95 (*0-02-864776-9*) S&S Trade.

Reflections from the Light of Christ: 5 Quaker Classics. James R. Newby. LC 80-7477. 126p. 1980. pap. 7.95 (*0-913408-55-7*) Friends United.

Reflections from the North Country. Sigurd F. Olson. (Illus.). 1976. 25.00 (*0-394-40265-0*) Knopf.

Reflections from the North Woods. LeRoy Larson. LC 86-62069. (Orig.). 1986. write for info. (*0-9617181-0-2*) Banjar Pubns.

***Reflections from the Pen of C. Gordon K.** C. Gordon Kershner. 20p. (Orig.). 1996. pap. 4.95 (*0-9656015-0-1*) C G Kershner.

Reflections from the Third Day: Photographic Revelations of Plant Design. J. V. Brindle & J. J. White. (Illus.). 60p. (Orig.). 1978. pap. 6.00 (*0-913196-20-7*) Hunt Inst Botanical.

Reflections from the Workplace. Rex P. Gatto. 1995. pap. text ed. 10.95 (*0-945997-28-0*) GTA Pr.

Reflections II - Treasures from the Heart. 1994. write for info. (*0-9648125-0-9*) W H Ross.

Reflections II - Treasures from the Heart. 1994. audio write for info. (*0-9648125-9-2*) W H Ross.

Reflections III - Treasures from the Heart. 1994. write for info. (*0-9648125-1-7*) W H Ross.

Reflections in a Clockshop. Nell Maiden. (Illus.). 48p. 1996. pap. 8.00 (*1-885912-06-4*) Sows Ear Pr.

Reflections in a Jaundiced Eye. Florence King. 208p. 1990. pap. 8.95 (*0-312-03978-6*) St Martin.

Reflections in a Male Eye: John Huston & the American Experience. Ed. by Gaylyn Studlar & David Desser. LC 92-43059. (Studies in the History of Film & Television). (Illus.). 272p. (C). 1993. text ed. 42.00 (*1-56098-194-6*); pap. text ed. 15.95 (*1-56098-292-6*) Smithsonian.

Reflections in a Private Eye. Josiah Thompson. 304p. 1988. 17.95 (*0-316-84175-7*) Little.

Reflections in a Tarnished Mirror: The Use & Abuse of the Great Lakes. Thomas C. Kuchenberg. LC 78-70548. (Illus.). 1978. pap. 9.50 (*0-933072-01-5*) Golden Glow.

Reflections in Black & White. Gloria Suggs. 96p. 1996. 10.00 (*0-8059-3763-3*) Dorrance.

***Reflections in Blood.** Michael Thomas. Ed. by Robert Pearce. LC 96-69187. (Illus.). 376p. (Orig.). 1996. pap. text ed. 23.50 (*1-883122-05-8*) Pearce Pub.

Reflections in Dark Glass: The Life & Times of John Wesley Hardin. Bruce McGinnis. LC 95-26599. 180p. 1996. 24.95 (*1-57441-008-3*) UNTX Pr.

Reflections in Rhyme: A Parson's Poetry. James W. Scarborough. 192p. 1992. pap. text ed. 9.95 (*0-8403-7375-9*) Kendall-Hunt.

Reflections in the Light: Daily Thoughts & Meditations. Shakti Gawain. LC 91-43198. 400p. 1988. pap. 9.95 (*0-931432-13-8*) New Wrld Lib.

Reflections in the Mind's Eye: Reference & Its Problematization in 20th-Century French Fiction. Brian T. Fitch. (Theory - Culture Ser.). 240p. 1991. 50.00 (*0-8020-5890-6*); pap. 19.95 (*0-8020-6822-7*) U of Toronto Pr.

***Reflections in the Mirror of Religion.** Ninian Smart. LC 96-43975. 1997. text ed. 45.00 (*0-312-17247-8*) St Martin.

Reflections in the Nile. J. Suzanne Frank. 432p. 1997. 22.00 (*0-446-52089-6*) Warner Bks.

***Reflections in the Nile.** J. Suzanne Frank. 1997. 22.00 (*0-614-27224-6*) Warner Bks.

Reflections in the Stocktank, 2 vols., Set. Dave Fisher. 1994. pap. 5.50 (*1-885766-13-0*) Brand Cross.

Reflections in Time. Elizabeth Crane. 1996. mass mkt., pap. text ed. 4.99 (*0-505-52089-3*, Love Spell) Dorchester Pub Co.

Reflections in Verse. Virgil Heskett. 80p. (Orig.). 1995. pap. write for info. (*1-57553-038-4*) Watermrk Pr.

Reflections of a Black Cowboy. Robert H. Miller. (Field Guides Ser.: Vol. I). (Illus.). 9p. (Orig.). (J). (gr. 5-7). 1988. pap. text ed. 9.95 (*0-929592-01-8*) Waterlinc Prodns.

Reflections of a Black Cowboy Series, 4 vols. Robert Miller. (Illus.). 416p. (J). (gr. 4-7). 1991. pap. 19.80 (*0-382-24083-9*); lib. bdg. 51.80 (*0-382-24078-2*) Silver Burdett Pr.

Reflections of a Boomtown: A Photographic Essay of the Burkburnett Oil Boom 1912-1982. Jeff Landrum. (Illus.). 1982. 24.95 (*0-9611894-0-1*) J Landrum Pub.

Reflections of a Catholic Theologian on Visiting an Abortion Clinic. Daniel C. Maguire. 11p. 1985. pap. 3.00 (*0-915365-10-3*) Cath Free Choice.

Reflections of a Cold Warrior: From Yalta to the Bay of Pigs. Richard M. Bissell, Jr. et al. LC 95-43084. 261p. (C). 1996. 30.00 (*0-300-06430-6*) Yale U Pr.

Reflections of a Confused Middle Class Black Youth. Illus. by Walt Carr. 68p. (Orig.). 1996. pap. 10.00 (*0-911849-05-X*) Comptex Assocs Inc.

Reflections of a Country Doctor. Barry Ladd. LC 95-77536. 200p. 1995. 20.95 (*0-944435-37-8*) Glenbridge Pub.

***Reflections of a Culture Broker: A View from the Smithsonian.** Richard Kurin. LC 97-6974. 1997. pap. write for info. (*1-56098-757-X*) Smithsonian.

***Reflections of a Culture Broker: A View from the Smithsonian.** Richard Kurin. LC 97-6974. 1997. text ed. 34.95 (*1-56098-789-8*) Smithsonian.

Reflections of a Digger: Fifty Years of World Archaeology. Froelich Rainey. LC 92-12150. (Illus.). 324p. 1992. 22.50 (*0-924171-15-4*) U PA Mus Pubns.

Reflections of a Family Doctor: Writings of Herbert J. Levin, M.D. Herbert J. Levin. 185p. (Orig.). (C). 1994. pap. text ed. 19.95 (*0-9642777-0-0*) Levin Family.

Reflections of a Fanatical Learner: Memories, Meanings, & Musings. Willard D. Callender, Jr. LC 94-26462. 318p. (C). 1994. pap. text ed. 36.50 (*0-8191-9672-X*); lib. bdg. 49.50 (*0-8191-9671-1*) U Pr of Amer.

Reflections of a Financier. Otto Kahn. 1972. 59.95 (*0-8490-0938-3*) Gordon Pr.

Reflections of a Ghost. deluxe limited ed. Andrews Lytle. 35.00 (*0-686-78139-2*) New London Pr.

Reflections of a Healing Heart. Linda Estela. LC 94-18880. 1994. pap. 4.95 (*0-9624626-8-3*) Astarte Shell Pr.

Reflections of a Legacy: The Bonnet House Story. Jayne Rice. Ed. by Jayme Robinson. (Illus.). 152p. 1989. 35.00 (*0-9624757-0-X*) Bonnet Hse.

Reflections of a Nonpolitical Man. Thomas Mann. Tr. by Walter D. Morris from GER. 452p. 1987. reprint ed. pap. 14.95 (*0-8044-6482-0*, F Ungar Bks) Continuum.

Reflections of a Nuclear Weaponeer. Frank H. Shelton. (Illus.). 830p. 1992. 120.00 (*1-881816-02-8*, TX 3 241 793) Shelton Ent.

Reflections of a Nuclear Weaponeer, Chap. 1: The Manhattan Project. Frank H. Shelton. (Illus.). 64p. 1992. pap. 10.00 (*1-881816-04-4*) Shelton Ent.

Reflections of a Nuclear Weaponeer, Chap. 10: Testing Moritorium 1958-1961. Frank H. Shelton. (Illus.). 80p. 1992. pap. 10.00 (*1-881816-13-3*) Shelton Ent.

Reflections of a Nuclear Weaponeer, Chap. 11: A Return to Testing 1961-1962. Frank H. Shelton. (Illus.). 90p. 1992. pap. 10.00 (*1-881816-14-1*) Shelton Ent.

Reflections of a Nuclear Weaponeer, Chap. 12: The Limited Test Ban Treaty 1963. Frank H. Shelton. (Illus.). 88p. 1992. pap. 10.00 (*1-881816-15-X*) Shelton Ent.

R

Reflections of a Nuclear Weaponeer, Chap. 2: Operation Crossroads - 1946. Frank H. Shelton. (Illus.). 72p. 1992. pap. 10.00 (*1-881816-05-2*) Shelton Ent.

Reflections of a Nuclear Weaponeer, Chap. 3: Operation Sandstone 1947-1948. Frank H. Shelton. (Illus.). 58p. 1992. pap. 10.00 (*1-881816-06-0*) Shelton Ent.

Reflections of a Nuclear Weaponeer, Chap. 4: Operation Greenhouse 1950-1951. Frank H. Shelton. (Illus.). 50p. 1992. pap. 10.00 (*1-881816-07-9*) Shelton Ent.

Reflections of a Nuclear Weaponeer, Chap. 5: Operation Ivy - 1952. Frank H. Shelton. (Illus.). 58p. 1992. pap. 10.00 (*1-881816-08-7*) Shelton Ent.

Reflections of a Nuclear Weaponeer, Chap. 6: Operation Castle 1954. Frank H. Shelton. (Illus.). 60p. 1992. pap. 10.00 (*1-881816-09-5*) Shelton Ent.

Reflections of a Nuclear Weaponeer, Chap. 7: Operation Redwing 1956. Frank H. Shelton. (Illus.). 78p. 1992. pap. 10.00 (*1-881816-10-9*) Shelton Ent.

Reflections of a Nuclear Weaponeer, Chap. 8: Operation Plumbbob 1957. Frank H. Shelton. (Illus.). 58p. 1992. pap. 10.00 (*1-881816-11-7*) Shelton Ent.

Reflections of a Nuclear Weaponeer, Chap. 9: Operation Hardtack 1958. Frank H. Shelton. (Illus.). 68p. 1992. pap. 10.00 (*1-881816-12-5*) Shelton Ent.

***Reflections of a Paleface from the Rosebud.** Helen Crosswait. 66p. 1992. per. 9.00 (*0-614-24757-8*) Tesseract SD.

Reflections of a Physicist. 2nd ed. Percy W. Bridgman. Ed. by I. Bernard Cohen. LC 79-3118. (Three Centuries of Science in America Ser.). 1980. reprint ed. lib. bdg. 53.95 (*0-405-12595-X*) Ayer.

Reflections of a Pilot. Len Morgan. (Illus.). 224p. (Orig.). 1987. 16.95 (*0-8306-2098-2*); pap. 12.95 (*0-8306-2398-1*) McGraw-Hill Prof.

Reflections of a Post-Auschwitz Christian. Harry J. Cargas. LC 88-26798. 160p. (C). 1989. pap. 15.95 (*0-8143-2096-1*) Wayne St U Pr.

Reflections of a Prairie Daughter. Illus. by Jolene Steffen. LC 89-91745. 150p. (Orig.). 1989. pap. 5.00 (*0-9623066-0-6*) Prairie Daughter.

Reflections of a Radical Moderate. Elliot Richardson. 288p. 1996. 24.00 (*0-679-42820-8*) Pantheon.

Reflections of a Rock Lobster: A Story about Growing up Gay. Aaron Fricke. (Illus.). 123p. (YA). (gr. 8-12). 1995. pap. 5.95 (*1-55583-607-0*) Alyson Pubns.

Reflections of a Romantic: Visions in Verse. Harry J. November. (Orig.). 1996. pap. write for info. (*1-57553-288-3*) Watermrk Pr.

Reflections of a Rotarian. Jack Pearce. LC 94-72593. 401p. 1994. 24.95 (*1-885373-03-1*); pap. 19.95 (*1-885373-04-X*) Emerald Ink.

Reflections of a Scandal in Bohemia. J. Decker. 98p. 1986. 20.00 (*0-685-35564-0*) Samson Pubs.

Reflections of a Schoolmistress. Nora Frye. Ed. by Janet S. Panger. LC 94-79184. (Illus.). 192p. (Orig.). 1994. pap. 10.95 (*0-9643799-0-2*) Aurinko Pubns.

Reflections of a Seismic Interpreter. Paul M. Tucker. 98p. 1990. 19.00 (*1-56080-012-7*, 572) Soc Expl Geophys.

Reflections of a Soul's Journey. Peter J. Prato. LC 95-69932. (Illus.). 160p. 1995. 16.95 (*1-56167-216-5*) Noble Hse MD.

Reflections of a Stereo Pioneer. Arthur C. Keller. (Illus.). 1985. 15.00 (*0-911302-52-2*) San Francisco Pr.

Reflections of a Time. Ed. by Dee Frances. 42p. (Orig.). 1992. pap. 7.95 (*0-9635341-2-2*) DDDD Pubns.

Reflections of a Warrior. F. D. Miller & E. C. Kureth. Ed. by Paul McCarthy. 256p. 1992. reprint ed. mass mkt. 5.50 (*0-671-75396-7*) PB.

Reflections of a Whale-Watcher. Michelle A. Gilders. LC 94-38745. (Illus.). 288p. 1995. pap. 16.95 (*0-253-20957-9*); text ed. 29.95 (*0-253-32572-2*) Ind U Pr.

Reflections of a White Bear. Carolyn E. Campbell. 40p. (Orig.). 1994. pap. 6.00 (*0-9628094-5-4*) Pearl Edit.

***Reflections of a World of Reality.** 2nd ed. Rodriguez H. Hollimon. 72p. 1997. reprint ed. pap. 10.00 (*1-57502-460-8*, P01379) Morris Pubng.

***Reflections of a Wounded Heart.** Craig Chitty. 130p. (Orig.). 1996. pap. write for info. (*1-57502-363-6*, P01167) Morris Pubng.

Reflections of a Young Woman. Dianne J. Morrissey. 1978. pap. 4.95 (*0-686-24550-4*) Aaron-Jenkins.

Reflections of an Affirmative Action Baby. Stephen L. Carter. LC 91-70054. 286p. 1992. pap. 14.50 (*0-465-06869-3*) Basic.

Reflections of an American Muslim. Shahid Athar. 256p. (Orig.). 1994. pap. 14.95 (*0-934905-26-6*) Kazi Pubns.

Reflections of an Angry Middle-Aged Editor. James A. Wechsler. LC 72-37152. (Essay Index Reprint Ser.). 1977. reprint ed. 18.95 (*0-8369-2524-6*) Ayer.

Reflections of an Elder Brother: Awakening from the Dream. Bartholomew. Ed. by M. Moore. 177p. (Orig.). 1989. pap. 10.95 (*0-9614010-5-2*) High Mesa Pr.

Reflections of an Enlightened Blond. Ann K. Cooper. 120p. (Orig.). 1988. pap. text ed. write for info. (*0-910463-07-7*) Edit Heliodor.

Reflections of an Hispanic Mennonite. Jose Ortiz. LC 89-11872. 96p. 1989. pap. 6.95 (*0-934672-78-4*) Good Bks PA.

Reflections of an Industrialist: From Mudhouse to Millionaire. Malik A. Nath. 187p. (C). 1992. text ed. 25.00 (*0-7069-6026-2*, Pub. by Vikas II) S Asia.

Reflections of an Oreo Cookie: Growing up Black in the 1960s. Gerald Thompson. LC 90-27116. 144p. 1991. 24.95 (*0-912526-53-X*) Lib Res.

Reflections of Arsulu. Marilyn Kaye. LC 92-53935. (Little Mermaid Novels Ser.). (Illus.). 80p. (J). (gr. 1-4). 1992. pap. 3.50 (*1-56282-248-9*) Disney Pr.

Reflections of Becca. Lynda Trent. (Superromance Ser.). 1993. mass mkt. 3.39 (*0-373-70536-0*, 1-70536-7) Harlequin Bks.

Reflections of Being. Peter Ralston. 80p. 1991. pap. 9.95 (*1-55643-119-8*) North Atlantic.

Reflections of California: The Athalie Richardson Irvine Clarke Memorial Exhibition. Donald B. Schewe. LC 94-76124. 185p. 1994. 40.00 (*0-9635468-3-X*) Irvine Mus.

Reflections of Change: Children's Literature since 1945. Ed. by Sandra L. Beckett. LC 96-22004. (Contributions to the Study of World Literature Ser.: 74). 224p. 1997. text ed. 55.00 (*0-313-30145-X*, Greenwood Pr) Greenwood.

Reflections of Change: Sociopolitical Commentary & Criticism in Malaysian Popular Music since 1950. Craig A. Lockard. (Crossroads Ser.: Ser. 6.1). 144p. (Orig.). 1991. pap. 6.00 (*1-877979-92-9*) SE Asia.

Reflections of Childhood: A Quotations Dictionary. Irving Weiss & Anne D. Weiss. LC 91-24746. 400p. 1991. lib. bdg. 50.00 (*0-87436-646-1*) ABC-CLIO.

Reflections of Dues. Dwayne Candler. 60p. (Orig.). 1996. pap. write for info. (*1-57553-035-X*) Watermrk Pr.

Reflections of Eden: My years with the orangutans of Borneo. LC 94-22948. 1995. 24.95 (*0-316-30181-7*) Little.

Reflections of Eden: My Years with the Orangutans of Borneo. Birute M. Galdikas. 1996. pap. 13.95 (*0-316-30186-8*); pap. 13.95 (*0-614-12556-1*) Little.

Reflections of Elegance: Cartier Jewels from the Lindemann Collection. John W. Keefe et al. (Illus.). 182p. 1987. pap. 39.95 (*0-89494-030-9*) New Orleans Mus Art.

Reflections of Emma. Buddy Youngreen. 145p. (Orig.). (C). 1993. 16.95 (*0-910523-42-8*) Grandin Bk Co.

Reflections of Emma. Buddy Youngreen. (Personal Enrichment Ser.). (Illus.). 142p. (Orig.). 1991. pap. write for info. (*0-929985-93-1*) Jackman Pubng.

Reflections of Eve & Her Daughters. Marsha Newman. (Illus.). 1981. 6.95 (*0-9608658-0-2*) Wellspring Utah.

Reflections of Faith: Houses of Worship in the Lone Star State. Willard B. Robinson. LC 94-20796. (Illus.). 268p. (Orig.). 1994. 45.00 (*0-918954-57-6*) Baylor Univ Pr.

Reflections of Family Expressions. Matty Barraclough. (Orig.). 1995. pap. write for info. (*1-57553-044-9*) Watermrk Pr.

Reflections of Five Public Officials. Ed. by Kenneth W. Thompson. (Papers on Presidential Transitions & Foreign Policy: Vol. V). 102p. (Orig.). (C). 1987. lib. bdg. 36.00 (*0-8191-5773-2*, Pub. by White Miller Center) U Pr of Amer.

Reflections of French River. June B. Smith. 48p. 1981. 5.95 (*0-920806-25-2*, Pub. by Penumbra Pr CN) U of Toronto Pr.

Reflections of Glory: Paul's Polemical Use of the Moses-Doxa Tradition in 2 Corinthians. Linda L. Belleville. (Journal for the Study of the New Testament, Supplement Ser.: Vol. 52). 351p. 70.00 (*1-85075-265-6*) CUP Services.

Reflections of Greatness: Ancient Egypt at the Carnegie Museum of Natural History. Diana C. Patch. LC 89-62543. (Illus.). 128p. (Orig.). (C). 1990. pap. text ed. 24.95 (*0-911239-14-6*) Carnegie Mus.

***Reflections of Hollywood.** Alan L. Gansberg. Date not set. write for info. (*0-688-08897-X*) Morrow.

Reflections of Interdependence: Issues for Economic Theory & U. S. Policy. M. Von Neumann Whitman. LC 78-53603. 338p. reprint ed. pap. 96.40 (*0-685-15973-6*, 2026317) Bks Demand.

Reflections of Internment: The Art of Hawaii's Hiroshi Honda. Franklin Odo et al. (Illus.). 33p. (Orig.). 1994. pap. 8.95 (*0-937426-27-X*) Honolu Arts.

Reflections of Ireland. Patricia Preston. 1991. 19.98 (*0-8317-4984-9*) Smithmark.

***Reflections of Ireland.** Patricia T. Preston. 1997. 14.95 (*1-85833-696-1*) BHB Intl.

Reflections of Joy: Acrylic Painting Techniques. Joyce Beebe. (Designer Ser.). (Illus.). 32p. (Orig.). 1986. pap. 8.95 (*0-917121-13-9*, 50-100) M F Weber Co.

Reflections of Kansas: A Prairie Postcard Album, 1900-1930. Frank Wood & Scott Daymond. LC 88-71928. (Illus.). 112p. (C). 1988. 23.95 (*0-9621273-0-2*) Daywood Pub Co.

Reflections of Lac du Flambeau: An Illustrated History of Lac du Flambeau, Wisconsin 1745-1995. Ed. by Michael J. Goc. (Illus.). 160p. 1994. 23.00 (*0-938627-26-0*) New Past Pr.

Reflections of Leisure: A Tribute. Robert L. Wilder. 96p. 1980. 12.50 (*0-943272-15-7*) Inst Recreation Res.

Reflections of Leisure: A Tribute. deluxe ed. Robert L. Wilder. 96p. 1980. 20.00 (*0-943272-16-5*) Inst Recreation Res.

Reflections of Life. Melvin Lars. 55p. (Orig.). 1993. pap. 10.00 (*0-9638218-0-6*) M Lars.

Reflections of Light. Sharonn D. Halderman. 1995. pap. 3.75 (*0-7880-0572-3*) CSS OH.

Reflections of Liquid Helium. E. L. Andronikashvili. Tr. by Robert Berman. (AIP Translation Ser.). (Illus.). 1989. 60.00 (*0-88318-575-X*) Am Inst Physics.

***Reflections of Loko Miwa: Les Chemins de Loco-Miroir.** Lilas Desquiron & Robin O. Bodkin. (CARAF Bks.). 1998. write for info. (*0-8139-1752-2*); pap. write for info. (*0-8139-1753-0*) U Pr of Va.

Reflections of Love. Carol A. Osley. 42p. (Orig.). 1982. pap. 4.25 (*0-910119-01-5*) SOCO Pubns.

Reflections of Madison County. Photos by Mark F. Heffron. (Illus.). 80p. 1994. 9.95 (*0-8317-4866-4*) Smithmark.

Reflections of Mind: Western Psychology Meets Tibetan Buddhism. Tarthang Tulku. LC 75-5254. (Illus.). 1975. 22.00 (*0-913546-15-1*); pap. 12.95 (*0-913546-14-3*) Dharma Pub.

Reflections of My Grandparents. Sylvia Healy. (Illus.). 80p. 1985. 24.95 (*0-939688-13-1*) Directed Media.

Reflections of My Life. William B. Andersen. (Orig.). 1995. pap. write for info. (*1-56167-283-1*) Watermrk Pr.

Reflections of My Life. Ellen G. Andrew. (Orig.). 1995. pap. write for info. (*1-57553-090-2*) Watermrk Pr.

Reflections of My Life. Helen P. Bell. (Orig.). 1995. pap. write for info. (*1-57553-078-3*) Watermrk Pr.

Reflections of My Life. Albert J. DeRoose. (Orig.). 1995. pap. write for info. (*1-57553-048-1*) Watermrk Pr.

Reflections of My Life. Paula J. Dibble. 60p. Date not set. pap. text ed. write for info. (*1-57553-018-X*) Watermrk Pr.

Reflections of My Life. Eleanor M. Dirksen. (Illus.). 60p. (Orig.). 1995. pap. write for info. (*1-57553-028-7*) Watermrk Pr.

Reflections of My Life. Mary J. Foster. 80p. (Orig.). 1995. pap. write for info. (*1-57553-010-4*) Watermrk Pr.

Reflections of My Life: The Apology of John the Baptist. Dennis Dallison. Ed. by Ruth E. Norman. (Illus.). 66p. (Orig.). 1982. pap. 5.00 (*0-932642-75-6*) Unarius Acad Sci.

Reflections of My Mind. Luella Hill. 44p. (YA). 1994. pap. write for info. (*0-9640181-2-8*) Straight From The Heart.

Reflections of Nature: Flowers in American Art. Ella M. Forshay. 1990. 29.95 (*0-685-33409-0*); pap. 17.99 (*0-517-69599-5*) Random Hse Value.

Reflections of Nazism: An Essay on Kitsch & Death. Saul Friedlander. Tr. by Thomas Weyr from FRE. LC 93-1012. 144p. 1993. reprint ed. 20.00 (*0-253-32434-3*); reprint ed. pap. 10.95 (*0-253-20846-7*) Ind U Pr.

Reflections of Nero: Culture, History, & Representation. Ed. by Jas Elsner & Jamie Masters. LC 93-34503. viii, 239p. (C). 1994. 45.00 (*0-8078-2143-8*) U of NC Pr.

Reflections of Old Cedarburg. 3rd ed. Robert T. Teske. (Illus.). 156p. 1994. pap. 14.95 (*0-9625597-2-5*) Cedarburg Cultural Ctr.

Reflections of One Army Nurse in World War II. Gladys Bonine. Date not set. 14.95 (*0-533-11625-2*) Vantage.

***Reflections of Our Past: A Pictorial History of Carlton County, Minnesota.** Francis M. Carroll et al. LC 97-9724. 1997. write for info. (*0-89865-991-4*) Donning Co.

Reflections of Ourselves: The Women's Movement in the Mass Media from 1963 to the Present. Sharon Howell. (American University Studies: Communications: Ser. XXVII, Vol. 1). 208p. (C). 1989. text ed. 46.95 (*0-8204-0523-X*) P Lang Pubng.

Reflections of Pearls & Swine. Stephen P. Schulz. LC 95-90970. 1996. 8.95 (*0-533-11796-8*) Vantage.

Reflections of Portland, Maine. Ed. by Dennis Griggs & Frederic L. Thompson. (Illus.). 124p. 1986. 29.95 (*0-9611320-1-9*) Congress Sq.

Reflections of Realism: Paradox, Norm, & Ideology in Nineteenth Century German Prose. Robert C. Holub. LC 90-49118. 258p. (C). 1991. text ed. 19.95 (*0-8143-2291-3*) Wayne St U Pr.

Reflections of Reality: Healing. Charlene Wiek. (Illus.). 87p. 1992. pap. 12.95 (*0-9633383-0-7*) Hermitage Pr.

Reflections of Reality in Japanese Art. Sherman E. Lee & Indiana University Staff. LC 82-45940. (Illus.). 304p. 1983. 35.00 (*0-910386-70-6*) Cleveland Mus Art.

Reflections of Renaissance England: Life, Thought, & Religion Mirrored in Illustrated Pamphlets. Marie-Helene Davies. LC 85-32028. (Princeton Theological Monographs: No. 1). 1986. pap. 18.00 (*0-915138-68-9*) Pickwick.

Reflections of Rosedown. Ola M. Ward & Helen Le Bourgeois. Ed. by Helen Le Bourgeois. (Illus.). 56p. pap. 9.95 (*0-614-06258-6*) Rosedown Plantation.

Reflections of Salem's Past. Dale E. Shaffer. (Illus.). 80p. (Orig.). 1984. pap. 3.95 (*0-915060-21-3*) D E Shaffer.

Reflections of Scenes, Sounds & Emotions of the Distant Past. R. E. Spencer. 136p. 1992. 12.00 (*0-9630830-0-7*) R E Spencer.

***Reflections of Self.** Kris Vantornhout. Ed. by Alisa B. Oliver. (Illus.). 176p. (Orig.). 1997. pap. 14.95 (*0-9641606-8-4*) Easy Break.

Reflections of Social Life in the Navaho Origin Myth. Katherine Spencer. LC 76-43850. (Univ. of New Mexico. Publications in Anthropology: No. 3). 1983. reprint ed. 34.50 (*0-404-15705-X*) AMS Pr.

Reflections of Tantras. Sudhakar Chattopadhyaya. 106p. 1979. 11.95 (*0-318-36386-0*) Asia Bk Corp.

Reflections of the Dream, 1975-1994: Twenty-One Years Celebrating the Life of Dr. Martin Jr. at the Massachusetts Institute of Technology. Ed. by Clarence G. Williams. 1995. 35.00 (*0-262-23187-5*); pap. text ed. 17.50 (*0-262-73115-0*) MIT Pr.

***Reflections of the Field at Gettysburg.** Bill Lonecke. (Illus.). 80p. (Orig.). 1997. mass mkt. 9.95 (*1-57532-102-5*) Press-Tige Pub.

Reflections of the Heart. Richard S. Becker. (Illus.). 53p. (C). 1989. pap. write for info. (*0-318-65862-3*) R S Becker.

Reflections of the Heart. Ron Rice. (Illus.). 28p. (Orig.). 1995. pap. 6.95 (*0-9646093-0-4*) Kerley Pub Servs.

***Reflections of the Holy Land & Africa from A to Z May 4-19, 1996.** Melinda G. Graves. (Illus.). vii, 36p. 1996. pap. 10.00 (*0-9656105-0-0*) M G Graves.

Reflections of the Law in Literature. Francis L. Windolph. LC 71-117863. (Essay Index Reprint Ser.). 1977. 16.95 (*0-8369-1739-1*) Ayer.

Reflections of the Past: Anthology of San Jose. Ed. by Judith Henderson. (Illus.). 400p. 1996. 49.95 (*1-886483-07-8*) Heritge Pubng.

Reflections of the Rav: Lessons in Jewish Thought Adapted from the Lectures of Rabbi Joseph B. Soloveitchik, Vol. 1. Abraham R. Besdin. 1993. 22.95 (*0-88125-330-8*) Ktav.

Reflections of the Rav: Man of Faith in the Modern World Adapted from the Lectures of Rabbi Joseph B. Soloveitchik, Vol. 2. Abraham R. Besdin. 1989. 19.95 (*0-88125-312-X*) Ktav.

Reflections of the Self: Poems of Spiritual Life. Swami Muktananda. Tr. by Swami Chidvilasananda. LC 80-50391. (Illus.). 200p. (Orig.). 1980. pap. 10.95 (*0-914602-50-0*) SYDA Found.

***Reflections of the South.** Bethany E. Bultman. 1997. 14.95 (*1-85833-697-X*) BHB Intl.

Reflections of the Weaver's World: The Gloria F. Ross Collection of Contemporary Navajo Weaving. Ann L. Hedlund. LC 92-72353. (Illus.). 112p. (C). 1993. pap. 29.95 (*0-295-97231-9*) U of Wash Pr.

Reflections of Women in Antiquity. H. P. Foley. 420, xviiip. 1992. pap. text ed. 26.00 (*2-88124-576-5*) Gordon & Breach.

Reflections of Women in Antiquity. Helene P. Foley. 420p. (C). 1982. text ed. 87.00 (*0-677-16370-3*) Gordon & Breach.

Reflections of Women in the New Kingdom: Ancient Egyptian Art from the British Museum. Gay Robins. (EUMILOP Ser.: No. 7). 24p. 1995. pap. 10.00 (*0-9638169-6-9*) M C Carlos Mus.

***Reflections of Yesterday.** Gladys Gard. Ed. by Kelly O'Donnell. (Illus.). 200p. 1997. pap. 12.95 (*1-57532-155-6*) Press-Tige Pub.

Reflections of Yesterday. Debbie Macomber. (Mira Bks.). 1995. mass mkt. 4.99 (*1-55166-070-9*, 1-66070-3, Mira Bks) Harlequin Bks.

Reflections of Yesterday, Vol. 1. Jesse Sarmiento. LC 86-90398. (Illus.). 88p. 1986. pap. 5.95 (*0-9615290-1-6*) Rainy Day FL.

Reflections on a Gift of Watermelon Pickle... And Other Modern Verse. large type ed. Compiled by Stephen Dunning et al. 1995. 50.50 (*0-614-09606-5*, L-78696-00) Am Printing Hse.

Reflections on a Gift of Watermelon Pickle & Other Modern Verse. Ed. by Stephen Dunning et al. LC 66-8763. (Illus.). 144p. (J). (gr. 7 up). 1967. 18.00 (*0-688-41231-9*) Lothrop.

Reflections on a Life. Norbert Elias. Tr. by Edmund Jephcott from DUT. (Illus.). 180p. (GER.). (YA). (gr. 12 up). 1994. text ed. 49.95 (*0-7456-1276-8*) Blackwell Pubs.

Reflections on a Life. Norbert Elias. Tr. by Edmund Jephcott. (Illus.). 180p. (YA). (gr. 12 up). 1994. pap. text ed. 19.95 (*0-7456-1383-7*) Blackwell Pubs.

Reflections on a Lifetime. Dale M. Bentz. 128p. 1991. pap. 9.95 (*0-944266-12-6*) Maecenas Pr.

Reflections on a Literary Revolution. Graham G. Hough. LC 60-2451. 133p. reprint ed. pap. 38.00 (*0-685-17849-8*, 2029509) Bks Demand.

***Reflections on a Marine Venus: A Companion to the Landscape of Rhodes.** Lawrence Durrell. 200p. pap. 10.95 (*1-56924-791-9*) Marlowe & Co.

Reflections on a Philosophy. Forrest C. Shaklee, Sr. LC 73-10833. pap. 3.95 (*0-87502-038-0*) Benjamin Co.

Reflections on a Rainy April Day. Chief Little Summer & Warm Night Rain. (Illus.). 23p. (J). (gr. 1-5). 1991. 8.95 (*1-880440-02-4*) Piqua Pr.

Reflections on a Troubled World Economy. Ed. by Fritz Machlup et al. (Essays in Honor of Herbert Giersch Ser.). 350p. 1983. text ed. 39.95 (*0-312-66741-8*) St Martin.

Reflections on a Western Town: An Oral History of Crested Butte, Colorado. Kelsey D. Wirth. 1996. 29.95 (*0-9649185-0-1*); pap. 19.95 (*0-9649185-2-8*) Oh-Be-Joyful.

Reflections on Afro-American Music. With Contributions from Richard L. Abrams & Others. Dominique-Rene De Lerma. LC 72-619703. 279p. reprint ed. pap. 79.60 (*0-685-16400-4*, 2027301) Bks Demand.

Reflections on Aging: A Spiritual Guide. Leo E. Missinne. LC 89-64247. 112p. (Orig.). 1990. pap. 3.95 (*0-89243-319-1*) Liguori Pubns.

Reflections on America. Jacques Maritain. LC 74-26882. 205p. 1975. reprint ed. 35.00 (*0-87752-166-2*) Gordian.

Reflections on American Brilliant Cut Glass. Bill Boggess & Louise Boggess. LC 95-5450. 256p. (Orig.). 1995. 39.95 (*0-88740-722-6*) Schiffer.

Reflections on an Aquarium. Louis Bernstein & Louis E. Garibaldi. Ed. by Vilma Barr. LC 92-70602. (Illus.). 96p. (Orig.). 1992. 26.95 (*0-9632150-0-0*) Drum Comns.

Reflections on an Aquarium. Louis Bernstein & Louis E. Garibaldi. Ed. by Vilma Barr. LC 92-70602. (Illus.). 96p. (Orig.). (YA). 1992. pap. text ed. 16.95 (*0-9632150-1-9*) Drum Comns.

Reflections on Architectural Practices in the Nineties. Ed. by William S. Saunders et al. (Illus.). 272p. (Orig.). 1996. pap. 18.95 (*1-56898-056-6*) Princeton Arch.

Reflections on Art. Susanne K. Langer. 1979. 25.95 (*0-405-10611-4*) Ayer.

Reflections on Artificial Intelligence. Blay Whitby. 192p. (Orig.). 1994. pap. text ed. 22.95 (*1-871516-68-4*, Pub. by Intellect Bks UK) Cromland.

Reflections on Becoming: Fifteen Literature-Based Units for a Young Adolescent. Ronnie L. Sheppard. 106p. (C). 1993. pap. text ed. 15.00 (*1-56090-077-6*) Natl Middle Schl.

Reflections on Behaviorism & Society. B. F. Skinner. (Century Psychology Ser.). (Illus.). 1978. text ed. 40.00 (*0-13-770057-1*) P-H.

Reflections on Biochemistry. Arthur Kornberg et al. 1976. 213.00 (*0-08-021011-2*, Pub. by Pergamon Repr UK) Franklin.

Reflections on Bioethic. David Bleich. 1995. write for info. (*0-88125-473-8*) Ktav.

Reflections on Biologic Research. Giulio Gabbiani et al. LC 67-26012. (Illus.). 256p. 1967. 8.90 (*0-87527-035-2*) Green.

Reflections on British Painting. Roger E. Fry. LC 76-99695. (Essay Index Reprint Ser.). 1977. 15.95 (*0-8369-1350-7*) Ayer.

An Asterisk (*) at the beginning of an entry indicates that the title is appearing in BIP for the first time.

Reflections on Church & State. James E. Wood, Jr. LC 95-75757. xxi, 774p. 1995. 39.95 (*0-929182-50-2*) Baylor U J M Dawson.

Reflections on Civilization, Reader, Vol. II. Ronald H. Fritze. (C). 1991. pap. text ed. 33.50 (*0-673-38404-7*) Addson-Wesley Educ.

Reflections on Commercial Life. Ed. by Murray. 496p. (C). 1997. pap. 24.95 (*0-415-91196-6*, Routledge NY) Routledge.

Reflections on Commercial Life. Ed. by Murray. 496p. (C). 1997. text ed. 74.95 (*0-415-91195-8*, Routledge NY) Routledge.

Reflections on Composing: Four American Composers. Frederick Koch. LC 78-59839. 1986. pap. 12.95 (*0-915604-20-5*) Carnegie-Mellon.

Reflections on Contemporary Nursing Practice. Judith Townshend & Margaret McMillan. 352p. 1995. pap. 45.00 (*0-7506-8911-0*) Buttrwrth-Heinemann.

Reflections on Counseling. Dryden. 118p. 1993. pap. 48.00 (*1-56593-262-5*, 0552) Singular Publishing.

Reflections on Crystal Waters. Mocoo Wollert. 66p. (C). 1990. pap. 40.00 (*0-86439-126-9*, Pub. by Boolarong Pubns AT) St Mut.

Reflections on Cultural Policy: Past, Present, Future. Ed. by Evan Alderson et al. (Calgary Institute for the Humanities Ser.). 160p. (C). 1993. text ed. 35.00 (*0-88920-215-X*) Wilfrid Laurier.

Reflections on Diabetes. American Diabetes Association Staff. LC 96-6157. 104p. 1996. pap. 9.95 (*0-945448-65-1*) Am Diabetes.

Reflections on Distance Education for India. P. Renga Ramanujam. (Illus.). 181p. 1995. 20.00 (*81-85445-93-1*, Pub. by Manak Pubns Pvt Ltd) Nataraj Bks.

Reflections on Economic Development: The Selected Essays of Michael P. Todaro. Michael P. Todaro. LC 94-28486. (Economists of the Twentieth Century Ser.). 528p. 1995. 85.00 (*1-85898-073-9*) E Elgar.

Reflections on Economic Development: Toward a New Latin American Consensus. Enrique V. Iglesias. (Inter-American Development Bank Ser.). 164p. 1992. 15.95 (*0-940602-52-0*) IADB.

Reflections on Elegance: Pasadena's Huntington Hotel Since 1906. rev. ed. Donald M. Decker & Mary L. Decker. (Illus.). 80p. 1991. pap. 4.95 (*0-918329-24-8*) Royal Lit.

Reflections on Equestrian Art. Nuno Oliveira. 130p. 1990. write for info. (*0-85131-461-9*, Pub. by J A Allen & Co UK) St Mut.

Reflections on Experimental Science. Martin L. Perl. LC 95-48852. (World Scientific Series in 20th Century Mathematics: Vol. 14). 580p. 1995. text ed. 84.00 (*981-02-2429-X*, GPPh-BR2901) World Scientific Pub.

***Reflections on Experimental Science: Selected Papers.** Martin L. Perl. 1995. pap. text ed. 38.00 (*981-02-2574-1*) World Scientific Pub.

Reflections on Faith & Inspiration. Ariel Books Staff. (Illus.). 40p. 1995. 6.95 (*0-8362-4744-2*) Andrews & McMeel.

***Reflections on Feminist Family Therapy Training.** Ed. by Kathy Weingarten & Michele L. Bograd. LC 96-30446. (Journal of Feminist Family Therapy: Vol. 8, No. 2). 89p. (C). 1996. 39.95 (*0-7890-0002-4*) Haworth Pr.

Reflections on Fieldwork in Morocco. Paul Rabinow. LC 77-71066. (Quantum Bks.: No. 11). 1977. pap. 13.95 (*0-520-03529-1*) U CA Pr.

Reflections on Frege's Philosophy. Reinhardt Grossmann. LC 77-78328. (Northwestern University Publications in Analytic Philosophy). 277p. reprint ed. 79.00 (*0-8357-9468-7*, 2010264) Bks Demand.

Reflections on Gender & Science. Evelyn F. Keller. LC 84-17327. 176p. 1986. pap. 12.00 (*0-300-03636-1*) Yale U Pr.

***Reflections on Gender & Science.** 10th anniversary ed. Evelyn F. Keller. 1996. 12.00 (*0-300-06595-7*) Yale U Pr.

Reflections on Giving, Receiving, & Serenity. Veronica Ray. (Hazelden Meditation Ser.). 1996. 5.99 (*0-517-15023-9*, Wings Books) Random.

Reflections on Growing up Disabled. Ed. by Reginald L. Jones. 103p. 1983. pap. text ed. 10.00 (*0-86586-134-X*, P258) Coun Exc Child.

Reflections on Hanging. Arthur Koestler. LC 82-45670. reprint ed. 30.00 (*0-404-62423-5*) AMS Pr.

***Reflections on Healing: A Central Nursing Construct.** LC 96-50950. (Pub. Ser.). 1996. write for info. (*0-88737-725-4*) Natl League Nurse.

Reflections on Higher Education: A Dean's View. Abraham L. Gitlow. 234p. (Orig.). (C). 1995. pap. text ed. 29.00 (*0-7618-0073-5*); lib. bdg. 49.00 (*0-7618-0072-7*) U Pr of Amer.

Reflections on History. Jacob Burckhardt. LC 78-24385. Orig. Title: Force & Freedom. 1979. reprint ed. 15.00 (*0-913966-37-1*); reprint ed. pap. 7.00 (*0-913966-38-X*) Liberty Fund.

Reflections on History & Historians. Theodore S. Hamerow. LC 86-22451. 288p. (C). 1986. text ed. 30.00 (*0-299-10930-5*) U of Wis Pr.

Reflections on History & Historians. Theodore S. Hamerow. LC 86-22451. 288p. 1991. pap. text ed. 14.95 (*0-299-10934-8*) U of Wis Pr.

Reflections on Human Development. Mahbub Ul Haq. 288p. 1995. 38.00 (*0-19-510191-X*); pap. 12.95 (*0-19-510193-6*) OUP.

Reflections on Human Nature. Arthur O. Lovejoy. LC 61-15700. 281p. 1968. reprint ed. pap. 13.95 (*0-8018-0395-0*) Johns Hopkins.

Reflections on Humanae Vitae. Pope John Paul, II. LC 84-28625. 96p. 1984. pap. 3.50 (*0-8198-6410-2*) Pauline Bks.

Reflections on International Administration. Alexander Loveday. LC 74-9168. 334p. 1974. reprint ed. text ed. 69.50 (*0-8371-7618-2*, LOIA, Greenwood Pr) Greenwood.

Reflections on International Arbitration & Litigation in the International Court of Justice. Shabtai Rosenne. (Forum Internationale Ser.: No. 9). 1987. 24.00 (*90-6544-351-7*) Kluwer Law Tax Pubs.

Reflections on Islamic History & Civilization: The Complete Collected Essays of Sir Hamilton Gibb, 4 vols., Set. Ed. by Lawrence I. Conrad. (Illus.). 2500p. 140.00 (*0-87850-054-5*) Darwin Pr.

Reflections on James Joyce: Stuart Gilbert's Paris Journal. Stuart Gilbert. Ed. by Thomas F. Staley & Randolph Lewis. LC 92-33233. (HRHRC Imprint Ser.). (Illus.). 117p. (C). 1993. text ed. 24.95 (*0-292-77671-3*) U of Tex Pr.

***Reflections on Jerusalem: City of David in Classical Texts.** Naftali Rothenberg et al. Ed. by Carol Diament. xiv, 125p. (Orig.). 1995. pap. 9.00 (*1-889525-03-0*) WZO.

***Reflections on Jesus & Socrates: Word & Silence.** Paul W. Gooch. 1997. 30.00 (*0-614-27565-2*) Yale U Pr.

Reflections on Kant's Philosophy. Ed. by William H. Werkmeister. LC 75-20376. 181p. 1975. 23.95 (*0-8130-0541-8*) U Press Fla.

Reflections on Kant's Philosophy. Ed. by William H. Werkmeister. LC 75-20376. 190p. reprint ed. pap. 54.20 (*0-7837-5066-8*, 2044762) Bks Demand.

Reflections on Kashmir Politics. Wani Gull Mohd. (C). 1993. 12.50 (*81-7024-580-X*, Pub. by Ashish II) S Asia.

Reflections on Kashmir Politics. Syed T. Hussain. (C). 1987. 31.00 (*0-8364-2139-6*, Pub. by Usha II); 31.00 (*0-8364-2231-7*, Pub. by Sundeep II) S Asia.

Reflections on Kashmir Politics. Gull M. Wani & Nasir A. Naqash. xi, 94p. 1993. 10.95 (*1-881338-25-8*) Nataraj Bks.

Reflections on Kurt Godel. Hao Wang. 368p. 1990. reprint ed. pap. 18.00 (*0-262-73087-1*) MIT Pr.

Reflections on Landscape: The Lives & Work of Six British Landscape Architects. Sheila Harvey. 200p. 1987. text ed. 67.95 (*0-291-39708-5*, Pub. by Gower UK) Ashgate Pub Co.

Reflections on Language Learning. Ed. by Leila Barbara & Mike Scott. LC 94-30329. 240p. 1994. 69.95 (*1-85359-258-7*); pap. 24.95 (*1-85359-257-9*) Taylor & Francis.

Reflections on Law Librarianship: A Collection of Interviews. Ed. by Marjorie A. Garson et al. (American Association of Law Libraries Publications Ser.: No. 29). xii, 262p. 1988. 35.00 (*0-8377-0128-7*) Rothman.

Reflections on Leadership: How Robert K. Greenleaf's Theory of Servant-Leadership Influenced Today's Top Manaagement Thinkers. Ed. by Larry C. Spears. LC 94-40297. 368p. 1995. text ed. 27.95 (*0-471-03686-2*) Wiley.

Reflections on Learning. Howard M. Jones. LC 69-17580. (Essay Index Reprint Ser.). 1977. 15.95 (*0-8369-0022-7*) Ayer.

Reflections on Lee: A Historian's Assessment. Charles P. Roland. LC 95-3685. (Illus.). 128p. 1995. 16.95 (*0-8117-0719-9*) Stackpole.

Reflections on Leisure, Play, & Recreation. David L. Jewell. LC 96-24838. 1997. pap. 14.95 (*0-8093-2114-9*) S Ill U Pr.

Reflections on Liberation. Daryl R. Grigsby. LC 84-72421. (Illus.). 176p. (Orig.). 1985. pap. 5.95 (*0-9614210-0-2*) Asante Pubns.

***Reflections on Life: A Student's Book of Poetry.** Christine M. Synowiec. 1995. pap. 9.95 (*1-885335-15-6*) Positive Support.

Reflections on Life after Life. Raymond A. Moody, Jr. 160p. 1985. mass mkt. 5.99 (*0-553-25227-5*) Bantam.

Reflections on Life & Death. Joseph Chiari. LC 77-4054. 141p. 1977. 35.00 (*0-87752-212-X*) Gordian.

Reflections on Life & How to Live It. H. R. Stevens. LC 93-86537. 154p. (Orig.). 1993. pap. text ed. 7.50 (*1-878579-07-X*) SUN Pub Co.

Reflections on Life & Love. James M. Richardson. 112p. (Orig.). 1995. pap. 10.00 (*0-9647901-0-6*) Harmattan Pr.

***Reflections on Literature & Morality.** Andre Gide & Paul Guillaume. Ed. & Intro. by Justin O'Brien. Date not set. write for info. (*0-8369-2396-0*) Ayer.

Reflections on Literature for Children. Ed. by Francelia Butler & Richard W. Rotert. LC 84-12554. xi, 281p. (C). 1984. pap. 27.50 (*0-208-02075-6*, Lib Prof Pubns) Shoe String.

Reflections on Logic, Politics & Reality: A Challenge to the Sacred Consensus of Contemporary American Thinking. Albert Murray. 256p. (C). 1989. 24.95 (*1-877586-00-5*) Braimanna Pubs.

Reflections on Lorca's Private Mythology: Once Five Years Pass & the Rural Plays. Beth Wellington. LC 91-38450. (Ars Interpretandi Ser.: Vol. 2). 150p. (C). 1994. text ed. 45.95 (*0-8204-1799-8*) P Lang Pubng.

Reflections on Love. Paul J. Lehman & Rani Ziegler. (Illus.). 80p. (Orig.). 1993. pap. 8.95 (*0-9622035-2-1*) Universal Oregon.

Reflections on Love, Religion, & Beyond. 2nd rev. ed. Donald W. Garner. LC 87-62644. 92p. (C). 1988. pap. 3.95 (*0-9618970-1-5*) Sea Crow Prodn.

Reflections on Man & the Human Condition. abr. ed. John Bourman. Ed. by Philip Kollas. 200p. 1995. 19.95 (*0-9650797-0-8*) J L Bowman.

***Reflections on Marriage.** William P. Steinhauser & Laurie A. Boyce. (Illus.). 72p. 1984. 2.75 (*0-940679-00-0*) CCOC.

Reflections on Mary's Help Hospital & Seton Medical Center, 1893-1985. Marie M. Mahoney. 180p. 1986. 25.00 (*0-9616516-0-1*) Seton Med Ctr.

Reflections on Medicine, Biotechnology, & the Law. Zelman Cowen. LC 86-1492. 68p. reprint ed. pap. 25.00 (*0-7837-1818-7*, 2042018) Bks Demand.

Reflections on Modern History: The Historian & Human Responsibility. Hans Kohn. LC 77-28495. 360p. 1978. reprint ed. text ed. 65.00 (*0-313-20232-X*, KORM, Greenwood Pr) Greenwood.

Reflections on Modern Psychiatry. Ed. by David J. Kupfer. LC 91-33208. 143p. 1992. text ed. 28.50 (*0-88048-516-7*, 8516) Am Psychiatric.

***Reflections on Moments in Time.** Frederick A. Mochel. (Orig.). 1997. pap. write for info. (*1-57553-549-1*) Watermrk Pr.

Reflections on Monetarism: Britain's Vain Search for a Successful Economic Strategy. Tim Congdon. 304p. 1992. pap. 24.95 (*1-85278-766-X*) E Elgar.

Reflections on Money. Ed. by David T. Llewellyn. LC 89-39231. 215p. 1990. text ed. 59.95 (*0-312-03997-2*) St Martin.

Reflections on Moral Re-Armament. Kenneth Belden. 1983. 4.25 (*0-901269-77-8*) Grosvenor USA.

***Reflections on Motherhood.** Katrina Fried. 1997. 15.95 (*0-8362-2657-7*) Andrews & McMeel.

Reflections on Multiculturalism. Ed. by Robert F. Eddy. LC 96-3043. 240p. (Orig.). 1996. pap. 19.95 (*1-877864-45-5*) Intercult Pr.

Reflections on Muscle. Andrew Huxley. LC 79-5480. (Sherrington Lectures: No. 14). (Illus.). 121p. reprint ed. pap. 34.50 (*0-8357-3702-0*, 2036426) Bks Demand.

***Reflections on Nature: Small Paintings by Arthur Dove, 1942-1943.** Charles C. Eldredge et al. LC 97-10942. 1997. write for info. (*1-885444-05-2*) Am Fed Arts.

Reflections on Nikolai Gogol. Marrianne Bogojavlensky. 69p. 1968. pap. 3.00 (*0-317-30452-6*) Holy Trinity.

Reflections on Our Age: UNESCO. Intro. by David J. Hardman. LC 74-128295. (Essay Index Reprint Ser.). 1977. 24.95 (*0-8369-2024-4*) Ayer.

Reflections on Our Common Systems of Morality: On Human Nature. Francis Hutcheson. Ed. by Thomas Mautner. LC 92-23820. 240p. (C). 1993. text ed. 49.95 (*0-521-43089-5*) Cambridge U Pr.

Reflections on Our Hymns. Max Wheeler. 1992. pap. 4.95 (*0-89137-604-6*) Quality Pubns.

Reflections on Our Times. P. N. Haksar. 119p. 1982. 19.95 (*0-318-37263-0*) Asia Bk Corp.

***Reflections on Parenting.** Carol G. Mooney. xii, 167p. (Orig.). 1996. pap. 14.95 (*0-9609466-2-4*) NEAEYC.

Reflections on Philosophy: Introductory Essays. Leemon McHenry & Frederick Adams. LC 92-50010. 227p. (C). 1992. pap. text ed. 15.00 (*0-312-06777-1*) St Martin.

Reflections on Political Economy (1771) Pietro Verri. Tr. by Barbara McGilvray & Peter Groenewegen from ITA. xxix, 120p. 1993. lib. bdg. 29.50 (*0-678-01459-0*) Kelley.

Reflections on Political Identity. Anne Norton. LC 88-45400. (Constitutional Thought Ser.). 192p. 1988. text ed. 36.50 (*0-8018-3694-8*) Johns Hopkins.

Reflections on Political Identity. Anne Norton. (Johns Hopkins Series in Constitutional Thought). 224p. (C). 1993. reprint ed. pap. text ed. 14.95 (*0-8018-4728-1*) Johns Hopkins.

Reflections on Population. 2nd ed. Rafael M. Salas. 256p. 1985. 78.00 (*0-08-032406-1*, Pergamon Pr) Elsevier.

Reflections on Racial Identity, Race Relations & Culture: Collected Works of Janet E. Helms. Ed. by Janet E. Helms & Jacalyn Mindell. 250p. (Orig.). (YA). (gr. 12 up). 1996. pap. text ed. 19.95 (*0-9633036-1-9*) Content Comms.

Reflections on Reasoning. Raymond S. Nickerson. 160p. (C). 1986. 29.95 (*0-89859-762-5*); pap. 18.50 (*0-89859-763-3*) L Erlbaum Assocs.

Reflections on Reasoning. Raymond S. Nickerson. (C). 1986. teacher ed. write for info. (*0-89859-764-1*) L Erlbaum Assocs.

***Reflections on Rebellion: Stories from the Indonesian Upheavals of 1948 & 1965.** Ed. by William H. Frederick. Tr. by John H. McGlynn & William H. Frederick. LC 83-60271. (Papers in International Studies: No. 60). 175p. 1983. reprint ed. pap. 49.90 (*0-608-04102-5*, 2064834) Bks Demand.

***Reflections on Regionalism: Report of the Study Group on International Trade.** Jaime Serra et al. LC 97-3701. 1997. write for info. (*0-87003-076-0*) Carnegie Endow.

Reflections on Relationships. (YA). (gr. 11-12). 1978. student ed. 9.64 (*0-13-770081-4*) P-H.

Reflections on Relaxation. Judy Loosmore. (Life Line Ser.). (Illus.). 158p. (Orig.). 1994. pap. 16.95 (*1-55059-081-2*) Temeron Bks.

Reflections on Revival. Charles G. Finney. LC 78-26527. 160p. 1979. pap. 7.99 (*0-87123-157-3*) Bethany Hse.

Reflections on Revolution: Images of Romanticism. Ed. by Alison Yarrington & Kelvin Everest. LC 92-13300. 216p. (C). (gr. 13). 1993. text ed. 62.95 (*0-415-07741-9*, A9804) Routledge.

Reflections on Richard Hartshorne's The Nature of Geography. T. H. Elkins et al. Ed. by Stanley D. Brunn. LC 89-83425. (Occasional Publications of the AAG). 170p. (Orig.). (C). 1989. pap. text ed. 10.00 (*0-89291-204-9*) Assn Am Geographers.

***Reflections on Riding & Jumping: Winning Techniques for Serious Riders.** William Steinkraus. LC 96-33561. (Illus.). 240p. 1997. pap. 17.95 (*1-57076-043-8*, Trafalgar Sq Pub) Trafalgar.

Reflections on Roberto. Phil Musick. 138p. 1994. pap. 14.95 (*0-9641355-0-7*) Pitts Pirates.

Reflections on Self Psychology. Ed. by Joseph D. Lichtenberg & Samuel Kaplan. (Psychoanalytic Inquiry Bk.: Vol. 1). 448p. 1983. text ed. 49.95 (*0-88163-001-2*) Analytic Pr.

Reflections on Shamanism: The Tribal Healer & the Technological Trance. John Grim. (Teilhard Studies: No. 6). 20p. (Orig.). 1981. pap. 3.50 (*0-89012-029-3*) Am Teilhard.

Reflections on Shattered Windows: Promises & Prospects for Asian American Studies. Ed. by Shirley Hune et al. LC 87-31725. (Association for Asian American Studies Ser.). 238p. (C). 1988. pap. 20.00 (*0-87422-039-4*) Wash St U Pr.

Reflections on Simplicity. Elaine M. Prevallet. LC 82-80439. 31p. 1982. pap. 3.00 (*0-87574-244-0*) Pendle Hill.

Reflections on Society. Jack Friedland. 128p. (Orig.). 1996. pap. 8.95 (*0-9642390-4-3*) New Gateway Pr.

***Reflections on Sociology & Theology.** David Martin. 272p. 1997. 60.00 (*0-19-827384-3*) OUP.

Reflections on Spacetime: Foundations, Philosophy, History. Ed. by U. Majer & H. J. Schmidt. LC 95-37544. 1995. lib. bdg. 55.00 (*0-7923-3712-3*) Kluwer Ac.

Reflections on St. Paul. Burns K. Seeley. Ed. by Jerome F. Coniker. LC 82-72202. (Living Meditation & Prayerbook Ser.). (Illus.). 270p. (Orig.). 1982. pap. text ed. 5.00 (*0-932406-07-6*) AFC.

***Reflections on Statistics: Agendas for Learning, Teaching, & Assessment in K-12.** Ed. by Susanne P. Lajoie. LC 97-7357. (Studies in Mathematical Thinking & Learning). 350p. 1997. write for info. (*0-8058-1971-1*) L Erlbaum Assocs.

***Reflections on Statistics: Agendas for Learning, Teaching, & Assessment in K-12.** Ed. by Susanne P. Lajoie. LC 97-7357. (Studies in Mathematical Thinking & Learning). 350p. 1997. pap. write for info. (*0-8058-1972-X*) L Erlbaum Assocs.

***Reflections on Suicide.** 2nd ed. Perry H. Biddle, Jr. 36p. 1996. pap. 3.95 (*0-914733-22-2*) Desert Min.

Reflections on Suicide. Anne L. Stael-Holstein. LC 77-37724. reprint ed. 39.50 (*0-404-56838-6*) AMS Pr.

Reflections on Swami Vivekananda: Hundred Years after Chicago. Ed. by M. Sivaramkrishna & Sumita Roy. (C). 1993. 22.00 (*81-207-1603-5*, Pub. by Sterling Plns Pvt II) S Asia.

***Reflections on Symmetry: In Chemistry...& Elsewhere.** E. Heilbronner & J. Dunitz. (Illus.). vi, 154p. (C). 1993. 39.50 (*3-527-28488-5*, VCH) Wiley.

Reflections on Tashmoo. Ruth T. Cochrane & Marguerite L. Miller. (Illus.). 50p. 1994. pap. 8.95 (*0-9641966-0-3*) Cochrane-Miller.

Reflections on Television. Gene F. Jankowski & David C. Fuchs. (Illus.). 165p. 1995. 25.00 (*0-19-507487-4*) OUP.

Reflections on Texas. (Illus.). 30p. 1979. pap. 2.95 (*0-933164-42-4*) U of Tex Inst Tex Culture.

Reflections on That Other America. Ivan H. Nothdurft. LC 95-95357. 120p. (Orig.). 1996. pap. 8.00 (*0-934426-66-X*) NAPSAC Reprods.

Reflections on the Aesthetics of Futurism, Dadaism, & Surrealism: A Prosody Beyond Words. Eric Sellin. LC 93-33960. 168p. 1993. 79.95 (*0-7734-9361-1*) E Mellen.

Reflections on the American Institutions: Selections from the American Commonwealth. James Bryce. 1990. 14.50 (*0-8446-0517-4*) Peter Smith.

Reflections on the Beginnings of Prestressed Concrete in America. 368p. 1981. pap. 30.00 (*0-937040-18-5*, JR-H-81) P-PCI.

***Reflections on the Big Red Bombs: U. S. S. R. Nuclear Weapons.** Frank H. Shelton. Ed. by Jolene Schneider. (Illus.). 156p. 1997. 15.00 (*1-881816-17-6*) Shelton Ent.

***Reflections on the Body, Cremation, & Catholic Funeral Rites.** Committee on the Liturgy, National Conference of Catholic Bishops. 16p. 1997. pap. text ed. 1.50 (*1-57455-033-0*) US Catholic.

Reflections on the Book, "The Doctrine of Nova Hierosolyma Concerning the Sacred Scripture" Philip N. Odhner. 86p. 1987. 12.50 (*1-883270-07-3*) Swedenborg Assn.

Reflections on the Brazilian Counter-Revolution: Essays. Florestan Fernandes. Tr. by Michel Vale & Patrick M. Hughes from POR. LC 80-5456. 199p. reprint ed. pap. 56.80 (*0-685-23737-0*, 2032778) Bks Demand.

Reflections on the Catechism of the Catholic Church. Ed. by James Socias. 250p. 1993. pap. 9.95 (*0-933932-67-7*) Scepter Pubs.

Reflections on the Civil War. Bruce Catton. Ed. by John Leekley. 272p. 1987. mass mkt. 6.99 (*0-425-10495-8*) Berkley Pub.

Reflections on the Civil War. Bruce Catton. Ed. by John Leekley. 272p. 1994. reprint ed. pap. 12.00 (*0-425-14141-1*, Berkley Trade) Berkley Pub.

Reflections on the Creed. Hugh Lavery. (C). 1988. 39.00 (*0-85439-213-0*, Pub. by St Paul Pubns UK) St Mut.

***Reflections on the Cross.** 76p. 1985. 8.99 (*0-8341-9642-5*) Lillenas.

Reflections on the Cross. Contrib. by Eleanor Whitsett. 1985. 9.99 (*0-685-71351-2*, MB-549) Lillenas.

Reflections on the Cuban Missile Crisis. rev. ed. Raymond L. Garthoff. 170p. 1989. pap. text ed. 12.95 (*0-8157-3053-5*) Brookings.

***Reflections on the Cultural Revolution: Canons & Disciplinary Change.** Jan Gorak. (Wellesley Studies in Critical Theory). 300p. Date not set. text ed. 45.00 (*0-8153-0889-2*) Garland.

Reflections on the Death of a Porcupine & Other Essays. D. H. Lawrence. Ed. by Michael Herbert. (Cambridge Edition of the Works of D. H. Lawrence). 400p. 1988. text ed. 110.00 (*0-521-26622-X*); pap. text ed. 39.95 (*0-521-35847-7*) Cambridge U Pr.

Reflections on the Decline of Science in England: And on Some of the Causes. Charles Babbage. LC 77-115928. xv, 228p. 1970. reprint ed. 39.50 (*0-678-00645-8*) Kelley.

R

***Reflections on the Development of Modern Macroeconomics.** Brian Snowdon et al. LC 97-23219. 1997. write for info. (*1-85898-342-8*) E Elgar.

Reflections on the Encyclical: The Splendor of Truth. Albert J. Shamon. LC 94-66186. 64p. (Orig.). 1994. pap. 2.00 (*1-877678-28-7*) Riehle Found.

Reflections on the Failure of Socialism. Max Eastman. LC 82-2957. 128p. 1982. reprint ed. text ed. 55.00 (*0-313-23534-1*, EARE, Greenwood Pr) Greenwood.

Reflections on the Failure of the First West Indian Federation. Hugh W. Springer. LC 70-38762. (Harvard University. Center for International Affairs. Occasional Papers in International Affairs: No. 4). reprint ed. 27.50 (*0-404-54604-8*) AMS Pr.

Reflections on the Fantastic: Selected Essays from the Fourth International Conference on the Fantastic in the Arts. Ed. by Michael R. Collings. LC 86-12123. (Contributions to the Study of Science Fiction & Fantasy Ser.: No. 24). 124p. 1986. text ed. 45.00 (*0-313-25555-5*, CRF/) Greenwood.

Reflections on the Folklife Festival: An Ethnography of Participant Experience. Richard Bauman et al. (Special Publications: No. 2). (Illus.). 70p. (C). 1992. text ed. 22.50 (*1-879407-03-5*); pap. text ed. 9.95 (*1-879407-02-7*) IN Univ Folk Inst.

Reflections on the Formation & the Distribution of Riches. A. Robert Turgot. Tr. by William J. Ashley. LC 71-157514. (Reprints of Economic Classics Ser.). xxii, 112p. 1971. reprint ed. 29.50 (*0-678-00017-4*) Kelley.

Reflections on the French Revolution: A Hillsdale Symposium. Frwd. by Stephen Tonsor. LC 89-77161. (Illus.). 185p. 1990. 19.95 (*0-89526-750-0*) Regnery Pub.

Reflections on the Gospel, Vol. One: Daily Devotions for Radical Christian Living. John M. Talbot. 181p. 1994. reprint ed. pap. 8.00 (*1-883803-02-0*) Troubadour Lord.

Reflections on the Gospel, Vol. Two: Daily Devotions for Radical Christian Living. John M. Talbot. 152p. 1994. reprint ed. pap. 8.00 (*1-883803-03-9*) Troubadour Lord.

Reflections on the Hero As Quixote. Alexander Welsh. LC 80-8584. 255p. 1981. reprint ed. pap. 72.70 (*0-7837-8598-4*, 2049413) Bks Demand.

***Reflections on the History of Art: Views & Reviews.** E. H. Gombrich. Ed. by Richard Woodfield. (Illus.). 256p. Date not set. 29.95 (*0-7148-2493-3*, Pub. by Phaidon Press UK) Chronicle Bks.

Reflections on the History of Art: Views & Reviews. Ernest H. Gombrich. Ed. by Richard Woodfield. 256p. 1987. 40.00 (*0-520-06189-6*) U CA Pr.

Reflections on the International Monetary System. Ariel Buira. LC 95-1091. (Essays in International Finance Ser.: No. 195). 46p. 1995. pap. 8.00 (*0-88165-102-8*) Princeton U Int Finan Econ.

Reflections on the International Monetary System. Guillaume Guindey & Charles A. Coombs. (Per Jacobsson Lectures: 1980). 34p. reprint ed. pap. 25.00 (*0-317-29084-3*, 2019265) Bks Demand.

Reflections on the Jesus Prayer. 1985. 8.95 (*0-87193-070-6*) Dimension Bks.

Reflections on the Law of Love. James A. Griffin. LC 91-11889. 96p. (Orig.). 1991. pap. 4.95 (*0-8189-0608-1*) Alba.

Reflections on the Loma Prieta Earthquake of October 17, 1989. Structural Engineers Association of California Staff. (Illus.). 1991. 40.00 (*0-9628947-0-2*) Structl Eng.

Reflections on the March of the Living: April 26 - May 10, 1992. Alvin I. Schiff. 164p. (Orig.). (YA). (gr. 11-12). 1993. pap. 25.00 (*0-930029-07-0*) Central Agency.

Reflections on the May Fourth Movement. Ed. by Benjamin I. Schwartz. LC 77-183976. (East Asian Monographs: No. 44). 140p. 1972. pap. 14.00 (*0-674-75230-9*) HUP.

Reflections on the Mental Side of Sports. Marie Dalloway. LC 94-66323. 143p. 1994. pap. text ed. 14.95 (*0-9634933-4-5*) Optimal Perf.

Reflections on the Modernization of Spain. Rodrigo Botero. LC 92-8644. 32p. 1992. 6.95 (*1-55815-199-0*) ICS Pr.

Reflections on the Motive Power of Fire. Sadi Carnot. (Illus.). 1990. 14.50 (*0-8446-1809-8*) Peter Smith.

Reflections on the Occasion of the Fiftieth Anniversary. Ed. by Richard G. Cunningham. 66p. (Orig.). 1988. pap. 4.00 (*0-943616-41-7*) Canon Law Soc.

Reflections on the Okinawan Experience: Essays Commemorating 100 Years of Okinawan Immigration. Ed. by Ronald Y. Nakasone. LC 96-84002. (Illus.). 135p. 1996. 28.00 (*0-9623086-3-3*); pap. 14.00 (*0-9623086-4-1*) Dharma Cloud Pubs.

Reflections on the Philosophy of the History of Mankind. Johann G. Herder. LC 68-24012. (Classic European Historians Ser.). 418p. reprint ed. pap. 122.30 (*0-8357-7007-9*, 2056771) Bks Demand.

***Reflections on the Pool: California Designs for Swimming.** I. B. Melchior. LC 96-44236. (Illus.). 160p. 1997. 45.00 (*0-8478-2014-9*) Rizzoli Intl.

Reflections on the Priesthood. Anthony M. Coniaris. 1993. pap. 10.95 (*0-937032-94-8*) Light&Life Pub Co MN.

Reflections on the Principles of Psychology: William James after a Century. Ed. by Michael G. Johnson & Tracy B. Henley. 344p. 1990. 89.95 (*0-8058-0205-3*) L Erlbaum Assocs.

Reflections on the Problem of Relevance. Alfred Schutz. Ed. by Richard M. Zaner. LC 82-11850. xxiv, 186p. 1982. reprint ed. text ed. 39.75 (*0-313-22820-5*, SCRER, Greenwood Pr) Greenwood.

Reflections on the Psalms. C. S. Lewis. LC 58-10910. 1964. pap. 8.00 (*0-15-676248-X*, Harvest Bks) HarBrace.

Reflections on the Revolution in Europe. Ralf Dahrendorf. 176p. 1990. 17.95 (*0-8129-1883-5*, Times Bks) Random.

Reflections on the Revolution in France. Edmund E. Burke. LC 92-27564. (World's Classics Ser.). 352p. (Orig.). 1993. 7.95 (*0-19-281844-9*) OUP.

Reflections on the Revolution in France. Edmund E. Burke. Ed. by J. G. Pocock. LC 86-31894. (HPC Classics Ser.). 294p. (Orig.). (C). 1987. pap. text ed. 9.95 (*0-87220-020-5*) Hackett Pub.

Reflections on the Revolution in France. Edmund E. Burke. Ed. by J. G. Pocock. LC 86-31894. (HPC Classics Ser.). 294p. (Orig.). (C). 1987. lib. bdg. 29.95 (*0-87220-021-3*) Hackett Pub.

Reflections on the Revolution in France. Edmund E. Burke. (Great Books in Philosophy). 253p. (Orig.). 1988. pap. 7.95 (*0-87975-411-7*) Prometheus Bks.

Reflections on the Revolution of Our Time. Harold J. Laski. 367p. 1968. reprint ed. 25.00 (*0-7146-1564-1*, Pub. by F Cass Pubs UK) Intl Spec Bk.

Reflections on the Revolution of Our Times. Harold J. Laski. LC 68-14931. 367p. 1968. reprint ed. 45.00 (*0-678-05063-5*) Kelley.

Reflections on the River. Stephen Cassettari. (Illus.). 48p. 1994. 10.00 (*0-207-18210-8*, Pub. by Angus & Robertson AT) HarpC.

Reflections on the Role of the Principal. Ed. by Robert J. Kealey. 73p. (Orig.). 1989. pap. 5.00 (*1-55833-013-5*) Natl Cath Educ.

***Reflections on the Rubaiyat.** John W. Nutter. 204p. (Orig.). 1996. pap. write for info. (*1-883938-34-1*) Dry Bones Pr.

Reflections on the Run: One Hundred Meditations on Faith, Growth & Commitment. Charles B. Fulton, Jr. LC 94-2810. 128p. 1994. pap. 8.99 (*0-87788-818-3*) Shaw Pubs.

Reflections on the Spirituality of Gregorian Chant. Jacques Hourlier. Ed. by Richard J. Pugsley. Tr. by Dom G. Casprini & Robert J. Edmonson from FRE. 79p. (C). 1995. pap. 6.95 (*1-55725-096-0*) Paraclete MA.

Reflections on the Study of Religion. Jacques Waardenburg. (Religion & Reason Ser.: No. 15). 1978. text ed. 64.65 (*90-279-7604-X*) Mouton.

***Reflections on the Swan Sea.** Gary G. Swancey. 299p. (Orig.). 1998. pap. 12.95 (*1-889501-41-7*, Appaloosa) Sovereign.

Reflections on the Tantras. Sudhakar Chattopadhyaya. (C). 1990. 14.00 (*81-208-0691-3*, Pub. by Motilal Banarsidass II) S Asia.

***Reflections on the Third Millennium: An Alternative Vision to Postmodernism.** Juan A. Blanco. 1997. pap. 15.95 (*1-876175-03-6*) Ocean Pr.

Reflections on the Thoughts of a Young Black Male: Collection of My Childhood Poetry. David R. Burgest. (Illus.). 127p. (Orig.). 1992. pap. write for info. (*0-9624077-0-4*) Self-Taught Pubs.

Reflections on the Tibetan Terrier: A Collection of Writings about the Tibetan Terrier. 2nd ed. Jane Reif. LC 95-68069. (Illus.). 120p. 1995. 22.00 (*0-913337-25-0*) Southfarm Pr.

Reflections on the Transformation of Industrial Relations. Ed. by James Chelius & James R. Dworkin. LC 89-48376. (Institute of Management & Labor Relations Ser.: No. 1). (Illus.). 233p. 1990. 29.50 (*0-8108-2259-8*) Scarecrow.

Reflections on the Vietnam War. Cao Van Vien & Dong Van Khuyen. 165p. 1989. reprint ed. pap. 18.50 (*0-923135-06-5*) Dalley Bk Service.

Reflections on the Wall. Michael Posey. 1994. 9.95 (*1-881116-31-X*) Black Forest Pr.

Reflections on the Water: Understanding God & the World Through the Batpism of Believers. Ed. by Paul S. Fiddes. LC 96-14324. (Regent's Study Guides Ser.: Vol. 4). 152p. 1996. pap. 13.95 (*1-57312-052-9*) Smyth & Helwys.

Reflections on the Way to the Gallows: Rebel Women in Pre-War Japan. Tr. & Intro. by Mikiso Hane. 340p. (C). 1988. 35.00 (*0-520-06259-0*); pap. 14.95 (*0-520-08421-7*) U CA Pr.

Reflections on the Women's Movement in India: Religion, Ecology, Development. Gabriele Dietrich. xiv, 145p. 1992. 25.00 (*81-85487-01-4*, Pub. by Horizon India Bks II) Advent Bks Div.

Reflections on the Work of Edward Said: Secular Criticism & the Gravity of History. Pearson E. Ansell & Ed B. Parry. (C). 1996. pap. write for info. (*0-85315-840-1*, Pub. by Lawrence & Wishart UK) NYU Pr.

Reflections on the World Economic Crisis. Andre G. Frank. LC 80-29270. 192p. 1981. 23.00 (*0-85345-563-5*); pap. 10.00 (*0-85345-564-3*) Monthly Rev.

Reflections on the 1988-1990 March of the Living. Ed. by P. Miles et al. (Illus.). 139p. (Orig.). 1991. pap. 25.00 (*0-930029-04-6*) Central Agency.

***Reflections on Theology & Gender.** Ed. by Fokkelien Van Dijk-Hemmes & Athalya Brenner. 107p. 1994. pap. 26.95 (*90-390-0111-1*, Pub. by KOK Pharos NE) Eisenbrauns.

Reflections on Therapeutic Storymaking: Like a Piece of Uncast Wood. Alida Gersie. 140p. 1995. pap. 19.95 (*1-85302-272-1*) Taylor & Francis.

Reflections on Things at Hand: The Neo-Confucian Anthology. Tr. by Wing-Tsit Chan. LC 65-22548. (Records of Civilization: Sources & Studies). 441p. 1967. text ed. 70.00 (*0-231-02819-9*) Col U Pr.

Reflections on Tibetan Culture: Essays in Memory of Turrell v. Wylie. Ed. by Richard Sherburne. LC 89-48515. (Studies in Asian Thought & Religion: Vol. 15). 368p. 1989. lib. bdg. 99.95 (*0-88946-064-7*) E Mellen.

Reflections on Toscanini. Harvey Sachs. 208p. 1993. pap. 14.95 (*1-55958-315-0*) Prima Pub.

Reflections on Vietnam. Robert G. Kaiser et al. 52p. (Orig.). 1991. pap. write for info. (*0-9630136-0-2*) Dialogue.

Reflections on Violence. John Keane. 192p. (C). 1996. text ed. 60.00 (*1-85984-979-2*, Pub. by Vrso UK); pap. text ed. 18.00 (*1-85984-115-5*, Pub. by Vrso UK) Norton.

Reflections on Violence. Georges Sorel. 1993. 23.00 (*0-8446-1416-5*) Peter Smith.

Reflections on Violence. Georges Sorel. LC 70-180432. reprint ed. 35.00 (*0-404-56165-9*) AMS Pr.

Reflections on Women in Monarchies & Democracies: Exploring Leadership Through the Study of Five Great Lives. Sally J. Patton. (Creative Lives Ser.). (Illus.). 68p. (Orig.). 1991. teacher ed., pap. 18.00 (*0-913705-41-1*) Zephyr Pr AZ.

Reflections on World Civilizations, 1. Ronald H. Fritze. (C). 1992. 26.50 (*0-673-46664-7*) Addson-Wesley Educ.

Reflections on World Civilizations, 2. Ronald H. Fritze. (C). 1992. 28.00 (*0-673-46665-5*) Addson-Wesley Educ.

Reflections, Sharing Thoughts: One-on-One. Alvin M. O'Hanlon. LC 86-61409. 1986. 17.50 (*0-9616898-0-3*) Phoenix Pr FL.

Reflections, Sketches, & Provocations: Essays & Commentary 1981-1987. Bob Avakian. 225p. 1989. 15.00 (*0-89851-102-X*); pap. 5.95 (*0-89851-101-1*) RCP Pubns.

Reflections Symphony No. 2: For Orchestra Full Score. K. Huska. 80p. 1992. pap. 40.00 (*0-7935-1590-4*) H Leonard.

Reflections Then & Now. Mildred Crombie. Ed. by Marion Perry. LC 81-52041. (Illus.). 55p. (Orig.). 1981. pap. 4.95 (*0-938838-07-5*) Textile Bridge.

Reflections Through a Glass. Anna G. Curzio. 80p. 1987. 45.00 (*0-7212-0777-4*, Pub. by Regency Press UK) St Mut.

Reflections Through a Moving Lens. Joseph S. Salzburg. 369p. 1985. 12.50 (*0-9614715-0-6*) Sovereign MD.

Reflections Through Time. S. B. Jones-Hendrickson. 63p. 1989. 7.95 (*0-932831-00-1*) Eastern Caribbean Inst.

***Reflections to Hold on To: I Hold Dear These "Reflections" & Have Chosen to Share Them with You. Ruth.** Ruth Wallin. (Illus.). 64p. 1996. spiral bd., pap. 14.95 (*1-880470-44-6*) Creative Des.

Reflections upon Ancient & Modern Learning. William Wotton. (Anglistica & Americana Ser.: No. 12). 359p. 1968. reprint ed. 89.70 (*0-685-66531-3*, 05101980) G Olms Pubs.

Reflective Approach to Teaching Physical Education. Donald R. Hellison & Thomas J. Templin. LC 90-20654. (Illus.). 208p. (C). 1991. text ed. 30.00 (*0-87322-311-X*, BHEL0311) Human Kinetics.

***Reflective Approaches to European Governance.** Ed. by Knud E. Jorgensen. 272p. 1997. text ed. 65.00 (*0-312-17257-5*) St Martin.

Reflective Cracking in Pavements: State of the Art & Design Recommendations. Ed. by J. M. Rigo et al. LC 93-7255. (RILEM Proceedings Ser.: No. 20). 1993. write for info. (*0-419-18220-9*, E & FN Spon) Routledge Chapman & Hall.

Reflective Expressions. Garry Martin. 36p. (Orig.). pap. 4.98 (*0-9639912-1-3*) Southeast Pubns.

Reflective Faculty Evaluation: Enhancing Teaching & Determining Faculty Effectiveness. John A. Centra. LC 93-19504. (Higher Education Ser.). 266p. text ed. 31.95 (*1-55542-579-8*) Jossey-Bass.

Reflective Helping in HIV & AIDs. Ed. by Charles Anderson & Patricia Wilkie. 256p. 1991. 95.00 (*0-335-15632-0*, Open Univ Pr); pap. 39.00 (*0-335-15631-2*, Open Univ Pr) Taylor & Francis.

Reflective Learning for Social Work. Ed. by Nick Gould & Imogen Taylor. 176p. 1996. 55.95 (*1-85742-320-8*, Pub. by Arena UK); pap. 28.95 (*1-85742-321-6*, Pub. by Arena UK) Ashgate Pub Co.

Reflective Optics. Dietrich G. Korsch. (Illus.). 358p. 1991. text ed. 122.00 (*0-12-421170-4*) Acad Pr.

Reflective Planning, Teaching, & Evaluation, K-12. Judy W. Eby. Ed. by Edward Kujawa. 384p. (C). 1993. pap. text ed. 55.00 (*0-02-331331-5*, Macmillan Coll) P-H.

***Reflective Planning, Teaching & Evaluation K 12.** 2nd ed. Judy W. Eby. LC 96-40427. 1997. 51.00 (*0-13-496480-2*, Merrill Coll) P-H.

Reflective Practice for Educators: Improving Schooling Through Professional Development. Karen F. Osterman & Robert B. Kottkamp. LC 92-37083. 224p. 1993. 47.95 (*0-8039-6046-8*); pap. 21.95 (*0-8039-6047-6*) Corwin Pr.

Reflective Practice in Nursing: The Growth of the Professional Practitioner. Ed. by Anthony M. Palmer et al. LC 93-38307. (Illus.). 193p. 1994. pap. 24.95 (*0-632-03597-8*) Blackwell Sci.

Reflective Practitioner. Donald A. Schon. 384p. 1995. pap. 25.95 (*1-85742-319-4*, Pub. by Arena UK) Ashgate Pub Co.

Reflective Practitioner: How Professionals Think in Action. Donald A. Schon. LC 82-70855. 374p. 1984. pap. 19.00 (*0-465-06878-2*) Basic.

***Reflective Principal: Leading the School Development Process.** David Stewart et al. LC 97-10140. (Illus.). 320p. (Orig.). 1997. pap. 26.95 (*1-57274-038-8*) R Owen Pubs.

Reflective Professional in Education. Ed. by Carmel Jennings & Elizabeth Kennedy. 220p. 1995. pap. 29.95 (*1-85302-330-2*, Pub. by J Kingsley Pubs UK) Taylor & Francis.

Reflective Researcher: Social Workers' Theories of Practice Research. Jan Fook. 224p. 1996. pap. 27.95 (*1-86448-033-5*, Pub. by Allen Unwin AT) Paul & Co Pubs.

Reflective Roles of the Classroom Teacher. D. John McIntyre & Mary J. O'Hair. 353p. (C). 1996. text ed. 46.95 (*0-534-17136-2*) Wadsworth Pub.

Reflective Supervision: A Relationship for Learning, 2 bks., Set. Linda Gilkerson & Rebecca S. Shanok. Ed. by Linda Eggbeer. 80p. (Orig.). (C). 1995. pap. text ed. 125.00 incl. vhs (*0-943657-36-9*) Zero To Three.

***Reflective Supervisor: A Practical Guide for Educators.** Raymond L. Calabrese & Sally J. Zepeda. LC 97-3483. (Illus.). 250p. 1997. write for info. (*1-883001-38-2*) Eye On Educ.

***Reflective Teach, Vol. 1.** Zeichner. Date not set. pap. text ed. write for info. (*0-312-08066-2*) St Martin.

Reflective Teacher Education: Cases & Critiques. Ed. by Linda Valli. LC 90-30789. (SUNY Series, Teacher Preparation & Development). 281p. (C). 1992. text ed. 64.50 (*0-7914-1131-1*); pap. text ed. 21.95 (*0-7914-1132-X*) State U NY Pr.

Reflective Teaching. 2nd ed. Newman. 1996. student ed., pap. text ed. 12.00 (*0-13-459645-5*) P-H.

Reflective Teaching: An Introduction. Kenneth M. Zeichner. 104p. 1996. pap. 12.95 (*0-8058-8050-X*) L Erlbaum Assocs.

Reflective Teaching: The Study of Your Constructivist Practices. 2nd ed. Ed. by James G. Henderson. 288p. (C). 1996. pap. text ed. 31.00 (*0-02-353521-0*, Macmillan Coll) P-H.

Reflective Teaching for Student Empowerment: Elementary Curriculum & Methods. Dorene D. Ross et al. (Illus.). 496p. (Orig.). (C). 1992. pap. text ed. 54.00 (*0-02-403960-8*, Macmillan Coll) P-H.

Reflective Teaching in Second Language Classrooms. Jack C. Richards & Charles Lockhart. (Language Education Ser.). 256p. (C). 1994. pap. 18.95 (*0-521-45803-X*); text ed. 44.95 (*0-521-45181-7*) Cambridge U Pr.

***Reflective Teaching in the Postmodern World: A Manifesto for Education in Postmodernity.** Stuart Parker. LC 96-28699. 1997. write for info. (*0-335-19586-5*, Open Univ Pr); pap. write for info. (*0-335-19585-7*, Open Univ Pr) Taylor & Francis.

Reflective Teaching in the Primary School. 2nd ed. Andrew Pollard & Sarah Tann. (Education Ser.). (Illus.). 224p. 1993. text ed. 70.00 (*0-304-32618-6*); pap. text ed. 24.95 (*0-304-32620-8*) Cassell.

Reflective Thinking: The Method of Education. Henry G. Hullfish & Phillip G. Smith. LC 77-16064. 273p. 1978. reprint ed. text ed. 59.75 (*0-313-20005-X*, HURT, Greenwood Pr) Greenwood.

Reflective Traveler. 48p. 1994. pap. 14.95 (*0-00-255445-3*) Collins SF.

Reflective Turn: Case Studies in & on Educational Practice. Ed. by Donald A. Schon. 384p. (C). 1990. text ed. 49.00 (*0-8077-3046-7*); pap. text ed. 24.95 (*0-8077-3045-9*) Tchrs Coll.

Reflective Wisdom: Richard Taylor on Issues That Matter. Ed. by John Donnelly. 380p. 1989. 36.95 (*0-87975-522-9*) Prometheus Bks.

Reflector & Lens Antennas: Analysis & Design Using Personal Computers. Ed. by Carlyle J. Sletten. LC 88-10452. (Illus.). 452p. reprint ed. pap. 128.90 (*0-7837-4376-9*, 2044116) Bks Demand.

Reflector & Lens Antennas: Analysis & Design Using Personal Computers - Software, User's Manual & Example Book, Version 2.0. 2nd ed. Carlyle J. Sletten. (Artech House Antenna Software Library). 250p. 1991. write for info. incl. disk (*0-89006-557-8*) Artech Hse.

Reflejos: An Intermediate Reader for Communication. 2nd ed. Patricia Boylan et al. 226p. (SPA.). (C). 1983. pap. text ed. 32.25 (*0-03-061346-9*) HB Coll Pubs.

***Reflets.** Robert E. Vicars & Catherine Merillou. 381p. (FRE.). (C). 1996. pap. text ed. 39.56 (*0-669-35260-8*) HM College Div.

***Reflets.** annot. ed. Robert E. Vicars & Catherine Merillou. (FRE.). (C). 1996. teacher ed., text ed. 39.56 (*0-669-35261-6*) HM College Div.

Reflets du Monde Francais. 2nd ed. Mary S. Metz. 1978. Instr's. manual. teacher ed., pap. text ed. write for info. (*0-07-041792-X*) McGraw.

Reflets, les Echos & les Ombres Chez Henri Bosco: Une Etude Du Double Obscur. Sandra L. Beckett. LC 93-15152. 296p. (FRE.). 1993. 89.95 (*0-7734-2898-4*) E Mellen.

Reflex. Dick Francis. 320p. 1986. mass mkt. 5.95 (*0-449-21173-8*, Crest) Fawcett.

***Reflex.** Dick Francis. 1997. mass mkt. write for info. (*0-449-45727-3*) Fawcett.

Reflex & Bone Structure. Clarence Major. LC 96-11532. 144p. 1996. reprint ed. pap. 12.95 (*1-56279-084-6*) Mercury Hse Inc.

Reflex Control of the Circulation. Irving H. Zucker & Joseph P. Gilmore. 1073p. 1991. 217.95 (*0-8493-8801-5*, QP109) CRC Pr.

Reflex Seizures & Reflex Epilepsies. Benjamin Zifkin. 400p. 1997. text ed. 115.00 (*0-397-51627-4*) Lppncott-Raven.

Reflex Sympathetic Dystrophy: A Reappraisal. Ed. by Wilfrid Janig & Michael D. Stanton-Hicks. LC 95-45160. (Progress in Pain Research & Management Ser.: Vol. 6). (Illus.). 268p. 1996. 55.00 (*0-931092-13-2*) Intl Assn Study Pain.

Reflex Sympathetic Dystrophy: Pathophysiological Mechanisms & Clinical Implications. Ed. by Robert F. Schmidt & Wilfrid Janig. LC 92-49653. 306p. 1992. 97.00 (*1-56081-284-2*, VCH) Wiley.

Reflex Testing Methods for Evaluating CNS Development. 2nd ed. Mary R. Fiorentino. (Illus.). 72p. 1981. 25.95 (*0-398-02584-3*) C C Thomas.

Reflex Zone Therapy of the Feet. Hanne Marquardt. 160p. (Orig.). 1984. pap. 14.95 (*0-89281-234-6*) Inner Tradit.

Reflexes & Motor Integration: Sherrington's Concept of Integrative Action. Judith P. Swazey. LC 69-13768. (Monographs in the History of Science). 291p. 1969. 26.50 (*0-674-75240-6*) HUP.

Reflexion und Determination. Joachim Kopper. (Kantstudien Ergaenzungsheft Ser.: Vol. 108). (C). 1976. text ed. 92.35 (*3-11-006617-3*) De Gruyter.

An Asterisk (*) at the beginning of an entry indicates that the title is appearing in BIP for the first time.

***Reflexion und Freiheit: Zum Verhaltnis von Philosophie und Poesie in Rilkes und Holderlins Spatwerk.** Stefan Offenhauser. 240p. (GER.). 1996. 44.95 (3-631-30945-7) P Lang Pubng.

Reflexiones De un Agricultor. Joaquin P. Rodriguez. 1978. pap. 10.00 (0-89729-203-0) Ediciones.

Reflexiones Eticas. Henry Stob. 260p. (SPA.). 1982. pap. 10.95 (0-939125-42-0) Evangelical Lit.

Reflexiones para el Enfermo y su Familia. Jorge L. Denton. 130p. 1991. pap. 6.50 (0-9630759-4-2) J L H Denton.

Reflexiones Sobre el Desarrollo Economico. Enrique V. Iglesias. 180p. 1992. 15.95 (0-940602-51-2) IADB.

Reflexions: Poems by Avonne Shani Abnathya-Arnold. Avonne S. Abnathya-Arnold. LC 91-90694. (Illus.). 66p. (Orig.). 1991. pap. 6.95 (0-9631147-0-0) A S Abrathyn-Arnold.

Reflexions d'un Solitaire, 4 vols. Andre E. Gretry. Ed. by Lucien Solvay & Ernest Closson. LC 76-43920. (Music & Theatre in France in the 17th & 18th Centuries Ser.). reprint ed. 245.00 (0-404-60190-1) AMS Pr.

Reflexions et Prieres dans L'espace-temps. Pierre Teilhard De Chardin. 13.95 (0-685-36601-4) Fr & Eur.

***Reflexions on the Longitudinal Distribution Factor KHb on the ISO Procedure.** Georges Henriot. (Technical Papers). 1981. pap. text ed. 30.00 (1-55589-188-8) AGMA.

Reflexions ou Sentences et Maxims Morales: Reflexions Diverses. Francois De La Rochefoucauld. 286p. 1967. write for info. (0-318-63585-2) Fr & Eur.

Reflexions Sur la Philosophie Ancienne et Moderne, et Sur l'Usage Qu'on En Doit Faire Pour la Religion. Rene Rapin. xx, 263p. reprint ed. write for info. (0-318-71396-9) G Olms Pubs.

Reflexions Sur la Poesie. Paul Claudel. 192p. (FRE.). 1963. 6.95 (0-8288-9115-X, F94480) Fr & Eur.

Reflexions Sur la Poetique d'Aristote, et Sur les Ouvrages Des Poetes Anciens et Modernes. Rene Rapin. xx, 257p. 1973. reprint ed. write for info. (3-487-04818-3) G Olms Pubs.

Reflexions sur la Question Juive. Jean-Paul Sartre. (Folio Essais Ser.: No. 10). (FRE.). 1962. pap. 9.95 (2-07-032287-4) Schoenhof.

Reflexions sur l'Amerique. Jacques Maritain. 224p. (FRE.). 1958. pap. 9.95 (0-7859-5536-4) Fr & Eur.

Reflexions Sur les Idees De Saint-Martin & La Philosophie Mystique en France A la Fin Du Eighteenth Siecle, Vol. VII. Louis Moreau & Adolphe Franck. Ed. by Robert Amadou. 228p. reprint ed. write for info. (0-318-71418-3) G Olms Pubs.

Reflexive Communication in the Culturally Diverse Workplace. John K. Kikoski & Catherine K. Kikoski. LC 95-45398. 248p. 1996. text ed. 59.95 (0-89930-955-0, Quorum Bks) Greenwood.

Reflexive Epistemology. Danilo Zolo. 208p. (C). 1989. lib. bdg. 110.00 (0-7923-0320-2, Pub. by Klwr Acad Pubs NE) Kluwer Ac.

Reflexive Language: Reported Speech & Metapragmatics. Ed. by John A. Lucy. (Illus.). 408p. (C). 1993. text ed. 80.00 (0-521-35164-2) Cambridge U Pr.

Reflexive Modernization: Politics, Tradition, & Aesthetics in the Modern Social Order. Ulrich Beck. 230p. (C). 1995. 39.50 (0-8047-2471-7); pap. 14.95 (0-8047-2472-5) Stanford U Pr.

Reflexive Novel: Fiction as Critique. Michael Boyd. LC 81-72029. 320p. 1983. 39.50 (0-8387-5029-X) Bucknell U Pr.

Reflexive Paradoxes. T. S. Champlin. 224p. 1988. lib. bdg. 59.95 (0-415-00083-1) Routledge.

Reflexive Structures. L. E. Sanchis. xii, 233p. 1988. 54.00 (0-387-96728-1) Spr-Verlag.

Reflexive Thesis: Writing Sociology of Scientific Knowledge. Malcolm Ashmore. LC 89-4728. (Illus.). 320p. 1989. 34.95 (0-226-02968-9) U Ch Pr.

Reflexive Universe: Evolution of Consciousness. Arthur M. Young. (Illus.). 293p. 1985. reprint ed. pap. 16.95 (0-9609850-6-9) Rob Briggs. Twentieth-century developments in quantum physics, together with an emerging science of consciousness, have created the need for a new cosmology, or model of the universe. The theory of process contained in THE REFLEXIVE UNIVERSE places consciousness within the context of contemporary science. One of the central themes of this extraordinary work is that each successive organization of matter, from fundamental particles in physics to living organisms, expresses a particular stage in the evolution of mind. Starting with the photon, the basic unit of light, & moving through atomic physics, molecular chemistry, the morphology of plants & animals & finally to levels of human evolution, Young develops his theory in vivid step-by-step detail. Consciousness, in his point of view, is not isolated from the material universe. It exists in a continuum, one in which physical & nonphysical realms can be linked & the teachings of mythology & religion can be integrated. To order: Call: 24 hour Visa & MasterCard only: 800-447-7814. Or write: Robert Briggs Associates, c/o Publishers Services, P.O. Box 2510, Novato, CA 94948. Trade STOP orders 40% plus postage. ***Publisher Provided Annotation.***

***Reflexivity.** S. J. Bartlett. xii, 510p. 1992. 148.75 (0-444-89092-0, North Holland) Elsevier.

Reflexivity & Revolution in the New Novel: Claude Ollier's Ficional Cycle. Cecile Lindsay. 215p. 1990. 50.00 (0-8142-0527-5) Ohio St U Pr.

Reflexivity & the Crisis of Western Reason. Barry Sandywell. LC 95-137118. (Logological Investigations Ser.: Vol. 1). 528p. (C). (gr. 13). 1996. text ed. 125.00 (0-415-08756-2) Routledge.

***Reflexivity & Voice.** Ed. by Rosanna Hertz. LC 97-4619. 240p. 1997. 46.00 (0-7619-0383-6); pap. 21.95 (0-7619-0384-4) Sage.

Reflexivity in Film & Literature: From Don Quixote to Jean-Luc Godard. Robert Stam. 320p. 1992. pap. text ed. 16.00 (0-231-07945-1) Col U Pr.

Reflexivity in Film & Literature: From Don Quixote to Jean-Luc Godard. Robert Stam. LC 84-24155. (Studies in Cinema: No. 31). (Illus.). 299p. reprint ed. pap. 85.30 (0-8357-1607-4, 2070578) Bks Demand.

Reflexivity in Tristram Shandy: An Essay in Phenomenological Criticism. James E. Swearingen. LC 77-5515. 285p. reprint ed. pap. 81.30 (0-8357-3759-4, 2036485) Bks Demand.

Reflexology. Anya Gore. (Alternative Health Ser.). 96p. 1993. pap. 12.95 (0-8048-1836-3) C E Tuttle.

***Reflexology.** Vicki Pitman & Kay Jehan. 256p. (Orig.). 1997. pap. 42.50 (0-7487-2867-8, Pub. by Stanley Thornes UK) Trans-Atl Phila.

Reflexology. Maybelle Segal. (Illus.). 1976. 7.95 (0-87426-040-X) Whitmore.

Reflexology. Maybelle Segal. 1976. pap. 7.00 (0-87980-358-4) Wilshire.

Reflexology. Chris Stormer. (Headway Lifeguides Ser.). (Illus.). 128p. 1995. pap. 15.95 (0-340-55594-7, Pub. by Headway UK) Trafalgar.

Reflexology: A Definitive Guide to Self-Treatment. Chris Stormer. 160p. 1995. pap. 11.95 (0-340-62038-2, Pub. by Headway UK) Trafalgar.

Reflexology: A Way to Better Health. 6th ed. Nicola M. Hall. (Illus.). 186p. (Orig.). 1988. reprint ed. pap. 12.95 (0-946551-73-1, Pub. by Gateway Books UK) ACCESS Pubs Network.

Reflexology: Art, Science & History. Christine Issel. (Illus.). 204p. (Orig.). 1990. pap. 14.95 (0-9625448-0-9) New Frntr Pub.

***Reflexology: The A-Z Guide to Healing with Pressure Points.** Judh Sachs & Judith Berger. Date not set. write for info. (0-440-22255-9) Dell.

Reflexology & Color Therapy Workbook: Combining the Healing Benefits of Two Complementary Therapies: A New Approach. Pauline Wills. (Home Library of Alternative Medicine). (Illus.). 160p. 1992. pap. 14.95 (1-85230-347-6) Element MA.

Reflexology for Good Health. Anna Kaye & Don C. Mathan. 1980. pap. 10.00 (0-87980-383-5) Wilshire.

Reflexology for Kids: Helping Your Child Overcome Illness. Kevin Kunz & Barbara Kunz. LC 97-7680. 1997. pap. write for info. (0-517-88845-9, Harmony) Crown Pub Group.

Reflexology Manual: An Easy-to-Use Illustrated Guide to Healing Zones of the Hands & Feet. Pauline Wills. LC 95-12387. (Illus.). 144p. 1995. pap. 19.95 (0-89281-547-7, Heal Arts VT) Inner Tradit.

Reflexology Partnership: A Healing Bond. Suzanne Adamson & Eilish Harris. (Illus.). 160p. 1996. pap. 13.95 (1-85626-149-2, C Kyle) Trafalgar.

Reflexology Today: The Stimulation of the Body's Healing Forces Through Foot Massage. Doreen E. Bayly. 64p. (Orig.). 1984. pap. 8.95 (0-89281-284-2) Inner Tradit.

Reflexology Workout. Stephanie Rick. 1995. pap. 14.00 (0-517-88485-2) Random Hse Value.

Reflexology Workout: Hand & Foot Massage for Super Health & Rejuvenation. Stephanie Rick. (Illus.). 1986. pap. 12.00 (0-517-56176-X, Harmony) Crown Pub Group.

Reflowering of the Goddess. Gloria F. Orenstein. (Athene Ser.). 256p. (C). 1990. text ed. 47.50 (0-8077-6243-1); pap. text ed. 17.95 (0-8077-6242-3) Tchrs Coll.

Reflowering of the Goddess: Contemporary Journeys & Cycles of Empowerment. Gloria F. Orenstein. (Athene Ser.). (Illus.). 250p. 1990. text ed. 47.50 (0-08-035179-4, 2707, Pub. by PPI UK); pap. text ed. 17.95 (0-08-035178-6, Pub. by PPI UK) Elsevier.

Reflux Diagnosis with Doppler Ultrasound. Ehrenburg Schultz. 1993. pap. text ed. 29.95 (3-7945-1303-7) Wiley.

Reflux Nephropathy Update: 1983. Ed. by C. J. Hodson et al. (Contributions to Nephrology Ser.: Vol. 39). (Illus.). xvi, 388p. 1984. 79.25 (3-8055-3807-3) S Karger.

Refocusing Educational Psychology. Ed. by Neville Jones & Norah Frederickson. 255p. 1990. 60.00 (1-85000-492-7, Falmer Pr); pap. 33.00 (1-85000-493-5, Falmer Pr) Taylor & Francis.

Refocusing the Corporation. Al Ries. 1996. 25.00 (0-614-15438-3) Harper Busn.

Reforestation in Arid Lands. rev. ed. Fred R. Weber & Carol Stoney. Ed. by Margaret Crouch. 335p. 1987. English, 335 pp. 14.95 (0-86619-264-6); French, 340 pp. 14.95 (0-86619-285-9) Vols Tech Asst.

***Reforestation Industry: Market Segment Specialization Program - Audit Technique Guide.** 140p. (Orig.). 1996. pap. 47.00 (1-57402-122-2) Athena Info Mgt.

Reforestation of the High Andes with Local Species. J. Brandbyge & L. B. Holm-Nielsen. (Reports from the Botanical Institute, University of Aarhus: No. 13). (Illus.). 114p. (C). 1986. pap. 12.95 (87-87600-16-1, Pub. by Aarhus Univ Pr DK) David Brown.

Reforesting the Earth. Sandra Postel & Hori Heise. (Papers). 64p. (Orig.). (C). 1988. pap. 5.00 (0-916468-84-4) Worldwatch Inst.

***Reforging... Transatlantic Relations.** Barry. 1997. pap. 15.00 (1-57906-027-7) NYU Pr.

Reforging the Iron Cross: The Search for Tradition in the West German Armed Forces. Donald Abenheim. (Illus.). 266p. 1989. text ed. 52.50 (0-691-05534-3) Princeton U Pr.

Reform see Crime & Justice in American History

Reform & Abolition of the Traditional Chinese Examination System. Wolfgang Franke. (East Asian Monographs: No. 10). 108p. 1960. pap. 11.00 (0-674-75250-3) HUP.

Reform & Adaptation in Nigerian University Curricula, 1960-1992: Living on the Credit Line. Abdalla U. Adamu. LC 93-36834. (African Studies: Vol. 33). 304p. 1993. text ed. 99.95 (0-7734-9422-7) E Mellen.

Reform & Authority in the Medieval & Reformation Church. Ed. by Guy F. Lytle. LC 79-17380. 351p. reprint ed. pap. 100.10 (0-685-17824-2, 2029496) Bks Demand.

Reform & Change in Higher Education: International Perspectives. Ed. by James E. Mauch & Paula L. Sabloff. LC 94-31729. (Garland Studies in Higher Education: No. 2). (Illus.). 336p. 1994. text ed. 50.00 (0-8153-1706-9, SS961) Garland.

Reform & Counterreform: Dialects of the Word in Western Christianity since Luther. Ed. by John C. Hawley. LC 94-5576. (Religion & Society Ser.: No. 34). x, 243p. (C). 1994. lib. bdg. 61.55 (3-11-014016-0, 114-94) Mouton.

Reform & Development in Deng's China. Ed. by Shao-Chuan Leng. LC 94-4725. (Miller Center Series on Asian Political Leadership: Vol. 4). 214p. (C). 1994. pap. text ed. 26.00 (0-8191-9504-9); lib. bdg. 54.50 (0-8191-9503-0) U Pr of Amer.

Reform & Development in Rural China. Du Runsheng. Ed. by Thomas R. Gottshang. LC 94-12854. (Studies on the Chinese Economy). 1994. text ed. 85.00 (0-312-12282-9) St Martin.

Reform & Development of Higher Education in Europe: France, the Netherlands & Poland (UNESCO) (Education Studies & Documents: No. 49). (Orig.). 1963. pap. 25.00 (0-8115-1373-4) Periodicals Srv.

Reform & Insurrection in Bourbon New Granada & Peru. Ed. by John R. Fisher et al. LC 90-35704. (Illus.). 360p. 1991. text ed. 47.50 (0-8071-1569-X); pap. text ed. 18.95 (0-8071-1654-8) La State U Pr.

Reform & Insurrection in Russian Poland, 1856-1865. R. F. Leslie. LC 72-91767. 272p. 1970. reprint ed. text ed. 35.00 (0-8371-2415-8, LERI, Greenwood Pr) Greenwood.

Reform & Intellectual Debate in Victorian England, 1830-1880. Barbara Dennis & David Skittoa. Ed. by Isobel Armstrong. (World & Word Ser.). 240p. 1987. 67.50 (0-685-19165-6, Pub. by Croom Helm UK); pap. text ed. 16.95 (0-7099-5428-X, Pub. by Croom Helm UK) Routledge Chapman & Hall.

Reform & Market Democracy. George Macesich. LC 91-10179. 160p. 1991. text ed. 45.00 (0-275-93989-8, C3989, Praeger Pubs) Greenwood.

Reform & Punishment: Essays on Criminal Sentencing. Michael H. Tonry & Franklin E. Zimring. LC 83-6504. (Studies in Crime & Justice). 218p. 1983. 30.00 (0-226-80816-5) U Ch Pr.

Reform & Reaction: The Big City Public Library in American Life. Rosemary R. DuMont. LC 77-71864. (Contributions in Librarianship & Information Science Ser.: No. 21). 153p. 1977. text ed. 49.95 (0-8371-9540-3, DRR/, Greenwood Pr) Greenwood.

Reform & Reaction in Post-Mao China: The Road Through Tiananmen. Richard Baum. 208p. (C). 1991. pap. 17.95 (0-415-90318-1, A4598, Routledge NY) Routledge.

Reform & Reaction in the Platine Provinces, 1810-1852. David Bushnell. LC 83-10490. (University of Florida Social Sciences Monographs: No. 69). viii, 182p. (Orig.). 1983. pap. 24.95 (0-8130-0757-7) U Press Fla.

Reform & Reaction in Twentieth Century American Politics. John J. Broesamle. LC 89-11751. (Contributions in American History Ser.: No. 137). 500p. 1990. text ed. 69.50 (0-313-26799-5, BTB/, Greenwood Pr) Greenwood.

Reform & Reconstruction: Britain after the War, 1945-1951. Ed. by Stephen Brooke. LC 94-23922. (Documents in Contemporary History Ser.). 1995. text ed. 59.95 (0-7190-4504-5, Pub. by Manchester Univ Pr UK); text ed. 24.95 (0-7190-4505-3, Pub. by Manchester Univ Pr UK) St Martin.

***Reform & Reformation.** write for info. (0-7131-5953-7, Pub. by E Arnold UK) Routledge Chapman & Hall.

Reform & Reformation: England, 1509-1558. Geoffrey R. Elton. LC 77-6464. (New History of England Ser.: No. 146, The New History of England). 432p. 1979. pap. 17.50 (0-674-75248-1) HUP.

Reform & Reformers in the Progressive Era. Ed. by David R. Colburn & George E. Pozzetta. LC 82-6140. (Contributions in American History Ser.: No. 101). (Illus.). xi, 196p. 1982. text ed. 49.95 (0-313-22907-4, CRP/, Greenwood Pr) Greenwood.

Reform & Regicide: The Reign of Peter III of Russia. Carol S. Leonard. LC 92-5176. (Indiana-Michigan Series in Russian & East European Studies). 244p. 1993. 35.00 (0-253-33322-9) Ind U Pr.

Reform & Regulation: American Politics from Roosevelt to Wilson. 3rd rev. ed. Lewis L. Gould. (Illus.). 243p. (C). 1996. pap. text ed. 11.95 (0-88133-899-0) Waveland Pr.

Reform & Regulation in Long Term Care. Ed. by Valerie LaPorte & Jeffrey Rubin. LC 79-9761. 230p. 1979. text ed. 55.00 (0-275-90379-6, C0379, Praeger Pubs) Greenwood.

Reform & Regulation of Property Rights see Property Rights in American History: From the Colonial Era to the Present

Reform & Renewal: Essays on Authority, Ministry & Social Justice in the American Church. Anthony T. Padovano. LC 89-63119. 144p. (Orig.). (C). 1990. pap. 9.95 (1-55612-266-7) Sheed & Ward MO.

Reform & Renewal: The Cato Lecture. Jane D. Douglass. 32p. (Orig.). 1995. pap. 7.50 (1-86407-073-0, Pub. by JBCE AT) Morehouse Pub.

Reform & Renewal in Higher Education: Implications for Library Instruction. Ed. by Carolyn Kirkendall. LC 80-81485. (Library Orientation Ser.: No. 10). 1979. 25.00 (0-87650-124-2) Pierian.

Reform & Resistance: An Ethnographic View of School Reform. Donna E. Muncey & Patrick J. McQuillan. LC 95-43603. 1996. write for info. (0-300-06108-0) Yale U Pr.

***Reform & Retribution: A Pictorial History of American Prisons.** John Roberts. LC 96-39441. (Illus.). 200p. 1997. 54.95 (1-56991-054-5) Am Correctional.

Reform & Revolution. E. A. Smith. LC 92-21682. 1992. 38.00 (0-7509-0187-X, Pub. by Sutton Pubng UK) Bks Intl VA.

Reform & Revolution: The Life & Times of Raymond Robins. Neil V. Salzman. LC 90-5358. (Illus.). 486p. 1991. 35.00 (0-87338-426-1) Kent St U Pr.

Reform & Revolution in China: The 1911 Revolution in Hunan & Hubei. Joseph W. Esherick. LC 75-17297. (Center for Chinese Studies, University of Michigan: No. 5). 1976. pap. 17.00 (0-520-05734-1) U CA Pr.

Reform & Revolution in Communist Systems. Gary K. Bertsch. 240p. (C). 1990. pap. text ed. 40.00 (0-02-309125-8, Macmillan Coll) P-H.

Reform & Revolution in France, 1774-1791: An Essay in the Politics of Transition. P. M. Jones. (Illus.). 285p. (C). 1995. text ed. 59.95 (0-521-45322-4); pap. text ed. 18.95 (0-521-45942-7) Cambridge U Pr.

Reform & Transformation in Communist Systems: Comparative Perspectives. Ed. by Ilpyong J. Kim & Jane S. Zacek. LC 91-61757. 380p. (C). 1991. pap. 19.95 (0-88702-059-3) Washington Inst Pr.

Reform & Transformation in Eastern Europe: Soviet-Type Economies on the Threshold of Change. Ed. by Janos M. Kovacs & Marton Tardos. LC 91-25207. 320p. (C). (gr. 13). 1992. text ed. 79.95 (0-415-06630-1, A6743) Routledge.

Reform As Reorganization: Papers. Royce Hanson & Julius Margolis. LC 73-19348. (Governance of Metropolitan Regions Ser.: No. 4). 139p. reprint ed. pap. 39.70 (0-317-09382-7, 2020967) Bks Demand.

Reform Calculus, Vol. 1. Stewart. (Mathematics Ser.). 1997. student ed., pap. 28.95 (0-534-34435-6) Wadsworth Pub.

Reform Calculus, Vol. 1. Stewart. (Mathematics Ser.). 1998. student ed., pap. 24.95 (0-534-34439-9) Wadsworth Pub.

Reform Calculus-Single Variable. Stewart. LC 97-6620. (Mathematics Ser.). 1997. text ed. 77.95 (0-534-34450-X) Wadsworth Pub.

Reform Decade in China: From Hope to Despair. Ed. by Marta Dassu & Anthony J. Saich. 220p. 1991. pap. 16.95 (0-7103-0417-X, A5505) Routledge Chapman & Hall.

Reform, Distortions, & Credibility. Guillermo A. Calvo. 24p. 1991. write for info. (0-940602-42-3) IADB.

Reform in Administration of Justice. American Academy of Political & Social Science Staff. LC 79-156961. (Foundations of Criminal Justice Ser.). reprint ed. 34.50 (0-404-09101-6) AMS Pr.

Reform in Administrator Preparation Programs: Individual Perspectives. Michael et al. Ed. by Frederick C. Wendel & Miles T. Bryant. 83p. (Orig.). (C). 1990. pap. text ed. 7.00 (1-55996-143-0) Univ Council Educ Admin.

Reform in Administrator Preparation Programs: Myths, Realities & Proposals. Frank et al. Ed. by Frederick C. Wendel. 66p. (Orig.). (C). 1991. pap. text ed. 7.00 (1-55996-146-5) Univ Council Educ Admin.

Reform in America: The Continuing Frontier. Robert H. Walker. LC 85-15711. (Illus.). 280p. 1986. 30.00 (0-8131-1549-3) U Pr of Ky.

Reform in America - The Reform Spirit in America. Robert H. Walker. 984p. 1990. 39.00 (0-89464-464-5) Krieger.

Reform in China. Jan S. Prybyla. 372p. Date not set. 37.75 (0-8447-3717-8, AEI Pr) Am Enterprise.

Reform in China: Challenges & Choices - A Summary & Analysis of the CESRRI Survey. Chinese Economic System Reform Research Institute Staff. Ed. by Bruce L. Reynolds. LC 87-23537. 240p. (C). (gr. 13). 1987. pap. text ed. 30.95 (0-87332-459-5, East Gate Bk) M E Sharpe.

Reform in China: Huang Tsun-Hsien & the Japanese Model. Noriko Kamachi. (East Asian Monographs: No. 95). 400p. (C). 1981. 26.00 (0-674-75278-3) HUP.

Reform in Detroit: Hazen S. Pingree & Urban Politics. Melvin G. Holli. LC 81-6347. xvi, 269p. 1981. reprint ed. text ed. 59.75 (0-313-22671-7, HORI, Greenwood Pr) Greenwood.

Reform in Eastern Europe. Oliver J. Blanchard & Rudiger Dornbusch. (Illus.). 120p. 1991. 20.00 (0-262-02328-8) MIT Pr.

Reform in Eastern Europe. Olivier Blanchard et al. 128p. 1993. pap. 11.00 (0-262-52181-4) MIT Pr.

Reform in Empowerment, Choice & Adult Learning. Bacilious et al. (Orig.). (C). 1992. pap. text ed. 7.00 (1-55996-154-6) Univ Council Educ Admin.

Reform in Graduate & Professional Education. Lewis B. Mayhew & Patrick J. Ford. LC 73-20968. (Jossey-Bass Higher Education Ser.). 270p. reprint ed. pap. 77.00 (0-685-16184-6, 2027762) Bks Demand.

Reform in Modern Russian History: Progress or Cycle? Ed. by Theodore Taranovski. (Woodrow Wilson Center Press Ser.). 416p. (C). 1995. text ed. 69.95 (0-521-45177-9) Cambridge U Pr.

Reform in New York City: A Study in Urban Progressivism. Augustus Cerillo, Jr. (Modern American History Ser.). 272p. 1991. text ed. 20.00 (0-8240-1893-1) Garland.

Reform in Nineteenth-Century China. Ed. by Paul A. Cohen & John E. Schrecker. (East Asian Monographs: No. 72). 349p. 1976. 14.00 (0-674-75281-3) HUP.

R

Reform in Oaxaca, 1856-76: A Microhistory of the Liberal Revolution. Charles R. Berry. LC 80-15378. (Illus.). 302p. reprint ed. pap. 86.10 (*0-8357-3788-8*, 2036519) Bks Demand.

Reform in Reverse: Human Rights in the People's Republic of China, No. 6. Ta-Ling Lee & John F. Copper. 150p. 1987. 8.00 (*0-942182-86-3*, 83) Occasional Papers.

Reform in Russia & the U. S. S. R. Past & Prospects. Ed. by Robert O. Crummey. LC 88-39451. 328p. 1990. pap. text ed. 16.95 (*0-252-06176-4*) U of Ill Pr.

Reform in School Mathematics & Authentic Assessment. Ed. by Thomas A. Romberg. (SUNY Series, Reform in Mathematics Education). 291p. 1995. text ed. 59.50 (*0-7914-2161-9*); pap. text ed. 19.95 (*0-7914-2162-7*) State U NY Pr.

Reform in Sung China: Wang An-Shih, 1021-1086, & His New Policies. James T. Liu. LC 59-9281. (East Asian Monographs: No. 3). 1959. 5.00 (*0-674-75300-3*) HUP.

Reform in Teacher Education: A Sociological View. 1990. 18.00 (*0-89333-059-0*) AACTE.

Reform in the House of Commons: The Select Committee System. Michael Jogerst. LC 92-22420. (Comparative Legislative Studies). 256p. (C). 1993. text ed. 35.00 (*0-8131-1805-0*) U Pr of Ky.

Reform in the Ottoman Empire, 1856-1876. Roderic H. Davison. LC 63-12669. 493p. reprint ed. pap. 140.60 (*0-317-09287-1*, 2000890) Bks Demand.

Reform in the Ottoman Empire, 1856-1876. Roderic H. Davison. LC 73-148618. 503p. (C). 1973. reprint ed. 75.00 (*0-87752-135-2*) Gordian.

Reform in the Provinces: The Government of Stuart England. Anthony Fletcher. LC 86-1684. 386p. 1986. text ed. 40.00 (*0-300-03673-6*) Yale U Pr.

Reform in the Soviet Union: Glasnost & the Future. John Sallnow. LC 89-28880. 160p. 1990. text ed. 39.95 (*0-312-04076-8*) St Martin.

Reform in Trade Union Discrimination in the Construction Industry: Operation Dig & Its Legacy. Irwin Dubinsky. LC 72-12974. (Special Studies in U. S. Economic, Social & Political Issues). 1973. 49.50 (*0-275-07080-8*) Irvington.

Reform Jewish Ethics & the Halakhah: An Experiment in Decision Making. Ed. by Eugene B. Borowitz. 1995. 29.95 (*0-87441-571-3*) Behrman.

Reform Judaism in America: A Biographical Dictionary & Sourcebook. Ed. by Kerry M. Olitzky et al. LC 92-25794. (Jewish Denominations in America Ser.). 75p. 1993. text ed. 79.50 (*0-313-24628-9*, SUJ, Greenwood Pr) Greenwood.

Reform Judaism Today. Eugene B. Borowitz. 800p. 1983. pap. text ed. 15.95 (*0-87441-315-X*) Behrman.

Reform, Labor, & Feminism: Margaret Dreier Robins & the Women's Trade Union League. Elizabeth A. Payne. LC 87-10794. (Women in American History Ser.). (Illus.). 234p. 1988. text ed. 24.95 (*0-252-01445-6*) U of Ill Pr.

Reform Movements & Social Transformation in India. Anita Mattoo. 134p. 1991. text ed. 25.00 (*81-85047-72-3*, Pub. by Reliance Pub Hse II) Apt Bks.

Reform of Civil Procedure: Essays on "Access to Justice" Ed. by Ross Cranston & Adrian A. Zuckerman. 472p. 1996. 90.00 (*0-19-826092-X*); pap. 35.00 (*0-19-826093-8*) OUP.

***Reform of Common Agriculture.** Ingersent. Date not set. pap. 69.95 (*0-312-21009-4*) St Martin.

Reform of Criminal Law in Pennsylvania: Selected Enquiries 1787-1819. Ed. by Morton J. Horwitz et al. LC 73-37983. 1972. 34.95 (*0-405-04026-1*) Ayer.

Reform of Education. Giovanni Gentile. Tr. by Dino Bigongiari. LC 78-63672. (Studies in Fascism: Ideology & Practice). 264p. reprint ed. 37.50 (*0-404-16935-X*) AMS Pr.

Reform of Elementary School Education: A Report on Elementary Schools in America & How They Can Be Changed to Improve Teaching & Learning. B. Frank Brown. 168p. 1992. 22.50 (*0-89464-475-0*) Krieger.

Reform of FBI Intelligence Operations: Written under the Auspices of the Police Foundation. John T. Elliff. LC 78-70290. 261p. 1979. reprint ed. pap. 74.40 (*0-7837-9333-2*, 2060074) Bks Demand.

Reform of Health Care Systems: A Comparative Analysis of Seven OECD Countries. 216p. (Orig.). 1992. pap. 46.00 (*92-64-13791-2*) OECD.

Reform of Health Care Systems: A Review of Seventeen OECD Countries. OECD Staff. 344p. (Orig.). 1994. pap. 86.00 (*92-64-14250-9*) OECD.

Reform of Housing in Eastern Europe & the Soviet Union. Ed. by Bengt Turner et al. LC 91-23422. 352p. (C). (gr. 13). 1992. text ed. 74.95 (*0-415-07068-6*, A6732) Routledge.

Reform of Intergovernmental Fiscal Relations in Developing & Emerging Market Economies. Anwar Shah. LC 94-11503. (Policy & Research Ser.: Vol. 23). 100p. 1994. 7.95 (*0-8213-2836-0*, 12836) World Bank.

Reform of International Institutions. C. Fred Bergsten et al. (Triangle Papers: No. 11). 1976. 15.00 (*0-318-02786-0*); pap. 6.00 (*0-318-02787-9*) Trilateral Comm.

Reform of King Josiah & the Composition of the Deuteronomistic History. Erik Eynikel. LC 95-49106. (Oudtestamentische Studien: Vol. 33). 1995. 119.00 (*90-04-10266-3*) E J Brill.

Reform of Legal Procedure. Moorfield Storey. 263p. 1986. reprint ed. lib. bdg. 27.50 (*0-8377-1140-1*) Rothman.

Reform of Local Government Finance in Britain. S. J. Bailey. 208p. (C). 1988. text ed. 55.00 (*0-415-00530-2*) Routledge.

Reform of Prisoners, 1830-1900. W. J. Forsythe. LC 86-28022. 256p. 1987. text ed. 39.95 (*0-312-00466-4*) St Martin.

***Reform of Property Law.** Ed. by Paul Jackson & David C. Wilde. LC 97-7849. 416p. 1997. text ed. 72.95 (*1-85521-884-4*, Pub. by Ashgate UK) Ashgate Pub Co.

Reform of Public Spending for Agriculture. Bonni Van Blarcom et al. LC 93-34173. (Discussion Paper Ser.: No. 216). 118p. 1993. 7.95 (*0-8213-2667-8*, 12667) World Bank.

Reform of Renewal. Benedict Groeschel. LC 90-81769. 227p. (Orig.). 1990. pap. 12.95 (*0-89870-286-0*) Ignatius Pr.

Reform of Rural Land Markets in Latin America & the Caribbean: Research, Theory, & Policy Implications. Eric B. Shearer et al. (LTC Research Papers: No. 141). 104p. (Orig.). 1991. pap. 10.00 (*0-685-49241-9*) U of Wis Land.

Reform of Schooling: The Saga of Transformation vs. Tinkering or Whatever Happened to I. G. E.? rev. ed. Bernard J. Fleury. 354p. (Orig.). (C). 1994. pap. text ed. 38.50 (*0-8191-9650-9*) U Pr of Amer.

Reform of State Legislatures & the Changing Character of Representation. Eugene W. Hickok, Jr. (Illus.). 178p. (C). 1992. pap. 32.00 (*0-8191-8535-3*); lib. bdg. 57.50 (*0-8191-8534-5*) U Pr of Amer.

Reform of the Criminal Law & Procedure. Ed. by Robert M. Fogelson. LC 74-3816. (Criminal Justice in America Ser.). 1974. reprint ed. 20.95 (*0-405-06165-X*) Ayer.

Reform of the Hebrew Alphabet. Michael Landmann. Tr. by David J. Parent. LC 76-14595. (Illinois Language & Culture Ser.: Vol. 1). 345p. reprint ed. pap. 98.40 (*0-317-09443-2*, 2013715) Bks Demand.

Reform of the Liturgy, 1948-1975. Annibale Bugnini. Tr. by Matthew J. O'Connell from ITA. 1008p. 1990. 59.50 (*0-8146-1571-6*) Liturgical Pr.

***Reform of the Rake.** George. 1997. mass mkt. 3.25 (*0-373-03484-9*) Harlequin Bks.

***Reform of the Rake.** large type ed. George. 1997. mass mkt. 3.25 (*0-373-15730-4*) Harlequin Bks.

***Reform of the Socialist System in Central & Eastern Europe.** Martin J. Bull & Mike Ingham. LC 97-22992. 1997. write for info. (*0-312-17732-1*) St Martin.

Reform of the Taxation of Mergers, Acquisitions & Leveraged Buyouts. Samuel C. Thompson, Jr. LC 92-76163. 292p. 1993. 50.00 (*0-89089-534-1*) Carolina Acad Pr.

Reform of the United Nations: A Report, 2 vols. Joachim W. Muller. LC 91-50824. 1992. lib. bdg. 130.00 (*0-379-20671-4*) Oceana.

Reform of the Venezuelan Fiscal System. Ed. by T. E. Batalla. LC 88-37957. 441p. 1989. reprint ed. pap. 125.70 (*0-608-00144-9*, 2060925) Bks Demand.

Reform of Undergraduate Education. Arthur Levine & John R. Weingart. LC 73-7154. (Jossey-Bass Higher Education Ser.). 176p. reprint ed. 50.20 (*0-8357-9343-5*, 2013960) Bks Demand.

***Reform of Wholesale Payment Systems & Its Impact on Financial Markets.** David Folkerts-Landau et al. (Occasional Papers: Vol. 51). 60p. (Orig.). 1996. pap. 20.00 (*1-56708-096-0*) Grp of Thirty.

Reform or Revolution. Daniel De Leon. 1977. pap. 0.50 (*0-935534-37-7*) NY Labor News.

Reform or Revolution. Rosa Luxemburg. 1973. 250.00 (*0-87968-069-5*) Gordon Pr.

Reform or Revolution. Rosa Luxemburg. Tr. by Integer. LC 73-79783. 79p. 1970. reprint ed. pap. 9.95 (*0-87348-303-0*); reprint ed. lib. bdg. 30.00 (*0-87348-302-2*) Pathfinder NY.

Reform Papers see Writings of Henry D. Thoreau

Reform, Planning & City Politics: Montreal, Winnipeg, Toronto. Harold Kaplan. 768p. 1981. 50.00 (*0-8020-5543-5*) U of Toronto Pr.

Reform, Protest & Social Transformation. Satish K. Sharma. (C). 1987. 31.50 (*81-7024-098-0*, Pub. by Ashish II) S Asia.

Reform, Recovery, & Growth: Latin America & the Middle East. Ed. by Rudiger Dornbusch & Sebastian Edwards. LC 94-27934. (National Bureau of Economic Research Project Reports). 436p. 1994. 65.00 (*0-226-15845-4*) U Ch Pr.

Reform Response: Recent Reform Responses. Solomon B. Freehof. LC 72-12300. 246p. reprint ed. pap. 70.20 (*0-317-41851-3*, 2026179) Bks Demand.

Reform, Revolution & Reaction: Archbishop John Thomas Troy & the Catholic Church in Ireland 1787-1817. Vincent J. McNally. 268p. (C). 1995. lib. bdg. 44.50 (*0-8191-9999-0*) U Pr of Amer.

Reform Rule in Czechoslovakia: The Dubcek Era, 1968-1969. Galia Golan. LC 72-83587. 335p. reprint ed. pap. 95.50 (*0-317-26401-X*, 2024458) Bks Demand.

Reform the People: Changing the Attitudes Towards Popular Education in Early Twentieth-Century China. Paul Bailey. 320p. 1993. pap. 30.00 (*0-7486-0281-X*, Pub. by Edinburgh U Pr UK) Col U Pr.

Reform Thought in Sixteenth Century Italy. Elisabeth G. Gleason. Ed. by James A. Massey. LC 81-5648. (American Academy of Religion, Texts & Translations). 136p. (C). 1981. pap. text ed. 16.95 (*0-89130-498-3*, 01-02-04) Scholars Pr GA.

Reform Through Community: Resocializing Offenders in the Kibbutz. Michael Fischer & Brenda Geiger. LC 91-12837. (Kibbutz Study Ser.: No. 3). 256p. 1991. text ed. 55.00 (*0-313-27931-4*, FRD, Greenwood Pr) Greenwood.

Reform Without Liberalization: China's National People's Congress & the Politics of Institutional Change. Kevin J. O'Brien. (Illus.). 324p. (C). 1990. text ed. 54.95 (*0-521-38086-3*) Cambridge U Pr.

***Reform Work, Reform Welfare.** Joel F. Handler. LC 97-17475. 1997. 35.00 (*0-300-07248-1*); pap. text ed. 16.00 (*0-300-07250-3*) Yale U Pr.

Reforma Contributiva de Puerto Rico: Edicion Especial. Ed. by Butterworth Staff. 170p. 1992. pap. 18.00 (*0-88063-513-4*) MICHIE.

***Reforma, Recuperacion y Crecimiento: America Latina y Medio Oriente.** Ed. by Rudiger Dornbusch & Sebastian Edwards. 494p. (SPA.). 1996. pap. text ed. 24.00 (*1-886938-05-9*) IADB.

***Reformability of China's State Sector.** Tien-Ching Hsu & Guo C. Wen. LC 96-35406. 1997. write for info. (*981-02-2655-1*) World Scientific Pub.

Reformas a la Seguridad Social En Chile. Ed. by Mario Marcel & Alberto Arenas. 1991. write for info. (*0-940602-41-5*) IADB.

***Reformas Economicas e Trabalhistas na America Latina e no Caribe.** 40p. (POR.). 1995. 6.95 (*0-8213-3502-2*, 13502) World Bank.

Reformas Economicas En Chile. Ed. by Oscar Munoz. 1992. write for info. (*0-940602-49-0*) IADB.

***Reformas Laborales y Economicas en America Latina y el Caribe.** 40p. (SPA.). 1995. 6.95 (*0-8213-3501-4*, 13501) World Bank.

Reformatio Legum Ecclesiasticarum. James C. Spalding. (Sixteenth Century Essays & Studies). 340p. 1992. 40.00 (*0-940474-19-0*) Sixteenth Cent.

Reformatio Perennis: Essays on Calvin & the Reformation in Honor of Ford Lewis Battles. Ed. by Brian Gerrish. LC 81-1007. (Pittsburgh Theological Monographs: No. 32). 1981. pap. 15.00 (*0-915138-41-7*) Pickwick.

Reformation. Owen Chadwick. 1990. pap. 12.95 (*0-14-013757-2*, Viking) Viking Penguin.

Reformation. Will Durant & Ariel Durant. (Story of Civilization Ser.: Vol. 6). (Illus.). 1040p. 1983. 35.00 (*0-671-61050-3*) S&S Trade.

Reformation. Sarah Flowers. LC 95-8822. (World History Ser.). (Illus.). 112p. (J). (gr. 5-12). 1996. lib. bdg. 17.96 (*1-56006-243-6*) Lucent Bks.

Reformation. Michael A. Mullett. (Rigby Interactive Library - History). (J). 1996. lib. bdg. write for info. (*1-57572-011-6*) Rigby Interact Libr.

***Reformation.** Ernest G. Schwiebert. 600p. 1996. 99.00 (*0-8006-2836-5*, Fortress Pr) Augsburg Fortress.

Reformation. Jonathan W. Zophy. 304p. (C). 1996. pap. text ed. 26.40 (*0-13-181561-X*) P-H.

Reformation. rev. ed. George L. Mosse. (Illus.). 64p. (C). 1991. pap. text ed. 2.25 (*1-877891-02-9*) Paperbook Pr Inc.

Reformation. George P. Fisher. LC 83-45660. reprint ed. 54.50 (*0-404-19810-4*) AMS Pr.

Reformation, Vol. 3. Owen Chadwick. (History of the Church Ser.). (Orig.). 1964. mass mkt. 6.95 (*0-14-020504-7*, Penguin Bks) Viking Penguin.

Reformation, Vol. VI. Will Durant. (Story of Civilization Ser.: Vol. 6). (Illus.). 1994. 17.98 (*1-56731-017-6*, MJF Bks) Fine Comms.

Reformation: A Comedy Acted at the Dukes Theater. Joseph Arrowsmith. LC 92-23808. (Augustan Reprints Ser.: Nos. 237-238). 1986. reprint ed. 21.50 (*0-404-70237-6*, PR3316) AMS Pr.

Reformation: Basic Interpretations. 2nd ed. Ed. by Lewis W. Spitz. (Problems in European Civilization Ser.). 252p. (C). 1972. pap. text ed. 16.76 (*0-669-81620-5*) HM College Div.

***Reformation: Education & History.** Lewis W. Spitz. LC 97-6852. (Variorum Collected Studies Ser.: Vol. 555). 336p. 1997. text ed. 94.95 (*0-86078-546-7*, Pub. by Ashgate UK) Ashgate Pub Co.

Reformation: Roots & Ramifications. Heiko A. Oberman. 288p. (Orig.). 1994. pap. text ed. 30.00 (*0-8028-0825-5*) Eerdmans.

Reformation see Renaissance & Reformation

Reformation & Catholicity. Gustaf E. Aulen. Tr. by Eric H. Wahlstrom from SWE. LC 78-25981. 1979. reprint ed. text ed. 65.00 (*0-313-20809-3*, AURC, Greenwood Pr) Greenwood.

Reformation & Latin Literature in Northern Europe. Ed. by Inger Ekrem et al. 254p. 1996. 48.00 (*82-00-22636-0*) Scandnvan Univ Pr.

Reformation & Renaissance. Jean M. Stone. LC 83-45670. (Illus.). reprint ed. 76.50 (*0-404-19820-1*) AMS Pr.

Reformation & Resistance in Tudor Lancashire. Christopher Haigh. LC 73-88308. 391p. reprint ed. pap. 111.50 (*0-317-29372-9*, 2024476) Bks Demand.

Reformation & Revolt in the Low Countries. Alastair Duke. 330p. 1991. boxed 60.00 (*1-85285-021-3*) Hambledon Press.

Reformation & Rural Society: The Parishes of Brandeburg-Ansbach-Kulmbach, 1528-1603. C. Scott Dixon. (Studies in Early Modern History). 250p. (C). 1996. text ed. 49.95 (*0-521-48311-5*) Cambridge U Pr.

Reformation & Society in Guernsey. D. M. Ogier. (Illus.). 242p. 1997. 71.10 (*0-85115-603-7*) Boydell & Brewer.

Reformation & the English People. J. J. Scarisbrick. 214p. 1986. pap. text ed. 23.95 (*0-631-14755-1*) Blackwell Pubs.

Reformation & the People. Thomas A. Lacey. LC 83-45583. reprint ed. 22.00 (*0-404-19901-1*) AMS Pr.

Reformation & the Visual Arts: The Protestant Image Question in Western & Eastern Europe. Sergiusz Michalski. LC 92-13311. (Christianity & Society in the Modern World Ser.). 272p. (C). 1993. text ed. 59.95 (*0-415-06512-7*, A7874) Routledge.

Reformation Biblical Drama in England: Mary Magdalegne & the History of Jacob & Esau. Ed. by Paul W. White. LC 92-17420. (Renaissance Imagination Ser.). (Illus.). 232p. 1992. text ed. 62.00 (*0-8153-0460-9*) Garland.

***Reformation Era Pamphlet in the Ambrose Swasey Library: An Annotated Bibliography.** Paul Schrodt. (Illus.). 224p. 1997. lib. bdg. 46.00 (*0-7618-0514-1*) U Pr of Amer.

Reformation Europe: A Guide to Research. Ed. by Steven E. Ozment. 390p. 1982. 18.50 (*0-910345-01-5*) Center Reform.

Reformation Europe: Age of Reform & Revolution. Delamar Jensen. 480p. (C). 1981. pap. text ed. 29.16 (*0-669-03626-9*) HM College Div.

Reformation Europe: Age of Reform & Revolution. 2nd ed. Delamar Jensen. 525p. (C). 1992. pap. text ed. 29.16 (*0-669-20009-3*) HM College Div.

***Reformation in Eastern & Central Europe.** Ed. by Karin Maag. LC 96-41760. (Saint Andrew's Studies in Reformation History). (Illus.). 288p. 1997. text ed. 68.95 (*1-85928-358-6*, Pub. by Ashgate UK) Ashgate Pub Co.

Reformation in England, 2 vols. Merle D'Aubigne. 1977. 39.99 (*0-85151-488-X*) Banner of Truth.

Reformation in England. Gustave L. Constant. Tr. by R. E. Scantlebury. LC 83-45576. reprint ed. 85.00 (*0-404-19895-3*) AMS Pr.

Reformation in England, 2 vols., 1. Merle D'Aubigne. 1977. pap. 21.99 (*0-85151-486-3*) Banner of Truth.

Reformation in England, 2 vols., 2. Merle D'Aubigne. 1977. pap. 21.99 (*0-85151-487-1*) Banner of Truth.

Reformation in England: Religio Depapilate. Philip Hughes. (Modern Revivals in History, Reformation in England Ser.: Vol. 2). 397p. 1993. 69.95 (*0-7512-0152-9*, Pub. by Gregg Pub UK) Ashgate Pub Co.

Reformation in England: The King's Proceedings. Philip Hughes. (Modern Revivals in History Ser.: Vol. 1). 430p. 1993. 69.95 (*0-7512-0151-0*, Pub. by Gregg Pub UK) Ashgate Pub Co.

Reformation in England: True Religion Now Established. Philip Hughes. (Modern Revivals in History, Reformation in England Ser.: Vol. 3). 460p. 1993. 74.95 (*0-7512-0153-7*, Pub. by Gregg Pub UK) Ashgate Pub Co.

***Reformation in England to the Accession of Elizabeth I.** write for info. (*0-7131-5270-2*, Pub. by E Arnold UK) Routledge Chapman & Hall.

Reformation in Germany. Henry C. Vedder. 1977. lib. bdg. 59.95 (*0-8490-2506-0*) Gordon Pr.

Reformation in Germany. Henry C. Vedder. LC 83-45671. reprint ed. 52.50 (*0-404-19821-X*) AMS Pr.

Reformation in Germany & Switzerland. Pamela Johnston & Bob Scribner. (Cambridge Topics in History Ser.). (Illus.). 128p. (C). 1993. pap. text ed. 17.95 (*0-521-40607-2*) Cambridge U Pr.

Reformation in Historical Thought. A. G. Dickens et al. 456p. 1985. 45.00 (*0-674-75311-9*) HUP.

***Reformation in Ireland 1400-16.** Meigs. LC 97-10259. 1997. text ed. 65.00 (*0-312-17582-5*) St Martin.

Reformation in Its Literature. Arthur Smellie. LC 83-45669. reprint ed. 38.00 (*0-404-19819-8*) AMS Pr.

Reformation in Lithuania: Religious Fluctuations in the Sixteenth Century. Antanas Musteikus. (East European Monographs: No. 246). 125p. 1988. text ed. 38.00 (*0-88033-143-7*) East Eur Monographs.

Reformation in National Context. Ed. by Bob Scribner et al. 260p. (C). 1994. pap. text ed. 18.95 (*0-521-40960-8*) Cambridge U Pr.

Reformation in National Context. Ed. by Bob Scribner et al. 260p. (C). 1994. text ed. 59.95 (*0-521-40155-0*) Cambridge U Pr.

Reformation in Poland. Paul Fox. LC 72-136395. reprint ed. 29.50 (*0-404-02544-7*) AMS Pr.

Reformation in Scotland, Causes, Characteristics, Consequences: Stone Lectures at Princeton Theological Seminary, 1907-1908. Ed. by David H. Fleming. LC 83-45579. reprint ed. 67.50 (*0-404-19897-X*) AMS Pr.

Reformation in the Cities: The Appeal of Protestantism to Sixteenth-Century Germany & Switzerland. Steven E. Ozment. LC 75-8444. 248p. 1980. pap. 14.00 (*0-300-02496-7*) Yale U Pr.

Reformation into Nonconformity. LC 97-13950. 1997. write for info. (*0-8386-3667-5*) Fairleigh Dickinson.

Reformation of Machismo: Evangelical Conversion & Gender in Colombia. Elizabeth E. Brusco. LC 94-21340. (Illus.). 224p. (C). 1995. pap. 14.95 (*0-292-70821-1*); text ed. 35.00 (*0-292-70820-3*) U of Tex Pr.

Reformation of Reform Judaism. Ed. by Jacob Neusner. LC 92-33290. (Judaism in Cold War America, 1945-1990 Ser.: Vol. 6). 272p. 1993. text ed. 25.00 (*0-8153-0076-X*) Garland.

***Reformation of Ritual: Interpretation of Early Modern Germany.** Susan C. Karant-Nunn. (Christianity & Society in the Modern World Ser.). 344p. (C). 1997. text ed. 74.95 (*0-415-11337-7*) Routledge.

Reformation of Society Through Adequate Education. C. Antonio Provost. LC 94-69192. 1996. 15.95 (*0-8158-0511-X*) Chris Mass.

Reformation of the Bible: The Bible of the Reformation. David Price et al. LC 95-38683. 1996. 45.00 (*0-300-06667-8*); pap. write for info. (*0-941881-18-0*) Yale U Pr.

Reformation of the Church: A Collection of Reformed & Puritan Documents on Church Issues. Iain H. Murray. 416p. (C). 1987. reprint ed. 16.99 (*0-85151-118-X*) Banner of Truth.

Reformation of the Ecclesiastical Laws of England, 1552. Thomas Cramer et al. Tr. & Intro. by James C. Spalding. (Sixteenth Century Essays & Studies: Vol. 19). (Illus.). 320p. 1992. 35.00 (*0-685-61092-6*) Sixteenth Cent.

Reformation of the Parishes: The Ministry & the Reformation in Town & Country. Ed. by Andrew Pettegree. LC 93-17868. (C). 1993. text ed. 69.95 (*0-7190-4005-1*, Pub. by Manchester Univ Pr UK) St Martin.

Reformation of the Sixteenth Century. Roland Bainton. 1990. 27.00 (*0-8446-1581-1*) Peter Smith.

An Asterisk (*) at the beginning of an entry indicates that the title is appearing in BIP for the first time.

Reformation of the Sixteenth Century in Its Relation to Modern Thought & Knowledge. Charles A. Beard. LC 80-12915. xxviii, 450p. 1980. reprint ed. text ed. 45.50 (*0-313-22410-2*, BERF, Greenwood Pr) Greenwood.

Reformation of the Sixteenth Century in Its Relations to Modern Thought & Knowledge. Charles Beard. LC 77-27168. (Hibbert Lectures: 1883). reprint ed. 59.50 (*0-404-60404-8*) AMS Pr.

Reformation of the Subject: Spenser, Milton, & the English Protestant Epic. Linda Gregerson. (Studies in Renaissance Literature & Culture: No. 6). 260p. (C). 1995. text ed. 54.95 (*0-521-46277-0*) Cambridge U Pr.

***Reformation of the Twelfth Century.** Giles Constable. (Illus.). 448p. 1997. text ed. 64.95 (*0-521-30514-4*) Cambridge U Pr.

Reformation Principles & Practice: Essays in Honour of A. G. Dickens. Ed. by Peter N. Brooks. 1980. 72.95 (*0-85967-579-3*, Pub. by Scolar Pr UK) Ashgate Pub Co.

Reformation Refugees As an Economic Force. Frederick A. Norwood. LC 83-45668. reprint ed. 39.50 (*0-404-19818-X*) AMS Pr.

Reformation Roots. Ed. by John B. Payne & Barbara B. Zikmund. (Living Theological Heritage of the United Church of Christ Ser.: Vol. 7). 696p. 1996. 50.00 (*0-8298-1143-5*) Pilgrim OH.

Reformation Spirituality: The Religion of George Herbert. Gene E. Veith, Jr. LC 83-46176. 288p. 1985. 40.00 (*0-8387-5071-0*) Bucknell U Pr.

Reformation Studies. A. G. Dickens. 624p. (C). 1983. text ed. 70.00 (*0-907628-04-4*) Hambledon Press.

Reformation Thought: An Introduction. 2nd ed. Alister E. McGrath. LC 92-12336. 272p. (Orig.). (C). 1995. pap. 19.99 (*0-8010-2053-0*) Baker Bks.

Reformation Thought: An Introduction. 2nd ed. Alister E. McGrath. LC 92-12336. 272p. (Orig.). 1993. pap. 26.95 (*0-631-18651-4*) Blackwell Pubs.

Reformation To Revolution. Margp Todd. (Rewriting Histories Ser.). (Illus.). 296p. (C). 1995. pap. 17.95 (*0-415-09692-8*, Routledge NY) Routledge.

Reformation to Revolution: Politics & Religion in Early Modern England. Ed. by Margo Todd. LC 94-11831. (Rewriting Histories Ser.). 296p. (C). (gr. 13). 1994. text ed. 62.95 (*0-415-09691-X*) Routledge.

Reformation to the Present see History of Christianity

Reformation und Neuzeit: Three-Hundred Jahre Theologie in Halle. Ed. by Udo Schnelle. 458p. (GER.). (C). 1994. lib. bdg. 136.95 (*3-11-014588-X*) De Gruyter.

Reformational Theology: A New Paradigm for Doing Dogmatics. Gordon J. Spykman. xiv, 576p. 1995. pap. 30.00 (*0-8028-0525-6*) Eerdmans.

***Reformations.** Felipe Fernandez-Armesto. LC 96-40940. 1997. 29.50 (*0-684-83104-X*) S&S Trade.

Reformations Old & New: Essays on the Socio-Economic Impact of Religious Change c. 1470-1630. Ed. by Beat A. Kumin. (St. Andres Studies in Reformation History). (Illus.). 288p. 1996. 74.95 (*1-85928-220-2*, Pub. by Scolar Pr UK) Ashgate Pub Co.

Reformatory Prison Discipline As Developed by the Rt. Hon. Sir Walter Crofton in the Irish Convict Prisons. Mary Carpenter. LC 67-26667. (Criminology, Law Enforcement, & Social Problems Ser.: No. 2). 1967. reprint ed. 13.00 (*0-87585-002-2*) Patterson Smith.

Reformatory Schools for the Children of the Perishing & Dangerous Classes. Mary Carpenter. LC 75-5684. (Social History of Education Series 1: No. 2). xi, 353p. 1969. reprint ed. 45.00 (*0-678-08451-3*) Kelley.

Reformatory Schools for the Children of the Perishing & Dangerous Classes & for Juvenile Offenders: With Index Added. Mary Carpenter. LC 72-108223. (Criminology, Law Enforcement, & Social Problems Ser.: No. 106). 1970. reprint ed. lib. bdg. 15.00 (*0-87585-106-1*) Patterson Smith.

***Reformdefizite der Deutschen Hochschule: Zum Dilemma der Staatlichen Universitat im Spannungsfeld Zwischen Normativer Theorie & Politischer Realitat 2., Durchgesehene Auflage.** Andreas Rosigkeit. (Illus.). 348p. (GER.). 1996. 61.95 (*3-631-30879-5*) P Lang Pubng.

Reforme Intellectuelle et Morale de la France. Ernest Renan. (FRE.). 1990. pap. 24.95 (*0-7859-3333-6*, 2870273614) Fr & Eur.

Reforme Sociale En France Deduite De L'observation Comparee Des Peuples Europeens: Social Reform in France Deduced from the Comparative Observation of the European Peoples, 2 Vols. Frederick Le Play. LC 74-25766. (European Sociology Ser.). 936p. 1975. reprint ed. 74.95 (*0-405-06520-5*) Ayer.

Reformed America: The Middle & Southern States, 1783-1837. Fred J. Hood. LC 79-23984. 264p. 1980. pap. 75.30 (*0-7837-8383-3*, 2059193) Bks Demand.

Reformed & Catholic: Selected Theological Writings of Phillip Schaff. Ed. by Charles Yrigoyen, Jr. & George H Bricker. LC 79-17391. (Pittsburgh Original Texts & Translations Ser.: No. 4). 1979. pap. text ed. 15.75 (*0-915138-40-9*) Pickwick.

Reformed & Feminist: A Challenge to the Church. Johanna W. Van Wijk-Bos. 132p. (Orig.). 1991. pap. 12.00 (*0-664-25194-3*) Westminster John Knox.

Reformed Calculus. Stewart. (Mathematics Ser.). (C). 1998. text ed. 45.95 (*0-534-34330-9*) Brooks-Cole.

Reformed Christians & Mormom Christians: Let's Talk. Roger R. Keller. 155p. 10.95 (*0-317-62513-6*) Pryor Pettengill.

Reformed Church in China, 1842-1951. Gerald F. De Jong. LC 92-18046. (Historical Series of the Reformed Church in America: Vol. 22). 1992. pap. 25.00 (*0-8028-0661-9*) Eerdmans.

Reformed Church Roots. Arie R. Brouwer. write for info. (*0-685-62275-4*) Reformed Church.

Reformed Confessionalism in Nineteenth-Century America: Essays on the Thought of John Williamson Nevin. Ed. by Sam Hamstra & Arie J. Griffioen. LC 95-32364. (ATLA Monographs: No. 38). (Illus.). 280p. 1995. 42.50 (*0-8108-3058-2*) Scarecrow.

Reformed Doctrine of Predestination. Loraine Boettner. 1991. pap. 9.99 (*0-87552-112-6*, Pub. by Evangelical Pr) Presby & Reformed.

Reformed, Evangelical, Catholic Theology: The Contribution of the World Alliance of Reformed Churches, 1875-1982. Alan P. Sell. LC 90-45927. 316p. reprint ed. pap. 90.10 (*0-7837-5561-9*, 2045336) Bks Demand.

Reformed Faith. Loraine Boettner. 1983. pap. 2.50 (*0-87552-122-3*, Pub. by Evangelical Pr) Presby & Reformed.

Reformed Faith & Economics. Ed. by Robert L. Stivers. LC 89-30054. 262p. (Orig.). (C). 1989. pap. text ed. 24.00 (*0-8191-7381-9*, Presby US); lib. bdg. 43.00 (*0-8191-7380-0*, Presby US) U Pr of Amer.

Reformed Faith & Politics: Essays Prepared for the Advisory Council on Church & Society of the United Presbyterian Church in the U. S. A. & the Council on Theology & Culture of the Presbyterian Church in the U. S. Ed. by Ronald H. Stone. LC 83-10513. 210p. (Orig.). (C). 1983. pap. text ed. 21.50 (*0-8191-3296-9*); lib. bdg. 43.00 (*0-8191-3295-0*) U Pr of Amer.

Reformed Librarie-Keeper with a Supplement to the Reformed-School, As Subordinate to Colleges in Universities. John Dury. LC 92-24284. (Augustan Reprints Ser.: No. 220). 1983. reprint ed. 14.50 (*0-404-70220-1*, Z665) AMS Pr.

Reformed Pastor. Richard Baxter. 1979. pap. 5.99 (*0-85151-191-0*) Banner of Truth.

Reformed Presbyterian Ministers: 1950-1993. Ed. by Charles McBurney. 225p. 1994. 25.00 (*1-884527-05-1*); pap. 15.00 (*1-884527-09-4*) Crown & Covenant.

***Reformed Protestant Dutch Church of Bergen (Jersey City) New Jersey, 1666-1788.** The Holland Society of New York Staff. (Illus.). 1997. reprint ed. pap. 23.00 (*0-7884-0635-3*, H546) Heritage Bk.

Reformed Reader: A Sourcebook in Christian Theology: Classical Beginnings 1519-1799, Vol. 1. Ed. by William S. Johnson & John H. Leith. 416p. 1993. text ed. 30.00 (*0-664-21957-8*) Westminster John Knox.

Reformed Reader: A Sourcebook in Christian Theology: Contemporary Trajectories 1799-Present, Vol. 2. Ed. by George Stroup. 336p. 1994. text ed. 30.00 (*0-664-21958-6*) Westminster John Knox.

Reformed Roots of the English New Testament: The Influence of Theodore Beza on the English New Testament. Irena Backus. LC 80-17915. (Pittsburgh Theological Monographs: No. 28). 1980. pap. 10.00 (*0-915138-36-0*) Pickwick.

Reformed Social Ethics & the Korean Church. Nak-Heong Yang. LC 94-30285. (Asian Thought & Culture Ser.: Vol. 21). 1995. write for info. (*0-8204-2622-9*) P Lang Pubng.

Reformed Spirituality: An Introduction for Believers. Howard L. Rice. 192p. (Orig.). 1991. pap. 17.00 (*0-664-25230-3*) Westminster John Knox.

***Reformed Theology in America: A History of Its Modern Development.** Ed. by David F. Wells. (C). 1997. pap. text ed. 19.99 (*0-8010-2148-0*) Baker Bks.

***Reformed Theology Today.** Loius I. Hodges. 19.95 (*0-614-26620-3*) Columbia Intl Univ.

Reformed Zion-Pine Church Record, 1788-1827. George M. Smith. Ed. by Klaus Wust & Ilse Martin. 1984. pap. 9.95 (*0-917968-12-3*) Shenandoah Hist.

Reformer Vagy Forradalmar Volt-e Nagy Imre? Niklos Molnar & Laszlo Nagy. LC 83-61981. 160p. (HUN.). 1983. pap. 10.00 (*0-930888-22-7*) Brooklyn Coll Pr.

Reformers: Living History. Michael Ryan. (C). 1988. 59.00 (*0-946139-52-0*) St Mut.

Reformers - Wycliffe, Hus, Savonarola, & Knox, Vol. 2 of 7. (Men Who Changed the World Ser.: Vol. 2). 1972. 1.50 (*0-89985-255-6*) Christ for the Nations.

***Reformers & Activists.** Nancy J. Nielsen. LC 96-41254. (American Indian Lives Ser.). (YA). 1997. 17.95 (*0-8160-3440-0*) Facts on File.

Reformers & Revivalists: The History of The Wesleyan Church. Ed. by Wayne E. Caldwell & Wesleyan Church, History Committee Staff. (Wesleyan History Ser.). 718p. 1992. 17.95 (*0-89827-095-2*, BKJ09) Wesleyan Pub Hse.

Reformers & the Theology of Reformation. William Cunningham. 1979. 31.99 (*0-85151-013-2*) Banner of Truth.

Reformers & Their Stepchildren. Leonard Verduin. 1995. 22.00 (*0-8028-3791-3*) Eerdmans.

Reformers & War: American Progressive Publicists & the First World War. John A. Thompson. LC 86-26329. xi, 300p. 1987. text ed. 59.95 (*0-521-25289-X*) Cambridge U Pr.

Reformer's Apprentice: A Novel of Old San Francisco. Harriet Rochlin. 224p. 1996. 19.95 (*1-56474-167-2*) Fithian Pr.

***Reformer's Apprentice: A Novel of Old San Francisco.** Harriet Rochlin. 222p. 1997. reprint ed. pap. 11.95 (*1-56474-237-7*) Fithian Pr.

Reformers Before the Reformation, Set. Emile de Bonnechose. Tr. by Campbell Mackenzie. LC 78-63194. (Heresies of the Early Christian & Medieval Era Ser.: Second Ser.). reprint ed. 44.50 (*0-404-16190-1*) AMS Pr.

Reformers Before the Reformation in Germany & the Netherlands, 2 vols. C. Ullmann. 1977. lib. bdg. 200.00 (*0-8490-2507-9*) Gordon Pr.

Reformers, Corporations, & the Electorate: An Analysis of Arizona's Age of Reform. David R. Berman. (Illus.). 304p. 1992. 35.00 (*0-87081-249-1*) Univ Pr Colo.

Reformers, Rebels, & Revolutionaries: The Western Canadian Radical Movement, 1899-1919. A. Ross McCormack. (Reprints in Canadian History Ser.). 256p. 1992. pap. 18.95 (*0-8020-7682-3*) U of Toronto Pr.

Reformers, Rebels, & Revolutionaries: The Western Canadian Radical Movement, 1899-1919. Andrew R. McCormack. LC 77-4338. 246p. reprint ed. pap. 70.20 (*0-317-27019-2*, 2023646) Bks Demand.

Reforming Administrator Preparation Programs. Ammentrop et al. (Orig.). (C). 1992. pap. text ed. 7.00 (*1-55996-153-8*) Univ Council Educ Admin.

Reforming Adult Services for Persons with Developmental Disabilities. John Kregel. 272p. 1990. text ed. 38.00 (*0-9626521-8-0*, Andover Med Pubs) Buttrwrth-Heinemann.

Reforming Agricultural Commodity Policy. Brian D. Wright & Bruce L. Gardner. (Studies in Agricultural Policy). 168p. 1995. 29.95 (*0-8447-3906-5*) Am Enterprise.

***Reforming America's Schools.** Baker & Mendelsohn. 248p. (C). 1997. per. 25.95 (*0-7872-3952-6*) Kendall-Hunt.

***Reforming & Conforming: NASDC Principals Discuss School Accountability Systems.** New American Schools Development Corp. Staff et al. LC 96-43663. 1996. pap. 15.00 (*0-8330-2440-X*, MR-716-NASDC) Rand Corp.

Reforming & Restructuring of Education. English et al. Ed. by Frederick C. Wendel. 90p. (Orig.). (C). 1992. pap. text ed. 7.00 (*1-55996-151-1*) Univ Council Educ Admin.

Reforming Asian Socialism: The Growth of Market Institutions. Ed. by John McMillan & Barry Naughton. LC 96-4313. (C). 1996. 62.50 (*0-472-10661-9*) U of Mich Pr.

***Reforming Australia's Unions.** Michael Costa & Mark Hearn. 290p. 1997. pap. 29.00 (*1-86287-248-1*, Pub. by Federation Pr AU) Gaunt.

Reforming Bureaucracy: The Politics of Institutional Choice. Jack H. Knott & Gary J. Miller. (Illus.). 304p. (C). 1987. pap. text ed. 46.00 (*0-13-770090-3*) P-H.

Reforming Central & Eastern European Economies: Initial Results & Challenges. Ed. by Vittorio Corbo et al. 318p. 1991. 29.95 (*0-8213-1893-4*, 11893) World Bank.

Reforming Chicago Public Schools: The Intended & Unintended Consequences. Rose Vasquez. LC 94-19839. 225p. 1994. lib. bdg. 15.95 (*1-879528-03-7*) LEPS Pr.

Reforming Chicago Schools: The Intended & Unintended Consequences. Rosetta Vasquez. LC 94-19839. 225p. 1994. reprint ed. pap. 64.20 (*0-608-01710-8*, 2062365) Bks Demand.

***Reforming China's Financial System.** Zhu Huayou. 168p. 1996. 9.95 (*7-119-01341-6*, Pub. by Foreign Lang CH) China Bks.

Reforming China's Public Finances. Ed. by Ehtisham Ahmad et al. 1995. 24.00 (*1-55775-511-6*) Intl Monetary.

Reforming Church...Gift & Task: Essays from a Free Conference. Ed. by Charles P. Lutz. LC 95-34890. 256p. 1995. pap. 14.95 (*1-886513-02-3*) Kirk Hse Pubs.

***Reforming Dairy Policy.** 75p. 1996. 19.00 (*92-64-14911-2*, Pub. by Org for Econ FR) OECD.

Reforming Defense: The State of American Civil-Military Relations. David C. Hendrickson. LC 87-17003. 176p. 1988. text ed. 30.00 (*0-8018-3550-X*) Johns Hopkins.

Reforming Economic Systems in Developing Countries. Ed. by Dwight H. Perkins & Michael Roemer. (Institute for International Development Ser.). 492p. 1991. 29.95 (*0-674-75319-4*, PERREF) HUP.

Reforming Economics: Calvinist Studies on Methods & Institutions. Ed. by John P. Tiemstra. LC 90-6050. (Toronto Studies in Theology: Vol. 48). 344p. 1990. lib. bdg. 99.95 (*0-88946-924-5*) E Mellen.

Reforming Education: The Emerging Systemic Approach. Stephen L. Jacobson & Robert Berne. LC 93-6442. 296p. 1993. 49.95 (*0-8039-6098-0*) Corwin Pr.

Reforming Education: The Opening of the American Mind. Mortimer J. Adler. 320p. 1990. pap. 8.95 (*0-02-030175-8*) Macmillan.

Reforming Education & Changing Schools: Case Studies in Policy Sociology. Stephen J. Ball et al. 224p. (C). 1992. pap. 19.95 (*0-415-07790-7*, A7716) Routledge.

Reforming Farm Policy: Toward a National Agenda. Willard W. Cochrane & C. Ford Runge. LC 92-11113. (Illus.). 288p. 1992. text ed. 39.95 (*0-8138-0448-5*) Iowa St U Pr.

Reforming Federal-Provincial Fiscal Arrangements: Towards Sustainable Federalism. Frances St. Hilaire. 85p. 1994. pap. 13.95 (*0-88645-153-1*, Pub. by Inst Res Pub CN) Ashgate Pub Co.

Reforming Federal Regulation. Robert E. Litan & William D. Nordhaus. LC 83-3622. (Yale Fastback Ser.: No. 27). 224p. 1983. text ed. 42.00 (*0-300-03045-2*) Yale U Pr.

Reforming Financial Institutions in the United States: Towards Rebuilding a Safe & More Efficient System. Ed. by George G. Kaufman. LC 93-2298. 208p. (C). 1993. lib. bdg. 99.00 (*0-7923-9383-X*) Kluwer Ac.

***Reforming Financial Systems: Historical Implications for Policy.** Ed. by Gerard Caprio, Jr. & Dimitri Vittas. (Illus.). 200p. (C). 1997. text ed. 49.95 (*0-521-58115-X*) Cambridge U Pr.

Reforming Florida's Sentencing Guidelines: Balancing Equity, Justice, & Public Safety. Roger B. Handberg & N. Gary Holten. 144p. 1993. per. 36.69 (*0-8403-8738-5*) Kendall-Hunt.

Reforming Fundamentalism: Fuller Seminary & the New Evangelicalism. George M. Marsden. LC 95-10335. 1995. pap. 15.00 (*0-8028-0870-0*) Eerdmans.

Reforming Fundamentalism: Fuller Seminary & the New Evangelicalism. George M. Marsden. LC 87-22243. 331p. reprint ed. pap. 94.40 (*0-7837-3185-X*, 2042789) Bks Demand.

Reforming Health Care: A Market Prescription. (CED Statement on National Policy Ser.). 114p. 1987. pap. 9.50 (*0-87186-084-8*); lib. bdg. 11.50 (*0-87186-784-2*) Comm Econ Dev.

Reforming Health Care: The Philosophy & Practice of International Health Reform. Ed. by David Seedhouse. LC 94-44374. 242p. 1995. pap. text ed. 29.95 (*0-471-95325-3*) Wiley.

Reforming Health Care Systems. Ed. by Joshua Shemer & Mikko Vienonen. 240p. (Orig.). 1995. pap. text ed. 60.00 (*965-229-121-8*, Pub. by Gefen Pub Hse IS) Gefen Bks.

Reforming Health Care Systems: Experiments with the NHS. Ed. by A. J. Culyer & Adam Wagstaff. LC 95-42419. (Section F Series, British Association for the Advancement of Science). (Illus.). 192p. 1996. 80.00 (*1-85898-329-0*) E Elgar.

Reforming Human Services: Change Through Participation. Hans Toch & J. Douglas Grant. (Library of Social Research: Vol. 142). (Illus.). 240p. 1982. pap. 24.95 (*0-8039-1887-9*) Sage.

Reforming Human Services: Change Through Participation. Hans Toch & J. Douglas Grant. LC 82-10527. (Sage Library of Social Research: Vol. 142). 272p. 1982. reprint ed. pap. 77.60 (*0-608-00822-2*, 2061611) Bks Demand.

***Reforming Indian Economy: The Narasimha Rao & Manmohan Singh Era.** R. J. Venkateswaran. (C). 1996. 16.00 (*81-259-0043-8*, Pub. by Vikas II) S Asia.

Reforming Justice in Russia, 1864-1996: Power, Culture, & the Limits of Legal Order. Ed. by Peter H. Solomon, Jr. LC 97-11590. 416p. (C). (gr. 13). 1997. text ed. 82.95 (*1-56324-862-X*) M E Sharpe.

Reforming Juvenile Detention: No More Hidden Closets. Ed. by Ira M. Schwartz & William H. Barton. 192p. 1995. 45.00 (*0-8142-0635-2*) Ohio St U Pr.

Reforming Kings: Cult & Society in First Temple Judah. Lowery. (Journal for the Study of the Old Testament Supplement Ser.: No. 120). 236p. (C). 1991. 45.00 (*1-85075-318-0*, Pub. by Sheffield Acad UK) CUP Services.

Reforming Libel Law. Ed. by John Soloski & Randall P. Bezanson. LC 92-5660. (Communication Ser.). 380p. 1992. lib. bdg. 47.50 (*0-89862-317-0*) Guilford Pr.

Reforming Lord Ragsdale. Carla Kelly. (Regency Romance Ser.). 224p. 1995. pap. 3.99 (*0-451-18465-3*, Sig) NAL-Dutton.

Reforming Marlowe: The Nineteenth-Century Canonization of a Renaissance Dramatist. Thomas W. Dabbs. LC 89-46399. 1991. 32.50 (*0-8387-5192-X*) Bucknell U Pr.

***Reforming Marriage.** Douglas Wilson. 144p. (Orig.). 1995. pap. 9.50 (*1-885767-45-5*) Canon Pr ID.

Reforming Mathematics Education in America's Cities: The Urban Mathematics Collaborative Project. Norman L. Webb. (Ways of Knowing in Science Ser.). 256p. (C). 1994. text ed. 46.00 (*0-8077-3383-0*); pap. text ed. 21.95 (*0-8077-3382-2*) Tchrs Coll.

***Reforming Medicaid.** James R. Cantwell. 14p. 1995. pap. 10.00 (*1-56808-062-X*, 197) Natl Ctr Pol.

***Reforming Medicare with Medical Savings Accounts.** Gary Robbins & Aldona Robbins. 16p. 1995. pap. 10.00 (*1-56808-060-3*, 195) Natl Ctr Pol.

Reforming Mexico's Agrarian Reform. Ed. by Laura Randall. LC 95-25771. (Columbia University Seminar Ser.). 320p. (gr. 13). 1996. text ed. 69.95 (*1-56324-643-0*); pap. text ed. 24.95 (*1-56324-644-9*) M E Sharpe.

Reforming Money & Finance: Toward a New Monetary Regime. 2nd ed. Ed. by Robert Guttmann. LC 96-31863. 288p. (C). (gr. 13-13). 1996. text ed. 64.95 (*1-56324-770-4*) M E Sharpe.

Reforming Money & Finance: Toward a New Monetary Regime. 2nd ed. Ed. by Robert Guttmann. LC 96-31863. 288p. (C). 1996. pap. text ed. 28.95 (*1-56324-771-2*) M E Sharpe.

Reforming of General Education. Daniel Bell. (Foundations of Higher Education Ser.). 1996. write for info. (*1-56000-591-2*) Transaction Pubs.

Reforming Open & Distance Education: Critical Reflections from Practice. Ed. by Terry Evans & Daryl Nation. 224p. 1992. 70.00 (*0-7494-0822-7*) St Martin.

Reforming Open & Distance Education: Critical Reflections from Practice. Ed. by Terry Evans & Daryl Nation. LC 92-43316. 240p. 1993. text ed. 45.00 (*0-312-09484-1*) St Martin.

***Reforming Our Thinking on Welfare: Strategies for State Action.** Sally Tyler et al. 32p. (Orig.). 1996. pap. 5.00 (*1-877966-33-9*) Ctr Women Policy.

***Reforming Personnel Preparation in Early Intervention.** Winton. LC 97-16420. 1997. pap. text ed. 35.00 (*1-55766-286-X*) P H Brookes.

Reforming Planned Economies in an Integrating World Economy. Ed. by Barry P. Bosworth & Gur Ofer. (Integrating National Economies Ser.). 186p. (C). 1995. 34.95 (*0-8157-1048-8*); pap. 14.95 (*0-8157-1047-X*) Brookings.

***Reforming Power of the Scriptures: A Biography of the English Bible.** Mary M. Trammell & Willilam G. Dawley. LC 96-86014. (Illus.). 250p. 1996. 39.95 (*0-87510-314-6*) Christian Sci.

Reforming Private Health Insurance. Mark A. Hall. LC 94-14779. 150p. 1994. 19.95 (*0-8447-3862-X*, AEI Pr); pap. 12.95 (*0-8447-3863-8*, AEI Pr) Am Enterprise.

Reforming Products Liability. W. Kip Viscusi. 270p. (C). 1991. 40.00 (*0-674-75323-2*) HUP.

Reforming Protestantism: Christian Commitment in Today's World. Douglas F. Ottati. LC 95-10454. 192p. (Orig.). 1995. pap. 20.00 (*0-664-25604-X*) Westminster John Knox.

R

An Asterisk (*) at the beginning of an entry indicates that the title is appearing in BIP for the first time.

Reforming Public Administration for Development: Experiences from Eastern Africa. Gelase Mutahaba. LC 89-24550. (Library of Management for Development). xv, 183p. 1989. pap. 24.50 (*0-931816-93-9*) Kumarian Pr.

Reforming Public Welfare: A Critique of the Negative Income Tax Experiment. Peter H. Rossi & Katharine C. Lyall. LC 75-41509. 208p. 1976. 29.95 (*0-87154-754-6*) Russell Sage.

Reforming Regulation: An Evaluation of the Ash Council Proposals. Roger G. Noll. LC 75-179326. (Studies in the Regulation of Economic Activity). 116p. 1971. pap. 8.95 (*0-8157-6107-4*) Brookings.

Reforming Retirement Policies. LC 81-15207. (CED Statement on National Policy Ser.). 66p. 1981. pap. 5.00 (*0-87186-073-2*) Comm Econ Dev.

Reforming Rural Russia: State, Local Society, & National Politics, 1855-1914. Francis W. Wcislo. (Studies of the Harriman Institute, Columbia University). (Illus.). 376p. (C). 1990. text ed. 62.50 (*0-691-05574-2*) Princeton U Pr.

Reforming School Finance. Robert D. Reischauer. LC 73-1080. (Brookings Institution Studies in Social Experimentation). 199p. reprint ed. pap. 56.80 (*0-317-26349-8*, 2025401) Bks Demand.

Reforming Science Education: Project 2061. (State Legislative Reports: Vol. 15, No. 1). 12p. 1990. 5.00 (*1-55516-257-6*, 7302-1501) Natl Conf State Legis.

Reforming Science Education: Social Perspectives & Personal Reflections. Rodger W. Bybee. LC 93-17231. (Ways of Knowing in Science Ser.: Vol. 1). 216p. (C). 1993. 43.00 (*0-8077-3261-3*); pap. 19.95 (*0-8077-3260-5*) Tchrs Coll.

*__Reforming Sex: The German Movement for Birth Control & Abortion Reform.__ Atina Grossman. (Illus.). 304p. 1997. reprint ed. pap. 17.95 (*0-19-512124-4*) OUP.

Reforming Sex: The German Movement for Birth Control & Abortion Reform, 1920-1950. Atina Grosmann. (Illus.). 352p. 1995. text ed. 49.95 (*0-19-505672-8*) OUP.

Reforming State-Local Relations: A Practical Guide. Steven Gold. Ed. by Sharon Schwoch. 159p. (Orig.). 1989. pap. 20.00 (*1-55516-545-1*, 5315) Natl Conf State Legis.

Reforming Teacher Education: Issues & New Directions. Joseph A. Braun, Jr. LC 89-7876. (Source Books on Education: Vol. 20). 380p. 1989. text ed. 55.00 (*0-8240-3712-X*) Garland.

Reforming Teacher Education: The Impact of the Holmes Group Report. Jonas F. Soltis. 144p. (C). 1987. pap. text ed. 14.95 (*0-8077-2871-3*) Tchrs Coll.

*__Reforming Teacher Education: The Impact of the Holmes Group Report.__ Ed. by Jonas F. Soltis. LC 87-6427. (Special Issues from the Teachers College Record Ser.). 145p. pap. 41.40 (*0-608-05100-4*, 2065656) Bks Demand.

Reforming Teacher Education in South Dakota. Robert Emans. 1985. 5.00 (*1-55614-105-X*) U of SD Gov Res Bur.

Reforming the "Bad" Quartos: Performance & Provenance of Six Shakespearean First Editions. Kathleen O. Irace. LC 92-56612. 1994. 37.50 (*0-87413-471-4*) U Delaware Pr.

Reforming the Bank Regulatory Structure. Andrew S. Carron. LC 84-45847. (Studies in the Regulation of Economic Activity). 52p. 1985. pap. 8.95 (*0-8157-1303-7*) Brookings.

Reforming the Civil Justice System. Ed. by Larry Kramer. LC 96-10869. 480p. (C). 1996. 65.00 (*0-8147-4665-9*) NYU Pr.

Reforming the Civil Service. Geoffrey K. Fry. 320p. 1993. text ed. 70.00 (*0-7486-0412-X*, Pub. by Edinburgh U Pr UK) Col U Pr.

Reforming the Constitution. Ed. by Subhash C. Kashyap. (C). 1992. text ed. 33.00 (*81-85674-53-1*, Pub. by UBS Pubs Dist II) S Asia.

Reforming the CYA: How to End Crowding, Diversify Treatment & Protect the Public Without Spending More Money. Paul DeMuro et al. 132p. 1988. pap. 5.95 (*0-943004-04-7*) Common Knowledge.

Reforming the Economies of Central & Eastern Europe. Organization for Economic Cooperation & Development Staff. 119p. (Orig.). 1992. pap. 21.00 (*92-64-13613-4*) OECD.

Reforming the Energy Sector in Transtion Ecomonies: Selected Experience & Lessons, Vol. 296. Dale Gray. LC 95-34359. (World Bank Discussion Papers). 126p. 1995. 8.95 (*0-8213-3424-7*, 13424) World Bank.

Reforming the Federal Pay System. (Government Employee Relations Special Report Ser.). 17p. 1989. pap. 25.00 (*1-55871-160-0*) BNA Plus.

Reforming the Forest Service. Randal O'Toole. (Illus.). 248p. (Orig.). 1988. 34.95 (*0-933280-49-1*); pap. 19.95 (*0-933280-45-9*) Island Pr.

Reforming the Health Care Market: An Interpretive Economic History. David F. Drake. LC 94-13475. 240p. 1994. 42.50 (*0-87840-567-4*); pap. 16.95 (*0-87840-568-2*) Georgetown U Pr.

Reforming the International Monetary System: From Roosevelt to Reagan. Robert D. Hormats. LC 87-80815. (Headline Ser.: No. 281). 1987. pap. 5.95 (*0-87124-113-7*) Foreign Policy.

Reforming the Labor Market in a Liberalized Economy. Ed. by Gustavo Marquez. (Inter-American Development Bank Ser.). 256p. (Orig.). 1996. pap. text ed. 18.50 (*0-940602-96-2*) IADB.

Reforming the Law: Impact of Child Development Research. Ed. by Gary B. Melton. LC 87-31. (Guilford Law & Behavior Ser.). 307p. 1987. lib. bdg. 42.00 (*0-89862-278-6*) Guilford Pr.

*__Reforming the Law of Takings in Michigan.__ Donald J. Kochan. (Illus.). 34p. (Orig.). 1996. pap. 5.00 (*0-9647703-5-0*, S96-03) Mackinac Ctr Public Pol.

Reforming the Law of the Sea Treaty: Opportunities Missed, Precedents Set, & U. S. Sovereignty Threatened. Peter M. Leitner. 386p. 1996. pap. text ed. 42.00 (*0-7618-0394-7*); lib. bdg. 62.00 (*0-7618-0393-9*) U Pr of Amer.

*__Reforming the Military Retirement System.__ Beth J. Asch et al. LC 96-37426. Date not set. pap. write for info. (*0-8330-2463-9*) Rand Corp.

Reforming the Philippine Electoral Process: Developments 1986-88. National Democratic Institute for International Affairs Staff. 86p. 1991. pap. 8.95 (*1-880134-10-1*) Natl Demo Inst.

Reforming the Ruble: Monetary Aspects of Perestroika. Ed. by Michael P. Claudon & Josef C. Brada. 328p. (C). 1990. text ed. 36.00 (*0-8147-1447-1*) NYU Pr.

Reforming the Russian Legal System. Gordon B. Smith. (Soviet Paperbacks Ser.: No. 11). 260p. (C). 1996. text ed. 59.95 (*0-521-45052-7*); pap. text ed. 21.95 (*0-521-45669-X*) Cambridge U Pr.

Reforming the Schools--for Teachers. John W. Friesen. LC 87-13361. 164p. (Orig.). 1987. pap. text ed. 19.00 (*0-8191-6480-1*); lib. bdg. 44.00 (*0-8191-6479-8*) U Pr of Amer.

Reforming the Secret State. Patrick Birkinshaw. (Studies in Law & Politics Ser.). 96p. 1991. pap. 20.00 (*0-335-09631-X*, Open Univ Pr) Taylor & Francis.

Reforming the Soviet Economy: Equality vs. Efficiency. Ed A. Hewett. LC 87-29500. 404p. (C). 1988. 39.95 (*0-8157-3604-5*); pap. 18.95 (*0-8157-3603-7*) Brookings.

Reforming the Treaty on European Union: The Legal Debate. Jan A. Winter & T.M.C. Asser Institute Staff. LC 96-9072. 1996. lib. bdg. 225.00 (*90-411-0133-0*) Kluwer Ac.

Reforming the United Nations. David W. Felder. 52p. 1996. pap. text ed. 8.95 (*0-910959-79-X*, B&G 26E) Wellington Pr.

Reforming the United Nations: The Challenge of Relevance. K. P. Saksena. LC 92-559. 256p. (C). 1993. text ed. 32.00 (*0-8039-9445-1*) Sage.

*__Reforming the Welfare State.__ Ed. by Herbert Giersch. LC 97-2292. (Illus.). 300p. 1997. 94.00 (*3-540-61493-1*) Spr-Verlag.

Reforming the Workplace: A Study of Self-Regulation in Occupational Safety. Joseph V. Rees. LC 88-20822. (Law in Social Context Ser.). 320p. (C). 1988. text ed. 44.95 (*0-8122-8132-2*) U of Pa Pr.

Reforming Urban Land Policies & Institutions in Developing Countries. Catherine Farvacque & Patrick McAuslan. (Urban Management Program Policy Paper Ser.: No. 5). 133p. 1992. pap. 9.95 (*0-8213-2092-0*, 12092) World Bank.

Reforming World Agricultural Trade: A Policy Statement by Twenty-Nine Professionals from Seventeen Countries. Institute for International Economics Staff. LC 88-149720. 42p. reprint ed. pap. 25.00 (*0-7837-4214-2*, 2043903) Bks Demand.

Reforming World Trade: The Social & Environmental Priorities. Caroline LeQuesne. (Oxfam Insight Ser.). 80p. 1996. pap. 7.95 (*0-85598-346-9*, Pub. by Oxfam UK) Humanities.

Reformism & Revisionism in Africa's Political Economy in the 1990s: The Dialectics of Adjustment. Timothy M. Shaw. 230p. (C). 1993. text ed. 65.00 (*0-312-07977-X*) St Martin.

Reformist Apocalypticism & Piers Plowman. Kathryn Kerby-Fulton. (Cambridge Studies in Medieval Literature: No. 7). 272p. (C). 1990. text ed. 69.95 (*0-521-34298-8*) Cambridge U Pr.

Reformperspektiven fur die Industriegesellschaft. Ulrich Heyder. 304p. 1995. pap. text ed. 36.00 (*3-7186-5669-8*, Harwood Acad Pubs) Gordon & Breach.

Reformpolitik & Sozialer Wandel in der Sowjetunion, 1970-1980. Klaus Von Beyme. 212p. (GER.). 1988. pap. 36.00 (*3-7890-1647-0*, Pub. by Nomos Verlags GW) Intl Bk Import.

Reforms for Women: Future Options. Ed. by Najma Heptulla. (C). 1992. 36.00 (*81-204-0688-5*, Pub. by Oxford IBH II) S Asia.

Reforms of Peter the Great: Progress Through Coercion in Russia. Evgenii V. Anisimov. Tr. by John T. Alexander from RUS. LC 92-22280. (New Russian History Ser.). 344p. (gr. 13). 1993. text ed. 69.95 (*1-56324-047-5*); pap. text ed. 26.95 (*1-56324-048-3*) M E Sharpe.

Reforms of the Council of Constance (1414-1418) Phillip H. Stump. LC 93-31994. (Studies in the History of Christian Thought: Vol. 53). 1993. 180.00 (*90-04-09930-1*) E J Brill.

Reformulated Motor Gasoline: Markets, Technologies, Industry Ramifications. Forman. 216p. 1995. 2,650.00 (*0-614-10878-0*, E-071) BCC.

*__Reformulating Reformed Theology: Jesus Christ - The Theology of Hugh Ross MacKintosh.__ Robert R. Redman, Jr. 304p. 1997. 40.00 (*0-7618-0515-X*) U Pr of Amer.

Refounding: A Franciscan Provincial Experiment. Anthony Carrozzo. (Spirit & Life Refounded Ser.). 135p. 1994. pap. 8.00 (*1-57659-037-2*) Franciscan Inst.

Refounding Democratic Public Administration: Modern Paradoxes, Postmodern Challenges. Ed. by Gary L. Wamsley & James F. Wolf. (C). 1996. pap. 25.95 (*0-8039-5977-X*); 55.00 (*0-8039-5976-1*) Sage.

Refounding the Church: Dissent for Leadership. Gerald A. Arbuckle. LC 93-19668. 288p. 1993. pap. 20.00 (*0-88344-896-3*) Orbis Bks.

Refracted Dreams. Pat Tennant et al. Ed. by Jamie Teasley. LC 89-51425. 83p. 1989. pap. 5.95 (*1-55523-273-6*) Winston-Derek.

Refracting America: Gender, Race, Ethnicity, & the Environment in American History to 1877. Barbara M. Posadas & Robert McColley. (American History to Eighteen Seventy-Seven Ser.: Vol. 1). (Illus.). 224p. (Orig.). (C). 1993. pap. text ed. 11.96 (*1-881089-16-9*) Brandywine Press.

Refraction Seismics Vol. 13: Lateral Resolution Structure & Seismic Velocity. D. Palmer & K. Helbig. (Handbook of Geophysical Exploration Ser.). 1986. 129.00 (*0-946631-13-1*, Pub. by Pergamon Repr UK) Franklin.

Refractional Influences in Astrometry & Geodesy. Ed. by Erik Tengstrom & George Teleki. (International Astronomical Union Symposia Ser.: No. 89). 1979. pap. text ed. 70.50 (*90-277-1038-4*); lib. bdg. 129.50 (*90-277-1037-6*) Kluwer Ac.

Refractions. Octavio Armand. Tr. by Carol Maier from SPA. (Orig.). 1994. pap. 15.00 (*0-930829-21-2*) Lumen Inc.

Refractions. Robert L. Smith. LC 79-53012. (Living Poets' Library: Vol. 21). 1979. pap. 3.50 (*0-934218-11-0*) Dragons Teeth.

Refractions. Alois Vogel. Tr. by Walter L. Kreeger. LC 94-19456. (Studies in Austrian Literature, Culture, & Thought). 235p. 1995. pap. 21.95 (*0-929497-97-X*) Ariadne CA.

Refractions: Poems. Frederick Morgan. 1981. 25.00 (*0-317-40789-9*) Abattoir.

Refractive Anomalies. Theodore Grosvenor & Merton C. Flom. (Illus.). 433p. 1990. 90.00 (*0-409-90149-0*) Buttrwrth-Heinemann.

Refractive Keratotomy for Cataract Surgery & the Correction of Astigmatism. Ed. by Robert M. Kershner. LC 94-15787. 158p. 1994. 79.00 (*1-55642-237-7*) SLACK Inc.

Refractive Lamellar Keratoplasty. Ed. by George W. Rozakis. LC 94-4393. 178p. 1994. 89.00 (*1-55642-229-6*) SLACK Inc.

Refractive Management of Ametropia. Ed. by Kenneth E. Brookman. (Illus.). 240p. 1996. pap. text ed. 35.00 (*0-7506-9569-2*) Buttrwrth-Heinemann.

Refractive Nonlinearity of Wide Band Semiconductors & Applications, Vol. 9. A. A. Borshch et al. Ed. by V. S. Letokhov. (Laser Science & Technology Ser.: Vol. 9). xiv, 142p. 1990. pap. text ed. 155.00 (*3-7186-4971-3*) Gordon & Breach.

Refractive Surgery. Azar. 672p. 1996. text ed. 225.00 (*0-8385-8276-1*) Appleton & Lange.

Refractive Surgery. Olivia N. Serdarevic. 1994. 39.00 (*0-316-78067-7*) Little.

*__Refractive Surgery: Current Techniques & Management.__ Olivia N. Serdarevic. LC 96-29391. (Illus.). 368p. 1996. 158.50 (*0-89640-325-4*) Igaku-Shoin.

*__Refractive Surgery for Eyecare Professionals.__ Johnny L. Gayton & Robert M. Kershner. LC 97-10167. (Basic Bookshelf for Eyecare Professionals Ser.). 1997. write for info. (*1-55642-337-3*) SLACK Inc.

Refractive Surgery for Primary Care Optometrists. Arthur Medina, Jr. 250p. 1996. 40.00 (*1-55642-277-6*) SLACK Inc.

Refractories. 4th ed. F. H. Norton. LC 67-20660. (Illus.). 462p. (C). 1985. reprint ed. text ed. 75.00 (*1-878907-06-9*, RAN) TechBooks.

Refractories: Production & Properties. J. H. Chesters. 562p. (Orig.). 1973. pap. text ed. 52.50 (*0-904357-62-7*, Pub. by Inst Materials UK) Ashgate Pub Co.

Refractories: The Hidden Industry. Corrinne Krause. 256p. 1987. 38.00 (*0-916094-94-4*, REFRAC) Am Ceramic.

Refractories, Carbon & Graphite Products, Activated Carbon, Advanced Ceramics see 1997 Annual Book of ASTM Standards: General Products, Chemical Specialties, & End Use Products, Section 15

Refractories for Iron & Steelmaking. J. H. Chesters. 502p. 1974. text ed. 52.50 (*0-900497-89-0*, Pub. by Inst Materials UK) Ashgate Pub Co.

Refractories for the Chemical Process Industries. (MTI Manual Ser.: No. 9). (Illus.). 392p. 1984. 131.00 (*0-685-39502-2*) NACE Intl.

Refractories in the Glass Industry. Alexis G. Pincus. LC 78-55364. (Provessing in the Glass Industry Ser.). 280p. 1980. 24.95 (*0-911993-09-6*) Ashlee Pub Co.

Refractories Manual. 2nd ed. 200p. 60.00 (*0-87433-114-5*, GM8902) Am Foundrymen.

Refractories-Silk see Encyclopedia of Chemical Technology

Refractory Alloying Elements in Superalloys. Ed. by John K. Tien & Steven Reichman. LC 83-73688. (Conference Proceedings - American Society for Metals Ser.). (Illus.). 189p. reprint ed. pap. 53.90 (*0-8357-3514-1*, 2034321) Bks Demand.

Refractory Concrete. Symposium on Refractory Concrete Staff. LC 78-67102. (ACI Publication Ser.: SP-57). (Illus.). 313p. reprint ed. pap. 89.30 (*0-8357-3072-7*, 2039329) Bks Demand.

Refractory Concrete: State-of-the Art Report. 224p. 1979. 98.50 (*0-317-32086-6*, 547R-79(89)BOW6) ACI.

Refractory Depression: Current Strategies & Future Directions. William A. Nolen et al. LC 93-49532. 235p. 1994. text ed. 84.95 (*0-471-94315-0*) Wiley.

Refractory Glaucomas. Ed. by Fathi El-Sayyad et al. LC 95-7750. (Illus.). 320p. 1995. 95.00 (*0-89640-284-3*) Igaku-Shoin.

Refractory Husbands. Mary S. Cutting. LC 79-128729. (Short Story Index Reprint Ser.). 1977. 17.95 (*0-8369-3620-5*) Ayer.

Refractory Linings: Thermomechanical Design & Applications. Charles A. Schacht. LC 94-24950. (Mechanical Engineering Ser.: Vol. 95). 504p. 1995. 185.00 (*0-8247-9560-1*) Dekker.

Refractory Men, Fanatical Women. Edwin Bannon. 209p. 1992. pap. 14.95 (*0-85244-226-2*, Pub. by Gracewing UK) Morehouse Pub.

Refractory Metals: State of the Art, 1988: Proceedings of a Symposium Held on Refractory Metals, State-of-the-Art, Sponsored by the TMS Refractory Metals Committee, Held During the TMS Fall Meeting, Chicago, Illinois, September 27, 1988. fac. ed. Minerals, Metals & Materials Society Staff. Ed. by R. L. Ammon & P. K. Kumar. LC 89-60380. (Illus.). 207p. 1989. pap. 59.00 (*0-7837-8608-5*, 2052539) Bks Demand.

Refractory Metals & Alloys: Proceedings. Ed. by M. Semchyshen. LC 61-9444. (Metallurgical Society Conference Ser.: Vol. 11). 635p. reprint ed. pap. 180.00 (*0-317-10265-6*, 2000674) Bks Demand.

Refractory Metals & Alloys III: Applied Aspects. Ed. by Robert I. Jaffee. LC 65-24869. (Metallurgical Society Conference Ser.: Vol. 30). 1038p. reprint ed. pap. 180.00 (*0-317-10849-2*, 2001518) Bks Demand.

Refractory Metals & Alloys IV: Research & Development. Ed. by Robert I. Jaffee et al. LC 68-21965. (Metallurgical Society Conference Ser.: Vol. 41). 1384p. reprint ed. pap. 180.00 (*0-317-10586-8*, 2001530) Bks Demand.

Refractory Metals & Their Industrial Applications-STP 849. ASTM Committee B-10. Ed. by Robert E. Smallwood. LC 84-70136. (Illus.). 115p. 1984. pap. text ed. 19.00 (*0-8031-0203-8*, 04-849000-05) ASTM.

Refrainformen im Chansonnier de L'Arsenal. Herta Orenstein. (Wissenschaftliche Abhandlungen-Musicological Studies: Vol. 19). 120p. (GER.). 1972. lib. bdg. 54.00 (*0-912024-89-5*) Inst Mediaeval Mus.

Refrains chez les trouveres du XIIe siecle au debut du XIVe. Eglal Doss-Quinby. LC 84-47878. (American University Studies: Romance Languages & Literature: Ser. II, Vol. 17). 316p. (C). 1984. text ed. 32.00 (*0-8204-0153-6*) P Lang Pubng.

Reframing: A New Method in Pastoral Care. Donald Capps. LC 89-37499. 192p. (Orig.). 1990. pap. 16.00 (*0-8006-2413-0*, 1-2413) Augsburg Fortress.

Reframing: Neuro-Linguistic Programming & the Transformation of Meaning. Richard Bandler & John Grinder. Ed. by Steve Andreas & Connirae Andreas. 215p. (Orig.). 1982. 14.00 (*0-911226-24-9*); pap. 10.50 (*0-911226-25-7*) Real People.

Reframing Abstract Expressionism: Subjectivity & Painting in the 1940s. Michael Leja. LC 92-32992. (Illus.). 448p. (C). 1993. text ed. 60.00 (*0-300-04461-5*) Yale U Pr.

*__Reframing Abstract Expressionism: Subjectivity & Painting in the 1940s.__ Michael Leja. (Illus.). 400p. 1997. pap. 25.00 (*0-300-07082-9*) Yale U Pr.

Reframing America. Andrei Codrescu & Alexander Alland. (Points of Entry Ser.). 96p. 1995. pap. 19.95 (*0-938262-27-0*) Ctr Creat Photog.

Reframing & Reform: Perspectives on Organization, Leadership, & School Change. Robert Carlson. LC 95-11579. 343p. (Orig.). (C). 1996. pap. text ed. 23.16 (*0-8013-1106-3*) Longman.

Reframing Culture: The Case of the Vitagraph Quality Films. William Uricchio & Roberta E. Pearson. LC 93-16641. (Illus.). 272p. 1993. pap. text ed. 17.95 (*0-691-02117-1*) Princeton U Pr.

Reframing Diversity in Education: Educational Leadership for the 21st Century. Joan P. Shapiro et al. Ed. by William J. Bailey. LC 94-62046. (Educational Leadership for the 21st Century Ser.). 182p. 1995. 39.95 (*1-56676-240-5*, 762405) Technomic.

Reframing Educational Policy: Democracy, Community, & the Individual. Joseph Kahne. LC 95-42598. (Advances in Contemporary Educational Thought Ser.: Vol. 16). 208p. (C). 1996. text ed. 48.00 (*0-8077-3493-4*); pap. text ed. 22.95 (*0-8077-3492-6*) Tchrs Coll.

Reframing Human Resource Management: Power, Ethics & the Subject at Work. Barbara Townley. 240p. 1994. 65.00 (*0-8039-8493-6*) Sage.

Reframing Human Resource Management: Power, Ethics & the Subject at Work. Barbara Townley. 1994. pap. 21.95 (*0-8039-8496-0*) Sage.

*__Reframing International Development: Globalism, Postmodernity, & Difference.__ Nelson W. Keith. LC 97-4764. 1997. write for info. (*0-8039-7061-7*); pap. write for info. (*0-8039-7062-5*) Sage.

Reframing Japanese Cinema: Authorship, Genre, History. Ed. by Arthur Nolletti, Jr. & David Desser. LC 91-33659. (Illus.). 384p. 1992. 39.95 (*0-253-34108-6*); pap. 18.95 (*0-253-20723-1*, MB-723) Ind U Pr.

Reframing of Performance Anxiety: A Constructivist View. Joan S. Ingalls. 170p. (C). 1994. pap. 24.95 (*0-9643645-4-9*) Mind Plus Muscle.

Reframing of Realism: Galdos & the Discourses of the Nineteenth-Century Spanish Novel. Hazel Gold. LC 92-39376. 255p. 1993. text ed. 43.95 (*0-8223-1334-0*); pap. text ed. 18.95 (*0-8223-1367-7*) Duke.

Reframing Organizational Culture. Ed. by Peter J. Frost et al. 416p. (C). 1991. 62.00 (*0-8039-3650-8*); pap. 27.50 (*0-8039-3651-6*) Sage.

Reframing Organizations: Artistry, Choice, & Leadership. Lee G. Bolman & Terrence E. Deal. LC 90-46853. (Management-Social & Behavioral Science Ser.). 520p. (Orig.). text ed. 38.95 (*1-55542-299-3*); pap. text ed. 26.95 (*1-55542-323-X*) Jossey-Bass.

*__Reframing Organizations: Artistry, Choice & Leadership.__ 2nd ed. Lee B. Bolman & Terrence E. Deal. LC 96-53592. (Jossey-Bass Higher & Adult Education Ser.). 1997. write for info. (*0-7879-0822-3*) Jossey-Bass.

*__Reframing Organizations: Artistry, Choice & Leadership.__ 2nd ed. Lee G. Bolman & Terrence E. Deal. LC 96-53592. (Jossey-Bass Higher & Adult Education Ser.). 1997. pap. write for info. (*0-7879-0821-5*) Jossey-Bass.

Reframing Religious Life: An Expanded Vision for the Future. Diarmuid O'Murchu. 159p. 1994. pap. 35.00 (*0-85439-499-0*, Pub. by St Paul Pubns UK) St Mut.

Reframing the Renaissance: Visual Culture in Europe & Latin America, 1450-1650. Ed. & Intro. by Claire Farago. LC 95-12148. (Illus.). 1995. 45.00 (0-300-06295-8) Yale U Pr.

Reframing Women's Health: Multidisciplinary Research & Practice. Ed. by Alice Dan. LC 94-7456. 1994. 55.00 (0-8039-5773-4); pap. text ed. 28.00 (0-8039-5860-9) Sage.

Reframings: New American Feminist Photography. Ed. by Diane Neumaier. LC 94-46914. (Illus.). 1996. 49.95 (1-56639-331-0) Temple U Pr.

Refranes: Southwestern Spanish Proverbs. rev. ed. Ruben Cobos. (Illus.). 192p. 1985. pap. 11.95 (0-89013-177-5) Museum NM Pr.

Refranes en el "Quijote" Texto y Contexto. M. Cecilia Colombi. 1990. 40.50 (0-916379-66-3) Scripta.

***Refranes Mas Usados en Puerto Rico.** Maria E. Diaz De Rivera. 174p. (SPA.). 1994. pap. 6.00 (0-8477-0064-X) U of PR Pr.

Refranes O Proverbios Castellanos Traduzidos En Lingua Francesca. Cesar Oudin. 256p. reprint ed. write for info. (0-318-71627-5) G Olms Pubs.

Refrano General Ideologico Espanol. 3rd ed. Luis M. Kleiser. 816p. (SPA.). 1989. pap. 105.00 (0-7859-5058-3) Fr & Eur.

Refresh My Heart. Brownlow. (Easelette Miniatures Ser.). (Illus.). 1995. spiral bd. 4.99 (1-877719-82-X) Brownlow Pub Co.

Refresh My Heart: A Daily Prayer Journal. Paul C. Brownlow. 1991. spiral bd. 7.99 (1-877719-18-8) Brownlow Pub Co.

Refresh My Heart: A Daily Prayer Journal. deluxe ed. Paul C. Brownlow. 1994. spiral bd. 7.99 (1-877719-22-6) Brownlow Pub Co.

***Refresh My Heart - Victorious Spirit.** 10.35 (1-877719-73-0) Brownlow Pub Co.

***Refresh My Heart in Spring.** Jack Countryman. (Illus.). 1998. 12.99 (0-8499-5337-5) Word Pub.

Refresh, Renew, Revive. Ed. by H. B. London. (Pastor to Pastor Resource Ser.). 1996. 14.99 (1-56179-467-8) Focus Family.

Refresh Your Greek: Pratical Helps for Reading the New Testament. Wesley J. Perschbacher. 1989. text ed. 74. 99 (0-8024-3352-9) Moody.

***Refresh Your Life in the Spirit: How the Holy Spirit Can Empower You Every Day.** Ursula Bleasdell. 1997. pap. text ed. 10.99 (1-56955-022-0) Servant.

Refreshed by the Word: Cycle B. John E. O'Brien. 160p. 1996. pap. 10.95 (0-8091-3649-X, 3649-X) Paulist Pr.

Refreshed by the Word: Cycle C. John E. O'Brien. 144p. 1994. pap. 10.95 (0-8091-3506-X) Paulist Pr.

Refreshed by the Word, Cycle A, Cycle A. John E. O'Brien. 160p. (Orig.). 1995. pap. 10.95 (0-8091-3597-3, 1995) Paulist Pr.

Refresher Course in Gregg Shorthand. Madeline S. Strony et al. (Diamond Jubilee Ser.). 1970. text ed. 24.95 (0-07-062205-1) McGraw.

Refresher Course in Gregg Shorthand Simplified. Madeline S. Strony et al. 1962. text ed. 24.95 (0-07-062248-5) McGraw.

Refresher Guide for the Safety Professional, 4 vols. 1995. Set. 339.95 (0-939874-48-2) ASSE.

***Refresher Mathmatics.** 10th ed. 1988. pap. text ed. 17.50 (0-13-771122-0) P-H.

Refreshing Pauses: Coca-Cola & Human Rights in Guatemala. Henry J. Frundt. LC 87-16001. 288p. 1987. text ed. 45.00 (0-275-92764-4, C2764, Praeger Pubs) Greenwood.

Refreshing the Parts: Electoral Reform & British Politics. Ed. by Smyth. (C). 1992. pap. 19.95 (0-85315-753-7, Pub. by Lawrence & Wishart UK) NYU Pr.

Refreshings: A Book of Renewal. Illus. by Ricky Lindley. 210p. (Orig.). 1990. pap. 9.95 (0-942727-18-5) NC Yrly Pubns Bd.

Refreshment in the Desert: Spiritual Connections in Daily Life. Gilbert Padilla. LC 85-50663. 128p. (Orig.). 1992. pap. 7.95 (0-89622-228-4) Twenty-Third.

Refreshments Now & Then: Colonial, Victorian, & Contemporary Sweets. Patricia B. Mitchell. 1995. pap. 4.00 (0-925117-79-X) Mitchells.

Refrigeracion Industrial. Wilbert F. Stoecker. LC 91-45884. 352p. (SPA.). 1992. 39.95 (0-912524-68-5) Busn News.

Refrigerant Containment Technician Certification Test. (Career Examination Ser.). pap. 29.95 (0-8373-3776-3, C3776) Nat Learn.

Refrigerant Management: The Recovery, Recycling & Reclaiming of CFCs. Billy C. Langley. LC 92-40577. 155p. 1994. pap. 37.95 (0-8273-5590-4) Delmar.

Refrigerant Manual: Managing the Phase-Out of CFCs. Building Owners & Managers Assn. Int. Staff. 136p. (Orig.). 1993. pap. text ed. 85.00 (0-943130-05-0) Build Own & Man.

Refrigerant Recovery Book. Ed. by Mildred Geshwiler. 220p. 1993. pap. 49.00 (1-883413-11-7) Am Heat Ref & Air Eng.

Refrigerating Machine Mechanic. Jack Rudman. (Career Examination Ser.: C-1451). 1994. pap. 27.95 (0-8373-1451-8) Nat Learn.

Refrigerating Machine Operator. Jack Rudman. (Career Examination Ser.: C-670). 1994. pap. 27.95 (0-8373-0670-1) Nat Learn.

Refrigeration, Pt. I. Ed. by A. Ross Sabin. (Illus.). 144p. (gr. 11). 1974. 20.00 (0-938336-01-0) Whirlpool.

Refrigeration, Pt. II. Ed. by A. Ross Sabin. (Illus.). 208p. (gr. 11). 1974. 20.00 (0-938336-02-9) Whirlpool.

Refrigeration: A Practical Manual for Apprentices. 3rd ed. G. H. Reed. (Illus.). 153p. 1974. reprint ed. 32.50 (0-85334-605-4, Pub. by Elsevier Applied Sci UK) Elsevier.

Refrigeration: Home & Commercial. 2nd ed. Edwin P. Anderson. Ed. by Rex Miller. (Illus.). 1984. 19.95 (0-685-08249-0) Macmillan.

Refrigeration: Home & Commercial. 4th ed. Edwin P. Anderson. 768p. 1990. 36.00 (0-02-584875-5) Macmillan.

Refrigeration: Vending Mechanic. NAMA Staff. 160p. 1995. pap. text ed., spiral bd. 33.50 (0-7872-0989-9) Kendall-Hunt.

***Refrigeration & AC Tech Acetales.** Whitman & Johnson. 100p. 1996. text ed. 120.00 (0-8273-8217-0) Delmar.

Refrigeration & AC Techniques - Signature. 2nd ed. Whitman. (Heating, Ventilation & Air Conditioning Ser.). 1991. 2.95 (0-8273-5666-8) Delmar.

Refrigeration & Air Conditioning. Whitman. (Heating, Ventilation & Air Conditioning Ser.). 1989. lab manual ed., pap. 17.95 (0-8273-3486-9) Delmar.

Refrigeration & Air Conditioning. 2nd ed. Air-Conditioning & Refrigeration Institute Staff. (Illus.). 779p. 1986. text ed. 77.00 (0-13-770181-0) P-H.

Refrigeration & Air Conditioning. 2nd ed. Air-Conditioning & Refrigeration Institute Staff. (Illus.). 779p. 1987. student ed., pap. text ed. 25.00 (0-13-770223-X) P-H.

Refrigeration & Air Conditioning. 2nd ed. Wilbert F. Stoecker & J. W. Jones. 464p. 1982. text ed. write for info. (0-07-061619-1) McGraw.

Refrigeration & Air Conditioning. 2nd ed. A. R. Trott. (Illus.). 820p. 1989. 99.95 (0-408-03789-X) Buttrwrth-Heinemann.

***Refrigeration & Air Conditioning.** 3rd ed. 1997. text ed. 66.67 (0-13-323775-3) P-H.

Refrigeration & Air Conditioning. 3rd ed. William M. Johnson & William C. Whitman. LC 94-30065. 1152p. 1995. text ed. 48.45 (0-8273-5646-3) Delmar.

Refrigeration & Air Conditioning. 3rd ed. Billy C. Langley. 1985. text ed. 86.00 (0-8359-6629-1, Reston) P-H.

Refrigeration & Air Conditioning. 7th ed. Whitman. (Heating Ventilation/Air Conditioning Ser.). 1989. lab manual ed., pap. 125.00 (0-8273-3483-4) Van Nos Reinhold.

Refrigeration & Air Conditioning Dictionary. A. M. Abd-El-Wahed. 395p. (ARA, ENG, FRE & GER.). 1979. 75. 00 (0-8288-4833-5, M9756) Fr & Eur.

Refrigeration & Air Conditioning SG & LM. 3rd ed. Whitman. 400p. 1995. 20.95 (0-8273-7038-5) Delmar.

***Refrigeration & Air Conditioning Tech - Class Manager.** Whitman & Johnson. 1996. text ed. 199.95 (0-8273-8215-4) Delmar.

Refrigeration & Air-Conditioning Technology. Rex Miller. 1983. teacher ed. 6.64 (0-02-665550-0); text ed. 26.00 (0-02-665540-3); student ed. 6.64 (0-02-665560-8) Glencoe.

Refrigeration & Air Conditioning Technology. Whitman. (Heating, Ventilation & Air Conditioning Ser.). 1986. 13. 95 (0-8273-2417-0) Delmar.

Refrigeration & Air Conditioning Technology. 2nd ed. William C. Whitman & William M. Johnson. 1024p. 1991. student ed., pap. 19.95 (0-8273-4445-7) Delmar.

Refrigeration & Air Conditioning Technology. 2nd ed. William C. Whitman & William M. Johnson. 1024p. 1991. pap. 104.95 (0-8273-4764-2) Delmar.

Refrigeration & Air Conditioning Technology. 2nd ed. William C. Whitman & William M. Johnson. 1024p. 1991. vhs 349.95 (0-8273-4777-4) Delmar.

Refrigeration & Air Conditioning Technology. 2nd ed. William C. Whitman & William M. Johnson. 1024p. 1991. pap. 41.95 (0-8273-4443-0); student ed., pap. 17. 95 (0-8273-4444-9) Delmar.

Refrigeration & Air Conditioning Technology. 3rd ed. Whitman. (Heating, Ventilation & Air Conditioning Ser.). 1995. pap. 41.95 (0-8273-7207-8) Delmar.

Refrigeration & Air Conditioning Technology: Concepts, Procedures & Troubleshooting Techniques. William Johnson & William C. Whitman. LC 86-16506. 960p. (C). 1988. pap. 13.95 (0-8273-3479-6) Delmar.

Refrigeration & Air Conditioning Technology CTB. 3rd ed. Whitman. (Heating, Ventilation & Air Conditioning Ser.). 1995. 132.95 (0-8273-7056-3) Delmar.

Refrigeration & the Environment: Typical Applications for Air Conditioning. BSRIA Staff. (C). 1994. 110.00 (0-86022-365-5, Pub. by Build Servs Info Assn UK) St Mut.

Refrigeration at Sea. 2nd ed. R. Munton & J. R. Stott. (Illus.). 238p. 1978. 79.25 (0-85334-766-2, Pub. by Elsevier Applied Sci UK) Elsevier.

Refrigeration Equipment: A Servicing & Installation Handbook. A. C. Bryant. (Illus.). 190p. 1991. pap. 38. 95 (0-7506-0007-1) Buttrwrth-Heinemann.

Refrigeration For Pleasureboats: Installation, Maintenance & Repair. Nigel Calder. (Illus.). 192p. 1990. text ed. 24. 95 (0-87742-286-9) Intl Marine.

Refrigeration for Pleasureboats: Installation, Maintenance & Repair. Nigel Calder. 1990. text ed. 24.95 (0-07-157998-2) McGraw.

Refrigeration Fundamentals: A Workbook Approach. William Gorman. LC 90-49621. 1991. 19.95 (0-912524-58-8) Busn News.

Refrigeration License Examinations. Antonio Mejias. LC 93-6800. 1993. pap. 25.00 (0-671-86705-9, Arco) Macmillan Gen Ref.

Refrigeration Licenses Unlimited. 2nd ed. Clayton H. Carrico. LC 92-11928. 250p. 1992. 27.95 (0-912524-72-3) Busn News.

Refrigeration Principles & Systems: An Energy Approach. Edward G. Pita. LC 91-14219. 1991. 32.95 (0-912524-61-8) Busn News.

Refrigeration Reference Notebook. Don Swenson. Ed. by Joanna Turpin. LC 94-34529. 180p. (Orig.). 1995. pap. text ed. 7.95 (0-912524-98-7) Busn News.

Refrigeration Servicing. Paul F. Goliber. LC 75-6064. 91p. 1976. pap. 24.95 (0-8273-1005-6) Delmar.

Refrigerator - Freezer Energy Efficiency Slide Rule. 1985. 5.00 (0-317-03099-X) Consumer Energy Coun.

Refrigerator & Air Conditioning. 2nd ed. William C. Whitman. 1991. pap. 49.95 (0-8273-5664-1) Delmar.

Refrigerator & Air Conditioning. 3rd abr. ed. Whitman. 368p. 1995. teacher ed., text ed. 39.95 (0-8273-7037-7) Delmar.

Refrigerator & the Universe: Understanding the Laws of Energy. Martin Goldstein & Inge F. Goldstein. 445p. 1993. text ed. 29.95 (0-674-75324-0) HUP.

Refrigerator & the Universe: Understanding the Laws of Energy. Martin Goldstein & Inge F. Goldstein. (Illus.). 445p. 1995. pap. 15.95 (0-674-75325-9, GOLREX) HUP.

Refrigerator Art. Guy Wise. (Real Life Adventures Collection). (Illus.). 112p. (Orig.). 1996. pap. 7.95 (0-8362-2137-0) Andrews & McMeel.

Refrigerator Art Quilts: Preserving Your Child's Art in Fabric. Jennifer Paulson. LC 95-26024. (Illus.). 44p. (Orig.). 1996. pap. 14.95 (1-56477-132-6, B249) That Patchwork.

***Refrigerator Door Gallery: Cartoons from the News-Press.** Doug MacGregor. (Illus.). 192p. (Orig.). 1996. pap. 12. 95 (0-9654843-0-0) D MacGregor.

Refuge. Lisa T. Bergren. 336p. 1994. pap. text ed. 8.99 (0-88070-875-1, Multnomah Bks) Multnomah Pubs.

Refuge. Liane I. Brown. (Illus.). 211p. (Orig.). 1987. pap. 10.50 (0-89084-392-9, 032177) Bob Jones Univ Pr.

Refuge. Sami Michael. Tr. by Edward Grossman from HEB. 376p. 1988. 22.50 (0-8276-0308-8) JPS Phila.

***Refuge.** Mark Olsen. 180p. (Orig.). 1996. pap. 9.95 (0-9639465-2-8) Sardis Pr.

Refuge. Belle Waring. LC 90-33961. (Poetry Ser.). 88p. 1990. 19.95 (0-8229-3655-0); pap. 10.95 (0-8229-5441-9) U of Pittsburgh Pr.

Refuge: A Novel. Gopal Gandhi. 1989. 14.00 (0-86311-064-9, Pub. by Ravi Dayal II) S Asia.

Refuge: Unnatural History. Terry T. Williams. 1992. pap. 12.00 (0-679-74024-4, Vin) Random.

Refuge & the Cave. Arthur M. Weinberg. 142p. (YA). (gr. 5 up). 1984. pap. 7.95 (0-900125-48-9) Bahai.

Refuge at la Source. Jean Daniel. (FRE.). 1979. pap. 10.95 (0-7859-1895-7, 2070371212) Fr & Eur.

Refuge Denied: Problems in the Protection of Vietnamese & Cambodians in Thailand & the Admission of Indochinese Refugees into the United States. Al Santoli & Laurence Eisenstein. Ed. by Roni Rubenstein & Arthus C. Helton. (Illus.). 120p. (Orig.). 1989. pap. text ed. 10.00 (0-934143-20-X) Lawyers Comm Human.

Refuge for All Ages: Immigration in Louisiana History. Ed. by Carl A. Brasseaux. LC 95-83196. (Louisiana Purchase Bicentennial: Vol. X). 716p. 1996. 40.00 (1-887366-01-6) U of SW LA Ctr LA Studies.

***Refuge of Night Vol. 1: A Modern Vampire Myth with a Bonus Tale of Renaissance Terror.** Mike Cervello. LC 96-96817. (Illus.). 70p. (Orig.). 1996. pap. 4.95 (0-9654364-0-3) C V K Publishing.

Refuge of the Apocalypse. Elizabeth Van Buren. 188p. 1986. 25.95 (0-85207-181-7, Pub. by C W Daniel UK) Natl Bk Netwk.

Refuge of the Apocalypse: Doorway into Other Dimensions. Elizabeth Van Buren. (Illus.). 348p. 38.95 (0-8464-4282-5) Beekman Pubs.

Refuge of the Honored: Social Organization in a Japanese Retirement Community. Yasuhito Kinoshita & Christie W. Kiefer. (C). 1993. 35.00 (0-520-07595-1) U CA Pr.

Refugee. Piers Anthony. (Bio of a Space Tyrant Ser.: Vol. I). 320p. 1983. mass mkt. 4.50 (0-380-84194-0) Avon.

Refugee. Asif Currimbhoy. (Writers Workshop Bluebird Ser.). 38p. 1971. 4.80 (0-88253-785-7) Ind-US Inc.

Refugee Aid & Development: Theory & Practice. Ed. by Robert F. Gorman. LC 92-45086. (Studies in Social Welfare Policies & Programs: No. 17). 248p. 1993. text ed. 59.95 (0-313-28580-2, GRE, Greenwood Pr) Greenwood.

Refugee & Immigrant Resource Directory. 3rd ed. Alan E. Schorr. 256p. 1994. pap. 47.50 (0-938737-28-7) Denali Press.

Refugee Children: Theory, Research, & Services. Ed. by Frederick L. Ahearn, Jr. & Jean L. Athey. LC 90-25554. (Series in Contemporary Medicine & Public Health). 240p. 1991. text ed. 42.50 (0-8018-4160-7) Johns Hopkins.

***Refugee Children Around the World.** Austcare. 1991. pap. text ed. write for info. (0-582-87486-6, Pub. by Longman UK) Longman.

Refugee Communities: A Comparative Field Study. Steven Gold. (Series on Race & Ethnic Relations: Vol. 4). 288p. (C). 1992. 52.00 (0-8039-3796-2); pap. 24.00 (0-8039-3797-0) Sage.

***Refugee Communities: Comparative Field Study.** Steven J. Gold. LC 91-14695. (Sage Series on Race & Ethnic Relations: No. 4). (Illus.). 271p. 1992. reprint ed. pap. 77.30 (0-608-04309-5, 2065088) Bks Demand.

Refugee Empowerment & Organization Change: A Systems Perspective. Ed. by Peter W. Van Arsdale. LC 92-36236. 1992. write for info. (0-913167-53-3) Am Anthro Assn.

Refugee from Heaven. Cora Evans. 450p. 1994. pap. 22.00 (0-9640323-0-9) Kallima Pubng.

Refugee Girl. Dirouhi K. Highgas. LC 86-71863. 1986. write for info. (0-936893-01-X) Baikar.

Refugee in International Law. 2nd ed. Guy S. Goodwin-Gill. 624p. 1996. 90.00 (0-19-826019-9); pap. 35.00 (0-19-826020-2) OUP.

***Refugee Law & Policy: Cases & Materials.** Karen Musalo et al. LC 97-11885. 950p. (C). 1997. text ed. 75.00 (0-89089-870-7) Carolina Acad Pr.

Refugee Law & Policy: International & U. S. Responses. Ed. by Ved P. Nanda. LC 89-11901. (Studies in Human Rights: No. 9). 238p. 1989. text ed. 59.95 (0-313-26870-3, NRP/, Greenwood Pr) Greenwood.

Refugee Mental Health in Resettlement Countries. Ed. by Carolyn L. Williams & Joseph Westermeyer. (Clinical & Community Psychology Ser.). 267p. 1986. text ed. 73.95 (0-89116-445-6) Hemisp Pub.

Refugee Ministry in the Local Congregation. John R. Mummert & Jeff Bach. LC 91-42220. 128p. (Orig.). 1992. pap. 9.99 (0-8361-3580-6) Herald Pr.

Refugee Policy: Canada & the United States. Ed. by Howard Adelman. 375p. 1991. pap. 14.50 (0-934733-64-3) CMS.

Refugee Protection: An Analysis & Action Proposal. 1983. write for info. (0-318-60437-X) US Comm Refugees.

Refugee Protection in Africa: Current Trends. 1985. write for info. (0-318-60434-5) US Comm Refugees.

Refugee Question in Mid-Victorian Politics. Bernard Porter. LC 78-73947. 254p. reprint ed. pap. 72.40 (0-317-55484-0, 2029224) Bks Demand.

Refugee Refoulement: The Forced Return of Haitians under the U. S. - Haitian Interdiction Agreement. Lawyers Committee for Human Rights Staff. 64p. 1990. lib. bdg. 8.00 (0-934143-30-7) Lawyers Comm Human.

***Refugee Reports.** annuals 45.00 (0-614-25341-1) US Comm Refugees.

***Refugee Resettlement Program: Report to Congress (1992)** 200p. (Orig.). 1996. reprint ed. pap. 25.00 (0-7881-2946-5) DIANE Pub.

Refugee Scholars in America: Their Impact & Their Experiences. Lewis A. Coser. LC 84-40193. 369p. reprint ed. pap. 105.20 (0-7837-7139-8, 2080296) Bks Demand.

Refugee Village. Herman Tambe. 1993. pap. 9.95 (0-931848-88-1) Dryad Pr.

Refugee Women. Compiled by Susan F. Martin. LC 92-5754. 140p. (C). 1991. pap. 17.50 (1-85649-001-7, Pub. by Zed Bks Ltd UK); text ed. 49.95 (1-85649-000-9, Pub. by Zed Bks Ltd UK) Humanities.

Refugee Women & Reproductive Health Care: Reassessing Priorities. Deirdre Wulf. 77p. 1994. pap. write for info. (0-9637711-1-6) Intl Rescue Comm.

***Refugee Women & Reproductive Health Care: Reassessing Priorities.** Deirdre Wulf et al. 77p. (Orig.). 1997. pap. text ed. 35.00 (0-7881-3841-3) DIANE Pub.

Refugee Women & Their Mental Health: Shattered Societies, Shattered Lives. Ed. by Ellen Cole et al. LC 92-24548. (Women & Therapy Ser.: Vol. 13, Nos. 1-2 & Vol. 13, No. 3, 1992). (Illus.). 376p. 1993. 49.95 (1-56024-372-4); pap. 14.95 (1-56023-030-4) Haworth Pr.

Refugees. W. Lewis. write for info. (0-275-90020-7, C0020, Praeger Pubs) Greenwood.

Refugees. Carole Seymour-Jones. LC 92-14803. (Past & Present Ser.). (Illus.). 48p. (YA). (gr. 6 up). 1992. lib. bdg. 12.95 (0-02-735402-4, Mac Bks Young Read) S&S Childrens.

Refugees. Rachel Warner. LC 96-16164. (Global Issues Ser.). (J). 1997. lib. bdg. 24.26 (0-8172-4547-2) Raintree Steck-V.

Refugees: A Challenge to Solidarity: Proceedings of the International Round Table on the Question of Refugees. LC 94-10226. (Proceedings of the International Round Table on the Question of Refugees Ser.). 370p. 1994. 14. 50 (0-934733-78-3) CMS.

Refugees: A World Report. Ed. by Lester A. Sobel et al. LC 79-16981. 188p. reprint ed. pap. 53.60 (0-685-24017-7, 2031610) Bks Demand.

Refugees: Extended Exile. W. R. Smyser. LC 87-20957. (Washington Papers: No. 129). 158p. 1987. text ed. 45. 00 (0-275-92877-2, C2877, Praeger Pubs); pap. text ed. 11.95 (0-275-92878-0, B2878, Praeger Pubs) Greenwood.

Refugees: Holdings of the CMS Library-Ctr. Migration Archives. Compiled by Diana Zimmerman. ix, 423p. 1987. 35.00 (0-934733-34-1) CMS.

***Refugees: Seeking a Safe Haven.** Kem K. Sawyer. LC 94-41425. (Multicultural Issues Ser.). (Illus.). 128p. (YA). (gr. 6 up). 1995. lib. bdg. 18.95 (0-89490-663-1) Enslow Pubs.

Refugees: The New International Politics of Displacement. Kathleen Newland. LC 81-50523. (Worldwatch Papers). 1981. pap. 5.00 (0-916468-42-9) Worldwatch Inst.

Refugees: The Trauma of Exile. Ed. by D. Miserez. (C). 1989. lib. bdg. 125.50 (0-7923-0112-9) Kluwer Ac.

Refugees: Viewpoints, Case Studies & Theoretical Considerations on the Care & Management of Refugees. F. Souza. (Illus.). 136p. 1980. pap. 23.00 (0-08-025460-8, Pergamon Pr) Elsevier.

Refugees & Development in Africa. Ed. by Peter Nobel. (Scandinavian Institute of African Studies: No. 19). 121p. 1987. 42.00 (91-7106-272-6, Pub. by Nordisk Afrikainstitutet SW) Coronet Bks.

Refugees & Development in Africa: The Case of Eritrea. Gaim Kibreab. LC 86-63776. (Illus.). 300p. 1987. 35.00 (0-932415-26-1); pap. 11.95 (0-932415-27-X) Red Sea Pr.

Refugees & the Asylum Dilemma in the West. Ed. by Gilburt D. Loescher. 184p. 1992. pap. 13.95 (0-271-00856-3) Pa St U Pr.

Refugees & World Politics. Ed. by Elizabeth G. Ferris. LC 85-495. 240p. 1985. text ed. 38.95 (0-275-90099-1, C0099, Praeger Pubs) Greenwood.

Refugees As Immigrants: Cambodians, Laotians & Vietnamese in America. Ed. by David W. Haines. LC 87-26637. (Illus.). 210p. (C). 1989. lib. bdg. 58.50 (0-8476-7553-X, R7553) Rowman.

An Asterisk (*) at the beginning of an entry indicates that the title is appearing in BIP for the first time.

R

Refugees Convention, 1951: The Travaux Preparatoires Analysed with a Commentary by Dr. Paul Weis. Paul Weis. (Cambridge International Documents Ser.: No. 7). 300p. (C). 1995. text ed. 125.00 (*0-521-47295-4*) Cambridge U Pr.

Refugees from Irian Jaya in Papua New Guinea: A Trip Report. 1985. write for info. (*0-318-60431-0*) US Comm Refugees.

Refugees from Laos - In Harm's Way. Joseph Cerquone. Ed. by Virginia Hamilton. (Issue Papers). 1986. pap. 2.00 (*0-685-14150-0*) US Comm Refugees.

Refugees from Militarism: Draft-Age Americans in Canada. Renee G. Kasinsky. LC 75-46232. 350p. 1976. 39.95 (*0-87855-113-1*) Transaction Pubs.

Refugees from Nowhere. George Bourland. pap. 4.00 (*0-912136-04-9*) Twowindows Pr.

Refugees from Slavery in Canada West: Report to the Freedmen's Inquiry Commission. Samuel G. Howe. LC 69-18540. (American Negro: His History & Literature. Series 2). 1968. reprint ed. 12.95 (*0-405-01872-X*) Ayer.

Refugees from Vietnam. Carol Dalglish. Ed. by Jo Campling. LC 89-30607. 224p. 1989. text ed. 49.95 (*0-312-03165-3*) St Martin.

Refugees in America: Committee for the Study of Recent Immigration from Europe. Ed. by Maurice Davie. LC 74-1513. (Illus.). 453p. 1974. reprint ed. text ed. 75.00 (*0-8371-7390-6*, DARA, Greenwood Pr) Greenwood.

Refugees in America in the 1990s: A Reference Handbook. Ed. by David W. Haines. LC 95-50902. 480p. 1996. text ed. 79.50 (*0-313-29344-9*, Greenwood Pr) Greenwood.

Refugees in Inter-War Europe: The Emergence of a Regime. Claudena Skran. (Illus.). 328p. 1995. text ed. 59.00 (*0-19-827392-4*) OUP.

Refugees in International Politics. Leon Gordenker. LC 87-11688. 256p. 1987. text ed. 45.00 (*0-231-06624-4*) Col U Pr.

Refugees in the Age of Total War. Ed. by Anna C. Bramwell. 432p. 1988. text ed. 60.00 (*0-04-445194-6*) Routledge Chapman & Hall.

Refugees in the United States: A Reference Handbook. Ed. by David W. Haines. LC 84-12794. (Illus.). viii, 243p. 1985. text ed. 59.95 (*0-313-24068-X*, HRU/, Greenwood Pr) Greenwood.

Refugees in Uganda & Rwanda: The Banyarwandan Tragedy. 1983. write for info. (*0-318-60436-1*) US Comm Refugees.

***Refugees into Citizens: Palestinians & the End of the Arab-Israeli Conflict.** Donna E. Arzt. 230p. 1996. pap. 18.95 (*0-87609-194-X*) Coun Foreign.

Refugees of a Hidden War: The Aftermath of Counterinsurgency in Guatemala. Beatriz Manz. LC 87-10169. (SUNY Series in Anthropological Studies of Contemporary Issues). (Illus.). 283p. 1987. pap. text ed. 24.95 (*0-88706-676-3*) State U NY Pr.

Refugees of a Hidden War: The Aftermath of Counterinsurgency in Guatemala. Beatriz Manz. LC 87-10169. (SUNY Series in Anthropological Studies of Contemporary Issues). (Illus.). 283p. 1988. text ed. 74.50 (*0-88706-675-5*) State U NY Pr.

Refugees of Revolution. Carl F. Wittke. LC 74-100255. 384p. 1970. reprint ed. text ed. 65.00 (*0-8371-2988-5*, WIRR, Greenwood Pr) Greenwood.

Refugees of 1776 from Long Island to Connecticut. Frederic G. Mather. (Illus.). 1204p. 1995. pap. 75.00 (*0-614-09997-8*, 3820) Clearfield Co.

Refugees or Migrant Workers? Diana Kay. LC 91-22828. (Critical Studies in Racism & Migration). 240p. (C). (gr. 13 up). 1992. text ed. 85.00 (*0-415-04790-0*, Routledge NY) Routledge.

Refugees or Settlers? Area Studies, Development Studies, & the Future of Asian Studies. Bruce Koppel. LC 95-8224. (Occasional Papers: No. 1). 1995. write for info. (*0-86638-172-4*) EW Ctr HI.

Refugees: Rationing the Right to Life: The Crisis in Emergency Relief. David Keen. LC 92-31342. 128p. (C). 1992. pap. 17.50 (*1-85649-092-0*, Pub. by Zed Bks Ltd UK); text ed. 49.95 (*1-85649-091-2*, Pub. by Zed Bks Ltd UK) Humanities.

Refugees South of the Sahara: An African Dilemma. Ed. by Hugh C. Brooks & Yassin El-Ayouty. LC 71-105994. (Contributions in Afro-American & African Studies: No. 14). 307p. 1970. text ed. 65.00 (*0-8371-3324-6*, BSS&, Greenwood Pr) Greenwood.

Refugees unto the Third Generation: U. N. Aid to the Palestinians. Benjamin Schiff. LC 94-27339. (Middle East Studies). 400p. 1995. text ed. 49.95 (*0-8156-2589-8*) Syracuse U Pr.

Refugees Without Refuge: Formation & Failed Implementation of U. S. Political Asylum Policy in the 1980's. Barbara M. Yarnold. 294p. (Orig.). (C). 1990. pap. text ed. 25.50 (*0-8191-7845-4*); lib. bdg. 46.00 (*0-8191-7844-6*) U Pr of Amer.

Refuges. Augustin Buzura. 460p. 1994. 65.00 (*0-88033-296-4*) East Eur Monographs.

Refugiados. Angel Castro. 1971. pap. text ed. 4.00 (*0-685-48630-3*) E Torres & Sons.

Refugio, They Named You Wrong. Susan C. Schofield. 216p. 1991. 17.95 (*0-945575-60-2*) Algonquin Bks.

Refugium Botanicum or Figures & Descriptions from Living Specimens of Little Known or New Plants of Botanical Interest, Vol. II. Illus. by W. H. Fitch. (Orchid Ser.). 1980. reprint ed. text ed. 27.50 (*0-930576-19-5*) E M Coleman Ent.

Refulgent Peregrinations. Astara, pseud. LC 96-92180. 112p. (Orig.). 1996. pap. 11.95 (*1-885226-21-7*) StarLineage.

Refunding Periodicals, Books, Clubs, Associations: A How to Find or Locate Workbook. rev. ed. Data Notes Staff. 63p. 1992. student ed., ring bd. 24.95 (*0-911569-06-5*) Prosperity & Profits.

Refunds under Central Excise & Customs. Vidya B. Mishra. (C). 1990. 100.00 (*0-89771-225-0*) St Mut.

Refurbishing Offices for People with Disabilities: A Design & Assessment Guide for Owners, Occupiers, Developers & Advisers. Jack Rostron & Murray Fordham. 128p. 1996. text ed. 46.95 (*1-85742-345-3*, Pub. by Arena UK) Ashgate Pub Co.

Refurbishing Our Foundations: Elementary Linguistics from an Advanced Point of View. C. F. Hockett. LC 87-29961. (Current Issues in Linguistic Theory Ser.: Vol. 56). ix, 181p. (C). 1987. 41.00 (*90-272-3550-3*) Benjamins North Am.

Refurbishment & Alteration Work. RICS Staff. (C). 1983. text ed. 29.00 (*0-85406-181-9*, Pub. by Surveyors Pubns) St Mut.

Refusal & Transgression in Joyce Carol Oates' Fiction. Marilyn C. Wesley. LC 92-39467. (Contributions in Women's Studies: No. 135). 192p. 1993. text ed. 47.95 (*0-313-28462-8*, WRQ/) Greenwood.

Refusal of the Shadow: Surrealism & the Carribean. Michael Richardson. 256p. 1996. pap. 20.00 (*1-85984-018-3*, Pub. by Vrso UK) Norton.

Refusal of the Shadow: Surrealism & the Carribean. Ed. by Michael Richardson. Tr. by Krzysztof Fijalkowski. 256p. (C). 1996. text ed. 65.00 (*1-85984-997-0*, Pub. by Vrso UK) Norton.

Refusal Skills: Preventing Drug Use in Adolescents. Arnold P. Goldstein et al. LC 90-60924. 176p. (Orig.). 1990. pap. text ed. 14.95 (*0-87822-323-1*, 4422) Res Press.

Refusals to Deal & Exclusive Distributorships. Antitrust Law Section Members. 64p. 1983. pap. 20.00 (*0-685-10017-0*, 503-0047) Amer Bar Assn.

Refuse & Garbage Disposal: Index of New Information with Authors & Subjects. Bernice R. Schindler. 180p. 1993. 47.50 (*1-55914-902-7*); pap. 44.50 (*1-55914-903-5*) ABBE Pubs Assn.

Refuse Record Book for U. S. Oceangoing Vessels. 68p. 1994. pap. text ed. 7.80 (*1-879778-25-4*, BK-0326) Marine Educ.

Refuse Recycling & Recovery. John R. Holmes. LC 80-42145. (Institution of Environmental Sciences Ser.). (Illus.). 196p. reprint ed. pap. 55.90 (*0-685-20676-9*, 2030465) Bks Demand.

***Refuse to Lose.** J. Calipari & D. Weiss. 1997. mass mkt. write for info. (*0-345-40802-0*) Ballantine.

Refuse to Lose. John Calipari & Dick Weiss. (Illus.). 288p. 1996. 23.00 (*0-345-40801-2*) Ballantine.

***Refusing Nazi Orders to Kill.** Kitterman. 1998. 46.00 (*1-85973-107-4*, Pub. by Berg Pubs UK); pap. 19.50 (*1-85973-112-0*) NYU Pr.

Refusing to Be a Man: Essays on Sex & Justice. John Stoltenberg. 240p. 1990. pap. 11.95 (*0-452-01043-8*, Mer) NAL-Dutton.

Refutatio Omnium Haeresium. Hippolytus. Ed. by Paul Wendland. xxiii, 337p. 1977. reprint ed. write for info. (*3-487-06330-1*) G Olms Pubs.

Refutation of Arrow's Theorem. Howard Delong. 102p. (C). 1991. lib. bdg. 37.00 (*0-8191-8250-8*) U Pr of Amer.

Refutation of Preparing for Child Custody Cases. Duane Magnani. 1988. 11.95 (*1-883858-18-6*) Witness CA.

Refutation of the Christian Principles. Hasdai Crescas. Tr. by Daniel J. Lasker. LC 91-15118. (SUNY Series in Jewish Philosophy). 156p. 1992. text ed. 59.50 (*0-7914-0965-1*); pap. text ed. 19.95 (*0-7914-0966-X*) State U NY Pr.

Refutation of the Sects. Yeznik Koghbatsi. Ed. by Thomas J. Samuelian. (Armenian Church Classics Ser.). (Illus.). 1986. pap. 5.00 (*0-934728-13-5*) D O A C.

Refuting the Critics: Evidences of Book of Mormon Authenticity. Michael T. Griffith. 176p. 1993. 17.98 (*0-88290-462-0*, 1032) Horizon Utah.

Reg & Ethel. Robert Huxter. (C). 1989. pap. 23.00 (*1-85072-109-2*, Pub. by W Sessions UK) St Mut.

***Reg Parnell: The Quiet Man Who Helped.** Graham Gould. (Illus.). 208p. 1996. 39.95 (*1-85260-561-8*, Pub. by J H Haynes & Co UK) Motorbooks Intl.

Regain. Jean Giono. 192p. (FRE.). 1958. 10.95 (*0-8288-9788-3*, F103770) Fr & Eur.

Regain. Marcel Pagnol. 254p. (FRE.). 1973. 11.95 (*0-8288-9750-6*, 2877060632) Fr & Eur.

Regain see Oeuvres Romanesques

***Regain Security: A Guide to the Costs of Disposing of Plutonium & Highly Enriched Uranium.** William J. Weida. (Studies in Green Research). (Illus.). 250p. 1997. text ed. 59.95 (*1-85972-516-3*, Pub. by Avebury Pub UK) Ashgate Pub Co.

Regaining Compassion: For Humanity & Nature. Charles Birch. 250p. (Orig.). 1993. pap. 17.99 (*0-8272-3214-4*) Chalice Pr.

Regaining Compassion for Humanity & Nature. Charles Birch. 251p. 1993. pap. 19.95 (*0-86840-213-3*, Pub. by New South Wales Univ Pr AT) Intl Spec Bk.

Regaining Competitiveness: Putting The Goal To Work. rev. ed. Mokshagundam L. Srikanth & Harold E. Cavallaro. (Illus.). 207p. (Orig.). 1990. pap. 24.95 (*0-943953-00-6*) Spectrum CT.

Regaining Consciousness in the Western World: Radical Essays on the Human Experience. Maya S. Devi et al. (Illus.). 96p. 1990. 14.95 (*0-9625744-0-6*); teacher ed. write for info. (*0-318-66966-8*); pap. 9.95 (*0-318-50017-5*); lib. bdg. 14.95 (*0-318-50016-7*) Dawn Rose Pr.

Regaining Excellence in Education. Mario D. Fantini. LC 85-63035. 253p. reprint ed. pap. 72.20 (*0-8357-8756-7*, AU00371) Bks Demand.

***Regaining Faith after Boston: An Insider's Views.** Sharen Meyers. 83p. (Orig.). 1997. pap. 6.95 (*1-56794-119-2*, C-2438) Star Bible.

Regaining Marxism. Ken Post. LC 95-32641. 1996. text ed. 65.00 (*0-312-12973-4*) St Martin.

Regaining Paradise: Milton & the Eighteenth Century. Dustin Griffin. (Illus.). 300p. 1986. text ed. 69.95 (*0-521-30913-1*) Cambridge U Pr.

Regaining Paradise Lost. Thomas N. Corns. LC 94-2146. (Medieval & Renaissance Library). 168p. (C). 1994. text ed. 58.95 (*0-582-06621-2*, 76863, Pub. by Longman UK); pap. text ed. 19.50 (*0-582-06620-4*, 76862, Pub. by Longman UK) Longman.

Regaining the High Ground: NATO's Stake in the New Talks on Conventional Forces in Europe. Barry M. Blechman et al. LC 89-36434. 240p. 1990. text ed. 39.95 (*0-312-03642-6*); text ed. 14.95 (*0-312-03643-4*) St Martin.

Regaining Wholeness Through the Subtle Dimensions: Where Science Meets Magic. Don Paris. (Illus.). 160p. (Orig.). 1993. pap. 12.95 (*1-884246-00-1*) Liv from Vis.

Regal see History of Roman Private Law

Regal Beagle. David Lesterson. Ed. by Beverly Hoffman et al. LC 93-70504. (Illus.). 29p. (J). (gr. 3). Date not set. write for info. (*0-9634122-3-X*) Feather Fables.

***Regal Image of Richard II & the Wilton Diptych.** Ed. by Dillian Gordon et al. (Illus.). 368p. 1996. text ed. 95.00 (*1-872501-72-9*, Pub. by Harvey Miller UK) Gordon & Breach.

Regal Reports: Super Money Making Ideas. 1987. lib. bdg. 64.00 (*0-8490-3910-X*) Gordon Pr.

Regal Rome, an Intro to Roman History. Francis W. Newman. 1952. 20.00 (*0-8196-1556-0*) Biblo.

Regal Trumpet. 1984. pap. 7.95 (*0-7935-2782-1*, 8369) H Leonard.

Regala de Navidad. Richard Paul Evans. 1995. pap. 12.95 (*0-684-81554-0*, Fireside) S&S Trade.

Regalia of Scotland. Walter Scott. 1991. pap. 5.95 (*0-89979-056-9*) British Am Bks.

Regalo. Danielle Steel. 224p. 1994. 9.95 (*0-385-31327-6*) Delacorte.

Regalo de Arrullos Para Ninos. Ed. by J. Aaron Brown. Tr. by Sysy Pineda. (Illus.). 14p. (SPA.). (J). (ps). 1988. Book with cassette. 12.95 incl. audio (*0-927945-02-9*) Someday Baby.

Regalo de Dios. (Libros Nueva Vida). (SPA.). 1986. 1.00 (*0-685-74978-9*, 490279) Editorial Unilit.

***Regalo de Dios.** (Serie Libros Nueva Vida - New Life Bks.). 12p. (SPA.). 1986. write for info. (*0-614-27129-0*) Editorial Unilit.

***Regalo de Tiempo.** Evans. 1998. pap. 10.00 (*0-684-83298-4*) S&S Trade.

Regalo de Tiempo. Richard P. Evans. 240p. 1996. 18.00 (*0-684-82426-4*, Simon Aguilar) S&S Trade.

Regalo de Un Nino. Marion Stroud. 16p. (SPA.). 1987. 8.99 (*0-8423-6318-1*, 497601) Editorial Unilit.

Regalo del Cesar. Rene De Goscinny & M. Uderzo. (Illus.). (SPA.). (J). 19.95 (*0-8288-4900-5*) Fr & Eur.

Regalo Magico - The Magic Shell. Nicholasa Mohr. 96p. (SPA.). (J). 1996. pap. 2.99 (*0-590-50210-7*) Scholastic Inc.

Regalos de Wali Dad. Shepard. (J). 1998. 16.00 (*0-689-80419-9*, Atheneum Bks Young) S&S Childrens.

***Regalos en Cofres de Plata - Silver Boxes.** Florence Littauer. (SPA.). write for info. (*1-56063-759-5*) Editorial Unilit.

***Regalos en la Primera Navidad.** (Serie Libros Despegables - Accordian Puzzle Books Ser.). 10p. (SPA.). 1987. write for info. (*0-614-27130-4*) Editorial Unilit.

***Regalos en la Primera Navidad - First Christmas Present.** (Serie Libros Despegables - Accordian Puzzle Books Ser.). 10p. (SPA.). (J). 1987. write for info. (*0-614-24400-5*) Editorial Unilit.

Regalos Que Puden Romper. Steve Chapman. (SPA.). pap. 6.99 (*0-88113-103-2*) Edit Betania.

Regan's Pride. Diana Palmer. (Silhouette Romance Ser.). 1994. pap. 2.75 (*0-373-19000-X*, 5-19000-4) Harlequin Bks.

Regan's Pride. Diana Palmer. (Romance Ser.). 1994. pap. 2.75 (*0-373-91000-2*, 5-91000-5) Silhouette.

Regan's Raiders. Rich Buckler & Monroe Arnold. (Illus.). 96p. 1987. 6.95 (*1-55601-005-2*) Great Sky.

Regard du Roi. Camara Laye. (FRE.). 1975. pap. 8.95 (*0-7859-3251-8*, 2266046705) Fr & Eur.

Regard et L'excedent. Jacques Taminiaux. (Phaenomenologica Ser.: No. 75). 193p. 1978. lib. bdg. 100.50 (*90-247-2028-1*, Pub. by M Nijhoff NE) Kluwer Ac.

Regardez-moi, Je Continue a Parler! Look, I'm Still Talking, Vol. 3. Blaine Ray & Joe Neilson. (Look, I Can Talk! Ser.). (Illus.). 78p. (Orig.). (FRE.). (YA). (gr. 9-12). 1993. pap. text ed. 12.95 (*0-929724-25-9*, 25-9) Command Performance.

Regardez-moi, Je Parle Vraiment! Look, I'm Truly Talking! Blaine Ray et al. (Look, I Can Talk! Ser.: Vol. 4). (Illus.). (Orig.). (FRE.). (YA). (gr. 10-12). pap. text ed. 12.95 (*0-929724-26-7*, 26-7); audio 9.95 (*0-929724-27-5*) Command Performance.

***Regardies 1997 Washington Desk Diary.** William Regardie. 144p. 1996. 24.95 (*0-9655227-0-9*) Regardie & Regardie Pr.

Regarding Animals. Arnold Arluke & Clinton R. Sanders. LC 95-43062. (Animals, Culture & Society Ser.). 211p. (C). 1996. pap. 16.95 (*1-56639-441-4*); lib. bdg. 54.95 (*1-56639-440-6*) Temple U Pr.

Regarding Children: A New Respect for Childhood & Families. Herbert Anderson & Susan B. Johnson. (Family Living in Pastoral Perspective Ser.). 144p. (Orig.). 1994. pap. 13.00 (*0-664-25125-0*) Westminster John Knox.

Regarding Electra. Maurice Valency. 1976. pap. 5.25 (*0-8222-0941-1*) Dramatists Play.

Regarding Malcolm X. Paula Giddings. 1994. 22.95 (*1-56743-049-X*) Amistad Pr.

Regarding Nature: Industrialism & Deep Ecology. Andrew McLaughlin. LC 92-14076. (SUNY Series in Radical, Social & Political Theory). 280p. 1993. pap. 19.95 (*0-7914-1384-5*) State U NY Pr.

Regarding Nature: Industrialism & Deep Ecology. Andrew McLaughlin. LC 92-14076. (SUNY Series in Radical, Social & Political Theory). 280p. 1993. text ed. 59.50 (*0-7914-1383-7*) State U NY Pr.

***Regarding Penelope: From Character to Poetics.** Nancy Felson. LC 97-18809. 232p. 1997. pap. 14.95 (*0-8061-2961-1*) U of Okla Pr.

Regarding Penelope: From Character to Poetics. Nancy Felson-Rubin. LC 93-4159. (Illus.). 232p. (C). 1993. text ed. 42.50 (*0-691-03228-9*) Princeton U Pr.

Regarding Politics: Essays on Political Theory, Stability, & Change. Harry Eckstein. LC 91-18245. 412p. (C). 1992. 50.00 (*0-520-07167-0*); pap. 17.00 (*0-520-07722-9*) U CA Pr.

Regarding Religious Education. Mary K. Cove & Mary L. Mueller. LC 77-10873. 181p. (Orig.). 1977. pap. 2.95 (*0-89135-011-X*) Religious Educ.

Regarding Remy: Southern Knights. Marilyn Pappano. (Intimate Moments Ser.). 1994. mass mkt. 3.50 (*0-373-07609-6*, 1-07609-0) Silhouette.

Regarding Television: Critical Approaches-An Anthology. Ed. by E. Ann Kaplan. LC 83-17015. 176p. (C). 1983. text ed. 42.95 (*0-313-27009-0*, U7009); pap. text ed. 12. 95 (*0-313-26992-0*, P6992) Greenwood.

Regarding the Borgo Pio: Between a Rock & a High Place. Martha Sutherland. 1996. 35.00 (*1-55728-413-X*) U of Ark Pr.

***Regarding the Proper, Vol. 9.** Ed. by Michael Benedikt. 1995. 15.50 (*0-292-71163-8*) Ctr Study of Amer Archit.

Regarding Wave. Gary Snyder. LC 72-122107. 1970. pap. 7.95 (*0-8112-0196-1*, NDP306) New Directions.

Regards from Camp, No. 3. Shifra Weinberg. LC 93-72599. 110p. (J). (gr. 6). 1993. 11.95 (*1-56062-232-6*) CIS Comm.

Regards from Camp: Search Party Sunday, No. 4. M. C. Millman. LC 94-69038. 150p. (J). (gr. 5-8). write for info. (*1-56062-284-9*) CIS Comm.

Regards from Camp 2: Deepwater Dilemma. Shifra Weinberg. LC 93-72270. (J). (gr. 5-8). 1993. write for info. (*1-56062-200-8*) CIS Comm.

Regards Sur la France Des Annees 1980: Le Roman. Ed. by J. Brami et al. (Stanford French & Italian Studies: No. 80). 256p. (FRE.). 1995. pap. 46.50 (*0-915838-96-6*) Anma Libri.

Regards sur le Monde Actuel. Paul Valery. (Folio Essais Ser.: No. 106). pap. 9.95 (*2-07-032494-X*) Schoenhof.

Regards sur le Monde Actuel, et Autres Essais. Paul Valery. (FRE.). 1988. pap. 12.95 (*0-7859-3380-8*) Fr & Eur.

Regards to the Czar. Margaret Coombs. LC 87-23177. 186p. (Orig.). 1989. pap. 15.95 (*0-7022-2108-2*, Pub. by Univ Queensland Pr AT) Intl Spec Bk.

Regards to the Man in the Moon. Ezra J. Keats. LC 86-28774. (Illus.). 32p. (J). (gr. k-3). 1987. reprint ed. pap. 3.95 (*0-689-71160-3*, Aladdin Paperbacks) S&S Childrens.

Regas 75th Commemorative History. Ed. by Dwain L. Kitchel. 80p. text ed. write for info. (*1-882194-10-1*) TN Valley Pub.

Regathering: The Church from "They" to "We" Esther B. Bruland. LC 94-43326. 154p. 1994. pap. text ed. 15.00 (*0-8028-0866-2*) Eerdmans.

Regatta Mystery & Other Stories. Agatha Christie. 224p. 1986. pap. text ed. 5.50 (*0-425-10041-3*) Berkley Pub.

***Regeln fur Die Deutsche Rechtschreibung.** 77p. (GER.). 1969. 4.40 (*3-296-40100-8*, Pub. by Weidmann GW) Lubrecht & Cramer.

Regeln und Sprache Des Sports, 2 vols. Mannheim. (GER.). 55.00 (*3-411-01362-1*, M-7601) Fr & Eur.

Regelrecht One. 7th ed. F. Kuiken. 119p. 1991. pap. 22.00 (*90-5383-075-8*) IBD Ltd.

Regelrecht Two. 4th ed. F. Kuiken. 108p. 1991. pap. 22.00 (*90-6256-971-4*) IBD Ltd.

Regelung der Arbeits-Verhaltnisse Im Kriege. Ed. by Ferdinand Hanusch & Emanuel Adler. (Wirtschafts-Und Sozialgeschichte des Weltkrieges (Osterreichische Und Ungarische Serie)). (GER.). 1927. 150.00 (*0-317-27539-9*) Elliots Bks.

Regelung der Volks-Ernahrung im Kriege. Hans Loewenfeld-Russ. (Wirtschafts-Und Sozialgeschichte des Weltkrieges (Osterreichische Und Ungarische Serie)). (GER.). 1926. 150.00 (*0-317-27542-9*) Elliots Bks.

Regenbogen Fisch Komm Wilf Mir! see Arc-en-ciel Et Le Petit Poisson Perdu: Rainbow Fish to the Rescue!

Regenbogenfisch. Marcus Pfister. (Illus.). (GER.). (J). 1992. 18.95 (*3-314-00581-4*) North-South Bks NYC.

Regenbogenfisch, Komm Hilf Mir. Marcus Pfister. (Illus.). 32p. (GER.). (J). (gr. k-3). 1995. 18.95 (*3-314-20716-6*) North-South Bks NYC.

Regency Charade. Margaret Mayhew. LC 86-9110. 192p. 1986. 15.95 (*0-8027-0912-5*) Walker & Co.

Regency Christmas: Five Stories. Mary Balogh et al. 1989. pap. 3.99 (*0-451-16484-9*, Sig) NAL-Dutton.

Regency Christmas: Five Stories, Vol. III. Mary Balogh et al. 352p. 1991. pap. 4.50 (*0-451-17086-5*, Sig) NAL-Dutton.

***Regency Christmas Carol.** Mary Balogh et al. LC 97-14804. 1997. pap. 5.99 (*0-451-19387-3*, Sig) NAL-Dutton.

Regency Christmas Feast. Mary Balogh & Heath. 1996. pap. 5.99 (*0-451-19046-7*, Sig) NAL-Dutton.

Regency Companion. Sharon Laudermilk & Teresa Hamlin. LC 88-28203. 368p. 1989. text ed. 35.00 (*0-8240-2249-1*, H841) Garland.

Regency Design, 1790-1840: Gardens, Buildings, Interiors, Furniture. John Morley. LC 92-28364. (Illus.). 448p. 1993. 150.00 (*0-8109-3768-9*) Abrams.

An Asterisk (*) at the beginning of an entry indicates that the title is appearing in BIP for the first time.

R

Regency Diamonds: Azalea & The Cyprian's Sister. Brenda Hiatt & Paula Marshall. (Regency Romance Ser.). 1994. mass mkt. 4.99 (*0-373-31214-8*, 1-31214-9) Harlequin Bks.

Regency England: The Age of Lord Liverpool. John Plowright. LC 95-32719. (Lancaster Pamphlets Ser.). 112p. (C). 1996. pap. 9.95 (*0-415-12140-X*) Routledge.

***Regency Etiquette: The Mirror of Graces (1811)** Ed. by R. L. Shep. LC 97-19223. (Illus.). 256p. (Orig.). 1997. pap. 17.95 (*0-914046-24-1*) R L Shep.

Regency Furniture. Frances Collard. (Illus.). 348p. 1996. 89.50 (*0-907462-51-0*) Antique Collect.

Regency Gardens: A New Garden History. Mavis Batey. 96p. 1995. pap. 35.00 (*0-7478-0289-0*, Pub. by Shire UK) St Mut.

Regency Gold. Marion Chesney. 1980. pap. 1.75 (*0-449-50002-0*, Coventry) Fawcett.

***Regency Gold: A Novel.** Marion Chesney. LC 97-22563. 1997. write for info. (*0-7862-1186-5*) Thorndike Pr.

Regency Morning. Elizabeth Law. 1990. mass mkt. 2.95 (*0-8217-3152-1*, Zebra Kensgtn) Kensgtn Pub Corp.

Regency Morning. Elizabeth Law. 224p. 1988. 17.95 (*0-8027-1043-3*) Walker & Co.

Regency Quartet. (Regency Romance Ser.). 1993. mass mkt. 2.99 (*0-373-31200-8*, 1-31200-8) Harlequin Bks.

Regency Rose. Miriam Lynch. 1980. pap. 1.75 (*0-449-50031-4*, Coventry) Fawcett.

Regency Sting. Elizabeth Mansfield. 240p. 1996. mass mkt. 4.99 (*0-515-08773-4*) Jove Pubns.

Regency Style. Steven Parissien. (Illus.). 240p. 1995. pap. 35.00 (*0-7148-3454-8*, Pub. by Phaidon Press UK) Chronicle Bks.

Regency Style. Steven Parissien. (Illus.). 240p. 1992. 60.00 (*0-89133-172-7*) Natl Trust Hist Pres.

Regency Summer. Mary Balogh et al. 352p. 1992. 4.50 (*0-451-17401-1*) NAL-Dutton.

Regency Valentine. Kitty Grey. 234p. 1991. 19.95 (*0-8027-1131-6*) Walker & Co.

Regency Valentine, No. 2. Edith Layton et al. 352p. 1992. pap. 4.50 (*0-451-17167-5*, Sig) NAL-Dutton.

Regency Valentine, Vol. 2. large type ed. Emma Lange et al. (Nightingale Series Large Print Bks.). 296p. 1992. pap. 14.95 (*0-8161-5272-1*, GK Hall) Thorndike Pr.

Regendering the School Story: Sassy Sissies & Tattling Tomboys. Jack D. Zipes. LC 96-19804. (Children's Literature & Culture Ser.: Vol. 3). (Illus.). 312p. 1996. text ed. 45.00 (*0-8153-2116-3*, SS1060) Garland.

Regenerate Lyric: Theology & Innovation in American Poetry. Elisa New. LC 92-23412. (Cambridge Studies in American Literature & Culture: No. 64). (Illus.). 288p. (C). 1993. text ed. 65.00 (*0-521-43021-6*) Cambridge U Pr.

***Regenerating Agriculture: Policies & Practice for Sustainability & Self-Reliance.** Jules N. Pretty. 320p. 1995. 44.95 (*0-309-05248-3*, Joseph Henry Pr) Natl Acad Pr.

Regenerating Agriculture: Policies & Practice for Sustainability & Self-Reliance. Jules N. Pretty. 320p. 1995. pap. 24.95 (*0-309-05246-7*, Joseph Henry Pr) Natl Acad Pr.

Regenerating the Coalfields: Policy & Politics in the 1980s & Early 1990s. Royce Turner. 276p. 1993. 59.95 (*1-85628-414-X*, Pub. by Avebury Pub UK) Ashgate Pub Co.

***Regenerating Town Centres.** Evans. 1997. text ed. 59.95 (*0-7190-4718-8*, Pub. by Manchester Univ Pr UK) St Martin.

Regeneration. Pat Barker. 252p. 1993. pap. 11.95 (*0-452-27007-3*, Dutton-W Abrahams Bk) NAL-Dutton.

Regeneration. large type ed. Pat Barker. LC 96-5286. 1996. 25.95 (*1-56895-320-8*, Compass) Wheeler Pub.

Regeneration. Sidney A. Weltmer. 43p. 1959. reprint ed. spiral bd. 7.00 (*0-7873-0950-8*) Hlth Research.

Regeneration: Being Part Two of the Temple of the Rosy Cross (1900) F. B. Dowd. 158p. 1996. reprint ed. pap. 17.95 (*1-56459-554-4*) Kessinger Pub.

Regeneration: Part II of the Temple of the Rosy Cross. F. B. Dowd. 144p. 1964. reprint ed. spiral bd. 7.00 (*0-7873-0291-0*) Hlth Research.

Regeneration & Networks of Queues. Gerald S. Shedler. (Applied Probability Ser.). (Illus.). viii, 224p. 1986. 58.95 (*0-387-96425-8*) Spr-Verlag.

Regeneration & Plasticity in the Mammalian Visual System, Vol. 4. Ed. by Dominic M. Lam & Garth M. Bray. (Illus.). 276p. 1992. 78.00 (*0-262-12169-7*, Bradford Bks) MIT Pr.

Regeneration & Transplantation, 2 vols., 3 pts. Eugene Korschelt. (Resources in Medical History Ser.). (Illus.). 1300p. (C). 1991. write for info. (*0-88135-095-8*, Sci Hist); write for info. (*0-88135-096-6*, Sci Hist) Watson Pub Intl.

Regeneration & Transplantation, 2 vols., 3 pts., Set. Eugene Korschelt. (Resources in Medical History Ser.). (Illus.). 1300p. (C). 1991. 85.00 (*0-88135-097-4*, Sci Hist) Watson Pub Intl.

Regeneration of Selected Tropical Tree Species in Corcovado National Park, Costa Rica. Stanley R. Herwitz. LC 80-26413. (University of California Publications in Social Welfare: No. 24). (Illus.). 161p. reprint ed. pap. 45.90 (*0-685-23994-2*, 2031577) Bks Demand.

Regeneration of the Coalfield Areas: Anglo-German Perspectives. Ed. by Has Critcher et al. LC 95-3375. 194p. 1995. 69.95 (*1-85567-205-7*) St Martin.

Regeneration of Vertebrate Sensory Receptor Cells. CIBA Foundation Staff. LC 91-21619. (CIBA Foundation Symposium Ser.: No. 160). 341p. 1991. text ed. 84.95 (*0-471-92960-3*, Wiley-Interscience) Wiley.

Regeneration of Woody Legumes in Sahel. Knud Tybirk. (AAU Reports: No. 27). 80p. (C). 1991. pap. 12.95 (*87-87600-35-8*, Pub. by Aarhus Univ Pr DK) David Brown.

Regeneration Stated & Explained According to Scripture & Antiquity with a Summary View of the Doctrine of Justification (1829) Daniel Waterland. 79p. 1996. pap. 12.00 (*1-56459-587-0*) Kessinger Pub.

Regeneration Through Violence: The Mythology of the American Frontier, 1600-1860. Richard Slotkin. LC 95-42509. 688p. 1996. pap. 20.00 (*0-06-097682-9*) HarpC.

Regenerative Design for Sustainable Development. John T. Lyle. 338p. 1994. text ed. 59.95 (*0-471-55582-7*) Wiley.

***Regenerative Design for Sustainable Development.** John T. Lyle. LC 93-21637. 1996. pap. text ed. 29.95 (*0-471-17843-8*) Wiley.

Regenerative Diet. John R. Christopher. LC 90-205281. 275p. 1982. per. 7.95 (*1-879436-00-0*, 99111) Christopher Pubns.

Regenerative Inventory Systems: Operating Characteristics & Optimization. I. Sahin. Ed. by O. Oral. (Bilkent University Lectures). (Illus.). x, 175p. 1990. 53.95 (*0-387-97134-3*) Spr-Verlag.

Regenerative Phenomena. John Kingman. LC 70-39143. (Wiley Series in Probability & Mathematical Statistics). 202p. reprint ed. pap. 57.60 (*0-317-26124-X*, 2024279) Bks Demand.

Regenerative Simulation of Response Times in Network of Queues. D. L. Iglehart & Gerald S. Shedler. (Lecture Notes in Control & Information Sciences Ser.: Vol. 26). 204p. 1980. pap. 23.00 (*0-387-09942-5*) Spr-Verlag.

Regenerative Spirit. Diane Elmeer. (Illus.). 8p. 1992. 4.00 (*1-879293-05-6*) Contemp Art Mus.

Regenerative Stochastic Simulation. Gerald S. Shedler. LC 92-23205. (Statistical Modeling & Decision Science Ser.). (Illus.). 400p. 1992. text ed. 73.00 (*0-12-639360-5*) Acad Pr.

Regenerators: Social Criticism in Late Victorian English Canada. Ramsay Cook. 304p. 1984. pap. 19.95 (*0-8020-6609-7*) U of Toronto Pr.

Regenerators: Social Criticism in Late Victorian English Canada. Ramsay Cook. LC 86-194918. (Illus.). 301p. reprint ed. pap. 85.80 (*0-8357-4136-2*, 2036908) Bks Demand.

Regenesis. Julia Ecklar. 288p. (Orig.). 1995. mass mkt. 4.99 (*0-441-00189-0*) Ace Bks.

Regenesis. large type ed. Alexander Fullerton. 608p. 1984. 27.99 (*0-7089-8224-7*) Ulverscroft.

Regenritual und Jahwetag im Joelbuch: Kanaanaischer Hintergrund, Kolometrie, Aufbau und Symbolik Eines Prophetenbuches. Oswald Loretz. (Ugaritisch-Biblische Literatur Ser.: Vol. 4). 189p. (GER.). 1986. text ed. 45.00 (*3-88733-068-4*, Pub. by UGARIT GW) Eisenbrauns.

Regent. Dale Perelman. LC 89-71381. (Illus.). 144p. (Orig.). 1990. pap. 8.95 (*0-931832-47-0*) Fithian Pr.

Regent. Arnold Bennett. LC 74-17073. (Collected Works of Arnold Bennett: Vol. 70). 1977. reprint ed. 25.95 (*0-518-19151-6*) Ayer.

***Regent Redux: A Life of the Statesman-Scholar Ichijo Kaneyoshi.** Steven D. Carter. (Michigan Monographs in Japanese Studies: Vol. 16). xv, 279p. 1996. 44.95 (*0-939512-75-0*) U MI Japan.

Regenta. Leopoldo Alas. Tr. & Intro. by John Rutherford. 736p. 1985. pap. 15.95 (*0-14-044346-0*, Penguin Classics) Viking Penguin.

Regente. Renee Massip. (FRE.). 1972. pap. 8.95 (*0-7859-3998-9*) Fr & Eur.

Regents - Prentice Hall Office Handbook. 3rd ed. Rita C. Kutie & Virginia Huffman. LC 92-26399. 480p. 1993. pap. text ed. 23.80 (*0-13-720020-X*) P-H.

Regents - Prentice Hall Textbook of Cosmetology. 3rd ed. Mary Healy. LC 92-46324. 1993. text ed. 22.75 (*0-13-690009-7*) Prentice ESL.

Regents College Proficiency Examination Series (CPEP) Jack Rudman. (Entire Ser.). 1994. pap. write for info. (*0-8373-5400-5*) Nat Learn.

Regents Competency Test in Science: Practice Book. Ed. by Mark Fisch. 158p. 1988. student ed. 7.95 (*0-910307-21-0*) Comp Pr.

Regents English Workbook, No. 1. 2nd ed. Robert J. Dixson. 1995. pap. text ed. 8.95 (*0-13-199001-2*) P-H.

Regents English Workbook 2. 2nd ed. Robert J. Dixson. 1995. pap. text ed. 8.95 (*0-13-199101-9*) P-H.

Regents English Workbook 3: Advanced. 2nd ed. Robert J. Dixson & Alan Dart. LC 94-47009. 1995. pap. text ed. 8.95 (*0-13-199268-6*) P-H.

Regents Exams & Answers French Level 3 (Comprehensive French) Barrons Staff. (FRE.). 1995. pap. text ed. 12.95 incl. audio (*0-8120-8316-4*) Barron.

Regents Exams & Answers Physics. 2nd ed. Gerwitz. 1997. pap. text ed. 5.95 (*0-8120-3349-3*) Barron.

Regents External Degree Series (REDP) Jack Rudman. (Entire Ser.). 1994. pap. write for info. (*0-8373-5600-8*) Nat Learn.

Regents Illustrated Classics: Teacher's Manuals. 1987. Beginning Level. pap. text ed. 8.00 (*0-13-770959-5*, 20646); Intermediate Level. pap. text ed. 6.25 (*0-88345-484-X*, 20658) Prentice ESL.

Regents of Nations: A Systematic Chronology of States & their Political Representatives in Past & Present, 4 vols. Peter Truhart. 4258p. 1988. lib. bdg. 650.00 (*3-598-10491-X*) K G Saur.

Regents of Seven Spheres. H. K. Challoner. 1976. pap. 10.00 (*0-7229-5009-8*) Theos Pub Hse.

***Regent's Passware: Computer Software Package - Earth Science.** 1997. pap. 19.95 incl. disk (*0-614-27597-0*) Barron.

***Regent's Passware: Computer Software Package - Global Studies.** 1997. pap. 19.95 incl. disk (*0-614-27598-9*) Barron.

***Regent's Passware: Computer Software Package - Sequential Mathematics, Course I.** 1997. pap. 19.95 incl. disk (*0-614-27599-7*) Barron.

***Regent's Passware: Computer Software Package - Sequential Mathematics, Course II.** 1997. pap. 19.95 incl. disk (*0-614-27600-4*) Barron.

Regents Power Pack: Biology. 1990. pap. 11.95 (*0-8120-7670-2*) Barron.

Regents Power Pack: Chemistry, 2 bks. 1993. pap. 12.95 (*0-8120-8011-4*) Barron.

Regents Prentice Hall TOEFL Prep Book. 2nd ed. Linford Lougheed. 432p. 1992. pap. text ed. write for info. (*0-13-714072-X*) P-H.

Regents Prentice Hall TOEFL Prep Book. 2nd ed. Linford Lougheed. 1993. pap. 17.25 (*0-13-782632-X*) P-H.

Regents Scholarship & College Qualification Test (RSE) Jack Rudman. (Admission Test Ser.: ATS-42). 1994. pap. 29.95 (*0-8373-5042-5*) Nat Learn.

***Regesta Pontificum Romanorum Ivbente Regai Societate Gottingensi Congessit Pavlvs Fridolinvs Kehr: Kalabrien - Sizilien I - Sizilien II.** Contrib. by Paulus F. Kehr. xliii, 492p. (ITA.). 1975. write for info. (*3-296-20912-3*, Pub. by Weidmann GW) Lubrecht & Cramer.

***Regesta Pontificum Romanorum Ivbente Regai Societate Gottingensi Congessit Pavlvs Fridolinvs Kehr Vol. II, Pt. I: Provincia Maguntinensis.** Contrib. by Albertus Brackmann. 260p. 1960. write for info. (*3-296-20802-X*, Pub. by Weidmann GW) Lubrecht & Cramer.

***Regesta Pontificum Romanorum Ivbente Regai Societate Gottingensi Congessit Pavlvs Fridolinvs Kehr Vol. II, Pt. II: Provincia Maguntinensis.** Contrib. by Albertus Brackmann. 320p. (GER.). 1960. write for info. (*3-296-20803-8*, Pub. by Weidmann GW) Lubrecht & Cramer.

***Regesta Pontificum Romanorum Ivbente Regai Societate Gottingensi Congessit Pavlvs Fridolinvs Kehr Vol. II, Pt. III: Provincia Maguntinensis.** Contrib. by Albertus Brackmann. 328p. (GER.). 1960. write for info. (*3-296-20804-6*, Pub. by Weidmann GW) Lubrecht & Cramer.

***Regesta Pontificum Romanorum Ivbente Regai Societate Gottingensi Congessit Pavlvs Fridolinvs Kehr Vol. VI, Pt. I: Liguria Sive Provincia Mediolanensis.** Contrib. by Paulus F. Kehr. xliv, 419p. (ITA.). 1961. write for info. (*3-296-20906-9*, Pub. by Weidmann GW) Lubrecht & Cramer.

***Regesta Pontificum Romanorum Ivbente Regai Societate Gottingensi Congessit Pavlvs Fridolinvs Kehr Vol. VI, Pt. II: Liguria Sive Provincia Mediolanensis.** Contrib. by Paulus F. Kehr. xxxviii, 392p. (ITA.). 1961. write for info. (*3-296-20907-7*, Pub. by Weidmann GW) Lubrecht & Cramer.

***Regesta Pontificum Romanorum Ivbente Regai Societate Gottingensi Congessit Pavlvs Fridolinvs Kehr Vol. VII, Pt. I: Venetiae & Histria.** Contrib. by Paulus F. Kehr. xxxiv, 54p. (ITA.). 1961. write for info. (*3-296-20908-5*, Pub. by Weidmann GW) Lubrecht & Cramer.

***Regesta Pontificum Romanorum Ivbente Regai Societate Gottingensi Congessit Pavlvs Fridolinvs Kehr Vol. VII, Pt. II: Venetiae & Histria.** Contrib. by Paulus F. Kehr. xxviii, 263p. (ITA.). 1961. write for info. (*3-296-20909-3*, Pub. by Weidmann GW) Lubrecht & Cramer.

***Regesta Pontificum Romanorum Ivbente Regai Societate Gottingensi Congessit Pavlvs Fridolinvs Kehr Vol. I: Provincia Salisburgensis.** Contrib. by Albertus Brackmann. 412p. (GER.). 1960. write for info. (*3-296-20801-1*, Pub. by Weidmann GW) Lubrecht & Cramer.

***Regesta Pontificum Romanorum Ivbente Regai Societate Gottingensi Congessit Pavlvs Fridolinvs Kehr Vol. I: Roma.** Contrib. by Paulus F. Kehr. xxvi, 202p. (ITA.). 1961. write for info. (*3-296-20901-8*, Pub. by Weidmann GW) Lubrecht & Cramer.

***Regesta Pontificum Romanorum Ivbente Regai Societate Gottingensi Congessit Pavlvs Fridolinvs Kehr Vol. II: Latium.** Contrib. by Paulus F. Kehr. xxx, 230p. (ITA.). 1961. write for info. (*3-296-20902-6*, Pub. by Weidmann GW) Lubrecht & Cramer.

***Regesta Pontificum Romanorum Ivbente Regai Societate Gottingensi Congessit Pavlvs Fridolinvs Kehr Vol. III: Etruria.** Contrib. by Paulus F. Kehr. 492p. (ITA.). write for info. (*3-296-20903-4*, Pub. by Weidmann GW) Lubrecht & Cramer.

***Regesta Pontificum Romanorum Ivbente Regai Societate Gottingensi Congessit Pavlvs Fridolinvs Kehr Vol. IV: Umbria, Picenum, Marsia.** Contrib. by Paulus F. Kehr. xxxiv, 336p. (ITA.). 1961. write for info. (*3-296-20904-2*, Pub. by Weidmann GW) Lubrecht & Cramer.

***Regesta Pontificum Romanorum Ivbente Regai Societate Gottingensi Congessit Pavlvs Fridolinvs Kehr Vol. IX: Samnium - Apulia - Lucania.** Contrib. by Paulus F. Kehr. (ITA.). 1962. write for info. (*3-296-20911-5*, Pub. by Weidmann GW) Lubrecht & Cramer.

***Regesta Pontificum Romanorum Ivbente Regai Societate Gottingensi Congessit Pavlvs Fridolinvs Kehr Vol. V: Aemilia Sive Provincia Ravennas.** Contrib. by Paulus F. Kehr. liv, 534p. (ITA.). 1961. write for info. (*3-296-20905-0*, Pub. by Weidmann GW) Lubrecht & Cramer.

***Regesta Pontificum Romanorum Ivbente Regai Societate Gottingensi Congessit Pavlvs Fridolinvs Kehr Vol. VIII: Regnum Normannorum - Campania.** Contrib. by Paulus F. Kehr. lii, 479p. (ITA.). 1961. write for info. (*3-296-20910-7*, Pub. by Weidmann GW) Lubrecht & Cramer.

***Regesta Regum Anglo-Normannorum: The Acta of William I 1066-1087.** Ed. by David Bates. 752p. 1997. 180.00 (*0-19-820674-7*) OUP.

Reggae - the Man Who Named the Music: Why Do the Heathen Rage. Ricardo A. Scott. (Reggae Book of Light Ser.). (Illus.). 73p. (Orig.). (YA). pap. write for info. (*1-883427-25-8*) Crnerstone GA.

Reggae - 101: Each One Teach One. Ricardo A. Scott. (Ras Crado Speaks - Reggae Education Ser.). (Illus.). 75p. (Orig.). Date not set. pap. write for info. (*1-883427-75-4*) Crnerstone GA.

Reggae & the Homeless: Lying with the Sheep. Ricardo A. Scott. (Reggae Book of Light Ser.). (Illus.). 65p. (Orig.). pap. write for info. (*1-883427-33-9*) Crnerstone GA.

Reggae Bloodlines: In Search of the Music & Culture of Jamaica. 3rd ed. Photos by Peter Simon. (Illus.). 224p. 1992. reprint ed. pap. 16.95 (*0-306-80496-4*) Da Capo.

Reggae Legends Dance Steps: How Legends Skank. Ricardo A. Scott. (Illus.). 50p. (Orig.). (YA). 1994. write for info. (*1-883427-12-6*) Crnerstone GA.

Reggae Lyrics, Slangs, & Interpretations: Reggae Phraseology Explained. Ricardo A. Scott. 85p. (Orig.). 1994. write for info. (*1-883427-14-2*) Crnerstone GA.

Reggae Music? - Your Right to Know: The Book of Truth - the Bible on Reggae. Ricardo A. Scott. (Ras Cardo Speaks on Reggae Truths Ser.: Vol. GRTS7391). (Illus.). 55p. (Orig.). Date not set. pap. write for info. (*1-883427-76-2*) Crnerstone GA.

Reggae on CD: The Essential Guide. Lloyd Bradley. 224p. 1995. pap. 19.95 (*1-85626-177-8*, C Kyle) Trafalgar.

Reggae or Not! Amiri Baraka. (Chapbook Ser.). (Illus.). 32p. 1982. pap. 3.00 (*0-936556-04-8*) Contact Two.

Reggae, Origin of the Word & Incorporation into Music: The Trench-Town Experience & Beyond. Ricardo A. Scott. (Illus.). 85p. (Orig.). write for info. (*1-883427-07-X*) Crnerstone GA.

Reggae Philosophy, Reggae Reality. Ricardo A. Scott. (Illus.). 100p. (Orig.). write for info. (*1-883427-19-3*) Crnerstone GA.

Reggae, Rastafricans Revolution: Jamaican Music from Ska to Dub. Pottash. LC 97-19893. 1997. 22.00 (*0-02-864728-9*) Mac Lib Ref.

***Reggae Songbook.** 108p. 1997. pap. 16.95 (*0-8256-1502-X*, AM 931392) Music Sales.

Reggaeration to Build a Black Nation: Why We Must Begin to Love & Trust Each Other or Perish. Ricardo A. Scott. (Ras Cardo Reggae Prophesies Ser.: Vol. GRTS7391). (Illus.). 65p. (Orig.). (YA). Date not set. pap. write for info. (*1-883427-82-7*) Crnerstone GA.

Reggae's Healing Effects: A Reggae Education for a Healing of the Nations. Ricardo A. Scott. (Illus.). 80p. (Orig.). 1994. write for info. (*1-883427-21-5*) Crnerstone GA.

Regge Poles in Particle Physics. P. D. Collins & E. J. Squires. (Tracts in Modern Physics Ser.: Vol. 45). 1968. 73.95 (*0-387-04339-X*) Spr-Verlag.

Reggie: A Portrait of Reginald Turner. Stanley Weintraub. LC 79-8085. reprint ed. 29.50 (*0-404-18393-X*) AMS Pr.

***Reggie: Making the Message Simple.** Joseph B. Strauss. (Illus.). 262p. 1997. 25.00 (*1-890419-01-X*) Fnd Chiropractic Educ.

Reggie Jackson. Norman L. Macht. LC 94-228. (Baseball Legends Ser.). (Illus.). 64p. (J). (gr. 3 up). 1994. lib. bdg. 15.95 (*0-7910-2169-6*) Chelsea Hse.

Reggie Jackson Super. pap. 1.95 (*0-590-05396-5*) Scholastic Inc.

Reggie Lewis: Quiet Grace. Craig Windham. LC 95-10448. (Illus.). 201p. 1995. 15.50 (*1-56698-164-6*) Actex Pubns.
At age 27, Boston Celtic Captain, Reggie Lewis, was on the verge of superstar status. His career & his life were cut short by a heart condition. This book does not dwell on the controversy or sensationalism that characterized Reggie's death, rather, it explores the life of this outstanding human being. Reggie Lewis was more than just a fine basketball player. He was an outstanding young man - warm, caring & generous. This is the story of Reggie's roots. You will learn of the family members, friends & forces that helped shape him & the quiet grace that helped him rise above the violence & poverty of his childhood Baltimore neighborhood. A review by John Bisney of ASSOCIATED PRESS states: "Heartfelt & compelling...QUIET GRACE vividly portrays Reggie's qualities & accomplishments. This straightforward account shows that the truth of Reggie's life outshines any unproven speculation about his death." The book contains a collection of photographs & Reggie's career stats in both college & the NBA. The writing style is gentle & conversational, written from interviews with family members & teammates. Young & old can benefit from the fine example of Reggie's life but the major audience is adolescents & young adults, including some who do not read very many books. To this end, the hardcover is priced at $15.50 & proceeds from the sale of this book will be donated in honor of Reggie Lewis to civic & charitable organizations. For information contact the publisher ACTEX Publications, 140 Willow Street, P.O. Box 974, Winstead, CT 06098, Phone (800) 282-2839, FAX (860) 738-3152, e-mail: retail@actexmadriver.com. Distributed by: Publishers Distribution Service, 6893 Sullivan Road, Grawn, MI 49637, Phone (616) 276-5196, FAX (616) 276-5197. ***Publisher Provided Annotation.***

An Asterisk (*) at the beginning of an entry indicates that the title is appearing in BIP for the first time.

R

***Reggie Miller.** Barry Wilner. LC 97-14224. (Basketball Legends Ser.). (Illus.). 64p. (J). (gr. 3 up). 1997. lib. bdg. 15.95 (0-7910-4384-3) Chelsea Hse.

Reggie Miller: Basketball Sharpshooter. Ted Cox. LC 95-1105. (Sports Stars Ser.). 48p. (J). (gr. 2-8). 1995. lib. bdg. 17.50 (0-516-04393-5) Childrens.

Reggie Miller: Basketball Sharpshooter. Ted Cox. (Sports Stars Ser.). (Illus.). 48p. (J). (gr. 2-8). 1996. reprint ed. pap. 4.50 (0-516-44393-3) Childrens.

***Reggie the Veggie.** Cambria Gordon. 1998. pap. 3.99 (0-679-88848-9); lib. bdg. 11.99 (0-679-98848-3) Random Bks Yng Read.

Reggie White: In the Trenches. Reggie White. 272p. 1996. 22.99 (0-7852-7252-6, J Thoma Bks) Nelson.

Reggie White: Star Defensive Lineman. Bill Gutman. LC 93-38960. (Millbrook Sports World Ser.). (Illus.). 48p. (J). (gr. 3-6). 1994. lib. bdg. 14.90 (1-56294-461-4) Millbrook Pr.

Reggie White: see In the Trenches: The Autobiography

Regia Marina, Italian Battleships of WWII. Erminio Bagnasco & Mark Grossman. LC 86-60436. (Illus.). 76p. 1986. pap. 7.95 (0-933126-75-1) Pictorial Hist.

Regicide: Or James the First, of Scotland, a Tragedy. Tobias G. Smollett. LC 78-67542. reprint ed. 37.50 (0-404-17205-9) AMS Pr.

Regicide & Restoration: English Tragicomedy, 1660-1671. Nancy K. Maguire. (Illus.). 280p. (C). 1993. text ed. 69.95 (0-521-41622-1) Cambridge U Pr.

Regicide & Revolution: Speeches at the Trial of Louis XVI. Tr. by Marian Rothstein. LC 92-39235. 240p. (C). 1993. pap. 16.50 (0-231-08259-2, Mrngside); text ed. 45.00 (0-231-08258-4, Mrngside) Col U Pr.

Regicide & Revolution: Speeches at the Trial of Louis XVI. Ed. by M. Walzer. LC 73-94370. (Cambridge Studies in the History & Theory of Politics). 233p. reprint ed. pap. 66.50 (0-317-27090-7, 2024556) Bks Demand.

Regicides. A. Rowse. 32.95 (0-7156-2607-8, Pub. by Duckworth UK) Focus Pub-R Pullins.

***Regie's Antics.** (J). pap. 5.00 (0-614-18225-5, PS02) Let Us Tch Kids.

Regime Administratif de l'Eau du Nil: Dans l'Egypte Grecque, Romaine & Byzantine. Danielle Bonneau. (Probleme der Agyptologie Ser.: No. 8). 340p. (FRE.). 1993. 95.25 (90-04-09687-6) E J Brill.

Regime & Discipline: Democracy & the Development of Political Science. Ed. by David Easton et al. 326p. 1995. text ed. 52.50 (0-472-10444-6) U of Mich Pr.

Regime Changes: Macroeconomic Policy Regimes & Financial Regulation in Europe from the 1930s to the 1990s. Ed. by Douglas J. Forsyth & Ton Notermans. LC 96-26895. 320p. 1997. 59.95 (1-57181-043-9) Berghahn Bks.

Regime Feodal De l'Italie Normande. Claude Cahen. LC 80-1995. reprint ed. 25.00 (0-404-18555-X) AMS Pr.

Regime for the Exploitation of Transboundary Marine Fisheries Resources. Ellen Hey. (C). 1989. lib. bdg. 125.50 (0-7923-0458-6) Kluwer Ac.

Regime for the High-Seas Fisheries: The Status & Prospects. (Law of the Sea Ser.). 48p. 1992. 10.00 (92-1-133435-7) UN.

Regime of Anastasio Somoza, 1936-1956. Knut Walter. LC 93-12467. (Illus.). xx, 304p. 1993. pap. text ed. 18.95 (0-8078-4427-6) U of NC Pr.

Regime of Islands in International Law. Hiran W. Jayewardene. (C). 1990. lib. bdg. 234.00 (0-7923-0130-7) Kluwer Ac.

***Regime of Straits in International Law.** Bing Jia. (Oxford Monographs in International Law). 320p. 1997. 95.00 (0-19-826556-5) OUP.

Regime of the Brother: After the Patriarchy. Juliet F. MacCannell. LC 90-8982. (Opening Out Ser.). 208p. (C). (gr. 13). 1991. pap. text ed. 15.95 (0-415-05435-4, A5613) Routledge.

Regime of the International Rivers: Danube & Rhine. Joseph P. Chamberlain. LC 68-57565. (Columbia University. Studies in the Social Sciences: No. 237). reprint ed. 29.50 (0-404-51237-2) AMS Pr.

Regime Politics: Governing Atlanta, 1946-1988. Clarence N. Stone. LC 89-35634. (Studies in Government & Public Policy). (Illus.). xiv, 314p. 1989. pap. 16.95 (0-7006-0416-2) U Pr of KS.

***Regime Theory in the Post-Cold War World: Rethinking Neoliberal Approaches to International Relations.** Robert M. Crawford. (Illus.). 250p. 1996. text ed. 62.95 (1-85521-848-8, Pub. by Dartmth Pub UK) Ashgate Pub Co.

Regime Transformations & Global Realignments: Indo-European Dialogues on the Post-Cold War World. Ed. by Kanta Ahuja et al. (Indo-Dutch Studies on Development Alternatives: Vol. 11). (Illus.). 390p. (C). 1993. text ed. 39.95 (0-8039-9131-2) Sage.

Regime Transitions, Spillovers & Buffer Stocks: Analysing the Swiss Economy by Means of a Disequilibrium Model. P. Stalder. Ed. by Martin J. Beckmann & W. Krelle. (Lecture Notes in Economics & Mathematical Systems Ser.: Vol. 360). (Illus.). vi, 193p. 1991. 33.95 (0-387-54056-3) Spr-Verlag.

Regimen De la Propiedad Privada En el Estado Libre Asociado De Puerto Rico (Intervencionismo, Dirigismo, Socializacion) Alberto Blanco. LC 78-1748. 125p. (SPA.). 1978. pap. 2.80 (0-8477-3016-6) U of PR Pr.

Regimen for Weight Control in Retired Couples & Others Who Want to Control Weight Happily. Charles N. Aronson. LC 73-88985. (Illus.). (C). 1973. 5.00 (0-915736-03-9) C N Aronson.

Regiment. John Dalmas. 416p. 1991. reprint ed. mass mkt. 5.99 (0-671-72065-1) Baen Bks.

Regiment: Let the Citizens Bear Arms. Harry M. Kemp. (Illus.). 408p. 1991. 24.95 (0-89015-836-3) Sunbelt Media.

Regiment for the Sea & Other Writings on Navigation. William Bourne. Ed. by E. G. Taylor. (Hakluyt Society Second Ser.: Vol. 121). (Illus.). 500p. 1996. 63.00 (0-85115-990-7, Pub. by Hakluyt Soc UK) Boydell & Brewer.

Regiment of Women. Thomas Berger. (Orig.). 1991. pap. 10.95 (0-316-09242-8) Little.

***Regiment Remembered: The 157th New York Volunteers.** unabridged ed. William Saxton. Ed. by Mary A. Kane. 160p. 1996. pap. 20.00 (0-9647244-2-1) Cortland NY.

Regiment (Sic) of Life, Newly Corrected & Enlarged. John Goeurot. LC 76-57385. (English Experience Ser.: No. 802). 1977. reprint ed. lib. bdg. 28.00 (90-221-0802-3) Walter J Johnson.

Regimental Badges of New Zealand. D. A. Corbett. (Illus.). 320p. (C). 1987. 140.00 (0-317-90381-0, Pub. by Picton UK) St Mut.

Regimental Badges of New Zealand. D. A. Corbett. 320p. (C). 1990. 90.00 (0-908596-05-7, Pub. by Picton UK) St Mut.

Regimental Histories of the American Civil War: A Guide to the Microfiche Collection, Unit 1. iii, 69p. 1992. pap. 20.00 (0-8357-2177-9) Univ Microfilms.

Regimental Histories of the American Civil War: A Guide to the Microfiche Collection, Unit 2. iii, 86p. 1992. pap. 20.00 (0-8357-2184-1) Univ Microfilms.

Regimental History of Cromwell's Army, 2 vols. Charles Firth. 816p. 1991. 175.00 (0-19-821217-8, 12275) OUP.

Regimental Losses in the American Civil War, 1861-1865. unabridged ed. William F. Fox. 595p. 1985. reprint ed. text ed. 60.00 (0-89029-007-5) Morningside Bkshop.

Regimental Strengths & Losses at Gettysburg. 3rd ed. John W. Busey & David G. Martin. 351p. 1994. 20.00 (0-944413-32-3) Longstreet Hse.

Regiments at Antietam. John W. Schildt. (Illus.). 170p. 1992. pap. write for info. (0-936772-10-7) Antietam.

Regiments of All Nations: A History of Britain Ltd. Lead Soldiers 1946-66. Joseph T. Wallis. LC 81-90044. (Illus.). 260p. (Orig.). 1981. pap. 25.00 (0-9605950-0-7) J Wallis.

Regiment's War. John Dalmas. 368p. 1993. mass mkt. 4.99 (0-671-72155-0) Baen Bks.

Regimes & Oppositions. Ed. by Robert A. Dahl. LC 79-151571. 415p. reprint ed. pap. 118.30 (0-8357-8757-5, 2033700) Bks Demand.

Regimes for the Ocean, Outer Space, & Weather. Seyom Brown et al. 257p. 1977. 26.95 (0-8157-1156-5); pap. 9.95 (0-8157-1155-7) Brookings.

Regimes in Crisis: The Post-Soviet Era & Implications for Development. Ed. by Barry Gills & Shahid Qadir. LC 94-41476. 320p. (C). 1995. pap. 29.95 (1-85649-256-7, Pub. by Zed Bks Ltd UK); text ed. 59.95 (1-85649-255-9, Pub. by Zed Bks Ltd UK) Humanities.

***Regimes, Politics, & Markets: Democratization & Economic Change in Southern & Eastern Europe.** Jose M. Maravall. Tr. by Justin Byrne. (Oxford Studies in Democratization). (Illus.). 288p. 1997. 58.00 (0-19-828083-1) OUP.

***Regimewandel Durch Groprojekte: Auf der Suche Nach Likaler Handlungsfahigkeit in Zurich und Wien.** Armin Kuhne. (Europaische Urbanitat-Politik der Stadte Ser.). (GER.). 1997. text ed. 70.00 (90-5708-007-9); pap. text ed. 31.00 (90-5708-008-7) Gordon & Breach.

Regimiento Contra la Peste: Biblioteca Nacional de Madrid I-51. Fernando Alvarez. Ed. by Maria Purificacion Zabia. (Medieval Spanish Medical Texts Ser.: No. 18). 6p. (SPA.). 1987. 10.00 incl. fiche (0-940639-14-9) Hispanic Seminary.

***Regina.** Antonio V. Pina. 600p. Date not set. pap. 27.95 (1-55978-785-6) R K Bks.

***Regina: An Illustrated History.** J. William Brennan. 34.95 (1-55028-250-6, Pub. by J Lorimer CN) Formac Dist Ltd.

Regina: From Pile O' Bones to Queen City of the Plains. William A. Riddell. 1980. 24.95 (0-89781-029-5, 5040) Am Historical Pr.

Regina: Vocal Score. M. Blitzstein. Ed. by Michael Lefferts. 252p. (Orig.). (C). 1997. pap. text ed. 55.95 (0-7935-1545-9, 00311578) H Leonard.

***Regina Calhoun Eats Dog Food.** Lynn Cullen. 1997. pap. 3.99 (0-380-78803-9) Avon.

***Regina Maria Anzenberger: Presents 20 Photographs.** Regina M. Anzenberger. 1997. 55.00 (3-908162-73-4) Dist Art Pubs.

Reginald Dalton: A Story of English University Life, 3 vols. in 2. John G. Lockhart. LC 79-8157. reprint ed. 84.50 (0-404-61987-8) AMS Pr.

Reginald Marsh - The Prints: Catalogue Raisonne. Norman Sasowsky. (Illus.). 288p. 1976. 125.00 (1-55660-264-2) A Wofsy Fine Arts.

Reginald Marsh's New York Paintings, Drawings, Prints & Photographs. Marylin Cohen. LC 83-6465. (Fine Art Ser.). (Illus.). 115p. (Orig.). 1983. pap. 9.95 (0-486-24594-2) Dover.

Reginald Pecock. Wendy Scase. Ed. by M. C. Seymour. (Authors of the Middle Ages Ser.). 64p. Date not set. pap. 17.95 (0-86078-428-2, Pub. by Variorum UK) Ashgate Pub Co.

***Reginald Rowe: A Retrospective, 1963-1995.** William J. Chiego. (Illus.). 76p. 1996. pap. 24.95 (0-916677-36-2) U of Tex Pr.

Reginald Turvey: Life & Art. Ed. by Lowell Johnson. 176p. (Orig.). 1986. pap. 19.50 (0-85398-238-4) G Ronald Pub.

Reginald's Science Fiction & Fantasy Awards: A Comprehensive Guide to the Awards & Their Winners. 3rd enl. rev. ed. Daryl F. Mallett & Robert Reginald. LC 92-24445. (Borgo Literary Guides Ser.: No. 1). 248p. 1993. pap. 23.00 (0-8095-1200-9); lib. bdg. 33.00 (0-8095-0200-3) Borgo Pr.

Regina's Big Mistake. Marissa Moss. (Illus.). 32p. (J). (gr. k-3). 1990. 16.00 (0-395-55330-X) HM.

Regina's Big Mistake. Marissa Moss. LC 90-32740. (Illus.). 32p. (J). (gr. k-3). 1995. pap. 4.95 (0-395-70093-0, Sandpiper) HM.

Regina's Dream. (Junior African Writers Ser.). (Illus.). 128p. (J). (gr. 5-6). 1995. pap. 5.00 (0-7910-3162-4) Chelsea Hse.

Regina's Vegetarian Table. Regina Campbell. LC 96-39849. 1998. 16.00 (0-7615-0697-7) Prima Pub.

Regiomontanus: His Life & Work. E. Zinner. Tr. by E. Brown from DUT. (Studies in the History & Philosophy of Mathematics: No. 1). 402p. 1990. 129.75 (0-444-88792-X, North Holland) Elsevier.

Regiomontanus: On Triangles - De Triangulis Omnimodis. Johannes R. Muller. Tr. & Intro. by Barnabas Hughes. LC 66-22861. 308p. (ENG & LAT.). 1967. reprint ed. pap. 87.80 (0-608-01882-1, 2062534) Bks Demand.

Regiomontanus Table of Houses. Justus & Assocs. Staff. Ed. by Carol A. Wiggers & Allen Edwall. 130p. (C). 1991. student ed. 18.00 (1-878935-14-3) JustUs & Assocs.

Region & Nation in Modern India. Ed. by Paul Wallace. 1985. 27.50 (0-8364-1245-1) S Asia.

Region & Regionalism in the United States: A Bibliographic Guide. rev. ed. Michael Steiner & Clarence Mondale. LC 83-48218. 514p. 1989. text ed. 82.00 (0-8240-9048-9) Garland.

Region & State in Honduras, 1870-1972: Reinterpreting the "Banana Republic" Dario A. Euraque. LC 96-6234. 1996. 39.95 (0-8078-2298-1); pap. 18.95 (0-8078-4604-X) U of NC Pr.

Region & State in Latin America's Past. Magnus Morner. LC 92-28774. (Symposia in Comparative History Ser.). 168p. 1993. text ed. 32.50 (0-8018-4478-9) Johns Hopkins.

Region As a Socio-Environmental System: An Introduction to a Systemic Regional Geography. Dov Nir. (C). 1990. lib. bdg. 115.50 (0-7923-0516-7) Kluwer Ac.

Region at Risk: The Third Regional Plan for the New York-New Jersey-Connecticut Metropolitan Area. Robert D. Yaro & Tony Hiss. 320p. (Orig.). (C). 1996. pap. text ed. 35.00 (1-55963-492-8) Island Pr.

Region Building in the Pacific. Gavin Boyd. (Policy Studies on International Politics). 280p. 1982. 74.00 (0-08-025985-5, Pergamon Pr) Elsevier.

Region Centre et Sud-Est see Dictionnaire des Eglises de France

Region, Class & Gender: A European Comparison. P. Cooke. (Illus.). 62p. 1984. pap. 22.00 (0-08-032303-0, Pergamon Pr) Elsevier.

Region, Economy, & Party: The Roots of Party Formation in Pennsylvania, 1820-1860. Ann M. Dykstra. (Nineteenth Century American Political & Social History Ser.). 400p. 1990. reprint ed. 25.00 (0-8240-4065-1) Garland.

Region in Transition: An Economic Atlas of Northeast Ohio. Ed. by Robert B. Kent. LC 91-22579. (Illus.). 183p. 1992. 39.95 (0-9622628-3-8) U Akron Pr.

Region of the Upper Columbia River & How I Saw It. Alfred Downing. 50p. 1980. 9.95 (0-87770-535-6); pap. 7.50 (0-87770-234-9) Ye Galleon.

Region of Unlikeness. Jorie Graham. 130p. (C). 1991. 17.95 (0-88001-271-4) Ecco Pr.

Region of Unlikeness. Jorie Graham. 1992. pap. 11.95 (0-88001-290-0) Ecco Pr.

Region ouest de Paris, Paris et ses environs, Bretagne, Normandie see Dictionnaire des Eglises de France

***Region, Race, & Cities: Interpreting the Urban South.** David R. Goldfield. LC 97-18547. 336p. 1997. text ed. 37.50 (0-8071-2189-4) La State U Pr.

***Region, Race, & Cities: Interpreting the Urban South.** David R. Goldfield. 336p. 1997. pap. 16.95 (0-8071-2244-0) La State U Pr.

Region Sud-Ouest see Dictionnaire des Eglises de France

Region vs. Nation: Cuyo in the Crosscurrents of Argentine Development, 1861-1914. William J. Fleming. LC 86-29919. 82p. 1987. text ed. 25.00 (0-87918-066-8) ASU Lat Am St.

Regional Accounts for Policy Decision: Papers Presented at the Conference on Regional Accounts, 1964. Conference on Regional Accounts Staff. Ed. by Werner Z. Hirsch. LC 66-23000. 244p. reprint ed. pap. 69.60 (0-7837-3127-2, 2042860) Bks Demand.

Regional Acidification Models. Ed. by Juha Kamari et al. (Illus.). viii, 306p. 1989. 79.95 (0-387-51825-8) Spr-Verlag.

Regional Advantage: Culture & Competition in Silicon Valley & Route 128. AnnaLee Saxenian. LC 93-39416. 240p. 1994. text ed. 24.95 (0-674-75339-9) HUP.

Regional Advantage: Culture & Competition in Silicon Valley & Route 128. AnnaLee Saxenian. (Illus.). 240p. 1996. pap. 14.95 (0-674-75340-2) HUP.

Regional Anaesthesia for Babies & Children. Jane M. Peutrell & Stephen J. Mather. (Illus.). 120p. (C). 1997. text ed. 65.00 (0-19-262425-3) OUP.

Regional Analysis & the New International Division of Labor. Frank Moulaert & Wilson Salinas. (Studies in Applied Regional Science). 1982. lib. bdg. 61.00 (0-89838-107-X) Kluwer Ac.

Regional Analysis of Prehistoric Ceramic Variation: Contemporary Studies of the Cibola Whitewares. Ed. by A. Sullivan & J. Hantman. (Anthropological Research Papers: No. 31). (Illus.). vi, 149p. 1984. pap. 15.00 (0-685-73907-4) AZ Univ ARP.

Regional & Adjustment Aspects of Trade Liberalization. Harry E. English. LC 74-1303. (Canada in the Atlantic Economy Ser.: No. 5). 374p. reprint ed. pap. 106.60 (0-8357-8299-9, 2034002) Bks Demand.

Regional & County-by-County Assessment of Archaeological Survey Coverage in Maryland. Maryland Historical Trust Staff. (White Papers Series on Preservation Planning: No. 1). 50p. 1987. 2.00 (1-878399-19-5) Div Hist Cult Progs.

Regional & County-by-County Assessment of Historic Standing Structures Survey Coverage in Maryland. Maryland Historical Trust Staff. (White Papers Series on Preservation Planning: No. 2). 37p. 1987. 2.00 (1-878399-20-9) Div Hist Cult Progs.

Regional & Interregional Input-Output Analysis: An Annotated Bibliography. Frank Giarrantani. LC 75-45868. 127p. 1976. 10.00 (0-89092-008-7) West Va U Pr.

Regional & Local Economic Analysis for Practitioners. 4th ed. Avron Bendavid-Val. LC 90-41092. 264p. 1991. text ed. 59.95 (0-275-93520-5, C3520, Praeger Pubs); pap. text ed. 22.95 (0-275-93751-8, B3751, Praeger Pubs) Greenwood.

Regional & Metropolitan Growth & Decline in the United States. William Frey & Alden Speare, Jr. LC 87-43098. (Population of the United States in the 1980s: A Census Monograph Ser.). 400p. 1988. text ed. 70.00 (0-87154-293-5) Russell Sage.

***Regional & National Identities in Europe in the Nineteenth & Twentieth Centuries.** Heinz G. Haupt & Michael G. Muller. LC 97-20722. (European Forum Ser.). (ENG & FRE.). 1997. write for info. (90-411-0875-0) Kluwer Law Tax Pubs.

Regional & State Water Resources Planning & Management: Proceedings of a Symposium Held in San Antonio, Texas. Ed. by Randall J. Charbeneau & Barney P. Popkin. LC 84-73194. (American Water Resources Association Technical Publication Ser.: No. TPS-83-1). 374p. reprint ed. pap. 106.60 (0-8357-7927-0, 2036353) Bks Demand.

Regional & Urban Development Policies: A Latin American Perspective. Guillermo Geisse. LC 78-103483. (Latin American Urban Research Ser.: Vol. 2). 298p. reprint ed. pap. 85.00 (0-317-29678-7, 2021904) Bks Demand.

***Regional & Urban Economics, Pts. 1 & 2.** Ed. by Richard Arnott. 1296p. 1997. text ed. 250.00 (3-7186-5410-5, ECU192, Harwood Acad Pubs) Gordon & Breach.

Regional Anesthesia: An Atlas of Anatomy & Techniques. Ed. by Marc B. Hahn et al. LC 95-31275. 400p. (C). (gr. 13). 1995. text ed. 140.00 (0-8151-4121-1) Mosby Yr Bk.

Regional Anesthesia: An Illustrated Procedural Guide. 2nd ed. LC 95-4493. (Illus.). 327p. 1995. pap. text ed. 69.95 (0-316-58906-3) Lppncott-Raven.

Regional Anesthesia & Analgesia. David L. Brown. Ed. by Richard Zorab. 800p. 1996. text ed. 139.00 (0-7216-5654-4) Saunders.

Regional Antineoplastic Drug Delivery in the Management of Malignant Disease. Maurie Markman. LC 90-15596. (Series in Contemporary Medicine & Public Health). 220p. 1991. text ed. 65.00 (0-8018-4166-6) Johns Hopkins.

Regional Appraisal of the International Development Strategy. 82p. 1992. 3.00 (92-1-121032-1) UN.

Regional Approaches to Confidence & Security-Building Measures. (Disarmament Topical Papers: No.17). 147p. Date not set. pap. 13.50 (92-1-142203-5, E.94.IX.5) UN.

Regional Approaches to Disarmament, Security, & Stability: Security & Stability. Ed. by Jayantha Dhanapala. LC 93-21137. (U. N. Institute for Disarmament Research (UNIDIR) Ser.). 256p. 1993. 59.95 (1-85521-363-X, Pub. by Dartmth Pub UK) Ashgate Pub Co.

Regional Approaches to Mortuary Analysis: Alexander. Ed. by Lane A. Beck. LC 94-49728. (Interdisciplinary Contributions to Archaeology Ser.). 280p. 1995. pap. 45.00 (0-306-44931-5, Plenum Pr) Plenum.

***Regional Approaches to Water Pollution in the Environment: NATO Advanced Research Workshop, Liblice, Czech Republic, September 5-10, 1995.** V. Elias. Ed. by P. E. Rijtema. LC 96-35770. (NATO Advanced Science Institutes Ser.). 328p. (C). 1996. lib. bdg. 156.00 (0-7923-4250-X) Kluwer Ac.

Regional Aquifer Systems of the United States, Aquifers of the Atlantic & Gulf Coastal Plain: Papers Presented at 22nd Annual AWRA Conference & Symposium, November 9-14, 1986, Atlanta GA. American Water Resources Association Staff. Ed. by John Vecchioli & A. Ivan Johnson. (AWRA Monograph Ser.: No. 9). 179p. reprint ed. pap. 51.10 (0-8357-4078-1, 2036768) Bks Demand.

Regional Aquifer Systems of the United States, Aquifers of the Caribbean Islands: Papers Presented at AWRA International Symposium on Tropical Hydrology, July 23-27, 1990, San Juan, Puerto Rico. fac. ed. Ed. by Fernando Gomez-Gomez & Vicente Quinones-Aponte. (AWRA Monograph Ser.: No. 15). 119p. 1991. reprint ed. pap. 34.00 (0-608-00998-9, 2061856) Bks Demand.

Regional Archaeology in Northern Manabi, Ecuador, Vol. 1: Environment, Cultural Chronology, & Prehistoric Subsistence in the Jama River Valley. Ed. by James A. Zeidler & Deborah M. Pearsall. Tr. by Ana M. Boza-Arlotti & Alvaro Higueras-Hare. LC 93-49512. (University of Pittsburgh Memoirs in Latin American Archaeology Ser.: No. 8). (Illus.). xxiv, 224p. (ENG & SPA.). 1994. pap. 20.00 (1-877812-10-2) UPLAAP.

Regional Archaeology in the Muisca Territory: A Study of the Fuquene & Susa Valleys - Arqueologia Regional en el Territorio Musica: Estudio de los Valles de Fuquene y Susa. Carl H. Langeback. Tr. by Roxanna M. Jones. LC 95-21919. (University of Pittsburgh Memoirs in Latin American Archaeology Ser.: No. 9). (ENG & SPA.). 1995. pap. 21.00 (1-877812-34-X) UPLAAP.

Regional Archaeology in the Valle de la Plata, Colombia: A Preliminary Report on the 1984 Season of the Projecto Arqueologico Valle de la Plata. Ed. by Robert Drennan. Tr. by Veronica Kennedy. (Technical Reports: No. 16). (Illus.). 195p. (Orig.). (ENG & SPA.). 1985. pap. 8.00 (*0-915703-06-8*) U Mich Mus Anthro.

Regional Architecture of the Early South. Ed. by Lisa C. Mullins. (Architectural Treasures of Early America Ser.). (Illus.). 245p. 1987. 19.95 (*0-918678-21-8*) Natl Hist Soc.

Regional Arts of the Early South: A Sampling from the Collection of the Museum of Early Southern Decorative Arts. John Bivins, Jr. & Forsyth Alexander. LC 91-60524. (Illus.). 176p. (C). 1991. pap. text ed. 24.95 (*0-945578-02-4*) Mus South Deco.

Regional Aspects of Carbonate Deposition: A Symposium. Ed. by Rufus J. Le Blanc & Julia G. Breeding. LC 57-2837. (Society of Economic Paleontologists & Mineralogists, Special Publication Ser.: No. 5). 215p. reprint ed. pap. 61.30 (*0-317-27104-0*, 2024732) Bks Demand.

Regional Association Five (South-West Pacific) - Abridged Final Report of the Tenth Session: Singapore, 14-24 November, 1989. World Meteorological Organization Staff. (WMO Ser.: No. 730). 118p. 1990. pap. 26.00 (*92-63-10730-0*, Pub. by Wrld Meteorological SZ) Am Meteorological.

Regional Association Four (North & Central America) - Abridged Final Report of the Tenth Session: Tegucigalpa, 3-12 May, 1989. World Meteorological Organization Staff. (WMO Ser.: No. 719). 137p. 1989. pap. 31.00 (*92-63-10719-X*, Pub. by Wrld Meteorological SZ) Am Meteorological.

Regional Association Two (Asia) - Abridged Final Report of the Ninth Session (1988) World Meteorological Organization, Staff. (WMO Ser.: No. 711). xii, 144p. 1989. pap. 38.00 (*92-63-10711-4*, Pub. by Wrld Meteorological SZ) Am Meteorological.

Regional Atlas of Bone Disease: A Guide to Pathologic & Normal Variation in the Human Skeleton. Robert W. Mann & Sean P. Murphy. (Illus.). 224p. 1990. pap. 32.95 (*0-398-06267-6*) C C Thomas.

Regional Atlas of Bone Disease: A Guide to Pathologic & Normal Variation in the Human Skeleton. Robert W. Mann & Sean P. Murphy. (Illus.). 224p. (C). 1990. text ed. 44.95 (*0-398-05675-7*) C C Thomas.

Regional Block: A Handbook for Use in the Clinical Practice of Medicine & Surgery. 4th ed. Daniel C. Moore. (Illus.). 532p. 1981. 46.95 (*0-398-01337-3*) C C Thomas.

*__Regional Blocs.__ Bhalla. LC 97-9155. 1997. text ed. 69.95 (*0-312-17528-0*) St Martin.

Regional Blood Flow & Clinical Considerations. Ed. by B. M. Altura & S. Halevy. (Cardiovascular Actions of Anesthetics & Drugs Used in Anesthesia Ser.: Vol. 2). (Illus.). viii, 296p. 1987. 172.00 (*3-8055-4158-9*) S Karger.

Regional Cancer Treatment. Ed. by K. R. Aigner et al. (Beitraege zur Onkologie, Contributions to Oncology Ser.: Vol. 29). (Illus.). viii, 312p. 1988. 60.00 (*3-8055-4762-5*) S Karger.

Regional Centers in Archaeology: Prospects & Problems. Ed. by William H. Marquardt. LC 77-82743. (Research Ser.: No. 14). (Illus.). 40p. 1977. pap. 4.00 (*0-943414-15-6*) MO Arch Soc.

Regional Chemotherapy. Ed. by U. Laffer. (Antibiotics & Chemotherapy Ser.: Vol. 40). (Illus.). viii, 100p. 1988. 71.25 (*3-8055-4670-X*) S Karger.

*__Regional Climates of the British Isles.__ Dennis Wheeler & Julian Mayes. LC 96-27477. 332p. (C). 1997. pap. write for info. (*0-415-13931-7*); text ed. write for info. (*0-415-13930-9*) Routledge.

Regional Co-Operation & Integration in Asia. OECD Staff. Ed. by K. Fukasaku. 260p. (Orig.). 1995. pap. 48.00 (*92-64-14645-8*, Pub. by Org for Econ FR) OECD.

Regional Conflict & National Policy. Ed. by Kent A. Price. LC 82-47983. xviii, 142p. 1982. pap. 12.95 (*0-8018-2919-4*) Resources Future.

Regional Conflict & U. S. Policy: Angola & Mozambique. Ed. by Richard J. Bloomfield. LC 88-23461. (Illus.). (C). 1988. pap. 12.95 (*0-917256-46-8*); text ed. 24.95 (*0-917256-45-X*) Ref Pubns.

Regional Conflicts & Security Issues Bk. Two. J. Mohan Malik. (Asian Defense Policies Ser.: Bk. 2). 263p. (C). 1995. pap. 72.00 (*0-7300-1720-6*, Pub. by Deakin Univ AT) St Mut.

Regional Conflicts Around Geneva. Adda B. Bozeman. LC 49-10185. (Augustana College Library Publications: No. 20). 432p. 1949. 7.00 (*0-910182-15-9*) Augustana Coll.

Regional Consumption Patterns: A System-Wide Approach. Saroja Selvanathan & E. A. Selvanathan. 235p. 1994. 59.95 (*1-85628-622-3*, Pub. by Avebury Pub UK) Ashgate Pub Co.

Regional Cookbook, Recipe & Cookbook Research Correspondence Course. Cookbook Consortium Educational Division Staff. 1985. ring bd. 26.95 (*0-318-04321-1*) Prosperity & Profits.

Regional Cooperation: Planning & Implementing a Strategy for Economic Development. James Unger. Ed. by Jenny Murphy. 52p. (Orig.). 1988. pap. 18.00 (*0-317-04809-0*) Natl Coun Econ Dev.

Regional Cooperation & Development in South Asia, Vol. I. Bhabani S. Gupta. 1986. 19.00 (*81-7003-065-X*) S Asia.

Regional Cooperation & Development in South Asia, Vol. II. Bhabani S. Gupta. 1986. 19.00 (*81-7003-066-8*) S Asia.

*__Regional Cooperation & Growth Triangles in ASEAN.__ Ed. by Toh M. Heng & Linda Low. 256p. 1993. pap. write for info. (*981-210-021-0*, Pub. by Times Academic SI) Intl Spec Bk.

*__Regional Cooperation & Integration Within Industry & Trade in Southern Africa: General Approaches, SADCC & the World Bank.__ Jens Haarlov. (Making of Modern Africa Ser.). 280p. 1997. text ed. 68.95 (*1-85972-412-4*, Pub. by Avebury Pub UK) Ashgate Pub Co.

Regional Cooperation for Development & the Peaceful Settlement of Disputes in Latin America. Ed. by Jack Child. No. 26. 1987. write for info. (*0-318-61801-X*) Intl Peace.

Regional Cooperation for Development & the Peaceful Settlement of Disputes in Latin American. Ed. by International Peace Academy Staff. 1987. lib. bdg. 79.50 (*0-89838-927-5*) Kluwer Ac.

Regional Cooperation in Export Credit & Export Credit Guarantees. 85p. 1995. 17.00 (*92-1-127035-9*, E.95.II.F.98) UN.

Regional Cooperation in South Asia. Ed. by Bimal Prasad. viii, 221p. 1989. text ed. 27.95 (*0-7069-4264-7*, Pub. by Vikas II) S Asia.

Regional Correlation, Bibliography of East & Southeast Asia, Summary of French Literature on the Quarternary of Cambodia, Lao People's Democratic Republic & Vietnam. 104p. 1993. 35.00 (*92-1-119620-5*, E.93.II.F.15) UN.

Regional Creative Ojo Book. Diane Thomas. LC 75-44654. 1976. pap. 2.95 (*0-918126-02-9*) Hunter Ariz.

Regional, Cultures, Managerial Behavior, & Entrepreneurship: An International Perspective. Ed. by Joseph W. Weiss. LC 87-32278. 216p. 1988. text ed. 55.00 (*0-89930-327-7*, WRI/, Quorum Bks) Greenwood.

Regional Cycles of Manufacturing Employment in the United States, 1914-1953. George H. Borts. (Occasional Papers: No. 73). 57p. 1960. reprint ed. 20.00 (*0-87014-387-5*) Natl Bur Econ Res.

Regional Dances of the Mexico. Edith Johnston. (Illus.). 64p. (J). (gr. 3 up). 1994. pap. 8.95 (*0-8442-7509-3*, Natl Textbk) NTC Pub Grp.

Regional Decline of a National Party: Liberals on the Prairies. David E. Smith. (Canadian Government Ser.). 184p. 1981. pap. 10.95 (*0-8020-6430-2*) U of Toronto Pr.

Regional Decline of a National Party: Liberals on the Prairies. David E. Smith. LC 81-195832. (Canadian Government Ser.: No. 21). 206p. reprint ed. pap. 58.80 (*0-8357-8300-6*, 2034063) Bks Demand.

Regional Depositional Systems Tracts, Paleogeography, & Sequence Stratigraphy, Upper Pennsylvanian & Lower Permian Strata, North- & West-Central Texas. L. F. Brown, Jr. et al. (Report of Investigations Ser.: RI 197). (Illus.). 116p. 1990. pap. 25.00 (*0-317-03122-8*) Bur Econ Geology.

Regional Desparities in India: Rural & Industrial Dimensions. Dietmar Rothermund et al. (C). 1991. 22.00 (*0-8364-2734-3*, Pub. by Manohar II) S Asia.

Regional Development. D. V. Rao & Mudda Vinay. 1990. 20.00 (*81-7001-075-6*, Pub. by Chanakya II) S Asia.

Regional Development: Experiences & Prospects in South & Southeast Asia. Louis Lefeber et al. LC 72-152080. (Regional Planning Ser.: No. 1). 278p. 1971. text ed. 33.85 (*90-279-6914-0*) Mouton.

Regional Development: Experiences & Prospects in the United States of America. John H. Cumberland. 170p. 1971. text ed. 25.00 (*90-279-7266-4*) Mouton.

Regional Development: The USSR & After. Oksana Dmitrieva. LC 95-268. 256p. 1996. text ed. 49.95 (*0-312-12839-8*) St Martin.

Regional Development & Contemporary Industrial Response: Extending Flexible Specialisation. Ed. by Huib Ernste. 256p. 1992. text ed. 65.00 (*1-85293-214-7*) St Martin.

Regional Development & Contemporary Industrial Response: Extending Flexible Specialization. Ed. by Huib Ernste & Verena Meier. LC 00-91. 296p. 1992. text ed. 64.95 (*0-470-21924-6*) Halsted Pr.

Regional Development & the International Division of Labour. G. Van Den Broek et al. (C). 1989. 16.00 (*81-7022-283-4*, Pub. by Concept II) S Asia.

Regional Development & the Local Community: Planning, Politics, & Social Context. Clyde Weaver. LC 83-21640. (Illus.). 215p. reprint ed. pap. 61.30 (*0-8357-7547-X*, 2036269) Bks Demand.

Regional Development in a Modern European Economy: The Case of Tuscany. Ed. by Robert Leonardi & Rafaella Y. Nanetti. 256p. 1994. 49.00 (*1-85567-155-7*) St Martin.

Regional Development in Britain. 2nd ed. Gerald Manners et al. LC 79-42901. (Illus.). 440p. reprint ed. pap. 125.40 (*0-685-20595-9*, 2030529) Bks Demand.

Regional Development in Europe: Recent Initiatives & Experiences - Proceedings of the Fourth International Conference on Science Parks & Innovation Centres Held in Berlin, Nov. 12-13, 1987. Ed. by Jurgen Allesch. xiv, 368p. (C). 1989. lib. bdg. 111.55 (*3-11-011815-7*) De Gruyter.

Regional Development in the Nineteen Nineties: The British Isles in Transition. Ed. by Peter Townroe & Ron Martin. (Regional Policy & Development Ser.: No. 4). 250p. 1992. 57.00 (*1-85302-139-3*) Taylor & Francis.

Regional Development in the U. S. S. R. Trends & Prospects. LC 79-91195. (NATO Colloquium Publications). 1979. 30.00 (*0-89250-115-4*) Orient Res Partners.

Regional Development Problems & Policies in Canada. OECD Staff. 67p. (Orig.). 1994. pap. 20.00 (*92-64-14193-6*) OECD.

Regional Development Problems & Policies in the United Kingdom. OECD Staff. 90p. (Orig.). 1994. pap. 20.00 (*92-64-14194-4*) OECD.

Regional Development Strategies: A European Perspective. Ed. by Jeremy Alden & Philip Boland. LC 95-44356. (Regional Policy & Development Ser.: Vol. 15). 325p. 1996. 34.95 (*1-85302-356-6*, Pub. by J Kingsley Pubs UK) Taylor & Francis.

Regional Development Theories & Their Application. Benjamin Higgins & Donald J. Savoie. LC 93-45849. 356p. (C). 1994. 49.95 (*1-56000-160-7*) Transaction Pubs.

Regional Differences in Family Structure in India. Pauline Kolenda. 400p. 1987. 49.95 (*81-7033-029-7*) Asia Bk Corp.

*__Regional Dimension of R&D & Innovation Statistics - Regional Manual.__ Eurostat Staff. 98p. 1996. pap. 25.00 (*92-827-7003-6*, CA95-96-124-ENC, Pub. by Europ Com UK) Bernan Associates.

*__Regional Dimension of the European Union: Towards a 'Third Level' in Europe?__ Ed. by Charlie Jeffery. LC 96-47846. 240p. (Orig.). 1997. pap. text ed. 19.50 (*0-7146-4306-8*, Pub. by F Cass Pubs UK) Intl Spec Bk.

*__Regional Dimension of the European Union: Towards a 'Third Level' in Europe?__ Ed. by Charlie Jeffery. LC 96-47846. 240p. (Orig.). 1997. text ed. 37.50 (*0-7146-4748-9*, Pub. by F Cass Pubs UK) Intl Spec Bk.

Regional Dimension of Transformation in Central Europe. Grzegorz Gorzelak. (Regional Policy & Development Ser.: No. 10). 300p. 1995. pap. 34.95 (*1-85302-301-9*) Taylor & Francis.

Regional Directory of Minority- & Woman-Owned Businesses, 1992: Central Edition. Ed. by Thomas D. Johnson & Lisa G. Osborn. 750p. (Orig.). 1992. pap. 145.00 (*0-933527-30-6*) Business Research.

Regional Directory of Minority- & Woman-Owned Businesses, 1992: Eastern Edition. Ed. by Thomas D. Johnson & Lisa G. Osborn. 800p. (Orig.). 1992. pap. 145.00 (*0-933527-29-2*) Business Research.

Regional Directory of Minority- & Woman-Owned Businesses, 1992: Western Edition. Ed. by Thomas D. Johnson & Lisa G. Osborn. 725p. (Orig.). 1992. pap. 145.00 (*0-933527-31-4*) Business Research.

Regional Directory of Minority & Woman Owned Business Firms: Central Edition. 6th ed. Ed. by Thomas D. Johnson. 750p. (Orig.). 1994. pap. 175.00 (*0-933527-40-3*) Business Research.

Regional Directory of Minority & Woman Owned Business Firms: Western Edition. 6th ed. Ed. by Thomas D. Johnson. 700p. (Orig.). 1994. pap. 175.00 (*0-933527-41-1*) Business Research.

Regional Directory of Minority-Women Owned Business Firms 1990: Center. 1992. write for info. (*0-8103-9729-3*) Gale.

Regional Directory of Minority-Women Owned Business Firms 1990: East. 1992. write for info. (*0-8103-9730-7*) Gale.

Regional Directory of Minority-Women Owned Business Firms 1990: West. 93th ed. 1994. 628.00 (*0-8103-9901-6*) Gale.

Regional Disaggregation of National Policies & Plans. Ed. by Antoni Kuklinski. (Regional Planning Ser.: No. 8). 1974. text ed. 43.85 (*90-279-7921-9*) Mouton.

Regional Disparities & Development in India. Ed. by Rama S. Tripathi & R. P. Tewari. (Illus.). xxiv, 336p. 1993. 39.00 (*81-7024-599-0*, Pub. by Ashish Pub Hse II) Nataraj Bks.

Regional Disparities & Regional Development: Planning of West Bengal. Firma K. Mukh & Sachi G. Dastidar. (C). 1991. 24.00 (*0-8364-2645-2*, Pub. by Firma KLM II) S Asia.

Regional Dissector of the Cat. Louis J. Zanella. (C). 1993. student ed. 8.81 (*1-56870-047-4*) RonJon Pub.

Regional Distribution of Federal Receipts & Expenditures in the 19th Century: A Quantitative Study. John B. Legler. Ed. by Stuart Bruchey. LC 76-39833. (Nineteen Seventy-Seven Dissertations Ser.). (Illus.). 1977. lib. bdg. 23.95 (*0-405-09913-4*) Ayer.

Regional Diversity: Growth in the United States, 1960-1990. Gregory Jackson et al. LC 81-12768. 216p. 1981. text ed. 21.00 (*0-86569-107-X*, T107, Auburn Hse) Greenwood.

Regional Dynamics, 2 vols. Ed. by Kingsley E. Haynes et al. LC 96-32421. (Modern Classics in Regional Science Ser.: No. 4). 1192p. 1996. 360.00 (*1-85898-111-5*) E Elgar.

Regional Dynamics: Studies in Adjustment Theory. Gordon L. Clark et al. 350p. (C). 1986. text ed. 75.00 (*0-04-330353-6*); pap. text ed. 29.95 (*0-04-330354-4*) Routledge Chapman & Hall.

*__Regional Dynamics: The Basis of Electoral Support in Britain.__ William H. Field. LC 97-1303. 208p. 1997. 42.50 (*0-7146-4782-9*, Pub. by F Cass Pubs UK); pap. 19.50 (*0-7146-4336-X*, Pub. by F Cass Pubs UK) Intl Spec Bk.

Regional Dynamics of Language Differentiation in Belgium: A Study in Cultural-Political Geography. Alexander B. Murphy. (Research Papers: No. 227). 1988. pap. 12.00 (*0-89065-132-9*) U Ch Pr.

Regional Earth Science Information in Local Water Management. Murray B. McPherson. 185p. 1975. pap. 14.00 (*0-87262-151-0*) Am Soc Civil Eng.

Regional Econometric. M. Ray Perryman. 1987. lib. bdg. 95.50 (*0-89838-216-5*) Kluwer Ac.

Regional Economic Analysis of Innovation & Incubation. E. J. Davelaar. 349p. 1991. text ed. 76.95 (*1-85628-139-6*, Pub. by Avebury Pub UK) Ashgate Pub Co.

Regional Economic Co-Operation in South Asia. M. R. Aggarwal. 155p. 1979. 16.95 (*0-318-37268-1*) Asia Bk Corp.

Regional Economic Co-Operation in South Asia. T. Nirmala Devi. 1989. 26.00 (*81-85076-83-9*) S Asia.

Regional Economic Development. O. J. Firestone. LC 75-307808. (Social Science Studies: Vol. 9). 286p. 1974. reprint ed. pap. 81.60 (*0-608-02191-1*, 2062861) Bks Demand.

Regional Economic Development: Canada's Search for Solutions. 2nd ed. Donald J. Savoie. 320p. 1992. 50.00 (*0-8020-2781-4*); pap. 19.95 (*0-8020-6830-8*) U of Toronto Pr.

Regional Economic Development: Canada's Search for Solutions. Donald J. Savoie. LC 86-182040. (Illus.). 222p. reprint ed. pap. 63.30 (*0-8357-6389-7*, 2035744) Bks Demand.

Regional Economic Development: Essays in Honour of Francois Perroux. Donald J. Savoie. (Illus.). 352p. (C). 1987. text ed. 29.95 (*0-04-338155-3*) Routledge Chapman & Hall.

Regional Economic Development: The Federal Role. Gordon C. Cameron. LC 77-86390. (Resources for the Future Ser.). reprint ed. 37.50 (*0-404-60329-7*) AMS Pr.

Regional Economic Development: The Federal Role. Gordon C. Cameron. LC 70-142108. 225p. reprint ed. pap. 64.20 (*0-7837-3576-6*, 2043435) Bks Demand.

*__Regional Economic Development: Theories & Strategies for Developing Countries.__ Marguerite N. Abd El-Shahid. 49p. 1994. pap. 10.00 (*0-86602-304-6*, Sage Prdcls Pr) Sage.

Regional Economic Development in Italy. Lloyd B. Saville. LC 67-21707. 205p. reprint ed. pap. 58.50 (*0-317-20419-X*, 2023444) Bks Demand.

Regional Economic Development in the Middle East: A Survey. James R. Prescott & Bakir Abu-Kishk. (Studies in Technology & Social Change: No. 3). 61p. (Orig.). (C). 1988. pap. 6.00 (*0-945271-03-4*) ISU-CIKARD.

Regional Economic History: The Mid-Alantic Area since 1700. Glenn Porter. 92p. 1976. pap. write for info. (*0-914650-13-0*) Hagley Museum.

Regional Economic Impact from Construction of a Nuclear Electric Generating Plant. Gene Steiker & James Strathman. (Discussion Paper Ser.: No. 91). 1976. pap. 10.00 (*1-55869-105-7*) Regional Sci Res Inst.

Regional Economic Integration & Transnational Corporations in the 1990s: Europe 1992, North America, & Developing Countries. 52p. 1990. 12.50 (*92-1-104343-3*, 90.II.A.14) UN.

Regional Economic Long Waves: Employment Dynamics in the Tri-State Region. James W. Hughes & Joseph J. Seneca. (Rutgers Regional Reports). 366p. 1996. pap. 39.95 (*0-88285-155-1*) Ctr Urban Pol Res.

Regional Economic Modeling: A Systematic Approach to Forecasting & Policy Analysis. George I. Treyz. LC 93-22947. 544p. (C). 1993. lib. bdg. 126.00 (*0-7923-9382-1*) Kluwer Ac.

Regional Economic Modeling in the Soviet Union. Misha V. Belkindas. Ed. by Anne H. Johnson. (Illus.). ix, 102p. (Orig.). 1989. pap. text ed. 75.00 (*1-55831-089-4*) Delphic Associates.

Regional Economic Modeling in Theory & in Practice. Curtis C. Harris, Jr. & Mehrzad Nadji. LC 87-10444. 174p. (Orig.). 1987. lib. bdg. 43.50 (*0-8191-6389-9*) U Pr of Amer.

Regional Economic Policy. Hendrik Folmer. 1986. lib. bdg. 101.50 (*90-247-3308-1*) Kluwer Ac.

Regional Economic Structure & Environmental Pollution. B. E. Coupe. (Studies in Applied Regional Science: No. 5). 1977. pap. text ed. 60.00 (*90-207-0646-2*) Kluwer Ac.

Regional Economics. Marion Temple. LC 94-7206. 1994. text ed. 55.00 (*0-312-12225-X*, Pub. by Macm UK) St Martin.

Regional Effects of U. S. Direct Investment Abroad. Norman J. Glickman & Geoffrey J. Bannister. (Working Paper Ser.: No. 47). 42p. 1988. pap. 5.00 (*0-89940-528-2*) LBJ Sch Pub Aff.

Regional Emigration & Remittances in Developing Countries: The Portuguese Experience. Rick L. Chaney. LC 85-19382. 270p. 1986. text ed. 55.00 (*0-275-92018-6*, C2018, Praeger Pubs) Greenwood.

Regional Employment Programme for Latin America & the Caribbean: Employment in Latin America. LC 78-19459. (Praeger Special Studies). 208p. 1978. text ed. 55.00 (*0-275-90309-5*, C0309, Praeger Pubs) Greenwood.

*__Regional Energy & Economic Self-Sufficiency Indicators in the Southeastern United States.__ Skip Laitner & Marshall Goldberg. (Illus.). 76p. (Orig.). (C). 1997. pap. text ed. 30.00 (*0-7881-3744-1*) DIANE Pub.

Regional Flood Frequency Analysis. Ed. by Vijay P. Singh. (C). 1987. lib. bdg. 156.50 (*90-277-2575-6*) Kluwer Ac.

*__Regional Foods of Northern Italy: Recipes & Remembrances.__ Marlena Di Blasi. LC 97-14389. 1997. 20.00 (*0-7615-0905-4*) Prima Pub.

Regional French Cuisines: From Normandy to Provence. Janet K. Fletcher & Hallie Herron. LC 94-28048. (Kitchen Arts Ser.). 128p. 1995. pap. 11.95 (*1-56426-070-4*) Cole Group.

Regional French of County Beauce, Quebec. Raleigh Morgan, Jr. LC 74-78061. (Janua Linguarum, Series Practica: No. 177). 128p. 1975. pap. text ed. 64.65 (*90-279-3107-0*) Mouton.

*__Regional Frequency Analysis: An Approach Based on L-Moments.__ J. R. Hosking & James R. Wallis. LC 97-4007. (Illus.). 224p. (C). 1997. text ed. 69.95 (*0-521-43045-3*) Cambridge U Pr.

Regional Futures & Transatlantic Economic Relations. Miles Kahler. LC 95-41303. 100p. (Orig.). 1996. pap. 15.95 (*0-87609-182-6*) Coun Foreign.

Regional Garden Design in the United States. Ed. by Therese O'Malley & Marc Trieb. LC 93-23720. (Colloquium on the History of Landscape Architecture Ser.: No. 15). 1995. 50.00 (*0-88402-223-4*) Dumbarton Oaks.

R

R

Regional Geography see International Geography - 76

***Regional Geography of Africa.** Senior. 1983. pap. text ed. write for info. (0-582-60390-0, Pub. by Longman UK) Longman.

***Regional Geography of the United States & Canada.** 2nd ed. Tom L. McKnight. LC 96-46115. (Illus.). 576p. (C). 1997. text ed. 63.00 (0-13-456484-7) P-H.

Regional Geography of the World. Wheeler. (C). 1990. student ed., suppl. ed., pap. text ed. 34.00 (0-03-032629-X) HB Coll Pubs.

Regional Geography of United States & Canada. Tom L. McKnight. 608p. 1991. text ed. 63.00 (0-13-352956-8) P-H.

Regional Geology of Africa. S. W. Petters. (Lecture Notes in Earth Sciences Ser.: Vol. 40). (Illus.). xxii, 722p. 1991. 110.00 (0-387-54528-X) Spr-Verlag.

Regional Geology of Czechoslovakia, Pt. 1: The Bohemia Massif. Ed. by J. Svoboda. (Illus.). 668p. 1966. 55.00 (3-510-99065-X) Lubrecht & Cramer.

Regional Geology of Czechoslovakia, Pt. 2: The West Carpathians. Ed. by M. Mahel & T. Buday. (Illus.). 723p. 1968. 45.50 (3-510-99066-8) Lubrecht & Cramer.

Regional Geology of Eastern Idaho & Western Wyoming. Ed. by P. K. Link et al. (Memoir Ser.: No. 179). (Illus.). 1992. 44.38 (0-8137-1179-7) Geol Soc.

Regional Ground Water Quality. W. Alley. 1993. text ed. 109.95 (0-442-00937-2) Van Nos Reinhold.

Regional Growth ... Local Reaction: The Enactment & Effects of Local Growth Control & Management Measures in California. Madelyn Glickfeld & Ned Levine. (Illus.). 160p. (Orig.). 1992. pap. text ed. 15.00 (1-55844-119-0) Lincoln Inst Land.

Regional Growth & Decline in the United States. 2nd ed. Bernard L. Weinstein & John Rees. LC 85-6319. 176p. 1985. text ed. 49.95 (0-275-90184-X, C0184, Praeger Pubs) Greenwood.

***Regional Growth & Regional Policy Within the Framework of European Integration.** Ed. by K. Peschel. (Contributions to Economics Ser.). (Illus.). 197p. 1996. pap. 67.00 (3-7908-0957-8) Spr-Verlag.

Regional Health Facility System Planning: An Access Opportunity Approach. Jerry B. Schneider & John G. Symons, Jr. (Discussion Paper Ser.: No. 48). 1971. pap. 10.00 (1-55869-106-5) Regional Sci Res Inst.

Regional History of the Railways of Great Britain, Vol. 5: Eastern Counties. Donald I. Gordon. Ed. by David J. Thomas. LC 76-385595. (Illus.). 256p. 1968. 24.95 (0-678-05734-6) Kelley.

Regional Holding Companies Refocus Channel Efforts: Returning to Home Regions & Telecon Products. Market Intelligence Staff. 341p. (Orig.). 1992. 1,295.00 (1-56753-049-4) Frost & Sullivan.

Regional Housing & Labour Markets. Ed. by Manfred M. Fischer et al. LC 96-27870. (Modern Classics in Regional Science Ser.: No. 5). 584p. 1996. 185.00 (1-85898-112-3) E Elgar.

Regional Housing Opportunities for Lower Income Households: A Resource Guide to Affordable Housing & Regional Mobility Strategies. Robert W. Burchell et al. 236p. (Orig.). (C). 1995. pap. text ed. 45.00 (0-7881-2134-0) DIANE Pub.

Regional Human Rights: A Comparative Study of the West European & Inter-American Systems. A. Glenn Mower, Jr. LC 91-28. (Studies in Human Rights: No. 12). 192p. 1991. text ed. 55.00 (0-313-27235-2, MRF, Greenwood Pr) Greenwood.

***Regional Hydrological Response to Climate Change.** Ed. by J. A. Jones. LC 96-49481. (GeoJournal Library). 440p. (C). 1997. lib. bdg. 199.00 (0-7923-4329-8) Kluwer Ac.

***Regional Identity & Economic Change: THe Upper Rhine 1450-1600.** Tom Scott. (Illus.). 270p. 1997. 75.00 (0-19-820644-5) OUP.

Regional Identity under Soviet Rule: The Case of the Baltic States. Ed. by Dietrich A. Loeber et al. (Illus.). xx, 469p. 1989. 50.00 (0-685-29788-8) Assn Advan Baltic Studies.

Regional Imagination: The South & Recent American History. Dewey W. Grantham. LC 78-26556. 283p. reprint ed. pap. 80.70 (0-685-17860-9, 2029468) Bks Demand.

***Regional Immunology.** J. Wayne Streilein. 1988. pap. text ed. 40.00 (0-471-61047-X) Wiley.

Regional Impact of Community Policies in Europe. Willem Molle & Riccardo Cappellin. 210p. 1988. text ed. 76.95 (0-566-05587-2, Pub. by Avebury Pub UK) Ashgate Pub Co.

***Regional Impact of the Channel Tunnel Throughout the Community.** 315p. 1996. pap. 60.00 (92-826-8804-6, CX85-94-559-ENC, Pub. by Europ Com UK) Bernan Associates.

Regional Impacts of Global Climate Change: Assessing Change & Response at the Scales That Matter. Ed. by S. J. Ghan. LC 95-46745. 1996. 57.50 (1-57477-017-9) Battelle.

Regional Impacts of U. S. - Mexican Relations. Intro. by Ina Rosenthal-Urey. (Monographs: No. 16). 152p. (Orig.). (C). 1986. pap. 12.50 (0-935391-67-3, MN-16) UCSD Ctr US-Mex.

Regional Imperative: Regional Planning & Governance in Britain, Europe & the United States. Urlan A. Wannop. LC 95-4118. (Regional Policy & Development Ser.: Vol. 9). 450p. 1995. pap. 49.95 (1-85302-292-6) Taylor & Francis.

Regional Imperatives in Utilization & Management of Resources: India & the U. S. S. R. Manzoor Alam & Atiya H. Kidwai. 1987. 58.50 (0-8364-2256-2, Pub. by Concept II) S Asia.

Regional Incentives & the Quality, Vol. 41/1. Amin et al. (Progress in Polymer Science Ser.: No. 41/1). 120p. 1994. pap. 61.00 (0-08-042481-3, Pergamon Pr) Elsevier.

Regional Income. (Studies in Income & Wealth: No. 21). 419p. 1957. reprint ed. 109.00 (0-87014-177-5) Natl Bur Econ Res.

Regional Income Inequality & Poverty in the UK: An Analysis Based on the 1985 Family Expenditure Survey. Vani K. Borooah et al. 208p. 1991. text ed. 55.95 (1-85521-075-4, Pub. by Dartmth Pub UK) Ashgate Pub Co.

Regional Incomes in the United States, 1929-1967: Level, Distribution, Stability, & Growth. Philip M. Lankford. LC 72-91224. (University of Chicago Department of Geography Research Paper Ser.: Vol. 145). 150p. 1972. reprint ed. pap. 42.80 (0-608-02433-3, 2063076) Bks Demand.

Regional Industrial Co-Operation: Experiences & Perspectives of ASEAN & the Andean Pact. 102p. 1986. 9.00 (92-1-106204-7, E.85.II.B.5) UN.

***Regional Innovation Systems: The Role of Governances in a Globalized World.** Ed. by Philip Cooke et al. 272p. 1996. 75.00 (1-85728-689-8, Pub. by UCL Pr UK); pap. 26.95 (1-85728-690-1, Pub. by UCL Pr UK) Taylor & Francis.

Regional Input Output Model & Economic Multipliers for the San Francisco Bay Region: 1987. 40p. 1991. 35.00 (0-318-22684-7) Assn Bay Area.

Regional Input-Output Modelling: New Developments & Interpretations. J. H. Dewhurst et al. 282p. 1991. text ed. 72.95 (1-85628-119-1, Pub. by Avebury Pub UK) Ashgate Pub Co.

***Regional Integration, Vol. 1.** Oyejide. LC 96-49387. 1997. text ed. 69.95 (0-312-17321-0) St Martin.

Regional Integration: The West European Experience. William Wallace. (Integrating National Economies Ser.). 142p. (C). 1995. 34.95 (0-8157-9224-7); pap. 14.95 (0-8157-9223-9) Brookings.

Regional Integration: Theory & Research. Ed. by Leon N. Lindberg & Stuart A. Scheingold. LC 77-139717. (Illus.). 439p. 1971. pap. 15.95 (0-674-75327-5) HUP.

Regional Integration among Developing Countries: Opportunities, Obstacles & Options. Rolf J. Langhammer & Ulrich Hiemenz. 112p. (Orig.). (C). 1992. pap. text ed. 34.50 (0-472-10376-8) U of Mich Pr.

Regional Integration Among the Asian Nations: A Computable General Equilibrium Model Study. Innwon Park. LC 94-37884. 156p. 1995. text ed. 57.95 (0-275-94981-8, Praeger Pubs) Greenwood.

***Regional Integration & Cooperation in West Africa: A Multidimensional Perspective.** Real P. Lavergne. LC 97-4957. 1997. pap. text ed. 21.95 (0-86543-567-7) Africa World.

***Regional Integration & Cooperation in West Africa: A Multidimensional Perspective.** Real P. Lavergne. LC 97-4957. 1997. write for info. (0-86543-566-9) Africa World.

Regional Integration & Developing Countries. OECD Staff. 96p. (Orig.). 1993. pap. 28.00 (92-64-13909-5) OECD.

***Regional Integration & Global Free Trade: Addressing the Fundamental Conflicts.** Mark S. LeClair. 128p. 1997. text ed. 49.95 (1-85972-574-0, Pub. by Avebury Pub UK) Ashgate Pub Co.

Regional Integration and Industrial Relations in North America. Ed. by Maria L. Cook & Harry C. Katz. LC 94-23338. 1994. pap. 28.95 (0-87546-851-9, ILR Press) Cornell U Pr.

Regional Integration & the Asia Pacific. Ed. by Bijit Bora & Christopher Findlay. 272p. 1996. 85.00 (0-19-553635-5) OUP.

Regional Integration & the Global Trading System. Ed. by Kym Anderson & Richard Blackhurst. LC 93-10640. 1993. text ed. 45.00 (0-312-10065-5) St Martin.

Regional Integration & the Multilateral Trading System: Synergy & Divergence. 92p. (Orig.). 1995. pap. 19.00 (92-64-14432-3, Pub. by Org for Econ FR) OECD.

***Regional Integration & Transition Economies: The Case of the Baltic Rim.** OECD Staff. 212p. (Orig.). 1996. pap. 29.00 (92-64-14929-5, 14-96-11-1, Pub. by Org for Econ FR) OECD.

Regional Integration in East & West. Christopher T. Saunders. LC 83-9796. 280p. 1983. text ed. 32.50 (0-312-66917-8) St Martin.

Regional Integrations in the New World Economic Environment. Andras Inotaj. 286p. (C). 1986. 60.00 (963-05-4353-2, Pub. by Akad Kiado HU) St Mut.

Regional Interest Magazines of the United States: Historical Guides to the World's Periodicals & Newspapers. Ed. by Sam G. Riley & Gary W. Selnow. LC 90-36739. 432p. 1990. text ed. 99.50 (0-313-26840-1, RRI, Greenwood Pr) Greenwood.

***Regional Italian Cooking.** Diane Seed. Date not set. write for info. (0-688-12789-4) Morrow.

Regional Italian Kitchen. Nika Hazelton. LC 78-3717. (Illus.). 370p. 1978. 18.95 (0-87131-252-2) M Evans.

Regional Italian Seafood: Authentic Italian Kitchen. Pietro Semino. Tr. & Intro. by Michael Sola. (Authentic Italian Kitchen Ser.). (Illus.). 136p. 1995. 15.95 (0-9642027-1-9) Strawpaper Pr.

Regional Italian Specialties. Renato Rudatis. Ed. by Sonia Allison. (Gourmet Cookshelf Ser.). (Illus.). 64p. 1992. 13.95 (0-572-01707-3, Pub. by W Foulsham UK) Trans-Atl Phila.

Regional Landscapes of the United States & Canada. 4th ed. Stephen S. Birdsall & John W. Florin. LC 91-14787. 528p. (C). 1991. text ed. 46.00 (0-471-61646-X) Wiley.

Regional Language in France. Ed. by Andree Tabouret-Keller. (International Journal of the Sociology of Language Ser.: No. 29). 1980. pap. text ed. 60.00 (3-11-000343-0) Mouton.

Regional Levies Handbook. 2nd ed. T. S. Emslie. 176p. 1991. pap. 41.00 (0-409-07680-5, SA) MICHIE.

Regional Long Waves, Uneven Growth & the Cooperative Alternative. Douglas E. Booth. LC 87-2348. 126p. 1987. text ed. 47.95 (0-275-92567-6, C2567, Praeger Pubs) Greenwood.

Regional Management of Metropolitan Floodplains. Ed. by Rutherford H. Platt. (Program on Environment & Behavior Monograph Ser.: No. 45). 334p. (Orig.). (C). 1987. pap. 10.00 (0-685-28119-1) Natural Hazards.

Regional Markets & Agrarian Transformation in Bolivia: Cochabamba, 1539-1960. Robert H. Jackson. LC 94-18693. (Illus.). 294p. 1994. 29.95 (0-8263-1533-X) U of NM Pr.

Regional Metamorphism of Ore Deposits & Genetic Implications. Ed. by P. G. Spry & L. T. Bryndzia. (Illus.). 252p. 1990. 105.00 (90-6764-126-X, Pub. by VSP NE) Coronet Bks.

Regional Migrations, Ethnicity & Security. Lok Raj Baral. (South Asian Case Ser.). 1989. text ed. 27.95 (81-207-1103-3, Pub. by Sterling Pubs II) Apt Bks.

Regional Ministers: Power & Influence in the Canadian Cabinet. Herman Bakvis. 416p. 1991. 60.00 (0-8020-2622-2); pap. 22.95 (0-8020-6698-4) U of Toronto Pr.

Regional Models of Trade & Development. B. S. Berendsen. (Studies in Development & Planning: Vol. 7). 1978. lib. bdg. 65.00 (90-207-0753-1) Kluwer Ac.

***Regional Myocardial Blood Flow & Metabolism in Chronic & Acute Heart Disease: A Study with Positron Emission Tomography.** Alex Maes. (Acta Biomedica Loveniensia Ser.: No. 131). (Illus.). 129p. (Orig.). 1996. pap. 39.50 (90-6186-747-9, Pub. by Leuven Univ BE) Coronet Bks.

Regional Network for Latin America on Animal Disease Diagnosis Using Immunoassay & Labelled DNA Probe Techniques. (Illus.). 196p. (Orig.). (C). 1993. pap. text ed. 50.00 (1-56806-391-1) DIANE Pub.

Regional Oceanography: An Introduction. Matthias Tomczak & J. Stuart Godfrey. LC 93-30118. 432p. 1994. text ed. 135.00 (0-08-041021-9, Pergamon Press); pap. text ed. 39.95 (0-08-041020-0, Pergamon Press) Buttrwrth-Heinemann.

Regional Opioid Analgesia. J. De Castro et al. (Developments in Anesthesiology & Critical Care Ser.). (C). 1990. lib. bdg. 319.00 (0-7923-0162-5) Kluwer Ac.

***Regional Orders: Building Security in a New World.** David A. Lake & Patrick M. Morgan. LC 96-50186. 1997. 55.00 (0-271-01703-1); pap. 19.95 (0-271-01704-X) Pa St U Pr.

Regional Organisations: A Third World Perspective. Ed. by Rama S. Melkote. 220p. 1990. text ed. 27.95 (81-207-1130-0, Pub. by Sterling Pubs II) Apt Bks.

Regional Organization of the Hohokam in the American Southwest: A Stylistic Analysis of Red-on-Buff Pottery. Jill E. Neitzel. LC 90-28291. (Evolution of North American Indians Ser.). 215p. 1991. reprint ed. text ed. 20.00 (0-8240-2509-1) Garland.

Regional Organization of the Social Security Administration. John A. Davis. LC 68-59254. (Columbia University. Studies in the Social Sciences: No. 571). reprint ed. 32.50 (0-404-51571-1) AMS Pr.

Regional Peacekeeping & International Enforcement: The Liberian Crisis. Ed. by Marc Weller. (International Documents Ser.: No. 6). (Illus.). 493p. (C). 1994. text ed. 95.00 (0-521-47754-9) Cambridge U Pr.

Regional Perspective on Dry Farming. Salahudin Qureshi. (C). 1989. 34.00 (81-7033-072-6, Pub. by Rawat II) S Asia.

Regional Perspectives on the Puerto Rican Experience. Ed. by Carlos E. Cortes. LC 79-6231. (Hispanics in the United States Ser.). 1981. lib. bdg. 81.95 (0-405-13178-X) Ayer.

Regional Petroleum Geology of the World Vol. 21, Part 1: Europe & Asia. Ed. by Holger Kulke. (Beitraege Zur Regionalen Geologie Der Erde). (Illus.). 931p. 1994. lib. bdg. 225.00 (0-614-01283-X, Pub. by Shire Pubns UK) Lubrecht & Cramer.

Regional Petroleum Geology of the World, Pt. 1, Europe & Asian: Regionale Erdoel und Erdgasgeologie der ErdeTeil, Pt. 1, Europe und Asien. Holger Kulke. (Beitraege Zur Regionalen Geologie der Erde Ser.: Vol. 21). (Illus.). xxii, 936p. 1994. lib. bdg. 210.00 (3-443-11021-5) Lubrecht & Cramer.

Regional Physical Mapping. Ed. by Kay E. Davies & Shirley M. Tilghman. (Genome Analysis Ser.: Vol. 5). (Illus.). 200p. (C). 1993. text ed. 25.00 (0-87969-413-0) Cold Spring Harbor.

Regional Plan of New York & Its Environs: The Graphic Regional Plan, Set. Ed. by Richard C. Wade. Incl. Building of the City by Thomas Adams. LC 73-2914. 1974. (0-318-50879-6); LC 73-2914. (Metropolitan America Ser.). 930p. 1974. reprint ed. 57.95 (0-405-05413-0) Ayer.

***Regional Plan of NY, Vol. 1.** Date not set. 28.95 (0-405-05412-2) Ayer.

Regional Planner. Jack Rudman. (Career Examination Ser.: C-694). 1994. pap. 27.95 (0-8373-0694-9) Nat Learn.

Regional Planning: Introduction and Explanation. Melville C. Branch. LC 87-27314. 222p. 1988. text ed. 59.95 (0-275-92403-3, C2403, Praeger Pubs); pap. text ed. 19.95 (0-275-92539-0, B2539, Praeger Pubs) Greenwood.

Regional Planning Guidance for the West Midlands Region. H. M. S. O. Staff. 70p. 1995. pap. 20.00 (0-11-753141-3, HM31413, Pub. by Stationery Ofc UK) Bernan Associates.

Regional Policies in Nigeria, India & Brazil. Ed. by Antoni Kuklinski. (Regional Planning Ser.: Vol. 9). 1978. text ed. 61.55 (90-279-7842-5) Mouton.

Regional Policy. Nigel Copperthwaite & Colin Mellors. (Spicers European Policy Reports). 240p. (C). 1990. pap. text ed. 150.00 (0-415-03828-6, A4394) Routledge.

Regional Policy. Ed. by Jill Preston. (Spicers European Union Policy Briefings Ser.). 228p. 1994. 150.00 (1-56159-083-5, Stockton Pr) Groves Dictionaries.

Regional Policy: A European Approach. Norbert Vanhove & Leo H. Klaassen. LC 79-55648. 540p. 1980. text ed. 60.00 (0-916672-49-2, R3416) Rowman.

Regional Policy & Local Governments: Studies in English. Gy Horvath. (Illus.). 215p. (C). 1991. pap. 120.00 (963-8371-58-7, Pub. by Akad Kiado HU) St Mut.

Regional Policy & Local Governments: Studies in English. Gy Horvath. 215p. (C). 1991. pap. 140.00 (963-05-7158-7, Pub. by Akad Kiado HU) St Mut.

Regional Policy & Regional Integration. Ed. by Niles Hansen et al. LC 96-27872. (Modern Classics in Regional Science Ser.: No. 6). 672p. 1996. 200.00 (1-85898-113-1) E Elgar.

Regional Policy & Technology Transfer: A Cross-National Perspective. K. Clement et al. 113p. 1995. pap. text ed. 40.00 (0-11-515357-8, HM53578, Pub. by Stationery Ofc UK) Bernan Associates.

Regional Policy in a Changing World. N. Hansen et al. LC 89-29566. (Environment, Development, & Public Policy: Public Policy & Social Services Ser.). (Illus.). 325p. 1990. 54.50 (0-306-43300-1, Plenum Pr) Plenum.

Regional Policy in Europe. S. S. Artobolevskiy. 300p. 1995. pap. text ed. 39.95 (1-85302-308-6) Taylor & Francis.

Regional Policy, Transport Networks & Communications. OECD Staff. (ECMT Round Table Ser.). 140p. (Orig.). 1994. pap. 22.00 (92-821-1191-1) OECD.

Regional Politics: America in a Post City Era. H. V. Savitch & Ronald K. Vogel. (Urban Affairs Annual Review Ser.: Vol. 45). 336p. 1996. 58.00 (0-8039-5890-0); pap. 24.95 (0-8039-5891-9) Sage.

Regional Power Rivalries in the New Eurasia: Russia, Turkey, & Iran. Ed. by Alvin Z. Rubinstein & Oles M. Smolansky. LC 95-6805. 304p. (C). (gr. 13). 1995. text ed. 69.95 (1-56324-622-8) M E Sharpe.

Regional Power Rivalries in the New Eurasia: Russia, Turkey, & Iran. Ed. by Alvin Z. Rubinstein & Oles M. Smolansky. LC 95-6805. 304p. (C). (gr. 13). 1995. pap. text ed. 26.95 (1-56324-623-6) M E Sharpe.

Regional Powers & Small State Security: India & Sri Lanka, 1977-1990. K. M. De Silva. (Woodrow Wilson Center Press Ser.). (Illus.). 400p. 1995. text ed. 48.50 (0-8018-5149-1) Johns Hopkins.

Regional Price Formation in Eastern Europe. Jozef M. Van Brabant. (C). 1987. lib. bdg. 156.50 (90-247-3540-8) Kluwer Ac.

***Regional Problems & Policies in Japan.** 72p. (Orig.). 1996. pap. 22.00 (92-64-15334-9, 04-96-06-1, Pub. by Org for Econ FR) OECD.

***Regional Problems & Policies in the Czech Republic & the Slovak Republic.** 143p. 1996. 30.00 (92-64-14828-0, 14-96-09-1, Pub. by Org for Econ FR) OECD.

Regional Problems, Problem Regions & Public Policy in the U. K. Ed. by Peter Damesick & Peter H. Wood. (Illus.). 288p. 1987. 69.00 (0-19-823257-8) OUP.

Regional Pulmonary Function in Health & Disease. Ed. by B. L. Holman & J. F. Lindeman. (Progress in Nuclear Medicine Ser.: Vol. 3). 196p. 1973. 56.00 (3-8055-1425-5) S Karger.

Regional Reporter Citations. Shepard's Citation, Inc. Staff. 1989. write for info. (0-318-59341-6) Shepards.

Regional Reporters. write for info. (0-318-57503-5) West Pub.

Regional Residuals Environmental Quality Management Modeling. Ed. by Blair T. Bower. LC 77-92413. (Resources for the Future, RFF Research Paper Ser.: NO. R-7). 244p. reprint ed. pap. 69.60 (0-317-26044-8, 2023786) Bks Demand.

Regional Review of the Stock of Hospital Floorspace. G. Samuelsson-Brown & S. Whittome. 1992. 400.00 (0-86022-321-3, Pub. by Build Servs Info Assn UK) St Mut.

Regional Roots of Indian Nationalism: Gunarat, Maharashtra & Rajasthan. Ed. by Markand Mehta. (C). 1990. 42.00 (0-8364-2485-9, Pub. by Criterion II) S Asia.

Regional Russian Recipes. Susan Ward. 1993. 12.98 (1-55521-905-5) Bk Sales Inc.

***Regional Sales Handbook.** unabridged ed. Woody Totcove & Gloria Leacox. 300p. (Orig.). 1996. pap. 295.00 (1-890299-02-2) Gov Technology.

Regional Satellite Oceanography. Serge Victorov. 256p. 1996. 79.95 (0-7484-0273-X); pap. 44.95 (0-7484-0274-8) Taylor & Francis.

Regional Science: Perspectives for the Future. Ed. by Manas Chatterji. 464p. 1997. text ed. 79.95 (0-312-15930-7) St Martin.

Regional Science: Retrospect & Prospect. Ed. by D. E. Boyce et al. (Illus.). viii, 505p. 1991. 123.95 (0-387-53493-8) Spr-Verlag.

Regional Science in Developing Countries. Ed. by Manas Chatterji & Kaizhong Yang. LC 96-30370. 432p. 1997. text ed. 79.95 (0-312-12981-5) St Martin.

Regional Security after the Cold War. Ed. by James E. Goodby. (SIPRI Publication). 280p. 1995. 49.95 (0-19-829171-X) OUP.

Regional Security & Confidence-Building Processes: The Case of Southern Africa. (Disarmament Topical Papers: No. 16). 57p. Date not set. pap. 13.00 (92-9045-079-7, E.GV.93.0.6) UN.

Regional Security in the Middle East. Ed. by Charles R. Tripp. LC 83-40155. (Adelphi Library). 192p. 1984. text ed. 29.95 (0-312-66940-2) St Martin.

***Regional Security in the Middle East: Past, Present & Future.** Zeev Maoz. LC 97-22900. 1997. write for info. (0-7146-4808-6, Pub. by F Cass Pubs UK); pap. write for info. (0-7146-4375-0, Pub. by F Cass Pubs UK) Intl Spec Bk.

An Asterisk (*) at the beginning of an entry indicates that the title is appearing in BIP for the first time.

Regional Security Regimes: Israel & Its Neighbors. Ed. by Efraim Inbar. LC 94-5046. (SUNY Series in Israeli Studies). 313p. (C). 1995. text ed. 59.50 (*0-7914-2323-9*); pap. text ed. 19.95 (*0-7914-2324-7*) State U NY Pr.

Regional Shopping Centres: Out-of-Town Versus In-Town. Mark Thompson & Peter McGoldrick. 211p. 1992. 63.95 (*1-85628-114-0*, Pub. by Avebury Pub UK) Ashgate Pub Co.

Regional Silviculture of the United States. 3rd ed. John W. Barrett. 643p. 1994. text ed. 89.95 (*0-471-59817-8*) Wiley.

Regional Sketches. Harriet Beecher Stowe. Ed. by John R. Adams. (Masterworks of Literature Ser.). 1972. 18.95 (*0-8084-0024-X*); pap. 14.95 (*0-8084-0025-8*) NCUP.

Regional Specialization, Employment & Economic Growth in Belgium from 1846 to 1970. Guido L. De Brabander. Ed. by Stuart Bruchey. LC 80-2797. (Dissertations in European Economic History Ser.). (Illus.). 1981. lib. bdg. 30.95 (*0-405-13981-0*) Ayer.

Regional Statistics: A Guide to Information Sources. Ed. by M. Balachandran. LC 80-14260. (Economics Information Guide Ser.: Vol. 13). 272p. 1980. 68.00 (*0-8103-1463-0*) Gale.

Regional Stock Exchanges in a Central Market System: Conference Volume. (Explorations in Economic Research Two Ser.: No. 3). 183p. 1975. reprint ed. 35.00 (*0-685-61386-0*) Natl Bur Econ Res.

Regional Strategy for Environmental Protection & Rational Use of Natural Resources. 52p. 1988. 9.00 (*92-1-116431-1*, E. 88. II.E.26) UN.

Regional Strategy for Health Care of the Elderly in the Eastern Mediterranean Region: 1992-2001. (Regional Advisory Panel on Health Care of the Elderly Ser.). 22p. 1994. pap. text ed. 6.00 (*92-9021-188-1*, 1440009) World Health.

Regional Stratigraphy of North America. W. J. Frazier & D. R. Schwimmer. LC 87-7019. (Illus.). 744p. 1987. 165. 00 (*0-306-42324-3*, Plenum Pr) Plenum.

Regional Structural Change: Experience & Prospects in Two Mature Economies. Lay J. Gibson & Robert J. Stimson. Ed. by Benjamin H. Stevens. (Monograph Ser.: No. 8). (Illus.). 161p. (C). 1989. pap. 23.00 (*1-55869-136-7*) Regional Sci Res Inst.

Regional Structural Change & Industrial Policy in International Perspective: United States, Great Britain, France, Federal Republic of Germany. Ed. by Joachim J. Hesse. 600p. 1988. 168.00 (*3-7890-1508-3*, Pub. by Nomos Verlags GW) Intl Bk Import.

Regional Structure of Development & Growth in India, 2 vols., 1. Ed. by G. P. Mishra & A. Joshi. 1985. 38.00 (*0-8364-1446-2*, Pub. by Ashish II) S Asia.

Regional Studies: The Interplay of Land & People. Ed. by Glen E. Lich. LC 91-4133. (Elma Dill Russell Spencer Series in the West & Southwest: No. 12). (Illus.). 198p. 1992. 33.95 (*0-89096-477-7*) Tex A&M Univ Pr.

Regional Studies & Specific Developments see Handbook of Strata-Bound & Stratiform Ore Deposits

Regional Studies, Methods & Analyses: Selected Papers Submitted at the International Geographical Union's European Regional Conference, Budapest. I. Bencze & Gy Bora. 416p. (C). 1974. 78.00 (*963-05-0417-0*, Pub. by Akad Kiado HU) St Mut.

Regional Studies of Europe. Russell Ivy. 196p. (C). 1995. pap. text ed., spiral bd. 31.44 (*0-7872-0430-7*) Kendall-Hunt.

Regional Studies of the Potwar Plateau Area, Northern Pakistan. Ed. by Peter D. Warwick & Bruce R. Wardlaw. LC 95-9726. (Bulletin Ser.: Vol. 2078). 1995. write for info. (*0-615-00607-8*) US Geol Survey.

Regional Studies, Vol. 5 see Handbook of Strata-Bound & Stratiform Ore Deposits

Regional Survey of New York & Its Environs, 10 Vols. Ed. by Richard C. Wade. (Metropolitan America Ser.). (Illus.). 1974. 204.00 (*0-405-05439-4*) Ayer.

Regional Systems: IGU Congress, Moscow, 1976, Proceedings, Pt. 2. Ed. by Yuri Medvedkov. 1977. pap. 23.00 (*0-08-021323-5*, Pergamon Pr) Elsevier.

Regional Technology Guide: Central U. S. 1997. 175.00 (*0-936507-88-8*) CorpTech.

Regional Technology Guide: Eastern Lakes. annuals 1997. 175.00 (*0-936507-87-X*) CorpTech.

Regional Technology Guide: Great Lakes. annuals 1997. 175.00 (*0-936507-86-1*) CorpTech.

Regional Technology Guide: Mid Atlantic. annuals 1997. 175.00 (*0-936507-78-0*) CorpTech.

Regional Technology Guide: Midwest. annuals 1997. 175.00 (*0-936507-85-3*) CorpTech.

Regional Technology Guide: New England. annuals 1996. 175.00 (*0-936507-81-0*) CorpTech.

Regional Technology Guide: New York Metro. annuals 1996. 175.00 (*0-936507-77-2*) CorpTech.

Regional Technology Guide: NJ & Delaware Valley. annuals 1996. 175.00 (*0-936507-83-7*) CorpTech.

Regional Technology Guide: Northern California. 1996. 175.00 (*0-936507-90-X*) CorpTech.

Regional Technology Guide: Northwest U. S. 1997. 175.00 (*0-936507-89-6*) CorpTech.

Regional Technology Guide: Southeast U. S. annuals 1996. 175.00 (*0-936507-84-5*) CorpTech.

Regional Technology Guide: Southern California. 1996. 175.00 (*0-936507-91-8*) CorpTech.

Regional Technology Guide: Southwest U. S. 1996. 175.00 (*0-936507-92-6*) CorpTech.

Regional Tectonic Synthesis of Northwestern New England & Adjacent Quebec. Wallace M. Cady. LC 77-98020. (Geological Society of America, Memoir Ser.: No. 120). 248p. reprint ed. pap. 70.70 (*0-317-28385-5*, 2025466) Bks Demand.

Regional Theatre: The Revolutionary Stage. Joseph W. Zeigler. LC 76-51780. (Quality Paperbacks Ser.). 1977. reprint ed. pap. text ed. 6.95 (*0-306-80056-X*) Da Capo.

***Regional Theatre Directory 1997-98.** annuals Ed. by Jill Charles. 180p. 1997. pap. 16.95 (*0-933919-36-0*) Theatre Directories.

Regional Trade Arrangements. Augusto De la Torre & Margaret R. Kelly. LC 91-45766. (Occasional Paper Ser.: No. 93). v, 54p. 1992. pap. 15.00 (*1-55775-227-3*) Intl Monetary.

Regional Trade Blocs, Multilateralism & the GATT: Complementary Paths to Free Trade? Ed. by Till Geoger. LC 96-6322. 192p. 1996. 45.95 (*1-85567-407-6*, Pub. by Pntr Pubs UK) Bks Intl VA.

Regional Trading Arrangements among Developing Countries: The ASEAN Example. Dean A. DeRosa. (Research Report - International Food Policy Research Institute Ser.: Vol. 103). 1995. write for info. (*0-89629-106-5*) Intl Food Policy.

Regional Trading Blocs: A Threat to the Multilateral Trading System? (Committee for Development Planning Ser.). 41p. 1990. 10.00 (*92-1-130141-6*, 90. IV.5) UN.

Regional Trading Blocs in the World Economic System. Jeffrey A. Frankel. LC 96-2660. 350p. (Orig.). 1996. pap. 22.00 (*0-88132-202-4*) Inst Intl Eco.

***Regional Trading Blocs, Mobile Capital & Exchange Rate Co-ordination.** Tamim A. Bayoumi. (Bank of England, Working Paper Ser.: No. 12). (Illus.). 48p. pap. 25.00 (*0-608-04965-4*, 2065544) Bks Demand.

Regional Transformation & Industrial Revolution: A Geography of the Yorkshire Woollen Industry. Derek Gregory. LC 83-191000. 309p. reprint ed. pap. 88.10 (*0-7837-2954-5*, 2057500) Bks Demand.

Regional Transit Authorities: A Policy Analysis of Massachusetts. Barbara P. Glacel. LC 83-2139. 300p. 1983. text ed. 65.00 (*0-275-90987-5*, C0987, Praeger Pubs) Greenwood.

Regional Transit Guide: San Francisco Bay Area. Marilyn M. Reynolds. Ed. by Brenda Kahn. (Illus.). 128p. (Orig.). 1989. pap. 3.95 (*0-9624272-0-9*) Metro Trans Comm.

Regional Transit Guide 1991: San Francisco Bay Area. Marilyn M. Reynolds. Ed. by Brenda Kahn. (Illus.). 128p. 1990. pap. 3.95 (*0-9624272-1-7*) Metro Trans Comm.

***Regional Trends No. 31: 1996.** HMSO Staff. 232p. 1996. pap. 75.00 (*0-11-620773-6*, HM07736, Pub. by Stationery Ofc UK) Bernan Associates.

Regional Trends Geology. Schenk. 1983. lib. bdg. 165.00 (*90-277-1679-X*) Kluwer Ac.

Regional Trends 1994, No. 29. HMSO Staff. 232p. 1994. pap. 55.00 (*0-11-620649-7*, HM06497, Pub. by Stationery Ofc UK) Bernan Associates.

Regional Underpinnings of the U. S.-Japan Partnership, 1987: An Analysis of Japan-Related Activities in Georgia. J. Alexander Heslin & Cedric L. Suzman. 1990. 5.00 (*0-685-34497-5*) Southern Ctr Intl Stud.

Regional Variations in the Economic Development of Germany During the Nineteenth Century. Frank B. Tipton. LC 76-6857. 284p. reprint ed. pap. 81.00 (*0-7837-0223-X*, 2040531) Bks Demand.

Regional Vegetational History of the High Peaks (Adirondack Mountains) New York. Donald R. Whitehead & Stephen T. Jackson. (Bulletin Ser.: No. 478). (Illus.). 27p. (Orig.). (C). 1990. pap. text ed. 6.00 (*1-55557-195-6*) NYS Museum.

Regional Voices: Collections of Poems by Writers in Maryland, Virginia & the District of Columbia. Compiled by Joseph D. Adams. (Poet's Domain Ser.: Vol. 1). xiv, 50p. (Orig.). 1990. pap. 4.95 (*1-880016-02-8*) Road Pubs.

Regional Volume Table for Gmelina Arborea. A. Greaves. 1978. 60.00 (*0-85074-044-4*) St Mut.

Regional Welfare Effects of U. S. Import Restraints on Apparel, Petroleum, Steel & Textiles. Michael Metzger et al. 173p. 1996. 51.95 (*1-85972-317-9*, Pub. by Avebury Pub UK) Ashgate Pub Co.

***Regional World: Territorial Development in a Global Economy.** LC 97-16062. (Perspectives on Economic Change Ser.). 1997. lib. bdg. 32.50 (*1-57230-258-5*, C0258) Guilford Pr.

Regionale Chemotherapie der Leber. Ed. by K. Aigner. (Beitraege zur Onkologie, Contributions to Oncology Ser.: Vol. 21). (Illus.). viii, 140p. 1985. 63.25 (*3-8055-4014-0*) S Karger.

***Regionale Entwicklungspolitik Vol. XVI: Konzeption Einer Dezentralisierten und Integrierten Regionalpolitik.** Burkhard Scherer. (Hohenheimer Volkswirtschaftliche Schriffen Ser.: Bd. 24). (Illus.). 292p. (GER.). 1997. pap. 57.95 (*3-631-30877-9*) P Lang Pubng.

Regionalisation & Labour Flows in Pacific Asia. Pang Eng Fong. 92p. (Orig.). 1993. pap. text ed. 18.00 (*92-64-14008-5*, 41-93-16-1) OECD.

Regionalisation in the Sudan. Beshir M. Osman. (C). 1986. 29.00 (*0-685-30259-8*, Pub. by Oxford Polytechnic UK) St Mut.

Regionalisation of Indian Politics. Prabhat Datta. (C). 1993. 16.00 (*81-207-1493-8*, Pub. by Sterling Plns Pvt II) S Asia.

Regionalism. Li K. Shaw. (Illus.). 238p. 1990. pap. text ed. 30.00 (*0-9607806-7-X*) Li Kung Shaw.

Regionalism: The New Geography of Opportunity. Henry G. Cisneros. 29p. (Orig.). 1995. pap. text ed. 15.00 (*0-7881-2202-9*) DIANE Pub.

***Regionalism & Africas Development.** Asante. LC 97-18971. 1997. text ed. 65.00 (*0-312-17697-X*) St Martin.

Regionalism & Change in the Economy of Independent Delos. Gary Reger. LC 93-22738. (Hellenistic Culture & Society Ser.: Vol. 14). 1994. 55.00 (*0-520-08460-8*) U CA Pr.

Regionalism & Its Place in the Multilateral Trading System. OECD Staff. 275p. (Orig.). 1996. pap. 46.00 (*92-64-14831-0*, Pub. by Org for Econ FR) OECD.

Regionalism & Nationalism in the United States: The Attack on Leviathan. Donald Davidson. 388p. (C). 1990. pap. 24.95 (*0-88738-372-6*) Transaction Pubs.

Regionalism & Regional Devolution in Comparative Perspective. Mark O. Rousseau & Raphael Zariski. LC 87-47735. 303p. 1987. text ed. 65.00 (*0-275-92546-3*, C2546, Praeger Pubs) Greenwood.

Regionalism & Rivalry: Japan & the U. S. in Pacific Asia. Ed. by Jeffrey A. Frankel & Miles Kahler. (National Bureau of Economic Research Conference Report Ser.). (Illus.). 488p. 1993. 63.00 (*0-226-25999-4*) U Ch Pr.

Regionalism & the Female Imagination: A Collection of Essays. Ed. by Emily Toth. 205p. (C). 1985. 45.95 (*0-89885-168-8*); pap. 20.95 (*0-89885-169-6*) Human Sci Pr.

Regionalism & the Musical Heritage of Latin America. Joseph Arbena et al. (Latin American Curriculum Units for Junior & Community Colleges Ser.). v, 84p. (Orig.). (C). 1980. pap. text ed. 4.95 (*0-86728-006-9*) U TX Inst Lat Am Stud.

Regionalism & the New International Economic Order: Studies Presented to the UNITAR-CEESTEM Club of Rome Conference at the United Nations. Ed. by Davidson Nicol et al. LC 80-23706. (Policy Studies on International Development). 448p. 1981. pap. text ed. 46.00 (*0-08-026331-3*, Pergamon Pr) Elsevier.

Regionalism & the Pacific Northwest. Ed. by William G. Robbins et al. LC 83-2416. 256p. 1983. 24.95 (*0-87071-337-X*); pap. 15.95 (*0-87071-338-8*) Oreg St U Pr.

Regionalism & the South: Selected Papers of Rupert Vance. Rupert Vance. Ed. by John Reed et al. LC 81-16235. xxii, 353p. 1982. 39.95 (*0-8078-1513-6*) U of NC Pr.

Regionalism & the United Nations. B. Andemichael. 623p. 1979. lib. bdg. 105.50 (*90-286-0109-0*) Kluwer Ac.

Regionalism & World Order. Ed. by Andrew Gamble & Anthony J. Payne. LC 95-53125. 256p. 1996. text ed. 55.00 (*0-312-15987-0*) St Martin.

Regionalism & World Order. Ed. by Andrew Gamble & Anthony J. Payne. LC 95-53125. 256p. 1996. text ed. 19.95 (*0-312-15988-9*) St Martin.

Regionalism & World Trade: A Study of Regional Arrangements & Article XXIV of GATT. J. A. McMahon & J. C. Woodliffe. 256p. Date not set. 70.00 (*1-85567-252-9*, Pub. by Pntr Pubs UK) Bks Intl VA.

Regionalism, Business Interests & Public Policy. Ed. by William D. Coleman & Henry J. Jacek. (Studies in Neo-Corporatism). 256p. (C). 1989. text ed. 49.95 (*0-8039-8227-5*); pap. text ed. 19.95 (*0-8039-8272-0*) Sage.

Regionalism in a Converging World: Discussion for Lisbon Meeting. Toyoo Gyohten. LC 93-30080. (Triangle Papers: No. 42). 1993. pap. 6.00 (*0-930503-68-6*) Trilateral Comm.

Regionalism in America. Ed. by Merrill Jensen. LC 51-6901. 439p. reprint ed. pap. 125.20 (*0-7837-1659-1*, 2041956) Bks Demand.

Regionalism in Indian Perspective. Bharati Mukherjee. 1992. 13.00 (*81-7074-123-8*, Pub. by KP Bagchi IA) S Asia.

Regionalism in Late-Medieval Manuscripts & Texts: Essays Celebrating the Publication of a Linguistic Atlas of Late Medieval England. Ed. by Felicity Riddy. (York Manuscripts Conferences: II). 222p. (C). 1991. 79.00 (*0-85991-311-2*) Boydell & Brewer.

Regionalism, Multilateralism & Deeper Integration. Robert Z. Lawrence. LC 95-26205. (Integrating National Economies: Promise & Pitfalls Ser.). 158p. 1996. 34.95 (*0-8157-5182-6*); pap. 14.95 (*0-8157-5181-8*) Brookings.

Regionalism or Globalism? A Report of the September 1994 Seminar: Transatlantic Trade & Investment: Factors for Stability. Peter S. Rashish. 76p. (Orig.). 1995. pap. 15. 00 (*0-9628287-0-X*) European Inst.

Regionalism Reconsidered: New Approaches to the Field. Ed. by David M. Jordan & William Cain. LC 94-20701. (Wellesley Studies in Critical Theory: Vol. 5). 232p. 1994. text ed. 39.00 (*0-8153-1289-X*, H1698) Garland.

Regionalism, State & the Emerging Political Patterns in India. Ajeya Sarkar. (C). 1991. 12.75 (*0-8364-2643-6*, Pub. by Firma KLM II) S Asia.

***Regionalism vs. Multilateral Trade Arrangement.** Takatoshi Ito et al. LC 97-7794. (NBER-East Asia Seminar on Economics Ser.). 1997. 59.00 (*0-226-38672-4*) U Ch Pr.

Regionalist Art, Thomas Hart Benton, John Steuart Curry, Grant Wood: A Guide to the Literature. Mary S. Guedon. LC 82-3334. 199p. 1982. 22.50 (*0-8108-1543-5*) Scarecrow.

Regionalization: Issues in Intensive Care for High Risk Newborns & their Families. Claire S. Rudolph & Susan R. Borker. LC 87-15136. 208p. 1987. text ed. 65.00 (*0-275-92547-1*, C2547, Praeger Pubs) Greenwood.

***Regionalization & Labour Market.** Campbell. LC 97-18984. 1997. text ed. 69.95 (*0-312-17703-8*) St Martin.

***Regionalization in the World Economy NAFTA: The Americas, & Asia-Pacific.** Ed. by Van R. Whiting. 310p. 1996. pap. 19.95 (*0-333-92401-0*) Asia Bks CA.

Regionalization of Warfare: The Falkland Islands, Lebanon & the Iran-Iraq Conflict. Ed. by James Brown & William P. Snyder. (Illus.). 266p. (C). 1984. 39.95 (*0-88738-022-0*); pap. 24.95 (*0-87855-985-X*) Transaction Pubs.

Regionalization of Water Management: A Revolution in England & Wales. Daniel A. Okun. (Illus.). 377p. 1977. 74.00 (*0-85334-738-7*, Pub. by Elsevier Applied Sci UK) Elsevier.

***Regionalization World Economy.** Frankel. LC 97-15325. 1997. 43.00 (*0-226-25995-1*) U Ch Pr.

Regionalized Systems as an Approach to Perinatal Health Care: Annotated Bibliography. Barbara Pearce. (CPL Bibliographies Ser.: No. 54). 81p. 1981. 10.00 (*0-86602-054-3*, Sage Prdcls Pr) Sage.

Regions- Nomenclature of Territorial Units for Statistics NUTS March 1995. Eurostat Staff. 82p. 1995. pap. text ed. 20.00 (*92-827-4491-4*, CA-59-95-001-EN, Pub. by Commiss Europ Commun BE) Bernan Associates.

***Regions & Distances of France Map.** 1996. 8.95 (*2-06-700910-9*, 910) Michelin.

Regions & European Integration. Ed. by Robert Leonardi & Rafaella Y. Nanetti. 1992. text ed. 39.00 (*0-86187-149-9*) St Martin.

Regions & Global Warming: Impacts & Response Strategies. Ed. by Jurgen Schmandt & Alan Jones. (Illus.). 416p. 1992. 70.00 (*0-19-507586-2*) OUP.

Regions & Industries: A Perspective on the Industrial Revolution in Britain. Ed. by Pat Hudson. (Illus.). 320p. (C). 1989. text ed. 59.95 (*0-521-34106-X*) Cambridge U Pr.

Regions & Regionalism in the United States. Michael Bradshaw. LC 87-17917. 186p. 1988. 35.00 (*0-87805-339-5*); pap. 15.95 (*0-87805-340-9*) U Pr of Miss.

Regions & Repertoires: Topics in South African Politics & Culture. Ed. by Stephen Clingman. (South African Studies: Vol. 6). 222p. (Orig.). (C). 1992. pap. text ed. 24.95 (*0-86975-411-4*, Pub. by Ravan Pr ZA) Ohio U Pr.

Regions & Resources: Strategies for Development. David T. Kresge et al. (Joint Center for Urban Studies). (Illus.). 264p. 1984. 35.00 (*0-262-11091-1*) MIT Pr.

Regions & the European Community: The Regional Response to the Single Market in the Underdeveloped Areas. Ed. by Robert Leonardi. LC 92-28756. 1992. 37. 50 (*0-7146-3460-3*, Pub. by F Cass Pubs UK) Intl Spec Bk.

Regions & the New Europe: Patterns in Core & Periphery Development. Ed. by Martin Rhodes. LC 95-4963. (European Policy Research Unit Studies: No. 1). 1996. text ed. 75.00 (*0-7190-4251-8*, Pub. by Manchester Univ Pr UK) St Martin.

Regions at Risk: Comparisons of Threatened Environments. Jeanne X. Kasperson et al. (Studies pm Critical Evironmental Regions). 598p. 1995. pap. text ed. 50.00 (*92-808-0848-6*, UNUP-0848, Pub. by UN Univ JA) Bernan Associates.

Region's Growth. (Illus.). 143p. 1967. 10.00 (*0-318-16380-2*) Regional Plan Assn.

Regions in Question: Space Development Theory & Regional Policy. C. G. Gore. (Development & Underdevelopment Ser.). 304p. 1984. pap. text ed. 15.95 (*0-416-31420-1*, 4021) Routledge Chapman & Hall.

Regions in Recession & Resurgance. Michael Chisholm. (Illus.). 256p. (C). 1990. pap. text ed. 22.95 (*0-04-330063-4*) Routledge Chapman & Hall.

Regions in Recession & Resurgance. Michael Chisholm. (Illus.). 256p. (C). 1990. text ed. 55.00 (*0-685-46014-2*) Routledge Chapman & Hall.

Region's Money Flows: The Government Accounts, Vol. 1. 88p. 1977. 10.00 (*0-318-16382-9*, 127) Regional Plan Assn.

Regions Northwest: A Wine & Food Yearbook. Ed. by Judy Peterson-Nedry. (Illus.). 102p. (Orig.). 1996. per. 8.95 (*0-9651260-0-5*) Regions NW.

Regions of France: A Reference Guide to History & Culture. Wayne Northcutt. LC 96-5806. 336p. 1997. text ed. 55.00 (*0-313-29223-X*, Greenwood Pr) Greenwood.

Regions of Infiltration. Louis R. Massa. (Illus.). 32p. 1995. pap. 11.00 (*0-8059-3677-7*) Dorrance.

Regions of Memory: Uncollected Prose, 1949-1982. W. S. Merwin. Ed. by Ed Folsom & Cary Nelson. LC 86-1358. 376p. 1987. text ed. 29.95 (*0-252-01241-0*) U of Ill Pr.

Regions of Recent Star Formation. Ed. by R. S. Roger & P. E. Dewdney. 1982. lib. bdg. 165.00 (*90-277-1383-9*) Kluwer Ac.

***Regions of Risk: Hazards, Vulnerability & Disaster.** Kenneth Hewitt. (C). 1996. pap. text ed. 24.95 (*0-582-21005-4*) Addison-Wesley.

Regions of Silence: Studies on the Difficulty of Communicating. Maria G. Ciani. (London Studies in Classical Philology: Vol. 17). viii, 160p. (C). 1987. 40.00 (*90-70265-17-6*, Pub. by Gieben NE) Benjamins North Am.

Regions of Spain: A Reference Guide to History & Culture. Robert W. Kern. LC 95-6481. 432p. 1995. text ed. 55.00 (*0-313-29224-8*, Greenwood Pr) Greenwood.

Regions of the Imagination: The Development of British Rural Fiction. W. J. Keith. 200p. 1988. 35.00 (*0-8020-2654-0*) U of Toronto Pr.

Regions of the Mind: Brain Research & the Quest for Scientific Certainty. Susan L. Star. LC 89-4432. (Illus.). 304p. 1989. 37.50 (*0-8047-1673-0*) Stanford U Pr.

Regions of the New Europe 1995. Ernst & Young. 1995. 710.00 (*1-85564-452-5*, Pub. by Euromoney UK) Am Educ Systs.

Regions of the World Today. 2nd ed. John Benhart & C. Rober Scull. 320p. (C). 1995. per. 26.19 (*0-8403-8329-0*) Kendall-Hunt.

Regions Reconsidered: Economic Networks, Innovation & Local Development. Ed. by Edward Bergman et al. (Illus.). 320p. 1991. text ed. 90.00 (*0-7201-2108-6*, Mansell Pub) Cassell.

Regions Statistical Yearbook: 1994. 211p. 1995. pap. 30.00 (*92-826-8298-6*, CA-83-94-7815EC, Pub. by Europ Com UK) Bernan Associates.

***Regions Statistical Yearbook 1995.** 211p. 1996. pap. 45.00 (*92-827-5948-2*, CA91-95-924-4MC, Pub. by Europ Com UK) Bernan Associates.

R

Regis & Kathie Lee: Their Lives Together & Apart. Norman King. LC 95-19246. 240p. 1995. 19.95 (*1-55972-307-6*, Birch Ln Pr) Carol Pub Group.

Regis & Kathie Lee: Their Lives Together & Apart, Vol. 1. Norman King. 1996. mass mkt. 5.99 (*0-312-96063-8*) St Martin.

Regis Debray: The Writing of Commitment. Keith Reader. LC 95-14373. (Modern European Thinkers Ser.). 1995. 40.00 (*0-7453-0821-X*, Pub. by Pluto Pr UK); pap. 13.95 (*0-7453-0822-8*, Pub. by Pluto Pr UK) LPC InBook.

Regis Debray & the Latin American Revolution: A Collection of Essays. Ed. by Leo Huberman & Paul M. Sweezy. LC 68-8077. 144p. reprint ed. pap. 41.10 (*0-318-34969-8*, 2030767) Bks Demand.

*__Regis Santos: Thirty Years of Collecting.__ Thomas J. Steele. Ed. by Paul Rhetts & Barbe Awalt. LC 97-70979. (Illus.). 120p. 1997. 54.95 (*0-9641542-4-2*) LPD Pr.

*__Regis Santos: Thirty Years of Collecting.__ Thomas J. Steele. Ed. by Paul Rhetts & Barbe Awalt. LC 97-70979. (Illus.). 120p. 1997. pap. 39.95 (*0-9641542-7-7*) LPD Pr.

*__Regisseur und die Aufzeichnungspraxis der Opernregie im 19. Jahrhundert.__ Arne Langer. Ed. by Jurgen Maehder & Jurg Stenzl. (Perspektiven der Opernforschung Ser.: Bd. 4). 454p. (GER.). 1997. 76.95 (*3-631-31224-5*) P Lang Pubng.

Register. Norbert Gstrein. LC 95-1619. (Studies in Austrian Literature, Culture, & Thought). 265p. 1995. pap. 21.50 (*1-57241-012-4*) Ariadne CA.

Register: Information Directory for the Russian Far East. Jeff B. Wheeler. (Illus.). 220p. (Orig.). 1994. pap. 25.00 (*0-9642408-0-7*) D Vostok Ltd.

Register Allocation in Optimizing Compilers. Bruce W. Leverett. LC 83-18297. (Computer Science: Systems Programming Ser.: No. 19). 234p. reprint ed. pap. 66.70 (*0-685-20449-9*, 2070313) Bks Demand.

Register Analysis: Theory & Practice. Ed. by Mohsen Ghadessy. (Open Linguistics Ser.). 288p. 1993. text ed. 79.00 (*1-85567-123-9*) St Martin.

Register Book for the Parish Prince Frederick Winyaw: Anno Domini 1713. National Association Colonial Dames of America Staff. (Illus.). 270p. 1982. reprint ed. 25.00 (*0-89308-299-6*) Southern Hist Pr.

Register in Puerto Rico, Nineteen Hundred & Three to Nineteen Hundred & Five, 2 vols. Charles Hartzell. (Puerto Rico Ser.). 1979. lib. bdg. 200.00 (*0-8490-2994-5*) Gordon Pr.

Register-Index for the Gmelin Handbuch Dev Anorganischen Chemie. Planck, Max, Society for the Advancement of Science, Gmelin Institute for Inorganic Chemistry Staff. (Gmelin Handbuch der Anorganischen Chemie Ser.: Vol. 1, Ac-Au). 254p. 1975. 270.00 (*0-387-93295-X*) Spr-Verlag.

Register of Albemarle Parish, Surry & Sussex Counties, 1739-1788. National Society of Colonial Dames of America Staff. Ed. by Gertrude R. Richards. (Illus.). 275p. 1984. reprint ed. 32.50 (*0-89308-545-6*) Southern Hist Pr.

Register of American Malacologists. R. Tucker Abbott. LC 86-72678. 180p. 1987. 12.00 (*0-915826-18-6*) Am Malacologists.

Register of American Yachts 1988-89: The Yacht Owners Register. Yacht Owners Register, Inc. Staff. Ed. by Gary R. Dougherty. (Illus.). 370p. 1989. 110.00 (*0-915953-01-3*) Yacht Owners.

Register of American Yachts, 1990: The Yacht Owners Register. Yacht Owners Register, Inc. Staff. Ed. by Gary R. Dougherty. (Illus.). 400p. 1990. 110.00 (*0-915953-02-1*) Yacht Owners.

Register of Americans of Prominent Descent, Vol. I. Compiled by Sue M. O'Brien. LC 81-69243. 545p. 1982. 35.00 (*0-686-36318-3*) Morten Pub.

Register of Artists, Engravers, Booksellers, Bookbinders, Printers & Publishers in New York City, 1821-42. Sidney F. Huttner & Elizabeth S. Huttner. (Illus.). 299p. 1993. 50.00 (*0-914930-15-X*, 40525) Biblio Soc Am.

Register of Australian Herbage Plant Cultivars. 3rd ed. Ed. by R. N. Oram. 300p. 1990. pap. 75.00 (*0-643-05054-X*, Pub. by CSIRO AT) Aubrey Bks.

Register of Baptisms of the French Protestant Refugees Settled at Thorney, Cambridgeshire, 1654-1727. Ed. by Henry Peet. Bd. with Letters of Denization. Ed. by William A. Shaw. ; Registers of the French Church of Portarlington, Ireland. Ed. by Thomas P. Le Fanu. ; Registers of the French Churches of Bristol. Ed. by Charles E. Lart. ; Register of the French Church at Thorpe-le-Spoken. Ed. by William C. Waller. (Huguenot Society of London Publications: Vols. 17-20). 1974. reprint ed. (*0-8115-1650-4*) Periodicals Srv.

Register of Canadian Honours. 1991. 65.00 (*1-895021-01-4*) Gale.

Register of Development Activities of the U. N. System, 1988: ACCIS. 916p. 1990. 40.00 (*92-1-100347-4*, E.GV.89.0.10) UN.

Register of Development Activities of the United Nations System. 1064p. 1990. 42.00 (*92-1-100356-3*, GV.90.0.13) UN.

Register of Development Activities of the United Nations System. 6th ed. ACCIS Staff. 1105p. 1994. 45.00 (*92-1-100674-0*) UN.

Register of Development Activities of the United Nations System 1987. 752p. 1988. 30.00 (*92-1-100341-5*, E.88.0.4) UN.

Register of Development Research Projects in Africa. OECD Staff. 360p. (Orig.). 1992. pap. 58.00 (*92-64-03699-7*) OECD.

Register of Development Research Projects in Latin America. OECD Staff. 455p. (Orig.). 1993. pap. 75.00 (*92-64-03076-X*) OECD.

Register of Development Research Projects in Selected European Countries. OECD Staff. 362p. (Orig.). (ENG & FRE.). 1992. pap. 58.00 (*92-64-03532-X*) OECD.

Register of Educational Research in the UK. 436p. (C). 1996. pap. text ed. 350.00 (*0-415-13243-6*) Routledge.

Register of English Theatrical Documents, 1660-1737. Ed. by Robert D. Hume. LC 90-42095. 1056p. (C). 1991. 90.00 (*0-8093-1270-0*) S Ill U Pr.

Register of Environmental Engineering Graduate Programs. 5th ed. Ed. by Gary L. Amy & William R. Knocke. LC 84-70854. 626p. 1984. pap. 30.00 (*0-917567-00-5*) Assn Environ Eng.

Register of Florida CSA Pension Applications. Virgil D. White. LC 89-62132. 1989. 36.00 (*0-945099-13-4*) Natl Hist Pub.

Register of Free Blacks, Rockingham County, Virginia, 1807-1859. Dorothy A. Boyd-Rush. 252p. (Orig.). 1992. pap. 22.00 (*1-55613-658-7*) Heritage Bk.

Register of Higher Education 1996: The Source Book for Higher Education. 9th ed. 1099p. 1995. pap. 32.95 (*1-56079-519-0*) Petersons.

Register of Higher Education 1997: The Who's Who of Higher Education. 10th rev. ed. Ed. by Peterson's Staff. 1100p. 1996. pap. 49.95 (*1-56079-658-8*) Petersons.

Register of Holy Trinity, Coventry, Warickshire. (C). 1987. 35.00 (*0-317-89875-2*, Pub. by Birmingham Midland Soc UK) St Mut.

Register of Indexers. 1994. pap. text ed. 15.00 (*0-936547-24-3*) Am Soc Index.

Register of Invalid Pensions, Revolutionary Service, 1789. Bob Closson & Mary Closson. 16p. 1987. reprint ed. pap. text ed. 2.50 (*0-933227-67-1*) Closson Pr.

Register of John Catterick, Bishop of Coventry & Lichfield 1415-19. Ed. by R. N. Swanson. (Canterbury & York Society Ser.). 112p. 1991. 50.00 (*0-907239-35-8*) Boydell & Brewer.

Register of John Kirkby, Bishop of Carlisle I 1332-1353 & the Register of John Ross, Bishop of Carlisle, 1325-1332. Ed. by R. L. Storey. (Canterbury & York Society Ser.: No. 79). 192p. (C). 1993. 59.00 (*0-907239-48-X*, Canterbury & York Soc) Boydell & Brewer.

Register of John Kirkby Bishop of Carlisle, 1332-1352, No. II. Ed. by R. L. Storey. (Canterbury & York Society Ser.: No. 81). 147p. (C). 1995. 53.00 (*0-907239-50-1*, Canterbury & York Soc) Boydell & Brewer.

Register of John Morton II, Archbishop of Canterbury, 1486-1500, II. Ed. by Christopher Harper-Bill. (Canterbury & York Society Ser.: No. 78). 268p. (C). 1992. 50.00 (*0-907239-47-1*) Boydell & Brewer.

Register of John Waltham, Bishop of Salisbury, 1388-1395. Ed. by T. C. Timmins. (Canterbury & York Society Ser.: Vol. 80). (Illus.). 355p. (C). 1994. 45.00 (*0-907239-49-8*, Canterbury & York Soc) Boydell & Brewer.

Register of Laws of the Arabian Gulf: Basic Work & 1988 Supplement Service. W. M. Ballantyne. (C). 1988. 935.00 (*1-85333-089-2*, Pub. by Graham & Trotman UK); ring bd. 935.00 (*1-85333-090-6*, Pub. by Graham & Trotman UK) Kluwer Ac.

Register of Laws of the Arabian Gulf: Main Work & Supplement Service, 1990. Ed. by W. M. Ballantyne. (C). 1990. 1,528.00 (*1-85333-333-6*, Pub. by Graham & Trotman UK) Kluwer Ac.

Register of Laws of the Arabian Gulf: 1989 Basic Work & 1989 Supplement Service. W. M. Ballantyne. (C). 1989. pap. text ed. 27.00 (*1-85333-253-4*, Pub. by Graham & Trotman UK) Kluwer Ac.

Register of Laws of the Arabian Gulf: 1991 Main Work & 1991 Supp Service. W. M. Ballantyne. (C). 1991. ring bd. 1,230.00 (*1-85333-491-X*, Pub. by Graham & Trotman UK); Quarterly suppl. suppl. ed. 267.00 (*0-685-39302-X*, Pub. by Graham & Trotman UK) Kluwer Ac.

Register of Laws of the Arabian Gulf: 1992 Main Work & 1992 Supplement Service. W. M. Ballantyne. 700p. 1992. ring bd. 1,185.00 (*1-85333-639-4*, Pub. by Graham & Trotman UK) Kluwer Ac.

Register of Laws of the Arabian Gulf: 1993 Main Work & 1993 Supplement Service. Ed. by W. M. Ballantyne. (C). 1993. ring bd. 1,301.00 (*1-85333-810-9*, Pub. by Graham & Trotman UK) Kluwer Ac.

Register of Lawyers. 4th ed. Stephen Gillers. 1995. 51.00 (*0-316-31458-7*) Little.

*__Register of Management Consultants.__ Date not set. 34.95 (*0-8464-4416-X*) Beekman Pubs.

Register of Middle English Religious & Didactic Verse. Carleton F. Brown. 1977. 57.95 (*0-8369-7155-8*, 7987) Ayer.

Register of Ministers, Exhorters & Readers & of Their Stipends. Church of Scotland Staff. LC 71-174310. (Maitland Club, Glasgow. Publications: No. 5). reprint ed. 32.50 (*0-404-52929-1*) AMS Pr.

Register of My Favorite Recipes. rev. ed. Barbara Deede. (Illus.). 144p. 1995. student ed., spiral bd. 8.95 (*0-9622412-4-5*) Pickle Point.

Register of National Recreation Trails. 1994. lib. bdg. 250.95 (*0-8490-9045-8*) Gordon Pr.

Register of New Netherland, 1626-1674. Edmund B. O'Callaghan. 198p. 1996. reprint ed. pap. 21.50 (*0-614-16544-X*, 9294) Clearfield Co.

Register of North American Insurance Companies. American Preeminent Registry Staff. 420p. (Orig.). 1993. 125.00 (*0-9633783-1-7*) Am Preeminent Reg.

Register of Officers of the Confederate States Navy 1861-1865. John M. Carroll. Date not set. pap. 19.95 (*0-8488-0046-X*, J M C & Co); lib. bdg. 29.95 (*0-8488-0011-7*, J M C & Co) Amereon Ltd.

Register of One Name Studies. 5th ed. (C). 1987. 30.00 (*0-317-89895-7*, Pub. by Birmingham Midland Soc UK) St Mut.

Register of Overwharton Parish, Stafford County, Virginia, 1723-1758. George H. King. (Illus.). 296p. 1985. reprint ed. 30.00 (*0-89308-576-6*) Southern Hist Pr.

Register of Oxyrhynchites 30 BC - AD 96. John Whitehorne & Brian Jones. LC 81-18494. (BASP Supplements Ser.). 292p. (C). 1983. 35.50 (*0-89130-529-7*, 31-00-25) Scholars Pr GA.

Register of Pennsylvania Biologists. 2nd ed. Ed. by T. D. Jacobsen & Sharon M. Tomasic. (Special Publications: No. 16). 120p. (Orig.). 1992. pap. 11.00 (*0-911239-41-3*) Carnegie Mus.

Register of Polish American Scholars, Scientists, Writers & Artists. Ed. by Damian Wandycz. 80p. 1969. pap. 4.00 (*0-940962-38-1*) Polish Inst Art & Sci.

Register of Regulations. Ed. by Butterworth Staff. ring bd. 255.00 (*0-614-05955-0*) MICHIE.

*__Register of Reporting Labor Organizations.__ 1997. lib. bdg. 250.95 (*0-8490-7637-4*) Gordon Pr.

Register of Research: Investigation in Adult Education. ERIC Staff & Adult Education Association of the U. S. A. Staff. 1968. 2.30 (*0-88379-012-2*); 8.00 (*0-88379-030-0*) A A A C E.

Register of Research: Investigation in Adult Education. ERIC Staff & Adult Education Association of the U. S. A. Staff. 1970. 6.90 (*0-88379-013-0*) A A A C E.

Register of Research, 1987. Ed. by John Purcell. 96p. (C). 1987. 60.00 (*0-85292-399-6*) St Mut.

Register of Revolutionary Soldiers & Patriots Buried in Litchfield County. LC 76-42089. 1976. 9.65 (*0-914016-32-6*) Phoenix Pub.

Register of Royal & Baronial Domestic Minstrels, 1272-1327. Constance Bullock-Davies. 243p. 1986. 70.00 (*0-85115-431-X*) Boydell & Brewer.

Register of Saint Paul's Parish 1715-1776, Stafford County 1715-1776, King George County, Virginia, 1777-1798. George H. King. (Illus.). 192p. 1985. reprint ed. 27.50 (*0-89308-577-4*) Southern Hist Pr.

Register of Ships of the U. S. Navy, 1775-1990: Major Combatants. K. Jack Bauer & Stephen S. Roberts. LC 91-25241. 376p. 1991. text ed. 89.50 (*0-313-26202-0*, BRK, Greenwood Pr) Greenwood.

Register of St. Augustine's Abbey, Canterbury: Commonly Called the Black Book, 2 pts., Pt. 1. Ed. by G. J. Turner & H. E. Salter. (British Academy, London, Records of the Social & Economic History of England & Wales Ser.: Vol. 2). 1974. reprint ed. pap. 60.00 (*0-8115-1242-8*) Periodicals Srv.

Register of St. Augustine's Abbey, Canterbury: Commonly Called the Black Book, 2 pts., Pt. 2. Ed. by G. J. Turner & H. E. Salter. (British Academy, London, Records of the Social & Economic History of England & Wales Ser.: Vol. 2). 1974. reprint ed. pap. 50.00 (*0-8115-1243-6*) Periodicals Srv.

Register of St. Kenelm's Clifton upon Teme Worcestershire. (C). 1987. 35.00 (*0-317-89857-4*, Pub. by Birmingham Midland Soc UK) St Mut.

Register of St. Mary, Oldswinford, Worcestershire. (C). 1987. 35.00 (*0-317-89872-8*, Pub. by Birmingham Midland Soc UK) St Mut.

Register of St. Michael & All Angels, Adbaston, Staffs. (C). 1987. 35.00 (*0-317-89850-7*, Pub. by Birmingham Midland Soc UK) St Mut.

Register of St. Modwen, Burton-on-Trenton Staffs. (C). 1987. 50.00 (*0-317-89862-0*, Pub. by Birmingham Midland Soc UK) St Mut.

Register of St. Peter de Witton, Droitwich, Worcestershire. (C). 1987. 35.00 (*0-317-89874-4*, Pub. by Birmingham Midland Soc UK) St Mut.

Register of St. Philip's the Cathedral Church of Birmingham. (C). 1987. 35.00 (*0-317-89870-1*, Pub. by Birmingham Midland Soc UK) St Mut.

Register of the Abbey of St. Thomas, Dublin. Ed. by John T. Gilbert. (Rolls Ser.: No. 94). 1974. reprint ed. 70.00 (*0-8115-1171-5*) Periodicals Srv.

Register of the Baptisms in the Dutch Church at Colchester from 1645 to 1728: Edited for the Huguenot Society of London. W. J. Moens. 177p. 1994. pap. text ed. 30.00 (*1-55613-998-5*) Heritage Bk.

Register of the Church of St. Giles, Sheldon, Pt. 2. (C). 1987. 35.00 (*0-317-89848-5*, Pub. by Birmingham Midland Soc UK) St Mut.

Register of the Confederate Debt. Raphael P. Thian. 224p. 1994. reprint ed. text ed. 45.00 (*0-88000-148-8*) Quarterman.

Register of the French Church at Thorpe-le-Spoken see Register of Baptisms of the French Protestant Refugees Settled at Thorney, Cambridgeshire, 1654-1727

Register of the Great Seal of Scotland, 11 vols. Aberdeen Rare Books Staff. (C). 1988. 2,150.00 (*0-685-30215-6*, Pub. by Aberdeen Rare Bks UK) St Mut.

Register of the Hills Bros. Coffee, Inc. Collections, ca. 1856-1988. Vanessa Broussard-Simmons & Wendy A. Shay. 1996. write for info. (*0-614-10099-2*) Natl Mus Am.

Register of the Marriages Celebrated in Greenbrier County (West) Virginia from 1781-1849. Compiled by Norma P. Evans. LC 82-82599. 84p. 1983. pap. 15.00 (*0-937418-07-2*) N P Evans.

Register of the Middlebrook Family, Descendants of Joseph Middlebrook of Fairfield, Connecticut. L. F. Middlebrook. (Illus.). 411p. 1989. reprint ed. pap. 61.50 (*0-8328-0871-7*); reprint ed. lib. bdg. 69.50 (*0-8328-0870-9*) Higginson Bk Co.

Register of the Milwaukee (Wis.) Mayor: Records of the Henry W. Maier Administration, 1960-1988. Ed. by Mark A. Vargas. (Milwaukee Ser.: No. 44). (Illus.). 150p. 1993. pap. write for info. (*1-879281-07-4*) G Meir Lib.

Register of Thetford Priory Pt. 2: 1518-1540. Ed. by David Dymond. (Records of Social & Economic History, New Series British Academy: No. 25). (Illus.). 500p. 1997. 95.00 (*0-19-726161-2*) OUP.

Register of Vital Records of Roman Catholic Parishes from the Region Beyond the Bug River. Edward A. Peckwas. 44p. 5.95 (*0-317-57777-8*) Polish Genealog.

Register of Walter Bronescombe, Bishop of Exeter 1258-1280 No. I. Ed. by O. F. Robinson. (Canterbury & York Society Ser.: Vol. 82). 208p. (C). 1995. 45.00 (*0-907239-51-X*, Canterbury & York Soc) Boydell & Brewer.

*__Register of William Bateman, Bishop of Norwich 1344-1355, Vol. I.__ Ed. by Phyllis E. Pobst. (Canterbury & York Society Ser.: Vol. 84). 168p. 1997. 53.10 (*0-907239-54-4*) Boydell & Brewer.

*__Register of William Melton, Archbishop of York, 1317-1340.__ Ed. by Reginald Brocklesby. (Canterbury & York Society Ser.: Vol. IV). 224p. 1997. 53.00 (*0-907239-56-0*) Boydell & Brewer.

*__Register of Wooden Yachts 1996-1997: A List of North American Wooden Yachts, Boats, Vessels, & Their Owners.__ Woodenboat Magazine Editors. 598p. 1996. 55.00 (*0-937822-38-8*) WoodenBoat Pubns.

Register of York Freemen 1680-1986. Ed. by M. Phil. 1200p. (C). 1988. 75.00 (*1-85072-054-1*, Pub. by W Sessions UK) St Mut.

Register over Dast Magazin Vols. I-XV: Sept. 1968-Dec. 1982. Iwan Erichsson. LC 85-11366. 146p. 1985. reprint ed. lib. bdg. 29.00 (*0-89370-875-5*) Borgo Pr.

Register to "Genera Siphonogamarum" K. W. Von Dalla Torre & H. Harms. 1958. reprint ed. 68.00 (*3-7682-0072-8*) Lubrecht & Cramer.

*__Register Zu Gottfried Wilhelm Leibniz.__ Joseph E. Hofmann. (Olms Paperbacks Ser.: Bd. 49). (GER.). 1977. write for info. (*3-487-06451-0*) G Olms Pubs.

Register, 510(k), 1992, 2 vols. 1992. per. 239.00 (*0-914176-44-7*) Wash Busn Info.

*__Registered Firms Directory ISO9000/AS9000 1996.__ (C). 1996. pap. text ed. 14.00 (*1-55989-966-2*) Underwrtrs Labs.

*__Registered Firms Directory ISO9000/AS9000 1996.__ 2nd ed. (C). 1996. pap. text ed. 14.00 (*1-55989-967-0*) Underwrtrs Labs.

Registered Places of New Mexico: The Land of Enchantment. Cotton Mather & George F. Thompson. 1995. 19.95 (*0-9643841-0-8*) NMex Geograp.

Registered Professional Nurse. Jack Rudman. (Career Examination Ser.: C-671). 1994. pap. 27.95 (*0-8373-0671-X*) Nat Learn.

*__Registered Professional Nurses & Unlicensed Assistive Personnel.__ 2nd ed. American Nurses Association Staff. 96p. 1996. 14.95 (*1-55810-132-2*, NP-89A) Am Nurses Pub.

*__Registered Representative.__ 5th ed. Philip Meyers. 1998. 44.95 (*0-02-862196-4*) Macmillan.

Registered Representative: Stockbroker's Exam. 2nd ed. Philip Meyers. (Illus.). 448p. 1992. pap. 35.00 (*0-13-770702-9*, Arco) Macmillan Gen Ref.

Registered Representative (RR) (Stockbroker) Jack Rudman. (Admission Test Ser.: ATS-1). 1994. pap. 39.95 (*0-8373-5001-8*) Nat Learn.

Registered Representative Stockbroker. 4th ed. Phillip Meyers. 494p. 1996. 39.95 (*0-02-860594-2*) Macmillan.

Registered Technologist, R.T. (AR-RT) Jack Rudman. (Career Examination Ser.: C-680). 1994. pap. 29.95 (*0-8373-0680-9*) Nat Learn.

Registering Agent Services for Delaware Incorporators & Other States: A How to Find or Locate Reference. Compiled by Bibliotheca Press Research Division Staff. 150p. 1992. ring bd. 23.95 (*0-939476-87-8*) Prosperity & Profits.

Registering Title to Land: A Series of Lectures Delivered at Yale. Jacques Dumas. 106p. 1985. reprint ed. lib. bdg. 20.00 (*0-8377-0522-3*) Rothman.

Registers. Clark Coolidge. 88p. (Orig.). (C). 1994. pap. 9.95 (*0-939691-10-8*) Avenue B.

Registers of Allerton Mauleverer & Askham Richard, County York, England: The Publications of the Yorkshire Parish Register Society, Vol. XXXI. F. William Slingsby. 140p. 1995. reprint ed. pap. text ed. 13.00 (*0-7884-0226-9*) Heritage Bk.

Registers of Birth, Winchester, Virginia, 1853-1860. Dola S. Tylor. vi, 108p. (Orig.). 1991. pap. 20.00 (*1-55613-379-0*) Heritage Bk.

Registers of Birth, Winchester, Virginia, 1865-1891. Dola S. Tylor. vi, 304p. (Orig.). 1991. pap. 35.00 (*1-55613-380-4*) Heritage Bk.

Registers of Free Negroes, Botetourt County, Virginia, 1802-1836. Dorothy A. Boyd-Rush. xi, 75p. 1993. pap. 10.00 (*0-8095-8674-6*); lib. bdg. 29.00 (*0-8095-8274-0*) Borgo Pr.

Registers of Hanbury, Worcestershire. (C). 1987. 35.00 (*0-317-89861-2*, Pub. by Birmingham Midland Soc UK) St Mut.

Registers of North Farnham Parish, 1663-1814, & Lunenburg Parish, 1783-1800, Richmond County, Virginia. George H. King. (Illus.). 240p. 1985. reprint ed. 28.50 (*0-89308-580-4*) Southern Hist Pr.

Registers of Park Lane Presbyterian Church, Cradley, Worcestershire. (C). 1987. 35.00 (*0-317-89849-3*, Pub. by Birmingham Midland Soc UK) St Mut.

Registers of St. John the Baptist, Halesowen Worcestershire. (C). 1987. 35.00 (*0-317-89860-4*, Pub. by Birmingham Midland Soc UK) St Mut.

Registers of St. John the Baptist, Wasperton. (C). 1987. 35.00 (*0-317-89856-6*, Pub. by Birmingham Midland Soc UK) St Mut.

Registers of St. Mary Kingswinford, Staffs. (C). 1987. 35.00 (*0-317-89853-1*, Pub. by Birmingham Midland Soc UK) St Mut.

Registers of St. Mary, Swynnerton, Staffs. (C). 1987. 35.00 (*0-317-89871-X*, Pub. by Birmingham Midland Soc UK) St Mut.

An Asterisk (*) at the beginning of an entry indicates that the title is appearing in BIP for the first time.

Registers of St. Michael & All Angels, GT Witley, Worcestershire. (C). 1987. 35.00 (*0-317-89859-0*, Pub. by Birmingham Midland Soc UK) St Mut.

Registers of St. Nicholas, Kings Norton Worcestershire. (C). 1987. 35.00 (*0-317-89866-3*, Pub. by Birmingham Midland Soc UK) St Mut.

Registers of the Chapelry of St. Michael & All Angles, Little Witley, Worcestershire. (C). 1987. 50.00 (*0-317-89869-8*, Pub. by Birmingham Midland Soc UK) St Mut.

Registers of the Church of St. Editha, Church Eaton, Staffs. (C). 1987. 30.00 (*0-317-89851-5*, Pub. by Birmingham Midland Soc UK) St Mut.

Registers of the French Church see Letters of Denization & Acts of Naturalization for Aliens in England, 1509-1603

Registers of the French Church of Portarlington, Ireland see Register of Baptisms of the French Protestant Refugees Settled at Thorney, Cambridgeshire, 1654-1727

Registers of the French Churches of Bristol see Register of Baptisms of the French Protestant Refugees Settled at Thorney, Cambridgeshire, 1654-1727

Registers of the French Conformed Churches of St. Patrick & St. Mary, Dublin see Despatches of Michele Suriand & Marc'Antonio Barbaro, Venetian Ambassadors at the Court of France, 1560-1563

Registers of Wednesfield, Staff: Baptists. & Burials, 1751 to 1837. (C). 1987. 35.00 (*0-317-89854-X*, Pub. by Birmingham Midland Soc UK) St Mut.

Registers of Written English: Situational Factors & Linguistic Features. Mohsen Ghadessy. (Open Linguistics Ser.). 265p. 1992. 55.00 (*0-86187-989-9*) St Martin.

Registra Quorundam Abbatum Monasterii S. Albani Qui Saeculo XVMO Floruere see Chronica Monasterii S. Albani

Registrar. Jack Rudman. (Career Examination Ser.: C-1452). 1994. pap. 27.95 (*0-8373-1452-6*) Nat Learn.

Registrar's Guide to Facilities Planning & Management. American Association of Collegiate Registrars & Admissions Officers Staff. 61p. reprint ed. pap. 25.00 (*0-317-26608-X*, 2024074) Bks Demand.

Registrasie van Aktes Wet Forty-Seven van 1937: Deeds Registries Act 47 of 1937. ring bd. write for info. (*0-7021-1642-4*, Pub. by Juta SA) Gaunt.

Registration Act. 4th ed. R. Rustomji. (C). 1989. 265.00 (*0-685-27901-4*) St Mut.

Registration & the Draft. Ed. by Martin Anderson. (Publication Ser.: No. 242). 415p. (C). 1982. 7.98 (*0-8179-7421-0*) Hoover Inst Pr.

Registration Examination for Dieticians (RED) Jack Rudman. (Admission Test Ser.: ATS-41). 1994. pap. 39.95 (*0-8373-5041-7*) Nat Learn.

***Registration Methods for Small History Museums.** 3rd ed. Daniel B. Reibel. LC 96-51217. (AASLH Ser.). (Illus.). 192p. 1997. pap. 17.95 (*0-7619-8905-6*) AltaMira Pr.

***Registration Methods for the Small Museums.** 3rd ed. Daniel B. Reibel. LC 97-4593. (AASLH Ser.). (Illus.). 300p. 1997. 49.00 (*0-7619-8904-8*) AltaMira Pr.

***Registration of Baroque Organ Music.** Barbara Owen. LC 96-33081. 1997. write for info. (*0-253-33240-0*); pap. write for info. (*0-253-21085-2*) Ind U Pr.

Registration of City School Children: A Consideration of the Subject of the City School Census. John D. Haney. LC 76-176836. (Columbia University. Teachers College. Contributions to Education Ser.: No. 30). reprint ed. 37.50 (*0-404-55030-4*) AMS Pr.

Registration of J. S. Bach's Organ Works. Thomas Harmon. (Illus.). vi, 372p. (Orig.). 1978. pap. 83.00 (*0-913746-25-8*) Organ Lit.

Registration Techniques. 26p. 17.95 (*0-914951-18-1*) LERN.

Registro Bibliografico: Las Impresiones Digitales de un Libro. Florencio O. Santillan. (Illus.). 77p. (Orig.). (SPA.). (C). 1989. pap. text ed. 12.00 (*0-929928-01-6*) Fog Pubns.

***Registro de Clase.** (SPA.). 1998. pap. 2.25 (*1-890219-26-6*) Life Pubs Intl.

***Registro de General.** 1997. write for info. (*1-890219-27-4*) Life Pubs Intl.

Registro de Reglamentos. Ed. by Butterworth Staff. ring bd. 255.00 (*0-614-05956-9*) MICHIE.

Registros y Analisis De Accidentes De Trabajo. 38p. 10.00 (*0-317-04650-0*) Inter-Am Safety.

Registrum Cartarum Ecclesie Sancti Egidii De Edinburgh. Ed. by David Laing. LC 76-174803. (Bannatyne Club, Edinburgh. Publications: No. 105). reprint ed. 47.50 (*0-404-52860-0*) AMS Pr.

Registrum De Dunfermelyn. Ed. by Cosm N. Innes. LC 70-164810. (Bannatyne Club, Edinburgh. Publications: No. 74). reprint ed. 65.00 (*0-404-52793-0*) AMS Pr.

Registrum Domus De Soltre. Ed. by David Laing. LC 77-171638. (Bannatyne Club, Edinburgh. Publications: No. 109). reprint ed. 42.50 (*0-404-52863-5*) AMS Pr.

Registrum Episcopatus Aberdonensis: Ecclesie Cathedralis Aberdonensis Regesta Que Extant in Unum Collecta, 2 vols. Aberdeen, Scotland (Diocese Staff). Ed. by Cosmo N. Innes. LC 77-38504. (Maitland Club, Glasgow. Publications: No. 63). 1845. 165.00 (*0-404-53065-6*) AMS Pr.

Registrum Episcopatus Brechinensis, 2 vols. Ed. by Patrick Chalmers & John I. Chalmers. LC 72-39524. (Bannatyne Club, Edinburgh. Publications: No. 102). reprint ed. 155.00 (*0-404-52855-4*) AMS Pr.

Registrum Episcopatus Glasguensis, 2 vols., Set. Ed. by Cosmo N. Innes. (Maitland Club, Glasgow Ser.: No. 61). reprint ed. 95.00 (*0-404-52794-9*) AMS Pr.

Registrum Episcopatus Moraviensis. Ed. by Cosmo N. Innes. LC 71-172742. (Bannatyne Club, Edinburgh. Publications: No. 58). reprint ed. 57.50 (*0-404-52768-X*) AMS Pr.

Registrum Epistolarum Fratris Johannis Peckham, Archiepiscopi Cantuanriensis, 3 vols. Ed. by Charles Martin. (Rolls Ser.: No. 77). 1974. reprint ed. 210.00 (*0-8115-1147-2*) Periodicals Srv.

Registrum epistolarum Stephani de Lexinton abbatis de Stannlegia et de Saviagnaco see Stephen of Lexington: Letters from Ireland, 1228-1229

Registrum Honoris De Morton, 2 Vols. Ed. by Thomas Thomson et al. LC 76-173002. 1853. 95.00 (*0-404-52836-8*) AMS Pr.

Registrum Malmesburiense: The Register of Malmesbury Abbey, 2 vols. Ed. by J. S. Brewer & Charles T. Martin. (Rolls Ser.: No. 72). 1974. reprint ed. 140.00 (*0-8115-1140-5*) Periodicals Srv.

Registrum Metellanum, I. Maitland Club Staff. LC 72-967. (Maitland Club, Glasgow. Publications: No. 11). reprint ed. 27.50 (*0-404-52941-0*) AMS Pr.

Registrum Monasterii De Passelet. Paisley Abbey Staff. Ed. by Cosmo N. Innes. LC 75-174311. (Maitland Club, Glasgow. Publications: No. 17). reprint ed. 67.50 (*0-404-52954-2*) AMS Pr.

Registrum Palatinum Dunelmense: The Register of Richard de Kellawe...1311-1316, 4 vols. Ed. by Thomas D. Hardy. (Rolls Ser.: No. 62). 1974. reprint ed. 280.00 (*0-8115-1130-8*) Periodicals Srv.

Registrum S. Marie De Neubotle. Newbattle Abbey Staff. Ed. by Cosmo N. Innes. LC 74-173074. (Bannatyne Club, Edinburgh. Publications: No. 89). reprint ed. 52.50 (*0-404-52819-8*) AMS Pr.

Registrum Sive Liber Irrotularius Et Consuetudinarius Prioratus Beatae Mariae Wigorniensis. William H. Hale. LC 17-1258. (Camden Society, London. Publications, First Ser.: No. 91). reprint ed. 65.00 (*0-404-50191-5*) AMS Pr.

***Registry.** 1997. 39.99 (*0-672-30992-0*) Macmillan.

Registry of California Wineries: A Complete Guide to California Wines & Wineries. Leslie K. Brown. LC 88-71590. (Illus.). 346p. (Orig.). 1988. pap. text ed. 22.00 (*0-9621771-0-5*) Colwyn Corp.

Registry of Death. Peter Lamb. LC 96-22478. (Illus.). 56p. 1996. pap. 15.95 (*0-87816-448-0*) Kitchen Sink.

Registry of Deeds, Dublin, Abstract of Wills, 1708-1745 & 1746-1785 Vol. I & II, 2 vols., Set. Ed. by P. Beryl Eustace. 883p. 1996. reprint ed. pap. 65.00 (*0-614-16539-3*, 9179) Clearfield Co.

Registry of Mass Spectral Data. 5th ed. Fred W. McLafferty. 1989. reel tape 6,000.00 (*0-471-51593-0*) Wiley.

Registry of Mass Spectral Data with Structures, CD-ROM. 5th ed. Fred W. McLafferty. 1989. pap. text ed. 3,995.00 incl. cd-rom (*0-471-51297-4*) Wiley.

Registry of Professional Reporters & Membership Directory. 350p. pap. 50.00 (*0-318-15866-3*, 184) Natl Ct Report.

Registry of Toxic Effects of Chemical Substances, RTECS: A Comprehensive Guide. Ed. by Doris V. Sweet. 70p. (Orig.). (C). 1994. pap. text ed. 30.00 (*0-7881-0565-5*) DIANE Pub.

Registry of Women in Religious Studies, 1981-1982. Ed. by Lorine M. Getz. 1982. pap. 49.95 (*0-88946-277-1*) E Mellen.

Registry Review for Computed Tomography. Daniel N. DeMaio. Ed. by Lisa Biello. LC 95-49210. 240p. 1996. pap. 25.00 (*0-7216-6285-4*) Saunders.

Regius Manuscript: The Earliest Masonic Document. Frederick M. Hunter. 100p. 1996. pap. 15.95 (*1-56459-526-9*) Kessinger Pub.

Regla Kimbisa del Santo Cristo del Buen Viaje. 2nd ed. Lydia Cabrera. (Coleccion del Chichereku). 85p. (SPA.). 1986. reprint ed. pap. 6.95 (*0-89729-396-7*) Ediciones.

Regla Papers: An Indexed Guide to the Papers of the Romero de Terreros Family & Other Colonial & Early National Mexican Families. Ed. by John F. Guido & Lawrence R. Stark. (Illus.). 140p. 1995. pap. 28.00 (*0-87422-111-0*) Wash St U Pr.

Reglamento Para El Servicio De Correos De La Republica.. .1877. (Guatemala Postal History Pamphlet Ser.: No. 3). (Illus.). 68p. 1984. reprint ed. pap. 6.00 (*0-913129-05-4*) La Tienda.

Reglamentos Por Agencia. Ed. by Butterworth Staff. ring bd. 60.00 (*0-614-05957-7*) MICHIE.

Reglas De Catalogacion Angloamericanas. 395p. (SPA.). 1970. 8.00 (*0-8270-3075-4*) OAS.

Reglas de Congo: Palo Monte-Mayombe. Lydia Cabrera. LC 79-50627. (Coleccion del Chichereku). 225p. (Orig.). (SPA.). 1986. pap. 18.00 (*0-89729-398-3*) Ediciones.

Reglas De Evidencia, 1979: Edicion Especial. 170p. (SPA.). 1979. pap. 20.00 (*0-88063-504-5*) MICHIE.

***Reglas de los Buenos Principios Corrientes de Fabricacion para los Farmaceuticos Completados (RBPCFs), Vol. 8204.** LC 87-3892. 1992. pap. 3.95 (*0-614-30069-X*) Keystone Pr.

Reglas de los Buenos Principios de Fabricacion para Fabricacion, el Empacar, el Almacenaje, y la Instalacion de Aparatos Medicos (BFSs de Aparatos), Vol. 8205. 3rd ed. 1994. pap. 3.95 (*0-940701-49-9*) Keystone Pr.

Reglas De Procedimiento Civil, 1979: Edicion Especial. 250p. (SPA.). 1979. pap. 16.00 (*0-88063-527-4*) MICHIE.

Reglas Para la Ordenacion Alfabetica De los Catalogos. (Manuales del Bibliotecario Ser.: No. 8). 1978. reprint ed. pap. text ed. 3.00 (*0-8270-3080-0*) OAS.

Reglas Parlamentarias. H. F. Kerfoot. Tr. by Jose M. Sanchez from ENG. 88p. (SPA.). 1986. reprint ed. 3.99 (*0-311-11012-6*) Casa Bautista.

Reglas y Consejos Sobre Investigacion Cientifica. Santiago Ramon y Cajal. (Nueva Austral Ser.: Vol. 232). (SPA.). 1991. pap. text ed. 24.95 (*84-239-7232-1*) Elliots Bks.

Regle de l'Homme. Joseph Kessel. (Folio Ser.: No. 2092). (FRE.). pap. 6.95 (*2-07-038180-3*) Schoenhof.

Regle de l'Homme. Joseph Kessel. 124p. (FRE.). 1984. pap. 10.95 (*0-7859-2575-9*, 2070381803) Fr & Eur.

Regle du Jeu, Vol. 1: Biffures. Michel Leiris. (FRE.). 1991. pap. 16.95 (*0-7859-2947-9*) Fr & Eur.

Regle du Jeu, Vol. 2: Fourbis. Michel Leiris. (FRE.). 1991. pap. 15.95 (*0-7859-3395-6*) Fr & Eur.

Regle du Jeu, Vol. 3: Fibrilles. Michel Leiris. (FRE.). 1991. pap. 16.95 (*0-7859-2953-3*) Fr & Eur.

Regle du Jeu, Vol. 4: Frele Bruit. Michel Leiris. (FRE.). 1991. pap. 19.95 (*0-7859-2954-1*) Fr & Eur.

Reglen der Dt. Rechtschreibung. (Duden-Taschenbuch Ser.: No. 3). 160p. 1993. 12.25 (*3-411-04933-2*, Pub. by Bibliogr Inst Brockhaus GW) Langenscheidt.

Regles Utiles et Claires Pour la Direction De L'Esprit et la Recherche De la Verite. Rene Descartes. (Archives Internationales d'Histoire des Idees (International Archives of the History of Ideas) Ser.: No. 88). 364p. 1978. lib. bdg. 165.00 (*90-247-1907-0*, Pub. by M Nijhoff NE) Kluwer Ac.

Regnal Formulas in Byzantine Egypt. Roger S. Bagnall & K. A. Worp. LC 79-1316. (Bulletin of the American Society of Papyrologists Supplements Ser.: No. 2). 102p. reprint ed. pap. 29.10 (*0-7837-5419-1*, 2045183) Bks Demand.

Regole Armoniche see Monuments of Music & Music Literature in Facsimile

Regolith Exploration Geochemistry in Arctic & Temperate Terrains. Ed. by L. K. Kauranne et al. LC 92-11570. (Handbook of Exploration Geochemistry Ser.: Vol. 5). 444p. 1992. 213.00 (*0-444-89154-4*) Elsevier.

Regolith, Soils & Landforms. Cliff Ollier & Colin Pain. 316p. 1996. text ed. 105.00 (*0-471-96121-3*) Wiley.

Regreening Australia: Caring for Young Trees 2. Nan Oates. (Illus.). 76p. 1990. pap. 15.00 (*0-643-05088-4*, Pub. by CSIRO AT) Aubrey Bks.

Regreening the National Parks. Michael Frome. LC 91-17477. 289p. (Orig.). 1991. pap. 21.00 (*0-8165-1288-4*) U of Ariz Pr.

Regresar Quiere Decir Seguir Adelante. June F. Esparza. Ed. by Anna Ramirez-Pekarsky & Carmen DeLuna. Tr. by Carmen DeLuna & Maria Montalvo. (Illus.). 208p. (Orig.). (SPA.). (C). 1997. pap. 14.95 (*0-9647161-1-9*) Thgts in Motion.

***Regreso a Sion - The Return to Zion: Cronicas III.** Bodie Thoene. 364p. (SPA.). 1987. write for info. (*1-56063-512-6*) Editorial Unilit.

Regreso al Colegio. Charles M. Schulz. (Peanuts Ser.). 64p. (SPA.). (J). 1971. 4.95 (*0-8288-4509-3*) Fr & Eur.

Regreso Al Paraiso. Raye Morgan. (Silhouette Deseo Ser.: No. 148). 1996. mass mkt. 3.50 (*0-373-35148-8*, 1-35148-5) Harlequin Bks.

Regressed Patient. L. B. Boyer. LC 82-24363. 368p. 1983. 35.00 (*0-87668-626-9*) Aronson.

Regression. John M. Bennett. 1988. pap. 2.00 (*0-935350-18-7*) Luna Bisonte.

Regression: A Second Course on Statistics. Thomas H. Wonnacott & Ronald J. Wonnacott. LC 86-14384. 576p. (C). 1986. reprint ed. text ed. 54.50 (*0-89874-970-0*) Krieger.

Regression Analysis. Graybill. (Statistics Ser.). 1994. lab manual ed., pap. 20.95 (*0-534-19870-8*) Wadsworth Pub.

Regression Analysis. Graybill. (Statistics Ser.). 1994. lab manual ed., pap. 20.95 (*0-534-19871-6*) Wadsworth Pub.

Regression Analysis. Graybill. (Statistics Ser.). 1994. student ed., pap. 20.95 (*0-534-19876-7*) Wadsworth Pub.

Regression Analysis: Concepts & Applications. Franklin A. Graybill & Hariharan K. Iyer. 701p. 1994. text ed. 75.95 (*0-534-19869-4*) Wadsworth Pub.

Regression Analysis: Theory, Methods & Applications. Amartya K. Sen. (Texts in Statistics Ser.). (Illus.). xv, 347p. 1995. 52.95 incl. disk (*0-387-97211-0*) Spr-Verlag.

Regression Analysis & Its Application: A Data-Oriented Approach. R. F. Gunst & R. L. Mason. (Statistics: Textbooks & Monographs: Vol. 34). 424p. 1980. 85.00 (*0-8247-6993-7*) Dekker.

Regression Analysis by Example. 2nd ed. Samprit Chatterjee & Bertram Price. LC 91-11046. (Probability & Mathematical Statistics Ser.: Applied Probability & Statistics Section Ser.). 304p. 1991. text ed. 64.95 (*0-471-88479-0*) Wiley.

Regression Analysis of Prior Experiences of Key Production Personnel As Predictors of Revenues from High-Grossing Motion Pictures in American Release. Thomas S. Simonet. Ed. by Garth S. Jowett. LC 79-6685. (Dissertations on Film, 1980 Ser.). 1980. lib. bdg. 22.95 (*0-405-12917-3*) Ayer.

Regression Analysis with Application. Ed. by G. Barrie Wetherill. (Monographs on Statistics & Applied Probability). 250p. 1986. pap. 35.00 (*0-412-27490-6*, 9984) Chapman & Hall.

Regression & Apocalypse: Studies in North American Literary Expressionism. Sherrill E. Grace. 1990. 45.00 (*0-8020-5816-7*) U of Toronto Pr.

Regression & Econometric Methods. David S. Huang. LC 80-12646. 288p. 1980. reprint ed. lib. bdg. 27.50 (*0-89874-181-5*) Krieger.

Regression & Factor Analysis in Econometrics. H. F. Schilderinck. (Tilburg Studies in Econometrics: No. 1). 1978. lib. bdg. 65.00 (*90-207-0664-0*) Kluwer Ac.

Regression & Linear Models. Richard B. Darlington. 576p. 1990. text ed. write for info. (*0-07-015372-8*) McGraw.

Regression Diagnostics. John Fox. (Quantitative Applications in the Social Sciences Ser.: Vol. 79). 96p. (C). 1991. pap. text ed. 9.95 (*0-8039-3971-X*) Sage.

Regression Diagnostics: Identifying Influential Data & Sources of Collinearity. David A. Belsley et al. LC 79-19876. (Probability & Mathematical Statistics Ser.). 320p. 1980. text ed. 117.00 (*0-471-05856-4*) Wiley.

Regression Estimation from Grouped Observations. Y. Haitovsky. 1973. 21.95 (*0-85264-219-9*) Lubrecht & Cramer.

***Regression Hypnotherapy: Transcripts of Transformation.** Randal Churchill. Ed. by Cheryl Canfield. 320p. 39.95 (*0-9656218-1-2*) Transforming Pr.

***Regression Methods Applied.** John Harraway. 1996. 49.95 (*0-908569-92-0*, Pub. by U Otago Pr NZ) Intl Spec Bk.

Regression Models: Censored, Sample Selected, or Truncated Data. Richard Breen. (Quantitative Applications in the Social Science Ser.: Vol. 111). 96p. 1996. pap. 9.95 (*0-8039-5710-6*) Sage.

***Regression Models for Categorical & Limited Dependent Variables: Analysis & Interpretation.** J. Scott Long. (Advanced Quantitative Techniques in the Social Sciences Ser.: Vol. 7). 416p. 1997. 45.00 (*0-8039-7374-8*) Sage.

Regression, Stress, & Readjustment in Aging: A Structured, Bio-Psychosocial Perspective on Coping & Professional Support. Zeev Ben-Sira. LC 91-17302. 184p. 1991. text ed. 49.95 (*0-275-94078-0*, C4078, Praeger Pubs) Greenwood.

Regression Therapy: A Handbook for Professionals, 2 vols. Winafred B. Lucas. 1175p. 1993. 49.50 (*1-882530-00-4*) Deep Forest Pr.

Regression Therapy: A Handbook for Professionals, 2 vols., Vol. I. Winafred B. Lucas. 1175p. 1993. write for info. (*1-882530-01-2*) Deep Forest Pr.

Regression Therapy: A Handbook for Professionals, 2 vols., Vol. II. Winafred B. Lucas. 1175p. 1993. write for info. (*1-882530-02-0*) Deep Forest Pr.

***Regression Therapy Using Hypnosis: How Reliving Early Experiences Can Improve Your Life.** Ursula Markham. (Orig.). pap. 12.95 (*0-7499-1530-7*, Pub. by Piatkus Bks UK) London Brdge.

Regression Therapy Using Hypnosis: How Reliving Early Experiences Can Improve Your Life. Ursula Markham. 126p. (Orig.). 1996. pap. text ed. 12.95 (*0-7499-1032-1*, Pub. by Piatkus Bks UK) London Brdge.

Regression to Dependence: A Second Opportunity for Ego Integration & Developmental Progression. Robert C. Van Sweden. LC 94-11404. 256p. 1994. 35.00 (*1-56821-279-8*) Aronson.

Regression with Dummy Variables. Melissa A. Hardy. (Quantitative Applications in the Social Sciences Ser.: Vol. 93). (Illus.). 96p. (C). 1993. pap. text ed. 9.95 (*0-8039-5128-0*) Sage.

Regressive Sets & the Theory of Isols. Thomas G. McLaughlin. LC 82-5115. (Lecture Notes in Pure & Applied Mathematics Ser.: No. 66). 383p. reprint ed. pap. 109.20 (*0-7837-5172-9*, 2044902) Bks Demand.

Regret. Janet Landman. 320p. 1993. 30.00 (*0-19-507178-6*) OUP.

Regret Not a Moment. Nicole McGehee. 528p. 1994. mass mkt. 5.99 (*0-446-60071-7*) Warner Bks.

Regrets et autres oeuvres poetiques. Joachim Du Bellay. Ed. by Jolliffe. Bd. with Antiquitez de Rome Plus un Songe ou Vision sur le Mesme Subject. (Textes Litteraires Francais Ser.). 8.75 (*0-685-34184-4*) Fr & Eur.

Regrets, Les Antiquites de Rome, Defense et Illustration, Etc. Joachim Du Bellay. (Poesie Ser.). 317p. (FRE.). 1967. pap. 9.95 (*2-07-032147-9*) Schoenhof.

Regrets Only. Sally Quinn. 672p. 1987. mass mkt. 5.99 (*0-345-34459-6*) Ballantine.

Regrowing the American Economy. Ed. by G. William Miller. LC 83-3171. 192p. 1983. 11.95 (*0-13-771022-4*); pap. 4.95 (*0-13-771014-3*) Am Assembly.

Regrowing the American Economy. American Assembly Staff. LC 83-3171. 191p. reprint ed. pap. 54.50 (*0-685-20468-5*, 2029866) Bks Demand.

Regsgeskiedenis. De Vos. 314p. 1991. write for info. (*0-7021-2762-0*, Pub. by Juta SA); pap. write for info. (*0-7021-2671-3*, Pub. by Juta SA) Gaunt.

Regula Musice Plane. fac. ed. Bonaventura Da Brescia. (Monuments of Music & Music Literature in Facsimile Ser., Series II: Vol. 77). (Illus.). 46p. (ITA.). 1975. lib. bdg. 20.00 (*0-8450-2277-6*) Broude.

Regulae Ad Directionem Ingenii: Texte Critique Etabli Par G. Crapulli avec la Version Hollandaise du XVIIieme Siecle. Rene Descartes. (International Archives of the History of Ideas Ser.: No. 12). 278p. 1966. lib. bdg. 82.50 (*90-247-0188-0*, Pub. by M Nijhoff NE) Kluwer Ac.

Regular & Chaotic Dynamics. 2nd ed. A. J. Lichtenberg & M. A. Lieberman. Ed. by F. John & Jerrold E. Marsden. (Applied Mathematical Sciences Ser.: Vol. 38). Orig. Title: Regular & Stochastic Motion. (Illus.). 656p. 1994. 72.95 (*0-387-97745-7*) Spr-Verlag.

Regular & Stochastic Motion. A. J. Lichtenberg & M. A. Lieberman. (Applied Mathematical Sciences Ser.: Vol. 38). (Illus.). 499p. 1989. 56.00 (*0-387-90707-6*) Spr-Verlag.

Regular & Stochastic Motion see Regular & Chaotic Dynamics

Regular B-Groups, Degenerating Riemann Surfaces, & Spectral Theory. D. Hejhal. LC 91-1171. (Memoirs Ser.: Vol. 88/437). 138p. 1990. pap. text ed. 22.00 (*0-8218-2499-6*, MEMO/88/437) Am Math.

Regular Complex Polytopes. 2nd ed. H. S. Coxeter. (Illus.). 224p. (C). 1991. text ed. 64.95 (*0-521-39490-2*) Cambridge U Pr.

Regular Confession: An Exercise in Sacramental Spirituality. Arthur B. Chappell. LC 91-44337. (American University Studies: Theology & Religion: Ser. VII, Vol. 130). 202p. (C). 1992. text ed. 40.95 (*0-8204-1813-7*) P Lang Pubng.

An Asterisk (*) at the beginning of an entry indicates that the title is appearing in BIP for the first time.

R

Regular Cycles of Money, Inflation, Regulation & Depression. Ravi Batra. LC 85-50598. (Illus.). 192p. (C). 1985. 20.00 (*0-939352-04-4*) Venus Bks.

Regular Dad: Making Fatherhood Fun. Ron G. Woods. LC 86-81572. 175p. (Orig.). 1986. pap. 12.98 (*0-88290-313-6*) Horizon Utah.

Regular Differential Forms. Ed. by E. Kunz & R. Waldi. LC 88-28825. (Contemporary Mathematics Ser.: No. 79). 153p. 1988. pap. 23.00 (*0-8218-5085-7*, CONM/79) Am Math.

Regular Dirichlet-Voronoi Partitions for the Second Triclinic Group: Proceedings. M. I. Stogrin. LC 75-23284. (Proceedings of the Steklov Institute of Mathematics Ser.: No.123). 116p. 1975. pap. 55.00 (*0-8218-3023-6*, STEKLO/123) Am Math.

Regular Economic Cycles: Money, Inflation, Regulation & Depressions. Ravi Batra. 192p. 1989. text ed. 24.95 (*0-312-03260-9*) St Martin.

Regular Education Initiative: Alternative Perspectives on Concepts, Issues, & Methods. Ed. by J. W. Lloyd et al. (Illus.). 320p. (C). 1991. text ed. 36.95 (*0-9625233-3-X*) Sycamore Pub.

Regular Exercise: A Handbook for Clinical Practice. Steven Jonas. LC 94-42548. 264p. 1995. 34.95 (*0-8261-8860-5*) Springer Pub.

Regular Figures. Ian N. Sneddon. LC 63-10121. (International Series of Monographs on Pure & Applied Mathematics: Vol. 48). 1964. 160.00 (*0-08-010058-9*, Pub. by Pergamon Repr UK) Franklin.

Regular Flood of Mishap. Tom Birdseye. LC 93-9888. (Illus.). 32p. (J). (ps-3). 1994. lib. bdg. 15.95 (*0-8234-1070-6*) Holiday.

***Regular Flood of Mishap.** Tom Birdseye. (Illus.). 1997. pap. 6.95 (*0-8234-1338-1*) Holiday.

Regular Guy. Mona Simpson. 1996. 25.00 (*0-679-45091-2*) McKay.

Regular Guy. Mona Simpson. 1997. pap. 13.00 (*0-679-77271-5*) McKay.

***Regular Guy.** Mona Simpson. 372p. 25.00 (*0-614-23185-X*) Knopf.

Regular Mappings & the Space of Homeomorphisms on a 3-Manifold. M. E. Hamstrom. (Memoirs of the American Mathematical Society Ser.: Vol. 40). 42p. 1986. reprint ed. 16.00 (*0-8218-1240-8*, MEMO/1/40C) Am Math.

Regular Polytopes. H. S. Coxeter. (Illus.). 321p. 1973. reprint ed. pap. 8.95 (*0-486-61480-8*) Dover.

Regular Respite: An Evaluation of a Shoptial Rota Bed Scheme for Elderly People. Ed. by Michael Nolan & Gordon Grant. 312p. (C). 1992. 75.00 (*0-86242-115-2*, Pub. by Age Concern Eng UK) St Mut.

Regular Rolling Noah. George E. Lyon. LC 90-39984. (Illus.). 32p. (J). (gr. k-3). 1991. reprint ed. pap. 4.95 (*0-689-71449-1*, Aladdin Paperbacks) S&S Childrens.

Regular Structures: Lectures in Pattern Theory III. U. Gronander. (Applied Mathematical Sciences Ser.: Vol. 33). 569p. 1981. 85.95 (*0-387-90560-X*) Spr-Verlag.

Regular Variation. N. H. Bingham et al. (Encyclopedia of Mathematics & Its Applications Ser.: No. 27). (Illus.). 500p. 1987. text ed. 125.00 (*0-521-30787-2*) Cambridge U Pr.

Regular Variation. N. H. Bingham et al. (Encyclopedia of Mathematics & Its Applications Ser.: No. 27). (Illus.). 516p. (C). 1989. pap. text ed. 49.95 (*0-521-37943-1*) Cambridge U Pr.

Regularity Problem for Quasilinear Elliptic & Parabolic Systems, Vol. XXI. Alexander A. Koshelev. Ed. by A. Dold & F. Takens. LC 95-37502. (Lecture Notes in Mathematics Ser.: Vol. 1614). 255p. 1995. 53.95 (*3-540-60251-8*) Spr-Verlag.

Regularity Theory & Stochastic Flows for Parabolic SPDES. F. Flandoli. (Stochastics Monographs). 87p. 1995. text ed. 30.00 (*2-88449-045-0*) Gordon & Breach.

Regularity Theory for Quasilinear Elliptic Systems & Monge-Ampere Equations in Two Dimensions. F. Schulz. Ed. by A. Dold et al. (Lecture Notes in Mathematics Ser.: Vol. 1445). xv, 123p. 1990. 31.95 (*0-387-53103-3*) Spr-Verlag.

Regularization Methods for Ill-Proposed Problems. Morozov. 272p. 1993. 81.00 (*0-8493-9311-6*) CRC Pr.

Regularization of Business Investment. Universities-National Bureau Staff. (Conference Ser.: No. 4). 539p. 1954. reprint ed. 140.20 (*0-87014-195-3*) Natl Bur Econ Res.

Regularization of Inverse Problems. Heinz W. Engl et al. LC 96-28672. (Mathematics & Its Applications Ser.). 1996. lib. bdg. 160.00 (*0-7923-4157-0*) Kluwer Ac.

Regulars in the Redwoods: The U. S. Army in Northern California 1852-1861. William F. Strobridge. LC 94-71442. (Frontier Military Ser.: Vol. XVII). (Illus.). 283p. 1994. 29.95 (*0-87062-214-5*) A H Clark.

***Regulated Chemicals Directory 1993 Autumn Supplement.** (C). (gr. 13 up). 1993. text ed. write for info. (*0-412-04301-7*) Chapman & Hall.

***Regulated Chemicals Directory 1993 Spring Supplement.** (C). (gr. 13 up). 1993. text ed. write for info. (*0-412-04281-9*) Chapman & Hall.

***Regulated Chemicals Directory 1993 Summer Supplement.** (C). (gr. 13 up). 1993. text ed. write for info. (*0-412-04291-6*) Chapman & Hall.

***Regulated Chemicals Directory 1994.** ChemADVISOR Inc. Staff. (Illus.). 1600p. (Orig.). (C). (gr. 13 up). 1994. pap. text ed. 299.95 (*0-412-05281-4*) Chapman & Hall.

Regulated Chemicals Directory 1995. Chemical Advisor Inc. Staff. (Environmental Engineering Ser.). 1988p. 1995. text ed. 329.95 (*0-442-02124-0*) Van Nos Reinhold.

Regulated Credit: The Credit & Security Aspects. A. J. Duggan et al. lx, 848p. 1989. 127.50 (*0-455-20832-8*, Pub. by Law Bk Co AT) Gaunt.

Regulated Credit: The Sale Aspect. A. J. Duggan. xxxix, 407p. 1986. 82.00 (*0-455-20691-0*, Pub. by Law Bk Co AT) Gaunt.

Regulated Deregulation of the Financial System in Korea. Ismail Dalla & Deena Khatkhate. LC 95-30168. (Discussion Papers: Vol. 292). 42p. 1995. 6.95 (*0-8213-3356-9*, 13356) World Bank.

Regulated Economy: A Historical Approach to Political Economy. Ed. by Claudia D. Goldin & Gary D. Libecap. LC 94-4931. (National Bureau of Economic Research Project Report Ser.). 320p. 1994. 56.00 (*0-226-30110-9*) U Ch Pr.

Regulated Enterprise: Natural Gas Pipelines & Northeastern Markets, 1938-1954. Christopher J. Castaneda. LC 92-23827. (Historical Perspectives on Business Enterprise Ser.). 208p. 1993. 35.00 (*0-8142-0590-9*) Ohio St U Pr.

Regulated Industries. Jones. 1976. text ed. 38.00 (*0-88277-509-X*) Foundation Pr.

Regulated Industries. Paul W. MacAvoy. (C). 1979. pap. text ed. 4.95 (*0-393-95094-8*) Norton.

Regulated Industries in a Nutshell. 3rd ed. Richard J. Pierce & Ernest Gellhorn. LC 94-8849. (Nutshell Ser.). 374p. 1994. pap. 17.00 (*0-314-03660-1*) West Pub.

Regulated Landscape: Lessons on Statewide Land Use Planning from Oregon. Gerrit Knaap & Arthur C. Nelson. (Illus.). 243p. 1992. pap. text ed. 20.00 (*1-55844-120-4*) Lincoln Inst Land.

Regulated Power Supplies. 4th ed. Irving M. Gottlieb. 1992. pap. text ed. 28.95 (*0-07-023922-3*) McGraw.

Regulated Power Supplies. 4th ed. Irving M. Gottlieb. 472p. 1992. 39.95 (*0-8306-2540-2*, 3991); pap. 24.95 (*0-8306-2539-9*, 3991) McGraw-Hill Prof.

Regulated Rewriting in Formal Language Theory. J. Dassow & G. Paun. (EATCS Monographs on Theoretical Computer Science: Vol. 18). (Illus.). 308p. 1990. 93.95 (*0-387-51414-7*) Spr-Verlag.

***Regulated Riparian Model Water Code: Final Report of the Water Laws Committee of the Water Resources Planning & Management Division of the American Society of Civil Engineers.** American Society of Civil Engineers Staff & Joseph W. Dellapenna. LC 97-158. 1997. write for info. (*0-7844-0226-4*) Am Soc Civil Eng.

Regulated Streams. Ed. by J. F. Craig & J. B. Kemper. LC 87-16596. (Advances in Ecology Ser.). (Illus.). 444p. 1987. 120.00 (*0-306-42674-9*, Plenum Pr) Plenum.

Regulating a New Economy: Public Policy & Economic Change in America, 1900-1933. Morton Keller. (Illus.). 300p. 1990. 34.50 (*0-674-75362-3*) HUP.

Regulating a New Economy: Public Policy & Economic Change in America 1900-1933. Morton Keller. (Illus.). 312p. 1996. pap. 18.95 (*0-674-75363-1*) HUP.

Regulating a New Society: Public Policy & Social Change in America, 1900-1933. Morton Keller. LC 93-47567. (Illus.). 410p. (C). 1979. text ed. 49.95 (*0-674-75366-6*, KELREN) HUP.

Regulating Agriculture. Ed. by Philip Lowe et al. 190p. 1995. text ed. 95.00 (*0-471-95932-4*) Wiley.

Regulating Agriculture, Vol. 5. (C). 1992. 95.00 (*1-85346-202-0*, Pub. by D Fulton Pubs UK) St Mut.

Regulating America, Regulating Sweden: A Comparative Study of Occupational Safety & Health Policy. Steven Kelman. 280p. 1981. 32.50 (*0-262-11076-8*) MIT Pr.

Regulating Big Business: Antitrust in Great Britain & America, 1880-1990. Tony Freyer. 384p. (C). 1992. text ed. 69.95 (*0-521-35207-X*) Cambridge U Pr.

Regulating Birth see **Making Midwives Legal: Childbirth, Medicine, & the Law**

Regulating Bodies: Essays in Medical Sociology. Bryan S. Turner. LC 92-4229. 256p. (C). 1992. pap. 16.95 (*0-415-08264-1*, A7759); text ed. 79.95 (*0-415-06963-7*, A7755) Routledge.

Regulating British Medicine: The General Medical Council. M. Stacey. LC 92-5579. 293p. 1992. text ed. 84.95 (*0-471-93189-6*, Wiley-L) Wiley.

Regulating Broadcast Programming. Thomas G. Krattenmaker & Lucas A. Powe, Jr. (AEI Studies in Telecommunication Deregulation). (Illus.). 350p. 1994. 32.50 (*0-262-11195-0*) MIT Pr.

Regulating Business: The Search for an Optimum. Institute for Contemporary Studies Staff. 260p. 1978. pap. text ed. 21.95 (*0-917616-27-8*) Transaction Pubs.

Regulating Business by Independent Commission. Marver H. Bernstein. LC 77-2985. 306p. 1977. reprint ed. text ed. 45.00 (*0-8371-9563-2*, BERB, Greenwood Pr) Greenwood.

Regulating Campaign Finance. Ed. by Lloyd N. Cutler et al. LC 85-72102. (Annals of the American Academy of Political & Social Science Ser.: Vol. 486). 200p. (Orig.). 1986. text ed. 26.00 (*0-8039-2542-5*); pap. text ed. 17.00 (*0-8039-2543-3*) Sage.

Regulating Confusion: Samuel Johnson & the Crowd. Thomas Reinert. LC 95-32412. 208p. 1996. text ed. 45.95 (*0-8223-1707-9*); pap. text ed. 15.95 (*0-8223-1717-6*) Duke.

Regulating Corporate Groups in Europe. Ed. by David Sugarman & Gunther Teubner. 551p. 1990. 134.00 (*3-7890-1903-8*, Pub. by Nomos Verlags GW) Intl Bk Import.

Regulating Covert Action: Practices, Contexts, & Policies of Covert Coercion Abroad in International & American Law. W. Michael Reisman & James Baker. 256p. (C). 1992. text ed. 35.00 (*0-300-05059-3*) Yale U Pr.

Regulating Danger: The Struggle for Mine Safety in the Rocky Mountain Coal Industry. James Whiteside. LC 89-39702. (Illus.). xvi, 279p. 1990. text ed. 42.50 (*0-8032-4752-4*) U of Nebr Pr.

Regulating Drinking Water in the 1990s. Gilbert. 352p. 1991. 99.95 (*0-87371-595-0*) CRC Pr.

Regulating DSM Program Evaluation. 132p. 1994. 25.00 (*0-614-06942-4*) NARUC.

Regulating Employment & Welfare: Company & National Policies of Labour Force Participation at the End of Worklife in Industrial Countries. Ed. by Frieder Naschold & Bert De Vroom. LC 93-35001. (Studies in Organization: No. 53). x, 496p. (C). 1993. lib. bdg. 98.95 (*3-11-013513-2*) De Gruyter.

Regulating Europe. Ed. by Giandomenico Majone. LC 96-7015. (European Public Policy Ser.). 328p. (C). 1996. pap. 24.95 (*0-415-14296-2*); text ed. 74.95 (*0-415-14295-4*) Routledge.

***Regulating Finance: The Political Economy of Spanish Financial Policy from Franco to Democracy.** Arvid J. Lukauskas. LC 97-4888. (C). 1997. 54.50 (*0-472-10836-0*) U of Mich Pr.

Regulating Flood-Plain Development. Francis C. Murphy. LC 59-16022. (University of Chicago, Department of Geography, Research Paper Ser.: No. 56). 216p. reprint ed. pap. 61.60 (*0-7837-0383-X*, 2040703) Bks Demand.

Regulating for Competition: Government, Law, & the Pharmaceutical Industry in the United Kingdom & France. Leigh Hancher. (Government-Industry Relations Ser.: No. 5). 448p. 1990. 125.00 (*0-19-827570-6*) OUP.

Regulating Forum Selection in International Litigation: The 14th Sokol Colloquium. Ed. by Jack L. Goldsmith. LC 96-39260. 1997. lib. bdg. 95.00 (*0-941320-74-X*) Transnatl Pubs.

Regulating Fraud: White-Collar Crime & the Criminal Process. Michael Levi. 416p. 1990. 55.00 (*0-422-61160-3*, A0718) Routledge Chapman & Hall.

Regulating International Business Through Codes of Conduct. Raymond J. Waldmann. LC 80-19846. (AEI Ser.: No. 287). 152p. reprint ed. pap. 43.40 (*0-7837-1086-0*, 2041618) Bks Demand.

Regulating International Financial Markets: Issues & Policies. Ed. by Franklin R. Edwards. 352p. (C). 1991. lib. bdg. 90.00 (*0-7923-9155-1*) Kluwer Ac.

Regulating Labor: The State & Industrial Relations Reform in Postwar France. Chris Howell. (Illus.). 320p. 1992. text ed. 47.50 (*0-691-07898-X*) Princeton U Pr.

Regulating Media: The Experience of Six Countries. Wolfgang Hoffmann-Riem. (Guilford Communication Ser.). 424p. 1996. lib. bdg. 45.00 (*1-57230-029-9*, 0029) Guilford Pr.

***Regulating Medical Progress: The Growth of FDA Controls over Health Care Technology.** John E. Calfee. 125p. 1998. 29.95 (*0-8447-4034-9*) Am Enterprise.

***Regulating Medical Progress: The Growth of FDA Controls over Health Care Technology.** John E. Calfee. 125p. 1998. pap. 14.95 (*0-8447-4035-7*) Am Enterprise.

Regulating Medical Work: Formal & Informal Controls. Judith Allsop & Linda Mulcahy. LC 96-17728. (Health Services Management Ser.). 224p. 1996. pap. 27.00 (*0-335-19404-4*, Open Univ Pr) Taylor & Francis.

***Regulating Medical Work: Formal & Informal Controls.** Judith Allsop & Linda Mulcahy. (Health Services Management Ser.). 224p. 1996. 89.00 (*0-335-19405-2*, Open Univ Pr) Taylor & Francis.

Regulating Pesticides in Food: The Delaney Paradox. National Research Council Staff. LC 87-61095. (Illus.). 288p. reprint ed. pap. 82.10 (*0-7837-5984-3*, 2045791) Bks Demand.

Regulating Pesticides in Texas. Contrib. by Susan Hadden & Thomas McGarity. LC 84-82118. (Policy Research Project Report: No. 66). 283p. 1984. pap. 8.50 (*0-89940-668-8*) LBJ Sch Pub Aff.

***Regulating Pollution: Does the U. S. System Work?** J. Clarence Davies & Jan Mazurek. LC 97-7159. (Illus.). 56p. 1997. pap. 9.95 (*0-915707-85-3*) Resources Future.

Regulating Power: The Economics of Electricity in the Information Age. Carl Pechman. LC 93-10053. (Topics in Regulatory Economics & Policy Ser.: Vol. 15). 256p. (C). 1993. lib. bdg. 105.00 (*0-7923-9347-3*) Kluwer Ac.

Regulating Privacy: Data Protection & Public Policy in Europe & the United States. Colin J. Bennett. LC 91-30559. 288p. 1992. pap. 18.95 (*0-8014-8010-8*) Cornell U Pr.

Regulating Regional Power Systems. Clinton J. Andrews. LC 94-21702. 416p. 1995. text ed. 75.00 (*0-89930-943-7*, Quorum Bks) Greenwood.

***Regulating Regional Power Systems: Case Studies & Perspectives on Emerging Competition.** Clinton Andrews. 416p. 1995. pap. 59.95 (*0-7803-1139-6*, PP5369) Inst Electrical.

Regulating Reproduction. Robert H. Blank. 272p. (C). 1992. pap. text ed. 16.00 (*0-231-07017-9*) Col U Pr.

Regulating Reproduction in India's Population: Efforts, Results & Recommendations. K. Srinivasan. LC 95-11725. 348p. 1995. 38.00 (*0-8039-9239-4*) Sage.

Regulating Residential Care: A Case Study of a Voluntary Home. Sally Sainsbury. (Occasional Papers on Social Administration). 172p. 1989. text ed. 59.95 (*0-566-07039-1*, Pub. by Avebury Pub UK) Ashgate Pub Co.

Regulating Risk: The Science & Politics of Risk. Ed. by Thomas A. Burke et al. LC 93-61119. (Illus.). 102p. 1993. pap. 25.00 (*0-944398-13-8*) ILSI.

Regulating Safety & Health: A Working Model. Leo Teplow. 255p. 1987. pap. 13.95 (*0-939874-78-4*) ASSE.

Regulating Securities Firms: Capital Adequacy Rules & the Level Playing Field. Richard Dale. LC 95-53020. 1996. text ed. 80.00 (*0-471-95781-X*) Wiley.

***Regulating Sexually Oriented Businesses.** David W. Owens. (Special Ser.: Vol. 15). 15p. (Orig.). 1997. pap. text ed. 15.00 (*1-56011-304-9*) Institute Government.

Regulating the Automobile. Robert W. Crandall et al. LC 85-48171. (Studies in the Regulation of Economic Activity). 202p. 1986. 29.95 (*0-8157-1594-3*) Brookings.

Regulating the City: Competition, Scandal & Reform. Michael Clarke. LC 85-29715. 192p. 1986. 69.00 (*0-335-15381-X*, Open Univ Pr); pap. 25.00 (*0-335-15382-8*, Open Univ Pr) Taylor & Francis.

Regulating the Environment: An Overview of Federal Environmental Laws. Neil Stoloff. (Legal Almanacs 2D Ser.). 101p. 1991. lib. bdg. 22.50 (*0-379-11173-X*) Oceana.

Regulating the Future: The Creative Balance. Ed. by Carol T. Foreman. 200p. 1991. 45.00 (*0-944237-34-7*); pap. 19.50 (*0-944237-35-5*) Ctr National Policy.

Regulating the Intellectuals: Perspectives on Academic Freedom in the 1980's. Ed. by Craig Kaplan & Ellen W. Schrecker. LC 83-17836. 272p. 1983. text ed. 49.95 (*0-275-91021-0*, C1021, Praeger Pubs) Greenwood.

Regulating the Lives of Women: Social Welfare Policy from Colonial Times to the Present. rev. ed. Mimi Abramovitz. LC 96-9172. 412p. 1996. 40.00 (*0-89608-552-X*); pap. 22.00 (*0-89608-551-1*) South End Pr.

Regulating the New Financial Services Industry. Cynthia A. Glassman et al. LC 88-14085. 90p. (Orig.). (C). 1988. pap. text ed. 13.75 (*0-944237-25-8*); lib. bdg. 29.00 (*0-944237-26-6*) Ctr National Policy.

Regulating the Poor: The Functions of Public Welfare. Ed. by Frances F. Piven & Richard A. Cloward. LC 93-17460. 1993. pap. 14.00 (*0-679-74516-5*, Vin) Random.

Regulating the Regulators: An Introduction of the Legislative Oversight. James R. Bowers. LC 89-36697. 156p. 1990. text ed. 45.00 (*0-275-93354-7*, C3354, Praeger Pubs) Greenwood.

Regulating the Social: The Welfare State & Local Politics in Imperial Germany. George Steinmetz. LC 92-44333. (Studies in Culture - Power - History). (Illus.). 404p. (C). 1993. text ed. 52.50 (*0-691-03240-8*) Princeton U Pr.

Regulating Toxic Substances: A Philosophy of Science & the Law. Carl F. Cranor. (Environmental Ethics & Science Policy Ser.). (Illus.). 272p. 1993. 55.00 (*0-19-507436-X*) OUP.

***Regulating Toxic Substances: A Philosophy of Science & the Law.** Carl F. Cranor. (Environmental Ethics & Science Policy Ser.). (Illus.). 272p. 1997. reprint ed. pap. 18.95 (*0-19-511378-0*) OUP.

Regulating Toxic Substances in Surface Waters. Foran. 192p. 1993. 67.95 (*0-87371-498-9*, L498) Lewis Pubs.

Regulating Traffic Safety. Martin L. Friedland et al. 176p. (Orig.). 1990. pap. 16.95 (*0-8020-6764-6*) U of Toronto Pr.

Regulating U. S. Intelligence Operations: A Study in Definition of the National Interest. John M. Oseth. LC 84-22105. 254p. reprint ed. pap. 72.40 (*0-7837-2421-7*, 2042567) Bks Demand.

Regulating Unfair Trade. Pietro S. Nivola. 284p. (C). 1993. 34.95 (*0-8157-6090-6*); pap. 14.95 (*0-8157-6089-2*) Brookings.

Regulating Utilities with Management Incentives: A Strategy for Improved Performance. Kurt A. Strasser & Mark F. Kohler. LC 89-10191. 206p. 1989. text ed. 59.95 (*0-89930-375-7*, SPU/, Quorum Bks) Greenwood.

Regulating Womanhood: Reproduction & Motherhood. Carol Smart. 256p. (C). 1992. pap. text ed. 17.95 (*0-415-07405-3*, Routledge NY) Routledge.

Regulation: Economic Theory & History. Ed. by Jack High. (Illus.). 200p. (C). 1991. text ed. 45.00 (*0-472-10272-9*) U of Mich Pr.

Regulation: Legal Form & Economic Theory. Anthony I. Ogus. (Clarendon Law Ser.). 350p. 1994. 69.00 (*0-19-825443-1*); pap. 32.00 (*0-19-825934-4*) OUP.

Regulation & Control of Cell Proliferation. K. Lapis & A. Jeney. 512p. (C). 1984. 162.00 (*963-05-3246-8*, Pub. by Akad Kiado HU) St Mut.

Regulation & Control of Complex Biological Processes by Biotransformation. Ed. by Klaus Ruckpaul & Horst Rein. LC 93-44152. (Frontiers in Biotransformation Ser.: Vol. 9). 1994. 135.00 (*3-05-501367-0*, Pub. by Akademie Verlag GW) Wiley.

Regulation & Deregulation. Jules Backman. (ITT Key Issues Lecture Ser.). 188p. (Orig.). 1981. pap. text ed. write for info. (*0-672-97879-2*) Macmillan.

***Regulation & Deregulation, Cases & Materials.** Jeffrey L. Harrison et al. LC 97-625. (American Casebook Ser.). 561p. 1997. text ed. write for info. (*0-314-21171-3*) West Pub.

***Regulation & Deregulation, Cases & Materials, Teacher's Manual to Accompany.** Jeffrey L. Harrison et al. (American Casebook Ser.). 100p. 1997. pap. text ed. write for info. (*0-314-22689-3*) West Pub.

Regulation & Deregulation in the Trucking Industry: A Research Report. (Illus.). 30p. (Orig.). (C). 1993. pap. text ed. 25.00 (*1-56806-797-6*) DIANE Pub.

Regulation & Deregulation of the Motor Carrier Industry. Ed. by John R. Felton & Dale G. Anderson. LC 88-9366. (Illus.). 224p. 1989. reprint ed. pap. 63.90 (*0-608-00152-X*, 2060933) Bks Demand.

Regulation & Development: India's Policy Experience of Controls over India. 2nd ed. Sharad S. Marathe. 340p. (C). 1990. text ed. 16.95 (*0-8039-9628-4*) Sage.

Regulation & Functional Significance of T-Cell Subsets. Ed. by R. L. Coffman. (Chemical Immunology Ser.: Vol. 54). (Illus.). x, 218p. 1992. 182.75 (*3-8055-5577-6*) S Karger.

Regulation & Its Reform. Stephen Breyer. LC 81-6753. (Illus.). 486p. 1982. 40.00 (*0-674-75375-5*) HUP.

Regulation & Its Reform. Stephen Breyer. 486p. 1984. pap. 22.50 (*0-674-75376-3*) HUP.

Regulation & Labor. Robert J. Lalonde. (Case; Hb - Economics Ser.). 1997. text ed. 4.95 (*0-538-85804-4*) S-W Pub.

An Asterisk (*) at the beginning of an entry indicates that the title is appearing in BIP for the first time.

Regulation & Macroeconomic Performance. Brian Goff. LC 95-42637. (Topics in Regulatory Economics Ser.: Vol. 21). 145p. (C). 1995. lib. bdg. 79.95 (*0-7923-9684-7*) Kluwer Ac.

Regulation & Markets. Daniel F. Spulber. 712p. 1989. 65.00 (*0-262-19275-6*) MIT Pr.

Regulation & Policies of American Shipping. Ernst G. Frankel. LC 81-12721. 352p. 1982. text ed. 55.00 (*0-86569-099-5*, Auburn Hse) Greenwood.

Regulation & Prevention of Economic Crime Internationally: A Handbook for Government Agencies, Financial Institutions, & Business Corporations. Ed. by Jonathan Reuvid. 250p. 1995. 70.00 (*0-7494-1539-8*, Pub. by Kogan Pg UK) Cassell.

Regulation & Public Law. Ed. by Robert Baldwin & Christopher McCrudden. (Law in Context Ser.). xx, 399p. 1987. 47.50 (*0-297-78780-2*) Rothman.

Regulation & Repression. Anne Edwards. 288p. 1989. pap. text ed. 19.95 (*0-04-332136-4*, Pub. by Allen Unwin AT) Paul & Co Pubs.

Regulation & Revolution in United States Farm Productivity. Sally H. Clarke. (Studies in Economic History & Policy: The United States in the Twentieth Century). (Illus.). 304p. (C). 1994. text ed. 64.95 (*0-521-44117-X*) Cambridge U Pr.

Regulation & Specificity of the Polycation-Stimulated Protein Phosphates. E. Waelkens. No. 6. 113p. (Orig.). 1988. pap. 32.50 (*90-6186-273-6*, Pub. by Leuven Univ BE) Coronet Bks.

Regulation & Supervision of Financial Institutions. David T. Llewellyn. 1986. 50.00 (*0-85297-174-5*, Pub. by Inst Bankers UK) St Mut.

***Regulation & Supervision of Financial Institutions in the NAFTA Countries & Beyond.** Ed. by George M. Von Furstenberg. LC 96-52830. 288p. (C). 1997. lib. bdg. 105.00 (*0-7923-9866-1*) Kluwer Ac.

Regulation & Taxation of Commercial Banks During the International Debt Crisis. Jonathan Hay & Nirmaljit Paul. (Technical Paper Ser.: No. 158). 230p. 1991. 13.95 (*0-8213-1942-6*, 11942) World Bank.

Regulation & the Courts: The Case of the Clean Air Act. R. Shep Melnick. LC 83-7694. 404p. 1983. 36.95 (*0-8157-5662-3*); pap. 16.95 (*0-8157-5661-5*) Brookings.

Regulation & the Informal Economy: Microenterprises in Chile, Ecuador, & Jamaica. Ed. by Victor E. Tokman & Emilio Klein. LC 95-33096. 211p. 1995. lib. bdg. 49.95 (*1-55587-608-0*) Lynne Rienner.

Regulation & the Nature of Postal & Delivery Services. Ed. by Michael A. Crew & Paul R. Kleindorfer. LC 92-34657. (C). 1992. lib. bdg. 103.00 (*0-7923-9301-5*) Kluwer Ac.

Regulation & the Reagan Era. Ed. by Roger E. Meiners & Bruce Yandle. LC 89-7594. (Independent Studies in Political Economy). 250p. (C). 1989. 49.50 (*0-8419-1174-6*); pap. 19.95 (*0-8419-1271-8*) Holmes & Meier.

Regulation CC Service Directory. annuals Ed. by Thomson Financial Publishing Staff. 1991. pap. 54.00 (*1-56310-006-1*) Amer Bank Bond Buyer.

***Regulation D.** Randolph H. Elkins & Larry M. Meeks. (Corporate Practice Ser.: No. 51). 1994. ring bd. 95.00 (*1-55871-304-2*) BNA.

Regulation, Deregulation, Reregulation: The Future of the Banking, Insurance, & Securities Industries. Alan Gart. 422p. 1993. text ed. 59.50 (*0-471-58052-X*) Wiley.

Regulation for Revenue: The Political Economy of Land Use Exactions. Alan A. Altshuler et al. 175p. (C). 1993. 34.95 (*0-8157-0356-2*); pap. 14.95 (*0-8157-0355-4*) Brookings.

Regulation in Metabolism. E. A. Newsholme & C. Start. LC 72-5721. (Illus.). 363p. reprint ed. pap. 103.50 (*0-7837-5205-9*, 2044933) Bks Demand.

Regulation in Perspective: Historical Essays. Thomas K. McCraw. 1982. pap. text ed. 10.95 (*0-07-103282-7*) McGraw.

Regulation in Texas: Its Impact, Processes & Institutions, 2 vols. Contrib. by Leigh Boske & Dennis Thomas. (Policy Research Project Report: No. 76). 1986. pap. 18.00 (*0-89940-678-5*) LBJ Sch Pub Aff.

Regulation in Texas: Its Impact, Processes & Institutions, 2 Vols., Vol. : Case Studies. Contrib. by Leigh Boske & Dennis Thomas. (Policy Research Project Report: No. 76). 221p. 1986. Vol. 2: Case Studies, 221 pps. pap. 10.00 (*0-89940-680-7*) LBJ Sch Pub Aff.

Regulation in Texas: Its Impact, Processes & Institutions, 2 Vols., Vol. 1: Overview. Contrib. by Leigh Boske & Dennis Thomas. (Policy Research Project Report: No. 76). 271p. 1986. pap. 10.00 (*0-89940-679-3*) LBJ Sch Pub Aff.

Regulation in the Reagan-Bush Era: The Eruption of Presidential Influence. Barry D. Friedman. LC 95-8654. (Policy & Institutional Studies). 312p. 1996. 39.95 (*0-8229-3878-2*) U of Pittsburgh Pr.

Regulation in the White House: The Johnson Presidency. David M. Welborn. Ed. by Emmette S. Redford & James E. Anderson. LC 93-19982. (Administrative History of the Johnson Presidency Ser.). 384p. (C). 1993. text ed. 45.00 (*0-292-79078-3*) U of Tex Pr.

Regulation of Accountants under Federal Securities Law. 96p. 1992. pap. 15.00 (*0-685-67026-0*, 4801) Commerce.

***Regulation of Acid-Base Balance.** Ed. by Donald W. Seldin & Gerhard H. Giebisch. LC 86-40396. 615p. 1989. reprint ed. pap. 175.30 (*0-608-03449-5*, 2064150) Bks Demand.

Regulation of Agrochemicals: A Driving Force in Their Evolution. Ed. by Gino J. Marco et al. LC 91-19736. (Illus.). 188p. 1991. 44.95 (*0-8412-2089-1*); pap. 34.95 (*0-8412-2085-9*) Am Chemical.

Regulation of Air Pollutant Emissions from Motor Vehicles. Lawrence J. White. LC 82-6647. (AEI Studies: No. 356). 120p. reprint ed. pap. 34.20 (*0-8357-4527-9*, 2037399) Bks Demand.

Regulation of Aldostorone Biosynthesis. 2nd rev. ed. J. Muller. (Monographs on Endocrinology: Vol. 29). (Illus.). 300p. 1987. 158.00 (*0-387-17907-0*) Spr-Verlag.

***Regulation of Alternative Processing of the Sarco/ Endoplasmic Reticulum Ca (2+)-ATPase Gene 2 Transcript During Muscle Differentiation.** Luc Mertens. (Acta Biomedica Lovaniensia Ser.: Vol. 120). 122p. (Orig.). 1995. pap. 36.50 (*90-6186-721-5*, Pub. by Leuven Univ BE) Coronet Bks.

Regulation of American Federalism. Donald F. Kettl. LC 86-46272. 224p. 1987. reprint ed. pap. text ed. 13.95 (*0-8018-3508-9*) Johns Hopkins.

***Regulation of Angiogenesis.** I. D. Goldberg & E. M. Rosen. (Experientia Supplementum Ser.: Vol. 79). (Illus.). 430p. 1996. 168.00 (*3-7643-5309-0*) Birkhauser.

Regulation of Antibody Products by IGG Binding Structrues. Gergley. 1995. write for info. (*0-8493-4951-6*) CRC Pr.

Regulation of Bacterial Differentiation. Ed. by Patrick J. Piggot et al. LC 93-29794. (Illus.). 300p. (C). 1993. text ed. 72.00 (*1-55581-066-7*) Am Soc Microbio.

***Regulation of Banking: Cases & Materials on Depository Institutions & Their Regulators.** Michael P. Malloy. LC 92-9473. 1106p. 1992. text ed. 65.00 (*0-87084-575-6*) Anderson Pub Co.

Regulation of Banks & Other Depository Institutions in Malaysia - A Study in Monetary, Prudential & Other Controls. Lee. 385p. 1992. boxed 171.00 (*0-409-99601-7*) MICHIE.

Regulation of Blood Flow & Tissue Oxygen Supply: G. Westerlander Gesprach, Erwin Reisch-Symposium, Westerland. Ed. by Jurgen Grote et al. (Funktion Analyse Biologischer Systeme Ser.: No. 22). 290p. (Orig.). 1994. pap. 75.00 (*3-437-30776-2*, Pub. by G Fischer Verlag GW) Lubrecht & Cramer.

Regulation of Body Fluid Volumes by the Kidney: Proceedings of the Natriuretic Hormone Symposium, Czechoslovakia, June, 1969. Natriuretic Hormone Symposium Staff. Ed. by J. H. Cort & B. Lichardus. (Illus.). 192p. 1970. 54.50 (*3-8055-0772-0*) S Karger.

Regulation Of Body Weight: Biological & Behavioral Mechanisms. Ed. by C. Bouchard & G. A. Bray. (Dahlem Workshop Reports Life Science). 327p. 1996. text ed. 89.95 (*0-471-96373-9*) Wiley.

Regulation of Breathing. 2nd expanded rev. ed. Ed. by Jerome A. Dempsey & Allan I. Pack. (Lung Biology in Health & Disease Ser.: Vol. 79). 1250p. 1994. 195.00 (*0-8247-9227-0*) Dekker.

Regulation of Breathing Part 1. Thomas F. Hornbein. LC 80-29164. (Lung Biology in Health & Disease Ser.: No. 17). 693p. 1981. reprint ed. pap. 180.00 (*0-7837-8319-1*, 2049105) Bks Demand.

Regulation of Breathing Part 2. Thomas F. Hornbein. LC 80-29164. (Lung Biology in Health & Disease Ser.: No. 17). 733p. 1981. reprint ed. pap. 180.00 (*0-7837-8320-5*, 2049105) Bks Demand.

Regulation of Building Operations Act, 1958 (with Rules & Regulations & Urban Planning & Development Act, 1973. U. P. Shankar. 396p. 1980. 135.00 (*0-317-57740-9*) St Mut.

Regulation of Carbohydrate Metabolism, 2 vols., Vol. 1. Rivka Beitner. LC 84-12060. 176p. 1985. Vol. I, 176p. 105.00 (*0-8493-5262-2*, QP701, CRC Reprint) Franklin.

Regulation of Carbohydrate Metabolism, 2 vols., Vol. 2. Ed. by Rivka Beitner. LC 84-12060. 224p. 1985. Vol. II, 224p. 132.00 (*0-8493-5263-0*, QP701, CRC Reprint) Franklin.

Regulation of Carbon & Nitrogen Reduction & Utilization in Maize. Ed. by Jack C. Shannon et al. LC 86-72906. 382p. (Orig.). 1986. pap. text ed. 20.00 (*0-943088-09-7*) Am Soc of Plan.

Regulation of Carbon Partitioning in Photosynthetic Tissue. Ed. by Robert L. Heath & Jack Preiss. 396p. 1985. pap. text ed. 20.00 (*0-943088-07-0*) Am Soc of Plan.

Regulation of Cardiac Function: Molecular, Cellular, & Pathophysiological Aspects. International Society & Federation of Cardiology Staff. Ed. by Lionel H. Opie et al. 342p. 1984. lib. bdg. 135.00 (*90-6764-035-2*, Pub. by VSP NE) Coronet Bks.

***Regulation of Cell Growth & Activation.** Ed. by James J. Mond et al. LC 89-10328. (Advances in Regulation of Cell Growth Ser.). reprint ed. pap. 86.70 (*0-608-04666-3*, 2065387) Bks Demand.

Regulation of Cellular Signal Transduction Pathways by Desensitization & Amplification. Ed. by David Sibley & Miles D. Houslay. (Molecular Pharamcology of Cell Regulation Ser.: Vol. 3). 368p. 1994. text ed. 155.00 (*0-471-94154-9*) Wiley.

Regulation of Cellular Systems. Reinhart Heinrich & Stefan Schuster. LC 96-1594. 416p. (gr. 13). 1996. text ed. 89.95 (*0-412-03261-9*, Chap & Hall NY) Chapman & Hall.

Regulation of Cerebral Blood Flow. John W. Phillis. 448p. 1993. 209.00 (*0-8493-5096-4*, QP108) CRC Pr.

Regulation of Cerebral Circulation: Proceedings of the 4th Tbilisi Symposium on Cerebral Circulation, Tbilist, 19-21 April, 1978. G. I. Mchedlishvili et al. 266p. (C). 1979. 60.00 (*963-05-2209-8*, Pub. by Akad Kiado HU) St Mut.

Regulation of Choloroplast Biogenesis. Ed. by J. H. Argyroudi-Akoyunoglo. (NATO ASI Series A, Life Sciences: Vol. 226). (Illus.). 605p. (C). 1992. 145.00 (*0-306-44184-5*, Plenum Pr) Plenum.

Regulation of Commerce under the Federal Constitution. Thomas H. Calvert. (Studies in Constitutional Law). xiv, 380p. 1981. reprint ed. lib. bdg. 32.50 (*0-8377-0429-4*) Rothman.

Regulation of Coronary Blood Flow. Ed. by M. Inoue et al. (Illus.). 336p. 1992. 108.00 (*0-387-70072-2*) Spr-Verlag.

Regulation of Corporate Disclosure. J. Robert Brown, Jr. 1995. write for info. (*1-56706-160-5*) Panel Pubs.

Regulation of Corporate Disclosures. write for info. (*0-318-66845-9*) P-H.

Regulation of Corporate Political Activity. 3rd ed. Gregory K. Merryman. (Corporate Practice Series Portfolio: No. 16). 1988. 92.00 (*0-87179-998-7*) BNA.

Regulation of Desire: Homo & Hetero Sexualities. Gary Kinsman. LC 95-79359. 423p. 1996. 52.99 (*1-55164-041-4*, Pub. by Black Rose Bks CN); pap. 23.99 (*1-55164-040-6*, Pub. by Black Rose Bks CN) Consort Bk Sales.

Regulation of Direct Broadcasting from Satellites: The U. N. Involvement. Benno H. Signitzer. LC 76-14372. (Special Studies). (Illus.). 175p. 1976. text ed. 45.00 (*0-275-90252-8*, C0252, Praeger Pubs) Greenwood.

Regulation of DNA Replication & Transcription. M. Beljanski. (Experimental Biology & Medicine Ser.: Vol. 8). (Illus.). x, 190p. 1983. pap. 99.25 (*3-8055-3631-3*) S Karger.

***Regulation of Enzymatic Systems Detoxifying Xenobiotics in Plants.** Kriton K. Hatzios. LC 97-24672. (NATO ASI Series: Partnership Sub-Series 3). 1997. write for info. (*0-7923-4646-7*) Kluwer Ac.

Regulation of Enzyme Activity: In Focus. J. H. Ottaway. (In Focus Ser.). (Illus.). 100p. 1988. pap. 17.95 (*1-85221-072-9*, IRL Pr) OUP.

Regulation of Enzyme Synthesis & Activity in Higher Plants. Harold Smith. 1978. text ed. 199.00 (*0-12-650850-X*) Acad Pr.

Regulation of Erythropoiesis. Ed. by E. D. Zanjani et al. (Illus.). 608p. 1988. 175.00 (*0-89335-307-8*) PMA Pub Corp.

Regulation of Financial Markets in the 1990s: Issues & Problems in an Age of Innovation. David Gowland. (Illus.). 152p. 1990. text ed. 70.00 (*1-85278-177-7*) E Elgar.

Regulation of Financial Planners. John P. Moriarty & Curtlan R. McNeily. LC 91-26315. (Securities Law Ser.). 1991. ring bd. 145.00 (*0-87632-816-8*) Clark Boardman Callaghan.

Regulation of Flood Hazard Areas to Reduce Flood Losses, Vol. 3. Jon Kusler. (Special Publications: No. 2). 300p. (Orig.). (C). 1982. pap. 8.00 (*0-685-28086-1*) Natural Hazards.

Regulation of Food Law by the EC. Charles Lister. 300p. 1992. pap. text ed. 175.00 (*0-406-01305-5*, UK) MICHIE.

Regulation of Foreign Banking in the United States. Ibrahim A. Warde. (International Banking Ser.). 1992. pap. text ed. 95.00 (*0-88115-101-7*) I B P C Inc.

Regulation of Foreign Banks: United States & International. Ralph Reisner & Michael Gruson. 750p. 1993. 160.00 (*0-88063-287-9*); suppl. ed. 35.00 (*0-685-74147-8*) MICHIE.

Regulation of Foreign Lawyers. 3rd ed. Sydney M. Cone & ABA, Committee on Comparative Procedure & Practice. LC 84-72263. 110p. 1984. pap. 15.00 (*0-89707-155-7*, 525-0035) Amer Bar Assn.

Regulation of Gene Expression & Brain Function. Ed. & Contrib. by Paul J. Harrison. LC 93-26907. (Basic & Clinical Aspects of Neuroscience Ser.: Vol. 6). 1994. 39.95 (*0-387-57156-6*) Spr-Verlag.

Regulation of Gene Expression by Hormones. Ed. by Kenneth W. McKerns. LC 83-6310. (Biochemical Endocrinology Ser.). 278p. 1983. 85.00 (*0-306-41204-7*, Plenum Pr) Plenum.

Regulation of Gene Expression in Animal Viruses. Ed. by L. Carrasco et al. (NATO ASI Series A, Life Sciences: Vol. 240). (Illus.). 338p. (C). 1993. 105.00 (*0-306-44408-9*, Plenum Pr) Plenum.

***Regulation of Gene Expression in Escherichia Coli.** Edmund C. Lin. Ed. by A. Simon Lynch. LC 95-43432. 592p. 1996. 99.95 (*0-412-10291-9*, 71068) Chapman & Hall.

Regulation of Gene Expression in Escherichia Coli: Special Edition. Edmund C. Lin & A. Simon Lynch. LC 95-43432. 296p. 1996. 99.95 (*1-57059-315-9*) R G Landes.

Regulation of Growth Hormone & Somatic Growth: Proceedings of the International Meeting on Regulation of Somatic Growth, Lugo, Spain, 14-16 October 1991. Ed. by Luis F. De La Cruz. LC 92-49289. (International Congress Ser.: No. 996). 1992. 170.75 (*0-444-89192-7*, Excerpta Medica) Elsevier.

Regulation of Growth in Neoplasia. Ed. by G. V. Sherbet. (Illus.). x, 202p. 1981. 93.00 (*3-8055-2305-X*) S Karger.

Regulation of Heme Biosynth by Drugs, Hormones & Toxicants. Piper. 1994. 139.95 (*0-8493-6834-0*) CRC Pr.

Regulation of Heme Protein Synthesis. Ed. by Hiroyoshi Fujita. LC 93-50106. 1994. 45.00 (*1-880854-18-X*) AlphaMed Pr.

Regulation of Hemoglobin Switching. Ed. by George Stamatoyannopoulos & Arthur W. Nienhuis. LC 91-20808. (Series in Contemporary Medicine & Public Health). (Illus.). 576p. 1991. text ed. 125.00 (*0-8018-4253-0*) Johns Hopkins.

Regulation of Hemoglobin Synthesis. J. Neuwirt & P. Ponka. 1977. lib. bdg. 70.50 (*90-247-1999-2*) Kluwer Ac.

Regulation of Hepatic Metabolism: Intra- & Intercellular Compartmentation. Ed. by Ronald G. Thurman et al. LC 85-30084. 510p. 1986. 125.00 (*0-306-42137-2*, Plenum Pr) Plenum.

Regulation of Hepatic Microsomal UDP-Glucuronosyltransferases & Nucleotide Sugar. X. Bossuyrt. No. 78. 161p. (Orig.). 1994. pap. 39.50 (*90-6186-601-4*, Pub. by Leuven Univ BE) Coronet Bks.

Regulation of Human Fertility. Harold C. Mack Symposium on the Physiology & Pathology of Reproduction Staff. Ed. by Kamran S. Moghissi & Tommy N. Evans. LC 75-29482. 319p. reprint ed. pap. 91.00 (*0-7837-3671-1*, 2043545) Bks Demand.

Regulation of Immune Gene Expression. Ed. by Marc Feldmann & Andrew McMichael. LC 86-10257. (Experimental Biology & Medicine Ser.: Vol. 13). (Illus.). 384p. 1986. 99.50 (*0-89603-104-7*) Humana.

Regulation of Immune Response Dynamics, 2 vols., Vol. I. Ed. by Charles Delisi & Jacques R. Hiernaux. 176p. 1982. 104.00 (*0-8493-6632-1*, QR186) Franklin.

Regulation of Immune Response Dynamics, 2 vols., Vol. II. Ed. by Charles Delisi & Jacques R. Hiernaux. 184p. 1982. 107.00 (*0-8493-6633-X*) Franklin.

Regulation of Imports & Exports of Hazardous Wastes & Commercial Products. Ed. by Heidi H. Bumpers & Stephen C. Jones. (Environmental Management Guides Ser.). 29p. 1994. pap. text ed. 25.00 (*0-86587-437-9*) Gov Insts.

Regulation of Insider Dealing in Britain. Jacqueline A. Suter. 464p. 1989. boxed 144.00 (*0-406-70069-9*, U.K.) MICHIE.

Regulation of Insurance. Justin L. Brady et al. LC 95-77159. (Illus.). 192p. (C). 1995. pap. text ed. 26.00 (*0-89462-092-4*, IR201) IIA.

Regulation of International Commercial Aviation: The International Regulatory Structure & Treaties, 2 binders. Ed. by James Fox. LC 83-19392. 1992. ring bd. 350.00 (*0-379-11819-X*) Oceana.

Regulation of International Trade. Robert Howse & Michael J. Trebilcock. LC 94-26221. 480p. (C). (gr. 13). 1995. text ed. 99.95 (*0-415-08162-9*) Routledge.

Regulation of International Trade: Political Economy & Legal Order. Michael J. Trebilcock & Robert Howse. LC 94-26221. 320p. (C). 1995. pap. 25.00 (*0-415-08163-7*, B4666) Routledge.

Regulation of Investment Advisers, 1995. Thomas Lemke & Gerald T. Lins. (Securities Law Ser.). 1991. pap. 137.50 (*0-614-07306-5*) Clark Boardman Callaghan.

Regulation of Investment Advisors. Clifford E. Kirsch. 400p. 1996. ring bd. 115.00 (*0-614-17134-2*, B1-1349) PLI.

Regulation of Investment Companies. Thomas P. Lemke et al. LC 95-11825. 1995. ring bd. write for info. (*0-8205-1022-X*) Bender.

Regulation of Isopentenoid Metabolism. Ed. by W. David Nes et al. LC 92-17807. (ACS Symposium Ser.: Vol. 497). (Illus.). 270p. 1992. 66.95 (*0-8412-2457-9*) Am Chemical.

Regulation of Lawyers: Problems of Law & Ethics. Stephen Gillers & Norman Dorsen. (C). 1985. 32.00 (*0-316-31380-7*) Little.

Regulation of Lawyers: Statutes & Standards. Stephen Gillers. 1989. 17.95 (*0-316-31338-6*) Little.

Regulation of Lawyers: Statutes & Standards with Recent Supreme Court Decisions. Stephen Gillers. 1990. 18.95 (*0-316-31421-8*) Little.

Regulation of Lawyers, Nineteen Eighty-Seven Supplement: Problems of Law & Ethics. Stephen Gillers & Norman Dorsen. 140p. 1987. 8.95 (*0-316-31343-2*) Little.

Regulation of Learning. Ed. by P. R. Simons & G. Beukhof. (Selecta Reeks Ser.: Vol. 77). viii, 202p. 1987. 30.00 (*90-6472-119-X*) Taylor & Francis.

Regulation of Low-Level Radioactive Waste Disposal Facilities: Certification of Proposal Sites & Disposal Methods. (Illus.). 43p. (Orig.). (C). 1993. pap. text ed. 20.00 (*1-56806-763-1*) DIANE Pub.

Regulation of Madness: Origins on Incarceration in France. Robert Castel. Tr. by W. D. Halls. (Medicine & Society Ser.: Vol. 1). 280p. 1988. 45.00 (*0-520-06306-6*) U CA Pr.

Regulation of Male Fertility. Ed. by G. R. Cunningham et al. (Clinics in Andrology Ser.: No. 5). (Illus.). 245p. 1980. lib. bdg. 171.00 (*90-247-2373-6*) Kluwer Ac.

Regulation of Media Ownership by the Federal Communications Commission: An Assessment. Stanley M. Besen & Leland L. Johnson. LC 84-26387. 77p. 1984. pap. 7.50 (*0-8330-0627-4*, R-3206-MF) Rand Corp.

Regulation of Membrane Lipid Metabolism. Guy A. Thompson, Jr. 256p. 1980. 132.00 (*0-8493-5427-7*, QH601, CRC Reprint) Franklin.

Regulation of Membrane Lipid Metabolism. 2nd ed. Guy A. Thompson, Jr. 256p. 1992. 105.00 (*0-8493-4561-8*, QP572) CRC Pr.

Regulation of Money Managers, 4 vols., 1. Tamar Frankel. LC 77-1577. 1978. 165.00 (*0-316-29191-9*) Little.

Regulation of Money Managers, 4 vols., 2. Tamar Frankel. LC 77-1577. 1978. 165.00 (*0-316-29192-7*) Little.

Regulation of Money Managers, 4 vols., 3. Tamar Frankel. LC 77-1577. 1980. 165.00 (*0-316-29193-5*) Little.

Regulation of Money Managers, 4 vols., 4. Tamar Frankel. LC 77-1577. 1980. 165.00 (*0-316-29194-3*) Little.

Regulation of Money Managers, 4 vols., Set. Tamar Frankel. LC 77-1577. 1980. suppl. ed. 295.00 (*0-316-29190-0*) Little.

Regulation of Money Managers, 1986 Supplement, Set. Tamar Frankel. LC 77-15717. 336p. 1986. Multi-vol. set. write for info. (*0-316-29202-8*) Little.

Regulation of Monopoly. Roger Sherman. (Illus.). 336p. (C). 1989. text ed. 80.00 (*0-521-36315-2*); pap. text ed. 26.95 (*0-521-36862-6*) Cambridge U Pr.

Regulation of Motor Vehicle & Traffic Safety. Glenn C. Blomquist. (C). 1988. lib. bdg. 75.00 (*0-89838-280-7*) Kluwer Ac.

Regulation of Nationality in International Law. 2nd ed. Ruth Donner. 450p. 1995. 95.00 (*0-941320-77-4*) Transnatl Pubs.

R

Regulation of Neuroendocrine Aging. Ed. by A. V. Everitt & Judie R. Walton. (Interdisciplinary Topics in Gerontology Ser.: Vol. 24). (Illus.). viii, 156p. 1988. 112.00 (*3-8055-4770-6*) S Karger.

Regulation of Ovarian & Testicular Function. Ed. by Virendra B. Mahesh et al. LC 87-22073. (Advances in Experimental Medicine & Biology Ser.: Vol. 219). (Illus.). 774p. 1987. 135.00 (*0-306-42676-5*, Plenum Pr) Plenum.

Regulation of Pesticides: Science, Law & the Media. Ed. by Richard C. Honeycutt. 197p. 1988. pap. text ed. 65.00 (*0-86587-740-8*) Gov Insts.

Regulation of Pharmaceuticals in Developing Countries: Legal Issues & Approaches. D. C. Jayasuriya. 118p. 1985. pap. text ed. 14.00 (*92-4-156089-4*, 1150236) World Health.

Regulation of Physical & Mental Systems: Systems Theory of the Philosophy of Science. Eugene G. D'Aquili. LC 89-12984. (Studies in Sociology: Vol. 4). 200p. 1990. lib. bdg. 89.95 (*0-88946-633-5*) E Mellen.

Regulation of Pituitary Function. Ed. by T. Van Wimersma Greidanus & W. J. Lamberts. (Frontiers of Hormone Research Ser.: Vol. 14). (Illus.). vi, 218p. 1985. 143.25 (*3-8055-4061-2*) S Karger.

Regulation of Political Conflict. Eduard A. Ziegenhagen. LC 86-91493. 244p. 1986. text ed. 55.00 (*0-275-92131-X*, C2131, Praeger Pubs) Greenwood.

Regulation of Porphyrin & Heme Biosynthesis: Proceedings of the International Research Conference, Marburg an der Lahn, June 28-July 1, 1973. rev. ed. International Research Conference Staff. Ed. by Manfred Doss. (Journal: Enzyme: Vol. 16, No. 1-6 & Vol. 17, No. 1-2). 384p. 1974. reprint ed. 113.75 (*3-8055-1652-5*) S Karger.

***Regulation of Potassium Balance.** Ed. by Donald W. Seldin & Gerhard Giebisch. LC 86-45986. reprint ed. pap. 109.50 (*0-608-04719-8*, 2065440) Bks Demand.

Regulation of Potassium Transport Across Biological Membranes. Ed. by Luis Reuss et al. (Illus.). 512p. (C). 1990. text ed. 60.00 (*0-292-77043-X*) U of Tex Pr.

Regulation of Professions: A Law & Economics Approach to the Regulation of Attorneys & Physicians in the U. S., Belgium, the Netherlands, Germany & the U. K. Ed. by Michael Faure et al. 425p. 1993. pap. 93.00 (*90-6215-334-8*, Pub. by Maklu Uitgevers BE) Gaunt.

***Regulation of Provider Risk Sharing & Other Limitations on Risk Bearing Provider Networks.** Randolph S. Jordan. (BNA's Health Law & Business Ser.: No. 2300). 1996. 125.00 (*1-55871-336-0*) BNA.

Regulation of Public Utilities: Theory & Practice. 3rd ed. Charles F. Phillips, Jr. 1025p. 1993. 65.00 (*0-910325-45-6*) Public Util.

Regulation of Railroad Abandonments. Charles R. Cherington. Ed. by Stuart Bruchey. LC 80-1299. (Railroads Ser.). (Illus.). 1981. reprint ed. lib. bdg. 27.95 (*0-405-13769-9*) Ayer.

Regulation of Reciprocal Insurance Exchanges. Reinmuth. (C). 1967. 10.50 (*0-256-00676-8*) Irwin.

***Regulation of Religious Organizations As Recipients of Governmental Assistance.** Carl H. Esbeck. LC 96-86601. 64p. (Orig.). (C). 1996. pap. 10.00 (*0-936456-03-5*) Ctr Pub Justice.

Regulation of Rural Electric Cooperatives. National Consumer Law Center, Inc. Staff. LC 93-84977. (Utility Law Practice Ser.). 208p. 1993. pap. 60.00 (*1-881793-08-7*) Nat Consumer Law.

Regulation of Secondary Metabolism in Actinomycetes. Ed. by Stuart Shapiro. 304p. 1989. 253.00 (*0-8493-6927-4*, QR82) CRC Pr.

Regulation of Secondary Metabolite Formation. H. Kleinkauf et al. 402p. 1985. 80.00 (*3-527-26475-2*, VCH) Wiley.

Regulation of Serum Lipids by Physical Exercise. Eino Hietanen. 192p. 1982. 109.00 (*0-8493-6330-6*, QP99, CRC Reprint) Franklin.

Regulation of Sexuality: Experiences of Family Planning Workers. Carole Joffe. LC 86-5824. 208p. (C). 1987. pap. 16.95 (*0-87722-510-9*) Temple U Pr.

Regulation of Smooth Muscle Contraction. Ed. by R. S. Moreland. (Advances in Experimental Medicine & Biology Ser.: Vol. 304). (Illus.). 542p. 1991. 140.00 (*0-306-44041-5*, Plenum Pr) Plenum.

Regulation of Target Cell Responsiveness. International Foundation for Biochemical Endocrinology Staff. Ed. by Kenneth W. McKerns et al. LC 83-24773. (Biochemical Endocrinology Ser.). 550p. 1984. 195.00 (*0-685-08419-1*, Plenum Pr) Plenum.

Regulation of Target Cell Responsiveness. Ed. by International Foundation for Biochemical Endocrinology Staff et al. LC 83-24773. (Biochemical Endocrinology Ser.). 564p. 1984. 195.00 (*0-685-08390-X*, Plenum Pr) Plenum.

Regulation of Target Cell Responsiveness, Vol. 1. International Foundation for Biochemical Endocrinology Staff. Ed. by Kenneth W. McKerns et al. LC 83-24773. (Biochemical Endocrinology Ser.). 550p. 1984. 125.00 (*0-306-41500-3*, Plenum Pr) Plenum.

Regulation of Target Cell Responsiveness, Vol. 2. Ed. by International Foundation for Biochemical Endocrinology Staff et al. LC 83-24773. (Biochemical Endocrinology Ser.). 564p. 1984. 125.00 (*0-306-41501-1*, Plenum Pr) Plenum.

Regulation of the Commodities Futures & Options Markets, 2 vols. Thomas A. Russo. LC 83-431. (Securities Law Publications). 1598p. 1983. text ed. 210.00 (*0-07-054348-8*) Shepards.

Regulation of the Commodities, Futures & Options Markets. 2nd rev. ed. Bob McKinney. LC 95-25784. 1995. write for info. (*0-07-172790-6*) Shepards.

Regulation of the Contractile Cycle in Smooth Muscle. Ed. by T. Nakano & D. J. Hartshorne. 239p. 1995. 133.00 (*3-540-70149-4*) Spr-Verlag.

Regulation of the Contractile Cycle in Smooth Muscle. Ed. by T. Nakano & D. J. Hartshorne. 1996. 133.00 (*0-387-70149-4*); 133.00 (*4-431-70149-4*) Spr-Verlag.

Regulation of the Electronic Mass Media: Law & Policy for Radio, Television, Cable & the New Video Technologies. 2nd ed. Douglas H. Ginsburg et al. (American Casebook Ser.). 657p. 1991. text ed. 48.50 (*0-314-82946-6*); pap. text ed. 10.00 (*0-314-85396-0*) West Pub.

Regulation of the Eukaryotic Cell Cycle. CIBA Foundation Staff. LC 92-28930. (CIBA Foundation Symposium Ser.: No. 170). 289p. 1992. text ed. 84.95 (*0-471-93446-1*) Wiley.

Regulation of the Gas Industry, 4 vols., Set. American Gas Association Staff. 1981. ring bd. write for info. (*0-8205-1311-3*) Bender.

***Regulation of the Healthcare Professions.** Ed. by Timothy S. Jost. LC 97-2634. 216p. (Orig.). 1997. pap. 38.00 (*1-56793-058-1*) Health Admin Pr.

Regulation of the IGE Antibody Response. Ed. by K. Ishizaka. (Progress in Allergy Ser.: Vol. 32). (Illus.). x, 346p. 1982. 170.50 (*3-8055-3470-1*) S Karger.

Regulation of the Life Insurance Business. Jon S. Hanson. LC 95-78625. 600p. (C). 1995. text ed. 71.00 (*0-943590-75-2*) Amer College.

Regulation of the Natural Gas Producing Industry. Ed. by Keith C. Brown. LC 71-186502. (Resources for the Future Ser.). (Illus.). 271p. 1972. pap. 10.00 (*0-8018-1383-2*) Johns Hopkins.

***Regulation of the RAS Signaling Network.** Hiroshi Maruta & Anthony W. Burgess. LC 96-35747. (Molecular Biology Intelligence Unit Ser.). 188p. 1996. 89.95 (*1-57059-404-X*) R G Landes.

Regulation of the Securities & Commodities Markets. Ralph S. Janvey. 1992. ring bd. 165.00 (*0-685-69645-6*, RSCM) Warren Gorham & Lamont.

Regulation of the Security Markets: An Original Anthology. Ed. by Vincent P. Carosso. LC 75-2662. (Wall Street & the Security Market Ser.). 1975. 35.95 (*0-405-06986-3*) Ayer.

Regulation of the Stock Exchange Members. Raymond Vernon. LC 70-38947. (FDR & the Era of the New Deal Ser.). 1972. reprint ed. 25.00 (*0-306-70451-X*) Da Capo.

Regulation of the Unit Trusts. J. W. Vaughn. 201p. 1990. 115.00 (*1-85044-162-6*) LLP.

Regulation of the Vascular Endothelium: Signals & Transduction Mechanisms. J. M. Boeynaems & S. Pirotton. (Molecular Biology Intelligence Unit Ser.). 118p. 1994. 89.95 (*1-57059-026-5*, LN9026) R G Landes.

***Regulation of Trading.** Zufferey. 1997. lib. bdg. write for info. (*90-411-0679-0*) Kluwer Law Tax Pubs.

Regulation of Vertebrate Limb Regeneration. Ed. by Raymond Sicard. (Illus.). 195p. 1985. 39.95 (*0-19-503604-2*) OUP.

Regulation of Water & Sewer Utilities. Frank F. Skillem. 68.00 (*0-685-52375-6*, B7) Sterling TX.

***Regulation of Wireless Communication Systems.** Frederick J. Day. LC 97-15293. 450p. 1997. text ed. 89.00 (*0-86587-586-3*) Gov Insts.

Regulation on Subdivision & Stability of Passenger Ships. IMO Staff. (C). 1974. English ed. 25.00 (*0-7855-0000-6*, IMO 823E, Pub. by Intl Maritime Org UK); French ed. 25.00 (*0-685-74494-9*, IMO 824F, Pub. by Intl Maritime Org UK); Spanish ed. 25.00 (*0-685-74495-7*, IMO 825S, Pub. by Intl Maritime Org UK) St Mut.

Regulation, Organizations, & Politics: Motor Freight Policy at the Interstate Commerce Commission. Lawrence S. Rothenberg. 326p. (C). 1993. text ed. 49.50 (*0-472-10443-8*) U of Mich Pr.

Regulation Reporter on Prepaid Legal Services. 1240p. suppl. ed. 275.00 (*0-317-46497-3*); 125.00 (*0-685-73790-X*) Am Prepaid.

Regulation Requirements for Hazardous Materials. Somendu Majumdar. LC 92-32345. 688p. 1993. text ed. 70.00i (*0-07-039761-9*) McGraw.

Regulation S: The Safe Harbor for Offshore Securities Transactions. Ronald Adee. (Corporate Practice Ser.: No. 58). 1991. ring bd. 92.00 (*1-55871-199-6*) BNA.

Regulation School: A Critical Introduction. Robert Boyer. 152p. 1990. text ed. 52.50 (*0-231-06548-5*) Col U Pr.

Regulation State-Pak. LC 02-15. 17.50 (*0-317-65823-9*) Am Prepaid.

Regulation Theory & Its Application to Trade Policy: A Study of ITC Decision-Making 1975-1985. Wendy L. Hansen. LC 90-3000. (Foreign Economic Policy of the United States Ser.). 125p. 1990. reprint ed. text ed. 15.00 (*0-8240-7469-6*) Garland.

Regulation Theory & the British State: The Case of the Urban Development Corporation. Mo O'Toole. 256p. 1996. 59.95 (*1-85972-305-5*, Pub. by Avebury Pub UK) Ashgate Pub Co.

Regulation Z Handbook. Stuart M. Bloch & William B. Ingersoll. 44p. 1982. 19.95 (*0-318-19283-7*) Land Dev Inst.

Regulation Z Truth-in-Lending: Comprehensive Compliance Manual. rev. ed. William J. O'Connor & Phillip S. Toohey. 524p. 1991. 254.00 incl. disk (*0-685-62690-3*) Am Bankers.

Regulations & Notes on the Uniform for the Navy & Marine Corp of the United States: 1852. Ed. by Jacques N. Jacobsen. 1989. 5.00 (*0-913150-88-6*) Pioneer Pr.

Regulations & Notes on the Uniform of the Army of the United States: 1847. Ed. by Jacques N. Jacobsen. 1989. 5.00 (*0-913150-74-6*) Pioneer Pr.

Regulations & Notes on the Uniform of the Army of the United States: 1851. Ed. by Jacques N. Jacobsen. 1989. 5.00 (*0-913150-77-0*) Pioneer Pr.

Regulations & Notes on the Uniform of the Army of the United States: 1857. Ed. by Jacques N. Jacobsen. 1989. 5.00 (*0-913150-78-9*) Pioneer Pr.

Regulations & Notes on the Uniform of the Army of the United States: 1861. Ed. by Jacques J. Jacobsen. 1989. 5.00 (*0-913150-79-7*) Pioneer Pr.

Regulations & Notes on the Uniform of the Army of the United States: 1872. Ed. by Jacques N. Jacobsen. 1989. 5.00 (*0-913150-80-0*) Pioneer Pr.

Regulations & Notes on the Uniform of the Army of the United States: 1882. Ed. by Jacques N. Jacobsen. 1989. 5.00 (*0-913150-81-9*) Pioneer Pr.

Regulations & Notes on the Uniform of the Army of the United States: 1888. Ed. by Jacques N. Jacobsen. 1989. 5.00 (*0-913150-82-7*) Pioneer Pr.

Regulations & Notes on the Uniform of the Army of the United States: 1899. Ed. by Jacques N. Jacobsen. 1989. 5.00 (*0-913150-83-5*) Pioneer Pr.

Regulations & Notes on the Uniform of the Army of the United States: 1902. Ed. by Jacques N. Jacobsen. 1989. 5.00 (*0-913150-84-3*) Pioneer Pr.

Regulations & Notes on the Uniform of the Army of the United States: 1912. Ed. by Jacques N. Jacobsen. 1989. 5.00 (*0-913150-85-1*) Pioneer Pr.

Regulations & Notes on the Uniform of the Army of the United States, Section 1 - Officers: 1917. Ed. by Jacques N. Jacobsen. 1989. 5.00 (*0-913150-86-X*) Pioneer Pr.

Regulations & Notes on the Uniform of the Army of the United States, Section 2 - Enlisted Men: 1917. Ed. by Jacques N. Jacobsen. 1989. 5.00 (*0-913150-87-8*) Pioneer Pr.

Regulations by Agency. Ed. by Butterworth Staff. ring bd. 60.00 (*0-614-05958-5*) MICHIE.

Regulations Concerning the International Carriage of Dangerous Goods by Rail: 1995 Edition. 662p. 1994. pap. 70.00 (*0-11-551266-7*, HM12667, Pub. by Stationery Ofc UK) Bernan Associates.

***Regulations Concerning the International Carriage of Dangerous Goods by Rail: 1997 Edition.** 540p. 1996. pap. 145.00 (*0-11-551840-1*, HM18401, Pub. by Stationery Ofc UK) Bernan Associates.

Regulations for the Control & Abatement of Air Pollution. 480p. (Orig.). (C). 1993. pap. text ed. 60.00 (*1-56806-744-5*) DIANE Pub.

Regulations for the Control of Pollution by Noxious Liquid Substances in Bulk (Annex 11, Marpol 73-78) International Maritime Organization Staff. 1986. text ed. 90.00 (*0-89771-949-2*, Pub. by Intl Maritime Org UK) St Mut.

Regulations for the Medical Department of the Army. 96p. 1989. reprint ed. 18.75 (*1-877791-00-8*) Bohemian Brigade.

Regulations for the Prevention of Pollution by Oil (Annex 1, Marpol 72-78) International Maritime Organization Staff. 1986. text ed. 55.00 (*0-89771-948-4*, Pub. by Intl Maritime Org UK) St Mut.

Regulations for the Prussian Infantry: To Which Is Added the Prussian Tactick. Prussia Kriegsministerium Staff. LC 68-54803. 444p. 1969. reprint ed. text ed. 38.50 (*0-8371-0625-7*, PRPI, Greenwood Pr) Greenwood.

Regulations for the Public Use of Records in the National Archives. 62p. (Orig.). (C). 1995. pap. text ed. 25.00 (*0-7881-2282-7*) DIANE Pub.

***Regulations for the Safe Transport of Radioactive Material: 1996 Edition.** (Safety Standards Ser.: No. ST-1). 220p. 1996. pap. 80.00 (*92-0-104996-X*, STI/PUB/998, Pub. by IAEA AU) Bernan Associates.

Regulations, Institutions, & Commitment: Comparative Studies of Telecommunications. Ed. by Brian Levy & Pablo T. Spiller. (Political Economy of Institutions & Decisions Ser.). (Illus.). 192p. (C). 1996. text ed. 54.95 (*0-521-55013-0*); pap. text ed. 19.95 (*0-521-55996-0*) Cambridge U Pr.

Regulations Made Easy for Private Pilots. Dick Doberstein. pap. text ed. 8.95 (*0-9607866-4-3*) Simplified Reg.

Regulations of the C. S. A. Medical Department: IN: Regulations for the Army of the Confederate States. Samuel P. Moore. (American Civil War Medical Ser.: No. 8). 420p. 1991. 50.00 (*0-930405-36-6*) Norman SF.

Regulations Pesticides: FIFRA Amendments of 1988. Janice L. Greene et al. 170p. 1989. 60.00 (*1-55871-032-9*, 45EDSR09) BNA Plus.

Regulations to Govern the Preservation of Records of Electric, Gas & Water Utilities. 55p. 1985. 5.00 (*0-317-01640-7*) NARUC.

Regulators. Richard Bachman. LC 96-8931. 496p. 1996. pap. 24.95 (*0-525-94190-8*) NAL-Dutton.

Regulators. Richard Bachman. 1996. pap. 29.95 (*0-14-086322-2*) Viking Penguin.

***Regulators.** Richard Bachman. 1997. mass mkt. 383.52 (*0-451-98396-3*, Sig) NAL-Dutton.

Regulators. Stephen King, pseud. 1996. pap. 24.95 (*0-670-87281-4*) Viking Penguin.

***Regulators.** large type ed. Richard Bachman. LC 96-31831. 1996. write for info. (*0-7862-0844-9*) Thorndike Pr.

***Regulators.** large type ed. Richard Bachman. LC 96-31831. 1997. pap. 24.95 (*0-7862-0845-7*) Thorndike Pr.

Regulators. William Degenhard. LC 80-54849. 598p. 1981. reprint ed. 24.95 (*0-933256-22-1*) Second Chance.

Regulators & the Market. Cento Veljanovski. 243p. (C). 1991. text ed. 70.00 (*0-255-36248-X*, Pub. by Inst Economic Affairs UK) St Mut.

Regulators Ltd. Richard Bachman. 1996. pap. 325.00 (*0-525-94224-6*) Viking Penguin.

Regulatory & Advanced Regulatory Control: Application Techniques. David W. Spitzer. LC 93-30758. 145p. 1993. pap. 45.00 (*1-55617-487-X*) ISA.

Regulatory & Advanced Regulatory Control: System Development. Harold L. Wade. LC 93-30759. 261p. 1993. pap. 68.00 (*1-55617-488-8*) ISA.

Regulatory Approach to Air Quality Management: A Case Study of New Mexico. Winston Harrington. LC 81-81368. 132p. 1981. 10.00 (*0-8018-2700-0*) Resources Future.

Regulatory Aspects of the Initial Public Offering of Securities. Alan S. Gutterman. (Corporate Practice Ser.: No. 60). 1991. ring bd. 95.00 (*1-55871-238-0*) BNA.

***Regulatory Burden: Measurement Challenges & Concerns Raised by Selected Companies.** Ed. by Curtis Copeland et al. (Illus.). 128p. (Orig.). (C). 1997. pap. text ed. 40.00 (*0-7881-4056-6*) DIANE Pub.

Regulatory Challenge. Ed. by Matthew Bishop et al. 472p. 1995. text ed. 79.00 (*0-19-877341-2*) OUP.

Regulatory Challenge. Ed. by Matthew Bishop et al. 472p. 1995. pap. text ed. 32.00 (*0-19-877342-0*) OUP.

Regulatory Choices: A Perspective on Developments in Energy Policy. Ed. by Richard J. Gilbert. LC 90-46760. (Illus.). 430p. 1991. 45.00 (*0-520-07056-9*) U CA Pr.

***Regulatory Compliance.** Mortgage Bankers Association of America Staff. 195p. (C). 1997. pap. 145.00 (*1-57599-020-2*) Mortgage Bankers.

Regulatory Compliance Desk Reference. 2nd ed. Regulatory Compliance Associates, Inc. Staff. LC 96-10712. (Illus.). 224p. (C). 1996. text ed. 75.00 (*0-7863-0967-9*) Irwin Prof Pubng.

Regulatory Control & Standardization of Allergenic Extracts. 2nd ed. Ed. by Reinhard Kurth & Gerhard Siefert. (Arbeiten aus dem Paul-Ehrlich Institut Ser.: Vol. 82). 269p. 1988. pap. 75.00 (*0-89574-268-3*, VCH) Wiley.

Regulatory Control & Standardization of Allergenic Extracts: Seventh International Paul-Ehrlich-Seminar, September 7-10, 1993, Langen, FRG. Ed. by Reinhard Kurth et al. (Arbeiten Aus dem Paul-Ehrlich-Institut Ser.: No. 87). (Illus.). viii, 321p. 1994. pap. 95.00 (*3-437-11622-3*, Pub. by G Fischer Verlag GW) Lubrecht & Cramer.

Regulatory Control & Standardization of Allergenic Extracts: Sixth International Paul-Ehrlich-Seminar, September 1990, Frankfurt, Main. Gerhard Siefert. (Arbeiten Aus dem Paul-Ehrlich-Institut Ser.: Vol. 85). (Illus.). 244p. (Orig.). 1992. pap. text ed. 67.00 (*1-56081-326-1*, Pub. by G Fischer Verlag GW) Lubrecht & Cramer.

Regulatory Cooperation in an Interdependent World. OECD Staff. 250p. (Orig.). 1994. pap. 50.00 (*92-64-14196-0*) OECD.

Regulatory Decision Making: The Virginia State Corporation Commission. Laurence J. O'Toole & Robert S. Montjoy. LC 84-5146. 405p. reprint ed. pap. 115.50 (*0-8357-2715-7*, 2039829) Bks Demand.

Regulatory Economics of Title Insurance. Nelson R. Lipshutz. LC 93-5440. 168p. 1994. text ed. 59.95 (*0-275-94742-4*, Praeger Pubs) Greenwood.

Regulatory Federalism, Natural Resources, & Environmental Management. Ed. by Michael S. Hamilton. 205p. 1990. 24.95 (*0-936678-15-1*) Am Soc Pub Admin.

Regulatory Finance. Roger Morin. 560p. 1994. pap. 89.00 (*0-910325-46-4*) Public Util.

Regulatory Finance: Financial Foundations of Rate of Return Regulation. (C). 1991. lib. bdg. 70.50 (*0-7923-9143-8*) Kluwer Ac.

Regulatory Flexibility in Schools: What Happens When Schools Are Allowed to Change the Rules? (Illus.). 57p. (Orig.). (C). 1995. pap. text ed. 20.00 (*0-7881-1850-1*) DIANE Pub.

Regulatory Function of Adenosine. Ed. by Robert M. Berne et al. 1983. 375.00 (*90-247-2779-0*) Kluwer Ac.

Regulatory Functions of Interferons, Vol. 350. Ed. by Jan Vilcek et al. LC 80-25207. (Annals Ser.). 641p. 1980. 126.00 (*0-89766-089-7*); pap. 126.00 (*0-89766-090-0*) NY Acad Sci.

Regulatory Guidance for the Federal Motor Carrier Safety Regulations. 1996. pap. text ed. 6.95 (*0-88711-229-3*) Am Trucking Assns.

***Regulatory Guidance for the Federal Motor Carrier Safety Regulations.** 1996. pap. text ed. 6.95 (*0-88711-348-6*) Am Trucking Assns.

Regulatory Gut Peptides in Paediatric Gastroenterology & Nutrition. Ed. by P. Heinz-Erian et al. (Frontiers of Gastrointestinal Research Ser.: Vol. 21). (Illus.). viii, 264p. 1992. 215.75 (*3-8055-5549-0*) S Karger.

Regulatory Impediments to the Private Industrial Sector Development in Asia: A Comparative Study. Deena Khatkhate. LC 92-23555. (Discussion Paper Ser.: No. 177). 220p. 1992. 11.95 (*0-8213-2221-4*, 12221) World Bank.

Regulatory Incentives for Demand-Side Management. Ed. by Steven M. Nadel et al. LC 92-28968. (Illus.). 302p. (Orig.). 1992. pap. 31.00 (*0-918249-16-3*) Am Coun Energy.

Regulatory Interventionism in the Utility Industry: Fairness, Efficiency, & the Pursuit of Energy Conservation. Barbara R. Barkovich. LC 88-15392. 181p. 1989. text ed. 55.00 (*0-89930-383-8*, BVY/, Quorum Bks) Greenwood.

Regulatory Issues since 1964: The Rise of the Deregulation Movement. Intro. by Robert F. Himmelberg. LC 93-47533. (Business & Government in America since 1870 Ser.: Vol. 11). 424p. 1994. text ed. 70.00 (*0-8153-1413-2*) Garland.

Regulatory Justice: Implementing a Wage-Price Freeze. Robert A. Kagan. LC 77-72498. 200p. 1978. 24.95 (*0-87154-425-3*) Russell Sage.

An Asterisk (*) at the beginning of an entry indicates that the title is appearing in BIP for the first time.

Regulatory Language Behavior. Betty L. Dubois & Isabel Crouch. (Edward Sapir Monograph Ser. in Language, Culture & Cognition: No. 13). xiv, 96p. (Orig.). 1985. pap. 20.00 (0-933104-19-7) Jupiter Pr.

Regulatory Management: A Guide to Cond. Environmental Affairs & Min. Liab. Egan. 256p. 1991. 81.95 (0-87371-455-5, L455) Lewis Pubs.

Regulatory Management & Compliance Audit Deskbook. 2nd ed. Nadolny & Young. 550p. 1992. 195.00 (1-55738-364-2) Irwin Prof Pubng.

Regulatory Management & Information Systems, 1994, No. 8. (Public Management Occasional Papers). 64p. (Orig.). (ENG & FRE.). 1995. pap. 19.00 (92-64-14566-4, Pub. by Org for Econ FR) OECD.

Regulatory Mechanisms Affecting Gonadal Hormone Action. Ed. by J. A. Thomas & R. L. Singhal. (Advances in Sex Hormone Research Ser.: Vol. 3). 356p. reprint ed. pap. 101.50 (0-317-27715-4, 2052098) Bks Demand.

Regulatory Mechanisms for Nursing Training & Practice: Meeting Primary Health Care Needs. (Technical Report Ser.: No. 738). 71p. 1986. pap. text ed. 10.00 (92-4-120738-8, 1100738) World Health.

Regulatory Mechanisms in Breast Cancer: Advances in Cellular & Molecular Biology of Breast Cancer. Ed. by Marc E. Lippman & Robert B. Dickson. (Cancer Treatment & Research Ser.). (C). 1991. lib. bdg. 196.00 (0-7923-0868-9) Kluwer Ac.

Regulatory Mechanisms in Gastrointestinal Function. Ed. by Timothy S. Gaginella. LC 95-8329. 320p. 1995. 136.95 (0-8493-9439-2, 9439) CRC Pr.

Regulatory Mechanisms in Insect Feeding. Ed. by Reginald F. Chapman & Gerrit de Boer. 320p. (gr. 13). 1995. text ed. 75.00 (0-412-03141-8) Chapman & Hall.

Regulatory Mechanisms of Human Neoplastic Cell Growth by Cytokines: Past & Future Prospect. Ed. by Fumimaro Takaku & Takeshi Ogura. LC 93-4563. (Gann Monograph on Cancer Research: No. 40). 1993. 72.00 (0-8493-7747-1) CRC Pr.

Regulatory Mechanisms of Neuron to Vessel Communication in the Brain. Ed. by S. Govoni et al. (NATO ASI Series H: Cell Biology: Vol. 33). (Illus.). xii, 416p. 1989. 150.95 (0-387-50379-X) Spr-Verlag.

Regulatory Peptides. Julia M. Polak. (BioSeries-EXS: No. 56). 400p. 1989. 193.00 (0-8176-1976-3) Birkhauser.

Regulatory Peptides & Amines During Ontogeny & in Non-Endocrine Cancers: Occurrence & Possible Functional Significance. Lars-Inge Larsson. LC 88-10967. (Progress in Histochemistry & Cytochemistry Ser.: Vol. 17, No. 4). 222p. 1988. pap. 125.00 (0-89574-263-2) G F Verlag.

Regulatory Peptides, from Molecular Biology to Function. fac. ed. Ed. by E. Costa & Marco Trabucchi. LC 81-40857. (Advances in Biochemical Psychopharmacology Ser.). (Illus.). 587p. pap. 167.30 (0-7837-7213-0, 2047085) Bks Demand.

Regulatory Peptides in Paraganglia. C. Heym & W. Kummer. LC 88-20475. (Progress in Histochemistry & Cytochemistry Ser.: Vol. 18, No. 2). 95p. 1988. pap. 75.00 (0-89574-270-5, Pub. by G Fischer Verlag GW); 65.00 (0-685-56005-8, Pub. by G Fischer Verlag GW) Lubrecht & Cramer.

Regulatory Policy Analysis. Ed. by Mel Dubnick & Alan Gitelson. (Orig.). (C). 1982. pap. 15.00 (0-918592-51-8) Pol Studies.

Regulatory Policy & Practices: Regulating Better & Regulating Less. Fred Thompson. LC 82-13131. 270p. 1982. text ed. 49.95 (0-275-90916-6, C0916, Praeger Pubs) Greenwood.

Regulatory Policy & the Social Sciences. Roger G. Noll. (California Series on Social Choice & Political Economy: No. 5). 1985. 55.00 (0-520-05187-4) U CA Pr.

Regulatory Politics & Electric Utilities. Douglas D. Anderson. LC 80-26943. 191p. 1981. text ed. 49.95 (0-86569-058-8, Auburn Hse) Greenwood.

Regulatory Politics in Japan: The Case of Foreign Banking. Louis W. Pauly. (Cornell East Asia Ser.: No. 45). 92p. (Orig.). 1987. pap. 7.00 (0-939657-45-7) Cornell East Asia Pgm.

Regulatory Politics in Transition. Marc A. Eisner. LC 92-40435. (Interpreting American Politics Ser.). 288p. (C). 1993. text ed. 45.00 (0-8018-4557-2); pap. text ed. 14.95 (0-8018-4558-0) Johns Hopkins.

Regulatory Practice for Biopharmaceutical Production. Ed. by Anthony S. Lubiniecki & Susan A. Vargo. 555p. 1994. text ed. 127.50 (0-471-04900-X) Wiley.

Regulatory Process, Accountability & Management Of. 185p. 1980. pap. text ed. 5.00 (1-56986-166-8) Federal Bar.

Regulatory Process in Allergy & Asthma. Ed. by K. Blaser. (Journal: International Archives of Allergy & Applied Immunology: Vol. 90, Suppl. 1). (Illus.). iv, 76p. 1990. pap. text ed. 33.25 (3-8055-5152-5) S Karger.

Regulatory Processes in Clinical Endocrinology. Ed. by Walter B. Essman. 300p. 1982. text ed. 40.00 (0-88331-193-3) Luce.

Regulatory Properties of the Mammalian Adenylyl Cyclases. Zhengui Xia & Daniel Storm. LC 96-22640. (Molecular Biology Intelligence Unit Ser.). 210p. 1996. 89.95 (1-57059-360-4) R G Landes.

***Regulatory Proteins: Techniques & Protocols.** Ed. by Hugh C. Hemmings. (Neuromethods Ser.: Vol. 30). (Illus.). 445p. 1996. 75.00 (0-89603-415-1) Humana.

Regulatory Proteins of the Complement System. Atkinson. 1992. write for info. (0-8493-6710-7, CRC Reprint) Franklin.

Regulatory Reform: Challenges for the Future. 265p. 1979. pap. text ed. 10.00 (1-56986-167-6) Federal Bar.

Regulatory Reform: Economic Analysis & British Experience. Mark Armstrong et al. 400p. 1994. 37.50 (0-262-01143-3) MIT Pr.

Regulatory Reform: Information on Costs, Cost-Effectiveness & Mandated Deadlines for Regulations. (Illus.). 49p. (Orig.). (C). 1995. pap. text ed. 20.00 (0-7881-2049-2) DIANE Pub.

Regulatory Reform: New Vision or Old Curse. Margaret N. Maxey & Robert L. Kuhn. LC 84-26261. 254p. 1985. text ed. 40.95 (0-275-90145-9, C0145, Praeger Pubs) Greenwood.

***Regulatory Reform & International Market Openness.** OECD Staff. 296p. (Orig.). 1996. pap. 37.00 (92-64-15313-6, 22-96-06-1, Pub. by Org for Econ FR) OECD.

Regulatory Reform, Current Issues. 304p. 1980. pap. text ed. 30.00 (1-56986-168-4) Federal Bar.

***Regulatory Reform in Mexico's Natural Gas Sector.** 224p. 1996. 60.00 (92-64-14926-0, Pub. by Org for Econ FR) OECD.

Regulatory Reform in Transport: Some Recent Experiences. Ed. by Jose Carbajo. LC 93-16712. (Symposium Ser.). 120p. 1993. 10.95 (0-8213-2331-8, 12331) World Bank.

Regulatory Reform of Stock & Futures Markets. Ed. by Franklin R. Edwards. (C). 1990. lib. bdg. 61.00 (0-7923-9067-9) Kluwer Ac.

Regulatory Reform, Privatisation & Competition Policy. OECD Staff. 134p. (Orig.). 1992. pap. 31.00 (92-64-13666-5) OECD.

Regulatory Reporting Compliance Handbook: 1994 Edition. 2nd ed. Price. 1994. per. 60.00 (1-55738-704-4) Irwin Prof Pubng.

Regulatory Reporting Compliance Handbook: 1995 Edition. 3rd ed. Price Waterhouse Staff. 124p. (C). 1995. per. 65.00 (1-55738-765-6) Irwin Prof Pubng.

***Regulatory Reporting Handbook, 1996-1997 Edition.** 4th ed. Price Waterhouse Staff. 160p. (C). 1996. per. 65.00 (0-7863-0955-5) Irwin Prof Pubng.

Regulatory Requirements for Laser Product Manufacturers, No. 111. 200p. 1996. 75.00 (0-685-30513-9) Laser Inst.

***Regulatory Risk Management Handbook, 1996-1997.** 208p. 1996. 65.00 (0-7863-1168-1) Irwin.

***Regulatory Risk Management Handbook 1996-1997 Edition.** Price Waterhouse Staff. 1997. per. 65.00 (0-7863-1201-7) Irwin.

Regulatory Role of the Nervous System in Aging. Ed. by H. T. Blumenthal. (Interdisciplinary Topics in Gerontology Ser.: Vol. 7). 1970. 41.75 (3-8055-0508-6) S Karger.

Regulatory Rulemaking to Implement Congressional Legislation: Lessons from the Powerplant & Industrial Fuel Use Act of 1978. Frank A. Camm. LC 83-11010. 1983. pap. 7.50 (0-8330-0510-3, R-2982-DOE/RC) Rand Corp.

Regulatory Status of Direct Food Additives. T. Furia. LC 80-11487. 288p. 1980. 164.00 (0-8493-6380-2) CRC Pr.

Regulatory Taking: The Limits of Land Use Controls. LC 90-81439. 422p. 1993. pap. 49.95 (0-89707-552-8, 533-0049) Amer Bar Assn.

***Regulatory Takings.** Steven J. Eagle. 772p. 1996. 105.00 (1-55834-329-6, 61876) MICHIE.

Regulatory Takings: Law, Economics, & Politics. William A. Fischel. LC 95-1361. (Illus.). 432p. (C). 1995. text ed. 45.00 (0-674-75388-7) HUP.

Regulatory Treatment of Embedded Costs. 114p. 1994. 30.00 (0-614-06943-2) NARUC.

***Regulierung des Mietwohnungsmarktes in der Bundesrepublik Deutschland: Eine Positive Okonomische Analyse.** Jutta Bison. (Illus.). 299p. (GER.). 1996. 57.95 (3-631-30997-X) P Lang Pubng.

Regulus vel Pueri Soli Sapiunt: (The Little Prince) Antoine de Saint-Exupery. Tr. by Augusto Haury from FRE. (Illus.). 96p. (LAT.). 1985. pap. 6.00 (0-15-676300-1, Harvest Bks) HarBrace.

Rehab: Drought & Famine in Ethiopia. Ed. by Abdul M. Hussein. LC 77-354221. (African Environment: Special Report Ser.: Vol. 2). 128p. 1976. reprint ed. pap. 36.50 (0-8357-3247-9, 2059141) Bks Demand.

Rehab Diary. Samuel. LC 88-91460. 1989. pap. 9.95 (0-87212-225-5) Libra.

***Rehab in Sports Medicine.** Canavan. LC 97-17095. 1997. text ed. 70.00 (0-8385-8313-X) P-H.

Rehab Index: Vocational Rehabilitation in California: a General Index & Desk Reference. 8th rev. ed. James T. Stewart. 250p. 1997. pap. 49.50 (0-9635814-5-7) J T Stewart.

Rehab Index 1993 Reform Supplement. James T. Stewart. 29p. 1994. pap. text ed. 19.50 (0-9635814-3-0) J T Stewart.

Rehab Rochester: A Sensible Guide for Old-House Maintenance, Repair & Rehabilitation. Steve Jordan. (Illus.). 95p. 1995. pap. 9.95 (0-9641706-4-7) Landmark Soc.

Rehab Your Way to Riches: Guide to High Profit - Low Risk Renovation of Residential Property. R. Dodge Woodson. 208p. (Orig.). 1992. pap. 14.95 (1-55870-247-4, Betrwy Bks) F & W Pubns Inc.

***Rehabilitated Buildings.** Links Editors. (Illus.). 238p. 1997. 85.00 (84-921606-9-1, Pub. by Links SP) Bks Nippan.

***Rehabilitated Estuarine Ecosystems: The Thames Estuary, Its Environment & Ecology.** Ed. by Attrill & Trett. (Illus.). 220p. (C). (gr. 13 up). 1997. text ed. 78.00 (0-412-49680-1, Chap & Hall NY) Chapman & Hall.

Rehabilitating Apartments: A Recycling Process. Robert A. Cagann. LC 93-27771. (Illus.). 194p. 1993. pap. 35.95 (0-944298-90-7, 800) Inst Real Estate.

Rehabilitating Blind & Visually Impaired People: A Psychological Approach. Dodds. 218p. 1993. pap. 47.75 (1-56593-153-X, 0465) Singular Publishing.

Rehabilitating Blind & Visually Impaired People: A Psychological Approach. Allan Dodds. LC 93-16158. 1993. write for info. (0-412-46970-7) Chapman & Hall.

Rehabilitating Criminal Sexual Psychopaths: Legislative Mandates, Clinical Quandries. Nathaniel J. Pallone. 140p. 1990. 34.95 (0-88738-340-8) Transaction Pubs.

Rehabilitating Damaged Ecosystems. Ed. by John Cairns, Jr. 1988. write for info. (0-318-62935-6, Q4541) CRC Pr.

Rehabilitating Damaged Ecosystems. Ed. by John Cairns, Jr. 448p. 1994. 79.95 (1-56670-043-4, L1043) Lewis Pubs.

Rehabilitating Damaged Ecosystems, Vol. I. Ed. by John Cairns, Jr. 192p. 1988. 202.95 (0-8493-4391-7) CRC Pr.

Rehabilitating Damaged Ecosystems, Vol. II. Ed. by John Cairns, Jr. 224p. 1988. 203.00 (0-8493-4392-5) CRC Pr.

Rehabilitating Government: Pay & Employment Reform in Africa. Ed. by David Lindauer & Barbara Nunberg. (World Bank Ser.). 256p. 1996. 68.95 (1-85972-226-1, Pub. by Avebury Pub UK) Ashgate Pub Co.

Rehabilitating Government: Pay & Employment Reform in Africa. Ed. by David L. Lindauer & Barbara Nunberg. LC 94-26924. (World Bank Regional & Sectoral Studies). 1994. 13.95 (0-8213-3000-4, 13000) World Bank.

Rehabilitating Juvenile Justice. Charles H. Shireman & Frederic G. Reamer. LC 86-6788. 188p. 1986. text ed. 41.50 (0-231-06328-8) Col U Pr.

Rehabilitating Juvenile Justice. Charles H. Shireman. 188p. 1989. pap. text ed. 17.00 (0-231-06329-6) Col U Pr.

Rehabilitating Oiled Seabirds: A Field Manual. Anne S. Williams. Ed. by Jeff Burridge & Meryl L. Kane. LC 85-73815. (Illus.). 50p. (Orig.). 1986. pap. text ed. 25.00 (0-89364-056-5, 841-44070) Am Petroleum.

Rehabilitating Older & Historic Buildings: Law, Taxation, Strategies. 2nd ed. S. L. et al. 88p. 1993. suppl. ed., pap. text ed. 48.00 (0-471-00185-6) Wiley.

Rehabilitating Older & Historic Buildings-Law-Taxation-Strategies. 2nd ed. Stephen L. Kass et al. LC 92-15741. (Real Estate Practice Library). 608p. 1992. text ed. 140.00 (0-471-57164-4) Wiley.

Rehabilitating the Narcotics Addict: Report. Institute on New Developments in the Rehabilitation of the Narcotics Addict Staff et al. Ed. by United States Public Health Service Division of Hospitals Staff. Tr. by United States Department of Health, Education, & Welfare Rehabilitation Administration Staff. (Illus.). 1968. reprint ed. 13.95 (0-405-00056-1, 16411) Ayer.

Rehabilitation. Fuzy. (C). Date not set. 19.95 (0-8273-7931-5) Delmar.

Rehabilitation. Fuzy. (C). 1996. teacher ed., pap. text ed. 12.00 (0-8273-7932-3) Delmar.

Rehabilitation: A Component of Comprehensive Cardiac Care. Ed. by Nanette K. Wenger. (Bibliotheca Cardiologica Ser.: No. 40). (Illus.). xii, 132p. 1986. 106.50 (3-8055-4359-X) S Karger.

Rehabilitation: Index of Modern Information with Bibliography. Keith S. Pittham. LC 88-47796. 150p. (Orig.). 1988. 44.50 (0-88164-884-1); pap. 39.50 (0-88164-885-X) ABBE Pubs Assn.

Rehabilitation: The Federal Government's Response to Disability, 1935 to 1954. Edward D. Berkowitz. Ed. by William R. Phillips & Janet Rosenberg. LC 79-6896. (Physically Handicapped in Society Ser.). 1980. lib. bdg. 36.95 (0-405-13107-0) Ayer.

Rehabilitation Activities Profile. G. J. Lankhorst et al. 80p. 1996. pap. 20.00 (90-5383-398-6, Pub. by VUB Univ Pr BE) Paul & Co Pubs.

Rehabilitation after Cardiovascular Diseases, with Special Emphasis on Developing Countries: Report of a WHO Expert Committee. (Technical Report Ser.: No. 831). viii, 122p. (CHI, ENG, FRE & SPA.). 1993. pap. text ed. 17.00 (92-4-120831-7, 1100831) World Health.

Rehabilitation after Myocardial Infarction: The European Experience. Ed. by Veikko Kallio & Elizabeth Clay. (Public Health in Europe Ser.: No. 24). 148p. 1985. pap. text ed. 13.00 (92-890-1160-2, 1320024) World Health.

Rehabilitation & Community Care. Stephen Pilling. (Strategies for Mental Health Ser.). 224p. (C). 1991. pap. text ed. 13.95 (0-415-01067-5, A5416) Routledge.

***Rehabilitation & Comprehensive Secondary Prevention after Acute Myocardial Infarction.** D. Dorossiev. (Euro Reports & Studies Ser.: No. 84). 99p. 1983. pap. text ed. 8.00 (92-890-1250-1) World Health.

Rehabilitation & Continuing Care in Cancer. Ronald W. Raven. 172p. 1986. 39.00 (1-85070-105-9) Prthnon Pub.

Rehabilitation & Disability: Psychosocial Case Studies. E. Davis Martin, Jr. & Gerald L. Gandy. 200p. 1990. pap. 26.95 (0-398-06269-2) C C Thomas.

Rehabilitation & Disability: Psychosocial Case Studies. E. Davis Martin, Jr. & Gerald L. Gandy. 200p. (C). 1990. text ed. 39.95 (0-398-05698-6) C C Thomas.

Rehabilitation & Handicapped Literature, 1982-1985 Update: A Bibliographic Guide to the Microfiche Collection. Ed. by Mary E. Morrison. (Orig.). 1987. 20.00 (0-8357-0732-6) Univ Microfilms.

Rehabilitation & Replacement of Bridges on Secondary Highways & Local Roads. (National Cooperative Highway Research Program Report Ser.: No. 243). 46p. 1981. 6.80 (0-309-03408-6) Transport Res Bd.

Rehabilitation & Restorative Care in the Community. Hoeman. (Illus.). 228p. (C). (gr. 13). 1990. pap. text ed. 27.95 (0-8016-2415-0) Mosby Yr Bk.

Rehabilitation & the Chronic Renal Disease Patient. Ed. by Nancy G. Kutner et al. LC 85-1866. 200p. 1985. text ed. 30.00 (0-89335-222-5) PMA Pub Corp.

***Rehabilitation & the Law: Liability & the OT Practitioner.** Steve Long & Rita Burghardt. 60p. (Orig.). 1996. pap. text ed. 21.00 (1-56900-040-9, 1145) Am Occup Therapy.

Rehabilitation Approaches to Drug & Alcohol Dependence. Behrouz Shahandeh. viii, 91p. 1988. pap. 13.50 (92-2-100526-7) Intl Labour Office.

Rehabilitation Aspects of Drug Dependence. Arnold J. Schecter. 192p. 1977. 112.00 (0-8493-5475-7, RC566, CRC Reprint) Franklin.

Rehabilitation Assistant. Jack Rudman. (Career Examination Ser.: C-545). 1994. pap. 29.95 (0-8373-0545-4) Nat Learn.

Rehabilitation Caseload Management: Concepts & Practice. Jack L. Cassell & S. Wayne Mulkey. LC 85-3385. 350p. 1985. pap. text ed. 34.00 (0-936104-67-8, 1275) PRO-ED.

Rehabilitation Center. David W. Felder. 44p. 1996. pap. text ed. 8.95 (0-910959-68-4, B&G 13D) Wellington Pr.

Rehabilitation Cost Analyst. Jack Rudman. (Career Examination Ser.: C-3121). 1994. pap. 34.95 (0-8373-3121-8) Nat Learn.

Rehabilitation Counseling: Basics & Beyond. 2nd ed. Ed. by Edna Szymanski & Randall M. Parker. LC 97-10241. 444p. (Orig.). 1992. pap. text ed. 36.00 (0-89079-518-5, 1409) PRO-ED.

Rehabilitation Counseling: Collected Papers. C. H. Patterson. 1969. pap. 7.80 (0-87563-015-4) Stipes.

***Rehabilitation Counseling: Profession & Practice.** Ed. by Dennis R. Maki & T. F. Riggar. LC 96-46426. (Springer Rehabilitation Ser.: Vol. 11). (Illus.). 375p. 1996. write for info. (0-8261-9510-5) Springer Pub.

Rehabilitation Counseling & Services: Profession & Process. Ed. by Gerald L. Gandy et al. (Illus.). 376p. (C). 1987. text ed. 49.95 (0-398-05282-4) C C Thomas.

Rehabilitation Counseling & Services: Profession & Process. Ed. by Gerald L. Gandy et al. (Illus.). 376p. 1987. pap. 33.95 (0-398-06143-2) C C Thomas.

Rehabilitation Counselling: Approaches in the Field of Disability. Ed. by Sharon E. Robertson & Roy I. Brown. LC 92-26462. (Rehabilitation Education Ser.: Vol. 5). 322p. 1992. pap. 44.75 (1-56593-017-7, 0260) Singular Publishing.

Rehabilitation Counselor. Jack Rudman. (Career Examination Ser.: C-672). 1994. pap. 29.95 (0-8373-0672-8) Nat Learn.

Rehabilitation Counselor Certification Examination (CRC) Jack Rudman. (Admission Test Ser.: ATS-92). 1994. pap. 29.95 (0-8373-5092-1) Nat Learn.

Rehabilitation Counselor Supervisor. Jack Rudman. (Career Examination Ser.: C-1980). 1994. pap. 34.95 (0-8373-1980-3) Nat Learn.

Rehabilitation Counselor Trainee. Jack Rudman. (Career Examination Ser.: C-1783). 1994. pap. 27.95 (0-8373-1783-5) Nat Learn.

Rehabilitation Detectives: Doing Human Service Work. Paul C. Higgins. LC 85-1849. (Sociological Observations Ser.: No. 16). 240p. reprint ed. pap. 68.40 (0-7837-4557-5, 2044085) Bks Demand.

Rehabilitation Engineering. Mann. Date not set. write for info. (0-7506-9537-4) Buttrwrth-Heinemann.

Rehabilitation Engineering. Ed. by Smith. 576p. 1990. 286.00 (0-8493-6951-7, RM950) CRC Pr.

Rehabilitation Engineering: Proceedings. Economic Commission for Europe Staff. 148p. 1994. pap. 25.00 (92-1-116595-4, RA790) UN.

Rehabilitation Engineering Applied to Mobility & Manipulation. Rory A. Cooper. LC 95-38066. (Medical Science Ser.). (Illus.). 516p. 1995. 190.00 (0-7503-0343-3, RM950) IOP Pub.

Rehabilitation Equipment & Product Market--1995 Update: Effective Technology Leads to Improved Patient Compliance. Frost & Sullivan Staff. 381p. 1996. write for info. (0-7889-0418-3, 5313-58) Frost & Sullivan.

Rehabilitation Evaluation: Some Application Guidelines. Ed. by James A. Bitter & Don L. Goodyear. LC 75-9719. 1975. text ed. 29.50 (0-8422-5223-1); pap. text ed. 9.95 (0-8422-0502-0) Irvington.

Rehabilitation for Mental Health Problems: An Introduction Handbook. 2nd ed. Clephane A. Hume & Ian Pullen. LC 93-18261. 288p. 1993. pap. text ed. 43.00 (0-443-04554-2) Churchill.

Rehabilitation for Traumatic Brain Injury. Baontke et al. Date not set. 40.00 (0-7506-9581-1) Buttrwrth-Heinemann.

***Rehabilitation Hospital: Role Play Peacegame.** David W. Felder. 52p. 1997. pap. text ed. 8.95 (1-57501-106-9, 13D) Wellington Pr.

Rehabilitation in Community Mental Health. H. Richard Lamb. LC 76-168989. (Jossey-Bass Behavioral Science Ser.). 222p. reprint ed. pap. 63.30 (0-685-16195-1, 2027760) Bks Demand.

Rehabilitation in Ischemic Heart Disease. Ed. by William Blocker, Jr. & David Cardus. LC 80-22840. (Illus.). 500p. 1983. text ed. 80.00 (0-88331-194-1) Luce.

Rehabilitation in Mental Health: Goals & Objectives for Independent Living. Barbara J. Hemphill et al. LC 89-43121. 160p. 1991. pap. 27.00 (1-55642-143-5) SLACK Inc.

Rehabilitation in Parkinson's Disease. Caird. 144p. 1991. pap. 54.50 (1-56593-561-6, 0707) Singular Publishing.

Rehabilitation in Parkinson's Disease. Francis Caird. (Therapy in Practice Ser.: No. 25). pap. 29.95 (0-412-34600-1) Chapman & Hall.

Rehabilitation in Psychiatry: An Introductory Handbook. Clephane Hume & Ian Pullen. LC 85-11677. (Illus.). 256p. (Orig.). 1986. pap. text ed. 33.00 (0-443-02509-6) Churchill.

***Rehabilitation in the Aging.** Ed. by T. Franklin Williams. LC 83-42929. 389p. 1984. reprint ed. pap. 110.90 (0-608-03458-4, 2064159) Bks Demand.

Rehabilitation Inspector. Jack Rudman. (Career Examination Ser.: C-2639). 1994. pap. 34.95 (0-8373-2639-7) Nat Learn.

Rehabilitation International: Proceedings of the Fifteenth World Congress of Rehabilitation International, Held June 1984 in Lisbon, Portugal. 350p. 1984. 30.00 (0-317-19041-5) Rehab Intl.

Rehabilitation Interventions for the Institutionalized Elderly. Ed. by Ellen D. Taira. LC 88-18065. (Physical & Occupational Therapy in Geriatrics Ser.: Vol. 6, No. 2). (Illus.). 77p. 1989. text ed. 29.95 (*0-86656-833-6*) Haworth Pr.

Rehabilitation Interviewer. Jack Rudman. (Career Examination Ser.: C-2708). 1994. pap. 29.95 (*0-8373-2708-3*) Nat Learn.

***Rehabilitation into Independent Living: 30th Anniversary of Rehabilitation Gazette.** Ed. by Gini Laurie et al. 128p. (Orig.). 1989. write for info. (*0-614-28390-6*) Gazette Intl.

Rehabilitation Literature, 1950 to 1955: A Bibliographic Review of the Medical Care, Education, Employment, Welfare & Psychology of Handicapped Children & Adults. Earl C. Graham & Marjorie Mullen. Ed. by William R. Phillips & Janet Rosenberg. LC 79-6901. (Physically Handicapped in Society Ser.). 1980. reprint ed. lib. bdg. 61.95 (*0-405-13112-7*) Ayer.

Rehabilitation Medicine. Gerald F. Fletcher. (Illus.). 480p. 1992. text ed. 69.50 (*0-8121-1445-0*) Williams & Wilkins.

Rehabilitation Medicine: Principles & Practices. 2nd ed. Ed. by Joel A. DeLisa et al. LC 92-49401. 1,264p. 1993. text ed. 129.00 (*0-397-51262-7*) Lppncott-Raven.

Rehabilitation Medicine: Proceedings of the Sixth International Rehabilitation Medicine Association Congress, Madrid, 17-22 June, 1990. Ed. by A. Molina et al. (International Congress Ser.: No. 928). 312p. 1991. 134.50 (*0-444-81133-8*, Excerpta Medica) Elsevier.

Rehabilitation Methods in Neuropsychiatry. Nicholas L. Rock et al. LC 95-48870. (Illus.). 320p. (Orig.). 1996. pap. 49.95 (*1-56593-632-9*, 1310) Singular Publishing.

Rehabilitation, Music & Human Well-Being. Pref. by Mathew Lee. (Illus.). 282p. (Orig.). 1989. pap. 29.95 (*0-918812-59-3*, ST 190) MMB Music.

***Rehabilitation Nurse's Survival Guide.** Roslyn Heffner. (Illus.). 360p. (Orig.). 1994. pap. 20.00 (*0-9653317-0-9*) R Heffner Vocat.

Rehabilitation Nursing: Process & Application, 2. 2nd ed. Hoeman. 752p. (C). (gr. 13). 1995. text ed. 62.00 (*0-8016-7766-1*) Mosby Yr Bk.

Rehabilitation Nursing for the Neurological Patient. Marcia Hanak. LC 91-5189. 240p. (C). 1992. 32.95 (*0-8261-7660-7*) Springer Pub.

Rehabilitation of Brain Functions: Principles, Procedures & Techniques of Neurotraining. James F. Craine & Howard E. Gudeman. (Illus.). 358p. (C). 1981. spiral bd., pap. 53.95 (*0-398-04605-0*) C C Thomas.

Rehabilitation of Child Labourers in India. Rabindra N. Pati. (C). 1991. 30.00 (*81-7024-361-0*, Pub. by Ashish II) S Asia.

Rehabilitation of Clergy Alcoholics: Ardent Spirits Subdued. Joseph H. Fichter. LC 80-28447. 203p. 1982. 35.95 (*0-89885-009-6*) Human Sci Pr.

Rehabilitation of Cognitive Disabilities. Ed. by J. Michael Williams & Charles J. Long. (Illus.). 246p. 1987. 80.00 (*0-306-42594-7*, Plenum Pr) Plenum.

Rehabilitation of Damaged Buildings: Sick Building Syndrome. Ed. & Pref. by Sabah A. Rayes. (Illus.). 706p. (C). 1995. pap. text ed. 60.00 (*0-939493-12-8*) Coun Tall Bldg.

Rehabilitation of Degraded Forests in Asia. Ajit K. Banerjee. LC 94-40154. (World Bank Technical Paper: No. 270). 62p. 1995. pap. 6.95 (*0-8213-3119-1*, 13119) World Bank.

Rehabilitation of Degraded Land Ecosystem. A. S. Kolarkar et al. (C). 1992. text ed. 162.50 (*81-7233-036-7*, Pub. by Scientific Pubs II) St Mut.

Rehabilitation of Freshwater Fisheries. I. Cowx. 1994. 95.00 (*0-85238-195-6*) Blackwell Sci.

Rehabilitation of Jackson Webber Clark. LC 96-92282. 200p. (Orig.). 1996. pap. write for info. (*0-9652532-0-1*) C Nubin.

Rehabilitation of Late-Deafened Adults: Modular Program Manual. Jaclyn B. Spitzer et al. LC 93-14225. 256p. (gr. 13). 1993. pap. text ed. 35.00 (*0-8016-7788-2*) Mosby Yr Bk.

Rehabilitation of Lower Limb Amputees. 3rd ed. Humm. 1977. text ed. 31.00 (*0-7020-0650-5*) HarBrace.

Rehabilitation of Marginal Housing Stock in Urban Areas: A Selected Annotated Bibliography, No. 929-930. Ila M. Hallowell & Marilyn Gehr. 1975. 6.50 (*0-686-20378-X*, Sage Prdcls Pr) Sage.

Rehabilitation of Memory. Barbara A. Wilson. LC 86-7636. 259p. 1986. lib. bdg. 47.50 (*0-89862-678-1*) Guilford Pr.

Rehabilitation of Memory. Barbara A. Wilson. LC 86-7636. 259p. 1988. pap. text ed. 20.95 (*0-89862-513-0*) Guilford Pr.

Rehabilitation of Myth: Vico's New Science. Joseph Mali. 296p. (C). 1992. text ed. 69.95 (*0-521-41952-2*) Cambridge U Pr.

Rehabilitation of Offenders: A Guide to the Law. Brian Harris. 105p. (C). 1988. 110.00 (*1-85190-057-8*, Pub. by Fourmat Pub UK) St Mut.

***Rehabilitation of Older People: A Handbook for the Multidisciplinary Team.** Amanda J. Squires. (Illus.). 312p. (Orig.). 1996. pap. 47.95 (*1-56593-735-X*, 1430) Singular Publishing.

Rehabilitation of Persons with Rheumatoid Arthritis. Chang & Sutin. 300p. 1996. 66.00 (*0-8342-0679-X*, 20679) Aspen Pub.

Rehabilitation of Rivers. Ed. by Louise De Waal et al. Date not set. text ed. 90.00 (*0-471-95753-4*) Wiley.

Rehabilitation of the Adult & Child with Traumatic Brain Injury. 2nd ed. Ed. by M. Rosenthal et al. LC 89-7929. 652p. (C). 1990. text ed. 82.00 (*0-8036-7626-3*) Davis Co.

Rehabilitation of the Aging & Elderly Patient. Susan J. Garrison. Ed. by Gerald Felsenthal et al. LC 92-48558. (Illus.). 592p. 1993. 91.00 (*0-683-03125-2*) Williams & Wilkins.

Rehabilitation of the Body As a Means of Knowing in Pascal's Philosophy of Experience. Jennifer Yhap. LC 91-9020. (Studies in the History of Philosophy: Vol. 20). 108p. 1991. lib. bdg. 59.95 (*0-7734-9796-X*) E Mellen.

Rehabilitation of the Brain-Damaged Adult. Gerald Goldstein & Leslie Ruthven. (Applied Clinical Psychology Ser.). 280p. 1983. 54.50 (*0-306-40498-2*, Plenum Pr) Plenum.

Rehabilitation of the Cardiac Patient. Ed. by Nanette K. Wenger et al. (Advances in Cardiology Ser.: Vol. 33). (Illus.). xvi, 192p. 1987. 131.25 (*3-8055-4339-5*) S Karger.

Rehabilitation of the Coronary Patient. 3rd ed. Ed. by Nanette K. Wenger & Herman K. Hellerstein. 625p. 1991. text ed. 74.95 (*0-443-08765-2*) Churchill.

Rehabilitation of the Drunken Driver: A Corrective Course in Phoenix, Arizona, for Persons Convicted of Driving under the Influence of Alcohol. Ernest Stewart & James L. Malfetti. LC 73-137738. 265p. reprint ed. pap. 75.60 (*0-317-28974-8*, 2020326) Bks Demand.

Rehabilitation of the Foot. Anthony Sammarco. 450p. (C). (gr. 13). 1994. text ed. 82.00 (*0-8016-7771-8*) Mosby Yr Bk.

Rehabilitation of the Hand. 4th ed. James M. Hunter. 1400p. (C). (gr. 13). 1995. text ed. 210.00 (*0-8016-7125-6*) Mosby Yr Bk.

Rehabilitation of the Hearing Impaired Adult. Stephens & Goldstein. 856p. Date not set. write for info. (*0-407-00394-0*) Buttrwrth-Heinemann.

Rehabilitation of the Knee. 2nd ed. Letha Griffin. 350p. (C). (gr. 13). 1994. text ed. 105.00 (*0-8016-7556-1*) Mosby Yr Bk.

Rehabilitation of the Knee: A Problem Solving Approach. Ed. by Bruce H. Greenfield et al. LC 93-324. (Contemporary Perspectives in Rehabilitation Ser.: Vol. 11). (Illus.). 467p. (C). 1993. text ed. 41.00 (*0-8036-4335-7*) Davis Co.

***Rehabilitation of the Older Adult.** write for info. (*0-340-54825-8*, Pub. by E Arnold UK) Routledge Chapman & Hall.

***Rehabilitation of the Patient with Pulmonary Disease.** Neil S. Cherniack et al. 1997. pap. text ed. write for info. (*0-07-011649-0*) McGraw.

***Rehabilitation of the Physically Disabled Adult.** 2nd ed. C. John Goodwill. Ed. by M. Anne Chamberlain & Chris Evans. (Illus.). 580p. 1997. pap. 111.50 (*1-56593-320-6*, 0650) Singular Publishing.

Rehabilitation of the River Rhine. Van de Kraats. (Water Science & Technology Ser.). 424p. 1994. pap. 197.75 (*0-08-042530-5*, Pergamon Pr) Elsevier.

Rehabilitation of the Severely Brain Injured Adult: A Practical Approach. 2nd ed. G. Muir-Giles & J. Clark-Wilson. (Illus.). 272p. 1997. pap. 47.75 (*1-56593-319-2*, 0649) Singular Publishing.

Rehabilitation of the Spine: A Practitioner's Manual. Ed. by Craig Liebenson. 432p. 1995. 75.00 (*0-683-05032-X*) Williams & Wilkins.

Rehabilitation of the Surgical Knee. Ed. by George J. Davies. 100p. (Orig.). 1984. pap. 25.00 (*0-930269-00-4*) CyPr NY.

Rehabilitation of the Wounded. Ed. by Carl Kelsy et al. LC 79-6910. (Physically Handicapped in Society Ser.). 1980. reprint ed. lib. bdg. 19.95 (*0-405-13120-8*) Ayer.

Rehabilitation of Virtue: Foundations of Moral Education. Robert T. Sandin. LC 91-41535. 296p. 1992. text ed. 49.95 (*0-275-94159-0*, C4159, Praeger Pubs) Greenwood.

Rehabilitation of Whitehead: An Analytic & Historical Assessment of Process Philosophy. George R. Lucas, Jr. LC 88-22607. (SUNY Series in Philosophy). 261p. 1989. text ed. 24.50 (*0-88706-988-6*) State U NY Pr.

Rehabilitation of Workers' Compensation & Other Insurance Claimants: Case Management, Forensic, & Business Aspects. John D. Rasch. (Illus.). 222p. 1985. 41.95 (*0-398-05087-2*) C C Thomas.

Rehabilitation Policies & Programmes. S. D. Gokhale. 126p. 1986. 14.00 (*0-8364-1872-7*, Pub. by Somaiya II) S Asia.

Rehabilitation Practices with the Physically Disabled. James Garrett & Edna S. Levine. LC 72-13875. 569p. 1973. text ed. 75.00 (*0-231-03523-3*) Col U Pr.

Rehabilitation Psychology: Proceedings. National Conference on the Psychological Aspects of Disability Staff. Ed. by Walter S. Neff. LC 75-183150. 337p. reprint ed. pap. 96.10 (*0-7837-0492-5*, 2040816) Bks Demand.

Rehabilitation R&D Progress Reports: 1992-1993. Ed. by Tamara T. Sowell. 486p. (Orig.). (C). 1994. pap. text ed. 50.00 (*0-7881-1442-5*) DIANE Pub.

Rehabilitation, Recidivism & Research. Robert Martinson et al. 96p. 1976. 6.00 (*0-318-15372-6*) Natl Coun Crime.

Rehabilitation, Renovation, & Preservation of Concrete & Masonry Structures. Ed. by Gajanan M. Sabnis. LC 84-72964. (American Concrete Institute Publication Ser.: No. SP-85). (Illus.). 274p. reprint ed. pap. 78.10 (*0-7837-6672-6*, 2046288) Bks Demand.

Rehabilitation, Renovation, & Reconstruction of Buildings: Proceedings of a Workshop Sponsored by the National Science Foundation & ASCE. 105p. 1985. 15.00 (*0-87262-493-5*) Am Soc Civil Eng.

Rehabilitation Resource Manual: Vision. 4th ed. Resources for Rehabilitation Staff. 1993. pap. 39.95 (*0-929718-10-0*) Resc Rehab.

Rehabilitation Specialist's Handbook. Jules M. Rothstein et al. LC 90-14090. (Illus.). 1022p. 1991. pap. 29.95 (*0-8036-7629-8*) Davis Co.

Rehabilitation Specialist's Handbook. 2nd ed. Steven L. Wolf et al. LC 97-18584. (Illus.). 1375p. (C). 1997. pap. text ed. 38.95 (*0-8036-0047-X*) Davis Co.

***Rehabilitation Studies Handbook.** Ed. by Barbara A. Wilson & D. L. McLellan. (Illus.). 448p. (C). 1997. pap. text ed. 49.95 (*0-521-43713-X*) Cambridge U Pr.

Rehabilitation Surgery for Deformities Due to Poliomyelitis: Techniques for the District Hospital. Ed. by Edwin J. Krol & World Health Organization Staff. (Illus.). 112p. (CHI, ENG & FRE.). 1993. pap. text ed. 25.00 (*92-4-154457-0*, 1150403) World Health.

Rehabilitation Tax Credit: Market Segment Specialization Program-Audit Technique Guide. 226p. 1995. pap. 55.00 (*1-57402-104-4*) Athena Info Mgt.

Rehabilitation Techniques: Vocational Adjustment for the Handicapped. James S. Payne et al. 208p. (C). 1984. 35.95 (*0-89885-159-9*) Human Sci Pr.

Rehabilitation Techniques in Sports Medicine. Prentice. (C). 1993. pap. text ed. 54.95 (*0-8016-7819-6*); pap. text ed. 54.95 (*0-8016-7820-X*) Mosby Yr Bk.

Rehabilitation Technology. Glenn Hedman. LC 90-4593. (Physical & Occupational Therapy in Pediatrics Ser.: Vol. 10, No. 2). (Illus.). 181p. 1990. text ed. 39.95 (*1-56024-033-4*) Haworth Pr.

Rehabilitation Technology: Strategies for the European Union; Proceedings of the First Tide Congress, Apr 6-7, 1993, Brussels. E. Ballabio et al. LC 93-78138. (Studies in Health Technology & Informatics: Vol. 9). 271p. (gr. 12). 1993. 105.00 (*90-5199-131-2*, Pub. by IOS Pr NE) IOS Press.

***Rehabilitation Therapy & the Law.** annuals Steve Long & Rita Burghardt. 16p. (Orig.). 1996. pap. 60.00 (*1-56900-045-X*) Am Occup Therapy.

Rehabilitation with Brain Injury Survivors: An Empowerment Approach. Christiane C. O'Hara & Minnie Harrell. LC 90-1040. 504p. 1991. 118.00 (*0-8342-0180-1*) Aspen Pub.

***Rehabilitation with the Aid of a Horse: A Collection of Studies.** Ed. by Barbara T. Engel. (Illus.). ix, 260p. (Orig.). 1997. pap. text ed. write for info. (*0-9633065-2-9*) B E Therapy.

Rehabilitations & Other Essays. C. S. Lewis. LC 71-167377. (Essay Index Reprint Ser.). 1977. reprint ed. 18.95 (*0-8369-2559-9*) Ayer.

Rehabilitations & Other Essays. C. S. Lewis. reprint ed. 14.00 (*0-403-04233-X*) Somerset Pub.

Rehabilitative & Restorative Nursing in the Long Term Care Facility. Marguerite Bouvette. (Illus.). 122p. (Orig.). (C). 1989. pap. text ed. 9.50 (*1-877735-24-8*, 141) M&H Pub Co TX.

Rehabilitative Audiology for Children & Adults. 2nd ed. Jerome G. Alpiner & Patricia A. McCarthy. (Illus.). 544p. 1993. 49.00 (*0-683-00078-0*) Williams & Wilkins.

Rehearsal. Earl Reimer. (Christian Theatre Ser.). 23p. 1994. pap. 3.00 (*1-57514-138-8*, 1104) Encore Perform Pub.

Rehearsal: The Principles & Practice of Acting for the Stage. 6th ed. Miriam A. Franklin & James G. Dixon, III. (Illus.). 272p. 1982. pap. text ed. 67.00 (*0-13-771550-1*) P-H.

Rehearsal see Restoration Plays

Rehearsal for a Renaissance. Douglas W. Clark. 1992. mass mkt. 4.50 (*0-380-76310-9*, AvoNova) Avon.

Rehearsal for Living: Psychodrama Theory, Techniques, & Applications. Adaline Starr. LC 76-49045. 396p. reprint ed. pap. 112.90 (*0-7837-3640-1*, 2043507) Bks Demand.

Rehearsal for Murder. Richard Levinson & William Link. 1983. pap. 5.25 (*0-87129-279-3*, R36) Dramatic Pub.

Rehearsal for Reconstruction: The Port Royal Experiment. Willie L. Rose. 456p. 1976. reprint ed. pap. 14.95 (*0-19-519882-4*) OUP.

Rehearsal Guide for the Choral Director. Jack Boyd. LC 77-2051. (C). 1977. reprint ed. pap. text ed. 15.95 (*0-916656-03-9*, MFBK 03) Mark Foster Mus.

Rehearsal Management For Directors. David Alberts. LC 94-49122. 160p. 1995. pap. 15.95 (*0-435-08665-0*, 08665) Heinemann.

Rehearsal, 1671. George Villiers. Ed. by Edward Arber. 132p. 1984. pap. 15.00 (*0-87556-342-2*) Saifer.

Rehearsals for Fascism: Populism & Political Mobilization in Weimar Germany. Peter Fritzsche. (Illus.). 320p. 1990. 55.00 (*0-19-505780-5*) OUP.

Rehearsals for Growth: Theater Improvisation for Psychotherapists. Daniel J. Wiener. 288p. 1994. 32.00 (*0-393-70187-5*) Norton.

Rehearsals in Time: Poems & Dreams. deluxe ed. Judith H. Settle. Ed. by MaryBelle Campbell. 56p. 1992. per., pap. 10.00 (*1-879009-07-2*) S P-Persephone Pr.

***Rehearsals of Revolution: The Political Theater of Bengal.** Rustom Bharucha. LC 83-10470. (Illus.). 278p. 1983. reprint ed. pap. 79.30 (*0-608-04387-7*, 2065168) Bks Demand.

Rehearsing. Michael Craft. LC 92-70179. 120p. (Orig.). 1993. pap. 9.95 (*1-879603-09-8*) Los Hombres.

Rehearsing for Romance. Carolyn Keene. (Nancy Drew Files Ser.: No. 114). (YA). (gr. 6 up). 1996. mass mkt. 3.99 (*0-671-50355-3*, Archway) PB.

***Rehearsing with Rat.** Jonathan Potter. Ed. by William-Alan Landes. LC 97-5553. 55p. 1997. pap. 5.00 (*0-88734-371-6*) Players Pr.

***Rehema's Journey.** Barbara A. Margolies. (J). 1997. mass mkt. 4.99 (*0-590-42847-0*) Scholastic Inc.

Rehnquist Court: In Pursuit of Judicial Conservatism. Stanley H. Friedelbaum. LC 93-14122. (Contributions in Legal Studies: No. 76). 184p. 1993. text ed. 52.95 (*0-313-27990-X*, FRQ/, Greenwood Pr) Greenwood.

Rehnquist Court & Civil Rights. David Tucker. (Applied Legal Philosophy Ser.). 250p. 1995. text ed. 63.95 (*1-85521-310-9*, Pub. by Dartmth Pub UK) Ashgate Pub Co.

***Rehnquist Court & Criminal Punishment.** Christopher E. Smith. LC 97-10778. (Current Issues in Criminal Justice Ser.: No. 21). 176p. 1997. 35.00 (*0-8153-2573-8*) Garland.

***Rehoboth.** Angela E. Hunt. LC 97-162. (Keepers of the Ring Ser.: No. 4). 1997. pap. 11.99 (*0-8423-2015-6*) Tyndale.

Reich: The Nudes of Jon Reich. Jon Reich. LC 90-91911. (Illus.). 130p. 1991. 59.95 (*0-9627203-0-5*) Predictable Pr.

Reich & Nation: The Holy Roman Empire As Idea & Reality, 1763-1806. John G. Gaaliardo. LC 79-2170. 380p. reprint ed. pap. 108.90 (*0-685-44448-1*, 2056701) Bks Demand.

Reich Angel: A Novel. Anita Mason. LC 94-31322. 373p. 1995. 24.00 (*1-56947-033-2*) Soho Press.

Reich Angel: A Novel. Anita Mason. LC 94-31322. (Hera Ser.). 373p. 1997. pap. 13.00 (*1-56947-071-5*) Soho Press.

Reich for Beginners. David Z. Mairowitz. (Writers & Readers Documentary Comic Bks.). (Illus.). 176p. 1986. pap. 6.95 (*0-86316-031-X*) Writers & Readers.

Reich for Beginners. M. Mairowitz & German Gonzales. 1990. pap. 21.00 (*0-04-021032-4*, Pub. by Northcote UK) St Mut.

Reich, Jung, Regardie & Me: The Unhealed Healer. J. Marvin Spiegelman. LC 91-67382. 192p. (Orig.). 1991. pap. 12.95 (*1-56184-032-7*) New Falcon Pubns.

Reich Star Rulebook. Ken Richardson. Ed. & Illus. by Simon Bell. (Reich Star Ser.). 246p. (Orig.). 1990. pap. 19.95 (*0-9627428-0-5*) Creative Encounters.

Reichard Collection of Early Pennsylvania German Dialogues & Plays. Ed. by Albert F. Buffington. (Pennsylvania German Folklore Ser.: Vol. 61). 1962. 20.00 (*0-911122-15-X*) Penn German Soc.

Reichen & Robert: Transforming Space. Alain Pelissier. 1994. pap. 59.00 (*0-8176-5052-0*) Birkhauser.

***Reichen & Robert: Transforming Space.** Alain Pelissier. 1996. 65.00 (*3-7643-5052-0*) Birkhauser.

Reichenbach's Letters on OD & Magnetism (1852) F. D. O'Byrne. 119p. 1964. reprint ed. spiral bd. 12.50 (*0-7873-0639-8*) Hlth Research.

Reichian Growth Work: Melting the Blocks to Life & Love. Nick Totten & Em Edmondson. 160p. (Orig.). 1988. pap. 9.95 (*1-85327-016-4*, Pub. by Prism Pr UK) Assoc Pubs Grp.

Reichmans: Family, Faith, Fortune, & the Empire of Olympia & York. Anthony Bianco. (Illus.). 810p. 1997. 30.00 (*0-8129-2140-2*, Times Bks) Random.

***Reichpaper - A Guide to Civil & Paramilitary Identification & Membership Documents of the Third Reich, Vol. 1.** Bruce E. Kipp. (Illus.). 206p. (Orig.). 1995. spiral bd., pap. 29.95 (*0-9653843-0-6*) Mackerin Mrktg.

***Reichpaper - A Guide to Civil & Paramilitary Identification & Membership Documents of the Third Reich, Vol. 2.** Bruce E. Kipp. (Illus.). 210p. (Orig.). 1996. pap. 45.00 (*0-9653843-1-4*) Mackerin Mrktg.

Reichsrecht und Volksrecht in Den Ostlichen Provinzen Des Romiscshen Kaiserreichs. Ludwig Mitteis. xiv, 562p. 1984. reprint ed. write for info. (*3-487-00502-6*) G Olms Pubs.

Reid. Isabella Alden. (Grace Livingston Hill Ser.). 281p. 1995. mass mkt., pap. 4.99 (*0-8423-3181-6*) Tyndale.

Reid. Isabella Alden. (Grace Livingston Hill Ser.). 250p. 1995. mass mkt., pap. 5.99 (*0-8423-3182-4*) Tyndale.

Reid & His French Disciples: Aesthetics & Metaphysics. James W. Manns. (Brill's Studies in Intellectual History: Vol. 45). 250p. 1994. 77.00 (*90-04-09942-5*, NLG110) E J Brill.

Reid's Branson Instruction to Juries, 7 Vols. 3rd ed. 1991. suppl. ed. 110.00 (*0-87473-827-X*) MICHIE.

Reid's Branson Instruction to Juries, 7 vols. 3rd ed. A. H. Reid. 1966. suppl. ed. 250.00 (*0-672-84048-0*) MICHIE.

Reid's Controversy in Obstetrics & Gynecology 3. 3rd ed. Frederick P. Zuspan & C. Donald Christian. (Illus.). 672p. 1983. text ed. 139.00 (*0-7216-2565-7*) Saunders.

Reigen/Liebelei. Arthur Schnitzler. 168p. (GER.). 1995. pap. 13.50 (*3-596-27009-X*, Pub. by Fischer Taschbch Verlag GW) Intl Bk Import.

Reigersman Desirable World. 1974. pap. text ed. 82.50 (*90-247-1706-X*) Kluwer Ac.

Reign & Rejection of King Saul: A Case for Literary & Theological Coherence. V. Philips Long. 294p. 1989. 23.95 (*1-55540-391-3*, 06 21 18); pap. 11.95 (*1-55540-392-1*, 06 21 18) Scholars Pr GA.

***Reign in Hell.** William Diehl. 1997. 25.00 (*0-345-41144-7*) Ballantine.

Reign of Charles V, 1516-1558. William L. McElwee. LC 83-45657. reprint ed. 36.00 (*0-404-19807-4*) AMS Pr.

Reign of Christ the King. Michael Davies. LC 92-61180. 36p. (Orig.). 1992. pap. 1.25 (*0-89555-474-7*) TAN Bks Pubs.

Reign of Cnut. Ed. by Alexander Rumble. LC 94-16870. (Studies in the Early History of Britain). 1994. 46.50 (*0-8386-3605-5*) Fairleigh Dickinson.

Reign of Edward the Third: Crown & Political Society in England, 1327-1377. Mark Ormrod. (Illus.). 352p. (C). 1991. text ed. 38.00 (*0-300-04875-0*) Yale U Pr.

Reign of Elizabeth, Fifteen Fifty-Eight to Sixteen Three. 2nd ed. J. B. Black. (Oxford History of England Ser.). 1959. 65.00 (*0-19-821701-3*) OUP.

Reign of Elizabeth I: Court & Culture in the Last Decade. Ed. by John Guy. 300p. (C). 1995. text ed. 59.95 (*0-521-44341-5*) Cambridge U Pr.

Reign of Error. Edward Rooney. 24p. 1995. pap. 9.00 (*0-8059-3679-3*) Dorrance.

An Asterisk (*) at the beginning of an entry indicates that the title is appearing in BIP for the first time.

Reign of ETS: The Corporation That Makes up Minds. Ed. by Nairn, Allan & Associates Staff. LC 80-107761. (Ralph Nader Report on the Educational Testing Service Ser.). 554p. (Orig.). 1980. pap. 30.00 (*0-936486-00-7*) R Nader.

Reign of Fantasy: The Political Roots of Reagan's Star Wars Policy. Kerry L. Hunter. LC 91-32357. (American University Studies: Political Science: Ser. X, Vol. 34). 181p. (C). 1992. text ed. 35.95 (*0-8204-1771-8*) P Lang Pubng.

Reign of George Third, Seventeen Sixty to Eighteen Fifteen. J. Steven Watson. (Oxford History of England Ser.). 1960. 55.00 (*0-19-821713-7*) OUP.

Reign of German Militarism & the Disaster of 1918 see Sword & the Scepter: The Problem of Militarism in Germany

Reign of God. Jim McGuiggan. 120p. (Orig.). 1992. pap. 6.95 (*0-940999-88-9*, C2226) Star Bible.

Reign of God: An Introduction to Christian Theology from a Seventh-Day Adventist Perspective. Richard Rice. LC 85-70344. 424p. (C). 1985. text ed. 29.99 (*0-943872-90-1*) Andrews Univ Pr.

***Reign of God: An Introduction to Christian Theology from a Seventh-Day Adventist Perspective.** 2nd rev. ed. Richard Rice. 464p. (C). 1997. text ed. 34.95 (*1-883925-16-9*) Andrews Univ Pr.

Reign of Grace. Abrh Booth. 7.99 (*0-87377-014-5*) GAM Pubns.

Reign of Guilt. David C. Phillips. (Collected Works of David G. Phillips). 1988. reprint ed. lib. bdg. 59.00 (*0-7812-1329-0*) Rprt Serv.

Reign of Guilt. David G. Phillips. (American Author Ser.). 1981. reprint ed. lib. bdg. 49.00 (*0-686-71939-5*) Scholarly.

Reign of Henry Eighth from His Accession to the Death of Wolsey, 2 Vols. John S. Brewer. Ed. by James Gairdner. LC 70-52901. reprint ed. 95.00 (*0-404-01072-5*) AMS Pr.

Reign of Henry III. D. A. Carpenter. LC 96-5798. 480p. 1996. 65.00 (*1-85285-137-6*) Hambledon Press.

Reign of Henry Seventh from Contemporary Sources, 3 vols. Ed. by Albert F. Pollard. LC 73-181970. reprint ed. 145.00 (*0-404-05140-5*) AMS Pr.

Reign of Henry VIII: Politics, Policy, & Piety. Ed. by Diarmaid MacCulloch. LC 95-19514. (Problems in Focus Ser.). 256p. 1995. text ed. 49.95 (*0-312-12892-4*); text ed. 19.95 (*0-312-12900-9*) St Martin.

Reign of Ideology. Eugene Goodheart. LC 96-8330. 240p. 1996. 42.50 (*0-231-10622-X*); pap. 15.50 (*0-231-10623-8*) Col U Pr.

Reign of Jesus Thru Mary. Gabriel Denis. 1949. 6.00 (*0-910984-03-4*) Montfort Pubns.

***Reign of King Henry VI.** R. A. Griffiths. (History Paperbacks Ser.). (Illus.). 1024p. 1997. pap. 35.95 (*0-7509-1609-5*, Pub. by Sutton Pubng UK) Bks Intl VA.

Reign of King John. Sidney Painter. 1979. 33.95 (*0-405-10619-X*) Ayer.

Reign of King Pym. Jack H. Hexter. LC 41-4164. (Harvard Historical Studies: Vol. 48). 255p. 1941. reprint ed. pap. 72.70 (*0-608-01603-9*, AU00475) Bks Demand.

Reign of Law. James L. Allen. (Principle Works of James Lane Allen). 1989. reprint ed. lib. bdg. 79.00 (*0-7812-1734-2*) Rprt Serv.

Reign of Law: A Tale of the Kentucky Hemp Fields. James L. Allen. LC 77-164556. (American Fiction Reprint Ser.). 1977. reprint ed. 34.95 (*0-8369-7032-2*) Ayer.

***Reign of Law: Marbury V. Madison & the Construction of America.** Paul W. Kahn. LC 96-47844. 1997. write for info. (*0-300-06679-1*) Yale U Pr.

***Reign of Leo VI (886-912) Politics & People.** Shaun Tougher. LC 97-22089. (Medieval Mediterranean Ser.). 1997. write for info. (*90-04-10811-4*) E J Brill.

Reign of Louis XIV. Ed. by Paul Sonnino. LC 90-48479. (Illus.). 272p. (C). 1991. pap. 17.50 (*0-391-03705-6*) Humanities.

Reign of Mary I. 2nd ed. Robert Tihler. (C). 1992. pap. text ed. 13.50 (*0-582-06107-5*) Longman.

Reign of Mary Tudor. David M. Loades. (Illus.). 448p. (C). 1991. pap. text ed. 34.50 (*0-582-05759-0*, 78831) Longman.

Reign of Nabonidus, King of Babylon (556-539 BC) Paul-Alain Beaulieu. (C). 1990. text ed. 55.00 (*0-300-04314-7*) Yale U Pr.

Reign of Patti. Herman Klein. Ed. by Andrew Farkas. LC 76-29944. (Opera Biographies Ser.). (Illus.). 1977. reprint ed. lib. bdg. 46.95 (*0-405-09686-0*) Ayer.

Reign of Patti. Herman Klein. LC 77-17874. (Music Reprint Ser.: 1978). (Illus.). 1978. reprint ed. lib. bdg. 55.00 (*0-306-77530-1*) Da Capo.

***Reign of Quanity & the Sign of the Times.** Rene Guenon. 1996. pap. 15.95 (*0-614-21237-5*, 1066) Kazi Pubns.

Reign of Quantity & the Signs of the Times. 3rd ed. James R. Wetmore. (Perennial Wisdom Ser.). 402p. (FRE.). 1995. reprint ed. pap. text ed. 24.95 (*0-900588-14-4*) S Perennis.

Reign of Rabble: The St. Louis General Strike of 1877. David T. Burbank. LC 66-21658. 208p. 1966. 35.00 (*0-678-00186-3*) Kelley.

***Reign of Ramesses IV.** A. J. Peden. (Illus.). 148p. 1994. pap. 19.95 (*0-85668-622-0*, Pub. by Aris & Phillips UK) David Brown.

Reign of Reality: A Fresh Start for the Earth. Joyce Marshall & Gene W. Marshall. LC 87-90621. (Illus.). 267p. 1987. pap. 10.00 (*0-9611552-2-1*) Realistic Living.

Reign of Shadows. Deborah Chester. 1996. mass mkt. 5.99 (*0-441-00340-0*) Ace Bks.

Reign of Stephen: Kingship, Warfare, & Government in Twelfth-Century England. Keith J. Stringer. LC 93-18771. (Lancaster Pamphlets Ser.). 84p. (C). 1993. pap. 10.95 (*0-415-01415-8*, B2471) Routledge.

Reign of the Brown Magician. Lawrence Watt-Evans. 1996. mass mkt. 5.99 (*0-345-37247-6*, Del Rey) Ballantine.

Reign of the Dinosaurs. Jean-Guy Michard. (Discoveries Ser.). (Illus.). 144p. 1992. pap. 12.95 (*0-8109-2808-6*) Abrams.

***Reign of the Greyhound: A Popular History of the First Family of Dogs.** Cynthia Branigan. (Illus.). 192p. 1997. 24.95 (*0-87605-696-6*) Howell Bk.

Reign of the Horse: The Horse in Print, 1500-1715. Intro. by Anthony Dent. (Illus.). 64p. (Orig.). 1991. pap. 4.95 (*0-9629254-0-3*) Folger.

Reign of the House of Rothschild. E. Corti. 1973. 300.00 (*0-87968-171-3*) Gordon Pr.

Reign of the Phallus: Sexual Politics in Ancient Athens. Eva C. Keuls. LC 92-32765. (C). 1993. 45.00 (*0-520-07928-0*); pap. 18.00 (*0-520-07929-9*) U CA Pr.

Reign of the Pirates of British Origin: Twelve Buccaneers of the East & West Indies, 1670-1750. Archibald Hurd. 1977. pap. text ed. write for info. (*0-8490-2508-7*) Gordon Pr.

Reign of the Reptiles. Michael Benton. 1990. 17.99 (*0-517-02557-4*) Random Hse Value.

Reign of the Theatrical Director 1887-1924: French Theatre. Bettina Knapp. LC 87-51204. viii, 273p. 1988. 30.00 (*0-87875-358-3*) Whitston Pub.

Reign of Thutmose IV. Betsy M. Bryan. LC 90-27688. 416p. 1991. pap. 118.60 (*0-7837-7459-1*, 2049181) Bks Demand.

Reign of William Rufus & the Accession of Henry the First, 2 vols. Edward A. Freeman. reprint ed. 85.00 (*0-404-00620-5*) AMS Pr.

Reign of Women in Eighteenth Century France. Vera Lee. (Illus.). 140p. 1976. 18.95 (*0-87073-990-5*); pap. 14.95 (*0-87073-991-3*) Schenkman Bks Inc.

Reigning Cats & Dogs: Don't Let Your Pet Run Your Life. Herbert Tanzer. Ed. by Frank Reuter. 145p. 1991. reprint ed. text ed. 12.95 (*0-942540-05-0*) Breakthru Pub.

Reigning in Life As a King. John Osteen. 140p. (Orig.). 1984. pap. 4.95 (*0-912631-01-5*) J O Pubns.

***Reigning in the World.** Benjamin Schwarz. 1998. write for info. (*0-201-56559-5*) Addison-Wesley.

Reigning, Kolomna Icon of the Mother of God: Account of Appearance, Liturgical Service, Akathist Hymn. Tr. by Isaac E. Lambertsen from RUS. (Illus.). 48p. (Orig.). 1989. pap. 4.00 (*0-912927-37-2*, X037) St John Kronstadt.

Reigniting Love & Passion: 24 Marital Checkpoints. Guy Greenfield. LC 95-15304. 160p. (Orig.). (YA). (gr. 10). 1995. pap. 9.99 (*0-8010-5232-7*) Baker Bks.

***Reigns of Charles II & James VII & II.** Lionel K. Glassey. LC 96-33270. 1997. text ed. 45.00 (*0-312-16508-0*) St Martin.

***Reihe No. 2: Philosophischer Briefwechsel.** Gottfried W. Leibniz. (GER.). 1972. write for info. (*3-487-04102-2*) G Olms Pubs.

Reiki: A Torch in Daylight. Karyn K. Mitchell. 128p. 1994. student ed., pap. 14.95 (*0-9640822-1-7*) Mind Rivers.

Reiki: Beyond the Usui System. Karyn K. Mitchell. 256p. (Orig.). 1994. student ed., pap. 19.96 (*0-9640822-2-5*) Mind Rivers.

Reiki: E Geschichte von Hawayo Takata. Helen J. Haberly. Tr. by Birgitt Krause. (Illus.). 144p. (Orig.). (GER.). 1991. pap. 12.00 (*0-944135-07-2*) Archedigm Pubns.

Reiki: Hawayo Takata's Story. Helen J. Haberly. (Illus.). 128p. (Orig.). 1990. pap. 12.00 (*0-944135-06-4*) Archedigm Pubns.

Reiki: Het Verhaal Van Hawayo Takata. Helen J. Haberly. Tr. by Xavier Van Den Camp & Inger Droog. (Illus.). 142p. (Orig.). (DUT.). 1994. pap. 12.00 (*0-944135-01-3*) Archedigm Pubns.

Reiki: The Healer's Touch. Elizabeth F. Severino. (Illus.). 202p. 1995. pap. 19.95 (*1-888674-08-3*) Healing Connect.

Reiki - for First Aid: Reiki Treatment As Accompanying Therapy for Over 40 Types of Illness. With a Supplement on Natural Healing. Walter Lubeck. 154p. (Orig.). 1995. pap. 14.95 (*0-914955-26-8*) Lotus Pr WI.

Reiki - Hands That Heal. Joyce J. Morris. (Illus.). 200p. (Orig.). 1996. pap. 22.00 (*1-888196-05-X*) Ctr Bkstore.

A comprehensive manual for both the Reiki student & the inquisitive seeker of sacred knowledge. REIKI - HANDS THAT HEAL is an extremely definitive book that covers where Reiki came from, what it is, & what it is not, & what you can do with it. Other areas covered include - Reiki research, Reiki miracles, how to do treatments on both yourself & others, how to treat specific ailments, creating a healing environment, & how to tie Reiki into a personal growth path. The reader is given a new viewpoint of Reiki with the informative material given by William Morris, OMD, linking Reiki to Oriental medicine. The manual is illustrated with beautifully hand drawn sketches of hand positions for giving Reiki treatments, & clairvoyantly drawn sketches of the aura before & after Reiki initiations. Joyce was introduced to Reiki in 1981, & became the 44th Reiki Master in the United States. She is the founder & Director of the Reiki Center of Los Angeles, & is a member of The Alliance of Reiki Masters. As a leader in the Metaphysical field for many years, she has presented at numerous conferences & Expos around the country on Reiki, as well as other personal growth subjects. In addition to REIKI - HANDS THAT HEAL, Joyce has produced a series of guided visualization tapes & a workbook on her class on Feng Shui. Order from: The Center Bookstore, 16161 Ventura B #802, Encino, CA 91436. Tel. (818) 981-9100. ***Publisher Provided Annotation.***

Reiki - Metaphysics, Science & Philosophy. 160p. (Orig.). 1995. pap. 15.00 (*0-9645944-0-4*) Parama Wisdom.

Reiki - Universal Life Energy: Heals Body, Mind & Spirit - A Holistic Method Suitable for Self-Treatment & the Home, Professional Practice, Teleotherapeutics-Spiritual Healing. Bodo Baginski & Shalila Sharamon. Tr. by Chris Baker & Judith Harrison from GER. (Illus.). 211p. (Orig.). 1988. pap. 12.95 (*0-940795-02-7*) LifeRhythm.

Reiki - Way of the Heart: The Reiki Path of Initiation. Walter Lubeck. (Illus.). 208p. (Orig.). 1996. pap. 14.95 (*0-941524-91-4*) Lotus Light.

Reiki & Beyond: Healing Manual: One Planet - One People. S. Jeanne Gunn. (Illus.). 156p. (Orig.). 1994. student ed., pap. 17.95 (*0-9643412-0-4*) Reiki & Beyond Spirt.

Reiki & Medicine. Nancy Eos. LC 95-90006. (Illus.). 108p. (Orig.). 1995. pap. 14.95 (*0-9644923-0-X*) Nancy Eos.

Reiki & Other Rays of Touch Healing. Kathleen A. Milner. (Orig.). 165.00 incl. audio, vhs (*1-886903-99-9*) K Milner.

Reiki & Other Rays of Touch Healing. 2nd ed. Kathleen Milner. (Healing Art Ser.). (Illus.). 152p. (Orig.). (C). 1995. pap. 15.95 (*1-886903-97-2*) K Milner.

Traces the ancient art of hands-on-healing from before the time of Christ to the present. The book explains in simple language how the manifestation of healing transformations takes place by explaining how elemental healing rays emanating from the Creator are channeled through the healer. Healing techniques & concrete examples are given in self-healing, as well as facilitating healing for others, animals & Mother Earth. The chapter on symbols includes exercises in how to use them in healing. There are also chapters on how to use these same elemental rays in magic & Feng Shui (the Chinese art of altering life's circumstances by altering one's environment). Two of the companion videos, HEALING HANDS & SYMBOLS IN HEALING were released before the book & reviewed in the August 1994 issue of BODY MIND SPIRIT magazine. HEALING ANIMALS shows comparative anatomy & corresponding healing techniques. Five audio tapes guide the mediator through exercises discussed in the book. REIKI & OTHER RAYS OF TOUCH HEALING has been reviewed by several new age publications & is available through the following distributors: Baker & Taylor 1-800-233-3657, Bookpeople 1-800-684-0431, New Leaf 1-800-430-0501, Moving Books, Samuel Weisser 1-800-423-7087 & DeVorss & Co. ***Publisher Provided Annotation.***

Reiki Class: First & Second Degree Audio Cassette Tapes. William L. Rand. 1994. pap. 29.95 incl. audio (*1-886785-01-5*) Vision Pub.

Reiki Energy Medicine: Bringing the Healing Touch into Home, Hospital, & Hospice. Libby Barnett et al. (Illus.). 192p. 1996. pap. 12.95 (*0-89281-633-3*, Heal Arts VT) Inner Tradit.

***Reiki Fire: New Information about the Origin of the Reiki Power a Complete Method.** Frank A. Petter. (Illus.). 144p. (Orig.). 1997. pap. 12.95 (*0-914955-50-0*) Lotus Light.

Reiki Healing Yourself & Others: A Photo-Instructional Art Book. Marsha J. Burack. 160p. 1995. pap. text ed. 24.95 (*1-880441-39-X*) Reiki Heal.

Reiki I Manual. 2nd ed. Karen Miller. 88p. (Orig.). 1993. spiral bd. 12.95 (*0-9630439-5-1*) Bayrock.

Reiki II Manual. 2nd ed. Karen Miller. (Illus.). 124p. (Orig.). 1993. spiral bd. 12.95 (*0-9630439-6-X*) Bayrock.

Reiki in Everyday Living: How Universal Energy Is a Natural Part of Life, Medicine, & Personal Growth. 2nd ed. Earlene F. Gleisner. 104p. (Orig.). 1993. pap. 12.95 (*1-880357-07-0*) WFP.

***Reiki Mystery School: Transformational Reiki.** Karyn Mitchell et al. (Illus.). 200p. (Orig.). 1997. pap. text ed. 16.95 (*0-9640822-5-X*) Mind Rivers.

Reiki Plus Natural Healing: A Manual for First Degree Reiki Natural Healing. 5th rev. ed. David G. Jarrell. Ed. by Richard Levitt. (Illus.). 96p. 1983. per. 15.00 (*0-9634690-0-2*) Reiki Plus.

Reiki Plus Professional Practitioner's Manual for Second Degree: "Now What Do I Do That I'm Second Degree" 2nd ed. David G. Jarrell. 96p. 1996. 22.00 (*0-9634690-1-0*) Reiki Plus.

Reiki the Healing Touch: First & Second Degree Manual. William L. Rand. 44p. 1992. 12.95 (*0-9631567-0-5*) Vision Pub.

***Reiki with Gemstones: Activating Your Self-Healing Powers by Connecting the Universal Life Force & Gemstone Therapy.** Ursula Klinger-Omenka. (Illus.). 128p. (Orig.). 1997. pap. 12.95 (*0-914955-29-2*) Lotus Light.

Reilly of the White House. Michael Reilly. (American Autobiography Ser.). 248p. 1995. reprint ed. lib. bdg. 79.00 (*0-7812-8623-9*) Rprt Serv.

Reilly's Bride. Patricia Thayer. (Romance Ser.). 1996. mass mkt. 3.25 (*0-373-19146-4*, 1-19146-9) Silhouette.

Reilly's Luck. Louis L'Amour. 224p. 1985. mass mkt. 3.99 (*0-553-25305-0*) Bantam.

***Reilly's Luck.** large type ed. Louis L'Amour. LC 96-35015. (West-Hall Ser.). 359p. 1997. lib. bdg. 24.95 (*0-7838-1950-1*, GK Hall) Thorndike Pr.

***Reilly's Return.** Amelia Autin. 1997. mass mkt. 3.99 (*0-373-07820-X*, 1-07820-3) Silhouette.

Reilly's Woman. Janet Dailey. (Janet Dailey Americana Ser.: No. 878). 1992. mass mkt. 3.59 (*0-373-89878-9*, 1-89878-2) Harlequin Bks.

Reilly's Woman. large type ed. Janet Dailey. (Nightingale Ser.). 200p. 1990. pap. 14.95 (*0-8161-4964-X*, GK Hall) Thorndike Pr.

Reimaging the Pariah City: Urban Development in Belfast & Detroit. William J. Neill et al. 251p. 1995. 59.95 (*1-85628-480-8*, Pub. by Avebury Pub UK) Ashgate Pub Co.

Reimagining America: A Theological Critique of the American Mythos & Biblical Hermeneutics. Charles Mabee. LC 84-27335. xvi, 156p. 1985. 15.95 (*0-86554-148-5*, MUP/H139) Mercer Univ Pr.

Reimagining American Theatre. Robert Brustein. 324p. 1992. reprint ed. pap. 12.95 (*0-929587-99-5*, Elephant Paperbacks) I R Dee.

Reimagining Canada: Language, Culture, Community, & the Canadian Constitution. Jeremy Webber. 368p. 1994. 55.00 (*0-7735-1146-6*, Pub. by McGill CN); pap. 19.95 (*0-7735-1152-0*, Pub. by McGill CN) U of Toronto Pr.

Reimagining Christian Origins: A Colloquium Honoring Burton L. Mack. Ed. by Elizabeth A. Castelli & Hal Taussig. LC 96-12472. 352p. 1996. 35.00 (*1-56338-171-0*); pap. 25.00 (*1-56338-172-9*) TPI PA.

Reimagining Computers & Composition: Teaching & Research in the Virtual Age. Ed. by Gail Hawisher & Paul J. LeBlanc. LC 92-5502. 240p. 1992. pap. text ed. 27.50 (*0-86709-307-2*, 0307) Boynton Cook Pubs.

***Reimagining Culture.** MacDonald. 1997. 46.50 (*1-85973-980-6*, Pub. by Berg Pubs UK); pap. 19.50 (*1-85973-985-7*, Pub. by Berg Pubs UK) NYU Pr.

Reimagining Denominationalism: Interpretive Essays. Ed. by Robert B. Mullin & Russell E. Richey. LC 93-31858. (Religion in America Ser.). 320p. 1994. 39.95 (*0-19-508778-X*) OUP.

Reimagining God: The Case for Scriptural Diversity. Johanna W. Van Wijk-Bos. LC 94-36909. 144p. (Orig.). 1995. pap. 13.00 (*0-664-25569-8*) Westminster John Knox.

***Reimagining the Bible: The Storytelling of the Rabbis.** Howard Schwartz. 288p. 1997. 45.00 (*0-19-510499-4*); pap. 18.95 (*0-19-511511-2*) OUP.

Reimagining the Modern American West: A Century of Fiction, History, & Art. Richard W. Etulain. LC 96-10109. (Modern American West Ser.). 241p. 1996. 45.00 (*0-8165-1133-0*); pap. 17.95 (*0-8165-1683-9*) U of Ariz Pr.

Reimagining the Nation. Ed. by Marjorie Ringrose & Adam Lerner. LC 92-47424. 1993. 85.00 (*0-335-19150-9*, Open Univ Pr) Taylor & Francis.

Reimagining Thoreau. Robert Milder. (Cambridge Studies in American Literature & Culture: No. 85). 350p. (C). 1995. text ed. 59.95 (*0-521-46149-9*) Cambridge U Pr.

Reimagining Women: Representations of Women in Culture. Ed. by Shirley Neuman & Glennis Stephenson. 352p. 1993. 60.00 (*0-8020-2777-6*); pap. 24.95 (*0-8020-6825-1*) U of Toronto Pr.

***Reimann Fantasy, No. 2.** Reimann. Date not set. 22.95 (*0-312-86008-0*) St Martin.

Reimarus: Fragments. Ed. by Charles H. Talbert. (Reprints & Translations Ser.). 279p. (C). 1985. pap. 16.95 (*0-89130-858-X*, 00-07-07) Scholars Pr GA.

Reimbursable Geriatric Service Delivery: A Functional Maintenance Therapy System. Joan K. Glickstein & Gail K. Neustadt. 258p. ring bd. 143.00 (*0-8342-0268-9*, S45) Aspen Pub.

Reimbursement & Fiscal Management in Rehabilitation. Brian Rasmussen. 230p. (Orig.). 1995. pap. 69.95 (*0-912452-99-4*, P-117) Am Phys Therapy Assn.

***Reimbursement & Insurance Coverage for Nutritions Services.** American Dietetic Association Staff. LC 91-26128. 207p. 1991. reprint ed. pap. 59.00 (*0-608-03030-9*, 2063481) Bks Demand.

Reimbursement Manual: How To Get Paid for Your Advanced Practice Nursing Services. Ed. by Pamela Middlestadt. LC 93-9420. 186p. 1993. 44.95 (*1-55810-085-7*, NP-84) Am Nurses Pub.

***Reimbursement Manual for Medical Equipment in Managed Care.** Brian Rasmussen. LC 97-16282. 1997. 159.00 (*0-8342-0868-7*, S440) Aspen Pub.

Reimbursement Manual for the Medical Office. 3rd ed. James B. Davis. 400p. 1996. pap. text ed. 49.95 (*1-57066-025-5*) Practice Mgmt Info.

Reimbursement Strategies: Master the Payment Cycle in 1994. 4th ed. 156p. 1994. 49.95 (*1-56337-141-3*) Medicode Inc.

***Reims City Plan.** (Grafocarte Maps Ser.). 1994. 8.95 (*2-7416-0033-3*, 80033) Michelin.

Reina de la Paz: Eco de la Palabra Eterna. Tomislav Pervan. 55p. 1988. pap. 3.50 (*0-940535-16-5*, UP114) Franciscan U Pr.

Reina de las Americas. Patrick Flores. (Illus.). 69p. (SPA.). write for info. (*0-614-04877-X*) Mex Am Cult.

R

R

***Reina de las Americas: Works of Art from the Museum of the Basilica de Guadalupe.** Jaime Cuadriello et al. (Illus.). 136p. (Orig.). (ENG & SPA.). 1996. pap. 24.95 (*1-889410-01-2*) Mexican Fine Arts.
Reinaldo Arenas. Gary Soto. 1998. 23.95 (*0-8057-4554-8*, Twayne) Scribnrs Ref.
Reinaldo Arenas: Recuerdo y Presencia. Ed. by Reinaldo Sanchez. LC 92-73984. (Coleccion Polymita). (Illus.). 235p. (Orig.). (SPA.). 1994. pap. 25.00 (*0-89729-656-7*) Ediciones.
Reinaldo Arenas: The Pentagonia. Francisco Soto. (Illus.). 216p. 1994. lib. bdg. 34.95 (*0-8130-1315-1*) U Press Fla.
Reincarnation. Swami Abhedananda. 1947. 4.95 (*0-87481-604-1*, Pub. by Advaita Ashrama II) Vedanta Pr.
Reincarnation. Douglas M. Baker. 1981. pap. 12.50 (*0-906006-57-0*, Pub. by Baker Pubns UK) New Leaf Dist.
Reincarnation. George B. Brownell. 153p. 1981. pap. 14.00 (*0-89540-107-X*, SB-107) Sun Pub.
Reincarnation. F. Homer Curtiss. 62p. 1993. pap. 6.00 (*0-89540-260-2*, SB-260) Sun Pub.
Reincarnation. Papus, pseud. Tr. by Marguerite Vallior. (Illus.). 132p. (Orig.). 1991. pap. 6.95 (*0-922802-10-6*) Kessinger Pub.
Reincarnation. Friedrich Rittelmeyer. 164p. 1990. pap. 12. 95 (*0-86315-515-4*, 1304, Pub. by Floris Books UK) Anthroposophic.
Reincarnation. Katherine Tingley. 72p. 1981. pap. 8.00 (*0-89540-111-8*, SB-111) Sun Pub.
Reincarnation. 11th ed. Annie Besant. 1980. 7.50 (*81-7059-234-8*) Theos Pub Hse.
Reincarnation: A Critical Examination. Paul Edwards. 313p. 1996. 28.95 (*1-57392-005-3*) Prometheus Bks.
Reincarnation: A Lost Chord in Modern Thought. Leoline L. Wright et al. Ed. by Emmett Small & Helen Todd. (Theosophical Manual Ser.). 122p. 1975. pap. 4.95 (*0-913004-76-6*) Point Loma Pub.
Reincarnation: A New Horizon in Science, Religion, & Society. Sylvia Cranston & Carey Williams. LC 93-30942. 399p. (Orig.). (C). 1993. reprint ed. pap. 15.00 (*1-55700-025-5*) Theos U Pr.
Reincarnation: A Selected Annotated Bibliography. Lynn Kear. LC 96-10546. (Bibliographies & Indexes in Religious Studies). 336p. 1996. text ed. 75.00 (*0-313-29597-2*, Greenwood Pr) Greenwood.
Reincarnation: An Annotated Bibliography. Joel Bjorling. LC 95-19357. (Sects & Cults in America Ser.: Vol. 18). 194p. 1995. text ed. 35.00 (*0-8153-1129-X*, SS874) Garland.
Reincarnation: An Inquiry into Its Possibility & Significance. Peter Preuss. LC 88-32604. (Problems in Contemporary Philosophy Ser.: Vol. 14). 266p. 1989. lib. bdg. 89.95 (*0-88946-342-5*) E Mellen.
Reincarnation: Anthology & Quotations. 1994. lib. bdg. 255.95 (*0-8490-5668-3*) Gordon Pr.
Reincarnation: Claiming Your Past, Creating Your Future, an Edgar Cayce Reader. Lynn E. Sparrow. 1995. mass mkt. 4.99 (*0-312-95754-8*) Tor Bks.
Reincarnation: Cycle of Opportunity. Robert G. Chaney. LC 84-72387. (Adventures in Esoteric Learning Ser.). (Illus.). 56p. 1984. pap. 4.95 (*0-918936-13-6*) Astara.
Reincarnation: Illusion or Reality. Edmond Robillard. Tr. by K. D. Whitehead from FRE. LC 82-1638. 190p. (Orig.). 1982. pap. 9.95 (*0-8189-0432-1*) Alba.
Reincarnation: Opposing Viewpoints. Michael Arvey. LC 89-37443. (Great Mysteries Ser.). (Illus.). 112p. (J). (gr. 5-8). 1989. lib. bdg. 17.96 (*0-89908-067-7*) Greenhaven.
Reincarnation: Physical, Astral & Spiritual Evolution. Tr. by Papus & Marguerite Vallior. 142p. 1967. reprint ed. spiral bd. 8.50 (*0-7873-0654-1*) Hlth Research.
***Reincarnation: Remembering Past Lives.** Stephen Paulson & Genevieve L. Paulson. (Illus.). 208p. (Orig.). 1997. pap. 7.95 (*1-56718-511-8*, K-511-8) Llewellyn Pubns.
Reincarnation: The Boy Lama. 2nd rev. ed. Vicki Mackenzie. LC 95-51032. (Illus.). 200p. 1996. pap. 16. 95 (*0-86171-108-4*) Wisdom MA.
Reincarnation: The Cycle of Necessity. Manly P. Hall. 1978. pap. 14.95 (*0-89314-387-1*) Philos Res.
Reincarnation: The Inheritance of a Soul. Frank E. Richelieu. 32p. (Orig.). 1991. pap. 3.50 (*0-941992-25-X*) Los Arboles Pub.
***Reincarnation: The Missing Link in Christianity.** Elizabeth C. Prophet. 1997. pap. text ed. 12.95 (*0-922729-27-1*) Summit Univ.
***Reincarnation: The Missing Link in Christianity.** Elizabeth C. Prophet. 1997. 14.95 (*0-614-27551-2*) Summit Univ.
Reincarnation: The Phoenix Fire Mystery. Sylvia Cranston. LC 93-43965. 640p. 1994. reprint ed. pap. 19.00 (*1-55700-026-3*) Theos U Pr.
Reincarnation - A Biblical Doctrine? Whose Time Has Come for the Evangelical Christian. Marilynn McDirmit. 118p. (Orig.). (C). 1990. pap. 9.95 (*0-9623953-1-5*) Eagle Pubn Co.
Reincarnation & Biology: A Contribution to the Etiology of Birthmarks & Birth Defects, 2 vols. Ian Stevenson. Incl. Birthmarks. LC 95-30542. 1248p. 1997. text ed. 195.00 (*0-275-95283-5*, Praeger Pubs); Vol. 2. Birth Defects & Other Anomalies. LC 95-30542. 1120p. 1997. text ed. 195.00 (*0-275-95284-3*, Praeger Pubs); LC 95-30542. 2080p. 1997. Set text ed. 195.00 (*0-275-95282-7*, Praeger Pubs) Greenwood.
Reincarnation & Christianity. Robert A. Morey. LC 80-24497. 64p. 1980. pap. 4.99 (*0-87123-493-9*) Bethany Hse.
Reincarnation & Immortality. 3rd ed. Rudolf Steiner. LC 77-130817. 224p. 1970. pap. 5.95 (*0-89345-221-1*, Steinerbks) Garber Comm.
***Reincarnation & Immortality.** 3rd ed. Rudolf Steiner. LC 77-130817. 224p. 1970. pap. 5.95 (*0-8334-1706-1*, Steinerbks) Garber Comm.
Reincarnation & Its Phenomena. Filippo Liverziani. 192p. (C). 1989. pap. 39.00 (*0-7212-0789-8*, Pub. by Regency Press UK) St Mut.
Reincarnation & Karma: Two Fundamental Truths of Human Existence. Rudolf Steiner. Tr. by Dorothy S. Osmond et al. LC 92-28594. 1992. 10.95 (*0-88010-366-3*) Anthroposophic.
Reincarnation & Law of Karma. William W. Atkinson. 13. 50 (*0-911662-26-X*) Yoga.
Reincarnation & the Law of Karma. W. W. Atkinson. 1991. lib. bdg. 79.75 (*0-8490-4284-4*) Gordon Pr.
Reincarnation & the Law of Karma. William W. Atkinson. 249p. 1936. reprint ed. spiral bd. 8.50 (*0-7873-0059-4*) Hlth Research.
Reincarnation & Translation. Jim Lewis. 31p. (Orig.). 1981. pap. 3.00 (*0-942482-02-6*) Unity Church Denver.
***Reincarnation Controversy: Uncovering the Truth in the World Religions.** Steven J. Rosen. LC 97-18655. 140p. (Orig.). 1997. pap. 11.95 (*1-887089-11-X*) Torchlght Pub.
Reincarnation Explained. unabridged ed. Chris Butler. LC 83-61000. (Illus.). 288p. 1984. 12.95 (*0-88187-000-5*) Science Identity.
Reincarnation Explored. John Algeo. LC 87-40130. 166p. (Orig.). 1987. pap. 7.95 (*0-8356-0624-4*, Quest) Theos Pub Hse.
Reincarnation, Fact or Fallacy. rev. ed. Geoffrey Hodson. LC 67-4405. 1967. reprint ed. pap. 4.50 (*0-8356-0046-7*, Quest) Theos Pub Hse.
Reincarnation for the Christian. 2nd ed. Quincy Howe, Jr. LC 87-40132. 114p. 1987. pap. 6.95 (*0-8356-0626-0*, Quest) Theos Pub Hse.
Reincarnation in Christianity. Geddes MacGregor. (Orig.). 1989. pap. 9.95 (*0-8356-0501-9*, Quest) Theos Pub Hse.
Reincarnation in the New Testament. James M. Pryse. 92p. 1965. reprint ed. spiral bd. 8.00 (*0-7873-0682-7*) Hlth Research.
Reincarnation in the New Testament. James M. Pryse. 92p. 1994. reprint ed. pap. 14.95 (*1-56459-451-3*) Kessinger Pub.
Reincarnation Is Making a Comeback. Dan S. Ward. LC 90-63688. 220p. (Orig.). 1991. pap. 12.95 (*0-924608-07-2*, Whitford Pr) Schiffer.
Reincarnation of John Wilkes Booth. Dell Leonardi. LC 74-27952. 1975. 18.95 (*0-8159-6716-0*) Devin.
Reincarnation of John Wilkes Booth: A Study in Hypnotic Regression. Dell Leonardi. LC 74-27952. 180p. reprint ed. pap. 51.30 (*0-317-08182-9*, 2022710) Bks Demand.
Reincarnation of Russia: Struggling with the Legacy of Communism, 1990-1994. John Lowenhardt. LC 94-38510. 256p. 1995. text ed. 42.50 (*0-8223-1606-4*); pap. text ed. 15.95 (*0-8223-1623-4*) Duke.
Reincarnation, Theosophical Manual No. 2. Annie Besant. 73p. 1972. reprint ed. spiral bd. 4.50 (*0-7873-0103-5*) Hlth Research.
Reincarnation (1919) Annie Besant. 73p. 1996. pap. 11.95 (*1-56459-704-0*) Kessinger Pub.
Reincarnations. Richard Kostelanetz. 1981. pap. 5.00 (*0-918406-23-4*) Future Pr.
Reincarnations. deluxe ed. Richard Kostelanetz. 1981. 50. 00 (*0-918406-22-6*) Future Pr.
Reindeer. Caroline Arnold. LC 93-12981. (Illus.). (J). (gr. 4-7). 1993. pap. 3.95 (*0-590-46943-6*) Scholastic Inc.
Reindeer. Emery Bernhard. LC 93-45327. (Illus.). 32p. (J). (ps-3). 1994. lib. bdg. 15.95 (*0-8234-1097-8*) Holiday.
Reindeer. Emilie U. Lepthien. LC 93-33513. (New True Bks.). (Illus.). 48p. (J). (gr. k-4). 1994. lib. bdg. 19.00 (*0-516-01059-X*) Childrens.
Reindeer. Emilie U. Lepthien. LC 93-33513. (New True Bks.). (Illus.). 48p. (J). (gr. k-4). 1994. pap. 5.50 (*0-516-41059-8*) Childrens.
Reindeer & Caribou. C. C. Georgeson. (Shorey Historical Ser.). (Illus.). 24p. reprint ed. pap. 2.95 (*0-8466-0159-1*, S159) Shorey.
Reindeer & Gold. Murray. 1988. pap. 10.95 (*1-882008-02-2*) WWU CPNS.
Reindeer & Its Domestication. Berthold Laufer. LC 18-12075. (American Anthropological Association Memoirs Ser.). 1917. pap. 25.00 (*0-527-00517-7*) Periodicals Srv.
Reindeer & the Easter Bunny. Jim Olson. Ed. by Jane Van Vleck & Sally Olson. (Illus.). 18p. (Orig.). (J). (gr. 1-4). 1981. pap. 6.95 (*0-943806-00-3*) Neahtawanta Pr.
Reindeer Baby. Cynthia Alvarez. LC 94-69484. (J). 1995. 3.99 (*0-679-87123-3*) Random.
Reindeer Christmas. Morozuoi & Price. 32p. 1993. 18.95 (*0-385-25401-6*) Doubleday.
***Reindeer Christmas.** Price. (J). 1997. pap. write for info. (*0-15-201570-1*, HB Juv Bks) HarBrace.
Reindeer Christmas. Atsuko Morozumi & Price. 32p. 1995. pap. 9.95 (*0-385-25547-0*) Doubleday.
Reindeer, Dogs, & Snow-Shoes: A Journal of Siberian Travel & Explorations Made in the Years 1865, 1866 & 1867. Richard J. Bush. LC 72-115514. (Russia Observed Ser., No. 1). (Illus.). 1970. reprint ed. 29.95 (*0-405-03011-8*) Ayer.
Reindeer Hunters: A Prehistoric Novel of Passion & Adventure. Joan Wolf. 464p. 1995. pap. 5.99 (*0-451-17878-5*, Onyx) NAL-Dutton.
Reindeer Moon. Elizabeth M. Thomas. 1991. pap. 6.50 (*0-671-74189-6*) PB.
Reindeer on South Georgia: The Ecology of an Introduced Population. N. Leader-Williams. (Studies in Polar Research). (Illus.). 275p. 1988. 69.95 (*0-521-24271-1*) Cambridge U Pr.
Reindeer People. Ted Lewin. LC 93-19252. (Illus.). 40p. (J). 1994. text ed. 14.95 (*0-02-757390-7*, Mac Bks Young Read) S&S Childrens.
Reindeer Soup. Joe Pintauro. 1996. pap. 5.25 (*0-8222-1533-0*) Dramatists Play.
Reindeer Surprise. Rita A. Walsh. (J). (ps). 1994. pap. 1.50 (*0-8167-3509-3*) Troll Communs.
Reindeer's Shoe & Other Stories. Karle B. Wilson. LC 88-2292. (Illus.). 112p. (J). (ps-12). 1988. 17.95 (*0-936650-07-9*) E C Temple.
Reindustrialization: Implication for U. S. Industrial Policy. Ed. by Robert J. Thornton et al. LC 84-47777. (Contemporary Studies in Economic & Financial Analysis: Vol. 46). 160p. 1984. 73.25 (*0-89232-485-6*) Jai Pr.
Reindustrialization: The Menace Behind the Promise. Sam Marcy. 56p. 1981. pap. 3.50 (*0-89567-045-3*) World View Forum.
Reindustrialization & Technology. Roy R. Rothwell & Walter Zegveld. LC 85-2064. 288p. (gr. 13). 1985. pap. text ed. 25.95 (*0-87332-331-9*) M E Sharpe.
Reindustrialization Policy: Implications for Large Cities. 130p. 1981. 20.00 (*0-318-17321-2*, IB/81-908) Pub Tech Inc.
Reindustrializing New York State: Strategies, Implications, Challenges. Ed. by Morton Schoolman & Alvin Magid. LC 85-14771. 443p. 1986. text ed. 64.50 (*0-88706-177-X*); pap. text ed. 21.95 (*0-88706-178-8*) State U NY Pr.
Reine des Pommes. Chester Himes. 256p. (FRE.). 1987. pap. 10.95 (*0-7859-2543-0*, 2070378535) Fr & Eur.
Reine Margot. Alexandre Dumas. (FRE.). 1992. pap. 16.95 (*0-7859-3287-9*, 2277232793) Fr & Eur.
***Reine Margot.** Alexandre Dumas. Ed. by David Coward. (World's Classics). 432p. 1998. pap. 12.95 (*0-19-283302-2*) OUP.
Reine Margot. unabridged ed. Dumas. (FRE.). pap. 8.95 (*2-87714-188-8*, Pub. by Bookking Intl FR) Distribks Inc.
Reine Margot: Dame De Monsoreau: Les Quarante-Cinq. Alexandre Dumas. 1680p. (FRE.). 1988. pap. 65.00 (*0-7859-2192-3*, 2715213638) Fr & Eur.
Reine Morte. Henry De Montherlant. 1957. write for info. (*0-318-63586-0*) Fr & Eur.
Reine Morte. Henry De Montherlant. (Folio Ser.: No. 12). (FRE.). 1957. pap. 6.95 (*2-07-036012-1*) Schoenhof.
Reine Morte. Henry De Montherlant. (FRE.). 1972. pap. 10.95 (*0-8288-3754-6*, F115800) Fr & Eur.
Reiner Ruthenbeck: Photographs 1956-1976. (Illus.). 204p. 1992. 50.00 (*3-89322-232-4*, Pub. by Edition Cantz GW) Dist Art Pubs.
Reines de la France. Jean Cocteau. 168p. 1952. 18.95 (*0-686-54557-5*) Fr & Eur.
Reines Denken: Zur Kritik der Teleologischen Denkform. Jens Brockmeier. LC 92-3565. (Schriften Zur Philosophie der Differenz Ser.: No. 5). (GER.). 1992. 97.00 (*90-6032-320-3*, Pub. by Gruner NE) Benjamins North Am.
Reinflamando la Llama. Tr. by Salvador C. Alday. 30p. (SPA.). 1991. pap. 1.95 (*0-8146-5023-6*) Liturgical Pr.
***Reinforced & Prestressed Concrete.** 3rd ed. Kong & Evans. (Illus.). 528p. (Orig.). (C). (gr. 13 up). Date not set. pap. text ed. 45.50 (*0-412-37760-8*, Chap & Hall NY) Chapman & Hall.
***Reinforced & Prestressed Concrete Design.** E. O'Brien. (C). 1995. pap. text ed. 50.95 (*0-582-21883-7*, Pub. by Longman UK) Longman.
***Reinforced Concerted Action on Reactor Safety, FISA 95: EU Research on Severe Accidents, EUR 16896.** 668p. 1996. 80.00 (*92-827-6980-1*, CG91-95-196-ENC, Pub. by Europ Com UK) Bernan Associates.
***Reinforced Concerted Action on Reactor Safety (1990-1994) Final Progress Report, EUR 17126.** European Commission. 552p. 1996. pap. 90.00 (*92-827-6942-9*, CG-NA-17126-ENC, Pub. by Europ Com UK) Bernan Associates.
Reinforced Concrete. George E. Wynne. (C). 1981. teacher ed. write for info. (*0-8359-6639-9*, Reston) P-H.
***Reinforced Concrete.** rev. ed. Warner et al. Date not set. text ed. write for info. (*0-85896-821-5*) Addison-Wesley.
Reinforced Concrete. 3rd ed. Jack C. McCormac. (C). 1993. text ed. 73.95 (*0-06-500491-4*) Addison-Wesley Educ.
***Reinforced Concrete.** 3rd ed. Warner. 1994. text ed. write for info. (*0-582-71226-2*, Pub. by Longman UK) Longman.
Reinforced Concrete: A Fundamental Approach. 3rd ed. Edward G. Nawy. LC 95-13792. 832p. 1995. text ed. 95.00 (*0-13-123498-6*) P-H.
Reinforced Concrete: Analysis & Design. S. S. Ray. LC 94-13306. (Illus.). 576p. 1994. 99.95 (*0-632-03724-5*, Pub. by Blckwell Sci Pubns UK) Blackwell Sci.
***Reinforced Concrete: Design Theory & Examples.** 2nd ed. Choo & T. J. MacGinley. (Illus.). 544p. (Orig.). 1990. pap. text ed. 46.95 (*0-419-13830-7*, E & FN Spon) Routledge Chapman & Hall.
Reinforced Concrete: Mechanics & Design. 3rd ed. James G. MacGregor. LC 96-14925. 950p. 1996. text ed. 95.00 (*0-13-233974-9*) P-H.
Reinforced Concrete After Cracking: State of Service, Ultimate Limit State, Ductility Failure Mechanism of Hyperstatic Structures. 2nd ed. Albert Fuentes. Tr. by M. M. Oberai from FRE. (Illus.). 150p. 1995. 55.00 (*90-5410-245-4*) Balkema RSA.
Reinforced Concrete Columns. American Concrete Institute Staff. LC 75-8454. (American Concrete Institute Publication Ser.: SP-50). (Illus.). 320p. reprint ed. pap. 91.20 (*0-317-10048-3*, 2022761) Bks Demand.
***Reinforced Concrete Deep Beams.** Ed. by F. Kong. 290p. 1990. text ed. 127.00 (*0-442-30298-3*, Osprey Bks) Chapman & Hall.
Reinforced Concrete Design. Kenneth M. Leet. (Illus.). 544p. (C). 1982. 36.00 (*0-07-037024-9*) McGraw.
***Reinforced Concrete Design.** 3rd ed. Kenneth M. Leet. 1996. text ed. write for info. (*0-07-037100-8*) McGraw.
Reinforced Concrete Design. 3rd ed. Leonard Spiegel & George F. Limbrunner. 448p. 1991. text ed. 86.00 (*0-13-772393-8*) P-H.
***Reinforced Concrete Design.** 4th ed. Spiegel & Limbrunner. 1997. text ed. 66.67 (*0-13-490202-5*) P-H.
Reinforced Concrete Design. 5th ed. C. K. Wang & Charles G. Salmon. (C). 1992. text ed. 90.00 (*0-06-046887-4*) Addson-Wesley Educ.
***Reinforced Concrete Design.** 6th ed. Wang. (C). 1998. text ed. write for info. (*0-673-98460-5*) Addison-Wesley.
***Reinforced Concrete Design.** 6th ed. Wang Chu-Kia & Charles G. Salmon. LC 97-20869. 1997. write for info. (*0-321-98460-9*) Addison-Wesley.
***Reinforced Concrete Design: Conforms to 1995 ACI Codes.** 3rd ed. Kenneth M. Leet & Dionisio Bernal. LC 96-31173. 1996. write for info. (*0-07-037101-6*) McGraw.
***Reinforced Concrete Design: Solutions Manual.** Wang. (C). 1998. teacher ed., pap. text ed. write for info. (*0-673-97858-3*) Addison-Wesley.
Reinforced Concrete Design for Architects. Ronald E. Shaeffer. 1992. text ed. write for info. (*0-07-056417-5*) McGraw.
Reinforced Concrete Design Handbook: Working Stress Method. 3rd ed. 1965. pap. 51.75 (*0-685-85089-7*, SP-3) ACI.
Reinforced Concrete Design Handbook: Working Stress Method in Accordance with ACI 318-63. 3rd ed. American Concrete Institute Staff. LC 65-16807. (American Concrete Institute Publication: Vol. SP-3). 271p. 1965. reprint ed. pap. 77.30 (*0-608-02421-X*, 2063064) Bks Demand.
Reinforced Concrete Designer's Handbook. C. E. Reynolds & James C. Steedman. (Illus.). 500p. 1988. text ed. 95.00 (*0-419-14530-3*, E & FN Spon) Routledge Chapman & Hall.
Reinforced Concrete Detailer's Manual. 2nd ed. Brian Boughton. (Illus.). 136p. 1971. 27.95 (*0-8464-0788-4*) Beekman Pubs.
Reinforced Concrete Floor Slabs: Research & Design. 224p. 10.00 (*0-318-17541-X*) Reinforced Res.
Reinforced Concrete Floor Slabs: Research & Design. American Society of Civil Engineers Staff. (Reinforced Concrete Research Council Bulletin Ser.: No. 20). 215p. reprint ed. pap. 61.30 (*0-317-27661-1*, 2019543) Bks Demand.
Reinforced Concrete Fundamentals. 5th ed. Phil M. Ferguson et al. LC 87-20727. 768p. 1988. text ed. 86.95 (*0-471-80378-2*) Wiley.
Reinforced Concrete Fundamentals. 5th ed. Phil M. Ferguson et al. 124p. 1988. teacher ed. 12.50 (*0-471-63823-4*) Wiley.
Reinforced Concrete Masonry Construction Inspector's Handbook. 3rd ed. James E. Amrhein & Michael W. Merrigan. (Illus.). 462p. (Orig.). 1995. pap. text ed. 29. 50 (*0-940116-24-3*) Masonry Inst Am.
Reinforced-Concrete Slab-Column Structures. A. Ajdukiewicz & W. Starosolski. (Developments in Civil Engineering Ser.: No. 27). 368p. 1989. 213.75 (*0-444-98856-4*) Elsevier.
Reinforced Concrete Structures. Robert Park & Thomas Paulay. 769p. 1975. text ed. 115.00 (*0-471-65917-7*, Wiley-Interscience) Wiley.
Reinforced Concrete Structures, 2 vols., Vols. 1 & 2. E. E. Sigalov. (C). 1983. Vol. 1 272p., Vol. 2 392p. 100.00 (*0-685-46651-5*, Pub. by Collets) St Mut.
Reinforced Concrete Structures in Seismic Zones. Symposium on Reinforced Concrete Structures in Seismic Zones (1974: San Francisco) Staff. LC 77-74267. (American Concrete Institute Publication Ser.: SP-53). (Illus.). 491p. reprint ed. pap. 140.00 (*0-8357-7521-6*, 2036016) Bks Demand.
Reinforced Concrete Structures Subjected to Wind & Earthquake Forces. American Concrete Institute Staff. LC 80-66852. (American Concrete Institute Publication Ser.: No. SP-63). (Illus.). 632p. reprint ed. pap. 180.00 (*0-7837-6670-X*, 2046286) Bks Demand.
Reinforced Concrete Technology. Samuel E. French. LC 92-26646. 427p. 1994. pap. 55.95 (*0-8273-5495-9*) Delmar.
Reinforced Earth. T. S. Ingold. 149p. 1982. 36.00 (*0-7277-0089-8*, Pub. by T Telford UK) Am Soc Civil Eng.
Reinforced Grouted Brick Masonry Construction. 13th ed. James E. Amrhein. 130p. 1991. pap. 15.00 (*0-940116-19-7*) Masonry Inst Am.
Reinforced Layered Systems. (Research Record Ser.: No. 1153). 45p. 1987. 7.50 (*0-309-04660-2*) Transport Res Bd.
Reinforced Masonry Design. 3rd ed. Robert R. Schneider & Walter L. Dickey. LC 93-16900. (International Series in Civil Engineering). 752p. (C). 1993. text ed. 95.00 (*0-13-011727-7*) P-H.
Reinforced Masonry Engineering Handbook Clay & Concrete Masonry. 5th ed. 469p. 1994. 75.00 (*0-940116-27-8*) Masonry Inst Am.
Reinforced Plastics. rev. ed. LC 80-53543. (Illus.). 114p. 1990. reprint ed. pap. 34.00 (*0-938648-01-2*, 0110) T-C Pr CA.
***Reinforced Plastics: Properties & Applications.** Raymond B. Seymour. LC 91-71393. (Illus.). 273p. 1991. reprint ed. pap. 77.90 (*0-608-02640-9*, 2063298) Bks Demand.
Reinforced Plastics: Update. Business Communications Co., Inc. Staff. (Illus.). 133p. 1986. pap. 1,750.00 (*0-89336-478-9*, P-055R) BCC.
Reinforced Plastics-Composites, Adhesives & Thermosets: SPE PACTEC 81. 1981. 32.50 (*0-938648-40-3*, 1507) T-C Pr CA.
Reinforced Plastics-Composites, Structural Foam, Plastics in Building: SPE PACTEC 80, Vol. III. 256p. 32.50 (*0-938648-41-1*, 1505) T-C Pr CA.

An Asterisk (*) at the beginning of an entry indicates that the title is appearing in BIP for the first time.

Reinforced Soil & Geotextiles: Proceedings of the Geotextiles, Conference Held at the Indian Institute of Technology, Bombay, India, 8-9 December 1988. 408p. (C). 1989. text ed. 90.00 (*90-6191-938-X*, Pub. by A A Balkema NE) Ashgate Pub Co.

Reinforced Thermoplastic. Business Communications Co., Inc. Staff. 270p. 1989. 2,450.00 (*0-89336-679-X*, P-109) BCC.

Reinforced Thermoplastics. W. V. Titow & B. J. Lanham. (Illus.). x, 295p. 1975. 61.25 (*0-85334-630-5*, Pub. by Elsevier Applied Sci UK) Elsevier.

Reinforcement Anchorages & Splices. 2nd ed. 32p. 1984. 10.00 (*0-318-20466-5*) Concrete Reinforcing.

***Reinforcement & Reconstruction of Foundations.** V. B. Shvets et al. Tr. by J. Jaganmohan from RUS. (Geotechnika Ser.: No. 14). (Illus.). 284p. (C). 1996. text ed. 85.00 (*90-5410-261-6*, Pub. by A A Balkema NE) Ashgate Pub Co.

Reinforcement & Review Activities. Dorothy L. Williams. (Values & Choices Ser.). 40p. 1989. pap. text ed. 10.00 (*1-57482-209-8*) Search Inst.

Reinforcement & the Organization of Behaviour. Ed. by Michael D. Zeiler & Peter Harzem. LC 78-31697. (Advances in Analysis of Behaviour Ser.: No. 1). (Illus.). 427p. reprint ed. pap. 121.70 (*0-685-44048-6*, 2030518) Bks Demand.

Reinforcement Detailing Manual. Robin Whittle & Ove Arup Partnership Committee. (Viewpoint Ser.). (Illus.). 120p. (C). 1981. spiral bd. 50.00 (*0-7210-1223-X*, Viewpoint) Scholium Intl.

Reinforcement, Impact Modification & Nucleation of Polymers: RETEC-SPE, February 25-27, 1990, Houston, TX. Society Of Plastics Engineers Staff. 248p. reprint ed. pap. 70.70 (*0-8357-2995-8*, 2039263) Bks Demand.

Reinforcement in Functional Systems. K. V. Sudakov. (Systems Research in Physiology Ser.). 234p. 1991. text ed. 176.00 (*2-88124-783-0*) Gordon & Breach.

Reinforcement Learning. Ed. by Richard S. Sutton. (International Series in Engineering & Computer Science, VLSI, Computer Architecture, & Digital Screen Processing). 172p. (C). 1992. lib. bdg. 122.50 (*0-7923-9234-5*) Kluwer Ac.

Reinforcement of Earth Slopes & Embankments. (National Cooperative Highway Research Program Report Ser.: No. 290). 323p. 1987. 40.00 (*0-309-04024-8*) Transport Res Bd.

Reinforcing Bar Detailing. 2nd ed. 265p. 1980. 30.00 (*0-318-20464-9*) Concrete Reinforcing.

Reinforcing Reference Skills. Rosemary R. Gallagher. (J). (gr. 4-6). 1987. pap. 7.99 (*0-8224-4672-3*) Fearon Teach Aids.

Reinforcing Steel in Masonry. James E. Amrhein. 75p. (Orig.). 1991. pap. text ed. 10.00 (*0-940116-18-9*) Masonry Inst Am.

Reingeneering Performance Measurement: How to Align Systems to Improve Processes, Products, & Profits. Archie Lockamy. 312p. 1993. text ed. 47.50 (*1-55623-916-5*) Irwin Prof Pubng.

Reinhabiting a Separate Country: A Bioregional Anthology of Northern California. Ed. by Peter Berg. (Illus.). 220p. (Orig.). 1978. pap. 7.00 (*0-937102-00-8*) Planet Drum Books.

***Reinhabiting the Earth.** Gideon Kossoff. (Media Studies). 1997. pap. text ed. 24.95 (*0-304-33202-X*) Cassell.

Reinhabiting the Earth: Biblical Perspectives & Eco-Spiritual Reflections. Mary L. Van Rossum. LC 94-7302. 224p. 1994. 18.95 (*0-89243-691-3*, Triumph Books) Liguori Pubns.

Reinhard Heydrich: Assassination! Ray R. Cowdery & Peter Vodenka. (Illus.). 96p. (Orig.). 1994. pap. 15.00 (*0-910667-42-X*) USM.

Reinhard Keiser, Vol. 1. Ed. by John Roberts. (Handel Sources Ser.). 1987. text ed. 35.00 (*0-8240-6475-5*) Garland.

Reinhard Keiser, Vol. 3. Ed. by John Roberts. (Handel Sources Ser.). 1987. text ed. 30.00 (*0-8240-6477-1*) Garland.

Reinhardt Schuhmann International Symposium on Innovative Technology & Reactor Design in Extraction Metallurgy: 1986: Colorado Springs, CO. Reinardt Schuhmann International Symposium on Innovative Technology & Reactor Design in Extraction Metallurgy Staff et al. Ed. by D. R. Gaskell et al. LC 86-23469. (Illus.). 1080p. reprint ed. pap. 180.00 (*0-8357-5545-2*, 2035160) Bks Demand.

Reinhart, Joseph Kosuth, Felix Gonzalez-Torres: Symptoms of Interference, Conditions of Possibility. Ed. by Joseph Kosuth. (Art & Design Ser.: No. 34). (Illus.). 120p. (Orig.). 1994. pap. 26.95 (*1-85490-217-2*) Academy Ed UK.

Reinhold Messner, Free Spirit: A Climber's Life. Reinhold Messner. (Illus.). 288p. 1991. 24.95 (*0-89886-290-6*) Mountaineers.

Reinhold Niebuhr. Nathan A. Scott. LC 63-64003. (University of Minnesota Pamphlets on American Writers Ser.: No. 31). 48p. (Orig.). reprint ed. pap. 25.00 (*0-7837-2866-2*, 2057589) Bks Demand.

Reinhold Niebuhr: A Biography. Richard W. Fox. LC 96-9225. 408p. 1996. 16.95 (*0-8014-8369-7*) Cornell U Pr.

Reinhold Niebuhr: A Political Account. Paul Merkley. LC 76-351874. 303p. reprint ed. pap. 86.40 (*0-7837-6912-1*, 2046742) Bks Demand.

Reinhold Niebuhr: A Prophetic Voice in Our Time. Ed. by Harold R. Landon. (Essay Index Reprint Ser.). 1977. reprint ed. 13.95 (*0-518-10150-9*) Ayer.

Reinhold Niebuhr: Prophet from America. D. R. Davies. (Select Bibliographies Reprint Ser.). 1977. 16.95 (*0-8369-5324-X*) Ayer.

Reinhold Niebuhr: Theologian of Public Life. Ed. by Larry L. Rasmussen. LC 91-14239. (Making of Modern Theology Ser.). 312p. 1991. pap. 18.00 (*0-8006-3407-1*, 1-3407) Augsburg Fortress.

Reinhold Niebuhr & Christian Realism. Robin W. Lovin. 263p. (C). 1995. text ed. 59.95 (*0-521-44363-6*); pap. text ed. 17.95 (*0-521-47932-0*) Cambridge U Pr.

Reinhold Niebuhr & John Dewey: An American Odyssey. Daniel F. Rice. LC 92-4270. (Illus.). 358p. 1993. pap. text ed. 21.95 (*0-7914-1346-2*) State U NY Pr.

Reinhold Niebuhr & John Dewey: An American Odyssey. Daniel F. Rice. LC 92-4270. (Illus.). 358p. 1993. text ed. 64.50 (*0-7914-1345-4*) State U NY Pr.

Reinhold Niebuhr & the Issues of Our Time. Reinhold Niebuhr. Ed. by Richard Harries. LC 86-180530. 215p. reprint ed. pap. 61.30 (*0-7837-3188-4*, 2042792) Bks Demand.

Reinhold Niebuhr Reader: Selected Essays, Articles, & Book Reviews. Compiled by Charles C. Brown. LC 92-28345. 208p. 1992. pap. 18.95 (*1-56338-043-9*) TPI PA.

Reinhold Niebuhr (1892-1971) A Centenary Appraisal. Ed. by Gary A. Gaudin & Douglas J. Hall. (McGill Studies in Religion: Vol. 3). 199p. 1994. pap. 36.95 (*0-7885-0042-2*, 65 00 03) Scholars Pr GA.

Reining. Al Dunning. Ed. by Pat Close. (Illus.). 144p. 1983. pap. 12.95 (*0-911647-02-3*) Western Horseman.

***Reining.** Al Dunning. 1996. pap. text ed. 12.95 (*0-911647-39-2*) Western Horseman.

Reining: The Art of Performance in Horses. Bob Loomis & Kathy Kadash. (Illus.). 240p. 1990. write for info. (*0-9625898-8-8*) EquiMedia.

Reinkarnation des Lesers als Autor: Ein Rezeptionsgeschichtlicher Versuch Uber den Einfluss der Altindischen Literatur auf Deutsche Schriftsteller um 1900. Kamakshi P. Murti. (Quellen und Forschungen zur Sprach und Kulturgeschichte der Germanischen Voelker Ser.: NF 96 (220)). vi, 156p. (C). 1990. lib. bdg. 60.00 (*3-11-012371-1*) De Gruyter.

Reinmar's Women: A Study of the Women's Song (" Frauenlied" & "Frauenstrophe") of Reinmar der Alte. William E. Jackson. (German Language & Literature Monographs: No. 9). xxiv, 374p. 1981. 78.00 (*90-272-4002-7*) Benjamins North Am.

Reino de Dios, Tomo I. Francis Breisch, Jr. (SPA.). 1978. 7.25 (*1-55955-098-8*) CRC Wrld Lit.

Reino de Dios, Tomo II. Francis Breisch, Jr. (SPA.). 1978. 7.25 (*1-55955-099-6*) CRC Wrld Lit.

Reino de Dios y el Ministerio Educativo de la Iglesia. Daniel S. Schipani. 213p. (SPA.). 1984. pap. 7.99 (*0-89922-232-3*) Edit Caribe.

Reino de Este Mundo. Alejo Carpentier. (SPA.). 7.50 (*0-8288-2557-2*, 5818) Fr & Eur.

Reino de Este Mundo. Alejo Carpentier. (Caribbean Collection). 1994. pap. 6.25 (*0-8477-0187-5*) U of PR Pr.

Reino de la Geometria. Jose R. Sanchez. (Cuentos con Alma Ser.). (Illus.). 24p. (SPA.). (J). 1993. 16.95 (*1-56492-109-3*) Laredo.

Reino de las Tinieblos. Dallas Witmer. (SPA.). 1979. pap. 1.25 (*0-686-32331-9*) Rod & Staff.

Reino Imaginal, 2 vols. Jean-Clarence Lambert. (Grandes Monografias). (Illus.). 358p. (SPA.). 1993. 225.00 (*84-343-0736-7*) Elliots Bks.

***Reino y el Poder.** Gary Greig. 249p. (SPA.). 1995. pap. write for info. (*0-614-27131-2*) Editorial Unilit.

***Reino y el Poder - The Kingdom & the Power.** Gary Greig. 249p. (SPA.). 1995. write for info. (*0-614-24401-3*) Editorial Unilit.

Reinos Originarios. Carlos Fuentes. 195p. (SPA.). 1971. 8.95 (*0-8288-7091-8*) Fr & Eur.

Reins of Danger. Rebecca Price-Janney. LC 94-43616. (Heather Reed Mystery Ser.: Vol. 8). (J). 1995. pap. 5.99 (*0-8499-3632-2*) Word Pub.

Reins of Life. John A. Davies. 176p. (C). 1990. 40.00 (*0-85131-449-X*, Pub. by J A Allen & Co UK) St Mut.

Reinscribing Moses: Heine, Kafka, Freud, & Schoenberg in a European Wilderness. Bluma Goldstein. 218p. 1993. 37.00 (*0-674-75406-9*) HUP.

Reinsman of the West: Bridles & Bits. Ed Connell. 1977. pap. 7.00 (*0-87980-333-9*) Wilshire.

***Reinstatement Cost Assessment & Insurance Claims.** RICS Books Staff. 1995. pap. 33.00 (*0-85406-685-3*, Pub. by R-I-C-S Bks UK) St Mut.

Reinsurance. Ed. by Robert W. Strain. LC 80-14442. 692p. 1980. text ed. 79.50 (*0-939727-00-5*) R W Strain.

Reinsurance: Fundamentals & New Challenges. rev. ed. Ed. by Ruth Gastel. LC 95-10814. 192p. 1995. 22.50 (*0-932387-43-8*) Insur Info.

Reinsurance: Principles & Practice, Vol. 1. K. Gerathewol. (C). 1980. 495.00 (*0-685-33715-4*, Pub. by Witherby & Co UK) St Mut.

Reinsurance Contract Wording. rev. ed. Ed. by Robert W. Strain. 815p. 1996. text ed. 195.00 (*0-939727-39-0*) R W Strain.

Reinsurance for the Beginner. 3rd ed. Witherby & Co. Ltd. Staff & R. Phillippe Bellerose. 96p. (C). 1987. pap. 75.00 (*0-948691-32-8*, Pub. by Witherby & Co UK) St Mut.

Reinsurance for the Professional, 2 vols. Adel S. Din. (C). 1986. 750.00 (*0-685-33716-2*, Pub. by Witherby & Co UK) St Mut.

Reinsurance Fundamentals: Treaty & Facultative. Ross Phifer. LC 95-49717. 311p. 1996. text ed. 89.95 (*0-471-13452-X*) Wiley.

Reinsurance in Practice. Robert Kiln. 400p. 1991. 250.00 (*1-85609-012-4*, Pub. by Witherby & Co UK) St Mut.

Reinsurance in Practice. 2nd ed. Robert Kiln. 372p. (C). 1987. 185.00 (*0-900886-98-6*, Pub. by Witherby & Co UK) St Mut.

Reinsurance in the Third World. J. O. Irukwu & F. I. Arb. 266p. (C). 1980. 135.00 (*0-685-36234-5*, Pub. by Witherby & Co UK) St Mut.

Reinsurance in the Third World. Witherby & Co. Ltd. Staff. 266p. (C). 1987. 110.00 (*0-317-92270-X*, Pub. by Witherby & Co UK) St Mut.

Reinsurance Law Casebook. Ed. by Geoffrey M. Hall. 1992. 225.00 (*0-9514449-0-5*, Pub. by Busn & Med UK) St Mut.

Reinsurance Law Reports, Vol. 1. Ed. by Geoffrey M. Hall. 1990. 375.00 (*0-9514449-4-8*, Pub. by Busn & Med UK) St Mut.

Reinsurance Litigation & Arbitration. (Commercial Law & Practice Course Handbook Ser.). 280p. 1994. pap. 99.00 (*0-614-17149-0*, A4-4479) PLI.

Reinsurance Office Practice. Carol Boland. (DYP Textbook Ser.). 230p. 1993. pap. 155.00 (*1-870255-86-0*) LLP.

Reinsurance Practice & the Law. Barlow, Lyde & Gilbert, Reinsurance Division Staff. ring bd. 250.00 (*1-85044-390-4*) LLP.

Reinsurance Practices, 2 vols. Robert C. Reinarz et al. LC 90-84892. 459p. (C). 1990. pap. 26.00 (*0-89462-057-6*, ARe142) IIA.

Reinsurance Practices: A Workbook with Cases. Ed. by Robert W. Strain. LC 82-71573. 471p. 1982. pap. text ed., spiral bd. 45.00 (*0-939727-52-8*) R W Strain.

Reinsurance Underwriting. Robert Kiln. (DYP Textbook Ser.). 154p. 1989. pap. 155.00 (*1-870255-45-3*) LLP.

Reintegrating Fragmented Landscapes: Towards Sustainable Production & Nature Conservation. Ed. by R. J. Hobbs & D. A. Saunders. (Illus.). 336p. 1992. 116.95 (*0-387-97806-2*) Spr-Verlag.

Reintegration Resource: Compensatory Bridges to Independence. Donna Miazga. 1995. pap. 35.00 (*0-930599-42-X*) Thinking Pubns.

Reintegration to School after Hospital Treatment: Needs & Services. Isobel Larcombe. 137p. (C). 1995. 51.95 (*1-85628-990-7*, Pub. by Avebury Pub UK) Ashgate Pub Co.

Reinterpretation of American History & Culture. William H. Cartwright. Ed. by Richard L. Watson. LC 73-84548. 574p. reprint ed. pap. 163.60 (*0-685-16458-6*, 2052192) Bks Demand.

Reinterpretation of the American Revolution, 1763 to 1789. Compiled by Jack P. Greene. LC 78-27785. 626p. 1979. reprint ed. text ed. 85.00 (*0-313-20930-8*, GRRE, Greenwood Pr) Greenwood.

Reinterpreting Christine de Pizan. Ed. by Earl J. Richards et al. LC 90-45959. (Illus.). 296p. 1992. 45.00 (*0-8203-1307-6*) U of Ga Pr.

Reinterpreting Galileo. Ed. by William A. Wallace. LC 84-23901. (Studies in Philosophy & the History of Philosophy: No. 15). 296p. reprint ed. pap. 84.40 (*0-7837-4637-7*, 2044361) Bks Demand.

Reinterpreting Menopause. Komesaroff. LC 96-28892. 240p. (C). 1997. pap. 19.95 (*0-415-91565-1*, Routledge NY); text ed. 69.95 (*0-415-91564-3*, Routledge NY) Routledge.

Reinterpreting Prehistory of Central America. Ed. by Mark M. Graham. (Illus.). 456p. 1993. 39.95 (*0-87081-255-6*) Univ Pr Colo.

Reinterpreting Property. Margaret J. Radin. LC 93-4908. 278p. 1994. 29.95 (*0-226-70227-8*) U Ch Pr.

Reinterpreting Property. Margaret J. Radin. LC 93-4908. 278p. 1996. reprint ed. pap. text ed. 15.95 (*0-226-70228-6*) U Ch Pr.

***Reinterpreting Russia: An Annotated Bibliography of Books on Russia, the Soviet Union & the Russian Federation, 1991-1996.** Steven D. Boilard. LC 96-38095. (Magill Bibliographies Ser.). 1997. write for info. (*0-8108-3298-4*) Scarecrow.

Reinterpreting Russian History: Readings, 860-1860's. Ed. by Gary Marker. LC 92-46294. 464p. 1994. 50.00 (*0-19-507857-8*); pap. 19.95 (*0-19-507858-6*) OUP.

Reinterpreting the Legacy of William James. Ed. by Margaret E. Donnelly. LC 92-32729. 371p. 1992. pap. text ed. 29.95 (*1-55798-180-9*) Am Psychol.

Reinterpreting the Spanish American Essay: Women Writers of the 19th & 20th Centuries. Ed. by Doris Meyer. LC 94-17119. (Texas Pan American Ser.). 272p. (C). 1995. text ed. 37.50 (*0-292-75167-2*) U of Tex Pr.

Reintroduction Biology of Australian & New Zealand Fauna. Ed. by Melody Serena. 276p. 1995. 150.00 (*0-949324-56-6*, Pub. by Surrey Beatty & Sons AT) St Mut.

***Reinvent Yourself: A Lesson in Personal Leadership.** John J. Murphy. LC 95-61979. 188p. (Orig.). 1996. per. 12.00 (*0-9639013-2-X*) Venture Mgmt.

Reinvented Workplace. John Worthington. LC 97-761. (Illus.). 192p. 1996. pap. 47.95 (*0-7506-2841-3*, Butterwrth Archit) Buttrwrth-Heinemann.

Reinventing a Region: Restructuring & Policy Response in West Yorkshire. Ed. by Graham Haughton & David Whitney. LC 94-24574. (Urban & Regional Planning Ser.: Vol. 1). 257p. 1994. 63.95 (*1-85628-910-9*, Pub. by Avebury Pub UK) Ashgate Pub Co.

Reinventing Acupuncture: A New Concept of Ancient Medicine. Felix Mann. LC 92-27735. 1993. pap. 37.50 (*0-7506-0844-7*) Buttrwrth-Heinemann.

Reinventing Africa: Museums, Material Culture, & Popular Imagination in Late Victorian & Edwardian England. Annie E. Coombes. (Illus.). 256p. 1994. 55.00 (*0-300-05972-8*) Yale U Pr.

***Reinventing Africa: Museums, Material Culture, & Popular Imagination in Late Victorian & Edwardian England.** Annie E. Coombes. (Illus.). 288p. 1997. pap. 25.00 (*0-300-06890-5*) Yale U Pr.

***Reinventing Allegory.** Theresa M. Kelley. (Cambridge Studies in Romanticism: No. 22). (Illus.). 390p. (C). 1997. text ed. 59.95 (*0-521-43207-3*) Cambridge U Pr.

Reinventing America: The Common Sense Domestic Agenda for the 90's. Michael Foudy. LC 92-8633. 1992. pap. 19.95 (*0-9632571-0-2*) Inst Am Democracy.

Reinventing America for the 21St Century. Michael Foudy. 1996. pap. text ed. 11.95 (*0-9632571-8-8*) Inst Am Democracy.

***Reinventing America for the 21st Century.** Michael Foudy. 240p. 1996. 14.95 (*0-9632571-7-X*) Inst Am Democracy.

Reinventing American Education. Ed. by Rudy A. Magnan. (Orig.). pap. write for info. (*0-943025-47-8*) Cummngs & Hath.

***Reinventing American Inorganic Chemistry, 1950-2000: Selected Papers of F. A. Cotton.** 750p. 1997. lib. bdg. 67.00 (*981-02-2766-3*) World Scientific Pub.

***Reinventing American Protestantism: Christianity in the New Millennium.** Donald E. Miller. LC 96-35140. 1997. write for info. (*0-520-20938-9*) U CA Pr.

Reinventing Biology: Respect for Life & the Creation of Knowledge. Ed. by Lynda Birke & Ruth Hubbard. LC 95-1443. (Race, Gender, & Science Ser.). 312p. 1995. 35.00 (*0-253-32909-4*); pap. 15.95 (*0-253-20981-1*) Ind U Pr.

Reinventing Celebration: The Art of Planning Public Events. Bob Gregson. (Illus.). 64p. (Orig.). 1992. pap. 10.95 (*0-9632604-0-5*) Shaman Pr.

Reinventing Charity. Janet Poppendieck. 1998. pap. 11.95 (*0-14-024556-1*) Viking Penguin.

Reinventing Christianity. John Parratt. 1995. pap. 15.00 (*0-8028-4113-9*) Eerdmans.

***Reinventing Christianity: African Theology Today.** John Parratt. 227p. 1996. 45.95 (*0-86543-522-7*); pap. 14.95 (*0-86543-523-5*) Africa World.

Reinventing Cities: Equity Planners Tell Their Stories. Norman Krumholz & Pierre Clavel. LC 93-42538. (Conflicts in Urban & Regional Development Ser.). (Illus.). 272p. (C). 1994. 59.95 (*1-56639-209-8*); pap. 22.95 (*1-56639-210-1*) Temple U Pr.

Reinventing Collective Action: From the Global to the Local. Ed. by Colin Crouch & David Marquand. (Political Quarterly Ser.). 144p. (Orig.). (C). 1995. pap. text ed. 19.95 (*0-631-19721-4*) Blackwell Pubs.

Reinventing Communication: A Guide to Using Visual Language for Planning, Problem Solving, & Reengineering. Larry Raymond. LC 94-18254. (Illus.). 167p. 1994. pap. 15.00 (*0-87389-288-7*, H0845) ASQC Qual Pr.

Reinventing Congress for the 21st Century: Beyond Local Representation & the Politics of Exclusion. Sol Erdman & Lawrence Susskind. LC 94-61496. 85p. (Orig.). 1995. pap. text ed. 9.95 (*0-9643317-0-5*) Frontier NY.

Reinventing Cotton Mather in the American Renaissance: Magnalia Christi Americana in Hawthorne, Stowe, & Stoddard. Christopher D. Felker. LC 93-42071. 288p. (C). 1994. text ed. 47.50 (*1-55553-187-3*) NE U Pr.

Reinventing Darwin: The Great Debate at the High Table of Evolutionary Theory. Niles Eldredge. LC 94-32861. (Illus.). 256p. 1995. text ed. 27.95 (*0-471-30301-1*) Wiley.

Reinventing Education. Louis V. Gerstner. 1995. pap. 11.95 (*0-452-27145-2*, Plume) NAL-Dutton.

***Reinventing Electric Utilities.** Ed Smeloff & Peter Asmus. 165p. 1996. 34.95 (*1-55963-454-5*) Island Pr.

Reinventing Electric Utilities. Ed Smeloff & Peter Asmus. 465p. (C). 1996. pap. text ed. 16.95 (*1-55963-455-3*) Island Pr.

Reinventing Electric Utility Regulation. Ed. by Gregory B. Enholm & J. Robert Malko. 350p. (Orig.). 1995. pap. 69.00 (*0-910325-61-8*) Public Util.

***Reinventing Energy: Making the Right Choices.** Sally B. Gentille. (Illus.). 99p. (Orig.). 1997. pap. text ed. 35.00 (*0-7881-3777-8*) DIANE Pub.

Reinventing Evangelism. Donald C. Posterski. LC 89-15363. 202p. (Orig.). 1989. pap. 10.99 (*0-8308-1269-5*, 1269) InterVarsity.

Reinventing Eve: Modern Woman in Search of Herself. 2nd ed. Kim Chernin. LC 93-40772. 208p. 1994. reprint ed. pap. 13.00 (*0-06-092503-5*, PL) HarpC.

Reinventing Family. Laura Benkov. 1994. 22.00 (*0-517-58743-2*, Crown) Crown Pub Group.

Reinventing Fatherhood. Jonathan Gould. 1993. pap. 10.95 (*0-8306-4219-6*) McGraw-Hill Prof.

***Reinventing Food Regulations: National Performance Review.** Bill Clinton & Al Gore. 27p. (Orig.). 1996. pap. 20.00 (*0-7881-3685-2*) DIANE Pub.

Reinventing Fundraising: Realizing the Potential of Women's Philanthropy. Sondra C. Shaw & Martha A. Taylor. LC 94-32448. (Nonprofit Ser.). 296p. text ed. 27.95 (*0-7879-0050-8*) Jossey-Bass.

Reinventing Germany: German Political Development since 1945. Anthony Glees. (Illus.). 352p. 1996. 52.95 (*1-85973-190-2*); pap. 22.95 (*1-85973-185-6*) Berg Pubs.

Reinventing Government. David Osborne & Ted Gaebler. 1992. 26.00 (*0-201-52394-9*) Addison-Wesley.

Reinventing Government: An Analysis & Annotated Bibliography. Robert L. Hollings. LC 95-49152. 175p. 1995. 59.00 (*1-56072-264-9*) Nova Sci Pubs.

Reinventing Government? Appraising the National Performance Review. Donald F. Kettl. LC 95-131139. (CPM Report Ser.: No. 94-2). 78p. 1995. pap. 7.95 (*0-8157-4911-2*) Brookings.

Reinventing Government: How the Entrepreneurial Spirit Is Transforming the Public Sector. David Osborne & Ted Gaebler. 432p. 1993. pap. 14.95 (*0-452-26942-3*, Plume) NAL-Dutton.

Reinventing Government or Reinventing Ourselves: The Role of Citizen Owners in Making a Better Government. Hindy L. Schachter. LC 96-12019. (SUNY Series in Public Administration). 192p. (C). 1996. text ed. 49.50 (*0-7914-3155-X*); pap. text ed. 16.95 (*0-7914-3156-8*) State U NY Pr.

Reinventing Healthcare. Jack J. Tawil & F. C. Bold. vii, 310p. 1994. 23.95 (*1-883021-12-X*) Research Ent.

Reinventing Human Services: Community & Family Centered Practice. Ed. by Kristine E. Nelson & Paul Adams. (Modern Applications of Social Work Ser.). 295p. 1995. lib. bdg. 49.95 (0-202-36097-0) Aldine de Gruyter.

Reinventing Human Services: Community & Family Centered Practice. Ed. by Kristine E. Nelson & Paul Adams. (Modern Applications of Social Work Ser.). 295p. 1995. pap. text ed. 24.95 (0-202-36098-9) Aldine de Gruyter.

Reinventing Inequality. Ron E. Roberts & Douglas Brintnall. 339p. 1983. text ed. 22.95 (0-87073-793-7); pap. text ed. 18.95 (0-87073-794-5) Schenkman Bks Inc.

Reinventing Juvenile Justice. Barry Krisberg & James F. Austin. (Illus.). 224p. (C). 1993. text ed. 42.00 (0-8039-4828-X); pap. text ed. 18.50 (0-8039-4829-8) Sage.

***Reinventing Leadership: Change in an Age of Anxiety; Discussion Guide.** Edwin H. Friedman. 51p. 1997. pap. 95.00 incl. vdisk (1-57230-950-4, HD57) Guilford Pr.

***Reinventing Leadership: Strategies to Empower the Organization.** Warren Bennis. 1997. pap. 14.00 (0-688-15126-4, Quill) Morrow.

Reinventing Man: The Robot Becomes Reality. Igor Aleksander & Piers Burnett. 1984. 17.95 (0-03-063857-7) H Holt & Co.

Reinventing Marxism. Howard J. Sherman. LC 95-11951. 416p. 1995. text ed. 55.00 (0-8018-5076-2); pap. text ed. 16.95 (0-8018-5077-0) Johns Hopkins.

Reinventing NASA. David Moore. (Illus.). 52p. (Orig.). (C). 1994. pap. text ed. 25.00 (0-7881-1403-4) DIANE Pub.

Reinventing Nature? Responses to Postmodern Deconstruction. Michael E. Soule. LC 94-22631. (Illus.). 176p. (C). 1995. text ed. 34.95 (1-55963-310-7); pap. text ed. 17.95 (1-55963-311-5) Island Pr.

Reinventing New Jersey: Innovative Approaches under Fiscal Pressure. Ed. by Kathe Callahan et al. 82p. (Orig.). (C). 1996. pap. text ed. 9.95 (1-57420-054-2); vhs 9.95 (1-57420-055-0) Chatelaine.

Reinventing Our Schools Guide. Agency for Instructional Technology Staff. (Orig.). 1993. pap. text ed. 7.75 (0-7842-0722-4) Agency Instr Tech.

Reinventing Physics: Logic & Physics, a Dialectical Approach to Physics. Patrick A. O'Dougherty. 144p. (C). 1993. lib. bdg. 10.99 (0-9626665-2-1) Hellenist Amer Co.

Reinventing Politics: Eastern Europe from Stalin to Havel. W. Vladimir Tismaneanu. 1993. pap. 16.95 (0-02-932606-0, Free Press) Free Pr.

Reinventing Pop-Subculture: The Impact of Andy Warhol. Van M. Cagle. 260p. 1995. text ed. 46.00 (0-8039-5743-2) Sage.

Reinventing Pop-Subculture: The Impact of Andy Warhol. Van M. Cagle. LC 94-48049. 240p. 1995. pap. 22.95 (0-8039-5744-0) Sage.

Reinventing Public Education. Paul T. Hill. xviii, 124p. 1995. pap. text ed. 15.00 (0-8330-1631-8, MR-312-LE/GGF) Rand Corp.

***Reinventing Public Education: How Contracting Can Transform America's Schools.** Paul T. Hill et al. LC 96-39542. (A Rand Research Study). 1997. pap. 16.95 (0-226-33652-2); lib. bdg. 45.00 (0-226-33651-4) U Ch Pr.

Reinventing Rationality: The Role of Regulatory Analysis in the Federal Bureaucracy. Thomas O. McGarity. (Illus.). 375p. (C). 1991. text ed. 80.00 (0-521-40256-5) Cambridge U Pr.

Reinventing Reality: Five Texas Photographers. Elizabeth Ward. (Illus.). 22p. 1990. pap. 3.00 (0-941193-05-5) U Houst Sarah.

Reinventing Reality: The Art & Life of Rouben Mamoulian. Mark Spergel. LC 93-34466. (Filmmakers Ser.: No. 37). 336p. 1993. 42.50 (0-8108-2721-2) Scarecrow.

Reinventing Retirement: Life Without Boundaries. John A. Pugsley. 200p. 1994. pap. 13.95 (0-9639629-3-0) Shot Tower.

***Reinventing Revolution.** Edward McCaughan. LC 97-20978. (C). 1997. text ed. 50.00 (0-8133-6907-X) Westview.

Reinventing Revolution: New Social Movements & the Socialist Tradition in India. Gail Omvedt. LC 92-46911. (Socialism & Social Movements Ser.). 384p. (C). (gr. 13). 1993. text ed. 69.95 (0-87332-784-5, East Gate Bk); pap. text ed. 25.95 (0-87332-785-3, East Gate Bk) M E Sharpe.

Reinventing Revolution: Value & Difference in New Social Movements & the Left. Tim Jordan. (Avebury Series in Philosophy). 174p. 1994. 59.95 (1-85628-865-X, Pub. by Avebury Pub UK) Ashgate Pub Co.

Reinventing Shakespeare: A Cultural History from the Restoration to the Present. Gary Taylor. 480p. 1991. pap. 14.95 (0-19-506679-0) OUP.

Reinventing Superfund. Paul Thompson. Ed. by Karen Glass. 92p. (Orig.). 1994. pap. text ed. 20.00 (1-55877-176-X) Natl Governor.

Reinventing Systems: Collaborations to Support Families. Mia MacDonald. Ed. by Harvard Family Research Project Staff. 92p. 1994. pap. text ed. 7.50 (0-9630627-3-5) Harvard Fam.

Reinventing Technology: Policies for Democratic Values. Michael Goldhaber. (Alternative Policies for America Ser.). 224p. 1986. text ed. 35.00 (0-7102-0906-1, RKP); pap. text ed. 13.95 (0-7102-0907-X, RKP) Routledge.

Reinventing Technology, Rediscovering Community. Ed. by Phil Agre & Douglas Schuler. LC 96-36613. (Illus.). 240p. 1997. pap. 39.50 (1-56750-259-8); text ed. 78.50 (1-56750-258-X) Ablex Pub.

Reinventing the American People: Unity & Diversity Today. Ed. by Robert Royal. 190p. 1995. pap. 17.00 (0-8028-0878-6) Eerdmans.

Reinventing the Americas: Comparative Studies of Literature of the United States & Spanish America. Ed. by B. G. Chevigny & G. Laguardia. 389p. 1986. 64.95 (0-521-30196-3) Cambridge U Pr.

Reinventing the Business. Harmon. 1996. 35.00 (0-02-913864-7, Free Press) Free Pr.

Reinventing the Business. Roy L. Harmon. (Illus.). 496p. 1996. 34.50 (0-684-82301-2) Free Pr.

Reinventing the CFO: Moving from Financial Management to Strategic Management. Henry Johansson et al. LC 96-31878. (Illus.). 240p. 1996. text ed. 34.95 (0-07-012945-2) McGraw.

Reinventing the Congregation for a New Mission Frontier. Loren B. Mead. LC 91-72968. (Once & Future Church Ser.). 100p. (Orig.). 1991. pap. 9.95 (1-56699-050-5, AL129) Alban Inst.

Reinventing the Corporation: IBM & Market-Driven Product Development. Roy A. Bauer et al. (Illus.). 384p. 1992. 30.00 (0-19-506754-1) OUP.

***Reinventing the Economy.** David Simmons. 1997. pap. 17.95 (1-897766-17-3, Pub. by Jon Pubng UK) LPC InBook.

Reinventing the Enemy's Language: Contemporary Native Women's Writing of North America. Joy Harjo. LC 96-36547. 448p. 1997. 27.50 (0-393-04029-1) Norton.

Reinventing the Factory: Productivity Breakthroughs in Manufacturing Today. Roy L. Harmon & Leroy D. Peterson. 303p. 1989. 45.00 (0-02-913861-2, Free Press) Free Pr.

Reinventing the Factory II Vol. 2: Managing the World Class Factory. Roy L. Harmon. (Illus.). 320p. 1991. 45.00 (0-02-913862-0, Free Press) Free Pr.

***Reinventing the Family.** Laura Benkov. Date not set. pap. 1.99 (0-517-17610-6) Random Hse Value.

Reinventing the Family. Laura Benkov. 1995. pap. 14.00 (0-517-88486-0) Random Hse Value.

***Reinventing the Family.** Laura Benkov. 1996. 5.99 (0-517-17187-2) Random Hse Value.

Reinventing the Filipino Sense of Being & Becoming. Arnold M. Azurin. (Illus.). 240p. 1996. pap. text ed. 24.00 (971-542-073-7, Pub. by U of Philippines Pr PH) UH Pr.

***Reinventing the Forest Industry.** Jean Mater. LC 96-78528. 280p. (Orig.). 1997. pap. 14.95 (1-885221-58-4) BookPartners.

Reinventing the Future: Conversations with the World's Leading Scientists. Thomas A. Bass. (Illus.). (C). 1993. 24.95 (0-201-62642-X) Addison-Wesley.

Reinventing the Future: Conversations with the World's Leading Scientists. Thomas A. Bass. 272p. (C). 1995. pap. 14.00 (0-201-40795-7) Addison-Wesley.

Reinventing the Left. Ed. by David Miliband. 250p. 1995. pap. text ed. 22.95 (0-7456-1391-8) Blackwell Pubs.

Reinventing the Newspaper: Essays. Frank Denton & Howard Kurtz. LC 93-9255. (Perspectives on the News Ser.: Vol. 3). (Orig.). 1993. pap. 9.95 (0-87078-350-5) TCFP-PPP.

Reinventing the Office: Management Issues. Amy D. Wohl. (KU - Office Procedures Ser.). 1992. 183.95 (0-538-70791-7) S-W Pub.

***Reinventing the Past & Restructuring the Present in Reunified Germany: Comparative Academic Politics & the Case of East German Historians.** Mark Ginsburg & John A. Weaver. Ed. by Mark B. Ginsburg. (Studies in Education & Politics). 300p. 1998. text ed. 60.00 (0-8153-2284-4) Garland.

Reinventing the Pentagon: How the New Public Management Can Bring Institutional Renewal. Fred Thompson & L. R. Jones. LC 94-7515. (Public Administration Ser.). 320p. 32.95 (1-55542-710-3) Jossey-Bass.

Reinventing the Retail Bank: Cross Marketing Investment Products to Create the Full Service. Lawrence E. Harb. 1993. text ed. 47.50 (1-55738-386-3) Irwin Prof Pubng.

Reinventing the Sales Team: Building an Effective Sales Organization for Top Line Growth. William O'Connell & Sibson & Company Staff. 240p. 1997. text ed. 34.95 (0-07-048216-0) McGraw.

Reinventing the Schools: A Radical Plan for Boston. Steven F. Wilson. Ed. by James Taranto. (Pioneer Paper Ser.: No. 7). 341p. (Orig.). 1992. pap. text ed. 15.00 (0-929930-09-6) Pioneer Inst.

***Reinventing the Sexes: Biomedical Construction of Femininity & Masculinity.** Marianne Van Den Wijngaard. LC 96-41378. (Race, Gender & Science Ser.). 1997. write for info. (0-253-33250-8); pap. write for info. (0-253-21087-9) Ind U Pr.

Reinventing the Soviet Self: Media & Social Change in the Former Soviet Union. Jennifer E. Turpin. LC 94-22651. 176p. 1995. text ed. 49.95 (0-275-95043-3) Greenwood.

Reinventing the Truth: Historical Claims of One of the World's Largest Nameless Sects. Kevin N. Daniel. 315p. (Orig.). 1993. pap. 9.45 (0-9639419-0-9) Res Info Servs.

Reinventing the University: A Radical Proposal for a Problem-Focused University. Lynn Johnson & Jan D. Sinnott. (Social & Policy Issues in Education Ser.). 211p. 1996. 45.00 (1-56750-221-0); pap. 24.50 (1-56750-222-9) Ablex Pub.

Reinventing the University: Managing & Financing Institutions of Higher Education. Coopers & Lybrand LLP Staff et al. Ed. by Sandra L. Johnson & Sean C. Rush. LC 94-45421. (Nonprofit Law, Finance & Management Ser.). 432p. 1995. text ed. 130.00 (0-471-10452-3) Wiley.

Reinventing the University: Managing & Financing Institutions of Higher Education 1996. Ed. by Sandra L. Johnson & Sean C. Rush. 1996. suppl. ed., pap. text ed. 57.00 (0-471-14032-5) Wiley.

Reinventing the Vehicle for Environmental Management: Summer 1995 - First Phase Report. National Environmental Policy Institute Staff. 122p. 1995. 20.00 (0-614-16679-9) Nat Environ Policy.

Reinventing the Warehouse: World Class Distribution Logistics. Roy L. Harmon. 320p. 1993. 45.00 (0-02-913863-9, Free Press) Free Pr.

Reinventing the Wheel: A Design for Student Achievement in the 21st Century. Laura L. Loyacono. 96p. 1992. pap. 25.00 (1-55516-220-7, 2110) Natl Conf State Legis.

Reinventing the Workplace: How Business & Employees Can Both Win. Ed. by David I. Levine. LC 94-24066. 222p. (C). 1995. 38.95 (0-8157-5232-6); pap. 16.95 (0-8157-5231-8) Brookings.

Reinventing Urban Education: Multiculturalism & the Social Context of Schooling. Francisco L. Rivera-Batiz. 300p. (C). 1994. pap. write for info. (0-9638459-0-X) IUME Pr.

Reinventing Womanhood. Carolyn G. Heilbrun. 1994. 21.00 (0-8446-6742-0) Peter Smith.

Reinventing Womanhood. Carolyn G. Heilbrun. 248p. 1993. pap. 9.95 (0-393-31076-0) Norton.

***Reinventing Your Board: A Step-by-Step Guide to Implementing Policy Governance.** John Carver & Miriam M. Carver. LC 97-4810. (Jossey-Bass Public Administration Ser.). 1997. write for info. (0-7879-0911-4) Jossey-Bass.

Reinventing Your Career: Following the 5 New Paths to Career Fulfillment. Created by Business Week Staff. (Illus.). 122p. 1996. pap. text ed. 14.95 (0-07-009434-9) McGraw.

Reinventing Your Career: Surviving a Layoff & Creating New Opportunities. Stephen P. Adams. 160p. 1996. pap. 9.99 (1-881273-61-X) Northfield Pub.

***Reinventing Your Life.** Jeffery E. Young & Janet S. Klosko. 368p. 3.98 (0-8317-3553-8) Smithmark.

Reinventing Your Life: How to Break Free from Negative Life Patterns. Jeffrey E. Young & Janet S. Klosko. LC 93-48711. 384p. 1994. pap. 12.95 (0-452-27204-1, Plume) NAL-Dutton.

Reinventing Your Self: 28 Strategies for Coping with Change. Mark Towers. Ed. by Kelly Scanlon. LC 95-69803. (Illus.). 72p. 1995. spiral bd., pap. 10.95 (1-878542-90-7, 12-0020) SkillPath Pubns.

Reinventing Yourself. Dick Sutphen. 180p. (Orig.). (C). 1993. pap. 9.98 (0-87554-499-1) Valley Sun.

Reinventing Yourself: Becoming the Person You Want to Be. Barnes Boffey. LC 92-50851. (Illus.). 150p. (Orig.). 1992. pap. 12.00 (0-944337-14-7, 147) New View Pubns.

Reinvention of Love: Poetry, Politics, & Culture from Sidney to Milton. Anthony Low. LC 93-18184. 240p. (C). 1993. text ed. 54.95 (0-521-45030-6) Cambridge U Pr.

***Reinvention of Politics: Rethinking Modernity in the Global Social Order.** Ulrich Beck. Tr. by Mark Ritter. LC 96-45035. 200p. (GER.). 1996. 52.95 (0-7456-1366-7); pap. 21.95 (0-7456-1758-1) Blackwell Pubs.

Reinvention of the World: English Writing 1650-1750. Douglas Chambers. LC 95-36365. (Writing in History Ser.). 192p. 1996. text ed. 16.95 (0-340-58478-5, Pub. by E Arnld UK) St Martin.

Reinvention of the World: English Writing 1650-1750. Douglas Chambers. LC 95-36365. (Writing in History Ser.). 192p. 1996. text ed. 49.95 (0-340-66242-5, Pub. by E Arnld UK) St Martin.

Reinvention of Work: A New Vision of Livelihood for Our Time. Matthew Fox. LC 93-38866. 352p. 1995. pap. 14.00 (0-06-063062-0) Harper SF.

Reinvention's Next Steps: Governing in a Balanced Budget World: National Performance Review. Contrib. by Al Gore. 42p. (Orig.). 1996. pap. text ed. 20.00 (0-7881-2906-6) DIANE Pub.

Reinvesting in America: The Grassroots Movements that Are Feeding the Hungry, Housing the Homeless, & Putting Americans Back to Work. Robin Garr. 288p. 1995. 23.00 (0-201-40756-6) Addison-Wesley.

Reinvesting in Childcare. Anne Hoskins. 62p. 1991. 12.00 (0-685-56600-5) CPA Washington.

Reinvesting in Communities: Policy Options for New Jersey. Anne Hoskins et al. 65p. 1991. 20.00 (0-685-56601-3) CPA Washington.

Reinvigorating Our Schools: A Challenge to Parents, Teachers, & Policymakers. Ed. by Ernest W. Lefever. 56p. 1985. pap. 10.50 (0-89633-094-X) Ethics & Public Policy.

Reise In Arabien, 2 vols. in 1. William G. Palgrave. xii, 646p. reprint ed. write for info. (0-318-71548-1) G Olms Pubs.

Reise In Hadhramaut, Beled Beny 'Yssa und Beled El Hadschar. Adolph Von Wrede. 375p. reprint ed. write for info. (0-318-71573-2) G Olms Pubs.

Reise Ins Chinesischeh: Yunan, Wu-I-Shan und Tibetische, 1936-1954. Hans Stubel. (Asian Folklore & Social Life Monographs: No. 87). (ENG & GER.). 15.00 (0-89986-295-0) Oriental Bk Store.

Reise Nach Innerarabien, Kurdistan und Armenien, 1892. Eduard Nolde. (Illus.). xvi, 272p. reprint ed. write for info. (0-318-71542-2) G Olms Pubs.

Reise Nach Salzburg. Gertrud Seidmann. (Illus.). 1975. pap. 4.50 (0-582-36188-5) Longman.

Reise Nach Sudarabien. Heinrich F. Maltzan. (Illus.). 422p. reprint ed. write for info. (0-318-71530-9) G Olms Pubs.

Reisen. Jean De Mandeville. (Deutsche Volksbucher in Faksimiledrucken, Reihe A: Pt. 21). xxxiii, 388p. 1991. reprint ed. write for info. (3-487-09430-4) G Olms Pubs.

Reisen auf den Highways Im Canyon Country. F. A. Barnes. LC 92-71599. (Canyon Country Ser.: No. 31). (Illus.). 80p. (Orig.). (GER.). 1993. pap. 10.00 (0-925685-06-2) Canyon Country Pubns.

Reisen Durch Syrien, Palastina, Phonicien, die Tranjordan-Lander, Arabia Petraea und Unter-Agypten, 4 vols. Ulrich J. Seetzen. cii, 1858p. reprint ed. write for info. (0-318-71564-3) G Olms Pubs.

Reisen In Arabien. Johann L. Burckhardt. (Illus.). xiv, 706p. reprint ed. write for info. (0-318-71495-7) G Olms Pubs.

Reisen in Griechenland (Travels in Greece, Deutscsh) Richard Chandler. xvi, 432p. 1985. reprint ed. 70.00 (3-487-05741-7) G Olms Pubs.

Reisen In Sub-Arabien, Mahra-Land und Hadramut. Leo Hirsch. (Illus.). 333p. reprint ed. write for info. (0-318-71517-1) G Olms Pubs.

Reisen in Sud-Afrika in den Jahren 1849-1857. Laszlo Magyar. (B. E. Ser.: No. 155). (GER.). 1859. 50.00 (0-8115-3073-6) Periodicals Srv.

***Reisen Nach Bayreuth.** Agostino Sunti & Walter Jens. Ed. by Ingo Toussaint. 407p. (GER.). 1994. write for info. (3-487-08354-X) G Olms Pubs.

Reiseziel Mond. Herge. (Illus.). 62p. (GER.). (J). pap. 19.95 (0-8288-5059-3) Fr & Eur.

Reishi: Ancient Herb for Modern Times. Kenneth Jones. (Illus.). 34p. (Orig.). 1992. pap. 5.95 (0-9625638-1-1) Sylvan Pr WA.

Reishi: Hierba Legendaria Para Tiempos Modernos. Kenneth Jones. 42p. (SPA.). 1996. pap. 5.95 (0-9625638-2-X) Sylvan Pr WA.

Reishi Mushroom: Herb of Spiritual Potency & Medical Wonder. rev. ed. Terry Willard. (Illus.). 167p. (Orig.). 1992. pap. 14.95 (0-9625638-0-3) Sylvan Pr WA.

Reishi Mushroom As a Healing Herb. 1996. lib. bdg. 250.75 (0-8490-5876-7) Gordon Pr.

Reiss Rules for Two-Hour Monopoly: Fun, Fast, Unofficial Way to Play America's Favorite Board Game. Stephen Reiss. LC 93-85455. (Illus.). 64p. (Orig.). (J). (gr. 1-12). 1994. pap. 6.95 (0-9637853-3-8) Prosprty Prtnrs.

Reiter Treponeme: A Review of the Literature. A. L. Wallace & A. D. Harris. 1967. pap. text ed. 12.00 (92-4-068362-3, 1033602) World Health.

Reithaus. Liliane Skalecki. (Studien Zur Kunstgeschichte Ser.: Bd. 76). 256p. (GER.). 1992. write for info. (3-487-09631-5) G Olms Pubs.

***Reitkunst Oder Grundliche Anweisung Zur Kenntnis der Pferde, Deren Erziehung, Unterhaltung, Abrichtung, Nach Ihrem Verschiedenen Gebrauch und Bestimmung.** Francois R. De La Gueriniere. (Documenta Hippologica Ser.). (Illus.). xxx, 332p. (GER.). 1996. reprint ed. write for info. (3-487-08288-8) G Olms Pubs.

***REITS: Building Profits with Real Estate Investment Trusts.** John A. Mullaney. LC 97-14586. (Investment Classics Ser.). 304p. 1997. 39.95 (0-471-19324-0) Wiley.

REITs Fall 1994: What You Need to Know Now. (Real Estate Law & Practice Course Handbook Ser.). 352p. 1994. pap. 99.00 (0-614-17220-9, N4-4586) PLI.

REITs 1994: What You Need to Know Now. (Corporate Law & Practice Course Handbook, 1985-86 Ser.). 352p. 1994. pap. 99.00 (0-614-17182-2, B4-7093) PLI.

Reitz: Family History & Record Book of the Descendants of Johan Friedrich Reitz, the Pioneer, Who Landed at Philadelphia, Sept. 7, 1748. J. J. Reitz. (Illus.). 288p. 1992. reprint ed. pap. 43.50 (0-8328-2713-4); reprint ed. lib. bdg. 53.50 (0-8328-2712-6) Higginson Bk Co.

Reitz: Family History & Record Book of the Descendants of Johan Friedrich Reitz, the Pioneer, Who Landed at Philadelphia, Sept. 7, 1748. J. J. Reitz. (Illus.). 289p. 1994. reprint ed. pap. 44.50 (0-8328-4054-8); reprint ed. lib. bdg. 54.50 (0-8328-4053-X) Higginson Bk Co.

***Reivating Early Care & Education: A Vision for a Quality System.** Sharon L. Kagan & Nancy E. Cohen. LC 96-25323. 1996. write for info. (0-7879-0319-1) Jossey-Bass.

Reivers. William Faulkner. 1962. 17.95 (0-394-44229-6) Random.

Reivers: A Reminiscence. William Faulkner. LC 92-50095. 320p. 1992. pap. 12.00 (0-679-74192-5, Vin) Random.

Reivers: A Reminiscence. large type ed. William Faulkner. LC 95-13847. 390p. 1995. lib. bdg. 21.95 (0-7838-1302-3, GK Hall) Thorndike Pr.

Reivers: Typescript Setting Copy. William Faulkner. Ed. by Polk & Michael Millgate. (William Faulkner Manuscripts). 416p. 1986. text ed. 50.00 (0-8240-6835-1) Garland.

***Reiver's Woman.** Catherine Creel. 1997. mass mkt. 5.99 (0-449-18282-7, GM) Fawcett.

Reivers (1962) William Faulkner. Ed. by Michael Millgate et al. (William Faulkner Manuscripts). 416p. 1986. text ed. 50.00 (0-8240-6834-3) Garland.

***Rejar.** Dara Joy. 400p. (Orig.). 1997. mass mkt. 5.99 (0-505-52178-4) Dorchester Pub Co.

***Reject Me - I Love It! 21 Secrets for Turning Rejection into Direction.** unabridged ed. John Fuhrman. 162p. (Orig.). 1997. pap. 10.95 (0-938716-28-X, Success Pubs) Markowski Intl.

Rejected: Leading Economists Ponder the Publication Process. George B. Shepherd. LC 94-77282. 151p. (Orig.). (C). 1994. pap. text ed. 19.95 (0-913878-53-7) T Horton & Dghts.

Rejected: Sketches of the Twenty-Six Men Nominated for the Supreme Court but Not Confirmed by the Senate. J. Myron Jacobstein & Roy M. Mersky. LC 93-22374. 188p. 1993. 28.00 (0-9634017-4-2) Toucan Valley.

Rejected Body: Feminist Philosophical Reflections on Disability. Susan Wendell. LC 95-51391. 224p. 1996. pap. 16.95 (0-415-91047-1, Routledge NY) Routledge.

Rejected Body: Feminist Philosophical Reflections on Disability. Susan Wendell. LC 95-51391. 224p. (C). 1996. text ed. 59.95 (0-415-91046-3, Routledge NY) Routledge.

Rejected Stone. Moncure D. Conway. (Works of Moncure Daniel Conway Ser.). 1990. reprint ed. lib. bdg. 79.00 (0-685-44755-3) Rprt Serv.

Rejected Suitor. large type ed. Margaret S. Taylor. 336p. 1994. 25.99 (*0-7089-3122-7*) Ulverscroft.

***Rejecting Rejection.** Steve Steinberg. 146p. (Orig.). 1997. pap. 6.00 (*1-57502-421-7*, PO1295) Morris Pubng.

***Rejecting Rejection: How to Take Control of Your Life in Uncontrolled Times.** Bette Price. 136p. 1996. per., pap. text ed. 14.95 (*0-7872-2681-5*) Kendall-Hunt.

Rejecting the Second Generation Hypothesis: Maintaining Estonian Ethnicity in Lakewood, New Jersey. M. Ann Walko. LC 88-35232. (Immigrant Communities & Ethnic Minorities in the U. S. & Canada Ser.: No. 44). 1989. 47.50 (*0-404-19454-0*) AMS Pr.

Rejection. James R. Sherman. LC 81-86079. 87p. (Orig.). 1982. pap. 4.95 (*0-935538-02-X*) Pathway Bks.

Rejection & Emancipation: Contemporary Writing in German-Speaking Switzerland: Literature in Context, 1945-1991. Ed. by Michael Butler & Malcolm Pender. 262p. 1991. 59.95 (*0-85496-748-6*) Berg Pubs.

Rejection: How to Bounce Back see IVP Booklets

Rejection of Consequentialism: A Philosophical Investigation of the Considerations Underlying Rival Moral Conceptions. rev. ed. Samuel Scheffler. 200p. 1994. reprint ed. 49.95 (*0-19-823510-0*); reprint ed. pap. 14.95 (*0-19-823511-9*) OUP.

Rejects: People & Products That Outsmarted the Experts. Nathan Aaseng. (Inside Business Ser.). (Illus.). 80p. (J). (gr. 5 up). 1989. lib. bdg. 18.95 (*0-8225-0677-7*, Lerner Publctns) Lerner Group.

Rejoice: A Biblical Study of Dance. Debbie Roberts. 212p. 1992. 7.99 (*0-938612-02-6*) Destiny Image.

Rejoice! And Other Stories. Carl Tighe. 160p. 1993. 23.95 (*0-224-03023-X*, Pub. by Jonathan Cape UK) Trafalgar.

Rejoice: Your're a Minister's Wife. Marion K. Rich. 184p. 1978. pap. 9.99 (*0-8341-0551-9*) Beacon Hill.

Rejoice & Be Glad. Lois Veals. 2.99 (*0-906731-79-8*, Pub. by Christian Focus UK) Spring Arbor Dist.

Rejoice & Be Glad! Meditations on Fifteen Psalms. Maureena Fritz. Ed. by Carl Koch. (Illus.). 88p. (Orig.). 1995. pap. 7.95 (*0-88489-305-7*) St Marys.

***Rejoice & Sing!** Sweet Publishing Staff. 1996. pap. 3.25 (*0-8344-0126-6*) Sweet Pub.

Rejoice! God Lives in Me. Zygmunt V. Szarnicki. 320p. 1991. pap. 19.95 (*0-939332-20-5*) J Pohl Assocs.

***Rejoice! His Promises Are Sure.** Ardeth G. Kapp. LC 96-50301. 1997. write for info. (*1-57345-233-5*) Deseret Bk.

***Rejoice in Hope.** Terry Matthews. pap. 2.99 (*0-89274-727-7*) Harrison Hse.

Rejoice in Remembering. Cindy McGrath. 8.00 (*0-945905-20-3*) Family Hstory Pubns.

Rejoice in the Lord: A Hymn Companion to the Scriptures. Reformed Church in America Staff. Ed. by Erik Routley. 608p. 1985. 15.00 (*0-8028-9009-1*) Eerdmans.

Rejoice Mary. Ed. by Giancarlo Bruni. 96p. (C). 1988. 30. 00 (*0-85439-278-5*, Pub. by St Paul Pubns UK) St Mut.

Rejoice, O My Soul: Resources for a Self-Directed Retreat. Michelle Bennett. LC 93-2303. 96p. 1993. pap. 9.95 (*0-8091-3408-X*) Paulist Pr.

***Rejoice or Cry - Diary of a Recon Marine - Vietnam 1967-68.** John Rhodes. (Illus.). 219p. (Orig.). 1996. pap. 7.95 (*0-9655655-0-5*) J Rhodes.

Rejoice Together. Helen R. Pickett. 1995. pap. 9.00 (*1-55896-298-0*, Skinner Hse Bks) Unitarian Univ.

Rejoice with Jerusalem. Ed. by Dov P. Elkins. 1972. pap. 2.95 (*0-87677-065-0*) Prayer Bk.

Rejoice...Always! John Gwyn-Thomas. 176p. (Orig.). 1990. pap. 7.99 (*0-85151-562-2*) Banner of Truth.

Rejoicing in Christ: The Biography of Robert Carlton Savage. Stephen E. Savage. (Illus.). 367p. (Orig.). 1990. pap. 8.95 (*0-9627848-0-X*) Shadow Rock Pr.

Rejoicing in Diversity. Alan Weiss. 1994. pap. 6.95 (*0-910924-01-5*) Macalester.

Rejoicings. Gerald Stern. LC 83-63291. 80p. 1984. reprint ed. 13.95 (*0-915371-00-6*); reprint ed. pap. 6.95 (*0-915371-01-4*) Metro Bk Co.

Rejuvenate: Looking Younger & Feeling Vital. Devra Z. Hill. 192p. (Orig.). pap. 7.95 (*0-89529-472-9*) Avery Pub.

Rejuvenating a Tradition: Reform & Revolution in Modern China. Young-Tsu Wong. LC 89-48081. (Asian Thought & Culture Ser.: Vol. 3). 232p. (C). 1990. text ed. 53.50 (*0-8204-1223-6*) P Lang Pubng.

Rejuvenating Plants of Tropical Africa: Aphrodisiacs, Sterility, Impotence, Infertility. Albert A. Enti. Ed. & Intro. by Anthony K. Andoh. LC 88-63959. (Illus.). 56p. (Orig.). 1988. pap. 9.95 (*0-916299-07-4*) North Scale Co.

Rejuvenating the Body Through Fasting with Spirulina Plankton. 2nd ed. Christopher Hills. (Illus.). 64p. 1980. pap. text ed. 4.95 (*0-916438-35-X*) Dr Hills Technol.

Rejuvenating the Humanities. Ed. by Ray B. Browne & Marshall W. Fishwick. LC 91-77025. (Illus.). 220p. (C). 1992. 39.95 (*0-87972-545-1*); pap. 19.95 (*0-87972-546-X*) Bowling Green Univ Popular Press.

Rejuvenating the Mature Business: The Competitive Challenge. Charles Baden-Fuller & John M. Stopford. LC 93-36706. 1994. 29.95 (*0-87584-476-6*) Harvard Busn.

Rejuvenating the Mature Business: The Competitive Challenge. Charles Baden-Fuller & John M. Stopford. LC 92-26237. 224p. 1992. 38.00 (*0-415-08987-5*, Routledge NY) Routledge.

Rejuvenating the Mature Business: The Competitive Challenge. Charles Baden-Fuller & John Stopford. LC 95-30382. 304p. 1996. pap. 19.95 (*0-415-13520-6*) Routledge.

Rejuvenating the Mature Business: The Competitive Challenge. Chrales Baden-Fuller & John M. Stopford. 1994. text ed. 29.95 (*0-07-103585-0*) McGraw.

Rejuvenation. Linda Clark. 1978. 12.95 (*0-8159-6718-7*) Devin.

Rejuvenation. Horst Rechelbacher. (Illus.). 224p. 1987. pap. 14.95 (*0-89281-248-6*) Inner Tradit.

Rejuvenation: Science's New Fountain of Youth. (Longevity Ser.). 1991. lib. bdg. 75.00 (*0-8490-4149-X*) Gordon Pr.

Rejuvenation & Regeneration. Bernard Jensen. 1988. pap. 4.95 (*0-932615-16-3*) B Jensen.

Rekeningkundige Grondslae vir Prokureurs. M. C. Faul et al. 281p. 1987. pap. write for info. (*0-7021-1912-1*, Pub. by Juta SA) Gaunt.

***Rekindle the Fire: Antidote to Burnout.** John P. Webster. 188p. 1997. per. 12.50 (*0-614-26140-6*) Gren Fell Read Ctr.

Rekindle Your Love for Jesus. David E. Rosage. 180p. 1996. pap. 9.99 (*0-89283-932-5*) Servant.

Rekindled: How to Keep the Warmth in Marriage. 2nd ed. Pat Williams et al. LC 95-6913. 176p. (gr. 10). 1995. 12. 99 (*0-8007-1713-9*) Revell.

Rekindled Lifestyles. Calvin J. Moore. 1993. 10.00 (*0-533-10629-X*) Vantage.

Rekindled Passion. Penny Jordan. 1990. pap. 2.50 (*0-373-11324-2*) Harlequin Bks.

Rekindled Passion. large type ed. Penny Jordan. 1990. reprint ed. lib. bdg. 18.95 (*0-263-12263-8*, Pub. by Mills & Boon UK) Thorndike Pr.

Rekindling Commitment: How to Revitalize Yourself, Your Work, & Your Organization. Dennis Jaffe et al. LC 94-9266. (Management Ser.). 302p. 27.00 (*1-55542-704-9*) Jossey-Bass.

***Rekindling Community: Place, Pride & the Renewal of Rural & Local Schooling.** Paul Theobald. LC 96-51814. 1997. text ed. 50.00 (*0-8133-2303-7*) Westview.

***Rekindling Community: Place, Pride & the Renewal of Rural & Local Schooling.** Paul Theobald. LC 96-51814. (C). 1997. pap. text ed. 17.95 (*0-8133-2302-9*) Westview.

Rekindling Development: Multinational Firms & Third World Debt. Ed. by Lee A. Tavis. LC 87-40619. 352p. 1988. text ed. 37.00 (*0-268-01634-8*) U of Notre Dame Pr.

Rekindling the Flame: American Jewish Chaplains & the Survivors of European Jewry, 1944-1948. Alex Grobman. LC 92-28678. (Illus.). 260p. (C). 1992. text ed. 29.95 (*0-8143-2413-4*) Wayne St U Pr.

Rekindling the Hope of the Manger: An Advent Study. Evan D. Howard. 124p. 1991. pap. 10.00 (*0-8170-1180-3*) Judson.

Rekindling the Passion: Liturgical Renewal in Your Community. Susan S. Jorgensen. LC 92-32396. 272p. (Orig.). (C). 1993. pap. text ed. 14.95 (*0-89390-236-5*) Resource Pubns.

Rekindling the Spirit in Work. Howard Schecter. 1995. pap. 11.95 (*1-886449-06-6*) Barrytown Ltd.

Rekindling the Word: In Search of Gospel Truth. Carston P. Thiede. LC 95-38673. 224p. (Orig.). (C). 1995. pap. 25.00 (*1-56338-136-2*) TPI PA.

***Rekindling Your Spirit: Messages to Live By.** William Gorvine. 1996. pap. text ed. 15.95 (*0-9651703-0-6*) Eagle Pr FL.

Relacion de Acuerdos Bilaterales: OEA Ser. B-II 1, 1949-1980. OAS, General Secretariat for Legal Affairs. (Serie Sobre Tratados: No. 59). 74p. (ENG, FRE, POR & SPA.). (C). 1980. 4.00 (*0-8270-1283-7*) OAS.

Relacion de las Cosas de Yucatan. Diego De Landa. Tr. by Alfred M. Tozzer. (Harvard University Peabody Museum of Archaeology & Ethnology Papers). 1974. reprint ed. 72.00 (*0-527-01245-9*) Periodicals Srv.

Relacion Hospedante-Parasito Mecanismo De Patogenicidad De los Microorganismos. Manuel R. Leiva. (Serie de Biologia: No. 14). 91p. (C). 1981. pap. 3.50 (*0-8270-1322-1*) OAS.

Relacion Mundo-Escritura en Textos de Reinaldo Arenas, Juan Jose Saer, Juan Carlos Martini. LC 93-72619. 272p. (SPA.). 1993. pap. text ed. 20.00 (*0-935318-20-8*) Edins Hispamerica.

Relacion o Naugragios de Alvar Nunez Cabeza de Vaca. Ed. by Martin A Favata & Jose B. Fernandez. 27.50 (*0-916379-35-3*) Scripta.

Relaciones Comerciales. Nanette R. Pascal & Maria P. Rojas. 352p. (SPA.). (C). 1995. pap. text ed. 33.16 (*0-669-32579-1*) HM College Div.

***Relaciones Comericales.** Nanette R. Pascal & Maria P. Rojas. (SPA.). (C). 1996. teacher ed., text ed. 2.66 (*0-669-41783-1*) HM College Div.

Relaciones de Don Juan de Persia. Juan De Persia. Ed. by Narciso Alonso Cortes. 280p. (SPA.). 1968. 100.00 (*0-614-00118-8*) Elliots Bks.

Relaciones Humanas. Rosemary T. Fruehling. 141p. 1982. text ed. 12.96 (*0-07-022540-0*) McGraw.

Relaciones Humanas en Prevencion de Accidentes. 383p. 40.00 (*0-318-17995-4*) Inter-Am Safety.

Relaciones Humanas, Sanas y Positivas. M. Ramos. (Serie Realidades - Realities Ser.). 31p. (SPA.). 1995. pap. 1.79 (*1-56063-125-2*, 498137) Editorial Unilit.

***Relaciones Intimas - Intimate Relations: Intimate Relations, Vol. 420.** Elizabeth Oldfield. (Harlequin Bianca Ser.). (SPA.). 1997. mass mkt. 3.50 (*0-373-33420-6*, 1-33420-0) Harlequin Bks.

Relais du Silence 1996. 288p. 1996. 14.95 (*0-7859-9863-2*) Fr & Eur.

Relais et Chateaux: Relais Gourmand 1994. Regis Bulot. 612p. (FRE.). 1994. 14.95 (*0-614-00405-5*, 2950788904) Fr & Eur.

Relais et Chateaux 1994. Pierre Monthule. (ENG, FRE & GER.). 1994. pap. 9.95 (*0-7859-7428-8*) Fr & Eur.

Relais et Chateaux 1995. 1995. pap. 14.95 (*0-7859-9029-1*) Fr & Eur.

Relais et Chateaux 1996. (Orig.). 1996. 19.95 (*0-7859-9951-5*) Fr & Eur.

***Relais et Chateaux, 1997.** Ed. by Relais et Chateaux Staff. 1997. pap. 19.95 (*0-7859-9396-7*) Fr & Eur.

Relapse. John Vanbrugh. Ed. by Bernard Harris. (New Mermaid Ser.). (C). 1976. pap. text ed. 4.95 (*0-393-90032-0*) Norton.

Relapse. John Vanbrugh. Ed. by Curt A. Zimansky. LC 70-107279. (Regents Restoration Drama Ser.). (Illus.). 183p. reprint ed. pap. 52.20 (*0-685-20490-1*, 2029927) Bks Demand.

Relapse: A Guide to Successful Recovery. Dennis C. Daley. Ed. by Lee M. Joiner. LC 87-24385. 48p. (Orig.). 1987. pap. text ed. 4.25 (*0-943519-02-0*, B1902) Sulzburger & Graham Pub.

Relapse: Conceptual, Research & Clinical Perspectives. Pref. by Dennis C. Daley. LC 89-15611. (Journal of Chemical Dependency Treatment: Vol. 2, No. 2). (Illus.). 257p. 1989. text ed. 39.95 (*0-86656-919-7*); pap. text ed. 14.95 (*0-86656-976-6*) Haworth Pr.

Relapse see Restoration Plays

Relapse & Addictive Behaviour. Michael Gossop. 224p. 1989. 35.00 (*0-415-02354-8*) Routledge.

***Relapse & Recovery Grid.** Hazelden Staff. 1996. pap. 3.50 (*0-89486-544-7*) Hazelden.

Relapse & Recovery in Drug Abuse. 1991. lib. bdg. 77.95 (*0-8490-4356-5*) Gordon Pr.

Relapse & Recovery in Drug Abuse: Research Analysis & Utilization System. 1992. lib. bdg. 95.00 (*0-8490-5498-2*) Gordon Pr.

Relapse & the Addict. Richard Dunn. 24p. (Orig.). 1986. pap. 2.00 (*0-89486-393-2*, 5410B) Hazelden.

Relapse Prevention. Dennis C. Daley. 1989. pap. 14.95 (*0-8306-9004-2*) Sulzburger & Graham Pub.

***Relapse Prevention.** Gregory L. Little. 40p. 1996. wbk. ed., pap. 10.00 (*0-9655392-1-0*) Advanced Trnging.

Relapse Prevention: Maintenance Strategies in the Treatment of Addictive Behaviors. Ed. by G. Alan Marlatt & Judith R. Gordon. LC 84-19319. (Guilford Clinical Psychology & Psychotherapy Ser.). 558p. 1985. lib. bdg. 52.00 (*0-89862-009-0*) Guilford Pr.

Relapse Prevention: Treatment Alternatives & Counseling Aids. Dennis C. Daley. Ed. by Lee M. Joiner. LC 88-873. 144p. (Orig.). 1988. pap. text ed. 14.95 (*0-943519-06-3*, B1906) Sulzburger & Graham Pub.

***Relapse Prevention for Addictive Behaviours.** S. Wanigaratne et al. (Illus.). 224p. 1990. write for info. (*0-632-02484-4*) Blackwell Sci.

Relapse Prevention in Drug & Alcohol Abuse. 1995. lib. bdg. 251.95 (*0-8490-6815-0*) Gordon Pr.

Relapse Prevention Therapy with Chemically Dependent Criminal Offenders Pt. 1: An Executive Briefing for Judges & Policymakers. Terence T. Gorski. 104p. (Orig.). 1995. pap. text ed. 9.00 (*0-8309-0646-0*, Indep Pr) Herald Hse.

Relapse Prevention Therapy with Chemically Dependent Criminal Offenders Pt. 2: A Guide for Counselors, Therapists, & Criminal Justice Professionals. Terence T. Gorski. (Orig.). 1994. pap. text ed. 12.00 (*0-8309-0644-4*, Indep Pr) Herald Hse.

Relapse Prevention Therapy with Chemically Dependent Criminal Offenders Pt. 3: The Relapse Prevention Workbook for the Criminal Offender. Terence T. Gorski. 155p. (Orig.). 1993. pap. text ed. 15.95 (*0-8309-0645-2*, Indep Pr) Herald Hse.

Relapse Prevention Treatment for Alcoholics & Other Addicted People. Maxie C. Maultsby, Jr. (Illus.). 233p. 1990. reprint ed. pap. 13.95 (*0-932838-03-0*) Tangrm Bks.

***Relapse Prevention with REBT.** F. Michler Bishop. wbk. ed. 19.95 incl. audio (*0-917476-26-3*, C050) Inst Rational-Emotive.

Relapse Prevention with Sex Offenders. Ed. by D. Richard Laws. LC 88-36840. 338p. 1989. lib. bdg. 42.00 (*0-89862-381-2*) Guilford Pr.

Relapse Prevention Workbook: For Recovering Alcoholics & Drug Dependent Persons. Dennis C. Daley. 32p. (Orig.). 1986. student ed., pap. 11.50 (*0-918452-88-0*, 880) Learning Pubns.

Relapse Prevention Workbook: Spanish Edition, for Recovering Alcoholics & Drug Dependent Persons. Dennis Daley. 1993. pap. 11.50 (*1-55691-096-7*, 967) Learning Pubns.

Relapse Prevention Workbook for Women. Karen Mattson. 48p. 1992. pap. 4.95 (*1-56246-030-7*, P187) Johnsn Inst.

Relapse Prevention Workbook for Youth in Treatment. Charlene Steen. Ed. by Euan Bear et al. (S. O. S. Ser.: No. 5). 160p. (Orig.). 1993. pap. 15.00 (*1-884444-02-4*) Safer Soc.

Relapse Risk Survey. Emil Chiauzzi. 1994. pap. 12.50 (*1-55691-112-2*, 122) Learning Pubns.

***Relapse Traps.** Robert D. Ramsey. 200p. (Orig.). Date not set. pap. text ed. 15.95 (*1-879899-00-0*) Newjoy Pr.

Related at Birth. Robert Davenport. pap. 12.00 (*0-517-88079-2*) Crown Pub Group.

Related Mathematics for Carpenters. 2nd ed. P. L. Reband. (Illus.). 218p. 1973. pap. 12.96 (*0-8269-2332-1*) Am Technical.

Related Sermons see Commentary on the Lord's Sermon on the Mount with Seventeen Related Sermons

***Related Strangers.** Wilson. Date not set. pap. 26.00 (*0-8006-2738-5*, Fortress Pr) Augsburg Fortress.

Related Strangers: Jews & Christians, 70-170 C.E. Stephen G. Wilson. LC 95-32217. 1995. pap. 26.00 (*0-8006-2950-7*) Augsburg Fortress.

Related Technical Subjects (Biological & Chemical), Sr. H. S. Jack Rudman. (Teachers License Examination Ser.: T-50). 1994. pap. 27.95 (*0-8373-8050-2*) Nat Learn.

Related Technical Subjects (Mechanical, Structural, Electrical), Sr. H. S. Jack Rudman. (Teachers License Examination Ser.: T-51). 1994. pap. 27.95 (*0-8373-8051-0*) Nat Learn.

Relatedness: Essays in Metaphysics & Theology. Harold H. Oliver. LC 84-1152. xvi, 178p. 1984. 14.50 (*0-86554-141-8*, MUP/H132) Mercer Univ Pr.

Relating. Judy Bisignano. 64p. (J). (gr. 3-8). 1985. student ed. 8.99 (*0-86653-331-1*, GA 678) Good Apple.

Relating. Mark Dunster. 16p. (Orig.). 1988. pap. 4.00 (*0-89642-162-7*) Linden Pubs.

Relating: An Astrological Guide to Living with Others on a Small Planet. Liz Greene. LC 83-145084. 289p. (Orig.). 1978. pap. 14.95 (*0-87728-418-0*) Weiser.

Relating: Dialogues & Dialectics. Leslie A. Baxter & Barbara M. Montgomery. 285p. 1996. lib. bdg. 42.00 (*1-57230-099-X*) Guilford Pr.

Relating: Dialogues & Dialectics. Leslie A. Baxter & Barbara M. Montgomery. LC 96-18281. (Guilford Communication Ser.). 285p. 1996. pap. text ed. 18.95 (*1-57230-101-5*, 0101) Guilford Pr.

Relating: Reflections of a Psychologist. Alan Rauchway. (Illus.). 108p. 1985. pap. 9.95 (*0-89529-290-4*) Avery Pub.

Relating & Interacting: An Introduction to Interpersonal Communication. Raymond S. Ross & Mark Ross. (Illus.). 320p. (C). 1982. pap. text ed. write for info. (*0-13-771923-X*) P-H.

Relating Curriculum & Transfer. Ed. by Arthur M. Cohen. LC 85-644753. (New Directions for Community Colleges Ser.: No. 86). 110p. (Orig.). 1994. pap. 19.00 (*0-7879-9958-X*) Jossey-Bass.

Relating Events in Narrative: A Crosslinguistic Developmental Study. Ruth A. Berman & Dan I. Slobin. LC 93-39190. 768p. 1994. text ed. 125.00 (*0-8058-1435-3*) L Erlbaum Assocs.

Relating Geophysical Structures & Processes: The Jeffreys Volume. Ed. by Keiiti Aki & Renata Dmowska. LC 93-28483. (Geophysical Monograph, Vol. 76; IUGG Ser.: Vol. 16). 133p. 1993. 27.00 (*0-87590-467-X*) Am Geophysical.

Relating Humanities & Social Thought. Abraham Edel. (Science, Ideology, & Values Ser.: Vol. IV). 314p. 1990. 44.95 (*0-88738-321-1*) Transaction Pubs.

Relating Knowledge to Teacher Education: Responding to NCATE's Knowledge Base & Related Standards. 1989. 18.00 (*0-89333-054-X*) AACTE.

Relating Mass & Volume. Conrad L. Stanitski & H. Anthony Neidig. (Modular Laboratory Program in Chemistry Ser.). 12p. (C). 1996. pap. text ed. 1.35 (*0-87540-484-7*, PROP 484-7) Chem Educ Res.

Relating Psychically: Psychic Influences on Relationships. Sandra Stevens. (Illus.). 152p. (Orig.). 1989. pap. 9.95 (*0-945946-01-5*) Cassandra Pr.

Relating Redefined: Discovering the New Language for Living. rev. ed. John Narciso & David Burkett. (Illus.). 127p. (C). 1994. pap. text ed. 12.95 (*1-879797-01-1*) Redman Wright.

***Relating Resources to Personnel Readiness: Use of Army Strength Management Models.** Rand Corp. Staff et al. LC 96-39448. (Illus.). xix, 91p. 1997. pap. 15.00 (*0-8330-2458-2*, 790-OSD) Rand Corp.

Relating Styles Participant Kit. Donald L. MacRae & Carl J. Hartleib. 1981. pap. text ed. 65.00 (*0-07-092327-2*) McGraw.

Relating Theory & Data: Essays on Human Memory in Honor of Bennet B. Murdock. Ed. by William Hockley & Stephen Lewandowsky. 576p. 1991. pap. 49.95 (*0-8058-0733-0*); text ed. 99.95 (*0-8058-0732-2*) L Erlbaum Assocs.

Relating to Others. Steve Duck. 174p. (C). 1989. pap. 25. 95 (*0-534-11106-8*); text ed. 34.95 (*0-534-11105-X*) Brooks-Cole.

***Relating to Others.** Steve Duck. Ed. by Anthony S. Manstead. (Mapping Social Psychology Ser.). 192p. 1988. 42.50 (*0-335-15339-9*, Open Univ Pr); pap. 13.99 (*0-335-15344-5*, Open Univ Pr) Taylor & Francis.

***Relating to People of Other Religions: What Every Christian Needs to Know.** M. Thomas Thangaraj. LC 97-1852. 112p. 1997. pap. 8.95 (*0-687-05139-8*) Abingdon.

***Relating to the Relatives: Breaking Bad News, Communication & Support.** Thurstan B. Brewin & Margaret Sparshott. LC 96-42946. 177p. 1996. pap. 24. 95 (*1-85775-081-0*, Radcliffe Med Pr) Scovill Paterson.

Relation. Diane Ward. (Roof Bks.). 64p. (Orig.). 1989. pap. 7.50 (*0-937804-32-0*) Segue NYC.

Relation als Vergleich: Die Relationstheorie Des Johannes Buridan im Kontext Seines Denkens Und Der Scholastik. Von Rolf Schonberger. LC 94-4097. (Studien und Texte zur Geistesgeschichte des Mittelalters Ser.: Vol. 43). 1994. 128.50 (*90-04-09854-2*) E J Brill.

Relation Analysis of the Fourth Gospel: A Study in Reader-Response Criticism. Philip B. Harner. LC 93-1708. (Biblical Press Ser.: Vol. 9). 192p. 1993. text ed. 79.95 (*0-7734-2364-8*, Mellen Biblical Pr) E Mellen.

Relation Between Association & the Higher Mental Processes. John W. Tilton. LC 71-177706. (Columbia University. Teachers College. Contributions to Education Ser.: No. 218). reprint ed. 37.50 (*0-404-55218-8*) AMS Pr.

Relation Between Factory Employment & Output since 1899. Solomon Fabricant. (Occasional Papers: No. 4). 40p. 1941. reprint ed. 20.00 (*0-87014-319-0*); reprint ed. mic. film 20.00 (*0-685-61222-8*) Natl Bur Econ Res.

Relation Between Final Demand & Income Distribution. C. Grootaert. (Lecture Notes in Economics & Mathematical Systems Ser.: Vol. 217). 105p. 1983. 27.00 (*0-387-12307-5*) Spr-Verlag.

Relation Between Grade School Record & High School Achievement: A Study of the Diagnostic Value of Individual Record Cards. Clay C. Ross. LC 70-177211. (Columbia University. Teachers College. Contributions to Education Ser.: No. 166). reprint ed. 37.50 (*0-404-55166-1*) AMS Pr.

Relation Between Laboratory & Space Plasmas. K. Kikuchi. 1981. lib. bdg. 129.50 (*90-277-1248-4*) Kluwer Ac.

R

Relation Between Linguistic Structure & Associative Interference in Artificial Linguistic Material. Dael L. Wolfle. (LM Ser.: No. 11). 1932. pap. 25.00 (*0-527-00815-X*) Periodicals Srv.

Relation Between Major World Problems & Systems Learning: Proceedings of the Society for General Systems Research, 1983. George E. Lasker. 800p. 1983. pap. text ed. 66.00 (*0-914105-28-0*) Intersystems Pubns.

Relation Between Physical & Mental Illness: The Physical Status of Psychiatric Patients at a Multiphasic Screening Survey. Ed. by Michael R. Eastwood. LC 74-76877. (Clarke Institute of Psychiatry, Monograph Ser.: No. 4). 133p. reprint ed. pap. 38.00 (*0-317-26915-1*, 2023611) Bks Demand.

Relation Between the Lord of a Mannor & the Coppy-Holder His Tenent, Etc. Charles Calthorpe. LC 74-38163. (English Experience Ser.: No. 440). 100p. 1972. reprint ed. 15.00 (*90-221-0440-0*) Walter J Johnson.

Relation Database Design. Charles J. Wertz. 1993. 46.95 (*0-8493-7450-2*, TK) CRC Pr.

Relation des Voyages a la Cote Occidentale d'Afrique d'Alvise de Ca' da Mosto 1455-1457. Charles M. Schefer. (B. E. Ser.: No. 161). (FRE.). 1895. 25.00 (*0-8115-3077-9*) Periodicals Srv.

***Relation Entre le Nombre des Enfants et de la Scolarisation: Le Cas de la Cote D'Ivoire et du Ghana.** Mark Montgomery et al. (LSMS Working Paper Ser.: No. 112-F). 108p. (FRE.). 1995. 8.95 (*0-8213-3374-7*, 13374) World Bank.

Relation Modules of Finite Groups. Karl W. Gruenberg. LC 76-3645. (CBMS Regional Conference Series in Mathematics: No. 25). 81p. 1976. pap. 23.00 (*0-8218-1675-6*, CBMS/25) Am Math.

Relation of Accelerated Normal & Retarded Puberty to the Height & Weight of School Children. Herman G. Richard. (SRCD M Ser.: Vol. 2, No. 1). 1937. pap. 25.00 (*0-527-01494-X*) Periodicals Srv.

Relation of Aging to Immunity. R. L. Walford et al. (Illus.). 220p. (C). 1973. text ed. 29.75 (*0-8422-7106-6*) Irvington.

Relation of Certain Anomalies of Vision & Lateral Dominance to Reading Disability. Philip W. Johnston. (SRCD M Ser.: Vol. 7, No. 2). 1942. 25.00 (*0-527-01523-7*) Periodicals Srv.

Relation of Certain Formal Attributes of Siblings to Attitudes Held Toward Each Other & Toward Their Parents. H. L. Koch. (SRCD M Ser.: Vol. 25, No. 4). 1960. 25.00 (*0-527-01586-5*) Periodicals Srv.

Relation of Coal Properties to Gasification Reactivity. Institute of Gas Technology Staff & J. L. Johnson. 270p. 1975. pap. 8.50 (*0-318-12688-5*, M60677) Am Gas Assn.

Relation of Cost to Output for a Leather Belt Shop. Joel Dean. (Technical Papers: No. 2). 80p. 1941. reprint ed. 20.00 (*0-87014-447-2*); reprint ed. mic. film 20.00 (*0-685-66190-3*) Natl Bur Econ Res.

Relation of Custom to Law. Gilbert T. Sadler. (Legal Reprint Ser.). viii, 86p. 1986. reprint ed. lib. bdg. 20.00 (*0-8377-2610-7*) Rothman.

Relation of Diu Krone to La Mule Sanz Frain. Lawrence L. Boll. LC 77-140018. (Catholic University Studies in German: No. 2). reprint ed. 37.50 (*0-404-50222-9*) AMS Pr.

Relation of Engineering Mechanics Research to the Practice of Civil Engineering: Engineering Mechanics Division Specialty Conference, Washington, D.C., October 12-14, 1966. American Society of Civil Engineers, Engineering Mechanics Division Staff. LC 67-1660. (Illus.). 867p. reprint ed. pap. 180.00 (*0-317-11018-7*, 2004904) Bks Demand.

Relation of Literature to Life. Charles D. Warner. 1977. 17.95 (*0-8369-7237-6*, 8036) Ayer.

***Relation of Load to Wear on Gear Teeth.** E. Buckingham. (Technical Papers). 1926. pap. text ed. 30.00 (*1-55589-237-X*) AGMA.

Relation of Maryland, 2 pts. LC 76-57399. (English Experience Ser.: No. 815). 1977. reprint ed. lib. bdg. 20.00 (*90-221-0815-5*) Walter J Johnson.

Relation of Moliere to the Restoration Comedy. John Wilcox. LC 64-14719. 1972. 23.95 (*0-405-09078-1*) Ayer.

***Relation of My Imprisonment.** Russell Banks. 128p. 1996. 29.00 (*0-8095-9195-2*) Borgo Pr.

Relation of My Imprisonment. Russell Banks. 128p. 1996. pap. 10.00 (*0-06-097680-2*) HarpC.

Relation of My Imprisonment. Russell Banks. LC 83-17873. 124p. 1984. 12.95 (*0-940650-25-8*) Sun & Moon CA.

Relation of My Imprisonment. deluxe limited ed. Russell Banks. LC 83-17873. 124p. 1984. 20.00 (*0-940650-24-X*) Sun & Moon CA.

Relation of Nature to Man in Aboriginal America. Clark Wissler. LC 75-160133. reprint ed. 45.00 (*0-404-07005-1*) AMS Pr.

Relation of Ore Deposition to Doming in the North American Cordillera. LC 60-2730. (Geological Society of America, Memoir Ser.: No. 77). 131p. reprint ed. pap. 37.40 (*0-317-10779-8*, 2007960) Bks Demand.

Relation of Parental Authority to Children's Behavior & Attitudes, Vol. 22. Marian J. Yarrow. LC 76-92312. 123p. 1969. reprint ed. text ed. 45.00 (*0-8371-2701-7*, YAPA, Greenwood Pr) Greenwood.

Relation of Proceedings Concerning the Affairs of the Kirk of Scotland. John L. Rothes. LC 79-174966. (Bannatyne Club, Edinburgh. Publications: No. 37). reprint ed. 38.50 (*0-404-52743-4*) AMS Pr.

Relation of Religion to Civil Government in the United States. Isaac J. Cornelison. LC 75-107409. (Civil Liberties in American History Ser.). 1970. reprint ed. lib. bdg. 45.00 (*0-306-71890-1*) Da Capo.

Relation of Sci-Tech Information to Environmental Studies. Ed. by Ellis Mount. LC 89-71657. (Science & Technology Libraries: Vol. 10, No. 2). 155p. 1990. text ed. 29.95 (*0-86656-988-X*) Haworth Pr.

Relation of Sensation to Other Categories in Contemporary Psychology. Carl Rahn. Bd. with Effect of Adaptation on the Temperature Difference. E. Abbott. ; No. 6. Iowa University Studies in Psychology. Carl E. Seashore. ; Exp'l & Introspective Study of the Human Learning Process in the Maze. F. A. Perrin. ; On the Psychophysiology of a Prolonged Fast. Herbert S. Langfeld. (Psychology Monographs General & Applied: Vol. 16). 1974. reprint ed. Set pap. 55.00 (*0-8115-1415-3*) Periodicals Srv.

Relation of Shell Form to Life Habits of the Bivalvia (Mollusca) Steven M. Stanley. LC 71-111441. (Geological Society of America, Memoir Ser.: No. 125). 310p. reprint ed. pap. 88.40 (*0-317-28382-0*, 2025463) Bks Demand.

Relation of Some Yeares Travaile Begunne Anno 1626, into Afrique & the Greater Asia. Thomas Herbert. LC 76-25706. (English Experience Ser.: No. 349). 1971. reprint ed. 50.00 (*90-221-0349-8*) Walter J Johnson.

Relation of the Executive Power to Legislation. Henry C. Black. LC 73-19130. (Politics & People Ser.). 192p. 1974. reprint ed. 15.95 (*0-405-05855-1*) Ayer.

Relation of the Expongnable Attempt & Conquest of the Ylande of Tercera. Alvaro De Bacan. LC 76-57352. (English Experience Ser.: No. 772). 1977. reprint ed. lib. bdg. 20.00 (*90-221-0772-8*) Walter J Johnson.

Relation of the Judiciary to the Constitution. William M. Meigs. LC 73-124896. (American Constitutional & Legal History Ser). 1971. reprint ed. lib. bdg. 35.00 (*0-306-71988-6*) Da Capo.

Relation of the Lord De-la-Warre, Lord Governour of the Colonie Planted in Virginea. Thomas West. LC 77-25508. (English Experience Ser.: No. 249). 20p. 1970. reprint ed. 15.00 (*90-221-0249-1*) Walter J Johnson.

Relation of the Mineral Salts of the Body to the Signs of the Zodiac. G. W. Carey. 1991. lib. bdg. 69.00 (*0-8490-4248-8*) Gordon Pr.

Relation of the Mineral Salts of the Body to the Signs of the Zodiac. George W. Carey et al. 50p. 1966. reprint ed. spiral bd. 7.00 (*0-7873-0146-9*) Hlth Research.

Relation of the People to the Land in Southern Iraq. Fuad Baali. LC 66-64914. (University of Florida Monographs: Social Sciences: No. 31). 74p. reprint ed. pap. 25.00 (*0-7837-5033-1*, 2044706) Bks Demand.

Relation of the Rate of Response to Intelligence see Influence of Intuition in the Acquisition of Skill

Relation of the Second Voyage to Guiana, No. 65. Lawrence Keymis. LC 76-6258. 48p. 1968. reprint ed. 20.00 (*90-221-0065-0*) Walter J Johnson.

Relation of the State to Private Education in Norway: A Study of the Historical Development of State Regulations Governing the Various Types of Private Education in Norway. Emma Arent. LC 74-176522. (Columbia University. Teachers College. Contributions to Education Ser.: No. 235). reprint ed. 37.50 (*0-404-55235-8*) AMS Pr.

Relation of the Successful Beginnings of the Lord Baltimore's Plantation in Mary-Land. Cecil Calvert & Baron Baltimore. LC 77-6864. (English Experience Ser.: No. 857). 1977. reprint ed. lib. bdg. 15.00 (*90-221-0857-0*) Walter J Johnson.

Relation of the Successfull Beginnings of the Lord Baltemore's Plantation in Mary-Land: Photographic Facsimile of 1634 Pamphlet. Intro. by Lois G. Carr. (Illus.). 64p. 1984. reprint ed. pap. 6.00 (*0-685-54617-9*) J C Brown.

Relation of the Swedish-American Newspaper to the Assimilation of Swedish Immigrants. Albert F. Schersten. LC 36-19550. (Augustana College Library Publication: No. 15). 102p. 1935. pap. 6.00 (*0-910182-10-8*) Augustana Coll.

Relation of the Synodical Month & Eclipses to the Maya Correlation Problem see Studies in Middle America

Relation of the Troubles Which Have Happened in New-England, by Reason of the Indians There from the Year 1614 to the Year 1675. Increase Mather. LC 78-141093. (Research Library of Colonial Americana). 1972. reprint ed. 16.95 (*0-405-03298-6*) Ayer.

Relation of Theoretical & Applied Linguistics. Ed. by O. M. Tomic & R. W. Shuy. LC 87-16198. (Topics in Language & Linguistics Ser.). (Illus.). 216p. 1987. 52.50 (*0-306-42630-7*, Plenum Pr) Plenum.

Relation of Theory to Practice in Psychotherapy. Ed. by Leonard D. Eron & Robert Callahan. LC 69-13705. 1969. 39.50 (*0-202-26017-8*) Irvington.

Relation of Thomas Jefferson to American Foreign Policy, 1783-1793. William K. Woolery. LC 78-64123. (Johns Hopkins University. Studies in the Social Sciences. Thirtieth Ser. 1912: 2). reprint ed. 37.50 (*0-404-61237-7*) AMS Pr.

Relation of Thomas Jefferson to American Foreign Policy, 1783-1793. William K. Woolery. (BCL1 - U. S. History Ser.). 128p. 1992. reprint ed. lib. bdg. 69.00 (*0-7812-6146-5*) Rprt Serv.

Relation of Thomas Jefferson to American Policy, 1783-1793. William K. Woolery. LC 70-131863. 1971. reprint ed. 9.00 (*0-403-00750-X*) Scholarly.

Relation of Two Trips to Peten: Made for the Conversion of the Heathen Ytzaex & Cehaches. Fray A. De Avendano y Loyola. Ed. by Frank E. Comparato. Tr. by Charles P. Bowditch & Guillermo Rivera. LC 86-80968. 84p. (Orig.). 1987. pap. 20.00 (*0-911437-06-1*) Labyrinthos.

Relation, or Journal, of a Late Expedition to the Gates of St. Augustine, on Florida: Conducted by the Hon. General James Oglethorpe, with a Detachment of His Regiment & from Georgia. Edward Kimber. LC 75-45209. (Floridiana Facsimile & Reprint Ser.). 1976. reprint ed. 9.95 (*0-8130-0412-8*) U Press Fla.

Relation or Journal of the Beginning of the English Plantation at Plymouth. LC 74-80210. (English Experience Ser.: No. 683). 1974. reprint ed. 20.00 (*90-221-0683-7*) Walter J Johnson.

Relation, or Rather a True Account of the Isle of England. Ed. by Charlotte A. Sneyd. LC 17-1218. (Camden Society, London Publications: No. 37). reprint ed. 35.00 (*0-404-50137-0*) AMS Pr.

Relational Aesthetic. Harold W. McSwain. LC 93-22887. (New Studies in Aesthetics: Vol. 18). 307p. (C). 1994. text ed. 58.95 (*0-8204-2185-5*) P Lang Pubng.

Relational Christianity: Experiencing Intimacy & Companionship with the Living God. Steve Meeks. (Orig.). 1991. pap. 5.00 (*0-9630425-0-5*) Calvary TX.

Relational Communication. 4th ed. William W. Wilmot. LC 94-32256. 1995. pap. text ed. 27.50 (*0-07-070740-5*) McGraw.

Relational Communication: Continuity & Change in Personal Relationships. Julia T. Wood. LC 94-22691. 326p. 1995. pap. 40.95 (*0-534-24306-1*) Wadsworth Pub.

Relational Concepts in Psychoanalysis: An Integration. Stephen A. Mitchell. LC 88-11168. 312p. 1988. 39.95 (*0-674-75411-5*) HUP.

Relational Data Base Management System. Andrew T. Hutt. LC 79-40516. (Wiley Series in Computing). (Illus.). 240p. reprint ed. pap. 68.40 (*0-7837-4390-4*, 2044130) Bks Demand.

Relational Database. Carter. (C). 1994. pap. text ed. 31.95 (*1-85032-255-4*) ITCP.

Relational Database. J. Carter. 1994. pap. 29.95 (*0-412-55090-3*, Blackie & Son-Chapman NY) Routledge Chapman & Hall.

Relational Database: Selected Writings. C. J. Date. (C). 1986. text ed. 43.25 (*0-201-14196-5*) Addison-Wesley.

Relational Database: Using dBASE III Plus. Will Price. 1988. Incl. 5.25" diskette. write for info. incl. disk (*0-07-556416-5*); pap. text ed. write for info. (*0-07-555426-7*) McGraw.

Relational Database Advisor: Elements of PC Database Design. Kimberly & Maughan Saunders. 256p. 1991. pap. 16.95 (*0-8306-2500-3*, Windcrest) TAB Bks.

Relational Database Design & Implementation Using Db2. Stephen L. Montgomery. 1990. text ed. 44.95 (*0-442-00134-7*) Van Nos Reinhold.

Relational Database Design & Programming. Carter. (ITCP-UK Computer Science Ser.). 1997. pap. 32.99 (*1-85032-272-4*) ITCP.

Relational Database (IBM 5.25 Using dBASE 3 Plus), Set. Price. 1988. text ed. write for info. (*0-07-556424-6*) McGraw.

Relational Database Management for Microcomputers: Design & Implementation. Jan L. Harrington. (C). 1988. text ed. 40.00 (*0-03-008542-X*) HB Coll Pubs.

Relational Database Management for Microcomputers: Design & Implementation. 2nd ed. Jan L. Harrington. 378p. (C). 1994. pap. text ed. 44.25 (*0-03-031588-3*) Dryden Pr.

Relational Database Management in the Unix Environment. Rod Manis et al. (Illus.). 576p. (C). 1988. pap. text ed. 28.00 (*0-13-771833-0*) P-H.

Relational Database Systems. Dan A. Simovico & Richard L. Tenney. LC 95-10873. (Illus.). 485p. 1995. text ed. 44.95 (*0-12-644375-0*) Acad Pr.

Relational Database Systems: Analysis & Comparison. Ed. by J. William Schmidt & M. L. Brodie. 618p. 1983. 49.00 (*0-387-12032-7*) Spr-Verlag.

Relational Database Technology. S. Alagic. (Texts & Monographs in Computer Science). (Illus.). 275p. 1986. 71.95 (*0-387-96276-X*) Spr-Verlag.

Relational Database Writings: 1985-1989. C. J. Date. (Illus.). 480p. (C). 1990. text ed. 43.25 (*0-201-50881-8*) Addison-Wesley.

Relational Database Writings: 1989-1991. C. J. Date. (Illus.). 544p. (C). 1992. text ed. 46.25 (*0-201-54303-6*) Addison-Wesley.

Relational Database Writings 1991-1994. C. J. Date. LC 94-34434. (Illus.). 544p. (C). 1995. text ed. 45.95 (*0-201-82459-0*) Addison-Wesley.

Relational Databases. Barry M. Eaglestone. 328p. (Orig.). 1991. pap. 42.50 (*0-7487-1176-7*, Pub. by Stanley Thornes UK) Trans-Atl Phila.

Relational Databases: Concepts & Systems. Georges Gardarin & Patrick Valduriez. (Illus.). 480p. (C). 1989. text ed. 31.25 (*0-201-09955-1*) Addison-Wesley.

Relational Databases: Concepts, Selection & Implementation. A. J. Page. 240p. (Orig.). 1990. pap. 37.50 (*1-85058-140-1*, Pub. by Sigma Press UK) Coronet Bks.

Relational Databases & SQL. Paul Mahler. (Illus.). 1993. pap. write for info. (*0-13-772310-5*) P-H.

***Relational Databases Explained.** Mark Whitehorn. 1997. pap. text ed. 34.95 (*3-540-76032-6*) Spr-Verlag.

Relational Directory: The Illinois Supplement. Ed. by Diana Hauman. 108p. 1993. 65.00 (*1-883760-04-6*) DDH Ent.

Relational Directory: Who Knows Whom in Chicago. 2nd ed. Ed. by Diana Hauman. 580p. 1993. Milwaukee. 195.00 (*1-883760-01-1*); Who Knows Whom in St. Louis, 25p. 185.00 (*1-883760-02-X*); Chicago. write for info. (*1-883760-03-8*) DDH Ent.

Relational Directory: Who Knows Whom in Detroit. Ed. by Diana Hauman. 250p. 1993. 185.00 (*1-883760-05-4*) DDH Ent.

Relational Directory: Who Knows Whom in Minnesota. Ed. by David Hauman & Diana Hauman. 1995. 245.00 (*1-883760-07-0*) DDH Ent.

Relational Directory: Who Knows Whom in Wisconsin. David Hauman & Diana Hauman. 380p. 1994. 245.00 (*1-883760-06-2*) DDH Ent.

Relational Grammar. Barry J. Blake. 208p. (C). 1990. pap. 17.95 (*0-415-04660-2*, A4010) Routledge.

Relational Grammar of Kinyarwanda. Alexandre Kimenyi. LC 78-57304. (University of California Publications in Social Welfare: No. 91). 264p. reprint ed. pap. 75.30 (*0-685-23810-5*, 2032917) Bks Demand.

Relational Matching. G. Vosselman. Ed. by G. Goos & J. Hartmanis. LC 92-25541. (Lecture Notes in Computer Science Ser.: Vol. 628). ix, 190p. 1992. 38.00 (*0-387-55798-9*) Spr-Verlag.

Relational Metaphysics. Harold H. Oliver. (Studies in Philosophy & Religion: No. 4). 242p. 1981. lib. bdg. 127.00 (*90-247-2457-0*, Pub. by M Nijhoff NE) Kluwer Ac.

Relational Model for Database Management. E. M. Codd. (Illus.). 400p. (C). 1990. text ed. 46.25 (*0-201-14192-2*) Addison-Wesley.

Relational Models of the Lexicon: Representing Knowledge in Semantic Networks. Ed. by Martha W. Evens. (Studies in Natural Language Processing). (Illus.). 400p. (C). 1989. 59.95 (*0-521-36300-4*) Cambridge U Pr.

Relational Perspectives in Psychoanalysis. Ed. by Neil J. Skolnick & Susan C. Warshaw. 392p. 1992. 49.95 (*0-88163-107-8*) Analytic Pr.

Relational Pulpit: Closing the Gap Between Preacher & Pew. Scott W. Alexander. LC 93-15201. 1993. 14.00 (*1-55896-309-X*) Unitarian Univ.

Relational Self: Theoretical Convergences of Psychoanalysis & Social Psychology. Ed. by Rebecca C. Curtis. LC 90-15734. 319p. 1991. lib. bdg. 41.95 (*0-89862-558-0*) Guilford Pr.

***Relational Systems Model for Family Therapy: Living in the Four Realities.** Donald R. Bardill. LC 96-4072. (Illus.). 274p. (C). 1996. pap. text ed. 24.95 (*0-7890-0183-7*) Haworth Pr.

Relational Systems Model for Family Therapy: Living in the Four Realities. Donald R. Bardill. LC 96-4072. (Illus.). 294p. (C). 1996. 34.95 (*0-7890-0074-1*) Haworth Pr.

Relational Theory of Computing. J. G. Sanderson. (Lecture Notes in Computer Science Ser.: Vol. 82). 147p. 1980. 23.00 (*0-387-09987-5*) Spr-Verlag.

Relational Transitions: The Evolution of Personal Relationships. Richard L. Conville. LC 91-4089. 208p. 1991. text ed. 49.95 (*0-275-93523-X*, C3523, Praeger Pubs) Greenwood.

Relational Typology. Ed. by Frans Plank. (Trends in Linguistics, Studies & Monographs: No. 28). xii, 443p. 1985. 161.55 (*0-89925-086-6*) Mouton.

Relational View of the Atonement: Prolegomenon to a Reconstruction of the Doctrine. David L. Wheeler. (American University Studies: Theology & Religion: Ser. VII, Vol. 54). 297p. (C). 1989. 51.95 (*0-8204-0883-2*) P Lang Pubng.

Relational Youth Ministry. Robert P. Stamschror. (Illus.). (Orig.). 1995. pap. 27.95 (*0-88489-351-0*) St Marys.

Relationes Historicae: Ein Bestandsverzeichnis der Deutschen Messrelationen Von 1583 Bis 1648. Ed. by Klaus Bender. (Beitraege Zur Kommunikationsgeschichte Ser.: Bd. 2). 294p. (GER.). (C). 1994. lib. bdg. 152.35 (*3-11-014045-4*) De Gruyter.

Relations: Family Portraits. Ed. by Kenneth Sherman. 144p. 1995. lib. bdg. 35.00 (*0-8095-4852-6*) Borgo Pr.

Relations & Graphs: Discrete Mathematics for Computer Scientists. G. Schmidt & T. Stohlein. Ed. by W. Brauer et al. (EATCS Monographs on Theoretical Computer Science). (Illus.). ix, 301p. 1993. 69.00 (*0-387-56254-0*) Spr-Verlag.

Relations & Representations: An Introduction to the Philosophy of Social Psychological Science. John D. Greenwood. 192p. (C). 1991. pap. 18.95 (*0-415-05515-6*, A5717) Routledge.

Relations & Revelations. David Herbert. 103p. 9300. 35.00 (*0-7206-0874-0*, Pub. by P Owen Ltd UK) Dufour.

Relations Between Arabs & Israelis Prior to the Rise of Islam. David S. Margoliouth. (British Academy, London, Schweich Lectures on Biblical Archaeology Series, 1930). 1974. reprint ed. pap. 25.00 (*0-8115-1263-0*) Periodicals Srv.

Relations Between Combinatorics & Other Parts of Mathematics. Ed. by D. Ray-Chaudhuri. LC 78-25979. (Proceedings of Symposia in Pure Mathematics Ser.: Vol. 34). 378p. 1979. reprint ed. pap. 44.00 (*0-8218-1434-6*, PSPUM/34) Am Math.

Relations Between Cultures. Ed. by George F. McLean & John Kromkowski. (Cultural Heritage & Contemporary Change Ser.: No. 4). 396p. (Orig.). 1991. 45.00 (*1-56518-009-7*, JC330.R45) Coun Res Values.

Relations Between Cultures. Ed. by George F. McLean & John Kromkowski. (Cultural Heritage & Contemporary Change Series VI: Foundations of Moral Education,: Vol. I, No. 4). 396p. (Orig.). 1991. pap. 17.50 (*1-56518-008-9*) Coun Res Values.

***Relations Between Freedom & Responsibility in the Evolution of Democratic Government.** Date not set. 17.95 (*0-405-05873-X*) Ayer.

Relations Between Freedom & Responsibility in the Evolution of Democratic Government. Arthur T. Hadley. LC 73-19151. (Politics & People Ser.). 186p. 1974. reprint ed. 10.00 (*0-685-49686-4*) Ayer.

***Relations Between Load Rating & Design Stresses of Gear Units.** C. B. Connell. (Technical Papers). 1936. pap. text ed. 30.00 (*1-55589-242-6*) AGMA.

Relations Between Normal Aging & Disease. Ed. by Horton A. Johnson. (Aging Ser.: Vol. 28). 270p. 1985. text ed. 119.00 (*0-88167-063-4*) Lppncott-Raven.

An Asterisk (*) at the beginning of an entry indicates that the title is appearing in BIP for the first time.

Relations Between Northern & Southern Baptists. rev. ed. Robert A. Baker. Ed. by Edwin S. Gaustad. LC 79-52590. (Baptist Tradition Ser.). 1980. reprint ed. lib. bdg. 25.95 (*0-405-12457-0*) Ayer.

Relations Between Psychopathological & Socio-Professional Factors in Out-Patient Department Psychiatry. Ed. by G. Leresche & J. Bovet. (Journal: Psychopathology: Vol. 19, Suppl. 1, 1986). (Illus.). 260p. 1986. pap. 62.50 (*3-8055-4332-8*) S Karger.

Relations Between Scholastic Achievement in a School of Social Work & Six Factors in Students Background. Thornton W. Merriam. LC 70-177072. (Columbia University. Teachers College. Contributions to Education Ser.: No. 616). reprint ed. 37.50 (*0-404-55616-7*) AMS Pr.

Relations Between State & Higher Education. Ed. by Roel I. Veld et al. LC 96-15020. (Legislating for Higher Education in Europe Ser.: Vol. 1). 1996. write for info. (*90-411-0245-0*) Kluwer Law Tax Pubs.

Relations Between Structure & Relations in Nuclear Physics: Proceedings. Ed. by Da-Hsuan Feng et al. 428p. 1987. text ed. 117.00 (*9971-5-0264-X*) World Scientific Pub.

Relations Between the Council of Europe & the U. N. (Regional Studies). pap. 3.00 (*92-1-157036-0*, E.75XV. RS-1) UN.

Relations Between the EC & International Organizations: Legal Theory & Practice. Rachel Frid. LC 95-45693. 1995. pap. text ed. 165.00 (*90-411-0155-1*) Kluwer Ac.

Relations Between the Laws of Babylonia & the Laws of the Hebrew Peoples. C. H. Johns. (British Academy, London, Schweich Lectures on Biblical Archaeology Series, 1930). 1974. reprint ed. pap. 25.00 (*0-8115-1254-1*) Periodicals Srv.

Relations Between the Netherlands Reformed Church & the Church of England since 1945. Peter Staples. LC 91-41521. 244p. 1992. lib. bdg. 89.95 (*0-7734-9639-4*) E Mellen.

Relations Between the Spanish-Americans & Anglo-Americans in New Mexico. Carolyn Zeleny. LC 73-14219. (Mexican American Ser.). (Illus.). 370p. 1975. 31.95 (*0-405-05692-3*) Ayer.

Relations, Bounds & Approximations for Order Statistics. Barry C. Arnold & N. Balakrishnan. (Lecture Notes in Statistics Ser.: Vol. 53). ix, 173p. 1989. 35.95 (*0-387-96975-6*) Spr-Verlag.

Relations in Industry. Jane Crolley. 464p. (C). 1989. pap. text ed. 74.00 (*0-13-445685-8*) P-H.

Relations into Rhetorics: Local Elite Social Structure in Norfolk England, 1540-1640. Peter S. Bearman. LC 92-35962. (Arnold & Caroline Rose Monograph Series of the American Sociological Association). 220p. (C). 1993. text ed. 40.00 (*0-8135-1968-3*) Rutgers U Pr.

Relations of Borehole Resistivity to the Horizontal Hydraulic Conductivity & Dissolved-Solids Concentration in Water of Clastic Coastal Plain Aquiferes in the Southeastern United States. Robert E. Faye & Winston G. Smith. 1994. write for info. (*0-318-70176-6*) US Geol Survey.

Relations of Development & Aging. Ed. by James E. Birren & Leon Stein. LC 79-8659. (Growing Old Ser.). (Illus.). 1980. reprint ed. lib. bdg. 30.95 (*0-405-12775-8*) Ayer.

***Relations of Language & Thought: The View from Sign Language & Deaf Children.** Ed. by Marc Marschark & Victoria Everhart. (Illus.). 224p. 1997. 39.95 (*0-19-510057-3*); pap. 19.95 (*0-19-510058-1*) OUP.

Relations of Literature & Science: A Selected Bibliography, 1930-1949. Ed. by Fred A. Dudley. LC 50-4895. 146p. reprint ed. pap. 41.70 (*0-317-10401-2*, 2000294) Bks Demand.

Relations of Literature & Science: An Annotated Bibliography of Scholarship, 1880-1980. Ed. by Walter Schatzberg et al. LC 87-26241. xix, 458p. 1987. pap. 8.00 (*0-87352-173-0*); lib. bdg. 12.00 (*0-87352-172-2*) Modern Lang.

Relations of Particles, Vol. 42: Lecture Notes in Physics. L. B. Okun. 168p. 1991. text ed. 48.00 (*981-02-0453-1*); pap. text ed. 23.00 (*981-02-0454-X*) World Scientific Pub.

Relations of Pennsylvania with the British Government, 1696-1765. Winfred T. Root. LC 71-99249. reprint ed. 51.50 (*0-404-00608-6*) AMS Pr.

Relations of Pennsylvania with the British Government, 1696-1765. Winfred T. Root. (BCL1 - United States Local History Ser.). 422p. 1991. reprint ed. lib. bdg. 99.00 (*0-7812-6278-X*) Rprt Serv.

Relations of Rescue: The Search for Female Moral Authority in the American West, 1874-1939. Peggy Pascoe. (Illus.). 328p. 1993. reprint ed. pap. 18.95 (*0-19-508430-6*) OUP.

Relations of Ruling: Class & Gender in Postindustrial Societies. Wallace Clement & John Myles. LC 93-90666. 320p. (C). 1994. 55.00 (*0-7735-1164-4*, Pub. by McGill CN); pap. text ed. 19.95 (*0-7735-1178-4*, Pub. by McGill CN) U of Toronto Pr.

Relations of Shirley's Plays to the Elizabethan Drama. Robert S. Forsythe. LC 65-19615. 1972. 30.95 (*0-405-08528-1*, Pub. by Blom Pubns UK) Ayer.

Relations of the Sexes. Eliza B. Duffey. LC 73-20619. (Sex, Marriage & Society Ser.). 320p. 1974. reprint ed. 26.95 (*0-405-05824-1*) Ayer.

Relations of the United States & Spain: The Spanish-American War, 2 vols., Set. French E. Chadwick. (History - United States Ser.). 1992. reprint ed. lib. bdg. 150.00 (*0-7812-6210-0*) Rprt Serv.

Relations Particularized see Universals & Property Instances

Relations Politiques de la France et de l' Espagne avec l' Ecosse au Seizieme Siecle, 5 vols. Ed. by Jean B. Teulet. Incl. Vol. 1. Correspondences Francais 1515-1560. LC 77-176145. 47.50 (*0-404-52891-0*); Vol. 2. Correspondences Francaises 1559-1573. LC 77-176145. 47.50 (*0-404-52892-9*); Vol. 3. Correspondences Francaises 1575-1585. LC 77-176145. 47.50 (*0-404-52893-7*); Vol. 4. Correspondences Francaises 1585-1603. LC 77-176145. 47.50 (*0-404-52894-5*); Vol. 5. Correspondences Espagnoles 1562-1588. LC 77-176145. 47.50 (*0-404-52895-3*); LC 77-176145. (Bannatyne Club, Edinburgh. Publications: No. B). (FRE.). reprint ed. 237.50 (*0-404-52890-2*) AMS Pr.

Relations, Vol. 66: From Having to Being Annual ACPA Proceedings, 1992. Ed. by Therese-Anne Druart. 1993. pap. 20.00 (*0-918090-26-1*) Am Cath Philo.

Relationshift. Jacinth I. Baublitz. 216p. (Orig.). 1983. pap. 15.95 (*0-9610316-0-3*) J I Baublitz.

Relationship. John H. Hyman. (Illus.). 251p. (YA). (gr. 7 up). 1995. 16.95 (*1-880664-14-3*) E M Pr.

Relationship: The Heart of Helping People. Helen H. Perlman. LC 78-19064. x, 246p. 1983. pap. text ed. 11.95 (*0-226-66036-2*) U Ch Pr.

***Relationship: The Story of a Mission in the Dominican Republic.** Troy White, Sr. (Illus.). 146p. (Orig.). 1997. pap. 10.00 (*1-57502-469-1*, P01400) Morris Pubng.

Relationship among the Mixe-Zoquean Languages of Mexico. Soren Wichmann. (Studies in Indigenous Languages of the Americas). 469p. (C). 1995. text ed. 55.00 (*0-87480-487-6*) U of Utah Pr.

Relationship Banking: Cross Selling the Banks Products & Services to Meet Your Customers. Dwight S. Ritter. 1993. text ed. 37.50 (*1-55738-381-2*) Irwin Prof Pubng.

Relationship Between Agricultural Policy & Forestry in the Southern Region of the United States. Bassam C. Hamdar. LC 92-27798. (Government & the Economy: Outstanding Studies & Recent Dissertations). 192p. 1993. text ed. 15.00 (*0-8153-1225-3*) Garland.

Relationship Between Attitude & Information Concerning the Japanese in America. Gwynn Nettler. Ed. by Robert K. Merton & Harriet Zuckerman. LC 79-9016. (Dissertations on Sociology Ser.). 1980. lib. bdg. 21.95 (*0-405-12984-X*) Ayer.

Relationship Between Child Antropometry & Mortality in Developing Countries: Implications for Policy, Progress, & Future Research. David L. Pelletier. (Monographs). (Illus.). 72p. (C). 1991. pap. text ed. 12.00 (*1-56401-012-0*) Cornell Food.

Relationship Between Chlorine in Waste Streams & Dioxin Emissions from Waste Combustor Stacks Vol. 36: The Relationship Between Chlorine in Waste Streams & Dioxin Emissions from Waste Combustor Stacks. H. G. Rigo et al. (CRTD Ser.: Vol. 36). 716p. 1995. 100.00 (*0-7918-1222-7*, I00385) ASME.

Relationship Between Christian Liberty & Love. Nelson D. Kloosterman. 152p. (Orig.). Date not set. pap. 10.90 (*0-921100-30-2*) Inhtce Pubns.

***Relationship Between Emotional Expression, Treatment, & Outcome in Psychotherapy: An Empirical Study.** Rita Rosner. LC 96-41164. (European University Studies: Series 6, Vol. 565). 137p. 1996. pap. text ed. 35.95 (*0-8204-2983-X*) P Lang Pubng.

Relationship Between Employment & Unemployment. M. J. Dicks & N. Hatch. (Bank of England Discussion Papers: Vol. 39). (Illus.). 56p. 1989. reprint ed. pap. 25.00 (*0-608-01648-9*, 2062300) Bks Demand.

Relationship Between Engine Oil Viscosity & Engine Performance: Symposium. T. W. Selby. LC 77-150198. (ASTM Special Technical Publication Ser.: Vol. 621). (Illus.). 116p. 1977. reprint ed. pap. 33.10 (*0-7837-9114-3*, 2049532) Bks Demand.

***Relationship Between Expenditure-Based Plans & Development Plans: With Specific Reference to Housing.** N. Carter et al. (Progress in Planning Ser.: Vol. 39). 69p. 1992. 66.25 (*0-08-042187-3*, Pergamon Pr) Elsevier.

Relationship Between Herodotus' History & Primary History. Sara Mandell & David N. Freedman. LC 93-16100. (USF Studies in the History of Judaism: No. 60). 207p. 1993. 44.95 (*1-55540-838-9*, 240060) Scholars Pr GA.

Relationship Between High-Temperature Oil Rheology & Engine Operation: A Status Report DS-62. James A. Spearot. LC 85-15747. (Illus.). 140p. 1985. pap. text ed. 16.00 (*0-8031-0448-0*, 05-894000-12) ASTM.

***Relationship Between HIV & Other Conditions.** write for info. (*0-340-58715-6*, Pub. by E Arnold UK) Routledge Chapman & Hall.

Relationship Between House Prices & Land Supply. 120p. 1992. pap. 30.00 (*0-11-752593-6*, HM25936, Pub. by Stationery Ofc UK) Bernan Associates.

Relationship Between Neoplatonism & Christianity. Ed. by Thomas Finan & Vincent Twomey. 192p. 1992. 37.50 (*1-85182-085-X*, Pub. by Four Cts Pr IE) Intl Spec Bk.

Relationship Between Parapsychology & Gravity. J. G. Gallimore. (Handbook of Unusual Energies Ser.: Vol. 3). 215p. 1977. reprint ed. spiral bd. 52.00 (*0-7873-1024-7*) Hlth Research.

Relationship Between Prefrontal & Limbic Cortex: A Comparative Anatomical Review. Ed. by R. Reep. (Journal: Brain, Behavior & Evolution: Vol. 25, Nos. 1-2). (Illus.). 80p. 1985. pap. 44.00 (*3-8055-4033-7*) S Karger.

Relationship Between Religion & Mental Health. Ed. by Dinesh Bhugra. LC 94-47489. 240p. (C). (gr. 13). 1996. text ed. 65.00 (*0-415-08955-7*, B4333) Routledge.

Relationship Between Safety & Key Highway Features. (State of the Art Reports: No. 6). 110p. 1987. 59.95 (*0-309-04502-9*) Transport Res Bd.

Relationship Between Science & Technology: An Anthology of Historical & Philosophical Articles from "Technology & Culture" Ed. & Contrib. by David F. Channell. 320p. 1995. pap. text ed. 19.95 (*0-226-10117-7*); lib. bdg. 42.00 (*0-226-10116-9*) U Ch Pr.

Relationship Between Site Design & Travel Behavior. Rebecca L. Ocken. LC 95-3538. (CPL Bibliographies Ser.). (Illus.). 31p. 1994. pap. 10.00 (*0-86602-312-7*, Sage Prdcls Pr) Sage.

Relationship Between Social & Cognitive Development. Ed. by Willis F. Overton. (Jean Piaget Society Ser.). 272p. (C). 1983. text ed. 49.95 (*0-89859-249-6*) L Erlbaum Assocs.

Relationship Between the Universal Priesthood of the Baptized & the Ministerial Priesthood of the Ordained in Vatican II & in Subsequent Theology No. 10: Understanding "Essentia et Non Gradu," Lumen Gentium. Melvin Michalski. LC 95-39806. (Understanding "Essentia Et Non Gradu Tantum," Lumen Gentium Ser.: No. 10). 290p. 1996. write for info. (*0-7734-2264-1*) E Mellen.

Relationship Between Theory & Practice in Social Work. Bernece K. Simon. 55p. 1960. pap. text ed. 8.95 (*0-87101-337-1*) Natl Assn Soc Wkrs.

Relationship Between User Interface Design & Human Performance. Jane Carey. LC 96-25518. (Human Factors in Information Systems Ser.: Vol. 4). 300p. Date not set. pap. 39.50 (*1-56750-285-7*) Ablex Pub.

***Relationship Between User Interface Design & Human Performance.** Jane Carey. (Human Factors in Information Systems Ser.: Vol. 4). 300p. Date not set. text ed. 73.25 (*1-56750-286-5*) Ablex Pub.

Relationship Book: The Adolescent's Guide for Learning the Relationship Skills. Richard D. Solomon & Elaine C. Solomon. 125p. 1987. pap. text ed. 12.95 (*0-9617198-4-2*) NIRT Inc.

Relationship Breakdown Wills & Probate. John Thurston. 80p. 1992. 33.00 (*1-85190-170-1*, Pub. by Tolley Pubng UK) St Mut.

Relationship Building & Transforming: The Levels of Platonic & Erotic Love. Terence T. Gorski. 111p. (Orig.). 1993. pap. text ed. 7.50 (*0-8309-0638-X*) Herald Hse.

Relationship Cards...How to Get along with the One That You Love. Deborah Thornton. 78p. 1994. student ed. 14.00 (*0-9636638-8-7*) Inspirat Prayer.

Relationship-Centered Counseling: An Integration of Art & Science. Eugene W. Kelly, Jr. 304p. 1994. 33.95 (*0-8261-8210-0*) Springer Pub.

Relationship Conflict: Conflict in Parent-Child, Friendship & Romantic Relationship. Daniel J. Canary et al. (Series on Close Relationships: Vol. 10). 200p. 1995. 38.00 (*0-8039-5129-9*); pap. 16.95 (*0-8039-5130-2*) Sage.

Relationship Dynamics: Theory & Analysis. James Musgrave & Michael Anniss. (Illus.). 256p. 1996. 26.00 (*0-684-82449-3*) Free Pr.

Relationship Enhancement: Skill-Training Programs for Therapy, Problem Prevention, & Enrichment. Bernard G. Guerney, Jr. LC 76-11884. (Social & Behavioral Science Ser.). (Illus.). 421p. 45.95 (*0-87589-310-4*) Jossey-Bass.

***Relationship Enhancement Family Therapy.** Barry G. Ginsberg. LC 96-46033. (Wiley Series in Couples & Family Dynamics & Treatment). 1997. text ed. 47.50 (*0-471-04955-7*) Wiley.

Relationship Fundraising. Ken Burnett. (Illus.). 332p. 1995. 40.00 (*0-9518971-0-1*) Bonus Books.

Relationship Investing: What Active Institutional Investors Want from Management. John W. Kensinger & John Martin. LC 95-60288. 122p. (Orig.). 1996. pap. text ed. 35.00 (*1-885065-05-1*, 096-03) Finan Exec.

Relationship Management of the Borderline Patient: From Understanding to Treatment. David L. Dawson & Harriet L. MacMillan. LC 93-18886. (Illus.). 240p. 1993. text ed. 30.95 (*0-87630-714-4*) Brunner-Mazel.

Relationship Marketing. Regis Mckenna. 288p. 1991. 19.95 (*0-201-56769-5*) Addison-Wesley.

***Relationship Marketing.** Merlin Stone & Neil Woodcock. (Personal Development Ser.). 1995. pap. 19.95 (*0-7494-1755-2*) Kogan Page Ltd.

Relationship Marketing: Bringing Quality, Customer Service & Marketing Together. Martin Christopher et al. (CIM Professional Development Ser.). 224p. 1993. pap. 32.95 (*0-7506-0978-8*) Buttrwrth-Heinemann.

Relationship Marketing: Successful Strategies for the Age of the Customer. Regis McKenna. 256p. 1993. pap. 15.00 (*0-201-62240-8*) Addison-Wesley.

Relationship Marketing: Theory & Practice. Ed. by Francis Buttle. 240p. 1996. pap. 34.95 (*1-85396-313-5*, Pub. by Paul Chapman UK) Taylor & Francis.

Relationship Marketing for Competitive Advantage: Winning & Keeping Customers. Martin Christopher et al. (Illus.). 350p. 1995. pap. 47.95 (*0-7506-2020-X*) Buttrwrth-Heinemann.

***Relationship Marketing in Professional Services: A Study of Agency-Client Dynamics in the Advertising Sector.** Aino Halinen. LC 96-7702. 336p. (C). 1996. text ed. 75.00 (*0-415-14607-0*) Routledge.

Relationship Morality. J. Kellenberger. LC 94-15347. 448p. 1995. 57.50 (*0-271-01404-0*); pap. 19.95 (*0-271-01405-9*) Pa St U Pr.

Relationship of Adaptation & Fun & Pleasure to Psychological Growth: An Appendix to Homosexuality: The Psychology of the Creative Process. Paul Rosenfels. LC 86-142926. (Ninth Street Center Monographs). (Orig.). 1975. pap. 3.95 (*0-932961-01-0*) Ninth St Ctr.

Relationship of Asphalt Cement Properties to Pavement Durability. (National Cooperative Highway Research Program Report Ser.: No. 59). 43p. 1979. 5.60 (*0-309-02911-2*) Transport Res Bd.

Relationship of Calvin to Process Theology As Seen Through His Sermons. Blair Reynolds. LC 93-32120. (Texts & Studies in Religion: Vol. 61). 112p. 1993. text ed. 59.95 (*0-7734-9355-7*) E Mellen.

Relationship of Histology to Cancer Treatment: Proceedings of the West Coast Cancer Symposium, 9th Annual, San Francisco, 1973. West Coast Cancer Symposium Staff. Ed. by J. M. Vaeth. (Frontiers of Radiation Therapy & Oncology Ser.: Vol. 9). 200p. 1974. 113.75 (*3-8055-1748-3*) S Karger.

Relationship of Library User Studies to Performance Measures: A Review of the Literature. Ronald R. Powell. (Occasional Papers: No. 181). (Orig.). 1988. pap. 2.50 (*0-685-34544-0*) U of Ill Grad Sch.

Relationship of Man & Nature in the Modern Age: Dominion over the Earth. Ed. by Denis C. Lehotay. LC 93-10128. (Illus.). 284p. 1993. 89.95 (*0-7734-9273-9*) E Mellen.

***Relationship of Measured Gear Noise to Measured Gear Transmission Errors.** Robert E. Smith. (1987 Fall Technical Meeting). 1987. pap. text ed. 30.00 (*1-55589-482-8*) AGMA.

Relationship of Oral & Literate Performance Processes in the Commedia Dell'Arte: Beyond the Improvisation-Memorisation Divide. Tim Fitzpatrick. LC 94-47053. (Illus.). 468p. 1995. text ed. 109.95 (*0-7734-9003-5*) E Mellen.

Relationship of Organic Matter & Mineral Diagenesis. Donald L. Gautier et al. (Short Course Notes Ser.: No. 17). 279p. 1985. pap. 24.00 (*0-918985-51-X*) SEPM.

Relationship of Painting & Literature: A Guide to Information Sources. Ed. by Eugene L. Huddleston & Douglas A. Noverr. LC 78-53436. (American Studies Information Guide: Vol. 4). 208p. 1978. 68.00 (*0-8103-1394-4*) Gale.

Relationship of Prices to Economic Stability & Growth. U. S. Congress, Joint Economic Committee. LC 79-90718. 1959. reprint ed. lib. bdg. 29.50 (*0-8371-2897-8*, REOP, Greenwood Pr) Greenwood.

Relationship of Reform: Immigrants & Progressives in the Far West. Leslie Koepplin. LC 90-3253. (European Immigrants & American Society Ser.). 224p. 1990. reprint ed. text ed. 15.00 (*0-8240-0259-8*) Garland.

***Relationship of Sympathy: The Writer & the Reader in British Romanticism.** Thomas J. McCarthy. LC 96-41036. (Nineteenth Century Ser.). 192p. 1997. text ed. 67.95 (*1-85928-315-2*, Pub. by Ashgate UK) Ashgate Pub Co.

Relationship of the Mineral Salts of the Body to the Signs of the Zodiac. George W. Carey. 50p. 1992. pap. 5.00 (*0-89540-208-4*, SB-208, Sun Bks) Sun Pub.

Relationship of the Tetracoralla to the Hexacoralla. W. I. Robinson. (Connecticut Academy of Arts & Sciences Ser., Trans.: Vol. 21). 1917. pap. 49.50 (*0-685-22842-8*) Elliots Bks.

Relationship of Theory & Research. 2nd ed. Jacqueline Fawcett & Florence S. Downs. (Illus.). 334p. 1992. text ed. 50.00 (*0-8036-3415-3*) Davis Co.

Relationship of Verbal & Non-Verbal Communication. Ed. by Mary R. Key. (Contributions to the Sociology of Language Ser.: No. 25). 1980. pap. text ed. 21.55 (*90-279-7637-6*) Mouton.

Relationship Play Therapy. Clark Moustakas. LC 96-9434. 232p. 1997. 35.00 (*0-7657-0029-8*) Aronson.

Relationship Renewal: Step up to Intimacy. Diane Anderson & Glenn Anderson. 179p. 1992. student ed. 15.00 (*0-9647544-0-1*) Wolf Song.

Relationship Renewal Kit: Getting to the Heart of What Matters Most, 2 wkbks. Mary S. Moore. LC 94-92391. 1995. pap. text ed. 11.95 (*1-885574-00-2*) Courage Press.

Relationship Restored: Trends in U. S. - China Educational Exchanges, 1978-1984. David M. Lampton & Joyce A. Madancy. LC 86-61028. 286p. reprint ed. pap. 81.60 (*0-7837-1797-0*, 2041998) Bks Demand.

Relationship Revolution: A Baby Boomers Guide to Finding Love. Phyllis Phipps. 1993. pap. 10.95 (*0-9638341-9-3*) Summer Hill.

Relationship Roller Coaster: Riding Out the Ups & Downs. Anthony Andrews-Speed. LC 94-66824. 176p. (Orig.). 1994. pap. 14.95 (*0-9638880-1-3*) Osmyrrah Pub.

Relationship Selling: Building Trust to Sell Your Service. 2nd rev. ed. Karen Johnston & Jean Withers. (Business Ser.). 120p. 1992. pap. 12.95 (*0-88908-529-3*) Self-Counsel Pr.

Relationship Skills. Roberta Damon. Ed. by Gina Howard. 68p. 1993. pap. text ed. 5.95 (*1-56309-082-1*, New Hope) Womans Mission Union.

Relationship Strategies: The E & P Attraction. John G. Kappas. Ed. by George Kappas. 336p. 1992. pap. 19.95 (*0-614-04956-3*) Panorama Van Nuys.

Relationship Systems of the Tlingit, Haida, & Tsimshian. Theresa M. Durlach. LC 73-3547. (American Ethnological Society Publications: No. 11). reprint ed. 31.50 (*0-404-58161-7*) AMS Pr.

***Relationship Tool Box: Empowering Tools for Your Every Day Interactions.** Robert Abel. (Illus.). 500p. (Orig.). 1997. pap. 18.95 (*0-9657666-2-4*) Valntne Pub.

Relationship Triangles. Philip J. Guerin et al. LC 96-33339. (Guilford Family Therapy Ser.). 1996. lib. bdg. 27.95 (*1-57230-143-0*, 0143) Guilford Pr.

Relationship Workbook for Teens: What You Can Do to Attract That Special Someone. Judy Zerafa. (Illus.). 58p. (Orig.). 1996. student ed., pap. 6.95 (*0-944815-01-4*) Confidence Build.

Relationships. (YouthTalk Ser.). 48p. (YA). 1994. 5.25 (*0-8066-0263-5*, 15-5218); teacher ed., pap. 4.95 (*0-8066-0264-3*, 15-5219) Augsburg Fortress.

***Relationships.** (YouthSearch: Small-Group Resources Ser.). 64p. 1995. pap. 4.95 (*0-687-00599-X*) Abingdon.

Relationships. Center for Learning Network Staff. (Junior High Religion Ser.). 48p. 1992. teacher ed., spiral bd. 7.95 (*1-56077-186-0*); student ed., per. 5.95 (*1-56077-232-8*) Ctr Learning.

*__Relationships.__ Anthony Cronin. 48p. 9400. pap. 10.95 (*1-874597-06-5*) Dufour.

Relationships. Dunn & Eyre. 1990. pap. 4.95 (*0-88494-748-3*) Bookcraft Inc.

Relationships. Robert J. McManimie. 106p. (C). 1992. pap. text ed. 9.95 (*0-9631253-1-1*) Devsyn.

Relationships. Elizabeth Tener. LC 94-31056. (Teen Hotline Ser.). 1995. lib. bdg. 25.68 (*0-8114-3818-X*) Raintree Steck-V.

Relationships: A Study Guide. Dean Sherman. (Illus.). 80p. 1985. audio, lp 24.95 (*0-935779-07-8*); vhs 69.95 (*0-935779-08-6*) Crown Min.

Relationships: A Workbook. Jean Kirkpatrick. 39p. 7.95 (*0-317-05941-6*) WFS.

Relationships: Adult Children of Alcoholics. Joseph F. Perez. LC 87-21105. 1989. 23.95 (*0-89876-150-6*) Gardner Pr.

Relationships: An Anthology of Contemporary Austrian Prose. Ed. by Adolf Opel. (Studies in Austrian Literature, Culture, & Thought. Translation Ser.). 362p. 1991. pap. 25.00 (*0-929497-05-8*) Ariadne CA.

Relationships: How to be a Winner! George B. Eager. (Illus.). (Orig.). (YA). (gr. 6-12). 1993. pap. 3.00 (*1-879224-08-9*) Mailbox.

Relationships: How to Have Relationships, God's Way. Ashley Lee. 96p. 1995. pap. 7.95 (*0-9643797-0-8*) Ashley Lee.

Relationships: New Work by Sandra Rowe. Charles Gaines. (University Art Gallery, 1990 Ser.: No. 2). 60p. 1990. pap. text ed. 10.00 (*0-932173-05-5*) Sweeney Art Gallery.

Relationships: No One Taught Us How to Live Happily Ever After. pap. write for info. (*0-9632072-0-2*) A M B Ent.

Relationships: The Art of Making Life Work. John-Roger. 200p. 1986. 15.00 (*0-914829-50-5*) Mandeville LA.

Relationships: The Heart of Youth Ministry. John Walters et al. (Illus.). 80p. 1994. student ed. 49.95 incl. vhs (*0-9638739-2-X*) Bd Christ Educ.

*__Relationships: Transforming Archetypes.__ Marina Valcarenghi. LC 96-52506. (Illus.). 288p. (Orig.). 1997. pap. 14.95 (*0-89254-034-6*) Nicolas-Hays.

*__Relationships: What It Takes to Be a Friend.__ Pamela Reeve. LC 96-44079. 96p. 1997. 10.99 (*1-57673-044-1*, Multnomah Bks) Multnomah Pubs.

Relationships: Yours-Mine-Ours. Ed. by Molli Nickell. (Celebration of Discovery Ser.: Vol. III). (Illus.). 192p. 1989. pap. 12.95 (*0-938283-02-2*) Spirit Speaks.

Relationships - Conclusions. Karlyn Kamm & Gerald Chastain, Jr. (Solar Reading - Flight One Ser.). (J). (gr. 3). 70.00 incl. disk (*0-912899-13-1*) Lrning Multi-Systs.

Relationships & Development. Ed. by William W. Hartup & Z. Rubin. 240p. 1986. text ed. 49.95 (*0-89859-621-1*) L Erlbaum Assocs.

Relationships & Life Cycles. 2nd rev. ed. Stephen Arroyo. (Illus.). 240p. 1993. pap. 12.00 (*0-916360-55-5*) CRCS Pubns CA.

Relationships & Mechanisms in the Periodic Table. (Topics in Current Chemistry Ser.: Vol. 150). (Illus.). 290p. 1989. 141.95 (*0-387-50045-6*) Spr-Verlag.

Relationships & Well-Being Over the Life Stages. Pat M. Keith & Robert B. Schafer. LC 91-11078. 192p. 1991. text ed. 49.95 (*0-275-93422-5*, C3422, Praeger Pubs) Greenwood.

Relationships at Risk: Assessing Your Kid's Drug Abuse Potential. Timothy Titus. LC 90-81091. (Illus.). 49p. 1990. student ed. 6.95 (*0-925190-02-0*) Fairview Press.

Relationships Between Active Galactic Nuclei & Starburst Galaxies. Ed. by A. Filippenko. (ASP Conference Series Proceedings: Vol. 31). 468p. 1992. 28.00 (*0-937707-50-3*) Astron Soc Pacific.

Relationships Between Expressed Preferences & Curricular Abilities of Ninth Grade Boys. Oliver K. Garretson. LC 76-176976. (Columbia University. Teachers College. Contributions to Education Ser.: No. 396). reprint ed. 37.50 (*0-404-55396-6*) AMS Pr.

Relationships Between Health & Social Education PSSC & HEc. 1976. 45.00 (*0-317-05771-5*, Pub. by Natl Inst Soc Work) St Mut.

*__Relationships Between Mechanical Properties of Fibres & Mechanical Properties of Yarns.__ J. Y. Drean et al. 1991. pap. 42.00 (*0-614-20950-1*, Pub. by Textile Inst UK) St Mut.

Relationships Between School Taxes & Town Taxes in Vermont Local Government. Leonard J. Tashman & Michael J. Munson. (Occasional Papers: No. 8). (Illus.). 38p. (Orig.). 1984. pap. text ed. 3.50 (*0-944277-13-6*, T24) U VT Ctr Rsch VT.

Relationships Between Score & Choreography in Twentieth-Century Dance: Music, Movement & Metaphor. Paul Hodgins. LC 92-10794. (Illus.). 240p. 1992. lib. bdg. 89.95 (*0-7734-9552-5*) E Mellen.

Relationships Between Structure & Function of Cytochrome P-450: Experiments, Calculations, Models. Ed. by Klaus Ruckpaul & Horst Rein. (Frontiers in Biotransformation Ser.: Vol. 7). 370p. 1993. 140.00 (*0-685-67332-4*, Pub. by Akademie Verlag GW) Wiley.

*__Relationships Between Women in Later Life.__ Ed. by Karen A. Roberto. LC 96-30653. (Journal of Women & Aging Ser.: Vol. 8, Nos. 3/4). 204p. (C). 1996. pap. 14.95 (*1-56023-091-6*, Haworth Pastrl) Harrington Pk.

*__Relationships Between Women in Later Life.__ Ed. by Karen A. Roberto. LC 96-30653. (Journal of Women & Aging: Vol. 8, Nos. 3/4). 204p. (C). 1996. 34.95 (*0-7890-0009-1*, Haworth Pastrl) Haworth Pr.

Relationships, Chronic Illness, & Disability. Renee F. Lyons et al. (Series on Close Relationships: Vol. 11). 176p. 1995. 38.00 (*0-8039-4703-8*); pap. 16.95 (*0-8039-4704-6*) Sage.

Relationships Handbook. George S. Pransky. 1991. 9.95 (*0-8306-3834-2*) McGraw-Hill Prof.

Relationships in Dermatology: The Skin & Mouth, Eye, Sarcoidosis, Porphyria. Ed. by Julian L. Verbov. (New Clinical Applications Dermatology Ser.). (C). 1988. lib. bdg. 79.00 (*0-7462-0097-8*) Kluwer Ac.

Relationships in Early Childhood: Helping Young Children Grow. Erna Furman. 150p. 1997. pap. 24.95 (*0-8236-8272-2*, 25788) Intl Univs Pr.

Relationships in Marriage & Family. 3rd ed. Nick Stinnet & Nancy Stinnet. 496p. (C). 1990. text ed. 79.00 (*0-02-417580-3*, Macmillan Coll) P-H.

Relationships in Old Age: Coping with the Challenge of Transition. Robert O. Hansson & Bruce N. Carpenter. LC 93-46488. (Guilford Series on Personal Relationships). 180p. 1994. lib. bdg. 27.95 (*0-89862-198-4*) Guilford Pubns.

*__Relationships in Progress: A Pocket Guide to Creating a Healthy Relationship with Yourself & for Yourself, Vol. 1.__ Pamela B. Brewer. 167p. (Orig.). 1997. pap. 9.95 (*0-9655484-0-6*) Twenty-Six by Two.

Relationships in Recovery: Healing Strategies for Couples & Families. Emily Marlin. LC 89-45687. 288p. 1990. pap. 8.95 (*0-00-001645-4*, PL) HarpC.

Relationships in the New Age of AIDS: Self Awareness Through Commitment. Betty Bethards. 55p. (Orig.). 1988. pap. 2.50 (*0-918915-12-0*) Inner Light Found.

Relationships of Chrysemyd Turtles of North America: Testudines: Emydidae. Joseph P. Ward. (Special Publications: No. 21). (Illus.). 50p. 1984. pap. 9.00 (*0-89672-121-3*) Tex Tech Univ Pr.

Relationships of Polymetric Structure & Properties. Ed. by I. Chudacek. (Progress in Colloid & Polymer Science Ser.: Vol. 78). 212p. 1989. 106.00 (*0-387-91338-6*) Spr-Verlag.

Relationships of the Amphiberingian Marmots: Mammalia: Sciuridae. Robert S. Hoffmann et al. (Occasional Papers: No. 83). 56p. 1979. pap. 1.00 (*0-317-04825-2*) U KS Nat Hist Mus.

Relationships of the Superorders Alectoromorphae & Charadriomorphae (Aves) A Comparative Study of the Avian Hand. Boris C. Stegmann. (Publications of the Nuttall Ornithological Club: No. 17). (Illus.). 119p. 1978. 10.00 (*1-877973-27-0*) Nuttall Ornith.

Relationships of Transportation & Land Use, Economic Development, & Intercity Bus Issues. (Research Record Ser.: No. 1125). 143p. 1987. 13.00 (*0-309-04506-1*) Transport Res Bd.

Relationships with Friends, Parents, & Teachers: Team Spirit. Scharlotte Rich. (Runners Power Pak Ser.: No. 3). (J). 1996. pap. 5.99 (*0-88070-925-1*, Gold & Honey) Multnomah Pubs.

Relationships, You - Me - & the Others. Luis Nunez. 160p. 1994. pap. 8.95 (*0-9640457-0-2*) Cerebral Impact.

*__Relationships...Relationships.__ 90p. (Orig.). 1996. pap. 6.95 (*0-9634014-1-6*) S Martinoli.

Relative. Herbert L. Beierle. 1990. 20.00 (*0-940480-22-0*) UNI Press.

Relative Act of Murder. C. F. Roe. 256p. (Orig.). 1995. mass mkt. 4.99 (*0-451-18183-2*, Sig) NAL-Dutton.

Relative Attraction. Celia A. Scott. (Romance Ser.). 1994. mass mkt. 2.99 (*0-373-03306-0*, 1-03306-7) Harlequin Bks.

Relative Baseball II. Merritt Clifton & Pete Palmer. 80p. 1985. 5.00 (*0-317-19196-9*) Samisdat.

Relative Betrayal. Anne Mather. 1990. pap. 2.50 (*0-373-11315-3*) Harlequin Bks.

Relative Biological Effectiveness of Radiations of Different Qualities. Intro. by Warren K. Sinclair. LC 89-13918. (Report Ser.: No. 104). 218p. (Orig.). 1990. pap. 45.00 (*0-929600-12-6*) NCRP Pubns.

Relative Category Theory & Geometric Morphisms: A Logical Approach. Johnathan Chapman & Frederick Rowbottom. (Oxford Logic Guides Ser.: No. 16). (Illus.). 224p. 1992. 79.00 (*0-19-853434-5*) OUP.

Relative Clauses in Spanish Without Overt Antecedents & Related Constructions. Susan Plann. LC 78-68838. (University of California Publications in Linguistics: No. 93). 208p. 1980. pap. 59.30 (*0-7837-8420-1*, 2049222) Bks Demand.

Relative Complexities of First Order Calculi. Elmar Eder. (Artificial Intelligence Ser.). vi, 173p. (C). 1992. pap. 42.00 (*3-528-05122-1*, Pub. by Vieweg & Sohn GW) Informatica.

Relative Connections, Vol. I. Gyeorgos C. Hatonn. (The Phoenix Journals). 223p. 1993. pap. 6.00 (*1-56935-016-7*) Phoenix Source.

Relative Danger. Charlotte Douglas. 1995. pap. 4.99 (*0-8217-5142-5*) NAL-Dutton.

Relative Deprivation & Social Comparison: The Ontario Symposium, Vol. 4. Ed. by James M. Olson et al. (Ontario Symposia on Personality Ser.). 272p. (C). 1986. text ed. 49.95 (*0-89859-704-8*) L Erlbaum Assocs.

Relative Dividend Yield: Common Stock Investing for Income & Appreciation. Anthony E. Spare. LC 91-31643. 304p. 1992. text ed. 49.95 (*0-471-53652-0*) Wiley.

*__Relative Freedom.__ large type ed. Denise Robertson. (Magna Large Print Ser.). 468p. 1997. 27.50 (*0-7505-1082-X*) Thorndike Pr.

Relative Freedoms: Women & Leisure. Ed. by Erica Wimbush & Margaret Talbot. 224p. 1989. 90.00 (*0-335-15569-3*, Open Univ Pr); pap. 32.00 (*0-335-15568-5*, Open Univ Pr) Taylor & Francis.

Relative Frequency of English Speech Sounds. rev. ed. Godfrey Dewey. (Studies in Education: No. 4). 199p. 1950. 15.00 (*0-674-75450-6*) HUP.

Relative Frequency of English Spellings. Godfrey Dewey. LC 71-118887. 154p. reprint ed. pap. 43.90 (*0-317-41995-1*, 2026005) Bks Demand.

Relative Frequency Tables, 1900-1949. LC 78-61158. 312p. 1978. 16.00 (*0-86690-053-5*, A1004-014) Am Fed Astrologers.

Relative Humidity: Thermodynamic Charts. Technical Association of the Pulp & Paper Industry Staff. reprint ed. pap. 20.00 (*0-317-26870-8*, 2025293) Bks Demand.

Relative Importance of Crop Pests in South Asia. A. M. Geddes & M. Iles. 102p. 1991. pap. 30.00 (*0-85954-284-X*, Pub. by Nat Res Inst UK) St Mut.

Relative Importance of Crop Pests in Sub-Saharan Africa. A. M. Geddes. 68p. 1990. pap. 40.00 (*0-85954-272-6*, Pub. by Nat Res Inst UK) St Mut.

Relative Importance of Pre-Harvest Crop Pests in Indonesia. A. M. Geddes. 70p. 1992. pap. 30.00 (*0-85954-295-5*, Pub. by Nat Res Inst UK) St Mut.

Relative Inefficiency of Quotas. James E. Anderson. 240p. 1988. 27.50 (*0-262-01103-4*) MIT Pr.

Relative Information: Theories & Applications. G. Jumarie. (Synergetics Ser.: Vol. 47). (Illus.). xxii, 258p. 1990. 108.95 (*0-387-51905-X*) Spr-Verlag.

Relative Invariants of Rings: The Commutative Theory. F. Van Oystaeyen & Alain Verschoren. (Pure & Applied Mathematics Ser.: Vol. 79). 272p. 1983. 130.00 (*0-8247-7043-9*) Dekker.

Relative Invariants of Rings: The Noncommutative Theory. F. Van Oystaeyen & Alain Verschoren. (Pure & Applied Mathematics Ser.: Vol. 86). (Illus.). 304p. 1984. 145.00 (*0-8247-7281-4*) Dekker.

Relative Merits: A Personal View of the Bandaranaike Family of Sri Lanka. Yasmine Gooneratne. LC 85-18386. (Illus.). 272p. 1986. text ed. 29.95 (*0-312-67037-0*) St Martin.

Relative Merits of Conventional & Imaginative Types of Problems in Arithmetic. Harry G. Wheat. LC 71-177643. (Columbia University. Teachers College. Contributions to Education Ser.: No. 359). reprint ed. 37.50 (*0-404-55359-1*) AMS Pr.

Relative Merits of Three Methods of Subtraction: An Experimental Comparison of the Decomposition Method of Subtraction with the Equal Additions Method & the Austrian Method. J. T. Johnson. LC 77-176914. (Columbia University. Teachers College. Contributions to Education Ser.: No. 738). reprint ed. 37.50 (*0-404-55738-4*) AMS Pr.

*__Relative Minor.__ Deanna Ferguson. 86p. 1993. 9.95 (*0-921331-18-5*, Pub. by Tsunami Edits CN) SPD-Small Pr Dist.

Relative Motion Sensitivity in the Visual System of Cats & Monkeys. G. Gulyas. No. 2. 173p. (Orig.). 1988. pap. 32.50 (*90-6186-277-9*, Pub. by Leuven Univ BE) Coronet Bks.

Relative Motions Between Oceanic & Continental Plates in the Pacific Basin. David C. Engebretson et al. LC 85-17640. (Geological Society of America, Special Paper Ser.: No. 206). 65p. reprint ed. pap. 25.00 (*0-7837-2686-4*, 2043063) Bks Demand.

*__Relative Noise Levels of Parallel Axis Gears Sets with Various Contact Ratios & Gear Tooth Forms.__ Raymond J. Drago & J. W. Lenski. (1993 Fall Technical Meeting Ser.: Vol. 11). 1993. pap. text ed. 30.00 (*1-55589-623-5*) AGMA.

Relative Permeability of Petroleum Reservoirs. Koderitz & Herbert Harvey. 152p. 1986. 132.00 (*0-8493-5739-X*, TN870) CRC Pr.

Relative Productivity, Factor Intensity & Technology in the Manufacturing Sectors of the U. S. & the U. K. During the Nineteenth Century. Asher Ephraim. Ed. by Stuart Bruchey. LC 76-39822. (Nineteen Seventy-Seven Dissertations Ser.). (Illus.). 1977. lib. bdg. 23.95 (*0-405-09902-9*) Ayer.

Relative Recipes. Ruby Schmieder. (Illus.). 155p. (Orig.). 1991. pap. 18.00 (*0-9626013-9-X*) Cordell Expeditions.

*__Relative Risk Analysis in Regulating the Use of Radiation-Emitting Medical Devices.__ 1996. lib. bdg. 254.99 (*0-8490-6379-5*) Gordon Pr.

Relative Sins. Anne Mather. 1996. mass mkt. 3.50 (*0-373-11845-7*, 1-11845-4) Harlequin Bks.

*__Relative Sins.__ Anne Mather. (Harlequin Romance Ser.). 1996. 19.95 (*0-263-14717-7*) Thorndike Pr.

Relative Sins. Cynthia Victor. 464p. 1993. reprint ed. pap. 5.99 (*0-451-17601-4*, Onyx) NAL-Dutton.

Relative Stranger. large type ed. Mary Street. (Linford Romance Library). 320p. 1989. pap. 15.99 (*0-7089-6660-8*, Linford) Ulverscroft.

Relative Stranger. Charles Baxter. (Contemporary American Fiction Ser.). 240p. 1991. reprint ed. pap. 11.95 (*0-14-015628-3*, Penguin Bks) Viking Penguin.

*__Relative Strangers.__ Kathy L. Emerson. (Loveswept Ser.: Vol. 860). 1997. mass mkt. 3.50 (*0-553-44584-7*, Loveswept) Bantam.

Relative Strangers. Jean Ferris. (YA). 1993. 16.00 (*0-374-36243-2*) FS&G.

Relative Strangers: Studies of Stepfamily Processes. Ed. by William R. Beer. LC 88-6697. 192p. (C). 1989. 52.00 (*0-8476-7570-X*) Rowman.

Relative Strength Index: Forecasting & Trading Strategies. Andrew Cardwell. Date not set. 55.00 (*0-471-59251-X*) Wiley.

Relative to Relativity. Joan Richardson. Date not set. pap. 22.00 (*0-670-83955-8*) Viking Penguin.

Relative Truths: East End Photography. Tracey R. Bashkoff. (Illus.). 5p. (Orig.). 1992. pap. 2.00 (*0-614-14070-6*) Guild Hall.

Relative Values. Steele. 1994. pap. 2.99 (*0-373-15554-9*) Harlequin Bks.

Relative Values. Jessica Steele. (Romance Ser.). 1994. mass mkt. 2.99 (*0-373-03308-7*, 1-03308-3) Harlequin Bks.

Relative Values: Determining Attorneys' Fees. 232p. 1985. text ed. 95.00 (*0-07-021162-0*) Shepards.

Relative Values: Or What's Art Worth? Louisa Buck & Philip Dodd. (Illus.). 176p. 1994. pap. 14.95 (*0-563-20749-3*, BBC-Parkwest) Parkwest Pubns.

Relative Values for Physicians: Computer Applications. 1995. ring bd. 1,750.00 (*0-07-600556-9*); ring bd. 1,750.00 (*0-07-809806-8*) Hlthcare Mgmt Grp.

Relative Values for Physicians: Computer Applications, Set. 1995. pap. 34.95 (*0-07-809977-3*) Hlthcare Mgmt Grp.

Relative Values for Physicians, 1995-1996. rev. ed. Relative Value Studies, Inc. Staff. 900p. 1995. ring bd. 249.00 (*0-07-600771-5*) Hlthcare Mgmt Grp.

Relative Values for Physicians, 1995-1996. rev. ed. Relative Value Studies, Inc. Staff. 900p. 1995. ring bd. 495.00 incl. disk (*0-07-810175-1*) Hlthcare Mgmt Grp.

Relative Values for Physicians, 1996-1997. 1996. 249.00 (*0-07-600822-3*) McGraw.

Relative Wage Trends, Women's Work & Family Income. Chinhui Juhn. (AEI Studies on Understanding Inequality). 32p. (Orig.). 1996. pap. 9.95 (*0-8447-7077-9*, AEI Pr) Am Enterprise.

Relative Wages & International Competitiveness in U. S. Industry. James K. Galbraith & Paulo Du Pin Calmon. (Working Paper Ser.: No. 56). 75p. 1990. pap. 5.50 (*0-89940-537-1*) LBJ Sch Pub Aff.

Relatively Speaking. Morton Cooper. (Illus.). 96p. (Orig.). 1989. pap. 3.95 (*1-877953-01-6*) Voice & Speech.

Relatively Speaking: Relativity, Black Holes, & the Fate of the Universe. Eric J. Chaisson. 1990. pap. 12.95 (*0-393-30675-5*) Norton.

Relatively Speaking: Three One-Acts & a Monologue about the Family. Jerald Cohagan. 1988. 8.99 (*0-685-68701-5*, MP-642) Lillenas.

Relatively Speaking see Your Family Tree Connection

Relatives. Tracy Voigt. (Orig.). (gr. 10 up). 1982. reprint ed. pap. write for info. (*0-318-56773-3*) T Voigt.

Relatives at Risk for Mental Disorder. David L. Dunner et al. LC 87-42919. (American Psychopathological Association Ser.). 336p. 1988. reprint ed. pap. 95.80 (*0-608-00330-1*, 2061047) Bks Demand.

Relatives Came. Cynthia Rylant. LC 85-10929. (Illus.). 32p. (J). (ps-2). 1985. lib. bdg. 16.00 (*0-02-777220-9*, Bradbury S&S) S&S Childrens.

Relatives Came. Cynthia Rylant. LC 92-41394. (Illus.). 32p. (J). (ps-2). 1993. reprint ed. pap. 5.99 (*0-689-71738-5*, Aladdin Paperbacks) S&S Childrens.

Relativism: Cognitive & Moral. Ed. by Jack W. Meiland & Michael Krausz. LC 81-19834. 272p. 1982. pap. 15.00 (*0-268-01612-7*) U of Notre Dame Pr.

Relativism: Interpretation & Confrontation. Ed. by Michael Krausz. LC 88-40325. (C). 1988. pap. text ed. 25.50 (*0-268-01637-2*) U of Notre Dame Pr.

Relativism: Thoughts & Aphorisms. W. J. Stankiewicz. (Illus.). 1972. 25.00 (*0-686-09043-8*) Girs Pr.

Relativism & Realism in Science. Ed. by Robert Nola. 312p. (C). 1988. lib. bdg. 139.50 (*90-277-2647-7*, Pub. by Klwr Acad Pubs NE) Kluwer Ac.

Relativism & Religion. Ed. by Charles M. Lewis. LC 94-43978. 1995. text ed. 49.95 (*0-312-12392-2*) St Martin.

Relativism & the Natural Left. William P. Kreml. 192p. (C). 1984. text ed. 26.00 (*0-8147-4584-9*); pap. text ed. 12.00 (*0-8147-4585-7*) NYU Pr.

Relativism & the Social Sciences. Ernest Gellner. 200p. 1985. 64.95 (*0-521-26530-4*) Cambridge U Pr.

Relativism & the Social Sciences. Ernest Gellner. 200p. 1987. pap. text ed. 17.95 (*0-521-33798-4*) Cambridge U Pr.

Relativism, Conceptual Schemes & Categorial Framework. Steven D. Edwards. (Avebury Series in the Philosophy of Science). 133p. 1990. text ed. 68.95 (*0-566-07133-9*, Pub. by Avebury Pub UK) Ashgate Pub Co.

Relativism, Knowledge, & Faith. Gordon D. Kaufman. LC 59-11620. 155p. reprint ed. pap. 44.20 (*0-685-15748-2*, 2026778) Bks Demand.

Relativism, Nihilism, & God. Philip E. Devine. LC 89-40387. 1989. text ed. 26.50 (*0-268-01640-2*) U of Notre Dame Pr.

*__Relativism, Suffering & Beyond: Essays in Memory of Bimal K. Matilal.__ Ed. by P. Bilimoria & J. N. Mohanty. 394p. 1997. 35.00 (*0-19-563858-1*) OUP.

Relativism under Fire: The Psychoanalytic Challenge. Robert Endleman. 208p. (Orig.). (C). 1995. text ed. 40.00 (*1-885809-04-2*); pap. text ed. 19.95 (*1-885809-05-0*) Psyche Pr NY.

Relativist & Absolutist: The Early Neoclassical Debate in England. Emerson R. Marks. LC 75-23348. 171p. 1975. reprint ed. text ed. 49.75 (*0-8371-8348-0*, MARAB, Greenwood Pr) Greenwood.

Relativistic Action at a Distance: Classical & Quantum Aspects, Barcelona, Spain 1981, Proceedings. Ed. by J. Llosa. (Lecture Notes in Physics Ser.: Vol. 162). 263p. 1982. 31.95 (*0-387-11573-0*) Spr-Verlag.

Relativistic & Electron Correlation Effects in Molecules & Solids. Ed. by G. L. Malli. (NATO ASI Series B, Physics: Vol. 318). (Illus.). 482p. 1994. 129.50 (*0-306-44625-1*, Plenum Pr) Plenum.

Relativistic Aspects of Nuclear Physics. Takeshi Kodama et al. 452p. (C). 1990. text ed. 113.00 (*981-02-0191-5*) World Scientific Pub.

Relativistic Aspects of Nuclear Physics. T. Kodaman et al. 500p. 1992. text ed. 109.00 (*981-02-0866-9*) World Scientific Pub.

Relativistic Aspects of Nuclear Physics: Proceedings of the Third International Workshop. Takeshi Kodama. 420p. 1995. text ed. 109.00 (*981-02-1720-X*) World Scientific Pub.

*__Relativistic Astrophysics.__ B. J. Jones. Ed. by D. Markovic. (Contemporary Astrophysics Ser.). (Illus.). 300p. (C). 1997. text ed. 69.95 (*0-521-62113-5*) Cambridge U Pr.

R

Relativistic Astrophysics. Ed. by Y. D. Kim et al. 224p. (C). 1988. text ed. 64.00 (*9971-5-0576-2*) World Scientific Pub.

Relativistic Astrophysics: Proceedings of the 13th Texas Symposium. Ed. by M. Ulmer. 656p. 1987. pap. 61.00 (*9971-5-0310-7*); text ed. 148.00 (*9971-5-0307-7*) World Scientific Pub.

Relativistic Astrophysics: Vol. 2, The Structure & Evolution of the Universe. Ya B. Zel'Dovich. LC 77-128549. (Illus.). 752p. (C). 1983. reprint ed. lib. bdg. 96.00 (*0-226-97957-1*) U Ch Pr.

***Relativistic Astrophysics & Cosmology: LaLaguna, Tenerife, Spain, 4-7 September 1995.** Ed. by J. Buitrago et al. 270p. 1997. 58.00 (*981-02-3189-X*) World Scientific Pub.

Relativistic Astrophysics & Cosmology: Proceedings of the Sir Arthur Eddington Centenary Symposium, Vol. 1. Ed. by Venzo De Sabbata et al. 256p. 1984. 64.00 (*9971-966-99-9*) World Scientific Pub.

Relativistic Astrophysics & Cosmology: Proceedings of the XIV Gift International Seminar Sant Feliu de Guixols, Spain, June 27-July 1, 1983. E. Verdaguer & X. Fustero. 312p. 1984. 60.00 (*9971-966-60-3*) World Scientific Pub.

Relativistic Astrophysics & Cosmology: Proceedings of the 10th Potsdam Seminar. S. Gottlober et al. 350p. 1992. text ed. 109.00 (*981-02-0944-4*) World Scientific Pub.

Relativistic Astrophysics Eighth Symposium, Texas, Vol. 302. Ed. by Michael D. Papagiannis. (Annals Ser.). 689p. 1977. 47.00 (*0-89072-048-7*) NY Acad Sci.

Relativistic Astrophysics Gravity-Wave Astronomy, Vol. 7. L. P. Grishchuk. (Soviet Scientific Reviews Ser.: Vol. 7, Pt. 3). 132p. 1989. pap. text ed. 119.00 (*3-7186-4927-6*) Gordon & Breach.

Relativistic Atomic Collisions. Jorg Eichler & Walter E. Meyerhof. (Illus.). 413p. 1995. boxed 74.95 (*0-12-233675-5*) Acad Pr.

Relativistic Channeling. Ed. by R. Carrigan & J. Ellison. LC 87-7318. (NATO ASI Series B, Physics: Vol. 165). (Illus.). 538p. 1987. 120.00 (*0-306-42689-7*, Plenum Pr) Plenum.

Relativistic Cosmology: An Introduction. Jean Heidmann. (Illus.). 168p. 1980. 53.95 (*0-387-10138-1*) Spr-Verlag.

Relativistic Deduction: Epistemological Implications of the Theory of Relativity with a Review by Albert Einstein. Emile Meyerson. Tr. by David A. Sipfle & Mary A. Sipfle. 290p. 1985. lib. bdg. 122.00 (*90-277-1699-4*, D Reidel) Kluwer Ac.

Relativistic Dynamics of a Charged Sphere: Updating the Lorentz-Abraham Model. Arthur D. Yaghjian. Ed. by W. Beiglbock et al. LC 92-20235. (Lecture Notes in Physics, New Series, Monographs: Vol. M11). xii, 115p. 1992. 48.95 (*0-387-97887-9*) Spr-Verlag.

***Relativistic Effects in Chemistry Pt. A: Theory & Techniques.** Krishnan Balasubramanian. LC 96-36641. 232p. 1997. text ed. write for info. (*0-471-30400-X*) Wiley.

***Relativistic Effects in Chemistry Pt. B: Applications.** Krishnan Balasubramanian. LC 96-36641. 565p. 1997. text ed. 79.95 (*0-471-17991-4*) Wiley.

Relativistic Effects in the Spectra of Atomic Systems. L. Labzowsky et al. (Illus.). 352p. 1993. 144.00 (*0-7503-0223-2*) IOP Pub.

Relativistic Electrodynamics & Differential Geometry. S. Parrott. (Illus.). 320p. 1986. 83.95 (*0-387-96435-5*) Spr-Verlag.

Relativistic Fluid Dynamics. Ed. by A. M. Anile & Y. Choquet-Bruhat. (Lecture Notes in Mathematics Ser.: Vol. 1385). v, 308p. 1989. 45.95 (*0-387-51466-X*) Spr-Verlag.

Relativistic Fluids & Magneto-Fluids: With Applications in Astrophysics & Plasma Physics. A. M. Anile. (Cambridge Monographs on Mathematical Physics). (Illus.). 348p. (C). 1990. text ed. 110.00 (*0-521-30406-7*) Cambridge U Pr.

Relativistic Gravitation: Proceedings of Symposium 15 of the COSPAR Twenty-Seventh Plenary Meeting Held in Espoo, Finland, 18-29 July 1988. Ed. by R. D. Reasenberg & R. F. Vessot. (Advances in Space Research Ser.: No. 9). (Illus.). 158p. 1989. pap. 92.75 (*0-08-040151-1*, 1702; 1709; 2308, Pergamon Pr) Elsevier.

***Relativistic Gravitation & Gravitational Radiation.** Ed. by J. A. Marck & J. P. Lasota. LC 97-1228. (Cambridge Contemporary Astrophysics Ser.). (Illus.). 540p. (C). 1997. text ed. 69.95 (*0-521-59065-5*) Cambridge U Pr.

Relativistic Gravitational Experiments in Space: First William Fairbank Meeting. Remo Ruffini & I. Ciufolini. (Advanced Series in Astrophysics & Cosmology). 500p. 1993. text ed. 121.00 (*981-02-1263-1*) World Scientific Pub.

Relativistic Gravity Research with Emphasis on Experiments & Observations. LC 92-33778. 1992. 86. 95 (*0-387-56180-3*) Spr-Verlag.

Relativistic Hadrons in Cosmic Compact Objects: Proceedings of a Workshop in Koniki - Suhora, Poland, 9-11 October 1990. Ed. by A. Zdzierski & M. Sikora. (Lecture Notes in Physics Ser.: Vol. 391). xii, 182p. 1991. 39.00 (*0-387-54789-4*) Spr-Verlag.

Relativistic Heavy-Ion Collisions, Vol. 7. Ed. by R. C. Hwa et al. xvi, 316p. 1990. 184.00 (*2-88124-734-2*) Gordon & Breach.

Relativistic Heavy Ion Physics. J. Bartke. 400p. 1998. text ed. 67.00 (*981-02-1231-3*) World Scientific Pub.

Relativistic Heavy Ion Physics, 2 vols. Ed. by L. P. Csernai & D. D. Strottman. 748p. (C). 1991. pap. 52.00 (*981-02-0672-0*); text ed. 150.00 (*981-02-0550-3*) World Scientific Pub.

Relativistic Kinetic Theory: Principles & Applications. S. R. De Groot et al. 418p. 1980. 207.50 (*0-444-85453-3*, North Holland) Elsevier.

Relativistic Mechanics, Time & Inertia. E. Tocaci. 1984. lib. bdg. 158.50 (*90-277-1769-9*) Kluwer Ac.

Relativistic Naturalism: A Cross-Cultural Approach to Human Science. Quin McLoughlin. LC 91-430. 280p. 1991. text ed. 59.95 (*0-275-93870-0*, C3870, Praeger Pubs) Greenwood.

Relativistic Nuclear Many-Body Physics: Proceedings. Ed. by Buny C. Clark et al. 608p. 1989. text ed. 131.00 (*9971-5-0680-7*) World Scientific Pub.

Relativistic Nuclear Physics: Theories of Structure & Scattering. L. C. Celenza & C. M. Shakin. (Lecture Notes in Physics Ser.: Vol. 2). 300p. 1986. text ed. 54.00 (*9971-5-0010-8*); pap. text ed. 30.00 (*9971-5-0011-6*) World Scientific Pub.

Relativistic Nuclear Physics & Quantum Chromodynamics. Ed. by A. M. Baldin et al. 670p. (C). 1991. text ed. 118. 00 (*981-02-0785-9*) World Scientific Pub.

Relativistic Nuclear Physics in the Light Front Formalism. Ed. by V. R. Garsevanishvili & Z. R. Menteshashvili. 152p. 1993. pap. 115.00 (*1-56072-093-X*) Nova Sci Pubs.

Relativistic, Quantum Electrodynamic & Weak Interaction Effects in Atoms. Ed. by Walter Johnson et al. LC 89-84431. (AIP Conference Proceedings Ser.: No. 189). 536p. 1989. lib. bdg. 80.00 (*0-88318-389-7*) Am Inst Physics.

Relativistic Quantum Fields. James D. Bjorken & S. D. Drell. (International Series in Pure & Applied Physics). 1965. text ed. write for info. (*0-07-005494-0*) McGraw.

Relativistic Quantum Fields. Charles Nash. 1979. text ed. 149.00 (*0-12-514350-8*) Acad Pr.

Relativistic Quantum Mechanics. James D. Bjorken & S. D. Drell. (International Series in Pure & Applied Physics). 1964. text ed. write for info. (*0-07-005493-2*) McGraw.

Relativistic Quantum Mechanics. 3rd ed. Walter Greiner & D. A. Bromley. LC 93-38485. (Theoretical Physics Ser.). 1994. write for info. (*0-387-57266-X*) Spr-Verlag.

***Relativistic Quantum Mechanics: Wave Equations.** 2nd ed. Walter Greiner. LC 97-20187. 1997. pap. text ed. 69. 00 (*3-540-61621-7*) Spr-Verlag.

Relativistic Quantum Mechanics & Field Theory. Franz Gross. LC 92-40605. 648p. 1993. text ed. 74.95 (*0-471-59113-0*) Wiley.

Relativistic Quantum Mechanics & Introduction to Field Theory. Fransicso J. Yndurain. 332p. 1996. 59.00 (*3-540-60453-7*) Spr-Verlag.

Relativistic Quantum Mechanics & Quantum Fields. Theodore Y. Wu et al. 420p. (C). 1991. text ed. 78.00 (*981-02-0608-9*); pap. text ed. 44.00 (*981-02-0609-7*) World Scientific Pub.

Relativistic Quantum Mechanics of Leptons & Fields. Walter T. Grandy, Jr. (Fundamental Theories of Physics Ser.). 456p. 1991. lib. bdg. 151.00 (*0-7923-1049-7*) Kluwer Ac.

***Relativistic Reality: A Modern View.** James D. Edmonds. LC 96-31700. (Knots & Everything Ser.). 1997. write for info. (*981-02-2851-1*) World Scientific Pub.

Relativistic Theory of Atoms & Molecules. P. Pyykko. (Lecture Notes in Chemistry Ser.: Vol. 41). ix, 389p. 1986. 62.95 (*0-387-17167-3*) Spr-Verlag.

Relativistic Theory of Atoms & Molecules 2: A Bibliography 1986-1992. P. Pyykko. LC 93-31082. (Lecture Notes in Chemistry Ser.: Vol. 60). 1993. 115.95 (*0-387-57219-8*) Spr-Verlag.

Relativistic Thermodynamics. Richard A. Weiss. LC 91-77536. (Illus.). 244p. (C). 1992. reprint ed. pap. 24.00 (*0-9624789-2-X*) K & W Pubns.

Relativity. Albert Einstein. 1988. 7.99 (*0-517-02961-8*) Random Hse Value.

Relativity. Albert Einstein. 1995. pap. 7.00 (*0-517-88441-0*) Random.

Relativity. Albert Einstein. Tr. by Robert W. Lawson. LC 95-6732. (Great Minds Ser.). 135p. 1995. pap. 8.95 (*0-87975-979-8*) Prometheus Bks.

Relativity: An Introduction to the Special Theory. Asghar Qadir. 140p. 1989. text ed. 36.00 (*9971-5-0612-2*) World Scientific Pub.

Relativity: Opposing Viewpoints. Clarice Swisher. LC 90-3910. (Great Mysteries Ser.). (Illus.). 128p. (J). (gr. 5-8). 1990. lib. bdg. 17.96 (*0-89908-076-6*) Greenhaven.

Relativity: The Special & General Theory. Albert Einstein. Tr. by Robert W. Lawson. 1961. pap. 4.95 (*0-517-02530-2*, Crown) Crown Pub Group.

Relativity: The Special & General Theory. Albert Einstein. 1990. 20.25 (*0-8446-1169-7*) Peter Smith.

Relativity: The Special Theory. 2nd ed. J. L. Synge. 1980. 170.75 (*0-444-10280-9*, North Holland) Elsevier.

Relativity: The Special Theory. 2nd ed. J. L. Synge. 1980. 170.75 (*0-7204-0064-3*, North Holland) Elsevier.

Relativity: The Theory & Its Philosophy. Roger B. Angel. (Foundations & Philosophy of Science & Technology Ser.). (Illus.). 320p. 1980. 125.00 (*0-08-025197-8*, Pub. by Pergamon Repr UK) Franklin.

Relativity & Common Sense: A New Approach to Einstein. Hermann Bondi. (Illus.). 177p. (C). 1980. reprint ed. pap. 4.95 (*0-486-24021-5*) Dover.

Relativity & Consciousness: A New Approach to Evolution. Kate Flores. LC 84-24674. 186p. (Orig.). (C). 1985. pap. 10.00 (*0-87752-230-8*) Gordian.

Relativity & Engineering. J. Van Bladel. (Electrophysics Ser.: Vol. 15). (Illus.). 420p. 1984. 59.95 (*0-387-12561-2*) Spr-Verlag.

Relativity & Geometry. unabridged ed. Roberto Torretti. LC 95-49003. (Illus.). 416p. reprint ed. pap. 12.95 (*0-486-69046-6*) Dover.

***Relativity & Gravitation.** Philippe Tourrenc. (Illus.). 264p. 1997. text ed. 74.95 (*0-521-45075-6*) Cambridge U Pr.

***Relativity & Gravitation.** Philippe Tourrenc. (Illus.). 264p. 1997. pap. text ed. 29.95 (*0-521-45685-1*) Cambridge U Pr.

Relativity & Gravitation - Classical & Quantum. Ed. by J. C. D'Olivo et al. 450p. (C). 1991. text ed. 104.00 (*981-02-0715-8*) World Scientific Pub.

Relativity & Gravitation (SILARG Six) Proceedings of the Sixth Latin-American Symposium on Relativity & Gravity. Ed. by M. Novello. 380p. (C). 1988. text ed. 121.00 (*9971-5-0436-7*) World Scientific Pub.

Relativity & Scientific Computing: Computer Algebra, Numerics, Visualization. Ed. by F. W. Hehl et al. LC 96-6021. (Illus.). 416p. 1996. student ed., pap. 89.95 (*3-540-60361-1*) Spr-Verlag.

Relativity & Space. C. P. Steinmetz. 1991. lib. bdg. 74.95 (*0-8490-4930-X*) Gordon Pr.

Relativity, As Explained by Professor Xargle. Jeanne Willis. LC 93-32606. (Illus.). (J). (gr. 5 up). 1994. pap. 13.99 (*0-525-45245-1*) Dutton Child Bks.

Relativity, Cosmology, Topological Mass & Supergravity: Proceedings of the 4th Silarg Symposium on Gravity, Gauge Theories & Supergravity, USB Campus, Caracas, Dec. 5-11, 1982. Ed. by C. Aragone. 304p. 1984. text ed. 89.00 (*9971-950-95-2*) World Scientific Pub.

Relativity, Groups & Topology: 1963 see Houches Lectures

Relativity in Astronomy, Celestial Mechanics & Geodesy. M. H. Soffel. (Astronomy & Astrophysics Library). (Illus.). xiv, 208p. 1989. 69.95 (*0-387-18906-8*) Spr-Verlag.

Relativity in Celestial Mechanics & Astrometry. Ed. by J. Kovalevsky & Victor A. Brumberg. (Publications of The International Astronomical Union-Proceedings of Symposia Ser.). (Orig.). 1986. pap. text ed. 69.00 (*90-277-2190-4*) Kluwer Ac.

Relativity in Celestial Mechanics & Astrometry. Jean Kovalevsky & Victor A. Brumberg. (Publications of The International Astronomical Union-Proceedings of Symposia Ser.). (Orig.). 1986. lib. bdg. 154.50 (*90-277-2189-0*) Kluwer Ac.

Relativity in Illustrations. Jacob T. Schwartz. (Illus.). 128p. 1989. pap. 7.95 (*0-486-25965-X*) Dover.

Relativity in Our Time. Mendel Sachs. 165p. 1993. 65.00 (*0-7484-0117-2*, Pub. by Tay Francis Ltd UK); pap. 19. 95 (*0-7484-0118-0*, Pub. by Tay Francis Ltd UK) Taylor & Francis.

Relativity of Wrong. Isaac Asimov. 1989. mass mkt. 3.95 (*1-55817-169-X*, Pinncle Kensgtn) Kensgtn Pub Corp.

Relativity of Wrong. Isaac Asimov. 256p. 1996. pap. 12.00 (*1-57566-008-3*) Kensgtn Pub Corp.

Relativity on Curved Manifolds. F. De Felice & C. J. Clarke. (Monographs on Mathematical Physics). 400p. (C). 1990. text ed. 125.00 (*0-521-26639-4*) Cambridge U Pr.

Relativity on Curved Manifolds. F. De Felice & C. J. Clarke. (Monographs on Mathematical Physics). 464p. (C). 1992. pap. text ed. 44.95 (*0-521-42908-0*) Cambridge U Pr.

Relativity, Philosophy & Mind: The Notebooks of Paul Brunton, Vol. 13. Paul Brunton. Ed. by Paul Cash & Timothy Smith. (Illus.). 550p. 1988. 29.95 (*0-943914-38-8*); pap. 19.95 (*0-943914-39-6*) Larson Pubns.

Relativity Physics. R. Turner. (Student Physics Ser.). (Illus.). 128p. (Orig.). (C). 1984. pap. text ed. 12.95 (*0-7102-0001-3*, RKP) Routledge.

***Relativity Simply Explained.** unabridged ed. Martin Gardner. (Illus.). 224p. 1996. reprint ed. pap. text ed. 8.95 (*0-486-29315-7*) Dover.

Relativity, Supersymmetry & Cosmology: Proceedings of the Fifth Latin-American Symposium on Relativity & Gravity - SILARG V, Bariloche, Argentina, January 1985. Ed. by O. Bressan et al. 368p. 1985. 60.00 (*9971-5-0003-5*) World Scientific Pub.

Relativity, Supersymmetry, & Strings. Ed. by A. Rosenblum. LC 87-21294. (Illus.). 136p. 1990. 65.00 (*0-306-42680-3*, Plenum Pr) Plenum.

Relativity Theory: Concepts & Basic Principles. Amos Harpaz. LC 93-4658. 232p. 1993. reprint ed. text ed. 44. 00 (*1-56881-026-1*) AK Peters.

Relativity Theory & Astrophysics: Galactic Structure, (Proceedings of the Cornell University, Summer Seminar, 1965), Vol. 9. Cornell University, Summer Seminar Staff. Ed. by J. Ehlers. LC 62-21481. (Lectures in Applied Mathematics). 220p. 1968. reprint ed. 35.00 (*0-8218-1109-6*, LAM/9) Am Math.

Relativity Theory & Astrophysics: Relativity & Cosmology. Ed. by J. Ehlers. LC 62-21481. (Lectures in Applied Mathematics: Vol. 8). 289p. 1968. reprint ed. pap. 36.00 (*0-8218-1108-8*, LAM/8) Am Math.

Relativity Theory & Astrophysics, Stellar Structure. Ed. by J. Ehlers. LC 62-21481. (Lectures in Applied Mathematics: Vol. 10). 136p. 1968. reprint ed. pap. 34. 00 (*0-8218-1110-X*, LAM/10) Am Math.

Relativity, Thermodynamics, & Cosmology. Richard C. Tolman. LC 83-45477. 1934. 49.50 (*0-404-20262-4*, QC6) AMS Pr.

Relativity, Thermodynamics & Cosmology. Richard C. Tolman. xv, 501p. 1987. reprint ed. pap. text ed. 12.95 (*0-486-65383-8*) Dover.

Relativity Today. Ed. by Z. Perjes. 308p. (C). 1992. text ed. 130.00 (*1-56072-028-X*) Nova Sci Pubs.

Relativity Today: Proceedings of the Fourth Hungarian Relativity Workshop. Ed. by R. P. Kerr & Z. Perjes. 176p. 1994. 28.00 (*963-05-6766-0*, Pub. by A K HU) Intl Spec Bk.

Relativity Today: Proceedings of the 2nd Hungarian Relativity Workshop. Ed. by Z. Perjes. 288p. (C). 1988. pap. 47.00 (*9971-5-0517-7*); text ed. 100.00 (*9971-5-0513-4*) World Scientific Pub.

Relativity Visualized. Lewis C. Epstein. LC 82-84280. (Illus.). 200p. 1994. pap. 17.95 (*0-935218-05-X*) Insight Pr CA.

Relativization & Nominalized Clauses in Huallaga (Huanuco) Quechua. David J. Weber. LC 83-1094. (University of California Publications in Linguistics: No. 103). 140p. 1983. pap. 39.90 (*0-7837-8434-1*, 2049236) Bks Demand.

Relativization & Nominalized Clauses in Huallaga (Huanuco) Quechua. David J. Weber. LC 83-1094. (Publications in Linguistics: Vol. 103). 144p. (C). 1984. pap. 14.00 (*0-520-09666-5*) U CA Pr.

Relativization in Hebrew: A Transformational Approach. Yehiel Hayon. (Janua Linguarum, Series Practica: No. 189). (Illus.). 238p. (Orig.). 1973. pap. text ed. 69.25 (*90-279-2391-4*) Mouton.

Relato de Babia. Luis Mateo Diez. (Nueva Austral Ser.: Vol. 213). (SPA.). 1991. pap. text ed. 24.95 (*84-239-7213-5*) Elliots Bks.

Relatos. Silverio Munoz. 250p. (Orig.). (SPA.). 1991. pap. text ed. 15.00 (*0-937985-06-6*) Ediciones Arauco.

***Relatos de Poder.** Carlos Castaneda. 1992. pap. text ed. 11.99 (*968-16-0341-9*) Fondo de Cultura Economica.

Relatos en Espiral. Spottorno J. Ortega. (Nueva Austral Ser.: Vol. 143). (SPA.). 1991. pap. text ed. 24.95 (*84-239-1943-9*) Elliots Bks.

Relaunching Videotex. Ed. by Harry Bouwman. (Diverse Ser.). 188p. (C). 1992. lib. bdg. 126.00 (*0-7923-1711-4*) Kluwer Ac.

Relax. Toni Goffe. (J). (ps-3). 1993. 7.99 (*0-85953-789-7*) Childs Play.

Relax: Dealing with Stress. Murray Watts & Cary L. Cooper. 192p. (Orig.). 1993. pap. 9.95 (*0-563-36362-2*, BBC-Parkwest) Parkwest Pubns.

Relax & Enjoy Your Baby, Vol. 1. Sylvia K. Olkin. (Illus.). 12p. 1996. 16.95 incl. audio (*1-55961-346-7*, BP7506) Relaxtn Co.

Relax & Enjoy Your Life. Carol Thompson. LC 90-92055. (Illus.). 80p. (Orig.). 1991. pap. 7.95 (*0-9627448-4-0*) Saara Pubns.

Relax & Lose Weight. Robert R. Wall. (Illus.). 100p. (Orig.). 1988. write for info. (*0-318-63681-6*) R R Wall.

Relax & Renew: Restful Yoga for Stressful Times. Judith Lasater. LC 95-68875. (Illus.). 240p. (Orig.). 1995. pap. 21.95 (*0-9627138-4-8*) Rodmell Pr.

***Relax & Renew: With the Kundalina Yoga & Meditations of Yogi Bhajan.** Rattana, pseud. & Ann M. Maxwell. (Illus.). 195p. 1995. spiral bd. 25.00 (*1-888029-04-8*, Yoga Tech Pr) Heart Quest.

***Relax, God Is in Charge: Humor & Wisdom for Living & Loving Life.** Meiji Stewart. 1997. pap. text ed. 6.95 (*0-9647349-0-7*) Keep Coming Back.

Relax, It's Good for You. Ed Bernd, Jr. 2.95 (*0-913343-35-8*) Inst Psych Inc.

Relax! It's Only Dinner: Eat Splendidly Anytime Without Losing Your Mind. Cheryl Merser. LC 95-16553. (Illus.). 224p. 1995. pap. 14.00 (*0-684-81166-9*, Fireside) S&S Trade.

Relax One, Two, Three. rev. ed. Carol Healy. (Illus.). 30p. 1985. pap. text ed. 4.95 (*0-932491-06-5*) Res Appl Inc.

Relax! With Self Therap-Ease: A Simple Illustrated Course. Bonnie Pendleton & Betty Mehling. (Illus.). 176p. 1984. pap. 7.95 (*0-13-772187-0*) P-H.

Relax! with Self-Therap-Ease: Whole-Body Acupressure. Bonnie Pendleton & Betty Mehling. (Illus.). 171p. 1976. lib. bdg. 15.95 (*0-917306-01-5*) Calif Pubns.

Relax with Vernon Sechriest. Vernon Sechriest. LC 85-81255. 100p. (Orig.). 1985. pap. 5.95 (*0-938828-02-9*) Falls Tar.

***Relax, You May Only Have a Few Minutes Left: How to Use the Power of Humor to Defeat Stress in Your Life & Work.** Loretta La Roche & Larry Rothstein. (Illus.). 256p. 1997. 22.95 (*0-7868-6309-9*) Hyperion.

***Relax, Your Life Is Predestined.** Raymond H. DuRussel. 200p. (Orig.). 1997. pap. write for info. (*1-882792-43-2*) Proctor Pubns.

Relaxation. Chrissie Gallagher-Mundy. 128p. 1995. write for info. (*1-57215-186-2*) World Pubns.

Relaxation. James Hewitt. (Teach Yourself Ser.). 184p. 1988. pap. 7.95 (*0-679-72117-7*) Random.

Relaxation: A Comprehensive Manual for Adults, Children, & Children with Special Needs. Joseph R. Cautela & June Groden. LC 78-62906. (Illus.). 108p. (Orig.). (C). 1978. spiral bd. 14.95 (*0-87822-186-7*, 1867) Res Press.

Relaxation & De-Sensitization Training, Set-RD. Russell E. Mason. 1975. Incl. Tape-1A, T-1, T-2, T-6, T-5A, T-9; Brief Outlines 1, Relaxation Trng.; Hierarchy; Clinical App. pap. 60.00 incl. audio (*0-89533-006-7*) F I Comm.

Relaxation & Meditation Companion: Take a Deep Breath... Relax. Carol R. Gaffney. 28p. (Orig.). 1996. 12.95 incl. audio (*1-887330-02-X*) Mind-Body Ctr.

Relaxation & Stress Reduction Workbook. 4th ed. Martha Davis et al. LC 94-68249. 256p. 1995. pap. 17.95 (*1-879237-82-2*) New Harbinger.

Relaxation & Stress Reduction Workbook. Martha Davis et al. 276p. 1995. reprint ed. 9.98 (*1-56731-075-3*, MJF Bks) Fine Comms.

Relaxation Dynamics: A Cognitive-Behavioral Approach to Relaxation. rev. ed. Jonathan C. Smith. LC 88-63564. Orig. Title: Relaxation Dynamics: Nine World Approaches to Self-Relaxation. 378p. 1988. pap. text ed. 21.95 (*0-87822-309-6*, 2448) Res Press.

Relaxation Dynamics: Nine World Approaches to Self-Relaxation see Relaxation Dynamics: A Cognitive-Behavioral Approach to Relaxation

Relaxation for Children. 2nd ed. Jenny Richard. 1995. pap. 60.00 (*0-86431-148-6*, Pub. by Aust Council Educ Res AT) St Mut.

Relaxation in Complex Systems & Related Topics. Ed. by I. A. Campbell & C. Giovannella. (NATO ASI Series B, Physics: Vol. 222). (Illus.). 324p. 1990. 95.00 (*0-306-43600-0*, Plenum Pr) Plenum.

R

Relaxation in Glass & Composites. George W. Scherer. LC 91-22974. 348p. (C). 1992. reprint ed. lib. bdg. 69.95 (*0-89464-643-5*) Krieger.

Relaxation in Movement. B. Bullivant. 1990. pap. 35.00 (*0-7121-1863-2*, Pub. by Northcote UK) St Mut.

***Relaxation in Optimization Theory & Variational Calculus.** Tomas Roubicek. LC 96-31728. (Series in Nonlinear Analysis & Applications: Vol. 4). xiv, 474p. (C). 1997. text ed. 158.95 (*3-11-014542-1*) De Gruyter.

Relaxation in Polymers. T. Kobayashi. 340p. 1993. text ed. 109.00 (*981-02-1373-5*) World Scientific Pub.

Relaxation Phenomena in Condensed Matter. Ed. by William Coffey. (Advances in Chemical Physics Ser.: Vol. 87). 766p. 1994. text ed. 195.00 (*0-471-30312-7*) Wiley.

Relaxation Phenomena in Polymers. Shiro Matsuoka. 322p. (C). 1992. text ed. 59.95 (*1-56990-060-4*) Hanser-Gardner.

Relaxation Processes in Molecular Excited States. Ed. by J. Funfschilling. (C). 1989. lib. bdg. 167.50 (*0-7923-0001-7*) Kluwer Ac.

Relaxation Response. Herbert Benson & Miriam Z. Klipper. 1976. mass mkt. 6.99 (*0-380-00676-6*) Avon.

Relaxation Sensation: The Number One Success Factor in Life. Lorenzo. (Illus.). 128p. (Orig.). 1981. pap. 9.95 (*0-941122-00-X*) Lorenzo Prema.

Relaxation Techniques: A Practical Handbook for the Health Care Professional. Rosemary A. Payne. LC 94-33408. 1995. write for info. (*0-443-04933-5*) Churchill.

Relaxation Techniques & Health Sciences: Medical Subject Analysis with Reference Bibliography. Sally M. Frost. LC 85-47860. 150p. 1987. 37.50 (*0-88164-396-3*); pap. 34.50 (*0-88164-397-1*) ABBE Pubs Assn.

Relaxation Techniques for the Simulation of VLSI Circuits. Jacob K. White & Alberto L. Sangiovanni-Vincentelli. 1986. lib. bdg. 69.50 (*0-89838-186-X*) Kluwer Ac.

***Relaxations of Excited States & Photo-Induced Structural Phase Transitions: Proceedings of the 19th Taniguchi Symposium, Kashikojima, Japan, July 18-23, 1996, Vol. 124.** K. Nasu. LC 96-29968. (Springer Series in Solid-State Sciences). 1997. 109.00 (*3-540-62473-2*) Spr-Verlag.

Relaxed Home School: A Family Production. Mary Hood. 107p. 1994. pap. 10.95 (*0-9639740-0-9*) Ambleside Educ.

Relaxed Hostess. Ann Seranne. LC 86-27372. (Illus.). 140p. (Orig.). 1987. 14.95 (*0-9615072-1-7*) Dog Museum.

Relaxed Parent: Helping Your Kids Do More As You Do Less. Tim Smith. 1996. pap. 10.99 (*1-881273-60-1*) Northfield Pub.

Relaxercise: Ten Effortless Techniques for a More Flexible, Energetic, Pain-Free, Stress-Free Body. David Zemach-Bersin et al. LC 89-45242. (Illus.). 176p. 1990. pap. 22.00 (*0-06-250992-6*, PL 4405) Harper SF.

Relaxin: Structure, Function & Evolution, Vol. 380. Ed. by Bernard G. Steinetz. 246p. 1982. 54.00 (*0-89766-149-4*); pap. 54.00 (*0-89766-150-8*) NY Acad Sci.

Relaxing & Contracting Factors. Ed. by P. Vanhoutte. LC 87-22541. (Endothelium Ser.). 1988. 99.50 (*0-89603-128-4*) Humana.

***Relaxing & Recreating: Ideas for Students.** Norman C. Tognazzini & Margie Sherman. (Illus.). 8p. (Orig.). 1995. pap. 2.50 (*1-884241-41-7*, SPS0304) Energeia Pub.

Relay: An Information Management Workflow. Boche. (KM - Office Procedures Ser.). 1991. 595.95 (*0-538-25530-7*) S-W Pub.

***Relay Bk. 4.** Williams. 1992. student ed., pap. text ed. write for info. (*0-17-556261-X*) Addison-Wesley.

Relay Control Systems. Yakov Z. Tsypkin. Tr. by C. Constanda. (Illus.). 450p. 1985. text ed. 125.00 (*0-521-24390-4*) Cambridge U Pr.

Relay Protection of High Voltage Networks. G. Atabekov. LC 59-13714. 1960. 251.00 (*0-08-013816-0*, Pub. by Pergamon Repr UK) Franklin.

Relearning Politics: Survival in the Next Century. Hughes & DeBow. 1993. pap. text ed. write for info. (*0-07-031128-5*) McGraw.

Relearning the Dark. Nan Fry. LC 90-25998. (Series Fifteen). (Illus.). 72p. (Orig.). 1991. pap. 9.00 (*0-931846-39-0*) Wash Writers Pub.

***Relearning to See: Naturally & Clearly.** Thomas R. Quackenbush. LC 96-54600. (Illus.). 521p. (Orig.). 1997. 35.00 (*1-55643-205-4*) North Atlantic.

Release. Folk. 1995. 195.00 (*0-316-28751-2*) Little.

***Release.** Michael Hewlings. 32p. 1972. pap. 7.95 (*0-900977-38-8*, Pub. by Anvil Press UK) Dufour.

Release: Healing from Wounds of Family, Church, & Community. Flora S. Wuellner. 112p. 1996. pap. 9.95 (*0-8358-0775-4*) Upper Room Bks.

Release From Bondage. large type ed. Jean Graham. 400p. 1987. 25.99 (*0-7089-1727-5*) Ulverscroft.

Release of Genetically Engineered & Other Microorganisms. Ed. by J. C. Fry & M. Day. (Plant & Microbial Biotechnology Research Ser.: No. 2). 194p. (C). 1993. text ed. 90.00 (*0-521-41756-2*) Cambridge U Pr.

Release of Genetically Engineered Microorganisms. Duncan E. Stewart-Tull et al. Ed. by G. H. Collins & Frederick A. Skinner. 306p. 1988. text ed. 95.00 (*0-12-677521-4*) Acad Pr.

Release of Genetically Engineered Microorganisms. Duncan E. Stewart-Tull et al. Ed. by G. H. Collins & Frederick A. Skinner. 306p. 1999. text ed. write for info. (*0-12-677522-2*) Acad Pr.

Release of Genetically Engineered Organisms: Planning Aspects. Lucy M. Rowland. (CPL Bibliographies Ser.: Vol. 324). 33p. 1995. pap. 10.00 (*0-86602-324-0*, Sage Prdcls Pr) Sage.

Release of Genetically Modified Microorganisms - REGEM 2. Ed. by Duncan E. Stewart-Tull & Max Sussman. LC 92-30222. (FEMS Symposium Ser.: No. 63). (Illus.). 250p. (C). 1992. 79.50 (*0-306-44302-3*, Plenum Pr) Plenum.

Release Prevention Control & Counter. Pollution Engineering Staff. 66p. 1994. 24.95 (*0-934165-17-3*) Gulf Pub.

Release the Past. large type ed. Ivy Preston. (Romance Ser.). 1989. 25.99 (*0-7089-2078-0*) Ulverscroft.

***Release the Poet Within: How to Launch & Improve Poetry Craft & Ministry.** Leona Choy. 101p. 1996. pap. 14.95 (*1-889283-02-9*) Golden Morning.

Release the Power of the Blood Covenent. Marilyn Hickey. 1994. pap. 4.95 (*1-56441-053-6*) M Hickey Min.

Release the Sun. William Sears. 536p. 1995. pap. 9.95 (*0-87743-003-9*) Bahai.

Release Your Brakes! James W. Newman. 304p. 1993. reprint ed. pap. 14.95 (*0-9638918-0-4*) Pace Orgztn.

***Release 2.0: A Design for Living in the Digital Age.** Esther Dyson. 224p. 1997. 25.00 (*0-7679-0011-1*) Broadway BDD.

Released from Bondage. Neil T. Anderson. LC 92-41366. (Orig.). 1993. pap. 12.99 (*0-8407-4388-2*) Nelson.

Released from Shame: Recovery for Adult Children of Dysfunctional Families. Sandra D. Wilson. LC 90-41846. 175p. (Orig.). 1991. pap. 10.99 (*0-8308-1601-1*, 1601) InterVarsity.

Released to Love. Alfred H. Ells. LC 93-40301. 1994. pap. 10.99 (*0-8407-6799-4*) Nelson.

Releasement: Spirituality for Ministry. Barbara Fiand. 120p. 1991. reprint ed. pap. 9.95 (*0-8245-1083-6*) Crossroad NY.

***Releases: More Poems.** Mildred P. Richards. (Illus.). 66p. (Orig.). 1996. pap. 5.00 (*0-9637521-4-6*) Arlington Pl.

Releasing: The Key to Physical Manifastion, No. 1. Tina Lucia. Ed. by Linda Craig. (Releasing Ser.). (Illus.). 30p. 1988. pap. 6.95 (*0-317-91334-4*) T Lucia.

***Releasing an Independent Record: How to Successfully Start & Run Your Own Record Label.** 6th ed. Gary Hustwit. 1997. pap. text ed. 24.95 (*1-884615-18-X*) Rockpress Pub.

Releasing an Independent Record: How to Successfully Start & Run Your Own Record Label in the 1990s. rev. ed. Gary Hustwit. LC 91-68497. 124p. 1992. pap. 26.95 (*0-9627013-2-7*) Rockpress Pub.

Releasing an Independent Record: How to Successfully Start & Run Your Own Record Label in the 1990s. 4th ed. Gary Hustwit. LC 93-83748. 150p. 1993. pap. 22.95 (*0-9627013-5-1*) Rockpress Pub.

Releasing an Independent Record: How to Successfully Start & Run Your Own Record Label in the 1990s. 5th rev. ed. Gary Hustwit. (Illus.). 200p. (Orig.). 1995. pap. 24.95 (*1-884615-02-3*) Rockpress Pub.

Releasing Anger. S. Richard. 20p. 1985. pap. 2.00 (*0-89486-249-9*, 1420B) Hazelden.

Releasing Arthritis: The Seven Year Plan. Linda F. Fleming. Ed. by Mary Abrams. LC 89-92230. 200p. (Orig.). 1990. pap. 11.00 (*1-877631-02-7*) LF Pub VA.

Releasing God's Power Through the Laying on Hands. John Eckhardt. 64p. (Orig.). 1992. pap. 3.00 (*0-9630567-4-3*) Crusaders Minist.

Releasing Hormones: Genetics & Immunology in Human Reproduction. Ed. by S. Shan Ratnam et al. (Advances in Fertility & Sterility Ser.: Vol. 3). 204p. 1987. 55.00 (*1-85070-153-9*) Prthnon Pub.

***Releasing of the Power.** Gary Barnhart. 225p. (Orig.). 1997. pap. 18.99 (*1-57502-410-1*, PO1273) Morris Pubng.

Releasing Power from Within & the Real You. Linwood E. Mooring, Jr. (Illus.). 230p. (Orig.). pap. write for info. (*0-9646104-0-X*) Mooring Hse Pr.

Releasing Resources to Achieve Health Gain. Ed. by Christopher Riley et al. 1995. 79.95 (*1-85775-018-7*, Radcliffe Med Pr) Scovill Paterson.

Releasing Serpents. Bernice Zamora. LC 93-11946. 128p. 1994. pap. 11.00 (*0-927534-39-8*) Biling Rev-Pr.

Releasing Strategy: For Personal Power & Peace of Mind. Sharon M. Cameron. LC 93-93813. 133p. (Orig.). 1993. pap. 11.95 (*0-9635820-6-2*) Watershed CA.

Releasing the Ability of God Through Prayer. Charles Capps. 159p. 1978. mass mkt. 5.99 (*0-89274-075-2*, HH-075) Harrison Hse.

Releasing the Godly Fragrance. Mona Johnian. Ed. by David L. Young. 144p. (Orig.). 1989. pap. 4.95 (*0-929685-01-6*) Superior Bks.

Releasing the Imagination: Essays on Education, the Arts, & Social Change. Maxine Greene. (Education Ser.). 233p. text ed. 29.95 (*0-7879-0081-8*) Jossey-Bass.

Releasing the Prayer Anointing. Larry Lea. 288p. 1996. 19.99 (*0-7852-7712-9*) Nelson.

Releasing the Spirit. Randy Shankle. Orig. Title: Merismos. 240p. 1993. mass mkt. 5.99 (*0-88368-461-6*) Whitaker Hse.

Releasing the Undiscovered Country: Rebirth of Revolution. Thomas Jefferson. (American Rebirth Flip Bks.). 110p. 24.95 (*1-888407-11-5*) Powerhse Publng.

Releasing Through Numerology, No. 3. Tina Lucia. Ed. by Linda Craig. (Releasing Ser.). (Illus.). 150p. 1988. 12.95 (*0-317-91330-1*); pap. 9.95 (*0-317-91331-X*) T Lucia.

Releasing Through Tarot, No. 2. Tina Lucia. Ed. by Linda Craig. (Releasing Ser.). 150p. 1988. 19.95 (*0-317-91332-8*); pap. 9.95 (*0-317-91333-6*) T Lucia.

Releasing Your Potential. Myles E. Munroe. 224p. (Orig.). (SPA.). 1994. pap. 8.99 (*1-56043-108-3*) Destiny Image.

Releasing Your Potential Workbook. Myles E. Munroe. 48p. 1993. pap. 6.99 (*1-56043-093-1*) Destiny Image.

***Relections & Conversations.** Stone. Date not set. text ed. 45.00 (*0-312-17727-5*) St Martin.

Relentless. Kris Franklin. 320p. 1993. mass mkt. 4.50 (*0-8217-4371-6*, Zebra Kensgtn) Kensgtn Pub Corp.

Relentless. J. D. Rage. (Illus.). 51p. (Orig.). 1994. pap. 4.00 (*1-886206-13-9*) Venom Pr.

Relentless: The Hard-Hitting History of Buffalo Bills Football. Sal Maiorana. (Illus.). 480p. 1994. 39.50 (*1-885758-00-6*) Quality Sports.

***Relentless: The Japanese Way of Marketing.** Johny K. Johansson. 1997. pap. 14.00 (*0-88730-860-0*) Harper Busn.

Relentless Flame. large type ed. Patricia Wilson. (Harlequin Romance Ser.). 287p. 1995. lib. bdg. 18.95 (*0-263-14105-5*, Pub. by Mills & Boon UK) Thorndike Pr.

***Relentless Growth: How Silicon Valley's Secrets Can Work for Your Business.** Christopher Meyer. 1997. 27.50 (*0-684-83446-4*) Free Pr.

Relentless Hunger: The Heart's Search for Love. James E. Sullivan. LC 93-44071. 288p. (Orig.). 1994. pap. 11.95 (*0-8091-3466-7*) Paulist Pr.

Relentless Pursuit Trophy Whitetail Hunting: The Official Trophy Hunter's Guide. Tim Wells. 190p. 1995. 19.95 (*1-886812-00-4*); lib. bdg. 14.95 (*1-886812-01-2*) R Wells.

Relentless Storm. Clarie Lorrimer. 1994. 19.00 (*0-7278-4580-2*) Severn Hse.

***Relentlessly Practical Guide to Raising Serious Money: Proven Strategies for Nonprofit Organizations.** David Lansdowne. LC 96-86273. 264p. (Orig.). 1997. pap. 34.95 (*1-889102-13-X*) Emerson & Church.

Relevance: Communication & Cognition. Daniel Sperber. (C). 1995. pap. 22.95 (*0-631-19878-4*) Blackwell Pubs.

Relevance: Communication & Cognition. Daniel Sperber. (Language & Thought Ser.). (Illus.). 287p. 1986. 34.50 (*0-674-75475-1*); pap. 15.95 (*0-674-75476-X*) HUP.

Relevance: Papers from the 1994 Fall Symposium. Ed. by Russ Greiner & Devika Subramanian. (Technical Reports). (Illus.). 200p. 1994. spiral bd. 25.00 (*0-929280-76-8*) AAAI Pr.

Relevance in Sociological Research. Ed. by S. L. Doshi. (C). 1991. 22.50 (*81-7033-135-8*, Pub. by Rawat II) S Asia.

Relevance in the Education of Today's Business Student, 1973. (Yearbook Ser.). 292p. 5.00 (*0-933964-10-2*) Natl Busn Ed Assoc.

Relevance Lost: The Rise & Fall of Management Accounting. H. Johnson & Robert S. Kaplan. 1987. text ed. 32.00 (*0-07-103244-4*) McGraw.

Relevance Lost: The Rise & Fall of Management Accounting. H. Thomas Johnson & Robert S. Kaplan. 296p. 1991. pap. 15.95 (*0-87584-254-2*) Harvard Busn.

Relevance Lost: The Rise & Fall of Management Accounting. H. Thomas Johnson & Robert S. Kaplan. 1991. text ed. 15.95 (*0-07-103304-1*) McGraw.

Relevance of a Decade: Essays to Mark the First Ten Years of the Harvard Business School Press. Ed. by Paula B. Duffy. LC 94-13037. 1994. 25.00 (*0-87584-576-2*) Harvard Busn.

Relevance of a Decade: Essays to Mark the First Ten Years of the Harvard Business School Press. Ed. by Paula B. Duffy. 384p. (C). 1996. pap. 14.95 (*0-87584-687-4*) Harvard Busn.

Relevance of a Decade: Essays to Mark the First Ten Years of the Harvard Business School Press. Ed. by Paula B. Duffy. 1996. pap. text ed. 14.95 (*0-07-103653-9*) McGraw.

Relevance of Ambedkarism in India. Ed. by K. S. Chalam. (C). 1993. 22.00 (*81-7033-216-8*) S Asia.

Relevance of Anarchism. Sam Dolgoff. 36p. pap. 4.00 (*0-88286-200-6*) C H Kerr.

Relevance of Ancient Social & Political Philosophy for Our Times: A Short Introduction to the Problem. Kurt Von Fritz. LC 74-78098. iv, 57p. 1974. pap. 7.95 (*3-11-004859-0*) De Gruyter.

Relevance of Animal Studies to the Evaluation of Human Cancer Risk. R. D'Amato et al. (Progress in Clinical & Biological Research Ser.). 482p. 1992. text ed. 227.95 (*0-471-56183-5*, Wiley-Interscience) Wiley.

Relevance of Anthropology: The Indian Scenario. B. G. Halda. (C). 1991. 44.00 (*0-685-59786-5*, Pub. by Rawat II) S Asia.

Relevance of Apocalyptic. 3rd rev. ed. H. H. Rowley. LC 64-12221. 240p. 1980. reprint ed. pap. text ed. 9.50 (*0-87921-061-3*) Attic Pr.

Relevance of Bliss. Nona Coxhead. 192p. 1986. pap. 6.95 (*0-312-67055-9*) St Martin.

Relevance of Canadian History: U. S. & Imperial Perspectives. Robin W. Winks. 116p. (C). 1988. reprint ed. lib. bdg. 15.00 (*0-8191-6831-9*) U Pr of Amer.

Relevance of Charles Peirce. Ed. by Eugene Freeman. (Monist Library of Philosophy). 412p. 1983. 39.95 (*0-914417-00-2*); pap. 18.95 (*0-914417-04-5*) Hegeler Inst.

***Relevance of Creation.** pap. 12.95 (*0-89051-141-1*) Master Bks.

Relevance of Culture. Morris Freilich et al. LC 89-17729. 256p. (Orig.). 1989. text ed. 55.00 (*0-89789-181-3*, H181, Bergin & Garvey); pap. text ed. 14.95 (*0-89789-180-5*, G180, Bergin & Garvey) Greenwood.

Relevance of Economic Theories. Josef Pajestka & Charles H. Feinstein. 1980. text ed. 39.95 (*0-312-67054-0*) St Martin.

Relevance of General Systems Theory. Ed. by Ervin Laszlo. LC 72-81355. 213p. 1972. 8.95 (*0-8076-0659-6*) Braziller.

Relevance of International Adjudication. Milton Katz. LC 68-21974. 175p. 1968. 22.00 (*0-674-75500-6*) HUP.

***Relevance of Keynesian Economic Policies Today.** Philip Arestis & Malcolm C. Sawyer. LC 96-32987. 1997. text ed. 69.95 (*0-312-16552-8*) St Martin.

Relevance of Metaethics to Ethics. Torbjorn Tannsjo. (Stockholm Studies in Philosophy). 226p. (Orig.). 1976. pap. 39.50 (*91-22-00068-2*) Coronet Bks.

Relevance of Philosophy to Life. John Lachs. LC 94-44987. (Vanderbilt Library of American Philosophy). 336p. 1995. 29.95 (*0-8265-1262-3*) Vanderbilt U Pr.

***Relevance of Revelation.** Brian Keen. 124p. (Orig.). 1997. mass mkt. 4.99 (*1-55197-916-0*, Pub. by Comnwlth Pub CN) Partners Pubs Grp.

Relevance of Rexroth. Ken Knabb. LC 90-82474. 88p. (Orig.). 1990. pap. 5.00 (*0-939682-02-8*) Bur Public Secrets.

Relevance of the Beautiful & Other Essays. Hans-Georg Gadamer. Ed. by Robert Bernasconi. 190p. 1987. pap. text ed. 19.95 (*0-521-33953-7*) Cambridge U Pr.

Relevance of the Couch in Contemporary Psychoanalysis Vol. 15, No. 3, 1995: A Special Issue of Psychoanalytic Inquiry. 1995. pap. 20.00 (*0-88163-994-X*) Analytic Pr.

Relevance of the Family to Psychoanalytic Theory. Theodore Lidz. LC 92-1477. 266p. (C). 1992. 35.00 (*0-8236-5784-1*) Intl Univs Pr.

Relevance of the Fathers. Emilianos Timiadis. 1994. pap. 9.95 (*1-885652-01-1*) Holy Cross Orthodox.

Relevance of the Kalevala. Helmi Kortes-Erkkila. 92p. (Orig.). 1994. pap. 9.95 (*0-9632975-9-7*) Sampo Pub.

Relevance of the Property Teaching of Pope Paul VI: An Ancient Teaching in a New Context. Mark G. Etling. LC 93-840. 272p. 1993. text ed. 89.95 (*0-7734-2218-8*, Mellen Univ Pr) E Mellen.

***Relevance of Whitehead: 1961 Edition.** Ed. by Ivor Leclerc. 384p. 1996. reprint ed. write for info. (*1-85506-233-X*) Bks Intl VA.

Relevance Rediscovered, Vol. 1: An Anthology of 25 Significant Articles from the NACA Bulletins & Yearbooks. Richard Vangermeersch. Ed. by Claire Barth. (Illus.). 400p. (Orig.). 1990. pap. 40.00 (*0-86641-182-8*, 89227) Inst Mgmt Account.

Relevance Regained: From Top-down Control to Bottom-up Empowerment. H. Thomas Johnson. 224p. 1992. 32.00 (*0-02-916555-5*, Free Press) Free Pr.

Relevance Relations in Discourse: A Study with Special Reference to Sissala. Regina Blass. (Cambridge Studies in Linguistics: No. 55). (Illus.). 300p. (C). 1990. text ed. 65.00 (*0-521-38515-6*) Cambridge U Pr.

Relevance Theory: Applications & Implications. Ed. by Robyn Carston et al. (Pragmatics & Beyond New Ser.: No. 37). 300p. 1996. 79.00 (*1-55619-330-0*) Benjamins North Am.

Relevance to Human Cancer of N-Nitroso Compounds, Tobacco Smoke & Mycotoxins. Ed. by I. K. O'Neill et al. (IARC Scientific Publications: No. 105). (Illus.). 642p. 1991. pap. 150.00 (*92-832-2105-2*) OUP.

Relevancy of Torah to the Social & Ethical Issues of Our Time. Dovid Cohen. (Annual Fryer Memorial Lectures). 1.00 (*0-914131-57-5*, B140) Torah Umesorah.

Relevant Accounting Concepts & Applications: The Writings & Contribution of C. Rufus Rorem. Harvey S. Hendrickson. LC 90-25874. (New Works in Accounting History). 576p. 1991. text ed. 15.00 (*0-8153-0008-5*) Garland.

Relevant Anabaptist Missiology for the Nineteen Nineties. Ed. by Calvin E. Shenk. 178p. (C). 1990. pap. text ed. 18.00 (*1-877736-11-2*) MB Missions.

***Relevant Business Statistics.** Gerbing. (Miscellaneous/Catalogs Ser.). Date not set. text ed. 55.95 (*0-314-12680-5*) S-W Pub.

Relevant Circumstances & Maritime Delimitation. Malcolm D. Evans. (Oxford Monographs in International Law). 280p. 1989. 85.00 (*0-19-825240-4*) OUP.

Relevant Financial Statements: Original Anthology. Joshua Ronen & George H. Sorter. Ed. by Richard P. Brief. LC 77-87318. (Development of Contemporary Accounting Thought Ser.). 1978. lib. bdg. 30.95 (*0-405-10930-X*) Ayer.

Relevant Logics & Their Rivals, One. Richard Routley. 460p. (C). 1983. pap. text ed. 30.00 (*0-917930-66-5*) Ridgeview.

Relevant Logics & Their Rivals, One, Vol. 1. Richard Routley. xv, 460p. (C). 1983. lib. bdg. 49.00 (*0-917930-80-0*) Ridgeview.

Relevant Research, Vol. II. 284p. 1992. pap. text ed. 14.95 (*0-87355-111-7*) Natl Sci Tchrs.

***Relevant Translations: History, Presentation, Criticism, Application.** Jutta Muschard. LC 96-10167. (European University Studies, Series XXI: Vol. 163). 253p. 1996. pap. 51.95 (*0-8204-3161-3*, P306) P Lang Pubng.

Relevant Word: Communicating the Gospel to Seekers. Robert G. Duffett. 160p. 1995. pap. 15.00 (*0-8170-1233-8*) Judson.

Relevanzlogik und Situationssemantik. Wolfgang Heydrich. (Grundlagen der Kommunikation und Kognition - Foundations of Communication & Cognition Ser.). viii, 328p. (GER.). (C). 1995. lib. bdg. 167.70 (*3-11-014399-2*) De Gruyter.

Releve du Matin. Henry De Montherlant. (FRE.). 1972. pap. 10.95 (*0-8288-3755-4*, F115810) Fr & Eur.

***Reliability.** Kales. 1997. text ed. 50.67 (*0-13-485822-0*) P-H.

Reliability: Probabilistic Models & Statistical Methods. Lawrence M. Leemis. LC 94-23068. (International Series in Industrial & Systems Engineering). 319p. 1994. text ed. 83.00 (*0-13-720517-1*) P-H.

Reliability Analysis & Prediction: A Methodology Oriented Treatment. Krishna B. Misra. LC 92-13149. (Fundamental Studies in Engineering: No. 15). 890p. 1992. 409.25 (*0-444-89606-6*) Elsevier.

Reliability Analysis for Engineers: An Introduction. Roger D. Leitch. (Illus.). 248p. 1995. 80.00 (*0-19-856372-8*); pap. 45.00 (*0-19-856371-X*) OUP.

Reliability Analysis in Engineering Applications. Shu-Ho Dai & Ming-O Wang. (Competitive Manufacturing Ser.). (Illus.). 448p. 1992. text ed. 77.95 (*0-442-00842-2*) Van Nos Reinhold.

R

Reliability Analysis of Water Distribution Systems. Ed. by Larry W. Mays. 544p. 1989. pap. text ed. 36.00 (*0-87262-712-8*, 712) Am Soc Civil Eng.

*__Reliability & Decision Making.__ Ed. by Barlow et al. (Illus.). 384p. (C). (gr. 13 up). 1993. text ed. 98.95 (*0-412-53480-0*, Chap & Hall NY) Chapman & Hall.

Reliability & Degradation: Semiconductor Devices & Circuits. Ed. by M. J. Howes & D. V. Morgan. LC 80-42310. (Wiley Series in Solid State Devices & Circuits). (Illus.). 456p. reprint ed. pap. 130.00 (*0-7837-6385-9*, 2046098) Bks Demand.

Reliability & Degradation of III-V Optical Devices. Osamu Ueda. LC 96-26600. 353p. 1996. 88.00 (*0-89006-652-3*) Artech Hse.

Reliability & Degradation of Semiconductor Lasers & LEDs. Mitsuo Fukuda. (Optoelectronics Library). 400p. 1991. text ed. 89.00 (*0-89006-465-2*) Artech Hse.

Reliability & Life Testing Handbook, Vol. 1. Dimitri Kececioglu. 960p. 1992. text ed. 89.00 (*0-13-772377-6*) P-H.

Reliability & Life Testing Handbook, Vol. 2. Dimitri Kececioglu. 600p. (C). 1993. text ed. 85.00 (*0-13-772369-5*) P-H.

Reliability & Maintainability Guideline for Manufacturing Machinery & Equipment. 61p. 1993. 19.00 (*1-56091-362-2*, M-110) Soc Auto Engineers.

Reliability & Maintainability of Redundant & Non-Redundant Systems. Michael Sparkman & David Heinzelmann. 32p. (Orig.). (C). Date not set. pap. 15.00 (*1-56946-014-0*) Motorola Univ.

Reliability & Maintainability Symposium, 1993. IEEE, Reliability Society Staff. Ed. by Institute of Electrical & Electronics Engineers, Inc. Staff. LC 78-132873. 600p. 1993. pap. text ed. write for info. (*0-7803-0943-X*); lib. bdg. write for info. (*0-7803-0944-8*, 93CH3257-3); fiche write for info. (*0-7803-0945-6*) Inst Electrical.

Reliability & Maintainability Symposium, 1994. IEEE, Reliability Society Staff. Ed. by IEEE Staff. LC 78-132873. 500p. 1994. pap. text ed. write for info. (*0-7803-1786-6*); lib. bdg. write for info. (*0-7803-1787-4*, 94CH3391-0); fiche write for info. (*0-7803-1788-2*) Inst Electrical.

Reliability & Maintenance of Complex Systems. Ed. by S. Ozekici. LC 96-13936. (NATO ASI Ser.: Vol. 154). 587p. 1996. 173.00 (*3-540-61109-6*) Spr-Verlag.

*__Reliability & Optimization of Structural Systems.__ Ed. by R. Rackwitz et al. (Illus.). 324p. 1995. text ed. 89.95 (*0-412-63630-1*, Chap & Hall NY) Chapman & Hall.

Reliability & Optimization of Structural Systems. Ed. by P. Thoft-Christensen. (Lecture Notes in Engineering Ser.: Vol. 33). (Illus.). vi, 474p. 1987. pap. 79.00 (*0-387-18570-4*) Spr-Verlag.

Reliability & Optimization of Structural Systems: Proceedings of the Fourth IFIP WG 7.5 Conference, Munich, Germany, September 11-13, 1991. Ed. by R. Rackwitz et al. LC 92-16815. (Lecture Notes in Engineering Ser.: Vol. 76). (Illus.). vii, 485p. 1992. 137.95 (*0-387-55403-3*) Spr-Verlag.

Reliability & Optimization of Structural Systems V. Ed. by P. Thoft-Christensen & H. Ishikawa. (IFIP Transactions B: Applications in Technology Ser.: Vol. B-12). 298p. 1993. pap. 119.25 (*0-444-81605-4*, North Holland) Elsevier.

*__Reliability & Optimization of Structural Systems 1996: Proceedings of the Seventh IFIP WG 7.5 Working Conference Reliability & Optimization of Structural Systems, 1996.__ Dan M. Frangopol et al. LC 96-37446. 363p. 1997. 207.00 (*0-08-042826-6*, Pergamon Pr) Elsevier.

Reliability & Optimization of Structural Systems '90: Proceedings of the 3rd IFIP WG 7.5 Conference Berkeley, CA, U. S. A., March 26-28, 1990. Ed. by A. D. Kiureghian & P. Thoft-Christensen. (Lecture Notes in Engineering Ser.: Vol. 61). (Illus.). viii, 405p. 1991. pap. 68.00 (*0-387-53450-4*) Spr-Verlag.

Reliability & Process Control: Proceedings of a Conference on Process Control & Reliability Analysis Held in Conjunction with ASM's Materials Week '85, Toronto, Ontario, Canada, 14-17 October 1985. Conference on Process Control & Reliability Analysis Staff. Ed. by C. Ravindran et al. LC 86-70845. (Illus.). 279p. reprint ed. pap. 79.60 (*0-8357-4100-1*, 2036866) Bks Demand.

Reliability & Quality Control: Proceedings IASTED Symposium, Paris, France, June 24-26, 1987. Ed. by M. H. Hamza. 235p. 1987. 82.50 (*0-88986-128-5*, 113) Acta Pr.

Reliability & Risk Analysis: Methods & Nuclear Power Applications. Norman J. McCormick. LC 81-2758. 1981. text ed. 95.00 (*0-12-482360-2*) Acad Pr.

Reliability & Risk in Pressure Vessels & Piping. Ed. by J. H. Phillips. (PVP Ser.: Vol. 251). 172p. 1993. 45.00 (*0-7918-0978-1*, H00810) ASME.

Reliability & Robustness of Engineering Software. Ed. by C. A. Brebbia & G. Keramidas. LC 87-62015. (RRES Ser.). 540p. 1987. 138.00 (*0-931215-61-7*) Computational Mech MA.

Reliability & Safety Assessment of Dynamic Process Systems. Ed. by T. Aldemir et al. (NATO ASI Series F: Computer & Systems Sciences, Special Programme AET: Vol. 120). 236p. 1994. 71.95 (*0-387-57148-5*) Spr-Verlag.

Reliability & Uncertainty Analyses in Hydraulic Design. Ed. by Ben-Chie Yen & Yeou-Koung Tung. LC 93-41048. 1993. 30.00 (*0-87262-993-7*) Am Soc Civil Eng.

Reliability & Validity Assessment. Edward G. Carmines & Richard A. Zeller. LC 79-67629. (Quantitative Applications in the Social Sciences Ser.: No. 17). (Illus.). 70p. 1979. pap. 9.95 (*0-8039-1371-0*) Sage.

Reliability & Validity in Neuropsychological Assessment. M. D. Franzen. (Critical Issues in Neuropsychology Ser.). (Illus.). 320p. 1989. 45.00 (*0-306-43065-7*, Plenum Pr) Plenum.

Reliability & Validity in Qualitative Research. Jerome Kirk & Marc L. Miller. (Qualitative Research Methods Ser.: Vol. 1). 96p. 1985. text ed. 22.95 (*0-8039-2560-3*); pap. text ed. 9.95 (*0-8039-2470-4*) Sage.

Reliability Assessment of Electrical Power Systems Using Monte Carlo Methods. Ed. by Roy Billinton & W. Li. (Illus.). 365p. (C). 1994. text ed. 89.50 (*0-306-44781-9*, Plenum Pr) Plenum.

Reliability Assessment of Large Electric Power Systems. Roy Billinton & Ronald N. Allan. (C). 1988. lib. bdg. 86.50 (*0-89838-266-1*) Kluwer Ac.

Reliability, Availability, & Productiveness of Systems. D. J. Sherwin & A. Bossche. LC 93-16765. 288p. (gr. 13). 1993. text ed. 66.95 (*0-412-39320-4*) Chapman & Hall.

Reliability, Availability, Maintainability & Safety Assessment: Assessment, Hardware, Software & Human Factors, 2 vols., 1. A. Villemeur. LC 91-14329. 368p. 1992. text ed. 120.00 (*0-471-93048-2*) Wiley.

Reliability, Availability, Maintainability & Safety Assessment: Assessment, Hardware, Software & Human Factors, 2 vols., Set. A. Villemeur. 1119p. 1992. text ed. 142.00 (*0-471-93050-4*) Wiley.

Reliability, Availability, Maintainability & Safety Assessment: Assessment, Hardware, Software & Human Factors, 2 vols., Vol. 2. A. Villemeur. LC 91-14329. 751p. 1992. text ed. 120.00 (*0-471-93049-0*) Wiley.

Reliability Based Design. Singiresu S. Rao. 1992. text ed. 60.00 (*0-07-051192-6*) McGraw.

*__Reliability-Based Design in Civil Engineering.__ unabridged ed. Milton E. Harr. LC 96-35382. (Illus.). 304p. 1997. reprint ed. pap. text ed. 11.95 (*0-486-69429-1*) Dover.

Reliability-Based Design of Engineered Wood Structures: Proceedings of the NATO Advanced Research Workshop, Florence, Italy 3-5 June 1991. Ed. by Jozsef Bodig. LC 92-15408. 208p. (C). 1992. lib. bdg. 106.00 (*0-7923-1801-3*) Kluwer Ac.

Reliability-Based Mechanical Design. Ed. by Thomas A. Cruse. LC 96-48240. (Mechanical Engineering Series of Reference Books & Textbooks: Vol. 108). 341p. 1997. 110.00 (*0-8247-9793-0*) Dekker.

Reliability by Design: CAE Techniques for Electronic Components & Systems. A. C. Brombacher. 275p. 1992. text ed. 67.95 (*0-471-93193-4*) Wiley.

Reliability-Centered Maintenance. Anthony M. Smith. 1993. text ed. 40.00 (*0-07-059046-X*) McGraw.

*__Reliability-Centered Maintenance.__ 2nd ed. John Moubray. LC 97-8176. 448p. 1997. 49.95 (*0-8311-3078-4*) Indus Pr.

Reliability Data Bases. Aniello Amendola & Alfred Z. Keller. (C). 1987. lib. bdg. 171.00 (*90-277-2549-7*) Kluwer Ac.

Reliability Data Collection & Analysis. Ed. by J. Flamm & T. Luisi. LC 92-5509. (Eurocourses: Reliability & Risk Analysis Ser.: Vol. 3). 336p. (C). 1992. lib. bdg. 133.00 (*0-7923-1591-X*) Kluwer Ac.

Reliability Data Collection & Use in Risk & Availability Assessment. V. Colombari. (Illus.). x, 898p. 1989. 170.00 (*0-387-50834-1*) Spr-Verlag.

Reliability Design for Vibroacoustic Environments: Papers Presented at the Winter Annual Meeting of the American Society of Mechanical Engineers, New York, NY, November 17-21, 1974. American Society of Mechanical Engineers Staff. Ed. by Daniel D. Kana & Thomas G. Butler. LC 74-81164. (Illus.). 193p. reprint ed. pap. 55.10 (*0-685-23449-5*, 2032704) Bks Demand.

Reliability Engineering. K. K. Aggarwal. (Topics in Safety, Reliability & Quality Ser.). 396p. (C). 1993. lib. bdg. 188.50 (*0-7923-2524-9*) Kluwer Ac.

Reliability Engineering. Ed. by Aniello Amendola & Amalio Saiz de Bustamante. (C). 1988. lib. bdg. 234.00 (*90-277-2762-7*) Kluwer Ac.

Reliability Engineering. Elsayed A. Elsayed. 960p. (C). 1996. text ed. 66.95 (*0-201-63481-3*) Addison-Wesley.

Reliability Engineering. Ed. by Patrick D. O'Connor. (Arab School of Science & Technology Ser.). 305p. 1987. 78.95 (*0-89116-684-X*) Hemisp Pub.

Reliability Engineering for Electrical Design. Fuqua. (Electrical Engineering & Electronics Ser.: Vol. 34). 406p. 1986. 130.00 (*0-8247-7571-6*) Dekker.

Reliability Engineering Handbook, Vol. 1. Dimitri Kececioglu. 720p. 1991. text ed. 73.00 (*0-13-772294-X*, 330208) P-H.

Reliability Engineering Handbook, Vol. 2. Dimitri Kececioglu. 560p. 1991. text ed. 73.00 (*0-13-772302-4*) P-H.

Reliability Engineering Nineteen Seventy-Eight: Proceedings of the SRE Reliability Symposium, Ottawa, Ontario, Canada, October, 1978. Canadian Reliability Engineers Staff. LC 78-10571. 1979. pap. 29.00 (*0-08-023228-0*, Pergamon Pr) Elsevier.

Reliability Engineering, 1975. Canadian Reliability Engineers Staff. 1976. pap. 35.00 (*0-08-019977-1*, Pergamon Pr) Elsevier.

Reliability Engineering 1980: Proceedings of the 1980 Canadian SRE Reliability Symposium, Ottawa, Ontario, Canada May 15-16 1980. Canadian Reliability Engineers Staff. 170p. 1981. pap. 43.00 (*0-08-026163-9*, Pergamon Pr) Elsevier.

Reliability Evaluation of Engineering Systems: Concepts & Techniques. 2nd ed. Roy Billinton & Ronald N. Allan. LC 92-10368. 475p. (C). 1992. 65.00 (*0-306-44063-6*, Plenum Pr) Plenum.

Reliability Evaluation of Power Systems. 2nd ed. Roy Billinton & Ronald N. Allan. (Illus.). 510p. (C). 1996. 89.50 (*0-306-45259-6*, Plenum Pr) Plenum.

Reliability Evaluation of Some Fault-Tolerant Computer Architectures. Shunji Osaki & T. Nishio. (Lecture Notes in Computer Science Ser.: Vol. 97). 129p. 1980. 21.00 (*0-387-10274-4*) Spr-Verlag.

Reliability for Engineers, an Introduction. Michael Beasley. (Illus.). 270p. (C). 1991. text ed. 90.00 (*0-333-54237-1*, Pub. by Macmill Educ UK); pap. text ed. 35.00 (*0-333-54238-X*, Pub. by Macmill Educ UK) Scholium Intl.

Reliability for the Social Sciences: Theory & Applications. Rose E. Traub. (Measurement Methods for the Social Sciences Ser.: Vol. 3). (C). 1994. text ed. 42.00 (*0-8039-4324-5*); pap. text ed. 19.50 (*0-8039-4325-3*) Sage.

Reliability for the Technologies. 2nd ed. Leonard A. Doty. (Illus.). 242p. 1989. 28.95 (*0-8311-3024-5*) Indus Pr.

Reliability Fundamentals. V. M. Catuneanu & A. N. Mihalache. (Fundamental Studies in Engineering: No. 10). 240p. 1990. 167.00 (*0-444-98879-3*) Elsevier.

Reliability Growth Processes & Management. LC 62-38584. 67p. 1989. pap. text ed. 80.00 (*0-915414-31-7*) Inst Environ Sci.

Reliability-Heavy Duty. 1983. 20.00 (*0-89883-304-3*, SP533) Soc Auto Engineers.

Reliability Improvement with Design of Experiments. Condra. (Quality & Reliability Ser.: Vol. 41). 384p. 1993. 69.75 (*0-8247-8888-5*) Dekker.

*__Reliability in Communication Technology.__ Chown. (Illus.). 304p. (C). 1997. text ed. write for info. (*0-412-61740-4*, Chap & Hall NY) Chapman & Hall.

Reliability in Computer System Design. Marvin V. Zelkowitz. LC 87-1164. (Ablex Series in Software Engineering). 296p. 1987. text ed. 78.50 (*0-89391-412-6*) Ablex Pub.

Reliability in Engineering Design. K. C. Kapur & L. R. Lamberson. 586p. 1977. Net. text ed. 61.00 (*0-471-51191-9*) Wiley.

Reliability in Instrumentation & Control. J. C. Cluley. LC 92-21340. (Industrial Instrumentation Ser.). (Illus.). 208p. 1993. 57.95 (*0-7506-0737-8*) Buttrwrth-Heinemann.

Reliability in Non-Destructive Testing: Proceedings of the 27th Annual British Conference on Non-Destructive Testing, Portsmouth, UK, 12-15 September 1988. Ed. by C. Brook & P. D. Hanstead. (Illus.). 521p. 1989. pap. 27.00 (*0-08-036961-8*, Pergamon Pr) Elsevier.

Reliability in Procurement & Use: From Specification to Replacement. Henry S. Blanks. LC 92-10301. 356p. 1992. text ed. 120.00 (*0-471-93488-7*) Wiley.

Reliability in the Acquisitions Process. DePriest & Launer. (Lecture Notes in Statistics Ser.: Vol. 4). 216p. 1983. 95.00 (*0-8247-1792-9*) Dekker.

Reliability in Water Resources Management. Ed. by Edward A. McBean et al. LC 79-64191. 1979. 30.00 (*0-918334-30-6*) WRP.

Reliability, Key to Industrial Success: Proceedings of ASM's 1987 Conference on Reliability--Key to Industrial Success, Los Angeles, CA, 24-26 March 1987. Conference on Reliability--Key to Industrial Success Staff & Dimitri Kececioglu. Ed. by S. Sundaresan. LC 87-71238. (Illus.). 216p. reprint ed. pap. 61.60 (*0-8357-4093-5*, 2036859) Bks Demand.

Reliability, Maintainability, & Availability Assessment. 2nd ed. Mitchell O. Locks. LC 94-40648. 348p. 1995. 68.00 (*0-87389-293-3*, H0849) ASQC Qual Pr.

Reliability, Maintainability, & Risk. 4th rev. ed. David J. Smith. LC 92-30889. 1993. pap. 45.95 (*0-7506-0854-4*) Buttrwrth-Heinemann.

Reliability, Maintainability, & Supportability: A Porbabilistic Approach. J. Knezevic. 1993. text ed. 80.00 (*0-07-707691-5*) McGraw.

Reliability, Maintainability, & Supportability: A Probabilistic Approach. J. Knezevic. LC 92-17578. 1992. 39.50 (*0-07-707423-8*) McGraw.

Reliability, Maintainability, & Supportability Guidebook. 3rd ed. (Miscellaneous Ser.). 588p. 1995. 79.00 (*1-56091-514-5*, M-102/95) Soc Auto Engineers.

Reliability Methods for Engineers. K. S. Krishnamoarthi. 189p. 1992. 29.00 (*0-87389-161-9*, H0699) ASQC Qual Pr.

Reliability Modeling in Electric Power Systems. J. Endrenyi. LC 78-6222. (Illus.). 352p. reprint ed. pap. 100.40 (*0-8357-4611-9*, 2037544) Bks Demand.

Reliability Modelling & Applications. A. G. Colombo & A. Z. Keller. (C). 1987. lib. bdg. 167.00 (*90-277-2566-7*) Kluwer Ac.

Reliability of Boiler Plant. Ed. by H. Buttler & C. Petts. (C). 1980. 100.00 (*0-86022-090-7*, Pub. by Build Servs Info Assn UK) St Mut.

Reliability of Computer & Communication Networks. F. Roberts et al. LC 91-9953. (DIMACS Ser.: Vol. 5). 259p. 1991. 45.00 (*0-8218-6592-7*, DIMACS/5) Am Math.

Reliability of Electronic Packages & Semiconductor Devices. Giulio Di Giacomo. LC 96-29181. (Illus.). 370p. 1996. text ed. 65.00 (*0-07-017024-X*) McGraw.

Reliability of Heating, Ventilating & Air Conditioning Equipment: Introduction & Literature Survey. A. Hasan. (C). 1969. 50.00 (*0-685-33900-9*, Pub. by Build Servs Info Assn UK) St Mut.

Reliability of Hydro-Reclamation Installations. T. E. Mirtskhulava. Tr. by V. S. Kothekar from RUS. 308p. (C). 1987. text ed. 90.00 (*90-6191-491-4*, Pub. by A A Balkema NE) Ashgate Pub Co.

Reliability of Hydro-Reclamation Installations. T. E. Mirtskhulava. (C). 1987. 33.00 (*81-204-0196-4*, Pub. by Oxford IBH II) S Asia.

Reliability of Mental Tests in the Division of an Academic Group see Two Studies in Mental Tests

Reliability of Metals in Electronics. H. S. Rathore. 1995. pap. 42.00 (*1-56677-097-1*, PV 95-3) Electrochem Soc.

Reliability of Non-Destructive Inspection: Assessing the Assessment of Structures under Stress. M. G. Silk et al. (Illus.). 224p. 1987. 23.00 (*0-85274-533-8*) IOP Pub.

Reliability of Semiconductor Devices - Interconnections & Dielectric Breakdown, Vol. 92-4. Ed. by H. S. Rathore et al. LC 92-70488. (Proceedings Ser.). 350p. 1992. 42.00 (*1-56677-003-3*) Electrochem Soc.

Reliability of Sense Perception. William P. Alston. LC 92-54964. 1993. 32.50 (*0-8014-2862-9*) Cornell U Pr.

Reliability of Sense Perception. William P. Alston. LC 92-54964. 160p. 1996. pap. 11.95 (*0-8014-8101-5*) Cornell U Pr.

Reliability of Software Intensive Systems. Michael A. Friedman et al. LC 94-23431. (Advanced Computing & Telecommunications Ser.). (Illus.). 404p. 1995. 64.00 (*0-8155-1361-5*) Noyes.

Reliability of Sub-Seabed Disposal Operations for High Level Waste. M. M. Sarshar. (C). 1986. pap. text ed. 118.00 (*0-86010-835-X*, Pub. by Graham & Trotman UK) Kluwer Ac.

Reliability of the Cognitive Mechanism: A Mechanist Account of Empirical Justification. W. J. Talbott. (Harvard Dissertations in Philosophy Ser.). 272p. 1990. reprint ed. text ed. 20.00 (*0-8240-3211-X*) Garland.

Reliability Problems: General Principles & Applications in Mechanics of Solids & Structures. Ed. by F. Casciati & J. B. Roberts. (CISM International Centre for Mechanical Sciences Ser.: Vol. 317). (Illus.). vi, 271p. 1991. 71.95 (*0-387-82319-0*) Spr-Verlag.

Reliability Problems of Semiconductor Lasers. P. G. Eliseev. 306p. (C). 1991. pap. text ed. 135.00 (*0-941743-94-2*) Nova Sci Pubs.

Reliability Related Research on Plastic IC-Packages: A Test Chip Approach. H. C. Van Gestel. 332p. (Orig.). 1994. pap. 67.50 (*90-6275-960-2*, Pub. by Delft U Pr NE) Coronet Bks.

Reliability, Safety & Risk Management. J. Cox & N. Tait. (Illus.). 256p. 1991. pap. 78.95 (*0-7506-1073-5*) Buttrwrth-Heinemann.

Reliability Specification. EEMUA Staff. 1986. 125.00 (*0-85931-118-X*, Pub. by EEMUA UK) St Mut.

Reliability Statistics. Robert A. Dovich. (Reliability Ser.). 93p. (Orig.). 1990. pap. 24.00 (*0-87389-086-8*, H0601) ASQC Qual Pr.

Reliability, Stress Analysis, & Failure Prevention Aspects of Composite & Active Materials: 1994 International Mechanical Engineering Congress & Exposition, Chicago, Illinois - November 6-11, 1994. Ed. by E. Sancaktar & J. S. Lee. (Design Engineering Ser.: Vol. 79). 140p. 1994. 60.00 (*0-7918-1447-5*, G00942) ASME.

Reliability, Stress Analysis, & Failure Prevention Issues in Emerging Technologies & Materials Vol. 87. Ed. by E. Sancaktar. (1995 ASME International Mechanical Engineering Congress & Exposition Ser.: DE-Vol. 87). 124p. 1995. 56.00 (*0-7918-1763-6*, H01035) ASME.

*__Reliability, Stress Analysis & Failure Prevention Issues in Fastening & Joining, Composite & Smart Structures, Numerical & FEA Methods & Risk Minimization: Proceedings, ASME International Mechanical Engineering Congress & Exposition, 1996, Atlanta, Georgia.__ Ed. by Erol Sancaktar & Shahriar Jahanian. LC 96-78688. (DE Ser.: Vol. 92). 133p. 1996. pap. text ed. 60.00 (*0-7918-1546-3*) ASME Pr.

Reliability, Stress Analysis & Failure Prevention Methods in Mechanical Design: International Conference on Reliability, Stress Analysis & Failure Prevention, 1980, San Francisco, CA. Ed. by Wayne D. Milestone. LC 80-66039. 327p. reprint ed. pap. 93.20 (*0-317-58253-4*, 2056393) Bks Demand.

Reliability, Stress Analysis, & Failure Prevention, 1993. R. J. Schaller. LC 91-75468. (DE Ser.: Vol. 55). 340p. 1993. 75.00 (*0-7918-1172-7*, G00816) ASME.

Reliability Technology. fac. ed. Albert E. Green & A. J. Bourne. LC 73-161691. (Illus.). 650p. pap. 180.00 (*0-7837-7373-0*, 2047183) Bks Demand.

Reliability Technology - 1992. Ed. by T. A. Cruse. (AD Ser.: Vol. 28). 276p. 1992. 62.50 (*0-7918-1095-X*, G00739) ASME.

Reliability Test Plans & Facilities Workshop Proceedings. LC 62-38584. 33p. 1976. pap. text ed. 30.00 (*0-915414-51-1*) Inst Environ Sci.

Reliability Theory & Applications: Proceedings of China-Japan Symposium. Ed. by Shunji Osaki & J. Cao. 448p. (C). 1987. text ed. 100.00 (*9971-5-0347-6*) World Scientific Pub.

Reliability Theory & Its Application in Structural & Soil Mechanics. Ed. by P. Thoft-Christensen. (NATO Advanced Study Institutes Series E, Applied Sciences). 1983. lib. bdg. 234.00 (*90-247-2859-2*) Kluwer Ac.

Reliability vs. Reality: Proceedings of the Annual Meeting of the Institute of Environmental Sciences, 10th, 1964. Annual Meeting of the Institute of Environmental Sciences Staff. LC 62-38584. (Illus.). 1964. pap. text ed. 75.00 (*0-915414-04-X*) Inst Environ Sci.

Reliable Characters in the Primary History. Paul J. Kissling. (JSOT Supplement Ser.: No. 224). 350p. 1996. 65.50 (*1-85075-617-1*, Pub. by Sheffield Acad UK) CUP Services.

Reliable Computer Systems: Design & Evaluation. 2nd ed. Daniel P. Siewiorek & Robert S. Swarz. (Computer Technology Ser.). (Illus.). 908p. 1992. 80.95 (*1-55558-075-0*, EY-H880E-DP, Digital DEC) Buttrwrth-Heinemann.

Reliable Data Structures in C. Thomas Plum. 200p. 1985. pap. text ed. 34.95 (*0-911537-04-X*) Plum Hall.

*__Reliable Design of Medical Devices.__ Richard C. Fries. LC 96-49203. 728p. 1997. 195.00 (*0-8247-9843-0*) Dekker.

Reliable Distributed Computing with the Isis Toolkit. Kenneth P. Birman & Robert V. Renesse. LC 93-39785. 416p. 1994. 57.00 (*0-8186-5342-6*, 5342) IEEE Comp Soc.

R

Reliable Distributed Systems, 13th Symposium On. LC 10-609857. 240p. 1994. pap. 50.00 (*0-8186-6575-0*) IEEE Comp Soc.

Reliable Distributed Systems, 14th Symposium on (SRDS-14) LC 10-609857. 256p. 1995. pap. 50.00 (*0-8186-7153-X*, PR07153) IEEE Comp Soc.

Reliable Distributed Systems, 15th Symposium On: SRDS 15. LC 10-609857. 272p. 1996. pap. 60.00 (*0-8186-7481-4*) IEEE Comp Soc.

Reliable Fuels for Liquid Metal Reactors: International Conference Proceedings, Tucson, AZ September 7-11, 1986. 919p. 1986. 75.00 (*0-89448-126-6*, 700112) Am Nuclear Soc.

Reliable Healthcare Companions: Understanding & Managing Arthritis. Ed. by John L. Decker. 192p. (Orig.). 1987. mass mkt. 6.95 (*0-380-75011-2*) Avon.

Reliable Healthcare Companions: Understanding & Managing Asthma. John L. Decker. Ed. by Michael A. Kaliner. 192p. 1988. mass mkt. 6.95 (*0-380-75427-4*) Avon.

Reliable Healthcare Companions: Understanding & Managing Diabetes. Ed. by John L. Decker & Phillip Gorden. 192p. 1987. mass mkt. 6.95 (*0-380-75247-6*) Avon.

Reliable Healthcare Companions: Understanding & Managing Hypertension. John L. Decker & Harry R. Keiser. 224p. 1987. mass mkt. 6.95 (*0-380-75248-4*) Avon.

Reliable Healthcare Companions: Understanding & Managing Osteoporosis. Ed. by John L. Decker. 176p. 1988. mass mkt. 6.95 (*0-380-75429-0*) Avon.

Reliable Healthcare Companions: Understanding & Managing Ulcers. John L. Decker & Paul N. Maton. 1988. mass mkt. 6.95 (*0-380-75428-2*) Avon.

Reliable Knowledge: An Exploration of the Grounds for Belief in Science. John M. Ziman. (Canto Book Ser.). (Illus.). 208p. (C). 1991. pap. text ed. 10.95 (*0-521-40670-6*) Cambridge U Pr.

Reliable Light. Meredith Steinbach. (Fiction Ser.). 200p. 1990. 18.95 (*0-8135-1531-9*) Rutgers U Pr.

Reliable Object-Oriented Software: Applying Analysis & Design. Ed Seidewitz & Mike Stark. LC 95-42034. (Advances in Object Technology Ser.: No. 11). 425p. 1995. pap. 45.00 (*1-884842-18-6*) SIGS Bks & Multimedia.

Reliable Plan Selection by Intelligent Machines. George N. Saridis et al. (Series in Intelligent Control & Intelligent Automation: Vol. 1). 175p. 1996. text ed. 34.00 (*981-02-2336-6*) World Scientific Pub.

***Reliable Rain: A Practical Guide to Landscape Irrigation & Efficient Water Use.** Howard Hendrix & Stuart Straw. (Illus.). 160p. 1998. pap. 19.95 (*1-56158-202-6*, 070327) Taunton.

***Reliable Roses.** New York Botanical Garden Staff. (Serious Gardner Ser.). (Illus.). 1997. pap. 23.00 (*0-614-27226-2*, C P Pubs) Crown Pub Group.

Reliable Software Technologies, Ada-Europe '96: Ada-Europe International Conference on Reliable Software Technologies, Montreux, Switzerland, June 10-14, 1996 Proceedings, Vol. 108. Alfred Strohmeier. LC 96-19935. (Lecture Notes in Computer Science Ser.). 513p. 1996. pap. 81.00 (*3-540-61317-X*) Spr-Verlag.

***Reliable Software Technologies-ADA-Europe '97: 1997 ADA-Europe International Conference on Reliable Software Technologies, London, U. K. June 2-6, 1997, Proceedings, Vol. 125.** Keith Hardy & Jim Briggs. LC 97-24990. (Lecture Notes in Computer Science). 1997. write for info. (*3-540-63114-3*) Spr-Verlag.

***Reliable Spectroradiometry.** Henry J. Kostkowski. (Illus.). 624p. 1997. text ed. 200.00 (*0-9657713-0-X*) Spectroradiometry.

***Reliance of the Traveler.** Al-Ahmad I. Misri. Tr. by Noah H. Keller. 1270p. 1996. 65.00 (*0-614-21207-3*, 1067) Kazi Pubns.

Reliance of the Traveller: The Classic Manual of Islamic Sacred Law 'Umdat al-Salik by Ahmad ibn al-Naqib in Arabic with Facing English Text, Commentary & Appendicies. rev. ed. Ahmad Ibn al-Naqib. Ed. & Tr. by Nuh H. Keller from ARA. LC 94-19018. xxii, 1232p. 1994. write for info. (*0-9638342-2-3*) Sunna Bks.

Reliaquiae Sacrae, 5 vols. Martinus J. Routh. lv, 2416p. 1974. reprint ed. write for info. (*3-487-05142-7*) G Olms Pubs.

Relic. Douglas Preston & Lincoln Child. 384p. (J). 1995. 22.95 (*0-312-85630-X*) Forge NYC.

Relic. Douglas Preston & Lincoln Child. 384p. 1996. mass mkt. write for info. (*0-614-05542-3*) Tor Bks.

Relic. Douglas Preston & Lincoln Child. 480p. (J). 1996. pap. 6.99 (*0-8125-4326-2*) Tor Bks.

Relic. Douglas Preston & Lincoln Child. 1996. pap. 6.99 (*0-614-12879-X*) Forge NYC.

Relic. Douglas Preston. 1996. mass mkt. 6.99 (*0-8125-6358-1*) Tor Bks.

Relic. large type ed. Evelyn Anthony. (General Ser.). 376p. 1992. pap. 16.95 (*0-8161-5380-9*, GK Hall) Thorndike Pr.

Relic. 2nd ed. Eca De Querioz. Ed. & Tr. by Margaret J. Costa from POR. (Dedalus European Classics Ser.). 281p. 1997. reprint ed. pap. 14.99 (*0-946626-94-4*, Pub. by Dedalus UK) Subterranean Co.

***Relic Hunter the Book.** Ed Fedory. Ed. by Mary Hand. 134p. (Orig.). 1994. pap. text ed. 9.95 (*1-882279-02-6*) Whites Elect.

***Relic, Icon or Hoax? Carbon Dating the Turin Shroud.** H. E. Gove. LC 96-30321. (Illus.). 344p. 1996. 35.00 (*0-7503-0398-0*) IOP Pub.

Relic of Empire. W. Michael Gear. (Forbidden Borders Ser.: No. 2). 624p. (Orig.). 1992. mass mkt. 5.99 (*0-88677-492-6*) DAW Bks.

Relic of Empire: To South Arabia & Beyond. Michael Crouch. 192p. 1994. text ed. 39.50 (*1-85043-739-4*, Pub. by I B Tauris UK) St Martin.

***Relic of the Lost Cause: The Story of South Carolina's Ordinance of Secession.** rev. ed. Charles H. Lesser. Ed. by Judith M. Andrews. 32p. 1996. pap. 9.00 (*1-880067-36-6*) SC Dept of Arch & Hist.

Relic of the Revolution. Charles Herbert. LC 67-29023. (Eyewitness Accounts of the American Revolution Ser., No. 1). 1968. reprint ed. 11.95 (*0-405-01114-8*) Ayer.

Relicarios: Devotional Miniatures from the Americas. Martha Egan. 144p. 1996. pap. text ed. 24.95 (*0-89013-254-2*) Museum NM Pr.

Relics. Joan C. Cruz. LC 84-60744. (Illus.). 352p. 1984. pap. 12.95 (*0-87973-701-8*, 701) Our Sunday Visitor.

Relics. John J. Desjarlais. 1993. pap. 10.99 (*0-8407-6735-8*) Nelson.

Relics. Michael J. Friedman. Ed. by Dave Stern. (Star Trek: The Next Generation Ser.). 1992. mass mkt. 5.50 (*0-671-86476-9*) PB.

Relics. John Selawsky. Ed. by Edward Mycue. (Took Modern Poetry in English Ser.: No. 30). (Illus.). 28p. (Orig.). 1993. pap. 4.00 (*1-879457-32-6*) Norton Coker Pr.

Relics, Apocalypse, & the Deceits of History: Ademar of Chabannes, 989-1034. Richard A. Landes. LC 94-39890. (Harvard Historical Studies). (Illus.). 416p. 1995. text ed. 55.00 (*0-674-75530-8*, LANREL) HUP.

Relics of Ancient China, from the Collection of Dr. Paul Singer. Asia Society Staff et al. Ed. by Asia House Gallery, New York. 1976. 35.95 (*0-405-06566-3*, 10761) Ayer.

Relics of Repentance: The Letters of Pontius Pilate & Claudia Procula. 2nd rev. ed. Ed. by James F. Forcucci. 21p. 1996. pap. 8.95 (*0-9625158-2-5*) Issana Pr.

Relics of Sherlock Holmes. 2nd ed. Gary Lovisi. (Illus.). 52p. (Orig.). 1989. reprint ed. 4.00 (*0-936071-16-8*) Gryphon Pubns.

***Relics, Prayer, & Politics in Medieval Venetia: Romanesque Painting in the Crypt of Aquileia Cathedral.** Thomas E. Dale. LC 97-386. (Illus.). 1997. write for info. (*0-691-01175-3*) Princeton U Pr.

Relics Recycled on Cloud Nine. Margaret R. Otis. LC 81-18286. (Illus.). 96p. 1981. pap. 4.95 (*0-915010-30-5*) Sutter House.

***Relics, Ritual, & Representation in Buddhism: Rematerialising the Sri Lankan Theravada Tradition.** Kevin Trainor. (Cambridge Studies in Religious Traditions: No. 10). 256p. 1997. text ed. 54.95 (*0-521-58280-6*) Cambridge U Pr.

Relics, Water & the Kitchen Sink: A Diver's Guide to Underwater Archeology. 2nd ed. Alan R. Rowe. 56p. 1988. reprint ed. pap. 6.95 (*0-9616399-1-1*) Sea Sports Pubns.

***Relief.** 2nd ed. Piller. 1990. pap. text ed. write for info. (*0-85121-514-9*) Addison-Wesley.

Relief & Reconstruction. Roger Wilson. (C). 1943. pap. 3.00 (*0-87574-022-7*) Pendle Hill.

Relief at Last: Neutralization for Food Allergy & Other Illnesses. Joseph B. Miller. (Illus.). 352p. 1987. pap. text ed. 42.95 (*0-398-06643-4*) C C Thomas.

Relief at Last: Neutralization for Food Allergy & Other Illnesses. Joseph B. Miller. (Illus.). 352p. (C). 1987. text ed. 57.95 (*0-398-05283-2*) C C Thomas.

Relief Book for Pressured Cookers. Leola Skeen. 100p. 1984. pap. 12.95 (*0-930047-00-1*) Goldenleaf Pub Co.

Relief Carving with Bob Lundy. Bob Lundy. LC 92-60641. (Illus.). 96p. 1992. pap. 14.95 (*0-88740-439-1*) Schiffer.

Relief for Hurting Parents: How to Fight for the Lives of Teenagers, How to Prepare Younger Children for Less Dangerous Journeys Through Teenage Years. Buddy Scott. LC 93-72385. 240p. 1994. reprint ed. pap. 12.95 (*0-9637645-0-0*) Allon Pub.

Relief from Back Pain: The Tollison Program. C. David Tollison. 253p. 1987. text ed. 24.95 (*0-89876-140-9*) Gardner Pr.

Relief from Candida: Allergies & Ill Health. Greta Sichel. 1994. pap. text ed. 9.95 (*1-86351-001-X*, Pub. by Sally Milner AT) Seven Hills Bk.

Relief from Hayfever & Other Allergies. Lesley Sussman. 160p. 1992. mass mkt. 4.99 (*0-440-21065-8*) Dell.

Relief from Headache. 2nd ed. Donald I. Peterson. LC 83-71941. (Illus.). 226p. 1990. pap. 9.95 (*0-913657-00-X*) D E Donel.

Relief from IBS: Irritable Bowel Syndrome. Elaine F. Shimberg. 240p. 1991. mass mkt. 5.99 (*0-345-36712-X*) Ballantine.

Relief from Insomnia: Getting the Sleep of Your Dreams. Charles M. Morin. LC 95-42442. 208p. 1996. pap. 11.95 (*0-385-47706-6*, Main St Bks) Doubleday.

Relief from PMS. Dell Medical Library Staff & Pamela P. Novotny. 160p. 1992. mass mkt. 4.99 (*0-440-21086-0*) Dell.

Relief from Premenstrual Syndrome. Celia Halas. 1988. 13.95 (*0-8119-0649-3*) LIFETIME.

Relief from Premenstrual Syndrome. Celia M. Halas. 145p. 1984. 13.95 (*0-8119-0691-4*) LIFETIME.

Relief from Sinusitis. Dell Medical Library Staff. 160p. 1993. mass mkt. 4.99 (*0-440-21361-4*) Dell.

Relief in Recovery: A Guide to a Joyful Sobriety that Lasts. Bernardo Du Blanc. (Illus.). (Orig.). 1995. pap. 19.95 (*1-887195-15-7*) Visual Bks.

Relief of Pain from Headaches & TMJ. Paula Mackowiak. LC 89-927914. (Illus.). 200p. (Orig.). 1989. pap. 11.95 (*0-9625508-2-5*) Solomon Bks.

Relief or Reform? Reagan's Regulatory Dilemma. George C. Eads & Michael Fix. LC 84-5283. (Changing Domestic Priorities Ser.). 283p. (Orig.). 1984. pap. text ed. 20.50 (*0-87766-333-5*) Urban Inst.

Relief Pitchers. Doug Marx. (Baseball Heroes Ser.). (J). 1991. 12.50 (*0-86593-131-3*); lib. bdg. 16.67 (*0-685-66096-6*) Rourke Corp.

***Relief Printmaking: A Manual of Techniques.** Colin Walklin. (Illus.). 176p. 1997. pap. 29.95 (*1-86126-071-7*, Pub. by Crowood Pr UK) Trafalgar.

Relief Recorder: Record Your Foods & Moods for Emotional Relief. Bernardo Du Blanc. (Illus.). 1995. pap. 10.95 (*1-887195-16-5*) Visual Bks.

Relief Systems Handbook. C. Parry. 220p. 1994. 45.00 (*0-88415-271-5*) Gulf Pub.

Relief Veterinarian's Manual. rev. ed. Carin A. Smith. 100p. (C). 1995. 59.00 (*1-885780-04-4*) Smith Vet Srvs.

Relief Woodcarving & Lettering. Ian Norbury. LC 88-2257. 157p. 1988. reprint ed. pap. 18.95 (*0-941936-11-2*) Linden Pub Fresno.

***Reliefgenesse des Harzes.** H. Nicke. (Naturwissenschaftliche Arbeiten, Regionale Darstellungen und Schriften Ser.: Vol. 1). 195p. (ENG & GER.). 1995. pap. 72.00 (*3-931251-00-4*, Pub. by Martina Galunder GW) Balogh.

Reliefs & Inscriptions at Karnak, IV: The Battle Reliefs of King Sety I. Epigraphic Survey Staff. LC 84-61870. (Oriental Institute Publications: No. 107). 1986. 150.00 (*0-918986-42-7*) Orient Inst.

Reliefs & Inscriptions at Luxor Temple Vol. 1: The Festival Procession of Opet in the Colonnade Hall. Epigraphic Survey Staff. LC 93-85923. (Oriental Institute Publications: No. 112). (Illus.). xxvi, 60p. 1994. pap. 350.00 (*0-918986-94-X*) Orient Inst.

Relieve Your Aching Head: Secrets for Soothing Head & Neck Aches. Eric A. Mein. (Natural Remedies for Common Ailments & Conditions Ser.). 85p. (Orig.). 1991. pap. 4.95 (*0-87604-280-9*, 365) ARE Pr.

***Relieved of Command.** Benjamin S. Persons. (Illus.). 264p. 1996. pap. 20.95 (*0-89745-204-6*) Sunflower U Pr.

Relieving Pain: A Basic Hypotherapeutic Approach. Donald W. Schaefer. 312p. 1995. pap. 40.00 (*1-56821-481-2*) Aronson.

Relieving Third World Debt: A Call for Co-Responsibility, Justice, & Solidarity. United States Catholic Conference, Administrative Board Statement Staff. (Illus.). 52p. (Orig.). 1989. pap. 3.50 (*1-55586-311-6*) US Catholic.

Religieuse. Denis Diderot. (FRE.). 1972. pap. 11.95 (*0-7859-1689-X*, 2070360571) Fr & Eur.

Religieuse. Denis Diderot. (Folio Ser.: No. 57). (FRE.). 1972. pap. 9.95 (*2-07-036057-1*) Schoenhof.

Religieuse. Denis Diderot. 1972. write for info. (*0-318-63587-9*) Fr & Eur.

Religieuse. unabridged ed. Denis Diderot. (FRE.). pap. 5.95 (*2-87714-189-6*, Pub. by Bookking Intl FR) Distribks Inc.

Religio Medici: Medicine & Religion in Seventeenth-Century England. Ed. by Ole P. Grell & Andrew Cunningham. LC 96-2822. (Illus.). 356p. (C). 1996. 84.95 (*1-85928-339-X*, Pub. by Scolar Pr UK) Ashgate Pub Co.

Religio Medici, Hydriotaphia & the Garden of Cyrus. Thomas Browne. Ed. by R. H. Robbins. 224p. 1972. pap. 17.95 (*0-19-871064-X*) OUP.

Religio Medici, Letter to a Friend, & Christian Morals. enl. ed. Thomas Browne. Ed. by W. A. Greenhill. 450p. 1990. reprint ed. pap. 16.95 (*0-89385-034-9*) Sugden.

Religion. (YouthTalk Ser.). 32p. (YA). 1994. teacher ed., pap. 4.95 (*0-8066-0260-0*, 15-5215) Augsburg Fortress.

Religion. (YouthTalk Ser.). 48p. (YA). 1995. pap. 5.25 (*0-8066-0259-7*, 15-5214) Augsburg Fortress.

***Religion.** Ed. by Eleanor C. Goldstein. (Social Issues Resources Ser.: Vol. 5). 1996. 19.00 (*0-89777-199-0*) Sirs Inc.

Religion. Myrtle Langley. LC 96-12236. (Eyewitness Bks.). (J). 1996. 19.00 (*0-679-88123-9*) Knopf.

Religion. Myrtle Langley. LC 96-12236. (Eyewitness Bks.). (J). 1996. lib. bdg. 20.99 (*0-679-98123-3*) Knopf.

***Religion.** Thompson & Morison. 1986. pap. text ed. write for info. (*0-582-35497-8*, Pub. by Longman UK) Longman.

Religion. 2nd ed. John F. Wilson & W. Royce Clark. 224p. (C). 1988. pap. text ed. 39.40 (*0-13-771957-4*) P-H.

Religion. Desmond Painter et al. Ed. by Malcolm Yapp et al. (World History Program Ser.). (Illus.). 32p. (YA). (gr. 6-11). 1980. reprint ed. pap. text ed. 4.72 (*0-89908-120-7*) Greenhaven.

Religion, Vol 3. Ed. by Eleanor C. Goldstein. (Social Issues Resources Ser.). 1991. Incl. 1986-1990 Supplements. suppl. ed. 95.00 (*0-89777-085-4*) Sirs Inc.

Religion, Vol. 5. Ed. by Charles R. Wilson. (Perspectives on the American South Ser.: Vol. 5). 185, xvp. 1991. text ed. 74.00 (*2-88124-394-0*) Gordon & Breach.

Religion: A Cross-Cultural Encyclopedia. David Levinson. LC 96-45172. (Encyclopedia of Human Experiences Ser.). 352p. 1996. lib. bdg. 49.50 (*0-87436-865-0*) ABC-CLIO.

Religion: A Dialogue, & Other Essays. 3rd ed. Arthur Schopenhauer. Tr. by T. Bailey Saunders. LC 72-488. (Essay Index Reprint Ser.). 1980. reprint ed. 16.95 (*0-8369-2820-2*) Ayer.

Religion: A Dialogue, & Other Essays. Arthur Schopenhauer. Tr. by T. Bailey Saunders. LC 72-11305. 140p. 1973. reprint ed. text ed. 38.50 (*0-8371-6652-7*, SCRE, Greenwood Pr) Greenwood.

Religion: A Humanist Interpretation. Raymond Firth. LC 95-1980. 256p. (C). 1995. pap. 18.95 (*0-415-12897-8*); text ed. 69.95 (*0-415-12896-X*) Routledge.

Religion: An Introduction. T. William Hall et al. LC 85-42777. 288p. (Orig.). (C). 1986. pap. 18.00 (*0-06-063573-8*) Harper SF.

Religion: Aspects of Britain. Central Office of Info. (Aspects of Britain Ser.). (Illus.). 84p. 1997. pap. 9.95 (*0-11-701704-3*, HM17043, Pub. by Statnry Ofc UK) Seven Hills Bk.

Religion: Foundation of the Free Society. Edmund A. Opitz. LC 95-83491. 272p. 1996. reprint ed. pap. 14.95 (*0-910614-92-X*) Foun Econ Ed.

Religion: North American Style. 3rd ed. Thomas E. Dowdy & Patrick H. McNamara. LC 96-18514. 250p. (C). 1997. text ed. 48.00 (*0-8135-2343-5*); pap. text ed. 16.95 (*0-8135-2344-3*) Rutgers U Pr.

Religion: The Disease. Garry De Young. 1993. 25.00 (*0-936128-06-2*) De Young Pr.

Religion: The Missing Dimension of Statecraft. Ed. by Douglas Johnston & Cynthia Sampson. (Illus.). 350p. 1995. pap. 17.95 (*0-19-510280-0*) OUP.

Religion: The Social Context. 3rd ed. Meredith B. McGuire. 340p. (C). 1992. pap. 24.00 (*0-534-16968-6*) Wadsworth Pub.

Religion: The Social Context. 4th ed. Meredith B. McGuire. (C). 1997. pap. text ed. 32.95 (*0-534-50572-4*) Wadsworth Pub.

Religion: What Is It? 2nd ed. William C. Tremmel. 372p. (C). 1984. text ed. 32.00 (*0-03-062834-2*) HB Coll Pubs.

Religion: What Is It? 3rd ed. William C. Tremmel. 448p. (C). 1996. pap. text ed. write for info. (*0-15-503040-X*) HB Coll Pubs.

Religion: What Is It, & What Has It Done to & for Humanity? Edward A. Walsh. 256p. (Orig.). 1997. pap. 14.95 (*1-56474-189-3*) Fithian Pr.

Religion Vol. 4: Incl. 1991-94 Supplements. Ed. by Eleanor C. Goldstein. (Social Issues Resources Ser.). 1995. 95.00 (*0-89777-167-2*) Sirs Inc.

Religion, Aging & Health: A Global Perspective. Ed. by William M. Clements. LC 88-16357. (Journal of Religion & Aging: Vol. 4, Nos. 3-4). (Illus.). 146p. 1989. text ed. 39.95 (*0-86656-803-4*) Haworth Pr.

Religion & Advanced Industrial Society. James A. Beckford. 160p. 1989. text ed. 34.95 (*0-04-301228-0*); pap. text ed. 16.95 (*0-04-301229-9*) Routledge Chapman & Hall.

Religion & Advanced Industrial Society. James A. Beckford. 200p. (C). 1989. pap. 18.95 (*0-415-08462-8*, Routledge NY) Routledge.

Religion & Aging in the Indian Tradition. Shrinivas Tilak. LC 88-30583. (McGill Studies in the History of Religions). 226p. 1989. text ed. 64.50 (*0-7914-0044-1*); pap. text ed. 21.95 (*0-7914-0045-X*) State U NY Pr.

Religion & American Culture. David Hackett. 550p. (C). 1995. text ed. 69.95 (*0-415-91218-0*, Routledge NY) Routledge.

Religion & American Culture. George M. Marsden. 288p. (C). 1990. pap. text ed. 17.50 (*0-15-576583-3*) HB Coll Pubs.

Religion & American Culture: A Reader. David Hackett. 550p. 1995. pap. 24.95 (*0-415-91219-9*) Routledge.

Religion & American Education: Rethinking an American Dilemma. Warren A. Nord. LC 94-4589. (H. Eugene & Lillian Youngs Lehman Ser.). 502p. 1994. pap. 19.95 (*0-8078-4478-0*); text ed. 49.95 (*0-8078-2165-9*) U of NC Pr.

Religion & American Life: Resources. Ed. by Anne T. Fraker. LC 88-19933. 256p. 1989. text ed. 24.95 (*0-252-01588-6*) U of Ill Pr.

Religion & American Political Behavior. Ed. by Ted G. Jelen. LC 88-32186. 324p. 1989. text ed. 65.00 (*0-275-93089-0*, C3089, Praeger Pubs) Greenwood.

Religion & American Politics: From the Colonial Period to the 1980s. Ed. by Mark A. Noll. (Illus.). 416p. (C). 1989. pap. text ed. 20.95 (*0-19-505881-X*) OUP.

Religion & Anglo-American Women. Ed. by M. De Jong. 1991. pap. text ed. 24.00 (*2-88124-519-6*) Gordon & Breach.

Religion & Art. Richard Wagner. Tr. by William A. Ellis. LC 94-28469. xxxii, 376p. 1994. pap. 15.00 (*0-8032-9764-5*, Bison Books) U of Nebr Pr.

Religion & Art. Paul Weiss. LC 63-13170. (Aquinas Lectures). 1963. 15.00 (*0-87462-128-3*) Marquette.

Religion & Art, & Other Essays. John L. Spalding. LC 72-86785. (Essay Index Reprint Ser.). 1977. 19.95 (*0-8369-1195-4*) Ayer.

Religion & Art in Ashanti. Robert S. Rattray. LC 76-44781. reprint ed. 34.50 (*0-404-15878-1*) AMS Pr.

Religion & Art NAS see Richard Wagner's Prose Works

Religion & Authority in Roman Carthage: From Augustus to Constantine. J. B. Rives. (Illus.). 352p. 1995. text ed. 65.00 (*0-19-814083-5*) OUP.

Religion & Capitalism: Allies, Not Enemies. 2nd ed. Edmund A. Opitz. 328p. 1992. reprint ed. pap. 24.95 (*0-910614-81-4*) Foun Econ Ed.

Religion & Ceremonies of the Lenape. Mark R. Harrington. LC 76-43731. (MAI. Indian Notes & Monographs. Miscellaneous). reprint ed. 39.50 (*0-404-15572-3*) AMS Pr.

Religion & Change in Contemporary Asia. Ed. by Robert F. Spencer. LC 76-139450. 189p. reprint ed. pap. 53.90 (*0-318-39666-1*, 2033235) Bks Demand.

Religion & Civilization. A. H. Nadvi. 4.00 (*0-933511-34-5*) Kazi Pubns.

Religion & Class Structure. Liston Pope. (Reprint Series in Social Sciences). (C). 1993. reprint ed. pap. text ed. 1.00 (*0-8290-3821-3*, S-225) Irvington.

Religion & Communist Society: Selected Papers from the Second World Congress for Soviet & East European Studies. Ed. by Dennis J. Dunn. 165p. (Orig.). 1983. pap. 12.00 (*0-933884-29-X*) Berkeley Slavic.

Religion & Conscience in Ancient Egypt. William F. Petrie. LC 72-83176. 1972. reprint ed. 26.95 (*0-405-08854-X*) Ayer.

An Asterisk (*) at the beginning of an entry indicates that the title is appearing in BIP for the first time.

Religion & Constitutional Government in the United States: A Historical Overview with Sources. John E. Semonche. (Constitutional Bookshelf Ser.). 250p. (Orig.). 1985. pap. 12.00 (*0-930095-09-X*) Signal Bks.

***Religion & Contemporary Liberalism.** Ed. by Paul J. Weithman. (Orig.). 1997. pap. 23.00 (*0-614-27628-4*) U of Notre Dame Pr.

***Religion & Contemporary Liberalism.** Paul J. Weithman. LC 97-1806. 1997. write for info. (*0-268-01658-5*); pap. write for info. (*0-268-01659-3*) U of Notre Dame Pr.

Religion & Creation. Keith Ward. 360p. 1996. 70.00 (*0-19-826393-7*); pap. 19.95 (*0-19-826394-5*) OUP.

Religion & Crime. Frank Swancara. 17.50 (*0-936128-23-2*) De Young Pr.

Religion & Culture. Christopher H. Dawson. LC 77-27183. (Gifford Lectures: 1947). 232p. reprint ed. 35.00 (*0-404-60498-6*) AMS Pr.

Religion & Culture: An Introduction to Anthropology of Religion. Annemarie De Waal Malefijt. (Illus.). 407p. (C). 1990. reprint ed. pap. text ed. 18.95 (*0-88133-483-9*) Waveland Pr.

Religion & Culture: Essays in Honor of Paul Tillich. Walter Leibrecht. LC 78-167376. (Essay Index Reprint Ser.). 1977. reprint ed. 26.95 (*0-8369-2558-0*) Ayer.

Religion & Culture in Ancient Israel. J. Andrew Dearman. LC 92-33068. (Illus.). 320p. 1992. 24.95 (*0-943575-90-7*) Hendrickson MA.

Religion & Culture in Canadian Family Law. Syrtash. 200p. 1992. boxed 52.00 (*0-409-90371-X*) MICHIE.

Religion & Culture in Early Modern Russia. Ed. by Samuel H. Baron & Nancy S. Kollmann. LC 96-22921. 240p. 1997. lib. bdg. 34.00 (*0-87580-218-4*) N Ill U Pr.

***Religion & Culture in Renaissance England.** Ed. by Claire McEachern & Debora Shuger. (Illus.). 277p. (C). 1997. text ed. 59.95 (*0-521-58425-6*) Cambridge U Pr.

Religion & Custom in a Muslim Society: The Berti of Sudan. Ladislav Holy. (Cambridge Studies in Social & Cultural Anthropology: No. 78). (Illus.). 232p. (C). 1991. text ed. 74.95 (*0-521-39485-6*) Cambridge U Pr.

Religion & Dance. Ed. by Dennis J. Fallon & Mary J. Wolbers. LC 83-189712. (Focus on Dance Ser.: No. 10). 96p. reprint ed. pap. 27.40 (*0-317-55536-7*, 2029558) Bks Demand.

Religion & Democracy in Latin America. Ed. by William H. Swatos. LC 94-47462. 1995. pap. 21.95 (*1-56000-805-9*) Transaction Pubs.

Religion & Devotion in Europe, c. 1215-c. 1515. R. N. Swanson. (Cambridge Medieval Textbooks Ser.). (Illus.). 435p. (C). 1995. text ed. 69.95 (*0-521-37076-0*); pap. text ed. 19.95 (*0-521-37950-4*) Cambridge U Pr.

Religion & Disability: Perspectives in Scripture, Theology & Ethics. Marilyn E. Bishop. LC 94-44885. 80p. (Orig.). 1995. pap. 6.95 (*1-55612-713-8*) Sheed & Ward MO.

Religion & Domestic Violence in Early New England: The Memoirs of Abigail Abbot Bailey. Ed. by Ann Taves. LC 87-46245. (Religion in North America Ser.). (Illus.). 208p. 1989. 31.50 (*0-253-35658-X*); pap. 11.95 (*0-253-20531-X*, MB-531) Ind U Pr.

Religion & Doubt: Toward a Faith of Your Own. 2nd ed. Richard E. Creel. 176p. (C). 1990. pap. text ed. 29.80 (*0-13-772286-9*) P-H.

Religion & Dramatics: The Relationship Between Christianity & the Theater Arts. Herbert Sennet. LC 94-30407. 1994. 51.00 (*0-8191-9705-X*) U Pr of Amer.

Religion & Dramatics: The Relationship Between Christianity & the Theater Arts. Herbert Sennet. 160p. (Orig.). (C). 1994. pap. text ed. 27.50 (*0-8191-9706-8*) U Pr of Amer.

Religion & Economic Action: The Protestant Ethic, the Rise of Capitalism, & the Abuses of Scholarship. Kurt Samuelsson. Tr. by E. Geoffrey French. (Renaissance Society of America Reprint Text Ser.). 170p. 1993. reprint ed. pap. 14.95 (*0-8020-7733-1*) U of Toronto Pr.

Religion & Economic Ethics. Ed. by Joseph F. Gower. (College Theology Society Publications: Vol. 31). 306p. (C). 1990. pap. text ed. 26.00 (*0-8191-7666-4*) U Pr of Amer.

Religion & Economic Ethics, Vol. 31. Ed. by Joseph F. Gower. (College Theology Society Publications: Vol. 31). 306p. (C). 1990. lib. bdg. 44.50 (*0-8191-7665-6*) U Pr of Amer.

Religion & Economic Justice. Ed. by Michael Zweig. (C). 1991. 49.95 (*0-87722-847-7*) Temple U Pr.

Religion & Economic Justice. Ed. by Michael Zweig. (C). 1992. pap. 19.95 (*1-56639-003-6*) Temple U Pr.

Religion & Empire: The Dynamics of Aztec & Inca Expansionism. Geoffrey W. Conrad & Arthur A. Demarest. LC 83-14414. (New Studies in Archaeology). 256p. 1984. pap. text ed. 25.95 (*0-521-31896-3*) Cambridge U Pr.

Religion & Empiricism. John E. Smith. LC 67-20684. (Aquinas Lectures). 1967. 15.00 (*0-87462-132-1*) Marquette.

Religion & Employment in Northern Ireland. David Eversley. (C). 1989. text ed. 45.00 (*0-8039-8203-8*) Sage.

Religion & Ethical Issues: Position Guides for Decision Making. Ed. by Victor Obenhaus. LC 91-73417. 262p. (Orig.). (C). 1991. pap. 12.95 (*0-913552-47-X*) Exploration Pr.

***Religion & Ethnicity: Minorities & Social Change in the Metropolis.** Ed. by Rohit Barot. 203p. 1993. pap. 35.00 (*90-390-0061-1*, Pub. by KOK Pharos NE) Eisenbrauns.

Religion & Ethnicity among Muslims. A. R. Saiyed. Ed. by V. V. Saiyed & Mohammad Talib. (C). 1995. 42.00 (*0-614-08708-2*, Pub. by Rawat II); pap. 42.00 (*0-614-10005-4*, Pub. by Har-Anand Pubns II) S Asia.

***Religion & Faction in Hume's Moral Philosophy.** Jennifer A. Herdt. (Studies in Religion & Critical Thought: Vol. 3). 330p. (C). 1997. text ed. 59.95 (*0-521-55442-X*) Cambridge U Pr.

Religion & Family Connection: Social Science Perspectives. Ed. by Darwin L. Thomas. (Specialized Monograph Ser.: Vol. 3). 1988. 12.95 (*0-88494-636-3*) Bookcraft Inc.

Religion & Freedom of Thought. Perry Miller et al. LC 78-128296. (Essay Index Reprint Ser.). 1977. 12.95 (*0-8369-2199-2*) Ayer.

Religion & Gender. Ed. by Ursula King. LC 94-10767. 288p. 1994. 60.95 (*0-631-19376-6*); pap. 24.95 (*0-631-19377-4*) Blackwell Pubs.

Religion & Global Order. Ed. by Roland Robertson & William P. Garrett. LC 90-44569. 1990. 29.95 (*0-89226-090-4*, New Era Bks); pap. 14.95 (*0-89226-091-2*, New Era Bks) Paragon Hse.

Religion & Globalization. Peter F. Beyer. (Theory, Culture & Society Ser.: Vol. 27). (C). 1994. text ed. 55.00 (*0-8039-8916-4*); pap. text ed. 21.95 (*0-8039-8917-2*) Sage.

Religion & Hopi Life in the Twentieth Century. John D. Loftin. LC 90-37968. (Religion in North America Ser.). 192p. 1991. 24.50 (*0-253-33517-5*) Ind U Pr.

Religion & Hopi Life in the Twentieth Century. John D. Loftin. LC 90-37968. (Religion in North America Ser.). 192p. 1994. pap. 10.95 (*0-253-20857-2*) Ind U Pr.

Religion & Human Auto. Brabander. 1972. lib. bdg. 64.50 (*90-247-1329-3*) Kluwer Ac.

Religion & Human Behavior. W. N. Schoenfeld. LC 93-73791. xxix, 205p. (Orig.). 1993. pap. 16.95 (*0-9623311-5-5*) Authors Coop.

Religion & Human Purpose. Ed. by William Horosz & Tad S. Clements. 320p. (C). 1986. lib. bdg. 129.50 (*90-247-3000-7*, Pub. by M Nijhoff NE) Kluwer Ac.

Religion & Human Rights. Project on Religion & Human Rights Staff. 144p. (Orig.). 1994. pap. 10.00 (*1-56432-141-X*) Hum Rts Watch.

Religion & Human Survival: An Essay. Eric A. Stone. 13p. (Orig.) (C). lib. bdg. 7.95 (*0-9631937-1-6*) BioPsych Pr.

Religion & Identity. Ed. by Patrick O'Sullivan. (Irish Studies). 240p. 1996. 69.00 (*0-7185-1424-6*, Pub. by Leicester Univ Pr) Bks Intl VA.

Religion & Irreligion in Victorian England. Ed. by R. W. Davis & Richard J. Helmstadter. LC 91-40384. 205p. (C). 1992. text ed. 99.95 (*0-415-07625-0*) Routledge.

***Religion & Its Clergy: Index of New Information with Bibliography.** Fred R. Shannon. 150p. Date not set. 47.50 (*0-7883-1438-6*) ABBE Pubs Assn.

***Religion & Its Clergy: Index of New Information with Bibliography.** Fred R. Shannon. 150p. Date not set. pap. 44.50 (*0-7883-1439-4*) ABBE Pubs Assn.

Religion & Judgment: An Essay on the Method & Meaning of Religion. Willard E. Arnett. LC 66-11680. (Century Philosophy Ser.). 1966. 49.50 (*0-89197-377-X*) Irvington.

Religion & Justice in the War over Bosnia. Ed. by G. Scott Davis. 192p. 1996. pap. 17.95 (*0-415-91520-1*, Routledge NY) Routledge.

Religion & Justice in the War over Bosnia. Ed. by G. Scott Davis. 192p. (C). 1996. text ed. 55.00 (*0-415-91519-8*, Routledge NY) Routledge.

Religion & Law: Biblical-Judaic & Islamic Perspectives. Ed. by Edwin B. Firmage et al. LC 89-34612. xii, 401p. (C). 1990. text ed. 45.00 (*0-931464-39-0*) Eisenbrauns.

Religion & Law: How Through Halakhah Judaism Sets Forth Its Theology & Philosophy. Jacob Neusner. LC 96-12381. (South Florida Studies in the History of Judaism: No. 135). 166p. (C). 1996. 69.95 (*0-7885-0251-4*, 240135) Scholars Pr GA.

Religion & Law in Independent India. Ed. by Robert D. Baird. (C). 1993. 32.00 (*81-7304-035-4*, Pub. by Manohar II) S Asia.

Religion & Legitimation of Power in Sri Lanka. Ed. by Bardwell L. Smith. LC 77-7449. 244p. 1978. pap. 14.50 (*0-89012-008-0*) Col U Pr.

Religion & Life: The Foundations of Personal Religion. William R. Inge et al. LC 68-22940. (Essay Index Reprint Ser.). 1977. 16.95 (*0-8369-0819-8*) Ayer.

Religion & Literature in Western England, 600-800. Patrick Sims-Williams. (Studies in Anglo-Saxon England: No. 3). (Illus.). 460p. (C). 1990. 79.95 (*0-521-38325-0*) Cambridge U Pr.

Religion & Magic in the Life of Traditional Peoples. Alice B. Child & Irvin L. Child. 288p. 1992. pap. text ed. 28.00 (*0-13-012451-6*) P-H.

Religion & Marx. Rick B. Wise. LC 88-6208. 267p. (Orig.). 1988. pap. 12.00 (*0-910309-51-5*, 5521) Am Atheist.

Religion & Mass Media: Audiences & Adaptations. Daniel A. Stout & Judith M. Buddenbaum. LC 95-41786. 294p. 1996. 48.00 (*0-8039-7173-7*); pap. 22.95 (*0-8039-7174-5*) Sage.

Religion & Medical Ethics: Looking Backward, Looking Forward. Allen Verhey. 158p. 1996. pap. text ed. 18.00 (*0-8028-0862-X*) Eerdmans.

Religion & Medicine: A Medical Subject Analysis & Research Index with Bibliography. Patricia S. Hurley. LC 83-71656. 148p. 1985. 37.50 (*0-88164-032-8*); pap. 34.50 (*0-88164-033-6*) ABBE Pubs Assn.

Religion & Medicine of the Ga People. Margaret J. Field. LC 76-44718. 1977. reprint ed. 37.50 (*0-404-15923-0*) AMS Pr.

Religion & Mental Health. Ed. by John F. Schumaker. (Illus.). 336p. 1992. 55.00 (*0-19-506985-4*) OUP.

Religion & Mental Illness. Carol R. Murphy. (C). 1955. pap. 3.00 (*0-87574-082-0*) Pendle Hill.

Religion & Modern Life. Harvard University, Phillips Brooks House Association Staff. LC 75-39104. (Essay Index Reprint Ser.). 1977. reprint ed. 23.95 (*0-8369-2713-3*) Ayer.

Religion & Modern Society. Joseph Chiari. 215p. 1964. 69.50 (*0-614-00168-4*) Elliots Bks.

Religion & Modernity: Modes of Coexistence. Ed. by Pal Repstad. 240p. 1996. 43.00 (*82-00-22656-5*) Scandnvan Univ Pr.

Religion & Modernization in Southeast Asia. Fred R. Von der Mehden. 232p. 1986. text ed. 45.00 (*0-8156-2360-7*); pap. text ed. 17.95 (*0-8156-2361-5*) Syracuse U Pr.

Religion & Moral Reason: A New Method for Comparative Study. Ronald M. Green. 302p. 1988. pap. text ed. 19.95 (*0-19-504341-3*) OUP.

Religion & Morality. Ed. by D. Z. Phillips. LC 95-17961. (Claremont Studies in the Philosophy of Religion). 1996. text ed. 45.00 (*0-312-12868-1*) St Martin.

Religion & Myth. James MacDonald. LC 74-82059. 240p. 1969. reprint ed. text ed. 35.00 (*0-8371-1550-7*, MAR&, Negro U Pr) Greenwood.

Religion & National Integration in Africa: Islam, Christianity & Politics in the Sudan & Nigeria. Intro. by John O. Hunwick. (Islam & Society in Africa Ser.). 230p. 1992. 54.95 (*0-8101-1037-7*) Northwestern U Pr.

Religion & Nationalism. Ed. by John Coleman & Miklos Tomka. 150p. (Orig.). 1995. pap. 15.00 (*0-88344-887-4*) Orbis Bks.

Religion & Nationalism in Southeast Asia: Burma, Indonesia, & the Philippines. Fred R. Von der Mehden. (Illus.). 272p. (C). 1968. pap. 9.95 (*0-299-02944-1*) U of Wis Pr.

Religion & Nationalism in Soviet & East European Politics. enl. rev. ed. Ed. by Pedro Ramet. LC 88-21132. 560p. (C). 1988. text ed. 74.95 (*0-8223-0854-1*); pap. text ed. 29.95 (*0-8223-0891-6*) Duke.

Religion & Nationalism in Soviet Ukraine after 1945. Vasyl Markus. 46p. 1994. write for info. (*0-9609822-6-4*) Ukrainian Studies Fund.

Religion & Neoplatonism in Renaissance Medicine. Walter Pagel. Ed. by Marianne Winder. (Collected Studies: No. CS226). (Illus.). 346p. (C). 1985. reprint ed. text ed. 98.95 (*0-86078-174-7*, Pub. by Variorum UK) Ashgate Pub Co.

Religion & Nothingness. Keiji Nishitani. Tr. by Jan Van Bragt from JPN. LC 81-4084. (Nanzan Studies in Religion & Culture: No. 1). 366p. 1982. pap. 14.95 (*0-520-04946-2*) U CA Pr.

Religion & Our Divided Denominations. Ed. by Willard L. Sperry. LC 74-128315. (Essay Index Reprint Ser.). 1977. 17.95 (*0-8369-2201-8*) Ayer.

Religion & Pastoral Care: Information Index with Bibliography. Louis D. Sankaran. LC 88-47620. 150p. 1990. 37.50 (*1-55914-174-3*); pap. 34.50 (*1-55914-175-1*) ABBE Pubs Assn.

Religion & Personal Autonomy: The Third Disestablishment in America. Phillip E. Hammond. Ed. by Frederick M. Denny. LC 91-46356. (Studies in Comparative Religion). 234p. 1992. text ed. 29.95 (*0-87249-820-4*) U of SC Pr.

Religion & Personality Integration. Nilsen Anker. (Psycholgia Religionum Ser.: No. 8). 174p. (Orig.). 1980. pap. 30.00 (*91-554-0991-1*, Pub. by Uppsala Univ Acta Univ Uppsaliensis SW) Coronet Bks.

Religion & Philosophy. Ed. by Martin Warner. (Royal Institute of Philosophy Supplements Ser.: No. 31). 175p. (C). 1992. pap. text ed. 21.95 (*0-521-42951-X*) Cambridge U Pr.

***Religion & Philosophy: 1916 Edition.** R. G. Collingwood. 238p. 1996. reprint ed. pap. write for info. (*1-85506-317-4*) Bks Intl VA.

Religion & Philosophy in Germany. Heinrich Heine. Tr. by John Snodgrass from GER. LC 85-27675. 177p. (Orig.). (C). 1986. text ed. 49.50 (*0-88706-282-2*); pap. text ed. 16.95 (*0-88706-283-0*) State U NY Pr.

Religion & Philosophy of the Veda & Upanishads. Arthur B. Keith. (C). 1989. 62.50 (*81-208-0646-8*) S Asia.

Religion & Pilgrim Taxes under the Company Raj. Nancy Cassels. LC 87-61956. (Illus.). 207p. 1988. 34.00 (*0-913215-26-0*) Riverdale Co.

Religion & Political Conflict in Latin America. Ed. by Daniel H. Levine. LC 85-24525. xiii, 266p. (C). 1986. 34.95 (*0-8078-1689-2*); pap. 13.95 (*0-8078-4150-1*) U of NC Pr.

Religion & Political Conflict in South Asia: India, Pakistan, & Sri Lanka. Ed. by Douglas Allen. LC 91-45627. (Contributions to the Study of Religion Ser.: No. 34). 240p. 1992. text ed. 55.00 (*0-313-27309-X*, ARP, Greenwood Pr) Greenwood.

Religion & Political Culture in Britain & Ireland: From the Glorious Revolution to the Decline of Empire. David Hempton. 208p. (C). 1996. text ed. 54.95 (*0-521-47375-6*); pap. text ed. 16.95 (*0-521-47925-8*) Cambridge U Pr.

Religion & Political Modernization. Ed. by Donald E. Smith. LC 73-86917. 350p. reprint ed. pap. 99.80 (*0-317-29714-7*, 2022041) Bks Demand.

Religion & Political Power. Ed. by Gustavo Benavides & M. W. Daly. LC 88-24861. 240p. 1989. text ed. 64.50 (*0-7914-0026-3*); pap. text ed. 21.95 (*0-7914-0027-1*) State U NY Pr.

Religion & Political Society. Johann B. Metz et al. LC 73-18424. (Symposium Ser.: Vol. 1). xi, 209p. 1976. reprint ed. 89.95 (*0-88946-953-9*) E Mellen.

Religion & Politics. Ed. by Myron J. Aronoff. (Political Anthropology Ser.: Vol. III). 145p. 1983. 39.95 (*0-87855-459-9*) Transaction Pubs.

Religion & Politics. V. R. Iyer. viii, 226p. (C). 1991. 27.50 (*81-220-0231-5*) Advent Bks Div.

Religion & Politics. William F. Sollmann. (C). 1983. pap. 3.00 (*0-87574-014-6*) Pendle Hill.

Religion & Politics. Ed. by James E. Wood, Jr. LC 83-71725. (Institute of Church-State Studies). 122p. (Orig.). 1983. pap. 6.95 (*0-918954-39-8*) Baylor Univ Pr.

Religion & Politics. Ed. by Fred E. Baumann & Kenneth M. Jensen. LC 88-34438. 124p. reprint ed. pap. 35.40 (*0-7837-3563-4*, 2043419) Bks Demand.

Religion & Politics: Bishop Valerian Trifa & His Times. Gerald J. Bobango. (East European Monographs: No. 92). 294p. 1981. text ed. 68.50 (*0-914710-86-9*) East Eur Monographs.

Religion & Politics: Major Thinkers on the Relation of Church & State. Garrett W. Sheldon. LC 90-36071. (American University Studies: Political Science: Ser. X, Vol. 28). 256p. (C). 1990. text ed. 42.95 (*0-8204-1333-X*) P Lang Pubng.

Religion & Politics in Africa. Jeffrey Haynes. LC 95-40141. 256p. (C). 1996. pap. 25.00 (*1-85649-392-X*, Pub. by Zed Bks Ltd UK); text ed. 65.00 (*1-85649-391-1*, Pub. by Zed Bks Ltd UK) Humanities.

Religion & Politics in America: Faith, Culture & Strategic Choices. R. Booth Fowler & Allen D. Hertzke. (Explorations Ser.). 256p. (C). 1995. pap. text ed. 22.00 (*0-8133-1852-1*) Westview.

Religion & Politics in Aristophanes' Clouds. Marie C. Marianetti. (Altertumswissenschaftliche Texte und Studien: Vol. 24). x, 140p. (GER.). 1992. pap. 22.35 (*3-487-09633-1*) G Olms Pubs.

Religion & Politics in Colonial South Carolina. John W. Brinsfield. (Illus.). 204p. 1983. 25.00 (*0-89308-333-X*, SC 69) Southern Hist Pr.

Religion & Politics in Comparative Perspective: Revival of Religious Fundamentalism in East & West. Ed. by Bronislaw Misztal & Anson Shupe. LC 92-12120. 240p. 1992. text ed. 55.00 (*0-275-94218-X*, C4218, Praeger Pubs) Greenwood.

Religion & Politics in Contemporary Iran. Shahrough Akhavi. LC 79-22084. 255p. 1980. text ed. 64.50 (*0-87395-408-4*); pap. text ed. 21.95 (*0-87395-456-4*) State U NY Pr.

Religion & Politics in East Africa: The Period since Independence. Ed. by Holger B. Hansen & Michael Twaddle. (Eastern African Studies). 320p. (C). 1994. pap. text ed. 19.95 (*0-8214-1086-5*) Ohio U Pr.

Religion & Politics in East Africa: The Period since Independence. Ed. by Holger B. Hansen & Michael Twaddle. (Eastern African Studies). 320p. (C). 1995. text ed. 44.95 (*0-8214-1085-7*) Ohio U Pr.

Religion & Politics in Iran: Shi'ism from Quietism to Revolution. Nikki R. Keddie. LC 82-17351. 288p. 1983. text ed. 37.00 (*0-300-02874-1*) Yale U Pr.

Religion & Politics in Iran: Shi'ism from Quietism to Revolution. Ed. by Nikki R. Keddie. LC 82-17351. 288p. 1984. reprint ed. pap. 15.00 (*0-300-03245-5*, Y-504) Yale U Pr.

Religion & Politics in Israel. Charles S. Liebman & Eliezer Don-Yehiya. LC 83-48172. (Jewish Political & Social Studies). 160p. 1984. reprint ed. pap. 45.60 (*0-7837-6104-X*, 2059150) Bks Demand.

Religion & Politics in Israel: The Interplay of Judaism & Zionism. Daniel J. Elazar & Janet Aviad. 32p. 1981. pap. 2.50 (*0-87495-033-3*) Am Jewish Comm.

Religion & Politics in Korea under the Japanese Rule. Wi J. Kang. LC 86-18262. (Studies in Asian Thought & Religion: Vol. 5). 1986. lib. bdg. 79.95 (*0-88946-056-6*) E Mellen.

Religion & Politics in Latin America: Liberation Theology & Christian Democracy. Edward A. Lynch. LC 90-48694. 216p. 1991. text ed. 49.95 (*0-275-93774-7*, C3774, Praeger Pubs) Greenwood.

Religion & Politics in Muslim Society: Order & Conflict in Pakistan. Abkar S. Ahmed. LC 82-14774. (Illus.). 225p. 1983. text ed. 85.00 (*0-521-24635-0*) Cambridge U Pr.

Religion & Politics in the Ancient Near East. Ed. by Adele Berlin & Bernard D. Cooperman. (Studies & Texts in Jewish History & Culture: No. 1). 1996. boxed 25.00 (*1-883053-24-2*) Univ Pr MD.

Religion & Politics in the Early Republic: Jasper Adams & the Church-State Debate. Daniel L. Dreisbach. LC 95-37861. (Illus.). 240p. 1996. pap. text ed. 16.95 (*0-8131-0880-2*) U Pr of Ky.

Religion & Politics in the Early Republic: Jasper Adams & the Church-State Debate. Daniel L. Dreisbach. LC 95-37861. (Illus.). 240p. (C). 1996. text ed. 42.95 (*0-8131-1950-2*) U Pr of Ky.

Religion & Politics in the Modern World. Ed. by Peter H. Merkl & Ninian Smart. 296p. (C). 1985. pap. text ed. 13.20 (*0-8147-5393-0*) NYU Pr.

Religion & Politics in the U. S. 2nd ed. Kenneth D. Wald. 380p. 1991. 23.95 (*0-87187-604-3*) Congr Quarterly.

Religion & Politics in the United States. 3rd ed. Kenneth D. Wald. LC 96-38169. 380p. 1996. pap. 23.95 (*1-56802-157-7*) Congr Quarterly.

Religion & Politics in Tibet. B. R. Burman. 180p. 1979. 14.95 (*0-7069-0801-5*) Asia Bk Corp.

***Religion & Politics under the Early 'Abbasids: The Emergence of the Proto-Sunni Elite.** Muhammad Q. Zaman. LC 96-6517. (Islamic History & Civilization, Studies & Texts Ser.: No. 16). 256p. 1997. 85.75 (*90-04-10678-2*, NLG 137) E J Brill.

***Religion & Postmodernity.** Paul Lakeland. LC 97-23817. 1997. pap. text ed. 13.00 (*0-8006-3098-X*, Fortress Pr) Augsburg Fortress.

Religion & Power: Pagans, Jews & Christians in the Greek East. Douglas R. Edwards. 256p. 1996. 39.95 (*0-19-508263-X*) OUP.

Religion & Power in Morocco. Henry Munson, Jr. LC 92-40202. (Illus.). 256p. 1993. 28.00 (*0-300-05376-2*) Yale U Pr.

R

Religion & Power in the Ancient Greek World: Proceedings of the Uppsala Symposium 1993. Ed. by Pontus Hellstrom & Brita Alroth. (Uppsala Studies in Ancient Mediterranean & Near Eastern Civilizations: No. 24). (Illus.). 204p. (Orig.). 1996. pap. 52.50 (*91-554-3693-5*, Pub. by Uppsala Univ Acta Univ Uppsaliensis SW) Coronet Bks.

Religion & Power Structure in Rural India: (A Study of Two Fishing Villages in Kerala) Poovar-Sakthikulangara. J. Murickan. (C). 1991. 18.00 (*81-7033-117-X*, Pub. by Rawat II) S Asia.

Religion & Practical Reason: New Essays in the Comparative Philosophy of Religions. Ed. by Frank E. Reynolds & David Tracy. LC 94-7298. (SUNY Series, Toward a Comparative Philosophy of Religions). 444p. (C). 1994. text ed. 64.50 (*0-7914-2217-8*); pap. text ed. 21.95 (*0-7914-2218-6*) State U NY Pr.

Religion & Prevention in Mental Health: Research, Vision & Action. Kenneth I. Pargament et al. LC 92-5887. (Prevention in Human Services Ser.: Vol. 9, No.2). (Illus.). 232p. 1992. text ed. 59.95 (*1-56024-225-6*); pap. text ed. 24.95 (*1-56024-226-4*) Haworth Pr.

***Religion & Prime Time Television.** Ed. by Michael Suman. LC 97-19231. 1997. text ed. write for info. (*0-275-96034-X*, Praeger Pubs) Greenwood.

***Religion & Psychoactive Sacraments: A Bibliographic Guide.** Ed. by Thomas B. Roberts & Paula J. Hruby. (Entheogen Project Ser.: Vol. 1). 327p. 1995. spiral bd. 28.00 (*1-889725-00-5*) Coun Sprtal Pract.

Religion & Psychology: A Dialogical Approach. Maurice Friedman. 240p. (C). 1992. pap. 16.95 (*1-55778-346-2*) Paragon Hse.

Religion & Psychology: A Medical Subject Analysis & Research Index with Bibliography. Nancy L. Alpert. LC 83-71657. 150p. 1985. 37.50 (*0-88164-034-4*); pap. 34.50 (*0-88164-035-2*) ABBE Pubs Assn.

Religion & Psychology in Transition: Psychoanalysis, Feminism & Theology. James W. Jones. LC 96-15777. (Illus.). 224p. 1996. 22.50 (*0-300-06769-0*) Yale U Pr.

Religion & Public Doctrine in Modern England, Vol. 2. Maurice Cowling. (Cambridge Studies in the History & Theory of Politics). 403p. 1985. text ed. 69.95 (*0-521-25959-2*) Cambridge U Pr.

***Religion & Race: African & European Roots in Conflict - a Jamaican Testament.** Winston Lawson. (Research in Religion & Family Ser.: Vol. 4). 240p. (C). 1996. pap. text ed. 29.95 (*0-8204-3093-5*) P Lang Pubng.

Religion & Race: Southern Presbyterians, 1946-1983. Joel L. Alvis, Jr. LC 93-23923. 208p. (Orig.). 1994. pap. 19.95 (*0-8173-0701-X*) U of Ala Pr.

Religion & Radical Empiricism. Nancy Frankenberry. LC 86-16558. 226p. 1987. text ed. 64.50 (*0-88706-408-6*); pap. text ed. 21.95 (*0-88706-409-4*) State U NY Pr.

Religion & Radical Politics: An Alternative Christian Tradition in the United States. Robert H. Craig. (Illus.). 320p. (C). 1992. 44.95 (*0-87722-973-2*) Temple U Pr.

Religion & Radical Politics: An Alternative Christian Tradition in the United States. Robert H. Craig. (Illus.). 320p. (C). 1995. pap. text ed. 18.95 (*1-56639-335-3*) Temple U Pr.

Religion & Rajput Women: The Ethic of Protection in Contemporary Narratives. Lindsey Harlan. (Illus.). 274p. 1994. 36.50 (*81-215-0613-1*, Pub. by M Manoharial II) Coronet Bks.

Religion & Rajput Women: The Ethic of Protection in Contemporary Narratives. Lindsey Harlan. LC 91-2389. (Illus.). 286p. 1991. 42.50 (*0-520-07339-8*) U CA Pr.

Religion & Rational Theology: Religion & Rational Theology. Immanuel Kant. Ed. by Allen Wood & George DiGiovanni. (The Cambridge Edition of the Works of Immanuel Kant). 528p. 1996. text ed. 70.00 (*0-521-35416-1*) Cambridge U Pr.

Religion & Reason: An Anthology. Ed. by Burton F. Porter. LC 92-50011. 576p. (C). 1992. pap. text ed. 35.50 (*0-312-04885-8*) St Martin.

***Religion & Rebellion.** Judith Devlin & Ronan Fanning. 232p. 1997. 59.95 (*1-900621-03-7*) Dufour.

Religion & Rebellion in Iran: The Iranian Tobacco Protest of 1891-1892. Nikki R. Keddie. 163p. 1966. 37.50 (*0-7146-1971-X*, Pub. by F Cass Pubs UK) Intl Spec Bk.

Religion & Reductionism: Essays on Eliade, Segal, & the Challenge of the Social Sciences for the Study of Religion. Ed. by Thomas A. Idinopulos & Edward A. Yonan. LC 93-34561. (Studies in the History of Religions: No. 62). 1993. 83.50 (*90-04-09870-4*) E J Brill.

Religion & Religious Practice in the Seleucid Kingdom. Ed. by Per Bilde et al. (Studies in Hellenistic Civilization: No. 1). (Illus.). 269p. (C). 1990. text ed. 35.00 (*87-7288-322-7*, Pub. by Aarhus Univ Pr DK) David Brown.

Religion & Republic: The American Circumstance. Martin E. Marty. LC 86-47755. 391p. 1989. pap. 17.00 (*0-8070-1207-6*) Beacon Pr.

Religion & Resistance Politics in South Africa. Lyn S. Graybill. LC 95-13895. 168p. 1995. text ed. 52.95 (*0-275-95141-3*, Praeger Pubs) Greenwood.

Religion & Respectability: Sunday Schools & Working Class Culture, 1780-1850. Thomas W. Laqueur. LC 75-29728. 308p. reprint ed. pap. 87.80 (*0-8357-8302-2*, 2033797) Bks Demand.

Religion & Revelation: A Theology of Revelation in the World's Religions. Keith Ward. 368p. 1994. 65.00 (*0-19-826466-6*); pap. 19.95 (*0-19-826375-9*) OUP.

Religion & Revolution in Early-Industrial England: The Halevy Thesis & Its Critics. Intro. & Notes by Gerald W. Olsen. LC 89-36361. 252p. (Orig.). (C). 1990. pap. text ed. 26.50 (*0-8191-7555-2*); lib. bdg. 44.50 (*0-8191-7554-4*) U Pr of Amer.

Religion & Revolution in the Modern World: Ali Sariati's Islam & Persian Revolution. Naghi Yousefi. LC 95-3473. 1995. 38.50 (*0-8191-9894-3*) U Pr of Amer.

Religion & Ritual see Gros Ventre of Montana

Religion & Ritual in Chinese Society. Ed. by Arthur P. Wolf. LC 73-89863. (Studies in Chinese Society). xiv, 378p. 1974. 47.50 (*0-8047-0858-4*) Stanford U Pr.

Religion & Ritual in Chinese Society. Ed. by Arthur P. Wolf. LC 73-89863. (Studies in Chinese Society). 111p. reprint ed. pap. 30.00 (*0-7837-6456-1*, 2046460) Bks Demand.

Religion & Ritual in Rural India: A Case Study in Kumaon. Tribhuwan Kapur. (C). 1988. 20.00 (*81-7017-238-1*, Pub. by Abhinav II) S Asia.

***Religion & Schooling in Contemporary America: Confronting Our Cultural Pluralism.** Thomas C. Hunt & James C. Carper. LC 97-2439. (Source Books on Education Ser.). 230p. 1997. text ed. 50.00 (*0-8153-2472-3*) Garland.

Religion & Science. F. V. Verbitsky. 1959. pap. 1.00 (*0-317-30432-1*) Holy Trinity.

***Religion & Science.** 2nd ed. Bertrand Russell. LC 96-48939. 272p. 1997. pap. text ed. 12.95 (*0-19-511551-1*) OUP.

Religion & Science. Bertrand Russell. 258p. 1961. reprint ed. pap. 11.95 (*0-19-500228-8*) OUP.

***Religion & Science: Historical & Contemporary Issues.** Ian G. Barbour. LC 97-6294. 1997. pap. write for info. (*0-06-060938-9*) Harper SF.

Religion & Science: History, Method, Dialogue. Ed. by W. Mark Richardson & Wesley Wildman. LC 95-47045. 480p. (C). 1996. pap. 29.95 (*0-415-91667-4*); text ed. 75.00 (*0-415-91666-6*) Routledge.

Religion & Scientific Method. George N. Schlesinger. 210p. 1977. lib. bdg. 78.00 (*90-277-0815-0*, D Reidel) Kluwer Ac.

***Religion & Secularization in Literature, 1800-1980.** R. L. Brett. 304p. 1997. text ed. 40.00 (*0-86554-544-8*) Mercer Univ Pr.

Religion & Self-Acceptance: A Study of the Relationship Between Belief in God & the Desire to Know. John F. Haught. LC 80-5872. 195p. 1980. lib. bdg. 49.00 (*0-8191-1296-8*) U Pr of Amer.

Religion & Sex. Chapman Cohen. LC 72-9631. reprint ed. 47.50 (*0-404-57430-0*) AMS Pr.

Religion & Sex: Index of New Information & Bibliography. Mary A. Mandel. 150p. 1997. 47.50 (*0-7883-1010-0*); pap. 44.50 (*0-7883-1011-9*) ABBE Pubs Assn.

Religion & Sexual Health: Ethical, Theological, & Clinical Perspectives. Ed. by Ronald M. Green. LC 92-10060. (Theology & Medicine Ser.: Vol. 1). 248p. (C). 1992. lib. bdg. 117.50 (*0-7923-1752-1*, Pub. by Klwr Acad Pubs NE) Kluwer Ac.

Religion & Sexuality: The Shakers, the Mormons, & the Oneida Community. Lawrence Foster. LC 83-18315. 384p. 1984. pap. text ed. 13.95 (*0-252-01119-8*) U of Ill Pr.

Religion & Sexuality in American Fiction. Ann-Janine Morey. (Cambridge Studies in American Literature & Culture: No. 57). 340p. (C). 1992. text ed. 59.95 (*0-521-41676-0*) Cambridge U Pr.

Religion & Social Change in Modern Turkey: The Case of Bediuzzaman Said Nursi. Serif Mardin. LC 89-4280. (SUNY Series in Near Eastern Studies). 267p. (C). 1989. text ed. 64.50 (*0-88706-996-7*); pap. text ed. 21.95 (*0-88706-997-5*) State U NY Pr.

Religion & Social Conflicts. Otto Maduro. Tr. by Robert R. Barr from SPA. LC 82-3439. Orig. Title: Religion y Lucha de Clase. 189p. (Orig.). reprint ed. pap. 53.90 (*0-7837-5512-0*, 2045282) Bks Demand.

Religion & Social Formation in Korea: Minjung & Millenarianism. Sang T. Lee. xv, 246p. 1996. lib. bdg. 109.65 (*3-11-014797-1*) Mouton.

Religion & Social Justice. Ramesh Thakur. 1996. text ed. 49.95 (*0-312-15936-6*) St Martin.

Religion & Social Order in Albany, New York: 1652-1836. David G. Hackett. (Religion in America Ser.). (Illus.). 256p. 1991. 42.00 (*0-19-506513-1*) OUP.

Religion & Social Organization in Central Polynesia. Robert W. Williamson. Ed. by Ralph Piddington. LC 75-35218. reprint ed. 52.50 (*0-404-14241-9*) AMS Pr.

Religion & Social Responsibility. Thomas B. Irving. pap. 3.00 (*0-933511-35-3*) Kazi Pubns.

Religion & Social Theory. 2nd ed. Bryan S. Turner. (Theory, Culture & Society Ser.). 288p. (C). 1991. text ed. 69.95 (*0-8039-8568-1*); pap. text ed. 19.95 (*0-8039-8569-X*) Sage.

Religion & Social Work Practice in Contemporary American Society. Frank M. Loewenberg. 184p. 1988. text ed. 29.50 (*0-231-06452-7*) Col U Pr.

Religion & Societies: Asia & the Middle East. Ed. by Carlo Caldarola. (Religion & Society Ser.: No. 22). 688p. 1982. text ed. 96.15 (*90-279-3259-X*) Mouton.

Religion & Societies: Asia & the Middle East. Ed. by Carlo Caldarola. (Religion & Society Ser.: No. 22). 688p. 1984. pap. 69.25 (*3-11-010021-5*) Mouton.

Religion & Society. Sarvepalli Radhakrishnan. (C). 1995. 9.50 (*81-7223-163-6*, Pub. by Indus Pub II) S Asia.

Religion & Society: The Role of Compassion, Selfless Service, & Social Justice in Five Major Faith Traditions. Lucinda A. Mosher. (Illus.). 175p. (Orig.). (YA). (gr. 8-12). 1996. pap. text ed. write for info. (*1-881678-56-3*) CRIS.

Religion & Society in Arab Sind. Derryl N. Maclean. LC 88-24064. (Monographs & Theoretical Studies in Sociology & Anthropology in Honour of Nels Anderson: Vol. 25). x, 191p. (Orig.). 1989. pap. text ed. 53.75 (*90-04-08551-3*) E J Brill.

***Religion & Society in Contemporary Korea.** Lewis R. Lancaster et al. LC 97-2424. (Korea Research Monographs). 1997. write for info. (*1-55729-055-5*) IEAS.

Religion & Society in Cotswold Vale: Nailsworth, Gloucestershire, 1780-1865. Albion M. Urdank. 1990. 50.00 (*0-520-06670-7*) U CA Pr.

Religion & Society in Early Modern England: A Sourcebook. Ed. by David Cressy & Lori A. Ferrell. LC 95-38690. 288p. (C). 1996. pap. 17.95 (*0-415-11849-2*); text ed. 59.95 (*0-415-11848-4*) Routledge.

Religion & Society in Eastern India: Eschmann Memorial Lectures. Ed. by Hermann Kulke & G. C. Tripathi. (C). 1994. text ed. 28.00 (*0-614-04132-5*, Pub. by Manohar II) S Asia.

Religion & Society in England: 1850-1914. Hugh McLeod. (Social History in Perspective Ser.). 256p. 1996. text ed. 39.95 (*0-312-15798-3*); text ed. 18.95 (*0-312-15805-X*) St Martin.

Religion & Society in Frontier California. Laurie R. Maffly-Kipp. LC 93-24808. (Yale Historical Publications). 256p. 1994. 30.00 (*0-300-05377-0*) Yale U Pr.

Religion & Society in Kent 1640-1914. Nigel Yates et al. LC 94-14000. (Kent History Project Ser.: No. 2). (Illus.). 272p. (C). 1994. 63.00 (*0-85115-556-1*, Boydell Pr) Boydell & Brewer.

Religion & Society in Modern Japan. Mark R. Mullins. LC 93-23877. (Nanzan Studies in Asian Religions: Vol. 5). 256p. (C). 1993. text ed. 50.00 (*0-89581-935-X*); pap. text ed. 25.00 (*0-89581-936-8*) Asian Humanities.

Religion & Society in Post-Emancipation Jamaica. Robert J. Stewart. LC 91-41997. (Illus.). 276p. (Orig.). 1992. pap. text ed. 19.95 (*0-87049-749-9*); lib. bdg. 42.50 (*0-87049-748-0*) U of Tenn Pr.

Religion & Society in Russia: The Sixteenth & Seventh Centuries. Paul Bushkovitch. 272p. 1992. 45.00 (*0-19-506946-3*) OUP.

Religion & Society in Spain, c. 1492. John Edwards. (Collected Studies: CS520). 368p. 1996. 97.95 (*0-86078-544-0*, Pub. by Variorum UK) Ashgate Pub Co.

Religion & Society in T'ang & Sung China. Ed. by Patricia B. Ebrey & Peter N. Gregory. LC 93-20371. (Illus.). 400p. (C). 1993. text ed. 35.00 (*0-8248-1512-2*) UH Pr.

Religion & Society in the American West: Historical Essays. Ed. by Carl Guarneri & David Alvarez. LC 87-10591. (Illus.). 508p. (Orig.). (C). 1987. pap. text ed. 38.50 (*0-8191-6432-1*) U Pr of Amer.

Religion & Society in the Himalayas. Tanka B. Subba. (C). 1991. 21.50 (*81-212-0334-1*, Pub. by Gian Publng Hse II) S Asia.

Religion & Society in Transition: The Church & Social Change in England, 1560-1850. Ernest E. Best. LC 82-21699. (Texts & Studies in Religion: Vol. 15). 353p. 1982. lib. bdg. 99.95 (*0-88946-804-4*) E Mellen.

***Religion & Society in Western Australia.** Ed. by John Tonkin. (Studies in Western Australian History: Vol. IX). pap. 14.95 (*0-614-25205-9*) Intl Spec Bk.

Religion & Spirituality. Eliot Deutsch. LC 94-33771. 151p. (C). 1995. text ed. 39.50 (*0-7914-2457-X*); pap. text ed. 12.95 (*0-7914-2458-8*) State U NY Pr.

Religion & Spirituality. Parthasarathi Rajagopalachari. 152p. 1992. 10.00 (*0-945242-18-2*) Shri Ram Chandra.

Religion & Sport: The Meeting of Sacred & Profane. Charles S. Prebish. LC 92-30020. (Contributions to the Study of Popular Culture Ser.: No. 36). 264p. 1992. text ed. 49.95 (*0-313-28729-5*, GM8729, Greenwood Pr) Greenwood.

***Religion & State in the American Jewish Experience: A Documentary History.** Jonathan D. Sarna. LC 96-27119. 368p. 1997. text ed. 40.00 (*0-268-01654-2*) U of Notre Dame Pr.

Religion & Statecraft among the Romans. Alan Wardman. LC 82-47928. 223p. reprint ed. pap. 63.60 (*0-685-15556-0*, 2026708) Bks Demand.

Religion & Suicide in the African-American Community. Kevin E. Early. LC 92-19425. (Contributions in Afro-American & African Studies: No. 158). 160p. 1992. text ed. 49.95 (*0-313-28470-9*, ERS, Greenwood Pr) Greenwood.

Religion & Superstition in the Plays of Ben Johnson & Thomas Middleton. Berril Johansson. LC 68-1346. 1970. reprint ed. 75.00 (*0-8383-0667-5*) M S G Haskell Hse.

Religion & Superstition in the Plays of Ben Johnson & Thomas Middleton. Berril Johansson. (Essays & Studies on English Language & Literature: Vol. 7). 1974. reprint ed. pap. 35.00 (*0-8115-0205-8*) Periodicals Srv.

***Religion & Technology: A Study in the Philosophy of Culture.** Jay Newman. LC 96-50321. 208p. 1997. text ed. 55.00 (*0-275-95865-5*, Praeger Pubs) Greenwood.

***Religion & the American Experience: A Social & Cultural History, 1765-1996.** Donald C. Swift. LC 97-25937. 320p. (C). (gr. 13). 1997. text ed. 66.95 (*0-7656-0133-8*); pap. text ed. 25.95 (*0-7656-0134-6*) M E Sharpe.

Religion & the American Experience, the Twentieth Century: A Bibliography of Doctoral Dissertations. Arthur P. Young & E. J. Holley. LC 94-36759. (Bibliographies & Indexes in Religious Studies: Vol. 31). 432p. 1994. text ed. 85.00 (*0-313-27748-6*, Greenwood Pr) Greenwood.

Religion & the American Experience, 1620-1900: A Bibliography of Doctoral Dissertations. Arthur P. Young & E. Jens Holley. LC 92-28450. (Bibliographies & Indexes in Religious Studies: No. 24). 496p. 1992. text ed. 79.50 (*0-313-27747-8*, YRE/, Greenwood Pr) Greenwood.

Religion & the American Revolution. Jerald Brauer. LC 76-9718. 89p. pap. 25.40 (*0-685-15492-0*, 2026888) Bks Demand.

Religion & the Authority of the Past. Ed. by Tobin Siebers. (RATIO: Institute for the Humanities Ser.). (Illus.). 350p. (C). 1993. text ed. 52.50 (*0-472-10489-6*) U of Mich Pr.

***Religion & the Body.** Ed. by Sarah Coakley. (Cambridge Studies in Religious Traditions: No. 8). (Illus.). 374p. 1997. text ed. 69.95 (*0-521-36669-0*) Cambridge U Pr.

Religion & the Challenge of Philosophy. J. E. Barnhart. (Quality Paperback Ser.: No. 291). 400p. (Orig.). 1975. pap. 9.95 (*0-8226-0291-1*) Littlefield.

***Religion & the Clinical Practice of Psychology.** Edward Shafranske & James A. Mulick. 1996. 39.95 (*1-55798-321-6*) Am Psychol.

Religion & the Constitution. Paul G. Kauper. LC 64-7898. 147p. reprint ed. pap. 41.90 (*0-317-29869-0*, 2051881) Bks Demand.

Religion & the Constitution: A Reinterpretation. Peter J. Ferrara. LC 83-81643. 172p. (Orig.). (C). 1983. pap. text ed. 18.25 (*0-942522-06-0*) Free Congr Res.

Religion & the Culture Wars: Dispatches from the Front. John C. Green et al. LC 96-15997. (Religious Forces in the Modern Political World). 400p. 1996. pap. text ed. 26.95 (*0-8476-8268-4*); lib. bdg. 69.50 (*0-8476-8267-6*) Rowman.

Religion & the Decline of Magic. Keith Thomas. 716p. 1975. pap. write for info. (*0-02-420200-2*, Macmillan Coll) P-H.

***Religion & the Decline of Magic.** Keith Thomas. 736p. 1997. pap. 19.95 (*0-19-521360-2*) OUP.

***Religion & the Enlightenment: From Descartes to Kant.** James M. Byrne. LC 97-20355. 1997. pap. text ed. 22.00 (*0-664-25760-7*) Westminster John Knox.

Religion & the Family: When God Helps. Laurel A. Burton. LC 91-23285. (Illus.). 224p. 1992. pap. 19.95 (*1-56024-197-7*); lib. bdg. 29.95 (*1-56024-192-6*) Haworth Pr.

Religion & the Framers: The Biographical Evidence. M. E. Bradford. (Illus.). 36p. (Orig.). 1991. pap. 3.95 (*0-942516-09-5*) Plymouth Rock Found.

Religion & the Greeks. R. Garland. (Classical World Ser.). 121p. 1994. pap. 14.95 (*1-85399-409-X*, Pub. by Brstl Class Pr UK) Focus Pub-R Pullins.

Religion & the HIV-AIDS Community: Index of New Information with Authors & Subjects. rev. ed. American Health Research Institute Staff. LC 94-34806. 109p. 1994. 47.50 (*0-7883-0448-8*); pap. 44.50 (*0-7883-0449-6*) ABBE Pubs Assn.

Religion & the Individual: A Jewish Perspective. Louis Jacobs. (Cambridge Studies in Religious Traditions: No. 1). 176p. (C). 1992. text ed. 65.00 (*0-521-41138-6*) Cambridge U Pr.

Religion & the Individual: A Social-Psychological Perspective. 2nd ed. C. Daniel Batson et al. LC 92-28606. 440p. (C). 1993. 51.95 (*0-19-506208-6*); pap. 26.95 (*0-19-506209-4*) OUP.

Religion & the Life of the Nation: American Recoveries. Ed. by Rowland A. Sherrill. 280p. 1990. text ed. 39.95 (*0-252-01693-9*); pap. text ed. 14.95 (*0-252-06111-X*) U of Ill Pr.

Religion & the Making of Society: Essays in Social Theology. Charles Davis. (Studies in Ideology & Religion: No. 4). 228p. (C). 1993. text ed. 59.95 (*0-521-44310-5*); pap. text ed. 18.95 (*0-521-44789-5*) Cambridge U Pr.

Religion & the Modern Mind. Walter T. Stace. LC 80-24093. 285p. 1980. reprint ed. text ed. 38.50 (*0-313-22662-8*, STRM, Greenwood Pr) Greenwood.

Religion & the Natural Sciences: The Range of Engagement. James Huchingson. LC 92-81266. 608p. (C). 1993. pap. text ed. 26.75 (*0-03-052253-6*) HB Coll Pubs.

Religion & the One: Philosophies East & West. Frederick Copleston. 288p. 1994. 45.00 (*0-85532-514-3*, Pub. by Srch Pr UK) St Mut.

Religion & the Order of Nature. Seyyed H. Nasr. 320p. 1996. 65.00 (*0-19-510274-6*); pap. 18.95 (*0-19-510823-X*) OUP.

***Religion & the People of Western Europe 1789-1990.** 2nd ed. Hugh McLeod. (Illus.). 192p. (Orig.). 1997. pap. 15.95 (*0-19-289283-5*) OUP.

Religion & the People, 800-1700. Ed. by James Obelkevich. LC 78-7847. (Illus.). 351p. reprint ed. pap. 100.10 (*0-8357-3889-2*, 2036621) Bks Demand.

***Religion & the Political Order: Politics in Classical & Contemporary Christianity, Islam & Judaism.** Ed. by Jacob Neusner. LC 96-30129. (University of South Florida Studies on Religion & the Social Order). 334p. 1996. 89.95 (*0-7885-0310-3*, 245015) Scholars Pr GA.

Religion & the Presidential Election. Paul Lopatto. LC 84-26281. (American Political Parties & Elections Ser.). 192p. 1985. text ed. 49.95 (*0-275-90138-6*, C0138, Praeger Pubs) Greenwood.

Religion & the Public Good: A Bicentennial Forum. William L. Miller et al. 139p. 1989. 35.00 (*0-86554-326-7*, MUP-H276) Mercer Univ Pr.

Religion & the Public Order: An Annual Review of Church & State & of Religion, Law, & Society. Ed. by Donald A. Giannella. LC 64-17164. 288p. reprint ed. pap. 82.10 (*0-317-20699-0*, 2024114) Bks Demand.

Religion & the Public Schools. Incl. Legal Issue: 1965. Paul A. Freund. LC 65-26011. 1965. (*0-318-53172-0*); Educational Issue. Robert Ulich. LC 65-26011. 1965. (*0-318-53173-9*); LC 65-26011. vi, 56p. 1990. pap. 4.00 (*0-674-75600-2*) HUP.

***Religion & the Public Schools: A Summary of the Law.** Marc A. Stern. 50p. (Orig.). 1997. pap. text ed. 25.00 (*0-7881-3621-6*) DIANE Pub.

Religion & the Public Schools in 19th Century America: Contribution of Orestes A. Brownson. Edward J. Power. LC 95-31263. 192p. (Orig.). 1996. pap. 13.95 (*0-8091-3612-0*) Paulist Pr.

An Asterisk (*) at the beginning of an entry indicates that the title is appearing in BIP for the first time.

***Religion & the Racist Right: The Origins of the Christian Identity Movement.** rev. ed. Michael Barkun. LC 96-28347. 352p. (C). (gr. 13). 1996. 39.95 (*0-8078-2328-7*); pap. 15.95 (*0-8078-4638-4*) U of NC Pr.

Religion & the Radical Republican Movement, 1860-1870. Victor B. Howard. LC 89-49233. 312p. 1990. 34.00 (*0-8131-1702-X*) U Pr of Ky.

Religion & the Rebel. Colin Wilson. LC 74-9134. 338p. 1974. reprint ed. text ed. 59.75 (*0-8371-7596-8*, WIRA, Greenwood Pr) Greenwood.

Religion & the Religions in the English Enlightenment. Peter Harrison. 300p. (C). 1990. text ed. 75.00 (*0-521-38530-X*) Cambridge U Pr.

Religion & the Rise of Capitalism. Richard H. Tawney. 1990. 14.50 (*0-8446-1446-7*) Peter Smith.

Religion & the Rise of Democracy. Graham Maddox. LC 95-19599. 304p. (C). 1996. text ed. 79.95 (*0-415-02603-2*) Routledge.

Religion & the Rise of Modern Science. R. Hooykaas. 162p. 1993. reprint ed. pap. 12.95 (*1-57383-018-6*) Regent College.

Religion & the Rise of Sport. Baker. 1994. 24.95 (*0-02-901185-X*) S&S Trade.

Religion & the Rise of Western Culture. Christopher H. Dawson. LC 77-27181. (Gifford Lectures: 1948-49). reprint ed. 46.50 (*0-404-60499-4*) AMS Pr.

Religion & the Romans. K. Dowden. (Classical World Ser.). 110p. 1992. pap. 14.95 (*1-85399-180-5*, Pub. by Brstl Class Pr UK) Focus Pub-R Pullins.

Religion & the Sciences of Life: With Other Essays on Allied Topics. William McDougall. LC 70-39108. (Essay Index Reprint Ser.). 1977. reprint ed. 23.95 (*0-8369-2700-1*) Ayer.

***Religion & the Social Order, Vol. 3, Pt. A.** Ed. by David G. Bromley. 292p. 1993. 73.25 (*0-614-24145-6*) Jai Pr.

***Religion & the Social Order, Vol. 3, Pt. B.** Ed. by David G. Bromley. 229p. 1993. 73.25 (*1-55938-715-7*) Jai Pr.

***Religion & the Social Order, Vol. 7.** Ed. by David G. Bromley. 1997. 73.25 (*0-614-24144-8*) Jai Pr.

Religion & the Social Order: Between Sacred & Secular, Vol. 4. Ed. by David G. Bromley. 321p. 1994. 73.50 (*1-55938-763-7*) Jai Pr.

Religion & the Social Order: New Developments in Theory & Research, Vol. 1. Ed. by David G. Bromley. 283p. 1991. 73.25 (*1-55938-291-0*) Jai Pr.

Religion & the Social Order: Sex, Lies & Sanctity, Vol. 5. Ed. by David G. Bromley. 269p. 1995. 73.25 (*1-55938-904-4*) Jai Pr.

Religion & the Social Order: The Handbook on Cults & Sects in America, 2 vols., Vol. 3. Ed. by David G. Bromley. 1993. 146.50 (*1-55938-477-8*) Jai Pr.

Religion & the Social Order: The Issue of Authenticity in the Study of Religions, Vol. 6. Ed. by David G. Bromley. 279p. 1996. 73.25 (*0-7623-0038-8*) Jai Pr.

Religion & the Social Order: Vatican II & U. S. Catholicism, Vol. 2. Ed. by David G. Bromley. 284p. 1991. 73.25 (*1-55938-388-7*) Jai Pr.

Religion & the Social Order: What Kinds of Lessons Does History Teach? Jacob Neusner. LC 94-33696. (South Florida-Rochester-Saint Louis Studies on Religion & the Social Order: Vol. 11). 302p. 1995. 89.95 (*0-7885-0054-6*, 24 50 11) Scholars Pr GA.

***Religion & the Social Sciences: An Encyclopedia.** William H. Swatos. 800p. Date not set. text ed. 120.00 (*0-8153-1637-2*) Garland.

Religion & the Social Sciences: Essays on the Confrontation. Robert A. Segal. (Studies in Religion). 184p. 1989. 45.95 (*1-55540-295-X*, 14 70 03) Scholars Pr GA.

Religion & the Sociology of Knowledge: Modernization & Pluralism in Christian Thought & Structure. Ed. by Barbara Hargrove. LC 83-22149. (Studies in Religion & Society: Vol. 8). 412p. 1984. lib. bdg. 109.95 (*0-88946-872-9*) E Mellen.

Religion & the State: Essays in Honor of Leo Pfeffer. Ed. by James E. Wood, Jr. 596p. 1985. 39.95 (*0-918954-29-0*) Baylor Univ Pr.

Religion & the State: The Making & Testing of an American Tradition. Evarts B. Greene. LC 75-41122. reprint ed. 22.50 (*0-404-14548-5*) AMS Pr.

Religion & the State: The Struggle for Legitimacy & Power. Ed. by Robert J. Myers. LC 85-72100. (Annals of the American Academy of Political & Social Science Ser.: Vol. 483). 1986. text ed. 26.00 (*0-8039-2538-7*); pap. text ed. 17.00 (*0-8039-2539-5*) Sage.

Religion & the Transformation of Society: A Study in Social Change in Africa. Monica H. Wilson. LC 73-134622. (Scott Holland Memorial Lectures: 15; 1969). 173p. reprint ed. pap. 49.40 (*0-317-27081-8*, 2024562) Bks Demand.

Religion & the Transformations of Capitalism: Comparative Approaches. Ed. by Richard H. Roberts. LC 94-28913. 464p. (C). 1995. text ed. 99.95 (*0-415-11917-0*, B4332) Routledge.

Religion & the Unconscious. 2nd ed. Barry Ulanov & Ann B. Ulanov. LC 75-16302. 288p. 1985. pap. 16.00 (*0-664-24657-5*, Westminster) Westminster John Knox.

Religion & the Variety of Culture: A Study in Origin & Practice. Lamin Sanneh. LC 96-8088. (Christian Mission & Modern Culture Ser.). 96p. 1996. pap. 8.00 (*1-56338-166-4*) TPI PA.

Religion & the Western Mind. Ninian Smart. LC 86-10578. 142p. (C). 1987. text ed. 64.50 (*0-88706-382-9*); pap. text ed. 21.95 (*0-88706-383-7*) State U NY Pr.

Religion & the Working Class in Antebellum America. Jama Lazerow. LC 95-8600. 464p. 1995. text ed. 39.50 (*1-56098-544-5*) Smithsonian.

Religion & Truth. Donald Wiebe. 295p. 1981. text ed. 57.70 (*90-279-3149-6*) Mouton.

Religion & Twentieth-Century American Intellectual Life. Ed. by Michael J. Lacey. (Woodrow Wilson Center Ser.). 224p. (C). 1989. text ed. 54.95 (*0-521-37560-6*) Cambridge U Pr.

Religion & Twentieth-Century American Intellectual Life. Ed. by Michael J. Lacey. (Woodrow Wilson Center Ser.). 224p. (C). 1991. pap. text ed. 15.95 (*0-521-40775-3*) Cambridge U Pr.

Religion & Ultimate Well-Being: An Explanatory Theory. Martin Prozesky. LC 84-3340. 224p. 1984. text ed. 29.95 (*0-312-67057-5*) St Martin.

Religion & Urban Change: Croydon, 1840-1914. J. N. Morris. LC 92-27759. (Royal Historical Society: Studies in History: No. 65). (Illus.). 248p. (C). 1993. 63.00 (*0-86193-222-6*, Royal Historical Soc) Boydell & Brewer.

Religion & Violence. 2nd ed. Robert M. Brown. LC 87-10476. (Illus.). 144p. (Orig.). (C). 1987. pap. 10.00 (*0-664-24078-X*, Westminster) Westminster John Knox.

Religion & Western. Christopher H. Dawson. 240p. 1991. pap. 12.50 (*0-385-42110-9*) Doubleday.

Religion & Wine: A Cultural History of Wine Drinking in the United States. Robert C. Fuller. LC 95-4379. (Illus.). 152p. 1996. text ed. 30.00 (*0-87049-910-6*); pap. text ed. 15.00 (*0-87049-911-4*) U of Tenn Pr.

Religion & Women. Ed. by Arvind Sharma. LC 92-40320. (McGill Studies in the History of Religions). 291p. 1993. text ed. 59.50 (*0-7914-1689-5*); pap. text ed. 19.95 (*0-7914-1690-9*) State U NY Pr.

***Religion Around Us Bk. 1.** Dodd. 1990. pap. text ed. write for info. (*0-05-004254-8*) Addison-Wesley.

Religion As a Province of Meaning: The Kantian Foundations of Modern Theology. Adina Davidovich. LC 93-28255. (Harvard Theological Studies: Vol. 37). 362p. (Orig.). (C). 1993. pap. 19.00 (*0-8006-7090-6*) TPI PA.

***Religion As a Source of Violence: Concilium Journal.** Ed. by Karl-Josef Kuschel et al. 150p. 1997. pap. 15.00 (*1-57075-129-3*) Orbis Bks.

Religion as Anxiety & Tranquillity: An Essay in Comparative Phenomenology of the Spirit. J. G. Arapura. (Religion & Reason Ser.: No. 5). 1973. 29.25 (*90-279-7180-3*) Mouton.

Religion As Art: An Interpretation. Thomas R. Martland. LC 80-27104. (SUNY Series in Philosophy). 221p. 1981. text ed. 49.50 (*0-87395-520-X*) State U NY Pr.

Religion As Art: An Interpretation. Thomas R. Martland. LC 80-27104. (SUNY Series in Philosophy). 221p. 1982. pap. text ed. 16.95 (*0-87395-521-8*) State U NY Pr.

Religion As Belonging: A General Theory of Religion. John S. Cumpsty. 528p. (Orig.). (C). 1991. pap. text ed. 39.50 (*0-8191-8359-8*); lib. bdg. 69.50 (*0-8191-8358-X*) U Pr of Amer.

Religion As Creative Insecurity. Peter A. Bertocci. LC 73-1836. 128p. 1973. reprint ed. text ed. 45.00 (*0-8371-6803-1*, BECI, Greenwood Pr) Greenwood.

Religion As Critique. Robert J. Ackermann. LC 84-16471. 184p. 1985. lib. bdg. 25.00 (*0-87023-462-5*) U of Mass Pr.

Religion As Language-Game: A Critical Study with Special Regard to D. Z. Phillips. Lars Haikola. (Studia Philosophiae Religionis: Vol. 4). 1977. pap. 33.50 (*91-40-04596-X*) Coronet Bks.

Religion as Poetry. Andrew Greeley. 281p. 1996. pap. text ed. 21.95 (*1-56000-899-7*) Transaction Pubs.

Religion As Poetry. Andrew M. Greeley. LC 94-16035. 253p. (C). 1994. 39.95 (*1-56000-183-6*) Transaction Pubs.

Religion As Social Vision: The Movement Against Untouchability in 20th-Century Punjab. Mark Juergensmeyer. LC 80-24187. (Center for South & Southeast Asia Studies, UC Berkeley: No. 34). (Illus.). 350p. 1982. 52.50 (*0-520-04301-4*) U CA Pr.

Religion As Story. Ed. by James B. Wiggins. 218p. 1985. reprint ed. pap. text ed. 21.50 (*0-8191-4682-X*) U Pr of Amer.

Religion Behind the Iron Curtain. George N. Shuster. LC 78-13547. 281p. 1978. reprint ed. text ed. 59.75 (*0-313-20634-1*, SHRB, Greenwood Pr) Greenwood.

***Religion, Belief & Unbelief: A Psychological Study.** A. Vergote. 344p. (Orig.). 1996. pap. 72.50 (*90-6186-751-7*, Pub. by Leuven Univ BE) Coronet Bks.

Religion, BL-BX. Ed. by James Larrabee. LC 85-6863. (LC Cumulative Classification Ser.). 1000p. 1985. fiche write for info. (*0-933949-15-4*) Livia Pr.

Religion, BL-BX, Set. Ed. by James Larrabee. LC 85-6863. (LC Cumulative Classification Ser.). 1000p. 1985. ring bd. 105.00 (*0-933949-11-1*) Livia Pr.

Religion, BL-BX, Vol 1. Ed. by James Larrabee. LC 85-6863. (LC Cumulative Classification Ser.). 1000p. 1985. write for info. (*0-933949-12-X*); fiche write for info. (*0-933949-16-2*) Livia Pr.

Religion, BL-BX, Vol. 2. Ed. by James Larrabee. LC 85-6863. (LC Cumulative Classification Ser.). 1000p. 1985. write for info. (*0-933949-13-8*); fiche write for info. (*0-933949-17-0*) Livia Pr.

Religion, Body & Gender in Early Modern Spain. Ed. by Alain Saint-Saens. LC 91-39461. 184p. 1992. lib. bdg. 79.95 (*0-7734-9868-0*) E Mellen.

Religion Bouiti: Art Sacre. Stanislaw Swiderski. Ed. by Leonard G. Sbrocchi. (Culture of Gabon Ser.: Vol. 4). (Illus.). 308p. (Orig.). (FRE.). (C). 1989. pap. 60.00 (*0-921252-05-6*) LEGAS.

Religion Bouiti: Encyclopedie. Stanislaw Swiderski. Ed. by Leonard G. Sbrocchi. (Culture of Gabon Ser.: Vol. 5). (Illus.). 324p. (Orig.). (FRE.). 1990. pap. 39.00 (*0-921252-06-4*) LEGAS.

Religion Bouiti: Histoire I (1840-1948) Stanislaw Swiderski. Ed. by Leonard G. Sbrocchi. (Culture of Gabon Ser.: Vol. 1). (Illus.). 400p. (Orig.). (FRE.). (C). 1990. pap. 35.00 (*0-921252-02-1*) LEGAS.

Religion Bouiti: Histoire II (1948-1990) Stanislaw Swiderski. Ed. by Leonard G. Sbrocchi. (Culture of Gabon Ser.: Vol. 2). (Illus.). 354p. (Orig.). (FRE.). (C). 1990. pap. 35.00 (*0-921252-03-X*) LEGAS.

Religion Catholique et Appartenance Franco-Americaine: Franco-Americans & Religion: Impact & Influence. Intro. by Claire Quintal. 202p. (Orig.). (ENG & FRE.). (C). 1993. pap. text ed. 11.95 (*1-880261-01-4*) FI Assump Coll.

Religion, Civil Society & the State: A Study of Sikhism. J. P. Uberoi. (Illus.). 190p. 1996. 18.95 (*0-19-563691-0*) OUP.

Religion, Class & Identity: The State, the Catholic Church & the Education of the Irish in Britain. Mary Hickman. (Research in Ethnic Relations Ser.). 304p. 1995. 63.95 (*1-85628-534-0*, Pub. by Avebury Pub UK) Ashgate Pub Co.

***Religion, Class & Identity: The State, the Catholic Church & the Education of the Irish in Britain.** Mary Hickman. (Research in Ethnic Relations Ser.). 304p. 1997. pap. 34.95 (*1-85972-697-6*, Pub. by Avebury Pub UK) Ashgate Pub Co.

Religion Coming of Age. Roy W. Sellars. LC 75-3362. reprint ed. 32.50 (*0-404-59359-3*) AMS Pr.

Religion, Commerce, & the Integration of the Mandingo in Liberia. Augustine Konneh. LC 96-14958. 188p. 1996. lib. bdg. 48.00 (*0-7618-0354-8*); lib. bdg. 16.50 (*0-7618-0355-6*) U Pr of Amer.

Religion Confronting Science: And There Was Light. Donivan Bessinger. (Illus.). 176p. 1991. 17.95 (*0-9628594-0-0*); pap. 10.95 (*0-9628594-1-9*) Orchard Pk Pr.

Religion, Culture & Methodology: Papers of the Groningen Working-Group for the Study of Fundamental Problems & Methods of Science of Religion. Ed. by T. P. Van Baaren & H. J. Driljvers. 1973. text ed. 26.95 (*90-279-7249-4*) Mouton.

Religion, Culture, & Psychology in Arab-Israeli Relations. Ed. by Ian S. Lustick. LC 93-48221. (Arab-Israeli Relations Ser.: Vol. 5). (Illus.). 416p. 1994. reprint ed. text ed. 75.00 (*0-8153-1585-6*) Garland.

Religion, Culture, & Society in Early Modern Britain: Essays in Honour of Patrick Collinson. Ed. by Anthony Fletcher & Peter Roberts. LC 93-32407. (Illus.). 350p. (C). 1994. text ed. 64.95 (*0-521-41821-6*) Cambridge U Pr.

Religion, Culture & Society in the Early Middle Ages. Ed. by Thomas F. Noble & John J. Contreni. LC 87-5709. (Studies in Medieval Culture: No. 23). 1987. pap. 15.95 (*0-918720-84-2*); boxed 32.95 (*0-918720-83-4*) Medieval Inst.

Religion, Culture & Values: A Cross-Cultural Analysis of Motivational Factors in Native Irish & American Irish Catholicism. Bruce F. Biever. LC 76-6322. (Irish Americans Ser.). 1976. 68.95 (*0-405-09319-5*) Ayer.

Religion de la Poesia (Poetria) pap. 50.00 (*0-318-72521-5*) Instit Nacional.

***Religion, Democracy & Israeli Society.** Charles S. Liebman. (The Sherman Lecture Ser). 1997. text ed. 20.00 (*90-5702-012-2*, Harwood Acad Pubs) Gordon & Breach.

Religion der Aegypter. Adolf Erman. (Illus.). (C). 1978. reprint ed. 78.25 (*3-11-005187-7*) De Gruyter.

Religion der Griechen, Bd. 1: Von Den Anfangen Bis Hesiod. Otto Kern. xiii, 308p. 1963. write for info. (*3-296-13911-7*) G Olms Pubs.

Religion der Griechen, Bd. 2: Die Hochblute Bis Zum Ausgange Des 5. Jahrhunderts. Otto Kern. 319p. 1963. write for info. (*3-296-13912-5*) G Olms Pubs.

Religion der Griechen, Bd. 3: Von Platon Bis Kaiser Julian. Otto Kern. 352p. 1963. write for info. (*3-296-13913-3*) G Olms Pubs.

Religion des Cathares: Etude sur le Gnosticisme de la Basse Antiquite et du Moyen Age. Hans Soderberg. LC 77-84720. reprint ed. 57.50 (*0-404-16124-3*) AMS Pr.

Religion des Geistes. Salomon Formstecher. Ed. by Steven Katz. LC 79-7129. (Jewish Philosophy, Mysticism & History of Ideas Ser.). 1980. reprint ed. lib. bdg. 44.95 (*0-405-12251-9*) Ayer.

Religion des Romischen Heeres. Alfred Von Domaszewski. LC 75-10634. (Ancient Religion & Mythology Ser.). (Illus.). (GER.). 1976. reprint ed. 25.95 (*0-405-07012-8*) Ayer.

Religion, Development & African Identity, No. 17. Kirsten Holst Petersen. (Scandinavian Institute of African Studies). 163p. 1987. text ed. 46.00 (*91-7106-263-7*, Pub. by Nordisk Afrikainstitutet SW) Coronet Bks.

Religion, Deviance & Social. Bainbridge. 256p. (C). 1997. text ed. 55.00 (*0-415-91528-7*, Routledge NY) Routledge.

Religion, Deviance and Social. Bainbridge. 256p. (C). 1997. pap. 19.95 (*0-415-91529-5*, Routledge NY) Routledge.

Religion, Education & The U. S. Constitution. NSBA Council of School Attorneys Staff. 194p. (Orig.). 1994. reprint ed. pap. 25.00 (*0-88364-183-6*) Natl Sch Boards.

Religion et Culture. Jacques Maritain. 174p. (FRE.). 1991. pap. 12.95 (*0-7859-1447-1*, 2220031578) Fr & Eur.

Religion, Ethnicity & Politics: Ratifying the Constitution of Pennsylvania. Owen S. Ireland. LC 94-42605. 288p. 1995. 50.00 (*0-271-01433-4*); pap. 18.95 (*0-271-01434-2*) Pa St U Pr.

***Religion, Ethnicity, & Self-Identity: Nations in Turmoil.** Ed. by Martin E. Marty & R. Scott Appleby. LC 96-37268. 151p. 1997. 25.00 (*0-87451-815-6*) U Pr of New Eng.

Religion Factor: An Introduction to How Religion Matters. Ed. by William S. Green & Jacob Neusner. LC 96-21466. 269p. (Orig.). (C). 1996. pap. 17.00 (*0-664-25688-0*) Westminster John Knox.

Religion, Family, & the Life Course: Explorations in the Social History of Early America. Gerald F. Moran & Maris A. Vinovskis. 326p. (C). 1992. text ed. 47.50 (*0-472-10312-1*) U of Mich Pr.

***Religion, Federalism, & the Struggle for Public Life: Cases from Germany, India, & America.** William J. Everett. 240p. 1997. 45.00 (*0-19-510374-2*) OUP.

Religion, Feminism & Freedom of Conscience: A Mormon-Humanist Dialogue. Ed. by George D. Smith. 162p. (C). 1994. 23.95 (*0-87975-887-2*) Prometheus Bks.

Religion, Feminism, & Freedom of Conscience: A Mormon/Humanist Dialogue. Ed. by George D. Smith. LC 94-8606. xxiii, 162p. (Orig.). 1994. pap. 14.95 (*1-56085-048-5*) Signature Bks.

Religion, Feminism, & the Family. Ed. by Anne E. Carr & Mary S. Van Leeuwen. LC 96-8618. (Studies in the Family, Religion, & Culture). 400p. (Orig.). 1996. pap. 33.00 (*0-664-25512-4*) Westminster John Knox.

Religion for a Change, Bk. 2. J. O'Brien et al. (C). 1991. text ed. 45.00 (*0-7487-0474-4*, Pub. by Stanley Thornes UK) Trans-Atl Phila.

Religion for a Change, Bk. 3. J. O'Brien et al. (C). 1991. text ed. 45.00 (*0-7487-0475-2*, Pub. by Stanley Thornes UK) Trans-Atl Phila.

Religion for a Change: An Integrated Course in Religious & Personal Education. Joanne O'Brien et al. 96p. (Orig.). (C). 1991. pap. 35.00 (*0-7478-0475-3*, Pub. by Stanley Thornes UK) Trans-Atl Phila.

Religion for a Change: An Integrated Course in Religious & Personal Education, Bk. 1. Joanne O'Brien et al. 96p. (Orig.). (C). 1991. pap. 35.00 (*0-7478-0473-7*, Pub. by Stanley Thornes UK) Trans-Atl Phila.

Religion for a Change: An Integrated Course in Religious & Personal Education, Bk. 2. Joanne O'Brien & Liz Breuilly. 80p. (Orig.). (C). 1991. pap. text ed. 35.00 (*0-7478-0474-5*, Pub. by Stanley Thornes UK) Trans-Atl Phila.

Religion for a Change: An Integrated Course in Religious & Personal Education, 3 vols., Set. Martin E. Palmer et al. (Illus.). 272p. (Orig.). (J). (gr. 7-10). 1991. pap. 42.50 (*0-7487-0473-6*, Pub. by Stanley Thornes UK) Trans-Atl Phila.

Religion for a Change: An Integrated Course in Religious & Personal Education Teacher's Book. Joanne O'Brien et al. (C). 1991. pap. 35.00 (*0-7478-0476-1*, Pub. by Stanley Thornes UK) Trans-Atl Phila.

Religion for a Change Teacher's Book for Books 1 & 2. J. O'Brien et al. (C). 1991. text ed. 50.00 (*0-7487-0476-0*, Pub. by Stanley Thornes UK) Trans-Atl Phila.

Religion for a New Generation. 2nd ed. Jacob Needleman et al. Ed. by Kenneth J. Scott. 592p. (C). 1977. pap. text ed. 34.60 (*0-02-385990-3*, Macmillan Coll) P-H.

Religion for Free Minds. Julius S. Bixler. LC 75-3048. (Philosophy in America Ser.). 1976. reprint ed. 18.00 (*0-404-59045-4*) AMS Pr.

Religion for Mankind. Horace Holley. 248p. 1956. 16.50 (*0-87743-011-X*) G Ronald Pub.

Religion for Peace: Unabridged Proceedings. World Conference on Religion & Peace, 1st Assembly. Ed. by Jack A. Homer. 391p. 1973. 6.00 (*0-317-61732-X*); pap. 4.50 (*0-317-61731-1*) World Confer Rel & Peace.

Religion from Tolstoy to Camus. Ed. by Walter Kaufmann. 482p. (C). 1993. pap. text ed. 24.95 (*1-56000-706-0*) Transaction Pubs.

Religion Fundamentalista. Eva Jayaprakash & Joshi Jayaprakash. Ed. by Stephen Hayner & Gordon Aeschliman. (Global Issues Bible Study Ser.). 48p. (Orig.). 1990. wbk. ed. 4.99 (*0-8308-4910-6*, 4910) InterVarsity.

***Religion Fundamentalista.** Eva Jayaprakash. (Orig.). 1.50 (*0-8297-1954-7*) Life Pubs Intl.

Religion, Government & Education. Ed. by William W. Brickman & Stanley Lehrer. LC 77-24684. 292p. 1977. reprint ed. text ed. 59.75 (*0-8371-9749-X*, BRRG, Greenwood Pr) Greenwood.

Religion, Health, & Aging: A Review & Theoretical Integration. Harold G. Koenig et al. LC 88-17779. (Contributions to the Study of Aging Ser.: No. 10). 240p. 1988. text ed. 55.00 (*0-313-26208-X*, KRH/, Greenwood Pr) Greenwood.

Religion (Hellenistisches Judentum in Romischer Zeit): Philon & Josephus see Aufstieg und Niedergang der Roemischen Welt: Selection 2, Principat

Religion (Hellenistisches Judentum in Romischer Zeit): Philon & Josephus (Fortsetzung) see Aufstieg und Niedergang der Roemischen Welt: Selection 2, Principat

Religion, Homosexuality & Literature. Gary D. Comstock et al. Ed. by Michael L. Stemmeler & Michael Clark. LC 92-24252. (Gay Men's Issues in Religious Studies: Vol. 3). (Illus.). viii, 106p. 1992. pap. 10.00 (*0-930383-28-1*) Monument Pr.

Religion, Homosexuality & Literature. Gary D. Comstock et al. Ed. by Michael L. Stemmeler. LC 92-24252. (Gay Men's Issues in Religious Studies: Vol. 3). v, 106p. 1992. pap. 10.00 (*0-930383-29-X*) Monument Pr.

Religion, Ideology & Heidegger's Concept of Falling. Gregory Tropea. LC 87-17685. (American Academy of Religion Academy Ser.). 261p. 1987. 21.95 (*1-55540-041-8*, 01-01-54); pap. 15.95 (*1-55540-042-6*) Scholars Pr GA.

Religion in a Free Society. Sidney Hook. LC 67-11242. 132p. reprint ed. pap. 37.70 (*0-8357-4218-0*, 2037000) Bks Demand.

Religion in a Religious Age. Ed. by S. D. Goitein. 12.50 (*0-87068-268-7*); write for info. (*0-685-02925-5*) Ktav.

Religion in a Revolutionary Age: Perspectives on the American Revolution. Peter J. Albert. Ed. by Ronald Hoffman. LC 93-13544. 1994. text ed. 39.50 (*0-8139-1448-5*) U Pr of Va.

R

An Asterisk (*) at the beginning of an entry indicates that the title is appearing in BIP for the first time.

R

Religion in a Technical Age. Samuel H. Miller. LC 68-17628. 158p. reprint ed. pap. 45.10 (*0-7837-3848-X*, 2043670) Bks Demand.

Religion in a Tswana Chiefdom. Berthold A. Pauw. LC 85-21881. (Illus.). xii, 274p. 1985. reprint ed. text ed. 95.00 (*0-313-24974-1*, PRTC, Greenwood Pr) Greenwood.

Religion in Aboriginal Australia: An Anthology. Ed. by Max Charlesworth et al. LC 83-23437. (Illus.). 458p. (C). 1984. pap. text ed. 19.95 (*0-7022-2008-6*) Intl Spec Bk.

Religion in Africa. Ed. by Thomas D. Blakely et al. 528p. 1994. write for info. (*0-318-72744-7*) D M Kennedy Ctr Brigham.

Religion in Africa: Experience & Expression. Ed. by Thomas D. Blakely et al. LC 92-30302. (Monograph Series of the David M. Kennedy Center for International Studies at Brigham Young University: Vol. 4). 512p. (C). 1994. pap. 24.95 (*0-435-08083-0*, 08083) Heinemann.

Religion in Aging & Health: Theoretical Foundations in Methodological Frontiers. Ed. by Jeffrey S. Levin. (Focus Editions Ser.: Vol. 166). (Illus.). 320p. (C). 1993. text ed. 54.00 (*0-8039-5438-7*); pap. text ed. 24.95 (*0-8039-5439-5*) Sage.

Religion in America. Ed. by Gillian Lindt. LC 75-54571. (Great Contemporary Issues Ser.). 1977. lib. bdg. 27.95 (*0-405-09865-0*) Ayer.

Religion in America. 2nd ed. George C. Bedell et al. LC 81-8239. 560p. (C). 1982. text ed. 61.00 (*0-02-307810-3*, Macmillan Coll) P-H.

Religion in America. 3rd ed. Corbett. 352p. (C). 1996. pap. text ed. 36.60 (*0-13-476029-8*) P-H.

Religion in America. 5th rev. ed. Winthrop S. Hudson & John Corrigan. (Illus.). 464p. (C). 1992. pap. text ed. 44.00 (*0-02-357830-0*, Macmillan Coll) P-H.

Religion in America, 38 vols. Ed. by Edwin S. Gaustad. 1969. reprint ed. 2,510.50 (*0-405-00229-7*) Ayer.

Religion in America: Ser. 2, 40 Vols., Set. Ed. by Edwin S. Gaustad. 1972. reprint ed. 830.00 (*0-405-04050-4*) Ayer.

***Religion in American History: A Reader.** Ed. by Jon Butler & Harry S. Stout. 512p. (C). 1997. pap. text ed. 27.95 (*0-19-509776-9*) OUP.

Religion in American History: What to Teach & How. Charles C. Haynes. LC 90-33535. 173p. (Orig.). 1990. pap. text ed. 20.95 (*0-87120-166-6*, 611-90084) Assn Supervision.

Religion in American Life. Nelson R. Burr. LC 70-136219. (Goldentree Bibliographies Series in American History). (C). 1971. text ed. write for info. (*0-88295-507-1*) Harlan Davidson.

Religion in American Public Life. A. James Reichley. LC 85-21312. 402p. 1985. 42.95 (*0-8157-7378-1*); pap. 18.95 (*0-8157-7377-3*) Brookings.

Religion in an African City. Geoffrey Parrinder. LC 74-142921. (Illus.). 211p. 1973. reprint ed. text ed. 45.00 (*0-8371-5947-4*, PAC&, Negro U Pr) Greenwood.

Religion in an Age of Science. Ian G. Barbour. LC 89-45552. (Gifford Lectures Ser.: Vol. 1). 1990. pap. 18.00 (*0-06-060383-6*) Harper SF.

Religion in Ancient Egypt: Gods, Myths, & Personal Practice. Byron E. Shafer. 1991. 39.95 (*0-8014-2550-6*); pap. 14.95 (*0-685-72463-8*) Cornell U Pr.

Religion in Antebellum Kentucky. John B. Boles. LC 95-12711. 160p. 1995. pap. 9.95 (*0-8131-0844-6*) U Pr of Ky.

Religion in Appalachia. Ed. by John D. Photiadis. 1979. 10.75 (*0-686-26337-5*) W Va U Ctr Exten.

Religion in Australia. Roger Thompson. (Australian Retrospectives Ser.). 176p. 1995. pap. text ed. 32.00 (*0-19-553516-2*) OUP.

Religion in Britain: Since Nineteen Forty-Five. Grace Davie. (Making Contemporary Britain Ser.). (Illus.). 240p. 1994. pap. 23.95 (*0-631-18444-9*) Blackwell Pubs.

Religion in Calabar: The Religious Life & History of a Nigerian Town. Rosalind I. Hackett. (Religion & Society Ser.: No. 27). xviii, 481p. (C). 1989. lib. bdg. 126.95 (*0-89925-394-6*) Mouton.

Religion in Childhood & Adolescence: A Comprehensive Review of the Research. Kenneth E. Hyde. LC 90-42006. 529p. 1990. 32.95 (*0-89135-076-4*) Religious Educ.

Religion in China. Robert Orr. 144p. (Orig.). 1980. 4.95 (*0-318-16788-3*) US-China Peoples Friendship.

Religion in China Today: Policy & Practice. MacInnis. LC 89-38900. 450p. 1989. pap. 21.00 (*0-88344-645-6*) Orbis Bks.

Religion in China Today: Policy & Practice. Donald E. MacInnis. LC 89-38900. 450p. 1989. 40.00 (*0-88344-594-8*) Orbis Bks.

Religion in Chinese Society: A Study of Contemporary Social Functions of Religion & Some of Their Historical Factors. C. K. Yang. 473p. (C). 1991. reprint ed. pap. text ed. 18.95 (*0-88133-621-1*) Waveland Pr.

Religion in Contemporary Europe. Ed. by John Fulton & Peter Gee. LC 94-21169. 196p. 1994. text ed. 79.95 (*0-7734-9028-0*) E Mellen.

Religion in Contemporary Japan. Ian Reader. 320p. 1991. pap. text ed. 18.00 (*0-8248-1354-5*) UH Pr.

Religion in Contemporary Society. 3rd ed. H. Paul Chalfant et al. LC 93-86173. 502p. (C). 1994. boxed 40.00 (*0-87581-382-8*) Peacock Pubs.

Religion in Context: Cults & Charisma. I. M. Lewis. (Essays in Social Anthropology Ser.). (Illus.). 160p. 1986. pap. text ed. 16.95 (*0-521-31596-4*) Cambridge U Pr.

Religion in Context: Cults & Charisma. 2nd ed. I. M. Lewis. (Illus.). 190p. (C). 1996. text ed. 49.95 (*0-521-56234-1*) Cambridge U Pr.

Religion in Context: Cults & Charisma. 2nd ed. I. M. Lewis. (Illus.). 190p. (C). 1996. pap. text ed. 16.95 (*0-521-56634-7*) Cambridge U Pr.

Religion in Context: Recent Studies in Lonergan. Ed. by Timothy P. Fallon & Philip B. Riley. LC 88-21772. (College Theology Society Resources in Religion Ser.: No. 4). 216p. (Orig.). (C). 1988. lib. bdg. 45.00 (*0-8191-7137-9*) U Pr of Amer.

Religion in Crisis & Custom: A Sociological & Psychological Study. Anton T. Boisen & John Leary. LC 72-10977. 271p. 1973. reprint ed. text ed. 35.00 (*0-8371-6642-X*, BORC, Greenwood Pr) Greenwood.

Religion in Economics: A Study of John B. Clark, Richard T. Ely & Simon N. Patten. J. Rutherford Everett. xiii, 160p. 1982. reprint ed. lib. bdg. 29.50 (*0-87991-866-7*) Porcupine Pr.

Religion in Essence & Manifestation, Vol. 1. G. Van Der Leeuw. 1967. 14.50 (*0-8446-1457-2*) Peter Smith.

***Religion in Europe: Contemporary Perspectives.** Ed. by Sean Gill et al. 213p. 1994. pap. 27.95 (*90-390-0508-7*, Pub. by KOK Pharos NE) Eisenbrauns.

Religion in Film. Ed. by John R. May & Michael Bird. LC 81-23983. (Illus.). 276p. 1982. text ed. 29.00 (*0-87049-352-3*); pap. text ed. 16.00 (*0-87049-368-X*) U of Tenn Pr.

Religion in Greek Literature: A Sketch in Outline. Lewis Campbell. LC 79-148874. (Select Bibliographies Reprint Ser.). 1977. reprint ed. 24.95 (*0-8369-5645-1*) Ayer.

Religion in Higher Education among Negroes. Richard I. McKinney. LC 75-38785. (Religion in America, Ser. 2). 186p. 1975. reprint ed. 20.95 (*0-405-04075-X*) Ayer.

***Religion in History.** Troeltsch. pap. 31.95 (*0-567-29192-8*, Pub. by T & T Clark UK) Bks Intl VA.

Religion in History. Ernst Troeltsch. Tr. by James L. Adams & Walter E. Bense from GER. LC 89-37498. (Fortress Texts in Modern Theology Ser.). 352p. (Orig.). 1990. pap. 29.00 (*0-8006-3208-7*, 1-3208) Augsburg Fortress.

Religion in History/La Religion dans l'Histoire: The Word, the Idea, the Reality/Le Mot, l'Idee, la Realite. Ed. by Michael Despland & Gerard Vallee. (Editions SR Ser.: Vol. 13). 336p. (C). 1992. pap. 19.95 (*0-88920-211-7*) Wilfrid Laurier.

Religion in Human Experience: A Comparative Study. John R. Everett. 1977. lib. bdg. 59.95 (*0-8490-2509-5*) Gordon Pr.

Religion in Human Life: Anthropological Views. Edward Norbeck. 74p. (C). 1988. reprint ed. pap. text ed. 7.95 (*0-88133-354-9*) Waveland Pr.

Religion in India. Ed. by Triloki N. Madan. (Oxford in India Readings in Sociology & Social & Cultural Anthropology Ser.). 464p. 1993. reprint ed. pap. 14.95 (*0-19-563092-0*) OUP.

Religion in Indian Society: The Dimensions of 'Unity in Diversity' Boris Klyuev. x, 164p. 1989. text ed. 25.00 (*81-207-1037-1*, Pub. by Sterling Pubs II) Apt Bks.

Religion in Indiana: A Guide to Historical Resources. L. C. Rudolph & Judith E. Endelman. LC 84-43186. 247p. reprint ed. pap. 70.40 (*0-7837-4204-5*, 2059054) Bks Demand.

Religion in Industrial Society: Oldham & Saddleworth 1740-1865. M. A. Smith. (Historical Monographs). (Illus.). 360p. 1994. 59.00 (*0-19-820451-5*) OUP.

Religion in Japan: Arrows to Heaven & Earth. Ed. by Peter F. Kornicki & I. J. McMullen. (University of Cambridge Oriental Publications: No. 50). (Illus.). 350p. (C). 1996. text ed. 64.95 (*0-521-55028-9*) Cambridge U Pr.

Religion in Japanese Culture: Where Living Traditions Meet a Changing World. Ed. by Noriyoshi Tamaru & David Reid. 268p. 1996. 28.00 (*4-7700-2054-6*) Kodansha.

Religion in Japanese History. Joseph M. Kitagawa. LC 65-23669. 475p. 1966. text ed. 59.50 (*0-231-02834-2*) Col U Pr.

Religion in Japanese History: Lectures on the History of Religions. Joseph M. Kitagawa. 475p. 1990. pap. text ed. 19.50 (*0-231-02838-5*) Col U Pr.

***Religion in Late Roman Britain: Forces of Change.** Dorothy Watts. LC 97-19773. 1998. write for info. (*0-415-11855-7*) Routledge.

Religion in Leeds. Ed. by Alistair Mason. LC 94-22149. 1994. 50.00 (*0-7509-0581-6*, Pub. by Sutton Pubng UK); pap. 24.00 (*0-7509-0580-8*, Pub. by Sutton Pubng UK) Bks Intl VA.

Religion in Life at Louisbourg, 1713-1758. A. J. Johnston. 288p. 1984. 49.95 (*0-7735-0427-3*, Pub. by McGill CN) U of Toronto Pr.

Religion in Livy. D. S. Levene. LC 93-11077. (Mnemosyne Ser.: Supplement 127). xi, 257p. 1993. 89.00 (*90-04-09617-5*) E J Brill.

Religion in Modern Britain. Bruce. 160p. 1995. 39.95 (*0-19-878090-7*) OUP.

Religion in Modern India. Ed. by Robert D. Baird. (C). 1989. 36.00 (*0-945921-03-9*) South Asia Pubns.

Religion in Modern India. Ed. by Robert D. Baird. (C). 1995. reprint ed. 54.00 (*81-85054-64-9*, Pub. by Manohar II) S Asia.

Religion in Modern New Mexico. Ed. by Ferenc M. Szasz & Richard W. Etulain. LC 96-9995. 1997. 60.00 (*0-8263-1766-9*) U of NM Pr.

***Religion in Modern New Mexico.** Ed. by Ferenc M. Szasz & Richard W. Etulain. LC 96-9995. 1997. pap. 19.95 (*0-8263-1791-X*) U of NM Pr.

Religion in Montana Vol. 2: Pathways to the Present. Lawrence F. Small. LC 92-82842. 530p. 1995. pap. 24.95 (*1-56044-297-2*) Falcon Pr MT.

Religion in Montana Vol. I: Pathways to the Present. Ed. by Lawrence F. Small. LC 92-82842. (Illus.). 380p. (Orig.). 1992. pap. 19.95 (*1-56044-175-5*) Falcon Pr MT.

Religion in Native North America. Ed. by Christopher Vecsey. LC 89-78337. (Illus.). 208p. (Orig.). (C). 1990. pap. 16.95 (*0-89301-135-5*) U of Idaho Pr.

Religion in Personal Development: An Analysis & a Prescription. Harold A. Buetow. LC 91-21225. (American University Studies: Theology & Religion: Ser. VII, Vol. 108). 446p. (C). 1992. text ed. 65.95 (*0-8204-1580-4*) P Lang Pubng.

Religion in Plato & Cicero. John E. Rexine. LC 68-28581. 72p. 1968. reprint ed. text ed. 45.00 (*0-8371-0198-0*, RERP, Greenwood Pr) Greenwood.

***Religion in Politics.** Michael J. Perry. 192p. 1997. 29.95 (*0-19-510675-X*) OUP.

Religion in Politics. Arun Shourie. (C). 1987. 16.50 (*0-8364-2149-3*, Pub. by Roli Books) S Asia.

Religion in Politics: A World Guide. Ed. by Stuart Mews. 332p. 1990. 75.00 (*1-55862-051-6*) St James Pr.

Religion in Postwar China: A Critical Analysis & Annotated Bibliography. Ed. by David C. Yu. LC 93-28461. (Bibliographies & Indexes in Religious Studies: No. 28). 392p. 1993. text ed. 85.00 (*0-313-26732-4*, Greenwood Pr) Greenwood.

Religion in Practice. Swami Prabhavananda. 1960. 8.95 (*0-87481-016-7*) Vedanta Pr.

Religion in Primitive Culture. Edward Tylor. (Primitive Culture Ser.: Pt. 2). 1990. 19.25 (*0-8446-0946-3*) Peter Smith.

Religion in Primitive Cultures: A Study in Ethnophilosophy. Wilhelm Dupre. (Religion & Reason Ser.: No. 9). 366p. 1975. text ed. 56.95 (*90-279-7531-0*) Mouton.

Religion in Psychodynamic Perspective: The Contributions of Paul W. Pruyser. Ed. by H. Newton Malony & Bernard Spilka. 254p. 1991. 42.00 (*0-19-506234-5*) OUP.

Religion in Public Education. Vivian T. Thayer. LC 78-12385. 212p. 1979. reprint ed. text ed. 55.00 (*0-313-21212-0*, THRP, Greenwood Pr) Greenwood.

Religion in Public Life. Ed. by Daniel Cohn-Sherbok & David McLellan. LC 91-32830. 135p. 1992. text ed. 59.95 (*0-312-07279-1*) St Martin.

Religion in Public Life: A Dilemma for Democracy. Ronald F. Thiemann. LC 95-42085. 200p. 1996. 55.00 (*0-87840-609-3*); pap. 17.95 (*0-87840-610-7*) Georgetown U Pr.

Religion in Radical Transition. Ed. by Jeffrey K. Hadden. 166p. 1973. reprint ed. 29.95 (*0-87855-070-4*); reprint ed. pap. 18.95 (*0-87855-567-6*) Transaction Pubs.

Religion in Recent Art. 3rd ed. Peter T. Forsyth. LC 73-148780. reprint ed. 47.50 (*0-404-02515-3*) AMS Pr.

Religion in Relation: Method, Application, & Moral Location. Ivan Strenski. Ed. by Frederick M. Denny. LC 92-16153. (Studies in Comparative Religion). 267p. 1992. text ed. 34.95 (*0-87249-866-2*) U of SC Pr.

Religion in Shoes. Hunter B. Blakely. 199p. (Orig.). 1989. reprint ed. pap. text ed. 5.00 (*0-87651-992-3*) Southern U Pr.

Religion in Society: A Sociology of Religion. 5th ed. Ronald L. Johnstone. 384p. (C). 1996. pap. text ed. 37.33 (*0-13-125436-7*) P-H.

Religion in Sociological Perspective. Bryan R. Wilson. 198p. 1982. pap. 16.95 (*0-19-826664-2*) OUP.

Religion in Sociological Perspective. 2nd ed. Keith A. Roberts. 400p. (C). 1990. text ed. 42.95 (*0-534-12102-0*) Wadsworth Pub.

Religion in Sociological Perspective. 3rd ed. Keith A. Roberts. 465p. 1995. text ed. 53.95 (*0-534-20466-X*) Wadsworth Pub.

Religion in South Asia. Ed. by G. A. Oddie. 204p. 1991. 22.95 (*81-85425-46-9*) Asia Bk Corp.

Religion in South Asia: Religious Conversion & Revival Movements in South Asia in Medieval & Modern Times. Ed. by G. A. Oddie. (C). 1991. text ed. 24.00 (*0-945921-18-7*, Pub. by S Asia Pubs II) S Asia.

Religion in South Carolina. Ed. by Charles H. Lippy. LC 92-46310. 247p. 1993. text ed. 24.95 (*0-87249-891-3*) U of SC Pr.

Religion in Soviet Russia, Nineteen Seventeen to Nineteen Forty-Two. Nicholas S. Timasheff. LC 78-23615. 171p. 1980. reprint ed. text ed. 49.75 (*0-313-21040-3*, TIRS, Greenwood Pr) Greenwood.

Religion in Tennessee, 1777-1945. Herman A. Norton. LC 81-1562. (Tennessee Three Star Ser.). (Illus.). 136p. 1981. pap. 5.50 (*0-87049-318-3*) U of Tenn Pr.

Religion in the Age of Decline: Organisation & Experience in Industrial Yorkshire, 1870-1920. S. J. Green. (Illus.). 448p. (C). 1996. text ed. 69.95 (*0-521-56153-1*) Cambridge U Pr.

Religion in the Age of Exploration: The Case of Spawn & New Spawn. Ed. by Bryan F. Le Beau & Menachem Mor. (Studies in Jewish Civilization). 284p. 1996. 30.00 (*1-881871-21-5*) Creighton U Pr.

Religion in the Age of Romanticism: Studies in Early Nineteenth Century Thought. Bernard M. Reardon. 320p. 1985. text ed. 80.00 (*0-521-30088-6*); pap. text ed. 29.95 (*0-521-31745-2*) Cambridge U Pr.

Religion in the Ancient Greek City. Louise B. Zaidman & Pauline S. Pantel. Tr. by Paul Cartledge. (Illus.). 288p. (C). 1993. text ed. 59.95 (*0-521-41262-5*); pap. text ed. 20.95 (*0-521-42357-0*) Cambridge U Pr.

Religion in the Andes: Vision & Imagination in Early Colonial Peru. Sabine MacCormack. (Illus.). 531p. 1991. text ed. 69.50 (*0-691-09468-3*); pap. text ed. 21.95 (*0-691-02106-6*) Princeton U Pr.

Religion in the Contemporary South: Diversity, Community, & Identity. Ed. by O. Kendall White, Jr. & Daryl White. LC 94-9727. (Southern Anthropological Society Proceedings Ser.: No. 28). 184p. 1995. 40.00 (*0-8203-1675-X*); pap. 20.00 (*0-8203-1676-8*) U of Ga Pr.

Religion in the Japanese Experience. 2nd ed. H. Byron Earhart. (Illus.). 350p. 1997. pap. 25.95 (*0-534-52461-3*) Wadsworth Pub.

Religion in the Japanese Experience: Sources & Interpretations. Ed. by H. Byron Earhart. 270p. (C). 1974. pap. 18.50 (*0-8221-0104-1*) Wadsworth Pub.

Religion in the Lives of English Women, 1760-1930. Ed. by Gail Malmgreen. LC 86-45172. (Illus.). 224p. (C). 1986. 31.50 (*0-253-34973-7*) Ind U Pr.

Religion in the Making. rev. ed. Alfred N. Whitehead. x, 175p. 1996. 29.95 (*0-8232-1645-4*) Fordham.

Religion in the Medieval West. Bernad Hamilton. 224p. 1995. text ed. 16.95 (*0-7131-6461-1*, Pub. by E Arnld UK) St Martin.

Religion in the Megacity: Portraits from Two Latin American Cities. Phillip Berryman. LC 96-33367. 200p. (Orig.). 1996. pap. 18.00 (*1-57075-083-1*) Orbis Bks.

Religion in the Middle East: Three Religions in Concord & Conflict, Vol. 2: Islam. Ed. by Arthur J. Arberry. LC 76-11080. 764p. reprint ed. pap. 180.00 (*0-318-34756-3*, 2031615) Bks Demand.

Religion in the Modern World: From Cathedrals to Cults. Steve Bruce. (Illus.). 272p. 1996. 65.00 (*0-19-878152-0*) OUP.

Religion in the Modern World: From Cathedrals to Cults. Steve Bruce. (Illus.). 272p. 1996. pap. 14.95 (*0-19-878151-2*) OUP.

Religion in the New Age. J. Donald Walters. 72p. 1993. 2.95 (*1-56589-051-5*) Crystal Clarity.

Religion in the New World: The Shaping of Religious Traditions in the United States. Richard E. Wentz. LC 90-31425. 400p. (Orig.). 1990. pap. 22.00 (*0-8006-2424-6*, 1-2424) Augsburg Fortress.

Religion in the Old South. Donald G. Mathews. LC 77-587. 294p. 1979. pap. text ed. 16.95 (*0-226-51002-6*, P819) U Ch Pr.

Religion in the Philosophy of William James. Julius S. Bixler. LC 75-3049. reprint ed. 42.50 (*0-404-59046-2*) AMS Pr.

Religion in the Poetry & Drama of the Late Middle Ages: J. A. W. Bennett Memorial Lectures, Perugia, 1988. Ed. by Piero Boitani & Anna Torti. (J. A. W. Bennett Memorial Lectures). 248p. 1991. 70.00 (*0-85991-303-1*) Boydell & Brewer.

Religion in the Popular Prints 1600-1832. J. Miller. LC 85-5938. (English Satirical Print Ser.). 372p. 1986. lib. bdg. 100.00 (*0-85964-170-8*) Chadwyck-Healey.

Religion in the Post-War World. Ed. by Willard L. Sperry et al. LC 76-142698. (Essay Index Reprints - Religion & Education Ser.: Vol. 4). 1977. reprint ed. 17.95 (*0-8369-2202-6*) Ayer.

Religion in the Public Schools: An Introduction. Richard C. McMillan. LC 84-9147. x, 301p. 1984. 21.95 (*0-86554-093-4*, MUP/H085) Mercer Univ Pr.

Religion in the Public Square: Convictions in Political Debate. Robert Audi & Nicholas Wolterstorff. LC 96-44646. (Point/Counterpoint: Philosophers Debate Contemporary Issues Ser.: No. 94). 176p. 1997. 52.50 (*0-8476-8341-9*); pap. 16.95 (*0-8476-8342-7*) Rowman.

Religion in the Reich. Michael Power. LC 78-63706. (Studies in Fascism: Ideology & Practice). 1979. reprint ed. 41.50 (*0-404-16976-7*) AMS Pr.

Religion in the Schools. James J. Jurinski. (Contemporary World Issues Ser.). 1997. lib. bdg. 39.50 (*0-87436-868-5*) ABC-CLIO.

Religion in the Soviet Union: A Bibliography, 1980-1989. Boris Korsch. LC 92-10129. 672p. 1992. text ed. 105.00 (*0-8240-7096-8*, SS659) Garland.

Religion in the Soviet Union: An Archival Reader. Ed. by Felix Corley. (Illus.). 352p. (C). 1996. 55.00 (*0-8147-1539-7*) NYU Pr.

Religion in the Struggle for Power: A Study in the Sociological Study of Religion. Milton J. Yinger. Ed. by Harriet Zuckerman & Robert K. Merton. LC 79-9040. (Dissertations on Sociology Ser.). 1980. reprint ed. lib. bdg. 29.95 (*0-405-13007-4*) Ayer.

Religion in the Struggle for World Community: Proceedings of the Unabridged World Conference on Religion & Peace, 3rd Assembly. World Conference on Religion & Peace Staff. Ed. by Homer A. Jack. (Orig.). 1980. pap. 6.95 (*0-935934-05-7*) World Confer Rel & Peace.

Religion in the U. S. A., 2 vols. Robert Baird. (Works of Rev. Robert Baird). 1985. reprint ed. lib. bdg. 89.00 (*0-932051-57-X*) Rprt Serv.

Religion in the United States of America. Robert Baird. LC 70-83411. (Religion in America, Ser. 1). 1975. reprint ed. 42.95 (*0-405-00232-7*) Ayer.

Religion in the West. Ed. by Ferenc M. Szasz. (Illus.). 108p. 1984. pap. text ed. 15.00 (*0-89745-050-7*) Sunflower U Pr.

Religion in Third World Politics. Jeff Haynes. LC 93-11091. (Issues in Third World Politics Ser.). 166p. (C). 1994. pap. text ed. 18.95 (*1-55587-456-8*) Lynne Rienner.

***Religion in Third World Politics.** Jeff Haynes. Ed. by Vicky Randall. (Issues in Third World Politics Ser.). 176p. 1993. 42.50 (*0-335-15701-7*, Open Univ Pr); pap. 13.99 (*0-335-15700-9*, Open Univ Pr) Taylor & Francis.

Religion in Transition. Ed. by Vergilius T. Ferm. LC 68-29204. (Essay Index Reprint Ser.). 1977. 17.95 (*0-8369-0074-X*) Ayer.

Religion in Twentieth Century America. Herbert W. Schneider. LC 52-8219. (Library of Congress Series in American Civilization). (Illus.). 254p. reprint ed. pap. 74.10 (*0-8357-8301-4*, 2056797) Bks Demand.

Religion in Victorian Britain, Vol. I: Traditions. Ed. by Gerald Parsons. 256p. 1989. text ed. 19.95 (*0-7190-2511-7*, Pub. by Manchester Univ Pr UK) St Martin.

Religion in Victorian Britain, Vol. II: Controversies. Ed. by Gerald Parsons. LC 88-12359. (Illus.). 256p. 1989. text ed. 19.95 (*0-7190-2513-3*, Pub. by Manchester Univ Pr UK) St Martin.

An Asterisk (*) at the beginning of an entry indicates that the title is appearing in BIP for the first time.

Religion in Victorian Britain, Vol. III: Sources. Ed. by James R. Moore. LC 88-12359. 592p. 1989. text ed. 89.95 (*0-7190-2943-0*, Pub. by Manchester Univ Pr UK); text ed. 27.95 (*0-7190-2944-9*, Pub. by Manchester Univ Pr UK) St Martin.

Religion in Victorian Britain, Vol. IV: Interpretations. Ed. by Gerald Parsons. 208p. 1989. text ed. 17.95 (*0-7190-2946-5*, Pub. by Manchester Univ Pr UK) St Martin.

Religion in Vijayanagara Empire. Konduri S. Devi. 348p. 1990. text ed. 40.00 (*0-685-45138-0*, Pub. by Sterling Pubs II) Apt Bks.

Religion in Western Civilization Since the Reformation: Select Readings. Ed. by Jon Alexander & Giles Dimock. 184p. (C). 1983. pap. text ed. 16.00 (*0-8191-3391-4*) U Pr of Amer.

Religion, Intergroup Relations, & Social Change in South Africa. Gerhardus C. Oosthuizen et al. LC 88-15430. (Contributions in Ethnic Studies: No. 24). 249p. 1988. text ed. 49.95 (*0-313-26360-4*, HSG/, Greenwood Pr) Greenwood.

***Religion, Interpretation, & Diversity of Belief: The Framework Model for Kant to Durkheim to Davidson.** Terry F. Godlove, Jr. LC 96-37192. 208p. (Orig.). 1996. pap. text ed. 18.00 (*0-86554-541-3*) Mercer Univ Pr.

Religion, Interpretation & Diversity of Belief: The Framework Model from Kant to Davidson. Terry F. Godlove, Jr. 224p. (C). 1989. text ed. 64.95 (*0-521-36179-6*) Cambridge U Pr.

Religion Is a Personal Matter. Philip A. Verhalen. LC 89-28144. (American University Studies: Education: Ser. XIV, Vol. 29). 255p. (C). 1990. text ed. 55.95 (*0-8204-1195-7*) P Lang Pubng.

***Religion Is a Queer Thing: A Guide to the Christian Faith for Lesbian, Gay, Bisexual & Transgendered People.** Elizabeth Stuart. LC 97-2321. (Lesbian & Gay Studies). 192p. 1997. pap. 25.95 (*0-304-33749-8*) Cassell.

Religion Journals & Serials: An Analytical Guide. Compiled by Eugene C. Fieg, Jr. LC 87-32276. (Annotated Bibliographies of Serials: A Subject Approach Ser.: No. 13). 232p. 1988. text ed. 59.95 (*0-313-24513-4*, FRJ/, Greenwood Pr) Greenwood.

Religion: Judentum: Allgemeines, Palastinensisches Judentum FS see Aufstieg und Niedergang der Roemischen Welt: Selection 2, Principat

Religion, Kinship & Economy in Luapula, Zambia. Karla O. Poewe. LC 88-26643. (African Studies: Vol. 9). 253p. 1989. lib. bdg. 89.95 (*0-88946-190-2*) E Mellen.

Religion, Law & Learning in Classical Islam. George Makdisi. (Collected Studies: No. CS 347). 336p. 1991. text ed. 89.95 (*0-86078-301-4*, Pub. by Variorum UK) Ashgate Pub Co.

Religion, Law, & Power: The Making of Protestant Ireland 1660-1760. S. J. Connolly. (Illus.). 360p. 1995. pap. 26.00 (*0-19-820587-2*) OUP.

***Religion, Law & Society: A Christian-Muslim Discussion.** Ed. by Tarek Mitri. 138p. 1995. pap. 20.25 (*90-390-0514-1*, Pub. by KOK Pharos NE) Eisenbrauns.

Religion, Learning & Science in the 'Abbasid Period. Ed. by M. J. Young. (History of Arabic Literature Ser.). (Illus.). 592p. (C). 1991. text ed. 120.00 (*0-521-32763-6*) Cambridge U Pr.

***Religion Literacy Indicator.** Mary A. O'Neill. 1996. 9.95 (*1-55612-110-5*, SS1110) Sheed & Ward MO.

Religion, Literature, & Politics in Post-Reformation England: 1540-1688. Ed. by Donna B. Hamilton & Richard Strier. 276p. (C). 1996. text ed. 59.95 (*0-521-47456-6*) Cambridge U Pr.

***Religion Morality: An Introduction.** Paul W. Diener. LC 97-14698. 1997. pap. text ed. 22.00 (*0-664-25765-8*) Westminster John Knox.

Religion, Morality, & the Law. Ed. by J. Roland Pennock & John W. Chapman. (Nomos Ser.: Vol. 30). 356p. (C). 1988. 45.00 (*0-8147-6606-4*) NYU Pr.

Religion, Morality & the "New Right" Ed. by Melinda Maidens. LC 82-2333. (Illus.). 224p. reprint ed. pap. 63.90 (*0-8357-4242-3*, 2037030) Bks Demand.

Religion, Mortality & Politics According to Mahatma Gandhi. L. C. Prasad. (C). 1991. 27.50 (*81-7054-128-X*, Pub. by Classics India Pubns II) S Asia.

Religion, My Own: The Literary Works of Najib Mahfuz. Mattityahu Peled. LC 82-17582. 268p. 1983. 44.95 (*0-87855-135-2*) Transaction Pubs.

Religion, Myth, & Folklore in the World's Epics: The Kalevala & its Predecessors. Ed. by Lauri Honko. (Religion & Society Ser.: No. 30). xii, 588p. (C). 1990. lib. bdg. 183.10 (*3-11-012253-7*) Mouton.

Religion o Cristo? M. R. DeHaan. Orig. Title: Religion or Christ. 64p. (SPA.). 1970. mass mkt. 2.75 (*0-8254-1153-X*, Edit Portavoz) Kregel.

Religion of Ancient Egypt. W. M. Petrie. (African Heritage Classical Research Studies). 98p. reprint ed. 20.00 (*0-938818-38-4*) ECA Assoc.

Religion of Ancient Greece. Thaddeus Zielinski. Tr. by George R. Noyes. LC 76-107838. (Select Bibliographies Reprint Ser.). 1977. 19.95 (*0-8369-5222-7*) Ayer.

Religion of Ancient Palestine in the Light of Archaeology. S. A Cook. (British Academy, London, Schweich Lectures on Biblical Archaeology Series, 1930). 1974. reprint ed. pap. 30.00 (*0-8115-1267-3*) Periodicals Srv.

Religion of Ancient Scandinavia. W. A. Craigie. 1972. 59.95 (*0-8490-0939-1*) Gordon Pr.

Religion of Ancient Scandinavia. William A. Craigie. LC 74-99657. (Select Bibliographies Reprint Ser.). 1977. 18.95 (*0-8369-5086-0*) Ayer.

Religion of Art. Sangharakshita. 170p. 1996. pap. 11.95 (*0-904766-31-4*) Windhorse Pubns.

Religion of Art in Proust. Barbara J. Bucknall. LC 78-83546. (Illinois Studies in Language & Literature: No. 60). 224p. reprint ed. pap. 63.90 (*0-8357-3515-X*, 2034429) Bks Demand.

Religion of Beauty in Woman: Essays on Platonic Love in Poetry & Society. Jefferson B. Fletcher. LC 68-925. (Studies in Poetry: No. 38). 1969. reprint ed. lib. bdg. 75.00 (*0-8383-0550-4*) M S G Haskell Hse.

Religion of Burma & Other Papers. Ananda-Maitreya. LC 77-87482. reprint ed. 45.00 (*0-404-16790-X*) AMS Pr.

Religion of Capital. 9th ed. Paul Lafargue. 1961. pap. 0.50 (*0-935534-38-5*) NY Labor News.

Religion of China. Max M. Weber. 1968. pap. 19.95 (*0-02-934450-6*, Free Press) Free Pr.

Religion of Christ by Means of the Secret Symbols of the Rosicrucians. Franz Hartmann. 105p. 1969. reprint ed. spiral bd. 34.50 (*0-7873-1048-4*) Hlth Research.

Religion of Dr. Johnson. William T. Cairns. LC 71-93324. (Essay Index Reprint Ser.). 1977. 19.95 (*0-8369-1279-9*) Ayer.

Religion of Egypt. A. Mallon. (African Heritage Classical Research Studies). pap. 10.00 (*0-938818-37-6*) ECA Assoc.

Religion of Egypt. A. Mallon. (African Studies). reprint ed. 10.00 (*0-685-56712-5*) ECA Assoc.

Religion of George Fox: As Revealed in His Epistles. Howard H. Brinton. LC 68-57978. (Orig.). 1968. pap. 3.00 (*0-87574-161-4*) Pendle Hill.

Religion of Humanity. Octavius B. Frothingham. (Notable American Authors Ser.). 1992. reprint ed. lib. bdg. 75.00 (*0-7812-2903-0*) Rprt Serv.

Religion of Humanity: The Impact of Comtean Positivism on Victorian Britain. T. R. Wright. (Illus.). 325p. 1986. text ed. 80.00 (*0-521-30671-X*) Cambridge U Pr.

Religion of India: The Sociology of Hinduism & Buddhism. Max Weber. (C). 1992. 29.00 (*81-215-0571-2*, Pub. by Munshiram Manoharial II) S Asia.

Religion of Irish Dessent, 1650-1800. Ed. by Kevin Herlihy. 128p. 1996. 30.00 (*1-85182-236-4*, Pub. by Four Cts Pr IE) Intl Spec Bk.

Religion of Islam. Khurshid Ahmad. 28p. (Orig.). 1985. pap. 3.00 (*1-56744-370-2*) Kazi Pubns.

Religion of Islam. Samina. 14.95 (*0-913321-23-0*) Ahmadiyya Anjuman.

Religion of Islam. Muhammad A. Maulana. 617p. 1992. reprint ed. 20.95 (*0-913321-32-X*) Ahmadiyya Anjuman.

Religion of Islam: Aspects of Muslim Theology & Law. F. A. Klein. 252p. (C). 1989. pap. 29.95 (*0-7007-0190-7*, Pub. by Curzon Pr UK) Paul & Co Pubs.

Religion of Islam & Nation of Islam: What Is the Difference? Mustafa El-Amin. 70p. 1991. pap. text ed. 5.95 (*0-9638597-0-6*) El-Amin Prods.

***Religion of Israel: A Short History.** William J. Doorly. LC 97-154. (Orig.). 1997. pap. 16.95 (*0-8091-3705-4*) Paulist Pr.

Religion of Japan's Korean Minority: The Preservation of Ethnic Identity. Helen Hardacre. LC 84-80604. (Korea Research Monographs: No. 9). (Illus.). 74p. (Orig.). (C). 1985. pap. text ed. 6.00 (*0-912966-67-X*) IEAS.

Religion of Java. Clifford Geertz. LC 75-18746. xvi, 416p. 1976. reprint ed. pap. text ed. 19.95 (*0-226-28510-3*, P658) U Ch Pr.

Religion of Jesus the Jew. Geza Vermes. LC 93-18058. 1993. 16.00 (*0-8006-2797-0*, 1-2797) Augsburg Fortress.

Religion of Julian the Apostate. J. Stokes. 1993. reprint ed. pap. 5.95 (*1-55818-239-X*) Holmes Pub.

Religion of Love. Swami Vivekananda. 114p. 1919. pap. 3.95 (*0-87481-129-5*, Pub. by Advaita Ashrama II) Vedanta Pr.

Religion of Man. Rabindranath Tagore. 128p. 1988. pap. 9.95 (*0-04-200014-9*) Routledge Chapman & Hall.

Religion of Man. Rabindranath Tagore. LC 77-27145. (Hibbert Lectures: 1930). 248p. reprint ed. 35.00 (*0-404-60426-9*) AMS Pr.

Religion of Nature Delineated, 1724 & Related Commentaries. William Wollaston. LC 74-1469. 1974. 50.00 (*0-8201-1127-9*) Schol Facsimiles.

Religion of New Zealanders. Peter Donovan. (Illus.). 272p. 1990. pap. 29.95 (*0-86469-125-4*) Intl Spec Bk.

Religion of Philosophers. James H. Dunham. LC 78-80386. (Essay Index Reprint Ser.). 1977. 23.95 (*0-8369-1059-1*) Ayer.

Religion of Pots & Pans? Modes of Philosophical & Theological Discourse in Ancient Judaism. Jacob Neusner. LC 88-30828. (Brown Judaic Studies). 228p. 1989. 41.95 (*1-55540-283-6*, 140156) Scholars Pr GA.

Religion of Protestants: The Church in English Society 1559-1625. Patrick Collinson. 312p. 1984. pap. 26.00 (*0-19-820053-6*) OUP.

Religion of Reason: Out of the Sources of Judaism. Tr. & Intro. by Simon Kaplan. LC 95-4448. (Texts & Translations Ser.: No. 7). 570p. 1995. 34.95 (*0-7885-0102-X*, 010207) Scholars Pr GA.

Religion of Science Fiction. Frederick A. Kreuziger. LC 86-72543. 166p. 1986. 20.95 (*0-87972-366-1*); pap. 10.95 (*0-87972-367-X*) Bowling Green Univ Popular Press.

Religion of Shakespeare. Richard Simpson. Ed. by Henry S. Bowden. LC 74-176025. reprint ed. 64.50 (*0-404-00961-1*) AMS Pr.

Religion of Socialism: Being Essays in Modern Socialist Criticism. Ernest Belfort Bax. LC 74-39668. (Essay Index Reprint Ser.). 1977. reprint ed. 20.95 (*0-8369-2743-5*) Ayer.

Religion of Socrates. Mark L. McPherran. LC 95-45059. 1996. 35.00 (*0-271-01581-0*) Pa St U Pr.

Religion of Soldier & Sailor. Paul D. Moody et al. LC 45-3352. 123p. 1945. 13.95 (*0-674-75750-5*) HUP.

Religion of Solidarity. Edward Bellamy. (Institute of World Culture Ser.). 132p. 1984. pap. 8.75 (*0-88695-029-5*) Concord Grove.

***Religion of Technology: The Divinity of Man & the Spirit of Invention.** David F. Noble. LC 96-48019. 1997. 26.00 (*0-679-42564-0*) Knopf.

Religion of the Ancient Celts. John A. MacCulloch. 399p. 1992. pap. 27.50 (*0-09-471330-8*, Pub. by Constable Pubs UK) Trans-Atl Phila.

Religion of the Ancient Egyptians: Cognitive Structures & Popular Expressions. Ed. by Gertie Englund. (Uppsala Studies in Ancient Mediterranean & Near Eastern Civilizations: No. 20). (Illus.). 147p. (Orig.). 1989. pap. 43.00 (*91-554-2433-3*, Pub. by Umea U Bibl SW) Coronet Bks.

Religion of the Crow Indians. Robert H. Lowie. LC 74-7986. reprint ed. 39.50 (*0-404-11876-3*) AMS Pr.

Religion of the Future see Modern Essays

Religion of the Greeks & Romans. Karoly Kerenyi. LC 72-9823. (Illus.). 303p. 1973. reprint ed. text ed. 35.00 (*0-8371-6605-5*, KERG, Greenwood Pr) Greenwood.

Religion of the Heart. Hannah More. Ed. by Hal M. Helms. LC 93-84600. (Living Library). 226p. 1993. 8.95 (*1-55725-063-4*) Paraclete MA.

***Religion of the Heart.** Ed. by Seyyid H. Nasr. 330p. 1996. pap. 23.95 (*0-614-21329-0*, 1069) Kazi Pubns.

Religion of the Heart: Essays Presented to Frithjof Schuon on His Eightieth Birthday. Ed. by Seyyed H. Nasr & William Stoddart. 1991. pap. 23.95 (*0-9629984-0-0*) Foun Trad Studies.

Religion of the Hindus. Kenneth Morgan. 1987. reprint ed. 26.00 (*81-208-0387-6*, Pub. by Motilal Banarsidass II) S Asia.

Religion of the Hindus: Interpreted by Hindus. Ed. by Kenneth W. Morgan. LC 53-10466. 448p. reprint ed. 127.70 (*0-8357-9975-1*, 2015620) Bks Demand.

Religion of the Indians of California. fac. ed. A. L. Kroeber. (University of California Publications in American Archaeology & Ethnology: Vol. 4: 6). 38p. (C). 1907. reprint ed. pap. text ed. 3.70 (*1-55567-168-3*) Coyote Press.

Religion of the Kwakiutl Indians, 2 vols. Franz Boas. LC 72-82368. (Columbia Univ. Contributions to Anthropology Ser.: No. 10). reprint ed. 60.00 (*0-404-50560-0*) AMS Pr.

Religion of the Landless: The Social Context of the Babylonian Exile. Daniel L. Smith. LC 89-9211. 256p. (Orig.). 1989. pap. 19.95 (*0-940989-50-6*) Meyer Stone Bks.

Religion of the Luiseno Indians of Southern California. fac. ed. Constance G. DuBois. (University of California Publications in American Archaeology & Ethnology: Vol. 8: 3). 192p. (C). 1908. reprint ed. pap. text ed. 17.45 (*1-55567-182-9*) Coyote Press.

Religion of the Manichees: Donnellan Lectures for 1924. Francis C. Burkitt. LC 77-84698. reprint ed. 34.50 (*0-404-16105-7*) AMS Pr.

Religion of the People: Methodism & Popular Religion c. 1750-1900. David Hempton. LC 95-32861. 256p. (C). 1996. text ed. 65.00 (*0-415-07714-1*) Routledge.

***Religion of the Poor: Rural Missions in Europe & the Formation of Modern Catholicism, c. 1500-1800.** Louis Chatellier. (Illus.). 304p. (C). 1997. text ed. 59.95 (*0-521-56201-5*) Cambridge U Pr.

Religion of the Republic. Elwyn A. Smith. LC 70-130326. 304p. reprint ed. pap. 86.70 (*0-685-15796-2*, 2026890) Bks Demand.

Religion of the Russian People. Pierre Pascal. LC 76-24462. 130p. 1976. pap. 8.95 (*0-913836-30-3*) St Vladimirs.

Religion of the Sikh Gurus. Teja Singh. 52p. 1989. reprint ed. pap. 3.50 (*0-89540-173-8*, SB-173) Sun Pub.

Religion of the Sikhs. Gopal Singh. (C). 1987. reprint ed. 16.00 (*8-8364-2737-8*, Pub. by Allied II) S Asia.

Religion of the Sufis. David Shea & Anthony Troyer. 1979. 18.00 (*0-900860-68-5*, Pub. by Octagon Pr UK) ISHK.

Religion of the Veda. Hermann Oldenberg. Tr. by Shridhar B. Shrotri. (C). 1988. 42.50 (*81-208-0392-2*, Pub. by Motilal Banarsidass II) S Asia.

Religion of the Veda. Maurice Bloomfield. LC 70-94310. (BCL Ser. II). reprint ed. 34.50 (*0-404-00912-3*) AMS Pr.

Religion of the Yoruba: A Study of Symbology. J. O. Kayode. LC 82-16197. (Illus.). 300p. 1983. pap. 25.00 (*0-943324-06-8*) Omenana.

Religion of Tibet. Charles A. Bell. 1975. lib. bdg. 250.00 (*0-87968-482-8*) Krishna Pr.

Religion of Tibet. Charles Bell. (Illus.). 235p. 1990. reprint ed. pap. 16.00 (*957-9482-20-9*) Oriental Bk Store.

Religion of Tibet. Charles Bell. 1987. reprint ed. 42.50 (*81-7069-002-1*, Pub. by Munshiram Manoharial II) S Asia.

Religion of Tibet: Study of Lamaism. J. E. Ellam. 1972. 59.95 (*0-8490-0940-5*) Gordon Pr.

Religion of Truth. A. A. Maududi. pap. 3.00 (*0-933511-36-1*) Kazi Pubns.

Religion of Wordsworth. A. D. Martin. LC 72-8965. (Studies in Wordsworth: No. 29). 1973. reprint ed. lib. bdg. 42.95 (*0-8383-1680-8*) M S G Haskell Hse.

Religion on Capitol Hill: Myths & Realities. Peter L. Benson & Dorothy Hill. LC 86-16434. (Illus.). 223p. 1986. pap. 18.95 (*0-19-504168-2*) OUP.

Religion on the Prairie: The History of First Baptist Church of Jacksonville, Illinois, Its Pastors & Its People, in Context, 1841-1991. Edward E. Ferguson. LC 94-73372. (Illus.). 380p. (Orig.). 1995. 50.00 (*0-9644238-0-4*); 20.00 (*0-9644238-1-2*) Frst Baptist Church.

Religion or Christ see Religion o Cristo?

Religion, Order, & Law: A Study in Pre-Revolutionary England. David Little. LC 84-2611. 284p. (C). 1984. pap. text ed. 13.50 (*0-226-48546-3*) U Ch Pr.

Religion, Our True Interest. Thomas Watson. 129p. (C). 1992. pap. 8.99 (*0-9511484-1-9*) Revival Lit.

Religion Paysanne et Religion Urbaine et Toscane (c. 1280-1450) Charles M. De la Ronciere. (Collected Studies: No. CS 458). (Illus.). 350p. 1994. 98.95 (*0-86078-445-2*, Pub. by Variorum UK) Ashgate Pub Co.

Religion, Personality & Mental Health. Ed. by L. B. Brown. (Recent Research in Psychology Ser.). (Illus.). 225p. 1993. write for info. (*3-540-97773-2*) Spr-Verlag.

Religion, Personality, & Mental Health. Ed. by Laurence B. Brown. LC 93-15258. (Recent Research in Psychology Ser.). 1994. 83.95 (*0-387-97773-2*) Spr-Verlag.

Religion, Philosophy & Literature of Bengal Vaishnavism. Durgadas Mukhopadhyay. 1990. 17.50 (*81-7018-597-1*, Pub. by BR Pub II) S Asia.

Religion, Philosophy Yoga. Jean Filliozat. Tr. by Maurice Shukla. (C). 1991. 28.00 (*81-208-0718-9*, Pub. by Motilal Banarsidass II) S Asia.

Religion, Politics, & Communism: The South Asian Experience. Ed. by Rakhahari Chatterji. (C). 1994. 17.00 (*81-7003-174-5*, Pub. by S Asia Pubs II) S Asia.

Religion, Politics, & Higher Learning: A Collection of Essays. Morton G. White. LC 59-6163. 154p. reprint ed. pap. 43.90 (*0-317-08991-9*, 2001621) Bks Demand.

Religion, Politics, & Oil. Charles A. Kimball. 1992. pap. 2.98 (*0-687-35973-2*) Abingdon.

Religion, Politics & Preferment in France since Eighteen Ninety: "La Belle Epoque" & Its Legacy. Maurice Larkin. 220p. (C). 1995. text ed. 49.95 (*0-521-41916-6*) Cambridge U Pr.

Religion, Politics, & the Law: Commentaries & Controversies. Peter Schooten & Dennis Stevens. LC 95-16439. 385p. (C). 1995. pap. text ed. 28.00 (*0-534-19488-5*) HarBrace.

Religion, Politics, & the Moral Life. Michael Oakeshott. Ed. by Timothy Fuller. 160p. 1993. 25.00 (*0-300-05643-5*) Yale U Pr.

Religion Power & Protest in Local Communities: The Northern Shore of the Mediterranean. Ed. by Eric R. Wolf. LC 84-8407. (Religion & Society Ser.: No. 24). 287p. 1984. 84.65 (*3-11-009777-X*) Mouton.

Religion, Public Life, & the American Polity. Ed. by Luis E. Lugo. LC 93-38721. 320p. 1994. text ed. 39.00 (*0-87049-830-4*) U of Tenn Pr.

Religion Rationality. Gascoigne. 1985. lib. bdg. 162.50 (*90-247-2992-0*, Pub. by M Nijhoff NE) Kluwer Ac.

Religion, Reason & Man. Fritz Marti. LC 74-9353. 127p. 1974. 6.30 (*0-87527-141-3*) Green.

Religion, Reason & Revelation. 3rd rev. ed. Gordon H. Clark. Ed. & Intro. by John W. Robbins. 264p. 1995. pap. 10.95 (*0-940931-86-9*) Trinity Found.

Religion, Reason, & Truth: Historical Essays in the Philosophy of Religion. Sterling M. McMurrin. LC 82-4813. 302p. reprint ed. pap. 86.10 (*0-685-20459-6*, 2029852) Bks Demand.

Religion, Rebellion, Revolution: An Interdisciplinary & Cross-Cultural Collection of Essays. Ed. by Bruce Lincoln. LC 85-1992. 312p. 1985. text ed. 39.95 (*0-312-67061-3*) St Martin.

Religion, Reform & Revolution: Labor Panaceas in the Nineteenth Century. Ed. by Leon Stein & Philip Taft. LC 79-89743. (American Labor, from Conspiracy to Collective Bargaining Ser., No. 1). 581p. 1971. 31.95 (*0-405-02151-8*) Ayer.

***Religion, Religiosity & Communialism.** Praful Bidwai et al. 1996. 34.00 (*81-7304-132-6*, Pub. by Manohar II) S Asia.

Religion, Revelation & Reason. Eric C. Rust. LC 81-2760. vi, 192p. (C). 1981. pap. 12.50 (*0-86554-058-6*, MUP-P009) Mercer Univ Pr.

Religion Revolucionaria de Marx: La Regeneracion por Medio del Caos. Gary North. Tr. by Paul Howden & Jose L. Gonzalez from ENG. 292p. (SPA.). 1990. pap. 6.95 (*0-930464-37-0*) Inst Christian.

Religion, Revolution & English Radicalism: Nonconformity in Eighteenth Century Politics & Society. James E. Bradley. 470p. (C). 1990. text ed. 69.95 (*0-521-38010-3*) Cambridge U Pr.

Religion, Revolution, & Regional Culture in Eighteenth-Century France: The Ecclesiastical Oath of 1791. Timothy Tackett. LC 85-43317. (Illus.). 448p. 1986. text ed. 75.00 (*0-691-05470-3*) Princeton U Pr.

Religion, Rights & Laws. Anthony Bradney. LC 92-42154. 185p. 1993. 49.00 (*0-7185-1366-5*, Pub. by Leicester Univ Pr) St Martin.

Religion Romaine D'Auguste Aux Antonins, 2 vols. in 1. Gaston Boissier. xi, 917p. 1979. reprint ed. lib. bdg. 190.00 (*3-487-06702-1*) G Olms Pubs.

Religion, Science, & Magic: In Concert & in Conflict. Ed. by Jacob Neusner et al. 288p. 1992. reprint ed. pap. 19.95 (*0-19-507911-6*) OUP.

Religion, Science & Naturalism. William B. Drees. 330p. (C). 1996. text ed. 59.95 (*0-521-49708-6*) Cambridge U Pr.

Religion, Science, & Society in the Modern World. Alexander D. Lindsay. LC 70-37847. (Essay Index Reprint Ser.). 1977. reprint ed. 15.95 (*0-8369-2604-8*) Ayer.

Religion, Science & Worldview: Essays in Honor of Richard S. Westfall. Ed. by Margaret J. Osler & Paul L. Farber. 320p. 1985. text ed. 69.95 (*0-521-30452-0*) Cambridge U Pr.

Religion Social Change & Fertility Behavior: A Study of Kerala. R. Jayasree. (C). 1989. 21.00 (*81-7022-252-4*, Pub. by Concept II) S Asia.

Religion, Society & Politics in France Since 1789. Ed. by Frank Tallett & Nicholas Atkin. 248p. 1991. boxed 55.00 (*1-85285-057-4*) Hambledon Press.

***Religion, Society & Psychoanalysis: Readings in Contemporary Theory.** Janet L. Jacobs. (C). 1997. text ed. 65.00 (*0-8133-2647-8*); pap. text ed. 22.00 (*0-8133-2648-6*) Westview.

R

An Asterisk (*) at the beginning of an entry indicates that the title is appearing in BIP for the first time.

Religion, Society, & the State in Arabia: The Hijaz under Ottoman Control, 1840-1908. William L. Ochsenwald. LC 84-7498. (Illus.). 257p. 1984. 47.50 (*0-8142-0366-3*) Ohio St U Pr.

Religion, Society, & Utopia in Nineteenth-Century America. Ira L. Mandelker. LC 84-47. 200p. 1984. lib. bdg. 27.50 (*0-87023-436-6*) U of Mass Pr.

Religion, State & Ethnic Group, Vol. 6. Ed. by Donald Kerr. 334p. (C). 1992. 80.00 (*0-8147-4609-8*) NYU Pr.

Religion, State & Politics in India. Ed. by Moin Shakir. (C). 1989. 57.50 (*81-202-0213-9*, Pub. by Ajanta II) S Asia.

Religion, State, & Politics in the Soviet Union & the Successor States, 1953-1993. John Anderson. LC 93-44304. 224p. (C). 1994. text ed. 54.95 (*0-521-46231-2*); pap. text ed. 19.95 (*0-521-46784-5*) Cambridge U Pr.

Religion, State & Society in Contemporary Africa: Nigeria, Sudan, South Africa, Zaire, & Mozambique. Ed. by Austin M. Ahanotu. LC 91-28472. (American University Studies: Theology & Religion: Ser. VII, Vol. 111). 208p. (C). 1992. text ed. 39.95 (*0-8204-1755-6*) P Lang Pubng.

Religion, State & Society in Modern Britain. Ed. by Paul Badham. LC 89-36710. (Texts & Studies in Religion). 416p. 1989. lib. bdg. 109.95 (*0-88946-832-X*) E Mellen.

Religion, State & the Burger Court. Leo Pfeffer. LC 84-43056. 310p. 1985. 34.95 (*0-87975-275-0*) Prometheus Bks.

Religion-State Relationship & Constitutional Rights in India. V. P. Bhartiya. (C). 1987. 54.00 (*81-7100-009-6*, Pub. by Deep II) S Asia.

Religion That Works. Mark Finley & Steven R. Mosley. LC 96-10758. 1996. pap. 1.49 (*0-8163-1348-2*) Pacific Pr Pub Assn.

Religion, the Courts, & Public Policy. Robert F. Drinan. LC 78-6124. 261p. 1978. reprint ed. text ed. 59.75 (*0-313-20444-6*, DRRE, Greenwood Pr) Greenwood.

Religion, the Independent Sector, & American Culture. Ed. by Rowland A. Sherrill & Conrad Cherry. (American Academy of Religion, Studies in Religion). 204p. (C). 1992. 34.95 (*1-55540-584-3*, 010063); pap. 19.95 (*1-55540-585-1*) Scholars Pr GA.

Religion, the Missing Dimension of Statecraft. Ed. by Douglas Johnston & Cynthia Sampson. LC 93-21648. (Center for Strategic & International Studies Ser.). (Illus.). 350p. 1994. 38.00 (*0-19-508734-8*) OUP.

Religion, the State, & Education. Ed. by James E. Wood, Jr. LC 84-81477. (Institute of Church-State Studies). 151p. 1984. pap. 6.95 (*0-918954-32-0*) Baylor Univ Pr.

Religion, Theology, & American Public Life. Linell E. Cady. LC 92-3097. 202p. 1993. pap. text ed. 21.95 (*0-7914-1304-7*) State U NY Pr.

Religion, Theology, & American Public Life. Linell E. Cady. LC 92-3097. (SUNY Series in Religious Studies). 202p. 1993. text ed. 64.50 (*0-7914-1303-9*) State U NY Pr.

Religion, Tradition & Renewal. Ed. by Armin W. Geertz & Jeppe S. Jensen. 240p. (Orig.). (C). 1991. pap. 27.00 (*87-7288-213-1*, Pub. by Aarhus Univ Pr DK) David Brown.

Religion und Christentum in Fichtes Spaetphilosophie 1810-1813. Dirk Schmid. (Theologische Bibliothek Toepelmann Ser.: Bd. 71). x, 230p. (GER.). (C). 1995. lib. bdg. 129.25 (*3-11-014758-0*) De Gruyter.

***Religion und Gestaltung der Zeit.** Ed. by Dieter Georgi et al. 216p. 1994. pap. 39.00 (*90-390-0043-3*, Pub. by KOK Pharos NE) Eisenbrauns.

Religion under Bureaucracy: Policy & Administration for Hindu Temples in South India. Franklin A. Presler. (Cambridge South Asian Studies: No. 38). (Illus.). 220p. 1988. text ed. 59.95 (*0-521-32177-8*) Cambridge U Pr.

Religion under Socialism in China. Ed. by Luo Zhufeng. Tr. by Donald E. MacInnis & Zheng Xi'an from CHI. LC 90-33534. (Chinese Studies on China). 280p. (gr. 13). 1991. text ed. 63.95 (*0-87332-609-1*) M E Sharpe.

Religion vs. Television: Competitors in Cultural Context. Jay Newsman. LC 96-10439. (Media & Society Ser.). 168p. 1996. text ed. 55.00 (*0-275-95640-7*, Praeger Pubs) Greenwood.

Religion, Vol. 13 see History of Women in the United States: Topically Arranged Articles on the Evolution of Women's History in the United States

Religion, Vol. 16, Pt. I, Heidentum: Romische Religion, Allgemeines see Aufstieg und Niedergang der Roemischen Welt: Selection 2, Principat

Religion, Vol. 16, Pt. II, Heidentum: Romische Religion, Allgemeines FS see Aufstieg und Niedergang der Roemischen Welt: Selection 2, Principat

Religion, Vol. 17, Pt. I, Heidentum: Romische Gotterkulte, Orientalische Kulte in der Romische Welt see Aufstieg und Niedergang der Roemischen Welt: Selection 2, Principat

Religion, Vol. 17, Pt. II, Heidentum: Romische Gotterkulte, Orientalizche Kulte in der Romischen Welt, Fortsetzung see Aufstieg und Niedergang der Roemischen Welt: Selection 2, Principat

Religion, Vol. 17, Pt. III, Heidentum: Romische Gotterkulte, Orientalische Kulte in der Romischen Welt, Fortsetzung see Aufstieg und Niedergang der Roemischen Welt: Selection 2, Principat

Religion, Vol. 17, Pt. IV, Heidentum: Romische Gotterkulte, Orientalische Kulte in der Romische Welt, Fortsetzung see Aufstieg und Niedergang der Roemischen Welt: Selection 2, Principat

Religion, Vol. 18, Pt. II see Aufstieg und Niedergang der Roemischen Welt: Selection 2, Principat

Religion, Vol. 18, Pt. III see Aufstieg und Niedergang der Roemischen Welt: Selection 2, Principat

Religion, Vol. 19, Pt. I, Judentum: Allgemeines, Palastinensisches Judentum see Aufstieg und Niedergang der Roemischen Welt: Selection 2, Principat

Religion, Vol. 20, Pt. II see Aufstieg und Niedergang der Roemischen Welt: Selection 2, Principat

Religion, Vol. 23, Pt. I, Vorkonstantinisches Christentum: Verhaltnis zu Romischem Staat und Heidnischer Religion see Aufstieg und Niedergang der Roemischen Welt: Selection 2, Principat

Religion, Vol. 25, Pt. I, Vorkonstantinisches Christentum: Leben und Umwelt Jesu: Neues Testament Kanonische Schriften und Apokryphen see Aufstieg und Niedergang der Roemischen Welt: Selection 2, Principat

Religion, Vol. 25, Pt. III, Vorkonstantinisches Christentum: Leben und Umwelt Jesu; Neues Testament, Fortsetzung Kanonische Schriften und Apokryphen see Aufstieg und Niedergang der Roemischen Welt: Selection 2, Principat

Religion, Vol. 25, Pt. IV, Vorkonstantinisches Christentum: Leben und Umwelt Jesu; Neues Testament, Fortsetzung Kanonische Schriften und Apokryphen see Aufstieg und Niedergang der Roemischen Welt: Selection 2, Principat

Religion: Vorkonstantinisches Christentum: Leben und Umwelt Jesu; Neues Testament, Fortsetzung Kanonische Schriften und Apokryphen see Aufstieg und Niedergang der Roemischen Welt: Selection 2, Principat

Religion: Vorkonstantinisches Christentum: Verhaltnis zu Romischen Staat und Heidnischer Religion see Aufstieg und Niedergang der Roemischen Welt: Selection 2, Principat

Religion vs. Religion. Ali Shariati. Tr. by Laleh Bakhtiar from PER. 76p. (Orig.). (C). 1993. pap. 7.50 (*1-871031-00-1*) Abjad Bk.

***Religion vs. Religion.** Ali Shariati. Tr. by Laleh Bakhtiar. 75p. (Orig.). 1996. pap. 7.50 (*0-614-21444-0*, 1071) Kazi Pubns.

Religion with Medical, Psychological & Philosophical Aspects: Index of New Information & Bible of Progress. Gersten G. Panopolos. 160p. 1996. 47.50 (*0-7883-0226-4*); pap. 44.50 (*0-7883-0227-2*) ABBE Pubs Assn.

Religion Within Limits or Reason Alone. Immanuel Kant. 1960. pap. text ed. 14.00 (*0-06-130067-5*, TB67, Torch) HarpC.

Religion Without Revelation. Julian S. Huxley. LC 78-12065. 203p. 1979. reprint ed. text ed. 35.00 (*0-313-21225-2*, HURR, Greenwood Pr) Greenwood.

Religion Without Talking, No. 7: Religious Beliefs & Natural Belief in Hume's Philosophy of Religion Studies in European Thought. Beryl Logan. LC 93-16910. 184p. (C). 1993. text ed. 42.95 (*0-8204-2201-0*) P Lang Pubng.

***Religion Without Transcendence?** D. Z. Phillips & Timothy Tessin. LC 97-13671. (Claremont Studies in the Philosophy of Religion). 1997. write for info. (*0-312-17630-9*) St Martin.

***Religion y Cambio Social en P. R. (1898-1940)** Nelida A. Cintron. LC 96-85613. 168p. 1996. pap. 9.25 (*0-929157-39-7*) Ediciones Huracan.

Religion y Lucha de Clase see Religion & Social Conflicts

***Religion y Mitologia de los Uitotos, 2 vols.** Konrad T. Preuss. Incl. . (SPA.). 232p. 1994. pap. 25.00 (*958-17-0112-5*); . (SPA.). 917p. 1994. pap. 25.00 (*958-17-0113-3*); 50.00 (*958-17-0114-1*, IC004) UPLAAP.

Religion y Revolucion en Cuba. Manuel Fernandez. (Realidades Ser.). (Illus.). 250p. (SPA.). 1984. pap. 14.95 (*0-917049-00-4*) Saeta.

Religion Yesterday & Today. Henry S. Coffin. LC 75-117769. (Essay Index Reprint Ser.). 1977. 20.95 (*0-8369-1790-1*) Ayer.

***Religiones Del Mundo.** K. Brooks. (SPA.). 1.50 (*0-8297-0406-X*) Life Pubs Intl.

***Religiones, Sectas y Herejias.** J. Cabral. (SPA.). pap. 7.95 (*0-8297-1282-8*) Life Pubs Intl.

Religions: A Select, Classified Bibliography. Joseph F. Mitros. LC 77-183042. (Philosophical Questions Ser.: No. 8). 350p. 1973. 75.00 (*0-912116-08-0*) Learned Pubns.

Religions: Encountering People of Other Faiths. Charles Hambrick & Joy Lawler. (To the Point: Vol. 3). Orig. Title: Religions to the Point. 96p. (Orig.). 1995. pap. 8.95 (*0-687-43702-4*) Abingdon.

Religions: Values & Peak-Experiences. Abraham H. Maslow. 1983. 21.00 (*0-8446-6070-1*) Peter Smith.

Religions see Cultural Heritage of India

Religions & Languages: A Colloquium. Ed. by Bruce S. Alton. LC 91-18280. (Toronto Studies in Religion: Vol. 13). 163p. 1991. 39.95 (*0-8204-1695-9*) P Lang Pubng.

Religions & Teachings of Lalla: The Shaiva Yogini of Kashmir; Also Known as Laleshwari, Lalla Yogishwari & Lalishri. Richard C. Temple. 1990. reprint ed. 32.00 (*81-85326-28-2*, Pub. by Vintage II) S Asia.

Religions & the Status of Women. Jyotsna Chatterji. 1990. 17.50 (*81-85024-67-7*, Pub. by Uppal Pub Hse II) S Asia.

Religions & the Truth: Philosophical Reflections & Perspectives. Hendrik M. Vroom. (Currents of Encounter Ser.: Vol. 2). 392p. (Orig.). (C). 1989. pap. 28.00 (*0-8028-0502-7*) Eerdmans.

Religions & the Virtue of Religion, Vol. 65: Annual ACPA Proceedings, 1992. Ed. by Therese-Anne Druart & Marc Rasevic. 1992. pap. 20.00 (*0-918090-25-3*) Am Cath Philo.

Religions East & West. Fellows. 444p. (C). 1979. text ed. 42.00 (*0-03-019441-5*) HB Coll Pubs.

Religions East & West. 2nd ed. Fellows. (C). 1996. pap. text ed. write for info. (*0-15-503019-1*) HB Coll Pubs.

Religions for Human Dignity & World Peace: Unabridged Proceedings of the World Conference on Religion & Peace, 4th. World Conference on Religion & Peace Staff. Ed. by John B. Taylor & Gunther Gebhardt. 469p. 1986. pap. write for info. (*2-88235-000-7*) World Confer Rel & Peace.

Religions for Today. 3rd rev. ed. Roger Whiting. Orig. Title: Religions of Man. (Illus.). 270p. (YA). 9100. pap. 25.00 (*0-7487-0586-4*) Dufour.

***Religions in Conflict: Ideology, Cultural Contact & Conversions in Late Colonial India.** Antony Copley. (Illus.). 363p. 1997. 35.00 (*0-19-563676-7*) OUP.

Religions in Japan: Buddhism, Shinto, Christianity. Supreme Commander For The Allied Powers Staff. LC 77-13855. 194p. 1978. reprint ed. text ed. 35.00 (*0-8371-9874-7*, SURJ, Greenwood Pr) Greenwood.

***Religions in Korea: Beliefs & Cultural Values.** Ed. by Earl H. Phillipws & Eui-Young Yu. 127p. 1982. pap. 15.00 (*0-8420-2225-2*) Scholarly Res Inc.

Religions of America. Ed. by Leo Rosten. LC 74-11705. 672p. 1975. pap. 17.00 (*0-671-21971-5*) S&S Trade.

Religions of Ancient China. H. A. Giles. 1972. 59.95 (*0-8490-0941-3*) Gordon Pr.

Religions of Ancient China. Herbert A. Giles. LC 79-95067. (Select Bibliographies Reprint Ser.). 1977. 19.95 (*0-8369-5069-0*) Ayer.

Religions of Ancient China. rev. ed. H. A. Giles. 69p. 1989. reprint ed. pap. 3.95 incl. reel tape (*9971-4-9157-5*) Heian Intl.

Religions of Ancient Egypt & Babylonia. Archibald H. Sayce. LC 77-27223. (Gifford Lectures: 1902). reprint ed. 57.50 (*0-404-60457-9*) AMS Pr.

Religions of Ancient India. Louis Renou. 1972. 16.00 (*0-8364-2614-2*, Pub. by Munshiram Manoharial II) S Asia.

Religions of Antiquity. Ed. by Robert M. Seltzer. (Readings from the Encyclopedia of Religion Ser.). (C). 1989. 15.95 (*0-02-897373-9*) Macmillan.

Religions of Asia. Ninian Smart. 272p. (C). 1992. pap. text ed. 39.00 (*0-13-772427-6*) P-H.

Religions of Asia. 3rd ed. John Y. Fenton et al. Ed. by Grace G. Burford. LC 92-50026. (Illus.). 400p. (C). 1993. pap. text ed. 25.00 (*0-312-05753-9*) St Martin.

Religions of Atlanta: Religious Diversity in the Centennial Olympic City. Ed. by Gary Laderman. (American Academy of Religion - The Religions Ser.: No. 1). 365p. 1996. pap. 19.95 (*0-7885-0250-6*, 011201) Scholars Pr GA.

Religions of China. Daniel L. Overmyer. LC 85-42789. 128p. (Orig.). 1986. pap. 11.00 (*0-06-066401-0*) Harper SF.

Religions of China in Practice. Ed. by Donald S. Lopez, Jr. LC 95-41332. (Readings in Religions Ser.). 472p. 1996. text ed. 59.50 (*0-691-02144-9*); pap. text ed. 19.95 (*0-691-02143-0*) Princeton U Pr.

Religions of Democracy. Finkelstein et al. 1941. 9.50 (*0-8159-6708-X*) Devin.

Religions of Immigrants from India & Pakistan: New Threads in the American Tapestry. Raymond B. Williams. (Illus.). 304p. 1988. text ed. 80.00 (*0-521-35156-1*); pap. text ed. 24.95 (*0-521-35961-9*) Cambridge U Pr.

Religions of India. A. Barth. 332p. 1989. 25.00 (*0-317-52150-0*, Pub. by S Chand II) St Mut.

Religions of India. 6th ed. A. Barth. Tr. by J. Wood from FRE. 309p. 1990. reprint ed. 24.95 (*0-940500-64-7*) Asia Bk Corp.

Religions of India. A. Barth. 1990. reprint ed. 11.00 (*81-85418-02-0*, Pub. by Low Price II) S Asia.

***Religions of India: Hinduism, Yoga, Buddhism.** Thomas M. Berry. LC 96-28514. 1996. write for info. (*0-231-10781-1*) Col U Pr.

Religions of India: Hinduism, Yoga, Buddhism. 2nd ed. Thomas Berry. LC 92-10005. 246p. 15.50 (*0-89012-067-6*, AN067-6) Col U Pr.

Religions of India in Practice. Daniel S. Lopez, Jr. LC 94-34695. (Princeton Readings in Religion Ser.). 648p. 1995. pap. text ed. 19.95 (*0-691-04324-8*) Princeton U Pr.

Religions of India in Practice. Ed. by Donald S. Lopez, Jr. LC 94-34695. (Princeton Readings in Religion Ser.). 648p. 1995. text ed. 65.00 (*0-691-04325-6*) Princeton U Pr.

Religions of Islam. Muhammad A. Maulana. 808p. 1986. 90.00 (*0-317-52151-9*, Pub. by S Chand II) St Mut.

Religions of Japan: From the Dawn of History to the Era of Meiji. William E. Griffis. LC 70-37469. (Essay Index Reprint Ser.). 1977. reprint ed. 23.95 (*0-8369-2550-5*) Ayer.

Religions of Japan: Many Traditions Within One Sacred Day. H. Byron Earhart. LC 84-47722. (Religious Traditions of the World Ser.: Vol. 1). (Illus.). 160p. 1984. pap. 12.00 (*0-06-062112-5*) Harper SF.

Religions of Japan from the Dawn of History to the Era of Meiji. William E. Griffis. (Notable American Authors Ser.). 1992. reprint ed. lib. bdg. 75.00 (*0-7812-2962-6*) Rprt Serv.

Religions of Man see Religions for Today

Religions of Mesoamerica. David Carrasco. LC 89-45990. 1990. pap. 12.00 (*0-06-061325-4*) Harper SF.

Religions of Modern Syria & Palestine. Frederick J. Bliss. LC 76-39454. reprint ed. 39.50 (*0-404-00897-6*) AMS Pr.

Religions of Mongolia. Walther Heissig. Tr. by Geoffrey Samuel from GER. LC 80-146381. 1980. 45.00 (*0-520-03857-6*) U CA Pr.

Religions of Oceania. Tony Swain et al. LC 94-16171. (Library of Religious Beliefs & Practices). 256p. (C). 1995. pap. 18.95 (*0-415-06019-2*, C0375) Routledge.

Religions of Oceania. Tony Swain et al. LC 94-16171. (Library of Religious Beliefs & Practices). 256p. (C). (gr. 13). 1995. text ed. 59.95 (*0-415-06018-4*, C0374) Routledge.

Religions of South Africa. David Chidester. LC 91-3329. (Library of Religious Beliefs & Practices). (Illus.). 224p. (Orig.). (C). 1992. text ed. 79.95 (*0-415-04779-X*, A6501) Routledge.

Religions of South Africa. David Chidester. LC 91-3329. (Library of Religious Beliefs & Practices). (Illus.). 224p. (Orig.). (C). 1992. pap. 27.95 (*0-415-04780-3*, A6505) Routledge.

Religions of the American Indians. Ake Hultkrantz. LC 73-90661. (Hermeneutics: Studies in the History of Religions: No. 5). 1979. pap. 16.00 (*0-520-04239-5*) U CA Pr.

Religions of the Ancient World. George Rawlinson. 180p. 1996. pap. 17.95 (*1-56459-895-0*) Kessinger Pub.

Religions of the Ancient World. George Rawlinson. reprint ed. spiral bd. 10.00 (*0-7873-0709-2*) Hlth Research.

Religions of the Book Vol. 38: The Annual Publication of the College Theology Society (1991) Ed. by Gerard S. Sloyan. 352p. 1996. pap. text ed. 39.00 (*0-7618-0259-2*); lib. bdg. 62.50 (*0-7618-0258-4*) U Pr of Amer.

Religions of the East. Lucius Boraks. 106p. 1988. pap. 7.95 (*1-55612-140-7*) Sheed & Ward MO.

Religions of the East-West: Teacher's Guide. Lucius Boraks. LC 86-63499. (Illus.). 92p. (Orig.). 1988. pap. 9.95 (*1-55612-155-5*) Sheed & Ward MO.

Religions of the Hindukush, Vol. I: The Kafirs. Karl Jettmar. 172p. (C). 1987. 32.00 (*81-204-0156-5*, Pub. by Oxford IBH II) S Asia.

Religions of the Orient: A Christian View. John A. Hardon. LC 71-108377. 221p. reprint ed. pap. 63.00 (*0-317-30169-1*, 2025351) Bks Demand.

Religions of the People in Sixteenth Century Champagne. A. N. Galpern. (Historical Studies: No. 92). 200p. 1976. 22.50 (*0-674-75836-6*) HUP.

Religions of the Roman Empire. John Ferguson. LC 71-110992. (Aspects of Greek & Roman Life Ser.). (Illus.). 296p. (C). 1970. pap. 16.95 (*0-8014-9311-0*) Cornell U Pr.

Religions of the West. Lucius Boraks. LC 87-63499. 116p. (Orig.). (YA). 1988. pap. 7.95 (*1-55612-141-5*) Sheed & Ward MO.

Religions of the West. Ninian Smart. 272p. (C). 1993. pap. text ed. 39.00 (*0-13-156811-6*) P-H.

Religions of the World. Carl C. Clemen et al. LC 69-17570. (Essay Index Reprint Ser.). 1977. 39.95 (*0-8369-0011-1*) Ayer.

Religions of the World. James Haskins. 300p. 1991. 14.95 (*0-87052-930-7*) Hippocrene Bks.

Religions of the World. Ed. by Scott Morris. LC 92-22282. (Using & Understanding Maps Ser.). (Illus.). 48p. (YA). (gr. 5 up). 1993. lib. bdg. 17.95 (*0-7910-1810-5*) Chelsea Hse.

***Religions of the World.** Martin Palmer et al. Ed. by Martin Marty. LC 97-22829. (Atlas Ser.). (Illus.). 160p. (J). 1997. 29.95 (*0-8160-3723-X*) Facts on File.

Religions of the World. rev. ed. F. H. Meade et al. (Illus.). (C). 1988. 90.00 (*0-7157-2355-3*) St Mut.

Religions of the World. 3rd ed. Nielsen. 1993. teacher ed., pap. text ed. 10.00 (*0-312-08079-4*) St Martin.

Religions of the World. 3rd ed. Niels C. Nielson, Jr. et al. LC 92-50025. (Illus.). 576p. (C). 1993. pap. text ed. 37.00 (*0-312-05023-2*) St Martin.

Religions of the World. 6th ed. Lewis M. Hopfe, Jr. LC 93-20448. (Illus.). 434p. (C). 1993. pap. text ed. 44.00 (*0-02-356931-X*, Macmillan Coll) P-H.

***Religions of the World.** 7th ed. Lewis M. Hopfe & Mark R. Woodward. (C). 1997. pap. text ed. 28.00 (*0-13-627928-7*) P-H.

***Religions of the World: Which One Should I Choose?** Larry W. Smith. (Illus.). 92p. 1996. pap. 7.95 (*1-57914-000-9*) Campbell-Smith.

***Religions of the World Explained.** Date not set. 18.95 (*0-614-18988-8*) H Holt & Co.

Religions of Tibet. Giuseppe Tucci. Tr. by Geoffrey Samuel. 1988. 40.00 (*0-520-03856-8*); pap. 16.00 (*0-520-06348-1*) U CA Pr.

***Religions of Tibet in Practice.** Donald S. Lopez. LC 96-31592. (Princeton Readings in Religion Ser.). 1997. pap. 22.50 (*0-691-01183-4*); text ed. 60.00 (*0-691-01184-2*) Princeton U Pr.

Religions on File. Diagram Group Staff. (Illus.). 200p. 1990. ring bd. 155.00 (*0-8160-2224-0*) Facts on File.

Religions-Partheien und Philosophen-Schulen (Al- Milal Wa- 'n-'ihal, Deutsch, 2 pts. in 1 vol. Abu'l-Fath Schahrastani. xxx, 763p. 1969. reprint ed. write for info. (*0-318-71561-9*) G Olms Pubs.

***Religions Philosophie Des Sohar und Ihr Verhaltnis Zur Allgemeinen Judischen Theologie.** David H. Joel. xxiv, 394p. (GER.). 1977. reprint ed. write for info. (*3-487-06355-7*) G Olms Pubs.

Religions to the Point see Religions: Encountering People of Other Faiths

Religions, Values, & Peak-Experiences. Abraham H. Maslow. 1976. mass mkt. 6.00 (*0-14-004262-8*, Penguin Bks) Viking Penguin.

Religions, Values & Peak Experiences. Abraham H. Maslow. 144p. 1994. pap. 10.95 (*0-14-019487-8*) Viking Penguin.

***Religionsbegriff bei Mircea Eliade.** Christian Wachtmann. xxviii, 251p. (GER.). 1996. 54.95 (*3-631-49843-8*) P Lang Pubng.

An Asterisk (*) at the beginning of an entry indicates that the title is appearing in BIP for the first time.

R

Religionsdidaktik Zwischen Kreuz Und Hakenkreuz: Versuche Zur Bestimmung Von Aufgaben, Zielen Und Inhalten Des Evangelischen Religionsunterrichts, Dargestellt An Den Richtlinienentwuerfen Zwischen 1993 Und 1939. Friedhelm Kraft. (Arbeiten zur Praktischen Theologie Ser.: No. 8). xxi, 282p. (GER.). (C). 1996. lib. bdg. 139.30 (3-11-014981-8) De Gruyter.

Religionsgeschichtliche Erklaerung des Neuen Testamentes: Die Abhaengigkeit des aeltesten Christentums von nichtjuedischen Religionen und philosophischen Systemen. Carl Clemen. 440p. (C). 1973. reprint ed. text ed. 150.00 (3-11-002412-8) De Gruyter.

Religionsgeschichtliche Untersuchungen. Hermann Usener. (Volkskundliche Quellen, Reihe I Ser.). xxxv, 764p. 1972. reprint ed. write for info. (3-487-04347-5) G Olms Pubs.

Religionsgespraech als Mittel der konfessionellen und politischen Auseinandersetzung im Deutschland des 16. Jahrhunderts. Marion Hollerbach. (European University Studies: Ser. 3, Vol. 165). (GER.). 1982. 53. 85 (3-8204-7015-8) P Lang Pubng.

Religionsphilosophie. Wolfgang Trillhaas. 278p. (C). 1972. 36.95 (3-11-003868-4) De Gruyter.

Religionsphilosophie. rev. ed. Heinrich Scholz. xi, 332p. (GER.). (C). 1974. reprint ed. 93.10 (3-11-002217-6) De Gruyter.

Religionsphilosophie der Juden. Samuel Hirsch. Ed. by Steven Katz. LC 79-7136. (Jewish Philosophy, Mysticism & History of Ideas Ser.). 1980. reprint ed. lib. bdg. 81.95 (0-405-12262-4) Ayer.

Religionsphilosophie des Sohar und Ihr Verhaltnis zur Allgemeinen Judischen Theologie. David H. Joel. Ed. by Steven Katz. LC 79-7139. (Jewish Philosophy, Mysticism & History of Ideas Ser.). 1980. reprint ed. lib. bdg. 37.95 (0-405-12265-9) Ayer.

***Religionsphilosophie Kants.** Albert Schweitzer. viii, 325p. (GER.). 1990. reprint ed. write for info. (3-487-05264-4) G Olms Pubs.

Religionsphilosophischen Lehren des Isaak Abravanel. Jacob Guttmann. Ed. by Steven Katz. LC 79-7134. (Jewish Philosophy, Mysticism & History of Ideas Ser.). 1980. reprint ed. lib. bdg. 17.95 (0-405-12260-8) Ayer.

***Religionsprozeb Gegen Den Zopfschulzen (1791-1799) Ein Beitrag Zur Protestantischen Lehrpflicht und Lehrzucht in Brandenburg-Preuben Gegen Ende des 18.** Johannes Tradt. (Rechtshistorische Reihe Ser.: Bd. 158). (Illus.). xxvi, 497p. (GER.). 1997. 82.95 (3-631-30866-3) P Lang Pubng.

Religionswissenschaft & das Christentum: Eine Historische Untersuchung uber das Verhaltnis von Religionswissenschaft & Theologie. Sigurd Hjelde. (Studies in the History of Religions: No. 61). 504p. (GER.). 1993. 128.50 (90-04-09922-0, NLG 195) E J Brill.

Religionswissenschaft Joachim Wachs. Rainer Flasche. (Theologische Bibliothek Toepelmann Ser.: Vol. 35). (C). 1978. 76.15 (3-11-007238-6) De Gruyter.

Religiose Allbegriff Des Aischylos. Wolfgang Kiefner. 153p. (GER.). 1965. write for info. (0-318-70612-1) G Olms Pubs.

Religiose Poesie der Juden in Spanien. Michael Sachs. Ed. by Steven Katz. LC 79-7150. (Jewish Philosophy, Mysticism & History of Ideas Ser.). 1980. reprint ed. lib. bdg. 40.95 (0-405-12285-3) Ayer.

Religiose Reden. Paul Tillich. 518p. (C). 1987. lib. bdg. 52. 35 (3-11-011486-0) De Gruyter.

Religiose Stromungen Judentum: Mit besonderer Berucksichtigung des Chassidismus. Samuel A. Horodezky. Ed. by Steven Katz. LC 79-7137. (Jewish Philosophy, Mysticism & History of Ideas Ser.). 1980. reprint ed. lib. bdg. 25.95 (0-405-12263-2) Ayer.

***Religioser Pluralismus und Interreligioses Lernen.** Ed. by Johannes A. Van der Ven & Hans-Georg Ziebertz. (Theologie & Empirie Ser.: Vol. 22). 292p. 1994. pap. 40.50 (90-390-0505-2, Pub. by KOK Pharos NE) Eisenbrauns.

Religious Accommodation in the Workplace: A Legal & Practical Handbook. 150p. 1987. 45.00 (0-87179-949-9, BSP-79) BNA Plus.

Religious Accommodations in the Workplace. Kathleen B. Hayward. LC 96-21822. 50p. 1996. spiral bd. 47.00 (0-925773-28-X) M Lee Smith.

***Religious Advocacy & American History.** Ed. by Bruce Kuklick & D. G. Hart. LC 96-40840. 232p. (Orig.). 1997. pap. 24.00 (0-8028-4260-7) Eerdmans.

Religious Aesthetics: A Theological Study of Making & Meaning. Frank B. Brown. 248p. 1990. text ed. 45.00 (0-691-07366-X); pap. text ed. 17.95 (0-691-02472-3) Princeton U Pr.

Religious Affections. Jonathan Edwards. Ed. by John E. Smith. LC 59-12702. (Works of Jonathan Edwards Ser.: Vol. 2). (Illus.). 1959. 75.00 (0-300-00966-6) Yale U Pr.

Religious Affections. Jonathan Edwards. 382p. 1994. reprint ed. pap. 13.99 (0-85151-485-5) Banner of Truth.

Religious Affections: A Christian's Character Before God. Jonathan Edwards & James Houston. 208p. 1996. pap. 9.99 (1-55661-829-8) Bethany Hse.

Religious & Anti-Religious Thought in Russia. George L. Kline. LC 68-54484. (Weil Lectures). reprint ed. 47.30 (0-317-09813-6, 2020097) Bks Demand.

Religious & Cosmic Beliefs of Central Polynesia, 2 vols. Robert W. Williamson. LC 75-35220. reprint ed. 87.50 (0-404-14300-8) AMS Pr.

Religious & Educational Philosophy of the Young Women's Christian Association. Grace H. Wilson. LC 70-177632. (Columbia University. Teachers College. Contributions to Education Ser.: No. 554). reprint ed. 37.50 (0-404-55554-3) AMS Pr.

Religious & Ethical Factors in Psychiatric Practice. Ed. by Don S. Browning et al. 313p. 1990. 33.95 (0-8304-1225-5); pap. text ed. 22.95 (0-8304-1265-4) Nelson-Hall.

Religious & Ethnic Minority Politics in South Asia. Dhirendra K. Vajpeyi. LC 88-63582. 203p. (C). 1990. 29.00 (0-913215-42-2) Riverdale Co.

Religious & Ethnic Movements in Medieval Islam. Wilfred Madelung. (Collected Studies: Vol. CS364). 352p. 1992. 98.95 (0-86078-310-3, Pub. by Variorum UK) Ashgate Pub Co.

***Religious & Human Promotion & the Contemplative Dimension of Religious Life.** Congregation for Institutes of Consecrated Life Staff & Societies of Apostolic Life Staff. 54p. pap. 0.50 (0-8198-6432-3) Pauline Bks.

Religious & Legal Thought of Samuel Ben Hofni Gaon. David Sklare. LC 96-20920. (Etudes Sur le Judaisme Medieval Ser.: No. 18). 350p. (ARA & ENG.). 1996. 105.00 (90-04-10302-3) E J Brill.

Religious & Romantic Origins of Psychoanalysis: Individuation & Integration in Post-Freudian Theory. Suzanne R. Kirschner. (Cultural Social Studies). 260p. (C). 1996. text ed. 54.95 (0-521-44401-2) Cambridge U Pr.

Religious & Romantic Origins of Psychoanalysis: Individuation & Integration in Post-Freudian Theory. Suzanne R. Kirschner. (Cultural Social Studies). 260p. (C). 1996. pap. text ed. 17.95 (0-521-55560-4) Cambridge U Pr.

Religious & Secular: Conflict & Accommodation Between Jews in Israel. Charles S. Liebman. 238p. 1990. pap. 8.95 (0-9623723-1-5) AVI CHAI.

Religious & Secular Forces in Late Tsarist Russia: Essays in Honor of Donald W. Treadgold. Ed. by Charles E. Timberlake. LC 91-44276. 376p. 1992. 35.00 (0-295-97198-3) U of Wash Pr.

Religious & Social Ritual: Interdisciplinary Explorations. Ed. by Michael B. Aune & Valerie DeMarinis. 323p. 1996. text ed. 59.50 (0-7914-2825-7); pap. text ed. 19.95 (0-7914-2826-5) State U NY Pr.

Religious & Spiritual Groups in Modern America. 2nd ed. Robert S. Ellwood, Jr. & Harry Partin. 384p. (C). 1987. pap. text ed. 44.00 (0-13-773045-4) P-H.

Religious Architecture in Louisiana. Robert W. Heck. LC 95-30434. (Illus.). 176p. (C). 1996. 29.95 (0-8071-1977-6) La State U Pr.

Religious Archives, a Complete Technical Look for the Layman. rev. ed. Kevin W. Sandifer. Ed. by Rowland P. Gill et al. (Archival Science Ser.: No. 2). 96p. (C). 1996. pap. 14.95 (0-910653-16-X, 8011C, Red River Pr) Archival Servs.

Religious Art: A Workbook for Artists & Designers. Robin Landa. 272p. 1985. 29.95 (0-13-773037-3); pap. 16.95 (0-13-773029-2) P-H.

Religious Art from the Twelfth to the Eighteenth Century. Emile Male. LC 82-47903. (Illus.). 256p. 1982. pap. text ed. 18.95 (0-691-00347-5) Princeton U Pr.

Religious Art in France: The Late Middle Ages: A Study of Medieval Iconography & Its Sources. Emile Male. Ed. by Harry Bober. Tr. by Marthiel Mathews. (Bollingen Ser.: Vol. XC, No. 3). 600p. 1986. text ed. 99.50 (0-691-09914-6) Princeton U Pr.

Religious Art in France: The Thirteenth Century-A Study of the Origins of Medieval Iconography. Emile Male. Ed. by Harry Bober. Tr. by Marthiel Mathews from FRE. LC 82-11210. (Bollingen Ser.: Vol. XC). (Illus.). 576p. 1983. text ed. 125.00 (0-691-09913-8) Princeton U Pr.

Religious Art in France: The Twelfth Century. Emile Male. LC 72-14029. (Bollingen Ser.: Vol. I, No. 90). 664p. 1978. text ed. 145.00 (0-691-09912-X) Princeton U Pr.

***Religious Art in France, the Twelfth Century: A Study of the Origins of Medieval Iconography.** Emile Male. LC 72-14029. (Bolligen Ser.: No. 1). 607p. 1978. reprint ed. pap. 173.00 (0-608-02552-6, 2063196) Bks Demand.

***Religious Art of Jacopo Bassano: Painting As Visual Exegesis.** Paolo Berdini. (Cambridge Studies in New Art History & Criticism). (Illus.). 240p. 1997. text ed. 60.00 (0-521-56170-1) Cambridge U Pr.

***Religious Arts Festival.** David Trembley & Lo-Ann Trembley. 18p. 1995. pap. 5.50 (1-877871-82-6, 3705) Ed Ministries.

Religious Aspects of Hindu Philosophy. Joseph Mullens. (C). 1991. reprint ed. 32.00 (81-7054-123-9, Pub. by Classical Pub II) S Asia.

Religious Aspects of Hypnosis. 2nd ed. William J. Bryan, Jr. Ed. by Joe Hauser. (Illus.). 80p. Date not set. reprint ed. pap. 12.95 (0-9615140-5-1) Relaxed Bks.

Religious Aspects of Swedish Immigration: A Study of Immigrant Churches. George M. Stephenson. LC 69-18790. (American Immigration Collection. Series 1). (Illus.). 1969. reprint ed. 24.95 (0-405-00539-3) Ayer.

Religious Aspects of the Conquest of Mexico. C. S. Braden. 1976. lib. bdg. 59.95 (0-8490-2510-9) Gordon Pr.

Religious Aspects of the Conquest of Mexico. Charles S. Braden. LC 74-181914. reprint ed. 54.50 (0-404-00925-5) AMS Pr.

Religious Attitude & Life in Islam. D. B. MacDonald. 336p. 1985. 230.00 (1-85077-050-6, Pub. by Darf Pubs Ltd UK) St Mut.

Religious Attitude & Life in Islam. Duncan B. Macdonald. LC 70-121277. reprint ed. 32.50 (0-404-04125-6) AMS Pr.

Religious Attitudes Toward Usury: Two Early Polemics. Ed. by Arno Press Staff & Leonard Silk. LC 79-38471. (Evolution of Capitalism Ser.). 1979. 28.95 (0-405-04135-7) Ayer.

Religious Authenticity in the Clergy. John C. Fletcher. pap. 6.75 (1-56699-088-2, OD70) Alban Inst.

Religious Autobiographies. Gary L. Comstock. LC 94-20555. 375p. 1995. pap. 31.95 (0-534-18780-3) Wadsworth Pub.

Religious Basis of Spenser's Thought. Virgil K. Whitaker. 70p. (C). 1950. reprint ed. pap. 39.95 (0-8383-0081-2) M S G Haskell Hse.

Religious Belief & Ecclesiastical Careers in Late Medieval England. Ed. by Christopher Harper-Bill. (Studies in the History of Medieval Religion: No. III). 256p. (C). 1991. 71.00 (0-85115-296-1) Boydell & Brewer.

Religious Belief & Emotional Transformation: A Light in the Heart. Paul Lauritzen. LC 91-55509. 128p. 1992. 29.50 (0-8387-5217-9) Bucknell U Pr.

Religious Belief & the Will. Louis P. Pojman. (Problems of Philosophy Ser.). 256p. (C). 1986. text ed. 44.00 (0-7102-0399-3, RKP) Routledge.

Religious Beliefs: Index of New Information with Authors, Subjects, Research Categories & References. Maxine M. Hildebrand. 160p. (Orig.). 1995. 47.50 (0-7883-0732-0); pap. 44.50 (0-7883-0733-9) ABBE Pubs Assn.

Religious Beliefs & Practices of the Sikhs in Rural Punjab. Clarence O. McMullen. (C). 1989. 18.50 (0-945921-09-8) S Asia.

Religious Beliefs of Our Presidents: From Washington to F. D. R. Franklin Steiner. LC 95-10599. (Freethought Library). 190p. 1995. pap. 16.95 (0-87975-975-5) Prometheus Bks.

Religious Bibliographies in Serial Literature: A Guide. Michael J. Walsh et al. LC 81-312. 216p. 1981. text ed. 49.95 (0-313-22987-2, WRB/, Greenwood Pr) Greenwood.

Religious Bigotry: A Threat to Ordered State. Madhu Limaye. (C). 1995. 18.00 (81-202-0409-3, Pub. by Ajanta II) S Asia.

Religious Bodies in the United States: A Directory. J. Gordon Melton. LC 91-41564. (Religious Information Systems Ser.: Vol. 1). 340p. 1992. text ed. 55.00 (0-8153-0806-X, H# 1568) Garland.

Religious Bodies of America. F. E. Mayer & Arthur C. Piepkorn. 616p. 1968. 21.95 (0-570-03294-6, 15-1714) Concordia.

Religious Books for Children: An Annotated Bibliography. rev. ed. Patricia Pearl. 40p. 1988. 8.25 (0-915324-21-0) CSLA.

Religious Books for Children: An Annotated Bibliography. 3rd rev. ed. Patricia P. Dole. LC 93-4930. (Bibliography Ser.). 40p. 1993. reprint ed. pap. 8.25 (0-915324-35-0) CSLA.

***Religious Books in Prints.** Whitaker. (C). 1989. write for info. (0-85021-191-3, Pub. by J Whitaker UK) Bowker.

Religious Books, 1876-1982, 4 vol. set. 4389p. 1983. 245.00 (0-8352-1602-0) Bowker.

Religious Celebration of the Quinceanera. M.A.C.C. Team Staff. 50p. (SPA.). 1980. write for info. (0-614-04881-8) Mex Am Cult.

Religious Challenge to the State. Ed. by Matthew C. Moen & Lowell S. Gustafson. (C). 1991. 54.95 (0-87722-856-6) Temple U Pr.

Religious Change & Continuity: Sociological Perspectives. Ed. by Harry M. Johnson. LC 79-83574. (Jossey-Bass Social & Behavioral Science Ser.). 379p. reprint ed. pap. 108.10 (0-685-16236-2, 2027756) Bks Demand.

Religious Change in America. Andrew M. Greeley. LC 88-29417. (Social Trends in the United States Ser.). (Illus.). 144p. 1989. 32.00 (0-674-75840-4) HUP.

Religious Change in America. Andrew M. Greeley. (Illus.). 152p. 1996. pap. 14.95 (0-674-75841-2) HUP.

***Religious Change in Europe 1650-1914: Essays for John McManners.** Ed. by Nigel Aston. 464p. 1997. 95.00 (0-19-820596-1) OUP.

Religious Change in Zambia: Exploratory Studies. Wim M. Van Binsbergen, pseud. (Monographs from the African Studies Centre, Leiden). (Illus.). 416p. 1981. 75.00 (0-7103-0000-X); pap. text ed. 19.50 (0-7103-0012-3) Routledge Chapman & Hall.

Religious Chastity: An Ethnological Study, by John Main (Pseud.) Elsie W. Parsons. LC 72-9672. reprint ed. 54. 00 (0-404-57489-0) AMS Pr.

Religious Clip Art Book. Claudia Ortega. (Illus.). 32p. (Orig.). 1989. pap. 24.95 (1-55612-311-6) Sheed & Ward MO.

Religious Colleges & Universities in America: A Selected Bibliography. Thomas C. Hunt. LC 88-14737. 380p. 1988. text ed. 66.00 (0-8240-6648-0) Garland.

Religious Concerns in Contemporary Education. Philip H. Phenix. LC 59-11329. 118p. reprint ed. 33.70 (0-8357-9605-1, 2016949) Bks Demand.

Religious Confessions & Confessants. Anna R. Burr. 1977. lib. bdg. 59.95 (0-8490-2511-7) Gordon Pr.

Religious Conflict in Social Context: The Resurgence of Orthodox Judaism in Frankfurt Am Main, 1838-1877. Robert Liberles. LC 84-27981. (Contributions to the Study of Religion Ser.: No. 13). xvi, 297p. 1985. text ed. 59.95 (0-313-24806-0, LRX/) Greenwood.

Religious Consciousness. Govind S. Ghurye. 383p. 1965. 24.95 (0-318-37153-7) Asia Bk Corp.

Religious Controversies of the Nineteenth Century. A. O. Cockshut. LC 66-18225. 271p. 1966. reprint ed. pap. 77. 30 (0-8357-3821-3, 2057031) Bks Demand.

Religious Controversy in British India: Dialogues in South Asian Languages. Ed. by Kenneth W. Jones. LC 90-24210. (SUNY Series in Religious Studies). 291p. (C). 1992. text ed. 64.50 (0-7914-0827-2); pap. text ed. 21.95 (0-7914-0828-0) State U NY Pr.

Religious Conversion Movements in South Asia: Continuities & Change, 1800-1990. Ed. by Geoffrey A. Oddie. (Religion & Society in South Asia Ser.). 280p. (C). 1997. text ed. 48.00 (0-7007-0472-8, Pub. by Curzon Press UK) UH Pr.

Religious Conversions in India. Brojendra N. Bannerjee. 384p. 1982. 29.95 (0-940500-28-0, Pub. by Harnam Pub II) Asia Bk Corp.

Religious Conviction. Grif Stockley. 1994. 21.00 (0-671-79869-3) S&S Trade.

Religious Conviction. Grif Stockley. 1995. reprint ed. mass mkt. 5.99 (0-8041-1255-X) Ivy Books.

Religious Convictions & Political Choice. Kent Greenawalt. 288p. 1987. 55.00 (0-19-504913-6) OUP.

Religious Convictions & Political Choice. Kent Greenawalt. 280p. 1991. reprint ed. pap. 19.95 (0-19-506779-7) OUP.

Religious Crises in Modern America. Martin E. Marty. LC 81-80740. (Charles Edmondson Historical Lectures). 40p. (Orig.). 1981. pap. 5.95 (0-918954-26-6) Baylor Univ Pr.

Religious Critic in American Culture. William Dean. LC 93-42683. 256p. (C). 1994. text ed. 54.50 (0-7914-2113-9); pap. text ed. 16.95 (0-7914-2114-7) State U NY Pr.

Religious Cults Associated with the Amazons. Florence M. Anderson. LC 73-158253. reprint ed. 37.50 (0-404-00749-X) AMS Pr.

Religious Cults Associated with the Amazons. F. M. Bennett. 84p. (C). 1987. reprint ed. lib. bdg. 30.00 (0-89241-204-6) Caratzas.

Religious Cults in America. Ed. by Robert E. Long. LC 94-16329. (Reference Shelf Ser.: Vol. 66, No. 4). 1994. 15. 00 (0-8242-0855-2) Wilson.

Religious Cults of the Pai-I along the Burma-Yunnan Border. Ju-Kang Tien. LC 87-137760. (Monograph - Southeast Asia Program, Cornell University Ser.). 144p. reprint ed. pap. 41.10 (0-8357-2557-X, 2040248) Bks Demand.

Religious Culture in the Sixteenth Century: Preaching, Rhetoric, Spirituality, & Reform. John W. O'Malley. (Collected Studies: No. CS 404). 294p. 1993. 82.95 (0-86078-369-3, Pub. by Variorum UK) Ashgate Pub Co.

***Religious Culture of North-Eastern India.** N. N. Bhattacharyya. (C). 1995. 22.00 (81-7304-116-4, Pub. by Manohar II) S Asia.

***Religious Cultures of the World: A Statistical Reference.** Philip M. Parker. LC 96-43833. (Cross-Cultural Statistical Encyclopedia of the World: Vol. 1). 160p. 1997. text ed. 69.50 (0-313-29768-1, Greenwood Pr) Greenwood.

Religious Dances in the Christian & in Popular Medicine. Eugene L. Backman. Ed. by E. Classen. LC 77-8069. 364p. 1977. reprint ed. text ed. 65.00 (0-8371-9678-7, BARD, Greenwood Pr) Greenwood.

Religious Denominations in the United States: Their Past History, Present Condition, & Doctrines. Israel D. Rupp. LC 72-2943. reprint ed. 115.00 (0-404-10709-5) AMS Pr.

Religious Design of Hemingway's Early Fiction. Larry E. Grimes. LC 85-1183. (Studies in Modern Literature: No. 50). 166p. reprint ed. pap. 47.40 (0-8357-1635-X, 2070435) Bks Demand.

Religious Development in Childhood & Adolescence. Ed. by Fritz K. Oser & W. George Scarlett. LC 85-644581. (New Directions for Child Development Ser.: No. CD 52). 1991. 19.00 (1-55542-788-X) Jossey-Bass.

Religious Dialectics of Pain & Imagination. Bradford T. Stull. LC 93-39435. (Rhetoric & Theology Ser.). 196p. 1994. pap. text ed. 19.95 (0-7914-2082-5) State U NY Pr.

Religious Dialectics of Pain & Imagination. Bradford T. Stull. LC 93-39435. (SUNY Series in Rhetoric & Theology). 196p. 1994. text ed. 59.50 (0-7914-2081-7) State U NY Pr.

Religious Dimension in Hispanic Los Angeles: A Protestant Case Study. Clifton L. Holland. LC 74-5123. 541p. (Orig.). 1974. pap. 11.95 (0-87808-309-X) William Carey Lib.

Religious Dimension in the Thought of Giambattista Vico 1668-1744, Pt. 1: The Early Metaphysics. John Milbank. LC 91-32629. (Studies in the History of Philosophy: Vol. 23). 364p. 1991. lib. bdg. 99.95 (0-7734-9694-7) E Mellen.

Religious Dimension in the Thought of Giambattista Vico (1668-1744), Vol. 11: Language, Law & History. John Milbank. LC 91-32629. 292p. 1993. text ed. 89.95 (0-7734-9215-1) E Mellen.

Religious Dimension of Education in a Catholic School: Guidelines for Reflection & Renewal. Vatican Congregation for Catholic Education Staff. 61p. (Orig.). 1988. pap. 3.95 (1-55586-231-4) US Catholic.

Religious Dimension of Education in Catholic School. Veritas Publications Staff. 1989. pap. 15.00 (1-85390-072-9, Pub. by Veritas IE) St Mut.

Religious Dimension of Jane Austen's Novels. Gene Koppel. Ed. by Juliet McMaster. LC 87-25540. (Nineteenth-Century Studies). 154p. reprint ed. 43.70 (0-8357-1858-1, 2070622) Bks Demand.

Religious Dimensions of Biblical Texts: Greima's Structral Semiotics & Biblical Exegesis. Daniel Patte. 410p. 1990. 31.95 (1-55540-385-9); pap. 20.95 (1-55540-386-7, 06 06 19) Scholars Pr GA.

***Religious Dimensions of Child & Family Life: Reflections on the UN Convention on the Rights of the Child.** Ed. by Harold Coward & Philip Cook. LC 96-910613. 203p. 1996. pap. 17.95 (1-55058-104-X) Wilfrid Laurier.

Religious Dimensions of Confucianism. Rodney L. Taylor. LC 89-21724. (SUNY Series in Religious Studies). 198p. 1990. text ed. 64.50 (0-7914-0311-4); pap. text ed. 21.95 (0-7914-0312-2) State U NY Pr.

Religious Discourse: Thanksgiving Day Sermon, November 26, 1789. Gershom M. Seixas. LC 77-7298. (Illus.). 1977. reprint ed. pap. 2.00 (0-916790-00-2) Jewish Hist.

***Religious Diversity & American Religious History: Studies in Traditions & Cultures.** Ed. by Walter H. Conser, Jr. & Sumner B. Twiss. LC 97-26767. 312p. 1997. text ed. 55.00 (0-8203-1917-1) U of Ga Pr.

An Asterisk (*) at the beginning of an entry indicates that the title is appearing in BIP for the first time.

R

*__Religious Diversity & American Religious History: Studies in Traditions & Cultures.__ Ed. by Walter H. Conser, Jr. & Sumner B. Twiss. LC 97-26767. 312p. 1997. pap. text ed. 25.00 (*0-8203-1918-X*) U of Ga Pr.

Religious Diversity & Human Rights. Irene Bloom. LC 96-18261. 368p. 1996. 49.50 (*0-231-10416-2*); pap. 18.50 (*0-231-10417-0*) Col U Pr.

Religious Diversity & Social Change: American Cities, 1890-1906. Kevin J. Christiano. (Illus.). 272p. 1988. text ed. 75.00 (*0-521-34145-0*) Cambridge U Pr.

*__Religious Diversity in Public Schools: A Suburban Case Study.__ Deborah J. Levine. 64p. (Orig.). 1996. spiral bd. write for info. (*0-9640706-9-3*) Cock-a-Hoop.

Religious Dogmatics & the Evolution of Societies. Niklas Luhmann. Tr. by Peter Beyer. LC 84-8976. (Studies in Religion & Society: Vol. 9). 192p. 1984. lib. bdg. 79.95 (*0-88946-866-4*) E Mellen.

Religious Drama: Ends & Means. Harold A. Ehrensperger & Stanley Lehrer. LC 77-22986. (Illus.). 287p. 1977. reprint ed. text ed. 45.00 (*0-8371-9744-9*, EHRD, Greenwood Pr) Greenwood.

Religious Drama, Vol. 1: Five Plays. Ed. by Marvin Halverson. 1990. 18.00 (*0-8446-2792-5*) Peter Smith.

Religious Drama, Vol. 2: 21 Medieval Mystery & Morality Plays. Ed. by E. Martin Browne. 1990. 18.00 (*0-8446-2793-3*) Peter Smith.

Religious Drama, Vol. 3. Ed. by Marvin Halverson. 1990. 18.00 (*0-8446-2794-1*) Peter Smith.

Religious Education: Chicago, 1906-1955. reprint ed. lib. bdg. 2,250.00 (*0-685-77259-4*) AMS Pr.

Religious Education: Philosophical Perspectives. John Sealey. Ed. by Philip Snelders & Colin Wringe. (Introductory Studies in Philosophy of Education). 120p. 1985. text ed. 34.95 (*0-04-370130-2*); pap. text ed. 14.95 (*0-04-370131-0*) Routledge Chapman & Hall.

Religious Education & Human Development. Michael Grimmitt. 424p. (C). 1988. 60.00 (*0-85597-401-X*, Pub. by McCrimmon Pub) St Mut.

*__Religious Education & the Law: A Handbook for Parish Catechetical Leaders.__ Mary A. Shaughnessy. 137p. (Orig.). 1996. pap. 12.00 (*1-55833-176-X*) Natl Cath Educ.

Religious Education & Theology. Ed. by Norma H. Thompson. LC 81-17852. 254p. (Orig.). 1982. pap. 16.95 (*0-89135-029-2*) Religious Educ.

Religious Education & Young Adults. Donal O'Leary & Teresa Sallnow. (C). 1988. 60.00 (*0-85439-229-7*, Pub. by St Paul Pubns UK) St Mut.

Religious Education As a Second Language. Gabriel Moran. LC 89-33871. 254p. (Orig.). 1989. pap. 18.95 (*0-89135-072-1*) Religious Educ.

Religious Education As Social Transformation. Ed. by Allen J. Moore. LC 88-36413. 258p. (Orig.). 1989. pap. 18.95 (*0-89135-069-1*) Religious Educ.

Religious Education at a Crossroads: Moving on in the Freedom of the Spirit. Francoise Darcy-Berube. LC 95-22291. 176p. 1996. 14.95 (*0-8091-0476-8*) Paulist Pr.

Religious Education, Catechesis & Freedom. Kenneth Barker. LC 81-13962. 255p. (Orig.). 1981. pap. 2.95 (*0-89135-028-4*) Religious Educ.

Religious Education Encounters Liberation Theology. Daniel S. Schipani. LC 88-13093. 276p. (Orig.). (C). 1988. pap. 19.95 (*0-89135-064-0*) Religious Educ.

Religious Education Five-Twelve. Derek Bastide. 1987. 55.00 (*1-85000-149-9*, Falmer Pr); pap. 29.00 (*1-85000-150-2*) Taylor & Francis.

Religious Education Handbook: A Practical Parish Guide. James P. Enswiler. LC 79-26008. 108p. (Orig.). 1980. pap. 4.95 (*0-8189-0398-8*) Alba.

Religious Education in German Schools: An Historical Approach. Ernst C. Helmreich. LC 59-11509. 381p. 1959. 37.00 (*0-674-75850-1*) HUP.

Religious Education in the Infant School. Hilda Johnson & Ann Byrne. (C). 1988. 50.00 (*0-85439-228-9*, Pub. by St Paul Pubns UK) St Mut.

Religious Education in the Primary School: Managing Diversity. Elizabeth Hughes. (Education Ser.). (Illus.). 160p. 1994. 70.00 (*0-304-32658-5*); pap. 19.95 (*0-304-32656-9*) Cassell.

Religious Education in the Secondary School: Prospects for Religious Literacy. Andrew Wright. 128p. 1993. pap. 23.00 (*1-85346-242-X*, Pub. by D Fulton UK) Taylor & Francis.

Religious Education in the Small Membership Church. Ed. by Nancy T. Foltz. 234p. (Orig.). 1990. pap. 16.95 (*0-89135-077-2*) Religious Educ.

Religious Education Ministry with Youth. Ed. by D. Campbell Wyckoff & Don Richter. LC 81-19239. 318p. (Orig.). (C). 1982. pap. 13.95 (*0-89135-030-6*) Religious Educ.

Religious Education, Nineteen Forty-Four to Nineteen Eighty-Four. Ed. by A. G. Wedderspoon. 238p. 1968. 4.95 (*0-87921-063-X*); pap. 2.50 (*0-87921-064-8*) Attic Pr.

Religious Education of Older Adults. Linda J. Vogel. LC 83-21109. 196p. (Orig.). (C). 1984. pap. 12.95 (*0-89135-040-3*) Religious Educ.

Religious Education of Preschool Children. Lucie W. Barber. LC 80-27623. 196p. (Orig.). 1981. pap. 2.95 (*0-89135-026-8*) Religious Educ.

Religious Education Seven-Eleven: Developing Primary Teaching Skills. Terence Copley. LC 94-2252. (Curriculum in Primary Practice Ser.). 112p. (Orig.). (YA). (gr. 7-11). 1994. pap. text ed. 17.95 (*0-415-10125-5*, B4413) Routledge.

Religious Education, 1960-1993: An Annotated Bibliography. D. Campbell Wyckoff & George Brown. LC 94-24125. (Bibliographies & Indexes in Religious Studies: Vol. 33). 325p. 1995. text ed. 75.00 (*0-313-28453-9*, Greenwood Pr) Greenwood.

Religious Enthusiasm in the New World: Heresy to Revolution. David S. Lovejoy. 295p. 1985. 37.00 (*0-674-75864-1*) HUP.

Religious Evolution. Robert N. Bellah. (Reprint Series in Sociology). (C). 1993. reprint ed. pap. text ed. 1.90 (*0-8290-2641-X*, S-546) Irvington.

Religious Experience. Wayne Proudfoot. LC 84-23928. 1985. pap. 14.95 (*0-520-06128-4*) U CA Pr.

Religious Experience. 5th ed. Ninian Smart. 1996. pap. text ed. 41.00 (*0-02-412141-X*, Macmillan Coll) P-H.

Religious Experience: Its Nature, Types, & Validity. Alan C. Bouquet. LC 75-40997. 140p. 1976. reprint ed. text ed. 55.00 (*0-8371-8714-1*, BORL, Greenwood Pr) Greenwood.

Religious Experience & Ecological Responsibility, Vol. 3. Ed. by Don Crosby & Charles Hardwick. (American Liberal Religious Thought Ser.). 664p. (C). 1995. 74.95 (*0-8204-2790-X*) P Lang Pubng.

Religious Experience & Lay Society in T'ang China: A Reading of Tai Fu's Kuang-i Chi. Glen Dudbridge. (Cambridge Studies in Chinese History, Literature & Institutions). (Illus.). 285p. (C). 1995. text ed. 59.95 (*0-521-48223-2*) Cambridge U Pr.

*__Religious Experience & Mysticism: Otherness As Experience of Transcendence.__ Jose C. Nieto. 288p. 1997. 57.50 (*0-7618-0765-9*) U Pr of Amer.

*__Religious Experience & Mysticism: Otherness As Experience of Transcendence.__ Jose C. Nieto. 288p. 1997. pap. 34.50 (*0-7618-0766-7*) U Pr of Amer.

Religious Experience & Religious Belief. George B. Wall. LC 94-25225. 348p. (C). 1995. pap. text ed. 39.50 (*0-8191-9833-1*); lib. bdg. 63.00 (*0-8191-9832-3*) U Pr of Amer.

Religious Experience & Religious Belief: Essays in the Epistemology of Religion. Ed. by Joseph Runzo & Graig K. Ihara. LC 86-1614. 160p. (C). 1986. pap. text ed. 19.50 (*0-8191-5293-5*) U Pr of Amer.

Religious Experience of John Humphrey Noyes. Ed. by George W. Noyes. 1923. 39.95 (*0-8156-8060-0*) Syracuse U Pr.

Religious Experience of John Humphrey Noyes, Founder of the Oneida Community. John H. Noyes. Ed. by George W. Noyes. (Select Bibliographies Reprint Ser.). 1977. reprint ed. 29.95 (*0-8369-5750-4*) Ayer.

Religious Experience of Mankind. 3rd ed. Ninian Smart. LC 83-20169. (Illus.). 634p. 1984. pap. text ed. write for info. (*0-02-412130-4*, Macmillan Coll) P-H.

Religious Experience of the Primitive Church Proir to the Influence of Paul. P. G. Hopwood. 1977. lib. bdg. 59.95 (*0-8490-2512-5*) Gordon Pr.

Religious Experiences of Tommy: An Adult Novel. Bernard Adams. LC 95-80596. 192p. (Orig.). 1996. pap. 9.95 (*0-910042-75-6*) Allegheny.

Religious Explanation & Scientific Ideology. Jesse Hobbs. LC 93-6954. (Toronto Studies in Religion: Vol. 17). 234p. (C). 1994. text ed. 45.95 (*0-8204-2197-9*) P Lang Pubng.

Religious Explanations: A Model from the Sciences. Edward L. Schoen. LC 84-24237. xiv, 226p. 1985. text ed. 35.95 (*0-8223-0616-6*) Duke.

*__Religious Facilities.__ Meisei Co., Ltd. Editors. (Illus.). 224p. 1997. 85.00 (*4-938812-27-4*, Pub. by Meisei Co Ltd JA) Bks Nippan.

Religious Factor: A Sociological Study of Religion's Impact on Politics, Economics, & Family Life. Gerhard E. Lenski. LC 77-1275. 381p. 1977. reprint ed. text ed. 38.50 (*0-8371-9506-3*, LERF, Greenwood Pr) Greenwood.

Religious Faith & World Culture. Ed. by Amandus W. Loos. LC 71-128270. (Essay Index Reprint Ser.). 1977. 23.95 (*0-8369-1976-9*) Ayer.

Religious Faith Meets Modern Science. Paulinus F. Forsthoefel. LC 94-14611. 160p. (C). 1994. pap. 9.95 (*0-8189-0704-5*) Alba.

Religious Faith of Great Men. Archer Wallace. LC 67-26792. (Essay Index Reprint Ser.). 1977. 19.95 (*0-8369-0968-2*) Ayer.

Religious Fanaticism. Hannah W. Smith. Ed. & Intro. by Ray Strachey. LC 72-8252. Orig. Title: Group Movements of the Past & Experiments in Guidance. reprint ed. 49.50 (*0-404-11005-3*) AMS Pr.

Religious Folk Songs of the Negro. Ed. by Robert N. Dett. LC 72-1595. reprint ed. 29.50 (*0-404-09920-3*) AMS Pr.

Religious Folk Songs of the Negro. Hampton Institute Staff. LC 72-1624. reprint ed. 20.00 (*0-404-08312-9*) AMS Pr.

Religious Foundations of Medieval Stamford. J. S. Haatley & A. Roger. (C). 1974. text ed. 40.00 (*0-685-22170-9*, Pub. by Univ Nottingham UK) St Mut.

Religious Foundations of the Jewish State: The Concept & Practice of Jewish Statehood from Biblical Times to the Modern State of Israel. Mendell Lewittes. LC 94-17488. 284p. 1994. pap. 24.95 (*1-56821-301-8*) Aronson.

Religious Freedom. L. Pfeffer. Ed. by Franklyn S. Haiman. (To Protect These Rights Ser.). 192p. 1991. pap. 12.95 (*0-8442-6001-0*, Natl Textbk) NTC Pub Grp.

Religious Freedom: Belief, Practice & the Public Interest. James C. Schott. (Public Issues Ser.). (Illus.). 68p. (Orig.). (YA). (gr. 9-12). 1991. pap. 3.00 (*0-89994-358-6*); teacher ed., pap. 2.00 (*0-89994-359-4*) Soc Sci Ed.

Religious Freedom: Separation & Free Exercise, 2 vols. Ed. by Paul L. Murphy. (Bill of Rights & American Legal History Ser.). 952p. 1990. reprint ed. text ed. 75.00 (*0-8240-5862-3*) Garland.

*__Religious Freedom & the Position of Islam in Western Europe: Opportunities & Obstacles in the Acquisition of Equal Rights.__ Ed. by W. A. Shadid & P. S. Van Koningsveld. 230p. 1995. pap. 37.50 (*90-390-0065-4*, Pub. by KOK Pharos NE) Eisenbrauns.

Religious Freedom in Spain: Its Ebb & Flow. John D. Hughey. LC 77-119935. (Select Bibliographies Reprint Ser.). 1977. reprint ed. 23.95 (*0-8369-5378-9*) Ayer.

Religious Freedom in the Education Process: A Research Guide to Religion in Education (1950-1992) Deborah Mayo-Jefferies. LC 94-8623. (Legal Research Guides Ser.). 1994. 32.50 (*0-89941-871-6*, 308170) W S Hein.

Religious Fringe: A History of Alternative Religions in America. Richard Kyle. LC 93-7443. 468p. (Orig.). 1993. pap. 17.99 (*0-8308-1766-2*, 1766) InterVarsity.

Religious Function of the Psyche. Lionel Corbett. LC 95-25778. 272p. (C). 1996. pap. 18.95 (*0-415-14401-9*); text ed. 59.95 (*0-415-14400-0*) Routledge.

Religious Fundamentalism & American Education: The Battle for the Public Schools. Eugene F. Provenzo, Jr. LC 89-4456. (SUNY Series, Frontiers in Education). 134p. 1990. text ed. 59.50 (*0-7914-0217-7*); pap. text ed. 19.95 (*0-7914-0218-5*) State U NY Pr.

Religious Fundamentalisms & Global Conflict. R. Scott Appleby. Ed. by Nancy L. Hoepli. (Headline Ser.: No. 301). (Illus.). 80p. (Orig.). 1994. pap. 5.95 (*0-87124-157-9*) Foreign Policy.

*__Religious Games to Sharpen Your Knowledge of the Roman Catholic Faith.__ unabridged ed. Mabel Conde. (Illus.). 20p. 1997. pap. write for info. (*0-9658473-0-6*) M Conde.

Religious Hierarchy & Feudal Structure in Medieval Life & Thought. Pref. by Bessie W. Jones. 198p. (Orig.). (C). 1989. pap. text ed. write for info. (*0-318-65404-0*) Liberal Arts Pr.

Religious Higher Education in the United States: A Source Book. Ed. by Thomas C. Hunt & James C. Carper. LC 95-36782. (Source Books on Education: Vol. 46). 648p. 1995. text ed. 99.00 (*0-8153-1636-4*, SS950) Garland.

Religious History of America. rev. ed. Edwin S. Gaustad. LC 89-45746. (Illus.). 381p. 1990. reprint ed. pap. 24.00 (*0-06-063094-9*) Harper SF.

Religious History of Julia Evelina Smith's 1876 Translation of the Holy Bible: Doing More Than Any Man Has Ever Done. Susan J. Shaw. LC 92-23479. 360p. 1992. text ed. 99.95 (*0-7734-9840-0*) E Mellen.

Religious History of the American People. S. E. Ahlstrom. LC 72-151564. (Illus.). 1174p. 1972. 60.00 (*0-300-01475-9*) Yale U Pr.

Religious History of the American People. S. E. Ahlstrom. LC 72-151564. (Illus.). 1174p. 1974. pap. 27.00 (*0-300-01762-6*) Yale U Pr.

Religious Holidays & Calendars: An Encyclopaedic Handbook. Ed. by Aidan A. Kelly. 350p. 1993. lib. bdg. 64.00 (*1-55888-348-7*) Omnigraphics Inc.

*__Religious Holidays & Calendars: An Encyclopedic Handbook.__ 2nd ed. Ed. by Karen Bellenir. LC 97-24845. 350p. 1997. lib. bdg. 70.00 (*0-7808-0258-6*) Omnigraphics Inc.

Religious Human Rights in Global Perspective: Legal Perspectives. John F. Witte, Jr. Ed. by Johan D. Van Der Vyver. LC 95-53024. 1996. lib. bdg. 192.50 (*90-411-0177-2*, Pub. by M Nijhoff NE) Kluwer Ac.

*__Religious Human Rights in Global Perspective: Legal Perspectives.__ Ed. by John F. Witte, Jr. & Johan D. Van der Vyver. pap. 29.95 (*90-411-0180-2*) Scholars Pr GA.

*__Religious Human Rights in Global Perspective: Religious Perspectives.__ Ed. by John F. Witte, Jr. & Johan D. Van der Vyver. pap. 29.95 (*90-411-0179-9*) Scholars Pr GA.

Religious Human Rights in Global Perspectives: Religious Perspectives. Ed. by John F. Witte, Jr. & Johan D. Van der Vyver. LC 95-53025. 1996. text ed. 192.50 (*90-411-0176-4*, Pub. by M Nijhoff NE) Kluwer Ac.

Religious Humor: 409 Bits of Humor for Preachers, Teachers & Public Speakers. Walter M. Buescher. LC 95-25439. 56p. (Orig.). 1996. pap. 9.95 (*0-7880-0707-6*) CSS OH.

Religious Ideas of Harriet Beecher Stowe: Her Gospel of Womanhood. Gayle Kimball. LC 82-20377. (Studies in Women & Religion: Vol. 8). 216p. (C). 1982. lib. bdg. 89.95 (*0-88946-544-4*) E Mellen.

Religious Imagery in the Theatre of Tirso de Molina. Ann N. Hughes. LC 84-10754. (Sesquicentennial Ser.). xii, 152p. 1984. 13.50 (*0-86554-131-0*, MUP/H122) Mercer Univ Pr.

Religious Imagination. James P. Mackey. 256p. 1986. 25.00 (*0-85224-512-2*, Pub. by Edinburgh U Pr UK) Col U Pr.

Religious Imagination & Language in Emerson & Nietzsche. Irena S. Makarushka. 1994. text ed. 49.95 (*0-312-12022-2*) St Martin.

Religious Imagination & the Body: A Feminist Analysis. Paula M. Cooey. LC 93-30807. (Illus.). 216p. 1994. 38.00 (*0-19-508735-6*) OUP.

Religious Imagination in New Guinea. Ed. by Gilbert Herdtand & Michele Stephen. LC 89-30376. 320p. (C). 1989. text ed. 48.00 (*0-8135-1457-6*); pap. text ed. 17.95 (*0-8135-1458-4*) Rutgers U Pr.

Religious Impact on the Nation State: The Nigerian Predicament. Pat Williams & Toyin Falola. 360p. (C). 1995. 68.95 (*1-85972-073-0*, Pub. by Avebury Pub UK) Ashgate Pub Co.

Religious Impulse: A Quest for Innocence. Terrence Webster-Doyle. (Sane & Intelligent Living Ser.). 116p. 1989. pap. 9.95 (*0-942941-14-4*) Atrium Soc Educ.

Religious Information Sources: A Worldwide Guide. J. Gordon Melton & Michael A. Koszegi. LC 91-47697. (Religious Information Systems Ser.: Vol. 2). 581p. 1992. text ed. 75.00 (*0-8153-0859-0*, H#1593) Garland.

Religious Institute in Transition: The Story of Three General Chapters. Luke Salm. LC 92-74818. (Illus.). 270p. 1992. pap. 10.00 (*0-9623279-8-0*) Lasallian Pubns.

Religious Institutions, Vol. 13. Ed. by Craig Calhoun. (Comparative Social Research Ser.). 248p. 1992. 73.25 (*1-55938-238-4*) Jai Pr.

Religious Institutions & Women's Leadership: New Roles Inside the Mainstream. Ed. by Catherine Wessinger & Frederick Denny. LC 95-40226. (Studies in Comparative Religion). 420p. 1996. pap. text ed. 24.95 (*1-57003-073-1*) U of SC Pr.

Religious Instruction of the Negroes in the United States. Charles C. Jones. LC 70-149869. (Black Heritage Library Collection). 1977. 25.95 (*0-8369-8718-7*) Ayer.

Religious Instruction of the Negroes in the United States. Charles C. Jones. LC 73-82466. 277p. 1970. reprint ed. text ed. 35.00 (*0-8371-1645-7*, JOI&, Greenwood Pr) Greenwood.

*__Religious Inventions: Four Essays.__ Max Charlesworth. LC 96-37027. 168p. (C). 1997. 54.95 (*0-521-59076-0*) Cambridge U Pr.

*__Religious Inventions: Four Essays.__ Max Charlesworth. LC 96-37027. 168p. (C). 1997. pap. 18.95 (*0-521-59927-X*) Cambridge U Pr.

Religious Investigations of William James. Henry S. Levinson. LC 80-26109. 323p. reprint ed. pap. 92.10 (*0-7837-3767-X*, 2043584) Bks Demand.

Religious Issues & Interreligious Dialogues: An Analysis & Sourcebook of Developments since 1945. Ed. by Charles W. Fu & Gerhard E. Spiegler. LC 88-21398. 703p. 1989. text ed. 135.00 (*0-313-23239-3*, FUI/, Greenwood Pr) Greenwood.

*__Religious Itinerary of a Ghanaian People: The Kasena & the Christian Gospel.__ Allison M. Howell. LC 97-6388. (Studies in the Intercultural History of Christianity). 1997. write for info. (*0-8204-3256-3*) P Lang Pubng.

Religious Judgement: A Developmental Perspective. Fritz K. Oser & Paul Gmunder. Tr. by Norbert F. Hahn from GER. Orig. Title: Der Mensch: Stufen Seiner Religiosen Entwicklung. 235p. (Orig.). 1991. pap. 18.95 (*0-89135-081-0*) Religious Educ.

Religious Kings of the Sheepfold. Paul Grier. 126p. (Orig.). 1994. per. 10.95 (*0-9632190-7-3*) Longwood.

Religious Knowledge. Paul F. Schmidt. LC 79-8726. ix, 147p. 1981. reprint ed. text ed. 52.50 (*0-313-22188-X*, SCRK, Greenwood Pr) Greenwood.

Religious Language & Complementarity. John Losee. 280p. (C). 1991. lib. bdg. 49.50 (*0-8191-8371-7*) U Pr of Amer.

Religious Language & the Problem of Religious Knowledge. Ed. by Ronald E. Santoni. LC 68-27352. 382p. (C). reprint ed. 108.90 (*0-8357-9238-2*, 2017640) Bks Demand.

Religious Language of Thomas Traherne's Centuries. Kenneth J. Ames. (Religion & Literature Ser.). 1979. lib. bdg. 250.00 (*0-87700-260-6*) Revisionist Pr.

Religious Law in the Israel Legal System. Izhark Englard. 243p. 1986. 40.00 (*1-57588-356-2*, 304410) W S Hein.

Religious Leaders of America. Ed. by J. Gordon Melton. 750p. 1991. 90.00 (*0-8103-4921-3*) Gale.

Religious Leaders of American: A Biographical Guide to Founders & Leaders of Religious Bodies, Churches, & Spiritual Groups in North America. 2nd ed. J. Gordon Melton. 700p. 1998. 90.00 (*0-8103-8878-2*, 008162) Gale.

Religious Leadership: Personality, History & Sacred Authority. Richard A. Hutch. LC 90-36161. (Toronto Studies in Religion: Vol. 10). 340p. (C). 1990. text ed. 54.95 (*0-8204-1347-X*) P Lang Pubng.

Religious Liberals Read the Bible. John A. Buehrens. 64p. (Orig.). 1989. pap. 8.00 (*0-9622111-4-1*) Unitarian Ch All Souls.

*__Religious Liberties: Paul VI & Dignitatis Humanae.__ Ed. by John T. Ford. 202p. (Orig.). (C). 1997. pap. text ed. 24.95 (*88-382-3721-2*) Cath U Pr.

Religious Liberties in the Crossfire of Creeds. Franklin H. Littell. 169p. (Orig.). 1978. 5.00 (*0-931214-01-7*) Ecumenical Phila.

*__Religious Liberty.__ Walter Shurden. LC 97-14477. (Proclaiming the Baptist Vision Ser.). 1997. write for info. (*1-57312-169-X*) Smyth & Helwys.

Religious Liberty: An Inquiry. M. Searle Bates. LC 77-166096. (Civil Liberties in American History Ser.). 1972. reprint ed. lib. bdg. 59.50 (*0-306-70235-5*) Da Capo.

Religious Liberty: Catholic Struggles with Pluralism. John C. Murray. Ed. by J. Leon Hooper. LC 92-17829. (Library of Theological Ethics). 256p. (Orig.). 1993. pap. 18.00 (*0-664-25360-1*) Westminster John Knox.

Religious Liberty: The Christian Roots of Our Fundamental Freedoms. E. Glenn Hinson. 144p. 1991. pap. 8.95 (*0-9629898-0-0*); lib. bdg. 22.95 (*0-9629898-1-9*) Glad River.

Religious Liberty & Human Rights in Nations & in Religions. Ed. by Leonard Swidler. 255p. (Orig.). 1986. pap. 9.95 (*0-931214-06-8*) Ecumenical Phila.

*__Religious Liberty & International Law in Europe.__ Malcolm Evans. (Studies in International & Comparative Law). 380p. (C). 1997. text ed. 85.00 (*0-521-55021-1*) Cambridge U Pr.

Religious Liberty & State Constitutions. Edd Doerr & Albert J. Menendez. 100p. 1993. 21.95 (*0-87975-839-2*) Prometheus Bks.

Religious Liberty & the Secular State: The Constitutional Context. John M. Swomley. 146p. 1987. 25.95 (*0-87975-373-0*); pap. 15.95 (*0-87975-398-6*) Prometheus Bks.

Religious Liberty in a Pluralistic Society. Michael S. Ariens & Robert A. Destro. LC 96-9431. 1020p. 1996. 80.00 (*0-89089-653-4*) Carolina Acad Pr.

Religious Liberty in Eastern Europe & the U. S. S. R. Before & after the Great Transformation. Ed. by Paul Mojzes. 400p. 1992. text ed. 81.00 (*0-88033-234-4*) Col U Pr.

Religious Liberty in the Supreme Court: Cases That Define the Debate over Church & State. Terry Eastland. 512p. 1993. 29.95 (*0-89633-178-4*) Ethics & Public Policy.

An Asterisk (*) at the beginning of an entry indicates that the title is appearing in BIP for the first time.

Religious Liberty in the Supreme Court: The Cases That Define the Debate over Church & State. Ed. by Terry Eastland. 528p. (Orig.). 1995. pap. 25.00 (*0-8028-0838-7*) Eerdmans.

Religious Liberty in the World's Constitutions. Albert Blaustein & James P. O'Brien. (Religion Reference Ser.). 500p. 1998. text ed. 75.00 (*0-8153-0798-5*) Garland.

Religious Liberty in Western Thought. Noel B. Reynolds & W. Cole Durham. LC 96-43774. (Emory University Studies in Law & Religion Ser.). 1996. pap. 21.95 (*0-7885-0320-0*) Scholars Pr GA.

Religious Liberty in Western Thought. Noel B. Reynolds & W. Cole Durham. LC 96-43774. (Emory University Studies in Law & Religion Ser.). 1996. write for info. (*0-7885-0319-7*) Scholars Pr GA.

Religious Life: A Prophetic Vision: Hope & Promise for Tomorrow. Diarmuid O'Murchu. LC 91-72859. 264p. (Orig.). 1991. pap. 9.95 (*0-87793-463-0*) Ave Maria.

Religious Life: Rebirth Through Conversion. Gerald Arbuckle & David L. Fleming. 142p. (Orig.). (C). 1990. text ed. 39.00 (*0-85439-341-2*, Pub. by St Paul Pubns UK) St Mut.

Religious Life: The Challenges of Tomorrow. Ed. by Cassian J. Yuhaus. LC 94-1893. 1994. pap. 14.95 (*0-8091-3476-4*) Paulist Pr.

Religious Life & the Poor: Liberation Theology Perspectives. Alejandro Cussianovich. Tr. by John Drury. LC 78-16740. Orig. Title: Desde los Pobres de la Tiera. 176p. (Orig.). reprint ed. pap. 50.20 (*0-8357-7008-7*, 2033573) Bks Demand.

Religious Life As Adventure: Renewal, Refounding or Reform? Albert S. Dilanni. LC 94-30399. 175p. (Orig.). 1994. pap. 9.95 (*0-8189-0716-9*) Alba.

Religious Life in the Twenty-First Century: A Contemporary Journey into Canaan. Catherine Harmer. LC 95-60063. 148p. (Orig.). 1995. pap. 9.95 (*0-89622-651-4*) Twenty-Third.

Religious Life of Fugitive Slaves & Rise of the Coloured Baptist Churches, 1820-1865, in What Is Now Ontario. James K. Lewis. Ed. by Edwin S. Gaustad. LC 79-52574. (Baptist Tradition Ser.). 1980. lib. bdg. 23.95 (*0-405-12442-2*) Ayer.

Religious Life of Richard III: Piety & Prayer in the North of England. Jonathan Hughes. (Illus.). 224p. 1997. 72.00 (*0-7509-1115-8*, Pub. by Sutton Pubng UK) Bks Intl VA.

Religious Life of Samuel Johnson. Charles R. Pierce, Jr. LC 82-13938. 184p. (C). 1982. lib. bdg. 32.00 (*0-208-01992-8*, Archon Bks) Shoe String.

Religious Life of Theological Students. Benjamin B. Warfield. 1983. pap. 1.99 (*0-87552-524-5*, Pub. by Evangelical Pr) Presby & Reformed.

Religious Life of Thomas Jefferson. Charles B. Sanford. LC 83-21649. 246p. 1985. pap. text ed. 16.50 (*0-8139-1131-1*) U Pr of Va.

Religious Life of Young Americans: A Compendium of Surveys on the Spiritual Beliefs & Practices of Teen-Agers & Young Adults. George H. Gallup, Jr. & Robert Bezilla. 84p. (Orig.). 1992. pap. 34.95 (*0-924455-01-2*) GHG Intl Inst.

Religious Literacy, Textbooks, & Religious Neutrality. Warren A. Nord. (Occasional Papers in Religion & Ethics: No. 1). 1990. 8.00 (*1-881678-41-5*) CRIS.

Religious Lyrics of the Thirteenth, Fourteenth, & Fifteenth Centuries, 3 vols. Carleton Brown. 1972. 300.00 (*0-8490-0942-1*) Gordon Pr.

Religious Medicine: The History & Evolution of Indian Medicine. Kenneth G. Zysk. LC 92-20088. 340p. (C). 1992. 49.95 (*1-56000-076-7*) Transaction Pubs.

Religious Melancholy & Protestant Experience in America. Julius H. Rubin. (Religion in America Ser.). 304p. 1994. 39.95 (*0-19-508301-6*) OUP.

Religious Metaphysics of Simone Weil. Miklos Veto. Tr. by Joan Dargan. LC 93-40293. (SUNY Series, Simone Weil Studies). 219p. (C). 1994. text ed. 57.50 (*0-7914-2077-9*); pap. text ed. 18.95 (*0-7914-2078-7*) State U NY Pr.

Religious Methods & Resources in Bioethics. Ed. by Paul F. Camenisch. LC 93-24817. (Theory & Medicine Ser.: Vol. 2). 356p. (C). 1993. lib. bdg. 170.50 (*0-7923-2102-2*, Pub. by Klwr Acad Pubs NE) Kluwer Ac.

Religious Militancy & Self-Assertion: Islam & Politics in Nigeria. Matthew H. Kukha & Toyin Falola. (Making of Modern Africa Ser.). 320p. 1996. text ed. 72.95 (*1-85972-474-4*, Pub. by Avebury Pub UK) Ashgate Pub Co.

Religious Minorities in Canada: A Sociological Study of the Japanese Experience. Mark R. Mullins. LC 88-1703. (Canadian Studies: Vol. 4). 220p. 1989. lib. bdg. 89.95 (*0-88946-195-3*) E Mellen.

Religious Mission of the Irish People & Catholic Colonization. John L. Spalding. 1978. 19.95 (*0-405-10859-1*, 11857) Ayer.

Religious Motive in Philanthropy. Henry B. Washburn. LC 72-105047. (Essay Index Reprint Ser.). 1977. 20.95 (*0-8369-1634-4*) Ayer.

Religious Movements in Contemporary America. Ed. by Irving I. Zaretsky & Mark P. Leone. LC 73-39054. 871p. reprint ed. pap. 180.00 (*0-7837-3875-7*, 2043717) Bks Demand.

Religious Movements in the Middle Ages. Herbert Grundmann. Tr. by Steven Rowan from GER. LC 94-15466. 462p. 1996. pap. text ed. 30.00 (*0-268-01653-4*) U of Notre Dame Pr.

Religious Music in the Schools. Music Educators National Conference Staff. 4p. (Orig.). (C). 1987. pap. write for info. (*1-56545-069-8*, 4010) Music Ed Natl.

Religious Mythology & the Art of War: Comparative Religious Symbolisms of Military Violence. James A. Aho. LC 80-23465. (Contributions to the Study of Religion Ser.: No. 3). 264p. 1981. text ed. 59.95 (*0-313-22564-8*, ARM/, Greenwood Pr) Greenwood.

Religious Nationalism: Hindus & Muslims in India. Peter Van der Veer. LC 93-28079. 1994. pap. 14.00 (*0-520-08256-7*) U CA Pr.

Religious Naturalism: The First Secular, Western Culture Religion in History. Jeffrey Walther. LC 91-66010. (Illus.). 130p. (Orig.). (C). 1991. pap. text ed. 35.50 (*0-942004-50-7*) Throwkoff Pr.

Religious Objects as Psychological Structures: A Critical Integration of Object Relations Theory, Psychotherapy, & Judaism. Moshe H. Spero. LC 91-845. (Illus.). 260p. 1992. 31.95 (*0-226-76939-9*) U Ch Pr.

Religious Opinions & Example of Milton, Locke, & Newton. Henry Acton. LC 71-158223. reprint ed. 34.50 (*0-404-00283-8*) AMS Pr.

Religious Orders of the Catholic Reformation. Ed. by Richard L. DeMolen. LC 93-23762. xix, 280p. (C). 1994. 30.00 (*0-8232-1512-1*) Fordham.

Religious Organizations & the Law, 2 vols. William Bassett. (Civil Rights Ser.). 1996. ring bd. write for info. (*0-614-06273-X*) Clark Boardman Callaghan.

Religious Organizations & the Law. William W. Bassett. LC 97-4503. 1997. write for info. (*0-8366-1119-5*) Clark Boardman Callaghan.

Religious Origins of the American Revolution. Ed. by Page Smith. LC 76-13157. (American Academy of Religion. Aids for the Study of Religion Ser.: No. 3). 257p. reprint ed. pap. 73.30 (*0-7837-5408-6*, 2045172) Bks Demand.

Religious Origins of the French Revolution: From Calvin to the Civil Constitution, 1560-1791. Dale K. Van Kley. LC 95-47072. 400p. (C). 1996. 35.00 (*0-300-06478-0*) Yale U Pr.

Religious Orthodoxy & Popular Faith in European Society. Ed. by Ellen Badone. 226p. (Orig.). 1990. text ed. 49.50 (*0-691-09450-0*); pap. text ed. 16.95 (*0-691-02850-8*) Princeton U Pr.

Religious Outsiders & the Making of Americans. R. Laurence Moore. 272p. 1987. pap. 18.95 (*0-19-505188-2*) OUP.

Religious Patterning in Shakespeare's Major Tragedies. Sherman Hawkins. (Transactions, the Connecticut Academy of Arts & Sciences Ser.: Vol. 50, Pt. 3). 38p. 1991. pap. 10.50 (*1-878508-03-2*) CT Acad Arts & Sciences.

Religious Performance in Contemporary Islam: Shii Devotional Rituals in South Asia. Vernon J. Schubel. LC 92-40889. (Studies in Comparative Religion). (Illus.). 213p. (C). 1993. text ed. 39.95 (*0-87249-859-X*) U of SC Pr.

Religious Periodicals Directory. Graham P. Cornish. (Clio Periodicals Directories Ser.). 330p. 1986. lib. bdg. 99.50 (*0-87436-365-9*) ABC-CLIO.

Religious Periodicals of the United States: Academic & Scholarly Journals. Ed. by Charles H. Lippy. LC 85-9861. (Historical Guides to the World's Periodicals & Newspapers Ser.). 626p. 1986. text ed. 79.50 (*0-313-23420-5*, LRP/, Greenwood Pr) Greenwood.

Religious Perplexities. 3rd ed. Lawrence P. Jacks. LC 77-27149. (Hibbert Lectures: 1922). reprint ed. 30.00 (*0-404-60421-8*) AMS Pr.

Religious Perspectives on War: Christian, Muslim, & Jewish Attitudes Toward Force after the Gulf War. David R. Smock. LC 92-31981. 1992. pap. text ed. 6.95 (*1-878379-20-8*) US Inst Peace.

Religious Philosophy of Josiah Royce. Josiah Royce. Ed. by Stuart G. Brown. LC 76-4496. 239p. 1976. reprint ed. text ed. 35.00 (*0-8371-8810-5*, RORP, Greenwood Pr) Greenwood.

Religious Philosophy of Nishitani Keiji: Encounter with Emptiness. Taitetsu Unno. LC 90-39111. (Nanzan Studies in Religion & Culture). 366p. 1989. reprint ed. pap. 104.40 (*0-608-01782-5*, 2062440) Bks Demand.

Religious Philosophy of Plotinus & Some Modern Philosophies of Religion. William R. Inge. 1977. lib. bdg. 59.95 (*0-8490-2513-3*) Gordon Pr.

Religious Philosophy of Tagore & Radhakrishnan: A Comparative & Analytical Study. Harendra P. Sinha. (C). 1993. text ed. 15.00 (*81-208-1062-7*, Pub. by Motilal Banarsidass II) S Asia.

Religious Philosophy of Tanabe Hajime: The Metanoetic Imperative. Ed. by Taitetsu Unno & James W. Heisig. LC 90-41500. (Nanzan Studies in Religion & Culture). 413p. 1990. reprint ed. pap. 117.80 (*0-608-01781-7*, 2062439) Bks Demand.

Religious Philosophy of Vladimir Solovyov. Jonathan Sutton. LC 87-20648. 256p. 1988. text ed. 45.00 (*0-312-01239-X*) St Martin.

Religious Pieces in Prose & Verse. Ed. by George G. Perry. (EETS, OS Ser.: No. 26). 1974. reprint ed. 35.00 (*0-527-00026-4*) Periodicals Srv.

Religious Pieces in Prose & Verse from R. Thornton's MS. Ed. by G. G. Perry. (Early English Text Society Original Ser.: No. 26). 1996. reprint ed. 36.00 (*0-85991-813-0*, Pub. by EETS UK) Boydell & Brewer.

Religious Platonism. James K. Feibleman. LC 78-161628. 236p. 1971. reprint ed. text ed. 55.00 (*0-8371-6184-3*, FERP, Greenwood Pr) Greenwood.

Religious Pluralism, Vol. 5. Ed. by Leroy S. Rouner. LC 84-7431. (Boston University Studies in Philosophy & Religion: Vol. 5). 256p. (C). 1984. text ed. 37.00 (*0-268-01626-7*) U of Notre Dame Pr.

Religious Pluralism & Christian Truth. Joseph S. O'Leary. 272p. 1996. 69.50 (*0-7486-0727-7*, Pub. by Edinburgh U Pr UK) Col U Pr.

Religious Pluralism & Religious Education. Ed. by Norma H. Thompson. LC 88-5394. 330p. (Orig.). 1988. pap. 18.95 (*0-89135-061-6*) Religious Educ.

Religious Pluralism & the Nigerian State. Simeon O. Ilesanmi. LC 96-33643. (Monographs in International Studies-Africa Ser.: Vol. 66). 250p. (Orig.). (C). 1996. pap. text ed. 26.00 (*0-89680-194-2*, Ohio U Ctr Intl) Ohio U Pr.

Religious Pluralism & Truth: Essays on Cross-Cultural Philosophy of Religion. Ed. by Thomas Dean. LC 93-40598. (SUNY Series in Religious Studies). 271p. (C). 1994. pap. text ed. 19.95 (*0-7914-2124-4*) State U NY Pr.

Religious Pluralism & Truth: Essays on Cross-Cultural Philosophy of Religion. Ed. by Thomas Dean. LC 93-40598. (SUNY Series in Religious Studies). 271p. (C). 1995. text ed. 59.50 (*0-7914-2123-6*) State U NY Pr.

Religious Pluralism in the West: An Anthology. Ed. by David Mullan. 440p. 1997. pap. text ed. 64.95 (*0-631-20669-8*) Blackwell Pubs.

Religious Pluralism in the West: An Anthology. Ed. by David Mullan. 440p. 1997. pap. text ed. 29.95 (*0-631-20670-1*) Blackwell Pubs.

Religious Plurality in Africa: Essays in Honor of John S. Mbiti. Ed. by Jacob K. Olupona & Sulayman S. Nyang. (Religion & Society Ser.: No. 32). xxi, 445p. (C). 1995. pap. text ed. 34.95 (*3-11-014789-0*) Mouton.

Religious Plurality in Africa: Essays in Honour of John S. Mbiti. Ed. by Jacob K. Olupona & Sulayman S. Nyang. LC 93-7392. (Religion & Society Ser.: No. 32). xxi, 455p. (C). 1993. lib. bdg. 175.40 (*3-11-012220-0*) Mouton.

Religious Poems for Today's World. J. Topham. LC 83-22402. 69p. 1991. reprint ed. pap. text ed. 9.95 (*0-933486-57-X*) Am Poetry & Lit.

Religious Poetry of Jorge de Montemayor. Bryant L. Creel. (Monografías A Ser.: Vol. LXXVIII). (Illus.). 270p. (C). 1981. 63.00 (*0-7293-0103-6*, Pub. by Tamesis Bks Ltd UK) Boydell & Brewer.

Religious Polemic and the Intellectual History of the Mozarabs, c.1050-1200. Thomas E. Burman. LC 94-33776. (Studies in Intellectual History: 52). 1994. 113.00 (*90-04-09910-7*) E J Brill.

Religious Policy in the Soviet Union. Ed. by Sabrina P. Ramet. 350p. (C). 1993. text ed. 75.00 (*0-521-41643-4*) Cambridge U Pr.

Religious Policy of the Bavarian Government During the Napoleonic Period. Chester P. Higby. LC 19-12150. (Columbia University. Studies in the Social Sciences: No. 196). reprint ed. 42.50 (*0-404-51196-1*) AMS Pr.

Religious Policy of the Mughal Emperors. Sri Ram Sharma. 216p. 1989. reprint ed. 27.50 (*81-215-0412-0*, Pub. by M Manoharial II) Coronet Bks.

Religious Politics: Men Pleasers or God Pleasers. rev. ed. Roberts Liardon. 34p. 1988. pap. 1.00 (*1-879993-02-3*) Embassy Pub.

Religious Politics in Global & Comparative Perspective. Ed. by William H. Swatos, Jr. LC 89-2165. (Contributions in Sociology Ser.: No. 81). 194p. 1989. text ed. 49.95 (*0-313-26392-2*, SUW/, Greenwood Pr) Greenwood.

Religious Potential of the Child: Experiencing Scripture & Liturgy with Young Children. Sofia Cavalletti. Tr. by Patricia M. Coulter & Julie M. Coulter. LC 92-19804. 248p. 1992. pap. 16.00 (*0-929650-67-0*, CHILD) Liturgy Tr Pubns.

Religious Poverty & the Profit Economy in Medieval Europe. Lester K. Little. LC 78-58630. 268p. 1983. pap. 15.95 (*0-8014-9247-5*) Cornell U Pr.

Religious Press in America. Martin E. Marty et al. LC 72-6844. 184p. 1973. reprint ed. text ed. 49.75 (*0-8371-6500-8*, MARP, Greenwood Pr) Greenwood.

Religious Press in Britain, 1760-1900. Josef L. Altholz. LC 89-1956. (Contributions to the Study of Religion Ser.: No. 22). 225p. 1989. text ed. 55.00 (*0-313-25738-8*, AHW, Greenwood Pr) Greenwood.

Religious Press in the South Atlantic States, 1802-1865. Henry S. Stroupe. (Duke University. Trinity College Historical Society. Historical Papers: No. 32). reprint ed. 30.00 (*0-404-51782-X*) AMS Pr.

Religious Progress on the Pacific Slope: Addresses & Papers at the Celebration of the Semi-Centennial Anniversary of Pacific School of Religion, Berkeley, California. Pacific School of Religion Staff. LC 68-22941. (Essay Index Reprint Ser.). 1977. reprint ed. 21.95 (*0-8369-0820-1*) Ayer.

Religious Propaganda & Missionary Competition in the New Testament World: Essays in Honor of Dieter Georgi. Ed. by Lukas Bormann et al. LC 94-9716. (Supplements to Novem Testamentum Ser.: Vol. 74). 1994. 152.00 (*90-04-10049-0*) E J Brill.

Religious Quest. Ed. by Whitfield Foy. 752p. 1988. pap. 19.95 (*0-415-02526-5*) Routledge.

Religious Quest in the Poetry of T. S. Eliot Vol. 14. Caroline Phillips. LC 94-38440. (Studies in Art & Religious Interpretation). 112p. 1995. text ed. 59.95 (*0-7734-9152-X*) E Mellen.

Religious Quests of the Graeco-Roman World: A Study in the Historical Background of Early Christianity. Samuel Angus. LC 66-30791. 1929. 32.00 (*0-8196-0196-9*) Biblo.

Religious Radicalism & Politics in the Middle East. Ed. by Emmanuel Sivan & Menachem Friedman. LC 89-4235. (SUNY Series in Near Eastern Studies). 244p. 1990. pap. text ed. 21.95 (*0-7914-0159-6*) State U NY Pr.

Religious Radicalism & Politics in the Middle East. Ed. by Emmanuel Sivan & Menachem Friedman. LC 89-4235. (SUNY Series in Near Eastern Studies). 244p. 1990. text ed. 64.50 (*0-7914-0158-8*) State U NY Pr.

Religious Radicalism in England, 1535-1565. C. J. Clement. LC 94-23546. (Rutherford Studies in Historical Theology). 444p. 1995. text ed. 109.95 (*0-7734-9121-X*) E Mellen.

Religious Radicalism in the Greater Middle East. Ed. by Bruce Maddy-Weitzman & Efraim Inbar. LC 96-42105. (Besa Study in Mideast Securitye). 272p. (C). 1997. text ed. 42.50 (*0-7146-4769-1*, Pub. by F Cass Pubs UK); pap. text ed. 22.50 (*0-7146-4326-2*, Pub. by F Cass Pubs UK) Intl Spec Bk.

Religious Radicals in Tudor England. J. W. Martin. 256p. 1989. text ed. 55.00 (*1-85285-006-X*) Hambledon Press.

Religious Radio & Television in the United States, 1921-1991: The Programs & Personalities. Hal Erickson. LC 92-50304. 240p. 1992. lib. bdg. 43.50 (*0-89950-658-5*) McFarland & Co.

Religious Reflections on the Human Body. Ed. by Jane M. Law. LC 94-4436. 336p. 1995. 35.00 (*0-253-33263-X*); pap. 15.95 (*0-253-20902-1*) Ind U Pr.

Religious Regimes & State Formation: Perspectives from European Ethnology. Ed. by Eric R. Wolf. LC 90-40609. 308p. 1991. text ed. 59.50 (*0-7914-0650-4*); pap. text ed. 19.95 (*0-7914-0651-2*) State U NY Pr.

Religious Regimes in Peru: Religion & State Development in a Long-Term Perspective & the Effects in the Andean Village of Zurite. Fred Spier. 328p. (C). 1995. pap. 47.50 (*90-5356-053-X*, Pub. by Amsterdam U Pr NE); text ed. 62.50 (*90-5356-052-1*, Pub. by Amsterdam U Pr NE) U of Mich Pr.

Religious Renewal of Jewry. Ed. by Jacob Neusner. LC 92-34799. (Judaism in Cold War America, 1945-1990 Ser.: Vol. 5). 344p. 1993. text ed. 25.00 (*0-8153-0080-8*) Garland.

Religious Reprobates & Saved Sinners. 40p. 1987. pap. 2.00 (*0-934803-63-3*) J Van Impe.

Religious Resurgence: Contemporary Cases in Islam, Christianity, & Judaism. Ed. by Richard T. Antoun & Mary C. Hegland. 288p. 1987. text ed. 45.00 (*0-8156-2409-3*) Syracuse U Pr.

Religious Resurgence & Politics in the Contemporary World. Ed. by Emile Sahliyeh. LC 89-29262. (SUNY Series in Religion, Culture, & Society). 374p. 1990. text ed. 64.50 (*0-7914-0381-5*); pap. text ed. 21.95 (*0-7914-0382-3*) State U NY Pr.

Religious Revolution in the Ivory Coast: The Prophet Harris & the Harrist Church. Sheila S. Walker. LC 81-13010. (Studies in Religion). 224p. reprint ed. pap. 63.90 (*0-7837-2461-6*, 2042614) Bks Demand.

Religious Right: A Reference Handbook. John W. Storey & Glenn H. Utter. LC 95-44344. (Contemporary World Issues Ser.). 298p. 1995. 39.50 (*0-87436-778-6*) ABC-CLIO.

Religious Right: The Assault & Pluralism in America. Schwartz. 1995. pap. (*0-385-47841-0*) Doubleday.

Religious Right & Israel: The Politics of Armageddon. Ruth W. Mouly. (Midwest Research Monographs: No. 2). 47p. 1985. pap. 4.50 (*0-915987-01-5*) Political Rsch Assocs.

Religious Rights in the Public Schools. James Feliciano. 233p. 1991. 24.95 (*0-685-59596-X*); pap. 16.95 (*1-880054-00-0*); pap. text ed. 16.95 (*0-685-59598-6*); lib. bdg. 24.95 (*0-685-59597-8*) PAZ Pr.

Religious Rites & Festivals of India. G. R. Sholapur. (C). 1990. 33.00 (*81-217-0068-X*, Pub. by Bharatiya Vidya Bhavan II) S Asia.

Religious Rock'n'Roll, A Wolf in Sheep's Clothing. Jimmy Swaggart & Robert P. Lamb. 1987. 12.95 (*0-935113-05-3*) Swaggart Ministries.

Religious Roots of American Sociology. Cecil E. Greek. LC 91-38373. (Library of Sociology: Vol. 23). 288p. 1992. text ed. 46.00 (*0-8153-0390-4*, SS786) Garland.

Religious Roots of Rebellion: Christians in Central American Revolutions. Phillip Berryman. LC 83-19343. 464p. 1984. reprint ed. pap. 132.30 (*0-7837-9801-6*, 2060530) Bks Demand.

Religious Routes to Gladstonian Liberalism: The Church Rate Question & the Making of the Gladstonian State. J. P. Ellens. LC 93-21927. 1994. 45.00 (*0-271-01036-3*, MR-245-A) Pa St U Pr.

Religious Scepticism: Contemporary Responses to Gibbon. Ed. & Intro. by David Womersley. (Key Issues Ser.: No. 15). 250p. 1997. 75.00 (*1-85506-509-6*); pap. 29.95 (*1-85506-510-X*) Thoemmes Pr.

Religious Schools & Sects in Medieval Islam. Wilferd Madelung. (Collected Studies: No. CS213). 352p. (C). 1985. reprint ed. lib. bdg. 98.95 (*0-86078-161-5*, Pub. by Variorum UK) Ashgate Pub Co.

Religious Schools in the United States, K-12: A Source Book. Thomas C. Hunt & James C. Carper. LC 93-8147. 528p. 1993. text ed. 83.00 (*0-8153-0874-4*, SS841) Garland.

Religious Science Hymnal. 3rd ed. Ed. by Irma Glen. 225p. 1982. reprint ed. 8.00 (*0-87516-489-7*) DeVorss.

Religious Sense. Luigi Giussani. Tr. by John Zucchi from ITA. 160p. 1997. pap. 14.95 (*0-7735-1626-3*, Pub. by McGill CN) U of Toronto Pr.

Religious Sentimentalism in the Age of Johnson: 1740-1780 see Religious Trends in English Poetry

Religious Sentiments of Charles Dickens: Collected from His Writings. Charles Dickens. Ed. by C. McKenzie. LC 73-7504. (Studies in Dickens: No. 52). 1973. reprint ed. lib. bdg. 75.00 (*0-8383-1697-2*) M S G Haskell Hse.

Religious Significance of Atheism. Alasdair MacIntyre & Paul Ricoeur. LC 68-28398. (Bampton Lectures in America: No. 18). 106p. reprint ed. pap. 30.30 (*0-8357-4569-4*, 2037479) Bks Demand.

Religious Signing. Elaine Costello. (Illus.). 176p. 1986. pap. 16.95 (*0-553-34244-4*) Bantam.

Religious Socialisation. Ed. by E. Henau & R. J. Schreiter. (Theologie & Empirie Ser.: Vol. 21). 117p. 1995. pap. 25.25 (*90-390-0064-6*, Pub. by KOK Pharos NE) Eisenbrauns.

An Asterisk (*) at the beginning of an entry indicates that the title is appearing in BIP for the first time.

R

Religious Sociology: Interfaces & Boundaries. Ed. by William H. Swatos, Jr. LC 87-353. (Contributions in Sociology Ser.: No. 64). 208p. 1987. text ed. 49.95 (*0-313-25528-8*, SWJ/, Greenwood Pr) Greenwood.

Religious Solution to the Social Problem. Howard H. Brinton. (C). 1934. pap. 3.00 (*0-87574-002-2*) Pendle Hill.

Religious Spectrum. Margaret Chatterjee. (Studies in an Indian Context). 196p. 1984. 24.95 (*0-317-39860-1*, Pub. by Allied Pubs II) Asia Bk Corp.

Religious Spirits. Jonas B. Clark. 54p. (Orig.). 1995. pap. 6.00 (*1-886885-01-X*) Spirit Life.

Religious-Spiritual Attitudes of College-University Students in U. S. A., Germany, & Korea: A Survey, includes German & Korean Survey Questions. Won Y. Ji et al. (Illus.). 154p. (Orig.). (C). 1994. pap. 6.85 (*0-911770-60-7*) Concordia Seminary.

Religious Stained Glass for Today. Bill Hillman. (Illus.). 60p. 1990. 16.95 (*0-935133-37-2*) CKE Pubns.

Religious Strife in Egypt: Crisis & Ideological Conflict in the Seventies. Nadia R. Farah. xvi, 134p. 1986. text ed. 74.00 (*2-88124-092-5*) Gordon & Breach.

Religious Studies: Issues, Prospects & Proposals. Ed. by Larry W. Hurtado & Klaus K. Klostermaier. 486p. 1991. 59.95 (*1-55540-623-8*, 78 00 02) Scholars Pr GA.

Religious Studies: The Making of a Discipline. Walter H. Capps. LC 95-6956. 1995. pap. 30.00 (*0-8006-2535-8*, Fortress Pr) Augsburg Fortress.

Religious Studies in Alberta: A State-of-the-Art Review. Ronald W. Neufeldt. (Study of Religion in Canada Ser.: Vol. 1). 160p. (C). 1983. pap. 8.50 (*0-919812-18-X*) Wilfrid Laurier.

Religious Studies in Manitoba & Saskatchewan: A State-of-the-Art Review. Gordon Harland et al. (Study of Religion in Canada Ser.: Vol. 4). 172p. (C). 1993. pap. 19.95 (*0-88920-223-0*) Wilfrid Laurier.

Religious Studies in Ontario: A State-of-the-Art Review. Daniel Fraikin et al. (Study of Religion in Canada: Vol. 3). 320p. (C). 1992. pap. 24.95 (*0-88920-206-0*) Wilfrid Laurier.

Religious Studies, Theological Studies, & the University Divinity School. Joseph M. Kitagawa. (Studies in Theological Education). 200p. (C). 1992. 39.95 (*1-55540-559-2*, 000807); pap. 24.95 (*1-55540-560-6*, 00 08 07) Scholars Pr GA.

Religious Study of Judaism: Context, Text, Circumstance, Vol. 3. Jacob Neusner. (Studies in Judaism). 234p. (Orig.). 1987. pap. 22.50 (*0-8191-6048-2*, Studies in Judaism); lib. bdg. 50.00 (*0-8191-6047-4*, Studies in Judaism) U Pr of Amer.

Religious Study of Judaism: Description, Analysis & Interpretation. Jacob Neusner. LC 85-30411. (Studies in Judaism: Vol. 1). 188p. (Orig.). (C). 1986. pap. text ed. 20.50 (*0-8191-5394-X*, Studies in Judaism) U Pr of Amer.

Religious Study of Judaism: Description, Analysis, Interpretation-The Centrality of Context. Jacob Neusner. LC 85-30411. (Studies in Judaism: Vol. 2). 230p. (Orig.). (C). 1986. pap. text ed. 23.00 (*0-8191-5451-2*, Studies in Judaism); lib. bdg. 50.00 (*0-8191-5450-4*, Studies in Judaism) U Pr of Amer.

Religious Study of Judaism Vol. IV: Description, Analysis, Intrepretation: Ideas of History Ethics, Ontology, & Religion in Formative Judaism. Jacob Neusner. LC 85-30411. (Studies in Judaism). 210p. (C). 1988. lib. bdg. 34.00 (*0-8191-7142-5*) U Pr of Amer.

Religious System of China, 6 vols. J. J. DeGroot. 1982. reprint ed. 195.00 (*0-89986-346-9*) Oriental Bk Store.

Religious System of the Amazulu. (Folk-Lore Society, London Monographs: Vol. 15). 1974. reprint ed. 50.00 (*0-8115-0506-5*) Periodicals Srv.

Religious Systems of the Mahanubhava Sect. Anne Feldhaus. 1983. 26.00 (*0-8364-1005-X*) S Asia.

Religious Teachers of Greece. James Adam. LC 72-2565. (Select Bibliographies Reprint Ser.). 1977. reprint ed. 37.95 (*0-8369-6843-3*) Ayer.

Religious Teachers of Greece. James Adam. LC 65-22806. (Library of Religious & Philosophical Thought). iv, 467p. 1966. reprint ed. lib. bdg. 49.50 (*0-678-09950-2*, Reference Bk Pubs) Kelley.

Religious Teachings for Children, Bk. 1. Shaikh M. Sarwar. 44p. pap. 2.00 (*0-941724-03-4*) Islamic Seminary.

Religious Teachings for Children, Bk. 2. Shaikh M. Sarwar. 66p. pap. 2.00 (*0-941724-04-2*) Islamic Seminary.

Religious Teachings for Children, Bk. 3. Shaikh M. Sarwar. 80p. (C). pap. 2.00 (*0-941724-05-0*) Islamic Seminary.

Religious Teachings for Children, Bk. 4. Shaikh M. Sarwar. 72p. 1981. pap. 2.00 (*0-941724-06-9*) Islamic Seminary.

Religious Television: Controversies & Conclusions. Robert Abelman & Stewart M. Hoover. Ed. by Brenda Dervin. LC 89-78101. (Communication & Information Science Ser.). 376p. (C). 1989. pap. 39.50 (*0-89391-644-7*) Ablex Pub.

Religious Television: Controversies & Conclusions. Ed. by Robert Abelman et al. LC 89-78101. (Communication & Information Science Ser.). 376p. (C). 1989. text ed. 78.50 (*0-89391-643-9*) Ablex Pub.

Religious Thought & the Modern Psychologies: A Critical Conversation in the Theology of Culture. Don S. Browning. LC 86-45205. 268p. 1988. pap. 20.00 (*0-8006-2322-3*, Fortress Pr) Augsburg Fortress.

Religious Thought in England from the Reformation to the End of the Last Century, 3 vols. John Hunt. LC 72-153593. reprint ed. 225.00 (*0-404-09480-5*) AMS Pr.

Religious Thought in the Greater American Poets. Elmer J. Bailey. LC 68-8436. (Essay Index Reprint Ser.). 1977. reprint ed. 18.95 (*0-8369-0167-3*) Ayer.

Religious Thought in the Last Quarter-Century. Ed. by Gerald B. Smith. LC 71-107739. (Essay Index Reprint Ser.). 1977. 15.95 (*0-8369-1583-6*) Ayer.

Religious Thought in the Reformation. 2nd ed. Bernard M. Reardon. LC 94-36908. (C). 1995. text ed. 50.95 (*0-582-25960-6*) Longman.

Religious Thought in the Victorian Age: A Survey from Coleridge to Gore. 2nd ed. Bernard M. Reardon. LC 95-15347. 400p. (C). 1995. text ed. 61.50 (*0-582-26514-2*, Pub. by Longman UK); pap. text ed. 26.50 (*0-582-26516-9*, Pub. by Longman UK) Longman.

Religious Thought of Jose Rizal. rev. ed. Eugene A. Hessel. 354p. (Orig.). 1984. pap. 17.50 (*971-10-0070-9*, Pub. by New Day Pub PH) Cellar.

Religious Thoughts in the Reformation. Bernard M. Reardon. (C). 1981. pap. text ed. 28.50 (*0-582-49031-6*, 73448) Longman.

Religious Toleration & Persecution in Ancient Rome. Simeon L. Guterman. LC 70-104269. 160p. 1971. reprint ed. text ed. 49.75 (*0-8371-3936-8*, GURT, Greenwood Pr) Greenwood.

Religious Toleration & Social Change in Hamburg, 1529-1819. Joachim Whaley. (Cambridge Studies in Early Modern History). 290p. 1985. text ed. 80.00 (*0-521-26189-9*) Cambridge U Pr.

Religious Traditions & the Limits of Tolerance. Ed. by Louis Hammann et al. LC 88-2441. 158p. 1988. pap. 14.50 (*0-89012-047-1*) Col U Pr.

Religious Traditions at Vijayanatgara: As Revealed Through Its Monuments. Anila Verghese. (C). 1995. 72.00 (*81-7304-086-9*, Pub. by Manohar II) S Asia.

Religious Traditions in South Asia: Interaction & Change. Ed. by Geoffrey A. Oddie. (Religion & Society in South Asia Ser.). 260p. (C). 1997. text ed. 45.00 (*0-7007-0421-3*, Pub. by Curzon Press UK) UH Pr.

Religious Traditions of Asia. Ed. by Joseph M. Kitagawa. (Readings from the Encyclopedia of Religion Ser.). 384p. (Orig.). (C). 1989. 15.95 (*0-02-897211-2*) Macmillan.

Religious Traditions of the World: A Journey Through Africa, Mesoamerica, North America, Judaism, Christianity, Islam, Hinduism, Buddhism, China, & Japan. Ed. by H. Byron Earhart. LC 91-55481. 1088p. 1992. 39.00 (*0-06-062115-X*) Harper SF.

Religious Transformations & Socio-Political Change: Eastern Europe & Latin America. Ed. by Luther H. Martin. LC 93-4333. (Religion & Society Ser.: No. 33). xiv, 457p. (C). 1993. lib. bdg. 152.35 (*3-11-013734-8*) Mouton.

Religious Trend in Early Islamic Iran. Wilferd Madelung. 1988. 30.00 (*0-88706-700-X*) Mazda Pubs.

Religious Trends in English Poetry, 6 vols. Hoxie N. Fairchild. Incl. Vol. 2. Religious Sentimentalism in the Age of Johnson: 1740-1780. LC 39-12839. 1942. text ed. 70.00 (*0-231-08822-1*); Vol. 4. Christianity & Romanticism in the Victorian Era: 1830-1880. LC 39-12839. 1957. text ed. 70.00 (*0-231-08824-8*); Vol. 6. Valley of Dry Bones: 1920-1965. LC 39-12839. 1968. text ed. 70.00 (*0-231-08826-4*); LC 39-12839. write for info. (*0-318-51412-5*) Col U Pr.

Religious Truth for Our Time. William M. Watt. 120p. 1995. pap. 9.95 (*1-85168-102-7*) Onewrld Pubns.

Religious Urge-Reverential Life: The Notebooks of Paul Brunton, Vol. 12. Paul Brunton. 384p. 1988. 29.95 (*0-943914-36-1*); pap. 16.95 (*0-943914-37-X*) Larson Pubns.

Religious Values in an Age of Violence. Marc H. Tanenbaum. (Pere Marquette Lectures). 1976. 15.00 (*0-87462-508-4*) Marquette.

***Religious Values of the Terminally Ill: A Handbook for Health Professionals.** Delfi Mondragon. LC 97-16793. 1997. write for info. (*0-940866-64-1*) U Scranton Pr.

Religious Violence & Abortion: The Gideon Project. Dallas A. Blanchard & Terry J. Prewitt. LC 92-39693. (Illus.). 368p. 1993. pap. 17.95 (*0-8130-1194-9*); lib. bdg. 39.95 (*0-8130-1193-0*) U Press Fla.

Religious Visionaries. Joanne Cubbs. (Illus.). 40p. 1991. pap. 19.95 (*0-932718-31-0*) Kohler Arts.

Religious Within Experience & Existence: A Phenomenological Investigation. Patrick L. Bourgeois. LC 89-38120. 170p. 1989. text ed. 23.95 (*0-8207-0214-5*); pap. text ed. 14.95 (*0-8207-0215-3*) Duquesne.

Religious World: Communities of Faith. 3rd ed. Richard C. Bush et al. (Illus.). 460p. (C). 1993. text ed. 52.67 (*0-02-317529-X*, Macmillan Coll) P-H.

***Religious World of Contemporary Judaism: Observations & Convictions.** Jacob Neusner. 226p. 1989. 57.95 (*1-55540-410-3*) Scholars Pr GA.

Religious World of Jesus: An Introduction to Second Temple Palestinian Judaism. Frederick J. Murphy. LC 90-21922. 1991. pap. 24.95 (*0-687-36049-8*) Abingdon.

Religious World of Kirti Sri: Buddhism, Art & Politics of Late Medieval Sri Lanka. John Clifford Bolt. (Illus.). 192p. 1996. pap. 17.95 (*0-19-510757-8*) OUP.

Religious World of Kirti Sri: Buddhism, Art, & Politics of Late Medieval Sri Lanka. John C. Holt. (Illus.). 192p. 1996. 39.95 (*0-19-509705-X*) OUP.

Religious Worlds: Primary Readings in Comparative Perspective. Crossan. 624p. (C). 1995. per. 34.59 (*0-8403-6950-6*) Kendall-Hunt.

Religious Worlds: The Comparative Study of Religion. 2nd ed. William E. Paden. LC 93-43025. 208p. (C). 1994. pap. 14.00 (*0-8070-1229-7*) Beacon Pr.

Religious Writer's Marketplace. William H. Gentz & Sandra H. Brooks. LC 93-22587. 224p. (Orig.). 1993. pap. 17.95 (*0-687-36052-8*) Abingdon.

Religious Writings & Religious Systems, Vol. 1. Ed. by Jacob Neusner et al. (Studies in Religion). 200p. 1989. 53.95 (*1-55540-296-8*, 14 70 01) Scholars Pr GA.

***Religious Writings & Religious Systems, Vol. Two.** Ed. by Ernest S. Frerichs et al. (Brown Studies in Religion). 201p. 1989. 49.95 (*1-55540-333-6*) Scholars Pr GA.

Religiously Mixed Marriage. Gary Beauchamp & Deanna Beauchamp. 1981. pap. 6.50 (*0-89137-528-7*) Quality Pubns.

Religiously Speaking: Plays & Poems for Children's Church. Ed. by Jill Morris-McKinsey. 48p. (Orig.). (J). 1992. pap. 7.98 (*1-877588-03-2*) Creatively Yours.

Religiousness in Yoga: Lectures on Theory & Practice. T. K. Desikachar. Ed. by Mary L. Skelton & J. R. Carter. LC 79-9643. (Illus.). 314p. 1980. pap. text ed. 28.00 (*0-8191-0967-3*) U Pr of Amer.

***Religious/Philosophical Dictionary & Phonetic History.** Max. 50p. (Orig.). 1997. pap. 30.00 (*0-922070-69-5*) M Tecton Pub.

***Relinking Life & Work: Toward a Better Future.** Ford Foundation Staff. LC 96-3414. 1996. write for info. (*0-916584-51-8*) Ford Found.

Relinking with Witchcraft: Cooperation with Nature Spirits. Rhuddlwm Gawr. LC 85-73745. (Illus.). 140p. 1989. 12.95 (*0-931760-37-2*, CP 10115); pap. 10.95 (*0-931760-15-1*) Camelot GA.

Reliquare. William L. Fox et al. LC 87-70382. (Windriver Ser.). (Illus.). 32p. (Orig.). 1987. pap. 10.00 (*0-916918-36-X*) Duck Down.

Reliquare. limited ed. William L. Fox et al. LC 87-70382. (Windriver Ser.). (Illus.). 32p. (Orig.). 1987. 25.00 (*0-916918-37-8*) Duck Down.

***Reliquary.** Douglas Preston & Lincoln Child. LC 96-53533. 1997. 24.95 (*0-312-86095-1*) St Martin.

***Reliquary.** Douglas Preston & Lincoln Child. 1997. 24.95 (*0-614-27906-2*) Forge NYC.

***Reliques of Ancient English Poetry.** Intro. by Nick Groom. 1316p. (C). 1996. text ed. 385.00 (*0-415-14381-0*) Routledge.

Reliques of Ancient English Poetry, 2 vols. Thomas Percy. (BCL1-PR English Literature Ser.). 1992. reprint ed. lib. bdg. 150.00 (*0-7812-7132-0*) Rprt Serv.

Reliques of Irish Poetry, 1789: A Memoir of Miss Brooke, 1816. Charlotte Brooke. Ed. by A. C. Seymour. 544p. 1970. 75.00 (*0-8201-1082-5*) Schol Facsimiles.

Reliques of the Rives. James R. Childs. (Illus.). 750p. 1994. pap. text ed. 45.00 (*0-7884-0091-6*) Heritage Bk.

Reliquiae. Antimachus Colophonius. lxxii, 106p. 1974. write for info. (*3-296-10410-0*) G Olms Pubs.

Reliquiae. Teles. cxxiv, 107p. 1969. reprint ed. write for info. (*0-318-71052-8*) G Olms Pubs.

Reliquiae Antiquae, 2 vols. Ed. by Thomas Wright & James O. Halliwell. LC 13-3962. reprint ed. 135.00 (*0-404-07047-7*) AMS Pr.

Reliquiae Celticae, 2 vols. Alexander Cameron. Ed. by Alexander MacBain & John K. Kennedy. LC 78-72621. (Celtic Language & Literature Ser.: Goidelic & Brythonic). reprint ed. Set. 84.50 (*0-404-17543-0*) AMS Pr.

Reliquiae Diluvianae: Observations on the Organic Remains Contained in Caves Fissures, & Diluvial Gravel. William Buckland. Ed. by Claude C. Albritton, Jr. LC 77-6510. (History of Geology Ser.). (Illus.). 1978. reprint ed. lib. bdg. 33.95 (*0-405-10433-2*) Ayer.

Reliquiae Juveniles: Miscellaneous Thoughts in Prose & Verse. Isaac Watts. LC 68-17018. 1968. reprint ed. 50.00 (*0-8201-1049-3*) Schol Facsimiles.

Reliquiae Selectae. rev. ed. Menander. Ed. by F. H. Sandbach. (Oxford Classical Texts Ser.). 376p. 1990. 35.00 (*0-19-814737-6*) OUP.

***Reliquienkult im Altertum, 2 vols. in 1.** Friedrich Pfister. xii, 686p. (GER.). (C). 1974. reprint ed. 189.30 (*3-11-002453-5*) De Gruyter.

Reliving the Civil War: A Reenactor's Handbook. R. Lee Hadden. LC 96-12860. (Illus.). 256p. 1996. pap. 17.95 (*0-8117-2915-X*) Stackpole.

Reliving the Passion. Walter Wangerin. 224p. 1994. mass mkt. 5.99 (*0-06-104306-0*, Harp PBks) HarpC.

Reliving the Passion: Meditations on the Suffering, Death & Resurrection of Jesus as Recorded in Mark. Walter Wangerin, Jr. 144p. 1992. 12.99 (*0-310-75530-1*) Zondervan.

Reliving the Past: The Worlds of Social History. Ed. by Olivier Zunz. LC 85-1065. 344p. reprint ed. pap. 98.10 (*0-7837-6855-9*, 2046684) Bks Demand.

Reloading for Shotgunners. 3rd ed. Edward A. Matunas. LC 81-65119. (Illus.). 288p. (Orig.). 1993. pap. 17.95 (*0-87349-151-3*, RFS3) DBI.

***Reloading for Shotgunners.** 4th ed. Kurt D. Fackler & M. L. McPherson. (Illus.). 320p. 1997. pap. 19.95 (*0-87349-197-1*, RFS4) Krause Pubns.

Reloading Tools, Sights & Telescopes. Gerald O. Kelver. 1995. pap. 12.50 (*1-877704-21-0*) Pioneer Pr.

Relocate in San Diego. William Carroll. (Explore San Diego County Ser.). (Illus.). 176p. (Orig.). 1997. pap. 16.95 (*0-910390-48-7*, Coda Pubns) Auto Bk.

***Relocated Lives: Displacement & Resettlement Within the Mahaweli Project, Sri Lanka.** (Sri Landa Studies: Vol. 3). 200p. 1997. pap. 29.50 (*90-5383-502-4*, Pub. by VUB Univ Pr BE) Paul & Co Pubs.

Relocating Cultural Studies: Developments in Theory & Research. Ed. by Valda Blundell et al. LC 92-38183. (International Library of Sociology). 208p. (C). 1993. pap. 17.95 (*0-415-07549-1*, B0215, Routledge NY) Routledge.

Relocating Cultural Studies: Developments in Theory & Research. Ed. by Valda Blundell et al. LC 92-38183. (International Library of Sociology). 208p. (C). (gr. 13). 1993. text ed. 62.95 (*0-415-07548-3*, B0211, Routledge NY) Routledge.

Relocating Eden: The Image & Politics of Inuit Exile in the Canadian Arctic. Alan R. Marcus. LC 95-3420. (Illus.). 290p. 1995. pap. 19.95 (*0-87451-659-5*) U Pr of New Eng.

Relocating in the Twin Cities: A Guide to Living in the Minneapolis-St. Paul Area. Ed. by Randy Salas. (Star Tribune Source Bks.). (Illus.). (Orig.). 1995. pap. 5.95 (*0-9647179-0-5*) Star MN.

Relocating Madness: From the Mental Patient to the Person. Peter Barham & Robert Hayward. 180p. (C). 1995. pap. 21.95 (*1-85343-307-1*) NYU Pr.

Relocating Middle Powers: Australia & Canada in a Changing World Order. Andrew F. Cooper et al. 248p. 1993. pap. 29.95 (*0-522-84589-4*, Pub. by Melbourne Univ Pr AT) Paul & Co Pubs.

Relocating Spouse's Guide to Employment: Options & Strategies in the U. S. & Abroad. Frances Bastress. LC 86-19230. (Illus.). 265p. (Orig.). 1986. pap. 12.95 (*0-937623-00-8*) Woodley Pubns.

Relocating Spouse's Guide to Employment: Options & Strategies in the U. S. & Abroad. rev. ed. Frances Bastress. LC 87-16045. 265p. (Orig.). 1987. pap. 12.95 (*0-937623-01-6*) Woodley Pubns.

Relocating Spouse's Guide to Employment: Options & Strategies in the U. S. & Abroad. 3rd rev. ed. Frances Bastress. LC 88-33772. 265p. (Orig.). 1989. pap. 12.95 (*0-937623-02-4*) Woodley Pubns.

Relocating the Japanese Worker: Geographical Perspectives on Personnel Transfers, Career Mobility & Economic Restructuring. Richard Wiltshire. (Japan Library). 240p. (C). 1995. text ed. 49.00 (*1-873410-31-X*, Pub. by Curzon Press UK) UH Pr.

Relocating to San Francisco & the Bay Area: Everything You Need to Know Before You Go--& Once You Get There! Christina Guinot. 256p. 1996. per., pap. 15.00 (*0-7615-0249-1*) Prima Pub.

Relocating Your Workplace: A User's Guide to Acquiring & Preparing Business Facilities. Wadman Daly. LC 92-54361. (Illus.). 365p. (Orig.). 1993. pap. 23.95 (*1-56052-186-4*) Crisp Pubns.

Relocation. Emma B. Donath. LC 88-70455. 284p. 1988. write for info. (*0-86690-335-6*, D2800-014) Am Fed Astrologers.

Relocation: A Practical Guide. Sue Shortland. 160p. (C). 1990. 80.00 (*0-685-35803-8*, Pub. by IPM Hse UK); 80.00 (*0-85292-441-0*, Pub. by IPM Hse UK) St Mut.

Relocation & Real Property Acquisitions. (Special Reports: No. 192). 51p. 1981. 5.80 (*0-309-03120-6*) Transport Res Bd.

Relocation Assistant. Jack Rudman. (Career Examination Ser.: C-1988). 1994. pap. 27.95 (*0-8373-1988-9*) Nat Learn.

Relocation of the North American Indian. John M. Dunn. (World History Ser.). (Illus.). 112p. (J). (gr. 5-9). 1995. lib. bdg. 17.96 (*1-56006-240-1*, 2401) Lucent Bks.

Relocation Program see U. S. War Relocation Authority

Relocation Program: A Guidebook for the Residents of Relocation Centers see U. S. War Relocation Authority

Relocation Sourcebook: Modern Gardens of Eden Where You Can Live the Good Life. 1991. lib. bdg. 75.95 (*0-8490-4688-2*) Gordon Pr.

Relocation Supervisor. Jack Rudman. (Career Examination Ser.: C-3057). 1994. pap. 29.95 (*0-8373-3057-2*) Nat Learn.

Relocation Tax Advisor. Arthur Layton. 36p. 1997. pap. 7.00 (*0-9636296-5-4*) Hessel Group.

Relocations of the Spirit. Leon Forrest. 408p. 1995. 24.95 (*1-55921-068-0*) Moyer Bell.

Reloj y Yo. Yanitzia Canetti. (Illus.). 12p. (Orig.). (J). (gr. k-3). Date not set. pap. 3.95 (*1-56492-213-8*) Laredo.

Reloj y Yo. Robert Nicholson. Tr. by Jose R. Araluce from ENG. (Raices Ser.). (Illus.). 32p. (SPA.). (J). 1993. 16.95 (*1-56492-092-5*) Laredo.

Reluctance Synchronous Machines & Drives. I. Boldea. (Monographs in Electrical & Electronic Engineering: No. 38). (Illus.). 240p. 1996. 115.00 (*0-19-859391-0*) OUP.

Reluctant Admiral: Yamamoto & the Imperial Navy. Hiroyuki Agawa. Tr. by John Bester. LC 79-84652. 397p. 1982. pap. 13.00 (*0-87011-512-X*) Kodansha.

Reluctant Adult: An Exploration of Choice. Jim Hall. 1994. pap. text ed. 14.95 (*1-85327-082-2*, Pub. by Prism Pr UK) Assoc Pubs Grp.

Reluctant Adventuress. Sylvia Thorpe. 224p. 1977. pap. 1.50 (*0-449-23426-6*, Crest) Fawcett.

Reluctant Adversaries: Canada & the People's Republic of China, 1949-70. Ed. by Paul M. Evans & B. Michael Frolic. 288p. 1991. 60.00 (*0-8020-5896-5*); pap. 19.95 (*0-8020-6852-9*) U of Toronto Pr.

Reluctant Aid: United States Food Policy & Ethiopian Famine Relief. Steven L. Varnis. 234p. (C). 1990. 34.95 (*0-88738-348-3*) Transaction Pubs.

Reluctant Alliance: Behaviorism & Humanism. Bobby Newman. 130p. (C). 1992. 24.95 (*0-87975-727-2*) Prometheus Bks.

Reluctant Ally: Austria's Policy in the Austro-Turkish War, 1737-1739. Karl A. Roider. LC 72-79336. 206p. 1972. pap. 58.80 (*0-7837-8521-6*, 2049330) Bks Demand.

Reluctant Ally: France & Atlantic Security. Michael M. Harrison. LC 80-8865. 320p. 1981. text ed. 45.00 (*0-8018-2474-5*) Johns Hopkins.

Reluctant Ally: United States Foreign Policy Toward the Jews from Wilson to Roosevelt. Frank W. Brecher. LC 91-45. (Contributions in Political Science Ser.: No. 278). 192p. 1991. text ed. 49.95 (*0-313-27900-4*, BLU, Greenwood Pr) Greenwood.

Reluctant Art: Five Studies in the Growth of Jazz. Benny Green. (Quality Paperbacks Ser.). 208p. 1991. reprint ed. pap. 11.95 (*0-306-80441-7*) Da Capo.

Reluctant Art: The Growth of Jazz. Benny Green. (New Reprints in Essay & General Literature Index Ser.). 1977. reprint ed. 22.95 (*0-518-10199-1*, 10199) Ayer.

Reluctant Attraction. large type ed. Valerie Parv. 1995. 21.50 (*0-263-14359-7*, Pub. by M & B UK) Ulverscroft.

Reluctant Belligerent: American Entry into World War II. 2nd ed. Robert A. Divine. 179p. (C). 1979. pap. text ed. write for info. (*0-07-554672-8*) McGraw.

Reluctant Bodyguard. Lorna Michaels. (Superromance Ser.). 1995. mass mkt. 3.75 (*0-373-70633-2*, 1-70633-2) Harlequin Bks.

***Reluctant Break with Britain from Stamp Act to Bunker Hill.** Gregory T. Edgar. viii, 321p. 1997. pap. 23.00 (*0-7884-0585-3*, E134) Heritage Bk.

***Reluctant Bride.** Mary Balogh. 320p. 1998. mass mkt. 6.99 (*0-515-12206-8*) Jove Pubns.

Reluctant Bride. Janis Flores. (Weddings by DeWilde Ser.). 1996. mass mkt. 4.50 (*0-373-82538-2*, 1-82538-9) Harlequin Bks.

***Reluctant Bride.** Deborah Gordon. mass mkt. write for info. (*0-06-108165-5*) HarpC.

Reluctant Bridegroom. Gilbert Morris. (House of Winslow Ser.: Vol. 7). 304p. (Orig.). 1990. pap. 9.99 (*1-55661-069-6*) Bethany Hse.

Reluctant Bridegrooms: My Lady Love; Darling Amazon. Paula Marshall & Sylvia Andrew. (Promo Ser.). 1995. mass mkt. 4.99 (*0-373-31218-0*, 1-31218-0) Harlequin Bks.

Reluctant Captive. (Orig.). 1992. mass mkt. 4.95 (*1-56333-022-9*) Masquerade.

Reluctant Captive. large type ed. Helen Bianchin. (Harlequin Ser.). 1993. 19.95 (*0-263-13403-2*) Thorndike Pr.

Reluctant Captive: Year down Under. Helen Bianchin. (Presents Ser.). 1993. mass mkt. 2.99 (*0-373-11601-2*, 1-11601-1) Harlequin Bks.

Reluctant Cavalier. Karen Harbaugh. 224p. 1996. pap. 5.50 (*0-451-19020-3*, Sig) NAL-Dutton.

Reluctant Confederates: Upper South Unionists in the Secession Crisis. Daniel W. Crofts. LC 88-6927. (Fred W. Morrison Series in Southern Studies). (Illus.). xxix, 502p. (C). 1993. reprint ed. pap. 22.50 (*0-8078-4430-6*) U of NC Pr.

Reluctant Cook. Jane Gibb. 160p. 1991. pap. 16.50 (*0-7136-3437-5*) Sheridan.

Reluctant Daddy. Helen Conrad. (Hometown Reunion Ser.). 1996. mass mkt. 4.50 (*0-373-82550-1*, 1-82550-4) Harlequin Bks.

Reluctant Deckhand. Jan Padgett. 128p. (Orig.). (J). 1995. pap. 7.95 (*1-895766-01-X*, Pub. by Pacific Educ Pr CN) Orca Bk Pubs.

Reluctant Desire. Catherine Grant. (Rainbow Romances Ser.). 160p. 1995. 14.95 (*0-7090-5493-9*, 921) Parkwest Pubns.

Reluctant Desire. large type ed. Catherine Grant. (Linford Romance Library). 272p. 1996. pap. 15.99 (*0-7089-7830-4*) Ulverscroft.

Reluctant Dragon. Steven C. Anderson et al. 59p. 1990. pap. 5.00 (*0-87129-066-9*, R50) Dramatic Pub.

Reluctant Dragon. Kenneth Grahame. LC 89-1658. (Illus.). 58p. (J). (gr. 3-6). 1938. 14.95 (*0-8234-0093-X*); pap. 6.95 (*0-8234-0755-1*) Holiday.

Reluctant Dragon. Kenneth Grahame. 23p. (Orig.). (J). (gr. 2-9). 1993. pap. 3.00 (*1-57514-228-7*, 1074) Encore Perform Pub.

Reluctant Dragon. Kenneth Grahame. LC 83-209. (Illus.). 48p. (Orig.). (J). (gr. 2-4). 1988. pap. 6.95 (*0-8050-0802-0*, Bks Young Read) H Holt & Co.

Reluctant Dragon. Kenneth Grahame. Ed. by I. M. Richardson. LC 87-10906. (Illus.). 32p. (Orig.). (J). (gr. k-4). 1988. lib. bdg. 11.89 (*0-8167-1059-7*) Troll Communs.

Reluctant Dragon. Kenneth Grahame. Ed. by I. M. Richardson. LC 87-10906. (Illus.). 32p. (Orig.). (J). (gr. k-4). 1997. pap. 3.95 (*0-8167-1060-0*) Troll Communs.

***Reluctant Dragon.** Mary H. Surface. (Orig.). (J). 1997. pap. 5.50 (*0-87602-361-8*) Anchorage.

Reluctant Emperor: A Biography of John Cantacuzene, Byzantine Emperor & Monk c. 1295-1383. Donald M. Nicol. (Illus.). 217p. (C). 1996. text ed. 39.95 (*0-521-55256-7*) Cambridge U Pr.

Reluctant Empress: A Biography of Elisabeth of Austria. Brigitte Hamann. LC 86-45512. 432p. 1986. 25.00 (*0-394-53717-3*) Knopf.

Reluctant Enemies. Vivian Vaughn. 384p. 1995. mass mkt. 4.99 (*0-8217-4933-1*, Pinncle Kensgtn) Kensgtn Pub Corp.

Reluctant Entrepreneurs. Ed. by Rob Paton. 192p. 1990. 95.00 (*0-335-09233-0*, Open Univ Pr); pap. 39.00 (*0-335-09232-2*, Open Univ Pr) Taylor & Francis.

Reluctant Exhibitionist. Martin Shepard. LC 83-63255. 280p. 1985. pap. 5.95 (*0-932966-57-8*) Permanent Pr.

Reluctant Exiles? Migration from Hong Kong & the New Overseas Chinese. Ed. by Ronald Skeldon. LC 94-9887. (Hong Kong Becoming China: the Transition to 1997 Ser.). 380p. (C). 1994. pap. text ed. 29.95 (*1-56324-432-2*, East Gate Bk) M E Sharpe.

Reluctant Exiles? Migration from Hong Kong & the New Overseas Chinese. Ed. by Ronald Skeldon. LC 94-9887. (Hong Kong Becoming China The Transition to 1997 Ser.). 380p. (C). (gr. 13). 1994. 75.95 (*1-56324-431-4*, East Gate Bk) M E Sharpe.

Reluctant Exiles: Migration from Hong Kong & the New Overseas Chinese. Ed. by Ronald Skeldon. 380p. 1994. pap. 49.50 (*962-209-334-5*) Coronet Bks.

Reluctant Expatriate: The Life of Harold Frederic. Robert M. Myers. LC 94-39267. (Contributions to the Study of World Literature Ser.: Vol. 59). 216p. 1995. text ed. 52.95 (*0-313-29256-6*, Greenwood Pr) Greenwood.

Reluctant Farmer: The Rise of Agricultural Extension to 1914. Roy V. Scott. LC 70-102023. 374p. reprint ed. pap. 106.60 (*0-317-28992-6*, 2020235) Bks Demand.

Reluctant Feminists in German Social Democracy, 1885-1917. Jean H. Quataert. LC 78-70411. 327p. reprint ed. pap. 93.20 (*0-8357-3850-7*, 2036583) Bks Demand.

Reluctant for Romance. large type ed. Pamela Fudge. (Linford Romance Library). 240p. 1995. pap. 15.99 (*0-7089-7792-8*, Linford) Ulverscroft.

***Reluctant Frontiersman: James Ross Larkin on the Sante Fe Trail, 1856-57.** James R. Larkin. Ed. & Anno. by Barton H. Barbour. LC 89-25073. (Illus.). 220p. 1990. reprint ed. pap. 62.70 (*0-608-04136-X*, 2064869) Bks Demand.

Reluctant Ghost. Sheila R. Allen. (Lovers of Steadford Abbey Ser.). 252p. 1989. 18.95 (*0-8027-1057-3*) Walker & Co.

Reluctant God. Pamela F. Service. 192p. 1990. mass mkt. 4.50 (*0-449-70339-8*, Juniper) Fawcett.

Reluctant Guest. large type ed. Rosalind Brett. 1990. 25.99 (*0-7089-2276-7*) Ulverscroft.

***Reluctant Gun.** John J. Howard. 236p. (Orig.). 1997. mass mkt. 4.99 (*1-55237-071-2*, Pub. by Comnwlth Pub CN) Partners Pubs Grp.

***Reluctant Healer.** Susana Stoica. 100p. (Orig.). 1996. pap. 8.95 (*0-9654575-0-8*) Healing Alternat.

Reluctant Heart. Lois Stewart. 352p. 1994. mass mkt. 3.99 (*0-8217-4696-0*, Zebra Kensgtn) Kensgtn Pub Corp.

Reluctant Heart. large type ed. Jane Lester. 416p. 1988. 25.99 (*0-7089-1802-6*) Ulverscroft.

Reluctant Heir. large type ed. Grace Richmond. (Linford Romance Library). 1990. pap. 15.99 (*0-7089-6948-8*, Trailtree Bookshop) Ulverscroft.

Reluctant Heiress. Evelyn Richardson. 1996. pap. 4.99 (*0-451-18766-0*, Sig) NAL-Dutton.

Reluctant Hero. Richard Anderson. 140p. 1990. pap. 9.95 (*1-55523-392-9*) Winston-Derek.

Reluctant Hero. Sandra Paul. 1994. pap. 2.75 (*0-373-91016-9*, 5-91016-1); pap. 2.75 (*0-373-19016-6*, 5-19016-0) Harlequin Bks.

Reluctant Hero: A Snowy Road to Salem in 1802. Philip Brady. 144p. (YA). (gr. 7 up). 1990. 16.95 (*0-8027-6972-1*); lib. bdg. 17.85 (*0-8027-6974-8*) Walker & Co.

Reluctant Heroine. Dawn Lindsey. (Signet Regency Romance Ser.). 224p. (Orig.). 1993. pap. 3.99 (*0-451-17525-5*, Sig) NAL-Dutton.

Reluctant Heroine. large type ed. Dawn Lindsey. LC 93-37451. (Orig.). 1994. lib. bdg. 19.95 (*0-7862-0097-9*) Thorndike Pr.

Reluctant Hostage. large type ed. Margaret Mayo. 1992. lib. bdg. 18.95 (*0-263-13126-2*, Pub. by Mills & Boon UK) Thorndike Pr.

Reluctant Hosts: Europe & Its Refugees. Ed. by Daniele Johy & Robin Cohen. (Illus.). 250p. 1989. text ed. 65.95 (*0-566-07106-1*, Pub. by Avebury Pub UK) Ashgate Pub Co.

Reluctant Hunk. Lorna Michaels. (Temptation Ser.: No. 523). 1995. mass mkt. 2.99 (*0-373-25623-X*, 1-25623-9) Harlequin Bks.

Reluctant Icon: Gladstone, Bulgaria, & the Working Classes, 1856-1878. Ann P. Saab. (Historical Studies: Vol. 109). 257p. (C). 1991. 39.95 (*0-674-75965-6*) HUP.

Reluctant King. L. Sprague De Camp. 256p. 1996. mass mkt. 6.99 (*0-671-87746-1*) Baen Bks.

Reluctant Lawman. Bob Terrell. LC 95-20579. (Illus.). 141p. 1995. pap. 9.95 (*1-57090-027-2*) Alexander Bks.

***Reluctant Lord.** Teresa Desjardien. 256p. 1997. mass mkt. 4.99 (*0-614-23651-7*, Zebra Kensgtn) Kensgtn Pub Corp.

Reluctant Lover. Katherine Arthur. 1993. mass mkt. 2.99 (*0-373-03282-X*, 1-03282-0) Harlequin Bks.

Reluctant Lovers. Elizabeth Chadwick. (Chicago Girls Ser.). 448p. (Orig.). 1993. mass mkt., pap. text ed. 4.99 (*0-8439-3540-5*) Dorchester Pub Co.

Reluctant Managers. Richard Scase & Robert Goffee. 224p. 1989. text ed. 55.00 (*0-04-305016-6*); pap. text ed. 19.95 (*0-04-305017-4*) Routledge Chapman & Hall.

***Reluctant Metropolis: The Politics of Urban Growth in Los Angeles.** William Fulton. LC 97-6374. (Illus.). 1997. 28.95 (*0-923956-22-0*) Solano Pr.

***Reluctant Mistress.** large type ed. Natalie Fox. (Magna Large Print Ser.). 222p. 1997. 27.50 (*0-7505-1173-7*) Thorndike Pr.

Reluctant Modernism: American Thought & Culture, 1880-1900. George Cotkin. (American Thought & Culture Ser.). 250p. (C). 1992. 28.95 (*0-8057-9054-3*, Twayne); pap. 15.95 (*0-8057-9059-4*, Twayne) Scribnrs Ref.

Reluctant Modernism of Hannah Arendt. Seyla Benhabib. LC 95-50247. (Modernity & Political Thought Ser.: Vol. 10). 336p. (C). 1996. 48.00 (*0-8039-3816-0*); pap. 22.95 (*0-8039-3817-9*) Sage.

Reluctant Modernist: Andrei Belyi & the Development of Russian Fiction, 1902-1914. Roger Keys. LC 95-45544. 288p. (C). 1996. 70.00 (*0-19-815160-8*, Clarendon Pr) OUP.

Reluctant Nation: Australia & the Allied Defeat of Japan, 1942-1945. David Day. (Illus.). 344p. 1992. 49.95 (*0-19-553242-2*) OUP.

Reluctant Naturalist: A Study of G.E. Moore's Principia Ethica. Dennis Rohatyn. 150p. (Orig.). (C). 1987. lib. bdg. 40.50 (*0-8191-5767-8*) U Pr of Amer.

Reluctant Neighbor: Turkey's Role in the Middle East. Henri J. Barkey. 1996. pap. text ed. 17.95 (*1-878379-64-X*) US Inst Peace.

Reluctant Odyssey. Edith Pargeter. 295p. 1991. pap. 13.95 (*0-7472-3336-5*, Pub. by Headline UK) Trafalgar.

Reluctant Partners: Implementing Federal Policy. Robert P. Stoker. LC 91-50112. (Policy & Institutional Studies). 232p. (C). 1992. text ed. 49.95 (*0-8229-3688-7*) U of Pittsburgh Pr.

Reluctant Partners: Nashville & the Union, July 1, 1863, to June 30, 1865. Walter T. Durham. (Illus.). 320p. 1987. 19.95 (*0-9615966-1-9*) TN His Soc.

Reluctant Partners? NGOs, the State & Sustainable Agricultural Development. John W. Farrington et al. LC 93-7407. (Non-Governmental Organizations Ser.). (Illus.). 256p. (C). 1993. pap. 19.95 (*0-415-08844-5*, A9833) Routledge.

Reluctant Partners? NGOs, the State & Sustainable Agricultural Development. John W. Farrington et al. LC 93-7407. (Non-Governmental Organizations Ser.). (Illus.). 256p. (C). (gr. 13). 1993. text ed. 74.95 (*0-415-08843-7*, A9829) Routledge.

Reluctant Pilgrim: Defoe's Emblematic Method & Quest for Form in Robinson Crusoe. J. Paul Hunter. LC 66-16045. 251p. reprint ed. pap. 71.60 (*0-7837-2650-3*, 2043004) Bks Demand.

Reluctant Pillar: New York & the Adoption of the Federal Constitution. 2nd ed. Ed. by Stephen L. Schechter. LC 84-22266. 255p. 1985. reprint ed. pap. 13.95 (*0-930309-00-6*) Madison Hse.

Reluctant Pioneer: Mary Vowell Adams. Beatrice L. Bliss. (Illus.). 256p. 1992. reprint ed. pap. 13.95 (*0-9622738-4-8*) M Bliss.

Reluctant Pioneers: Constraints & Opportunities in an Icelandic Fishing Community. Willy C. Van den Hoonaard. LC 91-41982. (American University Studies: Anthropology & Science: Ser. XI, Vol. 59). 173p. (C). 1992. text ed. 36.95 (*0-8204-1801-3*) P Lang Pubng.

***Reluctant Pitcher, 57 Vols., Vol. 54.** Matt Christopher. (Matt Christopher Sports Classics Ser.). 1997. pap. text ed. 3.95 (*0-316-14127-5*) Little.

Reluctant Playwright. Botha. (African Writers Ser.). 232p. (C). 1993. pap. 10.95 (*0-435-90589-9*, 90589) Heinemann.

Reluctant Prisoner. large type ed. Stephanie Howard. 302p. 1995. 25.99 (*0-7505-0743-8*, Pub. by Magna Print Bks UK) Ulverscroft.

Reluctant Proposal. Violet Hamilton. 256p. 1993. mass mkt. 3.99 (*0-8217-4232-9*, Zebra Kensgtn) Kensgtn Pub Corp.

Reluctant Queen: The Story of Anne of York. large type ed. Jean Plaidy. LC 94-919. 1994. lib. bdg. 22.95 (*0-8161-7426-1*, GK Hall) Thorndike Pr.

Reluctant Ratifiers: Virginia Considers the Federal Constitution. Edwin L. Shepard. (Illus.). 48p. (Orig.). 1988. pap. text ed. 1.00 (*0-945015-01-1*) VA Hist Soc.

Reluctant Reader: How to Get & Keep Kids Reading. Wendy M. Williams. (Orig.). 1995. pap. write for info. (*0-446-67120-7*) Warner Bks.

Reluctant Reader: How to Get & Keep Kids Reading. Wendy M. Williams. 224p. (Orig.). 1996. mass mkt. 5.99 (*0-446-60338-4*) Warner Bks.

Reluctant Realists: The CDU-CSU & West German Ostpolitik. Clay Clemens. LC 88-29340. 370p. (C). 1989. text ed. 59.95 (*0-8223-0900-9*) Duke.

Reluctant Rebel: The Secret Diary of Robert Patrick, 1861-1865. Ed. by F. Jay Taylor. LC 59-9083. (Illus.). 288p. (C). 1996. pap. 12.95 (*0-8071-2072-3*) La State U Pr.

Reluctant Rebel in Air Force Blues. J. Remy Theberge. LC 77-74192. (Illus.). 270p. 1977. 14.50 (*0-918862-01-9*) Golden Gambit.

Reluctant Rebels: Comparative Studies of Revolution & Underdevelopment. John Walton. LC 83-7698. 1984. text ed. 49.50 (*0-231-05728-8*); pap. text ed. 17.00 (*0-231-05729-6*) Col U Pr.

Reluctant Rebels see Lawful Revolution: Louis Kossuth & the Hungarians, 1848-1849

Reluctant Reformers: The Impact of Racism on American Social Reform Movements. Robert Allen. LC 73-85495. 1974. pap. 12.95 (*0-88258-026-4*) Howard U Pr.

Reluctant Reforms: The Cristiani Government & the International Community in the Process of Salvadoran Post-War Reconstruction. Peter Sollis. 57p. (Orig.). 1993. pap. 7.00 (*0-929513-25-8*) WOLA.

Reluctant Retreat: The Soviet & East German Departure from Central Planning. Phillip J. Bryson. (Illus.). 420p. 1995. text ed. 62.95 (*1-85521-523-3*, Pub. by Dartmth Pub UK) Ashgate Pub Co.

***Reluctant Reunion.** Jim MaJure. 304p. 1996. 19.95 (*0-9650474-7-4*) Winchester OR.

***Reluctant Revolutionaries: New York City & the Road to Independence, 1763-1776.** Joseph S. Tiedemann. LC 96-35249. (Illus.). 352p. 1996. 45.00 (*0-8014-3237-5*) Cornell U Pr.

Reluctant Revolutionary: An Essay on David Hume's Account of Necessary Connection. Alan Schwerin. (American University Studies: Philosophy: Ser. V, Vol. 62). 160p. (C). 1989. text ed. 28.95 (*0-8204-0757-7*) P Lang Pubng.

***Reluctant Rogue.** Pam McCutcheon. 1997. mass mkt. 3.75 (*0-373-16696-6*, 1-16696-6) Harlequin Bks.

Reluctant Rogue: or Mother's Day. John Patrick. 1984. pap. 5.25 (*0-8222-0942-X*) Dramatists Play.

Reluctant Santa: Christmas Has Been Cancelled. Daniel A. Birchmore. LC 95-20584. (Illus.). 32p. (J). (ps-3). 1997. 15.95 (*1-887813-00-4*) Cucumber Island.

Reluctant Shaman. Kay C. Whitaker. 1991. 16.95 (*0-00-002649-2*, HarpT) HarpC.

Reluctant Shaman: A Woman's First Encounters with the Unseen Spirits of the Earth. Kay C. Whitaker. LC 90-55404. 1991. reprint ed. pap. 14.00 (*0-06-250943-8*) Harper SF.

***Reluctant Sheriff: The United States after the Cold War.** Richard N. Haass. LC 97-11422. 148p. 1997. 24.95 (*0-87609-198-2*) Coun Foreign.

Reluctant Soloist: A Directors Guide to Developing Church Vocalists. Debi Tyree. 96p. (Orig.). 1994. pap. 9.95 (*0-687-00656-2*) Abingdon.

Reluctant Spy. James Melville. 224p. 1995. 20.00 (*0-7278-4773-2*) Severn Hse.

Reluctant Superpower: A History of America's Economic Global Reach. Richard Holt. Ed. by John Urda. 304p. 1995. 30.00 (*1-56836-038-X*) Kodansha.

***Reluctant Superpower: United States' Policy in Bosnia, 1991-1995.** Wayne Bert. LC 96-46168. 1997. text ed. 35.00 (*0-312-17252-4*) St Martin.

Reluctant Swordsman. Dave Duncan. 1988. mass mkt. 5.99 (*0-345-35291-2*, Del Rey) Ballantine.

Reluctant Treasures: The Practice of Analytic Psychotherapy. Gordon Warme. LC 93-47136. 288p. 1994. 40.00 (*1-56821-217-8*) Aronson.

Reluctant Valor: The Oral History of Captain Thomas J. Evans, United States Third Army, 4th Armored Division (Code Name--Harpoon), 704th Tank Destroyer Battalion, European Theatre of Operations: The Lorraine Tank Battles & the US Third Army's March to Czechoslovakia: Containing the Combat Diary of the 704th TD Company C by Walter E. Mullen & Norman E. Macomber. Ed. by Richard D. Wissolik et al. 1995. write for info. (*1-885851-05-7*) St Vincent Coll.

Reluctant Vegetarian Cookbook. Simon Hope. 216p. 1992. pap. 34.95 (*0-7506-0992-3*) Buttrwrth-Heinemann.

Reluctant Viking. Sandra Hill. 448p. (Orig.). 1994. mass mkt., pap. text ed. 4.99 (*0-505-51983-6*) Dorchester Pub Co.

Reluctant Vision: An Essay in the Philosophy of Religion. Thomas P. Burke. LC 73-88354. 142p. (Orig.). reprint ed. pap. 40.50 (*0-685-15427-0*, 2026883) Bks Demand.

Reluctant Warrior. Michael C. Hodgins. 1997. mass mkt. 5.99 (*0-8041-1120-0*) Ivy Books.

Reluctant Warrior: A True Story of Duty & Heroism in Vietnam. Michael C. Hodgins. 400p. 1997. 24.00 (*0-449-91059-8*) Fawcett.

Reluctant Warrior: The Soviet Union & Arms Control. Coit D. Blacker. LC 86-32011. (Political Science Ser.). (Illus.). 850p. (C). 1995. pap. text ed. write for info. (*0-7167-1862-6*) W H Freeman.

Reluctant Welfare State: A History of American Social Welfare Policies. 2nd ed. Bruce S. Jansson. 278p. (C). 1993. text ed. 36.00 (*0-534-16386-6*) Brooks-Cole.

Reluctant Welfare State: American Social Welfare Policies - Past, Present, & Future. 3rd ed. Bruce S. Jansson. LC 96-12028. (Social Work Ser.). 407p. (C). 1997. text ed. 36.95 (*0-534-34141-1*) Brooks-Cole.

Reluctant Widow. large type ed. Georgette Heyer. LC 92-10161. 449p. 1992. reprint ed. lib. bdg. 20.95 (*1-56054-205-5*) Thorndike Pr.

Reluctant Witnesses: Jews & the Christian Imagination. Stephen R. Haynes. LC 94-22554. 224p. (Orig.). 1995. pap. 19.00 (*0-664-25579-5*) Westminster John Knox.

Reluctantly Alice. Phyllis Reynolds Naylor. LC 90-37956. 192p. (J). (gr. 3-7). 1991. lib. bdg. 15.00 (*0-689-31681-X*, Atheneum Bks Young) S&S Childrens.

Reluctantly Single: You Can Stop Waiting for Life to Happen & Start to Live. Harold I. Smith. LC 94-11825. 160p. (Orig.). 1994. pap. 10.95 (*0-687-36048-X*) Abingdon.

Relying on the Holy Spirit. Charles Stanley. (In Touch Study Ser.: Vol. 4). 96p. 1996. pap. 5.99 (*0-7852-6292-X*, Oliver-Nelson) Nelson.

Relying on the Holy Spirit: Experience the Joy-Filled Walk with God under the Anointing of... Charles Stanley. (In Touch Study Ser.). 1996. pap. text ed. 6.99 (*0-7852-7260-7*) Nelson.

REM. David Harrington. (CD Bks.). (Illus.). 120p. 1994. pap. 7.99 (*1-886894-16-7*, MBS Paperbk) Mus Bk Servs.

R.E.M. Peter Hogan. (Complete Guides to the Music Of... Ser.). (Illus.). 114p. (Orig.). (C). pap. 7.95 (*0-7119-4901-8*, OP 47769) Omnibus NY.

***REM: CD Interview Book.** (Interview CD Bks.). (Illus.). Date not set. 14.99 (*1-57899-005-X*) Mus Bk Servs.

***R.E.M. In Their Own Words.** Peter Hogan. (Illus.). 96p. (Orig.). pap. 15.95 (*0-7119-6162-X*, OP47862) Omnibus NY.

REM: The "Rolling Stone" Files: The Ultimate Compendium of Interviews, Articles, Facts & Opinions from the Files of "Rolling Stone" Rolling Stone Editors. 208p. 1995. pap. 12.95 (*0-7868-8054-6*) Hyperion.

Rem - Automatic for the People: Automatic for the People. Ed. by Michael Lefferts. 72p. (Orig.). (C). 1997. pap. text ed. 20.95 (*0-7935-2746-5*, 00308203) H Leonard.

Rem - Out of Time: Out of Time. Ed. by Michael Lefferts. 72p. (Orig.). (C). 1997. pap. text ed. 20.95 (*0-7935-2748-1*, 00308202) H Leonard.

Rem Koolhaas: Conversations with Students. (Architecture at Rice Ser.: Vol. 30). (Illus.). 80p. (Orig.). 1996. pap. 14.95 (*1-885232-02-0*) Princeton Arch.

Rem Koolhaas-OMA: Architecture 1970-1990. Jacques Lucan. (Illus.). 176p. (Orig.). (FRE.). 1991. pap. 29.95 (*1-878271-55-5*) Princeton Arch.

Rem, Monster. 19.95 (*0-7935-4394-0*, 00690037) H Leonard.

R.E.M. Remarks. Tony Fletcher. (Illus.). 160p. pap. 17.95 (*0-7119-3221-2*, OP 47212) Omnibus NY.

REM Sleep. John W. Crisanti, Jr. LC 93-93507. 120p. (Orig.). 1994. pap. 6.95 (*1-56002-370-8*, Univ Edtns) Aegina Pr.

REM Sleep: Its Temporal Distribution. Ed. by Charles A. Czeisler & Christian Guilleminault. 156p. 1980. reprint ed. pap. 44.50 (*0-608-00419-7*, 2061134) Bks Demand.

Rema. (J). 1991. 12.95 (*1-56062-090-0*) CIS Comm.

Remagen & Other Rhine Crossings. Walter Niedermayer. (Illus.). 67p. 1993. 9.95 (*0-935648-45-3*) Halldin Pub.

Remain with Me. Sam Tiesi. 31p. 1990. pap. 3.50 (*0-940535-35-1*, UP135) Franciscan U Pr.

Remainder of My Bread. limited ed. Elisabeth Marshall. 64p. 1995. write for info. (*0-9649013-0-7*) Listning Post Pr.

Remainder of One. Elinor J. Pinczes. LC 94-5446. (Illus.). 32p. (J). (gr. k-3). 1995. 14.95 (*0-395-69455-8*) HM.

R

Remainder of Their Days: Domestic Policy & Older Families in the United States & Canada. Ed. by Carolyn J. Rosenthal & Jon Hendricks. LC 92-44317. 248p. 1993. text ed. 40.00 (*0-8153-0483-8*, SS795) Garland.

Remaines Concerning Britain. William Camden. LC 77-113572. (Illus.). reprint ed. 84.50 (*0-404-01367-8*) AMS Pr.

Remaines of Gentilisme & Judaisme, Sixteen Hundred Eighty-Six to Eighty-Seven. John Aubrey. Ed. by James Britten. (Folk-Lore Society, London Monographs: Vol. 4). 1974. reprint ed. pap. 35.00 (*0-8115-0501-4*) Periodicals Srv.

Remaining in Light: Ant Meditations on a Painting by Edward Hopper. John Taggart. LC 92-24809. (SUNY Series, The Margins of Literature). 143p. (C). 1993. text ed. 59.50 (*0-7914-1505-8*); pap. text ed. 19.95 (*0-7914-1506-6*) State U NY Pr.

Remains. W. D. Snodgrass. 1985. pap. text ed. 5.00 (*1-880238-11-X*) BOA Edns.

Remains: Stories of Vietnam. William Crapser. LC 88-6667. 175p. 1988. pap. 9.95 (*0-937584-14-2*) Sachem Pr.

Remains Concerning Britain. William Camden. Ed. by R. D. Dunn. 632p. 1984. 80.00 (*0-8020-2457-2*) U of Toronto Pr.

Remains Concerning Britain. William Camden & Edgar Mertner. (Anglistica & Americana Ser.: No. 74). ix, 446p. 1970. reprint ed. 120.00 (*0-685-66440-6*, 05102523) G Olms Pubs.

Remains of Animals in Quaternary Lake & Bog Sediments & Their Interpretation. Ed. by David G. Frey. (Limnology Report). (Illus.). 116p. (Orig.). 1964. pap. text ed. 20.00 (*3-510-47002-8*, Pub. by E Schweizerbartsche GW) Lubrecht & Cramer.

Remains of Christopher Columbus. Joseph R. Muratore. (Illus.). 91p. 1973. pap. 3.00 (*0-686-09021-7*) Muratore.

Remains of Distant Times Vol. 19: Archaeology & the National Trust. Ed. by David M. Evans et al. (Occasional Papers). (Illus.). 248p. 1996. 53.00 (*0-85115-671-1*) Boydell & Brewer.

Remains of Old Latin, 4 vols. Ed. by E. H. Warmington. Incl. Vol. 1. Ennius. Caecilius. (ENG & LAT.). 14.50 (*0-674-99324-1*); Vol. 2. Livius Andronicus, Naevius, Pacuvius, Accius. (ENG & LAT.). 14.50 (*0-674-99347-0*); Vol. 3. Lucilius. Laws of the XII Tables. (ENG & LAT.). 14.50 (*0-674-99363-2*); Vol. 4. Archaic Inscriptions. (ENG & LAT.). 14.50 (*0-674-99396-9*); (Loeb Classical Library: Nos. 294, 314, 329, 359). (ENG & LAT.). write for info. (*0-318-53174-7*) HUP.

Remains of the Day. Kazuo Ishiguro. 1989. 22.00 (*0-394-57343-9*) Knopf.

Remains of the Day. Kazuo Ishiguro. LC 90-50177. (Vintage International Ser.). 256p. 1990. pap. 12.00 (*0-679-73172-5*, Vin) Random.

Remains of the Day: A Novel. Kazuo Ishiguro. 1993. pap. 11.00 (*0-394-25134-2*, Vin) Random.

Remains of the Early Popular Poetry of England, 4 Vols. Ed. by William C. Hazlitt. reprint ed. 350.00 (*0-404-03240-0*) AMS Pr.

Remains of the Rev. James Marsh, D.D., Late President, & Professor of Moral & Intellectual Philosophy, in the University of Vermont: With a Memoir of His Life. James Marsh. (American Biography Ser.). 642p. 1991. reprint ed. lib. bdg. 109.00 (*0-7812-8269-1*) Rprt Serv.

Remains to Be Seen. Contrib. by John Luedke et al. (Illus.). 72p. 1983. pap. 18.95 (*0-932718-15-9*) Kohler Arts.

Remains to Be Seen. large type ed. Roy Hart. 1991. 25.99 (*0-7089-2535-9*) Ulverscroft.

Remains to Be Seen: Essays on Marguerite Duras. Ed. by Sanford S. Ames. (American University Studies: Romance, Languages & Literature: Ser. 2, Vol. 72). 298p. 1988. 44.00 (*0-8204-0596-5*) P Lang Pubng.

Remake. Christine Brooke-Rose. 160p. 1996. pap. 18.95 (*1-85754-222-3*, Pub. by Carcanet Pr UK) Paul & Co Pubs.

Remake. Connie Willis. 160p. 1996. mass mkt. 5.99 (*0-553-57441-8*) Bantam.

Remake. limited ed. Connie Willis. 1994. boxed 45.00 (*0-929480-48-1*) Mark Ziesing.

***Remake: As Time Goes By.** Stephen H. Bogart. LC 96-33982. 1997. 22.95 (*0-312-85666-0*) Forge NYC.

Remaking America: How the Benevolent Traditions of Many Cultures Are Transforming Our National Life. James A. Joseph. (Non Profit Sector Ser.). 278p. text ed. 24.95 (*0-7879-0095-8*) Jossey-Bass.

Remaking America: Public Memory, Commemoration, & Patriotism in the Twentieth Century. John Bodnar. 318p. (C). 1992. pap. text ed. 15.95 (*0-691-03495-8*) Princeton U Pr.

Remaking & Lost Harmony: Stories from the Hispanic Caribbean. Ed. by Margarite F. Olmos & Lizabeth Paravisini-Gebert. (Dispatches Ser.: Vol. 3). 250p. (Orig.). 1995. pap. 17.00 (*1-877727-36-9*) White Pine.

Remaking Australia: The State, the Market, & Australia's Future. Hugh Emy. 272p. 1994. pap. 19.95 (*1-86373-450-3*, Pub. by Allen Unwin AT) Paul & Co Pubs.

Remaking China Policy: U. S.-China Relations & Governmental Decisionmaking. Richard Moorsteen & Morton Abramowitz. LC 74-164428. (Rand Corporation Research Studies). 174p. 1971. 18.95 (*0-674-75981-8*) HUP.

Remaking Cities: Proceedings of the 1988 International Conference in Pittsburgh. Ed. by Barbara Davis. LC 89-60853. (Illus.). 200p. 1989. pap. 12.95 (*0-8229-6906-8*) U of Pittsburgh Pr.

Remaking Congress: Change & Stability in the 1990's. Ed. by James A. Thurber & Roger H. Davidson. LC 95-35110. 230p. 1995. 38.95 (*1-56802-160-7*) Congr Quarterly.

Remaking Congress: Change & Stability in the 1990's. Ed. by James A. Thurber & Roger H. Davidson. LC 95-35110. 230p. 1995. pap. 24.95 (*1-56802-161-5*) Congr Quarterly.

Remaking Dixie: The Impact of World War II on the American South. Ed. by Neil R. McMillen. 192p. 1997. text ed. 47.50 (*0-87805-927-X*); pap. text ed. 18.00 (*0-87805-928-8*) U Pr of Miss.

Remaking Eastern Europe - On the Political Economy of Transition. Jozef M. Van Brabant. (International Studies in Economics & Econometrics). 244p. 1990. lib. bdg. 141.50 (*0-7923-0955-3*) Kluwer Ac.

Remaking Health Care in America: Building Organized Delivery Systems. Stephen M. Shortell et al. LC 95-46557. (Health Ser.). 350p. Date not set. 35.95 (*0-7879-0227-6*) Jossey-Bass.

Remaking History. Ed. by Barbara Kruger & Philomena Mariani. LC 89-650815. (Discussions in Contemporary Culture Ser.: No. 4). 308p. (Orig.). 1989. pap. 10.95 (*0-941920-12-7*) Bay Pr.

Remaking History & Other Stories. Kim S. Robinson. 528p. 1994. pap. 14.95 (*0-312-89012-5*) Orb NYC.

Remaking Human Geography. Ed. by Audrey Kobayashi & Suzanne Mackenzie. LC 88-34304. 288p. (C). 1989. pap. 24.95 (*0-04-445325-6*) Routledge Chapman & Hall.

Remaking Ibieca: Life in Aragon under Franco. Susan F. Harding. LC 83-21884. (Illus.). vii, 348p. 1984. 37.50 (*0-8078-1594-2*) U of NC Pr.

Remaking Liberalism: The Intellectual Legacy of Adam Shortt, O. D. Skelton, W. C. Clark, & W. A. Mackintosh, 1890-1925. Barry Ferguson. 336p. 1993. 49.95 (*0-7735-1113-X*, Pub. by McGill CN) U of Toronto Pr.

***Remaking Men: Jung Spirituality & Social Change.** David Tacey. 240p. (C). 1997. pap. 18.95 (*0-415-14241-5*); text ed. 65.00 (*0-415-14240-7*) Routledge.

Remaking of France: The National Assembly, the Constitution of 1791, & the Reorganization of the French Polity, 1789-1791. Michael P. Fitzsimmons. LC 93-35732. 288p. (C). 1994. text ed. 59.95 (*0-521-45407-7*) Cambridge U Pr.

Remaking of Istanbul: Portrait of an Ottoman City in the Nineteenth Century. Zeynep Celik. LC 92-31825. 201p. 1993. 16.95 (*0-520-08239-7*) U CA Pr.

Remaking of Modern Armies. Basil H. Liddell-Hart. 1980. lib. bdg. 64.95 (*0-8490-3189-3*) Gordon Pr.

Remaking of Pittsburgh: Class & Culture in an Industrializing City, 1877-1919. Francis G. Couvares. LC 83-5044. 187p. 1984. text ed. 59.50 (*0-87395-778-4*); pap. text ed. 19.95 (*0-87395-779-2*) State U NY Pr.

Remaking of Radio. Vincent M. Ditingo. (Illus.). 160p. 1994. pap. 29.95 (*0-240-80174-1*, Focal) Buttrwrth-Heinemann.

***Remaking of Television New Zealand 1984-1992.** Barry Spicer et al. 224p. 1997. pap. 24.95 (*1-86940-151-4*, Pub. by Auckland Univ NZ) Paul & Co Pubs.

Remaking of the British Working Class, 1840-1940. Mike Savage & Andrew Miles. LC 93-38448. (Historical Connections Ser.). 112p. (C). 1994. pap. 11.95 (*0-415-07320-0*, B3938) Routledge.

Remaking Our Schools: What Has Gone Wrong & New Ways to Fix It. Edward C. Pino. 200p. (Orig.). (C). 1993. lib. bdg. 19.95 (*1-883732-01-8*) I G S.

Remaking Peasant China: Problems of Rural Development & Institutions at the Start of the 1990s. Ed. by Jorgen Delman et al. 226p. (Orig.). (C). 1991. 42.50 (*87-7288-294-8*, Pub. by Aarhus Univ Pr DK) David Brown.

***Remaking Planning: Politics of Urban Change.** 2nd ed. Tim Brindley & Yvonne Rydin. 240p. (C). 1996. pap. 24.95 (*0-415-09874-2*) Routledge.

Remaking Planning: The Politics of Urban Change in the Thatcher Years. Tim Brindley et al. 192p. (C). (gr. 13). 1989. text ed. 65.00 (*0-04-711021-X*) Routledge Chapman & Hall.

***Remaking Queen Victoria.** Ed. by Margaret Homans & Adrienne Munich. (Studies in Nineteenth-Century Literature & Culture: Vol. 10). (Illus.). 300p. (C). 1997. text ed. 59.95 (*0-521-57379-3*) Cambridge U Pr.

***Remaking Queen Victoria.** Ed. by Margaret Homans & Adrienne Munich. (Studies in Nineteenth-Century Literature & Culture: Vol. 10). (Illus.). 300p. (C). 1997. pap. text ed. 19.95 (*0-521-57485-4*) Cambridge U Pr.

Remaking Russia: Voices from Within. Heyward Isham. LC 94-38420. 358p. (gr. 13). 1995. pap. 26.95 (*1-56324-436-5*) M E Sharpe.

Remaking Russia: Voices from Within. Ed. by Heyward Isham. LC 94-38420. 358p. (gr. 13). 1995. 64.95 (*1-56324-435-7*) M E Sharpe.

Remaking Society. Murray Bookchin. 208p. 1989. 37.95 (*0-921689-03-9*, Pub. by Black Rose Bks CN); pap. 18.95 (*0-921689-02-0*, Pub. by Black Rose Bks CN) Consort Bk Sales.

Remaking Society: Pathways to a Green Future. Murray Bookchin. LC 89-21990. 222p. (Orig.). (C). 1990. 30.00 (*0-89608-373-X*); pap. 10.00 (*0-89608-372-1*) South End Pr.

Remaking the Agrarian Dream: New Deal Rural Resettlement in the Mountain West. Brian Q. Cannon. 208p. 1996. 40.00 (*0-8263-1716-2*) U of NM Pr.

Remaking the Argentine Economy. Felipe De La Balze. 150p. 1995. pap. text ed. 14.95 (*0-87609-171-0*) Coun Foreign.

Remaking the Balkans. Christopher Cviic. (Chatham House Papers). 144p. 1991. pap. 14.95 (*0-87609-114-1*) Coun Foreign.

Remaking the Balkans. 2nd ed. Christopher Cviic. (Chatham House Papers). 128p. 1995. 50.00 (*1-85567-294-4*, Pub. by Pntr Pubs UK); pap. 15.95 (*1-85567-295-2*, Pub. by Pntr Pubs UK) Bks Intl VA.

Remaking the Earth: A Creation Story from the Great Plains of North America. Paul Goble. LC 96-4243. (Illus.). 32p. (J). (gr. k-3). 1996. 15.95 (*0-531-09524-X*); lib. bdg. 16.99 (*0-531-08874-X*) Orchard Bks Watts.

Remaking the Economic Institutions of Socialism: China & Eastern Europe. Ed. by David Stark & Victor G. Nee. 424p. 1989. 52.50 (*0-8047-1494-0*); pap. 16.95 (*0-8047-1495-9*) Stanford U Pr.

Remaking the European Security Order: Scenarios for the Post-Cold War Era. Barry G. Buzan et al. 224p. 1990. text ed. 49.00 (*0-86187-142-1*); text ed. 14.50 (*0-86187-143-X*) St Martin.

Remaking the Hexagon: The New France in the New Europe. Ed. by Gregory Flynn. (C). 1995. pap. text ed. 21.50 (*0-8133-8927-5*) Westview.

Remaking the International Monetary System: The Rio Agreement & Beyond. Fritz Machlup. LC 68-31419. (Committee For Economic Development, CED Supplementary Papers: No. 24). 171p. reprint ed. pap. 48.80 (*0-317-19923-4*, 2023125) Bks Demand.

Remaking the International Monetary System - the Rio Agreement & Beyond. Fritz Machlup. LC 68-31419. 176p. 1968. pap. 3.00 (*0-87186-224-7*) Comm Econ Dev.

***Remaking the Italian Economy.** Ricahrd M. Locke. (Cornell Studies in Political Economy). 256p. 1996. pap. 14.95 (*0-8014-8421-9*) Cornell U Pr.

Remaking the Italian Economy: Policy Failures & Local Successes in the Contemporary Polity. Richard M. Locke. (Studies in Political Economy). 256p. 1995. 29.95 (*0-8014-2891-2*) Cornell U Pr.

***Remaking the Labour Party: From Gaitskell to Blair.** Tudor Jones. LC 96-26319. 1996. write for info. (*0-415-12549-9*); pap. write for info. (*0-415-12550-2*) Routledge.

***Remaking the Middle East.** Ed. by Paul J. White & William S. Logan. 288p. 1997. 50.00 (*1-85973-163-5*) NYU Pr.

***Remaking the Middle East.** Ed. by Paul J. White & William S. Logan. 288p. 1997. pap. 19.50 (*1-85973-168-6*) NYU Pr.

Remaking the Nation: Identity & Politics in Latin America. Sarah Radcliffe & Sallie Westwood. LC 95-26840. 216p. (C). 1996. pap. 19.95 (*0-415-12337-2*); text ed. 65.00 (*0-415-12336-4*) Routledge.

Remaking the Past: Musical Modernism & the Influence of the Tonal Tradition. Joseph N. Straus. (Illus.). 264p. 1990. 37.50 (*0-674-75990-7*) HUP.

Remaking the Past to Make the Future. (Illus.). 48p. 1986. 5.00 (*0-685-65640-3*) NY Pub Lib.

Remaking the Shopping Center. Dean Schwanke. LC 94-60390. 171p. 1994. pap. text ed. 44.95 (*0-87420-756-8*, R29) Urban Land.

Remaking the Welfare State: Swedish Urban Planning & Policy-Making in the 1990s. Ed. by A. Khakee et al. 307p. (C). 1995. 63.95 (*1-85972-051-X*, Pub. by Avebury Pub UK) Ashgate Pub Co.

Remaking the Working Class? An Examination of Shop Stewards' Experiences. Bruce Spencer. 129p. 1989. 42.50 (*0-85124-508-0*, Pub. by Spokesman Bks UK) Coronet Bks.

***Remaking the World: Adventures in Engineering.** Henry Petroski. 1998. 24.00 (*0-375-40041-9*) Knopf.

Remaking the World Bank. Barend A. De Vries. LC 87-23406. 184p. (Orig.). 1988. pap. 14.95 (*0-932020-49-6*) Seven Locks Pr.

Remanufacturing Proceedings: Doing It Better the Second Time. American Production & Inventory Control Society Staff. 122p. 1992. 25.00 (*1-55822-098-4*) Am Prod & Inventory.

Remanufacturing Proceedings: Real Solutions from Real People. American Production & Inventory Control Society Staff. 152p. 1993. 25.00 (*1-55822-103-4*) Am Prod & Inventory.

Remanufacturing Proceedings: Regenerating Resources Through Repair & Remanufacturing. American Production & Inventory Control Society Staff. 43p. 1991. 25.00 (*1-55822-082-8*) Am Prod & Inventory.

Remanufacturing Resource Book. American Production & Inventory Control Society Staff. 392p. 1996. 15.00 (*1-55822-100-X*) Am Prod & Inventory.

Remapping China: Fissures in Historical Terrain. Ed. by Gail Hershatter et al. LC 95-14164. (Illus.). 364p. 1996. pap. 17.95 (*0-8047-2510-1*) Stanford U Pr.

Remapping China: Fissures in Historical Terrain. Ed. by Gail Hershatter et al. LC 95-14164. (Illus.). 364p. 1996. 45.00 (*0-8047-2509-8*) Stanford U Pr.

Remapping Memory: Space, Time, & the Politics of Memory. Ed. by Jonathan Boyarin. LC 94-9358. 1994. text ed. 44.95 (*0-8166-2452-6*); pap. text ed. 18.95 (*0-8166-2453-4*) U of Minn Pr.

Remapping the Postfranco Cinema. Ed. by M. Kinder. 134p. 1991. pap. text ed. 8.00 (*3-7186-0544-9*) Gordon & Breach.

Remarkable Advancement of the Afro-American. Mae Blair. LC 94-61587. 66p. 1997. per., pap. 12.95 (*1-55523-735-5*) Winston-Derek.

Remarkable Aerial Voyage. Willem Bilderdijk. Tr. & Intro. by Paul Vincent. LC 87-70814. 88p. 8700. pap. 13.95 (*0-905075-24-2*, Pub. by Wilfion Bks UK) Dufour.

Remarkable Agaves & Cacti. Park S. Nobel. (Illus.). 224p. 1994. pap. 24.95 (*0-19-508415-2*) OUP.

Remarkable Beatrix Potter. Alexander Grinstein. 360p. 1995. 50.00 (*0-8236-5789-2*) Intl Univs Pr.

Remarkable Case of Dorothy L. Sayers. Catherine Kenney. LC 89-39714. 327p. 1992. pap. 14.00 (*0-87338-458-X*) Kent St U Pr.

Remarkable Christmas of the Cobbler's Son. Ruth Sawyer. (J). 1997. pap. 5.99 (*0-14-054916-1*) Viking Penguin.

Remarkable Christmas of the Cobbler's Sons. Ruth Sawyer. (Illus.). 32p. (J). (ps-3). 1994. pap. 14.99 (*0-670-84922-7*) Viking Child Bks.

Remarkable Conversions & Striking Illustrations. H. C. Morrison. pap. 3.99 (*0-88019-102-3*) Schmul Pub Co.

Remarkable Discoveries! Frank Ashall. LC 93-46796. (Illus.). 388p. (C). 1994. text ed. 27.95 (*0-521-43317-7*) Cambridge U Pr.

Remarkable Discoveries! Frank Ashall. (Illus.). 292p. 1996. pap. text ed. 16.95 (*0-521-58953-3*) Cambridge U Pr.

Remarkable GG-1. Karl Zimmermann. 1977. pap. 12.95 (*0-915276-16-X*) Quadrant Pr.

***Remarkable Healings.** Modi. 500p. (Orig.). 1997. pap. text ed. 15.95 (*1-57174-079-1*) Hampton Roads Pub Co.

Remarkable Howe Caverns Story. Dana Cudmore. (Illus.). 192p. 1990. 14.95 (*0-87951-387-X*) Overlook Pr.

Remarkable Incident at Carson Corners. Reginald Rose. 71p. 1955. pap. 5.00 (*0-87129-704-3*, R13) Dramatic Pub.

***Remarkable Influence.** Emilia Lopes. 96p. (YA). (ps-12). 1996. per. 7.95 (*1-57258-119-0*) Teach Servs.

***Remarkable Jewish Women: Rebels, Rabbis & Other Jewish Women.** 2nd rev. ed. Emily Taitz & Sondra Henry. (Illus.). 224p. 1997. pap. 19.95 (*0-8276-0643-5*) JPS Phila.

Remarkable Jewish Women: Rebels, Rabbis, & Other Jewish Women from Biblical Times to the Present. Emily Taitz & Sondra Henry. LC 95-51989. (Illus.). (J). (gr. 4 up). 1996. 29.95 (*0-8276-0573-0*) JPS Phila.

Remarkable Journey. Lloyd Alexander. 288p. (J). 1993. pap. 4.99 (*0-440-40890-3*) Dell.

Remarkable Journey of Prince Jen. Lloyd Alexander. LC 91-13720. 288p. (J). (gr. 5-10). 1991. pap. 15.99 (*0-525-44826-8*) Dutton Child Bks.

Remarkable Life of Victoria Drummond Marine Engineer. Cherry Drummond. 368p. 1994. 37.50 (*0-907206-54-9*) Info Today Inc.

Remarkable Lives of One Hundred Women Artists. Brooke Bailey. (Twentieth-Century Women Ser.). 1994. 12.00 (*1-55850-360-9*) Adams Media.

Remarkable Lives of One Hundred Women Healers & Scientists. Brooke Bailey. LC 94-8436. (Twentieth Century Women Ser.). 1994. 12.00 (*1-55850-361-7*) Adams Media.

Remarkable Lives of One Hundred Women Writers & Journalists. Brooke Bailey. (Twentieth-Century Women Ser.). 1994. 12.00 (*1-55850-423-0*) Adams Media.

Remarkable Miracles: Story of a Godly Man's Walk Producing Miracles. rev. ed. G. C. Bevington. LC 91-78269. 168p. 1992. pap. 8.95 (*0-88270-703-5*) Bridge-Logos.

Remarkable New Genus of Tetraodontiform Fish with Features of Both Balistids & Ostraciids from the Eocene of Turkmenistan. James C. Tyler & Alexandre F. Bannikov. LC 92-23372. (Smithsonian Contributions to Paleobiology Ser.: No. 72). (Illus.). 18p. reprint ed. pap. 25.00 (*0-7837-4379-3*, 2044119) Bks Demand.

Remarkable Occurrences. unabridged ed. Beverly Carradine. 176p. 1994. reprint ed. pap. 11.99 (*0-88019-323-9*) Schmul Pub Co.

Remarkable People: A Rhode Island Family Album. Stephen Brigidi. 230p. (Orig.). 1996. pap. write for info. (*0-9629642-0-4*) Bristol Wkshps.

Remarkable People! Ready-to-Use Biography Activities for Grades 4-8. Marguerite Lewis & Pamela J. Kudla. 256p. 1991. pap. 27.95 (*0-87628-792-5*, 710506) P-H.

***Remarkable Providences.** Increase Mather. 262p. (YA). Date not set. reprint ed. 24.95 (*1-880045-18-4*) Back Home Indust.

Remarkable Providences: Readings on Early American History. rev. ed. Ed. by John P. Demos. 455p. 1991. text ed. 47.50 (*1-55553-097-4*); pap. text ed. 16.95 (*1-55553-098-2*) NE U Pr.

Remarkable Providences Illustrative of the Earlier Days of American Colonisation. Increase Mather. Ed. by Richard M. Dorsen. LC 77-70610. (International Folklore Ser.). 1977. reprint ed. lib. bdg. 26.95 (*0-405-10107-4*) Ayer.

Remarkable Railroad Passes of Otto Mears. William K. Strong. (Illus.). 36p. (Orig.). 1988. pap. 3.95 (*0-9608000-6-9*) San Juan County.

Remarkable Rainforest: An Active-Learning Book for Kids. Toni Albert. LC 94-60401. (Illus.). 64p. (Orig.). (J). (gr. 3-8). 1994. pap. 10.95 (*0-9640742-0-6*) Trickle Creek.

Remarkable Ramsey. Barbara Rinkoff. (Illus.). (J). (gr. 2-6). 1990. 15.75 (*0-8446-6195-3*) Peter Smith.

Remarkable Recipes. Antoinette K. Hatfield. Ed. by Thomas K. Worcester. (Illus.). 156p. 7.95 (*0-911518-04-5*) Touchstone Oregon.

Remarkable Record of Job: The Ancient Wisdom, Scientific Accuracy & Life-Changing Message of an Amazing Book. Henry M. Morris. 152p. (C). 1988. 14.99 (*0-8010-6238-1*) Baker Bks.

Remarkable Records of Rev. Gideon Bostwick, 1770-1793, Great Barrington, Massachusetts. Arthur C. Kelly. 118p. 1989. lib. bdg. 25.00 (*1-56012-092-4*, 92) Kinship Rhinebeck.

Remarkable Recovery: What Extraordinary Healings Can Tell Us about Getting Well & Staying Well. Caryle Hirshberg. 384p. (Orig.). 1996. pap. 12.00 (*1-57322-530-4*, Riverhd Trade) Berkley Pub.

Remarkable Red Raspberry Cookbook. 2nd ed. Sibyl Kile & Danita Petek. (Illus.). 170p. 1990. pap. 12.95 (*0-9615201-6-7*) BCG Ltd.

Remarkable Red Raspberry Recipes. Sibyl Kile. (Illus.). 170p. (Orig.). 1985. pap. 7.95 (*0-9615201-2-4*) BCG Ltd.

Remarkable Remains of the Ancient Peoples of Guatemala. Jacques VanKirk & Parney Bassett-VanKirk. LC 96-8668. (Illus.). 288p. 1996. 49.95 (*0-8061-2866-6*) U of Okla Pr.

An Asterisk (*) at the beginning of an entry indicates that the title is appearing in BIP for the first time.

***Remarkable Remains of the Ancient Peoples of Guatemala.** Jacques Vankirk & Parney Bassett-VanKirk. LC 96-8668. (Illus.). 288p. 1997. pap. 19.95 (*0-8061-2901-8*) U of Okla Pr.

Remarkable Ride of the Abernathy Boys. rev. ed. Robert B. Jackson. Ed. by Molly L. Griffis. LC 88-82956. (Illus.). 69p. (J). (gr. 4 up). 1988. reprint ed. pap. 6.00 (*0-9618634-6-3*) Levite Apache.

Remarkable Riderless Runaway Tricycle. rev. ed. Bruce McMillan. (Illus.). 48p. (J). (gr. k-4). 1985. reprint ed. pap. 10.00 (*0-934313-00-8*) Apple Isl Bks.

Remarkable Rocks. Ron Cole. Ed. by Lauren Weidenman. (Ranger Rick Science Spectacular Ser.). 16p. (J). (gr. 2-4). 1996. pap. 14.95 (*1-56784-221-6*) Newbridge Comms.

Remarkable Rocks: Student Book. Ron Cole. Ed. by Lauren Weidenman. (Ranger Rick Science Spectacular Ser.). (Illus.). 16p. (Orig.). (J). (gr. 2-4). 1996. pap. write for info. (*1-56784-246-1*) Newbridge Comms.

Remarkable Rocks Theme Pack. Ron Cole. Ed. by Lauren Weidenman. (Ranger Rick Science Spectacular Ser.). (Illus.). 16p. (J). (gr. 2-5). 1996. pap. write for info. (*1-56784-282-8*) Newbridge Comms.

***Remarkable Story of Norton I, Emperor of the United States & Protector of Mexico.** John Cech. (Illus.). 192p. 1997. pap. 14.95 (*1-56924-775-7*) Marlowe & Co.

Remarkable Surgical Practice of John Benjamin Murphy. Ed. by Robert L. Schmitz & Timothy T. Oh. LC 92-524. (Illus.). 256p. 1993. text ed. 39.95 (*0-252-01958-X*) U of Ill Pr.

Remarkable Survivors: Insights into Successful Aging among Women. Alice T. Day. (Illus.). 340p. (C). 1991. pap. text ed. 24.50 (*0-87766-491-9*); lib. bdg. 55.00 (*0-87766-492-7*) Urban Inst.

Remarkable Susan. Tim Kelly. 1972. pap. 3.25 (*0-8222-0943-8*) Dramatists Play.

Remarkable, Unspeakable New York: A Literary History. Shaun O'Connell. LC 94-36415. 400p. 1995. 27.50 (*0-8070-5002-4*) Beacon Pr.

***Remarkable, Unspeakable New York: A Literary History.** Shaun O'Connell. 1997. pap. text ed. 14.00 (*0-8070-5003-2*) Beacon Pr.

Remarkable Women: Perspectives on Female Talent Development. Rena F. Subotnik et al. Ed. by Mark Rasneo. LC 95-45434. (Perspectives on Creativity Ser.). 448p. (Orig.). (C). 1996. pap. 29.95 (*1-57273-047-1*) Hampton Pr NJ.

Remarkable Women: Perspectives on Female Talent Development. Rena F. Subotnik et al. LC 95-45434. (Perspectives on Creativity Ser.). 448p. (Orig.). (C). 1996. text ed. 79.50 (*1-57273-046-3*) Hampton Pr NJ.

***Remarkable Women of Ancient Egypt.** 3rd rev. ed. Barbara S. Lesko. (Illus.). 68p. 1996. pap. 16.95 (*0-930548-13-2*) B C Scribe.

Remarkably Neat Church in the Village of Thibodaux: An Antebellum History of St. John's Episcopal Church. David D. Plater. LC 94-67900. (Illus.). 109p. (Orig.). 1994. pap. 10.00 (*0-940984-90-3*) U of SW LA Ctr LA Studies.

Remarks about Academic Matters. Rudolf Kurth. LC 81-40177. 124p. (Orig.). 1982. pap. text ed. 18.00 (*0-8191-1856-7*) U Pr of Amer.

Remarks & Observations on a Voyage Around the World from 1803-1807. Georg H. Von Langsdorff. Ed. by Richard A. Pierce. Tr. by Victoria J. Moessner from GER. (Alaska History Ser.: No. 41). (Illus.). 1993. 30.00 (*0-89590-100-5*) Limestone Pr.

Remarks, Critical & Illustrative, on the Text & Notes of the Last Edition of Shakspeare. Joseph Ritson. LC 73-174324. reprint ed. 32.50 (*0-404-05348-3*) AMS Pr.

Remarks, Critical, Conjectural & Explanatory upon the Plays of Shakespeare, 2 vols. E. H. Seymour. LC 74-175848. 1976. reprint ed. 115.00 (*0-404-05754-3*) AMS Pr.

Remarks During a Journey Through North America in the Years 1819, 1820 & 1821. Adam Hodgson. LC 76-107479. 335p. 1970. reprint ed. text ed. 52.50 (*0-8371-3755-1*, HRN&, Greenwood Pr) Greenwood.

Remarks in the British Theatre (1806-1809) Elizabeth S. Inchbald. LC 90-49322. 1991. reprint ed. 90.00 (*0-8201-1449-9*) Schol Facsimiles.

Remarks Made on a Tour to Prairie du Chien: Thence to Washington City in 1829. Caleb Atwater. LC 75-82. (Mid-American Frontier Ser.). 1975. reprint ed. 28.95 (*0-405-06851-4*) Ayer.

Remarks of Henry Brewster Stanton in the Representatives Hall. Henry B. Stanton. LC 77-82223. (Anti-Slavery Crusade in America Ser.). 1970. reprint ed. 15.95 (*0-405-00662-4*) Ayer.

Remarks of My Life: Pr. Me Hezekiah Prince. Ed. by Sally Hill & Arthur Spear. (Illus.). 126p. 1979. 20.00 (*0-929539-69-9*, 1169) Picton Pr.

Remarks on American Literature. William E. Channing. (Works of William Ellery Channing II). 1990. reprint ed. lib. bdg. 79.00 (*0-685-27614-7*) Rprt Serv.

Remarks on Clarissa, Addressed to the Author...with Some Reflections on the Character & Behaviour of Prior's Emma: Appendix: Henry Fielding's Letter to Richardson Regarding Clarissa. Sarah Fielding. LC 92-24891. (Augustan Reprints Ser.: Nos. 231-232). 1985. reprint ed. 21.50 (*0-404-70231-7*, PR3634) AMS Pr.

Remarks on Colour. Ludwig Wittgenstein. Ed. by G. E. Anscombe. Tr. by Linda L. McAlister & Margarete Schattle from GER. 1977. pap. 12.95 (*0-520-03727-8*) U CA Pr.

Remarks on Frazer's Golden Bough. Ludwig Wittgenstein. (C). 1989. 30.00 (*0-907839-25-8*, Pub. by Brynmill Pr Ltd UK) St Mut.

Remarks on John Locke: With Locke's Replies. Ed. by Thomas Burnet. (C). 1989. 60.00 (*0-907839-43-6*, Pub. by Brynmill Pr Ltd UK) St Mut.

Remarks on Marx. Michel Foucault. 1991. pap. 6.00 (*0-936756-33-0*) Autonomedia.

Remarks on Mister J. P. Collier's & Mister C. Knight's Edition of Shakespeare. Alexander Dyce. LC 79-164815. reprint ed. 44.50 (*0-404-02230-8*) AMS Pr.

***Remarks on Mr. Hume's Dialogue Concerning Natural Religion.** Thomas Hayter. 80p. 1996. reprint ed. write for info. (*1-85506-178-3*) Bks Intl VA.

Remarks on Pacific Fishes. V. Pietschmann. (BMB Ser.). 1974. reprint ed. pap. 25.00 (*0-527-02179-2*) Periodicals Srv.

Remarks on Prison & Prison Discipline in the United States: With Intro. & Index Added. 2nd ed. Dorothea L. Dix. LC 84-7714. (Criminology, Law Enforcement, & Social Problems Ser.: No. 4). iv, 113p. (C). 1984. reprint ed. lib. bdg. 20.00 (*0-87585-705-1*) Patterson Smith.

Remarks on Several Acts of Parliament Relating More Especially to the Colonies Abroad. Jonathan Blenman. LC 70-141127. (Research Library of Colonial Americana). 1972. reprint ed. 20.95 (*0-405-03331-1*) Ayer.

Remarks on Some Fundamental Doctrines of Political Economy. John Craig. LC 70-121321. (Reprints of Economic Classics Ser.). xi, 244p. 1970. reprint ed. lib. bdg. 39.50 (*0-678-00684-9*) Kelley.

Remarks on Some of the Characters of Shakespeare. 3rd ed. Thomas Whately. LC 76-96362. (Eighteenth Century Shakespeare Ser.: No. 17). 128p. 1970. reprint ed. lib. bdg. 35.00 (*0-678-05129-1*) Kelley.

Remarks on Some of the Characters of Shakespeare. 3rd ed. Thomas Whately. Ed. by Richard Whately. 152p. 1970. reprint ed. bds. 35.00 (*0-7146-2518-3*, Pub. by F Cass Pubs UK) Intl Spec Bk.

Remarks on Some of the Characters of Shakespere. 3rd ed. Thomas Whately. reprint ed. 29.50 (*0-404-06917-7*) AMS Pr.

Remarks on the Character & Writings of John Milton. 3rd ed. William E. Channing. LC 72-966. reprint ed. 34.50 (*0-404-01448-8*) AMS Pr.

Remarks on the Country Extending from Cape Palmas to the River Congo. John Adams. 265p. 1966. reprint ed. 40.00 (*0-7146-1783-0*, BHA-01783, Pub. by F Cass Pubs UK) Intl Spec Bk.

Remarks On the Development of Rhetoric: A Companion Volume to the Rhetoric of Western Thought. James Hikins. 128p. 1996. pap. text ed. 25.20 (*0-7872-2511-8*) Kendall-Hunt.

Remarks on the Differences in Shakespeare's Versification in Different Periods of His Life. Charles Bathurst. LC 75-113550. 1970. reprint ed. 34.50 (*0-404-00692-2*) AMS Pr.

Remarks on the Foundations of Mathematics. rev. ed. Ludwig Wittgenstein. Ed. by George H. Von Wright et al. Tr. by G. E. Anscombe. 448p. 1983. reprint ed. pap. 19.00 (*0-262-73067-7*) MIT Pr.

Remarks on the Life & Writings of Dr. Jonathan Swift. John Earl of Orrery. (Anglistica & Americana Ser.: No. 6). 339p. 1968. reprint ed. 63.70 (*0-685-66498-8*, 05101960) G Olms Pubs.

Remarks on the Life & Writings of William Shakespeare. John Britton. LC 79-39531. reprint ed. 24.50 (*0-404-01086-5*) AMS Pr.

Remarks on the Needed Reform of German Studies in the United States. John Van Cleve & A. Leslie Willson. LC 92-41038. (GERM Ser.). 112p. 1993. 26.90 (*1-879751-39-9*) Camden Hse.

Remarks on the Philosophy of Psychology, Vol. 1. Ludwig Wittgenstein. Ed. by G. E. Anscombe & George H. Von Wright. LC 80-52781. 424p. (C). 1980. lib. bdg. 48.00 (*0-226-90433-4*) U Ch Pr.

Remarks on the Philosophy of Psychology, Vol. 1. Ludwig Wittgenstein. Ed. by G. E. Anscombe & George H. Von Wright. 424p. 1988. pap. text ed. 22.50 (*0-226-90436-9*) U Ch Pr.

Remarks on the Philosophy of Psychology, Vol. 2. Ludwig Wittgenstein. Ed. by George H. Von Wright & Heikki Nyman. Tr. by C. G. Luckhardt & A. E. Aue. LC 80-52781. 271p. (C). 1980. lib. bdg. 33.00 (*0-226-90434-2*) U Ch Pr.

Remarks on the Philosophy of Psychology, Vol. 2. Ludwig Wittgenstein. Ed. by George H. Von Wright & Heikki Nyman. Tr. by C. G. Luckhardt & A. E. Aue. LC 80-52781. 269p. (C). 1988. pap. text ed. 17.95 (*0-226-90437-7*) U Ch Pr.

Remarks on the Review of Inchiquin's Letters. Timothy Dwight. 1972. reprint ed. text ed. 29.00 (*0-8422-8040-5*) Irvington.

Remarks on the Review of Inchiquin's Letters. Timothy Dwight. 1986. reprint ed. pap. text ed. 6.95 (*0-8290-1921-9*) Irvington.

Remarks on the Statistics & Political Institutions of the United States. William G. Ouseley. LC 70-117887. (Select Bibliographies Reprint Ser.). 1977. reprint ed. 21.95 (*0-8369-5340-1*) Ayer.

Remarks on the Theory of Prime Ends. H. D. Ursell & L. C. Young. (Memoirs of the American Mathematical Society Ser.: Vol. 3). 29p. 1978. reprint ed. pap. 16.00 (*0-8218-1203-3*, MEMO/1/3) Am Math.

***Remarks upon a Late Book Entituled, the Fable of the Bees: 1725 Edition.** William Law. 108p. 1996. reprint ed. write for info. (*1-85506-127-9*) Bks Intl VA.

Remarks upon Alchemy & the Alchemists: Indicating a Method of Discovering the True Nature of Hermetic Philosophy. Ethan A. Hitchcock. LC 75-36842. (Occult Ser.). 1976. reprint ed. 26.95 (*0-405-07955-9*) Ayer.

Remarques sur les Memoires Imaginaires. Georges Duhamel. 96p. (FRE.). 1934. pap. 16.95 (*0-7859-5563-1*) Fr & Eur.

Remarques Sur les Spacelariacees. C. Sauvageau. 1971. reprint ed. 120.00 (*3-7682-0717-X*) Lubrecht & Cramer.

Remarriage: A Review & Annotated Bibliography. Benjamin Schlesinger. (CPL Bibliographies Ser.: No. 115). 69p. 1983. 10.00 (*0-86602-115-9*, Sage Prdcls Pr) Sage.

Remarriage: In the Middle Years & Beyond. Phyllis S. Kamm. (Mature Reader Ser.). 184p. (Orig.). 1991. pap. 8.95 (*1-55867-027-0*) Bristol Pub Ent CA.

Remarriage after 50: What Women, Men & Adult Children Need to Know. Jane H. Barton. 86p. (Orig.). 1994. pap. 11.95 (*0-9639891-0-3*) Roger-Thomas.

Remarriage & Blended Families. Stephen R. Treat. (Looking up Ser.). 24p. 1988. pap. 1.95 (*0-8298-0775-6*) Pilgrim OH.

Remarriage & Stepparenting: Current Research & Theory. Ed. by Kay Pasley & Marilyn Ihinger-Tallman. LC 87-17718. (Perspectives on Marriage & the Family Ser.). 323p. 1987. pap. text ed. 21.95 (*0-89862-922-5*) Guilford Pr.

Remarriage Manual. Krysta Kavenaugh. 64p. 1994. pap. 4.00 (*0-936098-70-8*) Intl Marriage.

Remarriage Without Financial Risk: How to Do It Right the Next Time. Harley Gordon. 300p. 1992. pap. 19.95 (*0-9625667-3-X*) Financial Plan Inst.

Remarried Families. Lawrence H. Ganong & Marilyn Coleman. (Series on Close Relationships: Vol. 9). 176p. (C). 1994. text ed. 38.00 (*0-8039-5122-1*); pap. text ed. 16.95 (*0-8039-5123-X*) Sage.

Remarried Family: Challenge & Promise. Esther Wald. LC 80-205980. 254p. 1981. 11.95 (*0-87304-184-4*); pap. 8.95 (*0-87304-183-6*) Families Intl.

Remarried with Children: Questions & Answers for Happier Stepfamilies. Stephen H. Wilson et al. 170p. 1992. pap. text ed. 8.95 (*0-9632900-0-2*) Steve Wilson.

Remasculinization of America: Gender & the Vietnam War. Susan Jeffords. LC 88-46019. (Theories of Contemporary Culture Ser.). 240p. 1989. 35.00 (*0-253-33188-9*); pap. 13.95 (*0-253-20530-1*, MB-530) Ind U Pr.

Rembrances. Ed. by Robert Lawrence & Deborah A. Case. (Illus.). 312p. 1995. text ed. 49.95 (*1-885206-12-7*, Iliad Pr) Cader Pubng.

Rembrandt. (Album Ser.: No. 1). 1976. pap. 7.95 (*0-87130-051-6*) Eakins.

Rembrandt. Christopher Baker. 1993. 29.98 (*1-55521-856-3*) Bk Sales Inc.

***Rembrandt.** Benedikt Taschen Staff. 1996. pap. 8.99 (*3-8228-9498-2*) Taschen Amer.

***Rembrandt.** U. Bockemuhl. 1994. pap. text ed. 9.99 (*3-8228-0559-9*) Taschen Amer.

***Rembrandt.** Chelsea House Publishing Staff. (World's Greatest Artists Ser.). 1997. 17.95 (*1-85813-918-X*) Chelsea Hse.

Rembrandt. Gerhard Gruitrooy. 1993. 4.99 (*0-7852-8307-2*) Nelson.

Rembrandt. Annemarie V. Heijn. (Illus.). 128p. 1989. 25.00 (*1-870248-21-X*) Scala Books.

Rembrandt. Jessica Hodge. (Illus.). 112p. 1995. 14.98 (*0-8317-7165-8*) Smithmark.

Rembrandt. John Jacob. 1990. 6.98 (*1-55521-598-X*) Bk Sales Inc.

Rembrandt. Marc Le Bot. (CAL Art Ser.). (Illus.). 96p. 1991. 18.00 (*0-517-58535-9*, Crown) Crown Pub Group.

***Rembrandt.** Vladimir Loewinson-Lessing. (Great Painters Ser.). 1996. 40.00 (*1-85995-164-3*) Parkstone Pr.

Rembrandt, 2 vols. Emile Michel. 1972. 200.00 (*0-8490-0943-X*) Gordon Pr.

Rembrandt. Ludwig Munz & Bob Haak. (Masters of Art Ser.). 164p. 1984. 22.95 (*0-8109-1594-4*) Abrams.

Rembrandt. Random House Value Publishing Staff. 1996. 9.99 (*0-517-18227-0*) Random Hse Value.

***Rembrandt.** Cynthia P. Schneider. Date not set. 35.00 (*0-06-438517-5*, Icon Edns) HarpC.

Rembrandt. Gary Schwartz. (First Impressions Ser.). (Illus.). 92p. (YA). 1992. 19.95 (*0-8109-3760-3*) Abrams.

Rembrandt. Larry Silver. Ed. by Norma Broude. LC 91-33472. (Rizzoli Art Ser.). (Illus.). 24p. (Orig.). 1992. pap. 7.95 (*0-8478-1519-6*) Rizzoli Intl.

Rembrandt. Leonard J. Statkes. (Illus.). 1996. pap. 4.95 (*0-89659-134-4*) Abbeville Pr.

Rembrandt. Mike Venezia. LC 87-33014. (Getting to Know the World's Greatest Artists Ser.). (Illus.). 32p. (J). (ps-4). 1988. pap. 6.95 (*0-516-42272-3*); lib. bdg. 19.50 (*0-516-02272-5*) Childrens.

Rembrandt. Christopher White. LC 83-51330. (World of Art Ser.). (Illus.). (Orig.). (C). 1984. pap. 14.95 (*0-500-20195-1*) Thames Hudson.

Rembrandt. Michael Kitson. (Color Library). (Illus.). 128p. (C). 1994. reprint ed. pap. 14.95 (*0-7148-2743-6*, Pub. by Phaidon Press UK) Chronicle Bks.

Rembrandt: And Dutch Painting of the 17th Century. Claudio Pescio. (Masters of Art Ser.). (Illus.). 64p. (J). (gr. 6 up). 1995. lib. bdg. 22.50 (*0-87226-317-7*) P Bedrick Bks.

***Rembrandt: Etchings & Engravings.** Victoria S. Charles. (Temporis Ser.). (Illus.). 208p. 1997. 55.00 (*1-85995-311-5*) Parkstone Pr.

Rembrandt: Experimental Etcher. Ed. by Museum of Fine Arts Staff. LC 87-80024. 1988. reprint ed. lib. bdg. 60.00 (*0-87817-320-X*) Hacker.

Rembrandt: Master of the Portrait. Pascal Bonafoux. Tr. by Alexandra Campbell. (Discoveries Ser.). (Illus.). 176p. 1992. pap. 12.95 (*0-8109-2813-2*) Abrams.

Rembrandt: Masterworks. 1990. 15.99 (*0-517-01508-0*) Random Hse Value.

Rembrandt: The Master & His Workshop, 2 vols. Ed. by Christopher Brown et al. (Illus.). 640p. (C). 1991. Set. 140.00 (*0-300-05191-3*) Yale U Pr.

Rembrandt: The Master & His Workshop - Drawings & Etchings. Ed. by Christopher Brown et al. (Illus.). 360p. (C). 1991. 65.00 (*0-300-05151-4*) Yale U Pr.

Rembrandt: The Master & His Workshop, Paintings. Christopher Brown. (Illus.). 360p. 1991. 75.00 (*0-300-05149-2*) Yale U Pr.

Rembrandt: The Old Testament. Eagle Books Staff. 144p. 1996. 29.99 (*0-7852-7340-9*) Nelson.

***Rembrandt - The Painter at Work.** Ernst Van de Wetering. 1997. 79.50 (*90-5356-239-7*, Pub. by Amsterdam U Pr NE) U of Mich Pr.

Rembrandt & Angels. Michael Rubinstein. 47p. 1982. pap. 4.00 (*0-904674-18-5*, Pub. by Octagon Pr UK) ISHK.

***Rembrandt & Dutch Portraiture.** David Spence. (Great Artists Ser.). 1997. pap. 5.95 (*0-7641-0290-7*) Barron.

Rembrandt & His Critics Sixteen Thirty to Seventeen Thirty. Seymour Slive. LC 86-81978. (Illus.). xii, 240p. 1988. reprint ed. lib. bdg. 40.00 (*0-87817-311-0*) Hacker.

Rembrandt & Not Rembrandt: Aspects of Connoisseurship. Walter A. Liedtke & Hubert Von Sonnenburg. (Illus.). 256p. 1995. 65.00 (*0-8109-6493-7*) Abrams.

Rembrandt Bible Drawings. Rembrandt Van Rijn. LC 79-52975. (Fine Art Ser.). (Illus.). 64p. (Orig.). 1980. pap. 3.95 (*0-486-23878-4*) Dover.

Rembrandt Corpus Paintings. 1986. lib. bdg. 825.00 (*90-247-3339-1*, Pub. by M Nijhoff NE) Kluwer Ac.

Rembrandt Documents. Marjon Van Der Meulen & Walter L. Strauss. LC 78-53627. 668p. 1979. 115.00 (*0-913870-68-4*) Abaris Bks.

Rembrandt Drawings. B. Haak. Tr. by Elizabeth Willems-Treeman. LC 76-10073. (Illus.). 1976. 22.50 (*0-87951-047-1*) Overlook Pr.

Rembrandt Drawings. B. Haak. Tr. by Elizabeth Willems-Treeman. LC 76-10073. (Illus.). 1977. pap. 19.95 (*0-87951-051-X*) Overlook Pr.

Rembrandt Etchings: Forty-Five Plates. Rembrandt Van Rijn. (Illus.). 48p. 1988. pap. 3.50 (*0-486-25677-4*) Dover.

***Rembrandt Etchings: In the Norton Simon Museum.** Gloria Williams. (Illus.). 62p. 1991. pap. 8.95 (*0-915776-08-1*) NS Mus.

Rembrandt Harmensz Van Rijn: Paintings from Soviet Museums. V. Loewinson-Lessing & Zh Egorova. (Illus.). 183p. (C). 1987. text ed. 330.00 (*0-569-09129-2*, Pub. by Collets) St Mut.

Rembrandt in Eighteenth Century England. Christopher White et al. LC 83-50668. (Illus.). 153p. (Orig.). 1983. pap. 15.00 (*0-930606-44-2*) Yale Ctr Brit Art.

Rembrandt Landscape Drawings. Rembrandt Van Rijn. (Art Library). (Illus.). 64p. (Orig.). 1981. pap. 3.95 (*0-486-24160-2*) Dover.

Rembrandt, Life of Christ: Life of Christ. Illus. by Rembrandt. LC 95-18407. 144p. 1995. 29.99 (*0-7852-7687-4*) Nelson.

Rembrandt-Not Rembrandt in the Metropolitan Museum of Art: Aspects of Connoisseurship. 1995. pap. 49.50 (*0-87099-754-8*, 0-8109-6493-7) Metro Mus Art.

Rembrandt Paintings. 1986. lib. bdg. 944.50 (*90-247-3340-5*, Pub. by M Nijhoff NE) Kluwer Ac.

Rembrandt Paintings, Vol. 3. 1990. lib. bdg. 898.50 (*90-247-3782-6*, Pub. by M Nijhoff NE) Kluwer Ac.

Rembrandt Peale 1778-1860: A Life in the Arts. Carol Hevner. 121p. 1985. 19.95 (*0-910732-19-1*) Pa Hist Soc.

Rembrandt Returns. Robert R. Leichtman. (From Heaven to Earth Ser.). (Illus.). 96p. (Orig.). 1981. pap. 3.50 (*0-89804-064-7*) Ariel GA.

Rembrandt Studies. Julius S. Held. (Illus.). 296p. 1990. text ed. 85.00 (*0-691-04077-X*); pap. text ed. 32.50 (*0-691-00282-7*) Princeton U Pr.

Rembrandt Takes a Walk. Mark Strand. (Illus.). (J). (gr. 3 up). 1987. 14.95 (*0-517-56293-6*) Crown Bks Yng Read.

Rembrandt, the Man in the Golden Helmet. Louis R. Velasquez. LC 94-90892. (Illus.). 101p. 1995. pap. 19.95 (*0-9644921-1-3*) Vela Pr.

Rembrandt the Rocker. Sonny Brewer. (Illus.). 1994. 14.95 (*0-9643727-0-3*) Over the Transom.

Rembrandt's Beret. Johnny Alcorn. LC 90-42330. (Illus.). 32p. (J). (gr. 1 up). 1991. 13.95 (*0-688-10206-9*, Tambourine Bks) Morrow.

***Rembrandt's Engravings.** Parkstone Press Limited Staff. (Temporis Ser.). 1997. 55.00 (*1-85995-310-7*) Parkstone Pr.

Rembrandt's Enterprise: The Studio & the Market. Svetlana Alpers. (Illus.). 308p. 1988. 35.95 (*0-226-01514-9*) U Ch Pr.

Rembrandt's Enterprise: The Studio & the Market. Svetlana Alpers. LC 87-16161. (Illus.). 308p. 1990. pap. 24.95 (*0-226-01518-1*) U Ch Pr.

Rembrandt's Etchings: States & Values. G. W. Nowell-Usticke. LC 87-80028. (Illus.). 379p. 1988. reprint ed. lib. bdg. 60.00 (*0-87817-300-5*) Hacker.

Rembrandt's Etchings True & False. George Biorklund & Osbert H. Barnard. LC 87-80027. (Illus.). 200p. 1988. reprint ed. lib. bdg. 50.00 (*0-87817-319-6*) Hacker.

Rembrandt's Hat. Bernard Malamud. 224p. 1973. 11.95 (*0-374-24909-1*) FS&G.

Rembrandt's Landscapes. Cynthia P. Schneider. 312p. (C). 1990. text ed. 50.00 (*0-300-04568-9*) Yale U Pr.

Rembrandt's Landscapes: Drawings & Prints. Cynthia P. Schneider et al. (Illus.). 292p. (Orig.). 1990. 75.00 (*0-8212-1819-0*) Bulfinch Pr.

Rembrandt's Landscapes: Drawings & Prints. Cynthia P. Schneider et al. LC 90-5524. (Illus.). 304p. (Orig.). 1990. 10.99 (*0-89468-147-8*) Natl Gallery Art.

Rembrandts LP. Ed. by Jeannette DeLisa. (Illus.). 88p. (Orig.). 1995. pap. text ed. 18.95 (*0-89724-768-X*, PF9518) Warner Brothers.

Rembrandt's Mirror. Laurence Lerner. LC 86-32526. 80p. 1987. pap. 10.95 (*0-8265-1223-2*) Vanderbilt U Pr.

Rembrandt's Polish Nobleman. Otaker Odlozilik. 32p. 1963. 3.00 (*0-685-25019-9*) Polish Inst Art & Sci.

R

Rembrandt's Self-Portraits: A Study in Seventeenth-Century Identity. H. Perry Chapman. (Illus.). 328p. 1990. reprint ed. text ed. 59.50 (*0-691-04061-3*); reprint ed. pap. text ed. 29.95 (*0-691-00296-7*) Princeton U Pr.

Remedial Action Technology for Waste Disposal Sites. 2nd ed. Kathleen Wagner et al. LC 86-17992. (Pollution Technology Review Ser.: No. 135). (Illus.). 642p. 1987. 54.00 (*0-8155-1100-0*) Noyes.

Remedial Activities to Enhance Expressive & Receptive Vocabulary: Booklet of General Information. Morrison F. Gardner. 1989. pap. 10.95 (*0-931421-57-8*) Psychol Educ Pubns.

Remedial Activities to Enhance Expressive & Receptive Vocabulary: Identifying by Pointing to Groups of Pictures of Persons & Things. Morrison F. Gardner. 1989. pap. 10.95 (*0-931421-54-3*) Psychol Educ Pubns.

Remedial Activities to Enhance Expressive & Receptive Vocabulary: Identifying by Pointing to Pictures of Action. Morrison F. Gardner. 1989. pap. 10.95 (*0-931421-46-2*) Psychol Educ Pubns.

Remedial Activities to Enhance Expressive & Receptive Vocabulary: Identifying by Pointing to Single Pictures of Persons & Things. Morrison F. Gardner. 1989. pap. 10.95 (*0-931421-51-9*) Psychol Educ Pubns.

Remedial Activities to Enhance Expressive & Receptive Vocabulary: Identifying Verbally Groups of Pictures of Persons & Things. Morrison F. Gardner. 1989. pap. 10.95 (*0-931421-52-7*) Psychol Educ Pubns.

Remedial Activities to Enhance Expressive & Receptive Vocabulary: Identifying Verbally Pictures of Action. Morrison F. Gardner. 1989. pap. 10.95 (*0-931421-48-9*) Psychol Educ Pubns.

Remedial Activities to Enhance Expressive & Receptive Vocabulary: Identifying Verbally Single Pictures of Persons & Things. Morrison F. Gardner. 1989. pap. 10.95 (*0-931421-50-0*) Psychol Educ Pubns.

Remedial & Clinical Reading Instruction. 2nd ed. Sandra McCormick. (Illus.). 608p. (C). 1994. text ed. 68.00 (*0-02-379271-X*, Macmillan Coll) P-H.

Remedial Arithmetic. Fred Justus. (Math Ser.). 24p. (gr. 3-5). 1979. student ed. 5.00 (*0-8209-0112-1*, A-22) ESP.

Remedial Arithmetic 1A. Fred Justus. (Math Ser.). 24p. (gr. 2-3). 1978. student ed. 5.00 (*0-8209-0109-1*, A-19) ESP.

Remedial Arithmetic 1B. Fred Justus. (Math Ser.). 24p. (gr. 2-4). 1978. student ed. 5.00 (*0-8209-0110-5*, A-20) ESP.

Remedial Arithmetic 1C. Fred Justus. (Math Ser.). 24p. (gr. 3-5). 1978. student ed. 5.00 (*0-8209-0111-3*, A-21) ESP.

Remedial Drama. Sue Jennings. LC 74-77191. 1978. pap. 10.95 (*0-87830-563-7*, Thtre Arts Bks) Routledge.

Remedial English. Evan Smith. 32p. 1987. pap. 3.25 (*0-8222-0944-6*) Dramatists Play.

Remedial Law: When Courts Become Administrators. Ed. by Robert Wood. LC 89-35720. 208p. (C). 1990. lib. bdg. 27.50 (*0-87023-698-9*) U of Mass Pr.

Remedial Measures in Astrology. Gouri S. Kapoor. (C). 1990. 6.50 (*0-8364-2768-8*, Pub. by Ranjan Pubs II) S Asia.

Remedial Motor Activity for Children. Bryant J. Cratty. LC 74-26973. 335p. reprint ed. pap. 95.50 (*0-7837-1484-X*, 2057179) Bks Demand.

Remedial Options for Metals-Contaminated Sites. Jeffrey L. Means et al. 240p. 1995. 69.95 (*1-56670-180-5*, L1180) Lewis Pubs.

Remedial Processes for Contaminated Land. Ed. by Malcolm Pratt. 148p. 1993. pap. 30.00 (*0-85295-310-0*, 9CH88) Gulf Pub.

Remedial Reading Drills with Directions. Kirk Hegge. 1965. pap. 10.00 (*0-911586-12-1*) Wahr.

Remedial Reading for Elementary School Students. Carolyn Smith-McGowen. (Teaching Resources in the ERIC Database (TRIED) Ser.). (Illus.). 76p. (Orig.). 1990. pap. 14.95 (*0-927516-14-4*) ERIC-REC.

Remedial Reading Handbook. Bonnie Lass & Beth Davis. (Illus.). 224p. (C). 1985. pap. text ed. write for info. (*0-13-773474-3*) P-H.

Remedial Technologies for Leaking Underground Storage Tanks. L. M. Preslo et al. (Illus.). 728p. 1988. 91.00 (*0-87371-125-4*, L125) Lewis Pubs.

Remedial Treatment of Buildings. 2nd ed. Barry A. Richardson. LC 94-22800. (Illus.). 368p. 1995. pap. 39.95 (*0-7506-2158-3*) Buttrwrth-Heinemann.

Remediarium Conversorum: A Synthesis in Latin of "Moralia in Job" Gregory the Great. Ed. by Joseph Gildea. LC 84-3693. 504p. 1984. 35.00 (*0-8453-4507-9*) Assoc Univ Prs.

Remediating Reading Difficulties. Sharon J. Crawley & King Merritt. 160p. (C). 1991. per. write for info. (*0-697-11557-7*) Brown & Benchmark.

Remediating Reading Difficulties. 2nd ed. Sharon J. Crawley & King Merritt. 224p. (C). 1995. spiral bd. write for info. (*0-697-24130-0*) Brown & Benchmark.

***Remediating Reading Difficulties.** 2nd ed. Sharon J. Crawley & King Merritt. 240p. (C). 1997. student ed., spiral bd. write for info. (*0-07-114459-5*) McGraw.

Remediation & Management of Degraded River Basins with Emphasis on Central & Eastern Europe: With Emphasis on Central & Eastern Europe, Vol. XI. Ed. by Vladimir Novotny & Laszlo Somlyody. (NATO ASI Ser, Partnership Sub-Series 2: Vol. 3). (Illus.). 529p. 1995. 264.95 (*3-540-60115-5*) Spr-Verlag.

***Remediation & Management of Low Vision.** Ed. by Roy G. Cole & Bruce P. Rosenthal. (Mosby's Optometric Problem-Solving Ser.). 296p. 1996. pap. 31.95 (*1-888504-14-5*, P241) Lighthouse NYC.

Remediation & Management of Low Vision. Ed. by Roy G. Cole & Bruce P. Rosenthal. LC 95-39180. (Mosby's Optometric Problem Solving Ser.). 320p. (C). (gr. 13). 1995. pap. text ed. 36.95 (*0-8151-5204-3*) Mosby Yr Bk.

***Remediation Engineering: Design Concepts.** Suthan S. Suthersan. LC 96-33432. (Geraghty & Miller Environmental Science & Engineering Ser.). 384p. 1996. 69.95 (*1-56670-137-6*) Lewis Pubs.

***Remediation Equipment.** Richard K. Miller & Christy H. Gunter. (Market Research Survey Ser.: No. 287). 50p. 1996. 200.00 (*1-55865-312-0*) Future Tech Surveys.

Remediation Manual for Petroleum-Contaminated Sites. David Russell. LC 91-67570. 200p. 1992. pap. text ed. 59.95 (*0-87762-876-9*) Technomic.

***Remediation of Articulation Disorders (RAD) A Pragmatic Approach.** Jan Bieniosek. (Illus.). 92p. (Orig.). (J). (gr. 1-6). 1996. pap. text ed. 18.95 (*0-937857-69-6*, 1420) Speech Bin.

Remediation of PCB Spills. Mitchell D. Erickson. 160p. 1993. 71.95 (*0-87371-945-X*, L945) Lewis Pubs.

Remediation of Petroleum Contaminated Soils. Cole. 384p. 1994. 59.95 (*0-87371-824-0*, L824) Lewis Pubs.

Remediation of Petroleum Contaminated Soils. Eve Riser-Roberts. 1997. 69.95 (*0-87371-858-5*, L858) Lewis Pubs.

***Remediation of Soil & Groundwater Opportunities in Eastern Europe: Proceedings of the NATO Advanced Research Workshop on Remediation of Soil & Groundwater As a Technical, Institutional & Socio-Economic Problem - Opportunities in Eastern Europe, Prague, Czech Republic, November 6-10, 1995.** Jaroslav Balek et al. Ed. by Edward A. McBean. LC 96-30278. (NATO ASI Series, Partnership SubSeries 2). 480p. (C). 1996. lib. bdg. 220.00 (*0-7923-4182-1*) Kluwer Ac.

Remediation Technologies Screening Matrix & Reference Guide. 144p. (Orig.). (C). 1994. pap. text ed. 35.00 (*0-7881-1538-3*) DIANE Pub.

Remediation Technologies Screening Matrix & Reference Guide. Ed. by U. S. Air Force Staff & U. S. EPA Staff. (Illus.). (C). 1995. reprint ed. 49.95 (*1-883767-11-3*) Am Acad Environ.

Remediaton of Hazardous Waste Contaminated Soils. Ed. by Donald L. Wise & Debra J. Trantolo. LC 93-50098. (Environmental Science & Pollution Ser.: Vol. 8). 952p. 1994. 215.00 (*0-8247-9160-6*) Dekker.

Remedies. Michael Schwartz. (Smith's Review Ser.). Date not set. pap. text ed. 15.95 (*1-56542-161-2*) E Pub Corp.

Remedies. 2nd ed. Bruce Kercher & Michael Noone. liii, 589p. 1990. pap. 75.00 (*0-455-20945-6*, Pub. by Law Bk Co AT) Gaunt.

Remedies: Adaptable to Courses Utilizing Laycock's Casebook on Modern American Remedies. Casenotes Publishing Co., Inc. Staff et al. Ed. by Norman S. Goldenberg & Peter Tenen. (Legal Briefs Ser.). (Orig.). 1994. pap. text ed. write for info. (*0-87457-149-9*, 1254) Casenotes Pub.

Remedies: Adaptable to Courses Utilizing Leavell, Love, Nelson, & Kovacic-Fleisher's Casebook on Equitable Remedies & Restitution. Casenotes Publishing Co., Inc. Staff. Ed. by Norman S. Goldenberg et al. (Legal Briefs Ser.). 1994. pap. write for info. (*0-87457-120-0*, 1253) Casenotes Pub.

Remedies: Adaptable to Courses Utilizing Re & Re Casebook on Remedies. Casenotes Publishing Co., Inc. Staff. Ed. by Norman S. Goldenberg et al. (Legal Briefs Ser.). 1996. pap. write for info. (*0-87457-121-9*, 1252) Casenotes Pub.

Remedies: Adaptable to Courses Utilizing Shoben & Tabb's Casebook on Remedies. Casenotes Publishing Co., Inc. Staff et al. Ed. by Norman S. Goldenberg et al. (Legal Briefs Ser.). 1995. pap. write for info. (*0-87457-162-6*, 1255) Casenotes Pub.

Remedies: Adaptable to Courses Utilizing York, Bauman & Rendleman's Casebook on Remedies. Casenotes Publishing Co., Inc. Staff. Ed. by Norman S. Goldenberg & Peter Tenen. (Legal Briefs Ser.). 1992. pap. write for info. (*0-87457-122-7*, 1250) Casenotes Pub.

Remedies: Commentary & Materials. 2nd ed. Michael Noone et al. 1993. pap. 96.00 (*0-455-21158-2*, Pub. by Law Bk Co AT) Gaunt.

Remedies: Commentary & Materials. 2nd ed. Michael Tilbury et al. 1993. 130.00 (*0-455-21157-4*, Pub. by Law Bk Co AT) Gaunt.

Remedies: Damages, Equity & Restitution. 2nd ed. Thompson & John A. Sebert. 1989. teacher ed. write for info. (*0-8205-0312-6*) Bender.

Remedies: Public & Private, Cases & Materials on. David Schoenbrod et al. (American Casebook Ser.). 848p. 1990. text ed. 45.50 (*0-314-71016-7*) West Pub.

Remedies: Public & Private, Cases & Materials on, Teacher's Manual to Accompany. David Schoenbrod et al. (American Casebook Ser.). 163p. 1990. pap. text ed. write for info. (*0-314-77000-3*) West Pub.

Remedies: Public & Private, Teacher's Manual to Accompany. 2nd ed. David Schoenbrod et al. (American Casebook Ser.). 240p. 1996. pap. text ed. write for info. (*0-314-20176-9*) West Pub.

Remedies: Public & Private, 1994 Supplement To. David Schoenbrod et al. (American Casebook Ser.). 255p. (C). 1994. suppl. ed., pap. text ed. 13.50 (*0-314-04581-3*) West Pub.

Remedies Against the Plague. Arnold C. Klebs & Eugene Droz. LC 75-23732. reprint ed. 35.00 (*0-404-13290-1*) AMS Pr.

Remedies & Practical Background: Inns of Court School of Law. 432p. 1995. pap. 44.00 (*1-85431-427-0*, Pub. by Blackstone Pr UK) Gaunt.

Remedies & Rackets: The Truth about Patent Medicines Today. James Cook. LC 75-39284. (Getting & Spending: The Consumer's Dilemma Ser.). 1976. reprint ed. 23.95 (*0-405-08059-X*) Ayer.

Remedies & the Sale of Land. Perell. 352p. 1988. boxed 81.00 (*0-409-80534-3*) MICHIE.

Remedies, Cases & Materials. 3rd ed. Edward D. Re & Stanton D. Krauss. (University Casebook Ser.). 1296p. (C). 1991. text ed. 44.95 (*0-88277-945-1*) Foundation Pr.

Remedies, Cases & Materials On. 4th ed. Edward D. Re & Joseph R. Re. (University Casebook Ser.). 1336p. (C). 1995. text ed. 49.95 (*1-56662-308-1*) Foundation Pr.

***Remedies, Cases & Materials On.** 4th ed. Edward D. Re. (University Casebook Ser.). 225p. 1996. teacher ed., pap. text ed. write for info. (*1-56662-443-6*) Foundation Pr.

Remedies Cases & Materials On. 5th ed. Kenneth M. York et al. (American Casebook Ser.). 1270p. (C). 1993. reprint ed. text ed. 54.50 (*0-314-88137-9*) West Pub.

Remedies for Breach of Contract: A Comparative Account. Guenter H. Treitel. 472p. 1992. reprint ed. pap. 45.00 (*0-19-825744-9*) OUP.

Remedies for Breach of Contract in Islamic & Iranian Law. S. H. Amin. 254p. (C). 1984. 195.00 (*0-946706-21-2*, Pub. by Royston Ltd) St Mut.

***Remedies for Breach of EC Law.** Julian Lonbay & Andrea Biondi. LC 96-38722. (Wiley Series in European Law). 1996. write for info. (*0-471-97109-X*) Wiley.

***Remedies for Torts & Breach of Contract.** 2nd ed. A. S. Burrows. 525p. 1994. pap. 46.00 (*0-406-50713-9*, UK) MICHIE.

Remedies in a Nutshell. 2nd ed. John F. O'Connell. LC 84-19705. (Nutshell Ser.). 320p. 1985. reprint ed. pap. 15.00 (*0-314-85066-X*) West Pub.

Remedies in Arbitration. 2nd ed. Marvin F. Hill, Jr. & Anthony V. Sinicropi. 570p. 1990. text ed. 56.00 (*0-87179-658-9*, 0658) BNA Books.

Remedies in Contract & Tort. Donald Harris. (Law in Context Ser.). xxxvii, 411p. 1988. 55.00 (*0-297-79355-1*) Rothman.

Remedies in Contract & Tort. Donald Harris. (Law in Context Ser.). 456p. (C). 1994. pap. text ed. 31.95 (*0-297-79401-9*) Northwestern U Pr.

Remedies in Employment Discrimination Law. Robert Belton. (Employment Law Library). 736p. 1992. text ed. 135.00 (*0-471-80051-1*) Wiley.

***Remedies in Employment Discrimination Law. 1997 Cumulative Supplement.** Robert Belton. pap. text ed. write for info. (*0-471-16672-3*) Wiley.

Remedies, Potions & Razzmatazz. Ed. by Donald L. Roberts. (Illus.). 510p. (Orig.). 1991. reprint ed. pap. 15.95 (*0-9628676-0-8*) Nostalgia CA.

Remedies Teacher's Manual: Cases & Materials On. 5th ed. Kenneth M. York et al. (American Casebook Ser.). 195p. 1992. pap. text ed. write for info. (*0-314-00733-4*) West Pub.

Remedies, Teacher's Manual for Cases & Problems. Elaine W. Shoben & W. Murray Tabb. (University Casebook Ser.). 398p. 1989. pap. text ed. write for info. (*0-88277-775-0*) Foundation Pr.

Remedies, Teacher's Manual to Accompany Cases & Materials On. 3rd ed. Edward D. Re & Stanton D. Krauss. (University Casebook Ser.). 126p. 1992. pap. text ed. write for info. (*0-88277-988-5*) Foundation Pr.

Remedies Teacher's Manual to Accompany Problems In. 2nd ed. Dan B. Dobbs & Kathleen Kavanagh. (American Casebook Ser.). 311p. 1993. pap. text ed. write for info. (*0-314-02793-9*) West Pub.

Remedies 1996-97. 384p. 1996. pap. 38.00 (*1-85431-575-7*, Pub. by Blackstone Pr UK) Gaunt.

***Remedio de Dios para el Rechazo - God's Remedy for Rejection.** Prince. 68p. (SPA.). 1996. write for info. (*0-7899-0209-5*) Editorial Unilit.

***Remedio de la Preocupacion.** H. Adolph. (SPA.). 1.50 (*0-8297-1934-2*) Life Pubs Intl.

Remedio en la Desdicha. Lope De Vega. 272p. (SPA.). 1975. 15.95 (*0-8288-7184-1*, S19615) Fr & Eur.

Remedios: Traditional Herbal Remedies of the Southwest. Michael Moore. LC 90-61682. (Illus.). 120p. (Orig.). 1990. pap. 9.95 (*1-878610-06-6*) Red Crane Bks.

***Remedios Caseros.** G. Smalley. (SPA.). 8.95 (*0-8297-1946-6*) Life Pubs Intl.

***Remedios De la Naturaleza: Desde la Aromaterapia Hasta Layoga, la Gu la Maxima de Los Mejores Tratamientos Sin Medicamentos Todos Comprobados.** Michael Castleman. LC 97-24241. 1997. write for info. (*0-87596-502-4*) Rodale Pr Inc.

Remedy: Class, Race, & Affirmative Action. Richard D. Kahlenberg. 1996. write for info. (*0-614-95746-X*) Basic.

Remedy: Class, Race, & Affirmative Action. Richard D. Kahlenberg. 432p. 1996. 25.00 (*0-465-09823-1*) Basic.

***Remedy: Class, Race & Affirmative Action.** Richard D. Kahlenberg. 368p. 1997. pap. 20.00 (*0-465-09824-X*) Basic.

Remedy Box. Amy J. Conway. LC 94-7706. 48p. 1994. boxed 19.95 (*0-8048-3015-0*) C E Tuttle.

Remedy for Overproduction & Unemployment. Hugo Bilgram. 1979. lib. bdg. 250.00 (*0-87700-287-8*) Revisionist Pr.

Remember. Barbara Taylor Bradford. LC 91-52706. 1992. mass mkt. 6.99 (*0-345-37936-5*) Ballantine.

***Remember.** Barbara Taylor Bradford. 1997. pap. 12.00 (*0-345-41859-X*) Ballantine.

Remember. O. P. Kretzmann. 72p. 1975. 4.99 (*0-570-03300-4*, 12-2632) Concordia.

Remember?? Ray F. Zuker. 210p. 1993. pap. 10.00 (*1-882194-05-5*) TN Valley Pub.

***Remember: A Story for the Child Within Us All.** Nicole Daines-Gibeaut & Robert Daines-Gibeaut. LC 95-94022. (Illus.). 156p. 1996. 14.95 (*0-9645055-6-8*) Heart-Heart Pub.

Remember Anything You Want. Virginia P. Krymow. LC 77-75039. 1977. pap. 3.00 (*0-918838-00-2*) Arlotta.

Remember Eve: How the Deceiver Works in the Beleiver's Life. Thaddeus R. Barnum. 196p. (Orig.). 1995. pap. 8.95 (*1-883928-13-3*) Longwood.

Remember Everything You Read: The Evelyn Wood 7-Day Reading & Learning Program. Stanley D. Frank. 1990. 23.00 (*0-8129-1773-1*, Times Bks) Random.

Remember Everything You Read: The Evelyn Wood 7-Day Speed Reading & Learning Program. Stanley D. Frank. 224p. 1992. mass mkt. 5.99 (*0-380-71577-5*) Avon.

Remember Fonetnoy! The 69th New York & the Irish Brigade in the Civil War. Joseph G. Bilby. (Illus.). 269p. 1995. 28.00 (*0-944413-37-4*) Longstreet Hse.

Remember Goliad! A History of La Bahia. Craig H. Roell. LC 94-25973. (Fred Rider Cotten Popular History Ser.: No. 9). (Illus.). 108p. (Orig.). 1994. pap. 5.95 (*0-87611-141-X*) Tex St Hist Assn.

Remember Hungary 1956: A Pictorial History of the Hungarian Revolution. Francis Laping & Hans Knight. (Illus.). 381p. 1992. 45.00 (*0-912404-01-9*) Alpha Pubns.

Remember If You Will. large type ed. Compiled by Joan Duce. (Mainstream Ser.). 163p. 1988. reprint ed. 18.95 (*1-85089-260-1*, Pub. by ISIS UK) Transaction Pubs.

Remember Jesus. S. Motyer. Date not set. 7.99 (*1-85792-153-4*, Pub. by Christian Focus UK) Spring Arbor Dist.

Remember Kirkland Lake: The Gold-Miners' Strike of 1941-42. Laurel S. MacDowell. (State & Economic Life Ser.). 308p. 1983. 35.00 (*0-8020-5585-0*); pap. 14.95 (*0-8020-6457-4*) U of Toronto Pr.

Remember Kirkland Lake: The History & Effects of the Kirkland Lake Gold Miners' Strike, 1941-42. Laurel S. MacDowell. LC 83-132702. (State & Economic Life Ser.: No. 5). (Illus.). 308p. reprint ed. pap. 87.80 (*0-8357-6386-2*, 2035741) Bks Demand.

Remember Laughter: A Life of James Thurber. Neil A. Grauer. LC 94-2945. (Illus.). xxii, 226p. (C). 1995. pap. 10.00 (*0-8032-7056-9*, Bison Books) U of Nebr Pr.

Remember Lot's Wife: And Other Unnamed Women of the Bible. April Yamasaki. LC 90-48224. 128p. (Orig.). 1991. pap. 9.95 (*0-87178-734-2*, 8342) Brethren.

Remember Love. Stacey Dennis. 512p. 1992. mass mkt. 4.50 (*0-8217-3993-X*, Zebra Kensgtn) Kensgtn Pub Corp.

***Remember Love.** Susan Plunkett. (Time Passages Ser.). 368p. 1996. mass mkt. 5.99 (*0-515-11980-6*) Jove Pubns.

Remember Me. Danice Allen. 384p. (Orig.). 1996. mass mkt. 4.99 (*0-380-78150-6*) Avon.

Remember Me. Glester Campbell. 1989. write for info. (*0-318-65486-5*) Tri Cor.

Remember Me. Mary Higgins Clark. 1995. pap. 6.99 (*0-671-86709-1*) PB.

Remember Me. Mary Higgins Clark. 1994. 23.50 (*0-671-86708-3*) S&S Trade.

Remember Me. Suzanne Lipsett. LC 90-49382. 145p. 1991. 17.95 (*0-916515-98-2*) Mercury Hse Inc.

***Remember Me.** Mary McCarthy. 698p. 1996. pap. 12.95 (*1-85371-610-3*, Pub. by Poolbeg Pr IE) Dufour.

***Remember Me?** Jennifer Mikels. (Special Edition Ser.: No. 1107). 1997. mass mkt. 3.99 (*0-373-24107-0*, 1-24107-4) Silhouette.

Remember Me. Christopher Pike. Ed. by Pat MacDonald. 224p. (YA). (gr. 8 up). pap. 3.99 (*0-671-73685-X*, Archway) PB.

Remember Me. Christopher Pike. (YA). (gr. 8 up). 1994. 14.00 (*0-671-50041-4*, Archway) PB.

Remember Me? Joseph Sharp. Ed. by James C. Perin. 300p. (Orig.). 1996. pap. 5.95 (*0-9644656-3-9*) Deep Lingo.

Remember Me. Alice P. Smith. 1994. 10.00 (*0-533-10788-1*) Vantage.

Remember Me. Margaret Wild. LC 95-10080. (Albert Whitman Concept Bks.). (Illus.). 32p. (J). (ps-2). 1995. lib. bdg. 14.95 (*0-8075-6934-8*) A Whitman.

Remember Me. large type ed. Sheila Walsh. 585p. 1995. 25.99 (*0-7505-0751-9*, Pub. by Magna Print Bks UK) Ulverscroft.

Remember Me. Mary Higgins Clark. 1995. reprint ed. lib. bdg. 32.95 (*1-56849-589-7*) Buccaneer Bks.

Remember Me: A Sufi Prayer. Avideh Shashaani. 114p. 1995. pap. 12.50 (*0-938572-11-3*) Bunny Crocodile.

***Remember Me: A Sufi Prayer.** Avideh Shashaani. 100p. 1996. pap. 11.00 (*0-614-21330-4*, 1371) Kazi Pubns.

Remember Me: Slave Life in Coastal Georgia. Charles Joyner. (Georgia Humanities Council Publications). (Illus.). 84p. 1991. pap. 9.95 (*0-8203-1317-3*) U of Ga Pr.

Remember Me: Women & Their Friendship Quilts. Linda O. Lipsett. (Illus.). 150p. 1997. pap. 24.95 (*0-8442-2650-5*) Quilt Digest Pr.

***Remember Me - a Sufi Prayer.** 2nd ed. Avideh Shashaani. LC 96-72636. 113p. (Orig.). 1997. pap. 12.50 (*0-910735-81-6*) MTO Printing & Pubn Ctr.

***Remember Me Dancing.** Ken Pareijko. 1996. pap. 14.95 (*1-878569-36-8*) Badger Bks Inc.

***Remember Me, Irene.** Jan Burke. 304p. 1997. mass mkt. 5.50 (*0-06-104438-5*, Harp PBks) HarpC.

Remember Me Irene. large type ed. Jan Burke. LC 96-19211. (Cloak & Dagger Ser.). 1996. lib. bdg. 22.95 (*0-7862-0786-8*, Thorndike Lrg Prnt) Thorndike Pr.

Remember Me, Irene: An Irene Kelly Mystery. Jan Burke. 304p. 1996. 21.00 (*0-684-80343-7*) S&S Trade.

Remember Me to Harold Square. Paula Danziger. 144p. (J). (gr. k-12). 1988. mass mkt. 3.99 (*0-440-20153-5*, LLL BDD) BDD Bks Young Read.

Remember Me to Harold Square. Paula Danziger. LC 87-6844. 168p. (J). (gr. 7 up). 1987. 13.95 (*0-385-29610-X*) Delacorte.

Remember Me to Marcie. Martin Yoseloff. 6.95 (*0-8453-7696-9*, Cornwall Bks) Assoc Univ Prs.

Remember Me When This You See. Deirdre Corey. (Friends 4-Ever Ser.: No. 4). 144p. (J). (gr. 4-7). 1990. pap. 2.75 (*0-590-42624-9*) Scholastic Inc.

Remember Mobile. Caldwell Delaney. (Illus.). 242p. 1980. reprint ed. 20.00 (*0-940882-13-2*) HB Pubns.

An Asterisk (*) at the beginning of an entry indicates that the title is appearing in BIP for the first time.

R

***Remember Mother Earth.** Schim Schimmel. LC 97-9617. (Illus.). 32p. 1997. write for info. (*1-55971-640-1*) NorthWord.

Remember My Heart. Janis R. Hudson. 1995. mass mkt. 4.99 (*0-7860-0187-9*, Pinncle Kensgtn) Kensgtn Pub Corp.

Remember My Name. Sara H. Banks. LC 92-61905. (Council for Indian Education Ser.). (Illus.). 120p. (Orig.). (J). (gr. 4-8). 1993. pap. 8.95 (*1-879373-38-6*) R Rinehart.

Remember Not to Forget: A Memory of the Holocaust. Norman H. Finkelstein. LC 92-24603. (Illus.). 32p. (J). (gr. 2 up). 1993. reprint ed. pap. 4.95 (*0-688-11802-X*, Mulberry) Morrow.

Remember Pearl Harbor. Elizabeth L. Hamilton. (Illus.). 29p. (J). (gr. 3). 1981. pap. 2.95 (*0-9631388-4-7*) AZ Mem Mus.

Remember Pearl Harbor. 6th ed. Blake Clark. 266p. 1987. reprint ed. mass mkt. 4.95 (*0-935180-49-4*) Mutual Pub HI.

Remember Rafferty: Pet Loss for Children. Joy Johnson. (Illus.). 24p. 1991. pap. 4.95 (*1-56123-024-3*) Centering Corp.

Remember Reno: A Biographer of Major General Jesse Lee Reno. William F. McConnell. LC 96-16506. (Illus.). 144p. 1996. 19.95 (*1-57249-020-9*) White Mane Pub.

Remember Roberto: Clemente Recalled by Teammates, Family, Friends & Fans. Jim O'Brien. (Pittsburgh Proud Ser.). (Illus.). 448p. 1994. 24.95 (*0-916114-14-7*); pap. 14.95 (*0-916114-15-5*) J P OBrien.

Remember Sometimes the Seekers of Dreams. J. P. Ballard. 63p. (Orig.). 1988. pap. text ed. 6.95 (*0-9620563-1-6*) Common Mans Symposium.

Remember That. Leslea Newman. (Illus.). 32p. (J). (gr. k-3). 1996. 14.95 (*0-395-66156-0*, Clarion Bks) HM.

Remember That Ol' Horse? Ron Westmoreland. LC 89-35524. (Centennial Series of the Association of Former Students: No. 34). 128p. 1989. 14.95 (*0-89096-409-2*) Tex A&M Univ Pr.

Remember the Alamo. Amelia E. Barr. 329p. 1980. reprint ed. lib. bdg. 11.95 (*0-89968-215-4*, Lghtyr Pr) Buccaneer Bks.

Remember the Alibi. Elizabeth D. Squire. 272p. (Orig.). 1994. mass mkt. 4.99 (*0-425-14351-1*, Prime Crime) Berkley Pub.

***Remember the Autumn Leaves.** Sherry M. Smith. (Illus.). 208p. (Orig.). 1997. pap. 13.93 (*0-9657665-0-0*) Autumn Dist.

***Remember the Catskills: Tales by a Recovering Hotelkeeper.** Esterita C. Blumberg. (Illus.). 295p. (Orig.). 1996. pap. 19.50 (*0-935796-80-0*, 80) Purple Mnt Pr.

Remember the Days see This Rough New Land

Remember the Days of Old. Isadore Fishman. LC 79-100058. (Illus.). (J). (gr. 4-9). 1969. 4.95 (*0-87677-000-6*) Hartmore.

Remember the End. Agnes Turnbull. 1993. reprint ed. lib. bdg. 89.00 (*0-7812-5846-4*) Rprt Serv.

***Remember the Former Things: The Recollection of Previous Texts in Isaiah 40-55.** Patricia T. Willey. LC 97-21732. (Society of Biblical Literature Dissertation Ser.). 1997. write for info. (*0-7885-0364-2*) Scholars Pr GA.

Remember the Future: The Apollo Legacy. Ed. by Stan Kent. (Science & Technology Ser.: Vol. 50). 218p. 1980. pap. 15.00 (*0-87703-127-4*); lib. bdg. 25.00 (*0-87703-126-6*) Univelt Inc.

Remember the Future (the Prophecies of Nostradamus) The Prophecies of Nostradamus. Victor Baines. (Illus.). 208p. (Orig.). 1994. pap. 17.95 (*0-9631740-2-9*) Holographic Bks.

Remember the Holocaust: A Memoir of Survival. Helen Farkas. (Illus.). 160p. (Orig.). 1995. pap. 10.95 (*1-56474-125-7*) Fithian Pr.

Remember the Ladies. Lyn Lifshin. 1985. pap. 1.50 (*0-317-19794-0*) Ghost Dance.

Remember the Ladies: A Woman's Book of Days. Kirstin Olsen. LC 93-16868. 1993. 12.95 (*0-8061-2558-6*) U of Okla Pr.

Remember the Ladies: New Perspectives on Women in American History. Ed. by Carol George. (Illus.). 256p. (C). 1975. 34.95 (*0-8156-0110-7*) Syracuse U Pr.

Remember the Ladies: The First Women's Rights Convention. Norma Johnston. 176p. (J). (gr. 4-7). 1995. pap. 3.50 (*0-590-47086-8*) Scholastic Inc.

Remember the Light. Mary P. Fisher. (Illus.). 32p. (Orig.). (J). (gr. k-4). 1986. pap. 4.50 (*0-9615149-7-3*) Fenton Valley Pr.

Remember the MacCutcheon. James Eade. 86p. (Orig.). 1991. pap. 6.95 (*0-945470-12-6*) Chess Ent.

Remember the Moment. large type ed. Denise Robertson. 485p. 1993. 25.99 (*0-7505-0271-1*) Ulverscroft.

***Remember the Morning.** Thomas Fleming. LC 97-16643. 1997. 24.95 (*0-312-86308-X*) St Martin.

Remember the Promise. Alvin N. Rogness. LC 76-27082. 64p. 1977. kivar 6.99 (*0-8066-1567-2*, 10-5480, Augsburg) Augsburg Fortress.

Remember the Promise. deluxe ed. Alvin N. Rogness. LC 76-27082. 78p. 1977. 11.99 (*0-8066-1619-9*, 10-5481, Augsburg) Augsburg Fortress.

Remember the Raisin! Kentucky & Kentuckians in the Battles & Massacre at Frenchtown, Michigan Territory, in the War of 1812 Published with Notes on Kentucky Veterans of the War of 1812, 2 vols. in 1. G. Glenn Clift. 339p. 1995. reprint ed. pap. 26.50 (*0-614-09963-3*, 9123) Clearfield Co.

Remember the Secret. Elisabeth Kubler-Ross. LC 81-68454. (Illus.). 32p. (J). (ps up). 1995. pap. 9.95 (*0-89087-524-3*) Celestial Arts.

Remember the Tarantella. Finola Moorehead. pap. 13.95 (*0-7043-4376-2*, Pub. by Womens Press UK) Trafalgar.

Remember the Tender Years - A Story. Jacquie Ingram. (Lonna Price Bethwick: 1). 88p. 1994. per., pap. text ed. 4.99 (*0-9643383-1-9*) Rose of Sharon.

***Remember the Time.** Annette Reynolds. 1997. mass mkt. 5.50 (*0-553-57652-6*) Bantam.

***Remember the Time...? The Power & Promise of Family Storytelling.** Eileen S. Kindig. LC 97-12921. 204p. 1997. pap. 10.99 (*0-8308-1965-7*, 1965) InterVarsity.

***Remember the Valiant.** large type ed. Rose Meadows. (Large Print Ser.). 304p. 1996. 25.99 (*0-7089-3654-7*) Ulverscroft.

***Remember the Wonders: A Fifty-Year History of Grand Canyon Baptist Association.** Naomi R. Hunke. LC 96-69312. 224p. (Orig.). 1996. pap. 15.95 (*1-57736-006-0*) Providence Hse.

Remember This One? 128p. 1982. otabind 12.95 (*0-7935-1917-9*, 00384600) H Leonard.

Remember This Time. Gloria K. Broder & Bill Broder. LC 83-4249. 336p. 1991. 14.95 (*0-937858-23-4*) Newmarket.

***Remember Three Days in "1863"** unabridged ed. LC 96-138181. 70p. (Orig.). 1996. pap. 10.00 (*0-9654312-0-7*) J Williamson.

Remember to Dream: A History of Jewish Radicalism. Robert Wolfe. 380p. 1994. pap. 12.00 (*0-9642465-1-1*) Jewish Radical.

Remember to Keep Holy the Lord's Day, Vol. 4. John Villata. (Reflections on the Commandments Ser.). 62p. 1995. pap. 2.95 (*0-8198-6459-5*) Pauline Bks.

Remember to Remember Who You Are. D. Trinidad Hunt. Ed. by Michelle M. Jerin. (Illus.). 72p. (Orig.). 1992. pap. 5.95 (*1-881904-02-4*) Elan Pr HI.

Remember Us. Albert R. Booky. LC 90-71972. 168p. (Orig.). 1992. pap. 9.00 (*1-56002-032-6*, Univ Edtns) Aegina Pr.

Remember Us. Lucien T. Martin & Melba B. Martin. (Illus.). 298p. 1987. 30.00 (*0-9620005-0-7*) Martin Pubs.

Remember When...? Marjorie Daniels. (Illus.). 157p. (Orig.). 1988. pap. 4.95 (*0-940828-17-0*) D Youra Studios.

Remember When. Robin L. Hatcher. (Americana Ser.). 448p. (Orig.). 1994. mass mkt., pap. text ed. 4.99 (*0-8439-3683-5*) Dorchester Pub Co.

Remember When. Ideals Editorial Staff. (Illus.). 160p. 1992. 24.95 (*0-8249-4045-8*) Ideals.

Remember When. Anne Laurence. (Superromance Ser.). 1993. mass mkt. 3.39 (*0-373-70539-5*, 1-70539-1) Harlequin Bks.

***Remember When.** McNaught. 1997. mass mkt. 7.99 (*0-671-79555-4*) PB.

Remember When. Judith McNaught. 448p. 1996. 24.00 (*0-671-52570-0*, PB Hardcover) PB.

***Remember When.** Random House Staff. 1997. 6.99 (*0-679-88407-6*) Random Bks Yng Read.

Remember When. large type ed. Judith McNaught. LC 96-49645. 1997. pap. 25.95 (*0-7862-0569-5*) Thorndike Pr.

Remember When. large type ed. Judith McNaught. LC 96-49645. 704p. 1997. 27.95 (*0-7862-0568-7*, Thorndike Lrg Prnt) Thorndike Pr.

***Remember When.** unabridged ed. Carol O'Connor. (Illus.). 64p. (Orig.). 1996. pap. 9.95 (*0-9653922-2-8*) Vital Link.

Remember When, Pt. II. Tom Conner. Ed. by Virginia Nobels. (Illus.). 120p. (Orig.). 1993. pap. 9.95 (*1-882616-04-9*) Advertiser.

Remember When, Vol. I. Jerome M. Hall. 150p. 1985. 14.95 (*0-9614356-0-7*) Creative Concepts.

***Remember When: A Nostalgic Look at America's National Pastime.** Thomas S. Owens. 176p. 1996. 22.98 (*1-56799-392-3*, MetroBooks) M Friedman Pub Grp Inc.

Remember When? Anderson County History Highlights. Ernest Jones. (Illus.). 100p. (Orig.). 1989. write for info. (*0-318-64843-1*) Lo-Wano Bks.

Remember When? Monologs of the Middle School Experience. C. Michael Perry. (Scene Bks.). 32p. (YA). (gr. 7-12). 1994. pap. 6.95 (*1-57514-006-3*, 5015) Encore Perform Pub.

Remember Where You Started From. Susan P. Holway. 84p. 1992. pap. 9.95 (*1-880166-03-8*) C&D Pub OR.

***Remember Who You Are.** William H. Willimon. 13.35 (*0-687-60973-9*) Abingdon.

Remember Who You Are: Baptism, a Model for Christian Life. William H. Willimon. LC 79-93359. (Illus.). 128p. (Orig.). 1980. pap. 8.95 (*0-8358-0399-6*) Upper Room Bks.

Remember Who You Are: Stories about Being Jewish. large type ed. Esther Hautzig. 224p. 1991. reprint ed. pap. 12.95 (*0-8027-2663-1*) Walker & Co.

Remember with Advantages: A History of the 10th, 11th & Royal Hussars, 1945-1992. Keeping the Peace of the Cold War in Europe. Henry Keown-Boyd. (Illus.). 288p. 1994. 47.50 (*0-85052-382-6*, Pub. by L Cooper Bks UK) Trans-Atl Phila.

Remember Your Confirmation. 48p. 1977. pap. 4.99 (*0-570-03751-4*, 12-2655) Concordia.

Remember Your Essence. Paul Williams. 1990. pap. 7.95 (*0-517-57296-6*, Harmony) Crown Pub Group.

Remember Your First Time? Nick V. Bozanich. 211p. (Orig.). (C). 1993. pap. 9.95 (*0-9635071-0-9*) Dela Pr.

Remember Your Relations: The Elsie Allen Basket Collection. Suzanne Abel-Vidol & Dot Brovarney. (Illus.). 128p. 1996. 47.00 (*0-8095-4997-2*) Borgo Pr.

Remember Your Relations: The Elsie Allen Baskets, Family & Friends. Suzanne Abel-Vidor et al. (Illus.). 128p. 1996. pap. text ed. 20.00 (*0-930588-80-0*) Heyday Bks.

Remember Your Relatives: Yankton Sioux Images, 1865-1915, Vol. 2. Renee Sansom-Flood et al. 150p. (Orig.). (C). 1989. pap. 8.50 (*0-9621936-1-5*) Yankton Sioux Tribe.

Remember Your Relatives, Vol. 1: Yankton Sioux Images, 1851 to 1904. Renee Sansom-Flood & Shirley A. Bernie. Ed. by Leonard R. Bruguier. (Illus.). 55p. (Orig.). (YA). (gr. 12). 1985. pap. 8.50 (*0-9621936-0-7*) Yankton Sioux Tribe.

Rememberance. Jo-Ann Power. 400p. 1995. mass mkt. 4.99 (*0-8217-0101-0*, Zebra Kensgtn) Kensgtn Pub Corp.

***Rememberance & Other Poems.** 18p. 1997. reprint ed. pap. 10.00 (*0-9657885-0-4*) S Danaher.

Rememberances: World War II 286th Engr C Bn. unabridged ed. Louis Gerken. (Illus.). 200p. (Orig.). 1996. 40.00 (*0-9617163-5-5*) Amer Scientific.

Remembered Death. large type ed. Agatha Christie. 368p. 1992. lib. bdg. 19.95 (*0-8161-4597-0*, GK Hall) Thorndike Pr.

Remembered Drums: A History of the Puget Sound Indian War. J. A. Eckrom. 220p. 1988. 17.95 (*0-936546-14-X*) Pioneer Pr Bks.

Remembered Earth: An Anthology of Contemporary Native American Literature. Ed. by Geary Hobson. LC 80-54561. (Illus.). 428p. 1981. reprint ed. pap. 16.95 (*0-8263-0568-7*) U of NM Pr.

Remembered Future: A Study in Literary Mythology. Harold Fisch. LC 83-48899. 208p. 1985. 10.95 (*0-253-35003-4*) Ind U Pr.

***Remembered Kisses: An Illustrated Anthology of Irish Love Poetry.** Fleur Robertson. 1997. 12.95 (*1-85833-715-1*) BHB Intl.

Remembered Light. Albert Huffstickler. 32p. pap. 4.95 (*0-941720-05-5*) Slough Pr TX.

Remembered Lives: The Work of Ritual, Storytelling, & Growing Older. Barbara Myerhoff. 250p. (C). 1992. pap. 19.95 (*0-472-08177-2*); text ed. 47.50 (*0-472-10317-2*) U of Mich Pr.

Remembered Love. Laura Cassidy. 350p. 1995. 21.50 (*0-263-14191-8*, Pub. by M & B UK) Ulverscroft.

Remembered Moments. Joy Railing. 110p. 1993. 15.95 (*1-882188-03-9*) Magnolia Mktg.

Remembered Past: 1914-1945. large type ed. Ronald A. Alvarez & Susan C. Kline. Ed. by National Council on the Aging Staff. (Large Print Inspirational Ser.). (Illus.). 1988. pap. 11.95 (*0-8027-2627-5*) Walker & Co.

Remembered Present: A Biological Theory of Consciousness. Gerald M. Edelman. LC 89-42907. (Illus.). 384p. 1990. 38.00 (*0-465-06910-X*) Basic.

Remembered Self: Emotion & Memory in Personality. Jefferson A. Singer & Peter Salovey. LC 93-8017. 1993. 40.00 (*0-02-901581-2*, Free Press) Free Pr.

Remembered Spring. large type ed. Margaret Maddocks. (Ulverscroft). 400p. 1994. 25.99 (*0-7089-3062-X*) Ulverscroft.

Remembered Village. Mysore N. Srinivas. (Center for South & Southeast Asia Studies, UC Berkeley: No. 26). 1977. pap. 14.95 (*0-520-03948-3*) U CA Pr.

Remembered Village. Mysore N. Srinivas. LC 75-7203. (Illus.). 375p. reprint ed. pap. 106.90 (*0-7837-4683-0*, 2044430) Bks Demand.

Remembered with Love. large type ed. P. L. Jones. (Linford Romance Library). 1989. pap. 15.99 (*0-7089-6782-5*) Ulverscroft.

Remembering. F. C. Bartlett. (Illus.). 317p. (C). 1995. text ed. 54.95 (*0-521-48278-X*) Cambridge U Pr.

Remembering. F. C. Bartlett. (Illus.). 317p. (C). 1995. pap. text ed. 17.95 (*0-521-48356-5*) Cambridge U Pr.

Remembering. Wendell Berry. LC 88-61166. 144p. 1988. 14.95 (*0-86547-330-7*) Gnomon Pr.

Remembering. Wendell Berry. LC 88-61166. 124p. 1990. pap. 11.00 (*0-86547-331-5*, North Pt Pr) FS&G.

Remembering. Earlyne C. Chaney. LC 74-81047. 372p. 1987. pap. 11.95 (*0-89031-018-1*) Astara.

Remembering. Art Fettig. LC 81-90188. (Illus.). (J). (gr. k-7). 1981. pap. 3.95 (*0-9601334-2-9*) Growth Unltd.

***Remembering.** Nadia Giordana. 12p. 1995. pap. text ed. 7.00 (*1-886352-06-2*) Crow Feather.

Remembering. Michael C. Macpherson. LC 94-96488. 224p. (Orig.). 1995. pap. 12.00 (*0-9642136-0-5*) Green Duck Pr.

Remembering. Coleen M. Paratore. (Books Worth Writing). 128p. 1992. 24.95 (*0-9630250-0-7*) Bks Worth Writing.

Remembering. Wagner. (J). 1998. pap. 5.99 (*0-689-81285-X*) S&S Childrens.

Remembering, Bk. 1. 1993. 6.60 (*0-88336-350-X*) New Readers.

Remembering, Bk. 2. 1993. 6.60 (*0-88336-351-8*) New Readers.

Remembering, Bks. 1 & 2. 1993. teacher ed. 5.95 (*0-88336-352-6*) New Readers.

Remembering: A Gentle Reminder of Who You Are... Teresa Winter. Ed. by Caroline Tilton. 240p. (Orig.). 1994. pap. text ed. 13.95 (*0-9636992-3-7*) Tor Down Pub.

Remembering: A Phenomenological Study. Edward S. Casey. LC 85-45889. (Studies in Phenomenology & Existential Philosophy). 378p. 1987. 49.95 (*0-253-34942-7*); pap. 24.95 (*0-253-20409-7*) Ind U Pr.

Remembering: Reflections of Growing up Adopted. Jeffrey R. LaCure. 96p. (Orig.). 1995. pap. text ed. 12.95 (*0-9635717-1-0*) Adoption Advocate.

***Remembering: The Story of a Soldier.** Virginia Mayo. (Illus.). 32p. (J). (gr. 2-4). 1997. 19.95 (*0-09-176687-7*, Pub. by Hutchinson UK) Trafalgar.

Remembering America: A Voice from the Sixties. Richard N. Goodwin. 560p. 1988. 19.95 (*0-316-32024-2*) Little.

Remembering America: A Voice from the Sixties. Richard N. Goodwin. LC 89-45093. 560p. 1989. reprint ed. pap. 13.00 (*0-06-097241-6*, PL) HarpC.

Remembering & Forgetting: An Inquiry into the Nature of Memory. Edmund B. Bolles. 1988. 22.95 (*0-8027-1004-2*) Walker & Co.

Remembering & Forgetting: Legacies of War & Peace in East Asia. Ed. by Gerrit W. Gong. (Significant Issues Ser.). (C). 1996. pap. text ed. 15.95 (*0-89206-284-3*) CSI Studies.

Remembering & Other Poems. Myra C. Livingston. LC 89-2654. 64p. (J). (gr. 3-7). 1989. lib. bdg. 13.95 (*0-689-50489-6*, McElderry) S&S Childrens.

Remembering & Repeating: Biblical Creation in Paradise Lost. Regina M. Schwartz. (Illus.). 160p. 1989. text ed. 54.95 (*0-521-34357-7*) Cambridge U Pr.

Remembering & Repeating: On Milton's Theology & Poetics. Regina M. Schwartz. LC 92-34410. (Illus.). 158p. (C). 1993. reprint ed. pap. text ed. 14.50 (*0-226-74201-6*) U Ch Pr.

Remembering & Revealing. Hilda Finzi. 1994. pap. 8.95 (*0-533-10863-2*) Vantage.

Remembering & the Sound of Words: Mallarme, Proust, Joyce, Beckett. Adam Piette. 304p. (C). 1996. 65.00 (*0-19-818268-6*) OUP.

Remembering Anna O. Mikkel Borch-Jacobsen. 144p. 1996. pap. 14.95 (*0-415-91777-8*) Routledge.

Remembering Anna O. Mikkel Borch-Jacobsen. 144p. (C). 1996. text ed. 49.95 (*0-415-91776-X*) Routledge.

Remembering Babylon. David Malouf. 1994. pap. 11.00 (*0-679-74951-9*, Vin) Random.

Remembering Billy: The Story of a West Texas Marine, His Friends, His Family, & His Sacrifice - Told by Those Who Knew Him. Compiled & Intro. by Richard Havens. LC 94-71469. (Illus.). 432p. 1994. 22.95 (*0-9641166-0-X*) Flatland Pubng.

***Remembering Blue.** Connie M. Fowler. 1998. write for info. (*0-679-45717-8*) Random.

Remembering Box. Eth Clifford. (Illus.). 64p. (J). (gr. 2-5). 1985. 15.95 (*0-395-38476-1*) HM.

Remembering Box. Eth Clifford. Ed. by ALC Staff. LC 85-10851. 64p. (J). (gr. 5 up). 1992. pap. 4.95 (*0-688-11777-5*) Morrow.

Remembering Brad: On the Loss of a Son to AIDS. H. Wayne Schow. LC 94-4031. (Illus.). xii, 160p. 1995. 15.95 (*1-56085-070-1*) Signature Bks.

Remembering Buddy: The Definitive Biography of Buddy Holly. rev. ed. John Goldrosen & John Beecher. Orig. Title: Buddy Holly: His Life & Music. (Illus.). 210p. 1996. pap. 18.95 (*0-306-80715-7*) Da Capo.

Remembering Carlos Bulosan. P. C. Morantte. 164p. (Orig.). (C). 1984. pap. 15.00 (*971-10-0184-5*, Pub. by New Day Pub PH) Cellar.

Remembering Charles Rennie Mackintosh. Alistair Moffat. (Illus.). 160p. (Orig.). 1995. pap. 19.95 (*0-948661-08-9*, Pub. by Colin Baxter Ltd UK) Voyageur Pr.

Remembering Charlie Chaplin. large type ed. Jerry Epstein. 355p. 1990. 19.95 (*1-85089-351-9*, Pub. by ISIS UK) Transaction Pubs.

Remembering China, 1935-1945: A Memoir. Bea E. Liu. LC 95-71165. (Minnesota Voices Project Ser.: No. 76). 172p. (Orig.). 1996. 22.95 (*0-89823-170-1*) New Rivers Pr.

***Remembering Clayton.** Ruth Hanke. LC 97-90003. 1997. 10.95 (*0-533-12264-3*) Vantage.

Remembering Denny. Calvin Trillin. LC 92-41932. 1993. 19.00 (*0-374-22607-5*) FS&G.

Remembering Denny. Calvin Trillin. 224p. 1994. pap. 9.99 (*0-446-67032-4*) Warner Bks.

***Remembering Detroit's Old Westside - 1920-1950: A Pictorial History of the Westsiders.** Westsiders Staff. (Illus.). 240p. 1997. write for info. (*0-9657779-0-1*) Westsiders.

***Remembering Dixie.** Ignatus D'Aquila. Ed. by Mimi Pelton. (Illus.). 384p. 1997. 22.95 (*0-9659156-0-3*) Hot Aug Nights.

Remembering E. G. Peterson: His Life & Our Story. Elmer G. Peterson. LC 74-13517. (Illus.). 149p. reprint ed. pap. 42.50 (*0-7837-7066-9*, 2046878) Bks Demand.

Remembering Elizabeth Bishop: An Oral Biography. Gary Fountain & Peter Brazeau. LC 94-14811. (Illus.). 456p. (C). 1994. 40.00 (*0-87023-936-8*) U of Mass Pr.

Remembering Elizabeth Bishop: An Oral Biography. Gary Fountain & Peter Brazeau. LC 94-14811. (Illus.). 456p. (C). 1996. pap. 18.95 (*1-55849-016-7*) U of Mass Pr.

Remembering Esperanza: A Cultural-Political Theology for North American Praxis. Mark K. Taylor. LC 90-30183. 1992. reprint ed. pap. 19.50 (*0-88344-798-3*) Orbis Bks.

Remembering Essex: A Pictorial History of Essex County, New Jersey. John T. Cunningham & Charles F. Cummings. LC 95-35729. 1995. write for info. (*0-89865-949-3*) Donning Co.

Remembering Farley: A For Better or for Worse Special Edition. Lynn Johnston. (Illus.). 192p. (Orig.). 1996. pap. 9.95 (*0-8362-1309-2*) Andrews & McMeel.

Remembering for the Future: Working Papers & Addenda, 3 vols., Set. Yehuda Bauer et al. (Illus.). 3250p. 1989. 609.25 (*0-08-036754-2*, Pergamon Pr) Elsevier.

Remembering Forward. Harold G. Clarke. LC 94-42345. 234p. 1995. 25.00 (*0-86554-472-7*, MUP-H370) Mercer Univ Pr.

Remembering G & Other Stories. Makeda Silvera. Date not set. pr. 10.95 (*0-920813-60-7*, Pub. by Sister Vision CN) LPC InBook.

Remembering Galileo. Spencer K. Porter. LC 95-10747. 216p. (C). 1995. pap. text ed. 29.00 (*0-8191-9963-X*); lib. bdg. 48.50 (*0-8191-9962-1*) U Pr of Amer.

Remembering Gardens: Stages & Travels. Kurt Klinger. Tr. by Harvey I. Dunkle. (Studies in Austrian Literature, Culture, & Thought. Translation Ser.). 1990. 23.50 (*0-929497-22-8*); pap. 17.95 (*0-929497-25-2*) Ariadne CA.

Remembering God's Word. Ed Rehbein. (Orig.). 1991. pap. 5.99 (*0-89900-359-1*) College Pr Pub.

Remembering Grandad. Gianni Padoan. (J). 1989. 11.99 (*0-85953-311-5*) Childs Play.

R

Remembering Grandma Moses. Beth M. Hickok. (Illus.). 64p. 1994. pap. 12.95 (*1-884592-01-5*) Images from the Past.

***Remembering Grandma Moses.** Beth M. Hickok. 1997. pap. 22.00 incl. audio (*1-884592-07-4*) Images from the Past.

Remembering His Benefit. Daniel Nicholoson. 48p. 1988. pap. text ed. 2.95 (*0-88144-074-4*) Christian Pub.

Remembering Horowitz: 125 Pianists Recall a Legend. Ed. & Compiled by David Dubal. 383p. 1995. 16.00 (*0-02-860269-2*) Schirmer Bks.

***Remembering Ida Rolf.** Ed. by Rosemary Feitis & Louis Schultz. 250p. (Orig.). 1996. pap. 14.95 (*1-55643-238-0*) North Atlantic.

Remembering in Vain: The Klaus Barbie Trial & Crimes Against Humanity. Alain Finkielkraut. Tr. by Roxanne Lapidus & Sima Godfrey from FRE. (European Perspectives Ser.). 112p. (C). 1992. text ed. 20.50 (*0-231-07464-6*) Col U Pr.

Remembering is the Greatest Gift of All. Thomas B. Franklin. 1991. 9.95 (*0-925053-05-8*) Octagon CA.

Remembering Jack & Bobby: An Anthology. Ed. by Sheila Cassidy. LC 92-70109. 108p. (Orig.). 1992. pap. 12.95 (*0-9630485-2-X*) In Print.

Remembering Jackie: A Life in Pictures. Life Magazine Editors. (Illus.). 128p. 1994. 24.95 (*0-446-51944-8*) Warner Bks.

***Remembering James Agee.** 2nd ed. Ed. by David Madden & Jeffrey J. Folks. LC 97-8507. 1997. 29.95 (*0-8203-1913-9*) U of Ga Pr.

Remembering James Wright. Robert Bly. 44p. 1991. pap. 6.00 (*0-915408-44-9*) Ally Pr.

Remembering Kings Past: Monastic Foundation Legends in Medieval Southern France. Amy G. Remensnyder. (Illus.). 376p. 1996. 49.95 (*0-8014-2954-4*) Cornell U Pr.

***Remembering Lake Quinsigamond, from Steamboats to White City.** Michael Perna. LC 97-60311. 150p. (Orig.). 1997. pap. 19.95 (*1-886284-02-4*, Tatnuck) Databks.

Remembering Laughter. Wallace Stegner. 160p. 1996. pap. 10.95 (*0-14-025240-1*, Viking) Viking Penguin.

Remembering Light & Stone. Deirdre Madden. 192p. (Orig.). 1994. pap. 9.95 (*0-571-16946-5*) Faber & Faber.

Remembering Malcolm. Benjamin Karim et al. 1996. mass mkt. 5.99 (*0-345-40051-8*) Ballantine.

Remembering Malcolm: The Story of Malcolm X from Inside the Muslm Mosque by His Assistant Minister, Benjamin Karim. Benjamin Karim et al. (Illus.). 224p. 1992. 21.00 (*0-88184-901-4*) Carroll & Graf.

Remembering Margaret Mitchell: Author of Gone with the Wind. Ed. by Lucille T. Love et al. (Illus.). 212p. 1992. 29.95 (*0-9634245-0-5*) E Ross Pubs.

Remembering Matt Talbot. Mary Purcell. 142p. (Orig.). 1990. pap. 11.95 (*1-85390-185-7*, Pub. by Veritas Publns IE) Ignatius Pr.

Remembering Me: A Journal for You & Your Loved Ones. Danielle Light. 136p. 1986. pap. 7.95 (*0-9616478-0-9*) Mt Shasta Pubns.

Remembering Milton. Ed. by Mary Nyquist. (C). pap. text ed. 29.95 (*0-7870-0003-5*) Digital Print.

Remembering Milton: Essays on the Texts & Traditions. Ed. by Margaret Ferguson & Mary Nyquist. 440p. 1988. text ed. 47.50 (*0-416-39730-1*); pap. text ed. 16.95 (*0-416-39740-9*) Routledge Chapman & Hall.

Remembering Mog. Colby Rodowsky. LC 95-30616. 144p. (J). (gr. 7-10). 1996. 15.00 (*0-374-34663-1*) FS&G.

***Remembering Mountains.** Janice E. Bowers. LC 97-4659. 1997. 29.95 (*0-8165-1717-7*); pap. 12.95 (*0-8165-1718-5*) U of Ariz Pr.

Remembering Names: Improvement Is Easy. Arthur A. Merrill. (Illus.). 57p. 1985. 9.75 (*0-911894-50-0*) Analysis.

Remembering Norm: A Victim's Story. Harriet M. Savitz. (Illus.). 128p. 1995. text ed. 13.00 (*0-8059-3786-2*) Dorrance.

Remembering Our Past: Studies in Autobiographical Memory. Ed. by David C. Rubin. (Illus.). 400p. (C). 1996. text ed. 59.95 (*0-521-46145-6*) Cambridge U Pr.

Remembering Pa. Wallace L. Goldstein. (Illus.). 68p. (Orig.). 1993. pap. text ed. 11.00 (*1-880836-01-7*) Pine Isl Pr.

Remembering Paradise: Nativism & Nostalgia in Eighteenth-Century Japan. Peter Nosco. (Harvard-Yenching Institute Monographs: No. 31). 271p. 1990. 28.00 (*0-674-76007-7*) HUP.

Remembering Pearl Harbor: Eyewitness Accounts by U. S. Military Men & Women. Ed. by Robert S. La Forte & Ronald E. Marcello. LC 90-40179. (Illus.). 320p. 1991. 24.95 (*0-8420-2371-2*) Scholarly Res Inc.

Remembering Pearl Harbor: The Story of the U. S. S. Arizona Memorial. Michael Slackman. (Illus.). 1989. pap. 9.95 (*0-917859-18-9*) Sunrise SBCA.

Remembering Pearl Harbor: The Story of the U.S.S. Arizona Memorial. 7th rev. ed. Michael Slackman. (Illus.). 120p. 1993. reprint ed. pap. 8.95 (*1-880352-29-X*) AZ Mem Mus.

Remembering People: The Key to Success. Harry Lorayne. 1996. pap. 14.95 (*0-8128-8557-0*, Scrbrough Hse) Madison Bks UPA.

Remembering Peter Sellers. Graham Stark. LC 91-68051. (Illus.). 210p. 1996. pap. 12.95 (*0-86051-742-X*, Robson-Parkwest) Parkwest Pubns.

Remembering Randall. Mary Jarrell. 128p. 1997. 20.00 (*0-06-118011-4*, PL); pap. 10.00 (*0-06-118013-0*, PL) HarpC.

Remembering Ray: A Composite Biography of Raymond Carver. Ed. by William L. Stull & Maureen P. Carroll. LC 93-11053. (Illus.). 263p. (Orig.). 1993. pap. 14.95 (*0-88496-370-5*) Capra Pr.

Remembering Ray: A Composite Biography of Raymond Carver. Ed. by William L. Stull & Maureen P. Carroll. 263p. 1993. lib. bdg. 39.00 (*0-8095-4119-X*) Borgo Pr.

Remembering Reagan. Peter Hannaford & Charles D. Hobbs. (Illus.). 160p. 49.95 (*0-89526-514-1*) Regnery Pub.

Remembering Reconsidered: Ecological & Traditional Approaches to the Study of Memory. Ulric Neisser & Eugene Winograd. (Emory Symposia in Cognition Ser.: No. 2). (Illus.). 420p. 1988. text ed. 64.95 (*0-521-33031-9*) Cambridge U Pr.

Remembering Reconsidered: Ecological & Traditional Approaches to the Study of Memory. Ed. by Ulric Neisser & Eugene Winograd. (Emory Symposia in Cognition Ser.: No. 2). (Illus.). 399p. (C). 1995. pap. text ed. 25.95 (*0-521-48500-2*) Cambridge U Pr.

Remembering, Repeating & Working Through Childhood Trauma. Lawrence E. Hedges. LC 94-2266. 352p. 1994. 40.00 (*1-56821-228-3*) Aronson.

Remembering Rosario: A Personal Glimpse into the Life & Works of Rosario Castellanos. Oscar Bonifaz. Ed. & Tr. by Myralyn F. Allgood. 1990. 27.50 (*0-916379-72-8*) Scripta.

Remembering Rostock, 1972-1990: The Ahrenshoop Symposium of the Brown-Rostock Exchange Program, March, 1989. Hans-Joachim Bernhard & Duncan Smith. 156p. (C). 1991. lib. bdg. 39.50 (*0-8191-8370-9*) U Pr of Amer.

Remembering Satan. Lawrence Wright. LC 93-23561. 1994. 22.00 (*0-679-43155-1*) Knopf.

Remembering Satan. Lawrence Wright. 1995. pap. 12.00 (*0-679-75582-9*) Random.

Remembering Saugus: Growing up in a Small Town. Richard G. Provenzano. (Saugus Historical Society Booklet Ser.: Vol. 6). 1995. write for info. (*0-936363-09-6*) Saugus Hist.

Remembering Season: A Family Christmas Journal. Compiled by Anne C. Buchanan & Debra K. Klingsporn. (Illus.). 140p. 1995. 17.95 (*0-8358-0770-3*) Upper Room Bks.

Remembering Selena: A Tribute in Pictures & Words. Himilce Novas & Rosemary Silva. LC 95-38834. (Illus.). 128p. (ENG & SPA.). 1995. pap. 9.95 (*0-312-14160-2*, Griffin) St Martin.

Remembering Self: Construction & Accuracy in the Self-Narrative. Ed. by Ulric Neisser & Robyn Fivush. LC 93-40556. (Emory Symposia in Cognition Ser.: Vol. 6). 240p. (C). 1994. text ed. 52.95 (*0-521-43194-8*) Cambridge U Pr.

Remembering Signor Oscar. Rosalind Berwald. (Illus.). 44p. 1992. 45.00 (*0-930126-39-4*) Typographeum.

Remembering Song: Encounters with the New Orleans Jazz Tradition. 2nd rev. ed. Frederick W. Turner. LC 93-39778. (Illus.). 1994. reprint ed. pap. 12.95 (*0-306-80555-3*) Da Capo.

Remembering South Vietnam. Rick Graetz. (Illus.). 96p. (Orig.). 1990. pap. 2.00 (*0-938314-79-3*) Am Wrld Geog.

Remembering Spain: Hemingway's Civil War Eulogy & the Veterans of the Abraham Lincoln Brigade. Ed. by Cary Nelson. 40p. 1994. text ed. 13.95 (*0-252-02124-X*) U of Ill Pr.

Remembering Stalin's Victims: Popular Memory & the End of the U. S. S. R. Kathleen E. Smith. LC 95-41397. (Illus.). 240p. 1996. 29.95 (*0-8014-3194-8*) Cornell U Pr.

Remembering the American Dream: Hispanic Immigration & National Policy. Roberto Suro. LC 94-3744. 125p. (C). 1994. pap. 9.95 (*0-87078-194-4*) TCFP-PPP.

Remembering the Bone House: An Erotics of Place & Space. Nancy Mairs. LC 94-41563. 288p. 1995. pap. 12.95 (*0-8070-7069-6*) Beacon Pr.

Remembering the Christian Past. Robert L. Wilken. LC 95-17635. 189p. 1995. pap. 17.00 (*0-8028-0880-8*) Eerdmans.

Remembering the Dance: Writing by Older Minnesotans. Ed. by Mary Rockcastle. (Illus.). 224p. (Orig.). 1989. pap. 7.00 (*0-927663-00-7*) COMPAS.

Remembering the Derby. Jim Bolus. LC 93-34923. 1994. 18.95 (*1-56554-040-9*) Pelican.

Remembering the Future: The Challenge of the Churches in Europe. Ed. by Robert C. Lodwick. LC 94-39489. (Illus.). 128p. (Orig.). 1995. pap. 8.95 (*0-377-00290-9*) Friendship Pr.

***Remembering the Future Vol. XIV: Interviews from Personal Computer World.** Ed. by W. Grossman. LC 96-36954. 227p. 1996. pap. 29.95 (*3-540-76095-4*) Spr-Verlag.

Remembering the Good Old Days: Lively Reminiscent Group Starters. Marge Knoth. (Illus.). 132p. (Orig.). 13.99 (*0-927935-02-3*) Valley Pr IN.

Remembering the Good Times. Richard Peck. 192p. (J). (gr. 5-12). 1986. mass mkt. 4.50 (*0-440-97339-2*, LLL BDD) BDD Bks Young Read.

Remembering the Harlem Renaissance. Ed. by Cary D. Wintz. LC 96-17058. (Harlem Renaissance, 1920-1940 Ser.: Vol. 5). (Illus.). 450p. 1996. text ed. 79.00 (*0-8153-2216-X*) Garland.

Remembering the Hiragana. James W. Heisig. 1990. pap. 8.00 (*0-87040-765-1*) Japan Pubns USA.

***Remembering the Holocaust.** Michael E. Stevens & Ellen D. Goldlust-Gingrich. LC 97-16191. (Voices of the Wisconsin Past Ser.). 1997. pap. write for info. (*0-87020-293-6*) State Hist Soc Wis.

Remembering the Kanji: Hyperkanji! Tom Minehart & James W. Heisig. 114p. 1993. disk 160.00 (*0-87040-971-9*) Japan Pubns USA.

Remembering the Kanji, No. 2: A Systematic Guide to Reading Japanese Characters. James W. Heisig. 397p. (Orig.). 1990. pap. 37.00 (*0-87040-748-1*) Japan Pubns USA.

Remembering the Kanji Three: A Supplementary Guide to Writing & Reading. James W. Heisig & Tanya Sienko. (Illus.). 300p. 1994. pap. 43.00 (*0-87040-931-X*) Japan Pubns USA.

Remembering the Kanjii. James W. Heising. 1990. pap. 40.00 (*0-87040-739-2*) Japan Pubns USA.

Remembering the Katakana. Helmut Morsbach et al. 96p. 1990. Incl. suppl. "Learning How to Remember". suppl. ed., pap. 8.00 (*0-87040-860-7*) Japan Pubns USA.

Remembering the Maine. Peggy Samuels & Harold Samuels. LC 94-34649. 384p. 1995. 29.95 (*1-56098-474-0*) Smithsonian.

***Remembering the Osage Kid.** Mardi O. Medawar. 1997. mass mkt. 6.50 (*0-553-57675-5*) Bantam.

***Remembering the Ozark Jubilee.** Reta Spears-Stewart. (Illus.). 138p. 1993. pap. write for info. (*0-9638648-0-7*) Barnabs Pub.

Remembering the Phallic Mother: Psychoanalysis, Modernism, & the Fetish. Marcia Ian. LC 92-33381. 264p. 1993. 39.95 (*0-8014-2637-5*) Cornell U Pr.

Remembering the Phallic Mother: Psychoanalysis, Modernism, & the Fetish. Marcia Ian. LC 92-33381. 264p. 1996. pap. 18.95 (*0-8014-9941-0*) Cornell U Pr.

Remembering the Poor: The History of Paul's Collection for Jerusalem. Dieter Georgi. 1992. pap. 7.98 (*0-687-36117-6*) Abingdon.

Remembering the Present: Painting & Popular History in Zaire. Johannes Fabian. (Illus.). 385p. 1996. 60.00 (*0-520-20375-5*); pap. 24.95 (*0-520-20376-3*) U CA Pr.

Remembering the Soos. David Evans. 102p. 1986. pap. 5.95 (*0-317-54062-9*) Plains Press.

Remembering the University of Chicago: Teachers, Scientists, & Scholars. Ed. by Edward Shils. (Illus.). 616p. 1991. 28.95 (*0-226-75335-2*) U Ch Pr.

Remembering Things of the Good Old Days. Richard Marks. LC 93-73607. 48p. 1993. pap. text ed. 8.00 (*1-885935-01-3*) Appalchn Log.

Remembering to Say "Mouth" or "Face" Stories. Omar S. Castaneda. (Winner of the Nineteen Ninety-Three Charles H. & N. Mildred Nilon Award for Excellence in Minority Fiction Ser.). 156p. 1993. 18.95 (*0-932511-80-5*); pap. 8.95 (*0-932511-81-3*) Fiction Coll.

Remembering U. S. Memories: The Fate of the U. S. Semiconductor Production Consortium. Stefanie A. Lenway et al. (Pew Case Studies in International Affairs). 50p. (C). 1996. pap. text ed. 3.50 (*1-56927-722-2*, GU Schl Foreign) Geo U Inst Dplmcy.

Remembering Vietnam: After the War in the Gulf. Link Nelms. 188p. 1995. pap. 13.50 (*0-87012-531-1*) McClain.

Remembering War: A U. S.-Soviet Dialogue. Ed. by Helene Keyssar & Vladimir Posner. (Illus.). 280p. 1990. 27.95 (*0-19-505126-2*) OUP.

Remembering War the American Way. G. Kurt Piehler. LC 94-10755. (Illus.). 248p. 1995. text ed. 34.95 (*1-56098-461-9*) Smithsonian.

***Remembering Water.** Carolyn Maddux. 89p. (Orig.). 1996. pap. 10.00 (*0-944920-22-5*) Bellowing Ark Pr.

Remembering Who We Are: Observations of a Southern Conservative. M. E. Bradford. LC 84-22225. 200p. 1985. 25.00 (*0-8203-0766-1*) U of Ga Pr.

Remembering William Carlos Williams. James Laughlin. LC 95-15719. 64p. (Orig.). 1995. pap. 7.95 (*0-8112-1307-2*, NDP811) New Directions.

Remembering Williamsburg. Parke Rouse, Jr. 1989. pap. 14.95 (*0-87517-059-5*) Dietz.

Remembering with Granny. Alma D. Worthington. 176p. 1995. 15.95 (*0-9647755-0-6*) Derryberry Pubns.

Remembering with Love: Messages of Love for the First Year of Grieving & Beyond. Elizabeth Levang. 1995. pap. 11.95 (*0-925190-86-1*) Fairview Press.

***Remembering with Mary: Rosary Meditations.** Robert B. Heath. 60p. pap. 1.95 (*0-8198-6461-7*) Pauline Bks.

Remembering World War II. large type ed. Ed. by Carolyn D. Tozier & Sylvia R. Liroff. (Discovery Through the Humanities Ser.). (Illus.). 222p. 1994. 20.00 (*0-910883-73-4*, 135) Natl Coun Aging.

Remembering Yesterday's Hits. Reader's Digest Editors. (Illus.). 252p. 1986. spiral bd. 29.95 (*0-89577-249-3*, Random) RD Assn.

Remembering You. Kristen Stepp. 1996. pap. 12.95 (*0-9626118-1-6*) Paris Bks.

***Remembering You.** Penelope J. Stokes. LC 97-15052. (Faith on the Home Front Ser.). 1997. pap. write for info. (*0-8423-0857-1*) Tyndale.

***Remembering Your Destiny: The Twelve Practices.** Pamela Murray. LC 96-79216. 212p. 1997. pap. 14.95 (*1-885221-69-X*) BookPartners.

Remembering Your Story: Spiritual Autobiography. Richard L. Morgan. LC 96-5058. 160p. (Orig.). 1996. pap. 10.95 (*0-8358-0781-9*, UR781) Upper Room Bks.

Remembering...Reaching: A Vision for Service. Joel A. Wiebe. 215p. 1994. pap. 22.95 (*1-884397-01-8*) Fresno Pacific.

Remembering...the Good Ole Days: Lively Reminiscent Group Starters. Marge Knoth. (Illus.). 132p. (Orig.). 1995. pap. 13.99 (*0-927935-09-0*) Valley Pr IN.

Remembery Chips. Cathy F. Rudolph. (Illus.). 34p. (J). (ps-3). 1994. 15.00 (*0-9642360-0-1*) Wayward Fluffy.

Remembrance. LC 94-42981. 480p. 1981. 24.95 (*0-385-28843-3*) Delacorte.

Remembrance. Jude Deveraux. (Orig.). 1995. pap. 6.99 (*0-671-74460-7*, Pocket Books) PB.

***Remembrance.** Kendall F. Person. 252p. (Orig.). 1996. pap. 12.00 (*1-889214-00-0*) Brookins Ent.

Remembrance. Danielle Steel. 544p. 1983. mass mkt. 6.50 (*0-440-17370-1*) Dell.

Remembrance. large type ed. Jude Deveraux. LC 94-42981. (Orig.). 1995. pap. 19.95 (*0-7838-1172-1*, GK Hall) Thorndike Pr.

Remembrance. large type ed. Jude Deveraux. LC 94-42981. 601p. 1995. 25.95 (*0-7838-1171-3*, GK Hall) Thorndike Pr.

Remembrance: Healing Teachings & Stories. Jeshua et al. 40p. (Orig.). (C). 1994. pap. 5.95 (*1-878555-06-5*) Oakbridge Univ Pr.

Remembrance see Danielle Steel: Family Album; Remembrance; Thurston House

***Remembrance & Imagination: Patterns in the Historical & Literary Representation of Ireland in the Nineteenth Century.** Joseph T. Leerssen. LC 96-42459. (Critical Conditions Ser.). 1997. pap. text ed. write for info. (*0-268-01655-0*) U of Notre Dame Pr.

Remembrance & Light: Images of Martha's Vineyard. Henry B. Hough. LC 84-4595. (Illus.). 112p. 1984. pap. 14.95 (*0-916782-54-9*) Harvard Common Pr.

***Remembrance & Prayer: The Way of Prophet Muhammad.** Muhammad Al-Ghazali. Tr. by Yusuf T. De Lorenzo. 232p. 1996. pap. 14.95 (*0-614-21331-2*, 1072) Kazi Pubns.

***Remembrance & Prayer: The Way of the Prophet Muhammad.** Muhammad Ghazali. Tr. by Yusuf T. De Lorenzo. LC 96-38161. 1996. 11.75 (*0-915957-61-2*) amana pubns.

Remembrance & Recollection: Essays on the Centennial Year of Martin Niemoller & Reinhold Niebuhr & the Fiftieth Year of the Wannsee Conference, Vol. XII. Ed. by Hubert G. Locke & Marcia S. Littell. (Study in the Shoah). 138p. 1995. lib. bdg. 32.50 (*0-7618-0157-X*) U Pr of Amer.

Remembrance & Reconciliation: Encounters Between Young Jews & Germans. Bjorn Krondorfer. LC 94-28747. 1995. 27.50 (*0-300-05959-0*) Yale U Pr.

***Remembrance Framed.** Jane H. Lamb. 30p. 1992. pap. 2.00 (*0-614-24767-5*) Tesseract SD.

Remembrance of a Time Just Past - Memoris De un Pasado in Mediato: Poetry. Guillermo Arango. Ed. by Linden Lane Press Staff. Tr. by Hugh A. Harter from SPA. 96p. (Orig.). pap. 13.00 (*0-685-65348-X*) Linden Ln Pr.

Remembrance of Christ. Charles H. Spurgeon. 1977. mass mkt. 0.75 (*1-56186-332-7*) Pilgrim Pubns.

Remembrance of Crimes Past: Poems. Dannie Abse. LC 92-37208. 80p. (Orig.). 1993. pap. 9.95 (*0-89255-176-3*) Persea Bks.

***Remembrance of Death & the Afterlife.** Muhammad Al-Ghazali. Tr. by T. J. Winter. 350p. 1996. pap. 21.95 (*0-614-21189-1*, 1073) Kazi Pubns.

Remembrance of Death & the Afterlife. Al-Ghazali. Ed. & Tr. by T. J. Winter from ARA. (Al-Ghazali Ser.). 138p. 1995. reprint ed. 59.95 (*0-946621-09-8*, Pub. by Islamic Texts UK); reprint ed. pap. 24.95 (*0-946621-13-6*, Pub. by Islamic Texts UK) Intl Spec Bk.

Remembrance of Eden: Harriet Bailey Bullock Daniel's Memories of a Frontier Plantation in Arkansas, Eighteen Forty-Nine to Eighteen Seventy-Two. Ed. & Intro. by Margaret J. Bolsterli. LC 93-6787. (Illus.). 160p. 1993. 26.00 (*1-55728-290-0*) U of Ark Pr.

Remembrance of Father: Words to Heal the Heart. Jonathon Lazear. LC 94-48791. 1995. pap. 10.00 (*0-684-80201-5*, Fireside) S&S Trade.

Remembrance of Mother: Words to Heal the Heart. Jonathon Lazear. 128p. 1994. pap. 10.00 (*0-671-88696-7*, Fireside) S&S Trade.

Remembrance of Patria: Dutch Arts & Culture in Colonial America, 1609-1776. Roderic H. Blackburn. LC 88-14645. (Illus.). 318p. 1988. 65.00 (*0-939072-06-8*) Albany Hist & Art.

Remembrance of Things Past. Marcel Proust. 1982. pap. 22.00 (*0-394-71183-1*, Vin) Random.

Remembrance of Things Past, 3 vols. Marcel Proust. Tr. by C. K. Scott-Moncrieff et al. from FRE. LC 82-40052. (C). 1982. pap. 64.00 (*0-394-71243-9*, Vin) Random.

Remembrance of Things Past, 1. Marcel Proust. 1981. 25.00 (*0-394-50644-8*) Random.

Remembrance of Things Past, 2. Marcel Proust. 1981. 25.00 (*0-394-50645-6*) Random.

Remembrance of Things Past, 3. Marcel Proust. 1981. 25.00 (*0-394-50646-4*) Random.

Remembrance of Things Past, Set. Marcel Proust. 1981. boxed 75.00 (*0-394-50643-X*) Random.

Remembrance of Tucson's Past: Century Ago & More, & Less in Tucson Arizona. Kerson D. Diamos. 150p. (Orig.). 1985. pap. 14.00 (*0-9614985-1-X*) El Siglo Bks.

Remembrance, Reunion, & Revival: Celebrating a Decade of Appalachian Studies. Dorgan et al. (Proceedings of the Appalachian Studies Conference). (Orig.). (C). 1988. pap. text ed. 10.95 (*0-913239-52-6*) Appalach Consortium.

Remembrance Rock. Carl Sandburg. 1991. pap. 19.95 (*0-15-676390-7*); pap. 19.95 (*0-685-48721-0*, Harvest Bks) HarBrace.

Remembrances. William Corbett. 1987. 5.00 (*0-935724-29-X*) Figures.

Remembrances: The Experience of the Past in Classical Chinese Literature. Stephen Owen. 159p. 1986. 24.50 (*0-674-76015-8*) HUP.

Remembrances in Endocrinology: An Endocrine Society History of the Study of Endocrinology & Its Practitioners. (Illus.). 113p. (C). 1993. boxed 20.00 (*1-879225-09-3*) Endocrine Soc.

Remembrances of a Time Gone by: Growing Up in the South Carolina Low Country, 1910-1922. O. Davis Davis. LC 94-9219. 1994. 15.00 (*0-87152-480-5*) Reprint.

Remembrances of Concord & the Thoreaus: Letters of Horace Hosmer to Dr. S. A. Jones. Horace Hosmer. Ed. by George Hendrick. LC 77-24232. 183p. 1977. text ed. 19.95 (*0-252-00660-7*) U of Ill Pr.

***Remembrances of Elvis.** Lucille Bender. 34p. (Orig.). 1996. pap. 9.95 (*1-885206-43-7*) Cader Pubng.

Remembrances of Lawrence Kohlberg. John R. Snarey. (Orig.). (C). 1988. pap. 5.00 (*0-9621113-0-9*) Emory U Ctr Faith.

An Asterisk (*) at the beginning of an entry indicates that the title is appearing in BIP for the first time.

Remembrances of Rivers Past. Ernest Schwiebert. LC 84-45099. (Illus.). 288p. 1984. reprint ed. pap. 8.95 (*0-916870-71-5*) Creat Arts Bk.

Remembrances of Roy Grant August 10, 1882 - September 9, 1967. Roy Grant. 316p. pap. text ed. 49.95 (*1-879975-01-7*) Document Shop.

Remembrances of Spring: Collected Early Poems. Naomi L. Madgett. LC 93-34603. (Lotus Poetry Ser.: Vol. 1). 170p. 1993. 24.95 (*0-87013-345-4*) Mich St U Pr.

Remembrances of Things Passed. Bonnie S. Bailey. LC 92-73647. 320p. 1993. write for info. (*0-9634316-0-9*) Highland Gourmet.

Remf Diary. David Willson. 313p. 1988. 19.95 (*0-930773-05-5*); pap. 10.95 (*0-930773-06-3*) Black Heron Pr.

REMF Returns. David Willson. 160p. 1992. pap. 10.95 (*0-930773-22-5*); lib. bdg. 19.95 (*0-930773-21-7*) Black Heron Pr.

***Remi-Nissen.** Thelma Paulson. (Illus.). 304p. (Orig.). 1996. pap. 16.95 (*0-9653934-0-2*) Access Midwest.

Remick's Pennsylvania Orphans' Court Practice, 6 vols., 7 bks. rev. ed. Charles W. Frampton & Paul C. Heintz. LC 75-10730. 1995. text ed. 465.00 (*0-317-03824-9*) Bisel Co.

***Remifemin.** Frank Murray. 1996. pap. text ed. 3.95 (*0-87983-764-0*) Keats.

Remind Me to Murder You Later: Short Stories. James Boylan. LC 88-45417. 144p. 1988. 18.95 (*0-8018-3728-6*) Johns Hopkins.

Reminded of His Goodness Songbook. Gary L. Johnson & Carol Johnson. 32p. 1981. pap. 2.50 (*0-87123-779-2*) Bethany Hse.

Reminder List of Eligible Releases: 62nd Annual Academy Awards for Distinguished Achievements During 1989. Ed. by Byerly Woodward. 40p. (Orig.). 1990. pap. 5.00 (*0-942102-11-8*) Acad Motion Pic.

Reminder List of Eligible Releases - 61st Annual Academy Awards for Distinguished Achievements During 1988. Ed. by Byerly Woodward. 40p. 1989. pap. 5.00 (*0-942102-09-6*) Acad Motion Pic.

Reminder List of Eligible Releases--60th Annual Academy Awards for Distinguished Achievements During 1987. Ed. by Byerly Woodward. 40p. 1988. pap. 5.00 (*0-942102-06-1*) Acad Motion Pic.

Reminders for Company Secretaries. 25th ed. John Birds. 136p. 1986. 60.00 (*0-85308-077-1*) St Mut.

Reminders for the Electrician. Tom Henry. (Illus.). 60p. (Orig.). (C). 1993. pap. text ed. 12.00 (*0-945495-40-4*) T Henrys CECB.

Remington: The Science & Practice of Pharmacy, 2 vols. 19th ed. Ed. by Alfonso R. Gennaro. LC 60-53334. 2000p. 1995. pap. 125.00 (*0-912734-05-1*) Mack Pub.

***Remington & Russell.** William C. Ketchum. 1997. 15.98 (*0-7651-9486-4*) Smithmark.

Remington & Russell: The Sid Richardson Collection. rev. ed. Brian W. Dippie. LC 93-21260. (Illus.). 240p. 1994. 70.00 (*0-292-71569-2*); pap. 34.95 (*0-292-71568-4*) U of Tex Pr.

Remington Arms & History, 1816-1934 Vol. 1: Except Early Shotguns, 2 vols. LC 88-50357. (West Arms Library - Classics Bks.). (Illus.). 1988. Vol. 1, 1816-1934. 52.00 (*0-911614-17-6*) B West.

Remington Arms & History, 1934-1989 Vol. 2: All Arms. LC 88-50357. (West Arms Library - Classics Bks.). (Illus.). 1988. Vol. 2, 1934-1989. 52.00 (*0-911614-18-4*) B West.

Remington Arms Catalogues, 1877-1899. Bill West. LC 79-125420. (West Arms Library - Classic Bks.). (Illus.). 1970. pap. 10.00 (*0-911614-09-5*) B West.

Remington Contract. Raymond Obstfeld. 304p. (Orig.). 1988. mass mkt. 4.50 (*0-373-97095-1*) Harlequin Bks.

Remington Firearms: Golden Age of Collecting. Robert W. Ball. LC 95-79727. (Illus.). 194p. 1995. 29.95 (*0-87341-360-1*, GAR01) Krause Pubns.

Remington Gun Catalog 1877. reprint ed. 3.50 (*0-913150-17-7*) Pioneer Pr.

Remington-Lee Rifle. Eugene Myszkowski. (Illus.). 104p. (Orig.). 1994. pap. 22.95 (*1-880677-04-0*) Excalibur NY.

Remington No. 1: West of the Pecos. James C. Boone. 176p. 1987. pap. 2.50 (*0-380-75265-4*) Avon.

Remington, No. 6: Border Trouble. James C. Boone. 176p. 1988. pap. 2.75 (*0-380-75271-9*) Avon.

Remington, No. 7: Red River Revenge. James C. Boone. 160p. 1988. pap. 2.75 (*0-380-75559-9*) Avon.

Remington, No. 8: Six-Guns at Spanish Peak. James C. Boone. 176p. 1988. pap. 2.75 (*0-380-75560-2*) Avon.

Remington Rolling Block Firearms. Konrad F. Schreier, Jr. Ed. by Pioneer Press Staff. (Illus.). 1977. pap. 8.00 (*0-913150-39-8*) Pioneer Pr.

Remington Rolling Block Pistols. Jerry Landskron. LC 81-50481. (Illus.). 304p. 1981. 34.95 (*0-940028-01-8*) Rolling Block.

Remington Rolling Block Pistols. deluxe ed. Jerry Landskron. LC 81-50481. (Illus.). 304p. 1981. 39.95 (*0-940028-00-X*) Rolling Block.

Remington Warm-up Studies for Trombone. Donald Hunsberger. LC 80-67541. (Illus.). 1980. 12.50 (*0-918194-10-5*) Accura.

Remington 700: A History & User's Manual. John F. Lacy. LC 89-91161. (Illus.). 208p. 1989. 44.95 (*0-9622303-0-8*) J F Lacy.

Reminiscence: The Key to Healthy Aging. Carmel Sheridan. LC 90-83231. (Illus.). 168p. (Orig.). 1991. pap. 11.95 (*0-943873-10-X*) Elder Bks.

Reminiscence & Nursing Home Life. Donna E. Schafer. LC 93-48154. (Studies on the Elderly in America). (Illus.). 204p. 1994. text ed. 58.00 (*0-8153-1614-3*) Garland.

Reminiscence & Re-Creation in Contemporary American Fiction. Stacey Olster. 350p. (C). 1989. text ed. 59.95 (*0-521-36383-7*) Cambridge U Pr.

Reminiscence & Rote Learning see Studies in Clinical Psychology

Reminiscence & the Self in Old Age. Edmund Sherman. 288p. 1991. 35.95 (*0-8261-7550-3*) Springer Pub.

Reminiscence of a Stock Operator. Edwin Lefevre. 299p. 1994. text ed. 45.00 (*0-471-05968-4*); pap. text ed. 19.95 (*0-471-05970-6*) Wiley.

Reminiscence of a Town That Thought It Would Be a Metropolis: Delaware City, Delaware. William O. Wingate. LC 93-71509. (Illus.). 50p. (Orig.). 1993. pap. text ed. 3.00 (*0-685-66902-5*) Delaware HP.

Reminiscence of Isaac & Rachel (Budd) Collins, with Accounts of Some Descendants & History of a Reunion Held at Philadelphia, 1892. J. Collins et al. (Illus.). 164p. 1993. reprint ed. pap. 24.50 (*0-8328-1373-7*); reprint ed. lib. bdg. 34.50 (*0-8328-1372-9*) Higginson Bk Co.

Reminiscence, Reminiscence, Reminiscence. Eve Kiley. 16p. (Orig.). 1995. pap. write for info. (*1-885206-23-2*, Iliad Pr) Cader Pubng.

Reminiscence Reviewed: Perspectives, Evaluations, Achievements. Ed. by Joanna Bornat. LC 93-22968. (Rethinking Aging Ser.). 160p. 1993. 79.00 (*0-335-19042-1*, Open Univ Pr); pap. 29.50 (*0-335-19041-3*, Open Univ Pr) Taylor & Francis.

Reminiscence Work with Old People. Clare Gillies & Anne James. LC 94-71059. 144p. pap. 32.99 (*0-412-58070-5*) Chapman & Hall.

Reminiscence Work with Old People. A. James & C. Gillies. 152p. 1994. 35.95 (*1-56593-375-3*, 0722) Singular Publishing.

***Reminiscences.** Thomas Carlyle. Ed. by K. J. Fielding & Ian Campbell. (The World's Classics Ser.). 448p. 1997. pap. 14.95 (*0-19-281748-5*) OUP.

Reminiscences. Nicholas N. Poppe. Ed. by Henry G. Schwarz. LC 82-4544. (Studies on East Asia: Vol. 16). (Illus.). vii, 330p. 1983. 25.00 (*0-914584-16-2*) WWUCEAS.

Reminiscences. Rabindranath Tagore. 272p. 1912. 6.50 (*0-318-37006-9*) Asia Bk Corp.

Reminiscences, 2 vols. Thomas Carlyle. Ed. by James A. Froude. LC 71-144936. (Literature Ser.). 1972. reprint ed. 29.00 (*0-403-00898-0*) Scholarly.

Reminiscences. Julia W. Howe. (Notable American Authors Ser.). 1992. reprint ed. lib. bdg. 75.00 (*0-7812-3223-6*) Rprt Serv.

Reminiscences. Douglas MacArthur. (Quality Paperbacks Ser.). (Illus.). 1985. reprint ed. pap. 15.95 (*0-306-80254-6*) Da Capo.

Reminiscences. Gerald Van De Linde. Ed. by Richard P. Brief. LC 77-87290. (Development of Contemporary Accounting Thought Ser.). 1978. reprint ed. lib. bdg. 37.95 (*0-405-10917-2*) Ayer.

Reminiscences. Isaac Wise. Ed. by David Philipson. LC 73-2233. (Jewish People; History, Religion, Literature Ser.). 1973. reprint ed. 33.95 (*0-405-05294-4*) Ayer.

Reminiscences: A Lifetime of Spiritualism. Ursula Roberts. 115p. 1985. 35.00 (*0-7212-0726-X*, Pub. by Regency Press UK) St Mut.

Reminiscences: Discreet & Indiscreet. T. N. Kaul. (Illus.). 312p. 1982. 43.95 (*0-940500-84-1*) Asia Bk Corp.

Reminiscences: Story of an Emigrant. Hans Mattson. Ed. by Franklyn D. Scott. LC 78-15201. (Scandinavians in America Ser.). (Illus.). 1979. reprint ed. lib. bdg. 28.95 (*0-405-11651-9*) Ayer.

Reminiscences: The Story of an Emigrant. Hans Mattson. (American Biography Ser.). 314p. 1991. reprint ed. lib. bdg. 79.00 (*0-7812-8278-0*) Rprt Serv.

Reminiscences see Recollections

Reminiscences & ... Solomon Oudel & Owen Barfield. 1986. pap. 3.95 (*0-916786-89-7*, Saint George Pubns) R Steiner Col Pubns.

Reminiscences & Gospel Hymn Stories. George C. Stebbins. LC 74-144689. reprint ed. 24.50 (*0-404-07203-8*) AMS Pr.

Reminiscences & Memoirs of North Carolina & Eminent North Carolinians. John H. Wheeler. lxxiv, 478p. 1993. reprint ed. pap. 42.50 (*0-685-69955-2*, 6280) Clearfield Co.

Reminiscences & Other Stories. Adriana C. Alcantara. 132p. (Orig.). 1993. pap. 8.25 (*971-10-0493-3*, Pub. by New Day Pub PH) Cellar.

Reminiscences & Recollections of Huey P. Long. large type ed. Calvit L. Walker. (Illus.). 127p. (Orig.). 1996. pap. 10.00 (*1-887745-02-5*) Dogwood TX.

Reminiscences & Reflexions of a Mid & Late Victorian. Ernest Belfort Bax. LC 67-27466. 283p. 1967. reprint ed. 45.00 (*0-678-00313-0*) Kelley.

***Reminiscences, Anecdotes & Statistics of the Early Settlers & the "Olden Time" in the Town of Sherburne, Chenango County.** Joel Hatch, Jr. 104p. 1997. reprint ed. pap. 16.00 (*0-8328-6240-1*) Higginson Bk Co.

Reminiscences, Biographical & Historical. Randolph Clark & William E. Tucker. LC 86-1286. 92p. 1986. reprint ed. 25.00 (*0-87565-064-3*) Tex Christian.

Reminiscences, Eighteen Twenty-Seven to Eighteen Ninety-Seven. Robert M. McLane. LC 72-79831. (China Library). 1972. reprint ed. lib. bdg. 21.00 (*0-8420-1375-X*) Scholarly Res Inc.

***Reminiscences of A. B. Mackey.** Homer J. Adams. Ed. by Janice M. Greathouse. (Centennial Ser.: Vol. 1). 140p. 1997. write for info. (*0-9657278-0-7*) Trevecca Nazarene.

Reminiscences of a Colonial Judge. James S. Dowling. Ed. by Anthony Dowling. 218p. 1996. 44.00 (*1-86287-175-2*, Pub. by Federation Pr AU) Gaunt.

Reminiscences of a Dramatic Critic: With an Essay on the Art of Henry Irving. Henry A. Clapp. LC 72-5536. (Select Bibliographies Reprint Ser.). 1977. reprint ed. 23.95 (*0-8369-6902-2*) Ayer.

Reminiscences of a Fiddle Dealer. David Laurie. (Illus.). 1977. reprint ed. text ed. 22.00 (*0-918624-01-0*) Virtuoso.

Reminiscences of A. K. C. Thomas E. Crispe. xxi, 306p. 1996. reprint ed. 84.00 (*1-56169-208-5*) Gaunt.

Reminiscences of a Marine. John A. Lejeune. Ed. by Richard H. Kohn. LC 78-22384. (American Military Experience Ser.). (Illus.). 1980. reprint ed. lib. bdg. 37.95 (*0-405-11860-0*) Ayer.

Reminiscences of a Marine. John A. Lejeune. (Illus.). 488p. reprint ed. 8.95 (*0-686-30999-5*) Marine Corps.

Reminiscences of a Mosby Guerrilla. John W. Munson. (Illus.). 277p. 35.00 (*1-56013-012-1*) Olde Soldier Bks.

Reminiscences of a Pastorial Ministry. Horace M. Taylor. 67p. (Orig.). 1987. pap. 5.00 (*0-9617424-1-0*) H M Taylor.

Reminiscences of a Portrait Painter. G. P. A. Healy. LC 78-96439. (Library of American Art). (Illus.). 1970. reprint ed. lib. bdg. 39.50 (*0-306-71829-4*) Da Capo.

Reminiscences of a Ranchman. Edgar B. Bronson. LC 62-8407. (Bison Book Ser.: No. BB127). 384p. reprint ed. pap. 109.50 (*0-8357-6633-0*, 2035286) Bks Demand.

Reminiscences of a Ranger. Major H. Bell. 1992. reprint ed. lib. bdg. 75.00 (*0-7812-5008-0*) Rprt Serv.

***Reminiscences of a Rebel.** Wayland F. Dunaway. (Army of Northern Virginia Ser.). (Illus.). 170p. (C). 1996. reprint ed. 25.00 (*0-935523-56-1*) Butternut & Blue.

Reminiscences of a Russian Antiquarian Bookseller: Encounters with People & Books, 1924-1986. Lew A. Glazer. Tr. by Paula Israelewicz from RUS. 200p. (Orig.). 1997. pap. 18.95 (*0-88962-616-2*) Mosaic.

***Reminiscences of a Soldier's Wife: An Autobiography.** John A. Logan. LC 97-17322. (Shawnee Classic Ser.). 1997. write for info. (*0-8093-2157-2*) Southern Ill U.

***Reminiscences of a Stock Opera.** Fraser Publishing Staff. 1982. 16.95 (*0-681-17080-8*) Fraser.

Reminiscences of a Trip Across the Plains in 1846 & Early Days in California. Luella Dickenson. 48p. 1977. 14.95 (*0-87770-180-6*) Ye Galleon.

Reminiscences of a Very Old Man. John Sartain. LC 74-81559. (Illus.). 1972. reprint ed. 22.95 (*0-405-08916-3*) Ayer.

Reminiscences of a Very Old Man, 1808-1897. John Sartain. (American Biography Ser.). 297p. 1991. reprint ed. lib. bdg. 69.00 (*0-7812-8340-X*) Rprt Serv.

Reminiscences of a Viennese Psychoanalyst. Richard F. Sterba. LC 82-11149. (Illus.). 186p. 1982. 34.95 (*0-8143-1716-2*) Wayne St U Pr.

Reminiscences of a Vocal Teacher: American Autobiography. Emi DeBidoli. 97p. 1995. lib. bdg. 69.00 (*0-7812-8497-X*) Rprt Serv.

Reminiscences of Abraham Lincoln. Ed. by Allen T. Rice. LC 72-13766. (Concordance Ser.: No. 37). 1971. reprint ed. lib. bdg. 69.95 (*0-8383-1227-6*) M S G Haskell Hse.

Reminiscences of Adams, Jay & Randolph Cos., Ind., 1896. Martha Lynch. 363p. 1979. 19.00 (*0-686-27819-4*) Bookmark.

Reminiscences of Alexander Toponce. Alexander Toponce. (American Biography Ser.). 221p. 1991. reprint ed. lib. bdg. 69.00 (*0-7812-8394-9*) Rprt Serv.

Reminiscences of an American Scholar. John W. Burgess. LC 34-2217. reprint ed. 20.00 (*0-404-01236-1*) AMS Pr.

***Reminiscences of an Ancient Strategist: The Mind of Sun Tzu.** Foo Check Teck. (Illus.). 250p. 1997. pap. 34.95 (*0-566-07845-7*, Pub. by Gower UK) Ashgate Pub Co.

Reminiscences of an Army Chaplain. Horace M. Taylor. LC 86-1472. 123p. 1987. 4.50 (*0-9617424-0-2*) H M Taylor.

Reminiscences of an Australian Army Nurse. E. McQuade White. (C). 1990. pap. 21.00 (*0-86439-134-X*, Pub. by Boolarong Pubns AT) St Mut.

Reminiscences of an Island Teacher: Life in the Bahamas, 1948-1953. Jack Ford. Ed. by Jack Hardy. (Illus.). 1992. pap. 9.95 (*0-932265-24-3*) White Sound.

Reminiscences of an Islander. Bayard Dill. 57p. (C). 1989. text ed. 40.00 (*1-872795-19-6*, Pub. by Pentland Pr UK) St Mut.

***Reminiscences of an Old Timer.** George Hunter. lib. bdg. 36.95 (*0-8488-1901-2*) Amereon Ltd.

Reminiscences of an Unlettered Man: Robert Barclay 1850-1924: Farm Servant, Tailor & Postman in Forgue & Auchterless. Ed. by David Stevenson. (Centre for Scottish Studies). 96p. 1986. pap. text ed. 9.95 (*0-08-032442-8*, Pub. by Aberdeen U Pr) Macmillan.

Reminiscences of Big I. William N. Wood. (Illus.). 137p. 1992. reprint ed. 25.00 (*0-916107-47-7*) Broadfoot.

***Reminiscences of Brownfield: Short Sketches from the History of the Town.** E. A. Stickney. (Illus.). 69p. 1997. reprint ed. pap. 14.00 (*0-8328-5819-6*) Higginson Bk Co.

Reminiscences of Bureau County, Illinois. N. Matson. (Illus.). 406p. 1993. lib. bdg. 42.00 (*0-8328-3527-7*) Higginson Bk Co.

***Reminiscences of Candia.** Wilson Palmer. (Illus.). 345p. 1997. reprint ed. lib. bdg. 39.50 (*0-8328-5980-X*) Higginson Bk Co.

Reminiscences of Carl Schurz, 3 vols. Carl Schurz. 1988. reprint ed. lib. bdg. 150.00 (*0-685-21402-8*) Rprt Serv.

Reminiscences of Catskill: Local Sketches by the Late James D. Pinckney Together with Interesting Articles by Thurlow Weed, Edain Croswell, S. Sherwood Day & Joseph Hallock, Esq. Arthur C. Kelly. 88p. 1981. reprint ed. lib. bdg. 12.50 (*1-56012-054-1*, 53) Kinship Rhinebeck.

***Reminiscences of Chekhov: Chekhov's Notebooks: Reminiscences of Tolstoy.** Samuel S. Koteliansky et al. Tr. by Leonard Woolf from RUS. 200p. (Orig.). 1996. reprint ed. per., pap. 10.95 (*0-913006-60-2*) Puckerbrush.

Reminiscences of Col. Henry Ernst Dosch. Fred Tockley. 19p. 1972. pap. 3.50 (*0-87770-081-8*) Ye Galleon.

Reminiscences of Confederate Service 1861-1865. Francis W. Dawson. LC 79-26720. 214p. 1993. pap. 11.95 (*0-8071-1885-0*) La State U Pr.

Reminiscences of D. H. Lawrence. John M. Murry. LC 75-157349. (Select Bibliographies Reprint Ser.). 1977. reprint ed. 19.95 (*0-8369-5810-1*) Ayer.

Reminiscences of Edgar Allan Poe. Mary Nichols. LC 74-4041. (Studies in Poe: No. 23). 1974. lib. bdg. 22.95 (*0-8383-2068-6*) M S G Haskell Hse.

Reminiscences of Felix Mendelssohn-Bartholdy. Elise Polko. LC 87-81563. 222p. 1987. reprint ed. 24.95 (*0-944435-01-7*) Glenbridge Pub.

Reminiscences of Fifty Years in Texas. John J. Linn. LC 86-60968. (Illus.). 397p. 1986. reprint ed. 21.95 (*0-938349-00-7*) State House Pr.

Reminiscences of Frontier Life. 2nd ed. I. B. Hammond. LC 23-939860. (Illus.). 100p. 1980. pap. text ed. 4.95 (*0-939860-04-X*) Tremaine Graph & Pub.

Reminiscences of Fugitive Slave Law Days in Boston. Austin Bearse. LC 74-82170. (Anti-Slavery Crusade in America Ser.). 1976. reprint ed. 18.95 (*0-405-00609-8*) Ayer.

Reminiscences of General Basil W. Duke, C. S. A. Basil W. Duke. (Select Bibliographies Reprint Ser.). 1977. 36.95 (*0-8369-5150-6*) Ayer.

Reminiscences of General Herman Haupt. Herman Haupt. LC 80-1314. (Railroads Ser.). (Illus.). 1981. reprint ed. lib. bdg. 33.95 (*0-405-13786-9*) Ayer.

Reminiscences of General Herman Haupt. Herman Haupt. (American Biography Ser.). 331p. 1991. reprint ed. lib. bdg. 79.00 (*0-7812-8171-7*) Rprt Serv.

Reminiscences of Golf on St. Andrews. rev. ed. James Balfour. 1987. 28.00 (*0-940889-14-5*) Classics Golf.

Reminiscences of Gov. R. J. Walker: With the True Story of the Rescue of Kansas from Slavery. George W. Brown. LC 79-38010. (Black Heritage Library Collection). 1977. reprint ed. 21.95 (*0-8369-8978-3*) Ayer.

Reminiscences of H. P. Blavatsky. rev. ed. Constance Wachtmeister. LC 76-44810. 1977. pap. 8.50 (*0-8356-0488-8*, Quest) Theos Pub Hse.

Reminiscences of Henry Angelo, 2 Vols. Henry Angelo. LC 77-81198. (Illus.). 1972. 60.95 (*0-405-08207-X*) Ayer.

***Reminiscences of Henry Angelo, Vol. 1.** Henry Angelo. Date not set. write for info. (*0-405-19035-2*) Ayer.

***Reminiscences of Henry Angelo, Vol. 2.** Henry Angelo. Date not set. write for info. (*0-405-18118-3*) Ayer.

Reminiscences of Henry Clay Barnabee. Henry C. Barnabee. Ed. by George L. Varney. LC 73-169779. (Select Bibliographies Reprint Ser.). 1977. reprint ed. 46.95 (*0-8369-5999-X*) Ayer.

Reminiscences of Home. LC 95-90846. 1996. 10.00 (*0-533-11728-3*) Vantage.

Reminiscences of Irene Fisher Coon, R.N., about the Early History of Orthopaedic Surgery at Sioux Valley Hospital. Ed. by Robert E. Van Demark, Sr. LC 92-12679. 1992. write for info. (*0-931170-52-4*) Ctr Western Studies.

Reminiscences of James Burrill Angell. James B. Angell. LC 79-152970. (Select Bibliographies Reprint Ser.). 1977. reprint ed. 20.95 (*0-8369-5722-9*) Ayer.

Reminiscences of James Burrill Angell. James B. Angell. (American Biography Ser.). 258p. 1991. reprint ed. lib. bdg. 69.00 (*0-7812-8012-5*) Rprt Serv.

Reminiscences of James N. Glover. James N. Glover. (Illus.). 129p. 1985. 14.95 (*0-87770-356-6*); pap. 9.95 (*0-685-16499-3*) Ye Galleon.

Reminiscences of John B. Jervis: Engineer of the Old Croton. John B. Jervis. Ed. by Neal FitzSimons. LC 70-145552. (New York State Bks.). 1971. 29.95 (*0-8156-0077-1*) Syracuse U Pr.

Reminiscences of Joseph B. Cumming 1893-1983. LC 84-206046. 1983. pap. 12.00 (*0-937044-09-1*) Richmond Cty Hist Soc.

Reminiscences of Levi Coffin. Levi Coffin. Ed. by Ben Richmond. LC 79-113578. 390p. 1991. reprint ed. pap. 15.95 (*0-404-00143-2*) Friends United.

Reminiscences of Levi Coffin. Levi Coffin. (American Biography Ser.). 732p. 1991. reprint ed. lib. bdg. 119.00 (*0-7812-8083-4*) Rprt Serv.

Reminiscences of Levi Coffin. Levi Coffin. 1993. reprint ed. lib. bdg. 89.00 (*0-7812-5351-9*) Rprt Serv.

Reminiscences of Levi Coffin, the Reputed President of the Underground Railroad. Levi Coffin. LC 68-28991. (American Negro: His History & Literature. Series 1). 1968. reprint ed. 51.95 (*0-405-01810-X*) Ayer.

Reminiscences of Life As an Aid to the Understanding of Our Time. Walter J. Stein. 1987. pap. 8.50 (*0-916786-92-7*, Saint George Pubns) R Steiner Col Pubns.

Reminiscences of Linda Richards. Linda Richards. (American Autobiography Ser.). 121p. 1995. reprint ed. lib. bdg. 69.00 (*0-7812-8624-7*) Rprt Serv.

Reminiscences of Los Alamos: 1943-1945. Ed. by Lawrence Badash & H. P. Broida. (Studies in the History of Modern Science: No. 5). 209p. 1980. pap. text ed. 46.00 (*90-277-1098-8*, D Reidel); lib. bdg. 70.50 (*90-277-1097-X*, D Reidel) Kluwer Ac.

Reminiscences of Michael Kelly. Michael Kelly. Ed. by Theodore E. Hook. LC 72-88491. 439p. 1972. reprint ed. 26.95 (*0-405-08688-1*, Pub. by Blom Pubns UK) Ayer.

Reminiscences of Michael Kelly of the King's Theatre & Theatre Royal Drury Lane 2 Vols. 2nd ed. Michael Kelly. LC 68-16243. (Music Ser.). 1968. reprint ed. lib. bdg. 65.00 (*0-306-71094-3*) Da Capo.

Reminiscences of My Childhood & Youth. George M. Brandes. LC 74-27967. (Modern Jewish Experience Ser.). 1975. reprint ed. 37.95 (*0-405-06697-X*) Ayer.

Reminiscences of My Father. Charles Dickens, Jr. LC 72-6292. (Studies in Dickens: No. 52). (Illus.). 1972. reprint ed. lib. bdg. 75.00 (*0-8383-1626-3*) M S G Haskell Hse.

Reminiscences of My Life. Charles Santley. 1977. 30.95 (*0-405-09706-9*, 16755) Ayer.

R

Reminiscences of My Life. Charles Santley. LC 80-2297. reprint ed. 37.50 (*0-404-18865-0*) AMS Pr.

Reminiscences of My Life in Camp. Susie K. Taylor. (American Biography Ser.). 82p. 1991. reprint ed. lib. bdg. 59.00 (*0-7812-8379-5*) Rprt Serv.

Reminiscences of My Life in Camp with the 33rd U. S. Colored Troop Late First S.C. Volunteers. Susie K. Taylor. LC 68-29020. (American Negro: His History & Literature. Series 1). 1970. reprint ed. 12.95 (*0-405-01840-1*) Ayer.

***Reminiscences of New Hampton, Also a Genealogical Sketch of the Kelley & Simpson Families.** Frank H. Kelley. 147p. 1997. reprint ed. pap. 19.50 (*0-8328-6015-8*) Higginson Bk Co.

***Reminiscences of Old East Hampton by the Sea, As Given by One of Her Native Townsmen.** Thomas M. Edwards. 300p. 1997. reprint ed. lib. bdg. 35.00 (*0-8328-6132-4*) Higginson Bk Co.

Reminiscences of Peace & War. Roger A. Pryor. LC 77-126248. (Select Bibliographies Reprint Ser.). 1977. 25.95 (*0-8369-5475-0*) Ayer.

Reminiscences of Present-Day Saints. Francis G. Peabody. LC 74-37525. (Essay Index Reprint Ser.). 1977. reprint ed. 25.95 (*0-8369-2576-9*) Ayer.

Reminiscences of Quincy, Containing Historical Events, Anecdotes, Matters Concerning Old Settlers & Old Times. Henry Asbury. (Illus.). 224p. 1995. reprint ed. lib. bdg. 29.50 (*0-8328-4682-1*) Higginson Bk Co.

Reminiscences of Reading. Daphne Phillips. 128p. 1987. 30.00 (*0-905392-39-6*) St Mut.

***Reminiscences of Richard Paver.** Richard Paver. Ed. by A. H. Duminy. (Graham's Town Ser.: No. 5). 143p. 1979. 39.00 (*0-86961-110-0*, Pub. by A A Balkema NE) Ashgate Pub Co.

Reminiscences of Rimsky-Korsakov. V. V. Yastrebtsev. Ed. by Florence Jonas. LC 84-16967. (Illus.). 576p. 1985. text ed. 85.00 (*0-231-05260-X*) Col U Pr.

Reminiscences of Rudolf Steiner. Andrei Belyi et al. (Illus.). 148p. 1990. 15.50 (*0-932776-13-2*, 1320); pap. 11.50 (*0-685-38181-1*, 1323) Adonis Pr.

***Reminiscences of Rudolf Steiner & Marie Steiner-von Sivers.** Ilona Schubert. Tr. by John M. Wood. (Illus.). 96p. 1991. pap. write for info. (*0-904693-31-7*, Pub. by Temple Ldge Pub UK) Anthroposophic.

Reminiscences of Rufus Choate, the Great American Advocate. Edward G. Parker. Ed. by Roy M. Mersky & J. Myron Jacobstein. (Classics in Legal History Reprint Ser.: Vol. 16). 524p. 1972. reprint ed. lib. bdg. 45.00 (*0-89941-015-4*, 301130) W S Hein.

***Reminiscences of Saratoga.** Compiled by Cornelius E. Durkee. (Illus.). 316p. 1997. reprint ed. lib. bdg. 37.00 (*0-8328-6219-3*) Higginson Bk Co.

***Reminiscences of Saratoga & Ballston.** William L. Stone. (Illus.). 451p. 1997. reprint ed. lib. bdg. 47.50 (*0-8328-6222-3*) Higginson Bk Co.

Reminiscences of School Life & Hints on Teaching, Vol. 8. Tackson & Fanny J. Coppin. LC 94-19855. (African American Women Writers, 1910-1940 Ser.). 1995. 25.00 (*0-8161-1633-4*) G K Hall.

Reminiscences of Sea Island Heritage. Ronald Daise. LC 85-26201. (Illus.). 1986. 19.95 (*0-87844-081-X*) Sandlapper Pub Co.

Reminiscences of Swami Vivekananda. Eastern & Western Admirers Staff. 430p. 1989. pap. 6.95 (*0-87481-232-1*, Pub. by Advaita Ashrama II) Vedanta Pr.

Reminiscences of the Civil War. John B. Gordon. LC 93-1861. (Illus.). xxviii, 500p. (C). 1993. pap. 16.95 (*0-8071-1863-X*) La State U Pr.

Reminiscences of the Civil War. John B. Gordon. (Illus.). 506p. 1993. 35.00 (*0-89029-091-1*) Morningside Bkshop.

Reminiscences of the Civil War. J. W. Stevens. 26.00 (*0-8488-1181-X*) Amereon Ltd.

Reminiscences of the Cuban Revolutionary War. Ernesto Guevarar. Tr. by Victoria Ortiz. LC 68-13655. (Illus.). 293p. reprint ed. pap. 83.60 (*0-7837-3917-6*, 2043765) Bks Demand.

Reminiscences of the English Lake Poets. Thomas De Quincey. LC 83-45741. reprint ed. 31.50 (*0-404-20078-8*) AMS Pr.

Reminiscences of the English Lake Poets. Thomas De Quincey. (BCL1-PR English Literature Ser.). 355p. 1992. reprint ed. lib. bdg. 89.00 (*0-7812-7067-7*) Rprt Serv.

Reminiscences of the Hon. Galahad Threepwood. 263p. 1993. write for info. (*0-87008-146-2*) JAS Heineman.

Reminiscences of the Indians. Cephas Washburn. Ed. by Phillip A. Sperry. 243p. reprint ed. 34.95 (*1-56869-051-7*); reprint ed. pap. 19.95 (*1-56869-052-5*) Oldbuck Pr.

Reminiscences of the Last Sixty-Five Years. Ebenezer S. Thomas. LC 79-125719. (American Journalists Ser.). 1971. reprint ed. 28.95 (*0-405-01700-6*) Ayer.

Reminiscences of the Last Sixty-Five Years. Ebenezer S. Thomas. (American Biography Ser.). 300p. 1991. reprint ed. lib. bdg. 69.00 (*0-7812-8381-7*) Rprt Serv.

Reminiscences of the Opera. Benjamin Lumley. LC 76-15185. (Music Reprint Ser.). 448p. 1976. reprint ed. 55.00 (*0-306-70842-6*) Da Capo.

Reminiscences of the Revolution. A. Reid. 32p. 1995. reprint ed. pap. 6.50 (*0-910746-44-3*) Hope Farm.

Reminiscences of the Russian Ballet. Alexandre Benois. Tr. by Mary Britnieva. LC 77-7791. (Series in Dance). (Illus.). 1977. reprint ed. lib. bdg. 45.00 (*0-306-77426-7*) Da Capo.

Reminiscences of the Thirteenth Regiment New Jersey Infantry in the Civil War. Samuel Toombs. (Illus.). 300p. (C). 1994. 25.00 (*0-944413-08-0*) Longstreet Hse.

Reminiscences of the Twenty-Second Iowa Volunteer Infantry: Giving Its Organization, Marches, Skirmishes, Battles, & Sieges as Taken from the Diary of Lieutenant S. C. Jones. Samuel C. Jones. LC 92-97501. (Illus.). 180p. 1993. reprint ed. 25.00 (*0-9628936-4-1*) Pr Camp Pope.

Reminiscences of the Vienna Circle & the Mathematical Colloquium. Karl Menger. Ed. by Louise Golland. LC 94-5014. (Vienna Circle Collection: Vol. 20). 272p. (C). 1994. pap. text ed. 28.00 (*0-7923-2873-6*) Kluwer Ac.

Reminiscences of the Vienna Circle & the Mathematical Colloquium. Karl Menger. Ed. by Louise Golland. LC 94-5014. (Vienna Circle Collection: Vol. 20). 272p. (C). 1994. lib. bdg. 106.00 (*0-7923-2711-X*, Pub. by Klwr Acad Pubs NE) Kluwer Ac.

Reminiscences of the 123rd Regiment, N.Y.S.V., Giving a Complete History of Its Three Years Service in the War. Henry C. Morhous. (Illus.). 220p. 1995. 30.00 (*1-881868-01-X*) Wash Cnty Hist.

Reminiscences of Thomas Dibdin, 2 vols. Thomas J. Dibdin. LC 70-111769. reprint ed. 74.50 (*0-404-02124-7*) AMS Pr.

***Reminiscences of Thomas Stubbs.** Thomas Stubbs. Ed. by W. A. Maxwell & R. T. McGeogh. (Graham's Town Ser.: No. 4). 318p. 1978. 46.00 (*0-86961-092-9*, Pub. by A A Balkema NE) Ashgate Pub Co.

Reminiscences of Tolstoy, Chekhov, & Andreev. Maxim Gorky. Tr. by Katherine Mansfield et al. from RUS. 1998. 35.00 (*0-86527-424-X*) Fertig.

***Reminiscences of Troy from Its Settlement in 1790 to 1807, with Remarks on Its Commerce, Enterprise, Improvements...Etc.** 2nd ed. John Woodworth. (Illus.). 110p. 1997. reprint ed. pap. 16.00 (*0-8328-6265-7*) Higginson Bk Co.

Reminiscences of Walt Whitman. W. Sloane Kennedy. LC 72-4113. (Studies in Whitman: No. 28). 1972. reprint ed. lib. bdg. 75.00 (*0-8383-1605-0*) M S G Haskell Hse.

Reminiscences of Washington Territory. enl. ed. Charles Prosch. 128p. 1969. 14.95 (*0-87770-022-2*) Ye Galleon.

Reminiscences of Woodland Stalking. Leo Ritchie. 174p. (C). 1989. 49.00 (*0-7223-2290-9*, Pub. by A H S Ltd UK) St Mut.

Reminiscences of WWII: The Last Good War. Irvin D. Magin. 408p. 1995. mass mkt. 4.99 (*1-896329-13-6*, Pub. by Comnwlth Pub CN) Partners Pubs Grp.

Reminiscences, Sermons, & Correspondence: Proving Adherence to the Principle of Christian Science As Taught by Mary Baker Eddy. Augusta E. Stetson. LC 91-169371. (Illus.). xx, 1282p. 1989. reprint ed. 38.00 (*1-879135-05-1*) Emma Pub Soc.

***Reminiscences, Sporting & Otherwise, of Early Days in Rockford.** John H. Thurston. (Illus.). 117p. 1997. reprint ed. lib. bdg. 18.00 (*0-8328-5790-4*) Higginson Bk Co.

Reminiscences to School Life Hints Teaching. Gates. (African American Women Writers 1910-1940 Ser.). 1995. 14.95 (*0-7838-1396-1*, Hall Reference) Macmillan.

Reminiscences, 1819-1899. Julia W. Howe. (American Biography Ser.). 465p. 1991. reprint ed. lib. bdg. 89.00 (*0-7812-8200-4*) Rprt Serv.

Reminiscencias Cubanas. Rene A. Jimenez. LC 77-82225. 1977. pap. 6.00 (*0-89729-167-0*) Ediciones.

Reminiscenses of a Private: William E. Bevens of the First Arkansas Infantry. Ed. by Daniel Sutherland. (Illus.). 324p. 1992. 34.00 (*1-55728-223-4*) U of Ark Pr.

Reminiscent Scrutinies: Memory in Anthony Powell's A Dance to the Music of Time. Laurie A. Frost. LC 89-51480. 139p. 1990. 15.00 (*0-87875-392-3*) Whitston Pub.

Reminiscenzen: Seine Rede vor Richter Gary, Sozialpolitische Abhandlungen, Briefe, Notizen, etc. 1888. August Spies. Ed. by Patricia A. Herminghouse & Carol Poore. LC 83-49205. (Crosscurrents, Writings of German Political Emigres in 19th Century America Ser.: Section I, Vol. 5). 181p. (C). 1984. text ed. 33.15 (*0-8204-0044-0*) P Lang Pubng.

Reminiscing: Autobiographical Notes. Paul A. Schilpp & Madelon Golden Schilpp. LC 95-8961. 163p. (C). 1996. pap. 14.95 (*0-8093-2028-2*) S Ill U Pr.

Reminiscing about Next Week. Judy Stedman. Ed. by Edward Mycue. (Took Modern Poetry in English Ser.: No. 25). (Illus.). 28p. (Orig.). 1991. pap. 3.00 (*1-879457-26-1*) Norton Coker Pr.

Reminiscing in Tempo: The Life & Times of a Jazz Hustler. Teddy Reig & Edward Berger. LC 90-36355. (Studies in Jazz: No. 10). (Illus.). 238p. 1990. 29.50 (*0-8108-2326-8*) Scarecrow.

Reminisin' Leroy Watts. (Illus.). 128p. 1993. 20.00 (*0-9636993-1-8*) VXA Pubns.

Reminscences of a Mosby Guerrilla. John W. Munson. 1983. reprint ed. 25.95 (*0-89201-109-2*) Zenger Pub.

Remise de Peine. Patrick Modiano. (FRE.). 1989. pap. 10.95 (*0-7859-2712-3*) Fr & Eur.

Remittances & Returnees: The Cultural Economy of Migration in Ilocos. Ed. by Raul Pertierra. (Illus.). 162p. (Orig.). 1992. pap. 13.75 (*971-10-0476-3*, Pub. by New Day Pub PH) Cellar.

Remizov's Fictions, 1900-1921. Greta N. Slobin. LC 91-16967. (Illus.). 205p. 1992. lib. bdg. 30.00 (*0-87580-158-7*) N Ill U Pr.

Remme's Ride for the Gold. Thorn Bacon. (Illus.). 120p. (J). 1994. 12.95 (*1-885221-07-X*); pap. 8.95 (*1-885221-11-8*) BookPartners.

Remnant. Mark T. Barclay. 73p. (Orig.). 1988. pap. 5.00 (*0-944802-00-1*) M Barclay Pubns.

Remnant. Jacob Barosin. 1989. pap. 10.95 (*0-89604-129-8*, Holocaust Library) US Holocaust.

***Remnant.** Gilbert Morris. (Far Fields Ser.: Bk. 2). 192p. 1997. pap. 8.95 (*0-914984-91-8*) Starburst.

***Remnant.** Keith C. Terry & Wesley Jarvis. LC 96-49371. 1996. write for info. (*1-57734-056-6*) Covenant Comms.

Remnant. Mary LaCroix. 535p. 1987. reprint ed. pap. 16.95 (*0-87604-201-9*, 7610) ARE Pr.

Remnant: Biblical Reality or Wishful Thinking? Clifford Goldstein. LC 93-23217. 1994. pap. 8.99 (*0-8163-1192-7*) Pacific Pr Pub Assn.

***Remnant: Living in Triumph.** Priscilla D. Fritz. 275p. (Orig.). 1997. pap. write for info. (*0-9651886-4-7*) Crowne Emerald.

Remnant: The History & Theology of the Remnant Idea from Genesis to Isaiah. 3rd ed. Gerhard F. Hasel. (Andrews University Monographs). 488p. 1980. pap. 19.99 (*0-943872-05-7*) Andrews Univ Pr.

Remnant Church. Richard L. Carroll. 173p. pap. text ed. 9.95 (*0-9643572-0-8*) St Marg Mary Chur.

Remnant in Crisis. Jack W. Provonsha. LC 92-41459. 1992. 9.99 (*0-8280-0698-9*) Review & Herald.

Remnant Population. Elizabeth Moon. 352p. 1996. 22.00 (*0-671-87718-6*) Baen Bks.

***Remnant Population.** Elizabeth Moon. 352p. 1997. mass mkt. 5.99 (*0-671-87770-4*) Baen Bks.

Remnant Seeds of Creation: A Strategy for Survival, or the Preservation of Non-Favoured Races in the Struggle for Life. P. Penn. 256p. 1991. text ed. 24.95 (*0-9629024-1-1*); pap. text ed. 14.95 (*0-9629024-0-3*) Aahaa Bks.

***Remnant Wars: Vanishing Brethren.** William L. Parkinson. LC 96-92674. 242p. (Orig.). 1996. pap. 7.95 (*0-9655478-0-9*) Parkinson Pub.

Remnants: The R. E. M. Collector's Handbook & Price Guide. Gary S. Nabors. LC 93-70503. (Illus.). 271p. (Orig.). 1993. pap. 17.95 (*0-9636241-4-8*) Eclipse PA.

Remnants of an Unknown Woman. John Evans & Ursule Molinaro. LC 87-42541. 24p. (C). 1987. pap. 4.00 (*0-87376-059-X*) Red Dust.

Remnants of Change: Poems Inspired by the Lithographs of Ancel Nunn. Samuel C. Woolvin. LC 91-37402. (Illus.). 252p. 1991. write for info. (*0-9627096-1-1*) Whitehead TX.

Remnants of Meaning. Stephen Schiffer. 328p. 1987. reprint ed. 37.50 (*0-262-19258-6*) MIT Pr.

Remnants of Meaning. Stephen Schiffer. 328p. 1989. reprint ed. pap. 18.50 (*0-262-69134-5*) MIT Pr.

Remnants of Receding Tears: Narrative Poems. J. S. Olga. 58p. 1993. pap. 5.95 (*1-883683-99-8*) Metropolis Pubs.

Remnants of the First Earth. Ray A. Young Bear. 320p. 1996. 23.00 (*0-8021-1581-0*, Grove) Grove-Atltic.

Remodel! An Architect's Advice on Home Renovation. Greg Gibson. LC 95-46221. (Illus.). 272p. 1996. pap. text ed. 19.95 (*0-471-12260-2*) Wiley.

Remodelaciones de Cocinas. Cy DeCosse Incorporated Staff. (Black & Decker Home Improvement Library). 1994. 16.95 (*0-86573-736-3*) Cowles Creative.

Remodeled to Death. Valerie Wolzien. 1995. mass mkt. 5.99 (*0-449-14921-8*) Fawcett.

Remodelers Business Basics. Linda W. Case. LC 88-62780. 232p. 1989. pap. 36.00 (*0-86718-300-4*) Home Builder.

***Remodelers Cost of Doing Business.** 3rd ed. Steve Maltzman. LC 97-70029. (Illus.). 74p. (Orig.). 1997. pap. 24.50 (*0-86718-430-2*) Home Builder.

Remodeler's Guide to Making & Managing Money. Linda W. Case. LC 95-92481. 140p. 1996. pap. 24.95 (*0-9648587-4-6*) Remodelng Cnslting.

Remodelers Marketing PowerPak. Linda W. Case & Victoria L. Downing. LC 95-92480. 216p. 1995. pap. 24.95 (*0-9648587-3-8*) Remodelng Cnslting.

Remodeling - Repair Construction Costs, 1992. Ed. by Stanley J. Strychaz. (Illus.). (Orig.). 1992. pap. 49.95 (*0-931708-30-3*) Saylor.

Remodeling Contractor's Handbook. Dan Wong. 304p. (Orig.). 1990. pap. 18.25 (*0-934041-45-8*) Craftsman.

Remodeling Kitchens, Bathrooms, & Utility Rooms. Byron W. Maguire. 240p. 1991. text ed. 35.00 (*0-13-770330-9*) P-H.

Remodeling Production. rev. ed. Walter W. Stoeppelwerth. 172p. 1988. pap. 37.50 (*1-882379-07-1*) HomeTech Info Systs.

Remodeling-Repair Construction Costs 1994. Ed. by Stanley J. Strychaz. (Illus.). 430p. 1994. pap. 49.95 (*0-931708-39-7*) Saylor.

Remodeling-Repair Construction Costs, 1995. Ed. by Stanley J. Strychaz. 430p. 1995. pap. 49.95 (*0-931708-47-8*) Saylor.

Remodeling Your Home: An Insider's Guide. Doris M. Tennyson. LC 95-37194. (Illus.). 140p. (Orig.). 1996. pap. 19.95 (*0-86718-411-6*) Home Builder.

Remodeling Your Professional Office. Schwartz. 224p. 1985. boxed 42.95 (*0-87489-338-0*) Med Econ.

***Remodeling/Repair Construction Costs, 1997.** 7th ed. 1997. 49.95 (*0-931708-62-1*) Saylor.

Remodelling Geography. Ed. by Bill Macmillan. (Illus.). 320p. 1989. text ed. 67.95 (*0-631-16099-X*) Blackwell Pubs.

Remolding of Destinies. 2nd ed. Albert Steffen. Tr. by George Cragin et al. from GER. (Illus.). 86p. 1984. pap. 6.50 (*0-932776-08-6*) Adonis Pr.

Remorse. Alba de Cespedes. Tr. by William Weaver from ITA. LC 78-14003. 1979. text ed. 69.50 (*0-313-20731-3*, CERE, Greenwood Pr) Greenwood.

Remorse. Samuel Taylor Coleridge. LC 90-118417. 96p. 1989. reprint ed. 40.00 (*1-85477-015-2*, Pub. by Woodstock Bks UK) Cassell.

***Remota: Airmail Paintings.** Eugenio Dittborn et al. (Illus.). (ENG & SPA.). 1997. mass mkt. 37.95 (*0-614-25987-8*) New Mus Contemp Art.

Remote. David Shields. LC 95-21809. (Illus.). 224p. 1996. 22.00 (*0-679-44591-9*) Knopf.

Remote Access Essentials. Margaret Robbins. (Illus.). 250p. 1995. pap. 24.95 (*0-12-691410-9*) Acad Pr.

***Remote Access Networking.** Kim Lew & Wei Cheng. 1997. 50.00 (*1-57870-029-9*) Mac Comp Pub.

***Remote Access Networking.** Kim Lew & Wei Chang. 1997. 50.00 (*1-56205-815-0*) New Riders Pub.

Remote & Controlled: Media Politics in a Cynical Age. Matthew R. Kerbel. (Dilemmas in American Politics Ser.). (Illus.). 166p. (C). 1995. pap. text ed. 15.95 (*0-8133-2593-5*) Westview.

Remote Assessment of Ocean Color for Interpretation of Satellite Visible Imagery: A Review. H. R. Gordon & A. Y. Morel. (Lecture Notes on Coastal & Estuarine Studies: Vol. 4). (Illus.). 130p. 1983. pap. 44.00 (*0-387-90923-0*) Spr-Verlag.

***Remote Beyond Compare: Letters of don Diego de Vargas to His Family from New Spain & New Mexico, 1675-1706.** Diego De Vargas. Ed. by John L. Kessell. LC 88-27651. (Journals of don Diego de Vargas Ser.). (Illus.). 610p. 1989. reprint ed. pap. 173.90 (*0-608-04137-8*, 2064870) Bks Demand.

Remote Control. Stephen White. 1997. pap. 22.95 (*0-525-94269-6*) NAL-Dutton.

***Remote Control.** Stephen White. 1997. 22.95 (*0-614-27939-9*) NAL-Dutton.

***Remote Control: A Sensible Approach to Kids, TV & the New Electronic Media.** Leonard Jason & Libby K. Hanaway. LC 97-11472. 1997. write for info. (*1-56887-022-1*, Prof Resc Pr) Pro Resource.

***Remote Control: Dilemmas of Black Intervention in British Film & TV.** Ed. by June Givanni. (Distributed for the British Film Institute Ser.). (Illus.). 48p. 1996. pap. 17.50 (*0-85170-537-5*, Pub. by British Film Inst UK) Ind U Pr.

Remote Control: Power, Cultures & the World of Appearances. Barbara Kruger. (Illus.). 107p. 1993. pap. 22.50 (*0-262-11177-2*) MIT Pr.

Remote Control: Power, Cultures, & the World of Appearances. Barbara Kruger. (Illus.). 251p. 1994. 10.95 (*0-262-61106-6*) MIT Pr.

Remote Control: Television, Audiences, & Cultural Power. Ed. by Ellen Seiter et al. 336p. 1989. 47.50 (*0-415-03605-4*, A3716) Routledge.

Remote Control: Television Audiences & Cultural Power. Ed. by Ellen Seiter et al. 272p. (C). 1991. pap. 16.95 (*0-415-06505-4*, A5740) Routledge.

Remote Control in the New Age of Television. Ed. by James R. Walker & Robert V. Bellamy. LC 93-6774. 288p. 1993. text ed. 57.95 (*0-275-94396-8*, C4396, Praeger Pubs) Greenwood.

Remote Control Race Car Bible. James R. Taylor & Lynda L. Taylor. Ed. by Ellen Silge. (Illus.). 151p. (Orig.). 1986. pap. text ed. 10.95 (*0-9616670-1-X*) J R Taylor.

Remote Controlled: How TV Affects You & Your Family. Joe L. Wheeler. LC 93-18884. 192p. 1993. pap. 10.99 (*0-8280-0713-6*) Review & Herald.

Remote Controls Are Better Than Women Because: or What Men Would Say If They Could. Karen Rostoker-Gruber. LC 92-84004. (Illus.). 80p. 1993. pap. 5.95 (*1-56352-076-1*) Longstreet Pr Inc.

Remote Cooperation: CSCW Issues for Mobile & Tele-Workers. Ed. by Alan J. Dix & Russell Beale. LC 96-12820. (Computer Supported Cooperative Work Ser.). 1996. pap. 64.50 (*3-540-76035-0*) Spr-Verlag.

Remote Country of Women: A Novel by Bai Hua. Hua Bai. Tr. by Qingyun Wu & Thomas O. Beebee from CHI. (Fiction from Modern China Ser.). 344p. 1994. pap. 14.95 (*0-8248-1611-0*); text ed. 38.00 (*0-8248-1591-2*) UH Pr.

Remote Depossession. Irene Hickman. 1994. pap. 8.75 (*0-915689-08-1*) Hickman Systems.

Remote Education & Informatives - Teleteaching: Proceedings of the IFIP TC3 International Conference, Budapest, Hungary, 20-25 Oct., 1986. Ed. by F. B. Lovis. 254p. 1988. 107.00 (*0-444-70418-3*, North Holland) Elsevier.

Remote Geochemical Analysis: Elemental & Mineralogical Composition. Ed. by C. M. Pieters & P. A. Englert. LC 92-42655. (Topics in Remote Sensing Ser.: No. 4). (Illus.). 585p. (C). 1993. text ed. 90.00 (*0-521-40281-6*) Cambridge U Pr.

Remote Intrusion. Howard A. Olgin. 352p. 1996. mass mkt. 5.99 (*0-440-21879-9*) Dell.

Remote Kingdoms. rev. ed. Tertius Chandler. (Illus.). 111p. 1981. pap. 14.00 (*0-9603872-5-0*) Gutenberg.

Remote LAN Access: A Guide for Networkers & the Rest of Us. Jeffrey N. Fritz & Manning Publications Staff. 250p. (C). 1996. pap. text ed. 35.00 (*0-13-494451-8*) P-H.

Remote LAN Connection. William G. Wong. 1995. pap. 34.95 (*1-55851-438-4*, M&T Books) H Holt & Co.

***Remote Network Administrator's Guide.** Tim Outman. 600p. 1997. 49.99 (*0-7897-1236-9*) Que.

Remote People. Evelyn Waugh. (Ecco Travel Ser.). 192p. 1990. pap. 8.95 (*0-88001-256-0*) Ecco Pr.

Remote Procedure Call Programming: Writing Networked Applications. John R. Corbin. 1990. 53.95 (*0-387-97247-1*) Spr-Verlag.

Remote Sensing. Ed. by Norman H. Foster. (Treatise of Petroleum Geology Reprint Ser.: No. 19). (Illus.). 607p. 1992. pap. 10.00 (*0-89181-418-3*, 541) AAPG.

Remote Sensing. Richard K. Miller & Terri C. Walker. LC 88-84059. (Survey on Technology & Markets Ser.: No. 81). 50p. 1991. pap. text ed. 200.00 (*1-55865-111-X*) Future Tech Surveys.

Remote Sensing. Ed. by Ken Watson & Robert D. Regan. LC 82-60624. (Geophysics Reprint Ser.: No. 3). 581p. 1983. pap. 19.00 (*0-931830-23-0*, 463) Soc Expl Geophys.

Remote Sensing. 2nd ed. Floyd F. Sabins. LC 86-2144. 449p. (C). 1995. text ed. write for info. (*0-7167-1793-X*) W H Freeman.

Remote Sensing. 3rd ed. Floyd F. Sabins. LC 96-31940. 1996. text ed. write for info. (*0-7167-2442-1*) W H Freeman.

An Asterisk (*) at the beginning of an entry indicates that the title is appearing in BIP for the first time.

R

Remote Sensing, ser. vol. 7. Goward. (Advances in Space Research). 1988. pap. 56.00 (*0-08-036658-9*, Pergamon Pr) Elsevier.

Remote Sensing: Digital Image Analysis. J. A. Richards. (Illus.). 320p. 1986. 69.00 (*0-387-16007-8*) Spr-Verlag.

Remote Sensing: Proceedings of an EARSEL-ESA Symposium, Guildford, U. K., April 8-11. Ed. by Geoffrey K. Pardoe. (Illus.). 64p. 1985. pap. 39.00 (*0-08-032538-6*, Pub. by PPL UK) Elsevier.

Remote Sensing: Proceedings of the 27th International Geological Congress, Vol. 18. International Geological Congress Staff. 236p. 1984. lib. bdg. 85.00 (*90-6764-027-1*, Pub. by VSP NE) Coronet Bks.

Remote Sensing: The Image Chain Approach. John R. Schott. (Illus.). 480p. (C). 1996. text ed. 59.95 (*0-19-508726-7*) OUP.

Remote Sensing - Principles & Applications. A. N. Patel & S. Singh. (C). 1992. text ed. 40.00 (*81-7233-037-5*, Pub. by Scientific Pubs II) St Mut.

Remote Sensing & Ecosystem Management, 1994. 378p. 1994. 75.00 (*1-57083-010-X*) ASP & RS.

Remote Sensing & Forest Survey. M. K. Sharma. 210p. (C). 1986. 125.00 (*81-7089-043-8*, Pub. by Intl Bk Distr II) St Mut.

Remote Sensing & Geographic Information Systems: Geological Mapping, Mineral Exploration & Mining. Christopher Legg. LC 92-21708. (Ellis Horwood Library of Space Science & Space Technology). 256p. 1993. 59.95 (*0-13-772336-9*, Pub. by Tavistock-E Horwood UK) Routledge Chapman & Hall.

Remote Sensing & Geographic Information Systems: Geological Mapping, Mineral Exploration & Mining. Christopher Legg. (Wiley-Praxis Ser.). 166p. 1995. reprint ed. text ed. 80.00 (*0-471-95423-3*) Wiley.

Remote Sensing & Geoinformation Systems as Related to Regional Planning of Health Services. Ed. by L. D. Miller et al. (CPL Bibliographies Ser.: No. 51). 76p. 1981. 10.00 (*0-86602-051-9*, Sage Prdcls Pr) Sage.

***Remote Sensing & GIS Applications to Nonpoint Source Planning.** 124p. 1991. 15.00 (*0-614-30386-9*, PR1) Terrene Inst.

***Remote Sensing & GIS for Land & Marine Resources & Environment Management: Proceedings, Regional Workshop on Remote Sensing & GIS for Land & Marine Resources & Environment Management in the Pacific Subregion, 1995.** 159p. 1996. pap. 20.00 (*92-1-119722-8*, 68548) UN.

Remote Sensing & Global Climate Change. Ed. by Robin A. Vaughan & Arthur P. Cracknell. LC 94-36780. (NATO ASI Series I: Global Environmental Change: Vol. 24). 1994. 214.00 (*3-540-58471-4*) Spr-Verlag.

Remote Sensing & G's for Site Characterization No. 1279: Applications & Standards. Ed. by Ivan Johnson et al. LC 95-48094. (Special Technical Publications: Vol. 1279). (Illus.). 1996. text ed. 59.00 (*0-8031-2027-3*, 04-012790-38) ASTM.

Remote Sensing & Image Interpretation. 3rd ed. Thomas M. Lillesand & Ralph W. Kiefer. 750p. 1994. text ed. 53.50 (*0-471-57783-9*) Wiley.

Remote Sensing & Natural Resource Management: Proceedings of the Fourth Forest Service Remote Sensing Applications Conference. 456p. 1992. 20.00 (*0-944426-89-1*) ASP & RS.

Remote Sensing & Resource Exploration. Ed. by Farouk El-Baz et al. 308p. (C). 1989. text ed. 89.00 (*9971-5-0819-2*) World Scientific Pub.

Remote Sensing & Tropical Land Management. Ed. by M. J. Eden & J. T. Parry. LC 85-17932. (Illus.). 393p. reprint ed. pap. 112.10 (*0-8357-2913-3*, 2039152) Bks Demand.

Remote Sensing & Water Resources Management. Ed. by Keith P. Thomson et al. (American Water Resources Association Proceedings Ser.: No. 17). 445p. reprint ed. pap. 126.90 (*0-317-11249-X*, 2017815) Bks Demand.

Remote Sensing Application in Agriculture & Hydrology: Proceedings of a Seminar Held at the Joint Research Centre of the Commission of the European Communities, Ispra, Italy. Ed. by Georges Fraysse. 510p. (C). 1980. text ed. 195.00 (*90-6191-081-1*, Pub. by A A Balkema NE) Ashgate Pub Co.

Remote Sensing Applications for Consumptive Use (Evapotranspiration) Papers Presented at 21st Annual AWRA Conference & Symposium, August 11-16, 1985, Tucson, AZ. Ed. by Arnold I. Johnson & A. Rango. (AWRA Monograph Ser.: No. 6). (Illus.). 78p. reprint ed. pap. 25.00 (*0-8357-3172-3*, 2039435) Bks Demand.

Remote Sensing Applications in Marine Science & Technology. Ed. by Arthur P. Cracknell. 1983. lib. bdg. 211.50 (*90-277-1608-0*) Kluwer Ac.

Remote Sensing Applications in Meteorology & Climatology. Ed. by Robin A. Vaughan. (C). 1987. lib. bdg. 194.00 (*90-277-2502-0*) Kluwer Ac.

Remote Sensing by Fourier Transform Spectrometry. Reinhard Beer. LC 91-33607. (Chemical Analysis: A Series of Monographs on Analytical Chemistry & Its Applications). 176p. 1992. text ed. 87.95 (*0-471-55346-8*) Wiley.

Remote Sensing Calibration Systems: An Introduction. Hsi Chen. LC 96-29865. 250p. 1997. 64.00 (*0-937194-38-7*) A Deepak Pub.

Remote Sensing Digital Image Analysis. 2nd enl. rev. ed. J. A. Richards. LC 94-29196. 330p. 1995. 59.95 (*0-387-58219-3*) Spr-Verlag.

Remote Sensing Digital Image Analysis: An Introduction. 2nd ed. John A. Richards. LC 93-10179. (Illus.). 344p. 1993. 119.00 (*0-387-54840-8*) Spr-Verlag.

Remote Sensing for Geologists: A Guide to Image Interpretation. Gary L. Prost. LC 93-50702. 326p. 1994. text ed. 115.00 (*2-88449-101-5*) Gordon & Breach.

Remote Sensing for Hazard Monitoring & Disaster Assessment: Marine & Coastal Applications, Vol. 2. Ed. by E. C. Barrett. (Current Topics in Remote Sensing Ser.). 240p. 1991. text ed. 132.00 (*2-88124-809-8*) Gordon & Breach.

Remote Sensing for Monitoring the Changing Environment of Europe: Proceedings of the 12th EARSeL Symposium Eger, Hungary, 8-11 September 1992. Ed. by Peter Winkler. (Illus.). 300p. (C). 1993. text ed. 110.00 (*90-5410-311-6*, Pub. by A A Balkema NE) Ashgate Pub Co.

Remote Sensing for Oceanography, Hydrology, & Agriculture. Ed. by J. F. Gower et al. (Advances in Space Research Ser.: Vol. 13). 296p. 1993. pap. 190.25 (*0-08-042201-2*, Pergamon Pr) Elsevier.

Remote Sensing for Resources Development & Environmental Management: Proceedings of the 7th International Symposium, ISPRS Commission VII, Enschede, 25-29 August 1986, 3 vols., Set. Ed. by M. C. Damen et al. 1300p. (C). 1986. text ed. 355.00 (*90-6191-674-7*, Pub. by A A Balkema NE) Ashgate Pub Co.

Remote Sensing for Tropical Ecosystem: Management Proceedings of the Regional Remote Sensing Seminar, Bali, Indonesia, 23-28 September, 1994. 300p. 1995. 45.00 (*92-1-119690-6*, E.95.II.F.24) UN.

Remote Sensing from Satellites: Proceedings of Workshops I & IX of the COSPAR Interdisciplinary Scientific Commission A (Meetings A2) of the COSPAR 25th Plenary Meeting Held in Graz, Austria 25 June - 7 July 1974. Ed. by W. D. Carter & E. T. Engman. 264p. 1985. pap. 54.00 (*0-08-032751-6*, Pub. by PPL UK) Elsevier.

Remote Sensing Geology. R. P. Gupta. (Illus.). 376p. 1991. 163.95 (*0-387-52805-9*) Spr-Verlag.

Remote Sensing Image Analysis: An Introduction. 2nd ed. J. A. Richards. LC 94-29196. 1994. write for info. (*3-540-58219-3*) Spr-Verlag.

Remote Sensing Imagery for Natural Resources Monitoring: A Guide for First-Time Users. David S. Wilkie & John T. Finn. (Methods & Cases in Conservation Science Ser.). (Illus.). 241p. 1996. 49.50 (*0-231-07928-1*) Col U Pr.

Remote Sensing Imagery for Natural Resources Monitoring: A Guide for First-Time Users. David S. Wilkie & John T. Finn. (Methods & Cases in Conservation Science Ser.). (Illus.). 295p. 1996. pap. text ed. 27.50 (*0-231-07929-X*) Col U Pr.

Remote Sensing in Exploration Geology. Ed. by Lee. (IGC Field Trip Guidebooks Ser.). 64p. 1989. 21.00 (*0-87590-564-1*, T182) Am Geophysical.

***Remote Sensing in Hydrology.** Engman & Gurney. (Remote Sensing Applications Ser.). (Illus.). 225p. (C). (gr. 13 up). 1990. text ed. 97.50 (*0-412-24450-0*) Chapman & Hall.

Remote Sensing in Soil Science. M. A. Mulders. (Developments in Soil Science Ser.: No. 15). 380p. 1987. 189.00 (*0-444-42783-X*) Elsevier.

***Remote Sensing Laboratory Manual.** Floyd F. Sabins. 240p. (C). 1996. pap. text ed. 45.09 (*0-7872-2543-6*) Kendall-Hunt.

Remote Sensing Methods & Applications. R. Michael Hord. LC 86-9064. (Remote Sensing & Image Processing Ser.). 362p. 1986. text ed. 130.00 (*0-471-82824-6*) Wiley.

Remote Sensing Methods in Studying Tectonic Fractures in Oil- & Gas-Bearing Formations. G. I. Amurskii et al. Tr. by N. Venkat Rao from RUS. (Russian Translation Ser.: No. 86). (Illus.). 164p. (C). 1991. text ed. 60.00 (*90-6191-989-4*, Pub. by A A Balkema NE) Ashgate Pub Co.

Remote Sensing, Noncontact Sensing, & Image Processing. Richard K. Miller. 966p. 1991. pap. text ed. 485.00 (*0-89671-109-9*) SEAI Tech Pubns.

Remote Sensing of Atmosphere & Oceans. Ed. by Ehrhard Raschke et al. (Advances in Space Research Ser.: No. 9). 474p. 1989. pap. 70.00 (*0-08-040149-X*, 2208; 2307; 2309, Pergamon Pr) Elsevier.

Remote Sensing of Biosphere Functioning. Ed. by R. J. Hobbs & Harold A. Mooney. (Ecological Studies: Vol. 79). (Illus.). 350p. 1990. 98.00 (*0-387-97098-3*) Spr-Verlag.

Remote Sensing of Earth Resources: A Guide to Information Sources. Ed. by M. Leonard Bryan. LC 79-22792. (Geography & Travel Information Guide Ser.: Vol. 1). (Illus.). 200p. 1979. 68.00 (*0-8103-1413-4*) Gale.

***Remote Sensing of Earth's Surface & Atmosphere.** A. B. Kahle et al. (Advances in Space Research (RJ) Ser.: Vol. 14). 292p. 1994. 165.00 (*0-08-042477-5*, Pergamon Pr) Elsevier.

Remote Sensing of Forest Resources: Theory & Applications. J. A. Howard. (Remote Sensing Applications Ser.: No. 7). (Illus.). 432p. (gr. 13). 1991. text ed. 173.50 (*0-412-29930-5*) Chapman & Hall.

Remote Sensing of GIS in Ecosystem Management. Ed. by V. Alaric Sample. 400p. (C). 1994. text ed. 49.95 (*1-55963-284-4*); pap. text ed. 29.95 (*1-55963-285-2*) Island Pr.

Remote Sensing of Ice & Snow. Dorothy Hall & Jaroslav Martinec. 200p. 1986. 42.50 (*0-412-25910-9*, 9536) Chapman & Hall.

Remote Sensing of Sea Ice & Icebergs. Ed. by Simon Haykin et al. (Remote Sensing Ser.). 704p. 1994. text ed. 112.00 (*0-471-55494-4*) Wiley.

Remote Sensing of Soils & Vegetation. Paul J. Curran et al. 200p. 1990. 90.00 (*0-85066-402-0*) Taylor & Francis.

Remote Sensing of the Earth from Space: Atmospheric Correction. K. Ya Kondratyev et al. (Illus.). 480p. 1992. 272.95 (*0-387-54244-2*) Spr-Verlag.

Remote Sensing of the Earth's Surface: Proceedings of Symposium 2, the COSPAR Interdisciplinary Scientific Commission A (Meeting A3) & Workshop I of the COSPAR 27th Plenary Meeting Held in Espoo, Finland, July 18-29, 1988. Ed. by V. V. Salomonson et al. (Advances in Space Research Ser.: No. 9). (Illus.). 331p. 1989. pap. 70.00 (*0-08-037385-2*, Pergamon Pr) Elsevier.

***Remote Sensing of the Earth's Surface & Atmosphere.** R. P. Singh et al. (Advances in Space Research (RJ) Ser.: Vol. 12). 468p. 1992. 165.00 (*0-08-041853-8*, Pergamon Pr) Elsevier.

Remote Sensing of the Lower Atmosphere: An Introduction. Graeme L. Stephens. (Illus.). 544p. (C). 1994. text ed. 67.00 (*0-19-508188-9*) OUP.

Remote Sensing Thematic Accuracy Assessment: A Compendium, 1994. 420p. 1994. 70.00 (*1-57083-002-9*) ASP & RS.

Remote Sensing Using Infrared Radiation: A Special Issue of the International Journal of Remote Sensing, Vol. 5, No. 1. 1984. 29.00 (*0-85066-983-9*) Taylor & Francis.

Remote Sensing with Soviet Satellites & Results from Telephoto 82 & Gyunesh-84 Experiments, Vol. 3. T. K. Ismailov. Ed. by F. Becker. (Remote Sensing Reviews Ser.: Vol. 3, No. 3). 232p. 1988. pap. text ed. 117.00 (*3-7186-4823-7*) Gordon & Breach.

Remote Sensing Yearbook 1986. Arthur P. Cracknell. 300p. 1986. 165.00 (*0-85066-313-X*) Taylor & Francis.

Remote Sensing Yearbook 1987, Vol. 2. Ed. by Arthur P. Cracknell & L. W. Hayes. 690p. 1987. 210.00 (*0-85066-378-4*) Taylor & Francis.

Remote Sensing Yearbook 1988-1989. Ed. by Arthur P. Cracknell & L. W. Hayes. 731p. 1989. 210.00 (*0-85066-407-1*) Taylor & Francis.

Remote Sensing Yearbook 1990. Arthur P. Cracknell & L. W. Hayes. 1990. 130.00 (*0-85066-808-5*) Taylor & Francis.

***Remote Sensing '96 - Integrated Applications for Risk Assessment & Disaster Prevention for the Mediterranean: Proceedings of the 16th EARSeL Symposium, Malta, 20-23 May 1996.** Ed. by A. Spiteri. (Illus.). 380p. (C). 1997. text ed. 120.00 (*90-5410-855-X*, Pub. by A A Balkema NE) Ashgate Pub Co.

Remote Sounding of the Atmosphere from Space: Proceedings of the Committee on Space Research, 21st Plenary Meeting, Innsbruck, Austria, 1978. Ed. by H. J. Bolle. (Illus.). 1979. 76.00 (*0-08-023419-4*, Pergamon Pr) Elsevier.

Remote Station Protective Signaling Systems. (Seventy Ser.). 1993. pap. 32.25 (*0-685-58065-2*, 72-90) Natl Fire Prot.

Remote Systems & Robotics in Hostile Environments, Pasco, WA, Mar. 29 - Apr. 2, 1987: Proceedings. 669p. 1987. 70.00 (*0-89448-131-2*, 700120) Am Nuclear Soc.

Remote Viewers: The Secret History of the CIA & the Pentagon. Jim Schnabel. 1997. mass mkt. 5.99 (*0-440-22306-7*) Dell.

Remotely Operated Vehicles: Technology Requirements Present & Future (ROV'86) Ed. by Society for Underwater Technology Staff. (C). 1986. lib. bdg. 122.00 (*0-86010-815-5*, Pub. by Graham & Trotman UK) Kluwer Ac.

Remotely Operated Vehicles of the World. Oilfield Publications Limited Staff. (Vessels of the World Ser.). (Illus.). 296p. 1994. pap. 182.00 (*1-870945-59-X*, Pub. by Oilfld Pubns Ltd UK) Am Educ Systs.

Remotely Sensed Data: Technology, Management, & Markets. (Illus.). 194p. (Orig.). (C). 1995. pap. text ed. 40.00 (*0-7881-1647-9*) DIANE Pub.

Remous Revolutionnaires: Armee Francaise Republique Batave: La France & les Pays-Bas, Vol. III. Ed. by Annie Jourdan & Joep Leerssen. (Orig.). (FRE.). (C). 1995. pap. 34.50 (*90-5356-174-9*, Pub. by Amsterdam U Pr NE) U of Mich Pr.

Removable Appliance Fabrication. Witt et al. (Illus.). 266p. 1988. text ed. 79.00 (*0-86715-180-3*, 1803) Quint Pub Co.

Removable Denture Construction. 3rd ed. John Frederick Bates et al. 167p. 1991. pap. 75.00 (*0-7236-1667-1*) Buttrwrth-Heinemann.

Removable Denture Prosthodontics. 2nd ed. Alan A. Grant & Wesley Johnson. (Dental Ser.). (Illus.). 325p. (Orig.). 1992. pap. text ed. 66.00 (*0-443-04631-X*) Churchill.

***Removable Partial Denture Design.** Yoshimasa Igarashi. (Dental Technique Ser.: No. 8). (Illus.). 65p. 1997. pap. text ed. 30.00 (*1-56386-040-6*) Ishiyaku Euro.

Removable Partial Dentures. Renner & Boucher. (Illus.). 416p. 1987. text ed. 62.00 (*0-86715-189-7*, 1897) Quint Pub Co.

Removable Partial Dentures: Color Atlas of Dental Medicine. George Graber. (Color Atlas of Dental Medicine Ser.). (Illus.). 224p. 1988. 155.00 (*0-86577-276-2*) Thieme Med Pubs.

***Removable Partial Dentures on Osseointegrated Implants: Principles of Treatment Planning & Prosthetic Rehabilitation in Edentulous Mandible.** Christian Besimo. LC 97-3822. 1997. write for info. (*0-86715-329-6*) Quint Pub Co.

Removable Partial Prosthodontics. Alastair R. MacGregory & Sybille K. Lechner. LC 93-2006. (Case Oriented Manual of Treatment). 160p. (gr. 13). 1994. 46.00 (*0-7234-1960-4*) Mosby Yr Bk.

Removable Prosthodontic Techniques. John B. Sowter. Ed. by Roger E. Barton. LC 86-7065. (Dental Laboratory Technology Manuals Ser.). (Illus.). viii, 248p. 1987. pap. 37.50 (*0-8078-4166-8*) U of NC Pr.

Removable Tattoo. John Knoll. (Illus.). 63p. (Orig.). 1989. pap. text ed. 5.00 (*0-9623013-0-2*) Long Road Pr.

Removal Aftershock: The Seminoles' Struggles to Survive in the West, 1836-1866. Jane F. Lancaster. LC 94-129. (Illus.). 248p. (C). 1994. pap. text ed. 16.00 (*0-87049-846-0*); lib. bdg. 32.00 (*0-87049-845-2*) U of Tenn Pr.

Removal & Disinfection Efficiency of Lime Softening Processes for Giardia & Viruses. (Illus.). 168p. 1995. pap. 66.00 (*0-89867-751-3*, 90648) Am Water Wks Assn.

Removal & Return: The Socio-Economic Effects of the War on Japanese Americans. Leonard Bloom & Ruth Riemer. LC 49-9867. (University of California Publications in Social Welfare: Vol. 4). 276p. reprint ed. pap. 78.70 (*0-317-29103-3*, 2021393) Bks Demand.

Removal of Causes from State Courts to Federal Courts, with Forms Adapted to the Several Acts of Congress on the Subject. 3rd ed. John F. Dillon. xxiii, 168p. 1981. reprint ed. lib. bdg. 22.00 (*0-8377-0514-2*) Rothman.

Removal of Hazardous Waste in Wastewater Facilities - Halogenated Organics. Water Pollution Control Federation Staff. (Manual of Practice Ser.: No. MFD11). 111p. 1986. pap. 41.50 (*0-943244-65-X*) Water Environ.

Removal of Heavy Metals from Groundwaters. 1995. write for info. (*0-8493-6984-3*) CRC Pr.

Removal of Lead-Based Bridge Paints. (National Cooperative Highway Research Program Report Ser.: No. 265). 72p. 1983. 8.00 (*0-309-03606-2*) Transport Res Bd.

Removal of Lead-Based Bridge Paints: Report on FHWA Workshop. Bernard R. Appleman & L. M. Smith. 113p. 1988. pap. text ed. 40.00 (*0-938477-35-8*) SSPC.

Removal of Metals from Wastewater: Neutralization & Precipitation. G. C. Cushnie, Jr. LC 83-22142. (Pollution Technology Review Ser.: No. 107). (Illus.). 232p. 1984. 32.00 (*0-8155-0976-6*) Noyes.

Removal of Natural Organic Matter in Biofilters. (Illus.). 220p. 1995. pap. 59.00 (*0-89867-797-1*, 90670) Am Water Wks Assn.

Removal of Nitrogen Compounds from Wastewater. Srensen Halling & S. E. Jrgensen. LC 93-32255. (Studies in Environmental Science: Vol. 54). 456p. 1993. 269.25 (*0-444-89152-8*) Elsevier.

Removal of Smoke & Grease-Laden Vapors from Commercial Cooking Equipment. National Fire Protection Association Staff. 1991. 20.25 (*0-317-63298-1*, 96-91) Natl Fire Prot.

Removal of Teeth: A Self-Instructional Guide, Bk. 2. 3rd rev. ed. James R. Hooley & Robert J. Whitacre. (Illus.). 117p. 1983. pap. 19.95 (*0-89939-021-8*) Stoma Pr.

Removal of the Cherokee Indians from Georgia. Wilson Lumpkin. LC 79-90182. (Mass Violence in America Ser.). 1977. reprint ed. 50.95 (*0-405-01325-6*) Ayer.

Removal of the Choctaw Indians. Arthur H. DeRosier, Jr. (Illus.). 224p. 1970. pap. text ed. 15.95 (*0-87049-329-9*) U of Tenn Pr.

Removal of Volatile Organic Chemicals from Potable Water: Technologies & Costs. Environmental Science & Engineering, Inc. Staff. LC 86-17962. (Pollution Technology Review Ser.: No. 134). (Illus.). 231p. 1987. 36.00 (*0-8155-1099-3*) Noyes.

Removals: Nineteenth-Century American Literature & the Politics of Indian Affairs. Lucy Maddox. 216p. 1991. 48.00 (*0-19-506931-5*) OUP.

Remove a Concept, Set, Pts. 1 & 2. Peter Ganick. Ed. by Stephen Forth. 80p. 1990. Set. per. 10.00 (*0-685-56982-9*) SPD-Small Pr Dist.

Remove Not the Ancient Landmark: Public Monuments & Moral Values. Ed. by Donald M. Reynolds. (Documenting the Image Ser.: Vol. III). 256p. 1996. text ed. 65.00 (*2-88124-602-8*, ECU38, Harwood Acad Pubs); pap. text ed. 23.00 (*2-88449-204-6*, ECU18, Harwood Acad Pubs) Gordon & Breach.

Remove the Bodies. large type ed. Elizabeth X. Ferrars. 390p. 1989. 25.99 (*0-7089-1943-X*) Ulverscroft.

Removing a Badge of Slavery: The Record of Brown vs. Board of Education. Ed. & Intro. by Mark Whitman. 440p. (C). 1993. text ed. 49.95 (*1-55876-049-0*) Wiener Pubs Inc.

Removing a Badge of Slavery: The Record of Brown vs. The Board of Education. Mark Whitman. 320p. (C). 1992. pap. text ed. 18.95 (*1-55876-058-X*) Wiener Pubs Inc.

Removing Anti-Judaism from the Pulpit. Ed. by Howard C. Kee & Irwin J. Borowsky. 144p. 1996. pap. text ed. 19.95 (*0-8264-0927-X*) Continuum.

Removing Barriers in Places of Public Accommodation: The Americans with Disabilities Act. (Illus.). 27p. (Orig.). (C). 1993. pap. text ed. 20.00 (*1-56806-538-8*) DIANE Pub.

Removing College Price Barriers: What Government Has Done & Why It Hasn't Worked. Michael Mumper. LC 95-797. (SUNY Series, Social Context of Education & SUNY Series, Teacher Empowerment & School Reform). 304p. (C). 1995. pap. text ed. 24.95 (*0-7914-2704-8*) State U NY Pr.

Removing College Price Barriers: What Government Has Done & Why It Hasn't Worked. Michael Mumper. LC 95-797. (SUNY Series, The Social Context of Education & SUNY Series, Teacher Empowerment & School Reform). 304p. 1995. text ed. 74.50 (*0-7914-2703-X*) State U NY Pr.

Removing Managerial Barriers to Effective Police Leadership: A Study of Executive Leadership & Executive Management in Big-City Police Departments. Norman H. Stamper. LC 92-61460. 175p. (Orig.). 1992. pap. 18.00 (*1-878734-29-6*) Police Exec Res.

Removing Regulatory Barriers to Affordable Housing: How States & Localities Are Moving Ahead. Carol T. Robbins et al. 84p. (Orig.). (C). 1993. pap. text ed. 20.00 (*0-7881-0068-8*) DIANE Pub.

***Removing Stains.** DK Publishing, Inc. Staff. LC 96-6587. (101 Essential Tips Ser.: Vol. 25). 72p. 1997. pap. 6.95 (*0-7894-1459-7*) DK Pub Inc.

Removing Stains from Concrete. 28p. 1987. pap. 11.95 (*0-924659-21-1*, 3570) Aberdeen Group.

Removing the Barriers: Accessibility Guidelines & Specifications. Stephen R. Cotler. (Illus.). 125p. 1991. pap. 55.00 (*0-913359-59-9*) APPA VA.

Removing the Barriers: The Practice of Reconciliation. James Dallen & Joseph A. Favazza. 76p. (Orig.). 1991. pap. 5.95 (*0-929650-37-9*, REMBAR) Liturgy Tr Pubns.

***Removing the Homeless: Role Play Peacegame.** David W. Felder. 56p. 1997. pap. text ed. 8.95 (*1-57501-103-4*, 20C) Wellington Pr.

Removing the "Ites" from Your Promised Land. Dick Bernal. 82p. (Orig.). 1995. pap. 5.95 (*1-884920-03-9*) Jubilee Christian Ctr.

Removing the Roadblocks: Group Psychotherapy with Substance Abusers & Family Members. Marsha Vannicelli. LC 91-35427. (Substance Abuse Ser.). 325p. 1992. lib. bdg. 38.95 (*0-89862-174-7*) Guilford Pr.

Removing the Veil: Hidden Truths of the Past, Present & Future. Cathy E. Thompson. 100p. (Orig.). 1995. pap. 14.95 (*0-9646043-0-2*) Ecclesia Publns.

Removing Your Mask: No More Hiding from Your Truth. Marion Moss. Ed. by Rosemary Warden & Richard Hubbard. (Illus.). 320p. (Orig.). 1992. pap. 13.95 (*0-9631341-0-8*) Orion Pub.

Rempart. Jacques Audiberti. 144p. (FRE.). 1953. pap. 28.95 (*0-7859-0367-4*, F83900) Fr & Eur.

Rempart des Beguines. Francoise Mallet-Joris. 1951. 8.95 (*0-686-56312-3*); 10.95 (*0-8288-9842-1*, F110801) Fr & Eur.

Remparts Lointains: La Politique Francaise des Travaux Publics a Terre-Neuve & a Lile Royale, 1695-1758. Frederick J. Thorpe. LC 80-131438. (Cahiers d'Histoire de l'Universite d'Ottawa Ser.: No. 11). 195p. (FRE.). 1980. reprint ed. pap. 55.60 (*0-608-02174-1*, 2062843) Bks Demand.

Remuda Dust. Fred Engel. (Illus.). 80p. (Orig.). 1993. pap. 12.95 (*0-9637705-2-7*) Benchmark UT.

Remunerating General Practitioners in Western Europe. Peter P. Groerewegen et al. 131p. 1991. text ed. 55.95 (*1-85628-162-0*, Pub. by Avebury Pub UK) Ashgate Pub Co.

Remuneration of a Manager: Dilemma, Dimensions, Dissentions, Dichotomies, Directions. Anwar Divecha. 344p. 1991. text ed. 40.00 (*81-207-1192-0*, Pub. by Sterling Pubs II) Apt Bks.

Remus: A Roman Myth. T. P. Wiseman. (Illus.). 224p. (C). 1995. text ed. 54.95 (*0-521-41981-6*); pap. text ed. 18.95 (*0-521-48366-2*) Cambridge U Pr.

Remus Tales: Playscript. Stanley V. Longman. 40p. (Orig.). (J). 1991. Playscript. pap. 5.00 (*0-87602-293-X*) Anchorage.

Remy De Gourmont, Selections from All His Works. Remy De Gourmont. Ed. & Tr. by Richard Aldington from FRE. LC 77-10269. (Illus.). reprint ed. 49.50 (*0-404-16321-1*) AMS Pr.

Remy Zaugg: A Sheet of Paper. (Illus.). 98p. 1992. pap. 25.00 (*1-56466-032-X*) Archer Fields.

Remy Zaugg: Voir Mort. (Illus.). 90p. 1992. pap. 45.00 (*3-909158-36-6*, Pub. by Wiese Verlag SZ) Dist Art Pubs.

***Remy Zaugg-Herzog & De Meuron: A Dialogue.** 116p. 1997. pap. 24.95 (*3-89322-889-6*) Dist Art Pubs.

Remyelination in the Central Nervous System. Ed. by S. E. Pfeiffer & E. Barbares. (Journal: Developmental Neuroscience: Vol. 11, No. 2, 1989). (Illus.). 72p. 1989. pap. 29.00 (*3-8055-5033-2*) S Karger.

Ren & Stimpy. Nickelodeon Staff. 1996. pap. 14.00 (*0-671-00371-2*) PB.

Ren & Stimpy: Pick of the Litter. Dan Slott. (Illus.). 1993. pap. 9.95 (*0-87135-970-7*) Marvel Entmnt.

Ren & Stimpy: Seeck Leetle Monkeys. Dan Slott. (Ren & Stimpy Ser.). 96p. 1994. pap. 12.95 (*0-7851-0064-4*) Marvel Entmnt.

Ren & Stimpy: Tastes Like Chicken. 96p. 1993. 12.95 (*0-87135-982-0*) Marvel Entmnt.

Ren & Stimpy: Your Pals. Dan Slott. (Ren & Stimpy Ser.). 96p. 1994. pap. 12.95 (*0-7851-0037-7*) Marvel Entmnt.

Ren & Stimpy Show: Kids, Don't Try This at Home. Dan Slott. 1994. pap. 12.95 (*0-7851-0023-7*) Marvel Entmnt.

Rena: or The Snow Bird. Caroline L. Hentz. (Notable American Authors Ser.). 1992. reprint ed. lib. bdg. 75.00 (*0-7812-3087-X*) Rprt Serv.

Renacer En Estados Unidos: Guia Complete Para Obtener una Identidad Estadounidinse. Trent Sands. LC 94-77266. 150p. (Orig.). (C). 1994. pap. 15.00 (*1-55950-118-9*, 6144) Loompanics.

Renacimiento Romano y Veneciano: Siglo XVI. Jose Pijoan. (Summa Artis Ser.: Vol. 14). 600p. 1989. 295.00 (*84-239-5214-2*) Elliots Bks.

Renacimiento, Siglo XVI see Historia De la Literatura Espanola

Renaissance. Bellerophon Staff. (J). (gr. 1-9). 1992. pap. 3.95 (*0-88388-011-3*) Bellerophon Bks.

Renaissance. Alison Brown. (C). 1990. pap. text ed. 13.50 (*0-582-35383-1*) Addison-Wesley.

Renaissance. Burke. 1996. text ed. 10.95 (*0-333-37201-8*, Pub. by Macm UK) St Martin.

Renaissance. Alison Cole. LC 93-21264. (Eyewitness Art Ser.). (Illus.). 64p. (J). 1994. 16.95 (*1-56458-493-3*) DK Pub Inc.

Renaissance. Tracy E. Cooper. (Stylebooks Ser.). (Illus.). 96p. 1995. 12.95 (*0-7892-0023-6*) Abbeville Pr.

***Renaissance.** James A. Corrick. (World History Ser.). (Illus.). (J). (gr. 4-12). 1997. lib. bdg. 17.96 (*1-56006-311-4*) Lucent Bks.

Renaissance. Will Durant & Ariel Durant. (Story of Civilization Ser.: Vol. 5). (Illus.). 784p. 1983. 35.00 (*0-671-61600-5*) S&S Trade.

Renaissance. Iain Fenlon. 1990. text ed. 54.00 (*0-13-773409-3*) P-H.

***Renaissance.** Ruth Forman. LC 97-20611. 1998. write for info. (*0-8070-6840-3*) Beacon Pr.

***Renaissance.** Holmes. 1997. 35.00 (*0-312-15318-X*) St Martin.

Renaissance. Rosa M. Letts. (Cambridge Introduction to Art Ser.). 112p. (C). 1981. pap. text ed. 13.95 (*0-521-29957-8*) Cambridge U Pr.

Renaissance. Intro. by Adam Philips. (World's Classics Ser.). 192p. 1987. pap. 6.95 (*0-19-281737-X*) OUP.

Renaissance. Gloria Verges & Oriol Verges. (Journey Through History Ser.). (Illus.). 32p. (J). (gr. 2-4). 1988. pap. 6.95 (*0-8120-3396-5*); El Renacimiento. pap. 6.95 (*0-8120-3397-3*) Barron.

Renaissance. Tim Wood. (See Through History Ser.). (Illus.). 48p. (J). (gr. 3-7). 1993. pap. 14.99 (*0-670-85149-3*) Viking Child Bks.

Renaissance. rev. ed. Wallace K. Ferguson. (Illus.). 64p. (C). 1991. pap. text ed. 2.25 (*1-877891-01-0*) Paperbook Pr Inc.

***Renaissance.** 2nd ed. Peter Burke. LC 96-43456. (Studies in European History). 1997. text ed. 10.95 (*0-312-17230-3*) St Martin.

Renaissance. Intro. by Lawrence Evans. LC 77-12308. 239p. 1977. reprint ed. pap. 9.00 (*0-915864-35-5*) Academy Chi Pubs.

Renaissance, Vol. V. Will Durant. (Story of Civilization Ser.: Vol. 5). (Illus.). 1994. 17.98 (*1-56731-016-8*, MJF Bks) Fine Comms.

Renaissance: A Reconsideration of the Theories & Interpretations of the Age, Proceedings of the Symposium, University of Wisconsin, 1959. Renaissance Symposium Staff. Ed. by Tinsley Helton. LC 80-21869. xiii, 160p. 1980. reprint ed. text ed. 49.75 (*0-313-22797-7*, SYRE) Greenwood.

Renaissance: A Thematic Unit. Linda J. Larsen. Ed. by Sharon Coan & Ina M. Levin. (Thematic Units Ser.). (Illus.). 80p. (J). (gr. 5-8). 1994. student ed. 9.95 (*1-55734-580-5*) Tchr Create Mat.

***Renaissance: Artists & Writers.** Sarah Halliwell. LC 97-13925. (Who & When Ser.). (J). 1998. write for info. (*0-8172-4725-4*) Raintree Steck-V.

Renaissance: Basic Interpretations. 2nd ed. Ed. by Karl H. Dannenfeldt. (Problems in European Civilization Ser.). 220p. (C). 1974. pap. text ed. 16.76 (*0-669-90530-5*) HM College Div.

***Renaissance: Brunelleschi to Michelangelo.** Henry A. Millon. 1997. 75.00 (*0-8478-1997-3*) Rizzoli Intl.

Renaissance: European Painting, 1400-1600. Charles McCorquodale. 1995. 49.98 (*0-8317-1881-1*) Smithmark.

Renaissance: Studies in Art & Poetry. Ed. by Donald L. Hill. 1980. pap. 16.95 (*0-520-03664-6*) U CA Pr.

***Renaissance: The Rebirth of Liberty in the Heart of Europe.** Vaclav Klaus. LC 97-18539. 1997. 18.95 (*1-882577-47-7*); pap. text ed. 9.95 (*1-882577-48-5*) Cato Inst.

Renaissance A. D. 1300-1600. Jennifer Moreland. (Learning Packets - History Ser.). (Illus.). 60p. (J). (gr. k-8). 1992. pap. text ed. 19.95 (*0-913705-28-4*) Zephyr Pr AZ.

Renaissance Alphabet: Il Perfetto Scrittore, Parte Seconda. Giovanni F. Cresci. LC 77-121765. 80p. 1971. reprint ed. pap. 25.00 (*0-608-01937-2*, 2062592) Bks Demand.

Renaissance & Baroque. Heinrich Wolfflin. Tr. by Kathrin Simon. (Illus.). 197p. 1967. pap. 16.95 (*0-8014-9046-4*) Cornell U Pr.

Renaissance & Baroque Bronzes in the Frick Art Museum. Charles Avery. (Illus.). 144p. (Orig.). (C). 1993. pap. 39.95 (*1-881403-02-5*) U of Pittsburgh Pr.

Renaissance & Baroque Music: A Comprehensive Survey. Friedrich Blume. Tr. by M. Herter Norton. (Illus.). (Orig.). (C). 1967. pap. text ed. 9.95 (*0-393-09710-2*) Norton.

Renaissance & Baroque Paintings from the Sciarra & Fiano Collections. Richard E. Spear. LC 72-1141. (Illus.). 112p. 1973. 35.00 (*0-271-01156-4*) Pa St U Pr.

Renaissance & Baroque Poetry of Spain. Ed. by Elias L. Rivers. 351p. (C). 1988. reprint ed. pap. text ed. 14.95 (*0-88133-363-8*) Waveland Pr.

Renaissance & Golden Age Essays in Honor of D. W. McPheeters. Ed. by Bruno M. Damiani. (SPA.). 1984. 25.00 (*0-916379-10-8*) Scripta.

Renaissance & Later Sculpture: The Thyssen-Bornemisza Collection. Anthony Radcliffe et al. (Illus.). 400p. 1992. 250.00 (*0-85667-401-X*) Sothebys Pubns.

Renaissance & Mannerism in Europe: The History of Decorative Arts. Alain Gruber & Michele Bimbenet-Privat. Tr. by John Goodman from FRE. LC 94-11053. (History of Decorative Arts Ser.). (Illus.). 496p. 1996. 165.00 (*1-55859-821-9*) Abbeville Pr.

Renaissance & Mannerism in Italy. Alastair Smart. (History of Art Ser.). (Illus.). 252p. (C). 1971. pap. text ed. 17.50 (*0-15-576595-7*) HB Coll Pubs.

Renaissance & Mannerism in Northern Europe & Spain. Alastair Smart. (History of Art Ser.). (Illus.). 224p. (C). 1972. pap. text ed. 17.50 (*0-15-576596-5*) HB Coll Pubs.

Renaissance & Reformation, 2 vols. Incl. Vol. 1. Italian Renaissance. 1980. pap. 19.99 (*0-570-03818-9*, 12-2759); Vol. 2. Reformation. Lewis W. Spitz. 1980. pap. 19.99 (*0-570-03819-7*, 12-2760); 1980. Set pap. 34.99 (*0-570-03839-1*, 12-2802) Concordia.

Renaissance & Reformation. Trevor Cairns. (Cambridge Introduction to World History Topic Bks.: Bk. 6). (Illus.). 96p. (YA). (gr. 7 up). 1987. pap. text ed. 17.95 (*0-521-33685-6*) Cambridge U Pr.

Renaissance & Reformation. William R. Estep. 320p. (Orig.). 1986. pap. text ed. 23.00 (*0-8028-0050-5*) Eerdmans.

Renaissance & Reformation & the Rise of Science. Harold P. Nebelsick. 320p. 1992. pap. text ed. 33.95 (*0-567-09604-1*, Pub. by T & T Clark UK) Bks Intl VA.

Renaissance & Reformation Times. Dorothy Mills. LC 83-45667. reprint ed. 55.00 (*0-404-19817-1*) AMS Pr.

Renaissance & Renascences in Western Art. Erwin Panofsky. (Icon Editions Ser.). (Illus.). 380p. 1972. pap. text ed. 21.00 (*0-06-430026-9*, IN-26, Icon Edns) HarpC.

Renaissance & Renewal in the Twelfth Century. Ed. by Robert L. Benson & Giles Constable. (Medieval Academy Reprints for Teaching Ser.: No. 26). 848p. 1991. pap. 27.50 (*0-8020-6850-2*) U of Toronto Pr.

Renaissance & Revolt: Essays in the Intellectual & Social History of Early France. John H. Salmon. (Cambridge Studies in Early Modern History). 380p. 1987. text ed. 89.95 (*0-521-32769-5*) Cambridge U Pr.

Renaissance & Revolution: Humanists, Scholars, Craftsmen, & Natural Philosophers in Early Modern Europe. Ed. by Frank A. James. LC 93-6624. (Illus.). 350p. (C). 1994. text ed. 59.95 (*0-521-43427-0*) Cambridge U Pr.

Renaissance & the Reformation. Henry S. Lucas. LC 83-45665. reprint ed. 67.50 (*0-404-19815-5*) AMS Pr.

Renaissance Antichrist: Luca Signorelli's Orvieto Frescoes. Jonathan B. Riess. 248p. (C). 1995. text ed. 62.50 (*0-691-04086-9*) Princeton U Pr.

Renaissance Architecture. Bates Lowry. LC 61-13691. (Great Ages of World Architecture Ser.). (Illus.). 127p. 1965. pap. 9.95 (*0-8076-0335-X*) Braziller.

Renaissance Architecture. Peter Murray. LC 82-62749. (History of World Architecture Ser.). (Illus.). 220p. 1990. pap. 29.95 (*0-8478-0474-7*) Rizzoli Intl.

Renaissance Architecture: Patrons, Critics, & Luxury. David Thomson. LC 93-16088. 1993. text ed. 24.95 (*0-7190-3963-0*, Pub. by Manchester Univ Pr UK) St Martin.

Renaissance Architecture in Venice. Ralph Lieberman. LC 82-22606. (Illus.). 144p. 1982. 60.00 (*0-89659-310-X*) Abbeville Pr.

Renaissance Architecture of Central & Northern Spain. A. Whittlesey. 1976. lib. bdg. 75.00 (*0-8490-2514-1*) Gordon Pr.

Renaissance Argument: Valla & Agricola in the Traditions of Rhetoric & Dialectic. Peter Mack. LC 93-26623. (Brill's Studies in Intellectual History: Vol. 43). xi, 395p. 1993. 121.50 (*90-04-09879-8*) E J Brill.

Renaissance Art: A Topical Dictionary. Irene Earls. LC 87-250. 345p. 1987. text ed. 89.50 (*0-313-24658-0*, ERT/, Greenwood Pr) Greenwood.

Renaissance Artist at Work: From Pisano to Titian. Bruce Cole. LC 82-48102. (Icon Editions Ser.). (Illus.). 208p. 1984. pap. text ed. 16.00 (*0-06-430129-X*, IN-129, Icon Edns) HarpC.

Renaissance Artists: De Picture Veterum Libri Tres. Franciscus Junius. (Printed Sources of Western Art Ser.). 332p. (LAT.). 1981. reprint ed. pap. 60.00 (*0-915346-68-0*) A Wofsy Fine Arts.

Renaissance Bible: Scholarship, Sacrifice, & Subjectivity. Debora K. Shuger. LC 93-5892. (New Historicism Ser.: Vol. 29). 1993. 40.00 (*0-520-08480-2*) U CA Pr.

***Renaissance Bodies.** Lucy Gent. 1997. pap. text ed. 29.00 (*0-948462-08-6*, Pub. by Reaktion Bks UK) Consort Bk Sales.

Renaissance Bodies: The Human Figure in English Culture c. 1540-1660. Lucy Gent & Nigel Llewellyn. (Illus.). 200p. (Orig.). 1990. pap. 29.00 (*0-295-97056-1*) U of Wash Pr.

Renaissance Bologna: A Study in Architectural Form & Content. Naomi Miller. (University of Kansas Humanistic Studies). 218p. (C). 1989. text ed. 39.95 (*0-8204-0885-9*) P Lang Pubng.

***Renaissance Cardinals & Their Worldly Problems.** D. S. Chambers. LC 96-33155. (Collected Studies: No. CS559). 384p. 1997. 98.95 (*0-86078-614-5*, Pub. by Ashgate UK) Ashgate Pub Co.

Renaissance Cardinal's Ideal Palace. Kathleen Weil-Garris & John D'Amico. 105p. 1980. 22.00 (*0-271-00458-4*) Am Acad Rome.

***Renaissance Characters.** Eugenio Garin. 1997. pap. text ed. 16.95 (*0-226-28356-9*) U Ch Pr.

Renaissance City. Giulio Argan. LC 70-90409. (Planning & Cities Ser.). (Illus.). 128p. 1969. pap. 9.95 (*0-8076-0521-2*) Braziller.

Renaissance Comic Tales of Love, Treachery, & Revenge. Ed. by Robert L. Martone. Tr. by Valerie Martone & Robert L. Martone from ITA. LC 94-16287. (Illus.). 248p. (Orig.). 1994. pap. 15.00 (*0-934977-31-3*) Italica Pr.

Renaissance Concepts of the Commonplaces. Joan M. Lechner. LC 74-6153. 268p. 1974. reprint ed. text ed. 87.50 (*0-8371-7491-0*, LERC, Greenwood Pr) Greenwood.

Renaissance Court: Milan under Galeazzo Maria Sforza. Gregory Lubkin. LC 93-17529. 1994. 47.00 (*0-520-08146-3*) U CA Pr.

Renaissance Cross Stitch Samplers. Angela Wainwright. (Illus.). 96p. (Orig.). 1996. pap. 14.95 (*0-304-34694-2*, Pub. by Cassell UK) Sterling.

Renaissance Culture in Context: Theory & Practice. Ed. by Jean R. Brink & William F. Gentrup. LC 93-7203. 240p. 1993. 69.95 (*0-85967-950-0*, Pub. by Scolar Pr UK) Ashgate Pub Co.

Renaissance Culture in Poland: The Rise of Humanism, 1470-1543. Harold B. Segel. LC 89-30788. 304p. 1989. 39.95 (*0-8014-2286-8*) Cornell U Pr.

Renaissance Curiosa: Dee..., Cardano..., Trithemius..., Dalgarno. Wayne Shumaker. LC 81-14177. (Medieval & Renaissance Texts & Studies: Vol. 8). (Illus.). 216p. 1982. 24.00 (*0-86698-014-8*, MR8) MRTS.

Renaissance Debut. Contrib. by Maurice C. Whitney. 1974. 4.95 (*0-913334-19-7*, CM1023) Consort Music.

Renaissance des Eros Uranios. Benedict Friedlaender. LC 75-12316. (Homosexuality: Lesbians & Gay Men in Society, History & Literature Ser.). (GER.). 1975. reprint ed. 33.95 (*0-405-07362-3*) Ayer.

Renaissance des Hausarztes. Erdmann Strum. (Patient Allgemeinmedizin Ser.: Band 1). (Illus.). 290p. 1983. 29.00 (*3-540-12374-1*) Spr-Verlag.

Renaissance Des Islams. Adam Mez. iv, 492p. 1968. reprint ed. write for info. (*0-318-71533-3*) G Olms Pubs.

Renaissance Dialectic & Renaissance Piety: Benet of Canfield's "Rule of Perfection" Tr. by Kent Emery, Jr. LC 87-21960. (Medieval & Renaissance Texts & Studies: Vol. 50). (Illus.). 328p. 1987. 30.00 (*0-86698-034-2*, MR50) MRTS.

Renaissance Dialogue: Literary Dialogue in Its Social & Political Contexts, Castiglione to Galileo. Virginia Cox. (Studies in Renaissance Literature & Culture: No. 2). 266p. (C). 1992. text ed. 65.00 (*0-521-40538-6*) Cambridge U Pr.

Renaissance Diplomacy. Garrett Mattingly. 284p. 1988. reprint ed. pap. 8.95 (*0-486-25570-0*) Dover.

Renaissance Discourses of Desire. Ed. by Claude J. Summers & Ted-Larry Pebworth. (Illus.). 296p. (C). 1993. text ed. 44.95 (*0-8262-0885-1*) U of Mo Pr.

***Renaissance Dog.** Marlo. 1997. write for info. (*0-8092-3170-0*) Contemp Bks.

Renaissance Drama. Ed. by Frances E. Dolan. 260p. 1996. text ed. 59.95 (*0-8101-0688-4*) Northwestern U Pr.

Renaissance Drama: Disorder & Drama. Ed. by Mary B. Rose. (New Ser.: No. XXI). 260p. 1991. 59.95 (*0-8101-0684-1*) Northwestern U Pr.

Renaissance Drama: Dramatic Intertextuality & Theatrical Conditions. Ed. by Mary B. Rose. (New Ser.: No. XXII). (Illus.). 275p. 1993. 59.95 (*0-8101-0685-X*) Northwestern U Pr.

Renaissance Drama: New Series, No. XXIV. Ed. by Mary B. Rose. 270p. 1995. 59.95 (*0-8101-1195-0*) Northwestern U Pr.

Renaissance Drama & the English Church Year. Rudolph C. Hassel. LC 78-24233. (Illus.). 227p. 1979. reprint ed. pap. 64.70 (*0-7837-8884-3*, 2049595) Bks Demand.

Renaissance Drama by Women: Texts & Documents. Ed. by S. P. Cerasano & Marion Wynne-Davies. LC 95-14783. 288p. (gr. 13). 1996. pap. 16.95 (*0-415-09807-6*) Routledge.

Renaissance Drama by Women: Texts & Documents. Ed. by S. P. Cerasano & Marion Wynne-Davies. LC 95-14783. 288p. (C). (gr. 13). 1996. text ed. 59.95 (*0-415-09806-8*) Routledge.

Renaissance Drama in England & Spain: Topical Allusion & History Plays. John Loftis. (Illus.). 296p. 1987. text ed. 45.00 (*0-691-06706-6*) Princeton U Pr.

Renaissance Drama New Series, No. XX: Essays on Renaissance Dramatic Traditions. Ed. by Mary B. Rose. 238p. 1990. 59.95 (*0-8101-0681-7*) Northwestern U Pr.

Renaissance Drama New Series XIX: Essays on Texts of Renaissance Plays. Ed. by Mary B. Rose. 270p. 1989. 49.95 (*0-8101-0680-9*) Northwestern U Pr.

Renaissance Drama of Knowledge. Hilary Gatti. 256p. 1989. 66.50 (*0-415-03207-5*, A3254) Routledge.

Renaissance Drama, Vol. XXIII: Renaissance Drama in an Age of Colonization. Ed. by Mary B. Rose. 210p. 1994. 59.95 (*0-8101-0686-8*) Northwestern U Pr.

Renaissance Dulcimer. Carrie Crompton. 1993. 5.95 (*0-87166-964-1*, 93841) Mel Bay.

***Renaissance Earth.** William E. Key-Nee. 250p. 1997. pap. 20.00 (*0-9657034-1-X*, 2) Mr Future.

Renaissance Eloquence: Studies in the Theory & Practice of Renaissance Rhetoric. Ed. by James J. Murphy. LC 81-13128. 472p. (C). 1983. 19.95 (*0-520-04543-2*, Hermagoras) L Erlbaum Assocs.

Renaissance Englishwoman in Print: Counterbalancing the Canon. Ed. by Anne M. Haselkorn & Betty S. Travitsky. LC 89-32870. (Illus.). 376p. (C). 1990. lib. bdg. 45.00 (*0-87023-690-3*) U of Mass Pr.

***Renaissance Engravers.** Parkstone Press Limited Staff. (Temporis Ser.). 1996. 55.00 (*1-85995-278-X*) Parkstone Pr.

Renaissance Era see Source Readings in Music History

Renaissance Essays. Denys Hay. 435p. 1988. text ed. 60.00 (*0-907628-96-6*) Hambledon Press.

Renaissance Essays. Hugh R. Trevor-Roper. LC 85-2775. viii, 320p. 1985. 27.00 (*0-226-81225-1*) U Ch Pr.

Renaissance Essays. Hugh R. Trevor-Roper. LC 85-2775. viii, 320p. 1989. pap. text ed. 19.95 (*0-226-81227-8*) U Ch Pr.

Renaissance Essays. Ed. by Paul O. Kristeller & Philip P. Wiener. (Library of the History of Ideas: Vol. 9). (Illus.). 383p. (C). 1993. reprint ed. 55.00 (*1-878822-18-7*); reprint ed. pap. 19.95 (*1-878822-19-5*) Univ Rochester Pr.

Renaissance Essays for Kitty Scoular Datta. Ed. by Sukanta Chaudhuri. (Illus.). 296p. 1995. 27.00 (*0-19-563702-X*) OUP.

Renaissance Essays II. Ed. by William J. Connell. (Library of the History of Ideas: Vol. 10). 383p. (C). 1993. 63.00 (*1-878822-23-3*); pap. 19.95 (*1-878822-28-4*) Boydell & Brewer.

Renaissance Europe: Age of Recovery & Reconciliation. 2nd ed. Delamar Jensen. 467p. (C). 1992. pap. text ed. 29.16 (*0-669-20007-7*) HM College Div.

Renaissance Europe: The Individual & Society, 1480-1520. J. R. Hale. LC 77-73495. 1971. pap. 15.95 (*0-520-03471-6*) U CA Pr.

Renaissance Feminism: Literary Texts & Political Models. Constance Jordan. LC 89-46172. 384p. 1990. 49.95 (*0-8014-2163-2*); pap. 17.95 (*0-8014-9732-9*) Cornell U Pr.

An Asterisk (*) at the beginning of an entry indicates that the title is appearing in BIP for the first time.

Renaissance Fictions of Anatomy. Devon L. Hodges. LC 84-16343. (Illus.). 160p. 1985. lib. bdg. 22.50 (0-87023-470-6) U of Mass Pr.

Renaissance (Fifteen Fifty to Sixteen Sixty) Ed. by Gordon Campbell. LC 89-70174. (St. Martin's Anthologies of English Literature Ser.: Vol. No. 2). 443p. 1990. text ed. 20.00 (0-312-04478-X) St Martin.

Renaissance Florence. Gene A. Brucker. LC 82-40097. (Illus.). 320p. 1983. 50.00 (0-520-04919-5); pap. 14.95 (0-520-04695-1) U CA Pr.

***Renaissance Florence.** Turner. 1997. pap. text ed. write for info. (0-13-618448-0) P-H.

Renaissance Florence. Gene A. Brucker. LC 74-10921. 320p. 1975. reprint ed. lib. bdg. 24.50 (0-88275-184-0) Krieger.

***Renaissance Florence: The Invention of a New Art.** A. Richard Turner. LC 96-3330. (The Perspectives Ser.). (Illus.). 176p. 1997. 18.95 (0-8109-2736-5) Abrams.

Renaissance Garden in Britain. John Anthony. 1989. pap. 35.00 (0-7478-0130-4, Pub. by Shire UK) St Mut.

Renaissance Genres. Ed. by Barbara K. Lewalski. (English Studies: No. 14). 512p. 1986. 27.95 (0-674-76040-9); pap. 11.95 (0-674-76041-7) HUP.

Renaissance Guitar. Frederick M. Noad. (Illus.). 104p. 1974. pap. 16.95 (0-8256-9950-9, AM35882) Music Sales.

***Renaissance Hamlet: Issues & Responses in 1600.** Roland M. Frye. LC 83-42555. 415p. 1984. reprint ed. pap. 118. 30 (0-608-03346-4, 2064058) Bks Demand.

Renaissance Historicism: Selections from "English Literary Renaissance" Ed. by Arthur F. Kinney & Dan S. Collins. LC 87-6052. 432p. (Orig.). (C). 1988. pap. text ed. 19.95 (0-87023-598-2) U of Mass Pr.

Renaissance Humanism. Donald R. Kelley. (Twayne's Studies in Intellectual & Cultural History: No. 2). 176p. 1991. 14.95 (0-8057-8606-6, Twayne) Scribnrs Ref.

Renaissance Humanism: Studies in Philosophy & Poetics. Ernesto Grassi. (Medieval & Renaissance Texts & Studies: Vol. 51). 172p. 1988. 24.00 (0-86698-035-0, MR51) MRTS.

***Renaissance Humanism at the Court of Clement VII: Francesco Berni's Dialogue Against Poets in Context.** Ed. by Anne Reynolds & Raymond Waddington. LC 96-41561. (Garland Studies in the Renaissance: Vol. 7). (Illus.). 388p. 1997. text ed. 87.00 (0-8153-2020-5) Garland.

Renaissance Humanism in Papal Rome: Humanists & Churchmen on the Eve of the Reformation. John D'Amico. (Studies in Historical & Political Science). 352p. 1991. reprint ed. pap. text ed. 18.95 (0-8018-4224-7) Johns Hopkins.

Renaissance Humanism, Vols. 1-3: Foundations, Forms & Legacy, 3 vols., Vol. 2. Ed. by Albert Rabil, Jr. LC 87-13928. (Illus.). 430p. 1988. pap. 26.95 (0-8122-1373-4) U of Pa Pr.

Renaissance Humanism, Vols. 1-3: Foundations, Forms & Legacy, 3 vols., Vol. 3. Ed. by Albert Rabil, Jr. LC 87-13928. (Illus.). 508p. 1988. pap. 36.95 (0-8122-1374-2) U of Pa Pr.

Renaissance Idea of Wisdom. Eugene F. Rice, Jr. LC 72-12117. (Illus.). 220p. 1973. reprint ed. text ed. 35.00 (0-8371-6712-4, RIRI, Greenwood Pr) Greenwood.

Renaissance Imagination: Essays & Lectures. D. J. Gordon. Ed. by Stephen Orgel. LC 74-81432. 1976. pap. 13.95 (0-520-04092-9) U CA Pr.

Renaissance in Business. Alan D. Hammond. 15p. (Orig.). 1985. pap. 2.00 (0-935427-02-3) Foundation Hse.

Renaissance in Cyclooctatetraene Chemistry. Leo A. Paquette. Ed. by Barton et al. 1976. pap. 15.50 (0-08-020479-1, Pergamon Pr) Elsevier.

Renaissance in England: Non-Dramatic Prose & Verse of the Sixteenth Century. Ed. by Hyder Rollins & Herschel Baker. 1014p. (C). 1992. reprint ed. pap. text ed. 38.95 (0-88133-673-4) Waveland Pr.

Renaissance in France: Drawings from the Ecole des Beaux-Arts, Paris. Ed. by Emmanuelle Brugerolles & David Guillet. (Illus.). 346p. (C). 1995. pap. 45.00 (0-295-97459-1) U of Wash Pr.

Renaissance in France: Drawings from the Ecole des Beaux-Arts, Paris. Emmanuelle Brugerolles & David Guillet. Tr. by Judith Schub from FRE. (Illus.). 346p. (Orig.). 1995. pap. 45.00 (0-916724-86-7) Harvard Art Mus.

Renaissance in Historical Thought: Five Centuries of Interpretation. Wallace K. Ferguson. LC 77-74812. reprint ed. 45.00 (0-404-14887-5) AMS Pr.

Renaissance in Italy, 7 vols., Set. John A. Symonds. (Anglistica & Americana Ser.: Vol. 98). lxxxv, 3774p. 1972. reprint ed. 637.00 (3-487-04145-6) G Olms Pubs.

Renaissance in National Context. Ed. by Roy Porter & Mikulas Teich. 236p. (C). 1991. text ed. 59.95 (0-521-36181-8); pap. text ed. 19.95 (0-521-36970-3) Cambridge U Pr.

Renaissance in Rome. Charles L. Stinger. LC 83-49337. (Illus.). 464p. 1985. 39.95 (0-253-35002-6) Ind U Pr.

Renaissance in Scotland: Studies in Literature, Religion, History & Culture Offered to John Durkan. Ed. by A. A. MacDonald et al. LC 94-26032. (Studies in Intellectual History: 54). 1994. 108.50 (90-04-10097-0) E J Brill.

Renaissance in the North. W. Gore Allen. LC 79-111810. (Essay Index Reprint Ser.). 1977. 20.95 (0-8369-1590-9) Ayer.

Renaissance into Baroque: Italian Master Drawings by the Zuccari, 1550-1600. E. J. Mundy. (Illus.). 240p. (C). 1990. 95.00 (0-685-74173-7) Cambridge U Pr.

Renaissance Landscapes: English Lyrics in a European Tradition. H. M. Richmond. 1973. pap. text ed. 33.85 (90-279-2470-8) Mouton.

Renaissance Latin Drama in England, 19 vols., Set. Ed. by Marvin Spevack et al. (Second Ser.). 1987. pap. 1,471.60 (3-487-07852-X) G Olms Pubs.

Renaissance Latin Drama in England: Abraham Cowley, Naufragium Joculare; William Johnson, Valetudinarium. Ed. by Marvin Spevack et al. (Second Series: Plays Associated with the University of Cambridge: Vol. 18). 1991. reprint ed. 89.70 (3-487-07870-8) G Olms Pubs.

Renaissance Latin Drama in England: Abraham Fraunce or H. Hickman, Hymenaeus; Abraham Fraunce, Victoria; Laelia. Ed. by Marvin Spevack et al. (Second Series: Plays Associated with the University of Cambridge: Vol. 13). 1991. reprint ed. 63.70 (3-487-07865-1) G Olms Pubs.

Renaissance Latin Drama in England: Cancer (Printed 1648); Edmund Stubbe, Fraus Honesta (Played 1618-19) Ed. by Marvin Spevack et al. (Second Series: Plays Associated with the University of Cambridge: Vol. 2). 1987. reprint ed. 76.70 (3-487-07854-6) G Olms Pubs.

Renaissance Latin Drama in England: Christopher Wren, Sr., Physiponomachia (Acted 1609-1611); Philip Parsons, Atalanta (Acted 1612); Thomas Atkinson, Homo (Acted 1615-1621) Ed. by Marvin Spevack et al. (First Series: Plays Associated with Oxford University: Vol. 4). 166p. 1982. reprint ed. 54.60 (3-487-07204-1) G Olms Pubs.

Renaissance Latin Drama in England: Edward Forsett, Pedantius. Ed. by Marvin Spevack et al. (Second Series: Plays Associated with the University of Cambridge: Vol. 9). 213p. 1989. reprint ed. 63.70 (3-487-07861-9) G Olms Pubs.

Renaissance Latin Drama in England: George Ruggle, Ignoramus (Played 1614) Ed. by Marvin Spevack et al. (Second Series: Plays Associated with the University of Cambridge: Vol. 1). 192p. 1987. reprint ed. 63.70 (3-487-07853-8) G Olms Pubs.

Renaissance Latin Drama in England: Henry Bellamy, Iphis (Acted 1621-1633); Joseph Crowther, Cephalus et Procris (Acted 1626-1628) Ed. by Marvin Spevack et al. (First Series: Plays Associated with Oxford University: Vol. 10). 24186p. 1982. reprint ed. 54.60 (3-487-07210-6) G Olms Pubs.

Renaissance Latin Drama in England: John Blencowe, Mercurius Sive Literarum Lucta (Acted 1629-1638); George Wilde, Eumorphus Sive Cupido Adultus (Acted 1634-5) Ed. by Marvin Spevack et al. (First Series: Plays Associated with Oxford University: Vol. 3). 123p. 1982. reprint ed. 54.60 (3-487-07203-3) G Olms Pubs.

Renaissance Latin Drama in England: John Christopherson, Jephthes; William Goldingham, Herodes. Ed. by Marvin Spevack et al. (Second Series: Plays Associated with the University of Cambridge: Vol. 7). iv, 96p. 1988. reprint ed. 48.10 (3-487-07859-7) G Olms Pubs.

Renaissance Latin Drama in England: John Foxe, Titus et Gesippus (Acted 1544-1545); Samuel Bernard, Andronicus Commenus (Alexis Imperator) (Acted 1618) Ed. by Marvin Spevack et al. (First Series: Plays Associated with Oxford University: Vol. 6). 170p. reprint ed. 54.60 (3-487-07206-8) G Olms Pubs.

Renaissance Latin Drama in England: Leonard Hutton, Bellum Grammaticale Sive Nominum Verborumque Discordia Civilis (Printed 1635); Thomas Snelling, Thibaldus Sive Vindictae Ingenium (Printed 1640) Ed. by Marvin Spevack et al. (First Series: Plays Associated with Oxford University: Vol. 12). 80p. 1983. reprint ed. 54.60 (3-487-07212-2) G Olms Pubs.

Renaissance Latin Drama in England: Matthew Gwinne, Nero (Printed 1603) Ed. by Marvin Spevack et al. (First Series: Plays Associated with Oxford University: Vol. 13). 166p. 1983. reprint ed. 54.60 (3-487-07213-0) G Olms Pubs.

Renaissance Latin Drama in England: Matthew Gwinne, Vertumnus Sive Annus Recurrens (Printed 1607); Matthew Gwinne, Tres Sibyllae (Printed 1607) Ed. by Marvin Spevack et al. (First Series: Plays Associated with Oxford University: Vol. 5). 74p. 1983. reprint ed. 54.60 (3-487-07205-X) G Olms Pubs.

Renaissance Latin Drama in England: Meleager; Ulysses Redux; Panniculus Hippolyto Assutus. William Gager. Ed. by Marvin Spevack et al. (First Series: Plays Associated with Oxford University: Vol. 2). 187p. 1982. reprint ed. 54.60 (3-487-07202-5) G Olms Pubs.

Renaissance Latin Drama in England: Mercurius Rusticans (Written 1605-1618); Antonius Bassanius Caracalla (Acted 1617-1619) Ed. by Marvin Spevack et al. (First Series: Plays Associated with Oxford University: Vol. 7). 106p. 1983. reprint ed. 54.60 (3-487-07207-6) G Olms Pubs.

Renaissance Latin Drama in England: Microcosmus; Stoicus Vapulans; Robert Ward, Fucus Sive Histriomastix. Ed. by Marvin Spevack et al. (Second Series: Plays Associated with the University of Cambridge: Vol. 11). 194p. 1991. reprint ed. 89.70 (3-487-07863-5) G Olms Pubs.

Renaissance Latin Drama in England: Nicholas Grimald, Christus Redivivus (1543); Nicholas Grimald, Archipropheta (Printed 1548) Ed. by Marvin Spevack et al. (First Series: Plays Associated with Oxford University: Vol. 9). 163p. 1983. reprint ed. 54.60 (3-487-07209-2) G Olms Pubs.

Renaissance Latin Drama in England: Oedipus (Acted 1577-92); Dido (Acted 1583) William Gager. Ed. by Marvin Spevack et al. (First Series: Plays Associated with Oxford University: Vol. 1). 62p. 1982. reprint ed. 54.60 (3-487-07201-7) G Olms Pubs.

Renaissance Latin Drama in England: Pastor Fidus; Parthenia; Clytophon. Ed. by Marvin Spevack et al. (Second Series: Plays Associated with the University of Cambridge: Vol. 10). 166p. 1990. reprint ed. 96.20 (3-487-07862-7) G Olms Pubs.

Renaissance Latin Drama in England: Peter Hausted, Senile Odium; Senilis Amor.; Alphonsus. Ed. by Marvin Spevack et al. (Second Series: Plays Associated with the University of Cambridge: Vol. 17). 1991. reprint ed. 89.70 (3-487-07869-4) G Olms Pubs.

Renaissance Latin Drama in England: Risus Anglicanus; John Hacket, Loiola. Ed. by Marvin Spevack et al. (Second Series: Plays Associated with the University of Cambridge: Vol. 6). iv, 234p. 1988. reprint ed. 63.70 (3-487-07858-9) G Olms Pubs.

Renaissance Latin Drama in England: Robert Burton, Philosophaster (1606) Ed. by Marvin Spevack et al. (First Series: Plays Associated with Oxford University: Vol. 8). 90p. 1983. reprint ed. 54.60 (3-487-07208-4) G Olms Pubs.

Renaissance Latin Drama in England: Roger Morrell, Hispanus; Nathaniel Wibourne, Machiavellus; Silvanus. Ed. by Marvin Spevack et al. (Second Series: Plays Associated with the University of Cambridge: Vol. 19). 1991. reprint ed. 48.10 (3-487-07871-6) G Olms Pubs.

Renaissance Latin Drama in England: Samuel Brooke, Adelphe; Samuel Brooke, Scyros; Samuel Brooke, Melanthe. Ed. by Marvin Spevack et al. (Second Series: Plays Associated with the University of Cambridge: Vol. 15). 1991. reprint ed. 89.70 (3-487-07867-8) G Olms Pubs.

Renaissance Latin Drama in England: The Christmas Prince (Acted 1607-1608) Sansbury et al. Ed. by Marvin Spevack et al. (First Series: Plays Associated with Oxford University: Vol. 11). 260p. 1983. reprint ed. 54.60 (3-487-07211-4) G Olms Pubs.

Renaissance Latin Drama in England: Thomas Legge, Richardus Tertius. Ed. by Marvin Spevack et al. (Second Series: Plays Associated with the University of Cambridge: Vol. 8). 1989. reprint ed. 128.70 (3-487-07860-0) G Olms Pubs.

Renaissance Latin Drama in England: Thomas Vincent, Paria. Ed. by Marvin Spevack et al. (Second Series: Plays Associated with the University of Cambridge: Vol. 16). iv, 214p. 1991. reprint ed. 63.70 (3-487-07868-6) G Olms Pubs.

Renaissance Latin Drama in England: Thomas Watson, Absalom; John Foxe, Christus Triumphans. Ed. by Marvin Spevack et al. (Second Series: Plays Associated with the University of Cambridge: Vol. 5). iv, 268p. 1988. reprint ed. 63.70 (3-487-07857-0) G Olms Pubs.

Renaissance Latin Drama in England: Thomas Watson, Antigone; William Alabaster, Roxana; Peter Mease, Adrastus Parentans Sive Vindicta. Ed. by Marvin Spevack et al. (Second Series: Plays Associated with the University of Cambridge: Vol. 4). 1987. reprint ed. 63.70 (3-487-07856-2) G Olms Pubs.

Renaissance Latin Drama in England: Walter Hawkesworth, Leander; Walter Hawkesworth, Labyrinthus. Ed. by Marvin Spevack et al. (Second Series: Plays Associated with the University of Cambridge: Vol. 3). 1987. reprint ed. 89.70 (3-487-07855-4) G Olms Pubs.

Renaissance Latin Drama in England: Zelotypus; John Chappell, Susenbrotus, or Fortunia; Aquila Cruso, Euribates Pseudomagus; William Mewe, Pseudomagia. Ed. by Marvin Spevack et al. (Second Series: Plays Associated with the University of Cambridge: Vol. 14). 182p. 1991. reprint ed. 89.70 (3-487-07866-X) G Olms Pubs.

Renaissance Latin Verse: An Anthology. Ed. by Alessandro Perosa & John Sparrow. LC 78-10969. 590p. reprint ed. pap. 168.20 (0-7837-0301-5, 2040623) Bks Demand.

Renaissance Literary Theory & Practice. C. S. Baldwin. 1959. 14.50 (0-8446-1042-9) Peter Smith.

Renaissance Magic. Ed. by Brian P. Levack. LC 92-22912. (Articles on Witchcraft, Magic, & Demonology Ser.: Vol. 11). 336p. 1992. text ed. 62.00 (0-8153-1034-X) Garland.

Renaissance Magic & the Return of the Golden Age: The Occult Tradition & Marlowe, Jonson & Shakespeare. John S. Mebane. LC 88-22068. (Illus.). xviii, 317p. 1989. reprint ed. pap. text ed. 15.00 (0-8032-8179-X, Bison Books) U of Nebr Pr.

***Renaissance Man.** Diane Bernard. 304p. 1997. mass mkt. 4.99 (0-8217-5628-1, Zebra Kensgtn) Kensgtn Pub Corp.

***Renaissance Man & His Child.** Haas. Date not set. text ed. write for info. (0-312-17563-9) St Martin.

Renaissance Man from Louisiana: A Biography of Arna Wendell Bontemps. Kirkland C. Jones. LC 91-47062. (Contributions in Afro-American & African Studies: No. 151). 232p. 1992. text ed. 47.95 (0-313-28013-4, JAR, Greenwood Pr) Greenwood.

Renaissance Man, Medieval or Modern? 3rd ed. Ed. by Brian Tierney et al. (Historical Pamphlets Ser.). 1976. pap. text ed. write for info. (0-07-553612-9) McGraw.

Renaissance Master Bronzes from the Kunsthistorisches Museum, Vienna. Manfred Leithe-Jasper. (Illus.). 304p. 1986. lib. bdg. 35.00 (0-935748-69-5) Scala Books.

Renaissance Mathematics. Flegg Chuquet. 1984. lib. bdg. 146.00 (90-277-1872-5) Kluwer Ac.

***Renaissance Moon.** Francis M. Nevins. Date not set. 22. 95 (0-312-15200-0) St Martin.

***Renaissance Music.** Allan W. Atlas. LC 97-19816. (Norton Introduction to Music History Ser.). 1998. 35. 95 (0-393-97169-4) Norton.

Renaissance Music for the Harp. Deborah Friou. (Illus.). 32p. (Orig.). 1985. pap. 9.95 (0-9602990-9-2) Woods Mus Bks.

Renaissance New Testament, Vol. 15. Randolph O. Yeager. LC 79-28652. 672p. (C). 1985. 25.00 (0-88289-259-2) Pelican.

Renaissance New Testament, Vol. 16. Randolph O. Yeager. LC 79-28652. 672p. (C). 1985. 25.00 (0-88289-759-4) Pelican.

Renaissance New Testament, Vol. 17. Randolph O. Yeager. LC 79-28652. 672p. (C). 1985. 25.00 (0-88289-459-5) Pelican.

Renaissance Notion of Woman: A Study in the Fortunes of Scholasticism & Medical Science in European Intellectual Life. Ian Maclean. LC 79-52837. (Cambridge Monographs in the History of Medicine). 119p. 1983. pap. text ed. 15.95 (0-521-27436-2) Cambridge U Pr.

***Renaissance of American Steel: Lessons for Managers in Competitive Industries.** Roger S. Ahlbrandt et al. (Illus.). 192p. 1996. 25.00 (0-19-510828-0) OUP.

Renaissance of Canadian History: A Biography of A. L. Burt. Lewis H. Thomas. LC 74-79988. 205p. reprint ed. 58.50 (0-8357-9770-8, 2019425) Bks Demand.

Renaissance of Carbon & Carbro - The Pictorial Photographer's Handbook. Tracy Diers. (Illus.). 1980. write for info. (0-9617656-1-5) Tracy Diers.

Renaissance of General Relativity: A Survey to Celebrate the 65th Birthday of Dennis Sciama. Ed. by George Ellis et al. (Illus.). 344p. (C). 1994. text ed. 57.95 (0-521-43377-0) Cambridge U Pr.

Renaissance of Interstitial Brachytherapy: Proceedings of the Annual San Francisco Cancer Symposium, 12th, March 4-5, 1977. Annual San Francisco Cancer Symposium Staff. Ed. by J. M. Vaeth. (Frontiers of Radiation Therapy & Oncology Ser.: Vol. 12). (Illus.). 1977. 94.50 (3-8055-2706-3) S Karger.

Renaissance of Islam. S. K. Bukhsh. 1981. 29.00 (0-933511-39-6) Kazi Pubns.

Renaissance of Islam. Adam Mez. Tr. by Salahuddin K Bukhsl & D. S. Margoliovth. LC 70-180361. reprint ed. 45.00 (0-404-56293-0) AMS Pr.

Renaissance of Italian Cooking. Lorenza De'Medici. 1989. 30.00 (0-449-90364-8) Fawcett.

Renaissance of Italian Gardens. Lorenza De'Medici. 1990. 35.00 (0-449-90441-5) Fawcett.

Renaissance of Jewish Culture in Weimar Germany. Michael Brenner. LC 95-30449. 306p. 1996. 30.00 (0-300-06262-1) Yale U Pr.

Renaissance of Mark Twain's House. Wilson H. Faude. 1977. lib. bdg. 28.00 (0-89244-074-0, Queens House) Amereon Ltd.

Renaissance of Medicine in Italy. Arturo Castiglioni. LC 79-114967. 1979. 17.95 (0-405-10587-8) Ayer.

Renaissance of Modern Hebrew & Modern Standard Arabic: Parallels & Differences in the Revival of Two Semitic Languages. Joshua Blau. (Publications in Near Eastern Studies: Vol. 18). 1982. pap. 45.00 (0-520-09548-0) U CA Pr.

Renaissance of Rock: British Invasion - The Sixties. Stuart A. Kallen. Ed. by Bob Italia. LC 89-84917. (History of Rock n' Roll Ser.). (Illus.). 48p. (J). (gr. 4). 1989. lib. bdg. 12.94 (0-939179-75-X) Abdo & Dghtrs.

Renaissance of Rock: Sounds of America - The Sixties. Stuart A. Kallen. Ed. by Bob Italia. LC 89-84916. (History of Rock n' Roll Ser.). (Illus.). 48p. (J). (gr. 4). 1989. lib. bdg. 12.94 (0-939179-74-1) Abdo & Dghtrs.

Renaissance of Sciences in Islamic Countries - Muhammad Abdus Salam. H. Dalafi & M. H. Hassan. 376p. 1994. pap. text ed. 39.00 (9971-5-0713-7) World Scientific Pub.

Renaissance of Sciences in Islamic Countries - Muhammad Abdus Salam. H. Dalafi et al. 420p. (C). 1994. text ed. 78.00 (9971-5-0946-6) World Scientific Pub.

Renaissance of the Goths in Sixteenth-Century Sweden: Johannes & Olaus Magnus As Politicians & Historians. Kurt Johannesson. LC 90-11173. (Illus.). 298p. 1991. 45.00 (0-520-07013-5) U CA Pr.

Renaissance of the Greek Ideal. Diana Watts. 1976. lib. bdg. 59.95 (0-8490-2515-X) Gordon Pr.

Renaissance of the Lyric in French Romanticism: Elegy, "Poeme," & Ode. Laurence M. Porter. LC 78-52832. (French Forum Monographs: No. 10). 143p. (Orig.). 1978. pap. 9.95 (0-917058-09-7) French Forum.

Renaissance of the State Psychiatric System: A Special Issue of Psychiatric Quarterly. Ed. by Stephen L. Katz. 102p. 1985. 16.95 (0-89885-346-X) Human Sci Pr.

Renaissance of the Twelfth Century. Charles H. Haskins. x, 437p. pap. 15.95 (0-674-76075-1) HUP.

Renaissance of the Twelfth Century. Ed. by Stephen K. Scher. LC 68-56467. (Illus.). 197p. 1969. pap. 6.00 (0-911517-32-4) Mus of Art RI.

Renaissance of Tibetan Civilization. Christoph Furer-Haimendorf. (Illus.). 128p. (Orig.). (C). 1990. pap. 11.95 (0-907791-21-2) Synerg AZ.

Renaissance or Ruin: The Final Saga of a Once Great Church. Britt Minshall. 409p. 1995. pap. 14.95 (0-9642773-0-1) Renaissance Inst.

Renaissance Orientale. Raymond Schwab. LC 75-30012. reprint ed. 82.50 (0-404-14018-1) AMS Pr.

Renaissance Ornament Prints & Drawings. Janet S. Byrne. LC 81-18806. (Illus.). 144p. 1981. 14.95 (0-87099-288-0) Metro Mus Art.

Renaissance Papers, 6 vols. Southeastern Renaissance Conference Staff. LC 55-3551. 93p. 1974. pap. 26.60 (0-8357-4391-8) Bks Demand.

Renaissance Papers, 6 vols. Southeastern Renaissance Conference Staff. LC 55-3551. 111p. 1967. reprint ed. pap. 31.70 (0-8357-4389-6, 2052203) Bks Demand.

Renaissance Papers, 6 vols. Southeastern Renaissance Conference Staff. LC 55-3551. 95p. 1968. reprint ed. pap. 27.10 (0-8357-4390-X) Bks Demand.

Renaissance Papers, 6 vols. Southeastern Renaissance Conference Staff. LC 55-3551. 69p. 1975. reprint ed. pap. 25.00 (0-8357-4392-6) Bks Demand.

Renaissance Papers, 6 vols. Southeastern Renaissance Conference Staff. LC 55-3551. 75p. 1976. reprint ed. pap. 25.00 (0-8357-4393-4) Bks Demand.

Renaissance Papers, 6 vols. Southeastern Renaissance Conference Staff. LC 55-3551. 103p. 1985. reprint ed. pap. 29.40 (*0-8357-4394-2*) Bks Demand.

Renaissance Papers, 1983. Southeastern Renaissance Conference Staff. Ed. by A. Leigh Deneef & M. Thomas Hester. LC 55-3551. 117p. reprint ed. pap. 33.40 (*0-685-17874-9*, 2052203) Bks Demand.

Renaissance Papers, 1990. Southeastern Renaissance Conference Staff. Ed. by Dale B. Randall & Joseph A. Porter. LC 55-3551. 98p. reprint ed. pap. 28.00 (*0-7837-1436-X*, 2052203) Bks Demand.

***Renaissance Papers 1996.** Ed. by George W. Williams & Philip Rollinson. (RP Ser.). 140p. 1997. 35.95 (*1-57113-200-7*) Camden Hse.

Renaissance Paris: Architecture & Growth, 1475-1600. David Thomson. LC 84-40286. (Illus.). 216p. 1984. pap. 18.95 (*0-520-05359-1*) U CA Pr.

Renaissance Patterns for Lace & Embroidery. Federico Vinciolo. (Illus.). 1971. reprint ed. pap. 5.95 (*0-486-22438-4*) Dover.

Renaissance People. Sarah Howarth. LC 92-4990. (People & Places Ser.). (Illus.). 48p. (J). (gr. 4-6). 1992. lib. bdg. 16.40 (*1-56294-088-0*) Millbrook Pr.

Renaissance Perspectives in Literature & the Visual Arts. Murray Roston. LC 86-18681. (Illus.). 448p. (Orig.). 1987. text ed. 75.00 (*0-691-06683-3*); pap. text ed. 29.95 (*0-691-01486-8*) Princeton U Pr.

Renaissance Philosophy. Brian P. Copenhaver. (History of Western Philosophy Ser.: No. 3). (Illus.). 416p. 1992. pap. 21.00 (*0-19-289184-7*) OUP.

Renaissance Philosophy of Giordano Bruno. Irving L. Horowitz. LC 52-14845. 160p. reprint ed. pap. 45.60 (*0-8357-7009-5*, AU00355) Bks Demand.

Renaissance Philosophy of Man: Petrarca, Valla, Ficino, Pico, Pomponazzi, Vives. Ed. by Ernst Cassirer et al. LC 48-9358. 405p. 1956. pap. text ed. 14.95 (*0-226-09604-1*, P1) U Ch Pr.

Renaissance Places. Sarah Howarth. LC 92-7537. (People & Places Ser.). (Illus.). 48p. (J). (gr. 4-6). 1992. lib. bdg. 16.40 (*1-56294-089-9*) Millbrook Pr.

Renaissance-Poetik - Renaissance Poetics. Ed. by Heinrich F. Plett. 449p. (ENG & GER.). (C). 1994. lib. bdg. 155.75 (*3-11-013964-2*) De Gruyter.

Renaissance Poets: Critical Heritage, 4 vols. Incl. Andrew Marvell. Ed. by Donno. 240p. (C). 1996. text ed. 120.00 (*0-415-13414-5*); George Herbert. Ed. by C. A. Patrides. 410p. (C). 1996. text ed. 130.00 (*0-415-13413-7*); John Donne. Ed. by Smith. 529p. (C). 1996. text ed. 150.00 (*0-415-13412-9*); Thomas Wyatt. Ed. by Thomson. 196p. (C). 1996. text ed. 120.00 (*0-415-13411-0*); 1375p. (C). 1996. Set text ed. 459.00 (*0-415-13410-2*) Routledge.

Renaissance Portraits: European Portrait - Painting in the 14th, 15th, & 16th Centuries. Lorne Campbell. LC 89-22686. 252p. (C). 1990. 65.00 (*0-300-04675-8*) Yale U Pr.

Renaissance Print: 1471-1550. David Landau & Peter W. Parshall. (Illus.). 448p. 1994. 70.00 (*0-300-05739-3*) Yale U Pr.

Renaissance Print, 1470-1550. David Landau. 1996. pap. 35.00 (*0-300-06883-2*) Yale U Pr.

Renaissance Reader. Ed. by Kenneth J. Atchity. LC 95-26153. (Illus.). 400p. 1996. 35.00 (*0-06-270129-0*, Harper Ref) HarpC.

***Renaissance Reader: First-Hand Encounters with the Renaissance.** Kenneth J. Atchity. 1997. pap. 18.00 (*0-06-273503-9*, Harper Ref) HarpC.

Renaissance, Reform, Reflections in the Age of Durer, Bruegel, & Rembrandt. Shelley K. Perlove. (Illus.). 152p. (Orig.). 1994. pap. 18.00 (*0-933691-05-X*) U Mich-Dearborn.

Renaissance Rereadings: Intertext & Context. Ed. by Maryanne C. Horowitz et al. LC 87-27228. 312p. 1988. text ed. 29.95 (*0-252-01489-8*); pap. text ed. 12.50 (*0-252-06009-1*) U of Ill Pr.

Renaissance Revivals: City Comedy & Revenge Tragedy in the London Theatre, 1576-1980. Wendy Griswold. LC 86-7059. (Illus.). xviii, 302p. 1986. 29.95 (*0-226-30923-1*) U Ch Pr.

Renaissance-Rhetorik - Renaissance Rhetoric. Ed. by Heinrich F. Plett. ix, 391p. (ENG & GER.). (C). 1993. lib. bdg. 161.55 (*3-11-013567-1*) De Gruyter.

Renaissance Rome: A Portrait of a Society, 1500-1559. Peter Partner. 1976. pap. 15.00 (*0-520-03945-9*) U CA Pr.

Renaissance Rome: A Portrait of a Society, 1500-1559. Peter Partner. LC 75-13154. (Illus.). 285p. reprint ed. pap. 81.30 (*0-685-23637-4*, 2029057) Bks Demand.

Renaissance Sackbut & Its Use Today. Henry G. Fischer. LC 84-62233. (Illus.). 61p. (C). 1984. pap. 1.95 (*0-87099-412-3*) Metro Mus Art.

Renaissance Sackbut & Its Use Today: Further or Amended Information. 1985. 4.50 (*0-317-01001-8*, 05-016522) Henry Fischer.

Renaissance Scots Poetry. Heijnsber. 1998. 23.95 (*0-8057-4549-1*) Macmillan.

Renaissance Self-Fashioning: From More to Shakespeare. Stephen Greenblatt. LC 80-13837. (Illus.). x, 332p. 1983. pap. text ed. 13.95 (*0-226-30654-2*) U Ch Pr.

Renaissance Selling: Enduring Wisdom from the Italian Masters. Vince Pesce. LC 95-90608. 176p. 1996. 24.95 (*1-887951-11-3*) Fish Pubng.

Renaissance Singer. Ed. by Thomas Dunn. LC 75-20077. 1976. 9.00 (*0-911318-10-0*) E C Schirmer.

Renaissance Society & Culture: Essays in Honor of Eugene F. Rice, Jr. Ed. by John Monfasani & Ronald G. Musto. LC 90-55872. (Illus.). 334p. 1995. pap. 25.00 (*0-934977-34-8*) Italica Pr.

***Renaissance Spain in Its Literary Relations with England & France: A Critical Bibliography.** Hilda U. Stubbings. LC 70-89143. xv, 138p. (C). 1969. lib. bdg. 25.00 (*0-8265-1142-2*) Rubena Pr.

***Renaissance Swordsmanship: The Illustrated Use of Rapiers & Cut-&-Thrust Swords.** John Clements. (Illus.). 152p. 1997. pap. 25.00 (*0-87364-919-2*) Paladin Pr.

"Renaissance" Talk: An Ordinary Language Approach to Critical Problems. Stanley Stewart. LC 97-4871. (Language & Literature Ser.: Vol. 23). (Illus.). 250p. 1997. text ed. 48.00 (*0-8207-0273-0*); pap. text ed. 19.95 (*0-8207-0274-9*) Duquesne.

Renaissance Tarot. Brian Williams. (Illus.). 207p. 1995. pap. 17.95 (*0-88079-545-X*, BK115) US Games Syst.

Renaissance: The Invention of Perspective see Art for Children

Renaissance, the Protestant Revolution & the Catholic Reformation in Continental Europe. Edward M. Hulme. LC 83-45662. reprint ed. 62.50 (*0-404-19812-0*) AMS Pr.

Renaissance Theatre: A Historiographical Handbook. Ronald W. Vince. LC 83-13031. 224p. 1984. text ed. 49.95 (*0-313-24108-2*, VRE/, Greenwood Pr) Greenwood.

Renaissance Theory of Love: The Context of Giordano Bruno's Eroici Furori. John C. Nelson. LC 58-7170. 288p. reprint ed. pap. 82.10 (*0-317-09244-8*, 2005782) Bks Demand.

Renaissance Thinkers. LC 92-34276. 414p. 1993. 15.95 (*0-19-283106-2*) OUP.

Renaissance Thought & Its Sources. Paul O. Kristeller. Ed. by Michael Mooney. LC 79-15521. 352p. 1981. pap. text ed. 22.00 (*0-231-04513-1*) Col U Pr.

Renaissance Thought & the Arts: Collected Essays. Paul O. Kristeller. LC 79-5485. 248p. (Orig.). 1980. text ed. 39.50 (*0-691-07253-1*); pap. text ed. 15.95 (*0-691-02010-8*) Princeton U Pr.

Renaissance Thread Methods & Ideas. Patricia Merrell. 24p. 1994. pap. 6.95 (*1-883504-00-7*) Sew-Art Int.

Renaissance Town. Jacqueline Morley. (Inside Story Ser.). (Illus.). 48p. (YA). (gr. 5 up). 1996. lib. bdg. 18.95 (*0-87226-276-6*) P Bedrick Bks.

Renaissance Tragedy & the Senecan Tradition: Anger's Privilege. Gordon Braden. LC 84-21029. 256p. 1985. text ed. 32.00 (*0-300-03253-6*) Yale U Pr.

Renaissance Tragicomedy: Explorations in Genre & Politics. Ed. by Nancy K. Maguire. LC 85-48060. (Studies in the Renaissance: No. 20). 1986. 34.50 (*0-404-62290-9*) AMS Pr.

Renaissance Vistas. Maude Barnes. LC 68-55838. (Essay Index Reprint Ser.). 1977. 17.95 (*0-8369-0178-9*) Ayer.

Renaissance War Studies. J. R. Hale. (Illus.). 624p. (C). 1983. text ed. 70.00 (*0-907628-02-8*) Hambledon Press.

Renaissance Warrior & Patron: The Reign of Francis I. R. J. Knecht. (Illus.). 560p. (C). 1994. text ed. 80.00 (*0-521-41796-1*) Cambridge U Pr.

Renaissance Warrior & Patron: The Reign of Francis I. R. J. Knecht. (Illus.). 638p. 1996. pap. text ed. 29.95 (*0-521-57885-X*) Cambridge U Pr.

Renaissance Woman: Helisenne's Personal & Invective Letters. Ed. by Marianna M. Mustacchi & Paul J. Archambault. Tr. by Paul J. Arcambault from FRE. 96p. (Orig.). 1986. text ed. 34.95 (*0-8156-2347-X*) Syracuse U Pr.

Renaissance Woman - a Sourcebook: Constructions of Femininity in England. Ed. by Kate Aughterson. LC 95-9518. 336p. (C). 1995. pap. 16.95 (*0-415-12046-2*) Routledge.

Renaissance Woman - a Sourcebook: Constructions of Femininity in England. Ed. by Kate Aughterson. LC 95-9518. 336p. (C). (gr. 13). 1995. text ed. 59.95 (*0-415-12045-4*) Routledge.

Renaissance Women: The Plays for Elizabeth Carry & the Poems of Aemilia Lanyer. Ed. by Diane Purkiss. (Women's Classics Ser.). 256p. 1995. 39.95 (*1-85196-029-5*, Pub. by Pickering & Chatto UK) Ashgate Pub Co.

Renaissance Women Writers. Walker. 1996. 28.95 (*0-8057-7017-8*, Twayne) Scribnrs Ref.

Renaissance Women Writers: French Texts - American Contexts. Ed. by Anne R. Larsen & Colette H. Winn. LC 93-26577. (Illus.). 242p. 1994. text ed. 39.95 (*0-8143-2473-8*) Wayne St U Pr.

***Renaissance 2000: Liberal Arts Essentials for Tomorrow's Leaders.** Luigi Salvaneschi. 300p. (Orig.). 1997. pap. 22.95 (*1-55571-412-9*) Oasis Pr OR.

Renaissances Before the Renaissance: Cultural Revivals of Late Antiquity & the Middle Ages. Ed. by Warren T. Treadgold. LC 83-42793. (Illus.). 256p. 1984. 32.50 (*0-8047-1198-4*) Stanford U Pr.

Renaissances Before the Renaissance: Cultural Revivals of Late Antiquity & the Middle Ages. Ed. by Warren Treadgold. LC 83-42793. (Illus.). 111p. reprint ed. pap. 30.00 (*0-7837-4070-0*, 2044026) Bks Demand.

Renal Ammonia Metabolism. Ed. by R. L. Tannen et al. (Contributions to Nephrology Ser.: Vol. 31). (Illus.). x, 154p. 1982. 77.75 (*3-8055-3481-7*) S Karger.

Renal Ammoniagenesis: Journal: Mineral & Electrolyte Metabolism, Vol. 16, Nos. 5 & 6, 1990. Ed. by Ira Kurtz. (Illus.). iv, 100p. 1990. pap. 55.00 (*3-8055-5238-6*) S Karger.

Renal Ammoniagenesis & Interorgan Cooperation in Acid-Base Homeostasis. Ed. by A. Tizianello et al. (Contributions to Nephrology Ser.: Vol. 110). (Illus.). xii, 184p. 1994. 161.75 (*3-8055-5915-1*) S Karger.

Renal Anatomy Applied to Urology, Endourology, & Interventional Radiology. Francisco J. Sampaio & Renan Uflacker. LC 92-528. 1992. 77.00 (*0-86577-464-1*) Thieme Med Pubs.

Renal & Electrolyte Disorders. 3rd ed. Ed. by Robert W. Schrier. 1986. 37.50 (*0-316-77479-0*) Little.

Renal & Electrolyte Disorders. 4th ed. Robert W. Schrier. 1991. pap. text ed. 57.95 (*0-316-77494-4*) Lppncott-Raven.

***Renal & Electrolyte Disorders.** 5th ed. Robert W. Schrier. (Illus.). 832p. 1997. pap. text ed. 57.95 (*0-316-77454-5*) Lppncott-Raven.

Renal & Urologic Aspects of HIV Infection. Ed. by Paul L. Kimmel & Jeffrey S. Berns. LC 94-48435. (Contemporary Issues in Nephrology Ser.: Vol. 29). 1995. write for info. (*0-443-08952-3*) Churchill.

Renal Basement Membranes in Health & Disease. Ed. by Robert G. Price & Billy G. Hudson. 456p. 1987. text ed. 99.00 (*0-12-564725-5*) Acad Pr.

***Renal Biopsy.** Gary E. Striker et al. 336p. 1997. text ed. 79.00 (*0-7216-6412-1*) Saunders.

Renal Biopsy in Glomerular Diseases. E. Beregi et al. 334p. (C). 1978. 110.00 (*963-05-1356-0*) St Mut.

Renal Biopsy in Glomerular Diseases: Clinical Histological, Immunohistological & Electron-Microscopic Studies. F. Antoni & M. Staub. 164p. (C). 1978. 45.00 (*963-05-1562-8*, Pub. by Akad Kiado HU) St Mut.

Renal Biopsy Interpretation. Fred G. Silva et al. LC 96-18700. 1996. 95.00 (*0-443-07784-3*) Churchill.

Renal Cell Carcinoma. Klein et al. 368p. 1993. 185.00 (*0-8247-9033-2*) Dekker.

Renal Cells in Culture: Journal: Mineral & Electrolyte Metabolism, Vol. 12, No. 1, 1986. Ed. by Leon G. Fine. (Illus.). 84p. 1986. pap. 75.75 (*3-8055-4160-0*) S Karger.

Renal Complications of Neoplasia. Ed. by Thurman D. McKinney. 288p. 1985. text ed. 69.50 (*0-275-92031-3*, C2031, Praeger Pubs) Greenwood.

Renal Cortical Necrosis. F. A. Laszlo. (Contributions to Nephrology Ser.: Vol. 28). (Illus.). viii, 216p. 1981. pap. 60.00 (*3-8055-2109-X*) S Karger.

Renal Dialysis. Ed. by J. D. Briggs et al. (Illus.). 350p. (gr. 13). 1994. text ed. 104.95 (*0-412-31310-3*) Chapman & Hall.

Renal Disease: A Conceptual Approach. E. Kinsey Smith. Ed. by Elizabeth A. Brain. LC 86-26835. (Illus.). 143p. (Orig.). 1987. pap. text ed. 23.95 (*0-443-08504-8*) Churchill.

Renal Disease: A Conceptual Approach. Kinsey Smith. LC 86-26835. (Illus.). 151p. 1987. reprint ed. pap. 43.10 (*0-7837-9589-0*, 2060338) Bks Demand.

Renal Disease: Classification & Atlas of Glomerular Diseases. 2nd ed. Jacob Churg et al. LC 94-22200. (Illus.). 541p. 1995. 159.95 (*0-89640-257-6*) Igaku-Shoin.

***Renal Disease in Dogs & Cats.** Ed. by A. R. Michell. (Illus.). 174p. 1987. write for info. (*0-632-01818-6*) Blackwell Sci.

Renal Disease in Small Animal Practice. Intro. by Veterinary Learning Systems Co., Inc. Staff. (The Compendium Collection). 1994. pap. text ed. 63.00 (*1-884254-18-7*) Vet Lrn Syst.

Renal Disease in the Aged. Porush. 1991. 82.95 (*0-316-71401-1*) Little.

***Renal Disease Progression & Management: Role of Vasoactive Agents, Cytokines, Lipids & Nutrition.** Ed. by Morrell M. Avram & Saulo Klahr. (Illus.). 372p. 1996. write for info. (*0-7216-3833-3*) Saunders.

Renal Disorders. Dorothy Brundage. (Illus.). 256p. (C). (gr. 13). 1991. text ed. 32.95 (*0-8016-1685-9*) Mosby Yr Bk.

Renal Dysfunction: Mechanisms Involved in Fluid & Solute Imbalance. Heinz Valtin. 1979. 30.95 (*0-316-89554-7*) Little.

Renal Effects of Petroleum Hydrocarbons. Ed. by Myron A. Mehlman et al. (Advances in Modern Environmental Toxicology Ser.: Vol. 7). (Illus.). 320p. 1984. text ed. 65.00 (*0-911131-08-6*) Princeton Sci Pubs.

Renal Eicosanoids. Ed. by Michael J. Dunn. (Illus.). 438p. 1989. 105.00 (*0-306-43320-6*, Plenum Pr) Plenum.

Renal Failure. 224p. 1995. pap. 24.95 (*0-86542-430-6*) Blackwell Sci.

Renal Failure: Diagnosis & Treatment. Ed. by J. Gary Abuelo. LC 95-7920. (Developments in Nephrology Ser.: Vol. 37). 284p. (C). 1995. lib. bdg. 150.00 (*0-7923-3438-8*) Kluwer Ac.

Renal Function. 3rd ed. Heinz Valtin. 336p. 1994. pap. text ed. 31.95 (*0-316-89560-1*) Lppncott-Raven.

Renal Gourmet, or What to Cook When Your Kidneys Quit. Ed. by Mardy Peters. (Illus.). 196p. 1991. spiral bd. 17.80 (*0-9641730-0-X*) Emonar.

Renal Heterogeneity & Target Cell Toxicity: Proceedings of the Second International Symposium on Nephrotoxicity, University of Surrey, U. K., 6-9 August 1984. International Symposium on Nephrotoxicity (1981: University of Surrey) Staff. LC 85-3167. (Monographs in Applied Toxicology: No. 2). 589p. reprint ed. pap. 167.90 (*0-8357-6934-8*, 2037993) Bks Demand.

Renal Immunology. G. Lubec. (Contributions to Nephrology Ser.: Vol. 35). (Illus.). vi, 194p. 1983. pap. 77.75 (*3-8055-3587-2*) S Karger.

Renal Involvement in Systemic Vasculitis: Seminar, 1st, Vimercate, September 22, 1990. Ed. by Adalberto Sessa. (Contributions to Nephrology Ser.: Vol. 94). (Illus.). x, 206p. 1991. 172.25 (*3-8055-5422-2*) S Karger.

Renal Medicine: Concise Medical Textbook. 3rd ed. Roger Gabriel. (Illus.). 288p. 1988. text ed. 37.00 (*0-7020-1267-X*, Bailliere-Tindall) Saunders.

Renal Nerves: Journal: Mineral & Electrolyte Metabolism, Vol. 15, Nos. 1 & 2. Ed. by G. F. DiBona. (Illus.). 96p. 1989. pap. 67.25 (*3-8055-4887-7*) S Karger.

Renal Nuclear Magnetic Resonance. Ed. by Z. H. Endre & A. Iaina. (Journal: Renal Physiology & Biochemistry: Vol. 12, No. 3, 1989). (Illus.). 76p. 1989. pap. 47.25 (*3-8055-5063-4*) S Karger.

***Renal Nursing.** 3rd ed. Ed. by P. R. Uldall. (Illus.). 440p. 1987. pap. write for info. (*0-632-01728-7*) Blackwell Sci.

Renal Nutrition Case Study. Helen Sanders & Hamid Rabb. 115p. (Orig.). (C). 1992. pap. text ed. 100.00 (*1-880864-03-7*) F S H.

***Renal Osteodystrophy.** Ed. by David A. Bushinsky. (Illus.). 424p. 1998. text ed. write for info. (*0-397-51836-6*) Lppncott-Raven.

Renal Pathology. 2nd ed. Ed. by Frederick Dische. (Illus.). 240p. 1995. 120.00 (*0-19-263032-6*) OUP.

Renal Pathology: With Clinical & Functional Correlations. Ed. by C. Craig Tisher et al. LC 65-9434. (Illus.). 1728p. 1989. text ed. 225.00 (*0-397-50779-8*, Lippnctt) Lppncott-Raven.

Renal Pathology with Clinical & Functional Correlations, 2 vols., 1. 2nd ed. Ed. by C. Craig Tisher & Barry M. Brenner. 1993. write for info. (*0-397-51238-4*) Lppncott-Raven.

Renal Pathology with Clinical & Functional Correlations, 2 vols., 2. 2nd ed. Ed. by C. Craig Tisher & Barry M. Brenner. 1993. write for info. (*0-397-51239-2*) Lppncott-Raven.

Renal Pathology with Clinical & Functional Correlations, 2 vols., Set. 2nd ed. Ed. by C. Craig Tisher & Barry M. Brenner. 1,856p. 1993. text ed. 265.00 (*0-397-51240-6*) Lppncott-Raven.

Renal Pathophysiology. Burton D. Rose & Helmut G. Rennke. LC 93-13959. (Illus.). 352p. 1994. 27.00 (*0-683-07354-0*) Williams & Wilkins.

Renal Pathophysiology. 3rd ed. Alexander Leaf & Ramzi Cotran. (Illus.). 432p. 1985. pap. text ed. 26.95 (*0-19-503488-0*) OUP.

Renal Pathophysiology: A Problem-Oriented Approach. James A. Shayman. (Illus.). 250p. 1995. pap. text ed. 21.95 (*0-397-51372-0*) Lppncott-Raven.

Renal Pathophysiology: Recent Advances. fac. ed. Ed. by Alexander Leaf et al. LC 79-63038. (Illus.). 299p. pap. 85.30 (*0-7837-7290-4*, 2047016) Bks Demand.

Renal Patient's Guide to Good Eating. Judith A. Curtis. (Illus.). 214p. 1989. pap. 24.95 (*0-398-06083-5*) C C Thomas.

Renal Patient's Guide to Good Eating. Judith A. Curtis. (Illus.). 214p. (C). 1989. text ed. 38.95 (*0-398-05611-0*) C C Thomas.

Renal Physiology. fac. ed. Donald J. Marsh. LC 83-11117. (Illus.). 163p. pap. 46.50 (*0-7837-7516-4*, 2046989) Bks Demand.

Renal Physiology. 2nd ed. Bruce M. Koeppen & Bruce A. Stanton. LC 96-16798. 224p. (C). (gr. 13). 1996. pap. text ed. 28.95 (*0-8151-5202-7*) Mosby Yr Bk.

Renal Physiology. 2nd ed. E. Koushanpour & Wilhelm Kriz. (Illus.). xii, 390p. 1986. 118.00 (*0-387-96304-9*) Spr-Verlag.

Renal Physiology. 5th ed. Arthur L. Vander. (Illus.). 238p. 1994. pap. text ed. 27.00 (*0-07-067009-9*) McGraw-Hill HPD.

Renal Physiology. Donald J. Marsh. LC 83-11117. 163p. reprint ed. pap. 46.50 (*0-7837-7111-8*, 2046940) Bks Demand.

Renal Physiology: People & Ideas. Ed. by Carl W. Gottschalk et al. (American Physiological Society Book). (Illus.). 520p. 1988. 87.50 (*0-19-520702-5*) OUP.

Renal Physiology in Health and Disease. Barry M. Brenner et al. (Illus.). 190p. 1987. pap. text ed. 34.00 (*0-7216-1973-8*) Saunders.

Renal Problems in Critical Care. Ed. by Lynn Schoengrund & Pamela Balzer. LC 84-27075. (Critical Care Nursing Ser.). 309p. 1989. pap. text ed. 32.20 (*0-8273-4358-2*) Delmar.

***Renal Protective Effect of ACE Inhibition & Angiotensin II Blockade.** Ed. by Giuseppe Remuzzi. (Journal Ser.: Vol. 4, Supplement 1, 1996). (Illus.). iv, 62p. 1996. pap. 28.75 (*3-8055-6442-2*) S Karger.

Renal Radiology & Imaging. O. P. Fitzgerald-Finch. (Topics in Renal Disease Ser.). 96p. 1981. lib. bdg. 49.00 (*0-85200-423-0*) Kluwer Ac.

Renal Research: Clinical & Experimental Contributions from Japan. Ed. by K. Kobayashi et al. (Contributions to Nephrology Ser.: Vol. 6). 1977. 55.25 (*3-8055-2402-1*) S Karger.

Renal Scarring: A Multi-Organ Approach to Fibrosis. Ed. by A. M. El Nahas. (Journal: Vol. 3, No. 2-3, 1995). (Illus.). 84p. 1995. pap. 54.00 (*3-8055-6149-0*) S Karger.

Renal Sonography. 2nd rev. ed. Francis S. Weill et al. (Illus.). 225p. 1986. 171.00 (*0-387-15343-8*) Spr-Verlag.

Renal Stone Disease: Pathogenesis, Prevention, & Treatment. Ed. by Charles Y. Pak. (Topics in Renal Medicine Ser.). (C). 1987. lib. bdg. 134.00 (*0-89838-886-4*) Kluwer Ac.

Renal System Course. Competence Assurance Systems Staff. (Illus.). 1981. pap. text ed. 50.00 (*0-89147-074-3*) CAS.

Renal Tract Stone: Metabolic Basis & Clinical Practice. Ed. by J. E. Wickham & A. Colin Buck. (Illus.). 462p. 1990. text ed. 89.00 (*0-443-03803-1*) Churchill.

Renal Transplant Tolerance: Molecular Mechanisms of T Cell Regulation. Ed. by Giuseppe Remuzzi. (Journal: Experimental Nephrology: Vol. 1, No. 2, 1993). (Illus.). 76p. 1993. pap. 37.00 (*3-8055-5699-3*) S Karger.

Renal Transplantation. Ed. by Marvin R. Garovoy & Ronald D. Guttmann. (Illus.). 446p. 1986. text ed. 73.00 (*0-443-08263-4*) Churchill.

Renal Transplantation. Shapiro & T. E. Starzl. LC 96-28894. 1997. text ed. 100.00 (*0-8385-8383-0*) Appleton & Lange.

Renal Transplantation: Sense & Sensitization. S. M. Gore & B. A. Bradley. (Developments in Nephrology Ser.). (C). 1988. lib. bdg. 180.50 (*0-89838-370-6*) Kluwer Ac.

Renal Transport of Organic Substances. Ed. by R. Greger et al. (Proceedings in Life Sciences Ser.). (Illus.). 330p. 1981. 64.95 (*0-387-10904-8*) Spr-Verlag.

Renal Tubular Disorders: Pathophysiology, Diagnosis, & Management. Ed. by Harvey C. Gonick & Vardaman M. Buckalew, Jr. LC 85-16084. (Kidney Disease Ser.: No. 5). 640p. 1985. reprint ed. pap. 180.00 (*0-608-01319-6*, 2062063) Bks Demand.

An Asterisk (*) at the beginning of an entry indicates that the title is appearing in BIP for the first time.

R

Renal Vascular Disease. Novick. 1995. text ed. 102.00 (*0-7020-1814-7*) Saunders.
Rename Contest Catalog. Carol Stetser. (Illus.). 16p. (Orig.). 1992. reprint ed. pap. 11.00 (*0-917960-05-X*) Padma.
Renamed & Redeemed: Operating in the Name of Jesus. Rod Parsley. 69p. (Orig.). 1991. pap. text ed. 10.00 (*1-880244-02-0*) Wrld Harvest Church.
Renaming the Streets. Poems. John Stone. LC 85-11289. 49p. 1985. pap. 9.95 (*0-8071-1272-0*); text ed. 13.95 (*0-8071-1271-2*) La State U Pr.
Renamo. 2nd ed. Alex Vines. 1995. pap. 16.95 (*0-86543-461-1*) Africa World.
Renamo: Anti-Communist Insurgents in Mozambique: The Fight Goes On. Sibyl W. Cline. LC 89-52151. (Illus.). 68p. (C). 1989. pap. text ed. 10.50 (*0-943057-02-7*) US Global Strat.
RENAMO: From Terrorism to Democracy in Mozambique. Alex Vines. LC 95-975. 1995. write for info. (*0-86543-460-3*) Africa World.
Renamo: Terrorism in Mozambique. Alex Vines. LC 91-13285. (Illus.). 192p. 1991. 18.50 (*0-253-36253-9*); pap. 8.95 (*0-253-28880-0*) Ind U Pr.
Renan-Sciences see Grande Encyclopedie
Renard et la Boussole. 2nd ed. Robert Pinget. 245p. (FRE.). 1971. pap. 13.95 (*0-7859-1515-X*, 2707303453) Fr & Eur.
Renard the Fox. Tr. by Patricia Terry. (C). 1992. reprint ed. 35.00 (*0-520-07683-4*); reprint ed. pap. 14.95 (*0-520-07684-2*) U CA Pr.
Rena's Experiment. Mary J. Holmes. (Notable American Authors Ser.). 1992. reprint ed. lib. bdg. 75.00 (*0-7812-3152-3*) Rprt Serv.
Rena's Promise: A Story of Sisters in Auschwitz. Rena K. Gelissen & Heather D. Macadam. LC 95-10359. 275p. (C). 1995. 23.00 (*0-8070-7070-X*) Beacon Pr.
Rena's Promise: A Story of Sisters in Auschwitz. Rena K. Gelissen & Heather D. Macadam. 288p. 1996. pap. 14.00 (*0-8070-7071-8*) Beacon Pr.
Renascence & Other Poems. Edna St. Vincent Millay. LC 72-3092. (Granger Index Reprint Ser.). 1977. reprint ed. pap. 13.95 (*0-8369-8245-2*) Ayer.
Renascence & Other Poems. Edna St. Vincent Millay. (Thrift Editions Ser.). (Illus.). 64p. reprint ed. pap. 1.00 (*0-486-26873-X*) Dover.
Renascence of Sociological Theory: Classical & Contemporary. Ed. by Henry Etzkowitz & Ronald M. Glassman. LC 90-63132. 392p. (C). 1990. boxed 45.00 (*0-87581-344-5*) Peacock Pubs.
Renascence of the English Drama. Henry A. Jones. LC 75-3126. (Essay Index Reprint Ser.). 1977. reprint ed. 25.95 (*0-8369-2511-4*) Ayer.
Renascence Portraits. Paul Van Dyke. LC 69-17593. (Essay Index Reprint Ser.). 1977. 21.95 (*0-8369-0096-0*) Ayer.
Renascent Mexico. Hubert Herring. 1976. lib. bdg. 59.95 (*0-8490-0944-8*) Gordon Pr.
Renata Tebaldi: The Woman & the Diva. Victor I. Seroff. LC 70-136653. (Biography Index Reprint Ser.). 1980. reprint ed. 23.95 (*0-8369-8048-4*) Ayer.
Renate Ponsold - Robert Motherwell: Apropos Robinson Jeffers. Ed. by Constance W. Glenn. (Illus.). 50p. 1980. pap. 45.00 (*0-936270-18-7*) CA St U LB Art.
Renato Beluche, Smuggler, Privateer, & Patriot, 1780-1860. Jane L. De Grummond. LC 82-14969. 316p. 1983. pap. 90.10 (*0-7837-8506-2*, 2049314) Bks Demand.
Renaud. Antonio Sacchini. Ed. by Eugene Gigout. (Chefs-d'oeuvre classiques de l'opera francaise Ser.: Vol. 38). (Illus.). 296p. (FRE.). 1970. reprint ed. pap. 35.00 (*0-8450-1138-3*) Broude.
Renault Centre. Chris Abel. (Architecture in Detail Ser.). (Illus.). 60p. 1991. pap. 43.95 (*0-442-30826-4*) Van Nos Reinhold.
***Renault Centre: Swindon 1982 Foster Associates.** Chris Abel. (Architecture in Detail Ser.). (Illus.). 60p. (Orig.). Date not set. pap. 29.95 (*1-85454-776-3*, Pub. by Phaidon Press UK) Chronicle Bks.
Renault Formula 1 Motor Racing Book. Frank Williams & Flavio Briatore. 64p. (J). (ps-3). 1996. 16.95 (*0-7894-0440-0*) DK Pub Inc.
Renault FT Tank. Steven J. Zaloga. (Vanguard Ser.: No. 46). (Illus.). 48p. pap. 10.95 (*0-85045-852-8*, 9335, Pub. by Osprey UK) Stackpole.
***Renault, 1975-1985: Coupes, Sedans & Wagons.** Chilton Book Co. Staff. (New Total Car Care Ser.). 1997. pap. text ed. write for info. (*0-8019-9079-3*) Chilton.
Renault 1975-85. Chilton Automotives Editorial Staff. LC 84-45489. 192p. (Orig.). 1985. pap. 16.95 (*0-8019-7561-1*) Chilton.
Renaut De Bage: Le Bel Inconnu (Li Biaus Descouneus; The Fair Unknown) Ed. by Fresco Donagher. Tr. by Colleen P. Donagher. LC 92-8114. (Library of Medieval Literature: Vol. MLA77). 496p. 1992. text ed. 20.00 (*0-8240-0698-4*) Garland.
Rench: A Stratified Site in the Central Illinois River Valley. Ed. by Mark A. McConaughy. (Reports of Investigations Ser.: No. 49). (Illus.). 430p. 1993. pap. 20.00 (*0-89792-143-7*) Ill St Museum.
Rencontres: French Grammar in Action. Jean-Paul Valette & Rebecca M. Valette. LC 84-81479. 484p. (FRE.). (C). 1985. pap. text ed. 40.36 (*0-669-07648-1*); Wkbk. student ed. 28.36 (*0-669-07649-X*); Tapescript. 2.66 (*0-669-07651-1*); Demotape. 2.66 (*0-669-07652-X*); Cassettes. audio 31.16 (*0-669-07650-3*) HM College Div.
Render Me, Gender Me: Lesbians Talk Sex, Class, Color, Nation, Stud-Muffins. Kath Weston. LC 96-14888. (Between Men - Between Women Ser.). 256p. 1996. 24.95 (*0-231-09642-9*) Col U Pr.
Render Me My Song: African-American Women Writers from Slavery to the Present. Sandi Russell. 240p. 1992. pap. 9.95 (*0-312-07074-8*) St Martin.
Render Them Submissive: Responses to Poverty in Philadelphia, 1760-1800. John K. Alexander. LC 79-22638. 248p. 1980. lib. bdg. 30.00 (*0-87023-289-4*) U of Mass Pr.
Render unto Caesar: The Religious Sphere in World Politics. Ed. by Sabrina P. Ramet & Donald W. Treadgold. 463p. (C). 1995. pap. 29.95 (*1-879383-44-6*) Am Univ Pr.
Render unto Caesar: The Religious Sphere in World Politics. Ed. by Sabrina P. Ramet & Donald W. Treadgold. 474p. (C). 1995. 69.50 (*1-879383-43-8*) Am Univ Pr.
***Render up the Body: A Novel of Suspense.** Marianne Wesson. LC 97-15689. 1998. write for info. (*0-06-018292-X*) HarpC.
Renderbrook: A Century under the Spade Brand. Steve Kelton. LC 89-5193. 222p. 1990. pap. 10.95 (*0-87565-083-X*) Tex Christian.
Rendered Infamous: A Book of Political Reality. Stephen Gaskin. LC 81-70392. 268p. (Orig.). 1985. text ed. 18.95 (*0-89789-099-X*, Bergin & Garvey) Greenwood.
***Rendering French Realism.** Lawrence R. Schehr. LC 96-38205. 1997. write for info. (*0-8047-2787-2*) Stanford U Pr.
Rendering in Mixed Media. Joseph Ungar. (Illus.). 160p. 1985. pap. 18.95 (*0-8230-7427-7*, Watsn-Guptill) Watsn-Guptill.
Rendering in Pen & Ink. Arthur L. Guptill. Ed. by Susan E. Meyer. (Illus.). 256p. 1976. 29.95 (*0-8230-4530-7*, Watsn-Guptill) Watsn-Guptill.
Rendering of God in the Old Testament. Dale Patrick. LC 80-2389. (Overtures to Biblical Theology Ser.: No. 10). 174p. (Orig.). reprint ed. pap. 49.60 (*0-685-23638-2*, 2029110) Bks Demand.
Rendering Techniques '95: Proceedings of the Eurographics Workshop in Dublin, Ireland, June 12-14, 1995. Ed. by P. M. Hanrahan & W. Purgathofer. (Eurographics Ser.). (Illus.). 372p. 1995. pap. 98.00 (*3-211-82733-1*) Spr-Verlag.
***Rendering Techniques '96: Proceedings of the Eurographics Workshop in Porto, Portugal, June 17-19, 1996.** Ed. by X. Pueyo et al. (Eurographics Ser.). (Illus.). ix, 294p. 1996. pap. 89.50 (*3-211-82883-4*) Spr-Verlag.
Rendering Things Visible: Essays on South African Literary Culture. Ed. by Martin Trump. LC 90-25740. 416p. (C). 1991. text ed. 39.95 (*0-8214-0988-3*) Ohio U Pr.
Rendering Things Visible: Essays on South African Literary Culture of the 1970s & 1980s. Ed. by Martin Trump. LC 90-25740. 416p. (C). 1991. reprint ed. pap. text ed. 19.95 (*0-8214-0993-X*) Ohio U Pr.
***Rendering unto Caesar.** Gill. LC 97-19432. 1997. pap. text ed. 15.95 (*0-226-29385-8*); lib. bdg. 33.00 (*0-226-29383-1*) U Ch Pr.
Rendering, Visualization, & Rasterization Hardware. Ed. by A. Kaufman. LC 93-27514. (Focus on Computer Graphics Ser.). viii, 193p. 1993. 71.95 (*0-387-56787-9*) Spr-Verlag.
Rendering with Markers. Ronald Kemnitzer. (Illus.). 144p. 1983. pap. 18.95 (*0-8230-4532-3*, Watsn-Guptill) Watsn-Guptill.
***Rendering with Radiance.** Gregory Ward & Robert Shakespeare. 600p. 1997. pap. 79.95 (*1-55860-499-5*) Morgan Kaufmann.
Renderings. Jenna McRae. (Rose Cottage Papers). (Illus.). 34p. (Orig.). 1995. pap. 7.00 (*1-887106-00-6*) McRae Banker.
Renderings. James Sallis. 105p. (Orig.). 1995. pap. 10.95 (*0-930773-32-2*) Black Heron Pr.
Renderings from Worcester's Past: Nineteenth-Century Architectural Drawings from the American Antiquarian Society. Lisa Koenigsberg. (Illus.). 68p. 1987. reprint ed. pap. 13.50 (*0-912296-91-7*) Am Antiquarian.
Renderman Companion: Programmer's Guide to Realistic Computer Graphics. Steve Upstill. (Computer Science Ser.). (Illus.). (C). 1990. pap. text ed. 33.50 (*0-201-50868-0*) Addison-Wesley.
Renders & Their Relatives: Joshua Render of Charles County, Maryland; Orange County, Virginia, & His Descendants, 1720-1985. Pearl O. Smith. LC 85-50210. 300p. 1985. 17.00 (*0-9614492-0-9*) Weeks Pubs.
***Rendevous Skyes West.** Wheeler. LC 97-23604. Date not set. 23.95 (*0-312-86319-5*) St Martin.
Rendez-Vous. Lenard Robbe-Grillet. (FRE.). (C). 1981. pap. text ed. 25.00 (*0-03-056248-1*) HB Coll Pubs.
Rendez-Vous: An Invitation to French. 3rd ed. Judith A. Muyskens et al. 1988. teacher ed. write for info. incl. reel tape (*0-07-540877-5*) McGraw.
Rendez-Vous: An Invitation to French. 4th ed. Judith A. Muyskens et al. LC 93-35951. 1994. Wkbk. wbk. ed., pap. text ed. write for info. (*0-07-044339-4*) McGraw.
Rendez-Vous: An Invitation to French. 4th ed. Judith A. Muyskens et al. LC 93-35951. 1994. Lab manual. lab manual ed., pap. text ed. write for info. (*0-07-044340-8*) McGraw.
Rendez-Vous: An Invitation to French. 4th ed. Judith A. Muyskens et al. LC 93-35951. 1994. Tapescript. text ed. write for info. (*0-07-044342-4*) McGraw.
Rendez-Vous De Patmos. Michel Deon. 306p. (FRE.). 1977. pap. 10.95 (*0-7859-1859-0*, 2070369692) Fr & Eur.
Rendez-vous de Senlis see Pieces Roses
Rendez-Vous de Senlis Suivi de Leocadia. Jean Anouilh. (FRE.). 1973. pap. 10.95 (*0-7859-1743-8*, 2070363759) Fr & Eur.
Rendez-Vous de Senlis Suivi de Leocadia. Jean Anouilh. Incl. Cher Antoine. 1974. (*0-318-52202-0*); Ne Reveillez Pas, Madam. 1974. (*0-318-52203-9*); Directeur de l'Opera. 1974. (*0-318-52204-7*); 448p. (FRE.). 1974. 39.95 (*0-7859-0347-X*, F81784) Fr & Eur.
***Rendez-vous Troublant.** Chrystine Brouillet. (Novels in the Roman Plus Ser.). 160p. (FRE.). (YA). (gr. 8 up). 1996. pap. 7.95 (*2-89021-193-2*, Pub. by Les Editions CN) Firefly Bks Ltd.
***Rendezvous.** Bridget Anderson. 256p. 1998. mass mkt. 4.99 (*0-7860-0485-1*, Pinncle Kensgtn) Kensgtn Pub Corp.
***Rendezvous.** Justine Levy. LC 97-3150. 1997. 22.00 (*0-684-82579-1*) S&S Trade.
Rendezvous. Carlos Mendoza. LC 92-90877. 250p. (Orig.). 1992. pap. 10.00 (*0-9608420-1-2*) C Mendoza.
Rendezvous. Amanda Quick. 384p. 1991. mass mkt. 6.50 (*0-553-29325-7*) Bantam.
Rendezvous. Alain Robbe-Grillet. Ed. by David Walker. 176p. 1987. pap. 9.95 (*0-423-51520-9*, A3862) Routledge Chapman & Hall.
Rendezvous. large type ed. Nancy John. (Dales Romance Ser.). 391p. 1993. pap. 17.99 (*1-85389-320-X*, Medcom-Trainex) Ulverscroft.
Rendezvous. large type ed. Amanda Quick. LC 92-18581. (General Ser.). 463p. 1992. pap. 16.95 (*0-8161-5454-6*, GK Hall); lib. bdg. 20.95 (*0-8161-5453-8*, GK Hall) Thorndike Pr.
Rendezvous: Back to a Simpler Time. Bill Cunningham. (Illus.). 96p. 1995. pap. 19.95 (*0-87905-722-X*) Gibbs Smith Pub.
Rendezvous: Reliving the Fur Trading Era of 1750 to 1840. Kurt Rhody. Ed. by Rob Reilly. (Illus.). 80p. (Orig.). 1996. pap. 17.95 (*0-939365-49-9*) Sierra Pr CA.
Rendezvous & Other Stories. Patrick O'Brian. 240p. 1994. 22.00 (*0-393-03685-5*) Norton.
Rendezvous & Other Stories. Patrick O'Brian. 256p. 1995. pap. 11.00 (*0-393-31380-8*, Norton Paperbks) Norton.
Rendezvous at the Alamo: Highlights in the Lives of Bowie, Crockett, & Travis. Virgil E. Baugh. LC 85-8570. (Illus.). x, 251p. 1985. reprint ed. pap. 12.95 (*0-8032-6074-1*, Bison Books) U of Nebr Pr.
Rendezvous Cruising. Greg Steiner. 238p. 1993. 27.95 (*0-9637456-5-4*) Cobalt Blue.
Rendezvous de Senlis. Jean Anouilh. (Folio Ser.: No. 375). (FRE.). pap. 8.95 (*2-07-036375-9*) Schoenhof.
Rendezvous in Rome. Carolyn Keene. Ed. by Anne Greenberg. (Nancy Drew Files Series, Passport to Romance Trilogy: No. 73, No. 2). 160p. (Orig.). (YA). 1992. pap. 3.75 (*0-671-73077-0*, Archway) PB.
Rendezvous in Space: The Science of Comets. John C. Brandt. LC 91-41170. 1995. text ed. write for info. (*0-7167-2175-9*) W H Freeman.
***Rendezvous Reader: Tall, Tangled, & True Tales of the Mountain Men, 1805-15.** Ed. by James H. Maguire et al. LC 97-10969. (Illus.). 376p. 1997. 59.95 (*0-87480-538-4*); pap. 19.95 (*0-87480-539-2*) U of Utah Pr.
Rendezvous to Roundup: The First One Hundred Years of Art in Wyoming. Sarah E. Boehme. LC 90-82510. (Illus.). 56p. 1992. pap. 16.95 (*0-931618-30-4*, U of Wash Pr) Buffalo Bill Hist Ctr.
Rendezvous with Ada 95. 2nd ed. David Naiditch. 608p. 1995. pap. text ed. 49.95 (*0-471-01276-9*) Wiley.
Rendezvous with Death. large type ed. Margaret A. Pemberton. (Dales Large Print Ser.). 1994. pap. 17.99 (*1-85389-493-1*, Pub. by Magna Print Bks UK) Ulverscroft.
Rendezvous with Destiny. Leonard Rapport & Arthur Northwood, Jr. (Illus.). 1977. 20.00 (*0-686-26296-4*) One Hund First Air.
***Rendezvous with Destiny: A Sailor's War.** Theodore C. Mason. LC 96-44138. 1997. 29.95 (*1-55750-580-2*) Naval Inst Pr.
Rendezvous with Idaho History. Dorothy Dutton & Caryl Humphries. (Illus.). (J). 1994. 24.95 (*0-9642420-0-1*) Sterling Ties.
Rendezvous with Love. Lena Allen-Shore. (With Love to Life Ser.). 118p. (C). 1988. pap. write for info. (*0-922351-01-5*) L Allen-Shore.
Rendezvous with Rama. Arthur C. Clarke. LC 73-3497. 288p. 1990. mass mkt. 6.99 (*0-553-28789-3*, Spectra) Bantam.
Rendezvous with Rama. Arthur C. Clarke. LC 73-3497. 1993. reprint ed. lib. bdg. 26.95 (*0-89968-449-1*, Lghtyr Pr) Buccaneer Bks.
***Rendezvous with Revenge.** Miranda Lee. 1996. 20.95 (*0-263-14822-X*, Pub. by Mills & Boon UK) Thorndike Pr.
Rendicion. Metsy Hingle. (Deseo Ser.). 1996. mass mkt. 3.50 (*0-373-35154-2*) Harlequin Bks.
Rendicion de Breda en la Literatura Y el Arte de Espana. Simon A. Vosters. (Monagrafias A Ser.: Vol. XXIX). (Illus.). 217p. (Orig.). (SPA.). (C). 1973. pap. 53.00 (*0-900411-67-8*, Pub. by Tamesis Bks Ltd UK) Boydell & Brewer.
Rendille. Ronald G. Parris. LC 94-7246. (Heritage Library of African Peoples: Set 1). (Illus.). 64p. (YA). (gr. 7-12). 1994. lib. bdg. 15.95 (*0-8239-1763-0*) Rosen Group.
***Rending & Renewing the Social Order.** Ed. by Yeager Hudson. LC 96-48814. 492p. 1996. text ed. 109.95 (*0-7734-9687-4*) E Mellen.
Rending the Veil: Literal & Poetic Translations of Rumi. Rumi. Tr. by Shahram T. Shiva. LC 94-36971. 280p. (PER.). (C). 1995. 27.95 (*0-934252-46-7*) Hohm Pr.
***Rending the Veil: Literal & Poetic Translations of Rumi.** Shahram T. Shiva. 258p. 1996. 27.95 (*0-614-21332-0*, 1427) Kazi Pubns.
Rending the Veil Heaven. Ted Gibbons. (Keepsake Bookcards Ser.). 79p. 1990. pap. text ed. 4.95 (*0-929985-13-3*) Jackman Pubng.
Rending the Veil of Heaven. Ted Gibbons. (Simple Gifts - Bookcard Ser.). 77p. 1990. pap. text ed. 4.95 (*0-685-35555-1*) Jackman Pubng.
Rene. Rene De Chateaubriand. Ed. by Denis Canal. 165p. (FRE.). 1991. pap. write for info. (*0-7859-4664-0*) Fr & Eur.
Rene see Oeuvres Romanesques et Voyages
Rene see Atala
Rene Char. Mary A. Caws. (Twayne's World Authors Ser.). (C). 1977. lib. bdg. 17.95 (*0-8057-6268-X*) Irvington.
Rene Char: The Myth & the Poem. James R. Lawler. LC 77-85547. (Princeton Essays in Literature Ser.). 135p. 1978. reprint ed. pap. 38.50 (*0-7837-9369-3*, 2060112) Bks Demand.
Rene Crevel: Le Pays des Miroirs Absolus. Myrna B. Rochester. (Stanford French & Italian Studies: No. 12). x, 174p. 1979. pap. 46.50 (*0-915838-25-7*) Anma Libri.
Rene Daniels. (Illus.). 64p. 1992. pap. 15.00 (*1-56466-030-3*) Archer Fields.
Rene Daumal: Le Contre-Ciel. Tr. by Kelton W. Knight from FRE. LC 90-34492. (American University Studies: Romance Languages & Literature: Ser. II, Vol. 147). 200p. (C). 1990. text ed. 31.95 (*0-8204-1332-1*) P Lang Pubng.
***Rene Daumal: The Life & Work of a Mystic Guide.** rev. ed. Kathleen F. Rosenblatt. (SUNY Series in Western Esoteric Traditions). (Illus.). 176p. (C). 1998. text ed. 59.50 (*0-7914-3633-0*) State Univ of New York.
***Rene Daumal: The Life & Work of a Mystic Guide.** rev. ed. Kathleen F. Rosenblatt. (SUNY Series in Western Esoteric Traditions). (Illus.). 176p. (C). 1998. pap. text ed. 19.95 (*0-7914-3634-9*) State Univ of New York.
***Rene Daumal's Mugle: And the Silk.** Rene Daumal & Phil Powrie. LC 97-25495. (Studies in French Literature). 1997. write for info. (*0-7734-8580-5*) E Mellen.
Rene Descartes: Critical Assessments, 4 vols., Set. Ed. by Georges J. Moyal. 1696p. (C). (gr. 13). 1991. boxed, text ed. 545.00 (*0-415-02358-0*, A5795) Routledge.
Rene Descartes: Meditation on First Philosophy, with Selections from the Objections & Replies. rev. ed. Rene Descartes. Ed. by John Cottingham. (Texts in the History of Philosophy Ser.). 160p. (C). 1996. 34.95 (*0-521-55252-4*); pap. text ed. 12.95 (*0-521-55818-2*) Cambridge U Pr.
Rene Descartes: Principles of Philosophy. Rene Descartes. Tr. by Valentine R. Miller & Reese P. Miller. (Synthese Historical Library: No. 4). 353p. 1982. lib. bdg. 158.50 (*90-277-1451-7*) Kluwer Ac.
Rene Descartes: Principles of Philosophy. Tr. by Valentine R. Miller & Reese P. Miller. (Synthese Library: No. 4). 353p. 1984. pap. text ed. 44.50 (*90-277-1754-0*, D Reidel) Kluwer Ac.
Rene Descartes' Meditations on First Philosophy in Focus. Ed. by Stanley Tweyman. LC 92-47345. (Philosophers in Focus Ser.). 224p. (C). 1993. pap. 16.95 (*0-415-07707-9*, B2544) Routledge.
Rene Descartes' Meditations on First Philosophy in Focus. Ed. by Stanley Tweyman. LC 92-47345. (Philosophers in Focus Ser.). 224p. (C). (gr. 13). 1993. text ed. 69.95 (*0-415-07706-0*, B2540) Routledge.
Rene Fernandat, Poet & Critic: Catholic University of America. Mary H. Konkel. LC 71-128928. (Studies in Romance Languages & Literatures: No. 45). reprint ed. 37.50 (*0-404-50345-4*) AMS Pr.
Rene Girard ou la Christinaisation des Sciences Humanies. Francois Lagarde. LC 93-23078. (Sociocriticism: Literature, Society & History Ser.: Vol. 7). 212p. (C). 1994. text ed. 45.95 (*0-8204-2289-4*) P Lang Pubng.
Rene Gnam Direct Mail Workshop. Rene Gnam. 1990. pap. 18.95 (*0-13-773433-6*) P-H.
Rene Gnam's Direct Mail Workshop: 1,001 Ideas, Tips, Rulebreakers & Brainstormers for Improving Profits Fast. Rene Gnam. 352p. 1989. text ed. 49.95 (*0-13-636622-8*) P-H.
Rene Guenon: A Teacher for Modern Times. Julius Evola. Ed. by J. D. Holmes. Tr. by Guido Stucco from ITA. (Orig.). 1993. pap. 6.95 (*1-55818-229-2*, Sure Fire) Holmes Pub.
Rene Leys. Victor Segalen. Tr. by J. A. Underwood. LC 88-42723. 222p. 1988. 17.95 (*0-87951-324-1*) Overlook Pr.
Rene Leys. Victor Segalen. Tr. by J. A. Underwood. 222p. 1989. Tusk. pap. 10.95 (*0-87951-350-0*) Overlook Pr.
Rene Magritte. A. M. Hammacher. Tr. by James Brockway from FRE. LC 94-37476. (Illus.). 167p. 1995. pap. 19.98 (*0-8109-8137-8*, Abradale Pr) Abrams.
Rene Magritte. Ed. by Andreas Huneke. 100p. 1995. text ed. 15.00 (*3-364-00337-8*) Gordon & Breach.
Rene Magritte Catalogue Raisonne Vol. 1: Oil Paintings 1916-1930. Ed. by David Sylvester & Sarah Whitfeld. 384p. 1992. 180.00 (*0-85667-423-0*, Pub. by P Wilson Pubs) Sothebys Pubns.
Rene Magritte Catalogue Raisonne Vol. 2: Oil Paintings & Objects 1931-1948, Vol. 2. Ed. by David Sylvester & Sarah Whitfeld. 448p. 1992. 180.00 (*0-85667-424-9*, Pub. by P Wilson Pubs) Sothebys Pubns.
Rene Magritte Catalogue Raisonne Vol. 3: Oil Paintings, Objects & Sculpture 1949-1967. Sarah Whitfield & Michael Raeburn. Ed. by David Sylvester. (Illus.). 448p. 1993. 180.00 (*0-85667-426-5*, Pub. by P Wilson Pubs) Sothebys Pubns.
Rene Magritte Catalogue Raisonne, Vol. 4: Oil Temperas, Watercolors, Gouaches & Papier Colles 1920-1967. Sarah Whitfield & Michael Raeburn. Ed. by David Sylvester. (Illus.). 448p. 1993. 180.00 (*0-85667-427-3*) Sothebys Pubns.
Rene Magritte Poetic Images. Susan J. Barnes. LC 79-89280. (Illus.). 15p. (Orig.). 1979. pap. 4.00 (*0-943526-38-8*) Parrish Art.
***Rene Maran: The Black Frenchman: A Biocritical Study.** Femi Ojo-Ade. LC 81-51663. (Illus.). 277p. 1984. 12.00 (*1-57889-052-7*); pap. 8.00 (*1-57889-051-9*) Passeggiata.
Rene Marques (1919-1979) Ed. by Amilcar Tirado & Nelida Perez. (Puerto Rican Bibliographies Ser.). 39p. (C). 1986. pap. 1.00 (*1-878483-47-1*) Hunter Coll CEP.

R

Rene ou La Vie de Chateaubriand. Andre Maurois. (Coll. Diamant). 25.50 (*0-685-36957-9*) Fr & Eur.

Rene ou la Vie de Chateaubriand. Andre Maurois. 315p. (FRE.). 1985. pap. 39.95 (*0-7859-4613-6*) Fr & Eur.

Rene Ricard: Trusty Sarcophagus Co. deluxe limited ed. 1990. boxed 175.00 (*0-685-53381-6*) Inanout Pr.

Rene Ricard: Trusty Sarcophagus Co. limited ed. 1990. boxed 475.00 (*0-9625119-0-0*); boxed 325.00 (*0-685-53380-8*) Inanout Pr.

Rene Spitz: Dialogues from Infancy. Ed. by Robert N. Emde. LC 83-26461. 495p. 1984. 67.50 (*0-8236-5787-6*) Intl Univs Pr.

Rene Watt Lemaire: Recollections of Life in Lander County, Nevada; Battle Mountain Business; & the Nevada State Senate. Ed. by Mary E. Glass. 298p. 1970. lib. bdg. 48.50 (*1-56475-088-4*); fiche write for info. (*1-56475-089-2*) U NV Oral Hist.

Renealmia (Zingiberoceae-Zingiberoideae) Costoideae (Additions) (Zingiberaceae) Paul J. Maas. LC 77-72241. (Flora Neotropica Monographs: No. 18). (Illus.). 218p. 1977. pap. 21.00 (*0-89327-192-6*) NY Botanical.

Renee. Renee F. Schwartz. LC 90-50818. 151p. 1990. 17.95 (*0-88400-149-0*) Shengold.

Renee Green: World Tour. Jan Avgikos et al. (Focus Ser.). (Illus.). 61p. (Orig.). 1993. pap. 14.95 (*0-914357-31-X*) Los Angeles Mus Contemp.

Renegade. D. R. Benson. Ed. by Doug Grad. (Tracker Ser.). 224p. (Orig.). 1992. pap. 3.50 (*0-671-73837-2*) PB.

Renegade. Gene DeWeese. Ed. by Dave Stern. (Star Trek Ser.: No. 55). 288p. (Orig.). 1991. mass mkt. 4.95 (*0-671-65814-X*) PB.

Renegade. Margaret St. George. (Intrigue Ser.). 1996. mass mkt. 3.75 (*0-373-22358-7*, 1-22358-5) Harlequin Bks.

Renegade. large type ed. Lauran Paine. LC 94-45643. 219p. 1995. lib. bdg. 19.95 (*0-7862-0396-X*) Thorndike Pr.

Renegade: Battle for Jacob's Star: The Official Strategy Guide. Tom Basham. 1995. pap. text ed. 19.95 (*0-7615-0181-9*) Prima Pub.

Renegade & Other Tales. Martha Wolfenstein. LC 79-101824. (Short Story Index Reprint Ser.). 1977. 21.95 (*0-8369-3212-9*) Ayer.

Renegade Canyon. large type ed. Peter Dawson. LC 93-35501. (Large Type Ser.). 1993. lib. bdg. 17.95 (*1-56054-704-9*) Thorndike Pr.

Renegade Christmas. deluxe ed. William Everson. 30p. 1984. 150.00 (*0-935716-29-7*) Lord John.

Renegade Cowboy. large type ed. Nelson Nye. (Nightingale Ser.). 1996. pap. 17.95 (*0-7838-1616-2*) G K Hall.

Renegade Gambler. large type ed. Lee Floren. (Lindford Western Library). 304p. 1995. pap. 15.99 (*0-7089-7701-4*, Linford) Ulverscroft.

Renegade Girl. Mary A. Gibbs. 224p. 1981. pap. 1.50 (*0-449-50198-1*, Coventry) Fawcett.

*__Renegade Guns.__ large type ed. Sam Gort. (Linford Western Library). 256p. 1996. pap. 15.99 (*0-7089-7948-3*, Linford) Ulverscroft.

*__Renegade Heart.__ Madeline Baker. 1996. mass mkt. 5.99 (*0-8439-4085-9*, Leisure Bks) Dorchester Pub Co.

Renegade in the Hills. Andy Thompson. Ed. by Rebecca S. Moore. (Light Line Ser.). (Illus.). 135p. (Orig.). (J). (gr. 5-8). 1989. pap. 6.49 (*0-89084-494-1*, 046136) Bob Jones Univ Pr.

Renegade Justice. Judd Cole. (Cheyenne Ser.: No. 3). 176p. (Orig.). 1993. mass mkt., pap. text ed. 3.50 (*0-8439-3385-2*) Dorchester Pub Co.

*__Renegade Justice/Vision Quest, 2 vols. in 1.__ Judd Cole. (Cheyenne Ser.: Nos. 3 & 4). 352p. 1997. mass mkt. 4.99 (*0-8439-4309-2*, Leisure Bks) Dorchester Pub Co.

Renegade Kids, Suburban Outlaws: From Youth Culture to Delinquency. Wayne S. Wooden. LC 94-22113. 248p. 1995. pap. 26.95 (*0-534-24012-7*) Wadsworth Pub.

Renegade Lady. Sonya Birmingham. 384p. (Orig.). 1992. mass mkt. 4.50 (*0-380-76765-1*) Avon.

Renegade Lady. Kathryn Hockett. 384p. 1995. mass mkt. 4.99 (*0-8217-5042-9*, Zebra Kensgtn) Kensgtn Pub Corp.

Renegade Lady. large type ed. Frank Silvester. (Linford Western Library). 304p. 1996. pap. 15.99 (*0-7089-7883-5*, Linford) Ulverscroft.

Renegade Lawman. large type ed. Gordon D. Shirreffs. (Linford Western Library). 240p. 1988. pap. 15.99 (*0-7089-6610-1*, Linford) Ulverscroft.

Renegade Love. Katherine Sutcliffe. 352p. 1988. mass mkt. 5.99 (*0-380-75402-9*) Avon.

Renegade Lover. Barbara Bretton. (American Romance Ser.). 1993. mass mkt. 3.50 (*0-373-16493-9*, 1-16493-8) Harlequin Bks.

Renegade Nation. Jake McMasters. (Cheyenne Ser.: No. 15). 176p. (Orig.). 1995. mass mkt., pap. text ed. 3.99 (*0-8439-3891-9*) Dorchester Pub Co.

Renegade Poet, & Other Essays. Francis Thompson. LC 67-22122. (Essay Index Reprint Ser.). 1977. 18.95 (*0-8369-0934-8*) Ayer.

Renegade Psychiatrist's Story: An Introduction to the Science of Human Nature. Paul Rosenfels. LC 86-142970. (Ninth Street Center Monographs). (Orig.). 1979. pap. 3.95 (*0-932961-05-3*) Ninth St Ctr.

*__Renegade Regionalists: The Modern Independence of Grant Wood, Thomas Hart Benton, & John Steuart Curry As Independent Modernists.__ James M. Dennis. LC 97-9184. (Illus.). 288p. 1998. 45.00 (*0-299-15580-3*); pap. 19.95 (*0-299-15584-6*) U of Wis Pr.

Renegade Rifles. Jon Sharpe. (Trailsman Ser.: No. 119). 176p. (Orig.). 1991. pap. 3.50 (*0-451-17093-8*, Sig) NAL-Dutton.

Renegade Saint: A Story of Hope by a Child Abuse Survivor. Phil E. Quinn. 1989. pap. 12.95 (*0-687-36131-1*) Abingdon.

*__Renegade Siege.__ Judd Cole. (Cheyenne Ser.: No. 20). 176p. (Orig.). 1996. mass mkt. 3.99 (*0-8439-4123-5*) Dorchester Pub Co.

*__Renegade Son, Bk. 26.__ Lisa Jackson. (Born in the U. S. A. Ser.). 1998. 4.50 (*0-373-47176-9*, 1-47176-2) Harlequin Bks.

Renegade States: The Evolution of Revolutionary Foreign Policy. Ed. by Stephen Chan & Andrew J. Williams. LC 94-12636. 1994. text ed. 75.00 (*0-7190-3169-9*, Pub. by Manchester Univ Pr UK); text ed. 24.95 (*0-7190-3170-2*, Pub. by Manchester Univ Pr UK) St Martin.

Renegade Trail. Jake Logan. (Slocum Ser.: No. 201). 192p. (Orig.). 1995. pap. text ed. 4.50 (*0-515-11739-0*) Jove Pubns.

Renegade Tribe: The Palouse Indians & the Invasion of the Inland Pacific Northwest. Clifford E. Trafzer & Richard D. Scheuerman. LC 86-23398. 224p. 1986. pap. 17.95 (*0-87422-027-0*) Wash St U Pr.

Renegade War. James McPhee. (Survival Two Thousand Ser.: No. 2). 1991. mass mkt. 3.50 (*0-373-63202-9*) Harlequin Bks.

*__Renegade's Lady.__ Bobbi Smith. 400p. (Orig.). 1997. mass mkt. 5.99 (*0-8439-4250-9*, Leisure Bks) Dorchester Pub Co.

Renegades of Pern. Anne McCaffrey. LC 89-6694. 448p. 1989. pap. 19.95 (*0-345-34096-5*, Del Rey) Ballantine.

Renegades of Pern. Anne McCaffrey. 384p. 1989. text ed. 25.00 (*0-89366-284-4*) Ultramarine Pub.

Renegades of Pern. Anne McCaffrey. 352p. 1990. mass mkt. 6.99 (*0-345-36933-5*, Del Rey) Ballantine.

*__Renegades of Pern.__ Anne McCaffrey. 1997. pap. 12.95 (*0-345-41939-1*, Del Rey) Ballantine.

*__Renegade's Redemption.__ Lindsay Longford. (Intimate Moments Ser.). 1997. mass mkt. 3.99 (*0-373-07769-6*, 1-07769-2) Silhouette.

Renegotiating Cultural Diversity in American Schools. Ann L. Davidson & Patricia J. Phelan. LC 93-22720. 272p. (C). 1993. text ed. 44.00 (*0-8077-3288-5*) Tchrs Coll.

Renegotiating Cultural Diversity in American Schools. Patricia Phelan & Ann L. Davidson. LC 93-22720. 272p. (C). 1993. pap. text ed. 18.95 (*0-8077-3287-7*) Tchrs Coll.

Renegotiating Family Relationships: Divorce, Child Custody, & Mediation. Robert E. Emery. LC 94-12337. 230p. 1994. lib. bdg. 28.95 (*0-89862-214-X*, 2214) Guilford Pr.

Renegotiating Health Care: Resolving Conflicts to Build Collaboration. Leonard Marcus et al. (Health Ser.). 475p. text ed. 36.95 (*0-7879-0151-2*) Jossey-Bass.

Renegotiating International Debt: The "Young Plan" Conference of 1929. William C. McNeil. (Pew Case Studies in International Affairs). 50p. (C). 1993. pap. text ed. 3.50 (*1-56927-208-5*) Geo U Inst Dplmcy.

Renegotiating Local Values: Working Women & Foreign Industry in Malaysia. Merete Lie & Ragnhild Lund. (SIAS Studies in Asian Topics: No. 15). 288p. (C). 1994. pap. text ed. 35.00 (*0-7007-0280-6*, Pub. by Curzon Press UK) UH Pr.

Renegotiating Secondary School Mathematics: A Study of Curriculum Change & Stability. Barry Cooper. (Studies in Curriculum History Ser.: Vol. 3). 300p. 1984. 55.00 (*1-85000-014-X*, Falmer Pr); pap. 30.00 (*1-85000-013-1*, Falmer Pr) Taylor & Francis.

Renegotiation of the Social Contract. Nelson W. Polsby. 1976. 1.00 (*1-55614-106-8*) U of SD Gov Res Bur.

Rene's Flesh. Virgilio Pinera. Tr. by Mark Schafer. LC 89-83811. 256p. 1992. pap. 12.95 (*1-56886-017-X*, Eridanos Library) Marsilio Pubs.

Renew the Earth: A Guide to the Second Draft of the U. S. Bishops' Pastoral Letter on Catholic Social Teachings & the U. S. Economy. James E. Hug. (Illus.). 32p. (Orig.). 1985. pap. text ed. 1.50 (*0-934255-02-4*) Center Concern.

Renew Your Mind. Marilyn Hickey. 30p. (Orig.). pap. 1.00 (*1-56441-164-8*) M Hickey Min.

Renew Your Worship: A Study in Blending of Traditional & Contemporary Worship. Robert E. Webber. 125p. 1996. pap. 7.95 (*1-56563-256-7*) Hendrickson MA.

Renewable & Novel Energy Sources. S. L. Sah. 160p. 1995. pap. 225.00 (*81-85880-82-4*, Pub. by Print Hse II) St Mut.

Renewable Energies: Sources, Conversion & Application. Ed. by P. D. Dunn et al. (Energy Ser.). 373p. 1986. boxed 109.00 (*0-86341-039-1*, EN002) Inst Elect Eng.

Renewable Energies in Africa. Ed. by Ogunlade R. Davidson & Stephen Karekezi. LC 97-5701. (African Energy Policy Research Ser.). (Illus.). 240p. (C). 1997. text ed. 62.50 (*1-85649-089-0*, Pub. by Zed Bks Ltd UK) Humanities.

Renewable Energies in Europe. Ed. by Rodot. 210p. 1994. pap. text ed. 419.00 (*3-7186-5618-3*, Harwood Acad Pubs) Gordon & Breach.

Renewable Energy. Alan Collinson. LC 90-19791. (Facing the Future Ser.). (Illus.). 48p. (J). (gr. 5-8). 1991. lib. bdg. 24.26 (*0-8114-2802-8*) Raintree Steck-V.

Renewable Energy. Bent Sorensen. LC 79-50306. 1980. text ed. 174.00 (*0-12-656150-8*) Acad Pr.

Renewable Energy: A Concise Guide to Green Alternatives. Jennifer Carless. LC 92-35137. 224p. (YA). 1993. 19.95 (*0-8027-8214-0*) Walker & Co.

Renewable Energy: Environment & Development. Maheshwar Dayal. (Illus.). 256p. 1990. text ed. 30.00 (*81-220-0150-5*, Pub. by Konark Pubs Pvt Ltd II) Advent Bks Div.

Renewable Energy: Power for a Sustainable Future. Ed. by Godfrey Boyle. (Illus.). 496p. (C). 1996. pap. 45.00 (*0-19-856451-1*) OUP.

Renewable Energy: Power for a Sustainable Future. Godfrey Boyle. (Illus.). 496p. 1996. 90.00 (*0-19-856452-X*) OUP.

Renewable Energy: Progress, Prospects. Stephen W. Sawyer. (Resource Publications in Geography). 90p. (Orig.). 1986. pap. 15.00 (*0-89291-192-1*) Assn Am Geographers.

Renewable Energy: Project Finance Law & Practice. Tony Stockwell et al. (Environmental Law Ser.). 350p. 1996. 140.00 (*1-874698-75-9*, Pub. by Cameron May UK) Gaunt.

Renewable Energy: Sources for Fuels & Electricity. Ed. by Henry Kelly et al. LC 92-14194. 1160p. 1992. pap. 45.00 (*1-55963-138-4*); text ed. 85.00 (*1-55963-139-2*) Island Pr.

Renewable Energy: Today's Contribution, Tomorrow's Promise. Cynthia P. Shea. (Worldwatch Papers). 68p. (Orig.). 1988. pap. 5.00 (*0-916468-82-8*) Worldwatch Inst.

Renewable Energy Alternative: How the United States & the World Can Prosper Without Nuclear Energy or Coal. John O. Blackburn. LC 86-29273. xi, 201p. 1987. text ed. 42.95 (*0-8223-0687-5*); pap. text ed. 20.95 (*0-8223-0744-8*) Duke.

*__Renewable Energy Annual.__ 1997. lib. bdg. 251.95 (*0-8490-8177-7*) Gordon Pr.

Renewable Energy Assessments: An Energy Planner's Manual. Marcia Gowen. 227p. 1985. pap. 17.00 (*0-86638-065-5*) EW Ctr HI.

Renewable Energy Conference Proceedings. 422p. 1993. 15.00 (*0-317-05615-8*) NARUC.

Renewable Energy Dictionary. Ed. by Margaret Crouch. 500p. 1982. 29.75 (*0-86619-161-5*, 11073-BK) Vols Tech Asst.

Renewable Energy in India. P. P. Gusain. 1990. text ed. 25.00 (*0-7069-4940-4*, Pub. by Vikas II) S Asia.

*__Renewable Energy Information Sources Vol. 9: A Guide to Print & Electronic Information on Environmentally Safe Energy.__ F. S. Seiler. (Illus.). 192p. (Orig.). 1997. pap. 359.95 (*0-88016-089-6*) WindBks.

Renewable Energy Prospects: Proceedings of the Conference on Non-Fossil Fuel & Non-Nuclear Fuel Energy Strategies, Honolulu, USS, January 1979. Ed. by Wilfrid Bach et al. 340p. 1980. 29.00 (*0-08-024252-9*, Pergamon Pr) Elsevier.

Renewable Energy Resources. Tony Twidell & Tony Weir. 500p. 1985. text ed. 65.00 (*0-685-43429-X*, NO. 6832, E & FN Spon); pap. text ed. 29.95 (*0-685-43430-3*, E & FN Spon) Routledge Chapman & Hall.

Renewable Energy Series. Renewable Energy Series Staff. Date not set. write for info. (*0-08-044425-3*, Pergamon Pr) Elsevier.

Renewable Energy Sourcebook: A Primer for Action. Matthew Freedman et al. (Illus.). 242p. (Orig.). 1995. pap. 60.00 (*0-937188-10-7*) Pub Citizen Inc.

*__Renewable Energy Sourcebook Section II: Federal Government R & D-Wind & Ocean Thermal.__ Lisa Brooks & Matt Freedman. (Illus.). 24p. (Orig.). 1996. pap. 15.00 (*0-937188-28-X*) Pub Citizen Inc.

Renewable Energy Strategies for Europe. Michael Grubb. 350p. (C). 54.95 (*1-85353-218-5*); pap. 24.95 (*1-85353-206-1*) Brookings.

Renewable Energy Strategies for Europe, 5 vols., Set. Michael Grubb. 1995. pap. write for info. (*1-85383-218-9*, Pub. by Erthscan Pubns UK) Island Pr.

Renewable Energy Systems in Southeast Asia. Joanta H. Green. 167p. 1996. 89.95 (*0-87814-464-1*) PennWell Bks.

Renewable Energy Technologies. Ed. by M. J. Chadwick & Lars A. Kristoferson. 1986. 146.00 (*0-08-034061-X*, Pub. by PPL UK) Franklin.

Renewable Energy Technologies: A Review of the Status & Costs of Selected Technologies. Kulsum Ahmed. LC 93-46726. (Technical Paper Ser.: No. 240). 184p. 1994. 10.95 (*0-8213-2744-5*, 12744) World Bank.

Renewable Energy Technology & the Environment: Proceedings of the 2nd World Renewable Energy Congress, Reading, U. K. 13-18 September 1992. Ed. by A. A. Sayigh. LC 92-20446. 1992. pap. 100.00 (*0-08-041278-5*, Pergamon Pr) Elsevier.

Renewable Energy Technology & the Environment: Proceedings of the 2nd World Renewable Energy Congress, Reading, U. K. 13-18 September 1992, 1. Ed. by A. A. Sayigh. LC 92-20446. 3500p. 1992. 1,013.00 (*0-08-041268-8*, Pergamon Pr) Elsevier.

Renewable Energy 2000. Anna M. Rooney et al. (Illus.). 145p. 1993. write for info. (*3-540-56882-4*) Spr-Verlag.

Renewable Energy-2000. G. T. Writxon et al. LC 93-14275. 1994. 86.95 (*0-387-56882-4*) Spr-Verlag.

Renewable Natural Resources: Economic Incentives for Improved Management. OECD Staff. 156p. (Orig.). 1989. pap. 20.00 (*92-64-13194-9*) OECD.

Renewable Natural Resources & the Environment: Pressing Problems in the Developing World, Vol. 2. W. Manshard & Kenneth Ruddle. (Natural Resources & the Environment Ser.). (Illus.). 410p. 1981. pap. 65.00 (*0-907567-06-1*, Tycooly Pub); text ed. 105.00 (*0-907567-01-0*, Tycooly Pub) Weidner & Sons.

Renewable Resource Economy. Robert D. Hamrin. 208p. 1983. text ed. 55.00 (*0-275-90995-6*, C0995, Praeger Pubs) Greenwood.

Renewable Resource Management: Proceedings. Ed. by T. L. Vicent & J. M. Skowronski. (Lecture Notes in Biomathematics Ser.: Vol. 40). 236p. 1981. 34.95 (*0-387-10566-2*) Spr-Verlag.

Renewable Resource Management in Agriculture. (Operations Evaluation Study Ser.). 212p. 1989. 11.95 (*0-8213-1373-8*, 11373) World Bank.

Renewable-Resource Materials: New Polymer Sources. Leslie H. Sperling. (Polymer Science & Technology Ser.: Vol. 33). 342p. 1986. 89.50 (*0-306-42271-9*, Plenum Pr) Plenum.

Renewable Resource Policy: The Legal-Institutional Foundation. David A. Adams. LC 93-6543. (Illus.). 580p. (C). 1993. text ed. 75.00 (*1-55963-225-9*) Island Pr.

Renewable Resources for Regional Development. Ed. by Moonis Raza. (C). 1988. 52.00 (*81-7022-229-X*, Pub. by Concept II) S Asia.

Renewable Source: A National Directory of Resources, Contacts, & Companies. Public Citizen's Critical Mass Energy Project Staff. 240p. (C). 1994. pap. text ed. 40.00 (*0-937188-93-X*) Pub Citizen Inc.

Renewable Sources of Energy & the Environment. Ed. by Essam El-Hinnawi & Asit K. Biswas. (Natural Resources & the Environment Ser.: Vol. 6). 234p. 1982. text ed. 100.00 (*0-907567-05-3*, Tycooly Pub); pap. text ed. 50.00 (*0-907567-10-X*, Tycooly Pub) Weidner & Sons.

Renewables Are Ready: People Creating Renewable Energy Solutions. Nancy Cole & P. J. Skerrett. (Real Goods Independent Living Ser.). (Illus.). 239p. (YA). 1995. pap. 19.95 (*0-930031-73-3*) Chelsea Green Pub.

Renewal: A 30-Day Devotional. Warren W. Wiersbe. (Thirty Day Devotional Ser.). 72p. 1995. pap. 3.50 (*1-56476-401-X*, 6-3401, Victor Bks) Chariot Victor.

Renewal & Improvement of Secondary Education: Concepts & Practices. Herbert J. Klausmeier et al. (Illus.). 362p. (Orig.). (C). 1984. lib. bdg. 54.50 (*0-8191-3609-3*) U Pr of Amer.

Renewal & Recognition of Teachers: Fellowships for Independent Study. Council for Basic Education Staff. 22p. 1985. pap. 4.95 (*0-931989-26-4*) Coun Basic Educ.

Renewal & Reformation: Wales C. 1415-1642. Glanmor Williams. LC 92-28333. (Oxford History of Wales Ser.: Vol. 3). (Illus.). 544p. 1993. pap. 24.95 (*0-19-285277-9*) OUP.

Renewal at the Schoolhouse: Management Ideas for Library Media Specialists & Administrators. Ed. by Ben Carson & Jane B. Smith. LC 93-2997. (Illus.). xix, 156p. 1993. pap. text ed. 25.00 (*0-87287-914-3*) Libs Unl.

Renewal Era Cubs, 1985-1990. Eddie Gold & Art Ahrens. LC 90-80680. (Illus.). 184p. 1990. 15.95 (*0-929387-13-9*) Bonus Books.

Renewal for the Twenty-First Century Church. Waldo J. Werning. 160p. (Orig.). 1988. pap. 9.95 (*0-570-04490-1*, 12-3115) Concordia.

*__Renewal from the Roots? The Struggle for Democratic Development in Nigeria.__ Ed. by Adebayo Adedeji. 256p. (C). 1997. 55.00 (*1-85649-509-4*, Pub. by Zed Bks Ltd UK) Humanities.

*__Renewal from the Roots? The Struggle for Democratic Development in Nigeria.__ Ed. by Adebayo Adedeji. 256p. (C). 1997. pap. 25.00 (*1-85649-510-8*, Pub. by Zed Bks Ltd UK) Humanities.

Renewal in Late Life Through Pastoral Counseling. James N. Lapsley. LC 92-19818. (Integration Bks.). 128p. 1992. pap. 9.95 (*0-8091-3333-4*) Paulist Pr.

Renewal in Theological Education: Strategies for Change. Robert W. Ferris. (BGC Monograph). (Illus.). 234p. (Orig.). 1990. pap. 6.95 (*1-879089-03-3*) B Graham Ctr.

Renewal of Anglicanism. Alister E. McGrath. LC 93-35681. 144p. (Orig.). 1993. pap. 9.95 (*0-8192-1603-8*) Morehouse Pub.

Renewal of Civilization. rev. ed. David Hofman. 144p. 1969. pap. 9.95 (*0-85398-007-1*) G Ronald Pub.

Renewal of Classical General Equilibrium Theory & Complete Input-Output Models. Ezra Davar. LC 94-9577. 1994. 55.95 (*1-85628-677-0*, Pub. by Avebury Pub UK) Ashgate Pub Co.

Renewal of Epic: Responses to Homer in the Argonautica of Apollonius. Virginia Knight. (Mnemosyne Ser.: Suppl. 152). 400p. 1995. 108.50 (*90-04-10386-4*) E J Brill.

Renewal of Islamic Law: Muhammad Baqer As-Sadr, Najaf, & the Shi'i International. Chibli Mallat. LC 92-23821. (Cambridge Middle East Library: No. 29). 280p. (C). 1993. text ed. 54.95 (*0-521-43319-3*) Cambridge U Pr.

Renewal of Literature: Emersonian Reflections. Richard Poirier. LC 86-10232. 256p. 1987. 19.95 (*0-394-50140-3*) Random.

Renewal of Mathematics Teaching in Primary Schools. vi, 226p. 1985. pap. 36.75 (*90-265-0599-X*) Swets.

Renewal of Meaning in Education: Responses to the Cultural & Ecological Crisis of Our Times. Ed. by Ron Miller. 160p. (Orig.). (C). 1993. pap. text ed. 18.95 (*0-9627232-3-1*) Holistic Educ Pr.

Renewal of Spirit. Debbie Friedman. Ed. & Tr. by Randee Friedman. 34p. (ENG & HEB.). 1995. pap. 12.95 (*0-9626286-6-2*) Sounds Write.

*__Renewal of Spirit.__ Debbie Friedman. Ed. & Tr. by Randee Friedman. 1995. audio 10.95 (*1-890161-21-7*); audio compact disk 17.95 (*1-890161-22-5*) Sounds Write.

Renewal of the Body. Annie R. Militz. 166p. 1996. pap. 17.95 (*1-56459-862-4*) Kessinger Pub.

Renewal of the Body. Annie R. Militz. 166p. 1972. reprint ed. spiral bd. 13.50 (*0-7873-0613-4*) Hlth Research.

Renewal of the Heidegger Kant Dialogue: Action, Thought, & Responsibility. Frank Schalow. LC 91-25822. (SUNY Series in Contemporary Continental Philosophy). 457p. (C). 1992. text ed. 64.50 (*0-7914-1029-3*); pap. text ed. 21.95 (*0-7914-1030-7*) State U NY Pr.

Renewal of the Mind. John L. Sandford & R. Loren Sandford. 224p. (Orig.). 1991. pap. 9.95 (*0-932081-27-4*) Victory Hse.

*__Renewal of the Old.__ David Johnston. 30p. 1997. pap. text ed. 8.95 (*0-521-58756-5*) Cambridge U Pr.

Renewal of the Social Organism. Rudolf Steiner. 180p. (Orig.). 1985. 20.00 (*0-88010-126-1*, 582413); pap. 10.95 (*0-88010-125-3*) Anthroposophic.

Renewal of the Teacher-Scholar: Faculty Development in the Liberal Arts College. William C. Nelsen. LC 82-135931. 116p. (Orig.). reprint ed. pap. 33.10 (*0-7837-1649-4*, 2041946) Bks Demand.

An Asterisk (*) at the beginning of an entry indicates that the title is appearing in BIP for the first time.

Renormalization Group: Proceedings of the 1st Conference on Renormalization Group. Ed. by D. V. Shirkov. 480p. (C). 1988. pap. 61.00 (*9971-5-0574-6*); text ed. 125.00 (*9971-5-0573-8*) World Scientific Pub.

Renormalization Group Theory of Critical Phenomena. S. V. Menon. (IPA Monographs in Physics). 1995. write for info. (*81-224-0701-3*, Pub. by Wiley Estrn II) Franklin.

Renormalization in Area-Preserving Maps. R. S. MacKay. (Advanced Series in Nonlinear Dynamics). 324p. 1993. text ed. 61.00 (*981-02-1371-9*) World Scientific Pub.

Renormalization in Quantum Field Theory with a Cut-Off. R. L. Ingraham. xvi, 182p. 1967. text ed. 226.00 (*0-677-01410-4*) Gordon & Breach.

Renormalization of Quantum Field Theories with Non-Linear Field Transformations. Ed. by P. Breitenlohner et al. (Lecture Notes in Physics Ser.: Vol. 303). vi, 239p. 1988. 34.95 (*0-387-19263-8*) Spr-Verlag.

Renormalization Theory. Ed. by Arthur S. Wightman & G. Velo. LC 75-45277. (NATO Advanced Study Institute Ser.: No. 23). 1976. lib. bdg. 39.50 (*90-277-0668-9*) Kluwer Ac.

Renormalized Quantum Field Theory. O. I. Zavialov. (C). 1990. lib. bdg. 252.00 (*90-277-2758-9*) Kluwer Ac.

Renormalized Supersymmetry: The Perturbation Theory of N-1 Supersymmetric Theories in Flat Space-Time. O. Piquet & K. Sibold. (Progress in Physics Ser.: Vol. 12). 368p. 1986. 76.50 (*0-8176-3346-4*) Birkhauser.

Renouveau 1958-1962 see Memoires d'Espoir

Renovacion Interior. Luis Palau. (Serie Cruzada - Crusade Ser.). 26p. (SPA.). 1991. pap. write for info. (*1-56063-116-3*, 498016) Editorial Unilit.

Renovacion Interior (Interior Renewal) Moda Pasajera (Transient Fashion) Luis Palau. (SPA.). 1.79 (*0-685-74979-7*, 498012) Editorial Unilit.

Renovado Dia a Dia. Aiden W. Tozer. 384p. (Orig.). (SPA.). 1988. 14.95 (*0-88113-259-4*) Edit Betania.

Renovados De Dia En Dia. Witness Lee. 30p. (SPA.). 2.00 (*0-87083-490-8*, 13001002) Living Stream Ministry.

Renovascular & Renal Parenchymatous Hypertension. Ed. by Thomas F. Luscher & N. M. Kaplan. (Illus.). 560p. 1992. 187.00 (*0-387-53324-9*) Spr-Verlag.

Renovascular Hypertension. Ed. by J. Ian Robertson et al. (Journal: Nephron: Vol. 44, Suppl. 1, 1986). (Illus.). iv, 116p. 1986. pap. 33.75 (*3-8055-4387-5*) S Karger.

Renovascular Hypertension: Pathophysiology, Diagnosis, & Treatment. Ed. by Nicola Glorioso et al. LC 86-26104. 554p. 1987. reprint ed. pap. 157.90 (*0-608-00357-3*, 2061074) Bks Demand.

Renovated Waste Water: An Alternative Source of Municipal Water Supply in the United States. James F. Johnson. LC 72-182155. (University of Chicago, Department of Geography, Research Paper Ser.: No. 135). 169p. (Orig.). reprint ed. pap. 48.20 (*0-7837-0405-4*, 2040726) Bks Demand.

Renovating & Restyling Vintage Homes: The Professional's Guide to Maximum Value Remodeling. Lawrence Dworin. (Illus.). 416p. (Orig.). 1996. pap. 33.50 (*1-57218-029-3*) Craftsman.

Renovating Old Houses. George Nash. LC 95-44407. (Illus.). 352p. 1996. reprint ed. pap. 19.95 (*1-56158-128-3*, 070258) Taunton.

Renovating the Vietnamese Communist Party: Nguyen van Linh & the Programme for Organizational Reform, 1987-91. Lewis M. Stern. 190p. 1994. text ed. 49.95 (*0-312-12037-0*) St Martin.

Renovating with a Contractor: The Complete Homeowner's Guide to Updating or Adding on to Your House Using a Home Contractor. Kevin Brenner & Kate Kelly. LC 95-44167. 200p. 1996. pap. 12.95 (*0-87833-904-3*) Taylor Pub.

***Renovating Woman: A Woman's Guide to Home Repair, Maintenance & Finding a Real Man.** Allegra Bennett. LC 96-42414. 1997. 22.00 (*0-671-52771-1*) PB.

Renovating Your Golf Course. unabridged ed. (NGF Info Pacs Ser.). (Illus.). 118p. (Orig.). 1995. pap. 45.00 (*1-57701-004-3*) Natl Golf.

Renovating Your Home for Maximum Profit: Make up to 4, 000 Dollars for Every 1,000 Dollars You Invest. Dan Lieberman. 1991. pap. 14.95 (*1-55958-097-6*) Prima Pub.

Renovating Your Home for Maximum Profit: Make up to 4, 000 Dollars for Every 1,000 Dollars You Invest. Dan Lieberman & Paul Hoffman. 390p. 1994. 21.95 (*0-914629-93-X*) Prima Pub.

Renovating Your Home for Maximum Profit: Make up to 4000 Dollars for Every 1000 Dollars You Invest in Your House, Condo, Co-op, or Rental Property. 2nd rev. ed. Dan Lieberman & Paul Hoffman. LC 93-50094. 1994. pap. 14.95 (*1-55958-505-6*) Prima Pub.

Renovating Your Own Home: A Step-by-Step Guide. David Caldwell. (Illus.). 240p. (Orig.). 1996. pap. 19.95 (*0-7737-5802-X*, Pub. by Stoddart Pubng CN) Genl Dist Srvs.

Renovation: A Complete Guide. 2nd rev. ed. Michael W. Litchfield. 640p. 1990. boxed 38.00 (*0-13-159336-6*) P-H.

***Renovation: A Complete Guide.** 3rd ed. Michael W. Litchfield. LC 96-49513. 1997. write for info. (*0-8069-9775-3*) Sterling Pubng.

Renovation of Paintings in Tuscany, 1250-1500. Cathleen Hoeniger. (Illus.). 250p. (C). 1995. text ed. 55.00 (*0-521-46154-5*) Cambridge U Pr.

Renovation of Socialism. Burlatskiy. Date not set. text ed. write for info. (*0-08-036771-2*, Pergamon Pr) Elsevier.

Renovation of Socialism. Burlatskiy. Date not set. text ed. write for info. (*0-08-037102-7*, Pergamon Pr) Elsevier.

Rensselaer-Where Imagination Achieves the Impossible. Carl Westerdahl et al. 216p. 1995. 49.95 (*0-9648198-0-5*) Rensselaer NY.

Rensselaerville: An Old Village in the Helderbergs, Vol. 10, No. 4. W. A. Keller. 1993. reprint ed. lib. bdg. 89.00 (*0-7812-5324-1*) Rprt Serv.

***Rent.** Jonathan Larson. Ed. by Kate Giel. LC 97-1171. (Illus.). 160p. 1997. 38.00 (*0-688-15437-9*, R Weisbach Bks) Morrow.

Rent: What Every Tenant & Landlord Must Know. J. James Hasenau. LC 70-150794. (Illus.). (Orig.). 1973. 12.95 (*0-913042-00-5*) Holland Hse Pr.

Rent-a-Puppy, Inc. Richard Boughton. LC 93-41688. (J). 1995. pap. 3.95 (*0-689-71836-5*, Atheneum S&S) S&S Trade.

Rent a Third Grader. B. B. Hiller. 192p. (J). (gr. 2-4). 1988. pap. 3.50 (*0-590-40966-2*) Scholastic Inc.

Rent Almost Free, Mortgage Almost Free Housing: A Workbook. Center for Self-Sufficiency Staff. 65p. (Orig.). 1992. ring bd. 19.95 (*0-910811-22-9*) Ctr Self Suff.

Rent Boy. Gary Indiana. (High Risk Bks.). 128p. (Orig.). 1994. pap. 10.99 (*1-85242-324-2*) Serpents Tail.

Rent Control. Robert Albon & David Stafford. 144p. 1987. lib. bdg. 55.00 (*0-7099-5411-5*, Pub. by Croom Helm UK) Routledge Chapman & Hall.

Rent Control. Robert A. Carter. 30p. 1982. 5.00 (*0-318-22974-9*) NYS Library.

Rent Control: An International Bibliography on Economics & Public Policy. Robert M. Clatanoff & Marc A. Levin. (Bibliographic Ser.: No. 11). 107p. 1985. pap. 19.00 (*0-88329-143-6*) IAAO.

Rent Control: Concepts, Realities, & Mechanisms. Monica Lett. 294p. 1976. boxed 17.95 (*0-87855-152-2*) Transaction Pubs.

Rent Control Debate. Ed. by Paul L. Niebanck. LC 85-1181. (Urban & Regional Policy & Development Studies). 160p. reprint ed. pap. 45.60 (*0-7837-2468-3*, 2042621) Bks Demand.

Rent Control in North America & Four European Countries. Joel F. Brenner & Herbert M. Franklin. 78p. 1977. pap. 14.95 (*0-87855-733-4*) Transaction Pubs.

Rent Control Legislation in Malaysia. R. R. Sethu. 292p. 1986. 93.00 (*0-409-99523-1*) MICHIE.

Rent Examiner. Jack Rudman. (Career Examination Ser.: C-695). 1994. pap. 23.95 (*0-8373-0695-7*) Nat Learn.

Rent Heavens. R. B. Jones. pap. 2.99 (*1-56632-080-1*) Revival Lit.

Rent Inspector. Jack Rudman. (Career Examination Ser.: C-673). 1994. pap. 23.95 (*0-8373-0673-6*) Nat Learn.

Rent Policy in ECE Countries. 53p. 23.00 (*92-1-116486-9*) UN.

Rent Program Specialist. Jack Rudman. (Career Examination Ser.: C-3530). 1994. pap. 27.95 (*0-8373-3530-2*) Nat Learn.

Rent Research Assistant. Jack Rudman. (Career Examination Ser.: C-696). 1994. pap. 27.95 (*0-8373-0696-5*) Nat Learn.

Rent Seeking. Gordon Tullock. (Shaftesbury Papers: Vol. 2). 104p. 1993. pap. 12.95 (*1-85278-870-4*) E Elgar.

Rental Contracts: A Reference Guide for Terms & Conditions of Contracts for the Rental of Personal Property. William T. Stephens. 52p. 1989. pap. 150.00 (*0-685-45859-8*) Am Rent Assn.

***Rental Form Kit.** Self-Counsel Press Staff. 1994. pap. 4.95 (*1-55180-092-6*) Self-Counsel Pr.

***Rental Form Kit for Washington.** Self-Counsel Press Staff. 1990. pap. 5.95 (*0-88908-930-2*) Self-Counsel Pr.

Rental Homes: The Tax Shelter That Works & Grows for You. Zucchero. 1983. 15.00 (*0-8359-6644-5*, Reston) P-H.

Rental Housing. W. Paul O'Mara et al. LC 84-51908. 167p. reprint ed. pap. 47.60 (*0-7837-1008-9*, 2041318) Bks Demand.

Rental Housing: Is There a Crisis? Ed. by John S. Weicher. LC 81-53063. (Illus.). 113p. (C). 1981. lib. bdg. 34.00 (*0-87766-307-6*) Urban Inst.

Rental Housing: Use of Smaller Market Areas to Set Rent Subsidy Levels Has Drawbacks. (Illus.). 141p. (Orig.). (C). 1995. pap. text ed. 35.00 (*0-7881-1731-9*) DIANE Pub.

Rental Housing in California: Market Forces & Public Policies, the Third Annual Donald G. Hagman Commemorative Conference. Donald G. Hagman Commemorative Conference Staff et al. Ed. by LeRoy Graymer et al. LC 86-28540. (Lincoln Institute of Land Policy Book Ser.). 127p. reprint ed. pap. 36.20 (*0-7837-5757-3*, 2045419) Bks Demand.

Rental Housing in the 1980s. Anthony Downs. LC 83-10124. 202p. 1983. 32.95 (*0-8157-1922-1*); pap. 12.95 (*0-8157-1921-3*) Brookings.

Rental Management Made Easy. W. G. Roberts. (Illus.). 150p. 1992. pap. 14.95 (*0-9629979-1-9*) Tower Pub GA.

Rental Real Estate: Section 1031 Exchanges & "Bite-the-Bullet" Phase-Out. 2nd rev. ed. Holmes F. Crouch. Ed. by Irma J. Crouch. LC 95-80858. (Series 400 Tax Guides: Vol. 401). (Illus.). 224p. 1996. pap. 18.95 (*0-944817-28-9*, T G 401) Allyear Tax.

Rented Christmas. Norman C. Ahern, Jr. & Yvonne Ahern. 34p. (Orig.). 1993. pap. 4.00 (*1-57514-121-3*, 1079) Encore Perform Pub.

Renters' Revenge: (A Landlord's Nightmare) Don W. Roberts. LC 91-65693. (Illus.). 112p. (Orig.). 1991. pap. 6.95 (*0-9629979-0-0*) Tower Pub GA.

***Renters' Rights.** Janet Portman. (Quick & Legal Ser.). 1997. pap. text ed. 15.95 (*0-87337-411-8*) Nolo Pr.

***Renters Rights Handbook.** Robert Shemin. 160p. (Orig.). 1997. pap. 9.95 (*0-9649153-1-6*) Big Boy Pub.

Renter's Survival Kit. Ed Sacks. 243p. (Orig.). 1993. pap. 17.95 (*0-7931-0588-9*, 19131901) Dearborn Finan.

Rentier State in Africa: Oil Rent Dependency & Neocolonialism in the Republic of Gabon. Douglas A. Yates. LC 96-14980. 256p. 1996. 59.95 (*0-86543-520-0*); pap. 18.95 (*0-86543-521-9*) Africa World.

Renting Mailing Lists. 1987. lib. bdg. 79.95 (*0-8490-3929-0*) Gordon Pr.

***Renton's Royal.** large type ed. Nina Tinsley. (Magna Large Print Ser.). 593p. 1997. 27.50 (*0-7505-1165-6*) Thorndike Pr.

Rents. Michael Wilcox. (Methuen New Theatrescripts Ser.). 80p. (C). 1988. pap. 6.95 (*0-413-51810-8*, A0237, Pub. by Methuen UK) Heinemann.

Rents, Taxes, & Peasant Resistance: The Lower Yangzi Region, 1840-1950. Kathryn Bernhardt. (Illus.). 344p. (C). 1992. 45.00 (*0-8047-1880-6*) Stanford U Pr.

Renuevo Tras la Lluvia - Equilibrio del Ansia. Arminda Valdes-Ginebra. LC 93-83116. 40p. (Orig.). (SPA.). 1993. pap. 8.00 (*1-882573-02-1*) Serena Bay.

***Renunciation.** Julia E. Rodriguez. Tr. by Andrew Hurley. LC 97-23728. 136p. 1997. 18.00 (*1-56858-057-6*) FWEW.

***Renunciation : A Novel.** Julia E. Rodriguez & Andrew Hurley. LC 97-23728. 1997. write for info. (*92-3-103162-7*, Pub. by UNESCO FR) Bernan Associates.

Renunciation & Reformulation: A Study of Conversion in an American Sect. Harriet Whitehead. LC 86-16211. (Anthropology of Contemporary Issues Ser.). (Illus.). 304p. 1987. 42.50 (*0-8014-1849-6*) Cornell U Pr.

Renunciation As a Tragic Focus: A Study of Five Plays. Eugene H. Falk. 1988. reprint ed. lib. bdg. 49.00 (*0-7812-0144-6*) Rprt Serv.

Renunciation As a Tragic Focus: A Study of Five Plays. Eugene H. Falk. LC 72-78701. (American Guidebook Ser.). 1954. reprint ed. 29.00 (*0-403-04236-4*) Somerset Pub.

Renyi Bilingual Picture Dictionary Chinese. (Illus.). 192p. (CHI & ENG.). (J). (ps-12). 1995. 19.95 (*1-878363-39-5*) Forest Hse.

Renyi Bilingual Picture Dictionary English. (Illus.). 192p. (J). (ps-12). 1994. 19.95 (*1-878363-40-9*) Forest Hse.

Renyi Bilingual Picture Dictionary Estonian. (Illus.). 192p. (ENG & EST.). (J). (ps-12). 1994. 19.95 (*1-878363-41-7*) Forest Hse.

Renyi Bilingual Picture Dictionary French. (Illus.). 192p. (ENG & FRE.). (J). (ps-12). 1994. 19.95 (*1-878363-42-5*) Forest Hse.

Renyi Bilingual Picture Dictionary German. (Illus.). 192p. (ENG & GER.). (J). (ps-12). 1994. 19.95 (*1-878363-43-3*) Forest Hse.

Renyi Bilingual Picture Dictionary Greek. (Illus.). 192p. (ENG & GRE.). (J). (ps-12). 1994. 19.95 (*1-878363-44-1*) Forest Hse.

Renyi Bilingual Picture Dictionary Hebrew. (Illus.). 192p. (ENG & HEB.). (J). (ps-12). 1994. 19.95 (*1-878363-45-X*) Forest Hse.

Renyi Bilingual Picture Dictionary Italian. (Illus.). 192p. (ENG & ITA.). (J). (ps-12). 1994. 19.95 (*1-878363-46-8*) Forest Hse.

Renyi Bilingual Picture Dictionary Japanese. (Illus.). 278p. (ENG & JPN.). (J). (ps-12). 1995. 24.95 (*1-878363-47-6*) Forest Hse.

Renyi Bilingual Picture Dictionary Lithuanian. (Illus.). 192p. (ENG & LIT.). (J). (ps-12). 1994. 19.95 (*1-878363-49-2*) Forest Hse.

Renyi Bilingual Picture Dictionary Macedonian. (Illus.). 192p. (ENG & MAC.). (J). (ps-12). 1994. 19.95 (*1-878363-50-6*) Forest Hse.

Renyi Bilingual Picture Dictionary Polish. (Illus.). 192p. (ENG & POL.). (J). (ps-12). 1994. 19.95 (*1-878363-51-4*) Forest Hse.

Renyi Bilingual Picture Dictionary Portuguese. (Illus.). 192p. (ENG & POR.). (J). (ps-12). 1994. 19.95 (*1-878363-52-2*) Forest Hse.

Renyi Bilingual Picture Dictionary Russian. (Illus.). 192p. (ENG & RUS.). (J). (ps-12). 1994. 19.95 (*1-878363-53-0*) Forest Hse.

Renyi Bilingual Picture Dictionary Spanish. (Illus.). 192p. (ENG & SPA.). (J). (ps-12). 1994. 19.95 (*1-878363-54-9*) Forest Hse.

Renyi Bilingual Picture Dictionary Ukrainian. (Illus.). 192p. (ENG & UKR.). (J). (ps-12). 1994. 19.95 (*1-878363-55-7*) Forest Hse.

Renyi Bilingual Picture Dictionary W. Armenian. (Illus.). 192p. (ARM.). (J). (ps-12). 1994. 19.95 (*1-878363-56-5*) Forest Hse.

***Renzo Piano: Logbook.** Renzo Piano. LC 97-5774. (Illus.). 272p. 1997. pap. 29.95 (*1-885254-65-2*) Monacelli Pr.

Renzo Piano Building Workshop, Vol. 1. Peter Buchanan. (Illus.). 240p. (C). 1993. 75.00 (*0-7148-2809-2*, Pub. by Phaidon Press UK) Chronicle Bks.

Renzo Piano Building Workshop: Complete Works, Vol. 2. Peter Buchanan. (Illus.). 240p. (C). 1995. 75.00 (*0-7148-2859-9*, Pub. by Phaidon Press UK) Chronicle Bks.

Renzo Piano Building Workshop: Complete Works, Vol. 3. Peter Buchanan. (Illus.). 240p. 1997. 75.00 (*0-7148-3543-9*, Pub. by Phaidon Press UK) Chronicle Bks.

Renzo Piano, 1964-1988. (Architecture & Urbanism Extra Edition Ser.). (Illus.). 288p. (Orig.). (ENG & JPN.). (C). pap. text ed. 82.50 (*4-900211-26-5*, Pub. by Japan Architect JA) Gingko Press.

Renzo Piano, 1987-1994. Ed. by Vittorio M. Lampugnani. Tr. by David Kerr from ITA. LC 95-3228. (Illus.). 272p. 1995. 49.50 (*0-8176-5159-4*) Birkhauser.

***Renzo Piano, 1987-1994.** Vittorio M. Lampugnani. 1996. pap. 49.50 (*3-7643-5159-4*) Birkhauser.

Renzoni on Baccarat. Tommy Rezoni. LC 72-76844. 160p. 1974. 7.00 (*0-8184-0067-6*) Carol Pub Group.

Reopening of Closure: Organicism Against Itself. Murray Krieger. (Wellek Library Lectures). 128p. 1989. text ed. 29.50 (*0-231-07006-3*) Col U Pr.

Reopening the Back Door: Answers to Questions about Ministering to Inactive Members. rev. ed. Kenneth C. Haugk. 192p. 1992. pap. 9.95 (*0-9634093-0-1*) Tebunah Minist.

Reopening the Western Frontier. High Country News Staff. Ed. by Ed Marston. LC 89-2225. (Illus.). 322p. (Orig.). 1989. 24.95 (*1-55963-011-6*); pap. 16.95 (*1-55963-010-8*) Island Pr.

Reoperations in Cardiac Surgery. Ed. by J. Stark. (Illus.). 415p. 1989. 375.00 (*0-387-19552-1*) Spr-Verlag.

Reoperative Aesthetic & Reconstructive Plastic Surgery, 2 Vols., Set. Ed. by James C. Grotting. LC 94-39605. (Illus.). 1661p. 1995. 395.00 (*0-942219-25-2*) Quality Med Pub.

Reoperative General Surgery. 2nd ed. Humphrey & Donald G. McQuarrie. LC 96-46310. 950p. (C). (gr. 13). 1996. text ed. 180.00 (*0-8151-7028-9*) Mosby Yr Bk.

Reoperative Gynecologic & Obstetrics Surgery. 2nd ed. Nichols. 420p. (C). (gr. 13). 1997. text ed. 95.00 (*0-8151-6452-1*) Mosby Yr Bk.

Reoperative Neurosurgery. John R. Little & Issam A. Awad. (Illus.). 379p. 1992. 135.00 (*0-683-05080-X*) Williams & Wilkins.

Reoperative Surgery of the Abdomen. Ed. by Donald E. Fry. LC 86-1434. (Science & Practice of Surgery Ser.: No. 6). 447p. 1986. reprint ed. pap. 127.40 (*0-608-01293-9*, 2062039) Bks Demand.

Reoperative Urology. Ed. by Marc S. Cohen & Martin I. Resnick. LC 94-26648. (Illus.). 311p. 1995. text ed. 89.95 (*0-316-74061-6*) Lppncott-Raven.

Reoperative Vascular Surgery. Ed. by Hugh H. Trout, 3rd et al. LC 87-13458. (Science & Practice of Surgery Ser.: No. 14). 391p. 1987. reprint ed. pap. 111.50 (*0-608-01313-7*, 2062057) Bks Demand.

Reordering Marriage & Society in Reformation Germany. Joel F. Harrington. (Illus.). 320p. (C). 1995. text ed. 54.95 (*0-521-46483-8*) Cambridge U Pr.

Reordering of Power: A Socio-Political Reading of Mark's Gospel. Herman Waetjen. LC 88-45251. 224p. (Orig.). 1989. pap. 21.00 (*0-8006-2319-3*, Fortress Pr) Augsburg Fortress.

Reordering the World: Geopolitical Perspectives on the Twenty-First Century. Ed. by George J. Demko & William B. Wood. LC 94-976. (C). 1994. pap. text ed. 24.00 (*0-8133-1727-4*) Westview.

Reorganisation of British Central Government. James Radcliffe. 236p. 1991. text ed. 55.95 (*1-85521-176-9*, Pub. by Dartmth Pub UK) Ashgate Pub Co.

Reorganising the National Health Service: An Evaluation of the Griffiths Report. Manfred Davidmann. (C). 1988. text ed. 50.00 (*0-85192-046-2*) St Mut.

Reorganization: Issues, Implications & Opportunities for U. S. Natural Resources Policy: Symposium Proceedings, April 19-20, 1979. Ed. by Frank J. Convery et al. 212p. reprint ed. pap. 60.50 (*0-7837-6036-1*, 2045849) Bks Demand.

Reorganization & Reform in the Soviet Economy. Ed. by Susan Linz & William Moskoff. LC 87-35630. 150p. (gr. 13). 1988. text ed. 59.95 (*0-87332-472-2*) M E Sharpe.

Reorganization & Rescheduling of the Civilian High-Level Waste Program. (State Legislative Reports: Vol. 15, No. 9). 11p. 1990. 5.00 (*1-55516-265-7*, 7302-1509) Natl Conf State Legis.

Reorganization of Central-Local Relations in Housing. Ed. by Lisa J. Johnson. (C). 1982. 29.00 (*0-685-30282-2*, Pub. by Oxford Polytechnic UK) St Mut.

Reorganization of Local Government in England, 1972-1977: An Assessment. John M. DeGrove. 50p. 1978. pap. text ed. 21.95 (*0-932328-00-8*) Transaction Pubs.

Reorganization of Nursing Practice: Creating the Corporate Venture. Tim Porter-O'Grady. 258p. (C). 1989. 59.00 (*0-8342-0123-2*, 20123) Aspen Pub.

Reorganization of Soviet Foreign Trade: Legal Aspects. M. M. Boguslavsky & P. S. Smirnov. Ed. by Serge L. Levitsky. Tr. by Denis M. McCauley. LC 88-26348. 232p. (gr. 13). 1989. text ed. 102.00 (*0-87332-508-7*) M E Sharpe.

Reorganizations under Chapter Eleven of the Bankruptcy Code. Richard F. Broude. 800p. 1986. ring bd. 110.00 (*0-317-05387-6*, 00595) NY Law Pub.

Reorganizations under Chapter of the Bankruptcy Code. Richard F. Broude. 500p. 1986. ring bd. 85.00 (*0-318-19265-9*, 00595) NY Law Pub.

Reorganizations Under Chapter 11 of the Bankruptcy Code. Walter R. Phillips. 1980. write for info. (*0-318-66759-2*) Harrison Co GA.

Reorganize. Jim Stedt. Ed. by Steve Lawton. (Illus.). 200p. 1990. student ed. 49.95 (*0-9625771-0-3*); spiral bd. 39.95 (*0-685-33048-6*) Hartley & Assocs.

Reorganized National Health Service. R. Levitt et al. 320p. 1995. 38.25 (*0-614-10678-8*, 1220) Singular Publishing.

Reorganized National Health Service. 4th ed. Levitt. 146p. 1991. pap. 52.50 (*1-56593-016-9*, 0259) Singular Publishing.

Reorganizing Eastern Europe: European Institutions & the Refashioning of Europe's Security Architecture. Andrew J. Williams. 208p. 1994. 57.95 (*1-85521-394-X*, Pub. by Dartmth Pub UK) Ashgate Pub Co.

Reorganizing Work: The Evolution of Work Changes in the Japanese & Swedish Automobile Industries. Ben Sachs. LC 93-42756. (Studies on Industrial Productivity). 168p. 1994. text ed. 48.00 (*0-8153-1641-0*) Garland.

***Reorientation of Medical Education: Goal, Strategies & Targets, 2.** (SEARO Regional Publications Ser.: No. 18). 19p. 1989. pap. text ed. 3.00 (*92-9022-121-6*) World Health.

***Reorientation of Medical Education: Indicators for Monitoring & Evaluation, 3.** (SEARO Regional Publications Ser.: No. 18). 101p. 1989. pap. text ed. 5.00 (*92-9022-122-4*) World Health.

***Reorientation of Medical Education: The Rationale & Vision - A Springboard for Change, 1.** (SEARO Regional Publications Ser.: No. 18). 45p. 1989. pap. text ed. 3.00 (*92-9022-120-8*) World Health.

Reorientation of Medical Education Pt. 4: Guidelines for Developing National Plans for Action. (WHO Regional Publications, South-East Asia Ser.: No. 18). ii, 16p. 1991. pap. text ed. 3.00 (*92-9022-160-7*, 1564018) World Health.

Reorientation of Medical Education Pt. 5: Introducing Problem-Based Learning in the South-East Asia Region. P. Abeykoon et al. (WHO Regional Publications, South-East Asia Ser.: No. 18). viii, 42p. 1992. pap. 4.00 (*92-9022-164-X*, 1565018) World Health.

Reorientations: Critical Theories & Pedagogies. Ed. by Bruce Henricksen & Thais Morgan. 288p. 1990. text ed. 39.95 (*0-252-01688-2*); pap. text ed. 14.95 (*0-252-06109-8*) U of Ill Pr.

Reorientations/Arabic & Persian Poetry. Ed. by Suzanne P. Stetkevych. LC 93-6900. 292p. 1994. 35.00 (*0-253-35493-5*) Ind U Pr.

Reorienting Accounting Education: Reports on the Environment, Professoriate, & Curriculum of Accounting. Ed. by Joseph J. Schultz, Jr. (Accounting Education Ser.: No. 10). 212p. 1989. 17.00 (*0-86539-072-X*) Am Accounting.

Reorienting Rhetoric: The Dialectic of List & Story. John D. O'Banion. 312p. 1991. 35.00 (*0-271-00775-3*) Pa St U Pr.

***Reorienting the Cooperative Structure in Selected Eastern European Countries: Case-Study on Poland.** 54p. 1994. 12.00 (*92-5-103512-1*, F35121, Pub. by FAO IT) Bernan Associates.

Reorienting the Cooperative Structure in Selected Eastern European Countries Case-Study on Hungary, Vol. 4. FAO. 1994. pap. 10.00 (*92-5-103433-8*, F34338, Pub. by FAO IT) Bernan Associates.

Reorienting the Federal - State Employment Service. Arnold L. Nemore & Garth L. Mangum. (Policy Papers in Human Resources & Industrial Relations Ser.: No. 8). (Orig.). 1968. pap. 5.00 (*0-87736-108-8*) U of Mich Inst Labor.

Reouverture du Texte. Frederique Chevillot. LC 91-77569. (Stanford French & Italian Studies: Vol. 74). 128p. (FRE.). 1993. pap. 46.50 (*0-915838-90-7*) Anma Libri.

Reoviridae. Ed. by Wolfgang K. Joklik. LC 83-6276. (Viruses Ser.). 588p. 1983. 129.50 (*0-306-41233-0*, Plenum Pr) Plenum.

Rep.-Additional Advance & Impex Pass Book Licences. Paras Ram. (C). 1989. 125.00 (*0-685-27936-7*) St Mut.

***Repackage Yourself: Success Strategies for Your Career, Business & Life.** Corliss M. Tillman. 120p. (Orig.). 1996. pap. 14.95 (*0-9641819-1-6*) M Systs Pubng.

Repacking Your Bags: Lighten Your Load for the Rest of Your Life. Richard Leider & David Shapiro. LC 94-37974. 240p. 1996. pap. 14.95 (*1-881052-87-7*) Berrett-Koehler.

Repacking Your Bags: Lighten Your Load for the Rest of Your Life. Richard J. Leider & David A. Shapiro. LC 94-37974. (Illus.). 250p. 1995. 21.95 (*1-881052-67-2*) Berrett-Koehler.

Repair Aide. Jack Rudman. (Career Examination Ser.: C-1453). 1994. pap. 23.95 (*0-8373-1453-4*) Nat Learn.

Repair & Protection of Concrete Structures. N. P. Mailvaganam. 496p. 1991. 216.95 (*0-8493-4993-1*, TA681) CRC Pr.

Repair & Reclamation. Ed. by R. E. Dolby & K. G. Kent. (Illus.). 222p. 1986. pap. 125.00 (*0-85300-187-1*, Pub. by Woodhead Pubng UK) Am Educ Systs.

Repair & Reconstruction in the Orbital Region. 3rd ed. Ed. by John C. Mustarde. (Illus.). 565p. 1991. text ed. 175.00 (*0-443-04023-0*) Churchill.

Repair & Recovery: The Story of Hoff General Army Hospital 1940 to 1954. Justin M. Ruhge. (Illus.). 54p. 1990. pap. 6.00 (*0-9614807-6-9*) Quantum Imaging.

Repair & Regeneration of the Nervous System: Berlin, 1981 Proceedings. J. G. Nicholls. (Dahlem Workshop Reports: Vol. 24). 411p. 1982. 42.95 (*0-387-11649-4*) Spr-Verlag.

Repair & Rehabilitation II. 80p. 1992. 33.75 (*0-685-72538-3*, C-20BOW6) ACI.

Repair & Rehabilitation of Concrete Structures. 92p. 1990. 20.50 (*0-685-62959-7*, C-10BOW6) ACI.

Repair & Renewal: Journey Through the Mind & Body. Ed. by Robert Somerville. LC 94-18844. (Journey Through the Mind & Body Ser.). (Illus.). 144p. 1994. 17.95 (*0-7835-1048-9*); lib. bdg. 17.99 (*0-7835-1049-7*) Time-Life.

Repair & Upgrade Your Own PC. 2nd ed. Kenneth Hughes. (Popular Applications Ser.). 136p. (Orig.). 1993. pap. 15.95 incl. disk (*1-55622-403-6*) Wordware Pub.

Repair Crew Chief. Jack Rudman. (Career Examination Ser.: C-1454). 1994. pap. 29.95 (*0-8373-1454-2*) Nat Learn.

Repair Crew Worker. Jack Rudman. (Career Examination Ser.: C-2004). 1994. pap. 23.95 (*0-8373-2004-6*) Nat Learn.

Repair Garages. (Eighty-Ninety Ser.). 1991. pap. 16.75 (*0-685-58141-1*, 88B-91) Natl Fire Prot.

Repair Manual for Marx O Electric Locomotives & Accessories. Julio Del Castillo. (Illus.). 200p. (Orig.). 1994. pap. 29.95 (*0-9645454-0-3*) Top Hat Hobbies.

Repair Master: For All Makes & Models of All Major Household Appliances, 1990, 32 vols. Woody Wooldridge. Ed. by Barnee Schollnick. (Illus.). 4316p. (Orig.). 1990. pap. 860.00 (*1-56302-105-6*) R Longhurst.

Repair Master for D & M Automatic Dishwasher, Vol. 8: All D&M Makes & Models. Barnee Schollnick. Ed. by Woody Wooldridge. (Illus.). 79p. (Orig.). 1990. pap. 25.00 (*1-56302-021-1*, 5555) R Longhurst.

Repair Master for Domestic Automatic Ice Makers, Vol. 11: Repair & Service of Domestic (Household) Ice Maker Designs Used by All Leading Refrigeration Manufacturers. Woody Wooldridge. (Illus.). 166p. (Orig.). 1990. pap. 35.00 (*1-56302-030-0*, 7531) R Longhurst.

Repair Master for Domestic-Commercial Refrigeration, Vol. 17: Refrigerators, Freezers, Reach-Ins, Walk-Ins. Barnee Schollnick. (Illus.). 203p. (Orig.). 1990. pap. 35.00 (*1-56302-048-3*, 7552) R Longhurst.

Repair Master for Domestic (Household) Refrigeration, Vol. 16: Refrigerators & Freezers. Barnee Schollnick. (Illus.). 132p. (Orig.). 1990. pap. 35.00 (*1-56302-045-9*, 7551) R Longhurst.

Repair Master for Electric Ranges & Controls, Vol. 3: All Makes & Models. Woody Wooldridge. (Illus.). 169p. (Orig.). 1990. pap. 25.00 (*1-56302-006-8*, 3052) R Longhurst.

Repair Master for Franklin Gas & Electric Dryers, Vol. 24: All Models. Barnee Schollnick. Ed. by Bud Campbell. (Illus.). 42p. (Orig.). 1990. pap. 25.00 (*1-56302-069-6*, 8058) R Longhurst.

Repair Master for Frigidaire Automatic Washers, Vol. 29: Unimatic & Pulsamatic Design. Woody Wooldridge. (Illus.). 80p. (Orig.). 1990. pap. 25.00 (*1-56302-084-X*, 9009) R Longhurst.

Repair Master for Frigidaire Gas & Electric Dryers, Vol. 25: All Models. Woody Wooldridge. (Illus.). 66p. (Orig.). 1990. pap. 25.00 (*1-56302-072-6*, 8059) R Longhurst.

Repair Master for Frigidaire Roller-Matic Washers, Vol. 33: Plus 24 Inch Syncro-Swing Mechanism. Barnee Schollnick. (Illus.). 118p. (Orig.). 1990. pap. 25.00 (*1-56302-096-3*, 9016) R Longhurst.

Repair Master for Gas Ranges & Controls, Vol. 2: All Makes & Models. Woody Wooldridge. (Illus.). 61p. (Orig.). 1990. pap. 25.00 (*1-56302-003-3*, 3051) R Longhurst.

Repair Master for General Electric Automatic Dishwasher, Vol. 5: All Models. Woody Wooldridge. (Illus.). 134p. (Orig.). 1990. pap. 25.00 (*1-56302-012-2*, 5552) R Longhurst.

Repair Master for General Electric Automatic Washers, Vol. 27: All Models. Barnee Schollnick. (Illus.). 89p. (Orig.). 1990. pap. 25.00 (*1-56302-078-5*, 9003) R Longhurst.

Repair Master for General Electric Gas & Electric Dryers, Vol. 19: All Models. Woody Wooldridge. (Illus.). 85p. (Orig.). 1990. pap. 25.00 (*1-56302-054-8*, 8052) R Longhurst.

Repair Master for Kitchenaid Automatic Dishwasher, Vol. 6: All Models. Woody Wooldridge. (Illus.). 95p. (Orig.). 1990. pap. 25.00 (*1-56302-015-7*, 5553) R Longhurst.

Repair Master for Maytag Automatic Washers, Vol. 30: All Models. Woody Wooldridge. (Illus.). 81p. (Orig.). 1990. pap. 25.00 (*1-56302-087-4*, 9010) R Longhurst.

Repair Master for Maytag Gas & Electric Dryers Plus Porta-Dryer, Vol. 21: All Models. Barnee Schollnick. Ed. by Woody Wooldridge. (Illus.). 86p. (Orig.). 1990. pap. 25.00 (*1-56302-060-2*, 8055) R Longhurst.

Repair Master for Microwave Ovens & Ranges, Imported Models, Vol. 4: Panasonic, Sanyo, Sharp, Micro-Tronics, Astro Chef, Imperial, Maitre'D, Minichef, Richplan, Stranthony, United 747. Woody Wooldridge. (Illus.). 134p. (Orig.). 1990. pap. 25.00 (*1-56302-009-2*, 3053) R Longhurst.

Repair Master for Microwave Ovens & Ranges, Vol. 1: Amana, Frigidaire, General Electric, Litton Westinghouse. Barnee Schollnick. Ed. & Illus. by Woody Wooldridge. 137p. (Orig.). 1990. pap. 25.00 (*1-56302-000-9*, 3050) R Longhurst.

Repair Master for Norge-Fedders Automatic Washers, Vol. 32: Plus-Capacity. Woody Wooldridge. (Illus.). 87p. (Orig.). 1990. pap. 25.00 (*1-56302-093-9*, 9015) R Longhurst.

Repair Master for Speed Queen Gas & Electric Dryers, Vol. 23: All Models. Barnee Schollnick. Ed. by Woody Wooldridge. (Illus.). 61p. (Orig.). 1990. pap. 25.00 (*1-56302-066-1*, 8057) R Longhurst.

Repair Master for Westinghouse Automatic Dishwasher, Vol. 7: All Models. Woody Wooldridge. (Illus.). 108p. (Orig.). 1990. pap. 25.00 (*1-56302-018-1*, 5554) R Longhurst.

Repair Master for Westinghouse Front Loading Automatic Washers, Vol. 28: All Models. Woody Wooldridge. (Illus.). 89p. (Orig.). 1990. pap. 25.00 (*1-56302-081-5*, 9005) R Longhurst.

Repair Master for Westinghouse Gas & Electric Dryers, Vol. 22: All Models. Woody Wooldridge. (Illus.). 100p. (Orig.). 1990. pap. 25.00 (*1-56302-063-7*, 8056) R Longhurst.

Repair Master for Westinghouse Top Loading Automatic Washers, Vol. 34: All Models. Woody Wooldridge. (Illus.). 79p. (Orig.). 1990. pap. 25.00 (*1-56302-099-8*, 9017) R Longhurst.

Repair Master for Whirlpool Automatic Dishwasher, Vol. 9: All Models. Barnee Schollnick. (Illus.). 107p. (Orig.). 1990. pap. 25.00 (*1-56302-024-6*, 5556) R Longhurst.

Repair Master for Whirlpool-Kenmore Automatic Washers, Vol. 26: All Models. Woody Wooldridge. (Illus.). 89p. (Orig.). 1990. pap. 25.00 (*1-56302-075-0*, 9001) R Longhurst.

Repair Master for Whirlpool-Kenmore Gas & Electric Dryers, Vol. 18: All Models. Barnee Schollnick. (Illus.). 102p. (Orig.). 1990. pap. 25.00 (*1-56302-051-3*, 8051) R Longhurst.

Repair Master for Window Air Conditioners, Vol. 12: All Makes & Models. Woody Wooldridge. (Illus.). 85p. (Orig.). 1990. pap. 35.00 (*1-56302-033-5*, 7541) R Longhurst.

Repair of Concrete Structures. 2nd ed. Ed. by R. T. Allen et al. LC 93-135425. 212p. 1993. 125.00 (*0-7514-0086-6*, Pub. by Blackie Acad & Prof UK) Routledge Chapman & Hall.

Repair of the World: The Novels of Marge Piercy. Kerstin Westerlund-Shands. LC 94-5149. (Contributions in Women's Studies: Vol. 145). 224p. 1994. text ed. 49.95 (*0-313-29257-4*) Greenwood.

Repair of Vehicle Bodies. 3rd ed. Alan Robinson. (Illus.). 380p. 1993. pap. 41.95 (*0-7506-0955-9*) Buttrwrth-Heinemann.

Repair Shop Manager. Jack Rudman. (Career Examination Ser.: C-1801). 1994. pap. 29.95 (*0-8373-1801-7*) Nat Learn.

Repair Supervisor. Jack Rudman. (Career Examination Ser.: C-2615). 1994. pap. 27.95 (*0-8373-2615-X*) Nat Learn.

Repair Welding & Fabrication Welding of Steel Castings see Steel Casting Handbook Supplements

Repair Your Own Credit. Bob Hammond. 128p. 1995. pap. 7.99 (*1-56414-166-7*) Career Pr Inc.

***Repair Your Own Credit.** 2nd ed. Bob Hammond. LC 97-13338. 1997. pap. write for info. (*1-56414-308-2*) Career Pr Inc.

Repairable Lesions in Microorganisms. Ed. by A. Hurst & Anwar Nasim. 1985. text ed. 139.00 (*0-12-362690-0*) Acad Pr.

Repairable Systems Reliability Modeling, Inference, Misconceptions & Their Causes: Modelling, Inference, Misconceptions & Their Causes. Harold Ascher & Harry Feingold. (Lecture Notes in Statistics Ser.: Vol. 7). 240p. 1984. 69.75 (*0-8247-7276-8*) Dekker.

Repairers of the Breach. Rod Parsley. 320p. 1993. pap. 12.99 (*0-89274-636-X*, HH-636) Harrison Hse.

Repairers of the Breach: There Is Much to Be Gained by a Return to the Discarded Values of the Past. Rod Parsley. 410p. (Orig.). 1992. pap. 11.99 (*1-880244-09-8*) Wrld Harvest Church.

Repairing a Damaged World: An Outline for Ecological Restoration. D. A. Saunders et al. 1993. 20.00 (*0-949324-51-5*, Pub. by Surrey Beatty & Sons AT) St Mut.

***Repairing & Extending, 4 vols.** H. Simmons. 1990. text ed. 236.95 (*0-442-00439-7*, Osprey Bks) Chapman & Hall.

Repairing & Extending Doors & Windows: Metal, Wood, Entrances, Store Fronts, Curtain Walls... H. Leslie Simmons. 57.95 (*0-442-20618-6*) Van Nos Reinhold.

Repairing & Extending Finishes, Pt. I: Plaster, Gypsum Board, & Ceramic Tile. H. Leslie Simmons. (Illus.). 300p. 1990. text ed. 67.50 (*0-442-20612-7*) Van Nos Reinhold.

Repairing & Extending Finishes, Pt. II: Acoustical Treatment, Resilient Flooring, Paint & Transparent Finishes. H. Leslie Simmons. (Illus.). 300p. (gr. 13). 1989. text ed. 60.95 (*0-442-20613-5*) Chapman & Hall.

Repairing & Extending Nonstructural Metals. H. Leslie Simmons. 57.95 (*0-442-20615-1*) Van Nos Reinhold.

Repairing & Extending Weather Barriers. H. Leslie Simmons. (Illus.). 344p. (gr. 13). 1989. text ed. 60.95 (*0-442-20611-9*) Chapman & Hall.

Repairing & Maintaining Your Own Stereo System. Matthew Mandl. (Illus.). 176p. 1983. text ed. 45.00 (*0-13-773515-4*) P-H.

Repairing & Restoring Antique Furniture. John Rodd. (Illus.). 224p. 1995. 27.95 (*0-7153-0304-X*, Pub. by D & C Pub UK) Sterling.

Repairing Antique Clocks. Eric Smith. (Illus.). 192p. 1993. 24.95 (*0-7153-0106-3*, Pub. by D & C Pub UK) Sterling.

Repairing Appliances. (Home Repair & Improvement Ser.). (Illus.). 136p. 1981. 14.60 (*0-8094-3482-2*); lib. bdg. 20.60 (*0-8094-3483-0*) Time-Life.

Repairing Body Fluids: Principles & Practice. Kassirer et al. 176p. 1989. text ed. 59.00 (*0-7216-1149-4*) Saunders.

Repairing Bridge Substructures. OECD Staff. (Road Transport Research Ser.). 124p. (Orig.). pap. 34.00 (*92-64-14542-7*, Pub. by Org for Econ FR) OECD.

Repairing Christian Lifestyles. 2nd ed. Steve Clapp & Sue I. Mauck. (Repairing Christian Lifestyles Ser.). (Illus.). 174p. (YA). (gr. 7-12). 1983. pap. 6.00 (*0-914527-26-6*); teacher ed., pap. 5.00 (*0-914527-27-4*) C-Four Res.

Repairing Furniture. (Home Repair & Improvement Ser.). (Illus.). 136p. 1980. 14.60 (*0-8094-2440-1*); lib. bdg. 20.60 (*0-8094-2439-8*) Time-Life.

***Repairing Furniture.** Time-Life Books Editors. (Home Repair & Improvement Ser.). (Illus.). 128p. Date not set. write for info. (*0-7835-3910-X*) Time-Life.

Repairing IBM PCs & Compatibles: An Illustrated Guide. Michael F. Hordeski. (Illus.). 272p. 1992. 29.95 (*0-8306-3900-4*, 3759, Windcrest); pap. 19.95 (*0-8306-3899-7*, 3759, Windcrest) TAB Bks.

Repairing Intimacy: An Object Relations Approach to Couples Therapy. Judith Siegel. LC 92-11152. 296p. 1995. reprint ed. pap. 30.00 (*1-56821-762-5*) Aronson.

Repairing Major Home Appliances. Robert W. Wood. 1992. pap. text ed. 12.95 (*0-07-071746-X*) McGraw.

Repairing Major Home Appliances. Robert W. Wood. (All Thumbs Guide Ser.). 144p. 1992. pap. 9.95 (*0-8306-2549-6*) McGraw-Hill Prof.

Repairing Major Home Appliances: An All Thumbs Guide. Wood. 1992. 17.95 (*0-8306-2550-X*) McGraw-Hill Prof.

Repairing Old & Historic Windows: A Manual for Architects & Homeowners. New York Landmarks Conservancy Staff. (Illus.). 208p. (Orig.). 1995. pap. text ed. 24.95 (*0-471-14418-5*) Wiley.

Repairing Old China & Ceramic Tiles. 1995. 5.98 (*0-7858-0404-8*) Bk Sales Inc.

Repairing Old Clocks & Watches. Anthony J. Whiten. (Illus.). 280p. 1982. 35.00 (*0-7198-0190-7*, Pub. by NAG Press UK) Antique Collect.

Repairing Pottery & Porcelain: A Complete Guide. Lesley Acton & Paul McAulay. LC 95-48175. 1996. pap. 18.95 (*1-55821-486-0*) Lyons & Burford.

Repairing Quartz Watches. 2nd ed. Henry B. Fried. 1988. 26.00 (*0-918845-06-8*) Am Watchmakers.

Repairing the Breach. Ed. by Bobby W. Austin. LC 96-17532. 288p. 1996. 34.95 (*0-931712-21-1*) Alpine Guild.

Repairing the Breach: A Report from the National Task Force on African American Men & Boys. Bobby W. Austin. 272p. 1996. pap. text ed. 13.95 (*1-879360-45-4*) Noble Pr.

Repairing the Reed Organ & Harmonium. S. G. Earl. (Illus.). 32p. 1932. pap. 5.00 (*0-913746-06-1*) Organ Lit.

***Repairing the Ruins: The Classical & Christian Challenge to Modern Education.** Ed. by Douglas Wilson. 272p. (Orig.). Date not set. pap. 14.00 (*1-885767-14-5*) Canon Pr ID.

Repairing Watch Cases. W. Schwanatus & W. Fenimore. (Illus.). 48p. 1993. pap. 5.95 (*0-930163-71-0*) Arlington Bk.

Repairing Watch Cases: Schwanatus & Fenimore 1909. 1981. pap. 4.00 (*0-915706-14-8*) Am Reprints.

Repairing Your Flooded Home. (Illus.). 56p. (Orig.). 1993. pap. text ed. 20.00 (*0-7881-0132-3*) DIANE Pub.

***Repairing Your Marriage: A Guide for Hope & Healing after the Affair.** Emily Brown. 256p. 1997. per. 15.00 (*0-7615-0963-1*) Prima Pub.

Repairs. David Gordon. 100p. 1991. pap. 9.95 (*0-943373-15-8*) Natl Poet Foun.

Repairs. Walter J. Simmons. (Boatbuilding Ser.). (Illus.). 292p. 1995. pap. 34.95 (*0-924947-10-1*) Duck Trap Pr.

Repairs: Poems. G. E. Murray. LC 79-5379. (Devins Award Breakthrough Ser.). 96p. 1979. text ed. 18.95 (*0-8262-0290-X*) U of Mo Pr.

Repairs, Reuse, Recycling: First Steps Toward a Sustainable Society. Denis Hayes. 1978. pap. write for info. (*0-916468-22-4*) Worldwatch Inst.

Reparaciones Basicas (Basic Home Repairs) Para el Hogar. Sunset Staff. (Illus.). 96p. 1996. pap. 9.99 (*0-376-01589-6*) Sunset Bks Inc.

Reparaciones Frecuentes en el Hogar - Everyday Home Repairs: Black & Decker. Cy DeCosse Incorporated Staff. 1993. 16.95 (*0-86573-724-X*) Cowles Creative.

Reparaciones y Proyectos de Plomeria. Cy DeCosse Incorporated Staff. (Black & Decker Home Improvement Library). 1994. 16.95 (*0-86573-735-5*) Cowles Creative.

Reparation: Restoring the Damaged Self in Child & Adult Psychotherapy. Hugh G. Clegg. LC 95-13022. Orig. Title: The Reparative Motif in Child & Adult Therapy. 244p. 1995. reprint ed. pap. 35.00 (*1-56821-557-6*) Aronson.

Reparation: Universal Gravitation, a Universal Fake. C. S. DeFord. LC 92-28003. 1992. pap. 5.95 (*0-87770-512-7*) Ye Galleon.

Reparation in World Politics: France & European Economic Diplomacy, 1916-1923. Marc Trachtenberg. LC 79-26898. 1980. text ed. 59.50 (*0-231-04786-X*) Col U Pr.

Reparations: The Cure for America's Race Problem. Ida Hakim et al. 283p. (Orig.). 1994. pap. 12.00 (*1-56411-088-5*) Untd Bros & Sis.

Reparations Petition: For United Nations Assistance under Resolution 1503 (XLVIII) on Behalf of African-Americans in the United States of America. Silis Muhammad. 23p. (Orig.). pap. 5.00 (*1-56411-083-4*) Untd Bros & Sis.

Reparative Motif in Child & Adult Therapy see Reparation: Restoring the Damaged Self in Child & Adult Psychotherapy

Reparative Therapy of Male Homosexuality: A New Clinical Approach. Joseph Nicolosi. LC 91-4534. 376p. 1991. 40.00 (*0-87668-545-9*) Aronson.

Repartiendose en la Vina de Cristo see Constitutions of the Society of Jesus, Pt. VII, Missioning

Repartitions Four. Richard Kostelanetz. 20p. (Orig.). 1992. pap. 3.00 (*0-926935-67-4*) Runaway Spoon.

Repase y Escriba: Curso Avanzado de Gramatica y Composicion. 2nd ed. Maria C. Dominicis. 464p. 1994. pap. text ed. 39.50 (*0-471-58488-6*) Wiley.

Repaso Pratico y Cultural. 4th ed. Vincenzo Cioffari & Emilio Gonzalez. 301p. (ENG & SPA.). (C). 1977. text ed. 41.96 (*0-669-96461-1*) HM College Div.

Repaso Prepar de Examenes Cosmetologos. Kibbe. (Standard Texts of Cosmetology Ser.). (SPA.). 1985. pap. 12.95 (*0-87350-356-2*) Milady Pub.

Repatriates & Refugees in a Colonial Society: The Case of Kenya. Joseph E. Harris. (Illus.). 256p. 1987. 24.95 (*0-88258-148-1*) Howard U Pr.

Repeal of Reticence. Rochelle Gurstein. 352p. 1996. 27.50 (*0-8090-8069-9*) Hill & Wang.

Repeal of the Blues: How Black Entertainers Influenced Civil Rights. Alan Pomerance. (Illus.). 288p. 1988. 17.95 (*0-8065-1105-2*, Citadel Pr) Carol Pub Group.

Repeal of the Blues: How Black Entertainers Influenced Civil Rights. Alan Pomerance. 1991. pap. 10.95 (*0-8065-1244-X*, Citadel Pr) Carol Pub Group.

Repeal of the Combination Acts: 1825. LC 72-2540. (British Labour Struggles Before 1850 Ser.). 1974. 23.95 (*0-405-04432-1*) Ayer.

Repeal of the Missouri Compromise. Ray P. Orman. (History - United States Ser.). 315p. 1992. reprint ed. lib. bdg. 89.00 (*0-7812-6150-3*) Rprt Serv.

Repeat. Versie M. Smith. 120p. 1995. pap. 7.00 (*0-9635436-1-X*) M S Pub.

Repeat after Me II. Claudia Black. 190p. (Orig.). 1995. pap. 15.95 (*0-910223-22-X*) MAC Pub.

Repeat Business. Larry W. Dennis. 1993. pap. 12.95 (*0-9631766-0-9*) Rising Tide Pub.

Repeat Offender Programs for Law Enforcement. William Spelman et al. 292p. (Orig.). (C). 1990. pap. text ed. 11.00 (*1-878734-18-0*) Police Exec Res.

Repeatability Problem in Parapsychology. Ed. by Betty Shapin & Lisette Coly. LC 84-62647. (International Conference Proceedings Ser.). 264p. 1985. 18.00 (*0-912328-38-X*) Parapsych Foun.

R

Repeated Games with Incomplete Information. Robert J. Aumann & Michael B. Maschler. 368p. 1995. 37.50 (*0-262-01147-6*) MIT Pr.

Repeated Takes. Michael Chanan. 224p. (C). 1995. pap. text ed. 20.00 (*1-85984-012-4*, C0532, Pub. by Vrso UK) Norton.

Repeated Takes. Michael Chanan. 224p. (C). 1995. text ed. 65.00 (*1-85984-917-2*, C0531, Pub. by Vrso UK) Norton.

Repeater Directory, 1996-1997. 1996. pap. 8.00 (*0-87259-560-9*) Am Radio.

Repeating Island: The Caribbean & the Postmodern Perspective. Antonio Benitez-Rojo. Tr. by James E. Maraniss. LC 91-36098. (Post-Contemporary Interventions Ser.). 328p. 1992. pap. 17.95 (*0-8223-1221-2*); lib. bdg. 54.95 (*0-8223-1225-5*) Duke.

Repeating Island: The Caribbean & the Postmodern Perspective. 2nd ed. Antonio Benitez-Rojo. Tr. by James E. Maraniss. LC 96-14685. (Post-Contemporary Interventions Ser.). 376p. (SPA.). 1996. text ed. 49.95 (*0-8223-1860-1*); pap. text ed. 17.95 (*0-8223-1865-2*) Duke.

***Repeating the Words of the Buddha.** Tulku U. Rinpoche. 112p. 1996. pap. 12.95 (*962-7341-16-9*, Pub. by Rang Jung Yshe HK) Bookpeople.

Repentance. Bishop Chrysostomos. (Themes in Orthodox Patristic Psychology Ser.: Vol. III). 75p. (Orig.). 1986. pap. 5.00 (*0-911165-09-6*) Ctr Trad Orthodox.

Repentance. Ephraem. pap. 1.95 (*0-89981-076-4*) Eastern Orthodox.

***Repentance: A Comparative Perspective.** Ed. by Amitai Etzioini & David E. Carney. LC 96-51904. 224p. 1997. 54.50 (*0-8476-8470-9*); pap. 18.95 (*0-8476-8471-7*) Rowman.

Repentance: The Joy Filled Life. Basilea Schlink. LC 83-23774. 96p. 1984. pap. 5.99 (*0-87123-592-7*) Bethany Hse.

Repentance & Blessings Deut. No. 5 see Torah Anthology: Meam Lo'ez

***Repentance & Confession in the Orthodox Church.** John Chryssaugis. 102p. 1996. reprint ed. pap. 5.95 (*0-917651-56-1*) Holy Cross Orthodox.

Repentance & Revolt: A Psychological Approach to History. Richard R. Freeman. 247p. 1975. 34.50 (*0-8386-7471-2*) Fairleigh Dickinson.

Repentance & Twentieth Century Man. C. John Miller. (Orig.). 1993. pap. 5.95 (*0-87508-334-X*) Chr Lit.

Repentance, Bk. 2: A Study of the Elementary Principles of Christ. Ed. by Joe Oakley. (First Principles Ser.). 1990. student ed. 6.00 (*0-685-45027-9*); student ed. 6.00 (*0-923968-02-4*); pap. 6.00 (*0-685-32619-5*); 6.00 (*0-318-49989-4*) Shady Grove Ch Pubns.

Repentance in Jewish Ethics, Philosophy & Mysticism. Shimon Shokek. LC 95-15870. (Jewish Studies: vol. 15). 272p. 1996. text ed. 89.95 (*0-7734-9407-3*) E Mellen.

Repentance of Lorraine. 2nd ed. Andrei Codrescu. 1995. mass mkt. 6.95 (*1-56333-329-5*, Rhinoceros) Masquerade.

Repentance of Mary Magdalene. Lewis Wager. LC 70-133754. (Tudor Facsimile Texts. Old English Plays Ser.: No. 36). reprint ed. 59.50 (*0-404-53336-1*) AMS Pr.

Repentance to Redemption. J. Unterman. pap. 16.50 (*1-85075-109-9*, Pub. by Sheffield Acad UK) CUP Services.

Repentant Heart. Dudley J. Delffs. 150p. (Orig.). 1995. per., pap. 9.00 (*0-89109-877-1*) NavPress.

Repentant Job: A Ricoeurian Icon for Biblical Theology. Thomas F. Dailey. LC 94-21285. 256p. (Orig.). (C). 1994. reprint ed. pap. text ed. 32.50 (*0-8191-9590-1*); reprint ed. lib. bdg. 59.50 (*0-8191-9589-8*) U Pr of Amer.

Repercussions of the Kalam in Jewish Philosophy. Harry A. Wolfson. LC 78-9798. 250p. 1979. 32.00 (*0-674-76175-8*) HUP.

Reperfusion-Induced Arrhythmias: Control & Mechanisms. Arpad Tosaki. 105p. 1995. pap. 18.00 (*963-05-6851-9*, Pub. by A K HU) Intl Spec Bk.

Reperfusion Injuries & Clinical Capillary Leak Syndrome. Ed. by B. A. Zikria et al. LC 94-5629. (Illus.). 480p. 1994. 85.00 (*0-87993-583-9*) Futura Pub.

Repertoire, Vol. 1. Ed. by Wolfgang Hageney. (Illus.). 88p. (ENG, FRE, GER, ITA & SPA.). 1987. pap. 19.95 (*88-7070-096-8*) Belvedere USA.

Repertoire, Vol. 2. Ed. by Wolfgang Hageney. (Illus.). 88p. (ENG, FRE, GER, ITA & SPA.). 1987. pap. 19.95 (*88-7070-097-6*) Belvedere USA.

Repertoire, Vol. 3. Ed. by Wolfgang Hageney. (Illus.). 88p. (ENG, FRE, GER, ITA & SPA.). 1987. pap. 19.95 (*88-7070-098-4*) Belvedere USA.

Repertoire, Vol. 4. Ed. by Wolfgang Hageney. (Illus.). 88p. (ENG, FRE, GER, ITA & SPA.). 1987. pap. 19.95 (*88-7070-099-2*) Belvedere USA.

Repertoire, Vol. 5. Ed. by Wolfgang Hageney. (Illus.). 88p. (ENG, FRE, GER, ITA & SPA.). 1987. pap. 19.95 (*88-7070-100-X*) Belvedere USA.

Repertoire: Modern Interior Design 1928-1929. Ed. by Wolfgang Hageney. (Illus.). 312p. (ENG, FRE, GER, ITA & SPA.). 1986. 69.95 (*88-7070-068-2*) Belvedere USA.

Repertoire de la Cuisine. Louis Saulnier. 1977. text ed. 16.95 (*0-8120-5108-4*) Barron.

Repertoire de la Jurisprudence Arbitrale Internationale-Repertory of International Arbitral Jurisprudence, Vol. 3, No. 3. Ed. by Vincent Coussirat-Coustere. (C). 1990. lib. bdg. 585.00 (*0-7923-1083-7*) Kluwer Ac.

Repertoire de peintures du Moyen Age et de la renaissance (1280-1580), 6 Vols. Salomon Reinach. 1974. pap. 560.00 (*0-8115-0047-0*) Periodicals Srv.

Repertoire Des Imprimeurs Parisiens, Libraires, Foundeurs De Caracteres et Correcteurs De l'Imprimerie Depuis l'Introduction De l'Imprimerie (1470) Jusqu'a la Fin Du Xvie Siecle. H. Renouard. 61.95 (*0-685-35952-2*) Fr & Eur.

Repertoire des Livres de Langue Francaise Disponibles (1972), 2 tomes. 95.00 (*0-685-35972-7*) Fr & Eur.

Repertoire des References aux Arts et a la Litterature dans "A la Recherche du Temps Perdu" de Marcel Proust. Michele M. Magill. LC 91-65734. (Marcel Proust Studies: Vol. 2). 272p. (FRE.). 1991. lib. bdg. 38.95 (*0-917786-85-8*) Summa Pubns.

Repertoire des Sources Historiques Du Moyen Age: Bio-Bibliographie, 2 vols. 2nd ed. C. Ulysse Chevalier. 1907. 500.00 (*0-527-16700-2*) Periodicals Srv.

Repertoire des Sources Historiques du Moyen Age: Topo Bibliographie, 1894-1903, 2 vols. Cyr U. Chevalier. (FRE.). 1974. 420.00 (*0-527-16710-X*) Periodicals Srv.

Repertoire Des Traites De Paix, De Commerce, D'alliance Etc., 2 vols. Tetot. LC 10-16452. 1974. reprint ed. Set. 72.00 (*0-527-89200-9*) Periodicals Srv.

Repertoire des Vases Peints Grecs et Etrusques, 2 Vols. Salomon Reinach. 1974. 130.00 (*0-8115-4856-2*) Periodicals Srv.

Repertoire Internationale des Etudes Africaines see International Directory of African Studies Research

Repertoire Mondial des Crustaces Copepodes des Eaux Interieures, No. 3: Harpacticoides. B. Dussart & D. Defaye. LC 89-70852. (Crustaceana Supplements Ser.: No. 16). vii, 384p. (FRE.). 1990. pap. 92.75 (*90-04-09191-2*) E J Brill.

Repertoire of League of Nations Serial Documents, 1919-1947, 2 vols. Carnegie Endowment for International Peace Staff. Ed. by Victor Y. Ghebali & Catherine Ghebali. LC 73-7839. 773p. 1973. lib. bdg. 85.00 (*0-379-00371-6*) Oceana.

Repertoire of Practice of the Security Council. 275p. 1974. 17.00 (*92-1-137008-6*, E.79.VII.1) UN.

Repertoire of Security Council Practice, Supplement 1984. 364p. 1991. 35.00 (*92-1-137027-2*, 91.VII.1) UN.

Repertoire of Synonyms of the Italian Language: Repertorio dei Sinonimi della Lingua Italiana. R. Ferrari. 463p. (ITA.). 1980. 24.95 (*0-8288-1989-0*, M9181) Fr & Eur.

Repertoire of the Practice of the Security Council. Incl. 1946-1951. pap. 6.00 (*0-685-13111-4*, E.54.VII.1); 1952-1955. 3.00 (*0-685-13112-2*, E.57.VII.1); 1956-1958. pap. 3.00 (*0-685-13113-0*, E.59.VII.1); 1964-1965. pap. 6.00 (*0-685-13115-7*, E.68.VII.1); 1966-1968. pap. 5.50 (*0-685-13116-5*, E.71.VII.1); 1969-1971. pap. 17.00 (*0-685-13117-3*, E.76.VII.1); 1972-1974. pap. 17.00 (*0-685-13118-1*, E.79.VII.1); write for info. (*0-318-60628-3*) UN.

Repertoire of the Practice of the Security Council: Supplement, 1975-1980. 480p. 1986. 29.00 (*92-1-137026-4*, E.86.VII.1) UN.

Repertoires & Cycles of Collective Action. Ed. by Mark Traugott. LC 94-37271. (Illus.). 208p. 1995. text ed. 28.95 (*0-8223-1527-0*) Duke.

Repertoires & Cycles of Collective Action. Ed. by Mark Traugott. LC 94-37271. (Illus.). 208p. 1995. pap. text ed. 13.95 (*0-8223-1546-7*) Duke.

Repertorio Selecto del Teatro Hispanoamericano Contemporaneo. Erminio Neglia & Luis Ordaz. LC 79-15199. 111p. 1982. 1.00 (*0-87918-042-0*) ASU Lat Am St.

Repertorium see Theilheimer's Synthetic Methods of Organic Chemistry: Synthetische Methoden der Organischen Chemie

***Repertorium Bibliographicum, 4 vols.** Ludwig Hain. Incl. Vol. 1. . 598p. 1996. reprint ed. Not sold separately (*1-888262-15-X*); Vol. 2. . 568p. 1996. reprint ed. Not sold separately (*1-888262-16-8*); Vol. 3. . 560p. 1996. reprint ed. Not sold separately (*1-888262-17-6*); Vol. 4. . 552p. 1996. reprint ed. Not sold separately (*1-888262-18-4*); reprint ed. 195.00 (*1-888262-19-2*) Martino Pubng.

Repertorium der Chemiscshen Litteratur Von 494 Vor Christi Geburt Bis 1806 in Chronologischer Ordnung Aufgestellt, 2 vols. G. F. Fuchs. xxix, 1254p. 1974. reprint ed. write for info. (*3-487-05239-3*) G Olms Pubs.

Repertorium der Griechischen Christlichen Papyri II: Kirchenvaeter-Papyri, Teil 1: Beschreibungen. Ed. by Kurt Aland & Hans-Udo Rosenbaum. (Patristische Texte Und Studien: Bd. 42). cxxix, 580p. (GER.). (C). 1995. lib. bdg. 260.00 (*3-11-006798-6*) De Gruyter.

Repertorium der Griechischen Christlichen Papyri, Pt.1: Biblische Papyri, Altes Testament, Neues Testament, Varia, Apokryphen. Ed. by Kurt Aland. (Patristische Texte und Studien: Vol. 18). 473p. (C). 1976. 142.35 (*3-11-004674-1*) De Gruyter.

Repertorium fuer Kunstwissenschaft, 52 vols. Ed. by Wilhelm Waetzold et al. (GER.). (C). 1969. 11,873.00 (*3-11-002641-4*) De Gruyter.

***Repertorium Germanicum Bd. II, Lieferung 1: Einleitung und Regesten.** Deutschen Historischen Institut in Rom Staff. iv, 578p. (GER.). 1961. write for info. (*3-296-21002-4*, Pub. by Weidmann GW) Lubrecht & Cramer.

***Repertorium Germanicum Bd. II, Lieferung 2: Personenregister.** Deutschen Historischen Institut in Rom Staff. iv, 578p. (GER.). 1961. write for info. (*3-296-21003-2*, Pub. by Weidmann GW) Lubrecht & Cramer.

***Repertorium Germanicum Bd. II, Lieferung 3: Ortsregister.** Deutschen Historischen Institut in Rom Staff. iv, 578p. (GER.). 1961. write for info. (*3-296-21004-0*, Pub. by Weidmann GW) Lubrecht & Cramer.

***Repertorium Germanicum Bd. IV, Teilband 1: Martin V., 1417-1431.** Deutschen Historischen Institut in Rom Staff. x, 1492p. (GER.). 1991. reprint ed. write for info. (*3-615-00065-X*, Pub. by Weidmann GW) Lubrecht & Cramer.

***Repertorium Germanicum Bd. IV, Teilband 2: (I, J, Y)** Deutschen Historischen Institut in Rom Staff. iv, 1493p. (GER.). 1957. write for info. (*3-296-21007-5*, Pub. by Weidmann GW) Lubrecht & Cramer.

***Repertorium Germanicum Bd. IV, Teilband 3: (L-Z)** Deutschen Historischen Institut in Rom Staff. iv, 2569p. (GER.). 1958. write for info. (*3-296-21008-3*, Pub. by Weidmann GW) Lubrecht & Cramer.

***Repertorium Germanicum Bd. I: Clemens VII. von Avignon 1378-1394.** Deutschen Historischen Institut in Rom Staff. xvi, 182p. (GER.). 1991. reprint ed. write for info. (*3-615-00063-3*, Pub. by Weidmann GW) Lubrecht & Cramer.

***Repertorium Germanicum Bd. III: Alexander V., Johann XXIII., Konstanzer Konzil 1409-1417.** Deutschen Historischen Institut in Rom Staff. viii, 48p. (GER.). 1991. reprint ed. write for info. (*3-615-00064-1*, Pub. by Weidmann GW) Lubrecht & Cramer.

Repertorium Nominum Gentilium et Cognominum Latinorum. Ed. by Heikki Solin & Olli Salomies. (Alpha-Omega, Reihe A Ser.: Bd. LXXX). xii, 474p. (GER.). 1988. write for info. (*3-487-07986-0*) G Olms Pubs.

Repertorium Organorum Recentioris et Motetorum Vetustissimi Stili, 4 vols. Friedrich Lucwig. 1972. reprint ed. write for info. (*3-487-04197-9*) G Olms Pubs.

Repertorium Organorum Recentioris et Motetorum Vetustissimi Stili, Band I, 2: Handschiften in Mensuralnotation. Fredrich Ludwig. (Wissenschaftliche Abhandlungen-Musicological Studies: Vol. 26). 350p. (GER.). 1979. lib. bdg. 134.00 (*0-912024-37-2*) Inst Mediaeval Mus.

Repertorium Organorum Recentioris et Motetorum Vetustissimi Stili, Katalog. Friedrich Ludwig. Ed. by Luther Dittmer. (Wissenschaftliche Abhandlungen-Musicological Studies: Vol. 17). 128p. (GER.). 1971. lib. bdg. 54.00 (*0-912024-87-9*) Inst Mediaeval Mus.

Repertorium Repertorii. Clemens Blume. 315p. 1971. reprint ed. 80.00 (*3-487-04209-6*) G Olms Pubs.

Repertory Additions from Kent's Lectures on Homeopathic Materia Medica. Linda Johnston. 554p. (C). 1990. student ed. 55.00 (*1-877691-24-0*) C Kent Agency.

Repertory Grid Technique & Personal Constructs: Applications in Clinical & Educational Settings. Ed. by Nigel Beail. (Illus.). 407p. 1985. 20.00 (*0-914797-16-6*) Brookline Bks.

Repertory of Decisions of the International Court of Justice, 1947-1992. Ed. by Giovanni C. Bruno. LC 94-25721. 1994. lib. bdg. 471.50 (*0-7923-2993-7*, Pub. by M Nijhoff NE) Kluwer Ac.

Repertory of Homoeopathic Materia Medica. J. T. Kent. 1975. 45.00 (*0-685-76570-9*) Formur Intl.

Repertory of International Arbitral Jurisprudence. Ed. by Vincent Coussirat-Coustere & Pierre M. Eisemann. 1989. lib. bdg. 301.50 (*90-247-3762-1*) Kluwer Ac.

Repertory of International Arbitral Jurisprudence, 2 vols., Vol. 1. Ed. by Vincent Coussirat-Coustere & Pierre M. Eismann. (ENG & FRE.). 1989. Vol. III: Pt. 1, 1044p. lib. bdg. 279.50 (*90-247-3761-3*) Kluwer Ac.

Repertory of International Arbitral Jurisprudence, 2 vols., Vol. 2. Ed. by Vincent Coussirat-Coustere & Pierre M. Eismann. (ENG & FRE.). 1991. Vol. III: 1946-1988, 1040p. 287.00 (*0-318-68291-5*) Kluwer Ac.

Repertory of International Arbitral Jurisprudence, 2 vols., Vol. 3. Ed. by Vincent Coussirat-Coustere & Pierre M. Eismann. (ENG & FRE.). 1990. lib. bdg. 663.50 (*0-7923-1090-X*) Kluwer Ac.

Repertory of Practice of United Nations Organs, Suppl. No. 5, Vol. 2. 200p. 1985. 17.50 (*92-1-133270-2*, E.85.V.8) UN.

Repertory of Practice of United Nations Organs: Articles 1-111 of the Charter, Table of Contents & Subject Index, Suppl. Nos. 1-3. 11.00 (*0-317-52083-0*, E.79.V.2) UN.

Repertory of Practice of United Nations Organs: Articles 55-111 of the Charter, Suppl. No. 4, Vol. 2. 400p. 1982. 26.00 (*92-1-133199-4*, E.82.V.7) UN.

Repertory of Practice of United Nations Organs: Articles 92-111 of the Charter, Suppl. No. 5, vol. 5. 212p. 1986. 19.00 (*92-1-133283-4*, E.86.V.7) UN.

Repertory of Practice of United Nations Organs: Suppl. No. 5 Vol. 1 Articles 1-22 of the Charter Covering the Period 1 Jan. 1970 to 31 Dec. 1978. 300p. 1986. 27.00 (*92-1-133282-6*, E.86.V.6) UN.

Repertory of Practices of United Nations Organs: Articles 1-54 of the Charter, Suppl. No. 4, Vol. 1. 26.00 (*0-317-52084-9*, E.80.V.13) UN.

Repertory of Pregnancy, Parturition & Puerperium. Alberto Soler-Medina. 79p. (Orig.). 1989. pap. text ed. 12.00 (*3-7760-1097-5*, Pub. by K F Haug Pubs) Medicina Bio.

Repertory of Proper Names in Yuan Literary Sources, 3 vols. Igor De Rachewiltz & May Wang. lxiii, 2716p. (CHI.). 1988. 200.00 (*0-89986-367-1*) Oriental Bk Store.

Repertory of Shakespeare's Company, 1594-1613. Roslyn L. Knutson. 282p. 1991. 36.00 (*1-55728-191-2*) U of Ark Pr.

Repertory of the Comedies Humaines of Balzac. Anatole Cerfberr & Jules Christophe. 1972. 75.00 (*0-87968-319-8*) Gordon Pr.

Repertory of the Homoeopathic Materia Medica. 6th ed. J. T. Kent. 1992. reprint ed. 28.00 (*81-7021-083-6*, Pub. by Sarat) S Asia.

Repertory of Tropes at Winchester, 2 vols., Vol. 1. Alejandro E. Planchart. LC 76-3033. 407p. reprint ed. pap. 109.90 (*0-8357-3430-7*, 2039688) Bks Demand.

Repertory of Tropes at Winchester, 2 vols., Vol. 2. Alejandro E. Planchart. LC 76-3033. 408p. reprint ed. pap. 116.30 (*0-8357-3431-5*) Bks Demand.

Reperusals & Re-Collections. Logan P. Smith. LC 68-29249. (Essay Index Reprint Ser.). 1977. reprint ed. 23.95 (*0-8369-0884-8*) Ayer.

Repetition. Peter Handke. Tr. by Ralph Manheim from GER. LC 87-33065. 225p. 1988. 18.95 (*0-374-24934-2*) FS&G.

Repetition & Semiotics: Interpreting Prose Poems. Stamos Metzidakis. LC 86-60801. 175p. 1986. 21.95 (*0-917786-41-6*) Summa Pubns.

Repetition & Trauma: Toward a Teleonomic Theory of Psychoanalysis. Max M. Stern. Ed. by Liselotte B. Stern. 192p. 1988. text ed. 29.95 (*0-88163-073-X*) Analytic Pr.

Repetition in Arabic Discourse: Paradigms Sytagms, & the Ecology of Language. Barbara Johnstone. LC 90-23248. (Pragmatics & Beyond Ser.: Vol. 18). viii, 130p. 1991. 38.00 (*1-55619-284-3*) Benjamins North Am.

Repetition in Discourse Vol. 1: Interdisciplinary Perspectives. Ed. by Barbara Johnstone. LC 92-42685. (Advances in Discourse Processes Ser.: Vol. 47). 272p. 1994. pap. 42.50 (*0-89391-931-4*) Ablex Pub.

Repetition in Discourse Vol. 1: Interdisciplinary Perspectives, Vol. 1. Ed. by Barbara Johnstone. LC 92-42685. (Advances in Discourse Processes Ser.: Vol. 47). 272p. 1994. text ed. 78.50 (*0-89391-830-X*) Ablex Pub.

Repetition in Discourse Vol. 2: Interdisciplinary Perspectives. Ed. by Barbara Johnstone. LC 92-42685. (Advances in Discourse Processes Ser.: Vol. 48). 232p. 1994. text ed. 78.50 (*0-89391-831-8*) Ablex Pub.

Repetition in Discourse Vol. 2: Interdisciplinary Perspectives, Vol. 2. Ed. by Barbara Johnstone. LC 92-42685. (Advances in Discourse Processes Ser.: Vol. 48). 232p. 1994. pap. 42.50 (*0-89391-932-2*) Ablex Pub.

Repetition in Latin Poetry: Figures of Allusion. Jeffrey Wills. 528p. 1997. 90.00 (*0-19-814084-3*, Clarendon Pr) OUP.

Repetition of the Possessive Pronouns in the Septuagint Vol. 40. Raija Sollamo. LC 95-22934. (Society of Biblical Literature Septuagint & Cognate Ser.). 130p. (C). 1995. 39.95 (*0-7885-0149-6*, 060440) Scholars Pr GA.

Repetition ou l'Amour Puni. Jean Anouilh. (Folio Ser.: No. 444). (FRE.). pap. 6.95 (*2-07-036444-5*) Schoenhof.

Repetition ou l'Amour Puni. Jean Anouilh. write for info. (*0-318-63588-7*, 2383) Fr & Eur.

Repetition Ou l'Amour Puni. Jean Anouilh. 140p. (FRE.). 1973. pap. 10.95 (*0-7859-1755-1*, F81895) Fr & Eur.

Repetition ou L'amour Puni see Pieces Brillantes

Repetition Strain Injuries: Index of New Information with Authors, Subjects, References, & Research Categories. Sidney M. Hobwell. LC 96-12513. 1996. 47.50 (*0-7883-1186-7*); pap. 44.50 (*0-7883-1187-5*) ABBE Pubs Assn.

Repetitions: Poetry by Judge-Bruce Wright. LC 80-53692. 1980. 19.95 (*0-89388-207-0*); pap. 9.95 (*0-89388-208-9*) Okpaku Communications.

Repetitions: The Postmodern Occasion in Literature & Culture. William V. Spanos. LC 86-20041. 376p. 1987. text ed. 45.00 (*0-8071-1316-6*) La State U Pr.

***Repetitionstabellen zur Kurzgefabten Griechischen Schulgrammatik.** Adolf Kaegi. 48p. (GER.). 8.80 (*3-615-70200-X*, Pub. by Weidmann GW) Lubrecht & Cramer.

Repetitionstabellen Zur Kurzgefassten Griechischen Schulgrammatik. Adolf Kaegi. 48p. write for info. (*3-296-70200-8*) G Olms Pubs.

Repetitive Manufacturing Group Reprints: Crucial Issues. American Production & Inventory Control Society Staff. 216p. 1992. 16.50 (*1-55822-093-3*) Am Prod & Inventory.

***Repetitive Manufacturing Specific Industry Group Annotate Bibliography.** 3rd ed. Ed. by Raymond L. Martin. 50p. (Orig.). 1995. pap. 10.00 (*1-55822-157-3*) Am Prod & Inventory.

Repetitive Motion Disorders of the Upper Extremity. Ed. by Stephen L. Gordon et al. 554p. 1995. 105.00 (*0-89203-143-3*) Amer Acad Ortho Surg.

Repetitive Strain Industry. Wendy C. Mill. 128p. 1994. pap. 8.00 (*0-7225-2919-8*) Thorsons SF.

Repetitive Strain Injury: A Computer User's Guide. Emil Pascarelli & Deborah Quilter. 218p. 1994. pap. text ed. 15.95 (*0-471-59533-0*) Wiley.

***Repetitive Strain Injury Recovery Book.** Deborah Quitter. 224p. (Orig.). 1997. pap. 14.95 (*0-8027-7514-4*) Walker & Co.

***Repetitive Strain Injury Sourcebook.** 224p. 1997. 25.00 (*1-56565-791-8*, Anodyne) Lowell Hse.

Repha. Repha Buckman. Ed. & Intro. by Robert Lawson. (Illus.). 68p. (Orig.). 1986. 15.99 (*0-940559-03-X*); pap. 5.00 (*0-940559-00-5*); audio 6.95 (*0-940559-01-3*); lp 6.95 (*0-940559-02-1*) Tri Crown Pr.

Repicturing Abstraction. Arthur Danto et al. Ed. by George Cruger & Randee Humphrey. LC 94-72978. (Illus.). 108p. 1995. 15.00 (*0-935519-20-3*) Anderson Gal.

Repiecing the Past: Patterns for 12 Quilts from the Collection of Sara Rhodes Dillow. Sara R. Dillow. LC 95-38724. 1995. pap. 19.95 (*1-56477-129-6*, B206) That Patchwork.

Repin, Ilya. Gregory Sternin. (C). 1987. 100.00 (*0-685-34422-3*, Pub. by Collets) St Mut.

Repiratory Diseases & Disorders Sourcebook. Ed. by Allan R. Cook & Peter D. Dresser. LC 95-19214. (Health Reference Ser.: Vol. 6). 771p. 1995. lib. bdg. 75.00 (*0-7808-0037-0*) Omnigraphics Inc.

Replacement Cardiac Valves. Endre Bodnar & Robert W. Frater. (Illus.). 480p. 1991. 94.50 (*0-08-035773-3*, Pub. by PPI UK) McGraw.

An Asterisk (*) at the beginning of an entry indicates that the title is appearing in BIP for the first time.

Replacement Cost Accounting. Lawrence Revsine. (Contemporary Topics in Accounting Ser.). (Illus.). 224p. 1973. pap. text ed. write for info. (*0-13-773630-4*) P-H.

Replacement Cost Is the Basis. BSRIA Staff. (C). 1985. 90.00 (*0-685-33897-5*, Pub. by Build Servs Info Assn UK) St Mut.

Replacement Costs & Accounting Reform in Post World War I Germany. Frank Clarke & Graeme Dean. 1991. text ed. 10.00 (*0-8153-0006-9*) Garland.

Replacement of Renal Function by Dialysis. 4th ed. Ed. by Claude Jacobs. LC 95-31081. 1480p. (C). 1996. lib. bdg. 325.00 (*0-7923-3610-0*) Kluwer Ac.

Replacement of Renal Function by Dialysis: A Textbook of Dialysis. 3rd enl. ed. Ed. by John F. Maher. (C). 1989. lib. bdg. 348.50 (*0-89838-414-1*) Kluwer Ac.

Replacement, Reduction & Refinement of Animal Experiments in the Development & Control of Biological Products. Ed. by F. Brown et al. (Developments in Biological Standardization Ser.: Vol. 86, 1996). (Illus.). x, 374p. 1996. pap. 300.00 (*3-8055-6260-8*) S Karger.

Replacing. Ed. by Dennis Cooley. 323p. (C). 1980. pap. text ed. 3.75 (*0-920802-34-6*, Pub. by ECW Press CN) Genl Dist Srvs.

***Replacing Citizenship: Aids Activism & Radical Democracy.** LC 96-52388. 1997. pap. text ed. 18.95 (*1-57230-222-4*) Guilford Pubns.

***Replacing Citizenship: AIDS Activism & Radical Democracy.** Michael P. Brown. LC 96-52388. 1997. lib. bdg. 40.00 (*1-57230-210-0*) Guilford Pubns.

Replacing Dad. Shelley F. Mickle. 266p. 1993. 16.95 (*1-56512-017-5*) Algonquin Bks.

Replacing Dad. Shelley F. Mickle. 1995. mass mkt. 4.99 (*0-312-95413-1*) St Martin.

Replacing Gasoline: Alternative Fuels for Light-Duty Vehicles. 1991. lib. bdg. 69.95 (*0-8490-4957-1*) Gordon Pr.

Replacing Petrochemicals with Biochemicals: A Pollution Prevention Strategy for the Great Lakes Region. Irshad Ahmed & David Morris. LC 94-31806. 55p. (Orig.). 1994. 25.00 (*0-917582-96-9*) Inst Local Self Re.

***Replacing the Federal Income Tax with a Consumption-Based Tax System.** Nathan Associates, Inc. Staff. (Orig.). 1996. pap. 40.00 (*0-614-30166-1*) Nat Retail Fed.

Replacing the Income Tax: Framework for a New Tax System. Alexander T. Hunt. Ed. by Bradley Belt. LC 95-44332. (Report Ser.). 45p. (C). 1995. pap. text ed. 14.95 (*0-89206-281-9*) CSI Studies.

Replacing the Warrior: Cultural Ideals & Militarism. William A. Myers. LC 85-81253. 32p. (Orig.). 1985. pap. 3.00 (*0-87574-263-7*) Pendle Hill.

Replanning the Blitzed City Center: A Comparative Study of Bristol, Coventry & Southampton 1941-1950. Junichi Hasegawa. (Themes in the Twentieth Century Ser.). 192p. 1992. 95.00 (*0-335-15634-7*, Open Univ Pr); pap. 36.00 (*0-335-15633-9*, Open Univ Pr) Taylor & Francis.

Replanting the Tree of Life: Towards An International Agenda for Coconut Palm Research. Gabrielle J. Persley. (Illus.). 172p. 1992. 55.00 (*0-85198-815-6*) CAB Intl.

Replay. Ken Grimwood. 320p. 1992. mass mkt. 5.99 (*0-441-71592-3*) Ace Bks.

***Replica.** Lionel Saben. 1997. pap. 5.99 (*0-7860-0479-7*) Kensgtn Pub Corp.

Replica Shadowing & Freeze-Etching Techniques. rev. ed. M. Willison & Alan J. Rowe. (Practical Methods in Electron Microscopy Ser.: Vol. 8). 302p. 1980. pap. 52.00 (*0-444-80165-0*) Elsevier.

***Replicant Night, Vol. 3.** K. W. Jeter. (Blade Runner Ser.). 1997. mass mkt. 6.50 (*0-553-57775-1*) Bantam.

Replicating History: Guide to the Plaster Casts on View at the Michael C. Carlos Museum & in Michael C. Carlos Hall, Emory University. Carey F. Ross et al. 27p. 1994. pap. 4.50 (*0-9638169-5-0*) M C Carlos Mus.

Replication & Transcription of Chromatin. Tsameu. 288p. 1992. 232.00 (*0-8493-6803-0*, QH599) CRC Pr.

***Replication of a Model for Determining Community-Based Needs of American Indians with Disabilities Through Consumer Involvement in Community Planning & Change: Executive Summary.** C. A. Marshall et al. 10p. 1992. pap. text ed. write for info. (*1-888557-02-8*, 100083) No Ariz Univ.

***Replication of a Model for Determining Community-Based Needs of American Indians with Disabilities Through Consumer Involvement in Community Planning & Change: Final Report, Phase I.** C. A. Marshall et al. 78p. 1992. pap. text ed. write for info. (*1-888557-03-6*, 100084) No Ariz Univ.

***Replication of Anterior Teeth in the Four Seasons of Life.** Klaus Muterthies. (Illus.). 92p. 1991. text ed. 66.00 (*0-86715-236-2*) Quint Pub Co.

Replication of DNA. David T. Denhardt. Ed. by John J. Head. LC 83-71256. (Carolina Biology Readers Ser.: No. 120). (Illus.). 16p. (gr. 10 up). 1983. pap. 2.75 (*0-89278-320-6*, 45-9720) Carolina Biological.

Replication of DNA & RNA. (Landmark Ser.). 1979. 22.50 (*0-8422-4124-8*) Irvington.

Replication of DNA in Micro-Organisms. Cold Spring Harbor Symposia on Quantitative Biology Staff. LC 34-8174. (Cold Spring Harbor Symposia on Quantitative Biology Ser.: Vol. 33). (Illus.). 906p. 1968. pap. 180.00 (*0-7837-8980-7*, 2049761) Bks Demand.

Replication of Habitat Profiles for Birds. Richard F. Johnston. (Occasional Papers: No. 82). 11p. 1979. pap. 1.00 (*0-317-04610-1*) U KS Nat Hist Mus.

Replication of Mammalian Parvoviruses. Ed. by David C. Ward & Peter Tattersall. LC 77-90839. 559p. 1978. reprint ed. pap. 159.40 (*0-608-01799-X*, 2062452) Bks Demand.

Replication of Viral & Cellular Genomes. Ed. by Yechiel Becker. (Developments in Molecular Virology Ser.). 1983. lib. bdg. 135.00 (*0-89838-589-X*) Kluwer Ac.

Replication Research in the Social Sciences. Ed. by James W. Neuliep. 530p. 1991. 55.00 (*0-8039-4091-2*); pap. 25.95 (*0-8039-4092-0*) Sage.

***Replication Techniques in Distributed Systems.** Abdelsalam A. Helal et al. LC 96-31702. (International Series on Advances in Database Systems). 176p. (C). 1996. lib. bdg. 97.50 (*0-7923-9800-9*) Kluwer Ac.

Replications: A Robotic History of the Science Fiction Film. J. P. Telotte. LC 95-6586. (Illus.). 224p. (C). 1995. 15.95 (*0-252-06466-6*); text ed. 29.95 (*0-252-02177-0*) U of Ill Pr.

Replications: Archaeology, Art History, Psychoanalysis. Whitney Davis. Ed. by Richard W. Quinn. 1996. 65.00 (*0-271-01523-3*); pap. 28.50 (*0-271-01524-1*) Pa St U Pr.

***Replicator Run.** Rainer Rey. 1997. mass mkt. 5.99 (*0-449-18337-8*, GM) Fawcett.

Replies from Interested Parties on Copyright & Neighbouring Rights in the Information Society. European Commission Staff. 484p. 1995. pap. 100.00 (*92-827-0204-9*, C1-87-94-043ACAC, Pub. by Europ Com UK) Bernan Associates.

Replikation des MobilenIntros (piDNA) in Mitochondrien von Podaspora Anserina. Mechanismus ubd Auswirkung auf die Alterung des Pilzes. Marcus Wedde. (Bibliotheca Mycologica Ser.: Vol. 156). (Illus.). 93p. (GER.). 1994. pap. 45.00 (*3-443-59058-6*, Pub. by Cramer-Borntraeger GW) Lubrecht & Cramer.

Reply from Wilderness Island. Peter Balakian. 77p. 1988. pap. 10.95 (*0-935296-73-5*) Sheep Meadow.

Reply of Our Lady Teresa to the Poet Crashaw on the Occasion of His Having Written a Hymn for Her Sake a Few Years after Her Death. Marsha Campbell. (Illus.). 69p. (Orig.). 1996. pap. 12.00 (*0-9642457-0-1*) Goddesses We Aint.

Reply of the Orthodox Church to Roman Catholic Overtures on Reunion. enl. rev. ed. Anthimos. 64p. 1986. pap. 2.00 (*0-913026-62-X*) St Nectarios.

Reply of the Orthodox Church to Roman Catholic Overtures on Reunion. Chrysostomos H. Stratman. (Orig.). (GRE.). 1978. reprint ed. pap. 1.50 (*0-938366-35-1*) Orthodox Chr.

Reply Requested: Thirty Letters of Advice. R. Yerkey. 1981. text ed. 15.33 (*0-201-10078-9*) Addison-Wesley.

Reply to J. A. Hobson. C. H. Douglas. 1972. 59.95 (*0-8490-0945-6*) Gordon Pr.

Reply to the Essay on Population by the Rev. T. R. Malthus. William C. Hazlitt. LC 66-21678. (Reprints of Economic Classics Ser.). 378p. 1967. reprint ed. 49.50 (*0-678-00203-7*) Kelley.

Reply to the Observations of Lieut. General Sir William Howe, on a Pamphlet, Entitled "Letters to a Nobleman" In Which His Misrepresentations Are Detected. Joseph Galloway. LC 72-8751. (American Revolutionary Ser.). 1781. lib. bdg. 26.50 (*0-8398-0669-8*) Irvington.

Repo & Reverse Markets. Marcia L. Stigum. 396p. 1988. text ed. 75.00 (*0-87094-988-8*) Irwin Prof Pubng.

Reponse Biblique Aux Temoins D. David Reed. 160p. (FRE.). 1991. pap. 6.95 (*0-8297-1108-2*) Life Pubs Intl.

Reponses. Francoise Sagan. 192p. 1974. pap. 3.95 (*0-686-55396-9*) Fr & Eur.

Reponses a Paul Claudel: Avec: Lettres Ouvertes. Francois Mauriac. (Illus.). 12.50 (*0-686-55476-0*) Fr & Eur.

Report. Incl. 1975. pap. 4.80 (*0-686-16950-6*); Set pap. (*0-318-56496-3*) World Health.

Report. American Psychological Association, Committee on the Standardizing of Procedure in Experimental Tests. Ed. by R. S. Woodworth. Bd. with Tests of Practical Mental Classification. W. H. Healy. ; Some Types of Attention. H. C. McComas. ; On the Functions of the Cerebrum. S. I. Franz. (Psychology Monographs General & Applied: Vol. 13). 1974. reprint ed. Set pap. 55.00 (*0-8115-1412-9*) Periodicals Srv.

Report, Vol. I. TWMC Staff. 302p. (Orig.). 1995. 18.95 (*0-9649409-0-6*) TWMC Pubng.

Report, Vol. I. TWMC Staff. 302p. (Orig.). 1995. pap. 12.95 (*0-9649409-3-0*) TWMC Pubng.

Report, Vol. 10. Ed. by Lida F. Harshman. 1970. 5.00 (*0-935057-25-0*) OH Genealogical.

Report, Vol. 11. Ed. by Lida F. Harshman. 1971. 5.00 (*0-935057-26-9*) OH Genealogical.

Report, Vol. 12. Ed. by Lida F. Harshman. 1972. 3.75 (*0-935057-27-7*) OH Genealogical.

Report, Vol. 13. Ed. by Lida F. Harshman. 1973. 5.00 (*0-935057-28-5*) OH Genealogical.

Report, Vol. 14. Ed. by Lida F. Harshman. 1974. 2.50 (*0-935057-29-3*) OH Genealogical.

Report, Vol. 15. Ed. by Lida F. Harshman. 1975. 3.75 (*0-935057-30-7*) OH Genealogical.

Report, Vol. 16. Ed. by Lida F. Harshman. 1976. 5.00 (*0-935057-31-5*) OH Genealogical.

Report, Vol. 17. Ed. by Lida F. Harshman. 1977. 5.00 (*0-935057-32-3*) OH Genealogical.

Report, Vol. 18. Ed. by Cora H. Bartholow. 1978. 5.00 (*0-935057-33-1*) OH Genealogical.

Report, Vol. 19. Ed. by Cora H. Bartholow. 1979. 5.00 (*0-935057-34-X*) OH Genealogical.

Report, Vol. 20. Ed. by Cora H. Bartholow. 1980. 5.00 (*0-935057-35-8*) OH Genealogical.

Report, Vol. 21. Ed. by Cora H. Bartholow. 1981. 2.50 (*0-935057-36-6*) OH Genealogical.

Report, Vol. 22. Ed. by Cora H. Bartholow. 1982. 3.75 (*0-935057-37-4*) OH Genealogical.

Report, Vol. 23. Ed. by Carol W. Bell. 1983. 5.00 (*0-935057-38-2*) OH Genealogical.

Report, Vol. 24. Ed. by Carol W. Bell. 1984. 3.75 (*0-935057-39-0*) OH Genealogical.

Report, Vol. 25. Ed. by Carol W. Bell. 1985. 5.00 (*0-935057-40-4*) OH Genealogical.

Report, Vol. 26. Ed. by Carol W. Bell. 1986. 5.00 (*0-935057-42-0*) OH Genealogical.

Report, Vol. 27. Ed. by Carol W. Bell. 1987. 5.00 (*0-935057-66-8*) OH Genealogical.

Report, Vol. 28. Ed. by Carol W. Bell. 1988. 5.00 (*0-935057-54-4*) OH Genealogical.

Report, Vol. 29. Ed. by Carol W. Bell. 1989. 5.00 (*0-935057-55-2*) OH Genealogical.

Report, Vol. 30. Ed. by Carol W. Bell. 1990. 5.00 (*0-935057-59-5*) OH Genealogical.

Report, Vol. 31. Ed. by Carol W. Bell. 1991. 5.00 (*0-935057-64-1*) OH Genealogical.

Report, Vol. 32. Ed. by Carol W. Bell. 1992. 5.00 (*0-935057-68-4*) OH Genealogical.

Report, Vol. 33. Ed. by Phyllis B. Miller. 1993. 25.00 (*0-935057-71-4*) OH Genealogical.

Report, Vol. 34. Ed. by Phyllis B. Miller. 1994. 25.00 (*0-935057-76-5*) OH Genealogical.

Report, Vol. 35. Ed. by Phyllis B. Miller. 1995. 25.00 (*0-935057-79-X*) OH Genealogical.

Report, Vol. 36. Ed. by Phyllis Delaney. 1996. 27.00 (*0-935057-81-1*) OH Genealogical.

Report: Proceedings of the WHO Expert Committee on Biological Standardization, 21st, Geneva, 1968. WHO Staff. (Technical Report Ser.: No. 293). 86p. (ENG, FRE, RUS & SPA.). 1964. pap. text ed. 5.00 (*92-4-120293-9*, 1100293) World Health.

Report: Proceedings of the WHO Expert Committee on Biological Standardization, 21st, Geneva, 1968. WHO Staff. (Technical Report Ser.: No. 384). 384p. (ENG, FRE, RUS & SPA.). 1968. pap. 7.00 (*92-4-120384-6*, 1100384) World Health.

Report: Proceedings of the WHO Expert Committee on Biological Standardization, 21st, Geneva, 1968. WHO Staff. (Technical Report Ser.: No. 413). 106p. (ENG, FRE, RUS & SPA.). 1969. pap. text ed. 7.00 (*92-4-120413-3*, 1100413) World Health.

Report: Proceedings of the WHO Expert Committee on Biological Standardization, 21st, Geneva, 1968. WHO Staff. (Technical Report Ser.: No. 444). 132p. 1970. pap. text ed. 7.00 (*92-4-120444-3*, 1100444) World Health.

Report: Proceedings of the WHO Expert Committee on Biological Standardization, 21st, Geneva, 1968. WHO Staff. (Technical Report Ser.: No. 463). 91p. 1971. pap. text ed. 7.00 (*92-4-120463-X*, 1100463) World Health.

Report: Proceedings of the WHO Expert Committee on Filariais, 16th, Geneva, 1961. WHO Staff. (Technical Report Ser.: No. 233). 49p. (ENG, FRE, RUS & SPA.). 1962. pap. text ed. 3.00 (*92-4-120233-5*, 1100233) World Health.

Report: Proceedings of the WHO Expert Committee on Gonococcal Infections, 1st, Geneva, 1962. WHO Staff. (Technical Report Ser.: No. 262). 70p. (ENG, FRE, RUS & SPA.). 1963. pap. text ed. 5.00 (*92-4-120262-9*, 1100262) World Health.

Report: Proceedings of the WHO Expert Committee on Onchocerciasis, 2nd, Geneva, 1965. WHO Staff. (Technical Report Ser.: No. 335). 96p. (ENG, FRE, RUS & SPA.). 1966. pap. text ed. 5.00 (*92-4-120335-8*, 1100335) World Health.

Report: Proceedings of the WHO Expert Committee on Respiratory Virus Diseases, 1st, Stockholm, 1958. WHO Staff. (Technical Report Ser.: No. 170). 59p. (ENG, FRE & SPA.). 1959. pap. text ed. 3.00 (*92-4-120170-3*, 1100170) World Health.

Report: Proceedings of the WHO Expert Committee on Smallpox, Eradication, 2nd, 1972. WHO Staff. (Technical Report Ser.: No. 493). 64p. 1972. pap. 7.00 (*92-4-120493-1*, 1100493) World Health.

Report: Proceedings of the WHO Expert Committee on Yellow Fever, 3rd, 1971. WHO Staff. (Technical Report Ser.: No. 479). 56p. 1971. pap. 5.00 (*92-4-120479-6*, 1100479) World Health.

***Report: 14th Report, Geneva, 1967.** WHO Expert Committee on Malaria. (Technical Report Ser.: No. 382). 50p. (FRE & SPA.). 1968. pap. 2.00 (*92-4-120382-X*, 1077) World Health.

***Report: 15th Report, Geneva, 1970.** WHO Expert Committee on Malaria. (Technical Report Ser.: No. 467). 59p. (FRE & SPA.). 1971. pap. 2.00 (*92-4-120467-2*, 1078) World Health.

Report about the Dispute of a Man with His Ba: Papyrus Berlin 3024. Hans Goedicke. LC 70-131472. 256p. reprint ed. pap. 73.00 (*0-317-09898-5*, 2002277) Bks Demand.

Report after Action: The Story of the 103rd Infantry Division. Ralph Mueller & Jerry Turk. (Divisional Ser.: No. 1). (Illus.). 166p. 1978. reprint ed. 39.95 (*0-89839-010-9*) Battery Pr.

Report Analyzes Telecommunications Brokering Business. 250p. write for info. (*0-318-51317-X*) C C M I.

Report & Interim Report, 2 Vols. League of Nations, Financial Committee, Gold Delegation. Ed. by Mira Wilkins. LC 78-3929. (International Finance Ser.). 1979. reprint ed. lib. bdg. 23.95 (*0-405-11232-7*) Ayer.

Report & Proceedings of the Investigation of the New York City Police. 1971. 325.00 (*0-685-43157-6*, 713) Ayer.

Report & Proceedings of the Senate Committee Appointed to Investigate the Police Department of the City of New York: The Lexow Committee Report, 6 Vols., Set. LC 75-154600. 1971. reprint ed. 325.00 (*0-405-03399-0*) Ayer.

***Report & Recommendations: Commission on the Future of Worker-Management Relations.** 1997. lib. bdg. 250.95 (*0-8490-7636-6*) Gordon Pr.

Report & Recommendations of the Minnesota Interagency Exotic Species Task Force. (Illus.). 44p. (Orig.). (C). 1995. pap. text ed. 25.00 (*0-7881-2611-3*) DIANE Pub.

Report Card in Nutrition: A Personalized Diet Evaluation. 4th ed. B. L. Frye. 138p. 1993. pap. text ed. 28.00 (*0-89787-131-6*) Gorsuch Scarisbrick.

Report Card on Basal Readers. Kenneth S. Goodman et al. LC 88-15130. 167p. (Orig.). (C). 1988. pap. text ed. 10.95 (*0-913461-98-9*) R Owen Pubs.

Report Card on Report Cards: Alternatives to Consider. Elizabeth Schmar & Tara Azwell. LC 94-45704. 209p. 1995. pap. text ed. 19.50 (*0-435-08842-4*, 08842) Heinemann.

Report Card on School Reform: The Teachers Speak. Carnegie Foundation for the Advancement of Teaching Staff. 85p. 1988. pap. text ed. 5.00 (*0-931050-34-0*) Carnegie Fnd Advan Teach.

Report Cards: What Every Health Provider Needs to Know about HEDIS & other Performance Measures. Paul J. Kenkel. LC 95-4111. 182p. 1995. 150.00 (*0-8342-0615-3*) Aspen Pub.

Report Cards Handbook: A Guide to Grade Reporting Using the Mac School Student Information System. Geoffrey D. Hirsch. (Illus.). 250p. (Orig.). 1995. pap. 44.00 (*0-9637294-3-8*) Sugar Hill Pr.

***Report Connections.** Carolyn J. Brown. (Illus.). 68p. 1995. spiral bd. 25.00 (*1-890891-07-X*) Breakthrough Inc.

Report, Economic & Social Progress in Latin America. 482p. 1987. write for info. (*0-940602-14-8*) IADB.

Report, Economic & Social Progress in Latin America. 604p. 1988. write for info. (*0-940602-15-6*) IADB.

Report, Economic & Social Progress in Latin America. 521p. 1989. write for info. (*0-940602-17-2*) IADB.

Report, Economic & Social Progress in Latin America. 308p. 1990. write for info. (*0-940602-34-2*) IADB.

Report Factory. Murray Suid. (Illus.). 48p. (J). (gr. 2-6). 1991. teacher ed., pap. 7.95 (*1-878279-17-3*, MM 1934) Monday Morning Bks.

***Report for Murder.** Val McDermid. 160p. pap. 11.95 (*0-7043-4080-1*, Pub. by Womens Press UK) Trafalgar.

Report Form Roundup: Easy Forms for Gathering, Writing & Reporting Information. (Illus.). 84p. 1988. wbk. ed., pap. 8.95 (*1-56472-068-3*) Edupress.

Report Formatting, Microcomputer Keyboarding/Formatting Applications. Crawford et al. (TA - Typing/Keyboarding Ser.). 1986. pap. 13.95 (*0-538-26120-X*) S-W Pub.

Report from a Town under Siege. Herbert Zbigniew. Tr. by Buguslaw Rostworowski from POL. (Poetry Ser.). (Illus.). 16p. (Orig.). 1984. pap. 6.50 (*0-317-39888-1*) Seluzicki Fine Bks.

Report from a Town under Siege. limited ed. Herbert Zbigniew. Tr. by Buguslaw Rostworowski from POL. (Poetry Ser.). (Illus.). 16p. (Orig.). 1984. 10.00 (*0-317-39889-X*) Seluzicki Fine Bks.

Report from Banaran No. 55: The Story of the Experiences of a Soldier During the War of Independence. T. B. Simatupang. Tr. by Benedict Anderson & Elizabeth Graves from IND. 186p. 1972. pap. 6.50 (*0-87763-005-4*) Cornell Mod Indo.

Report from Engine Co. Eighty Two. Dennis Smith. 240p. 1991. reprint ed. lib. bdg. 27.95 (*0-89966-774-0*) Buccaneer Bks.

Report from Grimes Creek after a Hard Winter. Nancy Stringfellow. (Illus.). 48p. (Orig.). 1990. pap. 9.95 (*0-931659-07-8*) Limberlost Pr.

Report from Hokkaido: The Remains of Russian Culture in Northern Japan. George A. Lensen. LC 73-2878. (Illus.). 216p. 1974. reprint ed. text ed. 49.75 (*0-8371-6818-X*, LERH, Greenwood Pr) Greenwood.

Report from Iron Mountain: On the Possibility & Desirability of Peace. Leonard C. Lewin. 160p. 1996. 20.00 (*0-684-82390-X*) Free Pr.

Report from Iron Mountain: On the Possibility & Desirability of Peace. Leonard C. Lewin. 110p. 1993. reprint ed. lib. bdg. 25.95 (*0-89968-322-3*) Buccaneer Bks.

Report from Jerusalem: City at the Crossroads. J. Robert Moskin. LC 77-79877. (Illus.). 64p. 1977. pap. 1.50 (*0-87495-013-9*) Am Jewish Comm.

Report from Part One: An Autobiography. Gwendolyn Brooks. LC 72-77308. 192p. (YA). (gr. 12). 1972. 22.95 (*0-910296-82-0*) Broadside Pr.

Report from Part Two. Gwendolyn Brooks. 170p. 1996. pap. text ed. 14.95 (*0-88378-162-X*) Third World.

Report from Red China. Harrison Forman. LC 74-28417. (China in the 20th Century Ser.). (Illus.). iv, 250p. 1975. reprint ed. lib. bdg. 29.50 (*0-306-70676-8*); reprint ed. lib. bdg. 29.50 (*0-306-70776-4*) Da Capo.

Report from the Besieged City. Zbigniew Herbert. Tr. by John Carpenter & Bogdana Carpenter. 78p. 1986. pap. 8.50 (*0-88001-094-0*) Ecco Pr.

Report from the Drunk Driving Prevention Project. Steven Ungerleider et al. 48p. (Orig.). 1986. pap. write for info. (*0-318-62527-X*) Integrated Res Servs.

Report from the Secret Committee on Joint Stock Banks, 20 August 1836. Great Britain, Parliament, House of Commons Staff. LC 70-363560. (Illus.). xii, 251p. 1968. reprint ed. lib. bdg. 49.50 (*0-678-05228-X*) Kelley.

Report from the Select Committee on Police of the Metropolis. Select Committee on Police. LC 74-156286. (Police in Great Britain Ser.). 1971. reprint ed. 31.95 (*0-405-03397-4*) Ayer.

Report from the Select Committee on Public Libraries, 23 July 1849. Great Britain, Parliament, House of Commons Staff. LC 74-366370. (Illus.). xx, 317p. 1968. reprint ed. lib. bdg. 65.00 (*0-678-05231-X*) Kelley.

Report from the Select Committee on the Health of Towns. Great Britain, Parliament, House of Commons Staff. LC 68-111978. xxiv, 262p. 1968. reprint ed. lib. bdg. 49.50 (*0-678-05230-1*) Kelley.

R

Report from the Select Committee on the High Price of Gold Bullion. Parliamentary Debates, Great Britain Staff. Ed. by Mira Wilkins. LC 78-3915. (International Finance Ser.). 1979. reprint ed. lib. bdg. 33.95 (*0-405-11219-X*) Ayer.

Report from the Select Committee to Whom the Several Petitions Complaining of the Distressed State of the Agriculture in the United Kingdom Were Referred, 18 June 1821. Great Britain, Parliament, House of Commons Staff. LC 68-112457. 479p. 1968. reprint ed. lib. bdg. 65.00 (*0-678-05227-1*) Kelley.

Report from Vietnam & Kampuchea. Diane Wang & Steve Clark. 70p. 1984. pap. 4.00 (*0-87348-484-3*) Pathfinder NY.

Report from Xunwu. Mao Zedong. Tr. by Roger R. Thompson. LC 89-21776. (Illus.). 304p. 1990. 42.50 (*0-8047-1678-1*) Stanford U Pr.

Report from Xunwu. Mao Zedong. Tr. by Roger R. Thompson. xii, 278p. Date not set. pap. 14.95 (*0-8047-2182-3*) Stanford U Pr.

Report in Favor of the Abolition of the Punishment of Death by Law, Made to Legislature of the State of New York April 14, 1841. John L. O'Sullivan. LC 74-3846. (Criminal Justice in America Ser.). 1974. reprint ed. 20.95 (*0-405-06162-5*) Ayer.

Report in Regard to the Range & Ranch Cattle Business of the United States. Joseph Nimmo, Jr. LC 72-2860. (Use & Abuse of America's Natural Resources Ser.). 214p. 1972. reprint ed. 19.95 (*0-405-04524-7*) Ayer.

Report in the Form of a Journal, the March of the Regiment of Mounted Riflemen to Oregon in 1849. Osborne Cross. 1967. reprint ed. 24.95 (*0-87770-008-7*) Ye Galleon.

Report It in Writing. Goodman. 1995. pap. text ed. 29.80 (*0-13-440363-0*) P-H.

Report Made in the Royal Council of the Indies. Antonio De Leon Pinelo. Ed. by Frank E. Comparato. Tr. by Doris Z. Stone. LC 84-81818. 1986. reprint ed. pap. 10.00 (*0-911437-05-3*) Labyrinthos.

Report of a Committee to Investigate the Subject of Myxoedema. Clinical Society of London Staff. (Illus.). 250p. 1992. 19.95 (*0-318-68444-6*) F A Countway.

Report of a General Plan for the Promotion of Public & Personal Health. Lemuel C. Shattuck et al. LC 70-180589. (Medicine & Society in America Ser.). 554p. 1972. reprint ed. 31.95 (*0-405-03971-9*) Ayer.

***Report of a Murder.** Yoryis Yatromanolakis. Ed. by Andre N. Crumey. Tr. by Helen Cavanagh from GRE. 220p. (Orig.). 1997. pap. 13.99 (*1-873982-12-7*, Pub. by Dedalus UK) Subterranean Co.

Report of a Preliminary Scheme of Improvements: Staten Island. New York City Commission. LC 73-2910. (Metropolitan America Ser.). 118p. 1974. reprint ed. 11.95 (*0-405-05408-4*) Ayer.

Report of a Study Group: Toward Peace in the Middle East. LC 75-42846. 1975. pap. 6.95 (*0-8157-9751-6*) Brookings.

Report of a Visit to Some of the Tribes of Indians, Located West of the Mississippi River. John D. Lang & Samuel Taylor, Jr. 34p. 1973. 7.50 (*0-87770-123-7*) Ye Galleon.

Report of a Workshop on Expanding U. S. Air Force Noncombat Mission Capabilities. Carl Builder et al. LC 93-4946. 1993. pap. 13.00 (*0-8330-1402-1*, MR-246-AF) Rand Corp.

Report of an Archaeological Tour in Mexico in 1881. Adolf F. Bandelier. LC 76-24822. reprint ed. 42.50 (*0-404-58052-1*) AMS Pr.

Report of an Aspen Institute Seminar on the Corporation & Society. David Vogel. 4.00 (*0-686-26002-3*) Aspen Inst Human.

Report of Board on Tests of Revolvers & Automatic Pistols 1907. (Illus.). pap. 3.50 (*0-686-20763-7*) Sand Pond.

Report of Captain Ward & Danseker, Pirates. Andrew Barker. LC 68-54615. (English Experience Ser.: No. 21). 56p. 1968. reprint ed. 15.00 (*90-221-0021-9*) Walter J Johnson.

Report of Chas. A. Wetmore, Special U. S. Commissioner of Mission Indians of Southern California. Charles A. Wetmore. Ed. by Norman E. Tanis. (Northridge Facsimile Ser.: Pt. VII). 1977. pap. 10.00 (*0-937048-06-2*) Santa Susana.

Report of General J. G. Totten, Chief Engineer, on the Subject of National Defenses. Joseph G. Totten. Ed. by Richard H. Kohn. LC 78-22400. (American Military Experience Ser.). 1980. reprint ed. lib. bdg. 15.95 (*0-405-11876-7*) Ayer.

***Report of General Standardization Committee.** AGMA Technical Committee. (AGMA Technical Papers: Vol. P83B). 8p. 1930. pap. text ed. 30.00 (*1-55589-125-X*) AGMA.

Report of Her Majesty's Chief Inspector of Fire Services - for the Year 1994 - 93. (Command Papers: No. 2679). 65p. 1994. pap. 40.00 (*0-10-126792-4*, HM67924, Pub. by Stationery Ofc UK) Bernan Associates.

Report of HHS Commission on Evaluation of Pain. 190p. 1986. pap. 14.00 (*0-685-23189-5*, 40,901) NCLS Inc.

***Report of Infant Mortality Study in San Diego County.** Helen M. Wallace et al. (Illus.). 124p. (Orig.). 1993. pap. 19.95 (*0-89914-038-6*) Third Party Pub.

Report of Intensive Survey Instrumented Range Assembly Area, Fort Irwin, San Bernardino County, California: Addendum: Survey, Testing, & Documentation Assembly & Offense Areas, Fort Irwin, California. fac. ed. Contrib. by W. T. Eckhardt & M. Jay Hatley. (Fort Irwin, Miscellaneous Reports). 55p. (C). 1982. reprint ed. pap. text ed. 4.95 (*1-55567-521-2*) Coyote Press.

Report of Investigation: The Aldrich Ames Espionage Case. 232p. (Orig.). (C). 1995. pap. text ed. 45.00 (*0-7881-1618-5*) DIANE Pub.

Report of Mission to Uruguay in April-May, 1974. Niall MacDermot & Inger Fahlander. 10p. reprint ed. pap. 25.00 (*0-317-29849-6*, 2051908) Bks Demand.

Report of Mr. Kennedy, of Maryland: Proceedings of the U. S. Congress, 27th, 3rd Session, 1842. U. S. Congress Staff. LC 78-140879. (Black Heritage Library Collection). 1977. 54.95 (*0-8369-8759-4*) Ayer.

Report of Mr. S. Hoofien to the Joint Distribution Committee of the American Funds for Jewish War Sufferers,New York. Sigfried Hoofien. Ed. by Moshe Davis. LC 77-70702. (America & the Holy Land Ser.). (Illus.). 1977. reprint ed. lib. bdg. 19.95 (*0-405-10254-2*) Ayer.

Report of Occupational Injuries & Illnesses in the Gas Utility Industry & the Transmission Industry, 1977. 55p. 2.00 (*0-318-12689-3*, J00448) Am Gas Assn.

Report of Progress: Archaeological Research By the University of Missouri. Carl H. Chapman et al. (Special Publications: No. 1). (Illus.). 57p. (Orig.). 1957. pap. 3.00 (*0-943414-61-X*) MO Arch Soc.

***Report of Regional Consultation on Institutional Credit for Sustainable Fish Marketing.** (Fisheries Reports: No. 540). 150p. 1996. pap. 14.00 (*92-5-103859-7*, F38597, Pub. by FAO IT) Bernan Associates.

Report of Subcommittee on Settlement Conferences. 30p. 1987. pap. 4.50 (*0-317-02663-1*, 43,285) NCLS Inc.

Report of the Ad Hoc Consultation on the Role of RGNAL Fisheries Agencies in... FAO Staff. (Fisheries Reports: 500). 172p. 1994. pap. 17.00 (*92-5-103505-9*, F35059, Pub. by FAO IT) Bernan Associates.

Report of the Annual Round Table Meeting on Linguistics & Language Studies...Linguistics, 22nd: Developments of the Sixties - Viewpoints for the Seventies. fac. ed. Georgetown University Round Table on Languages & Linguistics Staff. Ed. by Richard J. O'Brien. LC 58-31607. (Monograph Series on Languages & Linguistics: Vol. 24). 330p. reprint ed. pap. 94.10 (*0-7837-7790-6*, 2047545) Bks Demand.

Report of the Annual Round Table Meeting on Linguistics & Language Studies...Sociolinguistics, 23rd: Current Trends & Prospects. fac. ed. Georgetown University Round Table on Languages & Linguistics Staff. Ed. by Robert W. Shuy. LC 58-31607. 362p. reprint ed. pap. 103.20 (*0-7837-7791-4*, 2047546) Bks Demand.

Report of the ARL Serials Prices Project. 1989. pap. 60.00 (*0-918006-16-3*) ARL.

Report of the Board of Fortifications or Other Defenses Appointed by the President of the U. S. under the Provisions of the Act of Congress, Approved March 3, 1885 & Plates to Accompany, 2 Vols. U. S. Congress, House of Representatives Staff. Ed. by Richard H. Kohn. LC 78-22408. (American Military Experience Ser.). (Illus.). 1980. reprint ed. lib. bdg. 80.95 (*0-405-11883-X*) Ayer.

Report of the Chief Signal Officer, U. S. Signal Corps. LC 74-4671. (Illus.). 544p. 1974. reprint ed. 51.95 (*0-405-06037-8*) Ayer.

Report of the Chilean National Commission on Truth & Reconciliation, 2 vols., Set. Tr. by Phillip E. Berryman from SPA. LC 93-13815. (C). 1993. text ed. 69.00 (*0-268-01645-3*); pap. text ed. 34.50 (*0-268-01646-1*) U of Notre Dame Pr.

Report of the Commission on Country Life. Commission on Country Life, Jr. Ed. by Dan C. McCurry & Richard E. Rubenstein. LC 74-30625. (American Farmers & the Rise of Agribusiness Ser.). 1975. reprint ed. 19.95 (*0-405-06787-9*) Ayer.

Report of the Commission on Old Age Pensions, Annuities & Insurance. Massachusetts Commission on Old Age Pensions, Annuities & Insurance. LC 75-17233. (Social Problems & Social Policy Ser.). (Illus.). 1976. reprint ed. 34.95 (*0-405-07502-2*) Ayer.

Report of the Commission on the Cost of Living. Massachusetts Commission on the Cost of Living. LC 75-17232. (Social Problems & Social Policy Ser.). (Illus.). 1976. reprint ed. 65.95 (*0-405-07501-4*) Ayer.

Report of the Commissioner of Corporations on the Petroleum Industry: Foreign Trade, Pt. 3. U. S. Department of Commerce & Labor Staff. Ed. by Stuart Bruchey & Eleanor Bruchey. LC 76-5040. (American Business Abroad Ser.). (Illus.). 1976. reprint ed. 66.95 (*0-405-09306-3*) Ayer.

Report of the Commissioner of Indian Affairs: Reports for the Years 1824-1899, 65 vols. U. S. Office of Indian Affairs Staff. (C). 1986. reprint ed. 945.00 (*0-404-07550-9*) AMS Pr.

Report of the Commissioner of Indian Affairs for the Territories of Washington & Idaho & the State of Oregon for the Year of 1870. 75p. 1981. 12.00 (*0-87770-247-0*) Ye Galleon.

Report of the Commissioners of Her Majesty's Customs & Excise for the Year: Year Ended 31 March 1994. HMSO Staff. (Command Papers: No. 2651). 97p. 1994. pap. 35.00 (*0-10-126512-3*, HM65123, Pub. by Stationery Ofc UK) Bernan Associates.

Report of the Committee Appointed Pursuant to House Resolutions 429 & 504 to Investigate the Concentration of Control of Money & Credit. Banking & Currency Committee. LC 75-2677. (Wall Street & the Security Market Ser.). 1975. reprint ed. 23.95 (*0-405-07239-2*) Ayer.

Report of the Committee of Fifteen on the Elementary School. William T. Harris. LC 73-89188. (American Education: Its Men, Institutions, & Ideas. Series 1). 1974. reprint ed. 16.95 (*0-405-01426-0*) Ayer.

Report of the Committee of the Senate upon the Relations Between Labor & Capital & Testimony Taken by the Committee, 4 Vols. United States Congress, Senate Committee on Foreign Relations. 297.00 (*0-405-07518-9*, 18381) Ayer.

Report of the Committee on Police Conditions of Service. Police Conditions of Service Committee. LC 76-156281. (Police in Great Britain Ser.). 1971. reprint ed. 21.95 (*0-405-03392-3*) Ayer.

Report of the Committee on Prices in the Bituminous Coal Industry. (Conference on Price Research Ser.: No. 1). 167p. 1938. reprint ed. 43.50 (*0-87014-187-2*); reprint ed. mic. film 21.80 (*0-685-61190-6*) Natl Bur Econ Res.

Report of the Committee on Secondary School Studies, Appointed at the Meeting of the National Education Association. National Education Association, Committee on Secondary School Studies. LC 70-89222. (American Education: Its Men, Institutions, & Ideas. Series 1). 1978. reprint ed. 21.95 (*0-405-01403-1*) Ayer.

Report of the Committee on the Criteria & Nomenclature of the Major Divisions of the Ocean Bottom. (Publications Scientifique Ser.). 124p. 1940. write for info. (*0-318-14529-4*) Intl Assoc Phys Sci Ocean.

Report of the Committee to Consider the Ethical Implications of Emerging Technologies in the Breeding of Farm Animals. HMSO Staff. 86p. 1995. pap. 30.00 (*0-11-242965-3*, HM29653, Pub. by Stationery Ofc UK) Bernan Associates.

Report of the Community Mental Health Practice - Education Project. Ed. by Mary G. Harm. 1978. 3.85 (*0-318-35361-X*) Coun Soc Wk Ed.

***Report of the Conference for the Adoption of a Draft Agreement for the Establishment of the Indian Ocean Tuna Commission, Rome, 1989.** 55p. (ENG, FRE & SPA.). 1989. 12.00 (*92-5-002852-0*, Pub. by FAO IT) Bernan Associates.

***Report of the Conference of FAO, 25th Session, Rome, 1989.** 260p. 1990. 27.00 (*92-5-102931-8*, F9318, Pub. by FAO IT) Bernan Associates.

***Report of the Conference of FAO, 26th Session, Rome, 1991.** 263p. 1992. 35.00 (*92-5-103165-7*, F6657, Pub. by FAO IT) Bernan Associates.

***Report of the Conference of FAO, 27th Session, Rome, 1993.** 356p. 1994. 30.00 (*92-5-103460-5*, Pub. by FAO IT) Bernan Associates.

Report of the Congressional Committees Investigating the Iran/Contra Affair. Lee H. Hamilton & Daniel K. Inouye. (Illus.). 690p. (Orig.). 1995. pap. text ed. 65.00 (*0-7881-2602-4*) DIANE Pub.

***Report of the Council of FAO: 104th Session, Rome, November 1993.** 118p. 1993. 12.00 (*92-5-103440-0*, F34400, Pub. by FAO IT) Bernan Associates.

***Report of the Council of FAO: 106th Session, Rome, May-June 1994.** 81p. 1994. 12.00 (*92-5-103535-0*, F35350, Pub. by FAO IT) Bernan Associates.

***Report of the Council of FAO 111th Session Rome October 1-10 1996.** FAO Staff. 41p. 1996. pap. 10.00 (*92-5-103897-X*, F3897X, Pub. by FAO IT) Bernan Associates.

Report of the Council of Hygiene & Public Health of the Citizens' Association of New York Upon the Sanitary Condition of the City. Citizens' Association of New York Staff. LC 77-112532. (Rise of Urban America Ser.). (Illus.). 1976. reprint ed. 51.95 (*0-405-02443-6*) Ayer.

Report of the Council of the Shakespeare Society to the Second Annual Meeting, 1843 see English Fairy Mythology: Illustrations of the Fairy Mythology of a Midsummer Night's Dream; with Oberon's Vision in the Midsummer Night's Dream, Illusustrated by a Comparison with Lylie's Endymion,

Report of the County of Lanark of a Plan for Relieving Public Distress & Removing Discontent by Giving Permanent, Productive Employment to the Poor & Working Classes. Robert Owen. LC 72-2942. reprint ed. 34.50 (*0-404-10708-7*) AMS Pr.

Report of the Crime Commission. 48.00 (*0-318-36248-1*) Ayer.

Report of the Crime Commission, 1925: Legislative Document Number 23. New York State Crime Commission. LC 74-3840. (Mass Violence in America Ser.). 1974. reprint ed. 53.95 (*0-405-06157-9*) Ayer.

Report of the CWLA Task Force on Children & HIV Infection: Initial Guidelines. 60p. 1988. pap. 1.00 (*0-87868-339-9*) Child Welfare.

Report of the Debates & Proceedings of the Convention for the Revision of the Constitution of the State of Indiana, 1850, Vol. I. 1935. 5.50 (*1-885323-40-9*) IN Hist Bureau.

Report of the Debates in the Convention of California on the Formation of the State Constitution, in Sept. & Oct., 1849. John R. Browne. LC 72-9431. (Far Western Frontier Ser.). 532p. 1973. reprint ed. 40.95 (*0-405-04962-5*) Ayer.

Report of the Decision of the Supreme Court of the United States & the Opinions of Judges Thereof, in the Case of Dred Scott vs. John F. A. Sanford. LC 69-11323. (Law, Politics & History Ser.). 240p. 1970. reprint ed. lib. bdg. 29.50 (*0-306-71183-4*) Da Capo.

Report of the Department of the Treasury on the Bureau of Alcohol, Tobacco & Firearms Investigation of Vernon Wayne Howell, Also Known as David Koresh, 2 vols. 1994. lib. bdg. 495.00 (*0-8490-8558-6*) Gordon Pr.

***Report of the Director: Quadrennial 1986-1989 Annual 1989.** (PAHO Official Document Ser.: No. 234). 169p. 1990. pap. text ed. 20.00 (*92-75-17234-X*) World Health.

Report of the Eighteenth Annual Round Table Meeting on Linguistics & Language Studies. Georgetown University Round Table Meeting on Linguistics & Language Studies Staff. Ed. by Edward L. Blansitt. LC 58-31607. (Monograph Series on Languages & Linguistics: No. 20). 209p. reprint ed. pap. 59.60 (*0-7837-6353-0*, 2046065) Bks Demand.

Report of the Ellis Island Committee. Carleton H. Palmer. LC 78-145478. (American Immigration Library). 149p. 1971. reprint ed. lib. bdg. 22.95 (*0-89198-021-0*) Ozer.

Report of the Experiments on Animal Magnetism: Proceedings of the Committee of the Medical Section of the French Royal Academy of Sciences, June 21-28, 1831. French Royal Academy of Sciences, Medical Section Committee & J. C. Colquhoun. LC 75-7371. (Perspectives in Psychical Research Ser.). 1975. reprint ed. 25.95 (*0-405-07022-5*) Ayer.

Report of the Expert Committee on the Public Health Aspects of Housing, 1st, Geneva, 1961. Expert Committee on the Public Health Aspects of Housing. (Technical Report Ser.: No. 225). 60p. (ENG, FRE & SPA.). 1961. pap. text ed. 3.00 (*92-4-120225-4*, 1100225) World Health.

***Report of the Expert Consultation on Utilization & Conservation of Aquatic Genetic Resources, Grottaferrata, Italy, 1992.** 63p. 1993. 10.00 (*92-5-103424-9*, Pub. by FAO IT) Bernan Associates.

Report of the Expert Panel on Blood Cholesterol Levels in Children & Adolescents. (Illus.). 119p. (Orig.). 1996. pap. text ed. 25.00 (*0-7881-2817-5*) DIANE Pub.

Report of the Expert Panel on Population Strategies for Blood Cholesterol Reduction. (Illus.). 139p. 1996. reprint ed. pap. text ed. 25.00 (*0-7881-2816-7*) DIANE Pub.

Report of the Exploring Expedition to the Rocky Mountains. John C. Fremont. (Notable American Authors Ser.). 1992. reprint ed. lib. bdg. 75.00 (*0-7812-2897-2*) Rprt Serv.

Report of the FDA Task Force on International Harmonization: Food & Drug Administration, December 1992. 1993. pap. write for info. (*1-880626-02-0*) FOI Services.

Report of the Federal Trade Commission on Agricultural Income Inquiry, 3 Vols., Set. Incl. Pt. 1. Principal Farm Products. Ed. by Federal Trade Commission et al. LC 74-30658. 1975. (*0-318-50880-X*); Vol. 2. Fruits & Vegetables. LC 74-30658. lib. bdg. (*0-318-50881-8*); Pt. 3. Supplementary Report. Ed. by Federal Trade Commission et al. LC 74-30658. 1975. (*0-318-50882-6*); LC 74-30658. (American Farmers & the Rise of Agribusiness Ser.). 1975. reprint ed. 145.95 (*0-405-06833-6*) Ayer.

Report of the Federal Trade Commission on Foreign Ownership in the Petroleum Industry. U. S. Federal Trade Commission Staff. Ed. by Mira Wilkins. LC 76-29746. (European Business Ser.). (Illus.). 1977. reprint ed. lib. bdg. 23.95 (*0-405-09763-8*) Ayer.

Report of the Federal Trade Commission on the Radio Industry: In Response to House Resolution 548, 67th Congress, Fourth Session, December 1, 1923. Federal Trade Commission. LC 74-4680. (Telecommunications Ser.). 360p. 1974. reprint ed. 33.95 (*0-405-06046-7*) Ayer.

Report of the Fifteenth Annual (First International) Round Table Meeting on Linguistics & Language Studies. Georgetown University Round Table Meeting on Linguistics & Language Studies Staff. Ed. by C. I. Stuart. LC 56-38540. (Monograph Series on Languages & Linguistics: No. 17). 242p. reprint ed. pap. 69.00 (*0-7837-6350-6*, 2046062) Bks Demand.

Report of the FIP Commission on Prestressed Lightweight Concrete. (PCI Journal Reprints Ser.). 28p. 1985. pap. 14.00 (*0-318-19738-3*, JR52) P-PCI.

Report of the First International Conference on Educational Research (UNESCO) (Education Studies & Documents: No. 20). 1974. reprint ed. pap. 25.00 (*0-8115-1344-0*) Periodicals Srv.

Report of the Fourteenth Annual Round Table Meeting on Linguistics & Language Studies. Georgetown University Round Table Meeting on Linguistics & Language Studies Staff. Ed. by Robert J. DiPietro. LC 56-38540. (Monograph Series on Languages & Linguistics: No. 16). 189p. reprint ed. pap. 53.90 (*0-7837-6349-2*, 2046061) Bks Demand.

***Report of the Gaming Board for Great Britain 1995-96.** 87p. 1996. pap. 30.00 (*0-10-281496-1*, HM14961, Pub. by Stationery Ofc UK) Bernan Associates.

Report of the Geology of the Henry Mountains: U. S. Geographical & Geological Survey of the Rocky Mountain Region. Grove K. Gilbert. Ed. by Claude C. Albritton, Jr. LC 77-6519. (History of Geology Ser.). (Illus.). 1978. reprint ed. lib. bdg. 23.95 (*0-405-10441-3*) Ayer.

Report of the Global Conference on the Sustainable Dvelopment of Small Island Developing States: Bridgetown, Barbados,26 April-6 May 1994. 91p. Date not set. 12.50 (*92-1-100538-8*, E.94.I.18 & COR) UN.

***Report of the Helical Gear Committee.** AGMA Technical Committee. (Technical Papers: Vol. 102). 30p. 1938. pap. text ed. 30.00 (*1-55589-132-2*) AGMA.

Report of the Incarceration Work Group. 65p. (Orig.). (C). 1993. pap. text ed. 25.00 (*1-56806-823-9*) DIANE Pub.

Report of the International Commission for Central American Recovery & Development. William L. Ascher. Ed. by Ann Hubbard. LC 89-1475. 148p. 1989. text ed. 40.95 (*0-8223-0897-5*) Duke.

Report of the International Commission for Central American Recovery & Development. William L. Ascher. Ed. by Ann Hubbard. LC 89-1475. 148p. 1989. pap. text ed. 16.95 (*0-8223-0933-5*) Duke.

***Report of the International Commission on the Balkans.** 197p. 1996. pap. 14.95 (*0-87003-118-X*) Carnegie Endow.

Report of the International Conference on Drug Abuse & Illicit Trafficking, Vienna, 17-26 June 1987. 143p. 1987. 17.00 (*92-1-100320-2*, E. 87.I.18) UN.

Report of the International Narcotics Control Board. 39p. 1989. 9.00 (*92-1-148078-7*, 89.XI.2) UN.

An Asterisk (*) at the beginning of an entry indicates that the title is appearing in BIP for the first time.

Report of the International Narcotics Control Board. 42p. 1990. 12.00 (92-1-148082-5) UN.

Report of the International Narcotics Control Board. 62p. 1994. 20.00 (92-1-148094-9, E.95.XI4.4) UN.

Report of the International Narcotics Control Board for 1988. 1988. 12.00 (92-1-148076-0, E.88.XI.4) UN.

Report of the International Workshop on a Framework Convention & Associated Protocols: A Non Governmental Perspective. John C. Topping, Jr. & Climate Institute Staff. 68p. 1990. pap. 10.00 (0-614-06732-4) Climate Inst.

Report of the Interregional Seminar to Promote the Implementation of the International Plan of Action on Aging. 46p. 1986. pap. 7.00 (92-1-130111-4, E.86.IV.5) UN.

Report of the Invitational Workshop on Data Integrity. (Computer Science Ser.). 1990. lib. bdg. 75.95 (0-8490-3994-0) Gordon Pr.

Report of the Joint Committee of the General Assembly Appointed to Investigate the Police Department of the City of St. Louis. Missouri General Assembly, Joint Committee of The General Assembly. LC 70-154587. (Police in America Ser.). 1971. reprint ed. 24.95 (0-405-03384-2) Ayer.

Report of the Joint Committee on Reconstruction: Proceedings of the U. S. Congress, 39th, 1st Session, 4 pts. U. S. Congress, House of Representatives Staff. Ed. by W. P. Fessenden et al. LC 78-168523. (Black Heritage Library Collection). 825p. 1977. reprint ed. 35.95 (0-8369-8875-2) Ayer.

Report of the Joint FAO-WHO Meeting, Rome, November-December 1982, 2 vols., Nos. 46 & 49. (Plant Production & Protection Papers). 79p. (ENG, FRE & SPA.). 1983. Evaluations. pap. 55.00 (92-5-101432-9, F2542) Bernan Associates.

Report of the Joint Special Committee on Investigation of the Affairs of the Maine State Prison: Made to the Fifty-Third Legislature. Maine Joint Special Committee. LC 74-3832. (Criminal Justice in America Ser.). 1974. reprint ed. 15.95 (0-405-06152-8) Ayer.

Report of the Joint Special Committee to Investigate Chinese Immigration. U. S. Senate Joint Special Committee. Ed. by Roger Daniels. LC 78-54836. (Asian Experience in North America Ser.). 1979. reprint ed. lib. bdg. 93.95 (0-405-11294-7) Ayer.

Report of the Kansas Judicial Study Advisory Committee: Recommendations for Improving the Kansas Judicial System. 120p. 1974. 1.00 (0-318-14443-3) IJA NYU.

Report of the Kingdom of Congo & of the Surroundings: Countries Drawn Out of the Writings of the Portuguese Duarte Lopez. Filippo Pigafetta. Ed. by Margarite Hutchinson. (Illus.). 174p. 1970. reprint ed. 45.00 (0-7146-1847-0, Pub. by F Cass Pubs UK) Intl Spec Bk.

Report of the Kingdome of Congo, Gathered by P. Pigafetta. Duarte Lopes. Tr. by A. Hartwell. LC 75-25675. (English Experience Ser.: No. 260). 1970. reprint ed. 65.00 (90-221-0260-2) Walter J Johnson.

Report of the Land Planning Committee, Vol. 2. Land Planning Committee, U.S. National Resources Board. LC 75-26322. (World Food Supply Ser.). (Illus.). 1976. reprint ed. 20.95 (0-405-07798-X) Ayer.

Report of the Manuscripts of Mrs. Stopford-Sackville of Drayton House, Northamptonshire, 2 vols., Set. Great Britain Historical Manuscripts Commission. Ed. by George Billias. LC 72-8813. (American Revolutionary Ser.). reprint ed. lib. bdg. 100.00 (0-8398-0803-8) Irvington.

Report of the Miller Center Commission on Presidential Disability & the Twenty-Fifth Amendment. Miller, White Burkett, Center of Public Affairs Staff & University of Virginia Staff. 44p. (Orig.). (C). 1988. pap. text ed. 8.00 (0-8191-6893-9, Pub. by White Miller Center) U Pr of Amer.

Report of the Missouri Task Force on Gender & Justice. 374p. (Orig.). (C). 1994. pap. text ed. 60.00 (0-7881-0698-8) DIANE Pub.

Report of the National Advisory Commission on Law Enforcement. 241p. (Orig.). (C). 1993. pap. text ed. 40.00 (1-56806-877-8) DIANE Pub.

Report of the National Commission on Superconductivity. (Illus.). 76p. (Orig.). (C). 1994. pap. text ed. 30.00 (0-7881-0304-0) DIANE Pub.

Report of the National Conservation Commission, 3 vols. Ed. by Henry Gannett. LC 72-2837. (Use & Abuse of America's Natural Resources Ser.). (Illus.). 1960p. 1972. reprint ed. #0-405-04544-1. 46.95 (0-405-04543-3) Ayer.

Report of the National Conservation Commission, 3 vols, Set. Ed. by Henry Gannett. LC 72-2837. (Use & Abuse of America's Natural Resources Ser.). (Illus.). 1960p. 1972. reprint ed. 139.95 (0-405-04506-9) Ayer.

Report of the National Task Force on Criminal History Record Disposition Reporting. 76p. (Orig.). (C). 1993. pap. text ed. 20.00 (1-56806-778-X) DIANE Pub.

Report of the Native Grievances Inquiry, 1913-1914. South Africa, Commissioner on Native Grievances Inquiry. LC 77-109362. 129p. 1970. reprint ed. text ed. 59.75 (0-8371-3851-5, NGI&, Negro U Pr) Greenwood.

*__Report of the Nevada Commission on Nuclear Projects.__ Grant Sawyer. 154p. 1996. reprint ed. pap. 40.00 (0-7881-3142-7) DIANE Pub.

Report of the New Jersey Attorney General's Task Force on the Use of Force in Law Enforcement. 137p. (Orig.). (C). 1994. pap. text ed. 35.00 (0-7881-0419-5) DIANE Pub.

Report of the New York State Commission on Relief for Widowed Mothers. New York State Commission on Relief for Widowed Mothers. LC 74-1696. (Children & Youth Ser.: Vol. 18). 602p. 1974. reprint ed. 48.95 (0-405-05973-6) Ayer.

*__Report of the NIST Workshop on Digital Signature Certificate Management.__ Ed. by Dennis K. Branstad. (Illus.). 177p. (C). 1996. reprint ed. pap. 35.00 (0-7881-3409-4) DIANE Pub.

Report of the North Carolina Geological Survey, No. 249 see Bulletins of American Paleontology: Vol. 56

Report of the Open-Ended AD HOC Group of Experts on Biosafety. 38p. (Orig.). (C). 1995. pap. text ed. 20.00 (0-7881-2547-8) DIANE Pub.

Report of the Open Government Through Public Telecommunications Study Commission. 25p. (Orig.). (C). 1993. pap. text ed. 25.00 (1-56806-754-2) DIANE Pub.

Report of the Organization & Campaigns of the Army of the Potomac: To Which Is Added an Account of the Campaign in Western Virginia, with Plans of Battle-Fields. George B. McClellan. LC 78-109629. (Select Bibliographies Reprint Ser.). 1977. 35.95 (0-8369-5238-3) Ayer.

Report of the Pennsylvania State Parole Commission to the Legislature, 1927 Part I, & Part Ii. Parole Commission, Commonwealth of Pennsylvania. LC 74-3849. (Criminal Justice in America Ser.). 1974. reprint ed. 28.95 (0-405-06163-3) Ayer.

Report of the Presidential Commission on the Space Shuttle Challenger Accident. (Illus.). 256p. (Orig.). (C). 1995. pap. text ed. 40.00 (0-7881-1912-5) DIANE Pub.

Report of the President's Commission on Aviation Security & Terrorism. 59p. (Orig.). (C). 1993. pap. text ed. 25.00 (1-56806-867-0) DIANE Pub.

Report of the President's Commission on Campus Unrest: Including the Killings at Jackson State & Kent State Tragedy. LC 71-139710. 537p. 1970. 5.95 (0-405-01712-X) Ayer.

Report of the Proceedings & Papers Read in Prince's Hall. Industrial Remuneration Conference Staff. LC 67-30064. (Reprints of Economic Classics Ser.). xxiv, 528p. 1968. reprint ed. 65.00 (0-678-00350-5) Kelley.

Report of the Public Lands Commission. U. S. House of Representatives, 46th Congress Staff. LC 72-2865. (Use & Abuse of America's Natural Resources Ser.). 796p. 1972. reprint ed. 60.95 (0-405-04532-8) Ayer.

Report of the Public Lands Commission with Appendix. LC 72-2864. (Use & Abuse of America's Natural Resources Ser.). 402p. 1972. reprint ed. 28.95 (0-405-04531-X) Ayer.

Report of the Railroads Committee upon Several Petitions for Legislative Aid to the Canajoharie & Catskill Railroad. 1973. reprint ed. pap. 5.00 (0-910746-24-9, CAC01) Hope Farm.

Report of the Royal Commission of 1552. Walter C. Richardson. LC 72-86893. 302p. 1974. 20.00 (0-937058-08-4) West Va U Pr.

Report of the Royal Commission on Capital Punishment: Presented to Parliament by Command of Her Majesty, Sept. 1953. Great Britain, Royal Commission on Capital Punishment. LC 79-25707. 505p. 1980. reprint ed. text ed. 79.50 (0-313-22121-9, GBCP) Greenwood.

Report of the Royal Commission on Chinese & Japanese Immigration. Canada Royal Commission on Chinese & Japanese Immigration. Ed. by Roger Daniels. LC 78-54812. (Asian Experience in North America Ser.). 1979. reprint ed. lib. bdg. 33.95 (0-405-11268-8) Ayer.

Report of the Royal Commission on Police Powers & Procedure. Royal Commission on Police Powers & Procedures. LC 73-156283. (Police in Great Britain Ser.). 1971. reprint ed. 16.95 (0-405-03394-X) Ayer.

*__Report of the Secretary of Defense to the President & the Congress: January 1994.__ Les Aspin. (Illus.). 340p. (Orig.). 1996. reprint ed. pap. text ed. 45.00 (0-7881-2992-9) DIANE Pub.

Report of the Secretary of State upon Weights & Measures: Prepared in Obedience to a Resolution of the House of Representatives of the Fourteenth of December, 1819. John Q. Adams. Ed. by I. Bernard Cohen. LC 79-7945. (Three Centuries of Science in America Ser.). 1980. reprint ed. lib. bdg. 25.95 (0-405-12526-7) Ayer.

Report of the Secretary of the Treasury on the Subject of Public Roads & Canals. Albert Gallatin. LC 68-20392. (Library of Early American Business & Industry: No. 19). 123p. 1968. reprint ed. 29.50 (0-678-00368-8) Kelley.

Report of the Select Commission on Western Hemisphere Immigration. Ed. by Carlos E. Cortes. LC 80-7574. (Hispanics in the United States Ser.). (Illus.). 1981. reprint ed. lib. bdg. 23.95 (0-405-13185-2) Ayer.

Report of the Select Committee of the Senate of the U. S. on the Sickness & Mortality on Board Emigrant Ships. Hamilton Fish. Ed. by Barbara G. Rosenkrantz. LC 76-25663. (Public Health in America Ser.). (Illus.). 1977. reprint ed. lib. bdg. 17.95 (0-405-09818-9) Ayer.

Report of the Seventeenth Annual Round Table Meeting on Linguistics & Language Studies. Georgetown University Round Table Meeting on Linguistics & Language Studies Staff. LC 58-31607. (Monograph Series on Languages & Linguistics: No. 19). 268p. reprint ed. pap. 76.40 (0-7837-6352-2, 2046064) Bks Demand.

Report of the Sixteenth Annual Round Table Meeting on Linguistics & Language Studies. Georgetown University Round Table Meeting on Linguistics & Language Studies Staff. Ed. by Charles W. Kreidler. LC 58-31607. (Monograph Series on Languages & Linguistics: No. 18). 220p. reprint ed. pap. 62.70 (0-7837-6351-4, 2046063) Bks Demand.

Report of the South Carolina General Assembly Joint Committee to Investigate Law Enforcement. South Carolina General Assembly Joint Committee to Investigate Law Enforcement. LC 74-3855. (Criminal Justice in America Ser.). 1974. reprint ed. 69.95 (0-405-06168-4) Ayer.

Report of the Special Commission on Investigation of the Judicial System, Commonwealth of Massachusetts: Under Chapter Sixty-Two of the Resolves of 1935. Massachusetts Special Commission on Investigation of the Judicial System. LC 74-3833. (Criminal Justice in America Ser.). 1974. reprint ed. 17.95 (0-405-06153-6) Ayer.

Report of the Special Committee of the New York City Board of Aldermen on the New York City Police Department: New York City Common Council Document, Vol. 53. New York City Common Council Staff. LC 72-154582. (Police in America Ser.). 1971. reprint ed. 26.95 (0-405-03378-8) Ayer.

Report of the Spongiform Encephalopathy Advisory Committee. HMSO Staff. 100p. 1995. pap. 75.00 (0-11-242987-4, HM29874, Pub. by Stationery Ofc UK) Bernan Associates.

Report of the State Commission to Investigate Provision for the Mentally Deficient. New York State Commission to Investigate Provision for the Mentally Deficient. LC 75-17234. (Social Problems & Social Policy Ser.). (Illus.). 1976. reprint ed. 96.95 (0-405-07503-0) Ayer.

Report of the Superintendent of the State Land Survey of the State of New York, 1898. Verplanck Colvin. (Illus.). 350p. 1989. 60.00 (0-685-29368-8) Assn Protect Adirondacks.

Report of the Symposium on Prevention of Marine Pollution from Ships. International Maritime Organization Staff. 1976. txt ed. 39.00 (0-89771-957-3, Pub. by Intl Maritime Org UK) St Mut.

Report of the Task Force on Administrative Adjudication. 225p. 1988. 28.50 (0-317-02664-X, 43,625) NCLS Inc.

Report of the Task Force on Child Abuse - Neglect System Safeguards. 52p. (Orig.). (C). 1992. pap. text ed. 20.00 (1-56806-094-7) DIANE Pub.

Report of the Task Force on Children. Ed. by Karen Glass & Mark Miller. (America in Transition, the International Frontier Ser.). 40p. (Orig.). 1989. pap. text ed. 10.95 (1-55877-033-X) Natl Governor.

Report of the Task Force on Disclosure Simplification: U. S. Securities & Exchange Commission. Philip K. Howard. (Illus.). 96p. (Orig.). (C). 1996. pap. 30.00 (0-7881-2917-1) DIANE Pub.

Report of the Task Force on Domestic Markets. Ed. by Mark Miller. (America in Transition, the International Frontier Ser.). 40p. (Orig.). 1989. pap. text ed. 10.95 (1-55877-048-8) Natl Governor.

Report of the Task Force on Foreign Markets. Ed. by Mark Miller. (America in Transition, the International Frontier Ser.). 42p. (Orig.). 1989. pap. text ed. 10.95 (1-55877-043-7) Natl Governor.

Report of the Task Force on International Education. Ed. by Mark Miller & Karen Glass. (America in Transition, the International Frontier Ser.). 40p. (Orig.). 1989. pap. text ed. 10.95 (1-55877-038-0) Natl Governor.

Report of the Task Force on Research & Technology. Ed. by Mark Miller. (America in Transition, the International Frontier Ser.). 40p. (Orig.). 1989. pap. text ed. 10.95 (1-55877-046-1) Natl Governor.

Report of the Task Force on the Quality of Audits of Governmental Units. American Institute of Certified Public Accountants Staff. 80p. reprint ed. pap. 25.00 (0-8357-4592-9, 2037523) Bks Demand.

Report of the Task Force on Transportation Infrastructure. Ed. by Mark Miller. (America in Transition, the International Frontier Ser.). 40p. 1989. pap. text ed. 10.95 (1-55877-050-X) Natl Governor.

Report of the Truth of the Fight about the Iles of Acores. Walter Raleigh. LC 72-26280. (English Experience Ser.: No. 183). 32p. 1969. reprint ed. 30.00 (90-221-0183-5) Walter J Johnson.

Report of the Twentieth Century Fund Task Force on Market Speculation & Corporate Governance. LC 92-34936. (Orig.). 1992. pap. 9.95 (0-87078-330-0) TCFP-PPP.

Report of the Twentieth Century Task Force on the Privatization of Public Housing. Michael Stegman. 128p. 1989. 18.95 (0-87078-306-8); pap. 8.95 (0-87078-307-6) TCFP-PPP.

Report of the U. N. Regional Cartographic Conference on Asia & the Pacific, 12th. 66p. 1991. 10.00 (92-1-100463-2, 91.I.42) UN.

Report of the U. S. Advisory Committee on Education. U. S. Advisory Committee on Education. LC 74-1711. (Children & Youth Ser.). 260p. 1974. reprint ed. 25.95 (0-405-05987-6) Ayer.

Report of the United Nation Conference on Environment & Development Vols. 1-3: Rio de Janeiro, 3-14 June, 1992. 1993. 50.00 (92-1-100498-5) UN.

Report of the United States Attorney General's National Committee to Study the Antitrust Laws. United States Attorney General's National Committee to Study the Antitrust Laws. LC 76-10980. xiii, 393p. 1976. reprint ed. text ed. 75.00 (0-8371-8822-9, USAL, Greenwood Pr) Greenwood.

Report of the Violence Prevention Advisory Task Force (Minn.) (Illus.). 65p. (Orig.). (C). 1995. pap. text ed. 25.00 (0-7881-2404-8) DIANE Pub.

Report of the Working Party on Courses for Animal Licensees. M. W. Smith. 1984. 30.00 (0-685-12472-X) St Mut.

*__Report of the Workshop on the Role of Financial Institutions in Strengthening Fisheries.__ Food & Agriculture Organization Staff. (Fisheries Reports: No. 549). 158p. 1997. pap. 17.00 (92-5-103930-5, F39305, Pub. by FAO IT) Bernan Associates.

Report of the Workshop on the Transfer & Development of Environmentally Sound Technologies (ESTs) 51p. 1994. 10.00 (92-1-112335-6) UN.

Report of the World Conference on Sanctions Against Racist South Africa: Paris, June 16-20, 1986. 79p. pap. 11.00 (92-1-100305-9, E.86.I.23) UN.

Report of the World Conference to Review & Appraise the Achievements of the United Nations Decade for Women: Equality, Development & Peace. 304p. 1985. 30.00 (92-1-130104-1) UN.

*__Report of the 14th Session of the Coordinating Working Party on Atlantic Fishery Statistics, Paris, 1990, & Report of the 2nd Ad Hoc Consultation on Global Tuna Statistics, La Jolla, California, 1987.__ 49p. 1990. 12.00 (92-5-102953-9, Pub. by FAO IT) Bernan Associates.

*__Report of the 1994-1996 Advisory Council on Social Security Vol. 1: Findings & Recommendations.__ Ed. by Edward M. Gramlich et al. (Illus.). 261p. (Orig.). 1997. pap. text ed. 50.00 (0-7881-4268-2) DIANE Pub.

Report of the 2010 Committee: The Future of Japan & the World Economy. (Illus.). 31p. (Orig.). (C). 1993. pap. text ed. 25.00 (1-56806-317-2) DIANE Pub.

Report of U. S. Select Commission on Immigration & Refugee Policy: A Critical Analysis. Ed. by Wayne A. Cornelius & Ricardo Anzaldua. (Research Reports: No. 32). 34p. (Orig.). (C). 1983. pap. 5.00 (0-935391-31-2, RR-32) UCSD Ctr US-Mex.

Report of Wenamum. Hans Goedicke. LC 74-6823. (Johns Hopkins Near Eastern Studies). 200p. reprint ed. pap. 57.00 (0-317-41825-4, 2025625) Bks Demand.

Report on a Journey to Riyadh (1865) Lewis Pelly. (Arabia Past & Present Ser.: Vol. 6). (Illus.). 1978. reprint ed. 26.95 (0-902675-64-8) Oleander Pr.

Report on a National Study of Parental Leaves. 1986. 25.00 (0-89584-153-3) Catalyst.

Report on a Negotiation: Helsinki-Geneva-Helsinki Nineteen Seventy-Two to Nineteen Seventy-Five. Ed. by Luigi V. Ferraris. Tr. by Marie-Claire Barber from ITA. (Collection De Relations Internationales Ser.). 439p. 1981. lib. bdg. 93.50 (90-286-0779-X) Kluwer Ac.

Report on a Workshop on Technology Choices, Work & Society's Future. Ed. by Aspen Institute Staff. 136p. (Orig.). 1987. pap. text ed. 16.00 (0-8191-5836-4, Aspen Inst for Humanistic Studies) U Pr of Amer.

Report on Afghanistan. Kuldip Nayar. 1981. 12.00 (0-8364-0690-7, Pub. by Allied II) S Asia.

Report on Afghanistan. Kuldip Nayyar. 212p. 1980. 15.95 (0-318-37264-9) Asia Bk Corp.

Report on American Manuscripts in the Royal Institution of Great Britain, 4 vols., Set. Great Britain Historical Manuscripts Commission. Ed. by George Billias. LC 72-8703. (American Revolutionary Ser.). 1979. reprint ed. lib. bdg. 200.00 (0-8398-0801-1) Irvington.

Report on an Acceleration of History: The Emergence of the European Economic Space: an Executive-Level Seminar Conducted by the European Institute March 16-18, 1990, Wye Plantation, Wye Maryland. Frwd. by Jacqueline Graphin. 30p. (Orig.). 1990. write for info. (0-9628287-1-8) European Inst.

Report on an Analysis of the Office of Pipeline Safety Annual Report Data for the Natural Gas Distribution Companies 1970-1975. Battelle Columbus Laboratories Staff et al. 83p. 1977. pap. 2.00 (0-318-12690-7, X50577) Am Gas Assn.

Report on an Income Tax in Texas. Melvin Greenhut. Ed. by Svetozar Pejovich & Henry Dethloff. (Series on Public Issues: No. 21). 1986. pap. 2.00 (0-86599-057-3) PERC.

Report on an Investigation of the Feasibility of Establishing a National Civil Engineering Software Center to the American Society of Civil Engineers for the Research Council on Computer Practices. Kenneth G. Medearis. LC 79-302366. 128p. reprint ed. pap. 36.50 (0-317-20732-6, 2023822) Bks Demand.

Report on Archaeological Work at Suwannet eth-Thaniya, Tananir, & Khirbet Minha. Ed. by George M. Landes. LC 75-30540. (American Schools of Oriental Research, Supplement Ser.: Vol. 21). 117p. 1975. text ed. 17.50 (0-89757-317-X); pap. text ed. 13.50 (0-89757-321-8) Am Sch Orient Res.

Report on Available Standard Samples, Reference Samples, & High-Purity Materials for Spectrochemical Analysis - DS 2. 156p. 1980. pap. 4.50 (0-685-00561-5, 05-002000-39) ASTM.

Report on Bengal. Famine Inquiry Commission of India. LC 75-26302. (World Food Supply Ser.). 1976. reprint ed. 23.95 (0-405-07781-5) Ayer.

Report on Blacklisting: Part One, the Movies. John Cogley. LC 79-169349. (Arno Press Cinema Program Ser.). 326p. 1979. reprint ed. 26.95 (0-405-03915-8) Ayer.

Report on Brunei in Nineteen Hundred Four. M. S. McArthur. LC 87-11218. (Monographs in International Studies, Southeast Asia Ser.: No. 74). 216p. 1987. pap. text ed. 15.00 (0-89680-135-7, Ohio U Ctr Intl) Ohio U Pr.

Report on Communion. Ed Conroy. 446p. 1990. mass mkt. 4.95 (0-380-70811-6) Avon.

*__Report on Competition Policy 1995, Vol. 25.__ 446p. 1996. pap. 35.00 (92-827-7081-8, CM94-96-429-ENC, Pub. by Europ Com UK) Bernan Associates.

Report on Confidential Enquiries into Maternal Deaths in the United Kingdom, 1988-1990. 164p. 1994. pap. 25.00 (0-11-321691-2, HM16912, Pub. by Stationery Ofc UK) Bernan Associates.

*__Report on Confidential Enquiries into Maternal Deaths in the United Kingdom, 1991-1993.__ HMSO Staff. 164p. 1996. pap. 30.00 (0-11-321983-0, HM19830, Pub. by Stationery Ofc UK) Bernan Associates.

Report on Corporate Library Spending. Primary Research Staff. 112p. 1995. pap. 80.00 (1-57440-000-2) Primary Research.

An Asterisk (*) at the beginning of an entry indicates that the title is appearing in BIP for the first time.

R

Report on Corporate State Tax Administrative Uniformity. American Institute of Certified Public Accountants Staff. LC 90-810. 58p. 1990. pap. 25.00 (*0-7837-8476-7*, 2049281) Bks Demand.

Report on County Consolidation in South Dakota with Special Reference to Buffalo & Jerauld Counties. W. O. Farber & William H. Cape. 1968. 5.00 (*1-55614-107-6*) U of SD Gov Res Bur.

Report on Dialectal Work see English Dialect Society Publications: Miscellanies

Report on Diesel & Gas Engines Power Costs, 1974: Data for 1972 & Previous Years. American Society of Mechanical Engineers Staff. 33p. reprint ed. pap. 25.00 (*0-317-08172-1*, 2013318) Bks Demand.

Report on Economic Conditions of the South: FDR & the Era of the New Deal. U. S. Emergency Council Staff. LC 70-172009. 1972. reprint ed. lib. bdg. 15.00 (*0-306-70438-2*) Da Capo.

Report on Education. Edward Seguin. LC 76-39942. (History of Psychology Ser.). 1976. reprint ed. 50.00 (*0-8201-1282-8*) Schol Facsimiles.

Report on Effective Psychotherapy: Legislative Testimony. Roberta Russell. Ed. by Suzanne Smith. LC 81-90112. 81p. (C). 1981. 30.00 (*0-940106-00-0*) Hillgarth Pr.

Report on Effective Psychotherapy: Legislative Testimony & Recommendations for Therapeutic Relationships in a Caring World. rev. ed. Roberta Russell. Ed. by Suzanne Smith. 120p. pap. text ed. 14.95 (*0-940106-54-X*) Hillgarth Pr.

Report on Elevated-Temperature Properties of Selected Superalloys, DS7-S1. 1968. pap. 11.00 (*0-8031-0814-1*, 05-007001-40) ASTM.

Report on Equipment Availability for the Ten-Year Period, 1967-1976. 50p. 1977. 18.75 (*0-317-34109-X*, 047764) Edison Electric.

Report on Forest Research 1995. 78p. 1995. pap. text ed. 40.00 (*0-11-710333-0*, HM03330, Pub. by Stationery Ofc UK) Bernan Associates.

Report on Government Procurement Practices. Stanley Fishner. LC 87-92078. 128p. 1989. 13.95 (*0-9606848-2-4*, Camelot Pubs) Fishner Bks.

Report on Great Lakes Water Quality: Report to the International Joint Commission, Presented at Toledo, Ohio, November 1987. fac. ed. Great Lakes Water Quality Board Staff. LC 89-79106. 252p. 1987. pap. 71.90 (*0-7837-8615-8*, 2075222) Bks Demand.

Report on Great Lakes Water Quality, 1987: Appendix A; Progress in Developing Remedial Action Plans for Areas of Concern in the Great Lakes Basin; Report to the International Joint Commission, Presented at Toledo, Ohio, November 1987. fac. ed. Great Lakes Water Quality Board Staff. 214p. 1987. pap. 61.00 (*0-7837-8616-6*, 2075223) Bks Demand.

Report on India's Food Crisis & Steps to Meet It. Agricultural Production Team Staff. LC 75-26294. (World Food Supply Ser.). 1976. reprint ed. 23.95 (*0-405-07767-X*) Ayer.

Report on Issues Surrounding Retention of Client Files in Law Firms. Gloria Zimmerman et al. 94p. 1993. pap. 36.00 (*0-933887-46-9*, A4593) ARMA Intl.

Report on Japanese Immigration & Alleged Discrimatory Legislation Against Japanese Residents in the U. S. U. S. Department of State Staff & Roland Morris. Ed. by Roger Daniels. LC 78-7081. (Asian Experience in North America Ser.). 1979. reprint ed. lib. bdg. 23.95 (*0-405-11295-5*) Ayer.

Report on Library Cooperation, 1989. 7th ed. Compiled by Jean E. Wilkins. LC 80-67287. 438p. 1990. 25.00 (*0-8389-7453-8*) ASCLA.

Report on National Legislation for the Equalization of Opportunities for People with Disabilities: Examples from 22 Countries & Areas. 42p. 1989. 12.00 (*92-1-130134-3*, 89.IV.6) UN.

Report on Natural Gas Cooling. 51p. 1993. 12.50 (*0-317-05196-2*) NARUC.

Report on Needs Assessment Methodology: Sources of Needs Assessments in Public Law. Anne M. Delaney et al. LC 79-102731. (American Foundation for the Blind Research Ser.). 223p. reprint ed. pap. 63.60 (*0-7837-0136-5*, 2040425) Bks Demand.

Report on Oceanographical Work from Ocean Weather Ships. S. F. Grace. (Publications Scientifiques Ser.: No. 16). write for info. (*0-614-17804-5*) Intl Assoc Phys Sci Ocean.

Report on Operational Programmes 1993. 1995. pap. 135.00 (*0-85954-395-1*, Pub. by Nat Res Inst UK) St Mut.

Report on PC Integration, 1991. Rational Data Systems, Inc. Staff. 118p. 1992. 5.00 (*1-881378-12-8*) Rational Data.

Report on PC Integration, 1992. Rational Data Systems, Inc. Staff. 136p. 1992. 24.95 (*1-881378-13-6*) Rational Data.

Report on Pipeline Location. (Manual & Report on Engineering Practice Ser.: No. 46). 86p. 1965. pap. 8.00 (*0-87262-040-9*) Am Soc Civil Eng.

Report on Planning, Policy Making & Research Activities. Resources for the Future, Inc. Staff. LC 61-14884. 46p. reprint ed. pap. 25.00 (*0-317-27688-3*, 2052106) Bks Demand.

Report on Portugal's War in Guinea-Bissau. Al Venter, Jr. (Illus.). 1973. 3.00 (*0-685-03457-7*) Munger Africana Lib.

Report on Probate & Estate Administration Statutes. 140p. (Orig.). (C). 1993. pap. text ed. 40.00 (*1-56806-951-0*) DIANE Pub.

Report on Profitability by Line by State. annuals 374p. (C). 1994. ring bd. 125.00 (*0-89382-313-9*) Nat Assn Insurance.

Report on Profitability by Line by State. rev. ed. Ed. by Jim Bugenhagen. (C). 1995. ring bd. 125.00 (*0-89382-368-6*, PBL-PB) Nat Assn Insurance.

Report on Profitability by Line by State, 1990. 270p. (C). 1991. pap. 100.00 (*0-89382-182-9*) Nat Assn Insurance.

Report on Profitability by Line by State 1992. 378p. 1994. pap. 125.00 (*0-89382-259-0*) Nat Assn Insurance.

Report on Radioactive Waste Disposal. IAEA Staff. (Technical Reports: No. 349). 104p. 1993. pap. 45.00 (*92-0-100393-5*, STI/DOC/349, Pub. by IAEA AU) Bernan Associates.

Report on Radionics. Edward W. Russell. 110p. 1973. pap. 19.95 (*0-85435-002-0*, Pub. by C W Daniel UK) Natl Bk Netwk.

Report on Radionics. 6th ed. Edward W. Russell. (Illus.). 256p. pap. 26.95 (*0-8464-4283-3*) Beekman Pubs.

Report on Releases of Hazardous Substances from Underground Storage Tanks in California 1991. 646p. (Orig.). (C). 1992. pap. text ed. 60.00 (*1-56806-023-8*) DIANE Pub.

Report on Self-Help Law: Its Many Perspectives. 111p. 1987. pap. 7.50 (*0-685-29727-6*, 351-0007-01) Amer Bar Assn.

Report on Ship Channel Design. Task Committee on Ship Channel Design for the Committee on Waterways, Waterways, Port, Coastal, & Ocean Division Staff. LC 93-31935. (Manual & Report on Engineering Practice Ser.: No. 80). 1993. 19.00 (*0-87262-981-3*) Am Soc Civil Eng.

Report on Single-Tier Trial Court System. 51p. (Orig.). (C). 1994. pap. text ed. 25.00 (*0-7881-1365-8*) DIANE Pub.

Report on Spiritualism: Together with the Evidence, Oral & Written. London Dialectical Society Staff. LC 75-36849. (Occult Ser.). 1976. reprint ed. 35.95 (*0-405-07965-6*) Ayer.

Report on State Public Health Work, Based on a Survey of State Boards of Health. Charles V. Chapin. Ed. by Barbara G. Rosenkrantz. LC 76-25657. (Public Health in America Ser.). (Illus.). 1977. reprint ed. lib. bdg. 23.95 (*0-405-09807-3*) Ayer.

Report on the Adoption of the Gold Standard in Japan. Masayoshi Matsukata. Ed. by Mira Wilkins. LC 78-3937. (International Finance Ser.). (Illus.). 1979. reprint ed. lib. bdg. 40.95 (*0-405-11238-6*) Ayer.

Report on the Affairs of British North America, 3 vols., Set. John G. Durham. LC 73-117388. 1970. reprint ed. lib. bdg. 150.00 (*0-678-00647-4*) Kelley.

Report on the American Workforce. (Illus.). 202p. (Orig.). (C). 1995. pap. text ed. 30.00 (*0-7881-1917-6*) DIANE Pub.

*__Report on the American Workforce.__ 1997. lib. bdg. 250.99 (*0-8490-7666-8*) Gordon Pr.

Report on the Archaeology of Maine: Being a Narrative of Explorations in That State, 1912-1920, Together with Work at Lake Champlain, 1917. Warren K. Moorehead. LC 76-43788. (Phillips Academy). reprint ed. 74.50 (*0-404-15643-6*) AMS Pr.

Report on the Australian Royal Commission on Aboriginal & Torres Strait Islander Deaths in Custody. Celia McGuinnes & Leo Whelan. Ed. by Minnesota Lawyers International Human Rights Committee Staff. 32p. (Orig.). 1988. pap. 3.00 (*0-929293-18-5*) MN Advocates.

Report on the Barracks & Hospitals of the United States Army, No. 4. John S. Billings. 1870. 102.00 (*0-914074-08-3*, J M C & Co) Amereon Ltd.

Report on the Chicago Strike of June - July, 1894: C. D. Wright, Chairman. United States Strike Commission. LC 68-27849. (Library of American Labor History). liv, 681p. 1972. reprint ed. 65.00 (*0-678-00882-5*) Kelley.

Report on the Commercial Statistics of Syria. John Bowring. LC 73-6271. (Middle East Ser.). 1973. reprint ed. 18.95 (*0-405-05326-6*) Ayer.

Report on the Condition of the Insane Poor in the County Poor Houses of New York. Sylvester D. Willard. LC 73-2430. (Mental Illness & Social Policy; the American Experience Ser.). 1973. reprint ed. 16.95 (*0-405-05238-3*) Ayer.

Report on the Condition of the South. Carl Schurz. LC 74-92238. (American Negro: His History & Literature. Series 3). 1970. reprint ed. 13.95 (*0-405-01938-6*) Ayer.

Report on the Construction of a Military Road from Fort Walla Walla to Fort Benton. John Mullan. (Illus.). 183p. 1994. 29.95 (*0-87770-102-4*) Ye Galleon.

Report on the Diplomatic Archives of the Department of State, 1789-1840. rev. ed. A. C. McLaughlin. (Cl Ser.). 1906. reprint ed. pap. 25.00 (*0-527-00682-3*) Periodicals Srv.

Report on the Diseases of Silk-Worms in India. A. Pringle Jameson. 168p. 1984. pap. 175.00 (*0-7855-0388-9*, Pub. by Intl Bks & Periodicals II) St Mut.

Report on the Elevated-Temperature Properties of Stainless Steels. Ward F. Simmons & John A. Van Echo. LC 65-21045. (ASTM Data Ser.: No. DS5-S1). 214p. reprint ed. pap. 61.00 (*0-7837-4413-7*, 2044157) Bks Demand.

Report on the Elevated-Temperature Properties of Stainless Steels, DS5-S1. 214p. 1981. pap. 6.00 (*0-8031-0555-X*, 05-005001-40) ASTM.

Report on the Excavation of Marin-374. Navato Senior High Archaeology Club Staff. (Illus.). 49p. (C). 1967. reprint ed. pap. text ed. 4.70 (*1-55567-411-9*) Coyote Press.

Report on the Excavations at Grime's Graves: Weeting, Norfolk, March - May, 1914. Prehistoric Society of East Anglia Staff. Ed. by W. G. Clarke. LC 77-86437. reprint ed. 28.00 (*0-404-16676-8*) AMS Pr.

Report on the Expedition. Therkel Mathiassen. LC 76-21664. (Thule Expedition, 5th, 1921-1924 Ser.: Vol. 1, No. 1). reprint ed. 39.50 (*0-404-58301-6*) AMS Pr.

Report on the Gaudiya Vaishnava Vedanta: Form of Vedic Ontology. Henry P. Stapp. LC 96-22681. (Illus.). 46p. (Orig.). 1995. pap. text ed. 3.00 (*0-941525-10-4*) Bhaktivdnta Institute.

*__Report on the Guatemala Review.__ Anthony S. Harrington et al. 67p. (Orig.). 1996. pap. 25.00 (*0-7881-3358-6*) DIANE Pub.

Report on the Hygiene of the United States Army, No. 8. John S. Billings. 1875. 102.00 (*0-914074-09-1*, J M C & Co) Amereon Ltd.

Report on the Improvement & Development of the Transportation Facilities of San Francisco. Bion J. Arnold. LC 73-11900. (Metropolitan America Ser.). (Illus.). 510p. 1974. reprint ed. 46.95 (*0-405-05383-5*) Ayer.

Report on the Insects of Massachusetts Injurious to Vegetation. Thaddeus W. Harris. LC 70-125746. (American Environmental Studies). 1971. reprint ed. 29.95 (*0-405-02671-4*) Ayer.

*__Report on the International Conference on Gearing, October 18-19, 1960.__ J. Erler. (Technical Papers). 1961. pap. text ed. 30.00 (*1-55589-351-1*) AGMA.

Report on the Island of Purto Rico. Henry K. Carroll. LC 74-14223. (Puerto Rican Experience Ser.). (Illus.). 817p. 1975. reprint ed. 65.95 (*0-405-06213-3*) Ayer.

Report on the Measurement of International Capital Flows. LC 92-24762. 128p. 1992. pap. 19.50 (*1-55775-307-5*) Intl Monetary.

Report on the Mound Explorations of the Bureau of Ethnology. rev. ed. Cyrus Thomas. (Classics of Smithsonian Anthropology Ser.: No. 7). (Illus.). 786p. (C). 1985. reprint ed. pap. text ed. 29.95 (*0-87474-915-8*, THRMP) Smithsonian.

Report on the Murder of the General Secretary. Karel Kaplan. Tr. by Karel Kovanda from CZE. (Illus.). 323p. 1990. 49.50 (*0-8142-0477-5*) Ohio St U Pr.

Report on the Nineteen Sixty-Nine Galaxy Conference of Adult Education Organizations. Alexander N. Charters. (Landmark Ser.: No. 1). 1971. pap. text ed. 2.00 (*0-87060-005-2*, LNH 1) Syracuse U Cont Ed.

Report on the Nineteen Thirty-One Powell Mound Excavations, Madison County, Illinois. Steven R. Ahler & Peter J. DePuydt. (Reports of Investigations Ser.: No. 43). (Illus.). 40p. (C). 1987. pap. 5.00 (*0-89792-111-9*) Ill St Museum.

Report on the Office of Environment, Safety & Health Special Review of Occupational Safety & Health Programs for the Hanford High-Level Waste Tanks. 117p. (Orig.). (C). 1993. pap. text ed. 35.00 (*1-56806-701-1*) DIANE Pub.

Report on the Pacific Wagon Roads. Albert H. Campbell. 1969. 24.95 (*0-87770-003-6*) Ye Galleon.

Report on the Penitentiaries of the United States: With Introduction Added. William Crawford. LC 69-16235. (Criminology, Law Enforcement, & Social Problems Ser.: No. 97). 1969. reprint ed. 50.00 (*0-87585-097-9*) Patterson Smith.

Report on the Penitentiary System in the United States. Society for the Prevention of Pauperism Staff. LC 74-3854. (Criminal Justice in America Ser.). 1974. reprint ed. 15.95 (*0-405-06172-2*) Ayer.

Report on the Perinatal Drug Exposure Task Force in Virginia. 51p. (Orig.). (C). 1993. pap. text ed. 20.00 (*0-7881-0151-X*) DIANE Pub.

Report on the Police, Vol. 14. National Commission on Law Observance & Enforcement Staff. LC 77-154578. (Police in America Ser.). 1971. reprint ed. 13.95 (*0-405-03376-1*) Ayer.

Report on the Poor & Insane in Rhode-Island. Thomas R. Hazard. LC 73-2403. (Mental Illness & Social Policy; the American Experience Ser.). 1973. reprint ed. 16.95 (*0-405-05209-X*) Ayer.

Report on the Potential Use of Small Dams to Produce Power for Low-Income Communities. International Science & Technology, Inc. Staff. Ed. by Mary M. Allen. (Illus.). 1979. 15.00 (*0-936130-02-4*) Intl Sci Tech.

*__Report on the Presidential Commission on the Space Shuttle Challenger Accident.__ (Illus.). 262p. 1986. pap. text ed. 50.00 (*1-57979-147-6*) BPI Info Servs.

Report on the Prisons & Reformatories of the United States & Canada. Theodore W. Dwight. (Notable American Authors Ser.). 1992. reprint ed. lib. bdg. 75.00 (*0-7812-2733-X*) Rprt Serv.

Report on the Prisons & the Reformatories of the United States & Canada, Made to the Legislature of New York, January, 1867. Enoch C. Wines & Theodore W. Dwight. LC 71-156036. reprint ed. 55.00 (*0-404-09138-5*) AMS Pr.

Report on the Progress of Nuclear Waste Isolation Feasibility Studies 1980 see Geology & Geohydrology of the Palo Duro Basin, Texas Panhandle

Report on the Progress of Nuclear Waste Isolation Feasibility Studies 1981 see Geology & Geohydrology of the Palo Duro Basin, Texas Panhandle

Report on the Progress of Nuclear Waste Isolation Feasibility Studies 1982 see Geology & Geohydrology of the Palo Duro Basin, Texas Panhandle

*__Report on the Russian Army & Its Campaigns in Turkey, 1877-1878.__ V. F. Greene. (European War Ser.: Vol. 8). (Illus.). 520p. 1996. reprint ed. 59.95 (*0-89839-252-7*) Battery Pr.

Report on the San Antonio Study of Legal Services Delivery Systems. 141p. 1989. pap. 10.00 (*0-89707-473-4*, 351-0008) Amer Bar Assn.

Report on the Sandstone of the Connecticut Valley, Especially Its Fossil Footmarks. Edward Hitchcock. LC 73-17825. (Natural Sciences in America Ser.). (Illus.). 256p. 1974. reprint ed. 31.95 (*0-405-05743-1*) Ayer.

Report on the Sanitary Condition of the Labouring Population of Great Britain, 1842. E. Chadwick. Ed. by M. Flinn. 443p. 1979. 28.00 (*0-85224-145-3*, Pub. by Edinburgh U Pr UK) Col U Pr.

Report on the Second Half of the Twentieth Century. Ken Norris. 1977. pap. 1.50 (*0-916696-05-7*) Cross Country.

Report on the Second Half of the Twentieth Century. Ken Norris. 1988. pap. 9.00 (*0-919349-84-6*) Guernica Editions.

Report on the Situation of Defence Lawyers in Argentina, March, 1975. Heleno C. Fragoso. 23p. reprint ed. pap. 25.00 (*0-317-29847-X*, 2051909) Bks Demand.

Report on the Situation of Human Rights in Paraguay-Informe Sobre la Situacion De los Derechos Humanos En Paraguay. 1978. pap. 3.00 (*0-8270-2595-5*); pap. 3.00 (*0-8270-2565-3*) OAS.

Report on the Situation of Human Rights in the Republic of Bolivia. OAS, General Secretariat, Inter-American Commission of Human Rights. 117p. (SPA.). (C). 1981. pap. 5.00 (*0-685-03623-5*) OAS.

Report on the Situation of Human Rights in the Republic of Colombia. OAS, General Secretariat, Inter-American Commission of Human Rights. 222p. (SPA.). (C). 1981. pap. 8.00 (*0-8270-1374-4*) OAS.

Report on the Situation of Human Rights in the Republic of Guatemala. OAS, General Secretariat, Inter-American Commission of Human Rights. (OAS Ser.: L/V/II.53 Doc 21, Rev. 3). 133p. (SPA.). (C). 1981. pap. 6.00 (*0-8270-1428-7*) OAS.

Report on the Situation of Human Rights in the Republic of Nicaragua. OAS, General Secretariat, Inter-American Commission of Human Rights. 171p. (SPA.). (C). 1981. pap. 7.00 (*0-8270-1373-6*) OAS.

Report on the Situation of Human Rights in Uruguay-Informe Sobre la Situacion de los Derechos Humanos en Uruguay. 1978. Eng. Ed. 3.00 (*0-8270-2585-8*); Span Ed. pap. 3.00 (*0-8270-2570-X*) OAS.

Report on the Social Statistics of Cities, 2 Vols., Set. George E. Waring, Jr. Incl. 1. New England & the Middle States. LC 70-112577. 1970. 88.95 (*0-405-02482-7*); Vol. 2. Southern of the Western States. LC 70-112577. 1970. 88.95 (*0-405-02483-5*); LC 70-112577. (Rise of Urban America Ser.). (Illus.). 1979. reprint ed. 177.95 (*0-405-02481-9*) Ayer.

Report on the Social Statistics of Cities: 10th Census, 1880 Census Reports, Vols. 18-19, 1970. U. S. Census Office Staff & George E. Waring, Jr. 1970. 80.50 (*0-685-11361-2*, 18805) Ayer.

Report on the Stoney Corals from the Red Sea. Georg Scheer & Gopinadha Pillai. (Zoologica Ser.: Heft 133). 198p. 1983. pap. text ed. 186.70 (*3-510-55019-6*) Lubrecht & Cramer.

Report on the Survey on the Image of Lawyers in Advertising. LC 90-81937. 106p. 1990. pap. 30.00 (*0-685-47181-0*, 406-0010) Amer Bar Assn.

Report on the Swanscombe Skull see Swanscombe Skull

Report on the "The Star Spangled Banner" Oscar G. Sonneck. LC 75-145993. 1972. reprint ed. pap. 5.95 (*0-486-22237-3*) Dover.

Report on the UNESCO La Breviere Seminar on Workers. Ed. by G. D. Cole & Andre Philip. (UNESCO Education Studies & Documents: No. 1). 1974. reprint ed. pap. 25.00 (*0-8115-1325-4*) Periodicals Srv.

Report on the United States & Mexican Boundary Survey, 2 vols. William Emory. 1993. reprint ed. lib. bdg. 150.00 (*0-7812-5878-2*) Rprt Serv.

Report on the United States Seafood Industry, 1994. Howard M. Johnson & Ian Dore. 108p. (Orig.). 1994. pap. 45.00 (*0-9636871-3-1*) Zeus Faber.

Report on the Violent Male. A. E. Van Vogt. 36p. (C). 1993. reprint ed. pap. 15.00 (*0-946650-40-3*) Borgo Pr.

Report on the Violent Male. Ed. by A. E. Van Vogt. 36p. (C). 1993. reprint ed. lib. bdg. 25.00 (*0-8095-6761-X*) Borgo Pr.

Report on the Vision of the Electronic Display Industry in the Year 2000. Ed. by David Andrews & Jack Bernstein. Tr. by Interlingua Staff from JPN. (Illus.). 224p. 1995. 795.00 (*1-884730-00-0*) JB & Me.

*__Report on the Vision of the Electronic Display Industry in the Year 2000.__ Tr. by David Andrews & Jack Bernstein from JPN. (Illus.). 87p. 1996. pap. 295.00 (*1-884730-06-X*, Interlingua) JB & Me.

Report on the West Coast Women's Studies Conference. Ed. by Women's Studies Committee & Joan H. Wilson. 1974. pap. 5.00 (*0-912786-35-3*) Know Inc.

Report on the World Social Situation. 226p. 1993. pap. 24.95 (*92-1-130155-6*, E.93.IV.2) UN.

Report on the World Social Situation, 1989. 126p. 21.00 (*92-1-130129-7*, E.89.IV.1) UN.

*__Report on the 1992 U. S. Tour of European Concrete Highways.__ Michael Darter. (Illus.). 147p. (C). 1996. reprint ed. pap. 30.00 (*0-7881-3556-2*) DIANE Pub.

Report on Theosophical Society. Society for Psychical Report Staff. LC 75-36920. (Occult Ser.). (Illus.). 1976. 29.95 (*0-405-07975-3*) Ayer.

Report on Title XX Social Services Block Grant Expenditures: July 1, 1981-June 30, 1982. Illinois Office of the Governor. write for info. (*0-318-58928-1*) Illinois Governor.

Report on U. S. Barriers to Trade & Investment (1994) 10th ed. 115p. (C). 1994. pap. text ed. 35.00 (*0-7881-1485-9*) DIANE Pub.

Report on U. S. Barriers to Trade & Investment (1995) (Illus.). 70p. (Orig.). (C). 1995. pap. text ed. 20.00 (*0-7881-2295-9*) DIANE Pub.

*__Report on U. S. Barriers to Trade & Investment, 1996.__ (Illus.). 53p. (Orig.). (C). 1996. pap. 30.00 (*0-7881-3487-6*) DIANE Pub.

Report on U. S. Trade & Investment Barriers (1993) Problems of Doing Business with the U. S. (Illus.). 90p. (Orig.). (C). 1994. pap. text ed. 25.00 (*0-7881-0266-4*) DIANE Pub.

Report on Unfair Trade Policies by Major Trading Partners. 212p. (Orig.). (C). 1993. pap. text ed. 50.00 (*1-56806-782-8*) DIANE Pub.

An Asterisk (*) at the beginning of an entry indicates that the title is appearing in BIP for the first time.

Report on University Adult Education in Australia & New Zealand. P. Sheats. 1967. 2.50 (*0-8156-7013-3*, NES 27) Syracuse U Cont Ed.

Report on Work of Prison Dept. April 1993-March 1994 see Prison Service Annual Report & Accounts

Report on Workshop on the Future of National Atmospheric Research. Ed. by Alfred K. Blackadar & Earl G. Droessler. 143p. (Orig.). 1977. pap. 11.00 (*0-933876-45-9*) Am Meteorological.

Report Options. Meredith M. Bell & Dennis E. Coates. 16p. 1994. pap. text ed. 5.00 (*1-886713-06-5*) Perform Support Systs.

Report Prepared for the Sixth International Conference of Labour Statisticians: Montreal, 4 to 12 August, 1948. Incl. Pt. I. Employment, Unemployment & Labor Force Statistics, a Study of Methods. 1948. (*0-318-58884-6*); Pt. II. Cost-of-Living Statistics, Methods & Techniques of the Post-War Period. 1947. (*0-318-58885-4*); Pt. III. Methods of Statistics of Industrial Injuries. 1947. (*0-318-58886-2*); Final Report: The Sixth International Conference of Labour Statisticians, Montreal, 4-12 August, 1948. 1974. (*0-318-58887-0*); (I.L.O. Studies & Reports New Ser.: No. 7). 1974. reprint ed. 45.00 (*0-8115-3332-8*) Periodicals Srv.

Report Presented 1909 see Study of Sensory Control in the Rat

Report Series Code Dictionary. 3rd ed. Ed. by Eleanor J. Aronson & Asta V. Kane. 647p. 1986. 180.00 (*0-8103-2147-5*) Gale.

Report Submitted to the Supreme Commander for the Allied Powers, Tokyo, March 30, 1946: Submitted to the Supreme Commander for the Allied Powers, Tokyo, March 30, 1946. United States Education Mission to Japan Staff. LC 76-48977. (U. S. Department of State, Pub. 2579 Far Eastern Ser.: No. 11). 62p. 1977. reprint ed. text ed. 45.00 (*0-8371-9331-1*, USRU) Greenwood.

Report That Dr. Miguel Ramos de Arizpe, Priest of Borbon, & Deputy in the Present General & Special Cortes of Spain for the Province of Coahuila, One of the Four Eastern Interior Provinces of the Kingdom of Mexico, Presents to the August Congress. Miguel Ramos-Arizpe. Tr. & Intro. by Nettie L. Benson. LC 69-19011. xiii, 61p. 1970. reprint ed. text ed. 49.75 (*0-8371-1036-X*, TLRR) Greenwood.

Report to the Attorney General: Department of Law Reorganization Study. 326p. 1979. 23.00 (*0-318-14444-1*) IJA NYU.

Report to the Brown Association, U. S. A. Columbus Smith. 126p. 1990. reprint ed. pap. 22.00 (*0-8328-0333-2*); reprint ed. lib. bdg. 30.00 (*0-8328-0332-4*) Higginson Bk Co.

Report to the Committee of the City Council Appointed to Obtain the Census of Boston for the Year 1845. Lemuel C. Shattuck. LC 75-17243. (Social Problems & Social Policy Ser.). (Illus.). 1976. reprint ed. 25.95 (*0-405-07514-6*) Ayer.

Report to the Dade County Grand Jury Regarding Guardianship. W. Schmidt. 1982. write for info. (*0-318-58138-8*) FSU CSP.

Report to the Governor on the Hawaii Statewide Drug Prevention & Control Strategy: An Overview & Action Plans. (Illus.). 165p. (Orig.). (C). 1994. pap. text ed. 35.00 (*0-7881-0271-0*) DIANE Pub.

Report to the Governor the Committee to Study P.R's Finances see Informe al Gobernador del Comite Para el Estudio de las Finanzas de Puerto Rico (Informe Tobin)

Report to the Interim Shareholders. Patricia Fillingham. (Illus.). 104p. (Orig.). 1991. pap. 10.00 (*0-942292-11-1*) Warthog Pr.

Report to the King: Colonel Juan Camargo y Cavallero's Account of New Spain, 1815. John S. Leiby. (American University Studies: History: Ser. IX, Vol. 3). 227p. (Orig.). 1984. pap. text ed. 22.70 (*0-8204-0050-5*) P Lang Pubng.

Report to the Lord Chancellor on H. M. Land Registry for the Year 1994-95. 63p. 1995. 30.00 (*0-10-256295-4*, HM62954, Pub. by Stationery Ofc UK) Bernan Associates.

***Report to the Lord Chancellor on Her Majesty's Land Registry for the Year, 1995-96.** annuals 63p. 1996. pap. 30.00 (*0-10-281196-2*, HM811962, Pub. by Stationery Ofc UK) Bernan Associates.

Report to the Nation on Crime & Justice. (Illus.). 50p. (Orig.). (C). 1993. pap. text ed. 20.00 (*1-56806-854-9*) DIANE Pub.

Report to the Nation on Crime & Justice. 2nd ed. (NCJ Ser.: No. 105506). (Illus.). 138p. (Orig.). 1988. pap. 11.00 (*0-16-003620-8*, S/N 027-000-01295-7) USGPO.

Report to the President for Transmittal to the Congress. U. S. Commission on Intergovernmental Relations. LC 77-74962. (American Federalism-the Urban Dimension Ser.). (Illus.). 1978. reprint ed. lib. bdg. 29.95 (*0-405-10505-3*) Ayer.

Report to the President on Implementing Recommendations of the Natl. Performance Review: A New Vision for Labor-Management Relations. 1995. lib. bdg. 250.00 (*0-8490-5858-9*) Gordon Pr.

Report to the Principal's Office! Jerry Spinelli. 144p. (J). (gr. 4-6). 1992. 3.50 (*0-590-46277-6*, Apple Paperbacks) Scholastic Inc.

Report to the Secretary of War of the U. S. on Indian Affairs. Jedidiah Morse. LC 70-108516. (Illus.). 400p. 1972. reprint ed. 69.00 (*0-403-00345-8*) Scholarly.

Report to the Stockholders & Other Poems. 3rd ed. John Beecher. LC 62-6046. (Illus.). 1971. reprint ed. 5.00 (*0-911234-02-0*) Red Mtn.

Report upon Pile-Structures in Naaman's Creek, Near Claymont, Delaware. H. T. Cresson. (Harvard University Peabody Museum of Archaeology & Ethnology Papers: HU. PMP Vol. 1, No. 4). 1974. reprint ed. pap. 25.00 (*0-527-01186-X*) Periodicals Srv.

Report upon the Colorado River of the West. Joseph C. Ives. LC 69-18459. (American Scene Ser.). (Illus.). 1969. reprint ed. lib. bdg. 52.50 (*0-686-85847-6*) Da Capo.

Report Upon the Illegal Practices of the United States Department of Justice. R. G. Brown et al. LC 73-90206. (Mass Violence in America Ser.). 1979. reprint ed. 17.95 (*0-405-01301-9*) Ayer.

Report... Upon the Settlement of the Revenues of Excise & Customs in Scotland A.D. MDCLVI. Thomas Tucker. LC 79-177574. (Bannatyne Club, Edinburgh. Publications: No. 7). reprint ed. 34.50 (*0-404-52708-6*) AMS Pr.

Report Writer. Steve Eckols. LC 80-82868. (Illus.). 106p. (C). 1980. pap. 17.50 (*0-911625-07-0*) M Murach & Assoc.

Report Writers Explained. Jeff Sims. (C). 1996. pap. text ed. 27.00 (*0-13-244989-7*) P-H.

Report Writer's Manual. Kathryn Hughes & Joan Vinall-Cox. 127p. 1995. lib. bdg. 39.00 (*0-8095-4854-2*) Borgo Pr.

Report Writer's Manual. Kathryn Hughes & Joan Vinall-Cox. 127p. 1989. reprint ed. pap. 14.95 (*0-88962-280-9*) Mosaic.

Report Writing. (General Aptitude & Abilities Ser.: CS-41). 1994. pap. 23.95 (*0-8373-6741-7*) Nat Learn.

Report Writing. Stephen Allender. (C). 1991. pap. 30.00 (*0-85171-095-6*, Pub. by IPM Hse UK) St Mut.

Report Writing. rev. ed. Judith Vidal-Hall. (C). 1988. 45.00 (*0-685-33714-6*, Pub. by Witherby & Co UK) St Mut.

Report Writing. 2nd ed. Joan Van Emden & Jennifer Easteal. LC 93-2659. 1993. 6.99 (*0-07-707606-0*) McGraw.

***Report Writing.** 2nd ed. Joan Van Emden & Jennifer Eastel. 109p. (Orig.). 1993. pap. 22.00 (*0-7487-1894-X*, Pub. by Stanley Thornes UK) Trans-Atl Phila.

Report Writing Correspondence Course, 2 vols., Set, Bks. I & II. American Correctional Association Staff. Ed. by Diane Geiman & Rosalie Rosetti. (Correspondence Courses Ser.). (Orig.). 1987. Set (Bks. I & II). pap. 54.00 (*0-942974-90-5*, 167) Am Correctional.

Report Writing for Architects. 3rd rev. ed. David Chappell. LC 96-5630. 180p. 1996. text ed. 49.95 (*0-632-04001-7*) Blackwell Sci.

Report Writing for Business. 8th ed. Raymond V. Lesikar, Sr. & John Pettit. 480p. (C). 1990. text ed. 56.95 (*0-256-06948-4*, 12-0420-08) Irwin.

Report Writing for Business. 9th ed. Raymond V. Lesikar & John D. Pettit. LC 94-12499. 480p. (C). 1994. per. 61.50 (*0-256-11565-6*) Irwin.

Report Writing for Business. 9th ed. Raymond V. Lesikar & John D. Petit, Jr. 1995. pap. write for info. (*0-256-18021-0*) Irwin.

Report Writing for Business & Industry. Steven P. Golen et al. LC 84-17256. (Business Communications Ser.). 526p. 1985. text ed. 39.95 (*0-471-80822-9*) P-H.

Report Writing for Criminal Justice Professionals. Clarice R. Cox & Jerrold G. Brown. LC 90-82310. 300p. (C). 1991. pap. text ed. 28.95 (*0-87084-166-1*) Anderson Pub Co.

Report Writing for Law Enforcement & Corrections. John C. Bowden. (Illus.). 108p. (Orig.). 1993. student ed. 14.00 (*1-887172-01-7*) G Bowden.

Report Writing for Law Enforcement & Corrections. John C. Bowden. (Illus.). 116p. (Orig.). 1993. pap. 24.00 (*1-887172-00-9*) G Bowden.

Report Writing for Law Enforcement & Corrections, No. 1. John C. Bowden. 218p. (Orig.). (C). 1995. teacher ed. 35.50 (*1-887172-04-1*) G Bowden.

Report Writing for Law Enforcement & Corrections, No. 2. John C. Bowden. 218p. (Orig.). (C). 1995. teacher ed. 128.50 (*1-887172-05-X*) G Bowden.

Report Writing for Law Enforcement & Corrections No. 3: Power Point Presentation. John C. Bowden. (Illus.). 510p. (Orig.). (C). 1995. teacher ed. 128.50 (*1-887172-06-8*) G Bowden.

Report Writing for Quality Assurance Analysts. William E. Perry. (Illus.). 1981. pap. 24.95 (*0-318-20494-0*) Quality Assurance.

Report Writing for Security Personnel. Christopher A. Hertig & Gary E. Bittner. 146p. 1991. pap. 27.95 (*0-409-90154-7*) Buttrwrth-Heinemann.

Report Writing in Assessment & Evaluation. Stephen W. Thomas. (Illus.). 188p. (Orig.). 1986. pap. 17.75 (*0-916671-56-9*) TRR.

***Report Writing in Business.** Trevor J. Bentley. (Business & Management Ser.). 1988. pap. 12.95 (*1-85091-352-8*) Kogan Page Ltd.

Report Writing in dBASE II. Marilyn McMahon et al. 15.95 (*0-317-06186-0*) P-H.

Report Writing in the Field of Communication Disorders: A Handbook for Students & Clinicians. 2nd ed. Kenneth J. Knepflar & Annette A. May. (Clinical Ser.: Vol. 4). 114p. (Orig.). 1992. pap. text ed. 7.00 (*0-910329-61-3*, 0310104) Am Speech Lang Hearing.

Report Writing Lesson Plan. Rosalie Rosetti. Ed. by Katherine Scott. 91p. 1991. 209.99 (*0-929310-65-9*, 142) Am Correctional.

Report Writing with Microcomputer Applications. Shirley Kuiper. (PS - Communication/English Ser.). 1992. text ed. 68.95 (*0-538-70200-1*) S-W Pub.

Reportage Journalism Vol. 1: International Reporting 128-1985. From the Activities of the League of Nations to Present-day Global Problems. Ed. by Heinz-Dietrich Fischer & Erika J. Fischer. (Pulitzer Prize Archive). 436p. 1987. 75.00 (*3-598-1049X-7*) K G Saur.

Reportage of Urban Culture: Robert Park & the Chicago School. Rolf Lindner. (Ideas in Context Ser.: No. 43). (Illus.). 256p. (C). 1996. text ed. 54.95 (*0-521-44052-1*) Cambridge U Pr.

Reportage uber Alcatraz: Die Geschichte der Gefangnisinsel erzaht von Fruheren Bewohnern. Jolene Babyak. Tr. by Renate Chestnut from ENG. (Illus.). 130p. (Orig.). (GER.). (YA). 1991. pap. 11.95 (*0-9618752-1-6*) Ariel Vamp Pr.

Reportaje De Vietnam y Kampuchea. Diane Wang & Steve Clark. (Illus.). 77p. (SPA.). 1987. pap. 6.95 (*0-87348-493-2*) Pathfinder NY.

Reporte de Quien Creeras? Marilyn Phillipps. Tr. by Carol O'Hara. 60p. (Orig.). 1995. teacher ed., pap. text ed. write for info. (*1-884794-20-3*) Eden Pubng.

Reporte of a Discourse Concerning Supreme Power in Affaires of Religion. John Hayward. LC 79-84116. (English Experience Ser.: No. 935). 64p. 1979. reprint ed. lib. bdg. 15.00 (*90-221-0935-6*) Walter J Johnson.

Reported Miracles: A Critique of Hume. J. Houston. 282p. (C). 1994. text ed. 65.00 (*0-521-41549-7*) Cambridge U Pr.

Reported Sightings: Art Chronicles, 1957-1987. John Ashbery. Ed. by David Bergman. LC 90-49781. (Illus.). 417p. 1991. pap. text ed. 16.95 (*0-674-76225-8*, ASHREX) HUP.

Reported Speech: Forms & Functions of the Verb. Ed. by Theo A. Janssen & Wim Van Der Wurff. LC 96-9656. (Pragmatics & Beyond Ser.: No. 43). x, 312p. 1996. lib. bdg. 79.00 (*1-55619-805-1*) Benjamins North Am.

Reporter -- A Tyewriting Simulation. Kushner. (PB - Keyboarding Ser.). (J). (gr. k-8). 1982. pap. 10.95 (*0-538-11620-X*) S-W Pub.

Reporter & the Law: Techniques of Covering the Courts. Lyle W. Denniston. LC 92-15053. 300p. 1992. pap. 16.50 (*0-231-08031-X*); text ed. 39.50 (*0-231-08030-1*) Col U Pr.

Reporter on the Job Vol. III. rev. ed. Beverly L. Ritter & Michael LaBorde. (Realtime Machine Shorthand Ser.). 160p. (C). 1992. teacher ed., pap. text ed. 26.75 (*0-938643-11-8*) Stenotype Educ.

Reporter on the Job Vol. III, Vol. III. rev. ed. Beverly L. Ritter & Michael LaBorde. (Realtime Machine Shorthand Ser.). 276p. (C). 1992. pap. text ed. 35.50 (*0-938643-09-6*) Stenotype Educ.

Reporter Reader. Reporter. Ed. by Max Ascoli. LC 74-93373. (Essay Index Reprint Ser.). 1977. 28.95 (*0-8369-1428-7*) Ayer.

Reporter Services & Their Use: How Reporter Services Can Help You in Law School & Beyond. 3rd ed. LC 92-40703. 1992. write for info. (*1-55871-287-9*) BNA.

Reporter Who Would Be King: A Biography of Richard Harding Davis. Arthur Lubow. (Illus.). 448p. 1992. text ed. 25.00 (*0-684-19404-X*) S&S Trade.

Reporters: Memoirs of a Young Newspaperman. Will Fowler. LC 91-17235. (Illus.). 336p. 1992. 21.95 (*0-915677-61-X*) Roundtable Pub.

Reporters Arranged & Characterized with Incidental Remarks. 4th enl. rev. ed. John W. Wallace. vi, ii, 654p. 1995. reprint ed. 85.00 (*0-89941-927-5*, 502170) W S Hein.

Reporter's Checklist & Notebook. Melvin Mencher. 160p. (C). 1995. spiral bd. write for info. (*0-697-29404-8*) Brown & Benchmark.

Reporter's Environmental Handbook. Bernadette West et al. (Illus.). 250p. (C). 1994. text ed. 45.00 (*0-8135-2148-3*); pap. text ed. 16.95 (*0-8135-2149-1*) Rutgers U Pr.

Reporters Handbook. 3rd ed. Weinberg. 1995. pap. text ed. 20.75 (*0-312-10153-8*) St Martin.

Reporters Handbook: An Investigators Guide to Documents & Techniques. John H. Ullmann. 1990. 25.95 (*0-312-05147-6*) St Martin.

Reporter's Handbook: An Investigator's Guide to Documents & Techniques. 2nd ed. Ed. by John H. Ullmann & Jan Colbert. LC 90-37266. 442p. (C). 1990. pap. text ed. 19.00 (*0-312-00435-4*) St Martin.

Reporter's Handbook: An Investigator's Guide to Documents & Techniques. 3rd ed. Steve Weinberg. 1995. 27.95 (*0-312-13596-3*) St Martin.

Reporter's Life. Walter Cronkite. (Illus.). 384p. 1996. 26.95 (*0-394-57879-1*) Knopf.

***Reporter's Life.** Walter Cronkite. 1997. pap. 14.00 (*0-345-41103-X*) Ballantine.

***Reporter's Life.** large type ed. Walter Cronkite. 1996. pap. 26.95 (*0-679-77414-9*) Random.

***Reporter's Life.** large type ed. Walter Cronkite. 1996. audio 24.00 (*0-679-45814-X*) Random Hse Lrg Prnt.

***Reporter's Life.** large type ed. Walter Cronkite. 1997. pap. 26.95 (*0-7838-8058-8*) Thorndike Pr.

Reporters Report Reporters. Curtis D. MacDougall. LC 68-15283. (Illus.). 193p. reprint ed. pap. 55.10 (*0-685-20340-9*, 2029781) Bks Demand.

Reporting: An Inside View. Lou Cannon. LC 77-79691. (C). 1977. 9.95 (*0-930302-12-5*); pap. 4.95 (*0-930302-13-3*) Cal Journal.

Reporting a Revolution: The Iranian Revolution & the NIICO Debate. J. V. Vilanilam. 204p. (C). 1989. text ed. 22.50 (*0-8039-9594-6*) Sage.

Reporting Africa. Olav S. Stokke. LC 76-163923. 250p. 1971. 27.50 (*0-8419-0090-6*, Africana) Holmes & Meier.

***Reporting & Writing.** Scanlan. (C). 1998. pap. text ed. 34.75 (*0-15-505378-7*) HB Coll Pubs.

Reporting & Writing the News. Evan Hill & John J. Breen. (Illus.). 318p. (C). 1988. reprint ed. pap. text ed. 20.95 (*0-88133-380-8*) Waveland Pr.

Reporting by Key Informants on Labour Markets: An Operational Manual. W. Mason & L. Richter. xi, 41p. (Orig.). 1985. pap. 11.25 (*92-2-105109-9*) Intl Labour Office.

Reporting Child Abuse: A Guide to Mandatory Requirements for School Personnel. Karen L. Michaelis. Ed. by Jerry J. Herman & Janice L. Herman. LC 93-28246. (Road Maps to Success Ser.). 72p. 1993. pap. 11.95 (*0-8039-6100-6*) Corwin Pr.

Reporting Child Abuse & Neglect in North Carolina. Janet Mason. 115p. 1996. pap. text ed. 8.00 (*1-56011-296-4*, 96.17) Institute Government.

Reporting Chronic Pain Episodes on Health Surveys. 71p. (Orig.). (C). 1993. pap. text ed. 25.00 (*1-56806-503-5*) DIANE Pub.

Reporting, Control & Analysis of Property, Plant, & Equipment. Michael J. Sandretto. Ed. by Claire Barth. 75p. (Orig.). 1990. pap. 20.00 (*0-86641-188-7*, 90249) Inst Mgmt Account.

Reporting Crime: The Media Politics of Criminal Justice. Philip Schlesinger & Howard Tumber. (Clarendon Studies in Criminology). 320p. 1994. pap. 23.00 (*0-19-825839-9*, Clarendon Pr) OUP.

Reporting Disaggregated Information. Paul Pacter. LC 93-70113. (Financial Accounting Standards Board Research Report Ser.). 423p. 1993. pap. 25.00 (*0-910065-54-3*) Finan Acct Found.

Reporting Experimental Data: Selected Reprints. Ed. by Howard J. White, Jr. LC 93-14521. (Illus.). 365p. 1993. 89.95 (*0-8412-2529-X*) Am Chemical.

Reporting for Radio. Chuck Crouse. 1992. 29.95 (*0-929387-88-0*) Bonus Books.

Reporting for Television. Carolyn D. Lewis. LC 83-7568. (Illus.). 192p. 1984. text ed. 35.00 (*0-231-05538-2*) Col U Pr.

Reporting for the Media. 6th ed. Fred Fedler et al. 640p. (C). 1996. pap. text ed. 44.25 (*0-15-503724-2*) HB Coll Pubs.

***Reporting for the Print.** 6th ed. Fred Fedler. (C). 1996. teacher ed., pap. text ed. 28.00 (*0-15-503882-6*) HarBrace.

Reporting for the Print Media. 4th ed. Fred Fedler. 694p. (C). 1988. pap. text ed. 29.50 (*0-15-576628-7*); pap. text ed. 34.00 (*0-15-576629-5*) HB Coll Pubs.

Reporting for the Print Media. 5th ed. Fred Fedler. 736p. (C). 1991. Media Writer manual. student ed., pap. text ed. 5.50 (*0-15-576635-X*) HB Coll Pubs.

Reporting for the Print Media. 5th ed. Fred Fedler. 736p. (C). 1993. pap. text ed. write for info. (*0-15-500602-9*); Media Writer software. disk write for info. (*0-15-576630-9*) HB Coll Pubs.

Reporting Foreign Operations. Samuel R. Hepworth. Ed. by Richard P. Brief. LC 80-1494. (Dimensions of Accounting Theory & Practice Ser.). 1980. reprint ed. lib. bdg. 25.95 (*0-405-13524-6*) Ayer.

Reporting from Corinth. Alice Friman. LC 83-173208. 88p. (Orig.). (C). 1984. pap. 6.95 (*0-935306-24-2*) Barnwood Pr.

***Reporting from the Field: SAS Software Experts Present Real-World Repot-Writing Applications.** 329p. (C). 1994. pap. 32.95 (*1-55544-644-2*) SAS Inst.

Reporting in Depth. Hiley H. Ward. LC 90-26595. 447p. (C). 1991. text ed. 47.95 (*0-87484-847-4*, 847); teacher ed., pap. text ed. write for info. (*1-55934-069-X*, 1069) Mayfield Pub.

Reporting Interest Rate Swaps: The Association of Disclosure Quality with Credit Risk & Ownership Structure. Barbara T. Uliss. LC 93-49429. (Financial Sector of the American Economy Ser.). 200p. 1994. text ed. 50.00 (*0-8153-1723-9*) Garland.

Reporting Manual. Larry L. Perry. 248p. 1987. ring bd. 95.00 (*0-13-773490-5*, Busn) P-H.

Reporting of Service Efforts & Accomplishments. Paul K. Brace et al. LC 80-84887. (Financial Accounting Standards Board Research Report Ser.). (Illus.). 114p. (Orig.). 1980. pap. 6.50 (*0-910065-09-8*) Finan Acct Found.

Reporting of Social Science in the National Media. Carol Weiss & Eleanor Singer. LC 87-43099. 320p. 1988. text ed. 34.95 (*0-87154-802-X*) Russell Sage.

Reporting of Summary Indicators: An Investigation of Research & Practice. Paul Frishkoff. LC 81-70208. (Financial Accounting Standards Board Research Report Ser.). 74p. (Orig.). 1981. pap. 6.00 (*0-910065-13-6*) Finan Acct Found.

Reporting on Chronic Pain Episodes on Health Surveys. LC 92-49423. (Vital & Health Statistics, Series 6: Cognition & Survey Measurement, No. 6: DHHS Publication: No. PHS 92-1081). 1992. write for info. (*0-8406-0466-1*) Natl Ctr Health Stats.

Reporting on Municipal Solid Waste: A Local Issue. (Illus.). 82p. (Orig.). (C). 1994. pap. text ed. 25.00 (*0-7881-1494-8*) DIANE Pub.

Reporting on Risk: A Journalist's Handbook on Environmental Risk Assessment. Michael Kamrin et al. LC 94-74349. 114p. 1995. spiral bd., pap. 8.00 (*1-885756-08-9*, MICHU-SG-95-600) MI Sea Grant.

Reporting on Risk: Getting It Right in an Age of Risk. Victor Cohn. LC 90-60505. 65p. (Orig.). (C). 1990. pap. 8.95 (*0-937790-42-7*, 4350) Media Institute.

Reporting on Risk: How the Mass Media Portray Accidents, Diseases, Disasters & Other Hazards. Eleanor Singer & Phyllis M. Endreny. 288p. 1993. 29.95 (*0-87154-801-1*) Russell Sage.

***Reporting on Risks: The Practice & Ethics of Health & Safety Communication.** William J. Willis & Albert A. Okunade. LC 96-37692. 1997. text ed. write for info. (*0-275-95296-7*, Praeger Pubs); pap. text ed. write for info. (*0-275-95298-3*, Praeger Pubs) Greenwood.

Reporting Public Affairs: Problems & Solutions. 2nd ed. Ronald P. Lovell. (Illus.). 506p. 1993. pap. text ed. 26.95 (*0-88133-696-3*) Waveland Pr.

Reporting, Recordkeeping & Disclosure Requirements for an Environmental Audit. Joseph G. Crist. (Environmental Audit Handbook Ser.: Vol. 2). 1989. pap. 49.95 (*1-55840-064-8*) Exec Ent Pubns.

Reporting, Recordkeeping, & Disclosure Requirements for an Environmental Audit. Joseph G. Crist. 1994. pap. text ed. 49.95 (*0-471-11260-7*) Wiley.

Reporting Religion: Facts & Faith. Ed. by Benjamin J. Hubbard. LC 89-29051. (Eagle Bk.). 210p. 1990. pap. 17.95 (*0-944344-10-0*) Polebridge Pr.

Reporting South Africa. Rich Mkhondo. LC 93-32149. 175p. (C). 1993. pap. 13.95 (*0-435-08089-X*, 08089) Heinemann.

Reporting Stenographer. Jack Rudman. (Career Examination Ser.: C-2125). 1994. reprint ed. pap. 23.95 (*0-8373-2125-5*) Natl Learn.

***Reporting Systems for Bank Man.** Bai. 1990. text ed. 40.00 (*0-07-413137-0*) McGraw.

***Reporting Technical Information.** 9th ed. Houp & Pearsall. LC 97-5734. 1997. pap. text ed. 47.00 (*0-205-27221-5*) P-H.

***Reporting the Arab Israeli Conflict: How Hegemony Works.** Tamar Liebes. (Routledge Research in Cultural & Media Studies). 192p. (C). 1997. text ed. 69.95 (*0-415-15465-0*) Routledge.

Reporting the Counterculture. Richard Goldstein. (Media & Popular Culture Ser.: No. 5). 208p. (C). (gr. 13). 1989. text ed. 44.95 (*0-04-445238-1*) Routledge Chapman & Hall.

***Reporting the Kennedy Assassination: Journalists Who Were There Recall Their Experiences.** Ed. by Laura Hlavach & Darwin Payne. LC 96-61385. (Illus.). 174p. (Orig.). 1996. pap. 10.00 (*0-9637629-2-3*) Three Forks.

Reporting the Nation's Business: Press-Government Relations During the Liberal Years, 1935-1957. Patrick H. Brennan. 328p. 1993. 45.00 (*0-8020-2977-9*); pap. 18.95 (*0-8020-7434-0*) U of Toronto Pr.

Reporting the War: The Journalistic Coverage of World War II. Frederick S. Voss. LC 93-36113. (Illus.). 208p. 1994. 39.95 (*1-56098-349-3*); pap. 24.95 (*1-56098-348-5*) Smithsonian.

***Reporting to Court under the Children Act: A Handbook for Social Services.** 90p. 1996. pap. 19.00 (*0-11-321968-7*, HM19687, Pub. by Stationery Ofc UK) Bernan Associates.

Reporting to Parents in English & Spanish. Barbara Thuro. LC 89-86000. 150p. (Orig.). (J). (ps-12). 1990. pap. 17.95 (*0-932825-03-6*) Ammie Enter.

Reporting Treasury Performance: A Framework for the Treasury Practitioner. International Federation of Accountants Staff. 46p. (Orig.). 1995. pap. text ed. 10.00 (*1-887464-05-0*) Intl Fed Accts.

***Reporting Waitangi: The Shaping of Television News.** Sue Abel. (Illus.). 176p. 1997. pap. 29.95 (*1-86940-176-X*, Pub. by Auckland Univ NZ) Paul & Co Pubs.

Reporting with Understanding. William L. Rivers & Gary Atkins. LC 86-22808. (Illus.). 248p. 1987. reprint ed. pap. 70.70 (*0-608-00061-2*, 2060827) Bks Demand.

Reporting World War II: American Journalism 1938-1946, 2 vols. Incl. Reporting World War II, 1938-1946 Pt. 1: American Journalism 1938-1944. LC 94-45463. (Illus.). 912p. 1995. 35.00 (*1-883011-04-3*); Reporting World War II, 1938-1946 Pt. 2: American Journalism 1944-1976. LC 94-45463. (Illus.). 970p. 1995. 35.00 (*1-883011-05-1*); 1995. 70.00 (*1-883011-12-4*) Library of America.

Reporting World War II, 1938-1946, Pt. 1, American Journalism 1938-1944 see Reporting World War II: American Journalism 1938-1946

Reporting World War II, 1938-1946, Pt. 2, American Journalism 1944-1976 see Reporting World War II: American Journalism 1938-1946

Reportorie of Records at Westminster. A. Agard. LC 72-225. (English Experience Ser.: No. 291). 1971. reprint ed. 30.00 (*90-221-0291-2*) Walter J Johnson.

***Reports & Certificates of Calibration.** (NCSL Recommended Practices Ser.: No. RP-11). 10.00 (*0-614-18750-8*) Natl Conf Stds Labs.

Reports & Papers on Botany. A. Henfrey. 514p. 1985. pap. 175.00 (*0-7855-0387-0*, Pub. by Intl Bks & Periodicals II) St Mut.

Reports & Proceedings - Rapports et Debates - Berichte und Verhandlungen - Informes y Debates - International Society for Labor Law & Social Security, 10th International Congress, Washington, DC, September 7-10, 1982, 3 vols., Vol. 1. International Society for Labor Law & Social Security, International Congress Staff. Ed. by Benjamin Aaron & Donald F. Farwell. LC 83-21018. 476p. (ENG, FRE, GER & SPA.). reprint ed. pap. 135.70 (*0-7837-4857-4*, 2044332) Bks Demand.

Reports & Proceedings - Rapports et Debates - Berichte und Verhandlungen - Informes y Debates - International Society for Labor Law & Social Security, 10th International Congress, Washington, DC, September 7-10, 1982, 3 vols., Vol. 2. International Society for Labor Law & Social Security, International Congress Staff. Ed. by Benjamin Aaron & Donald F. Farwell. LC 83-21018. 710p. (ENG, FRE, GER & SPA.). reprint ed. pap. 180.00 (*0-7837-4858-2*, 2044332) Bks Demand.

Reports & Proceedings - Rapports et Debates - Berichte und Verhandlungen - Informes y Debates - International Society for Labor Law & Social Security, 10th International Congress, Washington, DC, September 7-10, 1982, 3 vols., Vol. 3. International Society for Labor Law & Social Security, International Congress Staff. Ed. by Benjamin Aaron & Donald F. Farwell. LC 83-21018. 620p. (ENG, FRE, GER & SPA.). reprint ed. pap. 176.70 (*0-7837-4859-0*, 2044332) Bks Demand.

Reports Comprising the Survey of the Cook County Jail. Chicago Community Trust Staff. LC 73-3818. (Criminal Justice in America Ser.). (Illus.). 1974. reprint ed. 26.95 (*0-405-06139-0*) Ayer.

Reports! Formatting Applications. 2nd ed. Grill. (TA - Typing/Keyboarding Ser.). 1990. text ed. 18.95 (*0-538-60167-1*) S-W Pub.

Reports from Committees of the House of Commons 1715-1801 Printed But Not Inserted in the Journals of the House, General Index. 380p. 1973. reprint ed. 149.00 (*0-85964-000-0*) Chadwyck-Healey.

Reports from German Villages in the Ukraine of 1942-43: a Key to a Microfilm. Adam Giesinger. 27p. 1977. 7.50 (*0-914222-19-8*) Am Hist Soc Ger.

Reports from the Classroom: Cases for Reflective Teaching. Sarah Huyvaert. LC 94-9514. 1994. pap. text ed. 22.00 (*0-205-15514-6*) Allyn.

Reports from the Fields. (Liberal Learning & the Arts & Sciences Major Ser.: Vol. 2). xiii, 226p. (Orig.). (C). 1991. pap. text ed. 20.00 (*0-911696-50-4*) Assn Am Coll.

Reports from the Holocaust: The Making of an AIDS Activist. Larry Kramer. 368p. 1994. pap. 13.95 (*0-312-11419-2*, Stonewall Inn) St Martin.

***Reports from the Present: Selected Work: 1982-94.** Tom Leonard. 275p. 1997. pap. 19.95 (*0-224-03169-4*, Pub. by Jonathan Cape UK) Trafalgar.

Reports from the Select Committee on Police & Minutes of Evidence, Vol. 36. Select Committee on Police. LC 77-156284. (Police in Great Britain Ser.). 1971. reprint ed. 26.95 (*0-405-03395-8*) Ayer.

Reports, Minutes & Schedules. 2nd ed. Bartholomew. (TA - Typing/Keyboarding Ser.). 1984. pap. 15.95 (*0-538-20373-0*) S-W Pub.

Reports of Astronomy, Vol. 21A: Transactions of the International Astronomical Union. Ed. by Derek McNally. (C). 1991. lib. bdg. 202.00 (*0-7923-1172-8*) Kluwer Ac.

Reports of Cases: The Circuit Courts of the United States. Albert Brunner. xi, 742p. 1968. reprint ed. 40.00 (*0-89941-592-X*, 502100) W S Hein.

Reports of Cases Decided by Chief Justice Chase in the Circuit Court of the United States for the Fourth Circuit: 1865-1869. Bradley T. Johnson. LC 75-75292. (American Constitutional & Legal History Ser). 1972. reprint ed. lib. bdg. 75.00 (*0-306-71291-1*) Da Capo.

Reports of Cases Determined in the General Court of Virginia From 1730-1740, 1768-1772. Thomas Jefferson. LC 81-84431. viii, 145p. 1981. reprint ed. lib. bdg. 38.00 (*0-89941-143-6*, 302280) W S Hein.

Reports of Cases in the Vice Admiralty of the Province of New York & in the Courts of Admiralty of the State of New York, 1715-1788. Charles M. Hough. (Yale Historical Pubs., Manuscripts & Edited Texts Ser.: No. VIII). 1925. 97.50 (*0-685-89777-X*) Elliots Bks.

Reports of Commercial Cases 1895-1941, 46 vols. 1987. 3,200.00 (*0-86205-266-1*) MICHIE.

Reports of Commission Decisions Relating to Competition Articles 85, 86 & 90 of 1891-1985. 895p. 1994. pap. 50.00 (*92-826-6252-7*, CM-79-93-792-EN, Pub. by Commiss Europ Commun BE) Bernan Associates.

***Reports of Commission Decisions Relating to State Aid (Article 93, Para 2, Neg. Fin) 1973-1995.** European Communities Staff. 1223p. 1996. pap. 75.00 (*92-827-7751-0*, CM96-96-465-ENC, Pub. by Europ Com UK) Bernan Associates.

Reports of Current Work on Behavior of Materials at Elevated Temperatures: November 18-21, 1974, New York, N. Y. Held as Part of the 1974 ASME Winter Annual Meeting. Adolph O. Schaefer. LC 74-22198. 193p. reprint ed. pap. 55.10 (*0-317-08567-0*, 2016882) Bks Demand.

***Reports of Decisions in Probate (Coffey's Reports), 6 vols.** James V. Coffey. 1997. reprint ed. 495.00 (*1-57588-204-3*) W S Hein.

Reports of Economic Missions, 5 vols., Set. International Bank for Reconstruction & Development Staff. 1961. reprint ed. 287.50 (*0-404-60300-9*) AMS Pr.

Reports of Inspection Made in the Summer of 1877. William T. Sherman & Philip H. Sheridan. 1985. 19.95 (*0-87770-329-9*) Ye Galleon.

Reports of International Arbitral Awards. 85p. 1993. 40.00 (*92-1-033069-2*, JX1195) UN.

Reports of International Arbitral Awards, Vol. 17. 1980. 34.00 (*0-685-41529-5*, EF80.V.2 H) UN.

Reports of International Arbitral Awards, Vol. 18. 534p. 1980. 33.00 (*92-1-033009-9*, EF.80.V.7) UN.

Reports of International Arbitral Awards, Vol. 19. 352p. 1990. 39.50 (*92-1-033064-1*, 90.V.7) UN.

Reports of Ministers on the Secrete Meeting of the So Called "Chroncommittee" of the Government of Szalasi. Hungarian Historical Research Society Staff. LC 77-85228. 194p. 1980. pap. 11.95 (*0-935484-05-1*) Universe Pub Co.

Reports of My Death: An Autobiography, Vol. 2. Karl Shapiro. LC 88-6204. 304p. 1990. 22.95 (*0-945575-28-9*) Algonquin Bks.

Reports of ORCA on Water Fluoridation. Ed. by European Organization for Caries Research, Board. (Journal: Caries Research: Vol. 8, Suppl. 1). 36p. 1974. 13.75 (*3-8055-1707-6*) S Karger.

Reports of Patent Cases 1884-1986, 107 vols. 1988. write for info. (*0-86205-278-5*) MICHIE.

Reports of Randolph & Barradall on Decisions of the General Court of Virginia, 1728-1741, 2 vols., Set. R. T. Barton. 764p. 1994. lib. bdg. 65.00 (*0-8095-8269-4*) Borgo Pr.

Reports of Special Assistant Poor Law Commissioners on the Employment of Women & Children in Agriculture. Great Britain Poor Law Board Staff. LC 68-141609. xiv, 378p. 1968. reprint ed. lib. bdg. 65.00 (*0-678-05232-8*) Kelley.

Reports of Tax Cases 1875-1988, 60 vols., Set. boxed 5,000.00 (*0-86205-282-3*, UK) MICHIE.

Reports of the Commission Decisions Relating to Competition End 1990-1992. Eurostat. 252p. 1995. pap. 40.00 (*92-826-8538-1*, CV-84-94-387ENC, Pub. by Europ Com UK) Bernan Associates.

Reports of the Coxcatlan Project: First Annual Report. Edward B. Sisson. 1973. pap. 7.00 (*0-939312-13-1*) Peabody Found.

Reports of the Delegates of the Mosely Industrial Commission to the United States of America, Oct.-Dec., 1902. Mosely Industrial Commission. LC 73-2526. (Big Business; Economic Power in a Free Society Ser.). 1973. reprint ed. 19.95 (*0-405-05105-0*) Ayer.

Reports of the European Communities, 1952-1977: An Index to Authors & Chairmen. J. Neilson. 576p. 1981. text ed. 110.00 (*0-7201-1592-2*, Mansell Pub) Cassell.

Reports of the Immigration Commission, 41 Vols, Set. United States Immigration Commission. LC 76-85474. reprint ed. 1,128.00 (*0-405-00390-0*) Ayer.

Reports of the Industrial Commission on Immigration Including Testimony, with Review & Digest, & Special Reports on Education Including Testimony with Review & Digest. United States Industrial Commission. LC 70-129417. (American Immigration Collection. Series 2). 1970. reprint ed. 50.95 (*0-405-00571-7*) Ayer.

Reports of the Law of Civil Government in Territory Subject to Military Occupation by the Military Forces of the United States. 3rd ed. Charles E. Magoon. Ed. by Igor I. Kavass & Adolf Sprudzs. LC 72-75029. (International Military Law & History Ser.: Vol. 2). 808p. 1972. reprint ed. lib. bdg. 55.00 (*0-930342-39-9*, 300920) W S Hein.

Reports of the Magicians & Astrologers of Nineveh & Babylon in the British Museum, 2 vols., Set. Reginald C. Thompson. LC 73-18857. (Luzac's Semitic Text & Translation Ser.: Nos. 6-7). reprint ed. 41.50 (*0-404-11358-3*) AMS Pr.

Reports of the Mosely Education Commission to the United States of America, October-December, 1903. Mosely Education Commission. LC 73-89223. (American Education: Its Men, Institutions, & Ideas. Series 1: Its Men, Institutions & Ideas, Ser. 1). 1978. reprint ed. 20.95 (*0-405-01445-7*) Ayer.

Reports of the Princeton University Expeditions to Patagonia, 1896-1899, 8 vols. & supp. Ed. by W. B. Scott. (Illus.). 4948p. 1914. lib. bdg. 995.00 (*3-510-99068-4*, Pub. by E Schweizerbartsche GW) Lubrecht & Cramer.

Reports of the Prison Discipline Society, Boston: Reports 1-29, 1826-1854 (With Intro. essay & Analytical Index Added), 6 vols. Prison Discipline Society Boston Staff. LC 71-129322. (Criminology, Law Enforcement, & Social Problems Ser.: No. 155). (Illus.). 1972. 175.00 (*0-87585-155-X*) Patterson Smith.

Reports of the Proceedings & Debates of the New York Constitutional Convention, 1821. New York Constitutional Convention Staff. LC 72-133168. (Law, Politics & History Ser.). 1970. reprint ed. lib. bdg. 85.00 (*0-306-70069-7*) Da Capo.

Reports of the Royal Commission on Chinese Immigration. Ed. by Roger Daniels. LC 78-54810. (Asian Experience in North America Ser.). 1979. reprint ed. lib. bdg. 52.95 (*0-405-11267-X*) Ayer.

Reports of the Special Committee Appointed to Investigate the Official Conduct of the Members of the Board of Police Commissioners: City of Boston, Document No. 166. Joint Special Committee Staff. LC 78-156279. (Police in America Ser.). 1971. reprint ed. 16.95 (*0-405-03372-9*) Ayer.

Reports of the Special Masters of the United States Supreme Court in the Submerged Lands Cases, 1949-1987. Ed. by C. Thomas Koester & John Briscoe. (Illus.). 1066p. 1992. 110.00 (*0-910845-45-X*, 593) Landmark Ent.

***Reports of the Symposium on Social, Economic & Management Aspects of Recreational Fisheries.** Food & Agriculture Organization Staff. (Fisheries Reports: No. 541). 136p. 1997. suppl. ed., pap. 14.00 (*92-5-103926-7*, F39267, Pub. by FAO IT) Bernan Associates.

Reports of the United States Delegation to the Third United Nations Conference on the Law of the Sea. Ed. by M. Nordquist & C. H. Park. (Law of the Sea Occasional Papers: No. 33). 689p. 1983. 16.00 (*0-911189-07-6*) Law Sea Inst.

Reports of the XIV International Congress of the Historical Sciences Series. LC 77-81885. 1977. lib. bdg. 181.95 (*0-405-10517-7*) Ayer.

Reports on Astronomy. Ed. by Jacqueline Bergeron. LC 93-50750. (Transactions of the International Astronomical Union Ser.: Vol. 22A). 616p. 1994. lib. bdg. 200.50 (*0-7923-2709-8*) Kluwer Ac.

Reports on Astronomy. Ed. by Jean-Pierre Swings. (C). 1988. lib. bdg. 252.00 (*90-277-2734-1*) Kluwer Ac.

Reports on Astronomy. Patrick A. Wayman. 1982. lib. bdg. 182.50 (*90-277-1423-1*) Kluwer Ac.

Reports on Astronomy, 3 pts., Pt. 1. Ed. by G. Contopoulos. (Transactions of the International Astronomical Union Ser.: Vol. XVIA). 1976. lib. bdg. 129.50 (*90-277-0739-1*) Kluwer Ac.

Reports on Astronomy, 3 pts., Pt. 1. Ed. by Edith A. Muller. (Transactions of the International Astronomical Union Ser.: Vol. XVII A). 1979. lib. bdg. 80.00 (*90-277-1005-8*) Kluwer Ac.

Reports on Astronomy, 3 pts., Pt. 2. Ed. by Edith A. Muller. (Transactions of the International Astronomical Union Ser.: Vol. XVII A). 1979. lib. bdg. 80.00 (*90-277-1006-6*) Kluwer Ac.

Reports on Astronomy, 3 pts., Pt. 3. Ed. by G. Contopoulos. (Transactions of the International Astronomical Union Ser.: Vol. XVIA). 1976. lib. bdg. 129.50 (*90-277-0741-3*) Kluwer Ac.

Reports on Astronomy, 3 pts., Pt. 3. Ed. by Edith A. Muller. (Transactions of the International Astronomical Union Ser.: Vol. XVII A). 1979. lib. bdg. 80.00 (*90-277-1007-4*) Kluwer Ac.

Reports on Astronomy: Transactions of the International Astronomical Union Volume XIXA. Ed. by Richard M. West. 1985. lib. bdg. 206.50 (*90-277-2039-8*) Kluwer Ac.

***Reports on Astronomy: Transactions of the International Atronomical Union, Vol. XXIII-A.** 1997. lib. bdg. 315.00 (*0-7923-4540-1*) Kluwer Ac.

Reports on Ceftriaxone (RocephinR) Ed. by H. Schoenfeld. (Journal: Chemotherapy: Vol. 27, Suppl. 1). (Illus.). iv, 104p. 1981. pap. 23.25 (*3-8055-3034-X*) S Karger.

Reports on Communist China (October 1956-April 1961), Set, Vols. 1-37. Current Scene Staff. (China Classic & Contemporary Works in Reprint Ser.). 1995. reprint ed. Set. 65.00 (*0-404-19568-7*) AMS Pr.

Reports on Crime Investigation: 82nd Congress, First Session, Senate Reports. U. S. Senate Staff. LC 77-90207. (Mass Violence in America Ser.). 1969. reprint ed. 32.95 (*0-405-01336-1*) Ayer.

Reports on Happiness: A Pilot Study of Behavior Related to Mental Health. Norman M. Bradburn & David Caplovitz. LC 64-15605. (Monographs in Social Research: No. 3). 1965. 9.95 (*0-202-30020-X*) Natl Opinion Res.

Reports on Nationalism by a Study Group of Members of the Royal Institute of International Affairs: Proceedings. Royal Institute of International Affairs. 360p. 1963. 30.00 (*0-7146-1571-4*, Pub. by F Cass Pubs UK) Intl Spec Bk.

Reports on the Committee on Vision: 1947-1990. Committee on Vision, National Research Council Staff. 124p. 1990. pap. text ed. 15.00 (*0-309-04148-1*) Natl Acad Pr.

Reports on the Growth of Industry in New York. 670p. 1993. reprint ed. lib. bdg. 109.00 (*0-7812-5219-9*) Rprt Serv.

Reports on the Iconclass Workshop, November 1987 at Santa Monica, CA: A Special Issue of the Journal Visual Resources. Ed. by H. E. Roberts et al. x, 70p. 1988. text ed. 24.00 (*2-88124-371-1*) Gordon & Breach.

Reports on the Northeastern Part of the Quinghai-Xizang Plateau (Tibet) by Sino-West German Scientific Expedition. Ed. by J. Hoeverman & Wang Wenying. 510p. (C). 1987. 45.00 (*3-443-39075-7*) Lubrecht & Cramer.

Reports on the Second INCRA International Symposium on Automotive Radiators. 266p. 1967. 39.90 (*0-317-34542-7*, 99) Intl Copper.

Reports on the State of Certain Parishes in Scotland. Ed. by Alexander Macdonald. LC 79-175588. (Maitland Club, Glasgow. Publications: No. 34). reprint ed. 32.50 (*0-404-53003-6*) AMS Pr.

Reports Required by Congress 1994: CIS Guide to Executive Communications. Ed. by Congressional Information Service, Inc. Staff. 1995. 595.00 (*0-88692-337-9*) Cong Info.

Reports That Get Results: Guidelines for Executives. fac. ed. Ian Mayo-Smith. LC 89-24716. (Illus.). 45p. 1990. pap. 25.00 (*0-7837-7582-2*, 2047335) Bks Demand.

Reports to the Hon. George Stoneman, Governor of California, on Certain Claims of the State of California Against the United States, November 1, 1878, to November 1, 1886. John Mullin. Ed. by Stuart Bruchey. LC 78-56670. (Management of Public Lands in the U. S. Ser.). (Illus.). 1979. reprint ed. lib. bdg. 44.95 (*0-405-11345-5*) Ayer.

Reports Upon Insects Collected During Geographical & Geological Explorations & Surveys West of the One Hundredth Meridian, During the Years 1872, 1873, & 1874. Ed. by George M. Wheeler & Keir B. Sterling. LC 77-81109. (Biologists & Their World Ser.). (Illus.). 1978. reprint ed. lib. bdg. 24.95 (*0-405-10693-9*) Ayer.

Repos du Guerrier. Christiane Rochefort. (Idees Ser.). 280p. 1958. 12.50 (*0-686-55228-8*) Fr & Eur.

Repos Du Septieme Jour. Paul Claudel. 1973. 14.95 (*0-686-54429-3*) Fr & Eur.

Repositioning Feminism & Education: Perspectives on Educating for Social Change. Janice Jipson et al. LC 95-2083. (Critical Studies in Education & Culture). 296p. 1995. text ed. 62.95 (*0-89789-436-7*, Bergin & Garvey); pap. text ed. 19.95 (*0-89789-437-5*, Bergin & Garvey) Greenwood.

Repositioning for the Future: Baltimore County Public Library Long Range Plan 1994-1999. Eleanor J. Rodger. (Illus.). 32p. 1994. 20.00 (*0-937076-05-8*) Baltimore Co Pub Lib.

***Repositioning Higher Education.** Frank Coffield & Bill Williamson. LC 96-47781. 1997. write for info. (*0-335-19715-9*, Open Univ Pr); pap. write for info. (*0-335-19716-7*, Open Univ Pr) Taylor & Francis.

***Repositioning of U. S. Caribbean Relations in the New World Order.** Ed. by Ransford W. Palmer. LC 97-5591. 1997. text ed. write for info. (*0-275-95858-2*, Praeger Pubs) Greenwood.

Repositionings: Readings of Contemporary Poetry, Photography, & Performance Art. Ed. by Frederick Garber. LC 94-12433. 272p. 1995. 37.50 (*0-271-01408-3*); pap. 17.95 (*0-271-01409-1*) Pa St U Pr.

Repossessing Ernestine: A Granddaughter Uncovers the Secret History of Her Family. Marsha Hunt. 1996. write for info. (*0-614-96293-5*) HarpC.

An Asterisk (*) at the beginning of an entry indicates that the title is appearing in BIP for the first time.

Repossessing Ernestine: Uncovering the Secret History of an American Family. Marsha Hunt. LC 95-48436. 304p. 1996. 24.00 (*0-06-017443-9*) HarpC.

Repossession & You. 3.50 (*0-944253-77-6*) Inst Dev Indian Law.

Repossession of Aircraft & Insolvency in the European Community. Ed. by Sinclair Roche & Temperley. 162p. 1993. text ed. 350.00 (*1-85044-471-4*) LLP.

Repossession of Property on Mortagage Default. M. P. Thompson. 120p. 1993. 96.00 (*1-85190-194-9*, Pub. by Tolley Pubng UK) St Mut.

Repossessions: Selected Essays on the Irish Literary Heritage. Sean O. Tuama. 1995. 40.00 (*1-85918-044-2*, Pub. by Cork Univ IE); pap. 24.00 (*1-85918-045-0*, Pub. by Cork Univ IE) Intl Spec Bk.

***Repossessions & Foreclosures.** 3rd ed. National Consumer Law Center, Inc. Staff. LC 95-72045. (Consumer Credit & Sales Legal Practice Ser.). 334p. 1995. pap. 90.00 (*1-881793-38-9*) Nat Consumer Law.

Repphun Family: Circas: 1840-50s to 1988. Herman A. Neufeld. LC 88-192584. 57p. 1988. 15.00 (*0-945608-10-1*) C Joyce Gall.

Represas (Dams) J. Cooper. (Maravillas de la Humanidad (Man-Made Wonders) Ser.: Set VI). (SPA.). (J). 1991. 8.95 (*0-86592-924-6*) Rourke Enter.

Represent Yourself in Court: How to Prepare & Try a Winning Case. Paul Bergman & Sara J. Berman-Barrett. 384p. 1995. pap. 29.95 (*0-87337-222-0*) Nolo Pr.

***Represent Yourself in Court: How to Prepare & Try a Winning Case.** 2nd ed. Paul Bergman. 1997. pap. text ed. 29.95 (*0-87337-402-9*) Nolo Pr.

Representaciones en la Ensenanza de las Matematicas. Ana H. Quintero. LC 87-25573. 240p. 1988. pap. 16.00 (*0-8477-2750-5*) U of PR Pr.

Representaciones Palaciegas: 1603-1699 Estudia y Documentos. Ed. by N. D. Shergold & J. E. Varey. (Fuentes Para la Historia del Teatro en Espana, Series C: Vol. II). 276p. (Orig.). (SPA.). (C). 1982. pap. 35.00 (*0-7293-0132-X*, Pub. by Tamesis Bks Ltd UK) Boydell & Brewer.

***Representation: Cultural Representations & Signifying Practices.** Ed. by Stuart Hall. (Culture, Media & Identities Ser.: Vol. 2). 368p. (C). 1997. 75.00 (*0-7619-5431-7*, 74868); pap. 23.95 (*0-7619-5432-5*, 74876) Sage.

Representation: Relationship Betwen Language & Image. Stefano Levialdi & C. Bernardelli. 236p. 1994. text ed. 71.00 (*981-02-1690-4*) World Scientific Pub.

Representation & Acquisition of Lexical Knowledge: Polysemy, Ambiguity, & Generativity: Papers from the 1995 Spring Symposium. Ed. by Judith Klavans. (Technical Reports). (Illus.). 185p. 1995. spiral bd. 25.00 (*0-929280-84-9*) AAAI Pr.

Representation & Control of Infinite Dimensional Systems, Vol. 1. Alain Bensoussan et al. LC 92-10323. (Systems & Control: Foundations & Applications Ser.). (Illus.). 320p. 1992. 86.50 (*0-8176-3641-2*) Birkhauser.

Representation & Control of Infinite Dimensional Systems, Vol. 2. Alain Benoussan et al. (Systems & Control: Foundations & Applications Ser.). 343p. 1993. 92.00 (*0-8176-3642-0*) Birkhauser.

Representation & Derivation in the Theory of Grammar. Ed. by Hubert Hiader & Klaus Netter. (C). 1991. lib. bdg. 129.50 (*0-7923-1150-7*) Kluwer Ac.

Representation & Design: Tracing a Hermeneutics of Old English Poetry. Pauline E. Head. LC 96-2391. (SUNY Series in Medieval Studies). (Illus.). 166p. 1997. text ed. 59.50 (*0-7914-3203-3*); pap. text ed. 19.95 (*0-7914-3204-1*) State U NY Pr.

Representation & Development in Brazil, 1972-1973. 2nd ed. Youseff Cohen et al. LC 80-84095. 1980. write for info. (*0-89138-950-4*) ICPSR.

Representation & Form: A Study of Aesthetic Values in Representational Art. Walter Abell. 1988. reprint ed. pap. 3.95 (*0-685-21478-8*); reprint ed. lib. bdg. 49.00 (*0-7812-0220-5*) Rprt Serv.

Representation & Form: A Study of Aesthetic Values in Representational Art. Walter Abell. LC 36-17784. 172p. 1936. reprint ed. 16.00 (*0-403-08900-X*) Somerset Pub.

Representation & Its Discontents: The Critical Legacy of German Romanticism. Azade Seyhan. 196p. (C). 1992. 37.50 (*0-520-07675-3*); pap. 16.00 (*0-520-07676-1*) U CA Pr.

Representation & Party Politics. Bruce Graham. LC 93-14798. (Studies in Comparative Politics). 242p. 1993. 56. 95 (*0-631-17395-1*); pap. 23.95 (*0-631-17396-X*) Blackwell Pubs.

Representation & Policy Formation in Federal Systems: Canada & the United States. Ed. by David M. Olson & C. E. Franks. LC 93-19575. 325p. 1993. pap. 24.95 (*0-87772-340-0*) UCB IGS.

Representation & Presidential Primaries: The Democratic Party in the Post-Reform Era. James I. Lengle. LC 80-1791. (Contributions in Political Science Ser.: No. 57). (Illus.). xv, 133p. 1981. text ed. 49.95 (*0-313-22482-X*, LEP/, Greenwood Pr) Greenwood.

***Representation & Processing of Spatial Expressions.** Ed. by Patrick Olivier & Klaus-Peter Gapp. LC 97-4129. 250p. 1997. text ed. write for info. (*0-8058-2285-2*) L Erlbaum Assocs.

Representation & Reality. Hilary Putnam. (Illus.). 1991. pap. 11.95 (*0-262-66074-1*) MIT Pr.

Representation & Responsibility: Exploring Legislative Ethics. Ed. by Bruce Jennings & Daniel Callahan. 348p. 1985. 60.00 (*0-306-41994-7*, Plenum Pr) Plenum.

***Representation & Retrieval of Video Data in Multimedia Systems.** Ed. by HongJiang Zhang. 88p. (C). 1997. lib. bdg. 72.50 (*0-7923-9863-7*) Kluwer Ac.

***Representation & Retrieval of Visual Media in Multimedia Systems.** Philippe Aigrain & Dragutin Petkovic. Ed. by Hong J. Zhang. LC 96-38482. 104p. (C). 1996. lib. bdg. 75.00 (*0-7923-9771-1*) Kluwer Ac.

Representation & the Imagination: Beckett, Kafka, Nabokov, & Schoenberg. Daniel Albright. LC 80-26976. (Chicago Original Paperback Ser.). viii, 230p. (C). 1981. pap. text ed. 24.00 (*0-226-01252-2*) U Ch Pr.

Representation & the Mind-Body Problem in Spinoza. Michael Della Rocca. 240p. 1996. text ed. 39.95 (*0-19-509562-6*) OUP.

***Representation & the Text: Re-Framing the Narrative Voice.** Ed. by William G. Tierney & Yvonna S. Lincoln. LC 96-44385. 256p. 1997. pap. text ed. 19.95 (*0-7914-3472-9*) State U NY Pr.

***Representation & the Text: Re-Framing the Narrative Voice.** Ed. by William G. Tierney & Yvonna S. Lincoln. LC 96-44385. 256p. 1997. text ed. 59.50 (*0-7914-3471-0*) State U NY Pr.

Representation & Understanding. Bobrow. 1975. text ed. 61.00 (*0-12-108550-3*) Acad Pr.

Representation Before the Collection Division of the IRS. Robert E. Mckenzie. 1990. 95.00 (*0-318-41449-X*) Clark Boardman Callaghan.

Representation from Above: Members of Parliament & Representative Democracy in Sweden. Peter Esaiasson & Soren Holmberg. LC 96-11009. 370p. 1996. 67.95 (*1-85521-746-5*, Pub. by Dartmth Pub UK) Ashgate Pub Co.

***Representation Gap.** Brian Towers. (Illus.). 320p. 1997. pap. 19.95 (*0-19-829319-4*) OUP.

***Representation Gap.** Brian Towers. (Illus.). 320p. 1997. 70.00 (*0-19-828946-4*) OUP.

***Representation in Contemporary French Fiction.** Dina Sherzer. LC 85-5882. 212p. 1986. reprint ed. pap. 60.50 (*0-608-02682-4*, 2063335) Bks Demand.

Representation in Crisis: The Constitution, Interest Groups, & Political Parties. David K. Ryden. LC 95-39220. (SUNY Series in Political Party Development). 309p. (C). 1996. text ed. 65.50 (*0-7914-3057-X*); pap. text ed. 21.95 (*0-7914-3058-8*) State U NY Pr.

Representation in Ethnography: In Other Wor(l)ds. John Van Maanen. 240p. 1995. text ed. 45.00 (*0-8039-7162-1*); pap. text ed. 21.95 (*0-8039-7163-X*) Sage.

***Representation in Political Philosophy: A Classical Reader on the Foundations in Democracy.** (Illus.). 350p. (Orig.). (C). Date not set. pap. text ed. write for info. (*0-9649227-1-1*) Fla Inst Gov.

Representation in Scientific Practice. Ed. by Michael Lynch & Steve Woolgar. 320p. 1990. pap. 20.00 (*0-262-62076-6*) MIT Pr.

Representation in State Legislatures. Malcolm E. Jewell. LC 82-40174. 216p. 1982. 24.00 (*0-8131-1463-2*) U Pr of Ky.

Representation LIE Group, 3 vols. N. J. Vilenkin. 1992. lib. bdg. 1,371.00 (*0-7923-1494-8*) Kluwer Ac.

***Representation of Complex Stimuli in the Primate Visual Cortex.** Martin Tovee. 200p. 1997. 89.95 (*0-412-14101-9*) R G Landes.

Representation of Cumulus Convection in Numerical Models of the Atmosphere. (Meteorological Monograph: Vol. 24, No. 46). 1992. 65.00 (*1-878220-13-6*) Am Meteorological.

Representation of Deities of the Maya Manuscripts. P. Schellhas. (Harvard University Peabody Museum of Archaeology & Ethnology Papers: Vol. 4, No. 1). (Illus.). 1904. pap. 25.00 (*0-527-01198-3*) Periodicals Srv.

Representation of Features in Non-Linear Phonology: The Articulator Node Hierarchy. Elizabeth Sagey. LC 90-22758. (Outstanding Dissertations in Linguistics Ser.). 248p. 1991. text ed. 15.00 (*0-8153-0152-9*) Garland.

Representation of InDefiniteness. Eric J. Reuland & Alice G. Ter Meulen. (Current Studies in Linguistics: Vol. 14). 360p. 1987. 40.00 (*0-262-18126-6*) MIT Pr.

Representation of Knowledge & Belief. Myles Brand & Robert M. Harnish. LC 86-24961. (Arizona Colloquim on Cognition Ser.: No. 1). 368p. 1986. 56.00 (*0-8165-0971-9*) U of Ariz Pr.

Representation of Lie Groups & Special Functions: Classical & Quantum Groups & Special Functions. N. Ja Vielenkin. (Mathematics & Its Applications, Soviet Ser.: Vol. 3). 656p. (C). 1992. lib. bdg. 361.00 (*0-7923-1493-X*) Kluwer Ac.

Representation of Lie Groups & Special Functions: Recent Advances. N. J. Vilenkin. (Mathematics & Its Applications Ser.). 516p. (C). 1994. lib. bdg. 253.50 (*0-7923-3210-5*) Kluwer Ac.

Representation of Lie Groups, Special Functions, & Integral Transforms, Vol. 1: Simplest Lie Groups, Special Functions, & Integral Transforms. N. J. Vilenkin & A. U. Klimyk. 632p. 1900. lib. bdg. 371.00 (*0-7923-1466-2*) Kluwer Ac.

Representation of Mesmerism in Honore de Blazac's La Comedie Humaine, Vol. 6. Melissa Marcus. (New Connections Ser.). 128p. (C). 1995. text ed. 38.95 (*0-8204-1818-8*) P Lang Pubng.

***Representation of Places: Reality & Realism in City Design.** Peter Bosselmann. LC 97-81. 1997. write for info. (*0-520-20658-4*) U CA Pr.

Representation of Rings by Sections. John Dauns & Karl H. Hofmann. LC 52-42839. (Memoirs Ser.: No. 1/83). 180p. 1983. reprint ed. pap. 17.00 (*0-8218-1283-1*, MEMO/1/83) Am Math.

Representation of Slavery in Cuban Fiction. Lorna V. Williams. LC 94-6238. 232p. 1994. 34.95 (*0-8262-0957-2*) U of Mo Pr.

***Representation of Speech in Biblical Hebrew Narrative: A Linguistic Analysis.** Cynthia L. Miller. LC 96-32331. (Harvard Semitic Monographs). 460p. 1996. 44.95 (*0-7885-0248-4*, 040055) Scholars Pr GA.

Representation of the Past: Museums & Heritage in the Post-Modern World. Kevin Walsh. (Heritage: Care-Preservation-Management Program Ser.). 192p. (C). 1992. pap. 19.95 (*0-415-07944-6*, A7854) Routledge.

Representation of the Self in the American Renaissance. Jeffrey Steele. LC 87-4050. 236p. 1987. reprint ed. pap. 67.30 (*0-608-02066-4*, 2062719) Bks Demand.

Representation of the Self in the American Renaissance. Jeffrey Steele. LC 87-4050. xviii, 218p. (C). 1989. reprint ed. pap. text ed. 14.95 (*0-8078-4263-X*) U of NC Pr.

Representation of the Two Stones with the Characters Inscribed upon Them, That Were Found by D. Wyrick, During the Summer of 1860 Near Newark, Ohio. D. Wyrick. Tr. by J. W. McCarty from HEB. (Ohio History, Archaeological Fraud, Prehistoric Indians Ser.). (Illus.). 13p. 1994. reprint ed. pap. 1.95 (*1-56651-106-2*); reprint ed. spiral bd. 3.00 (*1-56651-110-0*) A W McGraw.

Representation of the United States Abroad. rev. ed. Ed. by Vincent M. Barnett. LC 65-15651. 1965. reprint ed. pap. 1.95 (*0-317-04630-6*) Am Assembly.

***Representation of the World: A Naturalized Semantics.** Arthur Melnick. (Revisioning Philosophy Ser.: Vol. 26). 368p. (C). 1997. text ed. 57.95 (*0-8204-3350-0*) P Lang Pubng.

Representation of Wild Animals in Hittite Texts. Billie J. Collins. pap. text ed. write for info. (*0-614-03992-4*, Pub. by Netherlands Inst NE) Eisenbrauns.

Representation of Witnesses Before Federal Grand Juries. 3rd ed. National Lawyers Guild Staff & Rikki Klieman. LC 83-15607. (Criminal Law Ser.). (C). 1984. ring bd. 145.00 (*0-87632-426-X*) Clark Boardman Callaghan.

Representation of Women in Fiction. Ed. by Carolyn G. Heilbrun & Margaret R. Higonnet. LC 82-12685. (Selected Papers from the English Institute; 1982-83, New Ser.: No. 7). 214p. reprint ed. pap. 61.00 (*0-685-20621-1*, 2030574) Bks Demand.

Representation of Women in the Novels of Juan Valera: A Feminist Critique. Teresia L. Taylor. LC 93-43219. (Wor(l)ds of Change Ser.: Vol. 4). 135p. (C). 1997. 35.95 (*0-8204-2417-X*) P Lang Pubng.

Representation Problem for Frechet Surfaces. J. T. Youngs. LC 52-42839. (Memoirs Ser.: No. 1/8). 143p. 1980. reprint ed. pap. 21.00 (*0-8218-1208-4*, MEMO/1/8) Am Math.

Representation Rights & the Burger Years. Nancy Maveety. 280p. (C). 1991. text ed. 47.50 (*0-472-10227-3*) U of Mich Pr.

Representation Theorems on Banach Function Spaces. Neil E. Gretsky. LC 52-42839. (Memoirs Ser.: No. 1/84). 56p. 1968. pap. 16.00 (*0-8218-1284-X*, MEMO/1/84) Am Math.

Representation Theory: A First Course. W. Fulton. (Graduate Texts in Mathematics Ser.: Vol. 129). (Illus.). xv, 551p. 1991. 49.50 (*0-387-97527-6*) Spr-Verlag.

Representation Theory: A First Course. W. Fulton. (Graduate Texts in Mathematics Ser.: Vol. 129). (Illus.). xv, 551p. 1996. 29.50 (*0-387-97495-4*) Spr-Verlag.

Representation Theory: Selected Papers. I. M. Gelfand. LC 82-4440. (London Mathematical Society Lecture Note Ser.: No. 69). 330p. 1982. pap. text ed. 52.95 (*0-521-28981-5*) Cambridge U Pr.

***Representation Theory & Algebraic Geometry.** Ed. by A. Martsinkovsky & G. Todorov. (London Mathematical Society Lecture Note Ser.: Vol. 238). 131p. (C). 1997. pap. 34.95 (*0-521-57789-6*) Cambridge U Pr.

Representation Theory & Anaysis on Homogeneous Spaces: Proceedings of a Conference in Memory of Larry Corwin, February 5-7, 1993, Rutgers University. Ed. by Simon G. Gindikin. LC 94-34420. (Contemporary Mathematics Ser.: Vol. 177). 1994. pap. 46.00 (*0-8218-0300-X*, CONM/177) Am Math.

Representation Theory & Automorphic Forms. Wallach & Paul J. Sally. 238p. 1993. pap. 62.00 (*0-8218-0720-X*, BULL RE/2) Am Math.

Representation Theory & Complex Geometry. Neil Chriss & Victor Ginzburg. LC 94-27574. 395p. 1997. 64.50 (*0-8176-3792-3*) Birkhauser.

Representation Theory & Dynamical Systems. A. M. Vershik. LC 91-640741. (Advances in Soviet Mathematics Ser.: Vol. 9). 267p. 1992. 116.00 (*0-8218-4108-4*, ADVSOV/9) Am Math.

Representation Theory & Harmonic Analysis: Proceedings: Conference in Honor of Ray A. Kunze on Representation Theory & Harmonic Analysis (1994: Cincinnati, Ohio), Vol. 191. Ed. by Kenneth I. Gross et al. LC 95-35225. (Contemporary Mathematics Ser.: No. 191). 272p. 1995. pap. 55.00 (*0-8218-0310-7*, CONM/191) Am Math.

Representation Theory & Harmonic Analysis of Semisimple Lie Groups. Paul J. Sally, Jr. & David A. Vegan. LC 88-10301. (Mathematical Surveys & Monographs: No. 31). 350p. 1989. 102.00 (*0-8218-1526-1*, SURV/31) Am Math.

Representation Theory & Noncommunitative Harmonic Analysis I: Fundamental Concepts, Representations of Cirasoro & Affine Algebras. LC 94-11597. (Encyclopedia of Mathematical Sciences Ser.: Vol. 22). 1994. 118.95 (*0-387-18698-0*) Spr-Verlag.

Representation Theory & Noncommutative Harmonic Analysis II. Ed. by A. A. Kirillov. LC 95-1411. (Encyclopedia of Mathematical Sciences Ser.: Vol. 59). 1995. 107.95 (*0-387-54702-9*) Spr-Verlag.

Representation Theory & Number Theory in Connection with the Local Langlands Conjecture. J. Ritter. LC 88-39030. (Contemporary Mathematics Ser.: Vol. 86). 266p. 1989. pap. 36.00 (*0-8218-5093-8*, CONM/86) Am Math.

Representation Theory, Group Rings, & Coding Theory (Papers in Honor of Professor S. D. German (1922-1987) Ed. by Isaacs et al. LC 89-6942. (Contemporary Mathematics Ser.: Vol. 93). 357p. 1989. pap. 57.00 (*0-8218-5098-9*, CONM/93) Am Math.

Representation Theory I: Finite Dimensional Algebras. G. O. Michler. (Lecture Notes in Mathematics Ser.: Vol. 1177). xv, 340p. 1986. 48.95 (*0-387-16432-4*) Spr-Verlag.

Representation Theory II: Groups & Orders. G. O. Michler. (Lecture Notes in Mathematics Ser.: Vol. 1178). xv, 370p. 1986. 48.95 (*0-387-16433-2*) Spr-Verlag.

Representation Theory of Algebras. Robert Gordon. (Lecture Notes in Pure & Applied Mathematics Ser.: Vol. 37). 480p. 1978. 165.00 (*0-8247-6714-4*) Dekker.

Representation Theory of Algebras: Proceedings of the 7th International Conference on Representations of Algebras, Held August 22-26, 1994. Ed. by Raymundo Bautista et al. (Conference Proceedings, Canadian Mathematical Society Ser.: Vol. 18). 749p. 1996. pap. 129.00 (*0-8218-0395-6*, CMSAMS/18) Am Math.

Representation Theory of Algebras & Related Topics: Proceedings of the Workshop on Representation Theory of Algebras & Related Topics. Ed. by Raymundo Bautista et al. LC 96-4255. (Conference Proceedings - Canadian Mathematical Society Ser.: Vol. 19). 406p. 1996. pap. 95.00 (*0-8218-0396-4*, CMSAMS/19) Am Math.

Representation Theory of Artin Algebras. Maurice Auslander et al. LC 93-43326. (Studies in Advanced Mathematics: No. 36). (Illus.). 500p. (C). 1995. 69.95 (*0-521-41134-3*) Cambridge U Pr.

***Representation Theory of Artin Algebras.** Maurice Auslander et al. (Cambridge Studies in Advanced Mathematics: No. 36). 440p. 1997. pap. 29.95 (*0-521-59923-7*) Cambridge U Pr.

Representation Theory of Finite Groups. W. Feit. (Mathematical Library: Vol. 25). 502p. 1982. 153.75 (*0-444-86155-6*, North Holland) Elsevier.

Representation Theory of Finite Groups. Martin Burrow. LC 92-39061. 184p. 1993. reprint ed. pap. 6.95 (*0-486-67487-8*) Dover.

Representation Theory of Finite Groups & Associative Algebras. Charles W. Curtis & Irving Reiner. (Classics Library). 689p. 1988. pap. text ed. 68.95 (*0-471-60845-9*) Wiley.

Representation Theory of Finite Groups & Finite-Dimensional Algebras. Claus M. Ringel & G. O. Michler. (Progress in Mathematics Ser.: Vol. 95). 532p. 1991. 99.00 (*0-8176-2604-2*) Spr-Verlag.

Representation Theory of Finite Groups & Related Topics: Proceedings of the Symposia in Pure Mathematics-Madison, Wis.-1970. Ed. by Irving Reiner. LC 79-165201. (Proceedings of Symposia in Pure Mathematics Ser.: Vol. 21). 178p. 1971. 41.00 (*0-8218-1421-4*, PSPUM/21) Am Math.

Representation Theory of Groups & Algebras. Jeffrey Adams et al. LC 92-43340. (Contemporary Mathematics Ser.: No. 145). 491p. 1993. pap. 50.00 (*0-8218-5168-3*, CONM/145) Am Math.

Representation Theory of Lie Groups. Michael F. Atiyah et al. LC 78-73820. (London Mathematical Society Lecture Note Ser.: No. 34). 1980. pap. 59.95 (*0-521-22636-8*) Cambridge U Pr.

Representation Theory of Lie Groups & Lie Algebras. T. Kawazoe et al. 256p. 1992. text ed. 67.00 (*981-02-1090-6*) World Scientific Pub.

Representation Theory of Semisimple Groups: An Overview Based on Examples. Anthony W. Knapp. LC 85-43295. (Mathematical Ser.: No. 36). 912p. 1986. text ed. 92.00 (*0-691-08401-7*) Princeton U Pr.

Representation Theory of the Symmetric Group. Gilbert Robinson. LC 63-424. (Mathematical Expositions Ser.: No. 12). 214p. reprint ed. pap. 61.00 (*0-317-09069-0*, 2014385) Bks Demand.

Representation Versus Direct Democracy in Fighting about Taxes. Lewis A. Dexter. 155p. 1982. pap. 21.95 (*0-87073-426-1*) Transaction Pubs.

Representational Approach to the Joint Determination of Housing Market Segmentation & Housing Preferences. Tony E. Smith. (Discussion Paper Ser.: No. 116). 1980. pap. 10.00 (*1-55869-107-3*) Regional Sci Res Inst.

Representational Ideas: From Plato to Patricia Churchland. Richard A. Watson. LC 95-11928. (Synthese Library: Vol. 250). 1995. lib. bdg. 99.00 (*0-7923-3453-1*, Pub. by Klwr Acad Pubs NE) Kluwer Ac.

***Representational Malaise of Nineteenth-Century German Realism: New Approaches to Theodor Fontane.** Ed. by Marion Doebeling. (GERM Ser.). 180p. 1998. 52.95 (*1-57113-143-4*) Camden Hse.

Representational Mind: A Study of Kant's Theory of Knowledge. Richard E. Aquila. LC 83-47918. (Studies in Phenomenology & Existential Philosophy). 224p. 1984. 31.50 (*0-253-35005-0*) Ind U Pr.

Representations: Essays on Literature & Society. Steven Marcus. 384p. 1990. text ed. 49.50 (*0-231-07400-X*); pap. text ed. 17.50 (*0-231-07401-8*) Col U Pr.

Representations: Images of the World in Ciceronian Oratory. Ann Vasaly. LC 92-18738. (Latinos in American Society & Culture Ser.: No. 1). (Illus.). 299p. 1993. 45.00 (*0-520-07755-5*) U CA Pr.

Representations: Images of the World in Ciceronian Oratory. Ann Vasaly. (Illus.). 301p. (C). 1996. pap. 14. 95 (*0-520-20178-7*) U CA Pr.

Representations: Social Constructions of Gender. Ed. by R. Unger. 336p. 1989. text ed. 39.95 (*0-89503-057-8*); pap. text ed. 29.96 (*0-89503-052-7*) Baywood Pub.

An Asterisk (*) at the beginning of an entry indicates that the title is appearing in BIP for the first time.

Representations & Characters of Finite Groups. M. J. Collins. (Cambridge Studies in Advanced Mathematics: No. 22). 242p. (C). 1990. text ed. 74.95 (*0-521-23440-9*) Cambridge U Pr.

Representations & Characters of Groups. Gordon D. James & Martin W. Liebeck. LC 92-30619. (Illus.). 350p. (C). 1993. text ed. 74.95 (*0-521-44024-6*); pap. text ed. 30.95 (*0-521-44590-6*) Cambridge U Pr.

Representations & Cohomology, Vol. 1: Basic Representative Theory of Finite Groups & Associative Algebra, Vol. I. D. J. Benson. (Studies in Advanced Mathematics: No. 30). 250p. (C). 1991. text ed. 49.95 (*0-521-36134-6*) Cambridge U Pr.

Representations & Cohomology, Vol. 2: Vol. 2: Cohomology of Groups & Modules. D. J. Benson. (Studies in Advanced Mathematics: No. 31). 250p. (C). 1992. text ed. 64.95 (*0-521-36135-4*) Cambridge U Pr.

***Representations & Contradictions: Ambivalence Towards Images, Theatre, Fiction, Relics & Sexuality.** Jack Goody. LC 96-40927. 288p. 1997. pap. 24.95 (*0-631-20526-8*) Blackwell Pubs.

***Representations & Invariants of the Classical Groups.** Roe Goodman & Nolan Wallach. (Studies in Advanced Mathematics: Vol. 59). (Illus.). 600p. (C). 1997. write for info. (*0-521-58273-3*) Cambridge U Pr.

Representations de Longeur Finie des Groupes de Lie Resolubles. Fokko Du Cloux. (Memoirs Ser.: Vol. 80/407). 78p. 1989. pap. 18.00 (*0-8218-2470-8*, MEMO/80/407) Am Math.

Representations in Archaeology. Ed. by Jean-Claude Gardin & Christopher Peebles. LC 91-24995. (Illus.). 412p. 1992. text ed. 70.00 (*0-253-32546-3*); pap. text ed. 31.50 (*0-253-20709-6*, MB-709) Ind U Pr.

Representations of Affine Hecke Algebras. Nanhua Axi. LC 09-22893. (Lecture Notes in Mathematics Ser.: 1587). 1994. 23.00 (*0-387-58389-0*) Spr-Verlag.

Representations of Affine Hecke Algebras, 31. Nanhua Xi. LC 09-22893. (Lecture Notes in Mathematics: Vol. 1587). 1994. 29.95 (*3-540-58389-0*) Spr-Verlag.

Representations of Algebraic Groups. Ed. by Jens C. Jantzen. (Pure & Applied Mathematics Ser.). 443p. 1987. text ed. 101.00 (*0-12-380245-8*) Acad Pr.

Representations of Algebras. Ed. by Sheila Brenner & H. Tachikawa. (London Mathematical Society Lecture Note Ser.: No. 168). (Illus.). 375p. (C). 1992. pap. text ed. 54.95 (*0-521-42411-9*) Cambridge U Pr.

Representations of Algebras: Proceedings of the Durham Symposium 1985. Ed. by P. J. Webb. (London Mathematical Society Lecture Note Ser.: No. 116). 275p. 1987. pap. text ed. 47.95 (*0-521-31288-4*) Cambridge U Pr.

Representations of Algebras: Sixth International Conference, August 19-22, 1992. Ed. by Vlastimil Dlab & Helmut Lenzing. LC 93-32528. (Canadian Mathematical Society, Conference Proceedings Ser.: No. 14). 478p. 1993. 81.00 (*0-8218-6019-4*, CMSAMS/14) Am Math.

Representations of Algebras, Locally Compact Groups, & Banach - Algebraic Bundles, Vol. 1: Basic Representation Theory of Groups & Algebras. Ed. by James M. Fell & Robert S. Doran. (Pure & Applied Mathematics Ser.). 746p. 1988. text ed. 180.00 (*0-12-252721-6*) Acad Pr.

Representations of Algebras, Locally Compact Groups, & Banach - Algebraic Bundles, Vol. 2: Induced Representations, the Imprivitivity Theorem, & the Generalized Mackey Analysis. Ed. by James M. Fell & Robert S. Doran. (Pure & Applied Mathematics Ser.). 738p. 1988. text ed. 180.00 (*0-12-252722-4*) Acad Pr.

Representations of Commonsense Knowledge. Ernest Davis. (Representation & Reasoning Ser.). 544p. (C). 1990. text ed. 54.95 (*1-55860-033-7*) Morgan Kaufmann.

Representations of Compact Lie Groups. T. Brocker & Tom T. Dieck. (Graduate Texts in Mathematics Ser.: Vol. 98). (Illus.). x, 313p. 1995. 49.95 (*0-387-13678-9*) Spr-Verlag.

Representations of Discrete Functions. Ed. by Tsutomu Sasao & Masahiro Fujita. 336p. (C). 1996. lib. bdg. 96.00 (*0-7923-9720-7*) Kluwer Ac.

Representations of Finite & Compact Groups. Barry Simon. LC 95-42958. (Graduate Studies in Mathematics: No. 10). 266p. 1995. 34.00 (*0-8218-0453-7*, GSM/10) Am Math.

Representations of Finite Chevalley Groups. George Lusztig. LC 78-24068. (CBMS Regional Conference Series in Mathematics: Vol. 39). 48p. 1979. reprint ed. 19.00 (*0-8218-1689-6*, CBMS/39C) Am Math.

Representations of Finite Dimensional Algebras. V. Dlab & H. Tachikawa. LC 91-24244. (Canadian Mathematical Society, Conference Proceedings Ser.: Vol. 11). 322p. 1991. 92.00 (*0-8218-6016-X*, CMSAMS/11) Am Math.

Representations of Finite Groups of Lie Type. Francois Digne & Jean Michel. (London Mathematical Society Student Texts Ser.: No. 21). 150p. (C). 1991. text ed. 59.95 (*0-521-40117-8*); pap. text ed. 22.95 (*0-521-40648-X*) Cambridge U Pr.

Representations of Groups: Annual Seminar, June 10-24, 1994, Banff, Alberta, Canada. Ed. by Bruce N. Allison & Gerald H. Cliff. (Canadian Mathematical Society, Conference Proceedings Ser.: Vol. 16). 1995. 110.00 (*0-8218-0311-5*, CMSAMS/16) Am Math.

Representations of Health, Illness & Handicap. Ed. by Ivana Markova & Robert Farr. 200p. 1995. pap. text ed. 20.00 (*3-7186-5658-2*, Harwood Acad Pubs) Gordon & Breach.

Representations of Health, Illness & Handicap. Ed. by Ivana Markova & Robert Farr. 200p. 1995. text ed. 58.00 (*3-7186-5657-4*, Harwood Acad Pubs) Gordon & Breach.

Representations of Infinite-Dimensional Groups. R. S. Ismagilov. LC 96-15810. (Translations of Mathematical Monographs: Vol. 152). 197p. 1996. 85.00 (*0-8218-0418-9*, MMONO/152) Am Math.

Representations of Innocence in Literatures of the World: Strategies of Multicultural Narrative. Carlee Lippman. LC 93-34509. 196p. 1993. text ed. 79.95 (*0-7734-9394-8*) E Mellen.

Representations of Integers As Sums of Squares. Ed. by Emil Grosswald. (Illus.). 200p. 1985. 107.95 (*0-387-96126-7*) Spr-Verlag.

Representations of Jews Through the Ages. Leonard J. Greenspoon & Bryan F. Le Beau. LC 96-17972. (Studies in Jewish Civilization: Vol. 8). 254p. (C). 1996. 25.00 (*1-881871-22-3*) Creighton U Pr.

Representations of Lie Groups & Lie Algebra. A. A. Kirillov. 225p. (C). 1985. 75.00 (*963-05-3542-4*, Pub. by Akad Kiado HU) St Mut.

Representations of Lie Groups & Related Topics, Vol. 7. Ed. by A. M. Vershik & D. M. Zhelobenko. xiv, 558p. 1990. text ed. 430.00 (*2-88124-678-8*) Gordon & Breach.

Representations of Motherhood. Ed. by Donna Bassin et al. LC 93-5933. (Illus.). 304p. 1994. 35.00 (*0-300-05762-8*) Yale U Pr.

Representations of Motherhood. Donna Bassin. 1996. pap. 16.00 (*0-300-06863-8*) Yale U Pr.

Representations of Musical Signals. Giovanni De Poli & Aldo Piccialli. (Illus.). 496p. 1991. 55.00 (*0-262-04113-8*) MIT Pr.

Representations of Nilpotent Lie Groups & Their Applications, Pt. 1. Frederick P. Greenleaf & Laurence Corwin. (Cambridge Studies in Advanced Mathematics: No. 18). 275p. (C). 1990. text ed. 85.00 (*0-521-36034-X*) Cambridge U Pr.

Representations of Old Age (DINROO) Notes Towards a Critique & Revision of Ageism in Nursing Practice. Heather Gibbs. (Research Monographs: No. 2). (C). 1990. pap. 24.00 (*0-7300-1447-9*, Pub. by Deakin Univ AT) St Mut.

Representations of Power: The Literary Politics of Medieval Japan. Michele Marra. LC 93-10236. (Illus.). 256p. (C). 1993. text ed. 36.00 (*0-8248-1535-1*); pap. text ed. 15.95 (*0-8248-1556-4*) UH Pr.

Representations of Preference Orderings. D. Bridges & G. Mehta. Ed. by G. Fandel & W. Trockel. (Lecture Notes in Economics & Mathematical Systems Ser.: Vol. 422). X, 162p. 1995. 52.00 (*3-540-58839-6*) Spr-Verlag.

Representations of Preference Orderings. Douglas Bridges & Ghanshyam Mehta. LC 94-45869. (Lecture Notes in Economics & Mathematical Systems: Vol. 422). 1995. write for info. (*0-387-58839-6*) Spr-Verlag.

Representations of Rank One Lie Groups 2: N-Cohomology. D. H. Collingwood. LC 88-10415. (Memoirs Ser.: No. 74/387). 101p. 1988. pap. 18.00 (*0-8218-2450-3*, MEMO/74/387) Am Math.

Representations of Rings over Skew Fields. A. H. Schofield. (London Mathematical Society Lecture Note Ser.: No. 92). (Illus.). 240p. 1985. pap. text ed. 47.95 (*0-521-27853-8*) Cambridge U Pr.

Representations of Rotation Lorentz Groups & Applications. I. Gelfand & R. Minlos. LC 62-9193. 1963. 168.00 (*0-08-010069-4*, Pub. by Pergamon Repr UK) Franklin.

Representations of Science & Technology in British Literature since 1880. Earl G. Ingersoll. LC 91-37132. (Worcester Polytechnic Institute Studies in Science, Technology, & Culture: Vol. 9). 320p. (C). 1992. text ed. 54.95 (*0-8204-1680-0*) P Lang Pubng.

Representations of Solvable Groups. Olaf Manz & Thomas R. Wolf. (London Mathematical Society Lecture Note Ser.: No. 185). 320p. (C). 1993. pap. text ed. 44.95 (*0-521-39739-1*) Cambridge U Pr.

Representations of the Crystallographic Space Groups: Irreducible Representations, Induced Representations, & Corepresentations. 2nd ed. O. V. Kovalek. Ed. by Harold T. Stokes & Doran M. Hatch. Tr. by Glen C. Worthey from RUS. LC 93-4825. 349p. 1993. text ed. 154.00 (*2-88124-934-5*) Gordon & Breach.

Representations of the Feminine in the Middle Ages. Ed. by Bonnie Wheeler. (Feminea Medievalia Ser.: Vol. 1). 378p. (C). 1995. 35.00 (*0-85115-650-9*) Boydell & Brewer.

Representations of the Hyperalgebra of a Semisimple Group. S. Donkin. (London Mathematical Society Lecture Note Ser.: No. 219). 250p. (C). Date not set. pap. text ed. 39.95 (*0-521-47251-2*) Cambridge U Pr.

Representations of the Intellectual. Edward W. Said. 1996. pap. 11.00 (*0-679-76127-6*) Random.

Representations of the Lie Group & Lie Algebras. A. A. Kirillov. 226p. (C). 1985. 168.00 (*0-685-36879-3*, Pub. by Collets) St Mut.

Representations of the Rotation & Lorentz Groups: An Introduction. Moshe Carmeli & S. Malin. LC 76-3337. (Lecture Notes in Pure & Applied Mathematics Ser.: No. 16). 133p. reprint ed. pap. 38.00 (*0-7837-4228-2*, 2043915) Bks Demand.

Representations of Vision: Trends & Tacit Assumptions in Vision Research. Ed. by Andrei Gorea et al. (Illus.). 351p. (C). 1991. text ed. 80.00 (*0-521-41228-5*) Cambridge U Pr.

Representations of Women: Nineteenth-Century British Women's Poetry. Kathleen Hickok. LC 83-13029. (Contributions in Women's Studies: No. 49). ix, 277p. 1984. text ed. 42.95 (*0-313-23837-5*, HIR/, Greenwood Pr) Greenwood.

Representations of Women in the Autobiographical Novels of Raymond Queneau. Madeleine Velguth. LC 89-13556. (American University Studies: Romance Languages & Literature: Ser. II, Vol. 133). 340p. 1990. text ed. 58.50 (*0-8204-1199-X*) P Lang Pubng.

Representations of Youth: The Study of Youth & Adolescence in Britain & America. Christine Griffin. LC 93-32894. (Feminist Perspectives Ser.). 256p. 1993. pap. 22.95 (*0-7456-0280-0*) Blackwell Pubs.

Representations, Targets, & Attitudes. Robert Cummins. (Representation & Mind Ser.). (Illus.). 168p. 1996. 25.00 (*0-262-03235-X*, Bradford Bks) MIT Pr.

***Representations 1 - Modulaires d'un Groupe Reductif P-adique Avec.** Marie-France Vigneras. LC 96-10919. (Progress in Mathematics Ser.: Vol. 137). 233p. 1996. 64.50 (*0-8176-3929-2*, QA174) Birkhauser.

***Representative Agent in Macroeconomics.** Hartley. (Routledge Frontiers of Political Economy Ser.). 240p. (C). 1997. text ed. 69.95 (*0-415-14669-0*, Routledge NY) Routledge.

Representative American Orations to Illustrate American Political History, 3 vols. Ed. by Alexander Johnston. (Notable American Authors Ser.). 1992. reprint ed. lib. bdg. 225.00 (*0-7812-3507-3*) Rprt Serv.

Representative & Responsible Government: An Essay on the British Constitution. Anthony H. Birch. LC 71-465276. 252p. reprint ed. pap. 71.90 (*0-685-15261-8*, 2026509) Bks Demand.

Representative Bodies. Thomas J. Pritchard. 213p. (C). 1988. 39.00 (*0-86383-403-5*, Pub. by Gomer Pr UK) St Mut.

Representative British Architects of the Present Day. Charles H. Reilly. LC 67-26774. (Essay Index Reprint Ser.). 1977. reprint ed. 15.95 (*0-8369-0818-X*) Ayer.

Representative Democracy: Public Policy & Midwestern Legislatures in the Late Nineteenth Century. Ballard C. Campbell. 267p. 1980. 32.00 (*0-674-76275-4*) HUP.

***Representative Democracy in Britain Today.** Colin Pilkington. LC 96-34391. (Politics Today Ser.). 1997. text ed. 59.95 (*0-7190-4817-6*, Pub. by Manchester Univ Pr UK); text ed. 19.95 (*0-7190-4818-4*, Pub. by Manchester Univ Pr UK) St Martin.

Representative English Comedies, 4 vols., Set. Ed. by Charles M. Gayley. LC 76-88240. reprint ed. 160.00 (*0-404-01950-1*) AMS Pr.

Representative English Novelists: Defoe to Conrad. Bruce McCullough. LC 72-5807. (Essay Index Reprint Ser.). 1977. reprint ed. 27.95 (*0-8369-7298-8*) Ayer.

Representative Essays: English & American. Ed. by John R. Moore. LC 72-284. (Essay Index Reprint Ser.). 1977. reprint ed. 23.95 (*0-8369-2808-3*) Ayer.

***Representative Form Accuracy of Gear Tooth Flanks on the Prediction of Vibration & Noise of Power Transmission.** A. Kubo & T. Nonaka. (1992 Fall Technical Meeting Ser.). 1992. pap. text ed. 30.00 (*1-55589-589-1*) AGMA.

Representative German Poems. K. Knortz. 1973. 59.95 (*0-8490-0946-4*) Gordon Pr.

Representative Government & Economic Power. David Coombes. (Policy Studies Institute). vi, 208p. 1982. text ed. 53.95 (*0-435-83180-1*, Pub. by Dartmth Pub UK); pap. text ed. 23.95 (*0-435-83181-X*, Pub. by Dartmth Pub UK) Ashgate Pub Co.

Representative Government & Environmental Management. Edwin T. Haefele. LC 73-16106. (Illus.). 208p. reprint ed. pap. 59.30 (*0-8357-4681-X*, 2037628) Bks Demand.

Representative Government & the Revolution: The Maryland Constitutional Crisis of 1787. Ed. by Melvin Yazawa. LC 75-6546. 200p. reprint ed. pap. 57.00 (*0-685-15550-1*, 2026705) Bks Demand.

Representative Government in Early Modern France. J. Russell Major. LC 79-14711. 752p. 1980. text ed. 67.00 (*0-300-02300-6*) Yale U Pr.

Representative Government in Modern Europe. 2nd rev. ed. Michael Gallagher et al. LC 94-39621. Orig. Title: Representative Government in Western Europe. 1995. pap. text ed. 18.75 (*0-07-036687-X*) McGraw.

Representative Government in Western Europe see Representative Government in Modern Europe

Representative Institutions in Renaissance France, 1421-1559. James R. Major. LC 82-25305. ix, 182p. (C). 1983. reprint ed. text ed. 59.75 (*0-313-23569-4*, MAJR, Greenwood Pr) Greenwood.

Representative Irish Tales. Ed. by William Butler Yeats. 364p. 7900. 40.00 (*0-901072-83-4*, Pub. by Colin Smythe Ltd UK); pap. 15.95 (*0-901072-84-2*, Pub. by Colin Smythe Ltd UK) Dufour.

Representative Man. Ralph Waldo Emerson. (Notable American Authors Ser.). 1992. reprint ed. lib. bdg. 75.00 (*0-7812-2810-7*) Rprt Serv.

Representative Man: Ralph Waldo Emerson in His Time. Joel Porte. (Illus.). 361p. 1988. text ed. 67.50 (*0-231-06740-2*) Col U Pr.

Representative Medieval & Tudor Plays. Ed. by Roger S. Loomis & Henry W. Wells. LC 77-111109. (Play Anthology Reprint Ser.). 1977. 24.95 (*0-8369-8202-9*) Ayer.

Representative Men. Ralph Waldo Emerson. 1995. pap. 12.95 (*1-56886-015-3*) Marsilio Pubs.

Representative Men: Seven Lectures. Ralph Waldo Emerson. 192p. 1996. pap. 15.95 (*0-674-76105-7*) Belknap Pr.

***Representative Men & Old Families of Rhode Island: Genealogical Records & Historical Sketches of Prominent & Representative Citizens & of Many of the Old Families, 3 vols.** (Illus.). 2336p. 1997. reprint ed. lib. bdg. 238.50 (*0-8328-6472-2*) Higginson Bk Co.

Representative Men of Puerto Rico. F. E. Jackson. (Puerto Rico Ser.). 1979. lib. bdg. 75.00 (*0-8490-2995-3*) Gordon Pr.

Representative Modern Preachers. Lewis O. Brastow. LC 68-57306. (Essay Index Reprint Ser.). 1977. 23.95 (*0-8369-0101-0*) Ayer.

Representative Phi Beta Kappa Orations: Second Series. Clark S. Northup. (BCL1-PS American Literature Ser.). 553p. 1992. reprint ed. lib. bdg. 99.00 (*0-7812-6658-0*) Rprt Serv.

Representative Phi Beta Kappa Orations, Ser. 1. 2nd ed. Ed. by Clark S. Northup. reprint ed. 45.00 (*0-404-04795-5*) AMS Pr.

Representative Phi Beta Kappa Orations, Ser. 2. Ed. by Clark S. Northup. LC 74-173800. reprint ed. 45.00 (*0-404-04796-3*) AMS Pr.

Representative Photoplays Analyzed. Scott O'Dell. 1972. 44.95 (*0-8490-0947-2*) Gordon Pr.

Representative Plays, 4 vols. Henry A. Jones. 1988. reprint ed. lib. bdg. 295.00 (*0-7812-0180-2*) Rprt Serv.

Representative Plays, 4 vols. Henry A. Jones. LC 72-145116. 1925. reprint ed. 295.00 (*0-403-01054-3*); reprint ed. 75.00 (*0-318-68144-7*) Scholarly.

Representative Plays by American Dramatists. Montrose J. Moses. 1972. 132.00 (*0-685-43147-9*, 1026) Ayer.

Representative Plays by American Dramatists, 3 vols. Montrose J. Moses. (BCL1-PS American Literature Ser.). 1992. reprint ed. lib. bdg. 225.00 (*0-7812-6654-8*) Rprt Serv.

Representative Plays by American Dramatists, 3 vols., Vol. 1. Ed. by Montrose J. Moses. LC 64-14707. 678p. 1911. reprint ed. 145.95 (*0-405-08803-5*) Ayer.

Representative Plays by American Dramatists, 3 vols., Vol. 2. Ed. by Montrose J. Moses. 823p. 1972. 48.95 (*0-405-08805-1*) Ayer.

Representative Plays by American Dramatists, 3 vols., Vol. 3. Ed. by Montrose J. Moses. LC 64-14707. 926p. 1972. 48.95 (*0-405-08806-X*) Ayer.

Representative Selections. James Fenimore Cooper. (BCL1-PS American Literature Ser.). 350p. 1993. reprint ed. lib. bdg. 89.00 (*0-7812-6952-0*) Rprt Serv.

Representative Selections. Benjamin Franklin. (BCL1-PS American Literature Ser.). 544p. 1993. reprint ed. lib. bdg. 99.00 (*0-7812-6937-7*) Rprt Serv.

Representative Selections. Oliver W. Holmes. (BCL1-PS American Literature Ser.). 472p. 1993. reprint ed. lib. bdg. 99.00 (*0-7812-6970-9*) Rprt Serv.

Representative Selections. Francis Parkman. (BCL1-PS American Literature Ser.). 1993. reprint ed. lib. bdg. write for info. (*0-7812-6997-0*) Rprt Serv.

Representative Selections. Mark Twain, pseud. (BCL1-PS American Literature Ser.). 459p. 1993. reprint ed. lib. bdg. 99.00 (*0-7812-6950-4*) Rprt Serv.

Representative Selections, with Introduction, Bibliography & Notes. James Fenimore Cooper. Ed. by Robert E. Spiller. LC 76-48040. (Illus.). 350p. 1977. reprint ed. text ed. 35.00 (*0-8371-9317-6*, CORES, Greenwood Pr) Greenwood.

Representative Short Story Cycles of the Twentieth Century: Studies in a Literary Genre. Forrest L. Ingram. LC 75-159465. (De Proprietatibus Litterarum, Ser. Major: No. 15). 234p. 1971. text ed. 46.15 (*90-279-1848-1*) Mouton.

Representative Spanish Authors, Vol. 1: From the Middle Ages Through the Eighteenth Century. 3rd ed. Ed. by Walter T. Pattison & Donald W. Bleznick. (C). 1971. text ed. 28.95 (*0-19-501326-3*) OUP.

Representative Spanish Authors, Vol. 2: The Nineteenth Century to the Present. 3rd ed. Ed. by Walter T. Pattison & Donald W. Bleznick. 500p. (C). 1971. text ed. 31.95 (*0-19-501433-2*) OUP.

Representative Structures, Vol. 2. Ed. by Theon Wilkinson. 236p. (C). 1981. 102.00 (*0-85292-289-2*, Pub. by IPM Hse UK) St Mut.

Representative Supreme Court? The Impact of Race, Religion, & Gender on Appointments. Barbara A. Perry. LC 91-14336. (Contributions in Legal Studies: No. 66). 176p. 1991. text ed. 49.95 (*0-313-27777-X*, PRC, Greenwood Pr) Greenwood.

Representative Words: Politics, Literature, & the American Language, 1776-1865. Thomas Gustafson. (Cambridge Studies in American Literature & Culture: No. 60). 432p. (C). 1993. text ed. 74.95 (*0-521-39512-7*) Cambridge U Pr.

Representative Works, Nineteen Thirty-Eight-Nineteen Eighty-Five. Jackson MacLow. LC 85-61392. (Roof Bks.). 350p. (Orig.). 1985. 18.95 (*0-937804-19-3*); pap. 12.95 (*0-937804-18-5*) Segue NYC.

Representative Writings of the Early Nineteenth Century (1800-1839) see Millennium in America: From the Puritan Migration to the Civil War

Representative Writings of the Eighteenth Century: Scriptural Interpretations see Millennium in America: From the Puritan Migration to the Civil War

Representative Writings of the Eighteenth Century: Applications of Prophecy see Millennium in America: From the Puritan Migration to the Civil War

Representative Writings: 1840-1860 see Millennium in America: From the Puritan Migration to the Civil War

Representatives: The Real Nature & Function of Papal Legates. Mario Oliveri. LC 81-108272. 192p. (Orig.). (C). 1981. reprint ed. pap. 4.95 (*0-905715-20-9*) Wanderer Pr.

Representatives of the Lower Clergy in Parliament, 1295-1340. Jeffrey H. Denton & John P. Dooley. (Royal Historical Society: Studies in History: No. 50). 150p. 1987. 63.00 (*0-86193-207-2*) Boydell & Brewer.

Representatives of the People. Vernon Bogdanor. 350p. 1985. text ed. 59.95 (*0-566-00878-5*, Pub. by Dartmth Pub UK) Ashgate Pub Co.

***Representatives Plays by America Dramatists, Vol. 1.** Ed. by Montrose J. Moses. 678p. Date not set. write for info. (*0-405-08804-3*) Ayer.

R

Represented Discourse in the Novels of Francois Mauriac: Catholic University of America. Anne G. Landry. LC 70-128933. (Studies in Romance Languages & Literatures: No. 44). reprint ed. 37.50 (*0-404-50344-6*) AMS Pr.

Representing a Claimant in a Workers' Compensation Case. Joseph M. Burke. LC 93-86314. 154p. 1993. pap. text ed. 45.00 (*0-944490-56-5*) Mass CLE.

Representing a Plaintiff in an Unjust Dismissal Case. Nancy s. Shilepsky. LC 93-79674. 120p. 1993. pap. text ed. 45.00 (*0-944490-54-9*) Mass CLE.

Representing America: Experiences of U. S. Diplomats at the UN. Frwd. by Linda M. Fasulo & Elliot L. Richardson. LC 84-3477. 362p. reprint ed. pap. 103.20 (*0-8357-5601-7*, 2035243) Bks Demand.

Representing America: The Ken Trevey Collection of American Realist Prints. Bruce Robertson. LC 94-48298. (Illus.). 68p. (C). 1995. pap. 15.00 (*0-942006-26-7*) U of CA Art.

Representing America, 1900-1940: Paintings from the Permanent Collection of the Whitney Museum of American Art. LC 86-80643. (Illus.). 29p. 1986. pap. 4.00 (*0-685-14309-0*) Flint Inst Arts.

Representing & Acquiring Geographic Knowledge. Ed. by Ernest Davis. 240p. (C). 1986. pap. text ed. 180.00 (*0-273-08769-X*, Pub. by Pitman Pubng UK) St Mut.

Representing & Intervening: Introductory Topics in the Philosophy of Natural Science. Ian Hacking. LC 83-5132. 272p. 1983. pap. text ed. 20.95 (*0-521-28246-2*) Cambridge U Pr.

Representing & Reasoning with Probabilistic Knowledge: A Logical Approach to Probabilities. Fahiem Bacchus. 256p. 1991. 35.00 (*0-262-02317-2*) MIT Pr.

Representing Asylum Applicants: An Attorney's Guide to Law & Procedure. Ed. by George Black et al. 217p. 1995. pap. text ed. 50.00 (*0-934143-71-4*) Lawyers Comm Human.

Representing Battered Women in Custody Disputes in the District of Columbia: Litigating Custody As a Part of a Civil Protection Order. Women's Legal Defense Fund Staff. 12p. 1986. 5.00 (*0-317-67860-4*) Women's Legal Defense.

Representing Belief: Religion, Art, & Society in Nineteenth-Century France. Michael P. Driskel. (Illus.). 288p. 1992. text ed. 48.50 (*0-271-00747-8*) Pa St U Pr.

RePresenting Bisexualities: Subjects & Cultures of Fluid Desire. Ed. by Maria Pramaggiore & Donald E. Hall. LC 96-8977. 320p. (C). 1996. 55.00 (*0-8147-6633-1*); pap. 18.95 (*0-8147-6634-X*) NYU Pr.

Representing Black Culture: Race & Cultural Politics in the United States. Richard M. Merelman. 288p. (C). 1995. pap. 17.95 (*0-415-91075-7*, B4660) Routledge.

Representing Black Men. Marcellus Blount & George P. Cunningham. LC 94-31105. 288p. (C). (gr. 13). 1995. text ed. 59.95 (*0-415-90758-6*) Routledge.

Representing Black Men. Marcellus Blount & George P. Cunningham. 288p. (gr. 13). 1995. pap. 17.95 (*0-415-90759-4*, Pub. by Tavistock UK) Routledge Chapman & Hall.

Representing Blackness: Issues in Film & Video. Ed. by Valerie Smith. LC 96-36075. (Depth of Field Ser.). (Illus.). 250p. (C). 1997. 48.00 (*0-8135-2313-3*); pap. 17.95 (*0-8135-2314-1*) Rutgers U Pr.

Representing Children's Book Characters. Mary E. Wilson. LC 88-31286. (Illus.). 182p. 1989. 29.50 (*0-8108-2169-9*) Scarecrow.

Representing Clients with Tax Problems. 124p. 1985. pap. 10.00 (*0-317-02673-9*, 39,833) NCLS Inc.

Representing Concepts in Semantic Nets. Marcello Frixione et al. (Artificial Intelligence Ser.). 256p. 1991. 75.00 (*0-13-773797-1*, 270509) P-H.

Representing Consumers After Repossession. 31p. 1988. pap. 4.75 (*0-317-02674-7*, 43,585) NCLS Inc.

Representing Convicts: New Perspectives on Convict Forced Labour Migration. Ian Duffield & James Bradley. LC 96-24610. (New Historical Perspectives on Migration Ser.). 1997. write for info. (*0-7185-0075-X*, Pub. by Leicester Univ Pr) Bks Intl VA.

Representing Disability Claimants Before the Social Security Administration: A Primer for New Advocates. 154p. 1985. 12.00 (*0-685-30196-6*, 40,208) NCLS Inc.

Representing Femininity: Middle-Class Subjectivity in Victorian & Edwardian Women's Autobiographies. Mary J. Corbett. 252p. 1992. 48.00 (*0-19-506858-0*) OUP.

Representing God in Washington: The Role of Religious Lobbies in the American Polity. Allen D. Hertzke. LC 87-15144. 278p. 1988. pap. 16.00 (*0-87049-570-4*); lib. bdg. 35.00 (*0-87049-553-4*) U of Tenn Pr.

Representing Hinduism: The Construction of Religious Traditions & National Identity. Ed. by Vasudha Dalmia & Heinrich Von Stietencron. LC 95-7978. 468p. 1995. 42.00 (*0-8039-9194-0*) AltaMira Pr.

Representing Interests & Interest Group Representation. Ed. by William Crotty et al. LC 94-2298. 112p. 1994. 43.50 (*0-8191-9458-1*); pap. 19.00 (*0-8191-9459-X*) U Pr of Amer.

***Representing Interests in the European Union.** LC 96-36917. 1997. text ed. 55.00 (*0-312-17288-5*) St Martin.

***Representing Ireland: Gender, Class, Nationality.** Susan S. Sailer. (Illus.). 256p. 1997. 49.95 (*0-614-29835-0*) U Press Fla.

Representing Ireland: Literature & the Origins of Conflict 1534-1660. Ed. by Brendan Bradshaw et al. LC 92-37859. (Illus.). 256p. (C). 1993. text ed. 59.95 (*0-521-41634-5*) Cambridge U Pr.

Representing Jazz. Ed. by Krin Gabbard. LC 94-37347. (Illus.). 328p. 1995. text ed. 45.95 (*0-8223-1579-3*); pap. text ed. 16.95 (*0-8223-1594-7*) Duke.

Representing Kenneth Burke: Selected Papers from the English Institute. Ed. by Hayden White & Margaret Brose. LC 82-47972. (New Series: No. 6). 224p. 1983. 35.00 (*0-8018-2877-5*) Johns Hopkins.

Representing Lesbian Mothers & Gay Fathers in the District of Columbia, Maryland, & Virginia. Women's Legal Defense Fund Staff. 1986. 4.00 (*0-317-67859-0*) Women's Legal Defense.

Representing Mental States & Mechanisms: Papers from the 1995 Spring Symposium. Ed. by Michael T. Cox & Michael Freed. (Technical Reports). (Illus.). 141p. 1995. spiral bd. 25.00 (*0-929280-88-1*) AAAI Pr.

Representing Modern Texts. Ed. by George Bornstein. 250p. (C). 1991. text ed. 49.50 (*0-472-09439-4*); pap. text ed. 19.95 (*0-472-06439-8*) U of Mich Pr.

Representing Musical Structure. Ed. by Peter Howell et al. (Cognitive Science Ser.). (Illus.). 370p. 1991. text ed. 80.00 (*0-12-357171-5*) Acad Pr.

Representing Nonprofit Organizations. Marilyn E. Phelan. 1994. 95.00 (*0-318-72537-1*) Clark Boardman Callaghan.

***Representing O. J. Murder: Criminal Justice & Mass Culture.** Ed. & Pref. by Gregg Barak. (Illus.). 200p. (C). 1996. pap. text ed. 25.50 (*0-911577-37-8*) Harrow & Heston.

Representing Older Persons: An Advocates Manual. National Senior Citizen Law Center Staff. Ed. by Alfred J. Chiplin, Jr. 142p. 1990. reprint ed. 45.00 (*0-685-15260-X*, 38,950) NCLS Inc.

***Representing Order: Crime, Law & Justice in the News Media.** R. V. Ericson et al. 400p. 1991. 45.00 (*0-335-09753-7*, Open Univ Pr); pap. 16.99 (*0-335-09752-9*, Open Univ Pr) Taylor & Francis.

Representing Order: Crime, Law, & Justice in the News Media. Richard V. Ericson et al. 448p. 1991. 50.00 (*0-8020-2757-1*); pap. 19.95 (*0-8020-6804-9*) U of Toronto Pr.

Representing Others. Ed. by Gidley. (Illus.). 163p. 1993. pap. 19.95 (*0-85989-354-5*, Pub. by Univ Exeter Pr UK) Northwestern U Pr.

Representing Parents in Child Protection Cases. 21p. 1988. pap. 3.00 (*0-89707-385-1*, 549-0086-01) Amer Bar Assn.

Representing People with Disabilities. Ed. by Peter Danziger. LC 91-52548. 594p. 1991. ring bd. 95.00 (*0-942954-38-6*) NYS Bar.

***Representing Plaintiffs in Title VII Actions, 2 vols.** Kent Spriggs. pap. text ed. write for info. (*0-471-18221-4*) Wiley.

Representing Plaintiffs in Title VII Actions. Kent Spriggs. LC 93-39238. (Employment Law Library). 1994. text ed. 115.00 (*0-471-00753-6*) Wiley.

Representing Plaintiffs in Title VII Actions, Vol. 2. Kent Spriggs. (Employment Law Library). 1360p. 1994. text ed. 230.00 (*0-471-00235-6*) Wiley.

***Representing Plaintiffs in Title VII Actions, Vol. 2.** Kent Spriggs. 1994. text ed. 115.00 (*0-471-00754-4*) Wiley.

Representing Plans under Uncertainty: A Logic of Time, Chance, & Action. Peter Haddawy. LC 94-2105. (Lecture Notes in Computer Science, Lecture Notes in Artificial Intelligence Ser.: Vol. 770). x, 129p. 1994. 29.95 (*0-387-57697-5*) Spr-Verlag.

Representing Primary Caretaker Parents in Custody Disputes: A Manual for Attorneys. Women's Legal Defense Fund Staff. 69p. (Orig.). 1984. pap. 15.00 (*0-932689-01-9*) Women's Legal Defense.

Representing Professional Athletes & Teams, 1988. 943p. 1988. 17.50 (*0-685-69484-4*) PLI.

Representing Professional Athletes & Teams, 1990. 1034p. 1990. 65.00 (*0-685-69485-2*) PLI.

Representing Professional Athletes & Teams 1993, 2 vols. (Patents, Copyrights, Trademarks, & Literary Property Ser.: Vols. 357-358). 1116p. 1993. 80.00 (*0-685-65520-2*, G4-3896) PLI.

Representing Reality: Discourse, Rhetoric & Social Construction. Jonathan Potter. 240p. 1996. 65.00 (*0-8039-8410-3*); pap. 22.95 (*0-8039-8411-1*) Sage.

Representing Reality: Issues & Concepts in Documentary. Bill Nichols. LC 91-2637. (Illus.). 336p. 1992. 39.95 (*0-253-34060-8*); pap. 18.50 (*0-253-20681-2*, MB-681) Ind U Pr.

Representing Reality: Readings in Literary Nonfiction. Ed. by John Warnock. LC 88-60552. 623p. (Orig.). (C). 1989. pap. text ed. 18.50 (*0-312-00069-3*) St Martin.

Representing Revolution: French & British Images, 1789-1804. Sura Levine & Joan Landes. (Illus.). 56p. 1989. pap. 12.00 (*0-914337-13-0*) Mead Art Mus.

Representing School Boards in the Nineties. rev. ed. Council of School Attorneys Staff. 700p. 1993. ring bd. 200.00 (*0-88364-177-1*) Natl Sch Boards.

Representing Shakespeare: History, Theatre & the R. S. C. Robert Shaughnessy. 1995. pap. 34.00 (*0-13-342940-7*) P-H.

Representing Shakespeare: New Psychoanalytic Essays. Ed. by Murray M. Schwartz & Coppelia Kahn. LC 79-3682. 320p. reprint ed. pap. 91.20 (*0-7837-3392-5*, 2043350) Bks Demand.

Representing Super Doll. Richard Peck. 192p. (YA). (gr. 7 up). 1989. pap. 2.95 (*0-440-97362-7*, LLL BDD) BDD Bks Young Read.

***Representing Superdog.** Richard Peck. 1997. pap. 4.99 (*0-14-038555-X*) Viking Penguin.

Representing the Audited Taxpayer. Robert E. McKenzie et al. 1990. 69.95 (*0-685-31933-4*) Clark Boardman Callaghan.

Representing the Child Client. 1987. write for info. (*0-8205-1584-1*) Bender.

Representing the Debtor in a Chapter 13 Consumer Bankruptcy. Mark G. DeGiacomo. LC 94-73531. 1995. pap. text ed. write for info. (*0-944490-83-2*) Mass CLE.

Representing the Debtor in a Chapter 7 Business Bankruptcy, Pts. 1 & 2: Summer 1992 Action Guide, 2 pts. Iain A. Macdonald. Ed. by Marie Hagelstein & Elizabeth M. Johnson. 213p. 1992. pap. 52.00 (*0-88124-529-1*, BU-11311) Cont Ed Bar-CA.

Representing the Debtor in a Chapter 7 Consumer Bankruptcy. Mark G. DeGiacomo. LC 93-83631. 92p. 1993. pap. text ed. 45.00 (*0-944490-50-6*) Mass CLE.

***Representing the Elderly in Florida.** Jo H. Curris & Michael J. Virgadamo. (D & S Florida Practice Ser.). 1995. spiral bd. 95.00 (*1-55834-275-3*, 61115) MICHIE.

Representing the English Renaissance. Ed. by Stephen Greenblatt. (Representation Bks.: No. 2). 360p. 1987. pap. 18.95 (*0-520-06130-6*) U CA Pr.

Representing the French Revolution: Literature, Historiography, & Art. Ed. by James A. Heffernan. LC 91-50816. (Illus.). 304p. 1992. pap. 29.95 (*0-87451-586-6*) U Pr of New Eng.

Representing the Holocaust: History, Theory, Trauma. Dominick La Capra. LC 93-33885. 248p. 1994. 35.00 (*0-8014-2997-8*) Cornell U Pr.

Representing the Holocaust: History, Theory, Trauma. Dominick LaCapra. 248p. 1996. pap. 14.95 (*0-8014-8187-2*) Cornell U Pr.

Representing the Other: A Feminism & Psychology' Reader. Ed. by Sue Wilkinson & Celia Kitzinger. 208p. 1996. 65.00 (*0-7619-5228-4*); pap. 19.95 (*0-7619-5229-2*) Sage.

Representing the Other: Race, Text, & Gender in Spanish & Spanish American Narrative. Paul J. Smith. 248p. 1992. 65.00 (*0-19-815870-X*) OUP.

Representing the Residential Real Estate Client. Frank Taddeo, Jr. 144p. 1987. 29.95 (*0-13-773763-7*, Busn) P-H.

Representing the Secured Creditor in Chapter 11 Cases. (Commercial Law & Practice Ser.). 691p. 1991. pap. text ed. 17.50 (*0-685-56853-9*, A4-4350) PLI.

Representing the Secured Creditor in Chapter 11 Cases 1994. (Commercial Law & Practice Course Handbook Ser.). 488p. 1994. pap. 99.00 (*0-685-65479-6*, A4-4457) PLI.

Representing the Small Business. (Corporate Law & Practice Course Handbook, 1985-86 Ser.: Vol. 790). 359p. 1992. 70.00 (*0-685-65493-1*, B4-7016) PLI.

***Representing the South Pacific: Colonial Discourse from Cook to Gauguin.** Rod Edmond. (Illus.). 280p. (C). 1997. text ed. 54.95 (*0-521-55054-8*) Cambridge U Pr.

Representing the Terminated Employee in Ohio: Evaluating, Settling & Liquidating State & Federal Claims. James B. Helmer & Ann Lugbill. 410p. 1990. pap. text ed. 59.00 (*0-87084-347-8*) Anderson Pub Co.

Representing the Trade Creditor & Landlord in Chapter 11 Cases. (Commercial Law & Practice Course Handbook Ser.). 693p. 1992. pap. 70.00 (*0-685-69486-0*) PLI.

Representing the Woman: Cinema & Psychoanalysis. Elizabeth Cowie. LC 96-20752. 416p. (C). 1996. text ed. 47.95 (*0-8166-2912-9*); pap. text ed. 18.95 (*0-8166-2913-7*) U of Minn Pr.

Representing Time in Natural Language: The Dynamic Interpretation of Tense & Aspect. Alice G. Ter Meulen. (Illus.). 160p. 1995. 25.00 (*0-262-20099-6*, Bradford Bks) MIT Pr.

***Representing Time in Natural Language: The Dynamic Interpretation of Tense & Aspect.** Alice G. Ter Meulen. (Illus.). 176p. 1997. reprint ed. pap. 12.50 (*0-262-70066-2*, Bradford Bks) MIT Pr.

Representing Uncertain Knowledge: An AI Approach. Dominic Clark & Paul Krause. 288p. (Orig.). 1993. pap. text ed. 22.95 (*1-871516-17-X*, Pub. by Intellect Bks UK) Cromland.

Representing Uncertain Knowledge: An Artificial Intelligence Approach. Paul Krause. LC 93-27791. (DIVS-Diverse Ser.). 278p. (C). 1993. lib. bdg. 129.50 (*0-7923-2433-1*) Kluwer Ac.

***Representing War: Form & Ideology in First World War Narratives.** Evelyn Cobley. (Theory/Culture Ser.). 274p. 1996. pap. 19.95 (*0-8020-7894-X*) U of Toronto Pr.

Representing War: Form & Ideology in First World War Narratives. Evelyn Cobley. (Theory/Culture Ser.). 274p. (C). 1996. 45.00 (*0-8020-0537-3*) U of Toronto Pr.

***Representing Woman: Sande Masquerades of the Mende of Sierra Leone.** Ruth B. Phillips. 1995. pap. 50.00 (*0-930741-45-5*) UCLA Fowler Mus.

Representing Woman: Sande Masquerades of the Mende of Sierra Leone. Ruth B. Phillips. 1995. 50.00 (*0-930741-44-7*) UCLA Fowler Mus.

Representing Women: Law, Literature, & Feminism. Ed. by Susan S. Heinzelman & Zipporah Wiseman. LC 94-6023. (Post-Contemporary Interventions Ser.). (Illus.). 400p. 1994. text ed. 49.95 (*0-8223-1481-9*); pap. text ed. 19.95 (*0-8223-1495-9*) Duke.

Representing Women: Myths of Feminity in the Popular Media. Myra MacDonald. LC 95-17544. 1995. write for info. (*0-340-63221-6*, Pub. by E Arnold UK) Routledge Chapman & Hall.

Representing Women: Myths of Feminity in the Popular Media. Myra MacDonald. 1995. text ed. 16.95 (*0-340-58016-X*, Pub. by E Arnld UK) St Martin.

***Representing Women in Renaissance England.** Ed. by Claude J. Summers & Ted-Larry Pebworth. LC 97-10984. 288p. 1997. spiral bd. 44.95 (*0-8262-1104-6*) U of Mo Pr.

Representing Yourself: What You Can Do Without a Lawyer. 2nd ed. Kenneth Lasson. LC 94-46383. 1995. pap. 13.95 (*0-452-27451-6*, Plume) NAL-Dutton.

Representing...Battered Women Who Kill. Sara L. Johann & Frank Osanka. 416p. 1989. pap. 47.95 (*0-398-06184-X*) C C Thomas.

Representing...Battered Women Who Kill. Sara L. Johann & Frank Osanka. 416p. (C). 1989. text ed. 79.95 (*0-398-05567-X*) C C Thomas.

***Represion, Exilio y Democracia: La Cultura Uruguaya.** Text by Hugo Achugar et al. (SPA.). 1987. 15.00 (*0-614-23155-8*) Edins Hispamerica.

***Represion y Reconstruccion de una Cultura: El Caso Argentino.** Text by Osvaldo Bayer et al. (SPA.). 1988. 12.00 (*950-23-0406-3*) Edins Hispamerica.

Repressed Economy: Causes, Consequences, Reform. Deepak Lal. (Economists of the Twentieth Century Ser.). 624p. 1993. 95.00 (*1-85278-888-7*) E Elgar.

***Repressed Memories.** Ed. by David Spiegel. (Review of Psychiatry Ser.: Vol. 16, Sect. II). 176p. (Orig.). 1997. pap. text ed. 25.00 (*0-88048-446-2*, 8446) Am Psychiatric.

Repressed Memories: A Journey to Recovery from Sexual Abuse. Renee Fredrickson. (Fireside - Parkside Recovery Book Ser.). 256p. 1992. pap. 10.00 (*0-671-76716-X*, Fireside) S&S Trade.

Repressed Memories: Can You Trust Them? Arlys N. McDonald. LC 95-21481. 288p. (gr. 10). 1995. 16.99 (*0-8007-1715-5*) Revell.

Repressed Memories of Sexual Abuse. Adele Mayer. 1995. pap. 11.95 (*1-55691-117-3*, 173) Learning Pubns.

Repressible Conflict, 1830-1861. Avery O. Craven. LC 83-45425. reprint ed. 39.50 (*0-404-20070-2*) AMS Pr.

Repressible Conflict, 1830-1861. Avery O. Craven. (History - United States Ser.). 97p. 1993. reprint ed. lib. bdg. 59.00 (*0-7812-4904-X*) Rprt Serv.

Repression: Basic & Surplus Repression in Psychoanalytic Theory: Freud, Reich, & Marcuse. Gad Horowitz. LC 77-5006. 237p. reprint ed. pap. 67.60 (*0-317-27027-3*, 2023638) Bks Demand.

Repression & Association: Implications for Personality Theory, Psychopathology & Health. Jerome L. Singer. 536p. 1995. pap. text ed. 19.95 (*0-226-76106-1*) U Ch Pr.

Repression & Dissociation: Implications for Personality Theory, Psychopathology & Health. Ed. by Jerome L. Singer. (John D. & Catherine T. MacArthur Foundation Series on Mental Health & Development). (Illus.). 544p. 1990. 34.95 (*0-226-76105-3*) U Ch Pr.

***Repression & Expression: Literary & Social Coding in Nineteenth-Century France.** Ed. by Carrol F. Coates. (Studies on Themes & Motifs in Literature: Vol. 22). 342p. (C). 1996. text ed. 42.95 (*0-8204-2844-2*) P Lang Pubng.

Repression & Fear: New Approaches to Resolve the Crisis in Psychopathology. Yacov Rofe. 500p. 1989. 78.95 (*0-89116-056-6*) Hemisp Pub.

Repression & Recovery: Modern American Poetry & the Politics of Cultural Memory, 1910-1945. Cary Nelson. LC 89-40264. (Wisconsin Project on American Writers Ser.). (Illus.). 256p. 1989. text ed. 19.95 (*0-299-12340-5*) U of Wis Pr.

Repression & Recovery: Modern American Poetry & the Politics of Cultural Memory, 1910-1945. Cary Nelson. LC 89-40264. (Wisconsin Project on American Writers Ser.). (Illus.). 352p. (C). 1992. reprint ed. pap. 12.95 (*0-299-12344-8*) U of Wis Pr.

Repression & Resistance: Insiders' Account of Apartheid. Ed. by Robin Cohen et al. (African Discourse Ser.: Vol. 2). 320p. 1990. 65.00 (*0-905450-86-8*, Pub. by H Zell Pubs UK) Bowker-Saur.

Repression & Resistance in India. Ed. by A. R. Desai. 1990. 52.50 (*0-86132-225-8*, Pub. by Popular Prakashan II) S Asia.

Repression & Revolt: The Origins of the 1948 Communist Insurrection in Malaya & Singapore. Michael R. Stenson. LC 75-631242. (Papers in International Studies: Southeast Asia Ser.: No. 10). 69p. reprint ed. pap. 25.00 (*0-317-09490-4*, 2005116) Bks Demand.

Repression, Exile, & Democracy: Uruguayan Culture. Ed. by Saul Sosnowski & Louise B. Popkin. Tr. by Louise B. Popkin from SPA. LC 92-10650. (Latin America in Translation - En Traduccion - Em Traducao Ser.). 272p. 1992. text ed. 49.95 (*0-8223-1258-1*); pap. text ed. 18.95 (*0-8223-1268-9*) Duke.

Repression in China since June 4, 1989. Asia Watch Staff. LC 90-84977. 120p. 1991. 10.00 (*0-929692-74-8*, Asia Watch) Hum Rts Watch.

Repression in Latin America: A Report of the Russell Tribunal Session in Rome, 1974. Ed. by William Jerman. 163p. 1975. 32.50 (*0-85124-140-9*, Pub. by Spokesman Bks UK) Coronet Bks.

Repression in Taiwan: A Look at the Kaohsiung Rally & Trials. Herb Thomas. 34p. 1980. 2.00 (*0-686-36618-2*) Asia Resource.

Repression of Crime, Studies in Historical Penology. Harry E. Barnes. LC 69-14911. (Criminology, Law Enforcement, & Social Problems Ser.: No. 56). 1969. reprint ed. 24.00 (*0-87585-056-1*) Patterson Smith.

Repression of Psychoanalysis: Otto Fenichel & the Political Freudians. Russell Jacoby. LC 86-11358. xiv, 218p. (C). 1986. reprint ed. pap. 13.50 (*0-226-39069-1*) U Ch Pr.

Repressor of Overmuch Blaming of the Clergy, by Sometime Bishop of Chichester, 2 vols. Reginald Peacock. Ed. by Churchill Babington. (Rolls Ser.: No. 19). 1974. reprint ed. 140.00 (*0-8115-1025-5*) Periodicals Srv.

Reprieve. Jean-Paul Sartre. 1992. pap. 15.00 (*0-679-74078-3*, Vin) Random.

Reprieve: The Testament of John Resko. John Resko. LC 75-17464. 285p. 1975. reprint ed. text ed. 59.75 (*0-8371-8311-1*, RERE, Greenwood Pr) Greenwood.

Reprieve for the Iron Horse: Amtrack. William E. Thomas. 1974. 10.00 (*0-87511-120-3*) Claitors.

Reprint of Official Register of Land Lottery of Georgia 1827. Martha L. Houston. 308p. 1992. reprint ed. pap. 25.00 (*0-685-62595-8*, 2907) Clearfield Co.

Reprint of Q. 2, 1599 see Romeo & Juliet: Parallel Texts of the First 2 Quartos; Quarto 1, 1597 & Quarto 2, 1599

R

Reprint of Quarto 1, 1597 see Romeo & Juliet: Parallel Texts of the First 2 Quartos; Quarto 1, 1597 & Quarto 2, 1599

Reprint-Prehospital Emergency Care & Crisis Intervention. 4th ed. Brent Hafen & Keith J. Karren. 1993. pap. 32.75 (*0-89303-978-0*) P-H.

Reprinted Selected Top Articles Published 1976 - 1977. Ed. by G. H. Berlyne. (Karger Highlights, Nephrology One Ser.). (Illus.). 1978. pap. 12.00 (*3-8055-2938-4*) S Karger.

Reprinted Selected Top Articles Published 1977, No. 1. Compiled by H. M. Myers. (Karger Highlights, Oral Science One Ser.). 1979. 12.00 (*3-8055-3028-5*) S Karger.

Reprints. W. H. Bates. 100p. 1993. reprint ed. spiral bd. 9.00 (*0-7873-0079-9*) Hlth Research.

Reprints of Bette Hochberg's Textile Articles. 36p. 1982. pap. 4.95 (*0-9600990-7-7*) B Hochberg.

***Reprints of Old Rituals.** Albert Pike. 76p. 1996. pap. 24. 95 (*1-56459-983-3*) Kessinger Pub.

Reprints of Welsh Manuscripts, 7 vols., Set. Ed. by E. Stanton Roberts. Incl. Vol. 1. Llanstephan, Ms. 6. LC 78-72656. 24.50 (*0-404-18241-0*); Vol. 2. Peniarth, Ms. 67. LC 78-72656. 24.50 (*0-404-18242-9*); Vol. 3. Peniarth, Ms. 57. LC 78-72656. 24.50 (*0-404-18243-7*); Vol. 4. Peniarth, Ms. 76. LC 78-72656. 24.50 (*0-404-18244-5*); Vol. 5. Peniarth, Ms. 53. LC 78-72656. 24.50 (*0-404-18245-3*); Vol. 6. Peniarth, Ms. 49. LC 78-72656. 24.50 (*0-404-18246-1*); Vol. 7. Gwyneddon, Ms. 3. LC 78-72656. 24.50 (*0-404-18247-X*); LC 78-72656. (Celtic Language & Literature Ser.: Goidelic & Brythonic). reprint ed. 171.50 (*0-404-18240-2*) AMS Pr.

Reprisal. J. Ahern. 1985. pap. 2.95 (*0-8217-2393-6*) NAL-Dutton.

Reprisal. Jerry Ahern. (Survivalist Ser.: No. 11). 1986. mass mkt. 2.50 (*0-8217-1590-9*, Zebra Kensgtn) Kensgtn Pub Corp.

Reprise. Lela Gilbert. 1995. mass mkt. 5.99 (*0-8499-3878-3*) Word Pub.

Reprise: The Vera G. List Collection. Diana L. Johnson. (Twentieth Anniversary Exhibition Ser.). (Illus.). 64p. (Orig.). 1991. pap. 10.00 (*0-933519-21-4*) D W Bell Gallery.

Repro Lab: A Laboratory Manual for Animal Reproduction. 4th ed. A. M. Sorensen, Jr. (Illus.). 151p. 1979. pap. text ed. 14.95 (*0-89641-011-0*) American Pr.

Reproach of the Gospel: An Inquiry into the Apparent Failure of Christianity As a General Rule of Life & Conduct. James H. Peile. 1977. lib. bdg. 59.95 (*0-8490-2516-8*) Gordon Pr.

Reprobation Asserted. John Bunyan. pap. 1.29 (*0-87377-987-8*) GAM Pubns.

Reproduce Almost Anything: Basic Silicone Mold Making. Ben Ridge. (Illus.). 44p. (YA). (gr. 6 up). 1992. wbk. ed., pap. 39.95 incl. vhs (*0-9634267-0-2*) Cherokee Access.

Reproducibility & Accuracy of Mechanical Tests, STP- 626. Ed. by H. E. Bennett et al. (NBS Special Publication Ser.: No. 568). 152p. 1975. pap. 15.00 (*0-8031-0556-8*, 04-626000-23) ASTM.

***Reproducible Emergencies.** 1997. mass mkt. 10.95 (*0-590-33071-3*) Scholastic Inc.

Reproducible Posters for Children's Ministry. Ed. by Karen Brewer. (Illus.). 64p. (Orig.). 1995. pap. text ed. 5.99 (*0-7847-0250-0*, 03315) Standard Pub.

Reproducing Antique Furniture see Making Antique Furniture Reproductions: Instructions & Measured Drawings for 40 Classic Projects

Reproducing Families: The Political Economy of English Population History. David A. Levine. (Themes in the Social Sciences Ser.). 272p. 1987. pap. text ed. 20.95 (*0-521-33785-2*) Cambridge U Pr.

Reproducing Order: A Study of Police Patrol Work. Richard V. Ericson. (Canadian Studies in Criminology). 256p. 1982. pap. 20.95 (*0-8020-6475-2*) U of Toronto Pr.

Reproducing Persons: Issues in Feminist Bioethics. Laura M. Purdy. 304p. 1996. 42.50 (*0-8014-3243-X*); pap. 16. 95 (*0-8014-8322-0*) Cornell U Pr.

Reproducing Pianos Past & Present. Kent A. Holliday. LC 88-32561. (Studies in History & Interpretation of Music: Vol. 13). 240p. 1989. lib. bdg. 89.95 (*0-88946-438-3*) E Mellen.

Reproducing Rape: Domination Through Talk in the Courtroom. Gregory M. Matoesian. LC 92-40155. (Language & Legal Discourse Ser.). viii, 264p. 1993. pap. text ed. 15.95 (*0-226-51080-8*); lib. bdg. 40.00 (*0-226-51079-4*) U Ch Pr.

Reproducing the Future: Anthropology, Kinship, & the New Reproductive Technologies. Marilyn Strathern. 224p. (C). 1992. pap. 16.95 (*0-415-90556-7*, A7454, Routledge NY) Routledge.

Reproducing the Womb: Images of Childbirth in Science, Feminist Theory, & Literature. Alice E. Adams. (Illus.). 280p. 1994. 37.50 (*0-8014-2945-5*); pap. 15.95 (*0-8014-8161-9*) Cornell U Pr.

Reproduction. Ed. by Norman T. Adler et al. (Handbook of Behavioral Neurobiology Ser.: Vol. 7). 784p. 1985. 165. 00 (*0-306-41768-5*, Plenum Pr) Plenum.

Reproduction. Jenny Bryan. LC 93-2038. (Body Talk Ser.). (Illus.). 48p. (J). (gr. 5 up). 1993. lib. bdg. 13.95 (*0-87518-589-4*, Dillon Silver Burdett) Silver Burdett Pr.

Reproduction: Directory of Authors of New Medical & Scientific Reviews with Subject Index. Science & Life Consultants Association Staff. 160p. 1995. 47.50 (*0-7883-0610-3*); pap. 44.50 (*0-7883-0611-1*) ABBE Pubs Assn.

Reproduction: Endocrinology & Infertility. Yen. Date not set. text ed. write for info. (*0-7216-4454-6*) Saunders.

Reproduction & Aging. Andras Balazs et al. 331p. (C). 1974. text ed. 29.50 (*0-8422-7159-7*) Irvington.

Reproduction & Breeding Techniques for Laboratory Animals. Ed. by E. S. Hafez. LC 70-98498. 433p. reprint ed. pap. 123.50 (*0-317-29300-1*, 2055677) Bks Demand.

Reproduction & Culture of Milkfish. Ed. by Cheng-Sheng Lee & I-Chiu Liao. (Illus.). 226p. (Orig.). 1985. pap. write for info. (*0-9617016-1-7*) Oceanic Inst.

Reproduction & Development of Marine Invertebrates. Ed. by W. Herbert Wilson, Jr. et al. LC 93-41979. 1994. text ed. 75.00 (*0-8018-4777-X*) Johns Hopkins.

Reproduction & Development of Pacific Coast Marine Invertebrates. Megumi F. Strathmann. (Illus.). 640p. 1987. 50.00 (*0-295-96523-1*) U of Wash Pr.

Reproduction & Development of Sharks, Skates, Rays & Ratfishes. Ed. by Leo S. Demski. LC 93-30134. (Developments in Environmental Biology of Fishes Ser.: No. 14). 320p. (C). 1993. lib. bdg. 222.00 (*0-7923-2509-5*) Kluwer Ac.

Reproduction & Disease in Captive & Wild Animals. Ed. by G. R. Smith & J. P. Hearn. (Zoological Society of London Symposia Ser.). (Illus.). 224p. 1989. 79.00 (*0-19-854007-8*) OUP.

Reproduction & Social Organization in Sub-Saharan Africa. Ed. by Ron J. Lesthaeghe. 1989. 75.00 (*0-520-06363-5*) U CA Pr.

Reproduction & Succession: Studies in Anthropology, Law, & Society. Robin Fox. LC 92-13207. 270p. (C). 1992. 39.95 (*1-56000-067-8*) Transaction Pubs.

Reproduction & Succession: Studies in Anthropology, Law, & Society. Robin Fox. 270p. 1996. pap. text ed. 21.95 (*1-56000-924-1*) Transaction Pubs.

Reproduction, Ethics & the Law: Feminist Perspectives. Joan C. Callahan. LC 95-13722. 416p. 1995. 39.95 (*0-253-32938-8*); pap. 18.95 (*0-253-20996-X*) Ind U Pr.

Reproduction, Growth, & Development in Two Species of Cloud Forest Peromyscus from Southern Mexico. Eric A. Rickart. (Occasional Papers: No. 67). 22p. 1977. pap. 1.00 (*0-317-04907-0*) U KS Nat Hist Mus.

***Reproduction in Cattle.** 2nd rev. ed. A. R. Peters & P. J. Ball. (Illus.). 240p. (C). 1996. pap. text ed. 31.95 (*0-632-04109-9*) Iowa St U Pr.

Reproduction in Domestic Animals. 4th ed. Perry T. Cupps. 670p. (C). 1990. text ed. 79.00 (*0-12-196575-9*) Acad Pr.

Reproduction in Domestic Ruminants. Ed. by G. D. Niswender et al. (Journal of Reproduction & Fertility, Supplement Ser.: No. 34). 270p. 1987. 67.00 (*0-906545-12-9*) Portland FL.

Reproduction in Domesticated Animals. Ed. by G. J. King. (World Animal Science Ser.: Vol. B9). 590p. 1993. 357. 50 (*0-444-89530-2*) Elsevier.

Reproduction in Education, Society & Culture. 2nd ed. Pierre Bourdieu. (Theory, Culture & Society Ser.: Vol. 4). 256p. (C). 1990. text ed. 49.95 (*0-8039-8319-0*); pap. text ed. 22.00 (*0-8039-8320-4*) Sage.

Reproduction in Farm Animals. 6th ed. E. S. Hafez. (Illus.). 500p. 1993. text ed. 55.00 (*0-8121-1534-1*) Williams & Wilkins.

Reproduction in Fungi: Genetical & Physiological Aspects. Charles G. Elliot. LC 94-144585. 309p. (gr. 13). 1993. text ed. 66.95 (*0-412-49640-2*) Chapman & Hall.

Reproduction in Marginal Populations of the Hispid Cotton Rat (Sigmodon hispidus) Leroy R. McClenaghan & Michael S. Gaines. (Occasional Papers: No. 74). 16p. 1978. pap. 1.00 (*0-317-04888-0*) U KS Nat Hist Mus.

Reproduction in Poultry. Etches. 328p. 1996. pap. 50.00 (*0-85198-738-9*) OUP.

Reproduction in Sheep. Ed. by D. R. Lindsay & D. T. Pearce. 427p. 1985. text ed. 120.00 (*0-521-30659-0*) Cambridge U Pr.

Reproduction in the Female Mammal: Proceedings. Easter School in Agricultural Science (14th 1967, University of Nottingham) Staff. Ed. by G. E. Lamming & E. C. Amoroso. 595p. reprint ed. pap. 169.60 (*0-317-42116-6*, 2025756) Bks Demand.

Reproduction in the Pig. 2nd ed. Valley. (YA). Date not set. write for info. (*0-7506-1058-1*) Buttrwrth-Heinemann.

Reproduction in the United States, 1965. Charles F. Westoff. LC 78-120760. 423p. reprint ed. pap. 120.60 (*0-7837-0244-2*, 2040553) Bks Demand.

Reproduction, Larval Biology, & Recruitment of the Deep-Sea Benthos. Ed. by Craig M. Young & Kevin J. Eckelbarger. LC 93-38716. 1994. 95.00 (*0-231-08004-2*) Col U Pr.

Reproduction, Medicine & the Socialist State. Alena Hietlinger. 256p. 1987. text ed. 39.95 (*0-312-67403-1*) St Martin.

Reproduction of Color. 5th ed. R. W. Hunt. (Illus.). 814p. 1996. 90.00 (*0-86343-381-2*, Pub. by Fountain Pr UK) Fisher Bks.

Reproduction of Daily Life. Fredy Perlman. 1969. pap. 1.00 (*0-934868-17-4*) Black & Red.

Reproduction of Marine Invertebrates: General Aspects. Ed. by Arthur C. Giese et al. (Seeking Unity in Diversity Ser.). 1987. text ed. 65.00 (*0-940168-08-1*) Boxwood.

Reproduction of Marine Invertebrates: Lophorphorates, Echinoderms, Vol. VI. Ed. by Arthur C. Giese et al. 1991. reprint ed. text ed. 65.00 (*0-940168-09-X*) Boxwood.

Reproduction of Mothering: Psychoanalysis & the Sociology of Gender. Nancy Chodorow. 263p. 1978. pap. 16.00 (*0-520-03892-4*) U CA Pr.

Reproduction of Profiles. Rosmarie Waldrop. LC 87-110380. 96p. 1987. 19.95 (*0-8112-1044-8*); pap. 9.95 (*0-8112-1045-6*, NDP649) New Directions.

Reproduction of Social Control: A Study of Prison Workers at San Quentin. Barbara A. Owen. LC 87-36113. 168p. 1988. text ed. 49.95 (*0-275-92818-7*, C2818, Praeger Pubs) Greenwood.

Reproduction Photography for Lithography. Eric Chambers. 339p. reprint ed. pap. 96.70 (*0-7837-0362-7*, 2040684) Bks Demand.

Reproduction, Sexuality, & the Family. Ed. & Intro. by Karen Maschke. LC 96-39903. (Gender & American Law Ser.: Vol. 2). (Illus.). 375p. 1997. text ed. 74.00 (*0-8153-2516-9*) Garland.

Reproduction, Technology, & Rights. Ed. by James M. Humber & Robert F. Almeder. LC 84-640015. (Biomedical Ethics Reviews Ser.: No. 1995/96). 168p. 1996. 44.50 (*0-89603-326-0*) Humana.

Reproductions. James A. Stewart. 1966. pap. 0.89 (*1-56632-055-0*) Revival Lit.

Reproductions. 6th ed. Haddad's Fine Arts, Inc. Staff. LC 91-70862. (Illus.). 500p. 1991. 60.00 (*0-88445-021-X*) Haddads Fine Arts.

Reproductions of Reproduction: Imaging Symbolic Change. Judith Roof. LC 95-43749. 256p. (C). 1996. pap. 16.95 (*0-415-91243-1*); text ed. 59.95 (*0-415-91242-3*) Routledge.

***Reproductive Adaptation of Rice to Environmental Stress.** Y. Takeoka et al. (Developments in Crop Science Ser.: Vol. 22). 226p. 1992. 182.25 (*0-444-98678-2*) Elsevier.

Reproductive & Developmental Behavior in Sheep: An Anthology from "Applied Animal Ethology" Ed. by A. F. Fraser. (Developments in Animal & Veterinary Science Ser.: Vol. 18). 440p. 1985. 158.25 (*0-444-42444-X*) Elsevier.

Reproductive & Perinatal Epidemiology. Michele Kiely. 624p. 1990. 178.95 (*0-8493-5379-3*, RG627) CRC Pr.

Reproductive Anthropology: Descent Through Woman. Donald Gebbie. LC 80-42013. (Wiley-Medical Publication Ser.). (Illus.). 401p. reprint ed. pap. 114.30 (*0-8357-4549-X*, 2037448) Bks Demand.

Reproductive Behaviour of Insects: Individuals & Populations. Ed. by Winston J. Bailey & T. James Ridsdill-Smith. 400p. (gr. 13). 1991. text ed. 114.95 (*0-412-31280-8*, A4815) Chapman & Hall.

Reproductive Biology. Yu. 304p. 1994. 65.00 (*0-8493-4439-5*) CRC Pr.

Reproductive Biology & Evolution of Tropical Woody Angiosperms: A Symposium from the XIVth International Botanical Congress, Berlin, 1987. Ed. by Ghillean T. Prance. LC 89-13542. (Memoirs Ser.: No. 55). (Illus.). 195p. 1990. pap. 40.50 (*0-89327-348-1*) NY Botanical.

Reproductive Biology & Taxonomy of Vascular Plants: Report Conference Botanical Society of British Isles, Bir 1965. J. Hawkes. LC 66-17930. 1966. 88.00 (*0-08-013154-9*, Pub. by Pergamon Repr UK) Franklin.

Reproductive Biology of Invertebrates, Vol. 5. K. G. Adiyodi. Ed. by Rita G. Adiyodi. LC 88-645030. 511p. 1993. text ed. 275.00 (*0-471-93410-0*, Wiley-L) Wiley.

Reproductive Biology of Invertebrates: Asexual Propagation & Reproductive Strategies, Vol. 6. Ed. by K. G. Adiyodi & Rita G. Adiyodi. (Reproductive Biology of Invertebrates: Vol. 6, Pt. A). 410p. 1994. text ed. 237.00 (*0-471-94118-2*) Wiley.

Reproductive Biology of Invertebrates: Fertilization, Embryonic Development & Parental Care, Vol. 4. Ed. by K. G. Adiyodi & Rita G. Adiyodi. (Reproductive Biology of Invertebrates Ser.). 463p. 1989. text ed. 365. 00 (*0-471-92269-2*) Wiley.

Reproductive Biology of Invertebrates: Fertilization, Embryonic Development & Parental Care, Vol. 4. Ed. by K. G. Adiyodi & Rita G. Adiyodi. 527p. 1991. text ed. 275.00 (*0-471-92271-4*, Wiley-L) Wiley.

***Reproductive Biology of Invertebrates: Progress in Developmental Biology, Vol. 8.** Ed. by K. G. Adiyodi & Rita G. Adiyodi. text ed. write for info. (*0-471-96808-0*) Wiley.

Reproductive Biology of Invertebrates: Progress in Gamete & Accessory Sex Gland Biology, Vol. 7. Ed. by K. G. Adiyodi & Rita G. Adiyodi. (Reproductive Biology of Invertebrates Ser.). Date not set. text ed. 169.95 (*0-471-96648-7*) Wiley.

Reproductive Biology of Invertebrates Pt. B: Asexual Propagation & Reproductive Strategies, Vol. 6. Ed. by K. G. Adiyodi & Rita G. Adiyodi. LC 88-645030. 432p. 1995. text ed. 206.00 (*0-471-94119-0*) Wiley.

Reproductive Biology of Invertebrates, Vol. 1: Oogenesis, Oviposition & Oosorption. Ed. by K. G. Adiyodi & Rita G. Adiyodi. LC 81-16355. 796p. reprint ed. pap. 180.00 (*0-8357-6637-3*, 2035290) Bks Demand.

Reproductive Biology of Invertebrates, Vol. 2: Spermatogenesis & Sperm Function. Ed. by K. G. Adiyodi & Rita G. Adiyodi. LC 81-16355. (Illus.). 718p. reprint ed. pap. 180.00 (*0-7837-4728-4*, 2044512) Bks Demand.

Reproductive Biology of Invertebrates, Vol. 3: Accessory Sex Glands, Vol. 3. Ed. by K. G. Adiyodi & Rita G. Adyodi. 518p. 1993. text ed. 365.00 (*0-471-91466-5*) Wiley.

Reproductive Biology of Lizards on the American Samoan Islands. Terry D. Schwaner. (Occasional Papers: No. 86). 53p. 1980. 1.00 (*0-317-04887-2*) U KS Nat Hist Mus.

Reproductive Biology of South American Vertebrates. W. C. Hamlett. (Illus.). 400p. 1992. 130.95 (*0-387-97732-5*) Spr-Verlag.

Reproductive Biology of the Mare: Basic & Applied Aspects. 2nd rev. ed. O. J. Ginther. LC 91-75595. 642p. 1992. 93.00 (*0-9640072-1-5*) Equisrvs Pubng.

Reproductive Biology of the Primates. Ed. by P. Luckett. (Contributions to Primatology Ser.: Vol. 3). 284p. 1974. pap. 103.25 (*3-8055-1671-1*) S Karger.

Reproductive Change in Developing Countries: Insights from the World Fertility Survey. Ed. by John Cleland & John Hobcraft. (Illus.). 301p. 1985. 65.00 (*0-19-828465-9*) OUP.

Reproductive Cycles in Lizards & Snakes. Henry S. Fitch. (Miscellaneous Publications: No. 52). 247p. (C). 1970. reprint ed. pap. text ed. 29.95 (*0-89338-037-7*) U KS Nat Hist Mus.

***Reproductive Decisions: An Economic Analysis of Gelada Baboon Social Strategies.** Robin I. Dunbar. LC 84-42584. (Monographs on Behavior & Ecology). 276p. 1984. reprint ed. pap. 78.70 (*0-608-02925-4*, 2063990) Bks Demand.

Reproductive Ecology of Tropical Forest Plants. Ed. by K. S. Bawa & M. Hadley. (Man & the Biosphere Ser.: Vol. 7). (Illus.). 422p. 1990. 65.00 (*1-85070-268-3*) Prthnon Pub.

Reproductive Effects of Chemical, Physical, & Biologic Agents: REPROTOX. Armand Lione et al. LC 95-76708. 891p. 1995. text ed. 150.00 (*0-8018-5183-1*) Johns Hopkins.

Reproductive Endocrinology. Cowan. LC 96-28717. 448p. 1996. text ed. 79.00 (*0-397-51186-8*) Lppncott-Raven.

Reproductive Endocrinology. 4th ed. Yen. 1998. text ed. write for info. (*0-7216-6897-6*) Saunders.

Reproductive Endocrinology: Physiology, Pathophysiology & Clinical Management. 3rd ed. (Illus.). 1024p. 1991. text ed. 177.00 (*0-7216-3206-8*) Saunders.

Reproductive Endocrinology, Surgery, & Technology, 2 vols. Ed. by Eli Y. Adashi et al. (Illus.). 2560p. 1995. text ed. 299.00 (*0-7817-0203-8*) Lppncott-Raven.

Reproductive Endocrinology/Infertility Nursing. (Certified Nurse Examination Ser.: CN-23). pap. 23.95 (*0-8373-6123-0*) Nat Learn.

Reproductive Failure. Ed. by Alan H. DeCherney. LC 86-2654. (Illus.). 320p. reprint ed. pap. 91.20 (*0-7837-6253-4*, 2045965) Bks Demand.

Reproductive Fitness. 2nd ed. Ed. by C. R. Austin & R. V. Short. (Reproduction in Mammals Ser.: Bk. 4). (Illus.). 225p. 1985. pap. text ed. 25.95 (*0-521-31984-6*) Cambridge U Pr.

Reproductive Genetic Testing: Impact upon Women. Ed. by M. I. Evans. (Journal: Fetal Diagnosis & Therapy: Vol. 8, Suppl. 1, 1993). (Illus.). vi, 246p. 1993. pap. 42.75 (*3-8055-5715-9*) S Karger.

***Reproductive Hazards in the Workplace: Bibliography.** 166p. (C). 1996. reprint ed. pap. 30.00 (*0-7881-3380-2*) DIANE Pub.

Reproductive Hazards in the Workplace: Mending Jobs, Managing Pregnancies. Regina Kenan. LC 91-34582. 306p. 1993. pap. 19.95 (*1-56023-006-1*) Harrington Pk.

Reproductive Hazards in the Workplace: Mending Jobs, Managing Pregnancies. Regina Kenen. LC 91-34582. (Illus.). 302p. 1992. lib. bdg. 49.95 (*1-56024-154-3*) Haworth Pr.

Reproductive Hazards of Industrial Chemicals. Ed. by S. M. Barlow & F. M. Sullivan. 610p. 1982. text ed. 199.00 (*0-12-078960-4*) Acad Pr.

Reproductive Hazards of the Workplace. Frazier. LC 97-5940. (Industrial Health & Safety Ser.). 528p. 1997. text ed. 79.95 (*0-442-02042-2*) Van Nos Reinhold.

Reproductive Health: A Key to a Brighter Future: Special Programme of Research, Development, & Research Training in Human Reproduction Biennial Report 1990-1991. 20th anniversary ed. Ed. by J. Khanna et al. xiii, 171p. 1992. pap. text ed. 35.00 (*92-4-156153-X*, 1150385) World Health.

Reproductive Health: Global Issues. Ed. by S. Shan Ratnam et al. (F. I. G. O. Manual of Human Reproduction Ser.: Vol. 3). (Illus.). 224p. 1990. text ed. 35.00 (*1-85070-194-6*) Prthnon Pub.

Reproductive Health Care for Women & Babies: Policy & Ethics. Ed. by Richard Beard et al. (Illus.). 500p. 1995. 85.00 (*0-19-262530-6*) OUP.

***Reproductive Health in Developing Countries: Expanding Dimensions, Building Solutions.** Panel on Reproductive Health, National Research Council Staff. LC 97-4867. 420p. (C). 1997. text ed. 44.95 (*0-309-05644-6*, Joseph Henry Pr) Natl Acad Pr.

***Reproductive Health of Adolescents: A Strategy for Action: A Joint WHO/UNFPA/UNICEF Statement.** WHO Staff. 18p. 1989. 3.00 (*92-4-156125-4*) World Health.

***Reproductive Husbandry of Pythons & Boas.** Ross & Marzec. 27.00 (*0-614-29978-0*) Serpents Tale.

Reproductive Husbandry of Pythons & Boas. Richard Ross. (Illus.). 270p. 1990. 75.00 (*0-9631470-0-5*) Inst Herpeto Res.

Reproductive Immunology. Richard Bronson et al. 1000p. 1996. 199.95 (*0-86542-367-9*) Blackwell Sci.

***Reproductive Immunology.** Ed. by L. B. Olding. (Current Topics in Microbiology & Immunology Ser.: Vol. 222). (Illus.). 320p. 1997. 154.95 (*3-540-61888-0*) Spr-Verlag.

Reproductive Issues & the Aging Male. Ed. by Florence P. Haseltine et al. LC 93-37829. (AAAS Publications: No. 93-22S). 152p. 1994. pap. 39.95 (*0-87168-523-X*) AAAS.

Reproductive Issues for Persons with Physical Disabilities. Ed. by Florence P. Haseltine et al. (Illus.). 400p. (C). 1993. pap. text ed. 34.00 (*1-55766-111-1*, STK-1111) P H Brookes.

Reproductive Laws for the 1990s. Ed. by Sherrill Cohen & Nadine Taub. LC 88-25867. (Contemporary Issues in Biomedicine, Ethics, & Society Ser.). 480p. 1988. 39.50 (*0-89603-157-8*); pap. 19.50 (*0-89603-175-6*) Humana.

Reproductive Life: Advances in Research in Psychosomatic Obstetrics & Gynaecology. Ed. by K. Wijma & B. Von Schoultz. 708p. (C). 1992. text ed. 78.00 (*1-85070-446-5*) Prthnon Pub.

Reproductive Medicine & Surgery. Ed. by Edward E. Wallach & Howard A. Zacur. (Illus.). 1182p. (C). (gr. 13). 1994. text ed. 155.00 (*0-8016-7504-9*) Mosby Yr Bk.

An Asterisk (*) at the beginning of an entry indicates that the title is appearing in BIP for the first time.

R

Reproductive Medicine & the Law. Ed. by A. Templeton & D. Cusine. (Illus.). 167p. 1990. text ed. 71.00 (*0-443-04410-4*) Churchill.

Reproductive Neureoendocrinology of Aging & Drug Abuse. Ed. by Dipak K. Sarkar & Charles D. Barnes. 300p. 1994. 95.95 (*0-8493-2451-3*, 2451) CRC Pr.

Reproductive Pathology of Domestic Mammals. Kenneth McEntee. 401p. 1990. text ed. 119.00 (*0-12-483375-6*) Acad Pr.

Reproductive Physiology. Ed. by A. Rosenfield et al. (F. I. G. O. Manual of Human Reproduction Ser.: Vol. 1). (Illus.). 120p. 1990. text ed. 35.00 (*1-85070-192-X*) Prthnon Pub.

Reproductive Physiology of Marsupials. C. Hugh Tyndale-Biscoe & Marilyn Renfree. (Monographs on Marsupial Biology). (Illus.). 507p. 1987. text ed. 140.00 (*0-521-25285-7*); pap. text ed. 49.95 (*0-521-33792-5*) Cambridge U Pr.

Reproductive Physiology of Vertebrates. 2nd ed. Ari Van Tienhoven. (Comstock Bk.). (Illus.). 491p. 1983. 59.50 (*0-8014-1281-1*) Cornell U Pr.

Reproductive Potential & Fertility Control. Ed. by Anne Walker & Catherine A. Niven. (Psychology of Reproduction Ser.: Vol. 1). 208p. 1995. pap. 32.50 (*0-7506-2249-0*) Buttrwrth-Heinemann.

Reproductive Processes & Contraception. Ed. by Kenneth W. McKerns. LC 80-20744. (Biochemical Endocrinology Ser.). 752p. 1981. 120.00 (*0-306-40534-2*, Plenum Pr) Plenum.

Reproductive Revolution: The Role of Contraception & Education in Population & Development. Pramilla Senanayake. (Illus.). 144p. (Orig.). 1994. pap. 25.00 (*1-85070-650-6*) Prthnon Pub.

Reproductive Rights: A Bibliography. Ed. by Joan Nordquist. (Contemporary Social Issues: A Bibliographic Ser.: No. 9). 60p. 1988. pap. 15.00 (*0-937855-17-0*) Ref Rsch Serv.

Reproductive Rights & Wrongs: The Global Politics of Population Control. Betsy Hartmann. 400p. 1994. pap. 18.00 (*0-89608-491-4*) South End Pr.

Reproductive Rights & Wrongs: The Global Politics of Population Control. rev. ed. Betsy Hartmann. 400p. 1994. 40.00 (*0-89608-492-2*) South End Pr.

Reproductive Risks & Prenatal Diagnosis. Mark I. Evans. (Illus.). 369p. (C). 1991. text ed. 105.00 (*0-8385-8396-2*, A8396-2) Appleton & Lange.

Reproductive Rituals: Perceptions of Fertility in Britain from the Sixteenth Century to the Nineteenth Century. Angus McLaren. 208p. (Orig.). 1985. pap. 13.95 (*0-416-37460-3*, NO. 9340) Routledge Chapman & Hall.

Reproductive Science, Genetics, & Birth Control. Ed. by Philip K. Wilson. LC 96-794. (Childbirth Ser.: Vol. 4). (Illus.). 448p. 1996. reprint ed. text ed. 80.00 (*0-8153-2233-X*) Garland.

Reproductive Seasonality in Teleosts: Environmental Influence. Munro & Scott. 264p. 1990. 217.00 (*0-8493-6875-8*, QL) CRC Pr.

Reproductive Success: Studies of Individual Variation in Contrasting Breeding Systems. T. H. Clutton-Brock. (Illus.). 512p. 1988. pap. text ed. 35.00 (*0-226-11059-1*); lib. bdg. 90.00 (*0-226-11058-3*) U Ch Pr.

Reproductive System. Regina Avraham. (Encyclopedia of Health Ser.). (Illus.). 128p. (YA). (gr. 7 up). 1991. lib. bdg. 19.95 (*0-7910-0025-7*) Chelsea Hse.

Reproductive System. Braem. 1994. pap. text ed. 19.95 (*1-878576-32-1*) Flash Anatomy Inc.

Reproductive System. Virginia B. Silverstein. (Human Body Systems Ser.). (Illus.). 96p. (J). (gr. 5-8). 1994. lib. bdg. 16.98 (*0-8050-2838-2*) TFC Bks NY.

***Reproductive System: The Human Body.** Steve Parker. LC 96-29685. (J). 1997. 24.26 (*0-8172-4806-4*) Raintree Pr.

Reproductive System see CIBA Collection of Medical Illustrations

Reproductive System Course. Competence Assurance Systems Staff. (Illus.). 1984. pap. text ed. 45.00 (*0-89147-107-3*) CAS.

***Reproductive Technologies.** Annette Burfoot. 800p. Date not set. text ed. 100.00 (*0-8153-0148-0*) Garland.

Reproductive Technologies. Carol Wekesser. (Current Controversies Ser.). 192p. (J). (gr. 5-12). 1996. pap. text ed. 12.96 (*1-56510-376-9*); lib. bdg. 20.96 (*1-56510-377-7*) Greenhaven.

Reproductive Technologies, Marriage & the Church: Proceedings of 1988 Bishops' Workshop. Ed. by Donald G. McCarthy. LC 88-28997. 318p. (Orig.). 1988. pap. 17.95 (*0-935372-23-7*) Pope John Ctr.

Reproductive Technology: A Research Guide to the Legal Status of the Frozen Human Embryo. Timothy Coppo. LC 95-33288. (Legal Research Guides Ser.: Vol. 25). 61p. 1996. 39.50 (*0-89941-982-8*, 308900) W S Hein.

***Reproductive Tissue Banking: Scientific Principles.** Ed. by Armand Karow & John K. Critser. LC 96-43738. (Illus.). 472p. 1997. boxed 99.00 (*0-12-399770-4*, AP Prof) Acad Pr.

***Reproductive Toxicology.** Ed. by M. Richardson. (Illus.). iv, 306p. 1993. 125.00 (*3-527-28561-X*, VCH) Wiley.

Reproductive Toxicology & Infertility. Ed. by Anthony R. Scialli & Michael J. Zinaman. LC 92-49769. 352p. 1992. text ed. 85.00 (*0-07-105438-3*) McGraw-Hill HPD.

Reproductive Tract Infections. Ed. by A. Germain et al. (Reproductive Biology Ser.). (Illus.). (C). 1992. text ed. 105.00 (*0-306-44241-8*, Plenum Pr) Plenum.

Reproductive Versatility in the Grasses. G. P. Chapman. 286p. (C). 1990. text ed. 100.00 (*0-521-38060-X*) Cambridge U Pr.

Reproductively Active Chemicals. Richard J. Lewis, Sr. 1100p. 1991. text ed. 159.95 (*0-442-31878-2*) Van Nos Reinhold.

Reprogramming Pain: Transform Pain & Suffering into Health & Success. Barry B. Bittman. LC 95-42990. (Developments in Clinical Psychology Ser.). 220p. 1996. pap. 39.50 (*1-56750-208-3*); text ed. 73.25 (*1-56750-207-5*) Ablex Pub.

Reprographic Chemicals & Inks: Changing Environments. 181p. 1992. 2,450.00 (*0-89336-898-9*, C-153) BCC.

***Reprographic Methods.** K. Rowlatt. 1986. pap. text ed. write for info. (*0-582-41324-9*, Pub. by Longman UK) Longman.

Reprographic Services in Libraries: Organization & Administration. Charles G. LaHood & Robert C. Sullivan. LC 75-25585. (LTP Publication Ser.: No. 19). 80p. reprint ed. pap. 25.00 (*0-317-26573-3*, 2023954) Bks Demand.

Reprographics. 3rd ed. William R. Pasewark. (KH - Office Machines Ser.). 1984. pap. 16.95 (*0-538-11910-1*) S-W Pub.

Reprography & Copyright Law. L. H. Hattery & G. P. Bush. 1964. 12.50 (*0-934454-71-X*) Lubrecht & Cramer.

Repromulgation of Ordinances: A Fraud on the Constitution of India. D. C. Wadhwa. (Gokhale Institute Studies: No. 66). (Illus.). 281p. 1983. text ed. 35.00 (*0-86131-432-8*, Pub. by Orient Longman Ltd II) Apt Bks.

Reps! The World's Hottest Body-Building Routines. Robert Kennedy. LC 85-17223. (Illus.). 192p. (Orig.). 1985. pap. 12.95 (*0-8069-6250-X*) Sterling.

ReptAlphabet Encyclopedia. Keith A. McConnell. (NaturEncyclopedia Ser.). (Illus.). 48p. (Orig.). (J). (gr. 4 up). 1984. pap. 5.95 (*0-88045-045-2*) Stemmer Hse.

Reptile. Colin McCarthy & Nick Arnold. LC 90-4890. (Eyewitness Bks.: No. 27). (Illus.). 64p. (J). (gr. 5 up). 1991. 19.00 (*0-679-80783-7*) Knopf Bks Yng Read.

Reptile. Colin McCarthy & Nick Arnold. LC 90-4890. (Eyewitness Bks.: No. 27). (Illus.). 64p. (J). (gr. 5 up). 1991. lib. bdg. 20.99 (*0-679-90783-1*) Knopf Bks Yng Read.

***Reptile & Amphibian Magazine, 1996-1997 Directory: The Herpetology Sourcebook.** 20.00 (*0-614-30001-0*) Serpents Tale.

Reptile & Amphibian Parasites. Eric Rundquist. (Illus.). 64p. 1995. pap. 9.95 (*0-7938-0276-8*, RE123) TFH Pubns.

***Reptile & Amphibian Study.** (Illus.). 80p. (YA). (gr. 6-12). 1993. pap. 2.40 (*0-8395-3288-1*, 33288) BSA.

Reptile & Amphibian Variants: Colors, Patterns, & Scales. Bernard Bechtel. LC 94-6665. (Illus.). 224p. 1995. 64.50 (*0-89464-862-4*) Krieger.

***Reptile & the Amphibian Problem Solver: Practical & Expert Advice on Keeping Snakes & Lizards.** Robert Davies. 1997. 29.95 (*1-56465-194-0*) Tetra Pr.

Reptile Ball. Jacqueline K. Ogburn. LC 96-7468. (Illus.). (J). 1997. pap. 14.99 (*0-8037-1731-8*); lib. bdg. write for info. (*0-614-14342-X*) Dial Bks Young.

***Reptile Ball.** Jacqueline K. Ogburn. LC 96-9628. (Illus.). (J). 1997. pap. 14.89 (*0-8037-1732-6*) Dial Bks Young.

Reptile Care: An Atlas of Diseases & Treatments, Vols. I & II. Fredric L. Frye. (TS Ser.: No. 165). (Illus.). 637p. 1991. text ed. 199.95 (*0-86622-214-6*, TS-165) TFH Pubns.

Reptile Clinician's Handbook. Fredric L. Frye. LC 92-23869. 288p. 1995. pap. 28.50 (*0-89464-948-5*) Krieger.

Reptile Discovery Library, 6 bks., Set, Reading Level 2. Louise Martin. (Illus.). 144p. (J). (gr. k-5). 1989. Set. lib. bdg. 71.60 (*0-86592-573-9*) Rourke Corp.

Reptile Diseases. Rolf Hackbarth. Tr. by U. Erich Friese from GER. (KW Ser.). (Illus.). 128p. 1990. lib. bdg. 9.95 (*0-86622-824-1*, KW-197) TFH Pubns.

***Reptile Ear: Its Structure & Function.** Ernest G. Wever. LC 78-51204. 1037p. 1978. reprint ed. pap. 180.00 (*0-608-02924-6*, 2063989) Bks Demand.

Reptile Egg-Shells SEM Atlas. Hermann Schleich & Werner Kastle. LC 88-7220. (Illus.). 123p. 1988. lib. bdg. 65.00 (*0-89574-258-6*) G F Verlag.

Reptile Gardens Souvenir Book. (Orig.). pap. text ed. write for info. (*1-56944-066-2*) Terrell Missouri.

Reptile Journalism: The Official Polish-Language Press under the Nazis, 1939-1945. Lucjan Dobroszycki. LC 94-17013. 1995. 25.00 (*0-300-05277-4*) Yale U Pr.

Reptile Keeper's Handbook. Susan M. Barnard. (Illus.). 252p. (Orig.). (C). 1996. pap. 58.50 (*0-89464-933-7*) Krieger.

Reptile Medicine & Surgery. Douglas R. Mader. LC 95-9672. (Illus.). 624p. 1995. text ed. 93.00 (*0-7216-5208-5*) Saunders.

Reptile World. Ian F. Spellerberg. (Mysteries & Marvels Ser.). (Illus.). 32p. (J). (gr. 4-7). 1985. pap. 5.95 (*0-86020-845-1*, Usborne); lib. bdg. 14.95 (*0-88110-174-5*, Usborne) EDC.

Reptiles. (Science Safari Ser.). 20p. (J). (gr. k up). 1990. 4.95 (*0-88679-823-X*) Educ Insights.

***Reptiles.** (Eyewitness Bks.). (SPA.). (J). 1997. 19.99 (*84-372-3761-0*) Random.

Reptiles. B. Armstrong. (Science Ser.). 32p. (J). (gr. 1-6). 1988. 3.95 (*0-88160-164-0*, LW 269) Learning Wks.

Reptiles. Donna Bailey. LC 89-21756. (Facts about Ser.). (Illus.). 48p. (J). (gr. 2-5). 1990. pap. 4.95 (*0-8114-6627-2*); lib. bdg. 24.26 (*0-8114-2507-X*) Raintree Steck-V.

Reptiles. Lois Ballard. LC 81-38525. (New True Bks.). (Illus.). 48p. (J). (gr. k-4). 1982. pap. 5.50 (*0-516-41644-8*); lib. bdg. 19.00 (*0-516-01644-X*) Childrens.

Reptiles. June Chatfield. (Illus.). 16p. (J). 1995. 10.99 (*0-89577-801-7*) RD Assn.

Reptiles. Carson Creagh. LC 95-24477. (Discoveries Ser.). (Illus.). 64p. (J). (gr. 3 up). 1996. 15.00 (*0-8094-9247-4*) Time-Life.

***Reptiles.** Mark Lambert. LC 97-18505. 1997. write for info. (*0-7894-2046-5*) DK Pub Inc.

***Reptiles.** Beatrice MacLeod. LC 97-20188. (Wonderful World of Animals Ser.). (Illus.). 1997. lib. bdg. write for info. (*0-8368-1958-6*) Gareth Stevens Inc.

Reptiles. Jenny Markert. (Nature Bks.). 32p. (J). (gr. 2-6). 1992. lib. bdg. 22.79 (*0-89565-850-X*) Childs World.

Reptiles. Giuseppe Minelli. LC 86-32907. (History of Life on Earth Ser.). (Illus.). 64p. 1987. 15.95 (*0-8160-1558-9*) Facts on File.

Reptiles. Judy Nayer. (At Your Fingertips Ser.). (Illus.). 10p. (J). (ps-3). 1992. bds. 6.95 (*1-56293-220-9*) McClanahan Bk.

Reptiles. Edward R. Ricciuti. LC 93-19227. (Our Living World Ser.). (Illus.). 64p. (J). (gr. 4-8). 1993. lib. bdg. 18. 95 (*1-56711-047-9*) Blackbirch.

Reptiles. Joy Richardson. LC 92-32912. (Picture Science Ser.). (Illus.). 32p. (J). (gr. 2-4). 1993. lib. bdg. 20.00 (*0-531-14254-X*) Watts.

Reptiles. Eileen Spinelli. (Childrens' Nature Library). (Illus.). 64p. (J). (gr. k-4). 1992. lib. bdg. 14.95 (*1-878363-88-3*, HTS Bks) Forest Hse.

Reptiles. Philip Steele. LC 90-42017. (Pocket Facts Ser.). (Illus.). 32p. (J). (gr. 5-6). 1991. lib. bdg. 11.95 (*0-89686-582-7*, Crstwood Hse) Silver Burdett Pr.

Reptiles. Lynn M. Stone. LC 92-34488. (Predators Ser.). (J). 1993. 12.67 (*0-86625-437-4*); 9.50 (*0-685-66263-2*) Rourke Pubns.

***Reptiles.** Lynn M. Stone. LC 96-52188. (Animal Kingdom Ser.). (J). 1997. write for info. (*1-55916-190-6*) Rourke Bk Co.

***Reptiles.** Lynn M. Stone. LC 97-16384. (Desert Animals Ser.). (J). 1997. write for info. (*0-86625-630-X*) Rourke Pubns.

Reptiles: An Educational Coloring Book. Spizzirri Publishing Co. Staff. Ed. by Linda Spizzirri. (Illus.). 32p. (J). (gr. 1-8). 1981. pap. 1.99 (*0-86545-031-5*) Spizzirri.

Reptiles - Superdoodles. Beverly Armstrong. LC 93-80433. 32p. (J). (gr. 1-6). 1994. 4.95 (*0-88160-229-9*, LW324) Learning Wks.

Reptiles & Amphibians. Ed. by Christine J. Dillon. (My First Report Ser.). (Illus.). 36p. (J). (gr. 1-3). 1995. pap. 5.95 (*0-913717-77-0*, 2225) Hewitt Res Fnd.

Reptiles & Amphibians, 2 vols. Catherine H. Howell. LC 93-10735. (Nature Library). (J). (gr. 1-3). 1994. 10.50 (*0-87044-891-9*) Natl Geog.

Reptiles & Amphibians. Joanne Mattern. LC 92-20189. (Illus.). 24p. (J). (gr. 4-7). 1992. pap. 1.95 (*0-8167-2954-9*) Troll Communs.

Reptiles & Amphibians. Mark O'Shea. (C). 1992. 21.00 (*0-907649-52-1*, Pub. by Expedit Advisory Centre UK) St Mut.

Reptiles & Amphibians. Louis Sabin. LC 84-8445. (Illus.). 32p. (J). (gr. 3-6). 1985. pap. text ed. 3.50 (*0-8167-0295-0*) Troll Communs.

Reptiles & Amphibians. Herbert S. Zim & Hobart M. Smith. (Golden Guide Ser.). (Illus.). 160p. 1987. pap. 5.50 (*0-307-24057-6*, Golden Pr) Western Pub.

Reptiles & Amphibians: Birth & Growth. Andres L. Ruiz. (Illus.). 64p. (J). 1996. 17.95 (*0-8069-6127-9*) Sterling.

Reptiles & Amphibians: Care, Behavior, Reproduction. Elke Zimmerman. (PS Ser.). (Illus.). 384p. 1993. text ed. 39.95 (*0-86622-541-2*, PS876) TFH Pubns.

Reptiles & Amphibians: Care in Captivity. E. Rundquist. (Illus.). 192p. 1994. 29.95 (*0-7938-0298-9*, TS211) TFH Pubns.

Reptiles & Amphibians Coloring Book. Thomas C. Quirk. (Illus.). (J). (gr. k-3). 1981. pap. 2.95 (*0-486-24111-4*) Dover.

***Reptiles & Amphibians Eastern/Central N. America.** Conant & Collins. (Peterson Field Guide Ser.). 24.95 (*0-614-29998-5*) Serpents Tale.

***Reptiles & Amphibians Eastern/Central N. America.** Conant & Collins. (Peterson Field Guide Ser.). pap. 16. 95 (*0-614-29999-3*) Serpents Tale.

Reptiles & Amphibians of Alabama. Robert H. Mount. LC 95-46581. (Illus.). 368p. 1996. pap. text ed. 19.95 (*0-8173-0054-6*) U of Ala Pr.

Reptiles & Amphibians of Australia. 5th ed. Harold G. Cogger. LC 91-34103. (Illus.). 704p. 1992. 99.95 (*0-8014-2739-8*) Cornell U Pr.

Reptiles & Amphibians of South Australia. Edgar R. Waite. LC 93-83046. 290p. 1994. 32.00 (*0-916984-30-3*) Krieger.

Reptiles & Amphibians of the Great Lakes Basin. James Harding. (C). 1995. pap. 19.95 (*0-472-06628-5*) U of Mich Pr.

Reptiles & Amphibians of the West. Vinson Brown. LC 74-3204. (Illus.). 79p. 1974. pap. text ed. 7.95 (*0-87961-028-X*) Naturegraph.

Reptiles & Amphibians Punch-Out Stencils. John E. Cymerman. (Illus.). (J). (gr. 4-7). 1993. pap. 3.95 (*0-486-27665-1*) Dover.

Reptiles and Amphibians Sticker Book: Reptiles & Amphibians. Kathie B. Smith. (Wonder of Nature Ser.). (Illus.). 16p. (J). (gr. k-4). 1996. 2.99 (*0-689-80688-4*, Litl Simon S&S) S&S Childrens.

Reptiles & Herbivory. G. King. (Illus.). 220p. 1996. 69.95 (*0-412-46110-2*) Chapman & Hall.

Reptiles Do the Strangest Things. Leonora Hornblow & Arthur Hornblow. LC 70-106500. (Step-up Bks.: No. 20). (Illus.). (J). (gr. 2-4). 1970. 6.95 (*0-394-80074-5*) Random Bks Yng Read.

Reptiles Dot to Dot: Educational Activity-Coloring Book. Peter M. Spizzirri. Ed. by Linda Spizzirri. (Illus.). 32p. (J). (gr. k-3). 1992. pap. 1.25 (*0-86545-207-5*) Spizzirri.

***Reptiles of British Columbia.** Patrick T. Gregory & R. Wayne Campbell. (Illus.). 112p. 1984. pap. 9.95 (*0-7718-9457-0*, Pub. by U BC Pr) U of Wash Pr.

Reptiles of North America. Hobart M. Smith & Edmund Brodie. (Golden Field Guide Ser.). (Illus.). 240p. (Orig.). 1982. pap. 11.95 (*0-307-13666-3*) Western Pub.

Reptiles of North Carolina. William M. Palmer & Alvin L. Braswell. LC 94-5711. (Illus.). 1995. 49.95 (*0-8078-2158-6*) U of NC Pr.

***Reptiles of Oregon & Washington.** Ed. by Robert M. Storm & William P. Leonard. (Trailside Ser.). (Illus.). 176p. (Orig.). 1995. pap. 16.95 (*0-914516-12-4*) Seattle Audubon Soc.

Reptiles of Virginia. Joseph C. Mitchell. LC 93-42002. (Illus.). 384p. 1994. 40.00 (*1-56098-356-6*) Smithsonian.

***Reptiles of Virginia.** Joseph C. Mitchell. (Illus.). 368p. (Orig.). 1997. pap. 24.95 (*1-56098-754-5*) Smithsonian.

Reptiles Primitivos. Chelsea House Publishers Staff. 1996. lib. bdg. 15.95 (*0-7910-4034-8*) Chelsea Hse.

Reptilia & Amphibia: Loricata, TeStudines, Vol. 1. 2nd ed. Malcolm A. Smith. Ed. by A. B. Shipley. (Fauna of British India Ser.). (Illus.). xxviii, 185p. (C). 1981. reprint ed. 20.00 (*0-88065-216-0*, Messers Today & Tomorrow) Scholarly Pubns.

Reptilia & Amphibia: Sauria, Vol. 2. 2nd ed. Malcolm A. Smith. Ed. by A. B. Shipley. (Fauna of British India Ser.). (Illus.). ix, 440p. (C). 1981. reprint ed. 35.00 (*0-88065-217-9*, Messers Today & Tomorrow) Scholarly Pubns.

Reptilia & Amphibia: Serpentes, Vol. 3. 2nd ed. Malcolm A. Smith. Ed. by A. B. Shipley. (Fauna of British India Ser.). (Illus.). xii, 583p. (C). 1981. reprint ed. 50.00 (*0-88065-218-7*, Messers Today & Tomorrow) Scholarly Pubns.

Reptilia & Batrachia. John Anderson. (Zoology of Egypt Ser.: No. 1). (Illus.). 1965. reprint ed. 250.00 (*3-7682-0240-2*) Lubrecht & Cramer.

Republic. Mitchell. (Book Notes Ser.). (C). 1985. pap. 2.50 (*0-8120-3436-8*) Barron.

Republic. Plato. Ed. by Terence H. Irwin. Tr. by A. D. Lindsay. 404p. 1993. pap. 7.95 (*0-460-87382-2*, Everyman's Classic Lib) C E Tuttle.

Republic. Plato. Tr. by Robin A. Waterfield. LC 92-38853. (World's Classics Ser.). 558p. 1993. 30.00 (*0-19-212604-0*) OUP.

Republic. Plato. Tr. by Benjamin E. Jowett. 1955. pap. 6.95 (*0-394-70128-3*, Vin) Random.

Republic. Plato. Tr. by Alexander D. Lindsay. LC 92-52932. 368p. (ENG & GRE.). 1992. 17.00 (*0-679-41330-8*, Everymans Lib) Knopf.

Republic. Plato. Ed. & Tr. by Raymond Larson. LC 77-86034. (Crofts Classics Ser.). 336p. (C). 1979. pap. text ed. write for info. (*0-88295-118-1*) Harlan Davidson.

Republic. Plato. Tr. by Benjamin Jowett. (Great Books in Philosophy). 397p. 1986. pap. 9.95 (*0-87975-345-5*) Prometheus Bks.

Republic. Plato. Tr. by Benjamin E. Jowett. LC 41-51966. 397p. 1983. 15.50 (*0-394-60813-5*, Modern Lib) Random.

Republic. Plato. Tr. by Benjamin E. Jowett. LC 90-55688. 416p. 1991. pap. 10.00 (*0-679-73387-6*, Vin) Random.

Republic. R. Sterling & Scott. 320p. 1996. pap. 10.95 (*0-393-31467-7*, Norton Paperbks) Norton.

Republic. rev. ed. Plato. Tr. & Intro. by Desmond Lee. (Classics Ser.). 472p. (YA). (gr. 9 up). 1955. pap. 7.95 (*0-14-044048-8*, Penguin Classics) Viking Penguin.

Republic. 2nd ed. Plato. Tr. by G. M. Grube from GRE. LC 92-21578. 320p. (C). 1992. pap. text ed. 6.95 (*0-87220-136-8*); lib. bdg. 34.95 (*0-87220-137-6*) Hackett Pub.

Republic. Plato. Tr. & Intro. by Robin A. Waterfield. (World's Classics Ser.). (Illus.). 560p. 1994. reprint ed. pap. 6.95 (*0-19-282909-2*) OUP.

Republic, 2 vols., 1. Plato. (Loeb Classical Library: No. 237, 276). 552p. 1930. text ed. 18.95 (*0-674-99262-8*) HUP.

Republic, 2 vols., 2. Plato. (Loeb Classical Library: No. 237, 276). 614p. 1935. text ed. 18.95 (*0-674-99304-7*) HUP.

Republic, 2 vols., Vols. V & VI. Plato. No. 237, 276. write for info. (*0-318-53175-5*) HUP.

Republic: Decline & Future Promise. Archibald E. Roberts. 1975. write for info. (*0-318-61783-8*, Betsy Ross Pr) Comm Restore Const.

Republic: Odyssey of Philosophy. Jacob Howland. LC 93-17562. (Twayne's Masterwork Studies: No. 122). 160p. 1993. 23.95 (*0-8057-8354-7*, Twayne); pap. 13.95 (*0-8057-8378-4*, Twayne) Scribnrs Ref.

Republic see Roman Silver Coins

Republic & Other Works. Incl. Symposiums. Plato. Tr. by Benjamin E. Jowett. 1960. pap. (*0-318-51739-6*); Parmenides. Plato. Tr. by Benjamin E. Jowett. 1960. pap. (*0-318-51740-X*); Euthyphro. (*0-318-51741-8*); Apology. (*0-318-51742-6*); Crito. (*0-318-51743-4*); Phaedo. (*0-318-51744-2*); 560p. 1960. pap. 7.95 (*0-385-09497-3*, C12, Anchor NY) Doubleday.

Republic & the School: Horace Mann on the Education of Free Men. 7th ed. Ed. by Lawrence A. Cremin. LC 57-9102. (Classics in Education Ser.). (Orig.). 1957. pap. text ed. 7.00 (*0-8077-1206-X*) Tchrs Coll.

Republic Chapterplays: A Complete Filmography of the Serials Released by Republic Pictures Corporation, 1934-1955. R. M. Hayes. LC 92-50305. (Illus.). 176p. 1992. lib. bdg. 35.00 (*0-89950-665-8*) McFarland & Co.

Republic Expands see U. S. History - One

Republic Five. Plato. Ed. by Halliwell. 1992. pap. 24.95 (*0-85668-536-4*, Pub. by Aris & Phillips UK) David Brown.

Republic, If You Can Keep It: The Foundation of the American Presidency, 1700-1800. Michael P. Riccards. LC 86-29595. (Contributions in Political Science Ser.: No. 167). 242p. 1987. text ed. 55.00 (*0-313-25462-1*, RRE/, Greenwood Pr) Greenwood.

Republic in Danger: General Maurice Gamelin & the Politics of French Defence, 1933-1940. Martin S. Alexander. 560p. (C). 1993. text ed. 95.00 (*0-521-37234-8*) Cambridge U Pr.

Republic of Armenia Vol. 3: From London to Sevres, February - August 1920. Richard G. Hovannisian. LC 72-129613. (Illus.). 528p. 1995. 45.00 (*0-520-08803-4*) U CA Pr.

Republic of Armenia Vol. 4: Between Crescent & Sickle: Partition & Sovietization. Richard G. Hovannisian. LC 72-129613. (Illus.). 345p. 1995. 45.00 (*0-520-08804-2*) U CA Pr.

Republic of Art & Other Essays. T. J. Diffey. LC 90-192. (New Studies in Aesthetics: Vol. 6). 345p. (C). 1991. text ed. 49.95 (*0-8204-1433-6*) P Lang Pubng.

Republic of China in International Perspective. Ed. by Christopher J. Sigur. 63p. 1993. pap. (*0-87641-122-7*) Carnegie Ethics & Intl Affairs.

Republic of China on Taiwan 1949-1988. Ed. by Cecilia S. Chang. 229p. 1991. write for info. (*0-933423-03-9*) St Johns U Asian Studies.

Republic of China (Taiwan) A Study of the Educational System of the Republic of China & a Guide to the Academic Placement of Students in Educational Institutions of the United States. Patrick J. Kennedy. LC 78-324722. (World Education Ser.). 127p. reprint ed. pap. 36.20 (*0-317-26612-8*, 2024075) Bks Demand.

Republic of China Yearbook 1996. (Illus.). 1000p. 1996. 45.00 (*957-00-6659-8*, Pub. by Kwang Hwa MY) Intl Pubns Serv.

Republic of Choice: Law, Authority, & Culture. Lawrence M. Friedman. 256p. 1990. 34.50 (*0-674-76260-6*) HUP.

Republic of Choice: Law, Authority, & Culture. Lawrence M. Friedman. 256p. 1994. pap. text ed. 16.95 (*0-674-76261-4*, FRIREX) HUP.

Republic of Colombia: An Account of the Country, Its People, Its Institutions & Its Resources. Francis L. Petre. 1976. lib. bdg. 39.95 (*0-8490-2517-6*) Gordon Pr.

Republic of Costa Rica. Joaquin B. Calvo. (Costa Rica Ser.). 1979. lib. bdg. 59.95 (*0-8490-2996-1*) Gordon Pr.

Republic of Cousins: Women's Oppression in Mediterranean Society. Germaine Tillion. 182p. 1993. pap. 9.95 (*0-86356-010-5*, Pub. by Saqi Bks UK) Interlink Pub.

Republic of Cousins: Women's Oppression in Mediterranean Society. Germaine Tillion. 182p. 1996. 39.95 (*0-86356-100-4*, Pub. by Saqi Bks UK) Interlink Pub.

Republic of Cousins: Women's Oppression in Mediterranean Society. Germaine Tillion. Tr. by Quintin Hoare from FRE. Orig. Title: Le Harem et les Cousins. 181p. (Orig.). 1984. pap. 10.95 (*0-685-08871-5*) Evergreen Dist.

***Republic of Croatia: 1995 Election Observation Report.** Cathy Salay et al. LC 96-34859. 1996. write for info. (*1-879720-18-3*) Intl Fndt Elect.

Republic of De Gaulle, 1958-1969. Serge Berstein. Tr. by Peter Morris. (History of Modern France Ser.: No. 8). 264p. (C). 1993. text ed. 59.95 (*0-521-25239-3*) Cambridge U Pr.

Republic of Dreams: A Novel. Nelida Pinon. Tr. by Helen Lane from SPA. (Texas Pan American Ser.). 669p. 1991. reprint ed. pap. 17.95 (*0-292-77050-2*) U of Tex Pr.

Republic of Fear: Inside Story of Saddam's Iraq. Samir Al-Khalil. LC 90-52933. 336p. 1991. pap. 12.95 (*0-679-73502-X*) Pantheon.

Republic of Florida: The Most Embarrassing Book Ever Written. Mike Albergo. (Illus.). (Orig.). 1989. pap. write for info. (*0-318-64083-X*) M Albergo.

Republic of Florida: Title Says it All! Mike Albergo. 97p. (Orig.). 1993. pap. 7.95 (*0-9621364-0-9*) M Albergo.

***Republic of Genius: A Reconstruction of Nietzsche's Early Thought.** Quentin P. Taylor. 288p. 1997. 59.95 (*1-878822-94-2*) Univ Rochester Pr.

***Republic of Georgia: Assessment & Voter Information Campaign.** Scott Lansell et al. LC 96-3453. 1996. write for info. (*1-879720-17-5*) Intl Fndt Elect.

Republic of Haiti - Agroforestry & Watershed Management Project Artibonite River. 33.00 (*0-8270-3050-9*) OAS.

Republic of Images: A History of French Filmmaking. Alan L. Williams. (Illus.). 458p. 1992. 55.00 (*0-674-76267-3*); pap. text ed. 22.00 (*0-674-76268-1*) HUP.

Republic of India: Bourgeois Democracy in Transition. Achin Vanaik. 288p. (C). 1990. pap. 19.95 (*0-86091-504-2*, A4513, Pub. by Verso UK) Routledge Chapman & Hall.

Republic of India: The Development of its Laws & Constitution. Alan Gledhill. LC 77-98761. xii, 309p. 1970. reprint ed. text ed. 69.50 (*0-8371-2813-7*, GLRI, Greenwood Pr) Greenwood.

Republic of Ireland. rev. ed. Dennis B. Fradin. LC 83-20960. (Enchantment of the World Ser.). (Illus.). 128p. (J). (gr. 5-9). 1994. lib. bdg. 30.00 (*0-516-02767-0*) Childrens.

***Republic of Kazakstan: Transition of the State.** (Country Study Ser.). 288p. 1997. 16.95 (*0-8213-3902-8*, 13902) World Bank.

Republic of Korea: A Political & Economic Study. W. D. Reeve. LC 79-9857. 197p. 1979. reprint ed. text ed. 49.75 (*0-313-21265-1*, RERK, Greenwood Pr) Greenwood.

Republic of Korea 1984 Statistical Abstract, Vol. 1. Ed. by Thomas Stern. (Illus.). 45p. (Orig.). 1984. pap. 4.50 (*0-317-06992-6*) Korea Eco Inst.

Republic of Labor: Philadelphia Artisans & the Politics of Class, 1720-1830. Ronald Schultz. LC 92-21082. 328p. 1993. 55.00 (*0-19-507585-4*) OUP.

Republic of Letters, Vol. 1. James Smith. Date not set. write for info. (*0-393-03818-1*) Norton.

Republic of Letters, Vol. 2. James Smith. Date not set. write for info. (*0-393-03819-X*) Norton.

Republic of Letters, Vol. 3. James Smith. Date not set. write for info. (*0-393-03820-3*) Norton.

Republic of Letters: A Cultural History of the French Enlightenment. Dena Goodman. (Illus.). 352p. 1994. 45.00 (*0-8014-2968-4*) Cornell U Pr.

Republic of Letters: A Cultural History of the French Enlightenment. Dena Goodman. (Illus.). 352p. 1996. pap. 15.95 (*0-8014-8174-0*) Cornell U Pr.

Republic of Letters: A History of Postwar American Literary Opinion. Grant Webster. LC 79-4951. 400p. reprint ed. pap. 114.00 (*0-318-34951-5*, 2030748) Bks Demand.

Republic of Letters: Librarian of Congress Daniel J. Boorstin on Books, Reading, & Libraries, 1975-1987. Ed. by John Y. Cole. LC 88-600451. 128p. 1989. 17.50 (*0-8444-0629-5*) Lib Congress.

Republic of Letters: The Correspondence Between Thomas Jefferson & James Madison. Ed. by James M. Smith. (Illus.). 210p. 1995. 150.00 (*0-393-03691-X*) Norton.

Republic of Letters in America: The Correspondence of John Peale Bishop & Allen Tate. John P. Bishop. Ed. by Thomas D. Young & John J. Hindle. LC 80-5186. 240p. reprint ed. pap. 68.40 (*0-7837-5779-4*, 2045445) Bks Demand.

Republic of Love. Carol Shields. 368p. 1993. pap. 11.95 (*0-14-014990-2*, Penguin Bks) Viking Penguin.

Republic of Love. Carol Shields. Date not set. pap. write for info. (*0-14-099716-4*) NAL-Dutton.

Republic of Many Mansions: Foundations of American Religious Thought. Denise L. Carmody & John T. Carmody. 288p. (C). 1990. pap. 16.95 (*1-55778-392-6*) Paragon Hse.

Republic of Mass Culture: Journalism, Filmmaking, & Broadcasting in America since 1941. James L. Baughman. (American Moment Ser.). 256p. 1992. text ed. 40.00 (*0-8018-4276-X*); pap. text ed. 13.95 (*0-8018-4277-8*) Johns Hopkins.

***Republic of Mass Culture: Journalism, Filmmaking, & Broadcasting in America since 1941.** 2nd ed. James L. Baughman. LC 96-26395. (American Moment Ser.). 304p. 1997. text ed. 40.00 (*0-8018-5520-9*) Johns Hopkins.

***Republic of Mass Culture: Journalism, Filmmaking, & Broadcasting in America since 1941.** 2nd ed. James L. Baughman. LC 96-26395. (American Moment Ser.). 304p. 1997. pap. text ed. 14.95 (*0-8018-5521-7*) Johns Hopkins.

Republic of Mexico in Eighteen Seventy-Six: A Political & Ethnological Division of the Population, Character, Habits, Costumes & Vocations of Its Inhabitants. Antonio G. Cubas. (Mexico Ser.). 1979. lib. bdg. 59.95 (*0-8490-2997-X*) Gordon Pr.

Republic of Plato. Plato. 396p. 1951. pap. 9.95 (*0-19-500364-0*) OUP.

Republic of Plato. Tr. by Thomas Taylor. 309p. 1992. pap. 35.00 (*1-56459-024-0*) Kessinger Pub.

Republic of Plato. 2nd ed. Tr. & Intro. by Allan Bloom. LC 68-54141. 512p. 1991. pap. 15.00 (*0-465-06934-7*) Basic.

Republic of Rivers: Three Centuries of Nature Writing from Alaska & the Yukon. John A. Murray. (Illus.). 368p. 1990. 30.00 (*0-19-506102-0*) OUP.

Republic of Rivers: Three Centuries of Nature Writing from Alaska & the Yukon. Ed. by John A. Murray. (Illus.). 322p. 1992. pap. 9.95 (*0-19-507605-2*) OUP.

Republic of Signs: Liberal Theory & American Popular Culture. Anne Norton. LC 92-36749. 208p. (C). 1993. pap. text ed. 12.95 (*0-226-59513-7*); lib. bdg. 34.00 (*0-226-59512-9*) U Ch Pr.

Republic of St. Peter: The Birth of the Papal State, 680-825. Thomas F. Noble. LC 83-21870. (Middle Ages Ser.). (Illus.). 412p. 1984. pap. text ed. 20.95 (*0-8122-1239-8*) U of Pa Pr.

***Republic of Tajikistan: Recent Economic Developments.** Peter Keller. (IMF Staff Country Report Ser.: Vol. 96/55). (Illus.). 158p. pap. 45.10 (*0-608-04870-4*, 2065529) Bks Demand.

Republic of Tea: The Story of the Creation of a Business As Told Through the Personal Letters. Bill Rosenzweig. 336p. 1994. pap. 15.00 (*0-385-42057-9*) Doubleday.

Republic of Texas. Archie P. McDonald. (Texas History Ser.). (Illus.). 40p. (C). 1981. pap. text ed. 8.95 (*0-89641-073-0*) American Pr.

Republic of Texas, Second Class Headrights: March 2, 1836-October 1, 1837. Benjamin F. Purl. 261p. 1994. reprint ed. lib. bdg. 32.50 (*0-8328-3873-X*) Higginson Bk Co.

***Republic of the Dispossessed: The Exceptional Old-European Consensus in America.** Rowland Berthoff. LC 96-36884. 264p. 1997. spiral bd. 39.95 (*0-8262-1101-1*) U of Mo Pr.

Republic of the Future. Anna B. Dodd. 1968. reprint ed. lib. bdg. 19.75 (*0-8290-1922-7*) Irvington.

Republic of the Marshall Islands: An Emerging Nation - An Overview for Peace Corp Volunteers. Steve C. Smith. (Illus.). 81p. 1986. pap. 12.95 (*0-936731-03-6*) Devel Self Rel.

Republic of Turkey, an American Perspective: A Guide to U. S. Official Documents & Government-Sponsored Publications. Julian W. Witherell. LC 87-600428. 211p. 1988. 19.00 (*0-8444-0587-6*, 030-000-00208-3) Lib Congress.

Republic of Viet Nam Coins & Currency. Howard A. Daniel, III. LC 76-351167. (Catalog & Guidebook of Southeast Asian Coins & Currency Ser.: Vol. II, Pt. 2). (Illus.). 160p. (Orig.). 1992. pap. 29.95 (*1-879951-02-9*) Southeast Asian.

Republic of Vietnam Armed Forces. Dong Van Khuyen. 401p. 1994. pap. text ed. 39.50 (*0-923135-29-4*) Dalley Bk Service.

Republic of Whores. Josef Skvorecky. 1994. 21.00 (*0-88001-371-0*) Ecco Pr.

Republic of Whores. Josef Skvorecky. 1996. pap. 15.00 (*0-88001-428-8*) Ecco Pr.

***Republic of Wine.** Mo Yan. 1998. pap. 24.95 (*0-670-86965-1*) Viking Penguin.

Republic of Yemen: Health Sector Review. (Country Study Ser.). 96p. 1994. 7.95 (*0-8213-2777-1*, 12777) World Bank.

Republic or Empire: American Resistance to the Philippine War. D. B. Schirmer. (Illus.). 300p. 1972. pap. text ed. 18.95 (*0-87073-105-X*) Schenkman Bks Inc.

Republic P-47 Thunderbolt: The Final Chapter: Latin American Air Forces Service. Dan Hagedorn. Ed. by John W. Lambert. LC 91-62115. (Illus.). 64p. (C). 1991. pap. 14.95 (*0-9625860-1-3*) Phalanx Pub.

Republic Reborn: War & the Making of Liberal America, 1790-1820. Steven Watts. LC 87-4147. (New Studies in American Intellectual & Cultural History). 384p. 1989. reprint ed. pap. text ed. 16.95 (*0-8018-3941-6*) Johns Hopkins.

Republic, U. S. A. Cromwell Gibbons. 1965. 10.00 (*0-8159-6709-8*) Devin.

Republic vs. Autocracy: Poland-Lithuania & Russia, 1686-1697. Andrzej S. Kaminski. (Harvard Series in Ukrainian Studies). 350p. (C). 1992. 29.95 (*0-916458-45-8*); pap. 17.00 (*0-916458-49-0*) Harvard Ukrainian.

Republic 10. Plato. Ed. by Halliwell. (Classical Texts Ser.). 1986. 49.95 (*0-85668-405-8*, Pub. by Aris & Phillips UK); pap. 24.95 (*0-85668-406-6*, Pub. by Aris & Phillips UK) David Brown.

Republican & Fascist Germany: Themes & Variations in the History of Weimar & the Third Reich 1918-1945. John Hiden. 320p. (C). 1996. text ed. 66.50 (*0-582-49209-2*, Pub. by Longman UK); pap. text ed. 17.95 (*0-582-49210-6*, Pub. by Longman UK) Longman.

Republican Art & Ideology in Late Nineteenth- Century France. Miriam R. Levin. LC 85-21021. (Studies in the Fine Arts - Art Theory: No. 11). (Illus.). 355p. reprint ed. pap. 101.20 (*0-8357-1670-8*, 2070608) Bks Demand.

Republican Court. Rufus W. Griswold. LC 79-176498. (American History & Americana Ser.: No. 47). 1971. reprint ed. lib. bdg. 62.95 (*0-8383-1285-3*) M S G Haskell Hse.

Republican Crown: Lawyers & the Making of the State in Twentieth Century Britain. Joseph M. Jacob. 432p. 1996. text ed. 59.95 (*1-85521-725-2*, Pub. by Dartmth Pub UK) Ashgate Pub Co.

Republican Experiment, Eighteen Forty-Eight to Eighteen Fifty-Two. Maurice Agulhon. LC 82-23461. (Cambridge History of Modern France Ser.: No. 2). (Illus.). 211p. 1983. pap. text ed. 19.95 (*0-521-28988-2*) Cambridge U Pr.

Republican France: Divided Loyalties. Peggy A. Phillips. LC 92-45075. (Contributions in Political Science Ser.: No. 325). 208p. 1993. text ed. 52.95 (*0-313-27503-3*, PCJ, Greenwood Pr) Greenwood.

Republican Germany: A Political & Economic Study, 1919-1928. Hugh Quigley & R. J. Clark. 1976. lib. bdg. 69.95 (*0-8490-2518-4*) Gordon Pr.

Republican Iraq: A Study in Iraqi Politics Since the Revolution of 1958. Majid Khadduri. LC 80-1923. reprint ed. 37.00 (*0-404-18973-3*) AMS Pr.

***Republican Like Me: A Diary of My Presidential Campaign.** Sparrow. 88p. 1997. pap. write for info. (*1-887128-22-0*) Soft Skull Pr.

Republican Looks at His Party. Arthur Larson. LC 74-12630. 210p. 1974. reprint ed. text ed. 35.00 (*0-8371-7737-5*, LARE, Greenwood Pr) Greenwood.

Republican Manifesto. John Hirst. 180p. 1994. pap. 19.95 (*0-19-553649-5*) OUP.

Republican Moment: Struggles for Democracy in Nineteenth-Century France. Philip G. Nord. LC 95-10445. (Illus.). 352p. 1995. 49.95 (*0-674-76271-1*) HUP.

Republican Moment: Struggles for Democracy in Nineteenth-Century France. Philip G. Nord. (Illus.). 352p. (C). 1995. text ed. 49.95 (*0-614-07251-4*) HUP.

***Republican or Democrat...Who Cares?** Amit Kataria. LC 96-85262. (Illus.). 112p. (Orig.). 1996. pap. 9.95 (*0-9653121-7-8*) Batten Bks.

***Republican Paradoxes & Liberal Anxieties Retrieving Neglected Fragments of Political Theory.** Ronald J. Terchek. 320p. 1996. 67.50 (*0-614-19224-2*); pap. 24.95 (*0-614-19225-0*) Rowman.

Republican Party: A History of Its Fifty Years Existence, 2 vols. Francis Curtis. LC 75-41070. (BCL Ser. II). reprint ed. 95.00 (*0-404-14870-0*) AMS Pr.

Republican Party & Black America from McKinley to Hoover, 1896-1933. Richard B. Sherman. LC 72-96714. 286p. reprint ed. pap. 81.60 (*0-8357-3516-8*, 2034659) Bks Demand.

Republican Party & the South, 1855-1877. Richard H. Abbott. LC 85-16557. (Fred W. Morrison Series in Southern Studies). xiv, 303p. 1986. 37.50 (*0-8078-1680-9*) U of NC Pr.

Republican Party Reptile. P. J. O'Rourke. LC 86-26504. 240p. 1995. pap. 9.95 (*0-87113-622-8*, Atlntc Mnthly) Grove-Atltic.

Republican Portugal: A Political History, 1910-1926. Douglas L. Wheeler. LC 77-15059. (Illus.). 352p. 1978. 37.50 (*0-299-07450-1*) U of Wis Pr.

Republican Protestantism in Aztlan. E. C. Orozco. LC 80-82906. 261p. 1980. pap. 24.00 (*0-9606102-2-7*) Petereins Pr.

Republican Revolution: Ideology & Politics in Pennsylvania, 1776-1790. Douglas M. Arnold. (Outstanding Studies in Early American History). 388p. 1989. reprint ed. 25.00 (*0-8240-6171-3*) Garland.

Republican Right since Nineteen Forty-Five. David W. Reinhard. LC 82-40460. 304p. 1983. 30.00 (*0-8131-1484-5*) U Pr of Ky.

Republican Roman Army 2nd Century B. C. Nicholas V. Sekunda. (Illus.). 48p. 1996. pap. 12.95 (*1-85532-598-5*, Pub. by Osprey UK) Stackpole.

Republican Roosevelt. 2nd ed. John M. Blum. LC 54-5182. 177p. 1977. pap. 11.95 (*0-674-76302-5*) HUP.

Republican Superstitions. Moncure D. Conway. (Works of Moncure Daniel Conway Ser.). 1990. reprint ed. lib. bdg. 79.00 (*0-685-44752-9*) Rprt Serv.

Republican Synthesis Revisited. Milton M. Klein & Richard D. Brown. 165p. 1992. pap. 19.95 (*0-614-16146-0*) Oak Knoll.

Republican Synthesis Revisited: Essays in Honor of George Athan Billias. Milton M. Klein et al. 165p. (C). 1992. pap. 19.95 (*0-944026-34-6*) Am Antiquarian.

Republican Tradition in Europe. Herbert A. Fisher. LC 75-179519. (Select Bibliographies Reprint Ser.). 1977. reprint ed. 23.95 (*0-8369-6648-1*) Ayer.

Republican Virago: The Life & Times of Catharine Macaulay. Bridget Hill. 232p. 1992. 65.00 (*0-19-812978-5*) OUP.

***Republicanism: A Theory of Freedom & Government.** Philip Pettit. (Oxford Political Theory). 320p. 1997. 29.95 (*0-19-829083-7*) OUP.

Republicanism & Bourgeois Radicalism: Political Ideology in Late Eighteenth-Century England & America. Isaac Kramnick. LC 90-55133. 328p. 1990. 49.95 (*0-8014-2337-6*); pap. 16.95 (*0-8014-9589-X*) Cornell U Pr.

Republicanism Debate. Ed. by Wayne Hudson & David Carter. 290p. pap. 27.95 (*0-86840-277-X*, Pub. by New South Wales Univ Pr AT) Intl Spec Bk.

Republicanism in New Orleans see New Orleans Voter: A Handbook of Political Description

Republicanism in Nineteenth-Century France, 1814-1871. Pamela M. Pilbeam. LC 94-30651. (European Studies). 1995. text ed. 49.95 (*0-312-12420-1*) St Martin.

Republicanism in Nineteenth-Century France, 1814-1871. Pamela M. Pilbeam. LC 94-30651. (European Studies). 1995. text ed. 18.95 (*0-312-12421-X*) St Martin.

Republicanism in Reconstruction Texas. Carl H. Moneyhon. LC 79-14283. (Illus.). 335p. 1980. text ed. 22.50 (*0-292-77553-9*) U of Tex Pr.

Republicanism, Liberty, & Commercial Society, 1649-1776. Ed. by David Wootton. LC 93-50739. (Making of Modern Freedom Ser.). 512p. 1995. 49.50 (*0-8047-2356-7*) Stanford U Pr.

Republicanism, Representation, & Consent: Views of the Founding Era. Ed. by Daniel J. Elazar. LC 79-5466. 137p. (Orig.). 1979. pap. 21.95 (*0-87855-807-1*) Transaction Pubs.

Republicans: From Lincoln to Bush. Robert A. Rutland. LC 96-23180. (Illus.). 296p. (C). 1996. pap. 19.95 (*0-8262-1090-2*) U of Mo Pr.

***Republicans: The Modern Party of FDR.** Tony J. Kocolas. 153p. (Orig.). (C). 1996. pap. 7.95 (*0-9654521-0-7*) Danton Pub.

Republicans & Reconstruction in Virginia, 1856-1870. Richard Lowe. (C). 1991. text ed. 35.00 (*0-8139-1306-3*) U Pr of Va.

Republicans & Vietnam, Nineteen Sixty-One to Nineteen Sixty-Eight. Terry Dietz. LC 85-24764. (Contributions in Political Science Ser.: No. 146). (Illus.). 199p. 1986. text ed. 49.95 (*0-313-24892-3*, DRV/, Greenwood Pr) Greenwood.

Republicans Face the Southern Question: The New Departure Years, 1877-1897. Vincent P. DeSantis. LC 78-64231. (Johns Hopkins University. Studies in the Social Sciences. Thirtieth Ser. 1912: 1). reprint ed. 13.00 (*0-404-61336-5*) AMS Pr.

***Republic's A-10 Thunderbolt II: A Pictorial History.** Don Logan. (Illus.). 240p. 1997. 49.95 (*0-7643-0147-0*) Schiffer.

Republics Ancient & Modern Vol. I: The Ancient Regime in Classical Greece. Paul A. Rahe. LC 94-5728. 380p. 1994. pap. text ed. 22.95 (*0-8078-4473-X*) U of NC Pr.

Republics Ancient & Modern, Vol. II: New Modes & Orders in Early Modern Political Thought. Paul A. Rahe. LC 94-5728. 490p. (C). 1994. pap. text ed. 24.95 (*0-8078-4474-8*) U of NC Pr.

Republics Ancient & Modern, Vol. III: Inventions of Prudence: Constituting the American Regime. Paul A. Rahe. LC 94-5728. 380p. (C). 1994. pap. text ed. 19.95 (*0-8078-4475-6*) U of NC Pr.

Republics, Nations & Tribes: The Ancient City & the Modern World. Martin Thom. 380p. (C). 1995. text ed. 70.00 (*1-85984-920-2*, B4663, Pub. by Vrso UK); pap. text ed. 23.00 (*1-85984-020-5*, B4667, Pub. by Vrso UK) Norton.

Republics of Reality 1975-1995. Charles Berstein. (Classics Ser.: No. 144). 260p. (Orig.). 1997. pap. 14.95 (*1-55713-304-2*) Sun & Moon CA.

Republics of South America. Royal Institute of International Affairs. LC 76-29396. reprint ed. 39.50 (*0-404-15350-X*) AMS Pr.

Republic's P-47 Thunderbolt: From Seversky to Victory. Warren M. Bodie. Ed. by Jeffrey Ethell. (Illus.). 425p. 1994. 44.95 (*0-9629359-1-3*) Widewing Pubns.

Republic's Private Navy: The American Privateering Business As Practiced by Baltimore During the War of 1812. Jerome R. Garitee. LC 76-41487. (American Maritime Library: Vol. 8). (Illus.). xx, 356p. 1977. 19.95 (*0-8195-5004-3*) Mystic Seaport.

Republic's Private Navy: The American Privateering Business As Practiced by Baltimore During the War of 1812. limited ed. Jerome R. Garitee. LC 76-41487. (American Maritime Library: Vol. 8). (Illus.). xx, 356p. 1977. 35.00 (*0-8195-5005-1*) Mystic Seaport.

Republik Ohne Chance? Akzeplanz und Legitimation der Weimarer Republik in der Deutschen Tagespresse Zwischen 1918 und 1923. Burkhard Asmuss. (Beitraege Zur Kommunikationsgeschichte Ser.: No. 3). 639p. (GER.). (C). 1994. lib. bdg. 215.40 (*3-11-014197-3*) De Gruyter.

An Asterisk (*) at the beginning of an entry indicates that the title is appearing in BIP for the first time.

Republikaner Party in Germany: Right-Wing Menace or Protest Catchall? Hans-Joachim Veen et al. LC 92-38868. (Washington Papers: No. 162). 83p. 1993. text ed. 39.95 (0-275-94579-0, C4579, Praeger Pubs); pap. text ed. 14.95 (0-275-94580-4, B4580, Praeger Pubs) Greenwood.

Republique Des Lacedemoniens. Xenophon. Ed. by W. R. Connor. LC 78-18589. (Greek Texts & Commentaries Ser.). (Illus.). 1979. reprint ed. lib. bdg. 24.95 (0-405-11431-1) Ayer.

Republique en Marche, 2 vols. Emile Zola. 660p. (FRE.). 1967. pap. 13.95 (0-7859-1455-2, 2246209315) Fr & Eur.

Republique... Notre Royaume de France. Charles Peguy. pap. 7.95 (0-685-37037-2) Fr & Eur.

Repudation. Rachid Boudjedra. (FRE.). 1981. pap. 10.95 (0-7859-2898-7) Fr & Eur.

Repudiation. Rachid Boudjedra. 176p. 1995. 26.00 (0-89410-729-1, Three Contnts); pap. 14.00 (0-89410-730-5, Three Contnts) Lynne Rienner.

Repudiation. Rachid Boudjedra. (Folio Ser.: No. 1326). 251p. (FRE.). 1986. pap. 8.95 (2-07-037326-6) Schoenhof.

Repudiation of State Debts. William A. Scott. LC 77-137282. reprint ed. 29.50 (0-404-05642-3) AMS Pr.

Repugnant Warehouse: An Expose of the Federal Prison System. Jim Coyne. Ed. by Maryann Dec. 212p. (Orig.). 1995. pap. 12.95 (0-9648228-1-4) Elysium Pubng.

Repunits & Repetends. Samuel Yates. LC 82-50241. 215p. 1982. pap. 13.00 (0-9608652-0-9) S Yates.

Reputation: Realizing Value from the Corporate Image. Charles Fombrun. 1996. text ed. 29.95 (0-07-103636-9) McGraw.

Reputation: Realizing Value from the Corporate Image. Charles J. Fombrun. 464p. 1996. 29.95 (0-87584-633-5) Harvard Busn.

Reputation: Studies in the Voluntary Elicitation of Good Conduct. Ed. by Daniel B. Klein. LC 96-39403. (Orig.). 1996. pap. 19.95 (0-472-06596-3); text ed. 57.50 (0-472-09596-X) U of Mich Pr.

Reputation & Influence of William Godwin in America. O. Earle. 1972. 59.95 (0-8490-0948-0) Gordon Pr.

Reputation & International Politics. Jonathan Mercer. (Studies in Security Affairs). 264p. 1996. 35.00 (0-8014-3055-0) Cornell U Pr.

Reputation, Image & Impression Management. D. B. Bromley. 300p. 1993. text ed. 95.00 (0-471-93869-6) Wiley.

Reputation Is Everything: How to Safeguard Your Company's Image. Peter S. Green. 1994. 35.00 (0-7863-0111-2) Irwin Prof Pubng.

Reputation of Abraham Cowley: Sixteen Sixty - Eighteen Hundred. Arthur H. Nethercott. (English Literature Ser.: No. 33). 1970. reprint ed. pap. 22.95 (0-8383-0057-X) M S G Haskell Hse.

Reputation of Christopher Marlowe. Charles F. Brooke. (Connecticut Academy of Arts & Sciences Ser., Trans.: Vol. 25). 1922. pap. 49.50 (0-685-22824-X) Elliots Bks.

Reputation of Criseyde, 1155-1500. Gretchen Mieszkowski. (Connecticut Academy of Arts & Sciences Ser., Trans.: Vol. 43). 1971. pap. 39.50 (0-685-22886-X) Elliots Bks.

Reputation of Jonathan Swift 1781-1882. Donald M. Berwick. LC 65-21096. (Studies in Irish Literature: No. 16). 1969. reprint ed. lib. bdg. 49.95 (0-8383-0508-3) M S G Haskell Hse.

Reputation of the American Businessman. Sigmund Diamond. 1990. 17.00 (0-8446-0581-6) Peter Smith.

Reputation of the Metaphysical Poets During the Age of Johnson & the Romantic Revival. Arthur H. Nethercott. LC 72-98993. (English Literature Ser.: No. 33). 1970. reprint ed. pap. 22.95 (0-8383-0058-8) M S G Haskell Hse.

Reputation Risk Management. Peter S. Green. 224p. 1992. 105.00 (0-614-04091-4, Pub. by Pitman Pubng UK) St Mut.

Reputation Risk Management: How to Plan & React. Peter S. Green. (Financial Times Management Ser.). 224p. 1992. 82.50 (0-273-03869-9, Pub. by Pitman Pub Ltd UK) Trans-Atl Phila.

Reputations of Socrates: The Afterlife of a Gadfly. James W. Hulse. LC 94-26472. (Revisioning Philosophy Ser.: Vol. 23). 232p. (C). 1995. text ed. 48.95 (0-8204-2608-3) P Lang Pubng.

Reputations Ten Years After. Basil H. Liddell-Hart. LC 68-8478. (Essay Index Reprint Ser.). (Illus.). 1977. reprint ed. 23.95 (0-8369-0619-5) Ayer.

*Request for Proposal Handbook. unabridged ed. Michael Asner. 300p. (Orig.). 1996. pap. 295.00 (1-890299-00-6) Gov Technology.

Request Presented to the King of Spayn by the Inhabitants of the Lowe Countreyes, Protesting That They Will Live According to the Reformation of the Gospell. LC 71-26044. (English Experience Ser.: No. 266). 1970. reprint ed. 10.00 (90-221-0266-1) Walter J Johnson.

Requiem. Jean Cocteau. 180p. (FRE.). 1962. 45.00 (0-8288-9123-0, F96740) Fr & Eur.

Requiem. Michael J. Friedman & Kevin Ryan. (Star Trek: The Next Generation Ser.: No. 32). 288p. (Orig.). 1994. mass mkt. 5.50 (0-671-79567-8) PB.

Requiem. Robert A. Heinlein. 448p. 1994. mass mkt. 5.99 (0-8125-1391-6) Tor Bks.

*Requiem. Joyce. Date not set. pap. 6.99 (0-312-86452-3) St Martin.

*Requiem. Graham Joyce. 1997. mass mkt. 6.99 (0-614-27803-1) Tor Bks.

Requiem. Andrew Lloyd Webber. (Vocal Score Ser.). 080p. 1985. pap. 12.95 (0-88188-473-1, 00362640) H Leonard.

Requiem. Jerome McDonough. (Illus.). 41p. 1977. pap. 3.25 (0-88680-163-X) I E Clark.

Requiem. Toni Ortner. LC 91-10019. (Illus.). 40p. (Orig.). 1991. pap. 6.95 (0-941749-22-3) Black Tie Pr.

Requiem: A Book of Poems. Jan E. Probstein. (Illus.). 92p. (Orig.). (RUS.). 1994. pap. text ed. 8.00 (0-911971-86-6) Effect Pub.

Requiem: A Hallucination. Antonio Tabucchi. Tr. by Margaret J. Costa from POR. LC 93-46672. 128p. 1994. 15.95 (0-8112-1270-X) New Directions.

Requiem: A Novel. Shizuko Go. Tr. by Geraldine Harcourt from JPN. 132p. 1992. reprint ed. pap. 7.00 (4-7700-1618-2) Kodansha.

*Requiem: By the Photographers Who Died in the Vietnam & Indochina War. Horst Faas & Tim Page. 1997. 65.00 (0-679-45657-0) Random.

Requiem: Director's Script. Jerome McDonough. (Illus.). 41p. 1977. pap. 10.00 (0-88680-164-8) I E Clark.

Requiem: Grim Harvest. W. Connors & Lisa Smedman. 1996. 30.00 (0-7869-0431-3) TSR Inc.

Requiem: Music of Mourning & Consolation. Alec Robertson. LC 75-32462. 300p. 1976. reprint ed. text ed. 35.00 (0-8371-8552-1, RORE, Greenwood Pr) Greenwood.

Requiem: Variations on Eighteenth-Century Themes. Forrest McDonald & Ellen S. McDonald. LC 88-14033. xii, 220p. 1988. 25.00 (0-7006-0370-0) U Pr of KS.

Requiem: Vocal Score. G. Faure. 80p. (ENG & LAT.). 1986. pap. 5.25 (0-7935-5510-8, 50324670) H Leonard.

Requiem a Lament in Three Movements. Thomas C. Oden. LC 94-38524. 176p. (Orig.). 1995. 16.95 (0-687-01160-4) Abingdon.

Requiem a Lament in Three Movements. Thomas C. Oden. LC 94-38524. 176p. (Orig.). 1995. pap. 11.95 (0-687-02003-4) Abingdon.

Requiem, & Its Maquettes. Francis Warner. 8000. pap. 12.95 (0-86140-063-1, Pub. by Colin Smythe Ltd UK) Dufour.

Requiem for a Dove. large type ed. Marjorie Eccles. (Mystery Ser.). 384p. 1992. 25.99 (0-7089-2603-7) Ulverscroft.

Requiem for a Dream. Herbert Selby, Jr. (Classic Reprint Ser.). 280p. (C). 1988. reprint ed. pap. 12.95 (0-938410-56-3) Thunders Mouth.

Requiem for a Gambler. Ray Barberis. 32p. 1995. pap. 11.00 (0-8059-3789-7) Dorrance.

*Requiem for a Glass Heart. Daivd Lindsey. 448p. 1997. mass mkt. 6.99 (0-553-57594-5) Bantam.

Requiem for a Glass Heart. David Lindsey. LC 95-45464. 480p. 1996. 23.95 (0-385-42312-8) Doubleday.

Requiem for a Glass Heart. large type ed. David Lindsey. 684p. 1996. lib. bdg. 26.95 (0-7838-1885-8, GK Hall) Thorndike Pr.

Requiem for a Grand Design: The Demise of the European Union. Ed. by Center for Critical European Studies Staff. 350p. 1996. 80.00 (90-5711-001-6, Pub. by NeXed Edits NE) Intl Spec Bk.

Requiem for a Kingfish. Ed Reed. LC 86-71787. 250p. 1986. 24.95 (0-9617384-0-5) Award Pubns.

Requiem for a Mezzo. large type ed. Carola Dunn. 291p. 1996. pap. 21.95 (0-7838-1857-2, GK Hall) Thorndike Pr.

Requiem for a Mezzo: A Daisy Dalrymple Mystery. Carola Dunn. LC 95-41248. (Daisy Dalrymple Mystery Ser.). 240p. 1996. 20.95 (0-312-14036-3) St Martin.

Requiem for a Nobody. Gene Catrambone. 250p. 1993. pap. 15.00 (0-9637348-0-6) DeKalb St Pr.

Requiem for a Nun. William Faulkner. 1951. 13.95 (0-394-44274-1) Random.

Requiem for a Nun. William Faulkner. LC 74-17145. 256p. 1975. pap. 10.00 (0-394-71412-1, Vin) Random.

Requiem for a Nun (1951) Thomas Mchaney & Michael Millgate. (William Faulkner Manuscripts). 1987. text ed. 85.00 (0-8240-6827-0) Garland.

Requiem for a Nun (1951) Thomas Mchaney & Michael Millgate. (William Faulkner Manuscripts). 464p. 1987. text ed. 60.00 (0-8240-6826-2) Garland.

Requiem for a Nun (1951) Pre Materials, 2 vols. Thomas Mchaney & Michael Millgate. (William Faulkner Manuscripts). 1987. text ed. 80.00 (0-8240-6825-4) Garland.

Requiem for a People: The Rogue Indians & the Frontiersmen. Stephen D. Beckham. LC 96-22808. (Northwest Reprints Ser.). (Illus.). 232p. 1996. reprint ed. pap. 15.95 (0-87071-521-6) Oreg St U Pr.

Requiem for a Redcoat. Louise M. Sims. 306p. 1993. 25.00 (0-9639203-0-8) Angel Pr AL.

Requiem for a Rustler. R. C. House. Ed. by Doug Grad. 256p. (Orig.). 1993. mass mkt. 3.99 (0-671-76043-2) PB.

*Requiem for an Army: The Case of the East German Military. Dale R. Herspring. 256p. 1997. 64.00 (0-8476-8718-X) Rowman.

*Requiem for an Army: The Case of the East German Military. Dale R. Herspring. 256p. 1997. pap. 23.95 (0-8476-8719-8) Rowman.

*Requiem for Harlem. Roth. Date not set. 24.95 (0-312-16980-9) St Martin.

Requiem for Hitler: And Other New Perspectives on the German Church Struggle. Klaus Scholder. LC 89-4505. 224p. 1989. pap. 15.95 (0-334-02295-9) TPI PA.

Requiem for Karl Marx. Frank E. Manuel. LC 94-48452. (Illus.). 272p. (C). 1995. 24.95 (0-674-76326-2) HUP.

*Requiem for Karl Marx. Frank E. Manuel. 1997. pap. text ed. 15.95 (0-674-76327-0) HUP.

Requiem for Marx. Intro. by Yuri N. Maltsev. 301p. (Orig.). 1993. pap. text ed. 17.95 (0-945466-13-7) Ludwig von Mises.

*Requiem for Modern Politics: The Political Tragedy of the Enlightenment. William Ophuls. LC 96-34216. 1996. text ed. 30.00 (0-8133-3142-0) Westview.

Requiem for Moses. 1997. mass mkt. 5.99 (0-345-40291-X) Ballantine.

Requiem for Orpheus: An Elegy in Three Parts in Honor of Jaco Pastorius 45th Birthday. Adam W. Seligman et al. (Illus.). 29p. (Orig.). 1996. pap. 7.50 (0-9650733-3-5, EC40-004) Echolalia Pr.

*Requiem for Renee. Stowers. Date not set. write for info. (0-312-16981-7) St Martin.

Requiem for Revolution: The United States & Brazil, 1961-1969. Ruth Leacock. LC 89-20054. (American Diplomatic History Ser.: No. 3). (Illus.). 329p. 1990. 30.00 (0-87338-401-6); pap. 19.00 (0-87338-402-4) Kent St U Pr.

*Requiem for Sergei Grinkov. Gennadiy Samsonenko. 180p. (Orig.). (RUS.). 1996. pap. 10.95 (0-9655194-0-6) G Samsonenko.

Requiem for Sugar. George Grace. (Illus.). 1986. 2.00 (0-938838-28-8) Textile Bridge.

Requiem for the Card Catalog: Management Issues in Automated Cataloging. Ed. by Daniel Gore et al. LC 78-7129. (New Directions in Librarianship Ser.: No. 2). 200p. 1979. text ed. 35.00 (0-313-20608-2, GMI/, Greenwood Pr) Greenwood.

Requiem for the Conqueror. W. Michael Gear. (Forbidden Borders Ser.: No. 1). 544p. (Orig.). 1991. mass mkt. 6.99 (0-88677-477-2) DAW Bks.

Requiem for the Heartland: The Oklahoma City Bombing - A Book to Benefit Families & Survivors. Ed. by David Cohen. LC 95-22055. (Illus.). 124p. 1995. pap. 19.95 (0-00-649203-7) Collins SF.

Requiem for the Sudan: War, Drought & Disaster Relief on the Nile. J. Millard Burr & Robert O. Collins. LC 94-18552. (C). 1994. pap. text ed. 24.00 (0-8133-2121-2) Westview.

Requiem in C Minor: Vocal Score. M. Haydn. 72p. 1986. pap. 12.95 (0-7935-3805-X, 50325530) H Leonard.

Requiem Letters. Ronald Senator. LC 95-13119. 240p. 1995. 27.50 (0-7145-2999-0) M Boyars Pubs.

Requiem of a City Church. Leonard Urban. LC 90-81327. 184p. (Orig.). 1990. pap. 8.95 (0-9626432-0-3) Ancient Echoes.

Requiem of Stars: Song of the Stellar Wind. Tracy Hickman. 400p. (Orig.). 1996. mass mkt. 5.99 (0-553-57302-0) Bantam.

Requiem por Yarini. Carlos Felipe. 1978. pap. 3.00 (0-89729-029-1) Ediciones.

Required Dance. W. E. Butts. LC 90-85369. (Orig.). 1990. pap. 7.00 (0-9627891-0-0) Igneus Pr.

Required Photographic Documentation & Equipment. William Leisher & Richard Amt. 1980. 4.50 (0-933098-08-1) Am Inst Conser Hist.

*Required Reading: Why Our American Classics Matter Now. Andrew Delbanco. LC 97-11229. 1997. write for info. (0-374-23007-2) FS&G.

Required Writing: Miscellaneous Pieces 1955-1982. Philip Larkin. LC 84-4099. 336p. (C). 1984. pap. 9.95 (0-374-51840-8) FS&G.

*Requirements Certification. Tryneski. 1996. lib. bdg. 38.00 (0-226-81318-5) U Ch Pr.

Requirements Engineering. Linda Macaulay. LC 95-51545. (Applied Computing Ser.). 216p. 1996. pap. 34.95 (3-540-76006-7) Spr-Verlag.

*Requirements Engineering: A Good Practice Guide. Ian Sommerville & Pete Sawyer. 250p. 1997. pap. 34.99 (0-471-97444-7) Wiley.

Requirements Engineering: Frameworks for Understanding. Roel Wieringa. 500p. 1996. pap. text ed. 64.95 (0-471-95884-0) Wiley.

Requirements Engineering: Proceedings of the IEEE International Symposium on Requirements Engineering (2nd: 1995: York, England) LC 94-69615. 232p. 1995. pap. 60.00 (0-8186-7017-7, PR07017) IEEE Comp Soc.

Requirements Engineering: Social & Technical Issues. 2nd ed. Ed. by Marina Jirotka et al. (Computers & People Ser.). 304p. 1994. text ed. 56.00 (0-12-385335-4) Acad Pr.

Requirements Engineering 1994: International Conference On. LC 93-80706. 264p. 1994. pap. 50.00 (0-8186-5480-5, 5480) IEEE Comp Soc.

Requirements Engineering, 2nd International Conference on (ICRE '96) 232p. 1996. pap. 50.00 (0-8186-7252-8, PRO7252) IEEE Comp Soc.

*Requirements Engineering, 3rd International Symposium. LC 10-90705. 288p. 1997. pap. 60.00 (0-8186-7740-6, PR07740) IEEE Comp Soc.

Requirements for a Software Engineering Environment. Marvin V. Zelkowitz. LC 88-10357. (Software Engineering Ser.: Vol. 2). (Illus.). 192p. 1989. text ed. 78.50 (0-89391-447-9) Ablex Pub.

Requirements for an Enterprise Document Management System. Black Forest Group Staff. (Orig.). 1995. 15.00 (0-614-09905-6, R018) Assn Inform & Image Mgmt.

*Requirements for Biological Substances: 5 Requirements for Smallpox Vaccine. (Technical Report Ser.: No. 180). 24p. 1959. pap. text ed. 3.00 (92-4-120180-0) World Health.

*Requirements for Biological Substances: 7 Requirements For Poliomyelitis Vaccine. (Technical Report Ser.: No. 237). 29p. 1962. pap. text ed. 3.00 (92-4-120237-8) World Health.

Requirements for Certification of Teachers, Counselors, Librarians, Administrators for Elementary & Secondary Schools, 1996-97. annuals 61th ed. John Tryneski. 256p. 1996. lib. bdg. 37.00 (0-226-81317-7) U Ch Pr.

Requirements for Engineering. 1983. 34.00 (0-387-12692-9) Spr-Verlag.

Requirements for Engineering 1991. 1991. 31.00 (0-387-54025-3) Spr-Verlag.

Requirements for Establishing Land-Information Systems in Cities in Sub-Saharan Africa. Alain Durand-Lasserve. LC 92-27326. (Urban Management Program, Urban Management & Land Ser.: Vol. 8). 114p. (FRE.). 1994. 8.95 (0-8213-2267-2, 12267) World Bank.

Requirements for Faithfulness. 1981. 1.95 (0-89858-030-7) Fill the Gap.

Requirements for Greatness: Justice, Mercy & Humility. Lori Wilke. 182p. (Orig.). 1996. pap. 7.99 (1-56043-152-0) Destiny Image.

Requirements for Poultry Virus Vaccines: Proceedings of the International Symposium, Lyon, 1973. International Symposium on Requirements for Poultry Virus Vaccines Staff. Ed. by Ch Merieux et al. (Developments in Biological Standardization Ser.: Vol. 25). 1976. 30.50 (3-8055-2413-7) S Karger.

*Requirements Management. Davis. 1997. pap. text ed. 35.00 (0-13-632985-3) P-H.

Requirements of Ascorbic Acid, Vitamin D, Vitamin B12, Folate & Iron: Proceedings of the WHO Expert Committee, Geneva, 1969. WHO Staff. (Technical Report Ser.: No. 452). 75p. 1970. pap. text ed. 7.00 (92-4-120452-4, 1100452) World Health.

Requirements of Laws & Regulations Enforced by the U. S. Food & Drug Administration. (Illus.). 79p. (C). 1992. pap. text ed. 25.00 (1-56806-117-X) DIANE Pub.

Requirements of Vitamin A, Thiamine, Riboflavin & Niacin: Report of a Joint FAO-WHO Expert Group. (Nutrition Meetings Reports: No. 41). 86p. 1967. pap. 9.00 (92-5-100453-6, F1467, Pub. by FAO IT) Bernan Associates.

Requirements to Become a P.I. in the Fifty States & Elsewhere. Joseph J. Culligan. LC 92-64222. (Illus.). 576p. 1994. pap. 19.95 (0-9630621-1-5) FJA.

Requirements Under the Public Records Act When Using Information Technology. 60p. 1994. pap. 60.00 (0-11-330630-X, HM0630X, Pub. by Stationery Ofc UK) Bernan Associates.

Requisite Organization: A Total System for Effective Managerial Organization & Managerial Leadership for the 21st Century. 2nd rev. ed. Elliott Jaques. LC 97-19034. (Illus.). 336p. (C). 1996. lib. bdg. 48.00 (1-886436-03-7) Cason Hall & Co.

In the global business world, REQUISITE ORGANIZATION stands as a beacon for a scientific approach to organizing corporations. Based on Jaques's latest research, the forthcoming second edition is a thorough revision of REQUISITE ORGANIZATION, (1989), a book that has established itself as the outstanding contribution to the development of effective managerial leadership systems. Jaques challenges current methods & assumptions in the field of organization, leadership & management, & presents a unified total management system built upon a rigorous theoretical base, Stratified Systems Theory, that makes it possible to relate all aspects of leadership, work & human resourcing into a coherent whole. Elliott Jaques, M.D. (Johns Hopkins), Ph.D. (Harvard), Professor Emeritus of Social Science at Brunel University, England & qualified as a psychoanalyst at the British Psycho-Analytical Society, has continuously combined work with organizations & with individuals - in industry, commerce, public service, education, the Church of England & the U.S. Army. He is the author of eighteen books. In THE CHANGING CULTURE OF A FACTORY (1951), he introduced the concept of business culture. He is also recognized as the originator of the term "mid-life crisis," in a scholarly paper, DEATH & THE MID-LIFE CRISIS, originally published in 1965. Order from: Cason Hall & Co., 51 Monroe Street, Suite 608, Rockville, MD 20850. Editorial Offices: 301-738-8200, Orders 1-800-448-7357, FAX 301-738-8203. Publisher Provided Annotation.

Requisitos para un Avivamiento. Leonard Ravenhill. Tr. by Juan S. Araujo from ENG. 112p. (SPA.). (C). 1988. pap. 3.95 (0-88113-014-1) Edit Betania.

*Rerating Damaged Naval Ship Propulsion Gear. R. Coblenz & C. Reeves. (1991 Fall Technical Meeting). 1991. pap. text ed. 30.00 (1-55589-606-5) AGMA.

Rereading. Matei Calinescu. LC 92-28229. 336p. (C). 1993. text ed. 35.00 (0-300-05657-5) Yale U Pr.

Rereading Allegory: A Narrative Approach to Genre. Deborah L. Madsen. LC 94-25350. 1994. write for info. (0-312-12298-5) Martin Pr.

Rereading America. 3rd ed. Colombo et al. 1995. teacher ed., pap. text ed. 5.00 (0-312-10341-7) St Martin.

Rereading America. 4th ed. Colombo. Date not set. pap. text ed. write for info. (0-312-14837-2) St Martin.

Rereading America: Cultural Contexts for Critical Thinking & Writing. 2nd ed. Gary Colombo et al. 784p. (Orig.). (C). 1992. teacher ed. write for info. (0-318-68816-6) St Martin.

Rereading America: Cultural Contexts for Critical Thinking & Writing. 3rd ed. Gary Colombo et al. 848p. 1995. pap. text ed. 22.50 (0-312-10139-2) St Martin.

Rereading Aphra Behn: History, Theory, & Criticism. Ed. by Heidi Hutner. LC 93-12243. (Feminist Issues: Practice, Politics, Theory Ser.). 336p. 1993. pap. text ed. 19.50 (0-8139-1443-4) U Pr of Va.

Rereading Beowulf. Edward B. Irving, Jr. LC 88-33828. (Middle Ages Ser.). 192p. (C). 1989. pap. 14.50 (0-8122-1428-5) U of Pa Pr.

An Asterisk (*) at the beginning of an entry indicates that the title is appearing in BIP for the first time.

R

Rereading Capital. Ben Fine & Laurence Harris. LC 78-20912. 1979. text ed. 45.00 (0-231-04792-4) Col U Pr.

Rereading Cultural Anthropology. Ed. by George E. Marcus. LC 92-21908. 416p. 1992. text ed. 49.95 (0-8223-1279-4); pap. text ed. 16.95 (0-8223-1297-2) Duke.

Rereading Cultural Geography. Ed. by Kenneth E. Foote et al. LC 93-40072. (Illus.). 520p. (C). 1994. pap. 24.95 (0-292-72484-5); text ed. 55.00 (0-292-72483-7) U of Tex Pr.

Rereading Doris Lessing: Narrative Patterns of Doubling & Repetition. Claire Sprague. LC 86-30879. xii, 210p. (C). 1987. text ed. 34.95 (0-8078-1747-3); pap. text ed. 16.95 (0-8078-4187-0) U of NC Pr.

***Rereading Doris Lessing: Narrative Patterns of Doubling & Repetition.** Claire Sprague. LC 86-30879. 222p. pap. 63.30 (0-608-05218-3, 2065755) Bks Demand.

***Rereading German History: From Unification to Reunification 1800-1996.** Richard Evans. 272p. (C). 1997. pap. 19.95 (0-415-15900-8, Routledge NY); text ed. 69.95 (0-415-15899-0, Routledge NY) Routledge.

Rereading Jack London. Ed. by Leonard Cassuto & Jeanne C. Reesman. LC 96-17052. 1996. 45.00 (0-8047-2634-5) Stanford U Pr.

Rereading Middle English Romance: Manuscript Layout, Decoration, & the Rhetoric of Composite Structure. Murray J. Evans. (Illus.). 208p. 1995. 44.95 (0-7735-1237-3, Pub. by McGill CN) U of Toronto Pr.

Rereading Modernism: New Directions in Feminist Criticism. Intro. by Lisa Rado. LC 94-14784. (Wellesley Studies in Critical Theory, Literary History & Culture: Vol. 4). 408p. 1994. text ed. 65.00 (0-8153-1189-3) Garland.

Rereading Moliere: Mise en Scene from Antione to Vitez. Jim Carmody. (Theater: Theory - Text - Performance Ser.). 200p. (C). 1993. text ed. 42.50 (0-472-10466-7) U of Mich Pr.

Rereading Nadine Gordimer. Kathrin Wagner. LC 93-44183. 308p. 1994. 29.95 (0-253-36303-9) Ind U Pr.

Rereading of Romans: Justice, Jews, & Gentiles. Stanley K. Stowers. 360p. 1994. 42.50 (0-300-05357-6) Yale U Pr.

***Rereading of Romans: Justice, Jews, & Gentiles.** Stanley K. Stowers. 396p. 1997. pap. 18.00 (0-300-07068-3) Yale U Pr.

Rereading of the Renewed Liturgy. Adrien Nocent. Tr. by Mary M. Misrahi. LC 94-7253. 152p. (Orig.). (ENG & FRE.). 1994. pap. 11.95 (0-8146-2299-2, Liturg Pr Bks) Liturgical Pr.

Rereading Shepard: Contemporary Critical Essays on the Plays of Sam Shepard. Ed. by Leonard Wilcox. LC 92-9850. 1993. text ed. 45.00 (0-312-07479-4) St Martin.

Rereading the New: A Backward Glance at Modernism. Kevin J. Dettmar. LC 92-27427. 340p. (C). 1992. text ed. 42.50 (0-472-10290-7) U of Mich Pr.

***Rereading the Renaissance: Petrarch, Augustine, & the Language of Humanism.** Carol E. Quillen. (C). 1997. 37.50 (0-472-10735-6) U of Mich Pr.

Rereading the Sophists: Classical Rhetoric Refigured. Susan C. Jarratt. LC 90-47156. 176p. (C). 1991. 24.95 (0-8093-1616-1) S Ill U Pr.

Rereading the Spanish American Essay: Translations of 19th & 20th Century Women's Essays. Ed. by Doris Meyer. LC 95-3564. (Texas Pan American Ser.). (Illus.). 320p. (Orig.). 1995. 40.00 (0-292-75179-6); pap. 19.95 (0-292-75182-6) U of Tex Pr.

***Rereading the Stone: Desire & the Making of Fiction in Dream of the Red Chamber.** Anthony C. Yu. LC 97-2207. 1997. write for info. (0-691-01561-9) Princeton U Pr.

***Rereading Walter Pater.** William F. Shuter. (Cambridge Studies in Nineteenth-Century Literature & Culture Ser.: No. 9). 174p. (C). 1997. text ed. 49.95 (0-521-57221-5) Cambridge U Pr.

Rereadings: Eight Early French Novels. Philip Stewart. LC 83-50520. 315p. 1984. pap. 17.00 (0-917786-32-7) Summa Pubns.

Rerepresentation: Readings in the Philosophy of Mental Representation. Ed. by Stuart Silvers. 448p. (C). 1988. lib. bdg. 143.50 (0-7923-0045-9, Pub. by Klwr Acad Pubs NE) Kluwer Ac.

Rerforming Financial Systems: Policy Change & Privitization. Neal S. Zank et al. LC 91-20043. (Contributions in Economics & Economic History Ser.: No. 127). 176p. 1991. text ed. 49.95 (0-313-28100-9, ZPB, Greenwood Pr) Greenwood.

Rerolls - Restrikes: Supplement. Angelo A. Rosato. (Encyclopedia of the Modern Elongated Ser.). (Illus.). 40p. 1992. pap. text ed. 25.00 (0-9626996-3-2) Angros Pubs.

Rerouting the Protestant Mainstream: Sources of Growth & Opportunities for Change. C. Kirk Hadaway & David A. Roozen. LC 94-32942. 144p. (Orig.). 1994. pap. 13.95 (0-687-45366-6) Abingdon.

Rerum Gestarum Libri Qui Supersunt, Vol. II, 1. Maccellinus Ammianus. 1963. Pages iv, 389-604. 90.00 (3-296-10402-X) G Olms Pubs.

Rerum Gestarum Libri Qui Supersunt, Vols. I & II. Ammianus Marcellinus. (GER.). 1963. write for info. (0-318-70575-3); Vol. I: Libri 14-25, pages xii, 1-387. write for info. (3-296-10401-1); Vol. II: Libri 26-31, pages iv, 389-604. write for info. (0-318-70576-1) G Olms Pubs.

Rerum Musicarum see Monuments of Music & Music Literature in Facsimile

Rerum Novarum - A Symposium Celebrating 100 Years of Catholic Social Thought. Ed. by Ronald F. Duska. LC 91-47947. (Symposium Ser.: Vol. 29). (Illus.). 260p. 1992. lib. bdg. 89.95 (0-7734-9447-2) E Mellen.

Reruns. Jonathan Baumbach. LC 74-77780. 170p. 1974. pap. 5.95 (0-914590-01-4) Fiction Coll.

Reruns on File: Using Broadcast Archives. Donald G. Godfrey. (Communication Textbook Ser.). 376p. (C). 1991. text ed. 79.95 (0-8058-1146-X); pap. text ed. 45.00 (0-8058-1147-8) L Erlbaum Assocs.

Res: Anthropology & Aesthetics. Ed. by Francesco Pellizzi. (RES Monographs on Anthropology & Aesthetics: No. 26). (Illus.). 144p. (C). 1996. pap. text ed. 25.43 (0-521-47722-0) Cambridge U Pr.

RES: Anthropology & Aesthetics, No. 22. Ed. by Francesco Pellizzi. (Illus.). 160p. (C). 1992. pap. text ed. 24.95 (0-521-43760-1) Cambridge U Pr.

RES: Anthropology & Aesthetics, No. 23. Ed. by Francesco Pellizzi. (Illus.). 152p. (C). 1993. pap. text ed. 25.95 (0-521-44741-0) Cambridge U Pr.

RES: Anthropology & Aesthetics, No. 24. Ed. by Francescso Pellizzi. (RES Monographs on Anthropology & Aesthetics). (Illus.). 160p. (C). 1993. pap. text ed. 25.95 (0-521-44742-9) Cambridge U Pr.

RES: Anthropology & Aesthetics, No. 25. Ed. by Francesco Pellizzi. (Illus.). 152p. (C). 1994. pap. text ed. 25.95 (0-521-46663-6) Cambridge U Pr.

Res: Anthropology & Aesthetics, Vol. 28. Ed. by Francesco Pellizzi. (Res Monographs on Anthropology & Aesthetics). 144p. (C). Date not set. pap. text ed. 25.95 (0-521-55858-1) Cambridge U Pr.

Res No. 27: Anthropology & Aesthetics. Ed. by Francesco Pellizzi. (RES Monographs on Anthropology & Aesthetics: No. 27). (Illus.). 144p. (C). 1996. pap. text ed. 25.95 (0-521-48373-5) Cambridge U Pr.

Res Gestae Divi Augusti. Augustus. Ed. by P. A. Brunt & J. M. Moore. 96p. 1969. pap. 15.95 (0-19-831772-7) OUP.

Res Gestae Divi Augusti. Cynthia Damon. (Greek Commentaries Ser.). 60p. (C). 1995. pap. text ed. 5.00 (0-929524-84-5) Bryn Mawr Commentaries.

Res Gestae Divi Augusti. Paterculus Velleius. (Loeb Classical Library: No. 152). 452p. 1924. 18.95 (0-674-99168-0) HUP.

Res Judicata & Collateral Estoppel: Tools for Plaintiffs & Defendants. Warren Freedman. LC 87-7307. 131p. 1988. text ed. 65.00 (0-89930-277-7, FJD/, Quorum Bks) Greenwood.

Res Judicata & Collateral Estoppel in Paternity & Child Support Cases. John L. Saxon. (Special Ser.: No. 09). 16p. (Orig.). (C). 1993. pap. text ed. 6.00 (1-56011-253-0) Institute Government.

Res Judicatae, Vols. 1-7: The Journal of the Law Student Society of Victoria Faculty of Law, University of Melbourne, 4 bks. 1957. 480.00 (0-685-70758-X) Gaunt.

Res Publica. 1995. 70.00 (0-614-13285-1) Gaunt.

Res Publica: Roman Politics & Society According to Cicero (Scources in Translation) W. Lacey & B. Wilson. 343p. 1978. reprint ed. 25.95 (0-906515-09-2, Pub. by Brstl Class Pr UK) Focus Pub-R Pullins.

***Res Publica Conquassata: Readings on the Fall of the Roman Republic.** Ed. by James K. Finn & Frank J. Groten, Jr. (Classical Studies). (Illus.). 256p. (Orig.). (LAT.). (C). 1998. pap. text ed. 24.95 (0-8143-2678-1) Wayne St U Pr.

Resale of Restricted Securities under SEC Rules 144 & 144A. 2nd ed. Marvin E. Pollock. (Corporate Practice Ser.: Portfolio No. 46). 1990. ring bd. 92.00 (1-55871-193-7) BNA.

Resale Price Maintenance. Claudius T. Murchison. LC 68-56673. (Columbia University. Studies in the Social Sciences: No. 192). reprint ed. 20.00 (0-404-51192-9) AMS Pr.

Resale Price Maintenance: An Economic Study of the FTC's Case Against the Corning Glass Works. Pauline M. Ippolito & Thomas R. Overstreet, Jr. (Illus.). 81p. (Orig.). (C). 1994. pap. text ed. 35.00 (0-7881-1181-7) DIANE Pub.

Resale Price Maintenance in Practice. J. F. Pickering. LC 66-78485. 236p. 1966. 35.00 (0-678-06025-8) Kelley.

Resale Shop or Flea Market Business - A How to Find or Locate Merchandise Workbook. Data Notes Publishing Staff. 62p. (Orig.). 1992. ring bd. 24.95 (0-911569-83-9) Prosperity & Profits.

Resale Thrift Store Junkie's Guide. Abraham M. Rudolph. 1992. pap. 9.95 (0-9628752-3-6) Fifty-Six Palms.

Resampling-Based Multiple Testing: Examples & Methods for P-Value Adjustment. Peter H. Westfall & Sidney S. Young. LC 92-22194. (Probability & Mathematical Statistics: Applied Probability & Statistics Section Ser.). 360p. 1992. text ed. 74.95 (0-471-55761-7) Wiley.

***Resbalones.** F. Hartley. (SPA.). 6.95 (0-8297-2037-5) Life Pubs Intl.

Rescate en Un Dia de Lluvia. Barbara Davoll. 24p. (SPA.). (J). 1983. pap. 6.99 (1-56063-124-4, 490376) Editorial Unilit.

Rescheduling Creditworthiness & Market Prices. Evanor D. Palac-McMiken. 288p. 1995. 63.95 (1-85628-879-X, Pub. by Avebury Pub UK) Ashgate Pub Co.

***Reschooling the Thoroughbred: How To Buy & Retrain a Racehorse.** Peggy Pittenger. LC 97-2696. 1997. write for info. (0-939481-49-9) Half Halt Pr.

Rescousse. Joseph Conrad. 528p. (FRE.). 1985. pap. 13.95 (0-7859-2015-3, 2070376605) Fr & Eur.

Rescue. David Anderson. Ed. by Norm Rhorer. (Illus.). 65p. (Orig.). 1995. pap. 6.95 (0-9628303-6-4, FP 30357) Fellow Minist.

Rescue. Joseph Conrad. 384p. 1996. pap. 9.95 (0-14-018034-6) Penguin.

Rescue. Jeremiah Healy. Ed. by Jane Chelius. 368p. 1995. 20.00 (0-671-89877-9) PB.

Rescue. Jeremiah Healy. 1996. pap. 5.99 (0-671-89875-2) S&S Trade.

Rescue. Nancy N. Rue. (Christian Heritage Ser.: No. 1). 1995. pap. 5.99 (1-56179-346-9) Focus Family.

Rescue! Calvinism for a New Generation. Ed. by R. Horn. 8.99 (1-85792-147-X, Pub. by Christian Focus UK) Spring Arbor Dist.

***Rescue: Jesus & Salvation Today.** Peter Selby. 128p. 1995. pap. 12.95 (0-687-06605-0) Abingdon.

Rescue: The Story of How Gentiles Saved Jews in the Holocaust. Milton Meltzer. LC 87-47816. (Illus.). 224p. (YA). (gr. 7 up). 1988. lib. bdg. 15.89 (0-06-024210-8) HarpC Child Bks.

Rescue: The Story of How Gentiles Saved Jews in the Holocaust. Milton Meltzer. LC 87-47816. (Trophy Nonfiction Bk.). (Illus.). 176p. (YA). (gr. 7 up). 1991. pap. 6.95 (0-06-446117-3, Trophy) HarpC Child Bks.

Rescue Alert. Joan E. Lloyd & Edwin B. Herman. 240p. (Orig.). 1994. mass mkt. 4.99 (0-425-14052-0) Berkley Pub.

***Rescue & Recovery: Iskra's Ordeal in the Western Isles.** Frank Mulville. (Illus.). 180p. 1997. pap. 14.95 (1-57409-038-0) Sheridan.

Rescue & Romances: Popular Novels Before World War 1. Diana C. Reep. LC 82-61169. 144p. 1982. pap. 7.95 (0-87972-212-6) Bowling Green Univ Popular Press.

Rescue & Romances: Popular Novels Before World War 1. Diane C. Reep. LC 82-61169. 144p. 1982. 13.95 (0-87972-211-8) Bowling Green Univ Popular Press.

***Rescue Archaeology - What's Next?** Ed. by Harold Mytum & K. Waugh. 127p. 1987. 9.00 (0-946722-05-6, Pub. by U York Dept Archaeol UK) David Brown.

Rescue Archeology: Proceedings of the Second New World Conference on Rescue Archeology. Ed. by Rex L. Wilson. LC 87-4530. 272p. 1987. pap. 12.95 (0-87074-220-5) SMU Press.

Rescue as Resistance: How Jewish Organizations Fought the Holocaust in France. Lucien Lazare. Tr. by J. M. Green. LC 95-50615. 353p. (ENG & FRE.). 1996. 32.50 (0-231-10124-4) Col U Pr.

Rescue at Sea. 2nd ed. John M. Waters. 1990. 31.95 (0-87021-542-6) Naval Inst Pr.

Rescue! Community Oriented Preventive Education Handbook: Helping Children Cope with Stress. Ofra Ayalon. Ed. by Shuki Duchovni. (Illus.). 154p. 1992. reprint ed. pap. 19.00 (965-343-001-7, AYA1) Chevron Pub.

Rescue Company. Ray Downey. 328p. 1992. 35.95 (0-912212-25-X) Fire Eng.

Rescue Diver Manual. rev. ed. Alex Brylske et al. Ed. by Mary E. Hurrell & Tonya Palazzi. (Illus.). 170p. (C). 1991. reprint ed. pap. 23.95 (1-878663-09-7) PADI.

Rescue Dog. Freeman. (New Readers Ser.). 1993. pap. text ed. write for info. (0-15-599351-8) HB Schl Dept.

***Rescue Excavations at the Broch of Birsay, 1974-82.** J. Hunter. (Illus.). 240p. 1986. pap. 19.98 (0-903903-04-0) David Brown.

Rescue from Beyond Orion. Mayland Schurch. (Discovery Ser.). 29p. 1987. pap. 0.89 (0-8163-0774-1) Pacific Pr Pub Assn.

Rescue from the Darkside. Georgeann Dewitt. 1984. pap. 5.95 (0-88144-029-9, CPS029) Christian Pub.

***Rescue in Albania: One Hundred Percent of Jews in Albania Rescued from Holocaust.** Harvey Sarner. 106p. 1997. 29.00 (1-888521-09-0) Brunswick Pr.

***Rescue in Albania: One Hundred Percent of Jews in Albania Rescued from Holocaust.** Harvey Sarner. 106p. 1997. pap. 15.00 (1-888521-11-2) Brunswick Pr.

Rescue in Denmark. Harold Flender. (Illus.). 280p. reprint ed. pap. 12.95 (0-686-95083-6) ADL.

Rescue in the Pacific: The Story of Disaster & Survival in a Force 12 Storm. Tony Farrington. 400p. 1996. text ed. 21.95 (0-07-021367-4) McGraw.

Rescue Josh McGuire. Ben Mikaelsen. LC 91-71386. 272p. (YA). (gr. 5-9). 1991. lib. bdg. 14.89 (1-56282-100-8) Hyprn Child.

Rescue Josh McGuire. Ben Mikaelsen. LC 91-71386. 272p. (J). (gr. 5-9). 1993. pap. 4.50 (1-56282-523-2) Hyprn Child.

***Rescue Machines.** Snapshot Staff. (My First Board Bks.). (Illus.). 22p. (J). 1997. bds. 2.95 (0-7894-1539-9) DK Pub Inc.

Rescue Mission. 1996. 10.00 (0-679-85854-7) Random.

Rescue 911 Family First Aid & Emergency Care Book: Simple Step-by-Step Guide. Julie Motz. 1996. mass mkt. 5.99 (0-671-52514-X, PB Trade Paper) PB.

Rescue of Broken Arrow. Max Brand. 249p. 1976. reprint ed. lib. bdg. 20.95 (0-89190-207-4, Rivercity Pr) Amereon Ltd.

Rescue of Landmark: Frank Lloyd Wright's Darwin Martin House. Marge Quinlan. (Illus.). 112p. 1990. pap. 9.95 (0-9620314-7-X) Meyer Enter.

***Rescue of Memory.** Cheryl P. Sucher. LC 96-36489. 1997. 23.00 (0-684-81462-5, Scribners PB Fict) S&S Trade.

Rescue of Robby Robo. Roy J. Myers & Stephanie E. Myers. LC 93-79744. (The Robby Robo Ser.: No. 1). (Illus.). 20p. (Orig.). (J). (gr. k-6). 1995. pap. write for info. (1-884108-00-8) R J Myers Pub.

Rescue of Rusty Rabbit. Bonnie L. Scherer. Ed. by Mary Roberts & Janie Hendricks. LC 90-63373. (Illus.). 12p. (Orig.). (J). (gr. 1-6). 1991. pap. text ed. 3.50 (0-9622421-1-X) B Scherer.

Rescue of Sir Clyde the Clumsy. (J). 1991. pap. 1.97 (1-56297-114-X) Lee Pubns KY.

Rescue of the Black Family. Jim Smith. 176p. (Orig.). 1996. pap. 9.95 (1-882185-32-3) Crnrstone Pub.

Rescue of the Danish Jews: Moral Courage under Stress. Ed. by Leo Goldberger. (Illus.). 224p. (C). 1988. text ed. 32.00 (0-8147-3010-8) NYU Pr.

Rescue of the Danish Jews: Moral Courage under Stress. Ed. by Leo Goldberger. (Illus.). 224p. (C). 1988. pap. 20.00 (0-8147-3011-6) NYU Pr.

***Rescue of the Innocents.** Finucane. LC 96-52278. 1997. text ed. 39.95 (0-312-16213-8) St Martin.

Rescue of the Romanovs. Guy Richards. LC 74-27953. (Illus.). 1975. 12.95 (0-8159-6717-9) Devin.

Rescue of the Royal Dream Maker. Fred D. Hill. Ed. by Gloria A. Hill. LC 92-73364. (Illus.). 45p. (J). (ps up). 1994. 15.95 (1-883519-00-4) Charill Pubs.

Rescue of the Thrift Industry. Andrew S. Carron. LC 83-71590. (Studies in the Regulation of Economic Activity). 31p. 1983. pap. 7.95 (0-8157-1301-0) Brookings.

Rescue of the 1856 Handcart Companies. Rebecca Bartholomew & Leonard J. Arrington. LC 92-42327. (Charles Redd Monographs in Western History: No. 11). (Illus.). 63p. 1993. reprint ed. pap. 6.95 (0-941214-04-4, C Redd Ctr Wstrn Studies) Signature Bks.

***Rescue on Crocodile Isle.** Michael Teitelbaum. (Donkey Kong Country Ser.). (J). 1997. pap. 3.50 (0-8167-4270-7) Troll Communs.

Rescue on the Rapids & Other Stories. Billie T. Signer. (Wind Star Ser.). (Illus.). 112p. (Orig.). 1995. pap. 5.95 (0-8198-6454-4) Pauline Bks.

Rescue Party, Vol. 1. Nick Butterworth. (J). (ps-3). 1993. 14.95 (0-316-11923-7) Little.

Rescue Run. 1995. mass mkt. 3.50 (0-373-64204-0, 1-64204-0, Wrldwide Lib) Harlequin Bks.

Rescue Shop Within a Yard of Hell. S. Dinnen. 8.50 (1-85792-122-4, Pub. by Christian Focus UK) Spring Arbor Dist.

Rescue Swine 1-1: True Stories & Poems about Life at an Animal Sanctuary. Stephen Lawrence. Ed. by Jay Wrolstad & Emily R. Johnson. (Illus.). 88p. (Orig.). (J). (gr. 3-9). 1996. pap. 9.95 (0-9650379-0-8) Msty Valley NY.

Rescue Systems One. 731p. 1995. student ed., teacher ed. 250.00 (0-614-09650-2, AVA19437BB00CDL) Natl Tech Info.

Rescue Systems One. 326p. 1995. student ed. 140.00 (0-614-09651-0, AVA19438BB00CDL) Natl Tech Info.

***Rescue Technician: Operational Readiness for Rescue Providers.** Maryland Fire & Rescue Institute Staff. 328p. (gr. 13). 1997. pap. text ed. 32.95 (0-8151-8390-9) Mosby Yr Bk.

Rescue the Captors. Russell M. Stendal. Ed. by Bill Townsend. LC 84-17826. (Illus.). 188p. 1985. reprint ed. 10.95 (0-931221-00-5); reprint ed. pap. 4.95 (0-931221-01-3) Ransom Pr.

Rescue the Dead: Poems. David Ignatow. LC 68-16005. (Wesleyan Poetry Program Ser.: Vol. 37). 79p. 1968. pap. 11.95 (0-8195-1037-8, Wesleyan Univ Pr); text ed. 25.00 (0-8195-2037-3, Wesleyan Univ Pr) U Pr of New Eng.

***Rescue the Ethiopian Jews! A Memoir, 1955-1995.** Graenum Berger. Ed. by B. Michael Berger. LC 97-93722. 236p. 1997. pap. 19.95 (0-9635641-1-0) J W B Hampton.

Rescue the Perishing. Gibbons Ruark. LC 90-47142. 64p. 1991. pap. 7.95 (0-8071-1668-8); text ed. 14.95 (0-8071-1667-X) La State U Pr.

Rescue Towing, Vol. 1. Michael Hancox. (Oilfield Seamanship Ser.). (Illus.). 150p. 1993. pap. 135.00 (1-870945-39-5, Pub. by Oilfld Pubns Ltd UK) Am Educ Systs.

Rescue Vehicles. LC 94-23756. (Look Inside Cross-Sections Ser.). (Illus.). 32p. (J). (gr. 1-4). 1995. 5.95 (1-56458-879-3) DK Pub Inc.

***Rescue Vehicles.** (Illus.). (J). pap. 8.99 (0-590-24557-0) Scholastic Inc.

Rescue Your Child from Public School: The Powerful Case for Home Schooling. Landis. 1995. 19.95 (0-9640479-6-9) E Dalton Bks.

Rescue 911: Extraordinary Stories. Linda Maron. 320p. (Orig.). 1995. mass mkt. 4.99 (0-425-14382-1) Berkley Pub.

Rescued by C++ 2nd ed. Kris Jamsa. 256p. 1996. pap. 22.95 (1-884133-08-8) Jamsa Pr.

***Rescued by C++** 3rd ed. Kris Jamsa. 1997. pap. 24.95 (1-884133-59-2) Jamsa Pr.

Rescued by Excel 5.0 for Windows. Allen Wyatt. (DF - Computer Applications Ser.). 1996. pap. 30.95 (0-7895-0086-8) Course Tech.

Rescued by Love. Anne M. Duquette. 1993. pap. 2.89 (0-373-03253-6, 1-03253-1) Harlequin Bks.

Rescued by Love. Debra Hyldahl. 1994. 17.95 (0-8034-9074-7, 094422) Bouregy.

Rescued by Love. large type ed. Anne M. Duquette. LC 93-13223. 1993. lib. bdg. 14.95 (1-56054-760-X) Thorndike Pr.

***Rescued by Personal Computers.** Kris Jamsa. (Orig.). 1997. pap. 24.95 (1-884133-54-1) Jamsa Pr.

Rescued by Upgrading Your PC. 2nd ed. Kris Jamsa. 272p. 1996. pap. 24.95 (1-884133-24-X) Jamsa Pr.

Rescued by Windows 3.1. Jamsa. (DF - Computer Applications Ser.). 1996. pap. 30.95 (0-7895-0089-2) Course Tech.

Rescued by Word 6.0 for Windows. Allen Wyatt. (DF - Computer Applications Ser.). 1996. pap. 30.95 (0-7895-0085-X) Course Tech.

Rescued from Paradise. Robert L. Forward & Julie F. Fuller. 352p. (Orig.). 1995. mass mkt. 5.99 (0-671-87655-4) Baen Bks.

Rescued from the River. Linda P. Carlyle. (Child's Steps to Jesus Ser.). 25p. (J). 1992. 6.99 (0-8163-1093-9) Pacific Pr Pub Assn.

Rescued Heart. Melinda Mcrae. 1997. pap. 5.99 (0-451-40648-6, Onyx) NAL-Dutton.

Rescued Heart. large type ed. Rebecca Winters. 213p. 1992. reprint ed. lib. bdg. 13.95 (1-56054-400-7) Thorndike Pr.

Rescued Readings: A Reconstruction of Gertrude Stein's Difficult Texts. Elizabeth Fifer. LC 92-7291. 146p. (C). 1992. 29.95 (0-8143-2340-5) Wayne St U Pr.

***Rescuers.** Mouse Works Staff. 1997. 7.98 (1-57082-755-9) Mouse Works.

An Asterisk (*) at the beginning of an entry indicates that the title is appearing in BIP for the first time.

R

***Rescuers.** Mouseworks Staff. 1997. 7.98 (*1-57082-050-3*) Mouse Works.

Rescuers. Margery Sharp. (J). (gr. 4-7). 1994. 4.95 (*0-316-78355-2*) Little.

Rescuers: Portraits of Moral Courage in the Holocaust. Gay Block & Malka Drucker. LC 91-31499. (Illus.). 272p. 1992. 49.95 (*0-8419-1322-6*); pap. 29.95 (*0-8419-1323-4*) Holmes & Meier.

Rescuers Down Under. Walt Disney Productions Staff. (Penguin-Disney Ser.). (J). 1990. 6.98 (*0-8317-7389-8*) Viking Child Bks.

Rescuers in Action. Barry Smith. 000224p. (gr. 13). 1995. text ed. 14.95 (*0-8151-7902-2*) Mosby Yr Bk.

Rescuers of Cypress: Learning from Disaster. Cynthia M. Stuhlmiller. (International Healthcare Ethics Ser.: Vol. 2). 248p. (C). 1996. text ed. 53.95 (*0-8204-2800-0*) P Lang Pubng.

Rescues: The Lives of Heroes. Michael Lesy. 1991. 18.95 (*0-374-24947-4*) FS&G.

Rescuing a Neighborhood: The Bedford-Stuyvesant Volunteer Ambulance Corps. Robert Fleming. LC 94-28097. 48p. (J). (gr. 3-7). 1995. 15.95 (*0-8027-8329-5*); lib. bdg. 16.85 (*0-8027-8330-9*) Walker & Co.

Rescuing Capitalist Free Enterprise for the 21st Century. Gerald A. Cory, Jr. LC 91-77266. (Illus.). 160p. (Orig.). 1992. pap. 10.95 (*0-9631280-1-9*) Ctr Behav Ecol.

***Rescuing Christine.** Alyssa Dean. 1997. mass mkt. 3.50 (*0-373-25736-8*, 1-25736-9) Harlequin Bks.

Rescuing Claire. Thomas Johnson. Ed. by Jane Rosenman. 1993. reprint ed. pap. 10.00 (*0-671-75885-3*, WSP) PB.

Rescuing Creusa: New Methodological Approaches to Women in Antiquity. Ed. by Marilyn Skinner. 1987. pap. 9.00 (*0-89672-148-5*) Tex Tech Univ Pr.

Rescuing Endangered Species. Jean F. Blashfield. LC 94-18009. (Restoring Nature: Success Stories Ser.). (Illus.). 96p. (J). (gr. 3-6). 1994. lib. bdg. 24.70 (*0-516-05544-5*) Childrens.

Rescuing History from the Nation: Questioning Narratives of Modern China. Prasenjit Duara. LC 95-3205. 286p. 1995. 32.00 (*0-226-16721-6*) U Ch Pr.

Rescuing History from the Nation: Questioning Narratives of Modern China. Prasenjit Duara. x, 276p. 1996. pap. text ed. 17.95 (*0-226-16722-4*) U Ch Pr.

Rescuing Horace Walpole. Wilmarth S. Lewis. LC 78-7590. (Illus.). 1978. 50.00 (*0-300-02278-6*) Yale U Pr.

Rescuing Jesus from the Gospels. Patricia G. Eddy. LC 94-60971. 280p. (Orig.). 1994. pap. 12.95 (*1-55523-720-7*) Winston-Derek.

Rescuing Little Roundhead. Syl Jones. 225p. 1996. 18.95 (*1-57131-215-3*) Milkweed Ed.

***Rescuing Reconstruction: The Debate on Post-War Economic Recovery in El Salvador.** (Hemisphere Initiatives Ser.). 57p. 1994. pap. 4.50 (*0-614-25729-8*) WOLA.

Rescuing Robinson Crusoe: Reconnecting Schools with the Changing Economy. Murname. 1996. 26.00 (*0-02-874066-1*) Free Pr.

Rescuing Souls from Hell. Norvel Hayes. 160p. (Orig.). 1990. pap. 7.99 (*0-89274-705-6*, HH705) Harrison Hse.

Rescuing the American Dream: Public Policies & the Crisis in Housing. Rolf Goetze. LC 82-18748. 150p. (C). 1983. 33.00 (*0-8419-0855-9*); pap. 18.95 (*0-8419-0862-1*) Holmes & Meier.

Rescuing the Bible from Fundamentalism: A Bishop Rethinks the Meaning of Scripture. John S. Spong. LC 90-41697. 228p. 1992. pap. 13.00 (*0-06-067518-7*) Harper SF.

Rescuing the Bible from Fundamentalists: A Bishop Rethinks the Meaning of Scripture. John S. Spong. LC 94-33493. 1995. student ed., pap. 10.00 (*0-06-067552-7*) Harper SF.

Rescuing the Comprehensive Experience. Bernard Barker. LC 85-11505. (Innovations in Education Ser.). 176p. 1986. 85.00 (*0-335-15141-8*, Open Univ Pr); pap. 32.00 (*0-335-15116-7*, Open Univ Pr) Taylor & Francis.

Rescuing the Dinner Hour: Easy Meals for Busy People. Peggy K. Glass. LC 94-31718. 288p. (Orig.). 1994. pap. 15.95 (*1-883280-04-4*) Font & Ctr Pr.

Resculpting: Poems. Maura A. Bramkamp. LC 95-68524. (Illus.). 50p. (Orig.). 1995. pap. 7.95 (*0-9646251-1-3*) Paper Boat Pr.

Resealed Erythrocytes as Carriers & Bioreactors: Proceedings of the International Meeting, 3rd, Held at the Gwinn Estate, Cleveland, Ohio, U. S. A., 18-20 October, 1989. Ed. by R. Green & J. R. Deloach. (Advances in the Biosciences Ser.: Vol. 81). (Illus.). 262p. 1991. 165.00 (*0-08-041156-8*, Pergamon Pr) Elsevier.

Resealing Joints & Cracks in Rigid & Flexible Pavements. (National Cooperative Highway Research Program Report Ser.: No. 98). 62p. 1982. 7.20 (*0-309-03459-0*) Transport Res Bd.

Resealing of Buildings: A Guide to Good Practice. Ron Woolman. Ed. by Allan Hutchinson. LC 93-48893. (Illus.). 192p. 1994. pap. 54.95 (*0-7506-1859-0*) Buttrwrth-Heinemann.

***Resealing of Buildings: A Guide to Good Practice.** Ron Woolman. Ed. by Allan Hutchinson. LC 93-48893. (Illus.). 193p. 1994. reprint ed. pap. 55.10 (*0-608-04414-8*, 2065195) Bks Demand.

Research. Ed. by C. Hawkins & M. Sorgi. (Illus.). 195p. 1992. pap. 26.00 (*0-387-13992-3*) Spr-Verlag.

***Research.** 2nd ed. Veit. LC 97-12005. 1997. pap. text ed. 18.00 (*0-205-27338-6*) P-H.

Research: A National Resource, 3 Vols. U. S. National Resources Committee Staff. Ed. by I. Bernard Cohen. LC 79-7985. (Three Centuries of Science in America Ser.). (Illus.). 1980. reprint ed. lib. bdg. 98.95 (*0-405-12567-4*) Ayer.

***Research: Developments & Progress in Science, Life & Medicine Including Concerns & World-Wide Criticisms.** John C. Bartone. 185p. 1997. 44.95 (*0-7883-1020-8*) ABBE Pubs Assn.

***Research: Developments & Progress in Science, Life & Medicine Including Concerns & World-Wide Criticisms.** John C. Bartone. 185p. 1997. pap. 39.95 (*0-7883-1021-6*) ABBE Pubs Assn.

Research: Process & Product. Mildred Hillestad. (Service Bulletin Ser.: No. 1). (Illus.). 140p. (C). 1977. pap. 10.00 (*0-9603064-3-9*) Delta Pi Epsilon.

Research: Some Ground Rules. J. S. Lumley & W. Benjimen. (Illus.). 256p. 1995. 70.00 (*0-19-854823-0*); pap. 33.50 (*0-19-854822-2*) OUP.

Research: Successful Approaches. Elaine R. Monsen. LC 91-31303. 1991. pap. 29.95 (*0-88091-092-5*, 0180) Am Dietetic Assn.

Research: The Validation of Clinical Practice. 3rd ed. Otto D. Payton. LC 93-26828. (Illus.). 355p. (C). 1993. pap. text ed. 24.95 (*0-8036-6800-7*) Davis Co.

Research about Leisure: Past, Present & Future. 2nd ed. Ed. by Lynn A. Morris. 1994. pap. 24.95 (*0-915611-96-1*) Sagamore Pub.

***Research Abstracts: Southeast Asia Region, 1.** (WHO Regional Publications, South-East Asia Ser.: No. 16). 88p. 1987. pap. text ed. 10.00 (*92-9022-118-6*) World Health.

***Research Abstracts: Southeast Asia Region, 4.** (WHO Regional Publications, South-East Asia Ser.: No. 16). 102p. 1994. pap. text ed. 10.00 (*92-9022-165-8*) World Health.

Research Abstracts Vol. 3: South-East Asia Region. (WHO Regional Publications, South-East Asia Ser.: No. 16). iv, 109p. 1991. pap. text ed. 10.00 (*92-9022-161-5*, 1560016) World Health.

Research Abstracts of the Scientific Program. 3rd ed. Ed. by James Druzik. (GCI Scientific Program Reports Ser.). 275p. 1995. pap. text ed. 15.00 (*0-89236-244-8*, Getty Conservation Inst) J P Getty Trust.

***Research Abstracts, 1980-1988.** 92p. 1989. 8.00 (*0-614-23451-4*, 3006) Am Assn Coll Registrars.

Research Access Through New Technology. Ed. by M. E. Jackson. LC 88-34373. (Studies in Library & Information Science: No. 1). 1989. 32.50 (*0-404-64001-X*) AMS Pr.

***Research Across the Disciplines: A Resource Guide.** Kristin R. Woolever et al. 169p. (Orig.). (C). 1996. pap. text ed. 5.95 (*1-55934-728-7*, 1728) Mayfield Pub.

Research Act. 3rd ed. Norman K. Denzin. 352p. (C). 1988. pap. text ed. 48.00 (*0-13-774381-5*) P-H.

***Research, Action, & the Community: Experiences in the Prevention of Alcohol & Other Drug Problems.** Ed. by Norman Giesbrecht. (Illus.). 326p. (Orig.). (C). 1996. reprint ed. pap. 40.00 (*0-7881-2964-3*) DIANE Pub.

Research Advances in Alcohol & Drug Problems, Vol. 6. Ed. by Yedi Israel et al. LC 73-18088. 536p. 1981. 95.00 (*0-306-40672-1*, Plenum Pr) Plenum.

Research Advances in Alcohol & Drug Problems, Vol. 7. Ed. by Reginald G. Smart et al. LC 73-18088. 486p. 1983. 95.00 (*0-306-41218-7*, Plenum Pr) Plenum.

Research Advances in Alcohol & Drug Problems, Vol. 8. Ed. by Reginald G. Smart et al. 328p. 1984. 85.00 (*0-306-41551-8*, Plenum Pr) Plenum.

Research Advances in Alcohol & Drug Problems, Vol. 9. Ed. by Howard D. Cappell et al. 315p. 1986. 79.50 (*0-306-42426-6*, Plenum Pr) Plenum.

Research Advances in Alcohol & Drug Problems, Vol. 10. L. T. Kozlowski et al. LC 73-18088. (Illus.). 424p. 1990. 95.00 (*0-306-43295-1*, Plenum Pr) Plenum.

Research Advances in Alcohol & Drug Problems Vol. 11: Drug Testing in the Workplace. Ed. by Scott Macdonald & Paul M. Roman. (Research Advances in Alcohol & Drug Problems: Vol. 11). (Illus.). 315p. (C). 1994. 85.00 (*0-306-44557-3*, Plenum Pr) Plenum.

Research Advances in Alcohol & Drug Problems, Vol. 5: Alcohol & Drug Problems in Women. Oriana J. Kalant. LC 73-18088. 784p. 1980. 110.00 (*0-306-40394-3*, Plenum Pr) Plenum.

Research Advances in Alzheimer's Disease & Related Disorders. Ed. by Khalid Iqbal et al. LC 94-36061. 798p. 1995. text ed. 269.00 (*0-471-95236-2*) Wiley.

Research Advances in Sexual Harassment. Ed. by John B. Pryor & Kathleen McKinney. 136p. 1995. pap. 20.00 (*0-8058-9935-9*) L Erlbaum Assocs.

Research Advances in the Compositae. Tom J. Mabry & G. W. Wagenitz. (Plant Systematics & Evolution Ser.: Suppl. 4). (Illus.). 120p. 1990. 111.95 (*0-387-82174-0*) Spr-Verlag.

Research Agenda for Studying Rural Public Service Delivery Alternatives in the North Central Region. David J. O'Brien et al. 76p. 1994. pap. text ed. 4.00 (*0-936913-09-6*, RRD 167) NCRCRD.

Research Agendas in the Sociology of Emotions. Ed. by Theodore D. Kemper. LC 89-26193. (SUNY Series in the Sociology of Emotions). 335p. 1990. text ed. 74.50 (*0-7914-0269-X*); pap. text ed. 24.95 (*0-7914-0270-3*) State U NY Pr.

Research Aide. Jack Rudman. (Career Examination Ser.: C-1580). 1994. pap. 27.95 (*0-8373-1580-8*) Nat Learn.

Research Airplanes: Testing the Boundaries of Flight. Don Berliner. (Discovery! Ser.). (Illus.). 64p. (J). (gr. 5 up). 1988. lib. bdg. 21.50 (*0-8225-1582-2*, Lerner Publctns) Lerner Group.

***Research Alert Yearbook - 1996 the Year in Review.** (Illus.). 487p. write for info. (*1-885747-09-8*) EPM Communs.

Research Analyst. Jack Rudman. (Career Examination Ser.: C-1949). 1994. pap. 34.95 (*0-8373-1949-8*) Nat Learn.

Research & Application in the Assessment of Environmental Health. Ed. by David B. Peakall & Lee R. Shugart. LC 92-38833. (NATO ASI Series H: Cell Biology: Vol. 68). 1993. 122.95 (*0-387-54612-X*) Spr-Verlag.

***Research & Argumentation.** rev. ed. Ed. by Williams. (C). 1995. text ed. 20.95 (*0-673-99604-2*) Addison-Wesley.

Research & Change in Urban Community Health. Ed. by Bruce Nigel. 464p. 1995. 76.95 (*1-85972-159-1*, Pub. by Avebury Pub UK) Ashgate Pub Co.

Research & Composition in Philosophy. 2nd ed. Sebastian A. Matczak. (Philosophical Questions Ser.: No. 2). (C). 1971. pap. text ed. 55.00 (*0-912116-05-6*) Learned Pubns.

Research & Consulting As a Business. N. Y. Davis et al. (NAPA Bulletin Ser.: No. 4). 1987. 6.00 (*0-913167-21-5*) Am Anthro Assn.

Research & Cumulative Watershed Effects. Leslie M. Reid. (Illus.). 118p. (Orig.). (C). 1995. pap. text ed. 35.00 (*0-7881-1894-3*) DIANE Pub.

Research & Data Analysis in Leisure, Recreation, Tourism & Sport Management. Joe M. Shockley, Jr. LC 95-69634. (Illus.). 338p. 1995. 39.93 (*0-9650905-1-5*) Sigma Pr NM.

Research & Development, Vol. XXVII. R. A. Wilson & D. L. Bosworth. Ed. by W. F. Maunder & M. C. Fleming. (Reviews of U. K. Statistical Sources Ser.). 248p. (gr. 13). 1993. text ed. 163.95 (*0-412-35640-6*, A4392) Chapman & Hall.

Research & Development: Project Selection Criteria. rev. ed. Jackson E. Ramsey. Ed. by Richard Farmer. LC 86-16085. (Research for Business Decisions Ser.: No. 80). 222p. reprint ed. 63.00 (*0-8357-1708-9*, 2070412) Bks Demand.

Research & Development & School Change. Ed. by R. Glaser. 128p. 1978. 19.95 (*0-89859-449-9*) L Erlbaum Assocs.

***Research & Development Annual Statistics.** EC Staff. 113p. 1996. pap. 30.00 (*92-827-8923-3*, CA3A-96-316-3AC, Pub. by Europ Com UK) Bernan Associates.

Research & Development As a Determinant of U. S. International Competitiveness. Rachel McCulloch. LC 78-63432. (Committee on Changing International Realities Ser.). 60p. 1978. 3.00 (*0-89068-044-2*) Natl Planning.

Research & Development As a Pattern in Industrial Management: A Case Study of Institutionalization & Uncertainty. Harrison C. White. Ed. by Harriet Zuckerman & Robert K. Merton. LC 79-9037. (Dissertations on Sociology Ser.). 1980. lib. bdg. 30.95 (*0-405-13004-X*) Ayer.

Research & Development Conference: 1984, Proceedings. Technical Association of the Pulp & Paper Industry Staff. 307p. reprint ed. pap. 87.50 (*0-317-20749-0*, 2024781) Bks Demand.

Research & Development Conference, 1986: Quality Inn, Raleigh, NC, September 28-October 1. Technical Association of the Pulp & Paper Industry Staff. (TAPPI Proceedings Ser.). (Illus.). 207p. reprint ed. pap. 59.00 (*0-317-58142-2*, 2029691) Bks Demand.

Research & Development Directory. 31th ed. 416p. 1992. pap. 15.00 (*1-56868-007-4*) Gov Data Pubns.

Research & Development Expenditure in Industry 1973-1992. 230p. (Orig.). 1995. pap. 55.00 (*92-64-14402-1*, Pub. by Org for Econ FR) OECD.

Research & Development Expenditure in Industry 1973-93. OECD Staff. 322p. (Orig.). (ENG & FRE.). 1996. pap. 65.00 (*92-64-04764-6*, Pub. by Org for Econ FR) OECD.

Research & Development Growth Trends. 230p. 1992. pap. text ed. 325.00 (*1-878339-21-4*) Schonfeld & Assocs.

Research & Development Growth Trends. 230p. 1993. pap. text ed. 325.00 (*1-878339-27-3*) Schonfeld & Assocs.

Research & Development Growth Trends. 230p. 1994. pap. text ed. 325.00 (*1-878339-35-4*) Schonfeld & Assocs.

Research & Development Growth Trends: 1996 Edition. 270p. 1996. pap. text ed. 325.00 (*1-878339-49-4*) Schonfeld & Assocs.

***Research & Development Growth Trends: 1997 Edition.** 270p. 1997. pap. text ed. 345.00 (*1-878339-58-3*) Schonfeld & Assocs.

Research & Development Guidelines for the Food Industries. Wilbur A. Gould. (Illus.). 172p. 1991. 56.00 (*0-930027-17-5*) CTI Pubns.

Research & Development in Expert Systems, VII: Proceedings of the 10th Annual Technical Conference of the BCS Specialist Group, September, 1990. Ed. by T. R. Addis & R. M. Muir. (British Computer Society Workshop Ser.). (Illus.). 327p. (C). 1990. text ed. 69.95 (*0-521-40403-7*) Cambridge U Pr.

***Research & Development in Expert Systems VIII: Proceedings of 10th Annual Technical Conference of the BCS Specialist Group, September 1991.** 286p. 1991. text ed. 69.95 (*0-521-41838-0*) Cambridge U Pr.

Research & Development in Expert Systmes IX: Proceedings of 12th Annual Technical Conference of the BCS Specialist Group, December 1992. Max A. Bramer & R. W. Milne. (British Computer Society Workshop Ser.). (Illus.). 356p. (C). 1993. text ed. 85.00 (*0-521-44517-5*) Cambridge U Pr.

Research & Development in Industry (1989) (Illus.). 154p. (Orig.). (C). 1993. pap. text ed. 35.00 (*1-56806-688-0*) DIANE Pub.

Research & Development in Industry (1991) Funds, 1991; Scientists & Engineers, 1992. (Illus.). 125p. (Orig.). (C). 1995. pap. text ed. 35.00 (*0-7881-2012-3*) DIANE Pub.

Research & Development in U. S. Manufacturing. Albert N. Link. LC 80-21542. 144p. 1981. text ed. 45.00 (*0-275-90672-8*, C0672, Praeger Pubs) Greenwood.

Research & Development in Work & Technology. Ed. by H. Pornschlegel. (Illus.). xiv, 413p. 1992. pap. 89.00 (*0-387-91427-7*) Spr-Verlag.

Research & Development Management: From the Soviet Union to Russia. C. M. Schneider. (Contributions to Economics Ser.). (Illus.). xviii, 255p. 1994. 65.00 (*0-387-91481-1*) Spr-Verlag.

Research & Development of Proton-Exchange Membrane (PEM) Fuel Cell System for Transportation Applications (Nov. 1993) Initial Conceptual Design Report. General Motors, Allison Gas Turbine Division Staff. (Fuel Cell Information Ser.: Vol. VII). 72p. 1996. lib. bdg. 99.00 (*0-89934-290-6*, BT952) Bus Tech Bks.

***Research & Development of Proton-Exchange-Membrane (PEM) Fuel Cell Systems for Transportation Applications Fuel Cell Infrastructure & Commercialization Study (11/96)** Allison Gas Turbine Div. of General Motors. (Fuel Cell Information Ser.: Vol. XIII). 187p. 1997. lib. bdg. 145.00 (*0-89934-339-2*, BT971) Bus Tech Bks.

Research & Development of Radioactive Waste Management & Storage, Vol. 3. Ed. by Commission of European Communities. (Radioactive Waste Management Ser.: Vol. 12). 402p. 1984. pap. text ed. 185.00 (*3-7186-0191-5*) Gordon & Breach.

Research & Development of Vaccines & Pharmaceuticals from Biotechnology: A Guide to Effective Project Management, Patenting, & Product Registration. Jens-Peter Gregersen. 173p. 1995. 60.00 (*3-527-30059-7*, VCH) Wiley.

Research & Development on Radioactive Waste Management & Storage: First Annual Progress Report of the European Community Programme 1980-84. Ed. by Commission of European Communities. (Radioactive Waste Management Ser.: Vol. 4). 130p. 1982. text ed. 74.00 (*3-7186-0115-X*) Gordon & Breach.

Research & Development on Radioactive Waste Management & Storage: Second Annual Progress Report of the European Community Programme 1980-1984, Vol. 2. 310p. 1983. text ed. 147.00 (*3-7186-0148-6*) Gordon & Breach.

Research & Development Project Selection. Joseph P. Martino. LC 94-30753. (Engineering Managment Ser.). 266p. 1995. text ed. 64.95 (*0-471-59537-3*) Wiley.

Research & Development, Tax Incentives, & the Structure of Production & Financing. J. I. Bernstein. LC 86-94275. (Ontario Economic Council Research Studies: No. 31). viii, 108p. 1986. 11.95 (*0-8020-6629-1*) U of Toronto Pr.

Research & Development Trends. 270p. 1995. pap. text ed. 325.00 (*1-878339-42-7*) Schonfeld & Assocs.

***Research & Development Work on Gear Tooth Forms for Fuze Timing Devices.** C. H. Wickenberg. (Technical Papers). 1958. pap. text ed. 30.00 (*1-55589-208-6*) AGMA.

Research & Developments on Teacher Education in the Netherlands. Ed. by J. T. Voorbach & L. G. Prick. (Teacher Education 5 Series). 204p. 1989. pap. 24.50 (*90-6472-150-5*) Taylor & Francis.

Research & Discovery in Medicine: Contributions from Johns Hopkins. A. McGehee Harvey. LC 81-47647. (Illus.). 344p. 1981. text ed. 39.50 (*0-8018-2723-X*) Johns Hopkins.

Research & Discovery Series, 8 vols., 3. L. Ron Hubbard. 100.00 (*0-317-00015-2*) Church Scient NY.

Research & Discovery Series, 8 vols., 4. L. Ron Hubbard. 100.00 (*0-317-00016-0*) Church Scient NY.

Research & Discovery Series, Vol. 4. L. Ron Hubbard. 986p. 1994. 150.00 (*0-88404-949-3*) Bridge Pubns Inc.

Research & Discovery Series, Vol. 5. L. Ron Hubbard. 756p. 1995. 150.00 (*0-88404-994-9*) Bridge Pubns Inc.

Research & Discovery Series, Vol. 6. L. Ron Hubbard. 790p. 1995. 150.00 (*1-57318-011-4*) Bridge Pubns Inc.

Research & Discovery Series, Vol. 7. L. Ron Hubbard. 807p. 1995. 150.00 (*1-57318-016-5*) Bridge Pubns Inc.

Research & Discovery Series, Vol. 8. L. Ron Hubbard. 841p. 1995. 150.00 (*1-57318-018-1*) Bridge Pubns Inc.

Research & Discovery Series, Vol. 9. L. Ron Hubbard. 850p. 1996. 150.00 (*1-57318-021-1*) Bridge Pubns Inc.

Research & Discovery Series Vol. 1. L. Ron Hubbard. 838p. 1994. 150.00 (*0-88404-931-0*) Bridge Pubns Inc.

Research & Discovery Series Vol. 2. L. Ron Hubbard. 960p. 1994. 150.00 (*0-88404-935-3*) Bridge Pubns Inc.

Research & Discovery Series Vol. 3. L. Ron Hubbard. 764p. 1994. 150.00 (*0-88404-948-5*) Bridge Pubns Inc.

***Research & Documentation On-Line & in the Library.** Fowler. (C). 1998. student ed., pap. text ed. write for info. (*0-321-01960-1*) Addson-Wesley Educ.

Research & Education for the Development of Integrated Crop-Livestock-Fish Farming Systems in the Tropics. P. Edwards et al. (ICLARM Studies & Reviews: No. 16). 53p. 1988. pap. 6.00 (*971-10-2246-X*, Pub. by ICLARM PH) Intl Spec Bk.

***Research & Education Issues & the 1995 Farm Bill: Proceedings, 43rd Annual Meeting of the Agricultural Research Institute, September 19, 1994.** 171p. pap. 33.00 (*0-614-24230-4*) Agri Research Inst.

Research & Education Reform: Roles for the Office of Educational Research & Improvement. National Research Council Staff. Ed. by R. C. Atkinson & G. B. Jackson. 204p. (C). 1992. pap. text ed. 29.00 (*0-309-04729-3*) Natl Acad Pr.

Research & Educational Institutions: Guides to Pollution Prevention. (Illus.). 48p. (Orig.). (C). 1993. pap. text ed. 30.00 (*1-56806-663-5*) DIANE Pub.

Research & Evaluation: How to Plan Research Instruments & Use the Results to Evaluate Your Effectiveness & Guide Decisions. Cook Communications Ministries International Staff. (Interlit Imprint Ser.: Vol. 18). (Illus.). 40p. (Orig.). 1996. pap. 5.95 (*1-884752-27-6*, 44362) Cook Min Intl.

R

Research & Evaluation for Information Professionals. Robert M. Losee, Jr. & Karen A. Worley. (Library & Information Science Ser.). (Illus.). 239p. 1993. text ed. 30.00 (0-12-455770-8) Acad Pr.

Research & Evaluation in Recreation, Parks, & Leisure Studies. 2nd ed. Richard G. Kraus & Lawrence Allen. LC 96-18709. 412p. (C). 1996. pap. text ed. 38.95 (0-89787-632-6) Gorsuch Scarisbrick.

Research & Evaluation Methodology. Louise Gresham. 114p. (C). 1993. spiral bd. Not Set by Publisher (0-933195-09-5) CA College Health Sci.

Research & Evalution in Education & the Social Sciences. Mary-Lee Smith & Gene V. Glass. (Illus.). 416p. (C). 1986. text ed. 60.67 (0-13-774050-6) P-H.

Research & Extension in Agricultural Development. R. E. Evenson. 35p. 1992. pap. 9.95 (1-55815-183-4) ICS Pr.

Research & Higher Education: The United Kingdom & the United States. Ed. by Thomas G. Whiston & Roger L. Geiger. 192p. 1991. 95.00 (0-335-15641-X, Open Univ Pr) Taylor & Francis.

Research & International Co-Operation in Criminal Justice: Survey on Needs & Priorities of Developing Countries. 1987. 25.00 (92-9078-003-7, E.87.III.N.2) UN.

Research & Intervention: Preventing Substance Abuse in Higher Education. (Illus.). 132p. (Orig.). (C). 1995. pap. text ed. 30.00 (0-7881-1626-6) DIANE Pub.

Research & Invention in Outer Space: Liability & Intellectual Property Rights. Ed. by Said Mosteshar. LC 95-44. 1995. lib. bdg. 160.00 (0-7923-2982-1, Pub. by M Nijhoff NE) Kluwer Ac.

Research & Its Application. Ed. by James P. Smith. LC 94-2693. (Advanced Nursing Ser.). (Illus.). 224p. 1994. pap. 27.95 (0-632-03867-5, Pub. by Blckwell Sci Pubns UK) Blackwell Sci.

Research & Language Learning see Language Teaching: Broader Contexts

Research & Lawmakers: A Student Perspective. David F. Rider & Barry Salussolia. LC 84-621357. (Occasional Papers: No. 4). (Illus.). 1981. pap. text ed. 4.00 (0-944277-05-5) U VT Ctr Rsch VT.

Research & Management Techniques for Wildlife & Habitats. Ed. by Theodore A. Bookhout. LC 93-61624. (Illus.). 740p. (C). 1994. text ed. 40.00 (0-933564-10-4) Wildlife Soc.

Research & Medical Practice: Their Interaction. CIBA Foundation Staff. LC 76-24846. (CIBA Foundation Symposium: New Ser.: No. 44). 228p. reprint ed. pap. 65.00 (0-317-29782-1, 2022172) Bks Demand.

Research & Methodology in General Pediatrics: A Swiss Experience. Ed. by P. Girardet. (Journal: Paediatrician: Vol. 9, Nos. 5-6). (Illus.). 128p. 1981. pap. 56.00 (3-8055-2661-X) S Karger.

Research & Policy: The Uses of Qualitative Methods in Social & Educational Research. Janet Finch. (Social Research & Educational Studies: Vol. 2). 260p. 1986. 60.00 (1-85000-098-0, Falmer Pr); pap. 33.00 (1-85000-099-9) Taylor & Francis.

Research & Practical Issues in Databases: Proceedings of the 3rd Australian Database Conference. B. Srinivasan & J. Zeleznikow. 350p. 1992. text ed. 95.00 (981-02-0952-5) World Scientific Pub.

Research & Practice in Deafness: Issues & Questions in Education, Psychology, & Vocational Service Provision. Ed. by Olga M. Welch. LC 93-14775. (Illus.). 326p. (C). 1993. text ed. 61.95 (0-398-05861-X) C C Thomas.

Research & Practice in Deafness: Issues & Questions in Education, Psychology, & Vocational Service Provision. Ed. by Olga M. Welch. LC 93-14775. (Illus.). 326p. 1993. pap. 39.95 (0-398-06485-7) C C Thomas.

Research & Practice in Physical Education: Selected Papers from the 1976 Research Symposia of the AAHPER National Convention. Ed. by Robert E. Stadulis. LC 77-150410. 297p. reprint ed. pap. 84.70 (0-317-55500-6, 2029534) Bks Demand.

Research & Productivity: Endogenous Technical Change. Ryuzo Sato & Gilbert Suzawa. LC 82-6745. 200p. 1983. text ed. 39.95 (0-86569-068-5, Auburn Hse) Greenwood.

Research & Productivity in Asian Agriculture. Robert E. Evenson et al. LC 90-55750. (Food Systems & Agrarian Change Ser.). (Illus.). 448p. 1991. 72.50 (0-8014-2535-2) Cornell U Pr.

Research & Professional Resources in Children's Literature: Piecing a Patchwork Quilt. Ed. by Kathy G. Short. LC 94-43802. 240p. 1995. pap. 20.95 (0-87207-126-X) Intl Reading.

*__Research & Recipes on Dementia, Heart Disease, Osteoporosis & Cancer.__ Rosemary C. Fisher. 1997. 9.95 (0-87527-530-3) Green.

Research & Reference Guide to French Studies. 2nd ed. Charles B. Osburn. LC 81-5637. 570p. 1981. 42.50 (0-8108-1440-4) Scarecrow.

Research & Reflections in Archaeology & History: Essays in Honor of Doris Stone. E. W. Andrews. LC 85-62925. (Publications: No. 57). 217p. 1986. 35.00 (0-939238-87-X) Tulane MARI.

Research & Reflexivity. Ed. by Frederick Steier. (Inquiries in Social Construction Ser.). 272p. (C). 1991. text ed. 55.00 (0-8039-8238-0); pap. text ed. 22.50 (0-8039-8239-9) Sage.

Research & Relevant Knowledge: American Research Universities since World War II. Roger L. Geiger. LC 92-22148. 432p. 1993. 65.00 (0-19-505346-X) OUP.

Research & Report Writing for Business & Economics. Conrad Berenson & Raymond Colton. (Orig.). (C). 1970. pap. text ed. write for info. (0-394-30318-0) Random.

Research & Results in Plant Breeding. Ed. by Gosta Olsson. (Illus.). 292p. (Orig.). 1986. pap. text ed. 58.00 (91-36-88705-6, Pub. by LTs Forlag A B SW) Coronet Bks.

Research & Service, a Fifty Year Record: Bureau of Public Administration - Institute of Governmental Studies, University of California, Berkeley. Dorothy C. Tompkins. LC 77-169911. 168p. reprint ed. pap. 47.90 (0-7837-2132-3, 2042414) Bks Demand.

Research & Service Programs in the PHS: Challenges in Organization. Institute of Medicine Staff. 156p. 1991. pap. text ed. 19.00 (0-309-04581-9) Natl Acad Pr.

Research & Source Guide for Students in Speech Pathology & Audiology. Gordon F. Holloway & L. Michael Webster. LC 73-571. 112p. 1978. 8.00 (0-87527-154-5) Green.

*__Research & Statistical Methods in Communication Disorders.__ David L. Maxwell & Eiki Satake. LC 96-29698. 1997. write for info. (0-683-05655-7) Williams & Wilkins.

*__Research & Technological Development Activities of the European Union: Annual Report 1995.__ 112p. 1996. pap. 25.00 (92-827-6918-6, CG93-95-580-ENC, Pub. by Europ Com UK) Bernan Associates.

Research & Technology. Ed. by I. Bernard Cohen. LC 79-7982. (Three Centuries of Science in America Ser.). (Illus.). 1980. lib. bdg. 25.95 (0-405-12564-X) Ayer.

Research & Technology: Annual Report of the Marshall Space Flight Center, 1991. (Illus.). 263p. (Orig.). (C). 1993. pap. text ed. 60.00 (1-56806-649-X) DIANE Pub.

Research & Technology Development in Advanced Communications Technologies in Europe. (Illus.). 381p. (Orig.). (C). 1995. pap. text ed. 60.00 (0-7881-1875-7) DIANE Pub.

Research & Technology Development of Telematic Systems for Flexible & Distance Learning: Delta 1993. (Illus.). 150p. (Orig.). (C). 1994. pap. text ed. 60.00 (0-7881-0774-7) DIANE Pub.

Research & Technology Development on Telematic Systems for Rural Areas. 122p. (Orig.). (C). 1993. pap. text ed. 35.00 (1-56806-769-0) DIANE Pub.

Research & Technology 1991: NASA. (Illus.). 156p. (Orig.). (C). 1993. pap. text ed. 45.00 (1-56806-612-0) DIANE Pub.

Research & the Complex Causality of the Schizophrenias. Group for the Advancement of Psychiatry Staff. LC 84-9535. (Group for the Advancement of Psychiatry, Symposium Ser.: No. 116). 101p. reprint ed. pap. 28.80 (0-7837-2100-5, 2042376) Bks Demand.

*__Research & the Manuscript Tradition.__ Frank G. Burke. LC 97-15729. 1997. write for info. (0-8108-3348-4) Scarecrow.

Research & the Teacher: A Qualitative Introduction to School Based Research. Graham Hitchcock & David Hughes. 304p. 1989. 55.00 (0-415-02432-3); pap. 16.95 (0-415-02433-1) Routledge.

Research & the Teacher: A Qualitative Introduction to School-Based Research. 2nd ed. Graham Hitcock & David Hughes. LC 95-14757. 336p. (C). 1995. pap. 19.95 (0-415-10102-6) Routledge.

Research & Theory in Developmental Psychology: Awards Papers of the New York State Psychological Association. Ed. by Marguerite F. Levy. 1983. 27.50 (0-8290-1067-X) Irvington.

Research & Theory in Family Science. Randall D. Day. 661p. 1995. pap. 47.95 (0-534-21780-X) Brooks-Cole.

Research & Thought in Administrative Theory: Developments in the Field of Educational Administration. Ed. by Gladys S. Johnston & Carol C. Yeakey. LC 86-20196. (Illus.). 236p. (Orig.). (C). 1986. pap. text ed. 22.00 (0-8191-5623-X) U Pr of Amer.

Research & Writing. Yelin. 1995. wbk. ed., pap. 16.95 (0-316-96805-6) Little.

*__Research & Writing.__ Zimmerman. (C). 1992. pap. write for info. (0-15-576608-2) HB Coll Pubs.

Research & Writing in the Disciplines. Donald E. Zimmerman & Dawn Rodrigues. 300p. (C). 1992. pap. text ed. write for info. (0-318-69141-8) HB Coll Pubs.

Research Animal Anesthesia, Analgesia & Surgery. Ed. by Alison C. Smith & M. Michael Swindle. LC 94-68123. 170p. 1994. pap. 55.00 (0-614-06557-7) Scientists Ctr.

Research Animals & Concepts of Applicability to Clinical Medicine: Experimental Biology & Medicine, Vol. 7. Ed. by K. Gaertner et al. (Illus.). x, 234p. 1982. pap. 118.50 (3-8055-3492-2) S Karger.

Research Animals & Experimental Design in Nephrology. H. Stolte & Jeannette Alt. (Contributions to Nephrology Ser.: Vol. 19). (Illus.). x, 250p. 1980. pap. 65.75 (3-8055-3075-7) S Karger.

Research, Application, & Experience with Precast Prestressed Bridge Deck Panels. Prestressed Concrete Institute Staff. (PCI Journal Reprints Ser.). 24p. 1975. pap. 12.00 (0-318-19843-6, JR167) P-PCI.

Research Applications of Nuclear Pulsed Systems. (Panel Proceedings Ser.). (Illus.). 234p. 1967. pap. 30.00 (92-0-151067-5, ISP144, Pub. by IAEA AU) Bernan Associates.

Research Applications Workbook. Fred Pyrczak. 1983. pap. text ed. 14.75 (0-912736-28-3) EDITS Pubs.

Research Approaches to Movement & Personality. Philip Eisenberg et al. 1979. 26.95 (0-405-03146-7, 11041) Ayer.

Research as Empowerment: Feminist Links, Postmodern Interruptions. Janice L. Ristock & Joan Pennell. 168p. 1996. pap. 19.95 (0-19-541080-7) OUP.

Research As Praxisi Lesso: Lessons from Programmatic Research into Therapeutic Practice. Lisa L. Hoshmand & Jack Martin. (Counseling & Development Ser.). 272p. (C). 1995. pap. text ed. 24.95 (0-8077-3427-6) Tchrs Coll.

Research as Social Change: New Opportunities for Qualitative Research. Michael Schratz & Rob Walker. LC 94-48383. 208p. (C). 1995. pap. 17.95 (0-415-11869-7) Routledge.

Research as Social Change: New Opportunities for Qualitative Research. Michael Schratz & Rob Walker. LC 94-48383. 208p. (C). (gr. 13). 1995. text ed. 62.95 (0-415-11868-9) Routledge.

Research Assistant. Jack Rudman. (Career Examination Ser.: C-674). 1994. pap. 29.95 (0-8373-0674-4) Nat Learn.

*__Research Associates' Heat Stress.__ Kent Halstead. 68p. (Orig.). 1997. pap. text ed. 30.00 (1-883298-05-9) Res Assoc WA.

Research at the Hampstead Child-Therapy Clinic & Other Papers. Anna Freud. LC 67-9514. (Writings of Anna Freud: Vol. 5). 575p. 1969. 75.00 (0-8236-6874-6) Intl Univs Pr.

Research at the Marketing - Entrepreneurship Interface, 1987. Gerald E. Hills. 307p. 1987. 19.95 (1-884058-00-0) U Ill Chicago.

Research at the Marketing - Entrepreneurship Interface, 1989. Gerald E. Hills et al. 479p. 1989. 19.95 (1-884058-01-9) U Ill Chicago.

Research at the Marketing - Entrepreneurship Interface, 1990. Gerald E. Hills et al. 356p. 1990. 19.95 (1-884058-02-7) U Ill Chicago.

Research at the Marketing - Entrepreneurship Interface, 1992. Gerald E. Hills & Raymond W. Laforge. 330p. 1992. 19.95 (1-884058-04-3) U Ill Chicago.

Research at the Marketing - Entrepreneurship Interface, 1993. Daniel F. Muzyka et al. 1993. 19.95 (1-884058-05-1) U Ill Chicago.

Research at the Marketing - Entrepreneurship Interface, 1994. Gerald E. Hills & Raymond W. La Forge. 363p. 1991. 19.95 (1-884058-03-5) U Ill Chicago.

Research at the Marketing - Entrepreneurship Interface, 1994. Ed. by Gerald E. Hills et al. 1994. 19.95 (1-884058-06-X) U Ill Chicago.

Research at the Marketing - Entrepreneurship Interface 1995. Ed. by Daniel F. Muzyka et al. (Orig.). 1995. pap. 19.95 (1-884058-07-8) U Ill Chicago.

Research at the Marketing/Entrepreneurship Interface 1996. Ed. by Gerald E. Hills et al. (Orig.). 1996. pap. text ed. 29.95 (1-884058-08-6) U Ill Chicago.

Research Balloons: Exploring Hidden Worlds. Carole S. Briggs. (Discovery! Ser.). (Illus.). 64p. (J). (gr. 5 up). 1988. lib. bdg. 21.50 (0-8225-1585-7, Lerner Publctns) Lerner Group.

Research-Based Teacher Evaluation. Ed. by Richard Schwab. 128p. (C). 1990. lib. bdg. 61.00 (0-7923-9094-6) Kluwer Ac.

Research Basics: How to Write Research Reports & Theses. Rudolf E. Klimes. 83p. (C). 1994. per., pap. text ed. 5.95 (1-886304-02-5) LearnWell Pr.

Research Bibliography of California's Chinese Americans. Compiled by Anna Chan. 47p. 1991. pap. text ed. 20.00 (1-883638-17-8) Rose Inst.

Research Book for Gifted Programs K-8. Nancy Polette. (Illus.). 176p. 1984. pap. 14.95 (0-913839-28-0) Pieces of Lrning.

Research Book of the Fifty States. Nancy Polette. (Illus.). 48p. 1991. pap. 5.95 (1-879287-03-X) Pieces of Lrning.

Research Briefings, 1986. Committee on Science, Engineering & Public Policy et al. 62p. 1986. pap. text ed. 9.95 (0-309-03689-5) Natl Acad Pr.

Research Briefings 1987. Institute of Medicine Staff et al. 80p. 1988. pap. text ed. 9.95 (0-309-03828-6) Natl Acad Pr.

Research Catalog of Maps of America to 1860 in the W. L. Clements Library. University Staff. 1980. 330.00 (0-8161-1227-4, Hall Library) G K Hall.

Research Catalog of the Library of the American Museum of Natural History: Authors, 13 vols. Ed. by American Museum of Natural History Staff. 1977. 1,455.00 (0-8161-0064-0, Hall Library) G K Hall.

Research Catalog of the Library of the American Museum of Natural History: Classed Catalog. Reading Catalog of the Library of the American Museum of Natural History Staff. 1978. 1,270.00 (0-8161-0238-4, Hall Library) G K Hall.

Research Center Directory, 2 vols. 12th ed. Ed. by Peter D. Dresser. 2000p. 1987. 365.00 (0-8103-0678-6) Gale.

Research Center Directory, 2 vols. 15th ed. Ed. by Karen Hill. 2000p. 1990. 400.00 (0-8103-7350-5) Gale.

Research Center Directory, 2 vols. 16th ed. Piccirelli. 1991. 420.00 (0-8103-7353-X) Gale.

Research Center Directory, 2 vols. 17th ed. Annette Piccirelli. 1992. 435.00 (0-8103-7617-2) Gale.

Research Center Directory, 2 vols. 18th ed. Annette Piccirelli. 1993. 470.00 (0-8103-8159-1) Gale.

Research Center Directory, 2 Vols. 19th ed. Annette Piccirelli. 1994. 470.00 (0-8103-8356-X) Gale.

Research Center Directory, 2 Vols. 20th ed. Ed. by Tony Gerring. 2775p. 1995. 485.00 (0-8103-9094-9) Gale.

Research Center Directory, 2 vols. 21th ed. Gerring. 1996. 500.00 (0-8103-4942-6) Taft Group.

*__Research Center Directory, 2 vols.__ 22th ed. 1997. 520.00 (0-7876-0166-7, 00108876, Gale Res Intl) Gale.

*__Research Center Directory, 2 vols.__ 23th ed. 1997. 520.00 (0-7876-1341-X, 00156491, Gale Res Intl) Gale.

Research Center Directory, Vol. 1. 19th ed. Annette Piccirelli. 1994. write for info. (0-8103-8357-8) Gale.

Research Center Directory, Vol. 1. 20th ed. Gerring. 1995. write for info. (0-8103-9095-7) Gale.

Research Center Directory, Vol. 2. 19th ed. Annette Piccirelli. 1994. write for info. (0-8103-8358-6) Gale.

Research Center Directory, Vol. 2. 20th ed. Gerring. 1995. write for info. (0-8103-9096-5) Gale.

Research Center Directory, 1989, 2 vols. 13th ed. Ed. by Peter D. Dresser. 1500p. 1988. 380.00 (0-8103-2591-8) Gale.

Research Centers: The Pentagon Moves the High-Tech Battlefield on Campus. Greg LeRoy. (Illus.). 22p. (Orig.). 1988. pap. text ed. 3.00 (0-945210-01-9) Public Search.

Research Centers Directory, Nineteen Eighty-Seven, 2 vols. 11th ed. Ed. by Mary M. Watkins. 1770p. 1986. Set. 355.00 (0-8103-0472-4) Gale.

Research Centers Directory, 1990, 2 vols. 14th ed. Ed. by Peter D. Dresser & Karen Hill. 2062p. 1989. 390.00 (0-8103-4861-6) Gale.

Research Challanges. Melissa Donovan. (Illus.). 168p. (J). (gr. 4-8). 1985. student ed. 13.99 (0-86653-271-4, GA 660) Good Apple.

Research, Co-Operation & Evaluation of Educational Programmes in the Third World: Workshops Held by the Development Studies Association-Education in Developing Countries Study Group, University of Leeds, U. K., March 30, 1984 & IDS, University of Sussex, U. K., April 9-13, 1984. Ed. by K. Watson & J. Oxenham. 1985. pap. 26.00 (0-08-033395-8, Pub. by PPL UK) Elsevier.

Research Collaboration in Industry. Keith Dickson et al. 224p. 1990. text ed. 35.00 (0-86187-816-7) St Martin.

Research, Comparisons, & Medical Applications of Ericksonian Techniques. Ed. by Jeffrey K. Zeig & Stephen R. Lankton. LC 88-2896. (Ericksonian Monographs: No. 4). 132p. 1988. text ed. 28.95 (0-87630-510-9) Brunner-Mazel.

Research Councils in the Social Sciences see Survey on the Ways in Which States Interpret Their International Obligations

Research Councils in the Social Sciences Addenda see Survey on the Ways in Which States Interpret Their International Obligations

*__Research Craft: An Introduction to Social Research Methods.__ 2nd ed. John B. Williamson et al. (Illus.). 446p. (C). 1992. reprint ed. text ed. 65.00 (1-878907-60-3) TechBooks.

Research Design: Cultural Resources Inventory Program for the Marine Corps Air Ground Combat Center, Twentynine Palms, California. Jeffrey H. Altschul et al. (Statistical Research Technical Ser.: No. 17). 55p. 1989. spiral bd. 6.00 (1-879442-15-9) Stats Res.

Research Design: Cultural Resources Inventory Program for the Marine Corps Air Ground Combat Center, Twentynine Palms, California. fac. ed. Jeffrey Altschul et al. (Statistical Research (Tucson, Arizona) Technical Ser.: No. 17). (Illus.). 59p. 1989. reprint ed. pap. text ed. 5.30 (1-55567-572-7) Coyote Press.

Research Design: Data Recovery along Route N13, Navajo Indian Reservation. fac. ed. Steven D. Shelley. (Statistical Research (Tucson, Arizona) Technical Ser.: No. 16). (Illus.). 227p. 1988. reprint ed. pap. text ed. 20.00 (1-55567-571-9) Coyote Press.

Research Design: Qualitative & Quantitative Approaches. John W. Creswell. 200p. (C). 1994. text ed. 48.00 (0-8039-5254-6); pap. text ed. 19.95 (0-8039-5255-4) Sage.

*__Research Design: Strategies & Choices in the Design of Social Research.__ Catherine Hakim. 224p. 1987. pap. text ed. 27.95 (0-415-07911-X) Routledge.

Research Design: Strategies & Choices in the Design of Social Research. Catherine Hakim. (Contemporary Social Research Ser.: No. 13). 240p. 1987. text ed. 49.95 (0-04-312031-8) Routledge Chapman & Hall.

Research Design: Strategies & Choices in the Design of Social Research. Catherine Hakim. LC 86-13989. (Contemporary Social Research Ser.: No. 13). 240p. (C). 1987. pap. text ed. 27.95 (0-04-312032-6) Routledge Chapman & Hall.

Research Design & Evaluation in Speech-Language Pathology & Audiology. 3rd ed. Franklin H. Silverman. 400p. 1992. text ed. 69.00 (0-13-755448-6) P-H.

*__Research Design & Evaluation in Speech-Language Pathology & Audiology.__ 4th ed. Franklin H. Silverman. LC 97-6601. 1997. 57.33 (0-205-19799-X) Allyn.

Research Design & Methods: A Process Approach. 3rd ed. Kenneth S. Bordens & Bruce B. Abbott. LC 95-24591. 617p. (C). 1995. text ed. 56.95 (1-55934-409-1, 1409); teacher ed., pap. text ed. write for info. (1-55934-583-7, 1583); student ed., pap. text ed. 16.95 (1-55934-584-5, 1584); teacher ed., pap. text ed. write for info. (1-55934-585-3, 1585) Mayfield Pub.

*__Research Design & Methods: A Process Approach, 1996, Including Labstat Pkg.__ 3rd ed. Kenneth S. Bordens & Bruce B. Abbott. 617p. 59.95 (1-55934-767-8) Mayfield Pub.

*__Research Design & Methods: A Process Approach, 1996, Including Study Guide.__ 3rd ed. Kenneth S. Bordens & Bruce B. Abbott. 617p. 59.95 (1-55934-596-9) Mayfield Pub.

*__Research Design & Methods: A Process Approach, 1996, Including Study Guide & Labstat Pkg.__ 3rd ed. Kenneth S. Bordens & Bruce B. Abbott. 617p. 64.95 (1-55934-768-6) Mayfield Pub.

Research Design & Statistical Analysis. Jerome L. Myers & Arnold D. Well. LC 95-8542. 728p. 1995. reprint ed. 49.95 (0-8058-2067-1) L Erlbaum Assocs.

Research Design & Statistics for the Safety & Health Professional. Charles A. Cacha. LC 96-37475. (Industrial Health & Safety Ser.). (Illus.). 256p. 1997. text ed. 49.95 (0-442-02041-4) Van Nos Reinhold.

Research Design Explained. 2nd ed. Mark Mitchell & Janina Jolley. 450p. (C). 1992. text ed. 45.25 (0-03-055972-3) HB Coll Pubs.

Research Design Explained. 3rd ed. Mitchell. (C). 1995. suppl. ed., teacher ed., pap. text ed. 35.00 (0-15-503247-X) HB Coll Pubs.

Research Design Explained. 3rd ed. Mark Mitchell & Janina Jolley. 658p. (C). 1996. text ed. 53.25 (0-15-502828-6) HB Coll Pubs.

An Asterisk (*) at the beginning of an entry indicates that the title is appearing in BIP for the first time.

Research Design Explained: Test Bank. 3rd ed. Mitchell. (C). 1995. pap. text ed. 26.75 (*0-15-503249-6*) HB Coll Pubs.

Research Design for Program Evaluation: The Regression-Discontinuity Approach. William M. Trochim. LC 84-1969. (Contemporary Evaluation Research Ser.: No. 6). 272p. 1984. reprint ed. pap. 77.60 (*0-608-01461-3*, 2059505) Bks Demand.

Research Design for Social Work & the Human Services. Jean W. Anastas & MacDonald. LC 93-44863. 596p. 38.95 (*0-669-20937-6*, Lexington) Jossey-Bass.

Research Design for the Data Recovery of Archaeological Sites Within No Name West Basin, Fort Irwin, San Bernardino County, California. fac. ed. Contrib. by Claude N. Warren et al. (Fort Irwin Archaeology Project, Research Reports: No. 1). 81p. 1982. reprint ed. pap. text ed. 7.50 (*1-55567-523-9*) Coyote Press.

Research Design for the Data Recovery of Bow Willow Wash South (Site 4-SBr-4204), a Pavement Quarry Within Fort Irwin, San Bernardino County, California. fac. ed. K. A. Bergin & C. N. Warren. (Fort Irwin Archaeology Project, Research Reports: No. 9). (Illus.). 118p. 1983. reprint ed. pap. text ed. 10.65 (*1-55567-533-6*) Coyote Press.

Research Design for the Roosevelt Community Development Study. William H. Doelle et al. (Anthropological Papers: No. 12). (Illus.). 184p. (Orig.). 1992. pap. 12.00 (*1-886398-10-0*) Desert Archaeol.

***Research Design for the Testing of Interstate 10 Corridor Prehistoric & Historic Archaeological Remains Between Interstate 17 & 30th Drive: Group II, Las Colinas.** David A. Gregory & Thomas R. McGuire. (Archaeological Ser.: Vol. 157). (Illus.). 79p. 1982. 5.95 (*1-889747-32-7*) Ariz St Mus.

Research Design in Anthropology: Paradigms & Pragmatics in the Testing of Hypotheses. John A. Brim et al. 123p. (C). 1982. reprint ed. pap. text ed. 16.95 (*0-8290-0583-8*) Irvington.

Research Design in Clinical Psychology. 2nd ed. Alan E. Kazdin. 494p. (C). 1992. pap. text ed. 39.50 (*0-205-14587-6*, H45875) Allyn.

***Research Design in Clinical Psychology.** 3rd ed. Alan E. Kazdin. (C). 1997. pap. text ed. 39.75 (*0-205-26088-8*) Allyn.

Research Design in Clinical Psychology & Psychiatry. J. B. Chassan. 496p. 1982. text ed. 19.50 (*0-8290-1009-2*) Irvington.

Research Design in Counseling. P. Paul Heppner et al. 462p. (C). 1992. text ed. 60.95 (*0-534-16284-3*) Brooks-Cole.

Research Design in Counseling. 2nd ed. Heppner & Kivlighan. (Counseling Ser.). Date not set. text ed. 42.00 (*0-534-34517-4*) Course Tech.

Research Designs. Paul E. Spector. (Quantitative Applications in the Social Sciences Ser.: Vol. 23). (Illus.). 88p. (C). 1981. pap. 9.95 (*0-8039-1709-0*) Sage.

Research Designs & Methods in Psychiatry. Ed. by M. Fava & J. F. Rosenbaum. LC 92-49613. (Techniques in the Behavioral & Neural Sciences Ser.: Vol. 9). 324p. 1992. 229.25 (*0-444-89595-7*); pap. 123.50 (*0-444-89594-9*) Elsevier.

Research Designs for Political Science: Contrivance & Demonstration in Theory & Practice. David A. Bositis. LC 89-38397. 184p. (C). 1990. text ed. 29.95 (*0-8093-1600-5*) S Ill U Pr.

Research Developments in Drug & Alcohol Use, Vol. 362. LC 81-3973. 244p. 1981. 49.00 (*0-89766-117-6*); pap. 49.00 (*0-89766-118-4*) NY Acad Sci.

***Research Developments in Probability & Statistics.** Ed. by E. Brunner & M. Denker. (Illus.). 464p. 1996. 235.00 (*90-6764-209-6*, Pub. by VSP NE) Coronet Bks.

Research Dilemmas in Administration & Policy Settings. Ed. by Catherine Marshall. (Special Issues of the Anthropology & Education Quarterly Ser.: Vol. 15, No. 3). 1984. 7.50 (*0-317-66345-3*) Am Anthro Assn.

Research Directions for Multicultural Education. Carl A. Grant. 225p. 1992. 80.00 (*1-85000-476-5*, Falmer Pr); pap. 27.00 (*1-85000-477-3*, Falmer Pr) Taylor & Francis.

Research Directions for the Decade: 1990 Summer Study on High Energy Physics. E. L. Berger. 1000p. 1992. text ed. 178.00 (*981-02-0931-2*) World Scientific Pub.

Research Directions in Computational Mechanics: A Series. National Research Council Staff. 144p. (C). 1991. pap. text ed. 19.00 (*0-309-04648-3*) Natl Acad Pr.

Research Directions in Computer Control of Urban Traffic Systems. 393p. 1979. pap. 22.00 (*0-87262-179-0*) Am Soc Civil Eng.

Research Directions in Computer Science: An MIT Perspective. Ed. by Albert R. Meyer et al. 516p. 1991. 45.00 (*0-262-13257-5*) MIT Pr.

Research Directions in Concurrent Object-Oriented Programming. Ed. by Gul Agha et al. (Illus.). 350p. 1993. 57.50 (*0-262-01139-5*) MIT Pr.

Research Directions in Database Security. Ed. by T. F. Lunt. (Illus.). 288p. 1992. 60.95 (*0-387-97736-8*) Spr-Verlag.

Research Directions in High-Level Parallel Programming Languages: Mont Saint-Michel, France, June 17-19, 1991 Proceedings. Ed. by J. P. Banatre et al. (Lecture Notes in Computer Science Ser.: Vol. 574). viii, 387p. 1992. 52.95 (*0-387-55160-3*) Spr-Verlag.

Research Directions in Object-Oriented Programming. Ed. by Bruce Shriver & Peter Wegner. (Computer Systems Ser.). 500p. 1987. 70.00 (*0-262-19264-0*) MIT Pr.

Research Directions in Software Technology. Ed. by Peter Wegner. (MIT Computer Science & Artificial Intelligence Ser.: No. 2). (Illus.). 1979. 60.00 (*0-262-23090-9*) MIT Pr.

Research Directions of Black Psychologists. Anderson J. Franklin & J. Frank Yates. Ed. by A. Wade Boykin et al. LC 79-7348. 440p. 1980. 50.00 (*0-87154-254-4*) Russell Sage.

***Research Directory: Research Activities Within Medical Groups & Research Centers.** Ed. by Suzanne S. White & Donna L. Burman. 350p. (Orig.). 1996. pap. text ed. 35.00 (*1-56829-012-8*) Med Group Mgmt.

Research-Doctorate Programs in the United States: Continuity & Change. National Research Council, Commission on Physical Sciences, Mathematics, & Applications Staff. Ed. by Marvin Goldberger et al. LC 95-35154. 768p. (Orig.). (C). 1995. text ed. 59.95 (*0-309-05094-4*) Natl Acad Pr.

Research, Education & Public Policy, Vol. 3. Ed. by Barbara J. Brown. LC 93-24268. (Nursing Administration Quarterly Ser.). 304p. 1993. 40.00 (*0-8342-0509-2*, 20509) Aspen Pub.

Research Ethics: A Psychological Approach. Ed. by Barbara Stanley et al. LC 95-22886. x, 273p. 1996. text ed. 35.00 (*0-8032-4188-7*) U of Nebr Pr.

***Research Ethics: A Reader.** Ed. by Deni Elliott & Judy E. Stern. LC 96-34654. (Illus.). 333p. 1997. pap. text ed. 25.00 (*0-87451-797-4*) U Pr of New Eng.

Research Ethics: Cases & Materials. Ed. by Robin L. Penslar. LC 94-5971. 320p. 1995. 31.50 (*0-253-34312-7*); pap. 13.95 (*0-253-20906-4*) Ind U Pr.

Research Ethics Involving Human Subjects: Facing the 21st Century. Ed. by Harold Y. Vanderpool. 544p. 1996. 59.00 (*1-55572-036-6*) Univ Pub Group.

Research Ethics, Manuscript Review, & Journal Quality: Symposium on the Peer Review - Editing Process, San Antonio, Tex., 1990. LC 92-7753. (ACS Miscellaneous Publication Ser.). 94p. 1992. pap. 12.00 (*0-89118-109-1*, PN4888) Am Soc Agron.

Research Experience. Ed. by M. Patricia Golden. LC 75-17321. 528p. 1976. pap. text ed. 32.00 (*0-87581-188-4*) Peacock Pubs.

Research Experience for Nurses: Realities of Studies into Nursing. Jill Buckeldee. Ed. by Richard McMahon. LC 93-35414. 144p. 1994. pap. 41.50 (*1-56593-193-9*, 0508, Chap & Hall NY) Singular Publishing.

Research Experiences in Plant Physiology: A Laboratory Manual. 2nd ed. T. C. Moore. (Illus.). 348p. 1981. pap. 52.95 (*0-387-90606-1*) Spr-Verlag.

Research Explorations in Adult Attachments. Intro. by Karl Pottharst. (American University Studies: Psychology: Ser. VIII, Vol. 14). 353p. (C). 1989. text ed. 53.95 (*0-8204-1050-0*) P Lang Pubng.

***Research Facilities for the Future of Nuclear Energy: Proceedings of an ENS Class 1 Topical Meeting.** 572p. 1996. lib. bdg. 67.00 (*981-02-2779-5*) World Scientific Pub.

Research Facilities of the Future. Stanley Stark. LC 94-28061. write for info. (*0-89766-903-7*); pap. text ed. write for info. (*0-89766-904-5*) NY Acad Sci.

Research Fellow. large type ed. Alex Stuart. 352p. 1986. 25.99 (*0-7089-1425-X*) Ulverscroft.

Research Fields in Physics. 9th ed. Contrib. by Institute of Physics Staff. LC 94-48024. 115p. 1994. pap. 100.00 (*0-7503-0333-6*) IOP Pub.

Research Findings on Smoking of Abused Substances. Ed. by C. Nora Chiang & Richard L. Hawks. (Illus.). 178p. (Orig.). (C). 1994. pap. text ed. 30.00 (*0-7881-0372-5*) DIANE Pub.

Research Findings on the Effectiveness of State Welfare-to-Work Programs. Evelyn Glanzglass. Ed. by Karen Glass. 40p. (Orig.). 1994. pap. text ed. 15.00 (*1-55877-194-8*) Natl Governor.

Research for Business Decisions: Business Research Methods. 5th ed. Howard L. Balsley. 496p. 1991. 39.50 (*0-931541-26-3*) Mancorp Pub.

Research for Electric Energy Systems. Ed. by William E. Anderson. (Illus.). 97p. (Orig.). (C). 1992. pap. text ed. 30.00 (*1-56806-003-3*) DIANE Pub.

Research for Health Professionals: Design, Analysis, & Ethics. Robert P. Heaney & Charles J. Dougherty. LC 87-31129. (Illus.). 282p. 1988. text ed. 36.95 (*0-8138-1712-9*) Iowa St U Pr.

Research for Physiotherapists: Project Design & Analysis. 2nd ed. Carolyn M. Hicks. LC 94-25780. 253p. 1995. 34.95 (*0-443-04999-8*) Churchill.

Research for Profit. O. A. Battista. 1989. 39.95 (*0-915074-12-5*) Knowledge Bk Pubs.

Research for Profit: The Problem, the Solution, a Case History. Paul W. Bachman. LC 78-75633. (Illus.). 202p. reprint ed. pap. 57.60 (*0-317-09730-X*, 2012403) Bks Demand.

Research for Public Transit: New Directions. (Special Reports: No. 213). 146p. 1987. 16.00 (*0-309-04461-8*) Transport Res Bd.

Research for Romance. Erin Phillips. (First Love Ser.). 186p. (YA). (gr. 7 up). 1996. pap. 49.95 (*0-671-53396-7*) PB.

Research for School Library Media Specialists. Kent L. Gustafson & Jane B. Smith. LC 93-34864. (Information Management, Policies & Services Ser.). 1994. pap. 39.50 (*1-56750-087-0*); text ed. 73.25 (*1-56750-086-2*) Ablex Pub.

***Research for the Future Development of Aquaculture in Ghana.** Ed. by M. Prein et al. (ICLARM Conference Proceedings Ser.: No. 42). 94p. 1995. per. write for info. (*971-8709-43-6*, Pub. by ICLARM PH) Intl Spec Bk.

Research for the Health Professional: A Practical Guide. 2nd ed. Diana M. Bailey. LC 96-36840. (Illus.). 278p. (C). 1997. pap. text ed. 22.95 (*0-8036-0151-4*) Davis Co.

Research for the Helping Professions. William K. Wilkinson & Keith McNeil. 490p. 1996. text ed. 63.95 (*0-534-34003-2*) Brooks-Cole.

***Research for the Reorientation of National Health Systems.** (Technical Report Ser.: No. 694). 71p. 1983. pap. text ed. 7.00 (*92-4-120694-2*) World Health.

Research for Writers. Robert J. Murray & Kate White. 152p. (C). 1995. pap. 40.00 (*0-7300-0302-7*, Pub. by Deakin Univ AT) St Mut.

Research Foresight: Creating the Future. Ben Martin & John Irvine. 300p. 1989. text ed. 52.00 (*0-86187-510-9*) St Martin.

Research Foundations for Psychotherapy Practice. Ed. by Mark Aveline & David A. Shapiro. 332p. 1995. text ed. 66.95 (*0-471-95219-2*) Wiley.

Research Foundations Object Oriented. Cardenas. 1995. pap. text ed. 56.00 (*0-13-456476-6*) P-H.

Research Foundations of Graduate Education: Germany, Britain, France, United States, Japan. Ed. by Burton R. Clark. LC 92-13407. (C). 1993. 48.00 (*0-520-07997-3*) U CA Pr.

Research Framework for Traditional Fisheries. Ian R. Smith. (Illus.). 40p. 1983. pap. text ed. 6.50 (*0-89955-391-5*, Pub. by ICLARM PH) Intl Spec Bk.

Research Fraud in the Behavioral & Biomedical Sciences. Ed. by David J. Miller & Michel Hersen. LC 91-21625. 272p. 1992. text ed. 65.00 (*0-471-52068-3*) Wiley.

Research Frontiers: Implantable Defibrillator Surgery. Spotnitz. 120p. 1992. 94.00 (*1-879702-41-X*) CRC Pr.

Research Frontiers in Anthropology. Ember. (Illus.). (C). 1994. pap. text ed. 16.00 (*0-13-337478-5*) P-H.

Research Frontiers in Fluid Dynamics. Ed. by Raymond J. Seeger & G. Temple. LC 65-14246. (Interscience Monographs & Texts in Physics & Astronomy: Vol. 15). reprint ed. pap. 160.00 (*0-317-08477-1*, 2051478) Bks Demand.

Research Frontiers in Industrial Relations & Human Resources. Ed. by David Lewin et al. 1992. 22.50 (*0-913447-53-6*) Indus Relations Res.

Research Frontiers in Magnetochemistry. C. J. O'Connor. LC 93-16991. 424p. 1993. text ed. 109.00 (*981-02-1246-1*) World Scientific Pub.

Research Frontiers in Marketing: Dialogues & Directions: 1978 Educator's Proceedings. American Marketing Association Staff. Ed. by Subhash C. Jain. LC 78-8596. (American Marketing Association, Proceedings Ser.: 43). 455p. reprint ed. pap. 129.70 (*0-317-39638-2*, 2023364) Bks Demand.

Research Frontiers in Politics & Government. Stephen K. Bailey et al. LC 72-7820. 240p. 1973. reprint ed. text ed. 59.75 (*0-8371-6527-X*, BARF, Greenwood Pr) Greenwood.

Research Fundamentals in Home Economics. 3rd ed. Marjory L. Joseph & William D. Joseph. (Illus.). 1986. pap. 27.95 (*0-916434-33-8*) Plycon Pr.

Research Funding & Resource Manual: Mental Health & Addictive Disorders. American Psychiatric Association Office of Research Staff. Ed. by Harold A. Pincus. 432p. 1995. pap. text ed. 56.00 (*0-89042-216-8*, 2216) Am Psychiatric.

***Research Funding Guidebook: Getting It, Managing It & Renewing It.** Joanne B. Ries & Carl G. Leukefeld. LC 97-4829. 1997. write for info. (*0-7619-0230-9*); pap. write for info. (*0-7619-0231-7*) Sage.

Research Games. K. C. Bowen. 126p. 1978. 31.00 (*0-85066-169-2*) Taylor & Francis.

Research Groups in Dutch Sociology. Jos De Haan. 282p. 1994. pap. 26.50 (*90-5170-312-0*, Pub. by Thesis Pubs NE) IBD Ltd.

Research Guide: Surrogate Motherhood. Kathleen K. Bach. LC 87-37863. (Legal Research Guides Ser.: Vol. 6). 46p. 1987. lib. bdg. 30.00 (*0-89941-588-1*, 305420) W S Hein.

Research Guide for China's Response to the West: A Documentary Survey, 1839-1923. Teng Ssu-Ya et al. LC 53-5061. 94p. 1954. pap. 6.95 (*0-674-76350-5*) HUP.

Research Guide for Psychology. Raymond G. McInnis. LC 81-1377. (Reference Sources for the Social Sciences & Humanities Ser.: No. 1). (Illus.). 604p. 1982. text ed. 105.00 (*0-313-21399-2*, MCR/, Greenwood Pr) Greenwood.

Research Guide for Studies in Early Childhood. Enid E. Haag. LC 88-5690. (Reference Sources for the Social Sciences & Humanities Ser.: No. 8). 444p. 1988. text ed. 69.50 (*0-313-24763-3*, HRC/, Greenwood Pr) Greenwood.

***Research Guide for the Digital Age: A New Handbook to Research & Writing for the Serious Student.** Francis A. Burkle-Young & Saundra Maley. LC 97-16464. 1997. pap. write for info. (*0-7618-0779-9*) U Pr of Amer.

Research Guide for Undergraduates: English & American Literature. 4th ed. Nancy L. Baker & Nancy Huling. LC 95-31637. (Illus.). viii, 88p. 1995. pap. 10.00 (*0-87352-566-3*, S2013) Modern Lang.
Completely updated to include detailed information on using computer resources, the new edition of the popular RESEARCH GUIDE FOR UNDERGRADUATE STUDENTS helps the beginning researcher use the library & locate books & articles on English & American literature. The GUIDE explains how to use forty essential reference works - from the print & electronic forms of the MLA INTERNATIONAL BIBLIOGRAPHY to the OXFORD ENGLISH DICTIONARY - & reprints many illustrations from the materials discussed. ***Publisher Provided Annotation.***

Research Guide on Language. Edgar C. Polome. (Trends in Linguistics, Studies & Monographs: No. 48). xii, 564p. (C). 1990. lib. bdg. 190.80 (*3-11-012046-1*) Mouton.

Research Guide to American Historical Biography, Vol. 1-3. Ed. by Robert Muccigrosso. LC 88-19316. 1778p. 1988. lib. bdg. 189.00 (*0-933833-09-1*) Beacham Pub Corp.

Research Guide to American Historical Biography, Vol. 5. LC 88-19316. 610p. 1991. lib. bdg. 63.00 (*0-933833-24-5*) Beacham Pub Corp.

Research Guide to American Historical Biography, Vol. 4: Women & Minorities. Ed. by Suzanne Niemeyer. LC 88-19316. 572p. 1990. lib. bdg. 63.00 (*0-933833-21-0*) Beacham Pub Corp.

Research Guide to Andean History: Bolivia, Chile, Ecuador, & Peru. Ed. by John J. TePaske. LC 80-29365. xiii, 346p. 1981. text ed. 41.00 (*0-8223-0450-3*) Duke.

Research Guide to Biography & Criticism, Set, Vols. 1 & 2. Ed. by Walton Beacham. LC 85-2188. (Literature Ser.). 1386p. (C). 1985. lib. bdg. 99.00 (*0-933833-00-8*) Beacham Pub Corp.

Research Guide to Biography & Criticism, Vols. 5-6. Ed. by Walton Beacham. 1150p. 1992. Set. lib. bdg. 139.00 (*0-933833-27-X*) Beacham Pub Corp.

Research Guide to Biography & Criticism: World Drama. Ed. by Walton Beacham. 752p. 1986. lib. bdg. 69.00 (*0-933833-06-7*) Beacham Pub Corp.

Research Guide to Biography & Criticism, 1990 Update. Ed. by Walton Beacham & David Lowe. 650p. 1990. lib. bdg. 63.00 (*0-933833-23-7*) Beacham Pub Corp.

Research Guide to Central America & the Caribbean. Kenneth J. Grieb. LC 84-40496. 432p. 1985. text ed. 35.00 (*0-299-10050-2*) U of Wis Pr.

Research Guide to Central Party & Government Meetings in China, 1949-1986. 2nd ed. Kenneth Lieberthal & Bruce Dickson. LC 88-18527. 392p. (gr. 13). 1989. text ed. 97.95 (*0-87332-492-7*, East Gate Bk) M E Sharpe.

Research Guide to Congress: How to Make Congress Work for You. 2nd ed. Judith Manion et al. 204p. 1991. text ed. 75.00 (*1-880955-00-8*) Legi-Slate.

Research Guide to Corporate Acquisitions, Mergers, & Other Restructuring. Michael Halperin & Steven J. Bell. LC 91-24199. 232p. 1992. text ed. 55.00 (*0-313-27220-4*, HRJ, Greenwood Pr) Greenwood.

Research Guide to Critical Legal Studies. Richard W. Bauman. 279p. (C). 1996. text ed. 59.00 (*0-8133-8980-1*) Westview.

Research Guide to Current Military & Strategic Affairs. William M. Arkin. 232p. 1981. 19.95 (*0-89758-032-X*); pap. 9.95 (*0-89758-025-7*) Inst Policy Stud.

Research Guide to European Historical Biography, Vols. 1-4. Ed. by James Moncure. (Illus.). 2240p. 1992. lib. bdg. 299.00 (*0-933833-28-8*) Beacham Pub Corp.

Research Guide to European Historical Biography, Vols. 5-8. Ed. by James Moncure. 2995p. 1993. lib. bdg. 299.00 (*0-933833-30-X*) Beacham Pub Corp.

Research Guide to Human Sexuality. Kara Lichtenberg. LC 93-37236. 527p. 1994. text ed. 79.00 (*0-8153-0867-1*, SS836) Garland.

Research Guide to Libraries & Archives in the Low Countries. Compiled by Martha L. Brogan. LC 91-12598. (Bibliographies & Indexes in Library & Information Science: No. 5). 576p. 1991. text ed. 89.50 (*0-313-25466-4*, BNR, Greenwood Pr) Greenwood.

Research Guide to Loyalist Ancestors: A Directory to Archives, Manuscripts, & Published Sources. Paul J. Bunnell. 146p. (Orig.). 1990. pap. 17.00 (*1-55613-357-X*) Heritage Bk.

Research Guide to Modern Irish Dramatists. Compiled by E. H. Mikhail. LC 78-69874. 104p. 1979. 10.00 (*0-87875-166-1*) Whitston Pub.

Research Guide to Musicology. fac. ed. James W. Pruett & Thomas P. Slavens. LC 84-24379. (Sources of Information in the Humanities Ser.: No. 4). 178p. 1985. pap. 50.80 (*0-7837-7314-5*, 2047241) Bks Demand.

Research Guide to People's Daily Editorials, 1949-1975. Michel Oksenberg & Gail Henderson. LC 82-4408. 212p. (Orig.). 1982. pap. text ed. 20.00 (*0-89264-949-6*) Ctr Chinese Studies.

Research Guide to Philosophy. fac. ed. Terrence N. Tice & Thomas P. Slavens. LC 83-11834. (Sources of Information in the Humanities Ser.: No. 3). 620p. 1983. pap. 176.70 (*0-7837-7313-7*, 2047240) Bks Demand.

Research Guide to Religious Studies. fac. ed. John F. Wilson & Thomas P. Slavens. LC 81-22862. (Sources of Information in the Humanities Ser.: No. 1). 199p. 1982. pap. 56.80 (*0-7837-7315-3*, 2047242) Bks Demand.

Research Guide to the Health Sciences: Medical, Nutritional, & Environmental. Kathleen J. Haselbauer. LC 87-17592. (Reference Sources for the Social Sciences & Humanities Ser.: No. 4). 672p. 1987. text ed. 89.50 (*0-313-23530-9*, HHS/, Greenwood Pr); lib. bdg. 49.95 (*0-685-18904-X*, Greenwood Pr) Greenwood.

***Research Guide to the Records of MALDEF: Mexican American Legal Defense & Education Fun & PRLDEF Puerto Rican Legal Defense & Education Fund.** Ed. by Theresa M. Casey & Pedro Hernandez. 148p. (Orig.). 1996. pap. 15.00 (*0-911221-16-6*) Stanford U Libraries.

Research Guide to the Russian & Soviet Censuses. Ed. by Ralph S. Clem. LC 86-47638. (Cornell Studies in Soviet History & Science). 296p. 1986. 49.95 (*0-8014-1838-0*) Cornell U Pr.

Research Guide to the Turner Movement in the United States. Compiled by Eric L. Pumroy & Katja Rampelmann. LC 96-5846. (Bibliographies & Indexes in American History Ser.: No. 33). 400p. 1996. text ed. 85.00 (*0-313-29763-0*, Greenwood Pr) Greenwood.

Research Guidelines for Aluminum Product Applications in Transportation & Industry: Proceedings of the ASME Workshop, Clearwater, FL, 1993. Ed. by D. Weissman-Berman. (CRTD Ser.: Vol. 29). 224p. 1994. pap. 52.50 (*0-7918-1203-0*) ASME.

Research Guidelines for Computer-Assisted Instruction. A. E. Hickey. 115p. 1974. 20.00 (0-87567-102-0) Entelek.

Research Guidelines for Cookery, Sensory Evaluation & Instrumental Tenderness Measurements of Fresh Meat. National Live Stock & Meat Board Staff. (Illus.). 48p. (C). 1995. write for info. (0-614-10779-2) Natl Live Stock.

Research Guidelines for Evaluating the Safety & Efficacy of Herbal Medicines. v, 86p. 1993. pap. text ed. 7.50 (92-9061-110-3, 1520003) World Health.

Research Guides to the Humanities, Social Sciences, Sciences & Technology: An Annotated Bibliography of Guides to Library Resources & Usage, Arranged by Subject or Discipline of Coverage. Ed. by Martin H. Sable. LC 86-15049. (Basic Reference Guides Ser.: No. 1). 198p. 1986. pap. 35.00 (0-87650-214-1, 4140) Pierian.

Research Ideas for the Classroom: Early Childhood Education, 3 vols. Ed. by Robert J. Jensen. LC 92-5479. 400p. 1993. 25.00 (0-02-895791-1); 16.00 (0-02-895794-6) Macmillan.

Research Ideas for the Classroom: High School Mathematics, 3 vols., Vol. 3. Ed. by Sigrid Wagner. 320p. 1993. 16.00 (0-02-895796-2) Macmillan.

Research Ideas for the Classroom: Middle School Mathematics, 3 vols. Ed. by Sigrid Wagner. 368p. 1993. 25.00 (0-02-895792-X) Macmillan.

Research Ideas for the Classroom: Middle School Mathematics, 3 vols., Vol. 2. Ed. by Sigrid Wagner. 368p. 1993. 16.00 (0-02-895795-4) Macmillan.

Research in Accounting in Emerging Economies, Vol. 1. Ed. by R. S. Olusegun Wallace et al. 290p. 1991. 73.25 (1-55938-134-5) Jai Pr.

Research in Accounting in Emerging Economies, Vol. 2. Ed. by R. S. Olusegun Wallace et al. 397p. 1993. 73.25 (1-55938-419-0) Jai Pr.

Research in Accounting in Emerging Economies, Vol. 3. Ed. by R. S. Olusegun Wallace et al. 1995. 73.25 (1-55938-697-5) Jai Pr.

Research in Accounting in Emerging Economies, Vol. 4. Ed. by R. S. Olusegun Wallace et al. 1996. 73.25 (1-55938-995-8) Jai Pr.

Research in Accounting Regulation, Vol. 1. Ed. by Timothy S. Doupnik & Kenneth S. Most. 404p. 1987. 73.25 (0-89232-693-X) Jai Pr.

Research in Accounting Regulation, Vol. 1. Ed. by Gary J. Previts et al. 235p. 1987. 73.25 (0-89232-849-5) Jai Pr.

Research in Accounting Regulation, Vol. 2. Ed. by Gary J. Previts et al. 245p. 1988. 73.25 (0-89232-941-6) Jai Pr.

Research in Accounting Regulation, Vol. 3. Ed. by Gary J. Previts et al. 248p. 1989. 73.25 (0-89232-998-X) Jai Pr.

Research in Accounting Regulation, Vol. 4. Ed. by Gary J. Previts et al. 221p. 1990. 73.25 (1-55938-084-5) Jai Pr.

Research in Accounting Regulation, Vol. 5. Ed. by Gary J. Previts et al. 211p. 1991. 73.25 (1-55938-399-2) Jai Pr.

Research in Accounting Regulation, Vol. 6. Ed. by Gary J. Previts et al. 227p. 1992. 73.25 (1-55938-417-4) Jai Pr.

Research in Accounting Regulation, Vol. 7. Ed. by Gary J. Previts et al. 222p. 1993. 73.25 (1-55938-692-4) Jai Pr.

Research in Accounting Regulation, Vol. 8. Ed. by Gary J. Previts et al. 263p. 1994. 73.25 (1-55938-402-6) Jai Pr.

Research in Accounting Regulation, Vol. 9. Ed. by Gary J. Previts et al. 252p. 1995. 73.25 (1-55938-883-8) Jai Pr.

Research in Accounting Regulation, Vol. 10. Ed. by Gary J. Previts et al. 1996. 73.25 (1-55938-996-6) Jai Pr.

***Research in Accounting Regulation: In Preparation, Summer 1997, Vol. 11.** Ed. by Gary J. Previts. 73.25 (0-7623-0168-6) Jai Pr.

Research in Addiction: An Update. Ed. by Hanns Hippius et al. LC 94-26617. (Psychiatry in Progress Ser.: Vol. 2). (Illus.). 160p. 1995. text ed. 32.00 (0-88937-134-2) Hogrefe & Huber Pubs.

Research in Airport Pavements. (Special Reports: No. 175). 116p. 1978. 9.20 (0-309-02800-0) Transport Res Bd.

Research in Archives: The Use of Unpublished Primary Sources. Philip C. Brooks. LC 69-19273. (Midway Reprint Ser.). 138p. reprint ed. pap. 39.40 (0-685-23856-3, 2056641) Bks Demand.

Research in Asian Economic Studies, 2 vols., Vol. 1. Ed. by M. Dutta & Zhang Zhongli. 1989. 157.00 (0-89232-986-6) Jai Pr.

Research in Asian Economic Studies: Asian Industrialization: Changing Economic Structures, Vol. 1, Pt. A. Ed. by M. Dutta & Zhang Zhongli. 359p. 1989. 78.50 (0-89232-987-4) Jai Pr.

Research in Asian Economic Studies: Asian Industrialization: Changing Economic Structures, Vol. 1, Pt. B. Ed. by M. Dutta & Zhang Zhongli. 377p. 1989. 78.50 (0-89232-988-2) Jai Pr.

Research in Asian Economic Studies: Chinas Economic Reform, 1978-1988, Vol. 3. Ed. by M. Dutta & Zhang Zhongli. 300p. 1991. 78.50 (1-55938-314-3) Jai Pr.

Research in Asian Economic Studies Vol. 2: China's Modernization & Open Economic Policy. Ed. by M. Dutta et al. 449p. 1990. 78.50 (1-55938-033-0) Jai Pr.

Research in Asian Economic Studies Vol. 4: Asian Economic Regimes: An Adaptive Innovation Paradigm. Ed. by M. Dutta & Zhang Zhongli. 1992. 157.00 (1-55938-429-8) Jai Pr.

Research in Asian Economic Studies Vol. 5: Asia-Pacific Economics: 1990's & Beyond. Ed. by M. Dutta & Zhang Zhongli. 474p. 1994. 78.50 (1-55938-616-9) Jai Pr.

Research in Atomic Structure. S. Fraga. (Lecture Notes in Chemistry Ser.: Vol. 59). 155p. 1993. 47.95 (0-387-56237-0) Spr-Verlag.

Research in Basic Writing: A Bibliographic Sourcebook. Ed. by Michael G. Moran & Martin J. Jacobi. LC 89-38229. 268p. 1990. text ed. 69.50 (0-313-25564-4, MRB/, Greenwood Pr) Greenwood.

Research in Biochemical Kinetics. Ed. by Boris I. Kurganov & N. P. Pal'mina. 182p. 1994. lib. bdg. 73.00 (1-56072-118-9) Nova Sci Pubs.

Research in Biopolitics, Vol. 1: Sexual Politics & Political Feminism. Ed. by Albert Somit. 362p. 1991. 73.25 (1-55938-096-9) Jai Pr.

Research in Biopolitics, Vol. 2: Biopolitics & the Mainstream: Contribution. Ed. by Albert Somit. 1994. 73.25 (1-55938-440-9) Jai Pr.

Research in Biopolitics, Vol. 3: Human Nature & Politics. Ed. by Albert Somit. 305p. 1995. 73.25 (1-55938-866-8) Jai Pr.

Research in Biopolitics, Vol. 4. Ed. by Albert Somit & Steven A. Peterson. 1996. 73.25 (0-7623-0039-6) Jai Pr.

***Research in Biopolitics, Vol. 5.** Ed. by Albert Somit & Steven A. Peterson. 1997. 73.25 (0-7623-0271-2) Jai Pr.

Research in Black Child Development: Doctoral Dissertation Abstracts, 1927-1979. Compiled by Hector F. Myers et al. LC 81-13425. (Illus.). xxi, 737p. 1982. text ed. 59.95 (0-313-22631-8, FRC/, Greenwood Pr) Greenwood.

Research in Black History: A Guide to Resource in the Birmingham Public Library. Ed. by Don Veasey. LC 87-29958. (Illus.). 100p. (Orig.). (C). 1987. pap. 6.00 (0-942301-06-4) Birm Pub Lib.

Research in California Law. 2nd ed. Myron Fink. vii, 132p. 1962. 37.00 (0-89941-594-6, 501950) W S Hein.

Research in Chemical Kinetics. Ed. by R. G. Compton & G. Hancock. LC 93-38643. 398p. 1993. 244.50 (0-444-81751-4) Elsevier.

Research in Chemical Kinetics. Ed. by R. G. Compton & G. Hancock. (Research in Chemical Kinetics Ser.: Vol. 3). 336p. 1995. 278.50 (0-444-82036-1) Elsevier.

Research in Chemical Kinetics, Vol. 2. Ed. by R. G. Compton & G. Hancock. 378p. 1994. 259.25 (0-444-82024-8) Elsevier.

Research in Chronic Viral Hepatitis. Ed. by W. H. Gerlich. (Archives of Virology Ser.: No. 8). (Illus.). 200p. 1994. 200.00 (0-387-82497-9) Spr-Verlag.

***Research in Church & Mission.** Viggo B. Sogaard. LC 96-48337. (Illus.). 280p. (Orig.). 1996. pap. text ed. 9.95 (0-87808-271-9, WCL271-9) William Carey Lib.

Research in Classrooms: The Study of Teachers, Teaching & Instruction. Lorin W. Anderson & Robert B. Burns. (Illus.). 375p. (C). 1989. text ed. 65.00 (0-08-034060-1, Prgamon Press) Buttrwrth-Heinemann.

Research in Classrooms: The Study of Teachers, Teaching & Instruction. Lorin W. Anderson & Robert B. Burns. (Illus.). 375p. (C). 1990. pap. text ed. 36.95 (0-08-034059-8, Prgamon Press) Buttrwrth-Heinemann.

Research in Collegiate Mathematics Education, I. Ed. by Ed Dubinsky et al. (CBMS Issues in Mathematics Education Ser.: Vol. 4). 229p. 1994. pap. text ed. 42.00 (0-8218-3504-1, CBMATH/4) Am Math.

***Research in Collegiate Mathematics Education, II.** Ed. by James Kaput et al. (Issues in Mathematics Education Ser.: Vol. 6). 217p. 1996. pap. 37.00 (0-8218-0382-4, CBMATH/6) Am Math.

Research in Community & Mental Health, Vol. 2. Ed. by James R. Greenley & Roberta G. Simmons. 357p. 1981. 73.25 (0-89232-152-0) Jai Pr.

Research in Community & Mental Health, Vol. 3. Ed. by James R. Greenley. 317p. 1993. 73.25 (0-89232-299-3) Jai Pr.

Research in Community & Mental Health, Vol. 4. Ed. by James R. Greenley. 370p. 1984. 73.25 (0-89232-489-9) Jai Pr.

Research in Community & Mental Health, Vol. 5. Ed. by James R. Greenley. 350p. 1995. 73.25 (0-89232-548-8) Jai Pr.

Research in Community & Mental Health, Vol. 7. Ed. by James R. Greenley. 325p. 1992. 73.25 (1-55938-441-7) Jai Pr.

Research in Community & Mental Health, Vol. 8. Ed. by James R. Greenley. 1995. write for info. (0-614-96754-6) Jai Pr.

Research in Community & Mental Health, Vol. 8. Ed. by James R. Greenley. 1995. 73.25 (0-614-11011-4) Jai Pr.

Research in Community & Mental Health, Vol. 9. Ed. by James R. Greenley. 1996. 73.25 (1-55938-140-X) Jai Pr.

Research in Community & Mental Health Vol. 6: Mental Disorders in Social Context. Ed. by James R. Greenley. 436p. 1996. 73.25 (0-89232-726-X) Jai Pr.

Research in Community Sociology, Supp. 1: The Community of the Streets. Ed. by Danesh A. Chekki. 199p. 1994. 73.25 (1-55938-717-3) Jai Pr.

Research in Community Sociology, Vol. 1: Contemporary Community: Change & Challenge. Ed. by Danesh A. Chekki. 231p. 1990. 73.25 (1-55938-074-8) Jai Pr.

Research in Community Sociology, Vol. 2: Communities in Transition. Ed. by Danesh A. Chekki. 255p. 1992. 73.25 (1-55938-107-8) Jai Pr.

Research in Community Sociology, Vol. 3: The Ethnic Quest for Comm.: Searching for. Ed. by Danesh A. Chekki. 250p. 1993. 73.25 (1-55938-360-7) Jai Pr.

Research in Community Sociology, Vol. 4: Suburban Communities: Change & Policy Resp. Ed. by Danesh A. Chekki. 269p. 1994. 73.25 (1-55938-773-4) Jai Pr.

Research in Community Sociology, Vol. 6. Ed. by Danesh A. Chekki. 1996. 73.25 (0-7623-0040-X) Jai Pr.

Research in Community Sociology Vol. 5: Urban Poverty in Affluent Nations. Ed. by Danesh A. Chekki. 249p. 1995. 73.25 (1-55938-884-6) Jai Pr.

Research in Composition & Rhetoric: A Bibliographic Sourcebook. Ed. by Michael G. Moran & Ronald F. Lunsford. LC 83-22568. (Illus.). xviii, 506p. 1984. text ed. 89.50 (0-313-23308-X, MOR/, Greenwood Pr) Greenwood.

Research in Computer & Robot Vision. Ed. by Colin Archibald & Paul Kwok. LC 94-45576. 432p. 1995. text ed. 109.00 (981-02-2134-7) World Scientific Pub.

Research in Congenital Hypothyroidism. Ed. by F. Delange et al. (NATO ASI Series A, Life Sciences: Vol. 161). (Illus.). 380p. 1989. 105.00 (0-306-43141-6, Plenum Pr) Plenum.

Research in Consumer Behavior, Vol. 1. Ed. by Jagdish N. Sheth. 1983. 73.25 (0-89232-323-X) Jai Pr.

Research in Consumer Behavior, Vol. 1. Ed. by Clifford J. Shultz, 2nd et al. 321p. 1985. 73.25 (0-89232-553-4) Jai Pr.

Research in Consumer Behavior, Vol. 2. Ed. by Clifford J. Shultz, 2nd et al. 257p. 1987. 73.25 (0-89232-623-9) Jai Pr.

Research in Consumer Behavior, Vol. 3. Ed. by Clifford J. Shultz, 2nd et al. 360p. 1988. 73.25 (0-89232-913-0) Jai Pr.

Research in Consumer Behavior, Vol. 4. Ed. by Clifford J. Shultz, 2nd et al. 213p. 1990. 73.25 (1-55938-004-7) Jai Pr.

Research in Consumer Behavior, Vol. 5. Ed. by Clifford J. Shultz, 2nd et al. 213p. 1991. 73.25 (1-55938-338-0) Jai Pr.

Research in Consumer Behavior, Vol. 6. Ed. by Clifford J. Shultz, 2nd et al. 268p. 1993. 73.25 (0-614-09930-7) Jai Pr.

Research in Consumer Behavior, Vol. 8. Ed. by Clifford J. Shultz, 2nd et al. 1995. 73.25 (0-614-09931-5) Jai Pr.

***Research in Consumer Behavior, Vol. 8.** Ed. by Clifford J. Shultz, II et al. 1997. 73.25 (1-55938-494-8) Jai Pr.

Research in Consumer Behavior Vol. 7: Consumption in Marketizing Economies. Ed. by Clifford J. Shultz, 2nd et al. 292p. 1994. 73.25 (1-55938-783-1) Jai Pr.

Research in Corporate Social Performance & Policy, Vol. 1. Ed. by James E. Post et al. 291p. 1978. 73.25 (0-89232-069-9) Jai Pr.

Research in Corporate Social Performance & Policy, Vol. 2. Ed. by James E. Post et al. 353p. 1980. 73.25 (0-89232-133-4) Jai Pr.

Research in Corporate Social Performance & Policy, Vol. 3. Ed. by James E. Post et al. 250p. 1981. 73.25 (0-89232-184-9) Jai Pr.

Research in Corporate Social Performance & Policy, Vol. 4. Ed. by James E. Post et al. 261p. 1982. 73.25 (0-89232-259-4) Jai Pr.

Research in Corporate Social Performance & Policy, Vol. 5. Ed. by James E. Post et al. 256p. 1983. 73.25 (0-89232-412-0) Jai Pr.

Research in Corporate Social Performance & Policy, Vol. 6. Preston Lee. Ed. by James E. Post et al. 252p. 1984. 73.25 (0-89232-499-6) Jai Pr.

Research in Corporate Social Performance & Policy, Vol. 7. Ed. by James E. Post et al. 293p. 1985. 73.25 (0-89232-585-2) Jai Pr.

Research in Corporate Social Performance & Policy, Vol. 11. Ed. by James E. Post et al. 300p. 1989. 73.25 (1-55938-017-9) Jai Pr.

Research in Corporate Social Performance & Policy, Vol. 12. Ed. by James E. Post et al. 401p. 1991. 73.25 (1-55938-116-7) Jai Pr.

Research in Corporate Social Performance & Policy, Vol. 14. Ed. by James E. Post et al. 236p. 1994. 73.25 (1-55938-732-7) Jai Pr.

Research in Corporate Social Performance & Policy, Vol. 15. Ed. by James E. Post et al. 1996. 73.25 (1-55938-966-4) Jai Pr.

Research in Corporate Social Performance & Policy: Empirical Studies of Business Eth & Values, Vol. 9. Ed. by James E. Post et al. 240p. 1987. 73.25 (0-89232-742-1) Jai Pr.

Research in Corporate Social Performance & Policy No. 1: Sustaining the Natural Environment. Ed. by James E. Post et al. 388p. 1995. suppl. ed. 78.50 (1-55938-945-1) Jai Pr.

Research in Corporate Social Performance & Policy Vol. 8: Center Themes in CSR Research. Ed. by James E. Post et al. 378p. 1987. 73.25 (0-89232-679-4) Jai Pr.

Research in Corporate Social Performance & Policy Vol. 10: International & ComparativeStudies. Ed. by James E. Post et al. 303p. 1988. 73.25 (0-89232-915-7) Jai Pr.

Research in Corporate Social Performance & Policy Vol. 13: Markets Politics & Social Performance. Ed. by James E. Post et al. 244p. 1993. 73.25 (1-55938-521-9) Jai Pr.

Research in Counseling. Ed. by C. Edward Watkins & Lawrence J. Schneider. 328p. 1991. text ed. 69.95 (0-8058-0689-X) L Erlbaum Assocs.

***Research in Counseling & Psychotherapy: Practical Applications.** Ed. by Windy Dryden. 272p. 1996. 69.95 (0-8039-7840-5); pap. 22.95 (0-8039-7841-3) Sage.

Research in Critical Theory since Nineteen Eighty-Five: A Classified Bibliography. Compiled by Leonard D. Orr. LC 89-16863. (Bibliographies & Indexes in World Literature Ser.: No. 21). 480p. 1989. text ed. 85.00 (0-313-26388-4, ORC/, Greenwood Pr) Greenwood.

Research in Dance: A Guide to Resources. Mary S. Bopp. LC 92-42508. (Reference Ser.). 304p. 1993. 55.00 (0-8161-9065-8, Hall Reference) Macmillan.

Research in Dance IV. Ed. by Judith A. Gray. 128p. (Orig.). (C). 1992. pap. 25.00 (0-88314-528-6) AAHPERD.

Research in Dementia Precox. Nolan D. Lewis. Ed. by Gerald N. Grob. LC 78-22572. (Historical Issues in Mental Health Ser.). 1980. reprint ed. lib. bdg. 25.95 (0-405-11925-9) Ayer.

Research in Design Thinking. Ed. by Nigel Cross et al. (Illus.). 222p. (Orig.). 1992. pap. 67.50 (90-6275-796-0, Pub. by Delft U Pr NE) Coronet Bks.

Research in Distance Education. Terry Evans. (C). 1990. pap. 75.00 (0-7300-1434-7, Pub. by Deakin Univ AT) St Mut.

Research in Distance Education, Vol. 2. Terry Evans & Philip Juler. 217p. 1995. pap. 50.00 (0-7300-2012-6, Pub. by Deakin Univ AT) St Mut.

Research in Distance Education No. 3, Vol. 3. Terry Evans & David Murphy. 233p. 1995. pap. 60.00 (0-7300-2103-3, Pub. by Deakin Univ AT) St Mut.

Research in Domestic & International Agribusiness Management, Vol. 1. Ray A. Goldberg. 228p. 1981. 73.25 (0-89232-172-5) Jai Pr.

Research in Domestic & International Agribusiness Management, Vol. 2. Ray A. Goldberg. 152p. 1981. 73.25 (0-89232-236-5) Jai Pr.

Research in Domestic & International Agribusiness Management, Vol. 3. Ray A. Goldberg. 183p. 1983. 73.25 (0-89232-309-4) Jai Pr.

Research in Domestic & International Agribusiness Management, Vol. 4. Ray A. Goldberg. 217p. 1983. 73.25 (0-89232-413-9) Jai Pr.

Research in Domestic & International Agribusiness Management, Vol. 5. Ray A. Goldberg. 292p. 1985. 73.25 (0-89232-518-6) Jai Pr.

Research in Domestic & International Agribusiness Management, Vol. 6. Ray A. Goldberg. 304p. 1986. 73.25 (0-89232-704-9) Jai Pr.

Research in Domestic & International Agribusiness Management, Vol. 7. Ray A. Goldberg. 177p. 1987. 73.25 (0-89232-716-2) Jai Pr.

Research in Domestic & International Agribusiness Management, Vol. 8. Ray A. Goldberg. 310p. 1988. 73.25 (0-89232-794-4) Jai Pr.

Research in Domestic & International Agribusiness Managment, Vol. 9. Ray A. Goldberg. 175p. 1989. 73.25 (0-89232-942-4) Jai Pr.

Research in Domestic & International Agribusiness Managment, Vol. 10. Ray A. Goldberg. 232p. 1992. 73.25 (1-55938-035-7) Jai Pr.

Research in Domestic & International Agribusiness Managment, Vol. 11. Ray A. Goldberg. 1994. 73.25 (1-55938-587-1) Jai Pr.

Research in Economic Anthropology, Supp. 6: Long-Term Subsistence Change in Preh. Nor. Ed. by Barry L. Isaac. 452p. 1992. 73.25 (1-55938-529-4) Jai Pr.

Research in Economic Anthropology, Supp. 7: Econ. Aspects of Water Mgmt. in the Prehi. Ed. by Barry L. Isaac. 488p. 1994. 73.25 (1-55938-646-0) Jai Pr.

Research in Economic Anthropology, Vol. 1. Ed. by Barry L. Isaac & George Dalton. 338p. 1978. 73.25 (0-89232-040-0) Jai Pr.

Research in Economic Anthropology, Vol. 2. Ed. by Barry L. Isaac & George Dalton. 390p. 1979. 73.25 (0-89232-085-0) Jai Pr.

Research in Economic Anthropology, Vol. 3. Ed. by Barry L. Isaac & George Dalton. 400p. 1980. 73.25 (0-89232-114-8) Jai Pr.

Research in Economic Anthropology, Vol. 4. Ed. by Barry L. Isaac & George Dalton. 321p. 1982. 73.25 (0-89232-189-X) Jai Pr.

Research in Economic Anthropology, Vol. 5. Ed. by Barry L. Isaac & George Dalton. 348p. 1983. 73.25 (0-89232-221-7) Jai Pr.

Research in Economic Anthropology, Vol. 6. Ed. by Barry L. Isaac & George Dalton. 308p. 1984. 73.25 (0-89232-357-4) Jai Pr.

Research in Economic Anthropology, Vol. 7. Ed. by Barry L. Isaac. 368p. 1985. 73.25 (0-89232-526-7) Jai Pr.

Research in Economic Anthropology, Vol. 8. Ed. by Barry L. Isaac. 375p. 1987. 73.25 (0-89232-680-8) Jai Pr.

Research in Economic Anthropology, Vol. 9. Ed. by Barry L. Isaac. 353p. 1987. 73.25 (0-89232-744-8) Jai Pr.

Research in Economic Anthropology, Vol. 10. Ed. by Barry L. Isaac. 306p. 1988. 73.25 (0-89232-946-7) Jai Pr.

Research in Economic Anthropology, Vol. 11. Ed. by Barry L. Isaac. 303p. 1989. 73.25 (1-55938-020-9) Jai Pr.

Research in Economic Anthropology, Vol. 12. Ed. by Barry L. Isaac. 391p. 1990. 73.25 (1-55938-118-3) Jai Pr.

Research in Economic Anthropology, Vol. 13. Ed. by Barry L. Isaac. 386p. 1991. 73.25 (1-55938-365-8) Jai Pr.

Research in Economic Anthropology, Vol. 15. Ed. by Barry L. Isaac. 358p. 1994. 73.25 (1-55938-784-X) Jai Pr.

Research in Economic Anthropology, Vol. 16. Ed. by Barry L. Isaac. 419p. 1996. 73.25 (1-55938-987-7) Jai Pr.

Research in Economic Anthropology, Vol. 17. Ed. by Barry L. Isaac. 1996. 73.25 (0-7623-0151-1) Jai Pr.

***Research in Economic Anthropology, Vol. 18.** Ed. by Barry L. Isaac. 1997. 73.25 (0-7623-0273-9) Jai Pr.

Research in Economic Anthropology: Early Paleoindian Economies of Eastern North America, Sup. 5: Early Paleoindian Economies of Eastern Nor. Ed. by Barry L. Isaac. 355p. 1990. 73.25 (1-55938-207-4) Jai Pr.

Research in Economic Anthropology: Economic Aspects of Prehispanic Highland Mexico, Supp. 2. Ed. by Barry L. Isaac. 408p. 1986. Suppl. 2: Economic Aspects of Prehispanic Highland Mexico. suppl. ed. 73.25 (0-89232-527-5) Jai Pr.

Research in Economic Anthropology: Prehistoric Economies of the Pacific Northwest Coast, Supp. 3. Ed. by Barry L. Isaac. (Research in Economic Anthropology Ser.: Suppl. 3). 351p. 1988. 73.25 (0-89232-818-5) Jai Pr.

Research in Economic Anthropology: Prehistoric Maya Economies of Belize, Supp. 4: Prehistoric Maya Economics. Ed. by Barry L. Isaac. 372p. 1989. 73.25 (1-55938-051-9) Jai Pr.

Research in Economic Anthropology Suppl. 1: The Economic Organization of the Inka State. John V. Murra. Ed. by Barry L. Isaac & George Dalton. (Research in Economic Anthropology Ser.: Suppl. 1). 214p. 1980. 73.25 (0-89232-118-0) Jai Pr.

Research in Economic History, Vol. 1. Ed. by Roger L. Ransom et al. 371p. 1979. 73.25 (0-89232-001-X) Jai Pr.

Research in Economic History, Vol. 1. Ed. by Paul Uselding. 337p. 1977. 73.25 (0-89232-056-7) Jai Pr.

An Asterisk (*) at the beginning of an entry indicates that the title is appearing in BIP for the first time.

Research in Economic History, Vol. 4. Ed. by Roger L. Ransom et al. 356p. 1979. 73.25 (*0-89232-080-X*) Jai Pr.
Research in Economic History, Vol. 5. Ed. by Roger L. Ransom et al. 301p. 1980. 73.25 (*0-89232-117-2*) Jai Pr.
Research in Economic History, Vol. 6. Ed. by Roger L. Ransom et al. 254p. 1981. 73.25 (*0-89232-119-9*) Jai Pr.
Research in Economic History, Vol. 7. Ed. by Roger L. Ransom et al. 361p. 1982. 73.25 (*0-89232-198-9*) Jai Pr.
Research in Economic History, Vol. 8. Ed. by Paul Uselding. 250p. 1983. 73.25 (*0-89232-261-6*) Jai Pr.
Research in Economic History, Vol. 9. Paul Uselding. Ed. by Roger L. Ransom et al. 253p. 1984. 73.25 (*0-89232-415-5*) Jai Pr.
Research in Economic History, Vol. 10. Ed. by Roger L. Ransom et al. 308p. 1986. 73.25 (*0-89232-676-X*) Jai Pr.
Research in Economic History, Vol. 11. Ed. by Roger L. Ransom et al. 316p. 1988. 73.25 (*0-89232-677-8*) Jai Pr.
Research in Economic History, Vol. 12. Ed. by Roger L. Ransom et al. 239p. 1990. 73.25 (*1-55938-007-1*) Jai Pr.
Research in Economic History, Vol. 13. Ed. by Roger L. Ransom et al. 275p. 1992. 73.25 (*1-55938-151-5*) Jai Pr.
Research in Economic History, Vol. 14. Ed. by Roger L. Ransom et al. 381p. 1993. 73.25 (*0-614-09933-1*) Jai Pr.
Research in Economic History, Vol. 15. Ed. by Roger L. Ransom et al. 1995. 73.25 (*1-55938-604-5*) Jai Pr.
***Research in Economic History, Vol. 16.** Ed. by Alexander J. Field et al. 185p. 1996. 73.25 (*1-55938-652-5*) Jai Pr.
***Research in Economic History, Vol. 17.** Ed. by Alexander J. Field et al. 1997. 73.25 (*0-7623-0186-4*) Jai Pr.
Research in Economic History: An Annual Compilation of Research, Vol. 2. Ed. by Roger L. Ransom et al. LC 76-13771. 389p. (Orig.). 1977. 73.25 (*0-89232-036-2*) Jai Pr.
Research in Economic History: Emergence of the Modern Political Economy, Supplement 4, No. 4. Ed. by Roger L. Ransom et al. 224p. 1986. 73.25 (*0-89232-619-0*) Jai Pr.
Research in Economic History: Recent Developments in the Study of Economics & Business History: Essays in Memory of Herman E. Kroos. Ed. by Roger L. Ransom et al. LC 76-13956. (Research in Economic History Ser.: Suppl. 1). 315p. 1977. suppl. ed. 73.25 (*0-89232-035-4*) Jai Pr.
Research in Economic History: Supplement 3 - Technique, Spirit & Form in the Making of the Modern Economics: Essays in Honor of William N. Parker, No. 3: Technique, Spirit & Form in the Making of. Ed. by Roger L. Ransom et al. 300p. 1984. suppl. ed. 73.25 (*0-89232-414-7*) Jai Pr.
Research in Economic History Suppl. 2: Variations in Business & Economic History: Essays in Honor of Donald L. Kemmerer. Ed. by Roger L. Ransom et al. 217p. 1982. suppl. ed. 73.25 (*0-89232-262-4*) Jai Pr.
Research in Economic History Suppl. 5: Agrarian Organization in the Century of Industrialization, 2 vols., Set. Ed. by Roger L. Ransom et al. 542p. 1989. suppl. ed. 146.50 (*0-89232-855-X*) Jai Pr.
Research in Economic History Suppl. 6: The Vital One: Essays in Honor of Jonathan Hughes. Ed. by Roger L. Ransom et al. 348p. 1991. suppl. ed. 73.25 (*1-55938-150-7*) Jai Pr.
Research in Education. 3rd ed. James H. McMillan & Schumacher. (C). 1992. 59.50 (*0-673-52214-8*) Addson-Wesley Educ.
Research in Education. 3rd ed. James H. McMillan & Schumacher. (C). 1993. student ed. 12.00 (*0-673-52316-0*) Addson-Wesley Educ.
Research in Education. 4th ed. James H. McMillan & Sally Schumacher. LC 96-18832. (C). 1997. text ed. 58.50 (*0-673-99741-3*) Longman.
Research in Education. 6th ed. John W. Best & James V. Kahn. 400p. (C). 1989. Casebound. boxed write for info. (*0-13-774290-8*) P-H.
Research in Education. 7th ed. John W. Best & James V. Kahn. LC 92-20516. 1992. text ed. 60.67 (*0-205-14224-9*) Allyn.
***Research in Education.** 8th ed. John W. Best & James V. Kahn. LC 96-53399. 1997. 59.00 (*0-205-18697-1*) Allyn.
***Research in Education: A Conceptual Approach.** 4th ed. McMillan. (C). 1997. student ed., pap. text ed. 15.95 (*0-673-98515-6*) Addison-Wesley.
Research in Education: Management & Policy, Retrospect & Prospect. Ed. by Rene Saran & Vernon Trafford. 240p. 1990. 75.00 (*1-85000-726-8*); pap. 33.00 (*1-85000-727-6*) Taylor & Francis.
Research in Education & the Behavioral Sciences. Emanuel J. Mason & William J. Bramble. 512p. (C). 1996. text ed. write for info. (*0-697-17105-1*) Brown & Benchmark.
Research in Educational Settings. Geoffrey Maruyama & Stanley Deno. (Applied Social Research Methods Ser.: Vol. 29). 160p. (C). 1992. text ed. 39.95 (*0-8039-4207-9*); pap. text ed. 17.95 (*0-8039-4208-7*) Sage.
Research in Electric Power. Philip Sporn & R. Robinson. LC 66-16884. (Commonwealth & International Library). 1966. 41.00 (*0-08-011509-8*, Pub. by Pergamon Repr UK) Franklin.
Research in Emerging Fields of Education: Concepts, Trends & Prospects. Ed. by Y. P. Aggarwal. 350p. 1988. text ed. 35.00 (*0-685-21869-4*, Pub. by Sterling Pubs II) Apt Bks.
Research in Environmental Education: Engaging the Debate. Paul Hart & Ian M. Robottom. 81p. 1995. pap. 34.00 (*0-7300-1673-0*, ESC822, Pub. by Deakin Univ AT) St Mut.
Research in Experimental Economics, Vol. 1. Ed. by R. Mark Isaac & Vernon L. Smith. 374p. (Orig.). 1979. 73.25 (*0-89232-030-3*) Jai Pr.
Research in Experimental Economics, Vol. 3. Ed. by R. Mark Isaac & Vernon L. Smith. 248p. (Orig.). 1986. 73.25 (*0-89232-337-X*) Jai Pr.
Research in Experimental Economics, Vol. 4. Ed. by R. Mark Isaac & Vernon L. Smith. 318p. (Orig.). 1991. 73.25 (*0-89232-652-2*) Jai Pr.
Research in Experimental Economics, Vol. 5. Ed. by R. Mark Isaac. 228p. (Orig.). 1992. 73.25 (*1-55938-366-6*) Jai Pr.
Research in Experimental Economics, Vol. 6. Ed. by R. Mark Isaac. (Orig.). 1995. 73.25 (*1-55938-607-X*) Jai Pr.
Research in Experimental Economics Suppl. 1: An Experiment in Non-Cooperative Oligopoly. Ed. by R. Mark Isaac et al. (Research in Experimental Economics Supplement Ser.: No. 1). 216p. 1980. suppl. ed. 73.25 (*0-89232-121-0*) Jai Pr.
Research in Experimental Economics Vol. 2. Ed. by R. Mark Isaac & Vernon L. Smith. 250p. (Orig.). 1982. 73.25 (*0-89232-263-2*) Jai Pr.
Research in Family Planning. Ed. by J. Bonnar et al. (Studies in Fertility & Sterility). 1984. lib. bdg. 163.50 (*0-85200-813-9*) Kluwer Ac.
Research in Family Planning. Conference on Research in Family Planning (1960: New York). Ed. by Clyde V. Kiser. LC 62-7409. 680p. reprint ed. pap. 180.00 (*0-317-29432-6*, 2024297) Bks Demand.
Research in Finance, Vol. 1. Ed. by Andrew H. Chen et al. 310p. 1979. 73.25 (*0-89232-043-5*) Jai Pr.
Research in Finance, Vol. 2. Ed. by Andrew H. Chen et al. 237p. 1980. 73.25 (*0-89232-130-X*) Jai Pr.
Research in Finance, Vol. 3. Ed. by Andrew H. Chen et al. 184p. 1981. 73.25 (*0-89232-218-7*) Jai Pr.
Research in Finance, Vol. 4. Ed. by Andrew H. Chen et al. 215p. 1983. 73.25 (*0-89232-279-9*) Jai Pr.
Research in Finance, Vol. 5. Ed. by Andrew H. Chen et al. 261p. 1985. 73.25 (*0-89232-587-9*) Jai Pr.
Research in Finance, Vol. 6. Ed. by Andrew H. Chen et al. 277p. 1994. 73.25 (*0-89232-650-6*) Jai Pr.
Research in Finance, Vol. 7. Ed. by Andrew H. Chen et al. 64p. 1986. 73.25 (*89-23-23906-2*) Jai Pr.
Research in Finance, Vol. 7. Ed. by Andrew H. Chen. 1987. 73.25 (*0-89232-796-0*) Jai Pr.
Research in Finance, Vol. 8. Ed. by Andrew H. Chen et al. 270p. 1990. 73.25 (*0-89232-969-6*) Jai Pr.
Research in Finance, Vol. 9. Ed. by Andrew H. Chen et al. 248p. 1991. 73.25 (*1-55938-339-9*) Jai Pr.
Research in Finance, Vol. 10. Ed. by Andrew H. Chen et al. 260p. 1993. 73.25 (*1-55938-424-7*) Jai Pr.
Research in Finance, Vol. 11. Ed. by Andrew H. Chen et al. 226p. 1994. 73.25 (*1-55938-651-7*) Jai Pr.
Research in Finance, Vol. 12. Ed. by Andrew H. Chen et al. 1994. 73.25 (*1-55938-781-5*) Jai Pr.
Research in Finance, Vol. 13. Ed. by Andrew H. Chen et al. 1995. 73.25 (*1-55938-578-2*) Jai Pr.
Research in Finance: Supplement Management under Government Intervention, No. 1: Management under Government Intervention. Ed. by Andrew H. Chen et al. 301p. 1984. suppl. ed. 73.25 (*0-89232-427-9*) Jai Pr.
Research in Financial Services: Private & Public Policy, Vol. 1. Ed. by George G. Kaufman. 262p. 1989. 73.25 (*1-55938-027-6*) Jai Pr.
Research in Financial Services: Private & Public Policy, Vol. 3. Ed. by David D. Franks et al. 280p. 1995. 73.25 (*1-55938-142-6*) Jai Pr.
Research in Financial Services: Private & Public Policy, Vol. 3. Ed. by George G. Kaufman. 289p. 1991. 73.25 (*1-55938-278-3*) Jai Pr.
Research in Financial Services: Private & Public Policy, Vol. 4. Ed. by George G. Kaufman. 179p. 1992. 73.25 (*1-55938-481-6*) Jai Pr.
Research in Financial Services: Private & Public Policy, Vol. 5. Ed. by George G. Kaufman. 206p. 1994. 73.25 (*1-55938-601-0*) Jai Pr.
Research in Financial Services: Private & Public Policy, Vol. 6. Ed. by George G. Kaufman. 312p. 1994. 73.25 (*1-55938-842-0*) Jai Pr.
Research in Financial Services: Private & Public Policy, Vol. 7. Ed. by George G. Kaufman. 1995. 73.25 (*1-55938-244-9*) Jai Pr.
Research in Fouling. Heat Transfer Research, Incorporated Staff. 87p. 1972. 13.05 (*0-317-34543-5*, 144) Intl Copper.
Research in General Practice. 2nd ed. J. G. Howie. 256p. 1990. pap. 27.50 (*0-412-33730-4*, A4444) Chapman & Hall.
Research in Georgia: With a Special Emphasis Upon the Georgia Department of Archives & History. Robert S. Davis, Jr. (Illus.). 268p. 1991. pap. 30.00 (*0-89308-199-X*) Southern Hist Pr.
Research in Global Strategic Management, Vol. 6. Ed. by Alan M. Rugman & Alain Verbeke. 1996. 73.25 (*0-7623-0015-9*) Jai Pr.
Research in Global Strategic Management: Global Competition & the Eur Community, Vol. 2. Ed. by Alan M. Rugman & Alain Verbeke. 275p. 1991. 73.25 (*1-55938-277-5*) Jai Pr.
Research in Global Strategic Management: International Business Research for the Twenty- First Century; Canada's New Research Agenda, Vol. 1. Ed. by Alan M. Rugman & Alain Verbeke. 221p. 1990. 73.25 (*1-55938-131-0*) Jai Pr.
Research in Global Strategic Management Vol. 3: Corporate Response to Global Change. Ed. by Alan M. Rugman & Alain Verbeke. 241p. 1992. 73.25 (*1-55938-482-4*) Jai Pr.
Research in Global Strategic Management Vol. 4: Global Competition: Beyond the 3 Generics. Ed. by Alan M. Rugman & Alain Verbeke. 241p. 1993. 73.25 (*1-55938-619-3*) Jai Pr.
Research in Global Strategic Management Vol. 5: Beyond the Diamond. Ed. by Alan M. Rugman & Alain Verbeke. 282p. 1995. 73.25 (*1-55938-434-4*) Jai Pr.
Research in Governmental & Nonprofit Accounting, 2 vols., Set, Vol. 3. Ed. by James L. Chan et al. 1987. 146.50 (*0-89232-699-9*) Jai Pr.
Research in Governmental & Nonprofit Accounting, Vol. 1. Ed. by James L. Chan et al. 347p. 1985. 73.25 (*0-89232-517-8*) Jai Pr.
Research in Governmental & Nonprofit Accounting, Vol. 2. Ed. by James L. Chan et al. 273p. 1986. 73.25 (*0-89232-628-X*) Jai Pr.
Research in Governmental & Nonprofit Accounting, Vol. 3, Pt. A. Ed. by James L. Chan et al. 206p. 1987. 73.25 (*0-89232-785-5*) Jai Pr.
Research in Governmental & Nonprofit Accounting, Vol. 3, Pt. B. Ed. by James L. Chan et al. 280p. 1987. 73.25 (*0-89232-786-3*) Jai Pr.
Research in Governmental & Nonprofit Accounting, Vol. 4. Ed. by James L. Chan et al. 260p. 1988. 73.25 (*0-89232-787-1*) Jai Pr.
Research in Governmental & Nonprofit Accounting, Vol. 5. Ed. by James L. Chan et al. 310p. 1989. 73.25 (*0-89232-975-0*) Jai Pr.
Research in Governmental & Nonprofit Accounting, Vol. 6. Ed. by James L. Chan et al. 262p. 1990. 73.25 (*1-55938-119-1*) Jai Pr.
Research in Governmental & Nonprofit Accounting, Vol. 7. Ed. by James L. Chan et al. 240p. 1992. 73.25 (*1-55938-418-2*) Jai Pr.
Research in Governmental & Nonprofit Accounting, Vol. 8. Ed. by James L. Chan et al. 348p. 1994. 73.25 (*1-55938-544-8*) Jai Pr.
Research in Governmental & Nonprofit Accounting, Vol. 9. Ed. by James L. Chan et al. 1996. 73.25 (*1-55938-055-1*) Jai Pr.
***Research in Governmental & Nonprofit Accounting: In Preparation, Summer 1997, Vol. 10.** Ed. by James L. Chan. 78.50 (*0-7623-0169-4*) Jai Pr.
Research in Health Care: Design, Conduct & Interpretation of Health Services Research. I. K. Crombie & H. T. Davies. LC 95-42359. 312p. 1996. pap. text ed. 25.00 (*0-471-96259-7*) Wiley.
Research in Health Care Settings. Kathleen E. Grady & Barbara Strudler-Wallston. (Applied Social Research Methods Ser.: Vol. 14). 160p. (C). 1988. text ed. 39.95 (*0-8039-2874-2*); pap. text ed. 17.95 (*0-8039-2875-0*) Sage.
Research in Human Capital & Development. Alan L. Sorkin. (Research in Human Capital & Development Ser.: Vol. 1). 276p. 1981. suppl. ed. 73.25 (*0-89232-129-6*) Jai Pr.
Research in Human Capital & Development, Vol. 2. Alan L. Sorkin. 224p. 1981. 73.25 (*0-89232-098-2*) Jai Pr.
***Research in Human Capital & Development, Vol. 11.** Alan L. Sorkin. 1997. 73.25 (*0-7623-0193-7*) Jai Pr.
***Research in Human Capital & Development: American Indian Economic Development, Vol. 10.** Alan L. Sorkin. 200p. 1996. 73.25 (*0-7623-0183-X*) Jai Pr.
Research in Human Capital & Development: An Annual Compilation of Research, Vol. 1. Alan L. Sorkin. 258p. 1979. 73.25 (*0-89232-019-2*) Jai Pr.
Research in Human Capital & Development: Education, Human Capital & Development, Vol. 5. Ed. by Gary S. Fields. 1984. 73.25 (*0-89232-417-1*) Jai Pr.
Research in Human Capital & Development: Health Care in the Changing Economic & Social Environment, Vol. 7. Alan L. Sorkin. 391p. 1993. 73.25 (*1-55938-132-9*) Jai Pr.
Research in Human Capital & Development: Migration, Human Capital & Development, Vol. 4. Alan L. Sorkin. 285p. 1987. 73.25 (*0-89232-416-3*) Jai Pr.
Research in Human Capital & Development: Nutrition, Food Policy & Development, Vol. 8. Alan L. Sorkin. 353p. 1995. 73.25 (*1-55938-611-8*) Jai Pr.
Research in Human Capital & Development: Population & Development Transformations in the Arab World, Vol. 9. Alan L. Sorkin. 256p. 1996. 73.25 (*1-55938-927-3*) Jai Pr.
Research in Human Capital & Development: Public Health & Development. Alan L. Sorkin. (Research in Human Capital & Development Ser.: Vol. 5). 293p. 1988. 73.25 (*0-89232-508-9*) Jai Pr.
Research in Human Capital & Development Vol. 6: Female Labor Force Participation & Development. Alan L. Sorkin. 273p. 1991. 73.25 (*1-55938-032-2*) Jai Pr.
***Research in Human Reproduction: Biennial Report 1986-1987.** E. Diczfalusy & P. Griffin. 346p. 1988. 25.00 (*92-4-156120-3*) World Health.
***Research in Human Reproduction: Biennial Report 1988-1989.** WHO Staff. 191p. 1990. 31.00 (*92-4-156140-8*) World Health.
***Research in Human Reproduction: Strengthening of Resources in Developing Countries: Report of a WHO Study Group, 1978.** (Technical Report Ser.: No. 627). 16p. 1978. pap. text ed. 4.00 (*92-4-120627-6*, 1100627) World Health.
Research in Human Social Conflict, Vol. 1. Ed. by Joseph B. Gittler. 365p. 1995. 73.25 (*1-55938-923-0*) Jai Pr.
Research in Human Social Conflict, Vol. 2. Ed. by Joseph B. Gittler. 1996. 73.25 (*0-7623-0030-2*) Jai Pr.
Research in Humanities Computing, No. 2. Ed. by Susan Hockey & Nancy Ide. (Illus.). 352p. (C). 1994. 60.00 (*0-19-824039-2*, 3735) OUP.
Research in Humanities Computing 1. Ed. by Susan Hockey et al. 376p. 1991. 85.00 (*0-19-824251-4*) OUP.
Research in Humanities Computing 3: Papers from the 1991 ACH-ALLC Conference. Ed. by Susan Hockey & Nancy Ide. (Illus.). 320p. 1994. 65.00 (*0-19-824064-3*) OUP.
Research in Humanities Computing 4 Vol. 4: Selected Papers from the 1992 ALLC/ACH Conference. Ed. by Susan Hockey & Nancy Ide. (Illus.). 292p. 1996. 75.00 (*0-19-823547-X*) OUP.
Research in Humanities Computing 5 Vol. 5: Selected Papers from the 1995 ACH-ALLC Conference. Ed. by Giorgio Perissinotto. (Illus.). 272p. 1996. 75.00 (*0-19-823626-3*) OUP.
Research in Immunology: Report of 5 Scientific Groups Convened by the Director-General of the World Health Organization, Geneva, 1962. (Technical Report Ser.: No. 286). 97p. (ENG, FRE, RUS & SPA.). 1964. pap. text ed. 7.00 (*92-4-120286-6*, 1100286) World Health.
Research in Industry. M. J. Mulky et al. (C). 1987. 20.00 (*81-204-0273-1*, Pub. by Oxford IBH II) S Asia.
Research in Inequality & Social Conflict, Vol. 1. Ed. by Isidor Wallimann & Michael Dobkowski. 319p. 1989. 73.25 (*0-89232-745-6*) Jai Pr.
Research in Inequality & Social Conflict, Vol. 2. Ed. by Isidor Wallimann & Michael Dobkowski. 279p. 1992. 73.25 (*1-55938-093-4*) Jai Pr.
Research in International Business & Finance, Pt. A. Ed. by Larry Lang et al. 240p. 1994. 73.25 (*1-55938-780-7*) Jai Pr.
Research in International Business & Finance, Pt. B. Ed. by Larry Lang et al. 232p. 1994. 73.25 (*1-55938-860-9*) Jai Pr.
Research in International Business & Finance, Vol. 12. Ed. by Larry Lang et al. 1995. 73.25 (*1-55938-919-2*) Jai Pr.
Research in International Business & Finance: Technology Transfer & Economic Development, Vol. 2. Ed. by Larry Lang et al. (Research in International Business & Finance Ser.: Vol. 2). 320p. 1982. 73.25 (*0-89232-140-7*) Jai Pr.
Research in International Business & Finance: Uncle Sam As Host, Vol. 5. Ed. by Larry Lang et al. 381p. 1986. 73.25 (*0-89232-588-7*) Jai Pr.
Research in International Business & Finance Vol. 1: The Economic Effects of Multinational Corporations. Ed. by Larry Lang et al. (Research in International Business & Finance Ser.). 330p. 1979. 73.25 (*0-89232-031-1*) Jai Pr.
Research in International Business & Finance Vol. 3: The Internationalization of Financial Markets & National Economic Policy. Ed. by Larry Lang et al. (Research in International Business & Finance Ser.: Vol. 3). 352p. 1983. 73.25 (*0-89232-264-0*) Jai Pr.
Research in International Business & Finance Vol. 4: International Business Strategies in the Asia-Pacific Region. Ed. by Larry Lang et al. 1984. 146.50 (*0-89232-308-6*) Jai Pr.
Research in International Business & Finance Vol. 7: The Modern International Environment. Ed. by Larry Lang et al. 258p. 1989. 73.25 (*0-89232-906-8*) Jai Pr.
Research in International Business & Finance Vol. 8: Prospects for Canadian-United States Economic Relations under Free Trade. Ed. by Larry Lang et al. 240p. 1990. 73.25 (*1-55938-050-0*) Jai Pr.
Research in International Business & Finance Vol. 9: Emerging Challeges for the International Industry. Ed. by Larry Lang et al. 268p. 1993. 73.25 (*1-55938-234-1*) Jai Pr.
Research in International Business & Finance Vol. 11: Studies in the Financial Markets of the Pacific Basin, 2 vols., Set. Ed. by Larry Lang et al. 1994. 146.50 (*1-55938-617-7*) Jai Pr.
Research in International Business & International Relations Vol. 1: Multinational Corporations & State-Owned Enterprises: A New Challenge in International Business. Ed. by Manuel G. Serapio, Jr. et al. 336p. 1986. 73.25 (*0-89232-529-1*) Jai Pr.
Research in International Business & International Relations Vol. 2: Chinas Trade with the Industrialized Countries. Ed. by Manuel G. Serapio, Jr. et al. (Research in International Business & International Relations Ser.: Vol. 2). 268p. 1986. 73.25 (*0-89232-530-5*) Jai Pr.
Research in International Business & International Relations Vol. 3: Multinationals & Newly Industrialized Countries. Ed. by Manuel G. Serapio, Jr. et al. 272p. 1989. 73.25 (*0-89232-649-2*) Jai Pr.
Research in International Business & International Relations Vol. 4: China & India: Foreign Investment & Economic Development. Ed. by Manuel G. Serapio, Jr. et al. 202p. 1990. 73.25 (*1-55938-121-3*) Jai Pr.
Research in International Business & International Relations Vol. 5: Japanese Direct Investments in the U. S. Ed. by Manuel G. Serapio, Jr. et al. 307p. 1993. 73.25 (*1-55938-279-1*) Jai Pr.
Research in International Business & International Relations Vol. 6: Emerging Trends in Japanese Management. Ed. by Manuel G. Serapio, Jr. et al. 243p. 1994. 73.25 (*1-55938-603-7*) Jai Pr.
Research in International Marketing. Ed. by Peter W. Turnbull & Stanley J. Paliwoda. 400p. 1987. 59.95 (*0-685-30335-7*, Pub. by Croom Helm UK) Routledge Chapman & Hall.
Research in Japanese Sources: A Guide. Herschel Webb. LC 94-1095. (Michigan Classics in Japanese Studies: No. 11). x, 174p. 1994. pap. 13.95 (*0-939512-65-3*) U MI Japan.
Research in Labor Economics, No. 1: Evaluating Manpower Training Programs. Ed. by Solomon W. Polachek et al. 375p. 1979. suppl. ed. 73.25 (*0-89232-046-X*) Jai Pr.
Research in Labor Economics, No. 2: New Approaches to Labor Unions: Proceedings. Ed. by Solomon W. Polachek et al. 353p. 1983. suppl. ed. 73.25 (*0-89232-265-9*) Jai Pr.
Research in Labor Economics, 2 vols., Set, Vol. 8. Ed. by Solomon W. Polachek et al. 1987. 146.50 (*0-89232-653-0*) Jai Pr.
Research in Labor Economics, Vol. 1. Ed. by Solomon W. Polachek et al. 376p. 1977. 73.25 (*0-89232-017-6*) Jai Pr.

R

Research in Labor Economics, Vol. 2. Ed. by Solomon W. Polachek et al. 381p. 1979. 73.25 (*0-89232-097-4*) Jai Pr.

Research in Labor Economics, Vol. 3. Ed. by Solomon W. Polachek et al. 389p. 1980. 73.25 (*0-89232-157-1*) Jai Pr.

Research in Labor Economics, Vol. 4. Ed. by Ronald G. Ehrenberg. 350p. 1982. 73.25 (*0-89232-243-8*) Jai Pr.

Research in Labor Economics, Vol. 4. Ed. by Solomon W. Polachek et al. 488p. 1982. 73.25 (*0-89232-220-9*) Jai Pr.

Research in Labor Economics, Vol. 5. Ed. by Solomon W. Polachek et al. 368p. 1983. 73.25 (*0-89232-312-4*) Jai Pr.

Research in Labor Economics, Vol. 6. Ed. by Solomon W. Polachek et al. 400p. 1984. 73.25 (*0-89232-418-X*) Jai Pr.

Research in Labor Economics, Vol. 7. Ed. by Solomon W. Polachek et al. 376p. 1986. 73.25 (*0-89232-589-5*) Jai Pr.

Research in Labor Economics, Vol. 9. Ed. by Solomon W. Polachek et al. 73.25 (*0-89232-746-4*) Jai Pr.

Research in Labor Economics, Vol. 10. Ed. by Solomon W. Polachek et al. 336p. 1989. 73.25 (*1-55938-025-X*) Jai Pr.

Research in Labor Economics, Vol. 11: Labor Economics & Public Policy. Ed. by Solomon W. Polachek et al. 320p. 1991. 73.25 (*1-55938-080-2*) Jai Pr.

Research in Labor Economics, Vol. 12. Ed. by Solomon W. Polachek et al. 310p. 1992. 73.25 (*1-55938-381-X*) Jai Pr.

Research in Labor Economics, Vol. 13. Ed. by Solomon W. Polachek et al. 338p. 1993. 73.25 (*1-55938-473-5*) Jai Pr.

Research in Labor Economics, Vol. 14. Ed. by Solomon W. Polachek et al. 1995. 73.25 (*1-55938-610-X*) Jai Pr.

Research in Law & Economics, Vol. 1. Ed. by Richard O. Zerbe. 243p. 1979. lib. bdg. 73.25 (*0-89232-028-1*) Jai Pr.

Research in Law & Economics, Vol. 2. Richard O. Zerbe. 240p. 1980. lib. bdg. 73.25 (*0-89232-131-8*) Jai Pr.

Research in Law & Economics, Vol. 3. Ed. by Richard O. Zerbe, Jr. 225p. 1981. 73.25 (*0-89232-231-4*) Jai Pr.

Research in Law & Economics, Vol. 5. Ed. by Richard O. Zerbe, Jr. 325p. 1983. 73.25 (*0-89232-419-8*) Jai Pr.

Research in Law & Economics, Vol. 7: Normative Law & Economics. Ed. by Richard O. Zerbe, Jr. 179p. 1985. 73.25 (*0-614-17869-X*) Jai Pr.

Research in Law & Economics, Vol. 9. Ed. by Richard O. Zerbe, Jr. 207p. 1987. 73.25 (*0-89232-657-3*) Jai Pr.

Research in Law & Economics, Vol. 11. Ed. by Richard O. Zerbe, Jr. 264p. 1987. 73.25 (*0-89232-830-4*) Jai Pr.

Research in Law & Economics, Vol. 12. Ed. by Richard O. Zerbe, Jr. 277p. 1989. 73.25 (*1-55938-008-X*) Jai Pr.

Research in Law & Economics, Vol. 13. Ed. by Richard O. Zerbe, Jr. 231p. 1991. 73.25 (*1-55938-143-4*) Jai Pr.

Research in Law & Economics, Vol. 14. Ed. by Richard O. Zerbe, Jr. 281p. 1992. 73.25 (*1-55938-404-2*) Jai Pr.

Research in Law & Economics, Vol. 15. Ed. by Richard O. Zerbe, Jr. 188p. 1992. 73.25 (*1-55938-499-9*) Jai Pr.

Research in Law & Economics, Vol. 16. Ed. by Richard O. Zerbe, Jr. 216p. 1994. 73.25 (*1-55938-500-6*) Jai Pr.

Research in Law & Economics, Vol. 17. Ed. by Richard O. Zerbe, Jr. 278p. 1995. 73.25 (*1-55938-964-8*) Jai Pr.

Research in Law & Economics, Vol. 18. Ed. by Richard O. Zerbe, Jr. 1996. 73.25 (*0-7623-0121-X*) Jai Pr.

Research in Law & Economics: Antitrust & Regulation, Vol. 6. Richard O. Zerbe, Jr. 295p. 73.25 (*0-89232-474-0*) Jai Pr.

Research in Law & Economics: Normative Law & Economics, Vol 7. Richard O. Zerbe, Jr. 1985. 73.25 (*0-89232-590-9*) Jai Pr.

Research in Law & Economics: The Economics of Patents & Copyrights, Vol. 8. Richard O. Zerbe, Jr. 287p. 1986. 73.25 (*0-89232-654-9*) Jai Pr.

Research in Law & Policy Studies, Vol. 1. Ed. by Stuart S. Nagel. 200p. 1987. 73.25 (*0-89232-525-9*) Jai Pr.

Research in Law & Policy Studies, Vol. 2. Ed. by Stuart S. Nagel. 277p. 1988. 73.25 (*0-89232-662-X*) Jai Pr.

Research in Law & Policy Studies, Vol. 3. Ed. by Stuart S. Nagel. 1994. 73.25 (*1-55938-021-7*) Jai Pr.

Research in Law & Policy Studies, Vol. 4. Ed. by Stuart S. Nagel. 348p. 1995. 73.25 (*1-55938-112-4*) Jai Pr.

Research in Law & Policy Studies, Vol. 5. Ed. by Stuart S. Nagel. 1997. 73.25 (*0-7623-0041-8*) Jai Pr.

***Research in Law & Policy Studies, Vol. 6.** Ed. by Stuart S. Nagel. 1998. 73.25 (*0-7623-0274-7*) Jai Pr.

Research in Law & Sociology, Vol. 2. Ed. by Susan S. Silbey & Austin Sarat. 274p. 1979. 73.25 (*0-89232-111-3*) Jai Pr.

Research in Law & Sociology, Vol. 3. Ed. by Susan S. Silbey & Austin Sarat. 344p. 1981. 73.25 (*0-89232-186-5*) Jai Pr.

Research in Law, Deviance & Social Control, Vol. 4. Ed. by Rita J. Simon & Steven Spitzer. 325p. 1982. 73.25 (*0-89232-241-1*) Jai Pr.

Research in Law, Deviance & Social Control, Vol. 6. Ed. by Susan S. Silbey & Austin Sarat. 272p. 1985. 73.25 (*0-89232-512-7*) Jai Pr.

Research in Law, Deviance & Social Control, Vol. 7. Ed. by Susan S. Silbey & Austin Sarat. 293p. 1985. 73.25 (*0-89232-528-3*) Jai Pr.

Research in Law, Deviance & Social Control, Vol. 8. Ed. by Susan S. Silbey & Austin Sarat. 194p. 1987. 73.25 (*0-89232-536-4*) Jai Pr.

Research in Law, Deviance & Social Control, Vol. 9. Ed. by Susan S. Silbey & Austin Sarat. 206p. 1988. 73.25 (*0-89232-747-2*) Jai Pr.

Research in Library & Information Science in India. P. S. Kumar. 1987. 38.50 (*81-7022-016-5*, Pub. by Concept II) S Asia.

Research in Man-Machine Communications Using Time Shared Computer Systems. Butler W. Lampson. LC 77-131392. 73p. 1969. 19.00 (*0-403-04513-4*) Scholarly.

Research in Marketing, Vol. 2. Ed. by Jagdish N. Sheth et al. 375p. 1979. 73.25 (*0-89232-059-1*) Jai Pr.

Research in Marketing, Vol. 3. Ed. by Jagdish N. Sheth et al. 325p. 1980. 73.25 (*0-89232-060-5*) Jai Pr.

Research in Marketing, Vol. 4. Ed. by Jagdish N. Sheth et al. 294p. 1990. 73.25 (*0-89232-169-5*) Jai Pr.

Research in Marketing, Vol. 5. Ed. by Jagdish N. Sheth et al. 275p. 1981. 73.25 (*0-89232-211-X*) Jai Pr.

Research in Marketing, Vol. 6. Ed. by Jagdish N. Sheth et al. 300p. 1983. 73.25 (*0-89232-315-9*) Jai Pr.

Research in Marketing, Vol. 7. Ed. by Jagdish N. Sheth et al. 288p. 1984. 73.25 (*0-89232-420-1*) Jai Pr.

Research in Marketing, Vol. 9. Ed. by Jagdish N. Sheth et al. 306p. 1987. 73.25 (*0-89232-831-2*) Jai Pr.

Research in Marketing, Vol. 10. Ed. by Jagdish N. Sheth et al. 265p. 1990. 73.25 (*0-89232-920-3*) Jai Pr.

Research in Marketing, Vol. 11. Ed. by Jagdish N. Sheth et al. 263p. 1992. 73.25 (*1-55938-287-2*) Jai Pr.

***Research in Marketing, Vol 13, 1997.** Ed. by Jagdish N. Sheth & Atul Parvatiyar. 1997. 73.25 (*0-7623-0284-4*) Jai Pr.

Research in Marketing: Alternative Paradigms for Widening Marketing Theory, No. 2: Changing the Course of Marketing. Ed. by Jagdish N. Sheth et al. (Research in Marketing Ser.: Suppl. 2). 311p. 1986. suppl. ed. 73.25 (*0-89232-627-1*) Jai Pr.

Research in Marketing: An Annual Compilation of Research, Vol. 1. Ed. by Jagdish N. Sheth et al. (Annual Ser.). 330p. (Orig.). 1978. 73.25 (*0-89232-041-9*) Jai Pr.

Research in Marketing: Distribution Channels & Institutions, Vol. 8: Distribution Channels & Institutions. Ed. by Jagdish N. Sheth et al. (Research in Marketing Ser.: Vol. 8). 402p. 1986. 73.25 (*0-89232-549-6*) Jai Pr.

Research in Marketing No. 1: Choice Models for Buyer Behavior, No. 1: Choice Models for Buyer Behavior. Ed. by Jagdish N. Sheth et al. (Research in Marketing Ser.). 350p. 1982. suppl. ed. 73.25 (*0-89232-267-5*) Jai Pr.

Research in Marketing Suppl. 3: Reseller Assortment Decision Criteria. Ed. by Jagdish N. Sheth et al. 176p. 1988. suppl. ed. 73.25 (*0-89232-898-3*) Jai Pr.

Research in Marketing Suppl. 4: Marketing & Development: Toward Broader Dimensions. Ed. by Jagdish N. Sheth et al. 368p. 1989. suppl. ed. 73.25 (*0-89232-993-9*) Jai Pr.

Research in Marketing Suppl. 5: Spatial Analysis in Marketing: Theory, Methods & Application. Ed. by Jagdish N. Sheth et al. 275p. 1991. suppl. ed. 73.25 (*1-55938-380-1*) Jai Pr.

Research in Marketing Suppl. 6: Explorations in the History of Marketing. Ed. by Jagdish N. Sheth et al. 1994. suppl. ed. 73.25 (*1-55938-653-3*) Jai Pr.

Research in Mathematics Education. Ed. by Richard J. Shumway. LC 80-4. (Illus.). 487p. 1980. 27.00 (*0-87353-163-9*) NCTM.

Research in Medicine: A Guide to Writing a Thesis in the Medical Sciences. George Murrell et al. (Illus.). 120p. (C). 1990. text ed. 54.95 (*0-521-39043-5*); pap. text ed. 16.95 (*0-521-39925-4*) Cambridge U Pr.

Research in Mental Health Computing: The Next Five Years. Ed. by John H. Greist et al. LC 87-35269. (Computers in Human Services Ser.: Vol. 2, Nos. 3-4). 176p. 1988. text ed. 49.95 (*0-86656-648-1*) Haworth Pr.

Research in Mexican History: Topics, Methodology, Sources & a Practical Guide to Field Research. Ed. by Richard E. Greenleaf & Michael C. Meyer. LC 72-86020. 239p. reprint ed. pap. 68.20 (*0-7837-6109-0*, 2059155) Bks Demand.

Research in Micropolitics, Vol. 4: New Directions in Political Psychology. Ed. by Michael X. Delli Carpini et al. 243p. 1994. 73.25 (*1-55938-197-3*) Jai Pr.

Research in Micropolitics, Vol. 5. Ed. by Michael X. Delli Carpini et al. 1996. 73.25 (*1-55938-885-4*) Jai Pr.

***Research in Micropolitics, Vol. 6.** Ed. by Michael X. Delli Carpini et al. 1997. 78.50 (*0-7623-0227-5*) Jai Pr.

Research in Micropolitics: Voting Behavior, Vol. 1. Samuel Long. Ed. by Michael X. Delli Carpini et al. 293p. 1986. 73.25 (*0-89232-365-5*) Jai Pr.

Research in Micropolitics Vol. 2: Voting Behavior II. Ed. by Michael X. Delli Carpini et al. (Research in Micropolitics Ser.: Vol. II). 304p. 1988. 73.25 (*0-89232-562-3*) Jai Pr.

Research in Micropolitics Vol. 3: Public Opinion. Ed. by Michael X. Delli Carpini et al. 247p. 1990. 73.25 (*0-89232-791-X*) Jai Pr.

Research in Middle Level Education, Vol. 16, No. 1. Ed. by Judith L. Irvin. 186p. (C). pap. text ed. 15.00 (*1-56090-075-X*) Natl Middle Schl.

Research in Middle Level Education, Vol. 16, No. 2. David B. Strahan. 104p. (C). pap. text ed. 15.00 (*1-56090-079-2*) Natl Middle Schl.

Research in Middle Level Education, Vol. 17, No. 1. Ed. by Judith L. Irvin. 136p. (C). pap. text ed. 15.00 (*1-56090-080-6*) Natl Middle Schl.

Research in Middle Level Education, Vol. 17, No. 2. Ed. by Judith L. Irvin & Judith Brough. 78p. (C). pap. text ed. 15.00 (*1-56090-087-3*) Natl Middle Schl.

Research in Middle Level Education, Vol. 18, No. 1. Ed. by David L. Hough. 131p. (C). 1994. pap. text ed. 15.00 (*1-56090-092-X*) Natl Middle Schl.

Research in Middle Level Education Vol. 15, No. 2, Vol. 15, No. 1. Ed. by Joanne Arhar. 84p. (C). 1991. pap. text ed. 14.00 (*1-56090-062-8*) Natl Middle Schl.

***Research in Ministry: A Primer for the Doctor of Ministry Program.** rev. ed. William R. Myers. LC 96-84945. (Studies in Ministry & Parish Life). xvi, 87p. (C). 1997. pap. text ed. 10.95 (*0-913552-61-5*) Exploration Pr.

Research in Mood Disorders: An Update. rev. ed. Ed. by Hanns Hippius et al. LC 93-32542. (Psychiatry in Progress Ser.: Vol. I). (Illus.). 160p. 1994. text ed. 32.00 (*0-88937-102-4*) Hogrefe & Huber Pubs.

Research in Music Behavior: Modifying Music Behavior in the Classroom. Clifford K. Madsen et al. LC 74-16362. (Illus.). 285p. reprint ed. pap. 81.30 (*0-317-09961-2*, 2020325) Bks Demand.

Research in Music Education: An Introduction to Systematic Inquiry. Edward L. Rainbow & Hildegard C. Froehlich. (Illus.). 330p. (C). 1987. 47.00 (*0-02-870320-0*) Schirmer Bks.

Research in Nursing. 2nd ed. Holly S. Wilson. Ed. by Debra Hunter. 738p. (C). 1989. teacher ed. 9.95 (*0-201-17850-8*); text ed. 40.95 (*0-201-05946-0*) Addison-Wesley.

***Research in Nursing & Health.** Ed. by Margaret Grier. 1983. pap. text ed. 30.00 (*0-471-88976-8*) Wiley.

Research in Organizational Behavior, Vol. 1. Ed. by Barry M. Staw & L. L. Cummings. 478p. 1979. 73.25 (*0-89232-045-1*) Jai Pr.

Research in Organizational Behavior, Vol. 2. Ed. by Barry M. Staw & L. L. Cummings. 368p. 1980. 73.25 (*0-89232-099-0*) Jai Pr.

Research in Organizational Behavior, Vol. 3. Ed. by Barry M. Staw & Larry L. Cummings. 356p. 1981. 73.25 (*0-89232-151-2*) Jai Pr.

Research in Organizational Behavior, Vol. 4. Ed. by Barry M. Staw & Larry L. Cummings. 364p. 1982. 73.25 (*0-89232-147-4*) Jai Pr.

Research in Organizational Behavior, Vol. 5. Ed. by Barry M. Staw & Larry L. Cummings. 368p. 1983. 73.25 (*0-89232-271-3*) Jai Pr.

Research in Organizational Behavior, Vol. 6. Ed. by Barry M. Staw & Larry L. Cummings. 475p. 1984. 73.25 (*0-89232-351-5*) Jai Pr.

Research in Organizational Behavior, Vol. 7. Ed. by Barry M. Staw & Larry L. Cummings. 408p. 1985. 73.25 (*0-89232-497-X*) Jai Pr.

Research in Organizational Behavior, Vol. 8. Ed. by Barry M. Staw & Larry L. Cummings. 375p. 1986. 73.25 (*0-89232-551-8*) Jai Pr.

Research in Organizational Behavior, Vol. 9. Ed. by Barry M. Staw & Larry L. Cummings. 368p. 1987. 73.25 (*0-89232-636-0*) Jai Pr.

Research in Organizational Behavior, Vol. 10. Ed. by Barry M. Staw & Larry L. Cummings. 408p. 1988. 73.25 (*0-89232-748-0*) Jai Pr.

Research in Organizational Behavior, Vol. 11. Ed. by Barry M. Staw & Larry L. Cummings. 310p. 1989. 73.25 (*0-89232-921-1*) Jai Pr.

Research in Organizational Behavior: An Annual Series of Analytical Essays & Critical Reviews, Vol. 12. Ed. by Barry M. Staw & Larry L. Cummings. 336p. 1990. 73.25 (*1-55938-029-2*) Jai Pr.

Research in Organizational Behavior: An Annual Series of Analytical Essays & Critical Reviews, Vol. 13. Ed. by Barry M. Staw & Larry L. Cummings. 352p. 1991. 73.25 (*1-55938-198-1*) Jai Pr.

Research in Organizational Behavior: An Annual Series of Analytical Essays & Critical Reviews, Vol. 14. Ed. by Barry M. Staw & Larry L. Cummings. 348p. 1992. 73.25 (*1-55938-242-2*) Jai Pr.

Research in Organizational Behavior: An Annual Series of Analytical Essays & Critical Reviews, Vol. 15. Ed. by Barry M. Staw & Larry L. Cummings. 408p. 1993. 73.25 (*1-55938-522-7*) Jai Pr.

Research in Organizational Behavior: An Annual Series of Analytical Essays & Critical Reviews, Vol. 16. Ed. by Barry M. Staw & Larry L. Cummings. 369p. 1994. 73.25 (*1-55938-719-X*) Jai Pr.

Research in Organizational Behavior: An Annual Series of Analytical Essays & Critical Reviews, Vol. 17. Ed. by Barry M. Staw & Larry L. Cummings. 461p. 1995. 92.50 (*1-55938-743-2*) Jai Pr.

Research in Organizational Behavior: An Annual Series of Analytical Essays & Critical Reviews, Vol. 18. Ed. by Barry M. Staw & Larry L. Cummings. 1995. 78.50 (*1-55938-938-9*) Jai Pr.

***Research in Organizational Behavior Vol. 19: An Annual Series of Analytical Essays & Critical Reviews.** Ed. by Barry M. Staw & L. L. Cummings. 1996. 78.50 (*0-7623-0179-1*) Jai Pr.

***Research in Organizational Change & Development.** Ed. by Richard W. Woodman & William A. Pasmore. 287p. 1992. 73.25 (*0-614-22105-6*) Jai Pr.

Research in Organizational Change & Development, Vol. 1. Ed. by Richard W. Woodman & William A. Pasmore. 1987. 73.25 (*0-89232-749-9*) Jai Pr.

Research in Organizational Change & Development, Vol. 2. Ed. by Richard W. Woodman & William A. Pasmore. 236p. 1988. 73.25 (*0-89232-772-3*) Jai Pr.

Research in Organizational Change & Development, Vol. 3. Ed. by Richard W. Woodman & William A. Pasmore. 236p. 1989. 73.25 (*0-89232-978-5*) Jai Pr.

Research in Organizational Change & Development, Vol. 4. Ed. by Richard W. Woodman & William A. Pasmore. 305p. 1990. 73.25 (*1-55938-076-4*) Jai Pr.

Research in Organizational Change & Development, Vol. 5. Ed. by Richard W. Woodman & William A. Pasmore. 322p. 1992. 73.25 (*1-55938-250-3*) Jai Pr.

Research in Organizational Change & Development, Vol. 7. Ed. by Richard W. Woodman & William A. Pasmore. 320p. 1993. 73.25 (*1-55938-539-1*) Jai Pr.

Research in Organizational Change & Development, Vol. 8. Ed. by Richard W. Woodman & William A. Pasmore. 302p. 1995. 73.25 (*1-55938-871-4*) Jai Pr.

Research in Organizational Change & Development, Vol. 9. Ed. by Richard W. Woodman & William A. Pasmore. 1996. 73.25 (*0-7623-0016-7*) Jai Pr.

Research in Parapsychology 1972: Abstracts & Papers from the 15th Annual Convention of the Parapsychological Association, 1972. Parapsychological Association Staff. Ed. by William G. Roll et al. LC 66-28580. 249p. 1973. 12.50 (*0-8108-0666-5*) Scarecrow.

Research in Parapsychology 1977: Abstracts & Papers from the 20th Annual Convention of the Parapsychological Association, 1977. Parapsychological Association Staff. Ed. by William G. Roll. LC 66-28580. 279p. 1978. lib. bdg. 12.50 (*0-8108-1131-6*) Scarecrow.

Research in Parapsychology 1978. Parapsychological Association Staff. Ed. by William G. Roll. LC 66-28580. 238p. 1979. 12.50 (*0-8108-1195-2*) Scarecrow.

Research in Parapsychology 1979: Abstracts & Papers from the 22nd Annual Convention of the Parapsychological Association. Parapsychological Association Staff. Ed. by William G. Roll. LC 66-2858. 238p. 1980. 12.50 (*0-8108-1327-0*) Scarecrow.

Research in Parapsychology 1980: Abstracts & Papers from the Twenty-Third Annual Convention of the Parapsychological Association, 1980. Ed. by Parapsychological Association Staff et al. LC 66-28580. 173p. 1981. 12.50 (*0-8108-1425-0*) Scarecrow.

Research In Parapsychology 1981: Abstracts & Papers from the Twenty-Fourth Annual Convention of the Parapsychological Association, 1981. Parapsychological Association Staff. LC 66-28580. 252p. 1982. 12.50 (*0-8108-1550-8*) Scarecrow.

Research in Parapsychology 1982: Jubilee Centenary Issue: Abstracts & Papers from the Twenty-Fifth Annual Convention of the Parapsychological Association, 1982. Ed. by Parapsychological Association Staff et al. LC 66-28580. 382p. 1983. 12.50 (*0-8108-1627-X*) Scarecrow.

Research in Parapsychology, 1983: Abstracts & Papers from the Twenty-Sixth Annual Convention of the Parapsychological Association, 1983. Parapsychological Association Staff. LC 66-28580. 196p. 1984. 12.50 (*0-8108-1695-4*) Scarecrow.

Research in Parapsychology 1984: Abstracts & Papers from the Twenty-Seventh Annual Convention of the Parapsychological Association, 1984. Parapsychological Association Staff. LC 66-28580. 215p. 1985. 12.50 (*0-8108-1812-4*) Scarecrow.

Research in Parapsychology 1985: Abstracts & Papers from the Twenty-Eighth Annual Convention of the Parapsychological Association, 1985. Parapsychological Association Staff. LC 66-28580. (Illus.). 256p. 1987. 12. 50 (*0-8108-1936-8*) Scarecrow.

Research in Parapsychology 1986: Abstracts & Papers from the Annual Convention of the Parapsychological Association 1986 29th. Parapsychological Association Staff. LC 66-28580. 256p. 1987. 12.50 (*0-8108-2068-4*) Scarecrow.

Research in Parapsychology, 1987: Abstracts & Papers from the Thirtieth Annual Convention of the Parapsychological Association, 1987. Parapsychological Association Staff. LC 66-28580. 229p. 1988. 12.50 (*0-8108-2128-1*) Scarecrow.

Research in Parapsychology, 1988: Abstracts & Papers from the Thirty-First Annual Convention of the Parapsychological Association, 1988. Parapsychological Association Staff. LC 66-28580. (Illus.). 200p. 1989. 12. 50 (*0-8108-2214-8*) Scarecrow.

Research in Parapsychology 1989: Abstracts & Papers from the Thirty-Second Annual Convention of the Parapsychological Association, 1989. Parapsychological Association Staff. LC 66-28580. (Illus.). 186p. 1990. 25. 00 (*0-8108-2339-X*) Scarecrow.

Research in Parapsychology 1991: Abstracts & Papers from the Thirty-Fourth Annual Convention of the Parapsychological Association. Ed. by Emily W. Cook & Deborah L. Delanoy. LC 66-28580. (Illus.). 240p. 1994. 29.50 (*0-8108-2827-8*) Scarecrow.

Research in Parapsychology 1992: Abstracts & Papers from the Thirty-Fifth Annual Convention of the Parapsychological Association, 1992. Ed. by Emily W. Cook. LC 95-35064. 192p. 1996. 32.00 (*0-8108-3041-8*) Scarecrow.

Research in Pastoral Care & Counseling: Quantitative & Qualitative Approaches. Larry VandeCreek et al. (Illus.). 200p. (Orig.). 1994. pap. text ed. write for info. (*0-929670-10-8*) JPCP.

Research in Perinatal Medicine. Ed. by Peter W. Nathanielsz & Julian T. Parer. (Research in Perinatal Medicine Ser.: No. I). (Illus.). 246p. 1984. 67.50 (*0-916859-03-7*) Perinatology.

Research in Personnel & Human Resources Management, Vol. 1. Ed. by Gerald R. Ferris et al. 324p. 1983. 73.25 (*0-89232-268-3*) Jai Pr.

Research in Personnel & Human Resources Management, Vol. 2. Ed. by Gerald R. Ferris et al. 303p. 1984. 73.25 (*0-89232-483-X*) Jai Pr.

Research in Personnel & Human Resources Management, Vol. 3. Ed. by Gerald R. Ferris et al. 275p. 1985. 73.25 (*0-89232-498-8*) Jai Pr.

Research in Personnel & Human Resources Management, Vol. 4. Ed. by Gerald R. Ferris et al. 389p. 1986. 73.25 (*0-89232-606-9*) Jai Pr.

Research in Personnel & Human Resources Management, Vol. 5. Ed. by Gerald R. Ferris et al. 412p. 1987. 73.25 (*0-89232-750-2*) Jai Pr.

Research in Personnel & Human Resources Management, Vol. 6. Ed. by Gerald R. Ferris et al. 344p. 1988. 73.25 (*0-89232-856-8*) Jai Pr.

Research in Personnel & Human Resources Management, Vol. 7. Ed. by Gerald R. Ferris et al. 317p. 1990. 73.25 (*1-55938-005-5*) Jai Pr.

An Asterisk (*) at the beginning of an entry indicates that the title is appearing in BIP for the first time.

Research in Personnel & Human Resources Management, Vol. 8. Ed. by Gerald R. Ferris et al. 414p. 1990. 73.25 (*1-55938-193-0*) Jai Pr.

Research in Personnel & Human Resources Management, Vol. 9. Ed. by Gerald R. Ferris et al. 407p. 1991. 73.25 (*1-55938-340-2*) Jai Pr.

Research in Personnel & Human Resources Management, Vol. 10. Ed. by Gerald R Ferris et al. 389p. 1992. 73.25 (*1-55938-427-1*) Jai Pr.

Research in Personnel & Human Resources Management, Vol. 11. Ed. by Gerald R. Ferris et al. 382p. 1993. 73.25 (*1-55938-557-X*) Jai Pr.

Research in Personnel & Human Resources Management, Vol. 12. Ed. by Gerald R. Ferris et al. 324p. 1994. 73.25 (*1-55938-733-5*) Jai Pr.

Research in Personnel & Human Resources Management, Vol. 13. Ed. by Gerald R. Ferris et al. 298p. 1995. 73.25 (*1-55938-943-5*) Jai Pr.

Research in Personnel & Human Resources Management, Vol. 14. Ed. by Gerald R. Ferris et al. 440p. 1996. 78.50 (*0-7623-0017-5*) Jai Pr.

***Research in Personnel & Human Resources Management: In Preparation, Summer 1997, Vol. 15.** Ed. by Gerald R. Ferris. 1996. 73.25 (*0-7623-0157-0*) Jai Pr.

Research in Personnel & Human Resources Management: International Human Resources Management, No. 1. Ed. by Gerald R. Ferris et al. 389p. 1983. suppl. ed. 73.25 (*0-89232-985-8*) Jai Pr.

Research in Personnel & Human Resources Management: International Human Resources Management, No. 2. Ed. by Gerald R. Ferris et al. 320p. 1984. suppl. ed. 73.25 (*1-55938-259-7*) Jai Pr.

Research in Personnel & Human Resources Management No. 3: International Human Resources Management. Ed. by Gerald R. Ferris et al. 400p. 1993. suppl. ed. 73.25 (*1-55938-720-3*) Jai Pr.

Research in Philosophy & Technology, Vol. 1. Ed. by Carl Mitcham et al. 390p. 1978. 73.25 (*0-89232-022-2*) Jai Pr.

Research in Philosophy & Technology, Vol. 2. Ed. by Carl Mitcham et al. 403p. 1979. 73.25 (*0-89232-101-6*) Jai Pr.

Research in Philosophy & Technology, Vol. 3. Ed. by Carl Mitcham et al. 412p. 1981. 73.25 (*0-89232-102-4*) Jai Pr.

Research in Philosophy & Technology, Vol. 4. Ed. by Carl Mitcham et al. 305p. 1982. 73.25 (*0-89232-181-4*) Jai Pr.

Research in Philosophy & Technology, Vol. 5. Ed. by Carl Mitcham et al. 339p. 1983. 73.25 (*0-89232-322-1*) Jai Pr.

Research in Philosophy & Technology, Vol. 6. Ed. by Carl Mitcham et al. 282p. 1983. 73.25 (*0-89232-352-3*) Jai Pr.

Research in Philosophy & Technology, Vol. 7. Paul T. Durbin. Ed. by Carl Mitcham et al. 304p. 1984. 73.25 (*0-89232-505-4*) Jai Pr.

Research in Philosophy & Technology, Vol. 8. Ed. by Carl Mitcham et al. 280p. 1985. 73.25 (*0-89232-593-3*) Jai Pr.

Research in Philosophy & Technology, Vol. 10. Ed. by Carl Mitcham et al. 376p. 1990. 73.25 (*1-55938-062-4*) Jai Pr.

Research in Philosophy & Technology Vol. 9: Ethics & Technology. Ed. by Carl Mitcham et al. LC 86-3026. 306p. 1989. 73.25 (*0-318-62532-6*) Jai Pr.

Research in Philosophy & Technology Vol. 11: Technology & Politics. Ed. by Carl Mitcham et al. 422p. 1991. 73.25 (*1-55938-212-0*) Jai Pr.

Research in Philosophy & Technology Vol. 12: Technology & the Environment. Ed. by Carl Mitcham et al. 364p. 1992. 73.25 (*1-55938-456-5*) Jai Pr.

Research in Philosophy & Technology Vol. 13: Technology & Feminism. Ed. by Joan Rothchild et al. 395p. 1993. 73.25 (*1-55938-566-9*) Jai Pr.

Research in Philosophy & Technology Vol. 14: Technology & Everyday Life. Ed. by Carl Mitcham et al. 351p. 1994. 73.25 (*1-55938-712-2*) Jai Pr.

Research in Philosophy & Technology Vol. 15: Social & Philosophical Constructions of Technology. Ed. by Carl Mitcham et al. 423p. 1995. 73.25 (*1-55938-886-2*) Jai Pr.

Research in Philosophy & Technology Vol. 16: Technology & Social Action. Ed. by Carl Mitcham & Leonard J. Waks. 1996. 73.25 (*0-7623-0109-0*) Jai Pr.

Research in Photosynthesis: Proceedings of the IXth International Congress on Photosynthesis, Nagoya, Japan, August 30-September 4, 1992, 4 vols. Ed. by Norio Murata. LC 92-39162. 3512p. (C). 1993. lib. bdg. 0.01 (*0-7923-2073-5*) Kluwer Ac.

Research in Physical Education & Sport: Exploring Alternative Visions. Ed. by Andrew C. Sparkes. 310p. 1992. 95.00 (*0-7507-0074-2*, Falmer Pr); pap. 39.00 (*0-7507-0075-0*, Falmer Pr) Taylor & Francis.

Research in Physical Education, Exercise Science, & Sport. Charles F. Cicciarella. LC 96-24644. (Illus.). 350p. (C). 1996. per. 37.95 (*0-89787-631-8*) Gorsuch Scarisbrick.

Research in Physical Therapy. Ed. by Christopher E. Bork. (Illus.). 384p. 1993. text ed. 35.95 (*0-397-54803-6*) Lppncott-Raven.

Research in Political Economy, Vol. 1. Ed. by Paul Zarembka. 231p. 1978. 73.25 (*0-89232-020-6*) Jai Pr.

Research in Political Economy, Vol. 2. Ed. by Paul Zarembka. 289p. 1979. 73.25 (*0-89232-120-2*); 73.25 (*89-923212-0-1*) Jai Pr.

Research in Political Economy, Vol. 3. Ed. by Paul Zarembka. 290p. 1980. 73.25 (*0-89232-156-3*) Jai Pr.

Research in Political Economy, Vol. 4. Ed. by Paul Zarembka. 227p. 1981. 73.25 (*0-89232-205-5*) Jai Pr.

Research in Political Economy, Vol. 5. Ed. by Paul Zarembka. 298p. 1982. 73.25 (*0-89232-269-1*) Jai Pr.

Research in Political Economy, Vol. 6. Ed. by Paul Zarembka. 303p. 1983. 73.25 (*0-89232-350-7*) Jai Pr.

Research in Political Economy, Vol. 7. Ed. by Paul Zarembka. 283p. 1984. 73.25 (*0-89232-490-2*) Jai Pr.

Research in Political Economy, Vol. 8. Ed. by Paul Zarembka. 289p. 1985. 73.25 (*0-89232-595-X*) Jai Pr.

Research in Political Economy, Vol. 9. Ed. by Paul Zarembka. 252p. 1986. 73.25 (*0-89232-661-1*) Jai Pr.

Research in Political Economy, Vol. 10. Ed. by Paul Zarembka. 250p. 1987. 73.25 (*0-89232-751-0*) Jai Pr.

Research in Political Economy, Vol. 11. Ed. by Paul Zarembka. 280p. 1988. 73.25 (*0-89232-922-X*) Jai Pr.

Research in Political Economy, Vol. 12. Ed. by Paul Zarembka. 294p. 1991. 73.25 (*0-89232-990-4*) Jai Pr.

Research in Political Economy, Vol. 13. Ed. by Paul Zarembka. 283p. 1992. 73.25 (*1-55938-343-7*) Jai Pr.

Research in Political Economy, Vol. 14. Ed. by Paul Zarembka. 272p. 1994. 73.25 (*1-55938-605-3*) Jai Pr.

Research in Political Economy, Vol. 15. Ed. by Paul Zarembka. 1996. 73.25 (*1-55938-971-0*) Jai Pr.

***Research in Political Economy, Vol. 16.** Ed. by Paul Zarembka. 1997. 73.25 (*0-7623-0237-2*) Jai Pr.

Research in Political Sociology, Vol. 1. Ed. by Philo Wasburn & Richard G. Braungart. 321p. 1985. 73.25 (*0-89232-557-7*) Jai Pr.

Research in Political Sociology, Vol. 2. Richard G. Braungart. Ed. by Philo Wasburn. 332p. 1986. 73.25 (*0-89232-610-7*) Jai Pr.

Research in Political Sociology, Vol. 3. Ed. by Philo Wasburn & Richard G. Braungart. 357p. 1987. 73.25 (*0-89232-752-9*) Jai Pr.

Research in Political Sociology, Vol. 4. Ed. by Philo Wasburn. 360p. 1989. 73.25 (*0-89232-901-7*) Jai Pr.

Research in Political Sociology, Vol. 5. Ed. by Philo Wasburn. 390p. 1991. 73.25 (*1-55938-077-2*) Jai Pr.

Research in Political Sociology, Vol. 6. Ed. by Philo Wasburn. 256p. 1993. 73.25 (*1-55938-446-8*) Jai Pr.

Research in Political Sociology, Vol. 7. Ed. by Philo Wasburn. 365p. 1995. 73.25 (*1-55938-887-0*) Jai Pr.

Research in Political Sociology, Vol. 8. Ed. by Philo Wasburn. 1996. 73.25 (*0-7623-0042-6*) Jai Pr.

Research in Politics & Society, Vol. 5. Ed. by Gwen Moore & J. Allen Whitt. 294p. 1995. 73.25 (*1-55938-117-5*) Jai Pr.

Research in Politics & Society, Vol. 6. Ed. by Gwen Moore & J. Allen Whitt. 1996. 73.25 (*0-7623-0043-4*) Jai Pr.

Research in Population Economics, Vol. 1. Ed. by Julian L. Simon et al. 347p. 1978. 90.25 (*0-89232-018-4*) Jai Pr.

Research in Population Economics, Vol. 2. Ed. by Julian L. Simon et al. 474p. 1980. 90.25 (*0-89232-125-3*) Jai Pr.

Research in Population Economics, Vol. 3. Ed. by Kenneth I. Wolpin et al. 1984. 90.25 (*0-89232-207-1*) Jai Pr.

Research in Population Economics, Vol. 4. Ed. by Julian L. Simon et al. 368p. 1982. 90.25 (*0-89232-242-X*) Jai Pr.

Research in Population Economics, Vol. 5. Ed. by W. Boyd Littrell et al. LC 89-9383. 295p. 1983. 25.75 (*0-89232-421-X*) Jai Pr.

Research in Population Economics, Vol. 6. Ed. by Julian L. Simon et al. 447p. 1988. 90.25 (*0-89232-626-3*) Jai Pr.

Research in Population Economics, Vol. 7. Ed. by Julian L. Simon et al. 287p. 1991. 90.25 (*0-89232-943-2*) Jai Pr.

Research in Population Economics, Vol. 8. Ed. by Julian L. Simon et al. 1995. 90.25 (*1-55938-370-4*) Jai Pr.

***Research in Population Genetics of Primitive Groups.** (Technical Report Ser.: No. 279). 26p. 1964. pap. text ed. 3.00 (*92-4-120279-3*) World Health.

***Research in Practice.** write for info. (*0-340-66193-3*, Pub. by E Arnold UK) Routledge Chapman & Hall.

Research-in-Progress, 1986-87. Independent Sector Staff. 260p. 1988. 25.00 (*0-685-44129-6*) Ind Sector.

Research-in-Progress, 1987-88. Independent Sector Staff. 163p. 1989. 25.00 (*0-685-44128-8*) Ind Sector.

Research in Psychiatry: Issues, Strategies, & Methods. Ed. by L. K. Hsu & M. Hersen. (Critical Issues in Psychiatry Ser.). (Illus.). 500p. 1992. 69.50 (*0-306-44162-4*, Plenum Med Bk) Plenum.

Research in Psychoanalysis: Process, Development, Outcome. Ed. by Theodore Shapiro & Robert N. Emde. LC 94-3704. 447p. 1995. 62.50 (*0-8236-5795-7*) Intl Univs Pr.

Research in Psychology: Methods & Design. C. James Goodwin. 512p. 1995. text ed. write for info. (*0-471-59385-0*) Wiley.

Research in Psychophysiology. Peter H. Venables & Margaret J. Christie. LC 74-18266. 456p. reprint ed. pap. 130.00 (*0-317-27713-8*, 2052099) Bks Demand.

Research in Psychotherapy: Proceedings. Conference on Research in Psychotherapy Staff. Ed. by Eli A. Rubinstein & Morris B. Parloff. LC 59-9192. 303p. reprint ed. pap. 86.40 (*0-7837-0493-3*, 2040817) Bks Demand.

Research in Public Administration. Ed. by Jay D. White & Guy B. Adams. 323p. (C). 1994. text ed. 46.00 (*0-8039-5682-7*); pap. text ed. 19.95 (*0-8039-5683-5*) Sage.

Research in Public Administration, Vol. 1. Ed. by James L. Perry. 232p. 1991. 73.25 (*1-55938-114-0*) Jai Pr.

Research in Public Administration, Vol. 2. Ed. by James L. Perry. 270p. 1993. 73.25 (*1-55938-433-6*) Jai Pr.

Research in Public Administration, Vol. 3. Ed. by James L. Perry. 338p. 1994. 73.25 (*1-55938-734-3*) Jai Pr.

Research in Public Administration, Vol. 4. Ed. by James L. Perry. 1995. 73.25 (*1-55938-888-9*) Jai Pr.

Research in Public Administration, Vol. 5. Ed. by James L. Perry. 1996. 73.25 (*0-7623-0018-3*) Jai Pr.

Research in Public Policy Analysis & Management, Vol. 3. Ed. by Stuart S. Nagel. 270p. 1986. 73.25 (*0-89232-533-X*) Jai Pr.

Research in Public Policy Analysis & Management, Vol. 4. Ed. by Stuart S. Nagel. 299p. 1987. 73.25 (*0-89232-663-8*) Jai Pr.

Research in Public Policy Analysis & Management, Vol. 6. Ed. by Stuart S. Nagel. 1994. 73.25 (*1-55938-389-5*) Jai Pr.

Research in Public Policy Analysis & Management, Vol. 7. Ed. by Stuart S. Nagel. 285p. 1995. 73.25 (*1-55938-841-2*) Jai Pr.

Research in Public Policy Analysis & Management, Vol. 8. Ed. by Stuart S. Nagel. 1996. 73.25 (*0-7623-0044-2*) Jai Pr.

Research in Public Policy Analysis & Management: Command, Control, & Communications in Competing Military Organizations, Vol. 3. Ed. by John P. Crecine. 300p. 1983. 73.25 (*0-89232-216-0*) Jai Pr.

Research in Public Policy Analysis & Management: Mission Financing to Realign National Defense, Vol. 5. L. R. Jones & Glenn C. Bixler. Ed. by Stuart S. Nagel. LC 92-1756. (Research in Public Policy Analysis & Management Ser.: Vol. 5). 242p. 1992. 73.25 (*0-89232-916-5*) Jai Pr.

Research in Quantum Field Theory: Proceedings of the Lebedev Physics Institute, Vol. 214. Ed. by V. I. Man'ko & M. A. Markov. 217p. (C). 1995. lib. bdg. 96.00 (*1-56072-221-5*) Nova Sci Pubs.

Research in Quantum Optics. Ed. by A. S. Shumovsky et al. 247p. 1995. text ed. 78.00 (*1-56072-115-4*) Nova Sci Pubs.

Research in Race & Ethnic Relations, Vol. 1. Ed. by Rutledge Dennis et al. 199p. 1979. 73.25 (*0-89232-064-8*) Jai Pr.

Research in Race & Ethnic Relations, Vol. 2. Ed. by Rutledge Dennis et al. 163p. 1980. 73.25 (*0-89232-141-5*) Jai Pr.

Research in Race & Ethnic Relations, Vol. 3. Ed. by Rutledge Dennis. 154p. 1982. 73.25 (*0-89232-224-1*) Jai Pr.

Research in Race & Ethnic Relations, Vol. 4. Ed. by Rutledge Dennis. 191p. 1985. 73.25 (*0-89232-361-2*) Jai Pr.

Research in Race & Ethnic Relations, Vol. 5. Ed. by Rutledge Dennis. 267p. 1989. 73.25 (*0-89232-614-X*) Jai Pr.

Research in Race & Ethnic Relations, Vol. 6. Ed. by Rutledge Dennis. 182p. 1992. 73.25 (*1-55938-045-4*) Jai Pr.

Research in Race & Ethnic Relations, Vol. 7. Ed. by Rutledge Dennis. 319p. 1994. 73.25 (*1-55938-570-7*) Jai Pr.

Research in Race & Ethnic Relations, Vol. 8. Ed. by Rutledge Dennis. 243p. 1995. 73.25 (*1-55938-889-7*) Jai Pr.

Research in Race & Ethnic Relations, Vol. 9. Ed. by Rutledge Dennis. 1996. 73.25 (*0-7623-0045-0*) Jai Pr.

Research in Reading in English as a Second Language. Ed. by Joanne Devine et al. 192p. 1987. pap. 16.50 (*0-939791-30-7*) Tchrs Eng Spkrs.

***Research in Reading Recovery.** 1995. pap. text ed. write for info. (*0-435-07239-0*) Heinemann.

Research in Real Estate Vol. 2: Urban Housing Markets & Property Valuation. C. F. Sirmans. Ed. by Steven D. Kapplin et al. (Research in Real Estate Ser.: Vol. 2). 291p. 1982. 73.25 (*0-89232-270-5*) Jai Pr.

Research in Real Estate Vol. 2: Urban Housing Markets & Property Valuation, Vol. 1. C. F. Sirmans. Ed. by Arthur L. Schwartz, Jr. & Steven D. Kapplin. 336p. 1981. 73.25 (*0-89232-217-9*) Jai Pr.

Research in Real Estate Vol. 2: Urban Housing Markets & Property Valuation, Vol. 3. Ed. by Steven D. Kapplin et al. 261p. 1991. 73.25 (*0-89232-422-8*) Jai Pr.

Research in Real Estate Vol. 2: Urban Housing Markets & Property Valuation, Vol. 4. Ed. by Steven D. Kapplin & Arthur L. Schwartz, Jr. 1996. 73.25 (*1-55938-378-X*) Jai Pr.

Research in Reference Effectiveness: Proceedings of a Preconference. Ed. by Marjory E. Murfin & Jo B. Whitlatch. (RASD Occasional Papers: No. 16). 129p. (Orig.). 1993. pap. 25.00 (*0-8389-7704-9*) ALA.

Research in Religion & Health: Selected Projects & Methods. Academy of Religion & Mental Health Staff. LC 59-15767. (Proceedings of the Fifth Academy Symposium Ser.: 1961). 175p. reprint ed. pap. 49.90 (*0-7837-0436-4*, 2040759) Bks Demand.

Research in Religious Education. Ed. by Leslie J. Francis et al. LC 96-33860. 478p. 1996. pap. 28.99 (*1-57312-053-7*) Smyth & Helwys.

Research in Rural Sociology & Development, Vol. 2: Focus on Community. Ed. by Daniel C. Clay & Harry K. Schwarzweller. 280p. 1985. 73.25 (*0-89232-558-5*) Jai Pr.

Research in Rural Sociology & Development, Vol. 3: Third World Contexts. Ed. by Daniel C. Clay & Harry K. Schwarzweller. 280p. 1987. 73.25 (*0-89232-586-0*) Jai Pr.

Research in Rural Sociology & Development, Vol. 4: Rural Labor Markets. Ed. by Daniel C. Clay & Harry K. Schwarzweller. 281p. 1989. 73.25 (*0-89232-925-4*) Jai Pr.

Research in Rural Sociology & Development, Vol. 5: Household Strategies. Ed. by Daniel C. Clay & Harry K. Schwarzweller. 263p. 1991. 73.25 (*1-55938-058-6*) Jai Pr.

Research in Rural Sociology & Development, Vol. 6. Ed. by Daniel C. Clay & Harry K. Schwarzweller. 270p. 1995. 73.25 (*1-55938-458-1*) Jai Pr.

Research in Rural Sociology & Development, Vol. 7. Ed. by Harry K. Schwarzweller. 1996. 73.25 (*1-55938-998-2*) Jai Pr.

Research in Rural Sociology & Development: Focus on Agriculture, Vol. 1: Focus on Agriculture. Ed. by Daniel C. Clay & Harry K. Schwarzweller. 353p. 1985. 73.25 (*0-89232-332-9*) Jai Pr.

***Research in Schools: A Reflective Ethnography for Educators.** Duncan Waite. Ed. by Joe Kincheloe & Shirley R. Steinberg. (Critical Education Practice Ser.). 250p. Date not set. text ed. 38.00 (*0-8153-2037-X*); pap. text ed. 18.95 (*0-8153-2321-2*) Garland.

Research in Science Education in Europe. Ed. by K. Frey et al. xii, 394p. 1977. pap. 50.00 (*90-265-0266-4*) Swets.

Research in Science Education in Europe. Ed. by Geoff Welford et al. LC 96-18747. 288p. 1996. pap. 42.95 (*0-7507-0547-7*, Falmer Pr) Taylor & Francis.

Research in Science Education in Europe. Geoff Welford et al. LC 96-18747. 1996. write for info. (*0-7507-0546-9*, Falmer Pr) Taylor & Francis.

Research in Science Education, 1938-1947. Robert W. Boenig. LC 69-12581. (Reviews of Research in Science Education Ser.: Vol. 1: 1938-1947). 306p. reprint ed. pap. 87.30 (*0-317-41929-3*, 2025993) Bks Demand.

Research in Science Education, 1948-1952. Robert W. Boenig & Nathan J. Swift. LC 69-12581. (Reviews of Research in Science Education Ser.: Vol. 2). 203p. reprint ed. pap. 57.90 (*0-317-42231-6*, 2026073) Bks Demand.

Research in Science Education, 1953-1957. Elizabeth P. Lawlor. LC 69-12581. (Reviews of Research in Science Education Ser.). 120p. reprint ed. pap. 34.20 (*0-317-41897-1*, 2026040) Bks Demand.

Research in Second Language Learning: Focus on the Classroom. Ed. by James P. Lantolf et al. LC 86-22300. (Delaware Symposia on Language Studies: Vol. 6). 240p. (C). 1987. text ed. 73.25 (*0-89391-363-4*) Ablex Pub.

Research in Social Group Work. Ed. by Sheldon D. Rose & Ronald A. Feldman. LC 86-29526. (Social Work with Groups Ser.: Vol. 9, No. 3). 124p. 1987. text ed. 29.95 (*0-86656-645-7*) Haworth Pr.

Research in Social Movement, Conflicts & Change, Vol. 5. Ed. by Louis Kriesberg et al. 343p. 1983. 73.25 (*0-89232-301-9*) Jai Pr.

Research in Social Movement, Conflicts & Change, Vol. 10: Soc. Movements As a Factor of Change in t. Ed. by Louis Kriesberg et al. 286p. 1988. 73.25 (*0-89232-723-5*) Jai Pr.

Research in Social Movements, Conflicts & Change, Supp. 2: The Green Movement Worldwide. Ed. by Louis Kriesberg et al. 252p. 1992. 73.25 (*1-55938-530-8*) Jai Pr.

Research in Social Movements, Conflicts & Change, Vol. 2. Ed. by Louis Kriesberg et al. 293p. 1979. 73.25 (*0-89232-108-3*) Jai Pr.

Research in Social Movements, Conflicts & Change, Vol. 3. Ed. by Louis Kriesberg et al. 266p. 1981. 73.25 (*0-89232-182-2*) Jai Pr.

Research in Social Movements, Conflicts & Change, Vol. 4. Ed. by Louis Kriesberg et al. 385p. 1981. 73.25 (*0-89232-201-2*) Jai Pr.

Research in Social Movements, Conflicts & Change, Vol. 6. Ed. by Louis Kriesberg et al. 300p. 1984. 73.25 (*0-89232-311-6*) Jai Pr.

Research in Social Movements, Conflicts, & Change, Vol. 7. Louis Kreisberg. 73.25 (*0-89232-559-3*) Jai Pr.

Research in Social Movements, Conflicts & Change, Vol. 7. Ed. by Louis Kriesberg et al. 299p. 1984. 73.25 (*0-89232-496-1*) Jai Pr.

Research in Social Movements, Conflicts & Change, Vol. 8. Ed. by Louis Kriesberg et al. 205p. 1985. 73.25 (*0-89232-571-2*) Jai Pr.

Research in Social Movements, Conflicts & Change, Vol. 9. Ed. by Louis Kriesberg et al. 280p. 1986. 73.25 (*0-89232-594-1*) Jai Pr.

Research in Social Movements, Conflicts & Change, Vol. 11. Ed. by Louis Kriesberg et al. 339p. 1989. 73.25 (*0-89232-945-9*) Jai Pr.

Research in Social Movements, Conflicts & Change, Vol. 12. Ed. by Louis Kriesberg et al. 344p. 1990. 73.25 (*1-55938-065-9*) Jai Pr.

Research in Social Movements, Conflicts & Change, Vol. 13. Ed. by Louis Kriesberg et al. 319p. 1991. 73.25 (*1-55938-239-2*) Jai Pr.

Research in Social Movements, Conflicts & Change, Vol. 14: The Transformation of Europ. Communist So. Ed. by Louis Kriesberg et al. 313p. 1992. 73.25 (*1-55938-457-3*) Jai Pr.

Research in Social Movements, Conflicts & Change, Vol. 15. Ed. by Louis Kriesberg et al. 242p. 1993. 73.25 (*1-55938-532-4*) Jai Pr.

Research in Social Movements, Conflicts & Change, Vol. 16. Ed. by Louis Kriesberg et al. 199p. 1994. 73.25 (*1-55938-654-1*) Jai Pr.

Research in Social Movements, Conflicts & Change, Vol. 17. Ed. by Louis Kriesberg et al. 1994. 73.25 (*1-55938-890-0*) Jai Pr.

Research in Social Movements, Conflicts & Change, Vol. 18. Ed. by Louis Kriesberg et al. 334p. 1995. 73.25 (*1-55938-947-8*) Jai Pr.

Research in Social Movements, Conflicts & Change, Vol. 19. Ed. by Louis Kriesberg et al. 290p. 1996. 73.25 (*0-7623-0046-9*) Jai Pr.

***Research in Social Movements, Conflicts & Change, Vol. 20.** Ed. by Louis Kriesberg et al. 1997. 73.25 (*0-7623-0252-6*) Jai Pr.

Research in Social Movements, Conflicts & Change: Alive & Kicking, Supp. 1: The Alinsky Legacy: Alive & Kicking. Ed. by Louis Kriesberg et al. (Research in Social Movement, Conflicts & Change Ser.: Suppl. 1). 274p. 1987. 73.25 (*0-89232-722-7*) Jai Pr.

Research in Social Movements, Conflicts & Change: An Annual Compilation of Research, Vol. 1. Ed. by Louis Kriesberg et al. 350p. 1978. 73.25 (*0-89232-027-3*) Jai Pr.

Research in Social Policy, Vol. 1. Ed. by John H. Stanfield, 2nd. 227p. 1987. 73.25 (*0-89232-521-6*) Jai Pr.

R

Research in Social Policy, Vol. 2. Ed. by John H. Stanfield, 2nd. 225p. 1982. 73.25 (*0-89232-917-3*) Jai Pr.

Research in Social Policy, Vol. 3. Ed. by John H. Stanfield, 2nd. 207p. 1994. 73.25 (*1-55938-443-3*) Jai Pr.

Research in Social Policy, Vol. 4. Ed. by John H. Stanfield, 2nd. 1996. 73.25 (*1-55938-891-9*) Jai Pr.

Research in Social Policy, Vol. 5. Ed. by John H. Stanfield, 2nd. 1997. 73.25 (*0-7623-0047-7*) Jai Pr.

Research in Social Problems & Public Policy, Vol. 1. Ed. by William R. Freudenburg & Ted I. Youn. 224p. 1979. 73.25 (*0-89232-068-0*) Jai Pr.

Research in Social Problems & Public Policy, Vol. 2. Ed. by William R. Freudenburg & Ted I. Youn. 296p. 1982. 73.25 (*0-89232-195-4*) Jai Pr.

Research in Social Problems & Public Policy, Vol. 3. Ed. by William R. Freudenburg & Ted I. Youn. 300p. 1984. 73.25 (*0-89232-339-6*) Jai Pr.

Research in Social Problems & Public Policy, Vol. 4. Ed. by William R. Freudenburg & Ted I. Youn. 219p. 1987. 73.25 (*0-89232-560-7*) Jai Pr.

***Research in Social Problems & Public Policy, Vol. 5.** Ed. by William R. Freudenburg & Ted I. Youn. 312p. 1994. 73.25 (*0-614-24727-6*) Jai Pr.

Research in Social Problems & Public Policy, Vol. 6. Ed. by William R. Freudenburg & Ted I. Youn. 1995. 73.25 (*1-55938-369-0*) Jai Pr.

***Research in Social Problems & Public Policy, Vol. 7.** Ed. by William R. Freudenburg & Ted I. Youn. 1998. 73.25 (*0-7623-0278-X*) Jai Pr.

Research in Social Stratification & Mobility, Vol. 2. Ed. by Robert Althauser & Michael Wallace. 350p. 1983. 73.25 (*0-89232-302-7*) Jai Pr.

Research in Social Stratification & Mobility, Vol. 3. Ed. by Robert Althauser & Michael Wallace. 224p. 1984. 73.25 (*0-89232-331-0*) Jai Pr.

Research in Social Stratification & Mobility, Vol. 4. Ed. by Robert Althauser & Michael Wallace. 296p. 1985. 73.25 (*0-89232-563-1*) Jai Pr.

Research in Social Stratification & Mobility, Vol. 5. Ed. by Robert Althauser & Michael Wallace. 371p. 1986. 73.25 (*0-89232-660-3*) Jai Pr.

Research in Social Stratification & Mobility, Vol. 6. Ed. by Robert Althauser & Michael Wallace. 285p. 1987. 73.25 (*0-89232-717-0*) Jai Pr.

Research in Social Stratification & Mobility, Vol. 7. Ed. by Robert Althauser & Michael Wallace. 352p. 1989. 73.25 (*0-89232-897-5*) Jai Pr.

Research in Social Stratification & Mobility, Vol. 8. Ed. by Robert Althauser & Michael Wallace. 352p. 1990. 73.25 (*1-55938-019-5*) Jai Pr.

Research in Social Stratification & Mobility, Vol. 9. Ed. by Robert Althauser & Michael Wallace. 375p. 1991. 73.25 (*1-55938-205-8*) Jai Pr.

Research in Social Stratification & Mobility, Vol. 10. Ed. by Robert Althauser & Michael Wallace. 336p. 1991. 73.25 (*1-55938-403-4*) Jai Pr.

Research in Social Stratification & Mobility, Vol. 11. Ed. by Robert Althauser & Michael Wallace. 347p. 1993. 73.25 (*1-55938-491-3*) Jai Pr.

Research in Social Stratification & Mobility, Vol. 12. Ed. by Robert Althauser & Michael Wallace. 400p. 1993. 73.25 (*1-55938-542-1*) Jai Pr.

Research in Social Stratification & Mobility, Vol. 13. Ed. by Robert Althauser & Michael Wallace. 296p. 1994. 73.25 (*1-55938-735-1*) Jai Pr.

Research in Social Stratification & Mobility, Vol. 14. Ed. by Robert Althauser & Michael Wallace. 1995. 73.25 (*1-55938-892-7*) Jai Pr.

Research in Social Stratification & Mobility, Vol. 15. Ed. by Michael Wallace. 1996. 73.25 (*0-7623-0048-5*) Jai Pr.

***Research in Social Stratification & Mobility, Vol. 16.** Ed. by Kevin Leicht. 1998. 73.25 (*0-7623-0279-8*) Jai Pr.

Research in Social Stratification & Mobility: An Annual Compilation of Research, Vol. 1. Ed. by Robert Althauser & Michael Wallace. 319p. 1981. 73.25 (*0-89232-067-2*) Jai Pr.

Research in Social Work. William J. Reid & Audrey D. Smith. LC 81-2885. 416p. 1981. text ed. 49.50 (*0-231-04700-2*) Col U Pr.

Research in Social Work. 2nd ed. William J. Reid & Audrey D. Smith. 360p. 1989. text ed. 39.50 (*0-231-06420-9*) Col U Pr.

Research in Social Work: An Introduction. 2nd ed. Margaret Williams et al. LC 94-66868. 350p. 1994. pap. text ed. 26.00 (*0-87581-388-7*) Peacock Pubs.

Research in Sociology of Education & Socialization, Vol. 1: Longitud Perspec on Educational Attainment. Ed. by Alan C. Kerckhoff et al. (Research in Sociology of Education & Socialization Ser.). 271p. 1979. 73.25 (*0-89232-122-9*) Jai Pr.

Research in Sociology of Education & Socialization, Vol. 5. Ed. by Alan C. Kerckhoff et al. 350p. 1985. 73.25 (*0-89232-424-4*) Jai Pr.

Research in Sociology of Education & Socialization, Vol. 10. Ed. by Alan C. Kerckhoff et al. 259p. 1994. 73.25 (*1-55938-283-X*) Jai Pr.

Research in Sociology of Education & Socialization, Vol. 11. Ed. by Alan C. Kerckhoff et al. 259p. 1996. 73.25 (*1-55938-573-1*) Jai Pr.

***Research in Sociology of Education & Socialization, Vol. 12.** Ed. by Aaron M. Pallas. 339p. 1997. 78.50 (*0-7623-0256-9*) Jai Pr.

Research in Sociology of Education & Socialization: Personal Change over the Life Course, Vol. 4. Ed. by Alan C. Kerckhoff et al. 286p. 1983. 73.25 (*0-89232-303-5*) Jai Pr.

Research in Sociology of Education & Socialization: Policy Research, Vol. 3. Ed. by Alan C. Kerckhoff et al. 323p. 1981. 73.25 (*0-89232-187-3*) Jai Pr.

Research in Sociology of Education & Socialization: Research on Educational Organizations, Vol. 2. Ed. by Alan C. Kerckhoff et al. 316p. 1981. 73.25 (*0-89232-158-X*) Jai Pr.

Research in Sociology of Education & Socialization: Selected Methodological Issues, Vol. 8. Ed. by Alan C. Kerckhoff et al. 258p. 1989. 73.25 (*0-89232-929-7*) Jai Pr.

Research in Sociology of Education & Socialization Vol. 6: International Perspectives on Education. Ed. by Alan C. Kerckhoff et al. 302p. 1987. 73.25 (*0-89232-712-X*) Jai Pr.

Research in Sociology of Education & Socialization Vol. 7: Out of School. Ed. by Alan C. Kerckhoff et al. 312p. 1987. 73.25 (*0-89232-755-3*) Jai Pr.

Research in Sociology of Education & Socialization Vol. 9: Historical Approaches. Ed. by Alan C. Kerckhoff et al. 294p. 1990. 73.25 (*1-55938-059-4*) Jai Pr.

Research in South Carolina. Ge L. Hendrix. LC 92-10707. 1992. write for info. (*0-915156-66-0*) Natl Genealogical.

Research in Soviet Social Psychology. Ed. by L. H. Strickland et al. (Recent Research in Psychology Ser.). (Illus.). x, 99p. 1986. 59.95 (*0-387-96317-0*) Spr-Verlag.

Research in Space: The German Spacelab Missions. Ed. by P. R. Sahm et al. 1993. text ed. 77.00 (*3-89100-021-9*) Gordon & Breach.

Research in Strategic Management & Information Technology, Vol. 1. Ed. by N. Venkatraman & John Henderson. 184p. 1994. 73.25 (*1-55938-782-3*) Jai Pr.

Research in Strategic Management & Information Technology, Vol. 2. Ed. by N. Venkatraman & John Henderson. 1996. 73.25 (*0-7623-0008-6*) Jai Pr.

Research in Surface Forces: Three-Dimensional Aspects of Surface Forces, Vol. 2. Konferentsiia po Poverkhnostym Silam, Institut Fizicheskoi Khimii Akademii Nauk S. S. S. R. Staff. Tr. by Paul P. Sutton. LC 62-15549. 328p. reprint ed. pap. 93.50 (*0-317-08152-7*, 2003409) Bks Demand.

Research in Taxation: "Journal of Political Economy" 86, No. 2, Pt. 2. Ed. by Michael J. Boskin. (Other Conferences Ser.: No. 11). 150p. 1978. reprint ed. 40.00 (*0-685-61422-0*) Natl Bur Econ Res.

Research in Taxation: A Conference of the National Bureau of Economic Research. Conference on Research in Taxation & Michael J. Boskin. (National Bureau of Economic Research, Conference Reports: No. 11). 160p. reprint ed. pap. 45.60 (*0-317-55570-7*, 2056365) Bks Demand.

Research in Teacher Education: International Perspectives. Ed. by Richard P. Tisher. 250p. 1990. 75.00 (*1-85000-782-9*, Falmer Pr); pap. 35.00 (*1-85000-783-7*, Falmer Pr) Taylor & Francis.

Research in Teaching of Foreign Languages. Ed. by Mujibul H. Siddiqui. (Illus.). vii, 252p. 1993. 32.00 (*81-7024-545-1*, Pub. by Ashish Pub Hse II) Nataraj Bks.

Research in Teaching of Literature. Ed. by Mujibul H. Siddiqui. (Illus.). vi, 191p. 1993. 25.00 (*81-7024-556-7*, Pub. by Ashish Pub Hse II) Nataraj Bks.

Research in Technical Communication: A Bibliographic Sourcebook. Ed. by Michael G. Moran & Debra Journet. LC 84-8977. xxviii, 512p. 1985. text ed. 89.50 (*0-313-23431-0*, MRT/, Greenwood Pr) Greenwood.

Research in Tennessee. Gale W. Bamman. LC 93-37251. (Research in the States Ser.). 1993. write for info. (*0-915156-72-5*) Natl Genealogical.

Research in Terrestrial Impact Structures. Ed. by Jean Pohl. (Earth Evolution Sciences Ser.). vi, 141p. 1987. 70.00 (*3-528-08940-7*, Pub. by Vieweg & Sohn GW) Informatica.

Research in Texas. Lloyd D. Bockstruck. LC 92-10706. (Research in the States Ser.). 1992. write for info. (*0-915156-70-9*) Natl Genealogical.

Research in the Classroom: Talk, Texts, & Inquiry. Ed. by Zoe Donoahue et al. 136p. (Orig.). 1996. pap. 18.00 (*0-87207-146-4*) Intl Reading.

Research in the Economics of Mental Health, Vol. 14. Ed. by Richard M. Scheffler et al. (Advances in Health Economics & Health Services Research Ser.). 264p. 1994. 73.25 (*1-55938-612-6*) Jai Pr.

***Research in the History of Economic Thought & Methodology, Archival Suppl. 6.** Ed. by Warren J. Samuels & Jeff E. Biddle. 1997. 73.25 (*0-7623-0286-0*) Jai Pr.

Research in the History of Economic Thought & Methodology, No. 2. Ed. by Warren J. Samuels et al. 255p. 1991. suppl. ed. 73.25 (*1-55938-245-7*) Jai Pr.

Research in the History of Economic Thought & Methodology, No. 3. Ed. by Warren J. Samuels et al. 204p. 1986. suppl. ed. 73.25 (*0-614-09936-6*) Jai Pr.

Research in the History of Economic Thought & Methodology, No. 4. Ed. by Warren J. Samuels et al. 274p. 1987. suppl. ed. 73.25 (*1-55938-757-2*) Jai Pr.

Research in the History of Economic Thought & Methodology, No. 5. Ed. by Warren J. Samuels et al. 1995. suppl. ed. 73.25 (*1-55938-094-2*) Jai Pr.

Research in the History of Economic Thought & Methodology, Vol. 2. Ed. by Warren J. Samuels et al. 246p. 1987. 73.25 (*0-89232-476-7*) Jai Pr.

Research in the History of Economic Thought & Methodology, Vol. 3. Ed. by Warren J. Samuels et al. 295p. 1995. 73.25 (*0-89232-616-6*) Jai Pr.

Research in the History of Economic Thought & Methodology, Vol. 4. Ed. by Warren J. Samuels et al. 376p. 1994. 73.25 (*0-89232-678-6*) Jai Pr.

Research in the History of Economic Thought & Methodology, Vol. 5. Ed. by Warren J. Samuels et al. 248p. 1987. 73.25 (*0-89232-832-0*) Jai Pr.

Research in the History of Economic Thought & Methodology, Vol. 6. Ed. by Warren J. Samuels et al. 283p. 1989. 73.25 (*0-89232-928-9*) Jai Pr.

Research in the History of Economic Thought & Methodology, Vol. 7. Ed. by Warren J. Samuels et al. 294p. 1990. 73.25 (*0-614-09934-X*) Jai Pr.

Research in the History of Economic Thought & Methodology, Vol. 8. Ed. by Warren J. Samuels et al. 288p. 1990. 73.25 (*1-55938-233-3*) Jai Pr.

Research in the History of Economic Thought & Methodology, Vol. 9. Ed. by Warren J. Samuels et al. 300p. 1992. 73.25 (*1-55938-428-X*) Jai Pr.

Research in the History of Economic Thought & Methodology, Vol. 10. Ed. by Warren J. Samuels et al. 270p. 1993. 73.25 (*0-614-09935-8*) Jai Pr.

Research in the History of Economic Thought & Methodology, Vol. 11. Ed. by Warren J. Samuels et al. 296p. 1993. 73.25 (*1-55938-502-2*) Jai Pr.

Research in the History of Economic Thought & Methodology, Vol. 12. Ed. by Warren J. Samuels et al. 260p. 1994. 73.25 (*1-55938-747-5*) Jai Pr.

Research in the History of Economic Thought & Methodology, Vol. 13. Ed. by Warren J. Samuels et al. 1995. 73.25 (*1-55938-095-0*) Jai Pr.

***Research in the History of Economic Thought & Methodology, Vol. 14, 1996.** Ed. by Warren J. Samuels & Jeff E. Biddle. 392p. 1996. 73.25 (*0-7623-0108-2*) Jai Pr.

Research in the History of Economic Thought & Methodology: Archival Supplement 1-Lectures by John Dewey: Moral & Political Philosophy. Ed. by Warren J. Samuels & Donald F. Koch. 248p. 1990. 73.25 (*1-55938-186-8*) Jai Pr.

Research in the History of Economic Thought & Methodology: The Craft of the Historian of Economic Thought, Vol. 1. Ed. by Warren J. Samuels et al. 275p. 1983. 73.25 (*0-89232-328-0*) Jai Pr.

Research in the Psychobiology of Human Behavior. Ed. by Eugene Meyer & Joseph V. Brady. LC 78-24710. (Illus.). 160p. reprint ed. pap. 45.60 (*0-8357-8303-0*, 2034152) Bks Demand.

Research in the Schizophrenic Disorders: The Stanley R. Dean Award Lectures, Vol. 1. Ed. by Robert Cancro & Stanley R. Dean. LC 84-20603. 291p. 1985. text ed. 47.50 (*0-89335-211-X*) PMA Pub Corp.

Research in the Schizophrenic Disorders: The Stanley R. Dean Award Lectures, Vol. 2. Ed. by Robert Cancro & Stanley R. Dean. LC 84-20603. 344p. 1985. text ed. 57.50 (*0-89335-212-8*) PMA Pub Corp.

***Research in the Social Sciences & Education: Principles & Process.** Manuel Martinez-Pons. LC 96-41348. 346p. 1996. pap. text ed. 34.50 (*0-7618-0526-5*) U Pr of Amer.

Research in the Social Scientific Study of Religion, Vol. 1. Ed. by Monty L. Lynn & David O. Moberg. 260p. 1989. 73.25 (*0-89232-882-7*) Jai Pr.

Research in the Social Scientific Study of Religion, Vol. 2. Ed. by Monty L. Lynn & David O. Moberg. 247p. 1990. 73.25 (*0-89232-933-5*) Jai Pr.

Research in the Social Scientific Study of Religion, Vol. 3. Ed. by Monty L. Lynn & David O. Moberg. 279p. 1991. 73.25 (*1-55938-276-7*) Jai Pr.

Research in the Social Scientific Study of Religion, Vol. 4. Ed. by Monty L. Lynn & David O. Moberg. 305p. 1992. 73.25 (*1-55938-359-3*) Jai Pr.

Research in the Social Scientific Study of Religion, Vol. 5. Ed. by Monty L. Lynn & David O. Moberg. 258p. 1993. 73.25 (*1-55938-301-1*) Jai Pr.

Research in the Social Scientific Study of Religion, Vol. 6. Ed. by Monty L. Lynn & David O. Moberg. 256p. 1994. 73.25 (*1-55938-762-9*) Jai Pr.

Research in the Social Scientific Study of Religion, Vol. 7. Ed. by Monty L. Lynn & David O. Moberg. 277p. 1996. 73.25 (*1-55938-893-5*) Jai Pr.

***Research in the Social Scientific Study of Religion, Vol. 8.** Ed. by Joanne M. Greer. 1997. 73.25 (*0-7623-0216-X*) Jai Pr.

Research in the Sociology of Health Care, Supp. 1: Organizational Constraints on Psychiatric. Ed. by Jennie J. Kronenfeld & Rose Weitz. (Research in the Sociology of Health Care Ser.: Supplement No. 1). 164p. 1981. 73.25 (*0-89232-176-8*) Jai Pr.

Research in the Sociology of Health Care, Vol. 1: Professional Control of Hlth. Serv. & Chal. Ed. by Jennie J. Kronenfeld & Rose Weitz. 377p. 1980. 73.25 (*0-89232-145-8*) Jai Pr.

Research in the Sociology of Health Care, Vol. 2: Changing Struct. of Hlth Serv. Occupations. Ed. by Jennie J. Kronenfeld & Rose Weitz. 352p. 1982. 73.25 (*0-89232-199-7*) Jai Pr.

Research in the Sociology of Health Care, Vol. 3: The Control of Costs & Performance of Med. Ed. by Jennie J. Kronenfeld & Rose Weitz. (Research in the Sociology of Health Care Ser.: Vol. 3). 350p. 1984. 73.25 (*0-89232-310-8*) Jai Pr.

Research in the Sociology of Health Care, Vol. 5: International Comparisons of Hlth Services. Ed. by Jennie J. Kronenfeld & Rose Weitz. (Research in the Sociology of Health Care Ser.: Vol. 5). 301p. 1987. 73.25 (*0-89232-597-6*) Jai Pr.

Research in the Sociology of Health Care, Vol. 6: The Experience & Mgmt. of Chronic Illness. Ed. by Jennie J. Kronenfeld & Rose Weitz. 321p. 1987. 73.25 (*0-89232-834-7*) Jai Pr.

Research in the Sociology of Health Care, Vol. 7. Ed. by Jennie J. Kronenfeld & Rose Weitz. 333p. 1988. 73.25 (*0-89232-883-5*) Jai Pr.

Research in the Sociology of Health Care, Vol. 8. Ed. by Jennie J. Kronenfeld & Rose Weitz. 341p. 1989. 73.25 (*1-55938-043-8*) Jai Pr.

Research in the Sociology of Health Care, Vol. 9. Ed. by Jennie J. Kronenfeld & Rose Weitz. 353p. 1991. 73.25 (*1-55938-098-5*) Jai Pr.

Research in the Sociology of Health Care, Vol. 10. Ed. by Jennie J. Kronenfeld & Rose Weitz. 287p. 1993. 73.25 (*1-55938-444-1*) Jai Pr.

Research in the Sociology of Health Care, Vol. 11: Agents of Health & Illness. Ed. by Jennie J. Kronenfeld & Rose Weitz. 208p. 1994. 73.25 (*1-55938-840-4*) Jai Pr.

Research in the Sociology of Health Care, Vol. 12. Ed. by Jennie J. Kronenfeld & Rose Weitz. 355p. 1995. 73.25 (*1-55938-894-3*) Jai Pr.

Research in the Sociology of Health Care, Vol. 13. Ed. by Jennie J. Kronenfeld. 1996. 73.25 (*0-7623-0049-3*) Jai Pr.

Research in the Sociology of Health Care: The Adoption & Social Consequences of Medical Technologies, Vol. 4: The Adoption & Social Consequences of Med. Ed. by Jennie J. Kronenfeld & Rose Weitz. 317p. 1986. 73.25 (*0-89232-492-9*) Jai Pr.

Research in the Sociology of Organizations, Vol. 1. Ed. by Samuel B. Bacharach et al. 352p. 1982. 73.25 (*0-89232-170-9*) Jai Pr.

Research in the Sociology of Organizations, Vol. 2. Ed. by Samuel B. Bacharach et al. 276p. 1983. 73.25 (*0-89232-203-9*) Jai Pr.

Research in the Sociology of Organizations, Vol. 3: The Social Psychological Processes. Ed. by Samuel B. Bacharach et al. 256p. 1984. 73.25 (*0-89232-340-X*) Jai Pr.

Research in the Sociology of Organizations, Vol. 4. Ed. by Samuel B. Bacharach et al. 377p. 1985. 73.25 (*0-89232-451-1*) Jai Pr.

Research in the Sociology of Organizations, Vol. 5. Ed. by Samuel B. Bacharach et al. 340p. 1987. 73.25 (*0-89232-637-9*) Jai Pr.

Research in the Sociology of Organizations, Vol. 6. Ed. by Samuel B. Bacharach et al. 344p. 1988. 73.25 (*0-89232-881-9*) Jai Pr.

Research in the Sociology of Organizations, Vol. 8: Organizations & Professions. Ed. by Samuel B. Bacharach et al. 297p. 1991. 73.25 (*1-55938-206-6*) Jai Pr.

Research in the Sociology of Organizations, Vol. 9. Ed. by Samuel B. Bacharach et al. 358p. 1991. 73.25 (*1-55938-398-4*) Jai Pr.

Research in the Sociology of Organizations, Vol. 10: Organizational Demography. Ed. by Samuel B. Bacharach et al. 220p. 1992. 73.25 (*1-55938-423-9*) Jai Pr.

Research in the Sociology of Organizations, Vol. 11. Ed. by Samuel B. Bacharach et al. 297p. 1993. 73.25 (*1-55938-462-X*) Jai Pr.

Research in the Sociology of Organizations, Vol. 12: Special Issue on Labor Relations & Unions. Ed. by Samuel B. Bacharach et al. 309p. 1994. 73.25 (*1-55938-736-X*) Jai Pr.

Research in the Sociology of Organizations, Vol. 14. Ed. by Samuel B. Bacharach et al. 1996. 73.25 (*0-7623-0019-1*) Jai Pr.

***Research in the Sociology of Organizations, Vol. 15.** Ed. by Samuel B. Bacharach. 1997. 78.50 (*0-7623-0180-5*) Jai Pr.

Research in the Sociology of Organizations: Structuring Participation in Organizations, Vol. 7. Ed. by Samuel B. Bacharach et al. 269p. 1990. 73.25 (*1-55938-009-8*) Jai Pr.

Research in the Sociology of Organizations: Studies of Organization in the Eur Tradit, Vol. 13. Ed. by Samuel B. Bacharach et al. 303p. 1995. 73.25 (*1-55938-895-1*) Jai Pr.

Research in the Sociology of Organizations: The Social Psychological Processes, Vol. 3. Ed. by Samuel B. Bacharach & Edward J. Lawler. 1984. 73.25 (*0-89232-450-3*) Jai Pr.

Research in the Sociology of Work, Vol. 1. Ed. by Ida H. Simpson & Richard L. Simpson. 481p. 1981. 73.25 (*0-89232-124-5*) Jai Pr.

Research in the Sociology of Work, Vol. 2: Peripheral Workers. Ed. by Ida H. Simpson & Richard L. Simpson. 379p. 1983. 73.25 (*0-89232-233-0*) Jai Pr.

Research in the Sociology of Work, Vol. 4: High Tech Work. Ed. by Ida H. Simpson & Richard L. Simpson. 333p. 1988. 73.25 (*0-89232-756-1*) Jai Pr.

Research in the Sociology of Work, Vol. 5: The Meaning of Work. Ed. by Ida H. Simpson & Richard L. Simpson. 304p. 1995. 73.25 (*0-89232-971-8*) Jai Pr.

Research in the Sociology of Work, Vol. 6. Ed. by Ida H. Simpson & Richard L. Simpson. 1997. 73.25 (*0-7623-0020-5*) Jai Pr.

Research in the Sociology of Work: Unemployment, Vol. 3: Unemployment. Ed. by Ida H. Simpson & Richard L. Simpson. 260p. 1986. 73.25 (*0-89232-564-X*) Jai Pr.

Research in the Twilight Zone. Neil Holbert. LC 76-45823. (American Marketing Association Monograph Ser.: No. 7). 32p. reprint ed. pap. 25.00 (*0-685-10859-7*, 2022483) Bks Demand.

Research in Therapeutic Recreation: Concepts & Methods. Ed. by Marjorie Malkin & Christine Z. Howe. LC 92-63340. 354p. (C). 1993. boxed 31.95 (*0-910251-53-3*) Venture Pub PA.

Research in Tibeto-Burman Languages. Everett A. Hale. (Trends in Linguistics Ser.). 213p. 1982. text ed. 70.80 (*90-279-3379-0*) Mouton.

Research in Transportation: Legal-Legislative & Economic Sources & Procedures. Ed. by Kenneth U. Flood. LC 72-118792. (Management Information Guide Ser.: No. 20). 132p. 1971. 68.00 (*0-8103-0820-7*) Gale.

Research in Transportation Economics, Vol. 1. Ed. by B. Starr McMullen & Theodore E. Keeler. 235p. 1983. 73.25 (*0-89232-272-1*) Jai Pr.

Research in Transportation Economics, Vol. 2. Theodore E. Keeler. Ed. by B. Starr McMullen. 259p. 1985. 73.25 (*0-89232-592-5*) Jai Pr.

An Asterisk (*) at the beginning of an entry indicates that the title is appearing in BIP for the first time.

Research in Transportation Economics, Vol. 3. Ed. by B. Starr McMullen & Andrew F. Daughety. 176p. 1994. 73.25 (*0-89232-691-3*) Jai Pr.

Research in Transportation Economics, Vol. 4. Ed. by B. Starr McMullen. 170p. 1996. 73.25 (*1-55938-915-X*) Jai Pr.

Research in Urban Economics, Vol. 1. Ed. by Robert D. Ebel et al. 276p. 1981. 73.25 (*0-89232-070-2*) Jai Pr.

Research in Urban Economics, Vol. 2. Ed. by Robert D. Ebel et al. 348p. 1982. 73.25 (*0-89232-212-8*) Jai Pr.

Research in Urban Economics, Vol. 3. Ed. by Robert D. Ebel et al. 313p. 1983. 73.25 (*0-89232-307-8*) Jai Pr.

Research in Urban Economics, Vol. 7. Ed. by Robert D. Ebel et al. 297p. 1988. 73.25 (*0-89232-690-5*) Jai Pr.

Research in Urban Economics, Vol. 8. Ed. by Robert D. Ebel et al. 159p. 1990. 73.25 (*1-55938-010-1*) Jai Pr.

Research in Urban Economics, Vol. 10. Ed. by Robert D. Ebel et al. 1995. 73.25 (*1-55938-856-0*) Jai Pr.

Research in Urban Economics Vol. 4: The Changing Economic & Fiscal Structure. Ed. by Robert D. Ebel et al. 322p. 1984. 73.25 (*0-89232-423-6*) Jai Pr.

Research in Urban Economics Vol. 5: Causes & Consequences of Urban Change in the World's Developed Countries. Ed. by Robert D. Ebel et al. 235p. 1985. 73.25 (*0-89232-446-5*) Jai Pr.

Research in Urban Economics Vol. 6: Urban Econometrics: Model Developments & Empirical Results. Ed. by Robert D. Ebel et al. 388p. 1986. 73.25 (*0-89232-671-9*) Jai Pr.

Research in Urban Economics Vol. 9: Structuring Direct Aid: People Versus Places. Ed. by Robert D. Ebel et al. 279p. 1994. 73.25 (*1-55938-282-1*) Jai Pr.

Research in Urban History: A Classified Survey of Doctoral & Masters' Theses. Richard Rodger. 281p. 1994. 78.95 (*1-85928-082-X*, Pub. by Scolar Pr UK) Ashgate Pub Co.

Research in Urban Policy, Vol. 1: Coping with Urban Austerity. Ed. by Terry N. Clark. 393p. 1984. 73.25 (*0-89232-325-6*) Jai Pr.

Research in Urban Policy, 2 vols. in 1, Vol. 2. Ed. by Terry N. Clark. 1986. 146.50 (*0-89232-729-4*) Jai Pr.

Research in Urban Policy, Vol. 2: Pt. A: Fiscal Austerity & Urban Management. Ed. by Terry N. Clark. 264p. 1986. 73.25 (*0-89232-534-8*) Jai Pr.

Research in Urban Policy, Vol. 2: Pt. B: Managing Cities. Ed. by Terry N. Clark. 280p. 1986. 73.25 (*0-89232-728-6*) Jai Pr.

Research in Urban Policy, Vol. 3: Decisions on Urban Dollars. Ed. by Terry N. Clark. 274p. 1989. 73.25 (*0-89232-757-X*) Jai Pr.

Research in Urban Policy, Vol. 4: Politics of Policy Innovation in Chicago. Ed. by Terry N. Clark. 232p. 1992. 73.25 (*1-55938-057-8*) Jai Pr.

Research in Urban Policy, Vol. 5: Local Admin. in the Policy Process: An Int. Ed. by Terry N. Clark. 290p. 1994. 73.25 (*1-55938-361-5*) Jai Pr.

Research in Urban Policy, Vol. 6. Ed. by Terry N. Clark. 1996. 73.25 (*1-55938-896-X*) Jai Pr.

Research in Urban Sociology, Vol. 1: Race, Class & Urban Change. Ed. by Ray Hutchison. 216p. 1989. 73.25 (*0-89232-758-8*) Jai Pr.

Research in Urban Sociology, Vol. 2: Gentrification & Urban Change. Ed. by Ray Hutchison. 222p. 1992. 73.25 (*0-614-09949-8*) Jai Pr.

Research in Urban Sociology, Vol. 3: Urban Sociology in Transition. Ed. by Ray Hutchison. 253p. 1993. 73.25 (*1-55938-580-4*) Jai Pr.

Research in Urban Sociology, Vol. 4. Ed. by Ray Hutchison. 1997. 73.25 (*1-55938-897-8*) Jai Pr.

Research Innovation & Business Enterprise: Venture Capital in Higher Education. Ed. by Allan Klingstrom. 159p. (Orig.). 1988. pap. 46.50 (*91-506-0670-0*, Pub. by Uppsala Universitet SW) Coronet Bks.

Research Institutions & Learned Societies. Ed. by Joseph C. Kiger. LC 81-6651. (Encyclopedia of American Institutions Ser.: No. 5). xxv, 551p. 1982. text ed. 55.00 (*0-313-22061-1*, KRE/, Greenwood Pr) Greenwood.

Research Instrumentation for the 21st Century. Ed. by Gary R. Beecher. (Beltsville Symposia in Agricultural Research Ser.). (C). 1988. lib. bdg. 211.50 (*90-247-3595-5*) Kluwer Ac.

Research Interviewing: Context & Narrative. Elliot G. Mishler. 208p. 1991. pap. 15.95 (*0-674-76461-7*, MISREX) HUP.

Research into Environmental Pollution: A Report of 5 WHO Scientific Groups. (Technical Report Ser.: No. 406). 83p. 1968. pap. text ed. 6.00 (*92-4-120406-0*, 1100406) World Health.

Research into Nurse Education. Ed. by Bryn D. Davis. 208p. 1983. pap. 22.00 (*0-7099-0825-3*, Pub. by Croom Helm UK) Routledge Chapman & Hall.

Research into Personal Development. Ed. by A. Duner. 192p. 1978. pap. 32.75 (*90-265-0284-2*) Swets.

Research into Practice: A Reader for Nurses & the Caring Professions. Ed. by Roger Sapsford & Pamela Abbott. 160p. 1992. 85.00 (*0-335-09743-X*, Open Univ Pr); pap. 29.00 (*0-335-09742-1*, Open Univ Pr) Taylor & Francis.

***Research into Practice: A Reader for Nurses & the Caring Professions.** 2nd ed. Pamela Abbott & Roger Sapsford. LC 96-49631. (Social Science for Nurses & the Caring Professions Ser.). 1997. write for info. (*0-335-19696-9*, Open Univ Pr); pap. write for info. (*0-335-19695-0*, Open Univ Pr) Taylor & Francis.

Research into Primary Education. viii, 204p. 1985. pap. 32.50 (*90-265-0616-3*) Swets.

Research into Secondary Education: Report of the Colloquy of Directors of Educational Research Institutions Held in San Marino, September 1991. Ed. by R. Stradling. viii, 232p. 1993. 45.75 (*90-265-1319-4*) Swets.

Research into Secondary School Curricula: Report of the Educational Research Workshop Held in Malta, October 1992. Ed. by Paul Heywood et al. LC 94-2888. (European Meetings on Educational Research Ser.: Vol. 31). vi, 176p. 1994. 44.25 (*90-265-1390-9*) Swets.

***Research into Spinal Deformities.** Ed. by J. S. Sevastik. LC 96-79139. (Studies in Health Technology & Informatics: Vol. 36). 500p. (YA). (gr. 12 up). Date not set. 122.00 (*90-5199-308-0*, 308-0) IOS Press.

Research into Student Learning in Distance Education. Alistair Morgan. (C). 1991. pap. 24.00 (*0-7300-1352-9*, IDE806, Pub. by Deakin Univ AT) St Mut.

***Research into Vehicle Dynamics & Simulation, 1997.** 1997. 61.00 (*1-56091-940-X*) Soc Auto Engineers.

***Research Issues in Aluminum Toxicity.** Robert A. Yokel & Mari S. Golub. LC 96-51984. 1997. write for info. (*1-56032-648-4*) Hemisp Pub.

Research Issues in Child Development. Ed. by Chris Pratt et al. 208p. (C). 1986. pap. text ed. 29.95 (*0-86861-414-9*) Routledge Chapman & Hall.

Research Issues in Data Engineering - Active Database Systems (RIDE-ADS '94) LC 93-80491. 200p. 1994. pap. text ed. 50.00 (*0-8186-5360-4*, 5360) IEEE Comp Soc.

Research Issues in Data Engineering, 5th International Workshop (RIDE-DOM '95) LC 94-73916. 168p. 1995. pap. 40.00 (*0-8186-7056-8*, PR07056) IEEE Comp Soc.

Research Issues in Data Engineering, 6th International Workshop on (RIDE-NDS '96) LC 95-81852. 184p. 1996. pap. 50.00 (*0-8186-7289-7*, PRO7289) IEEE Comp Soc.

***Research Issues in Data Engineering, 7th International Workshop on (RIDE '97) High Performance Database Management for Large Scale Applications.** LC 97-70592. 200p. 1997. pap. 80.00 (*0-8186-7849-6*, PR07849) IEEE Comp Soc.

Research Issues in Human Behavior & Sexually Transmitted Diseases in the AIDS Era. Ed. by Judith N. Wasserheit et al. (Illus.). 401p. 1991. 48.00 (*1-55581-036-5*) Am Soc Microbio.

Research Issues in Learning Disabilities: Theory, Methodology, Assessment, & Ethics. Ed. by Sharon Vaughn. LC 93-24815. (Illus.). 351p. 1993. 92.95 (*0-387-94079-0*) Spr-Verlag.

Research Issues in Psychological Dimensions of Cancer see Psychosocial Aspects of Cancer

Research Issues in Public Librarianship: Trends for the Future. Ed. by Joy M. Greiner. LC 93-40175. (Contributions in Librarianship & Information Science Ser.). 248p. 1994. text ed. 59.95 (*0-313-27867-9*, Greenwood Pr) Greenwood.

Research Issues in the Assessment of Birth Settings: Report of a Study. Committee on Assessing Alternative Birth Settings (U. S.). LC 82-22481. 191p. 1983. reprint ed. pap. 54.50 (*0-608-02342-6*, 2062983) Bks Demand.

Research Issues in the Learning & Teaching of Algebra. Ed. by Sigrid Wagner & Carolyn Kieran. (Research Agenda for Mathematics Education Ser.: Vol. 4). 296p. (C). 1989. text ed. 49.95 (*0-8058-0354-8*) L Erlbaum Assocs.

Research Issues in the Learning & Teaching of Algebra. Ed. by Sigrid Wagner & Carolyn Kieran. (Research Agenda in Mathematics Education Ser.: Vol. 4). (Illus.). 289p. 1989. pap. 15.00 (*0-87353-268-6*) NCTM.

Research Issues in Undergraduate Mathematics Learning: Preliminary Analyses & Reports. Ed. by James Kaput & Ed Dubinsky. (Notes Ser.: Vol. 33). 150p. 1994. pap. 34.95 (*0-88385-090-7*, NTE-33) Math Assn.

Research Issues on Bicycling, Pedestrians, & Older Drivers (TRR 1438) Ed. by Naomi Kassabian. (Transportation Research Record Ser.). (Illus.). 104p. 1994. pap. text ed. 25.00 (*0-309-05519-9*) Transport Res Bd.

***Research Issues Related to Strategic Planning for United States Agriculture in a Global Setting: Proceedings, 36th Annual Meeting of the Agricultural Research Institute, October 7-9, 1987.** 247p. pap. 25.00 (*0-614-24236-3*) Agri Research Inst.

Research It! Write It! A Step-by-Step Guide to Research & Writing. Diana Barnett. 32p. 1989. pap. 3.95 (*0-913853-07-0*, 32510, Alleyside) Highsmith Pr.

Research Libraries: The Past Twenty-Five Years, the Next Twenty-Five Years: Papers for a Festschrift Honoring L. W. Anderson, Director of Libraries, Colorado State University. Ed. by Taylor E. Hubbard. LC 86-2327. 108p. reprint ed. pap. 30.80 (*0-8357-5506-1*, 2035121) Bks Demand.

Research Libraries - Yesterday, Today, & Tomorrow: A Selection of Papers Presented at the International Seminars, Kanazawa Institute of Technology, Library Center, Kanazawa, Japan, 1982-1992. Ed. by William J. Welsh. LC 93-10377. (Contributions in Librarianship & Information Science Ser.: No. 77). 504p. 1993. text ed. 95.00 (*0-313-28966-2*, GM8966, Greenwood Pr) Greenwood.

Research Libraries & Their Implementation of AACR2: Foundations in Library & Information Science, Vol. 22. Ed. by Judith Hopkins & John A. Edens. LC 85-23825. (Foundations in Library & Information Science: Vol. 22). 360p. 1986. 73.25 (*0-89232-641-7*) Jai Pr.

Research Library Cooperation in the Caribbean: Papers of the First & Second Conferences of the Association of Caribbean University & Research Libraries. Ed. by Alma T. Jordan. LC 73-4218. 157p. reprint ed. pap. 44.80 (*0-317-27849-5*, 2024217) Bks Demand.

Research Library of Colonial Americana, 54 bks. Ed. by Richard C. Robey. 1972. 2,012.00 (*0-405-03270-6*) Ayer.

Research Library Statistics, 1907-08, 1987-88. 1989. pap. write for info. (*0-918006-17-1*) ARL.

Research Made Easy. Ginger Carey. 88p. 1996. teacher ed. 10.00 (*1-56417-846-3*, GA1553) Good Apple.

Research Made Simple: A Handbook for the Human Services. Raymond Mark. 411p. 1996. 58.00 (*0-8039-7426-4*); pap. 27.95 (*0-8039-7427-2*) Sage.

***Research Management in Forestry.** 126p. 1992. 15.00 (*92-5-103202-5*, F32025, Pub. by FAO IT) Bernan Associates.

Research Manual for ESL. Hatch & Lazarton. 1991. pap. 31.95 (*0-8384-2672-7*) Heinle & Heinle.

Research Manual for the Health Information Management Profession. Margret K. Amatayakul & Makhdoom A. Shah. 80p. 1992. 29.50 (*0-317-05439-2*) Am Hlth Info.

Research Manual for the HIM Professional. Margret K. Amatayakul. 1992. teacher ed. 5.00 (*0-318-19164-4*, 1021) Am Hlth Info.

Research Materials for the Study of Latin-America at the University of Texas. Lota M. Spell. LC 71-144116. 107p. 1969. reprint ed. text ed. 55.00 (*0-8371-5033-7*, TLSR, Greenwood Pr) Greenwood.

Research Materials in Music. Phillip Rehfeldt. (Music History Ser.). 98p. (C). 1990. pap. text ed. 20.00 (*0-933251-11-4*) Mill Creek Pubns.

Research Materials in the Social Sciences. 2nd ed. Jack A. Clarke. LC 67-25948. 64p. reprint ed. pap. 25.00 (*0-317-27035-4*, 2023629) Bks Demand.

Research Mathematical Papers. Florentin Smarandache. Ed. by V. Boju. (Illus.). 200p. (Orig.). (C). 1991. pap. 15.99 (*1-879585-02-2*) Erhus Univ Pr.

Research Matters. Hamp-Lyons & Courter. 1984. pap. 25.95 (*0-8384-3085-6*, Newbury) Heinle & Heinle.

Research Memorandum on Crime in the Depression. Thorsten D. Sellin. LC 79-162837. (Studies in the Social Aspects of the Depression). 1980. reprint ed. 19.95 (*0-405-00853-8*) Ayer.

Research Memorandum on Education in the Depression. Educational Policies Commission. LC 72-162838. (Studies in the Social Aspects of the Depression). 1974. reprint ed. 19.95 (*0-405-00841-4*) Ayer.

Research Memorandum on Internal Migration in the Depression. Warren S. Thompson. LC 70-162840. (Studies in the Social Aspects of the Depression). 98p. 1974. reprint ed. 18.95 (*0-405-00843-0*) Ayer.

Research Memorandum on Minority Peoples in the Depression. Donald Young. LC 74-162841. (Studies in the Social Aspects of the Depression). 1974. reprint ed. 19.95 (*0-405-00844-9*) Ayer.

Research Memorandum on Recreation in the Depression. Jesse F. Steiner. LC 78-162842. (Studies in the Social Aspects of the Depression). 1974. reprint ed. 19.95 (*0-405-00845-7*) Ayer.

Research Memorandum on Religion in the Depression. Samuel C. Kincheloe. LC 71-162843. (Studies in the Social Aspects of the Depression). 1974. reprint ed. 19.95 (*0-405-00846-5*) Ayer.

Research Memorandum on Rural Life in the Depression. Dwight Sanderson. LC 75-162844. (Studies in the Social Aspects of the Depression). 1974. reprint ed. 19.95 (*0-405-00847-3*) Ayer.

Research Memorandum on Social Aspects of Consumption in the Depression. Roland S. Vaile. LC 79-162845. (Studies in the Social Aspects of the Depression). 1974. reprint ed. 19.95 (*0-405-00848-1*) Ayer.

Research Memorandum on Social Aspects of Health in the Depression. Selwyn D. Collins & Clark Tibbitts. LC 72-162846. (Studies in the Social Aspects of the Depression). 1974. reprint ed. 19.95 (*0-405-00849-X*) Ayer.

Research Memorandum on Social Aspects of Reading in the Depression. Douglas Waples. LC 76-162847. (Studies in the Social Aspects of the Depression). 1974. reprint ed. 19.95 (*0-405-00850-3*) Ayer.

Research Memorandum on Social Aspects of Relief Policies in the Depression. R. Clyde White & Mary K. White. LC 70-162848. (Studies in the Social Aspects of the Depression). 1974. reprint ed. 19.95 (*0-405-00851-1*) Ayer.

Research Memorandum on Social Work in the Depression. Francis S. Chapin & Stuart A. Queen. LC 73-162849. (Studies in the Social Aspects of the Depression). 1974. reprint ed. 19.95 (*0-405-00852-X*) Ayer.

Research Memorandum on the Family in the Depression. Samuel A. Stouffer & Paul F. Lazarsfeld. LC 76-162839. (Studies in the Social Aspects of the Depression). 1973. reprint ed. 19.95 (*0-405-00842-2*) Ayer.

Research Method & Methodology in Finance & Accounting. R. J. Ryan et al. (Illus.). 224p. 1991. pap. 50.00 (*0-12-605065-1*); pap. text ed. 44.00 (*0-12-605064-3*) Acad Pr.

Research Methodologies in Human Diabetes. Ed. by C. E. Mogensen & E. Standl. LC 93-50659. 470p. 1994. 129.25 (*3-11-014248-1*) De Gruyter.

***Research Methodology: An Introduction for Science & Engineering Students.** S. Melville & W. Goddard. 175p. 1996. pap. 23.60 (*0-7021-3562-3*, Pub. by Juta & Co SA) Intl Spec Bk.

Research Methodology & African Studies, Vol. 1. Ed. by Abdul K. Bangura. LC 93-45512. 274p. (C). 1994. pap. text ed. 32.50 (*0-8191-9394-1*) U Pr of Amer.

Research Methodology & African Studies, Vol. 1. Ed. by Abdul K. Bangura. LC 93-45512. 274p. (C). 1994. lib. bdg. 59.00 (*0-8191-9393-3*) U Pr of Amer.

Research Methodology in Anthropology. Ajit K. Danda. (C). 1992. 17.00 (*81-210-0295-8*, Pub. by Inter-India Pubns) S Asia.

Research Methodology in Applied Economics: Organizing, Planning, & Conducting Economic Research. Don Ethridge. LC 94-36457. (Illus.). 282p. 1995. text ed. 44.95 (*0-8138-2514-8*) Iowa St U Pr.

Research Methodology in Commerce & Management. K. V. Rao. 1992. 30.00 (*81-207-1422-9*, Pub. by Sterling Pubs II) Apt Bks.

Research Methodology in Management. Arvindrai N. Desai. 1990. 22.50 (*81-7024-290-8*, Pub. by Ashish II) S Asia.

Research Methodology in Second-Language Acquisition. Ed. by Elaine E. Tarone et al. 360p. 1994. pap. 36.00 (*0-8058-1424-8*); text ed. 69.95 (*0-8058-1423-X*) L Erlbaum Assocs.

Research Methodology in Social Sciences in India. L. P. Vidyarthi & A. Haldar. xiii, 246p. 1985. 25.00 (*1-55528-049-8*, Pub. by Today & Tomorrows P & P II) Scholarly Pubns.

***Research Methods.** write for info. (*0-340-64629-2*, Pub. by E Arnold UK) Routledge Chapman & Hall.

Research Methods. Roger L. Dominowski. 1980. text ed. write for info. (*0-13-774315-7*) P-H.

***Research Methods.** Matsumoto. 1997. text ed. 57.00 (*0-205-19768-X*) P-H.

Research Methods. Jack R. Nation. LC 96-41289. 544p. (C). 1996. text ed. 59.00 (*0-02-386132-0*, Macmillan Coll) P-H.

***Research Methods.** Stangor. (C). Date not set. text ed. 58.76 (*0-395-74582-9*) HM.

Research Methods. 2nd ed. Anthony M. Graziano & Michael L. Raulin. (C). 1992. 55.00 (*0-06-501090-6*) Addson-Wesley Educ.

Research Methods. 2nd ed. Anthony M. Graziano & Michael L. Raulin. (C). 1993. student ed. 22.50 (*0-06-501091-4*) Addson-Wesley Educ.

Research Methods. 2nd ed. Patrick McNeill. (Society Now Ser.). 160p. (Orig.). (C). 1990. pap. text ed. 11.95 (*0-415-04126-0*, Routledge NY) Routledge.

Research Methods. 3rd ed. Donald H. McBurney. LC 93-5651. 410p. 1994. text ed. 64.95 (*0-534-17646-1*) Brooks-Cole.

***Research Methods.** 4th ed. McBurney. (Psychology Ser.). (C). 1998. text ed. 59.95 (*0-534-35510-2*) Brooks-Cole.

Research Methods. 5th ed. Nachmias. Date not set. pap. text ed. 47.95 (*0-312-13774-5*) St Martin.

Research Methods: A Process of Inquiry. 2nd ed. Anthony M. Graziano & Michael L. Raulin. LC 92-26256. 1992. 55.50 (*0-685-71885-9*) Addson-Wesley Educ.

***Research Methods: A Process of Inquiry.** 3rd ed. Ed. by Graziano. (C). 1997. student ed., pap. text ed. 19.95 (*0-673-98042-1*) Addison-Wesley.

Research Methods: A Process of Inquiry. 3rd ed. Anthony M. Graziano & Michael L. Raulin. LC 95-48877. 1996. write for info. (*0-673-98041-3*) HarpC.

***Research Methods: Guidance for Postgraduates.** Ed. by Tony Greenfield. 1996. pap. text ed. 24.95 (*0-470-23618-3*) Wiley.

Research Methods see Handbook of Social Psychology

Research Methods & Audit in General Practice. David Armstrong & John Grace. (Oxford General Practice Ser.: No. 29). (Illus.). 240p. 1995. pap. text ed. 45.00 (*0-19-262454-7*) OUP.

Research Methods & Casual Modeling in Marketing: AMA Winter Educators' Conference 1983. AMA Winter Educators' Conference Staff. Ed. by William R. Darden et al. LC 83-3713. (American Marketing Association, Proceedings Ser.). (Illus.). 288p. reprint ed. pap. 82.10 (*0-7837-2495-0*, 2042660) Bks Demand.

Research Methods & Communication in the Social Sciences. Tesfa G. Gebremedhin & Luther G. Tweeten. LC 94-13731. 184p. 1994. text ed. 49.95 (*0-275-94930-3*, Praeger Pubs) Greenwood.

Research Methods & Data Analysis in the Social Sciences. Thomas Herzog. LC 95-40976. 400p. (C). 1996. text ed. 58.50 (*0-673-99106-7*) Addson-Wesley Educ.

Research Methods & Organization Studies. Alan Bryman. (Contemporary Social Research Ser.: No. 20). 224p. 1989. pap. 19.95 (*0-04-445213-6*) Routledge Chapman & Hall.

Research Methods & Organization Studies. Alan Bryman. (Contemporary Social Research Ser.). 224p. (C). 1989. pap. text ed. 22.95 (*0-415-08404-0*, Routledge NY) Routledge.

Research Methods & Statistics for Psychology. Wendy A. Schweigert. LC 93-24216. 348p. 1994. text ed. 67.95 (*0-534-21756-7*) Brooks-Cole.

Research Methods & Statistics for Psychology: Instructor's Manual with Test Items. Wendy A. Schweigert. Date not set. teacher ed. write for info. (*0-534-21759-1*) Brooks-Cole.

***Research Methods & Statistics in Health Care.** write for info. (*0-7131-4522-6*, Pub. by E Arnold UK) Routledge Chapman & Hall.

Research Methods & Statistics in Psychology. Hugh Coolican. 320p. 1993. pap. 16.95 (*0-340-52404-9*, B0100, Pub. by E Arnold UK) Routledge.

Research Methods & Statistics in Psychology. 2nd ed. Hugh Coolican. 512p. 1995. text ed. 16.95 (*0-340-60082-9*, Pub. by E Arnld UK) St Martin.

Research Methods & the New Media, Vol. II. Frederick Williams et al. 224p. 1988. pap. 18.95 (*0-02-935331-9*, Free Press) Free Pr.

***Research Methods DOS.** 5th ed. Nachmias. 1996. pap. text ed. 25.00 (*0-312-15304-X*) St Martin.

Research Methods for Behavioral Scientists. Fred Leavitt. 448p. (C). 1993. per. write for info. (*0-697-23737-0*) Brown & Benchmark.

Research Methods for Business: A Skill-Building Approach. 2nd ed. Uma Sekaran. LC 91-33872. 448p. (C). 1992. Net. text ed. 46.00 (*0-471-61889-6*) Wiley.

***Research Methods for Clinical Social Workers: Empirical Practice.** John S. Wodarski. LC 96-40362. (Social Work Ser.). (Illus.). 280p. 1997. 39.95 (*0-8261-9650-0*) Springer Pub.

R

Research Methods for Communication Science. James H. Watt & Sjef Van Den Berg. LC 94-32092. 1995. text ed. 58.00 (0-205-14026-2) Allyn.

Research Methods for Community Health & Welfare: An Introduction. Karl E. Bauman. 160p. 1980. pap. 17.95 (0-19-502699-3) OUP.

*Research Methods for Construction. Richard Fellows & Anita Liu. LC 97-21932. 1997. pap. write for info. (0-632-04244-3) Blackwell Sci.

Research Methods for Criminal Justice. Michael G. Maxfield. (Criminal Justice Ser.). 1995. student ed., pap. 18.95 (0-534-23157-8) Wadsworth Pub.

*Research Methods for Criminal Justice. 2nd ed. Michael G. Maxfield. (Criminal Justice Ser.). (C). 1998. pap. 18.95 (0-534-52165-7) Wadsworth Pub.

Research Methods for Criminal Justice. 4th ed. Hagan. 496p. 1996. 55.00 (0-205-19351-X) Allyn.

Research Methods for Criminal Justice & Criminology. Dean J. Champion. LC 92-24748. 500p. 1992. text ed. 86.00 (0-13-572876-2) P-H.

Research Methods for Criminal Justice & Criminology. Michael G. Maxfield & Earl Babbie. LC 94-37944. 395p. 1995. text ed. 54.95 (0-534-23154-3) Wadsworth Pub.

*Research Methods for Criminal Justice & Criminology. 2nd ed. Michael G. Maxfield & Earl Babbie. (Criminal Justice Ser.). (C). 1997. text ed. 54.95 (0-534-52164-9) Wadsworth Pub.

Research Methods for Elite Studies. Ed. by George Moyser & Margaret Wagstaff. (Contemporary Social Research Ser.: No. 14). 240p. (C). 1987. text ed. 55.00 (0-04-312035-0); pap. text ed. 19.95 (0-04-312036-9) Routledge Chapman & Hall.

*Research Methods for English Language Teachers. Jo McDonough & Steven H. McDonough. LC 96-35143. 1997. text ed. 18.95 (0-340-61472-2) St Martin.

Research Methods for General Practitioners. David Armstrong et al. (Oxford General Practice Ser.: No. 16). (Illus.). 208p. 1990. pap. 32.50 (0-19-261822-9) OUP.

Research Methods for Generalist Social Work. Christine Marlow. 352p. (C). 1993. pap. 42.95 (0-534-14838-7) Brooks-Cole.

*Research Methods for Generalist Social Work. 2nd ed. Christine Marlow. LC 97-9557. 1998. 42.95 (0-534-34953-6) Brooks-Cole.

Research Methods for Health Sciences. D. A. Brodie et al. LC 94-1258. 210p. 1994. pap. text ed. 22.00 (3-7186-5527-6) Gordon & Breach.

Research Methods for Managers. John Gill & Phil Johnson. 176p. 1991. pap. 21.00 (1-85396-119-1, Pub. by P Chapman Pub UK) Taylor & Francis.

Research Methods for Multi-Mode Data Analysis. Ed. by Henry G. Law et al. 272p. 1984. text ed. 95.00 (0-275-91210-8, C1210, Praeger Pubs) Greenwood.

Research Methods for Nurses & the Caring Professions. Roger Sapsford & Pamela Abbott. 160p. 1992. 80.00 (0-335-09621-2, Open Univ Pr); pap. 27.00 (0-335-09620-4, Open Univ Pr) Taylor & Francis.

Research Methods for Public Administrators. 2nd ed. Elizabethann O'Sullivan & Gary R. Rassel. 576p. (C). 1995. text ed. 56.50 (0-8013-1172-1) Longman.

*Research Methods for Public Administrators. 3rd ed. Elizabethann O'Sullivan. (C). 1998. text ed. write for info. (0-8013-1851-3) Addison-Wesley.

Research Methods for Social Work. 2nd ed. Allen Rubin & Earl Babbie. 752p. (C). 1993. text ed. 56.95 (0-534-17478-7) Brooks-Cole.

Research Methods for Social Work. 3rd ed. Allen Rubin & Earl Babbie. (C). 1997. student ed., text ed. 17.95 (0-534-34498-4) Brooks-Cole.

Research Methods for Social Work. 3rd ed. Allen Rubin & Earl Babbie. LC 96-17903. (Social Work Ser.). 750p. (C). 1997. text ed. 58.95 (0-534-26388-7) Brooks-Cole.

Research Methods for Social Workers. 2nd ed. Bonnie L. Yegidis & Robert W. Weinbach. LC 95-22635. (Orig.). 1995. pap. text ed. 43.00 (0-205-15766-1) Allyn.

Research Methods for the Health Sciences. David Brodie. 210p. 1994. text ed. 43.00 (3-7186-5609-4, Harwood Acad Pubs) Gordon & Breach.

Research Methods for the Social Sciences: Practice & Applications. Robert J. Mutchnick & Bruce L. Berg. LC 95-11824. 283p. 1995. pap. text ed. 28.00 (0-02-385451-0, Macmillan Coll) P-H.

*Research Methods for Therapists. A. Drummond. (Illus.). 176p. (Orig.). 1996. pap. 47.75 (1-56593-207-2, 0521) Singular Publishing.

Research Methods in Anthropology: Qualitative & Quantitative Approaches. 2nd ed. H. Russell Bernard. 586p. (C). 1995. 65.00 (0-8039-5244-9); pap. 32.00 (0-8039-5245-7) AltaMira Pr.

Research Methods in Applied Behavior Analysis: Issues & Advances. Ed. by Alan Poling & R. Wayne Fugua. (Applied Clinical Psychology Ser.). 352p. 1986. 59.50 (0-306-42127-5, Plenum Pr) Plenum.

Research Methods in Business Education. Padmakar M. Sapre. (Service Bulletin Ser.: No. 4). 152p. 1990. pap. 15.00 (0-9603064-9-8) Delta Pi Epsilon.

Research Methods in Business Studies: A Practical Guide. Pervez N. Ghauri et al. LC 94-31964. 350p. 1995. pap. text ed. 46.00 (0-13-015710-4) P-H.

*Research Methods in Clinical & Counselling Psychology. Chris Barker et al. (Clinical Psychology Ser.). 1996. pap. text ed. 32.95 (0-471-96297-X) Wiley.

Research Methods in Clinical Psychology. Alan S. Bellack. (C). 1984. 74.95 (0-205-14282-6, H4282); pap. 29.95 (0-205-14281-8, H4281) Allyn.

Research Methods in Criminal Justice: An Introduction. 2nd ed. Jack D. Fitzgerald & Steven M. Cox. LC 93-35884. (Series in Law, Crime, & Justice). 343p. 1994. pap. text ed. 26.95 (0-8304-1384-7) Nelson-Hall.

Research Methods in Criminal Justice: Exploring Alternate Pathways. Ralph B. Taylor. LC 93-37861. 1994. text ed. write for info. (0-07-063001-1) McGraw.

Research Methods in Criminal Justice & Criminology. 3rd ed. Frank E. Hagan. (Illus.). 496p. (C). 1992. teacher ed. write for info. (0-318-69335-6) Macmillan.

Research Methods in Ecology. Frederic E. Clements. Ed. by Frank N. Egerton, 3rd. LC 77-74210. (History of Ecology Ser.). (Illus.). 1978. reprint ed. lib. bdg. 33.95 (0-405-10381-6) Ayer.

Research Methods in Education. 2nd ed. Louis Cohen & Lawrence Manion. LC 85-362. 383p. (Orig.). 1985. pap. 19.95 (0-7099-3438-6, Pub. by Croom Helm UK) Routledge Chapman & Hall.

Research Methods in Education. 4th ed. Louis Cohen & Lawrence Manion. LC 93-34390. 416p. (Orig.). (C). 1994. pap. 29.95 (0-415-10235-9, Routledge NY) Routledge.

Research Methods in Education. 6th ed. Wiersma. 1994. text ed. 60.67 (0-205-15654-1) Allyn.

Research Methods in Education. 6th ed. William Wiersma. LC 94-11080. 1995. write for info. (0-205-15658-4) Allyn.

Research Methods in Education: A Practical Guide. Robert E. Slavin. (Illus.). 384p. (C). 1984. text ed. write for info. (0-13-774364-5) P-H.

*Research Methods in Education & Psychology: Integrating Diversity with Quantitative & Qualitative Approaches. Donna M. Mertens. LC 97-4890. 560p. 1997. 69.95 (0-8039-5827-7) Sage.

*Research Methods in Education & Psychology: Integrating Diversity with Quantitative & Qualitative Approaches. Donna M. Mertens. LC 97-4890. 560p. 1997. pap. 34.00 (0-8039-5828-5) Sage.

Research Methods in Experimental Psychology. Loos. (C). 1995. text ed. 60.95 (0-673-99481-3) Addson-Wesley Educ.

Research Methods in Family Therapy. Ed. by Douglas H. Sprenkle & Sidney M. Moon. LC 96-21297. 1996. lib. bdg. 50.00 (1-57230-111-2) Guilford Pr.

Research Methods in Finance. George Tsetsekos. 120p. 1996. per. 23.04 (0-8403-8961-2) Kendall-Hunt.

*Research Methods in Health: Investigating Health & Health Services. Ann Bowling. LC 97-7997. 1997. write for info. (0-335-19886-4, Open Univ Pr); pap. write for info. (0-335-19885-6, Open Univ Pr) Taylor & Francis.

Research Methods in Human Development. Paul C. Cozby et al. LC 88-13714. 270p. (C). 1989. text ed. 39.95 (0-87484-788-5, 788) Mayfield Pub.

Research Methods in Human Resource Management. Richard J. Klimoski. (GC - Principles of Management Ser.). 1991. text ed. 38.95 (0-538-80246-4) S-W Pub.

Research Methods in Human Resource Management. Neal W. Schmitt & Richard J. Klimoski. 512p. (C). 1991. text ed. 37.95 (0-538-80123-9, GJ60AA) S-W Pub.

Research Methods in Language Learning. David Nunan. (Cambridge Language Teaching Library). (Illus.). 304p. (C). 1992. pap. text ed. 19.95 (0-521-42968-4) Cambridge U Pr.

Research Methods in Language Learning. David Nunan. (Cambridge Language Teaching Library). (Illus.). 304p. (C). 1992. text ed. 49.95 (0-521-41937-9) Cambridge U Pr.

Research Methods in Law & Business Studies. W. McLaughlin. 1987. 60.00 (0-946706-39-5, Pub. by Royston Ltd) St Mut.

Research Methods in Librarianship: Techniques & Interpretation. Ed. by Charles H. Busha & Stephen P. Harter. LC 79-8864. (Library & Information Science Ser.). 432p. 1980. text ed. 52.00 (0-12-147550-6) Acad Pr.

Research Methods In Neurochemistry, Vol. 5. Ed. by Neville Marks & Richard Rodnight. LC 72-222263. 334p. 1981. 79.50 (0-306-40583-0, Plenum Pr) Plenum.

Research Methods in Neurochemistry, Vol. 6. Ed. by Neville Marks & Richard Rodnight. 392p. 1985. 95.00 (0-306-41751-0, Plenum Pr) Plenum.

Research Methods in Nutritional Anthropology. 218p. 1989. 30.00 (92-808-0632-7) UN.

Research Methods in Occupational Epidemiology. Harvey Checkoway et al. (Monographs in Epidemiology & Biostatistics: No. 13). (Illus.). 368p. 1989. 45.00 (0-19-505224-2) OUP.

Research Methods in Park, Recreation, & Leisure Services. Ananda Mitra & Sam Lankford. (Illus.). 300p. (C). 1996. text ed. 37.95 (1-57167-030-0) Sagamore Pub.

Research Methods in Personality & Social Psychology. Ed. by Clyde Hendrick. (Review of Personality & Social Psychology Ser.: Vol. 11). 352p. (C). 1990. text ed. 54.00 (0-8039-3648-6); pap. text ed. 24.95 (0-8039-3649-4) Sage.

Research Methods in Personality & Social Psychology. Ed. by Clyde Hendrick & Margaret S. Clark. (Review of Personality & Social Psychology Ser.: Vol. 11). 351p. 1990. reprint ed. pap. 100.10 (0-608-01616-0, 2059595) Bks Demand.

Research Methods in Physical Activity. 3rd ed. Jerry R. Thomas & Jack K. Nelson. LC 95-25261. (Illus.). 512p. 1996. text ed. 49.00 (0-88011-481-9, BTHO0481) Human Kinetics.

Research Methods in Political Science: An Introduction Using Micro Case. 2nd ed. Michael Corbett. (Illus.). 254p. (C). pap. text ed. 22.50 (0-922914-02-8) MicroCase.

*Research Methods in Primary Care. Yvonne Carter & Cathryn Thomas. LC 96-53628. 1997. write for info. (1-85775-198-1, Radcliffe Med Pr) Scovill Paterson.

Research Methods in Psychiatry: A Beginner's Guide. 2nd ed. Ed. by Chris Freeman & Peter Tyrer. 320p. 1992. pap. text ed. 42.50 (0-88048-614-7, 8614, Pub. by Royal Coll Psych UK) Am Psychiatric.

Research Methods in Psychology. Ed. by Glynis Breakwell et al. 320p. 1995. 75.00 (0-8039-7764-6) Sage.

Research Methods in Psychology. Ed. by Glynis Breakwell et al. 320p. 1995. pap. 21.95 (0-8039-7765-4) Sage.

Research Methods in Psychology. Gary W. Heiman. (C). 1994. teacher ed. 11.96 (0-395-64620-0) HM.

Research Methods in Psychology. Gary W. Heiman. (C). 1994. text ed. 62.76 (0-395-64619-7) HM.

Research Methods in Psychology. 2nd ed. John J. Shaughnessy & Eugene B. Zechmeister. 1990. text ed. write for info. (0-07-072859-3) McGraw.

Research Methods in Psychology. 3rd ed. John J. Shaughnessy & Eugene B. Zechmeister. LC 93-18859. 1993. text ed. write for info. (0-07-056691-7) McGraw.

Research Methods in Psychology. 4th ed. David G. Elmes et al. Ed. by Schiller. 400p. (C). 1992. text ed. 54.25 (0-314-92999-1) West Pub.

Research Methods in Psychology. 4th ed. John J. Shaughnessy & Eugene B. Zechmeister. LC 96-22572. 1996. text ed. write for info. (0-07-057272-0) McGraw.

Research Methods in Psychology. 5th ed. David G. Elmes et al. LC 94-34602. 496p. (C). 1995. text ed. 58.75 (0-314-04458-2) West Pub.

*Research Methods in Psychology: A Handbook. Schweigert. LC 97-786. (Psychology Ser.). 1998. pap. 32.95 (0-534-34855-6) Brooks-Cole.

Research Methods in Psychology: A Primer. Siu L. Chow. 320p. (Orig.). (C). 1992. pap. text ed. 25.95 (1-55059-031-6) Temeron Bks.

Research Methods in Social Network Analysis. Linton C. Freeman et al. 530p. (C). 1991. pap. text ed. 29.95 (1-56000-569-6) Transaction Pubs.

Research Methods in Social Network Analysis. Ed. by Linton C. Freeman et al. 538p. (C). 1989. lib. bdg. 77.50 (0-913969-23-0, G Mason Univ Pr) Univ Pub Assocs.

Research Methods in Social Relations. 6th ed. Charles M. Judd et al. 600p. (C). 1991. text ed. 46.00 (0-03-031149-7) HB Coll Pubs.

Research Methods in Social Sciences. B. A. Sharma et al. 280p. 1984. text ed. 27.50 (0-86590-211-9, Pub. by Sterling Pubs II) Apt Bks.

Research Methods in Social Work. David Royse. 300p. 1990. pap. text ed. 20.95 (0-8304-1210-7) Nelson-Hall.

Research Methods in Social Work. 2nd ed. David Royse. LC 94-16190. (Social Work Ser.). 1995. pap. text ed. 26.95 (0-8304-1409-6) Nelson-Hall.

Research Methods in Special Education. Donna M. Mertens & John McLaughlin. (Applied Social Research Methods Ser.: Vol. 37). 168p. 1994. 39.95 (0-8039-4808-5) Sage.

Research Methods in Special Education. Donna M. Mertens & John McLaughlin. (Applied Social Research Methods Ser.: Vol. 37). 1994. pap. 17.95 (0-8039-4809-3) Sage.

Research Methods in Stress & Health Psychology. Ed. by Stanislav V. Kasl & Cary L. Cooper. (Studies in Occupational Stress). 344p. 1995. pap. text ed. 45.00 (0-471-95493-4) Wiley.

Research Methods in the Fields: Ten Anthropological Accounts. Ed. by Malcoln Crick & Bill Geddes. 263p. (C). 1995. pap. 54.00 (0-949823-31-7, Pub. by Deakin Univ AT) St Mut.

Research Methods in the Social & Behavioral Sciences. 2nd ed. Russell A. Jones. LC 95-37162. (Illus.). 369p. (Orig.). 1995. pap. text ed. 29.95 (0-87893-372-7) Sinauer Assocs.

Research Methods in the Social Sciences. Lee Ellis. 432p. (C). 1993. text ed. write for info. (0-697-14248-5) Brown & Benchmark.

Research Methods in the Social Sciences. Lee Ellis. 96p. (C). 1993. student ed., spiral bd. write for info. (0-697-17389-5) Brown & Benchmark.

Research Methods in the Social Sciences. 4th ed. Chara F. Nachmias & David Nachmias. LC 90-63540. 592p. (C). 1991. text ed. write for info. (0-312-06275-3) St Martin.

*Research Methods in the Social Sciences. 5th ed. write for info. (0-340-66226-3, Pub. by E Arnold UK) Routledge Chapman & Hall.

Research Methods in the Social Sciences. 5th ed. Nachmias. 1995. pap. text ed. 37.50 (0-312-10159-7) St Martin.

Research Methods in the Social Sciences. 5th ed. Nachmias. 1995. student ed., pap. text ed. 11.50 (0-312-10160-0) St Martin.

Research Methods in the Social Sciences. 5th ed. Nachmias. 1995. teacher ed., pap. text ed. 5.74 (0-312-10161-9) St Martin.

*Research Misconduct: Issues, Implements, & Strategies. Date not set. text ed. 73.25 (1-56750-340-3) Ablex Pub.

*Research Misconduct: Issues, Implements, & Strategies. Date not set. pap. 39.50 (1-56750-341-1) Ablex Pub.

Research Monograph, 27 vols. United States Works Progress Administration Staff. (FDR & the Era of the New Deal Ser.). 1971. lib. bdg. 385.00 (0-306-70359-9) Da Capo.

Research Monograph, 1988, No. 17. Ed. by Michael Legg. 70p. 1988. pap. 7.50 (1-879931-00-1) Natl Assoc Interp.

Research Needs & Opportunities in Friction. LC 94-71043. (CRTD Ser.: Vol. 28). 1994. pap. 25.00 (0-7918-1202-2) ASME.

*Research Needs for Health for All by the Year 2000. (SEARO Technical Publications Ser.: No. 2). 34p. 1983. pap. text ed. 4.00 (92-9022-141-0) World Health.

Research Needs for Radiation Protection. Intro. by Charles B. Meinhold. LC 93-34922. (Report Ser.: No. 117). 1993. pap. text ed. 30.00 (0-929600-32-0) NCRP Pubns.

Research Needs in Dam Safety: Proceedings of the First Conference, 3-6 December 1991, New Delhi, India. (Illus.). 306p. (C). 1992. text ed. 85.00 (90-6191-414-0, Pub. by A A Balkema NE) Ashgate Pub Co.

Research Needs in Non-Conventional Bioprocesses. Ed. by Linda Curran et al. LC 85-11065. 148p. 1985. 32.50 (0-935470-21-2) Battelle.

Research Needs in the Pulp & Paper Related Industries: A Report of an Industry Workshop. Technical Association of the Pulp & Paper Industry Staff. 95p. reprint ed. pap. 25.70 (0-8357-2958-3, 2039220) Bks Demand.

Research Needs Related to Intermodal Freight Transportation. (Transportation Research Circular Ser.: No. 338). 58p. 1988. 6.00 (0-685-38584-1) Transport Res Bd.

Research Needs Related to the Nation's Infrastructure: Proceedings of a Workshop Sponsored by the National Science Foundation & ASCE. 48p. 1984. 14.00 (0-87262-433-1) Am Soc Civil Eng.

Research Needs Report: Energy Conversion Research. American Society of Mechanical Engineers Staff. LC 77-367323. 137p. reprint ed. pap. 39.10 (0-8357-8758-3, 2033635) Bks Demand.

Research News, 34 issues. Arlene H. Eakle. 1990. Periodical, occasional. pap. write for info. (0-940764-20-2) Genealog Inst.

Research Notekeeping & Analysis of Evidence, Student Kit. Arlene H. Eakle. 35p. 1989. pap. 12.00 (0-940764-42-3) Genealog Inst.

Research Notekeeping Kit. Arlene H. Eakle. 53p. 1988. pap. 27.00 (0-940764-41-5) Genealog Inst.

Research Odyssey: Developing & Testing a Community Theory. George Hillery, Jr. 250p. 1981. 39.95 (0-87855-400-9) Transaction Pubs.

Research of Motivation in Education, Vol. 2: The Classroom Milieu. Carole Ames & Russell E. Ames. 1985. text ed. 95.00 (0-12-056702-4) Acad Pr.

Research of School Library Media Centers. Ed. by Blanche M. Woolls. 267p. 1990. 35.00 (0-931510-30-9) Hi Willow.

Research of the World Employment Programme: Future Priorities & Selective Assessment. Hans Singer. v, 136p. (Orig.). 1992. pap. 13.50 (92-2-107758-6) Intl Labour Office.

Research on Accounting Ethics, Vol. 1. Ed. by Lawrence A. Ponemon et al. 1995. 73.25 (1-55938-753-X) Jai Pr.

Research on Accounting Ethics, Vol. 2. Ed. by Lawrence A. Ponemon et al. 1996. 73.25 (1-55938-997-4) Jai Pr.

Research on Adolescence for Youth Service: An Annotated Bibliography on Adolescent Development, Educational Needs, & Media, 1978-1980. American Library Association Staff. Ed. by Gerald G. Hodges & Frances B. Bradburn. LC 83-25785. 160p. reprint ed. pap. 45.60 (0-7837-5956-8, 2045756) Bks Demand.

Research on Adulthood & Aging: The Human Science Approach. Ed. by L. Eugene Thomas. LC 88-31873. (SUNY Series in Aging). 249p. 1989. text ed. 64.50 (0-7914-0068-9) State U NY Pr.

Research on Adulthood & Aging: The Human Science Approach. Ed. by L. Eugene Thomas. LC 88-31873. (SUNY Series in Aging). 249p. 1989. pap. text ed. 21.95 (0-7914-0069-7) State U NY Pr.

Research on Advanced Television for Broadband ISDN. Bellcore Technical Personnel. (Illus.). 239p. (C). 1990. 520.00 (1-878108-11-5) Bellcore.

Research on Alcohol & Alcoholism. (Illus.). 105p. (Orig.). (C). 1993. pap. text ed. 30.00 (0-7881-0021-1) DIANE Pub.

Research on Alcoholics Anonymous: Opportunities & Alternatives. Barbara S. McCrady & William R. Miller. LC 92-63233. 440p. (Orig.). (C). 1993. pap. 25.95 (0-911290-24-9, BBK-139) Rutgers Ctr Alcohol.

Research on Changes of Chinese Society. Albert R. O'Hara. (Asian Folklore & Social Life Monographs: No. 20). 1971. 19.00 (0-89986-022-2) Oriental Bk Store.

Research on Chemical Kinetics. Ed. by G. E. Zaikov. 227p. 1994. pap. text ed. 89.00 (1-56072-094-8) Nova Sci Pubs.

Research on Chemical Lasers. Ed. by A. N. Orayevskiy. (Proceedings of the Lebedev Physics Institute Ser.: Vol. 193). 169p. 1992. 115.00 (1-56072-053-0) Nova Sci Pubs.

Research on Children. Ed. by Shirley Buttrick. 66p. 1992. 14.95 (0-87101-223-5) Natl Assn Soc Wkrs.

Research on Classroom Ecologies: Implications for Inclusion of Children with Learning Disabilities. Deborah L. Speece. 1996. pap. 27.50 (0-8058-1897-9); text ed. 59.95 (0-8058-1896-0) L Erlbaum Assocs.

Research on Computer-Based Instruction. J. M. Pieters et al. 176p. 1990. pap. 36.00 (90-265-1109-4) Swets.

Research on Culture & Values: The Intersection of Universities, Churches & Nations. Ed. by George F. McLean. LC 88-33914. (Cultural Heritage & Contemporary Life Series I. Culture & Values: Vol. 1). 196p. (Orig.). 1989. 45.00 (0-8191-7352-5); pap. 17.50 (0-8191-7353-3) Coun Res Values.

*Research on Democracy & Society, Vol. 4. Ed. by Frederick D. Weil. 1997. 73.25 (0-7623-0195-3) Jai Pr.

Research on Democracy & Society: Democratization in Eastern & Western Europe, Vol. 1. Ed. by Frederick D. Weil et al. 378p. 1993. 73.25 (1-55938-563-4) Jai Pr.

Research on Democracy & Society: Extremism, Protest, Social Movements & Democracy, Vol. 3. Ed. by Frederick D. Weil et al. 1995. 73.25 (1-55938-898-6) Jai Pr.

Research on Democracy & Society: Political Culture & Political Structure, Vol. 2. Ed. by Frederick D. Weil et al. 408p. 1994. 73.25 (1-55938-778-5) Jai Pr.

An Asterisk (*) at the beginning of an entry indicates that the title is appearing in BIP for the first time.

Research on Dietary Fibres. Gy Mozsik et al. 222p. (C). 1986. 75.00 (*963-05-4254-4*, Pub. by Akad Kiado HU) St Mut.

Research on Dolphins. Ed. by M. M. Bryden & Richard J. Harrison. (Illus.). 400p. 1986. 110.00 (*0-19-857606-4*) OUP.

Research on Economic Inequality, Vol. 1. Ed. by Daniel J. Slottje & Edward N. Wolff. 275p. 1989. 73.25 (*0-89232-938-6*) Jai Pr.

Research on Economic Inequality, Vol. 2. Ed. by Daniel J. Slottje & Edward N. Wolff. 237p. 1992. 73.25 (*1-55938-130-2*) Jai Pr.

Research on Economic Inequality, Vol. 3. Ed. by Daniel J. Slottje & Edward N. Wolff. 309p. 1992. 73.25 (*1-55938-590-1*) Jai Pr.

Research on Economic Inequality, Vol. 4. Ed. by Daniel J. Slottje & Edward N. Wolff. 260p. 1994. 73.25 (*1-55938-591-X*) Jai Pr.

Research on Economic Inequality Vol. 5: Inequality in the Labor Market: The Economics of Labor Market Segregation & Discrimination. Ed. by Daniel J. Slottje & Edward N. Wolff. 1994. 73.25 (*1-55938-643-6*) Jai Pr.

***Research on Educational Innovations.** 2nd ed. Arthur K. Ellis & Jeffrey T. Fouts. LC 97-10151. 259p. 1997. 39.95 (*1-883001-41-2*) Eye On Educ.

Research on Environments & People: Methods, Quality Assessment, New Directions. Swedish Council for Building Research Staff. Ed. by Roger S. Ulrich & Staffan Hygge. (Illus.). 148p. 1987. pap. 41.00 (*91-540-4757-9*) Coronet Bks.

Research on Ethics in Nursing Education. M. Silva & J. Sorrell. 192p. 1991. 22.95 (*0-88737-525-1*, 15-2409) Natl League Nurse.

Research on Foreign Students & International Study: An Overview & Bibliography. Philip G. Altbach et al. LC 85-3372. 416p. 1985. text ed. 59.95 (*0-275-90052-5*, C0052, Praeger Pubs) Greenwood.

***Research on Genetics in Psychiatry: Report of a WHO Scientific Group, 1966.** (Technical Report Ser.). 0020p. 1966. pap. text ed. 3.00 (*92-4-120346-3*, 1100346) World Health.

Research on Group Treatment Methods: A Selectively Annotated Bibliography. Bernard Lubin & C. Wilson. LC 96-23114. (Bibliographies & Indexes in Psychology Ser.: No. 9). 264p. 1996. text ed. 69.50 (*0-313-28339-7*, Greenwood Pr) Greenwood.

Research on Gynecological Endocrinology. Ed. by A. R. Genazzani et al. (Illus.). 687p. 1986. 68.00 (*1-85070-106-7*) Prthnon Pub.

Research on Health: A Medical Subject Analysis with Bibliography. Mary R. Bartone. LC 84-45738. 150p. 1987. 44.50 (*0-88164-254-1*); pap. 39.50 (*0-88164-255-X*) ABBE Pubs Assn.

***Research on Human Population Genetics: Report of a WHO Scientific Group, 1968.** (Technical Report Ser.: No. 387). 0032p. 1968. pap. text ed. 3.00 (*92-4-120387-0*, 1100387) World Health.

Research on Human Subjects: Problems of Social Control in Medical Experimentation. Bernard Barber et al. LC 70-83831. 264p. 1973. 40.00 (*0-87154-090-8*) Russell Sage.

Research on Human Subjects: Problems of Social Control in Medical Experimentation. Bernard Barber et al. LC 78-55938. 263p. 1979. reprint ed. pap. text ed. 24.95 (*0-87855-649-4*) Transaction Pubs.

Research on Instruction: Design & Effects. S. Dijkstra et al. LC 89-25682. 196p. 1990. 39.95 (*0-87778-221-0*) Educ Tech Pubns.

Research on Integrated Systems: Proceedings of the 93 Symposium. Gaetano Borriello & Carl Ebeling. (Illus.). 400p. 1993. 65.00 (*0-262-02357-1*) MIT Pr.

Research on International & Comparative Entrepreneurship, Vol. 1. Ed. by Dennis M. Ray. 1995. 73.25 (*1-55938-948-6*) Jai Pr.

Research on International & Comparative Entrepreneurship, Vol. 2. Ed. by Dennis M. Ray. 1996. 73.25 (*0-7623-0021-3*) Jai Pr.

Research on Intervention in Special Education. Ed. by Han Nakken et al. LC 92-7742. 452p. 1992. lib. bdg. 109.95 (*0-7734-9514-2*) E Mellen.

Research on Irrigation & Drainage Technologies: Fifteen Years of World Bank Experience. Raed Safadi & Herve Plusquellec. (Discussion Paper Ser.: No. 128). 68p. 1991. 7.95 (*0-8213-1891-8*, 11891) World Bank.

***Research on Judgment & Decision Making: Currents, Connections, & Controversies.** Ed. by William M. Goldstein & Robin M. Hogarth. (Cambridge Series on Judgment & Decision Making). (Illus.). 600p. (C). 1997. text ed. 80.00 (*0-521-48302-6*) Cambridge U Pr.

***Research on Judgment & Decision Making: Currents, Connections, & Controversies.** Ed. by William M. Goldstein & Robin M. Hogarth. (Cambridge Series on Judgment & Decision Making). (Illus.). 600p. (C). 1997. pap. text ed. 34.95 (*0-521-48334-4*) Cambridge U Pr.

Research on Laser Theory. Ed. by A. N. Orayevskiy. (Proceedings of the Lebedev Physics Institute Ser.: Vol. 171). 288p. (C). 1988. text ed. 125.00 (*0-941743-06-3*) Nova Sci Pubs.

Research on Mature-Age Students Returning to Study Mathematics at Tertiary Level. Ed. by Robyn Pierce. 67p. 1993. pap. 55.00 (*0-7300-2057-6*, Pub. by Deakin Univ AT) St Mut.

Research on Measurement Procedures with Individuals with Hearing Impairments. John Reiman & Michael Bollis. pap. text ed. write for info. (*0-944232-04-3*) Teaching Res.

Research on Men Who Batter: An Overview, Bibliography & Resource Guide. Edward W. Gondolf. Ed. by Lee M. Joiner. LC 87-34229. 104p. (Orig.). (C). 1988. pap. 11.95 (*0-943519-05-5*, B1905) Sulzburger & Graham Pub.

Research on Mental Illness & Addictive Disorders: Progress & Prospects: a Report. Institute of Medicine (U. S.), Board on Mental Health & Behavioral Medicine Staff. (Publication IOM Ser.: No. 84-07). 71p. reprint ed. pap. 25.00 (*0-8357-7694-8*, 2036045) Bks Demand.

Research on Modified Fertilizer Materials for Use in Developing-Country Agriculture. D. H. Parish et al. (Paper Ser.: No. P-2). 1980. pap. text ed. 4.00 (*0-88090-062-8*) Intl Fertilizer.

Research on Motivation in Education: Student Motivation, Vol. 1. Russell E. Ames & Carole Ames. LC 83-12315. 1984. text ed. 95.00 (*0-12-056701-6*) Acad Pr.

Research on Motivation in Education, Vol. 3: Goals & Cognitions. Ed. by Carole Ames & Russell E. Ames. 346p. 1989. text ed. 95.00 (*0-12-056703-2*) Acad Pr.

Research on Multipurpose Tree Species in Asia. Ed. by David Taylor & Kenneth G. MacDicken. 260p. 1991. pap. 27.50 (*0-933595-44-1*) Winrock Intl.

Research on Negotiation in Organizations, Vol. 1. Ed. by Roy J. Lewicki et al. 344p. 1986. 73.25 (*0-89232-638-7*) Jai Pr.

Research on Negotiation in Organizations, Vol. 2. Ed. by Roy J. Lewicki et al. 269p. 1990. 73.25 (*0-89232-639-5*) Jai Pr.

Research on Negotiation in Organizations, Vol. 3: Handbook of Negotiation Research. Ed. by Roy J. Lewicki et al. 332p. 1991. 73.25 (*1-55938-249-X*) Jai Pr.

Research on Negotiation in Organizations, Vol. 4. Ed. by Roy J. Lewicki et al. 240p. 1994. 73.25 (*1-55938-555-3*) Jai Pr.

Research on Negotiation in Organizations, Vol. 5. Ed. by Roy J. Lewicki et al. 276p. 1995. 73.25 (*1-55938-928-1*) Jai Pr.

Research on Negotiation in Organizations, Vol. 6. Ed. by Roy J. Lewicki et al. 1996. 73.25 (*0-7623-0022-1*) Jai Pr.

Research on Noise & Environmental Issues. (Transportation Research Record Ser.: No. 1176). 92p. 1988. 13.00 (*0-309-04715-3*) Transport Res Bd.

Research on Particle Detectors. Georges Charpak. (Twentieth Century Physics Ser.). 450p. 1995. text ed. 99.00 (*981-02-1902-4*); pap. text ed. 61.00 (*981-02-1903-2*) World Scientific Pub.

***Research on Professional Consultation & Consultation for Organizational Change: A Selectively Annotated Bibliography.** C. Dwayne Wilson & Bernard Lubin. LC 96-42164. (Bibliographies & Indexes in Psychology Ser.: Vol. 10). 160p. 1997. text ed. 59.95 (*0-313-28034-7*, Greenwood Pr) Greenwood.

Research on Reincarnation. Manly P. Hall. pap. 4.95 (*0-89314-349-9*) Philos Res.

Research on Religion & Aging: An Annotated Bibliography. Ed. by Harold G. Koenig. LC 94-44350. (Bibliographies & Indexes in Gerontology Ser.: No.27). 192p. 1995. text ed. 55.00 (*0-313-29427-5*, Greenwood Pr) Greenwood.

***Research on Russia & Eastern Europe, Vol. 3.** Ed. by Metta Spencer. 1997. 73.25 (*0-7623-0280-1*) Jai Pr.

Research on School Restructuring. Arthur K. Ellis & Jeffrey T. Fouts. LC 94-17750. 1994. 38.95 (*1-883001-09-9*) Eye On Educ.

Research on School-to-Work Transition Programs in the United States. David Stern et al. (Stanford Series on Education & Public Policy). 1995. write for info. (*0-7507-0428-4*, Falmer Pr); pap. write for info. (*0-7507-0429-2*, Falmer Pr) Taylor & Francis.

Research on Sentencing: The Search for Reform, 2 vols., Vol. I. National Research Council Panel on Sentencing Research & Alfred Blumstein. LC 83-4048. 315p. (C). 1983. pap. 29.95 (*0-309-03347-0*) Natl Acad Pr.

***Research on Social Work & Disasters.** Susan A. Murty. Ed. by Calvin L. Streeter. LC 96-40923. (Journal of Social Service Research: Vol. 22, Nos. 1/2). 160p. (C). 1996. 39.95 (*0-7890-0028-8*); pap. 14.95 (*0-7890-0303-1*) Haworth Pr.

Research on Socialization of Young Children in the Nordic Countries: An Annotated & Selected Bibliography. Ed. by Berit Elgaard et al. 194p. (C). 1989. pap. 16.95 (*87-7288-175-5*, Pub. by Aarhus Univ Pr DK) David Brown.

***Research on Strength of Gear Teeth.** ASME Staff. (Technical Papers). 1924. pap. text ed. 30.00 (*1-55589-265-5*) AGMA.

Research on Suicide: A Bibliography. Ed. by John L. McIntosh. LC 84-15706. (Bibliographies & Indexes in Psychology Ser.: No. 2). xiii, 323p. 1985. text ed. 75.00 (*0-313-23992-4*, MLR/, Greenwood Pr) Greenwood.

Research on Support for Parents & Infants in the Postnatal Period. C. F. Boukydis. LC 87-1349. 288p. 1987. text ed. 73.25 (*0-89391-333-2*) Ablex Pub.

Research on Teacher Thinking: Understanding Professional Development. Ed. by Christopher W. Day et al. 256p. 1993. 88.00 (*0-7507-0177-3*, Falmer Pr); pap. 33.00 (*0-7507-0178-1*, Falmer Pr) Taylor & Francis.

Research on Teachers' Thinking & Practice. Ed. by Ingrid Carlgren et al. LC 94-38648. 224p. 1995. pap. 26.00 (*0-7507-0431-4*, Falmer Pr); text ed. 75.00 (*0-7507-0430-6*, Falmer Pr) Taylor & Francis.

Research on Teaching: Concepts, Findings & Implications. Ed. by Penelope L. Peterson & Herbert J. Walberg. LC 78-62102. (Education Ser.). 1979. 33.00 (*0-8211-1518-9*) McCutchan.

Research on Technological Innovation, Management & Policy, Vol. 1. Ed. by Richard S. Rosenbloom & Robert A. Burgelman. 149p. 1983. 73.25 (*0-89232-273-X*) Jai Pr.

Research on Technological Innovation, Management & Policy, Vol. 2. Ed. by Richard S. Rosenbloom & Robert A. Burgelman. 224p. 1985. 73.25 (*0-89232-426-0*) Jai Pr.

Research on Technological Innovation, Management & Policy, Vol. 3. Ed. by Richard S. Rosenbloom & Robert A. Burgelman. 262p. 1987. 73.25 (*0-89232-688-3*) Jai Pr.

Research on Technological Innovation Management & Policy, Vol. 5. Ed. by Richard S. Rosenbloom & Robert A. Burgelman. 197p. 1994. 73.25 (*1-55938-083-7*) Jai Pr.

Research on Technological Innovation Management & Policy, Vol. 6. Ed. by Richard S. Rosenbloom & Robert A. Burgelman. 1996. 73.25 (*1-55938-984-2*) Jai Pr.

Research on Technological Innovation, Management & Policy: Tech, Competition, & Organization Theory, Vol. 4. Ed. by Richard S. Rosenbloom & Robert A. Burgelman. 296p. 1989. 73.25 (*0-89232-798-7*) Jai Pr.

Research on Thailand in the Philippines: An Annotated Bibliography of Theses, Dissertations, & Investigation Papers. Sida Chety. LC 77-152541. (Cornell University, Southeast Asia Program, Data Paper Ser.: No. 107). 100p. reprint ed. pap. 28.50 (*0-317-29630-2*, 2021849) Bks Demand.

Research on the African-American Family: A Holistic Perspective. Ed. by Wornie L. Reed & Robert B. Hill. LC 92-26624. 200p. 1993. text ed. 55.00 (*0-86569-019-7*, T019, Auburn Hse); pap. text ed. 17.95 (*0-86569-021-9*, R021, Auburn Hse) Greenwood.

Research on the African-American Family, Vol. II: A Holistic Perspective. Ed. by Robert B. Hill. (Assessment of the Status of African-Americans Ser.). 165p. (Orig.). (C). 1989. pap. 8.95 (*1-878358-02-2*) U MA W M Trotter Inst.

Research on the American West: Archaeology at Forts Cummings & Fillmore. Edward Staski. Ed. by June-el Piper & Stephen Fosberg. (Bureau of Land Management, New Mexico State Office Cultural Resources Ser.: Vol. 12). (Illus.). 350p. 1995. pap. 8.00 (*1-878178-13-X*) Bureau of Land Mgmt NM.

Research on the Bureaucracy of Pakistan: A Critique of Sources, Conditions, Issues, with Appended Documents. Ralph J. Braibanti. LC 66-14888. (Duke University, Commonwealth-Studies Center, Publication Ser.: No. 26). 610p. reprint ed. pap. 173.90 (*0-317-20091-7*, 2023371) Bks Demand.

***Research on the Education of Our Nation's Teachers: Teacher Education Yearbook V.** David M. Byrd & D. John McIntyre. (ATE Ser.). (Illus.). 288p. 1997. 69.95 (*0-8039-6512-5*); pap. 29.95 (*0-8039-6513-3*) Corwin Pr.

Research on the Ethiopian Flora: Proceedings of the First Ethiopian Flora Symposium Held in Uppsala, May 22-26, 1984. Ed. by Inga Hedberg. (Symbolae Botanicae Upsalienses Ser.). (Illus.). 212p. (Orig.). 1986. pap. text ed. 40.00 (*91-554-1956-9*, Pub. by Uppsala Univ Acta Univ Uppsaliensis SW) Coronet Bks.

Research on the Etiology of Schizophrenia. G. Malis. LC 61-11828. (International Behavioral Sciences Ser.). (Illus.). 207p. reprint ed. pap. 59.00 (*0-317-10350-4*, 2020657) Bks Demand.

Research on the Legal Profession: A Review of Work Done. 2nd ed. Olavi Maru. LC 86-70978. vii, 106p. 1986. pap. 25.00 (*0-910059-11-X*, 306040) W S Hein.

Research on the Manufacture & Use of Concrete. Ed. by Geoffrey Frohnsdorff. LC 86-82645. 244p. 1985. pap. text ed. 50.00 (*0-939204-32-0*) Eng Found.

***Research on the Menopause.** (Technical Report Ser.: No. 670). 120p. 1981. pap. text ed. 8.00 (*92-4-120670-5*) World Health.

***Research on the Menopause in the 1990s: Report of a WHO Scientific Group.** (WHO Technical Report Ser.: Vol. 866). 106p. 1996. pap. 20.00 (*92-4-120866-X*, 1100866) World Health.

Research on the Properties of Line Pipe: Summary Report. American Gas Association Pipeline Research Committee et al. 135p. 1962. pap. 3.00 (*0-318-12691-5*, L00290) Am Gas Assn.

Research on the Quality of Life. Ed. by Frank M. Andrews. 384p. text ed. 44.50 (*0-472-00700-9*) U of Mich Pr.

Research on the Quality of Life. Ed. by Frank M. Andrews. LC 86-15179. 384p. 1986. 42.00 (*0-87944-308-1*) Inst Soc Res.

Research on the Soviet Union & Eastern Europe, Vol. 1. Ed. by Anthony Jones. 249p. 1991. 73.25 (*1-55938-102-7*) Jai Pr.

Research on the Soviet Union & Eastern Europe, Vol. 2. Ed. by Anthony Jones. 1995. 73.25 (*1-55938-432-8*) Jai Pr.

Research on the Treatment of Narcotic Addiction. 1990. 250.00 (*0-87700-888-4*) Revisionist Pr.

Research on the Vegetation of NZ. 1986. 19.00 (*0-614-07540-8*, Pub. by Manaaki Whenua NZ) Balogh.

Research on the Viral Hypothesis of Mental Disorders. Ed. by P. V. Morozov. (Advances in Biological Psychiatry Ser.: Vol. 12). (Illus.). x, 178p. 1983. pap. 73.00 (*3-8055-3706-9*) S Karger.

Research on Transport Economics, Vol. XXVII. 450p. 1995. pap. 110.00 (*92-821-0207-6*, 74-95-01-3, Pub. by Org for Econ FR) OECD.

Research on Transport Economics Vol. XXVI. OECD Staff. 440p. (Orig.). (ENG & FRE.). 1994. pap. 100.00 (*92-821-0194-0*) OECD.

Research on Transport Economics Vol. XXVI, Vol. XXIV. OECD Staff. 407p. (Orig.). 1993. pap. text ed. 110.00 (*92-821-0175-4*, 74-92-02-3) OECD.

Research on Transport Economics Vol. XXVI, Vol. XXV. OECD Staff. 360p. (Orig.). 1993. pap. text ed. 90.00 (*92-821-0185-1*, 74-93-01-3) OECD.

Research on Transportation Facilities in Cold Regions. Ed. by Orlando B. Andersland & Francis H Sayles. LC 86-25920. 112p. 1986. pap. 16.00 (*0-87262-568-0*) Am Soc Civil Eng.

Research on U. S. Students Abroad. Ed. by Henry D. Weaver. 113p. (Orig.). 1989. pap. text ed. 12.00 (*1-882036-01-8*) NAFSA Washington.

***Research on Venous Outflow Reduction in Erectile Dysfunction.** Hubert Claes. (Acta Biomedica Lovaniensia Ser.: Vol. 108). 152p. (Orig.). 1995. pap. 39.50 (*90-6186-678-2*, Pub. by Leuven Univ BE) Coronet Bks.

Research on Whole Language: Support for a New Curriculum. Diane Stephens. LC 91-67299. 73p. (Orig.). (C). 1992. pap. text ed. 9.95 (*1-878450-13-1*) R Owen Pubs.

Research on Wole Soyinka. Ed. by Lindofrs & James Gibbs. 45.00 (*0-86543-218-X*); pap. 14.95 (*0-86543-219-8*) Africa World.

Research Opportunities for Materials with Ultrafine Microstuctures. National Research Council Staff. 130p. 1990. pap. text ed. 19.00 (*0-309-04183-X*) Natl Acad Pr.

Research Opportunities in American Cultural History. Ed. by John F. McDermott. LC 77-22111. 205p. 1977. reprint ed. text ed. 55.00 (*0-8371-9754-6*, MCRO, Greenwood Pr) Greenwood.

Research Opportunities in Auditing: The Second Decade. Ed. by Rashad Abdel-Khalik & Ira Solomon. 216p. 1989. 15.00 (*0-86539-070-3*) Am Accounting.

Research Opportunities in Renaissance Drama: The Reports of the Modern Language Association Conferences, 20 nos. in 8 vols., Set. Modern Language Association of America Staff. Incl. Vol. 1, No. 1. Chicago Conference, 1955. (*0-318-50700-5*); Vol. 1, No. 2. Washington Conference, 1956. (*0-318-50701-3*); Vol. 1, No. 3. Madison Conference, 1957. (*0-318-50702-1*); Vol. 2, No. 4. New York Conference, 1958. (*0-318-50703-X*); Vol. 2, No. 5. Chicago, 1959 & Philadelphia, 1960, Conferences. (*0-318-50704-8*); Vol. 2, No. 6. Chicago, 1961 & Washington, 1962, Conferences. (*0-318-50705-6*); reprint ed. 335.00 (*0-404-08063-4*) AMS Pr.

Research Organizer Handbook. 3rd ed. Prentice Hall Editorial Staff. 1993. pap. text ed. 5.33 (*0-13-813957-1*) P-H.

Research Paper: A Common-Sense Approach. Thomas E. Gaston & Bret H. Smith. (Illus.). 304p. 1987. pap. text ed. 28.60 (*0-13-774100-6*) P-H.

Research Paper: Process, Form, & Content. 6th ed. Audrey J. Roth. 300p. (C). 1989. pap. 15.95 (*0-534-09924-6*) Wadsworth Pub.

Research Paper: Process, Form, & Content. 7th ed. Audrey J. Roth. 300p. (C). 1995. pap. 21.95 (*0-534-17454-X*) Wadsworth Pub.

Research Paper Handbook. James D. Lester, Sr. & James D. Lester, Jr. (Illus.). 232p. (Orig.). 1991. pap. 7.95 (*0-673-36016-4*, GoodYrBooks) Addson-Wesley Educ.

Research Paper Made Easy. David Mendez. 29p. (Orig.). (C). 1990. pap. 3.00 (*1-56428-012-8*) Logos Intl Pub.

Research Paper Manual. 2nd ed. Martin H. Skoble. 54p. 1977. pap. 3.95 (*0-89529-008-1*) Avery Pub.

Research Paper Simplified. Taggart. (C). 1993. text ed. 9.50 (*0-06-501152-X*) Addson-Wesley Educ.

***Research Paper Smart.** Liz Buffa. 1997. pap. 10.00 (*0-679-78382-2*) Random.

Research Paper, Step-by-Step. 4th rev. ed. Edgar C. Alward. Orig. Title: Easing the Agony of the Research Paper. (Illus.). 182p. (YA). (gr. 7 up). 1996. wbk. ed., pap. text ed. 28.00 (*1-880836-11-4*) Pine Isl Pr.

***Research Paper, Step-By-Step: Simplified Method of Learning the Research Process. rev. ed. Edgar C. Alward. Orig. Title: Research Paper, Step-by-Step. 198p. 1996. pap. text ed. 35.00 (*1-880836-16-5*) Pine Isl Pr.**
Formerly titled RESEARCH PAPER, STEP-BY-STEP, this self-teaching, do-it-yourself textbook/workbook is designed to help students conceptualize & understand the complexity & nuances of the undergraduate research paper process. This instruction, offered in step-by-step order, will result in an effective research paper - one that is readable & concise because the student has made skilled use of the cross references in combination with the text detail & the worksheets. All instructions are in keeping within the 1995 style recommendations from the MLA. By following the format painstakingly, the student writer is enabled to pave a smooth way for a reader to comprehend the information being communicated. This innovative program has been thoroughly classroom tested. Indeed, one of its most valuable features is that it saves precious classroom time needed for concentration on writing style & content. It is designed to procure a plagiarism-proof paper from any student at any level. Also included is up-to-date information on documentating Internet related sources & brainstorming techniques for computer users. A must for college freshmen. To order, write: Pine Island Press, 69 Pine Island Lake, Westhampton, MA 01027. Or call 1-800-209-3691. ***Publisher Provided Annotation.***

Research Paper, Step-by-Step see **Research Paper, Step-By-Step: Simplified Method of Learning the Research Process**

Research Paper Workbook. 3rd ed. Ellen Strenski & Madge Manfred. 340p. (C). 1992. teacher ed. write for info. (*0-8013-0853-4*, 78939); pap. text ed. 31.95 (*0-8013-0815-1*, 78883) Longman.

An Asterisk (*) at the beginning of an entry indicates that the title is appearing in BIP for the first time.

R

Research Paper Workbook. 4th ed. Ellen Strenski. (C). 1998. pap. text ed. write for info. (0-8013-1632-4) Addison-Wesley.

Research Papers, 5 vols. in 6 bks. Private Philanthropy & Public Need Commission. 1986. reprint ed. lib. bdg. 312.00 (0-89941-446-X, 303990) W S Hein.

Research Papers: A Complete Guide for High School Students. Patricia Terry & Carolyn Bogart. 62p. 1991. 9.95 (0-9627259-0-0) Discovery Dix.

Research Papers: A Guided Writing Experience for Senior High Students. 2nd rev. ed. Richard Corbin & Jonathan Corbin. 1978. pap. text ed. 2.00 (0-930348-00-1) NY St Eng Coun.

Research Papers: A New Guide. Samuel Draper. 140p. 1994. per. 16.74 (0-8403-6675-2) Kendall-Hunt.

Research Papers in Violin Acoustics: 1973-1995. Carleen M. Hutchins & Virginia Benade. LC 96-16826. 1996. write for info. (1-56396-608-5) Acoustical Soc Am.

Research Papers in Violin Acoustics, 1973-1995. Carleen M. Hutchins & Virginia Benade. LC 96-16826. 1996. write for info. (1-56396-609-3); write for info. (1-56396-604-2) Acoustical Soc Am.

Research Papers, Plain & Simple. Laipson & Connell. 1992. pap. text ed. write for info. (0-07-035852-4) McGraw.

Research Paradigms in Psychosomatic Medicine. Ed. by T. N. Wise & G. Fava. (Advances in Psychosomatic Medicine Ser.: Vol. 17). (Illus.). viii, 272p. 1987. 140.00 (3-8055-4484-7) S Karger.

Research Parks & Other Ventures: The University-Real Estate Connection. Ed. by Rachelle Levitt. LC 85-52744. 113p. (C). 1985. pap. 42.95 (0-87420-633-2, R18) Urban Land.

***Research Perspectives in Accounting.** Ahmed Riahi-Belkaoui. LC 97-1697. 176p. 1997. text ed. 59.95 (1-56720-100-8, Quorum Bks) Greenwood.

Research Perspectives in Adult Education. Ed. by D. Randy Garrison. LC 93-32730. 230p. (C). 1994. lib. bdg. 27.50 (0-89464-716-4) Krieger.

Research Perspectives on the Transition from School to Work. Ed. by Guy Neave. 144p. 1978. pap. 23.50 (90-265-0278-8) Swets.

Research Philosophy & Techniques: Selected Readings. 2nd ed. Ed. by Christine L. Lewis. LC 92-71748. 172p. 1992. pap. text ed. 18.00 (0-89462-070-3, ARP101) IIA.

Research Planes. David Baker. (Military Aircraft Library). (Illus.). 48p. (J). (gr. 3-8). 1987. 13.95 (0-685-67595-5); lib. bdg. 18.60 (0-86592-354-X) Rourke Corp.

***Research Policies for Health for All.** (European Health For All Ser.: No. 2). 1988. pap. text ed. 8.00 (92-890-1053-3) World Health.

Research Potential of Anthropological Museum Collections. Ed. by Anne M. Cantwell et al. (Annals Ser.: Vol. 376). 585p. 1981. pap. 115.00 (0-89766-142-7); lib. bdg. 115.00 (0-89766-141-9) NY Acad Sci.

***Research Primer for Occupational & Physical Therapy.** Charlotte B. Royeen. 360p. (Orig.). (C). 1997. pap. text ed. 55.00 (1-56900-063-8); lib. bdg. 75.00 (1-56900-062-X) Am Occup Therapy.

Research Primer for Pastoral Care & Counseling. Larry VandeCreek. 96p. (Orig.). 1988. pap. text ed. 6.95 (0-929670-00-0) JPCP.

Research Priorities for Conservation Biology. Michael E. Soule & Kathryn A. Kohm. LC 89-15385. (Island Press Critical Issues Ser.). (Illus.). 97p. (Orig.). 1989. pap. 9.95 (0-933280-99-8) Island Pr.

Research Priorities on Alcohol: Proceedings of a Symposium. Ed. by Mark Keller. (Journal of Studies on Alcohol: Suppl. No. 8). 1979. 10.00 (0-911290-03-6) Rutgers Ctr Alcohol.

Research Problem Statements: Design & Construction of Transportation Facilities. (Transportation Research Circular Ser.: No. 363). 143p. 1990. 15.00 (0-685-38585-X) Transport Res Bd.

Research Problem Statements: Hydrology, Hydraulics & Water Quality. (Transportation Research Circular Ser.: No. 327). 54p. 1988. 6.00 (0-685-38586-8) Transport Res Bd.

***Research Process.** 3rd ed. Gary D. Bouma. (Illus.). 252p. 1997. 35.00 (0-19-553938-9) OUP.

Research Process: Books & Beyond. Myrtle Bolner & Gayle Poirier. 346p. (C). 1996. per., pap. text ed. 28.29 (0-7872-1915-0) Kendall-Hunt.

Research Process in Educational Settings: Ten Case Studies. Ed. by Robert G. Burgess. 275p. 1984. pap. 33.00 (0-905273-91-5, Falmer Pr) Taylor & Francis.

Research Process in Nursing. 2nd ed. D. F. Cormack. (Illus.). 334p. 1991. pap. 32.95 (0-632-02891-2) Blackwell Sci.

Research Process in Nursing. 2nd ed. Patricia A. Dempsey & Arthur D. Dempsey. (Nursing-Health Science Ser.). 320p. (C). 1986. pap. 32.50 (0-86720-350-1) Jones & Bartlett.

Research Process in Nursing. 3rd ed. Desmond F. Cormack. 432p. 1996. 29.95 (0-632-04019-X) Blackwell Sci.

Research Process in Nursing. 3rd ed. Dempsey. (Nursing-Health Science Ser.). 336p. (C). 1992. 40.00 (0-86720-449-4) Jones & Bartlett.

***Research Program of the New Partnership for a New Generation of Vehichles: Third Report.** 156p. 1997. pap. 32.00 (0-309-05776-0) Natl Acad Pr.

Research Project: How to Write It. 3rd rev. ed. Ralph Berry. LC 94-9071. 128p. (C). 1994. pap. 14.95 (0-415-11090-4, B4782, Routledge NY) Routledge.

Research Project Book. 2nd ed. Nancy Polette. (Illus.). 128p. (J). (gr. 4-9). 1992. pap. 12.95 (1-879287-06-4) Pieces of Lrning.

***Research Projects: Research Projects Within Medical Groups & Research Centers.** Ed. by Suzanne S. White & Donna L. Burman. 137p. (Orig.). 1996. pap. text ed. 20.00 (1-56829-013-6) Med Group Mgmt.

Research Projects for College Students: What to Write Across the Curriculum. Marilyn Lutzker. LC 87-37549. 152p. 1988. text ed. 42.95 (0-313-25149-5, LRW/, Greenwood Pr) Greenwood.

Research Proposals: A Guide to Success. 2nd ed. Thomas E. Ogden & Israel A. Goldberg. 464p. 1995. pap. text ed. 49.00 (0-7817-0313-1) Lppncott-Raven.

Research Quarterly. 55p. (C). 1995. pap. 150.00 (0-89382-311-2) Nat Assn Insurance.

Research Quarterly. 58p. (Orig.). (C). 95.00 (0-89382-370-8) Nat Assn Insurance.

Research Quarterly. rev. ed. Ed. by Michael Barth. (Illus.). 66p. (Orig.). 1996. pap. 100.00 (0-89382-387-2) Nat Assn Insurance.

***Research Quarterly, Vol. II, Issue 4.** Ed. by Mike Barth. 60p. (Orig.). (C). 1997. pap. 100.00 (0-89382-440-2, RSH-ZS) Nat Assn Insurance.

***Research Quarterly, Vol. II, No. 3.** rev. ed. Ed. by Michael Barth. 58p. (C). 1996. pap. 100.00 (0-89382-418-6, RSH-2S) Nat Assn Insurance.

***Research Quarterly, Vol. III, Issue 1.** Ed. by Mike Barth. 52p. (Orig.). (C). 1997. pap. 50.00 (0-89382-459-3, RSH-ZS) Nat Assn Insurance.

***Research Quarterly, Vol. III, Issue 2.** Ed. by Mike Barth. 50p. (Orig.). (C). 1997. pap. 50.00 (0-89382-460-7, RSH-ZS) Nat Assn Insurance.

Research Quarterly Vol. 1: Issue 3. 62p. (Orig.). (C). 1995. pap. 30.00 (0-89382-355-4) Nat Assn Insurance.

***Research Quarterly, April 1996.** rev. ed. Ed. by Michael Barth. 62p. (Orig.). (C). 1996. pap. write for info. (0-89382-406-2) Nat Assn Insurance.

Research Readings in Rehabilitation Counseling. H. Moses & C. H. Patterson. 1973. pap. 9.80 (0-87563-054-5) Stipes.

Research Recommendations to Facilitate Distributed Work. National Research Council, Technology & Telecommunications; Issues & Impact Committee. 84p. (Orig.). (C). 1994. pap. text ed. 25.00 (0-309-05185-1) Natl Acad Pr.

Research Relationship: Practice & Politics in Social Policy Research. Ed. by G. Clare Wenger. (Contemporary Social Research Ser.: No. 15). 240p. 1987. text ed. 60.00 (0-04-312037-7); pap. text ed. 19.95 (0-04-312038-5) Routledge Chapman & Hall.

Research Reports: A Guide for Middle & High School Students. Helen Sullivan & Linda Sernoff. LC 95-21489. 128p. (YA). (gr. 5 up). 1996. lib. bdg. 17.40 (1-56294-694-3) Millbrook Pr.

***Research Reports to Knock Your Teacher's Socks Off!** Nancy Polette. (Illus.). 48p. (Orig.). (J). (gr. 3-9). 1997. pap. 7.95 (1-880505-56-8, CLC0206) Pieces of Lrning.

Research Review (Ethical) Committees for Animal Experimentation. D. P. Britt. 1985. 30.00 (0-317-43890-5) St Mut.

Research Services Directory. 3rd ed. Ed. by Robert J. Huffman. 641p. 1986. 290.00 (0-8103-0246-2) Gale.

Research Services Directory. 5th ed. Annette Piccirelli. 1992. 325.00 (0-8103-7631-8) Gale.

Research Services Directory. 6th ed. Annette Piccirelli. 1995. 340.00 (0-8103-7905-8) Gale.

Research Shortcuts. Judi Kesselman-Turkel & Franklynn Peterson. 120p. 1982. pap. 8.86 (0-8092-5749-1) Contemp Bks.

Research Skills. Annie S. Barnes. 308p. 1994. per. 41.94 (0-8403-9030-0) Kendall-Hunt.

Research Solutions to the Financial Problems of Depository Institutions. J. Austin Murphy. LC 91-47641. 168p. 1992. text ed. 55.00 (0-89930-705-1, MRX, Quorum Bks) Greenwood.

Research Sourcebook. 2nd ed. Wilson. (C). 1995. pap. text ed. 16.75 (0-15-501716-0) HB Coll Pubs.

Research Sourcebook. 2nd ed. Wilson. (C). 1995. teacher ed., pap. text ed. 32.00 (0-15-501717-9) HB Coll Pubs.

***Research Strategies for Moving Beyond Reporting.** Sharron L. McElmeel. LC 96-34558. (Professional Growth Ser.). 181p. 1996. pap. 29.95 (0-938865-54-4) Linworth Pub.

Research Strategies for Small Businesses. rev. ed. Donald E. Gudmundson. LC 95-52987. (Studies in Entrepreneurship). 145p. 1996. text ed. 44.00 (0-8153-2335-2) Garland.

Research Strategies for the U. S. Global Change Research Program. National Research Council, Committee on Vision Staff. 294p. 1990. pap. text ed. 28.00 (0-309-04348-4) Natl Acad Pr.

Research Strategies in Alcoholism Treatment Assessment. Pref. by Dan J. Lettieri. LC 88-7212. (Drugs & Society Ser.: Vol. 2, No. 2). (Illus.). 123p. 1989. text ed. 29.95 (0-86656-782-8) Haworth Pr.

Research Strategies in Human Biology: Field & Survey Studies. Ed. by Gabriel W. Lasker & C. G. Mascie-Taylor. (Studies in Biological Anthropology: No. 14). (Illus.). 200p. (C). 1993. text ed. 69.95 (0-521-43188-3) Cambridge U Pr.

Research Strategies in Human Communication Disorders. 2nd ed. Donald G. Doehring. LC 90-22481. 216p. (Orig.). (C). 1996. pap. text ed. 29.00 (0-89079-644-0, 7803) PRO-ED.

Research Strategies in Psychotherapy. Edward S. Bordin. LC 74-11272. (Wiley Series on Personality Processes). 284p. reprint ed. pap. 81.00 (0-317-08426-7, 2051569) Bks Demand.

Research Strategies in Technical Communication. William Coggin & Lynnette R. Porter. 416p. 1995. pap. text ed. 34.95 (0-471-11994-6) Wiley.

Research Student's Guide to Success. Pat Cryer. 192p. 1996. 75.00 (0-335-19612-8, Open Univ Pr); pap. 23.95 (0-335-19611-X, Open Univ Pr) Taylor & Francis.

***Research Submersibles & Undersea Technologies.** unabridged ed. Richard J. Seymour. (WTEC Panel Reports). (Illus.). 315p. 1994. pap. write for info. (1-883712-33-5) Intl Tech Res.

Research Summary: The Census of Horticultural Specialties. David S. Stump. (Illus.). 76p. (C). 1982. pap. text ed. 20.00 (0-935336-01-X) Horticult Research.

Research Symposia: WEF 1992 Annual Conference, Vol. 1. 1992. pap. 150.00 (1-881369-04-8) Water Environ.

Research Symposium on the Male Adolescent Voice. Ed. by Maria Runfola & Lee Bash. (Proceedings Ser.). (Illus.). 182p. (Orig.). 1984. pap. 14.95 (0-931111-00-5) SUNY Buff Music.

Research Symposium, Vol. 1: WEF Annual Conference, 1993. 425p. 1993. pap. 150.00 (1-881369-41-2) Water Environ.

Research Teachings in Health Science. 2nd ed. James J. Neutens & Rubinson. 384p. 1996. 60.00 (0-205-17924-X) Allyn.

Research Technician. Jack Rudman. (Career Examination Ser.: C-1948). 1994. pap. 29.95 (0-8373-1948-X) Nat Learn.

Research Techniques for Clinical Social Workers. Ed. by Tony Tripodi & Irwin Epstein. LC 80-15516. 296p. 1980. text ed. 45.00 (0-231-04652-9) Col U Pr.

Research Techniques for High Pressure & High Temperature. Ed. by Gene C. Ulmer. (Illus.). 384p. 1971. 64.95 (0-387-05594-0) Spr-Verlag.

Research Techniques for Program Planning, Monitoring & Evaluation. Irwin Epstein & Tony Tripodi. LC 76-51825. 178p. 1977. text ed. 39.50 (0-231-03944-1) Col U Pr.

Research Techniques for the Social Sciences Manual. Edward Richardson. LC 83-10749. 123p. 1983. pap. 5.00 (0-913480-58-4) Inter Am U Pr.

Research Techniques in Coastal Environments. H. Jesse Walker. (Geoscience & Man Ser.: Vol. 18). (Illus.). 328p. 1977. pap. 18.00 (0-938909-17-7) Geosci Pubns LSU.

Research Techniques in Human Engineering. Jon Weimer. LC 94-36605. (C). 1995. text ed. 92.00 (0-13-097072-7) P-H.

Research Techniques in Human Engineering. Alfred R. E. Chapanis. LC 59-10765. 328p. reprint ed. pap. 93.50 (0-317-10928-6, 2002276) Bks Demand.

***Research That Makes a Difference: Complementary Methods for Examining Legal Issues in Education.** Ed. by David Schimmel. (Monograph: Vol. 56). (Illus.). 114p. (Orig.). 1996. pap. text ed. 18.95 (1-56534-068-X) Ed Law Assn.

Research Through Biotechnology: Institutional Impacts & Societal Concerns. Mack C. Shelley et al. (Bibliographies in Technology & Social Change Ser.: No. 1). 150p. (Orig.). (C). 1987. pap. 12.00 (0-945271-00-X) ISU-CIKARD.

Research to Practice? Implications of Research on the Challenging Behavior of People with Learning Disability. Ed. by Chris Kiernan. 400p. 1993. 42.00 (1-873791-25-9) Taylor & Francis.

Research-To-Practice Dilemma. Sharan B. Merriam. 13p. 1987. 3.00 (0-318-23414-9, OC123) Ctr Educ Trng Employ.

Research to Protect, Restore, & Manage the Environment. National Research Council Committee on Environmental Research. 256p. (Orig.). (C). 1993. pap. text ed. 28.00 (0-309-04929-6) Natl Acad Pr.

Research to the Point. Allan A. Metcalf. 224p. (C). 1991. pap. text ed. 14.75 (0-15-576604-X) HB Coll Pubs.

Research to the Point. 2nd ed. Allan A. Metcalf. 244p. (C). 1994. pap. text ed. 17.00 (0-15-501481-1) HB Coll Pubs.

Research to the Point. 2nd rev. ed. Metcalf. (C). 1995. pap. text ed. 18.50 (0-15-503709-9) HarBrace.

Research to Write. Maity Schrecengost. LC 94-2639. 56p. (J). (gr. 3-6). 1994. pap. 9.50 (0-917846-37-0, 33897, Alleyside) Highsmith Pr.

Research Toolkit: Putting It All Together. Friedman. LC 97-21796. (Social Work Ser.). 1998. pap. 17.95 (0-534-34409-7) Wadsworth Pub.

Research Tools for the Classics. Ed. by Roger S. Bagnall. LC 80-25766. (American Philological Association Pamphlet Ser.). 61p. (C). 1980. pap. 9.95 (0-89130-452-5, 40-06-06) Scholars Pr GA.

Research Tradition at UCSF: Conversations with Dr. Leslie Latty Bennett. Ed. by Andrea Richardson. (Oral History Ser.). (Illus.). 200p. (Orig.). 1992. pap. 20.00 (1-881525-00-7) Univ Calif SF.

Research Training: Present & Future. 226p. (Orig.). 1995. pap. 58.00 (92-64-14347-5, Pub. by Org for Econ FR) OECD.

Research, Training & Practice in Clinical Medicine of Aging. Ed. by L. Gitman & E. Woodford-Williams. (Interdisciplinary Topics in Gerontology Ser.: Vol. 5). 1970. 28.00 (3-8055-0505-1) S Karger.

Research Transformed into Practice Implementation of NSF Research: Proceedings of the Conference Sponsored by the National Science Foundation: Crystal City, Virginia, June 14-16, 1995. Ed. by James Colville & Amde M. Amde. 748p. 1995. 66.00 (0-7844-0094-6) Am Soc Civil Eng.

Research Trends in Fluid Dynamics: Report from the United States National Committee on Theoretical & Applied Mechanics. John L. Lumley. LC 95-25488. (Illus.). 328p. 1995. text ed. 50.00 (1-56396-459-7) Am Inst Physics.

Research Universities & Their Patrons. Robert M. Rosenzweig & Barbara Turlington. LC 81-19685. 200p. 1982. pap. 12.00 (0-520-04735-4) U CA Pr.

Research University in a Time of Discontent. Ed. by Jonathan R. Cole et al. 320p. 1994. text ed. 45.00 (0-8018-4957-8); pap. text ed. 15.95 (0-8018-4958-6) Johns Hopkins.

Research Utilization. Ed. by Carol Weiss. (C). 1976. pap. text ed. 15.00 (0-918592-14-3) Pol Studies.

Research Utilization in Social Work Education. Ed. by Scott Briar et al. 1981. 7.70 (0-318-35362-8) Coun Soc Wk Ed.

Research Utilization in the Social Services: Innovations in Practice & Administration. Ed. by Anthony J. Grasso & Irwin Epstein. LC 91-8447. (Illus.). 486p. 1992. pap. text ed. 39.95 (1-56024-071-7); lib. bdg. 69.95 (1-56024-070-9) Haworth Pr.

Research with Argonne Premium Coal Samples, Gasification Mechanisms, New Materials Derived from Hydrocarbon Fuels, Novel Analytical Techniques for Fossil Fuels, Posters - General & SCI-MIX: Preprints of Papers Presented at the 202nd ACS National Meeting, New York, NY, August 25-30, 1991. American Chemical Society, Division of Fuel Chemistry Staff. (Preprints of Papers: Vol. 36, No. 3, 1990). 563p. reprint ed. pap. 160.50 (0-7837-1009-7, 2041321) Bks Demand.

***Research with Disabled Children: Issues & Methods.** Stationery Office. 1997. pap. 30.00 (0-11-702148-2, HM021482, Pub. by Stationery Ofc UK) Bernan Associates.

Research with Farmers: Lessons from Ethiopia. Ed. by S. Franzel & Helen Van Houten. 320p. 1992. 70.00 (0-85198-814-8, Pub. by CAB Intntl UK) OUP.

***Research with Fission Fragments.** 380p. 1997. text ed. 47.00 (981-02-3140-7) World Scientific Pub.

Research with Hispanic Populations. Gerardo Marin & Barbara V. Marin. (Applied Social Research Methods Ser.: Vol. 23). (Illus.). 160p. 1991. 39.95 (0-8039-3720-2); pap. 17.95 (0-8039-3721-0) Sage.

Research Within Reach: Science Education. Ed. by David Holdzkom & Pamela B. Lutz. (Illus.). 236p. 1984. pap. 6.50 (0-317-65975-8) Natl Sci Tchrs.

Research Within Reach: Secondary School Reading: A Research Guided Response to Concerns of Reading Educators. Ed. by Donna E. Alvermann et al. LC 87-3928. 200p. reprint ed. pap. 57.00 (0-7837-1236-7, 2041373) Bks Demand.

Research Without Copying. 2nd ed. Nancy Polette. (Illus.). 48p. 1991. pap. 5.95 (0-913839-91-4) Pieces of Lrning.

Research Worker. Jack Rudman. (Career Examination Ser.: C-546). 1994. pap. 29.95 (0-8373-0546-2) Nat Learn.

Research Workout. Susan Martin & Harriet Green. (Illus.). 144p. (J). (gr. 4-9). 1984. student ed. 13.99 (0-86653-194-7, GA 551) Good Apple.

Research Writing Simplified. Raymond Clines & Elizabeth Cobb. LC 92-19492. (C). 1992. 9.50 (0-06-501044-2) Addson-Wesley Educ.

Research Writing Simplified: A Documentation Guide. 2nd ed. Raymond H. Clines & Elizabeth R. Cobb. LC 96-10579. (C). 1997. pap. text ed. 8.50 (0-673-98084-7) Addson-Wesley Educ.

Researcher Learns to Write: Selected Articles & Monographs. Donald H. Graves. LC 84-6525. 193p. (Orig.). 1984. pap. text ed. 20.00 (0-435-08213-2, 08213) Heinemann.

Researcher's Guide to American Genealogy. 2nd ed. Val D. Greenwood. LC 89-81464. (Illus.). 623p. 1990. 24.95 (0-8063-1267-X) Genealog Pub.

Researchers' Guide to Genealogical & Historical Records in Orange County, New York. Orange County Genealogical Society Staff. (Orig.). 1985. write for info. (0-9604116-6-6) Orange County Genealog.

Researcher's Guide to Scientific & Medical Illustrations. M. H. Briscoe. (Contemporary Bioscience Ser.). (Illus.). xi, 290p. 1990. pap. 19.95 (0-387-97199-8) Spr-Verlag.

Researcher's Guide to Sources on Soviet Social History in the 1930s. Ed. by Sheila Fitzpatrick & Lynne Viola. LC 89-10673. 312p. (gr. 13). 1990. text ed. 79.95 (0-87332-497-8) M E Sharpe.

Researcher's Guide to Sources on Soviet Social History in the 1930s. Ed. by Sheila Fitzpatrick & Lynne Viola. LC 89-10673. 360p. (C). (gr. 13). 1992. pap. text ed. 35.95 (1-56324-078-5) M E Sharpe.

Researchers Hooked on Teaching: Noted Scholars Discuss the Synergies of Teaching & Research. Ed. by Rae Andre & Peter J. Frost. (Foundations for Organizational Science Ser.). 332p. 1996. 45.00 (0-7619-0622-3); pap. 21.95 (0-7619-0623-1) Sage.

Researchers in Powder Metallurgy, Vol. 1. Zbigniew Michalewicz. LC 66-15306. 156p. reprint ed. pap. 44.50 (0-317-10429-2, 2020675) Bks Demand.

Researcher's Library of Georgia History, Genealogy, & Records Sources. Robert S. Davis, Jr. (Illus.). 450p. 1987. 42.50 (0-89308-535-9, GA 70) Southern Hist Pr.

Researcher's Library of Georgia History, Genealogy, & Records Sources, Vol. II. Robert S. Davis, Jr. (Illus.). 480p. 1990. 42.50 (0-89308-683-5, GA 87) Southern Hist Pr.

Researches in Anatolia: The Alishar Huyuk, Seasons of 1930-32, 29. Hans H. Von der Osten. LC 30-14678. (Oriental Institute Publications). 1973. lib. bdg. 18.00 incl. fiche (0-226-63939-8) U Ch Pr.

Researches in Anatolia: The Alishar Huyuk, Seasons of 1930-32, 30. Hans H. Von der Osten. LC 30-14678. (Oriental Institute Publications). 1973. lib. bdg. 18.00 incl. fiche (0-226-63940-1) U Ch Pr.

Researches in Asia Minor, Pontus & Armenia with Some Account of Their Antiquities & Geology, 2 vols. in 1. William J. Hamilton. (Illus.). xxxv, 1053p. 1983. reprint ed. lib. bdg. 128.70 (3-487-07370-6) G Olms Pubs.

Researches in Indian Archaeology, Art, Architecture, Culture & Religion, 2 vols., Set. Ed. by Phanikanta Mishra. (C). 1995. 200.00 (*81-85067-82-1*, Pub. by Sundeep Prakashan II) S Asia.

Researches in Indian Epigraphy & Numismatics. Jagannath Agrawal. (Illus.). xii, 133p. 1986. 18.00 (*0-685-67623-4*, Pub. by Sundeep Prak II) Nataraj Bks.

Researches in Manichaeism with Special Reference to the Turfan Fragments. Abraham V. Jackson. LC 32-9567. (Columbia University. Indo-Iranian Ser.: No. 13). reprint ed. 47.50 (*0-404-50483-3*) AMS Pr.

Researches in the Central Portion of the Usumatsintla Valley. T. Maler. (HU PMM Ser.). 1974. reprint ed. 50.00 (*0-527-01156-8*) Periodicals Srv.

Researches in the Phenomena of Spiritualism. William Crookes. 112p. 1972. reprint ed. spiral bd. 7.00 (*0-7873-0228-7*) Hlth Research.

Researches in the Uloa Valley, 1898. G. B. Gordon. (HU PMM Ser.). 1974. reprint ed. 30.00 (*0-527-01153-3*) Periodicals Srv.

Researches in the Usumatsintla Valley, Pt. 2. T. Maler. (HU PMM Ser.). 1974. reprint ed. 80.00 (*0-527-01157-6*) Periodicals Srv.

Researches into the Laws of Chemical Affinity. 2nd ed. Claude-Louis Berthollet. LC 65-23404. 1966. reprint ed. 27.50 (*0-306-70914-7*) Da Capo.

Researches into the Mathematical Principles of the Theory of Wealth. Augustin Cournot. LC 73-28986. (Reprints of Economic Classics Ser.). xxv, 213p. 1971. reprint ed. 35.00 (*0-678-00066-2*) Kelley.

Researches into the Physical History of Man. James C. Prichard. Ed. by George W. Stocking, Jr. LC 75-190425. (Classics in Anthropology Ser.). 716p. 1973. lib. bdg. 30.00 (*0-226-68120-3*) U Ch Pr.

Researches on Acupuncture & Moxibustion & Acupuncture Anaesthesia. Ed. by X. Zhang. (Illus.). 1179p. 1986. 112.00 (*0-387-10901-3*) Spr-Verlag.

Researches on Light. Robert Hunt. LC 72-9213. (Literature of Photography Ser.). 1973. reprint ed. 26.95 (*0-405-04921-8*) Ayer.

Researches on Organosulfur Compounds: Five Membered Tellurium-Containing Heterocycles, Vol. 6. Alexander Senning et al. (Sulfer Reports: Vol. 6, No. 1). 76p. 1986. pap. text ed. 76.00 (*3-7186-0369-1*) Gordon & Breach.

Researches on the United States. Philip Mazzei. Ed. & Tr. by Constance D. Sherman. LC 75-20037. (Illus.). 436p. reprint ed. 124.30 (*0-8357-9814-3*, 2016965) Bks Demand.

Researches on Waring's Problem. Leonard E. Dickson. LC 35-19856. (Carnegie Institution of Washington Publication Ser.: No. 464). 265p. reprint ed. pap. 75.60 (*0-317-09159-X*, 2015710) Bks Demand.

Researching American Culture: A Guide for Student Anthropologists. Ed. by Conrad P. Kottak. LC 81-23175. (C). 1982. pap. text ed. 18.95 (*0-472-08024-5*) U of Mich Pr.

***Researching Ancestors.** unabridged ed. Joseph A. Boyd, Jr. 60p. (Orig.). 1996. pap. text ed. write for info. (*1-888781-04-1*) J A Boyd.

Researching & Conceptualizing Drunk Driving: An Invitation to Criminologists & Criminal Law Scholars. James B. Jacobs. Ed. by Graham Hughes. (Occasional Papers: Vol. V). 17p. (Orig.). (C). 1988. pap. 5.00 (*1-878429-54-X*) NYU Ctr for Rsch in Crime Justice.

Researching & Finding Your German Heritage. 2nd enl. rev. ed. Marilyn Lind. LC 90-62026. (Illus.). 150p. (Orig.). 1991. reprint ed. pap. 13.25 (*0-937463-12-4*) Linden Tree.

Researching & Writing: Across the Curriculum. Christine A. Hult. LC 95-10390. 1995. pap. text ed. 19.00 (*0-205-16838-8*) Allyn.

Researching & Writing in History: A Practical Handbook for Student. F. N. McCoy. 1974. pap. 11.95 (*0-520-02621-7*) U CA Pr.

Researching & Writing in Sciences & Technology. Christine A. Hult. LC 95-21280. 1995. pap. text ed. 17.00 (*0-205-16840-X*) Allyn.

Researching & Writing in the Humanities & Arts. Christine A. Hult. LC 95-30218. 1995. pap. text ed. 17.00 (*0-205-16839-6*) Allyn.

Researching & Writing in the Social Sciences. Christine A. Hult. LC 95-23156. 1995. pap. text ed. 17.00 (*0-205-16841-8*) Allyn.

Researching & Writing Tribal Histories. Duane K. Hale. Ed. by M. T. Bussey. (Illus.). 84p. (Orig.). (C). pap. text ed. write for info. (*0-9617707-6-7*) Grnd Rpds Intertribal.

Researching Arkansas History: A Beginner's Guide. Tom W. Dillard & Valerie Thwing. (Illus.). 64p. 1980. pap. 5.00 (*0-914546-25-2*) Rose Pub.

Researching British Probates, 1354-1858: A Guide to the Microfilm Collection of the Family History Library, Northern England, Province of York. David H. Pratt. LC 92-18338. (Illus.). 240p. 1992. 75.00 (*0-8420-2420-4*) Scholarly Res Inc.

***Researching Business Markets.** Ed. by Ken Sutherland. (Marketing & Sales Ser.). 1994. pap. 29.95 (*0-7494-1497-9*) Kogan Page Ltd.

Researching Chicano Communities: Social-Historical, Physical, Psychological, & Spiritual Space. Irene I. Blea. LC 95-2224. 176p. 1995. text ed. 57.95 (*0-275-94974-5*, Praeger Pubs); pap. text ed. 17.95 (*0-275-95219-3*, Praeger Pubs) Greenwood.

***Researching Colleges on the World Wide Web.** Kerry Cochrane. LC 96-43513. 1997. pap. 16.00 (*0-531-11294-2*) Watts.

Researching Community Psychology: Issues of Theory & Methods. Ed. by Patrick Tolan et al. 259p. 1990. pap. text ed. 19.95 (*1-55798-234-1*) Am Psychol.

Researching Connection. Burgess. (C). 1995. pap. 24.36 (*0-395-73874-1*) HM.

Researching Constitutional Law. Albert P. Melone. (C). 1990. text ed. 27.95 (*0-673-52086-2*) Addson-Wesley Educ.

Researching Cultural Difference. Ed. by Kelleher. 256p. (C). 1996. text ed. 59.95 (*0-415-11182-X*) Routledge.

Researching Cultural Difference. David Kelleher & Sheila Hillier. 256p. (C). 1996. pap. 17.95 (*0-415-11183-8*) Routledge.

Researching Cultural Differences in Health. Ed. by David Kelleher & Sheila Hillier. LC 95-25980. 1996. write for info. (*0-04-151118-2*) Routledge.

Researching Culture: Qualitative Method & Cultural Studies. Pertti Alasuutari. 240p. (C). 1995. 65.00 (*0-8039-7830-8*); pap. 21.95 (*0-8039-7831-6*) Sage.

Researching Drama & Arts Education: Paradigms & Possibilities. Philip Taylor. LC 96-18744. 240p. 1996. 69.95 (*0-7507-0463-2*, Falmer Pr); pap. 24.95 (*0-7507-0464-0*, Falmer Pr) Taylor & Francis.

***Researching Education: Perspectives & Techniques.** Ed. by Gajendra V. Verma et al. 224p. 1996. 75.00 (*0-7507-0530-2*, Falmer Pr); pap. 24.95 (*0-7507-0531-0*, Falmer Pr) Taylor & Francis.

Researching Education Policy: Ethical & Methodological Issues. Ed. by David Halpin & Barry Troyna. LC 94-24820. (Social Research & Educational Studies: No. 15). 176p. 1994. 75.00 (*0-7507-0344-X*, Falmer Pr); pap. 27.50 (*0-7507-0345-8*, Falmer Pr) Taylor & Francis.

***Researching Family History: A Work Book.** Alexia S. Helsley. Ed. by Judith M. Andrews. 40p. 1996. wbk. ed., pap. 5.00 (*1-880067-38-2*) SC Dept of Arch & Hist.

Researching Health Care: Designs, Dilemmas, & Disciplines. Ed. by Jeanne Daly et al. LC 91-36911. 224p. (C). 1992. pap. 22.95 (*0-415-07078-3*, A7451); text ed. 85.00 (*0-415-07077-5*, A7447) Routledge.

Researching Health Risks. 1994. lib. bdg. 252.75 (*0-8490-5819-8*) Gordon Pr.

Researching Health Risks. (Illus.). 236p. (Orig.). (C). 1994. pap. text ed. 50.00 (*0-7881-1161-2*) DIANE Pub.

Researching Health Risks. 1995. lib. bdg. 251.95 (*0-8490-6693-X*) Gordon Pr.

Researching in Salt Lake City. rev. ed. Nancy E. Carlberg. 260p. (Orig.). 1993. pap. 20.00 (*0-944878-24-5*) Carlberg Pr.

Researching Industrial Markets: How to Identify, Reach, & Sell to Your Customers. Alan S. Krigman. LC 83-12832. 92p. 1983. reprint ed. pap. 26.80 (*0-7837-5130-3*, 2044858) Bks Demand.

Researching Language: Issues of Power & Method. Deborah Cameron et al. LC 91-30978. (Politics of Language Ser.). 192p. (C). 1992. pap. 16.95 (*0-415-05722-1*, A6839) Routledge.

Researching Language: Issues of Power & Method. Deborah Cameron et al. LC 91-30978. (Politics of Language Ser.). 176p. (C). 1992. text ed. 59.95 (*0-415-05721-3*, A6835) Routledge.

Researching Language & Literacy in Social Context. Ed. by David Graddol et al. LC 93-23198. 176p. 1993. 69.95 (*1-85359-222-6*, Pub. by Multilingual Matters UK); pap. 22.95 (*1-85359-221-8*, Pub. by Multilingual Matters UK) Taylor & Francis.

Researching Lived Experience: Human Science for an Action Sensitive Pedagogy. Max Van Manen. LC 89-48885. (SUNY Series, the Philosophy of Education). 202p. (C). 1990. text ed. 64.50 (*0-7914-0425-0*); pap. text ed. 21.95 (*0-7914-0426-9*) State U NY Pr.

Researching Local History. Mary Reed & Carole Simon-Smolinski. (Local History Technical Leaflets Ser.). (Illus.). 22p. (Orig.). 1985. pap. 1.50 (*0-931406-08-0*) Idaho State Soc.

Researching Local History: The Human Journey. Michael A. Williams. LC 95-45476. (Approaches to Local History Ser.). 1996. pap. text ed. write for info. (*0-582-04288-7*, Pub. by Longman UK) Longman.

Researching Local History: The Human Journey. Michael A. Williams. LC 95-45476. (Approaches to Local History Ser.). 1996. boxed write for info. (*0-582-04289-5*, Pub. by Longman UK) Longman.

Researching Markets, Industries & Business Opportunities, Edition II. 600p. 1995. 395.00 (*1-56365-037-1*) Wash Res.

Researching Modern Evangelicalism: A Guide to the Holdings of the Billy Graham Center, with Information on Other Collections. Compiled by Robert D. Shuster et al. LC 90-34009. (Bibliographies & Indexes in Religious Studies: No. 16). 384p. 1990. text ed. 69.50 (*0-313-26478-3*, SRQ/, Greenwood Pr) Greenwood.

Researching on the Internet: The Complete Guide to Organizing Searching & Qualifying... Robin Rowland. 1995. pap. 29.95 (*0-7615-0063-4*) Prima Pub.

Researching on World Wide Web. 2nd ed. Cynthia James-Catalano. 384p. 1996. per. 24.99 (*0-7615-0686-1*) Prima Pub.

Researching People. Maity Schrecengost. LC 96-15130. (Orig.). 1996. pap. write for info. (*0-917846-69-9*, Alleyside) Highsmith Pr.

Researching Persons with Mental Illness. Rosalind J. Dworkin. (Applied Social Research Methods Ser.: Vol. 30). 160p. (C). 1992. text ed. 39.95 (*0-8039-3603-6*); pap. text ed. 17.95 (*0-8039-3604-4*) Sage.

Researching Public Records: How to Get Anything on Anybody. Vincent Parco. LC 93-44224. 1994. 8.95 (*0-8065-1522-8*, Citadel Pr) Carol Pub Group.

Researching 'Race' & Teacher Education. Iram Siraj-Blatchford et al. 128p. 1995. 79.00 (*0-335-19428-1*); pap. 27.00 (*0-335-19427-3*) Taylor & Francis.

***Researching Racism in Education: Politics, Theory & Practice.** Paul Connolly & Barry Troyna. LC 97-23199. 1997. write for info. (*0-335-19663-2*, Open Univ Pr); pap. write for info. (*0-335-19662-4*, Open Univ Pr) Taylor & Francis.

Researching Reader: Source-Based Writing Across the Disciplines. Diane Dowdey. 608p. (C). 1990. teacher ed. write for info. (*0-03-028772-3*); pap. text ed. 20.00 (*0-03-028769-3*) HB Coll Pubs.

Researching Reincarnation from Creation to the Age of Aquarius. Leo M. Braun. 1991. 10.95 (*0-533-09282-5*) Vantage.

Researching Response to Literature & the Teaching of Literature: Points of Departure. Charles Cooper. LC 83-11826. 352p. 1985. pap. 39.50 (*0-89391-323-5*); text ed. 73.25 (*0-89391-184-4*) Ablex Pub.

Researching Sensitive Topics. Claire M. Renzetti & Raymond M. Lee. (Focus Editions Ser.: Vol. 152). (Illus.). 312p. (C). 1992. 54.00 (*0-8039-4844-1*); pap. 24.95 (*0-8039-4845-X*) Sage.

***Researching Sexual Behavior: Methodological Issues.** John Bancroft & Kinsey Institute for Research in Sex, Gender, & Reproduction Ser. LC 97-11417. (Kinsey Institute Ser.). 1997. write for info. (*0-253-33339-3*) Ind U Pr.

***Researching Sexual Violence Against Women: Methodological & Personal Perspectives.** Ed. by Martin D. Schwartz. LC 96-51226. 272p. 1997. 45.00 (*0-8039-7369-1*); pap. 19.95 (*0-8039-7370-5*) Sage.

Researching Social Gerontology: Concepts, Methods & Issues. Sheila M. Peace. Ed. by Peter G. Norton et al. 224p. (C). 1990. text ed. 47.50 (*0-8039-8284-4*); pap. text ed. 19.95 (*0-8039-8285-2*) Sage.

Researching Social Life. Nigel Gilbert. 352p. (C). 1993. text ed. 65.00 (*0-8039-8681-5*); pap. text ed. 22.95 (*0-8039-8682-3*) Sage.

Researching Social Processes in the Laboratory, Vol. 6. Carl J. Couch. LC 87-2758. (Contemporary Studies in Sociology: Vol. 6). 198p. 1987. 73.25 (*0-89232-823-1*) Jai Pr.

Researching the Accounting Curriculum: Strategies for Change. William Ferrara. (Studies in Accounting Education: Vol. 2). 227p. 1975. 12.00 (*0-86539-030-4*) Am Accounting.

Researching the Art of Teaching: Ethnography for Educational Use. Peter Woods. LC 96-2155. 208p. (C). 1996. pap. 17.95 (*0-415-13129-4*); text ed. 59.95 (*0-415-13128-6*) Routledge.

Researching the Country House: A Guide for Local Historians. E. Arthur Elton et al. (Illus.). 192p. 1992. 45.00 (*0-7134-6440-2*, Pub. by Batsford UK) Trafalgar.

Researching the Country House: A Guide for Local Historians. E. Arthur Elton et al. (Illus.). 192p. 1993. pap. 34.95 (*0-7134-6441-0*, Pub. by Batsford UK) Trafalgar.

Researching the Development of Lay Leadership in the Roman Catholic Church since Vatican II: Bibliographical Abstracts. L. Thomas Snyderwine. LC 87-12224. (Roman Catholic Studies: Vol. 1). 200p. 1987. lib. bdg. 79.95 (*0-88946-241-0*) E Mellen.

Researching the Early Years Continuum. Ed. by Pat Broadhead. (BERA Dialogues Ser.: No. 12). 194p. 1995. 79.00 (*1-85359-312-5*, Pub. by Multilingual Matters UK); pap. 29.95 (*1-85359-311-7*, Pub. by Multilingual Matters UK) Taylor & Francis.

Researching the Germans from Russia: An Annotated Bibliography of the "Germans from Russia Heritage Collection" Michael M. Miller. LC 86-61716. 224p. 1987. pap. 20.00 (*0-911042-34-2*) NDSU Inst Reg.

Researching the Old House. Ed. by Greater Portland Landmarks Research Committee. (Illus.). 72p. 1981. pap. 3.95 (*0-9600612-9-0*) Greater Portland.

Researching the People's Health. Ed. by Gareth Williams & Jenny Popay. LC 94-3184. 240p. (C). 1994. pap. 18.95 (*0-415-09972-2*, B4330) Routledge.

Researching the People's Health. Ed. by Gareth Williams & Jenny Popay. LC 94-3184. 192p. (C). (gr. 13). 1994. text ed. 69.95 (*0-415-09971-4*, B4326) Routledge.

Researching the Powerful in Education. Ed. by Geoffrey Walford. LC 94-42572. (Social Research Today Ser.: Vol. 4). 224p. 1994. 65.00 (*1-85728-133-0*, Pub. by UCL Pr UK); pap. 27.50 (*1-85728-134-9*, Pub. by UCL Pr UK) Taylor & Francis.

Researching the Presidency: Vital Questions, New Approaches. Ed. by George C. Edwards, III et al. LC 92-24940. (Series in Policy & Institutional Studies). 512p. (C). 1993. text ed. 49.95 (*0-8229-3737-9*); pap. text ed. 22.95 (*0-8229-5494-X*) U of Pittsburgh Pr.

Researching the Soul on Two Realms: Introduction to Religious Research. Julita M. Stone. LC 91-68238. (Illus.). 96p. (Orig.). 1992. pap. 5.95 (*0-915151-15-4*) Religious Res Pr.

***Researching Therapist: A Practical Guide to Planning, Performing & Communicating Research.** Sue Jenkins et al. LC 97-20081. 1997. write for info. (*0-443-05761-3*) Churchill.

Researching User Perspectives on Community Health Care. R. Heyman. (Illus.). 288p. 1994. pap. text ed. 44.95 (*1-56593-300-1*, 0624) Singular Publishing.

Researching Women's Lives from a Feminist Perspective. Ed. by Mary Maynard & June Purvis. LC 93-38801. 1994. write for info. (*0-7484-0152-0*, Pub. by Tay Francis Ltd UK); pap. write for info. (*0-7484-0153-9*, Pub. by Tay Francis Ltd UK) Taylor & Francis.

Researching, Writing & Publishing Your Church's History. Charles W. Deweese. (Resource Kit for Your Church's History Ser.). 8p. 1984. pap. 0.60 (*0-939804-19-0*) Hist Comm S Baptist.

Researching Your Family & Heritage. Marilyn Lind. LC 90-62025. (Illus.). 176p. (Orig.). (C). 1991. pap. 14.50 (*0-937463-13-2*) Linden Tree.

Researching Your Roots in New York, 4 vols. Arlene H. Eakle. 65p. 1991. pap. write for info. (*0-940764-55-5*) Genealog Inst.

Researching Your Way to a Good Job. Karmen N. Crowther. LC 92-9394. 240p. 1993. pap. text ed. 14.95 (*0-471-54827-8*) Wiley.

Resection & Plastic Surgery of Bronchi. Boris Petrovsky et al. Tr. by Mir Publishers Staff from RUS. (Illus.). 375p. (C). 1975. 27.95 (*0-8464-0790-6*) Beekman Pubs.

ResEdit Complete with Disk. Peter Alley. 1991. pap. 32.95 (*0-201-55075-X*) Addison-Wesley.

ResEdit Reference: For ResEdit Version 2.1. 2nd ed. Apple Computer, Inc. Staff. 192p. 1991. pap. 19.95 (*0-201-57767-4*) Addison-Wesley.

ResEdit Reference: For ResEdit Version 2.1. 2nd ed. Apple Computer, Inc. Staff. 192p. 1991. pap. 29.95 incl. disk (*0-201-57768-2*) Addison-Wesley.

Reselection of MPS. Alison Young. vi, 154p. (Orig.). 1983. pap. text ed. 29.95 (*0-435-83371-5*, Pub. by Dartmth Pub UK) Ashgate Pub Co.

Reseller Assortment Decision Criteria. Jerker Nilsson & Viggo Host. 181p. (Orig.). 1987. pap. 33.50 (*87-7288-079-1*, Pub. by Aarhus Univ Pr DK) David Brown.

Resemblance & Disgrace: Alexander Pope & the Deformation of Culture. Helen Deutsch. (Illus.). 304p. 1996. 39.95 (*0-674-76489-7*) HUP.

Resemblance & Identity: An Examination of the Problem of Universals. Panayot Butchvarov. LC 66-22437. 222p. reprint ed. 63.30 (*0-8357-9239-0*, 2015811) Bks Demand.

Resena Critica de una Introduccion al Antiguo Testament. Gleason L. Archer. 576p. (SPA.). 1982. pap. 16.99 (*0-8254-1033-9*, Edit Portavoz) Kregel.

***Resentment: A Comedy.** Gary Indiana. LC 96-46827. 1997. 22.95 (*0-385-48429-1*) Doubleday.

Resentment Against Achievement: Understanding the Assault upon Ability. Robert Sheaffer. 197p. 1988. 27.95 (*0-87975-447-8*) Prometheus Bks.

Reservation. Ted C. Williams. LC 75-46585. (Iroquois Bks.). (Illus.). 254p. 1985. pap. 14.95 (*0-8156-0197-2*) Syracuse U Pr.

Reservation: Policy, Programmes & Issues. Vimal P. Shah & Binod C. Agarwal. 210p. 1986. 31.00 (*0-8364-1912-X*, Pub. by Rawat II) S Asia.

Reservation Agent. (Career Examination Ser.: C-3653). pap. 27.95 (*0-8373-3653-8*) Nat Learn.

Reservation Blues. Sherman Alexie. 320p. 1996. pap. 12.99 (*0-446-67235-1*) Warner Bks.

Reservation of Title Clauses: Impact & Implications. Sally Wheeler. (Socio-Legal Studies). (Illus.). 240p. 1992. 65.00 (*0-19-825737-6*) OUP.

Reservation Policy & Anti-Reservationists. Ravinder S. Bains. (C). 1994. 20.00 (*81-7018-785-0*, Pub. by BR Pub II) S Asia.

Reservation Policy & Mandal Commission. C. Rupa. 168p. (C). 1992. text ed. 25.00 (*81-207-1384-2*, Pub. by Sterling Pubs II) Apt Bks.

Reservation Policy & Practice in India. Anirudh Prasad. (C). 1991. 67.50 (*81-7100-297-8*, Pub. by Deep II) S Asia.

Reservation Policy & Scheduled Castes in India. A. K. Vakil. 1986. 27.50 (*81-7024-016-6*, Pub. by Ashish II) S Asia.

Reservation Policy for Backward Classes. S. N. Singh. (C). 1996. 40.00 (*0-614-13262-2*, Pub. by Rawat II) S Asia.

Reservation Policy in India. K. S. Padhy & Jayashree Mahapatra. (C). 1988. 27.00 (*81-7024-195-2*, Pub. by Ashish II) S Asia.

Reservation, Problems & Prospects. Shayama N. Singh. (C). 1991. 36.00 (*81-85024-90-1*, Pub. by Uppal Pub Hse II) S Asia.

Reservation to City: Indian Migration & Federal Relocation. Elaine M. Neils. LC 78-144044. (University of Chicago, Department of Geography, Research Paper Ser.: No. 131). 214p. 1971. reprint ed. pap. 61.00 (*0-608-02282-9*, 2062923) Bks Demand.

Reservations. Henry Woodhead. LC 95-4967. (American Indians Ser.). (Illus.). 184p. Date not set. 19.95 (*0-8094-9737-9*) Time-Life.

Reservations: Poems. James Richardson. LC 76-45908. (Contemporary Poets Ser.). 75p. 1977. pap. 9.95 (*0-691-01334-9*) Princeton U Pr.

Reservations & Ticketing: Apollo. Carol Woodring & Gail S. Huck. 246p. 1991. text ed. 35.95 (*0-8273-3626-8*) Delmar.

Reservations & Ticketing: Apollo. Carol Woodring & Gail S. Huck. 246p. 1991. teacher ed. 11.00 (*0-8273-3627-6*) Delmar.

Reservations & Ticketing with SABRE. 2nd ed. Dennis L. Foster. LC 93-41610. 1994. write for info. (*0-02-801391-3*) Glencoe.

Reservations for Backward Classes: Mandal Commission Report of the Backward Classes Commission. Akalank Pub. Staff. (C). 1990. 53.00 (*0-89771-132-7*) St Mut.

Reservations for Scheduled Castes & Scheduled Tribes. H. C. Upadhyay. (C). 1991. text ed. 48.50 (*81-7041-485-7*, Pub. by Anmol II) S Asia.

Reservations in Unilateral Declarations Accepting the Compulsory Jurisdiction of the International Court of Justice. Stanimir A. Alexandrov. LC 94-35261. (Legal Aspects of International Organizations Ser.: Vol. 19). 1995. lib. bdg. 75.00 (*0-7923-3145-1*) Kluwer Ac.

Reservations Recommended: A Novel. Eric Kraft. LC 95-34775. 1995. pap. 12.00 (*0-312-13597-1*, Picador USA) St Martin.

Reservations to UN-Human Rights Treaties: Ratify & Ruin? Elizabeth Lijnzaad. LC 94-40864. (International Studies in Human Rights: Vol. 38). 1995. lib. bdg. 142.00 (*0-7923-3256-3*, Pub. by M Nijhoff NE) Kluwer Ac.

Reserve Analysis Tutorial: An Engineer's Perspective. Carl Sontz. 47p. 1992. pap. text ed. 50.00 (*0-9633097-0-6*) C Sontz.

R

An Asterisk (*) at the beginning of an entry indicates that the title is appearing in BIP for the first time.

R

Reserve Analysis Tutorial: An Engineer's Perspective. 2nd ed. Carl Sontz. 54p. pap. text ed. 50.00 (*0-9633097-1-4*) C Sontz.

***Reserve Component Linguists in Civil Affairs & Psychological Operations.** Ronald E. Sortor. (Illus.). 28p. 1996. pap. 6.00 (*0-8330-2451-5*, DB-186-A) Rand Corp.

Reserve Currencies in Transition. Study Group Staff. (Reports). 73p. 1982. pap. write for info. (*1-56708-058-8*) Grp of Thirty.

Reserve-Currency Diversification & the Substitution Account. Avraham Ben-Bassat. LC 84-581. (Studies in International Finance: No. 53). 42p. 1984. pap. text ed. 11.00 (*0-88165-225-3*) Princeton U Int Finan Econ.

***Reserve Forces Almanac.** Sol Gordon. 252p. 1997. 6.25 (*1-888096-55-1*) Uniformed Srvs.

Reserve Forces & the British Territorial Army: A Case Study for Nato in the 90's. Wallace E. Walker. 233p. (C). 1992. text ed. 59.00 (*1-85488-067-5*, Pub. by SPA Bks Ltd UK) St Mut.

Reserve Funds in Public School Finance. F. C. Ketler. LC 73-176964. (Columbia University. Teachers College. Contributions to Education Ser.: No. 456). reprint ed. 37.50 (*0-404-55456-3*) AMS Pr.

Reserve Mining Controversy: Science Technology & Environmental Quality. Robert V Bartlett. LC 79-48019. 312p. 1980. 18.95 (*0-253-14556-2*) Ind U Pr.

Reserve Mining Controversy: Science, Technology, & Environmental Quality. Robert V. Bartlett. LC 79-48019. 307p. 1980. reprint ed. pap. 87.50 (*0-608-01046-4*, 2059354) Bks Demand.

Reserve Officer Training Corps: Campus Paths to Service Commissions. Robert F. Collins. (Military Opportunities Ser.). (Illus.). 148p. (YA). (gr. 7-12). 1986. lib. bdg. 15.95 (*0-8239-0695-7*) Rosen Group.

Reserve Supply in the Post-Desert Storm Recruiting Environment. Beth J. Asch. LC 93-15861. 1993. pap. 13.00 (*0-8330-1382-3*, MR-224) Rand Corp.

Reserved Water Rights Settlement Manual. Peter W. Sly. LC 88-23148. 254p. 1988. 34.95 (*0-933280-72-6*); pap. 22.95 (*0-933280-71-8*) Island Pr.

Reserves of Crude Oil, Natural Gas Liquids, & Natural Gas in the United States & Canada, & U. S. Productive Capacity - December 31, 1974. 29th ed. 254p. 1975. pap. 5.00 (*0-318-12692-3*, F40074) Am Gas Assn.

Reserves of Crude Oil, Natural Gas Liquids, & Natural Gas in the United States & Canada, & U. S. Productive Capacity - December 31, 1975. 30th ed. 259p. 1976. pap. 6.00 (*0-318-12693-1*, F40075) Am Gas Assn.

Reserves of Crude Oil, Natural Gas Liquids, & Natural Gas in the United States & Canada As of Dec. 31, 1977. 32th ed. 265p. 1978. pap. 10.00 (*0-318-12695-8*, F40077) Am Gas Assn.

Reserves of Crude Oil, Natural Gas Liquids, & Natural Gas in the United States & Canada As of Dec. 31, 1978. 33th ed. 252p. 1979. pap. 13.00 (*0-318-12696-6*, F40078) Am Gas Assn.

Reserves of Crude Oil, Natural Gas Liquids, & Natural Gas in the United States & Canada As of December 31, 1976. 31th ed. 263p. 1977. pap. 10.00 (*0-318-12694-X*, F40076) Am Gas Assn.

Reserves of Crude Oil, Natural Gas Liquids, & Natural Gas in the United States & Canada As of December 31, 1979. 34th ed. 252p. 1980. pap. 15.00 (*0-318-12697-4*, F40079) Am Gas Assn.

***Reservist's Money Guide.** P. J. Budahn. LC 97-22437. 144p. 1997. pap. 11.95 (*0-8117-2917-6*) Stackpole.

Reservoir: Stories & Sketches. Janet Frame. 182p. 1993. pap. 10.95 (*0-8076-1305-3*) Braziller.

Reservoir Characterization. Larry W. Lake, Jr. & Herbert B. Carroll. 1986. text ed. 117.00 (*0-12-434065-2*) Acad Pr.

Reservoir Characterization III. Ed. by Bill Linville. LC 92-43076. 1056p. 1993. 125.95 (*0-87814-392-0*) PennWell Bks.

Reservoir Engineering Aspects of Fractured Formation. Louis H. Reiss. (Illus.). 120p. (C). 1980. 220.00 (*2-7108-0374-7*, Pub. by Edits Technip FR) St Mut.

Reservoir Engineering Aspects of Water Flooding. F. F. Craig, Jr. 134p. 1976. 21.00 (*0-89520-202-6*, 30403) Soc Petrol Engineers.

Reservoir Engineering Techniques Using FORTRAN. Mihir K. Sinha & Larry R. Padgett. LC 84-16106. (Illus.). 224p. 1984. text ed. 45.00 (*0-934634-50-5*) Intl Human Res.

Reservoir Eutrophication. Ed. by O. T. Lind. (Water Science & Technology Ser.: Vol. 28). 112p. 1993. pap. 114.25 (*0-08-042354-X*, Pergamon Pr) Elsevier.

***Reservoir Fisheries & Aquaculture Development for Resettlement in Indonesia.** Ed. by B. A. Costa-Pierce & O. Soemarwoto. (ICLARM Technical Reports: No. 23). 378p. 1990. per. write for info. (*971-10-2250-8*, Pub. by ICLARM PH) Intl Spec Bk.

Reservoir Fisheries Management: Strategies for the 80s. Ed. by G. E. Hall & M. J. Van Den Avyle. LC 84-62331. 327p. 1986. text ed. 19.00 (*0-913235-31-8*) Am Fisheries Soc.

Reservoir Flood Standards. 53p. 1975. 10.00 (*0-7277-0023-5*, Pub. by T Telford UK) Am Soc Civil Eng.

Reservoir Geophysics. Ed. by Robert E. Sheriff. LC 92-17973. (Investigations in Geophysics Ser.: No. 7). 408p. 1992. 85.00 (*1-56080-057-7*, 450) Soc Expl Geophys.

Reservoir Heterogeneity & Permeability Barriers in the Vicksburg S Reservoir, McAllen Ranch Gas Field. R. P. Langofrd et al. (Report of Investigations Ser.: No. RI 222). (Illus.). 64p. 1994. pap. 7.00 (*0-614-06201-2*) Bur Econ Geology.

***Reservoir Induced Earthquakes.** H. K. Gupta. (Developments in Geotechnical Engineering Ser.: Vol. 64). 364p. 1992. 201.25 (*0-444-88906-X*) Elsevier.

Reservoir Limnology: Ecological Perspectives. Kent W. Thornton et al. LC 89-24860. 256p. 1990. text ed. 79.95 (*0-471-88501-0*) Wiley.

Reservoir Management for Water Quality & THM Precursor Control. 412p. 1989. pap. 42.00 (*0-89867-489-1*, 90569) Am Water Wks Assn.

Reservoir Quality Assessment & Prediction in Clastic Rocks. M. D. Wilson et al. (Short Course Notes Ser.: No. 30). (Illus.). 460p. (Orig.). 1994. pap. 49.00 (*1-56576-007-7*) SEPM.

Reservoir Ravine. Hugh Hood. 238p. (C). 1979. 20.00 (*0-920802-50-8*, Pub. by ECW Press CN) Genl Dist Srvs.

Reservoir Ravine. Hugh Hood. 238p. 1985. pap. 4.95 (*0-7736-7100-5*) Genl Dist Srvs.

Reservoir Sedimentation. G. W. Annandale. (Developments in Water Science Ser.: No. 29). 222p. 1987. 128.00 (*0-444-42729-5*) Elsevier.

Reservoir Sedimentation Handbook: Design & Management of Dams, Reservoirs, & Watersheds for Sustainable Use. Gregory L. Morris & Fan Jiahua. (Illus.). 704p. 1997. text ed. 84.95 (*0-07-043302-X*) McGraw.

Reservoir Sedimentology. Ed. by Roderick W. Tillman & Koenraad J. Weber. (Special Publications: No. 40). 365p. 1987. 55.00 (*0-918985-69-2*) SEPM.

Reservoir Seismology: Geophysics in Nontechnical Language. Mamdouh R. Gadallah. LC 93-39214. 400p. 1994. 69.95 (*0-87814-411-0*) PennWell Bks.

Reservoir Sizing by Transition Probabilities. I. Zsuffa & A. Galai. LC 87-51100. 186p. 1987. Incl. 2 discs. 48.00 incl. disk (*0-918334-62-4*) WRP.

Reservoir Systems Operations. Ed. by G. H. Toebes & A. Sheppard. LC 81-70788. 601p. 1981. pap. 44.00 (*0-87262-288-6*) Am Soc Civil Eng.

Reservoir Trout Fishing with Tom Saville. Tom Saville. (Illus.). 256p. 1992. 34.95 (*0-85493-210-0*, Pub. by V Gollancz UK) Trafalgar.

Reservoirs in River Basin Development Proceedings. ICOLD Symposium on Reservoirs in River Basin Development Staff. Ed. by Leo Santbergen & Cees-Jan Van Westen. 525p. 1996. 80.00 (*90-5410-561-5*, Pub. by A A Balkema NE) Ashgate Pub Co.

Reset Your Appestat: A Successful Program for Achieving Permanent Weight Control Without Rigid Diets or Strenuous Exercise. Ben H. Douglas. LC 87-92249. (Illus.). 184p. (Orig.). 1988. 12.95 (*0-937552-21-6*, QRP Bks) Quail Ridge.

***Resetting the Clock: Five Anti-Aging Hormones That Improve & Extend Life.** Elmer Cranton. 1997. pap. text ed. 14.95 (*0-87131-823-7*) M Evans.

Resetting the Clock: 5 Anti-Aging Hormones That Are Revolutionizing the Quality & Length of Life. Elmer Cranton & William Fryer. LC 96-23750. 272p. 1996. 21.95 (*0-87131-801-6*) M Evans.

***Resetting the Margins: Russian Romantic Verse Tales & the Idealized Woman.** Luc J. Beaudoin. (Berkeley Insights in Linguistics & Semiotics Ser.: Vol. 23). 264p. (C). 1997. 47.95 (*0-8204-3048-X*) P Lang Pubng.

***Resettlement from Large Psychiatric Hospital to Small Community Residence: One Step to Freedom?** R. V. Forrester-Jones & Gordon Grant. (Avebury Studies in Care in the Community). 232p. 1997. text ed. 68.95 (*1-85972-363-2*, Pub. by Avebury Pub UK) Ashgate Pub Co.

***Resettlement of British Columbia: Essays on Colonialism & Geographical Change.** Cole Harris. (Illus.). 336p. 1996. 65.00 (*0-7748-0588-9*, Pub. by U BC Pr) U of Wash Pr.

***Resettlement of British Columbia: Essays on Colonialism & Geographical Change.** Cole Harris. 336p. 1997. pap. 24.95 (*0-7748-0589-7*, Pub. by U BC Pr) U of Wash Pr.

Resettlement of Indochinese Refugees in the United States: A Selective & Annotated Bibliography. Lawrence F. Ashmun. (Occasional Papers: No. 10). 207p. 1983. pap. 14.00 (*1-877979-10-4*) SE Asia.

Reshaping a Jealous Heart: How to Turn Dissatisfaction into Contentment. Alice Fryling. LC 93-42725. 144p. (Orig.). 1994. pap. 9.99 (*0-8308-1629-1*, 1629, Saltshaker Bk) InterVarsity.

***Reshaping America: Society & Institutions, 1945-1960.** Ed. by Robert H. Bremner & Gary W. Reichard. LC 82-3409. (U. S. A. 20-21: No. 1). 415p. 1982. reprint ed. pap. 118.30 (*0-608-04446-6*, 2064978) Bks Demand.

Reshaping Assessment Practices: Assessment in the Mathematical Sciences under Challenge. Max Stephens & John Izard. (C). 1990. 75.00 (*0-86431-127-3*, Pub. by Aust Council Educ Res AT) St Mut.

Reshaping Australian Education, 1960-1985. W. F. Connell. 1993. 150.00 (*0-86431-107-9*, Pub. by Aust Council Educ Res AT) St Mut.

Reshaping Central Government, Vol. I. Ed. by John Gretton & Anthony Harrison. (Reshaping the Public Sector Ser.). 224p. 1987. 34.95 (*0-946967-17-2*); pap. 21.95 (*0-946967-29-6*) Transaction Pubs.

Reshaping College Mathematics. Ed. by Lynn A. Steen. (MAA Notes Ser.). 135p. 1989. pap. 12.00 (*0-88385-062-1*, NTE-13) Math Assn.

Reshaping Curricula: Revitalization Programs at Three Land Grand Universities. Joyce P. Lunde. Ed. by Maurice Baker et al. 288p. (C). 1995. text ed. 34.95 (*1-882982-09-6*) Anker Pub.

Reshaping Dementia Care: Issues in Nursing Home Care. Ed. by Miriam K. Aronson & Donna C. Post. 176p. 1994. 35.00 (*0-8039-5159-0*); pap. 16.95 (*0-8039-5160-4*) Sage.

Reshaping Education in the 1990s: Perspectives on Primary Schooling. Rita Chawla-Duggan & Christopher J. Pole. LC 96-18406. 208p. 1996. 69.95 (*0-7507-0526-4*, Falmer Pr); pap. 25.95 (*0-7507-0527-2*, Falmer Pr) Taylor & Francis.

Reshaping Education in the 1990s: Perspectives on Secondary Schooling. Ed. by Christopher J. Pole & Rita Chawla-Duggan. 208p. 1996. 69.95 (*0-7507-0528-0*, Falmer Pr); pap. 24.95 (*0-7507-0529-9*, Falmer Pr) Taylor & Francis.

Reshaping Ethnic & Race Relations in Philadelphia: Immigrants in a Divided City. Judith Goode & Jo A. Schneider. LC 93-17959. 256p. 1994. pap. text ed. 19.95 (*1-56639-141-5*); lib. bdg. 59.95 (*1-56639-140-7*) Temple U Pr.

Reshaping Europe in the Twenty-First Century. Ed. by Patrick Robertson. LC 91-24191. 288p. 1992. text ed. 65.00 (*0-312-06889-1*) St Martin.

Reshaping European Defence. Ed. by Trevor Taylor. 128p. (C). 1994. pap. 14.95 (*0-905031-80-6*) Brookings.

Reshaping Government in Metropolitan Areas. LC 74-114417. 83p. 1970. pap. 1.50 (*0-87186-035-X*); lib. bdg. 2.50 (*0-87186-735-4*) Comm Econ Dev.

***Reshaping High School English.** Bruce Pirie. (Orig.). (YA). (gr. 8-12). 1997. 16.95 (*0-8141-5668-1*) NCTE.

***Reshaping Inpatient Care: Efficiency & Quality in New York City Hospitals.** Lynn Rogut. LC 96-45277. (Papers). 44p. 1996. 12.00 (*1-881277-29-1*) United Hosp Fund.

Reshaping IT for Business Flexibility: The IT Architecture as a Common Language for Dealing with Change. Mark Behrsin et al. LC 94-28194. (The IBM Ser.). 1994. write for info. (*0-07-707984-1*) McGraw.

Reshaping Labour: Organization, Work & Politics. John Holford. 288p. 1988. lib. bdg. 69.50 (*0-7099-4755-0*, Pub. by Croom Helm UK) Routledge Chapman & Hall.

Reshaping Life: Key Issues in Genetic Engineering. 2nd ed. R. Coppel & G. J. Nossal. (Illus.). (C). 1990. pap. 16.95 (*0-521-38969-0*) Cambridge U Pr.

Reshaping Life: Key Issues in Genetic Engineering. 2nd ed. G. J. Nossal & Ross L. Coppel. 192p. 1989. pap. 19.95 (*0-522-84381-6*, Pub. by Melbourne Univ Pr AT) Paul & Co Pubs.

Reshaping Local Government, Vol. III. Ed. by Michael Parkinson. (Reshaping the Public Sector Ser.). 256p. 1988. 34.95 (*0-946967-19-9*); pap. 21.95 (*0-946967-31-8*) Transaction Pubs.

Reshaping Local Worlds: Formal Education & Cultural Change in Rural Southeast Asia. Intro. by Charles F. Keyes. LC 89-52214. (Monograph Ser.: No. 36). 232p. 1991. 27.00 (*0-938692-43-7*); pap. 16.00 (*0-685-45591-2*) Yale U SE Asia.

Reshaping Ministry: Essays in Memory of Wesley Frensdorff. Ed. by Josephine Borgeson & Lynne Wilson. 286p. 1990. pap. 16.00 (*1-879145-00-6*) Jethro Pubns.

Reshaping Nationalized Industries, Vol. IV. Ed. by Christine Whitehead. (Reshaping the Public Sector Ser.). 303p. 1988. 34.95 (*0-946967-20-2*); pap. 21.95 (*0-946967-32-6*) Transaction Pubs.

Reshaping Nations to Cold War: Significant Events & the People Who Shaped Them, 8 vols. Joyce Moss & George Wilson. (Profiles in World History Ser.: Vol. 7). 223p. (J). 1995. 34.95 (*0-7876-0471-2*, 7 of 8, UXL) Gale.

Reshaping of America. D. Stanley Eitzen & Maxine Baca-Zinn. 416p. (C). 1988. pap. text ed. 27.60 (*0-13-774506-0*) P-H.

Reshaping of Everyday Life, 1790-1840. Jack Larkin. LC 87-46152. (Everyday Life in Early America). 384p. 1989. reprint ed. pap. 14.00 (*0-06-091606-0*, PL) HarpC.

Reshaping of French Democracy. Gordon Wright. LC 68-9654. 1970. reprint ed. 40.00 (*0-86527-167-4*) Fertig.

Reshaping of Plantation Society: The Natchez District, 1860-1880. Michael Wayne. LC 82-7817. xviii, 226p. 1983. text ed. 32.50 (*0-8071-1050-7*) La State U Pr.

Reshaping of Plantation Society: The Natchez District, 1860-1880. Michael Wayne. 240p. 1990. pap. text ed. 12.95 (*0-252-06127-6*) U of Ill Pr.

Reshaping of the National Labor Relations Board: National Labor Policy in Transition, 1937-1947. James A. Gross. (Illus.). 395p. reprint ed. pap. 112.60 (*0-8357-6581-4*, 2035976) Bks Demand.

Reshaping of Tradition: American Benedictine Women, 1852-1881. Ephrem Hollermann. 576p. 1993. pap. 19.95 (*0-9638734-0-7*) Sis Order St Benedict.

Reshaping Rural England: Social History 1850 - 1925. Alun Howkins. 272p. (C). 1991. pap. text ed. 22.95 (*0-04-445705-7*, Routledge NY) Routledge.

***Reshaping Rural England: Social History 1850-1925.** Alun Howkins. 272p. 1991. pap. text ed. 22.95 (*0-415-09066-0*) Routledge.

Reshaping Russian Architecture: Western Technology, Utopian Dreams. Ed. by William C. Brumfield. (Woodrow Wilson Center Ser.). (Illus.). 228p. (C). 1990. text ed. 80.00 (*0-521-39418-X*) Cambridge U Pr.

Reshaping School Mathematics: A Philosophy & Framework for Curriculum. 72p. 1990. pap. text ed. 7.95 (*0-309-04187-2*) Natl Acad Pr.

***Reshaping the City.** pap. write for info. (*0-340-60186-8*, Pub. by E Arnold UK) Routledge Chapman & Hall.

***Reshaping the City.** write for info. (*0-340-63214-3*, Pub. by E Arnold UK) Routledge Chapman & Hall.

Reshaping the City: A Critical Introduction to Urban Change. Mark Goodwin. 288p. 1996. text ed. 49.95 (*0-470-23549-7*, GE05); pap. text ed. 34.95 (*0-470-23548-9*) Halsted Pr.

Reshaping the Equity Markets: A Guide for the 1990s. Robert A. Schwartz. 1993. write for info. (*0-318-70154-5*) Irwin Prof Pubng.

Reshaping the Female Body: The Dilemma of Cosmetic Surgery. Kathy Davis. LC 94-19290. 224p. (C). (gr. 13). 1994. pap. 17.95 (*0-415-90632-6*, A7456, Routledge NY) Routledge.

Reshaping the German Right: Radical Nationalism & Political Change after Bismarck. Geoff Eley. 400p. 1990. pap. 26.95 (*0-472-08132-2*) U of Mich Pr.

Reshaping the German Right: Radical Nationalism & Political Change after Bismarck. Geoff Eley. LC 79-20711. 399p. reprint ed. pap. 113.80 (*0-8357-8304-9*, 2033716) Bks Demand.

Reshaping the Graduate Education of Scientists & Engineers. 1995. pap. text ed. 29.00 (*0-309-05285-8*) Natl Acad Sci.

Reshaping the Image of Appalachia. Ed. by Loyal Jones. (Illus.). (Orig.). 1986. pap. 7.50 (*0-938211-02-1*) Berea College Pr.

Reshaping the Media: Mass Communication in an Information Age. Everette E. Dennis. (Illus.). 300p. (C). 1989. text ed. 49.95 (*0-8039-3660-5*); pap. text ed. 24.00 (*0-8039-3661-3*) Sage.

Reshaping the National Health Service, Vol. II. Ed. by Robert Maxwell. (Reshaping the Public Sector Ser.). 256p. 1987. 34.95 (*0-946967-18-0*); pap. 21.95 (*0-946967-30-X*) Transaction Pubs.

Reshaping the Past: Jewish History & the Historians. Ed. by Jonathan Frankel. (Studies in Contemporary Jewry: Vol. X). 384p. 1994. 55.00 (*0-19-509355-0*) OUP.

Reshaping the Principalship: Insights from Transformational Reform Efforts. Ed. by Joseph Murphy & Karen S. Louis. LC 93-44470. 312p. 1994. 59.95 (*0-8039-6079-4*); pap. 27.95 (*0-8039-6080-8*) Corwin Pr.

Reshaping the Psychoanalytic Domain: The Work of Melanie Klein, W. R. D. Fairbairn, & D. W. Winnicott. Judith M. Hughes. 254p. (C). 1989. 42.50 (*0-520-06480-1*) U CA Pr.

Reshaping the Psychoanalytic Domain: The Work of Melanie Klein, W. R. D. Fairbairn & D. W. Winnicott. Judith M. Hughes. 256p. 1989. pap. 15.95 (*0-520-07188-3*) U CA Pr.

Reshaping the Self: Reflections on Renewal Through Therapy. Michael Eigen. 198p. 1995. 27.50 (*1-887841-00-8*, Psychosocial) Intl Univs Pr.

Reshaping the U. S. Left: Volume Three of the Year Left: Popular Struggles in the 1980's. Ed. by M. Davis & Michael Sprinkler. (Haymarket Ser.). 300p. 1988. 50.00 (*0-86091-193-4*, Pub. by Verso UK) Routledge Chapman & Hall.

Reshaping the U. S. Left: Volume Three of the Year Left: Popular Struggles in the 1980's. Ed. by M. Davis & Michael Sprinkler. (Haymarket Ser.). 300p. (C). 1988. pap. text ed. 20.00 (*0-86091-909-9*, Pub. by Vrso UK) Norton.

***Reshaping the World Trading System: A History of the Uruguay Round.** John Croome. (Illus.). 400p. (Orig.). (C). 1996. pap. 50.00 (*0-7881-3046-3*) DIANE Pub.

***Reshaping Western Security: The United States Faces a United Europe.** Richard N. Perle. Date not set. 22.95 (*0-8447-3790-9*) Am Enterprise.

Reshimas Mamarei Dach. Menachem M. Schneerson. 163p. (HEB.). reprint ed. 10.00 (*0-8266-5325-1*) Kehot Pubn Soc.

Reshimos Maamorei Dach. Shmuel Mattapash. 128p. 1981. reprint ed. 10.00 (*0-8266-5443-6*) Kehot Pubn Soc.

Reshimos Shiurim: Succah. Harold Reichman. Ed. by Y. Kuntz. (Notes on Jewish Talmud Ser.). 300p. (C). 1989. text ed. 10.00 (*0-685-29013-1*) Torah Study.

Reshimot, Vol. 1. Menachem M. Schneerson. 26p. (Orig.). (HEB.). 1995. 3.00 (*0-8266-5250-6*) Kehot Pubn Soc.

***Reshimot, Vol. 2.** Menachem M. Schneerson. 20p. (Orig.). (HEB.). 1994. pap. 3.00 (*0-8266-5251-4*) Kehot Pubn Soc.

Reshimot, Vol. 3. Menachem M. Schneerson. 49p. (Orig.). (HEB.). 1995. 5.00 (*0-8266-5252-2*) Kehot Pubn Soc.

Reshimot, Vol. 4. Menachem M. Schneerson. 27p. (Orig.). (HEB.). 1995. 3.00 (*0-8266-5253-0*) Kehot Pubn Soc.

Reshimot, Vol. 5. Menachem M. Schneerson. 38p. (Orig.). (HEB.). 1995. 3.00 (*0-8266-5254-9*) Kehot Pubn Soc.

Reshimot, Vol. 6. Menachem M. Schneerson. 31p. (Orig.). (HEB.). 1995. 3.00 (*0-8266-5155-0*) Kehot Pubn Soc.

Reshimot, Vol. 7. Menachem M. Schneerson. 85p. (Orig.). (HEB.). 1995. 5.00 (*0-8266-5156-9*) Kehot Pubn Soc.

Reshimot, Vol. 8. Menachem M. Schneerson. 25p. (Orig.). (HEB.). 1995. 3.00 (*0-8266-5157-7*) Kehot Pubn Soc.

Reshimot, Vol. 9. Menachem M. Schneerson. 20p. (Orig.). (HEB.). 1995. 2.00 (*0-8266-5158-5*) Kehot Pubn Soc.

Reshimot, Vol. 10. Menachem M. Schneerson. 45p. (Orig.). (HEB.). 1995. 3.00 (*0-8266-5159-3*) Kehot Pubn Soc.

Reshimot, Vol. 11. Menachem M. Schneerson. 22p. (Orig.). (HEB.). 1995. 2.00 (*0-8266-5160-7*) Kehot Pubn Soc.

Reshimot, Vol. 12. Menachem M. Schneerson. 54p. (Orig.). (HEB.). 1995. 3.00 (*0-8266-5161-5*) Kehot Pubn Soc.

Reshimot, Vol. 13. Menachem M. Schneerson. 46p. (Orig.). (HEB.). 1995. 3.00 (*0-8266-5162-3*) Kehot Pubn Soc.

***Reshimot, Vol. 14.** Menachem M. Schneerson. 30p. (Orig.). (HEB.). 1995. pap. 3.00 (*0-8266-5163-1*) Kehot Pubn Soc.

***Reshimot, Vol. 15.** Menachem M. Schneerson. 90p. (Orig.). (HEB.). 1995. pap. 5.00 (*0-8266-5164-X*) Kehot Pubn Soc.

Reshith Binah: A Hebrew Primer. Sidney M. Fish. 1976. pap. 3.95 (*0-8197-0035-5*) Bloch.

Resid & Heavy Oil Processing, Vol. 1. Jean-Francois Le Page et al. 188p. (C). 1992. 340.00 (*2-7108-0621-5*, Pub. by Edits Technip FR) St Mut.

Residence & Social Status: The Development of 17th-Century London. Gregg Carr. LC 91-9481. (Harvard Studies in Sociology: Outstanding Dissertations & Monographs Twenty-Two Distinguished Works from the Past Fifty Years). 248p. 1991. text ed. 20.00 (*0-8240-8423-3*) Garland.

Residence, Domicile & U. K. Taxation. 2nd ed. Neil D. Booth. 280p. 1998. pap. 135.00 (*0-406-12155-9*, U.K.) MICHIE.

An Asterisk (*) at the beginning of an entry indicates that the title is appearing in BIP for the first time.

Residence, Employment, & Mobility of Puerto Ricans in New York City. Terry J. Rosenberg. LC 73-77828. (University of Chicago, Department of Geography, Research Paper Ser.: No. 151). 244p. 1974. reprint ed. pap. 69.60 (*0-608-02279-9*, 2062920) Bks Demand.

Residence Hall Assistants in College: A Guide to Selection, Training, & Supervision. M. Lee Upcraft. LC 82-48075. (Higher & Adult Education Ser.). 298p. text ed. 38.95 (*0-87589-538-7*) Jossey-Bass.

Residence Life Programs & the First-Year Experience. 2nd ed. Ed. by William J. Zeller et al. (Freshman Year Experience Monograph: No. 5). (Orig.). 1996. pap. 30.00 (*1-889271-04-7*) Nat Res Ctr.

Residence of Twenty-One Years in the Sandwich Islands. Hiram Bingham. (Works of Hiram Bingham). 1989. reprint ed. lib. bdg. 79.00 (*0-7812-0305-8*) Rprt Serv.

Residence on Earth & Other Poems. Pablo Neruda. Tr. & Intro. by Donald D. Walsh. LC 72-93972. Orig. Title: Residencia en la Tierra. 1973. pap. 12.95 (*0-8112-0467-7*, NDP340) New Directions.

Residence on Earth & Other Poems: Bilingual Edition. Pablo Neruda. Tr. by Angel Flores. LC 76-75462. 205p. 1976. 40.00 (*0-87752-205-7*) Gordian.

Residences Des Souverains, 2 vols. in 1. Charles Percier & Pierre F. Fontaine. xi, 354p. 1973. reprint ed. write for info. (*3-487-04796-9*) G Olms Pubs.

Residencia de los Dioses. Rene De Goscinny & M. Uderzo. (Illus.). (SPA.). (J). 19.95 (*0-8288-4901-3*) Fr & Eur.

Residencia en la Tierra. 5th ed. Pablo Neruda. 160p. (SPA.). 1989. pap. 16.95 (*0-7859-4996-8*) Fr & Eur.

Residencia en la Tierra see Residence on Earth & Other Poems

Residency Director's Role in Specialty Certification. Ed. by John S. Lloyd. LC 85-70465. (Illus.). 255p. 1985. lib. bdg. 34.95 (*0-934277-05-2*) Am Bd Med Spec.

*__Residency Handbook.__ Lyle D. Victor. (Orig.). 15.95 (*0-614-19710-4*, OP045795WE) AMA.

Residency Handbook. Lyle D. Victor. LC 94-34495. (Clinical Handbook Ser.). (Illus.). 200p. (Orig.). (C). 1994. pap. text ed. 19.95 (*1-85070-583-6*) Prthnon Pub.

*__Resident Alien: The New York Diaries.__ Quentin Crisp. LC 97-1621. 232p. 1997. 21.95 (*1-55583-405-1*) Alyson Pubns.

Resident Aliens: Life in the Christian Colony. Stanley Hauerwas & William H. Willimon. LC 89-294. 176p. 1989. pap. 12.95 (*0-687-36159-1*) Abingdon.

Resident Aliens Live: Exercises for Christian Practice. Stanley Hauerwas & William H. Willimon. 1996. pap. write for info. (*0-614-97737-1*) Abingdon.

Resident Assessment Handbook: A Guide to Using the MDS. 2nd ed. Charlotte Eliopoulos. 137p. 1996. text ed. 39.95 (*1-882515-02-1*) Hlth Educ Netwk.

Resident Assistant: Case Studies & Exercises. Gregory S. Blimling. 256p. (C). 1994. per. 31.44 (*0-8403-9191-9*) Kendall-Hunt.

Resident Buildings Superintendent. Jack Rudman. (Career Examination Ser.: C-675). 1994. pap. 29.95 (*0-8373-0675-2*) Nat Learn.

Resident Commisioner Santiago Iglesias & His Times. Gonzalo F. Cordova. 1993. 28.50 (*0-8477-0899-3*) U of PR Pr.

Resident Engineer. 2nd ed. J. K. Ballantyne. 51p. 1986. 10.00 (*0-7277-0355-2*, Pub. by T Telford UK) Am Soc Civil Eng.

*__Resident Evil 2 - Totally Unauthorized.__ Brady Games, Staff. 112p. 1997. pap. 11.99 (*1-56686-685-5*) Macmillan.

Resident Guide to the Outpatient Care of Patients with HIV Disease. Scott M. Tenner. 78p. (Orig.). (C). pap. text ed. 6.00 (*1-883205-04-2*) Intl Med Pub.

Resident Orientals on the American Pacific Coast. Eliot G. Mears. Ed. by Roger Daniels. LC 78-54827. (Asian Experience in North America Ser.). 1979. reprint ed. lib. bdg. 40.95 (*0-405-11284-X*) Ayer.

Resident Peoples & National Parks: Social Dilemmas & Strategies in International Conservation. Ed. by Patrick C. West & Steven R. Brechin. LC 90-11300. (Illus.). 443p. 1991. 51.00 (*0-8165-1128-4*) U of Ariz Pr.

Resident Retention Revolution. Laurence C. Harmon & Kathleen M. McKenna-Harmon. LC 94-8456. (Illus.). 224p. 1994. text ed. 39.95 (*0-944298-97-4*, 740) Inst Real Estate.

Resident Rights QA Manual. W. H. Heaton. 400p. 1992. ring bd. 119.95 (*1-881057-00-3*) Heaton Pubns.

Residential. Rotovision S. A. Staff. 1996. pap. text ed. 35.00 (*0-8230-6492-1*) Watsn-Guptill.

Residential see Real Estate TaxPak (TM) USA

Residential & Extra-Familial Child & Youth Care: Recent International Developments. Ed. by Meir Gottesmann. 224p. 1994. 75.00 (*1-871177-73-1*, Pub. by Whiting & Birch UK); pap. 35.00 (*1-871177-74-X*, Pub. by Whiting & Birch UK) Paul & Co Pubs.

Residential & Inpatient Treatment of Children & Adolescents. Ed. by R. D. Lyman et al. (Illus.). 390p. 1989. 65.00 (*0-306-43161-0*, Plenum Pr) Plenum.

Residential & Light Construction from Architectural Graphic Standards. 8th ed. Charles G. Ramsey & Harold R. Sleeper. LC 90-29318. 467p. 1991. text ed. 125.00 (*0-471-54371-3*) Wiley.

Residential Apartheid: The American Legacy. Robert D. Bullard et al. (Urban Policies Ser.: Vol. 2). 250p. 1994. pap. text ed. 18.95 (*0-934934-43-6*) CAAS Pubns.

*__Residential Appraiser's Handbook.__ NAREA Staff. 158p. (Orig.). 1995. pap. 29.50 (*0-614-23692-4*) Todd Pub.

*__Residential Architecture.__ (Illus.). 230p. 1997. 85.00 (*84-921606-6-7*, Pub. by Links SP) Bks Nippan.

Residential Architecture of Henry Sprott Long & Associates. William R. Mitchell, Jr. (Illus.). 104p. 1992. 40.00 (*0-932958-13-3*) Golden Coast.

Residential Boilers & Heating Systems. Weinberger. (Heating, Ventilation & Air Conditioning Ser.). 1995. teacher ed., pap. 10.00 (*0-8273-5753-2*) Delmar.

*__Residential Broadband.__ 1997. 55.00 (*1-57870-020-5*) Macmillan Tech.

*__Residential Broadband.__ George Abe. 1997. 50.00 (*1-56205-813-4*) New Riders Pub.

*__Residential Building: Design & Construction.__ Jack H. Willenbrock et al. 700p. (C). 1997. pap. text ed. 90.00 (*0-13-375874-5*) P-H.

*__Residential Buildings: Snip 2.08.01-89.__ Russia's Minstroy Staff. (Snip Building Codes of Russia Ser.). (Illus.). iv, 33p. (Orig.). 1996. ring bd. 139.95 (*1-57937-013-6*) Snip Register.

Residential Care: The Provision of Quality Care in Residential & Educational Group Care Setting. Alan Davison. 432p. 1995. 76.95 (*1-85742-309-7*, Pub. by Arena UK) Ashgate Pub Co.

Residential Care: Your Role in the Health Care Team. Harvey K. Swenson & Jay S. Luxenberg. LC 95-48453. (Illus.). 350p. (Orig.). 1996. pap. text ed. 19.95 (*1-886657-06-8*) B Cracom Pub.

Residential Care for Elderly People: Using Research to Improve Practice. National Institute for Social Work Staff. (C). 1988. text ed. 45.00 (*0-902789-49-X*, Pub. by Natl Inst Soc Work) St Mut.

Residential Care for the Elderly: Critical Issues in Public Policy. Sharon A. Baggett. LC 89-2152. (Contributions to the Study of Aging Ser.: No. 13). 185p. 1989. text ed. 57.95 (*0-313-26759-6*, BRZ/, Greenwood Pr) Greenwood.

*__Residential Care Handbook: A Practical Guide to Caring & Staying in Business.__ 2nd ed. Ray Schwartz. LC 97-67326. 250p. 1997. ring bd. 30.00 (*0-89089-920-7*) Carolina Acad Pr.

Residential Care Services for the Elderly: Business Guide for Home-Based Eldercare. Doris K. Williams. LC 91-34626. (Journal of Housing for the Elderly: Vol. 8, No. 2). 106p. 1996. 39.95 (*1-56024-152-7*); pap. 14.95 (*0-7890-0066-0*) Haworth Pr.

Residential Child Care: An International Reader. Meir Gottesman. (Illus.). 300p. 1992. pap. 27.95 (*1-871177-17-0*, Pub. by Whiting & Birch UK) Paul & Co Pubs.

Residential Child Care: Team Development Programme. Joan Walton. 1994. 114.00 (*0-902789-90-2*, Pub. by Natl Inst Soc Work) St Mut.

Residential Child Care in America: Western Edition 93-94. 2nd ed. Ed. by Robert R. Cesena. 387p. 1993. per. 36.00 (*1-878817-01-9*) Services West Pub.

Residential Child Care in America, National Edition 1995-96: A Comprehensive Guide to Residential Treatment Options for Children in Need. Robert R. Cesena. 400p. (Orig.). 1994. pap. 44.00 (*1-878817-02-7*) Services West Pub.

Residential Circumstances of the Urban Poor in Developing Countries. United Nations Centre for Human Settlements (HABITAT) Staff. LC 81-1516. 320p. 1981. text ed. 55.00 (*0-275-90736-8*, C0736, Praeger Pubs) Greenwood.

Residential Cluster Development. Mark A. Kury & Susan C. Geniesse. LC 95-6742. (CPL Bibliographies Ser.: Vol. 315). 21p. 1994. pap. 10.00 (*0-86602-315-1*, Sage Prdcls Pr) Sage.

Residential Concrete. 2nd rev. ed. NAHB Research Center Staff. LC 93-36745. (Illus.). 96p. 1994. pap. 20.00 (*0-86718-389-6*) Home Builder.

Residential Condominium see Real Estate TaxPak (TM) USA

Residential Construction & Estimating: An Addition to the Complete Arizona Contractors' Study Guide. Donald Currell. (Illus.). 97p. (Orig.). 1991. text ed. 75.00 (*1-879020-04-1*) ACS Assocs Pub.

Residential Construction Costs, 1990. 9th ed. Thomas Brucie. Ed. by Paul Felber. (Illus.). 193p. (Orig.). 1990. pap. 49.95 (*0-931708-22-2*) Saylor.

Residential Construction Costs, 1992. Ed. by Stanley J. Strychaz. (Illus.). 240p. (Orig.). 1992. pap. 54.95 (*0-931708-28-1*) Saylor.

Residential Construction Costs 1994. Ed. by Stanley J. Strychaz. (Illus.). 250p. 1994. pap. 54.95 (*0-931708-38-9*) Saylor.

Residential Construction Costs, 1995. Ed. by Stanley J. Strychaz. (Illus.). 250p. 1995. pap. 54.95 (*0-931708-46-X*) Saylor.

*__Residential Construction Costs, 1997.__ 16th ed. 1997. 54.95 (*0-931708-61-3*) Saylor.

Residential Construction Symbol Library Users Manual: PowerDraw. Robert C. White. (Powercadd Ser.). (Illus.). 47p. 1988. 195.00 (*1-878250-03-5*) Eng Soft NC.

Residential Continuing Education. Cyril O. Houle. LC 71-171883. (Notes & Essays Ser.: No. 70). 1971. text ed. 3.00 (*0-87060-045-1*, NES 70) Syracuse U Cont Ed.

Residential Contracting: Hands-On Project Management for the Builder. August W. Domel & Luigina Petrucci. LC 94-19862. 1995. pap. text ed. 34.95 (*0-07-911916-6*) McGraw.

Residential Cooling, Pt. 1. James H. Doolin. 50p. 1982. pap. 15.00 (*0-914626-04-3*) Doolco Inc.

Residential Cooling, Pt. 2. James H. Doolin. 91p. 1982. pap. 15.00 (*0-914626-05-1*) Doolco Inc.

Residential Cost Handbook. Fred Harding & Richard Vishanoff. 340p. 1993. write for info. (*1-56842-000-5*) Marshall & Swift.

Residential Cost Handbook. Marshall & Swift. 1996. ring bd. write for info. (*1-56842-058-7*) Marshall & Swift.

*__Residential Cost Handbook.__ Marshall & Swift. 1997. ring bd. write for info. (*1-56842-062-5*) Marshall & Swift.

Residential Cost Handbook. Marshall & Swift Staff. 1995. ring bd. 94.95 (*1-56842-039-0*) Marshall & Swift.

Residential Crowding & Design. Ed. by J. R. Aiello & Abe Baum. LC 79-357. (Illus.). 270p. 1979. 49.50 (*0-306-40205-X*, Plenum Pr) Plenum.

Residential Demand & Development Potential in the San Francisco Bay Area. 28p. 1991. 25.00 (*0-317-05661-1*, P91001PLN) Assn Bay Area.

Residential Density Patterns in the San Francisco Bay Area: Historical, Recent & Planned. 37p. 1991. 25.00 (*0-317-05662-X*, P91002PLN) Assn Bay Area.

Residential Development & the Planning System: A Study of the Housing Land System at the Local Level. Yvonne Rydin. (Illus.). 70p. 1985. pap. 22.00 (*0-08-032742-7*, Pub. by PPL UK) Elsevier.

Residential Development Handbook. 2nd ed. Lloyd W. Bookout, Jr. et al. LC 90-70875. 1990. 64.95 (*0-87420-705-3*) Urban Land.

Residential Development Handbook. Urban Land Institute Staff. LC 77-930497. (Community Builders Handbook Ser.). (Illus.). 352p. reprint ed. pap. 100.40 (*0-8357-3191-X*, 2039462) Bks Demand.

Residential Displacement in the United States, 1970-1977. Sandra J. Newman & Michael S. Owen. LC 82-12101. (Institute for Social Research, Research Report Ser.). 106p. reprint ed. pap. 30.30 (*0-685-17866-8*, 2029469) Bks Demand.

Residential Duct Systems. Ronald K. Yingling et al. (Illus.). 65p. 1981. pap. 17.00 (*0-86718-000-5*) Home Builder.

Residential Education As an Option for At-Risk Youth. Ed. by Jerome Beker & Douglas Magnuson. LC 96-12415. 133p. 1996. text ed. 24.95 (*1-56024-818-1*) Haworth Pr.

Residential Electric Bills, Winter 94-95. 215p. 1995. 37.50 (*0-317-04709-4*) NARUC.

Residential Electrical Design. rev. ed. John E. Traister. (Illus.). 256p. 1994. pap. 22.50 (*0-934041-95-4*) Craftsman.

Residential Electrical Estimating. John E. Traister. (Illus.). 320p. (Orig.). 1995. pap. 29.00 (*1-57218-013-7*) Craftsman.

Residential Electrical Wiring. Rex Miller. (Illus.). 300p. 1981. teacher ed. 5.60 (*0-02-665630-2*); text ed. 15.96 (*0-02-665620-5*); student ed. 6.40 (*0-02-665640-X*) Glencoe.

Residential Energy: Cost Savings & Comfort for Existing Buildings. John T. Krigger. Ed. by Paul Richards & Donna Rose. (Illus.). 260p. (Orig.). (C). 1994. pap. text ed. 30.00 (*1-880120-07-0*) Saturn Rsce.

*__Residential Energy Audit Manual.__ 2nd ed. Ed. by Dale Schueman. (Illus.). 495p. 58.00 (*0-88173-134-X*, 0272) Fairmont Pr.

Residential Environmental Preferences & Choice: Some Preliminary Empirical Results Relevant to Urban Form. Mark D. Menchik. (Discussion Paper Ser.: No. 46). 1971. pap. 10.00 (*1-55869-108-1*) Regional Sci Res Inst.

Residential Environments & Households in the Randstad. Helen Kruythoff. (Housing & Urban Policy Studies: Vol. 8). (Illus.). 241p. (Orig.). (C). 1993. pap. 52.50 (*90-6275-927-0*, Pub. by Delft U Pr NE) Coronet Bks.

Residential Erosion & Sediment Control: Objectives, Principles & Design Considerations. 64p. 1978. pap. 11.00 (*0-87262-133-2*) Am Soc Civil Eng.

Residential Erosion & Sediment Control: Objectives, Principles & Design Considerations. LC 78-63632. (Illus.). 63p. 1978. pap. 16.95 (*0-87420-584-0*, E09) Urban Land.

Residential Estimator for Europe: L'Estimatif Residenttiel Bauschatzpreise Fur Eigenheime. Pascal Lorthioir. 172p. 1993. write for info. (*1-56842-006-4*); disk write for info. (*1-56842-010-2*) Marshall & Swift.

Residential Fiber Optic Networks: An Engineering & Economic Analysis. David P. Reed. LC 91-36112. (Artech House Telecommunications Library). (Illus.). 367p. 1992. reprint ed. pap. 104.60 (*0-7837-9698-6*, 2060428) Bks Demand.

Residential Fiber Optic Netwroks: An Engineering & Economic Analysis. David P. Reed. (Telecommunications Library). 376p. 1992. text ed. write for info. (*0-89006-600-0*) Artech Hse.

Residential Framing: A Homebuilder's Construction Guide. William P. Spence. (Illus.). 288p. 1993. pap. 19.95 (*0-8069-8594-1*) Sterling.

Residential Gas Bills, Winter 94-95. 208p. 1995. 37.50 (*0-317-04256-4*) NARUC.

Residential Gas Heating. James H. Doolin. 75p. 1982. pap. 15.00 (*0-914626-06-X*) Doolco Inc.

Residential Group Care in Community Context: Insights from the Israeli Experience. Ed. by Zvi Eisikovits & Jerome Beker. LC 85-7682. (Child & Youth Services Ser.: Vol. 7, Nos. 3 & 4). 167p. 1986. text ed. 39.95 (*0-86656-186-2*) Haworth Pr.

Residential Heat Pumps: Installation & Troubleshooting. S. E. Sutphin. LC 93-28350. 237p. 1993. 62.00 (*0-88173-141-2*) Fairmont Pr.

Residential Heat Pumps: Installation & Troubleshooting. Susan E. Sutphin. (Illus.). 224p. 1987. text ed. 44.00 (*0-13-774613-X*) P-H.

Residential Heating Operations & Troubleshooting. John E. Traister. (Illus.). 240p. (C). 1985. text ed. 37.00 (*0-13-774696-2*) P-H.

Residential Housing. Clois E. Kicklighter & Joan C. Kicklighter. (Illus.). 398p. 1992. 39.96 (*0-87006-926-8*) Goodheart.

Residential Indoor Air Quality & Energy Efficiency. Peter Du Pont & John Morrill. (Illus.). 267p. 1989. pap. 25.00 (*0-918249-08-2*) Am Coun Energy.

Residential, Industrial & Institutional Pest Control: Pesticide Application Compendium 2. Ed. by Patrick J. Marer. (Illus.). 232p. (Orig.). 1991. pap. 25.00 (*0-931876-93-1*, 3334) ANR Pubns CA.

*__Residential Interiors.__ PBC International. Date not set. pap. write for info. (*0-688-13021-6*) Morrow.

Residential Investment & Insurance Practices. Jack J. Ruff. 54p. (Orig.). 1984. pap. 4.00 (*1-55719-030-5*) U NE CPAR.

Residential Kitchen Design: A Research-Based Approach. Thomas Koontz & Carol V. Dagwell. LC 93-3827. 1994. text ed. 44.95 (*0-442-01419-8*) Van Nos Reinhold.

*__Residential Land Development Practices: A Textbook on Developing Land into Finished Lots.__ David E. Johnson. LC 96-42407. 1996. 32.00 (*0-7844-0202-7*) Am Soc Civil Eng.

Residential Landscape Architecture: Design Process for the Private Residence. Norman K. Booth & James E. Hiss. 416p. 1991. text ed. 88.00 (*0-13-775354-3*) P-H.

Residential Landscape Design. Bridwell & Ingles. (Agriculture Ser.). 1997. teacher ed., wbk. ed. 13.95 (*0-8273-6540-3*) Delmar.

Residential Landscape Design. 5th ed. Ingels & Bridwell. (Agriculture Ser.). 176p. 1997. wbk. ed. 14.95 (*0-8273-6539-X*) Delmar.

Residential Landscapes: Graphics, Planning & Design. Gregory M. Pierceall. (Illus.). 468p. (C). 1994. reprint ed. text ed. 53.95 (*0-88133-788-9*) Waveland Pr.

Residential Leases, Vol. 1. Stuart Bridge. 326p. 1994. pap. text ed. 50.00 (*1-85431-356-8*, Blckstone AT) Gaunt.

Residential Lending & Property Law. Robert Souster. 350p. 1990. pap. 125.00 (*0-85297-385-3*, Pub. by Inst Bankers UK) St Mut.

*__Residential Lighting, Vol. 2.__ Randall Whitehead. (Illus.). 192p. 1997. 39.99 (*1-56496-397-7*) Rockport Pubs.

Residential Lighting: Creating Dynamic Living Spaces. Randall Whitehead. 192p. 1993. pap. 39.99 (*1-56496-032-3*); pap. 39.99 (*1-56496-145-1*) Rockport Pubs.

Residential Lighting: Creating Dynamic Living Spaces. Randall Whitehead. 192p. 1993. pap. 29.95 (*1-55835-130-2*) AIA Press.

Residential Location & Spatial Behavior of the Elderly: A Canadian Example. Stephen M. Golant. LC 72-77307. (University of Chicago, Department of Geography, Research Paper Ser.: No. 143). 243p. 1972. reprint ed. pap. 69.30 (*0-608-02251-9*, 2062892) Bks Demand.

Residential Location & Urban Housing Markets. Ed. by Gregory K. Ingram. LC 77-10831. (National Bureau of Economic Research. Conference on Research in Income & Wealth. Studies in Income & Wealth: Vol. 43). 429p. reprint ed. pap. 122.30 (*0-317-41723-1*, 2052055) Bks Demand.

Residential Location Determinants of the Older Population. Gundars Rudzitis. LC 82-10966. (University of Chicago, Department of Geography, Research Paper Ser.: No. 202). 130p. 1982. reprint ed. pap. 37.10 (*0-608-02286-1*, 2062927) Bks Demand.

Residential Masonry Fireplace & Chimney Handbook. James E. Amrhein. (Illus.). 235p. (Orig.). 1995. pap. 19.50 (*0-940116-29-4*) Masonry Inst Am.

Residential Mobility & Public Policy. Ed. by William A. Clark & Eric G. Moore. LC 80-12624. (Urban Affairs Annual Reviews Ser.: No. 19). (Illus.). 320p. reprint ed. pap. 91.20 (*0-8357-8487-8*, 2034757) Bks Demand.

Residential Mobility Patterns in Dallas-Fort Worth & San Antonio: Determinants of Move, Racial Succession & Female-Headed Households. Ardeshir Anjomani et al. 111p. (Orig.). 1985. pap. 15.00 (*0-936440-59-7*) U TX SUPA.

Residential Mortgage Banking Basics. William H. Brewster. 47p. 1995. pap. 20.00 (*0-945359-95-0*) Mortgage Bankers.

Residential Mortgage Lending. 393p. 1989. 43.00 (*0-89982-341-6*, 050120); teacher ed. 20.00 (*0-685-63180-X*, 250120) Am Bankers.

Residential Mortgage Lending. 1988. 195.00 (*0-935988-29-7*) Todd Pub.

Residential Mortgage Lending. Marshall W. Dennis. (C). 1985. teacher ed. write for info. (*0-8359-6662-3*, Reston); text ed. 33.00 (*0-8359-6654-2*, Reston) P-H.

Residential Mortgage Lending. 3rd ed. 254p. 1991. pap. 39.95 (*0-912857-64-1*) Inst Finan Educ.

Residential Mortgage Lending. 4th ed. Marshall W. Dennis & Michael J. Robertson. LC 94-28986. 384p. 1994. text ed. 61.00 (*0-13-183815-6*) P-H.

Residential Mortgage Lending: From Application to Servicing. 4th ed. 1994. 42.95 (*0-912857-72-2*) Inst Finan Educ.

*__Residential Mortgage Lending: Servicing.__ 7th ed. Institute of Financial Education Staff. 1995. pap. 49.95 (*0-912857-75-7*) Inst Finan Educ.

Residential Mortgage Lending: State Regulation Manual, 6 vols. Andrea L. Negroni & Larry Platt. 1990. Mid-Atlantic, Northeast, Southeast, North Central, South Central & West. 275.00 (*0-685-74210-5*) Clark Boardman Callaghan.

*__Residential Mortgage Lending: Underwriting.__ 2nd rev. ed. 1997. pap. text ed. write for info. (*0-912857-79-X*) Inst Finan Educ.

Residential Mortgage Lending Documentation. 1995. 109.95 (*0-912857-67-6*) Inst Finan Educ.

Residential Mortgage Lending Origination. 1995. 109.95 (*0-912857-66-8*) Inst Finan Educ.

Residential Mortgage Loan Underwriting Casebook. Mortgage Bankers Assn. of America Staff. (Illus.). 200p. (Orig.). (C). 1989. student ed., pap. 100.00 (*0-945359-02-0*) Mortgage Bankers.

Residential Oil Burners. Herb Weinberger. 1993. teacher ed., pap. 14.95 (*0-8273-5014-7*) Delmar.

Residential Oil Burners. Herb Weinberger. 333p. 1993. text ed. 48.95 (*0-8273-5013-9*) Delmar.

Residential Patterns in American Cities, 1960. Philip H. Rees. LC 78-12169. (University of Chicago, Department of Geography, Research Paper Ser.: No. 189). 425p. 1979. reprint ed. pap. 121.20 (*0-608-02263-2*, 2062904) Bks Demand.

R

R

***Residential Printreading.** 2nd ed. L. P. Toenjes. (Illus.). 316p. 1996. pap. 29.96 (*0-8269-0439-4*) Am Technical.

Residential Program Counselor. (Career Examination Ser.: C-3662). pap. 27.95 (*0-8373-3662-7*) Nat Learn.

Residential Program Manager. (Career Examination Ser.: C-3663). pap. 29.95 (*0-8373-3663-5*) Nat Learn.

Residential Property Acquisition Handbook: Checklists for Making Sure You Don't Overlook Anything Important When You Buy a House, Condo, Apartment Building. John T. Reed. 250p. 1991. pap. 39.95 (*0-939224-22-4*) John T Reed.

Residential Property Management Handbook. Kent B. Banning. 1992. text ed. 49.50 (*0-07-003605-5*) McGraw.

Residential Property Tax Relief in Ontario. Richard M. Bird & N. E. Slack. LC 79-322196. (Ontario Economic Council Research Studies: No. 15). 198p. reprint ed. pap. 56.50 (*0-8357-4030-7*, 2036722) Bks Demand.

Residential Real Estate: A Comprehensive Guide of the Profession: Dade County Edition. Doris V. Carter. 700p. (Orig.). 1995. pap. 149.00 (*0-9649865-0-7*) Miami Daily.

Residential Real Estate: Its Economic Position As Shown by Values, Rents, Family Incomes, Financing, & Construction, Together with Estimates for All Real Estate. David L. Wickens. (General Ser.: No. 38). 328p. 1941. reprint ed. 85.30 (*0-87014-037-X*); reprint ed. mic. film 42.70 (*0-685-61217-1*) Natl Bur Econ Res.

Residential Real Estate Appraisal. 2nd rev. ed. Anthony Schools Corporation Staff. (Real Estate College-Level Ser.). (Illus.). 320p. (C). 1990. pap. text ed. 39.95 (*0-941833-30-5*) Anthony Schools.

***Residential Real Estate Appraisal.** 3rd ed. George Miller. LC 97-10358. 1997. pap. 59.33 (*0-13-460635-3*) P-H.

Residential Real Estate Appraisal: An Introduction to Real Estate Appraising. George H. Miller & Kenneth W. Gidbeau. (Illus.). 1980. text ed. 29.67 (*0-13-774521-4*) P-H.

Residential Real Estate Appraiser's Portable Handbook. Leland R. Hill & Phyllis M. Hill. 550p. 1990. 49.95 (*0-13-775321-7*) P-H.

Residential Real Estate Basics in Massachusetts. Ed. by Kathleen M. O'Donnell. 1995. ring bd. write for info. (*0-944490-93-X*) Mass CLE.

Residential Real Estate Contracts & Closings. (Real Estate Law & Practice Course Handbook Ser.). 232p. 1994. pap. 99.00 (*0-685-69755-X*, N4-4590) PLI.

Residential Real Estate Law & Practice in New Jersey. 3rd ed. Arthur S. Horn. 1000p. 1992. 150.00 (*0-685-65978-X*) NJ Inst CLE.

Residential Real Estate Practice. F. Peter Wigginton. LC 78-832. 1978. text ed. 18.95 (*0-672-97102-X*, Bobbs) Macmillan.

Residential Real Estate Transactions. annuals rev. ed. Caryl A. Yzenbaard. LC 91-73237. 1991. Revised annually with supplement. suppl. ed. 135.00 (*0-87632-891-5*) Clark Boardman Callaghan.

***Residential Remodeling & Universal Design: Making Homes More Comfortable & Accessible.** Carol Schaake et al. 122p. (Orig.). 1996. pap. text ed. 40.00 (*0-7881-3752-2*) DIANE Pub.

Residential Sales: How to List & Sell the Resale Home. Kelly. 312p. 1990. pap. 25.00 (*0-409-89140-1*) MICHIE.

Residential Sales Council Marketing Tools Yearbook, 1992. 1991. pap. 39.95 (*0-913652-77-6*, TR7610) Realtors Natl.

Residential School or Mainstreaming? A Guide for Parents of the Visually Impaired Child. Richard W. Webster. LC 89-83520. 116p. (Orig.). 1989. pap. text ed. 8.00 (*0-9622460-0-X*) Katan Pubns.

Residential Services & Developmental Disabilities in the U.S. A National Survey of Staff Compensation, Turnover & Related Issues. David Braddock & Dale Mitchell. (Orig.). (C). 1992. pap. 38.95 (*0-940898-28-4*) Am Assn Mental.

Residential Spaces of the World, Vol. 1. Images Publ. Group Staff. (Illus.). 256p. 1994. 59.95 (*1-875498-23-0*, Pub. by Images Publ AT) Bks Nippan.

***Residential Spaces of the World Vol. 2: A Pictorial Review.** (Illus.). 224p. 45.00 (*1-875498-46-X*) AIA Press.

Residential Special Education: The Current & Future Roles for Special Boarding Schools. Ted Cole. LC 86-8569. 176p. 1986. 90.00 (*0-335-15125-6*, Open Univ Pr); pap. 32.00 (*0-335-15124-8*, Open Univ Pr) Taylor & Francis.

Residential Sprinklers: A Primer. Ed. by Gary Courtney et al. (Illus.). 16p. 1986. pap. text ed. 6.00 (*0-685-59454-8*) IFSTA.

Residential Square Foot Building Costs 1994. Ed. by Stanley J. Strychaz. (Illus.). 200p. 1994. pap. 29.95 (*0-931708-41-9*) Saylor.

Residential Square Foot Building Costs, 1995. Ed. by Stanley J. Strychaz. (Illus.). 200p. 1995. pap. 29.95 (*0-931708-49-4*) Saylor.

***Residential Square Foot Building Costs, 1997.** 5th ed. 1997. 29.95 (*0-931708-64-8*) Saylor.

Residential Steel Faming Construction Guide, Vol. 1. E. N. Lorre. (Illus.). 234p. (Orig.). 1993. pap. 39.95 (*0-9651302-0-7*) Technical Pub.

Residential Steel Framing Handbook. Walls & Ceilings Magazine Editors. 1996. text ed. 49.95 (*0-07-057231-3*) McGraw.

Residential Storm Water Management: Objectives, Principles & Design Considerations. 64p. 1975. 8.00 (*0-87262-160-X*) Am Soc Civil Eng.

Residential Streets. 2nd ed. ASCE Staff et al. 90p. 1990. pap. text ed. 23.95 (*0-87420-700-2*, R07) Urban Land.

Residential Streets. 2nd enl. rev. ed. LC 89-49486. 104p. 1990. reprint ed. pap. text ed. 23.00 (*0-87262-746-2*) Am Soc Civil Eng.

Residential Tenancies. 2nd ed. Andrew Alston. 126p. 1993. pap. 63.00 (*0-409-78969-0*, NZ) MICHIE.

Residential Tenancies. 2nd ed. Richard Colbey. (Practice Notes Ser.). 104p. 1990. pap. write for info. (*0-85121-694-3*, Pub. by Cavendish UK) Gaunt.

***Residential Tenancies.** 3rd ed. Richard Colbey. (Cavendish Practice Notes Ser.). 1996. pap. 32.00 (*1-85941-293-9*, Pub. by Cavendish UK) Gaunt.

Residential Tenancies Law & Practice (N. S. W.) 2nd ed. Andrew G. Lang. xxiii, 328p. 1990. pap. 39.00 (*0-455-20798-4*, Pub. by Law Bk Co AT) Gaunt.

Residential Treatment: A Cooperative, Competency-Based Approach to Therapy & Program Design. Michael Durrant. 240p. (C). 1993. 27.95 (*0-393-70154-9*) Norton.

Residential Treatment: A Tapestry of Many Therapies. Ed. by Vera Fahlberg. LC 90-6790. 320p. (Orig.). 1990. pap. 24.95 (*0-944934-02-1*) Perspect Indiana.

Residential Treatment & the Sexually Abused Child. Thomas A. Plach. LC 93-7334. 170p. 1993. pap. 26.95 (*0-398-06324-9*) C C Thomas.

Residential Treatment & the Sexually Abused Child. Thomas A. Plach. LC 93-7334. 170p. (C). 1993. text ed. 38.95 (*0-398-05864-4*) C C Thomas.

Residential Treatment of Adolescents & Children: Issues, Principles & Techniques. John A. Stein. LC 94-26034. 1995. pap. text ed. 32.95 (*0-8304-1378-2*) Nelson-Hall.

Residential Treatment of Felon Drug Addicts: State Agents As Therapists. Sethard Fisher. (American University Studies: Anthropology & Science: Ser. XI, Vol. 13). 209p. (C). 1987. text ed. 32.90 (*0-8204-0502-7*) P Lang Pubng.

Residential Unit Supervisor. Jack Rudman. (Career Examination Ser.: C-3312). 1994. pap. 29.95 (*0-8373-3312-1*) Nat Learn.

Residential Water Problems: Prevention & Solutions. Alvin Sacks. Ed. by Dorris Tennyson. (Illus.). 96p. (Orig.). 1994. 20.00 (*0-86718-395-0*) Home Builder.

Residential Water Use Patterns. (Illus.). 124p. 1993. pap. 58.50 (*0-89867-686-X*, 90613) Am Water Wks Assn.

Residential Windows: A Guide to New Technology & Energy Performance. John Carmody et al. LC 96-28781. (Illus.). 192p. 1996. pap. 22.00 (*0-393-73004-2*, Norton Paperbks) Norton.

Residential Wiring. Thomas E. Proctor & Gary Rockis. (Illus.). 260p. 1994. 21.96 (*0-8269-1652-X*) Am Technical.

***Residential Wiring: Special Purpose Circuits.** (YA). (gr. 10 up). 1996. wbk. ed., pap. 7.00 (*0-8064-1286-0*, E46) Bergwall.

Residential Wiring to the 1996 NEC. 3rd rev. ed. Jeff Markell. (Illus.). 352p. (Orig.). 1995. pap. 24.50 (*1-57218-023-4*) Craftsman.

Residents: Freak Show, the Residents. Kyle Baker et al. (Illus.). 80p. (Orig.). 1992. pap. 9.95 (*1-878574-32-9*) Dark Horse Comics.

Residents: Freak Show, the Residents. limited ed. Kyle Baker et al. (Illus.). 80p. (Orig.). 1992. 79.95 (*1-56971-001-5*) Dark Horse Comics.

Residents: The Perils & Promise of Educating Young Doctors. David E. Duncan. 304p. 1996. 23.00 (*0-684-19709-X*) S&S Trade.

Residents As Teachers: A Guide to Educational Practice. Thomas L. Schwenk & Neal A. Whitman. 84p. (Orig.). (C). 1984. reprint ed. pap. text ed. 15.00 (*0-940193-03-5*) Univ UT Sch Med.

Residents Bad Day on the Midway: The Official Strategy Guide. Jeff Sengstack. 1995. pap. 19.95 (*0-7615-0348-X*) Prima Pub.

Resident's Guide for the Handling of Gynecological Tissue Specimens. Chhandra Bewtra. (Orig.). 1996. pap. text ed. 6.95 (*1-880906-15-5*) IDI Pubns.

Resident's Guide to Ambulatory Care. 2nd rev. ed. Michael B. Weinstock & Daniel M. Neides. (Illus.). 300p. Date not set. pap. 24.50 (*0-9646891-5-4*) Anadem Pubng.

Resident's Guide to Starting in Medical Practice. Ed. by C. James Holliman. LC 94-36733. (Illus.). 320p. 1994. 25.00 (*0-683-04125-8*) Williams & Wilkins.

Resident's Guide to Treatment of People with Chronic Mental Illness. Group for Advancement of Psychiatry, Committee on Psychiatry & the Community Staff. LC 92-48698. (GAP Reports: No. 136). 230p. 1993. text ed. 30.00 (*0-87318-204-9*, 7204) Am Psychiatric.

Resident's Handbook of Neonatology. Perlman & Kirpalani. 304p. (gr. 13). 1991. pap. text ed. 28.95 (*1-55664-114-1*) Mosby Yr Bk.

Resident's Neurology Book. Orrin Devinsky et al. LC 96-48408. (Illus.). 282p. (C). 1997. pap. text ed. 24.95 (*0-8036-0186-7*) Davis Co.

Residents of Farms & Rural Areas: A Statistical Profile. (Illus.). 64p. (Orig.). (C). 1994. pap. text ed. 25.00 (*0-7881-0241-9*) DIANE Pub.

Resident's Quick Reference to Internal Medicine. Berg. (Illus.). 210p. 1990. spiral bd. 19.95 (*0-397-51083-7*) Lppncott-Raven.

Resident's Recollections, Bk. 1. Lloyd E. Klos. LC 87-18918. (Illus.). 192p. (Orig.). 1987. pap. 9.95 (*0-932334-58-X*, NY76063, Empire State Bks) Hrt of the Lakes.

Resident's Recollections, Bk. 2. Lloyd E. Klos. LC 89-18918. (Illus.). 224p. (Orig.). 1988. pap. 9.95 (*1-55787-028-4*, NY76065, Empire State Bks) Hrt of the Lakes.

Resident's Recollections, Bk. 3. Lloyd E. Klos. LC 87-18918. (Illus.). 208p. (Orig.). 1989. pap. 9.95 (*1-55787-043-8*, NY76067, Empire State Bks) Hrt of the Lakes.

Resident's Recollections, Bk. 4. Lloyd E. Klos. LC 87-18918. (Illus.). 232p. (Orig.). 1990. pap. 9.95 (*1-55787-071-3*, NY76069, Empire State Bks) Hrt of the Lakes.

Resident's Recollections, Bk. 5. Lloyd E. Klos. LC 87-18918. (Illus.). 224p. (Orig.). 1991. pap. 9.95 (*1-55787-081-0*, NY76071, Empire State Bks) Hrt of the Lakes.

Resident's Recollections, Bk. 6. Lloyd E. Klos. LC 87-18918. (Illus.). 288p. (Orig.). 1993. pap. 9.95 (*1-55787-094-2*, NY76073, Empire State Bks) Hrt of the Lakes.

Residents' Rights: A Strategy for Action in Houses for Older People. Norman Baldwin et al. 215p. 1993. 59.95 (*1-85628-366-6*, Pub. by Avebury Pub UK) Ashgate Pub Co.

Residual & Unspecified Elements in Steel. Ed. by Albert S. Melilli & Edward G. Nisbett. LC 89-32224. (Special Technical Publication Ser.: No. STP 1042). (Illus.). 320p. 1989. text ed. 64.00 (*0-8031-1259-9*) ASTM.

Residual Lease Rates. Financial Publishing Co. Staff. 64p. 1974. pap. 8.00 (*0-87600-730-2*) Finan Pub.

Residual Lease Rates: Table III. Financial Publishing Co. Staff. 64p. 1980. pap. 8.00 (*0-87600-528-8*) Finan Pub.

Residual Lease Rates, Sixteen & a Quarter to Twenty-Five Percent. Ed. by Financial Publishing Co. Staff. (Illus.). 44p. 1973. pap. 8.00 (*0-87600-729-9*) Finan Pub.

Residual Lease Rates Two to Sixteen Percent. Ed. by Financial Publishing Co. Staff. 64p. 1973. pap. 8.00 (*0-87600-728-0*) Finan Pub.

Residual Markets - Automobile Insurance. Roger K. Kenney. 20p. 1993. pap. text ed. 15.00 (*1-887271-15-5*) Alliance Am Insurers.

Residual Markets - Guaranty Fund Assessments. Roger K. Kenney. 20p. 1994. pap. text ed. 15.00 (*1-887271-03-1*) Alliance Am Insurers.

***Residual Markets - Guaranty Fund Assessments.** rev. ed. Roger Kenney. (Illus.). 6p. 1996. pap. 15.00 (*1-887271-31-7*) Alliance Am Insurers.

Residual Markets - Property Insurance. Roger K. Kenney. 12p. 1993. pap. text ed. 15.00 (*1-887271-14-7*) Alliance Am Insurers.

***Residual Markets - Property Insurance.** rev. ed. Roger Kenney. (Illus.). 19p. 1996. pap. 15.00 (*1-887271-29-5*) Alliance Am Insurers.

Residual Markets - Workers Compensation. Roger K. Kenney. 9p. 1994. pap. text ed. 15.00 (*1-887271-04-X*) Alliance Am Insurers.

***Residual Markets - Workers Compensation.** rev. ed. Roger Kenney. (Illus.). 11p. 1996. pap. 15.00 (*1-887271-30-9*) Alliance Am Insurers.

Residual Markets Automobile Insurance. rev. ed. Roger K. Kenney. (Illus.). 20p. 1994. pap. text ed. 15.00 (*1-887271-21-X*) Alliance Am Insurers.

Residual Markets Guaranty Fund Assessments. rev. ed. Roger K. Kenney. (Illus.). 8p. 1994. pap. text ed. 15.00 (*1-887271-22-8*) Alliance Am Insurers.

Residual Markets-Property Insurance. rev. ed. Roger K. Kenney. (Illus.). 14p. (Orig.). 1995. pap. text ed. 15.00 (*1-887271-23-6*) Alliance Am Insurers.

Residual Markets Workers Compensation. rev. ed. Roger K. Kenney. (Illus.). 12p. (Orig.). 1995. pap. text ed. 15.00 (*1-887271-24-4*) Alliance Am Insurers.

Residual Stress. I. C. Noyan & J. B. Cohen. (Materials Research & Engineering Ser.). (Illus.). 300p. 1987. 105.95 (*0-387-96378-2*) Spr-Verlag.

Residual Stress Effects in Fatigue-- STP 776. Ed. by H. S. Reemsnyder & J. F. Throop. 241p. 1982. 26.50 (*0-8031-0711-0*, 04-776000-30) ASTM.

Residual Stress for Designers & Metallurgists: Proceedings of a Conference Held 9-10 April 1980, Chicago, IL. American Society for Metals Staff. Ed. by Larry J. Vande Walle. LC 81-4876. (Materials-Metalworking Technology Ser.). 255p. reprint ed. pap. 72.70 (*0-685-15489-0*, 2027033) Bks Demand.

Residual Stress in Design, Process, & Materials Selection: Proceedings of ASM's Conference on Residual Stress - in Design, Process, & Materials Selection: Cincinnati, Ohio, U. S. A., 27-29 April 1987. Conference on Residual Stress - in Design, Process, & Materials Selection Cincinnati, OH Staff. Ed. by William B. Young. LC 87-71686. (Illus.). 219p. pap. 62.50 (*0-7837-1871-3*, 2042072) Bks Demand.

Residual Stress in Rails, 2 vols. Ed. by Oscar Orringer. (Engineering Application of Fracture Mechanics Ser.). 492p. (C). 1992. lib. bdg. 282.50 (*0-7923-1651-7*) Kluwer Ac.

Residual Stresses: Papers Presented at the 1992 European Conference. Ed. by V. Hauk et al. (Illus.). 1040p. 1993. 200.00 (*3-88355-192-9*, Pub. by DGM Metallurgy Info GW) IR Pubns.

Residual Stresses - Measurement, Calculation, Evaluation: Proceedings of a 1990 Symposium. Ed. by V. Hauk et al. (Illus.). 252p. 1991. 73.00 (*3-88355-169-4*, Pub. by DGM Metallurgy Info GW) IR Pubns.

Residual Stresses & Their Effect. (Illus.). 56p. 1981. pap. 79.00 (*0-85300-141-3*, Pub. by Woodhead Pubng UK) Am Educ Systs.

Residual Stresses in CBN & Corundum Ground Gear Tooth Flanks As the Determining Factor in Abrasive Wheel Selections. Peter Moeckli. (Fall Technical Meeting Papers). (Illus.). 14p. 1986. pap. text ed., pap. 30.00 incl. audio compact disk (*1-55589-475-5*, 86FTM11) AGMA.

Residual Stresses in Composites: Measurement, Modeling & Effects on Thermo-Mechanical Behavior. Ed. by E. V. Barrera & I. Dutta. (Illus.). 330p. 1993. 20.00 (*0-87339-216-7*, 2167) Minerals Metals.

***Residual Stresses in Design Fabrication Assessment & Repair.** Ed. by R. W. Warke. 201p. 1996. pap. text ed. 100.00 (*0-7918-1774-1*, N6280) ASME Pr.

***Residual Years: Poems 1934-1948.** William Everson. 375p. 1997. pap. 17.50 (*1-57423-055-7*) Black Sparrow.

***Residual Years: Poems 1934-1948.** William Everson. 375p. 1997. 27.50 (*1-57423-056-5*) Black Sparrow.

***Residual Years: Poems 1934-1948.** limited ed. William Everson. 375p. 1997. 35.00 (*1-57423-057-3*) Black Sparrow.

Residuals & Influence in Regression. R. D. Cook & S. Weisberg. (Monographs on Statistics & Applied Probability). 200p. 1982. 42.50 (*0-412-24280-X*, NO. 6718) Chapman & Hall.

Residuals Management in Industry: A Case Study of Petroleum Refining. Clifford S. Russell. LC 72-12367. (Resources for the Future Ser.). (Illus.). 208p. 1973. 18.00 (*0-8018-1497-9*) Johns Hopkins.

Residuals Management in Industry: A Case Study of Petroleum Refining. Clifford S. Russell. LC 72-12367. (Illus.). 211p. reprint ed. pap. 60.20 (*0-685-23707-9*, 2032163) Bks Demand.

Residuation Theory. T. S. Blyth & M. F. Janowitz. LC 77-142177. 380p. (C). 1972. 170.00 (*0-08-016408-0*, Pub. by Pergamon Repr UK) Franklin.

Residue Currents & Bezout Identities. Carlos A. Berenstein et al. LC 93-30493. 172p. 1993. 49.50 (*0-8176-2945-9*) Birkhauser.

Residue Number System Arithmetic: Modern Applications to Digital Signal Processing. M. A. Soderstrand et al. LC 86-10516. 430p. 1986. 69.00 (*0-87942-204-1*, PC01982) Inst Electrical.

Residue Reviews. Ed. by Francis A. Gunther & J. Davies Gunther. (Illus.). 166p. 1982. 84.95 (*0-387-90750-5*) Spr-Verlag.

Residue Reviews, Vol. 51. Ed. by Francis A. Gunther. viii, 203p. 1974. 116.95 (*0-387-90079-9*) Spr-Verlag.

Residue Reviews, Vol. 58. LC 62-18595. 180p. 1975. 95.95 (*0-387-90135-3*) Spr-Verlag.

Residue Reviews, Vol. 62. G. E. Carmen et al. LC 62-18595. (Illus.). 176p. 1976. 91.95 (*0-387-90158-2*) Spr-Verlag.

Residue Reviews, Vol. 71. (Illus.). 1979. 89.95 (*0-387-90389-5*) Spr-Verlag.

Residue Reviews, Vol. 72. Ed. by Francis A. Gunther & J. Davies Gunther. (Illus.). 1979. 75.95 (*0-387-90418-2*) Spr-Verlag.

Residue Reviews, Vol. 73. 1980. 77.95 (*0-387-90470-0*) Spr-Verlag.

Residue Reviews, Vol. 74. (Illus.). 150p. 1980. 95.95 (*0-387-90503-0*) Spr-Verlag.

Residue Reviews, Vol. 75. Ed. by Francis A. Gunther. (Illus.). 189p. 1980. 103.95 (*0-387-90534-0*) Spr-Verlag.

Residue Reviews, Vol. 76. Ed. by Francis A. Gunther. (Illus.). 218p. 1980. 103.95 (*0-387-90535-9*) Spr-Verlag.

Residue Reviews, Vol. 78. (Illus.). 143p. 1981. 89.95 (*0-387-90566-9*) Spr-Verlag.

Residue Reviews, Vol. 79. Ed. by Francis A. Gunther. (Illus.). 280p. 1981. 89.95 (*0-387-90539-1*) Spr-Verlag.

Residue Reviews, Vol. 82. Ed. by Francis A. Gunther. (Illus.). 240p. 1982. 89.95 (*0-387-90678-9*) Spr-Verlag.

Residue Reviews, Vol. 83. Ed. by Francis A. Gunther & J. Davies Gunther. (Illus.). 174p. 1982. 77.95 (*0-387-90679-7*) Spr-Verlag.

Residue Reviews, Vol. 85. Ed. by Francis A. Gunther. (Illus.). 307p. 1982. 124.95 (*0-387-90751-3*) Spr-Verlag.

Residue Reviews, Vol. 86. Ed. by Francis A. Gunther. (Illus.). 133p. 1983. 72.95 (*0-387-90778-5*) Spr-Verlag.

Residue Reviews, Vol. 87. Ed. by Francis A. Gunther. (Illus.). 152p. 1983. 64.95 (*0-387-90781-5*) Spr-Verlag.

Residue Reviews, Vol. 94. (Illus.). 160p. 1985. 77.95 (*0-387-96130-5*) Spr-Verlag.

Residue Reviews, Vol. 95. (Illus.). ix, 130p. 1985. 54.00 (*0-387-96165-8*) Spr-Verlag.

Residue Reviews, Vol. 96. (Illus.). 140p. 1985. 79.95 (*0-387-96194-1*) Spr-Verlag.

Residue Reviews, Vol. 97. Ed. by Francis A. Gunther. (Illus.). xv, 151p. 1986. 89.95 (*0-387-96294-8*) Spr-Verlag.

Residue Reviews: Residues of Pesticides & Other Contaminants in the Total Environment, Vol. 73. Ed. by Francis A. Gunther & J. Davies Gunther. (Illus.). 140p. 1980. 35.00 (*3-540-90470-0*) Spr-Verlag.

Residues & Effluents: Processing & Environmental Considerations: Proceedings of an International Symposium Sponsored by Extraction & Process Division of TMS & the Iron & Steel Society at the 1992 TMS Annual Meeting, San Diego, California, U. S. A., March 1-5, 1992. Minerals, Metals & Materials Society Staff. Ed. by Ramana G. Reddy et al. LC 91-51084. (Illus.). 915p. 1991. reprint ed. pap. 180.00 (*0-7837-9136-4*, 2049936) Bks Demand.

Residues & Traces of Differential Forms Via Hochschild Homology. Joseph Lipman. LC 86-28698. (Contemporary Mathematics Ser.: Vol. 61). 95p. 1987. pap. 22.00 (*0-8218-5070-9*, CONM/61) Am Math.

Residues of Justice: Literature, Law, Philosophy. Wai C. Dimock. LC 95-39867. 291p. (C). 1996. 48.00 (*0-520-20243-0*) U CA Pr.

***Residues of Justice: Literature, Law, Philosophy.** Wai Chee Dimock. 1997. pap. text ed. 17.95 (*0-520-20244-9*) U CA Pr.

Residues of Pesticides & Other Contaminants in the Total Environment. Ed. by Francis A. Gunther. (Residue Reviews Ser.: Vol. 91). (Illus.). 160p. 1984. 89.95 (*0-387-90998-2*) Spr-Verlag.

Residues of Pesticides & Other Contaminants in the Total Environment. Ed. by Francis A. Gunther. (Residue Reviews Ser.: Vol. 92). (Illus.). 210p. 1984. 80.95 (*0-387-96018-X*) Spr-Verlag.

Residues of Pesticides & Other Contaminants in the Total Environment. Ed. by Francis A. Gunther. (Residue Reviews Ser.: Vol. 93). (Illus.). 255p. 1984. 80.95 (*0-387-96019-8*) Spr-Verlag.

Residues of Pesticides & Other Contaminants in the Total Environment. A. A. Jensen. (Residue Reviews Ser.: Vol. 89). 155p. 1983. 84.95 (*0-387-90884-6*) Spr-Verlag.

An Asterisk (*) at the beginning of an entry indicates that the title is appearing in BIP for the first time.

Residues of Pesticides & Other Contaminants in the Total Environment. M. Spindler et al. (Residue Reviews Ser.: Vol. 90). 145p. 1983. 89.95 (*0-387-90905-2*) Spr-Verlag.

***Residues of Some Veterinary Drugs in Animals & Foods: Albendazole, Dimetridazole, Diminazene Aceturate, Ipronidazole, Isometamidium Chloride, Metronidazole, Ronidazole, Sulfadimidine, Sulfathiazole, Trenbolone Acetate, 34th Meeting of JECFA, Geneva, 1989.** 112p. 1990. 14.00 (*92-5-102933-4*, F0293, Pub. by FAO IT) Bernan Associates.

***Residues of Some Veterinary Drugs in Animals & Foods: Azaperone, Carazolol, Febantel, Fenbendazole, Oxfendazole, Propionylpromazine, Spiramycin, Tylosin.** (Monographs, 38th Meeting of JECFA, Rome, 1991). 148p. 1991. 17.00 (*92-5-103096-0*, Pub. by FAO IT) Bernan Associates.

***Residues of Some Veterinary Drugs in Animals & Foods: Benzyl Penicillin, Carbadox, Closantel, Ivermectin, Levamisole, Olaquindox, Oxytetracycline, 36th Meeting of JECFA, Rome, 1990.** 129p. 1991. 17.00 (*92-5-103061-8*, F0618, Pub. by FAO IT) Bernan Associates.

***Residues of Some Veterinary Drugs in Animals & Foods: Chloramphenicol, Dexamethasone, Diminazene, Levamisole, Olaquindox, Spectinomycin, 42nd Meeting of JECFA, Rome, 1994.** 97p. 1994. 12.00 (*92-5-103553-9*, Pub. by FAO IT) Bernan Associates.

***Residues of Some Veterinary Drugs in Animals & Foods - Food & Nut Paper No. 41: Abamectin, Ceftiofur Sodium, Chlorte Tracycline, Diclazuril Doramectin, Vol. 8.** 130p. 1996. pap. 19.00 (*92-5-103839-2*, F38392, Pub. by FAO IT) Bernan Associates.

***Resilience: How to Bounce Back When the Going Gets Tough.** Frederic Flach. LC 97-7161. Orig. Title: Resilience: Discovering a New Strength at Times of Stress. 288p. 1997. reprint ed. pap. 14.95 (*1-886330-95-6*) Hatherleigh.

***Resilience: Rebounding When Life's Upsets Knock You Down.** H. Norman Wright. LC 97-3296. 224p. 1997. 16.99 (*0-89283-939-2*, Vine Bks) Servant.

Resilience & Growth Through Sustained Adjustment: The Moroccan Experience. Saleh M. Nsouli et al. LC 94-44348. (Occasional Paper Ser.: No. 117). 130p. 1995. pap. 15.00 (*1-55775-422-5*) Intl Monetary.

Resilience: Discovering a New Strength at Times of Stress see Resilience: How to Bounce Back When the Going Gets Tough

Resilience Enhancement for the Resident Physician. Edward Messner. 163p. 1993. pap. 7.95 (*0-929240-57-X*) EMIS.

Resilience of Christianity in the Modern World. Joseph B. Tamney. LC 90-22086. (SUNY Series in Religion, Culture, & Society). 178p. (C). 1991. pap. text ed. 21.95 (*0-7914-0822-1*) State U NY Pr.

Resilience of Christianity in the Modern World. Joseph B. Tamney. LC 90-22086. (SUNY Series in Religion, Culture, & Society). 178p. (C). 1992. text ed. 64.50 (*0-7914-0821-3*) State U NY Pr.

Resiliency: How to Bounce Back Faster, Stronger, Smarter. Tessa A. Warshaw & Dee Barlow. 224p. 1995. 21.95 (*1-57101-021-1*) MasterMedia Pub.

***Resiliency: How to Bounce Back Faster, Stronger, Smarter.** Tessa A. Warshaw & Dee Barlow. 224p. 1995. pap. 13.95 (*1-57101-043-2*) MasterMedia Pub.

Resiliency in Ethnic Minority Families: African American Families, Vol. 2. Ed. by Hamilton I. McCubbin et al. LC 94-61816. 350p. (Orig.). (C). 1995. pap. text ed. 30.00 (*0-9639334-3-4*) U of Wis CEFM.

Resiliency in Ethnic Minority Families: Native & Immigrant American Families, Vol. 1. Ed. by Hamilton I. McCubbin et al. 453p. (Orig.). 1994. pap. text ed. 30.00 (*0-9639334-2-6*) U of Wis CEFM.

Resiliency in Schools: Making It Happen for Students & Educators. Nan Henderson & Mike M. Milstein. LC 95-53339. 152p. 1996. 42.95 (*0-8039-6351-3*); pap. 18.95 (*0-8039-6352-1*) Corwin Pr.

Resilient Adults: Overcoming a Cruel Past. Gina O. Higgins. LC 94-7283. (Psychology Ser.). 399p. 1994. pap. 27.50 (*1-55542-673-5*) Jossey-Bass.

Resilient Adults: Overcoming a Cruel Past. Gina O. Higgins. (Psychology Ser.). 399p. 1996. reprint ed. pap. 19.95 (*0-7879-0253-5*) Jossey-Bass.

Resilient Chld: Preparing Today's Youth for Tomorrow's World. J. M. Joseph. (Illus.). 334p. 1994. 25.95 (*0-306-44646-4*, Plenum Insight) Plenum.

Resilient Europe: A Study of the Years 1870-2000. Peter Calvocoressi. 240p. (C). 1991. pap. text ed. 28.50 (*0-582-07854-7*, 78918) Longman.

Resilient Moduli of Soils: Laboratory Conditions. Ed. by David J. Elton & Richard P. Ray. LC 89-39535. 78p. 1989. pap. text ed. 14.00 (*0-87262-734-9*, 734) Am Soc Civil Eng.

Resilient Pioneers: A History of the Elastic Rail Spike Company. John Milligan. (Illus.). 1977. 24.95 (*0-8464-0791-4*) Beekman Pubs.

Resilient Self: How Survivors of Troubled Families Rise above Adversity. Stephen J. Wolin & Sybil Wolin. LC 92-50493. 1993. 23.00 (*0-394-58357-4*, Villard Bks) Random.

Resin Microscopy & On-Section Immunocytochemistry. G. R. Newman & J. A. Hobot. LC 93-14253. (Laboratory Ser.). 221p. 1993. 60.95 (*0-387-56429-2*) Spr-Verlag.

***Resin Transfer Molding For Aerospace Applications.** Kruckenburg. (Illus.). 528p. 1997. text ed. write for info. (*0-412-73150-9*, Chap & Hall NY) Chapman & Hall.

***Resin Transfer Moulding.** K. Potter. (Illus.). 208p. 1997. 64.95 (*0-412-72570-3*, Chap & Hall NY) Chapman & Hall.

Resins. Ed. by Michael Ash & Irene Ash. (What Every Chemical Technologist Wants to Know About...Ser.: Vol. V). 392p. 1990. 75.00 (*0-8206-0331-7*) Chem Pub.

Resins for Aerospace. Ed. by Clayton A. May. LC 80-15342. (ACS Symposium Ser.: No. 132). 1980. 54.95 (*0-8412-0567-1*) Am Chemical.

***Resins for Aerospace.** Ed. by Clayton A. May. LC 80-15342. (ACS Symposium Ser.: No. 132). (Illus.). 511p. 1980. reprint ed. pap. 145.70 (*0-608-03234-4*, 2063753) Bks Demand.

***Resins for Coatings: Chemistry, Properties & Applications.** Dieter Stoye et al. LC 96-36116. 458p. 1996. 169.50 (*1-56990-209-7*) Hanser-Gardner.

Resins for Surface Coatings. Peter K. Oldring & G. Hayward. (C). 1989. 305.00 (*0-685-36806-8*, Pub. by Fuel Metallurgical Jrnl UK); 900.00 (*0-86108-200-1*, Pub. by Fuel Metallurgical Jrnl UK) St Mut.

Resins for Surface Coatings, Vol. I. 2nd ed. Peter K. Oldring & G. Hayward. (Illus.). 230p. 1989. text ed. 99.00 (*0-947798-04-8*, Pub. by SITA Tech UK) Scholium Intl.

Resins for Surface Coatings, Vol. II. 2nd ed. C. J. Standen. (Illus.). 256p. 1987. text ed. 120.00 (*0-947798-05-6*, Pub. by SITA Tech UK) Scholium Intl.

Resins for Surface Coatings, Vol. III. 2nd ed. M. J. Husbands et al. (Illus.). 220p. 1987. text ed. 120.00 (*0-947798-06-4*, Pub. by SITA Tech UK) Scholium Intl.

Respiratory Care Calculations. David W. Chang. LC 93-38719. 276p. 1994. pap. 20.95 (*0-8273-6148-3*) Delmar.

***Resist! Essays Against a Homophobic Culture.** Ed. by Mona Oikawa et al. 242p. pap. 13.95 (*0-88961-197-1*, Pub. by Wmns Pr CN) LPC InBook.

***Resist & Masking Techniques.** Peter Beard. (Illus.). 128p. 1997. pap. 22.50 (*0-8122-1611-3*) U of Pa Pr.

Resist Me if You Can. Janis R. Hudson. 1996. mass mkt. 3.99 (*0-373-24037-6*, 1-24037-3) Silhouette.

Resist Much, Obey Little: Remembering Ed Abbey. Ed. by James R. Hepworth & Gregory McNamee. 272p. 1996. pap. 14.00 (*0-87156-879-9*) Sierra.

Resist Not Evil. Clarence Darrow. 1994. lib. bdg. 250.95 (*0-8490-8839-9*) Gordon Pr.

Resist Not Evil. 3rd rev. ed. Clarence Darrow. LC 94-76998. 188p. 1994. pap. 11.95 (*1-55950-115-4*, 99099) Loompanics.

Resist Not Evil. Clarence S. Darrow. LC 78-172567. (Peace Movement in America Ser.). 179p. 1972. reprint ed. lib. bdg. 22.95 (*0-89198-065-2*) Patterson Smith.

Resist Not Evil: With Intro. & Index Added. Clarence Darrow. LC 78-172567. (Criminology, Law Enforcement, & Social Problems Ser.: No. 148). 200p. 1972. reprint ed. pap. 10.00 (*0-87585-903-8*); reprint ed. lib. bdg. 20.00 (*0-87585-148-7*) Patterson Smith.

Resist the Devil: A Pastoral Guide to Deliverance Prayer. Charles W. Harris. LC 88-83043. viii, 118p. (Orig.). 1989. pap. 6.95 (*0-937779-07-5*) Greenlawn Pr.

Resistable Appeal of Fortress Europe. Martin Wolf. 100p. (Orig.). 1994. pap. 10.00 (*0-8447-3871-9*, AEI Pr) Am Enterprise.

***Resistance.** Deborah Bachrach. (Holocaust Library). (Illus.). (J). (gr. 4-12). 1997. lib. bdg. 17.96 (*1-56006-092-1*) Lucent Bks.

Resistance. Anita Shreve. LC 94-39269. 222p. 1995. 21.95 (*0-316-78999-2*) Little.

***Resistance.** Anita Shreve. 1997. pap. 12.95 (*0-316-78984-4*) Little.

Resistance. large type ed. Anita Shreve. 398p. 1995. 24.95 (*0-7862-0506-7*) Thorndike Pr.

Resistance: Moving Beyond the Barriers to Change. Price Pritchett. 34p. 1996. pap. 5.95 (*0-944002-18-8*) Pritchett Assocs.

Resistance: Psychodynamic & Behavioral Approaches. Ed. by Paul L. Wachtel. LC 81-23494. 288p. 1982. 42.50 (*0-306-40769-8*, Plenum Pr) Plenum.

Resistance: Selected Poems. Victor Serge. Tr. by James Brook from FRE. 112p. (Orig.). 1989. pap. 5.95 (*0-87286-225-9*) City Lights.

Resistance: Ten Years of Pop Culture That Shook the World. Armond White. 300p. 1995. 26.95 (*0-87951-586-4*) Overlook Pr.

Resistance Against the Third Reich 1933-1990. Ed. by Michael Geyer & John W. Boyer. 368p. (C). 1994. pap. 15.95 (*0-226-06959-1*); lib. bdg. 35.95 (*0-226-06958-3*) U Ch Pr.

***Resistance & Change: The Struggle of Guyanese Workers (1964-1994) with Emphasis on the Sugar Industry.** Nanda K. Gopaul. 275p. (Orig.). Date not set. pap. text ed. write for info. (*0-9656445-0-2*) Inside News.

Resistance & Conformity in the Third Reich. Martyn Housden. LC 96-18379. (Sources in History Ser.). 240p. (C). 1997. pap. 18.95 (*0-415-12134-5*); text ed. 65.00 (*0-415-12133-7*) Routledge.

***Resistance & Contradiction: Miskitu Indians & the Nicaraguan State, 1894-1987.** Charles R. Hale. 1996. pap. 17.95 (*0-8047-2800-3*) Stanford U Pr.

Resistance & Contradiction: Miskitu Indians & the Nicaraguan State, 1894-1988. Charles R. Hale. LC 93-17944. xviii, 296p. 1994. 45.00 (*0-8047-2255-2*) Stanford U Pr.

Resistance & Integration: Peronism & the Argentine Working Class, 1946-1976. Daniel James. (Cambridge Latin American Studies: No. 64). 300p. 1988. text ed. 80.00 (*0-521-34635-5*) Cambridge U Pr.

Resistance & Integration: Peronism & the Argentine Working Class, 1946-1976. Daniel James. (Cambridge Latin American Studies: No. 64). 320p. (C). 1994. pap. text ed. 17.95 (*0-521-46682-2*) Cambridge U Pr.

Resistance & Reaction: University Politics in Post-Mao China. Shirin Rai. LC 91-28959. 224p. 1991. text ed. 65.00 (*0-312-07187-6*) St Martin.

Resistance & Reconstruction. Chiang Kai-Shek. LC 71-111819. (Essay Index Reprint Ser.). 1977. 26.95 (*0-8369-1597-6*) Ayer.

Resistance & Reform in Tibet. Ed. by Robert Barnett & Shirin Akiner. LC 93-3072. (Illus.). 320p. 1994. 39.95 (*0-253-31131-4*) Ind U Pr.

Resistance & Reformation in Nineteenth-Century African-American Literature: Brown, Wilson, Jacobs, Delany, Douglass, & Harper. John Ernest. LC 95-17113. 352p. 1995. text ed. 45.00 (*0-87805-816-8*); pap. text ed. 17.95 (*0-87805-817-6*) U Pr of Miss.

Resistance & Renewal. Haig-Brown. 1994. per. 11.95 (*0-88978-189-3*, Pub. by Arsenal Pulp CN) LPC InBook.

Resistance & Revenge: The Armenian Assassination of the Turkish Leaders Responsible for the 1915 Massacres & Deportations. Jaques Derogy. 180p. (C). 1990. 34.95 (*0-88738-338-6*) Transaction Pubs.

Resistance & Revolution in China: The Communists & the Second United Front. Tetsuya Kataoka. LC 73-84386. (Center for Chinese Studies, UC Berkeley: No. 11). (Illus.). 1974. 55.00 (*0-520-02553-9*) U CA Pr.

Resistance & Revolution in Mediterranean Europe, 1939-1945. Tony Judt. 304p. 1989. 45.00 (*0-415-01580-4*, A3255) Routledge.

Resistance Arteries. Ed. by William Halpern et al. LC 88-19552. (Illus.). 1988. 92.50 (*0-916859-75-4*) Perinatology.

Resistance Arteries: Integration of the Regulatory Pathways. Ed. by William Halpern et al. LC 94-34398. (Experimental Biology & Medicine Ser.: Vol. 26). 384p. 1994. 109.50 (*0-89603-303-1*) Humana.

Resistance, Chaos & Control: Taiping Rebels, Taiwanese Ghosts, & Tiananmen. Robert P. Weller. LC 93-20037. 272p. 1993. 49.50 (*0-295-97285-8*) U of Wash Pr.

Resistance, Electronic & Magnetic Thermometry: Controls & Calibration; Bridges see Temperature: Its Measurement & Control in Science & Industry

Resistance Free Riding. Richard Shrake. 1993. 27.95 (*0-914327-51-8*) Breakthrgh NY.

Resistance Free Riding. Richard Zambeck. 27.95 (*0-914327-49-6*) Breakthrgh NY.

Resistance in Austria, 1938-1945. Radomir V. Luza. LC 83-6714. 383p. reprint ed. pap. 109.20 (*0-7837-2936-7*, 2057518) Bks Demand.

Resistance in the Desert: Moroccan Responses to French Imperialism, 1881-1912. Ross E. Dunn. 292p. 1977. text ed. 35.00 (*0-299-07360-2*) U of Wis Pr.

Resistance Literature. Barbara Harlow. LC 86-31149. (New Accents Ser.). 210p. 1987. 42.50 (*0-416-39950-9*, 1106); pap. 12.95 (*0-416-39960-6*, A0392) Routledge Chapman & Hall.

Resistance of Concrete to Freezing & Thawing. Donald J. Janssem & Mark B. Snyder. (SHRP Ser.: No. C-391). 224p. (Orig.). (C). 1994. pap. text ed. 15.00 (*0-309-05773-6*) SHRP.

Resistance of Pseudomonas Aeruginosa. Ed. by Michael R. Brown. LC 74-30224. 342p. reprint ed. pap. 97.50 (*0-317-07742-2*, 2016181) Bks Demand.

Resistance of Reference: Linguistics, Philosophy, & the Literary Text. Ora Avni. LC 90-30585. 352p. 1990. text ed. 48.50 (*0-8018-3993-9*) Johns Hopkins.

Resistance of the Air to Stone-dropping Meteors. Harry Nelson. LC 53-12359. (Augustana College Library Publications: No. 24). 37p. 1953. pap. 6.00 (*0-910182-19-1*) Augustana Coll.

Resistance of the Heart. Nathan Stolzfus. LC 95-50107. (Illus.). 352p. 1996. 30.00 (*0-393-03904-8*) Norton.

***Resistance of Vectors & Reservoirs of Disease to Pesticides: Tenth Report of the WHO Expert Committee on Vector Biology & Control.** WHO Staff. (Technical Report Ser.: No. 737). 87p. 1986. 12.00 (*92-4-120737-X*) World Health.

***Resistance of Vectors of Disease to Pesticides.** (Technical Report Ser.: No. 655). 82p. 1980. pap. text ed. 6.00 (*92-4-120655-1*) World Health.

Resistance of Woods to Marine Borers in Hawaiian Waters. C. H. Edmondson. (BMB Ser.). 1974. reprint ed. 25.00 (*0-527-02325-6*) Periodicals Srv.

***Resistance Parody 1895-1910.** Krasner. LC 97-10207. 1997. text ed. 39.95 (*0-312-17363-6*) St Martin.

Resistance, Rebellion, & Consciousness in the Andean Peasant World, 18th to 20th Centuries. Ed. by Steve J. Stern. LC 87-40152. (Illus.). 416p. (C). 1987. text ed. 45.00 (*0-299-11350-7*); pap. text ed. 15.00 (*0-299-11354-X*) U of Wis Pr.

Resistance, Rebellion & Death. Albert Camus. LC 73-14867. 1974. pap. 9.00 (*0-394-71966-2*, V-966, Vin) Random.

Resistance, Rebellion & Death. Albert Camus. 1995. pap. 12.00 (*0-679-76401-1*) Random.

***Resistance, Representation & Community.** Peter Blickle. (Origins of the Modern State in Europe, 13th to 18th Centuries). (Illus.). 304p. 1997. 95.00 (*0-19-820548-1*) OUP.

Resistance Through Rituals: Youth Subcultures in Post-War Britain. Ed. by Stuart Hall & Tony Jefferson. (Centre for Contemporary Studies Ser.). 287p. 1990. pap. text ed. 19.95 (*0-04-445609-3*) Routledge Chapman & Hall.

Resistance Through Rituals: Youth Subcultures in Postwar Britain. Stuart Hall & Tony Jefferson. (Illus.). 296p. (C). 1990. pap. 19.95 (*0-415-09916-1*, Routledge NY) Routledge.

***Resistance to Antineoplastic Agents Is Multifaceted: 3rd International Meeting on Drug Resistance, Aachen 1993.** Ed. by Rainhard Osieka. (Journal Ser.: Vol. 19, Supplement 1, 1996). (Illus.). vi, 38p. 1996. pap. 28.75 (*3-8055-6429-5*) S Karger.

Resistance to Antineoplastic Drugs. Ed. by David Kessel. LC 87-33744. 432p. 1989. 254.00 (*0-8493-4800-5*, RC271, CRC Reprint) Franklin.

Resistance to Antitumor Agents: Laboratory & Clinical Studies. Antonio L. Zichichi. (Ettore Majorana International Life Sciences Ser.: Vol. 7). 322, xp. 1989. pap. text ed. 155.00 (*3-7186-4956-X*) Gordon & Breach.

Resistance to Culture in Moliere, Laclos, Flaubert, & Camus: A Post-Modernist Approach. Larry W. Riggs. LC 92-32474. (Studies in French Literature: Vol. 13). 228p. 1992. text ed. 89.95 (*0-7734-9159-7*) E Mellen.

Resistance to Disease & Pests in Forest Trees. H. M. Heybroeck. 514p. 1990. 300.00 (*81-7089-124-8*, Pub. by Intl Bk Distr II) St Mut.

***Resistance to New Technology: Nuclear Power, Information Technology & Biotechnology.** 436p. 1997. pap. text ed. 39.95 (*0-521-59948-2*) Cambridge U Pr.

Resistance to New Technology: Nuclear Power, Information Technology, Biotechnology. Ed. by Martin Bauer. (Illus.). 360p. (C). 1995. text ed. 74.95 (*0-521-45518-9*) Cambridge U Pr.

Resistance to Plane-Stress Fracture (R-Curve Behavior) of A572 Structural Steel - STP591. 1976. pap. 5.25 (*0-8031-0557-6*, 04-591000-30) ASTM.

Resistance to Theory. Paul De Man. LC 85-28820. (Theory & History of Literature Ser.: Vol. 33). 156p. (Orig.). 1986. pap. text ed. 14.95 (*0-8166-1294-3*) U of Minn Pr.

Resistance to Tuberculosis: Experimental Studies in Native & Acquired Defense Mechanisms. Max B. Lurie. LC 64-25055. (Commonwealth Fund Publications). (Illus.). 410p. 1965. 37.00 (*0-674-76516-8*) HUP.

Resistance to Viral Diseases of Vegetables: Genetics & Breeding. Ed. by Molly Kyle. LC 92-8777. 272p. 1993. text ed. 39.95 (*0-88192-256-0*) Timber.

Resistance Training with Machines. Gene Power & Shawn Stratton. (Illus.). 116p. 1994. pap. text ed. 10.95 (*0-87563-531-8*) Stipes.

Resistance Vasculature. Ed. by John A. Bevan et al. LC 91-20884. (Vascular Biomedicine Ser.). (Illus.). 488p. 1991. 89.50 (*0-89603-212-4*) Humana.

Resistance Vessels: Physiology, Pharmacology & Hypertensive Pathology. Ed. by M. J. Mulvany et al. (Mikrozirkulation in Forschung und Klinik; Progress in Applied Microcirculation Ser.: Vol. 8). (Illus.). x, 236p. 1985. pap. 112.00 (*3-8055-4052-3*) S Karger.

Resistance Warfare 1940-45. Carlos Caballero Jurado. (Men-at-Arms Ser.: No. 169). (Illus.). 48p. pap. 11.95 (*0-85045-638-X*, 9101, Pub. by Osprey UK) Stackpole.

Resistance Welding Manual. 4th rev. ed. Ed. by James F. Deffenbaugh. LC 89-63296. (Illus.). 1989. text ed. 80.00 (*0-9624382-0-0*) Resistance Welder.

Resistant Essays. Jesse Bier. LC 93-24546. 228p. (Orig.). (C). 1993. pap. text ed. 28.50 (*0-8191-9272-4*); lib. bdg. 53.00 (*0-8191-9271-6*) U Pr of Amer.

Resistant Interactions: Child, Family, & Psychotherapist. Robert J. Marshall. LC 96-7483. (Master Works). 232p. 1997. reprint ed. pap. 25.00 (*1-56821-860-5*) Aronson.

Resistant Prices. Paul A. Brooke. 120p. 1975. 5.00 (*0-614-16161-4*) CEP.

***Resistant Structures: Particularity, Radicalism, & Renaissance Texts.** Richard Strier. LC 94-35106. (New Historicis Ser.). 1997. pap. 15.95 (*0-520-20905-2*) U CA Pr.

Resistant Structures: Particularity, Radicalism, & Renaissance Texts, 34. Richard Strier. LC 94-35106. (New Historicism Ser.). 256p. 1995. 38.00 (*0-520-08915-4*) U CA Pr.

Resistenzproblem bei der Chemo-und Radiotherapie Maligner Tumoren. Ed. by S. Seeber et al. (Beitraege zur Onkologie, Contributions to Oncology Ser.: Vol. 18). (Illus.). viii, 474p. 1984. 110.50 (*3-8055-3801-4*) S Karger.

Resisters see Japanese American World War II Evacuation

Resisting Bodies: The Negotiation of Female Agency in Twentieth-Century Women's Fiction. Helga Druxes. (Kritik Ser.). 232p. 1996. 34.95 (*0-8143-2534-3*) Wayne St U Pr.

Resisting Boundaries: The Subject of Naturalism in Brazil. Eva P. Bueno. LC 95-3923. (Latin American Studies: Vol. 6). 208p. 1995. text ed. 35.00 (*0-8153-1789-1*) Garland.

Resisting Discrimination: Affirmative Strategies for Principals & Teachers. Louis F. Miron. LC 96-28059. 160p. 1996. 42.95 (*0-8039-6422-6*); pap. 18.95 (*0-8039-6423-4*) Corwin Pr.

***Resisting Hostile Takeovers: The Case of Gillette.** Rita Ricardo-Campbell. LC 97-12811. 1997. text ed. write for info. (*0-275-95830-2*, Praeger Pubs) Greenwood.

Resisting Images: Essays on Cinema & History. Ed. by Robert Sklar & Charles Musser. (Culture & the Moving Image Ser.). (Illus.). 320p. 1990. pap. 18.95 (*0-87722-738-1*) Temple U Pr.

Resisting Novels: Ideology & Fiction. Lennard J. Davis. 248p. 1987. 39.50 (*0-416-37820-X*, 9097); pap. 13.95 (*0-416-37830-7*, 9098) Routledge Chapman & Hall.

Resisting Peer Pressure. Brown & Keller. 1990. 4.95 (*1-56456-108-9*, 405X) W Gladden Found.

Resisting Peer Pressure, 25 bks., Set. Brown & Keller. 1990. 57.75 (*1-56456-109-7*, 405) W Gladden Found.

***Resisting Protectionism: Global Industries & Politics of International Trade.** Helen V. Milner. LC 88-9945. 343p. 1988. reprint ed. pap. 97.80 (*0-608-02918-1*, 2063982) Bks Demand.

Resisting Reader: A Feminist Approach to American Fiction. Judith Fetterley. LC 78-3242. 224p. 1978. 29.95 (*0-253-31078-4*) Ind U Pr.

Resisting Reader: A Feminist Approach to American Fiction. Judith Fetterley. LC 78-3242. 224p. 1981. pap. 6.95 (*0-253-20247-7*, MB-247) Ind U Pr.

Resisting Reagan: The U. S. Central America Peace Movement. Christian Smith. (Illus.). 384p. 1996. pap. text ed., pap. 19.95 (*0-226-76336-6*); lib. bdg. 55.00 (*0-226-76335-8*) U Ch Pr.

Resisting Reform: A Policy Analysis of the Israeli Health Care Delivery System. Gerald Steinberg & Etta Bick. 260p. (C). 1992. lib. bdg. 56.00 (*0-8191-8654-6*, Pub. by Jerusalem Ctr Public) U Pr of Amer.

R

***Resisting Reform in English Studies: An Essay on Language & Limits.** Myron C. Tuman. (Literacy, Culture, & Learning Ser.). 394p. (C). 1998. text ed. 59.50 (*0-7914-3651-9*) State U NY Pr.

***Resisting Reform in English Studies: An Essay on Language & Limits.** Myron C. Tuman. (Literacy, Culture, & Learning Ser.). 394p. (C). 1998. pap. text ed. 19.95 (*0-7914-3652-7*) State U NY Pr.

***Resisting Regimes: Myth, Memory & the Shaping of a Muslim Identity.** Shail Mayaram. (Illus.). 481p. 1997. 29.95 (*0-19-563955-3*) OUP.

***Resisting Regionalism: Gender & Naturalism in American Fiction, 1885-1915.** Donna Campbell. LC 96-45666. 200p. 1997. text ed. 36.95 (*0-8214-1177-2*) Ohio U Pr.

Resisting Representation. Elaine Scarry. (Illus.). 192p. 1994. pap. 17.95 (*0-19-508964-2*) OUP.

Resisting State Violence: Radicalism, Gender, & Race in the U. S. Culture. Joy James. LC 96-19868. 280p. (C). 1996. pap. 18.95 (*0-8166-2813-0*); text ed. 47.95 (*0-8166-2812-2*) U of Minn Pr.

***Resisting Texts: Authority & Submission in Constructions of Meaning.** Peter L. Shillingsburg. (C). 1997. 39.50 (*0-472-10864-6*) U of Mich Pr.

Resisting the Anomie. Kawame Dawes. 112p. 1995. pap. 10.95 (*0-86492-147-0*, Pub. by Goose Ln Edits CN) Genl Dist Srvs.

Resisting the Serpent: Palau's Struggle for Self-Determination. Ched Myers & Robert Aldridge. (Illus.). 211p. (Orig.). 1990. pap. 9.95 (*1-879175-05-3*) Fortkamp.

Resisting the Virtual Life: The Culture & Politics of Information. Ed. by James Brook & Iain Boal. (Illus.). 256p. (Orig.). 1995. pap. 15.95 (*0-87286-299-2*) City Lights.

Resisting Writings (& the Boundaries of Composition) Derek Owens. LC 93-18752. (SMU Studies in Composition & Rhetoric). 212p. 1994. text ed. 24.95 (*0-87074-343-0*) SMU Press.

Resistive & Reactive Circuits. Albert P. Malvino. (Illus.). 640p. (C). 1974. text ed. 38.95 (*0-07-039856-9*) McGraw.

Resistive Circuit Theory. Robert Spence. 1979. pap. text ed. 18.00 (*0-917326-12-1*) APL Pr.

Resistive Weight Training. Norman Grant. 192p. (C). 1996. per., pap. text ed. 15.69 (*0-7872-1840-5*) Kendall-Hunt.

Resistive Weight Training. Norman G. Grant. 176p. (C). 1994. per. 15.64 (*0-8403-8504-8*) Kendall-Hunt.

***Resistivities & Chemical Analyses of Selected Oil & Gas Field, Water Well, & Spring Waters, Utah.** J. Wallace Gwynn. (Circular of the Utah Geological Survey Ser.: Vol. 87). (Illus.). 142p. (Orig.). 1995. pap. 9.50 (*1-55791-292-0*, C87) Utah Geological Survey.

Resistor Handbook. Cletus J. Kaiser. LC 94-94500. (Illus.). 100p. (Orig.). (C). 1994. pap. text ed. 19.95 (*0-9628525-1-1*) CJ Publng.

Resists in Microlithography & Printing. 2nd rev. ed. Bednar Bohumil et al. LC 92-5585. (Materials Science Monographs: Vol. 76). 1993. 175.00 (*0-444-98846-7*) Elsevier.

Resituating Writing: Constructing & Administering Writing Programs. Ed. by Joseph Janangelo & Kristine Hansen. LC 95-31501. (Crosscurrents Ser.). 163p. 1995. pap. text ed. 24.50 (*0-86709-366-8*, 0366) Boynton Cook Pubs.

Resizing for Organizational Effectiveness: A Report of a Workshop. Eli Ginzberg. 43p. 1985. pap. 20.00 (*0-685-13954-9*) CU Ctr Career Res.

Reskilling the I.T. Professional. James Martin. 300p. 1993. 35.95 (*0-13-090929-7*) P-H.

***Resmethrins: Resmethrin, Bioresmethrin, Cisresmethrin.** WHO Staff. (Environmental Health Criteria Ser.: No. 92). 79p. 1989. 16.00 (*92-4-154292-6*) World Health.

***Resmethrins Health & Safety Guide.** WHO Staff. (Health & Safety Guides: No. 25). 28p. 1989. 5.00 (*92-4-154346-9*) World Health.

Resoluciones de la Junta de Personal de Puerto Rico, 3 vols. Compiled by Irma Garcia de Serrano. LC 80-26437. (Illus.). (SPA.). 1980. 120.00 (*0-8477-2218-X*) U of PR Pr.

Resoluciones de la Junta de Personal de Puerto Rico, 3 vols., I. Compiled by Irma Garcia de Serrano. LC 80-26437. (Illus.). (SPA.). 1980. 30.00 (*0-8477-2227-9*) U of PR Pr.

Resoluciones de la Junta de Personal de Puerto Rico, 3 vols., III. Compiled by Irma Garcia de Serrano. LC 80-26437. (Illus.). (SPA.). 1980. 30.00 (*0-8477-2223-6*) U of PR Pr.

Resoluciones de la Junta de Personal de Puerto Rico, 3 vols., IV. Compiled by Irma Garcia de Serrano. LC 80-26437. (Illus.). (SPA.). 1980. 30.00 (*0-8477-2224-4*) U of PR Pr.

Resolute & Undertaking Characters: The Lives of Wilhelm & Otto Struve. Alan H. Batten. (C). 1988. lib. bdg. 116.50 (*90-277-2652-3*) Kluwer Ac.

Resolute Heart: Selected Writing from Lowell's Cambodian Community. Ed. & Tr. by George Chigas from CAM. LC 94-94026. 112p. 1994. pap. 7.00 (*0-9630295-1-7*) Mealea Pubns.

***Resolution.** Hobbie. 1998. 25.00 (*0-8050-5492-8*) H Holt & Co.

Resolution: A Critique of Video Art. Intro. by Patti Podesta. (Illus.). 131p. (Orig.). (C). 1986. pap. 10.00 (*0-937335-01-0*) LA Contemp Exhib.

Resolution As It Relates to Photographic & Electronic Imaging. 18p. 1993. pap. 45.00 (*0-89258-253-7*, TR26) Assn Inform & Image Mgmt.

***Resolution Calculus.** Alexander Leitsch. LC 96-39706. (Texts in Theoretical Computer Science Ser.). 302p. 1997. 45.95 (*3-540-61882-1*) Spr-Verlag.

***Resolution de Conflits Pour les Enfants, Grade 4.** Fran Schmidt & Alice Friedman. (Illus.). 84p. (Orig.). (ENG & FRE.). Date not set. teacher ed., pap. text ed. 23.95 (*1-878227-29-7*) Peace Educ.

Resolution Methods for the Decision Problem. C. Fermuller et al. LC 93-29010. (Lecture Notes in Artificial Intelligence Ser.: Vol. 679). viii, 205p. 1993. 39.95 (*0-387-56732-1*) Spr-Verlag.

Resolution of Conflict: Constructive & Destructive Processes. Morton Deutsch. LC 73-80080. (Carl Hovland Memorial Lectures). (Illus.). 448p. 1977. pap. 22.00 (*0-300-02186-0*) Yale U Pr.

Resolution of Inner Conflict: An Introduction to Psychoanalytic Therapy. Frank Auld & Marvin Hyman. 267p. (Orig.). 1991. text ed. 39.95 (*1-55798-116-7*) Am Psychol.

Resolution of Poverty in America. 2nd ed. Craig C. White. 256p. (C). 1995. per., pap. text ed. 30.39 (*0-7872-0566-4*) Kendall-Hunt.

Resolution of Prison Riots: Strategies & Policies. Bert Useem et al. (Illus.). 240p. 1996. 39.95 (*0-19-509324-0*) OUP.

Resolution of Surface Singularities. V. Cossart et al. (Lecture Notes in Mathematics Ser.: Vol. 1101). vii, 132p. 1985. 29.95 (*0-387-13904-4*) Spr-Verlag.

Resolution on CPC History (1949-81) Communist Party of China. 126p. 1981. pap. 6.50 (*0-317-66867-6*, Pergamon Pr) Elsevier.

Resolution Principle for a Logic with Restricted Quantifiers. H. J. Burckert. Ed. by Joerg H. Siekmann. (Lecture Notes in Artificial Intelligence Ser.: Vol. 568). x, 116p. 1991. 30.00 (*0-387-55034-8*) Spr-Verlag.

Resolution Proof Systems: An Algebraic Theory. Zbigniew Stachniak. (Automated Reasoning Ser.: Vol. 4). 224p. (C). 1996. lib. bdg. 120.00 (*0-7923-4017-5*) Kluwer Ac.

Resolution Trust Corporation: Cancellation of Indebtedness: Market Segment Specialization Program-Audit Technique Guide. 75p. 1995. pap. 27.50 (*1-57402-116-8*) Athena Info Mgt.

***Resolution Trust Corporation: Implementation of the Management Reforms in the RTC Completion Act.** (Illus.). 70p. 1996. reprint ed. pap. 20.00 (*0-7881-3263-6*) DIANE Pub.

***Resolutions.** Maxine Barry. 400p. (Orig.). 1997. mass mkt. 3.99 (*1-85487-903-0*, Pub. by Scarlet Bks UK) London Brdge.

Resolutions: Contemporary Video Practices. Ed. by Michael Renov & Erika Suderberg. 512p. 1995. text ed. 59.95 (*0-8166-2327-9*); pap. text ed. 21.95 (*0-8166-2330-9*) U of Minn Pr.

Resolutions & Decisions of the Communist Party of the Soviet Union. Incl. Vol. 1. Russian Social Democratic Labour Party, 1898-October, 1917. Ed. by Ralph C. Elwood. LC 74-81931. pap. 85.50 (*0-317-27011-7*); Vol. 2. Early Soviet Period, 1917-1929: PB. Ed. by Richard Gregor. LC 74-81931. pap. 98.50 (*0-317-27012-5*); Vol. 3. Stalin Years, 1929-1953: PB. Ed. by Robert H. McNeal. LC 74-81931. pap. 72.50 (*0-317-27013-3*); LC 74-81931. reprint ed. write for info. (*0-318-59271-1*, 2023650) Bks Demand.

Resolutions & Decisions of the Communist Party of the Soviet Union: Vol. 5, the Brezhnev Years, 1964-1981. Donald V. Schwartz. 296p. 1982. 42.50 (*0-8020-5552-4*) U of Toronto Pr.

Resolutions & Other Decisions of the Assembly 17th Session 1991. International Maritime Organization Staff. (C). 1992. 150.00 (*0-7855-0036-7*, IMO 142-E, Pub. by Intl Maritime Org UK) St Mut.

Resolutions & Recommendations: 19th Session of the General Assembly of IUCN, the World Conservation Union, Buenos Aires, Argentina 17-26 January 1994. 80p. (Orig.). (C). 1994. pap. text ed. 5.00 (*2-8317-0206-2*, Pub. by IUCN SZ) Island Pr.

Resolutions & Statements of the United Nations Security Council, 1946-1992: A Thematic Guide. 2nd enl. ed. Ed. by Karel C. Wellens. 1000p. (C). 1993. lib. bdg. 224.00 (*0-7923-2379-3*) Kluwer Ac.

Resolutions for Funeral, Welcome Addresses, & Responses for Special Occasions & Annual Days. J. R. Mosley, Sr. 1990. pap. text ed. 2.50 (*0-9627958-1-X*) J R Mosleys Pr.

Resolutions of the Eighteenth National Convention of the Communist Party, U. S. A. 1967. pap. 1.25 (*0-87898-018-0*) New Outlook.

Resolutions of the United Nations Security Council. Renata Sonnenfeld. (C). 1988. lib. bdg. 93.50 (*90-247-3567-X*) Kluwer Ac.

Resolved: Your Dead. Clay Coleman. (Horror High Ser.: No. 2). 160p. (YA). 1995. mass mkt. 3.50 (*0-06-106019-4*, PL) HarpC.

Resolved to (Re) Marry. Carole Buck. 1997. mass mkt. 3.50 (*0-373-76049-3*, 1-76049-5) Silhouette.

Resolves, a Duple Century. 3rd ed. Owen Feltham. LC 74-28853. (English Experience Ser.: No. 734). 1975. reprint ed. 55.00 (*90-221-0734-5*) Walter J Johnson.

Resolving Association Disputes. rev. ed. Vivian G. Walker. LC 91-33432. (C). 1991. pap. 14.50 (*0-941301-17-6*) CAI.

Resolving Complaints. Leebov. (gr. 13). 1995. 5.95 (*0-8151-5312-0*) Mosby Yr Bk.

Resolving Conflict. Ed. by Margaret S. Herrman. (Practical Management Ser.). (Illus.). 220p. (Orig.). (C). 1994. pap. text ed. 23.95 (*0-87326-071-6*) Intl City-Cnty Mgt.

Resolving Conflict: A Practical Approach. Gregory Tillett. (Sydney University Press Publication). (Illus.). 188p. 1993. reprint ed. pap. 27.00 (*0-424-00179-9*) OUP.

Resolving Conflict: Learning How You Both Can Win & Keep Your Relationship. Dale R. Olen. (Illus.). 212p. (Orig.). 1992. pap. text ed. 5.95 (*1-56583-012-1*) JODA.

Resolving Conflict: With Others & Within Yourself. Gini G. Scott. 252p. (Orig.). 1990. pap. 13.95 (*0-934986-81-9*) New Harbinger.

***Resolving Conflict across Cultures: Talking It Out to Mediation.** Selma Myers & Barbara Filner. 90p. 1997. 21.95 (*1-883998-19-0*) Amherst Educ.

Resolving Conflict in Africa: The Fermeda Workshop. Ed. by Leonard W. Doob. LC 71-123396. 228p. reprint ed. pap. 65.00 (*0-317-11303-8*, 2021995) Bks Demand.

Resolving Conflict in Black Male-Female Relationships. Lafrancis Rodgers-Rose. LC 85-51272. 70p. (Orig.). 1985. pap. 10.95 (*0-934185-00-X*) Traces Inst.

Resolving Conflict in the Blended Family. Tom Frydenger & Adrienne Frydenger. LC 91-18028. 192p. (Orig.). (gr. 10). 1991. pap. 8.99 (*0-8007-9182-7*) Chosen Bks.

***Resolving Conflict Once & for All: A Practical How-to-Guide to Mediating Disputes.** Mark Stein & Dennis J. Ernst. 140p. (Orig.). 1997. pap. 19.95 (*0-9656429-0-9*) Mediation First.

Resolving Conflict Successfully: Needed Knowledge & Skills. Neil Katz & John W. Lawyer. Ed. by Jerry J. Herman & Janice L. Herman. LC 93-44469. (Road Maps to Success Ser.). 72p. 1994. pap. 11.95 (*0-8039-6145-6*) Corwin Pr.

Resolving Conflict with Justice & Peace. Charles R. McCollough. LC 90-7869. 228p. (Orig.). 1991. pap. 14.95 (*0-8298-0870-1*) Pilgrim OH.

***Resolving Conflicts: How to Turn Conflict into Cooperation.** Wendy Grant. LC 97-17473. 1997. pap. 12.95 (*1-86204-126-1*) Onewrld Pubns.

Resolving Conflicts on the Job (A Worksmart Book) Jerry Wisinski. 80p. 1993. pap. 10.95 (*0-8144-7799-2*) AMACOM.

Resolving Corrosion Problems in Air Pollution Control Equipment - 1976. LC 75-38373. 117p. 1976. 10.00 (*0-915567-77-6*) NACE Intl.

Resolving Counterresistances in Psychotherapy. Herbert S. Strean. LC 92-49095. 240p. 1993. text ed. 33.95 (*0-87630-713-6*) Brunner-Mazel.

Resolving Development Disputes Through Negotiation. Timothy J. Sullivan. (Environment, Development, & Public Policy: Public Policy & Social Services Ser.). 238p. 1984. 49.50 (*0-306-41658-1*, Plenum Pr) Plenum.

Resolving Discriminatory Practices Against Minorities & Women in Steel & Auto - Los Angeles, California: 1936-1982. Myrna C. Donahoe. 47p. (Orig.). 1991. pap. 8.50 (*0-89215-165-X*) U Cal LA Indus Rel.

Resolving Disputes Between Nations: Coercion or Conciliation? Martin Patchen. LC 87-26845. xiii, 365p. (C). 1988. text ed. 49.95 (*0-8223-0764-2*); pap. text ed. 20.95 (*0-8223-0819-3*) Duke.

***Resolving Disputes over Life-Sustaining Treatment: A Health Care Provider's Guide.** Thomas L. Hafemeister & Paula L. Hannaford. 170p. (Orig.). 1996. pap. 20.00 (*0-89656-167-4*, R-186) Natl Ctr St Courts.

Resolving Divorce Issues: Heed "Warning Signals" & the Misdeeds of Spouse. 2nd rev. ed. Holmes F. Crouch. Ed. by Irma J. Crouch. LC 95-80856. (Series 100 Tax Guides: Vol. 104). (Illus.). 224p. 1996. pap. 18.95 (*0-944817-26-2*, T/G 104) Allyear Tax.

Resolving Drug Issues. Frank Elkouri & Edna A. Elkouri. LC 93-17519. 486p. 1993. text ed. 55.00 (*0-87179-776-3*) BNA Books.

Resolving Employment Disputes Without Litigation. Alan F. Westin & Alfred G. Feliu. LC 87-31989. 346p. 1988. text ed. 52.00 (*0-87179-558-2*, 0558) BNA Books.

Resolving Environmental Conflict: Towards Sustainable Community Development. Chris Maser. 200p. 1995. pap. 39.95 (*1-57444-007-1*) St Lucie Pr.

Resolving Environmental Regulatory Disputes. Lawrence Susskind et al. 260p. 1983. pap. 24.95 (*0-87073-145-9*) Schenkman Bks Inc.

Resolving Ethical Dilemmas: A Guide for Clinicians. Bernard Lo. LC 93-44523. (Illus.). 366p. 1994. 35.00 (*0-683-05138-5*) Williams & Wilkins.

Resolving Faculty Disputes. Irving Ladimer & Jane McCarthy. LC 81-67937. 80p. 1981. pap. 8.00 (*0-943001-12-9*) Am Arbitration.

Resolving Grievances in the Nursing Home: A Study of the Ombudsman Program. Abraham Monk et al. (Social Work & Social Issues Ser.). 1984. text ed. 49.50 (*0-231-05702-4*) Col U Pr.

***Resolving Homosexual Problems: A Guide for LDS Men.** Jason Park. 300p. (Orig.). 1997. pap. 15.95 (*0-941846-06-7*) Centry Pub.

***Resolving Identity-Based Conflict in Nations, Organizations, & Communities.** Jay Rothman. LC 97-4719. (Conflict Resolution Ser.). 1997. write for info. (*0-7879-0996-3*) Jossey-Bass.

Resolving Impasses in Therapeutic Relationships. Sue N. Elkind. LC 92-1692. 335p. 1992. lib. bdg. 36.95 (*0-89862-892-X*) Guilford Pr.

Resolving International Conflicts: The Theory & Practice of Mediation. Ed. by Jacob Bercovitch. 1995. 49.95 (*1-55587-474-6*); pap. 19.95 (*1-55587-601-3*) Lynne Rienner.

***Resolving International Disputes Through Win-Win or SOS Solutions.** Ed. by Stuart S. Nagel. (Advances in Developmental Policy Studies: Vol. 2). 1997. 73.25 (*0-7623-0192-9*) Jai Pr.

Resolving Interstate Child Custody Issues. John O. Williams. 20p. 1990. 2.95 (*1-56456-021-X*, 240) W Gladden Found.

Resolving Language Conflicts: A Study of the World's Constitution. Albert P. Blaustein & Dana Epstein. LC 86-52465. 105p. 1986. 45.00 (*0-934833-01-X*) US English.

Resolving Maps & the Dimension Group for Shifts of Finite Type. M. Boyle et al. LC 87-25475. (Memoirs Ser.: Vol. 70/377). 146p. 1987. pap. text ed. 25.00 (*0-8218-2440-6*, MEMO/70/377) Am Math.

Resolving Marital Conflicts. Herbert S. Strean. LC 96-849. 296p. 1996. reprint ed. pap. 35.00 (*1-56821-806-0*) Aronson.

Resolving Marital Conflicts: A Psychodynamic Perspective. Herbert S. Strean. (Personality Processes Ser.). 275p. 1985. text ed. 60.00 (*0-471-82504-2*) Wiley.

Resolving Nationality Conflicts: The Role of Public Opinion Research. Ed. by W. Phillips Davison & Leon Gordenker. LC 80-15128. 256p. 1980. text ed. 55.00 (*0-275-90467-9*, C0467, Praeger Pubs) Greenwood.

Resolving Patient Complaints: A Step-by-Step Guide to Effective Service Recovery. Liz Osborne. 212p. 1995. ring bd. 99.00 (*0-8342-0674-9*) Aspen Pub.

Resolving Public Conflict. Dukes. 1997. text ed. 69.95 (*0-7190-4512-6*); text ed. 19.95 (*0-7190-4513-4*) St Martin.

Resolving Quandaries in Dermatopathology. A. Bernard Ackerman et al. 308p. 1995. 75.00 (*0-9644798-0-X*) Promethean Med.

***Resolving Regional Conflicts.** Roger E. Kanet. LC 97-4802. 1998. write for info. (*0-252-02368-4*); pap. write for info. (*0-252-06671-5*) U of Ill Pr.

Resolving Relievances: A Practical Approach. Donald McPherson. (C). 1983. teacher ed. write for info. (*0-8359-6664-X*, Reston); pap. text ed. 21.00 (*0-8359-6663-1*, Reston) P-H.

Resolving Resistance in Group Psychotherapy. Leslie Rosenthal. LC 85-19940. 230p. 1994. reprint ed. pap. 35.00 (*1-56821-193-7*) Aronson.

Resolving Semantic Ambiguity. Ed. by D. S. Gorfein. (Cognitive Science Ser.). (Illus.). 360p. 1989. 106.95 (*0-387-96906-3*) Spr-Verlag.

Resolving Sexual Abuse. Yvonne M. Dolan. 1991. 29.95 (*0-393-70112-3*) Norton.

***Resolving Social Conflicts: And, Field Theory in Social Science.** LC 96-40386. 1997. 19.95 (*1-55798-415-8*) Am Psychol.

Resolving the Argentine Paradox: Politics & Development, 1966-1992. Davide G. Erro. LC 92-40793. 265p. 1993. lib. bdg. 43.00 (*1-55587-369-3*) Lynne Rienner.

Resolving the Fiscal-Year Dilemma. Bertil Westlin. 72p. (Orig.). 1988. pap. 10.00 (*0-318-33137-3*, 5244) Commerce.

Resolving the Global Economic Crisis: After Wall Street: A Statement by Thirty-Three Economists from Thirteen Countries. Institute for International Economics Staff. LC 87-83537. (Institute for International Economics. Special Report Ser.: No. 6). 30p. reprint ed. pap. 25.00 (*0-7837-4215-0*, 2043904) Bks Demand.

Resolving the Housing Crisis: Government Policy, Decontrol, & the Public Interest. Ed. by M. Bruce Johnson. LC 81-22917. (Urban & Social Policy Ser.). (Illus.). 426p. (C). 1982. 34.95 (*0-936488-58-1*); pap. 14.95 (*0-936488-59-X*) PRIPP.

Resolving the Illness Care Crisis. Dr. "H". LC 95-47513. 257p. 1996. 34.00 (*1-56072-284-3*); pap. 19.00 (*1-56072-271-1*) Nova Sci Pubs.

Resolving the Quality Quandary: Research! Initiate! Limit? Stephen Schmitt & Gary Morehead. 86p. (Orig.). 1994. pap. 69.00 (*1-889394-23-8*) Credit Union Execs.

Resolving the Security Dilemma in Europe: The German Debate on Non-Offensive Defence. Bjorn Moller. 339p. 1991. 56.00 (*0-08-041315-3*, Pub. by Brasseys UK) Brasseys Inc.

Resolving the Thrift Crisis. (Illus.). 93p. (Orig.). (C). 1993. pap. text ed. 35.00 (*1-56806-434-9*) DIANE Pub.

Resolving the Trauma of Incest: Reintegration Therapy with Survivors. Karin C. Meiselman. LC 89-43302. (Social & Behavioral Science Ser.). 342p. 32.95 (*1-55542-219-5*) Jossey-Bass.

Resolving Third World Conflict: Challenges for a New Era. Sheryl J. Brown & Kimber M. Schraub. LC 92-15433. 1992. pap. text ed. 21.95 (*1-878379-17-8*) US Inst Peace.

Resolving Traumatic Memories: Metaphors & Symbols in Psychotherapy. David J. Grove & B. I. Panzer. 277p. 1991. text ed. 52.95 incl. audio (*0-8290-2417-4*); audio 19.95 (*0-8290-2407-7*) Irvington.

Resolving Treatment Impasses: The Difficult Patient. Theodore Saretsky. LC 80-24661. 267p. 1981. 34.95 (*0-87705-088-0*) Human Sci Pr.

***Resolving Treatment Impasses: The Difficult Patient.** Theodore Saretsky. 288p. 1997. text ed. 40.00 (*0-7657-0095-6*) Aronson.

Resolving Unfinished Business: Assessing the Effects of Being Raised in a Dysfunctional Environment. Anthony S. Dallmann-Jones. 176p. (Orig.). 1996. pap. 12.95 (*1-881952-26-6*) Three Blue Herons.

***Resolving Violence: Anti-Violence Curriculum for Secondary Schools.** Jean Jenkin. 112p. 1997. pap. 29.95 (*0-86431-180-X*, Pub. by Aust Coun Educ Res AT) Paul & Co Pubs.

Resolving Water Disputes along the U. S. - Mexico Border: The Case of Paso del Norte. Janet Tanski & C. Richard Bath. 1995. 10.00 (*0-614-11102-1*, MG09) Border Res Inst.

Resonance Acoustic Spectroscopy. N. D. Veksler. Ed. by Herbert Uberall. LC 92-30272. (Wave Phenomena Ser.: Vol. 11). 1993. 97.95 (*0-387-55638-9*) Spr-Verlag.

Resonance Energy Transfer: Theory & Data. B. Wieb Van Der Meer et al. LC 94-5419. 177p. 1995. 95.00 (*1-56081-643-0*, VCH) Wiley.

Resonance Ionization Spectroscopy, 1984: Invited Papers from the Second International Symposium on Resonance Ionization Spectroscopy & Its Applications Held at Knoxville, Tennessee, on 16-20 June 1984. International Symposium on Resonance Ionization Spectroscopy & Its Applications Staff. Ed. by G. S. Hurst & M. G. Payne. LC 84-224632. (Conference Ser.: No. 71). 373p. reprint ed. pap. 106.40 (*0-7837-3246-5*, 2043265) Bks Demand.

An Asterisk (*) at the beginning of an entry indicates that the title is appearing in BIP for the first time.

R

Resonance Ionization Spectroscopy, 1992: Proceedings of the 6th International Symposium on Resonance Ionization Spectroscopy & Its Applications, Santa Fe, New Mexico, 24-29 May 1992. Ed. by C. Miller & J. E. Parks. (Institute of Physics Conference Ser.: No. 128). (Illus.). 376p. 1992. 170.00 (*0-7503-0230-5*) IOP Pub.

Resonance Ionization Spectroscopy 1994: Seventh International Symposium. Ed. by H. Jurgen Kluge et al. (AIP Conference Proceedings Ser.: No. 329). (Illus.). 544p. (C). 1995. text ed. 135.00 (*1-56396-437-6*) Am Inst Physics.

***Resonance Ionization Spectroscopy 1996: Eighth International Symposium.** Ed. by James E. Parks & Nicholas Winograd. (AIP Conference Proceedings Ser.: Vol. 388). 500p. 1997. text ed. 130.00 (*1-56396-611-5*) Am Inst Physics.

Resonance of Blood. Robert E. Vardeman. 224p. (Orig.). 1992. mass mkt. 4.50 (*0-380-75857-1*) Avon.

Resonance of Dust: Essays on Holocaust Literature & Jewish Fate. Edward Alexander. LC 79-15515. 276p. 1979. reprint ed. pap. 78.70 (*0-608-00912-1*, 2061706) Bks Demand,

Resonance Phenomena in Electron-Atom Collisions. V. I. Lengyel et al. (Atoms & Plasmas Ser.: Vol. 11). (Illus.). 200p. 1992. 92.95 (*0-387-54093-8*) Spr-Verlag.

Resonance Radiation & Excited Atoms. Allan C. Mitchell & Mark W. Zemansky. LC 62-5588. 352p. reprint ed. pap. 100.40 (*0-318-34827-6*, 2031696) Bks Demand.

Resonances. Ed. by E. Brandas & N. Elander. (Lecture Notes in Physics Ser.: Vol. 325). xviii, 564p. 1989. 93.95 (*0-387-50994-1*) Spr-Verlag.

Resonances: A Volume in Honor of Professor N. Bloembergen on His 70th Birthday. Ed. by M. D. Levenson et al. 512p. (C). 1990. text ed. 99.00 (*981-02-0377-2*); pap. text ed. 48.00 (*981-02-0378-0*) World Scientific Pub.

Resonances de l'Amour. Anne Philippe. (FRE.). 1985. pap. 8.95 (*0-7859-4223-8*) Fr & Eur.

***Resonances in Electron-Molecular Scattering, Van der Waals Complex, & Reactive Chemical Dynamics.** Ed. by Donald G. Truhlar. LC 84-16934. (ACS Symposium Ser.: No. 263). (Illus.). 536p. 1984. reprint ed. pap. 152.80 (*0-608-03255-7*, 2063774) Bks Demand.

Resonances in Electron-Molecule Scattering, Van Der Waals Complexes & Reactive Chemical Dynamics. Ed. by Donald G. Truhlar. LC 84-16934. (Symposium Ser.: No. 263). 522p. 1984. lib. bdg. 98.95 (*0-8412-0865-4*) Am Chemical.

Resonances Models & Phenomena. Sergio A. Albeverio et al. Ed. by L. S. Ferreira & Ludwig Streit. (Lecture Notes in Physics Ser.: Vol. 211). vi, 359p. 1984. 42.95 (*0-387-13880-3*) Spr-Verlag.

Resonant Anomalous X-Ray Scattering: Theory & Applications. Ed. by G. Materlik et al. LC 94-20905. 688p. 1994. 227.25 (*0-444-82025-6*, North Holland) Elsevier.

Resonant Gaps: Between Baudelaire & Wagner. Margaret Miner. LC 94-28793. 1995. 50.00 (*0-8203-1709-8*) U of Ga Pr.

Resonant Heterogeneous Processes in a Laser Field. V. A. Kravchenko et al. Tr. by S. A. Stewart from RUS. (Proceedings of the Institute of General Physics of the Academy of Sciences of the U. S. S. R. Ser.: Vol. 11). 253p. (C). 1989. text ed. 125.00 (*0-941743-70-5*) Nova Sci Pubs.

Resonant Lives: Sixty Figures of Consequence. Paul Greenberg. 210p. 1992. pap. 19.95 (*0-89633-153-9*) Ethics & Public Policy.

Resonant Lives: Sixty Figures of Consequence. Paul Greenberg. 1992. 19.95 (*0-89633-154-7*) Ethics & Public Policy.

Resonant Lives: Sixty Figures of Consequence. Paul Greenberg. LC 92-31380. 225p. 1992. pap. 11.95 (*0-89633-182-2*) Ethics & Public Policy.

Resonant Nonlinear Interactions of Light with Matter. V. S. Butylkin et al. (Illus.). 360p. 1989. 158.95 (*0-387-12109-9*) Spr-Verlag.

Resonant Power Converters. Marian K. Kazimierczuk & Dariusz Czarkowski. LC 94-31255. 481p. 1995. text ed. 74.95 (*0-471-04706-6*) Wiley.

***Resonant Power Converters: Solutions Manual.** Marian K. Kazimierczuk & Dariusz Czarkowski. 1995. teacher ed., pap. text ed. 25.00 (*0-471-12849-X*) Wiley.

***Resonant Recognition Model of Macromolecular Bioactivity: Theory & Applications.** Cosic. LC 96-43992. (Biomethods Ser.). 1996. write for info. (*0-8176-5487-9*) Birkhauser.

***Resonant Recognition Model of Macromolecular Bioactivity: Theory & Applications.** I. Cosic. LC 96-43992. (BioMethods Ser.: Vol. 8). (Illus.). 160p. 1997. 94.50 (*3-7643-5487-9*) Birkhauser.

Resonant Tunneling in Semiconductors: Physics & Applications. Ed. by Leroy L. Chang et al. (NATO ASI Series B, Physics: Vol. 277). (Illus.). 542p. 1992. 135.00 (*0-306-44048-2*, Plenum Pr) Plenum.

***Resonant Ultrasound Spectroscopy: Applications to Physics, Materials Measurements & Non-Destructive Evaluation.** Albert Migliori & John L. Sarrao. LC 96-29930. 1997. write for info. (*0-471-12360-9*) Wiley.

Resonare Christum: The Rome Years, Vol. III. John J. Wright. 598p. (Orig.). text ed. 18.95 (*0-89870-052-3*) Ignatius Pr.

Resonate with Stillness: Daily Contemplations. Contrib. by Swami Muktananda & Swami Chidvilasananda. LC 95-41463. 408p. 1995. pap. 14.95 (*0-911307-42-7*) SYDA Found.

Resorcinol: Its Uses & Derivatives. Hans Dressler. LC 94-30813. (Topics in Applied Chemistry Ser.). 487p. (C). 1995. 115.00 (*0-306-44850-5*, Plenum Pr) Plenum.

Resort City in the Sunbelt: Las Vegas, 1930-1970. Eugene P. Moehring. LC 89-9130. (Illus.). 344p. 1989. 29.95 (*0-87417-147-4*) U of Nev Pr.

Resort City in the Sunbelt: Las Vegas, 1930-1970. Eugene P. Moehring. LC 89-9130. (Illus.). 344p. 1995. pap. 17.95 (*0-87417-267-5*) U of Nev Pr.

***Resort Development.** Urban Land Institute Staff. (Community Builders Handbook Ser.). 350p. 1997. 69.95 (*0-87420-784-3*, R33) Urban Land.

***Resort Development & Management.** 2nd ed. Chuck Y. Gee. LC 88-21515. (Illus.). 554p. 1996. pap. write for info. (*0-86612-112-9*) Educ Inst Am Hotel.

Resort Hotel Photography. 1991. 4.95 (*0-89816-046-4*) Embee Pr.

Resort Properties - Coast to Coast: Condo & Villa Vacations, United States & Canada. 1992. pap. 20.00 (*1-881076-06-7*) Resort Prop Owners.

Resort Properties - Exotic Destinations: Villa & Condo Vacations: Hawaii, Mexico & Caribbean. Clinton Burr & Ellen Burr. 1992. pap. 20.00 (*1-881076-00-8*) Resort Prop Owners.

Resort Timeshare Industry in California. (Regional Studies). 82p. 1992. 65.00 (*0-614-04634-3*, 69004) ARDA.

Resort Timeshare Industry in Hawaii. (Regional Studies). 136p. 1992. 65.00 (*0-614-04632-7*, 69004) ARDA.

Resort Timeshare Industry in Mexico. (Regional Studies). 140p. 1994. 75.00 (*0-614-04631-9*, 43011) ARDA.

Resort Timeshare Industry in the Caribbean. (Regional Studies). 108p. 1994. 75.00 (*0-614-04635-1*) ARDA.

Resort Timeshare Industry in the United States. (Regional Studies). 59p. 1993. 75.00 (*0-614-04630-0*, 21300) ARDA.

Resort to Arms: International & Civil Wars, 1816-1980. 2nd ed. Melvin Small & J. David Singer. LC 81-18518. (Illus.). 373p. reprint ed. pap. 106.40 (*0-8357-8510-6*, 2034803) Bks Demand.

Resounding Praise. Dennis R. Johnson. 1987. 8.99 (*0-685-68336-2*, MB-589) Lillenas.

Resource: A Pro Bono Manual. American Bar Association, Special Commission on Dispute Resolution. LC 83-72985. 227p. 1983. ring bd. 10.00 (*0-89707-118-2*, 469-0002) Amer Bar Assn.

Resource - One Ondisc User Guide. Dennis Auld. 1989. incl. cd-rom (*0-914604-34-1*) UMI Louisville.

***Resource Allocation: Managing Money & People.** M. Scott Norton & Larry K. Kelly. LC 97-4940. (Illus.). 170p. 1997. text ed. write for info. (*1-883001-35-8*) Eye On Educ.

Resource Allocation in British Universities. Ed. by Michael Shattock & Gwynneth Rigby. 185p. 1983. 38.00 (*0-900868-97-X*, Open Univ Pr) Taylor & Francis.

Resource Allocation in Higher Education. William F. Massy. LC 95-48854. (Economics of Education Ser.). (C). 1995. 49.50 (*0-472-10686-4*) U of Mich Pr.

Resource Allocation Model for Public Health Planning: A Case Study of Tuberculosis Control. M. S. Feldstein et al. (WHO Bulletin Supplement Ser.: Vol. 48). 1973. pap. text ed. 16.00 (*92-4-068481-6*, 1034801) World Health.

Resource Allocation Problems: Algorithmic Approaches. Toshihide Ibaraki & Naoki Katoh. (Foundations of Computing Ser.). (Illus.). 338p. 1988. 40.00 (*0-262-09027-9*) MIT Pr.

***Resource Allocation to Fisheries Research in Asia.** Ed. by F. Brian Davy. (Asian Fisheries Society Spec. Publications: No. 7). 172p. 1993. per. write for info. (*971-8709-35-5*, Pub. by ICLARM PH) Intl Spec Bk.

***Resource & Environment Management.** Mitchell. (C). 1997. pap. text ed. 25.95 (*0-582-23796-3*, Pub. by Longman UK) Longman.

Resource & Environmental Economics. Brown. (HB - Economics Ser.). 1997. text ed. 59.95 (*0-538-83108-1*) S-W Pub.

Resource & Environmental Economics: Natural Resources & the Environment in Economics. Anthony C. Fisher. LC 81-9951. (Cambridge Surveys of Economic Literature Ser.). 256p. 1981. pap. text ed. 21.95 (*0-521-28594-1*) Cambridge U Pr.

Resource & Environmental Effects of U. S. Agriculture. Pierre R. Crosson & Sterling Brubaker. LC 82-47984. 255p. 1982. 16.95 (*0-8018-2920-8*) Resources Future.

Resource & Environmental Management in Canada: Addressing Conflict & Uncertainty. 2nd ed. Ed. by Bruce Mitchell. (Illus.). 456p. (C). 1995. pap. text ed. 35.00 (*0-19-541059-9*) OUP.

Resource & Output Trends in the United States since 1870. Moses Abramovitz. (Occasional Papers: No. 52). 23p. 1956. reprint ed. 20.00 (*0-87014-366-2*); reprint ed. mic. film 20.00 (*0-685-61306-2*) Natl Bur Econ Res.

***Resource Assessment in Forested Landscapes.** David D. Reed & Glen Mroz. LC 97-1735. 400p. 1997. 69.95 (*0-471-15582-9*) Wiley.

Resource Assistant. Jack Rudman. (Career Examination Ser.: C-1745). 1994. reprint ed. pap. 23.95 (*0-8373-1745-2*) Nat Learn.

Resource Atlas of the Apalachicola Estuary: SGR-55. Robert Livingston. 64p. 1983. write for info. (*0-318-60283-0*) U Fla Law.

Resource-Based & Evolutionary Theories of the Firm: Towards a Synthesis. Cynthia A. Montgomery. LC 95-3537. 288p. (C). 1995. lib. bdg. 87.50 (*0-7923-9562-X*) Kluwer Ac.

***Resource Based Learning.** Ed. by Sally Brown & Brenda Smith. 192p. 1996. pap. 34.95 (*0-7494-1932-6*) Taylor & Francis.

Resource Based Learning: Using Open & Flexible Learning Resources for Continuous Development. Julie Dorrell. LC 93-15715. (Training Ser.). 1993. write for info. (*0-07-707692-3*) McGraw.

Resource-Based Learning Activities: Information Literacy for High School Students. Ann Bleakley & Jackie Carrigan. LC 94-13857. 1994. pap. 30.00 (*0-8389-3443-9*) ALA.

Resource-Based View of the Firm. 200p. (C). 1995. pap. write for info. (*0-615-00555-1*) West Pub.

Resource Bibliography for the Decipherment of Maya Hieroglyphs & New Maya Hieroglyphs Readings. John F. Harris. LC 94-463. 1994. 7.95 (*0-924171-30-8*) U PA Mus Pubns.

Resource Bin Vol. I: Selected Reprints from Nuts & Volts. Don Lancaster. 154p. (Orig.). 1994. pap. 24.50 (*1-882193-11-3*) Synergetics Pr.

Resource Book: Directory of Organizations, Associations, Self Help Groups & Hotlines for Mental Health & Human Services Professionals & Their Clients. Robert L. Barker. LC 86-25765. 165p. 1987. text ed. 29.95 (*0-86656-622-8*) Haworth Pr.

Resource Book for HBJ Handwriting Book 2. Johnson. 1988. teacher ed., pap. 61.00 (*0-15-326073-4*) HB Schl Dept.

Resource Book for HBJ Handwriting Book 3. Johnson. 1988. teacher ed., pap. 61.00 (*0-15-326075-0*) HB Schl Dept.

Resource Book for HBJ Handwriting Book 4. Johnson. 1988. teacher ed., pap. 61.00 (*0-15-326076-9*) HB Schl Dept.

Resource Book for HBJ Handwriting Book 5. Johnson. 1988. teacher ed., pap. 61.00 (*0-15-326077-7*) HB Schl Dept.

Resource Book for HBJ Handwriting Book 6. Johnson. 1988. teacher ed., pap. 61.00 (*0-15-326078-5*) HB Schl Dept.

Resource Book for Senior Girl Scouts. Girl Scouts of the U. S. A. Staff. (Illus.). 192p. (Orig.). (YA). (gr. 9-12). 1995. pap. 9.95 (*0-88441-284-9*) Girl Scouts USA.

Resource Book for the Implementation of Applied Mathematics. Center for Occupational Research & Development Staff. (Applied Mathematics Ser.). (Illus.). 1993. pap. text ed. 30.00 (*1-55502-352-5*) CORD Commns.

Resource Book for the Kindergarten Teacher. Walter B. Barbe. (Illus.). (C). 1980. 39.95 (*0-88309-103-8*) Zaner-Bloser.

Resource Book for the Special Education Teacher. Virginia H. Lucas & Walter B. Barbe. (Illus.). 1982. 34.95 (*0-88309-117-8*) Zaner-Bloser.

Resource Book in Alumni Administration: Managing Alumni Programs I. Charles Webb & Paul Chewning. 1993. pap. 26.50 (*0-89964-301-9*, 29902) Coun Adv & Supp Ed.

Resource Book Math Unlimited 1991: Grade 5. Harcourt Brace Staff. 1991. teacher ed. 149.50 (*0-15-351584-8*) HB Schl Dept.

Resource Book Math Unlimited 1991: Grade 6. Harcourt Brace Staff. 1991. teacher ed. 149.50 (*0-15-351585-6*) HB Schl Dept.

Resource Book Math Unlimited 1991: Grade 7. Harcourt Brace Staff. 1991. teacher ed. 168.25 (*0-15-351586-4*) HB Schl Dept.

Resource Book Math Unlimited 1991: Grade 8. Harcourt Brace Staff. 1991. teacher ed. 168.25 (*0-15-372623-7*) HB Schl Dept.

Resource Book of Biochemistry. Moran & Scrimgeour. 1994. pap. text ed. 26.40 (*0-13-816679-X*) P-H.

Resource Book of Jewish Music: A Bibliographical & Topical Guide to the Book & Journal Literature & Program Materials. Compiled by Irene Heskes. LC 84-22435. (Music Reference Collection: No. 3). xiv, 302p. 1985. text ed. 49.95 (*0-313-23251-2*, HEJ/) Greenwood.

Resource Book of Rural Universities in the Developing Countries. Harold W. Hannah. LC 65-19571. 389p. reprint ed. pap. 110.90 (*0-317-28485-1*, 2019049) Bks Demand.

Resource Book of Sermons, 3 vols. 1987. pap. 23.99 (*0-88019-267-4*) Schmul Pub Co.

Resource Book of Sermons, 3 vols., 1. 1987. pap. 8.99 (*0-88019-212-7*) Schmul Pub Co.

Resource Book of Sermons, 3 vols., 2. 1987. pap. 8.99 (*0-88019-214-3*) Schmul Pub Co.

Resource Book of Sermons, 3 vols., 3. 1987. pap. 8.99 (*0-88019-219-4*) Schmul Pub Co.

Resource Book on Geography. Arthur Getis. 1984. 62.32 (*0-395-36547-3*) HM.

Resource Book on Progressive Pharmaceutical Services. 2nd ed. 200p. (Orig.). 1992. pap. text ed. write for info. (*1-879907-17-8*) Am Soc Hlth-Syst.

Resource Careers: Options & Opportunities in Environmental & Natural Resources Law. LC 79-55232. 107p. 1979. pap. 3.00 (*0-89707-012-7*, 535-0005) Amer Bar Assn.

Resource Communities: Settlement & Workforce Issues. Ed. by T. B. Brealey et al. 1988. pap. 60.00 (*0-643-04247-4*, Pub. by CSIRO AT) Aubrey Bks.

Resource Companion to Curriculum Initiative. Michael Eisenberg & Robert Berkowitz. Ed. by Peter Hernon & Charles R. McClure. LC 88-1598. (Information Management, Policies & Services Ser.: Vol. 7). 176p. 1988. pap. 39.50 (*0-89391-498-3*) Ablex Pub.

***Resource Competition.** Grover. (Illus.). 256p. 1997. text ed. write for info. (*0-412-74930-0*, Chap & Hall NY) Chapman & Hall.

Resource Competition & Community Structure. David Tilman. Ed. by Robert M. May. LC 81-47954. (Monographs in Population Biology: No. 17). (Illus.). 312p. 1982. pap. text ed. 24.95 (*0-691-08302-9*) Princeton U Pr.

Resource Competition & Community Structure. David Tilman. LC 81-47954. (Monographs in Population Biology: No. 17). (Illus.). 309p. 1982. reprint ed. pap. 88.10 (*0-7837-8184-9*, 2047889) Bks Demand.

Resource Conservation & Recovery Act (RCRA), 4 vols., Vol. 4, Module 1. Multimedia Development Services Staff. (Safety, Health & Environmental Fundamentals Ser.). (Illus.). (Orig.). (C). 1996. teacher ed., text ed. 65.00 (*1-57431-122-0*); pap. text ed. 30.00 (*1-57431-121-2*) Tech Trng Systs.

***Resource Conservation & Recovery Act (RCRA) Orientation Manual.** (Illus.). 209p. (C). 1996. reprint ed. pap. 40.00 (*0-7881-3164-8*) DIANE Pub.

Resource Conservation & Recovery Act (RCRA) Orientation Manual, 1990. rev. ed. (Illus.). 252p. 1990. per. 20.00 (*0-16-026038-8*, S/N055000003645) USGPO.

Resource Conservation Glossary. Soil Conservation Society of America Staff. LC 82-5830. 199p. reprint ed. pap. 56.80 (*0-7837-4614-8*, 2044335) Bks Demand.

Resource-Constrained Economies: The North American Dilemma. Frwd. by John Fraser. LC 80-16502. xvi, 307p. (Orig.). 1980. pap. text ed. 8.50 (*0-935734-05-8*) Soil & Water Conserv.

Resource-Constrained Project Scheduling: Exact Methods for the Multi-Mode Case. A. Sprecher. (Lecture Notes in Economics & Mathematical Systems: Vol. 409). xii, 142p. 1994. 47.95 (*0-387-57834-X*) Spr-Verlag.

Resource Development: Patterns, Problems & Prospects. V. Vidyanath. 407p. (C). 1991. 212.50 (*81-210-0280-X*, Pub. by Print Hse II) St Mut.

Resource Development in the Two-Year College. Ed. by David P. Mitzel. (C). 1988. text ed. 27.95 (*0-9619545-0-7*); pap. text ed. 17.95 (*0-9619545-1-5*) Natl Coun Res Dev.

Resource Development of the Lower Mississippi River: Conference Abstracts - Water Management of River Systems - RASA Abstracts. Ed. by Dhamo Dhamotharan et al. LC 91-75128. (Technical Publications: No. 91-3). (Illus.). 478p. (Orig.). 1991. pap. 45.00 (*1-882132-16-5*) Am Water Resources.

Resource Directory for Apple 2E. Widl. 1983. pap. 9.95 (*0-684-17934-2*) S&S Trade.

Resource Directory for Older People. 240p. (C). 1993. pap. text ed. 30.00 (*1-56806-942-1*) DIANE Pub.

***Resource Directory for Older People.** 1997. lib. bdg. 251.99 (*0-8490-6217-9*) Gordon Pr.

***Resource Directory for Older People.** 1997. lib. bdg. 250.95 (*0-8490-6245-4*) Gordon Pr.

***Resource Directory for Older People.** rev. ed. 274p. 1997. pap. text ed. 40.00 (*0-7881-3822-7*) DIANE Pub.

Resource Directory for the Disabled. Richard N. Shrout. 400p. 1991. 45.00 (*0-8160-2216-X*) Facts on File.

Resource Economics: An Economic Approach to Natural Resource & Environmental Policy. 2nd ed. Alan Randall. LC 87-4988. 448p. 1987. Net. text ed. write for info. (*0-471-87468-X*) Wiley.

Resource Economics: Selected Works of Orris C. Herfindahl. Ed. by David B Brooks. LC 74-6814. 316p. 1974. 27.50 (*0-8018-1645-9*) Resources Future.

Resource Economics for Foresters. Robinson G. Gregory. LC 87-16069. 477p. 1987. Net. text ed. 51.00 (*0-471-08521-9*) Wiley.

Resource Exchange Network for Eliminating Waste. (Illus.). 51p. (Orig.). (C). 1993. pap. text ed. 20.00 (*1-56806-476-4*) DIANE Pub.

Resource Extraction & Market Structure. M. Schafer. (Lecture Notes in Economics & Mathematical Systems Ser.: Vol. 263). xii, 154p. 1986. 25.95 (*0-387-16081-7*) Spr-Verlag.

Resource Focused Therapy. Wendel A. Ray & Bradford Keeney. (Systemic Thinking & Practice Ser.). 112p. 1993. pap. text ed. 22.95 (*1-85575-049-X*, Pub. by Karnac Bks UK) Brunner-Mazel.

Resource for Nonlawyers. 1985. pap. write for info. (*0-318-67346-0*) NCLS Inc.

Resource for the Study of Islam. Ney Rieber. 227p. 1993. pap. text ed. 9.95 (*1-56794-045-5*, C-2326) Star Bible.

Resource for Urban Educational Studies. (Urban Education Reports Ser.: No. 2). 12p. 1981. 2.00 (*0-317-13088-9*) I N Thut World Educ Ctr.

***Resource Guide: A Comprehensive Listing of Media for Further Study.** William L. Shulman. LC 97-19132. (Holocaust Ser.). 1997. lib. bdg. write for info. (*1-56711-208-0*) Blackbirch.

Resource Guide & Master Index. Time-Life Books Editors. Ed. by Marike Van der Veen. LC 95-18955. (Understanding Science & Nature Ser.). (Illus.). 152p. (YA). (gr. 7 up). 1995. teacher ed. write for info. (*0-8094-9716-6*) Time-Life.

Resource Guide for Child Care & Family Planning Services in the Maquiladora Industry. Paul Ganster & Dana Hamson. Tr. by Bertha Hernandez. (Illus.). 40p. (ENG & SPA.). 1995. pap. 7.00 (*0-925613-18-5*) SDSU Inst Reg Studies.

Resource Guide for Christian Counselors. Ed. by Douglas R. Flather. LC 95-37639. 410p. (Orig.). (gr. 10). 1996. pap. 17.99 (*0-8010-5249-1*) Baker Bks.

***Resource Guide for Christian Higher Education.** rev. ed. Orig. Title: Directory of Administrative Personnel 1993-94. 252p. 1996. ring bd. 25.00 (*0-9652730-2-4*) Coal Christian Coll.

Resource Guide for Creating Successful Communities. Conservation Foundation Staff et al. LC 89-15473. (Illus.). 206p. 1989. 39.95 (*1-55963-031-0*); pap. 24.95 (*1-55963-015-9*) Island Pr.

Resource Guide for Drug Management Programs for Older People. 124p. 1986. write for info. (*0-318-61579-7*) US HHS.

Resource Guide for Economics of Competition. C. H. Benjamin. (Illus.). 100p. (Orig.). pap. text ed. write for info. (*0-9631679-0-1*) GR Comm Col Edu TC.

Resource Guide for Elementary School Teaching. 3rd ed. Richard D. Kellough & Patricia L. Roberts. (Illus.). 480p. (C). 1993. pap. text ed. 46.00 (*0-02-362581-3*, Macmillan Coll) P-H.

R

*__Resource Guide for Elementary School Teaching.__ 4th ed. Richard D. Kellough. LC 97-787. 1997. pap. text ed. 47.00 (0-13-493354-0) P-H.

Resource Guide for Ergonomics. Ed. by Patricia Fernberg. (Illus.). 100p. (C). 1995. 29.95 (0-932905-08-0) Penton Pub.

Resource Guide for Fitness Programs for Older Persons. Alan Pardini & Connie Mahoney. 115p. 1986. write for info. (0-318-61580-0) US HHS.

Resource Guide for Injury Control Programs for Older Persons. 48p. 1987. write for info. (1-55672-023-8) US HHS.

Resource Guide for Nutrition Management for Older Persons. Marjorie Bogaert-Tullis & Sarah Samuels. 101p. 1986. write for info. (0-318-61578-9) US HHS.

*__Resource Guide for Older People.__ 1997. lib. bdg. 250.95 (0-8490-8205-6) Gordon Pr.

Resource Guide for People & Nations: World History 1987. Mazour. 1987. teacher ed., pap. text ed. 135.25 (0-15-373466-3) HR&W Schl Div.

*__Resource Guide for Practice in Foreign Markets.__ 1996. ring bd. 45.00 (1-879304-44-9, J352) AIA DC.

Resource Guide for Pre-Retirement Planning. Ed. by Eugene H. Seibert & Joanne S. Seibert. 132p. (Orig.). 1989. pap. 59.95 (0-939461-01-3) Seibert Assocs.

Resource Guide for Secondary School Teaching. 6th ed. Eugene C. Kim & Richard D. Kellough. 656p. (C). 1995. pap. text ed. 45.00 (0-02-363872-9, Macmillan Coll) P-H.

Resource Guide for Teaching: K-12. 2nd ed. Richard D. Kellough. LC 95-26560. 1996. pap. text ed. 50.00 (0-13-461963-3) P-H.

Resource Guide for the Communities of Columbus, New Mexico - Puerto Palomas, Chihuahua. Ed. by University of New Mexico Advanced Regional Planning Studio Staff. 120p. (SPA.). (C). 1992. pap. text ed. 10.00 (0-937795-04-6) Border Res Inst.

Resource Guide for the Consultant Dietitian. 3rd rev. ed. Consultant Dietitians in Health Care Facilities Staff. 209p. 1993. ring bd. 49.95 (1-884675-00-X) Cnslt Dietitians.

Resource Guide for Trainers & Facilitators of PLA, Vol. 1. Robert Leurs. 120p. (Orig.). 1996. pap. 15.95 (1-888753-00-5) PACT Pubns.

Resource Guide for Transportation Engineering Education. (Bibliography Ser.: No. 61). 57p. 1984. 8.20 (0-309-03651-8) Transport Res Bd.

Resource Guide for Transportation Engineering Education: Update. (Bibliography Ser.: No. 63). 48p. 1987. 10.00 (0-309-04462-6) Transport Res Bd.

Resource Guide for Trigonometry 1987. Coxford. 1987. teacher ed., pap. 57.00 (0-15-359371-7) HB Schl Dept.

Resource Guide for Women's Ministries. Linda R. McGinn. LC 89-71084. 176p. (Orig.). 1990. pap. 8.99 (0-8054-3005-9, 4230-05) Broadman.

Resource Guide for Working with Youth at Risk. Ed. by Robert C. Morris & Nelda Schultz. 263p. 1993. pap. 24.95 (1-56676-098-4) Technomic.

Resource Guide of Continence Products & Services. (Incontinence Ser.). 1991. lib. bdg. 75.00 (0-87700-962-7) Revisionist Pr.

Resource Guide on Blacks in Higher Education. National Association for Equal Opportunity in Higher Education Staff. 66p. (Orig.). (C). 1988. pap. text ed. 10.50 (0-8191-6949-8) NAEOHE.

Resource Guide, PACE: A Program for Acquiring Competence in Entrepreneurship. rev. ed. National Center for Research in Vocational Education Staff. 1983. 7.95 (0-318-67187-5, RD240D) Ctr Educ Trng Employ.

*__Resource Guide to Accompany Breastfeeding & Human Lactation.__ Riordan & Auerbach. 1996. 28.00 (0-7637-0220-X) Jones & Bartlett.

Resource Guide to Chiropractic: A Bibliography of Chiropractic & Related Areas, 1895-1981. Matthew J. Brennan. 155p. (C). 1981. pap. text ed. 18.00 (0-9606618-0-8, K-12) Am Chiro Assn.

Resource Guide to Doing Business in Central & Eastern Europe. 1992. lib. bdg. 79.99 (0-8490-5549-0) Gordon Pr.

Resource Guide to Information on Southern Africa. Margaret C. Lee. LC 88-50831. 54p. 1988. student ed. 3.95 (1-55523-163-2) Winston-Derek.

Resource Guide to Materials on the Arab World. Audrey Shabbas. (Illus.). 46p. (Orig.). 1987. pap. 6.95 (0-937694-74-6) Assn Arab-Amer U Grads.

Resource Guide to Public School Early Childhood Programs. Lilian G. Katz et al. LC 88-70536. 198p. (Orig.). (C). 1988. pap. 14.95 (0-87120-151-8, 611-88036) Assn Supervision.

Resource Guide to Special Education: Terms, Laws, Assessment, Procedures, Organizations. 2nd ed. William E. Davis. 329p. 1985. pap. text ed. 40.95 (0-205-08546-6, H85467) Allyn.

*__Resource Guide to Sustainable Landscapes & Gardens.__ 3rd ed. Wesley A. Gruesbeck & Jan Striffel. 486p. 1996. pap. 35.00 (0-9647109-1-9) Environ Resources.

Resource Guide to the State Environmental Management. 2nd ed. R. Steven Brown et al. 198p. 1990. pap. 40.00 (0-87292-097-6, C-184) Coun State Govts.

Resource Guide to Themes in Contemporary American Song Lyrics, 1950-1985. B. Lee Cooper. LC 85-21933. (Illus.). 481p. 1986. text ed. 79.50 (0-313-24516-9, CPI/, Greenwood Pr) Greenwood.

Resource Guide to Travel in Sub-Saharan Africa, 2 vols., Set. 800p. 1995. 200.00 (1-873836-55-4) Bowker-Saur.

Resource Guide to Travel in Sub-Saharan Africa, 2 vols., Vol. 2, Central & Southern Africa. 380p. 1997. 125.00 (1-873836-50-3) Bowker-Saur.

Resource Guide to Travel in Sub-Saharan Africa Vol. 1: East & West Africa, 2 vols., Vol. 1, East & West Africa. Louis Taussig. (Resource Guides to Travel: Vol. 1). 383p. 1995. 125.00 (1-873836-45-7, Pub. by H Zell Pubs UK) Bowker-Saur.

Resource Guide, 1987. 2nd ed. Ed. by Committee on Resource Sharing & Coordinated Acquisitions Staff. x, 56p. 1987. pap. 10.00 (0-938435-01-9) LI Lib Resources.

Resource Handbook for Satir Concepts. Johanna Schwab. 1990. pap. 12.95 (0-8314-0073-0) Sci & Behavior.

Resource Handbook on Performance Assessment & Measurement: A Tool for Students, Practitioners & Policymakers. Patricia Wheeler & Geneva Haertel. (Illus.). 261p. (Orig.). (C). 1993. pap. 24.95 (1-884690-15-7) Owl Press.

Resource Inventory & Baseline Study Methods for Developing Countries. Ed. by Francis Conant. LC 83-15493. (AAAS Publication Ser.: No. 83-3). 565p. reprint ed. pap. 161.10 (0-318-34729-6, 2031948) Bks Demand.

Resource Kit: Individual Sets in a Kit. Marion W. Stuart. student ed., text ed. write for info. (0-943343-50-X) Lrn Wrap-Ups.

Resource Kit for Managers of Volunteers. Betty B. Stallings. (Illus.). 300p. 1992. teacher ed., ring bd. 54.95 (0-9634560-0-8) Blding Better Skills.

Resource Letters, Bk. III. 1972. 26.00 (0-917853-82-2, RB19) Am Assn Physics.

Resource Letters, Bk. IV. 232p. 1982. 26.00 (0-917853-83-0, RB37) Am Assn Physics.

*__Resource Letters, Bk. V.__ 296p. 1994. 26.00 (0-917853-64-4, RB63) Am Assn Physics.

Resource Life Cycle Analysis: A Business Modeling Technique for IS Planning. Ronald G. Ross & Wanda I. Michaels. (Illus.). 90p. 1992. 39.95 (0-941049-01-9) Dbase Res Grp.

*__Resource List for ESL Practitioners: 1994 Able Curriculum Guide.__ 5th ed. Judy R. Roney et al. (Illus.). 48p. (C). 1996. reprint ed. pap. 20.00 (0-7881-3309-8) DIANE Pub.

Resource Management: Information Systems. Keith McCloy. 542p. 1995. 125.00 (0-7484-0119-9); pap. 59.00 (0-7484-0120-2) Taylor & Francis.

Resource Management & Agricultural Development in Jamaica: Lessons for a Participatory Approach. Harvey Blustain. (Special Series on Resource Management: No. 2). 151p. (Orig.). (C). 1982. pap. text ed. 9.00 (0-86731-083-9) Cornell CIS RDC.

Resource Management & Pastoral Institution Building in the West African Sahel. Nadarajah Shanmugaratnam et al. LC 92-29976. (Discussion Paper Ser.: No. 175). 89p. 1992. 7.95 (0-8213-2215-X, 12215) World Bank.

Resource Management Education. Fanatini. write for info. (0-275-90006-1, C0006, Praeger Pubs) Greenwood.

Resource Management for Distributed Multimedia Systems. Lars C. Wolf & Christian L. Wolf. LC 96-23058. 160p. (C). 1996. lib. bdg. 89.95 (0-7923-9748-7) Kluwer Ac.

Resource Management for Individuals & Families. Elizabeth B. Goldsmith. 325p. (C). 1996. text ed. 58.75 (0-314-04465-5) West Pub.

Resource Management in Amazonia. Ed. by Darrell A. Posey & William Balee. LC 89-9392. (Advances in Economic Botany Ser.: Vol. 7). (Illus.). 304p. 1989. pap. text ed. 59.00 (0-89327-340-6) NY Botanical.

Resource Management in Developing Countries. Peter H. Omara-Ojungu. (C). 1992. pap. text ed. 24.95 (0-582-30102-5) Addison-Wesley.

Resource Management in Developing Countries: Africa's Ecological & Economic Problems. Valentine U. James. LC 90-49217. 176p. 1991. text ed. 55.00 (0-89789-224-0, H224, Bergin & Garvey); pap. text ed. 17.95 (0-89789-227-5, G227, Bergin & Garvey) Greenwood.

Resource Manual: Social Workers & Social Work Services As Defined in Medicare Law & Regulation. 2nd ed. NASW Legislative Affairs Department Staff. 420p. 1992. 70.00 (0-87101-216-2) Natl Assn Soc Wkrs.

Resource Manual for Alcohol & Other Drug Abuse Education in Psychiatry. 35p. (Orig.). (C). 1995. pap. text ed. 20.00 (0-7881-2557-5) DIANE Pub.

*__Resource Manual for Campus-Based Youth Mentoring Programs.__ 200p. 1993. pap. 30.00 (0-614-30600-0) Ed Comm States.

*__Resource Manual for Providing Hospice Care to People Living with AIDS.__ National Hospice Organization AIDS Resource Committee. 109p. (Orig.). 1996. per., pap. 11.85 (0-931207-44-4) Natl Hospice.

Resource Manual for Texas Legal Services Programs Board of Directors. 76p. 1987. pap. 8.75 (0-317-03740-4, 42, 965) NCLS Inc.

Resource Manual for Typesetting with Your Computer. Al Beechick. LC 86-71983. 48p. 1986. pap. 9.95 (0-940319-03-9) Arrow Press.

Resource Materials: Banking & Commercial Lending Law, Vol. IV. 520p. (Orig.). 1983. pap. 25.00 (0-8318-0140-9, R140) Am Law Inst.

Resource Materials: Banking & Commercial Lending Law, Vol. V. Ed. by Richard T. Nassberg. 466p. (Orig.). 1984. pap. 25.00 (0-8318-0145-X, R145) Am Law Inst.

Resource Materials: Banking & Commercial Lending Law, Vol. VI. Ed. by Richard T. Nassberg. 449p. (Orig.). 1985. pap. 25.00 (0-8318-0152-2, R152) Am Law Inst.

Resource Materials: Banking & Commercial Lending Law, Vol. VII. Ed. by Richard T. Nassberg. 447p. (Orig.). 1986. pap. 25.00 (0-8318-0157-3, R157) Am Law Inst.

Resource Materials: Banking & Commercial Lending Law, Vol. VIII. Ed. & Intro. by Richard T. Nassberg. 328p. (Orig.). 1987. pap. 25.00 (0-8318-0162-X, R161) Am Law Inst.

Resource Materials: Banking & Commercial Lending Law, Vol. X. Ed. by Richard T. Smith & Nassberg. 641p. (Orig.). 1989. pap. text ed. 25.00 (0-8318-0169-7, R169) Am Law Inst.

Resource Materials: Banking & Commercial Lending Law, Vol. XII. Ed. by Richard T. Nassberg. xiii, 545p. (Orig.). 1991. pap. text ed. 30.00 (0-8318-0172-7, R174) Am Law Inst.

Resource Materials: Banking & Commercial Lending Law, Vol. XIV. Ed. by Richard T. Nassberg. 564p. (Orig.). 1993. pap. text ed. 80.00 (0-8318-0177-8, R179) Am Law Inst.

Resource Materials: Banking & Commercial Lending Law, Vol. XV. Pref. by Richard T. Nassberg. (Resource Materials Ser.). 610p. 1994. pap. text ed. 80.00 (0-8318-0182-4, R182) Am Law Inst.

Resource Materials: Banking & Commercial Lending Law, Vol. XI. Pref. by Richard T. Nassberg. 656p. (Orig.). 1990. pap. 25.00 (0-8318-0171-9, R171) Am Law Inst.

Resource Materials: Civil Practice & Litigation in Federal & State Courts, 2 vols. 4th ed. Ed. by Sol Schrieber. 2450p. 1987. pap. text ed. 47.50 (0-8318-0160-3, R160) Am Law Inst.

Resource Materials: Civil Practice & Litigation in Federal & State Courts, 2 vols. 5th ed. Ed. by Sol Schreiber. 2600p. 1992. ring bd. 200.00 (0-8318-0174-3, R178) Am Law Inst.

Resource Materials: Civil Practice & Litigation in Federal & State Courts, 2 vols., Set. 6th ed. Ed. by Sol Schreiber. 1994. pap. 175.00 (0-8318-0184-0, R184) Am Law Inst.

Resource Materials: Commercial Real Estate Financing, Including 1990 Supplement. 982p. (Orig.). 1989. suppl. ed., pap. 50.00 (0-8318-0168-9, R168/S474) Am Law Inst.

Resource Materials: Commercial Real Estate Financing, 1990 Supplement. 325p. (Orig.). 1990. Supplement 1990, 325 pgs. suppl. ed., pap. 50.00 (0-685-54036-7, S474) Am Law Inst.

Resource Materials: Condominium, Planned Unit Development & Conversion Documents. 4th ed. Frwd. by Paul A. Wolkin. 835p. (Orig.). 1988. suppl. ed., pap. 25.00 (0-8318-0138-7, R164) Am Law Inst.

Resource Materials: Employment & Labor Law. 7th ed. xviii, 1863p. 1995. pap. 150.00 (0-8318-0186-7, S983) Am Law Inst.

Resource Materials: Estate Planning in Depth, 2 vols. 8th ed. Ed. by Paul A. Wolkin. 1190p. (Orig.). 1984. pap. 37.50 (0-8318-0147-6, R147) Am Law Inst.

Resource Materials: Labor & Employment Law, 2 vols. 3rd ed. 1273p. 1986. 37.50 (0-8318-0156-5, R156) Am Law Inst.

Resource Materials: Labor & Employment Law, 2 vols. 4th ed. 1650p. 1988. 37.50 (0-8318-0163-8, R163) Am Law Inst.

Resource Materials: Labor & Employment Law, 2 vols. 5th ed. Ed. by Peter M. Panken. 1650p. 1990. pap. text ed. 50.00 (0-8318-0170-0, R170) Am Law Inst.

Resource Materials: Labor & Employment Law, 2 vols. 6th ed. Ed. by Peter M. Panken. 1812p. 1992. pap. text ed. 150.00 (0-8318-0176-X, R176) Am Law Inst.

Resource Materials: Modern Real Estate Transactions, 2 vols. 9th ed. 1098p. 1991. Set. pap. 60.00 (0-8318-0178-6, R172) Am Law Inst.

Resource Materials: Modern Real Estate Transactions, 2 vols. 10th ed. 2157p. 1993. pap. 150.00 (0-8318-0180-8, R181) Am Law Inst.

Resource Materials: Partnerships & Limited Liability Companies (LLCs), 2 vols., Set. 11th ed. xiv, 1159p. 1994. pap. 80.00 (0-8318-0183-2, R183) Am Law Inst.

Resource Materials: Partnerships: UPA, ULPA, Securities, Taxation, & Bankruptcy. 7th ed. (Resource Materials Ser.). 817p. 1987. pap. 25.00 (0-8318-0161-1, R162) Am Law Inst.

Resource Materials: Partnerships: UPA, ULPA, Securities, Taxation, & Bankruptcy. 9th ed. Ed. by James O. Hewitt. 928p. (Orig.). 1990. pap. text ed. 25.00 (0-8318-0173-5, R173) Am Law Inst.

Resource Materials: Partnerships: UPA, ULPA, Securities, Taxation, & Bankruptcy. 10th ed. xii, 1150p. 1992. pap. 40.00 (0-8318-0179-4, R177) Am Law Inst.

Resource Materials on the Middle East: A Bibliographic Guide. 1992. lib. bdg. 88.95 (0-8490-5432-X) Gordon Pr.

Resource Mobilization & Investment in an Islamic Economic Framework: Proceedings of the Third International Islamic Economics Seminar, 1990. Ed. by Zaidi Sattar. (Islamization of Knowledge Ser.: No. 13). 207p. (Orig.). 1992. pap. 10.00 (1-56564-048-9) IIIT VA.

Resource Mobilization for Drinking Water & Sanitation in Developing Nations. Ed. by F. W. Montenari et al. 768p. 1987. 62.00 (0-87262-629-6) Am Soc Civil Eng.

Resource Mobilization in Poor Countries: Implementing Tax Policies. Alex Radian. LC 79-66440. 226p. 1980. 34.95 (0-87855-304-5) Transaction Pubs.

Resource of Objectives for Training in Family Medicine: An Atlas. Compiled by STFM Task Force on Objectives Staff. 160p. 1979. 5.00 (0-942295-10-2) Soc Tchrs Fam Med.

Resource of War: The Credit of the Government Made Immediately Available - History of the Legal Tender Paper Money Issued During the Great Rebellion Being a Loan Without Interest & a National Currency. Elbridge G. Spaulding. LC 69-19681. (Money Markets Ser.). 213p. (C). 1971. reprint ed. text ed. 59.75 (0-8371-0662-1, SPRW) Greenwood.

Resource Pak. NCEET Staff. 436p. (C). 1996. 56.00 (0-7872-2235-6) Kendall-Hunt.

Resource Physiology of Conifers: Acquisition, Allocation & Utilization. Ed. by William K. Smith & Thomas M. Hinckley. (Physiological Ecology Ser.). (Illus.). 396p. 1994. boxed 74.95 (0-12-652870-5) Acad Pr.

Resource Pkg. see Deutsch Konkret, Level 1

Resource Pkg. see Deutsch Konkret, Level 2

Resource Planning Atlas. Brahm S. Ojha & Jasbir Singh. (C). 1993. text ed. 50.00 (81-85135-73-8) S Asia.

Resource Politics, Freshwater, & Regional Relations. Ed. by Caroline Thomas & Darryl Howlett. LC 92-42869. 1993. 95.00 (0-335-15775-0, Open Univ Pr) Taylor & Francis.

Resource Program: Organization & Implementation. J. Lee Wiederholt et al. LC 92-35594. 285p. (Orig.). (C). 1993. pap. text ed. 33.00 (0-89079-571-1, 0055) PRO-ED.

Resource Raising: The Role of Non-Cash Assistance in Corporate Philanthropy. Alex J. Plinio & Joanne B. Scanlon. 56p. 1986. pap. 10.00 (0-685-23210-7) Ind Sector.

Resource Recovery. Douglas Harbit. 8p. (Orig.). 1975. pap. 8.00 (0-317-04864-3) Natl Coun Econ Dev.

Resource Recovery & Recycling. Allan F. Barton. LC 78-13601. (Environmental Science & Technology Ser.). (Illus.). 429p. reprint ed. pap. 123.20 (0-7837-3520-0, 2057854) Bks Demand.

Resource Recovery & Solid Waste Management in Norway, Sweden, Denmark & Germany: Lessons for New York. 35p. (Orig.). (C). 1995. pap. text ed. 20.00 (0-7881-2565-6) DIANE Pub.

Resource Recovery & Utilization - STP592. 212p. 1975. 20.00 (0-8031-0558-4, 04-592000-41) ASTM.

Resource Recovery Economics: Methods for Feasibility Analysis. Stuart H. Russell. (Pollution Engineering & Technology Ser.: Vol. 22). (Illus.). 312p. 1982. 145.00 (0-8247-1726-0) Dekker.

Resource Recovery from Municipal Solid Wastes, 2 vols. Luis F. Diaz & Clarence G. Golueke. Incl. Vol. I. Primary Processing. 176p. 1982. 112.00 (0-8493-5613-X); Vol. II. Final Processing. 192p. 1982. 111.00 (0-8493-5614-8); 1982. write for info. (0-318-56976-0, TD794) CRC Pr.

Resource Recovery from Solid Wastes: Proceedings of a Conference in Miami Beach, Florida, May 10-12, 1982. Ed. by Subrata Sengupta & Kau-Fui V. Wong. LC 82-18145. 600p. 1982. 230.00 (0-08-028825-1, A125, Pergamon Pr) Elsevier.

Resource Recovery of Municipal Solid Wastes. Ed. by Peter J. Knox. LC 88-8052. (AIChE Symposium Ser.: Vol. 84, No. 265). 198p. 1988. pap. 25.00 (0-8169-0454-5, S-265) Am Inst Chem Eng.

Resource Recovery Through Incineration: Proceedings; Papers Presented at 1974 National Incinerator Conference, Miami, Florida, May 12-15, 1974. National Incinerator Conference Staff. LC 70-124402. 380p. reprint ed. pap. 108.30 (0-317-29795-3, 2016866) Bks Demand.

Resource Recovery Today & Tomorrow: Proceedings of 1980 National Waste Processing Conference, Ninth Biennial Conference: Papers Presented at 1980 National Waste Processing Conference, Washington, DC, May 11-14, 1980. National Waste Processing Conference Staff. LC 70-124402. 633p. reprint ed. pap. 180.00 (0-8357-8759-1, 2033649) Bks Demand.

Resource Recovery Today & Tomorrow: Supplement: Discussions: Papers Presented at 1980 National Waste Processing Conference, Washington, DC, May 11-14, 1980: Ninth Biennial Conference. National Waste Processing Conference Staff. LC 70-124402. 215p. reprint ed. pap. 61.30 (0-8357-8760-5, 2033650) Bks Demand.

Resource Rents & Public Policy in Western Canada. Ed. by Thomas Gunton & John Richards. 261p. 1987. pap. text ed. 20.00 (0-88645-049-7, Pub. by Inst Res Pub CN) Ashgate Pub Co.

Resource Room. Hammill. 1975. text ed. 28.00 (0-8089-0895-2) Saunders.

Resource Room: A Guide for Special Educators. Barry E. McNamara. LC 88-20086. 148p. (C). 1989. text ed. 74.50 (0-88706-983-5); pap. text ed. 24.95 (0-88706-984-3) State U NY Pr.

Resource Scarcity & the Hmong Response: Patterns of Settlement & Economy in Transition. R. G. Cooper. 328p. 1985. 42.50 (9971-69-070-5, Pub. by Sgapore Univ SI) Coronet Bks.

Resource Sector in an Open Economy. Ed. by Horst Siebert. (Lecture Notes in Economics & Mathematical Systems Ser.: Vol. 200). 161p. 1983. 31.00 (0-387-12700-3) Spr-Verlag.

Resource Selection by Animals: Statistical Design & Analysis for Field Studies. Bryan F. Manly et al. LC 92-36062. 192p. (gr. 13). 1993. text ed. 60.95 (0-412-40140-1) Chapman & Hall.

*__Resource Sharing in Biomedical Research.__ Division of Health Policy, Institute of Medicine Staff. 104p. (Orig.). 1996. pap. text ed. 35.00 (0-309-05582-2, Joseph Henry Pr) Natl Acad Pr.

Resource Sharing in Libraries: Why, How, When, Next Action Steps: Based on Papers Presented at the Conference Held April 11-12, 1973 at Pittsburgh, Pennsylvania. Ed. by Allen Kent. LC 73-90724. (Books in Library & Information Science: Vol. 8). (Illus.). 405p. reprint ed. pap. 115.50 (0-317-07889-5, 2051863) Bks Demand.

Resource Strategies in the 90s: Trends in ARL University Libraries. A. Melville. (Occasional Papers). 40p. 1994. pap. 25.00 (0-918006-72-4) ARL.

Resource Teacher: A Guide to Effective Practices. 2nd ed. J. Lee Wiederholt et al. LC 83-4642. (Illus.). 414p. 1983. pap. text ed. 36.00 (0-936104-33-3, 0085) PRO-ED.

Resource Technology '90. 830p. 1991. 15.00 (0-944426-45-X) ASP & RS.

An Asterisk (*) at the beginning of an entry indicates that the title is appearing in BIP for the first time.

R

Resource Theory: Explorations & Applications. Ed. by Uriel G. Foa et al. (Illus.). 304p. 1992. text ed. 58.00 (*0-12-261310-4*) Acad Pr.

Resource Track: Applying Biblical Principles to Personal Finances. Chip Reed. (Illus.). 74p. (Orig.). 1989. student ed., pap. 10.00 (*0-9621353-1-3*) C Reed Assocs.

Resource Transfer & Debt Trap, Vol. V, Pts. I & II. (C). 1988. 90.00 (*0-8364-2343-7*, Pub. by Ashish II) S Asia.

Resource Trends & Population Policy: A Time for Reassessment. Lester R. Brown. LC 79-64839. (Worldwatch Papers). 1979. pap. 5.00 (*0-916468-28-3*) Worldwatch Inst.

Resource Units in Hawaiian Culture. rev. ed. Donald D. Mitchell. (Illus.). 303p. 1992. pap. text ed. 21.95 (*0-87336-016-8*) Kamehameha Schools.

Resource Use by Chaparral & Matorral: A Comparison of Vegetation Function in Two Mediterranean Type Ecosystems. Ed. by P. C. Miller. (Ecological Studies: Vol. 39). (Illus.). 416p. 1981. 141.95 (*0-387-90556-1*) Spr-Verlag.

Resource Writer, 3 Vols. Barnwell. (C). 1994. pap. 34.36 (*0-395-68479-X*) HM.

*__Resourceful Caregiver: Helping Family Caregivers Help Themselves.__ National Family Caregivers Association Staff. 208p. (C). (gr. 13). 1996. pap. text ed. 12.95 (*0-8151-5556-5*, 30587) Mosby Yr Bk.

*__Resourceful Celeste, Incl. doll.__ Gordon Henderson. (Illus.). 32p. (J). 1995. pap. 30.00 (*1-890414-08-5*) Bow Tie.

*__Resourceful Reader.__ 4th ed. Webb. (C). 1997. pap. text ed. 21.75 (*0-15-505603-4*) HB Coll Pubs.

Resourceful Rehab: A Guide for Historic Buildings in Dade County, Florida. Metropolitan Dade County, Historic Preservation Division, OCED Staff & Charles E. Chase. (Illus.). (Orig.). 1987. pap. 9.95 (*0-9618373-0-6*) MDC-Hist Preserv Div.

Resourceful Woman. Shawn Brennan et al. (Illus.). 833p. 1994. pap. 17.95 (*0-8103-8594-5*) Gale.

*__Resourceful Writer.__ 3rd ed. Webb. (C). 1994. pap. write for info. (*0-15-501238-X*) HB Coll Pubs.

*__Resourceful Writer: A Basic Writing Course, 3 Vols.__ 3rd ed. William H. Barnwell & Robert Dees. (C). 1995. teacher ed., text ed. 31.56 (*0-395-68480-3*) HM.

Resourceful Writer: Readings to Accompany the Harbrace College Handbook. 2nd ed. Suzanne S. Webb. 514p. (C). 1989. pap. text ed. 21.50 (*0-15-576633-3*); pap. text ed. 3.00 (*0-15-576634-1*) HB Coll Pubs.

*__Resources.__ Julian Rowe & Molly Perham. (MapWorlds Ser.). (J). 1997. lib. bdg. 18.60 (*0-531-14387-2*) Watts.

Resources: A New Directory of New York City Directories. 2nd ed. Patricia A. Friedland & Rabina Naraine. LC 89-656336. 49p. 1996. pap. 9.00 (*0-88156-171-1*) Comm Serv Soc NY.

Resources: Environment & Policy. John Fernie & Alan S. Pitkethly. 352p. (C). 1986. 60.00 (*0-06-318314-5*, Pub. by P Chapman Pub UK) St Mut.

Resources: Handbook of Aid & Benefits for People with AIDS - ARC - HIV-Positive in Syracuse & Onondaga County. Compiled by Michael Welch. 90p. (Orig.). 1991. pap. text ed. 10.00 (*0-936826-36-3*) PS Assocs Croton.

Resources Allocation in Divisionalized Groups: A Study of Investment Manuals & Corporate Level Means of Control. Esbjorn Segelod. 240p. 1995. 59.95 (*1-85972-250-4*, Pub. by Avebury Pub UK) Ashgate Pub Co.

Resources & Attractions of Idaho Territory. Robert E. Strahorn. LC 90-48371. (Idaho Yesterdays Ser.). (Illus.). 104p. (C). 1990. reprint ed. pap. 6.95 (*0-89301-138-X*) U of Idaho Pr.

Resources & Development: Natural Resource Policies & Economic Development in an Interdependent World. Wisconsin Seminar on Natural Resource Policies Staff. Ed. by Peter Dorner & Mahmoud A. El-Shafie. LC 80-10577. 517p. 1980. reprint ed. pap. 147.40 (*0-608-01947-X*, 2062602) Bks Demand.

Resources & Development of Mexico. H. H. Bancroft. 1976. lib. bdg. 59.95 (*0-8490-2519-2*) Gordon Pr.

Resources & Environment in Asia's Marine Sector. Ed. by James B. Marsh. 504p. 1992. 105.00 (*0-8448-1708-2*) Taylor & Francis.

*__Resources & Environmental Issues Relevant to Mediterranean Fisheries Management.__ (GFCM Studies & Reviews: No. 66). 150p. 1996. pap. 17.00 (*92-5-103826-0*, F38260, Pub. by FAO IT) Bernan Associates.

Resources & Higher Education. Alfred Morris & John Sizer. 226p. 1983. 29.00 (*0-900868-90-2*, Open Univ Pr) Taylor & Francis.

Resources & Industry. Ed. by F. E. Hamilton. (Illustrated Encyclopedia of World Geography Ser.). (Illus.). 256p. 1992. 45.00 (*0-19-520943-5*) OUP.

Resources & Needs of American Diplomacy. Thorsten D. Sellin. LC 68-57759. (Annals Ser.: Vol. 380). 1968. 28.00 (*0-87761-111-4*); pap. 18.00 (*0-87761-110-6*, 380) Am Acad Pol Soc Sci.

Resources & People in East Kentucky: Problems & Potentials of a Lagging Economy. Mary J. Bowman & W. Warren Haynes. LC 83-11766. (Resources for the Future, Inc. Publications). 480p. reprint ed. 78.50 (*0-404-60328-9*) AMS Pr.

Resources & People in East Kentucky: Problems & Potentials of a Lagging Economy. Mary J. Bowman & W. Warren Haynes. LC 63-17668. 477p. reprint ed. pap. 136.00 (*0-7837-3145-0*, 2042841) Bks Demand.

Resources & Population: Natural, Institutional, & Demographic Dimsensions of Development. Ed. by Bernardo Colombo et al. LC 95-38883. (Pointficiae Academiae Scientiarum Scripta Varia Ser.: Vol. 20). (Illus.). 368p. 1996. 70.00 (*0-19-828918-9*, Clarendon Pr) OUP.

Resources & Projects Book. Ollie Kasicki. 1992. pap. 20.95 (*0-8273-5265-4*) Delmar.

Resources & Prospects of America: Ascertained During a Visit to the States in the Autumn of 1865. S. Morton Peto. LC 73-2529. (Big Business; Economic Power in a Free Society Ser.). 1973. reprint ed. 29.95 (*0-405-05108-5*) Ayer.

Resources & References: Hazardous Waste & Hazardous Materials Management. Gayle Woodside & Donna S. Kocurek. LC 94-4803. 295p. 1994. 64.00 (*0-8155-1351-8*) Noyes.

Resources & Reimbursement Agent. Jack Rudman. (Career Examination Ser.: C-3157). 1994. pap. 27.95 (*0-8373-3157-9*) Nat Learn.

Resources & Society. J. Zucchetto & A. M. Jansson. (Ecological Studies: Vol. 56). (Illus.). x, 246p. 1985. 134.00 (*0-387-96151-8*) Spr-Verlag.

*__Resources & Strategy: A Reader.__ Ed. by Nicolai J. Foss. (Oxford Management Readers Ser.). (Illus.). 300p. 1997. 75.00 (*0-19-878180-6*); pap. 19.95 (*0-19-878179-2*) OUP.

Resources & Strategy: Vital Materials in International Conflict, 1600-Present Day. Ian O. Lesser. 280p. 1989. text ed. 49.95 (*0-312-02372-3*) St Martin.

*__Resources, Costs & Efficiency of Training in the Total Army System.__ Michael G. Shanley et al. LC 97-24646. 1997. write for info. (*0-8330-2516-3*) Rand Corp.

Resources, Deprivation & Poverty. Brian Nolan & Christopher T. Whelan. LC 95-47230. (Illus.). 280p. 1996. 65.00 (*0-19-828785-2*, Clarendon Pr) OUP.

Resources Development, Environmental Land Management & Permitting, No. 3. (Mineral Law Ser.). 500p. 1996. text ed. 125.00 (*0-929047-60-3*) Rocky Mtn Mineral Law Found.

Resources Examiner. Jack Rudman. (Career Examination Ser.: C-1455). 1994. pap. 27.95 (*0-8373-1455-0*) Nat Learn.

*__Resources for American Indian Rehabilitation.__ Ed. by T. C. Thomason. 100p. 1995. pap. text ed. write for info. (*1-888557-08-7*, 100019) No Ariz Univ.

Resources for an Uncertain Future: Papers Presented at a Forum Marking the 25th Anniversary of Resources for the Future, 1977. Ed. by Charles J. Hitch. LC 77-18378. 117p. reprint ed. pap. 33.40 (*0-317-26464-8*, 2023800) Bks Demand.

Resources for Buddhist-Christian Encounter: An Annotated Bibliography. Society for Buddhist-Christian Studies Staff. Ed. by Harry L. Wells. LC 93-188865. 32p. 1993. pap. 4.25 (*0-9637372-9-5*) Multifaith Res.

Resources for Caring People. Phyllis J. Le Peau. (Caring People Bible Studies). 64p. (Orig.). 1991. wbk. ed., pap. 4.99 (*0-8308-1191-5*, 1191) InterVarsity.

Resources for Catechists & Chaplains. Ed. by Margaret McEntee. 216p. (Orig.). 1994. pap. 12.95 (*1-85607-108-1*, Pub. by Columba Pr IE) Twenty-Third.

Resources for Child Placement & Other Human Services: A Project CRAFT Publication. Armand Lauffer. LC 78-26352. (Sage Human Services Guides Ser.: No. 6). 192p. 1979. reprint ed. pap. 54.80 (*0-608-01468-0*, 2059512) Bks Demand.

Resources for Clinical Investigation: Report of a Study. Institute of Medicine, Division of Health Promotion & Disease Prevention Staff. (IOM Publication Ser.: No. 88-07). 93p. reprint ed. pap. 26.60 (*0-7837-3575-8*, 2043434) Bks Demand.

Resources for Creative Teaching in Early Childhood Education. 2nd ed. Darlene S. Hamilton et al. 672p. (C). 1990. pap. text ed. 36.00 (*0-15-576652-X*) HB Coll Pubs.

Resources for Development Education. 151p. 1990. pap. 12.00 (*0-944675-44-1*) Amer Forum.

Resources for Dramatic Play. Lois Brokering. (J). (ps). 1990. pap. 11.99 (*0-8224-5811-X*) Fearon Teach Aids.

Resources for Early Childhood: A Handbook. Ed. by Hannah Nuba et al. LC 93-5044. 576p. 1994. text ed. 80.00 (*0-8240-7395-9*, SS680) Garland.

Resources for Early Childhood Training: An Annotated Bibliography. Michele Porzel. LC 87-62944. 72p. 1987. pap. text ed. 5.00 (*0-935989-12-9*, NAEYC #790) Natl Assn Child Ed.

Resources for Educating Artistically Talented Students. Gilbert A. Clark & Enid D. Zimmerman. LC 86-23183. (Illus.). 192p. 1987. text ed. 34.95 (*0-8156-2401-8*) Syracuse U Pr.

Resources for Educational Testing & Measurement. Faite Mack. 352p. (Orig.). (C). 1994. pap. text ed. 19.80 (*0-87563-489-3*) Stipes.

Resources for Elders with Disabilities. 3rd large type ed. Resources for Rehabilitation Staff. (Orig.). 1996. pap. 48.95 (*0-929718-16-X*) Resc Rehab.

Resources for English As a Foreign Language (EFL) & English As a Second Language (ESL) a Guide. Domino Books Ltd Staff. 400p. (C). 1988. 150.00 (*1-85122-050-X*, Pub. by Domino Bks Ltd UK); pap. 100.00 (*1-85122-024-0*, Pub. by Domino Bks Ltd UK) St Mut.

Resources for Every Day in Every Way. Faraday Burditt & Cynthia Holley. 1989. pap. 17.99 (*0-8224-2508-4*) Fearon Teach Aids.

Resources for Freedom: A Report to the President by the President's Materials Policy Commission, June 1952, 2 Vols. United States President's Materials Policy Commission. Bd. with Vol. 1. Foundations for Growth & Security. Ed. by United States President's Materials Policy Commission. LC 72-2863.; Vol. 4. Promise of Technology. United States President's Materials Policy Commission. LC 72-2863. LC 72-2863. (Use & Abuse of America's Natural Resources Ser.). 434p. 1972. reprint ed. 42.95 (*0-405-04533-6*) Ayer.

Resources for Gifted Children in the New York Area. Darlene Freeman & Virginia Stuart. LC 79-91434. 350p. (Orig.). 1980. pap. 10.00 (*0-89824-005-0*) Trillium Pr.

Resources for Health: Technology Assessment for Policy Makings. Ed. by H. David Banta. LC 81-21079. 256p. 1982. text ed. 59.95 (*0-275-91358-9*, C1358, Praeger Pubs) Greenwood.

Resources for Health, Fitness & Learning. Ed. by David I. Weiss. LC 90-70268. viii, 216p. 1990. pap. 9.95 (*0-9618049-2-0*) D I Weiss.

*__Resources for Improving the Lives of Children.__ 48p. (C). 1996. per. write for info. (*0-697-36707-X*) Wm C Brown Pubs.

Resources for Jewish Genealogy in the Boston Area. Warren Blatt. (Illus.). 284p. 1996. text ed. 25.00 (*0-9652151-0-5*) Jewish Geneal Soc.

Resources for Latin American Jewish Studies: Essays on Using Jewish Reference Sources for the Study of Latin American Jewry; U. S. Library Collections on L. A. Jews; & U. S. Archival Resources for the Study of Jews in L. A. Thomas Niehaus et al. Ed. by Judith L. Elkin. LC 84-80219. (LAJSA Publication: No. 1). 59p. (Orig.). 1984. pap. text ed. 10.00 (*0-916921-00-X*) Lat Am Jewish Studies.

Resources for Living. Gaius G. Atkins. LC 77-117756. (Essay Index Reprint Ser.). 1977. 21.95 (*0-8369-1741-3*) Ayer.

Resources for Middle Childhood. Deborah L. Sheiman. LC 88-18046. 144p. 1988. text ed. 35.00 (*0-8240-7777-6*) Garland.

Resources for Ministry in Death & Dying. Roger G. Brandt & Larry A. Platt. LC 87-14298. (Orig.). 1988. pap. 14.99 (*0-8054-6945-1*, 4269-45) Broadman.

Resources for Nonlawyers. Nicala Carter. 14p. 1985. pap. write for info. (*0-318-64282-4*) NCLS Inc.

Resources for Optimal Care of the Injured Patient: 1993. rev. ed. American College of Surgeons, Committee on the Impaired Physician of the Board of Governors Staff. LC 93-11972. (Illus.). 1993. pap. text ed. 12.00 (*1-880696-03-7*) Am Coll Surgeons.

Resources for Outdoor Retreats: Journey into Nature, Journey into Heart. Robert P. Stamschror. (Illus.). 197p. (Orig.). 1994. spiral bd. 29.95 (*0-88489-320-0*) St Marys.

Resources for People with Disabilities & Chronic Conditions. 3rd ed. Resources for Rehabilitation Staff. 1996. pap. 49.95 (*0-929718-17-8*) Resc Rehab.

Resources for People with Disabilities 1991-92. (VCP Ser.). 192p. 1991. 60.00 (*0-909184-35-6*, Pub. by Deakin Univ AT) St Mut.

Resources for People with Special Needs 1994. Des Pickering. 247p. 1995. pap. 75.00 (*0-909184-43-7*, Pub. by Deakin Univ AT) St Mut.

Resources for Reproductive Rights Research. Intro. by Stephanie Aronson. LC 93-77744. (Orig.). 1993. pap. write for info. (*1-878428-10-1*) Inst Womens Policy Rsch.

Resources for Research in Legal Ethics. Todd W. Grant. LC 92-20434. (Legal Research Guides Ser.: Vol. 13). 58p. 1992. 35.00 (*0-89941-802-3*, 307550) W S Hein.

Resources for Science Literacy: Professional Development. American Association for the Advancement of Science Staff. LC 96-49376. 144p. 1997. pap. 49.95 (*0-19-510873-6*) OUP.

Resources for South Asian Language Studies in the United States: Report of a Conference Convened by the University of Pennsylvania for the United States Office of Education, January 15-16, 1960. Ed. by William N. Brown. LC 60-15611. 103p. reprint ed. pap. 29.40 (*0-317-11022-5*, 2002898) Bks Demand.

Resources for Teachers of Adults. John Cummins. 64p. (C). 1987. pap. 65.00 (*0-900559-60-8*) St Mut.

Resources for Teaching about the Social Impact of AIDS. Nancy J. Schmidt. 24p. 1990. 2.00 (*0-941934-62-4*) Indiana Africa.

Resources for Teaching Elementary School Science. Smithsonian Institution, National Academy of Sciences, National Science Resources Center Staff. 312p. (Orig.). 1996. pap. 17.95 (*0-309-05293-9*) Natl Acad Pr.

Resources for Teaching Home Economics. Virginia L. Clark & Dorothy E. Pomraning. 1986. 6.00 (*0-911365-26-5*, A261-08468) Family & Consumer Sci Educ.

Resources for Teaching Ideas. Bates. 1996. teacher ed., pap. text ed. 23.00 (*0-312-13805-9*) St Martin.

*__Resources for Teaching Linear Algebra.__ Ed. by David Carlson et al. LC 97-70503. (Notes Ser.: No. 42). 306p. (Orig.). (C). 1997. pap. 34.95 (*0-88385-150-4*, NTE-42/PMDS97) Math Assn.

*__Resources for Teaching Middle School Science.__ 400p. 1997. pap. 19.95 (*0-309-05781-7*) Natl Acad Pr.

*__Resources for Teaching Poetry, Vol. 1.__ Francis Meyer. Date not set. pap. text ed. write for info. (*0-312-11633-0*) St Martin.

Resources for Teaching the Freedom of Speech Course. Thomas L. Tedford & Dale A. Herbeck. 32p. 1998. pap. text ed. 3.00 (*0-9634489-6-X*) Strata Pub Co.

*__Resources for Teaching the Vietnam War: An Annotated Guide.__ Ed. by Ann L. Kelsey & Anthony O. Edmonds. vi, 90p. (Orig.). 1996. pap. 11.95 (*0-945919-19-0*) Ctr Social Studies.

Resources for Teaching Thinking: A Catalog. Janice Kruse. 520p. 1989. pap. 34.95 (*1-56602-030-1*) Research Better.

Resources for Teaching Young Children with Diverse Abilities: Birth Through Eight. 2nd ed. Penny L. Deiner. 544p. (C). 1993. pap. text ed. write for info. (*0-15-500094-2*) HB Coll Pubs.

Resources for Teaching Young Children with Special Needs. Penny L. Deiner. LC 82-84254. 564p. (C). 1983. text ed. 33.25 (*0-15-576627-9*) HB Coll Pubs.

Resources for the Future: An International Annotated Bibliography. Alan J. Mayne. LC 92-35820. (Bibliographies & Indexes in Economics & Economic History Ser.: No. 13). 288p. 1993. text ed. 75.00 (*0-313-28911-5*, GR8911) Greenwood.

Resources for the History of Physics: Guide to Books & Audiovisual Materials, Guide to Original Works of Historical Importance & Their Translations into Other Languages. Ed. by Stephen G. Brush. LC 70-186306. 192p. reprint ed. pap. 54.80 (*0-317-10599-X*, 2022324) Bks Demand.

Resources for the Implementation of Total Quality Management (TQM) in Education, in Nonprofits, & in the Service Sector. annot. ed. A. Blankenberger & M. Sullivan. 24p. 1992. pap. 10.00 (*0-918006-71-6*) ARL.

Resources for the Study of Economic History: A Preliminary Guide to Pre-Twentieth Century Printed Material in Collection. Dorothea D. Reeves. (Kress Library of Business & Economics Publication: No. 16). viiii, 62p. 1961. pap. 9.95 (*0-678-09917-0*, Kress Lib Business) Kelley.

Resources for the Welfare State: An Economic Introduction. John F. Sleeman. LC 78-41314. (Illus.). 197p. reprint ed. pap. 56.20 (*0-685-20314-X*, 2030354) Bks Demand.

*__Resources for Worship Planning.__ Date not set. pap. 19.99 (*0-8341-9404-X*) Lillenas.

Resources for Worship Planning: A Companion to the Hymnal "Sing to the Lord" Keith Schwanz. 200p. 1993. kivar 19.99 (*0-685-72851-X*, MB-671) Lillenas.

Resources for Writers. R. Baird Shuman. (Magill Bibliograhies Ser.). 167p. 1992. 40.00 (*0-8108-2799-9*) Scarecrow.

Resources Handbook: A Guide to Legal Studies for New South Wales. Larry Boyd. (Illus.). 168p. 1989. pap. 44.00 (*0-409-30134-5*, Austral) MICHIE.

Resources Handbook: A Guide to Legal Studies for Queensland, Vol. 1. M. J. Evans. 184p. 1993. pap. 54.00 (*0-409-30598-7*, Austral) MICHIE.

Resources Handbook: A Guide to Legal Studies for Queensland, Year 12. M. J. Evans. 232p. 1990. pap. 44.00 (*0-409-30332-1*, Austral) MICHIE.

Resources in America's Future: Patterns of Requirements & Availabilities 1960-2000. Hans H. Landsberg et al. LC 62-7233. 1017p. 1963. 50.00 (*0-8018-0357-8*) Resources Future.

Resources in Ancient Philosophy: An Annotated Bibliography of Scholarship in English, 1965-1989. Albert A. Bell, Jr. & James B. Allis. LC 91-39912. 818p. 1991. 85.00 (*0-8108-2520-1*) Scarecrow.

*__Resources in Cooperative Learning.__ Ed. by Harlan Rimmerman. (Illus.). 179p. 1996. pap. text ed. 25.00 (*1-879097-31-1*) Kagan Cooperative.

Resources in Early Literacy Development: An Annotated Bibliography. Ed. by Susan P. Burks & Muriel K. Rand. LC 92-28410. 64p. 1992. pap. 6.00 (*0-87207-342-4*) Intl Reading.

*__Resources in Early Literacy Development: An Annotated Bibliography.__ Ed. by Lesley M. Morrow et al. LC 92-28410. 58p. 1992. reprint ed. pap. 25.00 (*0-608-03472-X*, 2064182) Bks Demand.

Resources in Environment-Behavior Studies. rev. ed. University of Wisconsin Ph.D Faculty Staff & Gary T. Moore. (Publications in Architecture & Urban Planning: No. R87-5). vii, 137p. 1990. 13.00 (*0-938744-58-5*) U of Wis Ctr Arch-Urban.

Resources in Sacred Dance, 1991: Annotated Bibliography from Christian & Jewish Traditions. rev. ed. Kay Troxell. LC 91-187899. 56p. 1991. pap. 10.00 (*0-9623137-1-8*) Sacred Dance Guild.

Resources in Theatre & Disability. William E. Rickert & Jane Bloomquist. LC 88-5545. 208p. (Orig.). (C). 1988. pap. text ed. 25.00 (*0-8191-5749-X*); lib. bdg. 47.00 (*0-8191-5748-1*, Assn Theatre & Disabilty) U Pr of Amer.

Resources, Institutions & Strategies: Operation Flood & Indian Dairying. Ed. by Martin Doornbos & K. N. Nair. (IDPAD Ser.). 360p. (C). 1990. text ed. 35.00 (*0-8039-9648-9*) Sage.

Resources Interviewer. Jack Rudman. (Career Examination Ser.: C-1456). 1994. pap. 27.95 (*0-8373-1456-9*) Nat Learn.

*__Resources, Nations & Indigenous Peoples: Case Studies from Australasia, Melanesia & Southeast Asia.__ Ed. by Richie Howitt et al. (Illus.). 304p. 1996. pap. 45.00 (*0-19-553758-0*) OUP.

Resources, Needs & Outcomes in Community-Based Care. Andrew Bebbington & Davies Bleddyn. 497p. 1990. text ed. 64.95 (*1-85628-130-2*, Pub. by Avebury Pub UK) Ashgate Pub Co.

Resources of American Music History: A Directory of Source Materials from Colonial Times to World War II. Ed. by Donald W. Krummel et al. LC 80-14873. (Music in American Life Ser.). 463p. 1981. text ed. 70.00 (*0-252-00828-6*) U of Ill Pr.

Resources of Hope. Raymond Williams. 240p. 1988. 50.00 (*0-86091-229-9*, A3152, Pub. by Verso UK) Routledge Chapman & Hall.

Resources of Hope. Raymond Williams. 240p. (C). 1988. pap. text ed. 20.00 (*0-86091-943-9*, A3156, Pub. by Vrso UK) Norton.

Resources of Near-Earth Space. John S. Lewis et al. LC 93-23753. (Space Science Ser.). (Illus.). 977p. 1993. 82.00 (*0-8165-1404-6*) U of Ariz Pr.

Resources of Poverty: Women & Survival in Mexican Cities. Mercedes De La Rocha. (Studies in Urban & Social Change). (Illus.). 336p. (Orig.). 1993. pap. 25.95 (*0-631-19224-7*) Blackwell Pubs.

Resources of Rationality: A Response to the Postmodern Challenge. Calvin O. Schrag. LC 91-39551. (Studies in Continental Thought). 208p. 1992. 31.50 (*0-253-35054-9*); pap. 15.95 (*0-253-20733-9*, MB-733) Ind U Pr.

***Resources of Realism.** Norris. LC 97-6416. 1997. text ed. 65.00 (*0-312-17551-5*) St Martin.

Resources of the Earth. 2nd ed. James R. Craig & Vaughan. 472p. 1996. text ed. 66.00 (*0-13-457029-4*) P-H.

Resources of the Empire & Their Development see British Empire

Resources of the Southern Fields & Forests. Francis P. Porcher. LC 74-125758. (American Environmental Studies). 1974. reprint ed. 46.95 (*0-405-02684-6*) Ayer.

Resources of the Southern Fields & Forests, Medical, Economical, & Agricultural. Francis P. Porcher. (American Civil War Medical Ser.: No. 4). 601p. 1991. reprint ed. 75.00 (*0-930405-33-1*) Norman SF.

***Resources of the Third World.** Guy Arnold. LC 96-34108. 1997. write for info. (*0-304-33249-6*) Cassell.

***Resources of the Third World.** Guy Arnold. 352p. 1997. 100.00 (*0-304-33251-8*) Cassell.

Resources of the United Kingdom: Or the Present Distress Considered. William R. Pettman. LC 68-56563. (Reprints of Economic Classics Ser.). ix, 291p. 1970. reprint ed. 45.00 (*0-678-00661-X*) Kelley.

Resources Papers: Geography, Vol. 1. 1987. 200.00 (*0-317-62311-7*, Pub. by Scientific UK) St Mut.

Resources, Population, & the Philippines' Future: A Case Study. Gareth Porter & Delfin J. Ganapin, Jr. LC 88-51617. 78p. (Orig.). 1988. pap. text ed. 10.00 (*0-915825-34-1*) World Resources Inst.

Resources, Power & Interregional Interaction. Ed. by E. M. Schortman & P. A. Urban. (Interdisciplinary Contributions to Archaeology Ser.). (Illus.). 256p. 1992. 49.50 (*0-306-44068-7*, Plenum Pr) Plenum.

Resources, Power & Women: Proceedings of the African & Asian Inter-Regional Workshop on Strategies for Improving the Employment Conditions of Rural Women, Arusha, United Republic of Tanzania, August 20-25, 1984. Intro. by Dharam P. Ghai & Ibrahim Kaduma. ix, 82p. 1988. pap. 9.00 (*92-2-105009-2*) Intl Labour Office.

Resources, Society & Environmental Management. Gareth Jones & Graham Hollier. 384p. 1997. pap. 24.95 (*1-85396-234-1*, Pub. by Paul Chapman UK) Taylor & Francis.

Resources Supervisor. Jack Rudman. (Career Examination Ser.: C-1457). 1994. pap. 29.95 (*0-8373-1457-7*) Nat Learn.

Resources, Tariffs & Trade: Ontario's Stake. James R. Williams. LC 76-26043. (Ontario Economic Council Research Studies: No. 6). 125p. reprint ed. pap. 35.70 (*0-8357-4002-1*, 2036703) Bks Demand.

Resources to Riches. Jean Shafer & Lynne Deur. (Michigan Themes Ser.). (Illus.). 48p. (Orig.). 1995. teacher ed., ring bd. 19.95 (*0-938682-33-4*) River Rd Pubns.

***Resources, Values & Development.** Amartya Sen. 1997. pap. text ed. 19.95 (*0-674-76526-5*) HUP.

Resources, Values, & Development. Amartya K. Sen. 512p. 1985. 44.50 (*0-674-76525-7*) HUP.

Resourcing: Handbook for Special Education Resource Teachers. Mary Y. Jackson. 1992. pap. text ed. 12.00 (*0-86586-219-2*, P366) Coun Exc Child.

***RESPA & Real Estate Lending Strategies Guide.** 160p. 1993. pap. 25.00 (*0-614-26810-9*, BLS-3267) Commerce.

RESPA Compliance Manual: A Complete Guide to the Real Estate Settlement Procedures Act. T. Herbert Stevenson. 350p. 1991. 155.00 (*1-55738-319-7*) Irwin Prof Pubng.

RESPA Compliance Manual: The Complete Guide to Real Estate Settlement Procedures Act. 2nd rev. ed. T. Herbert Stevenson. 225p. (C). 1995. per. 65.00 (*1-55738-769-9*) Irwin Prof Pubng.

RESPA-Escrow Issues. Mitchel H. Kider. 112p. (Orig.). 1995. pap. 40.00 (*0-945359-46-2*) Mortgage Bankers.

***Respaesta de Dios Relociones.** K. Arthur. (SPA.). 6.95 (*0-8297-1506-1*) Life Pubs Intl.

Respect. Beverly Fiday. LC 87-36981. (Values to Live By Ser.). (Illus.). 32p. (J). (ps-2). 1988. lib. bdg. 21.36 (*0-89565-417-2*) Childs World.

***R.E.S.P.E.C.T.** Aretha Franklin. 1998. 25.00 (*0-375-50033-2*, Villard Bks) Random.

Respect, Reading Level 2. Elaine Goley. (Learn the Value Ser.: Set II). (Illus.). 32p. (J). (gr. 1-4). 1989. 11.95 (*0-685-58788-6*); lib. bdg. 14.60 (*0-86592-387-6*) Rourke Corp.

***Respect: Autobiography of Freddie Foreman.** Freddie Foreman & John Lisners. (Illus.). 240p. 1997. 40.00 (*0-7126-7688-0*, Pub. by Century UK) Trafalgar.

Respect & Protect: A Practical Step-by-Step Violence Prevention & Intervention Program for Schools & Communities. Carole Remboldt & Richard Zimman. LC 95-44082. 424p. (Orig.). 1995. pap. 99.95 (*1-56246-098-6*, P404) Johnsn Inst.

Respect Between the Sexes. Michael Dumond. (Illus.). 115p. (Orig.). (YA). (gr. 9-12). 1995. pap. 6.95 (*1-57515-084-0*) PPI Pubng.

Respect Black: The Writings & Speeches of Henry McNeal Turner. Ed. by Edwin S. Redkey. LC 79-138695. 1971. 11.95 (*0-405-01984-X*) Ayer.

Respect for Acting. Uta Hagen & Haskel Frankel. LC 72-2328. 227p. 1973. 18.95 (*0-02-547390-5*) Macmillan.

***Respect for Life in Medicine, Philosophy, & the Law.** Owsei Temkin et al. LC 76-47366. (Alvin & Fanny Blaustein Thalheimer Lectures: 1975). 128p. 1977. reprint ed. pap. 36.50 (*0-608-03658-7*, 2064484) Bks Demand.

Respect for Nature: A Theory of Environmental Ethics. Paul W. Taylor. LC 85-43318. (Studies in Moral, Political, & Legal Philosophy). 342p. 1986. pap. text ed. 17.95 (*0-691-02250-X*) Princeton U Pr.

Respect for Property. Barbara L. McCombs & Linda Brannan. (Skills for Job Success Ser.). (Illus.). 32p. (Orig.). 1990. student ed., pap. 4.95 (*1-56119-027-6*) Educ Pr MD.

Respect for Property. Barbara L. McCombs & Linda Brannan. (Skills for Job Success Ser.). (Illus.). 32p. (Orig.). (YA). (gr. 7-12). 1990. student ed., teacher ed. 44.95 (*1-56119-072-1*); teacher ed. 1.95 (*1-56119-028-4*); disk 39.95 (*1-56119-114-0*) Educ Pr MD.

Respect Life: Curriculum Guidelines. 109p. 1977. pap. 13.95 (*1-55586-924-6*) US Catholic.

***Respectability & Deviance.** Joeres. 1996. pap. text ed. 19.95 (*0-226-40066-2*) U Ch Pr.

Respectability of Mr. Bernard Shaw. A. Brinser. LC 75-22167. (Studies in George Bernard Shaw: No. 92). 1975. lib. bdg. 40.95 (*0-8383-2082-1*) M S G Haskell Hse.

Respectable Army: The Military Origins of the Republic, 1763-1789. James K. Martin & Mark E. Lender. Ed. by John H. Franklin & A. S. Eisenstadt. LC 81-173990. (American History Ser.). (Illus.). 256p. (Orig.). (C). 1982. pap. text ed. write for info. (*0-88295-812-7*) Harlan Davidson.

Respectable Folly: Millenarians & the French Revolution in France and England. Clarke Garrett. LC 74-24378. 252p. 1975. 33.00 (*0-8018-1618-1*) Johns Hopkins.

Respectable Lives: Social Standing in Rural New Zealand. Elvin Hatch. (C). 1992. 35.00 (*0-520-07472-6*) U CA Pr.

Respectable Lives: Social Standing in Rural New Zealand. Elvin Hatch. (Illus.). 221p. (C). 1994. pap. 14.95 (*0-520-07473-4*) U CA Pr.

Respectable Trade. Philippa Gregory. 1995. 25.00 (*0-06-017663-6*, GK Hall) Thorndike Pr.

Respectable Trade. Philippa Gregory. 480p. 1996. mass mkt. 5.99 (*0-06-109433-1*, Harp PBks) HarpC.

Respectable Trade. large type ed. Philippa Gregory. LC 95-30934. 682p. 1995. 26.95 (*0-7838-1477-1*, GK Hall) Thorndike Pr.

Respected Rebels. Mary A. Kearney & Edward Kearney. Ed. by Jean A. McConochie. 96p. 1987. pap. text ed. write for info. (*0-13-774598-2*, 21030) Prentice ESL.

Respected Sir. Naguib Mahfouz. 208p. 1990. pap. 7.95 (*0-385-26480-1*) Doubleday.

Respectful Educators - Capable Learners: Young Children's Rights & Early Education. Ed. by Cathy Nutbrown. 176p. 1996. pap. 24.95 (*1-85396-304-6*, Pub. by Paul Chapman UK) Taylor & Francis.

Respectful Rehabilitation: Answers to Your Questions about Old Buildings. National Park Service Staff. LC 96-21906. (Illus.). 200p. 1995. pap. text ed. 14.95 (*0-471-14419-3*) Wiley.

Respectfully Quoted: A Dictionary of Quotations from the Library of Congress. Ed. by Suzy Platt. 1992. 44.95 (*0-87187-687-6*) Congr Quarterly.

Respectfully Quoted: A Dictionary of Quotations with Subject Lists, Key Words & Author Index. 1991. lib. bdg. 79.95 (*0-8490-4580-0*) Gordon Pr.

Respectfully Yours, Mom & Dad. Glenn R. Stoutt & Marvyn Womack. Ed. by Kevin Nickols. 224p. (Orig.). 1987. pap. 12.95 (*0-932471-08-0*) Falsoft.

Respecting Diversity in the Classroom: Facilitator's Guide. 48p. (Orig.). 1995. pap. text ed. write for info. (*0-7842-0809-3*) Agency Instr Tech.

Respecting Our Differences: A Guide to Getting Along in a Changing World. Lynn Duvall. Ed. by Pamela Espeland. LC 94-7164. (Illus.). 208p. (Orig.). (YA). (gr. 7 up). 1994. pap. 12.95 (*0-915793-72-5*) Free Spirit Pub.

Respecting the Body: Affirming Today's Church. Timothy A. Johnson. 80p. (Orig.). 1996. pap. 5.00 (*1-57502-097-1*) Morris Pubng.

Respecting the Pupil, Essays on Teaching Able Students by Members of the Faculty of Phillips Exeter Academy. 2nd ed. Ed. by Donald B. Cole & Robert H. Cornell. LC 81-81104. (Illus.). 132p. 1981. pap. 13.95 (*0-939618-01-X*) Phillips Exeter.

Respecting the Rights of Others in a Violent Society: A Public Policy Perspective. Val J. Peter. (Boys Town National Family Home Program Informational Ser.). 9p. (Orig.). 1996. spiral bd., pap. 1.95 (*0-938510-93-2*, 19-206) Boys Town Pr.

***Respertorium Commentariorum Medii Aevi in Aristotelem Latinorum Quae in Bibliothecis Neerlandicis Asservantur.** L. M. De Rijk & O. Weijers. (Verhandelingen der Koninklijke Nederlandse Akademie van Wetenschappen, Afd. Letterkunde, Nieuwe Reeks Ser.: No. 109). 65p. 1981. pap. text ed. 22.00 (*0-444-85511-4*) Elsevier.

Respighi. (Portraits of Greatness Ser.). (ENG.). 1987. pap. 12.50 (*0-918367-09-3*) Elite.

Respira Con Facilidad: Guia Sobre el Asma Para Jovenes. Jonathan H. Weiss. 64p. (SPA.). (YA). 1996. pap. 9.95 (*0-945354-72-X*) Magination Pr.

Respiracion, la Mente y la Conciencia. Harish Johari. 96p. 1996. pap. 9.95 (*0-89281-474-8*) Inner Tradit.

***Respiration.** Abramoff. Date not set. 1.20 (*0-7167-9013-0*) W H Freeman.

Respiration. Paul Berghuis et al. (Biophysical Measurement Ser.). (Illus.). 170p. (Orig.). (C). 1992. 28.00 (*0-9627449-3-X*) SpaceLabs.

Respiration. Ed. by Wallace O. Fenn & Herman Rahn. (Handbook of Physiology Ser.: Pt. 3, Vols. 1 & 2). reprint ed. pap. 160.00 (*0-685-73767-5*, 2015381) Bks Demand.

Respiration & Crop Productivity. J. S. Amthor. (Illus.). 220p. 1989. 80.95 (*0-387-96938-1*) Spr-Verlag.

Respiration & Metabolism of Embryonic Vertebrates. Ed. by Roger Seymour. LC 84-9751. (Perspectives in Vertebrate Science Ser.). 1984. lib. bdg. 266.50 (*90-6193-053-7*) Kluwer Ac.

Respiration in Health & Disease. 3rd ed. Reuben M. Cherniack & Louis Cherniack. (Illus.). 480p. 1983. text ed. 54.00 (*0-7216-2527-4*) Saunders.

Respiration in Health & Disease: Lessons from Comparative Physiology, Bodchum, 16 to 20 August, 1992. Ed. by P. Scheid. (Funktions Analyse Biologischer System Ser.: Vol. 23). (Illus.). 390p. (Orig.). 1994. pap. 80.00 (*3-437-11552-9*, Pub. by G Fischer Verlag GW) Lubrecht & Cramer.

Respirators & Protective Clothing. E. C. Hyatt & J. M. White. (Safety Ser.: No. 22). (Illus.). 82p. 1967. pap. 30.00 (*92-0-123367-1*, ISP150, Pub. by IAEA AU) Bernan Associates.

Respiratory Allergy: Advances in Clinical Immunology & Pulmonary Medicine. Ed. by Gaetano Melillo et al. LC 93-15160. (International Congress Ser.: Vol. 1007). 288p. 1993. 170.50 (*0-444-89679-1*) Elsevier.

Respiratory Anatomy & Physiology. Martin & Youtsey. 288p. (gr. 13). 1987. pap. text ed. 19.95 (*0-8016-3175-0*) Mosby Yr Bk.

Respiratory & Alimentary Tract Disease. Ed. by H. S. Rosenberg & J. Bernstein. (Perspectives in Pediatric Pathology Ser.: Vol. 11). (Illus.). x, 218p. 1987. 176.00 (*3-8055-4435-9*) S Karger.

Respiratory & Infectious Disease. (Profile of Health & Disease in America Ser.). 240p. 1987. 40.00 (*0-8160-1458-2*) Facts on File.

Respiratory Autogenic Training & Obstetric Psychoprophylaxis. U. Piscicelli. 292p. 1987. pap. text ed. 25.00 (*1-57235-026-1*) Piccin NY.

Respiratory Burst & Its Physiological Significance. Ed. by Anthony J. Sbarra & R. R. Strauss. (Illus.). 466p. 1988. 120.00 (*0-306-42883-0*, Plenum Pr) Plenum.

Respiratory Care. Ed. by Jennifer A. Pryor. (International Perspectives in Physical Therapy Ser.: Vol. 7). (Illus.). 244p. 1991. pap. text ed. 39.95 (*0-443-03611-X*) Churchill.

***Respiratory Care.** Judy Tietsort. 232p. 1995. spiral bd. 105.00 (*1-879575-62-0*) Acad Med Sys.

Respiratory Care: A Clinical Approach. Gayle A. Traver & Gail F. Priestly. Ed. by Joyce T. Mitchell. LC 90-14524. 270p. 1991. text ed. 42.00 (*0-8342-0207-7*) Aspen Pub.

Respiratory Care: A Guide to Clinical Practice. 4th ed. George Burton. LC 96-40216. 1264p. 1997. text ed. 68.95 (*0-397-55165-7*) Lppncott-Raven.

Respiratory Care: Evolution of a Profession. Gary A. Smith et al. LC 89-81413. 233p. (Orig.). (C). 1989. 35.00 (*0-9624754-1-6*); pap. 17.50 (*0-9624754-0-8*) Applied Measurement.

Respiratory Care: Know the Facts. Howder. (Illus.). 279p. 1989. pap. text ed. 19.95 (*0-397-50940-5*) Lppncott-Raven.

Respiratory Care Assistant: Performance Evaluation Guide. California College for Health Sciences Staff. 60p. (C). 1992. write for info. (*0-933195-34-6*) CA College Health Sci.

Respiratory Care Assistant Program. 2nd ed. M. Jouett. LC 82-74058. 676p. (C). 1993. reprint ed. ring bd. write for info. (*0-933195-02-8*) CA College Health Sci.

Respiratory Care Certification Guide. 2nd ed. James R. Sills. LC 94-8962. (Illus.). 480p. (C). (gr. 13). 1994. pap. text ed. 36.95 (*0-8151-7515-9*) Mosby Yr Bk.

***Respiratory Care Competencies.** Judy Tietsort. 125p. 1994. spiral bd. 120.00 (*1-879575-46-9*) Acad Med Sys.

Respiratory Care Criteria Sourcebook Vol. 5: Supplement. William Yike & Gerry Stearns. 49p. (Orig.). 1991. pap. text ed. 7.00 (*0-916499-50-2*) Care Educ Grp.

Respiratory Care Drug Reference. Joseph L. Rau. 464p. (C). (gr. 13). 1996. pap. text ed. 26.95 (*0-8151-8456-5*) Mosby Yr Bk.

Respiratory Care Drug Reference. 2nd ed. Mclaughlin. LC 96-46968. 500p. 1996. 45.00 (*0-8342-0788-5*, 20788) Aspen Pub.

Respiratory Care Equipment. Richard D. Branson et al. (Illus.). 750p. 1993. text ed. write for info. (*0-397-50856-5*) Lppncott-Raven.

Respiratory Care Equipment. Ed. by Richard D. Branson et al. LC 94-22641. 592p. 1995. text ed. 53.95 (*0-397-54995-4*) Lppncott-Raven.

Respiratory Care Equipment. Goulet. 1997. text ed. write for info. (*0-7216-5193-3*) Saunders.

Respiratory Care Equipment. Mark Simmons. 168p. 1995. pap. text ed. 16.95 (*0-397-55193-2*) Lppncott-Raven.

Respiratory Care in Alternative Care Sites. Kenneth Wyka & William Clark. LC 97-20039. (Respiratory Care Ser.). 256p. 1997. pap. 23.95 (*0-8273-7679-0*) Delmar.

Respiratory Care of the Newborn & Child. 2nd ed. Clarie A. Aloan. LC 96-39478. 544p. 1997. pap. text ed. 39.95 (*0-397-54925-3*) Lppncott-Raven.

Respiratory Care Pharmacology. 4th ed. Joseph L. Rau. 350p. (gr. 13). 1993. pap. text ed. 43.00 (*0-8016-7184-1*) Mosby Yr Bk.

***Respiratory Care Pharmacology.** 5th ed. Joseph L. Rau. (Illus.). 448p. (C). (gr. 13). 1997. pap. text ed. 43.00 (*0-8151-2337-X*, 31046, Yr Bk Med Pubs) Mosby Yr Bk.

Respiratory Care Pharmacology: Quick Reference Guide. 4th ed. Joseph L. Rau. 40p. (gr. 13). 1993. pap. text ed. 9.95 (*0-8151-7078-5*) Mosby Yr Bk.

Respiratory Care Pharmacology & Aerosol, Vol. 4. Karen Milikowski. (Respiratory Care Workbook Ser.). 24p. (gr. 13). 1994. 8.95 (*0-8151-6308-8*, 26026) Mosby Yr Bk.

Respiratory Care Principles: A Programmed Guide to Entry-Level Practice. 3rd ed. Thomas A. Barnes. LC 91-9456. (Illus.). 515p. 1991. pap. text ed. 43.95 (*0-8036-0662-1*) Davis Co.

Respiratory Care Registry Guide. James R. Sills. 656p. (gr. 13). 1994. pap. text ed. 39.95 (*0-8016-6201-X*) Mosby Yr Bk.

Respiratory Care Sciences: An Integrated Approach. 2nd ed. William V. Wojciechowski. (Respiratory Care Ser.). 608p. 1996. pap. 37.95 (*0-8273-6661-2*) Delmar.

Respiratory Care Workbook. Howard B. Surkin & Anna W. Parkman. LC 89-16982. (Illus.). 372p. 1990. pap. text ed. 27.95 (*0-8036-8229-8*) Davis Co.

Respiratory Control: A Modeling Perspective. Ed. by G. D. Swanson & F. S. Grodins. (Illus.). 460p. 1990. 125.00 (*0-306-43366-4*, Plenum Pr) Plenum.

Respiratory Control: Peripheral & Central Mechanisms. Ed. by Dexter F. Speck et al. LC 92-13720. (Illus.). 248p. 1993. text ed. 80.00 (*0-8131-1788-7*) U Pr of Ky.

Respiratory Control & Lung Development in the Fetus & Newborn. Ed. by B. M. Johnston & P. D. Gluckman. LC 86-2556. (Reproductive & Perinatal Medicine Ser.: No. III). (Illus.). 424p. 1986. 77.50 (*0-916859-12-6*) Perinatology.

Respiratory Control Disorders in Infants & Children. Robert C. Beckerman et al. 448p. 1992. 72.00 (*0-683-00498-0*) Williams & Wilkins.

Respiratory Defense Mechanisms, Pt. 1. Brain et al. (Lung Biology in Health & Disease Ser.: Vol. 5). 512p. 1977. 185.00 (*0-8247-6381-5*) Dekker.

Respiratory Defense Mechanisms, Pt. 2. Brain et al. (Lung Biology in Health & Disease Ser.: Vol. 5). 760p. 1977. 230.00 (*0-8247-6532-X*) Dekker.

Respiratory Disease: Principles of Patient Care. Robert L. Wilkins & James R. Dexter. LC 92-48263. (Illus.). 414p. 1993. 37.95 (*0-8036-9326-5*) Davis Co.

Respiratory Disease: Principles of Patient Care. 2nd ed. Ed. by Robert L. Wilkins & James R. Dexter. LC 97-9419. (Illus.). 540p. (C). 1997. text ed. 39.95 (*0-8036-0155-7*) Davis Co.

Respiratory Disease in the Elderly Patient. Connolly. 344p. (gr. 13). 1995. text ed. 86.00 (*0-412-56830-6*) Chapman & Hall.

Respiratory Disorders. Springhouse Publication Co. Editors. (Nursing Timesavers Ser.). (Illus.). 344p. 1993. 33.95 (*0-87434-657-6*) Springhouse Pub.

Respiratory Disorders. 2nd ed. Susan Wilson & Thompson. (Illus.). 320p. (C). (gr. 13). 1990. text ed. 32.95 (*0-8016-5087-9*) Mosby Yr Bk.

Respiratory Distress Syndrome. (Landmark Ser.). 1979. 22.50 (*0-8422-4121-3*) Irvington.

Respiratory Distress Syndrome. Ed. by Kari O. Raivio et al. 1984. text ed. 119.00 (*0-12-576180-5*) Acad Pr.

Respiratory Distress Syndrome: Early Prediction of Outcome & Characterization of Two Types of Bronchopulmonary Dysplasia. S. Van Lierde. No. 79. 131p. (Orig.). 1994. pap. 36.50 (*90-6186-603-0*, Pub. by Leuven Univ BE) Coronet Bks.

Respiratory Distress Syndromes: Molecules to Man. Ed. by Mildred T. Stahlman. LC 90-13022. (Illus.). 300p. (C). 1990. text ed. 54.95 (*0-8265-1238-0*) Vanderbilt U Pr.

Respiratory Drug Delivery. Ed. by Peter R. Byron. 3304p. 1989. 158.00 (*0-8493-5344-0*, RM161) CRC Pr.

Respiratory Drug Therapy. Springhouse Publication Co. Editors. LC 94-33378. (Professional Quick Reference Ser.). (Illus.). 384p. 1995. 29.95 (*0-87434-731-9*) Springhouse Pub.

Respiratory Facts. John H. Riggs. LC 88-2057. (Illus.). 327p. (C). 1989. text ed. 18.95 (*0-8036-7333-7*) Davis Co.

***Respiratory Failure.** Horacio J. Adrogue & Martin J. Tobin. LC 96-9846. (Basics of Medicine Ser.). 248p. (Orig.). 1996. pap. text ed. 39.95 (*0-86542-478-0*) Blackwell Sci.

Respiratory Failure in the Child. Ed. by George A. Gregory. LC 81-38497. (Clinics in Critical Care Medicine Ser.). (Illus.). 217p. reprint ed. pap. 61.90 (*0-7837-2573-6*, 2042732) Bks Demand.

Respiratory Function in Disease. 3rd ed. David V. Bates. 560p. 1989. text ed. 73.50 (*0-7216-1592-9*) Saunders.

Respiratory Function in Speech & Song. Thomas J. Hixon. (Illus.). 448p. (C). 1991. reprint ed. pap. text ed. 45.00 (*1-879105-24-1*, A032) Singular Publishing.

Respiratory Function of the Upper Airway. Matthew & Sant'Ambrogio. (Lung Biology in Health & Disease Ser.: Vol. 35). 672p. 1988. 195.00 (*0-8247-7802-2*) Dekker.

Respiratory Health Effects of Passive Smoking: Lung Cancer & Other Disorders. (Illus.). 300p. (Orig.). (C). 1993. pap. text ed. 55.00 (*1-56806-738-0*) DIANE Pub.

***Respiratory Health Effects of Passive Smoking: Lung Cancer & Other Disorders, 2 vols.** 1997. lib. bdg. 600.95 (*0-8490-8144-0*) Gordon Pr.

Respiratory Health Effects of Passive Smoking: Lung Cancer & Other Disorders, 2 vols., Set. 1995. lib. bdg. 603.99 (*0-8490-6687-5*) Gordon Pr.

Respiratory Home Care. Patrick J. Dunne & Susan L. McInturff. LC 97-10615. (Illus.). 300p. (C). 1997. pap. text ed. 20.00 (*0-8036-0154-9*) Davis Co.

Respiratory Hypersensitivity: Its Cholinergic Background & Treatment. Masuicki Takino. 295p. (C). 1989. text ed. 70.00 (*0-946270-44-9*, Pub. by Pentland Pr UK) St Mut.

Respiratory Immune Defense in Children: Current Knowledge & Possible Therapeutic Interventions. Ed. by J. A. Bellanti & J. P. Boissel. (Journal: Respiration Ser.: Vol. 61, Suppl. 1, 1994). (Illus.). iv, 32p. 1994. pap. 15.75 (*3-8055-6077-X*) S Karger.

Respiratory Infections. Ed. by Merle A. Sande et al. (Contemporary Issues in Infectious Diseases Ser.: Vol. 5). (Illus.). 377p. 1986. text ed. 58.00 (*0-443-08450-5*) Churchill.

An Asterisk (*) at the beginning of an entry indicates that the title is appearing in BIP for the first time.

Respiratory Infections. fac. ed. Ed. by Merle A. Sande et al. LC 85-29932. (Contemporary Issues in Infectious Diseases Ser.: No. 5). (Illus.). 391p. 1986. reprint ed. pap. 111.50 (*0-7837-7893-7*, 2047649) Bks Demand.

Respiratory Infections: A Scientific Basis for Management. George A. Sarosi et al. LC 93-35615. (Illus.). 688p. 1994. text ed. 139.50 (*0-7216-4347-7*) Saunders.

Respiratory Infections: Diagnosis & Management. 3rd ed. Ed. by James E. Pennington. LC 93-48578. 832p. 1994. spiral bd. 99.00 (*0-7817-0173-2*) Lppncott-Raven.

Respiratory Infections in the Elderly. Ed. by Michael S. Niederman. 400p. 1991. text ed. 68.50 (*0-88167-817-1*) Lppncott-Raven.

Respiratory Intensive Care. Kenneth F. MacDonnell et al. 478p. 1987. 100.00 (*0-316-54193-1*) Little.

Respiratory Medicine. Ed. by Peter J. Barnes. (Illus.). 256p. 1993. text ed. 75.00 (*0-7506-0712-2*) Buttrwrth-Heinemann.

Respiratory Medicine, 2. 2nd ed. Brewis. 1995. text ed. 260.00 (*0-7020-1641-1*) Saunders.

Respiratory Medicine. 2nd ed. David C. Flenley & Douglas. (Illus.). 392p. (Orig.). 1990. pap. text ed. 39.00 (*0-7020-1342-0*, Bailliere-Tindall) Saunders.

Respiratory Medicine. P. N. Plowman. LC 87-31999. (Illustrated Lecture Ser.). 236p. reprint ed. pap. 67.30 (*0-7837-4772-1*, 2044527) Bks Demand.

Respiratory Medicine in the Tropics. Ed. by Janak N. Pande. (Illus.). 500p. 1997. 39.95 (*0-19-563311-3*) OUP.

Respiratory Monitoring. Martin J. Tobin. (Contemporary Management in Critical Care Ser.: Vol. 1, No. 4). (Illus.). 253p. 1992. text ed. 44.95 (*0-443-08831-4*) Churchill.

Respiratory Muscles in Chronic Obstructive Pulmonary Disease. Ed. by A. Grassino et al. (Current Topics in Rehabilitation Ser.). 200p. 1988. 65.95 (*0-387-19509-2*) Spr-Verlag.

Respiratory National Board. 2nd rev. ed. LC 94-23439. (C). 1994. pap. text ed. 37.95 (*0-8385-8414-4*) Appleton & Lange.

Respiratory Nursing. Delmar Staff & Mark B. Bauman. (Rapid Nursing Interventions Ser.). 224p. 1996. pap. 20.95 (*0-8273-7095-4*) Delmar.

Respiratory Pharmaceuticals Market: Demand for Non-Sedating Antihistamines Drives Market Growth. 210p. 1992. 1,995.00 (*1-56753-010-9*) Frost & Sullivan.

Respiratory Pharmacology & Toxicology. Mannfred A. Hollinger. (Illus.). 202p. 1985. text ed. 43.50 (*0-7216-1617-8*) Saunders.

Respiratory Physical Therapy & Pulmonary Care. Ulla Ingwersen. LC 76-27094. 176p. reprint ed. pap. 50.20 (*0-317-07783-X*, 2017410) Bks Demand.

Respiratory Physiology. J. A. Jacques. 1979. text ed. 35.00 (*0-07-032247-3*) McGraw.

Respiratory Physiology. fac. ed. Allan H. Mines. LC 80-5658. (Physiology Ser.). (Illus.). 176p. pap. 50.20 (*0-7837-7518-0*) Bks Demand.

Respiratory Physiology. 2nd fac. ed. Allan H. Mines. LC 86-607. (Physiology Ser.). (Illus.). 176p. pap. 47.60 (*0-7837-7282-3*, 2047024) Bks Demand.

Respiratory Physiology. 3rd ed. Allan H. Mines. LC 92-49692. (Series in Physiology). 192p. 1992. text ed. 72.50 (*0-88167-963-1*); pap. text ed. 34.00 (*0-88167-962-3*) Lppncott-Raven.

Respiratory Physiology: An Analytical Approach. Chang & Paiva. (Lung Biology in Health & Disease Ser.: Vol. 40). 896p. 1988. 250.00 (*0-8247-7855-3*) Dekker.

Respiratory Physiology: Basics & Applications. Alan R. Leff & Paul T. Schumacker. (Illus.). 224p. 1993. pap. text ed. 25.95 (*0-7216-3952-6*) Saunders.

Respiratory Physiology: People & Ideas. Ed. by John B. West. (Illus.). 320p. (C). 1996. text ed. 85.00 (*0-19-508081-5*) OUP.

Respiratory Physiology: The Essentials. 4th ed. John B. West. (Illus.). 195p. 1989. 26.00 (*0-683-08942-0*) Williams & Wilkins.

Respiratory Physiology: The Essentials. 5th ed. John B. West. LC 94-7758. (Illus.). 224p. 1994. 27.00 (*0-683-08937-4*) Williams & Wilkins.

Respiratory Physiology: Understanding Gas Exchange from Basic Principles to Applications. Henry D. Prange. LC 95-24639. 224p. (gr. 13). 1995. pap. text ed. 24.95 (*0-412-05211-3*) Chapman & Hall.

Respiratory Physiology of Animals. James N. Cameron. (Illus.). 368p. 1989. 65.00 (*0-19-506019-9*) OUP.

***Respiratory Proection.** Richard K. Miller et al. (Market Research Survey Ser.: No. 250). 50p. 1996. 200.00 (*1-55865-283-3*) Future Tech Surveys.

Respiratory Protection. Richard K. Miller & Marcia E. Rupnow. LC 90-83901. (Survey on Technology & Markets Ser.: No. 197). 50p. 1991. pap. text ed. 200.00 (*1-55865-221-3*) Future Tech Surveys.

Respiratory Protection, 4 vols., Vol. 1, Module 2. Multimedia Development Services Staff. (Safety, Health & Environmental Fundamentals Ser.). (Illus.). (Orig.). (C). 1996. pap. text ed. 30.00 (*1-57431-105-0*) Tech Trng Systs.

Respiratory Protection, 4 vols., Vol. 1, Module 2. Multimedia Development Services Staff. (Safety, Health & Environmental Fundamentals Ser.). (Illus.). (Orig.). (C). 1996. teacher ed., text ed. 65.00 (*1-57431-106-9*) Tech Trng Systs.

Respiratory Protection: A Manual & Guideline. 2nd ed. Ed. by C. E. Colton et al. 146p. 1991. 50.00 (*0-932627-45-5*) Am Indus Hygiene.

Respiratory Protection Handbook. Revoir. LC 96-47080. 464p. 1996. 69.95 (*0-87371-281-1*, L281) Lewis Pubs.

Respiratory Protection Monograph. AIHA Respiratory Protection Committee. 448p. 1985. 40.00 (*0-932627-20-X*) Am Indus Hygiene.

***Respiratory Protection Program.** Mark M. Moran. (OSHA Written Compliance Programs Ser.: No. 23). (Illus.). 50p. 1992. ring bd. 169.00 (*1-890966-17-7*) Moran Assocs.

Respiratory Protection Program for Industry. John Pritchard. 250p. 1992. pap. 77.95 (*0-442-00802-3*) Van Nos Reinhold.

Respiratory Role of the Upper Airways: A Selective Clinical & Pathophysiological Review. Philip Cole. LC 92-19173. 164p. (gr. 13). 1992. text ed. 49.00 (*1-55664-390-X*) Mosby Yr Bk.

Respiratory Sensation. Ed. by Adams & Guz. (Lung Biology in Health & Disease Ser.: Vol. 90). 464p. 1996. 165.00 (*0-8247-8846-X*) Dekker.

Respiratory Support. Springhouse Publication Co. Editors. LC 90-10418. (Clinical Skillbuilders Ser.). (Illus.). 210p. 1991. spiral bd. 26.95 (*0-87434-362-3*) Springhouse Pub.

***Respiratory Support.** Ed. by Keith Sykes. 256p. (Orig.). (C). 1995. pap. text ed. 57.00 (*0-7279-0830-8*, Pub. by BMJ Pubng Grp UK) Amer Coll Phys.

Respiratory Syncytial Virus. C. R. Pringle. (Perspectives in Medical Virology Ser.: Vol. 1). write for info. (*0-317-15191-6*) Elsevier.

Respiratory System. (Medical Ser.). (Illus.). 52p. 1983. pap. text ed. 9.95 (*0-935920-12-9*, Ntl Pubs Blck) P-H.

***Respiratory System.** LC 96-29746. (True Book Ser.). (J). 1997. write for info. (*0-516-20448-3*) Childrens.

Respiratory System. Braem. 1994. pap. text ed. 19.95 (*1-878576-31-3*) Flash Anatomy Inc.

Respiratory System. Ed. by T. C. Jones et al. LC 95-45938. (Monographs on Pathology of Laboratory Animals). (Illus.). 250p. 1996. 330.00 (*3-540-60383-2*) Spr-Verlag.

Respiratory System. Ed. by Thomas C. Jones et al. (Monographs on Pathology of Laboratory Animals). (Illus.). 320p. 1985. 288.00 (*0-387-13521-9*) Spr-Verlag.

Respiratory System. Mary Kittredge. (Encyclopedia of Health Ser.). (Illus.). 112p. (YA). (gr. 7 up). 1989. lib. bdg. 19.95 (*0-7910-0026-5*) Chelsea Hse.

Respiratory System. Virginia B. Silverstein. (Human Body Systems Ser.). (Illus.). 96p. (J). (gr. 5-8). 1994. lib. bdg. 16.98 (*0-8050-2831-5*) TFC Bks NY.

Respiratory System. 2nd ed. Ed. by T. C. Jones et al. LC 95-45938. (Monographs on Pathology of Laboratory Animals). (Illus.). 357p. 1996. 320.00 (*0-944398-69-3*) ILSI.

Respiratory System. 3rd ed. LC 92-48260. (Regents - Prentice-Hall Medical Assistant Kit Ser.). 1993. pap. 11.50 (*0-13-227026-9*) P-H.

Respiratory System see CIBA Collection of Medical Illustrations

Respiratory System Course. Competence Assurance Systems Staff. (Illus.). 1981. pap. text ed. 45.00 (*0-89147-105-7*) CAS.

Respiratory Systems Symposium. Ed. by M. A. Epstein & J. R. Ligas. (Illus.). 216p. 1990. 57.95 (*0-387-97404-0*) Spr-Verlag.

Respiratory Therapist Manual. Stanley Pincus. LC 74-79838. (Allied Health Ser.). 1975. pap. 7.05 (*0-672-61389-1*, Bobbs) Macmillan.

Respiratory Therapy Competency Evaluation Manual. Scanlan. 432p. (gr. 13). 1984. pap. text ed. 40.95 (*0-86542-015-7*, A-4324-4) Mosby Yr Bk.

Respiratory Therapy Equipment. 4th ed. Charles E. Spearman. (Illus.). 512p. 1990. student ed. 15.95 (*0-8016-3378-8*) Mosby Yr Bk.

Respiratory Therapy Equipment, No. 5. 5th ed. McPherson. 432p. (C). (gr. 13). 1994. text ed. 59.00 (*0-8016-7989-3*) Mosby Yr Bk.

Respiratory Therapy-Equipment & Disposables Market. (Market Research Reports: No. 316). 100p. 1994. 795.00 (*0-317-05483-X*) Theta Corp.

Respiratory Therapy Examination. Heath. (C). 1990. pap. text ed. 25.95 (*0-8385-8404-7*, A8404-4) Appleton & Lange.

***Respiratory Therapy Pearls.** Ed. by Frank A. Mazzagatti & Leon C. Lebowitz. LC 97-3043. (Pearls Ser.). (Illus.). 200p. (Orig.). 1997. pap. text ed. 39.00 (*1-56053-204-1*) Hanley & Belfus.

Respiratory Therapy Pharmacology. 3rd ed. Jospeh L. Rau, Jr. (Illus.). 316p. 1988. 29.95 (*0-685-34790-7*, Yr Bk Med Pubs) Mosby Yr Bk.

Respiratory Therapy Technician. (Career Examination Ser.: C-3422). 1994. pap. 29.95 (*0-8373-3422-5*) Nat Learn.

Respiratory Tract Mucus. CIBA Foundation Staff. LC 77-16019. (CIBA Foundation Symposium: New Ser.: No. 54). 342p. reprint ed. pap. 97.50 (*0-317-29774-0*, 2022179) Bks Demand.

Respiratory Viruses: Proceedings of the WHO Scientific Group, Geneva, 1967. WHO Staff. (Technical Report Ser.: No. 408). 100p. 1969. pap. text ed. 7.00 (*92-4-120408-7*, 1100408) World Health.

Respirometry of Activated Sludge. Milenko Ros. LC 93-60579. 155p. 1993. text ed. 69.95 (*1-56676-029-1*) Technomic.

Respite. Faith T. Allum. (Illus.). 48p. (Orig.). 1985. pap. 3.00 (*0-9613349-2-4*) F T Allum.

Respite & Other Korean Short Stories. Son Chang-sop et al. Ed. by Korean National Commission for UNESCO. Tr. by Kim Chong-un et al. from KOR. (Modern Korean Short Stories Ser.: No. 6). vii, 169p. 1983. 20.00 (*0-89209-207-6*) Pace Intl Res.

Respite Care: Programs, Problems & Solutions. Ed. by Lynn M. Tepper & John A. Toner. LC 92-48396. 240p. (Orig.). (C). 1993. pap. text ed. 24.95 (*0-914783-67-X*) Charles.

Respite Care: Time Out for Families. Epilepsy Foundation of America Staff. 66p. 1992. pap. 9.95 (*0-916570-06-1*) Epilepsy Foundation of America.

Respite for Caregivers of Alzheimer's Patients: Research & Practice. M. Powell Lawton et al. 176p. 1991. 24.95 (*0-8261-6610-5*) Springer Pub.

Respite Resource Guide. National Council on the Aging, Inc. Staff. 40p. 1990. pap. 8.00 (*0-910883-51-3*, 2040) Natl Coun Aging.

Resplendence of the Spanish Monarchy: Renaissance Tapestries & Armor from the Patrimonio. Antonio D. Ortiz. 1991. 49.50 (*0-8109-6408-2*) Abrams.

Resplendence of the Spanish Monarchy: Renaissance Tapestries & Armor from the Patrimonio. Antonio D. Ortiz et al. (Illus.). 172p. 1991. 9.95 (*0-87099-621-5*, 0-8109-6408-2) Metro Mus Art.

Resplendent Sites, Discordant Voices: Sri Lankans & International Tourism. Malcolm Crick. LC 94-1708. (Studies in Anthropology & History: Vol.8). 237p. 1994. text ed. 58.00 (*3-7186-5564-0*) Gordon & Breach.

Resplendent Themes. Billy E. Simmons. 70p. 1983. reprint ed. pap. 5.00 (*0-914520-19-9*) Insight Pr.

Respond - Mission: An Experience of Being Church. David M. Knight. (Spiritual Growth in Matthew's Gospel Ser.: Vol. 4). 80p. (Orig.). 1990. student ed., teacher ed. 4.95 (*0-942971-08-6*) His Way.

Respond-Conversion: An Experience of Conversion. David M. Knight. (Spiritual Growth in Matthew's Gospel Ser.: Vol. 2). 78p. (Orig.). 1990. student ed. 4.95 (*0-942971-04-3*) His Way.

Respond-Jesus: An Experience of Evangelization. David M. Knight. (Spiritual Growth in Matthew's Gospel Ser.: Vol. 1). 73p. (Orig.). 1990. student ed. 4.95 (*0-942971-02-7*) His Way.

Respond-The New Law: An Experience of Discipleship. David M. Knight. (Spiritual Growth in Matthew's Gospel Ser.: Vol. 3). 80p. (Orig.). 1990. student ed. 4.95 (*0-942971-06-X*) His Way.

***Respond to the AIDS Challenge.** Pye. Date not set. pap. text ed. write for info. (*0-582-06434-1*, Pub. by Longman UK) Longman.

***Respond to the Rhythms of Change: Using Biblical Principles.** Valerie L. Myers. 1997. pap. text ed. 12.95 (*1-880560-69-0*) DaBaR Srvs.

Respondent Spark: The Basics of Bible Study. Chuck Fager. 100p. (Orig.). 1981. pap. 9.95 (*0-945177-01-1*) Kimo Pr.

Respondent Spark: The Basics of Bible Study. 2nd rev. ed. Charles Fager. 80p. (Orig.). 1993. pap. 9.95 (*0-945177-09-7*) Kimo Pr.

Responding Democratically to Special Interest Groups. 4p. (Orig.). 1995. pap. 10.00 (*0-943397-28-6*, 160) Assn Calif Sch Admin.

Responding Differently to Writers & Writing. Julie Jochum. (Illus.). 76p. (Orig.). 1997. pap. 12.95 (*1-886979-09-X*) Practicl Pr.

Responding to Adolescent Needs. Ed. by Max Sugar. LC 79-26297. 273p. 1980. text ed. 30.00 (*0-88331-195-X*) Luce.

Responding to Adolescent Needs: A Pastoral Care Approach. P. Lowe. Ed. by Peter Mittler. (Special Needs in Ordinary Schools Ser.). 192p. 1988. pap. text ed. 22.50 (*0-304-31453-6*) Cassell.

Responding to Adolescent Suicide. Phi Delta Kappa Task Force on Adolescent Suicide Staff. LC 88-61773. 29p. (Orig.). 1988. pap. 3.50 (*0-87367-438-3*) Phi Delta Kappa.

Responding to AIDS: Psychosocial Initiatives. Ed. by Carl G. Leukefeld & Manuel F. Fimbres. LC 87-15211. 95p. 1987. 12.95 (*0-87101-148-4*) Natl Assn Soc Wkrs.

Responding to AIDS: The Healthcare Professional's Guide to Legal Issues & Responsibilities. Jonathan P. Tomes. 1994. text ed. 42.50 (*1-55738-613-7*) Irwin Prof Pubng.

Responding to America's Homeless: Public Policy Alternatives. F. Stevens Redburn & Terry F. Buss. LC 86-21186. 170p. 1986. text ed. 49.95 (*0-275-92231-6*, C2231, Praeger Pubs) Greenwood.

Responding to Changes in Sea Level: Engineering Implications. National Research Council Staff. LC 87-21965. 160p. 1987. pap. text ed. 24.95 (*0-309-03781-6*) Natl Acad Pr.

***Responding to Child Abuse: Procedures & Practice for Child Protection in Hong Kong.** Ed. by Charles O'Brian et al. 200p. (Orig.). 1997. pap. 29.95 (*962-209-429-5*, Pub. by HK Univ Pr HK) Intl Spec Bk.

Responding to Child Sexual Abuse: A Report to the 67th Session of the Texas Legislature. Glen A. Kercher. 60p. 1980. 2.00 (*0-318-02509-4*) S Houston Employ.

Responding to Children at Risk: A Guide to Recent Reports. Susan Austin & Gail Meister. 95p. 1990. pap. 21.95 (*1-56602-031-X*) Research Better.

Responding to Communities in Crisis: The Training Manual of the Crisis Response Team. NOVA (Young) Staff. 336p. 1996. spiral bd. 50.00 (*0-8403-9461-6*) Kendall-Hunt.

Responding to Community Outrage: Strategies for Effective Risk Communication. Peter M. Sandman. 124p. (C). 1993. pap. 25.00 (*0-932627-51-X*, 167-CC-93) Am Indus Hygiene.

Responding to Constraint: Policy & Management in Higher Education. John Pratt & Susanne Silverman. 160p. 1988. 95.00 (*0-335-09500-3*, Open Univ Pr) Taylor & Francis.

Responding to Crisis: A Planning Guide for Schools. Kendall Johnson. 96p. (Orig.). 1992. lib. bdg. 39.00 (*0-8095-6336-3*) Borgo Pr.

Responding to Defense Dependence: Policy Ideas & the American Defense Industrial Base. Erik R. Pages. LC 95-11275. 208p. 1996. text ed. 55.00 (*0-275-95313-0*, Praeger Pubs) Greenwood.

Responding to Defense Industrial Base Training Needs. Harold Starr. 35p. 1984. 4.25 (*0-318-22188-8*, RD248) Ctr Educ Trng Employ.

Responding to Disability Issues in Student Affairs. Ed. by Sue Kroeger & Judy Schuck. LC 85-644751. (New Directions for Student Services: No. 64). 126p. (Orig.). 1993. pap. 19.00 (*1-55542-681-6*) Jossey-Bass.

Responding to Disaster: A Guide for Mental Health Professionals. Ed. by Linda S. Austin. LC 91-44366. (Clinical Practice Ser.: No. 24). 256p. 1992. 31.00 (*0-88048-464-0*, 8464) Am Psychiatric.

Responding to Drug & Alcohol Problems in the Community: A Manual for Primary Health Care Workers, with Guidelines for Trainers. Ed. by M. Grant & R. Hodgson. viii, 109p. (CHI, ENG, FRE & SPA.). 1991. pap. text ed. 21.00 (*92-4-154427-9*, 1150366) World Health.

Responding to Drug Use & Violence: Helping People, Families & Communities: A Directory & Resource Guide of Public & Private-Sector Drug Control Grants. 157p. (C). 1996. pap. text ed. 30.00 (*0-7881-2912-0*) DIANE Pub.

***Responding to Drug Use & Violence: Helping People, Families, & Communities: A Directory & Resource Guide of Public & Private Sector Drug Control Grants.** 1997. lib. bdg. 250.95 (*0-8490-8222-6*) Gordon Pr.

Responding to Economic Change: Development Plans for Oxfordshire. Ed. by L. Hill & Vincent Nadin. (C). 1984. 29.00 (*0-685-30264-4*, Pub. by Oxford Polytechnic UK) St Mut.

Responding to Emergencies. 2nd ed. American Red Cross Staff. (gr. 13). 1996. pap. text ed. 25.00 (*0-8151-0351-4*) Mosby Yr Bk.

Responding to Global Warming: An Examination of the Prospects for Effective Action. Penny Eastwood. 133p. 1992. 23.00 (*0-85496-759-1*) Berg Pubs.

Responding to Global Warming: The Technology, Economics & Politics of Sustainable Energy. Peter Read. LC 93-18986. 256p. (C). 1994. pap. 25.00 (*1-85649-162-5*, Pub. by Zed Bks Ltd UK); text ed. 59.95 (*1-85649-161-7*, Pub. by Zed Bks Ltd UK) Humanities.

Responding to God. Martha Rowlett. 160p. (Orig.). 1996. pap. 12.95 (*0-8358-0783-5*, UR783) Upper Room Bks.

Responding to God's Challenge. Carolyn Spain & Eldred Spain. 1986. pap. 2.00 (*0-8309-0439-5*) Herald Hse.

***Responding to Grief: A Complete Resource Guide.** Richard Gilbert. 238p. 1997. ring bd. 79.00 (*1-889764-04-3*, Spirit of Hlth) A R K Co.

Responding to Hazardous Materials Incidents. 23p. 1992. 20.25 (*0-685-64970-9*, 471-92) Natl Fire Prot.

Responding to Human Needs: Community-Based Social Services, Vol. II. (Capitols & Communities Ser.). 32p. 1991. 15.00 (*1-55516-801-9*, 3902) Natl Conf State Legis.

Responding to Imperfection: The Theory & Practice of Constitutional Amendment. Ed. by Sanford Levinon. LC 94-27766. 352p. 1995. text ed. 59.50 (*0-691-08657-5*); pap. text ed. 19.95 (*0-691-02570-3*) Princeton U Pr.

Responding to Infants. Inez Moyer. LC 83-71345. 200p. (Orig.). (J). (ps). 1983. pap. 18.95 (*0-513-01769-0*) Denison.

Responding to Literature. 2nd ed. Judith A. Stanford. LC 95-40985. 1264p. (C). 1995. pap. text ed. 35.95 (*1-55934-538-1*, 1538) Mayfield Pub.

Responding to Literature: A Step-by-Step Guide for Student Writers. John S. Biays & Carol Wershoven. 496p. 1988. pap. text ed. write for info. (*0-07-005160-7*) McGraw.

Responding to Literature: Writing & Thinking Activities, Grades 1-3. Sandra M. Simons & Anne Maley. (Illus.). 136p. (Orig.). 1992. pap. text ed. 15.95 (*0-9627689-2-8*) Spring St OR.

Responding to Literature: Writing & Thinking Activities, Grades 4-8. Sandra M. Simons. 176p. 1990. pap. text ed. 15.95 (*0-9627689-0-1*) Spring St OR.

Responding to Literature Instructor's Manual. 2nd ed. Judith A. Stanford. 212p. (C). 1995. teacher ed., pap. text ed. write for info. (*1-55934-539-X*, 1539) Mayfield Pub.

Responding to Low-Intensity Conflict Challenges. Stephen Blank et al. (Illus.). 318p. (Orig.). (C). 1993. pap. text ed. 45.00 (*1-56806-436-5*) DIANE Pub.

Responding to Low-Intensity Conflict Challenges: "Small Wars" 1995. lib. bdg. 251.95 (*0-8490-7552-1*) Gordon Pr.

Responding to Mental Illness. Ed. by Gordon Horobin. LC 85-18379. (Research Highlights in Social Work Ser.). 170p. 1985. text ed. 29.95 (*0-312-67769-3*) St Martin.

***Responding to Money Laundering: International Perspectives.** Ernesto U. Savona. 304p. 1996. 65.00 (*90-5702-070-X*, Harwood Acad Pubs) Gordon & Breach.

Responding to New Realities in Disarmament. 124p. Date not set. 20.00 (*92-1-142208-6*, E.94.IX.8) UN.

Responding to Patients in Crisis. Springhouse Publishing Co. Editors. LC 93-1937. (Advanced Skills Ser.). (Illus.). 228p. 1993. 31.95 (*0-87434-557-X*) Springhouse Pub.

***Responding to Poverty: The Politics of Cash & Care.** Saul Becker. LC 96-50040. (Longman Social Policy in Britain Ser.). 1997. write for info. (*0-582-24322-X*, Pub. by Longman UK) Longman.

Responding to Probation & Parole Violations. Dale G. Parent & Dan Wentworth. 65p. (Orig.). (C). 1995. pap. text ed. 20.00 (*0-7881-2380-7*) DIANE Pub.

Responding to Prose: A Reader for Writers. Judith Fishman. (Illus.). 480p. (Orig.). (C). 1983. pap. text ed. 49.00 (*0-02-337900-6*, Macmillan Coll) P-H.

Responding to the Homeless: Policy & Practice. R. K. Schutt & Gerald R. Garrett. (Topics in Social Psychiatry Ser.). (Illus.). 246p. 1992. 39.50 (*0-306-44076-8*, Plenum Pr) Plenum.

Responding to the Mass Casualty Incident: A Guide for EMS Personnel. Alexander M. Butman. 1982. 14.50 (*0-940432-02-1*, Emergency Training) Educ Direction.

An Asterisk (*) at the beginning of an entry indicates that the title is appearing in BIP for the first time.

Responding to the Needs of Today's Minority Students. Ed. by Doris J. Wright. LC 85-644751. (New Directions for Student Services Ser.: No. SS 38). 1987. 19.00 (*1-55542-971-8*) Jossey-Bass.

Responding to the Screen: Reception & Reaction Processes. Dolf Zillmann. (Communication Ser.). 416p. (C). 1991. pap. 39.95 (*0-8058-1044-7*); text ed. 79.95 (*0-8058-0033-6*) L Erlbaum Assocs.

Responding to the Sexual Abuse of Adults with Learning Disabilities. Hilary Brown & Ann Craft. 200p. 1996. pap. 33.00 (*1-85302-204-7*, Pub. by J Kingsley Pubs UK) Taylor & Francis.

*__Responding to Troubled Youth.__ Malcolm W. Klein & Cheryl L. Maxson. (Studies in Crime & Public Policy). (Illus.). 256p. 1997. 39.95 (*0-19-509853-6*) OUP.

Responding to Violence on Campus. Ed. by Jan M. Sherrill & Dorothy G. Siegel. LC 85-644751. (New Directions for Student Services Ser.: No. SS 47). 1989. 19.00 (*1-55542-856-8*) Jossey-Bass.

Responding to Worldwide Needs. Ed. by Cornelius J. Dyck et al. LC 80-10975. (Mennonite Central Committee Story Ser.: Vol. 2). 155p. 1980. reprint ed. pap. 44.20 (*0-608-01758-2*, 2062416) Bks Demand.

Responding to Young Adult Literature. Virginia Monseau. LC 96-20. (Young Adult Literature Ser.). 103p. (YA). 1996. pap. text ed. 18.50 (*0-86709-401-X*, 0401) Boynton Cook Pubs.

Responding Voices: A Reader for Emerging Writers. Jan Ford & Elaine Hughes. LC 96-19889. 1996. pap. text ed. write for info. (*0-07-021526-X*) McGraw.

Responsa: Literary History of a Rabbinic Genre. Peter J. Haas. LC 96-7520. (Society of Biblical Literature Semeia Studies). 485p. 1996. 59.95 (*0-7885-0244-1*, 060631); pap. 39.95 (*0-7885-0245-X*, 06 06 31) Scholars Pr GA.

Responsa & Halakhic Studies. Isaac Klein. 20.00 (*0-87068-288-1*) Ktav.

Responsa Anthology. Avraham Y. Finkel. LC 90-39600. 232p. 1991. 45.00 (*0-87668-773-7*) Aronson.

Responsa Anthology. Avraham Y. Finkel. LC 90-39600. 232p. 1996. pap. 24.95 (*1-56821-942-3*) Aronson.

Responsa from the Holocaust. Ephraim Oshry. Tr. by Y. Leiman. 260p. 1983. 16.95 (*0-910818-55-X*) Judaica Pr.

Responsa of Modern Judaism. Sholom Klass. 610p. 1992. 22.95 (*1-882961-00-5*) Jewish Pr Pubns.

Responsa of Modern Judaism. Sholom Klass. 394p. 1994. 25.00 (*1-882961-02-1*) Jewish Pr Pubns.

Responsa of the Babylonian Geonim As a Source of Jewish History. Jacob Mann. LC 73-2215. (Jewish People; History, Religion, Literature Ser.). 1973. reprint ed. 25.95 (*0-405-05279-0*) Ayer.

Responsabilidad. Linda C. Johnson. (Helping Books in Spanish Ser.). (Illus.). 64p. (SPA.). (YA). (gr. 7-12). 1993. pap. 8.95 (*0-8239-1796-7*, D1796-7) Rosen Group.

Responsabilidad. Nancy Pemberton & Jeannie Williams. (Valores para la Vida Ser.). (Illus.). 32p. (SPA.). (J). (ps-2). 1988. lib. bdg. 21.36 (*0-89565-953-0*) Childs World.

*__Responsabilidad Civil Extracontractual: Un Estudio en las Decisiones del Tribunal Supremo de Puerto Rico.__ Carlos J. Irizarry-Yunque. 623p. (SPA.). 1996. pap. text ed. 40.00 (*1-881711-02-1*) Univ Interamrcna.

Responsabilidad Politica: Proclamando el Evangelio de la Vida, Protegiendo a los Mas Pequenos Entre Nosotros, y Buscando el Bien Comun. United States Catholic Conference Administrative Board Staff. Tr. by Oscar Reyes. 35p. (Orig.). (SPA.). 1995. pap. 1.75 (*1-57455-044-6*) US Catholic.

Responsabilidad Social del Creyente. Alfonso Lockward. 117p. (SPA.). 1992. pap. 4.50 (*1-56063-303-4*, 498523) Editorial Unilit.

Responsabilite de l'Artiste. Jacques Maritain. 128p. 1961. 9.95 (*0-686-56367-0*) Fr & Eur.

Response. Bahiyyih Nakhjavani. 144p. 1981. pap. 8.95 (*0-85398-107-8*) G Ronald Pub.

Response. Juliana Spahr. LC 96-36730. (New American Poetry Ser.: No. 32). 97p. (Orig.). 1997. pap. 10.95 (*1-55713-289-5*) Sun & Moon CA.

Response Analysis of A.C. Electrical Machines: Computer Models & Simulation. John R. Smith. LC 89-24303. 239p. 1990. text ed. 165.00 (*0-471-92488-1*) Wiley.

Response & Adaptation to Hypoxia: Organ to Organelle. Ed. by Sukhamay Lahiri et al. (Clinical Physiology Series - An American Physiological Society Book). (Illus.). 272p. 1991. 68.00 (*0-19-506244-2*) OUP.

Response & Analysis: Teaching Literature in Junior & Senior High School. Robert E. Probst. LC 87-24509. 279p. (Orig.). 1987. pap. text ed. 23.00 (*0-86709-203-3*, 0203) Boynton Cook Pubs.

Response & Stability: An Introduction to the Physical Theory. A. Brian Pippard. (Illus.). 238p. 1985. pap. text ed. 32.95 (*0-521-31994-3*) Cambridge U Pr.

Response & Stability: An Introduction to the Physical Theory. A. Brian Pippard. (Illus.). 238p. 1985. 74.95 (*0-521-26673-4*) Cambridge U Pr.

Response Effects in Surveys: A Review & Synthesis. Seymour Sudman & Norman M. Bradburn. LC 73-89510. (Monographs in Social Research: No. 16). 264p. 1974. 11.50 (*0-202-30270-9*) Natl Opinion Res.

Response Farming in Rainfed Agriculture. James I. Stewart. (Illus.). 110p. (Orig.). (C). 1988. pap. text ed. 17.95 (*0-9620274-0-5*) FWHARF.

Response Journals. Les Parsons. LC 90-117341. 90p. (Orig.). 1989. pap. text ed. 16.50 (*0-435-08517-4*, 08517) Heinemann.

Response Journals. Scholastic Books Staff. 80p. 1991. pap. 11.95 (*0-590-49137-7*) Scholastic Inc.

Response Manual for Combating Spills of Floating Hazardous Chemicals. A. Szluha et al. LC 91-43030. (Pollution Technology Review Ser.: No. 206). (Illus.). 436p. 1992. 64.00 (*0-8155-1292-9*) Noyes.

Response Models for Detection of Change. Amnon Rapoport et al. (Theory & Decision Library: No. 18). 1979. lib. bdg. 80.00 (*90-277-0934-3*) Kluwer Ac.

Response of Different Species to Total Body Irradiation. Ed. by J. J. Broerse & T. J. MacVittie. (Radiology Ser.). 1984. lib. bdg. 117.50 (*0-89838-678-0*) Kluwer Ac.

Response of Metals to High Velocity Deformation. Paul G. Shewmon. LC 61-9441. (Metallurgical Society Conference Ser.: Vol. 9). 503p. reprint ed. pap. 143.40 (*0-317-10938-3*, 2000672) Bks Demand.

Response of Multistory Concrete Structures to Lateral Forces. American Concrete Institute Staff. LC 72-93775. (American Concrete Institute Publication Ser.: SP-36). (Illus.). 320p. reprint ed. pap. 91.20 (*0-317-10936-7*, 2002352) Bks Demand.

Response of Natural Gas & Crude Oil Exploration & Discovery to Economic Incentives. Robert D. Spooner. Ed. by Stuart Bruchey. LC 78-22749. (Energy in the American Economy Ser.). (Illus.). 1979. lib. bdg. 23.95 (*0-405-12014-1*) Ayer.

Response of Nuclei under Extreme Conditions. Ed. by Ricardo A. Brogila & G. Bertsch. LC 87-32747. (Ettore Majorana International Science Series, Life Sciences: Vol. 28). (Illus.). 422p. 1988. 95.00 (*0-306-42571-8*, Plenum Pr) Plenum.

Response of Plants to Multiple Stresses. Ed. by Harold A. Mooney et al. (Physiological Ecology Ser.). (Illus.). 422p. 1991. text ed. 84.00 (*0-12-505355-X*) Acad Pr.

Response of Rav Moshe Feinstein: Translation & Commentary. Moses Feinstein & Moshe D. Tendler. LC 96-11212. 1996. write for info. (*0-88125-444-4*) Ktav.

Response of Social Work to the Depression. Jacob Fisher. 266p. 1980. pap. 18.95 (*0-87073-891-7*) Schenkman Bks Inc.

Response of the Catholic Church in the United States to Immigrants & Refugees see Pastoral Series

Response of the Nuclear System to External Forces: Proceedings of the Fifth La Rabida International Summer School on Nuclear Physics, Held at La Rabida, Huelva, Spain, 19 June to 1 July, 1994. Fifth La Rabida International Summer School on Nuclear Physics Staff. Ed. by Jose M. Arias et al. LC 95-4080. (Lecture Notes in Physics Ser.: Vol. 441). 1995. 85.95 (*3-540-59007-2*) Spr-Verlag.

Response of Western Forests to Air Pollution. Ed. by D. Binkley et al. LC 92-21992. (Ecological Studies: Vol. 97). (Illus.). xii, 532p. 1992. 109.95 (*0-387-97895-X*) Spr-Verlag.

Response Recordings: An Answer Song Discography, 1950-1990. B. Lee Cooper & Wayne S. Haney. LC 90-8728. 296p. 1990. 32.00 (*0-8108-2342-X*) Scarecrow.

Response Set in Personality Assessment. Ed. by Irwin A. Berg. LC 66-28342. 1967. 39.75 (*0-202-25019-9*) Irvington.

Response Spectrum Method. Gupte. 192p. 1992. 71.95 (*0-8493-8628-4*, QA) CRC Pr.

Response Surface Methodology: Process & Product Optimization Using Designed Experiments. Raymond H. Myers & Douglas C. Montgomery. LC 94-45548. (Series in Probability & Mathematical Statistics). 700p. 1995. text ed. 59.95 (*0-471-58100-3*) Wiley.

Response Surfaces. Khuri & Cornell. (Statistics: Textbooks & Monographs: Vol. 152). 536p. 1996. 75.00 (*0-8247-9741-8*) Dekker.

Response Time Testing of Nuclear-Safety-Related Instrument Channels in Nuclear Power Plants. 1986. pap. 25.00 (*0-87664-847-2*, S67.06) ISA.

Response Times: Their Role in Inferring Elementary Mental Organization. R. Duncan Luce. (Oxford Psychology Ser.: No. 8). (Illus.). 576p. 1986. 95.00 (*0-19-503642-5*) OUP.

Response Times: Their Role in Inferring Elementary Mental Organization. R. Duncan Luce. (Oxford Psychology Ser.: No. 8). (Illus.). 584p. 1991. reprint ed. pap. 55.00 (*0-19-507001-1*) OUP.

Response to Allen Ginsberg, 1926-1994: A Bibliography of Secondary Sources. Bill Morgan. LC 95-26449. 528p. 1996. text ed. 79.50 (*0-313-29536-0*, Greenwood Pr) Greenwood.

*__Response to Anti-Abortion Demonstrations: Cincinnati Police Division.__ Lesli Lord. 70p. 1996. reprint ed. pap. 35.00 (*0-7881-3421-3*) DIANE Pub.

Response to Disaster: Fact vs. Fiction & Its Perpetuation: The Sociology of Disaster. Henry W. Fischer, III. 160p. (C). 1994. pap. text ed. 22.00 (*0-8191-9553-7*); lib. bdg. 49.00 (*0-8191-9552-9*) U Pr of Amer.

Response to Imperialism: The United States & the Philippine-American War, 1899-1902. Richard E. Welch, Jr. LC 78-11403. (Illus.). xvi, 215p. (C). 1987. reprint ed. pap. 12.95 (*0-8078-4177-3*) U of NC Pr.

Response to Industrialism, 1885-1914. 2nd ed. Samuel P. Hays. Ed. by Daniel J. Boorstin. LC 95-18562. (Chicago History of American Civilization Ser.). 266p. 1995. pap. text ed. 13.95 (*0-226-32164-9*); lib. bdg. 39.95 (*0-226-32163-0*) U Ch Pr.

Response to Innovation: A Study of Popular Argument about New Mass Media. Robert E. Davis. Ed. by Garth S. Loweth. LC 75-21430. (Dissertations on Film Ser.). 1976. lib. bdg. 38.95 (*0-405-07533-2*) Ayer.

Response to Love. Ed. by Erica M. Purdie. (C). 1988. 35.00 (*0-7212-0825-8*, Pub. by Regency Press UK) St Mut.

Response to Marine Oil Spills. ITOPF Staff. (FRE.). (C). 1987. 100.00 (*0-948691-53-0*, Pub. by Witherby & Co UK); 100.00 (*0-948691-52-2*, Pub. by Witherby & Co UK); pap. 110.00 (*0-948691-51-4*, Pub. by Witherby & Co UK) St Mut.

Response to Meprobamate: A Predictive Analysis. fac. ed. John R. Wittenborn. LC 70-107228. 113p. pap. 32.30 (*0-7837-7355-2*, 2047164) Bks Demand.

Response to Modernity: A History of the Reform Movement in Judaism. Michael A. Meyer. LC 94-45560. 510p. 1995. reprint ed. pap. text ed. 18.95 (*0-8143-2555-6*) Wayne St U Pr.

Response to Need: A Case Study of Adult Education Graduate Program Development in the Southeast. Charles E. Kozoll. LC 72-57. (Occasional Papers: No. 28). 60p. 1972. pap. 2.25 (*0-87060-051-6*, OCP 28) Syracuse U Cont Ed.

Response to Occupational Health Hazards. J. Corn. 1992. text ed. 46.95 (*0-442-00488-5*) Van Nos Reinhold.

Response to Progressivism: The Democratic Party & New York Politics, 1902-1918. Robert F. Wesser. LC 86-5415. 288p. (C). 1986. text ed. 28.00 (*0-8147-9213-8*) NYU Pr.

Response to Progressivism: The Democratic Party & New York Politics, 1902-1918. Robert F. Wesser. LC 86-5415. 288p. (C). 1991. pap. 16.50 (*0-8147-9242-1*) NYU Pr.

Response to Prostitution in the Progressive Era. Mark T. Connelly. LC 79-24038. x, 261p. 1980. 37.50 (*0-8078-1424-5*) U of NC Pr.

Response to Revolution: Imperial Spain & the Spanish American Revolutions, 1810-1840. Michael P. Costeloe. (Cambridge Iberian & Latin American Studies). 256p. 1986. text ed. 69.95 (*0-521-32083-6*) Cambridge U Pr.

Response to Revolution: The United States & the Cuban Revolution, 1959-1961. Richard E. Welch, Jr. LC 84-25604. ix, 244p. 1985. 34.95 (*0-8078-1613-2*); pap. 13.95 (*0-8078-4136-6*) U of NC Pr.

Response to the End of History: Eschatology & Situation in Luke-Acts. John T. Carroll. LC 87-12699. (Society of Biblical Literature Ser.). 201p. 1988. 20.95 (*1-55540-148-1*, 06 01 92); pap. 13.95 (*1-55540-149-X*, 06 01 92) Scholars Pr GA.

Response to the Federalist: Contemporary Commentaries on a Political Masterwork, 1787-1788. Ed. & Intro. by Richard Leffler. (Constitutional Heritage Ser.: Vol. 3). 200p. write for info. (*0-945612-03-6*) Madison Hse.

Response to the Loma Prieta Earthquake. Janet A. McDonnell. (Illus.). 91p. (Orig.). (C). 1995. pap. text ed. 30.00 (*0-7881-2582-6*) DIANE Pub.

*__Response to the Paradoxes of Malestroit.__ Jean Bodin. Ed. & Tr. by Henry Tudor. (Primary Sources in Political Thought Ser.). 160p. 1997. 48.00 (*1-85506-532-0*) Thoemmes Pr.

*__Response to the Paradoxes of Malestroit.__ Jean Bodin. Ed. & Tr. by Henry Tudor. (Primary Sources in Political Thought Ser.). 160p. 1997. pap. 19.95 (*1-85506-533-9*) Thoemmes Pr.

Responses. David Cairns. LC 80-18152. (Music Ser.). 1980. reprint ed. 32.50 (*0-306-76047-9*) Da Capo.

*__Responses II: Prose Pieces.__ Richard Wilbur. LC 96-36229. 1997. 25.00 (*0-15-100254-1*) HarBrace.

Responses Magnetic: Selected Poems. Hajime Kijima. Ed. by Thomas Fitzsimmons. Tr. by Arthur Binard from JPN. LC 96-6817. (Asian Poetry in Translation: Japan Ser.: No. 18). (Illus.). 120p. 1996. text ed. 29.00 (*0-942668-47-2*); pap. text ed. 14.95 (*0-942668-48-0*) Katydid Bks.

*__Responses of Jamaican & American Deaf Groups to Stigma: A Critical Interpretive Approach.__ Jennifer M. Keane-Dawes. 146p. 1997. text ed. 34.50 (*0-7618-0652-0*) U Pr of Amer.

Responses of Mammalian Skin to Ultraviolet Irradiation: A Combined Morphological & Molecular Study. M. Garmyn. No. 64. 130p. (Orig.). 1993. pap. 39.50 (*90-6186-547-6*, Pub. by Leuven Univ BE) Coronet Bks.

Responses: On Paul de Man's Wartime Journalism. Ed. by Werner Hamacher et al. LC 88-29979. xxii, 477p. 1989. pap. text ed. 19.95 (*0-8032-7243-X*, Bison Books) U of Nebr Pr.

Responses to Changing Multiple-Use Demands: New Direction for Water Resources Planning & Management. Ed. by Michael J. Sale & Rita O. Wadlington. LC 94-70723. (Technical Publications: No. 94-2). (Illus.). 506p. (Orig.). 1994. pap. 36.00 (*1-882132-30-0*) Am Water Resources.

Responses to Christa Wolf: Critical Essays. Ed. by Marilyn S. Fries. LC 89-36490. 418p. (C). 1990. text ed. 45.00 (*0-8143-2130-5*) Wayne St U Pr.

Responses to Crime: An Introduction to Swedish Criminal Law & Administration. Alvar Nelson. Tr. by Jerome L. Getz from SWE. (New York University Criminal Law Education & Research Center Monograph: No. 6). vi, 90p. 1972. pap. text ed. 8.50 (*0-8377-0900-8*) Rothman.

Responses to Crime Vol. 3: Legislating with the Tide. Lord Windlesham. 488p. 1996. 75.00 (*0-19-826240-X*) OUP.

Responses to Crime, Vol. 2: Penal Policy in the Making. Lord Windlesham. 250p. 1993. 45.00 (*0-19-825416-4*) OUP.

Responses to Literature, Grades K-8. James H. Macon et al. 32p. 1990. pap. 5.95 (*0-87207-747-0*) Intl Reading.

Responses to One Hundred One Questions about Feminism. Denise L. Carmody. (Responses to 101 Questions Ser.). 144p. (Orig.). 1994. pap. 8.95 (*0-8091-3438-1*) Paulist Pr.

Responses to One Hundred One Questions About Jesus. Michael L. Cook. LC 93-25492. 144p. (Orig.). 1993. pap. 8.95 (*0-8091-3428-4*) Paulist Pr.

Responses to One Hundred One Questions on the Bible. Raymond E. Brown. 160p. 1990. pap. 8.95 (*0-8091-3188-9*) Paulist Pr.

Responses to One Hundred One Questions on the Dead Sea Scrolls. Joseph A. Fitzmyer. LC 92-21584. 224p. 1992. pap. 9.95 (*0-8091-3348-2*) Paulist Pr.

Responses to One Hundred One Questions on the Psalms & Other Writings. Ronald E. Murphy. LC 94-3739. 144p. 1995. pap. 8.95 (*0-8091-3526-4*) Paulist Pr.

Responses to Poetry. Alberta Turner. 321p. (Orig.). (C). 1990. pap. text ed. 25.50 (*0-8013-0150-5*, 75813) Longman.

Responses to Poverty: Lessons from Europe. Ed. by Robert Walker et al. LC 83-25351. 340p. 1984. 42.50 (*0-8386-3222-X*) Fairleigh Dickinson.

Responses to Poverty among Puerto Rican Women: Identity, Community, & Cultural Citizenship. Rina Benmayor et al. 118p. lib. bdg. 10.00 (*1-878483-06-4*) Hunter Coll CEP.

Responses to Rembrandt. Anthony Bailey. LC 93-15042. (Illus.). 160p. 1994. 21.95 (*0-943221-18-8*) Timken Pubs.

*__Responses to Shakespeare, 8 vols.__ Ed. & Intro. by John Adler. 1600p. (C). 1997. text ed. 925.00 (*0-415-16321-8*) Routledge.

Responses to Suffering in Classical Rabbinic Literature. David Kraemer. LC 93-47291. 304p. 1994. 52.00 (*0-19-508900-6*) OUP.

Responses to Takeover Bids. 2nd ed. Arthur Fleisher. (Corporate Practice Ser.: No. 6-2nd). 1985. 92.00 (*1-55871-262-3*) BNA.

*__Responses to Takeover Bids: Corporate, SEC, Tactical, & Fiduciary Considerations.__ Arthur Fleischer, Jr. & Alexander R. Sussman. (Corporate Practice Ser.: No. 6-3rd). 95.00 (*1-55871-357-3*) BNA.

Responses to the Barclay Report, England & Wales, Scotland. Compiled by Janie Thomas. 1984. 35.00 (*0-317-40613-2*, Pub. by Natl Inst Soc Work) St Mut.

Responses to 101 Questions on Business Ethics. George Devine. 144p. 1996. pap. 9.95 (*0-8091-3647-3*, 3647-3) Paulist Pr.

*__Responses to 101 Questions on Death & Eternal Life.__ Peter C. Phan. LC 97-19963. (Responses to 101 Questions...Ser.). 192p. (Orig.). 1997. pap. 9.95 (*0-8091-3711-9*) Paulist Pr.

Responses to 101 Questions on the Biblical Torah: Reflections on the Pentateuch. Roland E. Murphy. (Responses to 101 Questions Ser.). 144p. 1996. pap. 12.95 (*0-8091-3630-9*, 3630-9) Paulist Pr.

Responses to 101 Questions on the Church. Richard P. McBrien. LC 95-26172. (Responses to 101 Questions Ser.). 176p. 1996. pap. 9.95 (*0-8091-3638-4*, 3638-4) Paulist Pr.

*__Responsibilites & Liabilities of Bank & Bank Holding Company Directors.__ 4th ed. 204p. 1996. pap. 19.00 (*0-614-26811-7*, 13196BLS04) Commerce.

Responsibilities: Its Sources & Limits. Geoffrey Vickers. (Systems Inquiry Ser.). 142p. (Orig.). 1980. pap. text ed. 10.95 (*0-914105-18-3*) Intersystems Pubns.

*__Responsibilities & Liabilities of Accountants & Auditors: Proceedings of a Forum.__ United Nations Conference on Trade & Development Staff. 87p. 1996. pap. text ed. 25.00 (*92-1-104451-0*) UN.

Responsibilities & Liabilities of Bank & Bank Holding Company Directors. 3rd ed. Robert E. Barnett. 136p. pap. 15.00 (*0-685-59634-6*, 4877) Commerce.

Responsibilities of American Advertising: Private Control & Public Influence, 1920-1940. Otis Pease. LC 75-39266. (Getting & Spending: The Consumer's Dilemma Ser.). (Illus.). 1976. reprint ed. 23.95 (*0-405-08039-5*) Ayer.

Responsibilities of Corporate Officers & Directors under Federal Securities Laws, 1997. 192p. 1996. pap. 27.00 (*0-685-67027-9*, 5416) Commerce.

Responsibilities of Insurance Agents & Brokers, 3 vols. B. Harnett. 1974. write for info. (*0-8205-1362-8*) Bender.

Responsibilities of the American Book Community. Ed. by John Y. Cole. LC 81-607006. 88p. 1981. 7.95 (*0-8444-0328-8*) Lib Congress.

Responsibilities of the Novelist & Other Literary Essays. F. Norris. LC 68-26364. (Studies in Fiction: No. 34). 1969. reprint ed. lib. bdg. 75.00 (*0-8383-0269-6*) M S G Haskell Hse.

*__Responsibilities of the Professional Educator.__ Patricia Williams et al. 122p. (C). 1996. per., pap. text ed. 15.69 (*0-7872-2709-9*) Kendall-Hunt.

Responsibilities of Wealth. Ed. by Dwight F. Burlingame. LC 91-17000. (Philanthropic Studies). (Illus.). 164p. 1992. text ed. 19.95 (*0-253-31279-5*) Ind U Pr.

Responsibility. Linda C. Johnson. (Values Library). (Illus.). 64p. (YA). (gr. 7-12). 1990. lib. bdg. 15.95 (*0-8239-1107-1*) Rosen Group.

Responsibility. J. R. Lucas. (Illus.). 306p. 1995. pap. 23.00 (*0-19-823578-X*) OUP.

Responsibility. Nancy Pemberton. LC 87-37557. (Values to Live By Ser.). (Illus.). 32p. (J). (ps-2). 1988. lib. bdg. 21.36 (*0-89565-418-0*) Childs World.

Responsibility, Reading Level 2. Elaine Goley. (Learn the Value Ser.: Set II). (Illus.). 32p. (J). (gr. 1-4). 1989. 11.95 (*0-685-58789-4*); lib. bdg. 14.60 (*0-86592-394-9*) Rourke Corp.

Responsibility - Who Has It & Who Doesn't & What That Means to the Nation: Excerpts from the 1994 Harry Singer Foundation Essay Contest. Ed. by Margaret Bohannon-Kaplan. LC 94-60871. 160p. (Orig.). 1994. pap. 8.00 (*0-915915-27-8*) Wellington Pubns.

Responsibility & Christian Ethics. William Schweiker. (New Studies in Christian Ethics: No. 6). 290p. (C). 1995. text ed. 54.95 (*0-521-47527-9*) Cambridge U Pr.

*__Responsibility & Commitment: The Poetry of Edwin Thumboo.__ Ee T. Hong. Ed. by Leong L. Geok. 204p. (Orig.). 1997. pap. 39.50 (*9971-69-204-X*, Pub. by Sgapore Univ SI) Coronet Bks.

Responsibility & Criminal Liability. Christine Sistare. 192p. (C). 1989. lib. bdg. 114.50 (*0-7923-0396-2*, Pub. by Klwr Acad Pubs NE) Kluwer Ac.

Responsibility & Culture. L. P. Jacks. 1924. 39.50 (*0-685-89778-8*) Elliots Bks.

An Asterisk (*) at the beginning of an entry indicates that the title is appearing in BIP for the first time.

Responsibility & Evidence in Oral Discourse. Ed. by Jane H. Hill & Judith T. Irvine. (Studies in the Social & Cultural Foundations of Language: No. 15). (Illus.). 296p. (C). 1993. text ed. 69.95 (0-521-41515-2); pap. text ed. 23.95 (0-521-42529-8) Cambridge U Pr.

Responsibility & Liability of Public & Private Interests on Dams. 210p. 1976. pap. 13.00 (0-87262-167-7) Am Soc Civil Eng.

Responsibility & Morality: Helping Children Become Responsible & Morally Mature. Larry C. Jensen & Karen M. Hughston. LC 79-10727. (Illus.). 1979. pap. 7.95 (0-8425-1679-4) Frnds of the Libry.

Responsibility & Response. Clyde E. Hewitt. (Advent Christian History Ser.: Vol. 2). 269p. 1987. pap. write for info. (1-881909-17-4) Advent Christ Gen Conf.

Responsibility & Responsiveness. FESC. 1986. 45.00 (0-907659-31-4) St Mut.

Responsibility & the Moral Sentiments. R. Jay Wallace. LC 94-17255. 287p. 1994. text ed. 39.95 (0-674-76622-9, WALRES) HUP.

Responsibility & the University. Donald Kennedy. (Grace A. Tanner Lecture in Human Values Ser.). 21p. 1990. 7.50 (0-910153-07-8) E T Woolf.

Responsibility As Paradox Vol. 1: A Critique of Rational Discourse on Government. Michael M. Harmon. LC 95-7683. (Advances in Public Administration Ser.). (Illus.). 221p. 1995. 45.00 (0-8039-7007-2); pap. 19.95 (0-8039-7008-0) Sage.

Responsibility Center Budgeting: An Approach to Decentralized Management for Institutions of Higher Education. Edward L. Whalen. LC 91-14148. (Illus.). 228p. 1991. 24.50 (0-253-36480-9) Ind U Pr.

Responsibility, Character, & the Emotions: New Essays in Moral Psychology. Ed. by Ferdinand D. Schoeman. 400p. 1988. text ed. 80.00 (0-521-32720-2) Cambridge U Pr.

Responsibility, Character, & the Emotions: New Essays in Moral Psychology. Ed. by Ferdinand D. Schoeman. 400p. 1988. pap. text ed. 32.95 (0-521-33951-0) Cambridge U Pr.

Responsibility Factor: Steps Towards Wholeness. Gary L. Holmgren. LC 85-90307. 1985. 15.00 (0-932999-00-X) G L Holmgren Pubs.

Responsibility for Child Care: The Changing Role of Family & State in Child Development. Bernard Greenblatt. LC 76-50699. (Jossey-Bass Behavioral Science Ser.). 333p. reprint ed. pap. 95.00 (0-685-16248-6, 2027754) Bks Demand.

Responsibility for Crime: An Investigation of the Nature & Causes of Crime & a Means of Its Prevention. Philip A. Parsons. LC 75-76683. (Columbia University. Studies in the Social Sciences: No. 91). reprint ed. 29.50 (0-404-51091-4) AMS Pr.

Responsibility for Drug-Induced Injury. M. N. Dukes & B. Swartz. 500p. 1988. 253.25 (0-444-81005-6) Elsevier.

Responsibility for Rural-School Administration: Allocation of Responsibilities in the Administration of Schools in Rural Areas. Frank W. Cyr. LC 70-176703. (Columbia University. Teachers College. Contributions to Education Ser.: No. 579). reprint ed. 37.50 (0-404-55579-9) AMS Pr.

Responsibility in Health Care. George J. Agich. 318p. 1982. lib. bdg. 104.50 (90-277-1417-7, D Reidel) Kluwer Ac.

Responsibility in Mental Disease, Vol. 3. Henry Maudsley. Bd. with Treatise on Insanity. LC 77-72191. LC 77-72191. (Contributions to the History of Psychology Ser.: Vol. III, Pt. C, Medical Psychology). 603p. 1977. reprint ed. Set text ed. 95.00 (0-313-26942-4, U6942, Greenwood Pr) Greenwood.

Responsibility in the Classroom: A Teacher's Guide to Understanding & Motivating Students. Amy Lee & Betty L. Bettner. 49p. (Orig.). 1995. pap. 5.00 (0-9624841-5-6) Connex Pr.

Responsibility Matters. Peter A. French. LC 92-14728. xiv, 234p. 1992. 29.95 (0-7006-0556-8); pap. 14.95 (0-7006-0626-2) U Pr of KS.

Responsibility of Being Financially Free. S. Gregory Tiernan & Michael J. Pedro. (Orig.). 1988. pap. 14.95 (0-9621730-0-2) CRA Inc.

Responsibility of Forms. Roland Barthes. Tr. by Richard Howard. (Illus.). 320p. 1984. 22.95 (0-8090-8075-3) Hill & Wang.

Responsibility of Forms: Critical Essays on Music, Art, & Representation. Roland Barthes. Tr. by Richard Howard from FRE. (Illus.). 320p. 1991. pap. 13.95 (0-520-07238-3) U CA Pr.

Responsibility of Freedom: Keys to Move You from Suppression & Oppression to Liberty. Myles E. Munroe. 180p. (Orig.). 1997. pap. text ed. 16.99 (0-88419-393-4) Creation House.

Responsibility of Intellectuals: Selected Essays on Marxist Traditions in Cultural Commitment. Alan M. Wald. LC 91-37649. 272p. (C). 1995. pap. 17.50 (0-391-03943-1) Humanities.

Responsibility of International Organizations Toward Third Parties: Some Basic Principles. Moshe Hirsch. LC 94-44295. (Legal Aspects of International Organization Ser.: Vol. 20). 1995. lib. bdg. 105.00 (0-7923-3286-5) Kluwer Ac.

Responsibility of States for Acts of Unsuccessful Insurgent Governments. Haig Silvanie. LC 68-58622. (Columbia University. Studies in the Social Sciences: No. 457). reprint ed. 20.00 (0-404-51457-X) AMS Pr.

Responsibility of the Artist. Jacques Maritain. LC 70-150415. 120p. 1972. reprint ed. 30.00 (0-87752-145-X) Gordian.

Responsibility of the Christian Musician: Giving All to the One Who Gives Freely the Gift of Creativity. Glenn Kaiser et al. LC 94-24995. 75p. 1994. pap. 7.95 (0-940895-22-6) Cornerstone IL.

Responsibility of the Individual Within Organizations Environments. Thomas M. Heather. 123p. 1987. pap. text ed. 12.95 (0-939303-12-4) Educ Lrn Syst.

Responsibility or a Love Letter to My Son, the Hostage, from His Father, the Political Prisoner. (Analysis Ser.: No. 8). 1982. pap. 10.00 (0-686-42843-9) Inst Analysis.

Responsibility People: Eighteen Senior Leaders of Protestant Churches & National Ecumenical Agencies Reflect on Church Leadership. Ed. by William McKinney. LC 94-21600. 376p. 1994. pap. 25.00 (0-8028-0744-5) Eerdmans.

Responsibility Series. Alan C. Walter. Ed. by Beverly Miles. 152p. (Orig.). 1995. pap. text ed. 39.97 (1-57569-012-8) Wisdom Pubng.

Responsibility Skills: Lessons for Success. Jefferson, Thomas, Center Staff. (Success Through Accepting Responsibility - S. T. A. R. Ser.). 57p. 1987. Incl. set of 12 posters & audio tape. teacher ed. 69.95 incl. audio (0-938308-19-X) Jefferson Ctr.

Responsibility to Educate Girls for a Technologically Oriented Society. Deborah Towns. 92p. (C). 1985. 65.00 (0-7300-0117-2, Pub. by Deakin Univ AT) St Mut.

Responsibility Trap: A Blueprint for Treating the Alcoholic Family. Claudia Bepko & Jo-Ann Krestan. 320p. (C). 1985. 35.00 (0-02-902880-9, Free Press) Free Pr.

***Responsibilty of Freedom: Keys to Move You from Suppression & Oppression to Liberty.** Myles E. Munroe. 1996. 16.99 (0-88419-446-9) Creation House.

Responsible Administrator: An Approach to Ethics for the Administrative Role. 3rd ed. Terry L. Cooper. LC 90-5042. (Public Administration Ser.). 272p. 27.95 (1-55542-290-X) Jossey-Bass.

Responsible Alcohol Service: Instructor's Guide. Educational Foundation of the National Restaurant Association Staff. 72p. 1991. text ed. 25.00 (0-915452-61-8) Educ Found.

Responsible Alcohol Service: Leader's Guide. Educational Foundation of the National Restaurant Association Staff. 72p. (Orig.). 1991. pap. 25.00 (0-915452-62-6) Educ Found.

Responsible Alcohol Service: Manager's Coursebook. Educational Foundation of the National Restaurant Association Staff. 112p. (Orig.). 1991. pap. 50.00 (0-915452-59-6) Educ Found.

Responsible Alcohol Service: Server Guide. Educational Foundation of the National Restaurant Association Staff. 84p. (Orig.). 1991. pap. 10.95 (0-915452-60-X) Educ Found.

Responsible Alcohol Service: Video Guide: Intervention Techniques. Educational Foundation of the National Restaurant Association Staff. 24p. (Orig.). 1991. pap. write for info. (0-915452-64-2) Educ Found.

Responsible Alcohol Service: Video Guide: Responsibility & Monitoring. Educational Foundation of the National Restaurant Association Staff. 24p. (Orig.). 1991. pap. write for info. (0-915452-63-4) Educ Found.

Responsible Assertive Behavior: Cognitive-Behavioral Procedures for Trainers. Arthur J. Lange & Patricia Jakubowski. LC 76-1703. (Orig.). (C). 1976. pap. text ed. 24.95 (0-87822-174-3, 1743) Res Press.

Responsible Beverage Service: An Implementation Handbook for Communities. James F. Mosher. (Illus.). 108p. (Orig.). 1991. pap. 15.00 (1-879552-37-X) Stanford CRDP.

Responsible Biomedical Science: Text & Cases. Ed. by Francis L. Macrina. LC 94-46226. (Illus.). 300p. 1995. pap. write for info. (1-55581-069-1) Blackwell Sci.

Responsible Children in Today's World: A Guide for Parents. 2nd ed. Rachell N. Anderson. 1992. pap. text ed. 7.95 (0-9634548-6-2) Marriage & Fam LEC.

Responsible Christian: A Popular Guide for Moral Decision Making According to Classical Tradition. Vincent E. Rush. 288p. (C). 1984. 12.95 (0-8294-0448-1) Loyola Pr.

Responsible Citizenship: Ancient & Modern. Harvey C. Mansfield. LC 94-41697. (Kritikos Professorship in the Humanities Ser.). 1994. 5.00 (0-87114-228-7) U of Oreg Bks.

Responsible Classroom Management for Teachers & Students. J. Allen Queen. 320p. (C). 1996. pap. text ed. 31.00 (0-13-442336-4) P-H.

Responsible Communication: Ethical Issues in Business, Industry, & the Professions. James A. Jaksa & Michael S. Pritchard. LC 96-28081. (Hampton Press Communication Ser.). 416p. 1996. pap. text ed. 29.95 (1-57273-055-2) Hampton Pr NJ.

Responsible Communication: Ethical Issues in Business, Industry, & the Professions. James A. Jaksa & Michael S. Pritchard. LC 96-28081. (Hampton Press Communication Ser.). 416p. 1996. text ed. 76.50 (1-57273-054-4) Hampton Pr NJ.

Responsible Conduct of Research. Dore Beach. (Illus.). 150p. 1996. pap. 35.00 (3-527-29333-7, VCH) Wiley.

Responsible Conduct of Research in Health Sciences: Report of a Study. Institute of Medicine Staff. (Publication IOM Ser.: No. 89-01). 105p. reprint ed. pap. 30.00 (0-8357-8305-7, 2034174) Bks Demand.

Responsible Dog Ownership. Kathy D. Davis. LC 93-17581. (Illus.). 224p. 1994. pap. 21.95 (0-87605-801-2) Howell Bk.

Responsible Driving: Texas Edition. Kenel. 25.98 (0-02-635947-2) Glencoe.

Responsible Electorate: Rationality in Presidential Voting, 1936-1960. Valdimer O. Key et al. LC 66-13181. 184p. 1966. reprint ed. pap. 52.50 (0-7837-4113-8, 2057936) Bks Demand.

Responsible Evangelism: Relating Theory to Practice. Jon T. Murphree. 153p. (Orig.). (C). 1994. pap. write for info. (1-885729-00-6) Toccoa Falls.

Responsible Freedom in the Americas. Ed. by Angel Del Rio. 1969. reprint ed. text ed. 95.00 (0-8371-0199-9, RIFA, Greenwood Pr) Greenwood.

Responsible Grace: John Wesley's Practical Theology. Randy L. Maddox. (Kingswood Ser.). 400p. (Orig.). 1994. pap. 19.95 (0-687-00334-2) Abingdon.

Responsible Individualism. Wallace Johnson. LC 67-30828. 1967. 5.00 (0-8159-6710-1) Devin.

Responsible Judge: Readings in Judicial Ethics. Ed. by John T. Noonan, Jr. & Kenneth I. Winston. LC 92-31841. 416p. 1993. text ed. 75.00 (0-275-94022-5, C4022, Praeger Pubs); pap. text ed. 35.00 (0-275-94023-3, B4023, Praeger Pubs) Greenwood.

Responsible Manager: Practical Strategies for Ethical Decision Making. Michael Rion. 1996. pap. text ed. 19.95 (0-87425-351-9) HRD Press.

Responsible Parties. Jeffrey Sweet. 1985. pap. 5.25 (0-8222-0945-4) Dramatists Play.

Responsible Party Materials. 189p. 1988. 22.00 (0-685-30191-5, 43,928) NCLS Inc.

Responsible Pet Care, 6 bks., Reading Level 3. Pam Jameson & Tina Hearne. (Illus.). 192p. (J). (gr. 2-5). 1989. 71.70 (0-685-58765-7) Rourke Corp.

Responsible Pet Care, 6 bks., Set, Reading Level 3. Pam Jameson & Tina Hearne. (Illus.). 192p. (J). (gr. 2-5). 1989. Set. lib. bdg. 95.64 (0-86625-188-X) Rourke Corp.

Responsible Pet Care Series, 6 bks., Set II. Frisch. (J). 1991. 71.70 (0-86625-195-2) Rourke Pubns.

Responsible Physician & Thanatology. Ed. by Stewart G. Wolff, Jr. et al. (Current Thanatology Ser.). 100p. 1988. pap. 14.95 (0-930194-42-X) Ctr Thanatology.

Responsible Police Administration: Issues & Approaches. Lee W. Potts. LC 82-16059. 195p. 1983. pap. 55.60 (0-7837-8398-1, 2059209) Bks Demand.

Responsible Presidency. Landy. 1997. 24.95 (0-684-82796-4) Free Pr.

Responsible Presidency. Robert E. Landy. 1997. 24.95 (0-02-917777-4, Free Press) Free Pr.

Responsible Public Servant. Kenneth Kernaghan & John W. Langford. 220p. 1990. pap. text ed. 23.95 (0-88645-099-3, Pub. by Inst Res Pub CN) Ashgate Pub Co.

Responsible Rascal. Linda Schwartz. LC 90-62595. (J). (ps-3). 1991. pap. 4.95 (0-88160-188-8, LW1202) Learning Wks.

Responsible Reciprocity. Ed. by Julia A. White. LC 83-61311. (Papers on International Issues: No. 5). (Orig.). (C). 1983. pap. text ed. 5.00 (0-935082-04-2) Southern Ctr Intl Stud.

***Responsible Reporter.** 2nd ed. Bruce J. Evensen. LC 97-11650. 380p. (C). 1997. pap. text ed. 24.95 (1-885219-06-7) Vision AL.

Responsible Scholar: Ethical Considerations in the Humanities & Social Sciences. Ed. by Gerald Berthoud & Beat Sitter-Liver. LC 95-53708. 303p. 1996. 49.95 (0-88135-165-2) Watson Pub Intl.

Responsible Science Vol. II: Background Papers & Resource Documents. National Academy of Sciences, National Academy of Engineering, Institute of Medicine, Panel on Scientific Responsibility & the Conduct of Research Sta. 288p. 1993. pap. text ed. 35.00 (0-309-04788-9) Natl Acad Pr.

Responsible Science, Vol. I: The Ensuring Integrity of the Research Process. National Academy of Sciences Staff et al. 224p. 1992. pap. text ed. 24.95 (0-309-04731-5) Natl Acad Pr.

Responsible Self. H. Richard Niebuhr. LC 63-15955. 1978. pap. 11.00 (0-06-066211-5, RD 266) Harper SF.

Responsible Software Engineer: Selected Readings in IT Professionalism. Colin Myers et al. LC 96-9538. (Illus.). 360p. 1996. 64.95 (3-540-76041-5) Spr-Verlag.

Responsible Test Use: Case Studies for Assessing Human Behavior. Lorraine D. Eyde et al. 244p. (Orig.). 1993. pap. 24.95 (1-55798-203-1) Am Psychol.

Responsible Vision: The Philosophy of Julian Marfas. Harold Raley. 1980. 20.00 (0-89217-004-2); pap. 8.95 (0-89217-005-0) American Hispanist.

Responsible Workplace. Francis Duffy et al. LC 92-37496. (Illus.). 240p. 1993. pap. 69.95 (0-7506-0802-1, Butterwrth Archit) Buttrwrth-Heinemann.

Responsibly Slowing the Growth of Minnesota's Long Term Care Spending. 50p. (Orig.). (C). 1996. pap. text ed. 25.00 (0-7881-2770-5) DIANE Pub.

Responsio Ad Lutherum, 2 vols. Thomas More. Ed. by John M. Headley. LC 63-7949. (Complete Works of St. Thomas More Ser.: No. 5). 1969. 105.00 (0-300-01123-7) Yale U Pr.

Responsive Arts. Judy Nagle. LC 79-24450. 428p. (C). 1982. pap. text ed. 43.95 (0-87484-627-7, 627) Mayfield Pub.

Responsive Arts Instructor's Manual. Judy Nagle. 1982. pap. write for info. (0-614-17916-5, 212) Mayfield Pub.

Responsive Assessment: A New Way of Thinking about Learning. Mary Henning-Stout. LC 93-36593. (Education & Social & Behavioral Science Ser.). 323p. text ed. 32.95 (1-55542-645-X) Jossey-Bass.

Responsive Computer Systems. Y. Kakuda. Ed. by H. Kopetz. (Dependable Computing & Fault-Tolerant Systems Ser.: Vol. 7). (Illus.). 389p. 1993. 109.95 (0-387-82458-8) Spr-Verlag.

Responsive Computer Systems: Steps Toward Fault-Tolerant Real-Time System. Donald Fussell. Ed. by Miroslaw Malek. LC 95-34837. (Kluwer International Series in Engineering & Computer Science). 288p. (C). 1995. lib. bdg. 110.00 (0-7923-9563-8) Kluwer Ac.

Responsive Computing. Miroslaw Malek. LC 94-31249. 120p. (C). 1994. lib. bdg. 81.50 (0-7923-9511-5) Kluwer Ac.

Responsive Environments. Ian Bentley et al. (Illus.). 152p. 1985. pap. 49.95 (0-7506-0566-9, Butterwrth Archit) Buttrwrth-Heinemann.

Responsive Evaluation: Making Valid Judgments About Student Literacy. Ed. by Brian Cambourne & Jan Turbill. LC 94-29683. 144p. 1995. pap. text ed. 19.00 (0-435-08829-7, 08829) Heinemann.

Responsive Faith. Millard Erickson. LC 87-81478. 157p. (Orig.). 1987. pap. 4.95 (0-935797-29-7) Harvest IL.

Responsive Gels: Volume Transitions I. Ed. by K. Dusek. (Advances in Polymer Science Ser.: Vol. 109). (Illus.). 290p. 1993. 171.95 (0-387-56791-7) Spr-Verlag.

Responsive Gels: Volume Transitions II. Ed. by K. Dusek. (Advances in Polymer Science Ser.: Vol. 110). (Illus.). 260p. 1993. 145.00 (0-387-56970-7) Spr-Verlag.

Responsive Government: Service Quality Initiatives. Contrib. by OECD Staff. 319p. (Orig.). (ENG & FRE.). 1996. pap. 73.00 (92-64-14709-8, Pub. by Org for Econ FR) OECD.

Responsive Professional Education: Balancing Outcomes & Opportunities. Joan S. Stark et al. Ed. & Frwd. by Jonathan D. Fife. LC 86-82077. (ASHE-ERIC Higher Education Reports: No. 86-3). 128p. (C). 1986. pap. 18.75 (0-913317-30-6) GWU Grad Schl E&HD.

Responsive Public Library Collection: How to Develop & Market It. Sharon L. Baker. (Illus.). xi, 330p. 1993. lib. bdg. 45.00 (0-87287-911-9) Libs Unl.

Responsive Reader. Morgan. (C). 1995. teacher ed., pap. 26.75 (0-15-502171-0) HB Coll Pubs.

Responsive Reader. Morgan. (C). 1996. pap. text ed. write for info. (0-15-501182-0) HB Coll Pubs.

Responsive Regulation: Transcending the Deregulation Debate. Ian Ayres & John Braithwaite. (Oxford Socio-Legal Studies). (Illus.). 216p. 1992. 49.95 (0-19-507070-4) OUP.

Responsive Regulation: Transcending the Deregulation Debate. Ian Ayres & John Braithwaite. (Socio-Legal Studies). (Illus.). 216p. 1995. reprint ed. pap. 18.95 (0-19-509376-3) OUP.

Responsive Schools, Renewed Communities. Clifford W. Cobb. LC 92-18357. 320p. 1992. 34.95 (1-55815-205-9); pap. 19.95 (1-55815-216-4) ICS Pr.

Responsive Singing: Sabbath Morning Service. Robert A. Segal. 184p. 1972. 4.50 (0-8381-0218-2) USCJE.

Responsive Society: Collected Essays on Guiding Deliberate Social Change. Amitai Etzioni. LC 91-25603. (Management-Social & Behavioral Science Ser.). 497p. 45.95 (1-55542-378-7) Jossey-Bass.

Responsive Teaching: An Ecological Approach to Classroom Patterns of Language, Culture, & Thought. C. A. Bowers & David J. Flinders. (Advances in Contemporary Educational Thought Ser.). 288p. (C). 1990. text ed. 40.00 (0-8077-2998-1); pap. text ed. 19.95 (0-8077-2997-3) Tchrs Coll.

Responsive Therapy: A Systematic Approach to Counseling Skills. Sterling Gerber. LC 85-21869. 250p. 1986. 35.95 (0-89885-267-6); pap. 22.95 (0-89885-269-2) Human Sci Pr.

***Responsive University: Restructuring for High Performance.** William G. Tierney. 1997. 29.95 (0-8018-5715-5) Johns Hopkins.

Responsive Workplace: Employers & a Changing Labor Force. Sheila B. Kamerman & Alfred J. Kahn. LC 87-18223. 320p. 1987. text ed. 52.50 (0-231-06480-2) Col U Pr.

Responsive Workplace: Employers & a Changing Labor Force. Sheila B. Kamerman & Alfred J. Kahn. 320p. 1988. pap. text ed. 17.50 (0-231-06481-0) Col U Pr.

***Responsive Writer.** Siler. (C). 1997. lab manual ed. write for info. (0-15-504001-4) HB Coll Pubs.

Responsive Writer. Jocelyn Siler. 608p. (C). 1996. text ed. 35.00 (0-15-501167-7) HB Coll Pubs.

***Responsive Writer.** Jocelyn Siler. 608p. (C). 1996. pap. text ed. 31.00 (0-15-504003-0) HB Coll Pubs.

Responsiveness of Demand Policies to Balance of Payments: Postwar Patterns. Michael Michaely. (Studies in International Economic Relations: No. 5). 317p. 1971. reprint ed. 82.50 (0-87014-221-6) Natl Bur Econ Res.

Responsiveness of Kindergarten Children to the Behavior of Their Fellows. Esther K. Harris. (SRCD M Ser.: Vol. 11, No. 2). 1946. 25.00 (0-527-01538-5) Periodicals Srv.

Responsiveness, Responsibility, & Majority Rule. J. Roland Pennock. (Reprint Series in Social Sciences). (C). 1993. reprint ed. pap. text ed. 1.00 (0-8290-3603-2, PS-226) Irvington.

Responsorial Psalms for Sundays of the Year. Margaret Daly. 1989. pap. 22.00 (1-85390-118-0, Pub. by Veritas IE) St Mut.

Responsories & Versicles of the Latin Office of the Dead. Knud Ottosen. (Illus.). 512p. (C). 1993. 40.00 (87-7288-315-4, Pub. by Aarhus Univ Pr DK) David Brown.

Respublica. LC 79-133727. (Tudor Facsimile Texts. Old English Plays Ser.: No. 25). reprint ed. 49.50 (0-404-53325-6) AMS Pr.

Respublica: An Interlude for Christmas 1553 Attributed to Nicholas Udall. Ed. by W. W. Greg. (EETS Original Ser.: Vol. 226). 1971. reprint ed. 20.00 (0-19-722226-9, Pub. by EETS UK) Boydell & Brewer.

***Respuestas a La Alabanza Revisada.** M. Carothers. (SPA.). 7.95 (0-8297-2035-9) Life Pubs Intl.

Respuestas a Mis Amigos Catolicos. Thomas F. Heinz. LC 96-86272. 64p. (Orig.). (SPA.). 1996. pap. 3.50 (0-937958-53-0) Chick Pubns.

Respuestas a Preguntas Dificles. Josh McDowell & Don Stewart. 216p. (SPA.). 1986. pap. 7.95 (0-8297-0689-5) Life Pubs Intl.

***Respuestas al Colonialismo en la Politica Puertorriquena 1899-1929.** Rafael Bernabe. LC 96-85393. 320p. 1996. pap. 12.25 (0-929157-40-0) Ediciones Huracan.

An Asterisk (*) at the beginning of an entry indicates that the title is appearing in BIP for the first time.

R

Respuestas Al Cuaderno Practico Para Texto De Cosmetologia Milady - Answers to Milady's Standard Practical Workbook. 282p. (SPA.). 1992. teacher ed. 26.95 (*1-56253-098-4*) Milady Pub.

Respuestas Biblicas - Testigos D. David Reed. 144p. (SPA.). 1990. pap. 5.95 (*0-8297-0390-X*) Life Pubs Intl.

Respuestas Biblicas A 10 Preguntas Actuales. Victor Ricardo. (Estudio Biblico Para Mujeres Ser.). 57p. 1992. pap. 4.00 (*1-885630-27-1*) HLM Producciones.

Respuestas Catolicas a Preguntas Fundamentalistas. Philip St. Roman. Tr. by Olimpia Diaz. LC 87-81851. 96p. (Orig.). 1987. pap. 2.95 (*0-89243-275-6*) Liguori Pubns.

Respuestas Cuaderno Sobre el Arte y la Ciencia de la Manicura. 96p. (SPA.). 1990. pap. 34.84 (*0-87350-385-6*) Milady Pub.

Respuestas De Dios. deluxe ed. M. Countryman. 328p. (SPA.). 1989. ring bd. 12.95 (*0-937347-35-3*) C & D Intl.

Respuetas Al Cuaderno para la Tecnologia de las Unas de Milady. 125p. (SPA.). 1993. teacher ed., pap. 29.95 (*1-56253-208-1*) Milady Pub.

Ressentiment. Max F. Scheler. (Studies in Philosophy). 1994. pap. 20.00 (*0-87462-602-1*) Marquette.

***Ressources Halieutiques de la Mediterranee Pt. 1: Mediterranee Occidentale.** 141p. (FRE & SPA.). 1983. 17.00 (*92-5-201345-8*, FF18, Pub. by FAO IT) Bernan Associates.

Ressurection. Gina A. Bonati. 6p. 1994. pap. 3.00 (*1-886206-10-4*) Venom Pr.

Ressurection of Philosophy. Kevin Shepherd. 307p. (C). 1989. 110.00 (*0-9508680-3-5*, Pub. by Anthropographia UK) St Mut.

Rest. David Gordon. 155p. 1993. pap. 10.95 (*0-943373-26-3*) Natl Poet Foun.

Rest, Vol. 1. Palmer. 1995. 38.75 (*0-316-69028-7*) Little.

Rest, Vol. 2. Palmer. 1995. 38.75 (*0-316-69027-9*) Little.

Rest, Vol. 3. Palmer. 1995. 38.75 (*0-316-69026-0*) Little.

Rest, Vol. 4. Palmer. 1995. 38.75 (*0-316-69025-2*) Little.

Rest: Poetry. Aram Saroyan. 105p. 1986. 10.00 (*0-9606772-3-2*); pap. 5.00 (*0-9606772-2-4*) Blackberry Bks.

Rest: Poetry. deluxe ed. Aram Saroyan. 105p. 1986. Signed edit. 20.00 (*0-9606772-4-0*) Blackberry Bks.

***Rest & Relaxation.** J. N. Marquis & Cohen. Date not set. write for info. (*0-688-01121-7*) Morrow.

***Rest Area Guide to the United States & Canada, Vol. 5.** 5th rev. ed. Bill Cima. (Illus.). 248p. 1977. pap. 13.95 (*0-937877-25-5*) Cottage Pubns Inc.

Rest Areas, Wetlands, & Hydrology. (Research Record Ser.: No. 1224). 95p. 1989. 15.50 (*0-309-04818-4*) Transport Res Bd.

Rest Days: The Christian Sunday, the Jewish Sabbath & Their Historical & Anthropological Prototypes. Hutton Webster. 325p. 1992. reprint ed. lib. bdg. 36.00 (*1-55888-919-1*) Omnigraphics Inc.

Rest for the Wicked. Glyn Maxwell. 112p. 9600. pap. 16.95 (*1-85224-296-5*, Pub. by Bloodaxe Bks UK) Dufour.

Rest Harrow. Janice K. Keefer. 256p. (Orig.). 1993. pap. 12.00 (*0-00-647519-1*, Pub. by HarpC CN) HarpC.

Rest Here, My Heart. Maryhelen Clague. 1979. pap. 1.95 (*0-449-14284-1*, GM) Fawcett.

Rest in Peace. Pat Cook. 34p. 1976. pap. 3.00 (*0-87129-672-1*, R14) Dramatic Pub.

***Rest in Peace, Vol. 3.** Kathryn Reiss. (Ghost in the Dollhouse Ser.). (J). 1997. pap. text ed. 3.99 (*0-590-60362-0*, Apple Paperbacks) Scholastic Inc.

Rest in Pieces. large type ed. Rita Mae Brown & Sneaky P. Brown. LC 92-37866. 429p. 1993. reprint ed. lib. bdg. 20.95 (*1-56054-595-X*) Thorndike Pr.

Rest in Pieces. large type ed. Ralph McInerny. (Nightingale Ser.). 280p. 1991. lib. bdg. 13.95 (*0-8161-5107-5*, GK Hall) Thorndike Pr.

Rest in Pieces: A Mrs. Murphy Mystery. Rita Mae Brown. 368p. 1993. mass mkt. 5.99 (*0-553-56239-8*) Bantam.

Rest in the Day of Trouble. Kelley Varner. 252p. (Orig.). 1993. pap. 8.95 (*1-56043-119-9*) Destiny Image.

***Rest in the Lord.** Melva J. Harris. 65p. (Orig.). 1995. pap. text ed. 12.00 (*0-614-29915-2*) M J Harris.

Rest Is Prose. Samuel Hazo. LC 89-23638. 168p. 1990. text ed. 22.50 (*0-8207-0224-2*) Duquesne.

Rest Is Silence. Erico Verissimo. Tr. by L. C. Kaplan. LC 74-88994. 485p. 1970. reprint ed. text ed. 65.00 (*0-8371-2318-6*, VERS, Greenwood Pr) Greenwood.

Rest Is Silence: Death As Annihilation in the English Renaissance. Robert N. Watson. LC 93-45004. (C). 1995. 52.00 (*0-520-08494-2*) U CA Pr.

Rest Is Silence: The Powazki Cemetery in Warsaw. Waldorf Jerzy. (Illus.). 220p. 1990. 22.00 (*0-317-05092-3*) Szwede Slavic.

***Rest Lightly: An Anthology of Latin & Greek Tomb Inscriptions.** Tr. by Paul Shore from GEC. LC 97-19130. (Illus.). 80p. 1997. pap. text ed. write for info. (*0-86516-355-3*) Bolchazy-Carducci.

Rest of Faith. Karen Clemente. (Inter Acta Logos Ser.). (Illus.). 2p. (C). 1994. teacher ed., ring bd. write for info. (*1-885702-73-6*, 741-073t, Inter Acta); student ed., ring bd. 3.25 (*1-885702-72-8*, 741-073s, Inter Acta) WSN Pr.

Rest of Life: Three Novellas. Mary Gordon. (Contemporary American Fiction Ser.). 272p. 1994. pap. 10.95 (*0-14-014907-4*, Penguin Bks) Viking Penguin.

Rest of Life: Three Novellas. large type ed. Mary Gordon. LC 93-33493. 1994. lib. bdg. 23.95 (*0-8161-5907-6*, GK Hall) Thorndike Pr.

Rest of My Life. Laura R. Hunter & Polly H. Memhard. LC 81-85425. (Illus.). 112p. (Orig.). 1981. pap. 6.95 (*0-941834-01-8*) Growing Pains Pr.

Rest of Our Lives. Hall Bartlett. 1989. mass mkt. 4.95 (*0-8217-2674-9*, Zebra Kensgtn) Kensgtn Pub Corp.

Rest of Our Lives. Bartlett Hall. 1988. 19.95 (*0-394-56145-7*) Random.

Rest of Our Lives. Harvey Jackins. 522p. (Orig.). (C). 1986. 16.00 (*0-913937-05-3*); pap. 13.00 (*0-913937-06-1*) Rational Isl.

Rest of the Deer. Margaret Blanchard. LC 89-82511. 300p. 1989. 4.95 (*0-9624626-7-5*) Astarte Shell Pr.

Rest of the Dream: The Black Odyssey of Lyman Johnson. Wade Hall. LC 88-22660. 256p. 1988. 25.00 (*0-8131-1674-0*) U Pr of Ky.

Rest of the Earth. William H. Henderson. LC 97-12759. 1997. pap. 22.95 (*0-525-93981-4*) NAL-Dutton.

***Rest of the Road.** Don Blanding. Date not set. lib. bdg. 18.95 (*0-8488-1894-6*) Amereon Ltd.

Rest of the Story. Finis M. Bruington. LC 87-71127. (Illus.). 381p. 1987. 9.95 (*0-9616838-1-3*) F M Bruington.

Rest of the Way. J. D. McClatchy. 1992. pap. 10.00 (*0-679-74059-7*) McKay.

Rest of the Week. Kenneth J. Roberts. LC 73-87984. 191p. 1988. reprint ed. pap. text ed. 5.95 (*0-318-37581-8*) PAX Tapes.

***Rest of Us.** Jacquelyn Mitchard. 1997. pap. 22.95 (*0-670-87662-3*) Viking Penguin.

Rest of Us: The Rise of America's Eastern European Jews. Stephen Birmingham. 384p. 1984. 19.95 (*0-316-09647-4*) Little.

Rest of Your Life. Allen R. McGinnis. Ed. by Nancy V. Thompson. LC 85-23731. 175p. 1986. 10.00 (*0-9616042-0-4*) J & N Pubs.

Rest of Your Life. Patrick M. Morley. LC 92-515. 1992. 17.99 (*0-8407-6754-4*) Nelson.

Rest of Your Life Is the Best of Your Life. David Brown. 128p. 1993. pap. 9.95 (*0-942637-93-3*) Barricade Bks.

Rest of Your Life Is the Best of Your Life: David Brown's Guide to Growing Gray Disgracefully. David Brown. LC 91-19324. 128p. 1991. 14.95 (*0-942637-35-6*) Barricade Bks.

Rest Principle: A Neurophysiological Theory of Behavior. John D. Sinclair. LC 80-17396. 240p. 1981. text ed. 39.95 (*0-89859-065-5*) L Erlbaum Assocs.

Rest Stops for Single Mothers: Devotions to Encourage You on Your Journey. Susan T. Osborne & Lucille Moses. 240p. 1995. pap. 9.99 (*0-8054-5385-7*, 4253-85) Broadman.

Rest You Merry. Charlotte MacLeod. 224p. 1980. reprint ed. mass mkt. 4.99 (*0-380-47530-8*) Avon.

Restableciendo el Romance en el Matrimonio. Ed Wheat. (Serie Enfoque a la Familia - Focus on the Family Ser.). 68p. (SPA.). 1991. pap. 1.79 (*1-56063-187-2*, 497429) Editorial Unilit.

Restatement of Rabbinic Civil Law: Laws of Collection of Debts, Laws of Collection from Heirs, Laws of Mortgages, Laws of Agency, Laws of Guarantee, Laws of Presumption of Ownership of Personality, Chapters 97-139, Vol. 4. Emanuel Quint. LC 89-18546. 384p. 1993. 40.00 (*0-87668-197-6*) Aronson.

Restatement of Rabbinic Civil Law: Laws of Judges & Laws of Evidence, Chapters 1-38, Vol. 1. Emanuel Quint. LC 89-18546. 336p. 1990. 40.00 (*0-87668-799-0*) Aronson.

Restatement of Rabbinic Civil Law: Laws of Loans, Chapters 39-74, Vol. 2. Emanuel Quint. LC 89-18546. 352p. 1991. 40.00 (*0-87668-678-1*) Aronson.

Restatement of Rabbinic Civil Law: Laws of Partnerships, Laws of Agents, Laws of Sales, Acquisition of Personality, Vol. 6, Chapters 176-226. Emanuel Quint. LC 89-18546. 416p. 1995. 50.00 (*1-56821-319-0*) Aronson.

Restatement of Rabbinic Civil Law: Laws of Pleading, Chapters 75-96, Vol. 3. Emanuel Quint. LC 89-18546. 288p. 1993. 40.00 (*0-87668-396-0*) Aronson.

Restatement of Rabbinic Civil Law: Laws of Presumption of Ownership of Realty, Laws of Injuries to Neighbors, Laws of Joint Ownership of Realty, Laws of Partition of Realty, Chapters 140-175, Vol. 5. Emanuel Quint. LC 89-18546. 336p. 1994. 50.00 (*1-56821-167-8*) Aronson.

Restatement of Rabbinic Civil Law Vol. VII: Discrepancies in Sales, Gifts of a Healthy Person, Gifts Causa Mortis. Emanuel Quint. 304p. 1997. 50.00 (*1-56821-907-5*) Aronson.

***Restatement of Rabbinic Civil Law Vol. VIII: Laws of Lost & Found Objects, Laws of Inheritance, Laws of the Unpaid Bai.** Emanuel Quint. 1997. write for info. (*0-7657-9969-3*) Aronson.

Restatement of the Law. write for info. (*0-318-57507-8*) West Pub.

Restatement of the Law Citations. Shepard's Citation, Inc. Staff. 1986. 150.00 (*0-685-23135-6*) Shepards.

Restatement of the Law, First, Property: Future Interests, Vols. 2 & 3. 1940. 127.00 (*0-685-70565-X*, 5109) Am Law Inst.

Restatement of the Law, First, Property: Introduction & Freehold Interests, Vol. 1. 1936. 63.50 (*0-686-40949-3*, 5107) Am Law Inst.

Restatement of the Law, First, Property: Servitudes, Vol. 5. 1944. 63.50 (*0-614-00940-5*, 5111) Am Law Inst.

Restatement of the Law, First, Property Vol. 6: Appendix. xxxvii, 699p. 1993. 67.00 (*0-614-00941-3*, 5433) Am Law Inst.

Restatement of the Law, First, Restitution: Appendix, Vol. 2. xiv, 462p. 1988. text ed. 63.50 (*0-314-61453-2*, 5892) Am Law Inst.

Restatement of the Law, First, Restitution: Appendix, Vol. 3. xiv, 393p. 1988. text ed. 63.50 (*0-314-64924-7*, 5893) Am Law Inst.

Restatement of the Law, First, Restitution: Including Reporters' Notes. Warren A. Seavey & Austin W. Scott. ix, 208p. 1937. 63.50 (*0-686-90461-3*, 5118) Am Law Inst.

Restatement of the Law, Second: Complete Set & Individual Topics. American Law Institute. LC 65-5788. 1993. 3,592.50 (*0-317-01987-2*) Bisel Co.

Restatement of the Law, Second Vols. I & II: Conflict of Laws, 1988 Revisions, Permanent Pocket Parts, Set. 25.50 (*0-685-55291-8*, 5969) Am Law Inst.

Restatement of the Law, Second, Agency, 3 vols. 2031p. 1958. 190.50 (*0-686-40963-9*, 5127) Am Law Inst.

Restatement of the Law, Second, Agency: Appendix, Vol. 7. American Law Institute Staff. xxv, 686p. 1994. 67.00 (*0-314-02811-0*, 5434) West Pub.

Restatement of the Law, Second, Conflict of Laws, 4 Vols., Set Incl. 1988 Revisions & Vols. 1 & 2. 1971. Set, incl. 1988 revisions & Vols. 1 & 2. 254.00 (*0-317-30674-X*, 5140) Am Law Inst.

Restatement of the Law, Second Contracts: Appendix. 690p. 1990. 65.00 (*0-615-00345-1*, 5316) Am Law Inst.

Restatement of the Law, Second, Contracts: Appendix, Vol. 9. xxxix, 814p. 1993. 67.00 (*0-8140-1644-8*, 5417) Am Law Inst.

Restatement of the Law, Second, Contracts, Appendix, 3 vols., Set, Vols. 1-3. LC 81-50259. 1981. Set. 195.00 (*0-685-31121-X*, 5625) Am Law Inst.

Restatement of the Law, Second, Judgments: Official Draft & Vol. 3 of Appendix, 3 vols., Set. LC 81-70073. 1415p. 1982. 190.50 (*0-314-66807-1*, 5627) Am Law Inst.

Restatement of the Law, Second, Judgments, Appendix, Vol. 4. LC 81-70073. xv, 736p. 1988. 63.50 (*0-685-51831-0*, 5895) Am Law Inst.

Restatement of the Law, Second, Property: Donative Transfers: Official Draft, 4 vols., Vol. 1. LC 83-2563. xxxi, 407p. 1983. text ed. 63.50 (*0-314-73634-4*, 5687) Am Law Inst.

Restatement of the Law, Second, Property: Donative Transfers: Official Draft, 4 vols., Vol. 2. LC 83-2563. xxxv, 508p. 1986. text ed. 63.50 (*0-314-97073-8*, 5784) Am Law Inst.

Restatement of the Law, Second, Property: Donative Transfers: Official Draft, 4 vols., Vol. 3. LC 83-2563. xxxv, 550p. 1988. text ed. 63.50 (*0-314-39783-3*, 5968) Am Law Inst.

Restatement of the Law, Second, Property: Donative Transfers: Official Draft, 4 vols., Vol. 4. LC 83-2563. xxv, 436p. 1992. text ed. 63.50 (*0-685-67496-7*, 5335) Am Law Inst.

Restatement of the Law, Second, Property: Landlord & Tenant: Official Text, 2 vols. 1977. 127.00 (*0-686-40969-8*, 5179) Am Law Inst.

Restatement of the Law, Second, Torts, 4 vols. 1979. 254.00 (*0-686-91039-7*) Am Law Inst.

Restatement of the Law, Second, Trusts, 3 vols., Set. 1959. 190.50 (*0-685-41254-7*, 5214) Am Law Inst.

Restatement of the Law, Third: Foreign Relations Law of the United States, 2 Vols. Ed. by Louis Henkin. LC 86-20665. 1987. text ed. 190.50 (*0-314-30138-0*, 5898) Am Law Inst.

Restatement of the Law, Third: Suretyship & Guaranty. American Law Institute Staff. LC 96-14635. xx, 361p. (C). 1996. pap. 72.00 (*0-314-09422-9*, 5542) Am Law Inst.

Restatement of the Law, Third, Property (Donative Transfers) Tentative Draft No. 1. xxi, 202p. 1995. pap. 30.00 (*0-614-07323-5*, 5526) Am Law Inst.

Restatement of the Law, Third, Property (Mortgages) Tentative Draft No. 4. xxix, 315p. 1995. pap. 30.00 (*0-614-07324-3*, 5528) Am Law Inst.

Restatement of the Law, Third, Property (Servitudes) Tentative Draft No. 5. xvii, 82p. 1995. pap. 20.00 (*0-614-07325-1*, 5525) Am Law Inst.

Restatement of the Law, Third, Torts - Products Liability: Tentative Draft No. 2. xxix, 315p. 1995. pap. 45.00 (*0-614-07327-8*, 5529) Am Law Inst.

Restatement of the Law, Third, Trusts (Prudent Investor Rule) xix, 307p. 1992. 66.00 (*0-314-84246-2*, 5368) Am Law Inst.

Restatement of the Law, Third, Unfair Competition: Official Text. xviii, 682p. 1995. 85.00 (*0-314-04251-2*, 5473) Am Law Inst.

Restatements see Pimsleur's Checklists of Basic American Legal Publications

Restauracion de los Heridos. John White & Ken Blue. 264p. (SPA.). 1991. pap. 1.50 (*0-8297-0398-5*) Life Pubs Intl.

Restauracion del Ministerio Biblico. Frank Dietz. 112p. (SPA.). 1994. pap. 4.99 (*1-56063-594-0*, 497718) Editorial Unilit.

Restaurando el Mensaje De Pentecostes. B. H. Clendennen. Tr. by New Life Ministries International Staff et al. from ENG. 224p. (Orig.). (SPA.). 1991. pap. 6.95 (*1-878921-01-0*) Victory Temple.

***Restaurando Su Primer Amor.** Dave Hunt. 250p. (SPA.). pap. write for info. (*0-614-27132-0*) Editorial Unilit.

***Restaurando Su Primer Amor - Restoring Your First Love.** Dave Hunt. 250p. (SPA.). write for info. (*0-614-24402-1*) Editorial Unilit.

Restaurando Su Vida Deshecha. Gordon McDonald. 220p. (SPA.). 1990. pap. 7.99 (*1-56063-009-4*, 498458) Editorial Unilit.

***Restaurant: From Concept & Operation.** 2nd ed. Donald E. Lundberg & John Walker. 400p. 1993. teacher ed. 47.50 (*0-471-30618-5*) Wiley.

Restaurant: From Concept to Operation. 2nd ed. Donald E. Lundberg & John R. Walker. LC 92-39761. 384p. 1993. text ed. 29.00 (*0-471-57883-5*) Wiley.

Restaurant & Fast Food Site Selection. John C. Melaniphy. LC 91-34535. 400p. 1992. text ed. 54.95 (*0-471-55716-1*) Wiley.

Restaurant & Food Graphics. Hays Radice. (Illus.). 192p. 1996. pap. 34.95 (*0-86636-376-9*) Universe.

Restaurant & Institutional Food Industry: Update. Business Communications Co., Inc. Staff. 150p. 1988. pap. 1,750.00 (*0-89336-609-9*, GA039N) BCC.

***Restaurant at the Beginning of the Universe: Exploring the Wonderment of the World Through Physics.** Anthony P. Pitucco & Shawn Agut. LC 96-28581. (J). (gr. 5-12). 1996. 32.00 (*1-56976-056-X*) Zephyr Pr AZ.

Restaurant at the End of the Universe. Douglas Adams. 1995. mass mkt. 6.99 (*0-345-39181-0*) Ballantine.

Restaurant at the End of the Universe. Douglas Adams. 256p. 1982. 12.95 (*0-517-54535-7*, Harmony) Crown Pub Group.

***Restaurant at the End of the Universe.** Douglas Adams. 1997. pap. 11.00 (*0-345-41892-1*) Ballantine.

Restaurant Basics: Why Guests Don't Come Back...& What You Can Do about It. Bill Marvin. LC 91-29481. 240p. 1991. text ed. 39.95 (*0-471-55174-0*) Wiley.

Restaurant Biz is Show Biz: Why Marketing Is the Key to Your Success. Dave Steadman. Ed. by Dinah Witchel. (Illus.). 224p. 1991. 24.00 (*0-9628954-0-7*) Whittier Green.

Restaurant Companion: A Guide to Healthier Eating Out. 2nd ed. Hope S. Warshaw. LC 95-9953. 314p. (Orig.). 1995. pap. 13.95 (*0-940625-93-8*) Surrey Bks.

***Restaurant Design.** PBC International Staff. 1991. 55.00 (*0-688-10133-X*) Morrow.

***Restaurant Design.** 3rd ed. PBC International Staff. 1993. 59.95 (*0-688-12619-7*) Morrow.

Restaurant Finance: Handbook for Successful Management & Operations. John Ilich. 142p. reprint ed. pap. 15.95 (*0-935650-08-3*) Bengal Pr.

Restaurant Five Hundred: All-American Restaurant & Chef Yearbook. Camaro Editors. (Illus.). 1988. pap. 6.95 (*0-913290-71-8*) Camaro Pub.

Restaurant Franchising. Mahmood A. Khan. (Illus.). 452p. 1992. text ed. 52.95 (*0-442-23741-3*) Van Nos Reinhold.

Restaurant Franchising. 2nd ed. Mahmood A. Khan. (Hospitality, Travel & Tourism Ser.). (Illus.). 352p. 1996. text ed. 49.95 (*0-442-02244-1*) Van Nos Reinhold.

Restaurant Graphics, No. 2. Ed. by Rockport Publishers Editorial Staff. (Illus.). 160p. 1996. 34.99 (*1-56496-255-5*) Rockport Pubs.

Restaurant Graphics: From Matchbooks to Menus. (Illus.). 160p. 1993. 34.99 (*1-56496-047-1*, 30511) Rockport Pubs.

Restaurant Greetings to Duplicate & Use. A. Doyle. 1996. ring bd. 149.95 (*1-56820-181-8*) Story Time.

Restaurant Guide to the Finger Lakes. Charles DeMotte & Katherine W. Sundgren. (Illus.). 180p. 1991. pap. 8.95 (*0-935526-18-8*) McBooks Pr.

Restaurant Lover's Companion: A Handbook for Deciphering the Mysteries of Menus. Steve Ettlinger. (Illus.). 256p. 1995. pap. 14.95 (*0-201-40636-5*) Addison-Wesley.

Restaurant Lovers' Fat Gram Counter. Kalia Doner. 128p. (Orig.). 1995. pap. text ed. 6.99 (*0-425-14919-6*) Berkley Pub.

***Restaurant Management.** Mill. 1997. text ed. 48.00 (*0-13-201774-1*) P-H.

Restaurant Management. Nancy L. Scanlon. LC 92-11375. 260p. 1993. text ed. 52.95 (*0-442-00834-1*) Van Nos Reinhold.

Restaurant Management & Control: The Profitable Approach. Caesar Villano. (Orig.). 1985. pap. 22.95 (*0-86730-210-0*) Lebhar Friedman.

Restaurant Management Guide. Robert T. Gordon. LC 84-19814. 274p. 1984. 79.50 (*0-87624-511-4*, Inst Busn Plan) P-H.

Restaurant Manager's Handbook: How to Set up, Operate, & Manage a Financially Successful Restaurant. 3rd rev. ed. Douglas R. Brown. Ed. by Robert Montgomery. LC 88-84047. (Illus.). 300p. 1992. 59.95 (*0-910627-08-8*) Atlantic FL.

***Restaurant Maps: Washington, DC Metro Area Road Maps Showing the Locations of 808 Restaurants.** Ed. & Illus. by Donald R. Taylor. 210p. (Orig.). 1997. pap. 8.95 (*0-9637314-4-0*) Quick Study.

Restaurant Marketing. 2nd ed. William O. Smith. 1989. pap. 11.84 (*0-07-058543-1*) McGraw.

***Restaurant Newsletters That Pay Off.** Walter Mathews. LC 97-1969. 1996. text ed. 39.95 (*0-471-16912-9*) Wiley.

Restaurant Operations & Controls: A Practical Guide. Marcel R. Escoffier & Shirley D. Escoffier. 256p. 1986. text ed. 59.95 (*0-13-774803-5*) P-H.

Restaurant Owner's Handbook: Success Through Management Awareness. Jack C. Drewes. LC 87-32697. 356p. (Orig.). (C). 1988. text ed. 49.95 (*0-945034-01-6*); pap. text ed. 29.95 (*0-945034-00-8*) Posh Pubng.

Restaurant Pastries & Desserts. Yves Thuries. (Illus.). 432p. 1997. text ed. 89.95 (*0-442-01702-2*) Van Nos Reinhold.

***Restaurant Phenomenon: An Essential Guide.** Denny Offner. (Illus.). 114p. 1997. 24.95 (*1-882935-28-4*) Westphalia.

Restaurant Planning, Design & Construction: A Survival Manual for Owners, Operators & Developers. Jeff B. Katz. LC 96-18349. 1996. text ed. 49.95 (*0-471-13698-0*) Wiley.

Restaurant Planning Guide. Peter Rainsford & David H. Bangs, Jr. 176p. 1992. pap. 19.95 (*0-936894-35-0*) Upstart Pub.

Restaurant Planning Guide. 2nd ed. Peter Rainsford & David H. Bangs, Jr. 175p. 1996. pap. 22.95 (*1-57410-026-2*, 6100-2302) Upstart Pub.

Restaurant Purchasing: Principles & Practice. Hugh J. Kelly. LC 76-49750. 200p. 1985. pap. 28.95 (*0-912016-55-8*) Lebhar Friedman.

Restaurant Reality: A Manager's Guide. Michael M. Lefever. (Illus.). 304p. (Orig.). (C). 1989. pap. 32.95 (*0-442-25938-7*) Van Nos Reinhold.

***Restaurant Recipe Secrets.** 2nd ed. Gloria Pitzer. (Illus.). 60p. write for info. (*1-886138-09-5*) G Pitzers.

An Asterisk (*) at the beginning of an entry indicates that the title is appearing in BIP for the first time.

R

Restaurant Recycling Guide. John P. Allison. 24p. (Orig.). (C). 1992. pap. 7.95 (*0-9632789-3-2*) RMC Pub Grp.

Restaurant Redbook: Los Angeles, Vol. 1. Ed. by Garth W. Bishop. (Illus.). 1988. pap. 4.95 (*0-913290-89-0*) Camaro Pub.

Restaurant Redbook: San Francisco, Vol. 2. Ed. by Garth W. Bishop. (Illus.). 1987. pap. 4.95 (*0-913290-91-2*) Camaro Pub.

Restaurant Rose - The Menu Guide to Greater Pasadena. 8th rev. ed. Jan W. Castro. 88p. (Orig.). 1996. pap. 7.95 (*0-9624023-0-3*) J C West Prodns.

Restaurant Rose Six: The Menu Guide to Greater Pasadena. Jan W. Castro. 1992. pap. 8.95 (*0-9624023-4-6*) J C West Prodns.

Restaurant Server's Guide: To Quality Customer Service. rev. ed. William B. Martin. LC 85-73177. (Fifty-Minute Ser.). (Illus.). 71p. (Orig.). 1987. pap. 10.95 (*0-931961-08-4*) Crisp Pubns.

Restaurant Server's Guide to Quality Service. William Martin. 1988. 6.95 (*0-685-44003-6*, 110) Am Bartenders.

Restaurant Service: Beyond the Basics. Carol A. Litrides & Bruce H. Axler. 372p. 1994. text ed. 44.95 (*0-471-51476-4*) Wiley.

***Restaurant Start-Up Guide.** Peter Rainsford & David H. Bangs, Jr. LC 97-13871. 1997. pap. 22.95 (*1-57410-071-8*) Upstart Pub.

***Restaurant Style.** PBC International Staff. 1996. pap. 24.95 (*0-688-14927-8*) Morrow.

Restaurant Training Program: An Employee Training Guide for Managers. Karen A. Drummond. LC 92-47. 432p. 1992. pap. text ed. 75.00 (*0-471-55207-0*) Wiley.

***Restaurant 2000.** Wagner. LC 97-22351. 1997. 45.00 (*0-86636-586-9*) St Martin.

***Restaurant 2000: Dining Design III.** Christy Casamassima. LC 97-22351. 1997. pap. write for info. (*0-86636-587-7*) PBC Intl Inc.

Restaurants. Rotovision S. A. Staff. 1996. pap. text ed. 35.00 (*0-8230-6556-1*) Watsn-Guptill.

Restaurants - Conditions & Syndromes: Index of Actions & Reports. David S. Lehigh. LC 90-56273. 160p. 1991. 44.50 (*1-55914-328-2*); pap. 39.50 (*1-55914-329-0*) ABBE Pubs Assn.

Restaurants, Clubs & Bars: Planning, Design Investment for Food Service Facilities. rev. ed. Fred Lawson. (Illus.). 338p. 1995. pap. 62.95 (*0-7506-2076-5*, Butterwrth Archit) Buttrwrth-Heinemann.

***Restaurants of Detroit.** 7th ed. Mary Abraham. 1996. pap. 11.95 (*0-937247-65-0*) Detroit Pr.

Restaurants of New England. 2nd ed. Nancy Woodworth & Richard Woodworth. 490p. 1994. pap. 14.95 (*0-934260-75-3*) Wood Pond.

Restaurants of New Orleans. rev. ed. Roy F. Guste, Jr. 1991. 27.95 (*0-393-02838-0*) Norton.

Restaurants of Paris. Ed. by Gallimard Editions Staff. LC 94-8363. 1994. pap. 25.00 (*0-679-75578-0*) Knopf.

Restaurants of Pittsburgh. 1982. pap. 5.95 (*0-911479-00-7*) Dial Pub.

Restaurants That Work: Case Studies of the Best in the Industry. Martin E. Dorf. LC 92-11262. (Illus.). 224p. 1992. 55.00 (*0-8230-4540-4*, Whitney Lib) Watsn-Guptill.

Restauration et Gouvernement de Juillet see Histoire de l'Architecture Classique en France

***Restavec: From Haitian Slave Child to Middle-Class American.** Jean-Robert Cadet. LC 97-4832. 1998. write for info. (*0-292-71202-2*); pap. write for info. (*0-292-71203-0*) U of Tex Pr.

Restavek - Child Domestic Labor in Haiti: A Report by the MLIHRC. MLIHRC Delegate Staff et al. 51p. (Orig.). 1990. pap. 7.00 (*0-929293-06-1*) MN Advocates.

Restenosis after Intervention with New Mechanical Devices. Ed. by Patrick W. Serruys. (Developments in Cardiovascular Medicine Ser.). 528p. (C). 1992. lib. bdg. 290.50 (*0-7923-1555-3*) Kluwer Ac.

Restenosis after Percutaneous Transluminal Coronary Angioplasty: Detection, Assessment & Modes of Prevention. W. Desmet. No. 88. 168p. (Orig.). 1994. pap. 39.50 (*90-6186-626-X*, Pub. by Leuven Univ BE) Coronet Bks.

Restful Sleep: The Complete Mind-Body Program for Overcoming Insomnia. Deepak Chopra. (Perfect Health Library). 1994. 15.00 (*0-517-59923-6*, Harmony) Crown Pub Group.

Restful Sleep: The Complete Mind Body Program for Overcoming Insomnia. Deepak Chopra. (Perfect Health Library). 144p. 1996. pap. 11.00 (*0-517-88457-7*) Crown Pub Group.

Resting Bell: Collected Poems. Anthony Barnett. 384p. (Orig.). 1987. 28.00 (*0-907954-06-5*); Agneau 2 Paperbook Ser.: No. 4. pap. 16.00 (*0-907954-07-3*) SPD-Small Pr Dist.

Resting Places. Alta H. Hartfield. 1995. pap. 8.95 (*0-533-11522-1*) Vantage.

Resting Places in East Anglia. Walter Marsden. 1993. pap. 15.00 (*0-86025-897-1*, Pub. by Ian Henry Pubns UK) Empire Pub Srvs.

Resting Secure: Poems by David, Solomon, Isaiah & Habakkuk. Kathleen B. Nielson. (Challenge Bible Study Guides Ser.). 112p. (Orig.). (gr. 10). 1993. pap. 5.99 (*0-8010-6789-8*) Baker Bks.

Restitution. 2nd ed. Wade. Date not set. text ed. 17.50 (*0-88277-403-4*) Foundation Pr.

Restitution, 4 vols., 1. Pati Palmer. 1978. 165.00 (*0-316-69000-7*) Little.

Restitution, 4 vols., 2. Pati Palmer. 1978. 165.00 (*0-316-69001-5*) Little.

Restitution, 4 vols., 3. Pati Palmer. 1978. 165.00 (*0-316-69002-3*) Little.

Restitution: Criminal Justice or Social Control. Elmar Weitekamp. (C). 1998. text ed. 34.00 (*0-8133-2008-9*) Westview.

***Restitution: Developments in Unjust Enrichment.** Mitchell McInnes. 1996. pap. 85.00 (*0-455-21430-1*, Pub. by Cavendish UK) Gaunt.

***Restitution: Restructuring School Discipline.** Diane C. Gossen. 132p. teacher ed., pap. text ed. 25.00 (*0-944337-21-X*) Peytral Pubns.

Restitution: The Future. Peter Birks. 1992. 25.00 (*1-86287-088-8*, Pub. by Blackstone Pr UK) Gaunt.

***Restitution Vol. 1: Restructuring School Discipline.** 2nd rev. ed. Diane C. Gossen. LC 96-68623. 139p. (Orig.). 1996. pap. 12.95 (*0-944337-36-8*, 368) New View Pubns.

Restitution & the Conflict of Laws. Ed. by Francis Rose. 1995. pap. 48.00 (*0-9526499-0-X*, Pub. by Mansfield UK) Gaunt.

Restitution As a Criminal Sentence: A Selected Bibliography. Anthony G. White. 1977. 1.50 (*0-686-19112-9*, 1254, Sage Prdcls Pr) Sage.

Restitution of All Things. Andrew Jukes. 194p. 1976. reprint ed. pap. text ed. 7.00 (*0-910424-65-9*) Concordant.

Restitution of Decayed Intelligence: In Antiquities, Concerning the...English Nation. by the Studie & Travaile of R. Verstagen. Dedicated Unto the Kings Most Excellent Majestie. Richard Rowlands. LC 79-84134. (English Experience Ser.: No. 952). 380p. 1979. reprint ed. lib. bdg. 35.00 (*90-221-0952-6*) Walter J Johnson.

Restitution of Metaphysics. Errol E. Harris. 320p. (C). 1997. text ed. 60.00 (*0-391-04011-1*) Humanities.

Restless. Neesa Hart. 1996. pap. 4.99 (*0-7860-0259-X*) Kensgtn Pub Corp.

***Restless: The Memoirs of Labor & Consumer Advocate Esther Peterson.** Esther Peterson & Winifred Conkling. 193p. 1995. per. 15.00 (*1-886450-02-1*) Caring Pub.

Restless Caribbean: Changing Patterns of International Relations. Ed. by Richard L. Millett & W. Marvin Will. LC 78-19764. 330p. 1979. text ed. 55.00 (*0-275-90396-6*, C0396, Praeger Pubs) Greenwood.

Restless Centuries: A History of the American People. 2nd ed. Peter Carroll & David W. Noble. LC 78-67974. 1979. pap. text ed. write for info. (*0-8087-2920-9*) Burgess MN Intl.

Restless Dead: Ghostly Tales from Around the World. Daniel Cohen. (J). (gr. 3-6). 1996. pap. 3.50 (*0-671-53512-9*, Minstrel Bks) PB.

Restless Decade: John Gutmann's Photographs of the Thirties. Ed. by Lew Thomas. (Illus.). 160p. 1996. pap. 19.95 (*0-8109-2695-4*) Abrams.

Restless Dream. large type ed. Leila Mackinlay. 1988. 15.95 (*0-7089-1746-1*) Ulverscroft.

Restless Earth. Melvin Berger. Ed. by Susan Evento. (Ranger Rick Science Spectacular Ser.). 16p. (J). (gr. 2-4). 1995. pap. 14.95 (*1-56784-212-7*) Newbridge Comms.

***Restless Earth.** National Geographic Society (U. S.) Staff. LC 97-8115. 1997. denim write for info. (*0-7922-7006-1*) Natl Geog.

***Restless Earth.** National Geographic Society (U. S.) Staff. LC 97-8115. 1997. write for info. (*0-7922-7121-1*) Natl Geog.

***Restless Earth: Nature's Aw.** National Geographic Staff. LC 97-8115. 1997. 35.00 (*0-7922-7026-6*) Natl Geog.

Restless Earth: Student Book. Melvin Berger. Ed. by Susan Evento. (Ranger Rick Science Spectacular Ser.). (Illus.). 16p. (Orig.). (J). (gr. 2-4). 1996. pap. write for info. (*1-56784-237-2*) Newbridge Comms.

***Restless Earth: Theme Pack.** Melvin Berger. Ed. by Susan Evento. (Ranger Rick Science Spectacular Ser.). (Illus.). (Orig.). (J). (gr. 2-4). 1996. pap. write for info. (*1-56784-280-1*) Newbridge Comms.

***Restless Flame: Novel St. Augustine.** Louis De Wohl. 1997. pap. text ed. 12.95 (*0-89870-603-3*) Ignatius Pr.

***Restless from the Start.** Joei C. Hossack. LC 97-91654. (Illus.). 124p. (Orig.). 1997. pap. 10.95 (*0-9657509-0-6*) Skeena Pr.

Restless Genius: Robert Hooke & His Earthly Thoughts. Ellen T. Drake. (Illus.). 400p. 1996. 55.00 (*0-19-506695-2*) OUP.

Restless Guns. large type ed. William C. MacDonald. LC 94-35253. 300p. 1995. pap. 16.95 (*0-7838-1148-9*, GK Hall) Thorndike Pr.

***Restless Heart - Wheels & Highlights from Their First Album.** Ed. by Carol Cuellar. 84p. (Orig.). (C). 1987. pap. text ed. 12.95 (*0-7692-0543-7*, VF1400) Warner Brothers.

***Restless Hearts - Big Dreams in a Small Town.** Ed. by Carol Cuellar. 40p. (Orig.). (C). 1989. pap. text ed. 12.95 (*0-7692-0914-9*, VF1521) Warner Brothers.

Restless in Peace. John Mattera. 82p. 1987. pap. 5.00 (*0-87129-000-6*, R49) Dramatic Pub.

Restless Is the Wind. Kimberly Cates. 1989. mass mkt. 5.99 (*0-671-63395-3*) PB.

***Restless Land.** John Culp. Date not set. write for info. (*0-688-04488-3*) Morrow.

Restless Memories: Recollections of the Holocaust Years. 2nd rev. ed. Samuel P. Oliner. LC 85-82084. 215p. (Orig.). 1986. pap. 9.95 (*0-943376-28-9*) Magnes Mus.

Restless Messengers: Poems by Norman Finkelstein. Norman Finkelstein. LC 91-12701. (Contemporary Poetry Ser.). 88p. 1992. pap. 14.95 (*0-8203-1380-7*) U of Ga Pr.

Restless Mind: Alexis de Tocqueville on the Origin & Perpetuation of Human Liberty. Peter A. Lawler. 210p. (Orig.). (C). 1993. pap. text ed. 22.95 (*0-8476-7824-5*); lib. bdg. 58.50 (*0-8476-7823-7*) Rowman.

***Restless Mind: Essays in Honor of Amos Perlmutter.** Ed. by Benjamin Frankel. 250p. (C). 1996. text ed. 45.00 (*0-7146-4607-5*, Pub. by F Cass Pubs UK) Intl Spec Bk.

Restless Mind, Quiet Thoughts: A Personal Journal. Paul Eppinger & Charles Eppinger. LC 94-26201. 232p. 1994. pap. 12.95 (*1-883991-07-2*) Whte Cloud Pr.

***Restless Nation.** Alan Clements et al. (Illus.). 144p. 1996. 35.00 (*1-85158-884-1*, Pub. by Mnstream UK) Trafalgar.

***Restless Nights.** Tiffany White. (Temptation Ser.: No. 639). 1997. mass mkt. 3.50 (*0-373-25739-2*, 1-25739-3) Harlequin Bks.

Restless Planet: Tulburatoarg Lume. George Bajenaru. 160p. (Orig.). 1993. pap. 13.99 (*0-9619930-8-1*) Moonfall Pr VA.

***Restless Spirit.** large type ed. Jessica Blair. (Magna Large Print Ser.). 592p. 1997. 27.50 (*0-7505-1018-8*) Ulverscroft.

Restless Spirit: The Story of Robert Frost. Natalie S. Bober. (Illus.). 192p. (YA). (gr. 5 up). 1991. 19.95 (*0-8050-1672-4*, Bks Young Read) H Holt & Co.

Restless Spirits: Ghost Stories by American Women, 1872-1926. Ed. by Catherine A. Lundie. LC PS648.G48R47 1996. 328p. 1996. 55.00 (*1-55849-055-8*) U of Mass Pr.

Restless Spirits: Ghost Stories by American Women, 1872-1926. Ed. by Catherine A. Lundie. LC 96-19250. 328p. 1996. pap. 17.95 (*1-55849-056-6*) U of Mass Pr.

Restless Spirits from Japanese Noh Plays of the Fourth Group: Parallel Translations & Running Commentary. Chifumi Shimazaki. (Cornell East Asia Ser.: Vol. 76). (Illus.). 276p. (Orig.). (C). 1995. pap. 15.00 (*0-939657-76-7*, 76) Cornell East Asia Pgm.

Restless Spirits from Japanese Noh Plays of the Fourth Group: Parallel Translations & Running Commentary. Tr. by Chitumi Shimazaki from JPN. (Cornell East Asia Ser.: Vol. 76). (Illus.). 276p. (C). 1995. 25.00 (*0-939657-78-3*, 76) Cornell East Asia Pgm.

Restless Strangers: Nevada's Immigrants & Their Interpreters. Wilbur S. Shepperson. LC 78-117219. (Lancehead Ser.). (Illus.). xiv, 304p. 1970. 29.95 (*0-87417-028-1*) U of Nev Pr.

Restless Sun. Donat G. Wentzel. LC 88-18491. (Library of the Solar System: No. 3). (Illus.). 308p. 1989. 29.95 (*0-87474-982-4*) Smithsonian.

Restless Urban Landscape. Ed. by Paul L. Knox. LC 92-19473. 1992. text ed. 26.40 (*0-13-755414-1*) P-H.

***Restless Visionaries: The Social Roots of Antebellum Reform in Alabama & Michigan.** John W. Quist. (Illus.). 584p. 1998. text ed. 57.50 (*0-8071-2133-9*) La State U Pr.

Restless Water. Harriet Door. 70p. (Orig.). 1983. pap. 10.00 (*0-932662-47-1*) St Andrews NC.

Restless Wind. Nikki Benjamin. (Intimate Moments Ser.). 1993. mass mkt. 3.50 (*0-373-07519-7*, 5-07519-7) Silhouette.

Restless Wind. Dorothy Garlock. 384p. 1988. mass mkt. 5.99 (*0-445-20932-1*) Warner Bks.

Restless Years. Lucy Taylor. 432p. (Orig.). 1992. pap. 5.50 (*0-451-17333-3*, Sig) NAL-Dutton.

Restless Youth (Autobiography, Vol. 4, 1922-1929) Julian Green. Tr. by Euan Cameron. 256p. (FRE.). 1996. 29.95 (*0-7145-3002-6*) M Boyars Pubs.

Restless Youth in Ancient Rome. Emiel Eyben. LC 92-7227. 272p. (C). (gr. 13). 1993. text ed. 62.95 (*0-415-04366-2*, A5996) Routledge.

Reston Directory of Online Data Bases. Jay M. Shafritz & Louis Alexander. 1984. pap. 27.95 (*0-8359-6666-6*, Reston) P-H.

Reston Home Owners Association: A Case Study in New Community Management. Karl J. Ingebritsen. 53p. 1977. pap. 5.47 (*0-912104-26-0*, 851) Inst Real Estate.

***Restoration.** James Martin. 148p. (Orig.). 1996. pap. 10.00 (*1-57502-318-0*, P01080) Morris Pubng.

Restoration. Rose Tremain. 384p. 1991. pap. 8.95 (*0-14-012893-X*) Viking Penguin.

Restoration, Vol. 1. Jeff Swanson & Ruth E. Norman. (Illus.). 231p. (Orig.). 1981. pap. 10.00 (*0-932642-66-7*) Unarius Acad Sci.

Restoration, Vol. 2. Charles Spaegel & Ruth E. Norman. (Illus.). 188p. (Orig.). 1982. pap. 10.00 (*0-932642-67-5*) Unarius Acad Sci.

Restoration: Congress Term Limits & the Recovery of Deliberative Democracy. George F. Will. 150p. 1993. pap. 12.95 (*0-02-934713-0*, Free Press) Free Pr.

***Restoration: Discovering How All of God Meets Our Deepest Needs.** Navpress Publishing Staff. (Foundations for Christian Living Ser.). 1997. pap. text ed. 6.00 (*1-57683-009-8*) NavPress.

Restoration: The Winds of Change - Eighteenth Annual Spiritual Sword Lectureship. Ed. by Jim Laws. 1993. write for info. (*0-9615751-9-0*) Getwell Church.

Restoration: Tie-in Edition. Rose Tremain. 384p. 1994. pap. 10.95 (*0-14-024488-3*, Penguin Bks) Viking Penguin.

Restoration & Conservation of Islamic Monuments in Egypt. Ed. by Jere L. Bacharach. (World XEgypt Ser.). (Illus.). 240p. 1995. 35.00 (*977-424-356-0*, Pub. by Am Univ Cairo Pr UA) Col U Pr.

Restoration & Early Eighteenth-Century English Literature, 1660-1740: A Selected Bibliography of Resource Materials. Roger D. Lund. LC 79-87585. (Selected Bibliographies in Language & Literature Ser.: No. 1). 42p. (Orig.). 1980. pap. text ed. 10.00 (*0-87352-950-2*, SB001) Modern Lang.

Restoration & Eighteenth Century Comedy. Ed. by Scott McMillin. (Critical Editions Ser.). (C). 1973. pap. text ed. 14.95 (*0-393-09997-0*) Norton.

Restoration & Eighteenth-Century Comedy. 2nd ed. Ed. by Scott McMillin. LC 95-44942. (Critical Edition Ser.). (C). 1996. pap. text ed. 15.95 (*0-393-96334-9*) Norton.

Restoration & Eighteenth Century (Sixteen Sixty to Seventeen Ninety-Eight) Ed. by Ian McGowan. LC 89-70174. (St. Martin's Anthologies of English Literature Ser.: Vol. No. 3). 612p. 1990. text ed. 20.00 (*0-312-04477-1*) St Martin.

Restoration & Eighteenth Century Theatre Research Bibliography, 1961-68: 1961-1978. Carl J. Stratman et al. LC 75-79626. 241p. 1969. 10.50 (*0-87875-000-2*) Whitston Pub.

Restoration & Georgian England, 1660-1788. Ed. by David Thomas. (Theatre in Europe: a Documentary History Ser.). (Illus.). 448p. (C). 1989. text ed. 115.00 (*0-521-23380-1*) Cambridge U Pr.

Restoration & Management of Lakes & Reservoirs. G. Dennis Cooke et al. 560p. 1993. 69.95 (*0-87371-397-4*, L397) Lewis Pubs.

Restoration & Recovery of Shallow Eutrophic Lake Ecosystems in the Netherlands: Proceedings of a Conference Held in Amsterdam, The Netherlands, 18-19 April 1992. Ed. by Louis Van Liere & Ramesh D. Gulati. LC 92-12305. 308p. (C). 1992. lib. bdg. 216.00 (*0-7923-1697-5*) Kluwer Ac.

Restoration & Rehabilitation of the Desert Environment. Ed. by N. Al-Awadhi et al. LC 96-19949. 306p. 1996. 262.50 (*0-444-82471-5*) Elsevier.

Restoration & Renewal: The Church in the Third Millennium. Joseph F. Eagan. 480p. (Orig.). 1995. pap. 19.95 (*1-55612-763-4*) Sheed & Ward MO.

Restoration & the Augustans, 5 vols., Set. Incl. Jonathan Swift. Ed. by Williams. 357p. (C). 1996. text ed. 120.00 (*0-415-13908-2*); Alexander Pope. Ed. by Barnard. 560p. (C). 1996. text ed. 150.00 (*0-415-13432-3*); William Congreve. Erskine-Hill. 508p. (C). 1996. text ed. 150.00 (*0-415-13431-5*); John Dryden. Ed. by Kinsley. 424p. (C). 1996. text ed. 130.00 (*0-415-13430-7*); Earl of Rochester. Fairley-Hills. 287p. (C). 1996. text ed. 120.00 (*0-415-13429-3*); 1779p. (C). 1996. Set boxed, text ed. 539.00 (*0-415-13428-5*) Routledge.

Restoration & the Cat. 2nd ed. Edward Bond. 201p. (C). pap. 8.95 (*0-413-49920-0*, A0238) Heinemann.

Restoration & the Eighteenth Century. Ed. by Martin Price. (Illus.). 818p. 1973. pap. text ed. 25.00 (*0-19-501614-9*) OUP.

***Restoration & the England of Charles II.** 2nd ed. John Miller. LC 96-50299. 1997. pap. write for info. (*0-582-29223-9*) Longman.

Restoration & the July Monarchy. Jean Lucas-Dubreton. LC 29-16694. (National History of France Ser.: No. 8). reprint ed. 45.00 (*0-404-50798-0*) AMS Pr.

Restoration As a Response to the Holocaust. Teichtal. 1995. write for info. (*0-88125-441-X*) Ktav.

Restoration Cathedral Music: 1660-1714. Ian Spink. (Oxford Studies in British Church Music). (Illus.). 448p. 1996. text ed. 105.00 (*0-19-816149-2*) OUP.

Restoration Comedy: Crises of Desires & Identity. Edward Burns. 224p. 1987. text ed. 39.95 (*0-312-67789-8*) St Martin.

Restoration Comedy in Performance. J. L. Styan. (Illus.). 256p. 1986. pap. text ed. 23.95 (*0-521-27421-4*) Cambridge U Pr.

Restoration Comedy, 1660-1720. Bonamy Dobree. LC 81-1230. 182p. 1981. reprint ed. text ed. 42.50 (*0-313-22722-5*, DORC, Greenwood Pr) Greenwood.

***Restoration Court Stage 1660-1702.** Eleonore Boswell. LC 65-16227. (Illus.). 400p. Date not set. write for info. (*0-405-18138-8*) Ayer.

***Restoration Drama: An Annotated Bibliography.** Thomas J. Taylor. (Magill Bibliographies Ser.). 155p. 1989. 40.00 (*0-8108-2808-1*) Scarecrow.

Restoration Ecology: A Synthetic Approach to Ecological Research. Ed. by William R. Jordan, III et al. (Illus.). 352p. (C). 1990. pap. text ed. 35.95 (*0-521-33728-3*) Cambridge U Pr.

***Restoration Ecology & Sustainable Development.** Ed. by Krystyna Urbanska et al. LC 96-52176. (Illus.). 385p. (C). 1997. pap. write for info. (*0-521-59989-X*) Cambridge U Pr.

***Restoration Ecology & Sustainable Development.** Ed. by Krystyna Urbanska et al. LC 96-52176. (Illus.). 385p. (C). 1997. text ed. 85.00 (*0-521-58160-5*) Cambridge U Pr.

Restoration England. Patrick Morrah. LC 79-317995. 252p. reprint ed. pap. 71.90 (*0-318-34738-5*, 2031995) Bks Demand.

Restoration Europe 1814-1848. Broers. 172p. 1996. text ed. 69.95 (*0-7190-4722-6*) St Martin.

Restoration Europe 1814-1848. Michael Broers. 172p. 1996. text ed. 19.95 (*0-7190-4723-4*) St Martin.

***Restoration FOP: Gender Boundaries & Comic Characterization in Later Seventeenth Century Drama.** Andrew P. Williams. 206p. 1995. text ed. 89.95 (*0-7734-4193-X*) E Mellen.

Restoration Forestry: An International Guide to Sustainable Forestry Practices. Ed. by Michael Pilarski. (Illus.). 528p. (Orig.). (C). 1994. pap. 26.95 (*1-882308-51-4*) Kivaki Pr.

Restoration Forum, Vol. VIII. Ed. by Victor Knowles. 1990. pap. 6.99 (*0-89900-296-X*) College Pr Pub.

Restoration Forum, Vol. IX. 1992. pap. 6.99 (*0-89900-297-8*) College Pr Pub.

Restoration in Russia: Why Capitalism Failed. Boris Kagarlitsky. Tr. by Renfrey Clarke from RUS. LC 94-45850. 225p. (C). 1995. pap. text ed. 20.00 (*1-85984-072-8*, B4972, Pub. by Vrso UK) Norton.

Restoration in Russia: Why Capitalism Failed. Boris Kagarlitsky. Tr. by Renfrey Clarke from RUS. LC 94-45850. 225p. (C). (gr. 13). 1995. text ed. 65.00 (*1-85984-962-8*, B4968, Pub. by Vrso UK) Norton.

Restoration in the Church. 6.99 (*1-871676-02-9*, Pub. by Christian Focus UK) Spring Arbor Dist.

Restoration in the Church. Terry Virgo. 150p. (Orig.). 1989. reprint ed. pap. 5.95 (*0-939159-14-7*) Cityhill Pub.

Restoration Land Settlement in Co. Dublin, 1660-88. Lawrence J. Arnold. (Illus.). 224p. 1993. 45.00 (*0-7165-2503-8*, Pub. by Irish Acad Pr IE) Intl Spec Bk.

Restoration Literature, 1660-1700: Dryden, Bunyan, & Pepys. James R. Sutherland. (Oxford History of English Literature Ser.: Vol. VIII). 604p. 1990. 70.00 (*0-19-812234-9*) OUP.

R

Restoration Mind. LC 96-41595. 1997. write for info. (*0-87413-571-0*) U Delaware Pr.

Restoration Movement. Bob L. Ross. 1981. mass mkt. 3.00 (*1-56186-509-5*) Pilgrim Pubns.

Restoration Navy & English Foreign Trade 1674-1688: A Study in the Peacetime Use of Sea Power. Sari Hornstein. 352p. 1991. text ed. 72.95 (*0-85967-831-8*, Pub. by Scolar Pr UK) Ashgate Pub Co.

Restoration Newspaper & Its Development. James R. Sutherland. (Illus.). 264p. 1986. text ed. 75.00 (*0-521-32613-3*) Cambridge U Pr.

Restoration of All Things. Victor P. Abram. LC 62-18059. 149p. 1962. 6.00 (*0-910840-07-5*) Kingdom.

Restoration of American Politics see Politics in the Twentieth Century

Restoration of Aquatic & Terrestrial Systems. Ed. by R. W. Brocksen & Joe Wisniewski. (C). 1989. lib. bdg. 177.00 (*0-7923-0111-0*) Kluwer Ac.

Restoration of Aquatic Ecosystems: Science, Technology, & Public Policy. Ed. by Committee Staff on Restoration of Aquatic Ecosystems: Science, Technology, & Public Policy, National Research Council. 576p. 1992. text ed. 39.95 (*0-309-04534-7*) Natl Acad Pr.

Restoration of Brain Function by Tissue Transplantation. Ed. by O. Lindvall. LC 92-49462. (Basic & Clinical Aspects of Neuroscience Ser.: Vol. 5). 1993. 38.95 (*0-387-55823-3*) Spr-Verlag.

***Restoration of Carriages.** George L. Isles. (Illus.). 190p. 1996. pap. 24.95 (*0-941936-37-6*) Linden Pub Fresno.

Restoration of Carriages. George L. Isles. 190p. 1990. 68.00 (*0-85131-366-3*, Pub. by J A Allen & Co UK) St Mut.

Restoration of Dialogue: Readings in the Philosophy of Clinical Psychology. Ed. by Ronald B. Miller. 654p. 1992. 59.95 (*1-55798-157-4*); pap. 39.95 (*1-55798-166-3*) Am Psychol.

Restoration of Endangered Species: Conceptual Issues, Planning & Implementation. Ed. by Marilyn L. Bowles & Christopher J. Whelan. 416p. 1996. pap. text ed. 30.95 (*0-521-57422-6*) Cambridge U Pr.

Restoration of Endangered Species: Conceptual Issues, Planning, & Implementation. Ed. by Marlin L. Bowles & Christopher J. Whelan. LC 93-43593. (Illus.). 384p. (C). 1995. text ed. 74.95 (*0-521-41863-1*) Cambridge U Pr.

***Restoration of Forests: Environmental Challenges in Central & Eastern Europe.** LC 97-17694. 1997. text ed. 365.00 (*0-7923-4634-3*) Kluwer Ac.

Restoration of Function after Brain Injury. Aleksandr R. Luria & B. Haigh. LC 63-10016. 1963. 127.00 (*0-08-010130-5*, Pub. by Pergamon Repr UK) Franklin.

Restoration of Land: The Ecology & Reclamation of Derelict & Degraded Land. A. D. Bradshaw & M. J. Chadwick. LC 79-64658. 1980. 50.00 (*0-520-03961-0*) U CA Pr.

Restoration of Leningrad's Architectural Monuments. A. A. Kedrinskii et al. 312p. (RUS.). 1983. 100.00 (*0-317-57308-X*) St Mut.

Restoration of Lost & Obliterated Corners & Subdivision of Sections. 1979. reprint ed. 6.90 (*0-685-67581-5*, S240) Am Congrs Survey.

***Restoration of Love.** W. Ter Horst. LC 96-47554. 232p. (Orig.). 1997. pap. 18.00 (*0-8028-4141-4*) Eerdmans.

Restoration of Men. Karl Duff. 140p. (Orig.). 1990. pap. 8.99 (*1-56043-022-2*) Destiny Image.

Restoration of Motor Function in the Stroke Patient: A Physiotherapist's Approach. 3rd ed. Margaret Johnstone. LC 86-9554. (Illus.). 240p. (Orig.). 1987. pap. text ed. 29.95 (*0-443-03398-6*) Churchill.

Restoration of Normal Movement After Stroke. Margaret Johnstone. LC 94-41153. (Illus.). 1995. write for info. (*0-443-05247-6*) Churchill.

Restoration of Order: The Normalisation of Czechoslovakia, 1969. Milan Simecka. Tr. by A. G. Brain from CZE. 167p. 1985. text ed. 24.95 (*0-86091-081-4*, Pub. by Verso UK); pap. text ed. 12.95 (*0-86091-786-X*, Pub. by Verso UK) Routledge Chapman & Hall.

Restoration of Perfection: Labor & Technology in Medieval Culture. George Ovitt, Jr. 276p. 1987. text ed. 45.00 (*0-8135-1235-2*) Rutgers U Pr.

Restoration of Petroleum Contaminated Aquifers. Stephen M. Testa & Duane L. Winegardner. (Illus.). 240p. 1990. 87.00 (*0-87371-335-4*, L335) Lewis Pubs.

Restoration of Political Science & the Crisis of Modernity. Barry Cooper. LC 89-12335. (Studies in Social & Political Theory: Vol. 6). 320p. 1990. lib. bdg. 99.95 (*0-88946-106-6*) E Mellen.

Restoration of Politics: Interrogating History about a Civilization in Crisis. George Liska. 144p. (C). 1996. pap. 21.95 (*0-8476-8213-7*); lib. bdg. 52.50 (*0-8476-8212-9*) Rowman.

Restoration of Post-World War Two Cars. Peter Wallage. LC 77-94368. (Illus.). 168p. 1979. 16.50 (*0-8376-0145-2*) Bentley.

Restoration of Sewerage Systems: Conference Proceedings. 312p. 1982. 82.00 (*0-7277-0145-2*, Pub. by T Telford UK) Am Soc Civil Eng.

Restoration of Teeth. 2nd ed. T. R. Ford. (Illus.). 312p. 1992. pap. 49.95 (*0-632-03252-9*) Blackwell Sci.

Restoration of Temperate Wetlands. Ed. by Bryan D. Wheeler et al. LC 94-35414. 562p. 1995. text ed. 98.00 (*0-471-95105-6*) Wiley.

Restoration of Thailand under Rama I, 1782-1809. Klaus Wenk. LC 67-63491. (Association for Asian Studies, Monographs & Papers: No. 24). 161p. reprint ed. pap. 45.90 (*0-7837-0010-5*, 2020440) Bks Demand.

Restoration of the Interplanetary Confederation. Charles Spaegel & Ruth E. Norman. 506p. (C). 1987. 20.00 (*0-932642-90-X*) Unarius Acad Sci.

Restoration of the Jediah Hill Covered Bridge. (PCI Journal Reprints Ser.). 6p. 1985. pap. 10.00 (*0-318-19771-5*, JR262) P-PCI.

Restoration of the Monastery of Saint Martin of Tournai. Herman of Tournai. Tr. & Notes by Lynn H. Nelson. LC 95-40170. 248p. 1996. 34.95 (*0-8132-0850-5*); pap. 19.95 (*0-8132-0851-3*) Cath U Pr.

Restoration of the Orthodox Way of Life. Andrew of New Diveyevo. Tr. & Intro. by Seraphim Rose. (Illus.). 16p. (Orig.). 1987. pap. 2.00 (*0-912927-19-4*, X019) St John Kronstadt.

Restoration of the Self. Heinz Kohut. LC 76-45545. 345p. 1977. 55.00 (*0-8236-5810-4*) Intl Univs Pr.

Restoration of the State of Good in the World. Ilija Poplasen. (Illus.). 200p. (Orig.). 1980. 20.00 (*0-935352-02-3*) MIR PA.

Restoration of the State of Good in the World. Ilija Poplasen. 210p. (Orig.). 1982. 20.00 (*0-935352-08-2*) MIR PA.

Restoration of the Texas Capital. Michael Ward. 192p. 1995. 34.95 (*1-56352-196-2*) Longstreet Pr Inc.

Restoration of Tropical Forest Ecosystems. Ed. by Helmut Lieth & Martina Lohmann. LC 92-33607. (Tasks for Vegetation Science Ser.). 272p. 1993. lib. bdg. 192.50 (*0-7923-1945-1*) Kluwer Ac.

Restoration of Vintage & Thoroughbred Motorcycles. 2nd ed. Jeff Clew. (Illus.). 200p. 1991. 29.95 (*0-85429-853-3*, F185, Pub. by G T Foulis Ltd) Haynes Pubns.

Restoration of Walking for Paraplegics: Recent Advancements & Trends. Ed. by Maurizio Ferrarin & Antonio Pedotti. LC 92-53259. 387p. (gr. 12). 1992. pap. 110.00 (*90-5199-094-4*, Pub. by IOS Pr NE) IOS Press.

Restoration Plays. Incl. Rehearsal. George Villiers. 1966. (*0-318-54363-X*); Country Wife. William Wycherley. 1966. (*0-318-54364-8*); Man of Mode. George Etherege. 1966. (*0-318-54365-6*); All for Love: The World Well Lost. John Dryden. (Orig.). (*0-318-54366-4*); Venice Preserved. Thomas Otway. 1966. (*0-318-54367-2*); Relapse. John Vanbrugh. 1966. (*0-318-54368-0*); Way of the World. William Congreve. 1966. (*0-318-54369-9*); Beaux Strategem. George Farquhar. 1966. (*0-318-54370-2*); (Modern Library College Editions). (C). 1966. pap. text ed. write for info. (*0-07-553658-7*, T79) McGraw.

Restoration Plays. Ed. by Robert G. Lawrencee. 704p. 1994. 14.95 (*0-460-87432-2*, Everyman's Classic Lib) C E Tuttle.

Restoration Politics & Drama: The Plays of Thomas Otway, 1675-1683. Jessica Munns. LC 95-10377. 272p. 1996. 42.50 (*0-87413-548-6*) U Delaware Pr.

Restoration Promptbooks. Edward A. Langhans. LC 80-15626. 563p. 1981. 100.00 (*0-8093-0885-1*) S Ill U Pr.

Restoration Prose Fiction, 1666-1700: An Anthology of Representative Pieces. Ed. by Charles C. Mish. LC 76-98095. 305p. reprint ed. pap. 87.00 (*0-685-15680-X*, 2027338) Bks Demand.

Restoration Rake-Hero: Transformations in Sexual Understanding in Seventeenth-Century England. Harold Weber. LC 86-40063. 272p. 1986. text ed. 27.50 (*0-299-10690-X*) U of Wis Pr.

Restoration, Revolution, Reaction: Economics & Politics in Germany, 1815-1871. Theodore S. Hamerow. 360p. 1958. pap. text ed. 19.95 (*0-691-00755-1*) Princeton U Pr.

Restoration Scriptures: A Study of Their Textual Development. 2nd enl. rev. ed. Richard P. Howard. LC 95-17194. 320p. (C). Date not set. 30.00 (*0-8309-0693-2*) Herald Hse.

Restoration, Sixteen Sixty to Sixteen Eight-Eight: British History in Perspective. Paul Seaward. LC 90-40585. 180p. 1991. text ed. 49.95 (*0-312-04929-3*) St Martin.

***Restoration Stage Controversy, 6 vols.** Ed. by Yuji Kaneko. 1584p. (C). 1996. text ed. 625.00 (*0-415-14302-0*) Routledge.

Restoration Studies, No. III. Ed. by Maurice L. Draper. 1986. pap. 19.00 (*0-8309-0432-8*) Herald Hse.

Restoration Studies, Vol. I. Ed. by Maurice L. Draper. 1980. pap. 19.00 (*0-8309-0292-9*) Herald Hse.

Restoration Studies, Vol. II. Maurice L. Draper. 1983. pap. 19.00 (*0-8309-0362-3*) Herald Hse.

Restoration Studies IV. Ed. by Marjorie Troeh. 1988. pap. 19.00 (*0-8309-0515-4*) Herald Hse.

Restoration Studies VI: A Collection of Essays about the History, Beliefs, & Practice of the Reorganized Church of Jesus Christ of Latter Day Saints. Ed. by Paul M. Edwards et al. 224p. (C). Date not set. pap. text ed. 19.00 (*0-8309-0708-4*) Herald Hse.

***Restoration Theatre & Crisis.** Susan J. Owen. 240p. 1997. text ed. 76.00 (*0-19-818387-9*) OUP.

Restoration to Fellowship. Tony Palmisano. 32p. 1988. pap. 0.75 (*0-88144-126-0*) Christian Pub.

Restoration Tragedy: Form & the Process of Change. Eric Rothstein. LC 78-5529. 194p. 1978. reprint ed. text ed. 49.75 (*0-313-20472-1*, RORET, Greenwood Pr) Greenwood.

***Restoration Verse.** Harold Love. 1997. pap. 14.95 (*0-14-042407-5*) Viking Penguin.

***Restoration Wetlands.** Middletonb. (General Science Ser.). 1998. text ed. 54.95 (*0-442-02583-1*) Van Nos Reinhold.

Restorationist: Text One: A Collaborative Fiction by Jael B. Juba. Joyce Elbrecht & Lydia Fakundiny. LC 92-32586. (SUNY Series, The Margins of Literature). 429p. (C). 1993. 64.50 (*0-7914-1531-7*) State U NY Pr.

Restorationist: Text One: A Collaborative Fiction by Jael B. Juba. Joyce Elbrecht & Lydia Fakundiny. LC 92-32586. (SUNY Series, The Margins of Literature). 429p. 1994. pap. 21.95 (*0-7914-1532-5*) State U NY Pr.

Restorations of Masonic Geometry & Symbolry Being a Dissertation on the Lost Knowledge of the Lodge (1905) H. P. Bromwell. 617p. 1993. reprint ed. pap. 60.00 (*1-56459-417-3*) Kessinger Pub.

Restorative Approach for Nursing Home Social Workers. Marylou Hughes. 109p. (Orig.). (C). 1990. pap. text ed. 10.50 (*1-877735-28-0*, 159) M&H Pub Co TX.

Restorative Dental Materials. 10th ed. Craig. 600p. (C). (gr. 13). 1996. pap. text ed. 58.00 (*0-8151-1920-8*) Mosby Yr Bk.

Restorative Dental Materials: An Overview. Ed. by Joyce A. Reese & Thomas M. Valega. 331p. 1984. pap. text ed. 60.00 (*1-85097-003-3*, 1385) Quint Pub Co.

Restorative Dentistry: A Resume. Jerome M. Schweitzer. LC 85-70279. (Illus.). 367p. 1985. 85.00 (*0-9614591-0-7*) Garson Associates.

***Restorative Justice: An Annotated Bibliography--1997.** Ed. by Paul McCold. 185p. (Orig.). 1997. text ed. 20.00 (*1-881798-11-9*, Crimnal Justce) Willow Tree NY.

Restorative Justice: International Perspectives. Ed. by Burt Galaway & Joe Hudson. 530p. 1996. pap. text ed. 35.00 (*1-881798-07-0*) Willow Tree NY.

Restorative Justice on Trial - Pitfalls & Potentials of Victim-Offender Mediation: International Research Perspectives - Proceedings of the NATO Advanced Research Workshop on Conflict, Crime & Reconciliation: The Organization of Welfare Interventions in the Field of Restitutive Justice, Held in Il Ciocco, Lucca, Italy 8-12 April, 1991. Ed. by Heinz Messmer. 608p. (C). 1992. lib. bdg. 226.50 (*0-7923-1620-7*) Kluwer Ac.

Restorative Proctocolectomy. David C. Bartolo et al. LC 92-48681. (Illus.). 176p. 1993. 95.00 (*0-632-03333-9*) Blackwell Sci.

***Restorative Techniques in Paediatric Dentistry: An Illustrated Guide to the Restoration of Extensively Carious Primary Teeth.** Monty S. Duggal et al. (Illus.). 134p. 1995. write for info. (*0-7216-6007-X*) Saunders.

Restore Breathing: A Collection of Tales. Ben Sherman. LC 94-93952. 134p. 1994. pap. text ed. 11.00 (*0-9644164-0-9*) Sherman Trng.

Restore Me: Litanies, Prayers & Dialogues for Lent & Easter. Craig M. Sweet. LC 93-38011. 92p. 1993. pap. 8.50 (*1-55673-700-9*) CSS OH.

Restore My Soul. Nachman of Breslov & Nathan of Breslov. Tr. by Avraham Greenbaum from HEB. 128p. (Orig.). 1980. pap. 4.00 (*0-930213-13-0*) Breslov Res Inst.

Restore User's Manual. Dan Schultz-Ela & Ken Duncan. 75p. 1991. Requires Macintosh II or higher. pap. 249.95 incl. disk (*0-317-05181-4*, SW0001) Bur Econ Geology.

***Restored Hamilton County, Ohio, Marriages, 1860-1869.** Jeffrey G. Herbert. 652p. (Orig.). 1997. pap. 60.00 (*0-7884-0616-7*, H164) Heritage Bk.

Restored Hamilton County, Ohio Marriages 1870 - 1884, 2 vols., Set. Jeffrey G. Herbert. 1038p. (Orig.). 1995. pap. text ed. 95.00 (*0-7884-0139-4*) Heritage Bk.

Restored New Testament, 2 vols., Set. 3rd ed. James M. Pryse. 1971. reprint ed. spiral bd. 34.50 (*0-7873-0683-5*) Hlth Research.

Restored New Testament: The Hellenic Fragments, Freed from the Pseudo-Jewish Interpolations, Harmonized, & Done Into English Verse & Prose (1925): With Introductory Analyses, & Commentaries, Giving an Interpretation According to Ancient Philosophy & Psychology & a New Literal Translation of the Synoptic Gospels, with Commentaries & Illustrations. James M. Pryse. (Illus.). 840p. 1994. pap. 49.95 (*1-56459-433-5*) Kessinger Pub.

Restoree. Anne McCaffrey. 1987. mass mkt. 5.99 (*0-345-35187-8*, Del Rey) Ballantine.

Restorers. W. S. Di Piero. LC 91-29065. (Phoenix Poets Ser.). 86p. 1992. pap. 9.95 (*0-226-15347-9*) U Ch Pr.

Restorers. W. S. Di Piero. LC 91-29065. (Phoenix Poets Ser.). 86p. 1992. lib. bdg. 23.00 (*0-226-15346-0*) U Ch Pr.

Restorer's Classic Car Shop Manual. Jim Schild. LC 91-73273. (Illus.). 336p. (Orig.). 1991. pap. 24.95 (*0-9624958-4-0*) Auto Review Pub.

Restorer's Model A Shop Manual. Jim Schild. (Illus.). 224p. 1985. pap. 24.95 (*0-87938-194-9*) Motorbooks Intl.

***Restorers of Hope: Reaching the Poor in Your Community with Church-Based Ministries that Work.** Amy L. Sherman. LC 97-25330. 256p. (Orig.). 1997. pap. 13.99 (*0-89107-958-0*) Crossway Bks.

Restorers of the Lost Art. Robert Schmidt & Ellen Black. 350p. 1988. write for info. (*0-318-63129-6*) Golden Hind Pr.

Restoring a Loving Marriage. Jay Kesler. LC 92-2507. 144p. 1993. pap. 7.99 (*1-55513-666-4*, LifeJourney) Chariot Victor.

***Restoring America.** Jim Hightower. Date not set. write for info. (*0-688-12286-8*) Morrow.

Restoring America: The Second American Revolution. Roger H. Taylor. 340p. (Orig.). 1995. pap. 14.95 (*0-9649605-0-8*) Technlgy Mgmt.

***Restoring American Leadership: A U. S. Foreign & Defense Policy Blueprint.** Ed. by Kim R. Holmes & Thomas G. Moore. (Illus.). 288p. (Orig.). (C). 1996. pap. 19.95 (*0-89195-239-X*) Heritage Found.

Restoring America's Conscience. Ron Boehme. 256p. (Orig.). 1996. pap. 12.99 (*0-529-10696-5*, RAC) World Publng.

Restoring America's Future. Gene Gordon. (Illus.). 124p. (Orig.). 1996. pap. 9.95 (*1-888461-00-4*) Islewest Pub.

Restoring & Collecting Antique Reed Organs. 2nd ed. Horton Presley. LC 92-15651. (Illus.). 316p. 1987. reprint ed. pap. 16.95 (*0-911572-56-2*) Madison Bks UPA.

Restoring & Maintaining the Productivity of West African Soils: Key to Sustainable Development. Ed. by A. De Jheer et al. LC 96-13376. (Miscellaneous Fertilizer Studies: No. 14). (Illus.). 108p. (Orig.). 1996. pap. write for info. (*0-88090-112-8*) Intl Fertilizer.

Restoring & Protecting Marine Habitat: The Role of Engineering & Technology. National Research Council Staff. 212p. (Orig.). (C). 1994. pap. text ed. 27.00 (*0-309-04843-5*) Natl Acad Pr.

Restoring & Protecting the World's Lakes & Reservoirs. Ariel Dinar et al. LC 95-22293. (Technical Papers: No. 289). 130p. 1995. text ed. 8.95 (*0-8213-3321-6*, 13321) World Bank.

***Restoring Antique Beaded Purses.** Evelyn Haertig. (Illus.). (Orig.). (C). 1998. write for info. (*0-943294-02-9*) Gallery Graphics.

Restoring Antique Furniture: A Practical Guide. Richard Gethin. (Illus.). 120p. 1987. 15.95 (*0-900873-31-0*, Pub. by Bishopsgte Pr UK); pap. 11.95 (*0-900873-32-9*, Pub. by Bishopsgte Pr UK) Intl Spec Bk.

Restoring Antiques. Time-Life Books Editors. LC 94-49006. (Art of Woodworking Ser.). 144p. 1995. 19.95 (*0-8094-9929-0*) Time-Life.

Restoring At-Risk Communities: Doing It Together & Doing It Right. Ed. by John M. Perkins. LC 95-35456. (Illus.). 272p. (Orig.). (gr. 10). 1996. pap. 9.99 (*0-8010-5463-X*) Baker Bks.

Restoring Balance: Community-Directed Health Promotion for American Indians & Native Alaskans. Beth Howard-Pitney et al. Ed. by Prudence Breitrose. (Illus.). 131p. (Orig.). 1992. pap. 15.00 (*1-879552-39-6*) Stanford CRDP.

Restoring Balance in the Federal System. 61p. 1989. 30.00 (*0-685-38250-8*, C-158) Coun State Govts.

Restoring Balance to a Mother's Busy Life. Beth W. Saavedra. 192p. 1996. pap. 12.00 (*0-8092-3196-4*) Contemp Bks.

Restoring Bipartisanship in Foreign Affairs. American Bar Association Staff & Steven P. Soper. 74p. 1985. pap. 5.00 (*0-89707-208-1*, 355-0011) Amer Bar Assn.

Restoring Broken Vessels: Confronting the Attack on Female Sexuality. Victoria L. Johnson. Ed. by Clarinda Gipson. LC 95-72232. (Illus.). 290p. (Orig.). 1996. pap. 12.95 (*1-880560-65-8*) DaBaR Srvs.

***Restoring Classic & Collectible Cameras.** Thomas Tomosy. (Illus.). 172p. 1997. pap. 34.95 (*0-936262-59-1*) Amherst Media.

Restoring Diversity: Strategies for Reintroduction of Endangered Plants. Ed. by Donald A. Falk et al. 400p. (C). 1995. text ed. 39.95 (*1-55963-296-8*); pap. text ed. 27.50 (*1-55963-297-6*) Island Pr.

Restoring Dolls: A Practical Guide. Doreen Perry. (Illus.). 94p. 1987. 15.95 (*0-900873-59-0*, Pub. by Bishopsgte Pr UK); pap. 11.95 (*0-900873-61-2*, Pub. by Bishopsgte Pr UK) Intl Spec Bk.

Restoring Europe's Prosperity: Macroeconomic Papers from the Centre for European Policy Studies. Ed. by Oliver J. Blanchard et al. 208p. 1986. 25.00 (*0-262-02249-4*) MIT Pr.

Restoring Financial Flows to Latin America. Organization for Economic Cooperation & Development Staff. Ed. by Enrique V. Iglesias & Louis Emmerij. 251p. (Orig.). 1991. pap. 31.00 (*92-64-13476-X*) OECD.

Restoring God. Estella M. Pitt. 40p. 1994. pap. 4.95 (*0-9642764-0-2*) E Pitt.

Restoring Grandfather Clocks. Eric Smith. (Illus.). 224p. 1995. 40.00 (*0-7198-0270-9*, Pub. by R Hale Ltd UK) Antique Collect.

Restoring Growth in the Debt-Laden Third World. Martin Feldstein et al. (Triangle Papers: No. 33). 79p. (Orig.). 1987. pap. 6.00 (*0-930503-02-3*) Trilateral Comm.

Restoring Hardwood Floors. Mary Twitchell. LC 95-30706. (Storey Publishing Bulletin Ser.: No. A-136). 1995. pap. 2.95 (*0-88266-348-8*, Storey Pub) Storey Comm Inc.

***Restoring Harmony: A Guide for Managing Conflicts in Schools.** James L. Lee et al. LC 96-53393. 1997. 21.00 (*0-13-470313-8*, Merrill Coll) P-H.

***Restoring Hope: Conversations on the Future of Black America.** Ed. by Cornel West & Kelvin S. Sealey. LC 97-21797. 256p. 1997. 25.00 (*0-8070-0942-3*) Beacon Pr.

Restoring Hope in America: The Social Security Solution. Sam Beard. 220p. 1995. pap. text ed. 14.95 (*1-55815-489-2*) ICS Pr.

Restoring Iowa's Democracy: A Citizen's Guide for Improving Iowa's Government & Economic Future. Mark Edelman. vi, 145p. 1993. pap. 8.95 (*0-931209-52-8*) Mid-Prairie Bks.

Restoring Joy. Gordon MacDonald. 1996. pap. 6.99 (*0-88486-137-6*) Arrowood Pr.

Restoring Joy to Your Inner World. Gordon MacDonald. (Guidelines for Living Ser.). 1992. 10.98 (*0-88486-059-0*) Arrowood Pr.

***Restoring Justice.** Daniel V. Ness & Karen H. Strong. LC 97-71386. 228p. (C). 1997. pap. text ed. 24.95 (*0-87084-890-9*) Anderson Pub Co.

Restoring Mr. Lincoln's Home. Judith M. Winkelman. (Illus.). 48p. (Orig.). 1990. pap. 6.95 (*0-915992-50-7*) Eastern Acorn.

Restoring Oil Painting: A Practical Guide. Tim Aldridge. (Illus.). 80p. 1987. 15.95 (*0-900873-60-4*, Pub. by Bishopsgte Pr UK); pap. 11.95 (*0-900873-62-0*, Pub. by Bishopsgte Pr UK) Intl Spec Bk.

Restoring Oil Paintings. Tim Aldridge. 1985. 40.00 (*0-685-12456-8*, Pub. by Bishopsgate Pr Ltd UK); pap. 29.00 (*0-685-12457-6*, Pub. by Bishopsgte Pr UK) St Mut.

***Restoring Old Houses.** Nigel Hutchins. 1997. pap. text ed. 22.95 (*1-55209-144-9*) Firefly Bks Ltd.

An Asterisk (*) at the beginning of an entry indicates that the title is appearing in BIP for the first time.

R

Restoring Our Competitive Edge: Competing Through Manufacturing. Robert H. Hayes & Steven C. Wheelright. LC 84-3710. 427p. 1984. text ed. 42.50 (*0-471-05159-4*, Wiley-Interscience) Wiley.

Restoring Period Gardens. John Harvey. 1989. pap. 25.00 (*0-7478-0200-9*, Pub. by Shire UK) St Mut.

Restoring Personal Meaning in Reading Instruction: American Education's Greatest Need. Michael E. Walters. 45p. (Orig.). 1983. pap. text ed. 12.00 (*0-910609-03-9*) Gifted Educ Pr.

Restoring Persons in World Community. J. Andrew Bolton. 1986. pap. 12.00 (*0-8309-0461-1*) Herald Hse.

Restoring Pianolas & Other Self Playing Pianos. Arthur W. Ord-Hume. (Illus.). 160p. 1983. 45.00 (*0-04-789008-8*) Routledge Chapman & Hall.

Restoring Prairie Wetlands: An Ecological Approach. Susan M. Galatowitsch & Arnold Van Der Valk. LC 93-27825. (Illus.). 256p. 1994. text ed. 44.95 (*0-8138-2499-0*) Iowa St U Pr.

Restoring Praise & Worship. Douglas Christofell et al. 176p. 1991. 8.99 (*0-938612-40-9*) Destiny Image.

Restoring Praise & Worship to the Church. Ed. by David K. Blomgren et al. 220p. (Orig.). (C). 1989. pap. text ed. 7.95 (*0-317-94072-4*) Trumpet Pubns.

Restoring Pride: The Lost Virtue of Our Age. Richard Taylor. 232p. 1995. 23.95 (*1-57392-024-X*) Prometheus Bks.

Restoring Prosperity: Budget Choices for Economic Growth. 50p. 1992. pap. 14.50 (*0-87186-095-3*) Comm Econ Dev.

Restoring Prosperity: How Workers & Managers Are Forging a New Culture of Cooperation. Wellford W. Wilms. LC 95-43145. 288p. 1996. 25.00 (*0-8129-2030-9*, Times Business) Random.

Restoring Real Representation. Robert C. Grady. LC 92-18273. 184p. (C). 1993. text ed. 29.95 (*0-252-01967-9*) U of Ill Pr.

Restoring Shakespeare. Leon Kellner. LC 74-131761. (Illus.). xvi, 216p. 1972. reprint ed. 7.00 (*0-403-00648-1*) Scholarly.

Restoring Shakespeare: A Critical Analysis of the Misreadings in Shakespeare's Works. Leon Kellner. LC 78-77027. (Illus.). 1969. reprint ed. 30.00 (*0-8196-0244-2*) Biblo.

Restoring Shakespeare: A Critical Analysis of the Misreadings in Shakespeare's Works. Leon Kellner. (BCL1-PR English Literature Ser.). 216p. 1992. reprint ed. lib. bdg. 79.00 (*0-7812-7308-0*) Rprt Serv.

***Restoring Streams in Cities: A Guide for Planners, Policymakers & Citizens.** Ann L. Riley. 1997. pap. text ed. 35.00 (*1-55963-042-6*); pap. text ed. 55.00 (*1-55963-043-4*) Island Pr.

Restoring Texas: Raiford Stripling's Life & Architecture. Michael McCullar. LC 85-40052. (Illus.). 176p. 1985. 29.95 (*0-89096-254-5*) Tex A&M Univ Pr.

Restoring the American Dream. House Republicans. 1995. pap. 10.00 (*0-8129-2666-8*, Times Bks) Random.

***Restoring the Balance: A New Perspective on the Impact That the Imbalance Between Man & Nature Is Having on Our Economy, Our Society, & You.** Josef Shaw. LC 97-91932. (Illus.). viii, 203p. 1997. pap. 6.50 (*0-9658715-0-9*) J Shaw.

Restoring the Balance: A Pastor-Physician's Guide to Total Health & Healing. Jimmy Graham. 140p. 1995. pap. 10.95 (*1-882185-24-2*) Crnrstone Pub.

Restoring the Balance: State Leadership for America's Future. John H. Sununu et al. 130p. (Orig.). 1988. pap. text ed. 15.00 (*1-55877-014-3*) Natl Governor.

Restoring the Body. (Fitness, Health & Nutrition Ser.). (Illus.). 144p. 1988. 17.27 (*0-8094-6187-0*); lib. bdg. 23.27 (*0-8094-6188-9*) Time-Life.

Restoring the Christian Family. John Sandford & Paula Sandford. LC 79-64977. 336p. 1979. reprint ed. pap. 10.95 (*0-932081-12-6*) Victory Hse.

Restoring the Christian Soul: Overcoming Barriers to Completion in Christ Through Healing Prayer. Leanne Payne. LC 95-50955. 256p. (Orig.). (YA). (gr. 10). 1996. reprint ed. pap. 12.99 (*0-8010-5699-3*, Hamewith MI) Baker Bks.

Restoring the Color of Roses. Barrie J. Borich. LC 93-647. 168p. (Orig.). 1993. pap. 9.95 (*1-56341-027-3*); lib. bdg. 20.95 (*1-56341-028-1*) Firebrand Bks.

Restoring the Constitution, 1787-1987: Essays in Celebration of the Bicentennial. H. Wayne House et al. LC 87-29281. 350p. 1987. 14.99 (*0-945241-00-3*) Probe Bks.

Restoring the Diaspora: Discursive Structure & Purpose in the Epistle of James. Timothy B. Cargal. LC 93-10144. (Society of Biblical Literature Dissertation Ser.: No. 144). 260p. 1993. 29.95 (*1-55540-861-3*, 062144); pap. 19.95 (*1-55540-862-1*, 062144) Scholars Pr GA.

***Restoring the Earth: Visionary Solutions from the Bioneers.** Kenny Ausubel. LC 97-16958. 288p. 1997. pap. 12.95 (*0-915811-76-6*) H J Kramer Inc.

Restoring the Faith: The Assemblies of God, Pentecostalism, & American Culture. Edith L. Blumhofer. LC 92-23888. (Illus.). 304p. (C). 1993. pap. text ed. 17.95 (*0-252-06281-7*) U of Ill Pr.

Restoring the Fallen. Michael Smith. LC 91-62351. 160p. (Orig.). 1991. pap. 7.95 (*0-89221-215-2*) New Leaf.

Restoring the Fallen: A Team Approach to Caring, Confronting & Reconciling. Earl Wilson et al. LC 96-2808. 220p. 1997. pap. 11.99 (*0-8308-1619-4*, 1619) InterVarsity.

Restoring the Father to the Family. C. Russell Yates. LC 92-46254. 254p. (Orig.). 1993. pap. 15.00 (*0-944091-04-0*, Family Fnd Pubn) Intaglio Pr.

Restoring the Good Society: A New Vision for Politics & Culture. Don Eberly. LC 93-48973. 128p. 1994. pap. 6.99 (*0-8010-3226-1*, Hour Glass) Baker Bks.

Restoring the Image: An Introduction to Christian Caring & Counselling. Roger F. Hurding. 128p. 1986. reprint ed. pap. 8.95 (*0-85364-268-0*) Attic Pr.

Restoring the Jewishness of the Gospel: A Message for Christians. David H. Stern. (Illus.). 96p. (Orig.). 1989. pap. 5.95 (*965-359-001-4*) Jewish New Test Pubns.

Restoring the Jews to Their Homeland: Nineteen Centuries in the Quest for Zion. Joseph Adler. LC 96-20616. 472p. 1997. 40.00 (*1-56821-978-4*) Aronson.

Restoring the Land: Environmental Values, Knowledge & Action. Ed. by Laurie Cosgrove et al. 288p. 1994. pap. 29.95 (*0-522-84546-0*, Pub. by Melbourne Univ Pr AT) Paul & Co Pubs.

Restoring the Message of Pentecost. B. H. Clendennen. LC 90-90254. 224p. (Orig.). 1991. pap. 6.95 (*1-878921-00-2*) Victory Temple.

Restoring the Nation's Marine Environment. text ed. 45.00 (*0-943676-57-6*) MD Sea Grant Col.

Restoring the Original Bible. Ernest L. Martin. (Illus.). 504p. (Orig.). (C). 1994. pap. 19.95 (*0-945657-83-8*) Acad Scriptural Knowledge.

Restoring the Promise of American Labor Law. Ed. by Sheldon Friedman et al. LC 94-539. 376p. 1994. pap. 29.95 (*0-87546-326-6*, ILR Press) Cornell U Pr.

Restoring the Public Trust: A Fresh Vision for Progressive Government in America. Peter G. Brown. LC 93-7089. 240p. 1994. 15.00 (*0-8070-4306-0*) Beacon Pr.

Restoring the Queen. Laini Mataka. LC 91-74131. 65p. (Orig.). 1991. pap. 8.95 (*0-933121-80-6*) Black Classic.

Restoring the Soul of a Church: Congregations Wounded by Clergy Sexual Misconduct. Ed. by Mark Laasar & Nancy Hopkins. pap. 19.95 (*1-56699-164-1*) Alban Inst.

Restoring the Soul of a Church: Reconciling Congregations Wounded by Clergy Sexual Misconduct. Ed. by Mark R. Laaser & Nancy Hopkins. 280p. (Orig.). 1995. pap. 19.95 (*0-8146-2333-6*, Liturg Pr Bks) Liturgical Pr.

Restoring the Tallgrass Prairie: An Illustrated Manual for Iowa & the Upper Midwest. Shirley Shirley. LC 94-7374. (Bur Oak Original Ser.). (Illus.). 346p. 1994. pap. 16.95 (*0-87745-469-8*); text ed. 29.95 (*0-87745-468-X*) U of Iowa Pr.

Restoring the Village, Values & Commitment: Solutions for the Black Family. Jawanza Kunjufu. 1996. 19.95 (*0-913543-47-0*) African Am Imag.

Restoring the Vision: The Gospel & Modern Culture. Lawrence Osborn. 216p. 1995. pap. 18.95 (*0-264-67330-1*, Pub. by Mowbray-Cassell UK) Morehouse Pub.

Restoring the Vow of Stability: The Keys to Pastoral Longevity. Richard Brown. LC 93-70741. 250p. 1993. pap. 10.99 (*0-87509-532-1*) Chr Pubns.

Restoring the Wounded Woman: Recovering from Heartache & Discouragement. Melinda Fish. LC 92-44133. 248p. (Orig.). (gr. 10). 1993. pap. 9.99 (*0-8007-9196-7*) Chosen Bks.

Restoring the 10th Amendment: The American Federalist Agenda. Donald Devine. Ed. by Charles G. Gee. 350p. Date not set. text ed. 25.00 (*0-9645786-3-8*) VYTIS Pub.

Restoring Toys: A Practical Guide. Doreen Perry. (C). 1988. 35.00 (*1-85219-002-7*, Pub. by Bishopsgate Pr Ltd UK) St Mut.

Restoring Traditional Values: The Search for Human Theory. Edward H. Romney. 110p. 1995. 25.00 (*1-886996-51-2*); pap. 19.95 (*1-886996-50-4*) Hillcrst Pub.

Restoring, Tuning, & Using Classic Woodworking Tools. Michael Dunbar. LC 89-35456. (Illus.). 256p. 1989. pap. 19.95 (*0-8069-6670-X*) Sterling.

Restoring Vision: An Ethical Perspective on Doctors Curing Blindness Around the World. Tela Zasloff. 232p. (C). 1995. pap. text ed. 28.00 (*0-7618-0117-0*); lib. bdg. 54.00 (*0-7618-0116-2*) U Pr of Amer.

Restoring Wounded Warriors: Tools for Male Renewal. Linda H. Hollies. 120p. 1991. pap. 9.95 (*1-880299-03-8*) Woman to Woman.

***Restorying Our Lives: Personal Growth Through Autobiographical Reflection.** Gary M. Kenyon & William L. Randall. LC 97-5587. 1997. text ed. write for info. (*0-275-95663-6*, Praeger Pubs) Greenwood.

Restrained Response: American Novels of the Cold War & Korea, 1945-1962. Arne Axelsson. LC 89-11907. (Contributions in American Studies: No. 97). 239p. 1990. text ed. 59.95 (*0-313-26291-8*, AXR/, Greenwood Pr) Greenwood.

Restrained Trade: Cartels in Japan's Basic Materials Industries. Mark Tilton. 256p. 1996. 29.95 (*0-8014-3099-2*) Cornell U Pr.

Restraining the American Workforce. Kathleen Miller. 1989. 26.95 (*0-201-11585-9*) Addison-Wesley.

Restraining Trade to Invoke Investment: MITI & the Japanese Auto Producers. Simon Reich. (Pew Case Studies in International Affairs). 50p. (C). 1992. pap. text ed. 3.50 (*1-56927-150-X*) Geo U Inst Dplmcy.

Restraint. Sherry Sonnett. 352p. 1996. mass mkt., pap. 5.99 (*0-451-18642-7*, Sig) NAL-Dutton.

Restraint. Shery Sonnett. LC 94-29211. 1995. 21.00 (*0-671-87958-8*) S&S Trade.

Restraint & Handling of Wild & Domestic Animals. Murray E. Fowler. LC 78-5036. (Illus.). 338p. 1978. reprint ed. pap. 96.40 (*0-608-00128-7*, 2060906) Bks Demand.

***Restraint & Seclusion: Improving Practice & Conquering the JCHAO Standards.** Jack Zusman. (Orig.). 1996. pap. text ed. 77.00 (*1-885829-34-5*) Opus Communs.

Restraint of Domestic Animals. T. F. Sonsthagen. LC 90-813235. (Illus.). 250p. 1991. 21.50 (*0-939674-28-9*) Am Vet Pubns.

***Restraint of Domestic Animals.** 2nd ed. Quinn. 352p. (gr. 13). 1998. pap. text ed. 34.95 (*0-8151-3952-7*) Mosby Yr Bk.

***Restraint of Trade.** Michael M. Jefferson. 1996. text ed. 80.00 (*0-471-96271-6*) Wiley.

Restraint of Trade. Jacqueline Wilkinson. 230p. 1991. 69.00 (*1-85190-140-X*, Pub. by Tolley Pubng UK) St Mut.

Restraint or Retaliation? Israel's Response to the Iraqi Missile Attacks During the 1991 Gulf War. Laura Z. Eisenberg. (Pew Case Studies in International Affairs). 50p. (C). 1994. pap. text ed. 3.50 (*1-56927-361-8*, GU Schl Foreign) Geo U Inst Dplmcy.

Restraint Policy in Action: Housing in Dacorum & North Hertfordshire. Paul McNamara. (C). 1984. 29.00 (*0-685-30269-5*, Pub. by Oxford Polytechnic UK) St Mut.

Restraint Technologies: Front Seat Occupant Protection. 212p. 1987. 19.00 (*0-89883-961-0*, SP690) Soc Auto Engineers.

Restricted Activity Days & Other Problems Associated with Use of Marijuana or Cocaine among Persons 18-24 Years of Age: United States, 1991. National Center for Health Statistics Staff. (Advance Data Ser.: No. 246). 12p. write for info. (*0-614-02933-3*) Natl Ctr Health Stats.

Restricted Burnside Problem. 2nd ed. Michael Vaughan-Lee. (London Mathematical Society Monographs: New Series 8). 240p. 1993. 79.00 (*0-19-853786-7*) OUP.

Restricted Country. Joan Nestle. LC 87-26671. 192p. (Orig.). 1987. pap. 10.95 (*0-932379-37-0*); lib. bdg. 22.95 (*0-932379-38-9*) Firebrand Bks.

***Restricted Entry: Censorship on Trial, Second Edition.** 2nd ed. Janine Fuller & Stuart Blackley. 264p. 1996. pap. 16.95 (*0-88974-066-6*, Pub. by Press Gang CN) LPC InBook.

Restricted Environmental Stimulation: Research & Commentary. Ed. by John W. Turner, Jr. & Thomas H. Fine. (Illus.). 273p. 1990. lib. bdg. 30.00 (*0-944742-03-3*) Med Coll of OH Pr.

Restricted Environmental Stimulation: Theoretical & Empirical Developments in Flotation REST. Ed. by Peter Suedfeld et al. (Recent Research in Psychology Ser.). (Illus.). xix, 216p. 1990. 57.95 (*0-387-97348-6*) Spr-Verlag.

***Restricted Industrial Firms, Central & Eastern Europe.** pap. 7.95 (*0-8213-3729-7*, 13729) World Bank.

Restricted Orbit Equivalence. D. Rudolph. LC 84-28119. (Memoirs Ser.: No. 323). 149p. 1986. reprint ed. pap. text ed. 26.00 (*0-8218-2324-8*, MEMO/54/323) Am Math.

Restricted Three-Body Problem: Plane Periodic Orbits. Aleksandr D. Bryuno. Tr. by Balin Erdi. LC 94-27982. (Expositions in Mathematics Ser.: No. 17). (RUS.). 1994. 144.95 (*3-11-013703-8*) De Gruyter.

Restricting Handguns: The Case Against Gun Control Legislation. 1992. lib. bdg. 75.00 (*0-8490-5275-0*) Gordon Pr.

Restriction Fragment Length Polymorphism. Marie-Paule LeFranc & G. LeFranc. (Experimental & Clinical Immunogenetics Journal: Vol. 7, No. 1, 1990). (Illus.). 88p. 1989. pap. 37.75 (*3-8055-5113-4*) S Karger.

***Restriction Landmark Genomic Scanning (RLGS)** Y. Hayashizaki & S. Watanabe. LC 97-14839. (Lab Manual Ser.). 1997. lib. bdg. write for info. (*4-431-70193-1*) Spr-Verlag.

Restrictions Imposed on Contaminated Sites: A Status of State Actions. Barbara B. Wells. 175p. (Orig.). 1990. pap. text ed. 20.00 (*1-55877-122-0*) Natl Governor.

Restrictions Imposed on Contaminated Sites: A Status of State Actions. Barbara B. Wells. 200p. (Orig.). 1993. pap. text ed. 20.00 (*1-55877-171-9*) Natl Governor.

Restrictions Imposed on Contaminated Sites: A Status of State Actions, Vols. One & Two, 2 vols., Set. Ann Carroll. Ed. by Karen Glass. 472p. (Orig.). 1988. pap. text ed. 20.00 (*1-55877-003-8*) Natl Governor.

Restrictions of Foreign Real Estate Ownership. International Real Estate Institute Staff. LC 88-80366. (Illus.). 96p. 1988. pap. 28.50 (*0-935988-28-9*, 326) Todd Pub.

Restrictions on Use of Lie Detector Tests: Employee Polygraph Protection Act of 1988 Law & Explanation. 32p. 1988. pap. 3.00 (*0-685-67143-7*, 5194) Commerce.

Restrictive Business Practices, Transnational Corporations & Development. Frank Long. (Dimensions of International Business Ser.). 192p. 1981. lib. bdg. 61.00 (*0-89838-057-X*) Kluwer Ac.

Restrictive Policies for High Speed Police Pursuits. 60p. (Orig.). (C). 1993. pap. text ed. 20.00 (*1-56806-838-7*) DIANE Pub.

Restrictive Trade Practices: Commentary & Materials. Anne Hurley. xxv, 615p. 1991. 120.00 (*0-455-21007-1*, Pub. by Law Bk Co AT); pap. 89.00 (*0-455-21008-X*, Pub. by Law Bk Co AT) Gaunt.

Restrictive Trade Practices: Commentary & Materials. 2nd ed. Anne Hurley. 620p. 1995. pap. 76.00 (*0-455-21303-8*, Pub. by Law Bk Co AT) Gaunt.

Restrictive Trade Practices & Public Interest. R. K. Singh. (C). 1989. 230.00 (*0-685-36536-0*) St Mut.

Restrictive Trade Practices Law. Stephen Corones. 400p. 1994. 82.00 (*0-455-21271-6*, Pub. by Law Bk Co AT); pap. 62.00 (*0-455-21270-8*, Pub. by Law Bk Co AT) Gaunt.

Restrictiveness in Case Theory. Henry Smith. (Cambridge Studies in Linguistics: No. 78). 380p. (C). 1996. text ed. 59.95 (*0-521-46287-8*) Cambridge U Pr.

***Restrooms, Anyone? Plus: A Classic Lifshin Reader.** limited ed. Lyn Lifshin. Ed. by Joyce Carbone. 82p. (Orig.). 1997. pap. 8.95 (*1-878116-69-X*) JVC Bks.

Restructure: Four Historical Ideals in the Campbell-Stone Movement of the Polity of the Christian Church (Disciples of Christ) Anthony L. Dunnavant. LC 90-36892. (American University Studies: Theology & Religion: Ser. VII, Vol. 85). 265p. (C). 1991. text ed. 27.95 (*0-8204-1420-4*) P Lang Pubng.

Restructuring: American & Beyond: Proceedings: ASCE Structures Congress (13th: 1995: Boston, Mass.) ASCE Structures Congress Staff & ASCE Boston Civil Engineers Section Structural Group Staff. Ed. by Masoud Sanayei. LC 95-3639. 1886p. 1995. pap. 170.00 (*0-7844-0076-8*) Am Soc Civil Eng.

Restructuring: Place, Class & Gender. Paula Bagguley. 248p. (C). 1990. text ed. 45.00 (*0-8039-8214-3*) Sage.

Restructuring a Traditional Society: Construction Employment & Skills in Europe. Ed. by Helen Rainbird & Gerd Syben. 296p. 1991. 19.95 (*0-85496-585-8*) Berg Pubs.

Restructuring Administrative Policy in Public Schooling: Canadian & International Case Studies. Ed. by Yvonne M. Martin & R. J. Macpherson. 285p. (Orig.). (C). 1993. pap. text ed. 22.95 (*1-55059-054-5*) Temeron Bks.

Restructuring American Corporations: Causes, Effects & Implications. Abbass F. Alkharaji. LC 90-32699. 208p. 1990. text ed. 55.00 (*0-89930-573-3*, ARK, Quorum Bks) Greenwood.

Restructuring American Education: Innovations & Alternatives. Ed. by Ray C. Rist. LC 75-186712. 250p. 1972. 39.95 (*0-87855-037-2*); pap. text ed. 21.95 (*0-87855-533-1*) Transaction Pubs.

Restructuring American Foreign Policy. Ed. by John D. Steinbruner. 260p. 1988. 34.95 (*0-8157-8144-X*); pap. 14.95 (*0-8157-8143-1*) Brookings.

Restructuring an Urban High School. (Fastback Ser.: No. 323). 1991. 3.00 (*0-87367-323-9*) Phi Delta Kappa.

Restructuring & Managing the Telecommunications Sector. Ed. by Bjorn Wellenius et al. (Symposium Ser.). 160p. 1989. 14.95 (*0-8213-1198-0*, 11198) World Bank.

Restructuring & Privatization in Central Eastern Europe: Case Studies of Firms in Transition. Ed. by Saul Estrin et al. LC 95-3493. (Microeconomics of Transition Economics Ser.). (Illus.). 488p. (C). (gr. 13). 1995. text ed. 121.00 (*1-56324-611-2*) M E Sharpe.

***Restructuring & Quality: Issues for Tomorrow's Schools.** LC 96-47827. (Educational Management Ser.). 288p. (C). 1997. pap. write for info. (*0-415-13339-4*); text ed. write for info. (*0-415-13338-6*) Routledge.

Restructuring & Resizing: Strategies for Social Work & Other Human Services Administrators in Health Care. Candyce Berger. LC 92-33264. (Illus.). 84p. (Orig.). 1993. pap. 57.00 (*0-87258-626-X*, 187150) Am Hospital.

Restructuring Architectural Theory. Ed. by Marco Diani & Catherine A. Ingraham. (Studies in Phenomenology & Existential Philosophy). (Illus.). 128p. (Orig.). 1989. 32.95 (*0-8101-0834-8*); pap. 16.95 (*0-8101-0835-6*) Northwestern U Pr.

Restructuring Armed Forces in East & West. Ed. by Jan G. Siccama & Theo van den Doel. LC 94-15100. 141p. (C). 1994. pap. text ed. 46.50 (*0-8133-2476-9*) Westview.

Restructuring Arms Production in Western Europe. Ed. by Michael Brzoska & Peter Lock. (SIPRI Publication). 400p. 1992. 55.00 (*0-19-829147-7*) OUP.

Restructuring Banks & Enterprises: Recent Lessons from Transition Countries. Michael S. Borish et al. LC 94-49594. (World Bank Discussion Paper Ser.: No. 279). 84p. 1995. 7.95 (*0-8213-3193-0*, 13193) World Bank.

Restructuring Canada's Health Service System: How Do We Get There from Here? Ed. by Raisa B. Deber & Gail G. Thompson. 320p. (Orig.). 1992. pap. 25.00 (*0-8020-6005-6*) U of Toronto Pr.

Restructuring Corporate America. Clark. (C). 1996. text ed. 63.50 (*0-03-097667-7*) HB Coll Pubs.

Restructuring Corporate America. Clark. (C). 1996. teacher ed., pap. text ed. 36.75 (*0-03-006304-3*) HB Coll Pubs.

Restructuring Domination: Industrialists & the State in Ecuador. Catherine M. Conaghan. LC 88-1335. (Latin American Ser.). 216p. (C). 1988. 49.95 (*0-8229-3826-X*) U of Pittsburgh Pr.

Restructuring Early Childhood Education. (Fastback Ser.: No. 329). 1991. 3.00 (*0-87367-329-8*) Phi Delta Kappa.

Restructuring Economies in Distress: Policy Reform & the World Bank. Ed. by Vinod Thomas et al. (World Bank Publications). 580p. 1991. 68.00 (*0-19-520870-6*, 60870) OUP.

Restructuring Education: Issues & Strategies for Communities, Schools, & Universities. Robert J. Yinger & Kathryn M. Borman. LC 93-39853. 168p. (C). 1994. text ed. 45.00 (*1-881303-98-5*); pap. text ed. 19.95 (*1-881303-99-3*) Hampton Pr NJ.

Restructuring Education Through Technology. (Fastback Ser.: No. 326). 1991. 3.00 (*0-87367-326-3*) Phi Delta Kappa.

Restructuring Electricity Markets: A World Perspective. Charles J. Cicchetti & Kristina Sepetys. 209p. (Orig.). 1995. 64.00 (*1-885750-02-1*, REM-96) Visions Communs.

***Restructuring Engineering Education: A Focus on Change.** Ed. by Carolyn Meyers & Edward W. Ernst. (Illus.). 57p. (C). 1996. reprint ed. pap. 25.00 (*0-7881-3688-7*) DIANE Pub.

Restructuring for Caring & Effective Education: An Administrative Guide to Creating Heterogeneous Schools. Ed. by William Stainback et al. 384p. (Orig.). (C). 1992. pap. text ed. 30.00 (*1-55766-091-3*) P H Brookes.

Restructuring for Economic Flexibility. Paul Stewart et al. 193p. 1990. text ed. 68.95 (*1-85628-007-1*, Pub. by Avebury Pub UK) Ashgate Pub Co.

Restructuring for Innovation: The Making of the U. S. Semiconductor Industry. David P. Angel. LC 93-40423. (Perspectives on Economic Change Ser.). 216p. 1994. lib. bdg. 32.50 (*0-89862-297-2*, 2297) Guilford Pr.

***Restructuring for Integrative Education: Multiple Perspectives, Multiple Contexts.** Ed. by Todd E. Jennings. LC 96-37123. (Critical Studies in Education & Culture). 168p. 1997. text ed. 49.95 (*0-89789-496-0*, Bergin & Garvey) Greenwood.

R

Restructuring for Interdisciplinary Curriculum. Ed. by Daniel Tanner. 112p. (Orig.). (C). 1991. pap. text ed. 12.00 (*0-88210-251-6*) Natl Assn Principals.

*__Restructuring for Student Learning.__ Bruce G. Barnett & Kathryn S. Whitaker. (School Leader's Library). 195p. 1996. pap. 39.95 (*1-56676-382-7*, 764076) Technomic.

Restructuring for World Peace: Challenges for the Twenty-First Century. Ed. by Katharine Tehranian & Majid Tehranian. LC 92-15818. (Communication Series: Communication, Peace & Development). 392p. (C). 1992. text ed. 55.00 (*1-881303-84-5*); pap. text ed. 24.95 (*1-881303-85-3*) Hampton Pr NJ.

Restructuring Handbook: A Guide to School Revitalization. Kathryn S. Whitaker & Monte C. Moses. LC 93-13844. 224p. 1993. text ed. 41.95 (*0-205-14009-2*, Longwood Div) Allyn.

Restructuring Health Care: The Patient-Focused Paradigm. J. Philip Lathrop. LC 93-29550. (Health Ser.). 272p. text ed. 34.95 (*1-55542-594-1*) Jossey-Bass.

Restructuring Health Policy: An International Challenge. Ed. by John M. Virgo. 500p. (Orig.). 1986. pap. 25.00 (*0-914943-02-2*) IHEMI.

Restructuring Hegemony in the Global Political Economy. Ed. by Henk Overbeek. LC 92-35537. 272p. (C). (gr. 13). 1993. text ed. 79.95 (*0-415-05595-4*, A5933) Routledge.

*__Restructuring High Schools to Include All Students.__ Cheryl M. Jorgensen. LC 97-20065. 1997. write for info. (*1-55766-313-0*) P H Brookes.

*__Restructuring Higher Education: Cost Containment & Productivity Enhancement Efforts of North American Colleges & Universities.__ James Moses & Jay Weinstein. 1997. pap. 59.50 (*1-57440-006-1*) Primary Research.

Restructuring Higher Education: Proceedings of the Annual Conference, 1987. Heather Eggins. 226p. 1988. 95.00 (*0-335-09527-5*, Open Univ Pr) Taylor & Francis.

Restructuring Higher Education: What Works & What Doesn't in Reorganizing Governing Systems. Ed. by Terrence J. MacTaggart. LC 95-40654. (Higher & Adult Education Ser.). 286p. 1996. 31.95 (*0-7879-0193-8*) Jossey-Bass.

*__Restructuring in Eastern Europe: Microeconomics of Transition Process.__ Ed. by Soumitra Sharma. 208p. (C). 1997. text ed. 80.00 (*1-85898-576-5*) E Elgar.

Restructuring in the Classroom: Teaching, Learning, & School Organization. Richard F. Elmore et al. LC 95-46898. (Education Ser.). 288p. 1996. 28.95 (*0-7879-0239-X*) Jossey-Bass.

Restructuring in Virginia: A Case in Point. Margaret A. Miller. 1995. 10.00 (*0-614-13551-6*) SHEEO.

Restructuring Japan's Financial Markets. Ingo Walter. 432p. 1993. text ed. 60.00 (*1-55623-636-0*) Irwin Prof Pubng.

Restructuring Justice: The Innovations of the Ninth Circuit & the Future of the Federal Courts. Ed. by Arthur D. Hellman. LC 90-55129. (Illus.). 352p. 1991. pap. 18.95 (*0-8014-9686-1*) Cornell U Pr.

Restructuring Krakow: Desperately Seeking Capitalism. Jane Hardy & Al Rainnie. (Employment & Work Relations in Context Ser.). 256p. 1996. 100.00 (*0-7201-2231-7*, Mansell Pub) Cassell.

Restructuring Labour in the Enterprise. Ed. by Roger Blanpain. (Bulletin of Comparative Labour Relations Ser.: Vol. 15). 152p. 1987. pap. 62.00 (*90-6544-283-9*) Kluwer Law Tax Pubs.

*__Restructuring Large Industrial Firms in Central & Eastern Europe: An Empirical Analysis.__ Gherhard Pohl et al. LC 96-26383. (World Bank Technical Papers: No. 332). 48p. 1996. 7.95 (*0-8213-3712-2*, 13712) World Bank.

Restructuring Learning: Summer Institute Papers & Recommendations, 1990. 168p. 1993. pap. 12.50 (*1-884037-02-X*) Coun Chief St Schl Offs.

*__Restructuring Manufacturing.__ 1995. spiral bd. 90.00 (*0-614-20848-3*, Pub. by Textile Inst UK) St Mut.

*__Restructuring Manufacturing & Logistics in Multinationals: Application of a Design & Method in Five Case Studies.__ Bart Vos. 224p. 1997. 59.95 (*1-85972-489-2*, Pub. by Avebury Pub UK) Ashgate Pub Co.

*__Restructuring Networks in Post-Socialism: Legacies, Linkages & Localities.__ Ed. by Gernot Grabher & David Stark. (Illus.). 360p. 1997. 75.00 (*0-19-829020-9*) OUP.

Restructuring of America: A Futurist Projection. William S. Merwin. 104p. (Orig.). 1991. pap. 12.95 (*0-932863-13-2*) Clarity Pr.

Restructuring of American Religion: Society & Faith since World War II. Robert Wuthnow. Ed. by John F. Wilson. (Studies in Church & State). 392p. (Orig.). 1988. pap. text ed. 16.95 (*0-691-02057-4*) Princeton U Pr.

*__Restructuring of Hong Kong Industries & the Urbanization of Zhujiang Delta, 1979-1989.__ Francois Soulard. 1997. pap. text ed. 39.50 (*962-201-745-2*, Tung-hai) Cheng & Tsui.

Restructuring of International Relations Theory. Mark Neufeld. (Studies in International Relations: No. 43). 185p. (C). 1995. text ed. 54.95 (*0-521-47394-2*); pap. text ed. 16.95 (*0-521-47936-3*) Cambridge U Pr.

Restructuring of Library & Information Science Curriculum. A. Tejomurty. (C). 1994. text ed. 28.00 (*81-7022-499-3*, Pub. by Concept II) S Asia.

Restructuring of Physical Sciences in Europe & the U. S., 1945-1960. Ed. by M. De Maria & M. Grilli. 832p. (C). 1989. text ed. 166.00 (*9971-5-0740-4*) World Scientific Pub.

*__Restructuring of Romania's Economy: A Paradigm of Flexibility & Adaptability.__ Raphael Shen. LC 96-37689. 1997. text ed. write for info. (*0-275-95694-6*, Praeger Pubs) Greenwood.

Restructuring of Social & Political Theory. Richard J. Bernstein. LC 76-12544. 310p. (C). 1978. pap. 17.95 (*0-8122-7742-2*) U of Pa Pr.

Restructuring of the U. K. & European Defence Industry, Vol. 4, No. 2. Susan Willett. 90p. 1993. pap. text ed. 79.00 (*3-7186-5405-9*, Harwood Acad Pubs) Gordon & Breach.

Restructuring Our Schools: A Primer on Systemic Change. W. Patrick Dolan. 210p. 1994. pap. 19.95 (*0-9641690-0-2*) Systs & Organ.

Restructuring Patriarchy: The Modernization of Gender Inequality in Brazil, 1914-1940. Susan K. Besse. LC 95-23353. 1996. lib. bdg. 39.95 (*0-614-07953-5*) U of NC Pr.

Restructuring Patriarchy: The Modernization of Gender Inequality in Brazil, 1914-1940. Susan K. Besse. LC 95-23353. (Illus.). 300p. (C). 1996. pap. text ed. 16.95 (*0-8078-4559-0*) U of NC Pr.

Restructuring Patriarchy: The Modernization of Gender Inequality in Brazil, 1914-1940. Susan K. Besse. (Illus.). 300p. (C). 1996. lib. bdg. 39.95 (*0-8078-2252-3*) U of NC Pr.

*__Restructuring Personality Disorders: A Short-Term Dynamic Approach.__ Jeffrey J. Magnavita. LC 96-44159. (Assessment of Personality & Psychopathology Ser.). 1997. lib. bdg. 35.00 (*1-57230-185-6*, 0185) Guilford Pr.

Restructuring Personnel Selection: The Assessment Center Method. (Fastback Ser.: No. 327). 1991. 3.00 (*0-87367-327-1*) Phi Delta Kappa.

Restructuring Professional Standards to Achieve Professional Excellence in a Changing Environment: Report of the Special Committee on Standards of Professional Conduct for Certified Public Accountants. American Institute of Certified Public Accountants Staff. 72p. reprint ed. pap. 25.00 (*0-7837-0079-2*, 2040336) Bks Demand.

Restructuring Reform & Reality: What School Districts Are Really Doing. Kristen J. Amundson. (NSBA Best Practices Ser.). 79p. 1993. pap. 15.00 (*0-88364-175-5*) Natl Sch Boards.

Restructuring Schooling: Learning from Ongoing Efforts. Joseph Murphy & Philip Hallinger. LC 92-39720. 296p. 1993. 57.95 (*0-8039-6060-3*); pap. 26.95 (*0-8039-6061-1*) Corwin Pr.

Restructuring Schooling for Individual Students. William M. Bechtol & Juanita S. Sorenson. LC 92-15401. 429p. 1992. text ed. 53.95 (*0-205-13929-9*, Longwood Div) Allyn.

Restructuring Schools: An International Perspective on the Movement to Transform the Control & Performance of Schools. Ed. by Hedley Beare & William L. Boyd. LC 92-39836. 1993. 85.00 (*0-7507-0121-8*, Falmer Pr); pap. 29.00 (*0-7507-0122-6*, Falmer Pr) Taylor & Francis.

Restructuring Schools: Capturing & Assessing the Phenomena. Joseph Murphy. 144p. (C). 1991. text ed. 36.00 (*0-8077-3112-9*); pap. text ed. 16.95 (*0-8077-3111-0*) Tchrs Coll.

Restructuring Schools: Doing It Right. Mike M. Milstein. Ed. by Jerry J. Herman & Janice L. Herman. LC 93-17872. (Road Maps to Success Ser.). 80p. (C). 1993. pap. 11.95 (*0-8039-6072-7*) Corwin Pr.

Restructuring Schools: Promising Practices & Policies. Ed. by Maureen T. Hallinan. LC 95-37412. (Illus.). 260p. (C). 1995. 39.50 (*0-306-45034-8*) Plenum.

Restructuring Schools: The Next Generation of Educational Reform. Richard F. Elmore et al. LC 89-49292. (Education-Higher Education Ser.). 332p. text ed. 36.95 (*1-55542-234-9*) Jossey-Bass.

Restructuring Schools: Theory & Practice. Charles Reavis & Harry Griffith. LC 91-66130. 215p. 1991. text ed. 39.95 (*0-87762-849-1*) Technomic.

*__Restructuring Schools for Collaboration: Promises & Pitfalls.__ Ed. by Diana G. Pounder. LC 97-25123. (SUNY Series, Educational Leadership). 224p. (C). 1998. text ed. 59.50 (*0-7914-3745-0*); pap. text ed. 19.95 (*0-7914-3746-9*) State U NY Pr.

*__Restructuring Schools for Linguistic Diversity: Linking Decision Making to Effective Programs.__ Ed. by Ofelia Miramontes et al. (Language & Literacy Ser.). 320p. (C). 1997. text ed. 52.00 (*0-8077-3604-X*); pap. text ed. 23.95 (*0-8077-3603-1*) Tchrs Coll.

*__Restructuring Schools, Reconstructing Teachers: Responding to Change in the Primary School.__ Peter Woods. LC 97-8655. 1997. write for info. (*0-335-19816-3*, Open Univ Pr); pap. write for info. (*0-335-19815-5*, Open Univ Pr) Taylor & Francis.

Restructuring Schools with Technology. Linda R. Knapp & Allen D. Glenn. LC 95-5118. 1995. pap. text ed. 29.95 (*0-205-15799-8*) Allyn.

Restructuring Science Education: The Importance of Theories & Their Development. Richard Duschl. 176p. (C). 1990. text ed. 30.00 (*0-8077-3006-8*); pap. text ed. 16.95 (*0-8077-3005-X*) Tchrs Coll.

Restructuring Socialist Industry: Poland's Experience in 1990. Homi J. Kharas. (Discussion Paper Ser.: No. 142). 56p. 1992. 6.95 (*0-8213-1966-3*, 11966) World Bank.

Restructuring South Africa. Ed. by John D. Brewer. LC 93-29949. 1994. text ed. 59.95 (*0-312-10583-5*) St Martin.

Restructuring Teacher Education. (Fastback Ser.: No. 325). 1991. 3.00 (*0-87367-325-5*) Phi Delta Kappa.

*__Restructuring Telecommunication.__ Curwen. Date not set. text ed. write for info. (*0-312-21017-5*) St Martin.

Restructuring the American Financial System. Ed. by George G. Kaufman. (C). 1990. lib. bdg. 61.00 (*0-7923-9073-3*) Kluwer Ac.

*__Restructuring the American Health Market - Separating Myth Reality No. 1: Health Trends Issue Brief.__ Sylvia Fubini. 52p. (Orig.). 1996. pap. text ed. 110.00 (*1-887324-01-1*) Hlth Trends.

Restructuring the Automobile Industry: A Study of Firms & States in Modern Capitalism. Dennis P. Quinn. (Columbia Studies in Business, Government & Society). (Illus.). 416p. 1988. text ed. 56.50 (*0-231-06524-8*) Col U Pr.

Restructuring the Baltic Economies: Disengaging Fifty Years of U. S. S. R.'s Economic Integration. Raphael Shen. LC 94-18609. 256p. 1994. text ed. 55.00 (*0-275-94706-8*, Praeger Pubs) Greenwood.

Restructuring the Countryside: Environmental Policy in Practice. Ed. by Andrew W. Gilg. 150p. 1992. 68.95 (*1-85628-248-1*, Pub. by Avebury Pub UK) Ashgate Pub Co.

Restructuring the Education of Teachers: Commission on the Education of Teachers into the 21st Century. ATE Commission Staff. LC 90-28838. 1991. pap. 6.50 (*0-685-41083-8*) Assn Tchr Ed.

Restructuring the Education System: Agenda for the 1990s. Michael Cohen. 40p. 1988. pap. text ed. 7.50 (*1-55877-006-2*) Natl Governor.

Restructuring the French Economy: Government & the Rise of Market Competition since World War II. William J. Adams. 400p. 1989. 36.95 (*0-8157-0100-4*) Brookings.

Restructuring the GATT System. John H. Jackson. LC 89-71227. (Chatham House Papers). 128p. 1990. pap. 14.95 (*0-87609-076-5*) Coun Foreign.

*__Restructuring the Global Military Sector Vol. 1: New Wars.__ Mary Kaldor et al. LC 96-47165. (Illus.). 352p. 1997. 79.95 (*1-85567-427-0*, Pub. by Pntr Pubs UK) Bks Intl VA.

*__Restructuring the Global Military Sector Vol. 2: The End of Military Fordism.__ Mary Kaldor et al. 352p. 1997. 79.95 (*1-85567-428-9*) Cassell.

*__Restructuring the Human Resources Department: Objectives, Methods, & Results: A Report by the Saratoga Institute.__ Jac Fitz-Enz & Saratoga Institute Staff. LC 97-5778. 1997. write for info. (*0-8144-7967-7*) AMACOM.

Restructuring the Incentive System. Ed. by Judith B. Maxwell. LC 75-308268. (Policy Review & Outlook Ser.: No. 1975). 170p. 1974. reprint ed. pap. 48.50 (*0-608-01372-2*, 2062115) Bks Demand.

*__Restructuring the Labour Market: The South African Challenge.__ Guy Standing et al. 520p. 1996. pap. 40.50 (*92-2-109513-4*) Intl Labour Office.

Restructuring the Middle Level School: Implications for School Leaders. Sally N. Clark & Donald C. Clark. LC 93-26782. (SUNY Series, Middle Schools & Early Adolescents). 316p. 1994. pap. text ed. 21.95 (*0-7914-1922-3*) State U NY Pr.

Restructuring the Middle Level School: Implications for School Leaders. Sally N. Clark & Donald C. Clark. LC 93-26782. (SUNY Series, Middle Schools & Early Adolescents). 316p. 1994. text ed. 65.50 (*0-7914-1921-5*) State U NY Pr.

Restructuring the New York City Government. (Proceedings of the Academy of Political Science Ser.: Vol. 37, No. 3). 1989. pap. 14.95 (*0-614-04165-1*) Acad Poli Sci.

Restructuring the Schools: Problems & Prospects. Ed. by John J. Lane & Edgar G. Epps. LC 91-66584. (NSSE Series on Contemporary Educational Issues). 217p. 1992. 30.70 (*0-8211-1116-7*) McCutchan.

Restructuring the Science Curriculum for a Changing World: A Renewal Process. Bucks County Schools Intermediate Unit No. 22 Staff. Ed. by Elliot Seif. 179p. (Orig.). 1994. pap. 29.95 (*1-56602-057-3*) Research Better.

Restructuring the Soviet Economic Bureaucracy. Paul R. Gregory. (Soviet Interview Project Ser.). (Illus.). 192p. (C). 1990. text ed. 59.95 (*0-521-36386-1*) Cambridge U Pr.

Restructuring the Soviet Economy. David A. Dyker. 224p. (C). 1991. pap. text ed. 19.95 (*0-415-06761-8*, A6679) Routledge.

Restructuring the Soviet Economy. David A. Dyker. 224p. (C). (gr. 13). 1991. text ed. 79.95 (*0-415-05679-9*, A6675) Routledge.

Restructuring the Soviet Economy: In Search of the Market. Nicolas Spulber. 266p. (C). 1991. text ed. 49.50 (*0-472-10229-X*) U of Mich Pr.

*__Restructuring the Total Army School System.__ John D. Winkler et al. 27p. (Orig.). 1996. pap. text ed. 6.00 (*0-8330-2324-1*, DB-153-A) Rand Corp.

*__Restructuring the Welfare State Vol. VIII: Theory & Reform of Social Policy.__ Ed. by Peter Koslowski & Andreas Follesdal. LC 96-53579. (Studies in Economic Ethics & Philosophy). (Illus.). 402p. 1997. 119.00 (*3-540-62035-4*) Spr-Verlag.

Restructuring Through School Redesign. (Fastback Ser.: No. 322). 1991. 3.00 (*0-87367-322-0*) Phi Delta Kappa.

Restructuring Troubled Real Estate Loans: Guide to Workout Strategies & Procedures. Mark W. Patterson. LC 92-3890. (Real Estate Practice Library: No. 1836). 360p. 1992. text ed. 140.00 (*0-471-57466-X*) Wiley.

Restructuring Universities: Politics & Power in the Management of Change. Geoffrey Walford. 185p. 1989. 55.00 (*0-7099-3694-X*, Pub. by Croom Helm UK) Routledge Chapman & Hall.

Restructuring Urban Schools: A Chicago Perspective. G. Alfred Hess. (Series on School Reform). 264p. (C). 1995. text ed. 50.00 (*0-8077-3476-4*); pap. text ed. 23.95 (*0-8077-3475-6*) Tchrs Coll.

Restructuring Within a Labour Intensive Industry: The UK Clothing Industry in Transition. Ed. by Ian Taplin & Jonathan Winterton. 256p. 1996. 59.95 (*1-85972-322-5*, Pub. by Avebury Pub UK) Ashgate Pub Co.

Restructurings. Weil, Gotshal & Manges Staff. 375p. 1991. 245.00 (*1-85564-074-0*, Pub. by Euromoney UK) Am Educ Systs.

Restudy of the Fossil Scorpionida of the World, Vol. 55. E. N. Kjellesvig-Waering. 287p. 1986. 55.00 (*0-87710-401-8*) Paleo Res.

Resuemierende Auswahlbibliographie Zur Neueren Sowjetischen Sprachlehrforschung (Gesteuerter Fremdsprachenerwerb) Rupprecht S. Baur et al. (Language & Literary Ser. in Eastern Europe: No. 3). lxviii, 318p. 1980. 84.00 (*90-272-1504-9*) Benjamins North Am.

Resultado De La Dispensacion De La Trinidad Procesada Y La Transmision Del Cristo Que Lo Transciende Todo. Witness Lee. 106p. (SPA.). per. 3.75 (*0-87083-788-5*, 04023002) Living Stream Ministry.

*__Resulting Trusts.__ Robert Chambers. LC 96-54803. 288p. 1997. 65.00 (*0-19-876444-8*) OUP.

Results: The Key to Continuous School Improvement. Mike Schmoker. 1996. pap. 20.95 (*0-87120-260-3*) Assn Supervision.

Results & Evaluation of New Methodology in Cardiology: Proceedings of the Cardiovascular Disease Conference, 8th, Snowmass at Aspen, Colorado, Jan. 10-14, 1977. Cardiovascular Disease Conference Staff. Ed. by J. H. Vogel. (Advances in Cardiology Ser.: Vol. 22). 1977. 108.00 (*3-8055-2748-9*) S Karger.

Results & Trends in Theoretical Computer Science: Proceedings of a Colloquium in Honor of Arto Salmoaa, Graz, Austria, June 10-11, 1994. Ed. by J. Karhumaki et al. LC 94-20330. (Lecture Notes in Computer Science Ser.: Vol. 812). 1994. 65.95 (*0-387-58131-6*) Spr-Verlag.

Results from the Design Institute for Physical Property Data: Experimental Results & Data Compilation Procedures. Ed. by John R. Cunningham & Dennis K. Jones. LC 91-21323. (Symposium Ser.: Vol. 86, No. 279). 155p. (Orig.). 1990. pap. 30.00 (*0-8169-0496-0*) Am Inst Chem Eng.

Results from the Fourth Mathematics Assessment of the National Assessment of Educational Progress. Ed. by Mary M. Lindquist. LC 89-3335. (Illus.). 173p. 1989. pap. 15.00 (*0-87353-274-0*) NCTM.

*__Results from the Sixth Mathematics Assessment of the National Assessment of Educational Progress.__ Ed. by Patricia A. Kenney & Edward A. Silver. LC 97-5290. (Illus.). 296p. (Orig.). 1997. pap. 19.95 (*0-87353-429-8*) NCTM.

Results from the Wind Project Performance Reporting System. (Illus.). 35p. (Orig.). (C). 1993. pap. text ed. 25.00 (*1-56806-748-8*) DIANE Pub.

Results from Two National Surveys of Philanthropic Activity. James N. Morgan et al. 204p. (Orig.). 1979. pap. 12.00 (*0-87944-246-8*) Inst Soc Res.

Results from Two National Surveys of Philanthropic Activity. James N. Morgan et al. LC 79-53850. (Institute for Social Research, Research Report Ser.). 173p. (Orig.). reprint ed. pap. 49.40 (*0-7837-5254-7*, 2044991) Bks Demand.

Results in Education: 1988. National Governors' Association Staff. (Time for Results Ser.). (Orig.). 1988. pap. text ed. 12.50 (*1-55877-013-5*) Natl Governor.

Results in Education: 1989. Ed. by Karen Glass & Mark Miller. 50p. (Orig.). 1989. pap. text ed. 12.50 (*1-55877-056-9*) Natl Governor.

Results in Education: 1990. Ed. by Mark Miller. 80p. (Orig.). 1990. pap. text ed. 12.50 (*1-55877-080-1*) Natl Governor.

Results in Neuroanatomy, Motor Organization, Cerebral Circulation & Modelling: Recent Developments of Neurobiology in Hungary, Vol. 8. K. Lissak. (Recent Developments of Neurobiology in Hungary Ser.: No. 8). 242p. (C). 1979. 63.00 (*963-05-1594-6*, Pub. by Akad Kiado HU) St Mut.

Results in Neuroanatomy, Neurochemistry, Neurophysiology & Neuropathology: Recent Developments of Neurobiology in Hungary, Vol. 9. K. Lissak. (Recent Developments of Neurobiology in Hungary Ser.: No. 9). 232p. (C). 1982. 72.00 (*963-05-2947-5*, Pub. by Akad Kiado HU) St Mut.

Results in Neuroendocrinology, Neurochemistry & Sleep Research. K. Lissak. (Recent Developments of Neurobiology in Hungary Ser.: No. 7). 189p. (C). 1978. 50.00 (*963-05-1587-3*, Pub. by Akad Kiado HU) St Mut.

*__Results of a Survey of the American Indian Vocational Rehabilitation (Section 130) Projects Regarding Training & Technical Assistance Needs.__ G. L. Lonetree. 175p. 1989. pap. text ed. write for info. (*1-888557-34-6*, 100101) No Ariz Univ.

*__Results of an Experimental Program Utilized to Verify a New Tooth Strength Analysis.__ Raymond J. Drago. (Technical Papers). 60p. 1983. pap. text ed. 30.00 (*1-55589-070-9*) AGMA.

Results of Emancipation. Augustin Cochin. Tr. by Mary L. Booth. LC 76-83942. (Black Heritage Library Collection). 1977. 28.95 (*0-8369-8544-3*) Ayer.

*__Results of Regulatory Impact Survey of Industrial & Medical Materials Licensees of the Office of Nuclear Material Safety & Safeguards.__ 1997. lib. bdg. 250.95 (*0-8490-7705-2*) Gordon Pr.

Results of Search for Felt Reports for Selected Colorado Earthquakes. Robert M. Kirkham & Sherry D. Oakes. (Information Ser.: No. 23). 89p. (Orig.). 1986. pap. 6.00 (*1-884216-19-6*) Colo Geol Survey.

Results of Slavery. Augustin Cochin. Tr. by Mary L. Booth. LC 73-83960. (Black Heritage Library Collection). 1977. 38.95 (*0-8369-8698-9*) Ayer.

Results of Slavery: Work Crowned by the Institute of France. Augustin Cochin. Tr. by Mary L. Booth. LC 70-109619. (Select Bibliographies Reprint Ser.). 1977. 38.95 (*0-8369-5228-6*) Ayer.

An Asterisk (*) at the beginning of an entry indicates that the title is appearing in BIP for the first time.

Results of the Fifth George Vanderbilt Expedition (1941) Bahamas, Caribbean Sea, Panama, Galapagos Archipelago & Mexican Pacific Islands. George Vanderbilt et al. (Monograph: No. 6). (Illus.). 583p. (Orig.). 1944. pap. 20.00 (*0-910006-15-6*) Acad Nat Sci Phila.

Results of the First Workshop on Standards in Geothermics. Ed. by R. Haenel & M. Gupta. (Zentralblatt Fuer Geologie Ser.). (Illus.). 184p. 1983. pap. text ed. 63.70 (*0-945345-15-1*) Lubrecht & Cramer.

Results of the GATT Uruguay Round of Multilateral Trade Negotiations: Executive Summary. 52p. (Orig.). (C). 1994. pap. text ed. 30.00 (*0-7881-1128-0*) DIANE Pub.

Results of the School Health Education Evaluation. 68p. 1985. 10.50 (*0-685-16504-3*) Am Sch Health.

Results of the Seventh United Nations Population Inquiry among Governments. 175p. Date not set. pap. 20.00 (*92-1-151282-4*, E.95.XIII.11) UN.

*__Results of the Uruguay Round: Schedules for Goods & Services, Vol. 34.__ 150p. 1996. pap. 55.00 (*0-614-25778-6*, GATT/1994-7V.34, Pub. by Wrld Trade SZ) Bernan Associates.

*__Results of the Uruguay Round - Legal Texts.__ 200p. 1996. pap. 125.00 (*0-614-25779-4*, GATT/1994-4-A2, Pub. by Wrld Trade SZ) Bernan Associates.

Results of the Uruguay Round of Multilateral Trade Negotiations: Market Access for Goods & Services: Overview of the Results. (Illus.). 88p. (Orig.). (C). 1995. pap. text ed. 50.00 (*0-7881-1886-2*) DIANE Pub.

Results on Target. Bruce Dillman. (Illus.). 180p. (Orig.). 1989. pap. 12.50 (*0-944112-12-9*) Outcomes.

Results on the Uruguay Round Vol. 32: Schedules on Services. World Trade Organization Staff & Gatt. 558p. 1996. pap. 55.00 (*92-870-1121-4*, GATT/1994-7V32, Pub. by Wrld Trade SZ) Bernan Associates.

Results-Oriented Job Descriptions: More Than 225 Models to Use or Adapt - with Guidelines for Creating Your Own. Roger J. Plachy & Sandra J. Plachy. 300p. 1993. spiral bd. 65.00 (*0-8144-7806-9*) AMACOM.

Resume Adviser: How to Write & Design a Professional Resume. Thomas M. Sherman & Craig A. Stephan. LC 92-71018. 160p. 1992. pap. 11.95 (*0-9632159-7-3*) Barrister Hse.

*__Resume & Cover Letter Writing Guide.__ 2nd rev. ed. Carey E. Harbin. 36p. (Orig.). 1996. pap. text ed. 8.95 (*0-918995-05-1*) Voc-Offers.

*__Resume Catalog.__ rev. ed. Yana Parker. (Illus.). 288p. (Orig.). 1996. pap. 15.95 (*0-89815-891-5*) Ten Speed Pr.

Resume Doctor: How to Transform a Troublesome Work History into a Winning Resume. John J. Marcus. LC 95-21631. 192p. (Orig.). 1996. pap. 11.95 (*0-06-273369-9*, Harper Ref) HarpC.

Resume Guide for Women of the Nineties. Kim Marino. LC 92-13552. 132p. (Orig.). 1992. pap. 11.95 (*0-89815-504-5*) Ten Speed Pr.

Resume Handbook. 2nd ed. BMCC COOP Staff. 48p. 1995. 9.71 (*0-8403-8493-9*) Kendall-Hunt.

Resume Handbook: How to Write Outstanding Resume & Cover Letters for Every Situation. 3rd ed. Arthur Rosenberg & David V. Hizer. 176p. 1996. pap. 7.95 (*1-55850-616-0*) Adams Media.

Resume II: Artists, Galleries & Craftspersons of the Door Penisula. Jim Legault. (Illus.). 64p. (Orig.). 1982. 12.75 (*0-933072-02-3*); pap. 6.50 (*0-933072-03-1*) Golden Glow.

Resume Kit. 3rd ed. Richard H. Beatty. LC 95-16942. 320p. 1995. pap. text ed. 10.95 (*0-471-12403-6*) Wiley.

Resume Kit. 3rd ed. Richard W. Beatty. LC 95-16942. 320p. 1995. text ed. 29.95 (*0-471-12402-8*) Wiley.

Resume Kit, Do-It-Yourself. David J. Cillian. (Illus.). 9.95 (*1-880398-04-4*, 01014) SJT Enterprises.

Resume Makeover: The Resume Writing Guide That Includes Personalized Feedback. Jeffrey G. Allen. LC 94-34133. 276p. 1995. pap. text ed. 10.95 (*0-471-04624-8*) Wiley.

Resume of a Theory of Language. Louis Hjelmslev. Ed. & Tr. by Francis J. Whitfield. LC 75-33539. 312p. 1975. reprint ed. pap. 89.00 (*0-608-01886-4*, 2062538) Bks Demand.

Resume of the Bible. Eunice Kauffman. (Orig.). 1995. pap. 10.95 (*0-533-11312-1*) Vantage.

Resume Power: Selling Yourself on Paper. 5th ed. Tom Washington. 246p. 1996. pap. text ed. 12.95 (*0-931213-13-4*) Mount Vernon Pr.

Resume Pro: The Professional's Guide. Yana Parker. (Illus.). 416p. (Orig.). 1992. pap. 24.95 (*0-89815-466-9*) Ten Speed Pr.

Resume Reference Manual. Carl E. Gosmann. LC 93-71810. 101p. (C). 1993. pap. text ed. 14.95 (*0-9636758-2-6*) Career Connect.

Resume Repair Kit. William S. Frank. 200p. 1995. student ed. 19.95 (*1-884087-04-3*) CareerLab Bks.

*__Resume Shortcuts: How to Quickly Communicate Your Qualifications with Powerful Words & Phrases.__ Robbie M. Kaplan. LC 96-53562. 189p. (Orig.). 1997. pap. 14.95 (*1-57023-071-4*) Impact VA.

Resume Solution: How to Write & Use a Resume That Gets Results. 2nd rev. ed. David Swanson. LC 90-4904. 224p. 1995. pap. 12.95 (*1-56370-180-4*, J1804) JIST Works.

Resume Trainer's Manual. Kathryn K. Troutman. 1995. 200.00 (*0-615-00888-7*) Resume Place.

Resume with Monsters. William B. Spencer. 1996. pap. text ed. 5.99 (*1-56504-913-6*, 13351) White Wolf.

Resume Workbook: A Personal Career File for Job Applications. 5th ed. Carolyn N. Nutter. LC 77-17412. 128p. 1978. 9.95 (*0-910328-00-5*) Sulzburger & Graham Pub.

Resume Writer: Writing It Right. Bernard J. Poole et al. 128p. 1991. pap. text ed. 36.60 (*0-13-775388-8*) P-H.

Resume Writer: Your Professional Ghostwriter for Resumes. Tom Hayduk & Richard Young. Date not set. pap. text ed. 34.95 incl. disk (*0-538-85571-1*) S-W Pub.

Resume Writer's Handbook. Michael H. Smith. 240p. 1994. mass mkt. 4.99 (*0-06-109300-9*, Harp PBks) HarpC.

Resume Writer's Workbook. Stan Krantman. 107p. (C). 1992. teacher ed. 21.00 (*1-882942-02-7*); student ed. 18.00 (*1-882942-00-0*); pap. 25.00 incl. audio (*1-882942-04-3*); lib. bdg. 22.50 (*1-882942-01-9*); lib. bdg. 30.00 incl. audio (*1-882942-05-1*); audio 9.95 (*1-882942-03-5*) Capital Writers.

Resume Writer's Workbook. Stanley Krantman. 134p. 1995. student ed., pap. 23.95 (*0-8273-6943-3*) Delmar.

Resume Writer's Workbook. Stanley Krantman. 30p. 1995. teacher ed. 16.25 (*0-8273-6944-1*) Delmar.

Resume Writing: A Comprehensive How-to-Do-It Guide. 4th ed. Burdette E. Bostwick. LC 89-37360. 352p. 1990. pap. text ed. 14.95 (*0-471-51416-0*) Wiley.

Resume Writing for Results: A Workbook. 2nd ed. Pat Brett. 160p. (C). 1993. pap. 20.95 (*0-534-19980-1*) Wadsworth Pub.

Resume Writing for the Professional Nurse. rev. ed. Nancy Kuzmich. (Illus.). 110p. 1995. 39.95 (*0-916780-31-7*) CES Assocs.

Resume Writing, Interviewing & Roleplaying Skills for Salespeople Looking for New Jobs. Jack Bernstein. 64p. (Orig.). 1993. 12.50 (*0-9616226-5-2*) JB & Me.

Resume Writing Made Easy. 5th ed. Lola M. Coxford. LC 94-21096. 1994. per. 11.95 (*0-89787-821-3*) Gorsuch Scarisbrick.

*__Resume Writing Made Easy.__ 6th ed. Lola M. Coxford. 156p. 1997. pap. text ed. write for info. (*0-614-24125-1*) Gorsuch Scarisbrick.

*__Resume Writing Made Easy.__ 6th ed. Lola M. Coxford. LC 97-22038. 1998. write for info. (*0-13-679853-5*) P-H.

*__Resume Writing Made Easy: A Practical Guide to Resume Preparation & Job Search.__ 6th ed. Lola M. Coxford. 1997. pap. 12.95 (*0-89787-832-9*) Gorsuch Scarisbrick.

Resumes: Short & Sweet. Dinah Tallent. 135p. (YA). (gr. 7-12). 1992. pap. 6.95 (*1-57515-033-6*) PPI Pubng.

Resumes & Cover Letters for Transitioning Military Personnel. Ronald L. Krannich & Carl S. Savino. 179p. (Orig.). 1995. pap. 17.95 (*1-57023-040-4*) Impact VA.

Resumes & Cover Letters That Have Worked! A Book about Changing Careers & Jobs. Ed. by Anne McKinney. LC 95-19458. (Illus.). 272p. 1997. pap. 25.00 (*1-885288-04-2*) PREP Pubng.

Resumes & Cover Letters That Have Worked for Military Professionals: A Book That Translates Military Experience into Civilian Language. Ed. by Anne McKinney. LC 96-33822. (Illus.). 236p. (Orig.). 1996. pap. 25.00 (*1-885288-06-9*) PREP Pubng.

Resumes & Personal Statements for Health Professionals. James W. Tysinger. LC 94-30274. (Illus.). 195p. (Orig.). 1994. pap. 15.95 (*1-883620-19-8*) Galen AZ.

Resumes, Application Forms, Cover Letters & Interviews: How to Create Effective Resumes & Application Forms & How to Succeed in Tests & Interviews. 1991. lib. bdg. 69.95 (*0-8490-4391-3*) Gordon Pr.

Resumes Don't Get Jobs: The Realities & Myths of Job Hunting. Bob Weinstein. 1993. pap. text ed. 10.95 (*0-07-069144-4*) McGraw.

Resumes Don't Get Jobs: The Realities & Myths of Job Hunting. Robert Weinstein. 1993. text ed. 24.95 (*0-07-069143-6*) McGraw.

Resumes for Advertising Careers. VGM Career Horizons Editors. LC 92-24298. 160p. 1994. pap. 9.95 (*0-8442-4152-0*, VGM Career Bks) NTC Pub Grp.

Resumes for Architecture & Related Careers. VGM Career Horizons Editors. (Professional Resumes Ser.). 160p. (Orig.). 1996. pap. text ed. 9.95 (*0-8442-4398-1*, VGM Career Bks) NTC Pub Grp.

Resumes for Banking & Financial Careers. LC 93-1517. 160p. 1994. pap. 9.95 (*0-8442-4156-3*, VGM Career Bks) NTC Pub Grp.

Resumes for Better Jobs. 5th ed. Lawrence D. Brennan et al. 224p. 1992. pap. 9.00 (*0-13-773615-0*, Arco) Macmillan Gen Ref.

Resumes for Better Jobs. 6th ed. Lawrence Brennan. 1994. pap. 10.00 (*0-671-89195-2*) P-H.

Resumes for Better Jobs. 7th ed. Lawrence D. Brennan. 1996. 10.95 (*0-02-861189-6*) Macmillan.

Resumes for Business Management Careers. (VGM Professional Resumes Ser.). 160p. 1994. pap. 9.95 (*0-8442-8544-7*, VGM Career Bks) NTC Pub Grp.

Resumes for College Students & Other Recent Graduates. Passport Books Staff. 160p. 1994. pap. 9.95 (*0-8442-4150-4*, VGM Career Bks) NTC Pub Grp.

Resumes for Communications Careers. VGM Career Horizons Editors. LC 90-50723. (VGM Professional Resumes Ser.). 160p. (YA). (gr. 9 up). 1994. pap. 9.95 (*0-8442-8546-3*, VGM Career Bks) NTC Pub Grp.

Resumes for Computer Careers. LC 96-9316. (VGM Professional Resumes Ser.). 160p. 1996. pap. 9.95 (*0-8442-4523-2*, VGM Career Bks) NTC Pub Grp.

Resumes for Dummies. Joyce L. Kennedy. 1996. pap. 12.99 (*1-56884-396-8*) IDG Bks.

Resumes for Education. 160p. 1994. pap. 9.95 (*0-8442-8543-9*, VGM Career Bks) NTC Pub Grp.

Resumes for Educational Professionals. Kim Marino. 208p. 1994. pap. text ed. 14.95 (*0-471-31144-8*) Wiley.

Resumes for Engineering Careers. VGM Career Horizons Editors. LC 93-45474. 160p. 1994. pap. 9.95 (*0-8442-4160-1*, VGM Career Bks) NTC Pub Grp.

Resumes for Environmental Careers. VGM Career Horizons Editors. LC 93-45864. 160p. 1994. pap. 9.95 (*0-8442-4159-8*, VGM Career Bks) NTC Pub Grp.

Resumes for Ex-Military Personnel. VGM Career Horizons Editors. (VGM Professional Resumes Ser.). 160p. (Orig.). 1995. pap. 9.95 (*0-8442-4383-3*, VGM Career Bks) NTC Pub Grp.

Resumes for Executive Women. Laurie E. Lico. 128p. (Orig.). 1984. pap. 7.95 (*0-671-49758-8*) S&S Trade.

*__Resumes for Freelancers.__ Sheila Buff. 1996. pap. 5.50 (*1-880407-18-3*) Edit Freelancers.

Resumes for Government Careers. VGM Career Horizons Editors. (Professional Resumes Ser.). 160p. 1996. pap. text ed. 9.95 (*0-8442-4158-X*, VGM Career Bks) NTC Pub Grp.

Resumes for Health & Medical Careers. VGM Career Horizons Editors. LC 92-48533. (VGM Professional Resumes Ser.). 160p. 1995. pap. 9.95 (*0-8442-4154-7*, VGM Career Bks) NTC Pub Grp.

Resumes for High School Graduates. VGM Career Horizons Editors. LC 92-24300. 160p. 1994. pap. 9.95 (*0-8442-4151-2*, VGM Career Bks) NTC Pub Grp.

Resumes for High Tech Careers. (VGM Professional Resumes Ser.). 160p. 1994. pap. 9.95 (*0-8442-8542-0*, VGM Career Bks) NTC Pub Grp.

*__Resumes for Higher Paying Positions: A Complete Guide to Resume Writing for a More Rewarding Career.__ Cory Schulman. (Illus.). 187p. 1997. pap. text ed. 17.95 (*0-9642997-0-4*) Best Seller.

Resumes for Law Careers. 160p. (Orig.). 1995. pap. 9.95 (*0-8442-4388-4*, VGM Career Bks) NTC Pub Grp.

Resumes for Midcareer Job-Changers. 160p. 1994. pap. 9.95 (*0-8442-4155-5*, VGM Career Bks) NTC Pub Grp.

Resumes for Nursing Careers. LC 96-25596. (VGM Professional Resumes Ser.). 1996. 9.95 (*0-8442-4524-0*) NTC Pub Grp.

Resumes for Overseas & Stateside Jobs. Richard M. Zink. (Illus.). 80p. (Orig.). 1994. pap. 14.95 (*0-939469-41-3*) Zinks Career Guide.

Resumes for People Who Hate to Write Resumes: A Fast, Easy, Step-By-Step Method to Write Resumes & Cover Letters. Jack W. Wright. LC 91-50853. 77p. 1992. pap. 9.95 (*0-944020-01-1*) Shastar Pr.

Resumes for People Who Hate to Write Resumes: A Fast, Easy, Step-By-Step Method to Write Resumes & Cover Letters. 3rd ed. Jack W. Wright. 140p. 1994. pap. 12.95 (*0-944020-03-8*) Shastar Pr.

*__Resumes for Performing Arts Careers.__ LC 96-37069. (VGM Professional Resumes Ser.). 1997. write for info. (*0-8442-4521-6*) NTC Pub Grp.

Resumes for Re-Entering the Job Market. VGM Career Horizons Editors. (VGM Professional Resumes Ser.). 160p. (Orig.). 1995. pap. 9.95 (*0-8442-4390-6*, VGM Career Bks) NTC Pub Grp.

Resumes for Re-Entry: A Handbook for Women. 2nd ed. Charles Good. 180p. 1993. pap. 10.95 (*0-942710-85-1*) Impact VA.

Resumes for Sales & Marketing Careers. Jeffrey S. Johnson. 160p. 1994. pap. 9.95 (*0-8442-8545-5*, VGM Career Bks) NTC Pub Grp.

*__Resumes for Science Careers.__ LC 96-47683. 1997. write for info. (*0-8442-4522-4*) NTC Pub Grp.

Resumes for Scientific & Technical Careers. VGM Career Horizons Editors. LC 93-13307. (VGM Professional Resumes Ser.). 160p. 1994. pap. 9.95 (*0-8442-4157-1*, VGM Career Bks) NTC Pub Grp.

Resumes for Secretaries. Leonard Corwen. write for info. (*0-668-06250-9*) S&S Trade.

Resumes for Social Service Careers. VGM Career Horizons Editors. LC 94-12516. 160p. 1996. pap. 9.95 (*0-8442-4386-8*, VGM Career Bks) NTC Pub Grp.

Resumes for the Fifty Plus Job Hunter. 160p. (Orig.). 1994. pap. 9.95 (*0-8442-4389-2*, VGM Career Bks) NTC Pub Grp.

Resumes for the First-Time Job Hunter. VGM Career Horizons. LC 94-12509. 160p. 1996. pap. 9.95 (*0-8442-4387-6*, VGM Career Bks) NTC Pub Grp.

Resumes for the Health Care Professional. Kim Marino. LC 91-44718. 208p. 1993. pap. text ed. 14.95 (*0-471-55862-1*) Wiley.

Resumes for the Over-50 Job Hunter. Samuel N. Ray. LC 92-22988. 216p. 1993. pap. text ed. 16.95 (*0-471-57423-6*) Wiley.

Resumes for the Smart Job Search: The Ultimate Guide to Writing Resumes in the 90s. Marc L. Makos. LC 92-47008. 160p. 1993. pap. 14.95 (*0-9630394-9-0*) HD Pub.

Resumes for Women. Eva Shaw. LC 95-1127. 1995. pap. 10.00 (*0-671-89888-4*) Macmillan.

Resumes for Women: Job-Winning Resume Guidance for Every Situation. Eva Shaw. 192p. 1995. 9.95 (*0-02-860345-1*, Arco) Macmillan Gen Ref.

Resumes from Scratch: (A Workbook) Ralph French. 1990. 6.95 (*0-9627853-1-8*) Writers Help.

*__Resumes in Cyberspace: Your Complete Guide to a Computerized Job Search.__ Pat Criscito. 304p. 1997. pap. 14.95 (*0-8120-9919-2*) Barron.

Resumes Made Easy. Jan B. Mattia & Patti Marler. Ed. by Sarah Kennedy. (Made Easy Ser.). 96p. (Orig.). 1995. pap. 6.95 (*0-8442-4348-5*, VGM Career Bks) NTC Pub Grp.

Resumes! Resumes! Resumes! 2nd ed. Career Press Editors. 192p. 1995. pap. 9.99 (*1-56414-159-4*) Career Pr Inc.

*__Resumes! Resumes! Resumes!__ 3rd ed. Career Press, Inc. Staff. LC 97-17756. 1997. write for info. (*1-56414-309-0*) Career Pr Inc.

Resumes That Get Jobs. Brian Jud. Ed. by Charles Lipka. 20p. (Orig.). (C). 1995. student ed., pap. 1.45 (*1-880218-19-4*) Mktg Dir Inc.

Resumes that Get Jobs. Scope International Staff. 1998. 16.00 incl. disk (*0-02-861155-1*) Macmillan.

Resumes That Get Jobs. 8th ed. Ray Potter. 1996. 24.95 incl. disk (*0-02-860604-3*) Macmillan.

*__Resumes That Get Jobs.__ 9th ed. Jean Reed. 1998. 10.95 (*0-02-862206-5*) Macmillan.

*__Resumes That Get Jobs.__ 9th ed. Jean Reed. 1998. pap. 24.95 incl. disk (*0-02-862195-6*) Macmillan.

Resumes That Knock 'em Dead. 2nd ed. Martin J. Yate. LC 94-41686. 1994. pap. 10.95 (*1-55850-434-6*) Adams Media.

*__Resumes That Knock'em Dead.__ Martin Yate. Date not set. pap. 10.95 (*1-55850-817-1*) Adams Media.

Resumes That Mean Business. David R. Eyler. 1990. pap. 9.95 (*0-679-73120-2*) Random.

Resumes that Mean Business. rev. ed. David R. Eyler. LC 93-14761. 1993. pap. 10.00 (*0-679-74610-2*, Random Ref) Random.

Resumes that Mean Business. 2nd ed. D. Eyler. 208p. 1996. pap. 12.95 (*0-679-76973-0*) Random.

*__Resumes That Will Get You the Job You Want.__ Andrea Kay. LC 97-4922. 160p. 1997. pap. 12.99 (*1-55870-455-8*, Betrwy Bks) F & W Pubns Inc.

Resumes That Work. Tom Cowan. LC 83-8332. 192p. 1983. pap. 14.95 (*0-452-26213-5*, Plume) NAL-Dutton.

Resumes That Work: How to Sell Yourself on Paper. 2nd ed. Loretta D. Foxman. Ed. by Walter P. Polsky. LC 92-20595. 128p. 1992. pap. text ed. 14.95 (*0-471-57747-2*) Wiley.

Resummation of Divergent Perturbation Series: Introduction to Theory & Guide to Practical Applications. W. Janke & Hagen Kleinert. 300p. (C). 1998. text ed. 44.00 (*981-02-0198-2*) World Scientific Pub.

Resumption. Christopher Nicole. 352p. 1993. lib. bdg. 20.00 (*0-7278-4398-2*) Severn Hse.

Resupinate Aphyllophorales of the Northwestern Himalayas. S. S. Rattan. (Bibliotheca Mycologica Ser.: No. 60). (Illus.). 1977. lib. bdg. 78.00 (*3-7682-1172-X*) Lubrecht & Cramer.

*__Resupinate Non-Poroid Aphyllophorales of the Temperate Northern Hemisphere.__ J. A. Stalpers. (Verhandelingen der Koninklijke Nederlandse Akademie van Wetenschappen, Afd. Natuurkunde Ser.: No. 74). iv, 336p. 1980. pap. text ed. 81.25 (*0-444-85508-4*) Elsevier.

Resupinaten Phellinus-Arte in Mittel-Europa. mit Hinweisen auf die Respinaten Incnotus Arten. H. Jahn. (Bibliotheca Mycologica Ser.: Vol. 81). (Illus.). (GER.). 1981. reprint ed. pap. text ed. 32.00 (*3-7682-1307-2*) Lubrecht & Cramer.

Resureccion de la Verdadera Iglesia, Los Pobres Lugar Teologica de la Eclesiologia see True Church & the Poor

ReSurfacing: Techniques for Exploring Consciousness. Harry Palmer. 128p. (Orig.). 1994. student ed. 15.00 (*0-9626874-4-8*) Stars Edge.

Resurfacing with Portland Cement Concrete. (National Cooperative Highway Research Program Report Ser.: No. 99). 90p. 1982. 8.40 (*0-309-03460-4*) Transport Res Bd.

Resurgam. Dixie Atkins. 240p. (C). 1989. text ed. 50.00 (*1-872795-89-7*, Pub. by Pentland Pr UK) St Mut.

Resurgence & Uncertainty in Argentina, Brazil, & Chile. Sidney Weintraub. (Global Business White Paper Ser.). 1995. 20.00 (*0-614-13865-5*) CSI Studies.

*__Resurgence from the Abyss.__ Gloria L. Amos. LC 97-90042. (Orig.). 1997. pap. 14.95 (*0-533-12273-2*) Vantage.

Resurgence of Central Asia: Islam or Nationalism? Ahmed Rashid. (Politics in Contemporary Asia Ser.). 160p. (C). 1994. pap. 25.00 (*1-85649-132-3*, Pub. by Zed Bks Ltd UK); text ed. 59.95 (*1-85649-131-5*, Pub. by Zed Bks Ltd UK) Humanities.

Resurgence of Class Conflict in Western Europe Since 1968, 2 vols. Ed. by Colin Crouch & Alessandro Pizzorno. Incl. Vol. 1. . LC 77-16076. 1983. 49.50 (*0-8419-0355-7*); Vol. 2. . LC 77-16076. 1983. 49.50 (*0-8419-0356-5*); LC 77-16076. 1978. 49.50 (*0-685-02334-6*) Holmes & Meier.

Resurgence of Conservatism in Anglo-American Democracies. Ed. by Barry Cooper et al. LC 87-22270. vii, 468p. (C). 1987. text ed. 53.00 (*0-8223-0709-X*); pap. text ed. 20.95 (*0-8223-0793-6*) Duke.

Resurgence of Rajiv Gandhi: Assassination of Indira & After. Rai Singh. 203p. 1986. 24.95 (*0-318-36603-7*) Asia Bk Corp.

Resurgence of Regionalism in World Politics: Regional Organization & International Order. Ed. by Andrew Hurrell & Louise Fawcett. (Illus.). 360p. 1996. 65.00 (*0-19-827930-2*) OUP.

Resurgence of Regionalism in World Politics: Regional Organization & International Order. Ed. by Andrew Hurrell & Louise Fawcett. (Illus.). 360p. 1996. pap. 19.95 (*0-19-828067-X*) OUP.

Resurgence of Right-Wing Radicalism in Germany: New Forms of an Old Phenomenon? Ed. by Ulrich Wank. Tr. by James Knowlton from GER. 120p. (C). 1996. pap. 15.00 (*0-391-03959-8*) Humanities.

Resurgence of Right-Wing Radicalism in Germany: New Forms of an Old Phenomenon? Ed. by Ulrich Wank. Tr. by James Knowlton from GER. 120p. (C). 1996. text ed. 45.00 (*0-391-03958-X*) Humanities.

*__Resurgence of the Real: Body, Nature & Place in Hypermodern World.__ Charlene Spretnak. LC 96-52140. 1997. 22.00 (*0-201-53419-3*) Addison-Wesley.

Resurgent: New Writing by Women. Ed. by Lou Robinson & Camille Norton. 264p. 1992. text ed. 39.95 (*0-252-01835-4*); pap. text ed. 13.95 (*0-252-06203-5*) U of Ill Pr.

Resurgent Evangelicalism in the United States: Mapping Cultural Change since 1970. Mark A. Shibley. LC 95-50218. (Illus.). 180p. 1996. text ed. 24.95 (*1-57003-106-1*) U of SC Pr.

R

Resurgent Liberal & Other Unfashionable Prophecies. Robert Reich. 1989. 19.95 (0-8129-1833-9, Times Bks) Random.

Resurgent Liberal & Other Unfashionable Prophecies. Robert Reich. LC 90-50146. 320p. 1991. pap. 15.00 (0-679-73152-0, Vin) Random.

Resurgent Politics & Educational Progressivism in the New South: North Carolina, 1890-1913. H. Leon Prather, Sr. LC 77-74394. (Illus.). 186p. 1979. 40.00 (0-8386-2071-X) Fairleigh Dickinson.

Resurreccion Realidad o Ilusion? (Resurrection: Fact Or Fiction?) R. Beues. (SPA.). 1.50 (0-685-74980-0, 490257) Editorial Unilit.

*__Resurrected Holmes.__ Kaye. Date not set. pap. 14.95 (0-312-15639-1) St Martin.

Resurrected Holmes: New Cases from the Notes of John H. Watson, M. D. Ed. by Marvin Kaye. 353p. 1996. 24.95 (0-312-14037-1) St Martin.

*__Resurrecting Hope.__ George D. Perkin. pap. 16.30 (0-8307-1810-9) Regal.

Resurrecting Marx: The Analytical Marxists on Exploitation, Freedom, & Justice. David Gordon. 160p. (C). 1990. 39.95 (0-88738-390-4); pap. 21.95 (0-88738-878-7) Transaction Pubs.

Resurrecting the Body. Kenneth Arnold. 64p. (Orig.). 1992. pap. 2.20 (0-88028-130-8, 1166) Forward Movement.

Resurrecting the Past: A Joint Tribute to Adnan Bounni. Ed. by Paolo Matthiae et al. xxxvi, 407p. 1990. pap. text ed. 105.00 (90-6258-067-X, Pub. by Netherlands Inst NE) Eisenbrauns.

Resurrection. 1985. 10.00 (0-317-62132-7) St Mut.

Resurrection. Nicole Cooley. LC 96-2242. 96p. (C). 1996. pap. 10.95 (0-8071-2059-6) La State U Pr.

Resurrection. Florence DeGroat. LC 81-67782. (Universal Man Ser.: Vol. 2). (Illus.). 168p. (Orig.). 1981. pap. 6.50 (0-87516-456-0) DeVorss.

Resurrection. Margoe Jane. (Illus.). 64p. 1976. 4.00 (0-9602330-3-2) Margoe Jane.

Resurrection. Neville. 1966. pap. 10.95 (0-87516-076-X) DeVorss.

*__Resurrection.__ Ed. by Gerald O'Collins & Stephen T. Davis. 400p. 1997. 35.00 (0-19-815091-1) OUP.

*__Resurrection.__ David Remnick. 1998. pap. write for info. (0-375-75023-1, Vin) Random.

Resurrection. Leo Tolstoy. (Orig.). 1984. mass mkt. 4.95 (0-452-00718-6, Mer) NAL-Dutton.

Resurrection. Leo Tolstoy. Ed. by Richard F. Gustafson. (World's Classics Ser.). 528p. (Orig.). 1994. pap. 7.95 (0-19-283111-9) OUP.

Resurrection. Leo Tolstoy. Tr. by Vera Traill. (Classics Ser.). 576p. (Orig.). 1966. pap. 10.95 (0-14-044184-0, Penguin Classics) Viking Penguin.

Resurrection. William M. Valtos. 1988. 17.95 (0-931933-74-9, Univ Books) Carol Pub Group.

*__Resurrection.__ limited ed. A. C. Crispin. (Alien Ser.). 1997. mass mkt. 134.73 (0-446-16497-6, Aspect) Warner Bks.

Resurrection: A Short Play. Robert Villegas, Jr. (Lion Theatrical Ser.: No. 2). 1978. pap. 1.95 (0-930962-01-X) Villegas Pub.

*__Resurrection: A War Journey.__ Robin Gajdusek. LC 97-6150. 256p. 1997. pap. 16.00 (0-268-01660-7) U of Notre Dame Pr.

Resurrection: Interpreting the Easter Gospel. Rowan Williams. LC 93-48982. 144p. (Orig.). 1994. reprint ed. pap. 11.95 (0-8192-1615-1) Morehouse Pub.

Resurrection: Myth or Reality? John S. Spong. LC 93-25114. 1995. pap. 13.00 (0-06-067429-6) Harper SF.

Resurrection: The Confirmation of Clarence Thomas. John C. Danforth. 1994. text ed. 22.95 (0-02-906936-X, Free Press) Free Pr.

Resurrection: The Confirmation of Clarence Thomas. John C. Danforth. LC 94-25005. 1994. write for info. (0-453-03324-5, Viking) Viking Penguin.

*__Resurrection: The Ineffable Glory.__ E. M. Bounds. LC 96-79956. 142p. 1997. reprint ed. 12.95 (1-886787-03-4) Messengers Hope.

*__Resurrection: The Struggle for a New Russia.__ David Remnick. LC 96-47360. 398p. 1997. 25.95 (0-679-42377-X) Random.

Resurrection: True or False? Spiros Zodhiates. 129p. 1978. pap. 3.99 (0-89957-524-2) AMG Pubs.

Resurrection see Eleven Plays of William Butler Yeats

*__Resurrection, a War Journey: A Chronicle of Events During & Following the Attack on Fort Jeanne D'Arc at Metz, France, by F Company of the 379th Regiment of the 95th Infantry Division, November 14-21, 1944.__ Robin Gajdusek. LC 97-6150. 256p. 1997. 30.00 (0-268-01657-7) U of Notre Dame Pr.

Resurrection According to Matthew, Mark, & Luke. Norman Perrin. LC 76-47913. 96p. (Orig.). 1977. pap. 11.00 (0-8006-1248-5, 1-1248, Fortress Pr) Augsburg Fortress.

Resurrection According to Paul. John P. Mason. LC 92-47029. 168p. 1993. text ed. 79.95 (0-7734-2358-3) E Mellen.

Resurrection & Discipleship: Interpretive Models, Biblical Reflections, Theological Consequences. Thorwald Lorenzen. LC 95-31252. 225p. (Orig.). 1995. pap. 21.95 (1-57075-042-4) Orbis Bks.

Resurrection & Life. Bernard Sesboue. Tr. by Jane Burton. 112p. (Orig.). 1996. pap. text ed. 9.95 (0-8146-2267-4) Liturgical Pr.

Resurrection & Modern Man. Ignatius, IV. Tr. by Stephen Bigham from FRE. 96p. (Orig.). 1985. pap. 7.95 (0-88141-048-9) St Vladimirs.

Resurrection & Moral Order: An Outline for Evangelical Ethics. rev. ed. Oliver O'Donovan. 320p. (C). 1994. pap. 23.00 (0-8028-0692-9) Eerdmans.

Resurrection & Other Stories. Michael Lister. 150p. 1996. pap. 9.95 incl. audio (1-888146-01-X) St Matthews.

Resurrection & Parousia: A Traditional-Historical Study of Paul's Eschatology in I Corinthians 12. Joost Holleman. LC 96-5100. (Supplements to Novum Testamentum Ser.: No. 84). 233p. 1996. suppl. ed. 87.50 (90-04-10597-2) E J Brill.

Resurrection & Renewal: The Making of the Babi Movement in Iran, 1844-1850. Abbas Amanat. LC 88-47716. 528p. 1989. 57.50 (0-8014-2098-9) Cornell U Pr.

*__Resurrection & the Icon.__ Michel Quenot. LC 97-5312. 1997. write for info. (0-88141-149-3) St Vladimirs.

Resurrection at Sorrow Hill. Wilson Harris. 256p. 1994. 22.95 (0-571-16978-3) Faber & Faber.

*__Resurrection Chapter: I Corinthians 15.__ Fred Heyman. 24p. (Orig.). 1997. pap. 2.50 (1-880573-38-5) Grace WI.

Resurrection Day. (Mack Bolan Ser.: No. 3). 384p. 1985. mass mkt. 3.95 (0-373-61403-9) Harlequin Bks.

Resurrection Factor. Josh McDowell. 180p. 1992. pap. 10.99 (0-8407-4495-1) Nelson.

Resurrection (Five) Ed. by Chung H. Kwak. (Home Study Course). 40p. (Orig.). (C). 1980. pap. 4.00 (0-910621-14-4) HSA Pubns.

*__Resurrection from the Underground: Feodor Dostoevski.__ Rene Girard. Tr. by James G. Williams. LC 96-29582. 168p. 1997. 23.95 (0-8245-1608-7, Crossrd Herd) Crossroad NY.

Resurrection Hope. David A. Dean. 1992. student ed. write for info. (1-881909-00-X) Advent Christ Gen Conf.

Resurrection Hope: Leaders Guide. David A. Dean & Millie H. Griswold. 1992. teacher ed. write for info. (1-881909-01-8) Advent Christ Gen Conf.

*__Resurrection in the Cartoon.__ Robert Priest. 112p. 1997. pap. 12.00 (1-55022-313-5, Pub. by ECW Press CN) Genl Dist Srvs.

Resurrection Life & Power. Samuel L. Brengle. pap. 5.99 (0-88019-156-2) Schmul Pub Co.

Resurrection Life & Power. Samuel L. Brengle. 1978. reprint ed. 4.95 (0-86544-005-0) Salv Army Suppl South.

Resurrection Life, Bk. 6: A Study of the Elementary Principles of Christ. Ed. by Charles Cheatheam. (First Principles Ser.). (Orig.). 1992. student ed. 5.00 (0-923968-06-7) Shady Grove Ch Pubns.

Resurrection Life, Bk. 6: A Study of the Elementary Principles of Christ, Set. Ed. by Charles Cheatheam. (First Principles Ser.). (Orig.). 1992. 6.00 (0-685-54890-2) Shady Grove Ch Pubns.

Resurrection Love-Life. Barbara Dent. LC 93-1006. 160p. 1993. pap. 9.95 (0-8091-3405-5) Paulist Pr.

Resurrection Man. Eoin McNamee. 240p. 1996. pap. 12.00 (0-312-14716-3, Picador USA) St Martin.

Resurrection Man. Sean Stewart. LC 94-34587. 256p. (Orig.). 1995. 11.00 (0-441-00121-1) Ace Bks.

Resurrection Man. Sean Stewart. 1996. mass mkt. 5.99 (0-441-00339-7) Ace Bks.

Resurrection Man: A Novel. Eoin McNamee. LC 95-21825. 1995. 21.00 (0-312-13598-X, Picador USA) St Martin.

Resurrection Man: A Sarah Kelling & Max Bittersohn Mystery. large type ed. Charlotte MacLeod. LC 92-16313. 386p. 1992. reprint ed. lib. bdg. 18.95 (1-56054-457-0) Thorndike Pr.

Resurrection Mary: A Ghost Story. Kenan Heise. (Illus.). 200p. (Orig.). 1990. pap. text ed. 10.95 (0-924772-09-3) CH Bookworks.

Resurrection Narrative in Matthew: A Literary-Critical Examination. Keith H. Reeves. LC 93-36660. (Biblical Press Ser.: Vol. 19). 124p. 1993. text ed. 59.95 (0-7734-2384-2, Mellen Biblical Pr) E Mellen.

Resurrection of a Jenny. Chester L. Peek. (Illus.). 120p. (Orig.). 1994. per., pap. 19.95 (1-886196-00-1) Three Peaks.

Resurrection of a Kind. C. Rush. 112p. 1984. pap. text ed. 12.00 (0-08-030400-1, Pergamon Pr) Elsevier.

Resurrection of a Woman. Celeste Lasky. 465p. (Orig.). 1995. pap. 6.99 (0-9643331-0-4) Write On Pubns.

Resurrection of Anne Hutchinson. Robert H. Rimmer. LC 86-25472. 419p. 1986. 28.95 (0-87975-370-6) Prometheus Bks.

Resurrection of Aristocracy. Rudolph C. Evans. LC 87-83445. 336p. 1988. pap. 12.95 (0-915179-71-7, 94117) Loompanics.

Resurrection of Jesus. Gerd Luedemann. Tr. by John Bowden from GER. 224p. 1995. pap. 17.00 (0-8006-2792-X) Augsburg Fortress.

*__Resurrection of Jesus: New Considerations for Its Theological Interpretation.__ Kenan B. Osborne. LC 97-1669. 208p. (Orig.). 1997. pap. 14.95 (0-8091-3703-8) Paulist Pr.

Resurrection of Jesus Christ. Gerald O'Collins. (Pere Marquette Lectures). 1993. 15.00 (0-87462-548-3) Marquette.

Resurrection of Maltravers. Alexander Lernet-Holenia. Tr. by Joachim Neugroschel from GER. LC 88-80806. 223p. 1989. pap. 14.00 (0-941419-23-1, Eridanos Library) Marsilio Pubs.

Resurrection of Nature: Political Theory & the Human Character. J. Budziszewski. LC 86-6283. 224p. 1986. 37.50 (0-8014-1900-X) Cornell U Pr.

Resurrection of Rights in Poland. Jacek Kurczewski. LC 93-9237. 488p. 1993. Alk. paper. 75.00 (0-19-825685-X) OUP.

Resurrection of the American Spirit. Dean Sikes. 35p. (Orig.). 1995. pap. 6.95 (0-937539-13-9) Executive Bks.

Resurrection of the Black Phoenix: The Wizards of Nestalon, Bk. 1. G. K. Yancey. LC 93-93870. 64p. (Orig.). 1994. pap. 8.50 (1-56002-332-5, Univ Edtns) Aegina Pr.

Resurrection of the Body. Diana H. George. (Orig.). 1989. pap. 8.95 (0-938535-81-1) Salt-Works Pr.

Resurrection of the Body: Touch in D. H. Lawrence. Kathryn A. Walterscheid. LC 92-23320. (American University Studies: English Language & Literature: Ser. IV, Vol. 157). 144p. (C). 1994. text ed. 46.95 (0-8204-2019-0) P Lang Pubng.

Resurrection of the Body in Western Christianity, 200-1336. Caroline W. Bynum. LC 94-17299. (Lectures on the History of Religions Ser.: No. 15). 384p. 1995. 40.00 (0-231-08126-X) Col U Pr.

Resurrection of the Body in Western Christianity 200-1336. Caroline B. Walker. (Illus.). 384p. 1996. pap. 17.50 (0-231-08127-8) Col U Pr.

Resurrection of the Chinese Church. Tony Lambert. 368p. (C). 1991. pap. 12.99 (0-87788-728-4, OMF Books) Shaw Pubs.

Resurrection of the Chinese Church. Tony Lambert. 319p. (C). 1991. pap. 15.95 (0-340-54997-1) H & S Ltd.

Resurrection of the Dead. Karl Barth. Ed. by Robert J. Kastenbaum. LC 76-19559. (Death & Dying Ser.). 1979. reprint ed. lib. bdg. 25.95 (0-405-09555-4) Ayer.

Resurrection of the Dead: Blackman Is Spiritually Dead. Alfred Ali. 59p. 1993. reprint ed. pap. 5.95 (0-9636025-1-9) A Ali Lit Wrks.

Resurrection of the Lord: Mystery of Faith. Pierre R. Bernard. Tr. by Francis V. Manning from FRE. LC 96-785. 144p. (Orig.). 1996. pap. 7.95 (0-8189-0741-X) Alba.

Resurrection of the Republican Ideal. Charles S. Goodwin. LC 95-3474. 170p. (C). 1995. lib. bdg. 47.50 (0-8191-9898-6) U Pr of Amer.

Resurrection of the Republican Ideal. Ed. by Charles S. Goodwin. LC 95-3474. 170p. (C). 1995. pap. text ed. 28.00 (0-8191-9899-4) U Pr of Amer.

Resurrection of Vicky. Car & Parts Staff. (Illus.). 218p. 1995. pap. text ed. 12.95 (1-880524-12-0) Cars & Parts.

Resurrection or Reincarnation? Ed. by Johann B. Metz & Hermann Haring. (Concilium Ser.). 1993. 15.00 (0-88344-872-6) Orbis Bks.

Resurrection Promises. Leonard H. Budd & Roger G. Talbott. Ed. by Michael L. Sherer. LC 86-28314. (Orig.). 1987. pap. 6.55 (0-89536-850-1, 7809) CSS OH.

Resurrection Psychology: An Understanding of the Human Personality Based on the Life & Teachings of Jesus. Margaret G. Alter. LC 94-14928. 194p. (Orig.). (C). 1994. pap. 12.95 (0-8294-0782-0, ZCBALTER) Loyola Pr.

Resurrection Reconsidered. Gavin D'Costa. 240p. (Orig.). 1996. pap. 18.99 (1-85168-113-2, 577) Onewrld Pubns.

Resurrection Reconsidered: Thomas & John in Controversy. Gregory J. Riley. 1995. pap. 18.00 (0-8006-2846-2, Fortress Pr) Augsburg Fortress.

*__Resurrection Remember.__ Rowland. 6.30 (0-687-36169-9) Abingdon.

Resurrection Row. Anne Perry. 192p. 1986. mass mkt. 6.99 (0-449-21067-7, Crest) Fawcett.

Resurrection, Sex & God: Essays on the Foundations of Faith. Arthur F. Ide et al. LC 90-33786. (Illus.). 101p. (Orig.). 1990. pap. 5.00 (0-926899-01-5) Minuteman Pr.

Resurrection Tomb. E. Raymond Capt. LC 88-71638. (Illus.). 80p. 1988. pap. 3.00 (0-934666-24-5) Artisan Sales.

Resurrection 2027. J. G. Eccarius. 192p. (Orig.). 1995. pap. 7.00 (0-9622937-7-6) III Pub.

*__Resurrection Update: Collected Poems, 1975-1997.__ James Galvin. 1997. 25.00 (1-55659-121-7); pap. 16.95 (1-55659-122-5) Copper Canyon.

Resurrectionist. Thomas F. Monteleone. 416p. 1997. mass mkt. 6.50 (0-446-60399-6) Warner Bks.

Resurrectionists. Russell Working. LC 86-30754. (Iowa Short Fiction Award Ser.). 181p. 1987. text ed. 19.95 (0-87745-164-8) U of Iowa Pr.

Resurrections. David B. Axelrod. 118p. 1989. 20.00 (0-685-49063-7); pap. 10.00 (0-685-49064-5) Cross-Cultrl NY.

Resurrections. Simon Louvish. LC 94-10509. 252p. 1994. 18.95 (1-56858-014-2) FWEW.

Resurvey of the Fish Parasites of Western Lake Erie. Ralph V. Bangham. (Bulletin New Ser.: Vol. 4, No. 2). 1972. 2.00 (0-86727-061-6) Ohio Bio Survey.

Resuscitation: Key Data. 2nd ed. T. M. Craft. 112p. 1995. pap. 29.50 (1-85996-060-X, Pub. by Bios Scientific UK) Coronet Bks.

Resuscitation: Key Data: Treatment Protocols for Trauma, Burns, Cardiac Arrhythmias, Drug Overdose, Etc. M. J. Parr & T. M. Craft. 96p. (Orig.). 1994. pap. 29.50 (1-872748-53-8, Pub. by Bios Scientific UK) Coronet Bks.

Resuscitation & Artificial Hypothermia. Vladimir A. Negovskii. Tr. by Basil Haigh from RUS. LC 62-21589. 328p. reprint ed. pap. 93.50 (0-317-07804-6, 2020658) Bks Demand.

Resuscitation & Emergency Care. Royal Life Saving Society-Australia Staff. 96p. (gr. 13). 1994. pap. text ed. write for info. (0-8151-7322-9) Mosby Yr Bk.

Resuscitation Handbook. Raymond M. Fish. (Problems in Primary Care Ser.). 208p. 1989. text ed. 45.00 (0-87489-540-5) Med Econ.

Resuscitation of a Hanged Man. Denis Johnson. 1991. 19.95 (0-374-24949-0) FS&G.

Resuscitation of a Hanged Man. Denis Johnson. 272p. 1992. pap. 10.95 (0-14-016522-3, Penguin Bks) Viking Penguin.

Resynaptic Modulation of Postsynaptic Receptors in Mental Diseases. Intro. by Andre I. Salama. (Annals Ser.: Vol. 430). 137p. 1984. pap. 31.00 (0-89766-255-5); lib. bdg. 31.00 (0-89766-254-7) NY Acad Sci.

Resz Haladoknak, Vol. 2. Hegedus Lajos. 180p. pap. write for info. (0-318-55622-7, 094-1X) Saphrograph.

Resz Kezdoknek, Vol. 1. Hegedus Lajos. 184p. pap. write for info. (0-318-55621-9, 094-1) Saphrograph.

Ret. Mark Dunster. 12p. (Orig.). 1990. pap. 4.00 (0-89642-183-X) Linden Pubs.

RET: A Problem Solving Workbook. Alan Baldon & Albert Ellis. 116p. (Orig.). 1993. pap. 13.95 (0-917476-23-9) A Ellis Institute.

RET: Purchase & Sale of Real Property, 3 vols. C. Holtzschue. (Real Estate Transactions Ser.). 1987. Updates. ring bd. write for info. (0-8205-1658-9) Bender.

RET Resource Book for Practitioners. Ed. by Janet L. Wolfe & Michael E. Bernard. 275p. (Orig.). (C). 1993. pap. 39.95 (0-917476-22-0) A Ellis Institute.

Retablo de la Avaricia, la Lujuria y la Muerte. Ramon Del Valle-Inclan. Ed. by Ricardo Domenech. (Nueva Austral Ser.: Vol. 170). (SPA.). 1991. pap. text ed. 24.95 (84-239-1970-6) Elliots Bks.

Retahila. Alberto M. Herrera. LC 93-73852. (Coleccion Caniqui). 116p. (Orig.). (SPA.). 1994. pap. 9.95 (0-89729-711-3) Ediciones.

Retail Accounting & Financial Control. 5th ed. Robert Zimmerman. LC 89-22664. 412p. 1990. text ed. 120.00 (0-471-63218-X) Wiley.

Retail Ad Design. Clip Away Staff. 208p. 1991. pap. 19.95 (0-8306-3840-7, 3840, Liberty Hall Pr) TAB Bks.

Retail Advertising Manual. Ed. by Judy Y. Ocko. (Illus.). 300p. 1987. 89.95 (0-934590-18-4) Retail Report.

Retail & Restaurant. Compiled by Rockport Publishers Editorial Staff. (Design Library Ser.). (Illus.). 80p. 1996. pap. write for info. (1-56496-338-1) Rockport Pubs.

Retail Audit. Date not set. write for info. (0-88061-083-2) Intl Loss Cntrl.

Retail Banking: Serving the Financial Needs of Consumers. 1990. pap. 34.95 (0-912857-60-9) Inst Finan Educ.

*__Retail Banking: Survey Report.__ 100p. 1995. 145.00 (0-89982-432-3) Am Bankers.

*__Retail Banking: Survey Report.__ (Annual Ser.). 100p. (C). 1996. text ed. 218.00 (0-89982-008-5) Am Bankers.

Retail Banking in the 1990's. Ed. by D. Dassesse et al. (C). 1989. 85.00 (0-85297-294-6, Pub. by Inst Bankers UK) St Mut.

Retail Banking Revolution. Ed. by Peter Allen. 200p. 1985. pap. text ed. 295.00 (0-931634-60-1) FIND-SVP.

Retail Banking Series, 3 pts. Incl. Financial Performance of Banks. student ed. 18.00 (0-685-63286-5, 623400); Financial Performance of Banks. teacher ed. 27.00 (0-685-67740-0, 623401); Retail Management. student ed. 18.00 (0-685-63288-1, 622000); Retail Management. teacher ed. 24.00 (0-685-67741-9, 622001); Sales Management. student ed. 18.00 (0-685-63290-3, 623000); Sales Management. teacher ed. 24.00 (0-685-67742-7, 623001); write for info. (0-318-69954-0) Am Bankers.

Retail Banking Technology: Strategies & Resources That Seize the Competitive Advantage. Michael Violano. LC 92-10079. 256p. 1992. text ed. 85.00 (0-471-53174-X) Wiley.

Retail Business Management. 3rd rev. ed. Karen R. Gillespie et al. LC 82-21700. (Illus.). 480p. 1983. text ed. 32.80 (0-07-023228-8) McGraw.

*__Retail-Business Planning Guide.__ Warren G. Purdy. 350p. 1997. pap. 19.95 (1-880394-31-6) Inc Pub MA.

Retail Buying. 4th ed. Jay Diamond & Gerald Pintel. LC 92-24266. 384p. (C). 1992. text ed. 60.00 (0-13-755497-4) P-H.

Retail Buying. 5th ed. Jay Diamond & Gerald Pintel. LC 96-24452. 384p. 1996. 53.27 (0-13-496464-0) P-H.

Retail Buying: From Staples to Fashions to Fads. Richard Clodfelter. LC 92-19601. 372p. 1993. text ed. 38.50 (0-8273-5058-9) Delmar.

Retail Buying from Staples to Fashions to Fads Instructor's Guide. Richard Clodfelter. 106p. 1993. teacher ed., pap. 17.00 (0-8273-5059-7) Delmar.

Retail Change. Ed. by Rosemary Bromley & Colin Thomas. 1993. 75.00 (1-85728-059-8, Pub. by UCL Pr UK); pap. 25.00 (1-85728-060-1, Pub. by UCL Pr UK) Taylor & Francis.

Retail Detective Training Manual: How to Conduct the Observation, Surveillance, & Apprehension of Shop Lifters. Jim Walker. 100p. (Orig.). (C). 1997. pap. 35.00 (0-918487-15-3) Thomas Pubns TX.

Retail Development in the UK. Euromonitor Staff. 110p. (C). 1988. 1,125.00 (0-86338-316-5, Pub. by Euromonitor Pubns UK) Gale.

*__Retail Distribution Management.__ Ed. by John Fernie. (Transport & Logistics). 1991. 60.00 (0-7494-0030-7) Kogan Page Ltd.

Retail Distribution Strategies Two Thousand: Seven Leading Perspectives. 140p. 1992. pap. 124.00 (0-89982-345-9, 089500) Am Bankers.

*__Retail Entertainment.__ Retail Reporting Staff. Date not set. 39.95 (0-688-15720-3) Morrow.

Retail Environment. Ken Jones & Jim Simmons. LC 89-49763. (Illus.). 512p. (C). (gr. 13). 1990. text ed. 75.00 (0-415-04984-9, A5499) Routledge.

Retail Environment: Dynamics of Cash in the Payments System. Business Communications Co., Inc. Staff. 275p. 1983. 1,550.00 (0-89336-316-2, G-066A) BCC.

Retail Fashion Promotion & Advertising. Mary F. Drake et al. (Illus.). 368p. (C). 1991. text ed. 54.00 (0-02-330029-9, Macmillan Coll) P-H.

Retail Fee Income Opportunities. Gary W. Koeb. 1993. text ed. 195.00 (1-55738-723-0) Irwin Prof Pubng.

Retail Financial Services, Set. 218p. 170.00 (1-871682-91-6, Pub. by Euromoney UK) Am Educ Systs.

Retail Florist Business. 5th ed. Peter B. Pfahl & P. Blair Pfahl, Jr. 400p. 1994. 45.25 (0-8134-2967-6) Interstate.

Retail Flower Shop Operation. Redbook Florist Services Educational Advisory Committee. LC 91-73529. (Encycloflora Ser.). (Illus.). 478p. (Orig.). 1991. pap. text ed. 39.95 (1-56963-016-X) Redbk Florist.

An Asterisk (*) at the beginning of an entry indicates that the title is appearing in BIP for the first time.

Retail Image & Display. Vilma Barr & Katherine Field. LC 96-20790. 1996. 47.50 (*0-86636-339-4*); pap. write for info. (*0-86636-530-3*) PBC Intl Inc.

***Retail Image & Display.** PBC International Staff. Date not set. 47.50 (*0-688-15372-0*) Morrow.

Retail Image & Graphic Identity. Joan G. Salb. 208p. 1995. 49.95 (*0-934590-62-1*) Retail Report.

Retail in Detail: How to Start & Manage a Small Retail Business. Ronald L. Bond. Ed. by Linda Pinkham. LC 96-1648. (Successful Business Library). 184p. (Orig.). 1996. pap. 15.95 (*1-55571-371-8*) Oasis Pr OR.

***Retail in the Digital Age.** Nigel Cope. 1997. pap. text ed. 19.95 (*0-906097-59-2*, Pub. by Bowerdean Pubng UK) LPC InBook.

Retail Incubators: Linking Entrepreneurship & Commercial Development. Carol Patrylick. Ed. by Jenny Murphy. 38p. (Orig.). 1988. pap. 18.00 (*0-317-04810-4*) Natl Coun Econ Dev.

***Retail Industry Indicators.** NRF Staff. 85p. 1997. pap. 35.00 (*0-614-30167-X*) Nat Retail Fed.

Retail Jeweller's Guide. 5th ed. Kenneth Blakemore. (Illus.). 424p. 1994. pap. 38.95 (*0-7506-2042-0*) Buttrwrth-Heinemann.

Retail Jewellers Guide. 5th ed. Kenneth Blakemore. 416p. 1988. 62.95 (*0-408-02913-7*) Buttrwrth-Heinemann.

Retail Location: A Micro-Sale Perspective. Stephen Brown. 329p. 1992. 68.95 (*1-85628-049-7*, Pub. by Avebury Pub UK) Ashgate Pub Co.

***Retail Loss Control.** Peter Jones. 256p. 1997. pap. 34.95 (*0-7506-3188-0*) Buttrwrth-Heinemann.

Retail Loss Control. Peter H. Jones. (Illus.). 246p. 1990. 44.95 (*0-408-05562-6*) Buttrwrth-Heinemann.

Retail Management. (Study Units Ser.). 1977. pap. 9.00 (*0-89401-115-4*) Didactic Syst.

Retail Management. R. Cox & P. Brittain. 305p. (Orig.). (C). 1988. 90.00 (*0-685-39817-X*, Pub. by Inst Pur & Supply UK) St Mut.

Retail Management. Ronald W. Hasty & James Reardon. LC 96-15987. (Series in Marketing). 1996. text ed. write for info. (*0-07-027031-7*) McGraw.

Retail Management. Robert F. Lusch et al. 704p. (C). 1990. text ed. write for info. (*0-538-80294-4*, SF62AA) S-W Pub.

Retail Management. 2nd ed. Roger Cox & Paul Brittain. 320p. (Orig.). 1993. pap. 37.50 (*0-7121-1825-X*, Pub. by Pitman Pub Ltd UK) Trans-Atl Phila.

Retail Management. 2nd ed. Avijit Ghosh. LC 93-72475. 802p. (C). 1994. text ed. 70.50 (*0-03-076749-0*) Dryden Pr.

Retail Management. 2nd ed. Avijit Ghosh. (C). 1994. suppl. ed., teacher ed., pap. text ed. 49.75 (*0-03-094859-2*) HB Coll Pubs.

***Retail Management.** 3rd ed. Roger Cox & Paul Brittain. 320p. 1996. pap. 37.50 (*0-7121-1061-5*, Pub. by Pitman Pub Ltd UK) Trans-Atl Phila.

Retail Management. 3rd ed. Avijit Ghosh. 746p. (C). 1994. text ed. 56.00 (*0-03-021512-9*) Dryden Pr.

Retail Management. 6th ed. Berman & Evans. 800p. 1994. text ed. 77.33 (*0-02-308661-0*, Macmillan Coll) P-H.

Retail Management. 6th ed. Ronald W. Stampfl et al. LC 87-10555. 876p. 1988. Net. text ed. 49.50 (*0-471-85094-2*) Wiley.

Retail Management see Retail Banking Series

Retail Marketing. Ed. by Gary Akehurst & Nicholas Alexander. LC 96-14526. (Retailing Ser.). 200p. (Orig.). (C). 1996. pap. 21.00 (*0-7146-4175-8*, Pub. by F Cass Pubs UK) Intl Spec Bk.

Retail Marketing. 2nd ed. Robert F. Lusch et al. LC 92-2394. 1993. text ed. 75.95 (*0-538-82697-5*) S-W Pub.

Retail Marketing: For Employees, Managers & Entrepreneurs. Warren G. Meyer et al. 1988. pap. text ed. 7.68 (*0-07-002457-X*); pap. text ed. 7.68 (*0-07-002458-8*) McGraw.

Retail Marketing: For Employees, Managers & Entrepreneurs. 8th ed. Warren G. Meyer et al. 1988. text ed. 21.80 (*0-07-041698-2*) McGraw.

Retail Marketing Management. Ed. by W. Walter & W. White. 276p. (C). 1990. 150.00 (*0-685-39816-1*, Pub. by Inst Pur & Supply UK) St Mut.

Retail Marketing Plans. McDonald. 1993. 62.95 (*0-7506-0154-X*) Buttrwrth-Heinemann.

Retail Marketing Plans: How to Prepare Them, How to Use Them. Malcolm B. McDonald & Chrsitopher C. Tideman. 220p. 1996. pap. 24.95 (*0-7506-2021-8*) Buttrwrth-Heinemann.

Retail Marketing Strategy: Planning, Implementation, & Control. A. Coskun Samli. LC 87-37575. 373p. 1989. text ed. 69.50 (*0-89930-249-1*, SRG/, Quorum Bks) Greenwood.

Retail Merchandising. 10th ed. Samson. 1988. text ed. 43.95 (*0-538-19280-1*) S-W Pub.

Retail Merchandising. 11th ed. Samson. (SB - Marketing Education Ser.). 1993. 3.95 (*0-538-61328-9*) S-W Pub.

Retail Merchandising. 11th ed. Samson. (SB - Marketing Education Ser.). 1993. wbk. ed., pap. 13.95 (*0-538-61748-9*) S-W Pub.

Retail Merchandising - Consumer Goods. 10th ed. Samson. (SB - Marketing Education Ser.). 1988. 3.95 (*0-538-19283-6*) S-W Pub.

Retail Merchandising - Consumer Goods & Service. 11th ed. Samson. (SB - Marketing Education Ser.). 1993. student ed., text ed. 42.95 (*0-538-61326-2*) S-W Pub.

Retail Merchandising--Consumer Goods. 10th ed. Samson. (SB - Marketing Education Ser.). 1988. 186.95 (*0-538-28815-9*); 186.95 (*0-538-28816-7*) S-W Pub.

Retail Merchandising--Consumer Goods. 10th ed. Samson. (SB - Marketing Education Ser.). 1988. 186.95 (*0-538-28817-5*) S-W Pub.

Retail Merchandising & Selling, 3 vols., Vol. 1. 3rd rev. ed. Brooks Jensen. LC 95-92122. (Retailing to Win! Ser.). (Illus.). 240p. (Orig.). 1995. pap. 14.95 (*0-9645690-0-0*) Retail Sales.

Retail Merchandising, Consumer Goods. 11th ed. Samson. (SB - Marketing Education Ser.). 1993. wbk. ed., pap. 13.95 (*0-538-61749-7*) S-W Pub.

Retail Monitor Nineteen Ninety, 12 issues, Set. Euromonitor Staff. (C). 1989. 1,100.00 (*0-685-37366-5*, Pub. by Euromonitor Pubns UK) Gale.

Retail Monitor Nineteen Ninety-One, 12 issues, Set. Euromonitor Staff. (C). 1989. 1,200.00 (*0-685-37362-2*, Pub. by Euromonitor Pubns UK) Gale.

Retail Patronage Theory Proceedings. Ed. by Robert F. Lusch & William R. Darden. 1981. 17.00 (*0-931880-02-5*) U OK Ctr Econ.

***Retail Power Plays.** Wileman. LC 97-14139. 1997. 40.00 (*0-8147-9331-2*) NYU Pr.

Retail Price Cutting & Its Control by Manufacturers. Albert Haring. LC 75-39247. (Getting & Spending: The Consumer's Dilemma Ser.). (Illus.). 1976. reprint ed. 23.95 (*0-405-08021-2*) Ayer.

Retail Promotion Idea Book: 500 Creative Ways to Attract Customers to Stores & Shopping Centers. Ross Simmons. 272p. (Orig.). 1995. pap. 24.95 (*1-886514-00-3*) Prosprty Pub.

Retail Revolution: Market Transformation, Investment, & Labor in the Modern Department Store. Barry Bluestone et al. LC 80-26036. (Illus.). 160p. 1980. text ed. 49.95 (*0-86569-052-9*, Auburn Hse) Greenwood.

Retail Sales Tax: An Appraisal of New Issues. Daniel C. Morgan. (Illus.). 204p. 1964. 14.00 (*0-299-03100-4*) U of Wis Pr.

Retail Salesperson: A Programmed Text. 2nd ed. F. E. Hartzler. (Illus.). 1978. text ed. 14.68 (*0-07-026967-X*) McGraw.

Retail Sector: A Review of Floorspace, Building Type, Market Potential & Construction Activity, Great Britain. G. Samuelsson-Brown & S. Whittome. 1991. lib. bdg. 1,280.00 (*0-86022-315-9*, Pub. by Build Servs Info Assn UK) St Mut.

Retail Security & Loss Prevention. Read Hayes. 247p. 1991. 49.95 (*0-7506-9038-0*) Buttrwrth-Heinemann.

Retail Security & Shrinkage Protection. Philip P. Purpura. 336p. 1993. 42.95 (*0-7506-9274-X*) Buttrwrth-Heinemann.

Retail Security Policy Manual. K. R. Grover. 96p. 1992. 39.95 (*0-7506-9295-2*) Buttrwrth-Heinemann.

Retail Security vs. the Shoplifter: Confronting the Shoplifter While Protecting the Merchant. George L. Keckeisen. 102p. 1993. pap. 18.95 (*0-398-06198-X*) C C Thomas.

Retail Security vs. the Shoplifter: Confronting the Shoplifter While Protecting the Merchant. George L. Keckeisen. 102p. (C). 1993. text ed. 29.95 (*0-398-05830-X*) C C Thomas.

***Retail Side of Golf: Trends & Techniques.** unabridged ed. (NGF Info Pacs Ser.). (Illus.). 262p. (Orig.). 1996. pap. 45.00 (*1-57701-030-2*) Natl Golf.

Retail Store Planning & Design Manual. 2nd ed. Michael J. Lopez. LC 94-42640. (NRF Publishing Program Ser.). 224p. 1995. text ed. 135.00 (*0-471-07629-5*) Wiley.

Retail Structure. Ed. by Gary Akehurst & Nicholas Alexander. LC 96-14523. (Retailing Ser.). 200p. (Orig.). (C). 1996. pap. 21.00 (*0-7146-4176-6*, Pub. by F Cass Pubs UK) Intl Spec Bk.

Retail Structure in Europe. Euromonitor Staff. (C). 1990. write for info. (*0-318-67340-1*, Pub. by Euromonitor Pubns UK) Gale.

Retail Technology in Europe. Euromonitor Staff. 60p. (C). 1988. 825.00 (*0-86338-331-9*, Pub. by Euromonitor Pubns UK) Gale.

Retail Technology in the U. K. Euromonitor Staff. 130p. (C). 1988. 975.00 (*0-685-44989-0*, Pub. by Euromonitor Pubns UK) Gale.

Retail Tenant Directory, 1992. rev. ed. Ed. by Adrienne Toth et al. 1992. 325.00 (*0-911790-04-7*, Monitor Bk) Trade Dimensns.

Retail Tenant Directory, 1994. rev. ed. Ed. by Adrienne Toth et al. 1994. 325.00 (*0-911790-17-9*) Trade Dimensns.

Retail Tenant Directory, 1995. rev. ed. Ed. by Adrienne Toth et al. 1995. 325.00 (*0-911790-13-6*) Trade Dimensns.

Retail Trade in the U.K. 1987-88. Euromonitor Staff. 309p. (C). 1987. 825.00 (*0-86338-222-3*, Pub. by Euromonitor Pubns UK) Gale.

Retail Trade in the United Kingdom. 150p. 1985. 160.00 (*0-686-71956-5*, Pub. by Euromonitor Pubns UK) St Mut.

***Retail Wheeling: A Guide for End-Users.** 2nd ed. Peter C. Christensen. LC 96-9920. 1996. 89.95 (*0-87814-651-2*) PennWell Bks.

***Retail Working Papers: The Strategic Impact of Automated Systems on the Retail Enterprise.** Schreiber, Harry & Associates, Ltd. Staff. LC 96-77413. (Illus.). x, 172p. 1996. 32.00 (*0-9653165-0-5*, 101) Hexagon Pr Inc.

Retail/Commercial Building see Real Estate TaxPak (TM) USA

***Retailer's Guide to Loss Prevention & Security.** Donald J. Horan. 350p. 1996. 49.95 (*0-8493-8110-X*) CRC Pr.

Retailer's Manual. Samuel H. Terry. Ed. by Henry Assael. LC 78-316. (Century of Marketing Ser.). 1979. reprint ed. lib. bdg. 35.95 (*0-405-11179-7*) Ayer.

Retailing. Anderson. Date not set. teacher ed., pap. text ed. write for info. (*0-314-01310-5*) West Pub.

Retailing. Dickinson. (SB - Marketing Education Ser.). 1997. wbk. ed., pap. 12.95 (*0-538-82687-8*) S-W Pub.

***Retailing.** Dunne. (C). 1998. text ed. write for info. (*0-03-024758-6*); teacher ed., pap. text ed. 40.00 (*0-03-024819-1*) HB Coll Pubs.

Retailing. Patrick M. Dunne et al. (C). 1991. text ed. write for info. (*0-538-81443-8*, SF65AA) S-W Pub.

Retailing. Lucas. (C). 1994. suppl. ed., teacher ed., pap. 5.96 (*0-395-69237-7*) HM.

Retailing. Lucas. (C). 1994. student ed., pap. 19.16 (*0-395-56793-9*) HM.

Retailing. Lucas. (C). 1994. text ed. 70.36 (*0-395-56792-0*) HM.

Retailing. Lorraine Thornton. 1996. pap. 24.95 (*0-949142-56-5*, Pub. by Stirling Pr AT) Intl Spec Bk.

Retailing. 2nd ed. Dunne & Robert F. Lusch. (SB - Marketing Education Ser.). 1995. text ed. 72.95 (*0-538-84136-2*) S-W Pub.

Retailing. 4th ed. J. Barry Mason et al. (C). 1990. student ed., text ed. 21.95 (*0-256-09177-3*) Irwin.

Retailing. 4th ed. J. Barry Mason et al. 720p. (C). 1990. text ed. 60.95 (*0-256-08981-7*) Irwin.

Retailing. 5th ed. Dale M. Lewison. (Illus.). 912p. (C). 1993. text ed. 72.67 (*0-02-370530-2*, Macmillan Coll) P-H.

Retailing. 5th ed. J. Barry Mason et al. LC 93-21286. (Series in Marketing). 704p. (C). 1993. text ed. 69.95 (*0-256-12002-1*) Irwin Prof Pubng.

Retailing. 6th ed. Jay Diamond & Gerald Pintel. LC 95-22285. 417p. 1995. text ed. 75.00 (*0-13-448384-7*) P-H.

***Retailing.** 6th ed. Dale M. Lewison. LC 96-36764. (Illus.). 800p. (C). 1996. text ed. 72.67 (*0-13-461427-5*) P-H.

Retailing: Canadian Version. J. Barry Mason et al. 448p. (C). 1990. text ed. 54.95 (*0-256-07865-3*) Irwin.

Retailing: Case Problems. 2nd ed. A. Edward Spitz. 300p. 1989. teacher ed. write for info. (*0-318-66384-8*, H21272) P-H.

Retailing: Concepts, Strategy & Information. Carol H. Anderson. Ed. by Burvikovs. 800p. (C). 1993. text ed. 60.25 (*0-314-92052-8*) West Pub.

Retailing: New Perspectives. 2nd ed. Dorothy S. Rogers et al. 570p. (C). 1992. text ed. 55.25 (*0-03-054172-7*) Dryden Pr.

Retailing: Shopping, Society & Space. Larry O'Brien & Frank Harris. 224p. (C). 1990. 38.95 (*0-8464-1515-1*) Beekman Pubs.

Retailing: Theories & Practices for Today & Tomorrow: Proceedings of the Fourth Triennial National Retailing Conference Presented by the Academy of Marketing Science & the American Collegiate Retailing Association, Richmond, VA, October 22-24, 1994. National Retailing Conference (1994: Richmond, VA) Staff. Ed. by Robert L. King. (Special Conference Ser.: Vol. 7). 189p. 1994. reprint ed. pap. 53.90 (*0-608-00731-5*, 2061507) Bks Demand.

Retailing, Consumption, & Capital: Towards the New Retail Geography. Neil Wrigley. 1996. pap. 36.94 (*0-582-22824-7*) Addison-Wesley.

Retailing Environments in Developing Countries. Allan M. Findlay et al. LC 89-70143. 304p. (C). (gr. 13). 1990. text ed. 74.95 (*0-415-03739-5*, A4562) Routledge.

Retailing, International. 4th ed. J. Barry Mason et al. (C). 1992. student ed., text ed. 29.95 (*0-256-11410-2*) Irwin.

Retailing Management. Michael Levy & Barton A. Weitz. 864p. (C). 1991. text ed. 64.95 (*0-256-05989-6*) Irwin.

Retailing Management. 2nd ed. Michael Levy & Barton A. Weitz. LC 94-26274. (Marketing Ser.). 736p. (C). 1994. text ed. 69.95 (*0-256-13661-0*) Irwin.

***Retailing Management.** 3rd ed. Michael Levy. (Series in Marketing). 1997. write for info. (*0-256-22346-7*) Irwin Prof Pubng.

***Retailing Management.** 3rd ed. Michael Levy. LC 97-25683. (Series in Marketing). 1997. write for info. (*0-07-115387-X*) McGraw.

Retailing Management. William R. Davidson et al. LC 83-23378. (Illus.). 796p. reprint ed. pap. 180.00 (*0-7837-3505-7*, 2057838) Bks Demand.

***Retailing Management: A Planning Approach.** Larry D. Redinbaugh. (Illus.). 447p. (C). 1992. text ed. 60.00 (*1-878907-68-9*) TechBooks.

Retailing Merchandising & Control: Concepts & Problems. Robert J. Minichiello. 216p. (C). 1990. pap. text ed. 31.95 (*0-256-06767-8*) Irwin.

Retailing of Financial Services. Peter J. McGoldrick. LC 94-7269. 1994. write for info. (*0-07-707613-3*) McGraw.

Retailing Principles & Practices. 7th ed. Warren G. Meyer et al. LC 80-24885. (Illus.). 560p. (gr. 11-12). 1982. text ed. 25.16 (*0-07-041693-1*) McGraw.

Retailing Triumphs & Blunders: Victims of Competition in the New Age of Marketing Management. Ronald D. Michman & Alan J. Greco. LC 95-19469. 288p. 1995. text ed. 65.00 (*0-89930-869-4*, Quorum Bks) Greenwood.

Retained by the People: A History of American Indians & the Bill of Rights. John R. Wunder. LC 93-9804. 312p. 1994. pap. 18.95 (*0-19-505563-2*) OUP.

Retaining & Flood Walls. LC 94-244. (Technical Engineering & Design Guides As Adapted from the U. S. Army Corps of Engineers Ser.: No. 4). 1994. pap. 44.00 (*0-87262-968-6*, ASCE Press) Am Soc Civil Eng.

Retaining At-Risk Students: The Role of Career & Vocational Education. Lloyd W. Tindall. (Information Ser.: No. 335). 48p. 1988. 6.00 (*0-318-42052-X*) Ctr Educ Trng Employ.

Retaining Foodservice Employees. Karen Drummon. (Illus.). 224p. 1992. pap. 31.95 (*0-442-00571-7*) Van Nos Reinhold.

Retaining Structures. Ed. by C. R. Clayton. 840p. 1993. 134.00 (*0-7844-1932-9*) Am Soc Civil Eng.

Retaining Wall. Barry Seiler. LC 79-12883. 54p. 1979. pap. 3.75 (*0-934332-16-9*) LEpervier Pr.

Retaining Wall & Sound Attenuator. (PCI Journal Reprints Ser.). 6p. 1981. pap. 10.00 (*0-686-40146-8*, JR242) P-PCI.

Retaining What You Receive: How to Guard Your Goods. Charles R. Vance. 114p. (Orig.). 1994. pap. 7.95 (*0-9641578-0-2*, TX3-805-178) Spirit of Victory.

Retaliation: A Guide to State Regulatory Taxes, Fees, Deposits & Other Requirements. annuals 488p. (C). 1995. ring bd. 175.00 (*0-89382-318-X*) Nat Assn Insurance.

Retaliation: A Guide to State Retaliatory Taxes, Deposits & Other Requirements: State Tax Forms, 2 vols., Set. Ed. by Carolyn Johnson. 730p. 1996. ring bd. 250.00 (*0-89382-380-5*) Nat Assn Insurance.

Retaliation: A Guide to State Retaliatory Taxes, Fees, Deposits & Other Requirements. 500p. (C). 1992. ring bd. 175.00 (*0-89382-221-3*) Nat Assn Insurance.

Retaliation: A Guide to State Retaliatory Taxes, Fees, Deposits & Other Requirements. 470p. 1994. ring bd. 175.00 (*0-89382-258-2*) Nat Assn Insurance.

Retaliation: A Guide to State Retaliatory Taxes, Fees, Deposits & Other Requirements. 5th rev. ed. Ed. by Carolyn Johnson. 514p. (Orig.). 1995. ring bd. 250.00 (*0-89382-379-1*, RET-ZM) Nat Assn Insurance.

Retard. Diane O'Reilly. LC 88-83478. 200p. 1989. 18.95 (*0-944435-05-X*) Glenbridge Pub.

Retardation in Young Children: A Developmental Study of Cognitive Deficit. Sarah Broman et al. 376p. 1987. text ed. 69.95 (*0-89859-989-X*) L Erlbaum Assocs.

Retarded Isn't Stupid, Mom! Sandra Z. Kaufman. LC 87-29915. 256p. 1988. text ed. 18.00 (*0-933716-96-6*, 966) P H Brookes.

Retarded Kids Need to Play: A Manual for Parents & Other Teachers: Includes Ideas & Programs for Involving Retarded Children in Physical Activities. fac. ed. Cynthia C. Hirst & Elaine Michaelis. LC 82-83929. (Illus.). 288p. 1983. reprint ed. pap. 82.10 (*0-608-00944-X*, 2061736) Bks Demand.

Retarding America: The Imprisonment of Potential. Michael S. Brunner. LC 93-5889. 1993. 12.95 (*0-89420-292-8*, Halcyon) Natl Book.

Retargetable C Compiler. Chris Fraser & David Hansen. 500p. (C). 1995. text ed. 60.25 (*0-8053-1670-1*) Benjamin-Cummings.

***Retargetable Code Generation for Digital Signal Processors.** LC 97-17690. 1997. text ed. 245.00 (*0-7923-9958-7*) Kluwer Ac.

***Retargetable Compilers for Embedded Core Processors: Methods & Experiences in Industrial Applications.** LC 97-21895. Date not set. text ed. 200.00 (*0-7923-9959-5*) Kluwer Ac.

RETC Proceedings, Nineteen Eighty-One, 2 vols., Set. Ed. by R. L. Bullock & H. J. Jacoby. LC 81-65517. (Illus.). 1686p. 1981. 10.00 (*0-89520-285-9*) SMM&E Inc.

RETC Proceedings, Nineteen Seventy-Four, 2 vols. Ed. by Harry C. Pattison & Elio D'Appolonia. LC 74-84644. (Illus.). 1843p. 1974. reprint ed. 10.00 (*0-89520-024-4*) SMM&E Inc.

RETC Proceedings, 1985. Ed. by C. David Mann & Martin N. Kelley. LC 85-70960. (Rapid Excavation & Tunneling Conference Ser.). (Illus.). 1278p. 1985. 10.00 (*0-89520-441-X*, 441-X) SMM&E Inc.

RETC Proceedings, 1987, 2 vols. Intro. by J. M. Jacobs & R. S. Hendricks. LC 87-60888. (Rapid Excavation & Tunneling Conference Ser.). (Illus.). 1379p. 1987. 89.00 (*0-87335-065-0*) SMM&E Inc.

RETC Proceedings, 1989. Ed. by Robert A. Pond & Patrick B. Kenny. LC 89-60829. (Illus.). 881p. 1989. 68.00 (*0-87335-083-9*, 083-9) SMM&E Inc.

RETC Proceedings, 1991. Ed. by W. D. Wightman & D. C. McCarry. LC 91-60874. (Illus.). 954p. 1991. 68.00 (*0-87335-101-0*, 101-0) SMM&E Inc.

***Reteaching Worksheet, Skills for Life.** 11th ed. Couch. (CA - Career Development Ser.). 1997. pap. 13.95 (*0-314-20337-0*) S-W Pub.

RETEC Extrusion Technology for the 90's: Charlotte, NC, September 28-29, 1992. Society of Plastics Engineers Staff. 320p. reprint ed. pap. 91.20 (*0-7837-4496-X*, 2044273) Bks Demand.

Retech, Inc., Plasma Centrifugal Furnace: Applications Analysis Report. (Illus.). 39p. (Orig.). (C). 1993. pap. text ed. 30.00 (*1-56806-668-6*) DIANE Pub.

Retell Stories: From Words to Conversation with Meaning. Laura P. Goepfert. (Illus.). 50p. 1986. 17.95 (*0-937857-02-5*, 1441) Speech Bin.

Retelling - Rereading: The Fate of Storytelling in Modern Times. Karl Kroeber. LC 91-20383. (Illus.). 260p. (C). 1992. text ed. 35.00 (*0-8135-1765-6*) Rutgers U Pr.

***Retelling Tales: Essays in Honor of Russell Peck.** Ed. by Tom Hahn & Alan Lupack. LC 97-9919. (Illus.). 312p. 1997. 81.00 (*0-85991-477-1*) Boydell & Brewer.

Retelling U. S. Religious History. Ed. by Thomas A. Tweed. LC 96-8106. 311p. (C). 1997. 40.00 (*0-520-20569-3*); pap. 13.95 (*0-520-20570-7*) U CA Pr.

Retention & Drainage Short Course, 1989: Washington Hilton, Washington, DC, April 12-14. Technical Association of the Pulp & Paper Industry Staff. LC 89-151799. (TAPPI Notes Ser.). (Illus.). 109p. pap. 31.10 (*0-8357-6342-0*, 2035614) Bks Demand.

***Retention & Its Prevention.** Jim Grant. (Orig.). 1997. pap. 14.95 (*1-56762-066-3*) Modern Learn Pr.

Retention & Productivity Strategies for Nurse Managers. Huston & Bessie L. Marquis. (Nursing Management Ser.). (Illus.). 494p. 1989. text ed. 37.50 (*0-397-54739-0*) Lppncott-Raven.

Retention & Selectivity in Liquid Chromatography: Prediction, Standardisation, & Phase Comparisons. Ed. by Roger M. Smith. LC 95-118959. (Journal of Chromatography Library: Vol. 57). 478p. 1995. 278.50 (*0-444-81539-2*) Elsevier.

R

Retention & Stability in Orthodontics. Ed. by Ravindra Nanda & Charles J. Burstone. (Illus.). 176p. 1993. text ed. 75.50 (*0-7216-4342-6*) Saunders.

Retention As a Function of the Method of Measurement. Leo J. Postman & Lucy Rau. LC 57-9951. (California University, University of California Publications in Psychology: Vol. 8, No. 3). 56p. reprint ed. pap. 25.00 (*0-317-08156-X*, 2021417) Bks Demand.

Retention of African-American Males in High School: A Study of African-American Male High School Dropouts, African-American Seniors & White Male Seniors. Annie S. Barnes. 172p. (C). 1992. lib. bdg. 47.50 (*0-8191-8508-6*) U Pr of Amer.

Retention of Bank Records. rev. ed. American Bankers Association Staff. 223p. 1990. 95.00 (*0-685-57996-4*) Am Bankers.

Retention of Land for Agriculture: Policy, Practice & Potential in New England. Frank Schnidman et al. LC 87-5580. 358p. (C). 1990. pap. text ed. 17.50 (*1-55844-109-3*) Lincoln Inst Land.

Retention of Records: A Guide for Retention & Disposal of Student Records. American Association of Collegiate Registrars & Admissions Officers Staff. 67p. reprint ed. pap. 25.00 (*0-317-26604-7*, 2024073) Bks Demand.

Retention of Title: A Practical Guide to 19 National Legislations. International Chamber of Commerce Staff. 64p. (Orig.). (C). 1989. pap. text ed. 39.95 (*92-842-1082-8*, 501, Pub. by ICC Pub SA FR) ICC Pub.

Retention Theory for Teachers. Madeline C. Hunter. LC 95-6569. 1967. pap. 11.95 (*0-8039-6316-5*) Corwin Pr.

Rethinking Abortion: Equal Choice, the Constitution, & Reproductive Politics. Mark A. Graber. LC 95-25448. 246p. 1996. text ed. 29.95 (*0-691-01142-7*) Princeton U Pr.

Rethinking Active Learning Eight Through Sixteen. Norman Beswick. LC 86-29358. 150p. 1987. 55.00 (*1-85000-159-6*, Falmer Pr); pap. text ed. 29.00 (*1-85000-160-X*, Falmer Pr) Taylor & Francis.

Rethinking AIDS: The Tragic Cost of Premature Consensus. Robert S. Root-Bernstein. LC 92-26843. 532p. 1993. 35.00 (*0-02-926905-9*, Free Press) Free Pr.

Rethinking AIDS Prevention: Cultural Approaches. Ed. by Ralph Bolton & Merrill Singer. LC 92-13820. 367p. 1992. pap. text ed. 29.00 (*2-88124-552-8*) Gordon & Breach.

Rethinking America. Sokolik. 1992. pap. 26.95 (*0-8384-2277-2*) Heinle & Heinle.

Rethinking America: A New Game Plan from American Innovators: Schools, Business, People, Work. Hedrick Smith. 1995. 25.00 (*0-679-43551-4*) Random.

Rethinking America: An Innovative Blueprint for America's Schools, Businesses & People at Work. Hedrick Smith. 512p. 1996. pap. 15.00 (*0-380-72821-4*) Avon.

***Rethinking American Indian History: Analysis, Methodology, & Historiography.** Donald L. Fixico. LC 97-4745. 1997. 30.00 (*0-8263-1818-5*); pap. 16.95 (*0-8263-1819-3*) U of NM Pr.

***Rethinking American Literature.** Ed. by Lil Brannon & Brenda M. Green. LC 97-15044. (Orig.). 1997. 22.95 (*0-8141-4119-6*) NCTE.

Rethinking America's Security: Beyond Cold War to New World Order. Ed. by Graham T. Allison. (Illus.). 320p. (C). 1992. pap. text ed. 12.95 (*0-393-96218-0*) Norton.

Rethinking Anthropology. 5th ed. Edmund R. Leach. (London School of Economics Monographs on Social Anthropology: No. 22). 146p. (C). 1961. pap. 18.50 (*0-485-19622-0*, Pub. by Athlone Pr UK) Humanities.

Rethinking Appraisal & Assessment. Ed. by Helen Simons & John Elliott. 224p. 1989. 95.00 (*0-335-09518-6*, Open Univ Pr); pap. 39.00 (*0-335-09517-8*, Open Univ Pr) Taylor & Francis.

Rethinking Architecture: A Reader in Cultural Theory. Neil Leach. LC 96-19406. 416p. 1997. pap. 22.95 (*0-415-12826-9*) Routledge.

Rethinking Architecture: A Reader in Cultural Theory. Neil Leach. LC 96-19406. 416p. (C). 1997. text ed. 74.95 (*0-415-12825-0*) Routledge.

Rethinking Architecture: Design Students & Physically Disabled People. Ed. by Raymond Lifchez. 1986. pap. 14.95 (*0-520-05899-2*) U CA Pr.

Rethinking Art History: Meditations on a Coy Science. Donald Preziosi. (Illus.). 296p. (C). 1991. reprint ed. pap. text ed. 15.00 (*0-300-04983-8*) Yale U Pr.

***Rethinking Attention Deficit Disorders.** Miriam C. Julkowski et al. LC 97-6106. 350p. (Orig.). 1997. pap. 27.95 (*1-57129-037-0*) Brookline Bks.

Rethinking Bakhtin: Extensions & Challenges. Ed. by Gary S. Morson & Caryl Emerson. (Studies in Russian Literature & Theory). 330p. 1989. pap. 18.95 (*0-8101-0810-0*) Northwestern U Pr.

Rethinking Beckett: A Collection of Critical Essays. Ed. by Lance S. Butler & Robin J. Davis. LC 89-10596. 270p. 1990. text ed. 39.95 (*0-312-03594-2*) St Martin.

Rethinking Blake's Textuality. Molly A. Rothenberg. LC 93-13510. (Illus.). 176p. 1993. text ed. 34.95 (*0-8262-0901-7*) U of Mo Pr.

Rethinking Borders. Ed. by John C. Welchman. LC 95-45761. 1996. text ed. 49.95 (*0-8166-2868-8*) U of Minn Pr.

Rethinking Borders. Ed. by John C. Welchman. LC 95-45761. 1996. pap. text ed. 19.95 (*0-8166-2869-6*) U of Minn Pr.

Rethinking Bretton Woods: Towards Equitable, Sustainable, & Participatory Development: Conference Report & Recommendations. Ed. & Intro. by Jo M. Griesgraber. 38p. (Orig.). (C). 1994. pap. 5.95 (*0-934255-14-8*) Center Concern.

***Rethinking Business Strategies for Africa.** 1997. write for info. (*0-614-25469-8*) Econ Intel.

***Rethinking Business Strategy for Africa.** 1997. write for info. (*0-614-25486-8*) Econ Intel.

Rethinking Business to Business Marketing. Paul Sherlock. 188p. 1990. 27.95 (*0-02-928615-8*, Free Press) Free Pr.

Rethinking C. L. R. James. Ed. by Grant Farred. 320p. (C). 1995. 53.95 (*1-55786-598-1*) Blackwell Pubs.

Rethinking C. L. R. James: A Critical Reader. Ed. by Grant Farred. 320p. (C). 1995. pap. 21.95 (*1-55786-599-X*) Blackwell Pubs.

***Rethinking Camelot: JFK, the Vietnam War, & U. S. Political Culture.** Noam Chomsky. 172p. 48.99 (*1-895431-73-5*, Pub. by Black Rose Bks CN); pap. 19.99 (*1-895431-72-7*, Pub. by Black Rose Bks CN) Consort Bk Sales.

Rethinking Camelot: JFK, the Vietnam War, & U. S. Political Culture. Noam Chomsky. LC 93-297. 172p. 1993. 30.00 (*0-89608-459-0*); pap. 14.00 (*0-89608-458-2*) South End Pr.

Rethinking Careers Education & Guidance: Theory, Policy & Practice. A. G. Watts et al. LC 96-11770. 304p. (C). 1996. pap. 29.95 (*0-415-13975-9*); text ed. 79.95 (*0-415-13974-0*) Routledge.

Rethinking Christian Education: Explorations in Theory & Practice. Ed. by David S. Schuller. LC 92-32946. 160p. (Orig.). 1993. pap. 15.99 (*0-8272-3213-6*) Chalice Pr.

Rethinking Citizenship: Welfare, Ideology, & Change in Modern Society. Maurice Roche. LC 92-20497. 280p. 1992. pap. 22.95 (*0-7456-0307-6*) Blackwell Pubs.

Rethinking Class: Literary Studies & Social Formations. Ed. by Wai-chee Dimock & Michael T. Gilmore. LC 94-16980. (The Social Foundations of Aesthetic Forms Ser.). 285p. 1994. 49.50 (*0-231-07600-2*); pap. 16.50 (*0-231-07601-0*) Col U Pr.

Rethinking College Athletics. Ed. by Judith Andre & David N. James. 208p. 1991. 39.95 (*0-87722-716-0*) Temple U Pr.

Rethinking College Athletics. Judith Andre. 1992. pap. 19.95 (*1-56639-002-8*) Temple U Pr.

***Rethinking College Education.** George Allan. LC 97-11680. 240p. 1997. 29.95 (*0-7006-0842-7*) U Pr of KS.

Rethinking Communication Vol. 1: Paradigm Issues. Ed. by Brenda Dervin et al. LC 88-38979. 240p. 1989. pap. 68.40 (*0-7837-8961-0*, 2049742) Bks Demand.

Rethinking Communication Vol. 2: Paradigm Exemplars. Ed. by Brenda Dervin et al. LC 88-38979. 544p. 1989. reprint ed. pap. 155.10 (*0-608-01613-6*, 2059592) Bks Demand.

Rethinking Communication, Vol. 1: Paradigm Issues. Ed. by Brenda Dervin et al. 240p. (C). 1989. text ed. 27.50 (*0-8039-3029-1*) Sage.

Rethinking Communication, Vol. 2: Paradigm Exemplars. Ed. by Brenda Dervin et al. 544p. (C). 1989. text ed. 44.00 (*0-8039-3031-3*) Sage.

***Rethinking Confidence-Building Measures.** Marie-France Desjardins. (Adelphi Papers, No. 307; International Institute for Strategic Studies: No. 307). 71p. 1997. pap. 26.00 (*0-19-829321-6*) OUP.

Rethinking Constitutional Law: Originalism, Interventionism, & the Politics of Judicial Review. Earl M. Maltz. LC 93-30266. 158p. 1994. 27.50 (*0-7006-0653-X*) U Pr of KS.

Rethinking Context: Language As an Interactive Phenomenon. Ed. by Alessandro Duranti & Charles Goodwin. (Studies in the Social & Cultural Foundations of Language: No. 11). 384p. (C). 1992. pap. text ed. 29.95 (*0-521-42288-4*) Cambridge U Pr.

***Rethinking Corporate Strategies for the Middle East.** 1997. write for info. (*0-614-25468-X*) Econ Intel.

Rethinking Crime & Deviance Theory: The Emergence of a Structuring Tradition. Francis T. Cullen. LC 83-17796. 200p. 1987. pap. 22.50 (*0-8476-7551-3*); text ed. 50.00 (*0-86598-073-X*) Rowman.

Rethinking Criminal Law. George P. Fletcher. 1978. 42.00 (*0-316-28592-7*) Little.

Rethinking Criminology: The Realist Debate. Ed. by Roger Matthews & Jock Young. (Contemporary Criminology Ser.). (Illus.). 176p. 1992. 49.95 (*0-8039-8620-3*); pap. 19.95 (*0-8039-8485-5*) Sage.

Rethinking Critical Theory: Emancipation in the Age of Global Social Movements. Larry J. Ray. (Illus.). 256p. 1993. 69.95 (*0-8039-8363-8*); pap. 21.95 (*0-8039-8364-6*) Sage.

***Rethinking Culture.** Keyan Tomaselli. (Illus.). 152p. 1996. reprint ed. pap. 19.95 (*0-941702-44-8*) Lake View Pr.

Rethinking Curriculum: A Call for Fundamental Reform. 19p. 1988. 5.00 (*0-317-05340-X*) NASBE.

Rethinking Democracy: Freedom & Social Cooperation in Politics, Economy & Society. Carol C. Gould. 364p. (C). 1990. pap. text ed. 26.95 (*0-521-38629-2*) Cambridge U Pr.

Rethinking Democratic Education: The Politics of Reform. David M. Steiner. LC 93-49707. 1994. text ed. 32.95 (*0-8018-4842-3*) Johns Hopkins.

Rethinking Development: In Search of Humane Alternatives. Rajni Kothari. 248p. 1989. 28.50 (*0-945257-18-X*) Apex Pr.

Rethinking Development: Modernization, Dependency, & Post-Modern Politics. David E. Apter. 312p. (C). 1987. text ed. 49.95 (*0-8039-2971-4*); pap. text ed. 25.00 (*0-8039-2972-2*) Sage.

Rethinking Development Assistance for Renewable Electricity. Keith Kozloff & Olatokumbo Shobowale. 57p. (Orig.). 1994. pap. 12.95 (*1-56973-006-7*) World Resources Inst.

***Rethinking Development in a Gendered World.** Deborah A. Caro & Deborah S. Rubin. 192p. 1997. 32.00 (*1-55587-438-X*) Lynne Rienner.

***Rethinking Disputes: The Mediation Alternative.** Ed. by Julie MacFarlane. 392p. 1997. 120.00 (*0-614-30362-1*, Pub. by Cavendish UK) Gaunt.

Rethinking Disputes: The Mediation Alternative. Ed. & Intro. by Julie MacFarlane. (Lecture Notes...Ser.). 400p. 1996. write for info. (*1-85941-151-7*, Pub. by Cavendish UK) Gaunt.

Rethinking Domestic Violence: The Social Work & Probation Response. Audrey Mullender. LC 96-2572. 320p. (C). 1996. pap. 19.95 (*0-415-08055-X*); text ed. 65.00 (*0-415-08054-1*) Routledge.

Rethinking Dvorak: Views from Five Countries. Ed. by David R. Beveridge. (Illus.). 328p. 1996. text ed. 60.00 (*0-19-816411-4*) OUP.

Rethinking Early Greek Philosophy: Hippolytus of Rome & the Presocratics. Catherine Osborne. LC 87-47719. 400p. (C). 1987. 55.00 (*0-8014-2103-9*) Cornell U Pr.

Rethinking Economic Principles: Critical Essays on Introductory Textbooks. 2nd ed. Nahid Aslanbeigui & Michele I. Naples. 260p. (C). 1995. 49.95 (*0-256-17075-4*) Irwin Prof Pubng.

Rethinking Economics: Markets, Technology & Economic Evolution. Ed. by Geoffrey M. Hodgson & Ernesto Screpanti. 224p. 1991. text ed. 85.00 (*1-85278-416-4*) E Elgar.

Rethinking Economics: Reflections Based on a Study of the Indian Economy. C. T. Kurien. LC 96-6134. 272p. 1996. 32.00 (*0-8039-9309-9*) Sage.

Rethinking Education. Philip S. Gang. (Illus.). 164p. (Orig.). (C). 1989. pap. 13.95 (*0-9623783-0-5*) Dagaz Pr.

Rethinking Education in Ethiopia. Tekeste Negash. 118p. (Orig.). 1996. pap. 37.50 (*91-7106-383-8*, Pub. by Nordisk Afrikainstitutet SW) Coronet Bks.

***Rethinking Educational Change with Heart & Mind.** Ed. by Andy Hargreaves. 242p. (Orig.). 1997. pap. 23.95 (*0-87120-296-4*, 197000) Assn Supervision.

Rethinking Effective Schools. James Bliss et al. 224p. (C). 1990. text ed. 61.95 (*0-13-778804-5*) P-H.

Rethinking Elementary School Mathematics: Insights & Issues. Ed. by Terry Wood et al. LC 93-20649. (Journal for Research in Mathematics Education Monograph Ser.: No. 6). (Illus.). 122p. (Orig.). 1993. pap. 7.00 (*0-87353-362-3*) NCTM.

Rethinking Emergency Energy Policy. Richard Farmer. (Illus.). 52p. (Orig.). (C). 1994. pap. text ed. 35.00 (*0-7881-1548-0*) DIANE Pub.

Rethinking Employment Policy. Ed. by D. Lee Bawden & Felicity Skidmore. LC 88-39161. (Illus.). 282p. (Orig.). (C). 1989. pap. text ed. 24.00 (*0-87766-458-7*); lib. bdg. 57.00 (*0-87766-459-5*) Urban Inst.

Rethinking English. Ed. by Svati Joshi. (C). 1991. 28.50 (*81-900195-1-1*, Pub. by Manohar II) S Asia.

Rethinking Ethics in the Midst of Violence. Linda A. Bell. LC 93-2697. (New Feminist Perspectives Ser.). 320p. (Orig.). (C). 1993. 64.00 (*0-8476-7844-X*); pap. 23.95 (*0-8476-7845-8*) Rowman.

***Rethinking Ethnicity: Arguments & Explorations.** Richard Jenkins. 224p. 1997. 69.95 (*0-8039-7677-1*) Sage.

***Rethinking Ethnicity: Arguments & Explorations.** Richard Jenkins. 224p. 1997. pap. 23.95 (*0-8039-7678-X*) Sage.

Rethinking European Security. Ed. by Furio Cerutti & Rodolfo Ragionieri. 200p. 1990. 49.00 (*0-8448-1629-9*, Crane Russak) Taylor & Francis.

Rethinking Evangelism: A Theological Approach. Ben C. Johnson. LC 86-26787. 142p. (Orig.). 1987. pap. 11.00 (*0-664-24060-7*, Westminster) Westminster John Knox.

Rethinking Evidence: Exploratory Essays. William Twining. LC 93-47196. 416p. (C). 1994. pap. 19.95 (*0-8101-1142-X*) Northwestern U Pr.

Rethinking Federalism: Block Grants & Federal, State, & Local Responsibilities. Claude E. Barfield. LC 81-17602. 111p. reprint ed. pap. 31.70 (*0-7837-1087-9*, 2041619) Bks Demand.

Rethinking Foreign Language Writing. Virginia M. Scott. LC 95-46855. (Teaching Methods Ser.). 1996. pap. 25.95 (*0-8384-6600-1*); pap. 22.50 (*0-614-11913-8*) Heinle & Heinle.

Rethinking France: Plans for Renewal 1940-1946. Andrew Shennan. 344p. 1989. 85.00 (*0-19-827520-X*) OUP.

***Rethinking Generosity: Critical Theory & the Politics of Caritas.** Romand Coles. LC 97-18760. 272p. 1997. 39.95 (*0-8014-3341-X*) Cornell U Pr.

***Rethinking Generosity: Critical Theory & the Politics of Caritas.** Romand Coles. (Contestations Ser.). 272p. 1997. pap. 16.95 (*0-8014-8487-1*) Cornell U Pr.

Rethinking Genesis: The Sources & Authorship of the First Book of the Pentateuch. Duane Garrett. LC 91-2008. 280p. (Orig.). (C). 1991. pap. 13.99 (*0-8010-3837-5*) Baker Bks.

Rethinking German History. 1990. pap. text ed. 24.95 (*0-04-445720-0*) Routledge Chapman & Hall.

Rethinking German History: Nineteenth Century Germany & the Origins of the Third Reich. Richard J. Evans. 272p. (C). 1987. text ed. 65.00 (*0-04-943051-3*) Routledge Chapman & Hall.

Rethinking German History: 19th Century Germany & the Origins of the Third Reich. Richard J. Evans. 304p. (C). 1990. pap. text ed. 25.00 (*0-00-302090-8*) Routledge Chapman & Hall.

Rethinking Germanistik: Canon & Culture. Ed. by Robert Bledsoe et al. LC 90-6030. (Berkeley Insights in Linguistics & Semiotics Ser.: Vol. 6). 214p. (C). 1991. text ed. 46.95 (*0-8204-1373-9*) P Lang Pubng.

Rethinking "Gnosticism" An Argument for Dismantling a Dubious Category. Michael A. Williams. LC 96-6490. 334p. 1996. text ed. 49.50 (*0-691-01127-3*) Princeton U Pr.

Rethinking Goodness. Michael A. Wallach & Lise Wallach. LC 89-21570. (SUNY Series in Ethical Theory). 156p. 1990. text ed. 24.50 (*0-7914-0299-1*) State U NY Pr.

Rethinking Government - Reform & Reinvention? Proceedings of a Roundtable on Governance, June 1993, Montreal. Ed. by F. Leslie Seidle. 230p. 1993. pap. 15.95 (*0-88645-151-5*, Pub. by Inst Res Pub CN) Ashgate Pub Co.

Rethinking History. Keith Jenkins. 112p. (C). 1991. pap. 11.95 (*0-415-06778-2*, A6306) Routledge.

Rethinking History & Myth: Indigenous South American Perspectives on the Past. Ed. by Jonathan D. Hill. (Illus.). 344p. 1988. pap. text ed. 16.95 (*0-252-06028-8*) U of Ill Pr.

***Rethinking Home Economics: Women & the History of a Profession.** Ed. by Virginia B. Vincenti. (Illus.). 384p. 1996. pap. 18.95 (*0-8014-8175-9*) Cornell U Pr.

***Rethinking Home Economics: Women & the History of a Profession.** Ed. by Virginia B. Vincenti. LC 96-29976. (Illus.). 384p. 1997. 49.95 (*0-8014-2971-4*) Cornell U Pr.

Rethinking How We Age: A New View of the Aging Mind. C. G. Prado. LC 85-9862. (Contributions in Philosophy Ser.: No. 28). 185p. 1986. text ed. 49.95 (*0-313-24785-4*, PRA/, Greenwood Pr) Greenwood.

Rethinking Human Rights: Challenges for Theory & Action. Ed. by Smitu Kothari & Harsh Sethi. (Illus.). 187p. (Orig.). 1989. pap. 12.50 (*0-945257-07-4*) Apex Pr.

Rethinking Hypermedia: The Microcosm Approach. Wendy Hall. (Electronic Publishing Ser.). 216p. (C). 1996. lib. bdg. 85.00 (*0-7923-9679-0*) Kluwer Ac.

***Rethinking Identity & Metaphysics: From Frege to Marcus.** Claire O. Hill. LC 96-30387. 1997. write for info. (*0-300-06837-9*) Yale U Pr.

Rethinking Ideology: A Marxist Debate. Ed. by Sakari Hanninen & Leena Paldan. 160p. 1983. pap. 11.95 (*0-88477-015-X*) Intl General.

Rethinking Imagination: Culture & Creativity. Ed. by Gillian Robinson & John Rundell. LC 93-17209. 240p. (C). (gr. 13). 1993. text ed. 69.95 (*0-415-09192-6*) Routledge.

Rethinking Imagination: Culture & Creativity. Ed. by Gillian Robinson & John Rundell. LC 93-17209. 240p. (C). 1994. pap. 17.95 (*0-415-09193-4*) Routledge.

Rethinking Indian Law. Committee on Native American Struggles. 1983. 42.00 (*0-685-14957-9*) Natl Lawyers Guild.

Rethinking Innateness: A Connectionist Perspective on Development. Jeffery L. Elman et al. LC 96-15522. (Neural Networks & Connectionist Modeling Ser.). (Illus.). 475p. 1996. 45.00 (*0-262-05052-8*, Bradford Bks) MIT Pr.

Rethinking Institutional Analysis & Development: Issues, Alternatives & Choices. Ed. by Vincent Ostrom et al. LC 88-28421. 480p. 1988. text ed. 34.95 (*1-55815-024-2*) ICS Pr.

Rethinking Institutional Analysis & Development: Issues, Alternatives, & Choices. rev. ed. Ed. by Vincent Ostrom et al. LC 93-16940. 1993. pap. 19.95 (*1-55815-264-4*) ICS Pr.

Rethinking Instructional Supervision: Notes on Its Language & Culture. Duncan Waite. LC 94-36873. 175p. 1995. 75.00 (*0-7507-0379-2*, Falmer Pr); pap. 24.95 (*0-7507-0380-6*, Falmer Pr) Taylor & Francis.

Rethinking Intellectual History: Texts, Contexts, Language. Dominick LaCapra. LC 83-7218. 352p. 1983. pap. 18.95 (*0-8014-9886-4*) Cornell U Pr.

***Rethinking Intermarriage.** Gary Tobin & Katherine Simon. 1997. 25.00 (*0-614-27516-4*) Jossey-Bass.

Rethinking International Trade. Paul R. Krugman. 190p. 1990. 32.50 (*0-262-11148-9*) MIT Pr.

Rethinking International Trade. Paul R. Krugman. (Illus.). 292p. 1994. pap. 17.50 (*0-262-61095-7*) MIT Pr.

***Rethinking Islam.** Mohammed Arkoun. 139p. 1996. 59.95 (*0-614-21447-5*, 1075); pap. 3.95 (*0-614-21445-9*, 1411); pap. 19.95 (*0-614-21446-7*, 1075) Kazi Pubns.

Rethinking Islam: Common Questions, Uncommon Answers. Mohammed Arkoun. (C). 1994. pap. text ed. 19.95 (*0-8133-2294-4*) Westview.

Rethinking Japan Vol. I: Literature, Visual Arts & Linguistics. Ed. by Adriana Boscaro et al. (Illus.). 354p. (C). 1991. text ed. 59.00 (*0-904404-78-1*, Pub. by Curzon Press UK) UH Pr.

Rethinking Japan Vol. II: Social Sciences, Ideology & Thought. Ed. by Adriana Boscaro et al. 416p. (C). 1990. text ed. 59.00 (*0-904404-79-X*, Pub. by Curzon Press UK) UH Pr.

Rethinking Japan, Vol. I: Literature, Visual Arts & Linguistics. (Illus.). 350p. 1991. text ed. 49.95 (*0-312-04819-X*) St Martin.

Rethinking Japan, Vol. II: Social Sciences, Ideology & Thought. (Illus.). 400p. 1990. text ed. 49.95 (*0-312-04820-3*) St Martin.

Rethinking Jewish Faith: The Child of a Survivor Responds. Steven L. Jacobs. LC 93-20865. (SUNY Series in Modern Jewish Literature & Culture). 151p. (C). 1994. text ed. 57.50 (*0-7914-1957-6*); pap. text ed. 18.95 (*0-7914-1958-4*) State U NY Pr.

Rethinking Juvenile Justice. Barry Krisberg & Ira Schwartz. 1983. 7.00 (*0-318-02058-0*) Natl Coun Crime.

Rethinking Knowledge: Reflections across the Disciplines. Ed. by Robert F. Goodman & Walter R. Fisher. LC 94-14442. (SUNY Series in the Philosophy of the Social Sciences). 246p. 1995. text ed. 59.50 (*0-7914-2337-9*); pap. text ed. 19.95 (*0-7914-2338-7*) State U NY Pr.

Rethinking Labor History: Essays on Discourse & Class Analysis. Ed. by Leonard R. Berlanstein. LC 92-24297. (Illus.). 248p. (C). 1993. text ed. 39.95 (*0-252-01975-X*); pap. text ed. 12.95 (*0-252-06279-5*) U of Ill Pr.

***Rethinking Language & Gender Research: Theory & Practice.** Victoria Bergvall. 1996. pap. text ed. 29.59 (*0-582-25673-9*) Longman.

Rethinking Language & Gender Research: Theory & Practice. VictoriaL. Bergvall et al. LC 96-20024. (Real Language Ser.). 1996. write for info. (*0-582-26574-6*) Longman.

***Rethinking Language Arts: Passion & Practice.** Nina Zaragoza. Ed. by Joe Kincheloe & Shirley R. Steinberg. LC 96-34470. (Critical Education Practice Ser.: Vol. 9). 200p. 1997. pap. text ed. 18.95 (*0-8153-2322-0*) Garland.

***Rethinking Language Arts: Passion & Practice.** Nina Zaragoza. Ed. by Joe Kincheloe & Shirley R. Steinberg. LC 96-34470. (Critical Education Practice Ser.: Vol. 9). 200p. 1997. text ed. 39.00 (*0-8153-1958-4*) Garland.

Rethinking Lawrence. Ed. by Keith Brown. 256p. 1990. 85.00 (*0-335-09387-6*, Open Univ Pr); pap. 29.00 (*0-335-09388-4*, Open Univ Pr) Taylor & Francis.

Rethinking Leadership in Adult & Continuing Education. Ed. by Paul J. Edelson. LC 85-644750. (New Directions for Adult & Continuing Education Ser.: No. ACE 56). 130p. 1992. teacher ed. 19.00 (*1-55542-729-4*) Jossey-Bass.

Rethinking Legal Need: The Case of Criminal Justice. Paul Robertshaw. 259p. 1991. text ed. 59.95 (*1-85521-207-2*, Pub. by Dartmth Pub UK) Ashgate Pub Co.

Rethinking Liberal Education. Ed. by Nicholas H. Farnham & Adam Yarmolinsky. 176p. 1996. 35.00 (*0-19-509772-6*) OUP.

Rethinking Life & Death. Peter Singer. 320p. 1996. pap. 14.95 (*0-312-14401-6*) St Martin.

Rethinking Life & Death: The Construction of a New Ethic. Peter Singer. 1995. 22.95 (*0-312-11880-5*) St Martin.

Rethinking Linguistic Relativity. Ed. by John J. Gumperz & Stephen C. Levinson. (Studies in the Social & Cultural Foundations of Language: No. 17). 504p. (C). 1996. text ed. 74.95 (*0-521-44433-0*); pap. text ed. 27.95 (*0-521-44890-5*) Cambridge U Pr.

Rethinking Literacy Education: The Critical Need for Practice-Based Change. B. Allan Quigley. LC 96-21258. (Jossey-Bass Higher & Adult Education Ser.). 1996. write for info. (*0-7879-0287-X*) Jossey-Bass.

Rethinking Literary Biography: A Postmodern Approach to Tennessee Williams. Nicholas Pagan. LC 92-55117. 1993. 29.50 (*0-8386-3516-4*) Fairleigh Dickinson.

Rethinking Los Angeles. Ed. by Michael J. Dear et al. LC 96-10037. (Metropolis & Region Ser.: Vol. 2). 380p. 1996. 58.00 (*0-8039-7286-5*); pap. 26.95 (*0-8039-7287-3*) Sage.

Rethinking Marriage: Public & Private Perspectives. Ed. by Christopher Clulow. 136p. 1994. pap. text ed. 26.95 (*1-85575-046-5*, Pub. by Karnac Bks UK) Brunner-Mazel.

Rethinking Marx. Ed. by Sakari Hanninen & Leena Paldan. 200p. 1984. pap. 11.95 (*0-88477-021-4*) Intl General.

Rethinking Marxism. Ed. by Richard Wolff & Steven Resnick. 421p. Date not set. text ed. 13.00 (*0-936756-12-8*) Autonomedia.

Rethinking Masculinity: Philosophical Explorations in Light of Feminism. Ed. by Larry May et al. LC 92-22430. (New Feminist Perspectives Ser.). 244p. (C). 1992. 50.00 (*0-8476-7773-7*) Rowman.

Rethinking Masculinity: Philosophical Explorations in Light of Feminism. 2nd ed. Ed. by Larry May et al. LC 96-21390. 288p. 1996. 62.50 (*0-8476-8256-0*) Rowman.

Rethinking Masculinity: Philosophical Explorations in Light of Feminism. 2nd ed. Robert A. Strikwerda. 288p. 1996. pap. 16.95 (*0-8476-8257-9*) Rowman.

Rethinking Materialism: Perspectives on the Spiritual Dimension of Economic Behavior. Ed. by Robert Wuthnow. 296p. 1995. pap. 17.00 (*0-8028-0789-5*) Eerdmans.

Rethinking Media Literacy: A Critical Pedagogy of Representations. Peter McLaren et al. LC 94-40539. (Counterpoints Ser.: Vol. 4). 280p. (C). 1995. pap. text ed. 29.95 (*0-8204-1802-1*) P Lang Pubng.

***Rethinking Media, Religion, & Culture.** Ed. by Stewart M. Hoover & Knut Lundby. 336p. 1997. 55.00 (*0-7619-0170-1*); pap. 24.95 (*0-7619-0171-X*) Sage.

Rethinking Media Theory: Signposts & New Directions. Armand Mattelart & Michele Mattelart. Tr. by James A. Cohen & Marina Urquidi from FRE. (Media & Society Ser.: Vol. 5). 208p. (C). 1992. pap. text ed. 16.95 (*0-8166-1910-7*) U of Minn Pr.

Rethinking Metaphysics. L. Gregory Jones. 1995. pap. 24.95 (*0-631-19729-X*) Blackwell Pubs.

Rethinking Meter: A New Approach to the Verse Line. Alan Holder. 1995. 42.50 (*0-8387-5292-6*) Bucknell U Pr.

Rethinking Methods in Psychology. Ed. by Jonathan Smith et al. (Rethinking Psychology Ser.). 256p. (Orig.). 1995. 65.00 (*0-8039-7732-8*); pap. 21.95 (*0-8039-7733-6*) Sage.

Rethinking Middle East Politics. Simon Bromley. LC 93-34723. 216p. (Orig.). (C). 1994. pap. 16.95 (*0-292-70816-5*); text ed. 39.50 (*0-292-70815-7*) U of Tex Pr.

Rethinking Military Politics: Brazil & the Southern Cone. Alfred Stepan. 192p. 1988. pap. text ed. 13.95 (*0-691-02274-7*) Princeton U Pr.

Rethinking Modern Judaism. Eisen. 1997. 35.00 (*0-226-19528-7*) U Ch Pr.

Rethinking Modernity: The Ancients & the Moderns. Stanley Rosen. LC 88-26155. 272p. (C). 1989. 15.00 (*0-300-04331-7*) Yale U Pr.

***Rethinking Modernity & National Identity in Turkey.** Resat Kasaba. Ed. by Sibel Bozdogan. LC 96-51857. (Publications on the Near East). (Illus.). 304p. 1997. pap. 22.50 (*0-295-97597-0*) U of Wash Pr.

Rethinking Modernization. Ed. by John J. Poggie, Jr. & Robert N. Lynch. LC 72-826. 352p. 1974. text ed. 75.00 (*0-8371-6394-3*, POM/, Greenwood Pr) Greenwood.

***Rethinking Nationalism & Identity.** Wicker. 1997. 49.50 (*1-85973-926-1*, Pub. by Berg Pubs UK); pap. 19.50 (*1-85973-931-8*, Pub. by Berg Pubs UK) NYU Pr.

***Rethinking Nationalism in the Arab Middle East.** James P. Jankowski & I. Gershoni. LC 97-12826. 1997. write for info. (*0-231-10694-7*); pap. write for info. (*0-231-10695-5*) Col U Pr.

Rethinking Navajo Pueblitos. Patrick Hogan & Michael P. Marshall. (New Mexico Cultural Resources Ser.: Vol. 8). (Illus.). 338p. 1992. write for info. (*1-878178-09-1*) Bureau of Land Mgmt NM.

Rethinking Neural Networks: Quantum Fields & Biological Data. Ed. by Karl H. Pribram. 568p. 1993. pap. 95.00 (*0-8058-1466-3*) L Erlbaum Assocs.

Rethinking Nuclear Strategy. Stephen J. Cimbala. LC 87-28702. 288p. 1988. 40.00 (*0-8420-2294-5*) Scholarly Res Inc.

Rethinking Objectivity. Ed. by Allan Megill. LC 93-43023. (Post-Contemporary Interventions Ser.). 352p. 1994. text ed. 45.95 (*0-8223-1479-7*); pap. text ed. 16.95 (*0-8223-1494-0*) Duke.

Rethinking Obligation: A Feminist Method for Political Theory. Nancy J. Hirschmann. LC 91-55540. 384p. 1992. pap. 17.95 (*0-8014-9567-9*) Cornell U Pr.

Rethinking Organization: New Directions in Organization Theory & Analysis. Michael Reed & Michael Hughes. 320p. (C). 1992. text ed. 62.00 (*0-8039-8287-9*); pap. text ed. 22.00 (*0-8039-8288-7*) Sage.

Rethinking Our Centralized Monetary System: The Case for a System of Local Currencies. Lewis D. Solomon. LC 95-34441. 184p. 1996. text ed. 55.00 (*0-275-95376-9*, Praeger Pubs) Greenwood.

Rethinking Peace. Jennifer E. Turpin. 380p. (C). 1994. pap. text ed. 22.50 (*1-55587-488-6*); lib. bdg. 50.00 (*1-55587-482-7*) Lynne Rienner.

Rethinking Police Interrogation in England & Wales. John Baldwin. Ed. by Graham Hughes. (Occasional Papers: Vol. XI). 24p. (Orig.). 1992. pap. 5.00 (*1-878429-60-4*) NYU Ctr for Rsch in Crime Justice.

Rethinking Political Theory: Essays in Phenomenology & the Study of Politics. Hwa Y. Jung. (Series in Continental Thought). xvii, 292p. (C). 1993. text ed. 35.00 (*0-8214-1052-0*) Ohio U Pr.

Rethinking Popular Culture: Contemporary Perspectives in Cultural Studies. Ed. by Chandra Mukerji & Michael Schudson. LC 90-39009. 512p. 1991. pap. 17.95 (*0-520-06893-9*) U CA Pr.

Rethinking Power. Ed. by Thomas E. Wartenberg. LC 90-28586. (SUNY Series in Radical, Social & Political Theory). 353p. (C). 1992. text ed. 64.50 (*0-7914-0881-7*); pap. text ed. 21.95 (*0-7914-0882-5*) State U NY Pr.

Rethinking Progress: Movements, Forces & Ideas at the End of the Twentieth Century. Jeffrey C. Alexander & Piotr Sztompka. 256p. (C). (gr. 13). 1990. text ed. 62.95 (*0-04-445753-7*) Routledge Chapman & Hall.

Rethinking Prostitution: Purchasing Sex in the 1990s. Graham Scambler & Annette Scambler. LC 96-2138. 264p. (C). 1996. text ed. 65.00 (*0-415-12226-0*) Routledge.

Rethinking Prostitution: Purchasing Sex in the 1990s. Graham Scambler & Annette Scambler. LC 96-2138. 264p. (C). 1996. pap. 18.95 (*0-415-10207-3*) Routledge.

Rethinking Protestantism in Latin America. Ed. by David Stoll & Virginia Garrard-Burnett. LC 93-6582. 240p. 1993. Alk pbk. 49.95 (*1-56639-102-4*); Alk pbk. 19.95 (*1-56639-103-2*) Temple U Pr.

Rethinking Psychiatry: From Cultural Category to Personal Experience. Arthur Kleinman. 256p. 1988. text ed. 29.95 (*0-02-917441-4*, Free Press) Free Pr.

Rethinking Psychiatry from Cultural Category to Personal Experience. Arthur Kleinman. 1991. pap. 18.95 (*0-02-917442-2*, Free Press) Free Pr.

Rethinking Psychological Anthropology: Continuity & Change in the Study of Human Action. Philip D. Bock. (Illus.). 254p. (C). 1995. pap. text ed. 13.95 (*0-88133-851-6*) Waveland Pr.

Rethinking Psychology, Vol. 3. Ed. by Jonathan Smith et al. 256p. 1995. 65.00 (*0-8039-7734-4*); pap. 19.95 (*0-8039-7735-2*) Sage.

Rethinking Public Policy-Making: Questioning Assumptions, Challenging Beliefs. Ed. by Margaret Blunden & Malcom Dando. 240p. 1995. 55.00 (*0-8039-7602-X*) Sage.

Rethinking Pull-Out Services in Early Intervention: A Professional Resource. R. A. McWilliam. 384p. 1996. pap. text ed. 43.00 (*1-55766-242-8*, 2428) P H Brookes.

Rethinking Quaker Principles. Rufus M. Jones. (C). 1940. pap. 3.00 (*0-87574-008-1*) Pendle Hill.

Rethinking Race: Franz Boas & His Contemporaries. Vernon J. Williams, Jr. LC 95-34914. 168p. 1996. pap. 15.95 (*0-8131-0873-X*); text ed. 34.95 (*0-8131-1963-4*) U Pr of Ky.

Rethinking Radical Education: Essays in Honour of Brian Simon. Ed. by A. Rattansi. (C). 1992. pap. 19.95 (*0-85315-717-0*, Pub. by Lawrence & Wishart UK) NYU Pr.

Rethinking Realized Eschatology. Clayton Sullivan. LC 88-6612. viii, 152p. (C). 1988. 19.95 (*0-86554-302-X*, H266) Mercer Univ Pr.

Rethinking Reform: The Principal's Dilemma. NASSP Curiculum Council Staff. 80p. (Orig.). 1986. pap. 9.00 (*0-88210-193-5*) Natl Assn Principals.

Rethinking Religion: Connecting Cognition & Culture. E. Thomas Lawson & Robert N. McCauley. (Illus.). 203p. (C). 1993. pap. text ed. 19.95 (*0-521-43806-3*) Cambridge U Pr.

Rethinking Rental Housing. John I. Gilderbloom & Richard P. Appelbaum. 296p. 1987. 44.95 (*0-87722-498-6*) Temple U Pr.

Rethinking Rental Housing. John I. Gilderbloom & Richard P. Appelbaum. LC 87-1958. 296p. (C). 1987. pap. 19.95 (*0-87722-538-9*) Temple U Pr.

Rethinking Research on Land Degradation in Developing Countries. Yvan Biot et al. LC 95-22327. (Discussion Papers: Vol. 289). 152p. 1995. 9.95 (*0-8213-3329-1*, 13329) World Bank.

Rethinking Restructuring: Gender & Change in Canada. Ed. by Isabella Bakker. 320p. 1996. 55.00 (*0-8020-0702-3*); pap. 22.95 (*0-8020-7651-3*) U of Toronto Pr.

Rethinking Rights & Responsibilities: The Moral Bonds of Community. Arthur J. Dyck. LC 94-3889. 456p. 1994. pap. 21.95 (*0-8298-1006-4*) Pilgrim OH.

Rethinking Robin Hood. Kathy J. Hayes & Daniel J. Slottje. (Texas Study Ser.). (Illus.). 33p. (Orig.). 1993. pap. 10.00 (*1-56808-002-6*, 179) Natl Ctr Pol.

Rethinking Rural Development. Corporation for Enterprise Development Staff. 43p. 1993. pap. 17.50 (*1-883187-02-8*) Corp Ent Dev.

Rethinking Rural Poverty: Bangladesh As a Case Study. Ed. by Hossain Z. Rahman & Mahabub Hossain. LC 94-23400. 292p. 1995. 25.95 (*0-8039-9205-X*) Sage.

Rethinking Russia's National Interests. Ed. by Stephen R. Sestanovich. LC 93-40403. (Significant Issues Ser.). 127p. (Orig.). (C). 1994. pap. 16.00 (*0-89206-221-5*) CSI Studies.

Rethinking Sacraments: Holy Moments in Daily Living. Bill Huebsch. LC 88-51812. 204p. (Orig.). 1989. pap. 9.95 (*0-89622-393-0*) Twenty-Third.

Rethinking School Choice: Limits of the Market Metaphor. Jeffrey Henig. 287p. 1994. text ed. 35.00 (*0-691-03347-1*) Princeton U Pr.

Rethinking School Choice: Limits of the Market Metaphor. Jeffrey R. Henig. 312p. (C). 1994. pap. text ed. 16.95 (*0-691-04472-4*) Princeton U Pr.

Rethinking School Finance: An Agenda for the 1990s. Ed. by Allan R. Odden. LC 92-11512. (Education-Higher Education Ser.). 384p. text ed. 34.95 (*1-55542-451-1*) Jossey-Bass.

Rethinking School Improvement: Research, Craft & Concept. Ed. by Ann Lieberman. 240p. 1986. pap. text ed. 18.95 (*0-8077-2807-1*) Tchrs Coll.

Rethinking Schools: A Collection from the Leading Journal of School Reform. Ed. by David Levine et al. LC 94-34347. 304p. 1995. 25.00 (*1-56584-214-6*) New Press NY.

Rethinking Schools: A Collection from the Leading Journal of School Reform. Ed. by David P. Levine et al. LC 94-34347. 304p. 1995. pap. 16.00 (*1-56584-215-4*) New Press NY.

Rethinking Science As a Career: Perceptions & Realities in the Physical Sciences. Sheila Tobias et al. 1995. pap. 2.50 (*0-9633504-3-9*) Res Corp.

Rethinking Scripture: Essays from a Comparative Perspective. Ed. by Miriam Levering. LC 87-9919. 276p. 1988. text ed. 64.50 (*0-88706-613-5*); pap. text ed. 21.95 (*0-88706-614-3*) State U NY Pr.

***Rethinking Secularization: Reformed Reactions to Modernity.** Ed. by Gerard Dekkar et al. LC 96-48812. (Calvin Center Ser.). 312p. 1997. 64.50 (*0-7618-0645-8*); pap. 34.50 (*0-7618-0646-6*) U Pr of Amer.

Rethinking Sex: Social Theory & Sexuality Research. Ed. by R. W. Connell & Gary Dowsett. 182p. 1992. pap. 19.95 (*0-522-84487-1*, Pub. by Melbourne Univ Pr AT) Paul & Co Pubs.

Rethinking Sex: Social Theory & Sexuality Research. Ed. by R. W. Connell & G. W. Dowsett. 182p. 1993. 44.95 (*1-56639-072-9*); pap. 14.95 (*1-56639-073-7*) Temple U Pr.

Rethinking Sexual Harassment. Ed. by Clare Brant & Yun-Lee Too. LC 94-25614. (C). 69.69 (*0-7453-0837-6*, Pub. by Pluto Pr UK) LPC InBook.

Rethinking Sexual Harassment. Ed. by Clare Brant & Yun-Lee Too. (C). pap. 16.95 (*0-7453-0838-4*, Pub. by Pluto Pr UK) LPC InBook.

***Rethinking Sexuality: Foucault & Classical Antiquity.** David H. Larmour et al. LC 97-18650. 1997. write for info. (*0-691-01680-1*); pap. write for info. (*0-691-01679-8*) Princeton U Pr.

Rethinking Sisterhood: Unity in Diversity. Ed. by R. Duelli Klein. (Illus.). 100p. 1985. pap. 21.00 (*0-08-032679-X*, Pub. by PPL UK) Elsevier.

Rethinking Social Democracy in Western Europe. Ed. by Richard Gillespie & William E. Paterson. LC 93-6515. 1993. 37.50 (*0-7146-4525-7*, Pub. by F Cass Pubs UK); pap. 19.50 (*0-7146-4098-0*, Pub. by F Cass Pubs UK) Intl Spec Bk.

Rethinking Social Development: Theory, Research, & Practice. David Booth. 328p. (C). 1995. pap. 50.95 (*0-582-23497-2*, Pub. by Longman UK) Longman.

Rethinking Social History: English Society 1570-1920 & Its Interpretation. Ed. by Adrian Wilson. 352p. 1995. text ed. 24.95 (*0-7190-4650-5*, Pub. by Manchester Univ Pr UK) St Martin.

Rethinking Social Policy: Race, Poverty, & the Underclass. Christopher Jencks. 280p. (C). 1992. 35.00 (*0-674-76678-4*) HUP.

Rethinking Social Policy: Race, Poverty, & the Underclass. Christopher Jencks. LC 92-53407. 288p. 1993. reprint ed. pap. 14.00 (*0-06-097534-2*, PL) HarpC.

Rethinking Socialism: A Theory of Better Practice. Gavin Kitching. LC 83-12104. 176p. 1983. pap. 9.95 (*0-416-35840-3*, NO. 3981) Routledge Chapman & Hall.

Rethinking Socialist Economics: A New Agenda for Britain. Ed. by Peter Nolan & Suzanne Paine. LC 86-6682. 350p. 1986. text ed. 45.00 (*0-312-67806-1*) St Martin.

Rethinking Society. Hall. Date not set. 32.95 (*0-02-913632-6*, Free Press) Free Pr.

Rethinking Sorrow: Revelatory Tales of Late Medieval Japan. Margaret H. Childs. LC 89-25394. (Michigan Monographs in Japanese Studies: No. 6). xiv, 182p. 1991. 27.95 (*0-939512-42-4*) U MI Japan.

***Rethinking Sorrow: Revelatory Tales of Late Medieval Japan.** Margaret H. Childs. LC 89-25394. (Michigan Monographs in Japanese Studies: No. 6). xiv, 182p. 1996. pap. 14.95 (*0-939512-74-2*) U MI Japan.

Rethinking Sources International Law. G. J. Van Hoof. (Orig.). 1983. pap. text ed. 81.00 (*90-6544-085-2*) Kluwer Law Tax Pubs.

Rethinking Soviet Strategic Policy: Inputs & Implications. Dennis Ross. (CISA Working Papers: No. 5). 46p. (Orig.). 1977. pap. 15.00 (*0-86682-004-3*) Ctr Intl Relations.

Rethinking Special Needs in Mainstream Schools: Toward the Year 2000. Ed. by Alan Dyson & Charles Gains. 160p. 1993. pap. 32.50 (*1-85346-221-7*, Pub. by D Fulton UK) Taylor & Francis.

Rethinking State Development Policies & Programs. Jay Kayne & Molly Shonka. Ed. by Karen Glass. 40p. 1994. pap. text ed. 15.00 (*1-55877-181-6*) Natl Governor.

***Rethinking Strategic Management: Ways to Improve Competitive Performance.** Ed. by David E. Hussey. 1996. text ed. 55.00 (*0-471-95908-1*) Wiley.

***Rethinking Strategies in the Middle East.** 1997. 625.00 (*0-614-25485-X*) Econ Intel.

Rethinking Student Discipline: Alternatives That Work. Paula M. Short et al. LC 93-23415. 136p. 1994. 42.95 (*0-8039-6084-0*) Corwin Pr.

Rethinking Student Discipline: Alternatives That Work. Paula M. Short et al. LC 93-23415. 136p. 1995. pap. 18.95 (*0-8039-6085-9*) Corwin Pr.

Rethinking Symbolism. Daniel Sperber. LC 75-18433. (Studies in Social Anthropology: No. 11). 164p. 1975. pap. 16.95 (*0-521-09967-6*) Cambridge U Pr.

Rethinking Systems Analysis & Design. Gerald M. Weinberg. LC 88-5083. (Illus.). 208p. 1988. reprint ed. pap. 26.50 (*0-932633-08-0*) Dorset Hse Pub Co.

Rethinking Tax Fairness. John C. Goodman et al. (Illus.). 15p. (C). 1992. pap. 5.00 (*0-943802-93-8*, BG114) Natl Ctr Pol.

Rethinking Technologies. Ed. by Conley et al. LC 93-22415. 256p. 1993. text ed. 44.95 (*0-8166-2214-0*) U of Minn Pr.

Rethinking Technologies. Ed. by Verena A. Conley et al. LC 93-22415. 256p. 1993. pap. text ed. 17.95 (*0-8166-2215-9*) U of Minn Pr.

Rethinking the American Race Problem. Roy L. Brooks. 240p. 1990. 35.00 (*0-520-06886-6*) U CA Pr.

Rethinking the American Race Problem. Roy L. Brooks. 1992. pap. 15.95 (*0-520-07878-0*) U CA Pr.

Rethinking the Avant Garde. Jonathan Fineberg. LC 85-81548. (Illus.). 24p. 1985. pap. 7.50 (*0-915171-02-3*) Katonah Gal.

Rethinking the Balance: Government & Non-Governmental Organizations in the Netherlands. Ed. by Tymen J. Van der Ploeg & John W. Sap. 176p. 1996. pap. 30.00 (*90-5383-415-X*, Pub. by VUB Univ Pr BE) Paul & Co Pubs.

Rethinking the Borderlands: Between Chicano Culture & Legal Discourse. Carl Gutierrez-Jones. (Latinos in American Society & Culture Ser.). 1995. 40.00 (*0-520-08578-7*) U CA Pr.

Rethinking the Borderlands: Between Chicano Culture & Legal Discourse. Carl Gutierrez-Jones. (Latinos in American Society & Culture Ser.: Vol. 4). 1995. pap. 15.00 (*0-520-08579-5*) U CA Pr.

Rethinking the Center: Party Politics in Nineteenth- & Twentieth-Century Chile. Timothy R. Scully. 304p. 1992. 45.00 (*0-8047-1913-6*) Stanford U Pr.

***Rethinking the Church: A Challenge to Creative Redesign in an Age of Transition.** James E. White. LC 97-11010. 144p. (Orig.). 1997. pap. 11.99 (*0-8010-9039-3*) Baker Bks.

Rethinking the Clean Air Act Amendments. Kent Jeffrey. 1990. pap. 5.00 (*0-943802-86-5*, BG107) Natl Ctr Pol.

***Rethinking the Cold War.** Allen Hunter. LC 97-11618. 1997. write for info. (*1-56639-561-5*); pap. write for info. (*1-56639-562-3*) Temple U Pr.

Rethinking the Company: Forces Shaping Business in the Next Century. Thomas Clarke & Elaine Monkhouse. (Financial Times Management Ser.). 256p. 1994. 67.50 (*0-273-60713-8*, Pub. by Pitman Pub Ltd UK) Trans-Atl Phila.

Rethinking the Constitution: Perspectives on Canadian Constitutional Reform, Interpretation & Theory. Ed. by Anthony Peacock. 320p. 1996. pap. 35.00 (*0-19-541178-1*) OUP.

Rethinking the Corporation: The Architecture of Change. Robert M. Tomasko. 224p. 1993. 22.95 (*0-8144-5022-9*) AMACOM.

Rethinking the Corporation: The Architecture of Change. Robert M. Tomasko. 224p. 1995. pap. 16.95 (*0-8144-7890-5*) AMACOM.

Rethinking the Curriculum: Toward an Integrated, Interdisciplinary College Education. Ed. by Mary E. Clark & Sandra A. Wawrytko. LC 89-78404. (Contributions to the Study of Education Ser.: No. 40). 288p. 1990. text ed. 49.95 (*0-313-27306-5*, CRJ/, Greenwood Pr) Greenwood.

Rethinking the Delivery of Public Services to Citizens. Leslie F. Seidle. 200p. 1996. pap. 17.95 (*0-88645-178-7*, Pub. by Inst Res Pub CN) Ashgate Pub Co.

Rethinking the Development Experience: Essays Provoked by the Work of Albert O. Hirschman. Ed. by Lloyd Rodwin & Donald A. Schon. LC 94-12644. 369p. (C). 1994. 44.95 (*0-8157-7552-0*); pap. 19.95 (*0-8157-7551-2*) Brookings.

R

An Asterisk (*) at the beginning of an entry indicates that the title is appearing in BIP for the first time.

R

***Rethinking the Education of Deaf Students: Theory & Practice from a Teacher's Perspective.** LC 97-3501. 1997. pap. text ed. 24.00 (*0-435-07236-6*, 07236) Heinemann.

Rethinking the European Union. Landau. LC 96-18901. 1997. text ed. 59.95 (*0-312-16156-5*) St Martin.

Rethinking the Family: Some Feminist Questions. rev. ed. Ed. by Barrie Thorne & Marilyn Yalom. 272p. 1992. reprint ed. text ed. 42.50 (*1-55553-144-X*); reprint ed. pap. text ed. 15.95 (*1-55553-145-8*) NE U Pr.

Rethinking the Federal Lands. Ed. by Sterling Brubaker. LC 83-43261. 306p. (C). 1984. pap. 14.95 (*0-915707-01-2*); lib. bdg. 39.00 (*0-915707-00-4*) Resources Future.

Rethinking the Forms of Visual Expression. Robert Sowers. 1990. pap. 14.00 (*0-520-06992-7*) Random Hse Value.

Rethinking the French Revolution: Marxism & the Revisionist Challenge. George C. Comninel. 240p. (C). 1991. pap. text ed. 19.00 (*0-86091-890-4*, A4979, Pub. by Vrso UK) Norton.

Rethinking the French Revolution: Marxism & the Revisionist Challenge. George C. Comninel. 240p. 1987. text ed. 34.95 (*0-86091-179-9*, Pub. by Verso UK) Routledge Chapman & Hall.

Rethinking the Future: Rethinking Business, Principles, Competition, Control & Complexity, Leadership, Markets & the World. Ed. by Rowan Gibson. LC 96-25422. (Illus.). 288p. 1997. 25.00 (*1-85788-103-6*) Nicholas Brealey.

Rethinking the Future: The Correspondence Between Geoffrey Vickers & Adolph Lowe. Ed. by Jeanne Vickers. 239p. (C). 1991. text ed. 44.95 (*0-88738-412-9*) Transaction Pubs.

Rethinking the Henrician Era: Essays on Early Tudor Texts & Contexts. Ed. by Peter C. Herman. LC 93-12712. (Illus.). 320p. (C). 1994. text ed. 44.95 (*0-252-02034-0*); pap. text ed. 17.95 (*0-252-06340-6*) U of Ill Pr.

Rethinking the Latin American City. Ed. by Richard M. Morse & Jorge E. Hardoy. (Woodrow Wilson Center Press Ser.). 190p. 1992. text ed. 27.50 (*0-943875-43-9*) Johns Hopkins.

Rethinking the Materials We Use: A New Focus for Pollution Policy. Ed. by Ken Geiser & Frances H. Irwin. LC 92-44755. 145p. 1993. 12.50 (*0-89164-140-8*) World Wildlife Fund.

Rethinking the Museum & Other Meditations. Stephen E. Weil. LC 89-21985. 192p. 1990. pap. text ed. 15.95 (*0-87474-953-0*) Smithsonian.

Rethinking the Neolithic. Julian Thomas. (New Studies in Archaeology). (Illus.). 208p. (C). 1991. text ed. 80.00 (*0-521-40377-4*) Cambridge U Pr.

***Rethinking the New Deal Court: The Structure of a Constitutional Revolution.** Barry Cushman. 336p. 1998. pap. 24.95 (*0-19-512043-4*) OUP.

***Rethinking the New Deal Court: The Structure of a Constitutional Revolution.** Barry Cushman. 336p. 1998. 55.00 (*0-19-511532-5*) OUP.

Rethinking the Nineteenth Century: Contradictions & Movements. Ed. by Francisco O. Ramirez. LC 87-17791. (Contributions in Economics & Economic History Ser.: No. 76). 256p. 1988. text ed. 55.00 (*0-313-25997-6*, RRK/, Greenwood Pr) Greenwood.

Rethinking the Nuclear Weapons Dilemma in Europe. Ed. by P. Terrence Hopmann & Frank Barnaby. LC 87-12914. 392p. 1988. text ed. 59.95 (*0-312-67804-5*) St Martin.

Rethinking the Pacific. Gerald Segal. (Illus.). 416p. 1991. pap. 24.00 (*0-19-827379-7*) OUP.

Rethinking the Political. Ed. by Johanna Brenner et al. (Political Science & Gender Studies). 512p. 1995. lib. bdg. 39.95 (*0-226-07397-1*) U Ch Pr.

Rethinking the Political. Ed. by Johanna Brenner et al. (Political Science Gender Studies). 300p. 1995. pap. 19.95 (*0-226-07399-8*) U Ch Pr.

Rethinking the Politics of Commercial Society: The Edinburgh Review 1802-1832. Biancamaria Fontana. 264p. 1985. text ed. 59.95 (*0-521-30335-4*) Cambridge U Pr.

Rethinking the Progressive Agenda: The Reform of the American Regulatory State. Susan Rose-Ackerman. 1993. pap. 17.95 (*0-02-926845-1*, Free Press) Free Pr.

Rethinking the Rhetorical Tradition: From Plato to Postmodernism. James L. Kastely. LC 96-26861. 1997. write for info. (*0-300-06838-7*) Yale U Pr.

Rethinking the Role of the Automobile. Michael Renner. (Papers). 72p. (Orig.). (C). 1988. pap. 5.00 (*0-916468-85-2*) Worldwatch Inst.

Rethinking the Romance of the Rose: Text, Image, Reception. Ed. by Kevin Brownlee & Sylvia Huot. (Middle Ages Ser.). (Illus.). 400p. (Orig.). (C). 1992. text ed. 46.95 (*0-8122-3115-5*); pap. text ed. 19.95 (*0-8122-1395-5*) U of Pa Pr.

Rethinking the Russian Revolution. Edward Acton. (Reading History Ser.). 192p. 1990. 49.50 (*0-7131-6609-6*, A4334, Pub. by E Arnold UK) Routledge Chapman & Hall.

Rethinking the Russian Revolution. Edward Acton. (Reading History Ser.). 192p. 1995. text ed. 16.95 (*0-7131-6530-8*, A4338, Pub. by E Arnld UK) St Martin.

Rethinking the School: Subjectivity, Bureaucracy, Criticism. Ian Hunter. LC 93-49471. 1994. text ed. 45.00 (*0-312-12144-X*) St Martin.

Rethinking the Somali Political Experience. Hussein M. Adam. Date not set. pap. 18.95 (*0-932415-17-2*) Red Sea Pr.

Rethinking the South: Essays in Intellectual History. Michael O'Brien. LC 87-32482. 304p. 1988. text ed. 46.00 (*0-8018-3617-4*) Johns Hopkins.

Rethinking the South: Essays in Intellectual History. Michael O'Brien. LC 92-21424. (Brown Thrasher Bks.). (Illus.). 288p. 1993. reprint ed. pap. 20.00 (*0-8203-1525-7*) U of Ga Pr.

Rethinking the Soviet Experience: Politics & History since 1917. Stephen F. Cohen. 240p. 1986. pap. 8.95 (*0-19-504016-3*) OUP.

Rethinking the Soviet Experience: Politics & History Since 1917. Stephen F. Cohen. 288p. 1999. pap. 8.95 (*0-19-505714-7*) OUP.

Rethinking the Soviet Experience: Politics & History Since 1917. 2nd ed. Stephen F. Cohen. 288p. 1999. 29.95 (*0-19-506635-9*) OUP.

Rethinking the Spiritual Works of Mercy. Ed. by Francis A. Eigo. LC 93-13088. 1993. 8.95 (*0-87723-084-6*) Villanova U Pr.

***Rethinking the Sylph: New Perspectives on the Romantic Ballet.** rev. ed. Ed. by Lynn Garafola. LC 97-21728. (Illus.). 320p. 1997. reprint ed. text ed. 45.00 (*0-8195-6325-0*, Wesleyan Univ Pr) U Pr of New Eng.

***Rethinking the Sylph: New Perspectives on the Romantic Ballet.** rev. ed. Ed. by Lynn Garafola. LC 97-21728. (Illus.). 320p. 1997. reprint ed. pap. 19.95 (*0-8195-6326-9*, Wesleyan Univ Pr) U Pr of New Eng.

Rethinking the Theory of Organizational Communication: How to Read an Organization. James R. Taylor. LC 92-42916. (Communication & Information Science Ser.). 316p. 1993. pap. 39.50 (*1-56750-002-1*); text ed. 73.25 (*0-89391-885-7*) Ablex Pub.

Rethinking the Third World: Contributions Towards a New Conceptualization. Ed. by Rosemary Galli. 280p. 1991. 58.00 (*0-8448-1711-2*, Crane Russak); pap. 26.00 (*0-8448-1712-0*, Crane Russak) Taylor & Francis.

Rethinking the Transatlantic Partnership: Security & Economics in a New Era. Ed. by Gary L. Geipel & Robert A. Manning. 100p. (Orig.). 1996. pap. 12.95 (*1-55813-060-8*) Hudson Instit IN.

Rethinking the Trident Force. (Illus.). 78p. (Orig.). (C). 1993. pap. text ed. 40.00 (*1-56806-597-3*) DIANE Pub.

Rethinking the Unity of Luke & Acts. Mikeal C. Parsons & Richard I. Pervo. LC 93-9758. 1993. 19.00 (*0-8006-2750-4*, Fortress Pr) Augsburg Fortress.

Rethinking the Unthinkable: New Directions for Nuclear Arms. Ed. by Ivoh Daalder & Terry Terriff. 270p. 1993. text ed. 39.50 (*0-7146-4518-4*, Pub. by F Cass Pubs UK) Intl Spec Bk.

Rethinking the World: Discovery & Science in the Renaissance. (Illus.). 84p. 1992. 10.00 (*1-879598-12-4*) IN Univ Lilly Library.

Rethinking Third World Politics. Ed. by James Manor. 352p. (C). 1991. pap. text ed. 29.50 (*0-582-07458-4*, 78937) Longman.

Rethinking Today's Minorities. Ed. by Vincent N. Parrillo. LC 90-40733. (Contributions in Sociology Ser.: No. 93). 224p. 1991. text ed. 49.95 (*0-313-27537-8*, PRT, Greenwood Pr) Greenwood.

***Rethinking Tourism & Ecotravel: The Paving of Paradise & What You Can Do to Stop It.** Deborah McLaren. (Illus.). 224p. 1997. pap. 21.95 (*1-56549-065-7*) Kumarian Pr.

***Rethinking Tourism & Ecotravel: The Paving of Paradise & What You Can Do to Stop It.** Deborah McLaren. (Illus.). 224p. 1997. 48.00 (*1-56549-066-5*) Kumarian Pr.

***Rethinking Tradition: Integrating Service with Academic Study on College Campuses.** 200p. 1993. pap. 17.00 (*0-614-30599-3*) Ed Comm States.

Rethinking Tradition in Modern Islamic Thought. Daniel Brown. (Middle East Studies: No. 5). 250p. (C). 1996. text ed. 49.95 (*0-521-57077-8*) Cambridge U Pr.

Rethinking Translation: Discourse, Subjectivity, Ideology. Ed. by Lawrence Venuti. LC 91-30975. 204p. (Orig.). (C). 1992. pap. 16.95 (*0-415-06051-6*, A6620) Routledge.

Rethinking Ukrainian History. Ed. by Ivan L. Rudnytsky & John-Paul Himka. x, 268p. 1981. 14.95 (*0-920862-12-8*); pap. 9.95 (*0-920862-14-4*) Ukrainian Acad.

***Rethinking Unionism: An Alternative Vision for Northern Ireland.** Norman Porter. 252p. 9700. pap. 21.95 (*0-85640-585-X*, Pub. by Blackstaff Pr IE) Dufour.

Rethinking Urban Policy: Urban Development in An Advanced Economy. National Research Council Staff (U. S.). Ed. by Royce Hanson. LC 83-19422. 231p. reprint ed. pap. 65.90 (*0-7837-3738-6*, 2043430) Bks Demand.

***Rethinking Visual Anthropology.** Marcus Banks & Howard Morphy. LC 96-35202. 1997. write for info. (*0-300-06691-0*) Yale U Pr.

Rethinking Western Water Policy: Assessing the Limits of Legislation. Larry Morandi. 64p. 1994. pap. text ed. 10.00 (*1-55516-404-8*, 4339) Natl Conf State Legis.

Rethinking White Collar Crime. Tony G. Poveda. LC 94-1143. (Criminology & Crime Control Policy Ser.). 184p. 1994. text ed. 55.00 (*0-275-94586-3*, Praeger Pubs) Greenwood.

Rethinking Work Experience. Andrew Miller et al. 280p. 1991. 70.00 (*1-85000-895-7*, Falmer Pr); pap. 31.00 (*1-85000-896-5*, Falmer Pr) Taylor & Francis.

Rethinking Working-Class History: Bengal 1890-1940. Dipesh Chakrabarty. 300p. 1989. text ed. 47.50 (*0-691-05548-3*) Princeton U Pr.

Rethinking World History: Essays on Europe, Islam, & World History. Marshall G. Hodgson. LC 92-32575. (Studies in Comparative World History). 384p. (C). 1993. text ed. 54.95 (*0-521-43253-7*); pap. text ed. 19.95 (*0-521-43844-6*) Cambridge U Pr.

Rethinking Writing. Peshe C. Kuriloff. LC 88-60555. 229p. (Orig.). (C). 1989. teacher ed. write for info. (*0-312-01307-8*) St Martin.

Rethinking Writing. Joanne M. Podis & Leonard A. Podis. LC 95-23479. 1995. pap. text ed. 34.00 (*0-205-14805-0*) Allyn.

Rethinking Young Drivers. Ed. by J. Peter Rothe. 292p. 1989. pap. 21.95 (*0-88738-785-3*) Transaction Pubs.

***Rethinking Youth.** Johanna Wyn & Rob White. 208p. 1997. 69.95 (*0-7619-5521-6*); pap. 22.95 (*0-7619-5522-4*) Sage.

***Rethinking 1 Corinthians 11.2-16 Through Archaeological & Moral-Rhetorical Analysis.** David E. Blattenberger. LC 97-17799. (Studies in the Bible & Early Christianity). 1997. write for info. (*0-7734-8562-7*) E Mellen.

Rethymno As a Style of Life see Pandelis Prevelakis & the Value of a Heritage

Reticent Expansionism: The Foreign Policy of William McKinley. John M. Dobson. LC 87-34541. 212p. 1988. text ed. 26.50 (*0-8207-0202-1*) Duquesne.

Reticles in Electro Optical Devices. L. M. Biberman & R. Legault. LC 65-28562. (International Series of Monographs in Interdisciplinary & Advanced Topics: Vol. 1). 1966. 84.00 (*0-08-011683-3*, Pub. by Pergamon Repr UK) Franklin.

Reticulocyte. Samuel M. Rapoport. 256p. 1986. 218.00 (*0-8493-6538-4*, QP96) CRC Pr.

***Reticulocyte Counting by Flow Cytometry: Proposed Guideline (1993)** Contrib. by John A. Koepke. 1993. 75.00 (*1-56238-207-1*, H44-P) Natl Comm Clin Lab Stds.

Reticuloendothelial Structure & Function. Ed. by John H. Heller. LC 60-9817. 483p. reprint ed. 137.70 (*0-8357-9976-X*, 2012566) Bks Demand.

Reticuloendothelial System: A Comprehensive Treatise, Vol. 7A: Physiology. Ed. by Sherwood M. Reichard & James P. Filkens. LC 79-25933. 436p. 1984. 105.00 (*0-306-41422-8*, Plenum Pr) Plenum.

Reticuloendothelial System: A Comprehensive Treatise, Vol. 10: Infection. Ed. by Mario R. Escobar & J. P. Utz. LC 79-25933. (Illus.). 376p. 1988. 99.00 (*0-306-42846-6*, Plenum Pr) Plenum.

Reticuloendothelial System: A Comprehensive Treatise Vol. 9, Hypersensitivity. Ed. by S. Michael Phillips & Mario R. Escobar. LC 79-25933. 512p. 1986. 115.00 (*0-306-42305-7*, Plenum Pr) Plenum.

Reticuloendothelial System Vol. 3: A Comprehensive Treatise: Phylogeny & Ontogeny. Ed. by Nicholas Cohen & Michael Sigel. LC 79-25933. 790p. 1982. 135.00 (*0-306-40928-3*, Plenum Pr) Plenum.

Reticuloendothelial System Vol. 4: A Comprehensive Treatise: Immunopathology. Ed. by Noel R. Rose & Benjamin V. Siegel. LC 79-25933. 464p. 1983. 105.00 (*0-306-40979-8*, Plenum Pr) Plenum.

Reticuloendothelial System Vol. 5: A Comprehensive Treatise: Cancer. Ed. by Herman Friedman & Ronald B. Herberman. LC 79-25933. 376p. 1983. 95.00 (*0-306-41294-2*, Plenum Pr) Plenum.

Reticuloendothelial System Vol. 6: A Comprehensive Treatise: Immunology. Ed. by Joseph A. Bellanti & Herbert B. Herscowitz. LC 79-25933. 370p. 1984. 95.00 (*0-306-41421-X*, Plenum Pr) Plenum.

Reticuloendothelial System Vol. 7B: A Comprehensive Treatise: Physiology. Ed. by Sherwood M. Reichard & James P. Filkins. LC 79-25933. 558p. 1984. 115.00 (*0-306-41423-6*, Plenum Pr) Plenum.

Reticuloendothelial System Vol. 8: A Comprehensive Treatise: Pharmacology. Ed. by John W. Hadden & Andor Szentivanyi. LC 79-25933. 490p. 1985. 115.00 (*0-306-41792-8*, Plenum Pr) Plenum.

Reticuloendothelial System & Atherosclerosis: Proceedings. International Symposium on Atherosclerosis Staff. Ed. by N. R. Di Luzio & Rodolfo Paoletti. LC 67-17374. (Advances in Experimental Medicine & Biology Ser.: Vol. 1). 528p. reprint ed. pap. 150.50 (*0-685-15834-9*, 2026307) Bks Demand.

Retief! Jan Strnad & Dennis Fujitake. (Illus.). 192p. 1990. 14.95 (*0-927203-01-4*); pap. 14.95 (*0-927203-00-6*) Apple Pr PA.

Retin-A & Other Youth Miracles. Joseph P. Bark. 272p. 1990. reprint ed. pap. 9.95 (*1-55958-029-1*) Prima Pub.

Retina. Bressler. 1996. text ed. write for info. (*0-7216-6731-7*) Saunders.

Retina. 2nd ed. Ed. by Stephen J. Ryan. LC 93-40452. 2559p. (C). (gr. 13). 1994. text ed. 425.00 (*0-8016-8032-8*) Mosby Yr Bk.

Retina: An Approachable Part of the Brain. John E. Dowling. LC 87-152. (Illus.). 368p. 1987. 48.00 (*0-674-76680-6*) HUP.

Retina: The Fundamentals. Gloria Wu. (Illus.). 256p. 1995. text ed. 71.50 (*0-7216-6691-4*) Saunders.

Retina & Vitreous. Ed. by Rudolph M. Franklin. LC 93-12350. (Illus.). 1993. lib. bdg. 103.50 (*90-6299-091-6*) Kugler Pubns.

Retina & Vitreous: Section Four. (Basic & Clinical Science Course (1989-90) Ser.). 196p. (C). 1989. pap. text ed. 45.00 (*0-685-26048-8*) Am Acad Ophthal.

Retina & Vitreous: Textbook of Ophthalmology, Vol. 9. Federman & Gouras. 512p. 1993. 136.00 (*1-56375-100-3*) Gower-Mosby.

Retina Atlas. David R. Guyer et al. LC 94-31577. (Illus.). 800p. (C). (gr. 13). 1995. text ed. 260.00 (*0-8151-3432-0*) Mosby Yr Bk.

Retina, Vitreous & Choroid: Clinical Procedures. Robert L. Johnston. Ed. by Chris J. Cakanac. (Clinical Procedure Ser.). (Illus.). 136p. 1995. spiral bd. 40.00 (*0-7506-9615-X*) Buttrwrth-Heinemann.

Retina-Vitreous-Macula. Guyer. 1998. text ed. write for info. (*0-7216-6756-2*) Saunders.

Retinal Degeneration: Clinical & Laboratory Applications. Ed. by Joe G. Hollyfield et al. (Illus.). 352p. (C). 1994. 95.00 (*0-306-44570-0*, Plenum Pr) Plenum.

Retinal Degeneration & Regeneration: Proceedings of an International Symposium, Kanazawa, Japan, July 8-9, 1995. Ed. by Shinzi Kato et al. LC 96-1713. 1996. 90.00 (*90-6299-143-2*) Kugler Pubns.

Retinal Degenerations. Robert E. Anderson et al. (Illus.). 544p. 1991. 306.00 (*0-8493-0178-5*, RE551, CRC Reprint) Franklin.

Retinal Detachment. 5th ed. George F. Hilton et al. (Ophthalmology Monographs). (Illus.). 175p. (Orig.). 1989. pap. text ed. 37.50 (*0-685-26044-5*) Am Acad Ophthal.

Retinal Detachment: A Colour Manual of Diagnosis & Treatment. 2nd ed. Jack J. Kanski & Zdenek Gregor. (Colour Manuals in Ophthalmology Ser.). (Illus.). 179p. 1995. 75.00 (*0-7506-1768-3*) Buttrwrth-Heinemann.

Retinal Detachment: Diagnosis & Management. 2nd ed. William E. Benson. LC 65-10911. (Illus.). 224p. 1988. text ed. 68.25 (*0-397-50926-X*, Lppnctt) Lppncott-Raven.

Retinal Detachment: Principles & Practice. 2nd rev. ed. George F. Hilton et al. LC 94-43382. (Ophthalmology Monographs: Vol. 1). 1995. write for info. (*1-56055-028-7*) Am Acad Ophthal.

Retinal Detachment see Michels's Retinal Detachment

Retinal Detachment & Allied Diseases, 2 Vols., 1. Charles L. Schepens. (Illus.). 600p. 1983. text ed. 200.00 (*0-7216-7965-X*) Saunders.

Retinal Detachment & Allied Diseases, 2 Vols., 2. Charles L. Schepens. (Illus.). 600p. 1983. text ed. 200.00 (*0-7216-7966-8*) Saunders.

Retinal Detachment & Allied Diseases, 2 Vols., Set. Charles L. Schepens. (Illus.). 600p. 1983. text ed. 395.00 (*0-7216-7956-0*) Saunders.

Retinal Detachment Surgery. A. H. Chignell. (Illus.). 1980. 45.00 (*0-387-09475-X*) Spr-Verlag.

Retinal Diseases. Mark O. Tso. LC 65-8261. (Illus.). 480p. 1988. text ed. 85.00 (*0-397-50661-9*, Lppnctt) Lppncott-Raven.

Retinal Diseases: A Symposium on Differential Diagnostic Problems of Posterior Uveitis. Ed. by Samuel J. Kimura & Wayne M. Caygill. LC 66-16617. (Illus.). 395p. reprint ed. 112.60 (*0-8357-9420-2*, 2014557) Bks Demand.

Retinal Diseases: Pathogenesis, Laser Therapy, & Surgery. Jesse Sigelman. 1984. 130.00 (*0-316-79052-4*) Little.

Retinal Diseases Two. Ed. by R. Brancato et al. LC 87-22626. (Illus.). 392p. 1987. lib. bdg. 125.00 (*90-6299-037-1*, Pub. by Kugler NE) Kugler Pubns.

***Retinal Dystrophies & Degenerations.** Ed. by David A. Newsome. LC 84-42913. reprint ed. pap. 113.50 (*0-608-04744-9*, 2065465) Bks Demand.

Retinal Pigment Epithelial Transplantation. Devjani Lahiri-Munir & C. Garcia. LC 95-7452. (Medical Intelligence Unit Ser.). 133p. 1995. 69.00 (*1-57059-255-1*) R G Landes.

Retinal Pigment Epithelium. Ed. by M. Zingirian & F. C. Piccolino. LC 89-19878. (Illus.). 326p. 1990. lib. bdg. 106.50 (*90-6299-055-X*, Pub. by Kugler NE) Kugler Pubns.

Retinal Pigment Epithelium. Ed. by Keith M. Zinn & Michael F. Marmor. (Illus.). 531p. (C). 1979. 68.00 (*0-674-76684-9*) HUP.

Retinal Proteins. Ed. by Yu A. Ovchinnikov. 590p. 1987. lib. bdg. 179.00 (*90-6764-102-2*, Pub. by VSP NE) Coronet Bks.

Retinal Transmitters & Modulators: Models for the Brain, Vol. I. Ed. by William W. Morgan. 176p. 1985. 132.00 (*0-8493-5691-1*, QP479) CRC Pr.

Retinal Transmitters & Modulators: Models for the Brain, Vol. 2. William W. Morgan. LC 84-12068. 176p. 1984. 105.00 (*0-8493-5692-X*, QP479) Franklin.

***Retine, Vieillissement et Transplantation, Vol. 5.** Ed. by Y. Christen et al. 200p. 1994. 73.00 (*2-906077-42-9*) Elsevier.

***Retine, Vieillissement et Transplantation, Vol. 6.** Ed. by Y. Christen et al. 200p. 1995. 84.00 (*2-906077-60-7*) Elsevier.

Retinitis Pigmentosa: Proceedings of the 4th Congress of the International Retinitis Pigmentosa Association, Bad Nauheim 1986, FRG, Pt. 2. F. Brunsmann & R. Von Gyzicki. (Advances in the Biosciences Ser.: Vol. 63). 322p. 1988. 120.00 (*0-08-035725-3*, Pergamon Pr) Elsevier.

***Retinoid Protocols.** Ed. by Christopher Redfern. (Methods in Molecular Biology Ser.: Vol. 89). (Illus.). 350p. 1997. 69.50 (*0-89603-438-0*) Humana.

Retinoid Therapy: A Review of Clinical & Laboratory Research. Ed. by W. J. Cunliffe & A. Miller. 376p. 1983. text ed. 49.00 (*0-85200-740-X*) Kluwer Ac.

Retinoids: A Clinician's Guide. Nicholas Lowe & Ronald Marks. 1995. 75.00 (*0-614-06222-5*); 75.00 (*0-614-07390-1*, M Dunitz) Scovill Paterson.

Retinoids: Biology, Chemistry, & Medicine. 2nd ed. Ed. by Michael B. Sporn et al. LC 93-3451. 704p. 1993. text ed. 167.00 (*0-7817-0082-5*) Lppncott-Raven.

Retinoids: From Basic Science to Clinical Applications. Ed. by M. A. Livrea & G. Vidali. LC 94-16145. (Molecular & Cell Biology Updates Ser.). 1994. 116.00 (*0-8176-2812-6*) Birkhauser.

Retinoids: Progress in Research & Clinical Applications. M. A. Livrea & Packer. (Basic & Clinical Dermatology Ser.: Vol. 5). 672p. 1993. 225.00 (*0-8247-8758-7*) Dekker.

Retinoids: Ten Years On. Ed. by J. H. Saurat. (Illus.). x, 356p. 1991. 291.50 (*3-8055-5387-0*) S Karger.

Retinoids - Experimental & Clinical Results: Seventeenth World Congress of Dermatology, Berlin, May 1987, Journal: Dermatologica, Vol. 175, suppl. 1. Ed. by R. Stadler et al. (Illus.). iv, 204p. 1987. pap. 58.50 (*3-8055-4708-0*) S Karger.

An Asterisk (*) at the beginning of an entry indicates that the title is appearing in BIP for the first time.

Retinoids & Cell Differentiation. Ed. by Michael I. Sherman. 256p. 1986. 121.00 (0-8493-6322-5, QH607, CRC Reprint) Franklin.

Retinoids in Clinical Practice: The Risk-Benefit Ratio. Koren. (Medical Toxicology Ser.: Vol. 1). 296p. 1992. 140.00 (0-8247-8778-1) Dekker.

Retinoids in Cutaneous Malignancy. R. Marks. (Illus.). 215p. 1991. 135.00 (0-632-02646-4) Blackwell Sci.

Retinoids in Normal Development & Teratogenesis. Ed. by Gillian Morriss-Kay. (Illus.). 320p. 1992. 89.00 (0-19-854770-6) OUP.

Retinoids in Oncology. European School of Oncology Staff. Ed. by L. Degos & D. R. Parkinson. LC 95-14259. (ESO Monographs). (Illus.). 115p. 1995. 104.00 (3-540-59181-8) Spr-Verlag.

Retinoids in Oncology. Ed. by Hong & Lotan. LC 93-10155. (Basic & Clinical Oncology Ser.: Vol. 4). 352p. 1993. 160.00 (0-8247-9048-0) Dekker.

***Retinoids, Their Physiological Function & Therapeutic Potential.** Ed. by E. Edward Bittar & G. V. Sherbet. (Advances in Organ Biology Ser.: Vol. 3). 1997. 128.50 (0-7623-0285-2) Jai Pr.

Retinopathy of Prematurity. Ed. by Michael J. Shapiro et al. 1995. 94.00 (90-6299-125-4) Kugler Pubns.

Retinopathy of Prematurity: A Clinician's Guide. Ed. by J. T. Flynn & William S. Tasman. (Illus.). xiii, 162p. 1992. 95.00 (0-387-97635-3) Spr-Verlag.

Retinoscopy Book: An Introductory Manual for Eye Care Professionals. 4th ed. John M. Corboy et al. LC 79-65451. (Illus.). 160p. 1995. pap. text ed. 40.00 (1-55642-271-7, 62717) SLACK Inc.

***Retire a Millionaire.** Ken Kasel. 128p. 1997. pap. write for info. (1-886094-73-X) Chicago Spectrum.

Retire & Rejoice. Blackie Scott. 1995. pap. 6.95 (1-56145-112-6) Peachtree Pubs.

Retire & Thrive: Remarkable People Share Their Creative, Productive, & Profitable Retirement Strategies. Robert K. Otterbourg. 256p. 1995. pap. 15.00 (0-8129-2646-3) Kiplinger Bks.

***Retire at 55: Campbell Brown's Guide to Early Retirement.** Campbell Brown, Jr. Ed. by Mary C. Brown. (Orig.). 1997. pap. write for info. (0-614-28380-9) C Brown.

Retire Easy! A Blueprint for Building Personal Wealth. Thomas J. Nolan, Jr. (Illus.). 1984. 16.95 (0-13-778952-1, Busn); pap. 7.95 (0-13-778945-9, Busn) P-H.

Retire in Style: The Lifetime Security Planning Guide. Edward S. Soltesz. (Illus.). 1988. pap. 15.95 (0-8306-3017-1, 30017) McGraw-Hill Prof.

Retire Refired: A Guide to Dynamic Retirements. Elsie Perlmutter. 1988. pap. 12.95 (0-318-35152-8) Grad School.

Retire Richer with TIAA-CREF. Robert M. Soldofsky. Ed. by Bradley M. Loomer & Mary L. Snyder. LC 96-60593. 311p. (Orig.). 1996. pap. write for info. (0-9651682-0-4) Useful Pr IA.

Retire Smart: Sound Advice to Help You Make Your Retirement Years Happy, Healthy & Active. David Cleary & Virginia Cleary. LC 93-71917. 224p. (Orig.). 1993. pap. 12.95 (1-880559-09-9) Allworth Pr.

Retire to Fun & Freedom. Louise McCants & Cavett Robert. 192p. 1990. pap. 12.95 (0-446-39139-5) Warner Bks.

***Retire to Your Garden.** Margaret Davis. (Illus.). 80p. 1998. pap. 14.95 (0-86417-846-8, Pub. by Kangaroo Pr AT) Seven Hills Bk.

***Retired - Deal with It.** Jan B. King. Ed. by Cliff Carle. (Illus.). 64p. (Orig.). 1997. pap. 5.95 (1-57644-057-5) CCC Pubns.

Retired & Loving It. Bruce Cochran. 10p. 1995. write for info. (1-886386-29-3) Trisar.

Retired Dreams: Dom Casmurro, Myth & Modernity. Paul B. Dixon. LC 88-29081. 156p. (Orig.). 1989. pap. 10.95 (0-911198-98-9) Purdue U Pr.

Retired? Get Back in the Game! 37 Stories of Vibrant Men & Women (in Their 60s, 70s, 80s & 90s) Who Are Joyously Productive. Jack Wyman. 200p. 1994. pap. 14.95 (0-9639180-2-8) Doer Pubns.

***Retired Military Almanac.** Sol Gordon. 252p. 1997. 6.25 (1-888096-57-8) Uniformed Srvs.

Retiree Benefits: The Complete Guide to FASB Compliance & Health Care Cost Control, 1. 1989. write for info. (1-55871-120-1) BNA Plus.

Retiree Benefits: The Complete Guide to FASB Compliance & Health Care Cost Control, 2. 1989. write for info. (1-55871-121-X) BNA Plus.

Retiree Benefits: The Complete Guide to FASB Compliance & Health Care Cost Control, Set. 1989. 150.00 (1-55871-119-8) BNA Plus.

Retiree Health Benefits: Field Test of the FASB Proposal. Harold Dankner et al. LC 89-84509. (Illus.). 215p. 1989. pap. 25.00 (0-910586-74-8, 079-89) Finan Exec.

Retiree Health Benefits: How to Cope with the Accounting, Actuarial, & Management Issues. Murray S. Akresh et al. Ed. by Claire Barth & Jennifer Strand. (Bold Step Ser.). (Illus.). 134p. (Orig.). 1991. pap. 40.00 (0-86641-194-1, 91256) Inst Mgmt Account.

Retiree Health Benefits: What Is the Promise? 1989. 39.95 (0-86643-089-X) Empl Benefit Res Inst.

Retiree Health Care Crisis. Ed. by James H. Ballagh. (Current Issues Ser.: No. 12). 100p. (Orig.). 1989. pap. 10.00 (0-89215-159-5) U Cal LA Indus Rel.

Retiree Medical Liabilities, FAS 106, & Cost Containment: New Approaches to Redesign, Prefunding, & Disclosure. Cynthia Combe & Harold Dankner. (Tax Law & Estate Planning Course Handbook Ser.). 247p. 1992. pap. 17.50 (0-685-69487-9); audio 40.00 (0-685-69488-7) PLI.

Retiree Nonpension Benefits: Management Guidelines. E. Van Olson. (Current Issues Ser.: No. 2). 32p. 1993. reprint ed. 5.50 (0-89215-137-4) U Cal LA Indus Rel.

Retirees Handbook: Things to Do with All That Time Your Children Think You Have. Sue Schoening-Roess. 1995. pap. text ed. 5.95 (0-9645842-0-4) Blue Sky FL.

Retirement: A Consumer Guide for Planning & Housing New Jersey 1996. Barbara M. Lancaster. Ed. by Liane Gonzalez. 260p. 1995. pap. text ed. 24.95 (1-57108-011-2) Lancashire Intl.

Retirement: An Annotated Bibliography. Compiled by John J. Miletich. LC 86-9933. (Bibliographies & Indexes in Geronotology Ser.: No. 2). 164p. 1986. text ed. 42.95 (0-313-24815-X, MRI/, Greenwood Pr) Greenwood.

***Retirement: Beginning Your Best Years.** Ed. by Patrick Caton. 80p. 1997. spiral bd. 7.95 (1-56245-287-8) Great Quotations.

Retirement: Coping with Emotional Upheavals. Leland Bradford & Martha Bradford. LC 79-4101. 1979. 26.95 (0-88229-564-0) Nelson-Hall.

Retirement: Creating Promise out of Threat. Robert K. Kinzel. LC 78-32165. 141p. reprint ed. pap. 40.20 (0-317-26949-6, 2023584) Bks Demand.

Retirement: It's a Profession. Robert P. Hay. 24p. 1995. pap. 10.50 (0-8059-3666-1) Dorrance.

Retirement: Planned Liberation? Phil Long. 116p. (C). 1981. 102.00 (0-85292-294-9, Pub. by IPM Hse UK) St Mut.

Retirement: Planning Tomorrow Today. R. Stadt et al. LC 82-14799. 192p. 1983. pap. text ed. 12.75 (0-07-000404-8) McGraw.

Retirement: The Challenge of Change. E. Michael Brady. (Orig.). 1988. pap. 8.00 (0-939561-02-6) Univ South ME.

***Retirement: The Get Even Years.** Fred Sahner. Ed. by Cliff Carle. (Illus.). 96p. (Orig.). 1997. pap. 5.95 (1-57644-049-4) CCC Pubns.

Retirement: You're in Charge. Eleanor L. Furman. LC 84-3459. 176p. 1984. text ed. 49.95 (0-275-91159-4, C1159, Praeger Pubs) Greenwood.

Retirement-Age Policy: An International Perspective. Sara E. Rix & Paul Fisher. (Policy Studies on Social Policy). (Illus.). 176p. 1982. 56.00 (0-08-028840-5, K110, L115, Pergamon Pr) Elsevier.

Retirement (An Excerpt from the Tarnish on the Golden Years) Nona K. Carver. (Illus.). 22p. (Orig.). 1994. pap. 7.00 (0-9641195-1-X) Carver Cntry.

Retirement & Benefit Planning: Strategy & Design for Business & Tax-Exempt Organization. Randolph M. Goodman. 700p. 1994. ring bd. 105.00 (0-88063-331-X) MICHIE.

Retirement & Economic Behavior. Henry J. Aaron. 1984. pap. 16.95 (0-8157-0035-0) Brookings.

***Retirement & Estate Planning for Dummies.** Eric Tyson. 1997. pap. 19.99 (0-7645-5060-8) IDG Bks.

Retirement & Other Myths: Musings on the Leisurely Life with a Dash of Humor & Advice. Elliott Richman. LC 93-43072. 150p. 1994. pap. 9.95 (1-56875-074-9) R & E Pubs.

Retirement & Welfare Benefit Plans: A Guide to Understanding the Tax Implications. Michael G. Kushner et al. LC 89-36332. 610p. reprint ed. pap. 173.90 (0-7837-6419-7, 2046399) Bks Demand.

Retirement Angles: 1001 Ways to Make Your Life Better Today & Tomorrow. Donald J. Korn. 150p. 1994. pap. 15.95 (0-9639629-4-9) Shot Tower.

Retirement Association at the University of Washington: A History. Neal O. Hines. LC 90-12031. 140p. (Orig.). 1990. pap. 9.95 (0-295-96996-2) U of Wash Pr.

Retirement Begins at Forty. 69p. 1980. 2.00 (0-317-33899-4) Central Conf.

Retirement Benefits Examiner. Jack Rudman. (Career Examination Ser.: C-1558). 1994. pap. 29.95 (0-8373-1558-1) Nat Learn.

***Retirement Benefits Tax Guide.** 1800p. 1995. ring bd. 135.00 (0-8080-0060-8, 04695BLS05) Commerce.

Retirement Book. Herbert I. Kavet. 96p. 1993. 5.95 (0-88032-437-6) Ivory Tower Pub.

Retirement Careers: Combining the Best of Work & Leisure. DeLoss L. Marsh. Ed. by Susan Williamson & Roger Griffith. LC 91-2036. 192p. (Orig.). 1991. pap. 10.95 (0-913589-55-1) Williamson Pub Co.

Retirement Choices in North & South America, 2 vols., Set. 1991. lib. bdg. 128.95 (0-8490-4687-4) Gordon Pr.

Retirement Communities: An American Original. Ed. by Michael E. Hunt et al. LC 83-26506. (Journal of Housing for the Elderly: Vol. 1, Nos. 3-4). 278p. 1984. text ed. 49.95 (0-86656-267-2) Haworth Pr.

Retirement Communities: The Best Choices in Metro Washington. Peter Vandevanter. LC 91-32191. (Illus.). 255p. (Orig.). 1991. pap. 5.00 (0-939009-51-X) EPM Pubns.

Retirement Communities in Florida: A Consumer's Guide & Directory to Service-Oriented Facilities. Mary L. Brooks. LC 92-33930. 164p. 1993. pap. 12.95 (1-56164-024-7) Pineapple Pr.

***Retirement Community Movement: Some Contemporary Issues.** Ed. by Leon A. Pastalan. 81p. 1989. 24.95 (0-86656-925-1) Haworth Pr.

Retirement Counseling: A Handbook for Action. Jane E. Myers & Harold C. Riker. (Death Education, Aging & Health Care Ser.). 1989. 66.95 (0-89116-628-9) Hemisp Pub.

Retirement Counseling: A Handbook for Gerontology Practitioners. Virginia E. Richardson. LC 92-48349. (Life Styles & Issues in Aging Ser.: Vol. 1). 224p. 1993. 31.95 (0-8261-7020-X) Springer Pub.

Retirement Counselling: A Comprehensive Guide to Pre-Retirement Preparation & Training. Keith Hughes. LC 92-30639. 1992. 24.95 (0-07-707597-8) McGraw.

Retirement Decisions Made Easier: For Federal Employees under the Civil Service Retirement System. 4th ed. John W. Cooley. 200p. 1995. reprint ed. student ed., ring bd. 29.95 (1-883336-00-7) CCL.

***Retirement for Fun & Profit: "Supplement Your Income While Enjoying Your Retirement"** (Illus.). 350p. (Orig.). 1998. pap. 24.95 (1-56559-920-9) HGI Mrktng.

Retirement Guide for Canadians: An Overall Plan for a Comfortable Future. 12th rev. ed. Henry S. Hunnisett. (Retirement Ser.). 280p. 1993. pap. 9.95 (0-88908-288-X) Self-Counsel Pr.

Retirement Housing Markets: Project Planning & Feasibility Analysis. Susan Brecht & James F. Sherman. LC 90-25074. (Real Estate Practice Library). 352p. 1991. text ed. 140.00 (0-471-51630-9) Wiley.

Retirement in Industrialized Societies: Social, Psychological & Health Factors. Kyriacos C. Markides & Cary L. Cooper. 331p. 1987. text ed. 170.00 (0-471-91040-6) Wiley.

Retirement in Industrialized Societies: Social, Psychological, & Health Factors. Ed. by Kyriakos S. Markides & Cary L. Cooper. LC 86-19016. 343p. reprint ed. pap. 97.80 (0-7837-4766-7, 2044520) Bks Demand.

Retirement in the Twenty-First Century: Ready or Not? Employee Benefit Research Institute Staff. Ed. by Dallas L. Salisbury & Nora S. Jones. 1995. 29.95 (0-86643-081-4) Empl Benefit Res Inst.

Retirement Income Policy in Japan & the United States: United States - Japan Legislative Exchange Study Tour Report. Ronald K. Snell. 21p. 1993. pap. 5.00 (1-55516-526-5, 9321) Natl Conf State Legis.

Retirement Income Versus Family Responsibility: 10 Ways to Protect Working Women's Pension Benefits. (BNA Special Report Series in Work & Family: No. 29). 1990. write for info. (0-318-68057-2) BNA Plus.

Retirement Keys: Keys to Volunteering. Elizabeth Vierck. 1996. pap. text ed. 6.95 (0-8120-9507-3) Barron.

Retirement Life Planning: A Home Seminar for Husbands & Wives. rev. ed. William N. Cox. 82p. 1989. student ed. 59.95 (1-880429-01-2) CR & Assocs.

Retirement Living: A Guide to Housing Alternatives. fac. ed. Richard Forrest & Mary B. Forrest. LC 90-26863. 224p. 1991. reprint ed. pap. 63.90 (0-7837-8156-3, 2047861) Bks Demand.

Retirement Living: A Guide to the Best Residences in Northern California. Sally Ravel & Lee A. Wolfe. (Illus.). 256p. (Orig.). 1991. reprint ed. 35.00 (0-8095-5861-0) Borgo Pr.

***Retirement Made Easy.** 2nd ed. Rosemary Brown. (Careers & Testing Ser.). 1994. pap. 16.95 (0-7494-1099-X) Kogan Page Ltd.

Retirement Migration in America: An Analysis of the Size, Trends & Economic Impact of the Country's Newest Growth Industry. Charles F. Longino. Ed. & Frwd. by R. Alan Fox. LC 94-62150. (Illus.). 185p. (Orig.). 1995. pap. 39.95 (0-9644216-1-5) Vacation Pubns.

Retirement Myth: What You Must Know to Prosper in the Coming Meltdown of Job Security... Craig S. Karpel. 272p. 1996. pap. 12.50 (0-06-092737-2) HarpC.

Retirement of Revolutionaries in China: Public Policies, Social Norms, Private Interests. Melanie Manion. LC 92-32031. (Illus.). 224p. (C). 1993. text ed. 37.50 (0-691-08653-2) Princeton U Pr.

Retirement on a Shoestring. 2nd ed. John Howells. LC 95-15927. 216p. (Orig.). 1995. pap. 8.95 (0-933469-23-3) Gateway Bks.

Retirement, Pensions, & Social Security. Gary S. Fields & Olivia S. Mitchell. (Illus.). 192p. 1984. 24.00 (0-262-06091-4) MIT Pr.

Retirement Place Rated. Frommer Staff & David Savageau. (Illus.). 320p. 1995. 19.95 (0-02-860055-X) Macmillan.

Retirement Places Rated. David Savageau. 1995. pap. 20.00 (0-671-51750-3) S&S Trade.

Retirement Places Rated. 3rd ed. David Savageau. 288p. 1990. pap. 16.95 (0-13-778929-7) P-H.

Retirement Plan Alternatives: The Role of the Business Officer. Louis R. Morrell. LC 94-20948. 1994. 25.00 (0-915164-95-7) NACUBO.

Retirement Planning Alert: Will Your Plans Meet Your Life Style Needs? Richard J. Curtis. LC 87-36488. (Illus.). 62p. (Orig.). 1988. pap. 8.95 (0-945298-03-X) Curtis Pubns.

Retirement-Planning & Adjustment: A Selected Bibliography. John J. Miletich. (CPL Bibliographies Ser.: No. 117). 53p. 1983. 10.00 (0-86602-117-5, Sage Prdcls Pr) Sage.

Retirement Plans: A Users Guide for Employees & Retirees. Michael J. Pippin. LC 94-69148. 192p. 1995. pap. 12.95 (0-9644272-0-6) Pension Srv Design.

Retirement Plans: Basic Features & Defined Contribution Approaches - CEBS Study Manual: Course III. Wharton School Staff. 299p. (Orig.). 1992. student ed., pap. 65.00 (0-89154-450-X) Intl Found Employ.

Retirement Plans: Defined Benefit Approaches & Plan Administration - Study Manual - CEBS Course IV. Wharton School Staff. 272p. (Orig.). 1992. student ed., pap. 75.00 (0-89154-451-8) Intl Found Employ.

Retirement Retreats: or Which Concentration Camp Do You Prefer? Gyeorgos C. Hatonn. (The/Phoenix Journals). 223p. 1993. pap. 6.00 (1-56935-027-2) Phoenix Source.

Retirement Rights. Nancy Levitan. LC 93-49888. 512p. (Orig.). 1994. pap. 15.00 (0-380-76894-1) Avon.

Retirement Sample, Vol. 1. Public Employee Retirement Administration Staff. 113p. 1973. 7.00 (0-317-34952-X) Municipal.

Retirement Savings Plans: Design, Regulation, & Administration of Cash or Deferred Arrangments. David A. Littell et al. 90p. 1994. suppl. ed., pap. 47.00 (0-471-03581-5) Wiley.

Retirement Security: Planning a Sound Financial Future. David M. Walker. LC 96-24022. 320p. 1996. text ed. 29.95 (0-471-15207-2) Wiley.

Retirement Security & Tax Policy. Sophie M. Korczyk. LC 84-7975. 200p. (Orig.). 1984. 39.95 (0-86643-040-7); pap. 24.95 (0-86643-037-7) Empl Benefit Res Inst.

Retirement Systems for Public Employees. Thomas P. Bleakney. (Pension Research Council Publications). 232p. (C). 1991. text ed. 35.95 (0-256-01407-8) U of Pa Pr.

Retirement Systems in Japan. Robert L. Clark. (Pension Research Council Publications). 120p. (C). 1991. text ed. 32.50 (0-256-09141-2) U of Pa Pr.

Retirement 101: How TIAA-CREF Members Should Deal with the Dramatic Changes in Their Pensions. Willard F. Enteman. LC 92-18510. (Illus.). 244p. (Orig.). 1992. pap. 8.95 (0-299-13574-8) U of Wis Pr.

Retirement 901: A Comprehensive Seminar for Senior Faculty & Staff. Clay Schoenfeld. LC 92-62443. 249p. 1993. 27.95 (0-912150-25-4) Magna Pubns.

***Retirement...The Time for Real Happiness.** Walter O. Bachus. LC 96-94855. 160p. (Orig.). 1996. pap. 9.95 (0-9655395-0-4) W O Bachus.

Retiring First Class. Clint Combs & Larry Bradshaw. 144p. 1993. 9.98 (0-88290-470-1, 2050) Horizon Utah.

Retiring from Military Service: A Commonsense Guide. 2nd ed. K. C. Jacobsen. LC 94-7805. 320p. 1994. 25.95 (1-55750-401-6) Naval Inst Pr.

***Retiring in Arizona: Your One-Stop Guide to Living, Loving & Lounging under the Sun.** Dorothy Tegeler. LC 96-77468. (Illus.). 173p. 1996. pap. 10.95 (0-935182-89-6) Gem Guides Bk.

Retiring Old Cars: Programs to Save Petroleum & Reduce Emissions. 110p. (Orig.). (C). 1992. pap. text ed. 30.00 (1-56806-049-1) DIANE Pub.

Retiring on Your Own Terms: Your Total Retirement Planning Guide to Finances, Health, Life-Style, & Much, Much More. James W. Ellison et al. 1989. pap. 16.95 (0-517-57130-7, Crown) Crown Pub Group.

Retiring Right: Planning for a Successful Retirement. Lawrence J. Kaplan. LC 95-568. 352p. Date not set. pap. 14.95 (0-89529-655-1) Avery Pub.

***Retiring to Mexico.** Friedman. 340p. 1996. pap. 12.95 (0-9632111-1-0) Media Res.

Retiring to Your Own Business: How You Can Launch a Satisfying, Productive, & Prosperous Second Career. Gustav Berle. 300p. (Orig.). 1992. pap. 14.95 (0-940673-60-6) Puma Pub Co.

Reto en el Paraiso. Alejandro Morales. LC 82-73753. 381p. (ENG & SPA.). 1983. pap. 18.00 (0-916950-34-4) Biling Rev-Pr.

Retold in the Hills: A History of the Making & Recovery of Told in the Hills, the First Hollywood Feature Film Made in Idaho. Tom Trusky. (Illus.). 50p. 1990. pap. 5.95 (0-932129-11-0) Heming W Studies.

Retooling on the Run: The Executive Warrior. Stuart Heller & David S. Surrenda. LC 93-40411. (Illus.). 200p. (Orig.). (C). 1995. pap. 16.95 (1-883319-19-6) Frog Ltd CA.

Retooling Social Security for the 21st Century: Right & Wrong Approaches to Reform. C. Eugene Steuerle & Jon M. Bakija. (Illus.). 354p. (Orig.). 1994. pap. 18.95 (0-87766-602-4); lib. bdg. 66.00 (0-87766-601-6) Urban Inst.

Retooling the Science of Mind. B. Bernard Bane. 86p. 1987. pap. 5.00 (0-930924-26-6) BMB Pub Co.

Retorica de la Violencia en Tres Novelas Peruanas. Ismael P. Marquez. LC 92-27681. (University Texas Studies in Contemporary Spanish-American Fiction: Vol. 7). 130p. (C). 1994. text ed. 35.95 (0-614-00676-7) P Lang Pubng.

Retorno see Aguilas

Retouches a Mon Retour de l'URSS see Retour De l'URSS

Retouching from Start to Finish. 2nd ed. Veronica C. Weiss. LC 85-51179. 150p. 1986. reprint ed. 29.95 (0-935333-00-2) VC Pub.

Retouching Your Photographs. Jan W. Miller. (Illus.). 144p. 1986. pap. 18.95 (0-8174-3832-7, Amphoto) Watson-Guptill.

Retour Amont. Rene Char. 96p. (FRE.). 1966. 11.95 (0-7859-1104-9, 2070213773) Fr & Eur.

Retour au Palais Farnese: Avec: Choix de Lettres de Romain Rolland a sa Mere (1890-1891) Romain Rolland. (Illus.). 368p. (FRE.). 1956. pap. 8.95 (0-7859-5461-9) Fr & Eur.

Retour de l'Enfant Prodigue: Le Traite de Narcisse - La Tentative Amoureuse - El Hadj - Philoctete Bethsabe. Andre Gide. (FRE.). 1978. pap. 10.95 (0-8288-3686-8, M11015) Fr & Eur.

Retour de l'Enfant Prodigue: Recit. Andre Gide. (Folio Ser.: No. 1044). (FRE.). pap. 8.95 (2-07-037044-5) Schoenhof.

Retour de l'U. S. S. R. Retouches a Mon Retour de l'U. S. S. R. Andre Gide. (FRE.). 1978. pap. 10.95 (0-7859-2851-0) Fr & Eur.

Retour De l'URSS. Andre Gide. Incl. Retouches a Mon Retour de l'URSS. pap. (0-318-52237-3); (Idees Ser.). (FRE.). pap. 8.95 (2-07-035396-6) Schoenhof.

***Retour des Inactifs.** Denis Cote. (Novels in the Roman Plus Ser.). 160p. (FRE.). (YA). (gr. 8 up). 1996. pap. 7.95 (2-89021-142-8, Pub. by Les Editions CN) Firefly Bks Ltd.

***Retour Des Rats - The Rats Came Back.** (Picture Bks.). (Illus.). (FRE.). (J). 1996. lib. bdg. 16.95 (1-55037-460-5, Pub. by Les Editions CN) Firefly Bks Ltd.

Retour D'Imray. Rudyard Kipling. 280p. (FRE.). 1977. pap. 10.95 (0-7859-2385-3, 2070368955) Fr & Eur.

Retour du Divin. Jacques Audiberti. (FRE.). 1983. pap. 16.95 (0-7859-2740-9) Fr & Eur.

Retracing a Winter's Journey: Schubert's Winterreise. Susan Youens. LC 91-55234. 320p. 1991. 49.95 (0-8014-2599-9); pap. 18.95 (0-8014-9966-6) Cornell U Pr.

An Asterisk (*) at the beginning of an entry indicates that the title is appearing in BIP for the first time.

R

*Retracing Kipp Trails. James Arthur. 72p. (Orig.). 1997. pap. 12.95 (1-887804-10-2, News-Argus) Cent Mont Pubng.

Retracing Major Stephen H. Long's 1820 Expedition: The Itinerary & Botany. George J. Goodman & Cheryl A. Lawson. LC 94-42657. (American Exploration & Travel Ser.: Vol. 73). (Illus.). 384p. 1995. 39.95 (0-8061-2703-1) U of Okla Pr.

Retracing the Past, 2 Vols., I. 3rd ed. Gary B. Nash & Schultz. (C). 1994. text ed. 31.50 (0-06-501060-4) Addson-Wesley Educ.

Retracing the Past, 2 Vols., II. 3rd ed. Gary B. Nash & Schultz. (C). 1994. text ed. 31.50 (0-06-501061-2) Addson-Wesley Educ.

*Retracing the Past, Vol. 1. 4th ed. Ed. by Nash. LC 97-10816. (C). 1998. text ed. write for info. (0-673-98573-3) Addison-Wesley.

*Retracingt the Past, Vol. 2. 4th ed. Ed. by Nash. (C). 1998. text ed. write for info. (0-673-98574-1) Addison-Wesley.

Retractations. Augustine, Saint. Tr. by Mary I. Bogan. LC 67-30513. (Fathers of the Church Ser.: Vol. 60). 321p. 1968. 19.95 (0-8132-0060-1) Cath U Pr.

*Retraining: Teaching New Skills-Horse. Sharon B. Smith. 1998. 19.95 (0-87605-285-5) Howell Bk.

Retraining: Twenty-First Century Key to Success. Metro Resource Publications Staff. (Keep it Simple Ser.). (Illus.). 132p. (Orig.). pap. 14.95 (0-945376-99-5) Metro Resrc Pubns.

Retraining & Tradition: Skilled Worker in an Era of Change. Kentalle Miller & Isobel Miller. 192p. 1975. 27.95 (0-8464-1127-X) Beekman Pubs.

Retraining & Upgrading Workers: A Guide for Postsecondary Educators. Constance Faddis & Catharine P. Warmbrod. 208p. 1983. 12.50 (0-318-22191-8, RD235) Ctr Educ Trng Employ.

Retraining Cognition: Techniques & Applications. Rick Parente & Douglas Herrmann. LC 96-12260. 304p. 1996. 65.00 (0-8342-0764-8) Aspen Pub.

Retraining Memory Techniques & Applications. Rick Parente & Janet K. Anderson-Parente. (Illus.). (C). 1991. 49.95 (0-945541-02-3) CSY Pub Inc.

*Retraining the Nuclear Work Force. (Hazardous, Nuclear & Solid Waste Environmental Management Ser.: No. 6). 1996. pap. 10.00 (1-55516-516-8, 4663) Natl Conf State Legis.

Retraining the Unemployed. Ed. by Gerald Somers. LC 68-19575. 359p. reprint ed. pap. 102.40 (0-317-39634-X, 2023723) Bks Demand.

Retraite Sentimentale. Colette. (Folio Ser.: No. 135). (FRE.). pap. 8.95 (2-07-036135-7) Schoenhof.

Retraite Sentimentale. Sidonie-Gabrielle Colette. 256p. (FRE.). 1972. pap. 10.95 (0-7859-1702-0, 2070361357) Fr & Eur.

Retranca Del Ela. Luis D. Colon. 1996. pap. text ed. write for info. (1-56758-044-0) Edit Cultl.

Retrato de una Epoca. Carlos Cabezas. 212p. (Orig.). 1986. pap. 8.00 (0-917049-07-1) Saeta.

*Retrato del Amor del Cielo: Un Estudio Solore el Apostol Juan y Su Primera Epistola. Kirk Gilchrist. 150p. (Orig.). (SPA.). 1997. pap. write for info. (0-9647871-7-2, Hope of Israel) Hebron Minist.

Retratos Contemporaneos. Fernando Alegria. 256p. (C). 1979. pap. text ed. 18.75 (0-15-576680-5) HB Coll Pubs.

Retratos de Aves Tropicales. John S. Dunning. Tr. by John Guarnaccia & Mercedes Villamil from ENG. LC 85-24553. Orig. Title: Portraits of Tropical Birds. (Illus.). 174p. (SPA.). 1985. 30.00 (0-915180-28-6) Harrowood Bks.

Retratos de Hispanoamerica. Ed. by Eugenio Florit & Beatrice P. Patt. (SPA.). 1962. text ed. 16.95 (0-03-017135-0) Irvington.

Retratos del Salvador. Herbert Lockyer. 192p. (SPA.). 1986. pap. 1.50 (0-8297-0741-7) Life Pubs Intl.

Retratos Nuevomexicanos: A Collection of Hispanic New Mexican Photography. Steven A. Yates. (Illus.). 1987. pap. text ed. 5.95 (0-9609818-1-0) M Rogers Mus.

*Retreat. Aharon Appelfeld. 1998. pap. write for info. (0-8052-1096-2) Schocken.

*Retreat. Jason Sherman. LC 97-100342. 1997. pap. text ed. 10.95 (0-88754-511-4, Pub. by Playwrights CN Pr CN) Theatre Comm.

Retreat & Small Farm Management: Urban & Rural Survival. CWL. (Security & Survival Ser.). (Illus.). 48p. 1987. pap. 17.00 (0-939856-74-3) Tech Group.

Retreat Companion for Priests: Profound Insights for Priests about Their Life, Their Work, Their Spiritual Progress & Their Eternal Destiny. Francis P. Havey. LC 90-71099. 250p. 1990. reprint ed. pap. 7.50 (0-89555-406-2) TAN Bks Pubs.

Retreat from Africa. Patrick Mullins. 115p. (C). 1989. text ed. 49.00 (1-872795-37-4, Pub. by Pentland Pr UK) St Mut.

Retreat from China: British Policy in the Far East, 1937-1941. Nicholas Clifford. (China in the 20th Century Ser.). 1976. reprint ed. lib. bdg. 27.50 (0-306-70757-8) Da Capo.

Retreat from Class: A New 'True' Socialism. Ellen M. Wood. 202p. 1986. text ed. 44.95 (0-86091-128-4, Pub. by Verso UK); pap. text ed. 16.95 (0-86091-839-4, Pub. by Verso UK) Routledge Chapman & Hall.

*Retreat from Doomsday: The Obsolescence of Major War. John Mueller. xii,327p. 1996. reprint ed. pap. 24.95 (1-878822-88-8) Univ Rochester Pr.

Retreat from Empire? The First Nixon Administration. Robert E. Osgood et al. LC 72-12359. (America & the World Ser.: Vol. II). 360p. 1973. 52.00 (0-8018-1493-6); pap. 16.95 (0-8018-1499-5) Johns Hopkins.

Retreat from Injustice: Human Rights in Australian Law. Nick O'Neill & Robin Handley. 544p. 1994. pap. 59.00 (1-86287-121-3, Pub. by Federation Pr AU) Gaunt.

Retreat from Kabul: How Diplomacy Got the Russians Out of Afghanistan. Diego Cordovez & Selig S. Harrison. 400p. 1995. 35.00 (0-19-506294-9) OUP.

Retreat from Leningrad: Army Group North 1944-1945. Steven H. Newton. LC 95-67621. (Illus.). 320p. 1995. 24.95 (0-88740-806-0) Schiffer.

Retreat from Likeness in the Theory of Painting. 2nd ed. Frances M. Blanshard. LC 72-37913. (Select Bibliographies Reprint Ser.). 1977. reprint ed. 23.95 (0-8369-6733-X) Ayer.

Retreat from Love. Colette. Tr. by Margaret Crosland from FRE. 240p. 9600. pap. 23.00 (0-7206-0954-2, Pub. by P Owen Ltd UK) Dufour.

Retreat from Love. Sidonie-Gabrielle Colette. Tr. by Margaret Crosland. LC 79-19831. 226p. 1980. reprint ed. pap. 10.00 (0-15-676588-8, Harvest Bks) HarBrace.

*Retreat from New Jerusalem: British Politics, 1951-1964. Kevin Jeffreys. LC 96-34939. (British Studies). 1997. write for info. (0-312-16538-2) St Martin.

Retreat from Race: Asian Admissions & Racial Politics. Dana Y. Takagi. LC 92-13377. 260p. (C). 1993. text ed. 35.00 (0-8135-1913-6); pap. text ed. 16.00 (0-8135-1914-4) Rutgers U Pr.

Retreat from Reconstruction: 1869-1879. William Gillette. LC 79-12450. 1980. pap. text ed. 19.95 (0-8071-1006-X) La State U Pr.

Retreat from Reform: Labor Rights & Freedom of Expression in South Korea. Asia Watch Staff. LC 90-85381. 154p. 1990. pap. 10.00 (0-929692-75-6, Asia Watch) Hum Rts Watch.

*Retreat from Reform: Patterns of Political Behavior in Interwar Japan. Sharon Minichiello. LC 84-8535. 188p. 1984. reprint ed. pap. 53.60 (0-608-04391-5, 2065172) Bks Demand.

Retreat from Reform: The Prohibition Movement in the United States, 1890-1913. Jack S. Blocker, Jr. LC 76-5325. (Contributions in American History Ser.: No. 51). 263p. 1976. text ed. 38.50 (0-8371-8899-7, BRR/, Greenwood Pr) Greenwood.

Retreat from Revolution: The Dail Courts, 1920-1924. Mary Kotsonouris. 224p. 1994. 35.00 (0-7165-2511-9, Pub. by Irish Acad Pr IE) Intl Spec Bk.

*Retreat from Revolution: The Dail Courts, 1920-24. Mary Dotsonouris. 176p. 1996. 15.00 (0-7165-2613-1, Pub. by Irish Acad Pr IE) Intl Spec Bk.

Retreat from the Finland Station: Moral Odysseys in the Breakdown of Communism. Kenneth Murphy. 288p. 1992. text ed. 29.95 (0-02-922315-6, Free Press) Free Pr.

Retreat from the Modern. Nick Rengger. 128p. 1995. pap. 14.95 (0-906097-29-0) LPC InBook.

Retreat from the Regions: Corporate Change & the Closure of Factories. Stephen Fothergill & Nigel Guy. 216p. 1991. 57.00 (1-85302-101-6); pap. 29.95 (1-85302-100-8) Taylor & Francis.

Retreat Guide I. Steve Clapp. 20p. (Orig.). 1981. pap. 2.00 (0-914527-04-5) C-Four Res.

Retreat Guide II. Steve Clapp. (C-4 Journals Ser.). 29p. (Orig.). 1982. pap. 2.00 (0-914527-13-4) C-Four Res.

Retreat Handbook. Sandy Reimer & Larry Reimer. LC 86-21672. 192p. (Orig.). 1987. pap. 9.95 (0-8192-1393-4) Morehouse Pub.

Retreat, Hell! Jim Wilson. 352p. 1997. mass mkt. 4.50 (0-671-67866-3) PB.

Retreat into the Mind: Victorian Poetry & the Rise of Psychiatry. Ekbert Faas. 320p. 1991. pap. text ed. 14.95 (0-691-01511-2) Princeton U Pr.

Retreat of Representation: The Concept of Darstellung in German Critical Discourse. Martha B. Helfer. LC 95-18573. (SUNY Series, Intersections). 235p. 1996. pap. text ed. 14.95 (0-7914-2912-1) State U NY Pr.

Retreat of Representation: The Concept of Darstellung in German Critical Discourse. Martha B. Helfer. LC 95-18573. (SUNY Series, Intersections). 235p. 1996. text ed. 44.50 (0-7914-2911-3) State U NY Pr.

Retreat of Scientific Racism: Changing Concepts of Race in Britain & the United States Between the World Wars. Elazar Barkan. 384p. (C). 1993. pap. text ed. 20.95 (0-521-45875-7) Cambridge U Pr.

Retreat of Socialism in India: Two Decades Without Nehru, 1964-1984. R. C. Dutt. 219p. (C). 1987. 20.00 (81-7017-217-9, Pub. by Abhinav II) S Asia.

Retreat of the State: The Diffusion of Power in the World Economy. Susan Strange. (Studies in International Relations: No. 49). 200p. (C). 1996. pap. text ed. 16.95 (0-521-56440-9) Cambridge U Pr.

Retreat of the State: The Diffusion of Power in the World Economy. Susan Strange. (Studies in International Relations: No. 49). 200p. (C). 1997. text ed. 49.95 (0-521-56429-8) Cambridge U Pr.

Retreat of Turberculosis Eighteen Fifty to Nineteen Fifty. F. B. Smith. 288p. 1988. lib. bdg. 57.50 (0-7099-3383-5, Pub. by Croom Helm UK) Routledge Chapman & Hall.

Retreat to Commitment. W. W. Bartley, III. LC 84-14862. 285p. 1984. pap. 22.95 (0-8126-9127-X) Open Court.

Retreat to Moscow? Gorbachev & the East. Mark Almond. (C). 1990. 35.00 (0-907967-21-3, Pub. by Inst Euro Def & Strat UK) St Mut.

*Retreat to the Finger Lakes. Leona Jensen. (Illus.). 156p. 1992. pap. 8.95 (0-614-26435-9) Purple Mnt Pr.

Retreat with Francis & Clare of Assisi: Following Our Pilgrim Hearts. Murray Bodo & Susan S. Sing. 112p. (Orig.). 1996. pap. 7.95 (0-86716-238-4, B2384) St Anthony Mess Pr.

Retreat with Francis de Sales, Jane de Chantal & Aelred of Rievaulx: Befriending Each Other in God. Wendy M. Wright. 114p. (Orig.). 1996. pap. 7.95 (0-86716-239-2, B2392) St Anthony Mess Pr.

Retreat with Gerard Manley Hopkins & Hildegard of Bingen: Turning Pain into Power. Gloria Hutchinson. 136p. 1996. pap. text ed. 8.95 (0-86716-251-1) St Anthony Mess Pr.

Retreat with Jessica Powers: Loving a Passionate God. Robert F. Morneau. 104p. 1995. pap. 7.95 (0-86716-236-8) St Anthony Mess Pr.

Retreat with Job & Julian of Norwich: Trusting That All Will Be Well. Carol Luebering. 144p. 1995. pap. 9.95 (0-86716-227-9) St Anthony Mess Pr.

*Retreat with Mary of Magdala & Augustine: Rejoicing in Human Sexuality. Sidney Callahan. Ed. by Gloria Hutchinson. 1997. pap. write for info. (0-86716-262-7, B2627) St Anthony Mess Pr.

*Retreat with Oscar Romero & Dorothy Day: Walking with the Poor. Marie Dennis. Ed. by Gloria Hutchinson. 1997. pap. write for info. (0-86716-261-9, B2619) St Anthony Mess Pr.

*Retreat with Our Lady, Dominic & Ignatius: Praying with Our Bodies. Betsey Beckman et al. Ed. by Gloria Hutchinson. 192p. (Orig.). 1997. pap. 9.95 (0-86716-256-2, B2562) St Anthony Mess Pr.

Retreat with Pope John XXIII: Opening the Windows to Wisdom. Alfred A. McBride. 168p. (Orig.). 1996. pap. 9.95 (0-86716-258-9, B2589) St Anthony Mess Pr.

Retreat with Stillwell. Jack Belden. (China in the 20th Century Ser.). (Illus.). 368p. 1975. reprint ed. lib. bdg. 32.50 (0-306-70734-9) Da Capo.

Retreat with the Lord: A Popular Guide to the Spiritual Exercises of St. Ignatious of Loyola. John A. Hardon. 220p. (Orig.). 1993. pap. 10.99 (0-89283-833-7, Charis) Servant.

*Retreat with Thea Bowman & Bede Abram: Leaning on the Lord. Joseph A. Brown. Ed. by Gloria Hutchinson. 160p. (Orig.). 1997. pap. 9.95 (0-86716-277-5, B2775) St Anthony Mess Pr.

Retreat with Therese of Lisieux: Loving Our Way into Holiness. Elizabeth R. Obbard. 136p. (Orig.). 1996. pap. 8.95 (0-86716-242-2, B2422) St Anthony Mess Pr.

Retreat with Thomas Merton. M. Basil Pennington. (Retreat with Bks.). 128p. 1988. pap. 8.95 (0-916349-23-3) Amity Hse Inc.

Retreat with Thomas Merton: Becoming Who We Are. Anthony T. Padovano. 120p. 1996. pap. text ed. 7.95 (0-86716-229-5) St Anthony Mess Pr.

Retreat York: An Early Experiment in the Treatment of Mental Illness. Mary R. Glover. Ed. by Janet R. Glover. (C). 1988. 65.00 (0-900657-88-X, Pub. by W Sessions UK) St Mut.

Retreating from the Cold War: Germany, Russia, & the Withdrawal of the Western Group of Forces. David Cox. 160p. (C). 1996. 35.00 (0-8147-1528-1) NYU Pr.

*Retreating the Political. Jean-Luc Nancy & Philippe Lacoue-Labarthe. (Warwick Studies in European Philosophy). 232p. (C). 1997. text ed. 59.95 (0-415-15162-7) Routledge.

*Retreating the Political. Jean-Luc Nancy & Phillippe Lacoue-Labarthe. (Warwick Studies in European Philosophy). 232p. (C). 1997. pap. 18.95 (0-415-15163-5) Routledge.

*Retreats: Handmade Hideaways to Refresh the Spirit. G. Lawson Drinkard, 3rd. LC 97-1829. (Illus.). 144p. 1997. 39.95 (0-87905-798-X) Gibbs Smith Pub.

Retreats for Diocesan Priests. Bishops' Committee on Priestly Life & Ministry Staff & National Conference of Catholic Bishops Staff. 5p. (Orig.). 1990. pap. 1.25 (1-55586-344-2) US Catholic.

Retreats from Realism in Recent English Drama. Ruby Cohn. (Illus.). 250p. (C). 1991. text ed. 59.95 (0-521-40363-4) Cambridge U Pr.

*Retreats from the Edge: Youth Events to Build a Christian Community. Paul Harcey. 1997. pap. text ed. 9.95 (0-687-07581-5) Abingdon.

*Retrial Queues. Falin. 400p. 1997. text ed. write for info. (0-412-78550-1, Chap & Hall NY) Chapman & Hall.

Retribution. T. Michael Booth. (Orig.). 1994. mass mkt. 4.99 (0-345-37867-9) Ballantine.

Retribution. Michael Grant. LC 95-21753. 320p. 1995. 23.00 (0-06-017640-7, HarpT) HarpC.

Retribution. Michael Grant. 416p. 1996. mass mkt. 5.99 (0-06-109377-7, Harp PBks) HarpC.

Retribution. R. J. Pineiro. 1995. 23.95 (0-614-06177-6) Forge NYC.

Retribution. R. J. Pineiro. 384p. 1995. 23.95 (0-312-85940-6) Forge NYC.

Retribution. R. J. Pineiro. 1996. pap. 6.99 (0-614-98102-6) Tor Bks.

Retribution, Vol. 1. R. J. Pineiro. 1996. mass mkt. 6.99 (0-8125-4463-3) Tor Bks.

Retribution: Evil for Evil in Ethics, Law, & Literature. Marvin Henberg. 288p. 1990. 44.95 (0-87722-724-1) Temple U Pr.

Retribution & Eight Other Selected Plays. Wilfrido M. Guerrero. ix, 180p. (Orig.). (C). 1990. pap. 12.50 (971-10-0411-9, Pub. by New Day Pub PH) Cellar.

Retribution & Eschatology in Chronicles. Brian E. Kelly. (JSOT Supplement Ser.: No. 211). 280p. 1996. 50.00 (1-85075-579-5, Pub. by Sheffield Acad UK) CUP Services.

Retribution, Justice & Therapy. Jeffrie G. Murphy. 275p. 1979. pap. text ed. 39.00 (90-277-0999-8, D Reidel); lib. bdg. 82.50 (90-277-0998-X, D Reidel) Kluwer Ac.

Retribution: or The Vale of Shadows. Emma D. Southworth. LC 78-64099. reprint ed. 37.50 (0-404-17395-0) AMS Pr.

Retribution Reconsidered: More Essays in the Philosophy of Law. Jeffrie G. Murphy. LC 92-16624. (Philosophical Studies in Philosophy: Vol. 54). 244p. (C). 1992. lib. bdg. 109.50 (0-7923-1815-3, Pub. by Klwr Acad Pubs NE) Kluwer Ac.

Retrieval & Organizational Strategies in Conceptual Memory: A Computer Model. fac. ed. Janet L. Kolodner. LC 83-25387. (Artificial Intelligence Ser.). (Illus.). 277p. 1984. reprint ed. pap. 79.00 (0-7837-7833-3, 2047589) Bks Demand.

Retrieval from Semantic Memory. W. Noordman-Vonk. (Language & Communication Ser.: Vol. 5). (Illus.). 1979. 24.95 (0-387-09219-6) Spr-Verlag.

Retrieval of Geoscience Information: Proceedings of the Tenth Annual Meeting of the Geoscience Information Society, October 21, 1975, Salt Lake City, Utah. Geoscience Information Society Staff. (Geoscience Information Society Proceedings Ser.: Vol. 6). 202p. reprint ed. pap. 57.60 (0-7837-5626-7, 2045535) Bks Demand.

Retrieval of Information in the Humanities & the Social Sciences: Problems as Aids to Learning. 2nd ed. Slavens. (Books in Library & Information Science: Vol. 52). 200p. 1989. 55.00 (0-8247-8165-1) Dekker.

Retrieval of Medicinal Chemical Information. Ed. by W. Jeffrey Howe et al. LC 78-21611. (ACS Symposium Ser.: No. 84). 1978. 29.95 (0-8412-0465-9) Am Chemical.

*Retrieval of Medicinal Chemical Information. Symposium on Retrieval of Medicinal Chemical Information Staff. Ed. by W. Jeffrey Howe et al. LC 78-21611. (ACS Symposium Ser.: Vol. 84). 239p. 1978. reprint ed. pap. 68.20 (0-608-03945-4, 2064392) Bks Demand.

Retrieve: A New, Gentle Approach to Retriever Training. Bill Medcalf. (Illus.). 200p. 1990. 19.95 (0-9620226-0-8) Wildwood TX.

Retrieved Riches: Social Investigation in Britain 1840-1914. Ed. by David Englander & Rosemary O'Day. 448p. 1995. text ed. 76.95 (1-85928-118-4, Pub. by Scolar Pr UK) Ashgate Pub Co.

Retriever Puppy Training: The Right Start for Hunting. Clarice Rutherford & Cherylon Loveland. LC 88-3015. (Illus.). 110p. 1988. pap. 9.95 (0-931866-38-3) Alpine Pubns.

Retriever Shooting Dog. Mike Gould. (Illus.). 225p. 1998. write for info. (1-885106-39-4) Wild Adven Pr.

Retriever Training. Susan Scales. (Illus.). 176p. 1993. 29.95 (1-85310-331-4, Pub. by Swan Hill UK) Voyageur Pr.

Retriever Training for the Duck Hunter. R. Milner. (Illus.). 168p. 1993. 21.95 (0-940143-90-9) Safari Pr.

*Retriever Training Tests. 2nd rev. ed. James B. Spencer. LC 97-16859. (Illus.). 216p. 1997. pap. 16.95 (0-931866-95-2) Alpine Pubns.

Retriever Working Certificate Training. Rutherford et al. (Illus.). 120p. 1986. pap. 9.95 (0-931866-26-X) Alpine Pubns.

Retrievers: A Complete Pet Owner's Manual: Everything about Purchase, Care, Nutrition, Breeding, Behavior, & Training. Monika A. Wegler. LC 95-21995. (Illus.). 64p. 1996. pap. 6.95 (0-8120-9450-6) Barron.

Retrieving Democracy: In Search of Civic Equality. Philip Green. LC 84-23798. 288p. (C). 1985. 47.50 (0-8476-7405-3) Rowman.

Retrieving Fundamental Theology: The Three Styles of Contemporary Theology. Gerald O'Collins. LC 93-28251. 240p. (Orig.). (C). 1993. pap. 14.95 (0-8091-3418-7) Paulist Pr.

Retrieving the Human: A Christian Anthropology. Joseph Comblin. Tr. by Robert R. Barr from POR. LC 89-78416. (Theology & Liberation Ser.). 271p. 1990. reprint ed. pap. 77.30 (0-7837-9845-8, 2060574) Bks Demand.

Retrieving the Language of Compassion: The Education Professor in Search of Community. Maxine Greene. (DeGarmo Lectures: No. 15). 1990. 3.00 (0-685-41090-0) Soc Profs Ed.

Retrieving the Past: Essays on Archaeological Research & Methodology in Honor of Gus W. Van Beek. Ed. by Joe D. Seger. LC 95-48813. xxxiv, 310p. 1996. 39.50 (1-57506-012-4) Eisenbrauns.

Retrieving Women's History: Changing Perceptions of the Role of Women in Politics & Society. Ed. by S. Jay Kleinberg. 400p. 1992. pap. 16.95 (0-85496-682-X) Berg Pubs.

*Retro Hell: Life in the '70s & '80s from Afros to Zotz. Ben Is Dead Magazine Editors. 1998. pap. 12.95 (0-316-10282-2) Little.

Retro Lives. Lee Grimes. 208p. (Orig.). 1993. mass mkt. 4.50 (0-380-76913-1, AvoNova) Avon.

*Retro Renaissance Vol. 3: A Gracious Guide to Living It Up. Ed. by V. Vale & Marian Wallace. (V/Search Ser.: Vol. 3). (Illus.). (Orig.). Date not set. pap. write for info. (1-889307-02-5) V Search.

Retroactive. Catherine Howe. (Illus.). 20p. (Orig.). 1986. pap. write for info. (0-936739-02-9) Hallwalls Inc.

Retroactive Inhibition As Affected by Conditions of Learning. Edward Tolman. Bd. with No. 7. Iowa University Studies in Psychology. Ed. by Carl E. Seashore. ; Higher Scale of Mental Measurement & Its Application to Cases of Insanity. A. J. Rosanoff. ; Experimental Study of Attention. S. M. Fukuya. ; Interference of Will-Impluses with Application to Pedagogy. A. A. Roback. (Psychology Monographs General & Applied: Vol. 25). 1974. reprint ed. Set pap. 55.00 (0-8115-1424-2) Periodicals Srv.

*Retroactive Legislation. Daniel E. Troy. 1997. 29.95 (0-8447-4022-5) Am Enterprise.

Retroactive Legislation Affecting Interest in Land. John Scurlock. LC 54-62006. (Michigan Legal Publications). xv, 390p. 1982. reprint ed. lib. bdg. 42.00 (0-89941-175-4, 301400) W S Hein.

Retroactivity in Habeas Corpus Cases since Teague v. Lane. 37p. 1993. 15.00 (0-317-05925-4, PB-21) Natl Attys General.

*RetroAge: The Four Step Program to Reverse the Aging Process. Hattie & Sallie L. Batson. 176p. (Orig.). 1997. pap. 13.00 (0-425-15611-7, Berkley Trade) Berkley Pub.

An Asterisk (*) at the beginning of an entry indicates that the title is appearing in BIP for the first time.

Retrofit Opportunities for Energy Management & Cogeneration. Association of Energy Engineers Staff. Ed. by F. William Payne. LC 88-82219. 600p. 1988. pap. text ed. 62.00 (*0-88173-057-2*) Fairmont Pr.

***Retrofitting for Energy Conservation.** William Clark. LC 97-26079. (Illus.). 400p. 1997. text ed. 49.95 (*0-07-011920-1*) McGraw.

Retrofitting for Quick Die Change in America (With Supplement) Vernon G. Zunker. 128p. 1991. pap. 34.95 (*0-8403-6561-6*) Croydon Grp.

Retrofitting Fossil Plant Facilities - Structural Perspectives. LC 91-30047. 111p. 1991. pap. text ed. 15.00 (*0-87262-848-5*) Am Soc Civil Eng.

Retrofitting of Buildings for Energy Conservation. Ed. by Milton Meckler. LC 94-4801. 1994. write for info. (*0-88173-183-8*) Fairmont Pr.

Retrograde Condensation in Natural Gas Pipelines. American Gas Association Pipeline Research Committee et al. 512p. 1975. 12.00 (*0-318-12698-2*, L22277) Am Gas Assn.

Retrograde Condensation in Natural Gas Pipelines. David F. Bergman & M. Rasin Tek. LC 75-32098. 512p. reprint ed. pap. 146.00 (*0-8357-8306-5*, 2033961) Bks Demand.

Retrograde Mercury Workbook. C. J. Puotinen. 64p. 1982. pap. 4.95 (*0-930840-11-9*) Ninth Sign.

Retrograde Planets: Traversing the Inner Landscape. Erin Sullivan. (Contemporary Astrology Ser.). (Illus.). 438p. 1993. pap. 14.95 (*0-14-019329-4*, Arkana) Viking Penguin.

Retrogrades. Mohan Koparkar. 144p. pap. 6.95 (*0-918922-07-0*) Mohan Ents.

Retrolental Fibroplasia & Autistic Symptomatology: An Investigation into Some Relationships among Neonatal Environmental, Developmental & Affective Variables in Blind Prematures. Joan B. Chase. LC 72-155922. (American Foundation for the Blind Research Ser.: No. 24). 237p. reprint ed. pap. 67.60 (*0-7837-0137-3*, 2040426) Bks Demand.

***Retroperitoneal Laparascopy for the Urologist.** Durga D. Gaur. (Illus.). 412p. 1997. text ed. 99.50 (*0-19-564143-4*) OUP.

Retroperitoneum & Intestine. 2nd ed. Kenneth C. Suen. LC 94-4776. (Guides to Clinical Aspiration Biopsy Ser.). 236p. 1994. 98.50 (*0-89640-256-8*) Igaku-Shoin.

RetroSpace: Collected Essays on Chicano Literature. Juan Bruce-Novoa. LC 89-18371. 190p. (Orig.). 1990. pap. 11.00 (*1-55885-013-9*) Arte Publico.

Retrospect: An Anecdotal History of Sullivan County, New York. John Conway. LC 96-14374. (Illus.). 148p. (Orig.). 1996. pap. 15.00 (*0-935796-72-X*) Purple Mnt Pr.

Retrospect: The Origins of Catholic Belief & Practices. John Deedy. (Orig.). 1990. pap. 16.95 (*0-88347-260-0*) Res Christian Liv.

Retrospect & Prospect in Protein Research. Z. P. Li et al. 280p. 1991. text ed. 61.00 (*981-02-0518-X*) World Scientific Pub.

Retrospect of Early Quakerism: Being Extracts from the Records of Philadelphia Yearly Meeting & the Meetings Composing It. Ezra Michener. LC 91-66330. 434p. 1991. text ed. 35.00 (*0-9629841-0-8*) Cool Spring.

Retrospect of Fifty Years, 2 Vols. James C. Gibbons. LC 79-38447. (Religion in America, Ser. 2). 720p. 1972. reprint ed. 52.95 (*0-405-04066-0*) Ayer.

Retrospect of Forty Years. Edwin L. Godkin. (Notable American Authors Ser.). 1992. reprint ed. lib. bdg. 75.00 (*0-7812-2927-8*) Rprt Serv.

Retrospect of Rock: The Eighties. Stuart A. Kallen. Ed. by Bob Italia. LC 89-84919. (History of Rock n' Roll Ser.). (Illus.). 48p. (J). (gr. 4). 1989. lib. bdg. 12.94 (*0-939179-77-6*) Abdo & Dghtrs.

***Retrospect of Western Travel.** Harriet Martineau. (American History Through Literature Ser.). 240p. 1998. text ed. 62.95 (*0-7656-0213-X*); pap. text ed. 18.95 (*0-7656-0214-8*) M E Sharpe.

Retrospect of Western Travel, 2 Vols. Harriet Martineau. LC 68-24988. (American History & Americana Ser.: No. 47). 1969. reprint ed. lib. bdg. 150.00 (*0-8383-0165-7*) M S G Haskell Hse.

Retrospect of Western Travel, 3 vols., 1. Harriet Martineau. LC 68-57623. (Illus.). 1970. reprint ed. text ed. 55.00 (*0-8371-1969-3*, MAWU) Greenwood.

Retrospect of Western Travel, 3 vols., Set. Harriet Martineau. LC 68-57623. (Illus.). 1970. reprint ed. text ed. 125.00 (*0-8371-0967-1*, MAWT) Greenwood.

Retrospect of Western Travel, 3 vols., Set. Harriet Martineau. (BCL1 - U. S. History Ser.). 1991. reprint ed. lib. bdg. 225.00 (*0-7812-6013-2*) Rprt Serv.

Retrospect of Western Travel, 3 vols., Vol. 2. Harriet Martineau. LC 68-57623. (Illus.). 1969. reprint ed. text ed. 55.00 (*0-8371-0968-X*, MAWV) Greenwood.

Retrospect of Western Travel, 3 vols., Vol. 3. Harriet Martineau. LC 68-57623. (Illus.). 1970. reprint ed. text ed. 55.00 (*0-8371-0969-8*, MAWX) Greenwood.

RetroSpect: or Growing up in Blacksburg: And Other Tales Through a Long Life. Ellison A. Smyth. LC 93-11204. (Illus.). 208p. (Orig.). 1993. pap. 9.50 (*0-936015-22-5*) Pocahontas Pr.

Retrospection. Motohisa Honda. 136p. 1995. text ed. 13.00 (*0-8059-3704-8*) Dorrance.

Retrospection & Introspection. Mary Baker Eddy. reprint ed. pap. 10.00 (*0-87952-044-2*) Eddy Wrtngs M B Eddy.

Retrospection & Introspection. Mary M. Eddy. (Notable American Authors Ser.). 1992. reprint ed. lib. bdg. 75.00 (*0-7812-2752-6*) Rprt Serv.

Retrospection of America, 1797-1811. John Bernard. Ed. by Brander Matthews & Laurence Hutton. LC 73-83401. 392p. 1972. 26.95 (*0-405-08263-0*, Pub. by Blom Pubns UK) Ayer.

Retrospections of America 1797-1811. Ed. by John Bernard. 380p. 1987. reprint ed. pap. 19.50 (*1-55613-020-1*) Heritage Bk.

Retrospective. Ed. by Herbert Eimert & Karlheinz Stockhausen. Tr. by Cornelius Cardew & Ruth Koenig. (Reihe Ser.: No. 8). 1978. pap. 14.95 (*3-7024-0152-0*, UE26108E) Eur-Am Music.

Retrospective: Lawrence McKinin. Richard G. Baumann. (Illus.). 48p. (Orig.). 1983. pap. 5.00 (*0-910501-01-7*) U of Missouri Mus Art Arch.

Retrospective Bibliography of American Demographic History from Colonial Times to 1983. Ed. by Robert V. Wells. LC 88-32348. (Bibliographies & Indexes in American History Ser.: No. 11). 500p. 1989. text ed. 105.00 (*0-313-23130-3*, GDE/) Greenwood.

Retrospective Cataloguing in Europe: 15th-19th Century Printed Materials: Proceedings of the Int'l Conference, 1990. Ed. by Franz G. Kaltwasser & John M. Smethurst. 170p. 1992. 65.00 (*3-598-21131-7*) K G Saur.

Retrospective Conversion: From Cards to Computer. Anne G. Adler & Elizabeth A. Baber. LC 84-81656. (Library Hi Tech Monograph: No. 2). 324p. 1984. 45.00 (*0-87650-177-3*) Pierian.

Retrospective Conversion: History, Approaches, Considerations. Ed. by Brian Schottlaender. LC 92-19413. (Cataloging & Classification Quarterly Ser.: Vol. 14, Nos. 3-4). (Illus.). 167p. 1996. 39.95 (*1-56024-328-7*); pap. 19.95 (*0-7890-0055-5*) Haworth Pr.

Retrospective Miscue Analysis: Revaluing Readers & Reading. Yetta M. Goodman & Ann M. Marek. LC 95-23805. 256p. (Orig.). (C). 1996. pap. text ed. 24.95 (*1-878450-85-9*) R Owen Pubs.

Retrospective on the Bretton Woods System: Lessons for International Monetary Reform. Ed. by Michael D. Bordo & Barry Eichengreen. LC 92-30913. (National Bureau of Economic Research Project Report Ser.). (Illus.). 690p. (C). 1993. 82.00 (*0-226-06587-1*) U Ch Pr.

Retrospective on the Classical Gold Standard: 1821-1931. Ed. by Michael D. Bordo & Anna J. Schwartz. LC 84-2440. (National Bureau of Economic Research Conference Report Ser.). 694p. 1984. lib. bdg. 83.00 (*0-226-06590-1*) U Ch Pr.

***Retrospective Survey.** Tom Wesselmann. 1996. 45.00 (*3-89322-636-2*, Pub. by Edition Cantz GW) Dist Art Pubs.

Retrospective Technology Assessment, 1976. Ed. by J. A. Tarr. (Illus.). 1977. 10.00 (*0-911302-37-9*) San Francisco Pr.

Retrospectives for Piano. Kent Kennan. 40p. 1992. pap. 14.95 (*0-7935-1515-7*) H Leonard.

Retrospectives on Public Finance. Ed. by Lorraine Eden. LC 90-41461. (Fiscal Reform in the Developing World Ser.). 419p. 1991. text ed. 59.95 (*0-8223-1102-X*); pap. text ed. 25.95 (*0-8223-1115-1*) Duke.

Retrovectors for Human Gene Therapy. Clague P. Hodgson. LC 95-42550. (Medical Intelligence Unit Ser.). 122p. 1996. 59.00 (*1-57059-320-5*); 89.95 (*0-412-10241-2*) R G Landes.

Retroversion & Text Criticism: The Predictability Syntax in an Ancient Translation from Greek to Ethiopic. John R. Miles. (Society of Biblical Literature Septuagint & Cognate Studies Ser.). 224p. (C). 1985. 23.95 (*0-89130-878-4*, 06-04-17); pap. 15.95 (*0-89130-879-2*) Scholars Pr GA.

Retroviral Insertional Mutagenesis & Oncogene Activation. Ed. by H. J. Kung. (Current Topics in Microbiology & Immunology Ser.: Vol. 171). ix, 179p. 1991. 109.00 (*0-387-53857-7*) Spr-Verlag.

Retroviral Latency. Ed. by Mark A. Laughlin & Roger J. Pomerantz. (Medical Intelligence Unit Ser.). 115p. 1994. 89.95 (*1-57059-034-6*, LN9034) R G Landes.

Retroviral Reverse Transcriptases. Simon Litvak. (Molecular Biology Intelligence Unit Ser.). 205p. 1996. 89.95 (*0-412-10381-8*) R G Landes.

Retroviral Testing: Essentials of Quality Control & Lab Diagnosis. Constantine. 256p. 1992. 75.95 (*0-8493-4429-8*, RC607) CRC Pr.

Retroviridae, Vol. 1. Ed. by J. A. Levy. (Viruses Ser.). (Illus.). 316p. 1992. 95.00 (*0-306-44074-1*, Plenum Pr) Plenum.

Retroviridae, Vol. 2. Ed. by J. A. Levy. (Viruses Ser.). (Illus.). 480p. (C). 1993. 89.50 (*0-306-44369-4*, Plenum Pr) Plenum.

Retroviridae, Vol. 3. Ed. by J. A. Levy. (Viruses Ser.). (Illus.). 535p. (C). 1994. 110.00 (*0-306-44693-6*, Plenum Pr) Plenum.

Retroviridae, Vol. 4. Ed. by Jay A. Levy. (Viruses Ser.). 670p. (C). 1995. 129.50 (*0-306-45033-X*, Plenum Pr) Plenum.

Retrovirus Biology & Human Disease. Gallo & Flossie Wong-Staal. 432p. 1989. 150.00 (*0-8247-7874-X*) Dekker.

***Retroviruses.** Ed. by John M. Coffin et al. (Illus.). 900p. (C). 1997. text ed. 180.00 (*0-87969-497-1*) Cold Spring Harbor.

Retroviruses & Human Pathology. Ed. by Robert C. Gallo et al. LC 85-31692. (Experimental Biology & Medicine Ser.: Vol. 11). 576p. 1986. 119.50 (*0-89603-098-9*) Humana.

Retroviruses in Human Lymphoma-Leukemia: Proceedings of the 15th International Symposium of the Princess Takamatsu Cancer Research Fund, Japan, 1984. Ed. by M. Miwa et al. 352p. 1985. lib. bdg. 142.00 (*90-6764-057-3*, Pub. by VSP NE) Coronet Bks.

Retroviruses Infections of the Nervous System. Ed. by Michael B. Oldstone & Hilary Koprowski. (Current Topics in Microbiology & Immunology Ser.: Vol. 160). (Illus.). 176p. 1990. 105.00 (*0-387-51939-4*) Spr-Verlag.

Retroviruses of Human AIDS & Related Animal Diseases. M. Girard & B. Dodet. 384p. 88.00 (*2-906077-75-5*) Elsevier.

RetroWorlds: Selected Poems by Richard O'Connell. Richard O'Connell. 1993. pap. 25.00 (*3-7052-0804-7*) Atlantis Edns.

Rett Syndrome - Clinical & Biological Aspects: Studies on 130 Swedish Females. Bengt Hagberg. (Clinics in Developmental Medicine Ser.: No. 127). 130p. (C). 1993. text ed. 49.95 (*0-521-41283-8*) Cambridge U Pr.

Retter. Violet A. Garza. LC 87-40251. (Illus.). 315p. (Orig.). (J). 1987. pap. 12.95 (*1-55523-092-X*) Winston-Derek.

Retuara Syntax Studies in the Languages of Colombia, Vol. 3. Clayton L. Strom. LC 92-85042. 1992. pap. 18.00 (*0-88312-181-6*); fiche 16.00 (*0-88312-587-0*) Summer Instit Ling.

Retuning Culture: Musical Changes in Central & Eastern Europe. Ed. by Mark Slobin. LC 96-27983. 304p. 1996. pap. text ed. 17.95 (*0-8223-1847-4*) Duke.

Retuning Culture: Musical Changes in Central & Eastern Europe. Ed. by Mark Slobin. LC 96-27983. 304p. 1996. text ed. 49.95 (*0-8223-1855-5*) Duke.

***Returen to Glory: The Inside Story of the Green Bay Packers Return to Prominence.** Kevin Isaacson. 1996. pap. text ed. 16.95 (*0-87341-488-8*) Krause Pubns.

Return. Norman Ballinger. Ed. by Paulie Grissom. (Illus.). 72p. (Orig.). 1995. pap. text ed. 10.50 (*1-887294-00-7*) Black Ball Pr.

Return. James M. Cody. (Illus.). 1981. pap. 5.95 (*0-916908-04-6*); lib. bdg. 25.00 (*0-916908-31-3*) Place Herons.

Return. Joe De Mers. LC 95-35206. 416p. 1996. pap. 23.95 (*0-525-94097-9*) NAL-Dutton.

***Return.** Joe De Mers. 1997. pap. 6.99 (*0-451-40729-6*, Onyx) NAL-Dutton.

Return. Roger A. Faber. 67p. (YA). (gr. 9-12). 1994. spiral bd. 7.00 (*1-880122-03-0*, Almond Tree) White Stone.

Return. Diane Haeger. Ed. by Linda Marrow. 432p. (Orig.). 1993. mass mkt. 5.50 (*0-671-86480-7*) PB.

Return. Sonia Levitin. 192p. 1988. mass mkt. 4.50 (*0-449-70280-4*, Juniper) Fawcett.

Return. Sonia Levitin. LC 86-25891. 224p. (YA). (gr. 5 up). 1987. lib. bdg. 16.00 (*0-689-31309-8*, Atheneum Bks Young) S&S Childrens.

Return. Dan O'Neill. 146p. (Orig.). (C). 1984. pap. 2.50 (*0-931660-05-X*) R Oman Pub.

Return. Christopher Pike. Ed. by Patricia MacDonald. (Remember Me Two Ser.). 224p. (Orig.). (gr. 9 up). 1994. 14.00 (*0-671-87257-5*, Archway) PB.

Return. Christopher Pike. Ed. by Patricia MacDonald. (Remember Me Two Ser.). 224p. (Orig.). (YA). (gr. 9 up). 1994. pap. 3.99 (*0-671-87265-6*, Archway) PB.

***Return.** Al Sarrantonio. 1998. mass mkt. 5.99 (*0-451-45623-8*, ROC) NAL-Dutton.

Return. William Shatner. (Star Trek Ser.). 1996. 22.00 (*0-614-14678-X*) PB.

***Return.** Melanie Wallace. LC 89-62409. 88p. (Orig.). 1989. pap. text ed. 7.00 (*0-918618-39-8*) Pella Pub.

***Return.** Walter De la Mare. LC 97-23292. (Dover Horror Classics Ser.). 224p. 1997. reprint ed. pap. text ed. 8.95 (*0-486-29688-1*) Dover.

Return. Douglas A. Menville. LC 75-46266. (Supernatural & Occult Fiction Ser.). 1976. reprint ed. lib. bdg. 25.95 (*0-405-08124-3*) Ayer.

***Return: A Family Revisits Their Eastern European Roots.** Petru Popescu. LC 97-14270. 384p. 1997. 24.00 (*0-8021-1613-2*, Grove) Grove-Atltic.

Return: Chronicles of the Door. Gene Edwards. (View from Heaven Ser.: No. 5). 128p. 1996. pap. 8.99 (*0-8423-5601-0*) Tyndale.

Return: Poems Collected & New. Alurista. LC 81-68424. 176p. (ENG & SPA.). 1982. reprint ed. pap. 15.00 (*0-916950-24-7*) Biling Rev-Pr.

Return: The Spiritual Odyssey of a Soviet Scientist. Herman Branover. LC 95-23256. 264p. 1996. pap. 24.95 (*1-56821-529-0*) Aronson.

Return & Remembrance. Darwin O. Curtis. 1995. pap. 6.95 (*0-9646390-7-6*) Wind Word Pr.

Return & Tiger: And Other Short Stories. Hakob Karapents. Tr. by Tatul Sonentz-Papazian from ARM. LC 94-24231. 160p. (Orig.). 1995. pap. 20.00 (*0-9628715-9-1*) Blue Crane Bks.

Return Engagement. Elizabeth Bevarly. (Special Edition Ser.). 1993. mass mkt. 3.50 (*0-373-09844-8*, 5-09844-7) Silhouette.

Return Engagement. Violet Hamilton. 256p. 1992. mass mkt. 3.99 (*0-8217-3859-3*, Zebra Kensgtn) Kensgtn Pub Corp.

Return Engagement. Kay Hooper. 240p. 1995. pap. text ed. 4.99 (*0-515-11525-8*) Jove Pubns.

Return Engagement. Junior Board of the Quad City Symphony Orchestra Assn. Staff. Ed. by MaryKae Waytenick & Deb Giertz. (Illus.). 304p. spiral bd. 13.95 (*0-9621733-0-4*) JBQCS.

Return Engagement. large type ed. Carole Mortimer. (Harlequin Ser.). 1994. lib. bdg. 19.95 (*0-263-13717-1*) Thorndike Pr.

Return Engagement: (Presents Plus) Carole Mortimer. (Presents Ser.). 1994. mass mkt. 2.99 (*0-373-11671-3*, 1-11671-4) Harlequin Bks.

Return Engagement 1. Harry Turtledove. Date not set. pap. write for info. (*0-345-40615-X*) Ballantine.

Return Engagement 2. Harry Turtledove. Date not set. write for info. (*0-345-40561-7*); pap. write for info. (*0-345-40562-5*) Ballantine.

Return Engagement 3. Harry Turtledove. Date not set. write for info. (*0-345-40563-3*); pap. write for info. (*0-345-40564-1*) Ballantine.

Return Engagement 4. Harry Turtledove. Date not set. write for info. (*0-345-40565-X*); pap. write for info. (*0-345-40566-8*) Ballantine.

Return Fire. Charles Ingrid. (Sand Wars Ser.: Bk. 5). 1989. pap. 3.95 (*0-88677-363-6*) DAW Bks.

Return Fire - Rimfire Revenge. Kit Dalton. (Buckskin Double Edition Ser.). 352p. (Orig.). 1995. mass mkt., pap. text ed. 4.99 (*0-8439-3840-4*) Dorchester Pub Co.

Return from Avalon: A Study of the Arthurian Legend in Modern Fiction. Raymond H. Thompson. LC 84-10853. (Contributions to the Study of Science Fiction & Fantasy Ser.: No. 14). ix, 206p. 1985. text ed. 49.95 (*0-313-23291-1*, THR/, Greenwood Pr) Greenwood.

Return from Enlightenment. Forest K. Davis. LC 74-155656. 1971. write for info. (*0-912362-01-4*); pap. write for info. (*0-912362-02-2*) Adamant Pr.

***Return from Las Vegas.** Julian Loeb. 302p. (Orig.). 1996. pap. write for info. (*1-57502-269-9*, PO712) Morris Pubng.

Return from Madness: Psychotherapy with People Taking the New Antipsychotic Medications. Kathleen Degen & Ellen Nasper. LC 95-44617. 256p. 1996. 40.00 (*1-56821-625-4*) Aronson.

Return from Paradise. Edith R. Tjepkema. (Northwest Paradise Ser.: Vol.5). 100p. (Orig.). (J). 1992. pap. 4.95 (*0-9620280-4-5*) Northland Pr.

Return from Parnassus, Pt 2. LC 72-133728. (Tudor Facsimile Texts. Old English Plays Ser.: No. 111). reprint ed. 49.50 (*0-404-53411-2*) AMS Pr.

Return from Parnassus, Part 1 see Pilgrimage to Parnassus

Return from Rome. (Prince Valiant Ser.: Vol. 17). (Illus.). 48p. 1993. per. 16.95 (*1-56097-089-8*) Fantagraph Bks.

Return from the Inferno. Mack Maloney. (Wingman Ser.: No. 9). 1991. mass mkt. 3.95 (*0-8217-3510-1*, Zebra Kensgtn) Kensgtn Pub Corp.

Return from the Stars. Stanislaw Lem. 1989. pap. 7.95 (*0-15-676593-4*) HarBrace.

Return from Tomorrow. George G. Ritchie & Elizabeth Sherrill. LC 91-2552. 128p. (gr. 10). 1981. mass mkt. 3.99 (*0-8007-8412-X*, Spire) Revell.

Return Journey. Rosemary Kay. 256p. 1996. pap. 10.95 (*0-7472-5339-0*, Pub. by Headline UK) Trafalgar.

Return Migration to Puerto Rico. Jose Hernandez Alvarez. LC 76-4835. (Population Monograph: No. 1). (Illus.). 153p. 1976. reprint ed. text ed. 22.50 (*0-8371-8825-3*, ALRM, Greenwood Pr) Greenwood.

Return of a Champion: The Monica Seles Story. Joseph Layden. 1996. mass mkt. 5.99 (*0-312-96002-6*) St Martin.

Return of A. J. Raffles: An Edwardian Comedy in Three Acts Based Somewhat Loosely on E. W. Hornung's Characters in 'The Amateur Cracksman' Graham Greene. 92p. 1975. 12.50 (*0-89366-253-4*) Ultramarine Pub.

Return of Andromache. Richard M. Byers. LC 89-84943. (Illus.). 122p. 1990. 12.00 (*0-9602048-5-7*) Fairfield Hse.

Return of Astraea: An Astral-Imperial Myth in Calderon. Frederick A. De Armas. LC 86-7758. (Studies in Romance Languages: No. 32). 272p. 1986. reprint ed. pap. 77.60 (*0-608-02129-6*, 2062778) Bks Demand.

Return of B. B. Sidney J. Rauch. (Barnaby Brown Bks.: Bk. 2). (Illus.). 48p. (Orig.). (J). (gr. 2-4). 1989. pap. 4.95 (*1-55743-153-1*) Berrent Pubns.

Return of Brer Rabbit. G. A. Clay. (Illus.). 30p. (Orig.). 1995. pap. 12.00 (*0-9649903-0-X*, 1) Brer Rabbit.

Return of Caine O'Halloran. Joann Ross. 1994. 2.99 (*0-373-25589-6*) Harlequin Bks.

Return of Captain Conquer. Mel Gilden. (J). (gr. 5-8). 1985. 12.95 (*0-685-11811-8*) HM.

Return of Censorship in America. 1991. lib. bdg. 75.00 (*0-8490-4730-7*) Gordon Pr.

Return of Chase Cordell. Linda Castle. 1997. mass mkt. 4.99 (*0-373-28948-0*, 1-28948-7) Silhouette.

Return of Civil Society: The Emergence of Democratic Spain. Victor M. Perez-Diaz. LC 92-29941. 367p. 1993. 37.50 (*0-674-76688-1*) HUP.

Return of Claudia. large type ed. Rose Franken. 544p. 1983. 25.99 (*0-7089-1001-7*) Ulverscroft.

Return of Common Sense: A Chance to Begin Over Again. Eric Szuter. (Illus.). 153p. 1992. 19.95 (*0-9633602-9-9*) Sunrise Comn.

Return of Common Sense: The Demise of Relativity. Robert L. Henderson. 217p. (Orig.). 1992. pap. 15.00 (*0-9632656-0-1*) Com Sense AZ.

Return of Consciousness. Tawfig Al-Hakim. Tr. by Bayly Winder from ARA. (Studies in Near Eastern Civilization). 192p. (C). 1985. text ed. 40.00 (*0-8147-9202-2*) NYU Pr.

Return of Cord Navarro. Vella Munn. 1996. mass mkt. 3.99 (*0-373-07749-1*, 1-07749-4) Silhouette.

Return of Count Electric, & Other Stories. William B. Spencer. LC 92-34299. 220p. 1993. 22.00 (*1-877946-27-3*) Permanent Pr.

Return of Cultural Treasures. Jeanette Greenfield. (Illus.). 361p. (C). 1990. text ed. 79.95 (*0-521-33319-9*) Cambridge U Pr.

Return of Cultural Treasures. 2nd ed. Jeannette Greenfield. (Illus.). 270p. (C). 1996. text ed. 80.00 (*0-521-47170-2*) Cambridge U Pr.

Return of Cultural Treasures. 2nd ed. Jeannette Greenfield. (Illus.). 270p. (C). 1996. pap. text ed. 29.95 (*0-521-47746-8*) Cambridge U Pr.

Return of Culture & Identity in IR Theory. Ed. by Yosef Lapid & Friedrich Kiratochinil. LC 95-9033. (Critical Perspectives on World Politics Ser.). 255p. (Orig.). 1996. lib. bdg. 49.95 (*1-55587-522-X*, 87522X) Lynne Rienner.

***Return of Culture & Identity in IR Theory.** Ed. by Yosef Lapid & Friedrich Kratochwil. LC 95-9033. (Critical Perspectives Ser.). 253p. (Orig.). 1996. pap. 18.95 (*1-55587-727-3*, 877273) Lynne Rienner.

R

Return of Cyborg. Mel C. Thompson. (Illus.). 44p. (Orig.). 1991. pap. 3.95 (1-879665-05-0) Cyborg Prods.

***Return of Daniel's Father.** Janice Kaiser. (Temptation Ser.: No. 640). 1997. mass mkt. 3.50 (0-373-25740-6, 1-25740-1) Harlequin Bks.

Return of Dr. Fu Manchu. Sax Rohmer. 20.95 (0-89190-828-5) Amereon Ltd.

Return of Dr. Fu Manchu. Sax Rohmer. 1976. lib. bdg. 13.95 (0-89968-141-7, Lghtyr Pr) Buccaneer Bks.

Return of Dr. Sam Johnson, Detector. Lillian De La Torre. 200p. 1985. pap. 4.95 (0-930330-34-X) Intl Polygonics.

Return of Eden: Five Essays on Milton's Epics. Northrop Frye. LC 65-6968. (Canadian University Paperbooks Ser.: No. 166). 153p. reprint ed. pap. 43.70 (0-8357-4138-9, 2036911) Bks Demand.

Return of Eden McCall. Judith Duncan. (Intimate Moments Ser.). 1995. mass mkt. 3.75 (0-373-07651-7, 1-07651-2) Silhouette.

Return of Freddy LeGrand. Jon Agee. (J). (ps-3). 1992. 15.00 (0-374-36249-1) FS&G.

Return of Freddy LeGrand. Jon Agee. (Illus.). 32p. (J). (ps). 1994. pap. 4.95 (0-374-46230-5) FS&G.

***Return of Free Range Lanning.** Max Brand. 240p. 1997. reprint ed. mass mkt. 4.50 (0-8439-4294-0, Leisure Bks) Dorchester Pub Co.

Return of Free Range Lanning: A Western Trio. large type ed. Max Brand. LC 95-13853. 313p. 1995. 20.95 (0-7838-1289-2, GK Hall) Thorndike Pr.

Return of George Sutherland: Restoring a Jurisprudence of Natural Rights. Hadley Arkes. LC 94-219. 312p. (C). 1994. text ed. 45.00 (0-691-03472-9) Princeton U Pr.

***Return of George Sutherland: Restoring a Jurisprudence of Natural Rights.** Hadley Arkes. 312p. 1994. pap. text ed. 18.95 (0-691-01628-3) Princeton U Pr.

Return of Grand Theory in the Human Sciences. Ed. by Quentin Skinner. (Canto Book Ser.). 224p. (C). 1990. pap. text ed. 10.95 (0-521-39833-9) Cambridge U Pr.

Return of Hellecasters. 19.95 (0-7935-4963-9, 00690068) H Leonard.

Return of Herbert Bracewell & Why Am I Always Alone When I'm with You? Andrew Johns. 1985. pap. 5.25 (0-8222-0946-2) Dramatists Play.

Return of Jeeves. P. G. Wodehouse. 21.95 (0-8488-0332-9) Amereon Ltd.

Return of Jeeves: A Jeeves & Bertie Novel. P. G. Wodehouse. LC 85-42606. 231p. 1990. reprint ed. pap. 11.00 (0-06-096502-9, PL) HarpC.

Return of Jesus. Jesse Duplantis. (Mini-Bks.). 16p. 1993. pap. 0.75 (0-89274-647-5, HH-647) Harrison Hse.

***Return of Jimmie Lavender.** Vincent Starrett. (Vincent Starrett Memorial Library: Vol. 13). 306p. 1997. 25.00 (1-896648-04-5) Battered Silicon.

Return of Jupiter. Kenneth K. Wong. 48p. 1996. pap. 8.00 (0-8059-3835-4) Dorrance.

Return of King Arthur: The Legend Through Victorian Eyes. Debra N. Mancoff. LC 95-6473. (Illus.). 176p. 1995. 35.00 (0-8109-3782-4) Abrams.

***Return of Lanny Budd.** Upton Sinclair. lib. bdg. 31.95 (0-8488-2113-0) Amereon Ltd.

Return of Lono: A Novel of Captain Cook's Last Voyage. O. A. Bushnell. 300p. 1979. reprint ed. pap. 14.95 (0-87022-931-1) UH Pr.

Return of Lum. Rumiko Takahashi. (Illus.). 208p. 1995. pap. 15.95 (1-56931-035-1) Viz Commns Inc.

***Return of Lum Urusei Yatsura: Feudal Furor.** Rumiko Takahashi. 1997. pap. text ed. 15.95 (1-56931-210-9, Viz Comics) Viz Commns Inc.

Return of Lum-Urusei Yatsura: Lum in the Sun. Rumiko Takahashi. 1996. pap. text ed. 15.95 (1-56931-113-7) Viz Commns Inc.

***Return of Lum Urusei Yatsura: Trouble Times Ten.** Rumiko Takahashi. 1997. pap. text ed. 15.95 (1-56931-185-4, Viz Comics) Viz Commns Inc.

Return of Marilyn Monroe: A Novel about What Could Have Happened. Sam Staggs. 1992. pap. 4.99 (1-56171-181-0) Sure Seller.

Return of Martin Guerre. Natalie Z. Davis. (Illus.). 176p. 1983. 28.00 (0-674-76690-3) HUP.

Return of Martin Guerre. Natalie Z. Davis. LC 83-277. 162p. 1993. pap. text ed. 10.95 (0-674-76691-1) HUP.

Return of Merlin. Deepak Chopra. LC 95-1824. 448p. 1995. 24.00 (0-517-59849-3) Crown Pub Group.

Return of Merlin. Deepak Chopra. 432p. 1996. pap. 12.95 (0-449-91074-1) Fawcett.

Return of Merlin. large type ed. Deepak Chopra. LC 95-50039. 1996. 23.95 (1-56895-288-0) Wheeler Pub.

Return of Montezuma. Clarence W. Dawson. LC 91-29139. 128p. (Orig.). 1991. pap. 10.95 (0-86534-162-1) Sunstone Pr.

Return of Morris Schumsky. Steven Schnur. (Illus.). 48p. (J). (gr. 4-6). 1987. pap. 6.95 (0-8074-0358-X, 123927) UAHC.

Return of Mr. Campion. Margery Allingham. 192p. 1991. pap. 3.95 (0-380-71448-5) Avon.

Return of Mr. X. Mario Gilbert & Jaime Hernandez. Ed. by Dean Motter. (Limited-Signed Edition Ser.: No. 5). (Illus.). 114p. 1987. pap. 11.95 (0-685-17465-4) Graphitti Designs.

Return of Mr. X. Gilbert Hernandez et al. 1987. pap. 8.95 (0-446-38698-7) Warner Bks.

Return of Mr. X. deluxe limited ed. Mario Gilbert & Jaime Hernandez. Ed. by Dean Motter. (Limited-Signed Edition Ser.: No. 5). (Illus.). 114p. 1987. 34.95 (0-936211-03-2) Graphitti Designs.

Return of Nat Turner: History, Literature & Cultural Politics in Sixties America. Albert E. Stone. LC 90-28346. 432p. 1992. 35.00 (0-8203-1363-7) U of Ga Pr.

Return of Nathan Brazil, No. 4. Jack L. Chalker. 1986. mass mkt. 5.99 (0-345-34105-8, Del Rey) Ballantine.

Return of Native. Thomas Hardy. 448p. 1994. 13.00 (0-679-44108-5) Knopf.

Return of Native. Holt. 1989. student ed., pap. 10.00 (0-03-023459-X) HR&W Schl Div.

Return of Odysseus. Homer. LC 83-14234. (Tales from the Odyssey Ser.). (Illus.). 32p. (J). (gr. 4-8). 1984. pap. 3.95 (0-8167-0016-8) Troll Communs.

Return of O'Mahony. Harold Frederic. (Collected Works of Harold Frederic). 1988. reprint ed. lib. bdg. 59.00 (0-7812-1187-5) Rprt Serv.

Return of O'Mahony see Collected Works of Harold Frederic

Return of Owners of Land in Ireland: 1876 (32,614 Landowners Are Covered) 325p. 1995. reprint ed. lib. bdg. 39.50 (0-8328-5161-2) Higginson Bk Co.

Return of Owners of Land of One Acre & Upward: In the Several Counties, Counties of Cities, & Counties of Towns in Ireland, Showing the Names of Such Owners Arranged Alphabetically, Their Addresses, Etc. (Illus.). 323p. 1996. reprint ed. pap. 29.95 (0-8328-5160-4) Higginson Bk Co.

Return of Painting, The Pearl, & Orion: A Trilogy. Leslie Scalapino. 176p. 1991. pap. 16.95 (0-86547-469-9, North Pt Pr) FS&G.

***Return of Painting, the Pearl & Orion: A Trilogy.** Leslie Scalapino. 232p. 1997. 37.95 (1-883689-58-9); pap. 16.95 (1-883689-57-0) Talisman Hse.

Return of Philip Latinowicz. Miroslav Krleza. Tr. by Zora Depolo. LC 94-45996. (European Classics Ser.) (CRO & ENG.). 1995. write for info. (0-8101-1245-0); pap. 14.95 (0-8101-1246-9) Northwestern U Pr.

***Return of Philo T. McGiffin.** David C. Poyer. LC 97-46. (Bluejacket Bks.). 288p. 1997. pap. 14.95 (1-55750-689-2) Naval Inst Pr.

Return of Pleasure. Martha Elizabeth. LC 95-83068. 65p. 1996. 20.00 (1-881090-21-3); pap. 10.00 (1-881090-20-5) Confluence Pr.

Return of Pogo. Walt Kelly. 1976. 22.95 (0-8488-1067-8) Amereon Ltd.

Return of Pogo. Walt Kelly. (Pogo Collector's Edition Ser.). 192p. 1995. 19.95 (1-886460-04-3) Sunday Comics.

***Return of Rafe Mackade.** Nora Roberts. 1997. 20.95 (0-373-59766-5) Thorndike Pr.

Return of Rafe Mackade: (Heartbreakers) Nora Roberts. (Intimate Moments Ser.). 1995. mass mkt. 3.75 (0-373-07631-2, 1-07631-4) Silhouette.

Return of Raffles. Peter Tremayne. 1991. 18.00 (0-7278-4140-8) Severn Hse.

Return of Randal Morn. TSR Inc. Staff. (Advanced Dungeons & Dragons, 2nd Edition: Forgotten Realms Campaign World Ser.). 1995. 6.95 (0-7869-0170-5) TSR Inc.

Return of Retief. Keith Laumer. 1984. pap. 2.95 (0-685-09411-1, Baen Bks) PB.

Return of Rex & Ethel. Arnold Adoff. LC 91-23397. 1998. write for info. (0-15-266367-3) HarBrace.

Return of Rick Beanblos. Steve Thayer. 1998. pap. 22.95 (0-670-86572-9) Viking Penguin.

Return of Rinaldo, the Sly Fox. Ursel Scheffler. LC 93-17677. (Illus.). (J). (gr. 2-4). 1995. pap. 4.95 (1-55858-412-9) North-South Bks NYC.

***Return of Santa Paws.** Nicholas Edwards. (J). 1997. pap. text ed. 3.99 (0-590-94471-1) Scholastic Inc.

Return of Sarasvati: Translations of the Poetry of Prasad, Nirala, Pant & Mahadevi. Tr. & Intro. by David Rubin. LC 93-20404. (Studies on South Asia: No. 7). 201p. 1983. 25.00 (0-936115-08-4) U Penn South Asia.

Return of Scarcity: Strategies for an Economic Future. H. C. Coombs. 230p. (C). 1990. text ed. 59.95 (0-521-36373-X); pap. text ed. 18.95 (0-521-36896-0) Cambridge U Pr.

***Return of Se Norita Scorpion: A Western Trio.** large type ed. Les Savage. LC 97-24403. (Circle V Western Ser.). 1997. write for info. (1-57490-089-7) T T Beeler.

***Return of Second Thoughts.** John W. Hartman. LC 96-85108. (Illus.). 160p. 1997. 19.95 (1-885884-02-8) Cormorant Pr.

Return of Service. Stories. Jonathan Baumbach. LC 79-18102. (Illinois Short Fiction Ser.). 140p. 1979. text ed. 14.95 (0-252-00784-0) U of Ill Pr.

***Return of Sherlock Holmes.** (Heritage Literary Ser.). Date not set. pap. text ed. write for info. (0-582-34913-3, Pub. by Longman UK) Longman.

Return of Sherlock Holmes. Arthur Conan Doyle. 320p. 1987. pap. 2.95 (0-345-32713-6) Ballantine.

Return of Sherlock Holmes. Arthur Conan Doyle. Ed. by Richard L. Green. (Oxford Sherlock Holmes Ser.). 464p. (C). 1993. 11.00 (0-19-212317-3, 8952) OUP.

Return of Sherlock Holmes. Arthur Conan Doyle. 336p. 1982. pap. 5.95 (0-14-005708-0, Penguin Bks) Viking Penguin.

Return of Sherlock Holmes. Arthur Conan Doyle. 1987. pap. 3.50 (0-14-010026-1, Penguin Bks) Viking Penguin.

Return of Sherlock Holmes. Arthur Conan Doyle. (Sherlock Holmes Ser.). (Illus.). 200p. 1996. 9.98 (1-879582-13-9) Platinum Pr.

Return of Sherlock Holmes. Arthur Conan Doyle. Ed. & Intro. by Richard L. Green. (World's Classics Ser.). 464p. 1995. reprint ed. pap. 5.95 (0-19-282376-0) OUP.

Return of Sherlock Holmes: Based upon the Play by J. E. Harold Terry & Arthur Rose. Ernest Dudley. LC 93-1973. (Orig.). 1993. pap. 10.00 (0-88734-272-8) Players Pr.

Return of Silver Chief. Jack O'Brien. 21.95 (0-89190-398-4) Amereon Ltd.

Return of Simple. Langston Hughes. Ed. by Akiba S. Harper. 218p. 1995. pap. 9.95 (0-8090-1582-X) FS&G.

Return of Simple. Langston Hughes. Ed. by Akiba S. Harper. LC 93-45373. 1994. 20.00 (0-8090-8676-X) Hill & Wang.

Return of Sinta Claus: A Family Winter Solstice Tale. Mary Porter-Chase. (Illus.). (Orig.). (J). (gr. 3-12). 1991. pap. 6.00 (0-9630798-0-8) Samary Pr.

Return of Spirit: A Woman's Call to Spiritual Action. Josie RavenWing. 240p. 1996. pap. 11.95 (1-55874-385-5) Health Comm.

Return of Tarzan. Edgar Rice Burroughs. 222p. 1984. mass mkt. 4.99 (0-345-31575-8, Del Rey) Ballantine.

Return of the Actor. Alain Touraine. LC 87-13558. 196p. 1988. pap. text ed. 13.95 (0-8166-1594-2) U of Minn Pr.

Return of the Ainu: Cultural Mobilization & the Practice of Ethnicity in Japan, Vol. 9. Katarina Sjoberg. LC 03-16634. (Studies in Anthropology & History: Vol. 9). 221p. 1993. text ed. 53.00 (3-7186-5401-6) Gordon & Breach.

Return of the Amasi Bird: Black South African Poetry, 1891-1981. Ed. by Tim Couzens & Essop Patel. 411p. 1982. pap. text ed. 12.95 (0-86975-195-6, Pub. by Ravan Pr ZA) Ohio U Pr.

Return of the Ancestor. Richard A. Hughes. LC 91-35660. (American University Studies: Theology & Religion: Ser. VII, Vol. 129). 190p. (C). 1992. text ed. 37.95 (0-8204-1790-4) P Lang Pubng.

Return of the Ancients. F. Edward Butterworth. (Orig.). 1987. pap. 12.00 (0-941227-00-6) Cosmic Pr Chico.

Return of the Author. Eugen Simion. Tr. by James W. Newcomb. (Rethinking Theory Ser.). 280p. 1997. text ed. 54.95 (0-8101-1272-8) Northwestern U Pr.

Return of the Author. Eugen Simion. Tr. by James W. Newcomb. (Rethinking Theory Ser.). 280p. 1997. pap. text ed. 18.95 (0-8101-1273-6) Northwestern U Pr.

Return of the Bald Eagle. Priscilla M. Tucker. (Illus.). 128p. 1994. pap. 14.95 (0-8117-3059-X) Stackpole.

Return of the Benedictines to London: A History of Ealing Abbey from 1896 to Independence. Ed. by Rene Kollar. 300p. 1994. 55.00 (0-86012-175-5, Pub. by Srch Pr UK) St Mut.

Return of the Bird Tribes. Ken Carey. LC 90-56460. 252p. 1991. reprint ed. pap. 14.00 (0-06-250188-7) Harper SF.

Return of the Black Sheep: (Rebels & Rogues) Patricia Ryan. (Temptation Ser.). 1995. pap. 3.25 (0-373-25640-X, 1-25640-3) Harlequin Bks.

Return of the Brown Pelican. Dan Guravich. LC 83-901. (Illus.). 128p. 1983. reprint ed. pap. 36.50 (0-608-00865-6, 2061657) Bks Demand.

Return of the Buffalo: The Story Behind America's Indian Gaming Explosion. Ambrose I. Lane. LC 95-11677. (Illus.). 240p. 1995. text ed. 55.00 (0-89789-432-4, Bergin & Garvey) Greenwood.

Return of the Buffalo: The Story Behind America's Indian Gaming Explosion. Frwd. by Estaban E. Torres & Terry L. Pechota. LC 95-11677. (Illus.). 240p. 1995. pap. text ed. 18.95 (0-89789-433-2, Bergin & Garvey) Greenwood.

Return of the Buffaloes: A Plains Indian Story about Famine & Renewal of the Earth. Paul Goble. (Illus.). 32p. (J). (gr. 1-4). 1996. 15.95 (0-7922-2714-X) Natl Geog.

Return of the Comet. Dennis Schatz & Yasu Osawa. (Illus.). 42p. (J). (gr. 4-9). 1985. pap. 7.95 (0-935051-00-7) Pacific Sci Ctr.

Return of the Cowboy. Cheryl Biggs. 1997. mass mkt. 3.99 (0-373-07762-9, 1-07762-7) Silhouette.

Return of the Cuckoo. large type ed. Leslie Lance. 1990. 25.99 (0-7089-2124-8) Ulverscroft.

Return of the Dangerous Classes: Drug Prohibition & Policy Politics. Diana R. Gordon. LC 93-42535. 1994. 29.95 (0-393-03642-1) Norton.

Return of the Dead Gecko Vol. II: More Ways to Recycle a Dead Gecko. Kevin Sullivan. (Illus.). 96p. (Orig.). 1995. pap. 7.95 (0-9644149-2-9) Hawaya.

Return of the Democratic Party to Power in 1884. Harrison C. Thomas. LC 79-82245. (Columbia University. Studies in the Social Sciences: No. 203). reprint ed. 29.50 (0-404-51203-8) AMS Pr.

Return of the Dingbat Cat. Jean Richardson. LC 94-37571. (Illus.). (J). (gr. k-3). 1994. 12.95 (0-89015-972-6, Eakin Pr) Sunbelt Media.

***Return of the Dinosaurs.** Mike Resnick. 1997. mass mkt. 5.99 (0-88677-753-4) DAW Bks.

Return of the Dove. Margaret Storm. 300p. 1996. pap. 24.95 (1-56459-975-2) Kessinger Pub.

Return of the Dove. Margaret Storm. 293p. 1972. reprint ed. spiral bd. 25.50 (0-7873-0849-8) Hlth Research.

Return of the Dove: Empowerment to Ascension Is Written in Your Heart. 2nd ed. Diadra Price. 1995. pap. 12.95 (1-887884-00-9) Wings of Spirit.

Return of the Dove: Empowerment to Ascension Is Written in Your Heart, 3 Tapes, Set. Diadra Price. 1995. digital audio 15.95 (1-887884-01-7) Wings of Spirit.

Return of the Dream: An Analysis of the Probable Return on a National Investment in Individual Development Accounts. Daphne Clones et al. 90p. (Orig.). 1995. 15.00 (1-883187-06-0) Corp Ent Dev.

Return of the Eagle. Paul Buchanan. Ed. by Liz Parker. (Take Ten Bks.). (Illus.). 45p. (Orig.). (J). (gr. 6-12). 1992. pap. text ed. 3.95 (1-56254-052-1) Saddleback Pubns.

Return of the Eagle: How America Saved Its National Emblem. Greg Breining. LC 94-72402. (Illus.). 126p. (Orig.). 1994. pap. 19.95 (1-56044-300-6) Falcon Pr MT.

Return of the Emperor. Allan Cole & Chris Bunch. (Sten Adventure Ser.: No. 6). 1990. mass mkt. 5.99 (0-345-36130-X, Del Rey) Ballantine.

Return of the Evil Twin. Francine Pascal. (Sweet Valley High Magna Ser.). 352p. (YA). (gr. 7 up). 1995. mass mkt. 4.50 (0-553-56713-6, Sweet Valley) BDD Bks Young Read.

Return of the Evil Twin. Francine Pascal. (Sweet Valley Twins Ser.; Magna Edition: No. 5). 352p. (J). 1995. pap. 4.50 (0-553-57002-1) Bantam.

Return of the French Freud. Ed. by Todd Dufresne. 256p. (C). 1997. pap. 18.95 (0-415-91526-0, Routledge NY) Routledge.

Return of the French Freud. Ed. by Fufresne. 256p. (C). 1997. text ed. 59.95 (0-415-91525-2, Routledge NY) Routledge.

Return of the Furies: An Investigation into Recovered Memory Therapy. Hollida Wakefield & Ralph C. Underwager. 441p. 1994. pap. 19.95 (0-8126-9272-1) Open Court.

Return of the God of Wealth: The Transition to a Market Economy in Urban China. Charlotte Ikels. LC 95-34237. 380p. 1996. 49.50 (0-8047-2580-2); pap. 16.95 (0-8047-2581-0) Stanford U Pr.

Return of the Goddess. Elizabeth Cunningham. 1993. pap. 12.95 (0-88268-157-5) Station Hill Pr.

***Return of the Goddess.** Edward C. Whitmont. 288p. 1997. pap. text ed. 19.95 (0-8264-1020-0) Continuum.

Return of the Goddess: A Divine Comedy. Elizabeth Cunningham. LC 92-10395. 1992. 22.50 (0-88268-115-X) Station Hill Pr.

Return of the Goddess 1994: Engagement Calendar. (Illus.). 190p. (Orig.). 1993. spiral bd. 17.95 (0-9631468-1-5) Hands Goddess Pr.

Return of the Gods: A Philosophical-Theological Reappraisal of the Writings of Ernest Becker. Frederick Sontag. (American University Studies: Philosophy: Ser. V, Vol. 78). 154p. (C). 1989. text ed. 28.95 (0-8204-0909-X) P Lang Pubng.

***Return of the Gods: Evidence of Extraterrestrial Visitations.** Erich Von Daniken, pseud. 1997. pap. 21.95 (1-85230-961-X) Element MA.

Return of the Great Brain. John D. Fitzgerald. 180p. (J). (gr. 3-5). 1975. mass mkt. 3.99 (0-440-45941-9, YB BDD) BDD Bks Young Read.

***Return of the Great Goddess.** Burleigh Muten. LC 97-5529. (Illus.). 192p. 1997. pap. 14.95 (1-55670-608-1) Stewart Tabori & Chang.

***Return of the Guardians.** Marvine Lindberg. 194p. (Orig.). 1997. mass mkt. 4.99 (1-55237-234-0, Pub. by Comnwlth Pub CN) Partners Pubs Grp.

Return of the Home Run Kid. Matt Christopher. (J). (gr. 4-7). 1994. 3.95 (0-316-14273-5) Little.

Return of the Inca. Tr. by Grady L. Hillman & Guillermo Delgado from QUE. 60p. (Orig.). (C). 1984. lib. bdg. 35.00 (0-916908-11-9) Place Herons.

Return of the Indian. Lynne Reid Banks. LC 85-31119. (Illus.). 192p. (J). (gr. 4-6). 1986. 15.95 (0-385-23497-X) Doubleday.

Return of the Indian. Lynne Reid Banks. (Indian in the Cupboard Ser.). 192p. (J). (gr. 3-7). 1987. pap. 3.99 (0-380-70284-3, Camelot) Avon.

Return of the Indian. large type ed. Lynne Reid Banks. (Illus.). 196p. (J). (gr. 4-8). 1995. reprint ed. lib. bdg. 16.95 (1-885885-11-3, Cornerstone FL) Pages Inc FL.

Return of the Indian. Lynne Reid Banks. (Indian in the Cupboard Ser.). 192p. (J). 1995. reprint ed. mass mkt. 4.50 (0-380-72593-2, Flare) Avon.

Return of the Indian: Conquest & Revival in the Americas. Phillip Wearne. LC 96-9168. (Illus.). 256p. (C). 1996. 59.95 (1-56639-500-3); pap. 19.95 (1-56639-501-1) Temple U Pr.

Return of the Indian Spirit. Vinson Brown. Ed. by Phyllis Johnson. LC 81-65887. (Illus.). 64p. (YA). (gr. 5 up). 1995. pap. 6.95 (0-89087-401-8) Celestial Arts.

Return of the Individual: Rescue Attempts in a Bureaucratic Age. Wolfgang Kraus. Tr. by John Russell from GER. 187p. (C). 1985. text ed. 16.60 (0-8204-0194-3) P Lang Pubng.

Return of the Jedi. (J). Date not set. pap. 2.95 (0-590-32929-4) Scholastic Inc.

***Return of the Jedi.** (Star Wars Galaxy Guides Ser.: No. 5). 15.00 (0-87431-267-1, 40126) West End Games.

***Return of the Jedi.** Archie Goodwin. (Star Wars Ser.). 1997. pap. 9.95 (1-56971-235-2) Dark Horse Comics.

Return of the Jedi. James Kahn. 224p. 1983. mass mkt. 5.99 (0-345-30767-4, Del Rey) Ballantine.

Return of the Jedi. Elizabeth Levy. 1995. pap. 3.99 (0-679-87205-1) Random.

Return of the Jedi. George Lucas. 1995. 8.98 (1-57042-208-7) Warner Bks.

***Return of the Jedi: A Flip Book.** (Star Wars Ser.). 40p. (J). 1997. pap. text ed. 2.98 (1-57082-579-3) Mouse Works.

Return of the Jedi: The National Public Radio Dramatization. Brian Daley. 320p. 1996. pap. 11.00 (0-345-40782-2) Ballantine.

***Return of the Jedi: With Tattoos.** Golden Books Staff. (Star Wars Ser.). 1997. pap. text ed. 3.99 (0-307-13069-X, Golden Books) Western Pub.

***Return of the Jedi Storybook.** (J). 1997. mass mkt. 5.99 (0-590-06659-5) Scholastic Inc.

Return of the Killed & Wounded & Missing of the Army under the Immediate Command of Major General Winfield Scott, on the 19th & 20th of August, 1847, During the Mexican-American War. (Stokvis Studies in Historical Chronology & Thought). 100p. pap. write for info. (0-89370-427-X); lib. bdg. write for info. (0-89370-327-3) Borgo Pr.

Return of the King. J. R. R. Tolkien. (Illus.). 464p. 1992. 30.00 (0-395-64740-1) HM.

Return of the King. anniversary ed. J. R. R. Tolkien. Date not set. write for info. (0-395-31268-X) HM.

Return of the King. large type ed. J. R. R. Tolkien. (Lord of the Rings Ser.: Pt. 3). 544p. 24.95 (1-85089-424-8, Pub. by ISIS UK) Transaction Pubs.

Return of the King, Vol. 3. J. R. R. Tolkien. 544p. 1986. mass mkt. 5.99 (0-345-33973-8) Ballantine.

Return of the King: Being the Third Part of the Lord of the Rings. J. R. R. Tolkien. (Illus.). 450p. 1988. 21.95 (0-395-48930-X); pap. 11.95 (0-395-27221-1) HM.

***Return of the Living Dad.** Kate Orman. (Dr. Who New Adventures Ser.). 300p. 1996. mass mkt. 5.95 (0-426-20482-4, Pub. by Virgin Pub UK) London Brdge.

An Asterisk (*) at the beginning of an entry indicates that the title is appearing in BIP for the first time.

*Return of the Living Dead. John Russo. 1995. mass mkt. 5.99 (1-55197-508-4, Pub. by Comnwlth Pub CN) Partners Pubs Grp.

Return of the Lone Iguana: A Fox Trot Collection. Bill Amend. (Illus.). 128p. (Orig.). (YA). 1996. pap. 9.95 (0-8362-1027-1) Andrews & McMeel.

Return of the Massachusetts Loyalists. David E. Maas. (Outstanding Studies in Early American History). 596p. 1989. reprint ed. 35.00 (0-8240-6189-6) Garland.

Return of the Mentor: Strategies for Workplace Learning. Ed. by Brian J. Caldwell & Earl M. Carter. LC 93-2874. (Education Policy Perspectives Ser.). 1993. 85.00 (0-7507-0166-8, Falmer Pr); pap. 30.00 (0-7507-0167-6, Falmer Pr) Taylor & Francis.

Return of the Messiah. Richard Honorof. 220p. 1996. pap. 220.00 (0-9632375-2-7) Feed My Sheep.

Return of the Messiah. Robert W. Wilson. Ed. by Mary Caroland. LC 90-71228. 197p. 1991. pap. 8.95 (1-55523-384-8) Winston-Derek.

Return of the Mountain Man. William W. Johnstone. 1986. mass mkt. 2.25 (0-8217-1816-9, Zebra Kensgtn) Kensgtn Pub Corp.

*Return of the Mountain Man. William W. Johnstone. 1995. mass mkt. 4.99 (0-8217-5771-7, Zebra Kensgtn) Kensgtn Pub Corp.

*Return of the Mountain Man. William W. Johnstone. 192p. 1997. mass mkt. 4.99 (0-8217-5702-4, Zebra Kensgtn) Kensgtn Pub Corp.

Return of the Mountain Man. William W. Johnstone. 1996. mass mkt. 4.99 (0-8217-5298-7, Zebra Kensgtn) Kensgtn Pub Corp.

Return of the Mountain Man. William W. Johnstone. 1986. mass mkt. 2.25 (0-8217-4018-0, Zebra Kensgtn) Kensgtn Pub Corp.

Return of the Mummy. R. L. Stine. (Goosebumps Ser.: No. 23). 160p. (J). (gr. 4-6). 1994. pap. 3.99 (0-590-47745-5) Scholastic Inc.

Return of the Mummy. R. L. Stine. (Goosebumps TV Ser.: No. 4). (J). (gr. 4-7). 1996. pap. text ed. 3.99 (0-590-74589-1) Scholastic Inc.

*Return of the Native. Hardy. 1997. pap. text ed. 7.75 (0-03-051494-0) HR&W Schl Div.

Return of the Native. Thomas Hardy. (Airmont Classics Ser.). (J). (gr. 10 up). 1964. mass mkt. 3.50 (0-8049-0038-8, CL-38) Airmont.

Return of the Native. Thomas Hardy. Ed. by A. Walton Litz. LC 67-5356. (YA). (gr. 9 up). 1967. pap. 11.56 (0-395-05201-7, RivEd) HM.

Return of the Native. Thomas Hardy. Ed. by James Gindin. (Critical Editions Ser.). (Illus.). (C). 1969. pap. text ed. 12.95 (0-393-09791-9) Norton.

Return of the Native. Thomas Hardy. LC 92-52901. 1992. 20.00 (0-679-41730-3, Everymans Lib) Knopf.

*Return of the Native. Thomas Hardy. (Illustrated Classics Collection 4). 64p. 1994. pap. 4.95 (0-7854-0753-7, 40512) Am Guidance.

Return of the Native. Thomas Hardy. 384p. (YA). (gr. 9-12). 1982. 3.50 (0-553-21269-9, Bantam Classics) Bantam.

Return of the Native. Thomas Hardy. Ed. by Amanda Hodgson. 1995. pap. 4.95 (0-460-87531-0, Everyman's Classic Lib) C E Tuttle.

Return of the Native. Thomas Hardy. 414p. 1959. pap. 2.50 (0-451-52307-5, Sig Classics) NAL-Dutton.

Return of the Native. Thomas Hardy. (World's Classics Ser.). (Illus.). 512p. 1990. pap. 6.95 (0-19-282717-0) OUP.

Return of the Native. Thomas Hardy. Ed. by Dorothy Calhoun. (Now Age Illustrated IV Ser.). (Illus.). (J). (gr. 4-12). 1978. student ed. 1.25 (0-88301-343-6); pap. text ed. 2.95 (0-88301-319-3) Pendulum Pr.

Return of the Native. Thomas Hardy. LC 77-79923. (Hardy New Wessex Editions Ser.). 1979. pap. 2.95 (0-312-67901-7) St Martin.

Return of the Native. Thomas Hardy. Ed. by George Woodcock. (English Library). 496p. 1978. pap. 7.95 (0-14-043122-5, Penguin Classics) Viking Penguin.

Return of the Native. Thomas Hardy. 1959. mass mkt. 4.95 (0-451-52471-3, Sig Classics) NAL-Dutton.

Return of the Native. large type ed. Thomas Hardy. (Large-Print Ser.). 573p. 1992. reprint ed. lib. bdg. 24.00 (0-939495-36-8) North Bks.

Return of the Native. Thomas Hardy. reprint ed. lib. bdg. 28.95 (0-88411-561-5) Amereon Ltd.

Return of the Native. Thomas Hardy. 1992. reprint ed. lib. bdg. 24.95 (0-89968-264-2, Lghtyr Pr) Buccaneer Bks.

Return of the Native. Thomas Hardy. (BCL1-PR English Literature Ser.). 485p. 1992. reprint ed. lib. bdg. 99.00 (0-7812-7548-2) Rprt Serv.

Return of the Native: American Indian Political Resurgence. Stephen Cornell. 288p. 1990. pap. 17.95 (0-19-506575-1) OUP.

Return of the Native: Saint George Defeated. Brian Thomas. LC 94-44446. (Twayne's Masterwork Studies: No. 154). 1995. 23.95 (0-8057-8073-4, Twayne); pap. 13.95 (0-8057-8117-X, Twayne) Scribnrs Ref.

Return of the Native (Hardy) Flowers. (Book Notes Ser.). (C). 1984. pap. 2.50 (0-8120-3439-2) Barron.

Return of the Native Literature Guide. Johanna Wrinkle. 96p. 1992. pap. text ed. 10.95 (0-944459-57-9) ECS Lrn Systs.

Return of the Native Notes. Frank H. Thompson, Jr. 1966. pap. 3.75 (0-8220-1138-7) Cliffs.

*Return of the Native Readalong. Thomas Hardy. (Illustrated Classics Collection 4). 64p. 1994. pap. 14.95 incl. audio (0-7854-0769-3, 40514) Am Guidance.

Return of the Ninja. Jay Leibold. (Choose Your Own Adventure Ser.: No. 92). 128p. (J). 1989. pap. 3.50 (0-553-27968-8) Bantam.

Return of the Ninja. large type ed. Jay Leibold. LC 94-43432. (Choose Your Own Adventure Ser.: No. 92). (Illus.). 128p. (J). (gr. 4 up). 1995. lib. bdg. 15.93 (0-8368-1310-3) Gareth Stevens Inc.

*Return of the Plague: Concilium Journal. Ed. by Virgil Elizondo et al. 150p. 1997. pap. 15.00 (1-57075-130-7) Orbis Bks.

Return of the Plant That Ate Dirty Socks. Nancy McArthur. 128p. (Orig.). (J). (gr. 5-6). 1990. pap. 3.99 (0-380-75873-3, Camelot) Avon.

Return of the Political. Chantal Mouffe. 240p. (C). 1993. pap. text ed. 19.00 (0-86091-651-0, B2512, Pub. by Vrso UK) Norton.

Return of the Political. Chantal Mouffe. 240p. (C). (gr. 13). 1993. text ed. 60.00 (0-86091-486-0, B2508, Pub. by Vrso UK) Norton.

Return of the Portable Curmudgeon. Ed. & Compiled by Jon Winokur. (Illus.). 352p. 1995. pap. 10.95 (0-452-27030-8, Plume) NAL-Dutton.

Return of the Prodigal Son. Henri J. Nouwen. 176p. 1994. pap. 15.00 (0-385-47307-9) Doubleday.

Return of the Prodigal Son: A Story of Homecoming. Henri J. Nouwen. (Illus.). 152p. 1995. 29.00 (0-8264-0870-2) Continuum.

Return of the Puritans. 5th ed. LC 87-62433. 208p. 1987. pap. text ed. 5.00 (0-932050-38-7) New Puritan.

Return of the Rag Picker. large type ed. Og Mandino. 1993. 20.95 (1-56895-017-9) Wheeler Pub.

Return of the Ragpicker. Og Mandino. 160p. 1993. pap. 5.50 (0-553-29993-X) Bantam.

Return of the Rancher. Max Brand. 240p. 1995. mass mkt., pap. text ed. 3.99 (0-8439-3789-0) Dorchester Pub Co.

Return of the Reader: Reader-Response Criticism. Elizabeth Freund. (New Accents Ser.). 192p. 1987. 37.50 (0-416-34400-3, 9458); pap. 11.95 (0-416-34410-0, 9081) Routledge Chapman & Hall.

Return of the Real: The Avant-Garde. Hal Foster. LC 96-18323. (Illus.). 200p. 1996. 30.00 (0-262-06187-2, October Bk); pap. 17.50 (0-262-56107-7, October Bk) MIT Pr.

Return of the Remnant: The Rebirth of Messianic Judaism. Michael Schiffman. 192p. 1990. pap. 8.95 (1-880226-53-7) M J Pubs.

Return of the Rishi: A Doctor's Story of Spiritual Transformation & Ayurvedic Healing. Deepak Chopra. 224p. 1991. pap. 10.95 (0-395-57420-X) HM.

Return of the Runaway Bride. Donna Clayton. (Romance Ser.). 1994. pap. 2.75 (0-373-08999-6, 5-08999-0) Silhouette.

Return of the Seventh Carrier. Peter Albano. 400p. 1987. mass mkt. 3.95 (0-8217-2093-7, Zebra Kensgtn) Kensgtn Pub Corp.

Return of the Shadow: The History of the Lord of the Rings, Pt. 1. J. R. R. Tolkien & Christopher Tolkien. LC 88-22986. 1989. 29.95 (0-395-49863-5) HM.

Return of the Shadows. Norma Farber. LC 91-27517. (Laura Geringer Bk.). (Illus.). 40p. (J). (gr. k-3). 1992. lib. bdg. 14.89 (0-06-020519-9) HarpC Child Bks.

Return of the Slapstick Papyrus. Francois Deschamps. (Illus.). 132p. 1988. pap. 14.95 (0-89822-051-3) Visual Studies.

Return of the Soldier. Rebecca West. 200p. 1990. pap. 8.95 (0-88184-658-9) Carroll & Graf.

Return of the Soldier. Rebecca West. 192p. 1996. pap. 10.95 (0-7867-0347-4) Carroll & Graf.

Return of the Spanish. Don Coldsmith. 240p. 1993. pap. 4.50 (0-553-29681-7) Bantam.

Return of the Spirit. Taw P. Al-Hakim. Tr. by William Hutchins from ARA. 288p. (Orig.). 1990. reprint ed. 30.00 (0-89410-425-X, Three Contnts); reprint ed. pap. 15.00 (0-89410-426-8, Three Contnts) Lynne Rienner.

Return of the Straight Dope. Cecil Adams. 512p. (Orig.). 1994. pap. 10.00 (0-345-38111-4, Ballantine Trade) Ballantine.

Return of the Stranger. Reay Tannahill. 384p. 1996. 24.95 (0-312-14038-X) St Martin.

Return of the Sun: Native American Tales from the Northeast Woodlands. Joseph Bruchac. (Illus.). 200p. (Orig.). 1989. pap. 12.95 (0-89594-343-3) Crossing Pr.

Return of the Swallow. large type ed. Frances A. Bond. 648p. 1992. 25.99 (0-7505-0189-8) Ulverscroft.

Return of the Third-Grade Ghosthunters. Grace Maccarone. 64p. (J). 1989. pap. 2.99 (0-590-41944-7) Scholastic Inc.

*Return of the Tribal: A Celebration of Body Adornment. Rufus Camphausen. LC 97-17043. (Illus.). 160p. 1997. pap. 19.95 (0-89281-610-4) Inner Tradit.

Return of the Tribes to Peachtree. Jeff Galloway. (Illus.). 180p. (Orig.). 1995. pap. 13.95 (0-9647187-0-7) Phidippides.

Return of the Twelves. Pauline Clarke. 1990. reprint ed. lib. bdg. 25.95 (0-89966-675-2) Buccaneer Bks.

Return of the Vanishing American. Leslie Fiedler. LC 68-15433. pap. 2.95 (0-8128-1236-0, Scrbrough Hse) Madison Bks UPA.

Return of the Virginian. large type ed. David Robbins. LC 94-10669. 535p. 1994. lib. bdg. 20.95 (0-8161-5997-1, GK Hall) Thorndike Pr.

Return of the Visible in British Romanticism. William H. Galperin. LC 92-32622. (Illus.). 352p. 1993. text ed. 39.95 (0-8018-4505-X) Johns Hopkins.

Return of the White Indian see White Indian Boy

Return of the Whole Number of Persons Within the Several Districts of the United States, 1790. U. S. Census Office Staff. LC 75-22845. (America in Two Centuries Ser.). 1976. reprint ed. 16.95 (0-405-07715-7) Ayer.

Return of the Whole Number of Persons Within the Several Districts of the United States, 1800. U. S. Census Office Staff. LC 75-22846. (America in Two Centuries Ser.). 1976. reprint ed. 13.95 (0-405-07716-5) Ayer.

Return of the Whooping Crane. Robin W. Doughty. (Corrie Herring Hooks Ser.: No. 15). (Illus.). 192p. 1989. 24.95 (0-292-79041-4) U of Tex Pr.

Return of the Wolf. Steve Grooms. (Camp & Cottage Ser.). (Orig.). 1993. pap. 16.95 (1-55971-151-5) NorthWord.

Return of the Wolf. Dorothy H. Patent. LC 94-26798. (Illus.). (J). 1995. 15.95 (0-395-72100-8, Clarion Bks) HM.

*Return of the Wolf. Dorothy H. Patent. 1997. pap. 5.95 (0-395-84519-X, Clarion Bks) HM.

Return of the Wolf to Yellowstone. Thomas McNamee. 352p. 1997. 27.50 (0-8050-3101-4) H Holt & Co.

Return of the World. Todd Baron. 48p. 1988. 6.50 (0-929022-02-5) O Bks.

Return of Thematic Criticism. Ed. by Werner Sollors. LC 92-20083. (English Studies: No. 18). (Illus.). 321p. 1993. 32.50 (0-674-76686-5); pap. 15.95 (0-674-76687-3) HUP.

Return of Thrift: How the Coming Collapse of the Middle Class Welfare State Will Reawaken Values in America. Phillip Longman. 256p. 1996. 25.00 (0-684-82300-4) Free Pr.

Return of Valkyrie. Dixon et al. (Illus.). 1990. 29.95 (0-913035-59-9); pap. 9.95 (0-913035-60-2) Eclipse Bks.

*Return of Venegence. Wendy Rogers. 244p. (Orig.). 1997. mass mkt. 244.00 (1-55197-934-9, Pub. by Comnwlth Pub CN) Partners Pubs Grp.

Return of Viking II: Sequellae to: Atlantis 2, 3, 4, 5 & 1. Regina C. Rapier. 48p. 1995. reprint ed. 10.00 (0-614-06249-7) R C Rapier.

Return of William Shakespeare. Hugh Kingsmill. Ed. by R. Reginald & Douglas Melville. LC 77-84240. (Lost Race & Adult Fantasy Ser.). 1978. reprint ed. lib. bdg. 29.95 (0-405-10988-1) Ayer.

Return on Investment: Strategies for Profit. Robert Rachlin. LC 75-44668. 124p. 1976. 14.95 (0-938712-00-4) Marr Pubns.

Return on Investment in Training & Performance Improvement Programs. Jack Phillips. LC 97-12089. (Improving Human Performance Ser.). 320p. 1997. pap. 29.95 (0-88415-492-0, 5492) Gulf Pub.

*Return on Investment Manual: Tools & Applications for Managing Financial Results. Robert Rachlin. LC 97-12691. 352p. (C). (gr. 13). 1997. text ed. 59.95 (0-7656-0014-5, Sharpe Prof) M E Sharpe.

Return on Quality: Measuring the Financial Impact of Your Company's Quest for Quality. Roland T. Rust. 1993. text ed. 29.95 (1-55738-547-5) Irwin Prof Pubng.

Return on Vision: Collaborative Ventures in Training & Education. 1993. 8.50 (0-89215-183-8) U Cal LA Indus Rel.

Return Passage. Michael Harvey. 232p. (Orig.). (C). 1991. pap. 12.95 (1-878555-02-2) Oakbridge Univ Pr.

Return Passage. Ward. 19.95 (0-06-016794-7, HarpT) HarpC.

Return Passage of Multi-Stage Turbomachinery. Ed. by P. Nykorowitsch. 66p. 1983. pap. text ed. 8.00 (0-317-02644-5, G00225) ASME.

Return Targets & Shortfall Risks: Studies in Strategic Asset Allocation. Martil L. Leibowitz. 448p. 1995. text ed. 70.00 (1-55738-916-0) Irwin Prof Pubng.

Return the Innocent Earth. 2nd ed. Wilma Dykeman. 444p. 1994. pap. 14.95 (1-884450-01-6) Wakestone Bks.

Return Tickets to Scandinavia. L. Grace Dibble. 160p. (C). 1991. 35.00 (0-7223-1681-X, Pub. by A H S Ltd UK) St Mut.

Return Tickets to Southern Europe. L. Grace Dibble. 1981. 35.00 (0-7223-1423-X, Pub. by A H S Ltd UK) St Mut.

Return Tickets to Yugoslavia. L. Grace Dibble. 249p. (C). 1991. pap. 35.00 (0-7223-1809-X, Pub. by A H S Ltd UK) St Mut.

Return Ties of Existence. Ed. by Mehdi K. Nakosteen. 50p. (ENG & PER.). 1975. lib. bdg. 20.00 (0-936347-46-5) Iran Bks.

Return to a Dream. Mary Freeman. (Rainbow Romances Ser.: No. 897). 160p. 1994. 14.95 (0-7090-4969-2, Hale-Parkwest) Parkwest Pubns.

Return to Atlantis, Vol. 1. 2nd ed. Ruth E. Norman & Charles Spaegel. (Illus.). 323p. 1992. reprint ed. 25.00 (0-932642-51-9) Unarius Acad Sci.

Return to Atlantis, Vol. 3, Pt. 1. Ruth E. Norman & Charles Spaegel. (Illus.). 254p. (C). 1982. pap. 9.00 (0-932642-53-5) Unarius Acad Sci.

Return to Atlantis, Vol. 3, Pt. 2. Ruth E. Norman & Charles Spaegel. (Illus.). 334p. 1983. pap. 9.00 (0-932642-74-8) Unarius Acad Sci.

Return to Atlantis, Vol. 4. Ruth E. Norman & Charles Spaegel. 244p. 1987. pap. 9.00 (0-932642-70-5) Unarius Acad Sci.

Return to Avalon. Ed. by Jennifer Roberson. 400p. 1996. mass mkt. 5.99 (0-88677-679-1) DAW Bks.

Return to Aztlan: The Social Process of International Migration from Western Mexico. Douglas S. Massey et al. LC 87-5913. (Studies in Demography: Vol. 1). 354p. 1987. pap. 15.95 (0-520-06970-6) U CA Pr.

Return to Balandra. large type ed. Grace Driver. 1990. 25.99 (0-7089-2310-0) Ulverscroft.

Return to Beirut. Andree Chedid. Tr. by Ros Schwartss from FRE. 176p. (Orig.). 1990. pap. 10.95 (1-85242-149-5) Serpents Tail.

Return to Berry Meadow. Richard Scheuerman. 1995. 19.00 (0-914222-26-0) Am Hist Soc Ger.

Return to Bitter Creek. Doris B. Smith. 176p. (J). (gr. 3-7). 1988. pap. 4.99 (0-14-032223-X, Puffin) Puffin Bks.

Return to Bloodstone House. Jane Toombs. (Shadows Ser.: No. 5). 1993. mass mkt. 3.50 (0-373-27005-4) Silhouette.

Return to Bull Run: The Campaign & Battle of Second Manassas. John J. Hennessy. LC 92-1580. (Illus.). 624p. 1994. pap. 17.00 (0-671-88989-3, Touchstone Bks) S&S Trade.

Return to Camelot. Donna Grove. 352p. 1995. mass mkt. 4.50 (0-06-108303-8, Harp PBks) HarpC.

Return to Camelot: Chivalry & the English Gentleman. Mark Girouard. LC 81-51343. (Illus.). 320p. 1981. 22.00 (0-300-02739-7) Yale U Pr.

*Return to Camerein. Rick Shelley. 336p. 1998. mass mkt. 5.99 (0-441-00496-2) Ace Bks.

Return to Center. Bobbie Probstein. LC 85-70723. (Illus.). 256p. (Orig.). 1985. pap. 10.95 (0-87516-554-0) DeVorss.

Return to Center, That Address Now Known: A Little Guide Towards Evolution in the Light. Laura Cruger. 72p. 1994. pap. 8.00 (0-9643566-0-0) Awake VA.

Return to Chewandswallow: A Sequel to Cloudy with a Chance of Meatballs. Judith Barrett. LC 95-40510. (Illus.). (J). 1997. 16.00 (0-689-80104-1, Atheneum Bks Young) S&S Childrens.

*Return to Chewelah: A Story of Innocence & Loss. Janet G. May. LC 97-12093. 256p. 1997. pap. 11.95 (0-9641357-5-2) Storm Peak.

Return to Cheyne Spa. Daisy Vivian. 1990. mass mkt. 3.50 (0-8217-3247-1, Zebra Kensgtn) Kensgtn Pub Corp.

Return to Cheyne Spa. Daisy Vivian. 1988. 16.95 (0-8027-1019-0) Walker & Co.

Return to Child: Philosophy, Games & Techniques Developed by David Darling. David Darling. 36p. 1993. 9.00 (1-885617-00-3) Music for People.

Return to China upon the Shoulders of My Father. Belle Yang. LC 94-16410. 1994. 27.95 (0-15-100063-8) HarBrace.

*Return to Chipping Sodbury. Phyllis Martin. 240p. 1997. 21.95 (0-9656893-0-1) Credenda.

*Return to Christmas. Chris Heimerdinger. LC 97-21427. 1997. 14.95 (0-345-41916-2) Ballantine.

*Return to Christmas: Sometimes Miracles Come in Very Familiar Packages. Chris Heimerdinger. LC 96-45298. 1996. write for info. (1-57734-052-3) Covenant Comms.

Return to Community: Building Support Systems for People with Psychiatric Disabilities. Paul J. Carling. 348p. 1994. pap. text ed. 18.95 (0-89862-323-5) Guilford Pr.

Return to Community: Building Support Systems for People with Psychiatric Disabilities. Paul J. Carling. LC 94-29724. 348p. 1994. lib. bdg. 42.00 (0-89862-299-9) Guilford Pr.

Return to Cosmology: Postmodern Science & the Theology of Nature. Stephen E. Toulmin. 224p. (C). 1982. pap. 16.95 (0-520-05465-2) U CA Pr.

Return to Creation: A Survival Manual for Native & Natural People. Manitonquat (Medicine Story). (Illus.). 188p. (Orig.). (YA). (gr. 7 up). 1991. pap. 9.95 (0-943404-20-7) Bear Tribe.

Return to Cross Creek. W. Horace Carter. (Illus.). 308p. (Orig.). 1985. pap. text ed. 9.95 (0-937866-09-1) Atlantic Pub Co.

*Return to Cumorah: Piecing Together the Puzzle of Book of Mormon Geography. Duane R. Aston. LC 96-86571. (Illus.). VII, 175p. write for info. (0-9655167-0-9) Am River Pubns.

Return to Deadwood. J. R. Roberts. (Gunsmith Ser.: No. 146). 192p. (Orig.). 1994. pap. 3.99 (0-515-11315-8) Jove Pubns.

Return to Democracy in Sudan: Report of a Mission on Behalf of the International Commission of Jurists by Adib Halasa, John D. Cooke, Ustinia Dolgopol. International Commission of Jurists. LC 87-133414. (Illus.). 103p. reprint ed. pap. 29.40 (0-7837-5226-1, 2044959) Bks Demand.

Return to Derleth Vol. I: Selected Essays. Ed. by James P. Roberts. LC 93-93909. (Illus.). 74p. (Orig.). 1993. pap. 7.00 (0-9636544-0-3) White Hawk.

Return to Derleth Vol. II: Selected Essays. Ed. by James P. Roberts. LC 93-240396. (Illus.). 96p. (Orig.). 1995. pap. 7.00 (0-9636544-2-X) White Hawk.

Return to Diversity: A Political History of East Central Europe since World War II. 2nd ed. Joseph Rothschild. LC 92-35420. 320p. 1993. 41.95 (0-19-507381-9); pap. 17.95 (0-19-507382-7) OUP.

Return to Dragonshill. large type ed. Essie Summers. 352p. 1992. 25.99 (0-7089-2597-9) Ulverscroft.

Return to Eden. (Rainbow Romances Ser.: No. 894). 160p. 1994. 14.95 (0-7090-4946-3, Hale-Parkwest) Parkwest Pubns.

Return to Eden: A Journey Through the Promised Landscape of Amagalyuagba. David H. Turner. Ed. by Donald Wiebe. (Toronto Studies in Religion: Vol. 9). xxiii, 299p. 1989. 47.95 (0-8204-1118-3) P Lang Pubng.

Return to Eden: Elizabeth's Search for Answers. Barbara Michel. (Eden Ser.: Vol. 3). 240p. (Orig.). 1995. pap. 8.95 (0-936369-65-5) Son-Rise Pubns.

Return to Elysium. Joan M. Grant. 1980. 29.95 (0-405-11788-4) Ayer.

Return to Elysium. Joan M. Grant. 320p. 1987. pap. 9.95 (0-89804-145-7) Ariel GA.

*Return to Empire: Punjab under the Sikhs & British in the Mid-19th Century. Andrew Mafor. 1996. 34.00 (81-207-1806-2, Pub. by Sterling Plns Pvt II) S Asia.

Return to Equilibrium: The Secret of Behavior Revealed. Clifford A. White. LC 96-90214. (Orig.). 1996. pap. 8.95 (0-533-11954-5) Vantage.

Return to Essentials: Reflections on the Present State of Historical Study. Geoffrey R. Elton. 128p. (C). 1991. 34.95 (0-521-41098-3) Cambridge U Pr.

Return to Falling Heath. D. A. O'Connor. 344p. 1995. mass mkt. 5.99 (1-896329-31-4, Pub. by Comnwlth Pub CN) Partners Pubs Grp.

Return to Freedom. Ed. by Thomas H. Johnson. LC 75-134104. (Essay Index Reprint Ser.). 1977. 20.95 (0-8369-1966-1) Ayer.

Return to Garth Manor. large type ed. Beatrice Taylor. 1990. 25.99 (0-7089-2131-0) Ulverscroft.

R

R

Return to Genuses: Search for the Perfect Food in Today's Ultra-Chemicalized Environment. Ally O. Hing. (Handbook for Life Ser.). 36p. pap. 4.50 (0-614-04664-5) A Hing Foods.

Return to Ghost Hotel. Larry Weinberg. 160p. (Orig.). (J). (gr. 3-7). 1996. pap. 3.95 (0-8167-4016-X) Troll Communs.

Return to Gingerbread Inn. Betty Behringer. 112p. 1992. pap. 5.95 (0-932616-52-6) Brick Hse Bks.

***Return to Glory: The Leafs from Imlach to Fletcher.** Andrew Podnieks. (Illus.). 300p. 1997. pap. 19.95 (1-55022-242-2, Pub. by ECW Press CN) Genl Dist Srvs.

***Return to Glory: The Powerful Stirring of the Black Man.** Joel A. Freeman & Don B. Griffin. 126p. 1997. pap. 11.99 (0-9625605-7-X) Renais Prodns.

***Return to Glory Days.** Dean Gelfand. 1997. pap. 14.00 (0-671-56323-8, PB Trade Paper) PB.

Return to Grace: A Theology for Infant Baptism. Kurt Stasick. 328p. (Orig.). 1996. pap. 29.95 (0-8146-6155-6, Pueblo Bks) Liturgical Pr.

Return to Greatness: Strategies for Powerful Improvements in Our Schools. 62p. 1988. pap. text ed. 10.00 (0-943397-08-1) Assn Calif Sch Admin.

Return to Happiness. large type ed. Renee Shann. 345p. 1982. 25.99 (0-7089-0821-7) Ulverscroft.

Return to Hardath. large type ed. McFadden. (Dales Large Print Ser.). 1995. pap. 17.99 (1-85389-551-2, Dales) Ulverscroft.

Return to Harmony. Janette Oke & T. Davis Bunn. 224p. 1996. 15.99 (1-55661-901-4); pap. 8.99 (1-55661-878-6); audio write for info. (1-55661-903-0) Bethany Hse.

Return to Harmony. large type ed. Janette Oke & T. Davis Bunn. 280p. 1996. 12.99 (1-55661-902-2) Bethany Hse.

Return to Harmony: Creating Harmony & Balance Through the Frequencies of Sound. Nicole LaVoie. Ed. by Jill Lawrence et al. LC 96-92084. (Illus.). 260p. (Orig.). 1996. pap. 13.00 (0-9650387-4-2) Snd Wave Energy.

Return to Havana: The Decline of Cuban Society under Castro. Maurice Halperin. LC 93-41059. 212p. (C). 1994. 19.95 (0-8265-1250-X) Vanderbilt U Pr.

Return to Health. Jess Kraft. Ed. by Barbara A. Kraft. LC 87-60170. 140p. (Orig.). 1987. pap. 6.95 (0-9618099-0-6) Red Lantern Pr.

***Return to Hell's Acre.** large type ed. Damon Mills. (Dales Large Print Ser.). 243p. 1997. pap. 18.99 (1-85389-708-6) Ulverscroft.

Return to Herbal Medicine. LaDean Griffin. 1979. pap. 6.95 (0-89036-073-1) Hawkes Pub Inc.

Return to Howliday Inn. James Howe. 128p. (J). 1993. pap. 4.50 (0-380-71972-X, Camelot) Avon.

Return to Howliday Inn. James Howe. LC 91-29505. (Illus.). 176p. (J). (gr. 3-7). 1992. lib. bdg. 14.00 (0-689-31661-5, Atheneum Bks Young) S&S Childrens.

Return to Incomes Policy. Ed. by R. P. Dore et al. LC 94-13740. (Social Change in Western Europe Ser.). 1994. 45.00 (1-85567-247-2) St Martin.

Return to Incomes Policy. Ed. by Ronald Dore et al. LC 94-13740. (Social Change in Western Europe Ser.). 208p. 1994. pap. 24.95 (1-85567-225-1, Pub. by Pntr Pubs UK) Bks Intl VA.

Return to Increasing Returns. Ed. by James M. Buchanan & Yong J. Yoon. 376p. (C). 1993. text ed. 62.50 (0-472-10432-2) U of Mich Pr.

Return to Isis. Jean Stewart. 192p. (Orig.). 1992. pap. 9.99 (0-9628938-6-2) Rising NY.

***Return to Islamorada.** John F. Dillon. 277p. (Orig.). 1997. mass mkt. 4.99 (1-55197-794-X, Pub. by Comnwlth Pub CN) Partners Pubs Grp.

***Return to Ithaca.** Barbara Newborn. LC 96-37814. 144p. 1997. pap. 11.95 (1-85230-944-X) Element MA.

Return to Jerusalem. Hassan J. Husseini. 222p. 1993. 19.95 (0-7043-2735-X, Pub. by Quartet UK) Interlink Pub.

Return to Jerusalem. Ruth E. Norman et al. (Illus.). 286p. (Orig.). 1983. pap. 9.00 (0-932642-78-0) Unarius Acad Sci.

Return to Kandy. Vesak Nanayakkara. (C). 1994. 58.00 (81-7013-121-9, Pub. by Navrang) S Asia.

Return to Kashgar. Gunnar Jarring. Tr. by Eva Claeson. LC 86-1976. (Central Asia Book Ser.). (Illus.). xi, 252p. 1986. text ed. 37.95 (0-8223-0664-6) Duke.

Return to King's Mere. large type ed. Leslie Lance. 1976. 25.99 (0-85456-481-0) Ulverscroft.

Return to Krondor: Official Game Secrets. 208p. 1997. per., pap. 19.99 (0-7615-0709-4) Prima Pub.

***Return to Lankhmar Vol. 3: The Adventures of Fafhrd & the Grey Mouser.** rev. ed. Fritz Leiber. (Illus.). 1997. 21.99 (1-56504-928-4, 12002, Borealis) White Wolf.

Return to Laughter. Alice Bowen. 320p. 1964. pap. 9.95 (0-385-05312-6, Anchor NY) Doubleday.

Return to Lesbos. Valerie Taylor. 192p. 1982. pap. 3.95 (0-930044-33-9) Naiad Pr.

Return to Life: Two Imaginings of the Lazarus Theme. Ed. by Robert J. Kastenbaum. LC 76-19587. (Death & Dying Ser.). 1977. reprint ed. lib. bdg. 21.95 (0-405-09582-1) Ayer.

***Return to Life/Volver a Vivir.** Ed. & Photos by Suzanne Levine. LC 96-83386. (Illus.). 56p. (Orig.). 1996. pap. 16.00 (0-9620222-6-8) Chardon Pr.

Return to Love. Marianne Williamson. 336p. 1994. mass mkt. 6.50 (0-06-109290-8, PL) HarpC.

Return to Love. Marianne Williamson. pap. 6.98 (0-8317-0041-6) Smithmark.

***Return to Love.** large type ed. Mary Mackie. (Linford Romance Large Print Ser.). 208p. 1997. pap. 16.99 (0-7089-5116-3, Linford) Ulverscroft.

Return to Love. large type ed. Patricia Robins. 271p. 1994. pap. 17.99 (1-85389-460-5, Medcom-Trainex) Ulverscroft.

***Return to Love: A Novel.** Anita Stansfield. LC 97-23454. 1997. write for info. (1-57734-126-0) Covenant Comms.

Return to Love: Gift Edition. Marianne Williamson. 352p. 1996. 16.00 (0-06-018668-2) HarpC.

Return to Love: Reflections on the Principles of a Course in Miracles. Marianne Williamson. 352p. 1996. pap. 13.00 (0-06-092748-8) HarpC.

Return to Love: Reflections on the Principles of a Course in Miracles. Marianne Williamson. 352p. Date not set. 13.00 (0-06-092747-X) HarpC.

Return to Lower Cape Cod. A. F. Joy. Ed. by Paul Kemprecos. (Illus.). 100p. (Orig.). 1986. 5.00 (0-934703-03-5) Saturscent Pubns.

Return to Mathematical Circles. Howard W. Eves. 192p. (C). 1988. text ed. 55.95 (0-87150-105-8) PWS Pubs.

Return to Millboro: The Reincarnation Drama Continues. Marge Rieder. LC 95-41447. (Illus.). 256p. (Orig.). 1996. pap. 14.95 (0-931892-28-7) B Dolphin Pub.

Return to Mount Athos. Ed. by G. G. Arnakis. 171p. 1968. 9.00 (0-317-34062-X); pap. 6.00 (0-317-34063-8) Ctr Neo Hellenic.

Return to Murmansk. Henry Swain. 284p. 1996. 23.50 (0-85036-452-3) Sheridan.

Return to Nature: The True Natural Method of Healing & Living - Paradise Regained. A. Just. 1991. lib. bdg. 89.00 (0-8490-4540-1) Gordon Pr.

Return to Nature, Vol. 1: Paradise Regained. 2nd ed. Adolf Just. 303p. 1970. reprint ed. spiral bd. 12.00 (0-7873-0485-9) Hlth Research.

Return to Neveryon. Samuel R. Delany. LC 93-31051. (Return to Neveryon Ser.: Bk. 4). 293p. (C). 1994. reprint ed. pap. 14.95 (0-8195-6278-5, Wesleyan Univ Pr) U Pr of New Eng.

***Return to Normandy: Getting a Jump on History.** (Illus.). 150p. (YA). (gr. 8-12). 1997. 23.00 (0-614-29610-2) Skyspec Pub.

Return to Normandy: Still Brave at Heart. 2nd rev. ed. Robert L. Williams. LC 96-92321. Orig. Title: My Return to Normandy. (Illus.). 150p. (Orig.). 1996. 23.00 (0-9627534-2-4) Skyspec Pub.

Return to Numberville. Singin' Steve. (Smart Song Adventures Ser.). (Illus.). 16p. (J). (gr. k-1). 1996. bds. 9.95 incl. audio (1-882500-08-3) SmartSong.

Return to Oasis: War Poems & Recollections from the Middle East, 1940-1946. Ed. by Victor Selwyn et al. 288p. 1980. 18.95 (0-85683-047-X); pap. 9.95 (0-85683-051-8) Dufour.

Return to Paradise. Lenora Boneck & L. B. Self. 328p. 1987. pap. 12.95 (0-940415-01-1) B & K Pub Hse.

***Return to Paradise.** Breytenbac. 1996. write for info. (0-15-100216-9) HarBrace.

***Return to Paradise.** Breytenbac. (J). 1996. pap. write for info. (0-15-600373-2, HB Juv Bks) HarBrace.

Return to Paradise. Breyten Breytenbach. LC 94-18882. (Harvest Book Ser.). 1994. pap. 12.95 (0-15-600132-2) HarBrace.

Return to Paradise. James A. Michener. 416p. 1984. mass mkt. 5.99 (0-449-20650-5, Crest) Fawcett.

Return to Paradise. James A. Michener. 1951. 24.95 (0-394-44291-1) Random.

***Return to Paradise: A Biblical Foundation for Health.** Cheryl Townsley. 170p. (Orig.). 1996. pap. 12.00 (0-9644566-5-6) Lifestyle for Hlth.

***Return to Paradise: A Guide to South Sea Island Films.** Larry Langman. LC 96-47937. 320p. 1997. 48.00 (0-8108-3268-2) Scarecrow.

Return to Paradise: Continuity & Change in Hawaii. Wayne S. Wooden. LC 95-7953. 176p. (Orig.). (C). 1995. pap. text ed. 24.50 (0-8191-9920-6); lib. bdg. 49.50 (0-8191-9919-2) U Pr of Amer.

Return to Paradise Island. Louise Bergstrom. 1993. 17.95 (0-8034-9014-3) Bouregy.

Return to Peyton Place. Grace Metalious. 1995. reprint ed. lib. bdg. 29.95 (1-56849-649-4) Buccaneer Bks.

Return to Philosophy. Thomas Molnar. 113p. 1996. text ed. 24.95 (1-56000-251-4) Transaction Pubs.

Return to Philosophy: Being a Defence of Reason, an Affirmation of Values & a Plea for Philosophy. Cyril E. Joad. LC 75-41157. reprint ed. 37.50 (0-404-14559-0) AMS Pr.

Return to Planet Internet. Steve W. Rimmer. 304p. 1996. pap. text ed. 24.95 (0-07-053021-1) McGraw.

Return to Pleasant Valley: Louis Bromfield's Best from Malabar Farm & His Other Country Classics. Ed. by George DeVault. 317p. (Orig.). 1996. pap. 19.45 (0-929332-06-7) Amer Botanist.

Return to Powers. Michael Martone. 1985. 4.00 (0-317-19728-2) Windless Orchard.

Return to Reality: Some Essays on Contemporary Christianity. Ed. by Stanley G. Evans. 1954. 59.50 (0-317-07644-2) Elliots Bks.

Return to Reason: A Critique of Enlightment Evidentialism & a Defense of Reason & Belief. Kelly J. Clark. 1990. pap. 12.00 (0-8028-0456-X) Eerdmans.

Return to Region. Juan Benet. Tr. by Gregory Rabassa from SPA. LC 84-27467. (Twentieth-Century Continental Fiction Ser.). (Illus.). 320p. 1985. text ed. 45.00 (0-231-05456-4) Col U Pr.

Return to Region. Juan Benet. Tr. by Gregory Rabassa from SPA. LC 84-27467. (Twentieth-Century Continental Fiction Ser.). (Illus.). 320p. 1987. pap. text ed. 16.00 (0-231-05457-2) Col U Pr.

Return to Resistance: Breeding Crops to Reduce Pesticide Dependence. Raoul A. Robinson. LC 95-24667. 480p. 1996. pap. 29.95 (0-932857-17-5) Ag Access.

Return to Responsibility: Constraints on Autonomy in Higher Education. Paul L. Dressel & William H. Faricy. LC 70-186574. (Jossey-Bass Higher Education Ser.). 252p. reprint ed. pap. 71.90 (0-8357-9344-3, 2013936) Bks Demand.

Return to River Hospital. large type ed. Kathleen Treves. (Linford Romance Library). 320p. 1985. pap. 15.99 (0-7089-6066-9) Ulverscroft.

Return to Rocheworld. Robert L. Forward & Julie F. Fuller. 336p. 1993. mass mkt. 4.99 (0-671-72153-4) Baen Bks.

***Return to Sac Prairie.** August Derleth. 331p. 1996. 25.00 (1-896648-95-9) Battered Silicon.

***Return to Sac Prairie.** August Derleth. 331p. 1996. pap. 17.00 (1-896648-96-7) Battered Silicon.

Return to Scripture in Judaism & Christianity: Essays in Postcritical Scriptural Interpretation. Ed. by Peter Ochs. LC 93-24518. (Theological Inquiries Ser.). 384p. (Orig.). 1993. pap. 18.95 (0-8091-3425-X) Paulist Pr.

Return to Secret Party Funds. Perry Belmont. LC 73-19127. (Politics & People Ser.). 258p. 1974. reprint ed. 20.95 (0-405-05852-7) Ayer.

***Return to Sender.** Kevin Henkes. LC 96-52903. 1997. pap. 3.99 (0-14-038556-8) Viking Penguin.

Return to Sender. Rebecca Winters. 1995. mass mkt. 2.99 (0-373-03390-7, 1-03390-1) Harlequin Bks.

Return to Sender. large type ed. Rebecca Winters. (Harlequin Romance Ser.). 1996. 19.95 (0-263-14454-2, Pub. by Mills & Boon UK) Thorndike Pr.

Return to Sender: A Novel. Ann Slegman. Ed. by Gloria V. Hickok. LC 94-46360. 231p. (Orig.). 1995. pap. 12.95 (1-884235-10-7) Helicon Nine Eds.

Return to Sender: The Secret Son of Elvis Presley. Les Fox & Sue Fox. LC 95-90418. 350p. 1996. 21.95 (0-9646986-0-9) West Highland.

Return to Seward Park. Tom Tsutakawa. (J). 1994. 11.95 (0-533-10721-0) Vantage.

Return to Shiva. Shri Valmiki. (Sacred Texts Ser.). viii, 88p. (C). 1983. pap. 8.75 (0-88695-006-6) Concord Grove.

***Return to Silver City.** large type ed. Harold Lamb. (Dales Large Print Ser.). 224p. 1996. pap. 17.99 (1-85389-659-4, Dales) Ulverscroft.

Return to Sodom & Gomorrah: Bible Stories from Achaeologists. Charles R. Pellegrino. LC 94-2424. 1994. 25.00 (0-679-40006-0) Random.

Return to Sodom & Gomorrah: Bible Stories from Archaeologists. Charles R. Pellegrino. 424p. 1995. pap. 12.50 (0-380-72633-5) Avon.

Return to South Africa: The Ecstasy & the Agony. Trevor Huddleston. 150p. 1991. reprint ed. pap. 42.80 (0-7837-6560-6, 2046125) Bks Demand.

***Return to Spirit: After the Mythic Church.** Desmond Murphy. LC 97-14140. 1997. pap. write for info. (0-8245-1685-0) Crossroad NY.

***Return to Spirit Lake: Journey Through a Lost Landscape.** Christine Colasurdo. LC 97-16044. 288p. (Orig.). 1997. pap. 16.95 (1-57061-081-9) Sasquatch Bks.

***Return to Splendor in the World: The Christian Doctrine of Sin & Forgiveness.** Christof Gestrich. LC 97-10580. 1997. pap. write for info. (0-8028-4164-3) Eerdmans.

Return to Tahiti: Bligh's Second Breadfruit Voyage. Douglas L. Oliver. (Miegunyah Press Ser.: 1:2). 332p. 1988. 29.95 (0-522-84354-9, Pub. by Melbourne Univ Pr AT) Paul & Co Pubs.

Return to Tebel-Ayr: The Journey Continues. Colleen K. Snyder. LC 92-19565. 224p. (Orig.). 1993. pap. 8.99 (0-8054-6058-6, 4260-58) Broadman.

Return to Terra. Ann C. Ulrich. 209p. (Orig.). 1995. pap. 11.95 (0-944851-06-1) Earth Star.

***Return to the Carnival of Horrors, Vol. 22.** R. L. Stine. (Give Yourself Goosebumps Ser.). (J). 1997. pap. text ed. 3.99 (0-590-21062-9, Little Apple) Scholastic Inc.

Return to the Center. Bede Griffiths. 156p. 1976. pap. 11.95 (0-87243-112-6) Templegate.

Return to the Center. Otto Von Habsburg. Tr. by Carvel De Bussy. LC 92-46377. (Studies in Austrian Literature, Culture, & Thought. Translation Ser.). 227p. 1993. pap. 23.50 (0-929497-39-2) Ariadne CA.

Return to the Chateau. Pauline Reage. 1995. pap. 10.00 (0-345-39465-8) Ballantine.

***Return to the Child of Light.** Sheron L. Cook & Graciela B. Sholander. (Illus.). 150p. (Orig.). 1996. pap. 14.95 (0-9652299-0-4) Triangle Publng.

Return to the Darkest Days: Human Rights in Haiti since the Coup. Ed. by Human Rights Watch Staff. 24p. (Orig.). 1991. pap. 5.00 (1-56432-054-5) Hum Rts Watch.

Return to the Desert: A Journey from Mount Hermon to Mount Sinai. David Praill. (Illus.). 160p. 1995. pap. 10.00 (0-00-627830-2) Harper SF.

Return to the Final Four: How the UConn Women Carved Their Own Identity. Dom Amore. Ed. by Mark Leary. 144p. (Orig.). (YA). 1996. pap. text ed. 14.95 (0-9646638-2-1) Hartford Courant.

Return to the Garden. Shakti Gawain. 244p. 1993. reprint ed. pap. 11.95 (1-882591-04-6) Nataraj Pub.

Return to the Hamlets: A Sequel to Beyond the Sunset. Louise Hurren. 302p. (C). 1989. pap. 39.00 (0-7212-0815-0, Pub. by Regency Press UK) St Mut.

Return to the Heartland & Rebirth of the Old Order: Reconceptualizing the Environment of Strategies for East-Central Europe & Beyond. George Liska. LC 94-16108. 192p. (Orig.). 1994. pap. text ed. 17.00 (0-941700-87-9) JH FPI SAIS.

Return to the High Valley: Coming Full Circle. Kenneth E. Read. LC 85-16385. (Studies in Melanesian Anthropology: No. 4). (Illus.). 225p. 1986. 35.00 (0-520-05664-7); pap. 13.95 (0-520-06468-2) U CA Pr.

Return to the House of Usher. Robert Poe. LC 96-18270. 288p. 1996. 22.95 (0-312-86012-9) Forge NYC.

Return to the Joy of Health: Natural Medicine & Alternative Treatments for All Your Health Complaints. Zoltan P. Rona & Jeanne M. Martin. LC 95-910586. 424p. (Orig.). 1995. pap. 19.95 (0-920470-62-9) Alive Bks.

Return to the Jungle. Kathleen Hughes. 63p. 1983. 10.00 (0-936758-10-4) Ctr Responsive Law.

Return to the Kill. Ruth R. Moen. (Kathleen O'Shaughnessy Mystery Ser.: Bk. 3). 228p. (Orig.). 1996. pap. 6.95 (0-9635653-5-4) Flying Swan.

Return to the Landscape. Joseph C. Murphey. Ed. by Dave Oliphant. (Illus.). 1979. 8.00 (0-933384-02-5); pap. 5.00 (0-933384-01-7) Prickly Pear.

Return to the Lord: A Lenten Journey of Daily Reflections. Mark G. Boyer. LC 90-24013. 183p. 1991. pap. 8.95 (0-8189-0605-7) Alba.

***Return to the Misty Shore: A Novel, Vol. 3.** Bonnie Leon. (Northern Lights Ser.). 1997. pap. text ed. 10.99 (0-7852-7413-8) Nelson.

***Return to the Painted Cave.** Justin F. Denzel. LC 96-21127. (J). 1997. 15.95 (0-399-23117-X, Philomel Bks) Putnam Pub Group.

Return to the Primal Self: Identity in the Fiction of George Eliot. Alan D. Perlis. (American University Studies: English Language & Literature: Ser. IV, Vol. 71). 221p. (C). 1989. text ed. 35.50 (0-8204-0637-6) P Lang Pubng.

Return to the Promised Land. Corrine Benton. 32p. 1995. per., pap. 6.00 (0-8059-3637-8) Dorrance.

***Return to the Promised Land: The Story of Our Spiritual Recovery.** Grant R. Schnarr. LC 96-46221. 248p. (Orig.). 1997. pap. 12.95 (0-87785-179-4, Chrysalis Books) Swedenborg.

Return to the Red Planet. Eric Burgess. (Illus.). 222p. 1990. 37.00 (0-231-06942-1) Col U Pr.

Return to the River. James M. McCann. 176p. 1995. pap. 11.95 (0-9627530-1-7) Ridgetop Pr.

***Return to the River: A Story of the Chinook Run.** 3rd ed. Roderick Haig-Brown. LC 97-3074. (Illus.). 248p. 1997. reprint ed. pap. 14.95 (1-55821-581-6) Lyons & Burford.

Return to the Same City. Paco I. Taibo, II. Tr. by Laura Dail from SPA. LC 96-14425. 192p. 1996. 19.95 (0-89296-590-8) Mysterious Pr.

Return to the Same City. Paco I. Taibo, II. Tr. by Laura Dail. 176p. 1997. mass mkt. 5.99 (0-446-40520-5, Mysterious Paperbk) Warner Bks.

Return to the Source. Ed. by Dvora Kiel. 360p. 1984. 13.95 (0-87306-376-7); pap. 12.95 (0-87306-377-5) Feldheim.

Return to the Source: Selected Speeches by Amilcar Cabral. Amilcar Cabral. Ed. by Africa Information Service Staff. LC 74-7788. 110p. reprint ed. pap. 31.40 (0-7837-3918-4, 2043766) Bks Demand.

Return to the Springs. Jacob Trapp. Ed. & Intro. by John Buehrens. 92p. (Orig.). 1987. pap. 3.00 (0-933840-27-6, Skinner Hse Bks) Unitarian Univ.

Return to the Summit of Scouting: A Mid-Life Journey Back to Philmont. William Cass. LC 93-12448. (Illus.). 384p. (Orig.). 1993. pap. 12.95 (0-923568-29-8) Wilderness Adventure Bks.

***Return to the Tomb of Horrors.** 1997. 30.00 (0-7869-0732-0) TSR Inc.

Return to the Top: The Inside Story of North Carolina's 1993 NCAA Championship. Photos by Bob Donnan & Hugh Morton. (Illus.). 128p. 1994. 29.95 (1-880123-07-X) Village Sports.

Return to the Twilight Zone. Ed. by Carol Serling. (Orig.). 1996. 7.98 (1-56731-092-3, MJF Bks) Fine Comms.

***Return to the Valley.** Richard Booth. 1997. pap. 7.95 (1-57532-046-0) Press-Tige Pub.

Return to Theses Hills, The Vermont Years of Calvin Coolidge. Jane Curtis et al. LC 84-73356. (Illus.). 96p. 1985. 17.50 (0-930985-00-1); pap. 9.95 (0-930985-01-X) Curtis Lieberman.

Return to Thunder Road: The Story Behind the Legend. Alex Gabbard. (Illus.). 192p. (Orig.). 1992. pap. 11.95 (0-9622608-3-5) Gabbard Pubns.

Return to Thunder Road: The Story Behind the Legend. Alex Gabbard. (Illus.). 192p. (Orig.). 1993. 17.95 (0-9622608-4-3) Gabbard Pubns.

Return to Tibet. large type ed. Heinrich Harrer. (Illus.). 352p. 1986. 25.99 (0-7089-1488-8) Ulverscroft.

Return to Timberland. Sarah H. French. (Orig.). 1995. mass mkt. 5.95 (1-56333-257-4) Masquerade.

Return to Tsugaru: Travels of a Purple Tramp. Osamu Dazai. LC 87-48694. (Illus.). 236p. 1988. pap. 5.95 (0-87011-841-2) Kodansha.

Return to Vietnam. Raymond Depardon. 160p. (gr. 13). 1994. pap. 20.00 (0-86091-643-X, Pub. by Vrso UK) Norton.

Return to Vietnam. Jean-Claude Guillebaid. Tr. by John Simmons from FRE. LC 94-22121. (Illus.). 160p. (C). (gr. 13). 1994. text ed. 65.00 (0-86091-418-6, Pub. by Vrso UK) Norton.

Return to Virtue: Reflections on Living Wisely. James Bell, Jr. 1995. 12.99 (1-881273-04-0) Northfield Pub.

Return to Virtue: Reflections on Living Wisely. James S. Bell. 1995. 12.99 (0-8024-7304-0) Moody.

Return to Wallaby Creek. large type ed. Kerry Allyne. (Magna Romance Ser.). 266p. 1992. 25.99 (0-7505-0413-7) Ulverscroft.

Return to Wessex: Sequel to "Dorset Forever" Gwen Woodruff. LC 90-195176. (Illus.). 215p. 1983. 19.95 (0-9616165-1-2) Woodruff Pub.

Return to Whiskey Creek. June L. Pomerinke. LC 94-93851. (Illus.). 200p. (Orig.). 1994. pap. 5.50 (0-318-72778-1) Young Pr Idaho.

***Return to Wonder.** Arthur Gordon. 160p. 1997. pap. 14.99 (0-8054-5453-5) Broadman.

Return to Work after Coronary Artery Bypass Surgery. Ed. by Paul J. Walter. (Illus.). 480p. 1985. 62.00 (0-387-13591-X) Spr-Verlag.

Return to Work by Design: "Managing the Human & Financial Costs of Disability" Gene L. Dent. (Practical Management Ser.). 111p. (Orig.). 1990. pap. text ed. 24.00 (1-878403-00-1) Martin-Dennison Pr.

Return to Work Incentives: Lessons for Policymakers from Economic Studies. John A. Gardner. LC 89-8874. 1989. 25.00 (0-935149-19-8, WC-89-2) Workers Comp Res Inst.

Return to Work Process: A Case Management Approach. Richard Pimentel. Date not set. pap. text ed. 29.95 (0-942071-33-6) M Wright & Assocs.

An Asterisk (*) at the beginning of an entry indicates that the title is appearing in BIP for the first time.

*Return to Wuthering Heights. Nicola Thorne. 1996. 22.00 (0-7278-4913-1) Severn Hse.

Return to Yesterday. Annette Broadrick. (Western Lovers Ser.). 1995. mass mkt. 3.99 (0-373-88536-9, 1-88536-7) Harlequin Bks.

Return to Yesterday. Ford Madox Ford. 416p. 1972. reprint ed. 12.95 (0-87140-563-6) Liveright.

Return to Yesterday. Ford Madox Ford. 416p. 1983. reprint ed. pap. 7.95 (0-87140-271-8) Liveright.

Return to Yesterday: The History of Wardsboro, Vermont. C. S. Streeter. LC 80-15777. (Illus.). 248p. 1980. 15.00 (0-914016-71-7) Phoenix Pub.

Return to Zion. Bodie Thoene. LC 87-24244. (Zion Chronicles Ser.: Vol. 3). 352p. (Orig.). 1987. pap. 10.99 (0-87123-939-6) Bethany Hse.

Return to Zork: The Official Companion Guide. Peter Spear. 320p. 1994. 16.95 (1-56686-123-3) Brady Pub.

Return to Zork Adventurers Guide. Steve Schwartz. 1993. pap. 14.95 (1-55958-534-X) Prima Pub.

Return Trip Tango & Other Stories from Abroad. Ed. by Frank MacShane & Lori Carlson. (Columbia Collection). 320p. (C). 1992. pap. 16.00 (0-231-07993-1); text ed. 37. 50 (0-231-07992-3) Col U Pr.

Return Trips. Alice Adams. LC 85-40116. 179p. 1985. 14. 95 (0-394-53633-9) Knopf.

*Return via Rangoon. large type ed. Philip Stibbe. 480p. 1996. 25.99 (0-7089-3599-0) Ulverscroft.

*Return via Rangoon. 2nd ed. Philip Stibbe. 1997. pap. text ed. 16.95 (0-85052-476-8) Trans-Atl Phila.

Return Visit. Desmond Wilcx. (Illus.). 162p. 1992. pap. 15. 95 (0-563-36052-6, BBC-Parkwest) Parkwest Pubns.

Return with Honor. George Day. (Illus.). 288p. 1991. pap. 28.50 (0-912173-16-5) Champlin Museum.

Return with Honor. Especially for Youth Staff. 1995. pap. 7.95 (0-88494-991-5) Bookcraft Inc.

Return with Honor. Scott O'Grady & Jeff Coplon. 1995. 21.95 (0-385-48330-9) Doubleday.

Return with Honor. Scott O'Grady. 1995. 21.95 (0-8499-1321-7) Word Pub.

Return with Honor. Scott Ogrady. 208p. 1996. mass mkt. 6.99 (0-06-101147-9, Harp PBks) HarpC.

Return with Honor. large type ed. Scott O'Grady & Jeff Coplon. LC 96-6178. 1996. 26.95 (0-7862-0676-4) Thorndike Pr.

Returnable & Non-Returnable Packaging: The Management of Waste & Resources Towards an Eco-Social Market Economy. Gunther Poll & Friedrich Schneider. (Illus.). 160p. (Orig.). (C). 1993. pap. text ed. 45.00 (1-873936-25-7, Pub. by J & J Sci Pubs UK) Bks Intl VA.

Returned Battle Flags. Ed. by Richard Rollins. 1995. pap. 25.00 (0-9638993-4-1) Rank & File.

Returning. Ed. by Jonathan Magonet. LC 78-68143. 1978. pap. 3.95 (0-8197-0468-7) Bloch.

Returning. Dan Wakefield. Date not set. pap. write for info. (0-14-025493-5, Viking) Viking Penguin.

*Returning: A Spiritual Journey. Dan Wakefield. LC 97-1030. 1997. pap. 12.00 (0-8070-2711-1) Beacon Pr.

Returning a Borrowed Tongue. Ed. by Nick Carbo. 320p. (Orig.). (YA). (gr. 11-12). 1996. pap. 14.95 (1-56689-043-8) Coffee Hse.

Returning Alive from Hell. Naruko Wakimizu. 75p. 1988. per. 9.95 (0-89697-340-9) Intl Univ Pr.

Returning Back to Eden. Betty A. Peters. LC 94-61583. 128p. (Orig.). 1994. spiral bd. 9.95 (0-945383-55-X, 945-5838) Teach Servs.

Returning from the Light: Using Past Lives to Understand the Present & Shape the Future. Brad Steiger. 416p. 1996. pap. 5.99 (0-451-18623-0, Sig) NAL-Dutton.

Returning Home. (Victorian Era Ser.). 1993. mass mkt. 5.95 (0-929654-79-X, 96) Blue Moon Bks.

Returning Home: New Covenant & Second Exodus as the Context for 2 Corinthians 6.14-7.1. W. J. Webb. (Journal for the Study of the New Testament, Supplement Ser.: Vol. 85). 247p. 50.00 (1-85075-418-7, Pub. by Sheffield Acad UK) CUP Services.

Returning Home: Tao-Chi's Album of Landscapes and Flowers. Tr. & Intro. by Wen Fong. LC 76-15911. (Illus.). 91p. 1976. 15.00 (0-8076-1040-2); boxed 25.00 (0-8076-0827-0) Braziller.

*Returning Home: The Poetics of Whim & Fancy. Illus. by Tracy Porter. 48p. 1997. 6.95 (0-8362-3178-3) Andrews & McMeel.

*Returning Home for Easter: The Lenten Journey. Richard Gribble. 192p. (Orig.). 1996. pap. 9.95 (0-8198-6465-X) Pauline Bks.

Returning Nicholas. Deborah D. Desaix. LC 94-30328. (Illus.). 32p. (J). (ps-3). 1995. 16.00 (0-374-36251-3) FS&G.

Returning Remnant: Israel's Captivity & Return 605-430 B. C. Shawn E. Kauffled. LC 93-84831. 98p. (Orig.). 1994. pap. 7.99 (0-8100-0496-8, 15N0502) Northwest Pub.

Returning the Gaze: Essays on Racism, Feminism & Politics. Ed. by Himani Bannerji. 1993. per. 17.95 (0-920813-55-0, Pub. by Sister Vision CN) LPC InBook.

Returning the Gift: Poetry & Prose from the First North American Native Writers Festival. Ed. by Joseph Bruchac & Association for the Study of American Indian Literatures Staff. LC 94-4845. (Sun Tracks Ser.: Vol. 29). 369p. 1994. pap. 19.95 (0-8165-1486-0); lib. bdg. 45.00 (0-8165-1376-7) U of Ariz Pr.

Returning the Question. Trish Reeves. LC 88-71364. (CSU Poetry Ser.: No. XXV). 62p. (Orig.). 1988. 12.00 (0-914946-67-6); pap. 6.00 (0-914946-66-8) Cleveland St Univ Poetry Ctr.

Returning to A. Dorien Ross. (Illus.). 180p. (Orig.). 1995. pap. 9.95 (0-87286-307-7) City Lights.

Returning to A. Dorien Ross. (Illus.). 180p. (Orig.). 1995. 18.95 (0-87286-306-9) City Lights.

Returning to Care: Discharge & Reentry in Foster Care. Trudy Festinger. 1994. 12.95 (0-87868-591-X) Child Welfare.

Returning to Emotion. Maxwell Bodenheim. LC 73-18552. (BCL Ser.: I). reprint ed. 20.00 (0-404-11367-2) AMS Pr.

Returning to Learning: Getting Your G.E.D. Richard Conlow. Ed. by Phil Gerould. LC 89-81521. (Fifty-Minute Ser.). 66p. 1990. pap. 10.95 (1-56052-002-7) Crisp Pubns.

Returning to Nothing: The Meaning of Lost Places. Peter Read. 272p. (C). 1997. text ed. 59.95 (0-521-57154-5) Cambridge U Pr.

Returning to Seneca Falls - the First Women's Rights Convention & Its Meaning for Men Today: A Journey into the Historical Soul of America. Bradford Miller. 225p. 1995. pap. 17.95 (0-940262-71-1) Lindisfarne Bks.

Returning to Shakespeare. Brian Vickers. 256p. (C). 1989. text ed. 35.00 (0-415-03389-6, A3567) Routledge.

Returning to Silence: Zen Practice in Everyday Life. Dainin Katagiri. LC 87-28844. (Dragon Editions Ser.). 194p. (Orig.). 1988. pap. 15.00 (0-87773-431-3) Shambhala Pubns.

Returning to Sils-Maria: A Commentary to Nietzsche's "Also Sprach Zarathustra" Greg Whitlock. LC 89-27809. (American University Studies: Philosophy: Ser. V, Vol. 87). 328p. (C). 1990. text ed. 31.95 (0-8204-1198-1) P Lang Pubng.

*Returning to the Civil War: Grand Reenactments of an Anguished Time. Kent Courtney. LC 96-41231. (Illus.). 96p. 1997. 21.95 (0-87905-783-1) Gibbs Smith Pub.

Returning to the Homeland: Cherokee Poetry & Short Stories. MariJo Moore. LC 94-61389. (Illus.). 112p. (Orig.). 1995. pap. 9.95 (1-56664-073-3) WorldComm.

Returning to the Scene: Blake Edwards, Vol. 2. William Luhr & Peter Lehman. LC 80-28440. (Illus.). 320p. (C). 1989. 29.95 (0-8214-0917-4); pap. 14.95 (0-8214-0918-2) Ohio U Pr.

*Returning to the Source: The Way to the Experience of God. Wilson Van Dusen. LC 96-44858. 280p. (Orig.). 1996. 19.00 (0-911226-36-2); pap. 13.50 (0-911226-37-0) Real People.

Returning to the Source: Zen Discourses. Osho. 1995. pap. 14.95 (1-85230-700-5) Element MA.

Returning to Tradition: The Contemporary Revival of Orthodox Judism. M. Herbert Danzger. LC 88-27735. 384p. (C). 1989. 40.00 (0-300-03947-6) Yale U Pr.

Returning to Work: A Planning Book. Sandra L. Stark. LC 82-14892. 208p. 1983. pap. text ed. 13.65 (0-07-060887-3) McGraw.

Returning to Your First Love. Chris Harvey. 45p. 1994. pap. 5.00 (1-886357-00-5) C Harvey Minist.

Returning to Your First Love: Putting God Back in First Place. Tony Evans. 318p. 1995. 18.99 (0-8024-7908-1) Moody.

Returning What We Owed. Carolyne Wright. (Poetry Chapbook Ser.). 32p. (Orig.). 1980. pap. 4.00 (0-937669-00-8) Owl Creek Pr.

Returning Your Call: Poems. Leonard Nathan. LC 75-3485. (Contemporary Poets Ser.). 76p. 1975. pap. 9.95 (0-691-01321-7); text ed. 21.95 (0-691-06296-X) Princeton U Pr.

Returnings: Life After Death Experiences: A Christian View. John R. Aurelio. 112p. 1996. pap. text ed. 10.95 (0-8264-0877-X) Continuum.

Returns. Dennis Barone. (New American Fiction Ser.: No. 36). 112p. (Orig.). 1996. pap. 10.95 (1-55713-184-8) Sun & Moon CA.

Returns from Education to Employed Women in India. N. Shantha Mohan. (C). 1989. 30.00 (81-85024-63-4, Pub. by Uppal Pub Hse II) S Asia.

Returns in Over-the-Counter Stock Markets. Paul F. Jessup & Robert B. Upson. LC 73-77711. 125p. reprint ed. pap. 35.70 (0-317-39685-4, 2055883) Bks Demand.

Returns of History: Russian Nietzscheans after Modernity. Dragan Kujundzic. LC 96-18584. (SUNY Series, The Margins of Literature). 219p. (C). 1997. text ed. 59.50 (0-7914-3233-5); pap. text ed. 19.95 (0-7914-3234-3) State U NY Pr.

Returns to Scale & Elasticities of Substitution by Size of Establishment for Two-Digit U. S. Manufacturing Industries - 1958. Daniel Shefer. (Discussion Paper Ser.: No. 26). 1968. pap. 10.00 (1-55869-109-X) Regional Sci Res Inst.

Reuben. Mary C. Borntrager. LC 92-5432. (Ellie's People Ser.: Bk. 5). 160p. (Orig.). 1992. pap. 7.99 (0-8361-3593-8) Herald Pr.

Reuben. large type ed. Mary C. Borntrager. (Ellie's People Ser.: Bk. 5). 160p. (Orig.). 1993. pap. 8.99 (0-8361-3640-3) Herald Pr.

Reuben & Rachel: or Tales of Old Times, 2 vols. in one. Susanna Rowson. LC 78-64089. reprint ed. 37.50 (0-404-17074-9) AMS Pr.

Reuben & the Blizzard. Merle Good. LC 95-25411. (Illus.). 32p. (J). (gr. k-4). 1995. 14.95 (1-56148-184-X) Good Bks PA.

Reuben & the Fire. Merle Good. LC 93-1798. (Illus.). 32p. (J). (ps-3). 1993. lib. bdg. 14.95 (1-56148-091-6) Good Bks PA.

*Reuben & the Quilt. Merle Good. (Illus.). 32p. (J). 1997. 16.95 (1-56148-234-X) Good Bks PA.

Reuben Gold Thwaites: A Memorial Address. Frederick J. Turner. (BCL1 - U. S. History Ser.). 94p. 1991. reprint ed. lib. bdg. 59.00 (0-7812-6026-4) Rprt Serv.

Reuben Sachs: A Sketch. Amy Levy. LC 78-37699. reprint ed. 39.50 (0-404-56758-4) AMS Pr.

Reuben Snake: Your Humble Serpent. Jay C. Fikes. LC 94-43554. (Illus.). 277p. 1995. 24.95 (0-940666-60-X) Clear Light.

*Reuben Snake: Your Humble Serpent. Jay C. Fikes & Reuben Snake. (Illus.). 289p. 1997. pap. 14.95 (1-57416-007-9) Clear Light.

Reule of Crysten Religioun. R. Pecock. (EETS, OS Ser.: No. 171). 1974. reprint ed. 75.00 (0-527-00168-6) Periodicals Srv.

Reumes de Cours au College de France, 1952-60. Maurice Merleau-Ponty. (FRE.). 1982. pap. 16.95 (0-7859-2737-9) Fr & Eur.

Reunification of China: Pro-Taiwan Relations in Flux. Lai T. Lee. LC 90-44388. 200p. 1991. text ed. 49.95 (0-275-93772-0, C3772, Praeger Pubs) Greenwood.

Reunification of Germany. Ed. by Robert E. Long. LC 91-43545. (Reference Shelf Ser.: Vol. 64, No. 1). 132p. 1992. pap. 15.00 (0-8242-0825-0, DD262) Wilson.

Reunification of Germany. Diane Yancy. LC 93-17836. (Overview Ser.: World in Conflict). (J). (gr. 5-8). 1994. lib. bdg. 17.96 (1-56006-143-X) Lucent Bks.

Reunion. Jenne Andrews. LC 82-22928. 59p. (Orig.). 1983. pap. 7.00 (0-89924-038-0) Lynx Hse.

Reunion. Karen Ball. LC 96-26367. 250p. 1996. pap. 8.99 (0-88070-951-0, Palisades OR) Multnomah Pubs.

Reunion. Mark A. Boone. 224p. (Orig.). 1989. mass mkt. 2.95 (0-87067-331-9, BH331-9) Holloway.

Reunion. N. A. Diaman. LC 83-4051. (Illus.). 164p. (Orig.). 1983. pap. 8.95 (0-931906-04-0, Persona Pr) Persona Prod.

Reunion. Roger Essley. LC 93-12035. (J). (ps-6). 1994. 16. 00 (0-671-86722-9, S&S Bks Young Read) S&S Childrens.

*Reunion. Jerome McDonough. 30p. 1997. pap. 4.00 (0-88680-446-9) I E Clark.

Reunion. Lawrence Smale. 286p. (Orig.). 1991. pap. 19.95 (1-884690-08-4) Owl Press.

*Reunion. Fred Uhlman. 1997. pap. text ed. 10.00 (0-374-52515-3, Noonday) FS&G.

*Reunion. Photos by Irv Wieder. (Illus.). 104p. 1996. 29.00 (0-9654633-0-3) Upayah Pr.

Reunion. Rita Wrighton. LC 89-78207. 256p. 1990. 16.95 (0-931832-45-4) Fithian Pr.

Reunion. Michael J. Friedman. Ed. by Dave Stern. (Star Trek: The Next Generation Ser.). 352p. 1992. reprint ed. mass mkt. 5.99 (0-671-78755-1) PB.

*Reunion: A Love That Bridged Two Worlds. Jessica Ezell. 1996. pap. 14.95 (0-614-20469-0) Publishers Group.

Re*Union: Healing Our Victim & Offender Patterns. Dell M. Miller. (Illus.). 151p. (Orig.). (C). 1993. pap. 9.95 (0-9641650-0-7) Serenity Pubns.

Reunion: The Search for My Birth Family. Madelene Allen. 224p. 1992. 24.95 (0-7737-2588-1) Genl Dist Srvs.

Reunion Vol. 1: A Love That Bridged Two Worlds. Jessica Ezell. 208p. 1996. 18.95 (1-883478-17-0) Stillpoint.

Reunion & Dark Pony. David Mamet. LC 79-2319. 64p. 1990. pap. 8.95 (0-8021-5171-X, Grove) Grove-Atltic.

Reunion & Other Stories. Gershon Kranzler. (Illus.). 156p. (YA). reprint ed. 10.00 (0-8266-0327-0, Merkos LInyonei Chinuch) Kehot Pubn Soc.

Reunion & Reaction: The Compromise of 1877 & the End of Reconstruction. C. Vann Woodward. 1995. 21.50 (0-8446-6871-0) Peter Smith.

Reunion Book, Vol. 1. Mary J. Rillera. 216p. (Orig.). 1991. pap. 17.95 (0-910143-05-6) Pure CA.

Reunion Creole - French Dictionary: Dictionnaire Kreole Reunion-Francais. Alain Armand. 399p. (CRP & FRE.). 1987. pap. 105.00 (0-8288-1094-X, M970) Fr & Eur.

Reunion des Langues. P. Besnier. Ed. by V. L. Cascio. vi, 92p. 1985. 44.65 (90-6765-103-6); pap. 30.80 (90-6765-095-1) Mouton.

Reunion in Florence. (Orig.). 1992. mass mkt. 4.95 (1-56333-070-9, Badboy) Masquerade.

Reunion in Hell. Paul Caster. LC 82-62274. (Illus.). 80p. 1983. pap. 25.00 (0-937486-02-7) Perimeter Pr.

Reunion in Kentucky. Wanda Luttrell. LC 94-31114. (Illus.). 208p. (J). 1995. 12.99 (0-7814-0236-0, Chariot Bks) Chariot Victor.

Reunion in Kentucky. Wanda Luttrell. (Sarah's Journey Ser.: Vol. 3). (Illus.). 208p. (J). (gr. 4-7). 1995. pap. 5.99 (0-7814-0907-1) Chariot Victor.

Reunion in Renfrew. large type ed. W. E. Ross. (Linford Romance Library). 288p. 1992. pap. 15.99 (0-7089-7190-3, Trailtree Bookshop) Ulverscroft.

Reunion in San Jose. large type ed. Marshall Grover. (Linford Western Library). 272p. 1987. pap. 15.99 (0-7089-6352-8, Linford) Ulverscroft.

Reunion in Sicily. Jerre Mangione. LC 84-1855. (Morningside Bk.). 285p. 1984. reprint ed. text ed. 49.50 (0-231-05840-3); reprint ed. pap. text ed. 17.00 (0-231-05841-1) Col U Pr.

Reunion in Vienna. Edith Foster. (Studies in Austrian Literature, Culture & Thought; Translation Ser.). 180p. 1991. pap. 16.00 (0-929497-40-6) Ariadne CA.

Reunion of Isaac & Ishmael. Jack Cohen. 180p. pap. 12.95 (0-88962-396-1) Mosaic.

Reunion of Isaac & Ishmael. Jack Cohen. 169p. 1987. pap. 12.95 (0-88962-395-3) Mosaic.

Reunion of Trees: The Discovery of Exotic Plants & Their Introduction into North American & European Landscapes. Stephen A. Spongberg. LC 89-71743. (Illus.). 270p. (Orig.). 1990. 35.00 (0-674-76693-8) HUP.

Reunion of Trees: The Discovery of Exotic Plants & Their Introduction into North American & European Landscapes. Stephen A. Spongberg. (Illus.). 270p. (Orig.). (C). 1995. pap. 24.95 (0-674-76694-6) HUP.

Reunion on Neverend. John E. Stith. 352p. 1995. 4.99 (0-8125-1953-1) Tor Bks.

Reunion Planner. Phyllis A. Hackleman. (Illus.). 133p. 1995. pap. 12.95 (0-685-69920-X, 9575) Clearfield Co.

*Reunion Planner: For Windows. Linda J. Hoffman. 1996. pap. text ed. 29.95 (0-9630516-5-2) Goodman Lauren.

Reunion Planner: The Step-by-Step Guide Designed to Make Your Reunion a Social & Financial Success. Linda J. Hoffman & Neal Barnett. LC 91-73738. (Illus.). 147p. (Orig.). 1992. pap. 12.95 (0-9630516-2-8) Goodman Lauren.

Reuniones En Casa. Witness Lee. 102p. (SPA.). per. 3.50 (0-87083-235-2, 12007002) Living Stream Ministry.

*Reunions. Raymond Moody. 1997. pap. 12.00 (0-449-00119-9) Fawcett.

Reunions: How to Plan Yours. Harry McKinzie. 305p. pap. text ed. 16.95 (0-86626-002-1) McKinzie Pub.

Reunions: Visionary Encounters with Departed Loved Ones. Raymond Moody & Paul Perry. 1994. mass mkt. 5.99 (0-8041-1235-5) Ivy Books.

Reunions for Fun-Loving Families. Nancy F. Bagley. LC 94-11405. 128p. (Orig.). 1994. pap. 9.95 (0-918420-21-0) Brighton Pubns.

*Reunited! large type ed. Michael Johnstone. 304p. 1996. 25.99 (0-7089-3613-X) Ulverscroft.

Reunited States of America. David A. Heenan. LC 82-3936. 304p. (C). 1983. text ed. write for info. (0-201-10527-6) Addison-Wesley.

*Reuniting of America: Eleven Multicultural Dialogues. Donald Roy. (Major Concepts in Politics & Political Theory ser.: Vol. 11). 280p. (C). 1996. pap. text ed. 29. 95 (0-8204-3118-4) P Lang Pubng.

Reuniting Refugee Families: An Attorney's Guide to Law & Procedure. Ann E. Lewis. Ed. by Stephanie Marks & George Black. 200p. (Orig.). 1994. pap. text ed. 25.00 (0-934143-70-6) Lawyers Comm Human.

Reunitus: Building Bridges to Each Other Through Prayer Summits. Joe Aldrich. 210p. 1994. pap. 10.99 (0-88070-694-5) Multnomah Pubs.

Reupholstering at Home. Peter Nerovich. LC 91-67017. (Illus.). 176p. 1992. pap. 14.95 (0-88740-376-X) Schiffer.

Reupholstering at Home: A Do-It Yourself Manual for Turning Old Furniture into New Showpieces. Peter Nesovich. (Illus.). 1988. pap. 9.95 (0-517-53819-9, Crown) Crown Pub Group.

Reusable Ada Components Sourcebook. Antony Orme et al. (Ada Companion Ser.). (Illus.). 286p. (C). 1992. text ed. 69.95 (0-521-40351-0) Cambridge U Pr.

Reusable Launch Vehicle: Technology Development & Test Program. Committee on Reusable Launch Vehicle Technology & Test Program. 98p. 1996. pap. text ed. 27. 00 (0-309-05437-0) Natl Acad Pr.

*Reusable Software Components: Object-Oriented Embedded Systems Programming in C. Ted Van Sickle. LC 96-2941. 1996. 48.00 (0-13-613688-5) P-H.

*Reuse & Recycling of Contaminated Soil. Stephen M. Testa. LC 97-74. 1997. write for info. (1-56670-188-0) Lewis Pubs.

Reuse in SSADM Using Object Orientation. HMSO Staff. 174p. 1995. pap. 85.00 (0-11-330621-0, HM06210, Pub. by Stationery Ofc UK) Bernan Associates.

Reuse of Disposables: Implications for Quality Health Care & Cost Containment. Intro. by Ronald E. Easterling. (Illus.). 98p. (Orig.). 1983. pap. text ed. 30.00 (0-910275-27-0, TAR6-209) Assn Adv Med Instrn.

Reuse of Effluents - Methods of Wastewater Treatment & Health Safeguards: Proceedings of the WHO Expert Committee, Geneva, 1971. WHO Staff. (Technical Report Ser.: No. 517). 1973. pap. text ed. 7.00 (92-4-120517-2, 1100517) World Health.

Reuse of Hemodialyzer Blood Tubing. 48p. 1989. pap. 90. 00 (0-910275-83-1, TIR6-209) Assn Adv Med Instrn.

Reuse of Hemodialyzers. 2nd ed. 26p. 1993. pap. 82.00 (0-910275-15-7, RD47-209) Assn Adv Med Instrn.

Reuse of Sewage Effluent: Proceedings of a Symposium. Institution of Civil Engineers Staff. 332p. 1985. 42.00 (0-7277-0230-0, Pub. by T Telford UK) Am Soc Civil Eng.

Reuse of Sludge & Minor Wastewater Residuals. Alice Outwater. 192p. 1994. 59.95 (0-87371-677-9, L677) Lewis Pubs.

Reuse Operations: Community Development Through Redistribution of Used Goods. Michael Lewis et al. LC 95-31168. (Illus.). 60p. (Orig.). 1995. pap. text ed. 12.00 (0-917582-95-0) Inst Local Self Re.

Reuter Guide to Official Interest Rates. Ken Ferris. 1994. text ed. 55.00 (1-55738-815-6) Irwin Prof Pubng.

Reuters: The Story of a Century of News-Gathering. Graham Storey. LC 78-94619. 276p. 1970. reprint ed. text ed. 38.50 (0-8371-2571-5, STRE, Greenwood Pr) Greenwood.

Reuters Glossary: A Dictionary of International Economic & Financial Terms. Reuters Staff. 1989. pap. 12.95 (0-582-04286-0) Longman.

Reuters Glossary of International Economic & Financial Terms. 2nd ed. Compiled by Reuters, Ltd. Staff. 160p. 1995. 30.00 (1-56159-088-6, Stockton Pr) Groves Dictionaries.

Reuter's Guide to Official Interest Rates. 2nd ed. Ken Ferris & Mark Jones. 1996. text ed. 40.00 (1-55738-925-X) Irwin Prof Pubng.

Reuters Guide to World Bond Markets. Martin Essex & Ruth Pitchford. 256p. 1996. text ed. 80.00 (0-471-96046-2) Wiley.

Reuters Handbook for Journalists. Ian McDowell. LC 92-5673. 1992. pap. 47.95 (0-7506-0551-0) Buttrwrth-Heinemann.

Reutilization of Waste Materials: Selected Papers from the Third Recycling World Congress, Basle, Switzerland, 29 September-1 October 1980. Ed. by M. E. Henstock. 80p. 1981. pap. 29.00 (0-08-028743-3, Pergamon Pr) Elsevier.

R

***Reuven Shiloah - The Man Behind the Mossad: Secret Diplomacy in the Creation of Israel.** Haggai Eshed. Tr. by David Zinder & Leah Zinder from HEB. LC 97-11326. (Illus.). 368p. 1997. 57.50 (*0-7146-4812-4*, Pub. by F Cass Pubs UK); pap. 27.50 (*0-7146-4361-0*, Pub. by F Cass Pubs UK) Intl Spec Bk.

REV. Mike Root. LC 88-50590. 162p. (Orig.). 1989. pap. 8.00 (*0-916383-65-2*, Univ Edtns) Aegina Pr.

Rev It Up. 136p. 1991. otabind 19.95 (*0-7935-0320-5*, 00660196) H Leonard.

Reva K. Series & Other Works. Irwin Kremen. (Illus.). 32p. 1988. pap. 5.00 (*0-939351-06-4*) Temple U Tyler Gal.

***Revaluation: Tradition & Development in English Poetry.** F. R. Leavis. LC 97-17240. 294p. 1998. pap. 16.95 (*1-56663-171-8*) I R Dee.

Revaluation: Tradition & Development in English Poetry. Frank R. Leavis. LC 75-17192. 275p. 1975. reprint ed. text ed. 59.75 (*0-8371-8297-2*, LEREV, Greenwood Pr) Greenwood.

Revaluation of Women's Work. Sheila Lewenhak. 288p. 1988. lib. bdg. 57.50 (*0-415-01863-3*) Routledge.

Revaluations: Studies in Biography. Lascelles Abercrombie. 1977. 19.95 (*0-8369-0821-X*) Ayer.

Revaluations: Studies in Biography. Lascelles Abercrombie et al. LC 75-30773. (English Biography Ser.: No. 31). 1975. lib. bdg. 49.95 (*0-8383-2106-2*) M S G Haskell Hse.

Revaluations of Fixed Assets, 1925-1934. Solomon Fabricant. (NBER Bulletin Ser.: No. 62). 1936. reprint ed. 20.00 (*0-685-61178-7*) Natl Bur Econ Res.

Revaluing French Feminism: Critical Essays on Difference, Agency, & Culture. Ed. by Nancy Fraser & Sandra L. Bartky. LC 91-8415. 208p. 1992. 35.00 (*0-253-32436-X*); pap. 13.95 (*0-253-20682-0*, MB-682) Ind U Pr.

***Revanche D'Ani Croche.** Bertrand Gauthier. (Novels in the Roman Jeunesse Ser.). 96p. (FRE.). (J). (gr. 4-7). 1996. pap. 7.95 (*2-89021-078-2*, Pub. by Les Editions CN) Firefly Bks Ltd.

Revanche de Bozambo see Bozambo's Revenge

***Revanche d'Ishtar.** Ludmila Zeman. (Epic Of Gilgamesh Ser.). (Illus.). (FRE.). 1996. 19.95 (*0-88776-325-1*) Tundra Bks.

Reve. Emile Zola. (Coll. Diamant). 275p. (FRE.). 1986. pap. 10.95 (*0-7859-1376-9*, 2070377466) Fr & Eur.

Reve. Emile Zola. 1976. write for info. (*0-318-63589-5*) Fr & Eur.

Reve d'Alembert. 2nd ed. Denis Diderot & Jean Varloot. 248p. (FRE.). 1962. 11.95 (*0-8288-9745-X*, 2253034738) Fr & Eur.

Reve dans la Pavillon Rouge, Vol. 1. Xueqin Cao. (Pleiade Ser.). (FRE.). 1981. 110.00 (*0-8288-3450-4*, F78880) Fr & Eur.

Reve dans la Pavillon Rouge, Vol. 2. Xueqin Cao. (Pleiade Ser.). (FRE.). 1981. 110.00 (*0-7859-0641-X*, F79562) Fr & Eur.

Reve De Saxe. Michel Chaillou. 245p. (FRE.). 1988. pap. 11.95 (*0-7859-2090-0*, 2070380335) Fr & Eur.

Reve de Ti-Jean: (Ti-Jean's Dream) Oradel N. Morris. (Orig.). (ENG & FRE.). 1983. pap. 4.50 (*0-944064-02-7*) Paupieres Pub.

Reve et la Vie: A Theatrical Experiment by Gustave Flaubert. Katherine S. Kovacs. LC 81-70301. (Harvard Studies in Romance Languages: No. 38). (Orig.). (FRE.). 1981. pap. 12.50 (*0-940940-38-8*) Harvard U Romance Lang & Lit.

Reve et Son Interpretation. Sigmund Freud. (FRE.). 1985. pap. 10.95 (*0-7859-2793-X*, 2070322890) Fr & Eur.

Reve Mexicain. J. M. Le Clezio. (Folio Essais Ser.: No. 178). (FRE.). 1992. pap. 11.95 (*2-07-032680-2*) Schoenhof.

Reve Plus Long que la Nuit. Alain Jouffroy. 245p. (FRE.). 1978. pap. 10.95 (*0-7859-2403-5*, 2070370216) Fr & Eur.

Reveal & Conceal: Dress in Contemporary Egypt. Andrea B. Rugh. (Contemporary Issues in the Middle East Ser.). (Illus.). 192p. 1986. text ed. 44.95 (*0-8156-2368-2*) Syracuse U Pr.

Reveal the Magic of the Microwave. Chrissie Taylor. 128p. 1995. pap. 8.95 (*0-572-01491-0*, Pub. by Foulsham UK) Assoc Pubs Grp.

Reveal the Secrets in Doodles: Learn to Analyse Your Doodles. Patricia Marne. 214p. 1995. pap. 8.95 (*0-572-01427-9*, Pub. by Foulsham UK) Assoc Pubs Grp.

Reveal the Secrets of the Sacred Rose Tarot. Steven Culbert. 125p. 1988. pap. 9.95 (*0-88079-370-8*) US Games Syst.

Revealed Faith. Chris Sbravati. (Illus.). 104p. 1990. pap. write for info. (*0-318-68566-3*) Design Expressions.

Revealed Preference of Government. Kaushik Basu. LC 78-67300. 127p. reprint ed. pap. 36.20 (*0-318-34759-8*, 2031619) Bks Demand.

Revealed to Babes: Children in the Worship of God. Richard Bacon. 75p. (Orig.). pap. text ed. 7.95 (*0-9632557-3-8*) Old Paths Pubns.

Revealer of Secrets. Dov Taylor. LC 96-46569. (Modern Hebrew Classics Ser.). (C). 1996. pap. text ed. 23.00 (*0-8133-3213-3*) Westview.

***Revealing America: Image & Imagination in the Exploration of North America.** Ed. by James P. Ronda. 278p. (C). 1996. pap. text ed. 23.96 (*0-669-35175-X*) HM College Div.

Revealing Difference: The Fiction of Isabelle de Charriere. Jenene J. Allison. LC 94-48885. 176p. 1995. 33.50 (*0-87413-566-4*) U Delaware Pr.

Revealing Documents Guide to African American Manuscript Sources. Schlesinger Library Staff. 1993. 55.00 (*0-8161-0613-4*) G K Hall.

Revealing Hands: How to Read Palms. Richard Webster. LC 93-43198. (Illus.). 304p. 1994. pap. 14.95 (*0-87542-870-3*) Llewellyn Pubns.

Revealing Hidden Pictures. (Activity Bks.). (Illus.). 64p. (J). (gr. 2-5). 1990. pap. 1.99 (*0-671-72336-7*, Litl Simon S&S) S&S Childrens.

Revealing Image: Analytical Art Psychotherapy in Theory & Practice. Joy Schaverien. (Illus.). 256p. (C). 1991. pap. 19.95 (*0-415-04262-3*, A5915, Tavistock) Routledge.

Revealing Lives: Autobiography, Biography, & Gender. Ed. by Susan G. Bell & Marilyn Yalom. LC 89-26285. 255p. (C). 1990. pap. text ed. 24.95 (*0-7914-0436-6*) State U NY Pr.

Revealing Lives: Autobiography, Biography, & Gender. Ed. by Susan G. Bell & Marilyn Yalom. LC 89-26285. 255p. (C). 1990. text ed. 67.50 (*0-7914-0435-8*) State U NY Pr.

Revealing Moment & Other Plays. Oscar W. Firkins. LC 33-3099. 310p. reprint ed. pap. 88.40 (*0-317-39687-0*, 2055866) Bks Demand.

Revealing Prophets: Prophecy in Eastern African History. Ed. by David M. Anderson & Douglas H. Johnson. LC 94-10527. (Eastern African Studies). 320p. (C). 1994. pap. text ed. 17.95 (*0-8214-1089-X*) Ohio U Pr.

Revealing Prophets: Prophecy in Eastern African History. Ed. by David M. Anderson & Douglas H. Johnson. LC 94-10527. (Eastern African Studies). 320p. (C). 1995. text ed. 44.95 (*0-8214-1088-1*) Ohio U Pr.

Revealing Reveiling: Islamist Gender Ideology in Contemporary Egypt. Sherifa Zuhur. LC 91-3408. (SUNY Series in Middle Eastern Studies). 207p. (C). 1992. text ed. 59.50 (*0-7914-0927-9*); pap. text ed. 19.95 (*0-7914-0928-7*) State U NY Pr.

***Revealing Rural 'Others' Representation, Power & Identity in the British Countryside.** Paul Milbourne. LC 96-9773. (Rural Studies). 1997. write for info. (*1-85567-424-6*, Pub. by Pntr Pubs UK) Bks Intl VA.

***Revealing the American Language of Intelligence.** Jean-Marie Bonthous. 83p. 1996. pap. 35.00 (*0-9621241-3-3*) SCIP.

***Revealing the End of the World: To the Children of Light.** William B. Davis. LC 97-60418. 80p. (Orig.). 1997. pap. 7.99 (*1-57921-014-7*) WinePress Pub.

***Revealing the Holy Land: The Photographic Exploration of Palestine.** Kathleen S. Howe. LC 97-11157. 1997. write for info. (*0-89951-094-9*); pap. write for info. (*0-89951-095-7*) Santa Barbara Bd Realtors.

***Revealing the Revelation: A Guide to the Literature of the Apocalypse.** Bernie L. Calaway. 486p. 1997. pap. 54.95 (*1-57309-155-3*) Intl Scholars.

***Revealing the Revelation: A Guide to the Literature of the Apocalypse.** Bernie L. Calaway. 486p. 1997. 74.95 (*1-57309-156-1*) Intl Scholars.

***Revealing the Secrets of Anti-Aging: Ageless Vitality.** Linda R. Page. (Healthy Healing Library: Vol. 13). (Illus.). 32p. (Orig.). 1996. pap. 3.50 (*1-884334-13-X*) Hlthy Healing.

Revealing the Unknown to a Pair of Lovers. Ann L. Grunke. 1995. pap. 11.95 (*0-89823-161-2*) New Rivers Pr.

Revealing the World: An Interdisciplinary Reader for International Studies. Devorah A. Lieberman & Mel Gurtov. 304p. (C). 1994. per. 34.59 (*0-8403-7951-X*) Kendall-Hunt.

Revealing Word. 13th ed. Charles Fillmore. 228p. 1997. reprint ed. 12.95 (*0-87159-006-9*, 103) Unity Bks.

Reveiled Faith. Chris Sbravati. Ed. by Darielle E. Kraemmer. (Illus.). 105p. (Orig.). (C). 1989. pap. 8.95 (*0-685-29072-7*) Design Expressions.

Reveille: The Story of the Texas Aggie Mascot. Sharon Goertz. (Illus.). (J). (gr. 4-8). 1994. 9.95 (*0-89015-984-X*, Eakin Pr) Sunbelt Media.

Reveille for Radicals. Saul Alinsky. 1989. pap. 7.96 (*0-679-72112-6*, Vin) Random.

***Reveille in Washington.** Margaret Leech. 12.95 (*0-7867-0732-1*) Carroll & Graf.

Reveille in Washington, 1860-1865. Margaret Leech. 496p. 1991. pap. 12.95 (*0-88184-732-1*) Carroll & Graf.

Reveille Retreat. Eli A. Helmick. Ed. by James F. Gabelmann. (Illus.). 390p. 1996. text ed. 32.00 (*1-884680-03-8*) Gabelmann Pr.

Reveille till Taps: Soldier Life at Fort Mackinac, 1780-1895. Keith R. Widder. LC 73-159625. (Illus.). 116p. (Orig.). 1972. pap. 6.00 (*0-911872-12-4*) Mackinac St Hist Pks.

Reveilles de la Vie. Zoe Oldenbourg. (FRE.). 1974. pap. 11.95 (*0-7859-4035-9*) Fr & Eur.

Revel, Riot & Rebellion: Popular Politics & Culture in England 1603-1660. David Underdown. (Illus.). 352p. 1987. pap. 19.95 (*0-19-285193-4*) OUP.

***Revelacion Divina del Infierno.** Mary K. Baxter. write for info. (*0-614-28320-5*) Whitaker Dists.

Revelacion e Inspiracion de las Escrituras. John M. Lewis & Pablo A. Deiros. (Biblioteca de Doctrina Cristiana Ser.). 162p. (SPA.). 1986. pap. 7.99 (*0-311-09113-X*) Casa Bautista.

Revelaciones de una Gaviota: Un Encuentro Inesperado. Juan Suarez. 216p. (Orig.). 1994. pap. 12.95 (*0-9632334-4-0*) J Suarez.

Revelando el Futuro (Unlocking the Future) Lo Que-Horoscopo (What-Horoscope) Pedr Beckley. (SPA.). 1.50 (*0-685-74981-9*, 490256) Editorial Unilit.

Revelation. LC 88-70356. (Life Application Bible Study Guide). 112p. 1989. New Intl Version Text. 4.99 (*0-8423-2719-3*, 02-2719-3) Ldrship Minist Wrldwide.

Revelation. (LifeChange Ser.). 168p. 1989. pap. 7.00 (*0-89109-273-0*) NavPress.

***Revelation.** Balling. Date not set. 22.95 (*0-312-86314-4*) St Martin.

Revelation. Donald G. Barnhouse. 432p. 1985. pap. 22.99 (*0-310-20491-7*) Zondervan.

Revelation. Siegbert W. Becker. 1985. 23.99 (*0-8100-0190-X*, 15N0410) Northwest Pub.

Revelation. M. Eugene Boring. (Interpretation: a Bible Commentary for Preaching & Teaching Ser.). 240p. 1989. 24.00 (*0-8042-3150-8*) Westminster John Knox.

Revelation. David Y. Cho. LC 91-55228. 1991. pap. 9.99 (*0-88419-300-4*) Creation House.

Revelation. Concordia Publishing Staff. (God's Word for Today Ser.). 1994. pap. 4.99 (*0-570-09470-4*, 20-2640) Concordia.

***Revelation.** Daymon Duck. (God's Word for the Biblically-Inept Ser.: Vol. 1). (Illus.). 336p. 1997. pap. 16.95 (*0-914984-98-5*) Starburst.

Revelation. Walter M. Dunnett. (Survey of the Scriptures Study Guides Ser.). 1995. pap. 8.99 (*1-56570-006-6*) Meridian MI.

Revelation. Charles L. Feinberg. 1985. 14.99 (*0-88469-162-4*) BMH Bks.

Revelation. Tr. by J. Massyngberde Ford. LC 74-18796. (Anchor Bible Ser.: Vol. 38). (Illus.). 504p. 1975. 34.00 (*0-385-00895-3*) Doubleday.

***Revelation.** A. Garrow. (New Testament Readings Ser.). 176p. (C). 1997. pap. 16.95 (*0-415-14641-0*) Routledge.

Revelation. A. J. Garrow. LC 96-26318. (New Testament Readings Ser.). 176p. (C). 1997. text ed. write for info. (*0-415-14640-2*) Routledge.

***Revelation.** Catherine G. Gonzalez & Justo L. Gonzalez. (Bible Companion Ser.). 160p. (Orig.). 1997. pap. 16.00 (*0-664-25587-6*) Westminster John Knox.

Revelation. Wilfrid J. Harrington. (Sacra Pagina Ser.: No. 16). 296p. (Orig.). 1993. 29.95 (*0-8146-5818-0*) Liturgical Pr.

***Revelation.** C. M. Kempton Hewitt. (Genesis to Revelation Ser.). 1997. pap. text ed. 4.95 (*0-687-06237-3*) Abingdon.

Revelation. Henry A. Ironside. LC 96-1068. (Ironside Commentaries Ser.). 228p. 1996. pap. 9.99 (*0-87213-407-5*) Loizeaux.

Revelation. Irving L. Jensen. (Bible Self-Study Ser.). 124p. (Orig.). 1971. pap. 6.99 (*0-8024-4456-3*) Moody.

***Revelation.** J. Ramsey Michaels. LC 97-5276. (IVP New Testament Commentary Ser.: Vol. 20). 300p. 1997. 17.99 (*0-8308-1820-0*, 1820) InterVarsity.

Revelation. Robert H. Mounce. (New International Commentary on the New Testament Ser.). 426p. 1994. 32.00 (*0-8028-2519-2*) Eerdmans.

Revelation. Peggy Payne. LC 95-75417. 320p. 1995. pap. 12.95 (*0-9635967-1-3*) Banks Channel.

Revelation. Christopher Rowland. (Epworth Commentary Ser.). 176p. (Orig.). (C). 1994. pap. 16.00 (*0-7162-0493-2*, Epworth Pr) TPI PA.

Revelation. Charles C. Ryrie. (Orig.). 1996. pap. 9.99 (*0-8024-7108-0*) Moody.

Revelation. Lester Sumrall. 108p. (C). 1982. pap. text ed. 10.00 (*0-937580-58-9*) LeSEA Pub Co.

Revelation. John Sweet. Ed. by Dennis E. Nineham & Howard C. Kee. LC 90-31847. (New Testament Commentaries Ser.). 384p. (C). 1990. text ed. 24.95 (*0-334-02311-4*) TPI PA.

Revelation. Robert W. Wall. (New International Biblical Commentary Ser.). 320p. 1991. pap. 9.95 (*0-943575-49-4*) Hendrickson MA.

Revelation. John Westendorp. 204p. (Orig.). 1996. pap. write for info. (*1-57579-013-0*) Pine Hill Pr.

***Revelation.** F. Donald Williams. LC 94-90125. 120p. 1996. 11.95 (*0-533-11089-0*) Vantage.

Revelation. Geoffrey B. Wilson. 1985. pap. 5.99 (*0-85234-196-2*, Pub. by Evangelical Pr) Presby & Reformed.

***Revelation.** Ed. by Earl C. Wolf. (Beacon Small-Group Bible Studies). 88p. 1983. pap. 4.99 (*0-8341-0808-9*) Beacon Hill.

Revelation, No. 1. William Barclay. 196p. 1993. pap. 30.00 (*0-7152-0285-5*, Pub. by St Andrew UK) St Mut.

Revelation, No. 2. William Barclay. 244p. 1993. pap. 30.00 (*0-7152-0286-3*, Pub. by St Andrew UK) St Mut.

Revelation: A Book for the Rest of Us. Scott G. Sinclair. LC 92-8748. 156p. 1992. pap. 12.95 (*0-941037-19-3*) BIBAL Pr.

Revelation: A Call to Awaken. Sandra Altman. Ed. by Joanna Neff. 272p. (Orig.). 1991. pap. 15.95 (*1-880546-05-1*) Miracles Pr.

Revelation: A Commentary on the Book, Based on the Study of Twenty Four Psychic Discourses of Edgar Cayce. Edgar Cayce. (Twenty-Six Interpretive Readings Ser.). 214p. 1969. pap. 14.95 (*0-87604-003-2*, 215) ARE Pr.

Revelation: A Message of Hope for the New Millennium. rev. ed. Barbara M. Hubbard. (Illus.). 363p. 1995. pap. 16.95 (*1-882591-21-6*) Nataraj Pub.

Revelation: A Novel. Jean Grant. 1993. pap. 10.99 (*0-8407-3454-9*) Nelson.

Revelation: A Panorama of the Gospel Age. Fred P. Miller. 404p. 1991. pap. 19.95 (*1-883116-01-5*) Moellerhaus.

Revelation: A Panorama of the Gospel Age. 2nd rev. ed. Fred P. Miller. 424p. 1993. pap. text ed. 19.95 (*1-883116-00-7*) Moellerhaus.

Revelation: A Positive Perspective. Angeline Welk. Ed. by Carey Eyerly & Mary Westheimer. (Illus.). 144p. (Orig.). 1995. pap. write for info. (*1-885001-05-3*) Via Press.

Revelation: A Practical Commentary. L. Van Hartingsveld. LC 85-16075. (Text & Interpretation Ser.). 109p. reprint ed. pap. 31.10 (*0-7837-3191-4*, 2042795) Bks Demand.

Revelation: An Exposition of the First Eleven Chapters. James B. Ramsey. (Geneva Commentaries Ser.). 1977. 26.99 (*0-85151-256-9*) Banner of Truth.

Revelation: For a New Age. Dorothy Elder. LC 81-65477. 320p. (Orig.). 1981. pap. 14.00 (*0-87516-446-3*) DeVorss.

Revelation: From Metaphor to Analogy. Richard Swinburne. 248p. 1992. 68.00 (*0-19-823969-6*); pap. 24.00 (*0-19-823968-8*) OUP.

Revelation: Hope for the World in Troubled Times. Richard H. Lowery. LC 93-45777. (Covenant Bible Study Ser.). 86p. 1994. pap. 5.95 (*0-87178-739-3*, 8350) Brethren.

***Revelation: Illuminated Through Other Scripture.** Alfred Russ. 80p. (Orig.). 1996. pap. 8.00 (*1-57502-300-8*, P1030) Morris Pubng.

Revelation: Kingdoms in Conflict. Gene Fadeley. 89p. (Orig.). 1995. pap. 6.00 (*0-9646041-0-8*) Anchor Pubng.

Revelation: Leader's Guide. Leonard Doohan. (Scripture for Worship & Education Ser.). 48p. (Orig.). 1994. teacher ed., pap. 7.95 (*0-89390-308-6*) Resource Pubns.

Revelation: New International Version. large type ed. spiral bd. write for info. (*0-318-66323-6*) LBW.

Revelation: Our Crisis Is a Birth. Barbara M. Hubbard. Ed. by Noel McInnis. (Book of Co-Creation Ser.). 352p. 1993. 25.00 (*0-9631032-1-0*); pap. 16.95 (*0-9631032-0-2*) Foun Conscious Evol.

Revelation: Proclaiming a Vision of Hope. Wilfrid J. Harrington. LC 94-35073. (Scripture for Worship & Education Ser.). 168p. (Orig.). (C). 1994. pap. text ed. 14.95 (*0-89390-307-8*) Resource Pubns.

Revelation: Signs of the Times. L. E. Ashworth. (Illus.). 240p. (Orig.). (YA). (gr. 10). 1990. pap. 5.95 (*0-9627415-0-7*) Advent Times.

Revelation: The Lamb Who Is the Lion. Gladys Hunt. (Fisherman Bible Studyguide Ser.). 73p. 1973. pap. 4.99 (*0-87788-486-2*) Shaw Pubs.

Revelation: The New Astrology. Maxine Taylor. 52p. 1990. 10.00 (*0-86690-394-1*, T3124-014) Am Fed Astrologers.

Revelation: The Passover Key. Dan Juster. 140p. (Orig.). 1991. pap. 6.99 (*1-56043-044-3*) Destiny Image.

Revelation: The Prophecies-Apocalypse, & Beyond. Peter Lorie. LC 93-49383. 224p. 1995. 22.50 (*0-671-88872-2*) S&S Trade.

Revelation: The Road to Overcoming. Charles Neal. LC 89-51876. 214p. 1990. 8.95 (*0-87159-140-5*) Unity Bks.

Revelation: The Torah & the Bible. Jacob Neusner & Bruce D. Chilton. LC 95-37159. (Christianity & Judaism Ser.). 192p. (Orig.). 1995. pap. 17.00 (*1-56338-124-9*) TPI PA.

Revelation: The Triumph of God. Paul Stevens. (LifeGuide Bible Studies). 64p. (Orig.). 1987. wbk. ed., pap. 4.99 (*0-8308-1021-8*, 1021) InterVarsity.

Revelation: The UFO Conspiracy. David Bischoff. 368p. (Orig.). 1991. mass mkt. 5.99 (*0-446-35493-7*) Warner Bks.

Revelation: Things That Haven't Been Said. David Slankard. 223p. 1994. pap. 7.99 (*1-882449-25-8*) Messenger Pub.

Revelation: Vision of a Just World. Elisabeth S. Fiorenza. Ed. by Gerhard A. Krodel. LC 91-35271. (Proclamation Commentaries Ser.). 160p. 1992. pap. 13.00 (*0-8006-2510-2*, 1-2510, Fortress Pr) Augsburg Fortress.

Revelation: When All Things Become New. Joseph M. Stowell. (Great Books of the Bible). 64p. 1995. 4.99 (*0-310-49881-3*) Zondervan.

Revelation: Your Future Prophesied. Marjorie H. Russell. (Illus.). 80p. (Orig.). 1985. pap. 7.98 (*0-9614745-0-5*) Arcadia Ministry Pubns.

Revelation see Commentaries on the New Testament

Revelation see Apocalipsis

Revelation - the Last Book of the Bible. Edwin A. Schick. LC 76-62602. 80p. reprint ed. pap. 25.00 (*0-317-55548-0*, 2029617) Bks Demand.

Revelation - the Seer, the Saviour, & the Saved. rev. ed. James D. Strauss. (Bible Study Textbook Ser.). (Illus.). 582p. (C). 1972. 17.99 (*0-89900-048-7*) College Pr Pub.

Revelation, A Spiritual Study. Russell M. Woodard & George E. Smothermon. LC 95-71957. (Illus.). 745p. 1996. 54.95 (*0-9647493-0-0*) Read Write Pubns.

Revelation & Apocalyptic Symbols: Bible Stories of the Planets & Stars. Allen H. Bilderback. (Revelations of God's Glory & Hidden Identities Ser.). (Illus.). 180p. (YA). (gr. 8 up). 1992. 24.95 (*0-9630710-1-7*); pap. 10.00 (*0-9630710-0-9*) ABCO Pub.

Revelation & Divination in Ndembu Ritual. Victor Turner. LC 75-1623. (Symbol, Myth & Ritual Ser.). (Illus.). 352p. 1975. pap. 15.95 (*0-8014-9158-4*) Cornell U Pr.

Revelation & Experience. Carol R. Murphy. LC 64-22765. (Orig.). 1964. pap. 3.00 (*0-87574-137-1*) Pendle Hill.

Revelation & Faith: Theological Reflections on the Knowing & Doing of Truth. Theron D. Price. LC 86-33224. 192p. 1987. pap. 14.95 (*0-86554-261-9*, MUP P-45) Mercer Univ Pr.

Revelation & Love's Architecture. Martin C. D'Arcy. 90p. 1976. 8.00 (*0-89182-010-8*) Charles River Bks.

***Revelation & Mystery in Ancient Judaism & Pauline Christianity.** Markus Bockmuehl. LC 96-6813. 326p. 1997. pap. 25.00 (*0-8028-4277-1*) Eerdmans.

Revelation & Mystery in Ancient Judaism & Pauline Christianity. Markus N. Bockmuehl. (WissUNT Neuen Testament Ser.: No. 2-36). 250p. 1989. pap. 79.50 (*3-16-145339-5*, Pub. by J C B Mohr GW) Coronet Bks.

Revelation & Other Fiction from the Sewane Review: A Centennial Anthology. Ed. by George Core. LC 92-81354. 304p. 1992. 23.95 (*1-56469-012-1*) Harmony Hse Pub.

Revelation & Reason. Emil Brunner. 448p. 1984. reprint ed. pap. 19.95 (*0-913029-01-7*) Stevens Bk Pr.

Revelation & Reason in Islam. Arthur J. Arberry. LC 80-1936. (BCL Ser. I & II). reprint ed. 32.50 (*0-404-18952-0*) AMS Pr.

Revelation & Reconciliation: A Window on Modernity. Stephen N. Williams. 200p. (C). 1996. text ed. 54.95 (*0-521-48145-7*); pap. text ed. 16.95 (*0-521-48494-4*) Cambridge U Pr.

Revelation & Redemption: Jewish Documents of Deliverance from the Fall of Jerusalem to the Death of Nahmanides. George W. Buchanan. vi, 632p. 1978. text ed. 29.50 (*0-915948-04-4*) Eisenbrauns.

An Asterisk (*) at the beginning of an entry indicates that the title is appearing in BIP for the first time.

Revelation & Redemption at Colossae. Thomas J. Sappington. (JSNT Supplement Ser.: Vol. 53). 266p. (C). 1991. 52.50 (*1-85075-307-5*, Pub. by Sheffield Acad UK) CUP Services.

Revelation & Religion: Studies in the Theological Interpretation of Religious Types. Herbert H. Farmer. LC 77-27177. (Gifford Lectures: 1950). (Illus.). 256p. reprint ed. 34.50 (*0-404-60505-2*) AMS Pr.

Revelation & Response in the Old Testament. Cuthbert A. Simpson. LC 73-76022. reprint ed. 20.00 (*0-404-06056-0*) AMS Pr.

Revelation & Revolution: Basic Writings of Thomas Muntzer. Ed. & Tr. by Michael G. Baylor. LC 91-58965. 1993. 39.50 (*0-934223-16-5*) Lehigh Univ Pr.

***Revelation & Theology.** Rumscheidt. 37.95 (*0-521-08365-6*, Pub. by T & T Clark UK) Bks Intl VA.

Revelation & Truth: Unity & Plurality in Contemporary Theology. Thomas G. Guarino. LC 91-51143. 232p. 1993. 38.50 (*0-940866-18-8*) U Scranton Pr.

Revelation & Violence: A Study in Contextualization. Walter Brueggemann. LC 86-60473. (Pere Marquette Lectures). 72p. 1986. 15.00 (*0-87462-541-6*) Marquette.

Revelation Called the Badlands: Building a National Park, 1909-1939. Jay Shuler. (Illus.). 48p. (Orig.). 1989. pap. 4.00 (*0-912410-09-4*) Badlands Natl Hist.

Revelation Countdown: Stories by Cris Mazza. Cris Mazza & Ted Orland. (Black Ice Books Ser.). (Illus.). 151p. 1993. pap. 7.00 (*0-932511-73-2*) Fiction Coll.

***Revelation Dictionary of Gods, Religion, & Symbols.** Paul E. Hunter. (Illus.). 162p. (Orig.). Date not set. pap. 15.00 (*0-9642820-4-6*) Revelation NY.

Revelation 8-22. Robert L. Thomas. LC 95-4176. (Wycliffe Exegetical Commentary Ser.). 1995. 34.99 (*0-8024-9267-3*) Moody.

Revelation Explained. F. G. Smith. 464p. reprint ed. 5.50 (*0-686-29163-8*) Faith Pub Hse.

Revelation Explained: Not Setting Dates But Seeing Jesus. rev. ed. Lerry W. Fogle. LC 80-84975. 323p. (Orig.). 1995. pap. 9.95 (*0-88270-673-X*) Bridge-Logos.

Revelation Expounded. Finis J. Dake, Sr. 320p. 1989. 12.95 (*1-55829-027-3*) Dake Bible.

Revelation for Children. Dorie Erickson. (Illus.). 100p. (J). 1997. 29.95 (*0-937242-08-X*) Scandia Pubs.

Revelation for Laymen. James McKeever. 351p. (C). text ed. 14.99 (*0-931608-08-2*); pap. text ed. 7.95 (*0-931608-07-4*) Omega Pubns OR.

Revelation for Non-Hellenistic Millenia. Thomas Williams. 200p. 1995. 27.50 (*1-887495-04-5*) Coiny Pub.

Revelation for Teachers. Dorie Erickson. (Illus.). 300p. 1997. 29.95 (*0-937242-11-X*) Scandia Pubs.

Revelation for the Layman. Charles Scheibler. 235p. (Orig.). 1996. pap. 12.95 (*0-9650748-8-9*) Apogee Pubng.

Revelation for Today. James M. Efird. LC 88-22187. 1989. 11.95 (*0-687-36172-9*) Abingdon.

***Revelation: Four Views: A Parallel Commentary.** Steven Gregg. 608p. 29.99 (*0-8407-2128-5*) Nelson.

Revelation, History, & the Dialogue of Religions: A Study of Bhartrhari & Bonaventure. David A. Carpenter. LC 95-21567. (Faith Meets Faith Ser.). 250p. (Orig.). 1995. pap. 22.95 (*1-57075-039-4*) Orbis Bks.

Revelation-Illustrated & Made Plain. rev. ed. Tim LaHaye. 325p. 1974. pap. 10.99 (*0-310-26991-1*, 18073P) Zondervan.

Revelation in Indian Thought: A Festschrift in Honor of Professor T. R. V. Murti. Ed. by Harold Coward. LC 77-71192. 1977. 30.00 (*0-913546-52-6*) Dharma Pub.

Revelation in Jewish Wisdom Literature. John C. Rylaarsdam. (Midway Reprint Ser.). 140p. reprint ed. pap. 39.90 (*0-317-26582-2*, 2024065) Bks Demand.

***Revelation Mysteries: A Complete Study on End-Time Prophecy.** Steven D. Williams. LC 97-93417. (Illus.). 376p. (Orig.). 1998. pap. 20.00 (*1-886861-07-2*) Hosanna Pub Hse.

Revelation News: Bible Prophecy of the End-Time. 2nd ed. G. Wayne Cupp. (Illus.). 176p. 1992. reprint ed. pap. 9.95 (*1-889360-00-7*) Revel News.

Revelation of America in Prophecy: The Gospel-America's Power-the World's Hope. Sherlock Bally. 125p. (Orig.). (C). 1995. pap. text ed. write for info. (*1-885591-71-3*) Morris Pubng.

Revelation of Ares. Michel Potay. (ENG & FRE.). 1974. 49.95 (*0-614-14575-9*, Pub. by Assn pour la Diffsn) BookLink Distributors.

***Revelation of Ares.** Michel Potay. Ed. by Maison de la Revelation Staff. 777p. Date not set. 49.50 (*2-901821-07-3*, Pub. by Adira Pubs FR) BookWorld Dist.

Revelation of Baha'u'llah, 4 vols., Set. Adib Taherzadeh & R. T. Anderson. 1989. student ed., pap. 84.95 (*0-85398-311-9*) G Ronald Pub.

Revelation of Baha'u'llah: Mazra'ih & Bahji 1877-92, Vol. IV. Adib Taherzadeh. (Illus.). 504p. 1988. 33.50 (*0-85398-269-4*); pap. 21.25 (*0-85398-270-8*) G Ronald Pub.

Revelation of Baha'u'llah, Vol. I: Baghdad 1853-1863. Adib Taherzadeh. (Illus.). 384p. 1974. pap. 19.50 (*0-85398-057-8*) G Ronald Pub.

Revelation of Baha'u'llah, Vol. II: Adrianople, 1863-1868. Adib Taherzadeh. (Illus.). 492p. 1977. pap. 21.25 (*0-85398-071-3*) G Ronald Pub.

Revelation of Baha'u'llah Vol. III: Akka',the Early Years 1868-77. Adib Taherzadeh. (Illus.). 544p. 1983. pap. 21.25 (*0-85398-144-2*) G Ronald Pub.

Revelation of Christ's Glory: A Scientific Exposition of John's Apocalypse. Allen H. Bilderback. 93p. 1995. pap. text ed. 12.95 (*0-9630710-3-3*) ABCO Pub.

Revelation of Divine Love. Julian of Norwich Staff. Tr. & Intro. by M. L. Del Mastro. 224p. 1994. pap. 27.00 (*0-86012-232-8*, Pub. by Srch Pr UK) St Mut.

Revelation of Divine Love in Sixteen Showings: Made to Dame Julian of Norwich. Tr. & Intro. by M. L. Del Mastro. LC 94-338. 224p. (Orig.). 1994. pap. 10.95 (*0-89243-638-7*, Triumph Books) Liguori Pubns.

Revelation of Elchasai: Investigations into the Evidence for a Mesopotamian Jewish Apocalypse of the Second Century & Its Reception by Judeo-Christian Propagandists. Gerard P. Luttikhuizen. 263p. 1985. lib. bdg. 87.50 (*3-16-144935-5*, Pub. by J C B Mohr GW) Coronet Bks.

***Revelation of God and/as Human Reception: In the New Testament.** Dan O. Via. LC 97-1716. 256p. (Orig.). 1997. pap. 20.00 (*1-56338-198-2*) TPI PA.

Revelation of God in Nature. Bert Thompson & Wayne Jackson. (That You May Believe Ser.). 22p. (Orig.). 1985. pap. 3.50 (*0-932859-04-6*) Apologetic Pr.

Revelation of Hermes. Paracelsus. 1984. reprint ed. pap. 4.95 (*0-916411-81-8*) Holmes Pub.

Revelation of Jesus. Larry Wilson. 352p. (Orig.). 1992. pap. 12.00 (*0-945383-36-3*, 948-6107) Teach Servs.

Revelation of Jesus: Seeing Christ in Others. Tom Tiemens. LC 96-84799. (Orig.). 1996. pap. 6.95 (*0-88270-723-X*) Bridge-Logos.

Revelation of Jesus Christ. John F. Brug. 40p. (Orig.). 1985. pap. 3.50 (*0-8100-0088-1*, 22N0767) Northwest Pub.

Revelation of Jesus Christ. John F. Walvoord. LC 66-16227. (C). 1966. pap. 18.99 (*0-8024-7309-1*) Moody.

Revelation of Jesus Christ: A Commentary on the Book of Revelation. Jacob B. Smith. Ed. by J. Otis Yoder. LC 61-7091. 388p. reprint ed. pap. 110.60 (*0-8357-2656-8*, 2040191) Bks Demand.

Revelation of John. James Roberts. LC 73-20857. 1984. 12.95 (*0-915547-38-4*) Abilene Christ U.

***Revelation of John.** J. Roloff. 1993. 30.00 (*0-8006-9650-6*, Fortress Pr) Augsburg Fortress.

Revelation of John see Daily Study Bible - New Testament

Revelation of John see Daily Study Bible for the New Testament

***Revelation of Law in Scripture.** Patrick Fairbairn. 496p. 1996. 24.99 (*0-87552-868-6*) Presby & Reformed.

Revelation of Life Eternal: An Introduction to the Christian Message. Nicholas Arseniev. 144p. 1964. pap. 7.95 (*0-913836-00-1*) St Vladimirs.

***Revelation of Love.** Julian of Norwich Staff. Tr. by John Skinner. LC 96-39974. 188p. 1997. pap. 8.95 (*0-385-48756-8*, Image Bks) Doubleday.

Revelation of Love: Scripture, Prayers & Reflections for Eucharistic Adoration. David M. Turoldo. 180p. (Orig.). 1996. pap. 11.95 (*0-8198-6462-5*) Pauline Bks.

Revelation of Music: Learning to Love the Classics. Robert Danziger. LC 91-90208. (Illus.). 253p. (Orig.). (C). 1991. pap. text ed. 17.95 (*0-9613427-6-5*) Jordan Pr.

Revelation of Music: Learning to Love the Classics. 2nd enl. rev. ed. Robert Danziger. LC 95-75274. (Illus.). 312p. (Orig.). (C). 1995. pap. text ed. 27.95 incl. audio compact disk (*0-9613427-7-3*) Jordan Pr.

Revelation of Praise & Worship. Daphne A. Harris. 144p. (Orig.). (C). 1995. pap. 12.00 (*1-883893-07-0*) WinePress Pub.

Revelation of Prophetic Gesture. Marilyn J. Wright. (Illus.). 196p. (Orig.). (C). 1993. pap. text ed. write for info. (*0-9632748-1-3*) Majesty Pubns.

Revelation of Purgatory by an Unknown, 15th Century Woman Visionary: Introduction, Critical Text & Translation. Marta P. Harley. LC 85-28390. (Studies in Women & Religion: Vol. 18). 160p. 1985. lib. bdg. 69.95 (*0-88946-531-2*) E Mellen.

Revelation of Ramala. Centre. (Ramala Trilogy Ser.). 188p. 1978. pap. 17.95 (*0-85978-035-X*, Pub. by C W Daniel UK) Natl Bk Netwk.

Revelation of Ramala. 5th ed. 304p. pap. 20.95 (*0-8464-4284-1*) Beekman Pubs.

Revelation of Saint John - an Open Book. Irving C. Tomlinson. 285p. 1987. reprint ed. 12.95 (*0-942910-13-3*) Dynapress.

Revelation of St. John. George B. Caird. (Black's New Testament Commentary Ser.). 316p. 1993. 22.95 (*1-56563-018-1*) Hendrickson MA.

Revelation of St. John the Divine. W. Pascoe Goard. LC 89-81702. 112p. 1990. reprint ed. pap. 5.00 (*0-934666-38-5*) Artisan Sales.

Revelation of the Beast. Colin Deal. 118p. (Orig.). 1995. pap. 7.95 (*0-9646960-0-2*) New Life Assembly.

Revelation of the Secrets of the Birds & Flowers: Al Muqaddasi. Ed. by Denise Winn. Tr. by I. Hoare & D. Galy. 1980. 27.00 (*0-900860-75-8*, Pub. by Octagon Pr UK) ISHK.

Revelation of the Son of Man. Levi Khamor. xv, 328p. (Orig.). 1993. 23.95 (*0-9627925-1-9*); pap. 15.95 (*0-9627925-0-0*) BenYamin Pr.

Revelation of the True Minerva. Thomas Blenerhasset. LC 42-5954. 1978. reprint ed. 50.00 (*0-8201-1196-1*) Schol Facsimiles.

Revelation of the Unknowable God: Introduction, Text, Translation, & Notes. Karen L. King. 224p. 1996. 29.95 (*0-944344-44-5*) Polebridge Pr.

Revelation of Treasure Hid--Concerning Freedom, Concerning the Motherland, Concerning Justice, Apostolical Canons Respecting Baptism. Apostolos Makrakis. Ed. by Orthodox Christian Educational Society Staff. Tr. by Denver Cummings. 80p. (Orig.). 1952. pap. 3.95 (*0-938366-23-8*) Orthodox Chr.

Revelation Paralleled. Lorin W. Bristol. 220p. (Orig.). 1990. 12.95 (*0-9626302-0-9*); pap. 8.95 (*0-9626302-3-3*) Bristol CA.

Revelation Record. Henry M. Morris. 521p. 1983. 24.99 (*0-8423-5511-1*) Tyndale.

Revelation, Redemption, & Response: Calvin's Trinitarian Understanding of the Divine-Human Relationship. Philip W. Butin. LC 93-43173. 272p. (C). 1995. 39.95 (*0-19-508600-7*) OUP.

***Revelation Restored.** David W. Halivni. LC 97-8573. (Radical Traditions Ser.). 1997. text ed. 24.00 (*0-8133-3346-6*) Westview.

***Revelation Revealed.** Antiano D. Silvers. LC 96-90689. (Orig.). 1997. pap. 12.95 (*0-533-11687-2*) Vantage.

Revelation Revealed. Jack Van Impe. 282p. 1982. pap. 9.00 (*0-934803-09-9*) J Van Impe.

Revelation Revealed. rev. ed. Hal J. Chapel & Richard G. Clark. Ed. by Debbie Danielpour. (Orig.). 1987. pap. 45.00 (*0-941019-66-7*) Paradigm Hlth Care.

Revelation Revealed. rev. ed. Jack Van Impe. 311p. Date not set. pap. text ed. 9.00 (*0-614-07836-9*) J Van Impe.

Revelation Revealed: Simple Studies in Revelation for Simple Students by a Simple Teacher. Ivy Conner. 96p. (Orig.). 1991. pap. text ed. 7.95 (*1-878579-04-5*) SUN Pub Co.

Revelation Revealed Workbook: Simple Studies in Revelation for Simple Students by a Simple Teacher. Ivy Conner. 24p. (Orig.). 1991. pap. text ed. 4.95 (*1-878579-05-3*) SUN Pub Co.

Revelation Revisited: The Devil & Bobby Dyson, Period Five. Stephen Z. Surridge. LC 94-71928. (Illus.). 1184p. 1995. 48.00 (*0-9640711-7-7*) Elijah Hse.

Revelation, Rites, & Remembering: A Liturgy Text. Mary Collins. 160p. (Orig.). Date not set. pap. text ed. 9.95 (*0-8146-6127-0*) Liturgical Pr.

***Revelation Study Workbook.** Ernest L. Walker. 160p. (Orig.). 1995. pap. 5.95 (*1-56794-081-1*, C-2376) Star Bible.

Revelation Taught: The Paraclete in the Gospel of John. Eskil Franck. (New Testament Ser.: No. 14). 168p. (Orig.). 1985. pap. text ed. 42.50 (*91-40-05114-5*, Pub. by LiberUtbildning SW) Coronet Bks.

Revelation Through Reason: Religion in the Light of Science & Philosophy. Errol E. Harris. 1958. 49.50 (*0-317-27547-X*) Elliots Bks.

Revelation to John. Martin H. Franzmann. 148p. 1986. pap. 10.99 (*0-570-03728-X*, 12-2630) Concordia.

Revelation Unsealed. Donald A. Salerno, Jr. LC 95-69193. (Illus.). 250p. (Orig.). (C). 1995. pap. 14.95 (*0-9647152-0-1*) D A Salerno.

Revelation Visualized. Salem Kirban & Gary Cohen. (Prophecy Studies). 380p. 1990. pap. 13.99 (*0-89957-616-8*) AMG Pubs.

Revelation Visualized. Salem Kirban & Gary Cohen. 1971. pap. 14.95 (*0-912582-08-1*) Kirban.

Revelation, Vols. 1 & 2, 2 vols., Vol. 1. R. H. Charles. Ed. by Alfred Plummer & Charles A. Briggs. LC 21-5413. (International Critical Commentary Ser.). 568p. 1920. 39.95 (*0-567-05038-6*) Bks Intl VA.

Revelation, Vols. 1 & 2, 2 vols., Vol. 2. R. H. Charles. Ed. by Alfred Plummer & Charles A. Briggs. LC 21-5413. (International Critical Commentary Ser.). 506p. 1920. 39.95 (*0-567-05039-4*) Bks Intl VA.

Revelation X: The "Bob" Apocryphon: Hidden Teachings & Deuterocanonical Bob Dodds. Subgenius Foundation, Inc. Staff. 208p. 1994. pap. 14.95 (*0-671-77006-3*, Fireside) S&S Trade.

Revelation 1-12. David Aune. (Biblical Commentary Ser.: Vol. 52A). 600p. 1997. 29.99 (*0-8499-0251-7*) Word Pub.

Revelation 1-7. Robert L. Thomas. (Wycliffe Exegetical Commentary Ser.). 1992. text ed. 34.99 (*0-8024-9265-7*) Moody.

Revelation 13-22. David Aune. (Biblical Commentary Ser.: Vol. 52B). Date not set. 29.99 (*0-8499-0786-1*) Word Pub.

Revelations. Clive Barker. 1992. pap. 7.95 (*1-56060-129-9*) Eclipse Bks.

Revelations. Sophy Burnham. pap. write for info. (*0-345-38470-9*, Ballantine Trade) Ballantine.

Revelations. John Court. (New Testament Guides Ser.). 134p. pap. 9.95 (*1-85075-705-4*) CUP Services.

Revelations. David L. Dewey. 200p. 1994. 17.95 (*0-8059-3519-3*) Dorrance.

Revelations. Carl Hazlewood. (Illus.). 24p. (Orig.). 1987. pap. write for info. (*0-936739-07-X*) Hallwalls Inc.

***Revelations.** Ed Jones. 368p. 1997. pap. 8.95 (*1-85702-471-0*, Pub. by Fourth Estate UK) Trafalgar.

***Revelations.** Sherry Jones. LC 97-60777. 80p. 1997. 12.99 (*1-57921-028-7*) WinePress Pub.

***Revelations.** Wynonna Judd. pap. 14.95 (*0-7935-6572-3*) H Leonard.

Revelations. Phyliss McKinney. 20p. (Orig.). (YA). (gr. 5 up). 1992. pap. text ed. 4.95 (*1-877860-09-3*) Eula Intl Pub.

Revelations. Nick Mezins. Ed. by Jamie Teasley. LC 89-51757. 689p. 1990. 16.95 (*1-55523-819-X*) Winston-Derek.

Revelations. Charlotte Painter & Mary J. Moffat. Date not set. 8.99 (*0-517-15066-2*) Random Hse Value.

***Revelations.** Jacques Vallee. 1997. pap. 12.00 (*0-345-41944-8*) Ballantine.

***Revelations.** Ed. by Douglas E. Winter. 352p. 1997. 24.00 (*0-06-105246-9*, HarperPrism) HarpC.

Revelations: A Poet in Search of God. Patricia Caccavale. 58p. (Orig.). 1995. pap. text ed. 9.95 (*1-884707-12-2*) Lifestyles.

Revelations: Alabama's Visionary Folk Artists. Kathy Kemp. LC 94-6943. (Illus.). 224p. 1994. 60.00 (*1-881548-07-4*) Crane Hill AL.

Revelations: Alien Contact & Human Deception. Jacques Vallee. 1992. reprint ed. mass mkt. 5.99 (*0-345-37566-1*) Ballantine.

Revelations: American History, American Myths. Nathan I. Huggins. Ed. by Brenda S. Huggins. 320p. 1995. 25.00 (*0-19-508236-2*) OUP.

***Revelations: Art of the Apocalypse.** Nancy Grubb. LC 97-13228. (Illus.). 144p. 1997. 35.00 (*0-7892-0398-7*) Abbeville Pr.

***Revelations: Art of the Apocalypse.** Nancy Grubb. (Tiny Folio Ser.). (Illus.). 288p. 1997. 11.95 (*0-7892-0208-5*) Abbeville Pr.

Revelations: As It Is. Patricia Sri. Ed. by Morningland Publications, Inc. Staff. (Illus.). 635p. (Orig.). 1979. pap. 10.00 (*0-935146-08-3*) Morningland.

Revelations: Diaries of Women. Ed. by Mary J. Moffat & Charlotte Painter. 1975. pap. 10.00 (*0-394-71151-3*, Vin) Random.

Revelations: Drawing - America. Townsend Wolfe et al. 100p. 1988. 25.00 (*0-9612750-6-5*) Arkansas Art Ctr.

Revelations: Expository Essays by & about Blacks. Redd. 1991. 20.00 (*0-536-57971-7*) Ginn Pr.

Revelations: Gay Men's Coming Out Stories. Ed. by Adrien Saks & Wayne Curtis. 170p. (Orig.). 1994. pap. 7.95 (*1-55583-244-X*) Alyson Pubns.

Revelations: The Autobiography of Alvin Ailey. Alvin Ailey & A. Peter Bailey. LC 94-16684. 1994. 19.95 (*1-55972-255-X*, Birch Ln Pr) Carol Pub Group.

***Revelations: The Autobiography of Alvin Ailey.** Alvin Ailey & A. Peter Bailey. LC 96-39792. (Illus.). 192p. 1997. pap. 14.95 (*0-8065-1861-8*, Citadel Pr) Carol Pub Group.

***Revelations: The Autobiography of Alvin Ailey.** Alvin Ailey. 1997. pap. 14.95 (*0-614-28337-X*, Citadel Pr) Carol Pub Group.

***Revelations: The Autobiography of Alvin Ailey.** A. Peter Bailey. 184p. 4.98 (*0-7651-0184-X*) Smithmark.

Revelations: The Future Foretold. Keith L. Brooks. (Teach Yourself the Bible Ser.). 1962. pap. 5.99 (*0-8024-7308-3*) Moody.

Revelations: Wisdom of the Ages. Paul Roland. LC 95-61354. (Illus.). 160p. (Orig.). 1995. pap. 17.95 (*1-56975-047-5*) Ulysses Pr.

Revelations & Other Fiction from the Sewanee Review: A Centennial Anthology. Ed. by George Core. 304p. 1992. 24.95 (*1-56469-020-2*) Harmony Hse Pub.

Revelations Concerning Napoleon's Escape from St. Helena. Paul P. Ebeyer. 1947. 19.95 (*0-911116-75-3*) Pelican.

***Revelations for a New Millennium: Voices of Saints, Angels, & God.** Andrew Ramer. LC 96-36515. 1996. pap. 13.00 (*0-06-251470-9*) Harper SF.

Revelations from a Forty-Five Pound Purse. Cathy Guisewite. (Illus.). 128p. (Orig.). 1993. pap. 8.95 (*0-8362-1722-5*) Andrews & McMeel.

Revelations in a Schoolroom: And Other Recollections As Remembered in the Year 1984. Alma B. Gilman & Clarence R. Gilman. (Illus.). 56p. (Orig.). (YA). 1984. pap. 3.75 (*0-9613914-0-5*) A B Gilman.

Revelations of a Russian Diplomat: The Memoirs of Dmitrii I. Abrikossow. Dmitrii I. Abrikossow. Ed. by George A. Lensen. LC 64-18426. (Washington Paperbacks on Russia & Asia Ser.: No. 5). (Illus.). 351p. 1968. 20.00 (*0-295-73911-8*) U of Wash Pr.

Revelations of a Spirit Medium. Harry Price & Eric J. Dingwall. LC 75-7395. (Perspectives in Psychical Research Ser.). 1975. reprint ed. 31.95 (*0-405-07044-6*) Ayer.

Revelations of a Square Exhibiting a Graphic Display of the Savings & Doings or Eminent Free & Accepted Masons, from the Revival in 1717 by Dr. Desaguliers, to the Reunion in 1813 by Their R.H. The Duke of Kent & Sussex. George Oliver. 330p. 1995. reprint ed. pap. 24.95 (*1-56459-477-7*) Kessinger Pub.

Revelations of an International Spy. I. T. Lincoln. 1972. 59.95 (*0-8490-0949-9*) Gordon Pr.

Revelations of Antichrist. W. H. Burris. 1972. 59.95 (*0-8490-0950-2*) Gordon Pr.

Revelations of Antichrist: Concerning Christ & Christianity. William H. Burr. LC 79-161340. (Atheist Viewpoint Ser.). 448p. 1972. reprint ed. 31.95 (*0-405-03801-1*) Ayer.

Revelations of Brimstone: Ominous Portents of the Parousia of Christ. R. Henry Hall. (Illus.). 374p. (Orig.). 1984. pap. 6.95 (*0-930351-00-2*) Spirit Prophecy.

***Revelations of Divine Love.** (Great Devotional Classics Ser.). pap. 2.95 (*0-687-60977-1*) Abingdon.

Revelations of Divine Love. Julian. Tr. & Intro. by Clifton Wolters. 224p. 1982. pap. 10.95 (*0-14-044177-8*, Penguin Classics) Viking Penguin.

***Revelations of Divine Love.** Julian of Norwich Staff. pap. 2.00 (*0-8358-0184-5*) Upper Room Bks.

Revelations of Divine Love. Julian of Norwich Staff. Ed. by Roger L. Roberts. LC 82-80471. (Treasures from the Spiritual Classics Ser.). 64p. 1982. reprint ed. pap. 3.95 (*0-8192-1308-X*) Morehouse Pub.

Revelations of Divine Mercy: Daily Readings from the Diary of Blessed Faustina Kowalska. George W. Kosicki. 380p. (Orig.). 1996. pap. 14.99 (*0-89283-977-5*, Charis) Servant.

Revelations of Dr. Purcell: Stories from the Life of a Psychotherapist. Juana Culhane. LC 91-67750. 72p. 1993. pap. 9.95 (*0-685-66868-1*, Univ Edtns) Aegina Pr.

Revelations of HO: An Adventure in Self Realization. James Weldon. Ed. by Rod Charles & Elizabeth Pasco. 360p. (Orig.). (YA). (gr. 12). 1996. pap. 17.95 (*1-887472-09-6*) Sunstar Pubng.

Revelations of Margaret of Cortona. Ange-Marie Hiral. (Spirit & Life Ser.). vii, 87p. 1952. pap. 3.00 (*1-57659-093-3*) Franciscan Inst.

Revelations of Margery Kempe. John C. Hirsh. LC 88-7420. (Medieval & Renaissance Authors Ser.: Vol. 10). 128p. 1989. text ed. 46.50 (*90-04-08963-2*) E J Brill.

Revelations of Saint Birgitta. Ed. by W. P. Cumming. (EETS, OS Ser.: No. 178). 1974. reprint ed. 40.00 (*0-527-00175-9*) Periodicals Srv.

R

Revelations of Self: American Women in Autobiography. Ed. by Lois J. Fowler & David H. Fowler. LC 89-22039. 277p. 1990. text ed. 67.50 (*0-7914-0373-4*); pap. text ed. 24.95 (*0-7914-0374-2*) State U NY Pr.

Revelations of St. Bridget on the Life & Passion of Our Lord & the Life of His Blessed Mother. St. Bridget of Sweden. LC 83-51547. 81p. 1984. pap. 3.00 (*0-89555-233-7*) TAN Bks Pubs.

Revelations of the Hot Conquered Darling. Wayne Edwards. 44p. 1996. pap. 3.00 (*1-888283-05-X*) Merrimack Bks.

Revelations of the Metatron. Gary Sornson. Tr. by Lea Sornson et al. LC 95-15369. 244p. 1995. pap. 14.95 (*1-880090-21-X*) Galde Pr.

***Revelations of the Unseen: Futuh al-Ghayb.** Shaykh Jilani. 216p. 1996. pap. 18.00 (*0-614-21333-9*, 1445) Kazi Pubns.

Revelations of Women Mystics: From Middle Ages to Modern Times. Jose D. Vinck. LC 84-24485. 180p. (Orig.). 1985. pap. 7.95 (*0-8189-0478-X*) Alba.

***Revelations to the Shepherd of Hermas: A Book of Spiritual Visions.** Hermas. LC 96-39141. 96p. 1997. pap. 7.00 (*0-7648-0054-X*, Triumph Books) Liguori Pubns.

Revelatory Adventure. John Beaumont. 168p. (Orig.). 1992. pap. 7.99 (*1-56043-074-5*) Destiny Image.

Revelatory Text: Interpreting the New Testament As Sacred Scripture. Sandra M. Schneiders. LC 90-55810. 224p. 1991. pap. 22.00 (*0-06-067097-5*) Harper SF.

Revell Bible Dictionary. 2nd deluxe ed. Ed. by Lawrence O. Richards. LC 90-33022. (Illus.). 1168p. 1994. 39.99 (*0-8007-1594-2*) Revell.

Revell Concise Bible Dictionary. Ed. by Lawrence O. Richards. LC 91-21230. (Illus.). 704p. 1991. 14.99 (*0-8007-1658-2*) Revell.

Revelry. Samuel H. Adams. (BCL1-PS American Literature Ser.). 318p. 1992. reprint ed. lib. bdg. 89.00 (*0-7812-6914-8*) Rprt Serv.

Revels & Jests: Extracts from the Accounts of the Revels at Court in the Reigns of Queen Elizabeth & King James I. Ed. by P. Cunningham & J. O. Halliwell. Bd. with Tarlton's Jests & News Out of Purgatory. (Shakespeare Society of London Publications Ser.: Vol. 13). 1974. reprint ed. Set pap. (*0-8115-0175-2*) Periodicals Srv.

Revels Garland of Song: In Celebration of Spring, Summer & Autumn. Compiled & Intro. by John Langstaff. (Illus.). 176p. (Orig.). 1996. pap. 17.95 (*0-8256-9370-5*, RI 10096) Revels MA.

***Revels History of Drama, 8 vols.** Ed. by Clifford Leech et al. 3342p. (C). 1997. text ed. 775.00 (*0-415-14379-9*) Routledge.

Revels History of Drama in English, Vol. 2: 1500-1576. Thomas Craik et al. 1980. 59.95 (*0-416-13030-5*, NO. 6365) Routledge Chapman & Hall.

Revels History of Drama in English, Vol. 8: American Drama. Travis Bogard et al. (Illus.). 1978. 59.95 (*0-416-13090-9*, NO. 2101); pap. 27.50 (*0-416-81400-X*, NO. 2102) Routledge Chapman & Hall.

Revels in Jamaica, Sixteen Eighty-Two to Eighteen Thirty-Eight. Richardson L. Wright. LC 78-81202. (Illus.). 1972. reprint ed. 29.95 (*0-405-09105-2*) Ayer.

Revels of Fancy. William J. Vandyne. LC 71-179297. (Black Heritage Library Collection). 1977. reprint ed. 15.95 (*0-8369-8933-3*) Ayer.

Revenant. Louise Cooper. 320p. (Orig.). 1993. mass mkt. 4.99 (*0-8125-0807-6*) Tor Bks.

Revenant Christ. Friend Stuart. 28p. 1983. pap. 4.95 (*0-912132-15-9*) Dominion Pr.

Revenge. Natalie Fox. (Presents Ser.). 1995. pap. 2.99 (*0-373-11718-3*, 1-11718-3) Harlequin Bks.

Revenge. Diane Hoh. (Nightmare Hall Ser.: No. 26). 240p. (gr. 7-9). 1995. mass mkt. 3.50 (*0-590-25082-5*) Scholastic Inc.

Revenge. Noel Hynd. 1988. mass mkt. 3.95 (*0-8217-2529-7*, Zebra Kensgtn) Kensgtn Pub Corp.

***Revenge.** John Kerrigan, pseud. 224p. 1996. 22.00 (*0-7278-4928-X*) Severn Hse.

***Revenge.** Thompson & Helen. 1993. pap. text ed. write for info. (*0-17-556276-8*) Addison-Wesley.

Revenge. George Hayduke. 224p. 1984. reprint ed. pap. 9.95 (*0-8184-0353-5*) Carol Pub Group.

Revenge: Short Stories by Woman Writers. Ed. by Kate Saunders. 263p. 1992. pap. 12.95 (*0-571-12938-2*) Faber & Faber.

Revenge & Retribution. Josh Wilker. (Crime, Justice, & Punishment Ser.). (YA). (gr. 3 up). 1997. lib. bdg. 19.95 (*0-7910-4321-5*) Chelsea Hse.

Revenge at Lost Creek. Jon Sharpe. (Trailsman Ser.: No. 162). 176p. (Orig.). 1995. mass mkt. 3.99 (*0-451-18219-7*, Sig) NAL-Dutton.

Revenge at the Rodeo. Gilbert Morris. LC 92-591. (Danielle Ross Mystery Ser.). 320p. (Orig.). (gr. 10). 1993. pap. 9.99 (*0-8007-5457-3*) Revell.

Revenge Book. Bob Smith. (Illus.). 90p. 1980. pap. 10.00 (*0-87364-210-4*) Paladin Pr.

Revenge Book: The Chilling Sequel. Bob Smith. (Illus.). 80p. 1990. pap. 10.00 (*0-87364-539-1*) Paladin Pr.

***Revenge by Coincidence.** Peter Andrews. Ed. by Katherine Ludwig. 200p. (Orig.). 1997. pap. 7.99 (*1-885778-27-9*) Seaburn.

Revenge by Love. David Dooley. 90p. (Orig.). pap. 10.95 (*1-885266-06-5*) Story Line.

Revenge Encyclopedia. 120p. 1995. pap. 15.00 (*0-87364-851-X*) Paladin Pr.

Revenge for Love. Wyndham Lewis. LC 91-4269. (Illus.). 404p. (Orig.). (C). 1991. 25.00 (*0-87685-829-9*); pap. 15.00 (*0-87685-828-0*) Black Sparrow.

Revenge for Love. deluxe ed. Wyndham Lewis. LC 91-4269. (Illus.). 404p. (Orig.). (C). 1991. 30.00 (*0-87685-830-2*) Black Sparrow.

Revenge in Laredo. E. Adkins. 1987. pap. 2.50 (*0-8217-2173-9*) NAL-Dutton.

Revenge in Little Texas. Jason Manning. 1990. mass mkt. 2.95 (*0-8217-2898-9*, Zebra Kensgtn) Kensgtn Pub Corp.

Revenge in Rome. Patricia A. Stewart & Edna H. Maples. (Murder Mystery Parites Ser.). (Illus.). 52p. 1985. 8.00 (*0-317-38202-0*) Univ Games.

Revenge in the Classroom: Skool Kartoons for Everyone. Kent Grimsley. Ed. by Diane Parker. LC 92-50864. 100p. 1993. pap. 9.95 (*0-88247-966-0*) R & E Pubs.

***Revenge Is Sweet.** Jill Sheldon. (Scarlet Ser.). (Orig.). 1997. mass mkt. 3.99 (*1-85487-957-X*, Pub. by Scarlet Bks UK) London Brdge.

***Revenge Is Sweet: Dozens of Wicked Ways to Have the Last Laugh.** George Hayduke. 1997. pap. 14.95 (*0-8184-0594-5*) Carol Pub Group.

Revenge of Athena: Science, Exploitation & the Third World. Ed. by Z. Sardar. 378p. 1988. text ed. 90.00 (*0-7201-1891-3*, Mansell Pub) Cassell.

***Revenge of Goblins.** A. G. Cascone. 1996. pap. 42.00 (*0-8167-4191-3*) Viking Penguin.

***Revenge of God: The Resurgence of Islam, Christianity & Judaism in the Modern World.** Gilles Kepel. 220p. 1996. pap. 14.95 (*0-614-21679-6*, 1077) Kazi Pubns.

Revenge of God: The Resurgence of Islam, Christianity & Judaism in the Modern World. Gilles Kepel. Tr. by Alan Braley from FRE. 208p. (C). 1994. 35.00 (*0-271-01313-3*); 14.95 (*0-271-01314-1*) Pa St U Pr.

Revenge of History: Marxism & the East European Revolutions. Alex Callinicos. 161p. 1991. 30.00 (*0-271-00767-2*); pap. 13.95 (*0-271-00768-0*) Pa St U Pr.

Revenge of Ho-Tai. Thomas Hoobler. 208p. (J). (gr. 7 up). 1989. 15.95 (*0-8027-6870-9*) Walker & Co.

Revenge of Hothead Paisan: Homicidal Lesbian Terrorist. Diane DiMassa. (Illus.). 200p. 1995. pap. 16.95 (*1-57344-016-7*) Cleis Pr.

Revenge of Ishtar, Bk. II: Gilgamesh the King. Ludmila Zeman. LC 93-60332. (Illus.). 24p. (J). (gr. 3 up). 1993. 19.95 (*0-88776-315-4*) Tundra Bks.

Revenge of June Daley. Rina Keaton. 192p. (Orig.). 1996. mass mkt. 5.99 (*0-87067-970-8*, BH970-8) Holloway.

Revenge of Roadkill. B. Carlson. (Illus.). 117p. 1993. pap. 7.95 (*1-878488-42-2*) Quixote Pr IA.

Revenge of Seventh Carrier. Peter Albano. 1992. mass mkt. 3.99 (*0-8217-3631-0*, Zebra Kensgtn) Kensgtn Pub Corp.

Revenge of the Apple: Venganza de la Manzana. Alicia Partnoy. Tr. by Richard Schaaf & Regina Kreger from SPA. (Illus.). 100p. (Orig.). (ENG & SPA.). (C). 1992. pap. 8.95 (*0-939416-63-8*) Cleis Pr.

Revenge of the Baby-Sat. Bill Watterson. (Illus.). 128p. (Orig.). 1991. pap. 9.95 (*0-8362-1866-3*) Andrews & McMeel.

***Revenge of the Barbeque Queens.** Lou J. Temple. 1997. mass mkt. 5.99 (*0-312-96074-3*) St Martin.

Revenge of the Buffalo Hunter. Ralph Hayes. 1992. mass mkt. 3.99 (*1-55817-587-3*, Pinncle Kensgtn) Kensgtn Pub Corp.

Revenge of the Christmas Box: A Parody. Cathy Crimmins. 96p. 1996. pap. 9.95 (*0-7871-1037-X*, Dove Bks) Dove Audio.

Revenge of the Computer Phantoms. J. R. Black. (Shadow Zone Ser.). 132p. (J). (gr. 3-5). 1994. pap. 3.99 (*0-679-85407-X*, Bullseye Bks) Random Bks Yng Read.

Revenge of the Cootie Girls. Sparkle Hayter. LC 96-43984. 1997. pap. 20.95 (*0-670-86940-6*) Viking Penguin.

Revenge of the Crystal: Selected Writings by Jean Baudrillard on the Modern Object & Its Destiny, 1968-1983. Baudrillard. Ed. by Julian Pefanis & Paul Foss. 198p. (C). 55.50 (*0-7453-0298-X*, Pub. by Pluto Pr UK); pap. 17.95 (*0-7453-0305-6*, Pub. by Pluto Pr UK) LPC InBook.

Revenge of the Damned. Allan Cole & Chris Bunch. 1989. mass mkt. 5.99 (*0-345-33173-7*, Del Rey) Ballantine.

***Revenge of the Dinner Ladies.** large type ed. David Tinkler. (J). 1997. 16.95 (*0-7451-6969-4*, Galaxy Child Lrg Print) Chivers N Amer.

Revenge of the Dinosaurs. Tom B. Stone. (Graveyard School Ser.: No. 5). 112p. (J). (gr. 4-7). 1995. pap. 3.50 (*0-553-48227-0*) Bantam.

***Revenge of the Dog Robber.** Lane Riosley. (Lucky Hightops & the Cosmic Cat Patrol Ser.: No. 4). (Illus.). (J). (gr. 2-8). pap. 3.00 (*1-57514-270-8*, 1116) Encore Perform Pub.

Revenge of the Fishgod: Angling Adventures Around the World. Carl Von Essen. LC 96-22403. (Illus.). 192p. 1996. 21.95 (*0-8397-7115-0*) Eriksson.

Revenge of the Forty-Seven Samurai. Erik C. Haugaard. LC 94-7691. 240p. (J). (gr. 6 up). 1995. 14.95 (*0-395-70809-5*) HM.

Revenge of the Fox. Jack Jackson. 200p. 1995. pap. 13.00 (*0-8059-3587-8*) Dorrance.

Revenge of the Goblins. A. G. Cascone. (Deadtime Stories Ser.). 128p. (Orig.). (J). (gr. 3-7). 1996. pap. 3.50 (*0-8167-4139-5*) Troll Communs.

Revenge of the Grand Narrative: Marxist Perspective in Archaeology. Ed. by Tom Saunders. (Worldwide Archaeology Ser.: Vol. 3). 200p. 50.95 (*1-85628-702-5*, Pub. by Avebury Pub UK) Ashgate Pub Co.

Revenge of the Hairy Horror. E. W. Leroe. (Fiendly Corners Ser.: No. 3). 128p. (J). (gr. 3-7). 1996. pap. 3.95 (*0-7868-1097-1*) Hyprn Child.

Revenge of the Hawk. Leigh F. James. 374p. 1991. reprint ed. lib. bdg. 27.95 (*0-89966-880-1*) Buccaneer Bks.

Revenge of the Hound. Michael Hardwick. 1989. mass mkt. 3.95 (*1-55817-166-5*, Pinncle Kensgtn) Kensgtn Pub Corp.

Revenge of the Lawn: The Abortion: So the Wind Won't Blow It All Away. Richard Brautigan. 516p. 1995. pap. 14.95 (*0-395-70674-2*) HM.

Revenge of the Lawn Gnomes. R. L. Stine. (Goosebumps Ser.: No. 34). 160p. (gr. 4-6). 1995. pap. 3.99 (*0-590-48346-3*) Scholastic Inc.

Revenge of the Living Monolith. Marc Silvestri et al. 80p. 1985. 9.95 (*0-87135-083-1*) Marvel Entmnt.

Revenge of the Magic Chicken. Helen Lester. (Illus.). 32p. (J). (gr. k-3). 1990. 13.95 (*0-395-50929-7*) HM.

***Revenge of the Mount.** William Johnstone. 1997. mass mkt. 4.99 (*0-8217-5815-2*) Kensgtn Pub Corp.

Revenge of the Mountain Man. William W. Johnston. 256p. 1991. mass mkt. 3.55 (*0-8217-3821-6*, Zebra Kensgtn) Kensgtn Pub Corp.

Revenge of the Mountain Man. William W. Johnstone. 1995. pap. 4.50 (*0-8217-5176-X*) NAL-Dutton.

Revenge of the Mummy. A. E. Parker. (Clue Jr. Ser.: No. 13). (J). (gr. 4-7). 1996. pap. text ed. 3.50 (*0-590-62376-1*) Scholastic Inc.

Revenge of the Past: Nationalism, Revolution, & the Collapse of the Soviet Union. Ronald G. Suny. LC 93-10373. 224p. (C). 1993. 39.50 (*0-8047-2134-3*); pap. 14.95 (*0-8047-2247-1*) Stanford U Pr.

Revenge of the Philistines: Art & Culture 1972-1984. Hilton Kramer. 425p. 1985. 35.00 (*0-02-918470-3*, Free Press) Free Pr.

***Revenge of the Pirate Ghost.** Susan Saunders. (Black Cat Club Ser.: No. 5). (Illus.). 96p. (J). (gr. 1-5). 1997. pap. 3.95 (*0-06-442065-5*, Trophy) HarpC Child Bks.

***Revenge of the Red Raiders: The Illustrated History of the 22nd Bombardment Group in WW II.** Lawrence J. Hickey et al. (Eagles over the Pacific Ser.: Vol. 2). (Illus.). 480p. 1997. 75.00 (*0-913511-05-6*) Intl Res & Pub.

Revenge of the Rose. Michael Moorcock. 256p. 1994. mass mkt. 5.50 (*0-441-00106-8*) Ace Bks.

Revenge of the Shadow People. R. L. Stine. (R.L. Stien's Ghosts of Fear Street Ser.: no. 9). (J). (gr. 3-6). 1996. pap. 3.99 (*0-671-52949-8*) S&S Trade.

Revenge of the Small Small. Jean Little. (Illus.). 32p. (J). (ps-3). 1993. pap. 14.00 (*0-670-84471-3*) Viking Child Bks.

Revenge of the Son of the World's Tackiest Postcards. Klutz Press Staff. (World's Tackiest Postcards Ser.). 19p. (Orig.). 1989. pap. 5.95 (*0-932592-26-0*) Klutz Pr.

Revenge of the Space Pandas. David Mamet. 1978. 5.25 (*0-87129-532-6*, R26) Dramatic Pub.

Revenge of the Sports Widows: How to Cope with a Sports Fanatic. Kathleen L. Barry. 1991. pap. 6.95 (*1-56171-063-6*) Sure Seller.

***Revenge of the Wizards.** Peter Regan. Date not set. pap. 8.95 (*0-947962-61-1*) Dufour.

***Revenge of the Wizard's Ghost.** John Bellairs. 1997. pap. 3.99 (*0-14-038043-4*) Viking Penguin.

Revenge Ride. George G. Gilman. (Edge Ser.: No. 49). 192p. 1993. mass mkt. 3.50 (*1-55817-691-8*, Pinncle Kensgtn) Kensgtn Pub Corp.

Revenge Rider & the Long Roper. large type ed. Jim Wilmeth. 526p. 1983. 25.99 (*0-7089-1009-2*) Ulverscroft.

Revenge Techniques from the Master of Mayhem: Hardcore Hayduke. George Hayduke. LC 94-17110. 1994. 8.95 (*0-8184-0575-9*) Carol Pub Group.

Revenge Tragedy: Aeschylus to Armageddon. John Kerrigan. LC 95-36176. (Illus.). 432p. (C). 1996. 70.00 (*0-19-812186-5*, Clarendon Pr) OUP.

Revengers' Comedies. Alan Ayckbourn. 128p. 1991. pap. 12.95 (*0-571-14358-X*) Faber & Faber.

Revenger's Madness: A Study of Revenge Tragedy Motifs. Charles A. Hallett & Elaine S. Hallett. LC 80-13893. 361p. 1980. reprint ed. pap. 102.90 (*0-608-01847-3*, 2062497) Bks Demand.

Revenger's Tragedy. Cyril Tourneur. Ed. by R. A. Foakes. LC 95-25044. (Revels Student Editions Ser.). 144p. (C). 1996. text ed. 12.95 (*0-7190-4375-1*, Pub. by Manchester Univ Pr UK) St Martin.

Revenger's Tragedy. Cyril Tourneur. Ed. by Lawrence J. Ross. LC 66-12744. xxxii, 130p. 1966. pap. text ed. 5.95 (*0-8032-5284-6*, Bison Books) U of Nebr Pr.

Revenger's Tragedy. rev. ed. Ed. by Brian Gibbons. (New Mermaid Ser.). 109p. (C). 1991. pap. text ed. 6.95 (*0-393-90060-6*) Norton.

Revenger's Tragedy. Cyril Tourneur. Ed. by R. A. Foakes. (Revels Plays Ser.). 152p. 1988. reprint ed. text ed. 24.95 (*0-7190-1612-6*, Pub. by Manchester Univ Pr UK) St Martin.

Revenger's Tragedy: A Facsimile of the 1607-8 Quarto-Attributed to Thomas Middleton. MacDonald P. Jackson. LC 81-72052. 120p. 1983. 26.50 (*0-8386-3131-2*) Fairleigh Dickinson.

Revenger's Tragedy see Three Jacobean Tragedies

Revenge/Virgin's Vow/The Annuity. Aleksander Fredro. Tr. by Noel Clark. 224p. 1994. 15.95 (*0-948230-64-9*, Pub. by Absolute Classics UK) Theatre Comm.

Revenue Act 1993. Hoffman. Date not set. pap. text ed. write for info. (*0-314-03224-X*) West Pub.

Revenue Act '93. Hoffman. Date not set. student ed., pap. text ed. write for info. (*0-314-03225-8*) West Pub.

Revenue Agent. Jack Rudman. (Career Examination Ser.: C-3250). 1994. pap. 29.95 (*0-8373-3250-8*) Nat Learn.

Revenue Agent: Life & Death Exploits of a Prohibition Agent in West Virginia. 2nd ed. William G. Burleigh. Ed. & Photos by David B. Wallace. (Illus.). 52p. 1995. pap. 4.75 (*1-889074-00-4*) Elkhorn Pr.

Revenue & Reform: The Indian Problem in British Politics, 1757-1773. H. V. Bowen. 208p. (C). 1991. text ed. 54.95 (*0-521-40316-2*) Cambridge U Pr.

Revenue Base of the States: An Analysis of Recent Growth & Elasticity. 48p. 1993. pap. write for info. (*0-87292-980-9*, C-058-93) Coun State Govts.

Revenue Enhancement for Water & Wastewater Systems: Proceedings of the Session. Ed. by Jerry S. Rogers & William P. Bullock, Jr. LC 94-34443. 1994. 16.00 (*0-7844-0030-X*) Am Soc Civil Eng.

Revenue Equipment Maintainer. (Career Examination Ser.: C-3580). pap. 23.95 (*0-8373-3580-9*) Nat Learn.

Revenue Forecasting Made Easy for Local Governments. Cindy Hall. 107p. 1991. student ed. 29.95 (*1-882403-02-9*) The Innovation Grps.

Revenue Guide for Local Government. Robert L. Bland. 197p. (Orig.). 1989. pap. text ed. 32.00 (*0-87326-080-5*) Intl City-Cnty Mgt.

Revenue Instability & Conservation Rate Structures. (Illus.). 68p. 1995. pap. 35.00 (*0-89867-818-8*, 90681) Am Water Wks Assn.

Revenue Investigations & Appeals Manuals. 2nd ed. Leslie Beckett & B. E. Sabine. U.K. pap. 84.00 (*0-406-50152-1*, U.K.) MICHIE.

Revenue Law. 270p. (C). 1991. 72.00 (*1-85352-906-0*, Pub. by HLT Pubns UK); 90.00 (*1-85352-399-2*, Pub. by HLT Pubns UK); pap. text ed. 72.00 (*1-85352-862-5*, Pub. by HLT Pubns UK) St Mut.

Revenue Law. Susan Blake & Stephen W. Mayson. 710p. (C). 1990. 225.00 (*1-85431-052-6*, Pub. by Blackstone Pr UK) St Mut.

Revenue Law. M. Ramjohn. (Q & A Ser.). 320p. 1996. pap. write for info. (*1-874241-35-X*, Pub. by Cavendish UK) Gaunt.

Revenue Law. Philip Ridgway. (Lecture Notes...Ser.). 350p. 1996. pap. 36.00 (*1-874241-89-9*, Pub. by Cavendish UK) Gaunt.

Revenue Law. 13th ed. Susan Blake & Stephen W. Mayson. 1993. 64.00 (*1-85431-269-3*, Pub. by Blackstone Pr UK) Gaunt.

Revenue Law: Cases & Materials. Y. Grbich. 1100p. 1990. pap. 102.00 (*0-409-49516-6*, Austral); boxed 129.00 (*0-409-49515-8*, Austral) MICHIE.

***Revenue Law: Principles & Practice.** James Kirkbride & Abimbola A. Olowofoyeku. (Tudor-Law, Politics & Government Ser.). 1992. pap. 50.00 (*1-872807-70-4*) Kogan Page Ltd.

Revenue Law - Principles & Practice. 12th ed. Chris Whitehouse et al. 1994. pap. 27.50 (*0-406-03654-3*) MICHIE.

Revenue Law - Principles & Practice. 14th ed. Chris Whitehouse. 780p. 1996. pap. 51.00 (*0-406-05686-2*) MICHIE.

Revenue Law, 1992-93. 13th ed. Stephen W. Mayson & Susan Blake. 606p. 1993. pap. 58.00 (*1-85431-226-X*, Pub. by Blackstone Pr UK) Gaunt.

Revenue Management: Hard-Core Tactics for Market Domination. Robert G. Cross. LC 96-32457. 288p. 1997. pap. 27.50 (*0-553-06734-6*) Broadway BDD.

***Revenue Management: Hard-Core Tactics for Market Domination.** Robert G. Cross. (Illus.). 288p. 1997. reprint ed. pap. 15.00 (*0-7679-0033-2*) Broadway BDD.

Revenue Patterns in U. S. Cities & Suburbs: A Comparative Analysis. Susan A. MacManus. LC 77-27499. (Praeger Special Studies). 228p. 1978. text ed. 55.00 (*0-275-90304-4*, C0304, Praeger Pubs) Greenwood.

Revenue-Raising & Legitimacy: Tax Collection & Finance Administration in the Ottoman Empire, 1560-1660. Linda T. Darling. (Ottoman Empire & Its Heritage Ser.: Vol. 6). 1996. 116.25 (*90-04-10289-2*) E J Brill.

Revenue Reconciliation Act of 1990: Title XI Omnibus Budget Reconciliation Act of 1990, Public Law 101-508. Ed. by Bernard D. Reams & Faye L. Couture. LC 94-15648. 8748p. 1994. 760.00 (*0-89941-873-2*, 308180) W S Hein.

Revenue Reconciliation Act of 1990 Law & Explanation. 592p. 1990. pap. 19.50 (*0-685-67028-7*, 4970) Commerce.

Revenue Reconciliation Act of 1993 23 vols. A Legislative History of Title XIII Omnibus Budget Reconciliation Act of 1993, Public Law 103-66, 25 bks., Set. Ed. by Bernard D. Reams, Jr. 27,408p. 1995. 2,500.00 (*0-89941-930-5*, 308280) W S Hein.

Revenue Requirements, No. M35. 54p. 1990. pap. 40.00 (*0-89867-486-7*, 30035) Am Water Wks Assn.

Revenue Sharing: The Second Round. Richard P. Nathan & Charles F. Adams, Jr. LC 76-51884. 286p. reprint ed. pap. 81.60 (*0-317-26739-6*, 2025391) Bks Demand.

Revenue Sharing: Trick or Treat? William O. Farber. 1973. 1.00 (*1-55614-108-4*) U of SD Gov Res Bur.

Revenue Sharing & the City. Walter Heller et al. Ed. by Harvey S. Perloff & Richard P. Nathan. LC 77-86396. (Resources for the Future Ser.). 128p. reprint ed. 45.00 (*0-404-60333-5*) AMS Pr.

Revenue Stamps of the United States. Christopher West. LC 79-67395. (C. & S. Revenue Ser.). (Illus.). 144p. 1979. 21.95 (*0-9603498-0-4*) Castenholz Sons.

Revenue Statistics of OECD Member Countries 1965-1994. OECD Staff. 255p. (Orig.). (ENG & FRE.). 1995. pap. 64.00 (*92-64-04498-1*, Pub. by Org for Econ FR) OECD.

***Revenue Statistics, 1965-1995.** 300p. 1996. 63.00 (*92-64-04841-3*, Pub. by Org for Econ FR) OECD.

Revenue Unit Columns from the American Philatelist. Beverly S. King et al. LC 80-53091. 248p. 1981. reprint ed. lib. bdg. 35.00 (*0-88000-119-4*) Quarterman.

Revenue Words & Phrases Judicially Considered. J. L. Van Dorsten, pseud. 1021p. 1989. boxed 166.00 (*0-409-11026-4*, SA) MICHIE.

Revenuers & Moonshiners: Enforcing Federal Liquor Law in the Mountain South, 1865-1900. Wilbur R. Miller. LC 90-49549. (Illus.). xii, 251p. 1991. pap. 15.95 (*0-8078-4330-X*) U of NC Pr.

Reverberation Machines: The Later Plays & Essays. Richard Foreman. LC 85-17193. (Illus.). 256p. (Orig.). 1985. 19.95 (*0-88268-001-3*); pap. 10.95 (*0-88268-000-5*) Station Hill Pr.

An Asterisk (*) at the beginning of an entry indicates that the title is appearing in BIP for the first time.

Reverberation Mapping of the Broad-Line Region in Active Galactic Nuclei: Rutherford Appleton Laboratory Workshop on Astronomy & Astrophysics (10th, 1994: Abingdon, England) Ed. by P. M. Gondhalekar et al. LC 94-79685. (Conference Ser.: Vol. 69). 384p. 1994. 28.00 (0-937707-88-0) Astron Soc Pacific.

Reverberations: Across the Shimmering CASCADAS. Jeffner Allen. LC 93-31711. (Series in Feminist Philosophy). 204p. 1994. pap. 14.95 (0-7914-1898-7) State U NY Pr.

Reverberations: Across the Shimmering CASCADAS. Jeffner Allen. LC 93-31711. (SUNY Series in Feminist Philosophy). 204p. 1994. text ed. 44.50 (0-7914-1897-9) State U NY Pr.

Reverberations: Diptychs & Triptychs from the Southeast Museum of Photography. Alison D. Nordstrom. (Illus.). 16p. 1995. pap. text ed. 10.00 (1-887040-12-9) SE Mus Photo.

Reverberations: Explorations in the Canadian Short Story. Simone Vauthier. 208p. 1993. 26.95 (0-88784-164-3, Pub. by Hse of Anansi Pr CN); pap. 17.95 (0-88784-526-6, Pub. by Hse of Anansi Pr CN) Genl Dist Srvs.

Reverberations: Mothers & Daughters. Ed. & Illus. by Mildred Lachman-Chapin. 44p. (Orig.). 1995. pap. 19.95 (1-879260-32-8) Evanston Pub.

*__Reverberations: Mothers & Daughters.__ 2nd ed. Mildred Lachman-Chapin. (Illus.). 48p. 1996. reprint ed. pap. 19.95 (0-9643728-4-3) Perry Pubng.

Reverberations: Sound & Structure in the Novels of Virginia Woolf. Kathleen A. McCluskey. LC 85-21015. (Studies in Modern Literature: No. 54). (Illus.). 156p. reprint ed. pap. 44.50 (0-8357-1710-0, 2070508) Bks Demand.

Reverberations: The Memoirs of Dietrich Fischer-Dieskau. Tr. by Ruth Hein. (Illus.). 368p. 1990. pap. 14.95 (0-88064-122-3) Fromm Intl Pub.

Reverberator; Madame de Mauve; A Passionate Pilgrim: And Other Tales. Henry James. LC 70-158792. (Novels & Tales of Henry James Ser.: Vol. 13). xx, 549p. 1971. reprint ed. 45.00 (0-678-02813-3) Kelley.

Reverdy C. Ransom: Black Advocate of the Social Gospel. Calvin S. Morris. 212p. (Orig.). (C). 1990. lib. bdg. 44.50 (0-8191-7766-0) U Pr of Amer.

Revered by All. 2nd ed. Lester Eckman. LC 73-89418. 1976. 18.95 (0-88400-002-8) Shengold.

Reverence for Life. Albert Schweitzer. Tr. by Reginald H. Fuller. 1992. reprint ed. 21.95 (0-8290-2629-0) Irvington.

*__Reverence for Life: The Words of Albert Schweitzer.__ Compiled by Harold E. Robles. 212p. Date not set. 15.00 (0-88365-927-1) Galahad Bks.

Reverence for Wood. Eric Sloane. 111p. 1984. pap. 8.00 (0-345-31991-5, Ballantine Trade) Ballantine.

Reverence, Righteousness, & Rahamanut: Essays in Memory of Rabbi Dr. Leo Jung. Ed. by Jacob J. Schacter. LC 92-2566. 384p. 1992. 40.00 (0-87668-591-2) Aronson.

Reverend Beecher & Mrs. Tilton: Sex & Class in Victorian America. Altina L. Waller. LC 81-15982. (Illus.). 192p. 1982. lib. bdg. 27.50 (0-87023-356-4) U of Mass Pr.

Reverend Calvert R. Jones: Sunpictures Catalogue, No. 5. Larry J. Schaaf. (Illus.). 80p. (Orig.). 1990. pap. 25.00 (0-9621096-1-4) H P Kraus Jr.

Rev. Calvin Fairbank During Slavery Times: How He "Fought the Good Fight" to Prepare "the Way" Calvin Fairbank. (American Biography Ser.). 207p. 1991. reprint ed. lib. bdg. 69.00 (0-7812-8126-1) Rprt Serv.

Reverend Charles Owen Rice: Apostle of Contradiction. Patrick J. McGeever. LC 88-19766. (Illus.). 320p. 1989. 28.95 (0-8207-0209-9); pap. 18.00 (0-8207-0210-2) Duquesne.

Reverend Colonel Finch. Elizabeth Nitchie. LC 40-33650. reprint ed. 20.00 (0-404-04777-7) AMS Pr.

Reverend Devil. Ross Phares. (Illus.). 263p. 1974. 17.95 (0-88289-011-5) Pelican.

Reverend Elhanan Winchester: Biography & Letters. LC 72-38464. (Religion in America, Ser. 2). 358p. 1972. reprint ed. 29.95 (0-405-04090-3) Ayer.

Reverend Fun's Has Anybody Seen My Locust. Dennis M. Hengeveld. (Illus.). 96p. (Orig.). 1996. pap. 8.95 (1-55568-156-5) Gospel Films.

*__Reverend Gary Davis.__ Ed. by Aaron Stang. 84p. (Orig.). (C). 1993. pap. text ed. 18.95 (0-7692-0952-1, F3175GTXCD) Warner Brothers.

Rev. Gary Davis - Blues Guitar. Stefan Grossman. (Illus.). 140p. 1974. pap. 15.95 (0-8256-0152-5, OK63008, Oak) Music Sales.

Rev. John Moore of Newtown, of Newtown, Long Island, & Some of His Descendants. J. W. Moore. (Illus.). 541p. 1989. reprint ed. pap. 81.00 (0-8328-0881-4); reprint ed. lib. bdg. 89.00 (0-8328-0880-6) Higginson Bk Co.

Reverend John O'Hanlon's The Irish Emmigrant's Guide to the United States. Ed. by Edward J. Maguire. LC 76-6352. (Irish Americans Ser.). 1976. 25.95 (0-405-09346-2) Ayer.

Rev. John Shea Library, 5 vols., Set. John Shea. 1996. pap. 59.95 (0-88347-287-2, 7287) Res Christian Liv.

Reverend John Walker: Renaissance Man. Erving E. Beauregard. LC 89-39716. (American University Studies: History: Ser. IX, Vol. 87). 225p. (C). 1990. text ed. 42.95 (0-8204-1192-2) P Lang Pubng.

*__Reverend Joseph Tarkington: Methodist Circuit Rider - From Frontier Evangelism to Refined Religion.__ David L. Kimbrough. LC 96-51234. 1997. text ed. 35.00 (0-87049-979-3) U of Tenn Pr.

Reverend Randolph & Modern Miracles. Terrence L. Smith. 224p. 1988. 16.95 (0-399-13358-5, Putnam) Putnam Pub Group.

Reverend Smith, Sidney. Osbert Burdett. LC 72-144920. 303p. 1934. reprint ed. 39.00 (0-403-00883-2) Scholarly.

Rev. Thomas Barton (1728-1780) & Some of His Descendants & Some of Their In-Laws. Stuart E. Brown, Jr. 268p. 1988. Indexed. 37.50 (0-685-56618-8); pap. 27.50 (0-685-70054-2) VA Bk.

Reverend Thomas Bray: His Life & Selected Works Relating to Maryland. Ed. by Bernard C. Steiner. LC 79-39862. (Religion in America, Ser.: No. 2). 256p. 1972. reprint ed. 20.95 (0-405-04088-1) Ayer.

Reverend Thomas's False Teeth. Gayle Gillerlain. LC 93-39980. (Illus.). 32p. (J). (gr. k-3). 1995. pap. 14.95 (0-8167-3303-1) BrdgeWater.

Reverend Thomas's False Teeth. Gayle Gillerlain. LC 93-39980. (Illus.). 32p. (J). (gr. k-3). 1996. pap. 4.95 (0-8167-3304-X) BrdgeWater.

Reverend William Carwardine & the Pullman Strike of Eighteen Ninety-Four: The Christian Gospel & Social Justice. Stephen G. Cobb. LC 92-7603. 248p. 1992. lib. bdg. 89.95 (0-7734-9508-8) E Mellen.

Reverend William Proudfoot & the United Secession Mission in Canada. Stewart D. Gill. LC 91-41253. (Studies in History of Missions: Vol. 7). 236p. 1991. lib. bdg. 89.95 (0-7734-9446-4) E Mellen.

Reverent Discipline: Essays in Literary Criticism & Culture. George A. Panichas. LC 73-15749. 488p. 1974. 45.00 (0-87049-149-0) U of Tenn Pr.

Reverent Discipline: Essays in Literary Criticism & Culture. George A. Panichas. LC 73-15749. 488p. 1974. reprint ed. pap. 139.10 (0-7837-9507-6, 2060257) Bks Demand.

Reverie: Piano Solo. Claude Debussy. 8p. 1986. pap. 3.95 (0-7935-0586-0, 50281810) H Leonard.

*__Reverie & Interpretation: Sensing Something Human.__ Thomas H. Ogden. LC 97-9833. 1997. text ed. 40.00 (0-7657-0076-X) Aronson.

Reverie Jusqu'a Rousseau: Recherches sur un topos Litteraire. Robert J. Morrissey. LC 84-81406. (French Forum Monographs: No. 55). 184p. (Orig.). 1984. pap. 13.45 (0-917058-55-0) French Forum.

Reveries. Alexandra Grilikhes. 27p. (Orig.). 1994. pap. 7.00 (1-882827-04-X) Insight to Riot.

Reveries du Promeneur Solitaire. Jean-Jacques Rousseau. 288p. (FRE.). 1972. pap. 10.95 (0-7859-3989-X, 2070361861) Fr & Eur.

Reveries du Promeneur Solitaire. Jean-Jacques Rousseau. Ed. by S. Sylvestre de Sacy. (Folio Ser.: No. 186). 288p. 1972. 6.95 (2-07-036186-1) Schoenhof.

Reveries du Promeneur Solitaire. Jean-Jacques Rousseau. Ed. by S. Sylvestre De Sacy. 288p. 1972. write for info. (0-318-63590-9) Fr & Eur.

Reveries du Promeneur Solitaire. unabridged ed. Jean-Jacques Rousseau. (FRE.). pap. 5.95 (2-87714-224-8, Pub. by Bookking Intl FR) Distribks Inc.

Reveries of a Bachelor. Donald G. Mitchell. 1972. 59.95 (0-8490-0951-0) Gordon Pr.

*__Reveries of an Artist.__ Lou Burnett. 165p. (Orig.). (YA). 1996. pap. write for info. (1-57502-253-2, P0935) Morris Pubng.

Reveries of Raleigh. Emma S. McPherson. 286p. 1987. 75.00 (0-942179-02-1); pap. 35.00 (0-685-19192-3) Shelby Hse.

Reveries of the Solitary Walker. Jean-Jacques Rousseau. Tr. & Intro. by Peter France. (Classics Ser.). 160p. 1980. pap. 8.95 (0-14-044363-0, Penguin Classics) Viking Penguin.

Reveries of the Solitary Walker. Jean-Jacques Rousseau. Tr. & Notes by Charles E. Butterworth. LC 92-28212. 288p. (C). 1992. reprint ed. pap. text ed. 7.95 (0-87220-162-7); reprint ed. lib. bdg. 29.95 (0-87220-163-5) Hackett Pub.

Reversal Errors: Theories & Procedures. Kenneth A. Lane. Ed. by Sally M. Corngold. LC 88-50982. (Illus.). 153p. (Orig.). 1988. pap. 15.00 (0-929780-00-0) VisionExtension.

Reversal of Development in Argentina. Carlos H. Waisman. 344p. 1987. pap. text ed. 17.95 (0-691-02266-6) Princeton U Pr.

Reversal of Fortune. Alan M. Dershowitz. Ed. by Sally Peters. 360p. 1990. reprint ed. mass mkt. 4.99 (0-671-70724-8, Archway) PB.

Reversal of Fortune: Inside the Von Bulow Case. Alan M. Dershowitz. LC 85-25722. (Illus.). 1986. 19.95 (0-394-53903-6) Random.

Reversal of Multidrug Resistance in Cancer. Ed. by J. A. Kellen. 176p. 1993. 149.95 (0-8493-4744-0) CRC Pr.

Reversal Theory: Applications & Development. Ed. by M. F. Apter et al. 212p. (C). 1985. text ed. 39.95 (0-906449-74-X) L Erlbaum Assocs.

Reversal Theory: Motivation, Emotion & Personality. Michael J. Apter. 224p. 1989. 45.00 (0-415-01581-2) Routledge.

Reversals: A Personal Account of Victory over Dyslexia. Eileen M. Simpson. 246p. 1991. pap. 11.00 (0-374-52316-9, Noonday) FS&G.

Reversals of Fortune: Public Policy & Private Interests. Gary Mucciaroni. 225p. (C). 1995. 38.95 (0-8157-5876-6); pap. 16.95 (0-8157-5875-8) Brookings.

Reversals of the Earth's Magnetic Field. fac. ed. John A. Jacobs. LC 84-115850. (Illus.). 240p. reprint ed. pap. 68.40 (0-7837-8004-4, 2047760) Bks Demand.

Reversals of the Earth's Magnetic Field. 2nd ed. J. A. Jacobs. (Illus.). 356p. (C). 1995. text ed. 74.95 (0-521-45072-1) Cambridge U Pr.

Reverse Acronyms Initialisms & Abbreviations, 3 Vols., Vol. 3. 20th ed. Ed. by Mary R. Bonk. 1995. 320.00 (0-8103-5631-7) Gale.

Reverse Acronyms, Initialisms & Abbreviations Dictionary. 12th ed. 304p. 1987. 225.00 (0-8103-2507-1) Gale.

Reverse Acronyms, Initialisms & Abbreviations Dictionary, 3 pts. 21th ed. Mary R. Bonk. 3800p. 1996. 335.00 (0-8103-4889-6) Gale.

Reverse Acronyms, Initialisms & Abbreviations Dictionary, Vol. 2. 4th ed. Ed. by Mary R. Bonk. 1230p. 1997. 205.00 (0-8103-7438-2) Gale.

Reverse Acronyms, Initialisms & Abbreviations Dictionary, Vol. 3. 10th ed. Ed. by Julie E. Towell & Helen E. Sheppard. LC 84-643188. 2400p. 1985. 195.00 (0-8103-0684-0) Gale.

Reverse Acronyms, Initialisms, & Abbreviations Dictionary, Vol. 3. 15th ed. Ed. by Jennifer Mossman. LC 84-643188. 3642p. 1990. 250.00 (0-8103-5082-3) Gale.

Reverse Acronyms, Initialisms & Abbreviations Dictionary, 3 vols., Vol. 3. 16th ed. 1991. 260.00 (0-8103-5083-1) Gale.

Reverse Acronyms, Initialisms & Abbreviations Dictionary, 3 vols., Vol. 3. 17th ed. Ed. by Jennifer Mossman. (Acronyms, Initialisms & Abbreviations Dictionary Ser.). 1992. 270.00 (0-8103-7537-0, 030040) Gale.

Reverse Acronyms, Initialisms & Abbreviations Dictionary, 3 Pts., Vol. 3. 18th ed. Ed. by Jennifer Mossman. 3800p. 1993. 280.00 (0-8103-8207-5, 030044) Gale.

Reverse Acronyms, Initialisms & Abbreviations Dictionary, 3 Vols., Vol. 3. 19th ed. Jennifer Mossman. 1994. 310.00 (0-8103-5562-0) Gale.

*__Reverse Acronyms, Initialisms & Abbreviations Dictionary, 3 pts., Vol. 3.__ 23th rev. ed. Ed. by Mary R. Bonk. 3800p. 1997. 345.00 (0-7876-1319-3, 00156471, Gale Res Intl) Gale.

Reverse Acronyms, Initialisms & Abbreviations Dictionary, Vol. 3. 13th ed. Ed. by Julie E. Towell. (Acronyms, Initialisms & Abbreviations Dictionary Ser.: Vol. 3). 3300p. 1988. 230.00 (0-8103-2582-9) Gale.

Reverse Acronyms, Initialisms & Abbreviations Dictionary, 1989, Vol. 3. 14th ed. Ed. by Jennifer Mossman & Julie E. Towell. 3477p. 1989. 240.00 (0-8103-5081-5) Gale.

Reverse Acronyms, Initials & Abbreviations Part 1. 20th ed. Bonk. 1995. write for info. (0-8103-5632-5) Gale.

Reverse Acronyms, Initials & Abbreviations Part 2. 20th ed. Bonk. 1995. write for info. (0-8103-5633-3) Gale.

Reverse Acronyms, Initials & Abbreviations Part 3. 20th ed. Bonk. 1995. write for info. (0-8103-5634-1) Gale.

*__Reverse Aging: Scientific Health Methods, Easier & More Effective Than Diet & Exercise.__ Sang Whang. 123p. (Orig.). 1991. pap. 11.95 (0-614-30249-8) Siloam Enter.

Reverse Analytical Dictionary of Classical Armenian. Paul Jungmann & J. J. Weitenberg. LC 93-13334. (Trends in Linguistics, Documentation Ser.: No. 9). viii, 836p. (C). 1993. lib. bdg. 306.15 (3-11-012938-8) Mouton.

*__Reverse Dictionary.__ Reader's Digest Editors. (Illus.). 1997. pap. text ed. 16.95 (0-89577-951-X) RD Assn.

Reverse Dictionary. Beverly L. Ritter. (Realtime Machine Shorthand Ser.). 228p. (Orig.). (C). 1992. pap. text ed. 32.00 (0-938643-13-4) Stenotype Educ.

Reverse Dictionary of Urdu. Donald Becker. (URD.). 1980. 38.00 (0-8364-0656-7, Pub. by Manohar II) S Asia.

Reverse Discrimination: The Constitutional Debate. Ralph A. Rossum. LC 80-13777. (Political Science Ser.: No. 10). 240p. reprint ed. pap. 68.40 (0-8357-3517-6, 2034564) Bks Demand.

Reverse Discrimination Controversy: A Moral & Legal Analysis. Robert K. Fullinwider. 1980. 52.25 (0-317-05213-6); pap. 20.50 (0-317-05214-4) IPPP.

Reverse Discrimination Controversy: A Moral & Legal Analysis. Robert K. Fullinwider. (Philosophy & Society Ser.). 300p. 1980. pap. 22.50 (0-8476-6901-7) Rowman.

Reverse Effect: How Vitamins & Minerals Promote Health & Cause Disease. Walter A. Heiby. (Illus.). 1216p. (Orig.). 1988. 59.50 (0-938869-01-9) MediSci Pubs.

Reverse Engineering. Katheryn A. Ingle. 1994. text ed. 47.00 (0-07-031693-7) McGraw.

Reverse Engineering. Philip Newcomb. Ed. by Linda Wills. LC 96-26556. 184p. (C). 1996. lib. bdg. 105.00 (0-7923-9756-8) Kluwer Ac.

Reverse Engineering & Software Maintenance: A Practical Approach. Kevin Lano & Howard Haughton. LC 93-29541. (International Series in Software Engineering). 1993. write for info. (0-07-707897-7) McGraw.

Reverse Engineering, 2nd Working Conference on. LC 95-77097. 352p. 1995. pap. 70.00 (0-8186-7111-4, PR07111) IEEE Comp Soc.

Reverse Engineering, 3rd Working Conference on (WCRE '96) WCRE 96. LC 96-78442. 350p. 1996. pap. 100.00 (0-8186-7674-4) IEEE Comp Soc.

*__Reverse Fairy Tale.__ Linda G. Robiner. 32p. (Orig.). 1997. pap. 7.95 (0-614-30507-1) Pudding Hse Pubns.

Reverse Index of Greek Nouns & Adjectives Arranged by Terminations with Brief Historical Introduction. Carl D. Buck & W. Petersen. xvii, 765p. 1983. reprint ed. 160.00 (3-487-03203-1) G Olms Pubs.

Reverse Index of Manchu. William Rozycki & Rex Dwyer. Ed. by Denis Sinor. LC 81-52901. (Uralic & Altaic Ser.: Vol. 140). 189p. (Orig.). 1981. 14.00 (0-933070-08-X) Res Inst Inner Asian Studies.

Reverse International Acronyms, Initialisms & Abbreviations Dictionary. 2nd ed. Ed. by Helen E. Sheppard & Julie E. Towell. 907p. 1987. 180.00 (0-8103-2197-1) Gale.

Reverse International Acronyms, Initialisms & Abbreviations Dictionary, Vol. 2. 3rd ed. Ed. by Jennifer Mossman. 1178p. 1993. 205.00 (0-8103-7367-X, 009241) Gale.

Reverse Lexicon of Greek Proper Names. F. Dornseiff & Bernard Hansen. xiv, 340p. (GRE.). 1978. reprint ed. 35.00 (0-89005-251-4) Ares.

Reverse Licensing: International Technology Transfer to the United States. Manuchehr Shahrokhi. LC 86-25230. 192p. 1987. text ed. 55.00 (0-275-92258-8, C2258, Praeger Pubs) Greenwood.

Reverse Marketing. Michiel R. Leenders & David L. Blenkhorn. 1987. 45.00 (0-02-918381-2, Free Press) Free Pr.

Reverse Micelles: Biological & Technological Relevance of Amphiphilic Structures in Apolar Media. Ed. by Pier L. Luisi & B. E. Straub. 364p. 1984. 85.00 (0-306-41620-4, Plenum Pr) Plenum.

*__Reverse Mortgages & Other Senior Housing Options.__ David A. Bridewell & Charles Nauts. LC 96-42998. 1997. pap. write for info. (1-57073-406-2) Amer Bar Assn.

Reverse of the Medal. Patrick O'Brian. 288p. 1992. pap. 12.95 (0-393-30960-6) Norton.

Reverse of the Medal. Patrick O'Brian. 1994. 22.50 (0-393-03711-8) Norton.

Reverse Order. Steve Benson. 92p. (Orig.). 1989. pap. 9.00 (0-937013-25-0) Potes Poets.

Reverse Osmosis. Zahid Amjad. 384p. (C). (gr. 13). 1992. text ed. 84.95 (0-442-23964-5) Chapman & Hall.

Reverse Osmosis: A Practical Guide for Industrial Users. Wes Byrne. LC 95-60061. 461p. 1995. 90.00 (0-927188-03-1) Tall Oaks Pub.

Reverse Osmosis & Ultrafiltration. Ed. by S. Sourirajann & Takeshi Matsuura. (ACS Symposium Ser.: No. 281). 501p. 1985. lib. bdg. 98.95 (0-8412-0921-9) Am Chemical.

Reverse Osmosis Technology: Applications of High-Purity-Water Production. Parekh. (Chemical Industries Ser.: Vol. 35). 534p. 1988. 195.00 (0-8247-7985-1) Dekker.

Reverse Paintings on Glass: The Ryser Collection. Frieder Ryser. (Illus.). 192p. 1992. pap. 45.00 (0-87290-127-0) Corning.

Reverse Speech: A New Investigative Frontier. Ralph D. Thomas. (Private Investigator Ser.). 75p. 1991. pap. text ed. 38.00 (0-918487-58-7) Thomas Pubns TX.

*__Reverse Speech: Voices of the Unconscious.__ rev. ed. David J. Oates. 288p. (Orig.). 1996. pap. 19.95 (1-57901-000-8) Intl Promotions.

Reverse Symbolism Dictionary: Symbols Listed by Subject. Steven Olderr. LC 90-53517. 191p. 1992. lib. bdg. 32.50 (0-89950-561-9) McFarland & Co.

Reverse the Aging Process Naturally: How to Build the Immune System with Antioxidants, the Supernutrients of the Nineties. Gary Null & Martin Feldman. LC 92-56703. (Gary Null Health Library). 1993. pap. 12.00 (0-679-74509-2, Villard Bks) Random.

Reverse the Aging Process of Your Face: A Simple Technique That Works. Rachel Perry. LC 95-18688. 196p. pap. 13.95 (0-89529-625-X) Avery Pub.

Reverse the Charges: How to Save Money on Your Phone Bill. 4th ed. Sam Simon & Joe Waz, Jr. 1983. pap. 2.95 (0-394-71490-3) T R A C.

Reverse the Curse in Your Body & Emotions. Annette Capps. 106p. (Orig.). 1987. pap. 4.95 (0-9618975-0-3) Annette Capps.

Reverse the Curse in Your Life. Joan H. Robie. 176p. 1991. pap. 7.95 (0-914984-24-1) Starburst.

Reverse Thunder. Diane Ackerman. 96p. (Orig.). 1988. pap. 7.95 (0-930829-09-3) Lumen Inc.

Reverse Tradition: Postmodern Fictions & the Nineteenth Century Novel. Robert Kiely. LC 92-42333. 314p. 1993. text ed. 37.00 (0-674-76703-9) HUP.

Reverse Transcriptase. Ed. by Anna M. Skalka & Stephen P. Goff. LC 92-28740. (Monographs: Vol. 23). 448p. 1993. 49.00 (0-87969-382-7) Cold Spring Harbor.

Reverse Transcriptase PCR. Ed. by James A. Larrick & Paul D. Siebert. 346p. 1995. 140.00 (0-13-123118-9, Pub. by Tay Francis Ltd UK) Taylor & Francis.

Reversed Realities: Gender Hierarchies in Development Thought. Naila Kabeer. LC 94-7499. 346p. (C). 1994. pap. text ed. 19.00 (0-86091-584-0, Pub. by Vrso UK) Norton.

Reversed Realities: Gender Hierarchies in Development Thought. Naila Kabeer. LC 94-7499. 240p. (C). (gr. 13). 1994. text ed. 65.00 (0-86091-384-8, Pub. by Vrso UK) Norton.

Reversed Thunder: The Revelation of John & the Praying Imagination. Eugene H. Peterson. 1991. pap. 12.00 (0-06-066503-3) Harper SF.

Reversibility & Stochastic Networks. F. P. Kelly. LC 79-40515. (Probability & Mathematical Statistics Ser.). 230p. 1979. text ed. 219.00 (0-471-27601-4, Wiley-Interscience) Wiley.

Reversibility in Testicular Toxicity Assessment. Anthony R. Scialli. 192p. 1992. 118.00 (0-8493-5980-5, RA1224) CRC Pr.

Reversible Airway Obstruction: Neurohumoral Mechanisms & Treatment. Ed. by S. Bianco et al. (Journal: Respiration: Vol. 50, Suppl. 2, 1986). (Illus.). vi, 326p. 1987. pap. 94.50 (3-8055-4524-X) S Karger.

Reversible Crystal Plasticity. Vladimir S. Boyko et al. LC 93-32750. (Illus.). 294p. 1994. text ed. 85.00 (0-88318-869-4, AIP) Am Inst Physics.

Reversible Error. Robert K. Tanenbaum. 448p. 1993. reprint ed. pap. 5.99 (0-451-17519-0, Sig) NAL-Dutton.

Reversible Errors in Federal Criminal Cases. James R. Folsom. 575p. 1994. 150.00 (1-878337-36-X) Knowles Law.

Reversible Grammar in Natural Language Processing. Ed. by Tomek Strzalkowski. LC 93-38821. 476p. (C). 1993. lib. bdg. 161.00 (0-7923-9416-X) Kluwer Ac.

*__Reversible Map of France.__ 1996. 8.95 (2-06-700916-8, 916) Michelin.

Reversible Polymeric Gels & Related Systems. Ed. by Paul S Russo. LC 87-20305. (Symposium Ser.: No. 350). (Illus.). x, 324p. 1987. 71.95 (0-8412-1415-8) Am Chemical.

*__Reversible Polymeric Gels & Related Systems.__ Ed. by Paul S. Russo. LC 87-20305. (ACS Symposium Ser.: Vol. 350). 304p. 1987. reprint ed. pap. 86.70 (0-608-03873-3, 2064320) Bks Demand.

Reversible Systems. M. B. Sevryuk. (Lecture Notes in Mathematics Ser.: Vol. 1211). v, 319p. 1987. 40.95 (0-387-16819-2) Spr-Verlag.

Reversing Africa's Decline. Lester R. Brown & Edward C. Wolf. LC 85-51311. (Worldwatch Papers). 1985. pap. 5.00 (0-916468-65-8) Worldwatch Inst.

Reversing Ageing. Paul Galbraith. (Illus.). 236p. (C). 1995. pap. 12.95 (1-882330-37-4) Magni Co.

Reversing Asthma: Reduce Your Medications with This Revolutionary New Drug Program. Richard N. Firshein. 352p. 1996. 24.95 (0-446-51823-9) Warner Bks.

***Reversing Asthma: Reduce Your Medications with This Revolutionary New Drug Program.** Richard N. Firshein. 384p. 1998. pap. 12.99 (0-446-67363-3) Warner Bks.

Reversing Course: Carter's Foreign Policy, Domestic Politics, & the Failure of Reform. David G. Skidmore. LC 95-45293. 256p. (C). 1996. 29.95 (0-8265-1273-9) Vanderbilt U Pr.

Reversing Diabetes. Julian M. Whitaker. 1990. pap. 14.99 (0-446-38563-8) Warner Bks.

Reversing Discrimination: The Case for Affirmative Action. Gerald Horne. Ed. by Betty Smith. LC 92-20622. (Illus.). 132p. (Orig.). 1992. pap. 6.95 (0-7178-0695-2) Intl Pubs Co.

Reversing Heart Disease. Julian M. Whitaker. LC 84-40089. (Illus.). 272p. 1988. pap. 13.99 (0-446-38548-4) Warner Bks.

Reversing Human Aging. Michael Fossel. 1996. 25.00 (0-614-96996-4) Morrow.

Reversing Human Aging. Michael Fossel. LC 95-36636. 1996. 25.00 (0-688-14324-5) Morrow.

***Reversing Human Aging.** Michael Fossel. 320p. 1997. pap. 16.00 (0-688-15384-4, Quill) Morrow.

Reversing Industrial Decline? Industrial Structure in Britain & Her Competitors. Ed. by Paul Hirst & Jonathan Zeitlin. 303p. 1989. 38.95 (0-85496-029-5) Berg Pubs.

Reversing Landscape History: Power, Policy & Socialised Ecology in West Africa's Forest-Savanna Mosaic. Melissa Leach & James Fairhead. Date not set. text ed. 90.00 (0-471-96637-1) Wiley.

Reversing Language Shift: Theoretical & Empirical Foundations of Assistance to Threatened Languages. Joshua A. Fishman. (Multilingual Matters Ser.: No. 76). 500p. 1991. 99.00 (1-85359-122-X, Pub. by Multilingual Matters UK); pap. 36.00 (1-85359-121-1, Pub. by Multilingual Matters UK) Taylor & Francis.

Reversing Memory Loss: Medically Proven Methods for Regaining, Strengthening, & Preserving... Vernon H. Mark. 256p. 1993. pap. 12.95 (0-395-65371-1) HM.

Reversing Regional Economic Decline: A Supplement to Exchange Bibliography No. 1193. Nan C. Burg. 1977. 1.50 (0-686-19121-8, Sage Prdcls Pr) Sage.

Reversing the Aging Process. Gene Davis. 332p. (Orig.). 1987. pap. 29.95 (0-9618919-0-4) Life Res Found.

***Reversing the Aging Process: Twelve Steps Toward Growing Younger.** Kimberly Wittman. 95p. (Orig.). 1997. mass mkt. 9.95 (1-885351-22-4) Cheval Intl.

Reversing the Arms Race: How to Achieve & Verify Deep Reductions in the Nuclear Arsenals, Vol. 1. Ed. by F. Von Hippel & R. Z. Sagdeev. 432p. pap. text ed. 34.00 (2-88124-390-8) Gordon & Breach.

Reversing the Arms Race: How to Achieve & Verify Deep Reductions in the Nuclear Arsenals, Vol. 1. Ed. by F. Von Hippel & R. Z. Sagdeev. 432p. 1990. text ed. 68.00 (2-88124-436-X) Gordon & Breach.

Reversing the Conquest: History & Myth in Nineteenth-Century British Literature. Clare A. Simmons. LC 89-48882. 275p. (C). 1990. text ed. 45.00 (0-8135-1555-6) Rutgers U Pr.

***Reversing the Conquest: History & Myth in Nineteenth-Century British Literature.** Clare A. Simmons. LC 89-48882. 275p. (C). 1990. text ed. 45.00 (0-8135-1549-1) Rutgers U Pr.

Reversing the Flow: A Practical Guide to Bay Area Corporate Giving Programs. rev. ed. Intro. by Gary Delgado. 132p. (Orig.). 1993. pap. 49.95 (0-9636725-0-9) Appl Res Ctr.

Reversing the Nuclear Arms Race. Carla B. Johnson. 180p. (Orig.). (C). 1986. text ed. 18.95 (0-87047-032-9); pap. text ed. 11.25 (0-87047-033-7) Schenkman Bks Inc.

***Reversing the Spell: New & Selected Poems.** Eleanor Wilner. 1997. pap. 17.00 (0-614-29389-8) Copper Canyon.

***Reversing the Spell: New & Selected Poems.** Eleanor Wilner. 1997. pap. text ed. 16.00 (1-55659-082-2) Copper Canyon.

Reversing the Spiral: The Population, Agriculture, & Environment Nexus in Sub-Saharan Africa. Kevin M. Cleaver & Gotz A. Schreiber. LC 94-9060. (Directions in Development Ser.). 1994. 18.95 (0-8213-2769-0, 12769) World Bank.

Reversing Underachievement among Gifted Black Students: Promising Practices & Programs. Donna Y. Ford. LC 95-52527. (Education & Psychology of the Gifted Ser.: Vol. 11). 256p. (C). 1996. text ed. 52.00 (0-8077-3536-1); pap. text ed. 24.95 (0-8077-3535-3) Tchrs Coll.

Reversion: Piles of That. John M. Bennett. (Illus.). 252p. (Orig.). 1994. pap. 30.00 (0-935350-53-5) Luna Bisonte.

Reverting to Despotism: Human Rights in Haiti. Americas Watch Staff. 156p. 1990. 10.00 (0-929692-55-1, Am Watch) Hum Rts Watch.

***Reves De Gloire.** Andre Vanasse. (Novels in the Roman Plus Ser.). 160p. (FRE.). (YA). (gr. 8 up). 1996. pap. 7.95 (2-89021-234-3, Pub. by Les Editions CN) Firefly Bks Ltd.

Reveuse Bourgeoisie. Pierre Drieu La Rochelle. (FRE.). 1976. pap. 12.95 (0-7859-1793-4, 2070366200) Fr & Eur.

Revi-Lona: A Romance of Love in a Marvelous Land. Frank Cowan. Ed. by R. Reginald & Douglas Melville. LC 77-84216. (Lost Race & Adult Fantasy Ser.). 1978. reprint ed. lib. bdg. 24.95 (0-405-10971-7) Ayer.

Reviens, Snoopy. Charles M. Schulz. (Peanuts Ser.). 48p. (FRE.). (J). 1982. 10.95 (0-8288-4554-9) Fr & Eur.

Reviens, Snoopy: Presses Pocket. Charles M. Schulz. (Peanuts Ser.). 124p. (FRE.). (J). 1989. 10.95 (0-8288-4555-7) Fr & Eur.

***Review.** Ed. by James O. Hoge. 300p. 1997. text ed. 45.00 (0-8139-1769-7) U Pr of Va.

Review, Vol. 1. Ed. by James O. Hoge & James L. West, III. 345p. 1979. text ed. 40.00 (0-8139-0760-8) U Pr of Va.

Review, Vol. 2. Ed. by James O. Hoge & James L. West, III. 416p. 1980. text ed. 40.00 (0-8139-0865-5) U Pr of Va.

Review, Vol. 3. Ed. by James O. Hoge & James L. West, III. 346p. 1981. text ed. 40.00 (0-8139-0910-4) U Pr of Va.

Review, Vol. 4. Ed. by James O. Hoge & James L. West, III. 350p. 1983. text ed. 40.00 (0-8139-0974-0) U Pr of Va.

Review, Vol. 5. Ed. by James O. Hoge & James L. West, III. 224p. 1983. text ed. 40.00 (0-8139-1005-6) U Pr of Va.

Review, Vol. 6. Ed. by James O. Hoge & James L. West, III. xi, 332p. 1984. text ed. 40.00 (0-8139-1031-5) U Pr of Va.

Review, Vol. 7. Ed. by James O. Hoge & James L. West, III. xiv, 348p. 1985. text ed. 40.00 (0-8139-1076-5) U Pr of Va.

Review, Vol. 8. Ed. by James O. Hoge & James L. West, III. 304p. 1987. text ed. 40.00 (0-8139-1113-3) U Pr of Va.

Review, Vol. 9. Ed. by James O. Hoge & James L. West, III. 356p. (C). 1988. text ed. 40.00 (0-8139-1160-5) U Pr of Va.

Review, Vol. 11. Ed. by James O. Hoge, III & James L. West. x, 323p. 1989. text ed. 40.00 (0-8139-1252-0) U Pr of Va.

Review, Vol. 12. Ed. by James O. Hoge & James L. West, III. 326p. 1990. text ed. 40.00 (0-8139-1310-1) U Pr of Va.

Review, Vol. 14. Ed. by James O. Hoge & James L. West, III. 306p. (C). 1992. text ed. 40.00 (0-8139-1410-8) U Pr of Va.

Review, Vol. 16. Ed. by James O. Hoge. 335p. (C). 1994. text ed. 40.00 (0-8139-1535-X) U Pr of Va.

Review, Vol. 17. James O. Hoge. 310p. (C). 1995. text ed. 40.00 (0-8139-1635-6) U Pr of Va.

Review, Vol. 18. Ed. by James O. Hoge. 300p. 1996. text ed. 40.00 (0-8139-1691-7) U Pr of Va.

Review: A Book of Poems. Mark DeCarteret. (Illus.). 88p. (Orig.). 1995. pap. 8.95 (1-886963-01-0) Kettle of Fish.

Review: Fall 1989, Vol. 79-1. Yale. 1986. pap. text ed. 6.00 (0-300-09991-6) Yale U Pr.

Review: Spring 1990, Vol. 79-3. Yale. 1990. pap. text ed. 6.00 (0-300-09993-2) Yale U Pr.

Review: Winter 1989, Vol. 79-2. Yale. 1986. pap. text ed. 6.00 (0-300-09992-4) Yale U Pr.

Review & Abstract of the County Reports to the Board of Agriculture, 5 vols., Vols. 1-5. William Marshall. LC 69-11853. 1968. reprint ed. 295.00 (0-678-05613-7) Kelley.

Review & Analysis of the Progress Made in the Implementation of the SNPA in the Least Developed Countries in the ESCWA Region. 100p. 1991. 20.00 (92-1-128115-6, 90.II.L.5) UN.

***Review & Annotated Bibliography of Family Business Studies.** Pramodita Sharma & Jess H. Chua. Ed. by James J. Chrisman. LC 96-38175. 296p. (C). 1996. lib. bdg. 99.95 (0-7923-9783-5) Kluwer Ac.

Review & Appraisal of the World Population Plan of Action. 169p. 1986. pap. 14.00 (92-1-151158-5, E.86. XIII.2) UN.

Review & Appraisal of the World Population Plan of Action. 53p. 1989. pap. text ed. 5.50 (92-1-151185-2, E. 89.XIII.11) UN.

***Review & Appraisal of the World Population Plan of Action: 1994 Report.** Department for Economic & Social Information & Policy Analysis Staff. 149p. 1996. pap. 10.00 (92-1-151299-9, 68803) UN.

Review & Evaluation of Alternative Chemical Disposal Technologies. National Research Council, Panel on Review & Evaluation of Alternative Chemical Disposal Techs. 272p. (Orig.). (C). 1996. pap. text ed. 45.00 (0-309-05525-3) Natl Acad Pr.

Review & Evaluation of Appearance: Method & Techniques, STP 914. Ed. by Jay J. Rennilson & W. N. Hale, Jr. LC 86-7999. (Special Technical Publication Ser.). (Illus.). 112p. 1986. text ed. 24.00 (0-8031-0480-4, 04-914000-36) ASTM.

Review & Evaluation of Literature Pertaining to the Quantity & Control of Pollution from Highway Runoff & Construction. Michael E. Barrett et al. (Illus.). 140p. (Orig.). (C). 1995. pap. text ed. 35.00 (0-7881-1949-4) DIANE Pub.

Review & Evaluation of Smoking Cessation Methods: The U. S. & Canada, 1978-1985. Jerome L. Schwartz. (Illus.). 200p. (Orig.). (C). 1992. pap. text ed. 40.00 (1-56806-109-9) DIANE Pub.

Review & Index Through 1975 of Genus Candona (Ostracoda) in North America (Exclusive of Pre-Quaternary Species) Larry N. Stout. LC 76-47833. (Microform Publication: No. 6). (Illus.). 1976. 1.25 incl. mic. film (0-8137-6006-2) Geol Soc.

Review & Outlook for the World Oil Market. Shane S. Streifel. LC 95-24918. (World Bank Discussion Paper Ser.: Vol. 301). 170p. 1995. 10.95 (0-8213-3443-3, 13443) World Bank.

Review & Reduction of Real Property Assessments in New York. 3rd ed. Harry O. Lee et al. Ed. by Jill Nagy. LC 88-43298. 600p. 1988. 95.00 (0-942954-22-X, 4A1264) NYS Bar.

Review & Reduction of Real Property Assessments in New York-1994 Supplement. Harry O. Lee & Jill Nagy. 68p. 1994. pap. text ed. 25.00 (0-942954-70-X) NYS Bar.

Review & Synthesis of Research at Historical Sites see Final Report of the New Melones Archeological Project, California

Review & Synthesis of Research in Trade & Industrial Education. 3rd ed. Curtis R. Finch. 60p. 1983. 4.95 (0-318-22193-4, IN260) Ctr Educ Trng Employ.

Review Appraiser's Handbook: How to Review a Fannie Mae - Freddie Mac Residential Appraisal. 2nd ed. Henry S. Harrison. (Illus.). 432p. (C). 1990. pap. text ed. 34.95 (0-927054-04-3) H Sq Co.

***Review Book for Invasive CV Technology Vol. III: Hemodynamics.** 1997. spiral bd. 80.00 (0-9653568-5-X) Cardiac Self Assessmnt.

Review Book for MRA & MRT Certification Exam. Beth H. Anderson & Kimberly Suggs. (Health Services Administration Ser.). (Illus.). 200p. 1996. text ed. 23.95 (0-8273-6897-6) Delmar.

Review Book for the CLEP General Social Science Examination. Ann Garvin & Eileen Curristine. 335p. (C). 1996. pap. text ed. 12.95 (1-56030-002-7) Comex Systs.

Review Book for the CLEP Humanities Exam. Brian Eckert. (Illus.). 250p. (C). 1994. pap. text ed. 12.95 (1-56030-004-3) Comex Systs.

Review Book on Ophthalmology. S. Seal. (C). 1986. 49.00 (0-685-36206-X, Pub. by Current Dist II) St Mut.

***Review Course for the NESPA.** large type ed. Ed. by Chad Nye. (Illus.). 208p. 1997. 125.00 incl. audio (1-56593-741-4, 1440) Singular Publishing.

Review Cracking the GRE - Biology: 1997 Edition. Paul Johnson. (Princeton Review Ser.). 200p. 1996. pap. 18. 00 (0-679-76921-8, Random Ref) Random.

Review Cracking the SAT & PSAT: With Sample Tests on CD-ROM, 1997 Edition. Adam Robinson & John Katzman. (Princeton Review Ser.). 520p. 1996. pap. text ed., pap. 29.95 incl. cd-rom (0-679-77110-7, Villard Bks) Random.

***Review First Grade (Language)** Jo E. Moore. (Reading & Writing Ser.). (Illus.). 32p. (J). (gr. 1). 1996. teacher ed., pap. 2.95 (1-55799-431-5, 4033) Evan-Moor Corp.

Review for Anatomy & Physiology I Lecture-Lab with Illustrations. William C. Kleinelp. (Illus.). 8.50 (0-929941-19-5) Wood River Pubns.

Review for Anatomy & Physiology II Lecture-Lab with Illustrations. William C. Kleinelp. 8.50 (0-929941-20-9) Wood River Pubns.

Review for CLEP General English Composition. rev. ed. Rosemary Lewis. 245p. (C). 1996. pap. text ed. 12.95 (1-56030-001-9) Comex Systs.

Review for CLEP General Natural Science Exam. James R. Frendak. (Illus.). 192p. (C). 1996. pap. text ed. 12.95 (1-56030-003-5) Comex Systs.

Review for Danforth's Obstetrics & Gynecology. 7th ed. James R. Scott. LC 93-29365. 168p. 1994. Text & review. pap. text ed. 24.95 (0-397-51407-7) Lppncott-Raven.

Review for FMGENS. (National Medical Ser.). 1988. 37.00 (0-685-75188-0) Williams & Wilkins.

***Review for Intensive Care Medicine, Vol. 1.** Mark W. Sebastian et al. 400p. 1997. pap. text ed. 49.95 (0-316-73633-3, Little Med Div) Lppncott-Raven.

Review for Medicine of the Fetus & Mother. E. Albert Reece et al. LC 92-25643. 210p. 1992. pap. text ed. 19. 95 (0-397-51331-3) Lppncott-Raven.

***Review for Surgery: Scientific Principles & Practice.** 2nd ed. Greenfield et al. (Illus.). 528p. 1996. pap. text ed., pap. 39.95 incl. mac hd (0-397-51831-5) Lppncott-Raven.

Review for Surgery: Scientific Principles & Practice. 2nd ed. Lazar Greenfield. LC 96-26947. 496p. 1996. pap. text ed. 39.95 (0-397-51582-0) Lppncott-Raven.

Review for the CLEP General Examinations. Brian Eckert et al. (Review for the CLEP General Examinations Ser.). (C). 1995. pap. text ed. 64.75 (1-56030-088-4) Comex Systs.

This series of five study guides prepares a student for all the CLEP general examinations. There are separate books for each of the examinations: English Composition, Natural Science, Humanities, Social Science, & Mathematics. There is no better way to study for the CLEP examinations. Each book is complete. There is a subject matter review covering all the material on the examination. This allows a student to refresh knowledge that they have acquired during their life. Each book contains extensive exercises for a student to practice his knowledge. The best way to learn is by solving problems. Finally, each book has a sample test so that a student is able to see if he is ready to take the examination. The books can also be used in conjunction with Comex Systems, Inc.'s video tapes that help people prepare for the CLEP general examinations. Many libraries, military installations & colleges throughout the world have copies of the tapes available for students to use. Remember to think of Comex Systems, Inc. when you are considering test preparation materials. Our twenty years of experience & teacher tested materials make us the right choice.

Publisher Provided Annotation.

Review for the CLEP General Mathematics Examination. Michael O'Donnell. (Illus.). 192p. (C). 1997. pap. text ed. 12.95 (1-56030-000-0) Comex Systs.

***Review for the CLEP Introduction to Management Exam.** Donald Hovey. 196p. (C). 1994. pap. text ed. 12.95 (1-56030-091-4) Comex Systs.

Review for the College Entrance Examinations. student ed., pap. text ed. 12.95 (1-56030-009-4) Comex Systs.

Review for the GMAT. 1994. student ed., pap. text ed. 12. 95 (1-56030-082-5) Comex Systs.

Review for the Graduate Record Examination. Madeleine Argue et al. 350p. (C). 1992. pap. text ed. 12.95 (1-56030-011-6) Comex Systs.

Review for the Professional Engineer's Examination for Industrial Engineers. rev. ed. Donovan Young. LC 93-28424. 400p. 1996. 49.95 (0-89806-134-2) Eng Mgmt Pr.

Review for USMLA, Step 1. 3rd ed. (National Medical Ser.). 1994. 29.95 (0-685-75189-9) Williams & Wilkins.

***Review for USMLE.** 4th ed. John S. Lazo. (National Medical Ser.). 1996. pap. 33.00 (0-683-06276-X) Williams & Wilkins.

Review for USMLE, Step 2. 1994. 29.95 (0-685-75190-2) Williams & Wilkins.

Review for USMLE: United States Medical Licensing Examination, Step 1. John S. Lazo et al. LC 93-41661. (National Medical Series for Independent Study). (Illus.). 300p. 1994. 29.95 (0-683-06265-4) Williams & Wilkins.

Review for USMLE: United States Medical Licensing Examination, Step 1. 4th ed. Barbara Fadem et al. LC 93-41661. (National Medical Series for Independent Study). 102p. 1996. write for info. (0-683-02940-1) Williams & Wilkins.

Review for USMLE: United States Medical Licensing Examination, Step 2. Victor Gruber. LC 94-17360. (National Medical Series for Independent Study). 1994. 29.95 (0-683-06207-7) Williams & Wilkins.

***Review Kindergarten (Language)** Jo E. Moore. (Reading & Writing Ser.). (Illus.). 32p. (J). (gr. k). 1996. teacher ed., pap. 2.95 (1-55799-430-7, 4032) Evan-Moor Corp.

Review Manual for the National Nursing Home Administrators Examination. Robert W. Haacker. 127p. (C). 1987. 30.00 (0-929442-04-0) Publicare Pr.

Review Manual of Health Information: Management of Strategic Resources. Abdelhak. 1996. pap. text ed. 30. 00 (0-7216-5148-8) Saunders.

Review Materials for FLEX, National Board & Other Examinations: A Bibliography. 93p. (Orig.). (C). 1993. pap. text ed. 30.00 (1-56806-308-3) DIANE Pub.

Review of Ada Tasking. Alan Burns et al. (Lecture Notes in Computer Science Ser.: Vol. 262). viii, 141p. 1989. 22.00 (0-387-18008-7) Spr-Verlag.

Review of Administrative Action. Mark Aronson & Nicola Franklin. lxvii, 720p. 1987. 130.00 (0-455-20721-6, Pub. by Law Bk Co AT); pap. 94.50 (0-455-20722-4, Pub. by Law Bk Co AT) Gaunt.

Review of Administrative Acts: A Comparative Study of the Doctrine of Separation of Powers & Judicial Review in France & the U. S. Armin Uhler. LC 42-36733. (Michigan Legal Publications). xxxi, 207p. 1942. 43.50 (1-57588-357-0, 301710) W S Hein.

Review of Adult & Pediatric Urology. 3rd ed. Stuart S. Howards. 222p. (C). (gr. 13). 1995. pap. text ed. 46.95 (0-8151-4713-9) Mosby Yr Bk.

Review of African Granulites & Related Rocks. Tom N. Clifford. LC 74-84196. (Geological Society of America, Special Paper Ser.: No. 156). 54p. reprint ed. pap. 25.00 (0-317-28368-5, 2025471) Bks Demand.

Review of Agricultural Policies: Czech Republic. 298p. (Orig.). 1995. pap. 65.00 (92-64-14656-3, Pub. by Org for Econ FR) OECD.

***Review of Agricultural Policies: Estonia.** OECD Staff. 232p. (Orig.). 1996. pap. 50.00 (92-64-15348-9, 14-96-12-1) OECD.

Review of Agricultural Policies: Hungary. OECD Staff. 222p. (Orig.). 1994. pap. 49.00 (92-64-14055-7) OECD.

***Review of Agricultural Policies: Latvia.** OECD Staff. 240p. (Orig.). 1996. pap. 50.00 (92-64-15349-7, 14-96-13-1) OECD.

***Review of Agricultural Policies: Lithuania.** OECD Staff. 238p. (Orig.). 1996. pap. 50.00 (92-64-15350-0, 14-96-14-1) OECD.

Review of Agricultural Policies: Poland. 288p. (Orig.). 1995. pap. 56.00 (92-64-14310-6) OECD.

Review of Allied Health Education, Vol. 1. Ed. by Joseph Hamburg et al. LC 74-7876. 244p. 1974. reprint ed. pap. 69.60 (0-7837-5719-0, 2045442) Bks Demand.

Review of Allied Health Education, Vol. 2. Ed. by Joseph Hamburg et al. 200p. 1974. reprint ed. pap. 57.00 (0-318-71724-7, 2030052) Bks Demand.

Review of Allied Health Education, Vol. 3. Ed. by Joseph Hamburg. LC 74-7876. 167p. 1974. reprint ed. pap. 47. 60 (0-685-16439-X, 2027364) Bks Demand.

Review of Allied Health Education, Vol. 4. Ed. by Joseph Hamburg et al. LC 74-7876. 158p. 1974. reprint ed. Vol. 2, 158p. pap. 45.10 (0-7837-5720-4, 2045442) Bks Demand.

Review of Allied Health Education, Vol. 5. Ed. by Joseph Hamburg et al. LC 74-7876. 175p. 1994. reprint ed. pap. 49.90 (0-7837-5721-2, 2045442) Bks Demand.

***Review of Allium Section.** Brian Mathew. (Illus.). 1996. pap. 42.00 (0-947643-93-1, Pub. by Royal Botnic Grdns UK) Balogh.

Review of American Colonial Legislation by the King in Council. Elmer B. Russell. Ed. by R. H. Helmholz & Bernard D. Reams, Jr. LC 80-84869. (Historical Writings in Law & Jurisprudence Ser.: Title No. 21, Bk. 31). 230p. 1981. reprint ed. lib. bdg. 42.00 (*0-89941-083-9*, 302370) W S Hein.

Review of Amino Acid Transport Processes in Animal Cells & Tissues. Joseph Lerner. LC 78-55683. 1977. text ed. 8.00 (*0-89101-036-X*) U Maine Pr.

Review of Anglican Orders: The Problem & the Solution. George H. Tavard. (Theology & Life Ser.: Vol. 31). 170p. (C). 1990. pap. 14.95 (*0-8146-5800-8*) Liturgical Pr.

Review of Annulation. M. Jung. Ed. by Derek H. Barton. 1976. pap. 12.75 (*0-08-020621-2*, Pergamon Pr) Elsevier.

Review of Antitumor Substances Investigated in Organizations of the Former U. S. S. R. A. B. Syrkin & G. N. Apryshko. LC 92-75532. 98p. 1993. 430.00 (*0-927230-10-0*) Brandon Associates.

Review of Approaches to Viral Chemotherapy. Maxwell Gordon et al. 96p. 1981. 35.00 (*0-915340-08-9*) PJD Pubns.

Review of Austrian Economics, 1990, Vol. 4. Ed. by Murray N. Rothbard. (C). 1990. lib. bdg. 71.00 (*0-7923-9064-4*) Kluwer Ac.

Review of Automated Enforcement (for Traffic Safety) Kay Fitzpatrick. (Illus.). 57p. (Orig.). (C). 1994. pap. text ed. 30.00 (*0-7881-0305-9*) DIANE Pub.

Review of Behavior Therapy, Vol. 11: Theory & Practice. G. Terence Wilson et al. 404p. 1987. lib. bdg. 57.50 (*0-89862-751-6*) Guilford Pr.

Review of Behavior Therapy, Vol. 12: Theory & Practice. Cyril M. Franks et al. Ed. by G. Terence Wilson et al. 382p. 1990. lib. bdg. 57.50 (*0-89862-752-4*) Guilford Pr.

Review of Bible Critique. Johan E. Graae. 1993. 16.50 (*0-533-10355-X*) Vantage.

Review of Biostatistics. 3rd ed. Paul E. Leaverton. 128p. 1986. pap. 16.50 (*0-316-51853-0*) Little.

Review of Biostatistics: A Program for Self-Instruction. 3rd ed. Paul E. Leaverton. 1986. spiral bd. 12.00 (*0-316-51852-2*, Little Med Div) Little.

Review of Biostatistics: A Program for Self-Instruction. 5th ed. Paul E. Leaverton. LC 94-22888. 144p. 1995. spiral bd. 22.95 (*0-316-51883-2*) Lppncott-Raven.

Review of Canadian Securities: Quarterly. David Coghlan. 1995. 4.85 (*1-888279-00-1*) Re Can Sec.

*__Review of Canadian Securities-Quarterly.__ (Spring 97 Ser.: No. 3). 190p. (Orig.). (C). 1997. pap. 24.95 (*1-888279-06-0*) Re Can Sec.

Review of Caste in India. J. Murdoch. 110p. 1977. 14.95 (*0-318-36811-0*) Asia Bk Corp.

Review of Child Development Research, 2 vols., Set. Ed. by Martin L. Hoffman & Lois W. Hoffman. LC 64-20472. write for info. (*0-87154-383-4*) Russell Sage.

Review of Child Development Research, 2 Vols, Vol. 1. Ed. by Martin L. Hoffman & Lois W. Hoffman. LC 64-20472. 548p. 1964. 55.00 (*0-87154-384-2*) Russell Sage.

Review of Child Development Research, 2 Vols, Vol. 2. Ed. by Martin L. Hoffman & Lois W. Hoffman. LC 64-20472. 598p. 1966. 55.00 (*0-87154-385-0*) Russell Sage.

Review of Child Development Research, Vol. 3. Bettye M. Caldwell & Henry N. Ricciuti. 600p. 1976. pap. text ed. 10.00 (*0-226-09044-2*, P680) U Ch Pr.

Review of Child Development Research, Vol. 4. Frances D. Horowitz. 720p. 1975. lib. bdg. 30.00 (*0-226-35353-2*) U Ch Pr.

Review of Child Development Research, Vol. 6. Ed. by Willard W. Hartup. LC 64-20472. (Review of Child Development Research Ser.). 800p. (C). 1982. lib. bdg. 48.00 (*0-226-31873-7*) U Ch Pr.

Review of Child Development Research, Vol. 7. Ed. by Ross D. Parke. LC 64-20472. (Review of Child Development Research Ser.). x, 480p. 1985. lib. bdg. 36.00 (*0-226-64666-1*) U Ch Pr.

Review of Clinical Anesthesia. 2nd ed. David Silverman. LC 96-47931. 288p. 1997. pap. text ed. 39.95 (*0-397-58734-1*) Lppncott-Raven.

Review of Colombia's Agriculture & Rural Development Strategy. LC 96-2153. (Country Study Ser.). 134p. 1996. 9.95 (*0-8213-3622-3*, 13622) World Bank.

Review of Cosmic Rays: Sesquicentennial Celebration Proceedings. Thomas H. Johnson. (Connecticut Academy of Arts & Sciences Ser., Trans.: Vol. 38, Pt. 3). 1950. pap. 29.50 (*0-685-22899-1*) Elliots Bks.

Review of Cost-Effective Office Products, 1993: The Office Products on Today's Market That Improve Your Productivity & - or Reduce Your Costs. Al Toth. (Illus.). 352p. 1993. 29.95 (*1-881624-16-1*) PBM Pub.

Review of Country Case Studies on Climate Change. Jan Fuglestvedt et al. (Working Papers: No. 7). 61p. (Orig.). (C). 1994. pap. 6.95 (*1-884122-06-X*) Global Environ.

Review of Critical Care Nursing. Branum. (Illus.). 752p. (C). (gr. 13 up). 1996. pap. text ed. 36.95 (*0-8016-0128-2*) Mosby Yr Bk.

Review of Critical Care Nursing: Case Studies & Applications. Sheila D. Melander. Ed. by Barbara N. Cullen. 400p. 1996. pap. text ed. 30.00 (*0-7216-5537-8*) Saunders.

*__Review of Current Gear Tooth Cutting & Forming Equipment Symposium.__ AGMA Discussion Group. (Technical Papers: Vol. 129.14). 1961. pap. text ed. 30.00 (*1-55589-135-7*) AGMA.

Review of Dental Assisting. Hazel O. Torres & Lois E. Mazzucchi. (Illus.). 350p. 1983. pap. text ed. 35.95 (*0-7216-8883-7*) Saunders.

Review of Developments in Plane Strain Fracture Toughness Testing - STP 463. 275p. 1970. 18.25 (*0-8031-0037-X*, 04-463000-30) ASTM.

Review of Diagnosis, Oral Medicine, Radiology, & Treatment Planning. 3rd ed. Norman K. Wood. LC 92-12906. 373p. (C). (gr. 13). 1992. pap. text ed. 48.00 (*0-8016-6523-X*) Mosby Yr Bk.

Review of Diaphragm Walls. 152p. 1977. 18.00 (*0-7277-0045-6*, Pub. by T Telford UK) Am Soc Civil Eng.

Review of Doctor Johnson's New Edition of Shakespeare. W. Kenrick. LC 78-144647. reprint ed. 37.50 (*0-404-03659-7*) AMS Pr.

*__Review of Economic Doctrines: 1953 Edition.__ T. W. Hutchison. 480p. 1996. reprint ed. write for info. (*1-85506-240-2*) Bks Intl VA.

Review of Economic Doctrines, 1870-1929. Terence W. Hutchison. LC 74-9273. 456p. 1975. reprint ed. text ed. 41.50 (*0-8371-7637-9*, HURE, Greenwood Pr) Greenwood.

Review of Edwards's "Inquiry into the Freedom of the Will" Henry P. Tappan. LC 75-3412. reprint ed. 55.00 (*0-404-59406-9*) AMS Pr.

Review of Elementary Mathematics. Barnett Rich. (Schaum's Outline Ser.). (Orig.). 1977. pap. text ed. 11.95 (*0-07-052260-X*) McGraw.

Review of Environmental Contamination & Toxicology, Vol. 135. Ed. by G. W. Ware. (Illus.). 160p. 1994. 69.95 (*0-387-94192-4*) Spr-Verlag.

Review of Environmental Health Impacts in Developing Country Cities. David J. Bradley et al. LC 92-24094. (Urban Management Program Ser.: No. 6). 71p. 1992. 6.95 (*0-8213-2194-3*, 12194) World Bank.

Review of EPA's Environmental Monitoring & Assessment Program: Overall Evaluation. 1995. pap. text ed. 35.00 (*0-309-05286-6*) Natl Acad Sci.

*__Review of Eriope & Eriopidion (Labiatae)__ R. M. Harley. 107p. 1976. 15.00 (*0-614-21736-9*, Pub. by Royal Botnic Grdns UK) Balogh.

Review of Essentials of Accounting. Robert N. Anthony. (Illus.). (C). 1988. pap. text ed. 26.95 (*0-201-05905-3*) Addison-Wesley.

Review of Essentials of Accounting. 5th ed. Robert N. Anthony. LC 92-34805. (Illus.). 176p. (C). 1993. pap. text ed. 20.50 (*0-201-51287-4*) Addison-Wesley.

Review of Essentials of Accounting. 6th ed. Robert N. Anthony. Ed. by James Rigney. 192p. (C). 1997. pap. text ed. 20.50 (*0-201-44278-7*) Addison-Wesley.

Review of Fiscal, Monetary & Banking Policy in the ESCWA Region. (Economic & Social Commission for Western Asia (ESCWA) Publications). 90p. (ARA & ENG.). 1991. 10.00 (*92-1-128078-8*, AE.88.II.L.2) UN.

Review of Fisheries in OECD Countries: 1995 Edition. OECD Staff. 338p. (Orig.). 1996. pap. 106.00 (*92-64-14770-5*, Pub. by Org for Econ FR) OECD.

*__Review of Fisheries in OECD Countries, 1994 (1996 Edition)__ OECD Staff. 384p. 1996. pap. 104.00 (*92-64-15289-X*, Pub. by Org for Econ FR) OECD.

Review of Fluoride: Benefits & Risks: Report of the Ad Hoc Subcommittee on Fluoride. (Illus.). 240p. (Orig.). (C). 1994. pap. text ed. 50.00 (*0-7881-0729-1*) DIANE Pub.

*__Review of Food Consumption Surveys, 1985: Household Food Consumption by Economic Groups.__ 236p. 1986. 30.00 (*92-5-102375-1*, F2953, Pub. by FAO IT) Bernan Associates.

Review of Forecasts: Scaling & Analysis of Expert Judgments Regarding Cross-Impacts of Assumptions on Business Forecasts & Accounting Measures, Vol. 19. Robert E. Jensen. LC 83-70703. (Studies in Accounting Research). 235p. 1983. 15.00 (*0-86539-044-4*) Am Accounting.

*__Review of General Population Surveys of Drug Abuse.__ L. Johnston. (WHO Offset Publications: No. 52). 57p. 1980. 7.00 (*92-4-170052-1*) World Health.

Review of General Psychiatry. 4th ed. Howard H. Goldman. (C). 1994. pap. text ed. 36.95 (*0-8385-8421-7*, A8421-8) Appleton & Lange.

*__Review of General Semantics.__ Ed. by S. I. Hayakawa. (Illus.). 402p. Date not set. 24.95 (*0-8369-2495-9*) Ayer.

Review of Gross Anatomy. 6th ed. Ben Pansky. LC 95-18531. (Illus.). 688p. 1995. pap. text ed. 39.00 (*0-07-105446-4*) McGraw-Hill HPD.

Review of Hamlet. George H. Miles. LC 77-172730. reprint ed. 29.50 (*0-404-04324-0*) AMS Pr.

Review of Health & Social Services for Mentally Disordered Offenders (Mental Handicap) or Autism. HMSO Staff. (People with Learning Disabilities Ser.: Vol. 7). 206p. 1994. pap. 45.00 (*0-11-321701-3*, HM17013, Pub. by Stationery Ofc UK) Bernan Associates.

Review of Health Effects Basis for SOC & IOC Standards. (Illus.). 228p. 1993. pap. 63.00 (*0-89867-658-4*, 90609) Am Water Wks Assn.

*__Review of Hemodialysis for Nurses & Dialysis Patients, No. 6.__ Eutch. (C). (gr. 13). 1998. pap. text ed. 34.95 (*0-8151-2099-0*, 28866) Mosby Yr Bk.

Review of Hemodialysis for Nurses & Dialysis Personnel. 5th ed. C. F. Gutch. 313p. (C). (gr. 13). 1993. pap. text ed. 35.95 (*0-8016-6476-4*) Mosby Yr Bk.

Review of History: The Qajars & Their Time. Abou N. Azod. Ed. by Ardeshir Lotfalian. LC 95-51789. (Illus.). 544p. (PER.). 1996. 25.00 (*0-936347-75-9*) Iran Bks.

Review of Hogg's "Memoirs of Prince Alexy Haimatoff" 2nd ed. Percy Bysshe Shelley. Ed. by E. Dowden & Thomas J. Wise. Bd. with Extract from "Some Early Writings of Shelley". LC 74-30285. LC 74-30285. (Shelley Society, Second Ser.: No. 2). reprint ed. 22.50 (*0-404-11504-7*) AMS Pr.

Review of Human Physiology. 3rd ed. H. Frank Winter & Melvin L. Shourd. (Illus.). 250p. 1987. pap. text ed. 32.50 (*0-7216-2085-X*) Saunders.

Review of Imagery Uses in Twentieth Century Literature. Wilson Merck. (Orig.). 1990. pap. 9.90 (*0-913412-15-5*) Brandon Hse.

Review of Innovative Approaches to College Teaching. Beatrice Gross & Ronald Gross. 68p. 1980. 12.00 (*0-86539-036-3*) Am Accounting.

Review of Internal Medicine. David Schlossberg. LC 96-28657. 300p. 1996. pap. text ed. 39.95 (*0-397-51580-4*, Lippncott) Lppncott-Raven.

Review of Juniperus Chinensis et al. P. J. Van Melle. (Illus.). 1947. pap. 20.00 (*0-934454-72-8*) Lubrecht & Cramer.

Review of Labor Economics: A-Selection of Recent Articles in Labor Economics. Bruce Smith. 134p. (C). 1991. pap. text ed. 54.95 (*0-9627882-6-0*) Bradley Mann.

Review of Legal Education in the United States - Fall 1994: Law School & Bar Admission Requirements. 77p. 1993. pap. write for info. (*0-318-68950-2*, 529-0058) Amer Bar Assn.

Review of LPG Cargo Quantity Calculations. SIGTTO Staff. (C). 1985. 90.00 (*0-900886-99-4*, Pub. by Witherby & Co UK) St Mut.

Review of Lysander Spooner's Essay on the Unconstitutionality of Slavery. Wendell Phillips. LC 76-82220. (Anti-Slavery Crusade in America Ser.). 1970. reprint ed. 11.95 (*0-405-00648-9*) Ayer.

Review of Mainstream CFIDS Research in the USA: 1990 - June 1992. Kendra Dayger. 271p. 1992. pap. 21.00 (*0-317-05542-9*) CFIDS Rochester.

*__Review of Managing Quality & a Primer for the Certified Quality Manager Exam.__ Thomas J. Cartin & Donald J. Jacoby. LC 97-2864. 322p. 1997. 25.00 (*0-87389-358-1*, H0917) ASQC Qual Pr.

Review of Manufacturing Technologies for Antibodies. 116p. 1992. 1,250.00 (*0-89336-917-9*, C-088S) BCC.

Review of Maritime Transport: 1991. 94p. 1992. 28.00 (*92-1-112322-4*) UN.

Review of Maritime Transport: 1992. 121p. 1994. 30.00 (*92-1-112336-4*) UN.

Review of Maritime Transport Nineteen Eighty-Nine. 1990. 17.00 (*92-1-112292-9*, E 90.II.D.7) UN.

Review of Maritime Transport, 1987. 1988. 21.00 (*92-1-112246-5*, E.88.II.D.6) UN.

Review of Maritime Transport, 1988. 91p. 20.00 (*92-1-112282-1*, E.89.II.D.16) UN.

*__Review of Maritime Transport, 1995.__ United Nations Conference on Trade & Development Staff. 147p. 1996. pap. 30.00 (*92-1-112403-4*, JX4131) UN.

Review of Marketing, 1987. Ed. by Michael J. Houston. (Illus.). 505p. 1988. text ed. 60.00 (*0-685-24077-0*) Am Mktg.

Review of Marketing, 1987. American Marketing Association Staff. Ed. by Michael J. Houston. LC 78-649100. 515p. 1987. reprint ed. pap. 146.80 (*0-7837-9765-6*, 2060493) Bks Demand.

Review of Marketing, 1990 Edition, Vol. 4. Valarie A. Zeithaml. LC 78-649100. 551p. 1990. text ed. 60.00 (*0-685-40031-X*) Am Mktg.

Review of Maternal Child Nursing. Judith Green. 1978. text ed. 17.95 (*0-07-024302-6*) McGraw.

*__Review of Medical Physiology.__ Schneider. (Illus.). 200p. 1997. pap. text ed. 17.95 (*0-397-58403-2*) Lppncott-Raven.

Review of Medical Physiology. 17th ed. William Ganong. (C). 1995. pap. text ed. 36.95 (*0-8385-8431-4*, A8431-7) Appleton & Lange.

Review of Mental Health Nursing. P. Haring. 1979. text ed. 20.95 (*0-07-026415-5*) McGraw.

Review of NASA's Reimbursable Programs. unabridged ed. 40p. (Orig.). 1996. pap. 15.00 (*1-57744-000-5*) Nat Acad Public Admin.

Review of Neuroradiology. Val M. Runge. 160p. 1995. pap. text ed. 42.00 (*0-7216-5134-8*) Saunders.

Review of Neuroscience. 2nd ed. Ben Pansky et al. 576p. 1988. pap. text ed. 39.00 (*0-07-105304-2*) McGraw-Hill HPD.

*__Review of New York State Low-Level Radioactive Waste Siting Process.__ National Research Council Staff. 320p. (Orig.). 1996. pap. text ed. 35.00 (*0-309-05539-3*) Natl Acad Pr.

Review of North American Exomalopsis (Hymenoptera, Anthophoridae) Philip H. Timberlake. LC 78-66040. (University of California Publications in Social Welfare: No. 86). 164p. reprint ed. pap. 46.80 (*0-8357-6858-9*, 2035556) Bks Demand.

Review of Nuclear Fuel Experimental Data. 68p. (Orig.). 1995. pap. 17.00 (*92-64-14422-6*, Pub. by Org for Econ FR) OECD.

Review of Nuclear Medicine Technology. 2nd ed. Ann M. Stevens. Ed. by Eleanore Tapscott. LC 96-578. 141p. 1996. pap. 42.00 (*0-932004-45-8*) Soc Nuclear Med.

*__Review of Nurse Anesthesiology.__ Nagelhout. 1998. pap. text ed. write for info. (*0-7216-7531-X*) Saunders.

Review of Nursing Care of the Childbearing Family: A Study Guide. 2nd ed. Elaine Zimbler. 1995. pap. text ed. 23.95 (*0-8385-7093-3*, A7093-6, Medical Exam) Appleton & Lange.

Review of Ophthalmology. Kenneth C. Chern & Kenneth W. Wright. LC 96-20671. 1996. write for info. (*0-683-18239-0*) Williams & Wilkins.

Review of Ophthalmology. G. N. Seal. (C). 1989. 60.00 (*0-89771-363-X*, Pub. by Current Dist II) St Mut.

Review of Organic Functional Group: Introduction to Medicinal Organic Chemistry. 3rd ed. Thomas L. Lemke. LC 91-4855. (Illus.). 142p. 1991. pap. 25.95 (*0-8121-1428-0*) Williams & Wilkins.

Review of Orthopaedics. 2nd ed. Mark D. Miller. Ed. by Richard Lampert. LC 95-24469. (Illus.). 432p. 1996. pap. text ed. 49.95 (*0-7216-5901-2*) Saunders.

Review of Pain Medicine. Roger W. Davis. 148p. 1993. pap. 24.70 (*1-884401-00-7*) Pain Review.

Review of Pathology. rev. ed. Ivan Damjanov & Emanuel Rubin. Orig. Title: Pathology. 360p. 1993. reprint ed. pap. text ed. 27.95 (*0-397-51266-X*) Lppncott-Raven.

Review of Pathophysiology. Christian E. Kaufman, Jr. & Solomon Papper. 624p. (C). 1983. 40.00 (*0-316-48339-7*) Lppncott-Raven.

Review of Pediatric Critical Care. Sandra Czerwinski & Patricia A. Moloney-Harmon. Ed. by Barbara N. Cullen. (Illus.). 288p. 1996. pap. text ed. 32.00 (*0-7216-6159-9*) Saunders.

Review of Pediatric Over-the-Counter Drugs. Ed. by Peter Allen. 25p. 1989. pap. 250.00 (*0-941285-41-3*) FIND-SVP.

Review of Pediatrics. Burg. 1998. pap. text ed. write for info. (*0-7216-1754-9*) Saunders.

Review of Pediatrics. 4th ed. Richard D. Krugman. 1992. pap. text ed. 31.00 (*0-7216-3529-6*) Saunders.

Review of Personality & Social Psychology, 5 vols., 2. Review of Personality & Social Psychology Staff. Ed. by Ladd Wheeler. LC 80-649712. 295p. pap. 84.10 (*0-8357-8404-5*, 2034677) Bks Demand.

Review of Personality & Social Psychology, 5 vols., 3. Review of Personality & Social Psychology Staff. Ed. by Ladd Wheeler. LC 80-649712. 287p. pap. 81.80 (*0-8357-8405-3*, 2034677) Bks Demand.

Review of Personality & Social Psychology, 5 vols., 4. Review of Personality & Social Psychology Staff. Ed. by Ladd Wheeler. LC 80-649712. 328p. pap. 93.50 (*0-8357-8406-1*, 2034677) Bks Demand.

Review of Personality & Social Psychology, 5 vols., 5. Review of Personality & Social Psychology Staff. Ed. by Ladd Wheeler. LC 80-649712. 312p. pap. 89.00 (*0-8357-8407-X*, 2034677) Bks Demand.

Review of Personality & Social Psychology, 5 vols., Vol. 1. Review of Personality & Social Psychology Staff. Ed. by Ladd Wheeler. LC 80-649712. 352p. pap. 100.40 (*0-8357-8403-7*, 2034677) Bks Demand.

Review of Personality Theories. 2nd ed. Victor J. Drapela. LC 94-36205. (Illus.). 184p. (C). 1994. text ed. 36.95 (*0-398-05943-8*); pap. text ed. 22.95 (*0-398-05957-8*) C C Thomas.

Review of Pinus Caribaea. A. Greaves. 1980. 45.00 (*0-85074-052-5*) St Mut.

Review of Placement Services Within a Comprehensive Rehabilitation Framework: Survey Report. Richard J. Jacobsen et al. LC 78-72067. 76p. 1978. 5.00 (*0-686-38818-6*) Human Res Ctr.

Review of Plasma Physics, No. 18. Ed. by B. B. Kadomtsev. (Illus.). 325p. 1993. 110.00 (*0-306-11008-3*, Consultants) Plenum.

*__Review of Pollution in the African Environment.__ 125p. 1994. 15.00 (*92-5-103577-6*, F35776, Pub. by FAO IT) Bernan Associates.

Review of Private Approaches for Delivery of Public Services. Harry P. Hatry. LC 83-23299. (Illus.). 105p. (Orig.). 1983. pap. text ed. 16.00 (*0-87766-329-7*) Urban Inst.

*__Review of Problems Encountered by Small Users of Radioactive Substances.__ 50p. 1996. pap. 25.00 (*0-11-753238-X*, HM3238X, Pub. by Stationery Ofc UK) Bernan Associates.

Review of Progress in Quantitative Nondestructive Evaluation, Vol. 2. Ed. by Donald O. Thompson & Dale E. Chimenti. 1840p. 1983. 275.00 (*0-306-41350-7*, Plenum Pr) Plenum.

Review of Progress in Quantitative Nondestructive Evaluation, Vol. 5. Ed. by Donald O. Thompson & Dale E. Chimenti. 876p. 1986. 295.00 (*0-306-42269-7*, Plenum Pr) Plenum.

Review of Progress in Quantitative Nondestructive Evaluation, Vol. 6. Ed. by Donald O. Thompson & Dale E. Chimenti. (Illus.). 1820p. 1987. 295.00 (*0-306-42584-X*, Plenum Pr) Plenum.

Review of Progress in Quantitative Nondestructive Evaluation, Vol. 7. Ed. by Donald O. Thompson & Dale E. Chimenti. LC 82-9140. (Illus.). 1882p. 1988. 295.00 (*0-306-42837-7*, Plenum Pr) Plenum.

Review of Progress in Quantitative Nondestructive Evaluation, Vol. 8. Donald O. Thompson. Ed. by Dale E. Chimenti. (Illus.). 2348p. 1989. 345.00 (*0-306-43209-9*, Plenum Pr) Plenum.

Review of Progress in Quantitative Nondestructive Evaluation, Vol. 9. Donald O. Thompson. Ed. by Dale E. Chimenti. LC 82-9140. (Illus.). 2172p. 1990. 345.00 (*0-306-43535-7*, Plenum Pr) Plenum.

Review of Progress in Quantitative Nondestructive Evaluation, Vol. 10. Donald O. Thompson. Ed. by Dale E. Chimenti. (Illus.). 2238p. 1991. 345.00 (*0-306-43903-4*, Plenum Pr) Plenum.

Review of Progress in Quantitative Nondestructive Evaluation, Vol. 11. Donald O. Thompson. Ed. by Dale E. Chimenti. (Illus.). 2316p. (C). 1992. 345.00 (*0-306-44206-X*, Plenum Pr) Plenum.

Review of Progress in Quantitative Nondestructive Evaluation, Vol. 12. Ed. by Donald O. Thompson & Dale E. Chimenti. LC 82-9140. 2431p. 1993. 345.00 (*0-306-44483-6*, Plenum Pr) Plenum.

Review of Progress in Quantitative Nondestructive Evaluation, Vol. 13. Ed. by D. O. Thompson & D. E. Chimenti. (Illus.). 2270p. (C). 1994. text ed. 345.00 (*0-306-44731-2*, Plenum Pr) Plenum.

Review of Progress in Quantitative Nondestructive Evaluation: Proceeding of the 22nd Symposium Held in Seattle, Washington, July 30 - August 4, 1995, Vol 115. Ed. by Donald O. Thompson & Dale Chimenti. (Illus.). 2360p. (C). 1996. 375.00 (*0-306-45310-X*, Plenum Pr) Plenum.

Review of Progress in Quantitative Nondestructive Evaluation Vol. 14: Proceedings of the Twenty-First Annual Review Held in Snowmass Village, Colorado, July 31-August 5, 1994, 2 Pts., Vol. 14. Ed. by Donald O. Thompson & Dale E. Chimenti. LC 82-9140. 2480p. 1995. 365.00 (*0-306-45062-3*) Plenum.

R

R

*Review of Progress in Quantitative Nondestructive Evaluation Vol. 16: Proceedings of the Twenty-Third Symposium Held in Brunswick, Maine, July 28-August 2, 1996, 2 vols. Ed. by Donald O. Thompson & Dale E. Chimenti. 2256p. (C). 1997. 395.00 (0-306-45597-8, Plenum Pr) Plenum.

Review of Published Research on the Relationship of Some Personality Variables to ESP Scoring Level. Gordon L. Mangan. (Parapsychological Monographs: No. 1). 1958. pap. 5.00 (0-912328-03-7) Parapsych Foun.

*Review of Pulmonary Medicine & Critical Care. Reuben M. Cherniack. 1996. pap. text ed. 34.95 (1-55009-027-5, Pub. by B C Decker CN) Blackwell Sci.

Review of Radiation Risks & Uranium Toxicity with Applications to Decisions Associated with Decommissioning Clean-Up Criteria. (Illus.). 260p. (C). 1996. text ed. 49.00 (0-9630191-2-0) RSA Pubns.

Review of Radio Science 1990-1992. Ed. by W. Ross Stone. (Illus.). 750p. 1993. 110.00 (0-19-856376-0) OUP.

*Review of Radio Science 1993-1996. W. Ross Stone. (Illus.). 1032p. 1996. 175.00 (0-19-856532-1) OUP.

Review of Radiologic Physics. Huda & Slone. (Board Review Ser.). 1994. 25.00 (0-685-75160-0) Williams & Wilkins.

Review of Radiologic Physics. Walter Huda & Richard M. Sloan. LC 94-25711. 286p. 1994. 29.00 (0-683-04230-0) Williams & Wilkins.

Review of Radiology. 2nd ed. Ed. by Carl E. Ravin et al. LC 93-3351. (Illus.). 400p. 1993. pap. text ed. 55.00 (0-7216-5028-7) Saunders.

Review of Recent National Demographic Target Setting. 149p. 1989. 17.00 (92-1-151177-1, 89.X.III.5) UN.

Review of Research in Education, 3 vols. Incl. Vol. 9. . David C. Berliner. 1981. (0-935302-01-8); Vol. 10. . Ed. by Edmund Gordon. 432p. 1983. (0-935302-02-6); Vol. 11. . Ed. by Edmund Gordon. 1984. (0-935302-04-2); Vol. 12. . Ed. by Edmund Gordon. 1985. (0-935302-05-0); Vol. 13. . Ed. by Ernst Z. Rothkopf. 1986. (0-935302-06-9); 18.00 (0-317-31936-1); 25.00 (0-317-31937-X) Am Educ Res.

Review of Research in Education, No. 4. Ed. by Lee Shulman. LC 72-89719. 362p. reprint ed. pap. 103.20 (0-8357-9488-1, 2012294) Bks Demand.

Review of Research in Education, Vol. 16. Ed. by Courtney B. Cazden. LC 72-89719. 424p. 1990. text ed. write for info. (0-935302-11-5) Am Educ Res.

Review of Research in Education, Vol. 17. Ed. by Gerald Grant. 440p. 1991. text ed. write for info. (0-935302-12-3) Am Educ Res.

Review of Research in Nursing Education, Vol. I. Ed. by William L. Holzemer. 208p. 1986. pap. 19.95 (0-88737-340-2, 15-2170) Natl League Nurse.

Review of Research in Nursing Education, Vol. II. Ed. by William L. Holzemer. 208p. 1989. 22.95 (0-88737-399-2, 15-2219) Natl League Nurse.

Review of Research in Nursing Education, Vol. III. Ed. by Gloria Clayton & Pamela Baj. 192p. 1990. 22.95 (0-88737-486-7) Natl League Nurse.

Review of Research in Nursing Education, Vol. IV. Ed. by Pamela Baj & Gloria Clayton. 192p. 1991. pap. 22.95 (0-88737-504-9) Natl League Nurse.

Review of Research in Nursing Education, Vol. V. Ed. by Lois R. Allen. (C). 1992. pap. text ed. 24.95 (0-88737-542-1, 15-2448) Natl League Nurse.

Review of Research on Parent Influences on Child Personality. Family Service Association of America, Research Department Staff & Ruth V. Frankiel. LC 59-1935. 38p. reprint ed. pap. 25.00 (0-317-10343-1, 2050172) Bks Demand.

Review of Russellism, Et Cetera, Et Cetera. J. J. Mathis. 66p. 1988. reprint ed. pap. 2.95 (1-883858-41-0) Witness CA.

Review of Scottish Culture, Vol. 3. Alexander Fenton et al. 152p. (C). 1996. pap. 30.00 (0-85976-183-5, Pub. by J Donald UK) St Mut.

Review of Scottish Culture, Vol. 5. Alexander Fenton et al. 120p. (C). 1996. pap. 30.00 (0-85976-251-3, Pub. by J Donald UK) St Mut.

Review of Scottish Culture, Vol. 6. Alexander Fenton et al. 120p. (C). 1996. pap. 30.00 (0-85976-324-2, Pub. by J Donald UK) St Mut.

Review of Search & Reconnaisance Theory Literature. Michael L. Moore. LC 75-131015. 104p. 1970. 22.00 (0-403-04520-7) Scholarly.

Review of Selected North American Mitrate Stylophorans (Homalozoa: Echinodermata), Vol. 336. R. L. Parsley. 57p. 1991. 23.00 (0-87710-418-2) Paleo Res.

Review of Sports Medicine & Arthroscopy. Ed. by Mark D. Miller et al. LC 94-22156. (Illus.). 1995. pap. text ed. 54.00 (0-7216-5281-6) Saunders.

Review of Stathmonotus, with Redefinition & Phylogenetic Analysis of the Chaenopsidae: Teleostei: Blennioidei. Philip A. Hastings. LC 94-3192. (Smithsonian Contributions to Zoology Ser.: No. 558). 52p. 1994. pap. 25.00 (0-7837-7461-3, 2049183) Bks Demand.

*Review of Suicidology, 1997. Ed. by Ronald W. Maris et al. 1997. lib. bdg. 35.00 (1-57230-212-7, 0212) Guilford Pr.

Review of Surgery. 2nd ed. David C. Sabiston. Ed. by Lisette Bralow. 368p. 1996. pap. text ed. 35.00 (0-7216-8671-0) Saunders.

Review of Surgical Nursing. A. Descharnais. 1978. text ed. 21.95 (0-07-016560-2) McGraw.

Review of Taxation of Individuals: 1977-1992, 16 vols., Set. Bound set. 1,040.00 (0-8377-9136-7) Rothman.

Review of Telephone Network Reliability & Service Quality Standards. (Illus.). 130p. (C). 1994. reprint ed. pap. text ed. 35.00 (0-7881-1443-3) DIANE Pub.

Review of Textile Progress. Manchester & Bradford. 538p. 1972. 75.00 (0-686-63796-8) St Mut.

Review of Textile Progress: A Survey of World Literature, 1965-66, Vol. 17. LC 60-1460. 611p. reprint ed. pap. 174.20 (0-317-09916-7, 2020708) Bks Demand.

Review of the Activated Carbon Industry & Scope for Oil Palm Kernel Shell As a Raw Material. P. Reupke & A. Duff. 1993. pap. 25.00 (0-85954-326-9, Pub. by Nat Res Inst UK) St Mut.

Review of the Andean Leptodactylid Frog Genus Phrynopus. John D. Lynch. (Occasional Papers: No. 35). 51p. 1975. pap. 1.00 (0-686-80370-1) U KS Nat Hist Mus.

Review of the Broad-Headed Eleutherodactyline Frogs of South America (Leptodactylidae) John D. Lynch. (Occasional Papers: No. 38). 46p. 1975. pap. 1.00 (0-686-80371-X) U KS Nat Hist Mus.

Review of the Cattle Business in Johnson County Wyoming, Since 1822, & the Causes That Led to the Recent Invasion. Oscar H. Flagg. LC 79-90174. (Mass Violence in America Ser.). reprint ed. 6.50 (0-405-01309-4) Ayer.

Review of the Causes & Consequences of the Mexican War. William Jay. (Select Bibliographies Reprint Ser.). 1977. 26.95 (0-8369-5215-4) Ayer.

Review of the Causes & Consequences of the Mexican War. William Jay. LC 79-82202. (Anti-Slavery Crusade in America Ser.). 1978. reprint ed. 26.95 (0-405-00641-1) Ayer.

Review of the Centrolenid Frogs of Ecuador, with Descriptions of New Species. John D. Lynch & William E. Duellman. (Occasional Papers: No. 16). (Illus.). 66p. 1973. 1.00 (0-317-04877-5) U KS Nat Hist Mus.

Review of the Chemical & Biological Defence Program of Canada. 56p. (Orig.). (C). 1992. pap. text ed. 25.00 (1-56806-098-X) DIANE Pub.

Review of the Colonial Slave Registration Acts. African Institution, London Staff. LC 78-149860. (Black Heritage Library Collection). 1977. 18.95 (0-8369-8742-X) Ayer.

Review of the Convention on Contracts for the International Sale of Goods (Cisg) 1995. LC 96-8793. 1996. lib. bdg. 88.00 (90-411-0968-4) Kluwer Ac.

*Review of the Council's Work 42nd Review: 1 January-31 December 1994. 210p. 1996. pap. 30.00 (92-824-1272-5, BX51-95-002-ENC, Pub. by Europ Com UK) Bernan Associates.

Review of the Deep-Sea Fish Family Platytroctidae: Pisces: Salmoniformes. Tetsuo Matsui & Richard H. Rosenblatt. LC 86-25088. (Bulletin of the Scripps Institution of Oceanography, University of California, San Diego Ser.: No. 26). 169p. 1987. pap. 48.20 (0-7837-7492-3, 2049214) Bks Demand.

*Review of the Department of Defense's Program for Breast Cancer Research. 100p. 1997. pap. 20.00 (0-309-05780-9) Natl Acad Pr.

Review of the Department of Energy Classification. National Research Council Staff. 128p. (Orig.). (C). 1995. pap. text ed. 29.00 (0-309-05338-2) Natl Acad Pr.

Review of the Diseases & Treatments of Captive Turtles. James B. Murphy & Joseph T. Collins. LC 82-73100. pap. text ed. 16.00 (0-685-19240-7) Meseraule Prnting.

Review of the Fauna of the Marquesas Islands & Discussion of Its Origin. A. M. Adamson. (BMB Ser.: No. 159). 1974. reprint ed. 25.00 (0-527-02267-5) Periodicals Srv.

Review of the Fialuridine (FIAU) Clinical Trials. 1995. pap. text ed. 34.00 (0-309-05279-3) Natl Acad Sci.

Review of the Fiscal Impulse Measure. Peter S. Heller et al. LC 86-3027. (Occasional Paper Ser.: No. 44). 43p. 1986. pap. 7.50 (0-939934-60-4) Intl Monetary.

*Review of the Fisheries Resources of the Red Sea & Gulf of Aden. 144p. 1989. 13.00 (92-5-102832-X, Pub. by FAO IT) Bernan Associates.

Review of the Genera of New World Mymaridae: Hymenioptera: Chalcidoidea. Carl M. Yoshimoto. LC 89-70311. (Flora & Fauna Handbook Ser.: No. 7). x, 166p. 1990. 39.95 (1-877743-04-6) Sandhill Crane.

Review of the Genus Eunice (Polychaeta: Eunicidae) Based upon Type Material. Kristian Fauchald. LC 91-19518. (Smithsonian Contributions to Zoology Ser.: No. 523). 432p. reprint ed. pap. 123.20 (0-7837-2051-3, 2042326) Bks Demand.

*Review of the Habitat of the Earliest Vertebrates. Robert H. Denison. LC 56-14639. (Chicago Natural History Museum, Publication 814, Fieldiana, Anthropology Ser.: Vol. 11, No. 8). 100p. 1956. reprint ed. pap. 28.50 (0-608-03774-5, 2064616) Bks Demand.

Review of the Hermit Crabs of the Genus Xylopagurus A. Milne Edwards, 1880 (Crustacea: Decapoda: Paguridae), Including Descriptions of Two New Species. Rafael Lemaitre. LC 94-37724. (Smithsonian Contributions to Zoology Ser.: Vol. 570). 31p. 1995. reprint ed. pap. 25.00 (0-608-00511-8, 2061331) Bks Demand.

Review of the History of Infantry. Ernest M. Lloyd. LC 70-84277. 1982. reprint ed. text ed. 100.50 (0-8371-5015-9, LLHI, Greenwood Pr) Greenwood.

Review of the Labour Market in the Czech Republic. 143p. (Orig.). 1995. pap. 34.00 (92-64-14425-0, Pub. by Org for Econ FR) OECD.

Review of the Lectures of Wm. A. Smith DD, on the Philosophy & Practice of Slavery. John H. Power. 1977. 22.95 (0-8369-9172-9, 9046) Ayer.

*Review of the Legislation Regulation & Delivery of Methadone in 12 Member States: Final Report. 165p. 1996. pap. 45.00 (92-827-6094-4, CE91-95-592-ENC, Pub. by Europ Com UK) Bernan Associates.

Review of the Mexican War on Christian Principles: And an Essay on the Means of Preventing War. Philip A. Berry. LC 76-143427. (Peace Movement in America Ser.). ix, 87p. 1972. reprint ed. lib. bdg. 19.95 (0-89198-057-1) Ozer.

Review of the Municipal Pollution Abatement Programs in the Great Lakes Basin: Report to the Great Lakes Water Quality Board. fac. ed. Great Lakes Water Quality Board, Municipal Abatement Task Force Staff. LC 84-193419. (Illus.). 199p. 1983. pap. 56.80 (0-7837-8630-1, 2075247) Bks Demand.

Review of the Nature & Uses of Examinations in Medical Education. J. Charvat et al. (Public Health Papers: No. 36). 74p. 1968. pap. text ed. 7.00 (92-4-130036-1, 1110036) World Health.

Review of the Nearctic Alysiini (Hymenoptera, Braconidae) With Discussion of Generic Relationships Within the Tribe. Robert A. Wharton. LC 79-63592. (University of California Publications in Social Welfare: No. 88). (Illus.). 124p. reprint ed. pap. 35.40 (0-8357-6856-2, 2035554) Bks Demand.

Review of the Neonate. Carole A. Kenner. 1993. student ed., pap. text ed. 41.00 (0-7216-4204-7) HarBrace.

Review of the North American Eocene & Oligocene Apatemyidae: Mammalia: Insectivora. Robert M. West. (Special Publications: No. 3). (Illus.). 42p. 1973. pap. 5.00 (0-89672-028-4) Tex Tech Univ Pr.

Review of the North American Freshwater Snail Genus Pyrgulopsis (Hydrobiidae) Robert Hersler. LC 93-47246. (Smithsonian Contributions to Zoology Ser.: No. 554). 119p. 1994. pap. 34.00 (0-7837-7462-1, 2049184) Bks Demand.

Review of the North American Leptoconops: Diptera: Ceratopogonidae. Willis W. Wirth & William R. Atchley. (Graduate Studies: No. 5). (Illus.). 57p. (Orig.). 1973. pap. 3.00 (0-89672-012-8) Tex Tech Univ Pr.

Review of the North & Central American Species of Paravilla Painter (Diptera: Bombyliidae) Jack C. Hall. LC 80-19994. (University of California Publications in Social Welfare: No. 92). (Illus.). 208p. reprint ed. pap. 59.30 (0-685-24003-7, 2031588) Bks Demand.

Review of the Pelycosauria: Geological Society of American Special Papers, Vol. 28. Alfred S. Romer & Llewellyn I. Price. Ed. by Stephen J. Gould. LC 79-8346. (History of Paleontology Ser.). (Illus.). 1980. reprint ed. lib. bdg. 55.95 (0-405-12740-5) Ayer.

Review of the Phyllomedusa Buckleyi Group: Anura: Hylidae. David C. Cannatella. (Occasional Papers: No. 87). 40p. 1980. 1.00 (0-317-04840-6) U KS Nat Hist Mus.

Review of the Political Conflict in America, from the Commencement of the Anti-Slavery Agitation to the Close of Southern Reconstruction. Alexander Harris. LC 70-109328. 517p. 1970. reprint ed. text ed. 59.75 (0-8371-3594-X, HPC&, Greenwood Pr) Greenwood.

Review of the Prehistory of the Santa Clara Valley Region, California, No. 7. Albert B. Elsasser. Ed. by Gary S. Breschini & Trudy Haversat. (Archives of California Prehistory Ser.: No. 7). (Illus.). 117p. (Orig.). pap. 10.65 (1-55567-038-5) Coyote Press.

Review of the Principle Questions in Morals. Richard Price. (C). 1986. reprint ed. pap. text ed. 11.95 (0-935005-26-9); reprint ed. lib. bdg. 21.95 (0-935005-25-0) Lincoln-Rembrandt.

Review of the Publication, "Living Without Landfills" LC 89-35181. (Commentary Ser.: No. 5). 9p. 1989. pap. text ed. 20.00 (0-929600-06-1) NCRP Pubns.

Review of the Report, "Proposal for a Greater New Bedford, MA PCB Health Study" National Electrical Manufacturers Association, Power Equipment Division Staff. 15.00 (0-317-05981-5) Natl Elec Mfrs.

Review of the Southern African Species of Cyrtanthus. C. Reid & R. Allen Dyer. Ed. by R. Mitchel Beauchamp. (Illus.). 68p. (Orig.). 1984. pap. 12.00 (0-930653-00-9) Intl Bulb Soc.

Review of the Space Shuttle Costs: Reduction Goals & Procedures. unabridged ed. 40p. (Orig.). 1994. pap. 15.00 (1-57744-010-2) Nat Acad Public Admin.

*Review of the State of the Fisheries & the Environment of the Northeastern Mediterranean (Northern Levantine Basin) 80p. 1993. 10.00 (92-5-103392-7, Pub. by FAO IT) Bernan Associates.

Review of the State of World Marine Fishery Resources. FAO Staff. (Fisheries Technical Papers: 335). 142p. 1994. pap. 15.00 (92-5-103471-0, F34710, Pub. by FAO IT) Bernan Associates.

Review of the Structure & Operations of the SEC Practice Section: Report of the SECPS Review Committee. American Institute of Certified Public Accountants Staff. 86p. reprint ed. pap. 25.00 (0-317-27247-0, 2025097) Bks Demand.

Review of the Systemization of the Tooele Chemical Agent Disposal Facility. National Research Council Staff. 134p. (Orig.). 1996. pap. text ed. 34.00 (0-309-05486-9) Natl Acad Pr.

Review of the Taxonomy of the Sorex Vagrans Species Complex from Western North America. Darwen Hennings & Robert S. Hoffmann. (Occasional Papers: No. 68). 35p. 1977. pap. 1.00 (0-686-80294-2) U KS Nat Hist Mus.

Review of the Technological Efficacy of Some Antioxidants & Synergists. FAO-WHO Expert Committee on Food Additives. (WHO Food Additives Ser.: No. 3). 144p. 1972. pap. text ed. 8.00 (92-4-166003-1, 1270003) World Health.

Review of the United Nations Charter. U. S. Congress, Senate Committee on Foreign Relations. LC 68-55114. (Illus.). 365p. 1970. text ed. 35.00 (0-8371-3170-7, UNNC, Greenwood Pr) Greenwood.

Review of the USGS National Water Assessment Pilot Program. National Research Council Staff. 164p. 1990. pap. text ed. 15.00 (0-309-04292-5) Natl Acad Pr.

Review of Thrombolytic Therapy & Thromboembolic Disease. Ed. by William R. Bell & Arthur A. Sasahara. LC 88-64223. (Illus.). 128p. 1989. text ed. 28.95 (0-924428-00-7) Phys Sci Pub.

Review of Trends in Lake Erie Water Quality with Emphasis on the 1978-1979 Intensive Survey: Report to the Surveillance Work Group. fac. ed. Ed. by David E. Rathke & Clayton J. Edwards. LC 86-103207. (Illus.). 139p. 1985. pap. 39.70 (0-7837-8627-1, 2075241) Bks Demand.

Review of Tropical Plant Pathology, Suppl. No. 2. 1990. 49.00 (1-55528-233-4, Messers Today & Tomorrow) Scholarly Pubns.

Review of Tropical Plant Pathology, Vol. 6. 1990. 95.00 (0-685-59967-1, Pub. by Today & Tomorrows P & P II) Scholarly Pubns.

Review of Tropical Plant Pathology: Diseases of Cereals, Maize & Millet, Vol. 1. S. P. Raychaudhuri & J. P. Verma. (Illus.). 564p. 1984. 79.00 (1-55528-080-3, Pub. by Today & Tomorrows P & P II) Scholarly Pubns.

Review of Tropical Plant Pathology: Diseases of Fruits, Vol. 2. Ed. by S. P. Raychahduri & J. P. Verma. iv, 406p. 1986. 99.00 (1-55528-081-1, Pub. by Today & Tomorrows P & P II) Scholarly Pubns.

Review of Tropical Plant Pathology: Diseases of Plantation Crops & Forest Trees, Vol. IV. Ed. by S. P. Raychaudhuri & J. P. Verma. (Illus.). 350p. 1988. 99.00 (1-55528-092-7, Pub. by Today & Tomorrows P & P II) Scholarly Pubns.

Review of Tropical Plant Pathology: Diseases of Vegetables, Vol. 3. Ed. by S. P. Raychaudhuri & J. P. Verma. (Illus.). 586p. 1987. 95.00 (1-55528-144-3, Pub. by Today & Tomorrows P & P II) Scholarly Pubns.

Review of Tropical Plant Pathology, Vol. 5: Diseases of Fibre & Oilseed Crops. S. P. Raychaudhuri & J. P. Verma. (Illus.). vi, 316p. 1989. 95.00 (1-55528-173-7, Messers Today & Tomorrow) Scholarly Pubns.

Review of Undergraduate Physics. Benjamin F. Bayman & Morton Hamermesh. LC 85-26577. 336p. 1986. pap. text ed. 34.50 (0-471-81684-1) Wiley.

Review of Vascular Surgery. Ed. by William C. Krupski. 170p. 1994. pap. text ed. 33.50 (0-7216-4843-6) Saunders.

Review of Verbal Behavior by B. F. Skinner. Noam Chomsky. (Irvington Reprint Series in Anthropology). (C). 1991. reprint ed. pap. text ed. 2.90 (0-8290-2603-7, A-34) Irvington.

Review of Vinyl Technology II: Compounding, Processing, & Properties: Sheraton International at O'Hare, October 14-15, 1986. Society of Plastics Engineers Staff. (Illus.). 353p. pap. 100.70 (0-317-58188-0, 2029713) Bks Demand.

Review of Waste Management Organizations. John Grover. (Radioactive Waste Management & the Nuclear Fuel Cycle Ser.). 106p. 1984. pap. text ed. 101.00 (3-7186-0202-4) Gordon & Breach.

Review of Welding Cast Steels & Its Effects on Fatigue & Toughness Properties. 1979. 20.00 (0-686-45002-7) Steel Founders.

Review of Whole Numbers Through Algebra. Mary S. Charuhas. (Essential Mathematics for Life Ser.: No. 7). 1995. pap. text ed. 7.95 (0-02-802615-2) Glencoe.

Review Papers: International Solar-Terrestrial Physics Symposium, Sao-Paolo, June, 1974. Ed. by S. A. Bowhill. 212p. 1976. pap. 50.00 (0-08-019959-3, Pergamon Pr) Elsevier.

Review Questions & Answers. James Pratt. (Veterinary Board Ser.). (gr. 13). 1995. pap. text ed. 158.00 (0-8151-7388-1) Mosby Yr Bk.

Review Questions & Answers for Veterinary Boards: Ancillary Topics. Ed. by P. W. Pratt. LC 93-70151. 311p. 1993. 33.00 (0-939674-43-2) Am Vet Pubns.

*Review Questions & Answers for Veterinary Boards: Ancillary Topics. 2nd ed. Pratt. 352p. (gr. 13). 1997. pap. text ed. 36.95 (0-8151-7468-3) Mosby Yr Bk.

*Review Questions & Answers for Veterinary Boards: Basic Science. 2nd ed. Pratt. 352p. (gr. 13). 1997. pap. text ed. 36.95 (0-8151-7389-X) Mosby Yr Bk.

Review Questions & Answers for Veterinary Boards: Basic Sciences. Ed. by P. W. Pratt. LC 93-70147. 271p. 1993. 33.00 (0-939674-39-4) Am Vet Pubns.

Review Questions & Answers for Veterinary Boards: Clinical Sciences. Ed. by P. W. Pratt. LC 93-70148. 287p. 1993. 33.00 (0-939674-40-8) Am Vet Pubns.

*Review Questions & Answers for Veterinary Boards: Clinical Sciences. 2nd ed. Pratt. 352p. (gr. 13). 1997. pap. text ed. 36.95 (0-8151-7462-4) Mosby Yr Bk.

Review Questions & Answers for Veterinary Boards: Large Animal Medicine & Surgery. Ed. by P. W. Pratt. LC 93-70150. 313p. 1993. 33.00 (0-939674-42-4) Am Vet Pubns.

*Review Questions & Answers for Veterinary Boards: Large Animal Medicine & Surgery, No. 2. Pratt. 352p. (gr. 13). 1997. pap. text ed. 36.95 (0-8151-7466-7) Mosby Yr Bk.

Review Questions & Answers for Veterinary Boards: Small Animal Medicine & Surgery. Ed. by P. W. Pratt. LC 93-70149. 363p. 1993. 33.00 (0-939674-41-6) Am Vet Pubns.

*Review Questions & Answers for Veterinary Boards: Small Animal Medicine & Surgery, No. 2. Pratt. 352p. (gr. 13). 1997. pap. text ed. 36.95 (0-8151-7465-9) Mosby Yr Bk.

Review Questions & Answers for Veterinary Technicians. Ed. by P. W. Pratt. LC 93-70152. 409p. 1993. 29.00 (0-939674-44-0) Am Vet Pubns.

Review Questions & Answers for Veterinary Technicians. 2nd ed. Colville. 432p. (gr. 13). 1995. pap. text ed. 33.95 (0-8151-1850-3) Mosby Yr Bk.

Review Questions & Explanations in Computed Tomography. Lois E. Romans. LC 96-1773. 162p. 1996. pap. 24.95 (0-683-07330-3) Williams & Wilkins.

*Review Questions for CT. Euclid Seeram. LC 97-4140. 1997. pap. write for info. (0-86542-529-9) Blackwell Sci.

Review Questions for Embryology. T. R. Gest & J. M. Anderson. (Review Questions Ser.). (Illus.). 125p. (Orig.). (C). 1995. pap. text ed. 17.95 (*1-85070-591-7*) Prthnon Pub.

Review Questions for Gross Anatomy & Embryology. T. R. Gest et al. (Illus.). 400p. (C). 1993. pap. text ed. 21.95 (*1-85070-503-8*) Prthnon Pub.

***Review Questions for Human Anatomy: A Program of Study Through Regional Self-Assessment.** Patrick W. Tank. LC 96-2871. (Review Questions Ser.). 150p. (Orig.). 1996. pap. text ed. 21.95 (*1-85070-795-2*) Prthnon Pub.

Review Questions for Human Histology. E. Robert Burns. LC 95-17810. (Review Questions Ser.). 200p. (Orig.). 1995. 19.95 (*1-85070-594-1*) Prthnon Pub.

Review Questions for MRI. Carolyn Kaut & William Faulkner. LC 94-24135. 192p. 1994. 21.95 (*0-632-03905-1*) Blackwell Sci.

Review Questions for Neuroanatomy. William T. Mosenthal. LC 96-2843. (Review Questions Ser.). 133p. 1996. pap. 17.95 (*1-85070-653-0*) Prthnon Pub.

***Review Questions for the Health Information Management Examination: RRA & Art Examination Preparation.** Mary R. Burns et al. LC 96-29845. (Review Questions Ser.). 180p. 1997. pap. 19.95 (*1-85070-737-5*) Prthnon Pub.

***Review Questions for the NCLEX-PN.** 3rd ed. Sandra F. Smith. 1997. pap. text ed. 19.95 (*0-8385-8445-4*) Appleton & Lange.

***Review Questions for the Nuclear Medicine Examination.** Anna M. Gallo-Foss. LC 96-29859. (Review Questions Ser.). (Illus.). 180p. 1997. pap. 19.95 (*1-85070-703-0*) Prthnon Pub.

Review Questions Nclex RN. 8th ed. Smith. 1996. pap. text ed. 24.95 (*0-8385-8444-6*, Medical Exam) Appleton & Lange.

Review Radiography. 3rd ed. Dorothy A. Saia. LC 96-41411. 1996. pap. text ed. 32.95 (*0-8385-0280-6*) Appleton & Lange.

Review, Regulate or Reform? What Works to Control Workers' Compensation Medical Costs. Ed. by Thomas W. Grannemann. LC 94-32451. 1994. 75.00 (*0-935149-48-1*, WC-94-5) Workers Comp Res Inst.

***Review Second Grade (Language)** Jo E. Moore. (Reading & Writing Ser.). (Illus.). 32p. (J). (gr. 2). 1996. teacher ed., pap. 2.95 (*1-55799-432-3*, 4034) Evan-Moor Corp.

***Review Text in Podiatric Orthopedics & Primary Podiatric Medicine.** Marc A. Benard et al. LC 97-2759. 1997. write for info. (*1-57400-029-2*) Data Trace Pubng.

Review Text in United States History. 2nd ed. Paul M. Roberts. (YA). (gr. 7-9). 1989. pap. text ed. 16.67 (*0-87720-857-3*) AMSCO Sch.

***Review Third Grade (Language)** Phyllis Edwards. (Reading & Writing Ser.). (Illus.). 32p. (J). (gr. 3). 1996. teacher ed., pap. 2.95 (*1-55799-433-1*, 4035) Evan-Moor Corp.

Review, Vol. 13: 1991. Ed. by James O. Hoge & James L. West, III. 302p. (C). 1992. text ed. 40.00 (*0-8139-1371-3*) U Pr of Va.

Review, Vol. 15: 1993. Ed. by James O. Hoge & James L. West, III. 240p. 1993. text ed. 40.00 (*0-8139-1477-9*) U Pr of Va.

Review Workbook for Adult Education in Mathematics & English. Leonard S. Bennett et al. 1980. pap. 7.50 (*0-87738-001-5*) Youth Ed.

Review, 1988, Vol. 10. Ed. by James O. Hoge & James L. West, III. 304p. 1988. text ed. 40.00 (*0-8139-1217-2*) U Pr of Va.

Reviewbooks for the GED Test. Rosemary Lewis et al. (Reviewbooks for the GED Test Ser.). (Illus.). (YA). 1992. pap. text ed. 90.65 (*1-56030-089-2*) Comex Systs.

Reviewed Contents of Major Diabetes Congresses. F. Belfiore. (Frontiers in Diabetes Ser.: Vol. 1). xii, 162p. 1981. 71.25 (*3-8055-3414-0*) S Karger.

Reviewer's Guide, Vol. 1. Otto Tronowsky et al. LC 80-53456. 214p. 1981. text ed. 19.50 (*0-935988-20-3*, 306) Todd Pub.

Reviewing Apartment Leasing Techniques to Improve Profits. (Journal Reprint Ser.). 9.95 (*0-944298-45-1*, 892) Inst Real Estate.

ReViewing Asian America: Locating Diversity. Ed. by Soo-Young Chin et al. (Association for Asian American Studies: No. 6). 214p. (Orig.). 1995. pap. text ed. 29.00 (*0-87422-118-8*) Wash St U Pr.

Reviewing Basic Grammar. 3rd ed. Robert E. Yarber. (C). 1992. 28.00 (*0-673-46694-9*) Addson-Wesley Educ.

Reviewing Basic Grammar. 4th ed. Robert E. Yarber & Mary L. Yarber. LC 95-51008. 1996. write for info. (*0-06-739941-X*) Addson-Wesley Educ.

***Reviewing Basic Grammar.** 4th ed. Robert E. Yarber & Mary L. Yarber. LC 95-51008. 1996. write for info. (*0-673-99942-4*) Longman.

***Reviewing Basic Grammar.** 4th ed. Robert E. Yarber & Mary L. Yarber. LC 95-51008. (C). 1997. text ed. 28.95 (*0-673-99941-6*) Longman.

Reviewing Before the Edinburgh, 1788-1802. Derek Roper. LC 77-2446. (Illus.). 1978. 40.00 (*0-87413-128-6*) U Delaware Pr.

Reviewing Britain's Defence. Ian Bellany. (Illus.). 224p. (C). 1994. text ed. 59.95 (*1-85521-462-8*, Pub. by Dartmth Pub UK) Ashgate Pub Co.

Reviewing Condominium Projects. National Association of Review Appraisers & Mortgage Underwriters Staff & Fayette F. Arnold, III. LC 80-53455. (Illus.). 156p. 1981. 21.50 (*0-935988-21-1*) Todd Pub.

Reviewing German Grammar: A Self-Instructional Reference Book for Elementary German Grammar. Janet D. Rodewald. LC 84-21884. 364p. (Orig.). 1985. pap. text ed. 38.00 (*0-8191-4366-9*) U Pr of Amer.

Reviewing German Grammar & Building Vocabulary. Roselinde Konrad. LC 80-6238. 415p. (GER.). 1981. pap. text ed. 36.00 (*0-8191-1605-X*) U Pr of Amer.

***Reviewing Health Manpower Development: A Method of Improving National Health Systems.** M. Roemer. (Public Health Papers: No. 83). 149p. 1987. 13.00 (*92-4-130083-3*) World Health.

Reviewing Histories: Selections from New Latin American Cinema. Glauber Rocha et al. Ed. by Coco Fusco. Tr. by Jon Davis et al. (Illus.). 224p. (Orig.). 1987. pap. 8.00 (*0-936739-06-1*) Hallwalls Inc.

***Reviewing Kindergarten (Math)** Jo E. Moore. (Mathematics Ser.). (Illus.). 32p. (J). (gr. k). 1997. teacher ed., pap. 2.95 (*1-55799-482-X*, 4084) Evan-Moor Corp.

***Reviewing Orpheus: Essays on the Cinema & Art of Jean Cocteau.** Ed. by Cornelia A. Tsakiridou. LC 55-58217. (Review Ser.: Vol. 41, No. 1). 152p. 1997. 24.00 (*0-8387-5379-5*) Bucknell U Pr.

Reviewing Romanticism. Ed. by Philip W. Martin & Robin Jarvis. LC 91-24823. 244p. 1992. text ed. 55.00 (*0-312-06801-8*) St Martin.

Reviewing Sex: Gender & the Reception of Victorian Novels. Nicola D. Thompson. 260p. (C). 1996. 40.00 (*0-8147-8211-6*); pap. 17.50 (*0-8147-8212-4*) NYU Pr.

Reviewing the Arts. C. B. Titchener. 152p. 1988. 34.50 (*0-8058-0237-1*); pap. 17.50 (*0-8058-0397-1*) L Erlbaum Assocs.

***Reviewing the Personnel Function: A Toolkit for Development.** Nikki Fonda & Keith Buckton. 160p. 1995. 90.00 (*0-85292-576-X*, Pub. by IPM UK) St Mut.

***Reviewing the Safety of Existing Nuclear Power Plants: Proceedings.** IAEA Staff. 665p. 1997. pap. 215.00 (*92-0-105296-0*, STI/PUB/1005, Pub. by IAEA AU) Bernan Associates.

***Reviewing 1st Grade (Math)** Jo E. Moore. (Mathematics Ser.). (Illus.). 32p. (J). (gr. 1). 1997. teacher ed., pap. 2.95 (*1-55799-483-8*, 4085) Evan-Moor Corp.

***Reviewing 2nd Grade (Math)** Jo E. Moore. (Mathematics Ser.). (Illus.). 32p. (J). (gr. 2). 1997. teacher ed., pap. 2.95 (*1-55799-484-6*, 4086) Evan-Moor Corp.

Reviews & Articles: From Die Rote Fahne. Georg Lukacs. Tr. by Peter Palmer. (C). 1978. pap. 7.50 (*0-85036-281-4*, Pub. by Merlin Pr UK) Humanities.

Reviews & Critical Papers. Lionel P. Johnson. LC 67-22099. (Essay Index Reprint Ser.). 1977. 15.95 (*0-8369-0574-1*) Ayer.

Reviews & Essays of Austin Clarke. Gregory A. Schirmer. 370p. 1995. 75.00 (*0-86140-337-1*) Littlefield.

Reviews & Essays, 1936-55. Weldon Kees. (Poets on Poetry Ser.). (Orig.). 1988. 39.50 (*0-472-09383-5*); pap. 13.95 (*0-472-06383-9*) U of Mich Pr.

Reviews from Parent Coucil. Ed. by Carolyn Henebry. 248p. 9.95 (*0-9640274-2-9*) Parent Council.

Reviews from Parent Council, Vol. 3, No. 1. Ed. by Carolyn Henebry. iv, 237p. (Orig.). 1995. pap. 9.95 (*0-9640274-4-5*) Parent Council.

Reviews from Parent Council, Vol. 3, No. 2. Ed. by Carolyn Henebry. (Orig.). (J). 1996. pap. 11.95 (*0-9640274-5-3*) Parent Council.

***Reviews from Parent Council, Vol. 4, No. 1.** Carolyn L. Henebry. 224p. (Orig.). 1996. pap. text ed. 11.95 (*0-9640274-6-1*) Parent Council.

Reviews in Biotechnology & Bioengineering. Ed. by Harry W. Tyrer. LC 93-46296. (Critical Reviews of Biotechnology and Bioengineering Ser.: Vol. 1). 296p. 1994. text ed. 78.50 (*0-89391-581-5*) Ablex Pub.

Reviews in Complex Analysis, 1980-1986. LC 88-8145. 3064p. 1989. pap. 335.00 (*0-8218-0127-9*, REVCOM/86) Am Math.

***Reviews in Computational Chemistry.** Ed. by Kenny B. Lipkowitz & Donald B. Boyd. xix, 419p. 1990. 110.00 (*0-471-18728-3*) Wiley.

Reviews in Computational Chemistry, Vol. 1. Ed. by Kenneth B. Lipkowitz & Donald B. Boyd. LC 89-21466. (Illus.). xix, 419p. 1990. 115.00 (*0-89573-754-X*, VCH) Wiley.

Reviews in Computational Chemistry, Vol. 2. Ed. by Kenneth B. Lipkowitz & Donald B. Boyd. 520p. 1991. 110.00 (*1-56081-515-9*, VCH) Wiley.

***Reviews in Computational Chemistry, Vol. 2.** Ed. by Kenny B. Lipkowitz & Donald B. Boyd. xvi, 527p. 1991. 110.00 (*0-471-18810-7*) Wiley.

Reviews in Computational Chemistry, Vol. 3. Ed. by Donald B. Boyd & Kenneth B. Lipkowitz. LC 92-30192. 272p. 1993. 110.00 (*1-56081-619-8*, VCH) Wiley.

***Reviews in Computational Chemistry, Vol. 3.** Ed. by Kenny B. Lipkowitz & Donald B. Boyd. xvi, 271p. 1992. 110.00 (*0-471-18853-0*) Wiley.

Reviews in Computational Chemistry, Vol. 4. Donald B. Boyd & Kenneth B. Lipkowitz. 280p. 1993. 110.00 (*1-56081-620-1*, VCH) Wiley.

***Reviews in Computational Chemistry, Vol. 4.** Ed. by Kenny B. Lipkowitz & Donald B. Boyd. xix, 280p. 1993. 110.00 (*0-471-18854-9*) Wiley.

Reviews in Computational Chemistry, Vol. 5. Donald B. Boyd & Kenneth B. Lipkowitz. 458p. 1994. 110.00 (*1-56081-658-9*, VCH) Wiley.

***Reviews in Computational Chemistry, Vol. 5.** Ed. by Kenny B. Lipkowitz & Donald B. Boyd. xxii, 458p. 1993. 110.00 (*0-471-18866-2*) Wiley.

***Reviews in Computational Chemistry, Vol. 6.** Ed. by Kenneth B. Lipkowitz & Donald B. Boyd. (Illus.). 566p. 1995. 110.00 (*1-56081-667-8*, VCH) Wiley.

***Reviews in Computational Chemistry, Vol. 6.** Ed. by K. B. Lipowitz & D. B. Boyd. (Reviews in Computational Chemistry Ser.). 1995. text ed. 110.00 (*0-471-18596-5*) Wiley.

***Reviews in Computational Chemistry, Vol. 7.** Ed. by K. B. Lipowitz & D. B. Boyd. 1995. text ed. 110.00 (*0-471-18628-7*) Wiley.

Reviews in Computational Chemistry, Vol. 7. 7th ed. Ed. by Donald B. Boyd & Kenneth B. Lipkowitz. (Illus.). 585p. 1995. 110.00 (*1-56081-915-4*, VCH) Wiley.

Reviews in Computational Chemistry, Vol. 8. Ed. by Donald B. Boyd & Kenneth B. Lipkowitz. (Illus.). 350p. 1996. 110.00 (*1-56081-929-4*, VCH) Wiley.

***Reviews in Computational Chemistry, Vol. 8.** Ed. by K. B. Lipowitz & D. B. Boyd. 1996. text ed. 110.00 (*0-471-18638-4*) Wiley.

Reviews in Computational Chemistry, Vol. 9. Ed. by Donald B. Boyd & Kenneth B. Lipkowitz. (Illus.). 300p. 1996. 110.00 (*1-56081-930-8*, VCH) Wiley.

***Reviews in Computational Chemistry, Vol. 9.** Ed. by K. B. Lipowitz & D. B. Boyd. 1996. text ed. 110.00 (*0-471-18639-2*) Wiley.

***Reviews in Computational Chemistry, Vol. 10.** Ed. by K. B. Lipowitz & D. B. Boyd. xxiii, 334p. 1997. text ed. 120.00 (*0-471-18648-1*) Wiley.

Reviews in Environmental Contamination & Toxicology, Vol. 145. Ed. by G. W. Ware. (Illus.). 184p. 1995. 69.95 (*0-387-94584-9*) Spr-Verlag.

Reviews in Functional Analysis, 1980-1986, 4 vols. Intro. by William B. Johnson. LC 89-6708. 2461p. 1989. pap. 289.00 (*0-8218-0134-1*, REVFUA/86C) Am Math.

Reviews in Global Analysis, 1980-1986. LC 88-10565. (REVGLO Ser.: Vol. 86, Section 58). 3920p. 1988. pap. text ed. 355.00 (*0-8218-0104-X*, REVGLO-86) Am Math.

Reviews in Graph Theory, (1940-78), 4 vols., Set. Ed. by William G. Brown. LC 80-17817. 2035p. 1980. pap. 401.00 (*0-8218-0214-3*, REVGRAPH) Am Math.

Reviews in Graph Theory, (1940-78), 4 vols., Vol. 1. Ed. by William G. Brown. LC 80-17817. 588p. 1980. pap. 135.00 (*0-8218-0210-0*, REVGRA/1) Am Math.

Reviews in Graph Theory, (1940-78), 4 vols., Vol. 2. Ed. by William G. Brown. LC 80-17817. 546p. 1980. pap. 135.00 (*0-8218-0211-9*, REVGRA/2) Am Math.

Reviews in Graph Theory, (1940-78), 4 vols., Vol. 3. Ed. by William G. Brown. LC 80-17817. 574p. 1980. pap. 135.00 (*0-8218-0212-7*, REVGRA/3) Am Math.

Reviews in Graph Theory, (1940-78), 4 vols., Vol. 4. Ed. by William G. Brown. LC 80-17817. 327p. 1980. pap. 82.00 (*0-8218-0213-5*, REVGRA/4) Am Math.

Reviews in K-Theory, 1940-1984. Ed. by Bruce A. Magurn. LC 85-7481. 811p. 1985. pap. 321.00 (*0-8218-0088-4*, REVKC) Am Math.

Reviews in Library Book Selection. LeRoy C. Merritt et al. LC 58-62836. (Wayne State University Studies: Humanities: No. 3). 205p. reprint ed. pap. 58.50 (*0-7837-3821-8*, 2043641) Bks Demand.

Reviews in Macromolecular Chemistry, Vol. 3. Ed. by George B. Butler et al. LC 66-9971. (Illus.). 450p. reprint ed. pap. 128.30 (*0-685-23641-2*, 2027990) Bks Demand.

Reviews in Macromolecular Chemistry, Vol. 4. Ed. by George B. Butler et al. LC 66-9971. (Illus.). 427p. reprint ed. pap. 121.70 (*0-685-23640-4*, 2027991) Bks Demand.

Reviews in Macromolecular Chemistry, Vol. 5, Pt. 2. Ed. by George B. Butler et al. LC 66-9971. (Illus.). 242p. reprint ed. pap. 69.00 (*0-685-23642-0*, 2027989) Bks Demand.

Reviews in Macromolecular Chemistry, Vol. 6. Ed. by George B. Butler et al. LC 66-9971. (Illus.). 498p. reprint ed. pap. 142.00 (*0-685-23639-0*, 2027992) Bks Demand.

Reviews in Macromolecular Chemistry, Vol. 7. Ed. by George B. Butler et al. LC 66-9971. (Illus.). 313p. reprint ed. pap. 89.30 (*0-685-23643-9*, 2027988) Bks Demand.

Reviews in Macromolecular Chemistry, Vol. 11: 1974. Ed. by George B. Butler et al. LC 67-27715. (Illus.). 389p. reprint ed. pap. 110.90 (*0-7837-0779-7*, 2041093) Bks Demand.

Reviews in Macromolecular Chemistry, Vol. 12: 1975. Ed. by George B. Butler et al. LC 67-27715. (Illus.). 406p. reprint ed. pap. 115.80 (*0-7837-0780-0*, 2041094) Bks Demand.

Reviews in Macromolecular Chemistry, Vol. 8: 1972. Ed. by George B. Butler et al. LC 67-27715. (Illus.). 345p. reprint ed. pap. 98.40 (*0-7837-0921-8*, 2041226) Bks Demand.

Reviews in Macromolecular Chemistry, Vol. 9: 1973. Ed. by George B. Butler et al. LC 67-27715. (Illus.). 377p. reprint ed. pap. 107.50 (*0-7837-0777-0*, 2041091) Bks Demand.

Reviews in Mathematics & Mathematical Physics Vol. 10, No.1: Multidimensional Monge Ampere Equation, Vol. 10. Ed. by Novikov & Krichever. (Reviews in Mathematics & Mathematical Physics Ser.). 1995. pap. text ed. 35.00 (*3-7186-5831-3*) Gordon & Breach.

Reviews in Modern Astronomy, Vol. 4. Ed. by G. Klare. (Illus.). viii, 286p. 1991. 75.95 (*0-387-54245-0*) Spr-Verlag.

Reviews in Modern Astronomy Five: Variabilities in Stars & Galaxies. G. Klare. (Illus.). x, 271p. 1992. 82.95 (*0-387-55523-4*) Spr-Verlag.

Reviews in Modern Astronomy Three: Accretion & Winds. Ed. by G. Klare. viii, 371p. 1991. 59.00 (*0-387-53364-8*) Spr-Verlag.

Reviews in Modern Astronomy Two. Ed. by G. Klare. (Illus.). 400p. 1990. 62.95 (*0-387-51840-1*) Spr-Verlag.

Reviews in Number Theory: 1940-72, 6 vols., Set. Ed. by William J. LeVeque. LC 74-11335. 2931p. 1974. pap. 534.00 (*0-8218-0226-7*, REVNUM) Am Math.

Reviews in Number Theory: 1940-72, 6 vols., Vol. 1. Ed. by William J. LeVeque. LC 74-11335. 420p. 1974. pap. 123.00 (*0-8218-0203-8*, REVNUM/1) Am Math.

Reviews in Number Theory: 1940-72, 6 vols., Vol. 2. Ed. by William J. LeVeque. LC 74-11335. 672p. 1974. pap. 123.00 (*0-8218-0204-6*, REVNUM/2) Am Math.

Reviews in Number Theory: 1940-72, 6 vols., Vol. 3. Ed. by William J. LeVeque. LC 74-11335. 377p. 1974. pap. 123.00 (*0-8218-0205-4*, REVNUM/3) Am Math.

Reviews in Number Theory: 1940-72, 6 vols., Vol. 4. Ed. by William J. LeVeque. LC 74-11335. 582p. 1974. pap. 123.00 (*0-8218-0206-2*, REVNUM/4) Am Math.

Reviews in Number Theory: 1940-72, 6 vols., Vol. 5. Ed. by William J. LeVeque. LC 74-11335. 470p. 1974. pap. 123.00 (*0-8218-0207-0*, REVNUM/5) Am Math.

Reviews in Number Theory: 1940-72, 6 vols., Vol. 6. Ed. by William J. LeVeque. LC 74-11335. 410p. 1974. pap. 123.00 (*0-8218-0208-9*, REVNUM/6) Am Math.

Reviews in Number Theory, 1940-1983: Reviews in Number Theory, 1940-1972; Reviews in Number Theory, 1973-1983. pap. 1,263.00 (*0-8218-0146-5*, REVNUMSET) Am Math.

Reviews in Number Theory, 1973-83, 6 vols., Set. Ed. by Richard K. Guy. LC 84-11159. 3573p. 1990. pap. 899.00 (*0-8218-0218-6*, REVNUM/83) Am Math.

Reviews in Number Theory, 1973-83, 6 vols., Vol. 1. Ed. by Richard K. Guy. LC 84-11159. 460p. 1990. pap. 175.00 (*0-8218-0219-4*, REVNUM/83/1) Am Math.

Reviews in Number Theory, 1973-83, 6 vols., Vol. 2. Ed. by Richard K. Guy. LC 84-11159. 765p. 1990. pap. 175.00 (*0-8218-0220-8*, REVNUM/83/2) Am Math.

Reviews in Number Theory, 1973-83, 6 vols., Vol. 3. Ed. by Richard K. Guy. LC 84-11159. 344p. 1990. pap. 175.00 (*0-8218-0221-6*, REVNUM/83/3) Am Math.

Reviews in Number Theory, 1973-83, 6 vols., Vol. 4. Ed. by Richard K. Guy. LC 84-11159. 477p. 1990. pap. 175.00 (*0-8218-0222-4*, REVNUM/83/4) Am Math.

Reviews in Number Theory, 1973-83, 6 vols., Vol. 5. Ed. by Richard K. Guy. LC 84-11159. 699p. 1990. pap. 175.00 (*0-8218-0223-2*, REVNUM/83/5) Am Math.

Reviews in Number Theory, 1973-83, 6 vols., Vol. 6. Ed. by Richard K. Guy. LC 84-11159. 828p. 1990. pap. 175.00 (*0-8218-0224-0*, REVNUM/83/6) Am Math.

Reviews in Numerical Analysis, 1980-1986, 5 vols., Section 65. LC 87-25478. (REVNAN Ser.: Vol. 86). 3558p. 1987. pap. 303.00 (*0-8218-0102-3*, REVNAN/86) Am Math.

Reviews in Operator Theory, 1980-1986. LC 89-6551. (REVOPE Ser.: No. 86). 2639p. 1989. pap. 289.00 (*0-8218-0135-X*, REVOPE/86) Am Math.

Reviews in Partial Differential Equations, 1980-1986, 5 vols. Intro. by Murray H. Protter. LC 88-6681. 3998p. 1988. pap. 355.00 (*0-8218-0103-1*, REVPDE/86) Am Math.

Reviews in Particulate Materials, Vol. 4. Ed. by Animesh Bose et al. (Illus.). 300p. 1996. pap. 95.00 (*0-614-14709-3*) Metal Powder.

Reviews in Pediatric Hem-Oncology VI. Ed. by Carl Pochedly. LC 85-9547. 222p. 1985. text ed. 55.00 (*0-275-91306-6*, C1306, Praeger Pubs) Greenwood.

Reviews in Perinatal Medicine, Vol. 4. Emile M. Scarpelli. Ed. by Ermelando V. Cosmi. LC 75-38562. 544p. 1981. reprint ed. pap. 155.10 (*0-608-00268-2*, 2047143) Bks Demand.

Reviews in Perinatal Medicine Vol. 2. fac. ed. Ed. by Emile M. Scarpelli & Ermelando V. Cosmi. LC 75-38562. (Illus.). 405p. pap. 115.50 (*0-7837-7154-1*, 2047143) Bks Demand.

Reviews in Perinatal Medicine Vol. 3. fac. ed. Ed. by Emile M. Scarpelli & Ermelando V. Cosmi. LC 75-38562. (Illus.). 493p. pap. 140.60 (*0-7837-7153-3*, 2047143) Bks Demand.

Reviews in Ring Theory, 1960-1984: Reviews in Ring Theory, 1960-1979; Reviews in Ring Theory, 1980-1984, 2 vols. pap. 372.00 (*0-8218-0147-3*, REVRNG/60/84C) Am Math.

Reviews in Ring Theory, 1960-79. Lance W. Small. LC 81-10770. 1114p. 1981. pap. 334.00 (*0-8218-0215-1*, REVRING) Am Math.

Reviews in Ring Theory, 1980-1984. L. Small. LC 86-10907. (Reviews in Ring Theory Ser.: Vol. 84). 685p. 1986. pap. 108.00 (*0-8218-0097-3*, REVRNG/84) Am Math.

Reviews in Weed Science, Vol. 1. Ed. & Intro. by J. S. Bannon. 74p. 1985. text ed. 9.00 (*0-318-32863-1*) Weed Sci Soc.

Reviews in Weed Science, Vol. 2. Ed. & Intro. by C. L. Foy. 90p. 1986. text ed. 12.00 (*0-911733-06-X*) Weed Sci Soc.

Reviews of Creationist Books. 2nd ed. Ed. by Liz R. Hughes. (Illus.). 147p. 1992. pap. 10.00 (*0-939873-52-4*) Natl Ctr Sci Educ.

Reviews of Engineering Geology, Vol. 1. Geological Society of America Staff. Ed. by Thomas Fluhr & Robert F. Legget. LC 62-51690. (Illus.). 308p. reprint ed. pap. 80.10 (*0-685-23718-4*, 2032618) Bks Demand.

Reviews of English Language Proficiency Tests. Ed. by J. Charles Alderson et al. 88p. 1987. pap. 16.50 (*0-939791-31-5*) Tchrs Eng Spkrs.

Reviews of Environmental Contamination & Toxicology, 2 vols. Ed. by G. W. Ware. (Illus.). 1991. 54.00 (*0-387-97644-2*) Spr-Verlag.

Reviews of Environmental Contamination & Toxicology. Ed. by G. W. Ware. 160p. 1995. 69.95 (*0-387-94453-2*) Spr-Verlag.

Reviews of Environmental Contamination & Toxicology. Ed. by G. W. Ware. (Illus.). 184p. 1995. 69.95 (*0-387-94561-X*) Spr-Verlag.

Reviews of Environmental Contamination & Toxicology, 2 vols., Vol. 1. Ed. by G. W. Ware. (Illus.). 168p. 1990. 72.95 (*0-387-97444-X*) Spr-Verlag.

Reviews of Environmental Contamination & Toxicology, Vol. 98. Ed. by G. W. Ware. (Illus.). 185p. 1986. 85.95 (*0-387-96448-7*) Spr-Verlag.

Reviews of Environmental Contamination & Toxicology, Vol. 99. Ed. by G. W. Ware. (Illus.). 185p. 1987. 89.95 (*0-387-96498-3*) Spr-Verlag.

R

Reviews of Environmental Contamination & Toxicology, Vol. 100. Ed. by G. W. Ware. (Illus.). 170p. 1987. 83.95 (*0-387-96583-1*) Spr-Verlag.

Reviews of Environmental Contamination & Toxicology, Vol. 101. Ed. by G. W. Ware. 200p. 1987. 89.95 (*0-387-96593-9*) Spr-Verlag.

Reviews of Environmental Contamination & Toxicology, Vol. 102. Ed. by G. W. Ware. (Illus.). 195p. 1987. 77.95 (*0-387-96647-1*) Spr-Verlag.

Reviews of Environmental Contamination & Toxicology, Vol. 103. Ed. by G. W. Ware. (Illus.). 180p. 1988. 89.95 (*0-387-96693-5*) Spr-Verlag.

Reviews of Environmental Contamination & Toxicology, Vol. 104. 210p. 1988. 89.95 (*0-387-96725-7*) Spr-Verlag.

Reviews of Environmental Contamination & Toxicology, Vol. 105. 185p. 1988. 89.95 (*0-387-96723-0*) Spr-Verlag.

Reviews of Environmental Contamination & Toxicology, Vol. 108. Ed. by G. W. Ware. (Illus.). ix, 184p. 1988. 89.95 (*0-387-96902-0*) Spr-Verlag.

Reviews of Environmental Contamination & Toxicology, Vol. 110. Ed. by G. W. Ware. ix, 190p. 1989. 89.95 (*0-387-97158-0*) Spr-Verlag.

Reviews of Environmental Contamination & Toxicology, Vol. 112. Ed. by G. W. Ware. (Illus.). 168p. 1989. 89.95 (*0-387-97160-2*) Spr-Verlag.

Reviews of Environmental Contamination & Toxicology, Vol. 113. G. W. Ware. ix, 145p. 1989. 89.95 (*0-387-97206-4*) Spr-Verlag.

Reviews of Environmental Contamination & Toxicology, Vol. 114. G. W. Ware. (Illus.). ix, 171p. 1989. 89.95 (*0-387-97207-2*) Spr-Verlag.

Reviews of Environmental Contamination & Toxicology, Vol. 116. Ed. by G. W. Ware. ix, 205p. 1990. 89.95 (*0-387-97334-6*) Spr-Verlag.

Reviews of Environmental Contamination & Toxicology, Vol. 117. Ed. by G. W. Ware. (Illus.). 176p. 1990. 89.95 (*0-387-97403-2*) Spr-Verlag.

Reviews of Environmental Contamination & Toxicology, Vol. 118. Ed. by G. W. Ware. (Illus.). 168p. 1990. 89.95 (*0-387-97447-4*) Spr-Verlag.

Reviews of Environmental Contamination & Toxicology, 2 vols., Vol. 120. Ed. by G. W. Ware. (Illus.). 168p. 1990. 89.95 (*0-387-97445-8*) Spr-Verlag.

Reviews of Environmental Contamination & Toxicology, 2 vols., Vol. 122. Ed. by G. W. Ware. (Illus.). 168p. 1991. 89.95 (*0-387-97645-0*) Spr-Verlag.

Reviews of Environmental Contamination & Toxicology, Vol. 123. R. D. Wauchope et al. Ed. by G. W. Ware. (Illus.). 184p. 1991. 49.00 (*0-387-97726-0*) Spr-Verlag.

Reviews of Environmental Contamination & Toxicology, Vol. 124. R. D. Wauchope et al. Ed. by G. W. Ware. (Illus.). 168p. 1991. 64.95 (*0-387-97730-9*) Spr-Verlag.

Reviews of Environmental Contamination & Toxicology, Vol. 125. G. W. Ware. (Illus.). ix, 186p. 1991. 89.95 (*0-387-97762-7*) Spr-Verlag.

Reviews of Environmental Contamination & Toxicology, Vol. 126. Ed. by G. W. Ware. (Illus.). 160p. 1992. 89.95 (*0-387-97807-0*) Spr-Verlag.

Reviews of Environmental Contamination & Toxicology, Vol. 127. Ed. by G. W. Ware. 176p. 1992. 89.95 (*0-387-97829-1*) Spr-Verlag.

Reviews of Environmental Contamination & Toxicology, Vol. 128. Ed. by G. W. Ware. xiv, 124p. 1992. 89.95 (*0-387-97899-2*) Spr-Verlag.

Reviews of Environmental Contamination & Toxicology, Vol. 129. Ed. by G. W. Ware. xiv, 144p. 1992. 89.95 (*0-387-97900-X*) Spr-Verlag.

Reviews of Environmental Contamination & Toxicology, Vol. 130. Ed. by G. W. Ware. (Illus.). xi, 140p. 1992. 89.95 (*0-387-97931-X*) Spr-Verlag.

Reviews of Environmental Contamination & Toxicology, Vol. 131. Ed. by G. W. Ware. (Illus.). xi, 154p. 1992. 89.95 (*0-387-97925-5*) Spr-Verlag.

Reviews of Environmental Contamination & Toxicology, Vol. 132. Ed. by G. W. Ware. (Illus.). 168p. 1993. 69.95 (*0-387-94050-2*) Spr-Verlag.

Reviews of Environmental Contamination & Toxicology, Vol. 133. Ed. by G. W. Ware. (Illus.). 170p. 1993. write for info. (*3-540-94103-7*); 69.95 (*0-387-94103-7*) Spr-Verlag.

Reviews of Environmental Contamination & Toxicology, Vol. 134. G. W. Ware. 136p. 1993. 69.95 (*0-387-94178-9*) Spr-Verlag.

Reviews of Environmental Contamination & Toxicology, Vol. 136. Ed. by G. W. Ware. (Illus.). 168p. 1994. 69.95 (*0-387-94278-5*) Spr-Verlag.

Reviews of Environmental Contamination & Toxicology, Vol. 137. Ed. by G. W. Ware. (Illus.). 152p. 1994. 69.95 (*0-387-94283-1*) Spr-Verlag.

Reviews of Environmental Contamination & Toxicology, Vol. 138. Ed. by G. W. Ware. 160p. 1994. 69.95 (*0-387-94324-2*) Spr-Verlag.

Reviews of Environmental Contamination & Toxicology, Vol. 140. G. W. Ware. 216p. 1994. 69.95 (*0-387-94346-3*) Spr-Verlag.

Reviews of Environmental Contamination & Toxicology, Vol. 142. Ed. by G. W. Ware. (Illus.). 176p. 1995. 69.95 (*0-387-94548-2*) Spr-Verlag.

Reviews of Environmental Contamination & Toxicology, Vol. 144. Ed. by G. W. Ware. (Illus.). 176p. 1995. 69.95 (*0-387-94574-1*) Spr-Verlag.

Reviews of Environmental Contamination & Toxicology, Vol. 146. Ed. by G. W. Ware. (Illus.). 200p. 1996. 59.95 (*0-387-94703-5*) Spr-Verlag.

***Reviews of Environmental Contamination & Toxicology, Vol. 147.** Ed. by G. W. Ware. 168p. 1996. 59.95 (*0-387-94810-4*) Spr-Verlag.

***Reviews of Environmental Contamination & Toxicology, Vol. 148.** Ed. by G. W. Ware. (Illus.). 184p. 1996. 59.95 (*0-387-94842-2*) Spr-Verlag.

***Reviews of Environmental Contamination & Toxicology, Vol. 149.** G. W. Ware. (Illus.). 160p. 1996. 59.95 (*0-387-94863-5*) Spr-Verlag.

***Reviews of Environmental Contamination & Toxicology, Vol. 150.** Ed. by G. W. Ware. (Illus.). 184p. 1996. 59.95 (*0-387-94885-6*) Spr-Verlag.

***Reviews of Environmental Contamination & Toxicology, Vol. 152.** Ed. by G. W. Ware. (Illus.). 140p. 1997. 59.95 (*0-387-98277-9*) Spr-Verlag.

***Reviews of Environmental Contamination & Toxicology Vol. 151.** G. W. Ware. (Illus.). 176p. 1997. 59.95 (*0-387-98238-8*) Spr-Verlag.

Reviews of Environmental Contamination & Toxicology (Continuation of Residue Reviews), Vol. 115. Ed. by G. W. Ware. ix, 156p. 1990. 89.95 (*0-387-97289-7*) Spr-Verlag.

Reviews of Environmental Toxicology, Vol.111. Ed. by G. W. Ware. (Illus.). 168p. 1989. 89.95 (*0-387-97159-9*) Spr-Verlag.

Reviews of Immunoassay, 2 vols. Ed. by S. B. Pal. 1988. lib. bdg. write for info. (*0-318-63139-3*) Routledge Chapman & Hall.

Reviews of Immunoassay, 2 vols., Vol. 1. Ed. by S. B. Pal. 200p. 1988. lib. bdg. 89.95 (*0-412-01841-1*) Routledge Chapman & Hall.

Reviews of Immunoassay, 2 vols., Vol. 2. Ed. by S. B. Pal. 208p. 1988. lib. bdg. 89.95 (*0-412-01851-9*) Routledge Chapman & Hall.

Reviews of Infrared & Millimeter Waves: Optically Pumped Far-Infrared Lasers, Vol. 2. Franco Strumia. 492p. 1984. 135.00 (*0-306-41487-2*, Plenum Pr) Plenum.

Reviews of Lunar Sciences. Ed. by Joseph Chamberlain. (Illus.). 540p. 1977. reprint ed. pap. 5.00 (*0-87590-220-0*) Am Geophysical.

Reviews of National Policies for Education: Austria. OECD Staff. 106p. (Orig.). 1995. pap. 30.00 (*92-64-14394-7*, Pub. by Org for Econ FR) OECD.

***Reviews of National Policies for Education: Czech Republic.** OECD Staff. 160p. (Orig.). 1996. pap. 33.00 (*92-64-15307-1*, 91-96-09-1) OECD.

Reviews of National Policies for Education: France. 218p. (Orig.). (ENG & FRE.). 1996. pap. 53.00 (*92-64-14708-X*, Pub. by Org for Econ FR) OECD.

***Reviews of National Policies for Education: Greece.** OECD Staff. 216p. (Orig.). 1997. pap. 30.00 (*92-64-15365-9*, 91-97-03-1, Pub. by Org for Econ FR) OECD.

***Reviews of National Policies for Education: Mexico.** OECD Staff. 228p. (Orig.). 1997. pap. 29.00 (*92-64-15423-X*, 91-97-02-1, Pub. by Org for Econ FR) OECD.

Reviews of National Policies for Education: Netherlands. OECD Staff. 148p. (Orig.). 1992. pap. 31.00 (*92-64-13608-8*) OECD.

***Reviews of National Policies for Education: Poland.** 160p. 1996. 33.00 (*92-64-14897-3*, 91-96-07-1, Pub. by Org for Econ FR) OECD.

Reviews of National Policies for Education: Sweden. 244p. (Orig.). 1995. pap. 39.00 (*92-64-14380-7*, Pub. by Org for Econ FR) OECD.

Reviews of National Policies for Education Denmark "Educating Youth" OECD Staff. 126p. (Orig.). 1995. pap. 24.00 (*92-64-14475-7*, Pub. by Org for Econ FR) OECD.

Reviews of National Policies for Education Finland: Higher Education. OECD Staff. 246p. (Orig.). 1995. pap. 52.00 (*92-64-14442-0*, Pub. by Org for Econ FR) OECD.

Reviews of National Science & Technology Policy: Italy. OECD Staff. 163p. (Orig.). 1992. pap. 25.00 (*92-64-13614-2*) OECD.

Reviews of National Science & Technology Policy: Poland. Contrib. by OECD (Centre for Co-Operation with the Economies in Transition) Staff. 171p. (Orig.). (ENG & FRE.). 1996. pap. 30.00 (*92-64-14642-3*, Pub. by Org for Econ FR) OECD.

Reviews of National Science & Technology Policy: Portugal. OECD Staff. 180p. (Orig.). 1993. pap. 22.00 (*92-64-24042-X*) OECD.

Reviews of National Science & Technology Policy: Turkey. 128p. 1995. pap. 30.00 (*92-64-14641-5*, 92-95-14-1, Pub. by Org for Econ FR) OECD.

Reviews of National Science Policy: United States. OECD Staff. Ed. by I. Bernard Cohen. LC 79-7979. (Three Centuries of Science in America Ser.). 1980. reprint ed. lib. bdg. 55.95 (*0-405-12561-5*) Ayer.

Reviews of Neuroscience Vol. 3. fac. ed. Ed. by Seymour Ehrenpreis & Irwin J. Kopin. LC 74-80538. (Illus.). 238p. pap. 67.90 (*0-7837-7142-8*, 2047152) Bks Demand.

Reviews of Papers in Algebraic & Differential Topology, Topological Groups, & Homological Algebra 1940-67. Ed. by Norman E. Steenrod. LC 68-58968. 1448p. 1969. pap. 95.00 (*0-8218-0046-9*, REVTOP) Am Math.

Reviews of Physiology, Vol. 115. 1990. 90.00 (*0-387-51712-X*) Spr-Verlag.

Reviews of Physiology, Biochemistry & Pharmacology. Ed. by M. P. Blaustein et al. (Advances in Pharmacological Sciences Ser.: 126). 425p. 1994. 135.00 (*3-540-58477-3*) Spr-Verlag.

Reviews of Physiology Biochemistry & Pharmacology, Vol. 87. (Illus.). 250p. 1980. 71.00 (*0-387-09944-1*) Spr-Verlag.

Reviews of Physiology, Biochemistry, & Pharmacology, Vol. 88. Richard H. Adrian. (Illus.). 264p. 1981. 76.00 (*0-387-10408-9*) Spr-Verlag.

Reviews of Physiology, Biochemistry & Pharmacology, Vol. 89. Ed. by Richard H. Adrian. (Illus.). 260p. 1981. 70.00 (*0-387-10495-X*) Spr-Verlag.

Reviews of Physiology, Biochemistry & Pharmacology, Vol. 90. Ed. by Richard H. Adrian et al. (Illus.). 300p. 1981. 76.00 (*0-387-10657-X*) Spr-Verlag.

Reviews of Physiology, Biochemistry & Pharmacology, Vol. 91. Ed. by Richard H. Adrian et al. (Illus.). 240p. 1981. 67.00 (*0-387-10961-7*) Spr-Verlag.

Reviews of Physiology, Biochemistry, & Pharmacology, Vol. 92. Ed. by Richard H. Adrian et al. (Illus.). 220p. 1981. 67.00 (*0-387-11105-0*) Spr-Verlag.

Reviews of Physiology, Biochemistry & Pharmacology, Vol. 94. Ed. by Richard H. Adrian et al. (Illus.). 225p. 1982. 76.00 (*0-387-11701-6*) Spr-Verlag.

Reviews of Physiology, Biochemistry, & Pharmacology, Vol. 95. Ed. by Richard H. Adrian. (Illus.). 235p. 1982. 76.00 (*0-387-11736-9*) Spr-Verlag.

Reviews of Physiology, Biochemistry & Pharmacology, Vol. 96. Ed. by Richard H. Adrian et al. (Illus.). 194p. 1982. 72.00 (*0-387-11849-7*) Spr-Verlag.

Reviews of Physiology, Biochemistry & Pharmacology, Vol. 97. Ed. by Richard H. Adrian et al. (Illus.). 176p. 1983. 67.00 (*0-387-12135-8*) Spr-Verlag.

Reviews of Physiology, Biochemistry & Pharmacology, Vol. 98. H. Blashko et al. (Illus.). 260p. 1983. 93.00 (*0-387-12817-4*) Spr-Verlag.

Reviews of Physiology, Biochemistry, & Pharmacology, Vol. 110. (Illus.). v, 292p. 1988. 113.00 (*0-387-18736-7*) Spr-Verlag.

Reviews of Physiology, Biochemistry & Pharmacology, Vol. 113. Ed. by M. P. Blaustein et al. (Illus.). vi, 150p. 1989. 80.00 (*0-387-50948-8*) Spr-Verlag.

Reviews of Physiology, Biochemistry & Pharmacology, Vol. 114. Ed. by M. P. Blaustein et al. (Illus.). 272p. 1989. 113.00 (*0-387-51693-X*) Spr-Verlag.

Reviews of Physiology, Biochemistry & Pharmacology, Vol. 116. D. Pette et al. Ed. by M. P. Blaustein et al. (Illus.). 176p. 1990. 97.95 (*0-387-52880-6*) Spr-Verlag.

Reviews of Physiology, Biochemistry & Pharmacology, Vol. 118. Ed. by M. P. Blaustein et al. (Illus.). v, 128p. 1991. 76.00 (*0-387-54211-6*) Spr-Verlag.

Reviews of Physiology, Biochemistry & Pharmacology, Vol. 120. Ed. by M. P. Blaustein et al. (Illus.). 200p. 1992. 140.00 (*0-387-55364-9*) Spr-Verlag.

Reviews of Physiology, Biochemistry & Pharmacology, Vol. 122. Ed. by M. P. Blaustein et al. (Illus.). 290p. 1993. 143.00 (*0-387-56380-6*) Spr-Verlag.

Reviews of Physiology, Biochemistry & Pharmacology, Vol. 123. Ed. by M. P. Blaustein et al. v, 266p. 1994. 133.00 (*0-387-57536-7*) Spr-Verlag.

Reviews of Physiology, Biochemistry & Pharmacology, Vol. 125. Ed. by M. P. Blaustein et al. 1994. 124.00 (*0-387-57930-3*) Spr-Verlag.

Reviews of Physiology, Biochemistry & Pharmacology, Vol. 127. Ed. by M. P. Blaustein et al. (Illus.). 272p. 1995. 152.00 (*3-540-60135-X*) Spr-Verlag.

***Reviews of Physiology, Biochemistry & Pharmacology, Vol. 128.** Ed. by M. P. Blaustein et al. (Illus.). VI, 268p. 1996. 116.00 (*3-540-61343-9*) Spr-Verlag.

***Reviews of Physiology, Biochemistry & Pharmacology, Vol. 129.** Ed. by M. P. Blaustein et al. (Illus.). 80p. 1996. 74.95 (*3-540-61435-4*) Spr-Verlag.

***Reviews of Physiology, Biochemistry & Pharmacology, Vol. 130.** Ed. by M. P. Blaustein et al. (Illus.). 260p. 1997. 116.00 (*3-540-61762-0*) Spr-Verlag.

Reviews of Physiology, Biochemistry & Pharmacology: Special Issue on Signal Transduction, Vol. 119, Pt. I. Ed. by M. P. Blaustein et al. (Illus.). 264p. 1992. 147.00 (*0-387-55192-1*) Spr-Verlag.

Reviews of Physiology, Biochemistry & Pharmacology: Special Issue on Signal Transduction II, Vol. 121. Ed. by M. P. Blaustein et al. (Illus.). 216p. 1992. 140.00 (*0-387-55969-8*) Spr-Verlag.

Reviews of Physiology, Biochemistry & Pharmacology: The Superoxide-Forming NADPH Oxidase of Phagocytes: an Enzyme System Regulated by Multiple Mechanisms, Vol. 117. Ralph T. Seifert. 290p. 1991. 118.00 (*0-387-53663-9*) Spr-Verlag.

Reviews of Plasma Chemistry, Vol. 1. Ed. by Boris M. Smirnov. (Illus.). 340p. 1991. 105.00 (*0-306-11041-5*, Consultants) Plenum.

Reviews of Plasma Chemistry, Vol. 2. Ed. by Boris M. Smirnov. (Illus.). 349p. 1994. 110.00 (*0-306-11042-3*, Consultants) Plenum.

Reviews of Plasma Chemistry, Vol. 3. Ed. by Boris M. Smirnov. (Illus.). 300p. 1996. write for info. (*0-306-11043-1*) Plenum.

Reviews of Plasma Physics, Vol. 4, 1966. Ed. by M. A. Leontovich. Tr. by Herbert Lashinsky from RUS. LC 64-23244. (Illus.). 249p. reprint ed. pap. 71.00 (*0-8357-4388-8*, 2037243) Bks Demand.

Reviews of Plasma Physics, Vol. 9. Ed. by M. A. Leontovich. Tr. by A. B. Mikhailovskii et al. from RUS. LC 64-23244. 352p. 1986. 89.50 (*0-306-10999-9*, Consultants) Plenum.

Reviews of Plasma Physics, Vol. 10. Ed. by M. A. Leontovich. Tr. by Oleg H. Glebov from RUS. LC 64-23244. 526p. 1986. 125.00 (*0-306-11000-8*, Consultants) Plenum.

Reviews of Plasma Physics, Vol. 11. Ed. by M. A. Leontovich. Tr. by J. Hugill from RUS. LC 64-23244. 316p. 1986. 89.50 (*0-306-11001-6*, Consultants) Plenum.

Reviews of Plasma Physics, Vol. 12. Ed. by M. A. Leontovich et al. LC 64-23244. (Illus.). 364p. 1987. 95.00 (*0-306-11002-4*, Consultants) Plenum.

Reviews of Plasma Physics, Vol. 13. Ed. by B. B. Kadomtsev. Tr. by J. George Adashko from RUS. LC 64-23244. (Illus.). 396p. 1987. 105.00 (*0-306-11003-2*, Consultants) Plenum.

Reviews of Plasma Physics, Vol. 14. Ed. by B. B. Kadomtsev. Tr. by J. George Adashko from RUS. LC 64-23244. (Illus.). 258p. 1989. 95.00 (*0-306-11004-0*, Consultants) Plenum.

Reviews of Plasma Physics, Vol. 15. Ed. by B. B. Kadomtsev. LC 64-23244. (Illus.). 336p. 1990. 95.00 (*0-306-11005-9*, Consultants) Plenum.

Reviews of Plasma Physics, Vol. 16. B. B. Kadomtsev. LC 64-23244. (Illus.). 302p. 1990. 95.00 (*0-306-11006-7*, Consultants) Plenum.

Reviews of Plasma Physics, Vol. 17. Ed. by B. B. Kadomtsev. (Illus.). 300p. (C). 1993. 89.50 (*0-306-11007-5*, Consultants) Plenum.

Reviews of Plasma Physics, Vol. 19. Ed. by B. B. Kadomtsev. 260p. 1996. 95.00 (*0-306-11009-1*) Plenum.

Reviews of Renewable Energy Resources. Mahendra S. Sodha. (C). 1988. 44.00 (*0-85226-844-0*) S Asia.

Reviews of Weed Science, Vol. 3. Ed. by Chester L. Foy. 204p. 1987. text ed. 19.50 (*0-911733-07-8*) Weed Sci Soc.

Reviews on Analytical Chemistry: Euroanalysis VIII. Ed. by D. Littlejohn & D. Thorburn. 376p. 1994. 168.00 (*0-85186-982-3*, R6982) CRC Pr.

Reviews on Corrosion Inhibitor Science & Technology, Vol. 2. Ed. by A. Raman & P. Labine. (Illus.). 350p. (Orig.). 1996. pap. text ed. 90.00 (*1-57590-005-X*) NACE Intl.

Reviews on Corrosion Inhibitors Science & Technology. Ed. by A. Raman & P. Labine. LC 92-61226. 716p. 1993. pap. 120.00 (*1-877914-42-8*) NACE Intl.

Reviews on Finite Groups, 1940-1970. Ed. by Daniel Gorenstein. LC 74-771. 706p. 1974. pap. 135.00 (*0-8218-0202-X*, REVFINITEC) Am Math.

Reviews on Group Theory, 1940-1970: Reviews on Finite Groups, 1940-1970; Reviews on Infinite Groups, 1940-1970, 2 vols. pap. 267.00 (*0-8218-0148-1*, REVGRPC) Am Math.

Reviews on Infinite Groups, 1940-1970. Ed. by Gilbert Baumslag. LC 73-21521. 1062p. 1974. pap. 201.00 (*0-8218-0201-1*, REVINFINC) Am Math.

Reviling of the Great. Arnold Petersen. 112p. 1949. 1.50 (*0-935534-24-5*); pap. 0.75 (*0-935534-25-3*) NY Labor News.

***Revised Appreciation Certificates.** 2nd rev. ed. Patricia T. Kienzle. (Illus.). 46p. 1989. pap. 3.50 (*1-890798-07-X*) P T Kienzle.

Revised Basic Training in Camera Repair. Edward H. Romney. 132p. 1993. pap. text ed. 35.00 (*1-886996-52-0*) Hillcrst Pub.

Revised Checklist with Distribution Maps of the Turtles of the World. rev. ed. John B. Iverson. (Illus.). 363p. 1992. pap. 25.00 (*0-9617431-1-5*) J P Iverson.

Revised Classification of the Soils of Belize. I. C. Baillie et al. 71p. 1993. pap. 30.00 (*0-85954-344-7*, Pub. by Nat Res Inst UK) St Mut.

Revised Code of Washington Annotated. write for info. (*0-318-57501-9*) West Pub.

***Revised Common Lectionary: New Revised Standard Veresion 3 Year Cycle.** 599p. (Orig.). 1996. pap. text ed. 25.00 (*0-9618112-2-6*) St Marks Pr.

***Revised Common Lectionary in NRSV: For Sundays & Holidays.** Canon M. Perham. 1997. cd-rom 140.00 (*0-264-67456-1*) Cassell.

***Revised Common Lectionary in NRSV: For Sundays & Holidays.** Canon M. Perham. 1024p. 1997. 140.00 (*0-304-33697-1*) Cassell.

Revised Common Lectionary, 1992: The Report from the Consultation on Common Texts. LC 92-20507. 112p. 1992. pap. 13.95 (*0-687-36174-5*) Abingdon.

Revised Compleat Sinatra. rev. ed. Albert I. Lonstein & Vito R. Marino. LC 79-88307. (Illus.). 702p. 1980. 49.95 (*0-87990-000-8*) Lonstein Pubns.

Revised Correlation of Precambrian Rocks in the British Isles. Ed. by W. Gibbons & A. L. Harris. (Geological Society Special Reports Ser.: No. 22). 112p. (C). 1994. pap. 32.00 (*1-897799-11-X*, 209, Pub. by Geol Soc Pub Hse UK) AAPG.

Revised Correlation of Silurian Rocks in the British Isles. L. R. Cocks et al. (Geological Society Special Reports: No. 21). 32p. (C). 1991. pap. 24.00 (*0-903317-75-3*, 268, Pub. by Geol Soc Pub Hse UK) AAPG.

Revised Edition Quarto 2, 1599 see Romeo & Juliet: Parallel Texts of the First 2 Quartos; Quarto 1, 1597 & Quarto 2, 1599

Revised English Bible with Apocrypha. 1990. pap. 50.00 (*0-521-15153-8*) Cambridge U Pr.

Revised Foil. Charles A. Selberg. 164p. 1993. pap. 23.95 (*0-9638337-7-4*) Spotted Dog Pr.

Revised Handbook for Analyzing Jobs. 1996. lib. bdg. 250.95 (*0-8490-6903-3*) Gordon Pr.

***Revised Handbook for Analyzing Jobs.** 1997. lib. bdg. 250.99 (*0-8490-7667-6*) Gordon Pr.

Revised Handbook for Analyzing Jobs. U. S. Department of Labor, Employment & Training Administration Staff. 272p. 1992. pap. 19.95 (*1-56370-051-4*, HAJ) JIST Works.

Revised Handbook of the Flora of Ceylon, Vol. 7. Ed. by M. D. Dassanayake & F. R. Fosberg. (Illus.). 446p. (C). 1991. text ed. 70.00 (*90-6191-551-1*, Pub. by A A Balkema NE) Ashgate Pub Co.

***Revised Handbook to the Flora of Ceylon, Vol. 1.** Ed. by M. D. Dassanayake & F. R. Fosberg. 516p. 1980. 85.00 (*90-6191-064-1*, Pub. by A A Balkema NE) Ashgate Pub Co.

***Revised Handbook to the Flora of Ceylon, Vol. 2.** Ed. by M. D. Dassanayake & F. R. Fosberg. 518p. 1981. 85.00 (*90-6191-065-X*, Pub. by A A Balkema NE) Ashgate Pub Co.

***Revised Handbook to the Flora of Ceylon, Vol. 3.** Ed. by M. D. Dassanayake & F. R. Fosberg. 508p. 1981. 85.00 (*90-6191-066-8*, Pub. by A A Balkema NE) Ashgate Pub Co.

Revised Handbook to the Flora of Ceylon, Vol. 5. D. Dassanayake. (C). 1988. text ed. 60.00 (*0-685-22119-9*, Pub. by Scientific UK) St Mut.

An Asterisk (*) at the beginning of an entry indicates that the title is appearing in BIP for the first time.

***Revised Handbook to the Flora of Ceylon, Vol. 5.** Ed. by M. D. Dassanayake & F. R. Fosberg. 484p. 1985. 85.00 (*90-6191-068-4*, Pub. by A A Balkema NE) Ashgate Pub Co.

Revised Handbook to the Flora of Ceylon, Vol. 9. Ed. by M. D. Dassanayake. (Illus.). 494p. (C). 1995. text ed. 90.00 (*90-5410-267-5*, Pub. by A A Balkema NE) Ashgate Pub Co.

***Revised Handbook to the Flora of Ceylon, Vol. 10.** rev. ed. Ed. by M. D. Dassanayake & W. D. Clayton. (Illus.). 434p. (C). 1996. text ed. 85.00 (*90-5410-268-3*, Pub. by A A Balkema NE) Ashgate Pub Co.

Revised Handbook to the Flora of Ceylon, Vols. 1-4. D. Dassanayake. (C). 1988. text ed. 40.00 (*0-685-74019-6*, Pub. by Scientific UK) St Mut.

Revised Health Problems of the Horse. Robert M. Miller. Ed. by Gary Vorhes. (Illus.). 144p. (Orig.). 1987. pap. 12.95 (*0-911647-13-9*) Western Horseman.

Revised Key to the Adults of the British Species of Ephemeroptera. 2nd ed. D. E. Kimmins. 1972. 45.00 (*0-900386-17-7*) St Mut.

Revised Key to the British Water Bugs (Hempitera-Heteroptera) 2nd ed. T. T. Macan. 1976. 45.00 (*0-900386-07-X*) St Mut.

Revised List of Hawaiian Pteridophyta. C. Christensen. (BMB Ser.). 1974. reprint ed. pap. 25.00 (*0-527-02128-8*) Periodicals Srv.

Revised Medieval Latin Word-List from British & Irish Sources. Ed. by Ronald E. Latham. (British Academy Ser.). 548p. 1965. 58.00 (*0-19-725891-3*) OUP.

Revised Model Accreditation Plan for Asbestos. (State Legislative Reports: Vol. 19, No. 12). 6p. 1994. 5.00 (*1-55516-379-3*, 7302-1912) Natl Conf State Legis.

Revised Model Business Corporation Act (1984) 480p. 1985. 55.00 (*0-317-29376-1*, #H43880) HarBrace.

Revised Model Business Corporation Act (1984) 1985. write for info. (*0-318-65481-4*, H43899) P-H.

Revised Model Nonprofit Corporation Act. ABA, Business Law Staff. 454p. 1988. write for info. (*0-318-65479-2*, H77939) P-H.

Revised New General Catalogue of Nonstellar Astronomical Objects. Jack W. Sulentic & William G. Tifft. LC 73-83378. 384p. 1973. 56.00 (*0-8165-0421-0*) U of Ariz Pr.

Revised Nomenclature for Museum Cataloging: A Revised & Expanded Version of Robert G. Chenhall's System for Classifying Man-Made Objects. expanded rev. ed. James R. Blackaby et al. LC 95-50544. (American Association for State & Local History Book Ser.). 1995. 65.00 (*0-7619-9147-6*) AltaMira Pr.

***Revised Notes Towards a Bibliography of Austin Osman Spare.** Clive Harper. Ed. by A. R. Naylor. (Orig.). 1996. pap. 9.95 (*1-872736-53-X*, Pub. by Mandrake Pr UK) Holmes Pub.

Revised Prices, 1991: Political Buttons Encyclopedia Books I, II, III, 1789-1976. Theodore L. Hake. 96p. 1990. pap. 15.00 (*0-918708-11-7*) Hake.

Revised Professional's Complete Dowsing Course. Russ Simmons. LC 78-52300. 1993. 65.00 (*0-931740-00-2*) Dowsing Inst.

Revised Radiolarian Zonation for the Upper Jurassic of Western North America, Vol. 320. E. A. Pessagno, Jr. et al. 52p. 1984. 10.00 (*0-87710-396-8*) Paleo Res.

Revised RCRA Inspection Manual. U. S. Environmental Protection Agency, Office of Wetlands, Oceans, & Watersheds Staff. 689p. (Orig.). 1994. pap. text ed. 125.00 (*0-86587-395-X*) Gov Insts.

Revised Register of the Soldiers & Sailors of New Hampshire in the War of the Rebellion, 1861-1866. rev. ed. Ed. by Augustus D. Ayling. 1347p. 1994. reprint ed. lib. bdg. 129.50 (*0-8328-3966-3*) Higginson Bk Co.

Revised Roster of Vermont Volunteers & Lists of Vermonters Who Served in the Army & Navy of the United States During the War of the Rebellion, 1861-66. Compiled by Theodore S. Peck. 862p. 1995. reprint ed. lib. bdg. 89.00 (*0-8328-5122-1*) Higginson Bk Co.

Revised Shapley-Ames Catalog of Bright Galaxies. 2nd ed. Allan Sandage & G. A. Tammann. LC 80-68146. 1987. 35.00 (*0-87279-652-3*, 635) Carnegie Inst.

Revised Social Service Care Plans for Long Term Care Facilities. rev. ed. Marylou Hughes & Manuela Espinosa. 136p. (Orig.). (C). 1993. pap. text ed. 13.50 (*1-877735-11-6*, 114) M&H Pub Co TX.

Revised Soviet Union. Susan Finney. (Gifted Learning Ser.). 64p. teacher ed. 8.99 (*0-86653-738-4*, GA1453) Good Apple.

Revised Standards & Guidelines of Service for the Library of Congress Network of Libraries for the Blind & Physically Handicapped, 1984. Ed. by Association of Specialized & Cooperative Library Agencies, Headquaters Staff. LC 84-6356. 55p. 1984. pap. 5.00 (*0-8389-3306-8*) ALA.

Revised Stratigraphy & Correlations of the Niagaran Provincial Series (Medina, Clinton, & Lockport Groups) in the Type Area of Western New York. Carlton E. Brett. 1995. write for info. (*0-318-72667-X*) US Geol Survey.

Revised Taxonomic Procedures & Paleoecological Applications for Some North American Mississippian Fenestellidae & Polyporidae (Bryozoa), Vol. 57. E. M. Snyder. 275p. 1991. 60.00 (*0-87710-419-0*) Paleo Res.

Revised Teaching Notes to Accompany Studies in Contract Law. 4th ed. Ian Ayres. (University Casebook Ser.). 437p. 1995. pap. text ed. write for info. (*1-56662-268-9*) Foundation Pr.

Revised Technique of Ballroom Dancing. Alex Moore. (Ballroom Dance Ser.). 1986. lib. bdg. 79.95 (*0-8490-3311-X*) Gordon Pr.

Revised Technique of Ballroom Dancing. Alex Moore. (Ballroom Dance Ser.). 1984. lib. bdg. 79.95 (*0-87700-498-6*) Revisionist Pr.

Revised Technique of Latin American Dancing. Imperial Society of Teachers of Dancing Staff. (Ballroom Dance Ser.). 1984. lib. bdg. 79.95 (*0-87700-502-8*) Revisionist Pr.

Revised Transition State Spectrum for Concerted Bimolecular B - Eliminations. D. J. McLennan. 1976. pap. 15.50 (*0-08-020472-4*, Pergamon Pr) Elsevier.

Revised Yale Isochrones & Luminosity Functions. E. M. Green et al. 365p. 1987. pap. 30.00 (*0-317-61465-7*) Yale U Observ.

Revising Business Prose. 3rd ed. Richard A. Lanham. LC 91-11710. (Illus.). 160p. (C). 1991. pap. text ed. 24.00 (*0-02-367465-2*, Macmillan Coll) P-H.

Revising Fiction. David Madden. 1988. pap. 13.95 (*0-452-26414-6*, Plume) NAL-Dutton.

Revising Fiction: A Handbook for Writers. David Madden. 320p. 1988. pap. 8.95 (*0-452-26088-4*, Plume) NAL-Dutton.

Revising Herself: Women's Identity from College to Midlife. Ruthellen Josselson. 320p. 1996. 25.00 (*0-19-510839-6*) OUP.

Revising Life: Sylvia Plath's Ariel Poems. Susan R. Van Dyne. LC 92-31233. (Gender & American Culture Ser.). xvi, 208p. (C). 1993. 29.95 (*0-8078-2102-0*) U of NC Pr.

Revising Life: Sylvia Plath's Ariel Poems. Susan R. Van Dyne. LC 92-31233. (Gender & American Culture Ser.). 224p. (C). 1994. pap. 12.95 (*0-8078-4487-X*) U of NC Pr.

Revising Memory: Women's Fiction & Memoirs in Seventeenth-Century France. Faith E. Beasley. LC 90-31075. 296p. (C). 1991. text ed. 45.00 (*0-8135-1585-8*) Rutgers U Pr.

Revising Mythologies: The Composition of Thoreau's Major Works. Stephen Adams & Donald Ross. LC 88-801. 285p. 1988. reprint ed. pap. 81.30 (*0-608-01439-7*, 2062201) Bks Demand.

Revising Nonfiction. David Madden. Date not set. pap. 11.95 (*0-452-27456-7*, Plume) NAL-Dutton.

Revising Prose. 3rd ed. Richard A. Lanham. (Illus.). 144p. (C). 1991. pap. text ed. 24.00 (*0-02-367445-8*, Macmillan Coll) P-H.

Revising Prose Self-Teaching Exercise Book. Richard A. Lanham. 96p. (C). 1987. pap. text ed. 28.00 (*0-02-367490-3*, Macmillan Coll) P-H.

Revising Shakespeare. Grace Ioppolo. 247p. (C). 1991. 34.50 (*0-674-76696-2*) HUP.

Revising State Theory: Essays in Politics & Postindustrialism. Fred Block. 256p. (C). 1987. pap. 18.95 (*0-87722-524-9*) Temple U Pr.

Revising Technical & Business Writing: Principles & Applications. Kathryn Riley et al. 153p. 1992. pap. text ed. 19.95 (*0-9644636-0-1*) Parlay Enter.

Revising the Rules: Traditional Grammar & Modern Linguistics. Brock Haussamen. 160p. 1993. per. 19.95 (*0-8403-9032-7*) Kendall-Hunt.

***Revising the Rules: Traditional Grammar & Modern Linguistics.** Brock Haussamen. 176p. 1997. per., pap. text ed. 20.95 (*0-7872-3482-6*) Kendall-Hunt.

Revising the Tax Treatment of Employer-Provided Health Insurance. Sherry Glied. 44p. 1994. pap. 9.95 (*0-8447-7029-9*) Am Enterprise.

Revising the Word & the World: Essays in Feminist Literary Criticism. Ed. by Veve Clark et al. LC 93-10197. 288p. 1993. pap. 14.95 (*0-226-40064-6*) U Ch Pr.

Revising the Word & the World: Essays in Feminist Literary Criticism. Ed. by Veve Clark et al. LC 93-10197. 288p. 1993. lib. bdg. 35.00 (*0-226-40063-8*) U Ch Pr.

Revising the World: Modeling in Human Experience. James R. King. LC 96-4495. (Illus.). 320p. 1996. text ed. 39.95 (*0-252-02270-X*); pap. text ed. 17.95 (*0-252-06573-5*) U of Ill Pr.

Revising Wilde: Society & Subversion in the Plays of Oscar Wilde. Sos Eltis. (Oxford English Monographs). 240p. (C). 1996. 60.00 (*0-19-812183-0*) OUP.

Revising Your Resume. Nancy Schuman & William Lewis. LC 85-32320. 156p. 1986. pap. text ed. 12.95 (*0-471-84523-X*) Wiley.

Revisio Physolychnidum: Silene Subg. Physolychnis. Gilbert Bocquet. (Phanerogamarum Monographiae: Vol. 1). (Illus.). 1969. 120.00 (*3-7682-0624-6*) Lubrecht & Cramer.

***Revision: A Creative Approach to Writing & Rewriting Fiction.** David M. Kaplan. LC 96-29202. 240p. 1997. 18.95 (*1-884910-19-X*, Story Press) F & W Pubns Inc.

Revision & Amendment of State Constitutions. W. F. Dodd. LC 73-120854. (American Constitutional & Legal History Ser.). 1970. reprint ed. lib. bdg. 42.50 (*0-306-71959-2*) Da Capo.

Revision & Authority in Wordsworth: The Interpretation of a Career. William H. Galperin. LC 88-30325. 256p. (C). 1989. text ed. 39.95 (*0-8122-8140-3*) U of Pa Pr.

Revision & Cladistic Analysis of the Spider Family Pimoidae (Araneoidea: Araneae) Gustavo Hormiga. LC 93-24455. (Smithsonian Contributions to Zoology Ser.: No. 549). 108p. 1994. pap. 30.80 (*0-7837-7463-X*, 2049185) Bks Demand.

Revision & Romantic Authorship. Zachary Leader. 368p. (C). 1996. 75.00 (*0-19-812264-0*) OUP.

Revision & Updating in Knowledge Bases. Lea Sombe. 182p. 1994. text ed. 59.95 (*0-471-04062-2*) Wiley.

Revision Del Examen De Estado De Cosmetologia - State Exam Review for Cosmetology. Milady Publishing Company Staff. (SPA.). 1992. student ed., pap. 14.95 (*1-56253-099-2*) Milady Pub.

Revision del Genero Bistropogon L'Hrt. (Lamiaceae-Stachyoideae) Endemismo de la Region Macaronesica. Irene E. LaSerna Ramos. (Phanerogamarum Monographiae: Vol. 18). (Illus.). 380p. (SPA.). 1984. lib. bdg. 97.50 (*3-7682-1399-4*) Lubrecht & Cramer.

Revision der Gattung Pediastrum Meyen (Chlorophyta) Parra O. Barrientos. (Bibliotheca Phycologica Ser.: No. 48). (Illus.). 1979. 48.00 (*3-7682-1254-8*) Lubrecht & Cramer.

Revision der Gattung Pulicaria (Compositae Inuleae) fuer Afrika, Makaronesien und Arabian. E. Gamal-Eldin. (Phanerogamarum Monographiae: No. 14). (Illus.). 406p. (GER.). 1981. text ed. 65.00 (*3-7682-1294-7*) Lubrecht & Cramer.

Revision der Laubmoosgattung Mitthyridium (Mitten) Robinson Fuer Oreanien (Calymperaceae) H. Nowak. (Bryophytorum Bibliotheca Ser.: No. 20). (Illus.). (GER.). 1981. lib. bdg. 48.00 (*3-7682-1236-X*) Lubrecht & Cramer.

Revision der Lichenologischen Arten der Sammelgattung Rosellinia (Ascomycetes) M. Matzer et al. (Bibliotheca Lichenologica Ser.: Vol. 37). (Illus.). 146p. 1990. pap. 56.00 (*3-443-58016-5*, Pub. by Cramer-Borntraeger GW) Lubrecht & Cramer.

Revision der Niederlaendishen Heterobasidiomycetae und Homobasidiomycetae-Aphyllophoraceae, 2 parts in 1 vol. M. A. Donk. (Illus.). 1969. reprint ed. 64.00 (*3-7682-0621-1*) Lubrecht & Cramer.

Revision der Sektion Alopecuroideae DC. der Gattung Astragalus L. R. Becht. (Phanerogamarum Monographiae: No. 10). (Illus.). 1979. lib. bdg. 48.00 (*3-7682-1188-6*) Lubrecht & Cramer.

Revision der Sektion Chronopus Bge. der Gattung Astragalus. L. E. Ott. (Phanerogamarum Monographiae: No. 9). (Illus.). 1979. lib. bdg. 40.00 (*3-7682-1187-8*) Lubrecht & Cramer.

Revision Des Noostocacees Heterocystees: Contocacees Dans les Principaux Herbiers De France, Vol. 1. E. Bornet & C. Flahault. 1969. 48.00 (*3-7682-0002-7*) Lubrecht & Cramer.

Revision Einiger Calciphiler Formenkreise der Flechtengattung Lecidea. Hannes Hertel. (Illus.). 1967. pap. 48.00 (*3-7682-5424-0*) Lubrecht & Cramer.

Revision for MRCPsych, Pt. 1. Basant K. Puri & John Sklar. 232p. 1990. pap. text ed. 28.00 (*0-443-04331-0*) Churchill.

***Revision for Optics & Refraction.** Wai-Ching Leung. (An Arnold Publication). 144p. pap. 22.50 (*0-340-64613-6*, Pub. by E Arnold UK) Routledge Chapman & Hall.

Revision Hip Arthroplasty: A Practical Approach to Bone Stock Loss. Richard N. Villar & Derek McMinn. LC 96-9042. (Illus.). 192p. 1998. 135.00 (*0-7506-1640-7*) Buttrwrth-Heinemann.

Revision in Chemistry, No. I. D. P. Goel & S. P. Mittal. (Illus.). vi, 91p. (Orig.). 1983. pap. text ed. 5.95 (*0-86131-378-X*, Pub. by Orient Longman Ltd II) Apt Bks.

Revision in Physics, No. I. A. K. Bhargava. (Illus.). vi, 158p. (Orig.). 1983. pap. text ed. 7.95 (*0-686-44137-0*, Pub. by Orient Longman Ltd II) Apt Bks.

Revision in Strafsachen. 5th ed. Werner Sarstedt & Rainer Hamm. xl, 420p. 1983. 94.60 (*3-11-009712-5*) De Gruyter.

Revision Notes in Chemistry. E. N. Ramsden. (C). 1981. text ed. 40.00 (*0-85950-498-0*, Pub. by S Thornes Pubs UK) St Mut.

Revision Notes on Diagnostic Radiology. Hoe. 352p. Date not set. pap. write for info. (*0-7506-1474-9*) Buttrwrth-Heinemann.

Revision Notes on Surgical Care. P. J. Wormald & J. D. Knottenbelt. (Illus.). 384p. 1995. pap. 24.00 (*0-340-61377-7*, Pub. by Ed Arnold UK) OUP.

Revision of B. E. Dahlgren's Index of American Palms. S. F. Glassmann. (Phanerogamarum Monographiae: No. 6). 1972. 72.00 (*3-7682-0765-X*) Lubrecht & Cramer.

Revision of Colubrid Snakes of the Subfamily Homalopsinae. Ko Ko Gyi. (Museum Ser.: Vol. 20, No. 2). 177p. 1970. pap. 5.00 (*0-686-80361-2*) U KS Nat Hist Mus.

Revision of Crataegus Sect. Crataegus & Nothosect. Crataeguineae (Rosaceae-Maloideae) in the Old World. Knud I. Christensen. Ed. by Christiane Anderson. (Systematic Botany Monographs: Vol. 35). (Illus.). 199p. 1992. pap. 25.00 (*0-912861-35-5*) Am Soc Plant.

Revision of Cuphea Section Heterodon (Lythraceae) Shirley A. Graham. Ed. by Christiane Anderson. (Systematic Botany Monographs: Vol. 20). (Illus.). 168p. 1988. pap. 20.00 (*0-912861-20-7*) Am Soc Plant.

Revision of Cymbopetalum & Porcelia (Annonaceae) Nancy A. Murray. Ed. by Christiane Anderson. (Systematic Botany Monographs: Vol. 40). (Illus.). 121p. 1993. pap. 16.00 (*0-912861-40-1*) Am Soc Plant.

Revision of Dendrobium Section Oxyglossum (Orchidaceae) rev. ed. T. M. Reeve & P. J. Woods. Ed. by N. M. Gregory. (Notes from the Royal Botanic Garden Edinburgh Ser.: Vol. 46, No. 2, 1989). 1989. pap. 44.00 (*0-11-493502-5*, HM5025, Pub. by Royal Botanic Edinburgh UK) Balogh.

Revision of Far East Asia. Stary. (Sent Ser.). 1967. lib. bdg. 117.50 (*90-6193-113-4*) Kluwer Ac.

Revision of Haplostachys, Phyllostegia, & Stenogyne. E. E. Sherff. (BMB Ser.). 1974. reprint ed. pap. 25.00 (*0-527-02242-X*) Periodicals Srv.

Revision of Hieracium (Asteraceae) in Mexico & Central America. John H. Beaman. Ed. by Christiane Anderson. (Systematic Botany Monographs: Vol. 29). (Illus.). 77p. 1990. pap. 9.00 (*0-912861-29-0*) Am Soc Plant.

***Revision of Justice: A Benjamin Justice Mystery.** John M. Wilson. LC 97-17850. 288p. 1997. 21.95 (*0-385-48235-3*, Anchor NY) Doubleday.

***Revision of Leucomphalos Including Baphiastrum & Bowringia (Leguminosae-Papilionideae)** F. J. Breteler. (Wageningen Agricultural University Papers: No. 94-4). (Illus.). 41p. 1994. pap. 25.00 (*90-6754-362-4*, Pub. by Backhuys Pubs NE) Balogh.

***Revision of Macrotyloma (Leguminosae)** B. Verdcourt. (Illus.). 138p. 1982. pap. 22.00 (*0-614-21732-6*, Pub. by Royal Botnic Grdns UK) Balogh.

Revision of Melanconis, Pseudovalva, Prostecium & Titania. Lewis E. Wehmeyer. (University of Michigan Studies: No. 14). (Illus.). 1941. reprint ed. 40.00 (*3-7682-0929-6*) Lubrecht & Cramer.

Revision of Neotropical Menispermaceae Tribe Tinosporeae see Memoirs of the New York Botanical Garden: No. 20(2)

Revision of North American Liris Fabricius (Hymenoptera) Sphecoides, Larridae. Karl V. Krombein. LC 84-600998. (Smithsonian Contributions to Zoology Ser.: No. 404). 100p. reprint ed. pap. 28.50 (*0-317-30394-5*, 2024751) Bks Demand.

Revision of North American Tachysphex Wasps Including Central American & Caribbean Species: Hymenoptera: Sphecidae. Wojciech J. Pulawski. LC 88-70114. (Memoirs of the California Academy of Sciences Ser.: No. 10). (Illus.). 1988. pap. 30.00 (*0-940228-16-5*) Calif Acad Sci.

Revision of North American Trichodes (Herbst) Coleoptera: Cleridae. David E. Foster. (Special Publications: No. 11). (Illus.). 86p. 1976. pap. 4.00 (*0-89672-037-3*) Tex Tech Univ Pr.

Revision of Palicourea (Rubiaceae) in Mexico & Central America. Charlotte M. Taylor. Ed. by Christiane Anderson. (Systematic Botany Monographs: Vol. 26). (Illus.). 102p. 1989. pap. 12.50 (*0-912861-26-6*) Am Soc Plant.

Revision of Passiflora Subgenus Decaloba Section Pseudodysosmia, Passifloraceae. John M. MacDougal. Ed. by Christiane Anderson. (Systematic Botany Monographs: Vol. 41). (Illus.). 146p. 1994. pap. 19.00 (*0-912861-41-X*) Am Soc Plant.

Revision of R. P Whitfield's Types of Rugosan & Tabulate Corals in the Museum of Paleontology, University of California, & in the United States National Museum, No. 250 see Bulletins of American Paleontology: Vol. 56

Revision of Some Species Referred to Antinoe, Antinoella, Antinoana, Bylgides, & Harmothoe: Polychaeta: Polynoidae: Harmothinae. Marian H. Pettibone. LC 93-4229. (Smithsonian Contributions to Zoology Ser.: No. 545). (Illus.). 45p. reprint ed. pap. 25.00 (*0-7837-6292-5*, 2046007) Bks Demand.

Revision of Spathiphyllum (Araceae) G. S. Bunting. (Memoirs Ser.: Vol. 10 (3)). (Illus.). 54p. 1960. 8.00 (*0-89327-037-7*) NY Botanical.

***Revision of Tabernaemontana Vol. 1: The Old World Species.** A. J. Leeuwenberg. (Illus.). xii, 211p. 1991. pap. 40.00 (*0-947643-30-3*, Pub. by Royal Botnic Grdns UK) Balogh.

***Revision of Tabernaemontana Vol. 2: The New World Species & Stemmadenia.** A. J. Leeuwenberg. (Illus.). xvii, 237p. 1994. pap. 40.00 (*0-947643-74-5*, Pub. by Royal Botnic Grdns UK) Balogh.

Revision of Tetramolopium, Lipochaeta, Dubautia, & Railliardia. E. E. Sherff. (BMB Ser.). 1974. reprint ed. 25.00 (*0-527-02241-1*) Periodicals Srv.

Revision of the Adult & Larval Mosquitoes of Japan & Korea. Kazuo Tanaka et al. (Contributions Ser.: Vol. 16). (Illus.). 987p. 1979. 60.00 (*1-56665-041-0*) Assoc Pubs FL.

Revision of the Ahermatypic Scleractinia of the Philippine Islands & Adjacent Waters, Pt. 1. Stephen D. Cairns. LC 89-600214. (Smithsonian Contributions to Zoology Ser.: No. 486). (Illus.). 142p. reprint ed. pap. 40.50 (*0-8357-7906-8*, 2036334) Bks Demand.

Revision of the American Species of Epilobium Occurring North of Mexico. W. Trelease. 1977. reprint ed. 25.00 (*3-7682-1125-8*) Lubrecht & Cramer.

Revision of the American Species of Eriosema (Leguminosae-Lotoideae) J. W. Grear. (Memoirs Ser.: Vol. 20 (3)). (Illus.). 98p. 1970. 10.00 (*0-89327-069-5*) NY Botanical.

Revision of the American Species of Rourea Subgenus Rourea (Connaraceae) see Memoirs of the New York Botanical Garden: No. 26(1)

***Revision of the Antelope & "Latourea" Dendrobiums.** P. J. Cribb. (Illus.). 144p. 1989. pap. 24.00 (*1-878762-62-1*, Pub. by Royal Botnic Grdns UK) Balogh.

Revision of the Aphroditoid Polychaetes of the Family Acoetidae Kinberg (Polyodontidae Augener) & Reestablishment of Acoetes Audouin & Milne Edwards, 1832, & Euarche Ehlers, 1887. Marian H. Pettibone. LC 89-600058. (Smithsonian Contributions to Zoology Ser.: No. 464). 142p. reprint ed. pap. 40.50 (*0-8357-7530-5*, 2036240) Bks Demand.

Revision of the Atlantic Brisingida: Echinodermata: Asteriodea, with Description of a New Genus & Family. Maureen E. Downey. LC 86-6579. (Smithsonian Contributions to Zoology Ser.: No. 435). 61p. reprint ed. pap. 25.00 (*0-317-55530-8*, 2029553) Bks Demand.

Revision of the Cardinalfish Subgenera Pristiapogon & Zoramia (Genus Apogon) of the Indo-Pacific Region (Teleostei: Apogonidae) Thomas H. Fraser & Ernest A. Lachner. LC 84-600287. (Smithsonian Contributions to Zoology Ser.: No. 412). 51p. reprint ed. pap. 25.00 (*0-317-30175-6*, 2025357) Bks Demand.

Revision of the Classification of the Oscillatoriaceae. Francis Drouet. (Monograph: No. 15). (Illus.). 370p. 1968. lib. bdg. 8.00 (*0-910006-23-7*) Acad Nat Sci Phila.

Revision of the Corixidae of India & Adjacent Regions. G. Evelyn Hutchinson. (CT Academy of Arts & Science Transactions Ser.: Vol. 33). 1940. pap. 75.00 (*0-686-51302-9*) Elliots Bks.

Revision of the Dryinidae (Hymenoptera), 2 vols. M. Olmi. (Memoir Ser.: No. 37). (Illus.). 1938p. 1984. 130.00 (*1-56665-035-6*) Assoc Pubs FL.

An Asterisk (*) at the beginning of an entry indicates that the title is appearing in BIP for the first time.

Revision of the Echini. Alexander Agassiz. (Works of Alexander Agassiz). 1989. reprint ed. lib. bdg. 79.00 (*0-7812-1583-8*) Rprt Serv.

Revision of the Ektopodontidae (Mammalia, Marsupialia, Phalangeroidea) of the Australian Neogene. Ed. by M. O. Woodburne & W. A. Clemens. LC 85-16487. (University of California Publications in Geological Sciences: No. 131). 126p. 1986. pap. 36.00 (*0-7837-8436-8*, 2049238) Bks Demand.

Revision of the Family Seraphsidae (Gastropoda: Strombacea) see Palaeontographica Americana: Vol. 8

Revision of the Fungi Described As Gloesporium. J. A. Von Arx. 1970. 52.00 (*3-7682-0667-X*) Lubrecht & Cramer.

Revision of the Fungi Formerly Classified As Nectria Subgenus Hyphonectria. Gary J. Samuels. LC 66-6394. (Memoirs Ser.: Vol. 26, No. 3). (Illus.). 126p. 1976. pap. 9.00 (*0-89327-008-3*) NY Botanical.

Revision of the Genus Arcytophyllum Rubiaceae: Hedyotideae. Patricio V. Mena. LC 90-6284. (Memoirs Ser.: No. 60). (Illus.). 28p. 1990. pap. 7.25 (*0-89327-355-4*) NY Botanical.

Revision of the Genus Brachyotum (Tibouchineae Melastomataceae) see Memoirs of the New York Botanical Garden: No. 8(4)

***Revision of the Genus Cinchona (Rubiaceae-Cinchoneae)** Lennart Andersson. LC 97-24318. (Memoirs of the New York Botanical Garden Ser.). 1997. write for info. (*0-89327-416-X*) NY Botanical.

Revision of the Genus Declieuxia (Rubiaceae) Joseph H. Kirkbride, Jr. LC 66-6394. (Memoirs Ser.: Vol. 28, No. 4). (Illus.). 87p. 1976. pap. 11.00 (*0-89327-010-5*) NY Botanical.

Revision of the Genus Enallagma of the United States West of the Rocky Mountains & Identification of Certain Larvae by Discriminant Analysis: Odonata: Coenagrionidae. Rosser W. Garrison. LC 83-24105. (University of California Publications in Entomology: No. 105). 141p. 1984. pap. 40.20 (*0-7837-7482-6*, 2049204) Bks Demand.

Revision of the Genus Hackelia (Boraginaceae) in North America, North of Mexico see Memoirs of the New York Botanical Garden: No. 26(1)

***Revision of the Genus Hyparrhenia.** W. D. Clayton. (Kew Bulletin Additional Series II). (Illus.). 196p. 1969. pap. 15.00 (*0-11-240999-7*, Pub. by Royal Botnic Grdns UK) Balogh.

Revision of the Genus Hypochrysops C. & R. Felder: Lepidoptera-Lycaenidae. D. P. Sands. (Entomonography Ser.: No. 7). (Illus.). 116p. 1986. 48.00 (*90-04-08089-9*) Lubrecht & Cramer.

Revision of the Genus Hypoxylon. Yu-Ming Ju & Jack D. Roers. LC 96-83098. (Mycologia Memoir of the Mycological Society of America Ser.: No. 20). 382p. (C). 1996. text ed. 54.00 (*0-89054-214-7*) Am Phytopathol Soc.

Revision of the Genus Lespedeza Section Macrolespedeza: (Leguminosae) Shinobu Akiyama. (Illus.). 142p. 1988. 79.50 (*0-86008-429-9*, Pub. by U of Tokyo JA) Col U Pr.

Revision of the Genus Mapania. D. A. Simpson. (Illus.). vi, 189p. 1992. pap. 30.00 (*0-947643-53-2*, Pub. by Royal Botnic Grdns UK) Balogh.

Revision of the Genus Orthotricham in North America, North of Mexico. Dale H. Vitt. (Bryophytorum Bibliotheca Ser.: No. 1). (Illus.). 1973. 36.00 (*3-7682-0825-7*) Lubrecht & Cramer.

Revision of the Genus Pipiza Fallen (Diptera: Syrphidae) of America North of Mexico: With Notes on the Placement of the Tribe Pipizini. Gary A. Coovert. Ed. by Veda M. Cafazzo. LC 95-71128. (Bulletin Ser.: Vol. 11, No. 3). (Orig.). (C). 1996. pap. text ed., spiral bd. 15.00 (*0-86727-120-5*) Ohio Bio Survey.

Revision of the Genus Rhodocybe Maire (Agaricales) T. J. Baroni. (Nova Hedwigia Beiheft Ser.: No. 67). (Illus.). 300p. 1981. lib. bdg. 80.00 (*3-7682-5467-4*) Lubrecht & Cramer.

Revision of the Genus Sagittaria (Alismataceae) see Memoirs of the New York Botanical Garden: No. 9(2)

Revision of the Genus Stigeoclonium. A. K. Islam. (Illus.). 1963. pap. 48.00 (*3-7682-5410-0*) Lubrecht & Cramer.

Revision of the Grasshopper Genus Heteracris: Orthoptera, Acrididae, Eyprepocnemidinae. J. P. Grunshaw. 106p. 1991. pap. 50.00 (*0-85954-286-6*, Pub. by Nat Res Inst UK) St Mut.

Revision of the Grasshopper Genus Orthochtha & Allies: Orthoptera, Acrididae, Acridinae. G. B. Popov & L. D. Fishpool. 154p. 1992. pap. 60.00 (*0-85954-305-6*, Pub. by Nat Res Inst UK) St Mut.

Revision of the Hawaiian Species of Peperomia. T. G. Yuncker. (BMB Ser.). 1974. reprint ed. 25.00 (*0-527-02218-7*) Periodicals Srv.

Revision of the Indo-Australian Genus Attacus. Richard S. Peigler. LC 88-82574. (Illus.). 168p. (Orig.). (C). 1989. pap. text ed. 30.00 (*0-9611464-2-7*) Lepidoptera.

Revision of the Jumping Spider Genus Habronattus F. O. P. Cambridge (Araneae; Salticidae), with Phenetic & Cladistic Analyses. Charles E. Griswold. LC 86-11415. (University of California Publications in Entomology: No. 107). 356p. 1987. pap. 101.50 (*0-7837-7483-4*, 2049205) Bks Demand.

Revision of the Lichen Genus Xanthoparmelia in South America. T. H. Nash, 3rd et al. (Bibliotheca Lichenologica Ser.: Vol. 56). (Illus.). 156p. 1995. pap. 64.00 (*3-443-58035-1*, Pub. by Cramer-Borntraeger GW) Lubrecht & Cramer.

Revision of the Marine Nematodes of the Superfamily Draconematoidea Filipjev, 1918 (Nematoda: Draconematina) Merlin W. Allen. LC 77-83108. (University of California Publications in Social Welfare: No. 109). (Illus.). 141p. reprint ed. pap. 40.20 (*0-685-23996-9*, 2031579) Bks Demand.

Revision of the Mexican-Central American Species of Cavendishia (Vacciniaceae) James L. Luteyn. LC 66-6394. (Memoirs Ser.: Vol. 28, No. 3). (Illus.). 138p. 1976. pap. 5.00 (*0-89327-011-3*) NY Botanical.

Revision of the Mexican Species of Cyperus (Cyperaceae) Vol. 43. Gordon C. Tucker. Ed. by Christiane Anderson. (Systematic Botany Monographs). (Illus.). 213p. 1994. pap. 28.00 (*0-912861-43-6*) Am Soc Plant.

Revision of the Modern: The German Architecture Museum in Frankfurt. Ed. by Heinrich Klotz. (Academy Architecture Ser.). (Illus.). 88p. 1986. 14.95 (*0-312-67938-6*) St Martin.

Revision of the Neotropical Aquatic Beetle Genus Stegoelmis (Coleoptera, Elmidae) Paul J. Spangler. LC 90-10103. (Smithsonian Contributions to Zoology Ser.: No. 502). 56p. reprint ed. pap. 25.00 (*0-8357-2751-3*, 2039865) Bks Demand.

Revision of the New World Species of Psoraleeae Leguminosae: Papilionoideae. James W. Grimes. LC 90-6294. (Memoirs Ser.: No. 61). (Illus.). 109p. 1990. pap. 23.25 (*0-89327-356-2*) NY Botanical.

Revision of the North American Genus Argoporis: Coleoptera Tenebrionidae Cerenopini. Richard L. Berry. (Bulletin New Ser.: Vol. 6, No. 1). 1980. 10.00 (*0-86727-089-6*) Ohio Bio Survey.

Revision of the North American Genus Callirhoe (Malvaceae) Laurence J. Dorr. LC 89-13653. (Memoirs Ser.: No. 56). (Illus.). 84p. 1990. pap. 18.50 (*0-89327-349-X*) NY Botanical.

Revision of the North American Pleurocystitidae (Rhombifera-Cystoidea) R. L. Parsley. 82p. 1970. 4.00 (*0-87710-198-1*) Paleo Res.

Revision of the Nostocaceae with Constricted Trichomes. F. Drouet. (Beiheft zur Nova Hedwigia Ser.: No. 57). (Illus.). 1978. text ed. 120.00 (*3-7682-5457-7*) Lubrecht & Cramer.

Revision of the Order Phalangida of Ohio. Mary E. Walker. (Bulletin Ser.: No. 19). 1928. 2.00 (*0-86727-018-7*) Ohio Bio Survey.

Revision of the Pantropical Moss Genus Leucophanes Brid. N. S. Allen. (Bryophytorum Bibliotheca Ser.: Vol. 46). (Illus.). 280p. 1993. pap. text ed. 130.00 (*3-443-62018-3*, Pub. by Schweitzerbartsche GW) Lubrecht & Cramer.

Revision of the Polynesian Species of Peperomia. T. G. Yuncker. (BMB Ser.). 1974. reprint ed. 25.00 (*0-527-02251-9*) Periodicals Srv.

Revision of the Pteridophyta of Samoa. C. Christensen. (BMB Ser.). 1974. reprint ed. 25.00 (*0-527-02285-3*) Periodicals Srv.

Revision of the Sawfly Family Orussida for North & Central America (Hymenoptera: Symphyta, Orussidae) Woodrow W. Middlekauff. LC 83-1397. (University of California Publications in Entomology: No. 101). 58p. 1983. pap. 25.00 (*0-7837-7493-1*, 2049215) Bks Demand.

Revision of the Serphidae (Hymenoptera) Henry Townes & Marjorie Townes. (Memoir Ser.: No. 32). (Illus.). 541p. 1981. 65.00 (*1-56665-030-5*) Assoc Pubs FL.

Revision of the South American Genus Otachyrium: Poaceae: Panicoideae. Tatiana Sendulsky. LC 84-600087. (Smithsonian Contributions to Botany Ser.: No. 57). 28p. reprint ed. pap. 25.00 (*0-317-20823-3*, 2024794) Bks Demand.

Revision of the South American Species of Trachysphyrus -(Hymenoptera, Ichneumonidae) Charles Porter. (Memoir Ser.: No. 10). (Illus.). 387p. 1967. 45.00 (*1-56665-008-9*) Assoc Pubs FL.

Revision of the Stigonemataceae: With a Summary of the Classification of Blue-Green Algae. F. Drouet. (Nova Hedwigia Beiheft Ser.: No. 66). (Illus.). 300p. 1981. lib. bdg. 65.00 (*3-7682-5466-6*) Lubrecht & Cramer.

Revision of the Treaty. John Maynard Keynes. LC 73-37888. (Select Bibliographies Reprint Ser.). 1977. reprint ed. 18.95 (*0-8369-6725-9*) Ayer.

Revision of the Treaty see Collected Writings

Revision of the Tribe Antirrhineae, (Scrophulariaceae) David A. Sutton. (Illus.). 584p. 1988. 145.00 (*0-19-858520-9*) OUP.

Revision of the U. S. Standard Certificates & Reports, 1989: PHS 91-1465. (Documents & Committee Reports Ser. 4: No. 28). 34p. 1991. pap. 1.25 (*0-685-61571-5*, 017-022-01134-4) Natl Ctr Health Stats.

Revision of the World Species of Synophorus Foerster (Ichneumanidae) M. Sanborne. (Memoir Ser.: No. 38). (Illus.). 403p. 1984. 45.00 (*1-56665-036-4*) Assoc Pubs FL.

Revision of Tornatellinidae & Achatinellidae. C. M. Cooke, Jr. & Yasuo Kondo. (BMB Ser.: No. 221). 1974. reprint ed. 40.00 (*0-527-02329-9*) Periodicals Srv.

Revision of Tristerix (Loranthaceae) Job Kuijt. Ed. by Christiane Anderson. (Systematic Botany Monographs: Vol. 19). (Illus.). (Orig.). 1988. pap. 8.00 (*0-912861-19-3*) Am Soc Plant.

Revision of Twenty Genera of Gelini (Ichneumonidae) Henry Townes. (Memoir Ser.: No. 35). (Illus.). 281p. 1983. 35.00 (*1-56665-033-X*) Assoc Pubs FL.

Revision Otologic Surgery. Ed. by Vincent N. Carrasco & Harold C. Pillsbury. LC 97-1120. (Illus.). 304p. 1997. text ed. 89.00 (*0-86577-610-5*) Thieme Med Pubs.

***Revision Quest.** Sandra Lindow. 24p. (Orig.). 1997. pap. 5.00 (*1-886895-09-0*) Poetry Harbor.

***Revision Spine Surgery.** Margulies et al. (Illus.). 600p. (C). (gr. 13). 1998. text ed. 169.95 (*0-8151-4591-8*, 30029) Mosby Yr Bk.

Revision Surgery in Total Hip Arthroplasty. B. B. Wroblewski. xvii, 236p. 1990. 158.00 (*0-387-19618-8*) Spr-Verlag.

***Revision Surgery in Total Hip Arthroplasty.** Boguslaw M. Wroblewski. 236p. 1990. 144.00 (*3-540-19618-8*) Spr-Verlag.

Revision Taxonomica de Sideritis L., Subgenero Marrubiastrum, Moench, Mend.-Heuer, Endemismo Macaranesico. Perez De Paz et al. (Pherogamarum Monographiae Tomus Ser.: No. 20). (Illus.). 327p. (SPA.). 1992. text ed. 115.00 (*3-443-78002-4*, Pub. by Cramer-Borntraeger GW) Lubrecht & Cramer.

Revision Taxonomique et Possibilites d'Hybridation de Nematanthus Schrader (Gesneriaceae), Genre Endemique de la Foret Cotiere Bresilienne. Alain Chautems. (Dissertations Botanicae Ser.: Vol. 112). (Illus.). 230p. (FRE.). 1988. pap. 72.00 (*3-443-64024-9*) Lubrecht & Cramer.

***Revision Total Knee Arthroplasty.** Gerard A. Engh et al. LC 96-39068. 485p. 1997. 139.00 (*0-683-02827-8*) Williams & Wilkins.

Revision with White Tulip. Anne Bourdon. 50p. (Orig.). 1991. pap. 6.00 (*0-9629364-0-5*) Bourdon Pub.

Revisional Surgery in Rheumatoid Arthritis. Ed. by F. W. Hagena. (Rheumatology, the Interdisciplinary Concept Ser.: Vol. 13). (Illus.). x, 266p. 1990. 226.25 (*3-8055-4930-X*) S Karger.

Revisionary Interventions into the Americanist Canon. Ed. by Donald E. Pease. LC 93-49688. (New Americanists Ser.). 368p. 1994. text ed. 39.95 (*0-8223-1478-9*); pap. text ed. 15.95 (*0-8223-1493-2*) Duke.

Revisionary Play: Studies in the Spenserian Dynamics. Harry Berger, Jr. 494p. 1988. pap. 17.00 (*0-520-07180-8*) U CA Pr.

Revisionary Study of Leaf-Mining Flies: Agromyzidae of California. LC 81-70585. 496p. 1981. pap. text ed. 20.00 (*0-931876-53-2*, 3273) ANR Pubns CA.

Revisionder Europaeischen Arten der Flechtengattung Rhizocarpon mit Nichtgelbem Lager & Vielzelligen Sporen. T. Feuerer. (Bibliotheca Lichenologica Ser.: Vol. 39). 216p. (GER.). 1991. pap. 63.00 (*3-443-58018-1*, Pub. by Cramer-Borntraeger GW) Lubrecht & Cramer.

Revisioning Environmental Ethics. Daniel A. Kealey. LC 89-19678. 136p. 1990. text ed. 59.50 (*0-7914-0277-0*); pap. text ed. 19.95 (*0-7914-0278-9*) State U NY Pr.

Revisioning Evangelical Theology: A Fresh Agenda for the 21st Century. Stanley J. Grenz. LC 93-18090. 209p. (Orig.). 1993. pap. 16.99 (*0-8308-1772-7*, 1772) InterVarsity.

Revisioning Gita. Som P. Ranchan. 200p. 1991. text ed. 27.50 (*81-220-0216-1*, Pub. by Konark Pubs Pvt Ltd II) Advent Bks Div.

Revisioning History: Film & the Construction of the Past. Robert A. Rosenstone. 232p. 1994. pap. 16.95 (*0-691-02534-7*) Princeton U Pr.

***Revisioning Italy: National Identity & Global Culture.** Beverly Allen & Mary J. Russo. LC 97-20530. 1997. write for info. (*0-8166-2726-6*); pap. write for info. (*0-8166-2727-4*) U of Minn Pr.

Revisioning Men's Lives: Gender, Intimacy, & Power. Terry A. Kupers. 200p. 1993. pap. text ed. 18.95 (*0-89862-271-9*); lib. bdg. 42.00 (*0-89862-993-4*) Guilford Pr.

Revisioning Philosophy. Ed. by James Ogilvy. LC 91-30803. (SUNY Series in Philosophy). 318p. 1991. pap. text ed. 21.95 (*0-7914-0990-2*) State U NY Pr.

Revisioning Philosophy. Ed. by James Ogilvy. LC 91-30803. (SUNY Series in Philosophy). 318p. 1991. text ed. 64.50 (*0-7914-0989-9*) State U NY Pr.

Revisioning Psychology. James Hillman. LC 91-50502. 320p. 1992. reprint ed. pap. 11.00 (*0-685-52543-0*, PL) HarpC.

***Revisioning Science: Essays Toward a New Knowledge Base for Our Culture.** Susan E. Mehrtens. (Illus.). 304, xxiip. (Orig.). 1997. pap. 24.95 (*1-889919-00-4*) Potlatch Group Inc.

Revisioning Social Work Education: A Social Constructionist Approach. Intro. by Joan Laird. LC 94-2853. (Journal of Teaching in Social Work). (Illus.). 326p. 1994. lib. bdg. 49.95 (*1-56024-615-4*) Haworth Pr.

Revisioning the Church: Ecclesial Freedom in the New Paradigm. Peter C. Hodgson. LC 87-45894. 128p. 1988. pap. 12.00 (*0-8006-2072-0*, 1-2072, Fortress Pr) Augsburg Fortress.

Revisioning the DRE. Donald G. Emler. LC 89-34050. 257p. (Orig.). 1989. pap. 18.95 (*0-89135-071-3*) Religious Educ.

Revisioning the Political: Feminist Reconstructions of Traditional Concepts in Western Political Theory. Christine DiStefano. Ed. by Nancy J. Hirschmann. LC 96-28881. (Feminist Theory & Politics Ser.). 4p. (C). 1996. pap. text ed. 23.00 (*0-8133-8640-3*) Westview.

Revisioning the Political: Feminist Reconstructions of Traditional Concepts in Western Political Theory. Nancy J. Hirschmann & Christine DiStefano. (Feminist Theory & Politics Ser.). 4p. 1996. text ed. 64.00 (*0-8133-8639-X*) Westview.

Revisioning the Sacred: Essays in Baha'i Theology. Jack McLean. Ed. by Anthony A. Lee. (Studies in the Babi & Baha'i Religions: Vol. 8). 1996. 32.50 (*0-933770-95-2*); pap. 22.50 (*0-933770-96-0*) Kalimat.

Revisioning Writers' Talk: Gender & Culture in Acts of Composing. Mary A. Cain. LC 94-8007. (SUNY Series, Literacy, Culture, & Learning: Theory & Practice). 215p. 1995. text ed. 49.50 (*0-7914-2075-2*); pap. text ed. 16.95 (*0-7914-2076-0*) State U NY Pr.

Revisionism: A Key to Peace. Harry E. Barnes. 1971. 250.00 (*0-87700-192-8*) Revisionist Pr.

Revisionism: Essays on the History of Marxist Ideas. Ed. by Leopold Labedz. (Essay Index Reprint Ser.). 1977. reprint ed. 26.95 (*0-518-10166-5*) Ayer.

Revisionism & Brainwashing. Harry E. Barnes. 1971. 250.00 (*0-685-26298-7*) Revisionist Pr.

Revisionism & Empire: Socialist Imperialism in Germany 1897-1914. Roger Fletcher. (Illus.). 224p. 1984. text ed. 55.00 (*0-04-943031-9*) Routledge Chapman & Hall.

Revisionism & the Promotion of Peace. Harry E. Barnes. 1971. 59.95 (*0-87700-284-3*) Revisionist Pr.

Revisionist Bibliography. Keith Stimely. 1981. lib. bdg. 250.00 (*0-686-73186-7*) Revisionist Pr.

Revisionist Historians & German War Guilt. Warren B. Morris. 1976. lib. bdg. 250.00 (*0-87700-257-6*) Revisionist Pr.

Revisionist Hungary. S. Fenyes. 250p. 1988. write for info. (*0-937019-10-0*); pap. 20.00 (*0-937019-11-9*) Romanian Hist.

Revisionist Plays. John Harms. 1971. 250.00 (*0-685-26304-5*) Revisionist Pr.

Revisionist Resurrection Myhtologies Vol. 176: A Study of D. H. Lawrence's Italian Works. Jill Franks. (American University Studies: No. IV). 191p. (C). 1994. text ed. 45.95 (*0-8204-2414-5*) P Lang Pubng.

Revisionist Stage: American Directors Reinvent the Classics. Amy S. Green. (Cambridge Studies in American Theatre & Drama: No. 3). (Illus.). 224p. (C). 1994. text ed. 59.95 (*0-521-45343-7*) Cambridge U Pr.

Revisionist Viewpoints: Essays in a Dissident Historical Tradition. James J. Martin. LC 75-187779. 1977. pap. 5.95 (*0-87926-008-4*) R Myles.

***Revisions.** Willie Thompson. 1997. pap. text ed. 11.95 (*0-7453-0814-7*, Pub. by Pluto Pr UK) LPC InBook.

Revisions: Changing Perspectives in Moral Philosophy. Ed. by Stanley Hauerwas & Alasdair MacIntyre. LC 82-40386. (Revisions Ser.). 320p. (C). 1983. pap. text ed. 14.00 (*0-268-01617-8*) U of Notre Dame Pr.

Revisions: New Perspectives of Art Criticism. Howard J. Smagula. 192p. 1990. pap. text ed. 29.40 (*0-13-779364-2*) P-H.

Revisitations: Ten Little Pieces on Art Education. Harlan Hoffa. 80p. (Orig.). 1994. pap. text ed. 15.00 (*0-937652-70-9*, 205) Natl Art Ed.

Revisiting Blassingame's "The Slave Community" The Scholar's Respond. Ed. by Al-Tony Gilmore. LC 77-84765. (Contributions in Afro-American & African Studies: No. 37). 206p. 1978. text ed. 49.95 (*0-8371-9879-8*, GJB/, Greenwood Pr) Greenwood.

Revisiting Landscape. Reesey Shaw et al. LC 94-74123. 28p. (Orig.). 1995. pap. write for info. (*1-885088-01-9*) CA Ctr Arts.

Revisiting Literacy. Smith & Alcock. 1990. 80.00 (*0-335-09571-2*, Open Univ Pr); pap. 27.00 (*0-335-09570-4*, Open Univ Pr) Taylor & Francis.

Revisiting Mathematics Education: China Lectures. Hans Freudenthal. 216p. (C). 1991. lib. bdg. 97.00 (*0-7923-1299-6*) Kluwer Ac.

Revisiting My Pygmy Hosts. Paul Schebesta. Tr. by Gerald Griffin from GER. LC 74-15087. (Illus.). reprint ed. 49.50 (*0-404-12137-3*) AMS Pr.

Revisiting Talwar: A Study in the Royal Indian Navy Uprising of February 1946. Dipak Kumar Das. (C). 1994. 36.00 (*81-202-0349-6*, Pub. by Ajanta II) S Asia.

Revisiting the Americas: Teaching & Learning the Geography of the Western Hemisphere. T. Lee et al. Ed. by T. L. Martinson & Susan Brooker-Gross. (Pathways in Geography Ser.: No. 4). (Illus.). 260p. (Orig.). 1992. pap. text ed. 25.00 (*0-9627379-2-5*) NCFGE.

Revisiting "The Culture of the School & the Problem of Change" Seymour B. Sarason. LC 96-2143. (School Reform Ser.: Vol. 12). 416p. (C). 1996. text ed. 44.00 (*0-8077-3544-2*); pap. text ed. 19.95 (*0-8077-3543-4*) Tchrs Coll.

Revisiting the White City: American Art at the 1893 World's Fair. Carolyn K. Carr et al. LC 92-37218. (Illus.). 408p. 1993. 60.00 (*0-937311-01-4*); pap. 35.00 (*0-937311-02-2*) Natl Mus Amer Art.

Revisiting Wertheimer's Seminars, 2 vols. Abraham S. Luchins & Edith H. Luchins. Incl. Vol. 1. Value, Social Influence, & Power. LC 72-3525. 1978. 85.00 (*0-8387-1227-4*); Vol. 2. Problems in Social Psychology. LC 72-3525. 1978. 85.00 (*0-8387-1570-2*); LC 72-3525. 1046p. 1978. write for info. (*0-686-96685-6*) Bucknell U Pr.

***Revisiting Workers' Compensation in California: Administrative Inventory.** Carol A. Telles & Sharon E. Fox. LC 97-16421. 1997. write for info. (*0-935149-66-X*) Workers Comp Res Inst.

***Revisiting Workers' Compensation in Pennsylvania: Administrative Inventory.** Duncan S. Ballantyne. LC 96-54811. 1997. 29.00 (*0-935149-65-1*, WC-97-1) Workers Comp Res Inst.

Revisiting Workers' Compensation in Texas: Administrative Inventory. Peter S. Barth & Stacey M. Eccleston. LC 95-1658. 1995. 29.00 (*0-935149-51-1*, WC-95-1) Workers Comp Res Inst.

***Revisiting Workers' Compensation in Washington: Administrative Inventory.** Carol A. Telles & Sharon E. Fox. LC 96-35341. 1996. 29.00 (*0-935149-64-3*, WC-96-10) Workers Comp Res Inst.

Revista. Nancy Levy-Konesky & Karen Daggett. Ed. by Marilyn Perez-Abreu et al. 250p. (C). 1988. pap. text ed. 22.75 (*0-03-014214-8*) HB Coll Pubs.

Revista Interamericana de Bibliografia, Vol. XXX, No. 4, 1980. Oas General Secretariat Staff. 150p. (POR & SPA.). (C). 1980. pap. 2.00 (*0-686-74520-5*) OAS.

Revista Interamericana de Bibliografia, Vol. 31, No. 1. Oas General Secretariat Staff. 196p. (FRE, POR & SPA.). (C). 1981. pap. 3.00 (*0-686-75080-2*) OAS.

Revista Interamericana de Bibliografia: (Inter-American Review of Bibliography), Vol. XXX, No. 3. Oas General Secretariat Staff. 116p. (ENG & SPA.). 1980. pap. text ed. 2.00 (*0-686-69868-1*) OAS.

Revista Por el Imperio Del Derecho, No. 47: 1991. International Commission of Jurists. 75p. (SPA.). reprint ed. pap. 25.00 (*0-7837-7132-0*, 2052526) Bks Demand.

An Asterisk (*) at the beginning of an entry indicates that the title is appearing in BIP for the first time.

Revistas: An Annotated Bibliography of Spanish Language Periodicals for Public Libraries. Bibliotecas Para La Gente Periodical Committee. (Ethnic Studies Library Publications: No. 9). 31p. (Orig.). 1983. pap. 10.00 (*0-918520-07-X*) Chicano Stud Lib.

***Revisualizing Boundaries: A Plurilingual Ethos.** Lachman M. Khubchandani. LC 96-42037. (Language & Development Ser.: Vol. 3). 256p. (C). 1997. 32.50 (*0-8039-9353-6*, 93536) Sage.

Revitalising the Waterfront: International Dimensions of Dockland Redevelopment. Ed. by Brian S. Hoyle et al. LC 00-88. 265p. 1992. text ed. 64.95 (*0-470-21880-0*) Halsted Pr.

Revitalization Movements: Some Theoretical Considerations for Their Comparative Study. Anthony F. Wallace. (Irvington Reprint Series in Anthropology). (C). 1991. reprint ed. pap. text ed. 1.90 (*0-8290-2605-3*, A-230) Irvington.

Revitalization of Basic Business Education at All Instructional Levels. 160p. 1982. 5.00 (*0-933964-22-6*) Natl Busn Ed Assoc.

Revitalize Your Body with Nature's Secrets. Edwin Flatto. 1981. pap. 9.95 (*0-935540-14-8*) Plymouth Pr.

Revitalize Your Life: Improve Your Health, Your Sex Life, & Your Looks after Age Fifty. Jack Lalanne. 1995. pap. 13.95 (*0-8038-9356-6*) Hastings.

Revitalizing Agricultural Research in the Sahel: A Proposed Framework for Action. Jan Weijenberg et al. LC 93-30143. 108p. 1993. 7.95 (*0-8213-2598-1*, 12598) World Bank.

Revitalizing America's Business. Y. N. Chang. 256p. 1994. boxed 32.95 (*0-8403-9258-3*) Kendall-Hunt.

Revitalizing America's Cities: Neighborhood Reinvestment & Displacement. Ed. by Michael H. Schill & Richard P. Nathan. LC 83-396. (SUNY Series in Urban Public Policy). 184p. 1984. text ed. 64.50 (*0-87395-742-3*); pap. text ed. 21.95 (*0-87395-743-1*) State U NY Pr.

Revitalizing Antitrust in Its Second Century: Essays on Legal, Economic, & Political Policy. Ed. by Eleanor M. Fox et al. LC 91-6810. 568p. 1991. text ed. 69.50 (*0-89930-439-7*, FFF, Quorum Bks) Greenwood.

Revitalizing Apathetic Communities. 3rd ed. Carol Paul. (GAP Ser.: No. 16). 28p. 1996. pap. 17.50 (*0-944715-50-8*) CAI.

Revitalizing Apathetic Communities. 3rd rev. ed. Carol Paul. (GAP Report Ser.: No. 16). 16p. (C). 1994. pap. 17.50 (*0-944715-34-6*) CAI.

Revitalizing General Education in Time. Kanter & Gamson. LC 96-9703. 1996. 29.95 (*0-205-26257-0*) Allyn.

Revitalizing High Schools: What the School-to-Career Movement Can Contribute. Susan Goldberger & Richard Kazis. 38p. 1995. pap. text ed. 5.00 (*1-887410-79-1*) Jobs for Future.

Revitalizing Higher Education. Ed. by William F. Massy & Joel W. Meyerson. 120p. (Orig.). (C). 1995. 34.95 (*1-56079-642-1*) Petersons.

Revitalizing Higher Education. Ed. by Jamil Salmi & Adrian Verspoor. LC 94-27605. (Issues in Higher Education Ser.: No. 3). 450p. 1994. text ed. 90.75 (*0-08-041948-8*, Pergamon Pr) Elsevier.

Revitalizing Historic Urban Quaters. Tim Heath et al. (Illus.). 248p. 1996. pap. 37.95 (*0-7506-2890-1*) Buttrwrth-Heinemann.

Revitalizing International Law. Richard A. Falk. LC 88-21801. 261p. 1989. reprint ed. pap. 74.40 (*0-608-00046-9*, 2060812) Bks Demand.

Revitalizing Low-Income Neighborhoods: Recommendations from ULI Advisory Services Panels. Diane R. Suchman. LC 94-60414. 124p. 1994. pap. text ed. 35.95 (*0-87420-757-6*, R30) Urban Land.

Revitalizing Manufacturing: Text & Cases. Jan Klein. 656p. (C). 1992. 56.00 (*0-256-06809-7*) Irwin.

Revitalizing Remediation in the Middle Grades: An Invitational Approach. David B. Strahan. 22p. (Orig.). 1988. 4.00 (*0-88210-208-7*) Natl Assn Principals.

Revitalizing Residential Settings. Martin Wolins & Vochanan Wozner. LC 81-20804. (Jossey-Bass Social & Behavioral Science Ser.). 336p. reprint ed. pap. 95.80 (*0-8357-4926-6*, 2037856) Bks Demand.

Revitalizing Rural America: A Perspective on Collaboration & Community. Michael Murray & Larry Dunn. 1996. write for info. (*0-471-96349-6*) Wiley.

Revitalizing Rural America: A Perspective on Collaboration & Community. Michael Murray & Larry Dunn. 280p. 1996. pap. text ed. 35.00 (*0-471-96350-X*) Wiley.

Revitalizing Small Town America: State & Federal Initiatives for Economic Development. 314p. 1989. 25.00 (*0-317-05056-7*) Natl Coun Econ Dev.

Revitalizing Socialist Enterprise: A Race Against Time. Ed. by John Heath. LC 92-44128. 288p. (C). (gr. 13). 1993. text ed. 74.95 (*0-415-09122-5*, B2391, Routledge NY) Routledge.

Revitalizing State & Local Public Service: Strengthening Performance, Accountability, & Citizen Confidence. Ed. by Frank J. Thompson. LC 93-14559. (Public Administration Ser.). 474p. 39.95 (*1-55542-572-0*) Jossey-Bass.

Revitalizing Teacher Preparation in Science. Lynn Glass et al. 16p. 1993. pap. text ed. 4.00 (*0-87355-121-4*) Natl Sci Tchrs.

Revitalizing the Industrial City. Ed. by Ralph R. Widner & Marvin E. Wolfgang. (Annals Ser.: Vol. 488). 1986. 26.00 (*0-8039-2860-2*); pap. 17.00 (*0-8039-2861-0*) Sage.

Revitalizing the Retail Trade Sector in Rural Communities: Lessons from Three Midwestern States. Janet S. Ayres et al. Ed. by Julie Stewart. 50p. (C). 1992. pap. text ed. 3.50 (*0-936913-05-3*, RRD 162) NCRCRD.

Revitalizing the Sunday Morning Dinosaur: Making Sunday School the Fossil Fuel for Energizing Your Church. Ken Hemphill. LC 96-16399. 224p. 1996. 12.99 (*0-8054-6174-4*, 4261-74) Broadman.

Revitalizing the U. S. Economy. Ed. by Larry C. Ledebur et al. LC 85-30166. 242p. 1986. text ed. 55.00 (*0-275-92101-8*, C2101, Praeger Pubs) Greenwood.

Revitalizing the Waterfront: International Dimensions of Dockland Redevelopment. Ed. by B. S. Hoyle et al. LC 88-26219. (Belhaven Press Bk.). 265p. 1993. text ed. 85.00 (*0-471-94808-X*, Pub. by Pinter Publishers UK) Wiley.

Revitalizing U. S. Electronics: Lessons from Japan. John L. Sprague. (Illus.). 262p. 1993. 42.95 (*0-7506-9223-5*) Buttrwrth-Heinemann.

Revitalizing Undergraduate Science: Why Some Things Work & Most Don't. 192p. (Orig.). 1992. pap. 3.95 (*0-9633504-1-2*) Res Corp.

Revitalizing Urban Neighborhoods. Ed. by W. Dennis Keating et al. LC 96-18180. (Studies in Government & Public Policy). (Illus.). 288p. 1996. pap. 17.95 (*0-7006-0790-0*) U Pr of KS.

Revitalizing Urban Neighborhoods. Ed. by W. Dennis Keating et al. LC 96-18180. (Studies in Government & Public Policy). (Illus.). 288p. 1996. 35.00 (*0-7006-0789-7*) U Pr of KS.

Revitalizing Western Economies: A New Agenda for Business & Government. Russell L. Ackoff et al. LC 84-47977. (Joint Publication in the Jossey-Bass Management Series & the Jossey-Bass Social & Behavioral Science Ser.). 232p. reprint ed. pap. 66.20 (*0-7837-2509-4*, 2042668) Bks Demand.

***Revitalizing Your Board of Directors: A Q. & A. Guide to Getting the Most from Your Nonprofit Board.** James M. Hardy. LC 96-67925. pap. 24.95 (*1-889102-11-3*) Emerson & Church.

***Revival.** Neil T. Anderson. 1997. 17.99 (*0-614-27506-7*) Gospel Lght.

Revival. D. Martyn Lloyd-Jones. LC 86-72057. 320p. (Orig.). 1987. pap. 12.99 (*0-89107-415-5*) Crossway Bks.

Revival. Andrew Murray. 144p. (Orig.). 1990. pap. 7.99 (*1-55661-123-4*) Bethany Hse.

Revival. rev. ed. Richard O. Roberts. 159p. (C). 1991. reprint ed. pap. 8.95 (*0-940033-36-4*) R O Roberts.

Revival. 2nd rev. ed. Richard O. Roberts. 159p. (C). 1991. reprint ed. lib. bdg. 12.95 (*0-940033-37-2*) R O Roberts.

***Revival: A Study in Biblical Patterns.** D. B. Long. 1996. pap. 9.99 (*0-946351-38-4*, Pub. by John Ritchie UK) Loizeaux.

Revival: Its Principles & Personalities. Winkey Pratney. LC 93-61365. 240p. 1993. pap. 10.99 (*1-56384-058-8*) Huntington Hse.

Revival: Our Eternal Hope. Glenn Foster. 240p. 1994. per., pap. text ed. 10.95 (*0-8403-9777-1*) Kendall-Hunt.

Revival: Southern Writers in the Modern City. Ted R. Spivey. LC 85-29507. 224p. 1986. pap. 24.95 (*0-8130-0741-0*) U Press Fla.

***Revival: Southern Writers in the Modern City.** Ted R. Spivey. LC 85-29507. 235p. reprint ed. pap. 67.00 (*0-608-04463-6*, 2065207) Bks Demand.

Revival: Spoken Word from Lollapalooza 94. Ed. by Juliette Torrez et al. (Illus.). 230p. (Orig.). 1995. pap. 12.95 (*0-916397-41-6*) Manic D Pr.

Revival! The Current Spiritual Awakening in Brownwood, Fort Worth, Wheaton & Beyond. Ed. by John Avant et al. LC 95-22937. 176p. 1996. pap. 10.99 (*0-8054-6191-4*, 4261-91) Broadman.

Revival! A People Saturated with God. Brian H. Edwards. 1990. pap. 14.99 (*0-85234-273-X*, Pub. by Evangelical Pr) Presby & Reformed.

***Revival & Rebellion in Colonial Africa.** 1995. pap. 27.50 (*0-435-07418-0*) Heinemann.

Revival & Rebellion in Colonial Central Africa. Karen E. Fields. LC 84-42884. 346p. reprint ed. pap. 98.70 (*0-8357-3432-3*, 2039689) Bks Demand.

Revival & Religion Since 1700: Essays for John Walsh. Ed. by Jane Garnett & Colin Matthew. LC 93-31184. 342p. 1993. boxed 65.00 (*1-85285-093-0*) Hambledon Press.

Revival & Revivalism: The Making & Marring of American Evangelicalism 1750-1858. Iain H. Murray. 455p. 1994. 28.99 (*0-85151-660-2*) Banner of Truth.

Revival Architecture in Hungary: Classicism & Romanticism. Anna Zabor. 28p. 1985. 200.00 (*0-317-42871-3*) St Mut.

Revival Comes to Wales. Eifion Evans. 1979. pap. 6.95 (*1-85049-025-2*) Chr Lit.

Revival Fire. Wesley Duewel. 368p. 1995. pap. 14.99 (*0-310-49661-6*) Zondervan.

Revival Gods Way. Leonard Ravenhill. LC 83-15589. 160p. (Orig.). 1983. pap. 7.99 (*0-87123-620-6*) Bethany Hse.

Revival in the Rust Belt: Tracking the Evolution of an Urban Industrial Region. Daniel R. Denison & Stuart L. Hart. LC 87-26264. 224p. (Orig.). 1987. pap. text ed. 15.00 (*0-87944-322-7*) Inst Soc Res.

Revival in the Rust Belt: Tracking the Evolution of an Urban Industrial Region. Daniel R. Denison & Stuart L. Hart. LC 87-26264. 224p. (Orig.). reprint ed. pap. 63.90 (*0-7837-5246-6*, 2044981) Bks Demand.

Revival in Tin Town. Effie M. Williams. 84p. pap. 0.75 (*0-686-29164-6*) Faith Pub Hse.

Revival Literature: An Annotated Bibliography with Biographical & Historical Notices. Richard O. Roberts. xxxii, 575p. 1987. lib. bdg. 60.00 (*0-940033-27-5*) R O Roberts.

Revival Now Through Prayer & Fasting. Gordon Cove. 1988. pap. 9.99 (*0-88019-227-5*) Schmul Pub Co.

Revival of a Classical Tongue: Elizer Ben Yehuda & the Modern Hebrew Language. Jack Fellman. (Contributions to the Sociology of Language Ser.: No. 6). 1973. pap. text ed. 32.35 (*90-279-2495-3*) Mouton.

Revival of a Marblehead Mansion. Dorothy Miles. Ed. by Alexander MacDonald. 35p. 1982. reprint ed. pap. write for info. (*0-318-65392-3*) D Miles.

Revival of Aristocracy. Oscar Levy. 1972. 59.95 (*0-8490-0952-9*) Gordon Pr.

Revival of Buddhism in Modern India: The Role of B. R. Ambedkar & the Dalai Lama XIV. L. Kenadi. ix, 125p. (C). 1995. 13.00 (*81-7024-680-6*, Pub. by Ashish Pub Hse II) Nataraj Bks.

Revival of Constitutionalism. James W. Muller. LC 87-30177. 276p. 1988. reprint ed. pap. 78.70 (*0-7837-8908-4*, 2049619) Bks Demand.

Revival of Death. Tony Walter. LC 94-12148. 240p. (C). 1994. pap. 18.95 (*0-415-11854-9*, B4785) Routledge.

Revival of Death. Tony Walter. LC 94-12148. 240p. (C). (gr. 13). 1994. text ed. 62.95 (*0-415-08665-5*, B4104) Routledge.

Revival of Interest in the Dream. Robert Fliess. 164p. 1953. 27.50 (*0-8236-5820-1*) Intl Univs Pr.

Revival of Israel: Rome & Jerusalem, the Last Nationalist Question. Moses Hess. Tr. by Meyer Waxman. LC 95-5382. xvii, 265p. 1995. pap. 10.00 (*0-8032-7275-8*, Bison Books) U of Nebr Pr.

Revival of Nijinsky's Original l'Apres-Midi d'un Faune, Vol. 1, Part 3. Ed. by Jill Beck. 96p. 1991. pap. text ed. 23.00 (*3-7186-5117-3*, Harwood Acad Pubs) Gordon & Breach.

Revival of Pascal: A Study of His Relation to Modern French Thought. Dorothy M. Eastwood. LC 37-2631. (Oxford Studies in Modern Languages & Literature). 224p. reprint ed. pap. 63.90 (*0-317-08091-1*, 2051242) Bks Demand.

Revival of Religion. Burns et al. 449p. 1984. reprint ed. 24.99 (*0-85151-435-9*) Banner of Truth.

***Revival of Right Wing Extremism in the 90's.** Ed. by Peter H. Merkl et al. LC 97-2105. (Cass Series on Political Violence: No. 5). 304p. (C). 1997. 45.00 (*0-7146-4676-8*, Pub. by F Cass Pubs UK); pap. 19.50 (*0-7146-4207-X*, Pub. by F Cass Pubs UK) Intl Spec Bk.

Revival of Scholastic Philosophy in the Nineteenth Century. Joseph L. Perrier. LC 09-10966. reprint ed. 32.50 (*0-404-04994-X*) AMS Pr.

***Revival of the Democratic Intellect.** A. L. Walker. 1995. 24.00 (*0-7486-6188-3*, Pub. by Polygon UK) Subterranean Co.

Revival of Values Education in Asia & the West. S. Gopinathan. Ed. by W. K. Cummings & Y. Tomoda. LC 88-14037. (Pergamon Comparative & International Education Ser.: Vol. 7). (Illus.). 192p. (Orig.). (C). 1988. 92.00 (*0-08-035854-3*, Pub. by Pergamon Repr UK) Franklin.

***Revival of 1857-58: Interpreting an American Religios Awakening.** Kathryn T. Long. (Religion in America). (Illus.). 256p. 1997. 45.00 (*0-19-511293-8*) OUP.

Revival Power. Ronald Fowler. 1989. pap. 0.50 (*0-87162-585-7*, D1355) Warner Pr.

Revival Praying. Leonard Ravenhill. 176p. 1962. pap. 7.99 (*0-87123-482-3*) Bethany Hse.

Revival Preachers & Politics in Thirteenth-Century Italy: The Great Devotion of 1233. Augustine Thompson. LC 92-15169. 264p. 1992. 65.00 (*0-19-820287-3*, Clarendon Pr) OUP.

Revival, Revolution, & Religion in Early Virginia. Edwin S. Gaustad. (Illus.). 42p. 1994. pap. 9.95 (*0-87935-091-1*) Colonial Williamsburg.

Revival Sermon Outlines. Al Bryant. LC 91-41882. 64p. 1992. pap. 4.99 (*0-8254-2193-4*) Kregel.

Revival Sermon Outlines. Ed. by Charles R. Wood. 64p. 1969. pap. 4.99 (*0-8254-4005-X*) Kregel.

Revival Sermons. William C. Burns. 205p. 1981. pap. 7.99 (*0-85151-316-6*) Banner of Truth.

Revival Signs: Join the New Spiritual Awakening. Tom Phillips. 1995. 14.99 (*1-885305-15-X*) Multnomah Pubs.

Revival Styles in American Memorial Art. Peggy McDowell & Richard Meyer. LC 93-72851. (Illus.). 212p. 1994. 49.95 (*0-87972-633-4*); pap. 22.95 (*0-87972-634-2*) Bowling Green Univ Popular Press.

Revival We Need. rev. ed. Oswald J. Smith. Ed. by Chuck Dean. 144p. (YA). 1995. pap. 8.95 (*1-883893-04-6*) WinePress Pub.

***Revival Year Sermons: Preached in the Surrey Music Hall 1859.** C. H. Spurgeon. 96p. 1996. pap. 5.99 (*0-85151-703-X*) Banner of Truth.

Revival 2000! Don't Say "No" Until You Have Read This Book. Liberty S. Savard. 164p. (Orig.). 1995. pap. 7.95 (*0-929685-52-0*) Superior Bks.

Revival (3 Sermons) Charles H. Spurgeon. 1994. pap. 3.00 (*1-56186-430-7*) Pilgrim Pubns.

***Revivalism & Cultural Change.** Thomas. 1998. pap. text ed. 14.95 (*0-226-79586-1*) U Ch Pr.

Revivalism & Cultural Change: Christianity, Nation Building, & the Market in the Nineteenth-Century United States. George M. Thomas. (Illus.). 256p. 1989. 41.95 (*0-226-79585-3*) U Ch Pr.

Revivalism & Separatism in New England, 1740-1800: Strict Congregationalists & Separate Baptists in the Great Awakening. C. C. Goen. LC 87-18350. 401p. reprint ed. pap. 114.30 (*0-7837-0214-0*, 2040522) Bks Demand.

Revivalism & Social Reform: American Protestantism on the Eve of the Civil War. Timothy Smith. LC 80-8114. 272p. (C). 1980. reprint ed. pap. text ed. 14.95 (*0-8018-2477-X*) Johns Hopkins.

Revivalism, Social Conscience, & Community in the Burned-Over District: The Trial of Rhoda Bement. Glenn C. Altschuler & Jan M. Saltzgaber. (Illus.). 184p. 1983. pap. 11.95 (*0-8014-9246-7*) Cornell U Pr.

Revivals & Importations of French Comedies in England, 1749-1800. Willard A. Kinne. LC 40-3880. reprint ed. 32.50 (*0-404-03705-4*) AMS Pr.

Revivals & Roller Rinks: Religion, Leisure & Identity in Late-Nineteenth-Century Small-Town Ontario. Lynne Marks. (Studies in Gender & History). (Illus.). 376p. 1996. 55.00 (*0-8020-0751-1*); pap. 19.95 (*0-8020-7800-1*) U of Toronto Pr.

Revivals, Awakening, & Reform: An Essay on Religion & Social Change in America, 1607 to 1977. William G. McLoughlin. LC 77-27830. xvi, 256p. 1980. pap. text ed. 10.95 (*0-226-56092-9*, P891) U Ch Pr.

Revival's Children: A Religious History of Virginia's Eastern Shore. Kirk Mariner. LC 79-64801. (Illus.). 728p. 1979. reprint ed. 22.95 (*0-9648393-0-X*) Miona Pubns.

Revivals! Diverse Traditions: The History of Twentieth-Century American Craft, 1920-1945. Ed. by Janet Kardon. LC 94-11076. 1994. 49.50 (*0-8109-1955-9*) Abrams.

Revivals of the Eighteenth Century. Duncan MacFarlan. 312p. 1980. reprint ed. 16.00 (*0-939464-32-2*, Labyrinth) Baker Bks.

Revivals of the Eighteenth Century, Particularly at Cambuslang: With Three Sermons by the Rev. George Whitefield. Duncan Macfarlan. (Revival Library). (Illus.). 312p. (C). 1980. reprint ed. lib. bdg. 16.00 (*0-940033-14-3*) R O Roberts.

Revive Thy Work. Watchman Nee. Ed. by Herbert L. Fader. Tr. by Stephen Kaung from CHI. (Orig.). 1996. pap. 5.50 (*0-935008-81-0*) Christian Fellow Pubs.

***Revive Us Again: The Recovery of American Fundamentalism, 1925-1950.** Joel A. Carpenter. LC 97-13227. (Illus.). 384p. 1996. 25.00 (*0-19-505790-2*) OUP.

Revived Roman Empire & the Beast of the Apocalypse. Noah W. Hutchings. (Illus.). 140p. (Orig.). 1992. pap. 7.95 (*1-879366-31-2*) Hearthstone OK.

Reviving a Rural Industry: Silk Producers & Officials in India & Bangladesh. Willem Van Schendel. (C). 1995. 28.00 (*81-7304-125-3*, Pub. by Manohar II) S Asia.

Reviving Liberty: Radical Christian Humanism in Milton's Great Poems. Joan S. Bennett. LC 88-22682. (Illus.). 233p. 1988. 37.00 (*0-674-76697-0*) HUP.

Reviving Main Street. Ed. by Deryck Holdsworth. 256p. 1985. 25.00 (*0-8020-2542-0*); pap. 14.95 (*0-8020-6556-2*) U of Toronto Pr.

Reviving Old Houses: Over 500 Low-Cost Tips & Techniques. Alan D. Orme. LC 89-45220. (Illus.). 180p. 1989. 16.95 (*0-88266-582-0*, Garden Way Pub); pap. 12.95 (*0-88266-563-4*, Garden Way Pub) Storey Comm Inc.

Reviving Ophelia: Saving the Selves of Adolescent Girls. Mary Pipher. 320p. 1994. 24.95 (*0-399-13944-3*, Grosset-Putnam) Putnam Pub Group.

Reviving Ophelia: Saving the Selves of Adolescent Girls. Mary B. Pipher. 345p. 1995. pap. 12.95 (*0-345-39282-5*) Ballantine.

Reviving Primary Care: A U. S. - U. K. Comparison. John Fry et al. LC 95-15842. 1995. write for info. (*1-85775-001-2*, Radcliffe Med Pr) Scovill Paterson.

Reviving Private Investment in Developing Countries. Ed. by Ajay Chhibber et al. LC 92-12342. (Contributions to Economic Analysis Ser.: Vol. 208). 246p. 1992. 93.00 (*0-444-89395-4*, North Holland) Elsevier.

Reviving the American Dream: Stop "Just Getting By" & Build Real Wealth. Adam Starchild. 184p. 1994. pap. 14.00 (*0-87364-797-1*) Paladin Pr.

Reviving the American Dream: The Economy, the States, & the Federal Government. Alice M. Rivlin. 196p. (C). 1993. 34.95 (*0-8157-7476-1*); pap. 14.95 (*0-8157-7483-4*) Brookings.

Reviving the Ancient Faith: The Story of the Churches of Christ in America. Richard T. Hughes. 446p. (Orig.). 1996. pap. 30.00 (*0-8028-4086-8*) Eerdmans.

Reviving the Economy: Bush vs. the House Democrats. John C. Goodman et al. (Illus.). 17p. (C). 1992. pap. 5.00 (*0-943802-92-X*, BG113) Natl Ctr Pol.

Reviving the European Union. Ed. by C. Randall Henning et al. LC 93-50829. 176p. 1994. pap. 25.00 (*0-88132-208-3*) Inst Intl Eco.

Reviving the Everglades. David W. Felder. 48p. 1996. pap. text ed. 8.95 (*0-910959-71-4*, B&G 14B) Wellington Pr.

***Reviving the Renaissance: The Use & Abuse of the Past in Nineteenth-Century Italian Art & Decoration.** Rosanna Pavoni. (Cambridge Studies in Italian History & Culture). (Illus.). 288p. 1997. text ed. 69.95 (*0-521-48151-1*) Cambridge U Pr.

Reviving the Soul. Compiled by Robert Backhouse. 1995. pap. 10.99 (*0-551-02909-9*) Zondervan.

***Reviving the Spirit: A Generation of African Americans Goes Home to Church.** Beverly H. Lawrence. 192p. 1997. reprint ed. pap. 11.00 (*0-8021-3499-8*, Grove) Grove-Atltic.

Reviving the Stones: The Story of Nehemiah. David Hocking. Ed. by M. B. Steele. 192p. (Orig.). 1991. pap. 8.95 (*0-939497-23-9*) Promise Pub.

Reviving the Sustainable Metropolis: Guiding Bay Area Conservation & Development into the 21st Century. Larry Orman & Jim Sayer. (Illus.). 22p. (C). 1989. text ed. 5.00 (*0-685-45121-6*) Greenbelt.

Reviving the Tribe: Regenerating Gay Men's Sexuality & Culture in the Ongoing Epidemic. Eric Rofes. LC 95-35017. 318p. 1995. 29.95 (*1-56024-987-0*); pap. 14.95 (*1-56023-876-3*) Haworth Pr.

Reviving the World Court. Richard A. Falk. LC 85-31451. (Procedural Aspects of International Law Ser.: No. 18). 197p. (C). 1986. text ed. 50.00 (*0-8139-1084-6*, 306510) W S Hein.

Revnitel' Blagotchestija 19-go vjeka, Episkop Theofan Zatvornik. Priest Nikolai Deputatov. 71p. 1971. pap. 3.00 (*0-317-29261-7*) Holy Trinity.

Revocable Living Trust Sample. (Illus.). 240p. 1996. 89.00 (*1-885661-11-8*) Estate Protection.

Revocable Trusts. 3rd ed. George M. Turner. LC 95-44703. 1995. write for info. (*0-07-172738-8*) Shepards.

Revolt. S. Wise Bauer. 304p. 1996. pap. 12.99 (*0-8499-3935-6*) Word Pub.

Revolt Against Chemicals. Raymond W. Bernard. (Science of Organic Dietetics Ser.). 86p. 1955. reprint ed. spiral bd. 8.50 (*0-7873-1027-1*) Hlth Research.

R

Revolt Against Chivalry: Jesse Daniel Ames & the Women's Campaign Against Lynching. Jacquelyn D. Hall. 384p. (C). 1993. pap. 16.50 (*0-231-08283-5*); text ed. 52.50 (*0-231-08282-7*) Col U Pr.

Revolt Against Destiny: An Intellectual History of the United States. Paul A. Carter. 331p. 1989. text ed. 37.50 (*0-231-06616-3*) Col U Pr.

Revolt Against Dualism: An Inquiry Concerning the Existence of Ideas. Arthur O. Lovejoy. 424p. (C). 1996. pap. text ed. 29.96 (*1-56000-847-4*) Transaction Pubs.

Revolt Against Hitler. Fabian Von Schlabrendorff. LC 78-63714. (Studies in Fascism: Ideology & Practice). (Illus.). 184p. reprint ed. 39.50 (*0-404-16985-6*) AMS Pr.

Revolt Against Mechanism. Lawrence P. Jacks. LC 77-27140. (Hibbert Lectures: 1933). reprint ed. 32.50 (*0-404-60429-3*) AMS Pr.

Revolt Against Modernity: Leo Strauss, Eric Voegelin, & the Search for a Postliberal Order. Ted V. McAllister. LC 95-35016. (American Political Thought Ser.). (Illus.). 338p. (C). 1997. 35.00 (*0-7006-0740-4*) U Pr of KS.

***Revolt Against Modernity: Leo Strauss, Eric Voegelin, & the Search for a Postliberal Order.** Ted V. McAllister. (American Political Thought Ser.). (Illus.). 338p. 1997. pap. 16.95 (*0-7006-0873-7*) U Pr of KS.

Revolt Against Reason. Arnold H. Lunn. LC 72-108396. xiv, 273p. 1971. reprint ed. text ed. 49.75 (*0-8371-3819-1*, LURA, Greenwood Pr) Greenwood.

Revolt Against Regulation: The Rise & Pause of the Consumer Movement. Michael Pertschuk. LC 82-40108. 192p. 1982. pap. 13.00 (*0-520-05074-6*) U CA Pr.

Revolt Against Romanticism in American Literature. Sten Liljegren. (BCL1-PS American Literature Ser.). 60p. 1993. reprint ed. lib. bdg. 59.00 (*0-7812-6951-2*) Rprt Serv.

Revolt Against Romanticism in American Literature: As Evidenced in the Works of S. L. Clemens. Sten Liljegren. LC 65-15896. (Studies in Fiction: No. 34). (C). 1969. reprint ed. lib. bdg. 75.00 (*0-8383-0583-0*) M S G Haskell Hse.

Revolt Against Romanticism in American Literature As Evidenced in the Work of S. L. Clemens. S. B. Liljegren. 59p. 1983. pap. 12.50 (*0-87556-650-2*) Saifer.

Revolt Against Romanticism in American Literature As Evidenced in the Works of S. L. Clemens. S. B. Liljegren. (Essays & Studies on American Language & Literature: Vol. 1). 1974. reprint ed. pap. 25.00 (*0-8115-0183-3*) Periodicals Srv.

Revolt Against the Dead: The Modernization of a Mayan Community in the Highlands of Guatemala. D. E. Brintnall. (Library of Anthropology). 200p. 1979. text ed. 58.00 (*0-677-05170-0*) Gordon & Breach.

Revolt Against the Modern World: Politics, Religion, & Social Order in the Kali Yuga. Julius Evola. 288p. 1996. 29.95 (*0-89281-506-X*) Inner Tradit.

***Revolt among the Sharecroppers.** Howard Kester. LC 96-35712. (Illus.). 130p. 1997. pap. text ed. 14.50 (*0-87049-975-0*) U of Tenn Pr.

Revolt among the Sharecroppers. Howard Kester. LC 69-18576. (American Negro: His History & Literature. Series 2). 1969. reprint ed. 16.95 (*0-405-01876-2*) Ayer.

Revolt & Virginia. large type ed. Essie Summers. (Romance Ser.). 368p. 1993. 25.99 (*0-7089-2943-5*) Ulverscroft.

Revolt in Aspromonte. Corrado Alvaro. Tr. by Frances Frenaye from ITA. LC 62-12393. 128p. 1962. reprint ed. pap. 1.35 (*0-8112-0002-7*, NDP119) New Directions.

Revolt in Palestine the Eighteenth Century. Ahmad H. Joudah. LC 86-83198. (Leaders, Politics, & Social Change in the Islamic World Ser.: Vol. 6). 150p. 1987. 25.00 (*0-940670-11-9*) Kingston Pr.

Revolt in Prerevolutionary France: The Prince de Conti's Conspiracy Against Louis XV, 1755-1757. John D. Woodbridge. 264p. 1995. text ed. 39.95 (*0-8018-4945-4*) Johns Hopkins.

Revolt in the Desert. large type ed. T. E. Lawrence. 438p. 1990. 22.95 (*1-85089-401-9*, Pub. by ISIS UK) Transaction Pubs.

Revolt in the Netherlands: Brussels-Eighteen Thirty. John W. Rooney, Jr. 250p. (C). 1982. pap. text ed. 17.50 (*0-87291-156-X*) Coronado Pr.

Revolt in the Valley. Mari Williams. (YA). 1992. pap. 23.00 (*0-86383-778-6*, Pub. by Gomer Pr UK) St Mut.

Revolt in 2100. Robert A. Heinlein. 352p. 1986. reprint ed. mass mkt. 4.99 (*0-671-65589-2*) Baen Bks.

Revolt of Mamie Stover. William B. Huie. 1993. reprint ed. lib. bdg. 17.95 (*1-56849-205-7*) Buccaneer Bks.

Revolt of Mother. Mary E. Freeman. (Short Stories Ser.). (J). (gr. 5 up). 1992. lib. bdg. 13.95 (*0-88682-495-8*) Creative Ed.

Revolt of Naples. Rosario Villari. Tr. by James Newell. LC 92-34029. 250p. 1993. 38.95 (*0-7456-0724-1*) Blackwell Pubs.

Revolt of Nineteen Hundred & Five in Bengal. Benoy J. Ghosh. (C). 1987. 25.00 (*0-8364-2126-4*, KL Mukhopadhyay) S Asia.

Revolt of Nineteen-Sixteen in Russian Central Asia. Edward D. Sokol. LC 78-64219. (Johns Hopkins University. Studies in the Social Sciences. Thirtieth Ser. 1912: 1). reprint ed. 35.00 (*0-404-61323-3*) AMS Pr.

***Revolt of Owain Glyn Dwr.** R. R. Davies. (Illus.). 424p. 1997. reprint ed. pap. 16.95 (*0-19-285336-8*) OUP.

Revolt of the Admirals: The Fight for Naval Avation, 1945-1950. Jeffrey G. Barlow. LC 94-1937. 1994. 30.00 (*0-945274-24-6*) Naval Hist Ctr.

***Revolt of the Admirals: The Fight for Naval Aviation, 1945-1950, 2 vols.** 1997. lib. bdg. 600.25 (*0-8490-6152-0*) Gordon Pr.

Revolt of the Aesthetics: Ernesto Gimenez Caballero & the Origins of Spanish Fascism. Douglas W. Foard. (American University Studies: History: Ser. IX, Vol. 70). 257p. (C). 1989. text ed. 42.50 (*0-8204-0927-8*) P Lang Pubng.

Revolt of the Cockroach People. Oscar Z. Acosta. 256p. 1989. pap. 11.00 (*0-679-72212-2*, Vin) Random.

Revolt of the Communeros, 1721-1735: A Study in the Colonial History of Paraguay. Adalberto Lopez. 214p. 1976. 39.95 (*0-87073-124-6*) Transaction Pubs.

Revolt of the Conservation Democrats: An Essay on American Political Culture & Political Development, 1837-1844. Jean E. Friedman. LC 78-27449. (Studies in American History & Culture: No. 9). 159p. reprint ed. pap. 45.40 (*0-685-44073-7*, 2070119) Bks Demand.

Revolt of the Depression Generation: America's First Mass Student Movement, 1929-1941. Robby Cohen. LC 92-22733. 456p. 1993. 58.00 (*0-19-506099-7*) OUP.

Revolt of the Earth. SATPREM Staff. Tr. by Luc Venet from FRE. LC 90-5081. 200p. (Orig.). 1991. pap. text ed. 8.95 (*0-938710-24-9*) Inst Evolutionary.

Revolt of the Elites & the Betrayal of Democracy. Christopher Lasch. 276p. 1995. 22.00 (*0-393-03699-5*) Norton.

Revolt of the Elites & the Betrayal of Democracy. Christopher Lasch. 256p. 1995. pap. 12.95 (*0-393-31371-9*, Norton Paperbks) Norton.

Revolt of the Engineers: Social Responsibility & the American Engineering Profession. Edwin T. Layton, Jr. LC 85-23981. 312p. (Orig.). 1986. reprint ed. text ed. 37.50 (*0-8018-3286-1*) Johns Hopkins.

Revolt of the Judges: The Parlement of Paris & the Fronde, 1643-1652. Alanson L. Moote. LC 78-155003. 423p. reprint ed. pap. 120.60 (*0-8357-3851-5*, 2036584) Bks Demand.

Revolt of the Masses. Jose Ortega y Gasset. Ed. by Kenneth Moore. LC 81-40457. 240p. 1985. text ed. 33.50 (*0-268-01609-7*) U of Notre Dame Pr.

Revolt of the Masses. Jose Ortega y Gasset. 192p. 1994. pap. 8.95 (*0-393-31095-7*) Norton.

Revolt of the Middle-Aged Man. Edmund Bergler. LC 84-22396. xxi, 312p. 1985. 40.00 (*0-8236-5830-9*, 05830) Intl Univs Pr.

Revolt of the Mind. Tibor Meray. 449p. 1960. 8.75 (*0-685-55404-X*) Bookfinger.

Revolt of the Mind. Tamas Aczel & Tibor Meray. LC 74-20275. 449p. 1975. reprint ed. text ed. 65.00 (*0-8371-7851-7*, ACRM, Greenwood Pr) Greenwood.

Revolt of the Naked. D. V. Sadero. (Orig.). 1995. mass mkt. 4.95 (*1-56333-261-2*, Badboy) Masquerade.

Revolt of the Oppressed: Punnapra-Valalar 1946. P. K. Kaimal. (C). 1994. text ed. 20.00 (*81-220-0365-6*, Pub. by Konark Pubs II) S Asia.

Revolt of the Perverts (Gay Short Stories) Daniel Curzon. LC 77-83394. (Orig.). 1978. pap. 6.95 (*0-930650-01-8*) IGNA Books.

Revolt of the Provinces: The Regionalist Movement in America, 1920-1945. Robert L. Dorman. LC 92-31234. (H. Eugene & Lillian Youngs Lehman Ser.). xvi, 366p. (C). 1993. 49.95 (*0-8078-2101-2*) U of NC Pr.

Revolt of the Tenantry: The Transformation of Local Government in Ireland, 1872-1886. William L. Feingold. LC 84-4080. (Illus.). 318p. 1984. text ed. 45.00 (*0-930350-55-3*) NE U Pr.

Revolt of the Widows: The Social World of the Apocryphal Acts. Stevan L. Davies. LC 80-11331. 150p. 1980. 16.95 (*0-8093-0958-0*) S Ill U Pr.

Revolt on the Campus. James Wechsler. LC 73-8748. (Americana Library Ser.: No. 26). 258p. 1973. reprint ed. 25.00 (*0-295-95296-2*) U of Wash Pr.

Revolt on the Clyde. Gallacher. (C). 1978. pap. 15.00 (*0-85315-425-2*, Pub. by Lawrence & Wishart UK) NYU Pr.

***Revolt on Venus.** Jordan Gallader. 76p. (Orig.). 1997. pap. 8.95 (*1-882550-24-2*) Quiet Lion Pr.

Revolt, U. S. A. Lamar Middleton. LC 68-29232. (Essay Index Reprint Ser.). (Illus.). 1977. reprint ed. 20.95 (*0-8369-0708-6*) Ayer.

Revolte des Anges. Anatole France. (Coll. Bleue). pap. 14.50 (*0-685-34120-8*) Fr & Eur.

Revolte des Anges. Anatole France. 320p. (FRE.). 1972. 10.95 (*0-8288-9763-8*, F101351) Fr & Eur.

***Revolte Des Inactifs.** Denis Cote. (Novels in the Roman Jeunesse Ser.). 160p. (FRE.). (YA). (gr. 8 up). 1996. pap. 7.95 (*2-89021-127-4*, Pub. by Les Editions CN) Firefly Bks Ltd.

Revoltee. Guy Des Cars. 370p. (FRE.). 1985. pap. 11.95 (*0-7859-4798-1*) Fr & Eur.

Revoltes de la Bounty. Jules Verne. 96p. (FRE.). 1979. pap. 10.95 (*0-7859-1364-5*, 2070330907) Fr & Eur.

Revolting Recipes. Roald Dahl & Felicity Dahl. (J). 1997. pap. 6.99 (*0-14-037820-0*) Puffin Bks.

***Revolting Recipes 10.** Roald Dahl. 1997. pap. 69.90 (*0-14-774436-9*) Viking Penguin.

Revolting Reptiles. Steve Parker. LC 92-43725. (Creepy Creatures Ser.). (Illus.). 38p. (J). (gr. 3-6). 1992. lib. bdg. 22.83 (*0-8114-0692-X*) Raintree Steck-V.

Revolting Reptiles. Steve Parker. (Illus.). (J). 1995. pap. text ed. 5.95 (*0-8114-6335-4*) Raintree Steck-V.

Revolting Rhymes: Roald Dahl's Revolting Rhymes. Roald Dahl. LC 94-29459. (Illus.). 48p. (J). (gr. 1-8). 1995. pap. 4.99 (*0-14-037533-3*) Puffin Bks.

***Revolting Ronnie.** (Little Monsters Ser.). (J). 1997. write for info. (*0-614-21783-0*, Pub. by Splash UK) Assoc Pubs Grp.

Revolucija I Sloboda. Hrvoje Lun. 1978. pap. 16.00 (*0-9602138-1-3*) Plamen Pub.

Revolucion. Eduardo De Acha. LC 88-82485. (Coleccion Cuba y Sus Jueces). 88p. (Orig.). (SPA.). 1989. pap. 9.00 (*0-89729-508-0*) Ediciones.

Revolucion: Historia de la Iglesia Primitiva. Gene Edwards. (SPA.). 1993. 6.99 (*1-56063-377-8*, 498489) Editorial Unilit.

***Revolucion: Historia de la Iglesia Primitiva.** Gene Edwards. 271p. (SPA.). 1974. pap. write for info. (*0-614-27133-9*) Editorial Unilit.

Revolucion del Amor. George Verwer. 209p. (SPA.). 1990. pap. 3.99 (*1-56063-013-2*, 498460) Editorial Unilit.

Revolucion del Arte Moderno: Del Impresionismo Al Expresionismo. Esther Boix. (Del Arte Moderno Ser.: Vol. I). (Illus.). 128p. (SPA.). 1993. 100.00 (*84-343-0500-3*) Elliots Bks.

Revolucion En la Produccion: El Sistema SMED. Shigeo Shingo. (Illus.). 399p. (Orig.). (SPA.). 1990. pap. 65.00 (*84-87022-02-2*) Prod Press.

Revolucion es un Sueno Eterno. Andres Rivera. 1995. pap. 12.50 (*0-679-76335-X*, Vin) Random.

Revolucion Granadina, 1979-83. Maurice Bishop & Fidel Castro. 86p. (SPA.). 1984. pap. 6.95 (*0-87348-483-5*) Pathfinder NY.

Revolucion Psiquiatrica: Del Manicomio a la Comunidad. Ed. by Michael A. Woodbury. Tr. by Gallogo Mere & Lilita B. Diaz from ENG. 275p. (Orig.). (SPA.). 1987. pap. 40.00 (*0-9619117-0-0*) Veritas Ed Pub.

Revolucion Traicionada: Que es y a Donde Se Dirige la Union Sovietica?: The Revolution Betrayed: What Is the Soviet Union & Where Is It Going? Leon Trotsky. LC 91-68462. 255p. (Orig.). (SPA.). (C). 1992. reprint ed. pap. 18.95 (*0-87348-735-4*) Pathfinder NY.

Revolution. Truman Becker. 169p. (Orig.). 1987. pap. 12.50 (*971-10-0322-8*, Pub. by New Day Pub PH) Cellar.

Revolution: A Challenge of Love. Anthony G. Bottagaro. 272p. (Orig.). (C). 1988. write for info. (*0-9621433-1-6*); pap. write for info. (*0-9621433-0-8*) Interloc Pub.

Revolution: A Collection of Plays. Ed. by Gerald Weales & Robert J. Nelson. LC 74-23082. 312p. 1975. 16.95 (*0-679-50532-6*) Boulevard.

Revolution: A Sociological Interpretation. Michael S. Kimmel. 294p. 1990. 44.95 (*0-87722-736-5*); pap. 18.95 (*0-87722-741-1*) Temple U Pr.

Revolution: The Reagan Legacy. enl. rev. ed. Martin Anderson. (Publication Ser.: No. 399). 486p. (C). 1990. reprint ed. pap. text ed. 18.95 (*0-8179-8992-7*) Hoover Inst Pr.

Revolution: U. S. A. 2000. Ray Aman. LC 96-90149. (Orig.). 1996. pap. 14.95 (*0-533-11915-4*) Vantage.

Revolution: 500 Years of Struggle for Change. Mark Almond. LC 96-18647. (Illus.). 208p. 1996. 29.95 (*1-899883-74-6*, Pub. by DeAgostini Edits UK) Stewart Tabori & Chang.

Revolution - Inaugural Issue. Ed. by Natasha Perova & Arch Tait. (Glas Ser.: No. 1). (Illus.). 224p. pap. 14.95 (*0-939010-46-1*) I R Dee.

Revolution a Venir en Afrique Du Sud. 2nd ed. Jack Barnes. 196p. (FRE.). 1991. reprint ed. pap. 11.00 (*0-87348-645-5*) Pathfinder NY.

Revolution Aborted: The Lessons of Grenada. Ed. by Jorge Heine. LC 89-40583. (Latin American Ser.). 362p. 1990. 49.95 (*0-8229-3639-9*); pap. 19.95 (*0-8229-5433-8*) U of Pittsburgh Pr.

Revolution Administered: Agrarianism & Communism in Bulgaria. Nissan Oren. LC 72-8831. (Integration & Community Building in Eastern Europe Ser.: EE8). 224p. reprint ed. pap. 63.90 (*0-317-39640-4*, 2023108) Bks Demand.

Revolution Against the Church: From Reason to the Supreme Being. Michel Vovelle. Tr. by Alan Jose. (Illus.). 214p. 1992. 55.00 (*0-8142-0577-1*) Ohio St U Pr.

***Revolution, American Style: The Nineteen-Sixties & Beyond.** Paul N. Goldstene. Ed. by Victor Jones. (Publications in Political Science). 152p. (Orig.). 1997. pap. 11.95 (*0-88316-566-X*) Chandler & Sharp.

Revolution & After. Gordon Lindsay. (Old Testament Ser.: Vol.. 32). 1967. 1.95 (*0-89985-152-5*) Christ for the Nations.

Revolution & Change in Central & Eastern Europe. Roger East & Jolyon Pontin. 1996. pap. 18.95 (*1-85567-361-4*, Pub. by Pntr Pubs UK) Bks Intl VA.

Revolution & Change in Central & Eastern Europe. 2nd ed. Roger East & Jolyon Pontin. 286p. 1996. 62.00 (*1-85567-360-6*, Pub. by Pntr Pubs UK) Bks Intl VA.

Revolution & Change in Central & Eastern Europe: Political, Economic, & Social Challenges. Minton F. Goldman. LC 95-52512. 450p. (C). (gr. 13-13). 1997. text ed. 69.95 (*1-56324-757-7*) M E Sharpe.

Revolution & Change in Central & Eastern Europe: Political, Economic, & Social Challenges. Minton F. Goldman. LC 95-52512. 450p. (C). (gr. 13). 1997. pap. text ed. 32.95 (*1-56324-758-5*) M E Sharpe.

Revolution & Chinese Foreign Policy: Peking's Support for Wars of National Liberation. Peter Van Ness. (Center for Chinese Studies, UC Berkeley: No. 4). 1970. pap. 15.00 (*0-520-02055-3*) U CA Pr.

Revolution & Chinese Foreign Policy: Peking's Support for Wars of National Liberation. Peter Van Ness. LC 73-89893. 282p. reprint ed. pap. 80.40 (*0-685-23354-5*, 2032283) Bks Demand.

Revolution & Continuity: Essays in the History & Philosophy of Early Modern Science. Ed. by Peter Barker & Roger Ariew. LC 90-19633. (Studies in Philosophy & the History of Philosophy: Vol. 24). 222p. 1991. text ed. 42.95 (*0-8132-0738-X*) Cath U Pr.

Revolution & Convention in Modern Poetry: Studies in Ezra Pound, T. S. Eliot, Wallace Stevens, Edwin Arlington Robinson & Yvor Winters. Donald E. Stanford. LC 81-50342. 288p. 1983. 38.50 (*0-87413-197-9*) U Delaware Pr.

Revolution & Cosmopolitanism: The Western Stage & the Chinese Stages. Joseph R. Levenson. LC 73-121188. 196p. reprint ed. pap. 55.90 (*0-7837-4833-7*, 2044480) Bks Demand.

Revolution & Counter-Revolution. Said A. Arjomand. 300p. (C). 1990. pap. text ed. 14.95 (*0-226-02686-8*); lib. bdg. 34.95 (*0-226-02683-3*) U Ch Pr.

***Revolution & Counter Revolution.** Peter Calvert. Ed. by Frank Parkin. (Concepts in the Social Sciences Ser.). 96p. 1990. 32.50 (*0-335-15398-4*, Open Univ Pr); pap. 9.99 (*0-335-15397-6*, Open Univ Pr) Taylor & Francis.

Revolution & Counter-Revolution. Ed. by Ellen Rice. (Wolfson College Lectures). 240p. (C). 1991. text ed. 50.95 (*0-631-17816-3*) Blackwell Pubs.

Revolution & Counter-Revolution. 3rd ed. Tr. by Foundation for a Christian Civilization, Inc. Staff. 220p. 1993. pap. 8.95 (*1-877905-27-5*) Am Soc Defense TFP.

Revolution & Counter-Revolution: Mozambique's War of Independence, 1964-1974. Thomas H. Henriksen. LC 82-6132. (Contributions in Intercultural & Comparative Studies: No. 6). xii, 269p. 1983. text ed. 59.95 (*0-313-23605-4*, HER/) Greenwood.

Revolution & Counter-Revolution: The Revisionist Coup in China & the Struggle in the Revolutionary Communist Party, U. S. A. Revolutionary Communist Party, U. S. A. Staff. 1978. pap. 4.95 (*0-89851-016-3*) RCP Pubns.

Revolution & Counter-Revolution in Chile. Ed. by Paul M. Sweezy & Harry Magdoff. LC 73-90073. 160p. 1974. pap. 10.00 (*0-85345-325-X*) Monthly Rev.

Revolution & Counter-Revolution in China. M. N. Roy. 1972. lib. bdg. 59.95 (*0-8490-2520-6*) Gordon Pr.

Revolution & Counter-Revolution in Portugal. Martin Kayman. (C). 1987. pap. 17.50 (*0-85036-373-X*, Pub. by Merlin Pr UK) Humanities.

Revolution & Counter-Revolution in Spain. 2nd ed. Felix Morrow. LC 74-80372. 262p. 1974. reprint ed. pap. 17.95 (*0-87348-402-9*); reprint ed. lib. bdg. 50.00 (*0-87348-401-0*) Pathfinder NY.

Revolution & Counterrevolution: Change & Persistence in Social Structure. rev. ed. Seymour M. Lipset. 436p. 1987. pap. 24.95 (*0-88738-694-6*) Transaction Pubs.

Revolution & Counterrevolution in Guatemala, 1944-1963: An Annotated Bibliography of Materials in the Benson Latin American Collection. (Contributions to Librarianship Ser.: No. 9). 174p. 1984. pap. 20.00 (*0-930214-14-5*) U TX Austin Gen Libs.

Revolution & Counterrevolution in Guatemala, 1944-1963: An Annotated Guide to Street Literature in the Benson Latin American Collection. (Contributions to Librarianship Ser.: No. 10). 257p. Date not set. pap. 20.00 (*0-614-12905-2*) U TX Austin Gen Libs.

Revolution & Culture: The Bogdanov-Lenin Controversy. Zenovia A. Sochor. LC 87-25063. (Cornell Studies in Soviet History & Science). (Illus.). 258p. 1988. 37.50 (*0-8014-2088-1*) Cornell U Pr.

Revolution & Economic Transition: The Iranian Experience. Hooshang Amirahmadi. LC 90-33035. 420p. (C). 1990. pap. text ed. 24.95 (*0-7914-0510-9*) State U NY Pr.

Revolution & Economic Transition: The Iranian Experience. Hooshang Amirahmadi. LC 90-33035. 420p. (C). 1990. text ed. 74.50 (*0-7914-0509-5*) State U NY Pr.

Revolution & Empire: English Politics & the American Colonies in the Seventeenth Century. Robert M. Bliss. Ed. by John M. MacKenzie. LC 90-6462. (Studies in Imperialism). 320p. 1990. text ed. 79.95 (*0-7190-2383-1*, Pub. by Manchester Univ Pr UK) St Martin.

Revolution & Empire: English Politics & the American Colonies in the Seventeenth Century. Robert M. Bliss. (Studies in Imperialism). 320p. 1993. text ed. 19.95 (*0-7190-4209-7*, Pub. by Manchester Univ Pr UK) St Martin.

Revolution & English Romanticism: Politics & Rhetoric. Ed. by Keith Hanley & Raman Selden. LC 90-19423. 320p. 1991. text ed. 49.95 (*0-312-05770-9*) St Martin.

Revolution & Enlightenment in Europe. Timothy O'Hagan. (Enlightenment Rights & Revolution Ser.). 160p. 1991. pap. 37.90 (*0-08-040920-2*, Pub. by Aberdeen U Pr) Macmillan.

Revolution & Evolution in the Twentieth Century. James Boggs & Grace L. Boggs. LC 73-90076. 288p. 1975. reprint ed. pap. 11.00 (*0-85345-353-5*) Monthly Rev.

Revolution & Evolution 1848 in German-Jewish History. Werner E. Mosse et al. 443p. 1981. lib. bdg. 110.00 (*3-16-743752-9*, Pub. by J C B Mohr GW) Coronet Bks.

Revolution & Foreign Policy: The Case of South Yemen, 1967-1987. Fred Halliday. (Cambridge Middle East Library: No. 21). (Illus.). (C). 1990. 65.00 (*0-521-32856-X*) Cambridge U Pr.

Revolution & Genocide: On the Origins of the Armenian Genocide & the Holocaust. Robert Melson. LC 91-47944. 386p. 1992. 32.50 (*0-226-51990-2*) U Ch Pr.

Revolution & Genocide: On the Origins of the Armenian Genocide & the Holocaust. Robert Melson. (Illus.). 364p. 1996. reprint ed. pap. text ed. 16.95 (*0-226-51991-0*) U Ch Pr.

Revolution & History: Origins of Marxist Historiography in China, 1919-1937. Arif Dirlik. LC 77-80469. 1978. pap. 14.00 (*0-520-06757-6*) U CA Pr.

Revolution & Idealogy: Images of the Mexican Revolution in the United States. John Britton. (Illus.). 288p. 1995. text ed. 35.00 (*0-8131-1896-4*) U Pr of Ky.

Revolution & Independence. (C. C. Publications Social Studies). (Illus.). 64p. 1985. Incl. text, tchr's. guide, tests & ans. key. teacher ed. 7.30 (*0-685-10451-6*) SRA.

Revolution & International Politics. Peter Calvert. LC 83-9640. 250p. 1984. text ed. 35.00 (*0-312-67985-8*) St Martin.

Revolution & International Politics. 2nd ed. Peter Calvert. LC 96-17189. 1997. 62.00 (*1-85567-396-7*, Pub. by Pntr Pubs UK); pap. 18.95 (*1-85567-395-9*, Pub. by Pntr Pubs UK) Bks Intl VA.

An Asterisk (*) at the beginning of an entry indicates that the title is appearing in BIP for the first time.

Revolution & Intervention: U. S. - Cuban Relations in the 20th Century. Geoffrey Tegnell & Thomas Ladenburg. (SSEC American History Ser.). (Illus.). 176p. (Orig.). (YA). (gr. 9-12). 1992. pap. 21.95 (*0-89994-362-4*) Soc Sci Ed.

Revolution & Its Aftermath in Kampuchea: Eight Essays. Ed. by David P. Chandler & Ben Kiernan. LC 83-50326. (Monograph Ser.: No. 25). 319p. 1983. pap. 14.00 (*0-938692-05-4*) Yale U SE Asia.

Revolution & Land Reform in Ethiopia: Peasant Associations, Local Government & Rural Development. John M. Cohen et al. (Occasional Paper Ser.: No. 6). 127p. (Orig.). (C). 1976. pap. text ed. 4.80 (*0-86731-019-7*) Cornell CIS RDC.

Revolution & Madness: The Lives & Legends of Theroigne de Mericourt. Elisabeth Roudinesco. Tr. by Martin Thom. (Illus.). 296p. (gr. 13). 1992. pap. 19.00 (*0-86091-597-2*, A9770, Pub. by Vrso UK) Norton.

Revolution & Other Poems. Julia Vinograd. 1970. pap. 2.00 (*0-685-01028-7*) Oyez.

Revolution & Political Change. Ed. by Alexander J. Groth. LC 96-21474. (International Library of Politics & Comparative Government). 580p. 1996. text ed. 127.95 (*1-85521-684-1*, Pub. by Dartmth Pub UK) Ashgate Pub Co.

Revolution & Political Changes in the Third World. Ed. by Barry M. Schutz & Robert O. Slater. LC 90-8035. 275p. 1990. pap. text ed. 18.95 (*1-55587-216-6*); lib. bdg. 40.00 (*1-55587-153-4*) Lynne Rienner.

Revolution & Political Conflict in the French Navy 1789-1794. William S. Cormack. (Illus.). 336p. (C). 1995. text ed. 59.95 (*0-521-47209-1*) Cambridge U Pr.

Revolution & Politics in Russia: Essays in Memory of B. I. Nicolaevsky. Ed. by Alexander Rabinowitch et al. LC 79-183608. (Russian & East European Studies: No. 41). (Illus.). 428p. reprint ed. pap. 122.60 (*0-685-20433-2*, 2056435) Bks Demand.

Revolution & Reaction: Bolivia, 1964-1985. James M. Malloy & Eduardo A. Gamarra. 256p. 1987. 29.95 (*0-88738-159-6*) Transaction Pubs.

Revolution & Reaction: Bolivia, 1964-1992. 2nd ed. James M. Malloy & Eduardo A. Gamarra. 1992. 32.95 (*1-56000-032-5*) Transaction Pubs.

Revolution & Reaction in Cuba, 1933-1960: A Political Sociology from Machado to Castro. Samuel Farber. LC 76-7190. 302p. reprint ed. pap. 86.10 (*0-685-23465-7*, 2056660) Bks Demand.

Revolution & Reality: Essays on the Origin & Fate of the Soviet System. Bertram D. Wolfe. LC 80-16178. 423p. reprint ed. pap. 120.60 (*0-8357-3059-X*, 2039315) Bks Demand.

Revolution & Rebellion: State & Society in England in the Seventeenth & Eighteenth Centuries. J. C. Clark. 192p. 1986. pap. text ed. 19.95 (*0-521-33710-0*) Cambridge U Pr.

Revolution & Rebellion in the Early Modern World. Jack A. Goldstone. LC 89-49052. 600p. 1990. 40.00 (*0-520-06758-4*) U CA Pr.

Revolution & Rebellion in the Early Modern World. Jack A. Goldstone. 1993. pap. 17.95 (*0-520-08267-2*) U CA Pr.

Revolution & Reflection. Lee. 1974. pap. text ed. 59.00 (*90-247-1638-1*, Pub. by M Nijhoff NE) Kluwer Ac.

Revolution & Religion: American Revolutionary War & the Reformed Clergy. Keith L. Griffin. LC 92-38186. 176p. (C). 1993. text ed. 39.95 (*1-55778-590-2*) Paragon Hse.

Revolution & Religion: American Revolutionary War & the Reformed Clergy. Keith L. Griffin. 150p. 1994. 39.95 (*1-55778-580-5*) Paragon Hse.

Revolution & Religion in the Music of Liszt. Paul Merrick. (Illus.). 350p. 1987. text ed. 80.00 (*0-521-32627-3*) Cambridge U Pr.

Revolution & Repetition: Marx - Hugo - Balzac. Jeffrey Mehlman. LC 76-24589. (Quantum Bks.: No. 10). 1977. pap. 10.95 (*0-520-03531-3*) U CA Pr.

Revolution & Rescue in Grenada: An Account of the U. S.-Caribbean Invasion. Reynold A. Burrowes. LC 87-23704. (Contributions in Political Science Ser.: No. 203). 192p. 1988. text ed. 37.95 (*0-313-26066-4*, BWV/, Greenwood Pr) Greenwood.

Revolution & Restoration. Ed. by John Morrill. (History Today Bk.). (Illus.). 160p. 1993. pap. 22.95 (*1-85585-137-7*) Trafalgar.

Revolution & Restoration: The Rearrangement of Power in Argentina, 1776-1860. Mark D. Szuchman & Jonathan C. Brown. LC 94-4381. (Latin American Studies). (Illus.). x, 285p. 1994. text ed. 42.50 (*0-8032-4228-X*) U of Nebr Pr.

Revolution & Romanticism. Howard M. Jones. LC 73-84398. 490p. 1974. 27.95 (*0-674-76710-1*) Belknap Pr.

Revolution & Romanticism. Howard M. Jones. LC 73-84398. 501p. reprint ed. pap. 142.80 (*0-7837-3836-6*, 2043658) Bks Demand.

Revolution & Socialism in Ethiopia. Azinna Nwafor. Ed. by Omenana Collective Research Group Staff. (Etudes et Analyses Marxistes en Afrique Ser.). 55p. (Orig.). (C). 1987. reprint ed. pap. 3.00 (*0-686-88660-7*) Omenana.

Revolution & Subjectivity in Postwar Japan. J. Victor Koschmann. 280p. 1996. pap. text ed. 19.95 (*0-226-45122-4*); lib. bdg. 48.00 (*0-226-45121-6*) U Ch Pr.

Revolution & Survival: The Foreign Policy of Soviet Russia, 1917-18. Richard K. Debo. LC 78-9671. 476p. reprint ed. pap. 135.70 (*0-8357-4723-9*, 2037638) Bks Demand.

Revolution & Terror in France 1789-1795. 2nd ed. D. G. Wright. (C). 1990. pap. text ed. 13.50 (*0-582-00379-2*) Addison-Wesley.

Revolution & the Form of the British Novel, 1790-1825: Intercepted Letters, Interrupted Seductions. Nicola J. Watson. LC 93-30203. 232p. (C). 1994. 45.00 (*0-19-811297-1*, Clarendon Pr) OUP.

Revolution & the Meanings of Freedom in the Nineteenth Century. Ed. by Isser Woloch. (Making of Modern Freedom Ser.). 1996. 55.00 (*0-8047-2748-1*) Stanford U Pr.

***Revolution & the Millennium: China, Mexico & Iran.** James F. Rinehart. LC 97-4228. 1997. text ed. write for info. (*0-275-95931-7*, Praeger Pubs) Greenwood.

Revolution & the Multiclass Coalition in Nicaragua. Mark Everingham. (Latin American Ser.). 212p. (C). 1996. text ed. 45.00 (*0-8229-3933-9*); pap. text ed. 19.95 (*0-8229-5590-3*) U of Pittsburgh Pr.

Revolution & the Revolutionary Ideal. Robert Blackey & Clifford T. Paynton. 256p. 1976. 22.95 (*0-87073-986-7*) Schenkman Bks Inc.

Revolution & the Social System. Chalmers Johnson. LC 64-20987. (Studies Ser.: No. 3). 68p. 1964. pap. 5.95 (*0-8179-3032-9*) Hoover Inst Pr.

Revolution & the Twentieth Century Novel. Paul N. Siegel. Ed. by Frederick Stanton. LC 79-89424. 237p. 1979. pap. 16.95 (*0-913460-72-9*); lib. bdg. 50.00 (*0-913460-71-0*) Pathfinder NY.

Revolution & the Word: The Rise of the Novel in America. Cathy N. Davidson. (Illus.). 336p. 1988. pap. 12.95 (*0-19-505653-1*) OUP.

Revolution & Tradition in People's Poland: Education & Socialization. Joseph R. Fiszman. LC 70-166369. 400p. 1972. pap. text ed. 19.95 (*0-691-10009-8*) Princeton U Pr.

***Revolution & Tradition in People's Poland: Education & Socialization.** Joseph R. Fiszman. LC 70-166369. 404p. 1972. reprint ed. pap. 115.20 (*0-608-02872-X*, 2063936) Bks Demand.

Revolution & Tradition in Tientsin, 1949-1952. Kenneth G. Lieberthal. LC 79-64215. xiv, 234p. 1980. 35.00 (*0-8047-1044-9*) Stanford U Pr.

Revolution & Transition in East-Central Europe. 2nd ed. David S. Mason. (Dilemmas in World Politics Ser.). (C). 1996. pap. text ed. 16.95 (*0-8133-2835-7*) Westview.

Revolution & Urban Politics in Provincial France: Troyes & Reims, 1786-1790. Lynn A. Hunt. LC 76-48016. xii, 188p. 1978. 32.50 (*0-8047-0940-8*) Stanford U Pr.

Revolution & War. Stephen M. Walt. (Cornell Studies in Security Affairs). (Illus.). 392p. 1996. 35.00 (*0-8014-3205-7*); pap. 19.95 (*0-8014-8297-6*) Cornell U Pr.

Revolution & War in Spain, Nineteen Thirty-One to Nineteen Thirty-Nine. Ed. by Paul Preston. 320p. (Orig.). 1984. pap. 15.95 (*0-416-34970-6*, 9074) Routledge Chapman & Hall.

Revolution & World Order: The Revolutionary State in International Society. David Armstrong. LC 92-40619. 342p. (C). 1993. 65.00 (*0-19-827528-5*, Clarendon Pr) OUP.

Revolution As Theatre: Essays on Radical Style. Robert Brustein. 1970. pap. 1.95 (*0-87140-238-6*) Liveright.

Revolution As Tragedy: The Dilemma of the Moderate from Scott to Arnold. John P. Farrell. LC 79-26000. (Illus.). 304p. 1980. 42.50 (*0-8014-1278-1*) Cornell U Pr.

***Revolution at a Crossroads: Iran's Domestic Politics & Regional Ambitions.** David Menashri. LC 96-43152. (Policy Papers). 1996. write for info. (*0-944029-68-X*) Wash Inst NEP.

Revolution at Queretaro: The Mexican Constitutional Convention of 1916-1917. Eberhardt V. Niemeyer. (Latin American Monographs: No. 33). 319p. reprint ed. pap. 91.00 (*0-8357-7714-6*, 2036071) Bks Demand.

***Revolution at the Checkout Counter.** Stephen A. Brown. LC 97-2776. (Wertheim Publications in Industrial Relations). 1997. write for info. (*0-674-76720-9*) HUP.

Revolution at the Grassroots: Community Organizations in the Portuguese Revolution. Charles Downs. LC 88-31217. (SUNY Series in Urban Public Policy). 215p. 1989. text ed. 74.50 (*0-7914-0066-2*); pap. text ed. 24.95 (*0-7914-0067-0*) State U NY Pr.

Revolution at the Roots: Making Our Government Smaller, Better, & Closer to Home. William D. Eggers & John O'Leary. LC 95-9212. 256p. 1995. 25.00 (*0-02-874027-0*) Free Pr.

Revolution at the Table: Transformation of the American Diet. Harvey A. Levenstein. (Illus.). 320p. 1988. 30.00 (*0-19-504365-0*) OUP.

***Revolution Betrayed: Jurij Olesa's Envy.** Janet G. Tucker. 202p. 1996. 24.95 (*0-89357-263-2*) Slavica.

Revolution Betrayed: What Is the Soviet Union & Where Is It Going? Leon Trotsky. 322p. (C). 1991. pap. 18.95 (*0-929087-48-8*) Labor Pubns Inc.

Revolution Betrayed: What Is the Soviet Union & Where Is It Going? 5th ed. Leon Trotsky. Tr. by Max Eastman from RUS. LC 72-89900. 314p. (C). 1972. reprint ed. pap. 19.95 (*0-87348-226-3*); reprint ed. lib. bdg. 60.00 (*0-87348-225-5*) Pathfinder NY.

Revolution! British Reactions to the Belgian & Polish Upheavals of 1830: A Study of Diplomatic, Parliamentary, & Press Responses. Guy M. Townsend. (Stokvis Studies in Historical Chronology & Thought). 224p. pap. write for info. (*0-89370-929-8*); lib. bdg. write for info. (*0-89370-829-1*) Borgo Pr.

Revolution by Decree: Peru 1968-1975. Dirk Kruijt. 250p. 1994. 26.50 (*90-5538-004-0*, Pub. by Thesis Pubs NE) IBD Ltd.

***Revolution by the Book: The Rap Is Live.** Imam J. Al-Amin. 174p. 1996. pap. 12.00 (*0-614-21699-0*, 1078) Kazi Pubns.

Revolution by the Book: The Rap Is Live. Jamil Al-Amin. LC 93-2726. 174p. 1993. pap. 12.00 (*0-9627854-3-1*) Writers Inc.

Revolution, Confederation & Constitution. Ed. by Stuart G. Brown. LC 78-151607. (Literature of History Ser.). (C). 1971. 29.50 (*0-89197-384-2*); pap. text ed. 9.95 (*0-89197-385-0*) Irvington.

Revolution Disarmed: Chile, 1970-1973. Gabriel Smirnow. LC 79-83400. 170p. 1981. pap. 10.00 (*0-85345-486-8*) Monthly Rev.

Revolution Downeast: The War for American Independence in Maine. James S. Leamon. LC 92-17757. (Illus.). 320p. (Orig.). 1995. pap. 17.95 (*0-87023-959-7*) U of Mass Pr.

Revolution du Langage Poetique: L'Avant-Garde au Fin de Dix-Neuf Siecle. Julia Kristeva. (FRE.). 1985. pap. 21.95 (*0-7859-2701-8*) Fr & Eur.

Revolution, Economics & Religion: Christian Political Economy, 1798-1833. A. M. Waterman. 320p. (C). 1991. text ed. 69.95 (*0-521-39447-3*) Cambridge U Pr.

Revolution en Chantant. Robert Brecy. (Songs & Poetry Collection). (Illus.). 232p. (FRE.). 1995. 89.95 (*2-86808-031-6*) Intl Scholars.

Revolution et Empire see Histoire de l'Architecture Classique en France

Revolution et l'Empire see Histoire de la Langue Francaise des Origines a nos Jours

Revolution Falters: The Left in Philippine Politics after 1986. Ed. by Patricio Abinales. (Southeast Asia Program Ser.: SEAP 15). 182p. (Orig.). 1996. pap. 15.00 (*0-87727-132-1*, SEAP 15) Cornell SE Asia.

***Revolution for Export: 1849-1921.** Contrib. by Angelus Press Editors. (Puritans' Progress Ser.: Vol. 3). 155p. (Orig.). 1996. pap. 6.95 (*0-935952-38-1*) Angelus Pr.

Revolution for Nature: From the Environment to the Connatural World. Klaus M. Meyer-Abich. Tr. by Matthew Armstrong. (Philosophy & the Environment Ser.: No. 3). 145p. 1993. 25.00 (*0-929398-70-X*); pap. 15.95 (*0-929398-69-6*) UNTX Pr.

Revolution for the Hell of It. Abbie Hoffman. 1994. reprint ed. lib. bdg. 29.95 (*1-56849-293-6*) Buccaneer Bks.

Revolution Francais Dictionnaire General. Anne Manceron. 385p. (FRE.). 1989. 75.00 (*0-7859-8189-6*, 2877420329) Fr & Eur.

Revolution Francaise, Dictionnaire Biographique. Claude Manceron. 571p. (FRE.). 1989. 95.00 (*0-7859-8188-8*, 2877420086) Fr & Eur.

Revolution from Above: The Demise of the Soviet System. David Kotz & Fred Weir. 272p. (C). 1997. pap. 18.95 (*0-415-14317-9*); text ed. 69.95 (*0-415-14316-0*) Routledge.

Revolution from Above, Rebellion from Below: The Agrarian Transvaal At the Turn of the Century. Jeremy Krikler. LC 92-39144. (Oxford Studies in African Affairs). 280p. 1993. 59.00 (*0-19-820380-2*, Clarendon Pr) OUP.

Revolution from Abroad: The Soviet Conquest of Poland's Western Ukraine & Western Belorussia. Jan T. Gross. (Illus.). 380p. 1987. text ed. 52.50 (*0-691-09433-0*) Princeton U Pr.

Revolution from Below: Buddhist & Christian Movements for Justice in Asia: Four Case Studies from Thailand & Sri Lanka. Robert Bobilin. 190p. (Orig.). (C). 1988. pap. text ed. 20.00 (*0-8191-7038-0*) U Pr of Amer.

***Revolution from the Middle.** Samuel Francis. 250p. (Orig.). 1997. pap. 6.95 (*1-887898-01-8*) WTPI.

Revolution from the Right: Politics, Class, & the Rise of Nazism in Saxony, 1919-1933. Benjamin Lapp. LC 96-52073. (Studies in Central European History). (Illus.). 248p. (C). 1997. text ed. 55.00 (*0-391-04027-8*) Humanities.

Revolution from Within. Gloria Steinem. 1994. pap. 15.95 (*1-55800-605-2*) Dove Audio.

Revolution from Within: A Book of Self Esteem. Gloria Steinem. 1992. 22.95 (*0-316-81240-4*) Little.

Revolution from Within: A Book of Self-Esteem. Gloria Stienem. 1993. pap. 11.95 (*0-316-81247-1*) Little.

Revolution from Without: Yucatan, Mexico, & the United States, 1880-1924. Gilbert M. Joseph. LC 81-9958. (Cambridge Latin American Studies: No. 42). 416p. 1982. text ed. 95.00 (*0-521-23516-2*) Cambridge U Pr.

Revolution from Without: Yucatan, Mexico & the United States. 1880-1924. Gilbert M. Joseph. LC 87-32951. (Illus.). xviii, 405p. (C). 1988. pap. text ed. 19.95 (*0-8223-0822-3*) Duke.

Revolution from 1789 to 1906. Raymond Postgate. 1990. 14.50 (*0-8446-0332-5*) Peter Smith.

Revolution Gone Backward: The Black Response to National Politics, 1876-1896. Bess Beatty. LC 86-25747. (Contributions in Afro-American & African Studies: No. 105). 257p. 1987. text ed. 55.00 (*0-313-25533-4*, BRV/, Greenwood Pr) Greenwood.

Revolution Gottes. Eberhard Arnold. 110p. 1984. pap. 7.00 (*3-87173-689-9*) Plough.

Revolution, Idealism & Human Freedom: Schelling, Holderlin & Hegel & the Crisis of Early German Idealism. F. G. Nauen. (International Archives of the History of Ideas Ser.: No. 45). 113p. 1971. lib. bdg. 55.00 (*90-247-5117-9*) Kluwer Ac.

Revolution in Africa. K. Madhu Panikkar. LC 74-27428. 202p. 1975. reprint ed. text ed. 55.00 (*0-8371-7901-7*, PARA, Greenwood Pr) Greenwood.

Revolution in America, 1754-1788: Documents & Commentaries. Ed. by J. R. Pole. LC 70-126037. xxxii, 616p. 1970. 75.00 (*0-8047-0761-8*) Stanford U Pr.

***Revolution in American Drama.** Edmond M. Gagey. 315p. Date not set. 22.95 (*0-8369-2498-3*) Ayer.

Revolution in Arrears: The Development Crisis in Latin America. Leland M. Wooton. LC 87-36139. 224p. 1988. text ed. 55.00 (*0-275-92689-3*, C2689, Praeger Pubs) Greenwood.

Revolution in Asian Fertility: Dimensions, Causes, & Implications. Ed. by Richard Leete & Iqbal Alam. LC 92-30010. (International Studies in Demography). 348p. 1994. 59.00 (*0-19-828791-7*, Clarendon Pr) OUP.

Revolution in Banking & the Financial Services Industry. Donald R. Fraser. Ed. by Steve Pejovich & Henry Dethloff. (Series on Public Issues: No. 11). 26p. 1984. pap. 2.00 (*0-86599-021-2*) PERC.

Revolution in Biotechnology. Ed. by Jean L. Marx. (Illus.). 256p. 1989. text ed. 52.95 (*0-521-32749-0*) Cambridge U Pr.

Revolution in Central America. Daniel Fogel. LC 84-27805. (Illus.). 241p. 1985. pap. 6.00 (*0-910383-08-1*) Ism Pr.

Revolution in Central Europe 1918-1919. F. L. Carsten. 370p. 1988. pap. text ed. 19.95 (*0-7045-0586-X*, Pub. by Scolar Pr UK) Ashgate Pub Co.

Revolution in Clay: The Marer Collection of Contemporary Ceramics. Mary D. MacNaughton et al. (Ruth Chandler Williamson Gallery Ser.). (Illus.). 181p. 1994. 29.95 (*0-295-97405-2*) Williamson Gallery.

Revolution in Corporate Finance. 2nd ed. Ed. by Joel M. Stern & Donald H. Chew, Jr. LC 92-24567. 1992. pap. 29.95 (*0-631-18554-2*) Blackwell Pubs.

***Revolution in Corporate Finance.** 2nd rev. ed. Ed. by Joel M. Stern & Donald H. Chew. (Illus.). 514p. (C). 1997. pap. text ed. 32.95 (*1-57718-044-5*) Blackwell Pubs.

Revolution in Eastern Europe: Understanding the Collapse of Communism in Poland, Hungary, East Germany, Czechoslovakia, Romania & the Soviet Union. Peter Cipkowski. LC 90-26990. 184p. 1991. pap. text ed. 10.95 (*0-471-53968-6*) Wiley.

Revolution in El Salvador: Origins & Evolution. 2nd rev. ed. Tommie S. Montgomery. 344p. (C). 1994. pap. text ed. 24.00 (*0-8133-0071-1*) Westview.

Revolution in Fashion: European Clothing, 1715-1815. Kyoto Costume Institute Staff. (Illus.). 168p. 1990. 65.00 (*1-55859-072-2*) Abbeville Pr.

Revolution in Financial Services. Harold W. Gourgues, Jr. & Jeffery R. Lauterbach. LC 87-18390. (Illus.). 263p. reprint ed. pap. 75.00 (*0-7837-4610-5*, 2044329) Bks Demand.

Revolution in Form: Tampa Collects French Art, 1800-1950. Tampa Museum of Art Staff. Ed. by Ann S. Olson. (Illus.). 80p. (Orig.). 1991. write for info. (*1-878293-05-2*) Tampa Mus Art.

Revolution in France: The Era of the French Revolution & Napoleon 1789-1815. John Brooman. (Longman Origin Ser.). 1992. pap. text ed. 10.64 (*0-582-08254-4*) Longman.

Revolution in Glassmaking: Entrepreneurship & Technological Change in the American Industry, 1880-1920. Warren C. Scoville. LC 76-38264. (Evolution of Capitalism Ser.). 440p. 1972. reprint ed. 33.95 (*0-405-04144-6*) Ayer.

Revolution in Guinea: Selected Texts. Amilcar Cabral. LC 73-124084. 176p. reprint ed. pap. 50.20 (*0-318-34961-2*, 2030758) Bks Demand.

Revolution in History: The Jihad of Usman Dan Fodio. I. Sulaiman. 208p. 1986. text ed. 90.00 (*0-7201-1815-8*, Mansell Pub) Cassell.

Revolution in Hungary. Paul E. Zinner. LC 74-39215. (Select Bibliographies Reprint Ser.). 1977. reprint ed. 23.95 (*0-8369-6817-4*) Ayer.

Revolution in Iran. Daneshvar. LC 96-8633. 1996. text ed. 59.95 (*0-312-16270-7*) St Martin.

Revolution in Iran. A. Husain. (Flashpoints Ser.). (Illus.). 80p. (J). (gr. 7 up). 1988. lib. bdg. 18.60 (*0-86592-038-9*) Rourke Corp.

Revolution in Iran: The Politics of Countermobilization. Jerold Green. LC 82-11295. 218p. 1982. text ed. 55.00 (*0-275-90809-7*, C0809, Praeger Pubs) Greenwood.

Revolution in Iran: The Roots of Turmoil. Mehran Kamrava. 176p. (C). 1990. text ed. 59.95 (*0-415-03562-7*, A3914) Routledge.

***Revolution in Ireland.** Conor Kostick. 1997. pap. 16.95 (*0-7453-1123-7*, Pub. by Pluto Pr UK) LPC InBook.

Revolution in Ireland: Popular Militancy, 1917 to 1923. Conor Kostick. LC 96-16073. 1996. write for info. (*0-7453-1122-9*, Pub. by Pluto Pr UK) LPC InBook.

Revolution in Judaea: Jesus & the Jewish Resistance. Hyam Z. Maccoby. LC 80-16752. 256p. 1980. 9.95 (*0-8008-6784-X*) Taplinger.

Revolution in Land. Charles Abrams. Ed. by Stuart Bruchey. LC 78-56679. (Management of Public Lands in the U. S. Ser.). (Illus.). 1979. reprint ed. lib. bdg. 28.95 (*0-405-11316-1*) Ayer.

Revolution in Law: Contributions to the Development of Soviet Legal Theory, 1917-1938. Ed. by Piers Beirne. LC 89-29816. 216p. (gr. 13). 1990. text ed. 90.95 (*0-87332-560-5*) M E Sharpe.

Revolution in Manufacturing: The SMED System. Shigeo Shingo. Tr. by Andrew P. Dillon from JPN. LC 84-61450. (Illus.). 383p. 1985. 75.00 (*0-915299-03-8*) Prod Press.

Revolution in Measurement: Western European Weights & Measures Since the Age of Science. Ronald E. Zupko. LC 89-84666. (Memoirs Ser.: Vol. 186). (Illus.). 548p. (C). 1990. 30.00 (*0-87169-186-8*, M186-ZUR) Am Philos.

Revolution in Mexico: Years of Upheaval, 1910-1940. Ed. by James W. Wilkie & Albert L. Michaels. LC 84-8813. (Borzoi Books on Latin America). 332p. reprint ed. pap. 94.70 (*0-7837-1917-5*, 2042121) Bks Demand.

Revolution in Perception: The Ecological Psychology of James J. Gibson. Edward S. Reed. (C). 1989. 42.50 (*0-300-04289-2*) Yale U Pr.

Revolution in Perspective: Essays on the Hungarian Soviet Republic of 1919. Ed. by Andrew C. Janos & William B. Slottman. LC 74-138510. (Russian & East European Studies). 201p. reprint ed. pap. 57.30 (*0-685-23972-1*, 2031535) Bks Demand.

Revolution in Physics: A Non-Mathematical Survey of Quanta. Louis De Broglie. Tr. by Ralph W. Niemeyer. LC 76-95113. 310p. 1970. reprint ed. text ed. 65.00 (*0-8371-2582-0*, BRRP, Greenwood Pr) Greenwood.

An Asterisk (*) at the beginning of an entry indicates that the title is appearing in BIP for the first time.

R

Revolution in Poetic Language. Julia Kristeva. Tr. by Margaret Waller. LC 84-12181. (European Perspectives Ser.). 256p. 1984. text ed. 55.00 (*0-231-05642-7*); pap. text ed. 18.00 (*0-231-05643-5*) Col U Pr.

Revolution in Print: The Press in France, 1775-1800. Ed. by Robert Darnton & Daniel Roche. LC 88-20744. (Illus.). 367p. reprint ed. pap. 104.60 (*0-7837-4840-X*, 2044487) Bks Demand.

Revolution in Provincial France: Aquitaine, 1789-1799. Alan Forrest. LC 96-5762. (Illus.). 410p. 1996. 85.00 (*0-19-820616-X*, Clarendon Pr) OUP.

Revolution in Psychiatry. Ernest Becker. 1990. 18.25 (*0-8446-6276-3*) Peter Smith.

Revolution in Psychiatry. Hornstein. 1997. 25.00 (*0-02-914962-2*, Free Press) Free Pr.

Revolution in Psychiatry. Hornstein. 1997. 25.00 (*0-684-82792-1*) Free Pr.

Revolution in Real Estate: Extraordinary Listing & Selling Techniques That Dramatically Boost Income. Paul Christian. 1982. 100.00 (*0-13-780619-1*) Exec Reports.

Revolution in Real Estate Finance. Anthony Downs. LC 85-14941. 345p. 1985. 36.95 (*0-8157-1918-3*); pap. 16.95 (*0-8157-1917-5*) Brookings.

Revolution in Real Time: Managing Information Technology in the 1990s. Harvard Business Review Staff. (Harvard Business Review Book Ser.). 288p. 1990. 29.95 (*0-87584-242-9*) Harvard Busn.

Revolution in Real Time: MAnaging Information Technology in the 1990s. Harvard Business School Press Staff. 1991. text ed. 35.00 (*0-07-103296-7*) McGraw.

Revolution in Russia. Richard Brightfield. (Chronicles of Young Indiana Jones Ser.: Bk. 3). 128p. (J). 1992. 3.25 (*0-553-29784-8*) Bantam.

Revolution in Russia: Reassessments of 1917. Ed. by Edith R. Frankel et al. (Illus.). 368p. (C). 1992. pap. text ed. 21.95 (*0-521-40585-8*) Cambridge U Pr.

Revolution in Russia: Reassessments of 1917. Ed. by Edith R. Frankel et al. (Illus.). 368p. (C). 1992. text ed. 59.95 (*0-521-40523-8*) Cambridge U Pr.

Revolution in Science. I. Bernard Cohen. (Illus.). 704p. 1985. 42.50 (*0-674-76777-2*) Belknap Pr.

Revolution in Science. I. Bernard Cohen. LC 84-12916. (Illus.). 704p. 1987. pap. text ed. 16.95 (*0-674-76778-0*) Belknap Pr.

Revolution in Science. rev. ed. Time-Life Books Editors. (Understanding Computers Ser.). (Illus.). 128p. 1990. write for info. (*0-8094-7594-4*); lib. bdg. write for info. (*0-8094-7595-2*) Time-Life.

Revolution in Science Fifteen Hundred to Seventeen Fifty. A. Rupert Hall. LC 82-8978. (C). 1983. pap. text ed. 38.50 (*0-582-49133-9*, 73493) Longman.

Revolution in Siam, 1688: The Memoir of Father de Beze. Claude De Beze. Tr. by E. W. Hutchinson. LC 72-5773. 230p. reprint ed. pap. 65.60 (*0-8357-6666-7*, 2035334) Bks Demand.

Revolution in Spain: A Greenwood Archival Edition. Karl Marx & Friedric Engels. LC 74-27667. 255p. 1975. reprint ed. text ed. 52.50 (*0-8371-7909-2*, MARS, Greenwood Pr) Greenwood.

Revolution in Statecraft: Intervention in an Age of Interdependence. rev. ed. Andrew M. Scott. LC 82-9768. (Duke Press Policy Studies). xvii, 214p. 1982. reprint ed. pap. text ed. 14.95 (*0-8223-0494-5*) Duke.

Revolution in the Countryside: Rural Conflict & Agrarian Reform in Guatemala, 1944-1954. Jim Handy. LC 93-36112. xii, 272p. (C). 1994. text ed. 45.00 (*0-8078-2127-6*); pap. text ed. 16.95 (*0-8078-4438-1*) U of NC Pr.

Revolution in the Development of Capitalism. Mark Gould. LC 86-11310. 520p. 1987. pap. 15.95 (*0-520-06101-2*) U CA Pr.

Revolution in the Development of Capitalism: The Coming of the English Revolution. Mark Gould. LC 86-11310. (Illus.). 536p. reprint ed. pap. 152.80 (*0-7837-4805-1*, 2044452) Bks Demand.

Revolution in the Factory: The Birth of the Soviet Textile Industry, 1917-1920. William B. Husband. 237p. 1990. 45.00 (*0-19-506435-6*) OUP.

Revolution in the Head: The Beatles' Records & the Sixties. Ian Macdonald. 1995. pap. 14.95 (*0-8050-4245-8*) H Holt & Co.

Revolution in the House: Family, Class & Inheritance in Southern France, 1775-1825. Margaret H. Darrow. (Illus.). 389p. (C). 1990. text ed. 49.50 (*0-691-05562-9*) Princeton U Pr.

Revolution in the Hudson Highlands. Thomas A. Ware. 1965. pap. 8.95 (*0-910746-11-7*, RIT01) Hope Farm.

Revolution in the Mailbox: How Direct Mail Fundraising Is Changing the Face of American Society - & How Your Organization Can Benefit. Mal Warwick. (Illus.). 313p. 1994. 65.00 (*0-9624891-0-7*, 600201) Fund Raising.

Revolution in the Mind: Old Gods & the New Reason in Ancient Greece. rev. ed. W. K. Guthrie. (Illus.). 64p. (C). 1991. pap. text ed. 2.25 (*1-877891-09-6*) Paperbook Pr Inc.

Revolution in the Philippines. Ed. by Martin Wright. 1988. 25.00 (*1-55862-003-6*) St James Pr.

Revolution in the Physiology of the Living Cell & Beyond. Gilbert N. Ling. LC 89-11068. 404p. 1992. lib. bdg. 64.50 (*0-89464-398-3*) Krieger.

Revolution in the Revolution? Armed Struggle & Political Struggle in Latin America. Regis Debray. LC 80-19409. 126p. reprint ed. pap. 36.00 (*0-318-34963-9*, 2030760) Bks Demand.

Revolution in the Revolution? Armed Struggle & Political Struggle in Latin America. Regis Debray. Tr. by Bobbye Ortiz from FRE. LC 80-19409. 126p. 1980. reprint ed. text ed. 52.50 (*0-313-22669-5*, DERE, Greenwood Pr) Greenwood.

Revolution in the Sky: The Lockheeds of Aviation's Golden Age. Richard S. Allen. LC 88-9839. (Illus.). 256p. 1993. 37.50 (*0-88740-584-3*) Schiffer.

Revolution in the Theatre: French Romantic Theories of Drama. Barry V. Daniels. LC 83-1705. (Contributions in Drama & Theatre Studies: No. 7). xii, 249p. 1983. text ed. 59.95 (*0-313-22476-5*, DRT/, Greenwood Pr) Greenwood.

***Revolution in the U. S. Information Infrastructure.** 88p. 1995. pap. text ed. 12.00 (*0-309-05287-4*) Natl Acad Pr.

Revolution in the Village: Tradition & Transformation in North Vietnam, 1925-1988. Nguyen Dac Bang & Hy V. Luong. LC 91-40031. (Illus.). 286p. (C). 1992. text ed. 39.00 (*0-8248-1382-0*); pap. text ed. 17.95 (*0-8248-1399-5*) UH Pr.

Revolution in the Visual Arts & the Poetry of William Carlos Williams. Peter Halter. (Cambridge Studies in American Literature & Culture: No. 76). (Illus.). 304p. (C). 1994. text ed. 64.95 (*0-521-43130-1*) Cambridge U Pr.

Revolution in the World Petroleum Market. Mary A. Tetreault. LC 84-24931. (Illus.). xviii, 271p. 1985. text ed. 59.95 (*0-89930-012-X*, TWP/, Quorum Bks) Greenwood.

Revolution in the World-System. Ed. by Terry Boswell. LC 88-37518. (Contributions in Economics & Economic History Ser.: No. 94). 253p. 1989. text ed. 59.95 (*0-313-26726-X*, BRX/, Greenwood Pr) Greenwood.

Revolution in Time: Clocks & the Making of the Modern World. David S. Landes. (Illus.). 502p. 1985. pap. text ed. 12.95 (*0-674-76802-7*) Belknap Pr.

Revolution in Time: Clocks & the Making of the Modern World. David S. Landes. LC 83-8489. (Illus.). 502p. 1983. 32.00 (*0-674-76800-0*) HUP.

***Revolution in Time: The Case for a New Calendar.** Robert Wolfe. (Orig.). 1996. pap. 10.00 (*0-9642465-2-X*) Jewish Radical.

Revolution in U. S. Finance. Robert E. Litan. 55p. (C). 1991. pap. 7.95 (*0-8157-5279-2*) Brookings.

Revolution in Virginia, Seventeen Seventy-Five to Seventeen Eighty-Three. John E. Selby. LC 87-29983. (Illus.). 442p. 1988. text ed. 37.50 (*0-87935-075-X*, Pub. by Williamsburg) U Pr of Va.

Revolution in Warfare. Basil H. Liddell-Hart. LC 79-22632. 125p. 1980. reprint ed. text ed. 38.50 (*0-313-22173-1*, LHRW, Greenwood Pr) Greenwood.

Revolution in Warfare? Air Power in the Persian Gulf. Thomas A. Keaney & Eliot A. Cohen. LC 95-32745. (Illus.). 352p. 1995. 38.95 (*1-55750-131-9*) Naval Inst Pr.

Revolution in Words: Righting Women, 1868-1871. Ed. by Lana F. Rakow & Cheris Kramarae. (Women's Source Library). 304p. (C). (gr. 13). 1990. text ed. 49.95 (*0-415-90298-3*, A1693, Routledge NY) Routledge.

Revolution in World Missions. K. P. Yohannan. 205p. (Orig.). 1995. mass mkt. 5.99 (*0-88419-263-6*) Creation House.

Revolution in Writing. C. Day Lewis. LC 75-37952. (Studies in English Literature: No. 33). 1976. lib. bdg. 75.00 (*0-8383-2115-1*) M S G Haskell Hse.

Revolution in Writing: British Literary Responses to the French Revolution. Ed. by Kelvin Everest. 128p. 1991. pap. 29.00 (*0-335-09756-1*) Taylor & Francis.

Revolution, Life, & Labor: Soviet Porcelains (1917-1985) Deborah S. Shinn. (Illus.). 56p. 1993. pap. 15.95 (*0-295-97279-3*) U of Wash Pr.

Revolution, Life, & Labor: Soviet Porcelains (1918-1985) Deborah S. Shinn. Ed. by Nancy Aakre. LC 92-55010. (Illus.). 56p. (Orig.). 1992. pap. 15.95 (*0-910503-60-5*) Cooper-Hewitt Museum.

Revolution Machine: Musical Score. rev. ed. Donna M. Swajeski. (J). (gr. 3-12). 1985. pap. 15.00 (*0-88734-031-8*) Players Pr.

Revolution Machine: Playscript. rev. ed. Donna M. Swajeski. 55p. (Orig.). (J). (gr. 3-12). 1996. pap. 6.00 (*0-88734-511-5*) Players Pr.

Revolution Myth. Gene Fisher & Glen Chambers. (Illus.). 161p. (Orig.). 1981. pap. 7.00 (*0-89084-152-7*, 001818) Bob Jones Univ Pr.

Revolution oder Reform see Revolution or Reform: A Confrontation

Revolution of America. Guillaume T. Raynal. Ed. by George Billias. LC 72-10134. (American Revolutionary Ser.). 1979. reprint ed. lib. bdg. 39.50 (*0-8398-1774-6*) Irvington.

Revolution of Cola di Rienzo. 3rd rev. ed. Francisco Petrarca. Ed. by Ronald G. Musto. LC 86-80577. Orig. Title: Francesco Petrarca & the Revolution of Cola di Rienzo. 224p. 1996. pap. 17.50 (*0-934977-00-3*) Italica Pr.

Revolution of Conscience: Martin Luther King, Jr., & the Philosophy of Nonviolence. Greg Moses. LC 96-35442. (Critical Perspectives Ser.). 238p. 1996. lib. bdg. 23.95 (*1-57230-169-4*, 0169) Guilford Pr.

Revolution of Everyday Life. Raoul Vaneigem. Tr. by Donald Nicholson-Smith from FRE. Orig. Title: Traite de Savior-Vivre a l'usage des Jeunes Generationse. 279p. (Orig.). 1994. pap. 16.00 (*0-939306-06-9*) Left Bank.

Revolution of Little Girls. Blanche M. Boyd. 1992. pap. 12.00 (*0-679-73812-6*, Vin) Random.

Revolution of Moral Consciousness: Nietzsche in Russian Literature, 1890-1914. Edith W. Clowes. 288p. 1988. 29.00 (*0-87580-139-0*) N Ill U Pr.

Revolution of Nihilism: Warning to the West. Hermann Rauschning. Tr. by E. W. Dickes. LC 72-180666. reprint ed. 34.50 (*0-404-56402-X*) AMS Pr.

Revolution of Nihilism: Warning to the West. Hermann Rauschning. LC 72-4291. (World Affairs Ser.: National & International Viewpoints). 318p. 1972. reprint ed. 23.95 (*0-405-04583-2*) Ayer.

Revolution of Nineteen Hundred Five in Odessa: Blood on the Steppes. Robert Weinberg. LC 92-23096. (Indiana-Michigan Series in Russian & East European Studies). 272p. 1993. 29.95 (*0-253-36381-0*) Ind U Pr.

Revolution of Rock: The Seventies. Stuart A. Kallen. Ed. by Bob Italia. LC 89-84918. (History of Rock n' Roll Ser.). (Illus.). 48p. (J). (gr. 4). 1989. lib. bdg. 12.94 (*0-939179-76-8*) Abdo & Dghtrs.

Revolution of Sixteen Eighty-Eight & the Birth of the English Political Nation: Whig Triumph or Palace Revolution. 2nd ed. Ed. by Gerald M. Straka. (Problems in European Civilization Ser.). 254p. (C). 1973. pap. text ed. 16.76 (*0-669-82032-6*) HM College Div.

Revolution of Sixteen Eighty-Eight in England. James R. Jones. (Revolutions in the Modern World Ser.). (C). 1973. reprint ed. pap. text ed. 9.95 (*0-393-09998-9*) Norton.

Revolution of Sixteen Eighty-Eight to Sixteen Eighty-Nine: Changing Perspectives. Ed. by Lois G. Schwoerer. (Illus.). 304p. (C). 1992. text ed. 69.95 (*0-521-39321-3*) Cambridge U Pr.

Revolution of the Candles. Jorg Swoboda. Ed. by Richard V. Pierard. Tr. by Edwin Arnold. 232p. 1996. text ed. 22.95 (*0-86554-481-6*, MUP/P125) Mercer Univ Pr.

Revolution of the Dons: Cambridge & Society in Victorian England. Sheldon Rothblatt. LC 80-41865. 325p. reprint ed. pap. 92.70 (*0-685-20568-1*, 2030618) Bks Demand.

***Revolution of the Heart.** Bill Shore. 192p. 1996. pap. 12.00 (*1-57322-565-7*, Riverhd Trade) Berkley Pub.

Revolution of the Heart: Essays on the Catholic Worker. Ed. by Patrick G. Coy. LC 83-34910. (Illus.). 408p. (C). 1988. 37.95 (*0-87722-531-1*) Temple U Pr.

***Revolution of the Mind: Higher Learning among the Bolsheviks, 1918-1929.** Michael David-Fox. LC 96-47757. (Studies of the Harriman Institute). (Illus.). 256p. 1996. 39.95 (*0-8014-3128-X*) Cornell U Pr.

Revolution of the Mind: The Life of Andre Breton. Mark Polizzotti. LC 94-20166. (Illus.). 754p. 1995. 35.00 (*0-374-24982-2*) FS&G.

***Revolution of the Mind: The Life of Andre Breton.** Mark Polizzotti. LC 96-49484. (Illus.). 784p. 1997. reprint ed. pap. 20.95 (*0-306-80772-6*) Da Capo.

***Revolution of the Mystics: On the Social Aspects of Virasaivism.** John P. Schouten. 331p. 1991. pap. 40.00 (*90-242-3425-5*, Pub. by KOK Pharos NE) Eisenbrauns.

Revolution of the Saints: A Study in the Origins of Radical Politics. Michael Walzer. LC 65-22048. 352p. 1982. pap. 13.95 (*0-674-76786-1*) HUP.

Revolution of the Spirit: Crisis of Value in Russia, 1890-1924. 2nd ed. Ed. by Bernice G. Rosenthal & Martha Bohachevsky-Chomiak. LC 90-81779. 350p. 1990. reprint ed. 35.00 (*0-8232-1285-8*); reprint ed. pap. 19.95 (*0-8232-1286-6*) Fordham.

***Revolution of the Word: A Gathering of American Avant Garde Poetry, 1914-1945.** Jerome Rothenberg. 1997. pap. text ed. 15.95 (*1-878972-24-3*) Exact Change.

***Revolution of Their Own: Voices of Women in Soviet History.** Anastasia Posadskaia-Vanderbeck. Ed. by Barbara A. Engel. 1997. text ed. 65.00 (*0-8133-3365-2*) Westview.

***Revolution of Their Own: Voices of Women in Soviet History.** Anastasia Posadskaia-Vanderbeck. Ed. by Barbara A. Engel Barbara. (C). 1997. pap. text ed. 18.00 (*0-8133-3366-0*) Westview.

Revolution of Things. Miron Bialoszewski. Tr. by Bogdan Czaykowski & Andrzej Busza. LC 74-81212. 1974. 7.50 (*0-910350-01-9*) Charioteer.

Revolution of Wisdom: Studies in the Claims & Practice of Ancient Greek Science. G. E. Lloyd. 1988. pap. 15.95 (*0-520-06742-8*) U CA Pr.

Revolution of 1848. Price. 1996. text ed. 10.95 (*0-333-36609-3*, Pub. by Macm UK) St Martin.

Revolution of 1905: Authority Restored. Abraham Ascher. LC 87-26697. 472p. (C). 1992. 65.00 (*0-8047-1972-1*) Stanford U Pr.

Revolution of 1905: Authority Restored. Abraham Ascher. xvi, 444p. 1994. pap. 18.95 (*0-8047-2328-1*) Stanford U Pr.

Revolution of 1905: Russia in Disarray. Abraham Ascher. LC 87-26657. (Illus.). xvi, 424p. 1988. 65.00 (*0-8047-1436-3*) Stanford U Pr.

Revolution of 1905: Russia in Disarray. Abraham Ascher. xvi, 424p. 1994. pap. 18.95 (*0-8047-2327-3*) Stanford U Pr.

Revolution on Balance. Hugh Thomas. 1983. 2.00 (*0-317-90488-4*) Cuban Amer Natl Fndtn.

***Revolution on the Border: The United States & Mexico, 1910-1920.** Linda B. Hall & Don M. Coerver. LC 88-14222. (Illus.). 217p. 1990. reprint ed. pap. 61.90 (*0-608-04138-6*, 2064871) Bks Demand.

Revolution on the Rio Grande: Mexican Raids & Army Pursuits 1916-1919. Glenn Justice. (Southwestern Studies: No. 95). (Illus.). 110p. 1992. pap. 13.00 (*0-87404-186-4*) Tex Western.

Revolution on the Upper Ohio, 1775-1777. Reuben G. Thwaites & Louise P. Kellogg. (Illus.). xx, 275p. 1992. reprint ed. pap. text ed. 20.00 (*1-55613-639-0*) Heritage Bk.

Revolution on the Volga: 1917 in Saratov. Donald J. Raleigh. LC 85-12792. (Cornell Studies in Soviet History & Science). (Illus.). 376p. 1986. 45.00 (*0-8014-1790-2*) Cornell U Pr.

Revolution or Reform: A Confrontation. Herbert Marcuse & Karl R. Popper. LC 75-12192. (Studies in Ethics & Society Ser.: Vol. 2). Orig. Title: Revolution oder Reform. 120p. 1976. 16.95 (*0-89044-020-4*) Transaction Pubs.

Revolution Postponed: Women in Contemporary China. Margery Wolf. LC 83-40696. xii, 285p. 1985. reprint ed. 39.50 (*0-8047-1243-3*); reprint ed. pap. 12.95 (*0-8047-1348-0*) Stanford U Pr.

Revolution Principles: The Politics of Party 1689-1720. J. P. Kenyon. (Cambridge Studies in the History & Theory of Politics). 260p. (C). 1990. pap. text ed. 19.95 (*0-521-38656-X*) Cambridge U Pr.

Revolution Reassessed: Democracy & the Left in Contemporary Central America. Stephen R. Pelletier. 256p. (gr. 13). 1997. text ed. 62.95 (*1-56324-827-1*) M E Sharpe.

Revolution Reassessed: Democracy & the Left in Contemporary Central America. Stephen R. Pelletier. 256p. (gr. 13). 1997. pap. text ed. 24.95 (*1-56324-828-X*) M E Sharpe.

Revolution Reassessed: Revisions in the History of Tudor Government & Administration. Ed. by Christopher Coleman & David R. Starkey. 228p. 1986. 65.00 (*0-19-873064-0*) OUP.

Revolution, Rebellion & Religiousness. Bhagwan S. Rajneesh. LC 89-82415. 176p. (Orig.). 1990. pap. 12.95 (*0-941404-63-3*) New Falcon Pubns.

Revolution Reform & Social Justice: Studies in the Theory & Practice of Marxism. Sidney Hook. LC 74-21610. 307p. (C). 1975. text ed. 36.00 (*0-8147-3368-9*) NYU Pr.

Revolution, Reform & the Politics of American Taxation, 1763-1783. Robert A. Becker. LC 79-19729. 335p. 1980. reprint ed. pap. 95.50 (*0-608-00862-1*, 2061653) Bks Demand.

Revolution Remembered: The Memoirs & Selected Correspondence of Juan N. Seguin. Juan N. Seguin. Ed. by Jesus De la Teja. LC 91-23838. (Illus.). 230p. 1996. pap. 16.95 (*0-88051-034-X*) State House Pr.

Revolution Retrieved: Writings on Marx, Keynes, Capitalist Crisis & New Social Subjects (1967-83) Toni Negri. (Red Notes Italy Archive Ser.: Vol. 1). 274p. (Orig.). 1988. pap. 22.00 (*0-906305-10-1*, Pub. by Red Notes UK) AK Pr Dist.

Revolution Revisited: Effective Schools & Systemic Reform. Barbara O. Taylor & Pamela Bullard. LC 95-71480. 132p. (Orig.). 1995. pap. 12.00 (*0-87367-483-9*) Phi Delta Kappa.

Revolution, Romanticism, & the Afro-Creole Protest Tradition in Louisiana, 1718-1868. Caryn C. Bell. LC 96-35429. 328p. 1996. text ed. 35.00 (*0-8071-2096-0*) La State U Pr.

Revolution, Socialism & Nationalism in Viet Nam, Vol. 1: An Interrupted Revolution. Ken Post. 366p. 1989. 39.95 (*1-85521-037-1*, Pub. by Dartmth Pub UK) Ashgate Pub Co.

Revolution, Socialism & Nationalism in Viet Nam, Vol. 2: Viet Nam Divided. Ken Post. 1989. 39.95 (*1-85521-047-9*, Pub. by Dartmth Pub UK) Ashgate Pub Co.

Revolution, Socialism & Nationalism in Viet Nam, Vol. 3: Socialism in Half a Country. Ken Post. 397p. 1989. 39.95 (*1-85521-056-8*, Pub. by Dartmth Pub UK) Ashgate Pub Co.

Revolution, Socialism & Nationalism in Viet Nam, Vol. 4: The Failure of Counter-Insurgency in the South. Ken Post. 417p. 1989. 39.95 (*1-85521-091-6*, Pub. by Dartmth Pub UK) Ashgate Pub Co.

Revolution, Socialism & Nationalism in Viet Nam, Vol. 5: Winning the War & Losing the Peace, 5 vols. Ken Post. LC 93-21341. 416p. (C). 1994. text ed. 59.95 (*1-85521-097-5*, Pub. by Dartmth Pub UK) Ashgate Pub Co.

Revolution Surrealiste. No. One - Twelve. Ed. by Pierre Naville et al. LC 68-28660. (Contemporary Art Ser.). (Illus.). (FRE.). 1968. reprint ed. 74.95 (*0-405-00706-X*) Ayer.

***Revolution That Never Was.** W. Hutton. 1986. pap. text ed. write for info. (*0-582-29603-X*, Pub. by Longman UK) Longman.

Revolution, the Story of the Early Church. Gene Edwards. 1974. pap. text ed. 8.95 (*0-940232-02-2*) Seedsowers.

Revolution to Secession: Constitution Making in the Old Dominion. Robert P. Sutton. LC 89-30947. (Illus.). 304p. 1989. text ed. 39.50 (*0-8139-1215-6*) U Pr of Va.

Revolution to the Right: Criminal Procedure Jurisprudence During the Burger-Rehnquist Court Era. John F. Decker. LC 92-44251. (American Legal & Constitutional History Ser.). 136p. 1993. text ed. 40.00 (*0-8153-1250-4*) Garland.

Revolution to the Right: Criminal Procedure Jurisprudence During the Burger-Rehnquist Court Era. John F. Decker. LC 92-44251. (American Legal & Constitutional History Ser.). 136p. 1993. pap. text ed. 18.95 (*0-8153-1541-4*) Garland.

Revolution Today: Aspirations & Realities: Socialist Register 1989. Ed. by Ralph Miliband et al. 336p. (Orig.). (C). 1989. pap. 15.00 (*0-85345-784-0*) Monthly Rev.

Revolution Until Victory? The Politics & History of the PLO. Barry Rubin. LC 93-31651. 287p. 1994. text ed. 24.95 (*0-674-76803-5*) HUP.

Revolution until Victory? The Politics & History of the PLO. Barry Rubin. (Illus.). 288p. 1996. pap. 15.95 (*0-674-76804-3*) HUP.

Revolution, Violence & Equality. Ed. by Yeager Hudson & Creighton Peden. (Studies in Social & Political Theory: Vol. 10). 464p. 1991. lib. bdg. 89.95 (*0-88946-686-6*) E Mellen.

Revolution Wasn't Televised. Curtin. 320p. (C). 1997. text ed. 65.00 (*0-415-91121-4*, Routledge NY) Routledge.

Revolution Wasn't Televised. Lynn Spigel. 320p. (C). 1997. pap. 18.95 (*0-415-91122-2*, Routledge NY) Routledge.

An Asterisk (*) at the beginning of an entry indicates that the title is appearing in BIP for the first time.

Revolution Which Islam Created. Muhammad Masjidjamei. 64p. (Orig.). 1989. pap. text ed. 4.50 (*1-871031-16-8*) Abjad Bk.

Revolution Within the Revolution: Workers' Control in Rural Portugal. Nancy Bermeo. LC 85-42675. (Illus.). 264p. 1986. text ed. 45.00 (*0-691-07688-X*) Princeton U Pr.

Revolution X: A Survival Guide for Our Generation. Rob Nelson & Jon Cowan. 208p. 1994. pap. 9.95 (*0-14-023532-9*, Penguin Bks) Viking Penguin.

Revolutionaire Kriegswissenschaft. John Most. Bd. with Beast of Property. (History of Political Violence Ser.). 1985. reprint ed. Set lib. bdg. 30.00 (*0-527-41194-9*) Periodicals Srv.

***Revolutionaries.** LC 96-40155. (Rebels with a Cause Ser.). (J). 1998. write for info. (*0-8172-4656-8*) Raintree Steck-V.

Revolutionaries. deluxe ed. Time-Life Books Editors. Ed. by Russell B. Adams, Jr. LC 96-18598. (American Story Ser.). 192p. 1996. write for info. (*0-7835-6256-X*) Time-Life.

Revolutionaries see American Story

***Revolutionaries at Queen's Park: Ontario's Political Merry-Go-Round.** Ed. by Sidney Noel. (Illus.). 224p. 1997. pap. 19.95 (*1-55028-546-7*, Pub. by J Lorimer CN) Formac Dist Ltd.

***Revolutionaries at Queen's Park: Ontario's Political Merry-Go-Round.** Ed. by Sidney Noel. (Illus.). 224p. 1997. bds. 34.95 (*1-55028-547-5*, Pub. by J Lorimer CN) Formac Dist Ltd.

Revolutionaries in Modern Britain. Peter Shipley. 256p. 1976. 24.00 (*0-370-11311-X*) Transatl Arts.

Revolutionaries in the Theater: Meyerhold, Brecht, & Witkiewicz. Christine Kiebuzinska. Ed. by Oscar G. Brockett. LC 87-25516. (Theater & Dramatic Studies: No. 49). 192p. reprint ed. pap. 54.80 (*0-8357-1850-6*, 2070671) Bks Demand.

***Revolutionaries, Monarchists, & Chinatowns: Chinese Politics in the Americas & the 1911 Revolution.** L. Eve Ma. LC 89-28021. (Illus.). 240p. 1990. reprint ed. pap. 68.40 (*0-608-04392-3*, 2065173) Bks Demand.

***Revolutionaries of Realism: The Letters of John Sloan & Robert Henri.** John Sloan & Robert Henri. Ed. by Bennard B. Perlman. LC 96-27113. (Illus.). 376p. 1997. text ed. 35.00 (*0-691-04413-9*) Princeton U Pr.

Revolutionaries, Traditionalists & Dictators in Latin America. Harold E. Davis. LC 72-77988. 1973. lib. bdg. 46.00 (*0-8154-0420-4*) Cooper Sq.

Revolutionary. Andrew S. Swann. 1996. pap. 5.50 (*0-88677-699-6*) DAW Bks.

Revolutionary Age of Andrew Jackson. Robert V. Remini. 1987. pap. text ed. 13.00 (*0-06-132074-9*, Harp PBks) HarpC.

Revolutionary America, 1763-1789: A Bibliography, 2 vols. 1992. lib. bdg. 275.99 (*0-8490-8770-8*) Gordon Pr.

Revolutionary America, 1763-1789: A Bibliography, 2 vols., Set. LC 80-606802. 1672p. 1984. 38.00 (*0-8444-0359-8*, 030-000-00125-7) Lib Congress.

Revolutionary America, 1763-1800. Thomas L. Purvis. LC 93-38382. (Almanacs of Everyday Life Ser.). (Illus.). 383p. (YA). 1995. 70.00 (*0-8160-2528-2*) Facts on File.

Revolutionary & Dissident Movements. 3rd ed. (Revolutionary Movements of the World Ser.). 1992. 145.00 (*0-582-08692-2*, 076012, Pub. by Longman Grp UK) Gale.

Revolutionary & Dissident Movements: An International Guide. 2nd ed. Ed. by Henry W. Degenhardt. 600p. 1988. 140.00 (*0-8103-2056-8*, Pub. by Longman Grp UK) Gale.

Revolutionary & Other Stories. James Medley. (Orig.). 1996. mass mkt. 5.95 (*1-56333-417-8*, Badboy) Masquerade.

Revolutionary Approach to Successful Fly Fishing: Swimming Flies. Georges Odier. LC 83-51086. (Illus.). 222p. 1984. 19.95 (*0-913276-48-0*) Stone Wall Pr.

Revolutionary Armies: The Historical Development of the Soviet & the Chinese People's Liberation Armies. Jonathan R. Adelman. LC 79-7728. (Contributions in Political Science Ser.: No. 38). (Illus.). 230p. 1980. text ed. 55.00 (*0-313-22026-3*, ADR/) Greenwood.

Revolutionary Bishop Who Saw God at Work in Africa: An Autobiography. Ralph E. Dodge. LC 85-29092. (Illus.). 211p. (Orig.). 1986. pap. 8.95 (*0-87808-203-4*, WCL203-4) William Carey Lib.

Revolutionary Breakthroughs & National Development: The Case of Romania, 1944-1965. Kenneth Jowitt. LC 71-123625. 1971. 50.00 (*0-520-01762-5*) U CA Pr.

Revolutionary Brotherhood: Freemasonry & the Transformation of the American Social Order, 1730-1840. Steven C. Bullock. LC 95-39554. (Published for the Institute of Early American History & Culture Ser.). (Illus.). 512p. (C). 1996. text ed. 49.95 (*0-8078-2282-5*) U of NC Pr.

Revolutionary Career of Maximilien Robespierre. David P. Jordan. (Illus.). xii, 320p. 1989. pap. text ed. 23.95 (*0-226-41037-4*) U Ch Pr.

Revolutionary Census of New Jersey: An Index, Based on Rateables, of the Inhabitants of New Jersey During the Period of the American Revolution. rev. ed. Kenn Stryer-Rodda. 413p. 1986. reprint ed. lib. bdg. 25.00 (*0-912606-27-4*) Hunterdon Hse.

***Revolutionary Change.** Johnson. Date not set. pap. text ed. write for info. (*0-582-29642-0*, Pub. by Longman UK) Longman.

Revolutionary Change. 2nd ed. Chalmers A. Johnson. LC 81-85448. 232p. 1982. 35.00 (*0-8047-1144-5*); pap. 12.95 (*0-8047-1145-3*) Stanford U Pr.

Revolutionary Change in Cuba. Ed. by Carmelo Mesa-Lago. LC 73-158190. 560p. reprint ed. pap. 159.60 (*0-7837-2473-X*, 2042627) Bks Demand.

Revolutionary Changes in Understanding Man & Society: Scopes & Limits. Ed. by Johann G. Otschl. (Theory & Decision Library Series A: Vol. 21). 1995. lib. bdg. 156.00 (*0-7923-3627-5*, Pub. by Klwr Acad Pubs NE) Kluwer Ac.

Revolutionary Cholesterol Breakthrough: How to Eat Everything You Want & Have Your Heart Thank You for It. Robert E. Kowalski. 272p. 1996. 24.95 (*0-8362-1044-1*) Andrews & McMeel.

***Revolutionary Citizens: African Americans 1776-1804.** Daniel Littlefield. (The Young Oxford History of African Americans Ser.). (C). (gr. 12 up). 1997. 21.00 (*0-614-25377-2*) OUP.

Revolutionary Citizens: African Americans 1776-1804 see Young Oxford History of African Americans

Revolutionary Conservative: James Duane of New York. Edward P. Alexander. LC 78-38479. reprint ed. 20.00 (*0-404-00321-4*) AMS Pr.

Revolutionary Continuity: Birth of the Communist Movement, 1918-1922, Vol. 2. Farrell Dobbs. Ed. by Jack Barnes. LC 80-84850. 240p. 1983. pap. 16.95 (*0-913460-93-1*); lib. bdg. 50.00 (*0-913460-92-3*) Pathfinder NY.

Revolutionary Continuity, Vol. 1: Marxist Leadership in the U. S., 1848-1917. Farrell Dobbs. LC 80-84850. 220p. 1980. pap. 16.95 (*0-913460-84-2*); lib. bdg. 50.00 (*0-913460-85-0*) Pathfinder NY.

Revolutionary Cuba: A Bibliographical Guide, 1966. Ed. by Fermin Peraza. LC 68-21369. 1967. 10.95 (*0-87024-075-7*) U of Miami Pr.

Revolutionary Cuba: A Bibliographical Guide 1967. Ed. by Fermin Peraza. LC 75-92596. 1969. 10.95 (*0-87024-136-2*) U of Miami Pr.

Revolutionary Cuba: A Bibliographical Guide 1968. Ed. by Fermin Peraza. LC 68-21369. 1970. 10.95 (*0-87024-153-2*) U of Miami Pr.

Revolutionary Cuba & the End of the Cold War. David C. Jordan. LC 92-40550. 274p. (C). 1993. lib. bdg. 47.50 (*0-8191-8998-7*) U Pr of Amer.

Revolutionary Days: Recollections of Romanoffs & Bolsheviki 1914-1917. Princess Cantacuzene. LC 76-115515. (Russia Observed Ser., No. 1). 1970. reprint ed. 23.95 (*0-405-03012-6*) Ayer.

Revolutionary Diplomacy: Chinese Foreign Policy & the United Front Doctrine. J. D. Armstrong. LC 76-14315. 259p. 1977. pap. 13.00 (*0-520-04273-5*) U CA Pr.

Revolutionary Discourse in Mao's Republic. David E. Apter & Tony Saich. LC 94-4421. (Illus.). 423p. 1994. text ed. 49.95 (*0-674-76779-9*, APTREV); pap. text ed. 24.00 (*0-674-76780-2*, APTREX) HUP.

Revolutionary Dreams: Utopian Vision & Experimental Life in the Russian Revolution. Richard Stites. (Illus.). 344p. 1988. 49.95 (*0-19-505536-5*) OUP.

Revolutionary Dreams: Utopian Vision & Experimental Life in the Russian Revolution. Richard Stites. (Illus.). 344p. 1991. reprint ed. pap. 21.00 (*0-19-505537-3*) OUP.

Revolutionary Dynamics of Women's Liberation. George Novack. 1973. reprint ed. pap. 2.00 (*0-87348-120-8*) Pathfinder NY.

Revolutionary Education in China: Documents & Commentary. Peter J. Seybolt. LC 72-77204. 460p. reprint ed. pap. 131.10 (*0-317-29623-X*, 2021860) Bks Demand.

Revolutionary Ethiopia: From Empire to People's Republic. Edmond J. Keller. LC 87-46090. (Illus.). 320p. 1989. 35.00 (*0-253-35014-X*) Ind U Pr.

Revolutionary Ethiopia: From Empire to People's Republic. Edmond J. Keller. LC 87-46090. 320p. 1991. reprint ed. pap. 6.95 (*0-253-20646-4*, MB-646) Ind U Pr.

Revolutionary Exiles: The Russians in the First International & the Paris Commune. Woodford McClellan. (Illus.). 266p. 1979. 35.00 (*0-7146-3115-9*, Pub. by F Cass Pubs UK) Intl Spec Bk.

Revolutionary Feminism: The Mind & Career of Mary Wollstonecraft. Gary Kelly. 257p. 1996. text ed. 18.95 (*0-312-12904-1*) St Martin.

Revolutionary Figures (in Armenian) Mihran Damadian, Hambartzum Boyajian, Serob Aghbiur, Hrair-Dzhoghk, Gevorg Chavush, Sebastatsi Murad, Nigol Tuman. Antranig Chalabian. (Illus.). 464p. 1991. 25.00 (*0-9622741-2-7*) A Chalabian.

Revolutionary Forgiveness: Feminist Reflections on Nicaragua - the Amanecida Collective. Carter Heyward et al. LC 86-5434. 192p. reprint ed. pap. 54.80 (*0-8357-2691-6*, 2040227) Bks Demand.

Revolutionary France. Paul R. Hanson. 108p. (Orig.). (C). 1996. pap. 7.95 (*0-87411-814-X*) Copley Pub.

Revolutionary France: Liberty, Tyranny & Terror. Greg Hetherton. (History Programme Ser.). (Illus.). 64p. 1993. pap. text ed. 11.95 (*0-521-40914-4*) Cambridge U Pr.

Revolutionary France: 1770-1880. Francois Furet. Tr. by Antonia Nevill from FRE. (History of France Ser.). (Illus.). 630p. 1995. pap. 24.95 (*0-631-19808-3*) Blackwell Pubs.

Revolutionary Generation: Ideology, Politics & Culture in the Early Republic. 2nd ed. Linda K. Kerber. (New American History Essays Ser.). 30p. 1997. reprint ed. pap. 5.00 (*0-87229-052-2*) Am Hist Assn.

Revolutionary Government in Ireland: Dail Eireann 1919-22. Arthur Mitchell. 423p. (Orig.). 1978. pap. 75.00 (*0-7171-1481-3*, 307080, Pub. by Gill & MacMill IE) Irish Bks Media.

Revolutionary Government in Ireland: Dail Eireann 1919-22. Arthur Mitchell. 423p. (Orig.). 1995. pap. 37.95 (*0-7171-2015-5*, Pub. by Gill & MacMill IE) Irish Bks Media.

Revolutionary Grenada: A Study in Political Economy. Frederic L. Pryor. LC 86-8109. 415p. 1986. text ed. 65.00 (*0-275-92155-7*, C2155, Praeger Pubs) Greenwood.

***Revolutionary Guide to Access 2.0: Pro Developer's Edition.** Steve Wynkoop. 800p. 1994. pap. 44.95 incl. cd-rom (*1-874416-39-7*) Wrox Pr Inc.

***Revolutionary Guide to Assembly Language.** Maljugin et al. 1000p. 1993. pap. 39.95 incl. disk (*1-874416-12-5*) Wrox Pr Inc.

***Revolutionary Guide to Bitmapped Graphics.** Control Zed Staff. 550p. 1994. pap. 44.95 incl. cd-rom (*1-874416-31-1*) Wrox Pr Inc.

***Revolutionary Guide to COBOL with Compiler.** Handel et al. 650p. 1993. pap. 49.95 incl. disk (*1-874416-17-6*) Wrox Pr Inc.

***Revolutionary Guide to Delphi 2.** Brian Long et al. 800p. 1996. pap. 49.95 incl. cd-rom (*1-874416-67-2*) Wrox Pr Inc.

Revolutionary Guide to MFC 4 Programming with Visual C++ 2nd rev. ed. Mike Blaszczak. Ed. by Julian Dobson & Alex Stockton. 900p. (Orig.). 1996. pap. 49.95 (*1-874416-92-3*) Wrox Pr Inc.

***Revolutionary Guide to Office 95 Development.** Stephen Wynkoop. 1996. pap. 49.95 incl. cd-rom (*1-874416-69-9*) Wrox Pr Inc.

***Revolutionary Guide to OOP Using C++** V. Olshevky & A. Ponomarev. 600p. 1994. pap. 39.95 incl. disk (*1-874416-18-4*) Wrox Pr Inc.

***Revolutionary Guide to PowerBuilder 4.0.** Prasad Bodepuci. 860p. 1995. pap. 49.95 incl. cd-rom (*1-874416-60-5*) Wrox Pr Inc.

***Revolutionary Guide to QBasic.** Victor Djakonov et al. 550p. 1996. pap. 34.95 incl. disk (*1-874416-20-6*) Wrox Pr Inc.

***Revolutionary Guide to Turbo C Plus Plus.** Valery Sklyarov. 350p. 1992. pap. 34.95 incl. disk (*1-874416-10-9*) Wrox Pr Inc.

***Revolutionary Guide to Turbo Pascal.** Alexander N. Valvachov et al. 350p. 1993. pap. 34.95 incl. disk (*1-874416-11-7*) Wrox Pr Inc.

***Revolutionary Guide to Visual Basic 4 Professional.** Larry Roof. 700p. 1996. pap. 44.95 incl. cd-rom (*1-874416-37-0*) Wrox Pr Inc.

***Revolutionary Guide to Visual C Plus Plus.** Ben Ezzell. 550p. 1994. pap. 39.95 incl. disk (*1-874416-22-2*) Wrox Pr Inc.

***Revolutionary Guide to Visual FoxPro OOP.** Will Phelphs. 600p. 1996. pap. 46.95 incl. cd-rom (*1-874416-40-0*) Wrox Pr Inc.

Revolutionary Hamburg: Labor Politics in the Early Weimar Republic. Richard A. Comfort. x, 226p. 1966. 35.00 (*0-8047-0284-5*) Stanford U Pr.

***Revolutionary Hebrew, Empire & Crisis: Four Peaks in Hebrew Literature & Jewish Survival.** David Aberbach. LC 97-13467. 1997. 40.00 (*0-8147-0673-8*) NYU Pr.

Revolutionary Horizons: Regional Foreign Policy in Post-Khomeini Iran. John Calabrese. LC 93-44096. (International Political Economy Ser.). 1994. text ed. 49.95 (*0-312-12095-8*) St Martin.

Revolutionary Humanism & Historicism in Modern Italy. Edmund D. Jacobitti. LC 80-23619. 240p. 1981. text ed. 37.50 (*0-300-02479-7*) Yale U Pr.

Revolutionary Hungary: 1918-1921. Sander Szilassy. (Behind the Iron Curtain Ser.: No. 9). 1971. pap. 4.00 (*0-87934-005-3*) Danubian.

Revolutionary Idea in France, 1789-1871. 2nd ed. Godfrey E. Elton. LC 74-147116. reprint ed. 35.00 (*0-404-02325-8*) AMS Pr.

***Revolutionary Ideology & Chinese Reality: Dissonance under Mao.** Paul J. Hiniker. LC 77-7484. (Sage Library of Social Research: Vol. 47). 320p. 1977. reprint ed. pap. 91.20 (*0-608-02991-2*, 2059631) Bks Demand.

Revolutionary Imagination: The Poetry & Politics of John Wheelwright & Sherry Mangan. Alan M. Wald. LC 82-8498. xix, 288p. (C). 1983. text ed. 39.95 (*0-8078-1535-7*) U of NC Pr.

Revolutionary in Exile: The Emigration of Joseph Priestley to America, 1794-1804. Jenny Graham. LC 94-78516. (Transactions Ser.: Vol. 85, Pt. 2). (Illus.). 191p. (C). 1995. pap. 20.00 (*0-87169-852-8*, T852-grj) Am Philos.

***Revolutionary Incidents of Suffolk & Kings Counties, with an Account of the Battle of Long Island & the British Prisons & Prison-ships at New York.** Ed. by Henry Onderdonk, Jr. (Illus.). 268p. 1997. reprint ed. lib. bdg. 35.00 (*0-8328-6254-1*) Higginson Bk Co.

Revolutionary Industrial Unionism: The Industrial Workers of the World in Australia. Verity Burgmann. LC 95-3722. (Illus.). 328p. (C). 1997. text ed. 59.95 (*0-521-47123-0*) Cambridge U Pr.

Revolutionary Internationals, 1864-1943. Ed. by Milorad M. Drachkovitch. xv, 256p. 1966. 45.00 (*0-8047-0293-4*) Stanford U Pr.

Revolutionary Iran: Challenge & Response in the Middle East. Rouhollah K. Ramazani. LC 86-45440. 304p. 1987. text ed. 49.50 (*0-8018-3377-9*) Johns Hopkins.

Revolutionary Iran: Challenge & Response in the Middle East. Rouhollah K. Ramazani. LC 86-45440. 352p. 1988. reprint ed. pap. text ed. 14.95 (*0-8018-3610-7*) Johns Hopkins.

Revolutionary Journal of Colonel Jeduthan Baldwin, 1775-1778. Jeduthan Baldwin. Ed. by Thomas W. Baldwin. LC 73-140853. (Eyewitness Accounts of the American Revolution Ser., No. 1). (Illus.). 1971. reprint ed. 17.95 (*0-405-01223-3*) Ayer.

Revolutionary Justice in Paris, 1789-1790. Barry M. Shapiro. LC 92-10280. 312p. (C). 1993. text ed. 69.95 (*0-521-41598-5*) Cambridge U Pr.

Revolutionary Laughter: The World of Women Comics. Ed. by Roz Warren. (Illus.). 244p. 1995. pap. 16.95 (*0-89594-742-0*) Crossing Pr.

Revolutionary Law & Order: Politics & Social Change in the U. S. S. R. Peter H. Juviler. LC 76-12832. 1976. 27.95 (*0-02-916800-7*, Free Press) Free Pr.

Revolutionary Leadership. G. Terry Madonna. Ed. by Joseph E. Walker. LC 76-8955. (Lancaster County During the American Revolution Ser.). (Illus.). 56p. 1976. pap. 5.00 (*0-915010-07-0*) Sutter House.

Revolutionary Left in Spain: 1914-1923. Gerald H. Meaker. LC 73-80622. xii, 564p. 1974. 62.50 (*0-8047-0845-2*) Stanford U Pr.

Revolutionary Left in Spain, 1914-1923. Gerald H. Meaker. LC 73-80622. 1974. reprint ed. pap. 31.70 (*0-608-00525-8*, 2061404) Bks Demand.

Revolutionary Literature in China: An Anthology. John Berninghausen & Ted Huters. LC 76-51581. 109p. reprint ed. text ed. 31.10 (*0-317-30479-8*, 2024814) Bks Demand.

Revolutionary Marxism & Social Reality in the 20th Century: Collected Essays of Ernest Mandel. Ed. by Steve Bloom. LC 92-33943. (Revolutionary Studies). 224p. (C). 1994. pap. 18.50 (*0-391-03800-1*) Humanities.

***Revolutionary Medicine.** 2nd ed. C. Keith Wilbur. (Illustrated Living History Ser.). (Illus.). 144p. 1997. pap. 14.95 (*0-7627-0139-0*) Globe Pequot.

Revolutionary Medicine see Breakout: The Evolving Threat of Drug-Resistant Disease

Revolutionary Medicine, 1700-1800. C. Keith Wilbur. LC 80-82790. (Illustrated Living History Ser.). (Illus.). 80p. (Orig.). 1980. pap. 14.95 (*0-87106-041-8*) Globe Pequot.

***Revolutionary Medicine, 1700-1800.** Keith C. Wilbur. LC 96-43016. (Illustrated Living History Ser.). (Illus.). 1996. 19.95 (*0-7910-4532-3*, Am Art Analog) Chelsea Hse.

Revolutionary Mexico: The Coming & Process of the Mexican Revolution. John M. Hart. 1987. pap. 15.95 (*0-520-06744-4*) U CA Pr.

Revolutionary Mexico: The Coming & Process of the Revolution. John M. Hart. LC 87-5399. 478p. (C). 1987. 50.00 (*0-520-05995-6*) U CA Pr.

Revolutionary Mission: American Business in Latin America, 1900-1945. Thomas F. O'Brien. (Latin American Studies: No. 81). (Illus.). 352p. (C). 1996. text ed. 52.95 (*0-521-55015-7*) Cambridge U Pr.

Revolutionary Mission of Modern Art: Or Crud & Other Essays on Art. Margaret E. Stucki. 215p. 1973. pap. 20.00 (*0-686-14979-3*) Birds' Meadow Pub.

Revolutionary Movement in Italy, Austria, Hungary & Germany, 1848-49. Charles E. Maurice. LC 03-13471. 1968. reprint ed. 14.00 (*0-403-00075-0*) Scholarly.

Revolutionary Movement of Eighteen Forty-Eight to Forty-Nine in Italy, Austria-Hungary, & Germany. Charles E. Maurice. LC 68-25250. (World History Ser.: No. 48). (Illus.). 1969. reprint ed. lib. bdg. 75.00 (*0-8383-0215-7*) M S G Haskell Hse.

***Revolutionary Multiculturalism.** Peter McLaren. LC 97-15178. (C). 1997. pap. text ed. 20.00 (*0-8133-2571-4*) Westview.

Revolutionary Mystery. Spiros Zodhiates. (Illus.). 278p. 1974. pap. 6.99 (*0-89957-507-2*) AMG Pubs.

Revolutionary Mystery: First Corinthians 2. 8.99 (*0-89957-550-1*) AMG Pubs.

Revolutionary Mystique & Terrorism in Contemporary Italy. Richard Drake. LC 87-46410. (Illus.). 240p. 1989. 32.50 (*0-253-35019-0*) Ind U Pr.

Revolutionary New England, 1691-1776. James T. Adams. (BCL1 - United States Local History Ser.). 469p. 1991. reprint ed. text ed. 99.00 (*0-7812-6262-3*) Rprt Serv.

Revolutionary News: The Press in France, 1789-1799. Jeremy D. Popkin. Ed. by Keith M. Baker & Steven L. Kaplan. LC 89-28511. (Bicentennial Reflections on the French Revolution Ser.). 239p. (C). 1990. text ed. 39.95 (*0-8223-0984-X*); pap. text ed. 13.95 (*0-8223-0997-1*) Duke.

Revolutionary Organizations & Revolutionaries in Interbellum Poland: A Bibliographical Biographical Study. Compiled by Gabriele Simoncini. LC 92-7441. 356p. 1992. lib. bdg. 199.95 (*0-7734-9487-1*) E Mellen.

Revolutionary Origins of Modern Japan. Thomas M. Huber. LC 79-64214. 272p. 1990. 37.50 (*0-8047-1048-1*); pap. 14.95 (*0-8047-1755-9*) Stanford U Pr.

Revolutionary Outlaws: Ethan Allen & the Struggle for Independence on the Early American. Michael A. Bellesiles. 1993. pap. text ed. 17.50 (*0-8139-1603-8*) U Pr of Va.

Revolutionary Outlaws: Ethan Allen & the Struggle for Independence on the Early American Frontier. Michael A. Bellesiles. LC 92-31324. 428p. 1993. 47.50 (*0-8139-1419-1*) U Pr of Va.

Revolutionary Pamphlets. Piotr A. Kropotkin. Ed. by Roger N. Baldwin. LC 68-56519. 307p. 1972. reprint ed. 17.95 (*0-405-08720-9*, Pub. by Blom Pubns UK) Ayer.

Revolutionary Party: Essays in the Sociology of Politics. Feliks Gross. LC 72-806. (Contributions in Sociology Ser.: No. 12). 280p. 1974. text ed. 59.95 (*0-8371-6376-5*, GRV/, Greenwood Pr) Greenwood.

Revolutionary Party: Its Role in the Struggle. James P. Cannon. 1985. reprint ed. pap. 2.00 (*0-87348-346-4*) Pathfinder NY.

Revolutionary Path. Ed. by Kenneth Belden. 1975. 2.25 (*0-901269-14-X*) Grosvenor USA.

Revolutionary Patience. Dorothee Solle. Tr. by Rita Kimber & Robert Kimber. LC 77-24313. 90p. 1977. reprint ed. pap. 25.70 (*0-7837-9827-X*, 2060556) Bks Demand.

Revolutionary People at War: The Continental Army & American Character, 1775-1783. Charles Royster. LC 79-10152. (Institute of Early American History & Culture Ser.). (Illus.). xi, 452p. 1980. text ed. 39.95 (*0-8078-1385-0*) U of NC Pr.

Revolutionary People at War: The Continental Army & American Character, 1775-1783. Charles Royster. 463p. (C). 1996. pap. 17.95 (*0-8078-4606-6*) U of NC Pr.

R

Revolutionary People at War: The Continental Army & American Character, 1775-1783. Charles Royster. (Illus.). 512p. (C). 1982. reprint ed. pap. text ed. 12.95 (*0-393-95173-1*) Norton.

Revolutionary Petunias & Other Poems. Alice Walker. LC 72-88796. 70p. 1973. reprint ed. pap. 6.95 (*0-15-676620-5*, Harvest Bks) HarBrace.

***Revolutionary Poet: A Story about Phillis Wheatley.** Maryann N. Weidt & Mary O'Keefe-Young. LC 97-1566. (Creative Minds Book Ser.). (J). 1997. write for info. (*1-57505-037-4*, Carolrhoda); pap. write for info. (*1-57505-059-5*, Carolrhoda) Lerner Group.

Revolutionary Poet in the United States: The Poetry of Thomas McGrath. Ed. by Frederick C. Stern. LC 88-4846. 216p. 1989. text ed. 29.95 (*0-8262-0682-4*) U of Mo Pr.

Revolutionary Politics. Mehran Kamrava. LC 92-23060. 176p. 1992. text ed. 49.95 (*0-275-94444-1*, C4444, Praeger Pubs) Greenwood.

Revolutionary Politics & Locke's "Two Treatises of Government" Richard Ashcraft. LC 85-43269. 624p. 1986. pap. text ed. 24.95 (*0-691-10205-8*) Princeton U Pr.

Revolutionary Politics in Massachusetts: The Boston Committee of Correspondence & the Towns, 1772-1774. Richard D. Brown. LC 71-119072. (Illus.). 298p. 1970. 29.95 (*0-674-76781-0*) HUP.

Revolutionary Politics in the Long Parliament. John R. MacCormack. LC 72-93952. 352p. 1973. 32.00 (*0-674-76775-6*) HUP.

Revolutionary Popular Culture. Social Thought & Political Economy Junior Seminar II Staff. (Illus.). 180p. (C). 1989. pap. 6.75 (*0-924120-01-0*) Intl Oil Work.

Revolutionary Popular Culture: Sex, Race & Class in the Late Twentieth Century. Social Thought & Political Economy Seminar Staff. (Illus.). 100p. (C). 1988. pap. 5.00 (*0-685-24340-0*) Intl Oil Work.

Revolutionary Portugal. Vincente Braganca-Cunha. 1976. lib. bdg. 59.95 (*0-8490-2521-4*) Gordon Pr.

Revolutionary Power. Michael Pollard. Ed. by Rebecca Stefoff. LC 91-36504. (Pioneers in History Ser.). (Illus.). 48p. (J). (gr. 5-8). 1992. lib. bdg. 19.93 (*1-56074-039-6*) Garrett Ed Corp.

Revolutionary Process in Mexico. Ed. by Jaime E. Rodriguez. (Latin American Studies: Vol. 72). 374p. 1990. 34.50 (*0-87903-073-9*) UCLA Lat Am Ctr.

Revolutionary Prose of the English Civil War. Ed. by Howard Erskine-Hill & Graham Storey. LC 82-12904. (Cambridge English Prose Texts Ser.). (Illus.). 280p. 1983. text ed. 59.95 (*0-521-24404-8*) Cambridge U Pr.

Revolutionary Radicalism: Its History, Purpose & Tactics, 6 vols., Set. Ed. by New York State Legislature, Joint Committee Investigating Seditious Activities. 1980. lib. bdg. 1,200.00 (*0-8490-3152-4*) Gordon Pr.

Revolutionary Recipes. rev. ed. Patricia B. Mitchell. 1991. pap. 4.00 (*0-925117-42-0*) Mitchells.

Revolutionary Records of Maryland. Gaius M. Brumbaugh & Margaret R. Hodges. (Illus.). 56p. 1996. reprint ed. pap. 10.00 (*0-614-16633-0*, 760) Clearfield Co.

Revolutionary Records of the State of Georgia, 1769-1784, 3 vols., Set. Georgia General Assembly Staff. Ed. by Allen D. Candler. LC 72-965. reprint ed. 375.00 (*0-404-07300-X*) AMS Pr.

Revolutionary Reign of Terror: The Role of Violence in Political Change. Rosemary H. O'Kane. 320p. 1991. text ed. 80.00 (*1-85278-082-7*) E Elgar.

Revolutionary Religion: Christianity, Fascism, & Communism. Roger B. Lloyd. LC 78-63686. (Studies in Fascism: Ideology & Practice). reprint ed. 32.50 (*0-404-16903-1*) AMS Pr.

Revolutionary Road. Richard Yates. (Contemporaries Ser.). 1989. pap. 14.00 (*0-679-72191-6*, Vin) Random.

Revolutionary Road. Richard Yates. LC 70-163123. 337p. 1971. reprint ed. text ed. 59.75 (*0-8371-6221-1*, YARR, Greenwood Pr) Greenwood.

Revolutionary Roads. T. Lewis. 30.00 (*0-06-018231-8*, HarpT) HarpC.

Revolutionary Russia: 1917. John M. Thompson. 206p. 1981. pap. text ed. write for info. (*0-02-420700-4*, Macmillan Coll) P-H.

***Revolutionary Russia, 1917.** 2nd ed. John M. Thompson. (Illus.). 203p. (C). 1996. reprint ed. pap. text ed. 12.95 (*0-88133-932-6*) Waveland Pr.

Revolutionary Russian. Conference on the Russian Revolution Staff et al. Ed. by Richard Pipes. LC 68-15641. (Russian Research Center Studies: No. 55). 379p. reprint ed. pap. 108.10 (*0-7837-3840-4*, 2043662) Bks Demand.

Revolutionary Sarvodaya. Vinoba Bhave. Ed. & Tr. by Vasant Nargolkar from HIN. 64p. (Orig.). 1980. pap. 1.50 (*0-934676-23-2*) Greenlf Bks.

Revolutionary Services & Civil Life of General William Hull. Ed. by Maria Campbell. 1972. reprint ed. lib. bdg. 29.50 (*0-8422-8022-7*) Irvington.

Revolutionary Socialism in the Work of Ernst Toller. Richard Dove. Ed. by Gerhard P. Knapp & Luis Lorenzo-Rivero. (Utah Studies in Literature & Linguistics: Vol. 26). 496p. (C). 1987. lib. bdg. 49.50 (*0-8204-0382-2*) P Lang Pubng.

Revolutionary Socialist Development in the Third World. Ed. by Gordon White et al. LC 82-23705. 288p. 1983. 15.00 (*0-8131-1485-3*) U Pr of Ky.

Revolutionary Soldier, 1775-1781. rev. ed. C. Keith Wilbur. LC 92-40011. (Illustrated Living History Ser.). (Illus.). 96p. 1993. pap. 14.95 (*1-56440-166-9*) Globe Pequot.

***Revolutionary Soldier, 1775-1783.** Keith C. Wilbur. LC 96-43018. (Illustrated Living History Ser.). 1996. lib. bdg. 19.95 (*0-7910-4533-1*) Chelsea Hse.

Revolutionary Soldiers in Kentucky. Anderson C. Quisenberry. 206p. 1996. reprint ed. pap. 22.00 (*0-614-16599-7*, 4735) Clearfield Co.

Revolutionary Soldiers in Kentucky. Ed. by Anderson C. Quisenberry. 278p. 1994. reprint ed. pap. 29.50 (*0-8328-4013-0*) Higginson Bk Co.

Revolutionary Soldiers in Kentucky. Anderson C. Quisenberry. xix, 206p. 1985. reprint ed. lib. bdg. 39.00 (*0-685-10517-2*) Rprt Serv.

Revolutionary Soldiers of Onondaga County, New York. William M. Beauchamp. 307p. 1993. reprint ed. lib. bdg. 35.00 (*0-8328-3511-0*) Higginson Bk Co.

Revolutionary Soul. J. E. Owens. 51p. 1994. pap. text ed. 11.95 (*0-9642191-0-7*) Promiseland.

Revolutionary Soviet Film Posters. Mildred Constantine & Alan Fern. LC 74-6817. (Illus.). 112p. 1974. pap. 16.95 (*0-8018-1760-9*) Johns Hopkins.

Revolutionary Sparks: Freedom of Expression in Modern America. Margaret A. Blanchard. 624p. 1992. 59.00 (*0-19-505436-9*) OUP.

Revolutionary Spirit in France & America. Bernard Fay. Tr. by Ramon Guthrie. LC 66-26824. reprint ed. 65.00 (*0-8154-0067-5*) Cooper Sq.

***Revolutionary States, Leaders & Foreign Relations: A Comparative Study of China, Cuba & Iran.** Houman A. Sadri. LC 96-32468. 168p. 1997. text ed. 55.00 (*0-275-95321-1*, Praeger Pubs) Greenwood.

Revolutionary Strategy: A Handbook for Practitioners. Ernesto Betancourt. 196p. (C). 1991. 34.95 (*0-88738-411-0*) Transaction Pubs.

Revolutionary Struggle in the Philippines. Leonard Davis. LC 88-37946. (Illus.). 304p. 1989. text ed. 45.00 (*0-312-02818-0*) St Martin.

Revolutionary Suicide. Huey P. Newton. (Illus.). 350p. 1995. pap. 14.95 (*0-86316-326-2*) Writers & Readers.

Revolutionary Syndicalism: An International Perspective. Marcel Van Der Linden & Wayne Thorpe. 270p. 1990. text ed. 59.95 (*0-85967-815-6*, Pub. by Scolar Pr UK) Ashgate Pub Co.

Revolutionary Tales: African-American Women's Short Stories, from the First Story to the Present. Ed. by Bill Mullen. 554p. (Orig.). 1995. mass mkt. 6.50 (*0-440-22082-3*) Dell.

Revolutionary Theatre. Robert Leach. LC 93-35722. (Illus.). 256p. (C). (gr. 13). 1994. text ed. 62.95 (*0-415-03223-7*, B3719, Routledge NY) Routledge.

Revolutionary Theories of Louis-Auguste Blanqui. Alan B. Spitzer. LC 70-120198. (Columbia University Social Science Studies: No. 594). reprint ed. 20.00 (*0-404-51594-0*) AMS Pr.

Revolutionary Town. Louise K. Brown. LC 74-30897. (Illus.). 336p. 1975. 15.00 (*0-914016-14-8*) Phoenix Pub.

Revolutionary Tracings. James Jackson. LC 74-23242. 273p. 1974. pap. 3.50 (*0-7178-0452-6*) Intl Pubs Co.

Revolutionary Virginia: The Road to Independence, Vol. 5, Clash of Arms & the Fourth Convention, 1775-1776, a Documentary Record. Compiled by Robert L. Scribner & Brent Tarter. LC 72-96023. 471p. 1979. text ed. 19.50 (*0-8139-0806-X*) U Pr of Va.

Revolutionary Virginia Vol. 1: The Road to Independence: Forming Thunderclouds & the First Convention, 1763-1774: A Documentary Record. Ed. by Robert L. Scribner. LC 72-96023. 308p. 1973. text ed. 19.50 (*0-8139-0500-1*) U Pr of Va.

Revolutionary Virginia Vol. 2: The Road to Independence: The Committees & the Second Convention, 1773-75. A Documentary Record. Ed. by Robert L. Scribner. LC 72-96023. (Illus.). 418p. 1975. text ed. 19.50 (*0-8139-0601-6*) U Pr of Va.

Revolutionary Virginia, the Road to Independence, Vol, 3: Breaking Storm & the Third Convention, 1775 - a Documentary Record. Ed. by Robert L. Scribner & Brent Tarter. LC 72-96023. 548p. 1977. text ed. 19.50 (*0-8139-0685-7*) U Pr of Va.

Revolutionary Virginia, the Road to Independence, Vol. 4: The Committee of Safety & the Balance of Forces, 1775 a Documentary Record. Compiled by Robert L. Scribner & Brent Tarter. LC 72-96023. 543p. 1978. text ed. 19.50 (*0-8139-0748-9*) U Pr of Va.

Revolutionary Virginia, The Road to Independence, Vol. 6: The Time for Decision, 1776: A Documentary Record. Ed. by Robert L. Scribner & Brent Tarter. LC 72-96023. 594p. 1981. text ed. 19.50 (*0-8139-0880-9*) U Pr of Va.

Revolutionary Virginia, The Road to Independence, Vol. 7: Independence & the Fifth Convention, 1776, A Documentary Record, Vol. 7. Ed. by Robert L. Scribner & Brent Tarter. LC 72-96023. 1983. text ed. 24.50 (*0-8139-0968-6*) U Pr of Va.

Revolutionary War. (BipQuiz Ser.). (Illus.). 60p. (J). 1996. pap. 2.95 (*0-8069-4853-1*) Sterling.

Revolutionary War. Kathlyn Gay & Martin Gay. (Voices from the Past Ser.). (Illus.). 64p. (J). (gr. 5-8). 1995. lib. bdg. 15.98 (*0-8050-2844-7*) TFC Bks NY.

Revolutionary War. Gail B. Stewart. LC 91-29889. (America's Wars Ser.). (Illus.). 112p. (J). (gr. 5-8). 1991. lib. bdg. 20.96 (*1-56006-400-5*) Lucent Bks.

Revolutionary War. Ed. by Bill Yenne. (Making of America Ser.). (Illus.). 80p. (Orig.). 1996. pap. 6.95 (*0-912517-23-9*) Bluewood Bks.

Revolutionary War: A Sourcebook on Colonial America. Ed. by Carter Smith. LC 91-13938. (American Albums from the Collections of the Library of Congress). (Illus.). 96p. (J). (gr. 5-8). 1991. pap. 8.95 (*1-878841-69-6*); lib. bdg. 19.90 (*1-56294-039-2*) Millbrook Pr.

Revolutionary War: A Thematic Unit. John Carratello & Patty Carratello. (Thematic Units Ser.). (Illus.). 80p. (Orig.). (gr. 5-8). 1991. student ed. 9.95 (*1-55734-293-8*) Tchr Create Mat.

Revolutionary War: An Outline & Calendar. Arthur A. Merrill. (Illus.). (YA). (gr. 7 up). 1976. pap. 2.00 (*0-911894-35-7*) Analysis.

Revolutionary War: Korea & the Transformation of the Postwar World. Ed. by William J. Williams. (Military History Symposium Series of the United States Air Force Academy). 300p. (Orig.). 1993. pap. text ed. 24.95 (*1-879176-16-5*) Imprint Pubns.

Revolutionary War: The Pennsylvania-German in the Revolutionary War, 1775-1783. Henry M. Richards. (Illus.). 542p. 1991. reprint ed. 35.00 (*0-685-48614-1*, 4890) Genealog Pub.

Revolutionary War & Issachar Bates. John S. Williams. 14p. 1960. 0.50 (*0-937942-02-2*) Shaker Mus.

Revolutionary War Chronology & Almanac. Harv Hilowitz. 50p. pap. 7.50 (*0-910746-13-3*) Hope Farm.

***Revolutionary War Era Activity Book: Arts, Crafts, Cooking & Historical Aids.** Linda Milliken. Ed. by Kathy Rogers. (Illus.). 48p. (J). 1996. wbk. ed., pap. 5.95 (*1-56472-107-8*) Edupress.

Revolutionary War Genealogy. 104p. 1992. pap. 12.00 (*0-913857-04-1*) Genealog Sources.

Revolutionary War in the Hackensack Valley: The Jersey Dutch & Neutral Ground, 1775 - 1783. Adrian C. Leiby. 329p. 1980. reprint ed. pap. 14.95 (*0-8135-0898-3*) Rutgers U Pr.

Revolutionary War Journals of Henry Dearborn, 1775-1783. Ed. by Lloyd A. Brown & Howard H. Peckham. (Illus.). 264p. (Orig.). 1994. pap. text ed. 19.00 (*0-7884-0124-6*) Heritage Bk.

Revolutionary War Journals, 1775-1783. Henry Dearborn. Ed. by Lloyd A. Brown & Howard H. Peckham. LC 74-102233. (Select Bibliographies Reprint Ser.). 1977. 31.95 (*0-8369-5118-2*) Ayer.

***Revolutionary War Pensions of Soldiers Who Settled in Fayette Co., Kentucky.** Compiled by Annie W. Burns. 121p. 1996. reprint ed. pap. 17.00 (*0-8328-5198-1*) Higginson Bk Co.

Revolutionary War Records: Mecklenburg County, Virginia. (Katherine B. Elliott Books on Southern Virginia). 230p. 1964. 30.00 (*0-89308-422-0*, VA 62); pap. 25.00 (*0-89308-381-X*, VA 61) Southern Hist Pr.

Revolutionary War Records: Virginia. Gaius M. Brumbaugh. (Illus.). 707p. 1995. 45.00 (*0-08-630060-1*) Genealog Pub.

Revolutionary War Sermons. Ed. by David R. Williams. LC 84-14188. 1985. reprint ed. 75.00 (*0-8201-1400-6*) Schol Facsimiles.

Revolutionary War Soldier at Saratoga. (Soldier Ser.). 48p. (J). (gr. 5-6). 1991. lib. bdg. 17.80 (*1-56065-000-1*) Capstone Pr.

Revolutionary War Soldiers of Western North Carolina: Burke County, Vol. 1. Emmett R. White. 330p. 1984. 30.00 (*0-89308-536-7*) Southern Hist Pr.

Revolutionary War Veterans of Madison County, New York. Ed. by Isabel Bracy. 130p. (Orig.). 1987. pap. 10.00 (*0-932334-96-2*, NY27028) Hrt of the Lakes.

Revolutionary War Veterans Who Settled in Butler County, Pennsylvania. Paul W. Myers. 30p. 1987. per. 5.00 (*0-933227-69-8*) Closson Pr.

Revolutionary War Years. 2nd ed. W. Edmunds Claussen. (Illus.). 182p. 1974. 5.00 (*0-9616068-2-7*) Boyertown Hist.

Revolutionary Witness & Nobody Here but Us Chickens. Peter Barnes. (Methuen Modern Plays Ser.). 85p. (Orig.). (C). 1989. pap. 9.95 (*0-413-62170-7*, A0415, Pub. by Methuen UK) Heinemann.

Revolutionary Work in a Non-Revolutionary Situation: Report to the Second Plenary Session of the First Central Committee of the Revolutionary Communist Party, U. S. A. (1976) 70p. 1978. 1.00 (*0-89851-013-9*) RCP Pubns.

Revolutionary Years: West Africa Since 1800. 2nd ed. J. B. Webster & A. Adu Boahen. (Growth of African Civilization Ser.). (Illus.). (C). 1980. pap. text ed. 27.50 (*0-582-60332-3*, 74487) Longman.

Revolutionary's Quest. Ed. by Bimal Prasad. 406p. 1980. 29.95 (*0-318-37198-7*) Asia Bk Corp.

***Revolutionizing America's Schools.** Carl D. Glickman. LC 97-4826. (Jossey-Bass Education Ser.). 1997. write for info. (*0-7879-0944-0*) Jossey-Bass.

***Revolutionizing Christian Stewardship: Lessons from Copernicus.** Dan R. Dick. LC 96-72437. 112p. 1997. pap. 14.95 (*0-88177-212-7*, DR212) Discipleship Res.

Revolutionizing Higher Education in Agriculture: Framework for Change. Work Group on Systemic Change in Undergraduate Education in Agriculture Staff. Ed. by Harry O. Kunkel et al. LC 96-327. (Illus.). 168p. 1996. pap. text ed. 19.95 (*0-8138-2394-3*) Iowa St U Pr.

Revolutionizing Motherhood: The Mothers of the Plaza De Mayo. Marguerite G. Bouvard. LC 93-41428. (Latin American Silhouettes Ser.). 261p. 1994. 45.00 (*0-8420-2486-7*); pap. 15.95 (*0-8420-2487-5*) Scholarly Res Inc.

Revolutionizing Product Development: Quantum Leaps in Speed, Efficiency, & Quality. Steven C. Wheelwright & Kim B. Clark. (Illus.). 400p. 1992. 39.95 (*0-02-905515-6*, Free Press) Free Pr.

***Revolutionizing Workforce Performance: A Systems Approach.** Jack E. Bowsher. LC 97-21087. 1997. 39.95 (*0-7879-0798-7*, Pfffr & Co) Jossey-Bass.

Revolutions: Reflections on American Equality & Foreign Liberations. David B. Davis. LC 89-48924. (William E. Massey Sr. Lectures in the History of American Civilization). 130p. 1990. text ed. 23.50 (*0-674-76805-1*) HUP.

Revolutions: Theoretical, Comparative, & Historical Studies. Jack A. Goldstone. 343p. (C). 1986. pap. text ed. 20.00 (*0-15-576710-0*) HB Coll Pubs.

Revolutions: Theoretical, Comparative, & Historical Studies. 2nd ed. Jack A. Goldstone. 1993. pap. 20.00 (*0-15-500385-2*) HarBrace.

Revolutions & Dictatorships. Hans Kohn. LC 75-80388. (Essay Index Reprint Ser.). 1977. 28.95 (*0-8369-1145-8*) Ayer.

Revolutions & Interventions in Hungary & Its Neighbor States, 1918-1919. Ed. by Peter Pastor. 320p. 1988. text ed. 47.00 (*0-88033-137-2*) East Eur Monographs.

Revolutions & Military Rule in the Middle East: Egypt, Sudan, Yemen, Vol. 3. George M. Haddad. 14.95 (*0-8315-0061-1*) Speller.

Revolutions & Military Rule in the Middle East: The Northern Tier, Vol. 1. George M. Haddad. 12.95 (*0-8315-0059-X*) Speller.

Revolutions & Revolutionaries: Four Theories. Barbara Salert. LC 75-40652. 161p. 1981. text ed. 39.95 (*0-444-99021-6*, SRV/) Greenwood.

Revolutions & Revolutionaries: From Anarchism to Zhou Enlai. Van. 496p. 1996. 75.00 (*0-8160-3236-X*) Facts on File.

Revolutions & Revolutionary Movements. 2nd ed. James Defronzo. LC 96-8447. 363p. (C). 1996. pap. text ed. 24.00 (*0-8133-2394-0*) Westview.

***Revolutions & Revolutionary Waves.** Mark N. Katz. LC 97-11237. 1997. write for info. (*0-312-17322-9*) St Martin.

Revolutions for Freedom: The Mass Media in Eastern & Central Europe. Ed. by L. Earle Reybold. LC 91-19063. 250p. (Orig.). (C). 1991. pap. 10.95 (*0-943089-02-6*) U GA CFIMCTR.

Revolution's Godchild: The Birth, Death, & Regeneration of the Society of the Cincinnati in North Carolina. Curtis C. Davis. LC 76-7967. 319p. reprint ed. pap. 91.00 (*0-7837-2071-8*, 2042345) Bks Demand.

Revolutions in American's Lives: A Demographic Perspective on the History of Americans, Their Families, & Their Society. Robert V. Wells. LC 81-6949. (Contributions in Family Studies: No. 6). (Illus.). xvi, 311p. 1982. text ed. 59.95 (*0-313-23019-6*, WRA/) Greenwood.

Revolutions in Art & Ideas at the Turn of the Twentieth Century: A New Interpretation & Anthology. Intro. by David Galaty et al. 338p. (Orig.). (C). 1994. pap. text ed. 34.50 (*0-8191-9342-9*); lib. bdg. 59.50 (*0-8191-9341-0*) U Pr of Amer.

Revolutions in Eastern Europe. Roger East. (Illus.). 208p. 1992. text ed. 54.00 (*0-86187-169-3*); pap. text ed. 17.50 (*0-86187-179-0*) St Martin.

Revolutions in Eastern Europe: The Religious Roots. Niels C. Nielsen. LC 91-23592. 183p. 1991. reprint ed. pap. 52.20 (*0-7837-9855-5*, 2060584) Bks Demand.

Revolutions in Eastern Europe & the U. S. S. R. Promises vs. Practical Morality. Ed. by Kenneth W. Thompson. (Miller Center Series on a World in Change: Vol. 7). 186p. (Orig.). (C). 1995. pap. text ed. 22.50 (*0-7618-0050-6*); lib. bdg. 46.50 (*0-7618-0049-2*) U Pr of Amer.

Revolutions in Law & Legal Thought. Ed. by Zenon Bankowski. (Enlightenment Rights & Revolution Ser.: No. 6). 212p. 1991. pap. 37.90 (*0-08-040924-5*, Pub. by Aberdeen U Pr) Macmillan.

Revolutions in Mathematics. Ed. by Donald Gillies. (Illus.). 360p. (C). 1995. pap. 45.00 (*0-19-851486-7*) OUP.

Revolutions in Physics. Barry M. Casper & Richard J. Noer. (Illus.). (C). 1972. text ed. 26.95 (*0-393-09992-X*) Norton.

***Revolutions in Russia & China.** 2nd rev. ed. J. Zawacki. 1996. pap. text ed. write for info. (*0-07-021776-9*) McGraw.

Revolutions in Science: Their Meaning & Relevance. Ed. by William R. Shea. LC 88-31525. 304p. 1988. 40.00 (*0-88135-091-5*) Watson Pub Intl.

Revolutions in the Third World. Ed. by Quee-Young Kim. LC 90-23514. (International Studies in Sociology & Social Anthropology: No. 54). 151p. 1990. pap. 43.50 (*90-04-09355-9*) E J Brill.

Revolutions in Writing: Readings in Nineteenth-Century French Prose. Tr. & Selected by Rosemary Lloyd. (Indiana Masterpiece Editions Ser.). 448p. 1996. pap. 18.95 (*0-253-21069-0*); text ed. 49.95 (*0-253-33054-8*) Ind U Pr.

Revolutions of Civilization. W. M. Petrie. LC 73-158202. (World History Ser.: No. 48). (C). 1972. reprint ed. lib. bdg. 75.00 (*0-8383-1268-3*) M S G Haskell Hse.

Revolutions of the Heart. Marsha Qualey. LC 92-24528. 192p. (YA). (gr. 6 up). 1993. 14.95 (*0-395-64168-3*) HM.

Revolutions of the Word: Intellectual Contexts for the Study of Modern Literature. Charles G. Waugh. LC 96-18968. 1997. text ed. 19.95 (*0-340-64560-1*, Pub. by E Arnld UK) St Martin.

Revolutions of the Word: Intellectual Contexts for the Study of Modern Literature. Patricia Waugh. LC 96-18968. 1997. text ed. 59.95 (*0-340-64559-8*, Pub. by E Arnld UK) St Martin.

Revolutions of Wisdom: Studies in the Claims & Practice of Ancient Greek Science. Geoffrey E. Lloyd. LC 86-16055. (Sather Classical Lectures: No. 52). 480p. reprint ed. pap. 136.80 (*0-7837-4847-7*, 2044494) Bks Demand.

Revolutions of 1848: A Social History. Priscilla Robertson. 480p. 1952. pap. text ed. 19.95 (*0-691-00756-X*) Princeton U Pr.

Revolutions of 1848 Vol. 1: Political Writings, Vol. 1. Karl Marx. Ed. & Intro. by David Fernbach. 368p. 1993. pap. 11.95 (*0-14-044571-4*, Penguin Classics) Viking Penguin.

***Revolution's Other World: Communism & the Periphery, 1917-1939.** Ken Post. LC 97-18514. 1997. write for info. (*0-312-17631-7*) St Martin.

Revolutions Revisited: Two Faces of the Politics of Enlightenment. Ralph Lerner. LC 93-36438. xvi, 136p. (C). 1994. 22.50 (*0-8078-2136-5*) U of NC Pr.

Revolver De Maigret. Georges Simenon. pap. 3.95 (*0-685-11528-3*) Fr & Eur.

An Asterisk (*) at the beginning of an entry indicates that the title is appearing in BIP for the first time.

Revolver Rifles. Edsall James. 1974. 3.50 (*0-913150-30-4*) Pioneer Pr.

Revolving Culture: Notes from the Scottish Republic. Angus Calder. 256p. 1994. text ed. 15.95 (*1-85043-647-9*, Pub. by I B Tauris UK) St Martin.

Revolving Door Identification Model. Joseph S. Renzulli et al. (C). 1981. pap. 22.95 (*0-936386-16-9*) Creative Learning.

Revolving Doors: Sex Segregation & Women's Careers. Jerry A. Jacobs. LC 88-24986. xiv, 230p. 1989. 37.50 (*0-8047-1489-4*); pap. 12.95 (*0-8047-1814-8*) Stanford U Pr.

***Revolving Gridlock.** David Brady. LC 97-22279. (Transforming American Politics Studies Ser.). 2p. (C). 1997. text ed. 55.00 (*0-8133-2588-9*); pap. text ed. 16.95 (*0-8133-2589-7*) Westview.

Revolving Loan Funds. Mia Purcell. Ed. by Laurie B. Young. 40p. (Orig.). 1983. pap. 13.00 (*0-317-04848-1*) Natl Coun Econ Dev.

***Revolving Loan Funds & Credit Programmes for Fishing Communities: Management Guidelines.** 172p. 1992. 20. 00 (*92-5-102880-X*, F880X, Pub. by FAO IT) Bernan Associates.

Revolving Techniques: Clay - Glass - Metal - Wood. Albert B. LeCoff. Ed. by Tina C. LeCoff et al. (Illus.). 24p. (Orig.). 1992. pap. 6.00 (*0-9624385-4-5*) Wood Turn Ctr.

Revue de la Musique Dramatique en France. Felix Crozet. Bd. with Supplement a la Revue de la Musique Dramatique en France. LC 80-2270. LC 80-2270. reprint ed. 48.50 (*0-404-18833-8*) AMS Pr.

Revue de l'Histoire Juive en Egypte. Ed. & Intro. by Rene C. Bey. (Illus.). viii, 178p. 1987. pap. 35.00 (*0-9613805-2-7*) Halgo Inc.

Revue Du Cinema Anthology. Ed. by R. Gordon. 1976. lib. bdg. 75.00 (*0-8490-2522-2*) Gordon Pr.

Revue Internationale D'Histoire Militaire, No. 51: Belgrade. (Illus.). 455p. (FRE.). 1981. pap. 23.00 (*0-89126-182-6*) MA-AH Pub.

Revue Internationale D'Histoire Militaire, No. 52: Varsovie. 350p. (ENG & FRE.). 1982. pap. 23.00 (*0-89126-183-4*) MA-AH Pub.

Revue Internationale D'Histoire Militaire, No. 56: Madrid. (Illus.). 307p. (ENG & SPA.). 1984. pap. 23.00 (*0-89126-184-2*) MA-AH Pub.

Revue Internationale D'Histoire Militaire, No. 57: Stockholm. (Illus.). 214p. 1984. pap. 23.00 (*0-89126-185-0*) MA-AH Pub.

Revue Internationale D'Histoire Militaire, No. 60: Sofia. (Illus.). 310p. 1984. pap. 23.00 (*0-89126-186-9*) MA-AH Pub.

Revue Musicale 1827-1835, 2 vols., Set. Ed. by H. Robert Cohen. (Repertoire International de la Presse Musicale Ser.). (FRE.). 1991. lib. bdg. 240.00 (*0-8357-2147-7*) Univ Microfilms.

Revue Sommaire Le Doctrines Economiques. Augustin Cournot. LC 68-22372. (Reprints of Economic Classics Ser.). viii, 339p. 1968. reprint ed. 49.50 (*0-678-00377-7*) Kelley.

Reward & Recognition Process in Total Quality Management. Stephen B. Knouse. LC 94-36137. 164p. 1994. 32.00 (*0-87389-306-9*, H0863) ASQC Qual Pr.

***Reward for Loyalty.** Rabbi Nachman of Breslov. Ed. by Moshe Mykoff. (Illus.). 36p. (J). (gr. 1-4). 1996. 7.00 (*0-930213-63-7*) Breslov Res Inst.

Reward Management: A Handbook of Remuneration, Strategy & Practice. Michael Armstrong & Helen Murlis. 600p. 1993. pap. 175.00 (*0-7494-1009-4*, Pub. by IPM Hse UK) St Mut.

Reward Management: A Handbook of Salary Administration. Michael Armstrong & Helen Murlis. 550p. (C). 1988. 150.00 (*1-85091-335-8*) St Mut.

Reward Management: A Handbook of Salary Administration. Michael Armstrong & Helen Murlis. 592p. (C). 1991. pap. 100.00 (*0-7494-0220-2*, Pub. by IPM Hse UK) St Mut.

Reward Management: Employee Performance, Motivation & Pay. David A. Hume. (Illus.). 240p. (Orig.). (C). 1995. pap. 36.95 (*0-631-19623-4*) Blackwell Pubs.

***Reward of the Inheritance: A Black Man's Meditations on the Sacred Meaning of the Crown of Life.** Michael A. Williams. LC 96-80421. 416p. 1997. lib. bdg. 39.95 (*1-878527-49-5*) Black Phoenix Pr.

Reward, One Million Dollars. Leah Klein. (Operation Firestorm Ser.: Pt. 3). 179p. (J). (gr. 6-8). 9.95 (*1-56871-043-7*) Targum Pr.

Reward Plan Advantage: A Manager's Guide to Improving Business Performance Through People. Jerry L. McAdams. (Business & Management Ser.). 270p. 1993. 270.00 (*0-7879-0232-2*) Jossey-Bass.

Rewarding & Recognizing Employees: Ideas for Individuals, Teams & Managers. Joan P. Klubnik. LC 94-36127. (Briefcase Bks.). 1994. write for info. (*0-7863-0349-2*) Irwin Prof Pubng.

Rewarding & Recognizing Employees: Ideas for Individuals, Teams & Managers. Joan P. Klubnik. LC 94-36127. (Briefcase Bks.). 216p. 1996. text ed. 19.95 (*0-7863-0297-6*) Irwin Prof Pubng.

Rewarding Careers in the Nursery Industry. William Flemer, 3rd. 140p. (YA). (gr. 9-12). 1990. pap. 9.95 (*1-887632-51-4*) Amer Nurseryman Pub.

***Rewarding Group Performance: An Approach to Designing & Implementing Incentive Pay Programs.** Thomas B. Wilson & Carol C. Phalen. (Building Blocks Ser.: Vol. 28). (Illus.). 24p. (Orig.). 1996. pap. 24.95 (*1-57963-029-4*, A0228) Am Compensation.

Rewarding People: The Skill of Responding Positively. David Dickson et al. LC 92-27563. (International Series on Communication Skills). 240p. (C). 1993. pap. 19.95 (*0-415-04095-7*, A7811) Routledge.

Rewarding Results: Motivating Profit Center Managers. Kenneth A. Merchant. 1989. text ed. 35.00 (*0-07-103258-4*) McGraw.

Rewarding Speech. Julie A. Blonigen. (Illus.). 32p. 1993. 12.95 (*0-937857-40-8*, 1542) Speech Bin.

Rewarding the Sales Force. Ed. by Mike Langley. 100p. (C). 1987. 45.00 (*0-85292-380-5*) St Mut.

Rewarding Value Creation: A Practical Approach for Developing More Effective Pay Programmes. Gary Houriban et al. (Financial Times Management Ser.). 256p. 1997. 87.50 (*0-273-60706-5*, Pub. by Pitman Pub Ltd UK) Trans-Atl Phila.

***Rewarding Work: How to Restore Participation & Self-Support to Free Enterprise.** Edmund S. Phelps. LC 96-50204. 1996. write for info. (*0-674-09495-6*) HUP.

Rewards & Fairies. Rudyard Kipling. 1976. 27.95 (*0-8488-1070-8*) Amereon Ltd.

Rewards & Fairies. Rudyard Kipling. Ed. by Roger Lewis. 304p. 1988. pap. 3.95 (*0-14-043315-5*, Penguin Classics) Viking Penguin.

Rewards & Fairies. Rudyard Kipling. Ed. & Intro. by Roger Lewis. 304p. 1991. pap. 8.95 (*0-14-018437-6*, Penguin Classics) Viking Penguin.

Rewards & Punishments in the Arthurian Romances & Lyric Poetry of Medieval France. Ed. by Peter Davies & Angus J. Kennedy. 1987. 71.00 (*0-85991-250-7*) Boydell & Brewer.

Rewards & Reform: Creating Educational Incentives That Work. Ed. by Susan H. Fuhrman & Jennifer A. O'Day. (Education Ser.). 352p. 1996. 32.95 (*0-7879-0237-3*) Jossey-Bass.

Rewards at the Top: A Comparative Study of High Public Office. Ed. by Christopher Hood & B. Guy Peters. (Modern Politics Ser.). 256p. (C). 1994. text ed. 65.00 (*0-8039-7742-5*) Sage.

Rewards for Service: 1919. 1989. reprint ed. 5.00 (*0-913150-98-3*) Pioneer Pr.

Rewards of Hope. J. Norman Heard. LC 91-73206. 1992. 14.95 (*0-8158-0474-1*) Chris Mass.

Rewards of Merit. Patricia Fenn & Alfred P. Malpa. (Illus.). 224p. 1994. 39.95 (*0-943231-68-X*, 41591) Howell Pr VA.

Rewards Offered by the United States. Larry M. Dreyfus. Ed. by Estella Krebs. LC 88-90842. 160p. 1989. 14.95 (*0-88247-837-0*); pap. 9.95 (*0-88247-791-9*) R & E Pubs.

Rewards to Investors in Innovative Technology Applications: A Study of First Movers & Early Followers in ATMS. Brian L. Dos Santos & Ken Peffers. (Illus.). 58p. (Orig.). (C). 1993. pap. text ed. 30. 00 (*1-56806-917-0*) DIANE Pub.

Reweaving Religious Life: Beyond the Liberal Model. Mary J. Leddy. LC 90-70354. 200p. (Orig.). (C). 1990. pap. 9.95 (*0-89622-440-6*) Twenty-Third.

Reweaving the Family Tapestry: A Multigenerational Approach to Families. Ed. by Fredda H. Brown. 320p. (C). 1991. 32.95 (*0-393-70108-5*) Norton.

Reweaving the Urban Fabric: Approaches to Infill Housing. Marta Gutman et al. Ed. by Deborah Nørden. (Illus.). 160p. (Orig.). (C). 1989. pap. text ed. write for info. (*0-9621765-9-1*) NYSCA.

Reweaving the World: The Emergence of Ecofeminism. Irene Diamond & Gloria F. Orenstein. LC 89-29295. (Illus.). 324p. 1990. pap. 16.00 (*0-87156-623-0*) Sierra.

***Rewind.** Terry England. 1997. mass mkt. 5.99 (*0-380-78696-6*) Avon.

***Rewind & Search: Conversations with the Makers & Decision-Makers of CBS Television Drama.** Mary J. Miller. 562p. 1996. 49.95 (*0-7735-1365-5*, Pub. by McGill CN) U of Toronto Pr.

Rewinding the Reel. H. R. Coursen. Ed. by Napoleon St. Cyr. 80p. (Orig.). 1989. pap. 7.50 (*0-910380-07-4*) Cider Mill.

***Rewired.** Bruce Reinhart et al. 300p. 1997. write for info. (*1-57870-003-5*) Mac Comp Pub.

Rewired: A Parody. Tom Connor & Jim Downey. (Illus.). 80p. 1996. pap. text ed. 15.00 (*0-06-095184-2*) HarpC.

***Rewiring of America: The Fiber Optics Revolution.** David Chaffee. 49.95 (*0-614-18442-8*, B01023) Info Gatekeepers.

Rewiring of America: The Fiber Optics Revolution. G. David Chaffee. 256p. 1987. text ed. 60.00 (*0-12-166360-4*) Acad Pr.

***Rewiring the Corporate Brain: Using the New Science to Rethink How We Structure & Lead Organizations.** Danah Zohar. (Illus.). 250p. 1997. 27.95 (*1-57675-022-1*) Berrett-Koehler.

Rewoluja: Russian Poland, 1904-1907. Robert E. Blobaum. (Illus.). 320p. 1995. 35.00 (*0-8014-3054-2*) Cornell U Pr.

***Reworking Authority: Leading & Following in the Post-Modern Organization.** Larry Hirschhorn. LC 96-48420. 1997. 25.00 (*0-262-08258-6*) MIT Pr.

***Reworking Class.** Ed. by John R. Hall. 368p. 1997. pap. 19.95 (*0-8014-8321-2*) Cornell U Pr.

***Reworking Class: Cultures & Institutions of Economic Stratification.** Ed. by John R. Hall. LC 97-18765. 368p. 1997. 52.50 (*0-8014-3242-1*) Cornell U Pr.

Reworking Modernity: Capitalisms & Symbolic Discontent. Allan Pred & Michael J. Watts. LC 91-42894. (Hegemony & Experience Ser.). (Illus.). 265p. (C). 1992. text ed. 45.00 (*0-8135-1831-8*); pap. text ed. 17.00 (*0-8135-1832-6*) Rutgers U Pr.

***Reworking Success: New Communities at the Millenium.** Robert Theobald. 1997. 34.95 (*0-86571-366-9*) New Soc Pubs.

***Reworking Success: New Communities at the Millennium.** Robert Theobald. 1997. pap. text ed. 9.95 (*0-86571-367-7*) New Soc Pubs.

Reworking the Past: Hitler, the Holocaust, & the Historians' Debate. Ed. by Peter Baldwin. LC 88-43073. 316p. 1990. 15.00 (*0-8070-4302-8*) Beacon Pr.

Reworking the World: Organisations, Technologies, & Cultures in Comparative Perspective. Ed. by Jane Marceau. LC 92-32150. (Studies in Organization: No. 42). x, 514p. 1992. lib. bdg. 84.95 (*3-11-013158-7*) De Gruyter.

Reworlding: The Literature of the Indian Diaspora. Ed. by Emmanuel S. Nelson. LC 91-40939. (Contributions to the Study of World Literature Ser.: No. 42). 208p. 1992. text ed. 49.95 (*0-313-27794-X*, NLI, Greenwood Pr) Greenwood.

Rewrite Right! Jan Venolia. 128p. 1987. pap. 7.95 (*0-89815-202-X*) Ten Speed Pr.

ReWriter, Bk. I. Larry Berliner & Susan Berliner. (Illus.). 38p. (Orig.). (J). (gr. 5-8). 1985. pap. text ed. 17.95 (*0-913935-28-X*) ERA-CCR.

ReWriter, Bk. II. Larry Berliner & Susan Berliner. (Illus.). 38p. (Orig.). (J). (gr. 6-9). 1985. pap. text ed. 17.95 (*0-913935-29-8*) ERA-CCR.

Rewrites: A Memoir. Neil Simon. (Illus.). 400p. 1996. 25.00 (*0-684-82672-0*) S&S Trade.

Rewriting Caucasian History: The Medieval Armenian Adaptation of the Georgian Chronicles: The Original Georgian Texts & the Armenian Adaptation. Tr. & Comment by Robert W. Thomson. LC 95-40306. (Oxford Oriental Monographs: No. 3). (Illus.). 464p. (C). 1996. 98.00 (*0-19-826373-2*, Clarendon Pr) OUP.

Rewriting Chinese: Style & Innovation in Twentieth-Century Chinese Prose. Edward M. Gunn, Jr. LC 90-46362. 376p. 1991. 47.50 (*0-8047-1599-8*) Stanford U Pr.

Rewriting English: The Politics of Gender & Class. Janet Batsleer et al. (New Accents Ser.). 160p. (C). 1986. text ed. 27.50 (*0-416-38930-9*, 9473); pap. text ed. 12.95 (*0-416-38940-6*, 9474) Routledge Chapman & Hall.

Rewriting Family Scripts: From Secure Attachment to Systems Change. John Byng-Hall. LC 95-16208. (Family Therapy Ser.). 288p. 1995. lib. bdg. 35.00 (*0-89862-876-8*) Guilford Pr.

Rewriting Gender: Reading Contemporary Chinese Women. Ravni Thakur. 240p. (C). 1996. 55.00 (*1-85649-409-8*, Pub. by Zed Bks Ltd UK) Humanities.

Rewriting Gender: Reading Contemporary Chinese Women. Ravni Thakur. 240p. (C). 1996. pap. 19.95 (*1-85649-410-1*, Pub. by Zed Bks Ltd UK) Humanities.

Rewriting Greece: Queneau & the Agony of Presence. Constantin Toloudis. LC 94-11767. (AUS II: Vol. 211). 161p. (C). 1995. text ed. 35.95 (*0-8204-2488-9*) P Lang Pubng.

Rewriting History: The Original & Revised World War II Diaries of Curt Prufer, Nazi Diplomat. Ed. by Donald M. McKale. LC 88-12034. 277p. 1988. 24.00 (*0-87338-364-8*) Kent St U Pr.

***Rewriting Indian History.** Francois Gautier. (C). 1996. 20. 00 (*0-7069-9976-2*, Pub. by Vikas II) S Asia.

Rewriting Literacy: Culture & the Discourse of the Other. Ed. by Candace Mitchell & Kathleen Weiler. LC 91-15503. (Critical Studies in Education & Culture). 312p. 1991. text ed. 57.95 (*0-89789-225-9*, H225, Quorum Bks); pap. text ed. 18.95 (*0-89789-228-3*, G228, Quorum Bks) Greenwood.

Rewriting Literary History. Ed. by Tak-wai Wong & M. A. Abbas. 356p. (C). 1984. pap. text ed. 26.00 (*962-209-117-2*, Pub. by Hong Kong U Pr HK) St Mut.

Rewriting Literary History. International Conference on Literary Theory Staff. Ed. by Tak-Wai Wong & M. A. Abbas. LC 85-193865. 356p. 1984. reprint ed. pap. 101. 50 (*0-608-01392-7*, 2062153) Bks Demand.

Rewriting Love Stories: Brief Marital Therapy. Patricia O. Hudson & William H. O'Hanlon. 192p. 1994. pap. 11.95 (*0-393-31094-9*) Norton.

***Rewriting Melodrama: The Hidden Paradigm in Modern Spanish Theater.** Wadda C. Rios-Font. LC 96-47684. 240p. 1997. 36.50 (*0-8387-5342-6*) Bucknell U Pr.

Rewriting Network News - Wordwatching Tips from 345 TV & Radio Scripts. Mervin Block. 221p. 1990. 24.95 (*0-929387-15-5*) Bonus Books.

Rewriting Nursing History. Ed. by Celia Davies. 226p. 1980. 44.00 (*0-389-20153-7*, N6982) B&N Imports.

Rewriting of America's History. Catherine Millard. LC 91-73175. (Illus.). 1991. pap. 13.99 (*0-88965-092-6*, Pub. by Horizon Books CN) Chr Pubns.

***Rewriting Reality.** Fiddler. 1997. pap. 18.50 (*1-85973-143-0*, Pub. by Berg Pubs UK) NYU Pr.

Rewriting Reality: An Introduction to Elfriede Jelinek. Allyson Fiddler. Ed. by John Flower. (New Directions in European Writing Ser.). 200p. 1994. 45.95 (*0-85496-776-1*) Berg Pubs.

Rewriting Resemblance in Medieval French Romance: Ceci N' Est Pas un Graal. Paul V. Rockwell. LC 95-13705. (Garland Studies in Medieval Literature: Vol. 13). 264p. 1995. text ed. 50.00 (*0-8153-2035-3*, H1908) Garland.

Rewriting Shakespeare, Rewriting Ourselves. Peter Erickson. 239p. 1991. 30.00 (*0-520-07445-9*) U CA Pr.

Rewriting Shakespeare, Rewriting Ourselves. Peter Erickson. 228p. (C). 1994. pap. 14.00 (*0-520-08646-5*) U CA Pr.

Rewriting Techniques & Applications. Ed. by N. Dershowitz. (Lecture Notes in Computer Science Ser.: Vol. 355). vii, 579p. 1989. 61.00 (*0-387-51081-8*) Spr-Verlag.

Rewriting Techniques & Applications. Ed. by Jean-Pierre Jouannaud. 216p. 1988. pap. text ed. 41.00 (*0-12-390960-0*) Acad Pr.

Rewriting Techniques & Applications. Jean-Pierre Jouannaud. (Lecture Notes in Computer Science Ser.: Vol. 202). vi, 441p. 1985. 42.00 (*0-387-15976-2*) Spr-Verlag.

Rewriting Techniques & Applications. Ed. by P. Lescanne. (Lecture Notes in Computer Science Ser.: Vol. 256). vi, 285p. 1987. 36.00 (*0-387-17220-3*) Spr-Verlag.

Rewriting Techniques & Applications: Fourth International Conference, RTA-91 Como, Italy, April 10-12, 1991 Proceedings. Ed. by Ronald V. Book. (Lecture Notes in Computer Science Ser.: Vol. 488). vii, 458p. 1991. 47.95 (*0-387-53904-2*) Spr-Verlag.

Rewriting Techniques & Applications: Proceedings of the 5th International Conference, RTA '93, Montreal, Quebec, Canada, June 16-18, 1993. Ed. by C. Kirchner. (Lecture Notes in Computer Science Ser.: Vol. 690). xi, 488p. 1993. 65.95 (*0-387-56868-9*) Spr-Verlag.

Rewriting Techniques & Applications: Proceedings of the 6th International Conference, STA-95, Kaiserslautern, Germany, April 5-7, 1995. International Conference on Rewriting Techniques & Applications Staff. Ed. by Jieh Hsiang. LC 95-13007. (Lecture Notes in Computer Science Ser.: Vol. 914). 1995. write for info. (*0-387-59200-8*) Spr-Verlag.

***Rewriting Techniques & Applications: Proceedings, 8th International Conference, RTA-97, Sitges, Spain, June 2-5, 1997, Vol. 123.** Ed. by H. Comon. LC 97-18882. (Lecture Notes in Computer Science Ser.: Vol. 1232). xi, 339p. 1997. pap. 55.00 (*3-540-62950-5*) Spr-Verlag.

Rewriting Techniques & Applications: 6th International Conference, RTA-95, Kaiserslautern, Germany, April 5-7, 1995. Proceedings. Ed. by Jieh Hsiang et al. (Lecture Notes in Computer Science Ser.: Vol. 914). xii, 473p. 1995. 75.00 (*3-540-59200-8*) Spr-Verlag.

Rewriting Techniques & Applications: 7th International Conference, New Brunswick, N.J., July 1996 - Proceedings, Vol. 1103. H. Ganzinger. LC 96-26788. (Lecture Notes in Computer Science Ser.). 437p. 1996. pap. 68.00 (*3-540-61464-8*) Spr-Verlag.

Rewriting the Bible: Land & Covenant in Postbiblical Literature. Betsy Halpern-Amaru. LC 94-7383. 208p. (Orig.). (C). 1994. pap. 15.00 (*1-56338-091-9*) TPI PA.

Rewriting the Book. H. R. Coursen. Ed. by Napoleon St. Cyr. 48p. (Orig.). 1987. pap. 4.50 (*0-910380-06-6*) Cider Mill.

Rewriting the French Revolution: The Andrew Browning Lectures, 1989. Ed. by Colin Lucas. 224p. 1991. 59.00 (*0-19-821976-8*) OUP.

***Rewriting the Gender Curriculum.** Magda Lewis. Ed. by Joe Kincheloe & Shirley R. Steinberg. (Critical Education Practice Ser.). 200p. Date not set. text ed. 30. 00 (*0-8153-1185-0*) Garland.

***Rewriting the Gender Curriculum.** Mary Lewis. Ed. by Joe Kincheloe & Shirley R. Steinberg. 200p. Date not set. pap. text ed. 18.95 (*0-8153-2315-8*) Garland.

Rewriting the German Past: History & Identity in the New Germany. Ed. by Reinhard Alter & Peter Monteath. LC 96-49082. 304p. (C). 1997. pap. 18.50 (*0-391-04026-X*); text ed. 60.00 (*0-391-04025-1*) Humanities.

Rewriting the Good Fight: Critical Essays on the Literature of the Spanish Civil War. Ed. by Frieda S. Brown et al. LC 88-43431. 266p. (C). 1989. text ed. 26.00 (*0-87013-269-5*) Mich St U Pr.

***Rewriting the History of Ancient Greek Philosophy.** V. Tejera. LC 96-53521. (Contributions in Philosophy Ser.: 59). 1997. text ed. write for info. (*0-313-30357-6*, Greenwood Pr) Greenwood.

Rewriting the History of Madness: Studies in Foucault's "Histoire de la Folie" Ed. by Arthur Still & Irving Velody. LC 91-43296. 208p. (C). 1992. text ed. 110.00 (*0-415-06654-9*, A7402) Routledge.

Rewriting the History of the Judiciary Act of 1789: Exposing Myths, Challenging Premises & Using New Evidence. Wilfred J. Ritz. Ed. by Wythe Holt & L. H. LaRue. LC 89-37863. 288p. 1990. 35.00 (*0-8061-2239-0*) U of Okla Pr.

Rewriting the Renaissance: The Discourses of Sexual Difference in Early Modern Europe. Ed. by Margaret W. Ferguson et al. LC 85-28829. (Illus.). 464p. 1986. pap. text ed. 20.00 (*0-226-24314-1*) U Ch Pr.

Rewriting the Self: Histories from the Middle Ages to the Present. Ed. by Roy Porter. LC 96-15698. 296p. (C). 1996. pap. write for info. (*0-415-14280-6*); text ed. write for info. (*0-415-14279-2*) Routledge.

Rewriting the Self: History, Memory, Narrative. Mark P. Freeman. LC 92-15269. (Critical Psychology Ser.). 304p. (C). 1993. pap. 18.95 (*0-415-04198-8*, A7812, Routledge NY); text ed. 62.95 (*0-415-04197-X*, Routledge NY) Routledge.

Rewriting the Soul: Mutliple Personality & the Science of Memory. Ian Hacking. LC 94-41975. 336p. 1995. 27.50 (*0-691-03642-X*) Princeton U Pr.

***Rewriting the Thirties.** Keith Williams. (C). 1997. text ed. 49.95 (*0-582-29449-5*, Pub. by Longman UK); pap. text ed. 19.95 (*0-582-29448-7*, Pub. by Longman UK) Longman.

Rewriting the United States Constitution: An Examination of Proposals from Reconstruction to the Present. John R. Vile. LC 90-20854. 216p. 1991. text ed. 55.00 (*0-275-93842-5*, C3842, Praeger Pubs) Greenwood.

Rewriting the Victorians: Theory, History & Politics. Ed. by Linda M. Shires. LC 91-23416. 288p. (Orig.). (C). 1992. pap. 16.95 (*0-415-05525-3*, A4784) Routledge.

Rewriting the Victorians: Theory, History & Politics. Ed. by Linda M. Shires. LC 91-23416. 288p. (Orig.). (C). (gr. 13). 1992. text ed. 69.95 (*0-415-05524-5*, A4780) Routledge.

Rewriting Theatre: The Comedia & the Nineteenth-Century Refundicion. Charles Ganelin. LC 93-13479. 1994. 42. 50 (*0-8387-5259-4*) Bucknell U Pr.

Rewriting Writing. 2nd ed. Jo R. McCuen. (C). 1990. teacher ed., pap. text ed. 3.00 (*0-15-576720-8*) HB Coll Pubs.

Rewriting Writing: A Rhetoric & Reader. 2nd ed. Jo R. McCuen & Anthony C. Winkler. 733p. (C). 1990. teacher ed. write for info. (*0-318-67028-3*); pap. text ed. 22.75 (*0-15-576719-4*) HB Coll Pubs.

R

Rewriting Writing: A Rhetoric, Reader & Handbook. 2nd ed. Jo R. McCuen & Anthony C. Winkler. 835p. (C). 1990. teacher ed. write for info. (0-318-67021-6); text ed. 25.50 (0-15-576721-6) HB Coll Pubs.

Rex. Jack L. Stoll. 1981. 6.95 (0-918476-08-9) Cornerstone Pr.

Rex. large type ed. Joyce Stranger. 1974. 25.99 (0-85456-294-X) Ulverscroft.

Rex Allen: "My Life" Sunrise to Sunset - The Arizona Cowboy. Paula Simpson-Witt & Snuff Garrett. (Illus.). 126p. (Orig.). 1989. 27.95 (0-9625091-0-8); pap. 17.95 (0-9625091-1-6) Rex GarRus Pub.

Rex Allen: "My Life" Sunrise to Sunset - The Arizona Cowboy. limited ed. Paula Simpson-Witt & Snuff Garrett. (Illus.). 126p. (Orig.). 1989. 100.00 (0-9625091-2-4) Rex GarRus Pub.

Rex & Lilly Family Time. Laurene K. Brown. LC 93-24162. (J). 1995. lib. bdg. 12.95 (0-316-11385-9) Little.

***Rex & Lilly Family Time.** Laurie Krasny Brown. (Dino Easy Reader Ser.). 1997. pap. text ed. 3.95 (0-316-11109-0) Little.

Rex & Lilly Playtime. Laurene K. Brown. LC 93-25877. (Dino Easy Reader Ser.). (Illus.). (J). 1995. 12.95 (0-316-11386-7) Little.

***Rex & Lilly Playtime.** Laurie Krasny Brown. (Dino Easy Reader Ser.). 1997. pap. text ed. 3.95 (0-316-11110-4) Little.

Rex & Lilly Schooltime. Laurie K. Brown. LC 95-2912. (Illus.). 1997. 12.95 (0-316-10920-7) Bulfinch Pr.

***Rex & Lilly Schooltime.** Laurie K. Brown. (Dino Easy Reader Ser.). (Illus.). (J). (ps-1). 1997. 12.95 (0-614-28841-X) Little.

***Rex & Muffin Go Christmas Shopping.** Carol Lee. (Orig.). (J). (ps-3). 1997. pap. 6.95 (0-533-12297-X) Vantage.

Rex & the Saxophone. Sherrie S. Fagerstrom. (Barn Full of Tales Ser.). 20p. (J). (ps-6). 1995. pap. 6.50 (1-886466-17-3) Wee Folks Pubns.

Rex Barney's Thank Youuuu for 50 Years in Baseball from Brooklyn to Baltimore. Rex Barney & Norman L. Macht. LC 92-44664. (Illus.). 279p. 1993. 19.95 (0-87033-443-3, Tidewtr Pubs) Cornell Maritime.

Rex Beach. Abe C. Ravitz. (Western Writers Ser.: No. 113). (Illus.). 52p. 1994. pap. 4.95 (0-88430-112-5) Boise St U W Writ Ser.

Rex Harrison. Allen Eyles. (Illus.). 220p. 1986. 14.95 (0-491-03901-8) Carol Pub Group.

Rex Ingram: Master of the Silent Cinema. Liam O'Leary. (Illus.). 224p. 1994. pap. 23.95 (0-85170-443-3, Pub. by British Film Inst UK) Ind U Pr.

Rex Reed's Guide to Movies on TV & Video. Rex Reed. 640p. (Orig.). 1992. mass mkt. 6.99 (0-446-36206-9) Warner Bks.

Rex Stout: A Biography. John J. McAleer. LC 93-335. (Brownstone Mystery Guides Ser.: Vol. 6). (Illus.). x, 622p. 1994. pap. 49.00 (0-941028-10-0, Brownstone Bks); lib. bdg. 59.00 (0-941028-09-7, Brownstone Bks) Borgo Pr.

Rex Stout: Seven Complete Nero Wolfe Novels. Rex Stout. 1990. 13.99 (0-517-03753-X) Random Hse Value.

Rex Wayland's Fortune: The First Novel (1898) Ever Written about Seattle. H. A. Stanley. 400p. 1995. pap. 19.95 (1-881147-16-9) Lowell Print.

Rexford G. Tugwell: A Biography. Michael V. Namorato. LC 88-2397. 202p. 1988. text ed. 55.00 (0-275-92961-2, C2961, Praeger Pubs) Greenwood.

Rexrode Art. William F. Rexrode. (Illus.). 1966. 4.00 (0-87012-011-5) McClain.

***Rex's Dance: Level 2.** Catherine Peters. (Little Reader Ser.). (J). 1997. pap. text ed. 2.50 (0-395-88298-2) HM.

Rexx Cookbook: A Tutorial Guide to the Rexx Language in OS-2 & Warp on the IBM Personal Computer. Merrill Callaway. LC 94-62030. (Illus.). 320p. (Orig.). 1995. pap. 27.95 (0-9632773-4-0); 3.5 hd 14.95 (0-9632773-5-9) Whitestone NM.

REXX in the TSO Environment. rev. ed. Gabriel F. Gargiulo. 496p. 1993. text ed. 49.95 (0-471-56188-6) Wiley.

REXX Language: A Practical Approach to Programming. 2nd ed. Mike Cowlishaw. 1990. pap. text ed. 48.00 (0-13-780651-5) P-H.

REXX Reference Summary Handbook. 4th ed. Richard K. Goran. 270p. 1996. 31.95 (0-9639854-3-4) C F S Nevada.

REXX Tools & Techniques. Barry K. Nirmal. 264p. 1993. pap. text ed. 49.95 (0-471-58559-9, GD4175) Wiley.

Rey Colibri - the Hummingbird King: Una Leyenda Guatemalteca. Argentina Palacios. LC 92-21437. (J). (gr. 4-7). 1993. lib. bdg. 13.95 (0-8167-3122-5) Troll Communs.

Rey Colibri - the Hummingbird King: Una Leyenda Guatemalteca. Argentina Palacios. LC 92-21437. (J). (gr. 4-7). 1996. pap. 4.95 (0-8167-3071-7) Troll Communs.

Rey David. Penny Frank & Tony Morris. (Serie Historias de la Biblia - Children's Bible Story Books Ser.). 24p. (SPA.). (J). 1989. pap. 1.79 (0-945792-61-1, 490319) Editorial Unilit.

Rey de los Paganos. deluxe limited ed. Inclan R. Valle. (Ediciones Especiales y de Bibliofilo Ser.). (Illus.). 76p. (SPA.). 1993. 7,500.00 (84-343-0269-1) Elliots Bks.

Rey de Reyes: La Biblia en Cuadros. Jack T. Chick. (Illus.). 64p. (Orig.). (SPA.). (YA). (gr. 7-12). 1989. pap. 2.95 (0-937958-37-9) Chick Pubns.

Rey Gallo y Discursos de la Hormiga. Francisco Santos. Ed. by Victor Arizpe. (Textos B Ser.: No. 34). 320p. (C). 1991. 63.00 (1-85566-001-6, Pub. by Tamesis Bks Ltd UK) Boydell & Brewer.

Rey Lear. William Shakespeare. Ed. & Tr. by Angel-Luis Pujante. (Nueva Austral Ser.: Vol. 268). (SPA.). pap. text ed. 24.95 (84-239-7268-2) Elliots Bks.

Rey Mas Perfeto - The Perfect King. Antonio E. Gomez. Ed. & Tr. by Michael McGaha. LC 90-85335. 228p. 1991. pap. 22.00 (0-927534-10-X) Biling Rev-Pr.

Rey Muerto, Rey Puesto y Otros Relatos. Jose L. Heredia. LC 88-84140. (Coleccion Caniqui). 134p. (Orig.). (SPA.). 1989. pap. 9.95 (0-89729-521-8) Ediciones.

***Rey-Osterrieth Complex Figure Test Handbook: Clinical & Research Applications.** Ed. by Jeffrey Knight & Edith Kaplan. 700p. 1998. 75.00 (0-911907-30-0) Psych Assess.

Rey Siervo: Marcos. Marilyn Kunz & Katherione Schell. (Serie Encuentros Biblicos - Neighborhood Bible Study Ser.). 80p. (SPA.). 1989. pap. 1.50 (0-945792-87-5, 490455) Editorial Unilit.

***Reyes: Three Kings' Day.** Lori M. Carlson. LC 97-20937. (Illus.). (J). 1998. write for info. (0-525-67569-8) Dutton Child Bks.

Reyes Del Mambo Tocan Conciones de Amor: Novela. Oscar Hijuelos. LC 96-20227. 416p. 1996. pap. 13.00 (0-06-095214-8) HarpC.

Reykjavik: Results & Lessons. Mikhail S. Gorbachev. LC 86-31438. 87p. 1987. 19.95 (0-943071-06-2) Sphinx Pr.

Reykjavik & Beyond: Deep Reductions in Strategic Nuclear Arsenals & the Future Direction of Arms Control. National Academy of Sciences Staff. 80p. 1988. pap. text ed. 12.95 (0-309-03799-9) Natl Acad Pr.

Reykjavik Summit: Watershed or Washout? Melissa Williams. (Pew Case Studies in International Affairs). 50p. (C). 1993. pap. text ed. 3.50 (1-56927-438-X) Geo U Inst Dplmcy.

Reynard: The Story. Houghton Mifflin Company Staff. (Literature Experience 1993 Ser.). (J). (gr. 5). 1992. pap. 9.16 (0-395-61813-4) HM.

***Reynard Story: From Formula Ford to Indy Champions.** Mike Lawrence. (Illus.). 192p. 1997. 39.95 (1-85260-576-6) Haynes Pubns.

Reynard the Fox. Rachel Anderson & David Bradby. (Oxford Myths & Legends Ser.). (Illus.). 80p. (J). (gr. 5-8). 1987. 20.00 (0-19-274129-2) OUP.

Reynard the Fox. Arthur Fauquez. (J). 1962. 6.00 (0-87602-187-9) Anchorage.

Reynard the Fox. Illus. & Adapted by Alain Va Es. LC 94-8364. 1994. 16.95 (1-57036-055-3) Turner Pub GA.

Reynard the Fox in South Africa. Wilhelm H. Bleek. LC 78-67686. (Folktale Ser.). reprint ed. 24.50 (0-404-16055-7) AMS Pr.

Reyna's Reward: American Dreams. Wanda Dionne. 192p. (Orig.). (YA). 1996. pap. 3.99 (0-380-78476-9, Flare) Avon.

***Reynolda: An American Country House.** Barbara Mayer. 1997. 19.95 (0-89587-155-6) Blair.

Reynolds: History & One Line of Descendants of Robert & Mary Reynolds (1630? - 1928) of Boston, with the Hyatt Family of Princeton, New Jersey. M. H. Reynolds. (Illus.). 92p. 1993. reprint ed. pap. 18.00 (0-8328-3391-6); reprint ed. lib. bdg. 28.00 (0-8328-3390-8) Higginson Bk Co.

Reynolds: History & Some of the Descendants of Robert & Mary Reynolds (1630? - 1931) of Boston, Massachusetts. Compiled by M. H. Reynolds. (Illus.). 236p. 1993. reprint ed. pap. 37.50 (0-8328-3393-2); reprint ed. lib. bdg. 47.50 (0-8328-3392-4) Higginson Bk Co.

Reynolds Beal. 1989. pap. 34.95 (0-8386-3360-9) Fairleigh Dickinson.

Reynolds Beal: Impressionist Landscapes & Seacapes. Sidney Bressler. LC 87-45585. (Illus.). 1989. 65.00 (0-8386-3325-0) Fairleigh Dickinson.

Reynolds in Canada. Jennifer C. Watson. (Illus.). 84p. (C). 1988. text ed. 25.00 (0-88920-988-X) Wilfrid Laurier.

Reynolds Price: A Bibliography, 1949-1984. Stuart Wright & James L. West, III. LC 85-29463. (Linton R. Massey Descriptive Bibliography Ser.). xvi, 122p. (C). 1986. text ed. 25.00 (0-8139-1092-7) U Pr of Va.

Reynolds Price: From a Long & Happy Life to Good Hearts, with a Bibliography. Ed. by Lynn V. Sadler. xi, 154p. (Orig.). 1989. pap. 15.95 (1-878304-00-3) Methodist Coll Pr.

***Reynolds to the Rescue.** 64p. 1995. pap. 3.99 (0-8341-0993-X) Nazarene.

***Rez Road Follies: Canoes, Casinos, Computers, & Birch Bark Baskets.** Jim Northrup. 208p. 1997. 20.00 (1-56836-205-6) Kodansha.

Reza: A Moslem Sees Christ. Reza Sabri & Timothy Sheaff. 85p. 1991. pap. 4.95 (1-879882-00-0) WrldChangers.

***Reza: His Life & Times.** 1988. pap. 5.50 (0-8341-1241-8) Nazarene.

Rezando el Rosario Con Fray Angelico. Domenico Marcucci. Tr. by Dulce M. Jimenez-Abreu. (Illus.). 48p. (SPA.). 1991. pap. 2.50 (0-8189-0620-0) Alba.

Rezanov. Gertrude F. Atherton. LC 78-96873. (Illus.). 320p. reprint ed. lib. bdg. 29.00 (0-8398-0067-3) Irvington.

Rezanov. Gertrude F. Atherton. (Illus.). 320p. 1986. reprint ed. pap. text ed. 6.95 (0-8290-1924-3) Irvington.

Rezanov Voyage to Nueva California in 1806. limited ed. Nikolai P. Rezanov. 1988. 29.95 (0-87770-448-1) Ye Galleon.

Rezeption der Komodien des Plautus und Terenz im 19. Jahrhundert: Theorie - Bearbeitung - Buhne. Barbara R. Kes. 347p. (GER.). 1988. pap. 41.00 (90-6032-313-0, Pub. by B R Gruener NE) Benjamins North Am.

Rezeption des Artussotoffes in der Englischen und Amerikanischen Literatur Des 20: Jahrhunderts Bei Thomas Berger, Marion Zimmer Bradley, E. A. Robinson, Mary Stewart und T. H. White. Monika Essl. LC 95-1728. (Salzburger Studien Ser.). 248p. (GER.). 1995. text ed. 89.95 (0-7734-1243-3) E Mellen.

Rezeption, Interretation & Transformation Biblischer Motiv & Mythen in der DDR-Literatur & Ihre Bedeutung fuer die Theologie. Marie-Elisabeth Luedde. (Arbeiten zur Praktischen Theologie Ser.: Bd 4). vi, 178p. (GER.). (C). 1993. lib. bdg. 90.80 (3-11-013773-9) De Gruyter.

Rezeption und Interpretation der Aristotelischen Politica im Spaten Mittelalter, 2 vols., Set. Christoph Flueler. LC 92-37653. (Bochumer Studien zur Philosophie Ser.: No. 19, Bands 1 & 2). 1992. 144.00 (90-6032-337-8) Benjamins North Am.

Rezeption und Interpretation der Aristotelischen Politica im Spaten Mittelalter, 2 vols., Vol. 1. Christoph Flueler. LC 92-37653. (Bochumer Studien zur Philosophie Ser.: No. 19, Bands 1 & 2). xv, 335p. 1992. 59.00 (90-6032-335-1) Benjamins North Am.

Rezeption und Interpretation der Aristotelischen Politica im Spaten Mittelalter, 2 vols., Vol. 2. Christoph Flueler. LC 92-37653. (Bochumer Studien zur Philosophie Ser.: No. 19, Bands 1 & 2). vi, 209p. 1992. 85.00 (90-6032-336-X) Benjamins North Am.

Rezeption von Arthur Schnitzlers Reigen: Pressespiegel und Andere Zeitgenossische Kommentare. Gerd K. Schneider. (Studies in Austrian Literature, Culture & Thought; Translation Ser.). 634p. (GER.). 1995. 59.95 (1-57241-006-X) Ariadne CA.

RF & Microwave Circuit Design for Wireless Communications. Lawrence A. Larson. LC 95-49987. 1996. 89.00 (0-89006-818-6) Artech Hse.

RF & Microwave Digital Frequency Synthesizers: Theory & Design. Ulrich L. Rohde. LC 96-2841. 1996. text ed. write for info. (0-471-52019-5) Wiley.

RF & Microwave Matching Techniques. (Tech Edge Ser.). (Illus.). 125p. 1990. 25.00 (0-944916-14-7) Inter Con Tech.

***RF Circuit Design.** Chris Bowick. LC 96-51612. 1997. pap. write for info. (0-7506-9946-9) Buttrwrth-Heinemann.

RF Circuit Design. Christopher J. Bowick. LC 81-85517. 176p. 1982. 24.95 (0-672-21868-2) Buttrwrth-Heinemann.

RF Circuits: Practical Design & Layout for Wireless Communications. James S. Ussailis. (Illus.). 304p. 1997. text ed. 50.00 (0-07-065767-X) McGraw.

RF Design Guide: Systems, Circuits & Equations. Peter Vizmuller. LC 94-47188. 1995. 99.00 (0-89006-754-6) Artech Hse.

RF Plasma Heating in Toroidal Fusion Devices. V. E. Golant & V. I. Fedorov. Tr. by Donald H. McNeill from RUS. (Illus.). 202p. 1989. 89.50 (0-306-11021-0, Consultants) Plenum.

RF Radiation Safety Handbook. Ronald Kitchen. (Illus.). 336p. 1993. 69.95 (0-7506-1712-8) Buttrwrth-Heinemann.

RF Radiometer Handbook. G. Evans & C. W. McLeish. LC 77-501. 166p. reprint ed. pap. 47.40 (0-685-15293-6, 2027157) Bks Demand.

***RF Systems, Components, & Circuits Handbook.** Ferril Losee. LC 97-13330. (Microwave Engineering Ser.). 560p. 1997. 79.00 (0-89006-933-6) Artech Hse.

***RFC Communiques 1917-1918.** Ed. by Chaz Bowyer. (Illus.). 240p. 1998. 34.95 (1-898697-79-5, Pub. by Grub St Pubns UK) Seven Hills Bk.

RFC to the RAF India Nineteen Nineteen. John Ross. 122p. (Orig.). 1987. pap. 35.00 (0-7212-0792-8, Pub. by Regency Press UK) St Mut.

RFD Country! Mailboxes & Post Offices of Rural America. Sarah Thornbrook & Bill Thornbrook. LC 87-63477. (Illus.). 96p. 1988. pap. 14.95 (0-88740-121-X) Schiffer.

RFD No. 3. Harry W. Addison. LC 77-23069. 96p. 1977. audio 14.95 (0-88289-982-1) Pelican.

RFD #3. Harry Addison. 95p. (Orig.). 1994. pap. 7.95 (1-56554-114-6) Pelican.

RF/I Application 2000: A Guide to Understand & Using Radio Frequency Identification. unabridged ed. Jim Gerdeman. Ed. by Joanne LeRose. (Enabling Technology Ser.: No. 2). (Illus.). v, 229p. 1996. 42.50 (1-883872-01-4) Res Triangle.

***RFK.** David C. Heymann. 1998. pap. 24.95 (0-525-94217-3) NAL-Dutton.

RFK: Collected Speeches. Robert Kennedy. Date not set. pap. 12.00 (0-14-017656-X) Viking Penguin.

***RFP Process: Effective Management of the Acquisition of Library Materials.** Frances C. Wilkinson & Connie C. Thorson. 250p. 1997. lib. bdg. 30.00 (1-56308-481-3) Libs Unl.

RGCALC: Radar Range Detection Software & User's Manual. John Fielding. (Radar Library). 80p. 1987. 125.00 incl. disk (0-89006-270-6) Artech Hse.

RGP Lens Fitting. Carolyn Begly. (Contact Lens Update Ser.). 120p. 1997. 45.00 (0-7506-9677-X) Buttrwrth-Heinemann.

RGS Story Vol. 3: Over the Bridges, Vance Junction to Ophir. Russ Collman et al. (Illus.). 496p. 1993. 70.00 (0-913582-50-6, 0250) Sundance.

RGS Story Vol. 4: Over the Bridges, Ophir to Rico. Russ Collman et al. (Illus.). 496p. 1994. 70.00 (0-913582-58-1, 0252) Sundance.

RGS Story Vol. 5: Rico & the Mines. Russ Collman et al. (RGS Story Ser.: Vol. 5). (Illus.). 496p. 1996. 68.00 (0-913582-61-1, 0254) Sundance.

***RGS Story Vol. 6: Rico to Dolores.** Dell A. McCoy & Russ Collman. (Illus.). 480p. 1997. 70.00 (0-913582-63-8, 0256) Sundance.

Rgvedic Deities & Their Iconic Forms. Jyotsna Chawla. 1988. 56.00 (81-215-0082-6, Pub. by Munshiram Manoharial II) S Asia.

Rgvedic Deities & Their Iconic Forms. Jyotsna Chawla. (Illus.). 248p. 1990. reprint ed. 38.50 (81-215-0482-1, Pub. by M Manoharial II) Coronet Bks.

Rgvedic Society. Enric Aguilar i Matas. LC 90-21690. (Brill's Indological Library: Vol. 2). 174p. 1991. 64.50 (90-04-09352-4) E J Brill.

RH Dictionary-AMS. Date not set. pap. 5.99 (0-345-40524-2) Ballantine.

Rh Rhodium: Coordination Compounds with O- & N-Containing Ligands. 8th ed. (Gmelin Handbook of Inorganic & Organometallic Chemistry Ser.: Suppl. Vol. A1). (Illus.). xv, 275p. 1991. 1,050.00 (0-387-93639-4) Spr-Verlag.

RH Thesarus-AMS. Date not set. pap. 4.99 (0-345-40525-0) Ballantine.

Rhabdocline Needle Cast of Douglas Fir, No. 84. 1960. 0.80 (0-686-20696-7) SUNY Environ.

Rhabdomyosarcoma & Related Tumors in Children & Adolescents. Harold M. Maurer & Frederick B. Ruymann. (Illus.). 504p. 1991. 180.00 (0-8493-6902-9, RC281) CRC Pr.

Rhabdoviruses. Ed. by Robert R. Wagner. LC 87-12279. (Viruses Ser.). 562p. 1987. 135.00 (0-306-42453-3, Plenum Pr) Plenum.

Rhabdoviruses, Vol. I. David H. Bishop. 208p. 1979. 92.95 (0-8493-5913-9, QR415) CRC Pr.

Rhabdoviruses, 3 vols., Vol. II. David H. Bishop. 256p. 1980. 141.00 (0-8493-5914-7, QR415, CRC Reprint) Franklin.

Rhabdoviruses, 3 vols., Vol. III. David H. Bishop. 272p. 1980. 148.00 (0-8493-5915-5, CRC Reprint) Franklin.

Rhaeto-Romance Languages. John Haiman & Paola Beninca. LC 91-33772. (Romance Linguistics Ser.). 224p. (C). (gr. 13). 1992. text ed. 74.95 (0-415-04194-5, A6723) Routledge.

Rhamnus. Marshall A. Johnston & LaVerne A. Johnston. LC 78-16036. (Flora Neotropica Monographs: No. 20). (Illus.). 96p. 1978. pap. 10.00 (0-89327-209-4) NY Botanical.

Rhapsodie-On-The-Creek. Natalie L. Tawes. 120p. 1996. 12.00 (0-8059-3864-8) Dorrance.

***Rhapsodies: Poems from Hollywood.** Mark Dunster. 12p. (Orig.). (YA). (gr. 9-12). 1997. pap. 5.00 (0-89642-347-6) Linden Pubs.

***Rhapsodies in Black: Art of the Harlem Renaissance.** Richard J. Powell et al. LC 97-20475. 1997. write for info. (0-520-21263-0); pap. write for info. (0-520-21268-1) U CA Pr.

Rhapsodies of a Repeat Offender. Wayne Koestenbaum. 120p. 1995. pap. 12.95 (0-89255-212-3) Persea Bks.

Rhapsodies of a Repeat Offender: Poems. Wayne Koestenbaum. 120p. 1994. 22.95 (0-89255-200-X) Persea Bks.

Rhapsodist & Other Uncollected Writings. Charles B. Brown. LC 43-9591. 1977. 50.00 (0-8201-1203-8) Schol Facsimiles.

***Rhapsody.** Felicia Mason. 320p. 1997. mass mkt. 4.99 (0-7860-0404-5, Pinncle Kensgtn) Kensgtn Pub Corp.

Rhapsody. Arthur Schnitzler. Tr. by Otto P. Schinnerer. LC 70-175442. reprint ed. 37.50 (0-404-05614-8) AMS Pr.

***Rhapsody Developer's Guide.** Jesse Feiler. (Illus.). 350p. 1997. pap. 39.95 (0-12-251334-7, AP Prof) Acad Pr.

***Rhapsody from the Ground Up.** Harrington. 1998. pap. text ed. 27.95 (0-12-326424-3) Acad Pr.

***Rhapsody in Blue: The Chelsea Dream Team.** Rick Glanvill. (Illus.). 192p. 1997. 34.95 (1-85158-900-7, Pub. by Mnstream UK) Trafalgar.

Rhapsody in Blue & 45 Creative Piano Solos. 144p. (Orig.). 1994. pap. 14.95 (0-89724-317-X, PF0503) Warner Brothers.

***Rhapsody in D.** Todd Bruce. 96p. 1997. pap. 10.95 (0-88801-211-X, Pub. by Turnstone CN) LPC InBook.

***Rhapsody in St Stephen's Green: The Insect Play.** Flann O'Brien & Robert Tracy. 88p. 9400. pap. 12.95 (1-874675-27-9) Dufour.

Rhapsody in Time. Judith O'Brien. Ed. by Linda Marrow. 304p. (Orig.). 1994. mass mkt. 5.50 (0-671-87148-X) PB.

***Rhapsody of Scripture.** Richard M. Cromie. 48p. 1996. pap. 5.95 (0-914733-20-6) Desert Min.

Rhapsody on a Theme by Clement Marot. Douglas R. Hofstadter. (Grace A. Tanner Lecture in Human Values Ser.). 72p. 1995. 10.00 (0-910153-11-6) E T Woolf.

***Rhapsody's Song.** Patricia Hagan. 1998. mass mkt. 5.99 (0-451-40798-9, Onyx) NAL-Dutton.

RHCDS (FmHA) Housing Programs: Tenants' & Homeowners' Rights. 2nd rev. ed. National Housing Law Project Staff. 600p. 1995. pap. 95.00 (0-9606098-7-3) Natl Housing Law.

Rhea Complex: A Detour Around the Oedipus Complex. Akhter Ahsen. LC 84-72149. 279p. 1984. 35.00 (0-913412-24-4) Brandon Hse.

***Rhea County Tennessee Circuit Court Minutes: September 1815-March 1836.** Carol Wells. 172p. (Orig.). 1996. pap. 18.50 (0-7884-0468-7, W152) Heritage Bk.

***Rhea County, Tennessee Tax Lists 1832-1834, & County Court Minutes, 1829-1834: Minutes, 1829-1834, Vol. D.** Carol Wells. vi, 168p. (Orig.). 1996. pap. 20.00 (0-7884-0554-3, W153) Heritage Bk.

Rheatown, Tennessee. Rheatown United Methodist Women Staff. (Illus.). 113p. (YA). 1997. reprint ed. pap. text ed. 9.95 (0-932807-18-6) Overmountain Pr.

Rheingold: Libretto. Richard Wagner. 68p. (GER.). 1986. pap. 4.95 (0-7935-5610-4, 50340490) H Leonard.

***Rheingold: Translation & Commentary.** Richard Wagner. (Illus.). 1997. pap. 14.95 (0-7148-3651-6, Pub. by Phaidon Press UK) Chronicle Bks.

Rheinland Market: Poetry. Boria Sax. 32p. (Orig.). 1980. pap. 2.00 (0-938838-02-4) Textile Bridge.

Rhenish Massif: Structure, Evolution, Mineral Deposits & Present Geodynamics. Ed. by Andreas Vogel et al. (Earth Evolution Sciences Ser.). vi, 160p. 1987. 64.00 (3-528-08967-9, Pub. by Vieweg & Sohn GW) Informatica.

An Asterisk (*) at the beginning of an entry indicates that the title is appearing in BIP for the first time.

*Rhenish Wares. R. Symonds. (Illus.). 180p. 1992. pap. 50.00 (0-947816-23-2, Pub. by Oxford Univ Comm Arch UK) David Brown.

Rhenohercynian & Subvariscan Fold Belts. (Earth Evolution Science Ser.). 390p. 1993. 163.00 (3-528-06488-9) Informatica.

Rheo-Physics of Multiphase Polymer Systems: Characterization by Rheo-Optical Techniques. Ed. by K. Sondergaard & J. Lyngaae-Jorgensen. LC 95-61428. 600p. 1995. pap. text ed. 149.95 (1-56676-156-5) Technomic.

Rheological & Thermophysical Properties of Greases. G. B. Froishterer et al. Ed. by G. V. Vinogradov. 288p. 1988. text ed. 295.00 (2-88124-673-7) Gordon & Breach.

Rheological Fundamentals of Polymer Processing: Proceedings of the NATO Advanced Study Institute, Alvor, Portugal, September 16 - October 8, 1994. Ed. by J. A. Covas et al. (NATO Advanced Science Institutes Ser.: Series E). 463p. (C). 1995. lib. bdg. 218.00 (0-7923-3792-1) Kluwer Ac.

Rheological Methods in Food Process Engineering. James F. Steffe. LC 91-78360. 240p. (C). 1992. text ed. 65.00 (0-9632036-0-6) Freeman Pr.

Rheological Methods in Food Process Engineering. 2nd ed. James F. Steffe. LC 96-83538. 418p. 1996. text ed. 65.00 (0-9632036-1-4) Freeman Pr.

Rheological Modelling: Thermodynamical & Statistical Approaches: Proceedings of the Meeting Held at the Bellatara School of Thermodynamics, Autonomous University of Barcelona, Sant Feliu de Gu, Catalonia, Spain, 24-28 Sept. 1990. Ed. by J. Casas-Vazquez & D. Jou. x, 378p. 1991. 56.95 (0-387-53996-4) Spr-Verlag.

Rheological Parameters of Soils & Design of Foundations. Z. G. Ter-Martirosyan. Tr. by N. K. Mehta from RUS. (Russian Translation Ser.). (Illus.). 195p. (C). 1992. text ed. 75.00 (90-5410-211-X, Pub. by A A Balkema NE) Ashgate Pub Co.

Rheological Phenomena in Focus. D. V. Boger & K. Walters. (Rheological Ser.: Vol. 4). 166p. 1993. 156.25 (0-444-89473-X) Elsevier.

Rheological Properties of Cosmetics & Toiletries. Laba. (Cosmetic Science & Technology Ser.: Vol. 13). 440p. 1993. 199.00 (0-8247-9090-1) Dekker.

Rheological Properties of Lubricants. Jean Briant et al. (Illus.). 296p. (C). 1989. 530.00 (2-7108-0564-2, Pub. by Edits Technip FR) St Mut.

Rheology: Principles, Measurements, & Applications. Christopher W. Macosko. LC 93-31652. (Advances in Interfacial Engineering Ser.). 1994. 95.00 (1-56081-579-5, VCH) Wiley.

*Rheology: Principles, Measurements & Applications. Christopher W. Macosko. 1994. text ed. 95.00 (0-471-18575-2) Wiley.

Rheology & Elastohydrodynamic Lubrication. B. O. Jacobson. (Tribology Ser.: Vol. 19). 382p. 1991. 191.50 (0-444-88146-8, TRS 19) Elsevier.

*Rheology & Fluid Mechanics of Nonlinear Materials: Proceedings, ASME International Mechanical Engineering Congress & Exposition, 1996, Atlanta, Georgia. Ed. by Dennis A. Siginer & S. G. Advani. LC 96-78669. (AMD Ser.: Vol. 217). 315p. 1996. pap. text ed. 100.00 (0-7918-1526-9) ASME Pr.

Rheology & Non-Newtonian Flow. Ed. by Nicholas P. Cheremisinoff. (Encyclopedia of Fluid Mechanics Ser.: Vol. 7). 1184p. 1988. 195.00 (0-87201-540-8, 1540) Gulf Pub.

Rheology & Non-Newtonian Flow. John Harris. LC 76-49635. 376p. reprint ed. pap. 107.20 (0-317-27686-7, 2025217) Bks Demand.

*Rheology for Polymer Melt Processing. J. M. Piau & J. F. Agassant. LC 96-31377. (Rheological Ser.: Vol. 5). 434p. 1996. 240.75 (0-444-82236-4) Elsevier.

*Rheology of Fresh Cement & Concrete: Proceedings of an International Conference, Liverpool, 1990. Ed. by Banfill. (Illus.). 384p. 1990. text ed. 101.95 (0-419-15360-8, E & FN Spon) Routledge Chapman & Hall.

*Rheology of Industrial Polysaccharides: Theory & Applications. R. Lapasin & S. Pricl. (Illus.). 640p. 1995. text ed. 169.95 (0-7514-0211-7, Pub. by Blackie Acad & Prof UK) Routledge Chapman & Hall.

Rheology of Liquid Crystals. P. K. Khabibullaev et al. Ed. by Yu V. Gulyaev. 1994. 95.00 (0-89864-077-6) Allerton Pr.

Rheology of Lubricants. Ed. by T. C. Davenport. (Illus.). 148p. 1973. 39.75 (0-85334-473-6, Pub. by Elsevier Applied Sci UK) Elsevier.

*Rheology of Polymeric Systems: Principles & Applications. Pierre J. Carreau et al. LC 96-36329. 1997. write for info. (1-56990-218-6) Hanser-Gardner.

Rheology of Solids & of the Earth. Ed. by Shun-ichiro Karato & Mitsuhiro Toriumi. (Illus.). 448p. 1989. 115.00 (0-19-854497-9) OUP.

*Rheology of the Earth. 2nd ed. Giorgio Ranalli. (Illus.). 432p. (Orig.). 1995. pap. text ed. 45.00 (0-412-54670-1, Chap & Hall NY) Chapman & Hall.

Rheology of the Earth: Deformation & Flow Processes in Geophysics & Geodynamics. Giorgio Ranalli. LC 86-17311. 388p. 1987. text ed. 100.00 (0-04-551110-1); pap. text ed. 39.95 (0-04-551111-X) Routledge Chapman & Hall.

Rheometers for Molten Plastics: A Practical Guide to Testing & Property Measurement. John M. Dealy. 300p. (gr. 13). 1981. text ed. 82.95 (0-442-21874-5) Chapman & Hall.

Rheometry, Industrial Applications. Ed. by Kenneth Walters. LC 80-40956. (Materials Science Research Studies: No. 1). (Illus.). 426p. reprint ed. pap. 121.50 (0-8357-4555-4, 2037454) Bks Demand.

Rheophytes of the World: An Account of Flood - Resistant Flowering Plants & Ferns & the Theory of Autonomous Evolution. C. G. Van Steenis. 424p. 1981. lib. bdg. 175.00 (90-286-0840-0) Kluwer Ac.

Rheostasis: The Physiology of Change. Nicholas Mrosovsky. (Illus.). 192p. 1990. 60.00 (0-19-506184-5) OUP.

Rheotribology of Automotive Lubricants & Fluids. 220p. 1994. pap. 74.00 (1-56091-567-6, SP1055) Soc Auto Engineers.

RhErythropoietin in Cancer Supportive Treatment. Ed. by John F. Smyth et al. 288p. 1996. 99.75 (0-8247-9761-2) Dekker.

Rhesus see Euripides: Four Tragedies

Rhesus see Works

Rhetores Latini Minores. Ed. by C. Halm. (Classical Studies Ser.). (LAT.). reprint ed. lib. bdg. 49.00 (0-697-00038-9) Irvington.

Rhetoric. Peter Dixon. (Critical Idiom Ser.: Vol. 19). 1971. pap. 8.95 (0-416-66760-0, NO. 2166) Routledge Chapman & Hall.

Rhetoric. rev. ed. Covino & Jolliffe. 1995. pap. text ed. 50.00 (0-205-18462-6) P-H.

Rhetoric: Discovery & Change. Richard E. Young et al. 383p. (C). 1970. text ed. 24.00 (0-15-576895-6) HB Coll Pubs.

Rhetoric: Essays in Invention & Discovery. Richard McKeon. LC 86-28574. xxxiv, 220p. (C). 1987. 30.00 (0-918024-49-8) Ox Bow.

*Rhetoric Affirmative Resistance. Wolfreys. LC 96-50909. 1997. text ed. 49.95 (0-312-17330-X); text ed. 18.95 (0-312-17331-8) St Martin.

Rhetoric & American Poetry of the Early National Period. Gordon E. Bigelow. LC 60-63133. (University of Florida Humanities Monographs: No. 4). 86p. reprint ed. pap. 25.00 (0-7837-5027-7, 2044695) Bks Demand.

Rhetoric & American Statesmanship. Ed. by Glen E. Thurow & Jeffrey D. Wallin. LC 83-70310. 151p. 1984. pap. text ed. 12.50 (0-89089-255-5) Carolina Acad Pr.

Rhetoric & Argumentation. David L. Vancil. 352p. (C). 1992. text ed. 52.00 (0-205-13592-7) Allyn.

Rhetoric & Civility: Human Development, Narcissism, & the Good Audience. Harold Barrett. LC 90-32467. (SUNY Series in Speech Communication). 202p. (C). 1991. text ed. 64.50 (0-7914-0483-8); pap. text ed. 21.95 (0-7914-0484-6) State U NY Pr.

Rhetoric & Composition: A Sourcebook for Teachers & Writers. 3rd ed. Ed. by Richard Graves. LC 90-40515. 321p. (C). 1990. pap. text ed. 25.00 (0-86709-268-8, 0268) Boynton Cook Pubs.

Rhetoric & Criticism. Marie H. Nichols. LC 63-7958. 161p. 1963. pap. 45.90 (0-7837-8514-3, 2049323) Bks Demand.

Rhetoric & Culture in Lacan. Gilbert D. Chaitin. (Literature, Culture, Theory Ser.: No. 19). 264p. (C). 1996. text ed. 54.95 (0-521-49728-0); pap. text ed. 17.95 (0-521-49765-5) Cambridge U Pr.

Rhetoric & Death: The Language of Modernism & Postmodern Discourse Theory. Ronald Schleifer. 264p. 1990. text ed. 29.95 (0-252-01740-4) U of Ill Pr.

Rhetoric & Ethics: Historical & Theoretical Perspectives. Ed. by Victoria Aarons & Willis A. Salomon. LC 90-21255. 220p. 1991. lib. bdg. 89.95 (0-88946-212-7) E Mellen.

*Rhetoric & Hermeneutics in Our Time. Walter Jost & Michael J. Hyde. LC 96-45205. (Yale University Studies in Hermeneutics Ser.). 1997. write for info. (0-300-06836-0) Yale U Pr.

Rhetoric & History in Revolutionary New England. Donald Weber. 224p. 1988. 39.95 (0-19-505104-1) OUP.

Rhetoric & Homiletics in Fourth-Century Christian Literature: Prose Rhythm, Oratorical Style, & Preaching in the Works of Ambrose, Jerome, & Augustine. Steven M. Oberhelman. 199p. 1991. 29.95 (1-55540-617-3); pap. 19.95 (1-55540-618-1) Scholars Pr GA.

Rhetoric & Human Understanding. Ann Gill. 265p. (Orig.). (C). 1994. pap. text ed. 14.95 (0-88133-775-7) Waveland Pr.

Rhetoric & Irony: Western Literacy & Western Lies. C. Jan Swearingen. 344p. 1991. 42.00 (0-19-506362-7) OUP.

Rhetoric & Moral Philosophy see Florentine Codex, General History of the Things of New Spain

Rhetoric & Pedagogy: Its History, Philosophy, & Practice. Essays in Honor of James J. Murphy. Ed. by Winifred B. Horner & Michael C. Leff. 352p. 1995. text ed. 69.95 (0-8058-1821-9) L Erlbaum Assocs.

Rhetoric & Pedagogy: Its History, Philosophy, & Practice. Essays in Honor of James J. Murphy. Ed. by Winifred B. Horner & Michael C. Leff. 352p. 1995. pap. 34.50 (0-8058-1822-7) L Erlbaum Assocs.

Rhetoric & Philosophy. Ed. by Richard A. Cherwitz. 336p. (C). 1990. text ed. 49.95 (0-8058-0413-7) L Erlbaum Assocs.

Rhetoric & Philosophy in Conflict. Samuel Ijsseling. 142p. 1977. pap. text ed. 49.00 (90-247-1901-1, Pub. by M Nijhoff NE) Kluwer Ac.

Rhetoric & Philosophy in Hobbes's Leviathan. rev. ed. Raia Prokhovnik. LC 91-10709. (Political Theory & Political Philosophy Ser.). 268p. 1991. 20.00 (0-8153-0142-1) Garland.

Rhetoric & Pluralism: Legacies of Wayne Booth. Ed. by Frederick J. Antczak. 304p. 1995. 59.50 (0-8142-0642-5) Ohio St U Pr.

Rhetoric & Poetic in Thomas More's Utopia. A. F. Kinney. 36p. 1979. pap. 8.50 (0-89003-025-1) Undena Pubns.

Rhetoric & Poetics of Aristotle. Aristotle. (Modern Library College Editions). 250p. (C). 1984. pap. text ed. write for info. (0-07-554602-7) McGraw.

*Rhetoric & Political Culture in Nineteenth-Century America. Ed. by Thomas W. Benson. (Rhetoric & Public Affairs Ser.: No. 6). 215p. 1996. 31.95 (0-87013-468-X) Mich St U Pr.

*Rhetoric & Politics: Baltasar Gracian & the New World Order. Nicholas Spadaccini & Jenaro Talens. LC 96-39456. (Hispanic Issues Ser.). 1997. pap. text ed. 24.95 (0-8166-2911-0) U of Minn Pr.

*Rhetoric & Politics: Baltasar Gracian & the New World Order. Nicholas Spadaccini & Jenaro Talens. LC 96-39456. (Hispanic Issues Ser.). 1997. text ed. 62.95 (0-8166-2910-2) U of Minn Pr.

Rhetoric & Praxis: The Contribution of Classical Rhetoric to Practical Reasoning. Ed. by Jean D. Moss. LC 85-25449. 184p. reprint ed. pap. 52.50 (0-7837-4631-8, 2044354) Bks Demand.

Rhetoric & Public Address: A Bibliography, 1947-1961. James W. Cleary & Frederick W. Haberman. LC 64-7959. 506p. reprint ed. pap. 144.30 (0-317-10231-1, 2021132) Bks Demand.

Rhetoric & Reaction in Trito-Isaiah: The Structure, Growth & Authorship of Isaiah 56 - 66. P. A. Smith. LC 95-7526. (Supplements to Vetus Testamentum Ser.: Vol. 62). 1995. 68.00 (90-04-10306-6) E J Brill.

Rhetoric & Reality: Writing Instruction in American Colleges, 1900-1985. James A. Berlin. LC 86-20428. (Studies in Writing & Rhetoric). 236p. 1987. pap. text ed. 12.95 (0-8093-1360-X) S Ill U Pr.

Rhetoric & Reality in Environmental Policy: The Case of the Netherlands in Comparison with Britain. Ed. by Michael Wintle & Rachel Reeve. LC 94-15640. (Avebury Studies in Green Research). 1994. 55.95 (1-85628-927-3, Pub. by Avebury Pub UK) Ashgate Pub Co.

Rhetoric & Reality in Plato's Phaedrus. David A. White. LC 91-43967. (SUNY Series in Ancient Greek Philosophy). 340p. (C). 1993. pap. text ed. 21.95 (0-7914-1234-2) State U NY Pr.

Rhetoric & Reality in Plato's Phaedrus. David A. White. LC 91-43967. (SUNY Series in Ancient Greek Philosophy). 340p. (C). 1993. text ed. 64.50 (0-7914-1233-4) State U NY Pr.

Rhetoric & Reference in the Fourth Gospel. Margaret Davies. (JSNT Supplement Ser.: No. 69). 400p. 75.00 (1-85075-345-8, Pub. by Sheffield Acad UK) CUP Services.

*Rhetoric & Representation in Nonfiction Film. Carl R. Plantinga. (Studies in Film). 272p. (C). 1997. text ed. 54.95 (0-521-57326-2) Cambridge U Pr.

Rhetoric & Response: Great American Orators: Critical Studies, Speeches, & Sources, No. 3. Calvin M. Logue & Eugene Talmadge. LC 88-24748. 325p. 1989. text ed. 59.95 (0-313-25855-4, LUE, Greenwood Pr) Greenwood.

Rhetoric & Ritual in Colonial India: The Shaping of a Public Culture in Surat City, 1852-1928. Douglas Haynes. 400p. 1991. 55.00 (0-520-06725-8) U CA Pr.

Rhetoric & Ritual in the Theology of Philip Melanchthon: To Move the Heart. Michael B. Aune. 136p. 1995. 54.95 (1-883255-35-X); pap. 34.95 (1-883255-34-1) Intl Scholars.

*Rhetoric & Social Influence. Robert Rowland. 260p. (C). 1996. per., pap. text ed. 41.95 (0-7872-2605-X) Kendall-Hunt.

Rhetoric & Style: Strategies for Advanced Writers. Nevin K. Laib. LC 92-22827. 408p. (C). 1993. pap. text ed. 20.40 (0-13-478967-9) P-H.

Rhetoric & the Arts of Design. David S. Kaufer & Brian Butler. 232p. 1996. pap. 27.50 (0-8058-2146-5); text ed. 59.95 (0-8058-2145-7) L Erlbaum Assocs.

Rhetoric & the Founders. Arthur M. Schlesinger. LC 87-14260. (Exxon Education Foundation Series of Rhetoric & Political Discourse: Vol. 3). 102p. (Orig.). 1987. pap. text ed. 14.50 (0-8191-6466-6) U Pr of Amer.

Rhetoric & the New Testament: Essays from the 1992 Heidelberg Conference. Ed. by Stanley E. Porter & Thomas H. Olbricht. (Journal for the Study of the New Testament Supplement Ser.: No. 90). 538p. 80.00 (1-85075-449-7, Pub. by Sheffield Acad UK) CUP Services.

Rhetoric & the Origins of Medieval Drama. Jody Enders. LC 92-2798. (Rhetoric & Society Ser.). 304p. 1992. 37.50 (0-8014-2655-3) Cornell U Pr.

Rhetoric & the Poetics. Aristotle. Tr. by Ingram Bywater. LC 54-9971. 289p. 1977. 13.50 (0-394-60425-3, Modern Lib) Random.

Rhetoric & Theology: The Hermeneutic of Erasmus. Manfred Hoffmann. (Erasmus Studies). 248p. 1994. 70.00 (0-8020-0579-9) U of Toronto Pr.

Rhetoric As Philosophy: The Humanist Tradition. Ernesto Grassi. LC 79-25276. 1980. text ed. 25.00 (0-271-00256-5) Pa St U Pr.

Rhetoric As Social Imagination: Explorations in the Interpersonal Function of Language. George L. Dillon. LC 85-45069. 186p. (C). 1986. 26.95 (0-253-35011-5) Ind U Pr.

Rhetoric at Rome: A Historical Survey. rev. ed. M. L. Clarke. LC 96-3816. (Classical Studies). 224p. (C). 1996. pap. 18.95 (0-415-14156-7); text ed. 59.95 (0-415-14155-9) Routledge.

*Rhetoric Canon. Ed. by Brenda D. Schildgen. LC 97-16334. 280p. (Orig.). (C). 1997. pap. text ed. 24.95 (0-8143-2632-3) Wayne St U Pr.

Rhetoric, Comedy, & the Violence of Language in Aristophanes' Clouds. Daphne O'Regan. 432p. 1992. 55.00 (0-19-507017-8) OUP.

Rhetoric, Cultural Studies, & Literacy: Selected Papers from the 1994 Conference of the Rhetoric Society of America. Ed. by John F. Reynolds. 200p. 1995. 39.95 (0-8058-1608-9) L Erlbaum Assocs.

Rhetoric, Cultural Studies, & Literacy: Selected Papers from the 1994 Conference of the Rhetoric Society of America. Ed. by John F. Reynolds. 200p. 1995. pap. 19.95 (0-8058-1609-7) L Erlbaum Assocs.

Rhetoric for a Formation of Intention. Edward R. Heidt. LC 94-12137. (Catholic Scholars Press Ser.). 1995. 64.95 (1-883255-63-5); pap. 44.95 (1-883255-62-7) Intl Scholars.

Rhetoric for Academic Reasoning. Bensel-Meyers. (C). 1991. 10.00 (0-06-500403-5) Addson-Wesley Educ.

Rhetoric for Academic Reasoning. Bensel-Meyers. (C). 1992. teacher ed., text ed. 29.95 (0-06-040627-5) Addson-Wesley Educ.

*Rhetoric for Human Science. Hansen. 1997. pap. text ed. 26.67 (0-13-440272-3) P-H.

Rhetoric for Today. 6th ed. William F. Smith & Raymond D. Liedlich. 267p. (C). 1983. pap. text ed. 18.75 (0-15-577057-8) HB Coll Pubs.

Rhetoric for Writing Teachers. 3rd ed. Erika C. Lindemann. (Illus.). 320p. (C). 1995. pap. text ed. 21.95 (0-19-508844-1) OUP.

*Rhetoric, Hermeneutics & Translation in the Middle Ages: Academic Traditions & Vernacular Texts. 309p. 1995. pap. text ed. 23.95 (0-521-48365-4) Cambridge U Pr.

Rhetoric, Hermeneutics & Translation in the Middle Ages: Academic Traditions & Vernacular Texts. Rita Copeland. (Studies in Medieval Literature: No. 11). (Illus.). 350p. (C). 1991. text ed. 69.95 (0-521-38517-2) Cambridge U Pr.

Rhetoric in American Colleges, 1850-1900. Albert R. Kitzhaber. LC 90-52657. (SMU Studies in Composition & Rhetoric). 320p. 1990. text ed. 24.95 (0-87074-308-2); pap. text ed. 15.95 (0-87074-309-0) SMU Press.

*Rhetoric in an Antifoundational World: Language, Culture, & Pedagogy. Michael F. Bernard-Donals & Richard R. Glejzer. LC 97-19675. 1998. write for info. (0-300-07022-5) Yale U Pr.

Rhetoric in an Organizational Society: Managing Multiple Identities. George Cheney. Ed. by Thomas W. Benson. LC 90-20305. (Studies in Rhetoric & Communication). 213p. (C). 1991. text ed. 34.95 (0-87249-733-X) U of SC Pr.

Rhetoric in Greco-Roman Education. Donald L. Clark. LC 77-21723. 285p. 1977. reprint ed. text ed. 62.50 (0-8371-9790-2, CLRH, Greenwood Pr) Greenwood.

Rhetoric in Popular Culture. Barry Brummett. 256p. 1993. pap. text ed. 18.00 (0-312-06539-6) St Martin.

Rhetoric in the European Tradition. Thomas M. Conley. 325p. (C). 1990. text ed. 34.50 (0-8013-0256-0, 75909) Longman.

Rhetoric in the European Tradition. Thomas M. Conley. LC 93-32600. 336p. 1993. pap. text ed. 14.95 (0-226-11489-9) U Ch Pr.

Rhetoric in the New World: Rhetorical Theory & Practice in Colonial Spanish America. Don P. Abbott. LC 95-41775. (Studies in Rhetoric/Communication). (Illus.). 140p. 1996. text ed. 24.95 (1-57003-085-5) U of SC Pr.

Rhetoric in the War on Drugs: The Triumphs & Tragedies of Public Relations. Willian N. Elwood. LC 93-50065. 200p. 1994. text ed. 52.95 (0-275-94709-2, Praeger Pubs) Greenwood.

Rhetoric in Transition: Studies in the Nature & Uses of Rhetoric. Ed. by Eugene E. White. LC 79-15061. 1980. text ed. 30.00 (0-271-00223-9) Pa St U Pr.

Rhetoric, Innovation, Technology: Case Studies of Technical Communication in Technology Transfers. Stephen Doheny-Farina. (Illus.). 225p. 1992. 42.00 (0-262-04129-4) MIT Pr.

Rhetoric, Language, & Reason. Michel Meyer. LC 92-41696. (Literature & Philosophy Ser.). 192p. (C). 1994. 29.75 (0-271-01057-6); pap. text ed. 16.95 (0-271-01058-4) Pa St U Pr.

Rhetoric, Literature, & Interpretation. Ed. by Harry R. Garvin. LC 83-2553. (Bucknell Review Ser.: Vol. 28, No. 2). (Illus.). 184p. 1983. 22.00 (0-8387-5057-5) Bucknell U Pr.

Rhetoric Made Plain. 5th ed. Anthony C. Winkler & Jo R. McCuen. 555p. (C). 1988. text ed. 24.00 (0-15-577081-0); pap. text ed. 2.00 (0-15-577082-9) HB Coll Pubs.

Rhetoric Made Plain. 6th ed. Allan M. Winkler. (C). 1994. pap. text ed. 20.75 (0-15-501483-8) HB Coll Pubs.

Rhetoric of Agitation & Control. 2nd ed. John Bowers et al. (Illus.). 159p. (C). 1993. pap. text ed. 12.95 (0-88133-712-9) Waveland Pr.

Rhetoric of American Politics: A Study of Documents. William R. Smith. LC 71-95503. 464p. 1970. text ed. 75.00 (0-8371-1495-0, SMA/, Greenwood Pr) Greenwood.

*Rhetoric of American Romance: Dialectic & Identity in Emerson, Dickinson, Poe, & Hawthorne. Evan Carton. LC 84-27770. 301p. 1985. reprint ed. pap. 85.80 (0-608-03645-5, 2064471) Bks Demand.

Rhetoric of Antinuclear Fiction: Persuasive Strategies in Novels & Films. Patrick Mannix. LC 91-55466. 192p. 1992. 36.50 (0-8387-5218-7) Bucknell U Pr.

Rhetoric of Argument. 2nd ed. Jeanne Fahnestock & Marie Secor. 1990. pap. text ed. write for info. (0-07-557734-8) McGraw.

Rhetoric of Aristotle. Tr. by Lane Cooper. (Orig.). 1960. pap. text ed. 19.20 (0-13-780692-2) P-H.

Rhetoric of Aristotle, 2 Vols. Aristotle. Ed. by John E. Sandys. LC 72-9304. (Philosophy of Plato & Aristotle Ser.). (ENG & GRE.). 1980. reprint ed. 66.95 (0-405-04858-0) Ayer.

Rhetoric of Aristotle, 3 vols., Set. Ed. by John Edwin. 1970. reprint ed. 225.00 (0-685-66428-7) G Olms Pubs.

Rhetoric of Aristotle with a Commentary, 3 vols., 1. E. M. Cope. Ed. by John E. Sandys. (Classical Studies Ser.). (ENG & GRE.). reprint ed. lib. bdg. 59.00 (0-697-00033-8) Irvington.

R

Rhetoric of Aristotle with a Commentary, 3 vols., 2. E. M. Cope. Ed. by John W. Sandys. (Classical Studies Ser.). (ENG & GRE.). reprint ed. lib. bdg. 59.00 (0-697-00034-6) Irvington.

Rhetoric of Aristotle with a Commentary, 3 vols., 3. E. M. Cope. Ed. by John E. Sandys. (Classical Studies Ser.). (ENG & GRE.). reprint ed. lib. bdg. 59.00 (0-697-00035-4) Irvington.

Rhetoric of Aristotle with a Commentary, 3 vols., Set. E. M. Cope. Ed. by John E. Sandys. (Classical Studies Ser.). (ENG & GRE.). reprint ed. lib. bdg. 177.00 (0-89197-922-0) Irvington.

Rhetoric of Berkeley's Philosophy. Peter Walmsley. (Studies in Eighteenth-Century English Literature & Thought: No. 6). 288p. (C). 1990. text ed. 59.95 (0-521-37413-8) Cambridge U Pr.

Rhetoric of Black Power. Compiled by Robert L. Scott & Wayne Brockriede. LC 78-31755. 207p. 1979. reprint ed. text ed. 38.50 (0-313-20973-1, SCRB, Greenwood Pr) Greenwood.

Rhetoric of Blair, Campbell, & Whately: With Updated Bibliographies. James L. Golden & Edward P. Corbett. LC 89-11485. (Landmarks in Rhetoric & Public Address Ser.). 414p. (C). 1990. pap. 19.95 (0-8093-1602-1) S Ill U Pr.

Rhetoric of Bourgeois Revolution: The Abbe Sieyes & What Is the Third Estate? William H. Sewell, Jr. LC 94-16703. (Bicentennial Reflections on the French Revolution Ser.). 248p. 1994. text ed. 36.95 (0-8223-1528-9); pap. text ed. 11.95 (0-8223-1538-6) Duke.

Rhetoric of Change: Metaphor & Politics in the Commonwealth of Puerto Rico. J. Delgado-Figueroa. LC 94-96402. (Illus.). 364p. (Orig.). 1994. pap. 17.95 (0-9643486-0-8) Hispanic Caribbean.

Rhetoric of Church & State: A Critical Analysis of Religion Clause Jurisprudence. Frederick M. Gedicks. LC 95-10337. 184p. 1995. text ed. 49.95 (0-8223-1654-4); pap. text ed. 18.95 (0-8223-1666-8) Duke.

Rhetoric of Cicero's "Pro Cluentio" John T. Kirby. (London Studies in Classical Philology: Vol. 23). xii, 218p. 1990. pap. 47.00 (90-5063-044-8, Pub. by Gieben NE) Benjamins North Am.

Rhetoric of Concealment: Figuring Gender & Class in Renaissance Literature. Rosemary Kegl. 208p. 1994. 32.50 (0-8014-3016-X) Cornell U Pr.

Rhetoric of Confession: Shishosetsu in Early Twentieth Century Japanese Fiction. Edward Fowler. 1988. 45.00 (0-520-06064-4); pap. 16.00 (0-520-07883-7) U CA Pr.

Rhetoric of Conflict. Ed. by Kenneth R. Johnston. LC 79-97751. (Composition & Rhetoric Ser). (Orig.). (C). 1969. pap. write for info. (0-672-60905-3, CR19, Bobbs) Macmillan.

Rhetoric of Conservatism: The Virginia Convention of 1829-30 & the Conservative Tradition in the South. Dickson D. Bruce. LC 82-9224. (Illus.). 240p. reprint ed. pap. 68.40 (0-7837-6681-5, 2046297) Bks Demand.

Rhetoric of Courtship in Elizabethan Language & Literature. Catherine Bates. (Illus.). 262p. (C). 1992. text ed. 69.95 (0-521-41480-6) Cambridge U Pr.

Rhetoric of Curse in Galatians: Paul Confronts Another Gospel. Kjell A. Morland. LC 93-39947. (Emory University Studies in Early Christianity). 368p. (C). 1996. 44.95 (1-55540-923-7, 700605) Scholars Pr GA.

Rhetoric of David O. McKay: Mormon Prophet. Richard N. Armstrong. LC 93-17292. (American University Studies: Theology & Religion: Ser. VII, Vol. 92). 144p. (C). 1994. text ed. 35.95 (0-8204-2293-2) P Lang Pubng.

Rhetoric of Doing: Essays on Written Discourse in Honor of James L. Kinneavy. Ed. by Stephen P. Witte et al. 384p. (C). 1992. 29.95 (0-8093-1531-9); pap. 19.95 (0-8093-1532-7) S Ill U Pr.

Rhetoric of Doubtful Authority: Deconstructive Readings of Self-Questioning Narratives, St. Augustine to Faulkner. Ralph Flores. LC 83-15297. 176p. 1984. 32.50 (0-8014-1625-6) Cornell U Pr.

Rhetoric of Dreams. Bert O. States. LC 88-47766. 240p. 1988. 32.50 (0-8014-2198-5) Cornell U Pr.

Rhetoric of Economics. Donald N. McCloskey. LC 85-40373. (Rhetoric of the Human Sciences Ser.). 232p. 1987. reprint ed. pap. 14.95 (0-299-10384-6) U of Wis Pr.

Rhetoric of Electronic Communities. Ed. by Tharon W. Howard. (New Directions of Computers & Composition Studies). (Illus.). 220p. 1997. pap. 39.50 (1-56750-295-4); text ed. 73.25 (1-56750-294-6) Ablex Pub.

Rhetoric of Empire: Colonial Discourse in Journalism, Travel Writing, & Imperial Administration. David Spurr. LC 92-23232. 223p. (C). 1993. text ed. 42.95 (0-8223-1303-0); pap. text ed. 16.95 (0-8223-1317-0) Duke.

Rhetoric of Empiricism: Language & Perception, from Locke to I. A. Richards. Jules D. Law. LC 92-44276. 280p. (C). 1993. 37.50 (0-8014-2706-1) Cornell U Pr.

Rhetoric of English India. Sara Suleri. LC 91-13014. (Illus.). x, 240p. (C). 1992. pap. text ed. 12.95 (0-226-77983-1) U Ch Pr.

Rhetoric of Eugenics in Anglo-American Thought. Marouf A. Hasian, Jr. LC 95-13953. (University of Georgia Humanities Center Series on Science & the Humanities). 1996. 40.00 (0-8203-1771-3) U of Ga Pr.

Rhetoric of Everyday English Texts. Michael P. Jordan. (Illus.). 192p. (C). 1984. text ed. 49.95 (0-04-420047-1) Routledge Chapman & Hall.

Rhetoric of Failure: Deconstruction of Skepticism, Reinvention of Modernism. Ewa P. Ziarek. LC 95-1439. (SUNY Series, the Margins of Literature). 247p. 1995. text ed. 59.50 (0-7914-2711-0); pap. text ed. 19.95 (0-7914-2712-9) State U NY Pr.

Rhetoric of Fiction. 2nd ed. Wayne C. Booth. LC 82-13592. 576p. 1983. pap. text ed. 16.95 (0-226-06558-8) U Ch Pr.

Rhetoric of Gender Terms: 'Man', 'Woman', & the Portrayal of Character in Latin Prose. Francesca Santoro-L'Hoir. LC 91-34906. (Mnemosyne Ser.: Supplement 120). 216p. 1992. 78.50 (90-04-09512-8) E J Brill.

Rhetoric of Historical Representation: Three Narrative Histories of The French Revolution. Ann Rigney. 240p. (C). 1991. text ed. 59.95 (0-521-38152-5) Cambridge U Pr.

Rhetoric of History. Savoie Lottinville. LC 75-19418. 272p. 1976. pap. 13.95 (0-8061-2190-4) U of Okla Pr.

Rhetoric of Humanism: Spanish Culture After Ortega y Gasset. Thomas Mermall. LC 76-45293. 1976. pap. 12.00 (0-916950-16-6); lib. bdg. 20.00 (0-916950-02-6) Biling Rev-Pr.

Rhetoric of Identity in Isocrates: Text, Power, Pedagogy. Yun Lee Too. (Classical Studies). 260p. (C). 1995. text ed. 59.95 (0-521-47406-X) Cambridge U Pr.

Rhetoric of Imitation: Genre & Poetic Memory in Virgil & Other Latin Poets. Gian B. Conte. Ed. & Tr. by Charles Segal from ITA. LC 85-24316. (Cornell Studies in Classical Philology). 224p. (C). 1986. 35.00 (0-8014-1733-3) Cornell U Pr.

Rhetoric of Imitation: Genre & Poetic Memory in Virgil & Other Latin Poets. Gian B. Conte. Ed. by Charles Segal. (Studies in Classical Philology). 224p. 1996. pap. 15.95 (0-8014-8359-X) Cornell U Pr.

Rhetoric of Immediacy: A Cultural Critique of Chan-Zen Buddhism. Bernard Faure. 416p. 1991. pap. text ed. 18.95 (0-691-02963-6) Princeton U Pr.

Rhetoric of Independence: Myth & Reality of Social Policy in Thatcher's Britain. Barbara Waine. LC 90-28480. (Illus.). 181p. 1991. 19.95 (0-85496-311-1) Berg Pubs.

Rhetoric of Interpretation & the Interpretation of Rhetoric. Paul Hernadi. LC 89-7924. 210p. 1989. text ed. 37.95 (0-8223-1007-4); pap. text ed. 14.95 (0-8223-0934-3) Duke.

Rhetoric of Irony. Wayne C. Booth. LC 73-87298. xviii, 312p. 1975. reprint ed. pap. text ed. 15.95 (0-226-06553-7, P641) U Ch Pr.

Rhetoric of John Donne's Verse. W. F. Melton. 1972. 59.95 (0-8490-0953-7) Gordon Pr.

Rhetoric of Law. Ed. by Austin Sarat & Thomas R. Kearns. (Amherst Series in Law, Jurisprudence, & Social Theory). 300p. (Orig.). 1994. text ed. 49.50 (0-472-10525-6) U of Mich Pr.

Rhetoric of Law. Ed. by Austin Sarat & Thomas B. Kearns. (Orig.). 1995. pap. 19.95 (0-472-08386-4) U of Mich Pr.

Rhetoric of Leviathan: Thomas Hobbes & the Politics of Cultural Transformation. David Johnston. (Studies in Moral, Political, & Legal Philosophy). 256p. (C). 1989. text ed. 45.00 (0-691-07717-7); pap. text ed. 15.95 (0-691-02317-4) Princeton U Pr.

Rhetoric of Love. Ed. by Cristina Giorelli & Maria A. Stefanelli. 316p. reprint ed. pap. 22.50 (88-267-0196-2) Natl Poet Foun.

Rhetoric of Love: Das Menschenbild und die Form des Romans bei Iris Murdoch. Wolfram Volker. (Bochum Studies in English: No. 6). vi, 168p. (Orig.). 1978. pap. 27.00 (90-6032-099-9, Pub. by Gruner NE) Benjamins North Am.

***Rhetoric of Medieval Prefaces.** Dhira Mahoney. (Literature Reference Ser.). 200p. Date not set. text ed. 29.00 (0-8240-2946-1) Garland.

Rhetoric of Menachem Begin: The Myth of Redemption Through Return. Robert C. Rowland. 330p. (Orig.). 1985. pap. text ed. 25.50 (0-8191-4736-2); lib. bdg. 55.50 (0-8191-4735-4) U Pr of Amer.

Rhetoric of Modern Statesmanship, Vol. XVIII. Ed. by Kenneth W. Thompson. (Exxon Education Foundation Series on Rhetoric & Political Discourse). 262p. (Orig.). (C). 1992. pap. text ed. 27.50 (0-8191-8520-5); lib. bdg. 56.00 (0-8191-8519-1) U Pr of Amer.

Rhetoric of Moral Protest: Public Campaigns, Celebrity Endorsement, & Political Mobilization. Christian Lahusen. LC 96-24877. (Studies in Organization: Vol. 76). (Illus.). xvi, 425p. (C). 1996. text ed. 87.95 (3-11-015093-X, 134/96) De Gruyter.

Rhetoric of Morality & Philosophy: Plato's Gorgias & Phaedrus. Seth Benardete. 215p. 1991. 35.95 (0-226-04240-5) U Ch Pr.

Rhetoric of Motives. Kenneth Burke. LC 69-16742. 1969. reprint ed. pap. 16.00 (0-520-01546-0) U CA Pr.

Rhetoric of Pessimism & Strategies of Containment in the Short Stories of Guy de Maupassant. David Bryant. LC 93-27111. (Studies in French Literature: Vol. 7). 200p. 1993. text ed. 79.95 (0-7734-9344-1) E Mellen.

Rhetoric of Political Persuasion: The Narrative Artistry & Political Intentions of 2 Kings 9-11. Lloyd M. Barre. Ed. by Robert J. Karris. LC 87-15878. (Catholic Biblical Quarterly Monographs: No. 20). ix, 161p. 1988. pap. 5.00 (0-915170-19-1) Catholic Bibl Assn.

Rhetoric of Politics in the English Revolution, 1642-1660. Elizabeth Skerpan. 280p. (C). 1992. text ed. 42.50 (0-8262-0799-5) U of Mo Pr.

Rhetoric of Propaganda Vol. 28: A Tagmemic Analysis of Selected Documents of the Cultural Revolution in China. Xiao-Ming Yang. LC 93-17011. (American University Studies: No. XIII). 138p. (C). 1994. text ed. 38.95 (0-8204-2214-2) P Lang Pubng.

Rhetoric of Purity: Essentialist Theory & the Advent of Abstract Painting. Mark A. Cheetham. (New Art History & Criticism Ser.). (Illus.). 220p. (C). 1991. text ed. 64.95 (0-521-38546-6) Cambridge U Pr.

Rhetoric of Purity: Essentialist Theory & the Advent of Abstract Painting. Mark A. Cheetham. (Studies in New Art History & Criticism). (Illus.). 176p. (C). 1994. pap. text ed. 19.95 (0-521-47759-X) Cambridge U Pr.

Rhetoric of Racism. Mark L. McPhail. LC 93-8188. 170p. (C). 1994. lib. bdg. 41.00 (0-8191-9180-9) U Pr of Amer.

Rhetoric of Rage: Women in Dorothy Parker. Sondra Melzer. LC 95-36389. (Writing about Women Ser.: Vol. 22). 208p. (C). 1996. text ed. 44.95 (0-8204-3038-2) P Lang Pubng.

Rhetoric of Reaction: Perversity, Futility, Jeopardy. Albert O. Hirschman. LC 90-2361. (Belknap Ser.). 197p. 1991. pap. text ed. 12.00 (0-674-76868-X, HIRRHX) HUP.

Rhetoric of Reason: Writing & the Attractions of Argument. James Crosswhite. LC 95-44286. (Rhetoric of the Human Sciences Ser.). 344p. 1996. 58.00 (0-299-14950-1); pap. 24.95 (0-299-14954-4) U of Wis Pr.

***Rhetoric of Reception, Vol. 1.** Mailloux. Date not set. pap. text ed. write for info. (0-312-09219-9) St Martin.

Rhetoric of Religion: Studies in Logology. Kenneth Burke. 1970. pap. 14.00 (0-520-01610-6) U CA Pr.

Rhetoric of (Re)unification Vol. 20: Constructing Identity Through East & West German Newspapers. Beate C. Gilliar. LC 94-24567. (Berkeley Insights in Linguistics & Semiotics Ser.: 4). 136p. (C). 1996. text ed. 36.95 (0-8204-2614-8) P Lang Pubng.

Rhetoric of Righteousness in Romans. Campbell. (JSNT Supplement Ser.: No. 65). 280p. (C). 1992. 60.00 (1-85075-294-X, Pub. by Sheffield Acad UK) CUP Services.

Rhetoric of Righteousness in Romans 3:21-26. Douglas A. Campbell. (Journey for the Study of the New Testament Supplement Ser.: No. 66). 272p. (C). 1992. 60.00 (1-85075-350-4, Pub. by Sheffield Acad UK) CUP Services.

Rhetoric of Romans: Argumentative Constraint & Strategy & Paul's Dialogue with Judaism. Neil Elliott. (Journey for the Study of the New Testament Supplement Ser.: Vol. 45). 336p. pap. text ed. 70.00 (1-85075-261-3) CUP Services.

Rhetoric of Romanticism. Paul De Man. LC 84-3213. 327p. 1984. text ed. 55.00 (0-231-05526-9) Col U Pr.

Rhetoric of Romanticism. Paul De Man. LC 84-3213. 327p. 1986. pap. text ed. 17.50 (0-231-05527-7) Col U Pr.

Rhetoric of Science. Alan G. Gross. (Illus.). 248p. 1990. 37.00 (0-674-76873-6) HUP.

Rhetoric of Science. Alan G. Gross. (Illus.). 272p. 1996. pap. 17.95 (0-674-76876-0) HUP.

Rhetoric of Sexuality & the Literature of the French Renaissance. Lawrence D. Kritzman. (Cambridge Studies in French: No. 33). 208p. (C). 1991. text ed. 69.95 (0-521-35624-5) Cambridge U Pr.

Rhetoric of Sexuality & the Literature of the French Renaissance. Lawrence D. Kritzman. 262p. 1994. pap. 17.00 (0-231-08269-X) Col U Pr.

Rhetoric of Silence & Other Selected Writings. Lisa B. De Behar. LC 95-34481. (Approaches to Semiotics Ser.: No. 122). (C). 1995. lib. bdg. 152.35 (3-11-014425-5) Mouton.

Rhetoric of Social Research: Understood & Believed. Ed. by Albert Hunter. LC 90-31076. 248p. (C). 1990. text ed. 38.00 (0-8135-1596-3); pap. text ed. 16.00 (0-8135-1597-1) Rutgers U Pr.

***Rhetoric of Space: Literary & Artistic Representations of Landscape in Republican & Augustan Rome.** Eleanor W. Leach. LC 88-19668. (Illus.). 537p. 1988. reprint ed. pap. 153.10 (0-608-02500-3, 2063144) Bks Demand.

Rhetoric of Struggle: Public Address by African-American Women. Ed. by Robbie J. Walker. LC 91-40684. (Critical Studies in Black Life & Culture: Vol. 20). 467p. 1992. text ed. 66.00 (0-8240-7268-5, SS#701) Garland.

Rhetoric of Suffering: Reading the Book of Job in the Eighteenth Century. Jonathan Lamb. (Illus.). 352p. 1995. 65.00 (0-19-818264-3) OUP.

Rhetoric of Terrorism & Counterterrorism. Richard W. Leeman. LC 90-47522. (Contributions to the Study of Mass Media & Communications Ser.: No. 29). 232p. 1991. text ed. 55.00 (0-313-27587-4, LRT/, Greenwood Pr) Greenwood.

Rhetoric of the Babylonian Talmud, Its Social Meaning & Context. Jack N. Lightstone. (Studies in Christianity & Judaism: Vol. 6). 330p. (C). 1994. pap. 22.95 (0-88920-238-9) Wilfrid Laurier.

Rhetoric of the Book of Judges. Robert H. O'Connell. LC 95-48238. (Supplements to Vetus Testamentum Ser.: Vol. 63). 1995. 158.50 (90-04-10104-7) E J Brill.

Rhetoric of the Contemporary Lyric. Jonathan Holden. LC 79-3383. 160p. 1980. 6.95 (0-253-15667-X) Ind U Pr.

Rhetoric of the Frame: Essays on the Boundaries of the Artwork. Ed. by Paul Duro. LC 96-19427. (Cambridge Studies in New Art History & Criticism). (Illus.). 368p. (C). 1996. text ed. 80.00 (0-521-46148-0); pap. text ed. 29.95 (0-521-56629-0) Cambridge U Pr.

Rhetoric of the Human Sciences: Language & Argument in Scholarship & Public Affairs. John Nelson et al. LC 86-34030. (Illus.). 408p. 1990. pap. 16.95 (0-299-11024-9) U of Wis Pr.

Rhetoric of the "Other" Literature. W. Ross Winterowd. LC 89-33261. 192p. (C). 1990. text ed. 24.95 (0-8093-1587-4) S Ill U Pr.

Rhetoric of the People: The German Greens & the New Politics. William E. Coleman, Jr. & William E. Coleman, Sr. LC 92-28477. 168p. 1993. text ed. 45.00 (0-275-94083-7, C4083, Praeger Pubs) Greenwood.

Rhetoric of the Real: Studies in Post-Enlightenment Writing from 1790 to the Present. Simon Dentith. LC 90-46983. 200p. 1990. text ed. 39.95 (0-312-05659-1) St Martin.

Rhetoric of the Scene: Dramatic Narrative in the Early Middle Ages. Joaquin M. Pizarro. 280p. 1989. text ed. 40.00 (0-8020-5754-3) U of Toronto Pr.

Rhetoric of Valery's Prose Aubades. Ursula Franklin. LC 78-13044. 168p. reprint ed. pap. 47.90 (0-317-55687-8, 2029330) Bks Demand.

Rhetoric of Vision: Essays on Charles Williams. Peter J. Schakel. LC 95-36441. 360p. 1996. 41.50 (0-8387-5314-0) Bucknell U Pr.

Rhetoric of War: Training Day, the Militia, & the Military Sermon. Marie L. Ahearn. LC 89-1919. (Contributions in American Studies: No. 95). 223p. 1989. text ed. 55.00 (0-313-26619-0, ARW, Greenwood Pr) Greenwood.

Rhetoric of Western Thought. James L. Golden et al. 424p. (C). 1996. per., pap. text ed. 38.79 (0-7872-1968-1) Kendall-Hunt.

Rhetoric, Power & Community: An Exercise in Reserve. David Jasper. LC 92-18257. (Studies in Religion & Literature). 180p. (Orig.). 1993. pap. 20.00 (0-664-25434-9) Westminster John Knox.

Rhetoric, Prudence, & Skepticism in the Renaissance. Victoria Kahn. LC 84-21362. 248p. (C). 1985. 37.50 (0-8014-1736-8) Cornell U Pr.

Rhetoric, Reason, & Society: Rationality as Dialogue. George Muyerson. 160p. 1995. text ed. 69.95 (0-8039-7866-9); pap. text ed. 22.95 (0-8039-7867-7) Sage.

***Rhetoric Reclaimed: Aristotle & the Liberal Arts Tradition.** Janet M. Atwill. 248p. 1997. 35.00 (0-8014-3263-4) Cornell U Pr.

***Rhetoric Retold: Regendering the Tradition from Antiquity Through the Renaissance.** Cheryl Glenn. LC 97-7051. 1997. write for info. (0-8093-1929-2); pap. write for info. (0-8093-2137-8) S Ill U Pr.

***Rhetoric-Rhetoriqueurs-Rederijkers.** J. Koopmans et al. 292p. pap. 53.25 (0-444-85792-3) Elsevier.

Rhetoric, Scripture & Theology: Essays from the 1994 Pretoria Conference. Ed. by Stanley E. Porter & Thomas H. Olbricht. (JSNTS Ser.: No. 131). 460p. 1996. 79.50 (1-85075-607-4, Pub. by Sheffield Acad UK) CUP Services.

Rhetoric, Sophistry, Pragmatism. Ed. by Steven Mailloux. (Literature, Culture, Theory Ser.: No. 15). 290p. (C). 1995. text ed. 59.95 (0-521-46225-8) Cambridge U Pr.

Rhetoric, Sophistry, Pragmatism. Ed. by Steven Mailloux. (Literature, Culture, Theory Ser.: No. 15). 290p. (C). 1995. pap. text ed. 17.95 (0-521-46780-2) Cambridge U Pr.

Rhetoric, the Bible, & the Origins of Free Verse: The Early "Hymns" of Friedrich Gottlieb Klopstock. Katrin M. Kohl. (Quellen und Forschungen zur Sprach und Kulturgeschichte der Germanischen Voelker Ser.: NF 92 (216)). xiv, 322p. (C). 1990. lib. bdg. 121.55 (3-11-011999-4) De Gruyter.

Rhetoric Through Media. Thompson. 576p. 1996. pap. 32.00 (0-205-18918-0) Allyn.

***Rhetoric Through Media.** Gary Thompson. teacher ed., pap. write for info. (0-205-26644-4) Allyn.

Rhetorica, 2 vols. Marcus Tullius Cicero. Ed. by A. S. Wilkins. Incl. Vol. 1. Libros De Oratore Tres. 260p. 1922. 32.00 (0-19-814615-9); Vol. 2. Brutus, Orator, De Optimo Genere Oratorum, Partitiones Oratoriae, Topica. 276p. 1922. 29.95 (0-19-814616-7); (Oxford Classical Texts Ser.). write for info. (0-318-54887-9) OUP.

***Rhetorica.** Josef Kopperschmidt. (Philosophische Texte und Studien: Vol. 14). xii, 229p. (GER.). 1985. write for info. (3-487-07693-4) G Olms Pubs.

Rhetorica ad Alexandrum see Problems, Bks 22-38

Rhetorica of Philodemus. Philodemus of Garada. Tr. by Harry M. Hubbell. (Connecticut Academy of Arts & Sciences Ser., Trans.: Vol. 23). 1920. pap. 75.00 (0-685-22831-2) Elliots Bks.

Rhetorical Act. Karlyn K. Campbell. 310p. (C). 1982. text ed. 29.95 (0-534-01008-3) Wadsworth Pub.

Rhetorical Act. 2nd ed. Karlyn K. Campbell. LC 95-5414. 398p. 1996. text ed. 36.95 (0-534-16752-7) Wadsworth Pub.

Rhetorical Analysis of Popular American Film. Marc T. Newman. 400p. (C). 1993. pap. text ed. 36.69 (0-8403-9003-3) Kendall-Hunt.

Rhetorical Analysis of under the Volcano: Malcolm Lowry's Design Governing Postures. Dana Grove. LC 88-13971. (Studies in British Literature: Vol. 2). 404p. 1989. lib. bdg. 109.95 (0-88946-929-6) E Mellen.

Rhetorical & Critical Approaches to Public Relations. Ed. by Elizabeth L. Toth & Robert L. Heath. (Communication Textbook (Public Relations) Ser.). 344p. 1992. text ed. 69.95 (0-8058-0470-6) L Erlbaum Assocs.

Rhetorical Composition & Function of Hebrews 11. Michael R. Cosby. LC 88-27570. 132p. (C). 1989. 25.00 (0-86554-320-8, MUP/H273) Mercer Univ Pr.

Rhetorical Considerations: Essays for Analysis. 4th ed. Harry Brent & William Lutz. LC 83-19587. 496p. reprint ed. pap. 141.40 (0-7837-4745-4, 2044554) Bks Demand.

Rhetorical Criticism: A Study in Method. Edwin Black. LC 77-91050. 1978. reprint ed. pap. text ed. 13.95 (0-299-07554-0) U of Wis Pr.

Rhetorical Criticism: Context, Method, & the Book of Jonah. Phyllis Trible. LC 94-34616. (Guides to Biblical Scholarship Ser.). 1994. pap. 17.00 (0-8006-2798-9, 1-2798, Fortress Pr) Augsburg Fortress.

Rhetorical Criticism: Exploration & Practice. 2nd rev. ed. Sonja K. Foss. 553p. (C). 1995. pap. text ed. 28.95 (0-88133-873-7) Waveland Pr.

Rhetorical Criticism & the Poetry of the Book of Job. Pieter Van Der Lugt. LC 95-11575. (Oudtestamentische Studien: Vol. 32). 1995. 132.50 (90-04-10326-0) E J Brill.

Rhetorical Criticism of the Bible: A Comprehensive Bibliography with Notes on History & Method. Duane F. Watson & Alan J. Hauser. LC 93-35783. (Biblical Interpretation Ser.: Vol. 4). 1993. 74.50 (90-04-09903-4) E J Brill.

An Asterisk (*) at the beginning of an entry indicates that the title is appearing in BIP for the first time.

Rhetorical Designs for Professional & Technical Writing: A Teacher's Guide. William E. Tanner et al. LC 93-74070. 274p. (Orig.). 1993. pap. text ed. 24.95 (*0-9635769-1-7*) Caxtons Mod Art.

Rhetorical Dimensions of Popular Culture. Barry Brummett. LC 90-35565. 248p. 1991. text ed. 32.50 (*0-8173-0516-5*) U of Ala Pr.

***Rhetorical Ethics & Internetworked Writing.** Date not set. text ed. 73.25 (*1-56750-322-5*) Ablex Pub.

***Rhetorical Ethics & Internetworked Writing.** Date not set. pap. 39.50 (*1-56750-323-3*) Ablex Pub.

Rhetorical Grammar: Grammatical Choices, Rhetorical Effects. 2nd ed. Martha Kolln. LC 95-8300. 1995. pap. text ed. 26.00 (*0-02-365871-1*, Macmillan Coll) P-H.

Rhetorical Grammar, or Course of Lessons on Elocution. John Walker. (Anglistica & Americana Ser.: No. 21). xi, 348p. 1969. reprint ed. 57.20 (*0-685-66526-7*, 05102056) G Olms Pubs.

Rhetorical Hermeneutics: Invention & Interpretation in the Age of Science. Ed. by Alan G. Gross & William M. Keith. LC 95-52683. (SUNY Series in Speech Communication). 371p. 1996. text ed. 59.50 (*0-7914-3109-6*); pap. text ed. 19.95 (*0-7914-3110-X*) State U NY Pr.

Rhetorical Image. Marcia Tucker et al. Ed. by Deirdre Summerbell. (Illus.). 98p. 1990. 20.00 (*0-915557-71-1*) New Mus Contemp Art.

Rhetorical Interaction in I Corinthians 8 & 10: A Formal Analysis with Preliminary Suggestions for a Chinese, Cross-Cultural Hermeneutic. Khiok-Khng Yeo. LC 94-23481. (Biblical Interpretation Ser.: Vol. 9). 1994. 85.50 (*90-04-10115-2*) E J Brill.

Rhetorical Landscapes: The Poetry & Art Criticism of Jacques Dupin. Maryann De Julio. LC 91-73987. (Armstrong Monographs: No. 76). (Illus.). 115p. (Orig.). 1992. pap. 13.95 (*0-917058-80-1*) French Forum.

Rhetorical Logic of Henry James. Sheila Teahan. LC 95-30683. 184p. (C). 1995. text ed. 30.00 (*0-8071-2005-7*) La State U Pr.

Rhetorical Memory & Delivery: Classical Concepts for Contemporary Composition. Ed. by J. Frederick Reynolds. (Communications, Rhetoric & Public Address Ser.). 192p. 1993. pap. 19.95 (*0-8058-1293-8*); text ed. 39.95 (*0-8058-1292-X*) L Erlbaum Assocs.

Rhetorical Mosaic for a Kaleidoscope of Sound: Poetry As a Road to Understanding the Prose Voice. John F. Britt. LC 93-40295. (Am. Univ. Studies, V: Vol. 159). 192p. (C). 1994. text ed. 37.95 (*0-8204-2383-1*) P Lang Pubng.

Rhetorical Movement: Essays in Honor of Leland M. Griffin. Ed. by David Zarefsky. 350p. 1993. 49.95 (*0-8101-1092-X*) Northwestern U Pr.

Rhetorical Norms in Renaissance Literature. William J. Kennedy. LC 78-7391. 237p. reprint ed. pap. 67.60 (*0-8357-8307-3*, 2033778) Bks Demand.

Rhetorical Poetics: Theory & Practice of Figural & Symbolic Reading in Modern French Literature. Donald Rice & Peter Schofer. LC 83-47768. 256p. 1983. text ed. 22.50 (*0-299-09440-5*) U of Wis Pr.

Rhetorical Power. Steven Mailloux. LC 89-42878. 208p. 1989. 37.50 (*0-8014-2245-0*); pap. 14.95 (*0-8014-9602-0*) Cornell U Pr.

Rhetorical Presidency. Jeffrey K. Tulis. 224p. 1987. pap. text ed. 15.95 (*0-691-02295-X*) Princeton U Pr.

Rhetorical Purpose & the Political & Military Character of Philippians: A Call to Stand Firm. Timothy C. Geoffrion. LC 93-28219. (Biblical Press Ser.: Vol. 13). 280p. 1993. text ed. 89.95 (*0-7734-2374-5*) E Mellen.

Rhetorical Questions: Studies of Public Discourse. Edwin Black. LC 91-28534. 220p. 1992. 28.95 (*0-226-05501-9*) U Ch Pr.

Rhetorical Republic: Governing Representations in American Politics. Ed. by Frederick M. Dolan & Thomas L. Dumm. LC 92-41984. 304p. (C). 1993. pap. 17.95 (*0-87023-847-7*); lib. bdg. 40.00 (*0-87023-846-9*) U of Mass Pr.

Rhetorical Spaces: Essays on Gendered Locations. Lorraine Code. 224p. (C). 1995. pap. 16.95 (*0-415-90937-6*, B3863, Routledge NY) Routledge.

Rhetorical Spaces: Essays on Gendered Locations. Lorraine Code. 224p. (C). (gr. 13). 1995. text ed. 62.95 (*0-415-90936-8*, B3859, Routledge NY) Routledge.

Rhetorical Studies of National Political Debates: Nineteen Sixty to Nineteen Ninety-Two. 2nd ed. Ed. by Robert V. Friedenberg. LC 93-17665. (Praeger Series in Political Communication). 288p. 1993. text ed. 65.00 (*0-275-94339-9*, Praeger Pubs); pap. text ed. 18.95 (*0-275-94340-2*, Praeger Pubs) Greenwood.

***Rhetorical Studies of National Political Debates, 1996.** Ed. by Robert V. Friedenberg. LC 97-14470. 1997. pap. text ed. write for info. (*0-275-95738-1*, Praeger Pubs) Greenwood.

Rhetorical Study of the Speaking of Calvin Coolidge. Arthur F. Fleser. LC 89-38586. (Studies in 20th Century American History: Vol. 2). (Illus.). 193p. 1990. lib. bdg. 79.95 (*0-88946-321-2*) E Mellen.

Rhetorical Town. Sebastian Barry. 68p. 8500. pap. 11.95 (*0-85105-426-9*, Pub. by Colin Smythe Ltd UK) Dufour.

Rhetorical Tradition. 2nd ed. Bizzell. Date not set. pap. text ed. write for info. (*0-312-14839-9*) St Martin.

Rhetorical Tradition: Readings from Classical Times to the Present. Ed. by Patricia Bizzell & Bruce Herzberg. LC 88-63071. 1266p. (C). 1990. pap. text ed. 48.00 (*0-312-00348-X*, Bedford Bks) St Martin.

Rhetorical Tradition & Modern Writing. James J. Murphy et al. LC 82-2103. vii, 149p. 1982. pap. 19.75 (*0-87352-098-X*, J302P) Modern Lang.

Rhetorical Traditions & British Romantic Literature. Ed. by Don H. Bialostosky & Lawrence D. Needham. LC 94-19475. 320p. 1995. 39.95 (*0-253-31180-2*) Ind U Pr.

Rhetorical Traditions & the Teaching of Writing. Cyril H. Knoblauch & Lil Brannon. LC 83-15712. 171p. (Orig.). 1984. pap. text ed. 21.50 (*0-86709-105-3*, 0105) Boynton Cook Pubs.

Rhetorical Turn: Invention & Persuasion in the Conduct of Inquiry. Ed. by Herbert W. Simons. (Illus.). 460p. 1990. pap. text ed. 19.50 (*0-226-75902-4*); lib. bdg. 54.00 (*0-226-75901-6*) U Ch Pr.

Rhetorical Uses of the Authorizing Figure: Fidel Castro & Jose Marti. Donald E. Rice. LC 91-35027. 192p. 1992. text ed. 45.00 (*0-275-94214-7*, C4214, Praeger Pubs) Greenwood.

Rhetorical Voice of Psychoanalysis: Displacement of Evidence by Theory. Donald P. Spence. LC 93-6344. 240p. 1994. 32.00 (*0-674-76874-4*) HUP.

Rhetorical World of Augustan Humanism: Ethics & Imagery from Swift to Burke. Paul Fussell. LC 66-1724. 330p. reprint ed. pap. 94.10 (*0-317-29155-6*, 2055599) Bks Demand.

Rhetorics & Politics in Afghan Traditional Storytelling. Margaret A. Mills. LC 90-22019. (Publications of the American Folklore Society, Bibliographical & Special Ser.). 408p. (C). 1991. text ed. 33.95 (*0-8122-8199-3*) U of Pa Pr.

Rhetorics of Life-Writing in Early Modern Europe: Forms of Biography from Cassandra Fedele to Louis XIV. Ed. by Thomas F. Mayer & D. R. Woolf. LC 95-1859. (Studies in Medieval & Early Modern Civilization). 1995. text ed. 54.50 (*0-472-10591-4*) U of Mich Pr.

Rhetorics of Order-Ordering Rhetorics in English Neoclassical Literature. Ed. by J. Douglas Canfield & J. Paul Hunter. LC 88-40578. 200p. 1990. 36.50 (*0-87413-374-2*) U Delaware Pr.

Rhetorics of Popular Culture: Advertising, Advocacy & Entertainment. Robert L. Root, Jr. LC 86-14974. (Contributions to the Study of Popular Culture Ser.: No. 16). 192p. 1987. text ed. 45.00 (*0-313-24403-0*, Greenwood Pr) Greenwood.

Rhetorics of Reason & Desire: Vergil, Augustine, & the Troubadours. Sarah Spence. LC 87-47953. (Illus.). 192p. 1988. 35.00 (*0-8014-2129-2*) Cornell U Pr.

Rhetorics of Self Making. Ed. by Debbora Battaglia. LC 94-398. 1995. 30.00 (*0-520-08798-4*); pap. 14.00 (*0-520-08799-2*) U CA Pr.

Rhetorics of Thomas Hobbes & Bernard Lamy. John T. Harwood. LC 85-30448. (Landmarks in Rhetoric & Public Address Ser.). 422p. (Orig.). (C). 1986. text ed. 39.95 (*0-8093-1301-4*); pap. text ed. 14.95 (*0-8093-1302-2*) S Ill U Pr.

Rhetorics, Poetics & Cultures: Refiguring College English Studies. James A. Berlin. (Refiguring English Studies). 205p. (C). 1996. pap. 25.95 (*0-8141-4145-5*) NCTE.

***Rhetorik Als Pragmatisches System.** Regina Podlewski. (Philosophische Texte und Studien: Vol. 3). xiv, 271p. (GER.). 1982. write for info. (*3-487-06658-0*) G Olms Pubs.

Rhetorik der Araber, Nach Den Wichtigsten Quellen Dargestellt und Mit Angefugten Textauszugen. August F. Mehren. 144p. 1973. reprint ed. write for info. (*0-318-71532-5*) G Olms Pubs.

Rhetorik der Griechen und Romer. Richard Volkmann. xvi, 595p. 1987. reprint ed. write for info. (*3-487-00367-8*) G Olms Pubs.

Rhetorika - Schriften Zur Aristolelischen und Hellenistischen Rhetorik. 85.00 (*0-318-70803-5*) G Olms Pubs.

Rhetorique. Ed. by Marcel N. Muller. (Michigan Romance Studies: Vol. 13). 158p. (Orig.). 1993. pap. 10.00 (*0-939730-12-X*) Mich Romance.

Rhetorisches Argumentieren Bei Thukydides. Jurgen Gommel. iv, 90p. (GER.). 1966. write for info. (*0-318-70615-6*) G Olms Pubs.

Rheumaorthopadie. 1995. 139.00 (*3-540-60040-X*) Spr-Verlag.

Rheumatic & Skin Disease. Wyrnn Smith. (Profile of Health & Disease in America Ser.). (Illus.). 128p. 1988. 40.00 (*0-8160-1456-6*) Facts on File.

***Rheumatic & Skin Disease.** Wrynn Smith. LC 87-33090. (Profile of Health & Disease in America Ser.). 125p. 1988. reprint ed. pap. 35.70 (*0-608-02832-0*, 2063899) Bks Demand.

Rheumatic Diseases: Report of a WHO Scientific Group. (Technical Report Ser.: No. 816). vii, 59p. (CHI, ENG, FRE, RUS & SPA.). 1992. pap. text ed. 10.00 (*92-4-120816-3*, 1100816) World Health.

Rheumatic Diseases & Sports. Ed. by H. W. Baenkler. (Rheumatology Ser.: Vol. 16). (Illus.). vii, 232p. 1992. 191.50 (*3-8055-5425-7*) S Karger.

Rheumatic Diseases & the Heart. J. A. Cosh & J. L. Lever. (Illus.). 225p. 1989. 121.00 (*0-387-19524-6*) Spr-Verlag.

Rheumatic Fever. 2nd ed. Angelo Taranta & Milton Markowitz. (C). 1990. lib. bdg. 49.00 (*0-7462-0106-0*) Kluwer Ac.

Rheumatic Fever: A Symposium Held at the University of Minnesota on November 29, 30, & December 1, 1951. Minnesota Heart Association Staff. Ed. by Lewis Thomas. LC 52-11108. 359p. reprint ed. pap. 102.40 (*0-317-29474-1*, 2055922) Bks Demand.

***Rheumatic Fever & Rheumatic Heart Disease: Report on a WHO Study Group.** WHO Staff. (Technical Report Ser.: No. 764). 0058p. 1988. 8.00 (*92-4-120764-7*) World Health.

Rheumatism: A Consumer's Guide. large type ed. Geoffrey Littlejohn. (Illus.). 218p. 1992. 21.95 (*1-85695-005-0*, Pub. by ISIS UK) Transaction Pubs.

Rheumatoid Arthritis. Ed. by Michael Fischbach. (Contemporary Management in Internal Medicine Ser.: Vol. 1, No. 6). (Illus.). 228p. 1991. text ed. 35.00 (*0-443-08827-6*) Churchill.

Rheumatoid Arthritis. Edward D. Harris, Jr. Ed. by Richard Zorab. (Illus.). 432p. 1997. text ed. 125.00 (*0-7216-5249-2*) Saunders.

Rheumatoid Arthritis. Ed. by Michael Fischbach. LC 92-34535. (Contemporary Management in Internal Medicine Ser.: Vol. 1, No. 6). (Illus.). 243p. reprint ed. pap. 69.30 (*0-7837-6237-2*, 2045951) Bks Demand.

Rheumatoid Arthritis: Pathogenesis, Assessment, Outcome, & Treatment. Ed. by Wolfe & Pincus. 544p. 1994. 165.00 (*0-8247-8878-8*) Dekker.

Rheumatoid Arthritis: Recent Research Advances. Ed. by J. S. Smolen et al. LC 91-5068. 399p. 1992. 118.00 (*0-387-53315-X*) Spr-Verlag.

Rheumatoid Arthritis Surgery of the Complex Hand & Foot. Ed. by F. W. Hagena. (Rheumatology Ser.: Vol. 11). (Illus.). xiv, 190p. 1987. 141.75 (*3-8055-4408-1*) S Karger.

Rheumatoid Arthritis Surgery of the Elbow. Ed. by M. J. Hamalainen & F. W. Hagena. (Rheumatology, the Interdisciplinary Concept Ser.: Vol. 15). (Illus.). x, 130p. 1991. 108.00 (*3-8055-5327-7*) S Karger.

Rheumatoid Arthritis Surgery of the Shoulder. Ed. by A. W. Lattin & C. Petersson. (Rheumatology, the Interdisciplinary Concept Ser.: Vol. 12). (Illus.). xiv, 138p. 1989. 112.00 (*3-8055-4804-4*) S Karger.

Rheumatoid Hip. H. Thabe & Bad Kreuznach. (Illus.). xiii, 185p. 1990. 71.95 (*0-387-52884-9*) Spr-Verlag.

Rheumatology. H. Berry & Asm Jawad. 1985. lib. bdg. 61.00 (*0-85200-900-3*) Kluwer Ac.

Rheumatology. David M. Grennan. (Illus.). 255p. 1983. pap. text ed. 21.50 (*0-7020-0967-9*, Bailliere-Tindall) Saunders.

Rheumatology. J. M. Moll. (Colour Guide Ser.). (Illus.). 154p. 1992. pap. text ed. 19.95 (*0-443-04614-X*) Churchill.

***Rheumatology.** 2nd ed. J. M. Moll. LC 96-39719. (Colour Guide Ser.). 1997. write for info. (*0-443-05805-9*) Churchill.

Rheumatology: Problems in Primary Care. Matthew H. Liang et al. (Problems in Primary Care Ser.). 256p. 1990. pap. 39.95 (*0-87489-421-2*) Med Econ.

Rheumatology Disorders. Lawrence F. Layfer et al. (Illus.). 208p. 1988. pap. text ed. 49.00 (*0-7216-2385-9*) Saunders.

***Rheumatology Examination & Injection Techniques.** Michael Doherty et al. (Illus.). 143p. 1992. write for info. (*0-7020-1442-7*, Pub. by W B Saunders UK) Saunders.

Rheumatology for GPs. H. L. Currey & Sally Hull. (Oxford General Practice Ser.: No. 11). (Illus.). 272p. 1987. pap. 33.95 (*0-19-261657-9*) OUP.

Rheumatology for the Health Care Professional. Harry Spiera & Irwin Oreskes. 480p. (Orig.). (C). 1991. pap. 42.50 (*0-87527-464-1*) Green.

Rheumatology Guidebook. R. Ferrari et al. 200p. (Orig.). 1996. pap. 39.90 (*1-85996-215-7*, Pub. by Bios Sci UK) Bks Intl VA.

Rheumatology in Chinese Medicine. Gerard Guillaume & Mach Chieu. Tr. by David Vachon from FRE. (Illus.). 430p. (C). 1996. 95.00 (*0-939616-26-2*) Eastland.

Rheumatology in Primary Care. Juan J. Canoso. Ed. by Ray Kersey. LC 96-40174. 432p. 1997. text ed. 45.00 (*0-7216-6080-0*) Saunders.

Rheumatology Nursing: A Problem-Oriented Approach. Janice S. Pigg et al. LC 84-19551. 462p. 1989. text ed. 39.95 (*0-8273-4333-7*) Delmar.

***Rheumatology Pearls.** Ed. by Richard M. Silver & Edwin A. Smith. LC 96-49763. (Pearls Ser.). (Illus.). 220p. (Orig.). 1996. pap. text ed. 40.00 (*1-56053-201-7*) Hanley & Belfus.

Rheumatology Pocket Consultant. Campion & Dixon. 1989. pap. 34.95 (*0-632-01112-2*) Blackwell Sci.

Rheumatology Secrets. Ed. by Sterling West. LC 96-32241. (Secrets Ser.). (Illus.). 400p. (Orig.). 1996. pap. text ed. 34.95 (*1-56053-154-1*) Hanley & Belfus.

Rheumatology, State of the Art: Proceedings, 12th European Congress of Rheumatology, Budapest, Hungary, June 1991. Ed. by G. Balint et al. (International Congress Ser.: Vol. 984). xiv, 458p. 1992. 218.75 (*0-444-81212-1*) Elsevier.

Rhiannon. Shari Dodd. 240p. (Orig.). 1993. pap. 9.99 (*1-881542-09-2*) Blue Star Prodns.

Rhiannon. Roberta Gellis. (Roselynde Chronicles Ser.). 448p. 1994. mass mkt., pap. text ed. 5.99 (*0-8439-3695-9*) Dorchester Pub Co.

Rhiannon. Roscoe Howells. 152p. (C). 1987. pap. 20.00 (*0-86383-379-9*, Pub. by Gomer Pr UK) St Mut.

***Rhiannon: Truth Seeker. Susan R. Bockwinkel. Ed. by Paul Neimark. 293p. 1996. 25.00 (*0-87418-320-0*) Mind & Miracles.**
This visionary fiction teaches spiritual truths in a story that is simultaneously easy-to-read yet rich with meaning. Set in the eleventh century, RHIANNON is about a young girl who embarks on a spiritual journey, destined before her birth. She travels with her grandmother to a remote island to become a priestess-in-training in an order that honors the wisdom of many great traditions. The lessons she studies include the oneness of all, non-defensiveness, harmony, quieting the mind to hear the voice of the heart, surrender, forgiveness, non-judgement & healing. The fictional & historical frames of this book allow the reader permission & safety to suspend his own perceptions & beliefs & easily explore those of Rhiannon. The questions, fears & issues with which she struggles are the same as those in this century. RHIANNON is the archetypical journey of discovering universal truths which operate in all cultures & all times. To order or receive a free promotional booklet, call or write Mind & Miracles, 16363 Cammi Lane, Ft. Lauderdale, FL 954-389-8076. Or Rhiannon Books, P.O. Box 341, Northbrook, IL 60062. 847-604-2403. ***Publisher Provided Annotation.***

Rhin, 3 vols., Set. Victor Hugo. (Illus.). 900p. (FRE.). 1996. 130.00 (*0-614-97971-4*) Intl Scholars.

Rhin, Vol. 1. Victor Hugo. (Illus.). 300p. (FRE.). 1996. 59.95 (*2-86808-095-2*) Intl Scholars.

Rhin, Vol. 2. Victor Hugo. (Illus.). 300p. (FRE.). 1996. 59.95 (*2-86808-096-0*) Intl Scholars.

Rhin, Vol. 3. Victor Hugo. (Illus.). 300p. (FRE.). 1996. 59.95 (*2-86808-097-9*) Intl Scholars.

Rhind Mathematical Papyrus. Tr. & Comment by T. Eric Peet. 1990. reprint ed. 85.00 (*3-262-00839-7*) Periodicals Srv.

Rhind Mathematical Papyrus: An Ancient Egyptian Text. Gay Robins. 1990. pap. 8.95 (*0-486-26407-6*) Dover.

Rhine. (Panorama Bks.). (Illus.). (FRE.). 3.95 (*0-685-11529-1*) Fr & Eur.

Rhine. (Insight Guides Ser.). 1993. pap. 21.95 (*0-395-66199-4*) HM.

***Rhine.** M. Pollard. LC 97-3541. (Great Rivers Ser.). (Illus.). 32p. (J). (gr. 5-8). 1997. lib. bdg. 14.95 (*0-7614-0500-3*, Benchmark NY) Marshall Cavendish.

Rhine. Mark Smalley. LC 92-24041. (Rivers of the World Ser.). (Illus.). 48p. (J). (gr. 5-6). 1993. lib. bdg. 24.26 (*0-8114-3102-9*) Raintree Steck-V.

Rhine As Musical Metaphor: Cultural Identity in German Romantic Music. Cecelia H. Porter. LC 96-14967. (Illus.). 320p. 1996. text ed. 55.00 (*1-55553-284-5*) NE U Pr.

Rhine Flows into the Tiber: A History of Vatican II. Ralph M. Wiltgen. LC 82-50583. 304p. 1991. reprint ed. pap. 15.00 (*0-89555-186-1*) TAN Bks Pubs.

Rhine Valley. Berlitz Editors. (Pocket Guides Ser.). (Illus.). 1992. pap. 7.95 (*2-8315-2241-2*) Berlitz.

Rhinebeck, New York, Death Records of the Eighteenth & Nineteenth Centuries. Arthur C. Kelly. (Illus.). 190p. 1992. lib. bdg. 35.00 (*1-56012-123-8*, 119) Kinship Rhinebeck.

Rhinegold. Stephan Grundy. 848p. 1995. mass mkt. 6.99 (*0-553-56945-7*) Bantam.

Rhinegold. Richard Wagner. Ed. by Nicholas John. Tr. by Andrew Porter from GER. LC 85-52161. (English National Opera Guide Series: Bilingual Libretto, Articles: No. 35). (Illus.). 96p. (Orig.). (C). 1986. pap. 9.95 (*0-7145-4078-1*) Riverrun NY.

Rhinehart Reader Companion, Vols. I & II. Grace W. Ellis. (Illus.). 400p. (C). 1991. pap. text ed. 9.50 (*0-03-014224-X*); pap. text ed. 12.00 (*0-03-029407-X*) HB Coll Pubs.

Rhineland Inheritance. T. Davis Bunn. (Rendezvous with Destiny Ser.: No. 1). 224p. 1993. pap. 8.99 (*1-55661-347-4*) Bethany Hse.

Rhineland Inheritance. large type ed. T. Davis Bunn. 1995. 20.95 (*0-7838-1388-0*, GK Hall) Thorndike Pr.

Rhineland Radicals: The Democratic Movement & the Revolution Of 1848- 1849. Jonathan Sperber. (Illus.). 550p. 1991. pap. text ed. 24.95 (*0-691-00866-3*) Princeton U Pr.

Rhineland Radicals: The Democratic Movement & the Revolution of 1848-1849. Jonathan Sperber. (Illus.). 550p. 1991. text ed. 85.00 (*0-691-03172-X*) Princeton U Pr.

Rhineman Exchange. Robert Ludlum. 464p. 1989. mass mkt. 7.50 (*0-553-28063-5*) Bantam.

Rhinemann Exchange. Robert Ludlum. 464p. 1991. reprint ed. lib. bdg. 31.95 (*0-89966-778-3*) Buccaneer Bks.

Rhinestone Cowboy. Bethany Campbell. 1994. mass mkt. 3.99 (*0-373-82527-7*) Harlequin Bks.

Rhinestone Cowboy. Glen Campbell. 1994. 22.00 (*0-8499-1176-1*) Word Pub.

Rhinestone Cowboy: An Autobiography. Glenn Campbell. 1995. mass mkt. 5.99 (*0-312-95679-7*) Tor Bks.

Rhinestone Sharecropping. Bill Gunn. LC 81-52032. 194p. (Orig.). 1981. pap. 5.95 (*0-918408-19-9*) Reed & Cannon.

Rhinestones! Nancy N. Schiffer. LC 92-63100. (Illus.). 160p. (Orig.). 1993. pap. 16.95 (*0-88740-457-X*) Schiffer.

Rhinitis. 2nd ed. Ed. by Guy A. Settipane. LC 90-64470. (Illus.). 300p. 1991. text ed. 68.00 (*0-936587-04-0*) OceanSide Pubns.

***Rhinitis: Immunopathology & Pharmacotherapy.** D. Raeburn & Mark A. Giembycz. LC 96-37785. (Respiratory Pharmacology & Pharmacotherapy Ser.). 1997. write for info. (*3-7643-5301-5*) Birkhauser.

Rhinitis Mechanisms & Management. Ed. by I. S. MacKay. (Illus.). 230p. 1989. 38.00 (*1-85070-892-4*) Prthnon Pub.

Rhino. Caroline Arnold. LC 94-23904. (More Animal Favorites Ser.). (Illus.). 48p. (J). (gr. 2 up). 1995. 16.00 (*0-688-12694-4*, Morrow Junior); lib. bdg. 15.93 (*0-688-12695-2*, Morrow Junior) Morrow.

Rhino. Daryl Balfour & Sharna Balfour. (Illus.). 176p. 1992. text ed. 39.95 (*1-56757-001-1*) Appleton Comms.

Rhino. Sheila S. Klass. LC 92-35669. 160p. (J). (gr. 7-9). 1993. 13.95 (*0-590-44250-3*) Scholastic Inc.

Rhino. Sheila S. Klass. (J). 1996. mass mkt. 3.99 (*0-590-44251-1*) Scholastic Inc.

Rhino! Eduard Zingg. Ed. by Bob Italia. LC 93-7602. (African Animal Adventure Ser.). (J). 1993. lib. bdg. 15.98 (*1-56239-219-0*) Abdo & Dghtrs.

R

R

Rhino & Mouse. Todd S. Palmer. LC 93-33299. 40p. (J). (ps-3). 1994. pap. 12.99 (0-8037-1322-3); pap. 12.89 (0-8037-1323-1) Dial Bks Young.

***Rhino & Mouse.** Todd S. Palmer. 1997. pap. 3.50 (0-14-038433-2) Viking Penguin.

Rhino Comes to America. Thane Maynard. (Cincinnati Zoo Bks.). (Illus.). 40p. (J). (gr. 4-8). 1993. 15.95 (0-531-15258-8); lib. bdg. 22.70 (0-531-11173-3) Watts.

***Rhino History of Rock 'n' Roll: The 70s.** Preiss. 1997. 30.00 (0-671-01175-8, PB Hardcover) PB.

Rhino Man & Other Uncommon Environmentalists. Winthrop P. Carty & Elizabeth Lee. LC 92-9166. 178p. 1992. pap. 12.95 (0-929765-10-9) Seven Locks Pr.

Rhino-Otological Microsurgery of the Skull Base. Michael Portmann et al. LC 93-33094. (Practice of Surgery Ser.). (Illus.). 320p. 1994. 185.00 (0-443-04539-9) Churchill.

Rhino Ritz: An American Mystery. Keith Abbott. LC 78-23542. 1979. pap. 12.95 (0-912652-43-8) Blue Wind.

Rhino Ritz: An American Mystery. deluxe ed. Keith Abbott. LC 78-23542. 1979. 49.95 (0-912652-44-6) Blue Wind.

Rhino Stayed for Breakfast. large type ed. Rowena Lee. 1975. 25.99 (0-85456-371-7) Ulverscroft.

***Rhinoceros.** Mary Hull. (Overview Series). (Illus.). (J). (gr. 4-12). 1997. lib. bdg. 17.96 (1-56006-461-7) Lucent Bks.

Rhinoceros. Eugene Ionesco. 1959. write for info. (0-318-63591-7) Fr & Eur.

Rhinoceros. Eugene Ionesco. (FRE.). 1976. pap. 10.95 (0-8288-3693-0, F105991) Fr & Eur.

Rhinoceros. Eugene Ionesco. (Folio Ser.: No. 816). (FRE.). 1959. pap. 9.25 (2-07-036816-5) Schoenhof.

Rhinoceros. L. Martin. (Wildlife in Danger Ser.). (Illus.). 24p. (J). (gr. k-5). 1988. lib. bdg. 11.94 (0-86592-997-1) Rourke Corp.

Rhinoceros. Alison Tibbitts & Alan Roocroft. (Animals, Animals, Animals Ser.). (Illus.). 24p. (J). (ps-2). 1992. lib. bdg. 17.80 (1-56065-101-6) Capstone Pr.

Rhinoceros. 2nd ed. Eugene Ionesco. Ed. by Ellison et al. 320p. (FRE.). (C). 1976. text ed. write for info. (0-318-69158-2) HB Coll Pubs.

***Rhinoceros, Vol. 1.** George. (Illus.). (J). 1998. 14.95 (0-7868-3163-4) Disney Pr.

Rhinoceros & Other Plays. Eugene Ionesco. Tr. by Derek Prouse. 1990. 20.50 (0-8446-2293-1) Peter Smith.

Rhinoceros & Other Plays: The Leader, The Future Is in Eggs, It Takes All Kinds to Make a World. Eugene Ionesco. Tr. by Derek Prouse from FRE. LC 60-11090. 176p. (Orig.). 1988. pap. 10.00 (0-8021-3098-4, Grove) Grove-Atltic.

Rhinoceros Beetle to the Rescue. Linda Hartley. Ed. by Eril Hughes. LC 96-27085. (Shining Nature Ser.). (Illus.). 24p. (J). (ps-2). 1996. lib. bdg. 16.45 (1-56074-065-5) Garrett Ed Corp.

Rhinoceros from Durer to Stubbs: An Aspect of the Exotic. T. H. Clarke. LC 86-50086. (Illus.). 220p. 1988. pap. 29.95 (0-85667-326-9, Pub. by P Wilson Pubs) Sothebys Pubns.

Rhinoceros in the Classroom. R. Murray Schafer. 1975. pap. 14.95 (0-900938-44-7, UE26922) Eur-Am Music.

Rhinoceros Success. 62th ed. Scott Alexander. LC 80-51648. (Illus.). 123p. (Orig.). 1996. pap. 7.95 (0-937382-00-0) Rhinos Pr.

Rhinoceros Tap: And 14 Other Seriously Silly Songs. Sandra Boynton. (Illus.). 48p. (J). (ps up). 1996. 15.95 (0-7611-0593-X, 10593) Workman Pub.

Rhinoceroses. Amanda Harman. LC 96-10863. (Endangered! Ser.). (Illus.). (J). (gr. 3-5). 1996. lib. bdg. 14.95 (0-7614-0290-X, Benchmark NY) Marshall Cavendish.

Rhinocerotic Relativity. 15th ed. Scott R. Alexander. LC 83-60933. (Illus.). 120p. (Orig.). 1995. pap. 7.95 (0-937382-02-7) Rhinos Pr.

Rhinocerous Horn. Tr. by I. B. Horner et al. from PLI. (C). 1984. pap. 13.50 (0-86013-154-8, Pub. by Pali Text) Wisdom MA.

Rhinologic Diagnosis & Treatment. Thomas V. McCaffrey. (Illus.). 432p. 1996. text ed. 79.00 (0-86577-619-9) Thieme Med Pubs.

Rhinology: A State of the Art: Proceedings of the XVth Congress of the European Phinologic Society & the XIIIth International Symposium on Infection & Allergy of the Nose, Copenhagen, Denmark, June 19-23, 1994. Ed. by Mirkos Tos et al. 1995. 200.00 (90-6299-119-X) Kugler Pubns.

Rhinology & Nasal Allergy Yearbook 1996. David W. Kennedy & Paul A. Greenberger. (Illus.). 325p. 1996. 67.00 (0-936587-08-3) OceanSide Pubns.

Rhinology & Sinus Disease: A Problem-Oriented A... Steven D. Schaeffer. 352p. (C). (gr. 13). 1998. text ed. 99.95 (0-8016-7800-5) Mosby Yr Bk.

Rhinoplasty. Peter McKinney & Bruce Cunningham. (Illus.). 190p. 1988. text ed. 134.00 (0-443-08531-5) Churchill.

Rhinoplasty. Fernando Ortiz-Monasterio. LC 93-33891. (Illus.). 304p. 1994. text ed. 145.00 (0-7216-6786-4) Saunders.

Rhinoplasty: A Practical Guide to Functional & Aesthetic Surgery of the Nose. G. J. Nolst-Trenite. LC 92-48704. (Illus.). 200p. 1992. lib. bdg. 169.00 (90-6299-089-4) Kugler Pubns.

Rhinoplasty: State of the Art. Ed. by Ronald P. Gruber & George C. Peck. LC 92-18736. 391p. (C). (gr. 13). 1992. text ed. 189.00 (0-8016-6277-X) Mosby Yr Bk.

Rhinoplasty: The Art & the Science, 2 vols., Set. Eugene Tardy, Jr. Ed. by Larry McGrew. LC 95-41653. (Illus.). 912p. 1996. text ed. 395.00 (0-7216-8755-5) Saunders.

Rhinoplasty Tetrology: Corrective, Secondary, Congenital, Reconstructive. D. Ralph Millard, Jr. LC 96-1014. 1000p. 1996. text ed. 395.00 (0-316-57156-3) Lppncott-Raven.

***Rhinos.** Marianne Johnston. LC 96-37465. (Giant Animals Ser.). 1996. write for info. (0-8239-5144-8) Rosen Group.

Rhinos. Peter Murray. (Nature Bks.). 32p. (J). (gr. 2-6). 1992. lib. bdg. 22.79 (0-89565-838-0) Childs World.

Rhinos. Sally M. Walker. LC 96-228. (Illus.). (J). 1996. lib. bdg. 14.96 (1-57505-008-0, Carolrhoda) Lerner Group.

Rhinos. John B. Wexo. (Zoobooks Ser.). (J). 1991. lib. bdg. 14.95 (0-88682-333-1) Creative Ed.

Rhinos. Wildlife Education, Ltd. Staff. (Zoobooks Ser.). (Illus.). 20p. (Orig.). (J). (gr. 1-8). 1985. pap. 2.75 (0-937934-29-1) Wildlife Educ.

Rhinos: An Endangered Species. Malcolm Penny. (Illus.). 128p. 1988. write for info. (0-318-32664-7) Facts on File.

Rhinos for Lunch & Elephants for Supper! Tololwa M. Mollel. (Illus.). 32p. (J). (ps-3). 1992. 15.95 (0-395-60734-5, Clarion Bks) HM.

***Rhinos Who Snowboard.** Julie Mammano. LC 97-1349. (J). 1997. 11.95 (0-8118-1715-6) Chronicle Bks.

Rhinos Who Surf. Julie Mammano. 32p. (J). 1996. 11.95 (0-8118-1000-3) Chronicle Bks.

Rhizoctonia Solani: Biology & Pathology. Ed. by J. R. Parmeter. LC 69-16510. (Illus.). (C). 1970. 55.00 (0-520-01497-9) U CA Pr.

***Rhizoctonia Species: Taxonomy, Molecular Biology, Ecology, Pathology & Disease Control.** Buruch Sneh. LC 96-30327. 1996. lib. bdg. 224.00 (0-7923-3644-5, D Reidel) Kluwer Ac.

Rhizome & the Flower: The Perennial Philosophy--Yeats & Jung. James Olney. 1980. 52.50 (0-520-03748-0) U CA Pr.

Rhizophoracea & Gramineae see Forest Flora of the Bombay Presidency & Sind

Rhizosphere. E. A. Curl & B. Truelove. (Advanced Series in Agricultural Sciences: Vol. 15). (Illus.). 328p. 1985. 232.95 (0-387-15803-0) Spr-Verlag.

Rhizosphere. J. M. Lynch. LC 89-24819. (Environmental & Applied Microbiology Ser.). 458p. 1990. text ed. 265.00 (0-471-92548-9) Wiley.

Rhizosphere & Plant Growth. Donald L. Keister & Perry B. Cregan. (Beltsville Symposia in Agricultural Research Ser.). (C). 1991. lib. bdg. 242.00 (0-7923-1032-2) Kluwer Ac.

RHM: Robert Hunter Middleton: The Man & His Letters; Essays on His Life & Career. Ed. by Bruce Young & Bruce Beck. (Illus.). 1985. 25.00 (0-940550-08-3) Caxton Club.

Rhoda: A Life in Stories. Ellen Gilchrist. LC 95-8087. 432p. 1995. 13.95 (0-316-31464-1) Little.

Rhoda Sherbell: Sculpture. Clarissa H. Watson & Robert Myron. (Illus.). 13p. Date not set. 1.00 (0-614-10424-6) W Benton Mus.

Rhode College. William Strode. LC 85-81583. 112p. 1985. 30.00 (0-916509-03-6) Harmony Hse Pub.

Rhode Island. 1986. pap. 11.95 (0-393-30271-7) Norton.

***Rhode Island.** (Celebrate the States Ser.). (Illus.). 144p. (J). (ps up). 1998. lib. bdg. 22.95 (0-7614-0417-1, Benchmark NY) Marshall Cavendish.

Rhode Island. Dennis B. Fradin. (From Sea to Shining Sea Ser.). (Illus.). 64p. (J). (gr. 3-5). 1995. lib. bdg. 24.00 (0-516-03839-7) Childrens.

***Rhode Island.** Dennis B. Fradin. (From Sea to Shining Sea Ser.). 64p. (J). 1997. pap. 5.95 (0-516-26127-4) Childrens.

***Rhode Island.** Paul Joseph. LC 97-21417. (The United States Ser.). 1998. write for info. (1-56239-877-6) Abdo & Dghtrs.

Rhode Island. Kathleen Thompson. LC 95-44413. (Portrait of America Library). 48p. (J). (gr. 3 up). 1996. lib. bdg. 22.83 (0-8114-7385-6) Raintree Steck-V.

Rhode Island. Kathleen Thompson. LC 95-44413. (Portrait of America Library). 48p. (J). (gr. 3 up). 1996. pap. 5.95 (0-8114-7466-6) Raintree Steck-V.

Rhode Island. rev. ed. Ann Heinrichs. LC 89-25284. (America the Beautiful Ser.). (Illus.). 144p. (J). (gr. 4 up). 1992. lib. bdg. 28.30 (0-516-00485-9) Childrens.

Rhode Island: A Bibliography of Its History. Ed. by Roger Parks. LC 83-50139. (Bibliographies of New England History Ser.: No. 5). 263p. 1983. text ed. 45.00 (0-87451-284-0) U Pr of New Eng.

Rhode Island: A Guide to the Smallest State. Federal Writers' Project Staff & Writers Program-WPA Staff. (American Guide Ser.). 1989. reprint ed. lib. bdg. 79.00 (0-7812-1038-0, 1038) Rprt Serv.

Rhode Island: A Guide to the Smallest State. Federal Writers' Project Staff. (American Guidebook Ser.). 500p. 1937. reprint ed. 89.00 (0-403-02188-X) Somerset Pub.

Rhode Island: A Scenic Discovery. Steve Dunwell. Ed. by James B. Patrick. (Scenic Discovery Ser.). 120p. 1983. 25.00 (0-940078-03-1) Foremost Pubs.

Rhode Island: A Study in Separatism. Irving B. Richman. LC 72-3749. (American Commonwealths Ser.: No. 17). reprint ed. 42.50 (0-404-57217-0) AMS Pr.

Rhode Island: An Explorer's Guide. Phyllis Meras & Tom Gannon. (Explorer's Guide Ser.). (Illus.). 296p. (Orig.). 1995. pap. 16.00 (0-88150-308-8) Countryman.

***Rhode Island: An Explorer's Guide.** 2nd ed. Phyllis Meras & Tom Gannon. LC 97-24575. (Explorer's Guide Ser.). (Illus.). 396p. 1998. pap. 16.00 (0-88150-391-6) Countryman.

Rhode Island: Eight Poems. Michael S. Harper. 17p. (C). 1981. pap. 3.00 (0-913219-26-6) Pym-Rand Pr.

Rhode Island: Eight Poems. deluxe ed. Michael S. Harper. 17p. (C). 1981. 10.00 (0-913219-27-4) Pym-Rand Pr.

Rhode Island: Hello U. S. A. J. F. Warner. (J). (gr. 3-6). 1993. lib. bdg. 18.95 (0-8225-2731-6, Lerner Publctns) Lerner Group.

Rhode Island: Off the Beaten Path: A Guide to Unique Places. Paula Bodah. LC 95-43089. (Off the Beaten Path Ser.). (Illus.). 176p. (Orig.). 1995. pap. text ed. 10.95 (1-56440-651-2) Globe Pequot.

Rhode Island: The Independent State. George H. Kellner. 1982. 24.95 (0-89781-040-6) Am Historical Pr.

Rhode Island Actions & Remedies: Tort Law, 2 vols., Set. Daniel C. Pope & Ronald J. Resmini. 1180p. 1992. ring bd. 145.00 (1-56257-270-9) MICHIE.

***Rhode Island Album.** Don Bousquet. (Illus.). 160p. 1996. 24.95 (0-924771-78-X, Covered Brdge Pr) D C Press.

Rhode Island & Other State Greats (Biographies) Carole Marsh. (Carole Marsh Rhode Island Bks.). (Illus.). (J). 1994. pap. 19.95 (0-7933-1978-1); lib. bdg. 29.95 (0-7933-1977-3); disk 29.95 (0-7933-1979-X) Gallopade Pub Group.

Rhode Island & the Formation of the Union. Frank G. Bates. LC 68-1297. (Columbia University. Studies in the Social Sciences: No. 27). reprint ed. 35.00 (0-404-51027-2) AMS Pr.

Rhode Island & the Union, 1774-1795. Irwin H. Polishook. LC 69-18021. (Studies in History Ser.: No. 5). 280p. reprint ed. pap. 79.80 (0-8357-9469-5, 2013681) Bks Demand.

Rhode Island Appellate Practice. Joseph R. Weisberger. 190p. 1993. ring bd. 65.00 (0-614-05959-3) MICHIE.

Rhode Island Appellate Practice, 1985-1993. Joseph R. Weisberger. 190p. 1991. ring bd. 65.00 (0-88063-068-X) MICHIE.

Rhode Island Appellate Practice, 1985-1993. Joseph R. Weisberger. 190p. 1993. suppl. ed. 28.00 (0-88063-795-1) MICHIE.

Rhode Island Architecture. 2nd ed. Henry-Russell Hitchcock. LC 68-27725. (Architecture & Decorative Art Ser.: Vol. 19). (Illus.). 1968. reprint ed. lib. bdg. 42.50 (0-306-71037-4) Da Capo.

Rhode Island Arms Makers & Gunsmiths: 1643-1883. William O. Achtermier. LC 80-84583. (Illus.). 108p. 1980. 16.50 (0-917218-15-9) A Mowbray.

Rhode Island Bandits, Bushwackers, Outlaws, Crooks, Devils, Ghosts, Desperadoes & Other Assorted & Sundry Characters! Carole Marsh. (Carole Marsh Rhode Island Bks.). (Illus.). (J). 1994. pap. 19.95 (0-7933-0985-9); lib. bdg. 29.95 (0-7933-0986-7); disk 29.95 (0-7933-0987-5) Gallopade Pub Group.

Rhode Island Biographical & Genealogical Sketch Index. Compiled by J. Carlyle Parker. LC 90-25871. 1991. 29.95 (0-934153-08-6, OCLC 22859101) Marietta Pub.

Rhode Island Blue Ribbon Commission to Develop a Strategic Plan to Enhance Educational Programs & Opportunities for All. Christopher W. Wessells. (Illus.). 73p. (Orig.). (C). 1995. pap. text ed. 25.00 (0-7881-1574-X) DIANE Pub.

Rhode Island Bookstore Book: A Surprising Guide to Our State's Bookstores & Their Specialties for Students, Teachers, Writers & Publishers. Carole Marsh. (Rhode Island Bks.). (Illus.). 1994. pap. 19.95 (0-7933-2973-6); lib. bdg. 29.95 (0-7933-2972-8); disk 29.95 (0-7933-2974-4) Gallopade Pub Group.

***Rhode Island Business Directory 1997.** American Business Directories Staff. 544p. 1997. boxed 295.00 (1-56105-916-1) Am Busn Direct.

Rhode Island Campaign of 1778: Inauspicious Dawn of Alliance. Paul F. Dearden. LC 78-69820. (Illus.). 169p. 1980. 7.95 (0-917012-17-8) RI Pubns Soc.

Rhode Island Catholicism: A Historical Guide. Patrick T. Conley. 24p. (Orig.). 1984. pap. 2.95 (0-917012-56-9) RI Pubns Soc.

Rhode Island Census Index, 1782. (Illus.). lib. bdg. 49.00 (0-89593-476-0) Accelerated Index.

Rhode Island Census Index 1890: Union Veterans. Ronald V. Jackson. (Illus.). lib. bdg. 50.00 (0-89593-771-9) Accelerated Index.

Rhode Island Census, 1880. 1990. write for info. (0-89593-638-0) Accelerated Index.

Rhode Island Classic Christmas Trivia: Stories, Recipes, Activities, Legends, Lore & More! Carole Marsh. (Carole Marsh Rhode Island Bks.). (Illus.). (J). 1994. pap. 19.95 (0-7933-0988-3); lib. bdg. 29.95 (0-7933-0989-1); disk 29.95 (0-7933-0990-5) Gallopade Pub Group.

Rhode Island Coastales. Carole Marsh. (Carole Marsh Rhode Island Bks.). (Illus.). (J). 1994. pap. 19.95 (0-7933-1972-2); lib. bdg. 29.95 (0-7933-1971-4); disk 29.95 (0-7933-1973-0) Gallopade Pub Group.

Rhode Island Coastales! Carole Marsh. (Rhode Island Bks.). (J). 1994. lib. bdg. 29.95 (0-7933-7304-2) Gallopade Pub Group.

Rhode Island Colonial Census Index, 1742. Ronald V. Jackson. 1988. 30.00 (0-89593-819-7) Accelerated Index.

Rhode Island Colonial Census Index, 1747. Ronald V. Jackson. 1991. 49.00 (0-89593-820-0) Accelerated Index.

Rhode Island Colony. Dennis B. Fradin. LC 89-744. (Thirteen Colonies Ser.). (Illus.). 160p. (J). (gr. 4 up). 1989. lib. bdg. 28.00 (0-516-00391-7) Childrens.

Rhode Island Constitutional Development, 1636-1775: A Survey. Patrick T. Conley. 35p. 1968. reprint ed. pap. 2.75 (0-917012-42-9) RI Pubns Soc.

Rhode Island Cooks. American Cancer Society, Rhode Island Division Staff. LC 92-11048. 1992. spiral bd. 16.95 (0-87197-338-3) Favorite Recipes.

Rhode Island Corporations, Associations & Partnerships Laws Annotated, 1993 Edition. 20.00 (0-614-05960-7) MICHIE.

Rhode Island Court Rules Annotated, 1991-92. Michie Company Editorial Staff. 1216p. pap. 45.00 (0-87473-729-X) MICHIE.

Rhode Island Court Rules Annotated, 1994 Edition. Michie Butterworth Editorial Staff. 45.00 (1-55834-089-0) MICHIE.

Rhode Island Crime Perspective 1996. Ed. by Kathleen O. Morgan et al. 24p. 1996. pap. 19.00 (1-56692-538-X) Morgan Quitno Corp.

***Rhode Island Crime Perspective 1997.** Ed. by Kathleen O. Morgan & Scott E. Morgan. 24p. 1997. pap. 19.00 (1-56692-788-9) Morgan Quitno Corp.

Rhode Island Criminal & Traffic Law Manual, 1993 Edition. 30.00 (0-614-05961-5) MICHIE.

Rhode Island Criminal Procedure, 1988-1991. John A. MacFadyen & Barbara Hurst. 530p. 1993. ring bd. 125.00 (0-88063-075-2); suppl. ed. 55.00 (0-250-40700-0) MICHIE.

Rhode Island "Crinkum-Crankum" A Funny Word Book about Our State. Carole Marsh. (Rhode Island Bks.). (Illus.). (J). (gr. 3-12). 1994. 29.95 (0-7933-4925-7); pap. 19.95 (0-7933-4926-5); disk 29.95 (0-7933-4927-3) Gallopade Pub Group.

Rhode Island Dictionary. Mark Patinkin. (Illus.). 128p. 1993. pap. 8.95 (0-924771-45-3, Covered Brdge Pr) D C Press.

Rhode Island Dingbats! Bk. 1: A Fun Book of Games, Stories, Activities & More about Our State That's All in Code! for You to Decipher. Carole Marsh. (Rhode Island Bks.). (Illus.). (J). (gr. 3-12). 1994. pap. 19.95 (0-7933-3891-3); lib. bdg. 29.95 (0-7933-3890-5); disk 29.95 (0-7933-3892-1) Gallopade Pub Group.

Rhode Island Early Census, Vol. 1. Ronald V. Jackson. (Illus.). lib. bdg. 58.00 (0-89593-743-3) Accelerated Index.

Rhode Island Environmental Law Handbook. 2nd ed. McGovern et al. 231p. 1994. pap. text ed. 89.00 (0-86587-424-7) Gov Insts.

Rhode Island Facts & Factivities. Carole Marsh. (Carole Marsh State Bks.). (Illus.). 1996. 29.95 (0-614-11549-3, C Marsh); teacher ed., pap. 19.95 (0-7933-7925-3, C Marsh) Gallopade Pub Group.

Rhode Island Families, Genealogies of, from the New England Historical & Genealogical Register, 2 vols., Set. Intro. & Selected by Gary B. Roberts. 1989. 95.00 (0-8063-1218-1, 4883) Genealog Pub.

Rhode Island Federal Census Index: 1810. Ronald V. Jackson. LC 77-86092. (Illus.). 1976. lib. bdg. 40.00 (0-89593-122-2) Accelerated Index.

Rhode Island Federal Census Index, 1790. Ronald V. Jackson. (Illus.). lib. bdg. 35.00 (0-89593-770-0) Accelerated Index.

Rhode Island Federal Census Index, 1800. Ronald V. Jackson. LC 77-86085. (Illus.). 1972. lib. bdg. 40.00 (0-89593-127-3) Accelerated Index.

Rhode Island Federal Census Index, 1820. Ronald V. Jackson. LC 77-86091. (Illus.). 1976. lib. bdg. 38.00 (0-89593-123-0) Accelerated Index.

Rhode Island Federal Census Index, 1830. Ronald V. Jackson. LC 77-86092. (Illus.). 1976. lib. bdg. 50.00 (0-89593-124-9) Accelerated Index.

Rhode Island Federal Census Index, 1840. Ronald V. Jackson. LC 77-86093. (Illus.). 1977. lib. bdg. 54.00 (0-89593-125-7) Accelerated Index.

Rhode Island Federal Census Index, 1850. Ronald V. Jackson. LC 77-86084. (Illus.). 1976. lib. bdg. 63.00 (0-89593-126-5) Accelerated Index.

Rhode Island Federal Census Index, 1860. Ronald V. Jackson. 1985. 123.00 (0-89593-478-7) Accelerated Index.

Rhode Island Federal Census Index, 1870. Ronald V. Jackson. 200.00 (0-89593-477-9) Accelerated Index.

Rhode Island Festival Fun for Kids! Carole Marsh. (Rhode Island Bks.). (Illus.). (YA). (gr. 3-12). 1994. pap. 19.95 (0-7933-4044-6); lib. bdg. 29.95 (0-7933-4043-8); disk 29.95 (0-7933-4045-4) Gallopade Pub Group.

Rhode Island General Laws Annotated, 25 vols. write for info. (0-672-83449-9) MICHIE.

***Rhode Island Government! The Cornerstone of Everyday Life in Our State!** Carole Marsh. (Carole Marsh Rhode Island Bks.). (Illus.). (J). (gr. 3-12). 1996. pap. 19.95 (0-7933-6299-7); lib. bdg. 29.95 (0-7933-6298-9); disk 29.95 (0-7933-6300-4) Gallopade Pub Group.

Rhode Island Handbook. Mark Patinkin. (Illus.). 144p. 1994. pap. 9.95 (0-924771-49-6, Covered Brdge Pr) D C Press.

Rhode Island Health Care Perspective 1996. Ed. by Kathleen O. Morgan et al. 24p. 1996. pap. 19.00 (1-56692-638-6) Morgan Quitno Corp.

***Rhode Island Health Care Perspective 1997.** Ed. by Kathleen O. Morgan & Scott E. Morgan. 24p. 1997. pap. 19.00 (1-56692-738-2) Morgan Quitno Corp.

Rhode Island Historical & Biographical Index, Vol. 1. Ronald V. Jackson. LC 78-53715. (Illus.). 1984. lib. bdg. 30.00 (0-89593-198-2) Accelerated Index.

***Rhode Island History! Surprising Secrets about Our State's Founding Mothers, Fathers & Kids!** Carole Marsh. (Carole Marsh Rhode Island Bks.). (Illus.). (J). (gr. 3-12). 1996. pap. 19.95 (0-7933-6146-X); lib. bdg. 29.95 (0-7933-6145-1); disk 29.95 (0-7933-6147-8) Gallopade Pub Group.

Rhode Island Hot Air Balloon Mystery. Carole Marsh. (Carole Marsh Rhode Island Bks.). (Illus.). (J). (gr. 2-9). 1994. 29.95 (0-7933-2669-9); pap. 19.95 (0-7933-2670-2); disk 29.95 (0-7933-2671-0) Gallopade Pub Group.

Rhode Island in Perspective 1996. Ed. by Kathleen O. Morgan et al. 26p. 1996. pap. 19.00 (1-56692-588-6) Morgan Quitno Corp.

***Rhode Island in Perspective 1997.** Ed. by Kathleen O. Morgan & Scott E. Morgan. 26p. 1997. pap. 19.00 (1-56692-688-2) Morgan Quitno Corp.

An Asterisk (*) at the beginning of an entry indicates that the title is appearing in BIP for the first time.

Rhode Island in the Colonial Wars: A List of Rhode Island Soldiers & Sailors in King George's War, 1740-1748, & a List of Rhode Island Soldiers & Sailors in the Old French & Indian War, 1755-1762. Howard M. Chapin. 193p. 1994. 20.00 (*0-614-03804-9*, 945) Genealog Pub.

Rhode Island in the Colonial Wars: List of R. I. Soldiers & Sailors in King George's War, 1740-1748; & List of R. I. Soldiers in the Old French & Indian War, 1755-1762. H. M. Chapin. 193p. 1996. reprint ed. lib. bdg. 29.00 (*0-8328-5114-0*) Higginson Bk Co.

Rhode Island in the Continental Congress, 1765-1790. W. R. Staples. LC 71-153373. (Era of the American Revolution Ser.). 726p. 1971. reprint ed. lib. bdg. 75.00 (*0-306-70203-7*) Da Capo.

Rhode Island Indian Dictionary for Kids! Carole Marsh. (Carole Marsh State Bks.). (J). (gr. 2-9). 1996. 29.95 (*0-7933-7761-7*, C Marsh); pap. 19.95 (*0-7933-7762-5*, C Marsh) Gallopade Pub Group.

Rhode Island Jeopardy! Answers & Questions about Our State! Carole Marsh. (Rhode Island Bks.). (Illus.). (J). (gr. 3-12). 1994. pap. 19.95 (*0-7933-4197-3*); lib. bdg. 29.95 (*0-7933-4196-5*); disk 29.95 (*0-7933-4198-1*) Gallopade Pub Group.

Rhode Island "Jography" A Fun Run Thru Our State! Carole Marsh. (Carole Marsh Rhode Island Bks.). (Illus.). (J). 1994. pap. 19.95 (*0-7933-1955-2*); lib. bdg. 29.95 (*0-7933-1954-4*); disk 29.95 (*0-7933-1956-0*) Gallopade Pub Group.

Rhode Island Kid's Cookbook: Recipes, How-to, History Lore & More! Carole Marsh. (Carole Marsh Rhode Island Bks.). (Illus.). (J). 1994. pap. 19.95 (*0-7933-0997-2*); lib. bdg. 29.95 (*0-7933-0998-0*); disk 29.95 (*0-7933-0999-9*) Gallopade Pub Group.

***Rhode Island Land Evidences Vol. I: 1648-1696, Abstracts.** Rhode Island Historical Society Staff. (Illus.). 271p. 1996. reprint ed. pap. 25.00 (*0-614-23606-1*, 4880) Clearfield Co.

Rhode Island Library Book: A Surprising Guide to the Unusual Special Collections in Libraries Across Our State for Students, Teachers, Writers & Publishers - Includes Reproducible Mailing Labels Plus Activities for Young People! Carole Marsh. (Rhode Island Bks.). (Illus.). 1994. pap. 19.95 (*0-7933-3123-4*); lib. bdg. 29.95 (*0-7933-3122-6*); disk 29.95 (*0-7933-3124-2*) Gallopade Pub Group.

Rhode Island Media Book: A Surprising Guide to the Amazing Print, Broadcast & Online Media of Our State for Students, Teachers, Writers & Publishers - Includes Reproducible Mailing Labels Plus Activities for Young People! Carole Marsh. (Rhode Island Bks.). (Illus.). 1994. pap. 19.95 (*0-7933-3279-6*); lib. bdg. 29.95 (*0-7933-3278-8*); disk 29.95 (*0-7933-3280-X*) Gallopade Pub Group.

Rhode Island Military Census Index, 1776. (Illus.). lib. bdg. 49.00 (*0-89593-474-4*) Accelerated Index.

Rhode Island Military Census Index, 1777. (Illus.). 1988. lib. bdg. 64.00 (*0-89593-475-2*) Accelerated Index.

Rhode Island Mortality Schedule, 1860. Ronald V. Jackson. 1980. 63.00 (*0-89593-834-0*) Accelerated Index.

Rhode Island Mortality Schedule, 1870. Ronald V. Jackson. 1980. 74.00 (*0-89593-835-9*) Accelerated Index.

Rhode Island Mortality Schedule, 1880. Ronald V. Jackson. 1991. 80.00 (*0-89593-836-7*) Accelerated Index.

Rhode Island Mystery Van Takes Off! Book 1: Handicapped Rhode Island Kids Sneak Off on a Big Adventure. Carole Marsh. (Rhode Island Bks.). (Illus.). (J). (gr. 3-12). 1994. 29.95 (*0-7933-5078-6*); pap. 19.95 (*0-7933-5079-4*); disk 29.95 (*0-7933-5080-8*) Gallopade Pub Group.

Rhode Island Passenger Lists: Port of Providence 1798-1808; 1820-1872, Port of Bristol & Warren 1820-1871. Maureen A. Taylor. 232p. 1995. 25.00 (*0-8063-1459-1*) Genealog Pub.

Rhode Island Politics & the American Revolution, 1760-1776. David S. Lovejoy. LC 58-10478. (Brown University Studies: Vol. 23). 266p. reprint ed. pap. 75.90 (*0-685-44066-4*, 2030025) Bks Demand.

Rhode Island Practice: Tort Law & Personal Injury Practice, 2 vols. Ronald J. Resmini. 1300p. 1990. boxed 165.00 (*0-88063-408-1*) MICHIE.

Rhode Island Practice: Tort Law & Personal Injury Practice, 2 vols. Ronald J. Resmini. 1300p. 1993. suppl. ed. 37.00 (*0-685-74298-9*) MICHIE.

Rhode Island Practice: Tort Law & Personal Injury Practice. Ronald J. Resmini. 1300p. 1994. boxed 165.00 (*0-614-05962-3*) MICHIE.

Rhode Island Practice, Vol. 3: Wills, Trusts & Gifts. David T. Riedel. 1993. suppl. ed., ring.bd. 40.00 (*0-685-74272-5*) MICHIE.

Rhode Island Practice, Vol. 3: Wills, Trusts & Gifts, Vol. 3. David T. Riedel. 700p. 1994. boxed 125.00 (*0-88063-724-2*) MICHIE.

Rhode Island Quiz Bowl Crash Course! Carole Marsh. (Carole Marsh Rhode Island Bks.). (Illus.). (J). 1994. pap. 19.95 (*0-7933-1969-2*); lib. bdg. 29.95 (*0-7933-1968-4*); disk 29.95 (*0-7933-1970-6*) Gallopade Pub Group.

***Rhode Island Red, Vol. 1.** Charlotte Carter. LC 96-71368. (Mask Noir Ser.). 250p. (Orig.). 1997. 15.99 (*1-85242-564-4*, High Risk Bks) Serpents Tail.

Rhode Island Rollercoasters! Carole Marsh. (Rhode Island Bks.). (Illus.). (YA). (gr. 3-12). 1994. pap. 19.95 (*0-7933-5342-4*); lib. bdg. 29.95 (*0-7933-5341-6*); disk 29.95 (*0-7933-5343-2*) Gallopade Pub Group.

Rhode Island Rules of Evidence. Eric D. Green. 1993. suppl. ed., ring bd. 35.00 (*0-685-74349-7*) MICHIE.

Rhode Island Rules of Evidence. Eric D. Green. 400p. 1994. spiral bd. 95.00 (*0-88063-358-1*) MICHIE.

Rhode Island Scene. Ed. by Peter C. Crolius. (Illus.). 160p. (Orig.). 1986. pap. 10.95 (*0-934881-01-4*) Dutch Island.

Rhode Island School Trivia: An Amazing & Fascinating Look at Our State's Teachers, Schools & Students! Carole Marsh. (Carole Marsh Rhode Island Bks.). (Illus.). (J). 1994. pap. 19.95 (*0-7933-0994-8*); lib. bdg. 29.95 (*0-7933-0995-6*); disk 29.95 (*0-7933-0996-4*) Gallopade Pub Group.

Rhode Island Silly Basketball Sportsmysteries, Vol. 1. Carole Marsh. (Carole Marsh Rhode Island Bks.). (Illus.). (J). 1994. pap. 19.95 (*0-7933-0991-3*); lib. bdg. 29.95 (*0-7933-0992-1*); disk 29.95 (*0-7933-0993-X*) Gallopade Pub Group.

Rhode Island Silly Basketball Sportsmysteries, Vol. 2. Carole Marsh. (Carole Marsh Rhode Island Bks.). (Illus.). (J). 1994. pap. 19.95 (*0-7933-1981-1*); lib. bdg. 29.95 (*0-7933-1980-3*); disk 29.95 (*0-7933-1982-X*) Gallopade Pub Group.

Rhode Island Silly Football Sportsmysteries, Vol. 1. Carole Marsh. (Carole Marsh Rhode Island Bks.). (Illus.). (J). 1994. pap. 19.95 (*0-7933-1960-9*); lib. bdg. 29.95 (*0-7933-1959-5*); disk 29.95 (*0-7933-1961-7*) Gallopade Pub Group.

Rhode Island Silly Football Sportsmysteries, Vol. 2. Carole Marsh. (Carole Marsh Rhode Island Bks.). (Illus.). (J). 1994. pap. 19.95 (*0-7933-1963-3*); lib. bdg. 29.95 (*0-7933-1962-5*); disk 29.95 (*0-7933-1964-1*) Gallopade Pub Group.

Rhode Island Silly Trivia! Carole Marsh. (Carole Marsh Rhode Island Bks.). (Illus.). (J). 1994. pap. 19.95 (*0-7933-1952-8*); lib. bdg. 29.95 (*0-7933-1951-X*); disk 29.95 (*0-7933-1953-6*) Gallopade Pub Group.

Rhode Island State Rules of Evidence with Objections. Anthony J. Bocchino et al. 199p. 1995. pap. 16.95 (*1-55681-401-1*) Natl Inst Trial Ad.

Rhode Island Study Manual for Life & Accident & Health Insurance. 1990. pap. text ed. 7.95 (*0-7931-0051-8*, 5310-25) Dearborn Finan.

Rhode Island Timeline: A Chronology of Rhode Island History, Mystery, Trivia, Legend, Lore & More. Carole Marsh. (Rhode Island Bks.). (Illus.). (J). (gr. 3-12). 1994. pap. 19.95 (*0-7933-5993-7*); lib. bdg. 29.95 (*0-7933-5992-9*); disk 29.95 (*0-7933-5994-5*) Gallopade Pub Group.

Rhode Island Towns & Counties. Michael J. Denis. (New England Towns & Counties Ser.). 8p. (Orig.). 1983. pap. 2.00 (*0-935207-05-8*) Danbury Hse Bks.

Rhode Island 1777 Military Census. Mildred M. Chamberlain. LC 84-82485. 181p. 1985. 20.00 (*0-8063-1107-X*) Genealog Pub.

Rhode Island 1782 Census. Jay M. Holbrook. LC 78-78163. 241p. 1979. lib. bdg. 30.00 (*0-931248-00-0*) Holbrook Res.

Rhode Islanders Record the Revolution: The Journals of William Humphrey & Zuriel Waterman. Nathaniel N. Shipton & David Swain. LC 78-68840. (Rhode Island Revolutionary Heritage Ser.: Vol. 4). (Illus.). 131p. 1984. 8.95 (*0-917012-03-8*) RI Pubns Soc.

***Rhode Island's Mill Villages.** J. Fuoco. (Images of America Ser.). 1997. pap. 16.99 (*0-7524-0534-9*, Arcdia) Chalford.

Rhode Island's (Most Devastating!) Disasters & (Most Calamitous!) Catastrophies! Carole Marsh. (Carole Marsh Rhode Island Bks.). (Illus.). (J). 1994. pap. 19.95 (*0-7933-0982-4*); lib. bdg. 29.95 (*0-7933-0983-2*) Gallopade Pub Group.

Rhode Island's (Most Devastating!) Disasters & (Most Calamitous!) Catastrophies! Carole Marsh. (Carole Marsh Rhode Island Bks.). (Illus.). (J). 1997. disk 29.95 (*0-7933-0984-0*) Gallopade Pub Group.

Rhode Island's Road to Liberty. Patrick T. Conley & Albert T. Klyberg. (Illus.). 24p. (Orig.). 1987. pap. 3.50 (*0-917012-85-2*) RI Pubns Soc.

Rhode Island's Unsolved Mysteries (& Their "Solutions") Includes Scientific Information & Other Activities for Students. Carole Marsh. (Rhode Island Bks.). (Illus.). (J). (gr. 3-12). 1994. pap. 19.95 (*0-7933-5840-X*); lib. bdg. 29.95 (*0-7933-5839-6*); disk 29.95 (*0-7933-5841-8*) Gallopade Pub Group.

Rhodes. Berlitz Editors. (Pocket Guides Ser.). 1995. pap. 7.95 (*2-8315-1446-0*) Berlitz.

***Rhodes.** Thomas. LC 97-18588. 1997. 25.95 (*0-312-16982-5*) St Martin.

Rhodes: Travel Guide. Globe Pequot Press Staff. (Illus.). 128p. 1997. pap. text ed. 9.95 (*1-85368-435-X*) Globe Pequot.

***Rhodes & Barnato: Architects of Empire.** James Leasor. 1997. 32.95 (*0-85052-545-4*, Pub. by L Cooper Bks UK) Trans-Atl Phila.

Rhodes & Rhodesia: The White Conquest of Zimbabwe, 1884-1902. Arthur Keppel-Jones. (Illus.). 674p. 1983. text ed. 70.00 (*0-7735-0534-2*, Pub. by McGill CN) U of Toronto Pr.

***Rhodes & the Dodecanese.** Robin Barber. (Blue Guides Ser.). (Illus.). 256p. 1997. pap. 18.95 (*0-393-31582-7*) Norton.

Rhodes Family in America: A Genealogy & History, from 1497 to the Present Day. Howard J. Rhodes. (Illus.). 525p. 1992. reprint ed. pap. 79.00 (*0-8328-2391-0*); reprint ed. lib. bdg. 89.00 (*0-8328-2390-2*) Higginson Bk Co.

Rhodes in the Hellenistic Age. Richard M. Berthold. LC 83-23127. (Illus.). 243p. 1984. 39.95 (*0-8014-1640-X*) Cornell U Pr.

Rhodes, the Tswana, & the British: Colonialism, Collaboration, & Conflict in the Bechuanaland Protectorate, 1885-1899. Paul Maylam. LC 79-8582. (Contributions in Comparative Colonial Studies: No. 4). (Illus.). x, 245p. 1980. text ed. 79.50 (*0-313-20885-9*, MTB/) Greenwood.

Rhodesia: The Struggle for Freedom. Leonard T. Kapungu. LC 74-76966. 189p. reprint ed. pap. 53.90 (*0-8357-7010-9*, 2033533) Bks Demand.

Rhodesia Becomes Zimbabwe: The United States & the Internal Settlement & The Lancaster House Conference. Marc Levy. (Pew Case Studies in International Affairs). 50p. (C). 1989. pap. text ed. 3.50 (*1-56927-442-8*) Geo U Inst Dplmcy.

Rhodesia-Zimbabwe. Oliver Pollak & Karen Pollak. (World Bibliographical Ser.: No. 4). 195p. 1979. lib. bdg. 25.25 (*0-903450-14-3*) ABC-CLIO.

Rhodesian Ridgeback Champions, 1955-1980. Jan L. Pata. (Illus.). 97p. 1981. pap. 36.95 (*0-940808-04-8*) Camino E E & Bk.

Rhodesian Ridgeback Champions, 1981-1986. Camino E. E. & Bk. Co. Staff. (Illus.). 132p. 1988. pap. 28.95 (*0-940808-65-X*) Camino E E & Bk.

Rhodesian Ridgeback Champions, 1987-1992. Camino E. E. & Bk. Co. Staff. (Illus.). 150p. 1993. pap. text ed. 32.95 (*1-55893-027-2*) Camino E E & Bk.

Rhodesian Ridgebacks. Frank C. Lutman. (Illus.). 160p. 1994. lib. bdg. 9.95 (*0-7938-1101-5*, KW159) TFH Pubns.

Rhodesian Sellout. Robert Skimin. LC 77-79579. 1978. 6.95 (*0-87212-089-9*) Libra.

Rhodium. 1955. 180.00 (*0-387-93180-5*) Spr-Verlag.

Rhodium from Black Sands. Joe E. Champion. Ed. by Roger C. Briggs. (Illus.). 30p. 1993. spiral bd. 19.95 (*1-884928-11-0*) Discov Pubng.

Rhododendron Basics: Growing Healthy Plants. Harold E. Greer. (Illus.). 17p. (Orig.). 1996. pap. 3.50 (*0-910013-07-1*) Offshoot Pub.

Rhododendron Hybrids. 2nd ed. Homer E. Salley & Harold E. Greer. LC 91-44638. (Illus.). 442p. 1992. 59.95 (*0-88192-184-X*) Timber.

Rhododendron Portraits. D. M. Van Gelderen & J. R. Smith. LC 91-23264. (Illus.). 424p. 1992. 75.00 (*0-88192-194-7*) Timber.

Rhododendron Shedding Its Skin: Poems by Diane Frank. Diane Frank. LC 87-73215. (Illus.). 57p. (Orig.). 1988. pap. 10.00 (*0-9619744-0-0*) Blue Light Pr.

Rhododendron Species: Elepidotes Continued (Neriiflorum - Thomsonii, Azaleastrum & Camtschaticum), Vol. 3. H. H. Davidian. LC 81-23232. (Illus.). 429p. 1992. 54.95 (*0-88192-168-8*) Timber.

Rhododendron Species Vol. 4: Azaleas. H. H. Davidian. (Illus.). 184p. 1995. 54.95 (*0-88192-311-7*) Timber.

Rhododendron Species, Vol. II: Elepidotes (Arboreum-Lactaeum) H. H. Davidian. LC 81-23232. (Illus.). 392p. 1989. 54.95 (*0-88192-109-2*) Timber.

Rhododendrons in America. 2nd ed. Ted Van Veen. LC 77-104390. (Illus.). 192p. 1986. 39.95 (*0-8323-0450-6*); pap. 25.00 (*0-8323-0374-7*) Binford Mort.

Rhododendrons of China. Tr. by Judy D. Young & Lu-Sheng Chong from CHI. LC 80-68082. 690p. 1980. 25.00 (*0-8323-0373-9*) Binford Mort.

Rhododendrons of China, Vol. I. Ed. by Guo-Mei Feng. (Illus.). 196p. 1988. text ed. 97.50 (*7-03-000199-0*, Pub. by Sci Pr CH) Lubrecht & Cramer.

Rhododendrons of China, Vol. 2. Ed. by Guo-Mei Feng. (Illus.). 237p. 1992. lib. bdg. 97.50 (*7-03-002246-7*) Lubrecht & Cramer.

Rhododendrum of Sikkim Himalaya. J. D. Hooker. (C). 1988. text ed. 100.00 (*0-685-44248-9*, Pub. by Scientific UK) St Mut.

Rhodoendron of China, Vol. II. Guo-Mei Feng. 84p. 1992. text ed. 89.95 (*1-880132-01-X*) Sci Pr NY.

Rhodophylles des Forets Cotieres du Gabon et de la Cote d'Ivoire. Henri Romagnesi. (Nova Hedwigia Beiheft Ser.: No. 59). (Illus.). 1979. lib. bdg. 150.00 (*3-7682-5459-3*) Lubrecht & Cramer.

***Rhodophyta Pt. 1: Introduction, Nemaliales, Gigartinales.** Peter S. Dixon & Linda M. Irvine. (Seaweeds of the British Isles Ser.: Vol. 1, Pt. 1). (Illus.). 258p. 1997. pap. 49.95 (*0-11-310000-0*, Pub. by Statnry Ofc UK) Seven Hills Bk.

***Rhodophyta Pt. 2A: Cryptonemiales (Sensu Stricto) Palmariales, Rhodymeniales.** Linda M. Irvine. (Seaweeds of the British Isles Ser.: Vol. 1, Pt. 2A). (Illus.). 120p. 1997. pap. 24.95 (*0-11-310001-9*, Pub. by Statnry Ofc UK) Seven Hills Bk.

Rhodophyta Pt. 2B: Corallinales, Hildenbrandiales. Linda M. Irvine et al. (Seaweeds of the British Isles Ser.: Vol. 1, Pt. 2B). (Illus.). 288p. 1997. pap. 49.95 (*0-11-310016-7*, HM00167, Pub. by Statnry Ofc UK) Seven Hills Bk.

Rhodophyta Pt. 3A: Ceramiales. Christine A. Maggs & Max H. Hommersand. (Seaweeds of the British Isles Ser.: Vol. 1, Pt. 3A). (Illus.). 464p. 1997. pap. 59.95 (*0-11-310045-0*, HM00450, Pub. by Statnry Ofc UK) Seven Hills Bk.

Rhombus: The Cajun Unicorn. Timothy J. Edler. (Tim Edler's Tales from the Atchafalaya Ser.). (Illus.). 40p. (J). (gr. k up). 1984. pap. 10.00 (*0-931108-10-1*) Little Cajun Bks.

Rhomeo & Julietta see Romeus & Iuliet

***Rhonda the Rubber Woman.** Norma Peterson. LC 97-21535. 232p. 1998. write for info. (*1-57962-003-5*) Permanent Pr.

Rhone Renaissance: The Finest Rhone & Rhone-Style Wines from France & the New World. large type ed. Remington Norman. LC 95-61878. (Illus.). 386p. 1997. 50.00 (*0-932664-95-4*, 6848) Wine Appreciation.

Rhone Valley & Savoy. Rex Grizell & Arthur Eperon. (Regional Guides of France Ser.). (Illus.). 192p. 1992. reprint ed. pap. 16.95 (*0-8442-9945-6*, Passport Bks) NTC Pub Grp.

***RHS Gardener's Yearbook 1997.** Charles Quest-Ritson & Christopher Blair. (Illus.). 576p. (Orig.). 1997. pap. 36.50 (*0-333-67218-6*, Pub. by Macmlln UK) Trans-Atl Phila.

Rhubarb. Stephen Cosgrove. (Serendipity Ser.). (Illus.). 32p. (Orig.). (J). (ps-4). 1995. pap. 3.95 (*0-8431-3824-6*) Price Stern Sloan.

Rhubarb. Garrison Keillor. 1995. pap. 11.00 (*1-56511-112-5*) Viking Penguin.

Rhubarb for Good Measure. Jocelyne Kidston. 80p. 1987. 9.95 (*0-920806-82-1*, Pub. by Penumbra Pr CN) U of Toronto Pr.

***Rhubarb in the Catbird Seat.** Red Barber & Robert W. Creamer. LC 96-41632. 338p. 1997. pap. 14.95 (*0-8032-6136-5*, Bison Books) U of Nebr Pr.

Rhubarb in the Catbird Seat. Rowland Barber. 27.95 (*0-8488-1565-3*) Amereon Ltd.

***Rhubarb-O-Rama! Plays & Playwrights from the Rhubarb! Festival.** 2nd ed. Ed. by Franco Boni. 256p. 1997. pap. 16.95 (*0-921368-78-X*, Pub. by Blizzard Pub CN) Genl Dist Srvs.

Rhubarb Recipes. 2nd ed. Compiled by Jeanne DeMars. 111p. 1994. pap. 7.95 (*0-9627766-2-9*) Apple Blossom.

Rhudiprrt Collection. Dwight Decker & Teri S. Wood. 160p. 1996. pap. 13.95 (*1-883847-21-4*) MU Press.

Rhum. Blaise Cendrars. (FRE.). 1990. pap. 19.95 (*0-7859-3110-4*) Fr & Eur.

***Rhum: Mesolithic & Later Sites at Kinloch, Excavations 1984-1986.** Caroline Wickham-Jones. (Illus.). 182p. 1990. pap. 52.50 (*0-903903-07-5*) David Brown.

Rhum: The Natural History of an Island. Tim Clutton-Brock & Martim Ball. 160p. 1987. 35.00 (*0-85224-513-0*, Pub. by Edinburgh U Pr UK) Col U Pr.

Rhumbs. Ian Reid. Ed. by Peter Kaplan. LC 75-10586. 1975. 1.50 (*0-915176-07-6*) Pourboire.

***Rhy the Rhyming Detective Story Samphlet of Stories.** Story Time Staff. (Illus.). (Orig.). 1997. teacher ed., pap. 21.95 (*1-56820-193-1*) Story Time.

Rhy the Rhyming Detective Story Series, Set, Vols. 1-4. A. Doyle. (Orig.). (J). (gr. 4-11). 1996. pap. 59.95 (*1-56820-165-6*) Story Time.

Rhyder McClure's Short Course in Lotus 1-2-3. Rhyder McClure. pap. 22.67 (*0-13-780875-5*) P-H.

Rhyder McClure's Short Course in Paradox. Rhyder McClure. pap. 22.67 (*0-13-780883-6*) P-H.

Rhyder McClure's Short Course in Quattro Pro. Rhyder McClure. pap. 22.67 (*0-13-780891-7*) P-H.

Rhyme-along Board Books: Hey, Diddle, Diddle. Illus. by Dianne O. Burke. 12p. (J). (ps). 1994. 3.95 (*1-56565-097-2*) Lowell Hse.

Rhyme & Meaning in Crashaw. Mary E. Rickey. LC 72-5491. (Studies in Poetry: No. 38). 1972. reprint ed. lib. bdg. 45.95 (*0-8383-1603-4*) M S G Haskell Hse.

Rhyme & Meaning in the Poetry of Yeats. Marjorie Perloff. LC 78-102959. (De Proprietatibus Litterarum, Ser. Practica). (Illus.). 1970. pap. text ed. 53.85 (*90-279-0510-X*) Mouton.

Rhyme & Punishment: Random & Not So Academic Graffiti. S. Santhi. (Indian Poetry Ser.). 80p. 1975. 6.00 (*0-89253-015-4*) Ind-US Inc.

***Rhyme & Reason.** Jo A. Ferguson. 256p. 1998. mass mkt. 4.99 (*0-8217-5850-0*, Zebra Kensgtn) Kensgtn Pub Corp.

Rhyme & Reason. Ed. by Bob Jones. (Illus.). 222p. (Orig.). 1981. pap. 18.95 (*0-89084-142-X*, 017673) Bob Jones Univ Pr.

Rhyme & Reason: A Collection of Poems. Tom Catalano. 96p. (Orig.). 1993. pap. 9.95 (*1-882646-07-X*) Wordsmith Bks.

Rhyme & Reason: Pages from the Heart of a Songwriter. Jackson Leap. LC 96-70038. 160p. (Orig.). 1996. pap. 22.95 (*1-881576-91-4*) Providence Hse.

Rhyme & Reason: St. Thomas & Modes of Discourse. Ralph McInerny. LC 81-80234. (Aquinas Lectures). 84p. (C). 1981. 15.00 (*0-87462-148-8*) Marquette.

Rhyme & Reason in Reading & Spelling. Lynette Bradley & Peter Bryant. LC 84-24153. (International Academy for Research in Learning Disabilities Monograph Ser.: No. 1). (Illus.). 143p. reprint ed. pap. 40.80 (*0-7837-4713-6*, 2059065) Bks Demand.

Rhyme & Reason of Curt Sytsma. Curt L. Sytsma. LC 81-67557. (Illus.). 224p. 1982. 14.95 (*0-942170-05-9*) CSS Pubns.

Rhyme & Reason of Politics in Early Modern Europe: Collected Essays of Herbert H. Rowen. Ed. by Craig E. Harline. (Archives Internationales d'Histoire des Idees (International Archives of the History of Ideas) Ser.). 328p. (C). 1992. lib. bdg. 153.00 (*0-7923-1527-8*) Kluwer Ac.

Rhyme & Revolution in Germany. J. E. Legge. 1973. 59.95 (*0-8490-0954-5*) Gordon Pr.

Rhyme & Revolution in Germany: A Study in German History, Life, Literature & Character. James G. Legge. LC 72-126646. reprint ed. 33.45 (*0-404-03947-2*) AMS Pr.

Rhyme Bible: Read Aloud Stories from the Old & New Testaments. Linda J. Sattgast. (Illus.). 448p. (J). 1996. 17.99 (*0-88070-829-8*, Gold & Honey) Multnomah Pubs.

***Rhyme Bible: Read Aloud Stories from the Old & New Testaments.** Linda J. Sattgast. (Illus.). (J). (ps-3). 1997. audio 6.99 (*1-57673-051-4*, Gold & Honey) Multnomah Pubs.

***Rhyme Bible Activity.** Linda J. Sattgast. LC 96-51530. (Illus.). 64p. (J). (ps-3). 1997. student ed. 8.99 (*1-57673-050-6*, Gold & Honey) Multnomah Pubs.

***Rhyme Bible Prayer Book.** Linda J. Sattgast. LC 96-41976. (Illus.). 64p. (J). (ps-3). 1997. 8.99 (*1-57673-054-9*, Gold & Honey) Multnomah Pubs.

Rhyme of the Flying Bomb. Mervyn Peake. (Illus.). 43p. 1973. 10.95 (*0-317-61324-3*, Pub. by Colin Smythe Ltd UK) Dufour.

Rhyme of the Flying Bomb. Mervyn Peake. 43p. 7300. 18.95 (*0-900675-93-4*) Dufour.

Rhyme Stew. Roald Dahl. (J). Date not set. pap. 3.99 (*0-14-034365-2*, Viking) Viking Penguin.

R

Rhyme Theatre - Story Rhyme Plays & Skits. Story Time Stories That Rhyme Staff. 60p. (J). 1994. ring bd. 19.95 (*1-56820-117-6*) Story Time.

Rhyme Time. (Sesame Street Ser.: No. 15). (J). 1989. 1.49 (*0-553-18398-2*) Bantam.

Rhyme Time. Barbara B. Malley. 1992. pap. 10.99 (*0-86653-968-9*) Fearon Teach Aids.

Rhyme Time: A Beginner's Collection of Nursery Rhymes Translated into French. Marilyn Simundson-Olson. (Illus.). 52p. (FRE.). 1996. teacher ed., pap. 22.00 incl. digital audio, trans. (*1-888228-01-6*) Global Rhyme Time.

Rhyme Time: A Beginner's Collection of Nursery Rhymes Translated into French. Marilyn Simundson-Olson. (Illus.). 52p. (FRE.). (J). 1996. pap. 19.00 incl. audio, trans. (*1-888228-26-1*) Global Rhyme Time.

***Rhyme Time: A Beginner's Collection of Nursery Rhymes Translated into French.** 2nd ed. Marilyn Simundson-Olson. (Children's Edition Ser.: Vol. 1). (Illus.). 60p. (ENG & FRE.). (J). (ps-12). 1996. pap. write for info. (*1-888228-30-X*) Global Rhyme Time.

Rhyme Time: Original Story Poems for Children of All Ages. John Marinelli. 70p. (Orig.). (J). 1996. pap. 6.95 (*1-57502-137-4*) Morris Pubng.

Rhyme Time Vol. 1: A Beginner's Collection of Nursery Rhymes Translated into French. Marilyn Simundson-Olson. (Illus.). 52p. (Orig.). (FRE.). (J). (ps-8). 1995. pap. text ed. 19.00 (*1-888228-25-3*) Global Rhyme Time.

***Rhyme Time Vol. 3: A Global Approach to Enhance the Learning of French.** Marilyn Simundson-Olson. (Illus.). 60p. (ENG & FRE.). 1997. teacher ed. write for info. (*1-888228-15-6*) Global Rhyme Time.

Rhyme Time Books: Humpty Dumpty. Purnell. (J). 1989. 1.98 (*0-671-09369-X*) S&S Trade.

Rhyme Time, Nineteen Eighty-Eight: A Collection of Poetry by the Children of Oregon. Elementary School Children of Oregon. Ed. by Lillian E. Gillman. 104p. (Orig.). (J). (ps-6). 1988. 6.95 (*0-317-93374-4*) Other Eye.

Rhyme Tyme: Director's Guide. William-Alan Landes. LC 87-62593. (Wondrawhopper Ser.). 1988. teacher ed., pap. 30.00 (*0-88734-009-1*) Players Pr.

Rhyme Tyme: Music & Lyrics. rev. ed. William-Alan Landes & Jeff Rizzo. (Wondrawhopper Ser.). (J). (gr. 3-12). 1985. pap. text ed. 15.00 (*0-88734-008-3*) Players Pr.

Rhyme Tyme: Playscript. rev. ed. William-Alan Landes. LC 87-62593. (Wondrawhopper Ser.). (J). (gr. 3-12). 1985. pap. 6.00 (*0-88734-108-X*) Players Pr.

***Rhyme Will Shine: A Satirest Should Have Many to Choose from, Reading This Unique Book That Flows Without Interruption.** LC 96-94463. 180p. (Orig.). 1996. per., pap. 9.95 (*0-9653099-0-8*) J Lyon.

Rhymer & the Ravens: The Book of Fate. Jodie Forrest. LC 95-71656. 352p. (Orig.). 1996. reprint ed. pap. 13.95 (*0-9649113-0-2*) Seven Paws.

Rhymer's Club: Poets of the Tragic Generation. Norman Alford. LC 94-12834. 1994. text ed. 39.95 (*0-312-12341-8*) St Martin.

***Rhymers Club Poets of Tragic.** Alford. 1996. text ed. 17.95 (*0-312-16460-2*) St Martin.

Rhymers' Lexicon. Andrew Loring. 928p. 1998. reprint ed. 51.00 (*1-55888-218-9*) Omnigraphics Inc.

Rhymes. Vaudie V. Bonner. 1994. 8.95 (*0-533-11012-2*) Vantage.

***Rhymes.** Mary E. Millidge. (Orig.). 1996. pap. write for info. (*1-57553-313-8*) Watermrk Pr.

Rhymes & Ballads of London. Carole Tate. LC 72-90691. (Illus.). 32p. (J). (gr. k-4). 1973. 6.95 (*0-87592-042-X*) Scroll Pr.

***Rhymes & Reasons: An Annotated Collection of Mother Goose Rhymes.** LC 96-46815. (J). 1997. 19.95 (*0-86713-040-7*) Greenwich Wrkshop.

Rhymes & Riddles, Gags & Giggles. Walt Disney Productions Staff. (Walt Disney's Fun-to-Learn Library Ser.: Vol. 17). (Illus.). 44p. (J). (gr. 1-6). 1983. reprint ed. 3.49 (*1-885222-08-4*) Advance Pubs.

Rhymes & Stories. Burton Marks. LC 91-3663. (Read-a-Picture Ser.). (Illus.). 24p. (J). (gr. k-2). 1992. pap. 2.95 (*0-8167-2410-5*) Troll Communs.

Rhymes & Tales: Level 3. E. Evertts. (J). 1983. 15.75 (*0-03-061383-3*) HB Schl Dept.

Rhymes & Tales: Level 3 - 6. E. Evertts. (J). 1983. wbk. ed., pap. 15.50 (*0-03-061429-5*) HB Schl Dept.

***Rhymes & Tales Level 3.** Evertts. 1986. pap. text ed. 14.00 (*0-03-002318-1*) HR&W Schl Div.

***Rhymes & Verses, Vol. 1.** W. Delamare. Date not set. write for info. (*0-03-031710-X*) H Holt & Co.

Rhymes & Verses: Collected Poems for Young People. Walter J. De La Mare. LC 88-45278. (Illus.). 370p. (J). (gr. 2-4). 1988. 15.95 (*0-8050-0847-0*, Bks Young Read) H Holt & Co.

Rhymes for a Reason. large type ed. Christopher Messina. (Illus.). 49p. (J). (gr. 1-7). 1995. 39.50 (*1-57529-005-7*) Kabel Pubs.

Rhymes for Alice Bluelight. Walt Curtis. LC 83-23846. 66p. 1984. pap. 7.00 (*0-89924-040-2*) Lynx Hse.

Rhymes for Annie Rose. Shirley Hughes. LC 94-37544. (Illus.). 48p. (J). (ps up). 1995. 16.00 (*0-688-14220-6*) Lothrop.

Rhymes for Learning Times. Louise B. Scott. LC 82-73392. 145p. (Orig.). (J). (ps). 1984. pap. 15.95 (*0-513-01763-1*) Denison.

Rhymes for Muslim Children. Syed K. Hassan. Ed. by Saiyad F. Ahmad. (Illus.). 48p. (Orig.). (J). (ps up). 1992. pap. text ed. 5.00 (*1-56316-315-2*) Iqra Intl Ed Fdtn.

Rhymes for Talking Time. Lois B. Lee. 1973. text ed. 2.50 (*0-686-09389-5*) Expression.

Rhymes for the Quiet Times. George P. Schmidt. 56p. (Orig.). 1990. spiral bd. 5.95 (*1-877633-08-9*) Luthers.

Rhymes from the Books of Ham: Mormon Deceptions. Thomas Mariano. Ed. by Patricia Huhn. 105p. (Orig.). 1993. pap. 5.00 (*1-877637-09-2*) Mariano Pub.

Rhymes of a Bluejacket: Verses of a World War II Navy Vet. Robin R. Leatherman. LC 86-82065. (Illus.). 112p. (Orig.). 1986. pap. 6.95 (*0-939127-00-8*) Gulf Coast Pub.

Rhymes of a Family Doctor. Daniel R. Sullivan. 128p. (Orig.). 1994. pap. write for info. (*1-56167-163-0*) Am Literary Pr.

Rhymes of a Jerk. Larry Fagin. 7.00 (*0-686-09760-2*); pap. 3.50 (*0-686-09761-0*) Kulchur Foun.

***Rhymes of a Rexall Wrangler.** Dick Hart. (Bend Ser.: No. 0017). (Illus.). 50p. (Orig.). 1996. pap. 8.95 (*0-9643598-1-2*) Bend Pr CA.

Rhymes of Childhood. Edgar Guest. 190p. 1981. reprint ed. lib. bdg. 21.95 (*0-89968-220-0*, Lghtyr Pr) Buccaneer Bks.

Rhymes of the Ancient Manager: Leadership in the New Age. M. Scott Myers. (Illus.). 192p. (Orig.). 1994. 19.95 (*0-9639930-0-3*); pap. 14.95 (*0-9639930-1-1*) Choctaw Pubng.

Rhymes of the Raven Lady. P. J. Johnson. 1995. pap. 6.95 (*0-88839-366-0*) Hancock House.

Rhymes of the Times. Peter C. Milne. LC 91-67930. 149p. (Orig.). 1993. pap. 9.00 (*1-56002-189-6*, Univ Edtns) Aegina Pr.

***Rhymes of the Times II.** Audrey X. Flowers. (Orig.). (J). reprint ed. pap. 10.00 (*1-56411-146-6*) Untd Bros & Sis.

Rhymes on the Range. Mike Puhallo et al. 1995. pap. 6.95 (*0-88839-368-7*) Hancock House.

Rhyme's Reason. enl. ed. John Hollander. (C). 1989. pap. 9.00 (*0-300-04307-4*); text ed. 25.00 (*0-300-04306-6*) Yale U Pr.

Rhyme's Reason: A Guide to English Verse. John Hollander. LC 81-51342. (Illus.). 64p. (C). 1981. text ed. 20.00 (*0-300-02735-4*) Yale U Pr.

Rhymes, Riddles & Reasons, Vol. I: Genesis, A Devotional Book for Children. Barbara Westberg. LC 90-38218. (Illus.). 224p. (Orig.). (J). (gr. 3-7). 1991. pap. 7.99 (*0-932581-75-7*) Word Aflame.

Rhymes, Riddles & Reasons, Vol. 2: Exodus Through Judges. Barbara Westberg. LC 90-38218. (Illus.). 224p. (Orig.). (J). (gr. 3-7). 1992. pap. 7.99 (*0-932581-76-5*) Word Aflame.

Rhymes, Rounds & Riddles. Pamela C. Bye. 6.95 (*1-56222-819-6*, 94987) Mel Bay.

Rhymes to Count On. Ed. by Judy Nayer. (Storytime Bks.). (Illus.). 24p. (J). (ps-2). 1990. pap. 1.29 (*1-56293-104-0*) McClanahan Bk.

Rhymes to Predict the Weather. Don Haggerty. LC 84-52672. (Illus.). 132p. (Orig.). 1985. pap. 8.00 (*0-9614703-0-5*) Springmeadow Pub.

Rhymes We Like. Fay Robinson. LC 92-10754. (Bear & Alligator Tales Ser.). (Illus.). 32p. (J). (ps-2). 1993. lib. bdg. 17.00 (*0-516-02375-6*) Childrens.

***Rhymes with Orange.** Hilary B. Price. (Illus.). 128p. (Orig.). 1997. pap. 9.95 (*0-614-30607-8*) Andrews & McMeel.

***Rhymes with Oranges.** Hilary B. Price. 1997. pap. text ed. 9.95 (*0-8362-3655-6*) Andrews & McMeel.

Rhymin' Simon's Small Talk: Self Discovery Stress Management. Marilyn M. Dorsey. 83p. (J). (gr. 4 up). 1991. pap. 6.95 (*0-916369-18-8*) Magnolia Pr.

Rhyming. Carson & Dellosa. (Home Workbooks Ser.). (Illus.). 64p. (Orig.). (J). (gr. k-1). 1995. wbk. ed., pap. 2.49 (*0-88724-309-6*, CD6806) Carson-Dellos.

Rhyming Bible. Gordon Lindsay. 1967. 1.00 (*0-89985-250-5*) Christ for the Nations.

Rhyming Dictionary. 1991. lib. bdg. 75.00 (*0-8490-4143-0*) Gordon Pr.

Rhyming Dictionary. Rosalind Ferguson. 544p. 1986. pap. 13.95 (*0-14-051136-9*, Penguin Bks) Viking Penguin.

Rhyming Families. Barbara Gregorich. Ed. by Joan Hoffman. (I Know It! Bks.). (Illus.). 32p. (J). (gr. 1-3). 1981. student ed. 1.99 (*0-938256-38-6*) Sch Zone Pub Co.

Rhyming Gospels: A Poetic Paraphrase of Holy Scripture. Bernard Williams. Ed. by Mary G. Christmas & James C. Hefley. 180p. 1990. text ed. 9.95 (*0-929292-14-6*) Hannibal Bks.

Rhyming in the Rigging: Poems of the Sea. Ed. by Lahaina Harry. LC 77-80048. 174p. 1978. 20.00 (*0-918024-04-8*); pap. 8.95 (*0-918024-05-6*) Ox Bow.

Rhyming Pattern Reference One. Alpha Pyramis Research Division Staff. 8p. 1984. ring bd. 26.95 (*0-913597-46-5*) Prosperity & Profits.

Rhyming Pictures. Barbara Gregorich. Ed. by Joan Hoffman. (Get Ready! Bks.). (Illus.). tp. (J). (ps). 1980. student ed. 1.99 (*0-938256-53-X*) Sch Zone Pub Co.

Rhyming Rabbit. (Rabbit Tales Ser.: No. S899-3). (J). 1989. boxed 3.95 (*0-7214-5232-9*, Ladybrd) Penguin.

Rhyming Recipe & Cookbook, Vol. 1. Alpha Pyramis Research Division Staff. 21p. 1984. ring bd. 27.95 (*0-913597-50-3*) Prosperity & Profits.

Rhyming Techniques & Strategies. Pat Pattison. 76p. 1991. pap. 10.95 (*0-7935-1181-X*, 50481583, Berklee Pr) H Leonard.

Rhyming Thoughts. Lucy Fine-Drew. 108p. 1992. pap. 12.95 (*0-9636052-0-8*) Drew Pub WA.

***Rhyming Words.** Evan Kimble. (Play & Discover Ser.). (Illus.). (J). 1997. pap. 3.95 (*0-8069-9755-9*) Sterling.

***Rhyming Words.** Jo E. Moore. (Reading & Writing Ser.). (Illus.). 32p. (J). (gr. 1-2). 1997. teacher ed., pap. 2.95 (*1-55799-410-2*, 4012) Evan-Moor Corp.

Rhyming Words. Shereen G. Rutman. (Learn Today for Tomorrow Ser.). (Illus.). 32p. (J). (ps-1). 1992. student ed., pap. 2.25 (*1-56293-170-9*) McClanahan Bk.

***Rhyming Words.** Shereen G. Rutman. (J). 1997. wbk. ed., pap. text ed. 2.25 (*1-56293-955-6*) McClanahan Bk.

***Rhyming Words.** Scholastic, Inc. Staff. (Fun with Phonics Ser.). (J). 1997. pap. text ed. 6.95 (*0-590-76492-6*) Scholastic Inc.

Rhymney Memories. Thomas Jones. 173p. (C). 1970. pap. 20.00 (*0-86383-644-5*, Pub. by Gomer Pr UK) St Mut.

Rhynchota: Heteroptera, Vol. 1. W. L. Distant. (Fauna of British India Ser.). xxxviii, 438p. 1977. reprint ed. 25.00 (*0-88065-048-6*, Messers Today & Tomorrow) Scholarly Pubns.

Rhynchota: Heteroptera, Vol. 2. W. L. Distant. (Fauna of British India Ser.). xviii, 504p. 1977. reprint ed. 25.00 (*0-88065-049-4*, Messers Today & Tomorrow) Scholarly Pubns.

Rhynchota: Heteroptera - Appendix, Vol. 5. W. L. Distant. (Fauna of British India Ser.). xii, 362p. 1977. reprint ed. 20.00 (*0-88065-077-X*, Messers Today & Tomorrow) Scholarly Pubns.

Rhynchota: Heteroptera-Homoptera, Vol. 3. W. L. Distant. (Fauna of British India Ser.). iiv, 504p. 1977. reprint ed. 25.00 (*0-88065-075-3*, Messers Today & Tomorrow) Scholarly Pubns.

Rhynchota: Homoptera - Appendix, Vol. 4. W. L. Distant. (Fauna of British India Ser.). xiv, 502p. 1977. reprint ed. 25.00 (*0-88065-076-1*, Messers Today & Tomorrow) Scholarly Pubns.

Rhynchota: Homoptera - Appendix, Vol. 6. W. L. Distant. (Fauna of British India Ser.). viii, 250p. 1977. reprint ed. 15.00 (*0-88065-078-8*, Pub. by Today & Tomorrows P & P II) Scholarly Pubns.

Rhynchota: Homoptera - Appendix, Heteroptera - Addenda, Vol. 7. W. L. Distant. (Fauna of British India Ser.). viii, 212p. 1977. reprint ed. 15.00 (*0-88065-079-6*, Messers Today & Tomorrow) Scholarly Pubns.

Rhyolite Activity Book. Kari Coughlin. 48p. 1994. pap. 3.00 (*1-885770-02-2*) Frnds Rhyolite.

Rhyolite Activity Book. rev. ed. Kari Coughlin. (Illus.). 80p. 1994. pap. 10.00 (*1-885770-03-0*) Frnds Rhyolite.

Rhyolite-Death Valley's Ghost City of Golden Dreams. 11th ed. Harold O. Weight & Lucile Weight. 1988. pap. 2.95 (*0-912714-04-2*) Calico Pr.

Rhyolite Tour Guide. rev. ed. Kate Graves & Kari Coughlin. 25p. 1995. pap. 2.00 (*1-885770-01-4*) Frnds Rhyolite.

Rhyolite Tour Guide in German. Kate Graves & Paul Weller. 23p. 1994. pap. 2.00 (*1-885770-00-6*) Frnds Rhyolite.

Rhys, Stead, Lessing, & the Politics of Empathy. Judith K. Gardiner. LC 88-45460. (Everywoman). 200p. 1989. 18.50 (*0-253-35010-7*); pap. 5.25 (*0-253-20498-4*, MB-498) Ind U Pr.

Rhythm. 1993. pap. 19.95 incl. audio (*0-7935-1405-3*, 00660282) H Leonard.

Rhythm. 1993. pap. 24.95 incl. audio compact disk (*0-7935-1406-1*, 00660281) H Leonard.

***Rhythm: A Step-by-Step Guide to Understanding Rhythm for Guitar.** David Mead. 192p. pap. 17.95 incl. cd-rom (*1-86074-198-3*) Omnibus NY.

Rhythm: An Annotated Bibliography. Steven D. Winick. LC 74-14582. 1974. 25.00 (*0-8108-0767-X*) Scarecrow.

Rhythm & Beauty: The Art of Percussion. Rocky Maffit. LC 96-32627. (Illus.). 136p. 1996. 45.00 incl. audio compact disk (*1-886154-12-0*) Phoenix IL.

Rhythm & Blues. Lynn E. McCutcheon. (Illus.). 1971. 10.95 (*0-87948-028-9*) Beatty.

Rhythm & Blues Ballads. (Piano-Vocal-Guitar Ser.). 176p. (Orig.). 1988. pap. 14.95 (*0-88188-843-5*, HL 00360870) H Leonard.

Rhythm & Blues in New Orleans. John Broven. LC 77-13351. Orig. Title: Walking To New Orleans. (Illus.). 250p. 1983. pap. 13.95 (*0-88289-433-1*) Pelican.

Rhythm & Dues. 2nd ed. Linda M. Baron. 32p. 1981. 6.00 (*0-685-14557-3*) Harlin Jacque.

Rhythm & Life: The Work of Emile Jaques-Dalcroze. Irwin Spector. LC 89-28139. (Dance & Music Ser.: No. 3). (Illus.). 400p. 1989. text ed. 54.00 (*0-945193-00-9*) Pendragon NY.

Rhythm & Melodic Studies for Beginning Trumpet. William Bay. (Building Excellence Ser.). 1993. 4.95 (*1-56222-305-4*, 94709) Mel Bay.

Rhythm & Movement: Applications of Dalcroze Eurhythmics. Elsa Findlay. LC 71-169706. 96p. 1971. pap. 12.95 (*0-87487-078-X*) Summy-Birchard.

Rhythm & Noise: An Aesthetics of Rock. Theodore Gracyk. LC 95-44601. 304p. 1996. text ed. 49.95 (*0-8223-1734-6*); pap. text ed. 16.95 (*0-8223-1743-5*) Duke.

Rhythm & Pitch: An Integrated Approach to Sight Singing. Stevenson. 1985. pap. text ed. 57.33 (*0-13-780743-0*) P-H.

Rhythm & Pitch Notation Transparencies: 16 Rhythm & 16 Pitch Visuals with Booklet of Activities. Peg Hoenack & Kay Jones. (Music Literacy Ser.). (Illus.). 70p. 1993. ring bd. 54.95 (*0-913500-50-X*, C-2T) Peg Hoenack MusicWorks.

Rhythm & Resistance: Explorations in the Political Uses of Popular Music. Ray Pratt. LC 89-16197. (Media & Society Ser.). 248p. 1990. text ed. 55.00 (*0-275-92624-9*, C2624, Praeger Pubs) Greenwood.

Rhythm & Resistance: Political Uses of American Popular Music. Ray Pratt. LC 93-30228. 256p. 1994. pap. text ed. 16.95 (*1-56098-351-5*) Smithsonian.

Rhythm & Revolt: Tales of the Antilles. Ed. by Marcela Breton. LC 94-47254. 1995. pap. 12.95 (*0-452-27178-9*, Plume) NAL-Dutton.

Rhythm & Rhyme. Ronald Tamplin. LC 92-10506. (Open Guides to Literature Ser.). 1992. 75.00 (*0-335-09452-X*, Open Univ Pr); pap. 22.00 (*0-335-09451-1*, Open Univ Pr) Taylor & Francis.

Rhythm & Role Play. Carolyn Graham et al. 1991. audio 14.95 (*0-943327-09-1*) JAG Pubns.

Rhythm & Role Play. Carolyn Graham. (Illus.). 95p. 1991. pap. 10.95 (*0-943327-08-3*) JAG Pubns.

Rhythm & the Blues: A Life in American Music. Jerry Wexler & David Ritz. (Illus.). 352p. 1994. pap. 14.95 (*0-312-11376-5*) St Martin.

Rhythm & Touch: An Introduction to Craniosacral Therapy. Anthony P. Arnold. LC 95-22042. (Illus.). 156p. (Orig.). 1995. pap. 15.95 (*0-914732-35-8*) Bro Life Inc.

Rhythm & Writing. Robert S. Ochsner. LC 87-50836. 140p. 1989. 18.50 (*0-87875-347-8*) Whitston Pub.

Rhythm Book. Daniel Kazez. 1994. 14.00 (*0-918194-26-1*) Accura.

Rhythm Book: Studies in Rhythmic Reading & Principles. unabridged ed. Peter H. Phillips. LC 95-17333. (Illus.). 208p. 1995. reprint ed. pap. text ed. 10.95 (*0-486-28693-2*) Dover.

Rhythm, Content & Flavor: New & Selected Poems. Victor H. Cruz. LC 88-14542. 160p. (Orig.). 1989. pap. 8.00 (*0-934770-93-X*) Arte Publico.

Rhythm Factor in Human Behavior. Salvatore J. Garzino. LC 81-81611. 1982. 15.00 (*0-87212-151-8*) Libra.

Rhythm Games: For Perception & Cognition. Robert M. Abramson. 36p. 1997. pap. 19.95 incl. audio compact disk (*0-913650-08-0*, M0599CD) Warner Brothers.

***Rhythm Ghosts.** Tabourot. (Illus.). 237p. (Orig.). 1997. pap. write for info. (*1-881428-09-5*) Tactus Pr.

Rhythm Guitar. Harvey Vinson. (Orig.). 1969. pap. 17.95 (*0-8256-4061-X*, AM10687) Music Sales.

Rhythm Guitar Chord System. Bay, Mel, Publications, Inc. Staff. 1993. 4.95 (*0-87166-515-8*, 93214) Mel Bay.

Rhythm Guitar Vinson. Jim Gregory & Harvey Vinson. (Illus.). (Orig.). 1973. pap. 14.95 (*0-8256-4057-1*, AM10687) Music Sales.

Rhythm in Drama. Kathleen George. LC 79-24432. 1980. pap. 8.95 (*0-8229-5316-1*) U of Pittsburgh Pr.

Rhythm in Drama. Kathleen George. LC 79-24432. 206p. 1980. reprint ed. pap. 58.80 (*0-608-02056-7*, 2062709) Bks Demand.

Rhythm in Music: A Text-Book. George A. Wedge. 54p. 1990. reprint ed. lib. bdg. 59.00 (*0-7812-9135-6*) Rprt Serv.

Rhythm in Psychological, Linguistic & Musical Processes. Ed. by James R. Evans & Manfred Clynes. (Illus.). 302p. (C). 1986. 53.95 (*0-398-05235-2*) C C Thomas.

Rhythm in Psychological, Linguistic & Musical Processes. Ed. by James R. Evans & Manfred Clynes. (Illus.). 302p. 1986. pap. 35.95 (*0-398-06110-6*) C C Thomas.

Rhythm Incarnate: Tribute to Shanti Bardhan. Ed. by Gul Bardhan. (C). 1992. 58.00 (*81-7017-261-6*, Pub. by Abhinav II) S Asia.

***Rhythm Inside: Connecting Body, Mind, & Spirit Through Music.** Julia Schnebly-Black & Stephen E. Moore. 1997. pap. 18.95 (*0-614-27592-X*) Rudra Pr.

Rhythm Man: Fifty Years in Jazz. Steve Jordan & Tom Scanlan. (American Music Ser.). 184p. 1993. pap. 16.95 (*0-472-08202-7*) U of Mich Pr.

Rhythm, Music & Education. Emile Jaques-Dalcroze. LC 77-187829. (Illus.). 1972. reprint ed. 31.95 (*0-405-08666-0*, Pub. by Blom Pubns UK) Ayer.

Rhythm of Life. Richard Exley. 1987. 14.99 (*1-56292-469-9*, HB-469) Honor Bks OK.

Rhythm of Life. Leo Jung. 742p. 32.50 (*0-87559-145-0*) Shalom.

Rhythm of Life: And Other Essays. Alice C. Meynell. LC 78-37794. (Essay Index Reprint Ser.). 1977. reprint ed. 17.95 (*0-8369-2613-7*) Ayer.

***Rhythm of Life: Celtic Daily Prayer.** David Adam. 144p. 1997. pap. 8.95 (*0-8192-1715-8*) Morehouse Pub.

***Rhythm of Life's Emotion.** Nubia Levon. (Illus.). (Orig.). 1997. pap. 8.99 (*1-890254-16-9*) Innov Pub Concepts.

Rhythm of Live & the Psalms see Longing for God: Prayer & the Rhythms of Life

Rhythm of the Reef: A Day in the Life of the Coral Reef. Rick Sammon. LC 95-7378. (Illus.). 120p. 1995. 29.95 (*0-89658-311-2*) Voyageur Pr.

***Rhythm of the Seasons: A Journey Beyond Loss.** Marilyn Adams. LC 97-21495. (Illus.). 54p. 1997. 17.95 (*1-882835-38-7*) STA-Kris.

Rhythm of Twelfth-Century Polyphony. William G. Waite. LC 73-2648. (Illus.). 141p. 1973. reprint ed. text ed. 75.00 (*0-8371-6815-5*, WART, Greenwood Pr) Greenwood.

Rhythm of Wholeness. Dane Rudhyar. LC 83-70689. 268p. (Orig.). 1983. pap. 7.50 (*0-8356-0578-7*, Quest) Theos Pub Hse.

Rhythm on Record. Hilton R. Schleman. LC 77-28303. (Illus.). 333p. 1978. reprint ed. text ed. 59.75 (*0-313-20257-5*, SCRR, Greenwood Pr) Greenwood.

Rhythm Piano, 2 cass. Duane Shinn. (Illus.). 64p. 1988. per. 39.95 incl. audio (*0-912732-61-X*) Duane Shinn.

Rhythm Piano - Advanced, 4 cass. Duane Shinn. 1988. per. 49.95 incl. audio (*0-912732-63-6*) Duane Shinn.

Rhythm Quizlets: Self Assessment. Henry J. Marriott. LC 87-2802. (Illus.). 189p. 1987. pap. text ed. 29.00 (*0-8121-1110-9*) Williams & Wilkins.

Rhythm Quizlets: Self Assessment. 2nd ed. Henry J. Marriott. LC 87-2802. 300p. 1995. pap. 32.95 (*0-683-05582-8*) Williams & Wilkins.

Rhythm Reading. 2nd ed. Daniel Kazez. LC 96-21128. (C). 1997. pap. text ed. 17.95 (*0-393-97073-6*) Norton.

Rhythm Reading: Elementary Through Advanced Training. Daniel Kazez. LC 89-2774. 144p. (C). 1989. spiral bd. 21.95 (*0-87484-896-2*, 896) Mayfield Pub.

Rhythm, Rhyme & Read: Phonics. Karen M. Hilderbrand & Kim M. Thompson. 64p. (J). (ps-3). 1992. student ed. 6.99 (*0-9632249-0-5*, TWIN 205) Twin Sisters.

Rhythm, Rhyme & Read: States & Capitals. Kim M. Thompson & Karen M. Hilderbrand. (Illus.). 48p. (J). (gr. 3-6). 1992. 6.99 (*0-9632249-5-6*, TWIN 206) Twin Sisters.

An Asterisk (*) at the beginning of an entry indicates that the title is appearing in BIP for the first time.

Rhythm, Rhyme & Read Twinset: Phonics. Kim M. Thompson & Karen M. Hilderbrand. (Illus.). 64p. (J). (ps-3). 1993. student ed. 14.99 incl. audio (*1-882331-07-9*, TWIN 305) Twin Sisters.

Rhythm, Rhyme & Read Twinset: States & Capitals. Kim M. Thompson & Karen M. Hilderbrand. (Illus.). 48p. (J). (gr. 3-6). 1993. student ed. 14.99 incl. audio (*1-882331-08-7*, TWIN 306) Twin Sisters.

***Rhythm Riffs for Keyboards.** Jeff Hammer. 64p. pap. 9.95 incl. cd-rom (*0-7119-4512-8*) Omnibus NY.

Rhythm Sight-Reader, 2 bks., Bk. 1. Burton Kaplan. 96p. (Orig.). 1977. pap. 7.95 (*0-918316-01-4*) Percept Dev Tech.

Rhythm Sight-Reader, 2 bks., Bk. 2. Burton Kaplan. 96p. (Orig.). 1977. pap. 7.95 (*0-685-73781-0*) Percept Dev Tech.

Rhythm, Time, & Value. Mary L. Walker. (Music Ser.). 24p. (gr. 3 up). 1980. student ed. 5.00 (*0-8209-0278-0*, MU-7) ESP.

Rhythm Vision: A Guide to Visual Awareness. Dennis M. Roth. LC 90-30610. (Illus.). 128p. (Orig.). 1990. pap. 12.95 (*0-944091-02-4*) Intaglio Pr.

Rhythmic Activities & Dance. John P. Bennett & Pamela Coughenour. LC 94-38538. (Illus.). 176p. (Orig.). 1995. pap. text ed. 19.00 (*0-87322-718-2*, BBEN0718) Human Kinetics.

Rhythmic Aerobex see Prime Time Aerobics: Workbook

Rhythmic Alteration in 17th & 18th Century Music: Notes Inegales & Overdotting. Stephen E. Hefling. 232p. 1993. 38.00 (*0-02-871035-5*) Schirmer Bks.

Rhythmic & Synthetic Processes in Growth. Theodore T. Puck et al. Ed. by Dorothea Rudnick. LC 55-10678. (Society for the Study of Development & Growth, Symposium Ser.: 15th). 233p. reprint ed. pap. 66.50 (*0-7837-0245-0*, 2040554) Bks Demand.

Rhythmic Breathing Plus Olfactory Nerve Influence on Respiration. Richard B. Noble. 143p. 1971. reprint ed. spiral bd. 8.50 (*0-7873-1026-3*) Hlth Research.

Rhythmic Breathing Plus Olfactory Nerve Influence on Respiration (1908) Richard B. Noble. 165p. 1996. pap. 17.95 (*1-56459-835-7*) Kessinger Pub.

Rhythmic Breathings & Olfactory Nerve Influence on Respiration. Richard B. Noble. 1991. lib. bdg. 79.95 (*0-8490-4958-X*) Gordon Pr.

Rhythmic Cycle of Change. Ronald Robbins. LC 88-25446. 306p. (Orig.). 1989. pap. 24.95 (*0-9620928-1-9*) Neshama Pubns.

Rhythmic Gymnastics. Michi Fujimoto. 24p. (J). (ps up). 1996. pap. 7.95 (*0-8431-3988-9*) Price Stern Sloan.

***Rhythmic Gymnastics.** Tracy Maurer. LC 97-8394. (Let's Dance Ser.). (J). 1997. write for info. (*1-57103-171-5*) Rourke Pr.

Rhythmic Gymnastics: Instructor's Manual, Level 1-2. United States Gymnastics Federation Staff. 91p. 1993. pap. 15.00 (*1-885250-11-8*) USA Gymnastics.

Rhythmic Gymnastics: Instructor's Manual, Level 3-4. United States Gymnastics Federation Staff. (Illus.). 97p. 1993. pap. 15.00 (*1-885250-14-2*) USA Gymnastics.

Rhythmic Gymnastics: The Skills of the Game. Jenny Bott. (Illus.). 128p. 1995. pap. 19.95 (*1-85223-918-2*, Pub. by Crowood Pr UK) Trafalgar.

Rhythmic Gymnastics Rules & Policies 1993-94: Governing Competitions & Competitors Operating Code. United States Gymnastics Federation Staff. 70p. 1993. pap. 16.50 (*1-885250-03-7*) USA Gymnastics.

***Rhythmic Illusions.** Gavin Harrison. Ed. by Joe Testa. 72p. (Orig.). 1996. pap. text ed. 24.95 (*1-57623-687-0*, EL9655CD) Warner Brothers.

Rhythmic Integration. Ronald Robbins. 1990. pap. 13.95 (*0-88268-099-4*) Station Hill Pr.

Rhythmic Medicine - Music with a Purpose. Janalea Hoffman. 208p. (Orig.). 1995. pap. 14.95 (*1-886051-18-6*) Rhythmic Med.

Rhythmic Phrasing in English Verse. Richard Cureton. (English Language Ser.). 432p. (C). 1991. pap. text ed. 44.95 (*0-582-55267-2*) Longman.

Rhythmic Response of Negro & White Children Two to Six. Dorothy Van Alstyne & E. Osborne. (SRCD Ser.: Vol. 2, No.4). 1937. pap. 25.00 (*0-527-01497-4*) Periodicals Srv.

Rhythmic Structure of Music. Grosvenor Cooper & Leonard B. Meyer. LC 60-14068. 221p. 1963. pap. text ed. 14.95 (*0-226-11522-4*, P118) U Ch Pr.

Rhythmic Studies for Beginning Cello. Craig Duncan. (Building Excellence Ser.). 1993. 4.95 (*1-56222-242-2*, 94658) Mel Bay.

Rhythmic Studies for Beginning Viola. Craig Duncan. (Building Excellence Ser.). 1993. 4.95 (*1-56222-245-7*, 94661) Mel Bay.

Rhythmic Studies for Beginning Violin. Craig Duncan. (Building Excellence Ser.). 1993. 4.95 (*1-56222-163-9*, 94565) Mel Bay.

Rhythmic Training Workbook. Robert Starer. 1985. student ed., pap. 5.95 (*0-88188-458-8*, 00123559) H Leonard.

***Rhythmic Vocabulary: A Musician's Guide to Understanding & Improvising with Rhythm.** Alan Dworsky & Betsy Sansby. (Illus.). 220p. (Orig.). 1997. pap. text ed. 29.95 incl. audio compact disk (*0-9638801-2-8*) Dancing Hands.

Rhythmical Articulation: Complete Vocal Method. P. Bona. 76p. 1986. pap. 8.95 (*0-7935-0501-1*) H Leonard.

***Rhythms, Vol. 1.** Bruce Arnold. (Illus.). 150p. (Orig.). 1997. pap. 25.00 (*0-9648632-7-8*) MUSE EEK.

***Rhythms, Vol. 2.** Bruce Arnold. (Illus.). 150p. (Orig.). 1997. pap. 25.00 (*0-9648632-8-6*) MUSE EEK.

Rhythms: On the Work, Translation, & Psychoanalysis. Nicholas Abraham. Tr. by Benjamin Thigpen from GER. LC 94-42455. (Meridian: Crossing Aesthetics Ser.). 184p. 1995. 35.00 (*0-8047-2502-0*) Stanford U Pr.

Rhythms: On the Work, Translation, & Psychoanalysis. Nicolas Abraham. Tr. by Benjamin Thigpen from GER. LC 94-42455. (Meridian: Crossing Aesthetics Ser.). 184p. 1995. pap. 12.95 (*0-8047-2503-9*) Stanford U Pr.

Rhythms & Turning Points in the Life of the Child. Eugene M. Schwartz. 1990. pap. 11.50 (*0-685-54270-X*) R Steiner Col Pubns.

Rhythms Du Monde Francophone: Festival International de Louisiano. Ed. by Herman Mhire. (Illus.). 120p. (Orig.). 1996. 50.00 (*0-9651622-0-6*); pap. 30.00 (*0-614-14976-2*) Festival Intl.

Rhythms for Blues for Guitar: With Tablature. M. Wolfsohn. 16p. 1991. pap. 6.95 (*0-7935-0986-6*, 00699326) H Leonard.

***Rhythms from the Wild.** Art Wolfe. LC 96-45683. 1997. pap. 35.00 (*0-8174-5704-6*, Amphoto) Watsn-Guptill.

Rhythms in Fishes. Ed. by M. A. Ali. (NATO ASI, Series A: Life Sciences: Vol. 236). (Illus.). 351p. (C). 1993. 105.00 (*0-306-44318-X*, Plenum Pr) Plenum.

Rhythms in Physiological Systems: Proceedings of the International Symposium Schloss Elmau, 22-25 Oktober 1990. Ed. by H. Haken & H. P. Koepchen. (Synergetics Ser.: Vol. 55). ix, 363p. 1992. 89.95 (*0-387-54448-8*) Spr-Verlag.

Rhythms in Politics & Economics. Paul M. Johnson & William R. Thompson. (International Studies Association). 364p. 1985. text ed. 65.00 (*0-275-90123-8*, C0123, Praeger Pubs) Greenwood.

Rhythms of Academic Life. Ed. by Peter J. Frost & M. Susan Taylor. (Foundations for Organizational Science Ser.). 536p. 1996. 62.00 (*0-8039-7262-8*); pap. 29.95 (*0-8039-7263-6*) Sage.

Rhythms of Black Folk: Race, Religion & Pan-Africanism. Jon M. Spencer. 375p. (Orig.). (C). 1994. 49.95 (*0-86543-423-9*); pap. 16.95 (*0-86543-424-7*) Africa World.

Rhythms of English Poetry. Derek Attridge. 395p. (C). 1982. pap. text ed. 34.95 (*0-582-55105-6*) Longman.

Rhythms of Jazz: Keyboard Intermediate Level. L. Evans. 40p. 1984. pap. 5.95 (*0-7935-3999-4*, 00009046) H Leonard.

***Rhythms of Jewish Living.** Marc D. Angel. 1997. pap. write for info. (*0-7657-9983-9*) Aronson.

Rhythms of Jewish Living: A Sephardic Approach. Marc D. Angel. LC 86-25993. 208p. 1987. 14.95 (*0-87203-126-8*) Hermon.

Rhythms of Learning: Creative Tools for Developing Lifelong Skills. Don G. Campbell & Chris B. Brewer. 320p. (Orig.). 1991. pap. text ed. 30.00 (*0-913705-59-4*) Zephyr Pr AZ.

Rhythms of Life. 2nd ed. Lenore Turkeltaub. LC 87-83587. (Illus.). 72p. 1988. reprint ed. pap. 7.95 (*0-9614768-7-7*) Lenjalin Pubns.

Rhythms of Prayer. Ed. by Rachel Reeder. (Liturgy Ser.). 104p. (Orig.). 1990. pap. 8.95 (*0-918208-51-3*) Liturgical Conf.

Rhythms of Society. Ed. by Michael Young & Tom Schuller. (Reports of the Institute of Community Studies). 192p. (C). 1988. lib. bdg. 52.50 (*0-415-02533-8*) Routledge.

Rhythms of the Ecosystem. Janette Shetter. LC 76-26392. (Illus.). (Orig.). 1976. pap. 3.00 (*0-87574-208-4*) Pendle Hill.

Rhythms of the Inner Life. Howard R. Macy. LC 92-75661. 176p. 1992. pap. 9.95 (*0-913342-74-2*) Barclay Pr.

Rhythms of Vision: Changing Patterns of Myth & Consciousness. Lawrence Blair. (Illus.). 256p. 1991. reprint ed. pap. 12.95 (*0-89281-320-2*, Destiny Bks) Inner Tradit.

Rhythmusic. Ed. by Wolfgang Hageney. (Illus.). 248p. (ENG, FRE, GER, ITA & SPA.). 1982. pap. 39.95 (*88-7070-018-6*) Belvedere USA.

***Rhytismatales.** D. W. Minter. 500p. 1997. 115.00 (*0-85198-835-0*) CAB Intl.

RIA. Felix C. Forrest. 250p. 1987. reprint ed. 19.95 (*0-9618918-0-7*) Jwindz Pub.

RIA Complete Analysis of the Revenue Reconciliation Act of 1993. rev. ed. RIA In-House Professional Staff. 800p. 1993. pap. text ed. 34.95 (*0-7811-0078-X*) Res Inst Am.

RIA Federal Tax Handbook: (1994 Edition) rev. ed. RIA In-House Professional Staff. 760p. 1993. pap. text ed. 24.00 (*0-7811-0077-1*) Res Inst Am.

***RIA Federal Tax Handbook: 1997 Edition.** rev. ed. 896p. 1997. pap. text ed. 33.50 (*0-7811-0145-X*) Res Inst Am.

RIA Federal Tax Handbook 1995. rev. ed. RIA In-House Professional Staff. 765p. 1994. pap. text ed. 25.95 (*0-7811-0091-7*) Res Inst Am.

RIA Federal Tax Handbook (1996 Edition) rev. ed. 848p. 1995. pap. text ed. 28.95 (*0-7811-0114-X*) Res Inst Am.

RIA Federal Tax Regulations, Vols. I-IV. rev. ed. RIA In-House Professional Staff. 1996. pap. text ed. 55.95 (*0-7811-0125-5*) Res Inst Am.

RIA Federal Tax Regulations: (July 1993 Edition), 4 vols., Set. rev. ed. RIA In-House Professional Staff. 1993. pap. 54.00 (*0-7811-0076-3*) Res Inst Am.

RIA Federal Tax Regulations: January 1995 Edition, 4 vols., Set. rev. ed. RIA In-House Professional Staff. 8000p. 1995. pap. text ed. 55.95 (*0-7811-0101-8*) Res Inst Am.

RIA Federal Tax Regulations, January 1994, Vols. I-IV. RIA In-House Professional Staff. 1994. pap. text ed. 54.00 (*0-7811-0085-2*) Res Inst Am.

RIA Federal Tax Regulations (July 1995 Edition), Set, Vols. I-IV. rev. ed. RIA In-House Professional Staff. 1995. pap. text ed. 55.95 (*0-7811-0111-5*) Res Inst Am.

***RIA Federal Tax Regulations, July 1996, Vols. 1-4.** rev. ed. Research Inst. of America Staff. 8080p. 1996. pap. text ed. 56.95 (*0-7811-0142-5*) Res Inst Am.

RIA Federal Tax Regulations, 1993, 4 vols. RIA In-House Professional Staff. Incl. RIA Federal Tax Regulations, 1993 Vol. I. rev. ed. 2300p. 1993. pap. (*0-318-69995-8*); RIA Federal Tax Regulations, 1993 Vol. II. , 4 vols. rev. ed. 1850p. 1993. pap. (*0-318-69996-6*); RIA Federal Tax Regulations, 1993 Vol. III. , 4 vols. rev. ed. 2000p. 1993. pap. (*0-318-69997-4*); RIA Federal Tax Regulations, 1993 Vol. IV. , 4 vols. rev. ed. 2300p. 1993. pap. (*0-318-69998-2*); 1993. 52.00 (*0-7811-0067-4*) Res Inst Am.

RIA Federal Tax Regulations, 1993, Vol. I see RIA Federal Tax Regulations, 1993

RIA Federal Tax Regulations, 1993, Vol. II see RIA Federal Tax Regulations, 1993

RIA Federal Tax Regulations, 1993, Vol. III see RIA Federal Tax Regulations, 1993

RIA Federal Tax Regulations, 1993, Vol. IV see RIA Federal Tax Regulations, 1993

RIA Robotics Glossary. 80p. 1983. pap. 9.00 (*0-685-08461-2*) Robot Inst Am.

Rial Williams' Thirty-One Children. Dorothy Wilson. LC 95-78290. (Illus.). 148p. 1995. 23.00 (*0-938041-65-7*) Arc Pr AR.

Rialto Square Theatre. Dorothy L. Mavrich. (Illus.). 16p. 1993. 8.00 (*0-9635264-0-5*) D Mavrich.

***RIA's Complete Analysis of the Small Business, Health Insurance & Welfare Reform Acts of 1966.** 550p. (Orig.). 1996. pap. text ed. 45.00 (*0-7811-0144-1*) Res Inst Am.

***RIA's Complete Guide to Federal Income Tax Returns of Estates, Trusts & Decedents.** Stanley Gladstone. 384p. 1996. pap. text ed. 95.00 (*0-7811-0138-7*) Res Inst Am.

***RIA's Complete Guide to Independent Contractors & the Self-Employment Tax.** Sidney Weinman. 224p. (Orig.). 1996. pap. text ed. 50.00 (*0-7811-0136-0*) Res Inst Am.

***RIA's Complete Guide to the Federal Estate Tax Return.** Betsy McKenny & Suzanne Schmitt. 624p. (Orig.). 1996. pap. text ed. 125.00 (*0-7811-0137-9*) Res Inst Am.

***RIA's Complete Guide to 401(K) Plans.** Michael Einbinder. 400p. (Orig.). 1996. pap. text ed. 110.00 (*0-7811-0139-5*) Res Inst Am.

Riata & Spurs. Charles A. Siringo. 1993. reprint ed. lib. bdg. 75.00 (*0-7812-5902-9*) Rprt Serv.

Rib Baskets. Jean Finley. LC 86-60001. (Illus.). 80p. 1987. pap. 9.95 (*0-88740-087-6*) Schiffer.

Rib Cage. Larry Ketron. 1978. pap. 5.25 (*0-8222-0948-9*) Dramatists Play.

Rib Ticklers: A Book of Punny Animals. Teri Sloat & Robert Sloat. LC 93-48619. (Illus.). (J). Date not set. lib. bdg. write for info. (*0-688-12520-4*) Lothrop.

Rib Ticklers: A Book of Punny Animals. Teri Sloat & Robert Sloat. LC 93-48619. (Illus.). 32p. (J). (ps up). 1995. 15.00 (*0-688-12519-0*) Lothrop.

Ribald Tales: Stories Men Only Tell Other Men. Martin C. Sommers. 210p. 1996. pap. 13.95 (*0-9651872-1-7*) Gondola Pubng.

Ribbin', Jivin', & Playin' the Dozens: The Persistent Dilemma in Our School. 2nd ed. Herbert L. Foster. (Illus.). 359p. (C). 1990. pap. 18.95 (*0-9624847-0-9*) H L Foster Assocs.

Ribbing Him Rightly. Beneth P. Jones. (Illus.). 107p. (Orig.). 1987. pap. 7.00 (*0-89084-381-3*) Bob Jones Univ Pr.

Ribbon: A Celebration of Life. LC 85-80922. (Illus.). 160p. 1985. pap. 5.00 (*0-937274-24-0*) Lark Books.

Ribbon Accents. (Illus.). 28p. (Orig.). 1988. pap. 5.95 (*0-933491-35-2*) Hot off Pr.

Ribbon & a Star: The Third Marines at Bougainville. John Monks, Jr. LC 79-19749. (Illus.). 1980. reprint ed. 26.95 (*0-89201-077-0*) Zenger Pub.

Ribbon Around a Bomb. Lucinda Grey. 31p. (Orig.). 1994. pap. 6.95 (*0-9636545-4-3*) Wind Pubns.

Ribbon Around the Pentagon: Peace by Piecemakers. Linda Pershing. LC 95-32486. (Publications of the American Folklore Society Ser.). (Illus.). 242p. 1996. pap. text ed. 22.50 (*0-87049-923-8*); lib. bdg. 45.00 (*0-87049-922-X*) U of Tenn Pr.

Ribbon Basics: All the Stitches & Techniques of Silk Ribbon Work & Embroidery. Mary J. Hiney & Joy Anckner. 160p. 1996. pap. 16.95 (*0-8069-1295-2*) Sterling.

Ribbon Basics: All the Stitches & Techniques of Silk Ribbon Work & Embroidery. Mary Jo Hiney & Joy Anckner. LC 94-45684. (Illus.). 160p. 1995. 24.95 (*0-8069-1294-4*, Chapelle) Sterling.

Ribbon Bouquet: A Guide to French Ribbon Flowers & Silk Ribbon Embroidery. Kathy L. Pace. Ed. by Amber Sargent. (Illus.). 96p. (Orig.). 1995. pap. 11.00 (*1-887820-00-0*) Gooseberry Hill.

***Ribbon Design to Cherish.** Mary Jo Hiney. 1997. pap. text ed. 8.95 (*1-57933-004-5*) Craft Impressions.

***Ribbon Embroidery.** Daphne J. Ashby & Jackie Woolsey. (Illus.). 128p. 1997. 24.95 (*0-7153-0433-X*, Pub. by D & C Pub UK) Sterling.

Ribbon Embroidery by Machine. Marie Duncan & Betty Farrell. LC 96-20437. 96p. 1996. pap. 18.95 (*0-8019-8783-0*) Chilton.

***Ribbon Flowers to Brighten Your Home.** Marinda Stewart. 1997. pap. text ed. 8.95 (*1-57933-006-1*) Craft Impressions.

Ribbon for My Repute. large type ed. Alan Sewart. (Linford Mystery Library). 1989. pap. 15.99 (*0-7089-6748-5*) Ulverscroft.

Ribbon in the Sky. Dorothy Garlock. 352p. 1991. mass mkt. 5.99 (*0-446-35989-0*) Warner Bks.

Ribbon in the Sky. large type ed. Dorothy Garlock. LC 92-32528. (General Ser.). 437p. 1993. lib. bdg. 22.95 (*0-8161-5468-6*, GK Hall) Thorndike Pr.

Ribbon of Iron. Annette M. Meakin. LC 70-115540. (Russia Observed, Series I). 1970. reprint ed. 20.95 (*0-405-03050-9*) Ayer.

Ribbon of Sand: The Amazing Convergence of the Ocean & the Outer Banks. John R. Alexander & James D. Lazell, Jr. (Illus.). 256p. 1992. 18.95 (*0-945575-32-7*) Algonquin Bks.

Ribbon Trimmings: A Course in Six Parts. Woman's Institute of Domestic Arts & Sciences. 208p. 1992. reprint ed. pap. 19.95 (*0-9631893-0-1*) Sloane Pubns.

Ribbon Trimmings & Flowers: Instruction Paper with Examination Questions see Old-Fashioned Ribbon Trimmings & Flowers

Ribbon with Gold. Dorothy Robbie. (Lost Play Ser.). 1977. pap. 1.25 (*0-912262-41-9*) Proscenium.

Ribboncraft. Deena Beverley. (Illus.). 128p. 1996. 23.00 (*1-85732-789-6*) Antique Collect.

Ribbons. Jean S. Platt. (Illus.). 96p. (Orig.). 1992. pap. text ed. 11.95 (*0-9634688-0-4*) Persona Pr PA.

Ribbons. Laurence Yep. 192p. (J). (gr. 5-9). 1996. 15.95 (*0-399-22906-X*, Putnam) Putnam Pub Group.

Ribbons. Laurence Yep. (J). 1999. pap. 3.99 (*0-14-037422-1*, Viking) Viking Penguin.

Ribbons. Laurence Yep. Date not set. pap. 13.99 (*0-670-85929-X*) Viking Penguin.

***Ribbons.** Laurence Yep. 192p. (Orig.). (J). (gr. 5-8). 1997. pap. 5.95 (*0-698-11606-2*, Paperstar) Putnam Pub Group.

Ribbons: The Gulf War - A Poem. William Heyen. LC 91-66143. 56p. 1991. 18.95 (*1-877770-44-2*); pap. 12.50 (*1-877770-45-0*); audio 12.95 (*1-877770-47-7*) Time Being Bks.

***Ribbons & Roses.** D. B. Taylor. 1996. mass mkt. 4.99 (*1-55197-088-0*, Pub. by Comnwlth Pub CN) Partners Pubs Grp.

***Ribbons & Threads: Baltimore Style.** Bonnie Browning. LC 96-49792. 1996. write for info. (*0-89145-897-2*) Collector Bks.

Ribbons for Mikele. Terri Cohlene. (Illus.). (J). 1999. write for info. (*0-688-13093-3*, Morrow Junior); lib. bdg. write for info. (*0-688-13094-1*, Morrow Junior) Morrow.

Ribbons in the Wind. Margaret Brownley. 352p. 1996. mass mkt. 5.99 (*0-451-40717-2*) NAL-Dutton.

Ribbons in Time: Movies & Society since 1945. Paul Monaco. LC 86-42996. (Interdisciplinary Studies in History). 170p. reprint ed. pap. 48.50 (*0-7837-3719-X*, 2057897) Bks Demand.

Ribbons of Rainbows. Carolyn Blaylock. 160p. 1995. pap. 6.95 (*1-57071-079-1*) Sourcebks.

***Ribbons of Sand: Exploring Atlantic Beaches.** Larry Points & Andrea Jauck. (Illus.). 32p. (Orig.). (J). 1997. pap. 7.95 (*0-939365-57-X*) Sierra Pr CA.

Ribbons of Time. Marilyn Kleinhardt. 6p. 1993. pap. 6.00 (*1-884694-02-0*) Wood n Needle.

Ribbons, Roses & Ruffles. Paulette S. Jarvey. (Illus.). 28p. (Orig.). 1986. pap. 5.95 (*0-933491-11-5*) Hot off Pr.

Ribbons to Wrinkles. Bruce Cochran. (Illus.). 10p. 1994. write for info. (*1-886386-28-5*) Trisar.

***Ribcage: Israeli Women's Fiction.** Ed. by Carol Diament & Lily Rattok. xxxiv, 281p. (Orig.). 1994. pap. 15.00 (*1-889525-01-4*) WZO.

Ribofunk. Paul Di Filippo. LC 96-6902. 304p. 1996. 20.00 (*1-56858-062-2*) FWEW.

***Ribonucleases: Structures & Functions.** Ed. by Giuseppe D'Alessio & James F. Riordan. LC 96-41839. (Illus.). 670p. 1997. boxed 125.00 (*0-12-588945-3*, AP Prof) Acad Pr.

Ribonucleic Acids. 2nd ed. Ed. by P. R. Stewart & D. S. Letham. LC 77-4899. 1977. 95.95 (*0-387-90281-3*) Spr-Verlag.

Ribosomal RNA: Structure, Evolution, Processing, & Function in Protein Biosynthesis. Robert A. Zimmermann. 512p. 1995. 210.00 (*0-8493-8864-3*, TP8864, CRC Reprint) CRC Pr.

Ribosomal RNA & Group I Introns. Renee Schroeder & Rachel Green. LC 96-9499. (Molecular Biology Intelligence Unit Ser.). 239p. 1996. 89.95 (*1-57059-379-5*) R G Landes.

Ribosome: Structure, Function, & Evolution. Ed. by Walter E. Hill et al. (Illus.). 678p. 1990. 99.00 (*1-55581-020-9*) Am Soc Microbio.

Ribosomes. Ed. by Masayasu Nomura et al. LC 74-83791. (Monographs: Vol. 4). (Illus.). 930p. 1974. 79.00 (*0-87969-110-7*) Cold Spring Harbor.

Ribosomes & Protein Synthesis: A Practical Approach. Ed. by G. Spedding. (Practical Approach Ser.). (Illus.). 344p. 1990. pap. 49.95 (*0-19-963105-0*, IRL Pr) OUP.

Ribosomes & Protein Synthesis: A Practical Approach. Ed. by G. Spedding. (Practical Approach Ser.: 59). (Illus.). 344p. 1990. 79.00 (*0-19-963104-2*, IRL Pr) OUP.

Ribot No. 1: A Subversion. Ed. by Paul Vangelisti. 144p. 1994. pap. 9.95 (*1-55713-156-2*) Sun & Moon CA.

Ribot No. 3: A Subversion. Ed. by Paul Vangelisti. 144p. 1995. pap. 9.95 (*1-55713-241-0*) Sun & Moon CA.

Ribot No. 4: A Subversion. Ed. by Paul Vangelisti. 144p. (Orig.). 1996. pap. 9.95 (*1-55713-249-6*) Sun & Moon CA.

Ribot No.2: A Subversion. Ed. by Paul Vangelisti. 144p. 1995. pap. 9.95 (*1-55713-199-6*) Sun & Moon CA.

***Ribozyme Protocols.** Ed. by Philip C. Turner. LC 97-12062. (Methods in Molecular Biology Ser.: Vol. 74). (Illus.). 512p. 1997. 74.50 (*0-89603-389-9*) Humana.

Ribs: Over a Hundred All-American & International Recipes for Ribs & Fixings. Susan R. Friedland. (Harmony Particular Palate Cookbooks Ser.). 1988. pap. 6.95 (*0-517-55315-5*, Harmony) Crown Pub Group.

Ribs: Over 80 All-American and International Recipes for Ribs and Fixings. Susan R. Friedland. 128p. 1996. pap. 10.00 (*0-517-88725-8*, Crown) Crown Pub Group.

Ribs of Death: Poems. Paul Zimmer. 1968. 8.95 (*0-8079-0111-3*); pap. 4.95 (*0-8079-0112-1*) October.

Ribstone Pippins. Helen Wykham. 226p. (Orig.). 1996. pap. 14.95 (*0-7145-3017-4*) M Boyars Pubs.

An Asterisk (*) at the beginning of an entry indicates that the title is appearing in BIP for the first time.

R

Ribsy. Beverly Cleary. 144p. (J). 1992. pap. 4.50 (*0-380-70955-4*, Camelot) Avon.

Ribsy. Beverly Cleary. LC 64-13263. (Illus.). (J). (gr. 3-7). 1964. 16.00 (*0-688-21662-5*, Morrow Junior); lib. bdg. 15.93 (*0-688-31662-X*, Morrow Junior) Morrow.

Ribsy. Beverly Cleary. (J). 1996. mass mkt. 4.50 (*0-380-72803-6*) Avon.

Ribsy. Houghton Mifflin Company Staff. (Literature Experience 1993 Ser.). (J). (gr. 3). 1992. pap. 8.48 (*0-395-61791-X*) HM.

Ribwash. Colin Webber. 307p. 1995. pap. 10.95 (*0-575-05830-7*, Pub. by V Gollancz UK) Trafalgar.

Ric & Rac's Woodland Adventure. Norman Wright & Gary Oliver. (Wonder Woods Ser.). 32p. (J). 1995. 7.99 (*1-56476-459-1*, 6-3459, Victor Bks) Chariot Victor.

***Ric & Rac's Woodland Adventures.** (J). 1995. write for info. (*7-900882-26-X*, Chariot Bks) Chariot Victor.

Ric Masten Speaking. Ric Masten. LC 90-33891. (Illus.). 139p. (Orig.). 1990. pap. 8.00 (*0-918949-11-4*) Papier-Mache Press.

Ricardi di Cirenscestria Speculum Historiale de Gestis Regum Angliae, 2 vols. John E. Mayor. (Rolls Ser.: No. 30). 1974. reprint ed. Set. 110.00 (*0-8115-1058-1*); reprint ed. Vol. 1, 447-871. write for info. (*0-8115-1059-X*) Periodicals Srv.

Ricardian Economics. Mark Blaug. LC 73-9208. 269p. 1973. reprint ed. text ed. 38.50 (*0-8371-6982-8*, BLRE, Greenwood Pr) Greenwood.

Ricardian Politics. Murray Milgate & Shannon C. Stimson. 176p. 1992. text ed. 45.00 (*0-691-04278-0*) Princeton U Pr.

***Ricardian Socialists, 7 vols.** Ed. by Kenyon. LC 96-51595. 1568p. (C). 1997. text ed. 925.00 (*0-415-12213-9*) Routledge.

Ricardo - Diary of a Matinee Idol. Richard Alfieri. LC 89-34635. 256p. (Orig.). 1989. 18.95 (*0-936784-65-2*); pap. 9.95 (*0-936784-66-0*) J Daniel.

Ricardo & the Gold Standard: The Foundations of the International Money Order. Maria C. Marcuzzo & Annalisa Rosselli. 180p. 1991. text ed. 65.00 (*0-312-05327-4*) St Martin.

Ricardo & the Theory of Value Distribution & Growth. Giovanni A. Caravale & Domenico A. Tosato. (Modern Revivals in Economics Ser.). 240p. (C). 1993. text ed. 59.95 (*0-7512-0257-6*, Pub. by Gregg Revivals UK) Ashgate Pub Co.

Ricardo Flores Magon: A Chronology. V. Munoz. Tr. by W. Scott Johnson. (Libertarian & Anarchist Chronology Ser.). 1979. lib. bdg. 59.95 (*0-8490-3050-1*) Gordon Pr.

Ricardo Flores Magon: Apostle of the Mexican Social Revolution. Diego Abad de Santillan. (Mexico Ser.). 1979. lib. bdg. 59.95 (*0-8490-2998-8*) Gordon Pr.

Ricardo Flores Magon: Writings, 5 vols. Ricardo Flores Magon. 1979. Set. lib. bdg. 500.00 (*0-8490-2999-6*) Gordon Pr.

Ricardo Gullon: Sus Discipulos. Ed. by Adelaida Lopez de Martinez. (Homenajes de Aldeeu Ser.). (Illus.). 320p. (SPA.). (C). 1995. pap. 35.00 (*0-9626630-3-4*) Spanish Profs Amer.

***Ricardo Legorreta, Architect.** Ed. by John Mutlow. LC 96-47059. (Illus.). 240p. 1997. 65.00 (*0-8478-2023-8*) Rizzoli Intl.

Ricardo Mella: A Chronology. V. Munoz. Tr. by W. Scott Johnson. (Libertarian & Anarchist Chronology Ser.). 1979. lib. bdg. 59.95 (*0-8490-3037-4*) Gordon Pr.

Ricardo on Machinery. Albert Jeck & Heinz D. Kurz. 160p. 1997. lib. bdg. 35.00 (*0-678-01465-5*) Kelley.

Ricardo on Taxation. Carl S. Shoup. (Modern Revivals in Economics Ser.). 285p. 1992. 61.95 (*0-7512-0060-3*, Pub. by Gregg Pub UK) Ashgate Pub Co.

Ricardo Palma: Tradiciones Peruanas. Ed. by Peter Francis. LC 72-92110. (C). 1970. 5.80 (*0-08-006665-8*, Pergamon Pr) Elsevier.

Ricardo Story: The Autobiography of Sir Harry Ricardo, Pioneer of Engine Research. 282p. 1992. 19.00 (*1-56091-211-1*, R-116) Soc Auto Engineers.

Ricardo, the New View: Collected Essays, Vol. 1. Samuel Hollander. LC 96-7939. 400p. (C). (gr. 13). 1995. text ed. 85.00 (*0-415-11582-5*) Routledge.

Ricardo's Day. George Ancona. LC 94-725. (J). 1994. write for info. (*0-590-29257-9*) Scholastic Inc.

Ricardo's Economics: A General Equilibrium Theory of Distribution & Growth. Michio Morishima. (Illus.). 264p. (C). 1989. text ed. 69.95 (*0-521-36630-5*) Cambridge U Pr.

Ricardo's Economics: A General Equilibrium Theory of Distribution & Growth. Michio Morishima. (Illus.). 256p. (C). 1990. pap. text ed. 23.95 (*0-521-39688-3*) Cambridge U Pr.

Ricardo's Poetical Works: Poetry Truths & Rights. Ricardo A. Scott. (Illus.). 110p. (Orig.). write for info. (*1-883427-08-8*) Crnerstone GA.

Ricasoli & the Risorgimento in Tuscany. William K. Hancock. LC 68-9603. 1969. reprint ed. 48.00 (*0-86527-171-2*) Fertig.

Riccardo Muti: Twenty Years in Philadelphia. Ed. by Judith K. Kurnick. (Illus.). 112p. (Orig.). 1992. pap. text ed. 26.50 (*0-8122-1445-5*) U of Pa Pr.

Riccati Equation. Ed. by S. Bittanti et al. (Communications & Control Engineering Ser.). x, 338p. 1991. 149.95 (*0-387-53099-1*) Spr-Verlag.

Ricci & Levi-Civita's Tensor Analysis, Paper. Robert Hermann et al. LC 75-26206. (Lie Groups: History, Frontiers & Applications Ser.: No. 2). 260p. 1975. 45.00 (*0-915692-11-2*, 991600045) Math Sci Pr.

Rice. Nikky Finney. Date not set. pap. 15.95 (*0-920813-21-6*, Pub. by Sister Vision CN) LPC InBook.

Rice. S. J. Fretz. 36p. (Orig.). 1995. pap. 3.25 (*0-940844-50-8*) Wellspring.

Rice. Lynne Merrison. (Foods We Eat Ser.). (Illus.). 32p. (J). (gr. 1-4). 1990. lib. bdg. 17.50 (*0-87614-417-2*, Carolrhoda) Lerner Group.

***Rice.** Jillian Powell. LC 96-32831. (Everyone Eats Ser.). (J). 1997. lib. bdg. 21.40 (*0-8172-4758-0*) Raintree Steck-V.

Rice. Jerry Rice. 144p. 1996. 50.00 (*0-312-14796-1*) St Martin.

Rice. Jerry Rice & Michael Silver. LC 96-8685. 144p. 1996. pap. 25.00 (*0-312-14795-3*) St Martin.

***Rice.** Pam Robson. LC 97-6041. (What's for Lunch? Ser.). (J). 1997. write for info. (*0-516-20824-1*) Childrens.

Rice. Ruth Thomson. Ed. by Rebecca Stefoff. LC 90-40367. (Threads Ser.). (Illus.). 32p. (J). (gr. 3-5). 1990. lib. bdg. 15.93 (*0-944483-71-2*) Garrett Ed Corp.

Rice. Su Tong. 272p. 1996. pap. 11.95 (*0-14-025644-X*, Penguin Bks) Viking Penguin.

Rice. Su Tong. Tr. by Howard Goldblatt from CHI. LC 94-38307. 288p. 1995. 23.00 (*0-688-13245-6*) Morrow.

Rice, 2 vols. 2nd enl. rev. ed. Ed. by Bor S. Luh. (Illus.). 1024p. (gr. 13). 1991. text ed. 209.95 (*0-442-00735-5*) Chapman & Hall.

Rice, 2 vols., Vol. I: Production. 2nd enl. rev. ed. Ed. by Bor S. Luh. (Illus.). 1024p. (gr. 13). 1991. text ed. 133.95 (*0-442-00484-2*) Chapman & Hall.

Rice, 2 vols., Vol. II: Utilization. 2nd enl. rev. ed. Ed. by Bor S. Luh. (Illus.). 1024p. (gr. 13). 1991. text ed. 133.95 (*0-442-00485-0*) Chapman & Hall.

Rice, Vol. 14. Ed. by Y. P. Bajaj. (Biotechnology in Agriculture & Forestry Ser.). (Illus.). 648p. 1991. 330.00 (*0-387-51810-X*) Spr-Verlag.

Rice: A Food for All Seasons. H. D. Akins & Ellen F. Lew. (Illus.). 250p. 1989. pap. 10.00 (*0-9623005-0-0*) H D Akins.

Rice: A Food for All Seasons Cookbook. Ellen F. Lew & Harold D. Akins. (Illus.). 1989. 10.00 (*0-317-93880-0*) H D Akins.

Rice: Chemistry & Technology. 2nd ed. Ed. by B. O. Juliano. (Illus.). 774p. 1985. 145.00 (*0-913250-41-4*) Am Assn Cereal Chem.

Rice: Eighty-Five Irrestible Recipes from Risotto to Rifsstafel. Bonnie T. Leblang & Joanne L. Hayes. 128p. 1991. 14.00 (*0-517-57694-5*, Harmony) Crown Pub Group.

***Rice: From Jambalaya Risotto.** Clare Ferguson. (Illus.). 144p. 1997. 24.95 (*0-8478-2000-9*) Rizzoli Intl.

***Rice: Grain of the Ancients.** Marcia Eames-Sheavly. Ed. by Judy Stewart. (Illus.). 36p. (Orig.). (J). (gr. 4-7). 1996. pap. 7.75 (*1-57753-056-X*, 142LM18) Corn Coop Ext.

***Rice: Selected Aspects of Production, Trade & Price Policies.** 87p. 1985. 12.00 (*92-5-102329-8*, F2856, Pub. by FAO IT) Bernan Associates.

Rice: The Little Grain That Feeds the World. Raphaelle Brice. Tr. by Vicki Bogard from FRE. LC 90-50775. (Young Discovery Library). (Illus.). 38p. (J). (gr. k-5). 1991. 5.95 (*0-944589-30-8*, 308) Young Discovery Lib.

Rice & Barley Offerings in the Vedas. Jan Gonda. (Orientalia Rheno-Traiectina Ser.: No. 31). 140p. 1987. 60.25 (*90-04-08289-1*) E J Brill.

Rice & Beans & Tasty Things. Dora R. De Romano. Ed. by Jaime Romano. (Illus.). 484p. (Orig.). 1986. pap. write for info. (*0-9633449-1-9*) D R de Romano.

Rice & Man: Agricultural Ecology in Southeast Asia. Lucien M. Hanks. LC 92-21937. 174p. 1992. reprint ed. pap. text ed. 15.00 (*0-8248-1465-7*) UH Pr.

Rice & Slaves: Ethnicity & the Slave Trade in Colonial South Carolina. Daniel C. Littlefield. (Blacks in the New World Ser.). 216p. 1991. pap. text ed. 12.95 (*0-252-06214-0*) U of Ill Pr.

Rice & the Making of South Carolina: An Introductory Essay. Daniel C. Littlefield. 40p. 1995. pap. 5.00 (*1-880067-29-3*) SC Dept of Arch & Hist.

Rice As Self: Japanese Identities Through Time. Emiko Oknuki-Tierney. 198p. 1993. pap. text ed. 13.95 (*0-691-02110-4*) Princeton U Pr.

Rice Biotechnology. Ed. by Gurdev S. Khush & G. Toenniessen. (Biotechnology in Agriculture Ser.: No. 6). 336p. 1991. 110.00 (*0-85198-712-5*) CAB Intl.

Rice Blast Disease. P. S. Teng. 640p. 1994. 150.00 (*0-85198-935-7*) CAB Intl.

Rice Book: The Definitive Book on the Magic of Rice, with Hundreds of Exotic Recipes from Around the World. Sri Owen. (Illus.). 416p. 1994. 24.95 (*0-312-10532-0*) St Martin.

Rice Book: The Definitive Book on the Magic of Rice, with Hundreds of Exotic Recipes from Around the World. Sri Owen. 416p. 1996. pap. 15.95 (*0-312-14132-7*, Griffin) St Martin.

Rice, Chinese Home-Cooking. 1993. 17.95 (*0-941676-36-6*) Wei-Chuan Pub.

Rice Cookbook. Anne Dettmer & Victoria Lloyd-Davies. LC 93-32746. (Illus.). 96p. 1994. pap. 11.95 (*1-56440-360-2*) Globe Pequot.

***Rice Cookbook: 70 Classic & Contemporary Recipes Using One of Nature's Most Versatile Ingrediet.** Smithmark Staff. (Creative Cooking Library). 1996. 12.98 (*0-7651-9876-2*) Smithmark.

Rice Cooker. Ed. by Cole Group Staff. (Cooking Companion Ser.). (Illus.). 96p. (Orig.). 1995. pap. 7.95 (*1-56426-810-1*) Cole Group.

***Rice County, Minnesota, Military Personnel Vol. 1: War of 1812, Mexican War, Civil War, Spanish American War & World War I.** Compiled by John Dalby. 1995. reprint ed. pap. 20.00 (*0-915709-29-5*) Pk Geneal Bk.

Rice Diet Report. Judy Moscovitz. 224p. 1987. mass mkt. 5.99 (*0-380-70286-X*) Avon.

Rice Diseases. 3rd ed. S. H. Ou. 412p. 1985. 105.00 (*0-85198-545-9*, Pub. by CAB Intntl UK) OUP.

Rice Economics Research & Extension Programs at Texas A & M University. Ed. by M. Edward Rister et al. (Illus.). 65p. (Orig.). (C). 1993. pap. text ed. 30.00 (*1-56806-452-7*) DIANE Pub.

Rice Economies: Technology & Development in Asian Societies. Francesca Bray. LC 93-41318. 1994. 16.00 (*0-520-08620-1*) U CA Pr.

Rice Economy of Asia. Randolph Barker et al. LC 84-43086. 328p. 1985. pap. text ed. 24.95 (*0-915707-15-2*); lib. bdg. 35.00 (*0-915707-14-4*) Resources Future.

Rice Field Ecology in Northeastern Thailand. Charles W. Heckman. (Monographiae Biologicae: Vol. 34). (Illus.). 1979. lib. bdg. 100.50 (*90-6193-086-3*) Kluwer Ac.

***Rice-Fish Research & Development in Asia.** Ed. by C. R. Dela Cruz et al. (ICLARM Conference Proceedings Ser.: No. 24). 457p. 1992. per. write for info. (*971-10-2288-5*, Pub. by ICLARM PH) Intl Spec Bk.

***Rice Flooded Fields to Fabulous Meals: A Rice Country Collection.** Texas Rice Festival Staff. 240p. 1996. 19.95 (*0-9654028-5-1*) Texas Rice.

Rice for the Moon & Other Stories. Manuel S. Diaz. 117p. (Orig.). (C). 1986. pap. 7.50 (*971-10-0247-7*, Pub. by New Day Pub PH) Cellar.

Rice Hull Gasification: Theory & Praxis. A. Kaupp. (Illus.). 303p. (Orig.). 1984. 40.00 (*0-942914-05-8*); pap. 20.00 (*0-942914-04-X*); lib. bdg. 40.00 (*0-942914-06-6*) Tipi Wkshp Bks.

Rice in Human Nutrition. Bienvenido Juliano. 166p. 1994. pap. 35.00 (*92-5-103149-5*, F31495, Pub. by FAO IT) Bernan Associates.

Rice in South-East Asia: Cultures & Landscapes. Jacqueline M. Piper. (Images of Asia Ser.). (Illus.). 108p. 1994. 16.95 (*967-65-3038-7*) OUP.

Rice in the Storm: Faith in Struggle in the Philippines. Ed. by Rebecca C. Asedillo & B. David Williams. 1989. pap. 6.95 (*0-377-00192-9*) Friendship Pr.

Rice in West Africa: Policy & Economics. Scott R. Pearson et al. LC 80-50906. (Illus.). 512p. 1981. 62.50 (*0-8047-1095-3*) Stanford U Pr.

Rice Insects: Management Strategies. Ed. by E. A. Heinrichs & T. A. Miller. (Experimental Entomology Ser.). (Illus.). xiii, 347p. 1991. 159.95 (*0-387-97490-3*) Spr-Verlag.

Rice Is Nice: 108 Quick & Easy Brown Rice Recipes. Wendy Esko. (Illus.). 96p. (Orig.). (YA). 1995. pap. 8.95 (*1-882984-12-9*) One Peaceful World.

Rice Marketing in Indonesia: Methodology, Results & Implications of a Research Study. Ed. by P. Magrath et al. 1992. pap. 30.00 (*0-85954-311-0*, Pub. by Nat Res Inst UK) St Mut.

Rice Marketing System & Compulsory Levies in Andhra Pradesh: A Study of Public Intervention in Food Grain Marketing, India. K. Subbarao. 1979. 12.00 (*0-8364-0365-7*) S Asia.

Rice Meeting: 1990 Meeting of the Division of Particles & Fields of the American Physical Society. Ed. by B. E. Bonner & H. E. Miettinen. 1136p. (C). 1990. text ed. 161.00 (*981-02-0258-X*) World Scientific Pub.

***Rice, No Beans.** Minerva Martinez-Zanca. Ed. by Gloria Chavez. (Illus.). (Orig.). 1997. pap. text ed. 11.00 (*0-9655516-0-1*) Obra Hispana.

Rice-Paper Ceiling: Breaking Through Japanese Corporate Culture. Rochelle Kopp. LC 94-27608. 270p. 1994. 25.00 (*1-880656-14-0*) Stone Bridge Pr.

Rice Planters Recipes. David L. Gilbert, Jr. Tr. & Intro. by Dorothy M. Gilbert. (Illus.). 103p. (Orig.). (C). 1984. pap. 4.00 (*0-9615765-0-2*) Cane Patch.

Rice Policy in Indonesia. Scott R. Pearson et al. LC 90-55751. (Food Systems & Agrarian Change Ser.). (Illus.). 208p. 1991. 35.00 (*0-8014-2524-7*) Cornell U Pr.

Rice Powder. Sergio Galindo. Ed. by Bert Patrick & Lura L. Patrick. LC 78-51332. (Translation Ser.: No. 5). Orig. Title: Polvos De Arroz. 43p. 1978. pap. 10.00 (*0-912288-12-4*) Perivale Pr.

Rice Prices & Farmers' Welfare in Madagascar: A Non-Parametric Analysis. Christopher B. Barrett & Paul A. Dorosh. (Working Papers: No. 73). 31p. (C). 4195. pap. 7.00 (*1-56401-173-9*) Cornell Food.

Rice Production in Sri Lanka: A Combined Agronomic-Economic Study in the Intermediate & Dry Zones. Kenneth M. Menz. (C). 1990. text ed. 105.00 (*1-86320-022-3*, Pub. by ACIAR) St Mut.

Rice Program: Government Support Needs to Be Reassessed. (Illus.). 89p. (Orig.). (C). 1995. pap. text ed. 25.00 (*0-7881-1853-6*) DIANE Pub.

Rice Research in Asia: Progress & Priorities. Ed. by R. E. Evenson et al. 432p. 1996. 99.00 (*0-85198-997-7*) CAB Intl.

Rice, Rivalry & Politics: Managing Cambodian Relief. Linda Mason & Roger Brown. LC 82-40380. (Illus.). 240p. 1983. pap. 68.40 (*0-608-00882-6*, 2061676) Bks Demand.

Rice Room: Growing up Chinese-American - from Number Two Son to Rock 'N' Roll. Ben Fong-Torres. LC 93-28111. 272p. 1994. 22.95 (*0-7868-6002-2*) Hyperion.

Rice Room: Growing Up Chinese-American: From Number Two Son to Rock 'n' Roll. Ben Fong-Torrees. LC 94-43472. 1995. pap. 11.95 (*0-452-27412-5*, Plume) NAL-Dutton.

Rice, Rupees, & Ritual: Economy & Society among the Samosir Batak of Sumatra. D. George Sherman. LC 89-4408. (Illus.). 384p. 1990. 47.50 (*0-8047-1666-8*) Stanford U Pr.

Rice Science & Technology. Ed. by Marshall & Wadsworth. (Food Science & Technology Ser.: Vol. 59). 488p. 1993. 165.00 (*0-8247-8887-7*) Dekker.

Rice Sector of Peninsular Malaysia: A Rural Paradox. P. P. Courtenay. (ASAA Southeast Asia Publications Ser.). (Illus.). 208p. 1996. 29.95 (*1-86373-991-2*, Pub. by Allen & Unwin Aust Pty AT) Paul & Co Pubs.

Rice Societies: Asian Problems & Prospects. Ed. by Irene Norlund et al. (Studies on Asian Topics (Scandinavian Institute of Asian Studies): No. 10). 322p. (C). 1986. pap. 25.00 (*0-913215-17-1*) Riverdale Co.

Rice, the Amazing Grain: One Hundred Sixty Great Rice Dishes for Every Day. Marie Simmons. 304p. 1993. pap. 14.95 (*0-8050-2545-6*) H Holt & Co.

Rice, Traditional Chinese Cooking. 96p. 1993. 17.95 (*0-941676-43-9*) Wei-Chuan Pub.

Rice Tungro. V. D. Shukla. (Illus.). 240p. 1995. text ed. 76.00 (*1-886106-16-9*) Science Pubs.

Rice. "We Sought the Wilderness" (Memoirs of Some Descendants of Dea. Edmund Rice) C. S. Rice. 257p. 1991. reprint ed. pap. 39.50 (*0-8328-1976-X*); reprint ed. lib. bdg. 49.50 (*0-8328-1975-1*) Higginson Bk Co.

Rice without Rain. Minfong Ho. LC 86-33745. 236p. (J). (gr. 7 up). 1990. 16.00 (*0-688-06355-1*) Lothrop.

Riceland Spiders of South & Southeast Asia. Barrion & J. A. Litsinger. (Illus.). 736p. 1996. 225.00 (*0-85198-967-5*) OUP.

Ricerca della Lingua Perfetta Nella Cultura Europea see Search for the Perfect Language

***Ricercar a 6 for Two Keyboards: From the Musical Offering.** 2nd rev. ed. Ed. by Tamara Loring. ii, 28p. 1995. pap. text ed. 12.00 (*1-56571-126-2*) PRB Prods.

Ricercar & Aus Tiefer Noth for Six Viols. Johann Sebastian Bach. Ed. by Peter Ballinger. (Viol Consort Ser.: No. 1). 39p. 1991. pap. text ed. 12.00 (*1-56571-022-3*) PRB Prods.

Ricercar for Two Harpsichords. Johann Sebastian Bach. Ed. by Tamara Loring. (Early Keyboard Ser.: No. 1). ii, 28p. 1991. pap. text ed. 12.00 (*1-56571-018-5*) PRB Prods.

Riceyman Steps. Arnold Bennett. 393p. 1984. reprint ed. pap. 10.00 (*0-89733-093-5*) Academy Chi Pubs.

Rich! God Meeting Your Deepest Needs. Churches Alive, Inc. Staff. (God in You Bible Study Ser.). (Illus.). 72p. (Orig.). 1986. pap. 5.00 (*0-89109-094-0*) NavPress.

Rich: Joel Rich Ancestors & Descendants, from Dover, NH, Cape Cod & Gorham, ME to Jackson Plantation, Waldo County, 1677-1993. Frances M. DeMars. (Illus.). 175p. 1993. pap. 29.50 (*0-8328-3624-9*); lib. bdg. 39.50 (*0-8328-3623-0*) Higginson Bk Co.

Rich Against Poor: The Reality of Aid. C. R. Hensman. 308p. 1971. text ed. 18.95 (*0-87073-294-3*) Schenkman Bks Inc.

Rich & Famous. John Guare. 1977. pap. 5.25 (*0-8222-0949-7*) Dramatists Play.

Rich & Famous Baby Name Book Vol. 1: Ten Thousand Celebrity Names for Your Baby. Robert Davenport. 1994. mass mkt. 4.99 (*0-312-95407-7*) St Martin.

Rich & Famous Like My Mom. Hila Colman. LC 87-27448. 144p. (J). (gr. 4-7). 1988. 10.95 (*0-517-56836-5*) Crown Bks Yng Read.

***Rich & Famous Money Book: Investment Strategies of Leading Celebrities.** Jean S. Chatzky. LC 97-22835. 240p. 1997. 19.95 (*0-471-18540-X*) Wiley.

Rich & Judgment Proof. Harold E. Collins. 264p. (Orig.). 1995. pap. 20.00 (*1-886094-22-5*) Chicago Spectrum.

Rich & Poor. Glady N. Chianumba. 89p. 1990. 7.95 (*0-533-08270-6*) Vantage.

Rich & Poor Countries. 4th ed. Hans W. Singer & Javed A. Ansari. (Studies in Economics). 330p. 1988. pap. text ed. 22.95 (*0-04-445044-3*) Routledge Chapman & Hall.

Rich & Poor Countries. Hans W. Singer & Javed A. Ansari. LC 76-49137. (Studies in Economics: No. 12). 228p. reprint ed. pap. 65.00 (*0-317-42344-4*, 2025872) Bks Demand.

Rich & Poor Countries: Consequences of International Disorder. 4th ed. Hans W. Singer & Javed A. Ansari. LC 87-30632. 336p. (Orig.). (C). 1988. pap. 24.95 (*0-415-09459-3*, Routledge NY) Routledge.

Rich & Poor in the Shepherd of Hermas: An Exegetical-Social Investigation. Carolyn A. Osiek. Ed. by Bruce Vawter. LC 83-7385. (Catholic Biblical Quarterly Monographs: No. 15). xi, 184p. 1983. pap. 6.00 (*0-915170-14-0*) Catholic Bibl Assn.

Rich & Rare. Ed. by Sean McMahon. 380p. 8700. pap. 14.95 (*0-905169-86-7*, Pub. by Poolbeg Pr IE) Dufour.

Rich & Rare Land: Irish Poetry & Paintings. Fleur Robertson. (Illus.). 128p. 1995. 12.99 (*0-517-12169-7*) Random Hse Value.

Rich & Strange: Gender, History, Modernism. Marianne DeKoven. 257p. 1992. pap. text ed. 14.95 (*0-691-01496-5*) Princeton U Pr.

Rich & Super-Rich. Ferdinand Lundberg. 820p. reprint ed. pap. 14.95 (*0-8184-0486-8*) Carol Pub Group.

Rich & the Poor. Carl Kreider. LC 86-33614. 168p. (Orig.). 1987. pap. 9.99 (*0-8361-3433-8*) Herald Pr.

Rich & the Poor. Henry Parker. LC 77-7419. (English Experience Ser.: No. 882). 1977. reprint ed. lib. bdg. 75.00 (*90-221-0882-1*) Walter J Johnson.

Rich & the Super-Rich. Ferdinand Lundberg. Ed. by Eileen Brand. LC 67-10015. 1968. 15.00 (*0-8184-0069-2*) Carol Pub Group.

Rich Are Different. Susan Howatch. 704p. 1985. mass mkt. 6.99 (*0-449-20770-6*, Crest) Fawcett.

Rich Are Different. Ed. & Compiled by Jon Winokur. LC 96-6258. 272p. 1996. 20.00 (*0-679-44386-X*) Pantheon.

Rich As Sin. Anne Mather. (Presents Ser.). 1993. mass mkt. 2.99 (*0-373-11567-9*, 1-11567-4) Harlequin Bks.

Rich Cabinet Furnished with Varietie of Excellent Descriptions. Thomas Gainsford. LC 77-38417. (English Experience Ser.: No. 458). 368p. 1972. reprint ed. 45.00 (*90-221-0458-3*) Walter J Johnson.

Rich Christian in the Church of the Early Empire: Contradictions & Accommodations. L. William Countryman. LC 80-81884. (Texts & Studies in Religion: Vol. 7). viii, 248p. 1980. lib. bdg. 89.95 (*0-88946-970-9*) E Mellen.

Rich Colleges, Poor Colleges. D. Kent Halstead. 1996. pap. 75.00 (*1-883298-04-0*) Res Assoc WA.

An Asterisk (*) at the beginning of an entry indicates that the title is appearing in BIP for the first time.

R

Rich Detective. H. R. Keating. 256p. 1993. 18.95 (*0-89296-506-1*) Mysterious Pr.

***Rich Detective.** H. R. Keating. 1993. write for info. (*0-333-58520-8*, Pub. by Macmlln UK); pap. write for info. (*0-330-33298-8*, Pub. by Pan Books UK) Trans-Atl Phila.

Rich Detective. large type ed. H. R. Keating. LC 93-18808. 1993. lib. bdg. 17.95 (*1-56054-728-6*) Thorndike Pr.

Rich Die Richer: And You Can Too. William D. Zabel. LC 94-34368. 320p. 1995. 25.00 (*0-688-12350-3*) Morrow.

Rich Die Richer & You Can Too. William D. Zabel. 1996. pap. text ed. 17.95 (*0-471-15532-2*) Wiley.

Rich Dog: & The Story Of. Lydia Ugolini. Ed. by Susan R. Hall. Tr. by Anna Taraboletti-Segre from ITA. LC 96-75988. (Illus.). 130p. (J). (gr. 3-6). 1997. pap. 12.95 (*0-912339-04-7*, Beacon Hill Bks) Meridian Hse.

Rich Earth. large type ed. Pamela Oldfield. (Magna Large Print Ser.). 1994. 25.99 (*0-7505-0619-9*, Pub. by Magna Print Bks UK) Ulverscroft.

Rich Earth: Alaskas Mineral Industry. Alaska Geographic Society Staff. Ed. by L. J. Campbell & Penny Rennick. (Alaska Geographic Ser.: Vol. 22, No. 3). (Illus.). 96p. 1995. pap. 19.95 (*1-56661-027-3*) Alaska Geog Soc.

Rich Endowment: Government & Mining in Western Australia, 1829-1994. Ken Spillman. 1993. 39.95 (*1-875560-23-8*, Pub. by Univ of West Aust Pr AT) Intl Spec Bk.

Rich Farmer. Nick Butterworth & Mick Inkpen. (Best of the Bunch Two Ser.). (Illus.). 32p. (J). (ps-3). 1992. mass mkt. 3.99 (*0-551-02508-5*) HarpC.

Rich Fool. R. Woodman. (Look 'N See Ser.). (J). 1995. 0.99 (*1-85792-172-0*, Pub. by Christian Focus UK) Spring Arbor Dist.

Rich Forests, Poor People: Resource Control & Resistance in Java. Nancy L. Peluso. 1992. pap. 15.00 (*0-520-08931-6*) U CA Pr.

Rich Forests, Poor People: Resource Control & Resistance in Java. Nancy L. Peluso. 336p. (C). 1992. 50.00 (*0-520-07377-0*) U CA Pr.

Rich Friends. large type ed. Jacqueline Briskin. LC 94-32355. 704p. 1994. lib. bdg. 25.95 (*0-7838-1132-2*, GK Hall) Thorndike Pr.

***Rich Full Death.** Michael Dibdin. 1997. pap. write for info. (*0-375-70010-2*, Vin) Random.

***Rich Get Richer.** 2nd ed. Dennis D. Braun. LC 96-47169. 1997. pap. text ed. 27.95 (*0-8304-1433-9*) Nelson-Hall.

Rich Get Richer & Poor Get Poorer. 4th ed. Jeffrey H. Reiman. 1994. pap. text ed. 22.00 (*0-02-399252-2*, Macmillan Coll) P-H.

***Rich Get Richer & the Poor Get Prison: Ideology, Class, & Criminal Justice.** 5th ed. Jeffrey H. Reiman. 1997. 24. 00 (*0-205-26487-5*) Allyn.

Rich Get Richer & the Poor Write Proposals. Nancy Mitiguy. LC 79-624731. (Illus.). (Orig.). (C). 1978. pap. 7.00 (*0-934210-02-0*) Devlp Commy.

***Rich Girl.** R. L. Stine. (YA). 1997. mass mkt. 3.99 (*0-671-52962-5*, Archway) PB.

Rich Girl, Bad Boy. Audra Adams. (Desire Ser.). 1994. mass mkt. 2.99 (*0-373-05839-X*, 5-05839-1) Silhouette.

Rich Girl, Poor Girl. large type ed. Faith Baldwin. 323p. 1993. reprint ed. lib. bdg. 19.95 (*1-56054-274-8*) Thorndike Pr.

***Rich Girl/Sagas: Daughters of Silence.** R. L. Stine. (Fear Street Ser.). 1997. mass mkt. 119.70 (*0-671-85807-6*, Archway) PB.

***Rich Go to Heaven: Giving Charity in Jewish Thought.** Eli M. Shear & Chaim Miller. 1998. write for info. (*0-7657-5990-X*) Aronson.

Rich Grass & Sweet Water: Ranch Life with the Koch Matador Cattle Company. John Lincoln. LC 89-4434. (Centennial Series of the Association of Former Students: No. 32). (Illus.). 168p. 1989. 19.95 (*0-89096-387-8*) Tex A&M Univ Pr.

Rich Harvest: The History, Buildings, & People of Lincoln, Massachusetts. John C. MacLean. 680p. 1987. 30.00 (*0-944856-01-2*) Lincoln Hist Soc.

Rich Heritage of Quakerism. 2nd ed. Walter R. Williams, Jr. et al. LC 87-71513. (Illus.). 326p. 1987. reprint ed. pap. 13.95 (*0-913342-73-4*) Barclay Pr.

Rich in Love. Josephine Humphreys. 262p. 1988. pap. 9.00 (*0-14-010283-3*, Penguin Bks) Viking Penguin.

Rich in Love. Josephine Humphreys. 272p. 1992. pap. 10.95 (*0-14-017432-X*, Penguin Bks) Viking Penguin.

Rich Is Best. Julie Ellis. 720p. 1986. mass mkt. 4.50 (*0-8217-1924-6*, Zebra Kensgtn) Kensgtn Pub Corp.

Rich Is Better: How Women Can Bridge the Gap Between Wanting & Having It All. Tessa A. Warschaw. 287p. 1991. reprint ed. pap. 13.95 (*0-9630298-0-0*) TWG Pub NY.

Rich Kids: A Novel. Robert Westbrook. 320p. 1992. 18.95 (*1-55972-106-5*, Birch Ln Pr) Carol Pub Group.

Rich Land, a Poor People: Politics & Society in Modern Chiapas. 2nd abr. rev. ed. Thomas Benjamin. (Illus.). 400p. 1996. pap. 22.50 (*0-8263-1713-8*) U of NM Pr.

Rich Land, Poor Land. Stuart Chase. LC 70-92612. (Illus.). reprint ed. 57.50 (*0-404-01478-X*) AMS Pr.

Rich Law, Poor Law: Different Response to Tax & Supplementary Benefit Fraud. Dee Cook. 192p. 1989. 90.00 (*0-335-15878-1*, Open Univ Pr); pap. 32.00 (*0-335-15877-3*, Open Univ Pr) Taylor & Francis.

Rich Like Us. Nayantara Sahgal. LC 88-5306. 240p. 1988. reprint ed. pap. 8.95 (*0-8112-1078-2*, NDP665) New Directions.

Rich Lizard: And Other Poems. Deborah Chandra. 48p. (J). (gr. 4-7). 1996. 14.00 (*0-374-36274-2*) FS&G.

Rich Lizard: And Other Poems. Deborah Chandra. 48p. (J). (gr. 2-5). 1996. pap. 5.95 (*0-374-46289-5*, Sunburst Bks) FS&G.

Rich Man & Lazarus. William C. Nichols. (Proverbs 22:6 Ser.: No. 1). (Illus.). 40p. (J). (ps-4). 1996. pap. 8.00 (*0-9641803-4-0*) Internat Outreach.

Rich Man & Lazarus. Brownlow North. 1979. pap. 4.99 (*0-85151-121-X*) Banner of Truth.

Rich Man & Lazarus: The Intermediate State. E. W. Bullinger. LC 91-44383. 60p. 1992. pap. text ed. 3.50 (*1-880573-01-6*) Grace Wl.

Rich Man & Lazarus on the Reformation Stage: A Contribution to the Social History of German Drama. Stephen L. Wailes. LC 96-15361. 360p. 1997. 48.50 (*0-945636-88-1*) Susquehanna U Pr.

Rich Man & the Kingdom: John D. Rockefeller, Jr., & the Protestant Establishment. Albert F. Shenkel. LC 95-2580. (Harvard Theological Studies: Vol. 39). 192p. (Orig.). (C). 1995. pap. 14.00 (*0-8006-7092-2*) TPI PA.

Rich Man, Poor Man see Heinemann Guided Readers

Rich Man's Flowers. large type ed. Madeleine A. Polland. 576p. 1993. 27.99 (*0-7089-8697-8*) Ulverscroft.

Rich Man's Secret: An Amazing Formula for Success. Ken Roberts. LC 95-6490. 216p. 1995. pap. 9.95 (*1-56718-580-0*) Llewellyn Pubns.

Rich Nation, Strong Army: National Security & the Technological Transformation of Japan. Richard J. Samuels. LC 93-39156. (Cornell Studies in Political Economy). (Illus.). 480p. 1994. 49.95 (*0-8014-2705-3*) Cornell U Pr.

Rich Nation, Strong Army: National Security & the Technological Transformation of Japan. Richard J. Samuels. (Studies in Political Economy). (Illus.). 480p. 1996. pap. 19.95 (*0-8014-9994-1*) Cornell U Pr.

Rich Nations - Poor Nations: The Long Run Perspective. Ed. by Derek H. Aldcroft & Ross Catterall. LC 95-19498. (Illus.). 240p. 1996. 80.00 (*1-85898-059-3*) E Elgar.

Rich Neighbor Policy: Rockefeller & Kaiser in Brazil. Elizabeth A. Cobbs. (C). 1992. text ed. 35.00 (*0-300-05179-4*) Yale U Pr.

Rich Noble, Poor Noble. Michael L. Bush. 240p. 1988. text ed. 65.00 (*0-7190-2381-5*, Pub. by Manchester Univ Pr UK) St Martin.

Rich or Dead. Dan Kruger. 1990. 15.95 (*1-55972-024-7*, Birch Ln Pr) Carol Pub Group.

Rich Pay Late. Simon Raven. 1987. 15.95 (*0-8253-0415-6*) Beaufort Bks NY.

Rich, Rare & Red. Ben Howkins. 172p. 1987. pap. 9.95 (*0-932664-54-7*) Wine Appreciation.

Rich Register: A Directory of America's Wealthiest People, 1996. John D. Anderson. 240p. 1996. 395.00 (*0-9633933-0-8*) Rich Register.

***Rich Salt Place.** Photos by Marie V. Gery. 10p. 1986. per. 7.95 (*0-9614314-1-5*) Heywood Pr.

Rich Shall Inherit. Elizabeth Adler. 560p. 1990. mass mkt. 5.99 (*0-440-20639-1*) Dell.

Rich, the Well Born, & the Powerful: Elites & Upper Classes in History. Ed. by Frederic C. Jaher. LC 72-89605. 385p. 1973. reprint ed. pap. 109.80 (*0-8357-3518-4*, 2034445) Bks Demand.

Rich, the Wellborn, & the Powerful. Frederic C. Jaher. 384p. 1975. reprint ed. pap. 5.95 (*0-8065-0505-2*, Citadel Pr) Carol Pub Group.

Rich Timetable & Appendices; Feeling the Roof of a Mouth That Hangs Open, 2 bks. in 1. Sheila E. Murphy & Stacey Sollfrey. 1991. pap. 3.00 (*0-935350-30-6*); write for info. (*0-935350-31-4*) Luna Bisonte.

***Rich Wallace.** (Author Bios Ser.). (J). 1997. pap. write for info. (*0-676-76199-2*) Knopf Bks Yng Read.

Rich Wife. Peter H. Wyden. 1985. 17.95 (*0-02-631800-8*) Macmillan.

Rich with Years: Daily Meditations on Growing Older. Malcolm Boyd. LC 93-11337. 384p. 1993. pap. 13.00 (*0-06-250258-1*) Harper SF.

Rich World, Poor World. Geoffrey Lean. 1979. pap. 13.50 (*0-04-309012-5*) Routledge Chapman & Hall.

Richard A. Berman-Osterreicher, Demokrat, Weltburger: Ein Kapitel Deutsh-Osterreichischer Kulturgeschichte. Deutsche Bibliothek. 1995. 60.00 (*3-598-11297-1*) K G Saur.

Richard A. McCormick & the Renewal of Moral Theology. Paulinus I. Odozor. LC 94-15941. (C). 1995. text ed. 34. 95 (*0-268-01648-8*) U of Notre Dame Pr.

Richard Aldington. Thomas McGreevey. LC 74-1231. (Twayne's English Authors Ser.). (C). 1974. lib. bdg. 17. 95 (*0-8290-2404-2*) Irvington.

Richard Aldington. Thomas McGreevey. LC 74-1231. (English Biography Ser.: No. 31). 1974. lib. bdg. 43.95 (*0-8383-1785-5*) M S G Haskell Hse.

Richard Aldington: A Biography. Charles Doyle. LC 88-34922. (Illus.). 350p. (C). 1989. text ed. 39.95 (*0-8093-1566-1*) S Ill U Pr.

Richard Aldington: An Autobiography in Letters. Ed. by Norman T. Gates. 440p. 1992. 55.00 (*0-271-00832-6*) Pa St U Pr.

Richard Aldington: Selected Critical Writing, 1928-1960. Richard Aldington. Ed. by Alister Kershaw. LC 78-86189. (Crosscurrents-Modern Critiques Ser.). 158p. (C). 1970. 6.95 (*0-8093-0451-1*) S Ill U Pr.

Richard Aldington & H. D. The Early Years in Letters. Caroline G. Zilboorg. LC 91-70. (Illus.). 260p. 1992. 35. 00 (*0-253-36868-5*) Ind U Pr.

Richard Aldington & H. D. The Later Years in Letters. Richard Aldington. Ed. & Comment by Caroline C. Zilboorg. LC 94-24440. 1995. text ed. 79.95 (*0-7190-4570-3*, Pub. by Manchester Univ Pr UK) St Martin.

***Richard Aldington & Lawrence of Arabia: A Cautionary Tale.** Fred D. Crawford. LC 97-25418. 1998. write for info. (*0-8093-2166-1*) S Ill U Pr.

Richard Allen. Frederick E. Maser. 33p. 1976. pap. 1.00 (*1-880927-07-1*) Gen Comm Arch.

Richard Allen: An Apostle of Freedom. Charles H. Wesley. (YA). 1990. 12.95 (*0-87498-078-X*); pap. 9.95 (*0-87498-079-8*) Assoc Pubs DC.

Richard Allen: Religious Leader & Social Activist. Steve Klots. Ed. by Nathan I. Huggins. (Black Americans of Achievement Ser.). (Illus.). 112p. (YA). (gr. 5 up). 1991. lib. bdg. 19.95 (*1-55546-570-6*) Chelsea Hse.

Richard Allen: The First Exemplar of African American Education. E. Curtis Alexander. LC 83-85051. (African American Educator Ser.: Vol. III). (Illus.). 174p. (Orig.). 1985. pap. 9.95 (*0-938818-06-6*) ECA Assoc.

***Richard & Lindy's No-Nonsense Guide to Windows 95: An Anxiety-Free, Warm & Friendly Approach to Learning & Using Windows 95 for People Who Hate Software Manuals (& Those Who Love Them)** Richard A. Sherman & Lindy Root. 257p. (Orig.). 1997. pap. 19.95 (*1-881859-19-3*, P-95) Natl Ct Report.

Richard & Maria Cosway. Stephen Lloyd. (Illus.). 143p. 1995. pap. write for info. (*0-903598-53-1*, Pub. by Natl Galleries UK) Antique Collect.

Richard & Philip: The Burtons A Book of Memories. Philip Burton et al. 184p. 9300. 28.00 (*0-7206-0855-4*, Pub. by P Owen Ltd UK) Dufour.

Richard & Rhoda: Letters from the Civil War. Marion G. Phillips. 1981. 25.00 (*0-88082-038-1*, 1462) Picton Pr.

Richard & the Vratch. Beatrice Gormley. 144p. 1987. pap. 2.95 (*0-380-75207-7*, Camelot) Avon.

Richard Anuszkiewicz. Richard Armstrong. LC 76-43241. (Illus.). 40p. 1976. 10.00 (*0-686-99811-1*) Mus Contemp Art.

Richard Armour's Punctured Poems: Famous First & Infamous Second Lines. Richard Armour & Eric Gurney. LC 82-10989. (Illus.). 96p. 1982. pap. 3.95 (*0-912800-55-0*) Woodbridge Pr.

Richard Artschwager. (Parkett Art Magazine Ser.: No. 23). (Illus.). 200p. 1990. 19.50 (*3-907509-73-0*, Pub. by Parkett Pubs SZ) Dist Art Pubs.

Richard Artschwager. 1988. 40.00 (*0-393-02596-9*) Norton.

Richard Artschwager: PUBLIC (public) LC 91-75567. (Illus.). 80p. 1992. 19.95 (*0-932900-28-3*) Elvejhem Mus.

Richard B. Moore, Caribbean Militant in Harlem: Collected Writings, 1920-1972. Ed. by W. Burghardt Turner. LC 87-37382. (Blacks in the Diaspora Ser.). (Illus.). 336p. 1988. 57.50 (*0-253-31299-X*) Ind U Pr.

Richard B. Moore, Caribbean Militant in Harlem: Collected Writings, 1920-1972. Ed. by W. Burghardt Turner. LC 87-37382. (Blacks in the Diaspora Ser.). (Illus.). 336p. 1992. pap. 8.95 (*0-253-20759-2*, MB-759) Ind U Pr.

Richard B. Russell, Jr., Senator from Georgia. Gilbert C. Fite. LC 90-40277. (Fred W. Morrison Series in Southern Studies). (Illus.). xv, 567p. (C). 1991. 45.00 (*0-8078-1937-9*) U of NC Pr.

Richard Bach, 3 vols. Richard Bach. 1990. boxed 12.40 (*0-440-36006-4*) Dell.

Richard Baker's Companion to Music: A Personal A-Z Guide to Classical Music. Richard Baker. (Illus.). 208p. 1995. 27.95 (*0-563-36414-9*, BBC-Parkwest) Parkwest Pubns.

Richard Ball: Selected Poems, 1933-1993. Richard Ball. LC 94-60518. (Illus.). 160p. (Orig.). 1994. pap. 9.95 (*1-880964-07-4*) Zapizdat Pubns.

Richard Barnfield: Colin's Child. Harry Morris. LC 63-63443. (Florida State University Studies: No. 38). 217p. reprint ed. pap. 61.90 (*0-7837-4928-7*, 2044594) Bks Demand.

Richard Barnfield: The Complete Poems. Ed. by George Klawitter. LC 89-40776. (Illus.). 256p. 1991. 44.50 (*0-945636-15-6*) Susquehanna U Pr.

Richard Beacon, Solon His Follie: Or a Politique Discourse Touching the Reformation of Common-Weales Conquered, Declined or Corrupted. Richard Beacon. Ed. by Clare Carroll & Vincent Carey. (Medieval & Renaissance Texts & Studies: Vol. 154). 220p. 1996. 26. 00 (*0-86698-194-2*, MR154) MRTS.

Richard Beatty's Job Search Networking. Richard H. Beatty. LC 94-28765. 1994. pap. 9.95 (*1-55850-402-8*) Adams Media.

Richard Beer-Hofmann: His Life & Work. Esther N. Elstun. LC 82-14990. (Studies in German Literature). 225p. (C). 1983. 30.00 (*0-271-00335-9*) Pa St U Pr.

Richard Bennett's Early Days of Port Fairy. Ed. by Jan Critchett. 92p. 1984. pap. 45.00 (*0-949759-32-5*, Pub. by Deakin Univ AT) St Mut.

***Richard Berry Seager: Pioneer Archaeologist & Proper Gentleman.** Marshall J. Becker et al. LC 97-4625. 1997. write for info. (*0-924171-47-2*) U PA Mus Pubns.

***Richard Bingham's Poems & Short Stories.** Ed. & Compiled by Eileen Bingham. LC 96-90959. 1997. 13.95 (*0-533-12232-5*) Vantage.

Richard Boleslavsky: His Life & Work in the Theatre. J. W. Roberts. LC 81-16411. (Theater & Dramatic Studies: No. 7). (Illus.). 298p. reprint ed. pap. 85.00 (*0-8357-1250-8*, 2070279) Bks Demand.

Richard Bolitho - Midshipman. Alexander Kent. 1992. reprint ed. lib. bdg. 25.95 (*0-89966-971-9*) Buccaneer Bks.

Richard Bowman: Forty Years of Abstract Painting. Intro. by K. R. Eagles-Smith. (Illus.). 44p. (C). 1986. 24.95 (*0-9617486-1-3*) H A Parker.

Richard Branson, Virgin King: Inside Richard Branson's Business Empire. Tim Jackson. LC 95-39945. 1996. 24. 95 (*0-7615-0343-9*) Prima Pub.

Richard Brauer: Collected Papers, 3 vols., 1. Richard Brauer. Ed. by Warren J. Wong & Paul Fong. 1980. 80. 00 (*0-262-02135-8*) MIT Pr.

Richard Brautigan. Jay Boyer. LC 87-70030. (Western Writers Ser.: No. 79). (Illus.). 52p. (Orig.). 1987. pap. 4.95 (*0-88430-078-1*) Boise St U W Writ Ser.

Richard Brautigan: An Annotated Bibliography. John F. Barber. LC 89-43698. 244p. 1990. lib. bdg. 59.50 (*0-89950-525-2*) McFarland & Co.

Richard Brautigan's: A Confederate General from Big Sur, Dreaming of Babylon & the Hawkline Monster. Richard Brautigan. 608p. 1991. pap. 16.95 (*0-395-54703-2*) HM.

Richard Brome: A Study of His Life & Works. Clarence E. Andrews. LC 72-6665. (Yale Studies in English: No. 46). vi, 140p. (C). 1972. reprint ed. lib. bdg. 27.50 (*0-208-01122-6*, Archon Bks) Shoe String.

Richard Brown's New England. Richard Brown. (Illus.). 144p. 1996. 40.00 (*1-55209-070-1*) Firefly Bks Ltd.

Richard Burgin: A Life in Verse. Diana L. Burgin. (Illus.). 230p. (Orig.). 1989. pap. 19.95 (*0-89357-196-2*) Slavica.

Richard Burton: A Bio-Bibliography. Tyrone Steverson. LC 92-14592. (Bio-Bibliographies in the Performing Arts Ser.: No. 31). 352p. 1992. text ed. 49.95 (*0-313-27650-1*, SVX, Greenwood Pr) Greenwood.

Richard Burton: A Brother Remembered. David Jenkins. (Illus.). 240p. 1994. 29.95 (*0-7126-5768-1*, Pub. by Century UK) Trafalgar.

Richard Burton: A Life. Melvyn Bragg. (Illus.). 1989. 22.95 (*0-316-10595-3*) Little.

Richard Burton: So Much, So Little. Peter Stead. (Illus.). 129p. 1991. 30.00 (*1-85411-040-3*, Pub. by Seren Bks UK) Dufour.

Richard Cantillon: Pioneer of Economic Theory. Anthony Brewer. LC 91-36458. 224p. (C). (gr. 13). 1992. text ed. 69.95 (*0-415-07577-7*, A7304) Routledge.

Richard Cantillon (1680-1734) & Jacques Turgot (1727-1881) Mark Blaug. (Pioneers in Economics Ser.: Vol. 9). 320p. 1991. text ed. 125.00 (*1-85278-471-7*) E Elgar.

Richard Capes' Drawings Capture Siesta Key: An Artistic Tour of the Island. Richard Capes. Ed. by Julie Peelen & Marvin Whitley. (Illus.). 184p. (Orig.). 1992. 49.95 (*0-9635417-1-4*); pap. 24.95 (*0-9635417-0-6*) Capes Studio FL.

Richard Carvel. Winston Churchill. (BCL1-PS American Literature Ser.). 560p. 1992. reprint ed. lib. bdg. 99.00 (*0-7812-6687-4*) Rprt Serv.

Richard Chamberlain: An Actor's Life. Barbara Siegel. 1990. pap. 2.99 (*0-517-05924-X*) Random Hse Value.

Richard Clague: Eighteen Twenty-One to Eighteen Seventy-Three. LC 74-25157. (Illus.). 128p. 1974. pap. 5.00 (*0-913060-23-2*, New Orleans Mus Art) Norton Art.

Richard Clarke of Rowley, Mass., & His Descendants in the Line of Timothy Clark of Rockingham, Vermont, 1638-1904. T. B. Peck. (Illus.). 93p. 1993. reprint ed. lib. bdg. 28.00 (*0-8328-1354-0*) Higginson Bk Co.

Richard Clarke of Rowley, Mass., & His Descendants in the Line of Timothy Clark of Rockingham, Vermont, 1638-1904. Thomas B. Peck. (Illus.). 93p. 1993. reprint ed. pap. 18.00 (*0-8328-1355-9*) Higginson Bk Co.

Richard Clayderman: Hollywood & Broadway. 64p. 1987. pap. 9.95 (*0-7935-2678-7*, 00356391) H Leonard.

Richard Clayderman Hollywood & Broadway, Vol. 216. 80p. 1987. pap. 7.95 (*0-7935-4002-X*, 00101556) H Leonard.

Richard Clayderman Piano Solos: A Romantic Christmas. 48p. 1986. pap. 10.95 (*0-7935-2013-4*, 00356389) H Leonard.

Richard Clayderman Plays Love Songs of the World: Piano Solos. 48p. 1987. pap. 10.95 (*0-7935-2321-4*, 00356390) H Leonard.

Richard Cobden. Wendy Hinde. LC 86-26661. 376p. 1987. text ed. 47.50 (*0-300-03880-1*) Yale U Pr.

Richard Cobden: Independent Radical. Nicholas C. Edsall. (Illus.). 416p. 1987. 42.50 (*0-674-76879-5*) HUP.

***Richard Cocciante.** Ed. by Michael Lefferts. 72p. (Orig.). (C). 1997. pap. text ed. 34.95 (*0-7692-0838-X*, 01020631) Warner Brothers.

Richard Coeur de Lion: Kingship, Chivalry & War in the Twelfth Century. John Gillingham. LC 94-37250. 1994. 55.00 (*1-85285-084-1*) Hambledon Press.

Richard Corben's Art Book. (Illus.). 14.95 (*0-685-70821-7*) Fantagor Pr.

Richard Corben's Art Book. Richard Corben. (Illus.). 64p. (Orig.). 1990. pap. 14.95 (*0-9623841-2-7*) Fantagor Pr.

Richard Corben's Art Book, Vol. 2. 64p. 1994. 19.95 (*0-685-75277-1*) Fantagor Pr.

Richard Corben's Art Book Vol. 2. Richard Corben. (Illus.). 64p. (Orig.). 1994. pap. write for info. (*1-884924-00-X*) Fantagor Pr.

Richard Cory. A. R. Gurney. 1976. pap. 5.25 (*0-8222-1245-5*) Dramatists Play.

Richard Crashaw. Thomas F. Healy. (Medieval & Renaissance Authors Ser.: Vol. 8). x, 162p. 1986. 50.00 (*90-04-07864-9*) E J Brill.

Richard Crashaw: An Annotated Bibliography of Criticism, 1632-1980. John R. Roberts. LC 84-52264. 488p. 1985. text ed. 45.00 (*0-8262-0468-6*) U of Mo Pr.

Richard Crashaw & the Spanish Golden Age. R. V. Young. LC 82-1850. (Yale Studies in English: No. 191). 214p. reprint ed. pap. 61.00 (*0-7837-4544-3*, 2080326) Bks Demand.

Richard Daley: The Strong Willed Mayor of Chicago. Gerald Kurland. Ed. by D. Steve Rahmas. LC 70-190236. (Outstanding Personalities Ser.: No. 18). 32p. (Orig.). (J). (gr. 7-12). lib. bdg. 7.25 (*0-87157-518-3*) SamHar Pr.

Richard Daniels - Be Dangerous on Rock Guitar. Ed. by Mark Phillips. (Illus.). 146p. (Orig.). 1990. pap. text ed. 18.95 (*0-89524-314-8*) Cherry Lane.

Richard Deacon. John Caldwell et al. (Illus.). 96p. (Orig.). 1988. pap. 11.95 (*0-88039-018-2*) Mus Art Carnegie.

Richard Deacon. Jon Thompson. (Contemporary Artists Ser.). (Illus.). 160p. (Orig.). 1995. pap. 29.95 (*0-7148-3370-3*, Pub. by Phaidon Press UK) Chronicle Bks.

R

Richard Dehmels Gesammelte Werke, 10 Vols. in 3. Richard Dehmel. LC 76-163694. (BCL Ser. I). reprint ed. 110.00 (0-404-02070-4) AMS Pr.

Richard Diebenkorn. LC 96-52338. (Illus.). 1997. pap. write for info. (0-87427-107-X) Whitney Mus.

Richard Diebenkorn. Gerald Nordland. LC 87-42688. (Illus.). 248p. 1993. 75.00 (0-8478-0870-X) Rizzoli Intl.

Richard Diebenkorn: Small Paintings from Ocean Park. Intro. by Dore Ashton. LC 85-60997. 48p. 1986. 18.00 (0-939931-00-1) Houston Fine Art Pr.

Richard Diebenkorn: Works on Paper. Ed. & Intro. by Richard Newlin. LC 86-82665. 293p. 1987. 65.00 (0-940619-00-8) Houston Fine Art Pr.

Richard Diebenkorn: Works on Paper from the Harry W. & Margaret Anderson Collection. Susan Larsen et al. LC 92-73206. (Illus.). 96p. (Orig.). (C). 1993. pap. 15.00 (0-945192-11-8) USC Fisher Gallery.

Richard Doddridge Blackmore: His Life & Novels. Quincy G. Burris. (BCL1-PR English Literature Ser.). 219p. 1992. reprint ed. lib. bdg. 79.00 (0-7812-7440-0) Rprt Serv.

Richard Doyle. Rodney Engen. (Artist & the Critic Ser.: Vol. 2). 206p. 1983. 35.00 (0-904995-05-4, Pub. by Catalpa Pr Ltd UK) Oak Knoll.

Richard Durham's Destination Freedom: Scripts from Radio's Black Legacy, 1948-50. Ed. by J. Fred MacDonald. LC 88-35686. 280p. 1989. text ed. 59.95 (0-275-93138-2, C3138, Praeger Pubs) Greenwood.

Richard Eberhart. Ralph J. Mills. LC 66-63487. (University of Minnesota Pamphlets on American Writers Ser.: No. 55). 46p. (Orig.). reprint ed. pap. 25.00 (0-7837-2872-7, 2057583) Bks Demand.

Richard Eberhart: A Celebration. Ed. by Sydney Lea et al. 76p. (Orig.). (C). 1980. pap. 6.00 (0-917241-00-2) Kenyon Hill.

Richard Eberhart: A Descriptive Bibliography, 1921-1987. Stuart Wright. 450p. 1989. text ed. 85.00 (0-313-27708-7, WRT/, Greenwood Pr) Greenwood.

Richard Eberhart New & Selected Poems, 1930-1990. Richard Eberhart. 1990. pap. 8.95 (0-929654-91-9, North Star Line); text ed. 16.95 (0-929654-95-1, North Star Line) Blue Moon Bks.

Richard Erdoes Illustrated Treasury of Classic Unlaundered Limericks. Illus. by Richard Erdoes. LC 84-11014. 160p. 1984. pap. 14.95 (0-917439-01-5) Balsam Pr.

Richard F. S. Starr Memorial Volume. Ed. by David I. Owen & Gernot Wilhelm. LC 96-8532. (Studies on the Civilization & Culture of Nuzi & the Hurrians). viii, 478p. (C). 1996. 60.00 (1-883053-10-2) CDL Pr.

Richard Fairbanks: American Potter. Matthew Kangas. (Illus.). 128p. 1993. pap. 25.00 (0-295-97302-1) U of Wash Pr.

Richard Fairbanks 1929-1989: A Retrospective. Dixie Parker-Fairbanks et al. Ed. by Neeleke Nix. Tr. by Robert Goebel & Rita Alport from FIN. (Illus.). 50p. 1995. pap. 8.95 (1-881067-05-X) N Nelleke Studio.

Richard Farmer: Master of Emmanuel College, Cambridge, a Forgotten Shakespearean. Arthur Sherbo. LC 91-58086. 224p. (C). 1992. 35.00 (0-87413-444-7) U Delaware Pr.

*__Richard Fleischman: Spaces to be Shared.__ Maurizio Vitta. 1997. pap. text ed. 49.99 (88-7838-014-8, Pub. by Yeolrin Munhwa KO) Consort Bk Sales.

*__Richard Fleischman: Spaces to be Shared.__ Maurizio Vitta. 1997. pap. text ed. 49.99 (1-56496-358-6) Rockport Pubs.

*__Richard Fleischner: Projects.__ Diana L. Johnson & William H. Jordy. (Illus.). 48p. (Orig.). pap. 20.00 (0-933519-30-3) D W Bell Gallery.

Richard Fleischner Critical Distance. I. Michael Danoff. (Illus.). 39p. 1992. pap. 16.00 (1-879003-04-X) Edmundson.

Richard Garnett: The Scholar As Librarian. Barbara McCrimmon. LC 89-297. (ACRL Publications in Librarianship: No. 46). (Illus.). 224p. 1989. reprint ed. pap. 63.90 (0-7837-9685-4, 2060414) Bks Demand.

Richard Garwin on Arms Control. Ed. by Kenneth W. Thompson. LC 88-33936. (W. Alton Jones Foundation Series on Arms Control: Vol. XI). 224p. (Orig.). (C). 1989. pap. text ed. 22.00 (0-8191-7368-1, Pub. by White Miller Center); lib. bdg. 41.00 (0-8191-7367-3, Pub. by White Miller Center) U Pr of Amer.

*__Richard Gere: Man & Mystic.__ Bill Reed. Date not set. write for info. (0-688-05425-0) Morrow.

*__Richard Gere: The Flesh & the Spirit.__ John Parker. (Illus.). 282p. 1997. 24.95 (0-7472-1558-8, Pub. by Headline UK) Trafalgar.

*__Richard Gere: The Flesh & the Spirit.__ John Parker. (Illus.). 282p. 1997. pap. 11.95 (0-7472-5161-4, Pub. by Headline UK) Trafalgar.

Richard Gerstl - Oskar Kokoschka. Jane Kallir. (Illus.). 96p. (Orig.). 1992. pap. 18.00 (0-910810-26-5) Johannes.

Richard Guindon: 1981-1984. Christopher R. Young. (Illus.). 24p. (Orig.). 1985. pap. 3.50 (0-685-73703-9) Flint Inst Arts.

*__Richard Haag: Bloedel Reserve & Gasworks Park.__ Ed. by William S. Saunders. (Illus.). 64p. (Orig.). 1998. pap. 12.95 (1-56898-117-1) Princeton Arch.

Richard Hack's Complete Home Video Companion for Parents. Richard Hack. 320p. 1995. pap. 9.95 (0-7871-0292-X, Dove Bks) Dove Audio.

Richard Hamilton. David Sylvester & Richard Hamilton. (Illus.). 60p. 1991. 40.00 (0-947564-36-5, Pub. by A D'Offay Gallery UK) Dist Art Pubs.

Richard Hancox. (Art Gallery of Ontario Film Bks.). (Illus.). 48p. 1990. pap. 10.00 (0-919777-98-8) Wilfrid Laurier.

*__Richard Harding Davis: Great American Short Stories II.__ Illus. by James Balkovek. LC 94-75031. (Classic Short Stories Ser.). 80p. 1994. pap. 5.95 (0-7854-0584-4, 40030) Am Guidance.

Richard Harrington's Antarctic. Richard Harrington. LC 75-43581. (Alaska Geographic Ser.: Vol. 3, No. 3). (Illus.). 104p. 1976. Album Style. pap. 19.95 (0-88240-078-9) Alaska Geog Soc.

Richard Henrique: Memory Theatre. Ed. by Howard Shubert. (Illus.). 84p. 1994. pap. 15.95 (0-262-69168-X) MIT Pr.

Richard Henry Dana. Charles F. Adams, Jr. (Works of Charles Francis Adams Jr. (1835-1915)). 1989. reprint ed. lib. bdg. 79.00 (0-7812-1408-4) Rprt Serv.

Richard Higgins, a Resident & Pioneer Settler at Plymouth & Eastham, Mass, & at Piscataway, N. J., & His Descendants. Katherine C. Higgins. (Illus.). 799p. 1993. reprint ed. pap. 99.00 (0-8328-3038-0); reprint ed. lib. bdg. 109.00 (0-8328-3037-2) Higginson Bk Co.

Richard Hooker: A Selected Bibliography. Egil Grislis & W. Speed Hill. LC 79-32321. 1981. 5.50 (0-931222-03-6) Pitts Theolog.

*__Richard Hooker & the Construction of Christian Community.__ Ed. by A. S. McGrade. LC 96-40326. (Medieval & Renaissance Texts & Studies: Vol. 165). 440p. 1997. 32.00 (0-86698-206-X, MR165) MRTS.

*__Richard Hooker (1553/4-1600) Ecclesiastical Polity Selections.__ Ed. by Arthur Pollard. pap. write for info. (0-85635-860-6, Pub. by Carcanet Pr UK) Paul & Co Pubs.

Richard Hooker's Doctrine of the Royal Supremacy. W. J. Kirby. LC 89-71279. (Studies in the History of Christian Thought: Vol. LXIII). xi, 136p. 1990. 51.50 (90-04-08851-2) E J Brill.

Richard Hughes. Richard P. Graves. (Illus.). 491p. 1995. 40.00 (0-233-98843-2, Pub. by A Deutsch UK) Trafalgar.

Richard Hugo. Donna Gerstenberger. LC 82-74093. (Western Writers Ser.: No. 59). (Illus.). 50p. (Orig.). 1983. pap. 4.95 (0-88430-033-1) Boise St U W Writ Ser.

Richard Hunt. Judd Tully et al. (Illus.). 48p. (Orig.). 1989. pap. text ed. 6.00 (0-925941-01-8) Dorsky Gallery.

Richard Hurdis: Tale of Alabama. rev. ed. W. Gilmore Simms. LC 70-176021. reprint ed. 29.50 (0-404-06035-8) AMS Pr.

Richard Hurdis, A Tale of Alabama. William G. Simms. LC 94-37962. (Selected Fiction of William Gilmore Simms Ser.). 1995. 40.00 (1-55728-334-6) U of Ark Pr.

Richard Hurdis, a Tale of Alabama: A Tale of Alabama. William G. Simms. (Selected Fiction of William Gilmore Simms Ser.). 1995. pap. 24.00 (1-55728-347-8) U of Ark Pr.

Richard I in England, Eleven Eighty Nine & Eleven Ninety Four: Medieval People, Vol. 1. Harry S. Howser. LC 83-26598. (Illus.). 115p. (Orig.). 1986. pap. 10.00 (0-934667-04-7) Tangelwuld.

Richard II. Mark Dunster. 21p. (Orig.). (YA). 1995. pap. 5.00 (0-89642-287-9) Linden Pubs.

Richard II. Compiled by Kenneth Muir. 1988. pap. 3.50 (0-451-52217-6, Sig Classics) NAL-Dutton.

Richard II. William Shakespeare. (Classics Ser.). 192p. 1988. mass mkt. 3.95 (0-553-21303-2, Bantam Classics) Bantam.

Richard II. William Shakespeare. (BBC Television Plays Ser.). 1978. pap. 4.95 (0-563-17621-0, Pub. by BBC UK) Parkwest Pubns.

Richard II. William Shakespeare. Ed. by Louis B. Wright & Virginia A. LaMar. LC 78-24130. (Folger Edition). 288p. (YA). (gr. 9 up). 1984. pap. 3.50 (0-671-53142-5, WSP) PB.

Richard II. rev. ed. William Shakespeare. 1963. pap. 4.95 (0-451-52268-0, Sig Classics) NAL-Dutton.

Richard II. William Shakespeare. Ed. by Paul Werstine & Barbara A. Mowat. (New Folger Library). 320p. 1996. reprint ed. mass mkt. 3.99 (0-671-72283-2, Folger Lib) PB.

*__Richard II: A Sourcebook.__ expanded rev. ed. Keith Dockray. 192p. 1997. pap. 22.95 (0-7509-1479-3, Pub. by Sutton Pubng UK) Bks Intl VA.

Richard II: Power & Prerogative. James L. Gillespie. Ed. by Anthony Goodman. (Illus.). 480p. 1997. 70.00 (0-19-820189-3) OUP.

Richard II: Shakespeare: The Critical Tradition. William Shakespeare. Ed. by Charles R. Forker. (Shakespeare Ser.). 400p. (C). 1997. 160.00 (0-485-81002-6, Pub. by Athlone Pr UK) Humanities.

Richard II & Woodstock. Ed. by Brynmill Pr. Ltd. Staff. (C). 1989. 50.00 (0-907839-35-5, Pub. by Brynmill Pr Ltd UK) St Mut.

Richard II in the Early Chronicles. L. D. Duls. LC 73-80355. (Studies in English Literature: No. 79). 274p. 1975. pap. text ed. 46.15 (90-279-3326-X) Mouton.

Richard II Notes. Denis M. Calandra. (Cliffs Notes Ser.). 1982. pap. 3.95 (0-8220-0068-7) Cliffs.

Richard III. Mark Dunster. 26p. (Orig.). (YA). (gr. 5 up). 1995. pap. 6.00 (0-89642-263-1) Linden Pubs.

Richard III. Ed. by Mark Eccles. 1988. pap. 2.75 (0-451-51936-1, Sig Classics) NAL-Dutton.

*__Richard III.__ Margaret Healy. (Writers & Their Work Ser.). 80p. (Orig.). 1996. pap. 15.00 (0-7463-0845-0, Pub. by Nrthcote House UK) U Pr of Miss.

Richard III. Ian McKellen & Richard Loncraine. 304p. 1996. pap. 14.95 (0-87951-685-2) Overlook Pr.

Richard III. Charles L. Ross. LC 81-43381. (English Monarchs Ser.: No. 6). (Illus.). 263p. 1982. pap. 14.00 (0-520-05075-4) U CA Pr.

Richard III. William Shakespeare. (Classics Ser.). 240p. 1988. pap. 3.95 (0-553-21304-0, Bantam Classics) Bantam.

Richard III. William Shakespeare. (Book Notes Ser.). 1985. pap. 2.50 (0-8120-3537-2) Barron.

Richard III. William Shakespeare. Ed. by Mark Eccles. 1964. pap. 4.95 (0-451-52266-4, CE1833, Sig Classics) NAL-Dutton.

Richard III. William Shakespeare. (BBC Television Plays Ser.). 1983. pap. 7.95 (0-563-20022-7) Parkwest Pubns.

Richard III. large type ed. William Shakespeare. LC 95-39598. (Charnwood Large Print Ser.). 1991. pap. 24.95 (0-7089-4507-4, Charnwood) Ulverscroft.

Richard III. large type ed. William Shakespeare. 1992. pap. 24.95 (0-7089-4513-9) Ulverscroft.

Richard III. unabridged ed. William Shakespeare. LC 95-39598. (Thrift Editions Ser.). 106p. 1995. reprint ed. pap. write for info. (0-486-28747-5) Dover.

Richard III. William Shakespeare. Ed. by Paul Werstine & Barbara A. Mowat. (New Folger Library). 1996. reprint ed. mass mkt. 3.99 (0-671-72284-0, Folger Lib) PB.

Richard III & the Princes in the Tower. A. J. Pollard. (Illus.). 280p. (Orig.). 1993. pap. 26.00 (0-7509-0354-6, Pub. by Sutton Pubng UK) Bks Intl VA.

Richard III & the Princess in the Tower. A. J. Pollard. 1991. text ed. 39.95 (0-312-06715-1) St Martin.

Richard III Notes. James K. Lowers. (Cliffs Notes Ser.). 1966. pap. 3.95 (0-8220-0071-7) Cliffs.

Richard J. Daley: Politics, Race & the Governing of Chicago. Roger Biles. LC 94-48268. (Illus.). 305p. 1995. 32.00 (0-87580-199-4); pap. 18.00 (0-87580-566-3) N Ill U Pr.

Richard Jefferies: A Bibliographical Study. George Miller & Hugoe Matthews. 832p. 1993. 129.95 (0-85967-918-7, Pub. by Scolar Pr UK) Ashgate Pub Co.

Richard Kamler: Table of Voices. Richard Kamler et al. (Illus.). 32p. (Orig.). 1996. pap. text ed. 5.00 (0-930495-28-4) San Fran Art Inst.

Richard Kane, Gov of Minorca. write for info. (0-8386-3586-5) Fairleigh Dickinson.

*__Richard Keating.__ (Master Architect Ser.). 256p. 1996. 59.95 (1-875498-51-6) AIA Press.

Richard Kern: New York Girls. 208p. Date not set. pap. 29.95 (1-900106-10-8) Dist Art Pubs.

Richard King: Texas Cattle Rancher. William R. Sanford & Carl R. Green. LC 96-1892. (Legendary Heroes of the Wild West Ser.). (Illus.). 48p. (J). (gr. 4-10). 1997. lib. bdg. 14.95 (0-89490-673-9) Enslow Pubs.

Richard Knapwell - Quaestio Disputata de Unitate Formae: A Critical Edition. Ed. by Francis E. Kelley. LC 83-789. (Medieval & Renaissance Texts & Studies: Vol. 15p). 96p. 1982. pap. 25.00 (0-86698-022-9, MR15) MRTS.

*__Richard Korherr & His Reports: Secret German Statistical Reports on the Final Solution Originally Issued in 1943.__ (Holocaust Ser.). 1996. lib. bdg. 251.95 (0-8490-6051-6) Gordon Pr.

Richard Kostelanetz. Richard Kostelanetz. 1980. 25.00 (0-932360-55-6) Archae Edns.

Richard Lamb. Richard S. Wheeler. 1987. 16.95 (0-8027-4076-6) Walker & Co.

*__Richard Lieberson's Old-Time Fiddle Tunes for Guitar.__ 88p. 1997. pap. 14.95 (0-8256-2809-1, AM 16585) Music Sales.

Richard Lindner: Paintings & Watercolors 1948-1977. Peter H. Selz. (Illus.). 176p. 1996. 65.00 (3-7913-1486-6, Pub. by Prestel GW) te Neues.

*__Richard Lindner: Paintings & Watercolors, 1948-1977.__ Judith Zilczer et al. (Illus.). 172p. (Orig.). 1996. pap. 35.00 (0-9623203-6-6) Hirshhorn.

Richard Long. Hugh M. Davies. LC 89-63456. (Illus.). 24p. 1989. 12.00 (0-934418-33-0) Mus Contemp Art.

*__Richard Long: Circles, Cycles, Mud, Stones.__ Dana Friis-Hansen & Richard Brettell. 1997. 14.95 (0-936080-38-8) Cont Arts Museum.

Richard Long: Mountains & Waters. Richard Long. LC 92-54548. 65p. 1993. 35.00 (0-8076-1293-6) Braziller.

Richard Long: Walking in Circles. Anne Seymour et al. (Illus.). 264p. 1991. 90.00 (0-8076-1269-3) Braziller.

*__Richard Lovelace (1618-1658) Selected Poems.__ Ed. by Gerald Hammond. pap. write for info. (0-85635-673-5, Pub. by Carcanet Pr UK) Paul & Co Pubs.

Richard M. Nixon: Politician, President, Administrator. Ed. by Leon Friedman & William F. Levantrosser. LC 90-43378. (Contributions in Political Science Ser.: No. 269). 448p. 1991. text ed. 65.00 (0-313-27653-6, FNO/, Greenwood Pr) Greenwood.

Richard M. Nixon: Thirty-Seventh President of the United States. Rebecca Stefoff. Ed. by Richard G. Young. LC 89-39944. (Presidents of the United States Ser.). (Illus.). 128p. (J). (gr. 5-9). 1990. lib. bdg. 17.26 (0-944483-59-3) Garrett Ed Corp.

Richard M. Nixon: 37th President of the United States. Rebecca Stefoff. LC 95-18008. (J). 1995. write for info. (1-56074-063-9) Garrett Ed Corp.

Richard M. Nixon & His Family Paper Dolls. Tom Tierney. (Illus.). (J). (gr. k-3). 1992. pap. 3.95 (0-486-27354-7) Dover.

Richard M. Nixon, Jimmy Carter, Ronald Reagan. Edmund Lindop. (Presidents Who Dared Ser.). (Illus.). 64p. (J). (gr. 5-8). 1996. lib. bdg. 15.98 (0-8050-3405-6) TFC Bks NY.

Richard M. Nixon, President. Sallie Randolph. (Presidential Biography Ser.). 128p. (J). (gr. 5 up). 1989. 13.95 (0-8027-6848-2); lib. bdg. 14.85 (0-8027-6849-0) Walker & Co.

Richard M. Weaver, 1910-1963: A Life of the Mind. Fred D. Young. 232p. (C). 1995. 39.95 (0-8262-1030-9) U of Mo Pr.

Richard Mansfield, the Man & the Actor. Paul Wilstach. LC 79-107836. (Select Bibliographies Reprint Ser.). 1977. 30.95 (0-8369-5201-4) Ayer.

Richard Marx - Five of the Best. Ed. by Milton Okun. pap. 6.95 (0-89524-538-8) Cherry Lane.

Richard Marx - In Person. Ed. by Jon Chappell. pap. 9.95 (0-89524-499-3) Cherry Lane.

*__Richard Marx - Paid Vacation.__ Ed. by Carol Cuellar. 64p. (Orig.). (C). 1994. pap. text ed. 14.95 (0-7692-0480-5, P1066SMX) Warner Brothers.

Richard Marx - Repeat Offender. Ed. by Milton Okun. pap. 14.95 (0-89524-441-1) Cherry Lane.

Richard Marx - Rush Street. Ed. by Milton Okun. pap. 14.95 (0-89524-692-9) Cherry Lane.

Richard Marx (Piano - Vocal) Ed. by Milton Okun. (Illus.). 63p. (Orig.). 1990. pap. text ed. 14.95 (0-89524-346-6) Cherry Lane.

Richard Mather: Life, Journal & Selected Writings see Library of American Puritan Writings. The Seventeenth Century: The Seventeenth Century

Richard Mather of Dorchester. Barry R. Burg. LC 75-41987. 223p. reprint ed. pap. 63.60 (0-7837-5781-6, 2045447) Bks Demand.

Richard McKeon: A Study. George K. Plochmann. LC 89-28254. (Illus.). 276p. 1990. 35.95 (0-226-67109-7) U Ch Pr.

Richard Meier. Silvio Cassara. (Works & Projects Ser.). 1996. pap. text ed. 19.95 (84-252-1693-1) Watsn-Guptill.

Richard Meier. K. Frampton et al. (Illus.). 228p. 1990. 55.00 (0-85670-960-3) Academy Ed UK.

Richard Meier. Kenneth Frampton. 1990. pap. 55.00 (0-312-04526-3) St Martin.

*__Richard Meier.__ Philip Jodidioi. 1995. pap. 24.99 (3-8228-9256-4) Taschen Amer.

Richard Meier: Building for Art. Werner Blaser. 176p. 1989. 95.00 (0-8176-2326-4) Birkhauser.

*__Richard Meier: Building for Art.__ Werner Blaser. 176p. 1996. 135.00 (3-7643-2326-4) Birkhauser.

*__Richard Meier: Details.__ Werner Blaser. LC 96-46684. (Illus.). 168p. 1997. 98.00 (3-7643-5403-8) Birkhauser.

*__Richard Meier: Weishaupt Forum.__ Werner Blaser. 1996. 72.00 (3-7643-2847-9) Birkhauser.

Richard Meier, Architect. Compiled & Intro. by Joseph Rykwert. LC 83-42911. (Illus.). 412p. 1990. 65.00 (0-8478-0496-8) Rizzoli Intl.

Richard Meier, Architect. Compiled & Intro. by Joseph Rykwert. LC 83-42911. (Illus.). 412p. 1991. pap. 49.50 (0-8478-0497-6) Rizzoli Intl.

*__Richard Meier, Architect.__ 3rd ed. Richard Meier. 1997. 75.00 (0-8478-1996-5) Rizzoli Intl.

Richard Meier, Architect, Vol. 2. Richard Meier. LC 90-48765. (Illus.). 432p. 1991. 65.00 (0-8478-1320-7); pap. 49.50 (0-8478-1321-5) Rizzoli Intl.

*__Richard Meier, Architect, Vol. 3.__ Richard Meier. 1997. pap. 55.00 (0-8478-2048-3) Rizzoli Intl.

Richard Meier Collages. Lois Nesbitt. (Illus.). 48p. (Orig.). 1990. pap. 26.95 (1-85490-048-X) Academy Ed UK.

Richard Meier Collages. Lois Nesbitt. (Orig.). 1991. 24.95 (0-312-05672-9) St Martin.

Richard Meier Houses. Intro. by Paul Goldberger. LC 96-18492. (Illus.). 252p. 1996. 75.00 (0-8478-1931-0) Rizzoli Intl.

Richard Meier Sculpture. Lois Nesbit. (Illus.). 56p. 1994. pap. 25.00 (0-8478-1848-9) Rizzoli Intl.

Richard Meier, Weishaupt Forum. Werner Blaser. Tr. by D. O. Stephenson et al. LC 92-44680. v, 90p. (ENG, FRE & GER.). 1993. 69.50 (0-8176-2847-9) Birkhauser.

*__Richard Meier's Barcelona.__ Richard Meier. 1997. pap. 25.00 (1-885254-56-3) Monacelli Pr.

Richard Milhous Nixon: The Rise of an American Politician. Roger Morris. (Illus.). 944p. 1989. 29.95 (0-8050-1121-8) H Holt & Co.

Richard Milhous Nixon: The Rise of an American Politician. Roger Morris. (Illus.). 1024p. 1991. pap. 15.95 (0-8050-1834-4, Owl) H Holt & Co.

Richard Misrach. Richard Misrach. (Min Gallery Series of Contemporary American & Japanese Photography). (Illus.). 88p. 1989. pap. 30.00 (4-906265-17-0) Aperture.

Richard Monnier. Richard Monnier. (Illus.). 108p. (Orig.). 1993. pap. 25.00 (2-908257-07-6, Pub. by F R A C FR) Dist Art Pubs.

Richard Mulcahy. M. Valiulis. 1992. 37.50 (0-7165-2494-5, Pub. by Irish Acad Pr IE) Intl Spec Bk.

Richard Mulcahy. M. Valiulis. 1993. pap. 14.95 (0-7165-2510-0, Pub. by Irish Acad Pr IE) Intl Spec Bk.

Richard Mulcaster (c. 1531-1611) & Educational Reform in the Renaissance. Richard L. DeMolen. (Bibliotheca Humanistica & Reformatorica Ser.: No. XLIX). 242p. 1992. 72.50 (90-6004-415-0, Pub. by B De Graaf NE) Coronet Bks.

Richard Navin: The Mycenae Circle. Richard Navin. LC 80-1216. (Illus.). 20p. 1981. pap. 5.00 (0-89207-028-5) S R Guggenheim.

*__Richard Neutra.__ 2nd ed. D. Neurta. 192p. 1996. pap. 34.50 (3-7643-5588-3) Birkhauser.

Richard Neutra: Promise & Fulfillment, 1919-1932: Selections from the Letters & Diaries of Richard & Dione Neutra. Tr. & Compiled by Dione Neutra. LC 85-2245. 264p. 1986. 24.95 (0-8093-1228-X) S Ill U Pr.

Richard Neutra & the Search for Modern Architecture. Thomas S. Hines. LC 93-40782. 1994. 27.50 (0-520-08589-2) U CA Pr.

Richard Nixon. Roger Barr. LC 92-25566. (Importance of Ser.). (Illus.). 112p. (J). (gr. 5-8). 1992. lib. bdg. 17.96 (1-56006-035-2) Lucent Bks.

Richard Nixon. Dee Lillegard. LC 87-35185. (Encyclopedia of Presidents Ser.). (Illus.). 100p. (J). (gr. 3 up). 1988. lib. bdg. 22.00 (0-516-01356-4) Childrens.

Richard Nixon. C. Peter Ripley. (World Leaders - Past & Present Ser.). (Illus.). 112p. (YA). (gr. 5 up). 1988. lib. bdg. 19.95 (0-87754-585-5) Chelsea Hse.

Richard Nixon: One of Us. Tom Wicker. 1990. write for info. (0-318-66746-0) Random.

Richard Nixon: Rhetorical Strategist. Hal W. Bochin. LC 89-17193. (Great American Orators: Critical Studies, Speeches & Sources: No. 6). 237p. 1990. text ed. 47.95 (0-313-26108-3, BCQ/, Greenwood Pr) Greenwood.

*__Richard Nixon: The Enigmatic President.__ Martin Goldman. LC 97-19928. (Makers of America Ser.). 1997. 17.95 (0-8160-3397-8) Facts on File.

An Asterisk (*) at the beginning of an entry indicates that the title is appearing in BIP for the first time.

Richard Nixon: The Rise & Fall of a President. Rebecca Larsen. (Illus.). 160p. (YA). (gr. 9-12). 1991. lib. bdg. 22.70 (*0-531-10997-6*) Watts.
Richard Nixon: The Shaping of His Character. Fawn M. Brodie. 576p. (C). 1983. pap. text ed. 15.95 (*0-674-76880-9*) HUP.
Richard Nixon: The Shaping of His Character. Fawn M. Brodie. (Illus.). 1981. 18.95 (*0-393-01467-3*) Norton.
Richard Nixon & His America. Herbert S. Parmet. 1996. 14.98 (*0-8317-5947-X*) Smithmark.
Richard Norman Shaw. Andrew Saint. LC 75-4333. (Studies in British Art). (Illus.). 507p. reprint ed. pap. 144.50 (*0-7837-3309-7*, 2057711) Bks Demand.
***Richard O. Barnes: An Oral History.** Contrib. by Dianne Bridgman. (Illus.). xii, 97p. (Orig.). 1994. pap. write for info. (*1-889320-00-5*) WA St Oral Hist.
Richard Oastler: King of Factory Children, 1835-61. LC 72-2541. (British Labour Struggles Before 1850 Ser.). 1974. 25.95 (*0-405-04433-X*) Ayer.
Richard of Devizes: Chronicon Ricardi Divisiensis de Rebus Gestis Ricardi I Regis Angliae. Ed. by J. Stevenson. (English Historical Society Publications: Vol. 11). 1974. reprint ed. 30.00 (*0-8115-1536-2*) Periodicals Srv.
Richard of St. Victor: The Twelve Patriarchs, the Mystical Ark Book, Three of the Trinity. Ed. by Grover A. Zinn. LC 79-83834. (Classics of Western Spirituality Ser.). 448p. 1979. pap. 9.95 (*0-8091-2122-0*) Paulist Pr.
Richard of St. Victor's "Treatise on the Study of Wisdom That Men Call Benjamin" As Adapted in Middle English by the Author of "The Cloud of Unknowing" Together with "Treatise on Discretion of Spirits" & "Epistle on Discretion of Stirrings" Richard of St. Victor. Tr. by Dick Barnes from LAT. LC 90-39519. (Studies in Medieval Literature: Vol. 7). 120p. 1990. lib. bdg. 59.95 (*0-88946-294-1*) E Mellen.
***Richard Ogilvie: Illinois's Dynamic Reformer.** Taylor Pensoneau. LC 97-3816. 1997. write for info. (*0-8093-2148-3*) S Ill U Pr.
Richard Olney: Evolution of a Statesman. Gerald G. Eggert. LC 73-6878. (Illus.). 432p. 1974. 35.00 (*0-271-01162-9*) Pa St U Pr.
Richard Olney & His Public Service. Henry James. LC 70-87445. (American Scene Ser.). (Illus.). 1971. reprint ed. lib. bdg. 39.50 (*0-306-71516-3*) Da Capo.
***Richard Olney's French Wine & Food: A Wine Lover's Cookbook.** Richard Olney. LC 97-24713. 1997. write for info. (*1-56656-226-0*) Interlink Inc.
***Richard Orr's Nature Cross-Sections.** Richard Orr. (Illus.). (J). 22.99 (*0-590-24633-X*) Scholastic Inc.
Richard Owen: Victorian Naturalist. Nicolaas A. Rupke. LC 93-5739. (Illus.). 480p. 1994. 50.00 (*0-300-05820-9*) Yale U Pr.
Richard Parkes Bonington: On the Pleasure of Painting. Patrick J. Noon. LC 91-65083. (Illus.). 311p. 1991. pap. 39.95 (*0-930606-67-1*) Yale Ctr Brit Art.
Richard Parkes Bonington: On the Pleasures of Painting. Patrick J. Noon. (Illus.). 288p. (C). 1991. text ed. 90.00 (*0-300-05108-5*) Yale U Pr.
Richard Payne Knight: The Twilight of Virtuosity. Frank J. Messmann. 1974. text ed. 38.50 (*90-279-2628-X*) Mouton.
Richard Peters: Champion of the New South. Royce Shingleton. LC 84-22701. xiv, 258p. 1985. 21.95 (*0-86554-126-4*, MUP/H117) Mercer Univ Pr.
Richard Petty. Ron Frankl. LC 95-18216. (Race Car Legends Ser.). 64p. (J). (gr. 3 up). 1996. lib. bdg. 15.95 (*0-7910-3182-9*) Chelsea Hse.
Richard Pinkham of Old Dover, New Hampshire & His Descendants. Charles N. Sinnett. (Illus.). 308p. 1989. reprint ed. pap. 45.00 (*0-8328-0971-3*); reprint ed. lib. bdg. 53.00 (*0-8328-0970-5*) Higginson Bk Co.
Richard Pococke's Irish Tours. Ed. by John McVeagh. (Illus.). 240p. 1995. 39.50 (*0-7165-2539-9*, Pub. by Irish Acad Pr IE) Intl Spec Bk.
Richard Pousette-Dart. Ed. by Robert C. Hobbs & Joanne M. Kuebler. LC 90-82236. (Illus.). 196p. 1990. 39.95 (*0-936260-51-3*) Ind Mus Art.
Richard Pousette-Dart: Recent Paintings. (Illus.). 78p. (Orig.). 1991. pap. 25.00 (*0-925315-99-0*) ACA Galleries.
Richard Price & the Ethical Foundations of the American Revolution. Ed. by W. Bernard Peach. LC 77-91081. 350p. 1979. text ed. 39.95 (*0-8223-0400-7*) Duke.
***Richard, Prince of Thieves.** Antonio Jocson & J. E. Chon. (Illus.). 88p. (J). (gr. 1-5). 1997. 14.95 (*1-890963-25-9*) Lib Bell.
Richard Pryor. Joseph Nazel. 224p. (Orig.). 1981. mass mkt. 2.25 (*0-87067-013-1*, BH013) Holloway.
Richard R. Niebuhr on Christ & Religion: The Four-Stage Development of His Theology. Patrick Primeaux. LC 81-38369. (Toronto Studies in Theology: Vol. 4). (Illus.). xiv, 288p. 1981. lib. bdg. 89.95 (*0-88946-973-3*) E Mellen.
Richard Rawlinson: A Tercentenary Memorial: Tashjian, Tashjian & Enright. LC 89-13858. 1990. 29.95 (*0-932826-23-7*) New Issues MI.
Richard Redgrave. Susan P. Casteras & Ronald Parkinson. LC 87-51378. 224p. (C). 1988. text ed. 42.00 (*0-300-04221-3*) Yale U Pr.
***Richard Rodgers.** Lunden & Asch. (Pop Song Writers Ser.). 1998. 45.00 (*0-02-864842-0*) S&S Trade.
Richard Rodney Bennett: A Bio-Bibliography. Compiled by Stewart R. Craggs. LC 89-23674. (Bio-Bibliographies in Music Ser.: No. 24). 262p. 1990. text ed. 55.00 (*0-313-26179-2*, CGB/, Greenwood Pr) Greenwood.
***Richard Rogers.** Kenneth Powell. 1996. pap. 34.50 (*3-7643-5582-4*) Birkhauser.
Richard Rogers & Architects. Ed. by Andreas Papadakis. (Architectural Monographs: No. 10). (Illus.). 160p. 1985. 45.00 (*0-85670-862-3*); pap. 30.00 (*0-85670-786-4*) Academy Ed UK.
Richard Rogers & Partners: An Architectural Monograph. Contrib. by Peter Cook & Richard Rogers. (Academy Architecture Ser.). (Illus.). 160p. 1985. 45.00 (*0-312-68208-5*); pap. 30.00 (*0-312-68207-7*) St Martin.
Richard Rogers Partnership: Works & Projects. Richard Burdett. (Illus.). 276p. (Orig.). 1996. pap. 50.00 (*1-885254-32-6*) Monacelli Pr.
Richard Rogers, 1978-1988. (Architecture & Urbanism Extra Edition Ser.). (Illus.). 314p. (Orig.). (ENG & JPN.). (C). pap. text ed. 82.50 (*4-900211-25-7*, Pub. by Japan Architect JA) Gingko Press.
Richard Rohr: Illuminations of His Life & Work. Ed. by Andreas Ebert. 192p. 1993. 15.95 (*0-8245-1270-7*) Crossroad NY.
Richard Rolle: The English Writings. Ed. by Rosamund S. Allen. (Classics of Western Spirituality Ser.: Vol. 59). 256p. 1988. 16.95 (*0-8091-0401-6*); pap. 12.95 (*0-8091-3008-4*) Paulist Pr.
***Richard Rolle: The Fire of Love & the Mending of Life.** Ed. by Ruth Harvey. (Early English Text Society Original Ser.: No. 106). 1996. reprint ed. 45.00 (*0-85991-860-2*, Pub. by EETS UK) Boydell & Brewer.
Richard Rolle & the Invention of Authority. Nicholas Watson. (Studies in Medieval Literature: No. 13). 380p. (C). 1991. text ed. 90.00 (*0-521-39017-6*) Cambridge U Pr.
Richard Rorty: Prophet & Poet of the New Pragmatism. David L. Hall. LC 93-18515. (SUNY Series in Philosophy). 290p. 1993. pap. 18.95 (*0-7914-1772-7*) State U NY Pr.
Richard Rorty: Prophet & Poet of the New Pragmatism. David L. Hall. LC 93-18515. (SUNY Series in Philosophy). 290p. 1993. text ed. 54.50 (*0-7914-1771-9*) State U NY Pr.
Richard S. Hill: Tributes from Friends. Ed. by James B. Coover. LC 87-23292. (Detroit Studies in Music Bibliography: No. 58). xv, 397p. 1987. 45.00 (*0-89990-035-6*) Info Coord.
Richard Scarry. Julie Berg. LC 94-3392. (Tribute to the Young at Heart). 1994. pap. 4.95 (*1-56239-369-3*) Abdo & Dghtrs.
Richard Scarry. Julie Berg. LC 94-3392. (Tribute to the Young at Heart). (J). 1994. lib. bdg. 14.98 (*1-56239-358-8*) Abdo & Dghtrs.
Richard Scarry. Golden Puzzle Staff. (J). pap. 1.59 (*0-307-08244-X*, Golden Pr) Western Pub.
Richard Scarry. Golden Western Staff. (J). pap. 1.59 (*0-307-08246-6*, Golden Pr) Western Pub.
Richard Scarry Novelty. Richard Scarry. (J). (gr. 4 up). 1996. pap. 12.95 (*0-689-80905-0*, S&S Bks Young Read) S&S Childrens.
Richard Scarry's ABC Word Book. Richard Scarry. (Illus.). (J). (ps-2). 1971. lib. bdg. 5.99 (*0-394-92339-1*) Random Bks Yng Read.
Richard Scarry's Bedtime Stories. Richard Scarry. LC 86-484. (Pictureback Ser.). (Illus.). 32p. (J). (ps-1). 1986. pap. 3.25 (*0-394-88269-5*) Random Bks Yng Read.
Richard Scarry's Bedtime Stories. Richard Scarry. LC 86-484. (Richard Scarry's Best Book & Cassettes Ever! Ser.). (Illus.). 32p. (J). (ps-1). 1990. pap. 7.95 incl. audio (*0-679-80803-5*) Random Bks Yng Read.
Richard Scarry's Best Busy Year Ever. Richard Scarry. (Illus.). (J). (ps-1). 1991. 5.25 (*0-307-15748-2*, Golden Pr) Western Pub.
Richard Scarry's Best First Book Ever. Richard Scarry. LC 79-3900. (Illus.). (J). (ps-1). 1979. lib. bdg. 11.99 (*0-394-94250-7*) Random Bks Yng Read.
Richard Scarry's Best First Book Ever. Richard Scarry. LC 79-3900. (Illus.). (J). (ps-1). 1979. 14.00 (*0-394-84250-2*) Random Bks Yng Read.
Richard Scarry's Biggest Word Book Ever! Richard Scarry. (Illus.). 12p. (J). (ps-1). 1985. 34.95 (*0-394-87374-2*) Random Bks Yng Read.
Richard Scarry's Cars & Trucks from A to Z. Illus. by Richard Scarry. LC 89-64401. (Chunky Shape Bks.). 22p. (J). (ps). 1990. 3.99 (*0-679-80663-6*) Random Bks Yng Read.
Richard Scarry's Christmas Mice. (First Little Golden Bks.). (Illus.). 24p. (J). 1995. bds. 1.09 (*0-307-10125-8*, Golden Pr) Western Pub.
Richard Scarry's Color Book. Richard Scarry. LC 75-36465. (Illus.). 14p. (J). (ps-1). 1976. 4.99 (*0-394-83237-X*) Random Bks Yng Read.
Richard Scarry's Favorite Christmas Carols. Richard Scarry. (J). 1991. 17.95 (*1-55987-050-8*) J B Comns.
Richard Scarry's Find Your ABC's. Richard Scarry. (Pictureback Ser.). (Illus.). (J). (ps-1). 1973. pap. 3.25 (*0-394-82683-3*) Random Bks Yng Read.
Richard Scarry's Four Funniest Stories Ever! Richard Scarry. (Comes to Life Bks.). 16p. (J). (ps-2). 1994. write for info. (*1-883366-60-7*) YES Ent.
Richard Scarry's Getting Ready for School Workbook. Richard Scarry. (Richard Scarry's Best Workbook Ever! Ser.). (Illus.). 128p. (J). (ps-1). 1994. pap. 5.99 (*0-679-86554-3*) Random Bks Yng Read.
Richard Scarry's Hilda's Tea Party: Busy World of Richard Scarry. Richard Scarry. 32p. (J). (ps-3). 1996. pap. 3.25 (*0-689-80805-4*, S&S Bks Young Read) S&S Childrens.
***Richard Scarry's Iciest Day Ever.** Richard Scarry. (J). 1998. pap. 14.95 (*0-689-81846-7*) S&S Childrens.
***Richard Scarry's Just Right Word Book.** Richard Scarry. (Classic Board Bks.). (J). 1997. 5.99 (*0-679-88359-2*) Random Bks Yng Read.
Richard Scarry's Longest Book Ever. Richard Scarry. (J). 1995. 12.95 (*0-689-80134-3*, Litl Simon S&S) S&S Childrens.
Richard Scarry's Lowly Worm Storybook. Richard Scarry. LC 77-79842. (Pictureback Ser.). (Illus.). 32p. (Orig.). (J). (ps-1). 1986. pap. 3.25 (*0-394-88270-9*) Random Bks Yng Read.
Richard Scarry's Lowly Worm Word Book. Richard Scarry. LC 80-53103. (Chunky Bks.). (Illus.). 28p. (J). (ps). 1981. 3.99 (*0-394-84728-8*) Random Bks Yng Read.
Richard Scarry's Naughty Bunny. Richard Scarry. (Big Golden Bks.). (Illus.). 24p. (J). (ps-3). 1989. write for info. (*0-307-12092-9*, Golden Books) Western Pub.
Richard Scarry's Nursery Tales. Richard Scarry. (J). 1996. pap. text ed. 6.95 (*0-307-13075-4*, Golden Books) Western Pub.
Richard Scarry's One to Ten. Richard Scarry. (Golden Little Look-Look Bks.). (Illus.). 24p. (J). (ps-3). write for info. (*0-307-11615-8*, Golden Books) Western Pub.
Richard Scarry's Pig Will & Pig Won't. Richard Scarry. (Illus.). 1995. 4.99 (*0-679-86653-1*) Random Bks Yng Read.
Richard Scarry's Please & Thank You Book. Richard Scarry. LC 73-2441. (Pictureback Library Editions). (J). (ps-2). 1973. lib. bdg. 5.99 (*0-394-92681-1*) Random Bks Yng Read.
Richard Scarry's Please & Thank You Book. Richard Scarry. LC 73-2441. (Pictureback Library Editions). (J). (ps-2). 1973. pap. 3.25 (*0-394-82681-7*) Random Bks Yng Read.
Richard Scarry's Please & Thank You Book. Richard Scarry. LC 73-2441. (Richard Scarry's Best Book & Cassettes Ever! Ser.). (Illus.). 32p. (J). (ps-1). 1990. lib. bdg. 7.95 incl. audio (*0-679-80799-3*) Random Bks Yng Read.
Richard Scarry's Pop-Up Colors. Richard Scarry. (Illus.). (J). (ps-1). 1996. 8.99 incl. 5.25 hd (*0-689-80330-3*, Aladdin Paperbacks) S&S Childrens.
Richard Scarry's Pop-up Numbers. Richard Scarry. (J). (ps-1). 1996. 8.99 (*0-689-80331-1*, Litl Simon S&S) S&S Childrens.
Richard Scarry's Pop-Up Time. Richard Scarry. (J). 1997. 8.99 (*0-689-81077-6*) S&S Childrens.
Richard Scarry's Pop-Up Wheels. Richard Scarry. (J). 1997. 8.99 (*0-689-81076-8*) S&S Childrens.
Richard Scarry's Postman Pig & His Busy Neighbors. Richard Scarry. LC 77-91646. (Pictureback Ser.). (Illus.). (J). (ps-2). 1978. lib. bdg. 5.99 (*0-394-93898-4*) Random Bks Yng Read.
Richard Scarry's The Gingerbread Man. Richard Scarry. (Little Nugget Bks.). (Illus.). 28p. (J). 1994. write for info. (*0-307-12128-3*) Western Pub.
Richard Scarry's What Do People Do All Day? Richard Scarry. (Illus.). (J). (ps-3). 1968. 14.00 (*0-394-81823-7*) Random Bks Yng Read.
***Richard Scary's Best Flap Books Ever: Sneef Saves the Day.** Richard Scary. (Illus.). (J). (ps-k). 1997. 10.95 (*0-614-29097-X*, Litl Simon S&S) S&S Childrens.
Richard Second. William Shakespeare. Ed. by Kenneth Muir. pap. 2.50 (*0-451-51921-3*, CJ1518, Sig Classics) NAL-Dutton.
Richard Second. William Shakespeare. Ed. by Matthew W. Black. (Pelican Shakespeare Ser.). 140p. (YA). (gr. 9 up). 1957. pap. 5.95 (*0-14-071406-5*, Pelican Bks) Viking Penguin.
Richard Second. William Shakespeare. Ed. by Stanley Wells. (New Penguin Shakespeare Ser.). 288p. 1981. pap. 5.50 (*0-14-070719-0*, Penguin Classics) Viking Penguin.
Richard Selzer & the Rhetoric of Surgery. Charles M. Anderson. LC 88-26454. 160p. (C). 1989. 19.95 (*0-8093-1502-5*) S Ill U Pr.
Richard Serra: Afangar. Richard Serra & Dirk Reinartz. (Illus.). 78p. 1992. 29.95 (*3-907509-17-X*, Pub. by Parkett Pubs SZ) Dist Art Pubs.
Richard Serra: Deadweights, 1991-1992. Contrib. by Richard Serra. LC 92-80726. (Illus.). 34p. (Orig.). 1992. pap. write for info. (*1-878283-23-5*) PaceWildenstein.
Richard Serra: Drawings & Prints from Iceland. Told to Mark Rosenthal. (Illus.). 90p. 1992. text ed. 20.00 (*1-880146-03-7*) M Marks.
***Richard Serra: Intersection.** Martha Buskirk. (Illus.). 192p. 1996. 60.00 (*3-928762-52-4*, 620791, Pub. by Richter Verlag GW) Dist Art Pubs.
Richard Serra: Interviews, Etc. 1970-1980. Clara Weyergraf. 192p. 1980. pap. 25.00 (*0-9627767-5-0*) Archer Fields.
***Richard Serra: La Mormaire.** Dirk Reinartz. (Illus.). 120p. 1996. 70.00 (*3-928762-54-0*, 620792, Pub. by Richter Verlag GW) Dist Art Pubs.
Richard Serra: Props. Rosalind Krauss et al. (Illus.). 264p. 1995. pap. 70.00 (*3-928762-21-4*) Dist Art Pubs.
Richard Serra: Sculpture, 1987-1989. Intro. by Richard Serra. (Illus.). 82p. (Orig.). 1989. pap. write for info. (*1-878283-00-6*) PaceWildenstein.
Richard Serra - Sculpture. Rosalind E. Krauss et al. Ed. & Intro. by Laura Rosenstock. LC 85-62476. (Illus.). 184p. 1986. pap. 24.95 (*0-87070-590-3*) Mus of Modern Art.
Richard Shute of Boston, MA, 1631-1703 & Selected Progeny. Alan H. Shute & Clark H. Flint. 153p. (Orig.). 1995. pap. 25.00 (*0-7884-0348-6*) Heritage Bk.
Richard Simmons Farewell to Fat Cookbook: Homemade in the U. S. A. Richard Simmons. (Illus.). 192p. 1996. 19.95 (*1-57719-102-1*) GT Pubng Corp.
Richard Simmons' Never Give Up: Inspirations, Reflections, Stories of Hope. Richard Simmons. 384p. 1994. mass mkt. 5.99 (*0-446-60085-7*) Warner Bks.
***Richard Smallwood: Adoration.** Ed. by Jeannette DeLisa. 68p. (Orig.). (YA). 1996. pap. text ed. 16.95 (*1-57623-591-2*, PF9624) Warner Brothers.
Richard Smith's Guide to Getting Even: One Hundred Forty-Three Lessons in Etiquette for a World Gone Mad. Richard Smith. LC 93-14448. 160p. (Orig.). 1993. pap. 7.95 (*0-89480-478-2*, 1478) Workman Pub.
***Richard Spruce (1817-1893), Botanist & Explorer.** M. Seaward & S. FitzGerald. 359p. 1996. pap. 50.00 (*0-947643-94-X*, Pub. by Royal Botnic Grdns UK) Balogh.
Richard Steele. Austin Dobson. (BCL1-PR English Literature Ser.). 240p. 1992. reprint ed. lib. bdg. 79.00 (*0-7812-7408-7*) Rprt Serv.
Richard Steele. Austin Dobson. Ed. by Andrew Long. LC 72-108475. 1970. reprint ed. 39.00 (*0-403-00229-X*) Scholarly.
Richard Steele. Richard Steele. Ed. by George A. Aitken. LC 68-9714. 452p. 1971. reprint ed. text ed. 65.00 (*0-8371-4461-2*, STRS, Greenwood Pr) Greenwood.
Richard Steele. Richard Steele. (BCL1-PR English Literature Ser.). 452p. 1992. reprint ed. lib. bdg. 99.00 (*0-7812-7405-2*) Rprt Serv.
Richard Steele & the Sentimental Comedy. M. E. Hare. (Studies in Drama: No. 39). 1970. reprint ed. pap. 39.95 (*0-8383-0041-3*) M S G Haskell Hse.
Richard Stern. James Schiffer. (United States Authors Ser.). 200p. 1993. 23.95 (*0-8057-4007-4*, Twayne) Scribnrs Ref.
Richard Strauss. (Dent Master Musicians Ser.). (Illus.). (C). pap. write for info. (*0-19-816481-5*) OUP.
Richard Strauss. Henry T. Finck. 1972. 59.95 (*0-8490-0955-3*) Gordon Pr.
Richard Strauss. Michael Kennedy. 352p. 1995. 30.00 (*0-02-864517-0*) Schirmer Bks.
Richard Strauss. Ernest Newman. LC 79-94279. (Select Bibliographies Reprint Ser.). 1977. 21.95 (*0-8369-5053-4*) Ayer.
Richard Strauss. Ernest Newman. 144p. 1990. reprint ed. lib. bdg. 59.00 (*0-7812-9092-9*) Rprt Serv.
Richard Strauss: "Arabella" Kenneth Birkin. (Cambridge Opera Handbooks Ser.). (Illus.). 176p. (C). 1989. pap. text ed. 19.95 (*0-521-33577-9*) Cambridge U Pr.
Richard Strauss: "Der Rosenkavalier" Ed. by Alan Jefferson. (Cambridge Opera Handbooks Ser.). (Illus.). 178p. 1986. pap. 19.95 (*0-521-27811-2*) Cambridge U Pr.
Richard Strauss: "Salome" Ed. by Derrick Puffett. (Cambridge Opera Handbooks Ser.). 224p. 1989. pap. text ed. 19.95 (*0-521-35970-8*) Cambridge U Pr.
Richard Strauss: A Critical Commentary on His Life & Works, II. Norman Del Mar. LC 85-19033. (Illus.). 1986. pap. 19.95 (*0-8014-9318-8*) Cornell U Pr.
Richard Strauss: A Critical Commentary on His Life & Works, III. Norman Del Mar. LC 85-19033. (Illus.). 1986. pap. 19.95 (*0-8014-9319-6*) Cornell U Pr.
Richard Strauss: A Critical Commentary on His Life & Works, Vol. I. Norman Del Mar. LC 85-19033. (Illus.). 464p. 1986. 49.95 (*0-8014-1780-5*) Cornell U Pr.
Richard Strauss: A Critical Commentary on His Life & Works, Vol. II. Norman Del Mar. LC 85-19033. (Illus.). 480p. 1986. 49.95 (*0-8014-1781-3*) Cornell U Pr.
Richard Strauss: A Critical Commentary on His Life & Works, Vol. III. Norman Del Mar. LC 85-19033. (Illus.). 584p. 1986. 49.95 (*0-8014-1782-1*) Cornell U Pr.
Richard Strauss: Complete Catalog. Ernst Roth & Willi Schuh. LC 64-6063. 1964. pap. 5.25 (*0-913932-31-0*) Boosey & Hawkes.
Richard Strauss: Illustrated Lives of the Great Composers. David Nice. (Illustrated Lives of the Great Composers Ser.). (Illus.). 160p. 1996. 14.95 (*0-7119-1686-1*, OP 45038) Omnibus NY.
Richard Strauss: New Perspectives on the Composer & His Work. Ed. by Bryan Gilliam. LC 92-7675. (Sources of Music & Their Interpretation; Duke Studies in Music). (Illus.). 306p. 1992. text ed. 36.95 (*0-8223-1207-7*) Duke.
Richard Strauss & His World. Ed. by Bryan Gilliam. (Illus.). 444p. 1992. pap. text ed. 25.00 (*0-691-02762-5*) Princeton U Pr.
Richard Strauss et Romain Rolland. Romain Rolland & Richard Strauss. (Illus.). 248p. (FRE.). 1951. pap. 8.95 (*0-7859-5462-7*) Fr & Eur.
Richard Strauss's Elektra. Bryan Gilliam. (Studies in Musical Genesis & Structure). (Illus.). 192p. 1992. 75.00 (*0-19-313214-1*) OUP.
Richard Strauss's Elektra. Bryan Gilliam. (Studies in Musical Genesis & Structure). (Illus.). 288p. 1996. pap. 24.95 (*0-19-816602-8*) OUP.
Richard Tauber. Diana N. Tauber. LC 80-17085. (Music Ser.). 1980. reprint ed. 32.50 (*0-306-76049-5*) Da Capo.
Richard Tauber: Music Book Index. Diana N. Tauber. 237p. 1993. reprint ed. lib. bdg. 79.00 (*0-7812-9635-8*) Rprt Serv.
Richard Taylor: Soldier Prince of Dixie. T. Michael Parrish. LC 91-46467. (Illus.). xvi, 554p. (C). 1992. 37.50 (*0-8078-2032-6*) U of NC Pr.
Richard Taylor's U. S. Revenue Cutter Virginia, 1791-1797. Florence Kern. 1977. 3.95 (*0-913377-06-6*) Alised.
Richard the Liar-Hearted. Ron Dalrymple. 40p. (Orig.). 1979. pap. 2.95 (*0-935882-01-4*) Celestial Gifts.
Richard the Lionheart. John Gillingham. LC 78-63599. (Illus.). 1979. write for info. (*0-8129-0802-3*, Times Bks) Random.
***Richard II.** Nigel Saul. LC 96-36062. 1997. write for info. (*0-300-07003-9*) Yale U Pr.
Richard the Third. William Shakespeare. (Tudor Facsimile Texts. Old English Plays Ser.: No. 79). reprint ed. 59.50 (*0-404-53379-5*) Moonbeam Pubns.
Richard the Third: Crown & People. James Petre. (Illus.). 464p. 1993. text ed. 55.00 (*0-904893-11-1*, Pub. by Sutton Pubng UK) Bks Intl VA.
Richard the Third & His Rivals: Magnates & Their Motives in the Wars of the Roses. Michael Hicks. 460p. 1991. boxed 60.00 (*1-85285-053-1*) Hambledon Press.
Richard the Third & the Princes in the Tower. A. J. Pollard. 1995. text ed. 18.95 (*0-312-12640-9*) St Martin.
Richard Third. William Shakespeare. Ed. by G. Blakemore Evans. (Pelican Shakespeare Ser.). 192p. 1959. pap. 5.95 (*0-14-071416-2*, Pelican Bks) Viking Penguin.

R

Richard Third. William Shakespeare. Ed. by Ernst A. Honigmann. (New Penguin Shakespeare Ser.). 256p. 1981. pap. 5.95 (0-14-070712-3, Penguin Classics) Viking Penguin.

Richard Third. Jon Nichol. (Resource Units: Middle Ages, 1066-1485 Ser.). (Illus.). 24p. 1974. reprint ed. teacher ed., pap. text ed. 12.95 (0-582-39391-4) Longman.

Richard Third: A Study of Service. Rosemary Horrox. (Studies in Medieval Life & Thought, Fourth Ser.: No. 11). 368p. (C). 1991. pap. text ed. 22.95 (0-521-40726-5) Cambridge U Pr.

***Richard Thompson: The Biography.** Patrick Humphries. LC 96-37826. 1997. 26.00 (0-02-864752-1) Macmillan.

Richard Throssel: Crow Indian Photographer. Joanna C. Scherer. 1997. pap. 35.00 (0-8263-1755-3) U of NM Pr.

Richard Trevithick. James Hodge. 1989. pap. 25.00 (0-85263-177-4, Pub. by Shire UK) St Mut.

Richard Trilogy: Things As They Are. Everything to Live For. The Thin Mountain Air. Paul Horgan. LC 89-24872. 795p. 1990. pap. 24.95 (0-8195-6234-3, Wesleyan Univ Pr) U Pr of New Eng.

Richard Tuttle: Book & Cover. Richard Tuttle. (Illus.). 12p. 1992. text ed. write for info. (1-881138-03-8) Tallgrass Pr.

***Richard Upton: Landscape As God: The Drawings of Richard Upton.** David Shapiro. LC 96-61676. (Illus.). 60p. 1997. pap. 25.00 (0-9629503-2-7) Erebus Pr.

Richard Wagner. William H. Hadow. LC 74-24097. reprint ed. 29.00 (0-404-12942-0) AMS Pr.

Richard Wagner: "Parsifal" Lucy Beckett. (Cambridge Opera Handbooks Ser.). (Illus.). 220p. 1981. pap. text ed. 19.95 (0-521-29662-5) Cambridge U Pr.

Richard Wagner: Die Meistersinger von Nurnberg. Ed. by John Warrack. LC 93-39615. (Opera Handbooks Ser.). (Illus.). 225p. (C). 1994. text ed. 49.95 (0-521-44444-6); pap. text ed. 17.95 (0-521-44895-6) Cambridge U Pr.

Richard Wagner: His Life & His Dramas. 2nd rev. ed. William J. Henderson. LC 70-137240. reprint ed. 49.50 (0-404-03239-7) AMS Pr.

Richard Wagner: His Life in His Work. Paul Bekker. Tr. by M. M. Bozman. LC 70-107792. (Select Bibliographies Reprint Ser.). 1977. 35.95 (0-8369-5176-X) Ayer.

Richard Wagner: His Life in His Work. Paul Bekker. Tr. by M. M. Bozman. LC 74-106713. 522p. 1971. reprint ed. text ed. 35.00 (0-8371-3443-9, BERW, Greenwood Pr) Greenwood.

Richard Wagner: Mystic in the Making. Alan D. Aberbach. LC 90-26688. 223p. (C). 1991. text ed. 35.00 (0-89341-662-2, Longwood Academic) Hollowbrook.

Richard Wagner: Reverie d'un Poete Francais. Paul Claudel. 180p. 22.50 (0-686-54430-7) Fr & Eur.

Richard Wagner: Rienzi to Parsifal. Judith Gautier. LC 82-2344. (Music Reprint Ser.). (Illus.). 173p. (FRE.). 1982. reprint ed. lib. bdg. 27.50 (0-306-76172-6) Da Capo.

Richard Wagner: The Man, His Mind, & His Music. Robert W Gutman. 1990. pap. 12.95 (0-15-677615-4) HarBrace.

Richard Wagner: The Story of an Artist. Guy De Pourtales. Tr. by Lewis May from FRE. LC 76-138173. (Illus.). 1972. reprint ed. text ed. 75.00 (0-8371-5630-0, PORW, Greenwood Pr) Greenwood.

Richard Wagner: Theory & Theatre. Dieter Borchmeyer. Tr. by Stewart Spencer. 448p. 1991. 98.00 (0-19-315322-X) OUP.

Richard Wagner - His Life in His Work: Music Book Index. Paul Bekker. 522p. 1993. reprint ed. lib. bdg. 99.00 (0-7812-9797-6) Rprt Serv.

Richard Wagner - the Story of an Artist: Music Book Index. Guy De Comte Pourtales. 409p. 1993. reprint ed. lib. bdg. 99.00 (0-7812-9716-8) Rprt Serv.

Richard Wagner & Festival Theatre. Simon Williams. LC 93-34081. (Contributions in Drama & Theatre Studies: No. 53). 208p. 1994. text ed. 59.95 (0-313-27435-5, Greenwood Pr); pap. text ed. 16.95 (0-275-93608-2, Praeger Pubs) Greenwood.

Richard Wagner & the Anti-Semetic Imagination. Marc A. Weiner. LC 94-12187. (Texts & Contexts Ser.). (Illus.). xv, 441p. 1995. text ed. 45.00 (0-8032-4775-3) U of Nebr Pr.

***Richard Wagner & the Anti-Semitic Imagination.** Marc A. Weiner. LC 94-12187. (Illus.). xv, 447p. 1997. pap. 20.00 (0-8032-9792-0, Bison Books) U of Nebr Pr.

Richard Wagner & the English. Anne D. Sessa. LC 76-50287. 191p. 1979. 29.50 (0-8386-2055-8) Fairleigh Dickinson.

Richard Wagner & the Modern British Novel. John L. DiGaetani. 179p. 1978. 28.50 (0-8386-1955-X) Fairleigh Dickinson.

Richard Wagner & the Music of the Future. Franz Hueffer. LC 70-37122. (Essay Index Reprint Ser.). 1977. reprint ed. 22.95 (0-8369-2508-4) Ayer.

Richard Wagner & the Synthesis of the Arts. Jack M. Stein. LC 73-1840. (Illus.). 229p. 1973. reprint ed. text ed. 59.75 (0-8371-6806-6, STRX, Greenwood Pr) Greenwood.

Richard Wagner, His Life & His Dramas: A Biographical Study of the Man & an Explanation of His Work. William J. Henderson. 504p. 1990. reprint ed. lib. bdg. 99.00 (0-7812-9098-8) Rprt Serv.

Richard Wagner in Bayreuth: Unzeitgemaesse Betrachtungen, Nummer 4; Nachgelassene Fragmente, Anfang 1875 bis Fruehjahr, 1876 see Nietzsche Werke

Richard Wagner und die Indische Geisteswelt. Carl Suneson. LC 88-29776. xi, 124p. (Orig.). (GER.). 1989. pap. text ed. 28.75 (90-04-08859-8) E J Brill.

***Richard Wagner Unlined.** Paperblank Books Staff. (Great Composers Ser.). 1997. 10.95 (1-55156-059-3, Pub. by Paperblank Bk CN) Consort Bk Sales.

Richard Wagner's Music Dramas. Carl Dahlhaus. Tr. by Mary Whittall. 167p. (C). 1992. pap. 20.95 (0-521-42899-8) Cambridge U Pr.

Richard Wagner's Prose Works, 8 vols. Ed. by William A. Ellis. Incl. Vol. 4. Art & Politics. 1967. (0-318-51223-8); Vol. 5. Religion & Art NAS. 1967. (0-318-51224-6); Vol. 8. Posthumous. 1967. (0-318-51225-4); (GER.). 1966. reprint ed. lib. bdg. 250.00 (0-8450-2100-1) Broude.

Richard Wagner's Prose Works, 8 vols. Richard Wagner. 1988. reprint ed. lib. bdg. 800.00 (0-7812-0490-9) Rprt Serv.

Richard Wagner's Prose Works, 8 vols. Richard Wagner. Tr. by William A. Ellis. 1972. reprint ed. 695.00 (0-403-00255-9) Scholarly.

Richard Wagner's Prose Works, 8 vols., Vols. 7 & 8. Ed. by William A. Ellis. Incl. Vol. 4. Art & Politics. 1967. (0-318-51223-8); Vol. 5. Religion & Art NAS. 1967. (0-318-51224-6); Vol. 8. Posthumous. 1967. (0-318-51225-4); (GER.). 1967. reprint ed. 40.00 (0-685-00914-9) Broude.

Richard Wagner's Prose Works, Vol. 1: The Art-Work of the Future. Richard Wagner. Tr. by William A. Ellis. LC 78-107194. 1972. reprint ed. 100.00 (0-685-47618-9) Scholarly.

Richard Wagner's Prose Works, Vol. 2: Opera & Drama. Richard Wagner. Tr. by William A. Ellis. LC 78-107194. 1972. reprint ed. 100.00 (0-685-47619-7) Scholarly.

Richard Wagner's Prose Works, Vol. 3: The Theatre. Richard Wagner. Tr. by William A. Ellis. LC 78-107194. 1972. reprint ed. 100.00 (0-685-47620-0) Scholarly.

Richard Wagner's Prose Works, Vol. 4: Art & Politics. Richard Wagner. Tr. by William A. Ellis. LC 78-107194. 1972. reprint ed. 100.00 (0-685-47621-9) Scholarly.

Richard Wagner's Prose Works, Vol. 5: Actors & Singers. Richard Wagner. Tr. by William A. Ellis. LC 78-107194. 1972. reprint ed. 70.00 (0-685-47622-7) Scholarly.

Richard Wagner's Prose Works, Vol. 6: Religion & Art. Richard Wagner. Tr. by William A. Ellis. LC 78-107194. 1972. reprint ed. 100.00 (0-685-47623-5) Scholarly.

Richard Wagner's Prose Works, Vol. 7: In Paris & Dresden. Richard Wagner. Ed. by William A. Ellis. LC 78-107194. 1972. reprint ed. 100.00 (0-685-47624-3) Scholarly.

Richard Wagner's Prose Works, Vol. 8: Posthumous Etc. Richard Wagner. Tr. by William A. Ellis. LC 78-107194. 1972. reprint ed. 100.00 (0-685-47625-1) Scholarly.

***Richard Wagner's Religious Ideas: A Spiritual Journey.** Alan D. Aberbach,. LC 96-49363. 1996. write for info. (0-7734-8783-2) E Mellen.

Richard Warren Sears: Icon of Inspiration: Fable & Fact about the Founder & Spiritual Genius of Sears, Roebuck & Company. Frederick Asher. (Orig.). 1996. pap. 14.95 (0-533-11860-3) Vantage.

Richard Watson Gilder. Herbert F. Smith. LC 70-110705. (Twayne's United States Authors Ser.). 1970. pap. text ed. 6.95 (0-8290-0012-7); lib. bdg. 17.95 (0-89197-923-9) Irvington.

Richard Wetherill: Anasazi. rev. ed. Frank McNitt. LC 65-29102. (Illus.). 380p. 1974. reprint ed. pap. 14.95 (0-8263-0329-3) U of NM Pr.

Richard Widmark: A Bio-Bibliography. Kim R. Holston. LC 89-28648. (Bio-Bibliographies in the Performing Arts Ser.). 160p. 1990. text ed. 39.95 (0-313-26480-5, HRW/, Greenwood Pr) Greenwood.

Richard Widmark: The Man & His Movies. Allan Hunter. (Illus.). 94p. 1985. 14.95 (0-312-68217-4) St Martin.

Richard Wilbur: A Bibliographical Checklist. Notes by John P. Field & Richard Wilbur. LC 79-626237. (Serif Series: Bibliographies & Checklists: No. 16). 95p. reprint ed. pap. 27.10 (0-8357-5571-1, 2035198) Bks Demand.

Richard Wilbur: A Reference Guide. Frances Bixler. (Reference Guides to Literature Ser.). 459p. 1991. 50.00 (0-8161-7262-5, Hall Reference) Macmillan.

Richard Wilbur's Creation. Ed. by Wendy Salinger. (Under Discussion Ser.). 1983. pap. 16.95 (0-472-06348-0) U of Mich Pr.

Richard Wright. Robert Felgar. (United States Authors Ser.: No. 386). 192p. 1980. 21.95 (0-8057-7320-7, Twayne) Scribnrs Ref.

***Richard Wright.** Rowley. 1996. 37.50 (0-8050-4776-X) St Martin.

Richard Wright. Joan Urban. (Black American Ser.). (Illus.). 192p. (YA). 1990. reprint ed. mass mkt. 3.95 (0-87067-562-1, Melrose Sq) Holloway.

Richard Wright: A Collection of Critical Essays. Ed. by Arnold Rampersad. LC 94-19515. 216p. 1994. 12.95 (0-13-036120-8) P-H.

Richard Wright: An Introduction to the Man & His Works. Russell C. Brignano. LC 72-81667. (Critical Essays in Modern Literature Ser.). 217p. 1970. reprint ed. pap. 61.90 (0-608-00900-8, 2061694) Bks Demand.

Richard Wright: Author. Joan Urban. Ed. by Nathan I. Huggins. (Black Americans of Achievement Ser.). (Illus.). (YA). (gr. 5 up). 1989. lib. bdg. 19.95 (1-55546-618-4) Chelsea Hse.

Richard Wright: Books & Writers. Michel Fabre. LC 89-37020. 304p. 1990. 39.50 (0-87805-403-0) U Pr of Miss.

Richard Wright: Critical Perspectives Past & Present. K. A. Appiah. Ed. & Intro. by Henry L. Gates, Jr. LC 92-45754. (Literary Ser.). 476p. 1993. 24.95 incl. 5.25 hd (1-56743-014-7) Amistad Pr.

Richard Wright: Critical Perspectives Past & Present. Henry L. Gates, Jr. & K. A. Appiah. LC 92-45754. (Literary Ser.). 476p. 1993. pap. 14.95 (1-56743-027-9) Amistad Pr.

Richard Wright: Daemonic Genius. Margaret Walker. (Illus.). 428p. 1993. reprint ed. pap. 9.95 (1-56743-004-X) Amistad Pr.

Richard Wright: Myths & Realities. James C. Trotman. LC 88-26012. (Critical Studies in Black Life & Culture: Vol. 18). 180p. 1989. text ed. 33.00 (0-8240-7839-X, H892) Garland.

Richard Wright: Ordeal of a Native Son. Addison Gayle. 1983. 20.50 (0-8446-6000-0) Peter Smith.

Richard Wright see Modern Critical Views Series

Richard Wright & Racial Discourse. Yoshinobu Hakutani. 328p. (C). 1996. 34.95 (0-8262-1059-7) U of Mo Pr.

***Richard Wright & the Library Card.** William Miller. LC 97-6847. (Illus.). (YA). 1997. 15.95 (1-880000-57-1) Lee & Low Bks.

Richard Wright Bibliography: Fifty Years of Criticism & Commentary, 1933-1982. Compiled by Keneth Kinnamon. LC 87-27831. (Bibliographies & Indexes in Afro-American & African Studies: No. 19). 992p. 1988. text ed. 105.00 (0-313-25411-7, KRD/, Greenwood Pr) Greenwood.

***Richard Wright Reader.** Richard A. Wright et al. Ed. by Ellen Wright & Michel Fabre. LC 96-45124. (Illus.). 910p. 1997. reprint ed. pap. 22.50 (0-306-80774-2) Da Capo.

Richard Wright's Art of Tragedy. Joyce A. Joyce. LC 86-6906. 149p. (C). 1986. text ed. 18.95 (0-87745-148-6) U of Iowa Pr.

Richard Wright's Art of Tragedy. Joyce A. Joyce. LC 86-6906. 149p. 1986. reprint ed. pap. 9.95 (0-87745-320-9) U of Iowa Pr.

Richard Wright's Native Son see Bloom's Notes

Richard Wright's Native Son see Modern Critical Interpretations

Richard Wright's Native Son see Bloom's Notes

Richard Yates. large type ed. Castronovo. LC 96-38515. 1996. lib. bdg. 24.95 (0-8057-4031-7, Twayne) Scribnrs Ref.

Richards & Butler on Latent Damage. Robert Merkin. (C). 1987. 390.00 (0-685-32752-3, Pub. by Witherby & Co UK) St Mut.

Richard's Complete Bible Handbook. Lawrence O. Richards. 1987. pap. 17.99 (0-8499-3097-9) Word Pub.

Richard's Cycling for Fitness. John Schubert. (Orig.). 1988. pap. 11.00 (0-345-34117-1, Ballantine Trade) Ballantine.

Richard's Himself Again: A Stage History of "Richard III" Scott Colley. LC 91-36834. (Contributions in Drama & Theatre Studies: No. 46). 304p. 1992. text ed. 55.00 (0-313-26293-4, COR/, Greenwood Pr) Greenwood.

Richards on Rhetoric: Selected Essays, 1929-1974. I. A. Richards. Ed. by Ann E. Berthoff. (Illus.). 304p. (C). 1990. pap. text ed. 21.95 (0-19-506426-7) OUP.

Richards Ruben. Frederick Castle & Katherine B. Crum. 54p. 1994. pap. 20.00 (0-9638030-1-8) Mills Art Gal.

Richards' Ultimate Bicycle Book. Richard Ballantine & Richard Grant. LC 91-31540. (Illus.). 192p. 1992. 29.95 (1-56458-036-9) DK Pub Inc.

Richards' Ultimate Bicycle Repair Manual. Richard Ballantine & Richard Grant. LC 93-29836. (Illus.). 96p. 1994. pap. 8.95 (1-56458-484-4) DK Pub Inc.

Richard's Way. large type ed. Kate Thompson. 1978. 25.99 (0-7089-0214-6) Ulverscroft.

***Richardson: Plains Myths.** Jean Richardson. 1988. pap. text ed. 35.00 (0-936598-03-4) J Szoke Graphics.

***Richardson Coloring Book.** Tony Mollica & Bill Northrup. (Coloring the Classics Ser.). (Illus.). 28p. (J). 1994. 3.95 (1-883029-07-4) CHP NY.

Richardson Lakes: Jewels in the Rangeley Chain. Herbert P. Shirrefs. Ed. by Randall H. Bennett. (Illus.). 485p. 1996. 39.95 (0-9614153-4-7) Bethel Hist Soc.

Richardson Memorial, Comprising a Full History & Genealogy of the Posterity of Three Brothers, Ezekiel, Samuel, & Thomas Richardson. J. A. Vinton. (Illus.). 959p. 1989. reprint ed. pap. 144.00 (0-8328-1021-5); reprint ed. lib. bdg. 152.00 (0-8328-1020-7) Higginson Bk Co.

***Richardsons' Chartbook & Cruising Guide: Lake Huron.** 4th ed. Margaret Wells. Ed. by Christopher Collier. (Illus.). 198p. 1996. spiral bd. 74.95 (0-932647-16-2, LH4) Richardsons Marine.

***Richardsons' Chartbook & Cruising Guide: Lake Michigan.** 6th ed. Caroline Cannon & Elizabeth Hare. (Illus.). 128p. 1995. spiral bd. 69.95 (0-932647-15-4, LM6) Richardsons Marine.

***Richardsons' Chartbook & Cruising Guide: Lake Ontario, 5 vols.** 4th ed. Margaret Wells & Christopher Collier. 1997. spiral bd., pap. 69.95 (0-614-23153-1) Richardsons Marine.

***Richardsons' Chartbook & Cruising Guide: 1994 Lake Erie Edition.** 4th ed. Caroline Cannon & Elizabeth Hare. (Illus.). 140p. 1994. spiral bd. 69.95 (0-932647-13-8) Richardsons Marine.

***Richardsons' Chartbook & Cruising Guides: Lake Superior.** 2nd ed. 1994. 69.95 (0-932647-14-6) Richardsons Marine.

Richardson's "Clarissa & the Eighteenth-Century Reader" Tom Keymer. (Studies in Eighteenth-Century English Literature & Thought: No. 13). (Illus.). 283p. (C). 1992. 65.00 (0-521-39023-0) Cambridge U Pr.

Richardson's Guide to Negotiable Instruments. 8th ed. Jennifer James. 1991. pap. 30.00 (0-406-50920-4, U.K.) MICHIE.

Richart Commemorative Lectures: Proceedings. Ed. by Richard D. Woods & Geotechnical Engineeging Division Staff. 158p. 1985. 17.00 (0-87262-507-9) Am Soc Civil Eng.

Riche et Legere. Florence Delay. 252p. (FRE.). 1990. pap. 11.95 (0-7859-2143-5, 2070382575) Fr & Eur.

Riche, His Farewell to Militarie Profession: Pierce Penniless's Supplication to the Devil: Fooles & Jesters: A Nest of Ninnies see Early Prose & Poetical Tracts: Eight Novels Employed by English Dramatic Poets of the Reign of Queen Elizabeth

Riche Homme, La Folie De Maigret, La Disparition D'Odile. Georges Simenon. 864p. (FRE.). 1991. 49.95 (0-7859-0490-5, 2258033055) Fr & Eur.

Richelieu. R. J. Knecht. (Profiles in Power Ser.). (Illus.). 259p. (C). 1991. pap. text ed. 26.50 (0-582-55710-0, 78830) Longman.

Richelieu. Karl Federn. LC 72-132440. (World History Ser.: No. 48). 1970. reprint ed. lib. bdg. 75.00 (0-8383-1222-5) M S G Haskell Hse.

Richelieu & His Age. Ed. by Joseph Bergin & Laurence Brockliss. LC 92-35777. (Illus.). 312p. (C). 1992. 79.00 (0-19-820231-8, Clarendon Pr) OUP.

Richelieu & Olivares. John H. Elliott. LC 82-20929. (Studies in Early Modern History). 192p. 1984. 49.95 (0-521-26205-4) Cambridge U Pr.

Richelieu & Olivares. John H. Elliott. (Canto Book Ser.). (Illus.). 197p. (C). 1991. pap. text ed. 11.95 (0-521-40674-9) Cambridge U Pr.

Richelieu & Reason of State. William F. Church. LC 76-181518. 562p. reprint ed. pap. 160.20 (0-317-42020-8, 2025688) Bks Demand.

Richelieu & the Growth of French Power. James B. Perkins. LC 70-157353. (Select Bibliographies Reprint Ser.). 1977. reprint ed. 35.95 (0-8369-5814-4) Ayer.

Richelieu's Desmarets & the Century of Louis XIV. Hugh G. Hall. (Illus.). 416p. 1990. 95.00 (0-19-815157-8) OUP.

Richer by Tomorrow: It's How You Save That Counts! Lotty Polis. 52p. (Orig.). 1989. pap. 4.95 (0-9625247-0-0) Davric Corp.

Richer Entanglements: Essays & Notes on Poetry & Poems. Gregory Orr. LC 93-10796. (Poets on Poetry Ser.). 190p. (C). 1993. pap. 13.95 (0-472-06525-4); text ed. 39.50 (0-472-09525-0) U of Mich Pr.

Richer Fare for the Christian People: Reflections on the Sunday Readings, Cycles A, B, C. Ed. by Gail Ramshaw. 245p. 1990. pap. 18.50 (0-8146-6102-5, Pueblo Bks) Liturgical Pr.

Richer Harvest: New Horizons for Developing Countries. Sudhir Sen. LC 73-89988. 599p. reprint ed. pap. 170.80 (0-8357-7011-7, 2033535) Bks Demand.

Richer Life. Nikkyo Niwano. Tr. by Richard L. Gage from JPN. Orig. Title: Ningen Rashiku Ikiru. 138p. 1979. pap. 4.95 (4-333-00351-2, Pub. by Kosei Pub Co JA) C E Tuttle.

Richer Life see Richer Life for You in Christ: First Corinthians 1

***Richer Life for You in Christ: First Corinthians 1.** Spiros Zodhiates. (Exegetical Commentary Ser.). Orig. Title: Richer Life. 1972. pap. 8.99 (0-89957-442-4) AMG Pubs.

Richer Than Diamonds. large type ed. Joan Moules. 1990. pap. 15.99 (0-7089-6931-3, Trailtree Bookshop) Ulverscroft.

Richer, The Poorer: Stories, Sketches, & Reminiscences. Dorothy West. 272p. 1996. pap. 12.95 (0-385-47146-7, Anchor NY) Doubleday.

Richer Vision: The Development of Ethnic Minority Media in Western Democracies. Ed. by Charles Husband. 160p. 1994. pap. 35.00 (92-3-102941-X, U2941, Pub. by UNESCO FR) Bernan Associates.

Riches. Lee Blessing. 1986. pap. 5.25 (0-8222-1221-8) Dramatists Play.

Riches. Paul-Loup Sulitzer. (FRE.). 1993. pap. 14.95 (0-7859-3263-1, 2266055097) Fr & Eur.

Riches & Poverty: An Intellectual History of Political Economy in Britain, 1750-1834. Donald Winch. (Ideas in Context Ser.: No. 39). (Illus.). 440p. (C). 1996. text ed. 64.95 (0-521-55105-6); pap. text ed. 22.95 (0-521-55920-0) Cambridge U Pr.

Riches & Regrets: Betting on Gambling in Two Colorado Mountain Towns. Patricia A. Stokowski. LC 96-10138. (Illus.). 360p. 1996. 39.95 (0-87081-428-1) Univ Pr Colo.

Riches & Renunciation: Religion, Economy, & Society among the Jains. James A. Laidlaw. (Oxford Studies in Social & Cultural Anthropology). (Illus.). 448p. 1996. 89.00 (0-19-828031-9); pap. 29.95 (0-19-828042-4) OUP.

Riches, Class, & Power: The United States Before the Civil War. Edward Pessen. 467p. 1989. pap. 24.95 (0-88738-806-X) Transaction Pubs.

***Riches from Real Estate Technology.** Roald Marth. 240p. 1997. 24.95 (0-7931-1849-2, 1907-1801) Dearborn Finan.

Riches from the Earth: A Geologic Tour of the Dalton Highway. BLM Staff. (Illus.). 128p. 1995. pap. 9.95 (0-930931-10-6) Alaska Natural.

Riches Have Wings: A Tale for the Rich & Poor. Timothy S. Arthur. LC 77-137720. (American Fiction Reprint Ser.). 1977. reprint ed. 19.95 (0-8369-7019-5) Ayer.

Riches of Ancient Australia: An Indispensable Guide for Exploring Prehistoric Australia. 2nd ed. Josephine Flood. (Illus.). 373p. (C). 1990. reprint ed. pap. text ed. 29.95 (0-7022-2513-4, Pub. by Univ Queensland Pr AT) Intl Spec Bk.

Riches of British Archaeology. Andrew Selkirk. (Illus.). 208p. Date not set. text ed. write for info. (0-521-32132-8) Cambridge U Pr.

Riches of Eternity: Twelve Fundamental Doctrines from the Doctrine & Covenants. Ed. by John K. Challis & John G. Scott. LC 93-29480. 258p. 1993. 14.95 (1-56236-210-0) Aspen Bks.

Riches of Faith: The First Principle of the Gospel in the Lives of the Prophets & Saints. Ed. by John K. Challis & John G. Scott. LC 95-6363. 276p. 1995. pap. 9.95 (1-56236-214-3) Aspen Bks.

***Riches of France.** Clemente. Date not set. pap. 19.95 (0-312-15640-5) St Martin.

Riches of His Grace. Robert Menzies. 175p. 1956. 9.50 (0-227-67583-5) Attic Pr.

Riches of Holiness. Henry E. Brockett. pap. 4.99 (0-88019-169-4) Schmul Pub Co.

An Asterisk (*) at the beginning of an entry indicates that the title is appearing in BIP for the first time.

R

Riches of Prayer. Olavi Kaukola. Tr. & Pref. by Bernhard Hillila. 80p. (YA). 1991. reprint ed. pap. 7.95 (*0-8006-1861-0*) Polaris AZ.

Riches of Rag. Roger Grove. (Frances Clark Library for Piano Students). 16p. (Orig.). (J). (gr. k-12). 1976. pap. text ed. 5.95 (*0-87487-188-3*) Summy-Birchard.

Riches of the Heart. Margaret Johnson. LC 95-94885. 192p. 1995. 17.95 (*0-8034-9144-1*) Bouregy.

Riches of the West: A Sourcebook on the American West. Ed. by Carter Smith. LC 91-31127. (American Albums from the Collections of the Library of Congress). (Illus.). 96p. (J). (gr. 5-8). 1992. lib. bdg. 19.90 (*1-56294-132-1*) Millbrook Pr.

Riches of the West: A Sourcebook on the American West. Ed. by Carter Smith. LC 91-31127. (American Albums from the Collections of the Library of Congress). (Illus.). 96p. (J). (gr. 5-8). 1996. pap. 8.95 (*0-7613-0155-0*) Millbrook Pr.

Riches Stored in Secret Places. V. Davis. 1994. 12.99 (*0-8499-1166-4*) Word Pub.

***Riches Stored in Secret Places: A Devotional Guide for Those Who Hunger after the Deep Things of God.** Jennifer K. Dean. 159p. 1997. pap. 12.95 (*1-56309-203-4*, New Hope) Womans Mission Union.

Riches Stored in Secret Places see Let Me Grieve, but Not Forever

Riches to Rags: The Political Economy of Social Waste. Folke Dovring. 170p. 1984. 18.95 (*0-87073-514-4*); pap. 14.95 (*0-87073-515-2*) Schenkman Bks Inc.

Riches Within Your Reach. Robert Collier. 1984. 18.95 (*0-912576-14-6*); pap. 11.45 (*0-912576-13-8*) R Collier.

Richest Girl in the World. Stephanie Mansfield. 480p. 1994. mass mkt. 4.99 (*1-55817-792-2*, Pinncle Kensgtn) Kensgtn Pub Corp.

Richest Hole on Earth: A History of the Bingham Copper Mine. Leonard J. Arrington & Gary B. Hansen. LC 63-64592. (Utah State University. Monograph Ser.: Vol. 11, No. 1). 103p. (Orig.). reprint ed. pap. 29.40 (*0-8357-7908-4*, 2036336) Bks Demand.

Richest Kid in the World. Carol Gorman. LC 92-24935. (Tree House Kids Ser.: Bk. 3). (Illus.). 64p. (Orig.). (J). (gr. 1-4). 1993. pap. 3.99 (*0-570-04728-5*, 56-1687) Concordia.

Richest Kid in the World. Robert Hawks. 144p. (Orig.). (J). 1992. pap. 2.99 (*0-380-76241-2*, Camelot) Avon.

Richest Kid in the World: The Sixty Billion Dollar Fugitive. Robert Hawks. 160p. (Orig.). (J). (gr. 5). 1992. pap. 3.50 (*0-380-76242-0*, Camelot) Avon.

Richest Kids in Town. Peg Kehret. LC 93-47271. 128p. (J). (gr. 4 up). 1994. pap. 13.99 (*0-525-65166-7*, Cobblehill Bks) Dutton Child Bks.

***Richest Kids in Town.** Peg Kehret. (YA). 1997. mass mkt. 3.99 (*0-671-52940-4*, Minstrel Bks) PB.

Richest Lady in Town. rev. ed. Joyce L. Heatherley. 139p. 1992. pap. 7.95 (*0-929488-15-6*) Balcony Pub Inc.

Richest Man in Babylon. George S. Clason. pap. 6.95 (*0-8015-9006-X*, Dutton) NAL-Dutton.

Richest Man in Babylon. George S. Clason. 1989. pap. 10.95 (*0-452-26725-0*, Plume) NAL-Dutton.

Richest Man in Babylon. George S. Clason. 160p. 1988. pap. 3.50 (*0-451-15338-3*, Sig) NAL-Dutton.

Richest Man in Babylon. George S. Clason. 1988. pap. 4.99 (*0-451-16520-9*, Sig) NAL-Dutton.

Richest Man There Ever Was or Ever Will Be: The Financial Laws of Your Future. David L. Matthews, 3rd. Ed. by Mike Collins. LC 94-69820. 106p. 1994. pap. 14.95 (*0-9644282-0-2*) Stick To The Word.

Richest Vein: Eastern Tradition & Modern Thought. 2nd ed. James R. Wetmore. (Perennial Wisdom Ser.). 233p. 1995. reprint ed. pap. text ed. 19.95 (*0-900588-05-5*) S Perennis.

***Richest Vein: The Eastern Tradition & Modern Thought.** Charles Le Gai Eaton. 1996. pap. 18.95 (*0-614-21334-7*, 1079) Kazi Pubns.

Richey Clovis Cache: Earliest Americans along the Columbia River. Richard M. Gramly. LC 92-42771. (Monographs in Archaeology). (Illus.). 69p. (Orig.). (C). 1992. pap. text ed. 12.95 (*0-9615462-8-X*) Persimmon NY.

Richey Descendants. C. Edelbute. 93p. 1994. reprint ed. pap. 18.00 (*0-8328-4156-0*); reprint ed. lib. bdg. 28.00 (*0-8328-4157-9*) Higginson Bk Co.

***Richfield Springs & Vicinity: Historical, Biographical & Descriptive.** W. T. Bailey. (Illus.). 227p. 1997. reprint ed. lib. bdg. 29.50 (*0-8328-6212-6*) Higginson Bk Co.

Richie & the Fritzes. Marjorie W. Sharmat. LC 96-25798. (Trophy Chapter Bk.). Orig. Title: Chasing after Annie. (Illus.). 80p. (J). (gr. 3-6). 1997. pap. 3.95 (*0-06-442055-8*, Trophy) HarpC Child Bks.

Richie Benaud: Test Match Career. Spellmount Ltd. Publishers Staff. (C). 1992. 90.00 (*0-946771-99-5*, Pub. by Spellmount UK) St Mut.

Richie F. Dweebly Thunders On! Malcolm Yorke. LC 93-5003. (Teachers Secrets Ser.). (Illus.). 32p. (J). (gr. 1-4). 1994. 10.95 (*1-56458-199-3*) DK Pub Inc.

Richie Rich. Jordan Horowitz. 208p. (YA). 1994. pap. 3.50 (*0-590-25086-8*) Scholastic Inc.

Richie's Rocket. Joan Anderson. LC 92-38417. (Illus.). 32p. (J). (gr. k up). 1993. lib. bdg. 14.93 (*0-688-11305-2*, Morrow Junior) Morrow.

Richitos De Oro y los Tres Osos. (Spanish Well Loved Tales Ser.: No. 700-3). (SPA.). (J). (gr. 1). 1990. boxed 3.50 (*0-7214-1406-0*, Ladybrd) Penguin.

***Richland County, Ohio Newspapers: Abstracts & Extracts 1830-1849.** Ed. by Kerry L. Kimberly. LC 96-69412. 407p. 1996. 37.50 (*0-89725-265-9*, 1747) Picton Pr.

Richland Crossing: A Portrait of Texas Pioneers. Walter C. Dixson. 386p. 1994. pap. 25.00 (*0-9649936-0-0*) Peppermill Pub.

***Richland Home Centers, Inc. Annual Report: A Financial Analysis Case, 5 Vols.** 3rd ed. Marian Powers & Belverd E. Needles. (C). 1993. teacher ed., text ed. 11.96 (*0-395-65551-X*) HM.

***Richland Street.** Kevin O'Kelly. LC 96-61466. 283p. (Orig.). 1997. pap. 18.95 (*0-9653864-5-7*) Wacahoota Pr.

Richmond: A Pictorial History. Gertude Ward. (Indiana Pictorial History Ser.). (Illus.). 1994. write for info. (*0-943963-42-7*) G Bradley.

Richmond: The Story of a City. enl. rev. ed. Virginius Dabney. LC 89-38881. (Illus.). 436p. 1990. pap. 16.95 (*0-8139-1274-1*) U Pr of Va.

***Richmond: The Story of a City.** expanded rev. ed. Virginius Dabney. LC 89-38881. reprint ed. pap. 143.70 (*0-608-04567-5*, 2065306) Bks Demand.

Richmond - Rosenberg. San Antonio Cartographers Staff. 1996. 2.95 (*0-671-56293-2*) Macmillan.

Richmond & Kew Green: A Souvenir Guide. Nicholas Reed. 1992. pap. 29.95 (*0-9515258-6-7*, Pub. by Lilburne Pr UK) St Mut.

Richmond City & Henrico County, Virginia: 1850 U. S. Census. Virginia Genealogical Society Staff. 505p. 1981. pap. 20.00 (*0-89308-267-8*, VA 32) Southern Hist Pr.

Richmond County: Virginia Publick Claims. Janice L. Abercrombie & Richard Slatten. (Virginia Publick Claims Ser.). ix, 20p. 1991. pap. 5.00 (*0-8095-8676-2*) Borgo Pr.

Richmond County: Virginia Publick Claims. Janice L. Abercrombie & Richard Slatten. (Virginia Publick Claims Ser.). ix, 20p. (C). 1991. reprint ed. lib. bdg. 25.00 (*0-8095-8357-7*) Borgo Pr.

Richmond County, North Carolina Marriage Bonds & Certificates, 1783-1868. Francis T. Ingmire. 26p. 1994. pap. 8.00 (*0-8095-8675-4*); lib. bdg. 25.00 (*0-8095-8077-2*) Borgo Pr.

Richmond County, Virginia, Court Orders, 1721-1752: An Every-Name Index. 172p. 1996. spiral bd. 20.00 (*1-57445-022-0*) TLC Genealogy.

Richmond County, Virginia, Deeds and Bonds, 1721-1734. T.L.C. Genealogy Staff. LC 91-65234. 155p. (Orig.). 1991. spiral bd., pap. 14.00 (*1-57445-004-2*) TLC Genealogy.

Richmond County, Virginia Deeds, 1734-1741. T.L.C. Genealogy Staff. LC 91-65234. 101p. (Orig.). 1991. spiral bd. 14.00 (*1-57445-005-0*) TLC Genealogy.

Richmond County, Virginia Deeds, 1741-1750. T.L.C. Genealogy Staff. 107p. (Orig.). 1992. spiral bd. 14.00 (*1-57445-006-9*) TLC Genealogy.

Richmond County, Virginia Marriage Books, 1797-1853. Ed. by Anne W. Reddy & Andrew L. Riffe, IV. 158p. 1994. reprint ed. pap. 16.00 (*0-8328-4016-5*) Higginson Bk Co.

Richmond During the Revolution, 1775-1783. Harry M. Ward & Harold E. Greer, Jr. LC 77-22586. 205p. 1977. text ed. 30.00 (*0-8139-0715-2*) U Pr of Va.

Richmond During the War: Four Years of Personal Observation. Sallie B. Putnam. LC 96-20643. xxi, 373p. 1996. pap. 16.95 (*0-8032-8745-3*, Bison Books) U of Nebr Pr.

Richmond Eighteen Eighty-Seven: A Quaker Drama Unfolds. Mark Minear. LC 87-7603. 150p. 1987. pap. 6.95 (*0-913408-98-0*) Friends United.

Richmond Examiner During the War. John M. Daniel. LC 76-125690. (American Journalists Ser.). 1977. reprint ed. 23.95 (*0-405-01667-0*) Ayer.

Richmond Family Records, Vol. I: Maryland, Virginia, New England, Ireland & Somerset. H. I. Richmond. 232p. 1994. reprint ed. pap. 37.00 (*0-8328-4134-X*); reprint ed. lib. bdg. 47.00 (*0-8328-4133-1*) Higginson Bk Co.

Richmond Family Records, Vol. II: The Richmonds Alias Webb, of Wiltshire, England. H. I. Richmond. 265p. 1994. reprint ed. pap. 42.00 (*0-8328-6576-1*); reprint ed. lib. bdg. 52.00 (*0-8328-4132-3*) Higginson Bk Co.

Richmond Family Records, Vol. III: The Richmonds of Wiltshire, England. H. I. Richmond. 327p. 1994. reprint ed. pap. 49.50 (*0-8328-4130-7*); reprint ed. lib. bdg. 59.50 (*0-8328-4129-3*) Higginson Bk Co.

Richmond Family, 1594-1896, & Pre-American Ancestry, 1040-1594. J. B. Richmond. (Illus.). 633p. 1989. reprint ed. pap. 95.00 (*0-8328-1023-1*); reprint ed. lib. bdg. 103.00 (*0-8328-1022-3*) Higginson Bk Co.

Richmond, Fayette, Hampden, Thomas & Blount's Lynchburg Artillery. Robert H. Moore. (Virginia Regimental Histories Ser.). (Illus.). 178p. 1991. 19.95 (*1-56190-018-4*) H E Howard.

***Richmond, Fredericksburg & Potomac Railroad: The Capitol Cities Route.** William Griffin, Jr. (Illus.). 204p. 1996. 28.95 (*1-883089-12-3*) TLC VA.

***Richmond, Her Past & Present.** W. Asbury Christian. (Illus.). 618p. 1997. reprint ed. lib. bdg. 64.00 (*0-8328-6521-4*) Higginson Bk Co.

Richmond Hill Plantation, Eighteen Ten to Eighteen Sixty-Eight: The Discovery of Antebellum Life on a Waccamaw Rice Plantation. James L Michie. LC 89-24298. (Illus.). xx, 204p. 1990. 24.95 (*0-87152-441-4*) Reprint.

Richmond Howitzers. Lee Wallace. (Virginia Regimental Histories Ser.). (Illus.). 171p. 1994. write for info. (*1-56190-057-5*) H E Howard.

Richmond Howitzers in the War. Frederick S. Daniel. 1976. 27.95 (*0-8488-0974-2*) Amereon Ltd.

Richmond Illustrated: Unusual Stories of a City. David D. Ryan. (Illus.). 94p. 1993. 16.95 (*0-87517-071-4*) Dietz.

Richmond in Be-Gone Days: Being Reminiscences of an Old Citizen. Samuel Mordecai. LC 75-1861. (Leisure Class in America Ser.). 1975. reprint ed. 23.95 (*0-405-06927-8*) Ayer.

***Richmond in By-Gone Days, Being Reminiscences of an Old Citizen.** George M. West. (Illus.). 321p. 1997. reprint ed. lib. bdg. 32.00 (*0-8328-6523-0*) Higginson Bk Co.

Richmond in World War II. Francis E. Lutz. 1951. 7.50 (*0-87517-026-9*) Dietz.

Richmond Index to the Genera & Species of Birds. Smithsonian Institution Staff. 1992. 545.00 (*0-8161-1795-0*, Hall Library) G K Hall.

***Richmond Informer.** (Illus.). 300p. (Orig.). 1997. pap. 29.95 (*0-9656604-0-0*) Spectra Media.

***Richmond Is for Children.** 4th ed. Sabot School Richmond, Va. Staff. LC 97-18026. 1997. write for info. (*1-883522-19-6*) Rockbridge Pub.

Richmond Lecture: Its Purpose. John Tasker. (C). 1989. 25.00 (*0-9502723-0-2*, Pub. by Brynmill Pr Ltd UK) St Mut.

Richmond Reader, 1773-1983. Ed. by Maurice Duke & Daniel P. Jordan. LC 82-21921. (Illus.). xxii, 446p. 1983. 16.95 (*0-8078-1546-2*) U of NC Pr.

***Richmond Register, 1904 (Town History of Directory)** Compiled by Mitchell & Denning. (Illus.). 103p. 1997. reprint ed. pap. 15.00 (*0-8328-5903-6*) Higginson Bk Co.

Richmond School Decision. Merhige. LC 72-83394. pap. 6.00 (*0-912008-02-4*) Equity & Excel.

Richmond Stage, 1784-1812. Martin S. Shockley. LC 76-16866. (Illus.). 463p. reprint ed. pap. 132.00 (*0-8357-3142-1*, 2039405) Bks Demand.

Richmond Theater Fire, 1862. J. Wayne Beachy. (Illus.). 24p. (Orig.). (J). (gr. 5 up). 1987. pap. 3.00 (*0-9608084-3-4*) B Hawkins Studio.

Richmond Theatre, Yorkshire: A History of the Georgian Theatre, One of Only Four Remaining 18th Century English Playhouses. Sybil Rosenfield. (C). 1989. 34.00 (*0-900657-91-X*, Pub. by W Sessions UK) St Mut.

Richmond, Virginia: The Travel Guide for Kids. Lynn Evans. (J). 1991. pap. 5.00 (*0-945600-07-0*) Colormore Inc.

Richmond, Virginia - Home of the Confederate Navy, & its Aid to the Cause. L. Peter Wren. (Illus.). 80p. 1989. 7.95 (*0-685-35610-8*) L P Wren.

Richmond Volunteers: The Volunteer Companies of the City of Richmond & Henrico County, Virginia, 1861-1865. Louis H. Manarin & Lee A. Wallace, Jr. LC 72-100103. 312p. reprint ed. pap. 89.00 (*0-8357-9815-1*, 2014632) Bks Demand.

Richmond's Civil War Prisons. Sandra V. Parker. (Virginia Civil War Battles & Leaders Ser.). (Illus.). 101p. 1990. 19.95 (*0-930919-97-1*) H E Howard.

***Richmond's Fan District.** Drew St. J. Carneal. (Illus.). 1996. 35.00 (*1-889569-02-X*) Historic Richmond.

Richmondtown & Lighthouse Hill, NY. M. Ferrer. (Images of America Ser.). 128p. 1996. pap. 16.99 (*0-7524-0403-2*, Arcdia) Chalford.

Richmondtown Recipes - Three Centuries of Staten Island Cookery. Dorothy Fingado & Loretta McMillen. (Illus.). 1976. spiral bd. 6.00 (*0-9606756-3-9*) Staten Island.

***Richness of Contract Law: An Analysis & Critique of Contemporary Theories of Contract Law.** Robert A. Hillman. LC 96-49726. (Law & Philosophy Library). 300p. (C). 1997. lib. bdg. 115.00 (*0-7923-4336-0*) Kluwer Ac.

Rich/Poor Man's Guide to Pittsburgh. Dorthy Miller. Date not set. 12.95 (*0-944101-13-5*) New Pittsburgh.

***Rich's Business Guide to Silicon Valley & Northern California, 1996-97.** 808p. 1996. ring bd. 299.00 (*0-914189-43-3*) Busn Direct CA.

***Rich's Everyday Sales Prospecting Directory to Alameda County: 1997 Edition.** 323p. 1996. ring bd. 97.50 (*0-914189-44-1*) Busn Direct CA.

***Rich's Everyday Sales Prospecting Directory to Contra Costa County, 1996.** 214p. 1996. ring bd. 79.50 (*0-914189-42-5*) Busn Direct CA.

***Rich's Everyday Sales Prospecting Directory to San Francisco County, 1997.** rev. ed. 271p. 1997. ring bd. 79.50 (*0-914189-46-8*) Busn Direct CA.

***Rich's Everyday Sales Prospecting Directory to San Mateo County, 1997.** rev. ed. 248p. 1997. ring bd. 79.50 (*0-914189-45-X*) Busn Direct CA.

Richt Choice: A Complete Guide to Evaluating, Selecting, & Installing MRP II Software. Christopher D. Gray. 205p. 1995. text ed. 45.00 (*0-471-14246-8*) Wiley.

***Richter 10.** Mike Mcquay. 416p. 1997. mass mkt. 6.99 (*0-553-57333-0*) Bantam.

Richter und Sein Henker. Friedrich Durrenmatt. Ed. by William Gillis & J. J. Neumaier. (C). 1972. pap. 25.56 (*0-395-04499-5*) HM.

Richter 10. Arthur C. Clarke & Mike McQuay. LC 95-40649. 384p. 1996. 22.95 (*0-553-09708-3*, Spectra) Bantam.

Richter 10. large type ed. Arthur C. Clarke & Mike McQuay. LC 96-10457. 644p. 1996. 24.95 (*0-7862-0694-2*, Thorndike Lrg Prnt) Thorndike Pr.

***Richter's Anchor Stone Building Sets: Richter's Union Blocks.** George F. Hardy. (Illus.). 242p. 1993. 69.95 (*0-9656288-0-9*) G Hardy.

***Richters Anker-Steinbaukasten.** George F. Hardy. Tr. by Claus Ahlers. (Illus.). 242p. (GER.). 1995. 100.00 (*0-9656288-1-7*) G Hardy.

Richterzeit & Konigtum: Redaktionsgeschichtliche Studien zum Richterbuch. Uwe Becker. (Beiheft zur Zeitschrift fuer die Alttestamentliche Wissenschaft Ser.: Band 192). ix, 326p. (C). 1990. lib. bdg. 90.80 (*3-11-012440-8*) De Gruyter.

Richthofen: Beyond the Legend of the Red Barron. Peter Kilduff. (Illus.). 256p. 1995. pap. text ed. 17.95 (*0-471-12033-2*) Wiley.

Richtig Schreiben Leicht Gelemt. Mentor Lernhilfen. (GER.). 21.00 (*3-580-64120-4*) Langenscheidt.

Richtiges Deutsch. (Duden Ser.: Vol. 9). 803p. 1985. 33.50 (*3-411-20909-7*, Pub. by Bibliogr Inst Brockhaus GW) Langenscheidt.

Richtlinien zur Infusionstherapie mit Aminosaeuren. Ed. by P. Schoelmerich & H. Schoenborn. (Beitraege zur Infusionstherapie und Klinische Ernaehrung Ser.: Band 4). (Illus.). 1979. pap. 13.75 (*3-8055-3058-7*) S Karger.

Richtofen: Beyond the Legacy of the Red Baron. Peter Kilduff. 256p. 1994. text ed. 27.95 (*0-471-00877-X*) Wiley.

Ricitos de Oro - Little Book. Addison-Wesley Staff. (Spanish Elementary Ser.). (Illus.). 16p. (SPA.). (J). (gr. k-3). 1989. pap. text ed. 4.50 (*0-201-19707-3*) Addison-Wesley.

Ricitos De Oro y los Tres Ositos. (Illus.). 32p. (J). (ps-2). 1996. pap. 2.99 (*0-7214-5602-2*, Ladybrd) Penguin.

Ricitos de Oro y los Tres Osos. Illus. by Gill Guile. (Habia una Vez...Ser.). 24p. (ENG & SPA.). (J). (ps-1). 1995. 3.98 (*1-85854-356-8*) Brimax Bks.

Ricitos de Oro y los Tres Osos Big Book. Addison-Wesley Staff. (Spanish Elementary Ser.). (Illus.). 16p. (SPA.). (J). (gr. k-3). 1989. pap. text ed. 31.75 (*0-201-19935-1*) Addison-Wesley.

Ricitos Dorados y los Tres Osos. Illus. & Adapted by James Marshall. LC 95-22739. 32p. (J). (ps-3). 1996. pap. 14.99 (*0-8037-1990-6*) Dial Bks Young.

Rick & Jim's Real Reel Indians. Richard A. Payne. (Illus.). 32p. (Orig.). 1994. pap. text ed. 7.95 (*0-9636186-8-7*) Blue Sky Grap.

Rick & Po: Village Detectives, Bk. 1. Dorothy B. Artes. LC 86-50878. (Illus.). 98p. (Orig.). (J). (gr. 4-8). 1987. pap. 3.50 (*0-932433-28-6*) Windswept Hse.

Rick & Po, Special Agents, Bk. 2. Dorothy B. Artes. Ed. by Jane Weinberger. LC 87-51328. (Illus.). 66p. (Orig.). (J). (gr. 4-8). 1988. pap. 3.50 (*0-932433-39-1*) Windswept Hse.

Rick Barry's Pro Basketball Bible: 1995-96 Edition. Rick Barry & Jordan Cohn. (Illus.). 450p. (Orig.). 1995. pap. 18.95 (*0-9636385-7-2*) Basketball Bks.

***Rick Barry's Pro Basketball Bible (1996-97 Edition)** 8th ed. Rick Barry & Jordan Cohn. (Illus.). 400p. 1996. pap. 19.95 (*0-9636385-5-6*) Basketball Bks.

Rick Bayless' Mexican Kitchen. Rick Bayless & Deann G. Bayless. 416p. 1996. 35.00 (*0-684-80006-3*) S&S Trade.

Rick Goes to Little League. D. Walker. 1983. 3.95 (*0-89803-097-8*) Walker Pub Co.

Rick Heads for Soccer. D. Walker. 1985. 3.95 (*0-89803-115-X*) Walker Pub Co.

Rick Mather: Urban Approaches. Hugh Pearman. (Illus.). 112p. 1993. pap. 29.95 (*1-85702-007-3*, Pub. by Fourth Estate UK) Trafalgar.

Rick O'Shay: The Dailies, 1959-1960, No. 1. Stan Lynde. LC 94-69453. (Illus.). 168p. (Orig.). 1994. pap. 18.95 (*1-886370-00-1*, BK61) Cttnwd Pub.

Rick O'Shay: The Dailies, 1961-1962, No. 2. Stan Lynde. LC 95-68475. 160p. 1995. pap. text ed. 20.00 (*1-886370-01-X*, BK62) Cttnwd Pub.

Rick O'Shay, Hipshot & Me: A Memoir. 2nd ed. Stan Lynde. Ed. by Mike Gold. LC 90-82941. (Illus.). 264p. 1990. reprint ed. pap. 18.95 (*0-9626999-0-X*, BK02) Cttnwd Pub.

***Rick O'Shay, the Dailies: 1958.** Stan Lynde. (Illus.). 88p. (Orig.). 1996. reprint ed. pap. 14.95 (*1-886370-09-5*, BK-70) Cttnwd Pub.

Rick O'Shay, the Dailies: 1963-1964. Stan Lynde. (Illus.). 176p. 1996. reprint ed. pap. 18.95 (*1-886370-02-8*, BK-63) Cttnwd Pub.

Rick Spence's Clippper 5.2 Power Programmer's Guide. Rick Spence. LC 93-84823. 816p. 1993. 44.95 (*0-7821-1097-5*) Sybex.

Rick Spence's Guide to CA-Visual Objects. Rick Spence. LC 94-69704. 703p. 1995. pap. 29.99 incl. cd-rom (*0-7821-1668-X*) Sybex.

Rick Springfield. Simone Gillianti. (J). 1984. lib. bdg. write for info. (*0-671-53104-2*) S&S Trade.

***Rick Steves' Baltics & Russia, 1997.** Rick Steves & Ian Watson. 160p. 1997. pap. 9.95 (*1-56261-325-1*) John Muir.

***Rick Steves' Best of Europe, 1998.** rev. ed. Rick Steves. 576p. 1998. pap. 18.95 (*1-56261-384-7*) John Muir.

***Rick Steves' Europe Through the Back Door 1997.** 15th ed. Rick Steves. LC 96-30868. 512p. 1997. pap. 19.95 (*1-56261-333-2*) John Muir.

***Rick Steves' Europe Through the Back Door 1998.** rev. ed. Rick Steves. (Illus.). 512p. 1998. pap. 19.95 (*1-56261-392-8*) John Muir.

***Rick Steves' Europe, 1997.** Rick Steves. 576p. 1997. pap. 18.95 (*1-56261-326-X*) John Muir.

***Rick Steves' France, Belgium & the Netherlands, 1997.** Rick Steves & Steve Smith. 304p. 1997. pap. 15.95 (*1-56261-327-8*) John Muir.

***Rick Steves' France, Belgium & the Netherlands 1998.** rev. ed. Rick Steves & Steve Smith. 304p. 1998. pap. 15.95 (*1-56261-385-5*) John Muir.

Rick Steves' French, Italian & German Phrasebook & Dictionary. 2nd rev. ed. Rick Steves. (Illus.). 320p. (Orig.). (FRE, GER & ITA.). 1996. pap. 7.95 (*1-56261-314-6*) John Muir.

Rick Steves' French Phrasebook & Dictionary. 3rd rev. ed. Rick Steves. (Illus.). 192p. (Orig.). (FRE.). 1996. pap. 5.95 (*1-56261-311-1*) John Muir.

Rick Steves' German Phrasebook & Dictionary. 3rd rev. ed. Rick Steves. (Illus.). 192p. (Orig.). (GER.). 1996. pap. 5.95 (*1-56261-312-X*) John Muir.

***Rick Steves' Germany, Austria & Switzerland, 1997.** Rick Steves. 272p. 1997. pap. 14.95 (*1-56261-328-6*) John Muir.

***Rick Steves' Germany, Austria & Switzerland 1998.** rev. ed. Rick Steves. 272p. 1998. pap. 14.95 (*1-56261-386-3*) John Muir.

***Rick Steves' Great Britain & Ireland, 1997.** Rick Steves. 320p. 1997. pap. 15.95 (*1-56261-329-4*) John Muir.

R

***Rick Steves' Great Britain & Ireland 1998.** rev. ed. Rick Steves. 320p. 1998. pap. 15.95 (*1-56261-387-1*) John Muir.

Rick Steves' Italian Phrasebook & Dictionary. 3rd rev. ed. Rick Steves. (Illus.). 192p. (Orig.). (ITA.). 1996. pap. 5.95 (*1-56261-313-8*) John Muir.

***Rick Steves' Italy, 1997.** Rick Steves. 224p. 1997. pap. 13.95 (*1-56261-330-8*) John Muir.

***Rick Steves' Italy 1998.** rev. ed. Rick Steves. 224p. 1998. pap. 13.95 (*1-56261-388-X*) John Muir.

***Rick Steves' Russia & the Baltics 1998.** rev. ed. Rick Steves & Ian Watson. 160p. 1998. pap. 9.95 (*1-56261-389-8*) John Muir.

***Rick Steves' Scandinavia, 1997.** Rick Steves. 192p. 1997. pap. 13.95 (*1-56261-331-6*) John Muir.

***Rick Steves' Scandinavia 1998.** rev. ed. Rick Steves. 192p. 1998. pap. 13.95 (*1-56261-390-1*) John Muir.

***Rick Steves' Spain & Portugal, 1997.** Rick Steves. 240p. 1997. pap. 13.95 (*1-56261-332-4*) John Muir.

***Rick Steves' Spain & Portugal 1998.** rev. ed. Rick Steves. 240p. 1998. pap. 13.95 (*1-56261-391-X*) John Muir.

Rick Steves' Spanish & Portuguese Phrasebook & Dictionary. 3rd rev. ed. Rick Steves. (Illus.). 336p. (Orig.). (ENG, POR & SPA.). 1996. pap. 7.95 (*1-56261-315-4*) John Muir.

Rick Tees Off. David Walker. Ed. by Malcolm Wright. (Illus.). 112p. (Orig.). (J). (gr. 4-9). 1985. pap. text ed. 3.95 (*0-9614856-0-4*) Pro Golfers.

Rickahaw Beijing: City People & Politics in the 1920s. David Strand. 1993. pap. 15.95 (*0-520-08286-9*) U CA Pr.

Rickenbacker. Edward V. Rickenbacker. (Airlines History Project Ser.). (Illus.). reprint ed. 57.50 (*0-404-19332-3*) AMS Pr.

Rickenbacker: The History of the Rickenbacker Guitar. Richard R. Smith. LC 87-71571. (Illus.). 256p. 1987. pap. 29.95 (*0-931759-15-3*, 00000098) Centerstream Pub.

Rickenbacker Book: A Complete History of Rickenbacker Guitars. Tony Bacon & Paul Day. (Illus.). 96p. (Orig.). 1994. text ed. 19.95 (*0-87930-329-8*) Miller Freeman.

***Rickerson. The Diary of Achsa M. Tubbs-Rickerson, 1876-1901, Spring Creek, Warren Co., Pa.** Ed. by Don Rickerson, Jr. (Illus.). 137p. 1996. reprint ed. pap. 19.00 (*0-8328-5392-5*); reprint ed. lib. bdg. 29.00 (*0-8328-5391-7*) Higginson Bk Co.

Rickettsial & Chlamydial Diseases of Domestic Animals. Ed. by Zerai Woldehiwet & Miodrag Ristic. LC 92-34988. 1993. 160.00 (*0-08-040831-1*, Pergamon Pr) Elsevier.

***Rickettsial Infection & Immunity.** LC 97-22825. (Volume in Infectious Agents & Pathogenesis Ser.). (Illus.). (C). 1997. write for info. (*0-306-45528-5*, Plenum Pr) Plenum.

Rickey Henderson: Record Stealer. Ann Bauleke. (Sports Achievers Ser.). (Illus.). 48p. (J). (gr. 4-9). 1991. lib. bdg. 17.50 (*0-8225-0541-X*, Lerner Publctns) Lerner Group.

Rickey Henderson: Record Stealer. Ann Bauleke. (Illus.). 64p. (J). (gr. 4-9). 1992. pap. 4.95 (*0-8225-9597-4*, Lerner Publctns) Lerner Group.

Rickie. Frederick Flach. 1991. mass mkt. 5.99 (*0-345-37359-6*) Ballantine.

Rickover & the Nuclear Navy: The Discipline of Technology. Francis Duncan. LC 89-39097. 480p. 1990. 29.95 (*0-87021-236-2*) Naval Inst Pr.

Rickover Effect: How One Man Made a Difference. Theodore Rockwell. LC 92-3909. (Illus.). 411p. 1992. 32.95 (*1-55750-702-3*) Naval Inst Pr.

Rickover Effect: The Inside Story of How Adm. Hyman Rickover Built the Nuclear Navy. Theodore Rockwell. LC 95-19843. 411p. 1995. pap. text ed. 19.95 (*0-471-12296-3*) Wiley.

Ricks: History & Genealogy of the Ricks Family of America, Descendants of Isaac Ricks, born in England, 1638, & His Wife Kathren, & Allied Families. rev. ed. Compiled by Howard Ricks et al. (Illus.). 767p. 1994. reprint ed. pap. 109.00 (*0-8328-4089-0*); reprint ed. lib. bdg. 119.00 (*0-8328-4088-2*) Higginson Bk Co.

Rickshaw: The Novel Lo-t'o hsiang Tzu. Lao She. Tr. by Jean M. James from CHI. LC 79-10658. Orig. Title: Lo-to Hsiang Tzu. (C). 1979. pap. text ed. 10.00 (*0-8248-0655-7*) UH Pr.

Rickshaw Beijing: City People & Politics in the 1920s. David Strand. 1989. 45.00 (*0-520-06311-2*) U CA Pr.

***Ricky & the Hammond Cousins.** Wanda Yoder. 170p. (Orig.). (YA). (gr. 5 up). 1996. pap. 5.95 (*0-87813-562-6*) Christian Light.

Ricky Lee Jones - Flying Cowboys: Piano - Vocal. Ed. by Milton Okun. (Illus.). 67p. (Orig.). 1990. pap. text ed. 14.95 (*0-89524-505-1*) Cherry Lane.

Ricky Nelson, Vol. 11. CPP Belwin Staff. (Legendary Performer Ser.). 1990. pap. 14.95 (*0-89898-620-6*, TPF0153) Warner Brothers.

Ricky Skaggs Songbook. 80p. 1983. per. 12.95 (*0-7935-0905-X*, 00308084) H Leonard.

Ricky the Raccoon. (Frog Pond Ser.). (Illus.). (J). (ps-1). 2.98 (*0-517-46985-5*) Random Hse Value.

Ricky Van Shelton Songbook. (Piano-Vocal-Guitar Ser.). 80p. 1989. per. 12.95 (*0-7935-3401-1*, 00490188) H Leonard.

Ricky's Adventure in Alaska. James L. Jordan. (Ricky Shafer Ser.). (Illus.). 176p. (J). (gr. 4-6). 1995. pap. 4.95 (*0-9630534-1-8*) Living Water.

Ricky's Last Chance. James L. Jordan. 104p. (J). (gr. 4-6). 1991. pap. 3.95 (*0-9630534-0-X*) Living Water.

RICO, 2 vols., Vols. 1 & 2. David R. McCormack. 1988. Vol. 1, 350 pp., Vol. 2, 350 pp. ring bd. 185.00 (*1-878337-18-1*) Knowles Law.

RICO: Civil & Criminal, Law & Strategy. Ed. by Jed S. Rakoff & Howard W. Goldstein. 650p. 1989. ring bd. 110.00 (*0-317-05402-3*, 00609) NY Law Pub.

RICO in Business & Commercial Litigation. Kevin P. Roddy. 1840p. 1991. ring bd. 160.00 (*0-07-017989-1*) Shepards.

RICO in Business & Commercial Litigation. McGraw-Hill Staff Shepard's. 1991. text ed. 190.00 (*0-07-017898-4*) McGraw.

RICO Pleading Manual & Index. 1990. 30.00 (*0-317-05915-7*, PB16) Natl Attys General.

Rico You, the Writer. Barbara R. Rico. (C). 1997. 27.96 (*0-395-68635-0*) HM.

Ricochet. large type ed. Basil Copper. (Linford Mystery Library). 304p. 1993. pap. 15.99 (*0-7089-7382-5*, Linford) Ulverscroft.

Ricochet River. Robin Cody. 288p. 1994. reprint ed. pap. 11.95 (*0-936085-27-4*) Blue Heron OR.

Ricochets: Miniature Tales of Human Life. Andre Maurois. Tr. by Hamish Miles from FRE. LC 73-150551. (Short Story Index Reprint Ser.). 1977. reprint ed. 16.95 (*0-8369-3848-8*) Ayer.

Ricoeur & Kant: Philosophy of the Will. Pamela S. Anderson. LC 93-16101. (American Academy of Religion, Studies in Religion: Vol. 66). 165p. 1993. 29.95 (*1-55540-836-2*, 010066); pap. 19.95 (*1-55540-837-0*, 010066) Scholars Pr GA.

Ricoeur Reader: Reflection & Imagination. Paul Ricoeur. Ed. by Mario J. Valdes. 516p. 1991. 60.00 (*0-8020-5880-9*); pap. 24.95 (*0-8020-6814-6*) U of Toronto Pr.

Ricordi: Italian Text with English Translation. Franceseo Guicciardini. Tr. by Ninian H. Thomson. (C). 1949. 15.00 (*0-913298-41-7*) S F Vanni.

Ricordi: Things Remembered. Ed. by Minni. 1989. pap. 15.00 (*0-919349-97-8*) Guernica Editions.

Ricordi, Saggi e Testimonianze: Edizioni del Palazzo, Prato. Guiseppe Prezzolini et al. 300p. 1983. write for info. (*0-614-10138-7*) Am Inst Ital Stud.

Ricorso & Revelation: An Archetypal Poetics of Modernism. Evans L. Smith. (GERM Ser.). viii, 194p. 1995. 49.95 (*1-57113-066-7*) Camden Hse.

***Ricos en Cristo.** Warren W. Wiersbe. Ed. by Gary Hilliker. (New Testament Ser.). 169p. (SPA.). 1994. 7.95 (*1-879892-32-4*) Editorial Bautista.

***RICS Appraisal & Valuation Manual: The New Red Book.** RICS Books Staff. 300p. 1995. ring bd. 270.00 (*0-85406-699-3*, Pub. by R-I-C-S Bks UK) St Mut.

RICS Directory of International Practices. RICS Staff. 120p. (C). 1986. text ed. 75.00 (*0-685-40841-8*, Pub. by Surveyors Pubns) St Mut.

Riddall: Introduction to Land Law. 5th ed. J. G. Riddall. 592p. 1993. pap. 38.00 (*0-406-00589-3*, U.K.) MICHIE.

Riddall: Jurisprudence. J. G. Riddall. 1991. pap. 30.00 (*0-406-00064-3*) MICHIE.

Riddell of Rivermoon. large type ed. Miriam Macgregor. 1990. lib. bdg. 18.95 (*0-263-12348-0*, Pub. by Mills & Boon UK) Thorndike Pr.

Ridden Hard & Put up Wet. Keith Avery. LC 90-92078. (Illus.). vi, 62p. (Orig.). 1990. pap. 10.95 (*0-9624489-2-3*) G Logsdon Bks.

Ridden Hard & Put up Wet. limited ed. Keith Avery. LC 90-92078. (Illus.). vi, 62p. (Orig.). 1990. 50.00 (*0-9624489-3-1*) G Logsdon Bks.

Riddick's Rules of Procedure: A Modern Guide to Faster & More Efficient Meetings. Floyd M. Riddick & Miriam H. Butcher. LC 90-24274. 240p. 1991. reprint ed. pap. 14.95 (*0-8191-8064-5*) Madison Bks UPA.

Riddle. Mark Smith. (Illus.). vi, 78p. (Orig.). 1992. pap. 6.95 (*0-9634181-0-6*) Argo Pr.

Riddle. Neal Starkman. LC 89-25405. (Illus.). 50p. (Orig.). (J). (gr. 2-4). 1989. pap. 10.00 (*0-935529-13-6*) Comprehen Health Educ.

Riddle & Incest. Lawrence W. Markert. (New Poets Ser.: Vol. 3). 1974. pap. 1.95 (*0-932616-03-8*) Brick Hse Bks.

Riddle & Other Stories. Walter J. De La Mare. 1993. reprint ed. lib. bdg. 18.95 (*0-89968-423-8*, Lghtyr Pr) Buccaneer Bks.

Riddle & Other Tales. Walter J. De La Mare. 1976. 23.95 (*0-8488-0983-1*) Amereon Ltd.

***Riddle & the Rune.** Grace Chetwin. Date not set. write for info. (*0-688-05769-1*) Lothrop.

Riddle Book. Roy McKie. LC 77-85237. (Pictureback Ser.). (J). (ps-2). 1978. pap. 3.25 (*0-394-83732-0*); lib. bdg. 5.99 (*0-394-93732-5*) Random Bks Yng Read.

Riddle by the River. Marcia Vaughn. LC 93-46890. (Animal Fair Ser.). (J). (gr. 1 up). 1994. 14.95 (*0-382-24068-5*, Silver Pr NJ); lib. bdg. 10.95 (*0-382-24073-1*, Silver Pr NJ) Silver Burdett Pr.

Riddle by the River. Marcia Vaughn. LC 93-46890. (Animal Fair Ser.). (J). (gr. 1 up). 1994. pap. 4.95 (*0-382-24451-6*, Silver Pr NJ) Silver Burdett Pr.

Riddle City USA: A Book of Geography Riddles. Marco Maestro & Giulio Maestro. LC 93-16665. (Illus.). 64p. (J). (gr. 2-5). 1994. lib. bdg. 14.89 (*0-06-023369-9*) HarpC Child Bks.

Riddle-Day Saints. Rick Walton. LC 93-47423. 65p. (Orig.). 1993. pap. 5.95 (*0-87579-821-7*) Deseret Bk.

Riddle-Icious. J. Patrick Lewis. LC 93-43759. 40p. (J). (ps-4). 1996. 15.00 (*0-679-84011-7*); lib. bdg. 16.99 (*0-679-94011-1*) Knopf.

***Riddle-Icious.** J. Patrick Lewis. (J). 1997. pap. 6.99 (*0-679-88545-5*) Knopf.

***Riddle-icious.** J. Patrick Lewis. (Illus.). (J). (ps-3). 1997. reprint ed. pap. 6.99 (*0-614-28950-5*) Random Bks Yng Read.

Riddle in the Rare Book. Carolyn Keene. (Nancy Drew Ser.: No. 126). (J). (gr. 3-6). 1995. pap. 3.99 (*0-671-87209-5*, Minstrel Bks) PB.

Riddle King's Camp Riddles. Mike Thaler. LC 88-63193. (Riddle King Mini-Storybooks Ser.). (Illus.). 32p. (J). (gr. 1-5). 1989. pap. 1.25 (*0-394-83995-1*) Random Bks Yng Read.

Riddle King's Food Riddles. Mike Thaler. LC 88-63190. (Riddle King Mini-Storybooks Ser.). (Illus.). 32p. (J). (gr. 1-5). 1989. pap. 1.25 (*0-394-84041-0*) Random Bks Yng Read.

Riddle King's Pet Riddles. Mike Thaler. LC 88-63191. (Riddle King Mini-Storybooks Ser.). (Illus.). 32p. (J). (gr. 1-5). 1989. pap. 1.25 (*0-394-83977-3*) Random Bks Yng Read.

Riddle King's School Riddles. Mike Thaler. LC 88-63192. (Riddle King Mini-Storybooks Ser.). (Illus.). 32p. (J). (gr. 1-5). 1989. pap. 1.25 (*0-394-84004-6*) Random Bks Yng Read.

Riddle Me Ree. Martha B. King. (J). 1977. 5.00 (*0-87602-188-7*) Anchorage.

Riddle-Me Rhymes. Illus. by Rebecca Perry. LC 93-25179. 96p. (J). (gr. 3-7). 1994. lib. bdg. 13.95 (*0-689-50602-3*, McElderry) S&S Childrens.

Riddle of AIDS: Was AIDS Made in a Lab. 1992. lib. bdg. 75.00 (*0-8490-8708-2*) Gordon Pr.

***Riddle of Alabastar Royal.** Veryan. Date not set. 23.95 (*0-312-17121-8*) St Martin.

Riddle of Amish Culture. Donald B. Kraybill. LC 88-19868. (Illus.). 320p. 1989. 45.00 (*0-8018-3681-6*); pap. 12.95 (*0-8018-3682-4*) Johns Hopkins.

Riddle of Autism: A Psychological Analysis. George Victor. LC 95-31218. (Master Works). 356p. 1995. 40.00 (*1-56821-573-8*) Aronson.

Riddle of 'Contrapunctus XIX' Theologically Considered with a Conjectural Completion: Bach's Last Fugue. Paul Guggenheim. LC 92-7126. 120p. 1992. spiral bd. 39.95 (*0-7734-9820-6*) E Mellen.

***Riddle of Creation: Metaphor Structures in Old English Poetry.** Ruth C. Wehlau. (Studies in the Humanities: No. 24). 176p. (C). 1997. text ed. 39.95 (*0-8204-2897-3*) P Lang Pubng.

Riddle of Freud: Jewish Influences on His Theory of Female Sexuality. Estelle Roith. 250p. (C). 1987. lib. bdg. 55.00 (*0-422-61380-0*, Pub. by Tavistock UK) Routledge Chapman & Hall.

Riddle of Freud: Jewish Influences on His Theory of Female Sexuality. Estelle Roith. 250p. (C). 1987. pap. text ed. 16.95 (*0-422-61760-1*, Pub. by Tavistock UK) Routledge Chapman & Hall.

Riddle of Genesis. R. Koch. pap. 1.00 (*0-8199-0395-7*, Frncscn Herld) Franciscan Pr.

Riddle of Grace: Applying Grace to the Christian Life. Scott Hoezee. LC 95-45170. 175p. (Orig.). 1996. pap. 14.00 (*0-8028-4129-5*) Eerdmans.

Riddle of Gravitation. Peter G. Bergmann. LC 68-11537. 270p. 1977. text ed. 25.00 (*0-684-15378-5*) S&S Trade.

Riddle of Gravitation. rev. ed. Peter G. Bergmann. LC 92-22218. (Illus.). 256p. 1993. reprint ed. pap. text ed. 7.95 (*0-486-27378-4*) Dover.

Riddle of Hangar Eighteen. Timothy G. Beckley. 65p. 1987. spiral bd. 24.50 (*0-7873-1206-1*) Hlth Research.

Riddle of Justice: A Monograph Together with Suggestions for Much-Needed New Laws. James Mulligan. xvi, 155p. 1983. reprint ed. lib. bdg. 20.00 (*0-8377-0849-4*) Rothman.

Riddle of Liberty: Emerson on Alienation, Freedom & Obedience. Lou A. Lange. LC 86-6605. (Studies in Humanities). 142p. (C). 1986. 30.95 (*1-55540-019-1*, 00-01-11) Scholars Pr GA.

Riddle of MacArthur: Japan, Korea, & the Far East. John J. Gunther. LC 74-11880. 240p. 1975. reprint ed. text ed. 69.50 (*0-8371-7701-4*, GURM, Greenwood Pr) Greenwood.

Riddle of Man-Manly Love: The Pioneering Work on Male Homosexuality, 2 vols. Karl H. Ulrichs. Tr. by Michael A. Lombardi-Nash. (New Concepts in Human Sexuality Ser.). 712p. 1994. Set. 115.95 (*0-87975-866-X*) Prometheus Bks.

Riddle of Migration. William Rowan. 1977. lib. bdg. 59.95 (*0-8490-2523-0*) Gordon Pr.

Riddle of Penncroft Farm. Dorothea Jensen. (Great Episodes Ser.). 192p. (J). (gr. 3-7). 1989. 15.00 (*0-15-200574-9*, Gulliver Bks) HarBrace.

Riddle of Penncroft Farm. Dorothea Jensen. (Great Episodes Ser.). 192p. (J). (gr. 3-7). 1991. pap. 6.00 (*0-15-266908-6*, Gulliver Bks) HarBrace.

Riddle of Prehistoric Britain. Comyns Beaumont. (Illus.). 205p. 1996. pap. 19.95 (*1-56459-900-0*) Kessinger Pub.

Riddle of Prehistoric Britain. Comyns Beaumont. 208p. 1994. reprint ed. spiral bd. 24.50 (*0-7873-1205-3*) Hlth Research.

Riddle of Rattlesnake Gulch. Diane Woo. (Hidden Picture Hunt Ser.). (Illus.). 64p. (Orig.). (J). (gr. 2-6). 1992. pap. 3.95 (*1-56288-216-3*) Checkerboard.

***Riddle of Scheherezade.** Raymond Smullyian. LC 96-51505. 1997. 22.00 (*0-679-44634-6*) Knopf.

Riddle of Snoring. Marcus H. Boulware. 50p. 1969. reprint ed. spiral bd. 7.00 (*0-7873-1223-1*) Hlth Research.

***Riddle of St. Leonard's: A Medieval Mystery.** Candace M. Robb. LC 97-23035. 1997. write for info. (*0-312-16983-3*) St Martin.

Riddle of the Ages. Frank A. Peake. 80p. 1996. pap. 14.95 (*1-56459-974-4*) Kessinger Pub.

Riddle of the Ages. Frank A. Peake. 80p. 1975. reprint ed. spiral bd. 7.00 (*0-7873-0660-6*) Hlth Research.

Riddle of the Dinosaur. John N. Wilford. 1987. pap. 13.00 (*0-394-74392-X*, Vin) Random.

Riddle of the Floating Island. Paul Cox. LC 91-3853. (Adventures of Archibald the Koala on Rastepappe Island Ser.). (J). (ps-3). 1992. 16.00 (*0-671-77579-0*, Green Tiger S&S) S&S Childrens.

Riddle of the Fly & Other Stories. Elizabeth Enright. LC 70-121538. (Short Story Index Reprint Ser.). 1977. reprint ed. 19.95 (*0-8369-3494-6*) Ayer.

***Riddle of the Outlaw Bear.** John Leeper. (Illus.). 130p. (Orig.). (J). (gr. 1-8). 1996. pap. 7.99 (*1-889893-02-1*) Emerald House Group Inc.

Riddle of the Pacific. John M. Brown. 460p. 1996. pap. 18.95 (*0-932813-29-1*) Adventures Unltd.

Riddle of the Pacific. John M. Brown. LC 75-35177. reprint ed. 72.50 (*0-404-14205-2*) AMS Pr.

Riddle of the Painful Earth: Suffering & Society in W. D. Howell's Major Writings of the Early 1890's. Robert Mielke. (Illus.). 214p. (Orig.). 1994. lib. bdg. 57.00 (*0-943549-16-7*) TJU Pr.

Riddle of the Posicrucians. Manly P. Hall. 1996. pap. 4.95 (*0-89314-840-7*) Philos Res.

Riddle of the Red Purse. Patricia R. Giff. (Polka Dot Detective Ser.: No. 2). 80p. (Orig.). (J). (gr. k-6). 1987. pap. 3.50 (*0-440-47534-1*, YB BDD) BDD Bks Young Read.

Riddle of the Rock: The Only Successful Escape from Alcatraz. Don DeNevi. (Illus.). 245p. (C). 1991. 28.95 (*0-87975-647-0*) Prometheus Bks.

Riddle of the Rosetta Stone: Key to Ancient Egypt. James C. Giblin. LC 89-29289. (Illus.). 96p. (J). (gr. 3-7). 1990. lib. bdg. 5.95 (*0-690-04799-1*, Crowell Jr Bks) HarpC Child Bks.

Riddle of the Rosetta Stone: Key to Ancient Egypt. James C. Giblin. LC 89-29289. (Trophy Nonfiction Bk.). (Illus.). 96p. (J). (gr. 3-7). 1993. pap. 5.95 (*0-06-446137-8*, Trophy) HarpC Child Bks.

Riddle of the Sands. Erskine Childers. 352p. 1976. pap. 5.95 (*0-486-23280-8*) Dover.

Riddle of the Sands. Erskine Childers. Ed. by Jack Sweetman. LC 90-45843. (Classics of Naval Literature Ser.). 320p. 1991. 32.95 (*0-87021-601-5*) Naval Inst Pr.

Riddle of the Sands. Erskine Childers. (Crime Ser.). 336p. 1978. pap. 7.95 (*0-14-000905-1*, Penguin Bks) Viking Penguin.

Riddle of the Sands. Erskine Childers. Ed. by David Trotter. (Oxford Popular Fiction Ser.). (Illus.). 304p. 1995. pap. 7.95 (*0-19-282318-3*) OUP.

Riddle of the Sands. large type ed. Erskine Childers. (Large-Print Ser.). 543p. 1992. reprint ed. lib. bdg. 24.00 (*0-939495-38-4*) North Bks.

Riddle of the Sands. Erskine Childers. 1976. reprint ed. lib. bdg. 24.95 (*0-89190-240-6*, Rivercity Pr) Amereon Ltd.

Riddle of the Sands. Erskine Childers. 310p. 1990. reprint ed. lib. bdg. 23.95 (*0-89966-743-0*) Buccaneer Bks.

Riddle of the Sphinx: A Key to the Mysteries & a Synthesis of Philosophy. J. Munsell Chase. 1991. lib. bdg. 79.95 (*0-8490-4999-7*) Gordon Pr.

Riddle of the Sphinx: A Key to the Mysteries & a Synthesis of Philosophy. J. Munsell Chase. 87p. 1965. reprint ed. spiral bd. 5.50 (*0-7873-0166-3*) Hlth Research.

Riddle of the Sphinx: Thoughts about the Human Enigma. Jay G. Williams. 228p. (Orig.). (C). 1990. lib. bdg. 46.50 (*0-8191-7886-1*) U Pr of Amer.

Riddle of the Sphinx (1915) J. Munsell Chase. 86p. 1996. pap. 12.95 (*1-56459-934-5*) Kessinger Pub.

Riddle of the Stones. Daniel Cohen. LC 94-41802. (Illus.). (J). (gr. 3-9). 1995. pap. 2.95 (*1-85697-571-1*) LKC.

Riddle of the Tariff. Arthur C. Pigou. LC 74-1328. (Reprints of Economic Classics Ser.). xi, 107p. 1975. reprint ed. 25.00 (*0-678-01227-X*) Kelley.

Riddle of the Third Mile. 224p. 1988. mass mkt. 5.99 (*0-553-27363-9*) Bantam.

***Riddle of the Third Mile.** Colin Dexter. 1997. mass mkt. 5.99 (*0-8041-1488-9*) Ivy Books.

Riddle of the Universe. Ernst Haeckel. Tr. by Joseph McCabe from GER. (Great Minds Ser.). 391p. (Orig.). (C). 1991. pap. 10.95 (*0-87975-746-9*) Prometheus Bks.

Riddle of the Universe at the Close of the 19th Century. Ernst Haeckel. 1995. 18.00 (*0-403-00117-X*) Scholarly.

***Riddle of the Wayward Books.** Brad Strickland & Tom Fuller. (Wishbone Mysteries Ser.: Vol. 3). (Illus.). 128p. (Orig.). (J). (gr. 3-6). 1998. mass mkt. 3.99 (*1-57064-281-8*, Big Red) Lyrick Pub.

Riddle of This World. Sri Aurobindo. 98p. 1984. pap. 2.75 (*0-89071-306-5*, Pub. by SAA II) Aurobindo Assn.

Riddle Rhymes. Charles Ghigna. LC 94-18205. (Illus.). 32p. (J). (ps-3). 1995. 13.95 (*1-56282-479-1*) Hyprn Child.

Riddle Roundup: A Wild Bunch to Beef up Your Word Power. Giulio Maestro. LC 86-33404. (Illus.). 64p. (J). (gr. 2-5). 1989. pap. 6.95 (*0-89919-537-7*, Clarion Bks) HM.

Riddle Streak. Susan B. Pfeffer. (Illus.). 64p. (J). (gr. 2-4). 1995. pap. 4.95 (*0-8050-4260-1*, Redfeather BYR) H Holt & Co.

***Riddle Street.** Betty L. Kratoville. 64p. (Orig.). 1997. wbk. ed., pap. text ed. 12.00 (*1-57128-068-5*, 8068-5) High Noon Bks.

***Riddle Street, 5 vols., Set 2.** Elaine Pageler. Ed. by Betty L. Kratoville. (Illus.). 48p. (Orig.). (YA). (gr. 5 up). 1997. pap. text ed. 17.00 (*1-57128-061-8*, 8061-8) Acad Therapy.

Riddle Street Mystery Series: Wrong Robber Mystery, Market Stake-Out Mystery, Haunted Apartment House Mystery, Book Party Mystery, Radio Station Mystery, 5 bks. Elaine Pageler. Ed. by Betty L. Kratoville. (Illus.). 48p. (J). (gr. 1 up). 1994. pap. text ed. 17.00 (*0-87879-983-4*) High Noon Bks.

Riddlemaster of Hed, No. 1. Patricia A. McKillip. 240p. 1985. mass mkt. 5.99 (*0-345-33104-4*) Ballantine.

Riddler's Riddle Book. David Levin. 1991. pap. 3.50 (*0-8125-1353-3*) Tor Bks.

Riddles. Gary Chemielewski. LC 86-17720. (Smile-a-While Ser.). (Illus.). (J). (gr. 2-3). 1986. 9.95 (*0-685-58363-5*); lib. bdg. 13.27 (*0-86592-686-7*) Rourke Corp.

Riddles about Baby Animals. Jacqueline Ball. Ed. by Bonnie Brook. (What Can It Be? Ser.). (Illus.). 32p. (J). (ps-3). 1989. pap. 4.95 (*0-382-24235-4*, Silver Pr NJ); lib. bdg. 6.95 (*0-671-68576-7*, Silver Pr NJ) Silver Burdett Pr.

An Asterisk (*) at the beginning of an entry indicates that the title is appearing in BIP for the first time.

Riddles about Christmas. Jill Ashley. Ed. by Bonnie Brook. (What Can It Be? Ser.). (Illus.). 32p. (J). (ps-3). 1990. pap. 2.95 (*0-382-24383-8*); lib. bdg. 6.95 (*0-671-70552-0*) Silver Burdett Pr.
Riddles about Easter. Jill Ashley. (What Can It Be? Ser.). (Illus.). 32p. (J). (ps-3). 1991. pap. 2.95 (*0-382-24380-3*); lib. bdg. 6.95 (*0-671-72726-5*) Silver Burdett Pr.
Riddles about Hannukah. Susan C. Poskanzer. Ed. by Bonnie Brook. (What Can It Be? Ser.). (Illus.). 32p. (J). (ps-3). 1990. pap. 2.95 (*0-382-24384-6*) Silver Burdett Pr.
Riddles about Hannukah. Susan C. Poskanzer. Ed. by Bonnie Brook. (What Can It Be? Ser.). (Illus.). 32p. (J). (ps-3). 1990. lib. bdg. 6.95 (*0-671-70553-9*) Silver Burdett Pr.
Riddles about Our Bodies. Jacqueline Ball. Ed. by Bonnie Brook. (What Can It Be? Ser.). (Illus.). 32p. (J). (ps-3). 1989. pap. 4.95 (*0-382-24386-2*, Silver Pr NJ) Silver Burdett Pr.
Riddles about Our Bodies. Jacqueline Ball. Ed. by Bonnie Brook. (What Can It Be? Ser.). (Illus.). 32p. (J). (ps-3). 1989. lib. bdg. 6.95 (*0-671-68578-3*, Silver Pr NJ) Silver Burdett Pr.
Riddles about Passover. Susan C. Poskanzer. (What Can It Be? Ser.). (Illus.). 32p. (J). (ps-3). 1991. lib. bdg. 6.95 (*0-671-72724-9*) Silver Burdett Pr.
Riddles about Passover. Susan C. Poskanzer. (What Can It Be? Ser.). (Illus.). 32p. (J). (ps-3). 1991. pap. 2.95 (*0-382-24381-1*) Silver Burdett Pr.
Riddles about the Seasons. Jacqueline Ball. Ed. by Bonnie Brook. (What Can It Be? Ser.). (Illus.). 32p. (J). (ps-3). 1989. pap. 4.95 (*0-382-24387-0*, Silver Pr NJ) Silver Burdett Pr.
Riddles about the Seasons. Jacqueline Ball. Ed. by Bonnie Brook. (What Can It Be? Ser.). (Illus.). 32p. (J). (ps-3). 1989. lib. bdg. 6.95 (*0-671-68582-1*, Silver Pr NJ) Silver Burdett Pr.
Riddles about the Senses. Jacqueline Ball. Ed. by Bonnie Brook. (What Can It Be? Ser.). (Illus.). 32p. (J). (ps-3). 1989. lib. bdg. 6.95 (*0-671-68580-5*, Silver Pr NJ) Silver Burdett Pr.
***Riddles about the Senses.** Jacqueline Ball. Ed. by Bonnie Brook. (What Can It Be? Ser.). (Illus.). 32p. (J). (ps-3). 1989. pap. 2.95 (*0-382-24388-9*, Silver Pr NJ) Silver Burdett Pr.
Riddles & Jokes. (Illus.). (J). (ps-2). 1991. pap. 5.10 (*0-8136-5961-2*); lib. bdg. 7.95 (*0-8136-5203-0*) Modern Curr.
Riddles & Rhymes. Claudia Vumakes. (Illus.). 128p. 1993. pap. 12.95 (*1-878279-57-2*) Monday Morning Bks.
Riddles for a Naked Sailor. Mary Azrael. LC 91-66988. (Illus.). 48p. (Orig.). 1991. pap. 10.00 (*0-9631385-2-9*) Stonevale Pr.
Riddles for Clever Kids! Mark Dantzler. (Illus.). 26p. (J). 1994. pap. 9.50 (*0-930329-83-X*) Kabel Pubs.
Riddles in Filipino Folklore: An Anthropological Analysis. Donn V. Hart. LC 64-23338. 1964. 39.95 (*0-8156-2069-1*) Syracuse U Pr.
Riddles in Rhyme. Le Baron R. Briggs. 1972. 59.95 (*0-8490-0957-X*) Gordon Pr.
Riddles in Stone: Myths, Archaeology & the Ancient Britons. Richard Hayman. LC 96-29733. (Illus.). 288p. 1997. 40.00 (*1-85285-139-2*) Hambledon Press.
Riddles in Your Teacup. P. Ghose & D. Home. (Illus.). 192p. 1994. pap. 22.00 (*0-7503-0275-5*) IOP Pub.
Riddles of Aldhelm. James H. Pitman. LC 75-91189. (Yale Studies in English: No. 67). vii, 79p. (C). 1970. reprint ed. lib. bdg. 26.50 (*0-208-00910-8*, Archon Bks) Shoe String.
RIDDLES OF EROS: Exploring, Sex, Psyche & Culture. William Manson. LC 93-38164. 128p. (Orig.). (C). 1994. pap. text ed. 21.00 (*0-8191-9370-4*); lib. bdg. 42.00 (*0-8191-9369-0*) U Pr of Amer.
Riddles of Finnegans Wake. Patrick A. McCarthy. LC 79-24075. 184p. 1970. 29.50 (*0-8386-3005-7*) Fairleigh Dickinson.
Riddles of Jesus & Answers of Science: Modern Verification of His Wisdom & How It Can Help You. Osborn Segerberg, Jr. Ed. by Marcia Drennen. 272p. (Orig.). 1987. 21.95 (*0-9618626-0-2*); pap. 14.95 (*0-9618626-1-0*) Reges Bks.
Riddles of Nifiter. Hilda Sanderson. Ed. by Myrna Kemnitz. 130p. (Orig.). (YA). (gr. 7 up). 1996. pap. 6.99 (*0-88092-181-1*) Royal Fireworks.
Riddles of Science. John A. Thomson. LC 77-152218. (Essay Index Reprint Ser.). 1977. reprint ed. 23.95 (*0-8369-2257-3*) Ayer.
Riddles of the Inner Human Being: The Approach of the Michael Force. Rudolf Steiner. 15p. 1969. reprint ed. spiral bd. 4.50 (*0-7873-0835-8*) Hlth Research.
Riddles of the Russian People: A Collection of Riddles, Questions, Parables & Puzzles. Compiled by D. N. Sadovnikov. 566p. 1991. 15.50 (*0-88233-987-7*) Ardis Pubs.
Riddles of the Sphinx. Ferdinand C. Schiller. LC 70-126254. (Select Bibliographies Reprint Ser.). 1977. 26.95 (*0-8369-5481-5*) Ayer.
Riddles of the Sphinx & Other Mathematical Puzzle Tales. Martin Gardner. LC 87-62657. (New Mathematical Library: No. 32). (Illus.). 184p. 1987. pap. 15.00 (*0-88385-632-8*, NML-32) Math Assn.
Riddles of Venice: A Book of Six Treasure Hunts in Venice. Paul Stiga. Ed. by Beatrice H. Guthrie. (Illus.). 48p. 1989. write for info. (*0-9623364-0-8*) Save Venice.
***Riddles of Wipers.** John Ivelaw-Chapman. 1996. 29.95 (*0-85052-494-6*, Pub. by L Cooper Bks UK) Trans-Atl Phila.
***Riddles, Riddles, Riddles.** Ed. by Darwin A. Hindman. LC 96-54023. (Illus.). 64p. 1997. reprint ed. pap. text ed. 1.00 (*0-486-29654-7*) Dover.
Riddles to Stump You. J. Edward Thornberg. (Illus.). 48p. (Orig.). 1986. pap. 3.00 (*0-929082-10-9*) Natl Hall Humor.
Riddles to Take on Vacation. Joanne E. Bernstein & Paul Cohen. Ed. by Ann Fay. LC 87-2071. (Illus.). (J). (gr. 1-5). 1987. lib. bdg. 8.95 (*0-8075-6999-2*) A Whitman.
Riddles to Tell Your Cat. Caroline Levine. Ed. by Christy Grant. (Illus.). 32p. (J). (gr. 1-4). 1992. lib. bdg. 8.95 (*0-8075-7006-0*) A Whitman.
Riddles Today, Giggles Tomorrow. Joseph R. Carchia. 1992. 6.95 (*0-533-09337-6*) Vantage.
Riddley Walker. Russell Hoban. 214p. 1982. mass mkt., pap. 16.95 (*0-330-26645-4*) Trans-Atl Phila.
Riddling Thing: A Study of Time in Five Twentieth-Century Novels. Pauline W. Beard. LC 94-12985. 1996. 69.95 (*1-883255-71-6*); pap. 49.95 (*1-883255-70-8*) Intl Scholars.
Ride a Blue Horse: Playscript. Aurand Harris. 44p. (Orig.). (J). (gr. k-3). 1986. pap. 5.00 (*0-87602-264-6*) Anchorage.
Ride a Cock Horse. Vince Cross & Nick Sharratt. (J). write for info. (*0-19-279989-4*) OUP.
Ride a Cock Horse. Ed. by Gillian Mears. 164p. (C). 1990. 30.00 (*0-947087-12-5*, Pub. by Pascoe Pub AT) St Mut.
Ride a Cock Horse. Elma Williams. 1972. 12.00 (*0-7181-0930-9*) Transatl Arts.
Ride a Cock-Horse & Other Rhymes. (J). 1995. 13.95 (*0-679-44476-9*) Knopf.
Ride a Cockhorse. Raymond Kennedy. 1992. pap. 11.00 (*0-679-73835-5*, Vin) Random.
Ride a Dark Horse. Lynn Hall. 144p. 1988. pap. 2.95 (*0-380-75370-7*, Flare) Avon.
Ride a Hole Through the Wind. Judy Marshall. 92p. (Orig.). (YA). (gr. 9-12). 1994. pap. 5.00 (*0-88092-147-1*) Royal Fireworks.
Ride a Horse Not an Elevator. Lisa A. Saunders. LC 95-92719. (Illus.). 145p. (Orig.). (J). (gr. 1-6). 1995. pap. 6.95 (*0-9649403-0-2*) L Saunders.
Ride a Painted Pony. Jean Van Dyke. (Illus.). 338p. 1995. 22.00 (*0-9642734-1-1*) Squeek-by Grphs.
Ride a Pale Horse. Helen MacInnes. 384p. 1985. mass mkt. 5.99 (*0-449-20726-9*, Crest) Fawcett.
Ride a Purple Pelican. Jack Prelutsky. LC 84-6024. (Illus.). 64p. (J). (ps up). 1986. 17.95 (*0-688-04031-4*) Greenwillow.
***Ride a Purple Pelican.** Jack Prelutsky. Date not set. pap. 6.95 (*0-688-15625-8*) Morrow.
Ride a Storm. Quinn Wilder. 1993. pap. 2.89 (*0-373-03258-7*, 1-03258-0) Harlequin Bks.
Ride Across America: An Environmental Commitment. Lucian Spataro. Ed. by Tate Baird. LC 90-72061. (Illus.). 183p. (YA). (gr. 9 up). 1991. 12.95 (*0-914127-44-6*) Univ Class.
Ride Against the Wind. Terrell L. Bowers. LC 96-18656. 200p. 1996. 21.95 (*0-8027-4156-8*) Walker & Co.
***Ride Against the Wind.** large type ed. Terrell L. Bowers. LC 97-332. (Western Ser.). 288p. 1997. 20.95 (*0-7862-1076-1*, Thorndike Lrg Prnt) Thorndike Pr.
Ride All Around: Little Peek-in Book. Tr. by JoAnne Barkan from ITA. (Little Peek-in Bks.). (Illus.). 18p. (J). 1995. bds., spiral bd. 3.99 (*0-88705-784-5*, Wshng Well Bks) Joshua Morris.
Ride & Seek. L. Schwartz. (Just for Fun Ser.). (J). (gr. 3 up). 1987. 5.95 (*0-88160-159-4*, LW 103) Learning Wks.
Ride Down Mount Morgan. Arthur Miller. 128p. (Orig.). 1992. pap. 7.95 (*0-14-048236-9*, Penguin Bks) Viking Penguin.
Ride Down Mt. Morgan. deluxe limited ed. Arthur Miller. 1992. 80.00 (*0-89366-237-2*) Ultramarine Pub.
Ride Down the Wind. large type ed. Wayne Barton. LC 92-27527. (Nightingale Ser.). 320p. 1993. lib. bdg. 14.95 (*0-8161-5626-3*, GK Hall) Thorndike Pr.
Ride, Float, & Fly. Walt Disney Productions Staff. (Walt Disney's Fun-to-Learn Library Ser.: Vol. 15). (Illus.). 44p. (J). (gr. 1-6). 1983. reprint ed. 3.49 (*1-885222-06-8*) Advance Pubs.
Ride for Rimfire. Hank Edwards. 192p. 1995. mass mkt. 3.99 (*0-06-100748-X*, Harp PBks) HarpC.
Ride for the Brand: The Poetry & Songs of Red Steagall. Red Steagall. LC 92-28487. (Illus.). 128p. (C). 1993. 22.50 (*0-87565-112-7*); pap. 11.95 (*0-87565-115-1*) Tex Christian.
Ride for the High Points: The Real Story of Will James. Jim Bramlett. LC 92-39477. 272p. 1993. pap. 17.00 (*0-87842-288-9*) Mountain Pr.
Ride for Trinidad! Peter Field. 176p. 1988. pap. 2.75 (*0-380-70422-6*) Avon.
***Ride for Your Life.** large type ed. Johnny M. Bride. (Linford Western Large Print Ser.). 224p. 1997. pap. 16.99 (*0-7089-5001-9*, Linford) Ulverscroft.
Ride Guide: Hudson Valley New Bltz to Staten Island. Dan Goldfischer. LC 96-61364. (Illus.). 168p. (Orig.). 1997. pap. 10.95 (*0-933855-01-X*) White Meadow.
Ride Guide - North Jersey. 2nd ed. Dan Goldfischer & Karen Stratter. LC 94-60243. (Illus.). 170p. 1994. pap. 10.95 (*0-933855-08-7*) White Meadow.
Ride Guide Central Jersey. Dan Goldfischer. LC 89-50519. (Illus.). 90p. (Orig.). 1989. pap. 9.95 (*0-933855-03-6*) White Meadow.
Ride Guide to the Historic Alaska Railroad. Laura C. Zahn & Anita Williams. (Illus.). 64p. (Orig.). 1987. pap. 3.95 (*0-939301-01-6*) Down to Erth Pubns.
Ride Home. Judith Hemschemeyer. LC 87-50515. xx, 92p. 1987. 16.95 (*0-89672-153-1*) Tex Tech Univ Pr.
Ride in Morocco. F. MacNab. 400p. 1985. 220.00 (*1-85077-071-9*, Pub. by Darf Pubs Ltd UK) St Mut.
Ride in Pursuit of Happiness. Michael L. Clark. LC 95-92359. 204p. (Orig.). 1995. pap. 6.95 (*0-9647242-0-0*) Wet Saddleblankets Pubns.
Ride into Danger. Henry Treece. LC 59-12203. (Illus.). (J). (gr. 7-10). 1959. 24.95 (*0-87599-113-0*) S G Phillips.
Ride into Darkness. Kenyon McCann. LC 94-90229. 232p. (Orig.). 1995. pap. 10.95 (*1-56002-470-4*, Univ Edtns) Aegina Pr.
Ride into Morning. Mary Kennedy. 1969. 6.95 (*0-910664-15-3*) Gotham.
Ride into Morning: The Story of Tempe Wick. Ann Rinaldi. Ed. by Karen Grove. (Great Episodes Ser.). 368p. (YA). (gr. 7 up). 1991. 16.00 (*0-15-200573-0*, Gulliver Bks) HarBrace.
Ride into Morning: The Story of Tempe Wick. Ann Rinaldi. LC 90-49481. (Great Episodes Ser.). 368p. (YA). (gr. 7 up). 1995. pap. 6.00 (*0-15-200673-7*, Gulliver Bks) HarBrace.
Ride into Yesterday. Christopher Keegan. 137p. 1992. 18.95 (*0-8027-4132-0*) Walker & Co.
Ride It: The Complete Book of Motorcycle Trails. Don Smith. (Drive it! Ride it! Ser.). 133p. 14.95 (*0-85429-165-2*, F165, Pub. by G T Foulis Ltd) Haynes Pubns.
***Ride Like the Devil!** large type ed. Sam Gort. (Linford Western Large Print Ser.). 272p. 1997. pap. 16.99 (*0-7089-5007-8*) Ulverscroft.
***Ride New York: 35 Horse & Multiple-Use Trails in the Empire State.** Anne M. O'Dell. (Illus.). 270p. Date not set. pap. 14.95 (*0-9657744-0-6*) Crazy Horse Ranch.
***Ride of a Lifetime.** Albert Beurman. (Illus.). 48p. 1997. pap. 9.00 (*0-8059-4076-6*) Dorrance.
Ride of the Second Horseman: The Birth & Death of War. Robert L. O'Connell. (Illus.). 320p. 1995. 30.00 (*0-19-506460-7*) OUP.
***Ride of the Second Horseman: The Birth & Death of War.** Robert L. O'Connell. 320p. 1997. pap. 15.95 (*0-19-511920-7*) OUP.
***Ride of the Valkyries.** Richard Wagner. 1996. 15.95 (*0-486-29375-0*, 284323Q) Dover.
***Ride of Your Life: Being a Young Adventist Isn't for the Faint of Heart.** Alex Bryan et al. LC 96-46654. (J). 1996. write for info. (*0-8280-1066-8*) Review & Herald.
Ride on Mother's Back: A Day of Baby-Carrying Around the World. Emery Bernhard. (J). 1996. 15.00 (*0-15-200870-5*) HarBrace.
Ride on the Historical Virginia V. Sandy Renvold. (J). (gr. 2-3). 1995. pap. text ed. 7.95 (*0-9647088-0-9*) Keeper Bks.
Ride on the Political Merry-Go-Round. Elizabeth Snyder & Gabriel Meyer. LC 96-9600. 200p. 1996. 21.95 (*0-9629528-3-4*) Silverton Bks.
Ride on the Red Mare's Back. Ursula K. Le Guin. LC 91-21677. (Illus.). 48p. (J). (gr. 1-4). 1992. 16.95 (*0-531-05991-X*); lib. bdg. 17.99 (*0-531-08591-0*) Orchard Bks Watts.
Ride on the Red Mare's Back. Ursula K. Le Guin. LC 91-21677. (Illus.). 48p. (J). (gr. 1-4). 1996. pap. 6.95 (*0-531-07079-4*) Orchard Bks Watts.
Ride on the Wave of the Future: An Essay on Human Potential. Thomas Carlisle. LC 78-55736. (Illus.). 1978. 2.00 (*0-914580-08-6*) Angst World.
Ride on the Whirlwind. Sipho Sepamla. (African Writers Ser.). 244p. (C). 1984. reprint ed. pap. 8.95 (*0-435-90268-7*, 90268) Heinemann.
Ride on the Wind. Francis B. Chichester. Ed. by James B. Gilbert. LC 79-7236. (Flight: Its First Seventy-Five Years Ser.). (Illus.). 1980. reprint ed. lib. bdg. 26.95 (*0-405-12152-0*) Ayer.
Ride out the Wilderness: Geography & Identity in Afro-American Literature. Melvin Dixon. LC 86-30918. 200p. 1987. text ed. 24.95 (*0-252-01414-6*) U of Ill Pr.
Ride, Rebels, Ride. Randall Greenwood. (Orig.). mass mkt. 5.99 (*0-8125-3457-3*) Forge NYC.
Ride, Rebels, Ride. Randall Greenwood. (Orig.). 1996. mass mkt. 5.99 (*0-614-05518-0*) Forge NYC.
Ride Right: An Informative Training Manual for the Serious Rider That Wants to Improve. William G. Langdon, Jr. LC 93-91892. (Illus.). 122p. 1993. spiral bd. 29.95 (*1-883714-06-0*) Langdon Ent.
***Ride South!** C. H. Haseloff. 1996. 17.50 (*0-7451-4679-1*, Gunsmoke) Chivers N Amer.
Ride South! large type ed. Cynthia Haseloff. (Linford Western Library). 272p. 1985. pap. 15.99 (*0-7089-6142-8*) Ulverscroft.
Ride the Airwaves with Alfa & Zulu: Preparation for the Novice & No-Code Technician Amateur Radio Licenses. John Abbott. (Illus.). xii, 244p. (Orig.). 1996. pap. 14.95 (*0-9651088-0-5*) Abtronix.
Ride the Beast. Don Pendleton. (Executioner Ser.: No. 212). 1996. mass mkt. 3.75 (*0-373-64212-1*, 1-64212-3, Wrldwide Lib) Harlequin Bks.
Ride the Dark Trail. Louis L'Amour. 176p. 1984. mass mkt. 3.99 (*0-553-27682-4*) Bantam.
Ride the Devil Wind: A History of the Los Angeles County Forester & Fire Warden Department & Fire Protection Districts. David Boucher. Ed. by R. Dale Magee et al. 254p. 1991. lib. bdg. 55.00 (*0-941943-03-8*) Fire Pubns.
Ride the Devil's Trail. Dan Parkinson. 1990. mass mkt. 3.95 (*0-8217-2894-6*, Zebra Kensgtn) Kensgtn Pub Corp.
Ride the Eagle. Vita Vendresha. 304p. 1987. mass mkt. 3.95 (*0-373-97045-5*) Harlequin Bks.
Ride the Free Wind. F. Rosanne Bittner. (Savage Destiny Ser.: No. 2). 1989. mass mkt. 3.95 (*0-8217-2636-6*, Zebra Kensgtn) Kensgtn Pub Corp.
Ride the Free Wind. F. Rosanne Bittner. (Savage Destiny Ser.: No. 2). 448p. 1996. mass mkt. 5.99 (*0-8217-5343-6*, Zebra Kensgtn) Kensgtn Pub Corp.
***Ride the Lightning: A Novel.** Robert H. Mitchell. LC 96-44363. 304p. 1997. 26.95 (*0-8061-2917-4*) U of Okla Pr.
Ride the Morning Winds. Roberta G. Liddiard. LC 84-27354. 97p. (Orig.). 1985. pap. 5.95 (*0-933380-29-1*) Olive Pr Pubns.
Ride the Pink Horse. Dorothy B. Hughes. 208p. 1988. pap. 3.95 (*0-88184-385-7*) Carroll & Graf.
Ride the Rainbow Home. Susan Aylworth. LC 95-94894. 192p. 1995. 17.95 (*0-8034-9143-3*) Bouregy.
Ride the Razor's Edge: The Younger Brothers Story. Carl W. Breihan. LC 91-43547. (Illus.). 160p. 1992. 15.95 (*0-88289-879-5*) Pelican.
Ride the River, No. 17. Louis L'Amour. 192p. 1983. pap. 3.99 (*0-553-27683-2*) Bantam.
Ride the Shadow. David Lenson. LC 78-78115. 53p. 1979. pap. 3.75 (*0-934332-13-4*) LEpervier Pr.
Ride the Storm. Emma Darcy. (Presents Ser.: No. 1401). 1991. pap. 2.79 (*0-373-11401-X*) Harlequin Bks.
Ride the Storm. large type ed. Emma Darcy. 1993. 19.95 (*0-263-13315-X*) Thorndike Pr.
Ride the Thunder. Janet Dailey. 1993. mass mkt. 5.99 (*0-671-87511-6*) PB.
***Ride the Thunder.** Patricia Werner. 1997. pap. 3.75 (*0-373-22431-1*, 1-22431-0) Harlequin Bks.
Ride the Tiger. Lindsay McKenna. (Special Edition Ser.: No. 721). 1992. mass mkt. 3.29 (*0-373-09721-2*, 5-09721-7) Harlequin Bks.
Ride the Tiger to the Mountain: Tai Chi for Health. 1989. pap. 14.00 (*0-201-18077-4*) Addison-Wesley.
Ride the Waves Created by Institutional Investors: Tips for Making Money in the Stock Market. John Fung. Ed. by Diane Parker. LC 93-82497. 200p. (Orig.). 1994. pap. 10.95 (*1-56875-075-7*) R & E Pubs.
Ride the Wild Country. large type ed. Wade Hamilton. (Linford Western Library). 352p. 1994. pap. 15.99 (*0-7089-7503-8*, Linford) Ulverscroft.
Ride the Wild River. Gilbert Morris. LC 92-9437. (Jim Reno Westerns Ser.: No. 3). Orig. Title: The Runaway. 339p. 1992. 9.99 (*0-8423-5795-5*) Tyndale.
Ride the Wind. Katharine Kincaid. 1995. mass mkt. 5.50 (*0-8217-5132-8*, Zebra Kensgtn) Kensgtn Pub Corp.
***Ride the Wind.** Sylvia C. Pennywell. (Illus.). 25p. (Orig.). (YA). Date not set. pap. 15.00 (*0-9637324-4-7*) Silver Grace Pubs.
Ride the Wind. Lucia S. Robson. 1985. mass mkt. 5.99 (*0-345-32522-2*) Ballantine.
Ride the Wind: Airborne Journeys of Animals & Plants. Seymour Simon. LC 94-29052. (J). (gr. 1-8). 1997. 15.00 (*0-15-292887-1*) HarBrace.
***Ride the Wind: Airborne Journeys of Animals & Plants.** Seymour Simon. (Illus.). (J). (gr. 3 up). 1997. 15.00 (*0-614-28820-7*, Browndeer Pr) HarBrace.
Ride the Wind: U. S. A. to Africa. Anne Hillerman. LC 94-68083. (Illus.). 172p. (Orig.). (YA). 1995. pap. 13.95 (*0-9642561-7-7*) Rio Grande Pub.
Ride Through Rhyme & Other Cowboy Poems. R. P. Smith. Ed. by Jean Lukesh. (Illus.). 66p. (Orig.). 1995. pap. 7.95 (*0-614-07778-8*) Field Mouse Prodns.
Ride Through Rhyme & Other Cowboy Poems. R. P. Smith. Ed. by Jean Lukesh. (Illus.). 66p. (Orig.). 1995. pap. 7.95 (*0-9633651-2-6*) Orig Western.
***Ride to Khiva.** Frederick Burnaby. 416p. 1997. pap. 13.95 (*0-19-288050-0*) OUP.
Ride to Khiva: Travels & Adventures in Central Asia. Fred Burnaby. LC 79-115513. (Russia Observed Ser., No. 1). 1970. reprint ed. 23.95 (*0-405-03010-X*) Ayer.
Ride to Revenge. Eric Allen. (Orig.). 1979. mass mkt. 1.95 (*0-89083-551-9*, Zebra Kensgtn) Kensgtn Pub Corp.
Ride Western. Louis Taylor. 1979. pap. 7.00 (*0-87980-252-9*) Wilshire.
Ride Western Style: A Guide for Young Riders. Tommie Kirksmith. (Illus.). 192p. (J). (gr. 3-7). 1991. 16.95 (*0-87605-895-0*) Howell Bk.
Ride When You're Ready. Eve Bunting. (Author's Signature Collection). (Illus.). 64p. (J). (gr. 3-8). 1992. lib. bdg. 12.79 (*0-89565-776-7*) Childs World.
Ride with Huey the Engineer. 3rd ed. Jesse H. Stuart. (Illus.). 112p. (J). (gr. 3 up). 1988. reprint ed. 12.00 (*0-945084-11-0*); reprint ed. pap. 6.00 (*0-945084-10-2*) J Stuart Found.
Ride with Me, Mariah Montana. Ivan Doig. 384p. 1990. text ed. 18.95 (*0-689-12019-2*, Atheneum S&S) S&S Trade.
Ride with Me, Mariah Montana. Ivan Doig. (Contemporary American Fiction Ser.). 336p. 1991. reprint ed. pap. 11.95 (*0-14-015607-0*, Penguin Bks) Viking Penguin.
Ride with Me Through ABC. Susan Bond. LC 67-19376. (Illus.). 32p. (J). (ps). 6.95 (*0-87592-043-8*) Scroll Pr.
Ride with the Loomis Gang. E. Fuller Torrey. LC 96-8217. 1996. write for info. (*0-925168-56-4*) North Country.
***Ride with the Wind.** Charlotte Hamlin. (Orig.). 1997. pap. 12.99 (*0-8280-1129-X*) Review & Herald.
Ride with Your Mind: An Illustrated Masterclass in Right Brain Riding. Mary Wanless. (Illus.). 192p. 1992. 27.50 (*0-943955-52-1*, Trafalgar Sq Pub) Trafalgar.
Rideau. John De Visser & Larry Turner. 120p. 1995. 28.00 (*1-55046-136-2*, Pub. by Boston Mills Pr CN) Genl Dist Srvs.
Rideau Hall: An Illustrated History of Government House, Ottawa, from Victorian Times to the Present Day. R. H. Hubbard. (Illus.). 1977. 34.95 (*0-7735-0310-2*, Pub. by McGill CN) U of Toronto Pr.
Rideau Waterway. rev. ed. Robert F. Legget. LC 72-197084. 279p. reprint ed. pap. 79.60 (*0-317-27021-4*, 2023644) Bks Demand.
Rideau Waterway. 2nd ed. Robert F. Legget. (Illus.). 320p. 1986. 32.50 (*0-8020-2573-0*); pap. 17.95 (*0-8020-6591-0*) U of Toronto Pr.
Rideau Waterway. Robert F. Legget. LC 72-197084. 279p. reprint ed. pap. 79.60 (*0-318-34715-6*, 2031916) Bks Demand.
Rideaux et Tentures. Rene Briat. (FRE.). 1993. lib. bdg. 195.00 (*0-7859-3620-3*, 270590322) Fr & Eur.
Rider. Mark Rudman. LC 93-38326. (Wesleyan Poetry Ser.). 122p. (C). 1994. pap. 12.95 (*0-8195-1217-6*, Wesleyan Univ Pr) U Pr of New Eng.

An Asterisk (*) at the beginning of an entry indicates that the title is appearing in BIP for the first time.

R

Rider. Marian Wolbers. LC 96-3119. 192p. 1996. 21.95 (*0-312-14718-X*) St Martin.

Rider at the Gate. C. J. Cherryh. 496p. 1996. pap. 5.99 (*0-446-60345-7*, Aspect) Warner Bks.

Rider from Yonder. large type ed. Norman A. Fox. LC 93-34585. 1993. lib. bdg. 15.95 (*1-56054-711-1*) Thorndike Pr.

Rider Haggard & the Fiction of Empire: A Critical Study of British Imperial Fiction. Wendy R. Katz. 210p. 1988. text ed. 69.95 (*0-521-33425-X*) Cambridge U Pr.

Rider Haggard, Henry Miller & I: The Unpublished Writer. J. Marvin Spiegelman. LC 94-66059. 192p. (Orig.). 1997. pap. 14.95 (*1-56184-033-5*) New Falcon Pubns.

Rider of Asses: Poems. Gary D. Swaim. 64p. 1996. pap. 12.95 (*0-7734-2668-X*, Mellen Poetry Pr) E Mellen.

Rider of Distant Trails. large type ed. Romer Z. Grey. 1983. 15.95 (*0-7089-0929-9*) Ulverscroft.

Rider of Lost Creek. Louis L'Amour. 160p. (Orig.). 1982. mass mkt. 3.99 (*0-553-25771-4*) Bantam.

Rider of Ruby Hills. Louis L'Amour. 400p. 1986. 4.50 (*0-553-28112-7*) Bantam.

Rider on a White Horse. Brian Grattan. 1990. pap. 14.95 (*0-929385-18-7*) Light Tech Comns Servs.

Rider-Passenger Protection in Motorcycle Collisions. 220p. 1990. pap. 19.00 (*1-56091-057-7*, SP-827) Soc Auto Engineers.

Riders. Jilly Cooper. 928p. 1986. mass mkt. 9.99 (*0-552-12486-9*) Bantam.

Riders. Tim Winton. 377p. 1995. 23.00 (*0-684-80296-1*) S&S Trade.

Riders. Tim Winton. 384p. 1996. pap. 12.00 (*0-684-82277-6*) S&S Trade.

Riders. large type ed. Tim Winton. (Large Print Ser.). 392p. 1996. lib. bdg. 24.95 (*1-57490-036-6*, Beeler LP Bks) T T Beeler.

Rider's Aids. Pegotty Henriques. (Threshold Picture Guides Ser.). (Illus.). 24p. (Orig.). 1991. pap. 12.00 (*1-872082-23-8*, Pub. by Threshhold Bks UK) Half Halt Pr.

Riders along the Rio Grande: A Collection of Outlaws, Prostitutes & Vigilantes. Bob L'Aloge. LC 92-60658. (Illus.). 212p. 1992. pap. 9.95 (*1-881481-00-X*) Yucca Tree Pr.

***Riders by the Grey Lake.** Pauline Devine. 144p. Date not set. pap. 8.95 (*0-947962-99-9*) Dufour.

Rider's California: A Guidebook for Travelers. Fremont Rider. 1992. reprint ed. lib. bdg. 75.00 (*0-7812-5079-X*) Rprt Serv.

Rider's Guidebook. 2nd ed. Bill Cooper. (Illus.). 32p. 1994. pap. 4.95 (*1-884313-00-0*) Whitehorse NH.

Riders in the Chariot. Patrick White. (Fiction Ser.). 256p. 1985. pap. 8.95 (*0-14-002185-X*, Penguin Bks) Viking Penguin.

Riders in the Chariot. Patrick White. 496p. 1993. pap. 11.95 (*0-14-018634-4*, Penguin Classics) Viking Penguin.

Riders in the Shadowlands: Western Stories by H. A. Derosso. large type ed. Ed. by Bill Pronzini. Date not set. 20.00 (*0-7862-0760-4*, Thorndike Lrg Prnt) Thorndike Pr.

Riders of Black Dawn. Robin Gibson. 1993. 17.95 (*0-8034-8999-4*) Bouregy.

Riders of Death. large type ed. Lee Floren. 1991. pap. 15.99 (*0-7089-6958-5*) Ulverscroft.

Riders of High Rock. Louis L'Amour. 272p. 1994. mass mkt. 4.99 (*0-553-56782-9*) Bantam.

***Riders of High Rock: A Hopalong Cassidy Novel.** large type ed. Louis L'Amour. LC 96-36266. 1998. write for info. (*0-7838-1955-2*, GK Hall) Thorndike Pr.

Riders of Highrock. 5.98 (*0-8317-4692-0*) Smithmark.

***Riders of Rifle Range.** large type ed. Wade Hamilton. (Linford Western Library). 304p. 1997. pap. 16.99 (*0-7089-7988-2*, Linford) Ulverscroft.

Riders of Rohan. Christian Gehman. (Illus.). 48p. (YA). (gr. 10-12). 1985. pap. 12.00 (*0-915795-29-9*, 3100) Iron Crown Ent Inc.

Riders of the Pale Horse. T. Davis Bunn. 1994. pap. 9.99 (*1-55661-346-6*) Bethany Hse.

Riders of the Purple Sage. Zane Grey. 1976. 25.95 (*0-8488-1349-9*) Amereon Ltd.

Riders of the Purple Sage. Zane Grey. 384p. 1995. mass mkt. 5.50 (*0-06-101042-1*) HarpC.

Riders of the Purple Sage. Zane Grey. (Classics Ser.). 304p. 1990. pap. 9.95 (*0-14-018440-6*, Penguin Classics) Viking Penguin.

Riders of the Purple Sage. Zane Grey. Ed. by Lee C. Mitchell & David Trotter. (Oxford Popular Fiction Ser.). 304p. 1995. pap. 6.95 (*0-19-282443-0*) OUP.

Riders of the Purple Sage. Zane Grey. 1995. mass mkt. 4.99 (*0-671-45791-8*) PB.

Riders of the Purple Sage: The Authorized Edition. Zane Grey. LC 94-13798. (Illus.). xx, 337p. 1994. pap. 9.95 (*0-8032-7047-X*, Bison Books) U of Nebr Pr.

Riders of the Purple Sage - The Lone Star Ranger. Zane Grey. 736p. 1995. mass mkt. 4.99 (*0-06-100921-0*, Harp PBks) HarpC.

Riders of the Silver Rim. Brock Thoene & Bodie Thoene. (Saga of the Sierras Ser.: Vol. 2). 208p. (Orig.). 1990. pap. 7.99 (*1-55661-099-8*) Bethany Hse.

Riders of the Suwannee. Lee Gramling. LC 93-5215. 1993. 14.95 (*1-56164-046-8*); pap. 8.95 (*1-56164-043-3*) Pineapple Pr.

Riders of the Trojan Horse. Lauran Paine. 192p. 1991. 19.95 (*0-8027-4116-9*) Walker & Co.

Riders of the Trojan Horse. large type ed. Lauran Paine. 302p. 1991. reprint ed. lib. bdg. 17.95 (*1-56054-241-1*) Thorndike Pr.

Riders of the White Hell. large type ed. Cole Rickard. (Linford Western Library). 240p. 1993. pap. 15.99 (*0-7089-7363-9*, Linford) Ulverscroft.

Riders on Earth: Level 15. Evertts. 1983. 52.25 (*0-03-061398-1*) HB Schl Dept.

Riders on Earth: Level 15. E. Evertts. (J). 1983. wbk. ed., pap. 16.75 (*0-03-061441-4*) HB Schl Dept.

***Riders on Earth level 15.** Evertts. 1986. text ed. 46.50 (*0-03-002394-7*) HR&W Schl Div.

Riders on Earth 1986: Level 15. Evertts. (J). 1986. wbk. ed., pap. 13.75 (*0-03-002399-8*) HB Schl Dept.

Riders on the Storm: My Life with Jim Morrison & the Doors. John Densmore. 336p. 1991. pap. 13.95 (*0-385-30447-1*, Delta) Dell.

Riders Ready! A Book about BMX...with Advice from the Experts. Anne Perry. LC 85-50294. (Illus.). 130p. (Orig.). (J). (gr. 5-8). pap. 8.95 (*0-9615253-0-4*); 12.05 (*0-8479-9930-0*) Tadpole.

Riders to Cibola. Norman Zollinger. 1995. mass mkt. 4.99 (*0-8125-4845-0*) Forge NYC.

***Riders to the Sea.** John M. Synge. Ed. & Intro. by William-Allan Landes. LC 96-47095. 55p. (Orig.). 1996. pap. 6.00 (*0-88734-366-X*) Players Pr.

Riders to the Sea see Three Irish Plays

Riders to the Sea see Complete Plays of John M. Synge

Riders Up: Preparing for a Pony Race. Barbara Beirne. (J). (gr. 2-5). 1992. lib. bdg. 21.50 (*0-87614-714-7*, Carolrhoda) Lerner Group.

Riders West. large type ed. Ernest Haycox. LC 95-13692. 348p. 1995. 18.95 (*0-7862-0481-8*) Thorndike Pr.

Ridesharing & Transportation for the Disadvantaged. (Research Record Ser.: No. 1170). 86p. 1988. 13.00 (*0-309-04707-2*) Transport Res Bd.

Ridesharing Needs & Requirements: The Role of the Private & Public Sectors. (Special Reports: No. 193). 83p. 1981. 11.00 (*0-309-03223-7*) Transport Res Bd.

Ridge. Lisa W. Cantrell. 1989. mass mkt. 4.95 (*0-8125-0011-3*) Tor Bks.

Ridge: The Avenger (Sons & Lovers) Leanne Banks. (Desire Ser.). 1996. mass mkt. 3.50 (*0-373-05987-6*, 1-05987-2) Silhouette.

***Ridge Hill.** large type ed. Anna Jacobs. (Magna Large Print Ser.). 544p. 1996. 25.99 (*0-7505-0914-7*, Pub. by Magna Print Bks UK) Ulverscroft.

***Ridge-Pole Statues from the Late Archaic Temple at Satricum.** Patricia S. Lulof. 375p. 1996. 157.00 (*90-5170-355-4*, Pub. by Thesis Pubs NE) IBD Ltd.

Ridge Runner: The Story of a Maine Woodsman. Gerald Averill. LC 79-14339. (Illus.). 224p. 1979. reprint ed. pap. 8.95 (*0-945980-28-0*) Nrth Country Pr.

Ridgefield in Review. Silvio A. Bedini. (Illus.). 396p. 1994. reprint ed. lib. bdg. 42.50 (*0-8328-4026-2*) Higginson Bk Co.

Ridgefield to Color & Keep. Ridgefield Garden Club Coloring Book Committee Staff. Ed. by Lillian Willis. (Illus.). 44p. (Orig.). 1988. pap. 3.75 (*0-317-91201-1*) Ridgefield Garden Club.

Ridgeland Revealed: Guide to the Architecture of the Ridgeland-Oak Park Historic District. Oak Park Historic Preservation Commission Staff. Ed. by Arlene Sanderson. (Illus.). 110p. (Orig.). 1993. pap. 7.95 (*0-9616915-1-4*) Vil Oak Pk.

***Ridgeline Mysteries, No. 2.** 320p. 1998. write for info. (*1-56476-679-9*, Victor Bks) Chariot Victor.

***Ridgeline Mysteries, No. 3.** 320p. 1999. write for info. (*1-56476-680-2*, Victor Bks) Chariot Victor.

***Ridgeline Mysteries #1 Dr Death.** 320p. 1998. write for info. (*1-56476-678-0*, Victor Bks) Chariot Victor.

Ridgerunner. Richard Ripley. (Orig.). 1987. pap. 10.95 (*0-9603566-4-9*) Backeddy Bks.

Ridges & Valleys: A Mini-Encyclopedia of Anderson County, TN. 3rd ed. Ed. by Children's Museum of Oak Ridge, Tennessee Staff. (Illus.). 126p. (Orig.). (J). (gr. 5-12). 1990. pap. 5.50 (*0-9606832-5-9*) Chldrns Mus.

***Ridges in Image & Data Analysis.** David Eberly. LC 96-42118. (Computational Imaging & Vision Ser.). 228p. (C). 1996. lib. bdg. 117.00 (*0-7923-4268-2*) Kluwer Ac.

***Ridgeway.** Neil Curtis. (National Trail Guides Ser.). pap. 19.95 (*1-85410-268-0*, Pub. by Aurum Pr UK) London Brdge.

Ridgeway. Neil Curtis. (National Trail Guides Ser.). (Illus.). 168p. 1996. pap. 19.95 (*1-85410-019-X*, Pub. by Aurum Pr UK) London Brdge.

Ridgeway Ruby. large type ed. Prudence Bebb. 1995. 25.99 (*0-7089-3387-4*) Ulverscroft.

Ridgway Duels for Korea. Roy E. Appleman. LC 89-48499. (Military History Ser.: No. 18). (Illus.). 688p. 1990. 39.50 (*0-89096-432-7*) Tex A&M Univ Pr.

Ridicholas Nicholas: More Animal Poems. J. Patrick Lewis. LC 91-44349. (Illus.). 40p. (J). (gr. k-4). 1995. pap. 14.99 (*0-8037-1327-4*); pap. 14.89 (*0-8037-1328-2*) Dial Bks Young.

***Ridiculous!** Michael Coleman. LC 96-32964. (Illus.). (J). 1996. 12.95 (*1-888444-04-5*) Little Tiger.

Ridiculous History of World War II. Edwin J. Swineford. (Illus.). 232p. (Orig.). (C). 1994. pap. 12.00 (*0-9622670-1-5*) Kilroy Was There Pr.

Ridiculous Rhymes. Rozanne L. Williams. (Pick a Poem Ser.). (Illus.). 32p. (Orig.). (J). (gr. k-6). 1992. wbk. ed., pap. 11.98 (*1-57471-090-7*) Creat Teach Pr.

Ridiculous Rhymes from A to Z. John Walker. (Illus.). 64p. (J). (ps-2). 1995. 16.95 (*0-8050-1581-7*) H Holt & Co.

Ridiculous Riddles. Stuart A. Kallen. LC 92-14772. (J). 1992. lib. bdg. 13.98 (*1-56239-126-7*) Abdo & Dghtrs.

Ridiculous Theatre: Scourge of Human Folly: The Essays & Opinions of Charles Ludlam. Ed. by Steven Samuels. LC 92-2944. 320p. 1992. 24.95 (*1-55936-042-9*); pap. 14.95 (*1-55936-041-0*) Theatre Comm.

Ridiculous to the Delightful: Comic Characters in Sidney's New Arcadia. Robert N. Reeves. LC 73-91641. (LeBaron Russell Briggs Prize Honors Essays in English Ser.). 64p. 1974. pap. 2.50 (*0-674-76890-6*) HUP.

Ridiculously Easy to Use Pathway to Riches! Richard Starr. (Illus.). 220p. (Orig.). 1994. pap. 39.00 (*0-9640217-4-9*) Results Now.

Ridin' & Wreckin' Bob Wade. (Illus.). 32p. 1996. 9.95 (*0-87905-730-0*) Gibbs Smith Pub.

Ridin' Herd to Writing Symphonies: An Autobiography. Radie Britain. LC 95-6267. (Composers of North America Ser.: No. 12). 444p. 1996. 75.00 (*0-8108-2733-6*) Scarecrow.

Ridin'... Runnin'... Reminiscin' William H. Weatherford, Sr. & Brian Renner. (Illus.). 64p. 1985. 8.95 (*0-9614907-0-5*) Cowboy Poet.

Ridin' the Moon in Texas: Word Paintings. Ntozake Shange. (Illus.). 96p. 1988. pap. 9.95 (*0-312-02273-5*) St Martin.

Riding: A Guide for New Riders. Kate Delano & Condax Decker. (Illus.). 192p. 1995. 24.95 (*1-55821-381-3*) Lyons & Burford.

Riding: Buying Your First Horse. Marilyn Ross-Kinister. 124p. 1995. pap. 35.00 (*0-85131-625-5*, Pub. by J A Allen & Co UK) St Mut.

Riding a Dressage Test. Terry Colgate & Martin Diggle. 120p. 1990. pap. 30.00 (*0-85131-464-3*, Pub. by J A Allen & Co UK) St Mut.

Riding & Pony Care. Joanna Spector. (Horses Ser.). 32p. (J). (gr. 2 up). 1987. pap. 9.95 (*0-7460-0111-8*); lib. bdg. 17.95 (*0-88110-297-0*) EDC.

Riding & Roping: The Memoirs of J. Will Harris. Ed. by C. Virginia Matters. LC 74-78373. (Illus.). 211p. 1977. 20.00 (*0-913480-23-1*); pap. 6.00 (*0-913480-34-7*) Inter Am U Pr.

Riding Astride: The Frontier in Women's History. Patricia R. Dunlap. LC 95-21682. (Illus.). 220p. (C). 1996. 26.50 (*0-912869-17-8*); pap. 18.95 (*0-912869-18-6*) Arden Pr.

Riding Bicycles in the Rain. Lenore Balliro. Ed. by Alana Sherman & Lorraine DeGennaro. 20p. (Orig.). 1993. pap. 5.00 (*0-939689-16-2*) Alms Hse Pr.

Riding Book. Ginny L. Winter. (Illus.). (J). (gr. k-3). 1963. 8.95 (*0-8392-3031-1*) Astor-Honor.

Riding Camp. Bonnie Bryant. (Saddle Club Ser.: No. 10). 144p. (YA). 1990. mass mkt. 3.99 (*0-553-15790-6*) Bantam.

Riding Camp, Vol. 10. large type ed. Bonnie Bryant. LC 95-38625. (Saddle Club Ser.: No. 10). 144p. (J). (gr. 4 up). 1996. lib. bdg. 15.93 (*0-8368-1532-7*) Gareth Stevens Inc.

Riding Class. Bonnie Bryant. (Saddle Club Ser.: No. 52). 144p. (YA). 1996. mass mkt. 3.99 (*0-553-48362-5*) Bantam.

Riding Cross Country. Martin Diggle. 111p. 1990. 24.00 (*0-85131-426-0*, Pub. by J A Allen & Co UK) St Mut.

Riding Desire. Ed. by Tee A. Corinne. LC 91-3657. 160p. (Orig.). 1991. pap. 8.95 (*0-934411-44-1*, Banned Bks) Edward-William Austin.

Riding Down Dark. Ronald M. Pies. Ed. & Illus. by Carolyn Page. (Chapbook Ser.). 32p. (Orig.). 1992. pap. 6.00 (*1-879205-31-9*) Nightshade Pr.

Riding East: The SS Cavalry Brigade in Poland & Russia 1939-1942. Mark C. Yerger. (Illus.). 224p. 1996. 59.95 (*0-7643-0060-1*) Schiffer.

Riding Fence. June R. Welch. LC 83-80132. (Illus.). 200p. 1983. 18.95 (*0-912854-12-X*) Yellow Rose Pr.

Riding for a Fall. Lillian Roberts. 1996. mass mkt. 5.50 (*0-449-14985-4*) Fawcett.

Riding for Caesar: The Roman Emperors' Horse Guard. Michael P. Speidel. LC 93-23539. (Illus.). 243p. 1994. 27.95 (*0-674-76897-3*, SPERID) HUP.

***Riding for Ceasar: The Roman Emperor's Horse Guards.** Michael P. Speidel. 1997. pap. text ed. 16.95 (*0-674-76898-1*) HUP.

Riding for My Life. Julie Krone. LC 94-24976. 1995. 19.95 (*0-316-50477-7*) Little.

***Riding for Success: Both in & out of the Ring.** Gayle Lampe. (Illus.). 320p. 1996. text ed. 29.95 (*0-9655501-0-9*) Saddle & Bridle.

Riding for the Brand. Louis L'Amour. 256p. 1986. pap. 3.99 (*0-553-28105-4*) Bantam.

Riding for the Brand. Louis L'Amour. 192p. 1986. mass mkt. 2.95 (*0-88184-250-8*) Carroll & Graf.

***Riding for the Brand.** large type ed. Louis L'Amour. LC 96-42514. Date not set. 20.00 (*0-7838-1982-X*, GK Hall) Thorndike Pr.

Riding for the Rest of Us: A Practical Guide for Adult Riders. Jessica Jahiel. (Illus.). 224p. 1996. pap. 27.95 (*0-87605-909-4*) Howell Bk.

Riding High. Colleen R. Archer. 73p. (YA). (gr. 9-12). 1986. 7.95 (*0-920806-39-2*, Pub. by Penumbra Pr CN) U of Toronto Pr.

Riding High. Janet Dailey. LC 94-18547. (Janet Dailey's Love Scenes Ser.). 1994. pap. 3.50 (*1-56420-098-1*) New Readers.

Riding High. John Francome. 240p. 1996. mass mkt. 4.99 (*0-06-104291-9*, Harp PBks) HarpC.

Riding High. Michael Medved. 1999. pap. 23.95 (*0-525-93617-3*) NAL-Dutton.

Riding High: Scenes from a Lakeland Childhood. Barbara Sneyd. 22.95 (*0-7207-1711-6*) Viking Penguin.

Riding Home. Helen Potrebenko. 1996. pap. text ed. 10.95 (*0-88922-356-4*) Genl Dist Srvs.

Riding Home. Virginia Vail. LC 89-34548. (Horse Crazy Ser.). (Illus.). 128p. (J). (gr. 4-6). 1997. pap. 2.95 (*0-8167-1662-5*) Troll Communs.

Riding in a Point to Point. Anne Holland. 100p. 1990. pap. 24.00 (*0-85131-554-2*, Pub. by J A Allen & Co UK) St Mut.

***Riding Instructor's Handbook.** Monty Mortimer. 1997. pap. text ed. 14.95 (*0-7153-0622-7*) Sterling.

Riding Lawn Mower Service Manual. 4th ed. Intertec Publishing Staff. LC 86-83160. (Illus.). 300p. 1993. pap. text ed. 24.95 (*0-87288-525-9*, RLMS-4) Intertec Pub.

Riding Lesson. Bonnie Bryant. (Saddle Club Ser.: No. 36). 144p. (J). (gr. 4-7). 1994. 3.99 (*0-553-48151-7*) Bantam.

Riding Logic Available. Wilhelm Museler. 1985. 21.00 (*0-671-76492-6*) S&S Trade.

Riding Long Distance. Ann Hyland. 95p. (C). 1990. 29.00 (*0-85131-566-6*, Pub. by J A Allen & Co UK) St Mut.

Riding North One Summer. large type ed. Bettina Selby. 1991. 27.99 (*0-7089-8623-4*) Ulverscroft.

Riding on a Blue Note: Jazz & American Pop. Gary Giddins. 330p. 1981. 24.95 (*0-19-502835-X*) OUP.

Riding Out the Storms of Life. Howard L. Stimmel. 1996. 12.95 (*0-533-11614-7*) Vantage.

Riding out the Tropical Depression. Ellen Gilchrist. (Illus.). 35p. 1986. 125.00 (*0-317-46894-4*) Faust Pub Co.

Riding out the Tropical Depression. deluxe limited ed. Ellen Gilchrist. (Illus.). 35p. 1986. 50.00 (*0-917905-03-2*) Faust Pub Co.

Riding over Jumps. Martin Diggle. 188p. 1990. 29.00 (*0-85131-423-6*, Pub. by J A Allen & Co UK) St Mut.

Riding Recollections. G. J. Whyte-Melville. 248p. 1989. 19.95 (*0-948253-02-9*, Pub. by Sportsmans Pr UK) Trafalgar.

Riding School. Pam Dunning. 1989. pap. 16.95 (*0-8120-1883-4*) Barron.

***Riding School: Bind-Up.** Kate Needham & Lucy Smith. (Riding School Ser.). (Illus.). 128p. (Orig.). (YA). (gr. 3 up). 1997. pap. 14.95 (*0-7460-2929-2*, Usborne) EDC.

***Riding School: Bind-Up.** Kate Needham & Lucy Smith. (Riding School Ser.). (Illus.). 128p. (J). (gr. 3 up). 1997. lib. bdg. 22.95 (*0-88110-941-X*, Usborne) EDC.

***Riding Shotgun.** Rita M. Brown. 368p. 1997. mass mkt. 6.50 (*0-553-57224-5*) Bantam.

Riding Shotgun. Rita Mae Brown. LC 95-36103. 352p. 1996. 22.95 (*0-553-09605-2*, Bantam Trade Bks) Bantam.

Riding Shotgun. large type ed. Rita Mae Brown. LC 96-14352. (Large Print Bks.). 1996. pap. 23.95 (*1-56895-332-1*) Wheeler Pub.

Riding Side-Saddle. Janet W. MacDonald. 96p. 1995. 45.00 (*0-85131-621-2*, Pub. by J A Allen & Co UK) St Mut.

Riding Silver Star. Joanna Cole. (Illus.). (J). (gr. k-4). 1996. 15.00 (*0-688-13895-0*, Morrow Junior); lib. bdg. 14.93 (*0-688-13896-9*, Morrow Junior) Morrow.

Riding Teacher: A Basic Guide to Correct Methods of Classical Instruction. Alois Podhajsky. (Illus.). 204p. 1993. 22.95 (*0-943955-84-X*, Trafalgar Sq Pub) Trafalgar.

Riding the Airwaves with Alpha & Zulu. John Abbott et al. 208p. 1995. pap. 14.95 (*0-917963-14-8*) Artsci Inc.

Riding the Big Earth: Poems 1980-86. Joseph Richey. (Collected Poems Ser.). 64p. 1987. pap. 5.95 (*0-915032-89-9*) Natl Poet Foun.

Riding the Blue Silk. Marie W. Blair. 1994. 8.95 (*0-533-10902-7*) Vantage.

Riding the Bomb: True Stories of Young People Surviving the Insanity of World War. Charles R. Grizzle. LC 94-68809. 302p. 1995. 18.95 (*0-9644033-1-5*) Plateau Pubns.

Riding the Bull: How You Can Profit from the 1990's Stock Market Boom. Patrick McKeough. 148p. (Orig.). 1993. pap. 15.95 (*1-55013-522-8*, Pub. by Key Porter Bks CN) Firefly Bks Ltd.

Riding the Bull: My Year Inside the Madness at Merrill Lynch. Paul Stiles. LC 96-52232. 1997. 25.00 (*0-8129-2789-3*, Times Bks) Random.

Riding the Convection Connection: Teaching Energy: Hot Air Ballons. Donna S. Pfautsch. (Illus.). (Orig.). 1993. teacher ed., pap. 10.00 (*0-89824-216-9*) Trillium Pr.

Riding the Desert Trail. large type ed. Bettina Selby. 1990. 25.99 (*0-7089-2258-9*) Ulverscroft.

Riding the Dirt. Bob Sanford. (Illus.). 1973. 10.95 (*0-393-60018-1*) Norton.

Riding the Dragon: A Taoist Meditation Guide. 2nd ed. Liviu Argeseanu. LC 95-94551. (Illus.). 144p. (Orig.). 1996. pap. 19.95 (*0-9646988-9-7*) Apollo Pr NY.

Riding the Dragon: Myth & the Inner Journey. Roselle Angwin. LC 94-26671. 1995. pap. 11.95 (*1-85230-575-4*) Element MA.

Riding the Dragon: The Power of Committed Relationship. Rhea Powers & Gawain Bantle. LC 94-69882. 240p. 1995. pap. 14.95 (*1-880823-09-8*) N Star Pubns.

***Riding the Dutch Tiger: The Dutch East Indies Company & the Northeast Coast of Java, 1680-1743.** Luc Nagtegaal. (Verhandelingen Ser.: No. 171). (Illus.). 257p. (Orig.). 1996. pap. 37.00 (*90-6718-103-X*, Pub. by KITLV Pr NE) Cellar.

Riding the Ferry with Captain Cruz. Alice K. Flanagan. LC 96-17145. (Our Neighborhood Ser.). (Illus.). 32p. (J). 1996. lib. bdg. 18.00 (*0-516-20046-1*) Childrens.

***Riding the Ferry with Captain Cruz.** Alice K. Flanagan. (Our Neighborhood Ser.). 32p. (J). 1997. pap. 5.95 (*0-516-26059-6*) Childrens.

Riding the Gold Curve. Faye Morgan. 384p. 1994. 25.00 (*0-89672-326-7*) Tex Tech Univ Pr.

Riding the Gymkana Winner. Ed. by Bill Weikel. 1971. pap. 4.95 (*0-87505-379-3*) Borden.

Riding the Helix Express. Jan L. Harrington. (Illus.). 1992. ring bd. 39.95 (*0-9634291-0-8*) Black Gryphon.

***Riding the High Country.** Patrick T. Tucker. Ed. by Grace S. Coates. LC 87-27562. (Illus.). 165p. 1987. reprint ed. pap. 47.10 (*0-608-02979-3*, 2063447) Bks Demand.

Riding the Horse Backwards: Process Work in Theory & Practice. Arnold Mindell & Amy Mindell. 256p. (Orig.). 1992. pap. 11.95 (*0-14-019320-0*, Arkana) Viking Penguin.

Riding the Internet Highway. New Riders Publishing Staff. 1993. pap. 16.95 (*1-56205-192-X*) New Riders Pub.

Riding the Internet Highway. deluxe ed. Sharon Fisher & Bob Tidrow. 381p. 1994. Incl. diskette. pap. 24.99 incl. disk (*1-56205-315-9*) New Riders Pub.

***Riding the Iron Rooster.** Paul Theroux. 1997. pap. 12.95 (*0-449-00141-5*) Fawcett.

Riding the Iron Rooster. Paul Theroux. 1998. pap. 16.95 (*0-14-086166-1*) Viking Penguin.

Riding the Iron Rooster: By Train Through China. 480p. 1991. 5.99 (*0-517-03032-2*) Random Hse Value.

An Asterisk (*) at the beginning of an entry indicates that the title is appearing in BIP for the first time.

Riding the Iron Rooster: By Train Through China. Paul Theroux. 1989. mass mkt. 6.99 (0-8041-0454-9) Ivy Books.

Riding the Magic School Bus with Joanna Cole & Bruce Degen. Joanna Cole. (J). 1993. pap. 39.95 (0-590-45904-X) Scholastic Inc.

Riding the Mast Where It Swings. 2nd ed. Anne A. Paolucci. 1981. pap. 10.95 (0-918680-10-7) Bagehot Council.

Riding the Midnight River: Selected Poems of Pritish Nandy. Pritish Nandy. (Indian Poetry Ser.). 144p. 1975. 9.00 (0-89253-013-8) Ind-US Inc.

Riding the Northern Range: Poems from the Last Best-West. Ed. by Ted Stone. 160p. 1993. pap. 10.95 (0-88995-100-4, Pub. by Red Deer CN) Orca Bk Pubs.

Riding the One-Eyed Ford. 2nd ed. Diane Burns. (Poetry Ser.). (Illus.). 50p. (Orig.). (C). 1984. reprint ed. pap. 3.50 (0-936556-05-6) Contact Two.

Riding the Ox Home: A History of Meditation from Shamanism to Science. Willard Johnson. LC 86-47752. (Illus.). 262p. 1987. reprint ed. pap. 12.00 (0-8070-1305-6, BP-735) Beacon Pr.

Riding the Packet Boats & Other Stories. Mary V. Heuser. (Illus.). 32p. (Orig.). 1993. pap. write for info. (0-9634122-6-4) Feather Fables.

Riding the Rails: Tourist Guide to America's Scenic Train Rides. William C. Herow. LC 95-73314. (Illus.). 256p. (Orig.). 1996. pap. 14.95 (1-885464-25-8, 2010) Roundabout.

Riding the Rails: Trains, Then & Now. Steven Otfinoski. LC 96-19160. (Here We Go! Ser.). 32p. (J). (gr. 1 up). 1996. lib. bdg. 14.95 (0-7614-0404-X, Benchmark NY) Marshall Cavendish.

Riding the Range. Judy Mullican. (HighReach Learning Big Bks.). 8p. (J). (ps-k). 1994. pap. text ed. 10.95 (1-57332-011-0) HighReach Lrning.

Riding the Range. Judy Mullican. (Little Bks.). 8p. (J). (ps-k). 1995. pap. text ed. 10.95 (1-57332-014-5) HighReach Lrning.

Riding the Rap. Elmore Leonard. LC 94-38211. 304p. 1995. 22.95 (0-385-30847-7) Delacorte.

Riding the Rap. Elmore Leonard. 400p. 1996. mass mkt. 6.50 (0-440-21441-6) Dell.

Riding the Rap. Elmore Leonard. 336p. 1996. mass mkt. 6.50 (0-440-29539-4) Dell.

Riding the Rap. large type ed. Elmore Leonard. LC 95-10890. (Large Print Bks.). 1995. 26.95 (1-56895-224-4) Wheeler Pub.

Riding the Right Roads. Eva L. Mallory. (Illus.). 640p. 1989. ring bd. 25.00 (0-685-28999-0) Right Roads Pubns.

Riding the Runaway Horse: The Rise & Decline of Wang Laboratories. Charles Kenney. 1992. 22.95 (0-316-48919-0) Little.

Riding the Show Ring Hunter. Ed. by Bill Weikel. 1971. pap. 4.95 (0-87505-376-9) Borden.

***Riding the Snake.** Stephen Cannell. Date not set. write for info. (0-688-15805-6) Morrow.

Riding the Storm: A Play on Mahatma Gandhi. Shiva K. Ojha. 96p. 1989. text ed. 15.95 (81-207-0953-5, Pub. by Sterling Pubs II) Apt Bks.

***Riding the Tempest: A Biography of Teddy Roosevelt.** H. W. Brands. 480p. 1997. 30.00 (0-465-06958-4) Basic.

***Riding the Tempest: A Biography of Teddy Roosevelt.** H. W. Brands. 480p. 1998. pap. write for info. (0-465-06959-2) Basic.

***Riding the Tide of Change: Preparing for Personal & Planetary Transformation.** Martin F. Luthke. LC 97-90108. iv, 107p. (Orig.). 1997. pap. 9.95 (0-9656927-2-8) Expansion Pub.

Riding the Tiger: Doing Business in a Transforming World. Harrison Owen. LC 91-76873. 216p. (Orig.). 1992. pap. 20.00 (0-9618205-2-7) Abbott Pub.

Riding the Tiger: The Politics of Economic Reform in Post-Mao China. Gordon White. 300p. (C). 1993. 42.50 (0-8047-2148-3); pap. 15.95 (0-8047-2149-1) Stanford U Pr.

Riding the Tiger: Twenty Years on the Road: The Risks & Joys of Bringing Tibetan Buddhism to the West. Ole Nydahl. Ed. by Carol A. Aronoff. LC 92-6605. (Illus.). 512p. (Orig.). 1992. pap. 17.95 (0-931892-67-8) B Dolphin Pub.

Riding the Tiger's Back: A Footnote to the Assassination of JFK. Phillip Hemenway. LC 91-45719. (Illus.). 176p. 1992. 23.95 (0-918606-11-X) Heidelberg Graph.

Riding the Torch. Norman Spinrad. LC 84-12307. 166p. (Orig.). 1984. pap. 6.95 (0-89366-254-2) Ultramarine Pub.

Riding the Video Range: The Rise & Fall of the Western on Television. Gary A. Yoggy. LC 94-37472. (Illus.). 710p. 1995. lib. bdg. 65.00 (0-7864-0021-8) McFarland & Co.

Riding the Wave: Designing Your Organization's Architecture for Enduring Success. Keith Merron. 448p. 1994. text ed. 32.95 (0-442-01803-7) Van Nos Reinhold.

Riding the Waves of Change: Developing Managerial Competencies for a Turbulent World. Gareth Morgan. LC 87-46337. (Management Ser.). 230p. text ed. 28.95 (1-55542-093-1) Jossey-Bass.

Riding the Waves of Culture: Understanding Cultural Diversity in Business. Fons Trompenaars. LC 93-48785. 228p. 1994. text ed. 30.00 (0-7863-0290-9) Irwin Prof Pubng.

***Riding the Waves of Culture: Understanding Diversity in Global Business.** Fons Trompenaars. 1996. 34.95 (0-7863-1125-8) Irwin Prof Pubng.

Riding the Waves of Life. Tom Eggum. 126p. (Orig.). 1993. pap. 7.95 (1-883928-01-X) Longwood.

Riding the Whales. Victor Kelleher. LC 94-14868. (Illus.). (J). Date not set. pap. 14.99 (0-8037-1801-2) Dial Bks Young.

Riding the Whirlwind: An Ethiopian Story of Love & Revolution. Bereket H. Selassie. LC 92-32975. 340p. 1993. 21.95 (0-932415-75-X) Red Sea Pr.

***Riding the Whirlwind: An Ethiopian Story of Love & Revolution.** Bereket H. Selassie. 1997. pap. 14.95 (1-56902-047-7) Red Sea Pr.

Riding the White Horse Home: A Western Family Album. Teresa Jordan. 1994. pap. 12.00 (0-679-75135-1, Vin) Random.

Riding the Wind. Barbara G. Polikoff. (J). (gr. 4-7). 1995. 14.95 (0-8050-3492-7) H Holt & Co.

***Riding the Wind.** Barbara G. Polikoff. (J). (gr. 3-7). 1997. pap. 3.99 (0-614-28896-7, Puffin) Puffin Bks.

***Riding the Wind: Healing the Whole Person.** Robin Shapiro. LC 97-21680. 128p. (Orig.). 1997. pap. 12.95 (0-9639950-2-2) Tamarax Pr.

***Riding the Wind: Rural Leadership in Science & Mathematics Education.** 1997. lib. bdg. 250.95 (0-8490-8111-4) Gordon Pr.

***Riding the Wind & Other Tales.** James Hoggard. LC 97-14678. (Tarleton State University Southwestern Studies in the Humanities: No. 9). 176p. 1997. 19.95 (0-89096-781-4) Tex A&M Univ Pr.

Riding the Winds of Change: The Chronicles of Jack Hall. Jack Hall. (Illus.). 150p. 1994. pap. text ed. 14.95 (1-881116-51-4) Black Forest Pr.

Riding the Yellow Trolley Car. William P. Kennedy. (Illus.). 512p. 1994. pap. 12.95 (0-14-015992-4, Penguin Bks) Viking Penguin.

Riding Time. Rich Wallace. LC 95-20468. (J). 1996. pap. write for info. (0-679-87860-2) Knopf.

Riding Time Like a River: The Catholic Moral Tradition since Vatican II. Ed. by William J. O'Brien. LC 93-4394. 192p. 1993. 36.00 (0-87840-542-9) Georgetown U Pr.

Riding Time Like a River: The Catholic Moral Tradition since Vatican II. Ed. by William J. O'Brien. LC 93-4394. 126p. 1993. reprint ed. pap. 36.00 (0-608-01817-1, 2062466) Bks Demand.

Riding to Hounds. John Williams. 95p. 1990. pap. 30.00 (0-85131-463-5, Pub. by J A Allen & Co UK) St Mut.

Riding to Jerusalem. Bettina Selby. 1995. pap. text ed. 10.95 (0-316-78031-6) Little.

Riding to Music. Janet MacDonald. 95p. 1990. pap. 24.00 (0-85131-433-3, Pub. by J A Allen & Co UK) St Mut.

Riding Tough. large type ed. Jim Busbee. (Linford Western Library). 368p. 1985. pap. 15.99 (0-7089-6186-X) Ulverscroft.

Riding Towards the Light: An Apprenticeship in the Art of Dressage Riding. Paul Belasik. 152p. 1990. 40.00 (0-85131-509-7, Pub. by J A Allen & Co UK) St Mut.

***Riding Toys, Pre-1900 to Early 1990's.** 2nd rev. ed. (Illus.). 194p. 1996. pap. 29.95 (0-89538-012-9) L-W Inc.

Riding Western. Jane Lake. 88p. (C). 1990. pap. 21.00 (0-85131-432-5, Pub. by J A Allen & Co UK) St Mut.

Riding Whiskey. Carole S. Adler. LC 93-30196. (J). 1994. 13.95 (0-395-68185-5, Hills Med) HM.

Riding Wind. Barbara G. Polikoff. 1997. pap. 3.99 (0-14-038424-3) Viking Penguin.

***Riding with Custer: Recollections of a Cavalryman in the Civil War.** J. H. Kidd. LC 97-24450. (Illus.). 528p. 1997. pap. 19.95 (0-8032-7781-4, Bison Books) U of Nebr Pr.

***Riding with Rosser.** S. Roger Keller. (Illus.). 140p. Date not set. 19.95 (1-57249-066-7, Burd St Pr) White Mane Pub.

Riding with Stuart: Reminiscences of an Aide-de-Camp. Theodore S. Garnett. Ed. by Robert J. Trout. LC 93-48948. (Illus.). 124p. (C). 1994. 19.95 (0-942597-58-3) White Mane Pub.

Riding with the Dolphins: The Equinox Guide to Dolphins & Porpoises. Erich Hoyt. (Illus.). 64p. (J). (gr. 5 up). 1992. pap. 9.95 (0-921820-57-7, Pub. by Camden Hse CN); lib. bdg. 17.95 (0-921820-55-0, Pub. by Camden Hse CN) Firefly Bks Ltd.

Riding with the Lion: In Search of Mystical Christianity. Kyriacos C. Markides. 384p. 1996. pap. 13.95 (0-14-019481-9, Arkana) Viking Penguin.

Ridley's Law of Carriage of Goods by Land, Sea & Air. Jonathan Ignarski. 1988. pap. 135.00 (0-7219-0623-0, Pub. by Scientific UK) St Mut.

RIDT '94. Ed. by Jacques Andre et al. 312p. 1994. pap. text ed. 86.50 (0-471-94823-3) Wiley.

Ridvan (1993) Message for Children. Ed. by Australian Baha'i Children Education Task Force Staff. 13p. 1992. pap. 3.00 (0-909991-59-6) Bahai.

Rie Munoz: Alaskan Artist. Illus. by Rie Munoz. LC 90-663. 80p. 1984. pap. 19.95 (0-88240-257-9) Alaska Northwest.

***Riegel's Handbook of Industrial Chemistry.** Ed. by Kent. 1290p. 1992. text ed. 115.50 (0-412-99241-8, Chap & Hall NY) Chapman & Hall.

Riegel's Handbook of Industrial Chemistry. 9th ed. Ed. by James A. Kent. LC 92-22660. 1993. text ed. 99.95 (0-442-00175-4) Chapman & Hall.

***Riegle Community Development & Regulatory Improvement Act of 1994 - Law/Explanation/Conference Report.** 368p. 1994. pap. 19.90 (0-614-26812-5, BLS-3388) Commerce.

***Riegle-Neal Interstate Banking & Branching Efficiency Act of 1994.** 132p. 1994. pap. 19.00 (0-614-26813-3, BLS-3396) Commerce.

Riekert's Basic Employment Law. 2nd ed. J. Grogan. 180p. 1993. pap. write for info. (0-7021-2916-X, Pub. by Juta SA) Gaunt.

Riel Rebellions: A Cartographic History (Le Recit Cartographique des Affaires Riel) William A. Oppen. LC 80-453679. (Illus.). 119p. reprint ed. pap. 34.00 (0-8357-4000-5, 2036701) Bks Demand.

Riemann Approach to Integration. Washek F. Pfeffer. LC 93-18565. (Cambridge Tracts in Mathematics Ser.: No. 109). 292p. (C). 1994. text ed. 52.95 (0-521-44035-1) Cambridge U Pr.

Riemann Boundary Problem on Riemann Surfaces. Y. L. Rodin. (C). 1988. lib. bdg. 116.50 (90-277-2653-1) Kluwer Ac.

Riemann-Hilbert Problem: A Publication from the Steklov Institute of Mathematics, Adviser: Sergeev, Armen. D. V. Anosov & A. A. Bolibruch. (Aspects of Mathematics Ser.: Vol. 22). x, 191p. 1994. 46.00 (3-528-06496-X, Pub. by Vieweg & Sohn GW) Informatica.

Riemann Hypothesis & Hilberts Tenth Problem, Vol. 4. S. Chowla. (Mathematics & Its Applications Ser.). xvi, 120p. 1965. text ed. 161.00 (0-677-00140-1) Gordon & Breach.

***Riemann Legacy: Riemannian Ideas in Mathematics & Physics.** LC 97-17741. 1997. text ed. 595.00 (0-7923-4636-X) Kluwer Ac.

Riemann, Musiklexikon. Riemann. 108p. (GER.). 1967. 350.00 (0-8288-6690-2, M-7602) Fr & Eur.

Riemann-Roch Algebra. W. Fulton & Serge A. Lang. LC 84-26842. (Grundlehren der Mathematischen Wissenschaften Ser.: Vol. 277). x, 208p. 1985. 98.00 (0-387-96086-4) Spr-Verlag.

***Riemann Solvers & Numerical Methods for Fluid Dynamics: A Practical Introduction.** E. F. Toro. LC 97-23422. 1997. write for info. (3-540-61676-4) Spr-Verlag.

Riemann Surfaces. Ed. by E. Carvalho et al. 716p. (C). 1989. pap. 48.00 (9971-5-0903-2); text ed. 161.00 (9971-5-0902-4) World Scientific Pub.

Riemann Surfaces. 2nd ed. H. M. Farkas & I. Kra. Ed. by J. H. Ewing et al. (Graduate Texts in Mathematics Ser.: Vol. 71). (Illus.). xiv, 363p. 1995. 54.95 (0-387-97703-1) Spr-Verlag.

Riemann Surfaces: A View Towards Several Complex Variables. A. T. Huckleberry. (London Mathematical Society Lecture Note Ser.: No. 73). (Illus.). 260p. (C). 1993. pap. write for info. (0-521-28491-0) Cambridge U Pr.

Riemann Surfaces & Generalized Theta Functions. R. C. Gunning. (Illus.). 1976. 64.95 (0-387-07744-8) Spr-Verlag.

Riemann, Topology & Physics. Michael Monastyrsky. 1986. 39.50 (0-8176-3262-X) Birkhauser.

***Riemann, Topology & Physics.** 2nd ed. Michael Monastyrsky. 1996. 34.50 (0-8176-3789-3) Birkhauser.

Riemann-Type Integral That Includes Lebesgue-Stieltjes, Bochner & Stochastic Integrals. E. J. McShane. LC 52-42839. (Memoirs Ser.: No. 1/88). 54p. 1983. reprint ed. pap. 17.00 (0-8218-1288-2, MEMO/1/88) Am Math.

Riemann-Zeta Function. Anatoly A. Karatsuba & S. M. Voronin. Tr. by Neal Koblitz from RUS. LC 92-22817. (Expositions in Mathematics Ser.). xii, 396p. (C). 1992. lib. bdg. 115.95 (3-11-013170-6) De Gruyter.

Riemannian Foliations. Pierre Molino. (Progress in Mathematics Ser.: No. 73). 360p. 1987. 60.50 (0-8176-3370-7) Birkhauser.

Riemannian Geometry. Gerard Besson et al. Ed. by Miroslav Lovric et al. LC 95-47659. (Fields Institute Monographs: No. 4). 115p. 1996. 46.00 (0-8218-0263-1, FIM/4) Am Math.

Riemannian Geometry. Manfredo DoCarmo. 300p. 1994. 43.50 (0-8176-3490-8) Birkhauser.

***Riemannian Geometry.** Luther P. Eisenhart. (Princeton Landmarks in Mathematics & Physics Ser.). 1997. pap. text ed. 19.95 (0-691-02353-0) Princeton U Pr.

Riemannian Geometry. J. Lafontaine et al. (Universitext Ser.). x, 248p. 1987. pap. 29.00 (0-387-17923-2) Spr-Verlag.

Riemannian Geometry. Takashi Sakai. LC 96-6475. (Translations of Mathematical Monographs: No. 149). (Illus.). 358p. 1996. 119.00 (0-8218-0284-4, MMONO/149) Am Math.

Riemannian Geometry. T. J. Willmore. LC 92-45861. 336p. 1993. 75.00 (0-19-853253-9, Clarendon Pr) OUP.

Riemannian Geometry. rev. ed. Luther P. Eisenhart. 272p. 1950. text ed. 65.00 (0-691-08026-7) Princeton U Pr.

Riemannian Geometry. 2nd ed. S. Gallot et al. (Universitext Ser.). (Illus.). xiii, 284p. 1994. 39.00 (0-387-52401-0) Spr-Verlag.

Riemannian Geometry. 2nd rev. ed. Wilhelm Klingenberg. LC 95-2589. (De Gruyter Studies in Mathematics: Vol. 1). x, 410p. (C). 1995. lib. bdg. 79.95 (3-11-014593-6) De Gruyter.

***Riemannian Geometry.** T. J. Willmore. (Illus.). 336p. 1997. reprint ed. pap. text ed. 45.00 (0-19-851492-1) OUP.

***Riemannian Geometry, Vol. 171.** Peter Petersen. LC 97-5786. (Graduate Texts in Mathematics Ser.). 1997. write for info. (0-387-98212-4) Spr-Verlag.

Riemannian Geometry: A Beginner's Guide. Frank Morgan. LC 92-13261. (Illus.). 128p. (C). 1992. text ed. 30.00 (0-86720-242-4) AK Peters.

Riemannian Geometry: A Modern Introduction. Isaac Chavel. (Cambridge Tracts in Mathematics Ser.: No. 108). 350p. (C). 1994. text ed. 69.95 (0-521-43201-4) Cambridge U Pr.

Riemannian Geometry: A Modern Introduction. Isaac Chavel. (Tracts in Mathematics Ser.: No. 108). 400p. (C). 1995. pap. text ed. 27.95 (0-521-48578-9) Cambridge U Pr.

Riemannian Geometry & Geometric Analysis. Jurgen Jost. LC 95-2775. (Universitext Ser.). 1995. write for info. (3-540-57113-2) Spr-Verlag.

Riemannian Geometry & Geometric Analysis. Jurgen Jost. LC 95-2775. (Universitext Ser.). 400p. 1995. 59.95 (0-387-57113-2) Spr-Verlag.

Riemannian Geometry, Fibre Bundles, Kaluza-Klein Theories & All That. R. Coquereaux & A. Jadczyk. 360p. (C). 1988. text ed. 85.00 (9971-5-0426-X); pap. text ed. 49.00 (9971-5-0427-8) World Scientific Pub.

***Riemannian Manifolds: An Introduction to Curvature, Vol. 176.** John M. Lee. LC 97-14537. (Graduate Texts in Mathematics Ser.). 1997. write for info. (0-387-98271-X) Spr-Verlag.

***Riemannian Manifolds of Conullity Two.** 300p. 1996. lib. bdg. 48.00 (981-02-2768-X) World Scientific Pub.

Riemannian Symmetric Spaces of Rank One. Isaac Chavel. LC 72-76060. (Lecture Notes in Pure & Applied Mathematics Ser.: Vol. 5). 93p. reprint ed. pap. 26.60 (0-685-16260-5, 2027114) Bks Demand.

Riemann's Boundary Problem with Infinite Index. N. V. Govorov. Ed. by I. V. Ostrovskii. Tr. by Yu I. Lyubarskii. LC 93-50915. (Operator Theory: Advances & Applications Ser.: Vol. 67). 264p. (RUS.). 1994. 138.50 (0-8176-2999-8) Birkhauser.

Rien N'est Simple. Goscinny Sempe. (FRE.). 1978. pap. 10.95 (0-8288-3789-9, F16330) Fr & Eur.

Rien n'est Simple. Jean-Jacques Sempe. (Folio Ser.: No. 873). (FRE.). pap. 8.95 (2-07-036873-4) Schoenhof.

Rien Poortvliet's Horses. Rien Portvliet. (Illus.). 248p. 1995. 60.00 (1-55670-430-5) Stewart Tabori & Chang.

Rienzi: The Last of the Rome Tribune. Edward B. Lytton. LC 70-145150. 1971. reprint ed. 69.00 (0-403-01079-9) Scholarly.

Rienzi, the Last of the Roman Tribunes, 2 vols. in 1. Edward B. Lytton. (BCL1-PR English Literature Ser.). 1992. reprint ed. lib. bdg. 99.00 (0-7812-7591-1) Rprt Serv.

Riepetown Serb. Stanley Drakulich. Ed. by Thomas E. Shaw. (Illus.). 84p. 1996. pap. 12.95 (0-9633371-3-0) Carson St Pub.

Riera Cave: Stone Age Hunter-Gatherer Adaptations in Northern Spain, No. 36. Ed. by Lawrence G. Straus & Geoffrey A. Clark. LC 86-71561. (Anthropological Research Papers). (Illus.). xvii, 498p. (Orig.). (C). 1986. pap. 25.00 (0-9611932-4-7) AZ Univ ARP.

Riera I Arago. Gloria Picazo. (Great Monographs). (Illus.). 464p. 1993. 300.00 (84-343-0729-4) Elliots Bks.

Riesgo de Vivir. Lucia Fox. Ed. by Lucia Lockert. 55p. (SPA.). 1992. pap. 10.00 (1-880577-00-3) La Nueva Cronica.

Rietveld Method. Ed. by R. A. Young. (International Union of Crystallography: Monographs on Crystallography Ser.: Vol. 5). (Illus.). 312p. 1995. pap. text ed. 39.95 (0-19-855912-7) OUP.

Rietveld Method Tutorial, Seattle, 1989. (American Crystallographic Association Lecture Notes Ser.: No. 9). 1991. pap. 15.00 (0-685-51614-8) Polycrystal Bk Serv.

***RIF & the Federal Employee: What You Need to Know.** Susan M. Smith. (Illus.). 76p. 1996. pap. text ed. 9.95 (0-936295-66-X) FPMI Comns.

RIF Survival Handbook: How to Manage Your Money if You're Unemployed. John May. LC 82-80357. 132p. (Orig.). 1982. pap. 4.95 (0-9605750-2-2) Tilden Pr.

***Rife: Poems.** Stefanie Marlis. LC 97-10568. 96p. 1998. 20.95 (1-889330-11-6); pap. write for info. (1-889330-12-4) Sarabande Bks.

Riff Raff. Laurence Fishburne. 1997. pap. 5.25 (0-8222-1545-4) Dramatists Play.

Riff Tricks. Mick Barker. (Illus.). 48p. 1991. pap. 14.95 incl. audio (0-7119-2515-1, AM83163) Music Sales.

Riffraff Chronicles: Featuring Ray. Doug Manning. LC 95-94992. 104p. 1995. pap. 6.95 (0-9648690-1-2) Lowdown Bros.

Riff's Be Bop Book. Clements. (J). 1997. 3.99 (0-689-81304-X) S&S Childrens.

***Rifle.** Gary Paulsen. 112p. (YA). 1997. mass mkt. 4.50 (0-440-21920-5, LLL BDD) BDD Bks Young Read.

Rifle. Gary Paulsen. LC 95-730. 192p. (YA). (gr. 7 up). 1995. 16.00 (0-15-292880-4, HB Juv Bks) HarBrace.

Rifle, 2 vols. Intro. by Warren Greatbatch. (Illus.). 1990. reprint ed. 160.00 (0-916107-87-6) Broadfoot.

Rifle & Its Development for Big Game Hunting. S. Truesdell. (Illus.). 274p. 1992. 35.00 (0-940143-74-7) Safari Pr.

Rifle Guide. Sam Fadala. (Illus.). 288p. 1993. pap. 16.95 (0-88317-171-6) Stoeger Pub Co.

Rifle in America. Philip Sharpe. (Library Classics Ser.). (Illus.). 726p. 1987. reprint ed. 59.00 (0-935632-49-2) Wolfe Pub Co.

Rifle Markets in the United States: Statistical Analysis, 1991-1995: Bolt-Action, Single-Shot, Lever-Action Autoloader & Pump Action. Dennis M. Zogbi. 150p. (Orig.). 1991. pap. text ed. 1,195.00 (0-929717-01-5) Paumanok Pubns.

Rifle Operator's Manual. 1990. lib. bdg. 79.95 (0-8490-3989-4) Gordon Pr.

Rifle Shooting. Boy Scouts of America Staff. (Illus.). 96p. (Orig.). 1990. pap. 2.40 (0-8395-3330-6, 33330) BSA.

Rifle Volunteers, Eighteen Fifty-Nine to Nineteen Eight. Ray Westlake. 173p. (C). 1987. 70.00 (0-902633-79-1, Pub. by Picton UK) St Mut.

Rifleman Dodd. C. S. Forester. 1976. 18.95 (0-8488-1008-2) Amereon Ltd.

Rifleman Dodd. C. S. Forester. LC 89-63522. (Great War Stories Ser.). 160p. 1989. reprint ed. 19.95 (0-933852-76-2) Nautical & Aviation.

Rifleman of Ohio. Joseph Alsheler. 432p. 1981. reprint ed. lib. bdg. 25.95 (0-89968-226-X, Lghtyr Pr) Buccaneer Bks.

Rifleman of the Ohio. Joseph A. Altsheler. 25.95 (0-8488-1239-5) Amereon Ltd.

Rifleman of the Ohio. Joseph Altsheler. (Young Trailer Ser.). 319p. 1984. reprint ed. lib. bdg. 25.95 (0-89966-483-0) Buccaneer Bks.

Rifleman Went to War. Herbert W. McBride. 425p. 1987. reprint ed. 24.95 (0-935856-01-3) Lancer.

An Asterisk (*) at the beginning of an entry indicates that the title is appearing in BIP for the first time.

Rifleman's Handbook: A Shooter's Guide to Rifles, Reloading & Results. Illus. by Ken Clubb. 320p. (C). 1989. 21.95 (*0-9621148-2-0*) PJS Pubns.

Rifles: A Book of North American Landscapes. William T. Vollmann. (Seven Dreams Ser.: Vol. 6). 432p. 1995. pap. 11.95 (*0-14-017623-3*, Penguin Bks) Viking Penguin.

Rifles & Romance. Clint Berryhill. 200p. 1983. pap. 5.00 (*0-942698-09-6*) Trends & Events.

Rifles, Blankets, & Beads: Identity, History, & the Northern Athapaskan Potlatch. William E. Simeone. LC 94-48470. (Civilization of the American Indian Ser.: Vol. 216). (Illus.). 224p. 1995. 24.95 (*0-8061-2713-9*) U of Okla Pr.

Rifles for Watie. Harold Keith. LC 57-10280. (Trophy Keypoint Bk.). 352p. (YA). (gr. 7 up). 1987. pap. 3.95 (*0-06-447030-X*, Trophy) HarpC Child Bks.

Rifles for Watie. Harold Keith. LC 57-10280. 332p. (J). (gr. 7 up). 1991. lib. bdg. 14.89 (*0-690-04907-2*, Crowell Jr Bks) HarpC Child Bks.

Rifles for Watie: A Literature Unit. Michael Shepherd. Ed. by Patricia Miriani. (Literature Units Ser.). (Illus.). 48p. (Orig.). 1992. student ed. 7.95 (*1-55734-413-2*) Tchr Create Mat.

Rifles for Watie: A Study Guide. Linda Smoucha. Ed. by J. Friedland & R. Kessler. (Novel-Ties Ser.). (J). (gr. 5-8). 1996. pap. text ed. 15.95 (*1-56982-671-4*) Lrn Links.

Rifles of Revenge. Lewis B. Patten. 1979. mass mkt. 1.95 (*0-89083-568-3*, Zebra Kensgtn) Kensgtn Pub Corp.

Rifles of Revenge - Red Runs the River. Lewis B. Patten. 352p. 1994. mass mkt., pap. text ed. 4.99 (*0-8439-3598-7*) Dorchester Pub Co.

Rifles of the World. Jean-Noel Mouret. 1994. 17.98 (*1-55521-997-7*) Bk Sales Inc.

Rifles of the World. John Walter. LC 93-70481. (Illus.). 320p. (Orig.). 1993. pap. 20.95 (*0-87349-150-5*, ROW) DBI.

***Rift.** Peter Cole. 1997. pap. text ed. 9.95 (*1-886449-62-7*) Barrytown Ltd.

Rift. Peter Cole. 1989. pap. 6.95 (*0-88268-087-0*) Station Hill Pr.

Rift. Peter David. (Orig.). pap. 4.99 (*0-685-51957-0*) PB.

Rift. Peter David. Ed. by Dave Stern. (Star Trek Ser.: No. 57). 288p. (Orig.). 1991. mass mkt. 4.99 (*0-671-74796-7*) PB.

Rift. V. Y. Mudimbe. Tr. by Marjolijn De Jager. LC 92-44511. 128p. 1993. text ed. 16.95 (*0-8166-2312-0*) U of Minn Pr.

***Rift.** Walter Williams. 22.00 (*0-06-105294-9*, HarperPrism); mass mkt. 5.99 (*0-06-105794-0*, HarperPrism) HarpC.

Rift in the Clouds: Ugaritic & Hebrew Descriptions of the Divine. Marjo C. Korpel. (Ugaritisch-Biblische Literatur Ser.: Vol. 8). xii, 721p. 1990. text ed. 79.00 (*3-927120-07-3*, Pub. by UGARIT GW) Eisenbrauns.

Rift Valley Fever. Ed. by N. Goldblum et al. (Contributions to Epidemiology & Biostatistics Ser.: Vol. 3). (Illus.). xii, 196p. 1981. pap. 66.50 (*3-8055-1770-X*) S Karger.

***Rift Valley Fever: An Emerging Human & Animal Problem.** WHO Staff. (WHO Offset Publications: No. 63). 69p. 1982. 6.00 (*92-4-170063-7*) World Health.

Rift Valleys & Geology of East Africa. John W. Gregory. LC 76-44726. reprint ed. 47.50 (*0-404-15863-3*) AMS Pr.

Rifted Ocean-Continent Boundaries. Ed. by E. Banda et al. LC 95-15545. (NATO ASI Ser.: Series C, Mathematical & Physical Sciences: Vol. 463). 1995. lib. bdg. 185.00 (*0-7923-3505-8*) Kluwer Ac.

Rifter's Covenant No. 4: Exordium, No. 4. Sherwood Smith & David Trowbridge. 480p. (Orig.). 1995. 4.99 (*0-8125-2027-0*) Tor Bks.

Rifts Conversion Book. Kevin Siembieda. Ed. by Alex Marciniszyn & Thomas Bartold. (Illus.). 224p. (Orig.). (YA). (gr. 8 up). 1991. pap. 20.95 (*0-916211-53-3*, 803) Palladium Bks.

Rifts Japan. Kevin Siembieda. Ed. by Alex Marciniszyn et al. (Rifts World Bks.: No. 8). (Illus.). 200p. (Orig.). 1995. pap. 20.95 (*0-916211-88-6*, 818) Palladium Bks.

Rifts Mercenaries. J. Rosenstein. (Rifts RPG Ser.). (Illus.). 160p. (Orig.). 1994. pap. 16.95 (*0-916211-70-3*, 813) Palladium Bks.

Rifts Psyscape. C. J. Carella. Ed. by Kevin Siembieda & Alex Marcinszyn. (Rifts Worldbook Ser.: Vol. 12). (Illus.). 160p. (Orig.). 1997. pap. 16.95 (*0-916211-94-0*) Palladium Bks.

Rifts Role-Playing Game. Kevin Siembieda. Ed. by Alex Marciniszyn & Thomas Bartold. (Illus.). 256p. (Orig.). (YA). (gr. 8 up). 1990. pap. 24.95 (*0-916211-50-9*, 800) Palladium Bks.

Rifts Sourcebook. Kevin Siembieda. Ed. by Alex Marciniszyn & Thomas Bartold. (Rifts Sourcebook Ser.: No. 1). (Illus.). 112p. (Orig.). (YA). (gr. 8 up). 1991. pap. 11.95 (*0-916211-51-7*, 801) Palladium Bks.

Rifts South America, Vol. 2. Kevin Siembieda & C. J. Carella. Ed. by Kevin Kirsten & James Osten. (Rifts World Bks.: Vol. 9). (Illus.). 192p. (Orig.). (YA). (gr. 8 up). 1995. pap. 19.95 (*0-916211-89-4*, 819) Palladium Bks.

Rifts Undersea. Kevin Siembieda. (Rifts World Bks.: No. 7). (Illus.). 160p. (Orig.). 1995. pap. 15.95 (*0-916211-72-X*, 815) Palladium Bks.

Rig. John Collee. 384p. 1994. mass mkt. 4.99 (*0-06-104284-6*, Pub. by Haags Gemeentemuseum) HarpC.

Rig-Color Program: Computerized Harness-Container Color Pattern Selection. Gary Peek. 1995. 14.95 incl. disk (*0-915516-87-X*, PR-201) Para Pub.

Rig Equipment. fac. ed. Philip F. Lynch. LC 80-24533. (His a Primer in Drilling & Production Equipment: No. 2). (Illus.). 142p. pap. 40.50 (*0-7837-7426-5*, 2047221) Bks Demand.

Rig Veda. Bibek Debroy. (Great Epics of India Ser.: Veda 1). (C). 1992. pap. 3.00 (*0-8364-2778-5*, Pub. by BR Pub II) S Asia.

Rig Veda. Thomas Wyatt. Ed. & Tr. by Wendy D. O'Flaherty. (Classics Ser.). 502p. 1982. pap. 11.95 (*0-14-044402-5*, Penguin Classics) Viking Penguin.

Rig Veda, 4 pts, Pt. 4. Vedas. Ed. by Daniel H. Ingalls. LC 54-10046. (Oriental Ser.: No. 33-35). 300p. 1957. 16.50 (*0-674-76967-8*) HUP.

Rig Veda: A Metrically Restored Text with an Introduction & Notes. Ed. by Barend A. Van Nooten & Gary B. Holland. LC 94-37861. (Harvard Oriental Ser.: No. 50). 685p. 1994. text ed. 40.00 (*0-674-76971-6*, VANRIG) HUP.

Rig Veda Americanus. Ed. by Daniel G. Brinton. LC 73-83463. (Library of Aboriginal American Literature: No. 8). reprint ed. 44.00 (*0-404-52188-6*) AMS Pr.

Rig Veda Americanus: Sacred Songs of the Ancient Mexicans. D. Brinton. 1976. lib. bdg. 59.95 (*0-8490-2524-9*) Gordon Pr.

Rig-Veda-Samhita: The Sacred Hymns of the Brahmans, 4 vols., Set. 2nd ed. Friedrich M. Mueller. LC 73-18831. 1892. 176.00 (*0-404-11461-X*) AMS Pr.

Rig-Veda (Summary) 5.00 (*0-938924-29-X*) Sri Shirdi Sai.

Rig Warrior No. 2: Wheels of Death. William W. Johnstone. 1988. mass mkt. 2.95 (*0-8217-2331-6*, Zebra Kensgtn) Kensgtn Pub Corp.

Rig Your Dinghy Right: A Design & Installation Guide for Racing Sailors. Mark Chisnell. 1994. pap. text ed. 18.95 (*0-07-029123-3*) McGraw.

***Rigadoon.** Louis-Ferdinand Celine. Tr. by Ralph Manheim from FRE. LC 97-23297. 296p. 1997. reprint ed. pap. 13.50 (*1-56478-162-3*) Dalkey Arch.

Rigger Black Book: A Shadowrun Sourcebook. Philip McGregor. Ed. by Donna Ippolito & Sharon T. Mulvihill. (Shadowrun Ser.). (Illus.). 136p. (Orig.). 1991. pap. 15.00 (*1-55560-169-3*, 7108) FASA Corp.

Rigger's Apprentice. 2nd ed. Brian Toss. 1992. pap. text ed. 24.95 (*0-07-065075-6*) McGraw.

Rigger's Apprentice. 2nd ed. Brion Toss. (Illus.). 208p. 1992. pap. 24.95 (*0-87742-361-X*, 60360) Intl Marine.

Riggers Bible Handbook of Heavy Rigging. Robert P. Leach, Jr. 1983. reprint ed. 39.95 (*0-9600992-1-2*) Riggers Bible.

Rigger's Sourcebook. Deborah Blackmon. (Illus.). 3500p. (C). 1989. text ed. 350.00 (*0-318-41207-1*) Bravo Pub.

Rigging. 1991. lib. bdg. 72.95 (*0-8490-4126-0*) Gordon Pr.

Rigging Equipment & Outfit of Seagoing Ships, Pt. 1. J. P. De Haan. 464p. 1957. 310.00 (*0-85950-070-5*) St Mut.

Rigging Handbook: The Complete Illustrated Field Reference. Jerry Klinke. (Illus.). 110p. 1995. pap. 12.95 (*1-888724-00-5*) ACRA Pubng.

Rigging of Ships in the Days of the Spritsail Topmast, 1600-1720. R. C. Anderson. LC 93-43440. (Illus.). 320p. reprint ed. pap. 8.95 (*0-486-27960-X*) Dover.

Riggs: Our Pioneer Ancestors, Being a Record of Available Information As to the Riggs, Baldridge, Agnew, Earle, Kirkpatrick, Vreeland & Allied Families in the Ancestry of Samual Agnew Riggs & Catherine Doane Earle Riggs. H. E. Riggs. (Illus.). 230p. 1993. reprint ed. pap. 37.00 (*0-8328-3737-7*); reprint ed. lib. bdg. 47.00 (*0-8328-3736-9*) Higginson Bk Co.

Riggs Family of Maryland: A Genealogical & Historical Record Including Several of the Families in England. J. B. Riggs. (Illus.). 534p. 1993. reprint ed. pap. 81.00 (*0-8328-3735-0*); reprint ed. lib. bdg. 91.00 (*0-8328-3734-2*) Higginson Bk Co.

Right Actions in Sport: Ethics for Contestants. Warren P. Fraleigh. LC 83-83165. 208p. (C). 1984. pap. text ed. 18.00 (*0-87322-330-6*, BFRA0330) Human Kinetics.

Right after Sundown: Teaching Stories of the Navajo. Marilyne V. Mabery. 1991. pap. 14.95 (*0-912586-69-9*) Navajo Coll Pr.

Right & Democracy in Latin America. Ed. by Douglas A. Chalmers et al. LC 91-22940. 336p. 1992. text ed. 49.95 (*0-275-93822-0*, C3822, Praeger Pubs) Greenwood.

Right & Left: Essays on Dual Symbolic Classification. Ed. by Rodney Needham. LC 73-82982. 488p. reprint ed. pap. 139.10 (*0-685-23833-4*, 2056614) Bks Demand.

Right & Left & The Legend of the Holy Drinker. Joseph Roth. Tr. by Michael Hofmann. 320p. 1992. 23.95 (*0-87951-448-5*) Overlook Pr.

Right & Left & the Legend of the Holy Drinker. Joseph Roth. Tr. by Michael Hoffman. 304p. 1993. pap. 13.95 (*0-87951-456-6*) Overlook Pr.

Right & Left Hemispheres of the Animal Brain: Cerebral Lateralization of Function. V. L. Bianki. (Monographs in Neuroscience: Vol. 3). 423p. 1987. text ed. 155.00 (*2-88124-197-2*) Gordon & Breach.

Right & Might: The Dorr Rebellion & the Struggle for Equal Rights, 4 bks. Joyce M. Botelho. (Illus.). 103p. (Orig.). 1992. e. pap. 9.95 (*0-932840-10-8*) RI Hist Soc.

Right & the Good. W. D. Ross. LC 88-11019. 184p. (C). 1988. reprint ed. pap. 14.95 (*0-87220-058-2*); reprint ed. lib. bdg. 34.95 (*0-87220-059-0*) Hackett Pub.

Right & the Righteous: The Christian Right Confronts the Republican Party. Duane M. Oldfield. (Religious Forces in the Modern Political World). 304p. (C). 1996. 27.95 (*0-8476-8190-4*) Rowman.

Right & Wrong. Charles Fried. 288p. 1978. 29.00 (*0-674-76905-8*) HUP.

Right & Wrong. Charles Fried. 288p. 1979. pap. 12.50 (*0-674-76975-9*) HUP.

Right & Wrong: A Brief Guide to Understanding Ethics. Thomas I. White. 128p. 1987. pap. text ed. 27.20 (*0-13-781170-5*) P-H.

Right & Wrong: A Philosophical Dialogue Between Father & Son. Paul Weiss & Jonathan Weiss. LC 73-12702. (Arcturus Books Paperbacks). 222p. 1974. pap. 6.95 (*0-8093-0658-1*) S Ill U Pr.

Right & Wrong: Basic Readings in Ethics. Christina H. Sommers. 201p. (C). 1986. pap. text ed. 18.75 (*0-15-577110-8*) HB Coll Pubs.

Right & Wrong: Practical Ethics: A Fresh Look by a Retired Judge. Laurence R. Smith. LC 93-18433. 162p. (Orig.). (C). 1993. pap. text ed. 22.00 (*0-8191-9092-6*) U Pr of Amer.

Right & Wrong in Foreign Policy. James G. Eayrs. LC 66-4025. (Alan B. Plaunt Memorial Lectures: No. 1965). 65p. reprint ed. pap. 25.00 (*0-8357-8308-1*, 2033989) Bks Demand.

Right & Wrong of Compulsion by the State, & Other Essays. Auberon Herbert. LC 78-4879. 1978. 14.00 (*0-913966-41-X*); pap. 6.00 (*0-913966-42-8*) Liberty Fund.

Right & Wrong of Ushering. Andrew D. Phillips. Ed. by Marvin L. Smith. LC 92-71668. 84p. (Orig.). 1992. pap. text ed. 6.95 (*0-9625115-7-9*) Campbell Rd Pr.

Right & Wrong Thinking. 2nd ed. Kenneth E. Hagin. 1986. pap. 1.95 (*0-89276-004-4*) Hagin Ministries.

***Right Angle Countertop.** Larry Beers. 13p. (YA). (gr. 10 up). 1987. wbk. ed., pap. 7.00 (*0-8064-1409-X*, W30) Bergwall.

Right Angle Triangle: The Prince & the Singer. Ferdinand Voteur. 1977. 16.95 (*0-8369-9180-X*, 9053) Ayer.

Right Angles. J. O. Bledsoe. 200p. 1989. write for info. (*0-318-65356-7*) Nickajack Group.

Right Antenna: How to Select & Install Antennas for Entertainment & Communications Devices. rev. ed. Alvis J. Evans. (Illus.). 112p. (C). 1992. reprint ed. pap. 10.95 (*0-7906-1022-1*) Prompt Publns.

***Right Around That Corner: A Country Musical.** Joe Bell et al. 1992. pap. 5.00 (*1-57514-275-9*) Encore Perform Pub.

***Right at Home.** (Illus.). 8p. (J). (ps-1). 1995. 34.99 (*1-888074-38-8*) Pckts Lrning.

Right Behind the Flag. Kevin Heelen. 1989. pap. 5.25 (*0-8222-0950-0*) Dramatists Play.

***Right Book Right Time: Helping Children Cope.** Grindler et al. LC 96-43988. 1996. pap. 25.95 (*0-205-17272-5*) Allyn.

Right Brain - Left Brain Reflexology: A Self-Help Approach to Balancing Life Energies with Color, Sound, & Pressure-Point Techniques. Madeleine Turgeon. (Illus.). 221p. (Orig.). 1993. pap. text ed. 14.95 (*0-89281-432-2*, Heal Arts VT) Inner Tradit.

Right Brain & Religion: A Discussion of Religion in the Context of the Right-&-Left-Brain Theory. C. W. Dalton. Ed. by L. D. Garland. LC 90-81587. (Illus.). 1990. pap. 11.95 (*0-916969-02-9*) Big Blue Bks.

Right Brain & the Unconscious: Discovering the Stranger Within. R. Joseph. (Illus.). 390p. (C). 1992. 27.50 (*0-306-44330-9*, Plenum Pr) Plenum.

***Right-Brain Experience: An Intimate Program to Free the Powers of Your Imagination.** Marilee Zdenek. 1996. pap. text ed. 14.00 (*1-887697-00-4*) Two Roads Pubng.

Right-Brain Learning in Thirty Days: The Whole Mind Program. Keith Harary & Pamela Weintraub. (Higher Consciousness 30-Day Ser.). (Illus.). 112p. (Orig.). 1991. pap. 6.95 (*0-312-06452-7*) St Martin.

Right-Brain Sex: How to Reach the Heights of Sensual Pleasure by Releasing the Erotic Power of Your Mind. Carol G. Wells. 224p. 1991. reprint ed. mass mkt. 4.95 (*0-380-71348-9*) Avon.

Right Brain Vacation Photos: New Plays & Production Photographs from the Omaha Magic Theatre, 1972-1992. Ed. by JoAnn Schmidman et al. 152p. (Orig.). 1992. pap. 30.00 (*0-911382-13-5*) Simmons Boardman.

***Right-Brained Children in a Left-Brained World: Unlocking the Potential of Your ADD Child.** William J. Bennett. 1997. 23.00 (*0-684-84271-8*, S&S) S&S Trade.

Right by My Side. David Haynes. LC 92-64074. (Minnesota Voices Project Ser.). 176p. (Orig.). 1993. pap. 12.95 (*0-89823-147-7*) New Rivers Pr.

Right Cat for Me. Andrew De Prisco & James B. Johnson. (Illus.). 96p. 1996. 12.95 (*0-7938-1595-9*, KW238) TFH Pubns.

Right Center Left: Essays in American History. Leo P. Ribuffo. LC 91-5030. 325p. (C). 1992. text ed. 45.00 (*0-8135-1775-3*); pap. text ed. 16.95 (*0-8135-1776-1*) Rutgers U Pr.

***Right Chest, Wong Name.** Colleen Collins. (Love & Laughter Ser: No. 26). 1997. mass mkt. 3.50 (*0-373-44026-X*) Silhouette.

***Right Choice.** Elizabeth R. Achtemeier et al. Ed. by Paul T. Stallsworth. LC 96-51889. 144p. 1997. pap. 14.95 (*0-687-05079-0*) Abingdon.

***Right Choice.** Catherine George. (Harlequin Ser.). 1996. 19.95 (*0-263-14746-0*) Thorndike Pr.

Right Choice: A Complete Guide to Evaluating Selecting, & Installing MRP 11 Software. Christopher D. Gray. LC 86-63916. 250p. 1993. 107.00 (*0-939246-09-0*) Wiley.

Right Choice: Hires That Meet Your Agency Needs. Cleve Folger & Vince Peterson. 122p. (Orig.). 1993. pap. 12.95 (*1-56461-123-X*, 26050) Rough Notes.

Right Choice: Home Schooling. Christopher J. Klicka. 410p. 1992. text ed. 13.95 (*0-923463-83-6*) Noble Pub Assocs.

Right Choice, Vol. 1: A Guide to Missouri & Illinois Nursing Homes & Supportive Living Settings, 1989. Health Care Creative Services Staff. Ed. by Catherine L. Collins. 88p. (Orig.). 1988. pap. text ed. 6.95 (*0-923109-00-5*) Hlth Care Creat.

Right Choice, 1989, Vol. One: A Guide to Missour & Illinois Nursing Homes & Supportive Living Settings, 1989. Health Care Creative Services Staff. Ed. by Catherine L. Collins. 96p. (Orig.). 1988. pap. 6.95 (*0-685-44391-4*) Hlth Care Creat.

Right Choices: An Insider's Guide to Selecting a Nursing Home. Lynn Smith. 100p. 1992. pap. 9.95 (*0-9633706-0-X*) L Smith Ent.

Right Climate for Carbon Taxes: Creating Economic Inventives to Protect the Environment. Roger C. Dower & Mary B. Zimmerman. 40p. 1992. Large format. pap. 14.95 (*0-915825-78-3*, DODPP) World Resources Inst.

Right College. 6th ed. College Research Group of Concord, Mass. Staff. (Illus.). 1184p. 1992. pap. 22.00 (*0-13-781758-4*, Arco) Macmillan Gen Ref.

Right College. 7th ed. Ed. by College Research Group of Concord, Mass. Staff. 1994. pap. 22.00 (*0-671-89030-1*, Arco) Macmillan Gen Ref.

Right College. 8th ed. College Research Group of Concord, Mass. Staff. 1996. 22.95 (*0-02-861067-9*) Macmillan.

Right College 1990. Webster. 1989. pap. 16.95 (*0-13-981234-2*) Mac Pub USA.

Right Concept of Sin. Richard S. Taylor. 128p. 1945. pap. 7.99 (*0-8341-0139-4*) Beacon Hill.

Right Conduct: Theories & Applications. 2nd ed. Michael D. Bayles & Kenneth Henley. 432p. (C). 1988. pap. text ed. write for info. (*0-07-553966-7*) McGraw.

Right Data. Edwin Rubenstein. 409p. (Orig.). (C). 1993. pap. text ed. 17.95 (*0-9627841-3-3*) Natl Review.

***Right Deal.** Alex E. Halberstadt & Doug Rutledge. LC 96-90393. 1997. 13.95 (*0-533-12027-6*) Vantage.

Right Direction: A Casebook of General Jury Directions in Criminal Trials. J. L. Glissan & S. W. Tilmouth. 240p. 1990. boxed 96.00 (*0-409-49495-X*, Austral) MICHIE.

Right Distance. Samuel F. Pickering, Jr. LC 86-16012. 204p. 1987. 19.95 (*0-8203-0906-0*) U of Ga Pr.

Right Doctrine from the Wrong Texts? Essays on the Use of the Old Testament in the New. Ed. by G. K. Beale. LC 94-33709. 448p. (Orig.). (C). 1994. pap. 22.99 (*0-8010-1088-8*) Baker Bks.

Right Dog For You: Choosing a Breed that Matches Your Personality, Family & Lifestyle. Daniel F. Tortora. (Illus.). 384p. 1983. pap. 12.00 (*0-671-47247-X*, Fireside) S&S Trade.

Right Dose. Patricia Hausman. 1989. mass mkt. 5.95 (*0-345-35877-5*) Ballantine.

Right Down Your Alley, the Complete Book of Bowling. 4th ed. Vesma Grinfelds & Bonnie Hultstrand. (Illus.). 168p. 1996. pap. text ed. 15.95 (*0-89582-320-9*) Morton Pub.

Right Every Time. F. Price. 182p. (C). 1990. 270.00 (*0-685-39879-X*, Pub. by Inst Pur & Supply UK) St Mut.

Right Every Time. Frank Price. 200p. 1993. pap. 18.95 (*0-566-07419-2*, Pub. by Gower UK) Ashgate Pub Co.

Right Every Time: Using the Deming Approach. Price. 216p. 1990. 69.75 (*0-8247-8328-X*) Dekker.

***Right Fine Life: Kit Carson on the Santa Fe Trail.** Andrew Glass. (Illus.). 48p. (J). (gr. 1-5). 1997. lib. bdg. 16.95 (*0-8234-1326-8*) Holiday.

Right First Time: Using Quality Control for Profit. Frank Price. 296p. 1984. pap. 19.95 (*0-7045-0522-3*, Pub. by Gower UK); text ed. 67.95 (*0-566-02467-5*, Pub. by Gower UK) Ashgate Pub Co.

Right Fit: An Educator's Career Handbook & Employment Guide. Judy A. Strother & Darrel R. Marshall. 168p. (Orig.). 1989. pap. text ed. 14.95 (*0-89787-814-0*) Gorsuch Scarisbrick.

Right Fit: The Power of Ergonomics As a Competitive Strategy. Clifford M. Gross. (Illus.). 200p. 1996. 24.00 (*1-56327-111-7*) Prod Press.

Right Foot Guide to Indiana University Bloomington. 4th ed. Stephen G. Volan. (Right Foot College Guidebook Ser.). (Orig.). 1994. pap. 17.95 (*1-885387-05-9*) Tall Order Pr.

Right Foot Guide to the University of Illinois at Urbana-Champaign. Claire Sanders. Ed. by Stephen G. Volan. (Right Foot College Guidebook Ser.). 1994. pap. 17.95 (*1-885387-06-7*) Tall Order Pr.

Right Frame. Henry Heydenryk. (Illus.). 108p. 1993. pap. 16.95 (*1-55821-266-3*) Lyons & Burford.

Right from the Beginning. Patrick Buchanan. LC 87-35354. 1988. 18.95 (*0-316-11408-1*) Little.

Right from the Beginning. Patrick J. Buchanan. LC 90-43500. (Illus.). 400p. 1990. pap. 12.95 (*0-89526-745-4*) Regnery Pub.

Right from the Horse's Mouth. Sheridan. (College ESL Ser.). 1994. pap. 22.95 (*0-8384-3993-4*); teacher ed., pap. write for info. (*0-8384-4278-1*); suppl. ed. write for info. incl. audio (*0-8384-4277-3*) Heinle & Heinle.

Right from the Horse's Mouth: The Lives & Races of America's Great Thoroughbreds As Told in Their Own Words. John Devaney & Howard Liss. (Illus.). 192p. 1987. 4.99 (*0-517-56517-X*) Random Hse Value.

Right from the Start: Managing Your College Career. 2nd ed. Robert Holkeboer. (College Success Ser.). (C). 1996. pap. 30.95 (*0-534-21570-X*) Wadsworth Pub.

Right from the Start: Managing Your Way to College Success. Robert Holkeboer. 304p. (C). 1993. pap. 25.95 (*0-534-19290-4*) Wadsworth Pub.

Right from the Start: Report of the Early Childhood Education Task Force. 55p. 1988. 8.50 (*0-317-05329-9*) NASBE.

Right from the Start: Teaching Children Ages Three Through Eight. Bernard Spodek & Olivia N. Saracho. LC 93-36708. 1993. text ed. 61.00 (*0-205-15281-3*) Allyn.

Right from Wrong: What You Need to Know to Help Youth Make the Right Choices. Josh McDowell & Bob Hostetler. LC 94-27539. 336p. 1994. pap. 14.99 (*0-8499-3604-7*) Word Pub.

Right from Wrong: What You Need to Know to Help Youth Make the Right Choices. Josh McDowell & Bob Hostetler. LC 94-27539. 1994. 19.99 (*0-8499-1079-X*) Word Pub.

An Asterisk (*) at the beginning of an entry indicates that the title is appearing in BIP for the first time.

Right Fruteful Treatise for the Artificial Cure of Struma. William Clowes. LC 72-25835. (English Experience Ser.: No. 238). 68p. 1970. reprint ed. 15.00 (*90-221-0238-6*) Walter J Johnson.

Right Good People. Harold Warren. LC 73-93809. 1974. pap. 2.50 (*0-913239-20-8*) Appalach Consortium.

Right Guide: A Guide to Conservative & Right-of-Center Organizations. Ed. by Derk A. Wilcox et al. 456p. 1992. 74.95 (*0-914169-01-7*) Econ America.

Right Guide 1995: A Guide to Conservative & Right-of-Center Organizations. 2nd ed. Derk A. Wilcox. 484p. 74.95 (*0-914169-02-5*) Econ America.

Right Hand: Left-Handedness. Daniel Wilson. LC 78-72830. (Brainedness, Handedness, & Mental Abilities Ser.). reprint ed. 41.50 (*0-404-60898-1*) AMS Pr.

Right Hand & Left Hand Golfing. 2nd ed. Edward W. Eckhardt. (Illus.). 93p. 1994. 24.95 (*1-886759-00-6*) IntroTech.

Right-Hand Man. Connie Williams. Ed. by Christine Leaman. LC 92-19158. (Light Line Ser.). (Illus.). 100p. (J). 1992. pap. 6.49 (*0-89084-638-3*, 061614) Bob Jones Univ Pr.

Right-Hand Man: The Life of George W. Perkins. John A. Garraty. LC 77-18807. 433p. 1978. reprint ed. text ed. 41.50 (*0-313-20186-2*, GARH, Greenwood Pr) Greenwood.

***Right Hand Technique for Guitar.** Bruce Arnold. (Illus.). 175p. (Orig.). 1997. pap. 25.00 (*0-9648632-6-X*) MUSE EEK.

Right Hand Techniques. M. Wolfsohn. 16p. 1992. pap. 6.95 (*0-7935-0988-2*, 00699328) H Leonard.

Right Handbook: Grammar & Usage in Context. 2nd rev. ed. Patricia Belanoff et al. LC 92-28851. 294p. 1992. pap. text ed. 21.00 (*0-86709-316-1*, 0316) Boynton Cook Pubs.

Right Heart. Ed. by R. Leighton Fisk. LC 70-6558. (Cardiovascular Clinics Ser.: Vol. 17, No. 2). (Illus.). 273p. 1987. text ed. 55.00 (*0-8036-3572-9*) Davis Co.

Right Hemisphere: Neurology & Neuropsychology. Alfredo Ardila & Peggy Ostosky-Solis. (Monographs in Neuroscience). xvi, 278p. 1984. text ed. 194.00 (*2-88124-103-4*) Gordon & Breach.

Right Hemisphere & Verbal Communication. Yves Joanette et al. 312p. 1989. 112.95 (*0-387-97101-7*) Spr-Verlag.

Right Hemisphere Communication Disorders: Theory & Management. Connie Tompkins. (Illus.). 320p. (Orig.). (C). 1994. text ed. 45.00 (*1-56593-381-8*, 0770) Singular Publishing.

***Right Hemisphere Language Comprehension: Perspectives from Cognitive Neuroscience.** Mark Beeman & Christine Chiarello. LC 96-46733. 360p. 1997. pap. write for info. (*0-8058-1926-6*); text ed. write for info. (*0-8058-1925-8*) L Erlbaum Assocs.

Right Hemisphere Stroke: A Victim Reflects on Rehabilitative Medicine. Fred K. Johnson. LC 89-70612. (William Beaumont Hospital Speech & Language Pathology Ser.). 136p. (C). 1990. text ed. 19.95 (*0-8143-2172-0*) Wayne St U Pr.

Right Here on This Spot. Sharon H. Addy. LC 96-15382. (Illus.). (J). 1997. write for info. (*0-395-73091-0*) HM.

Right Ho, Jeeves. P. G. Wodehouse. 22.95 (*0-8488-0680-8*) Amereon Ltd.

Right Ho, Jeeves. P. G. Wodehouse. 256p. 1975. pap. 8.95 (*0-14-000934-5*, Penguin Bks) Viking Penguin.

***Right Honourable Gentleman.** pap. write for info. (*0-340-56275-7*, Pub. by E Arnold UK) Routledge Chapman & Hall.

Right Honourable Gentleman. Michael Dyne. 1967. pap. 5.25 (*0-8222-0951-9*) Dramatists Play.

Right Honourable Gentleman: Abubakar from the Black Rock. Trevor Clark. 896p. 1995. text ed. 55.00 (*0-340-56189-0*, Pub. by E Arnld UK) St Martin.

***Right Horse.** William Murray. LC 97-3208. 1997. 17.95 (*0-385-48353-8*) Doubleday.

Right Hours to Success. Lyman E. Stowe. 1970. reprint ed. spiral bd. 7.00 (*0-7873-1060-3*) Hlth Research.

***Right in France 1789-1996.** Atkin. Date not set. text ed. 59.50 (*1-86064-197-0*, Pub. by I B Tauris UK) St Martin.

***Right in the Middle.** 1996. text ed. 49.00 (*3-540-51242-X*) Spr-Verlag.

Right in the Middle. P. M. Davies. (Illus.). 288p. 1996. 49.00 (*0-387-51242-X*) Spr-Verlag.

Right in the Old Gazoo: A Lifetime of Scrapping with the Press. Alan K. Simpson. LC 96-25482. 269p. 1997. 24.00 (*0-688-11358-3*) Morrow.

Right in the Twentieth Century Vol. 1: Conservatism & Democracy. Girvin. 1994. 49.00 (*0-86187-981-3*) St Martin.

Right in Your Own Backyard: A Unit of Study for Local History. Jean Shafer. (Illus.). 48p. (Orig.). (J). (gr. 3-6). 1988. teacher ed., pap. 8.95 (*0-938682-16-4*) River Rd Pubns.

Right in Your Own Backyard: Nature Math. Time Life Inc Staff. Ed. by Elizabeth Ward et al. LC 92-27222. (I Love Math Ser.). (Illus.). 64p. (J). (gr. k-4). 1992. lib. bdg. write for info. (*0-8094-9963-0*) Time-Life.

Right in Your Own Backyard: Nature Math. Time Life Inc Staff. Ed. by Elizabeth Ward et al. LC 92-27222. (I Love Math Ser.). (Illus.). 64p. (J). (gr. 1-4). 1992. 16.95 (*0-8094-9962-2*) Time-Life.

Right Instrument for Your Child: The Key to Unlocking Musical Potential. Atarah Ben-Tovim & Douglas Boyd. 144p. 1996. pap. 13.95 (*0-575-05894-3*, Pub. by V Gollancz UK) Trafalgar.

Right Jack. Margaret Maron. 272p. (Orig.). 1995. mass mkt. 5.99 (*0-446-40417-9*, Mysterious Paperbk) Warner Bks.

Right Jack. large type ed. Margaret Maron. (Mystery Ser.). 480p. (Orig.). 1992. 25.99 (*0-7089-2730-0*) Ulverscroft.

Right Job for You. N. Nicholson & C. Clemie. (C). 1989. text ed. 29.95 (*0-948032-63-4*, Pub. by Rosters Ltd) St Mut.

Right Job for You! An Interactive Career Planning Guide. 2nd rev. ed. J. Michael Farr. 128p. (Orig.). 1991. pap. 9.95 (*1-56370-286-X*, RJ) JIST Works.

***Right Kind of Girl.** Betty Neels. 1997. pap. 3.25 (*0-373-15713-4*, 1-15713-0) Harlequin Bks.

***Right Kind of Girl.** Betty Neels. 1997. pap. 3.25 (*0-373-03467-9*, 1-03467-7) Harlequin Bks.

Right Kind of Girl. Betty A. Neels. 1996. 19.95 (*0-263-14579-4*, Pub. by Mills & Boon UK) Thorndike Pr.

Right Kind of Heroes: Coach Bob Shannon & the East St. Louis Flyers. Kevin Horrigan. LC 92-13723. 348p. 1992. 18.95 (*0-945575-70-X*) Algonquin Bks.

Right Kind of Man. large type ed. Florence Stuart. (Dales Romance Ser.). 195p. 1992. pap. 17.99 (*1-85389-333-1*) Ulverscroft.

Right Kind of Man (Holding Out for a Hero) Jessica Hart. (Romance Ser.). 1996. mass mkt. 3.25 (*0-373-03406-7*, 1-03406-5) Harlequin Bks.

Right Kind of War. John McCormick. 384p. 1994. pap. 4.99 (*0-451-40450-5*, Onyx) NAL-Dutton.

Right Kind of War. large type ed. John McCormick. LC 92-44777. (General Ser.). 548p. 1993. reprint ed. lib. bdg. 18.95 (*1-56054-663-8*) Thorndike Pr.

Right Kind of War: A Novel. John McCormick. LC 92-19546. 333p. 1992. 22.95 (*1-55750-574-8*) Naval Inst Pr.

Right Man. Marie Ferrarella. (Romance Ser.). 1993. pap. 2.69 (*0-373-08932-5*, 5-08932-1) Silhouette.

***Right Man.** large type ed. Sandra Field. (Magna Large Print Ser.). 309p. 1997. 27.50 (*0-7505-1127-3*) Ulverscroft.

Right Man for Loving. Kristina Logan. (Romance Ser.: No. 870). 1992. pap. 2.69 (*0-373-08870-1*, 5-08870-3) Silhouette.

Right Man for Loving. large type ed. Kristina Logan. 251p. 1992. reprint ed. lib. bdg. 13.95 (*1-56054-538-0*) Thorndike Pr.

***Right Man for the Job: A Novel.** Mike Magnuson. LC 96-28396. 256p. 1997. 23.00 (*0-06-018710-7*) HarpC.

Right Medicine: How to Make Health Care Reform Work Today. David Cundiff & Mary E. McCarthy. LC 94-27992. 256p. 1994. 24.50 (*0-89603-284-1*) Humana.

***Right Mind.** Robert Ornstein. LC 97-21659. 1997. write for info. (*0-15-100324-6*) HarBrace.

Right Mountain: Lessons from Everest on the Real Meaning of Success. Jim Hayhurst. 200p. 1996. text ed. 24.95 (*0-471-64150-2*) Wiley.

Right Moves. M. K. Kauffman. (YA). (gr. 7 up). 1987. pap. 2.25 (*0-373-98014-0*) S&S Trade.

Right Moves Vol. I: A Collection of Etiquette Strategies for Business. Ann C. Humphries. 116p. 1990. pap. 10.00 (*0-9644556-1-7*) ETICON.

Right Moves Vol. II: More Etiquette Strategies for Business. Ann C. Humphries. 128p. 1994. pap. 10.00 (*0-9644556-0-9*) ETICON.

Right Murder. Craig Rice. LC 90-84276. 312p. 1990. reprint ed. pap. 8.95 (*1-55882-078-7*) Intl Polygonics.

Right Name for Baby. Steven John. 128p. 1995. pap. 7.95 (*0-572-01430-9*, Pub. by Foulsham UK) Assoc Pubs Grp.

Right Notes: Twenty-Three Selected Essays by George Perle on Twentieth-Century Music. George Perle. 400p. 1995. lib. bdg. 46.00 (*0-945193-37-8*) Pendragon NY.

Right Number of Elephants. Jeff Sheppard. LC 90-4148. (Illus.). 32p. (J). (ps-3). 1990. 14.95 (*0-06-025615-X*); lib. bdg. 14.89 (*0-06-025616-8*) HarpC Child Bks.

Right Number of Elephants. Jeff Sheppard. LC 90-4148. (Trophy Picture Bk.). (Illus.). 32p. (J). (ps-3). 1992. pap. 4.95 (*0-06-443299-8*, Trophy) HarpC Child Bks.

Right Number of Elephants Big Book. Jeff Sheppard. LC 90-4148. (Trophy Picture Bk.). (Illus.). 32p. (J). (ps-3). 1993. pap. 19.95 (*0-06-443338-2*, Trophy) HarpC Child Bks.

Right of Appropriation & the Colorado System of Laws in Regard to Irrigation. Harvey Huston. 334p. 1983. reprint ed. lib. bdg. 27.50 (*0-8377-0649-1*) Rothman.

Right of Conquest: The Forcible Acquisition of Territory in International Law & Practices. Sharon Korman. 320p. 1996. text ed. 72.00 (*0-19-828007-6*) OUP.

Right of Innocent Passage & the Evolution of the International Law of the Sea: The Current Regime of "Free" Navigation in Coastal Waters of Third States. Frances Ngantcha. 256p. 1990. text ed. 49.00 (*0-86187-851-5*) St Martin.

Right of Nations to Self Determination: Selected Writings. Vladimir I. Lenin. LC 77-22314. 128p. 1977. reprint ed. text ed. 38.50 (*0-8371-9731-7*, LERN, Greenwood Pr) Greenwood.

Right of Passage: The Heroic Journey to Adulthood. Nancy G. Christopher. xii, 291p. (Orig.). 1996. pap. 15.00 (*0-9652719-2-7*) Cornell Press.

Right of Privacy: Its Constitutional & Social Dimensions; a Comprehensive Bibliography. David M. O'Brien. (Legal Bibliography Ser.: No. 21). 55p. (Orig.). 1980. pap. 15.00 (*0-935630-04-X*) U of Tex Tarlton Law Lib.

Right of Privacy in the Computer Age. Warren Freedman. LC 86-9362. 173p. 1987. text ed. 39.95 (*0-89930-187-8*, FRT/, Quorum Bks) Greenwood.

Right of Privatization in Hungary, 1989-1993. T. Sarkozy. 264p. 1994. pap. 35.00 (*963-05-6729-6*, Pub. by A K HU) Intl Spec Bk.

Right of Rights: The United States' Constitutional, Natural, Moral & Absolute Essential Right to Be. Daniel H. Devlin. 264p. 1995. pap. 19.95 (*1-886866-00-7*) Postrty Pr.

Right of Search & the Slave Trade in Anglo-American Relations, 1814-1862. Hugh G. Soulsby. LC 78-64149. (Johns Hopkins University. Studies in the Social Sciences. Thirtieth Ser. 1912: 2). reprint ed. 34.50 (*0-404-61260-1*) AMS Pr.

Right of Silence: The Case for Retention. James Wood & Adam Crawford. (C). 1988. 30.00 (*0-900137-32-0*, Pub. by NCCL UK) St Mut.

Right of Spoil of the Popes of Avignon, 1316-1415. Daniel Williman. LC 87-72870. (Transactions Ser.: Vol. 78, Pt. 6). (Illus.). 366p. (C). 1988. pap. 30.00 (*0-87169-786-6*, T786-WID) Am Philos.

Right of the Centre: An Autobiography of Cecil Parkinson. Cecil Parkinson. (Illus.). 312p. 1993. 39.95 (*0-297-81262-9*) Trafalgar.

Right of the People. William O. Douglas. LC 80-19135. 238p. 1980. reprint ed. text ed. 55.00 (*0-313-22640-7*, DORP, Greenwood Pr) Greenwood.

Right of the United States of America to the Northeastern Boundary Claimed by Them. Ed. by Albert Gallatin. LC 70-117876. (Select Bibliographies Reprint Ser.). 1977. 35.95 (*0-8369-5329-0*) Ayer.

Right of Way. Gilbert Parker. 1976. lib. bdg. 16.25 (*0-89968-079-8*, Lghtyr Pr) Buccaneer Bks.

Right-of-Way: A Guide to Abandoned Railroads in the United States. rev. ed. Waldo Nielson. (Illus.). 220p. 1992. pap. 19.95 (*0-89288-001-5*) Maverick.

Right of Way Agent. Jack Rudman. (Career Examination Ser.: C-3466). 1994. pap. 27.95 (*0-8373-3466-7*) Nat Learn.

Right-of-Way Aide. Jack Rudman. (Career Examination Ser.: C-2735). 1994. pap. 27.95 (*0-8373-2735-0*) Nat Learn.

Right-of-Way Surveying. LC 91-33896. 24p. 1991. pap. text ed. 10.00 (*0-87262-850-7*) Am Soc Civil Eng.

***Right On.** William M. Kunstler. Date not set. write for info. (*0-688-04938-9*) Morrow.

Right on the Edge of Crazy: On Tour with the U. S. Downhill Ski Team. Mike Wilson. 1993. pap. 11.00 (*0-679-74987-X*) Random.

Right on the Money: Messages for Spiritual Growth Through Giving. Brian K. Bauknight. LC 93-70967. 112p. 1994. pap. 11.95 (*0-88177-122-8*, DR122) Discipleship Res.

Right Opposition: The Lovestoneites & the International Communist Opposition of the 1930's. Robert J. Alexander. LC 80-1711. (Contributions in Political Science Ser.: No. 54). 320p. 1981. text ed. 59.95 (*0-313-22070-0*, AOP/, Greenwood Pr) Greenwood.

***"Right or Wrong, God Judge Me" Writings of John Wilkes Booth.** John W. Booth et al. LC 96-51249. 1997. 24.95 (*0-252-02347-1*) U of Ill Pr.

Right-Ordered Groups. Valerii M. Kopytov & Nikolai Y. Medvedev. Tr. by Scientific Books Staff. (Siberian School of Algebra & Logic Ser.). (Illus.). 260p. (C). 1996. 95.00 (*0-306-11060-1*, Consultants) Plenum.

Right over the Mountain: Travels with a Tibetan Medicine Man. Gill Marais. (Illus.). 160p. 1993. pap. 13.95 (*1-85230-150-3*) Element MA.

Right Path. Nora Roberts. (NR Flowers Ser.: No. 26). 1993. mass mkt. 3.59 (*0-373-51026-8*, 1-51026-2) Silhouette.

Right Path: The Autobiography of a Survivor. Edmund Mandel. LC 94-6632. 1994. 35.00 (*0-88125-498-3*) Ktav.

Right Person - Right Job Guess or Know: The Breakthrough Technologies of Performance Information. Chuck Russell. LC 95-74751. 114p. (Orig.). 1996. pap. 12.95 (*0-9647793-0-7*) Johnson & James.

***Right Person for the Job: How to Develop a Powerful Interview Questioning Plan Using Behavior Based Techniques.** Andrew S. Bargerstock. 60p. 1996. ring bd. 29.00 (*0-9639557-2-1*, Jacob-Cameron) A R K Co.

***Right Place.** Bryan H. Massam. 1993. 83.95 (*0-582-08116-5*, Pub. by Longman UK) Longman.

Right Place at the Right Time. John D. Roberts. (Illus.). 299p. 1990. 34.95 (*0-8412-1766-1*) Am Chemical.

Right Place at the Right Time: Everything You Need to Know about Retirement Housing. Joan Cleveland. 192p. 1996. pap. 10.95 (*0-14-025183-9*, Penguin Bks) Viking Penguin.

Right Plant, Right Place: The Indispensable Guide to the Successful Garden. Nicola Ferguson. (Illus.). 304p. (Orig.). 1984. pap. 18.00 (*0-671-52396-1*) Summit Bks.

***Right Plants for Dry Places: Native Plant Landscaping in Central Florida.** Suncoast Native Plant Society, Inc. Staff et al. LC 97-72213. (Illus.). 112p. (Orig.). 1997. pap. 12.95 (*0-8200-0416-2*) Great Outdoors.

Right Portfolio for the Right Job. Ed. by Supon Phornirunlit. (Illus.). 192p. 1994. 45.00 (*0-942604-36-9*) Madison Square.

Right Practical Reason: Aristotle & Aquinas on Prudence & Human Action. Daniel Westberg. LC 93-44415. (Theological Monographs). 294p. (C). 1994. 55.00 (*0-19-826731-2*, Clarendon Pr) OUP.

Right Promethean Fire: Imagination, Science, & Cultural Change. Ihab Hassan. LC 79-18844. 240p. 1980. text ed. 24.95 (*0-252-00753-0*) U of Ill Pr.

Right Questions? Ed. by Ayers Bagley. (SPE Monographs). 1983. 3.00 (*0-933669-20-8*) Soc Profs Ed.

Right Resolutions. 2nd ed. Swami Paramananda. 1981. pap. 1.95 (*0-911564-29-2*) Vedanta Ctr.

Right Road: A History of Right Wing Politics in Australia. Andrew Moore. (Australian Retrospective Ser.). 176p. 1995. pap. 24.95 (*0-19-553512-X*) OUP.

Right Seat. Avram Goldstein. (Illus.). 160p. 1986. pap. 10.95 (*0-938013-01-7*) Aviation.

Right Seat Guide: A White Knuckle Flier's Guide to Light Planes. Charles F. Spence. LC 94-20183. pap. 11.95 (*0-07-060148-8*) McGraw-Hill Prof.

Right-Seat Handbook: A Cockpit Passenger's Companion. Gordon Groene & Janet Groene. (Illus.). 144p. 1992. pap. 12.95 (*0-8306-4116-5*, 4222) McGraw-Hill Prof.

Right SF-170 Writer: The Complete Guide to Communicating Your Qualifications to Federal Employers. Ronald L. Krannich. 1992. pap. 19.95 (*0-942710-64-9*) Impact VA.

***Right Side of Forty Vol. 1: Celebrating Timeless Women.** Patricia Martin. LC 97-24308. (Illus.). 120p. 1997. 24.95 (*1-57324-095-8*) Conari Press.

Right Side Up. Mary A. Milam. 239p. (Orig.). 1991. pap. 5.95 (*0-9631187-0-6*) Marigold Pub.

Right Side Up. Mary A. Milam. 54p. (Orig.). 1994. pap. 3.95 (*0-9631187-1-4*) Marigold Pub.

Right Side Up! Reflections for Those Living with Serious Illness. Marlene Halpin. (Illus.). 80p. 1995. pap. 10.95 (*0-9641919-3-8*) Islewest Pub.

Right Sight Eye Exam. Edward Fradkin & Neil Fradkin. (Illus.). 64p. 1987. pap. 19.95 (*0-912159-01-4*) Center Pr CA.

***Right Start.** 1998. 19.95 (*0-87605-350-9*) Howell Bk.

***Right Start.** David Powers. 32p. (Orig.). Date not set. pap. 1.50 (*0-933672-32-2*, C-1506) Star Bible.

Right Start: Guidelines for Your Baby's Nutrition & Lifelong Health. Young. 224p. 1987. 17.95 (*0-8027-0968-0*) Walker & Co.

Right Start: Guidelines for Your Baby's Nutrition & Lifelong Health. Marcia E. Young. 224p. 1987. pap. 10.95 (*0-8027-7305-2*) Walker & Co.

Right Stats. Jerry R. Langone. (Illus.). 32p. 1994. 6.95 (*0-8059-3531-2*) Dorrance.

Right Stuff. Tom Wolfe. 384p. 1983. mass mkt. 6.99 (*0-553-27556-9*, Bantam Classics) Bantam.

Right Stuff. Tom Wolfe. LC 73-85731. 436p. 1979. 12.95 (*0-374-25032-4*) FS&G.

Right Stuff. Tom Wolfe. 436p. 1983. 30.00 (*0-374-25033-2*) FS&G.

Right Stuff for Guitar. D. Bennett. 48p. 1988. pap. 4.95 (*0-7935-5519-1*, 50488604) H Leonard.

Right Stuff for New Hang Glider Pilots. Erik Fair. LC 84-60909. (Illus.). 176p. 1987. pap. 9.95 (*0-913581-00-3*) Publitec.

Right Test. 3rd ed. Carl E. Speicher. 1998. pap. text ed. write for info. (*0-7216-5123-2*) Saunders.

Right Test: A Physician's Guide to Laboratory Medicine. 2nd ed. Carl E. Speicher. 256p. 1993. pap. text ed. 28.95 (*0-7216-3782-5*) Saunders.

Right Thing: Ten Years of Ethics Columns from the Healthcare Forum Journal. Emily Friedman. (Health Ser.). 250p. (Orig.). 1996. 28.95 (*0-7879-0225-X*) Jossey-Bass.

Right Thing to Do: Basic Readings in Moral Philosophy. James Rachels. 1989. pap. text ed. write for info. (*0-07-557002-5*) McGraw.

Right Thinking. Manly P. Hall. pap. 4.95 (*0-89314-812-1*) Philos Res.

Right Thinking: Conservative Common Sense Through the Ages. James D. Hornfischer. Ed. by Sue Carswell. 176p. (Orig.). 1996. pap. 12.00 (*0-671-53559-5*, PB Trade Paper) PB.

Right Thinking & Sacred Oratory in Counter-Reformation Rome. Frederick J. McGinness. LC 95-3104. 368p. 1995. text ed. 49.50 (*0-691-03426-5*) Princeton U Pr.

Right Time & Pace: A Microanalysis of Cross-Cultural Gatekeeping Interviews. Susan Fiksdal. Ed. by Cynthia Wallat. LC 90-265. (Language & Learning for Human Service Professions Ser.: Vol. 7). 192p. (C). 1990. pap. 39.50 (*0-89391-557-2*); text ed. 73.25 (*0-89391-556-4*) Ablex Pub.

Right Time, Right Place, Right Move, Right Now! Perry W. Buffington. 1992. pap. 14.95 (*0-9632379-0-X*) GoBuff Ent.

Right Time, the Right Place. Joseph S. Salzburg. 144p. 1978. 10.50 (*0-317-60907-6*) Sovereign MD.

Right Time, the Right Place. Joseph S. Salzburg. 144p. 1978. 7.50 (*0-682-49039-3*) Sovereign MD.

Right Time, the Right Place. Charles Wohlstetter. (Illus.). 288p. 1995. 24.95 (*1-55783-197-1*) Applause Theatre Bk Pubs.

Right to a Home. Labour Housing Group Staff. Ed. by David Griffiths. 194p. 1984. 42.50 (*0-85124-399-1*, Pub. by Spokesman Bks UK) Coronet Bks.

Right to Adequate Food as a Human Right. (Human Rights Studies: No. 1). 73p. 1989. pap. 9.00 (*92-1-154075-5*, E. 89.XIV.2) UN.

***Right to Be a Child.** Mason. 1998. write for info. (*0-201-14941-9*) Addison-Wesley.

Right to Be Greedy: A Situationist Synthesis of Communism & Stirnerite Egoism. 1984. lib. bdg. 250.00 (*0-87700-650-4*) Revisionist Pr.

Right to Be Greedy: Theses on the Practical Necessity of Demanding Everything. 1983. reprint ed. pap. 6.95 (*0-915179-35-0*) Loompanics.

Right to Be Human. Upendra Baxi. (C). 1987. 32.00 (*81-7062-021-X*, Pub. by Lancer II) S Asia.

Right to Be Human: A Biography of Abraham Maslow. Edward Hoffman. (Illus.). 382p. 1994. 24.95 (*0-9637902-2-6*) Four Worlds.

Right to Be Intelligent. Luis A. Machado. 85p. 1980. text ed. 40.00 (*0-08-025781-X*, CRC Reprint) Franklin.

Right to Be King: The Succession to the Crown of England, 1603-1714. Howard Nenner. LC 95-14389. (Studies in Legal History). 450p. (C). 1995. reprint ed. text ed. 39.95 (*0-8078-2247-7*) U of NC Pr.

Right to Be Lazy. Paul Lafargue. 1972. 250.00 (*0-87968-039-3*) Gordon Pr.

Right to Be Lazy. Intro. by Joseph Jablonski. (Revolutionary Classics Ser.). (Illus.). 128p. (C). reprint ed. pap. 9.00 (*0-88286-181-6*) C H Kerr.

An Asterisk (*) at the beginning of an entry indicates that the title is appearing in BIP for the first time.

R

Right to Be Merry. Mary Francis. LC 73-6850. 180p. 1973. reprint ed. pap. 6.50 (*0-8199-0506-2*, Frncscn Herld) Franciscan Pr.

Right to Bear Arms: State & Federal Bills of Rights & Constitutional Guarantees. Stephen P. Halbrook. LC 89-11722. (Contributions in Political Science Ser.: No. 243). 173p. 1989. text ed. 49.95 (*0-313-26539-9*, HRH/, Greenwood Pr) Greenwood.

Right to Bear Arms: The Rise of America's New Militias. Jonathan Karl. 192p. 1995. mass mkt. 5.99 (*0-06-101015-4*, Harp PBks) HarpC.

***Right to Belong 1940-60.** Weight. Date not set. pap. text ed. 39.50 (*1-86064-108-3*, Pub. by I B Tauris UK) St Martin.

Right to Buy in Rural Areas: An Investigation of Section 19 of the Housing Act, 1980. Neil Hawke. 33p. 1985. pap. 5.00 (*0-318-22772-X*, Pub. by Leicester Poly Law Schl) Pickering Pubns.

Right to Childhood: The U. S. Children's Bureau & Child Welfare, 1912-46. Kriste Lindenmeyer. LC 96-10031. 1997. text ed. 49.95 (*0-252-02275-0*); pap. text ed. 21.95 (*0-252-06577-8*) U of Ill Pr.

Right to Choose? M. Long. 9.99 (*1-85792-054-6*, Pub. by Christian Focus UK) Spring Arbor Dist.

Right to Communicate Decisions & Dissents: A Supreme Court Reader. Ed. by Mary E. Bezanson. LC 93-6015. 486p. (Orig.). (C). 1993. pap. text ed. 39.50 (*0-8191-9301-1*); lib. bdg. 69.50 (*0-8191-9300-3*) U Pr of Amer.

Right to Counsel in American Courts. William M. Beaney. LC 72-5275. (University of Michigan Publications History & Political Science Ser.: Vol. 19). 268p. 1972. reprint ed. text ed. 67.50 (*0-8371-5725-0*, BERC, Greenwood Pr) Greenwood.

Right to Counsel in Juvenile Court. 122p. 15.50 (*0-685-30177-X*, 44,200B) NCLS Inc.

Right to Development at the International Level. Rene-Jean Dupuy. 458p. 1980. lib. bdg. 129.00 (*90-286-0990-3*) Kluwer Ac.

Right to Development in International Law. Ed. by Subrata R. Chowdhurry. 432p. (C). 1992. lib. bdg. 153.00 (*0-7923-1682-7*) Kluwer Ac.

***Right to Die.** Margaret C. Jasper. (Oceana's Legal Almanac Ser.). 93p. (YA). (gr. 10-12). 1996. lib. bdg. 17.50 (*0-379-11230-2*) Oceana.

Right to Die. Elaine Landau. (Impact Bks.). (Illus.). 128p. (YA). (gr. 7-12). 1993. lib. bdg. 22.70 (*0-531-13015-0*) Watts.

Right to Die. Rex Stout. 208p. 1991. mass mkt. 4.99 (*0-553-24032-3*) Bantam.

Right to Die? Richard Walker. LC 96-24439. (J). 1997. lib. bdg. 18.60 (*0-531-14413-5*) Watts.

Right to Die. large type ed. Rex Stout. 224p. 1996. lib. bdg. 21.95 (*0-7838-1569-7*, GK Hall) Thorndike Pr.

Right to Die. Jeremiah Healy. Ed. by Jane Chelius. 288p. 1992. reprint ed. mass mkt. 4.99 (*0-671-70810-4*) PB.

Right to Die, 2 vols., Vol. 1. 2nd ed. Alan Meisel. LC 95-30540. 712p. 1995. text ed. 120.00 (*0-471-04674-4*) Wiley.

Right to Die, Vol. 2. Alan Meisel et al. 518p. 1994. suppl. ed., pap. 85.00 (*0-471-10644-5*) Wiley.

Right to Die, 2 vols., Vol. 2. 2nd ed. Alan Meisel. LC 95-30540. 1298p. 1995. text ed. 240.00 (*0-471-04672-8*); text ed. 120.00 (*0-471-04682-5*) Wiley.

Right to Die: A Two-Volume Anthology of Scholarly Articles, 2 vols., Set. Ed. by Melvin I. Urofsky & Philip E. Urofsky. LC 95-35829. 1995. text ed. 165.00 (*0-8153-2208-9*) Garland.

***Right to Die: Dax Cowart Case.** Cavalier & Covey. (C). 1997. teacher ed., pap. text ed. 14.95 (*0-415-15274-7*, Routledge NY) Routledge.

Right to Die: Decision & Decision Makers. Group for the Advancement of Psychiatry Staff. LC 84-45126. 96p. 1983. 15.00 (*0-87668-721-4*) Aronson.

Right to Die: Policy Innovation & Its Consequences. Henry R. Glick. 256p. 1992. text ed. 39.50 (*0-231-07638-X*) Col U Pr.

Right to Die: Policy Innovation & Its Consequences. Henry R. Glick. 1994. pap. 17.50 (*0-231-07639-8*) Col U Pr.

Right to Die: Public Controversy, Private Matter. Kathlyn Gay. LC 92-32201. (Issue & Debate Ser.). (Illus.). 128p. (YA). (gr. 7 up). 1993. lib. bdg. 17.90 (*1-56294-325-1*) Millbrook Pr.

***Right to Die: The New Consensus on What to Do When Stuck Between Two Worlds.** James M. Hoefler. LC 97-2593. 6p. 1997. text ed. 22.00 (*0-8133-2816-0*) Westview.

Right to Die: Understanding Euthanasia. Derek Humphry & Ann Wickett. 372p. 1990. pap. 10.00 (*0-9606030-9-3*) Hemlock Soc.

***Right to Die: 1997 Cumulative Supplement, Vol. 2.** 2nd ed. Alan Meisel. pap. text ed. write for info. (*0-471-16471-2*) Wiley.

Right to Die, No. 35: A Selective Bibliography. Compiled by Rhea A-L. Ballard. (Tarlton Law Library Legal Bibliography Ser.: No. 35). 40p. 1992. 20.00 (*0-935630-40-6*) U of Tex Tarlton Law Lib.

Right to Die with Dignity, Illinois Edition: The Living Will, the Power of Attorney for Health Care, & the Health Care Surrogate Act. Robert S. Hunter. (Klear-E-Lex Ser.). 168p. (Orig.). 1993. pap. 19.95 (*1-884177-05-0*) Justice IL.

Right to Dignity: Fidel Castro & the Nonaligned Nations Movement. 130p. 1993. pap. 9.95 (*1-875284-02-8*) Ocean Pr NY.

Right to Dream. Gaston Bachelard. Tr. by J. A. Underwood. LC 89-1302. (Bachelard Translation Ser.). 190p. 1989. pap. 17.00 (*0-911005-16-1*) Dallas Inst Pubns.

Right to Education: Anatomy of the Pennsylvania Case & Its Implications for Exceptional Children. Leopold D. Lippman & I. Ignacy Goldberg. LC 73-78038. (Teachers College Series in Special Education). 153p. reprint ed. pap. 43.70 (*0-685-20394-8*, 2030172) Bks Demand.

Right to Err: Selected Poems. Nina Iskrenko. Tr. by John High et al. (Illus.). 128p. (Orig.). 1995. 24.00 (*0-89410-806-9*, Three Contnts) Lynne Rienner.

***Right to Err: Selected Poems.** Nina Iskrenko. Tr. by John High et al. (Illus.). 128p. (Orig.). 1995. pap. 10.00 (*1-57889-031-4*) Passeggiata.

***Right to Fight.** 1996. lib. bdg. 250.99 (*0-8490-6368-X*) Gordon Pr.

***Right to Fight: African-American Marines in World War.** 1997. lib. bdg. 250.95 (*0-8490-6083-4*) Gordon Pr.

***Right to Fight: African-American Marines in World War II.** Bernard C. Nalty. (Illus.). 29p. 1996. reprint ed. pap. 25.00 (*0-7881-3531-7*) DIANE Pub.

Right to Food. Katarina Tomasevski. 1987. lib. bdg. 132.00 (*90-247-3365-0*, Pub. by M Nijhoff NE) Kluwer Ac.

Right to Forego Medical Treatment: What Are the Legal Limits. 46p. 1988. pap. 8.00 (*0-685-30153-2*, 40,910) NCLS Inc.

Right to Health As a Human Right: Colloquim 1978 of the Hague Academy of International Law. Ed. by Rene-Jean Dupuy. 513p. 1979. lib. bdg. 129.00 (*90-286-1028-6*) Kluwer Ac.

Right to Health Care: An Advocate's Guide to the Hill-Burton Uncompensated Care & Community Services Requirements. Armin Freifeld. 326p. (Orig.). 1986. pap. 15.00 (*0-941077-16-0*, 41,900) NCLS Inc.

Right to Health in the Americas: A Comparative Constitutional Study. Ed. by H. L. Fuenzalida-Puelma & S. S. Connor. (PAHO Scientific Publication Ser.: No. 509). xvii, 716p. (ENG & SPA.). 1989. pap. text ed. 60.00 (*92-75-11509-5*, 1610509) World Health.

Right to Home School: A Guide to the Law on Parents' Rights in Education. Christopher J. Klicka. LC 94-73846. 184p. 1995. pap. 7.50 (*0-89089-818-9*) Carolina Acad Pr.

Right to Hope: Crisis & Community. Melvin Rader. LC 81-51284. 148p. 1981. 25.00 (*0-295-95836-7*) U of Wash Pr.

Right to Housing: A Blueprint for Housing the Nation. Institute for Policy Studies, Working Group on Housing Staff & Dick Cluster. (Illus.). 72p. (Orig.). 1989. pap. 5.00 (*0-89758-046-X*) Inst Policy Stud.

Right to Imagination & Madness: An Essential Collection of Candid Interviews with U. K. Top Alternative Songwriters. Martin Roach. (Illus.). 384p. (Orig.). 1995. pap. 17.95 (*1-897783-03-5*, MR55576, Pub. by Indep Music Pr UK) Music Sales.

Right to Innocence: Healing the Trauma of Childhood Sexual Abuse. Beverly Engel. 272p. 1990. mass mkt. 5.99 (*0-8041-0585-5*) Ivy Books.

Right to Justice: The Political Economy of Legal Services in the United States. Charles K. Rowley. (John Locke Ser.). 432p. 1992. text ed. 80.00 (*1-85278-526-8*) E Elgar.

Right to Keep & Bear Arms: A Presentation of Both Sides. 1986. lib. bdg. 79.95 (*0-8490-3538-4*) Gordon Pr.

Right to Know. Ed. by Nancy Gruber. (Orig.). 1985. pap. write for info. (*1-880648-00-8*) DataCenter.

Right to Know, Vol. 1. Intro. by Zoia Horn. (Orig.). 1985. pap. 10.00 (*1-880648-01-6*) DataCenter.

Right to Know, Vol. 2. Intro. by Zoia Horn. (Orig.). 1988. pap. 15.00 (*1-880648-02-4*) DataCenter.

Right to Know, Vol. 3. Ed. by Nancy Gruber. (Orig.). 1990. pap. text ed. 20.00 (*1-880648-03-2*) DataCenter.

Right to Know, Vol. 4. Ed. by Zoia Horn et al. (Orig.). 1992. pap. write for info. (*1-880648-04-0*) DataCenter.

Right to Know: A Guide to Federal & State Requirements. 2nd ed. Interface Associates Staff. LC 86-21128. 270p. 1986. ring bd. 65.00 (*0-938135-07-4*) Interface Assocs.

Right to Know: Human Rights & Access to Reproductive Health Information. Ed. by Sandra Coliver. (Pennsylvania Studies in Human Rights). 416p. (Orig.). 1996. pap. text ed. 26.95 (*0-8122-1588-5*) U of Pa Pr.

Right to Know: The Inside Story of the Belgrano Affair. Clive Ponting. 1985. 25.00 (*0-317-54919-7*, Pub. by NCCL UK) St Mut.

Right to Know: The Promise of Low-Cost Public Inventions of Toxic Chemicals. 80p. 1994. pap. 18.00 (*0-89164-141-6*) World Wildlife Fund.

Right to Know a Compliance Encyclopedia for the Hazard Communication Standard. rev. ed. Neville C. Tompkins. 1986. ring bd. 129.95 (*1-55645-313-2*, 100017) Busn Legal Reports.

***Right to Know & the Right Not to Know.** Ed. by Ruth Chadwick et al. (Avebury Series in Philosophy). 112p. 1997. text ed. 55.95 (*1-85972-424-8*, Pub. by Avebury Pub UK) Ashgate Pub Co.

Right to Know Compliance Manual, 32M. rev. ed. Keller, J. J. & Assocs., Inc. Staff. Ed. by Linda Wereley. 280p. 1991. ring bd. 99.00 (*0-934674-66-3*, 271006) J J Keller.

Right to Know Handbook. John F. Brady. 480p. 1989. ring bd. 99.95 (*1-55645-327-2*) Busn Legal Reports.

Right to Know One's Human Rights: A Road Toward Marriage & Family. Vratislav Pechota. LC 83-72868. 52p. 1983. pap. 2.50 (*0-87495-056-2*) Am Jewish Comm.

Right-to-Know Pocket Guide for Construction Workers. Joseph O. Accrocco et al. 88p. 1993. 41.80 (*0-931690-31-5*) Genium Pub.

Right-to-Know Pocket Guide for Health Care Personnel. Ed. by Michael Cinquanti & Christine Gorman. (Illus.). 87p. (Orig.). 1991. pap. text ed. 41.80 (*0-931690-35-8*) Genium Pub.

Right-to-Know Pocket Guide for Laboratory Employees. Joseph O. Accrocco & M. Cinquanti. LC 89-71504. 88p. 1993. 41.80 (*0-931690-34-X*) Genium Pub.

Right-to-Know Pocket Guide for School & University Employees. Joseph O. Accrocco & R. A. Roy. 88p. 1990. 41.80 (*0-931690-33-1*) Genium Pub.

***Right to Learn.** Darling. LC 97-4736. 1997. 25.00 (*0-7879-0261-6*, 455167) Jossey-Bass.

Right to Learn: The Struggle for Education in South Africa. Pamela Christie. 256p. 1986. pap. 12.95 (*0-86975-286-3*, Pub. by Ravan Pr ZA) Ohio U Pr.

Right to Life. A. Delafield Smith. 1955. pap. 16.95 (*0-8084-0260-9*) NCUP.

***Right to Life in Japan.** Noel Williams. LC 96-43153. (Routledge/Nissan Institute Japanese Studies Ser.). 192p. (C). 1997. text ed. write for info. (*0-415-15617-3*) Routledge.

Right to Life Movement & Third Party Politics. Robert J. Spitzer. LC 86-14209. (Contributions in Political Science Ser.: No. 160). 167p. 1987. text ed. 45.00 (*0-313-25390-0*, SRT/, Greenwood Pr) Greenwood.

Right to Literacy. Ed. by Andrea A. Lunsford et al. LC 90-33855. iv, 306p. 1990. lib. bdg. 19.75 (*0-87352-197-8*, W430C) Modern Lang.

Right to Live. Russell Z. Bomberger. Ed. by Dorothy B. Gottshall. LC 89-90328. 104p. (Orig.). 1989. pap. 4.00 (*0-9623880-0-9*) Tussy B Zug Pubs.

Right to Live: The Right to Die. C. Everett Koop. 160p. 1981. reprint ed. pap. 4.95 (*0-919225-02-0*) Life Cycle Bks.

Right to Manage: A Study of Leadership & Reform in Employee Relations. W. W. Daniel & Neil McIntosh. 192p. 1972. 19.95 (*0-8464-0798-1*) Beekman Pubs.

Right to Manage: Industrial Relations Policies of American Business in the 1940s. Howell J. Harris. LC 81-69820. 312p. 1982. text ed. 25.00 (*0-299-08640-2*) U of Wis Pr.

Right to Membership of a Trade Union. R. W. Rideout. LC 75-17201. (Univ. of London Legal Ser.: No. 5). 243p. 1975. reprint ed. text ed. 59.75 (*0-8371-8295-6*, RIMTU, Greenwood Pr) Greenwood.

Right to Parenthood. William C. Gentry & William G. Karow. (Illus.). 136p. (Orig.). pap. text ed. 9.95 (*0-9636403-3-X*) LAX Prods.

Right to Play: Proceedings of the American Association for the Child's Right to Play. Marcey Guddemi & Tom Jambor. (Illus.). 140p. (Orig.). 1994. pap. 14.00 (*0-942388-09-7*) So Early Chldhood Assn.

***Right to Privacy.** E. Alderman & C. Kenne. 1997. 3.99 (*0-517-17964-4*) Random Hse Value.

***Right to Privacy.** E. Alderman & C. Kennedy. (YA). 1997. pap. 14.00 (*0-679-74434-7*, Vin) Random.

Right to Privacy. Caroline Kennedy & Ellen Alderman. LC 95-14286. 407p. (YA). 1995. 26.95 (*0-679-41986-1*) Knopf.

Right to Privacy. Adam C. Breckenridge. LC 73-88084. 163p. reprint ed. pap. 46.50 (*0-8357-3789-6*, 2036520) Bks Demand.

Right to Privacy: Gays, Lesbians, & the Constitution. Vincent J. Samar. 1992. pap. 18.95 (*0-87722-952-X*) Temple U Pr.

Right to Privacy & the Ninth Amendment. Ed. by Paul L. Murphy. (Bill of Rights & American Legal History Ser.: Vol. 7). 824p. 1990. reprint ed. text ed. 65.00 (*0-8240-5864-X*) Garland.

Right to Private Property. Waldron. 480p. 1991. 35.00 (*0-19-823937-8*) OUP.

Right to Property. A. L. Gandhi. 308p. 1985. 150.00 (*81-85046-22-0*, Pub. by Scientific UK) St Mut.

Right to Quality Child Care. Edward E. Gotts. 1988. pap. 1.50 (*0-87173-117-7*) ACEI.

***Right to Refuse Mental Health Treatment.** Bruce J. Winick. LC 96-42913. (Law & Public Policy Ser.). 432p. 1996. text ed. 59.95 (*1-55798-369-0*, 431-6770) Am Psychol.

Right to Religious Liberty: The Basic ACLU Guide to Religious Rights. rev. ed. Oliver S. Thomas. LC 94-13635. (ACLU Handbook Ser.). 176p. (C). 1995. 29.95 (*0-8093-1966-7*) S Ill U Pr.

Right to Rule & the Domain of the Sun. Kavalam N. Panikkar. (C). 1989. pap. 10.00 (*81-7046-071-9*, Pub. by Seagull Bks II) S Asia.

Right to Say No. Judith Todd. LC 72-93680. 224p. 1973. 24.95 (*0-89388-066-3*) Okpaku Communications.

Right to Self-Determination: Proceedings of the 8th World Congress of Right-to-Die-Societies. Ed. by A. O. Smook & B. De Vos-Schippers. 156p. 1993. pap. 24.50 (*90-6256-930-7*, Pub. by VU Univ Pr NE) Paul & Co Pubs.

Right to Silence. 3rd ed. Kiemann. 1989. pap. 15.95 (*0-687-36314-4*) Abingdon.

Right to Silence in Police Interrogation: Study of Some Issues Underlying Debate. Roger Leng. (Research Studies: No. 10). 86p. 1993. pap. 20.00 (*0-11-341063-8*, HM10638, Pub. by Stationery Ofc UK) Bernan Associates.

Right to Smoke? Emma Haughton. LC 96-417. (Viewpoints Ser.). (J). 1997. lib. bdg. 18.60 (*0-531-14412-7*) Watts.

Right to Speak: Working with the Voice. Patsy Rodenburg. LC 93-17448. 320p. (gr. 13). 1993. pap. 16.95 (*0-87830-055-4*) Routledge Chapman & Hall.

Right to Speak Out. David C. King. LC 96-21966. (Land of the Free Ser.). (Illus.). 48p. (J). (gr. 2-4). 1997. lib. bdg. 14.90 (*0-7613-0063-5*) Millbrook Pr.

Right to Strike. Kenneth D. Ewing. (Oxford Monographs on Labour Law). 208p. 1991. 55.00 (*0-19-825439-3*, 7935) OUP.

Right to Struggle. 2nd ed. Monte Melkonian. 240p. 1994. pap. 20.00 (*0-9641569-1-1*) Sardarabad.

Right to the Land: Essays on the Freedmen's Community. Edward Magdol. LC 76-39707. (Contributions in American History Ser.: No. 61). (Illus.). 290p. 1977. text ed. 59.95 (*0-8371-9409-1*, MFC/, Greenwood Pr) Greenwood.

Right to the Left: The Conservative's Lexicon of Liberalism. Jimmy Gigaditto. 98p. 1994. pap. 6.95 (*0-9643713-0-8*) ISL.

Right to the Whole Produce of Labour: The Origin & Development of the Theory of Labour's Claim to the Whole Product of Industry. Anton Menger. LC 68-54737. (Reprints of Economic Classics Ser.). cxviii, 271p. 1970. reprint ed. lib. bdg. 45.00 (*0-678-00714-4*) Kelley.

Right to Travel. 1992. lib. bdg. 75.00 (*0-8490-5276-9*) Gordon Pr.

Right to Travel under the Constitution. B. Errabbi. (C). 1989. 50.00 (*0-89771-765-1*, Pub. by Eastern Book II) St Mut.

Right to Travel Under the Constitution. B. Errabi. 1986. 75.00 (*0-317-90994-0*) St Mut.

Right to Treatment for Mental Patients. Ed. by Stuart Golann & William J. Fremouw. (Illus.). 320p. (C). 1976. 29.95 (*0-8290-0863-2*) Irvington.

Right to Treatment in Mental Health Law. W. Schmidt. 1976. write for info. (*0-318-58132-9*) FSU CSP.

Right to Vote. Nancy E. Allyn. LC 86-16480. (Milestone Documents in the National Archives Ser.). 26p. (Orig.). 1988. pap. text ed. 3.50 (*0-911333-51-7*, 200108) National Archives & Recs.

Right to Vote. Elaine Pascoe. LC 96-21965. (Land of the Free Ser.). (Illus.). 48p. (J). (gr. 2-4). 1997. lib. bdg. 14.90 (*0-7613-0066-X*) Millbrook Pr.

Right to Vote: Politics & the Passage of the 15th Amendment. William Gillette. LC 78-64243. (Johns Hopkins University. Studies in the Social Sciences. Thirtieth Ser. 1912: 1). reprint ed. 29.50 (*0-404-61348-9*) AMS Pr.

Right Tools for the Job: At Work in Twentieth-Century Life Sciences. Ed. by Adele E. Clarke & Joan H. Fujimura. (Illus.). 394p. 1992. text ed. 39.50 (*0-691-08581-1*) Princeton U Pr.

Right Touch: Understanding & Using the Language of Physical Contact. Stanley Jones. Ed. by Gary L. Kreps. LC 93-5499. (Speech Communication Association Applied Communication Ser.). 356p. 1993. text ed. 59.50 (*1-881303-41-1*); pap. text ed. 24.95 (*1-881303-42-X*) Hampton Pr NJ.

Right Track Writer: Beginning GED Essay Writing. John Fink & Carolyn Fink. LC 90-20182. (Cambridge Writing Ser.). 96p. (C). 1991. pap. text ed. 6.50 (*0-13-781659-6*, 640402) P-H.

Right Turn: William Bradford Reynolds, the Reagan Administration, & Black Civil Rights. Raymond Wolters. 454p. 1996. text ed. 49.95 (*1-56000-257-3*) Transaction Pubs.

Right under the Big Sky, I Don't Wear a Hat: The Haiku & Prose of Hosai Ozaki. Hosai Ozaki. Tr. by Hiroaki Sato from JPN. LC 93-3814. 144p. (Orig.). 1993. pap. 12.00 (*1-880656-05-1*) Stone Bridge Pr.

Right up Your Street. C. Groome. 5.99 (*1-85792-058-9*, Pub. by Christian Focus UK) Spring Arbor Dist.

Right v. Might: International Law & the Use of Force. 2nd ed. Louis Henkin et al. 160p. 1991. pap. 14.95 (*0-87609-109-5*) Coun Foreign.

Right Ventricle. Ed. by Marvin A. Konstam & Jeffrey M. Isner. (C). 1988. lib. bdg. 206.50 (*0-89838-987-9*) Kluwer Ac.

Right Ventricular Hypertrophy & Function in Chronic Lung Disease. Ed. by V. Jezek et al. LC 92-2330. (Current Topics in Rehabilitation Ser.). 1992. 69.95 (*0-387-19774-5*) Spr-Verlag.

Right Versus Privilege: The Open Admissions Experiment at the City University of New York. David E. Lavin et al. LC 80-69571. (Illus.). 1981. 35.00 (*0-02-918080-5*, Free Press) Free Pr.

***Right Vintage: A Wine Lover's Companion.** Simon Cadell. 1996. 24.95 (*0-86051-962-7*, Pub. by BBC UK) Parkwest Pubns.

***Right Vintage: A Wine Lover's Companion.** Simon Cadell. 224p. 1997. pap. 10.95 (*1-86105-069-0*, Pub. by Robson UK) Parkwest Pubns.

Right vs. Might: International Law & the Use of Force. Louis Henkin et al. LC 91-23136. 212p. 1991. reprint ed. pap. 60.50 (*0-608-02010-9*, 2062666) Bks Demand.

Right vs. Wrong: Solutions to the Amerian Nightmare. Harry Dent & Betty Dent. LC 92-18657. 1992. pap. 17.99 (*0-8407-3438-7*) Nelson.

Right Way the Safe Way Proved by Emancipation in the British West Indies, & Elsewhere. Lydia Maria Child. LC 76-82184. (Anti-Slavery Crusade in America Ser.). 1970. reprint ed. 20.95 (*0-405-00623-3*) Ayer.

Right Way to Invest in Mutual Funds. Walter L. Updegrave. 208p. (Orig.). 1996. pap. 9.99 (*0-446-67167-3*) Warner Bks.

Right Way to Live: Plato's Republic for Catholic Students. Richard Geraghty & Ronda De Sola Chervin. 124p. 1994. pap. text ed. 12.95 (*1-887582-01-0*) Chiaro Oscuro Pr.

Right Where You Are Sitting Now: Further Tales of the Illuminati. Robert A. Wilson. LC 82-4084. (Illus.). 208p. (Orig.). 1992. pap. 12.95 (*0-914171-45-3*) Ronin Pub.

Right Where You Live. Constance Brady. (Illus.). 188p. (Orig.). 1982. pap. 9.95 (*0-89087-242-2*) Conarc.

Right Wine. Tom Maresca. LC 90-43459. 368p. 1992. pap. 12.95 (*0-8021-3297-9*, Grove) Grove-Atltic.

Right Wing Conspiracy Theories. 1996. lib. bdg. 251.95 (*0-8490-6933-5*) Gordon Pr.

Right-Wing Extremism in Western Europe. Klaus Von Beyme. (Illus.). 116p. 1988. text ed. 32.00 (*0-7146-3345-3*, Pub. by F Cass Pubs UK) Intl Spec Bk.

Right Wing Individualist Tradition in America, 38 bks. Ed. by Murray N. Rothbard & Jerome Tuccille. 1972. 812.00 (*0-405-00410-9*) Ayer.

An Asterisk (*) at the beginning of an entry indicates that the title is appearing in BIP for the first time.

Right-Wing Military Government. Robert Pinkney. (Twayne's Themes in Right-Wing Ideology & Politics Ser.: No. 3). 256p. (C). 1990. 30.95 (0-8057-9554-5, Twayne); pap. 16.95 (0-8057-9555-3, Twayne) Scribnrs Ref.

Right-Wing Press in France, 1792-1800. Jeremy D. Popkin. LC 79-14067. 254p. reprint ed. pap. 72.40 (0-7837-0310-4, 2040632) Bks Demand.

Right-Wing Press in the French Revolution 1789-1792, No. 44. William J. Murray. (Royal Historical Society: Studies in History). 357p. 1986. 63.00 (0-86193-201-3) Boydell & Brewer.

Right-Wing Radicalism & Political Intolerance: A Study of Support for McCarthy in a New England Town. Martin A. Trow. Ed. by Harriet Zuckerman & Robert K. Merton. LC 79-9035. (Dissertations on Sociology Ser.). 1980. lib. bdg. 35.95 (0-405-13002-3) Ayer.

Right with God. rev. ed. John Blanchard. 126p. 1985. pap. 4.99 (0-85151-045-0) Banner of Truth.

***Right Word.** Buckley. 1998. pap. write for info. (0-15-600569-7) HarBrace.

***Right Word.** Fowler. 1992. student ed., pap. text ed. write for info. (0-17-555688-1) Addison-Wesley.

Right Word, No. III. rev. ed. American Heritage Dictionary Editors. 275p. 1990. 4.95 (0-395-53959-5) HM.

Right Word: A Collection of All-Occasion Romantic Verses. Darold Gholston. Ed. by Leon Golson. 90p. (Orig.). 1992. pap. 9.95 (0-9635488-9-1) Gholston Des.

Right Word in Chinese. 1986. 14.95 (0-318-36435-2, RIWOIN) China Bks.

***Right Word Wrong Word.** Alexander. Date not set. pap. text ed. write for info. (0-582-21860-8, Pub. by Longman UK) Longman.

Right Words: The Grace of Writing. Blair Adams & Joel Stein. LC 89-51226. (Illus.). 160p. 1993. pap. 19.95 (0-916387-28-3) Truth Forum.

Right Words, Right Places. Scott Rice. 445p. (C). 1993. pap. 31.95 (0-534-16038-7) Wadsworth Pub.

***Right You Are, If You Think You Are.** Luigi Pirandello. Tr. by Stanley Appelbaum. LC 96-36041. 64p. 1997. reprint ed. pap. text ed. 1.50 (0-486-29576-1) Dover.

Righte Merrie Christmasse!!! John Ashton. LC 68-56543. (Illus.). 261p. 1972. reprint ed. 18.95 (0-405-08225-8, Pub. by Blom Pubns UK) Ayer.

Righteous Cause: The Life of William Jennings Bryan. Robert W. Cherny. LC 94-10867. 238p. 1994. pap. 10.95 (0-8061-2667-1) U of Okla Pr.

***Righteous Cause or Tragic Folly: Changing Views of War in Modern Japanese Poetry.** Steve Rabson. LC 96-48385. (Michigan Monographs in Japanese Studies: No. 17). 1997. write for info. (0-939512-77-7) U MI Japan.

Righteous Discontent: The Women's Movement in the Black Baptist Church, 1880-1920. Evelyn B. Higginbotham. LC 92-19345. (Illus.). 320p. 1993. 38.50 (0-674-76977-5) HUP.

Righteous Discontent: The Women's Movement in the Black Baptist Church, 1880-1920. Evelyn B. Higginbotham. (C). 1994. pap. text ed. 15.95 (0-674-76978-3) HUP.

Righteous Gentile: The Story of Raoul Wallenberg, Missing Hero of the Holocaust. John Bierman. (Illus.). 264p. 1996. pap. 11.95 (0-14-024664-9, Penguin Bks) Viking Penguin.

***Righteous Gentiles.** Victoria Sherrow. (Holocaust Library). (Illus.). (J). (gr. 4-12). 1997. lib. bdg. 17.96 (1-56006-093-X) Lucent Bks.

Righteous Gentiles of the Holocaust: A Christian Interpretation. David P. Gushee. LC 94-29881. 1994. pap. 18.00 (0-8006-2838-1, Fortress Pr) Augsburg Fortress.

Righteous Gentiles of the Holocaust: A Christian Interpretation. David P. Gushee. LC 94-29881. 1994. 28.00 (0-8006-2902-7, Fortress Pr) Augsburg Fortress.

Righteous Lives: Narratives of the New Orleans Civil Rights Movement. Kim L. Rogers. (Illus.). 254p. (C). 1992. 45.00 (0-8147-7431-8) NYU Pr.

Righteous Lives: Narratives of the New Orleans Civil Rights Movement. Kim L. Rogers. (Illus.). 254p. (C). 1995. pap. 17.50 (0-8147-7456-3) NYU Pr.

Righteous Rakehell. Gayle Buck. 1988. pap. 3.99 (0-451-15668-4, Sig) NAL-Dutton.

Righteous Realists: Political Realism, Responsible Power, & American Culture in the Nuclear Age. Joel H. Rosenthal. LC 90-48592. (Political Traditions in Foreign Policy Ser.). 184p. 1991. text ed. 27.50 (0-8071-1649-1) La State U Pr.

***Righteous Rebel: Adam Cloud & the Natchez Intrigues, 1790-1795 : A Novel.** Catherine C. Templeton. LC 97-16100. 1997. write for info. (1-57168-163-9, Eakin Pr) Sunbelt Media.

***Righteous Rebel: Adam Cloud & the Natchez Intrigues, 1790-1795: A Novel.** Catherine C. Templeton. LC 97-16100. 1997. pap. 19.95 (1-57168-164-7, Eakin Pr) Sunbelt Media.

***Righteous Religion: Unmasking the Illusions of Fundamentalism & Authoritarian Catholicism.** Ed. by Kathleen Y. Ritter & Craig W. O'Neill. LC 96-4734. 212p. 1997. pap. 17.95 (0-7890-6017-5) Haworth Pr.

Righteous Religion: Unmasking the Illusions of Fundamentalism & Authoritarian Catholicism. Ed. by Kathleen Y. Ritter & Craig W. O'Neill. LC 96-4734. 212p. (C). 1997. 39.95 (0-7890-6016-7, Haworth Pastrl) Haworth Pr.

Righteous Remnant: The House of David. Robert S. Fogarty. LC 80-84666. (Illus.). 210p. 1989. reprint ed. pap. 12.50 (0-87338-393-1) Kent St U Pr.

Righteous Revenge. George Hayduke. LC 92-39507. 1993. 8.95 (0-8184-0569-4, L Stuart) Carol Pub Group.

Righteous Revenge: Getting Down to Getting Even. George Hayduke. (Illus.). 240p. 1991. 19.95 (0-87364-591-X) Paladin Pr.

Righteous Revenge of Artemis Bonner. Walter D. Myers. LC 91-42401. (Trophy Bk.). 144p. (J). (gr. 5-9). 1994. pap. 4.50 (0-06-440462-5, Trophy) HarpC Child Bks.

Righteous Rhymes, Vol. 1. Jamie S. Lash. (Illus.). 24p. (J). (gr. 2-7). 1983. pap. 2.95 (0-915775-00-X) Love Song Mess Assn.

Righteous Rhymes, Vol. 2. Ed. by Jamie S. Lash. (Illus.). 24p. (J). 1987. pap. 2.95 (0-915775-01-8) Love Song Mess Assn.

***Righteous Rogue.** Martha Kirkland. 1997. mass mkt. 4.99 (0-451-19278-8, Sig) NAL-Dutton.

Righteousness. Ronald D. Tucker. (Illus.). 48p. (Orig.). 1983. pap. 4.00 (0-933643-09-8) Grace Ch-St Louis.

Righteousness. 2nd ed. Ronald D. Tucker. 48p. (Orig.). 1995. pap. 4.00 (0-933643-42-X) Grace Ch-St Louis.

Righteousness Exalts a Nation. Harry R. Cyrus, pseud. Ed. by Barbara A. Klemm. 232p. pap. 15.00 (0-9639386-0-6) Fortune Prnting.

Righteousness in the Septuagint of Isaiah: A Contextual Study. John W. Olley. LC 78-3425. (Society of Biblical Literature. Septuagint & Cognate Studies: No. 8). 201p. reprint ed. pap. 57.30 (0-7837-5438-8, 2045203) Bks Demand.

Righteousness Inside Out: The Believer's Guide to Experiencing the Righteousness of Christ. Stuart Cedrone. LC 95-46991. 1996. pap. 8.99 (0-8163-1307-5) Pacific Pr Pub Assn.

Righteousness Inside Out: The Heart of the Problem & the Problem of the Heart. Mike Cope. 180p. 1988. pap. text ed. 6.99 (0-89225-333-9) Gospel Advocate.

Rightful Owner. 2nd ed. Jesse H. Stuart. (Illus.). 95p. (J). (gr. 3-6). 1989. reprint ed. 12.00 (0-945084-14-5); reprint ed. pap. 6.00 (0-945084-15-3) J Stuart Found.

Rightful Termination: Avoiding Litigation. Ron Visconti & Richard Stiller. Ed. by Sara Schneider. LC 93-73119. (Fifty-Minute Ser.). (Illus.). 88p. (Orig.). 1994. pap. 10.95 (1-56052-248-8) Crisp Pubns.

Rightful Termination: Defensive Strategies for Hiring & Firing in the Lawsuit-Happy 90's. James Walsh. (Taking Control Ser.). 330p. 1994. pap. 29.95 (1-56343-067-3) Merritt Pub.

Rightfully Mine. Doris Mortman. 736p. 1990. mass mkt. 6.50 (0-553-28416-9) Bantam.

Righthandedness & Lefthandedness: With Chapters Treating of the Writing Posture, the Rule of the Road, Etc. George M. Gould. LC 78-72794. reprint ed. 26.50 (0-404-60859-0) AMS Pr.

Righting. Ernest A. Joselovitz. 1977. pap. 3.25 (0-8222-0952-7) Dramatists Play.

Righting a Wrong: Japanese Americans & the Passage of the Civil Liberties Act of 1988. Leslie T. Hatamiya. LC 92-40402. (Asian America Ser.). 280p. 1994. 37.50 (0-8047-2144-0); pap. 14.95 (0-8047-2366-4) Stanford U Pr.

Righting the Educational Conveyor Belt. 2nd ed. Michael Grinder. Ed. by Lori Stephens. (Illus.). 256p. 1991. pap. 17.95 (1-55552-036-7) Metamorphous Pr.

***Righting Wrongs in East Euro.** Pogany. LC 97-20341. 1998. write for info. (0-7190-3042-0) St Martin.

Rightings! Diana Goure. (Illus.). 40p. (Orig.). 1989. pap. 4.00 (0-934852-58-8) Lorien Hse.

***Rightly Divided: Readings in Biblical Hermeneutics.** Ed. by Roy B. Zuck. LC 96-46208. 320p. (Orig.). 1996. pap. 14.99 (0-8254-4099-8) Kregel.

Rightly Dividing. Truman H. Etheridge. 1955. 6.00 (0-88027-017-9) Firm Foun Pub.

Rightly Dividing the Word of Truth. C. I. Scofield. LC 86-21085. 1896. Pkg. of 5. pap. 14.95 (0-87213-558-6); student ed., pap. 2.99 (0-87213-770-8) Loizeaux.

Rightly Dividing the Word of Truth. C. I. Scofield. (Christian Classics Ser.). 1995. pap. 3.49 (1-56570-013-9) Meridian MI.

Rightly Dividing the Word of Truth see Traza Bien la Palabra de Verdad

Rightly Dividing the Word, Vol. I: General Hermeneutics. Ed. by Terry M. Hightower. 532p. 10.00 (0-934916-13-6) Natl Christian Pr.

Rightly Teaching the Word of Your Truth: Studies in Faith & Culture, Church & Scriptures, Fathers & Worship, Hellenism & the Contemporary Scene in Honor of His Eminence Archbishop Iakovos. Ed. by Nomikos M. Vaporis. LC 94-39473. 1995. 37.50 (1-885652-10-0) Holy Cross Orthodox.

Rightness & Reasons: Interpretation in Cultural Practices. Michael Krausz. LC 93-12627. (Illus.). 192p. (C). 1993. 32.50 (0-8014-2846-7) Cornell U Pr.

Rightness vs Righteousness. Creflo A. Dollar, Jr. 20p. (Orig.). 1993. pap. 1.99 (0-9634781-5-X) Wrld Chang Minist.

Rights. Theodore M. Benditt. LC 81-23448. (Philosophy & Society Ser.). 158p. 1982. text ed. 50.00 (0-8476-6754-5) Rowman.

Rights. Michael Freeden. (Concepts in Social Thought Ser.). 128p. (C). 1991. pap. text ed. 13.95 (0-8166-1973-5) U of Minn Pr.

***Rights.** Michael Freeden. Ed. by Frank Parkin. (Concepts in the Social Sciences Ser.). 144p. 1991. pap. 9.99 (0-335-15572-3, Open Univ Pr) Taylor & Francis.

Rights. Lawrence Goldstone. LC 91-36047. 268p. 1992. 22.00 (1-877946-13-3) Permanent Pr.

Rights. Peter Jones. LC 94-32810. 1995. text ed. 55.00 (0-312-12403-1) St Martin.

Rights. Ed. by Carlos Nino. (International Library of Essays in Law & Legal Theory). 550p. (C). 1992. 150.00 (0-8147-5771-5) NYU Pr.

Rights across Borders: Immigration & the Decline of Citizenship. David Jacobson. LC 95-16657. 200p. 1995. text ed. 33.50 (0-8018-5150-5) Johns Hopkins.

***Rights Across Borders: Immigration & the Decline of Citizenship.** David Jacobson. 1997. pap. text ed. 14.95 (0-8018-5770-8) Johns Hopkins.

Rights & Christian Ethics. Kieran Cronin. (New Studies in Christian Ethics: No. 1). 349p. (C). 1993. text ed. 65.00 (0-521-41889-5) Cambridge U Pr.

Rights & Constitutionalism: The New South African Legal Order. John Dugard et al. 720p. 1994. 89.00 (0-7021-3285-3, Pub. by Juta SA) Gaunt.

Rights & Constitutionalism: The New South African Legal Order. Ed. by David Van Wyk et al. 550p. 1996. 115.00 (0-19-826225-6) OUP.

Rights & Decisions. Martin Van Hees. 1995. lib. bdg. 130.00 (0-7923-3754-9) Kluwer Ac.

Rights & Deprivation. Lesley A. Jacobs. 304p. (C). 1993. 45.00 (0-19-827767-9, 1927) OUP.

***Rights & Duties: Reflections on Our Conservative Constitution.** 2nd expanded rev. ed. Russell Kirk. LC 97-22262. 1997. write for info. (0-9653208-2-0) Spence Pub.

Rights & Ethics: Individual Rights & the Common Good. Pepper Worthington. (Memoirs of the National Honor Society of Phi Kappa Phi Symposium Ser.). (Illus.). 68p. (Orig.). 1993. pap. 6.00 (1-880994-07-0) Mt Olive Coll Pr.

Rights & Freedoms in Australia. Jude Wallace & Tony Pagone. 225p. 1989. pap. 31.00 (1-86287-026-8, Pub. by Federation Pr AU) Gaunt.

Rights & Goods: Justifying Social Action. Virginia Held. viii, 336p. 1989. reprint ed. pap. text ed. 18.00 (0-226-32588-1) U Ch Pr.

Rights & Liabilities of Public School Boards under Capital Outlay Contracts. Frank E. Henzlik. LC 76-176859. (Columbia University. Teachers College. Contributions to Education Ser.: No. 153). reprint ed. 37.50 (0-404-55153-X) AMS Pr.

Rights & Liabilities of Publishers, Broadcasters & Reporters, 2 vols. Slade R. Metcalf & Robin Bierstedt. LC 82-16839. (Individual Rights Ser.). 1549p. 1982. text ed. 200.00 (0-07-041685-0) Shepards.

Rights & Obligations in North-South Relations: Ethical Dimensions of Global Problems. Ed. by Moorhead Wright. LC 85-2212. 248p. 1986. text ed. 39.95 (0-312-68234-4) St Martin.

Rights & Obligations of Business in Singapore. Georgy T. Shenoy & Toh S. Kiat. 1996. write for info. (0-201-88913-7) Addison-Wesley.

Rights & Persons. A. I. Melden. LC 77-80180. 1978. pap. 11.00 (0-520-03839-8) U CA Pr.

Rights & Privileges of the Press. Fredrick S. Siebert. LC 70-100243. xvii, 429p. 1970. reprint ed. text ed. 65.00 (0-8371-4021-8, SIRP, Greenwood Pr) Greenwood.

***Rights & Realities: The Judicial Impact of the "Canadian Charter of Rights & Freedoms" on Education, Case Law & Political Jurisprudence.** Johathan L. Black-Branch. LC 97-7850. 236p. 1997. text ed. 63.95 (1-85521-936-0, Pub. by Ashgate UK) Ashgate Pub Co.

Rights & Reconciliation: U. N. Strategies in El Salvador. Ian Johnstone. LC 95-4614. (International Peace Academy Occasional Papers). 1995. 8.95 (1-55587-615-3) Lynne Rienner.

Rights & Regulation: Ethical, Political, & Economic Issues. Ed. by Tibor R. Machan & M. Bruce Johnson. LC 83-11309. (Illus.). 309p. (C). 1983. pap. 14.95 (0-936488-61-1) PRIPP.

Rights & Remedies under Federal Grants. Richard B. Cappalli. LC 79-12004. 414p. reprint ed. pap. 118.00 (0-685-15902-7, 2026795) Bks Demand.

Rights & Respect: What You Need to Know about Gender Bias & Sexual Harassment. Kathlyn Gay. LC 94-45501. (Illus.). 128p. (YA). (gr. 7 up). 1995. lib. bdg. 16.90 (1-56294-493-2) Millbrook Pr.

Rights & Responsibilities: International, Social & Individual Dimensions. Ed. by Nelson T. Horn. 300p. 1980. 39.95 (0-685-07092-1) Transaction Pubs.

Rights & Responsibilities: Using Your Freedom. Frances Shuker-Haines. LC 92-25732. (Good Citizenship Ser.). (Illus.). 48p. (J). (gr. 5-6). 1992. lib. bdg. 24.26 (0-8114-7355-4) Raintree Steck-V.

Rights & Responsibilities of Children & Youth in California. 220p. 1988. 25.00 (0-685-30182-6, 43,800) NCLS Inc.

Rights & Responsibilities of Landlords. (Legal Ser.). 1992. lib. bdg. 88.75 (0-8490-5316-1) Gordon Pr.

Rights & Responsibilities of Participants in Networked Communities. National Research Council, Steering Committee on Rights & Responsibilities in Networked Communities. Ed. by Dorothy E. Denning & Herbert S. Lin. 172p. (Orig.). (C). 1994. pap. text ed. 25.00 (0-309-05090-1) Natl Acad Pr.

Rights & the Common Good: The Communitarian Perspective. Amitai Etzioni. 288p. 1994. pap. text ed. 16.00 (0-312-08968-6) St Martin.

Rights & the Common Good: The Communitarian Perspective. Amitai Etzioni. 1995. text ed. 39.95 (0-312-10272-0) St Martin.

Rights & Their Foundations. Ed. by Jules L. Coleman. LC 93-33074. (Philosophy of Law Ser.: Vol. 2). 448p. 1994. text ed. 70.00 (0-8153-1398-5) Garland.

Rights & Wrongs: Coercion, Punishment, & the State. David A. Hokema. LC 84-40809. 160p. 1986. 32.50 (0-941664-07-4) Susquehanna U Pr.

Rights & Wrongs: Women's Struggle for Legal Equality. 2nd ed. Susan C. Nicholas et al. LC 86-2461. (Women's Lives - Women's Work Ser.). 112p. (Orig.). 1986. pap. 9.95 (0-935312-42-0) Feminist Pr.

Rights & Wrongs of Abortion. Ed. by M. Cohen et al. (Philosophy & Public Affairs Reader Ser.). 1974. pap. 11.95 (0-691-01979-7) Princeton U Pr.

Rights & Wrongs of Children. Daniel B. Freeman. (C). 1992. pap. text ed. 35.00 (0-86187-226-6) St Martin.

Rights at Work: Employment Relations in the Post-Union Era. Richard Edwards. 265p. (C). 1993. 42.95 (0-8157-2104-8); pap. 18.95 (0-8157-2105-6) Brookings.

Rights at Work: Pay Equity Reform & the Politics of Legal Mobilization. Michael W. McCann. LC 93-21278. (Language & Legal Discourse Ser.). 372p. 1994. pap. text ed. 18.95 (0-226-55572-0) U Ch Pr.

Rights at Work: Pay Equity Reform & the Politics of Legal Mobilization. Michael W. McCann. LC 93-21278. (Language & Legal Discourse Ser.). 372p. 1994. lib. bdg. 65.00 (0-226-55571-2) U Ch Pr.

Rights Based Fishing. Ed. by Philip A. Neher et al. (C). 1989. lib. bdg. 216.00 (0-7923-0246-X) Kluwer Ac.

Rights Debating Guide. Anthony C. Ibbott. 43p. 1990. pap. 2.50 (0-9625291-1-7) A C Ibbott Fndtn.

Rights, Emergencies & Judicial Review. Imtiaz Omar. 412p. 1996. 150.00 (90-411-0229-9) Kluwer Law Tax Pubs.

Rights for Animals? Deidre Rochford. (Viewpoints Ser.). (J). 1997. lib. bdg. 18.60 (0-531-14414-3) Watts.

Rights for Children. Jane S. Bauld. Tr. by Inlingua. (Illus.). 32p. (J). (gr. k-3). 1994. 17.95 (1-885340-00-1) Coming Age Pr.

Rights for Children. Jane S. Bauld. Tr. by Inlingua. (Illus.). 40p. (J). (gr. k-3). 1994. pap. 8.95 (0-9636274-7-3); 14.95 (1-885340-03-6) Coming Age Pr.

Rights, Freedoms, & Responsibilities of Students. Ed. by William A. Bryan & Richard H. Mullendore. LC 85-644751. (New Directions for Student Services Ser.: No. 59). 115p. (Orig.). 1992. pap. 19.00 (0-614-03602-X) Jossey-Bass.

Rights, Goods & Democracy. Ramon M. Lemos. LC 85-47801. 208p. 1986. 38.50 (0-87413-312-2) U Delaware Pr.

Rights in Conflict: The United Nations & South Africa. Louis B. Sohn. LC 93-39475. 195p. 1994. 85.00 (0-941320-89-8) Transnatl Pubs.

Rights in Moral Lives: A Historical-Philosophical Essay. A. I. Melden. 1988. 40.00 (0-520-06275-2) U CA Pr.

Rights in Patents & Technical Data: Course Manual. write for info. (0-318-61615-7) Fed Pubns Inc.

Rights in Security. S. Sheridan. 1990. 38.00 (0-7121-1859-4, Pub. by Northcote UK) St Mut.

Rights in Technical Data & Computer Software: The Department of Defense Rules. Matthew S. Simchak & David A. Vogel. 357p. (Orig.). 1995. per., pap. 65.00 (0-935165-34-7) GWU Gov Contracts.

***Rights in the Home.** Emma Haughton. LC 96-41658. (What Do We Mean By Human Rights? Ser.). (J). 1997. lib. bdg. write for info. (0-531-14436-4) Watts.

Rights in the Workplace: Employee's Guide to Legal Protection. Thomas J. Kennedy. 96p. 1992. pap. 9.95 (0-9630356-3-0) Makai.

Rights, Institutions & Impact of International Law According to the German Basic Law. Ed. by Christian Starck. 264p. 1987. pap. 54.00 (3-7890-1374-9, Pub. by Nomos Verlags GW) Intl Bk Import.

Rights, Justice, & Community. Ed. by Creighton Peden & John K. Roth. LC 92-27955. 496p. 1992. text ed. 109.95 (0-7734-9599-1) E Mellen.

Rights, Justice, & the Bounds of Liberty: Essays in Social Philosophy. Joel Feinberg. LC 79-48024. 335p. reprint ed. pap. 95.50 (0-7837-6775-7, 2046605) Bks Demand.

***Rights, Laws & Infallibility in Medieval Thought.** Brian Tierney. LC 97-8085. (Variorum Collected Studies Ser.: Vol. 578). 350p. 1997. text ed. 63.95 (0-86078-648-X, Pub. by Ashgate UK) Ashgate Pub Co.

Rights, Liability & Ethics in International Legal Practice: Ethics & Practice. Ed. by Mary C. Daly et al. LC 94-28869. 430p. 1994. 115.00 (0-929179-98-6) Juris Pubng.

Rights, Liberties, & Ideals: The Contributions of Milton R. Konvitz. David J. Danelski. viii, 182p. 1983. text ed. 19.50 (0-8377-0518-5) Rothman.

Rights, Liberties & Public Policy. Ernest Giglio. 225p. 1995. text ed. 59.95 (1-85972-045-5, Pub. by Avebury Pub UK) Ashgate Pub Co.

Rights of Access & Surface Use. 535p. 1984. ring bd. 80.00 (0-614-06617-4, RAS) Rocky Mtn Mineral Law Found.

Rights of Access to the Media. Ed. by Andras Sajo. LC 95-45921. 1996. write for info. (90-411-0166-7) Kluwer Law Tax Pubs.

Rights of Aliens & Refugees: The Basic ACLU Guide to Alien & Refugee Rights. 2nd rev. ed. David Carliner et al. LC 89-11570. 240p. (C). 1990. pap. 8.95 (0-8093-1598-X) S Ill U Pr.

Rights of Allah & Human Rights. M. I. Siddiqui. 1981. 15.95 (0-933511-40-X) Kazi Pubns.

Rights of an American Citizen. Benjamin L. Oliver. LC 76-119940. (Select Bibliographies Reprint Ser.). 1977. reprint ed. 25.95 (0-8369-5383-5) Ayer.

Rights of Assembly, Petition, Arms & Just Compensation. Ed. by Paul L. Murphy. (Bill of Rights & American Legal History Ser.). 764p. 1990. reprint ed. text ed. 60.00 (0-8240-5863-1) Garland.

Rights of Authors, Artists, & Other Creative People: The Basic ACLU Guide to Author & Artist Rights. 2nd rev. ed. Kenneth P. Norwick & Jerry S. Chasen. LC 91-23721. (ACLU Handbook Ser.). 293p. 1992. pap. 8.95 (0-8093-1773-7) S Ill U Pr.

Rights of Children. Ed. by D. D. Rawstron. (C). 1989. 39.00 (0-903534-35-5, Pub. by Brit Ag for Adopt & Fost UK) St Mut.

Rights of Citizenship. Ed. by Robert Blackburn. (Citizenship & the Law Ser.). 348p. 1993. pap. 29.95 (0-7201-2213-9, Mansell Pub) Cassell.

Rights of Citizenship. Ed. by Robert Blackburn. LC 92-43396. (Citizenship & the Law Ser.). 348p. 1993. 80.00 (0-7201-2124-8, Mansell Pub) Cassell.

R

An Asterisk (*) at the beginning of an entry indicates that the title is appearing in BIP for the first time.

R

Rights of Colonies Examined. Stephen Hopkins. Ed. by Paul Campbell. LC 74-20472. (Rhode Island Revolutionary Heritage Ser.: Vol. 2). (Illus.). 1975. reprint ed. 7.50 (*0-917012-02-X*) RI Pubns Soc.

Rights of Colored Men to Suffrage, Citizenship, & Trial by Jury. William Yates. LC 71-89437. (Black Heritage Library Collection). 1977. 12.95 (*0-8369-8695-4*) Ayer.

Rights of Creditors in Life Insurance Policies. Schwarzschild. (C). 1963. 11.50 (*0-256-00680-6*) Irwin.

Rights of Crime Victims. James Stark & Howard Goldstein. (ACLU Ser.). 448p. (Orig.). 1985. pap. 6.95 (*0-8093-9952-0*) S Ill U Pr.

Rights of Employees & Union Members: A Basic Guide to the Legal Rights of Non-Government Employees. rev. ed. Wayne N. Outten et al. LC 93-16895. (American Civil Liberties Union Handbook Ser.). 605p. (C). 1994. pap. 15.95 (*0-8093-1914-4*) S Ill U Pr.

Rights of Employees & Union Members: The Basic ACLU Guide to the Rights of Employees & Union Members. 2nd rev. ed. Wayne N. Outten et al. LC 93-16895. (American Civil Liberties Union Handbook Ser.). 604p. (C). 1994. 39.95 (*0-8093-1913-6*) S Ill U Pr.

Rights of Families: The Basic ACLU Guide to the Rights of Today's Family Members. Martin Guggenheim et al. LC 95-24832. (American Civil Liberties Union Handbook Ser.). 352p. (C). 1996. 34.95 (*0-8093-2051-7*); pap. 8.95 (*0-8093-2052-5*) S Ill U Pr.

Rights of Firefighters. Will Aitchison. 188p. 1991. pap. 29.95 (*1-880607-02-6*) Labor Rel Info.

Rights of Foster Parents. 72p. 1989. pap. 5.00 (*0-89707-460-2*, 549-0089-01) Amer Bar Assn.

Rights of Gun Owners. A. M. Gottlieb. (Law Enforcement Ser.). (Orig.). 1986. lib. bdg. 79.95 (*0-8490-3832-4*) Gordon Pr.

Rights of Gun Owners. rev. ed. Alan M. Gottlieb. xi, 235p. (Orig.). 1991. pap. 9.95 (*0-685-50062-4*) Merril Pr.

Rights of Indians & Tribes. Stephen L. Pevar. 1997. pap. 7.99 (*0-614-28296-9*, Puffin) Puffin Bks.

***Rights of Indians & Tribes.** Stephen L. Pevar. LC 97-20124. 1997. pap. 7.99 (*0-14-037783-2*) Puffin Bks.

Rights of Indians & Tribes: The Basic ACLU Guide to the Indian & Tribal Rights. 2nd rev. ed. Stephen L. Pevar. (ACLU Handbook Ser.). 335p. 1991. pap. 8.95 (*0-8093-1768-0*) S Ill U Pr.

Rights of Juveniles: The Juvenile Justice System. 2nd ed. Samuel M. Davis. LC 80-12465. (Civil Rights Ser.). (C). 1980. ring bd. 135.00 (*0-87632-104-X*) Clark Boardman Callaghan.

Rights of Law Enforcement Officers. 2nd ed. Will Aitchison. 430p. 1992. pap. 29.95 (*1-880607-07-7*) Labor Rel Info.

Rights of Lesbians & Gay Men: The Basic ACLU Guide to a Gay Person's Rights. 3rd rev. ed. Nan D. Hunter et al. LC 91-40607. (ACLU Handbook Ser.). 220p. 1994. pap. 15.95 (*0-8093-1634-X*) S Ill U Pr.

Rights of Lesbians & Gay Men in the Russian Federation. Masha Gessen. 124p. (Orig.). (ENG & RUS.). (C). pap. text ed. 15.00 (*1-884955-13-4*) Intl Gay & Lesbian.

Rights of Light & How to Deal with Them. John Anstey. 114p. (C). 1988. text ed. 85.00 (*0-85406-412-5*, Pub. by Surveyors Pubns) St Mut.

Rights of Man. Thomas Paine. 19.95 (*0-8488-1443-6*) Amereon Ltd.

Rights of Man. Thomas Paine. 1976. pap. 3.95 (*0-8065-0548-6*, Citadel Pr) Carol Pub Group.

Rights of Man. Thomas Paine. LC 92-20305. 226p. (C). 1992. pap. text ed. 6.95 (*0-87220-147-3*); lib. bdg. 27.95 (*0-87220-148-1*) Hackett Pub.

Rights of Man. Thomas Paine. 1994. 17.00 (*0-679-43314-7*) Random.

Rights of Man. Thomas Paine. 288p. 1993. pap. 6.95 (*0-460-87140-4*, Everyman's Classic Lib) C E Tuttle.

Rights of Man. Thomas Paine. LC 86-64007. (Great Books in Philosophy). 188p. pap. 7.95 (*0-87975-379-X*) Prometheus Bks.

Rights of Man. Thomas Paine. (Pelican Classics Ser.). 288p. 1984. pap. 9.95 (*0-14-039015-4*, Penguin Classics) Viking Penguin.

Rights of Man. Thomas Paine. 1989. reprint ed. lib. bdg. 18.95 (*0-89966-626-4*) Buccaneer Bks.

Rights of Man, Pt. I. Thomas Paine. LC 92-25538. 174p. 1992. reprint ed. 48.00 (*1-85477-109-4*, Pub. by Woodstock Bks UK) Cassell.

Rights of Man & Natural Law. Jacques Maritain. LC 74-150416. 120p. 1971. reprint ed. 25.00 (*0-87752-146-8*) Gordian.

Rights of Man, Common Sense, & Other Writings. Thomas Paine. Ed. & Intro. by Mark Philp. (The World's Classics Ser.). 544p. 1995. pap. 9.95 (*0-19-282865-7*) OUP.

***Rights of Memory: Essays on History, Science, & American Culture.** Ed. by Taylor Littleton. LC 85-13972. (The Franklin Lectures in the Sciences & Humanities). (Illus.). 238p. pap. 67.90 (*0-608-05136-5*, 2065697) Bks Demand.

Rights of Memory: Essays on History, Science & American Culture, Vol. V. Ed. by Taylor Littleton. LC 85-13972. (Franklin Lectures in the Sciences & the Humanities). (Illus.). 240p. 1986. text ed. 24.95 (*0-8173-0278-6*) U of Ala Pr.

Rights of Minority Cultures. Ed. by Will Kymlicka. 304p. 1995. text ed. 72.00 (*0-19-878100-8*) OUP.

Rights of Minority Cultures. Ed. by Will Kymlicka. 304p. 1995. pap. 19.95 (*0-19-878101-6*) OUP.

Rights of Nature: A History of Environmental Ethics. Roderick Nash. (History of American Thought & Culture Ser.). 320p. (C). 1989. pap. text ed. 14.95 (*0-299-11844-4*) U of Wis Pr.

Rights of Non-Muslims in Islamic State. A. A. Maududi. pap. 3.00 (*0-933511-41-8*) Kazi Pubns.

***Rights of Non Muslims in the Islamic State.** Mawlana Maudidi. 64p. 1996. pap. 3.00 (*0-614-21475-0*, 1607) Kazi Pubns.

Rights of Older Persons: A Basic Guide to the Legal Rights of Older Persons under Current Law. Robert N. Brown & Legal Counsel for the Elderly Staff. LC 88-2030. 413p. 1988. pap. 8.95 (*0-8093-1432-0*) S Ill U Pr.

Rights of Parties to Illegal Transactions. Neil Thompson. 240p. 1991. pap. 68.00 (*1-86287-036-5*, Pub. by Federation Pr AU) Gaunt.

Rights of Passage: How Women Can Find a New Freedom in Their Midyears. Elinor Lenz. 224p. 1993. pap. 14.95 (*1-56565-076-X*, Woman-Woman) Lowell Hse.

Rights of Passage: Social Change & the Transition from Youth to Adulthood. Sarah Irwin. (Cambridge Studies in Work & Social Inequality: Vol. 4). 1995. 65.00 (*1-85728-429-1*, Pub. by UCL Pr UK); pap. write for info. (*1-85728-430-5*, Pub. by UCL Pr UK) Taylor & Francis.

Rights of Passage: Struggles for Lesbian & Gay Legal Equality. Didi Herman. 192p. (C). 1994. 55.00 (*0-8020-0441-5*); pap. 19.95 (*0-8020-7231-3*) U of Toronto Pr.

Rights of Passage: The Past & Future of the ERA. Joan Hoff-Wilson. LC 85-45073. (Illus.). 160p. reprint ed. pap. 45.60 (*0-7837-3713-0*, 2057891) Bks Demand.

Rights of Patients: The Basic ACLU Guide to Patient Rights. 2nd rev. ed. George J. Annas. LC 88-29893. 328p. 1992. 29.50 (*0-89603-182-9*) Humana.

Rights of Patients: The Basic ACLU Guide to Patient Rights. 2nd rev. ed. George J. Annas. LC 88-29893. (ACLU Handbook Ser.). 312p. (C). 1989. pap. 9.95 (*0-8093-1527-0*) S Ill U Pr.

Rights of Patients in Europe: A Comparative Study. H. J. Leenen et al. LC 92-37647. 1992. 55.00 (*90-6544-671-0*) Kluwer Law Tax Pubs.

Rights of People Who Are HIV Positive: The Authoritative ACLU Guide to the Rights of People Living with HIV Disease & AIDS. William B. Rubenstein et al. LC 95-52122. 488p. (C). 1996. 34.95 (*0-8093-1991-8*) S Ill U Pr.

Rights of People Who Are HIV Positive: The Basic ACLU Guide to the Rights of People Living with HIV Disease & AIDS. William B. Rubenstein et al. LC 95-52122. 488p. (C). 1996. pap. 13.95 (*0-8093-1992-6*) S Ill U Pr.

Rights of People with Mental Disabilities: The Authoritative ACLU Guide to the Rights of People with Mental Illness & Mental Retardation. Robert M. Levy & Leonard S. Rubenstein. LC 95-36408. (American Civil Liberties Union Handbook Ser.). 424p. 1996. 34.95 (*0-8093-1989-6*) S Ill U Pr.

Rights of People with Mental Disabilities: The Basic ACLU Guide to the Rights of People with Mental Illness & Mental Retardation. Robert M. Levy & Leonard S. Rubenstein. LC 95-36408. (American Civil Liberties Union Handbook Ser.). 424p. (C). 1996. pap. 9.95 (*0-8093-1990-X*) S Ill U Pr.

Rights of Peoples. Ed. by James Crawford. 248p. 1992. pap. 26.00 (*0-19-825804-6*) OUP.

Rights of Prisoners. James J. Gobert & Neil P. Cohen. (Individual Rights Ser.). 548p. 1981. text ed. 95.00 (*0-07-011575-3*) Shepards.

Rights of Prisoners: A Comprehensive Guide to the Legal Rights of Prisoners under Current Law. 4th rev. ed. David Rudovsky et al. LC 87-23577. 127p. 1988. pap. 7.95 (*0-8093-1452-5*) S Ill U Pr.

Rights of Privacy. Michael F. Mayer. 251p. (C). 1972. text ed. 7.95 (*0-317-67878-7*) Law Arts.

Rights of Privacy. J. H. Shattuck. Ed. by Franklyn S. Haiman. (To Protect These Rights Ser.). 232p. 1991. pap. 12.95 (*0-8442-6002-9*, Natl Textbk) NTC Pub Grp.

Rights of Public Employees: The Basic ACLU Guide to the Rights of Public Employees. rev. ed. Robert M. O'Neil. LC 93-17474. (American Civil Liberties Union Handbook Ser.). 148p. (C). 1993. pap. 8.95 (*0-8093-1928-4*) S Ill U Pr.

Rights of Public Employees: The Basic ACLU Guide to the Rights of Public Employees. 2nd rev. ed. Robert M. O'Neil. LC 93-17474. (American Civil Liberties Union Handbook Ser.). 163p. (C). 1993. 24.95 (*0-8093-1927-6*) S Ill U Pr.

Rights of Publicity & Privacy. J. Thomas McCarthy. LC 86-21543. (Entertainment & Communication Law Ser.). 1987. ring bd. 145.00 (*0-87632-524-X*) Clark Boardman Callaghan.

Rights of Racial Minorities. Norman Dorsen. 1998. pap. 4.99 (*0-14-037785-9*) Viking Penguin.

Rights of Racial Minorities: The Basic ACLU Guide to Racial Minority Rights. rev. ed. Laughlin McDonald & John A. Powell. LC 93-15756. (American Civil Liberties Union Handbook Ser.). 288p. (C). 1993. pap. 8.95 (*0-8093-1888-1*) S Ill U Pr.

Rights of Racial Minorities: The Basic ACLU Guide to Racial Minority Rights. 2nd rev. ed. Laughlin McDonald & John A. Powell. LC 93-15756. (American Civil Liberties Union Handbook Ser.). 344p. (C). 1993. 34.95 (*0-8093-1899-7*) S Ill U Pr.

Rights of Reason. Ronald G. Aichele. Ed. & Illus. by Davies Group Staff. 150p. (C). 1995. pap. 11.20 (*0-9630076-8-8*) Davies Grp.

Rights of Reason: A Study of Kant's Philosophy & Politics. Susan M. Shell. LC 79-19801. 217p. reprint ed. pap. 61.90 (*0-8357-8309-X*, 2033979) Bks Demand.

Rights of Religious Persons in Public Education. rev. ed. John W. Whitehead. LC 93-15118. 384p. 1993. pap. 17.99 (*0-89107-737-5*) Crossway Bks.

Rights of Single People. Mitchell Bernard et al. (ACLU Ser.). 124p. (Orig.). 1985. pap. 4.95 (*0-8093-9956-3*) S Ill U Pr.

***Rights of Students.** Eve Cary. LC 97-18976. 1997. pap. 7.99 (*0-14-037784-0*) Viking Penguin.

Rights of Students: Basic ACLU Guide to Racial Minority Rights. Janet R. Price et al. LC 87-9890. (American Civil Liberties Union Handbook Ser.). 181p. 1988. pap. 8.95 (*0-8093-1423-1*) S Ill U Pr.

***Rights of Subordinated Peoples.** Ed. by Oliver Mendelsohn & Baxi Upendra. 388p. 1997. reprint ed. pap. 9.95 (*0-19-563928-0*) OUP.

Rights of Teachers. 2nd rev. ed. David Rubin & Steven Greenhouse. (ACLU Ser.). 366p. (Orig.). 1984. pap. 6.95 (*0-8093-9957-1*) S Ill U Pr.

Rights of the Accused in Law & Action. Ed. by Stuart S. Nagel. LC 72-84052. (Sage Criminal Justice System Annuals Ser.: No. 1). 320p. reprint ed. pap. 83.20 (*0-8357-8500-9*, 2034776) Bks Demand.

***Rights of the Child: A European Perspective.** 564p. 1996. pap. 30.00 (*92-871-3006-X*, Pub. by Council of Europe FR) Manhattan Pub Co.

Rights of the Child: International Instruments. Maria R. Saulle. 779p. (C). 1994. lib. bdg. 125.00 (*0-941320-86-3*) Transnatl Pubs.

Rights of the Child & the Changing Image of Childhood. Philip E. Veerman. (International Studies in Human Rights). 656p. (C). 1992. lib. bdg. 237.50 (*0-7923-1250-3*) Kluwer Ac.

***Rights of the Dying: A Companion for Life's Final Moments.** David Kessler. LC 97-1947. 1997. write for info. (*0-06-018753-0*) HarpC.

Rights of the Elderly & Retired: A Peoples' Handbook. William R. Wishard. LC 78-21123. 1979. 12.95 (*0-89666-002-8*); pap. 6.95 (*0-89666-003-6*) Cragmont Pubns.

Rights of the Hearing-Impaired Child. Ed. by Gary W. Nix. LC 77-85240. 1977. 2.95 (*0-88200-112-4*, P5543) Alexander Graham.

Rights of the Homeless. (Litigation & Administrative Practice Ser.). 825p. 1992. pap. text ed. 70.00 (*0-685-56923-3*, H4-5123) PLI.

Rights of the Middle Class: Advent of the Rebel Conservative. William J. Kelly. 177p. (Orig.). 1996. pap. 9.95 (*0-9647553-0-0*) rebel Promot.

Rights of the People. A. T. Jones. 380p. 1994. per. 11.95 (*0-945383-90-8*) Teach Servs.

***Rights of the Poor: The Authoritative ACLU Guide to Poor People's Rights.** Helen Hershkoff & Stephen Loffredo. LC 96-41433. (American Civil Liberties Union Handbks.). 1997. 39.95 (*0-8093-2117-3*); pap. 9.95 (*0-8093-2091-6*) S Ill U Pr.

***Rights of the Sick & Dying: A Practical Guide for Caregivers & Patients.** LC 97-21557. 1997. 14.95 (*0-02-861663-4*) Macmillan.

Rights of Way: Policy, Culture & Management. Ed. by Charles Watkins. LC 95-47479. (Rural Studies). (Illus.). 256p. 1996. pap. 100.00 (*1-85567-390-8*, Pub. by Pntr Pubs UK) Bks Intl VA.

***Rights of Women.** Norman Dorsen. 1998. pap. 4.99 (*0-14-037782-4*) Viking Penguin.

Rights of Women: A Comparative Study in History & Legislation. Moisei A. Ostrogorski. LC 80-21262. xv, 232p. 1980. reprint ed. lib. bdg. 37.50 (*0-87991-960-4*) Porcupine Pr.

Rights of Women: A Feminist Perspective. Ram Ahuja. (C). 1992. 20.00 (*81-7033-172-2*, Pub. by Rawat II) S Asia.

Rights of Women: An Action Guide to the U. N. Conventions of Special Relevance to Women. 120p. 1996. pap. 15.95 (*0-614-17320-5*) Int Wom Tribune Centre.

Rights of Women: The Basic ACLU Guide to Women's Rights. rev. ed. Susan D. Ross et al. 317p. (C). 1993. pap. 8.95 (*0-8093-1633-1*) S Ill U Pr.

Rights of Women: The Basic ACLU Guide to Women's Rights. 3rd rev. ed. Susan D. Ross et al. 336p. (C). 1993. 24.95 (*0-8093-1898-9*) S Ill U Pr.

Rights of Women in Islam. Asghar A. Engineer. 200p. 1992. text ed. 45.00 (*0-312-07584-7*) St Martin.

Rights of Women in Islam. Asghar A. Engineer. 196p. 1996. text ed. 18.95 (*0-312-16197-2*) St Martin.

Rights of Youth: American Colleges & Student Revolt, 1798-1815. Steven J. Novak. LC 76-43109. (Illus.). 230p. reprint ed. pap. 65.60 (*0-7837-5939-8*, 2045738) Bks Demand.

Rights on Trial: The Odyssey of a People's Lawyer. Arthur Kinoy. (Illus.). 375p. 1983. 37.50 (*0-674-77013-7*) HUP.

Rights on Trial: The Odyssey of a People's Lawyer. Arthur Kinoy. 368p. 1984. pap. text ed. 12.95 (*0-674-77014-5*) HUP.

Rights on Trial: The Odyssey of a People's Lawyer. 2nd ed. Arthur Kinoy. (Illus.). 340p. 1995. pap. 17.95 (*0-9641887-0-8*) Bernel Bks.

Rights, Politics, & Economics. James A. Diefenbeck. 256p. (C). 1995. lib. bdg. 39.50 (*0-7618-0096-4*) U Pr of Amer.

Rights Responsibilities & the Law. Judith Edmunds. 1982. 60.00 (*0-17-438190-5*, Pub. by NCCL UK) St Mut.

Rights, Restitution, & Risk: Essays in Moral Theory. Judith J. Thomson. Ed. by William A. Parent. (Illus.). 288p. 1986. pap. 15.95 (*0-674-76981-3*) HUP.

Rights Retained by the People: The History & Meaning of the Ninth Amendment. Ed. by Randy E. Barnett. 350p. (C). 1989. lib. bdg. 62.00 (*0-913969-22-2*, G Mason Univ Pr) Univ Pub Assocs.

Rights Retained by the People: The History & Meaning of the Ninth Amendment. Ed. by Randy E. Barnett. 350p. (C). 1991. pap. 16.95 (*0-913969-37-0*) Univ Pub Assocs.

Rights Retained by the People Vol. II: The History & Meaning of the Ninth Amendment. Ed. by Randy E. Barnett. 350p. (C). 1993. lib. bdg. 64.50 (*0-913969-44-3*) Univ Pub Assocs.

Rights Talk: The Impoverishment of Political Discourse. Mary A. Glendon. 218p. 1993. pap. 10.95 (*0-02-911826-3*, Free Press) Free Pr.

Rights Talk: The Impoverishment of Political Discourse. Mary A. Glendon. 1993. pap. 12.95 (*0-02-911823-9*, Free Press) Free Pr.

Rights to Health Care. Thomas J. Bole, III & William B. Bondeson. 318p. (C). 1991. lib. bdg. 141.50 (*0-7923-1137-X*, Pub. by Klwr Acad Pubs NE) Kluwer Ac.

Rights to Nature: Cultural, Economic, Political & Ecological Principles of Institutions for the Environment. Susan S. Hanna et al. 288p. (C). 1996. pap. text ed. 29.95 (*1-55963-490-1*) Island Pr.

Rights to Oceanic Resources. Ed. by Dorinda G. Dallmeyer & Louis DeVorsey, Jr. (C). 1989. lib. bdg. 95.50 (*0-7923-0019-X*) Kluwer Ac.

***Rights to Privacy.** Robert E. Long. LC 97-13914. (Reference Shelf Ser.). 1997. write for info. (*0-8242-0916-8*) Wilson.

Rights to Protest: The Basic ACLU Guide to Free Expression. Joel M. Gora et al. LC 90-19977. (American Civil Liberties Union Handbook Ser.). 344p. (C). 1991. pap. 8.95 (*0-8093-1699-4*) S Ill U Pr.

Rights To Responsibility: Multiple Approaches to Developing Character & Community. Alanda Greene. LC 96-25421. 1996. 30.00 (*1-56976-039-X*) Zephyr Pr AZ.

Rights v. Conspiracy: A Sociological Essay on the History of Labour Law in the United States. Anthony Woodiwiss. LC 89-35883. 341p. 1990. 19.95 (*0-85496-587-4*) Berg Pubs.

***Rights vs. Responsibilities: The Supreme Court & the Media.** Elizabeth B. Hindman. LC 96-38794. (Contributions to the Study of Mass Media and Communications: Vol. 50). 208p. 1997. text ed. 55.00 (*0-313-29922-6*, Greenwood Pr) Greenwood.

Rights, Welfare, & Mill's Moral Theory. David Lyons. 224p. 1994. pap. 18.95 (*0-19-508218-4*) OUP.

Rights You Possess. Anthony C. Ibbott. LC 89-92514. 100p. (Orig.). (C). 1990. pap. 10.00 (*0-9625291-0-9*) A C Ibbott Fndtn.

Rights You Possess. 2nd ed. Anthony C. Ibbott. 95p. (Orig.). 1993. pap. 5.00 (*0-9625291-4-1*) A C Ibbott Fndtn.

Rightsizing for Local Governments. Frank Benest. 94p. 1992. student ed. 29.95 (*1-882403-04-5*) The Innovation Grps.

Rightsizing New Enterprise. Kern & Johnson. 1996. text ed. 40.00 (*0-13-490384-6*) P-H.

Rightsizing Remedy: How Managers Can Respond to the Downsizing Dilemma. Charles F. Hendricks. 288p. 1992. text ed. 30.00 (*1-55623-654-9*) Irwin Prof Pubng.

Rightway Educational Services. Joseph Vollaro. (Review Book Ser.). 185p. 1992. Math Sequential I. pap. text ed. 12.95 (*0-9633309-0-X*); Math Sequential II. write for info. (*0-9633309-1-8*) Rightway Educ.

Rigid & Flexible Pavement Design & Analysis: Unbound Granular Materials, Tire Pressures, Backcalculation, & Design Methods. (Research Record Ser.: No. 1227). 224p. 1989. 32.00 (*0-309-04822-2*) Transport Res Bd.

Rigid-Chain Polymers: Hydrodynamic & Optical Properties in Solution. V. N. Tsvetkov. Tr. by E. A. Korolyova from RUS. LC 88-34423. (Macromolecular Compounds Ser.). (Illus.). 512p. 1989. 135.00 (*0-306-11020-2*, Consultants) Plenum.

Rigid Container Business. Business Communications Co., Inc. Staff. 336p. 1989. 2,650.00 (*0-89336-676-5*, P-077R) BCC.

Rigid Endoscope Systems Markets. (Market Research Reports: No. 512). 236p. 1996. 995.00 (*0-317-05469-4*) Theta Corp.

Rigid Fixation of the Craniomaxillofacial Skeleton. Michael J. Yaremchuk et al. Ed. by Joseph S. Gruss. 696p. 1992. text ed. 275.00 (*0-7506-9197-2*) Buttrwrth-Heinemann.

Rigid-Flex Printed Wiring Design for Production & Readiness. Rigling. (Electrical Engineering & Electronics Ser.: Vol. 47). 296p. 1988. 140.00 (*0-8247-7707-7*) Dekker.

Rigid-Ideal. 1980. 11.50 (*0-8176-0935-0*) Spr-Verlag.

Rigid Local Systems. Nicholas M. Katz. LC 95-44041. (Annals of Mathematics Studies: No. 139). 219p. 1996. text ed. 49.50 (*0-691-01119-2*); pap. text ed. 22.50 (*0-691-01118-4*) Princeton U Pr.

Rigid Medical Plastics. (Market Research Reports: No. 912). (Illus.). 161p. 1990. 295.00 (*0-317-05020-6*) Theta Corp.

Rigid Non-Packaging Transparent Plastics, No. P-053N. 1994. 2,650.00 (*1-56965-257-0*) BCC.

Rigid Polymer Networks, Vol. 118. S. M. Aharoni & S. F. Edwards. (Advances in Polymer Science Ser.). 256p. 1994. 150.00 (*0-387-58340-8*) Spr-Verlag.

Rigid Scrutiny: Critical Essays on the Old Testament. Ivan Engnell. Tr. by John T. Willis. LC 70-76166. 303p. 1969. 21.95 (*0-8265-1133-3*) Vanderbilt U Pr.

Rigoberta Menchu. Caroline Lazo. LC 93-8381. (Peacemakers Ser.). (Illus.). 64p. (J). (gr. 4 up). 1994. lib. bdg. 13.95 (*0-87518-619-X*, Dillon Silver Burdett) Silver Burdett Pr.

***Rigoberta Menchu: Champion of Human Rights.** Julie Schulze. (Contemporary Profiles & Policy Series for the Younger Reader). (YA). (gr. 8 up). write for info. (*0-934272-42-5*); pap. write for info. (*0-934272-43-3*) J G Burke Pub.

Rigodon. Louis-Ferdinand Celine. (FRE.). 1987. pap. 11.95 (*0-8288-3626-4*, M3190) Fr & Eur.

Rigodon. Louis-Ferdinand Celine. (Folio Ser.: No. 481). (FRE.). 9.95 (*0-685-57722-8*); pap. 8.95 (*2-07-036481-X*) Schoenhof.

An Asterisk (*) at the beginning of an entry indicates that the title is appearing in BIP for the first time.

Rigoletto. Giuseppe Verdi. Ed. by Nicholas John. Tr. by James Feuton from ITA. (English National Opera Guide Series: Bilingual Libretto, Articles: No. 15). (Illus.). 128p. (Orig.). 1982. pap. 9.95 (*0-7145-3939-2*) Riverrun NY.

Rigoletto: Libretto. Giuseppe Verdi. 44p. (ENG & ITA.). 1986. pap. 4.95 (*0-7935-2615-9*, 50340220) H Leonard.

Rigoletto: Melodrama in Three Acts, 2 vols., Vols. 1 & 2. Giuseppe Verdi. Ed. by Martin Chusid. LC 82-15985. (Works of Giuseppe Verdi: No. 1, Vol. 17). 516p. 1983. Set, Vol. 1, Score; Vol. 2, Commentary. lib. bdg. 250.00 (*0-226-85306-3*) U Ch Pr.

Rigor & Imagination: Essays on Human Communication from the Interactional View. John H. Weakland. LC 81-83995. 432p. 1981. text ed. 65.00 (*0-275-90741-4*, C0741, Praeger Pubs) Greenwood.

Rigor Mortis. large type ed. Mary Kittredge. LC 91-10952. 272p. 1991. reprint ed. lib. bdg. 19.95 (*1-56054-171-7*) Thorndike Pr.

Rigor Mortis. Mary Kittredge. 1992. reprint ed. mass mkt. 3.99 (*0-312-92865-3*) St Martin.

Rigor Mortis. Ralph McInerny, pseud. 1991. reprint ed. mass mkt. 3.99 (*0-373-26080-6*) Harlequin Bks.

***Rigorous Global Search: Continuous Problems.** R. Baker Kearfott. LC 96-35779. (Nonconvex Optimization & Its Applications Ser.: Vol. 13). 262p. (C). 1996. lib. bdg. 134.00 (*0-7923-4238-0*) Kluwer Ac.

Rigorous Results in Quantum Dynamics. Ed. by J. Dittrich & P. Exner. 344p. (C). 1991. text ed. 110.00 (*981-02-0561-9*) World Scientific Pub.

Rigveda. Edward V. Arnold. LC 73-139172. (Popular Studies in Mythology, Romance & Folklore: No. 9). reprint ed. 27.50 (*0-404-53509-7*) AMS Pr.

Rigveda, Vol. 3. Tr. by Acharya D. Martanda. 816p. (ENG, HIN & SAN.). 1984. 17.00 (*0-685-72920-6*, Pub. by Sarvadeshik Arya II) Nataraj Bks.

Rigveda, Vol. 4. Tr. by Acharya D. Deva. 808p. (ENG, HIN & SAN.). 1986. 17.00 (*0-685-72921-4*, Pub. by Sarvadeshik Arya II) Nataraj Bks.

Rigveda, Vol. 5. Ed. by Brahma D. Snatak & Surendra K. Hindi. Tr. by Acharya D. Deva & Vidya Martanda. viii, 720p. 1989. 17.00 (*0-685-72922-2*, Pub. by Sarvadeshik Arya II) Nataraj Bks.

Rigveda Brahmanas. Ed. by Arthur Keith. 1975. lib. bdg. 300.00 (*0-87968-440-2*) Krishna Pr.

Rigveda Samhita, 10 vols. Swami S. Prakash & Pandit S. Vidyalankar. 1986. 40.00 (*0-685-73822-1*) St Mut.

Rigveda, Vol. 1: With Maharishi Dayananda Sharaswati's Commentary. Tr. by Acharya D. Martanda. lx, 952p. 1974. 17.00 (*0-685-72918-4*, Pub. by Sarvadeshik Arya II) Nataraj Bks.

Rigveda, Vol. 2: With Maharshi Dayananda Saraswati's Commentary. Tr. by Swami D. Saraswati. 1012p. 1978. 17.00 (*0-685-72919-2*, Pub. by Sarvadeshik Arya II) Nataraj Bks.

Rigvedic Adityas. Joel P. Brereton. (American Oriental Ser.: Vol. 63). x, 356p. 1981. pap. 17.00 (*0-940490-63-3*) Am Orient Soc.

***Rikka: Soul of Japanese.** Y. Fujiwara. 1996. 79.95 (*4-07-972358-X*) Shufu no Tomo-Sha.

Rikki - Tikki - Taui. Rudyard Kipling. 20p. (Orig.). (J). (gr. 2-7). 1993. pap. 3.00 (*1-57514-258-9*, 1115) Encore Perform Pub.

Rikki-Tikki-Tavi. Rudyard Kipling. (Illus.). 44p. (J). (gr. 1 up). 1992. 17.00 (*0-15-267015-7*, HB Juv Bks) HarBrace.

Rikki Tikki Tavi. Rudyard Kipling. (Creative Short Stories Ser.). 1987. lib. bdg. 13.95 (*0-88682-126-6*) Creative Ed.

Rikki-tikki-tavi. Rudyard Kipling. LC 96-30540. (Little Treasures Ser.). (Illus.). 64p. (J). (gr. 3-9). 1997. 9.99 (*0-7636-0135-7*) Candlewick Pr.

***Rikki-Tikki-Tavi.** Jerry Pinkney & Rudyard Kipling. LC 96-51194. Date not set. 16.00 (*0-688-14320-2*, Morrow Junior) Morrow.

***Rikki-Tikki-Tavi.** Jerry Pinkney & Rudyard Kipling. LC 96-51194. (J). Date not set. lab manual ed., lib. bdg. 15.93 (*0-688-14321-0*, Morrow Junior) Morrow.

Riko Rabbit. Mei T. Nakano. LC 82-81737. (J). (gr. 2-5). 1982. pap. 5.95 (*0-942610-00-8*) Mina Pr.

Riland: Three Hundred Years of a Family Living, Being a History of the Rilands of Sutton Coldfield, England. W. K. Bedford. 175p. 1993. reprint ed. pap. 28.00 (*0-8328-3739-3*); reprint ed. lib. bdg. 38.00 (*0-8328-3738-5*) Higginson Bk Co.

Riley Child-Rhymes. James W. Riley. LC 74-121933. (Granger Index Reprint Ser.). 1977. 22.95 (*0-8369-6174-9*) Ayer.

Riley Child Rhymes with Hoosier Pictures. James W. Riley. (Illus.). 188p. (J). reprint ed. 20.00 (*1-878208-17-9*) Guild Pr IN.

Riley in Memoriam (1849-1916) A Sesquicentennial Celebrative Anthology by the Poets of Indiana. Ed. by John H. Morgan. LC 89-40432. (Illus.). 205p. 1989. pap. text ed. 24.95 (*1-55605-100-X*) Wyndham Hall.

Riley Inventory of Basic Learning Skills (RIBLS) Stanley R. Riley. 64p. 1991. pap. text ed. 17.00 (*0-87879-932-X*); student ed., vinyl bd. 50.00 (*0-87879-931-1*); student ed., vinyl bd. 50.00 (*0-87879-935-4*); student ed. 20.00 (*0-87879-933-8*); student ed. 20.00 (*0-87879-938-9*); 10.00 (*0-87879-934-6*); 10.00 (*0-87879-939-7*) Acad Therapy.

Riley on Business Interruption & Consequential Loss Insurance. David Cloughton. (C). 1985. 500.00 (*0-685-33713-8*, Pub. by Witherby & Co UK) St Mut.

Riley RM - Series. James Taylor. (Illus.). 200p. 1990. 39.95 (*0-947981-36-5*, Pub. by Motor Racing UK) Motorbooks Intl.

Riley's Annotated Bills of Exchange Act & Cheques & Payment Orders Act. 4th ed. Ken Robson. 320p. 1994. pap. 65.00 (*0-455-21294-5*, Pub. by Law Bk Co AT) Gaunt.

Riley's Flute Melodies, 2vols. in 1. Edward Riley. Ed. & Intro. by H. Wiley Hitchcock. LC 72-14213. (Earlier American Music Ser.: Vol. 18). 200p. 1973. reprint ed. lib. bdg. 27.50 (*0-306-70565-6*) Da Capo.

Riley's Sleeping Beauty. Sherryl Woods. (Special Edition Ser.). 1995. mass mkt. 3.75 (*0-373-09961-4*, 1-09961-3) Silhouette.

Rilhe on Black. Ken Bruen. (Mask Noir Ser.). 152p. (Orig.). 1997. pap. text ed. 12.99 (*1-85242-511-3*, Mask Noir) Serpents Tail.

Rilke. Art Beck. LC 82-84119. 70p. (Orig.). 1983. pap. 3.95 (*0-941692-06-X*) Elysian Pr.

Rilke: A Biography. Ralph Freedman. LC 87-42657. (Illus.). 1988. 24.95 (*0-394-52269-9*) Random.

Rilke: A Life. Wolfgang Leppmann. Tr. by Russell M. Stockman from GER. LC 84-6062. (Illus.). 421p. 1984. pap. 12.95 (*0-88064-015-4*) Fromm Intl Pub.

Rilke: Between Roots Selected Poems Rendered from German By Rika Lesser. Rainer M. Rilke. Tr. by Rika Lesser from GER. LC 85-43204. (Lockert Library of Poetry in Translation). 75p. 1986. pap. 9.95 (*0-691-01429-9*) Princeton U Pr.

Rilke & Benvenuta: An Intimate Correspondence. Ed. by Magda Von Hattingberg. Tr. by Joel Agee from GER. LC 87-15660. 148p. 1987. 16.95 (*0-88064-072-3*) Fromm Intl Pub.

Rilke & Russia: A Re-Evaluation. Daria A. Reshetylo-Rothe. (Studies in Modern German Literature: Vol. 18). 357p. (C). 1989. text ed. 62.50 (*0-8204-0560-4*) P Lang Pubng.

Rilke & the Visual Arts. Jennifer Liebnitz et al. Ed. by Frank Baron. (Illus.). 150p. 1982. 15.00 (*0-87291-153-5*) Coronado Pr.

Rilke, Europe, & the English-speaking World. Eudo C. Mason. LC 61-16153. 277p. reprint ed. pap. 79.00 (*0-317-20596-X*, 2024492) Bks Demand.

Rilke in Transition: An Exploration of His Earliest Poetry. James Rolleston. LC 73-99839. (Yale Germanic Studies: 4). 256p. reprint ed. pap. 73.00 (*0-317-29716-3*, 2022035) Bks Demand.

Rilke-Kommentar zu den "Aufzeichnungen des Malte Laurids Brigge" Kommentar Zu Den "Aufzeichnungen des Malte Laurids Brigge" William Small. (Germanic Languages & Literatures Ser.: No. 101). ix, 175p. 1983. lib. bdg. 29.95 (*0-8078-8101-5*) U of NC Pr.

Rilke on Love & Other Difficulties: Translations & Considerations of Rainer Maria Rilke. John J. Mood. 120p. 1994. pap. 9.95 (*0-393-31098-1*) Norton.

Rilke's Book of Hours: Love Poems to God. Rainer M. Rilke. Tr. by Anita Barrows. 176p. 1996. 21.00 (*1-57322-033-7*, Riverhead Books) Putnam Pub Group.

***Rilke's Book of Hours: Love Poems to God.** Tr. by Anita Barrows & Joanna Macy. 176p. 1997. reprint ed. pap. 8.00 (*1-57322-585-1*, Riverhd Trade) Berkley Pub.

Rilke's Duino Elegies. Ed. by Roger Paulin & Peter Hutchinson. (Studies in Austrian Literature, Culture & Thought; Translation Ser.). (Illus.). xii, 238p. 1996. 37.95 (*1-57241-032-9*) Ariadne CA.

Rilke's Duino Elegies. Rainer M. Rilke. Tr. by Alan F. Keele & Leslie Norris. (GERM Ser.: Vol. 65). (Illus.). x, 66p. 1993. 35.00 (*1-879751-01-1*) Camden Hse.

Rilke's Russia: A Cultural Encounter. Anna A. Tavis. (Studies in Russian Literature & Theory). 218p. 1994. 39.95 (*0-8101-1152-7*) Northwestern U Pr.

***Rilke's Russia: A Cultural Encounter.** Anna A. Tavis. (Studies in Russian Literature & Theory). 195p. 1997. pap. 14.95 (*0-8101-1466-6*) Northwestern U Pr.

Rilla of Ingleside. Lucy Maud Montgomery. (J). 1976. 23.95 (*0-8488-0592-5*) Amereon Ltd.

Rilla of Ingleside. Lucy Maud Montgomery. 288p. (J). 1985. pap. 3.50 (*0-553-26922-4*) Bantam.

Rilla of Ingleside. Lucy Maud Montgomery. 288p. (J). 1987. mass mkt. 3.95 (*0-7704-2185-7*) Bantam.

***Rilo Buru's Summer Vacation.** Marty Engle & Johnny R. Barnes, Jr. (Strange Matter Ser.: No. 31). 144p. (Orig.). (YA). (gr. 4 up). 1997. pap. 3.99 (*1-56714-090-4*) Montage Bks.

***Rim: A Novel of Virtual Reality.** Alexander Besher. 20.00 (*0-06-258613-0*) HarpC.

RIM: A Novel of Virtual Reality. Alexander Besher. 320p. 1996. mass mkt. 5.99 (*0-06-105669-3*) HarpC.

RIM: Fundamentals of Reaction Injection Molding. Christopher W. Macosko. 246p. (C). 1989. text ed. 49.95 (*1-56990-055-8*) Hanser-Gardner.

RIM: Growing up. Business Communications Co., Inc. Staff. 186p. 1987. pap. 1,950.00 (*0-89336-535-1*, P-054N) BCC.

Rim Country Mountain Biking: Great Rides along Arizona's Mogollon Rim. Jeffrey L. Stevenson. LC 95-3546. (Illus.). 257p. (Orig.). 1995. pap. 19.95 (*0-87108-856-8*) Pruett.

Rim of Christendom: A Biography of Eusebio Francisco Kino, Pacific Coast Pioneer. Herbert E. Bolton. LC 84-8814. 644p. 1984. reprint ed. 60.95 (*0-8165-0863-1*) U of Ariz Pr.

Rim of the Desert. Ernest Haycox. 305p. 1975. reprint ed. lib. bdg. 20.95 (*0-89190-974-5*, Rivercity Pr) Amereon Ltd.

Rim of the Prairie. Bess S. Aldrich. LC 25-19624. xii, 352p. 1966. pap. 12.95 (*0-8032-5002-9*, Bison Books) U of Nebr Pr.

***Rim of the Wheel.** Larry Caskey. LC 97-65964. 336p. 1997. 24.95 (*1-57197-061-4*) Pentland Pr.

Rim Poems. Joseph McLeod. 72p. 1990. pap. 9.95 (*0-921254-22-9*, Pub. by Penumbra Pr CN) U of Toronto Pr.

Rim Walkers. Vicki Grove. LC 92-36091. 224p. (YA). (gr. 5 up). 1993. 14.95 (*0-399-22430-0*, Putnam) Putnam Pub Group.

Rimani see Hanimations

Rimas. Archer M. Huntington. 1936. 7.00 (*0-87535-037-2*) Hispanic Soc.

Rimas. unabridged ed. Gustavo A. Becquer. (SPA.). pap. 7.95 (*84-410-0001-8*, Pub. by Bookking Intl FR) Distribks Inc.

Rimas of Gustavo Becquer. Gustavo A. Becquer. Tr. by Jules Renard. 1976. lib. bdg. 250.00 (*0-8490-2525-7*) Gordon Pr.

Rimas y Declaraciones Poeticas. Gustavo A. Becquer. 279p. (SPA.). 1989. 11.95 (*0-8288-7077-2*) Fr & Eur.

Rimas y Declaraciones Poeticas. Gustavo A. Bequer. Ed. by Estrada F. Lopez. (Nueva Austral Ser.: No. 6). (SPA.). 1991. pap. text ed. 11.95 (*84-239-1806-8*) Elliots Bks.

Rimas y Leyendas. Gustavo A. Becquer. (SPA.). 9.95 (*0-8288-2553-X*) Fr & Eur.

Rimas y Risas - Green Series: Small Book Classroom Set. (ENG & SPA.). 1992. teacher ed. 295.00 incl. audio (*1-56334-129-8*) Hampton-Brown.

Rimas y Risas - Red Series: Small Book Classroom Set. (Illus.). (ENG & SPA.). 1992. teacher ed. 295.00 incl. audio (*1-56334-128-X*) Hampton-Brown.

Rimas y Risas Green - English Supplement. (Rimas y Risas (Green) Ser.). (Illus.). (J). (ps-2). 1993. 253.00 (*1-56334-371-1*) Hampton-Brown.

Rimas y Risas Green - T. A. L. K. Manipulatives. (Rimas & Risas (Green) Ser.). (J). (ps-2). 1993. 140.00 (*1-56334-372-X*) Hampton-Brown.

Rimas y Risas Green Teacher's Activity Notebook. (Rimas y Risas Green Ser.). (Illus.). 144p. (ENG & SPA.). 1989. teacher ed., ring bd. 85.00 (*0-917837-07-X*) Hampton-Brown.

Rimas y Risas (Red) Series: Cuentitas Mios Classroom Set. (Illus.). (Orig.). (ENG & SPA.). (J). (gr. k-3). 1991. student ed. 277.00 (*1-56334-008-9*) Hampton-Brown.

Rimas y Risas (Red) Series: 4 Big Books. (Illus.). (Orig.). (ENG & SPA.). (J). (gr. k-3). 1991. 192.00 (*1-56334-007-0*) Hampton-Brown.

Rimas y Risas Red Teacher's Activity Notebook. (Rimas y Risas Red Ser.). (Illus.). 144p. 1990. teacher ed., ring bd. 85.00 (*0-917837-59-2*) Hampton-Brown.

Rimbaud. James G. Koch. (Illus.). 52p. (Orig.). 1996. pap. 4.95 (*1-884778-16-X*) Old Mountain.

Rimbaud. Pierre Petitfils. Tr. by Alan Sheridan from FRE. LC 87-6109. (Illus.). 400p. 1988. text ed. 40.00 (*0-8139-1142-7*) U Pr of Va.

Rimbaud. Wallace Fowlie. LC 65-20963. 288p. reprint ed. pap. 82.10 (*0-685-15513-7*, 2027211) Bks Demand.

Rimbaud: A Critical Introduction. C. A. Hackett. LC 80-40455. (Major European Authors Ser.). 250p. 1981. pap. 18.95 (*0-521-29756-7*); text ed. 59.95 (*0-521-22976-6*) Cambridge U Pr.

Rimbaud: The Boy & the Poet. Edgell Rickwood. LC 72-163208. (Studies in French Literature: No. 45). 1971. reprint ed. lib. bdg. 75.00 (*0-8383-1309-4*) M S G Haskell Hse.

Rimbaud: Visions & Habitations. Edward J. Ahearn. LC 82-2776. 383p. 1983. 55.00 (*0-520-04591-2*) U CA Pr.

Rimbaud & Jim Morrison: The Rebel As Poet. Wallace Fowlie. LC 93-37313. (Illus.). 128p. 1994. pap. text ed. 10.95 (*0-8223-1445-2*) Duke.

Rimbaud & Jim Morrison: The Rebel As Poet. Wallace Fowlie. LC 93-37313. (Illus.). 128p. 1994. text ed. 25.95 (*0-8223-1442-8*) Duke.

Rimbaud et le probleme des Illuminations. Henry D. Bouillane De Lacoste. LC 77-10253. reprint ed. 23.50 (*0-404-16303-4*) AMS Pr.

Rimbaud tel que je l'ai connu. Georges Izambard. LC 77-10271. reprint ed. 29.50 (*0-404-16323-8*) AMS Pr.

Rimbaud under the Steel Helmet. Helmut M. Soik. Tr. by George M. Gugelberger & Lydia Perera. 1976. pap. 4.00 (*0-88031-025-1*) Invisible-Red Hill.

Rimbaud's Theatre of the Self. James R. Lawler. 245p. (C). 1992. 42.50 (*0-674-77075-7*) HUP.

***Rime, 2 vols.** Ludovico Ariosto et al. 692p. 1995. write for info. (*3-487-10056-8*) G Olms Pubs.

***Rime, 3 vols., Vol. 2, 1, 2, 3.** Tasso et al. 1308p. (GER.). 1994. write for info. (*3-487-09910-1*) G Olms Pubs.

Rime & Punishment. Werner Low. (Poetry Ser.: No. 2). (Illus.). (Orig.). 1989. pap. 3.00 (*0-938823-02-7*) Pogment Pr.

Rime et la Raison: Les Collections Menil (Houston-New York) (Illus.). (FRE.). 1984. 45.00 (*2-7118-0258-2*) Inst for the Arts.

***Rime of Ancient Mariner, Vol. 1.** Fry. Date not set. pap. text ed. write for info. (*0-312-11223-8*) St Martin.

***Rime of the Ancient Mariner.** Samuel Coleridge. (Illus.). 88p. 1995. 19.95 (*1-879582-10-4*) Platinum Pr.

Rime of the Ancient Mariner. Samuel Taylor Coleridge. (Illus.). 1991. pap. 3.95 (*0-425-12763-X*) First Classics.

Rime of the Ancient Mariner. Samuel Taylor Coleridge. 1994. pap. 8.99 (*0-517-11849-1*) Random Hse Value.

Rime of the Ancient Mariner. Samuel Taylor Coleridge. Ed. by Gustave Dorbe. 1979. 19.95 (*0-405-11896-1*) Ayer.

Rime of the Ancient Mariner. Samuel Taylor Coleridge & Dean Motter. (Classics Illustrated Ser.). (Illus.). 52p. (YA). pap. 4.95 (*1-57209-024-3*) Classics Int Ent.

Rime of the Ancient Mariner. Samuel Taylor Coleridge. (Chatto Pocket Library). (Illus.). 44p. 1994. 13.95 (*0-7011-6051-9*, Pub. by Chatto & Windus UK) Trafalgar.

Rime of the Ancient Mariner. Hunt Emerson. (Illus.). 1990. pap. 9.95 (*1-56060-011-X*) Eclipse Bks.

Rime of the Ancient Mariner. Gustave Dore. (Illus.). 1970. reprint ed. pap. 4.95 (*0-486-22305-1*) Dover.

Rime of the Ancient Mariner: And Other Classic Stories in Verse. Samuel Taylor Coleridge. 224p. (J). 1996. pap. 3.99 (*0-14-037788-3*) Viking Penguin.

Rime of the Ancient Mariner: The Three Great Nineteenth Century Folios. 2nd ed. Samuel Taylor Coleridge. (Illus.). 112p. 1996. pap. 14.95 (*0-9631135-4-2*) MCE Publ Co.

Rime of the Ancient Mariner & Other Poems. Samuel Taylor Coleridge. 80p. 1992. reprint ed. pap. text ed. 1.00 (*0-486-27266-4*) Dover.

Rime of Verdancy: Poems of Nature. Jesse White. (Illus.). (Orig.). pap. 7.95 (*0-9637176-9-3*) Jesse White.

Rimers of Eldritch. Lanford Wilson. 1967. pap. 5.25 (*0-8222-0953-5*) Dramatists Play.

Rimfire Cartridge in the United States & Canada. John L. Barber. LC 86-72737. (Illus.). 221p. 1987. 39.95 (*0-9604982-6-5*) Armory Pubns.

Rimo: Mountain on the Silk Road. large type ed. Peter Hillary. (Illus.). 224p. 1992. 27.99 (*0-7089-8632-3*, Trail West Pubs) Ulverscroft.

Rimonah of the Flashing Sword: A North African Tale. Illus. by Omar Rayyan. LC 93-40091. 32p. (J). (ps-3). 1995. lib. bdg. 15.95 (*0-8234-1093-5*) Holiday.

Rimrock. Don P. Jenison. (Orig.). 1980. mass mkt. 1.95 (*0-89083-576-4*, Zebra Kensgtn) Kensgtn Pub Corp.

Rimrock. Gilbert Morris. LC 92-9439. (Jim Reno Westerns Ser.: Vol. 2). 257p. 1992. 9.99 (*0-8423-1059-2*) Tyndale.

Rimrock. large type ed. Luke Short. LC 95-24419. 1996. 21.95 (*0-7838-1465-8*, GK Hall) Thorndike Pr.

RIMS Symposia on Software Science & Engineering: Proceedings, Kyoto, Japan, 1982. Ed. by E. Goto et al. (Lecture Notes in Computer Science Ser.: Vol. 147). 232p. 1983. 29.90 (*0-387-11980-9*) Spr-Verlag.

RIMS Symposia on Software Science & Engineering II. Ed. by K. Araki. (Lecture Notes in Computer Science Ser.: Vol. 220). xi, 323p. 1986. 39.00 (*0-387-16470-7*) Spr-Verlag.

Rimskie Igre - Roman Games. Roman Gershgorin. 333p. (Orig.). (RUS.). 1992. pap. 3.00 (*1-881910-04-0*) Adventure NY.

Rimsky-Korsakov. Gerald E. Abraham. LC 75-41002. (BCL Ser.: No. II). reprint ed. 24.95 (*0-404-14500-0*) AMS Pr.

Rimsky-Korsakov. Montagu Montagu-Nathan. LC 74-24158. reprint ed. 29.50 (*0-404-13051-8*) AMS Pr.

Rimsky-Korsakov: Music Book Index. Gerald E. Abraham. 142p. 1993. reprint ed. lib. bdg. 69.00 (*0-7812-9623-4*) Rprt Serv.

Rimsky-Korssakow. Nikolaus V. Gilse Van Der Pals. viii, 692p. 1977. reprint ed. write for info. (*3-487-06427-8*) G Olms Pubs.

Rimwalkers. Vicki Grove. 224p. (J). (gr. 5-9). 1996. pap. 4.95 (*0-698-11423-X*, Paperstar) Putnam Pub Group.

Rin-Chen-Bzan-Po & the Renaissance of Buddhism in Tibet Around the Millenium: Indo-Tibetica II. Giuseppe Tucci. (C). 1988. 32.50 (*81-85179-21-2*, Pub. by Aditya Prakashan II) S Asia.

Rinaldo: Character & Intertext in Ariosto & Tasso. Michael Sherberg. LC 91-77570. (Stanford French & Italian Studies: Vol. 75). 216p. 1993. pap. 46.50 (*0-915838-91-5*) Anma Libri.

Rinaldo on the Run. Ursel Scheffler. 1996. pap. 5.95 (*1-55858-622-9*) North-South Bks NYC.

Rinaldo, the Sly Fox. Ursel Scheffler. (Illus.). 64p. (J). (gr. 2-4). 1994. pap. 4.95 (*1-55858-359-9*) North-South Bks NYC.

***Rina's Big Book of Sex Cartoons.** Rina Piccolo. (Illus.). 96p. (Orig.). 1997. pap. 8.95 (*1-889594-02-4*) Laugh Lines.

Rincon: A History of Corpus Christi Beach. Bill Walraven. (Illus.). 104p. (Orig.). 1990. 19.95 (*0-9626178-1-4*); pap. 6.95 (*0-9626178-0-6*) TX State Aquarium.

Rincon Hill & South Park: San Francisco's Fashionable Neighborhood 1853-1873. Albert Shumate. Ed. by Wayne Bonnett. (Illus.). 120p. 1988. 24.95 (*0-915269-08-2*) Windgate Pr.

Rincon Phase Seasonal Occupation in the Northern Tucson Basin. Mary Bernard-Shaw & Frederick W. Huntington. (Technical Reports: No. 90-2). (Illus.). 290p. (Orig.). 1990. pap. 12.00 (*1-886398-04-6*) Desert Archaeol.

Rinconete & Cortadillo. Miguel de Cervantes Saavedra. pap. 3.95 (*0-8283-1453-5*, Intl Pocket Lib) Branden Pub Co.

Rinderpest Virus see Cytomegloviruses

Rinds & Peels: A Recycling Reference. 1992. ring bd. 21.95 (*0-318-01302-9*) Prosperity & Profits.

Rinds, Roots & Stars: A Woman's Journal from the Great Flood. Cora V. Brooks. LC 96-26027. 64p. 1996. pap. 12.95 (*0-7734-2708-2*, Mellen Poetry Pr) E Mellen.

Rinehart: The Old Home, One Line of Descent from Abraham Rinehart & Catherine Brower. C. B. White. (Illus.). 72p. 1992. reprint ed. pap. 14.50 (*0-8328-2715-0*); reprint ed. lib. bdg. 24.50 (*0-8328-2714-2*) Higginson Bk Co.

Rinehart ESL Workbook. (C). 1990. teacher ed. write for info. (*0-03-032759-8*) HB Coll Pubs.

Rinehart Guide to Grammar: Exercises. 4th ed. Carter. (C). 1995. suppl. ed., pap. text ed. 5.00 (*0-15-503134-1*) HB Coll Pubs.

Rinehart Guide to Grammar & Style. 4th ed. Carter. (C). 1995. pap. text ed. 10.75 (*0-15-503561-4*) HB Coll Pubs.

Rinehart Guide to Grammar & Usage. 3rd ed. Bonnie Carter & Craig Skates. 464p. (C). 1993. pap. text ed. 14.00 (*0-15-500270-8*) HB Coll Pubs.

Rinehart Handbook for Writers. Bonnie E. Carter & Craig Skates. 800p. (C). 1990. teacher ed. write for info. (*0-03-032748-2*) HB Coll Pubs.

Rinehart Handbook for Writers. 2nd annot. ed. Bonnie E. Carter & Craig Skates. 800p. (C). 1990. teacher ed., text ed. write for info. (*0-03-032747-4*) HB Coll Pubs.

Rinehart Handbook for Writers. 2nd ed. Bonnie E. Carter & Craig Skates. 800p. (C). 1990. teacher ed. write for info. (*0-03-032754-7*); pap. text ed. 20.75 (*0-03-032744-X*); disk write for info. (*0-318-69144-2*) HB Coll Pubs.

R

Rinehart Handbook for Writers. 2nd ed. Bonnie E. Carter. 1990. 22.00 (*0-03-051107-0*) HB Coll Pubs.
Rinehart Handbook for Writers. 3rd ed. Bonnie Carter & Craig Skates. 752p. (C). 1993. text ed. 22.00 (*0-15-500269-4*) HB Coll Pubs.
Rinehart Handbook for Writers. 4th ed. Carter. (C). 1996. pap. text ed. 17.00 (*0-15-501984-8*) HB Coll Pubs.
*__Rinehart Handbook for Writers: Preparing for the CLAST.__ 4th ed. Jack S. Waugh. 64p. (C). Date not set. pap. text ed. write for info. (*0-15-503597-5*) HB Coll Pubs.
Rinehart Handbook with Guide Kit. (C). text ed. write for info. (*0-318-69145-0*) HB Coll Pubs.
Rinehart Lifts. R. R. Knudson. 88p. (J). (gr. 4-7). 1982. pap. 1.95 (*0-380-57059-9*, 57059-9, Camelot) Avon.
Rinehart Reader. 2nd ed. Rackham. (C). 1994. teacher ed. 33.75 (*0-15-501638-5*) HB Coll Pubs.
*__Rinehart Reader.__ 3rd ed. Jean Wyrick. (C). 1998. pap. text ed. 27.50 (*0-15-505512-7*) HB Coll Pubs.
*__Rinehart Reader, Vol. 1.__ 2nd ed. Wyrick. (C). 1993. pap. write for info. (*0-03-076693-1*) HB Coll Pubs.
Rinehart Reader, Vol. II. Jeff Rackham & Beverly J. Slaughter. 708p. (C). 1990. pap. text ed. 20.00 (*0-03-021609-5*) HB Coll Pubs.
Rinehart Reader Vol. II. Jean Wyrick & Beverly J. Slaughter. (Illus.). 608p. (C). 1989. text ed. 21.50 (*0-03-014243-1*) HB Coll Pubs.
Rinehart Reader Vol. II. 2nd ed. Jeff Rackham & Beverly J. Slaughter. LC 94-75161. (Illus.). 740p. (C). 1994. pap. text ed. 32.00 (*0-15-501621-0*) HB Coll Pubs.
Rinehart Reader Vol. II. 2nd ed. Jean Wyrick & Beverly J. Slaughter. 606p. (C). 1993. pap. text ed. 3.00 (*0-03-096516-0*) HB Coll Pubs.
Rinehart Shouts. R. R. Knudson. LC 86-29540. 115p. (J). (gr. 4 up). 1987. 13.00 (*0-374-36296-3*) FS&G.
Ring. 352p. 1980. 23.00 (*0-385-28872-7*) Delacorte.
*__Ring.__ Stephen Barkanic. 1998. pap. 23.95 (*0-525-94118-5*) NAL-Dutton.
Ring. Stephen Baxter. 512p. 1996. mass mkt. 5.99 (*0-06-105694-4*, HarperPrism) HarpC.
Ring. D. Duberley. (Spirals Ser.). (C). 1989. 30.00 (*0-09-144881-6*, Pub. by S Thornes Pubs UK) St Mut.
*__Ring.__ Sylvia Halliday. 416p. 1997. mass mkt. 5.50 (*0-8217-5597-8*, Zebra Kensgtn) Kensgtn Pub Corp.
Ring. Sylvia Halliday. 1996. pap. 21.95 (*0-8217-5252-9*) NAL-Dutton.
Ring. Lisa Maizlish. 24p. (J). (gr. k-3). 1996. 15.00 (*0-688-14217-6*) Greenwillow.
Ring. Lisa Maizlish. 32p. (J). Date not set. lib. bdg. write for info. (*0-688-14218-4*) Greenwillow.
Ring. Danielle Steel. 480p. 1983. mass mkt. 6.50 (*0-440-17392-2*) Dell.
Ring. Piers Anthony. 295p. 1989. reprint ed. pap. 3.95 (*0-8125-0104-7*) Tor Bks.
Ring: Anatomy of an Opera. Stephen Fay. LC 84-27825. (Illus.). 218p. 1985. 25.00 (*0-89341-532-4*, Longwood Academic) Hollowbrook.
Ring, a Horse & a Clown: An Eight Generation History of the Hannefords. John H. McConnell. (Illus.). 348p. (C). 1992. 29.95 (*0-9636019-0-3*, Astley & Ricketts) McConnell-Simmons.
*__Ring a Ring 'O Roses: Fingerplays for Preschool Children.__ 10th rev. ed. Ed. by Charles A. Hansen & Cynthia S. Stilley. 150p. 1996. spiral bd. 6.95 (*0-9654589-0-3*) Flint Pub Lib.
Ring-a-Ring o' Roses & a Ding, Dong Bell: A Collection of Nursery Rhymes. Ed. & Illus. by Alan Marks. LC 91-15222. 96p. (J). (gr. k up). 1991. pap. 19.95 (*0-88708-187-8*, Picture Book Studio) S&S Childrens.
Ring-a-Ring O'Roses & a Ding, Dong Bell. North South Books Staff. (Illus.). (J). Date not set. 19.95 (*1-55858-363-7*) North-South Bks NYC.
Ring & a Promise. Andrea Edwards. (Special Edition Ser.). 1995. pap. 3.50 (*0-373-09932-0*, 1-09932-4) Silhouette.
Ring & I. Jessica Richardson. Ed. by Jeffrey G. McAlister & Gary Udd. 225p. 1994. 16.95 (*0-9642398-0-9*) Jessica Richardson.
Ring & I. Jessica Richardson. Ed. by Jeffrey G. McAlister & Gary Udd. 225p. 1994. pap. 12.95 (*0-9642398-1-7*) Jessica Richardson.
Ring & Rejoice. Contrib. by Bill Ingram. 1986. 8.99 (*0-685-68372-9*, MB-565) Lillenas.
Ring & the Book. Robert Browning. Ed. & Intro. by Richard D. Altick. 712p. 1989. pap. 11.95 (*0-14-042294-3*, Penguin Classics) Viking Penguin.
Ring & the Book, 4 vols. Robert Browning. (BCL1-PR English Literature Ser.). 1992. reprint ed. lib. bdg. 300.00 (*0-7812-7460-5*) Rprt Serv.
*__Ring Around a Mystery.__ Vicki B. Erwin. LC 96-9634. (Elizabeth Bryan Mysteries Ser.). (J). 1997. 4.99 (*0-570-04886-9*, 12-3303) Concordia.
Ring Around a Rainbow: A Health Adventure. Sandra Robbins. (See-More's Stories Ser.). (Illus.). 32p. (Orig.). (J). (gr. k-5). 1993. pap. 4.95 (*1-882601-08-4*); pap. 9.98 incl. audio (*1-882601-05-X*) See-Mores Wrkshop.
Ring Around Max: The Correspondence of Ring Lardner & Maxwell Perkins. Ed. & Intro. by Clifford M. Caruthers. LC 72-6919. (Illus.). 192p. 1973. 22.50 (*0-87580-041-6*); pap. 12.50 (*0-87580-512-4*) N Ill U Pr.
Ring Around the Development Tree: Grow with Music & Movement. Joy Yelin. (Illus.). 35p. (Orig.). 1995. teacher ed. 7.95 (*0-9626150-1-3*) Musical Mosaics.
*__Ring Around the Moon: A Celebration of Life's Simple Pleasures.__ Lois E. Poole. LC 96-70132. xii, 148p. (Orig.). 1996. pap. 12.95 (*0-9653507-0-3*, P-1124-1) Pincushion Press.
Ring Around the Moon: Two Hundred Songs, Tongue Twisters, Riddles & Rhymes for Children. Edith Fowke. (Illus.). 160p. (J). (gr. k-5). 1987. reprint ed. pap. 12.95 (*1-55021-006-8*, Pub. by NC Press CN) U of Toronto Pr.
Ring Around the Rosie...! Gyeorgos C. Hatonn. 224p. (Orig.). 1995. pap. 6.00 (*1-56935-060-4*) Phoenix Source.
*__Ring Around the Sun.__ Clifford D. Simak. 3.95 (*0-7867-0852-2*) Carroll & Graf.
Ring Around the Sun. Clifford D. Simak. 208p. 1992. pap. 3.95 (*0-88184-852-2*) Carroll & Graf.
Ring Around the World. Early. 1983. text ed. 32.50 (*0-15-331259-9*) HB Schl Dept.
Ring Bearer's Big Day: A Child Has His First Experience Participating in a Wedding. Charlotte E. Thomas. LC 94-79366. (Illus.). 32p. (J). (ps-3). 1994. lib. bdg. 19.95 (*0-9633607-1-X*) Golden Rings.
Ring-Chain Tautomerism. Raimonds E. Valters & Wilhelm Flitsch. 270p. 1985. 85.00 (*0-306-41870-3*, Plenum Pr) Plenum.
Ring Cycle. Melvin Gorham. LC 79-64509. (Orig.). 1979. 12.00 (*0-914752-11-1*); pap. 7.00 (*0-914752-10-3*) Sovereign Pr.
*__Ring des Nibelungen: A Companion.__ Richard Wagner. (Illus.). 1997. pap. 14.95 (*0-7148-3650-8*, Pub. by Phaidon Press UK) Chronicle Bks.
Ring Enlargement in Organic Chemistry. Ed. by Manfred Hesse. 235p. 1991. 90.00 (*3-527-28182-7*, VCH) Wiley.
*__Ring for Tomb Service: In Edwardian England Murder Rings a Bell.__ Kate Kingsbury. 240p. 1997. mass mkt. 5.99 (*0-425-15857-8*, Prime Crime) Berkley Pub.
*__Ring Game.__ Pete Hautman. 1997. 22.00 (*0-684-83242-9*, S&S) S&S Trade.
Ring in a Case. Yuz Aleshkovsky. LC 95-10115. 248p. 1995. 24.95 (*0-8101-1138-1*) Northwestern U Pr.
Ring in a River. Eckhard Gerdes. LC 93-74792. (Illus.). 104p. (Orig.). 1994. pap. 9.95 (*1-884097-17-0*) Depth Charge.
Ring in Meiji. William Butler. 464p. 1965. 29.00 (*0-7206-7450-6*, Pub. by P Owen Ltd UK) Dufour.
Ring Lardner. Walton R. Patrick. (Twayne's United States Authors Ser.). 1963. pap. 13.95 (*0-8084-0261-7*, T32) NCUP.
Ring Lardner. Otto Friedrich. LC 65-64769. (University of Minnesota Pamphlets on American Writers Ser.: No. 49). 48p. reprint ed. pap. 25.00 (*0-317-29459-8*, 2055932) Bks Demand.
*__Ring Lardner: Great American Short Stories III.__ Illus. by James Balkovek. LC 95-76753. (Classic Short Stories Ser.). 80p. (YA). (gr. 6-12). 1995. pap. 5.95 (*0-7854-0628-X*, 40089) Am Guidance.
*__Ring Lardner: Selected Short Fiction.__ Ring Lardner. 1997. pap. 10.95 (*0-14-118018-8*) Viking Penguin.
Ring Lardner & the Other. Douglas H. Robinson. (Illus.). 336p. 1992. 60.00 (*0-19-507600-1*) OUP.
Ring Lardner Reader. Ring Lardner, Jr. Date not set. pap. 4.99 (*0-451-52586-8*, Sig Classics) NAL-Dutton.
Ring of Allaire. Susan Dexter. 224p. 1983. mass mkt. 4.99 (*0-345-31121-3*, Del Rey) Ballantine.
*__Ring of Bells: Poems of John Betjeman Selected for the Younger Reader.__ Irene Slade. (Illus.). 136p. (YA). (gr. 5-9). 1997. pap. 15.95 (*0-7195-0101-6*, Pub. by John Murray UK) Trafalgar.
Ring of Bone: Collected Poems 1950-1971. rev. ed. Lew Welch. Ed. by Donald Allen. LC 72-85644. (Illus.). 244p. (Orig.). 1979. pap. 12.95 (*0-912516-03-8*) Grey Fox.
*__Ring of Bright Water.__ Longman Publishing Staff. Date not set. pap. text ed. write for info. (*0-582-34591-X*, Pub. by Longman UK) Longman.
Ring of Bright Water. Gavin Maxwell. 236p. 1987. pap. 9.95 (*0-14-003923-6*, Penguin Bks) Viking Penguin.
Ring of Bright Water. Gavin Maxwell. (Illus.). 224p. 1987. pap. 10.95 (*0-14-024972-9*, Penguin Bks) Viking Penguin.
Ring of Bright Water. large type ed. Gavin Maxwell. 292p. 1991. 22.95 (*1-85089-591-0*, Pub. by ISIS UK) Transaction Pubs.
Ring of Brightest Angels Around Heaven. Rick Moody. 256p. 1996. pap. 11.99 (*0-446-67240-8*) Warner Bks.
Ring of Brightest Angels Around Heaven: A Novella & Stories. Rick Moody. LC 94-45903. 256p. 1995. 21.95 (*0-316-57929-7*) Little.
Ring of Charon. Roger M. Allen. 512p. 1990. mass mkt. 4.95 (*0-8125-3014-4*) Tor Bks.
Ring of Earth: A Child's Book of Seasons. Jane Yolen. LC 86-4800. (Illus.). 32p. (J). (ps up). 1986. 15.00 (*0-15-267140-4*, HB Juv Bks) HarBrace.
Ring of Endless Light. Madeleine L'Engle. 336p. (YA). (gr. 7 up). 1981. mass mkt. 4.99 (*0-440-97232-9*, LLL BDD) BDD Bks Young Read.
Ring of Evil, No. 1: Tagged for Terror. Franklin W. Dixon. Ed. by Anne Greenberg. (Hardy Boys Casefiles Ser.: No. 76). 160p. (Orig.). (J). (gr. 6 up). 1993. mass mkt. 3.99 (*0-671-73112-2*, Archway) PB.
Ring of Evil, No. 2: Survival Run. Franklin W. Dixon. Ed. by Ann Greenberg. (Hardy Boys Casefiles Ser.: No. 77). 160p. (Orig.). (J). (gr. 6 up). 1993. mass mkt. 3.99 (*0-671-79461-2*, Archway) PB.
Ring of Evil, No. 3: The Pacific Conspiracy. Franklin W. Dixon. (Hardy Boys Casefiles Ser.: No. 78). 160p. (Orig.). (YA). (gr. 6 up). 1993. mass mkt. 3.99 (*0-671-79462-0*, Archway) PB.
Ring of Fate. large type ed. Joyce Bentley. 370p. 1980. 25.99 (*0-7089-0553-6*) Ulverscroft.
Ring of Fire. Cinnamon Burke, pseud. 448p. (Orig.). 1995. mass mkt., pap. text ed. 5.99 (*0-505-52068-0*) Dorchester Pub Co.
Ring of Fire: An Indonesian Odyssey. Lawrence Blair & Lorne Blair. (Illus.). 272p. 1991. reprint ed. pap. 24.95 (*0-89281-430-6*, Park St Pr) Inner Tradit.
Ring of Fire Science Anytime Guide. HB Staff. 1995. pap. 8.00 (*0-15-306067-0*) HB Schl Dept.
Ring of Grass. large type ed. William Ellis. 688p. 1994. 25.99 (*0-7089-3075-1*) Ulverscroft.
*__Ring of Intrigue.__ Jane S. Fancher. 1997. pap. 6.99 (*0-88677-719-4*) DAW Bks.
*__Ring of Lead.__ Ken Pickering. 10p. 1997. pap. 2.50 (*0-88680-445-0*) I E Clark.
Ring of Liberation: Deceptive Discourse in Brazilian Capoeira. J. Lowell Lewis. (Illus.). 294p. 1992. pap. text ed. 17.95 (*0-226-47683-9*); lib. bdg. 38.50 (*0-226-47682-0*) U Ch Pr.
Ring of Lightning. Jane S. Fancher. (Dance of the Rings Ser.: Bk. 1). 544p. (Orig.). 1995. mass mkt. 5.50 (*0-88677-653-8*) DAW Bks.
*__Ring of Lions.__ Vasile I. Degereanu. 549p. (Orig.). 1997. mass mkt. 5.99 (*1-55197-897-0*, Pub. by Comnwlth Pub CN) Partners Pubs Grp.
Ring of Men. Adam Oliensis. 1995. pap. 3.25 (*0-8222-1468-7*) Dramatists Play.
Ring of Representation. Stephen D. Ross. LC 91-26923. (SUNY Series in Contemporary Continental Philosophy). 262p. (C). 1992. text ed. 59.50 (*0-7914-1109-5*); pap. text ed. 19.95 (*0-7914-1110-9*) State U NY Pr.
Ring of Return. Eva Martin. 306p. 1981. pap. 25.00 (*0-89540-109-6*, SB-109) Sun Pub.
Ring of Swords. Eleanor Arnason. 384p. 1994. pap. 13.95 (*0-312-89016-8*) Orb NYC.
Ring of Tall Trees. John Dowd. 128p. (YA). 1992. 14.95 (*0-920417-15-9*, Pub. by Raincoast Bks CN) Orca Bk Pubs.
Ring of Terror. Michael Gilbert. 256p. 1995. 20.00 (*0-7867-0193-5*) Carroll & Graf.
Ring of Terror. large type ed. Michael F. Gilbert. 1996. pap. 17.95 (*0-7838-1537-9*, GK Hall) Thorndike Pr.
Ring of the Dove. Ibn Hazm. 1953. 30.00 (*1-898942-02-1*, Pub. by Luzac Oriental UK) Weatherhill.
Ring of the Dove. Ibn Hazm. 1994. pap. 20.00 (*1-898942-03-X*, Pub. by Luzac Oriental UK) Weatherhill.
Ring of the Dove: A Treatise on the Art & Practice of Arab Love. Ali ibn Ahmad Ibn-Hazm. Tr. by A. J. Arberry. LC 78-63500. 288p. reprint ed. 34.50 (*0-404-17148-6*) AMS Pr.
Ring of the Farjumpers. Gary Hutchison. (Little People of the Ozark Mountains Ser.). 124p. 1995. pap. 8.95 (*1-885631-13-8*) G F Hutchison.
*__Ring of the Nibelung.__ Roy Thomas. 1997. pap. text ed. 24.95 (*0-932956-20-3*) Express Pr Ltd.
Ring of the Nibelung. Roy Thomas. 1991. pap. 14.99 (*0-446-39362-2*) Warner Bks.
Ring of the Nibelung. Richard Wagner. Tr. by Andrew Porter from GER. (Illus.). 1977. 17.50 (*0-393-02200-5*); pap. 14.95 (*0-393-00867-3*) Norton.
*__Ring of Tricks: Trickster Tales from America, the West Indies & Africa.__ Virginia Hamilton. LC 96-37543. (Illus.). (J). 1997. write for info. (*0-590-47374-3*) Scholastic Inc.
Ring of Truth. Teresa Bateman. LC 96-5336. (Illus.). 32p. (J). 1997. 15.95 (*0-8234-1255-5*) Holiday.
Ring of Truth. Vernon Scannel. 342p. (Orig.). 1988. pap. 9.95 (*0-86051-416-1*, Robson-Parkwest) Parkwest Pubns.
Ring of Truth: A Translator's Testimony. J. B. Phillips. LC 77-80627. 124p. 1977. pap. 7.99 (*0-87788-724-1*) Shaw Pubs.
Ring of Wessex Waters. John Ashley-Cooper. 224p. (C). 1989. 49.00 (*0-85493-198-8*, Pub. by Witherby & Co UK) St Mut.
Ring of Words: An Anthology of Song Texts. Intro. by Philip Miller. 544p. 1973. reprint ed. pap. 16.95 (*0-393-00677-8*) Norton.
Ring of Words in Medieval Literature. Ed. by Ulrich Goebel & David Lee. LC 93-39319. (Studies in German Language & Literature: Vol. 14). (Illus.). 356p. 1993. text ed. 99.95 (*0-7734-9387-5*) E Mellen.
Ring-Opening Polymerization. K. J. Ivin. 1984. 389.00 (*0-85334-211-3*, I-220-84) Elsevier.
Ring-Opening Polymerization. Ed. by Kurt C. Frisch & Sidney L. Reegen. LC 66-29483. (Kinetics & Mechanisms of Polymerization Ser.: No. 2). (Illus.). 542p. reprint ed. pap. 154.50 (*0-7837-0924-2*, 2041229) Bks Demand.
Ring-Opening Polymerization, 1. Ed. by K. J. Ivin & T. Saegusa. 1260p. 1984. write for info. (*0-85334-208-3*, Pub. by Elsevier Applied Sci UK) Elsevier.
Ring-Opening Polymerization, 2. Ed. by K. J. Ivin & T. Saegusa. 1260p. 1984. write for info. (*0-85334-209-1*, Pub. by Elsevier Applied Sci UK) Elsevier.
Ring-Opening Polymerization, 3. Ed. by K. J. Ivin & T. Saegusa. 1260p. 1984. write for info. (*0-318-57715-1*, Pub. by Elsevier Applied Sci UK) Elsevier.
*__Ring-Opening Polymerization: Kinetics, Mechanisms, & Synthesis: Developed from a Symposium.__ Ed. by James E. McGrath. LC 85-13352. (ACS Symposium Ser.: No. 286). (Illus.). 408p. 1985. reprint ed. pap. 116.30 (*0-608-04339-7*, 2065119) Bks Demand.
Ring-Opening Polymerization: Mechanism, Catalysis, Structure, Utility. Daniel J. Brunelle. 400p. (C). 1992. text ed. 118.00 (*1-56990-009-4*) Hanser-Gardner.
Ring Out the Old, Ring in the New Scrapbook. Nancy E. Krulik. (Saved by the Bell Ser.). 40p. (J). (gr. 4-7). 1994. pap. 4.95 (*0-590-48086-3*) Scholastic Inc.
Ring Resounding. John Culshaw. LC 87-2592. (Illus.). 276p. 1987. reprint ed. pap. 13.95 (*0-87910-101-6*) Limelight Edns.
Ring Round the Moon. adapted ed. Jean Anouilh. 1952. pap. 5.25 (*0-8222-0954-3*) Dramatists Play.
Ring, Sword & Unicorn. James M. Ward. 1983. 1.95 (*0-394-72314-7*) Random.
Ring-Tailed, Red-Eyed Sons o' Trouble. Damon Runyon. 24.95 (*0-8488-0144-X*) Amereon Ltd.
Ring the Banjar! The Banjo in America from Folklore to Factory. Robert L. Webb. (Illus.). 101p. 1995. reprint ed. pap. 24.95 (*1-57424-016-1*) Centerstream Pub.
Ring the Bells of Christmas. Contrib. by Bill Ingram. 1986. 7.99 (*0-685-68373-7*, MC-265) Lillenas.
Ring the Doorbell with Your Elbow: A Cookbook of "Portables" rev. ed. Wilma M. McCartney. LC 80-84349. (Illus.). 136p. 1981. pap. 8.95 (*0-933050-07-0*) New Eng Pr VT.
Ring Theory. Ed. by S. Jain. (Lecture Notes in Pure & Applied Mathematics Ser.: Vol. 25). 256p. 1977. 130.00 (*0-8247-6577-X*) Dekker.
Ring Theory. Ed. by F. M. Oystaeyen. (Lecture Notes in Mathematics Ser.: Vol. 1197). v, 231p. 1986. 32.95 (*0-387-16496-0*) Spr-Verlag.
Ring Theory. Louis H. Rowen. 623p. (C). 1991. Student ed. student ed., text ed. 78.00 (*0-12-599840-6*) Acad Pr.
Ring Theory. F. M. Van Oystaeyen. (Lecture Notes in Pure & Applied Mathematics Ser.: Vol. 51). 808p. 1979. 160.00 (*0-8247-6854-X*) Dekker.
Ring Theory: Nonsingular Rings & Modules. Kenneth R. Goodearl. (Pure & Applied Mathematics Ser.: Vol.33). 224p. 1976. 125.00 (*0-8247-6354-8*) Dekker.
Ring Theory: Proceedings of the Oklahoma Conference, 1st, University of Oklahoma. fac. ed. Ring Theory Conference Staff. Ed. by Bernard R. McDonald et al. LC 73-90768. (Lecture Notes in Pure & Applied Mathematics Ser.: No. 7). 315p. 1974. pap. 89.80 (*0-7837-7717-5*, 2047479) Bks Demand.
*__Ring Theory & Algebra III: Proceedings of the Third Oklahoma Conference, University of Oklahoma, 1979.__ Ring Theory Conference Staff. Ed. by Bernard R. McDonald. LC 80-17204. (Lecture Notes in Pure & Applied Mathematics Ser.: Vol. 55). reprint ed. pap. 127.20 (*0-608-04566-7*, 2065305) Bks Demand.
Ring Theory & Proceedings of the Biennial Ohio State-Denison Conference. Subodh K. Jain & S. T. Rizvi. 300p. 1993. text ed. 106.00 (*981-02-1385-9*) World Scientific Pub.
Ring Theory II: Proceedings of the Ring Theory Conference, 2nd, University of Oklahoma, 1975. Ring Theory Conference Staff. Ed. by Bernard R. McDonald & Robert A. Morris. LC 76-55134. (Lecture Notes in Pure & Applies Mathematics Ser.: Vol. 26). 315p. reprint ed. pap. 89.80 (*0-317-08349-X*, 2017693) Bks Demand.
Ring Theory 1989 in Honor of S. A. Amitsur. Ed. by Louis Rowen. (Israel Mathematical Conference Proceedings Ser.: Vol. 1). 430p. 1990. reprint ed. pap. 32.00 (*0-685-70699-0*, IMCP/1C, Bar-Ilan Univ) Am Math.
Ring! Tick Tock. Rich Cowley. (Snappy Sounds Ser.). (Illus.). 24p. (J). (ps). 1996. 3.95 (*1-55209-036-1*) Firefly Bks Ltd.
Ring up the Curtain. Ernest H. Short & Arthur Compton-Rickett. LC 78-114895. (Select Bibliographies Reprint Ser.). 1977. 24.95 (*0-8369-5299-5*) Ayer.
Ring W. Lardner: A Descriptive Bibliography. Matthew J. Bruccoli & Richard Layman. LC 75-9126. (Series in Bibliography). (Illus.). 488p. 1976. 100.00 (*0-8229-3306-3*) U of Pittsburgh Pr.
Ring-0-Roses. S. Slater. 1990. pap. 30.00 (*0-7463-0525-7*, Pub. by Northcote UK) St Mut.
Ringbom Stirling Engines. James R. Senft. (Illus.). 240p. 1993. 65.00 (*0-19-507798-9*) OUP.
Ringed Castle. Dorothy Dunnett. 1976. 32.95 (*0-8488-1302-2*) Amereon Ltd.
Ringed Castle. Dorothy Dunnett. 425p. 1983. reprint ed. lib. bdg. 37.95 (*0-89966-322-2*) Buccaneer Bks.
Ringed in Steel. Michael D. Mahler. 256p. 1987. mass mkt. 4.99 (*0-515-09074-3*) Jove Pubns.
Ringed Planet: Saturn. rev. ed. Isaac Asimov. LC 95-7879. (Isaac Asimov's Library of the Universe). Orig. Title: Saturn. (J). (gr. 3 up). 1995. lib. bdg. 18.60 (*0-8368-1223-9*) Gareth Stevens Inc.
Ringer. Marshall Terry. LC 87-70379. 239p. 1987. 16.95 (*0-931722-61-6*) Corona Pub.
Ringer on the Bell, Foot Through the Boards. K. C. Gerrish. 116p. (C). 1989. 30.00 (*0-7223-2250-X*, Pub. by A H S Ltd UK) St Mut.
Ringgold. Kent Conwell. 1993. 17.95 (*0-8034-8989-7*) Bouregy.
Ringing Ears Vol. 1: A Tinnitus Victim's Guide. John D. Griggs. Ed. by Cynthia M. Buddy et al. (Illus.). 60p. (Orig.). 1982. pap. 10.00 (*0-9612648-1-0*) Natl Tinn Fund.
Ringing in the Wilderness: Selections from the North Country Anvil. Ed. by Rhoda R. Gilman. (Illus.). 384p. (Orig.). 1996. pap. 14.95 (*0-930100-63-8*) Holy Cow.
*__Ringing the Changes in Europe: Regulatory Competition & the Transformation of the State, Britain, France, Germany.__ Adrienne Heritier et al. (Studies in Organization: Vol. 74). xiv, 363p. (C). 1996. text ed. 84.95 (*3-11-014765-3*) De Gruyter.
Ringing the Children In: Texas Country Schools. Thad Sitton & Milam C. Rowold. LC 86-14444. (Illus.). 256p. 1987. 19.95 (*0-89096-290-1*) Tex A&M Univ Pr.
Ringkomposition Bei Herodot und Ihre Bedeutung Fur die Beweistechnik. Ingrid Beck. iii, 136p. (GER.). 1971. 30.00 (*0-318-70627-X*) G Olms Pubs.
Ringle & Dingle: Santa's Christmas Elves. William E. Young. (Illus.). 32p. (Orig.). (J). 1991. pap. 5.95 (*0-9628122-1-8*) Pautuxet Pubns.
Ringling: The Florida Years, 1911-1936. David C. Weeks. LC 93-11189. (Illus.). 400p. 1993. pap. 24.95 (*0-8130-1243-0*); lib. bdg. 49.95 (*0-8130-1242-2*) U Press Fla.
Ringling Brothers: Circus Family *see* **Discovery Biographies**
Ringling by Any Other Name: The Story of John Ringling North & His Circus. Ernest J. Albrecht. LC 88-35639. (Illus.). 405p. 1989. 39.50 (*0-8108-2206-7*) Scarecrow.
Ringling Museum of Art Journal. Ed. by William H. Wilson. (Illus.). 16p. 1983. 10.00 (*0-916758-12-5*); pap. 10.00 (*0-685-07692-X*) Ringling Mus Art.

An Asterisk (*) at the beginning of an entry indicates that the title is appearing in BIP for the first time.

R

Ringmacher Thematic Catalogue (1773) Ed. by Barry S. Brook. (Thematic Catalogues Ser.: No. 14). (Illus.). 150p. 1988. lib. bdg. 70.00 (*0-918728-91-6*) Pendragon NY.

Ringmakers of Saturn. Norman R. Bergrun. Ed. by Meg Ross. LC 86-81530. (Illus.). 128p. 1986. 42.50 (*0-946270-33-3*, Pub. by Pentland Pr UK) Bergrun Res.

Ringmakers of Saturn. Norman R. Bergrun. 1986. 80.00 (*0-317-89940-6*, Pub. by Pentland Pr UK) St Mut.

Ringmaster. Morris L. West. 464p. 1901. mass mkt. 5.99 (*0-06-101080-4*, Harp PBks) HarpC.

Ringmaster's Secret. rev. ed. Carolyn Keene. LC 74-3867. (Nancy Drew Ser.: Vol. 31). (Illus.). 196p. (J). (gr. 4-7). 1954. reprint ed. 5.95 (*0-448-09531-9*, G&D) Putnam Pub Group.

Ringneck. Pheasants Forever Staff. LC 95-21968. (Illus.). 120p. 1995. 29.50 (*1-56044-350-2*) Falcon Pr MT.

***Ringnecked Parakeets & Their Mutations.** T. Bastiaan & G. J. Bastiaan. (Illus.). 128p. 1997. 79.00 (*0-614-30211-0*) Avian Pubns.

***Ringo: Straight Man of Joker?** Alan Clayson. 240p. pap. 14.95 (*1-86074-189-4*, Pub. by Sanctuary Pr UK) Music Sales.

Ringo Lake School. Florence N. Lovgren. LC 92-62006. 168p. 1993. pap. 9.00 (*1-56002-238-8*, Univ Edtns) Aegina Pr.

Ringolevio: A Life Played for Keeps. Emmett Grogan. 1990. pap. 12.95 (*0-8065-1168-0*, Citadel Pr) Carol Pub Group.

Ringo's Tombstone. William R. Garwood. LC 81-67729. 215p. 1981. 11.95 (*0-937618-01-2*) Bath St Pr.

Ringroad. Fay Hale. 304p. 1994. 24.95 (*0-9643112-1-6*) Arizona.

Rings: Discoveries from Galileo to Voyager. James C. Elliot & Richard Kerr. (Illus.). 224p. 1987. reprint ed. pap. 9.95 (*0-262-55013-X*) MIT Pr.

Rings: Five Passions in World Art. Intro. by J. Carter Brown. (Illus.). 296p. (Orig.). 1996. pap. write for info. (*0-614-10859-4*) High Mus Art.

Rings: Five Passions in World Art. Ed. by Michael Shapiro. LC 95-43959. 1996. pap. write for info. (*0-939802-81-3*) Abrams.

Rings: Five Passions in World Art. Ed. by Michael Shapiro. LC 95-43959. (Illus.). 320p. 1996. 49.50 (*0-8109-4429-4*) Abrams.

Rings: On the Life & Family of a Southern Boxer. Randolph Bates. 416p. 1992. 25.00 (*0-374-25047-2*) FS&G.

Rings: Symbols of Wealth, Power & Affection. Diana Scarisbrick. LC 92-29626. (Illus.). 224p. 1993. 60.00 (*0-8109-3775-1*) Abrams.

Rings & Categories of Modules. 2nd ed. Frank W. Anderson & Kent R. Fuller. Ed. by J. H. Ewing et al. LC 92-10019. (Graduate Texts in Mathematics Ser.: Vol. 13). 392p. 1992. 54.95 (*0-387-97845-3*) Spr-Verlag.

Rings & Fields. Graham Ellis. LC 92-15556. 184p. 1993. 48.00 (*0-19-853455-8*, Clarendon Pr); pap. 15.95 (*0-19-853454-X*, Clarendon Pr) OUP.

Rings & Geometry. Ed. by Rustem Kaya et al. 1985. lib. bdg. 206.50 (*90-277-2112-2*) Kluwer Ac.

***Rings & Radicals.** B.J. Gardner. (Pitman Research Notes in Mathematics Ser.). 1996. pap. 53.97 (*0-582-29281-6*) Longman.

Rings Around Your Mind: How to Program Your Mind to Control Stress, Fear, & Self-Destructive Behavior Patterns. Michael C. Giammatteo. (Illus.). (C). 1976. pap. text ed. 19.95 (*0-918428-08-4*) Sylvan Inst.

Rings, Clusters & Polymers of Main Group & Transition Elements. Ed. by H. W. Roesky. 560p. 1989. 179.50 (*0-444-88172-7*) Elsevier.

Rings, Clusters, & Polymers of the Main Group Elements. Ed. by Alan H. Cowley. LC 83-15462. (ACS Symposium Ser.: No. 232). 192p. 1983. lib. bdg. 36.95 (*0-8412-0801-8*) Am Chemical.

***Rings, Clusters, & Polymers of the Main Group Elements.** Ed. by Alan H. Cowley. LC 83-15462. (ACS Symposium Ser.: Vol. 232). 192p. 1983. reprint ed. pap. 54.80 (*0-608-03081-3*, 2063534) Bks Demand.

***Rings, Fields & Vector Spaces: An Approach to Geometric Constructability.** B. A. Sethuraman. LC 96-32220. (Undergraduate Texts in Mathematics Ser.). 200p. 1996. 34.95 (*0-387-94848-1*) Spr-Verlag.

Rings for the Finger. George F. Kunz. LC 78-172181. (Illus.). 512p. 1973. reprint ed. pap. 8.95 (*0-486-22226-8*) Dover.

Rings, Groups & Algebras. X. H. Cao. LC 96-22831. (Lecture Notes in Pure & Applied Mathematics Ser.: Vol. 181). 352p. 1996. pap. 150.00 (*0-8247-9733-7*) Dekker.

Rings in a Tree Trunk. S. Ramnath. (Writers Workshop Redbird Ser.). 46p. 1976. 8.00 (*0-86578-271-7*); text ed. 4.00 (*0-86578-272-5*) Ind-US Inc.

***Rings in Auctions Vol. X: An Experimental Approach, Vol. 447.** Angelo Artale. LC 96-46237. (Lecture Notes in Economics & Mathematical Systems Ser.). (Illus.). 172p. 1997. pap. 49.00 (*3-540-61930-5*) Spr-Verlag.

Rings in Time. Sam Gronning & Robert Kammen. (Rings in Time Ser.: Vol. 1). (Illus.). 370p. (Orig.). 1996. mass mkt. 7.95 (*0-932482-51-1*) Blue Feather.

***Rings, Modules, & Algebras in Stable Homotopy Theory.** Anthony Elmendorf et al. LC 96-35999. (Mathematical Surveys & Monographs Ser.: Vol. 47). 249p. 1996. 62.00 (*0-8218-0638-6*, SURV/47) Am Math.

Rings, Modules & Linear Algebra. B. Hartley & T. Hawkes. (Mathematics Ser.). 224p. (gr. 13). 1983. pap. text ed. 24.95 (*0-412-09810-5*, NO. 6144, Chap & Hall NY) Chapman & Hall.

Rings, Modules, & Preradicals. Ladislav Bican et al. LC 81-22209. (Lecture Notes in Pure & Applied Mathematics Ser.: No. 75). 255p. reprint ed. pap. 72.70 (*0-7837-0800-9*, 2041114) Bks Demand.

Rings of Burnished Brass & Other Stories. Yusuf Idris. Tr. by Catherine Cobham. 156p. 1992. pap. 9.95 (*977-424-248-3*, Pub. by Am Univ Cairo Pr UA) Col U Pr.

Rings of Continuous Function. Aull. (Lecture Notes in Pure & Applied Mathematics Ser.: Vol. 95). 336p. 1985. 140.00 (*0-8247-7144-3*) Dekker.

Rings of Continuous Functions. L. Gillman & M. Jerison. Ed. by J. H. Ewing et al. LC 76-20442. (Graduate Texts in Mathematics Ser.: Vol. 43). xiii, 300p. 1993. reprint ed. 49.95 (*0-387-90198-1*) Spr-Verlag.

Rings of Differential Operators on Classical Rings of Invariants. T. Levasseur & J. Stafford. LC 89-15147. (Memoirs Ser.: Vol. 81/412). 117p. 1989. pap. 21.00 (*0-8218-2475-9*, MEMO/81/412) Am Math.

Rings of Dimension II. Ed. by Wolmer Vasconcelos. (Lecture Notes in Pure & Applied Mathematics Ser.: Vol. 22). 120p. 1976. 110.00 (*0-8247-6447-1*) Dekker.

Rings of Empowerment: A Guide to Discovering & Fulfilling Your Life Purpose As Part of a Co-Creative Team. Carolyn Anderson. (Illus.). 168p. (Orig.). 1993. pap. text ed. 20.00 (*1-883208-00-9*) Global Family.

Rings of Faith. Mary M. Wrede. LC 85-91315. (Illus.). 160p. 1986. 9.95 (*0-9615969-0-2*) M M Wrede.

Rings of Fire: Primitive Affects & Object Relations in Group Psychotherapy. Ed. by Victor L. Schermer & Malcolm Pines. LC 93-34089. (International Library of Group Psychotherapy & Group Process). 336p. (C). 1994. pap. 19.95 (*0-415-06682-4*, Routledge NY); text ed. 62.95 (*0-415-06681-6*, Routledge NY) Routledge.

Rings of Green. Ann Peters. 84p. 8200. 19.95 (*0-86140-124-7*, Pub. by Colin Smythe Ltd UK); pap. 9.95 (*0-86140-129-8*, Pub. by Colin Smythe Ltd UK) Dufour.

Rings of Ice. Piers Anthony. 192p. 1974. pap. 3.50 (*0-380-00036-9*) Avon.

Rings of Life. Sally Bissell-Hadley. 48p. (Orig.). 1996. pap. 8.95 (*1-56167-300-5*) Am Literary Pr.

Rings of Quotients: An Introduction to Methods of Ring Theory. B. Stenstroem. LC 75-1003. (Grundlehren der Mathematischen Wissenschaften Ser.: Vol. 217). 315p. 1975. 97.95 (*0-387-07117-2*) Spr-Verlag.

Rings of Razor: Sunbat Closet. Matt Tilton. Ed. by Al H. Morrison. (Orig.). 1992. pap. write for info. (*0-9626761-1-X*) Al H Morrison.

Rings of Sand. large type ed. Tom McNab. 432p. 1985. 27.99 (*0-7089-8247-6*) Ulverscroft.

Rings on Woot-Kew's Tail: Indian Legends of the Origin of the Sun, Moon & Stars. Will Gerber et al. (Indian Culture Ser.). (J). (gr. 3-9). 1973. pap. 3.95 (*0-89992-059-4*) Coun India Ed.

***Rings, Roses...& Romance.** Barbara Benedict. 1997. mass mkt. 3.99 (*0-373-24104-6*, 1-24104-1) Silhouette.

Rings with Generalized Polynomial Identities. Ed. by Beidar et al. (Pure & Applied Mathematics Ser.: Vol. 196). 544p. 1995. 185.00 (*0-8247-9325-0*) Dekker.

Rings with Involution. Israel N. Herstein. LC 76-27861. (Chicago Lectures in Mathematics). 258p. 1976. pap. text ed. 15.00 (*0-226-32806-6*) U Ch Pr.

Rings with Morita Duality. Weimin Xue. Ed. by A. Dold et al. LC 92-23682. (Lecture Notes in Mathematics Ser.: Vol. 1523). x, 167p. 1992. 40.95 (*0-387-55770-9*) Spr-Verlag.

Ringside Seats. Katharine F. Gerould. LC 71-156647. (Essay Index Reprint Ser.). 1977. reprint ed. 20.95 (*0-8369-2318-9*) Ayer.

Ringstones & Other Curious Tales. John W. Wall. 1976. 23.95 (*0-405-08174-X*, 18500) Ayer.

Ringworld. Larry Niven. 352p. 1985. mass mkt. 5.99 (*0-345-33392-6*, Del Rey) Ballantine.

***Ringworld.** Larry Niven. 1997. pap. 11.00 (*0-345-41840-9*, Del Rey) Ballantine.

Ringworld Engineers. Larry Niven. 368p. 1985. mass mkt. 5.99 (*0-345-33430-2*, Del Rey) Ballantine.

***Ringworld Engineers.** Larry Niven. 1997. pap. 11.00 (*0-345-41841-7*, Del Rey) Ballantine.

Ringworld Throne. Larry Niven. LC 95-47882. 430p. 1996. 23.00 (*0-345-35861-9*, Del Rey) Ballantine.

***Ringworld Throne.** Larry Niven. 1997. mass mkt. 6.99 (*0-345-41296-6*, Del Rey) Ballantine.

Rinhart Handbook: Test Bank. 3rd ed. Carter. (C). 1993. pap. text ed. 8.00 (*0-15-501350-5*) HB Coll Pubs.

Rinkitink in Oz. L. Frank Baum. 22.95 (*0-8488-0735-9*) Amereon Ltd.

Rinkitink in Oz. L. Frank Baum. (Illus.). 336p. (J). (gr. 4 up). 1993. reprint ed. pap. text ed. 7.95 (*0-486-27756-9*) Dover.

***Rinkitink of Oz.** Peter Glassman. (J). Date not set. write for info. (*0-688-14720-8*, Morrow Junior) Morrow.

Rinkside Romance. Melissa Lowell. 176p. (J). 1996. pap. 3.99 (*0-553-48369-2*) Bantam.

Rinky Dinky Donkey. Christine H. Tangvald. (Illus.). 24p. (J). (ps-k). 1995. pap. 3.99 (*0-7847-0168-7*, 03928) Standard Pub.

Rinse Formula. Jacobus Rinse. (Good Health Guide Ser.). 32p. (Orig.). 1988. pap. 2.50 (*0-87983-465-X*) Keats.

Rinwood. Mark Dunster. 21p. (Orig.). 1984. pap. 4.00 (*0-89642-118-X*) Linden Pubs.

Rinzai: Master of the Irrational: The Present Day Awakened One Speaks on the Ancient Masters of Zen. Osho Rajneesh. Ed. by Swami Krishna Prabhu. (Zen Ser.). 202p. 1989. 14.95 (*3-89338-069-8*, Pub. by Rebel Hse GW) Osho America.

Rio. (Insight Guides Ser.). 1993. pap. 21.95 (*0-395-66295-8*) HM.

Rio. Doug Wildey. (Illus.). 64p. 1987. pap. 6.95 (*0-317-57743-3*) Graphitti Designs.

Rio. 2nd ed. Ana M. Ausejo. 198p. (SPA.). 1973. pap. 19.95 (*0-7859-4992-5*) Fr & Eur.

Rio, No. 6. limited ed. Doug Wildey. (Illus.). 64p. 1987. 34.95 (*0-936211-04-0*) Graphitti Designs.

Rio: Unravelling the Consequences. Ed. by Caroline Thomas. LC 93-50950. 1994. pap. 29.50 (*0-7146-4110-3*, Pub. by F Cass Pubs UK) Intl Spec Bk.

Rio Alive. 6th ed. Arnold Greenberg & Harriet Greenberg. (Alive Travel Ser.). (Illus.). 1988. pap. 10.95 (*0-935572-16-3*) Alive Pubns.

Rio Amazonas. Peter Murray. LC 93-7617. (Libro Vision Ser.). 32p. (SPA.). (J). (gr. 2-6). 1993. lib. bdg. 22.79 (*1-56766-039-8*) Childs World.

Rio Arriba. Elihu Blotnick. (Illus.). 342p. (Orig.). pap. 17.95 (*0-915090-24-4*) Calif Street.

Rio at Bay. Doug Wilder. (Illus.). 64p. 1993. pap. 6.95 (*1-878574-73-6*) Dark Horse Comics.

Rio Casino Intrigue. F. Van Wyck Mason. reprint ed. lib. bdg. 20.95 (*0-89190-356-9*, Rivercity Pr) Amereon Ltd.

Rio Claro: A Brazilian Plantation System, 1820-1920. Warren Dean. xx, 234p. 1976. 37.50 (*0-8047-0902-5*) Stanford U Pr.

Rio Contract. large type ed. William Newton. 1991. pap. 15.99 (*0-7089-7027-3*) Ulverscroft.

Rio de Janeiro: City Guide. Andrew Draffen. (Illus.). 280p. 1995. pap. 9.95 (*0-86442-315-2*) Lonely Planet.

Rio de Janeiro: In Eighty-Five Colorfotos. (Cities in Color Pictorial Guidebooks Ser.). (Illus.). 80p. (Orig.). 1992. pap. 10.95 (*0-9617959-4-8*) Cities in Color.

Rio de Janiero. Deborah Kent. LC 95-36157. (Cities of the World Ser.). (Illus.). 64p. (J). (gr. 4-6). 1996. lib. bdg. 24.00 (*0-516-00353-4*) Childrens.

Rio Del Norte: People of the Upper Rio Grande from Earliest Times to the Pueblo Revolt. Carroll L. Riley. (Illus.). 336p. (C). 1995. text ed. 29.95 (*0-87480-466-3*) U of Utah Pr.

Rio del Norte: People of the Upper Rio Grande from the Earliest Times to the Pueblo Revolt. Carroll L. Riley. (Illus.). 336p. (C). 1996. reprint ed. pap. text ed. 15.95 (*0-87480-496-5*) U of Utah Pr.

Rio Desperado. Gordon D. Shirreffs. 128p. 1988. pap. 2.50 (*0-380-70637-7*) Avon.

Rio Desperado. large type ed. Gordon D. Shirreffs. 1990. pap. 15.99 (*0-7089-6800-7*, Trailtree Bookshop) Ulverscroft.

Rio Diablo - Top Gun. Gordon D. Shirreffs. 368p. 1993. mass mkt., pap. text ed. 4.50 (*0-8439-3440-9*) Dorchester Pub Co.

Rio Grande. Richard Currey. Date not set. pap. 23.95 (*0-670-84966-9*) Viking Penguin.

***Rio Grande.** Harvey Fergusson. Date not set. write for info. (*0-688-04746-7*) Morrow.

Rio Grande. Joel Sherman. (Rivers West Ser.: Bk. 12). 304p. 1994. mass mkt. 4.99 (*0-553-29925-5*) Bantam.

Rio Grande: Scenic Line of the World. Dale Sanders. (Illus.). 128p. 1996. 39.95 (*0-9628699-8-8*) Hyrail Prods.

Rio Grande Blankets: Late Nineteenth-Century Textiles in Transition. Kellen K. McIntyre. LC 92-19989. (Illus.). 88p. 1992. pap. 22.50 (*0-9633710-0-2*) Adobe Gallery.

***Rio Grande Color Guide to Freight & Passenger Equipment.** Jim Eager. (Illus.). 1996. 49.95 (*1-878887-64-5*) Morning NJ.

Rio Grande do Sul & Brazilian Regionalism, 1882-1930. Joseph L. Love. LC 71-130829. (Illus.). xvi, 320p. 1971. 45.00 (*0-8047-0759-6*) Stanford U Pr.

Rio Grande Fall. Rudolfo A. Anaya. 368p. 1996. 23.00 (*0-446-51844-1*) Warner Bks.

Rio Grande Fall. Rudolfo A. Anaya. 352p. 1997. mass mkt. 6.99 (*0-446-60486-0*) Warner Bks.

Rio Grande High Style: Furniture Craftsmen. Elmo Baca. (Illus.). 176p. 1995. 39.95 (*0-87905-621-5*) Gibbs Smith Pub.

Rio Grande in Color: Colorado, XVol. 1. Ross B. Grenard. LC 92-80547. (Illus.). 128p. 1992. 45.00 (*1-878887-11-4*) Morning NJ.

Rio Grande Memories. John B. Norwood. LC 91-71587. (Illus.). 192p. 1991. 41.95 (*0-911581-21-9*) Heimburger Hse Pub.

Rio Grande Narrow Gauge. John B. Norwood. Ed. by Donald J. Heimburger & Marilyn M. Heimburger. LC 82-84384. (Illus.). 312p. 1983. 44.95 (*0-911581-00-6*) Heimburger Hse Pub.

Rio Grande Narrow Gauge Recollections. John B. Norwood. Ed. by Donald J. Heimburger & Marilyn M. Heimburger. LC 86-81505. (Illus.). 272p. 1986. 41.95 (*0-911581-07-3*) Heimburger Hse Pub.

***Rio Grande National Forest.** Outdoor Books & Maps Inc. Staff. 96p. 1997. 9.95 (*0-930657-15-2*) Outdr Bks & Maps.

Rio Grande Ransom. Jon Sharpe. (Canyon O'Grady Ser.: No. 19). 176p. (Orig.). 1992. pap. 3.50 (*0-451-17239-6*, Sig) NAL-Dutton.

Rio Grande Rift: Tectonics & Magmatism. Ed. by R. E. Riecker. (Special Publications). (Illus.). 438p. 1979. 25.00 (*0-87590-214-6*) Am Geophysical.

Rio Grande Riptide. large type ed. Roe Richmond. (Linford Western Library). 368p. 1993. pap. 15.99 (*0-7089-7359-0*, Linford) Ulverscroft.

***Rio Grande River Journal.** Craig Martin. 1997. pap. text ed. 15.95 (*1-57188-089-5*) F Amato Pubns.

Rio Grande Series. Rita D. Abbey. LC 96-23835. (Illus.). 96p. 1997. 29.95 (*0-9652870-0-9*) Gan Or.

Rio Grande Ski Train. Steve Patterson & Kenton Forrest. (Illus.). 64p. 1984. pap. 9.95 (*0-932497-00-4*) Tramway Pr.

Rio Grande Southern: An Ultimate Pictorial Study. Richard L. Dorman. LC 90-91619. (Illus.). 280p. 1990. 46.00 (*0-9616656-4-5*) RD Pubns.

Rio Grande Southern Album. Philip A. Ronfor. Ed. by Walter C. Lankenau. (Illus.). 36p. (Orig.). 1989. pap. 18.00 (*1-878343-01-7*) E Crist.

Rio Grande Southern II: An Ultimate Pictorial Study. Richard L. Dorman. LC 94-92171. (Illus.). 344p. 1994. 59.95 (*0-9616656-8-8*, 2500) RD Pubns.

Rio Grande Steam Locomotives: Standard Gauge. Donald J. Heimburger. (Illus.). 200p. 1996. 41.95 (*0-911581-16-2*) Heimburger Hse Pub.

Rio Grande Stories. Compiled by Carolyn Meyer. LC 93-33639. 224p. (J). (gr. 3-7). 1994. 11.00 (*0-15-200548-X*, Gulliver Bks); pap. 6.00 (*0-15-200066-6*, Gulliver Bks) HarBrace.

Rio Grande Textiles. Ed. & Compiled by Nora Fisher. LC 94-26549. 196p. 1994. pap. 29.95 (*0-89013-266-6*) Museum NM Pr.

***Rio Hondo.** Matt Braun. 1997. mass mkt. 5.99 (*0-312-96161-8*) St Martin.

Rio in the Time of the Viceroys. Luiz E. Costa. 1976. lib. bdg. 59.95 (*0-8490-2526-5*) Gordon Pr.

Rio in the Time of the Viceroys. Luiz Edmundo. LC 71-165628. (Select Bibliographies Reprint Ser.). 1977. reprint ed. 33.95 (*0-8369-5935-3*) Ayer.

Rio Maria: Song of the Earth. abr. ed. Ricardo F. Rezende. Ed. & Tr. by Linda Maloney. LC 93-49654. 180p. 1994. reprint ed. pap. 15.00 (*0-88344-960-9*) Orbis Bks.

Rio Negro: Rich Life in Poor Water. M. Goulding et al. (Illus.). xii, 200p. 1988. 50.00 (*90-5103-016-9*, Pub. by SPB Acad Pub NE) Balogh.

Rio Oro. Michael W. McCowen. LC 94-69824. 208p. (Orig.). 1995. pap. 11.95 (*0-9644823-0-4*) Capitan Pub.

Rio Rides Again. Doug Wildey. (Illus.). 72p. 1990. 8.95 (*0-87135-656-2*) Marvel Entmnt.

Rio Tigre & Beyond: The Amazon Jungle Medicine of Manuel Cordova. F. Bruce Lamb. (Illus.). 256p. (Orig.). 1985. pap. 14.95 (*0-938190-59-8*) North Atlantic.

***Riodinidae, Vol. 2.** Philip J. Devries. (Butterflies of Costa Rica Ser.). 368p. 1997. pap. text ed. 29.95 (*0-691-02889-3*) Princeton U Pr.

Riopelle in Conversation. Gilbert Erouart. 96p. (Orig.). 1995. pap. 11.95 (*0-88784-563-0*, Pub. by Hse of Anansi Pr CN) Genl Dist Srvs.

Rioplatnense Guitar: The Early Guitar & It's Context in Argentina & Uruguay, Vol. 1. Vladimir Bobri & Richard Pinnell. (Illus.). 500p. (Orig.). (C). pap. 17.95 (*0-933224-42-7*, T/38) Bold Strummer Ltd.

Rioplatnense Guitar: The Early Guitar & It's Context in Argentina & Uruguay, Vol. 1. Richard Pinnell. (Illus.). 500p. (Orig.). (C). 1993. pap. 35.00 (*0-933224-43-5*) Bold Strummer Ltd.

***Rios en la Soledad - Streams in the Midst of Loneliness.** Bertuzzi. 226p. (SPA.). write for info. (*1-56063-764-1*) Editorial Unilit.

Rios Redimidos. Jorge L. Morales. (Illus.). 55p. (C). 1969. 1.75 (*0-8477-3209-6*) U of PR Pr.

Rios y Lagos Internacionales-Utilizacion Para Fines Agricolas E Industriales: Documento De Antecedentes. 4th rev. ed. (Serie de Derecho y Relaciones Internacionales). (SPA.). 1971. 3.00 (*0-8270-5210-3*) OAS.

Rios y Palmas: Poesias. Oscar P. Moro. LC 85-80622. (Coleccion Espejo de Paciencia). 127p. (Orig.). (SPA.). 1985. pap. 8.95 (*0-89729-377-0*) Ediciones.

***Riot.** Casanova. 1998. pap. 4.95 (*0-7868-1249-4*) Hyprn Child.

Riot. Mary Casanova. 128p. (J). (gr. 4-7). 1996. 13.95 (*0-7868-0215-4*) Hyprn Child.

Riot. Mary Casanova. (J). (gr. 4-7). 1996. lib. bdg. 13.89 (*0-7868-2204-X*) Hyprn Child.

***Riot.** Satoshi Shiki. 1997. pap. text ed. 15.95 (*1-56931-196-X*, Viz Comics) Viz Commns Inc.

***Riot: Act Two.** Satoshi Shiki. 1997. pap. text ed. 15.95 (*1-56931-204-4*, Viz Comics) Viz Commns Inc.

Riot Act. Will Greene. 1963. pap. 5.25 (*0-8222-0955-1*) Dramatists Play.

***Riot Act.** Jon Stock. (Mask Noir Title Ser.). 1997. pap. text ed. 13.99 (*1-85242-557-1*) Serpents Tail.

Riot Control. 1992. lib. bdg. 255.95 (*0-8490-5586-5*) Gordon Pr.

***Riot in a Parrot Shoppe.** Helen Crosswait. 47p. 1991. pap. 7.50 (*0-614-24756-X*) Tesseract SD.

Riot in Heaven. Osonye T. Onwueme. (Musical Drama for the Voices of Color Ser.). 126p. (Orig.). (YA). (gr. 5 up). 1997. pap. 10.00 (*1-57579-054-8*, 2) Africana Leg Pr. RIOT IN HEAVEN is a powerful, allegorical drama about Traveler-X, a man of color who journeys to Heaven to find that he cannot make his passage into Heaven because the two gate-keepers (Stanley Livingstone & Jefferson Lugard) insist that he must produce a passport & visa to cross through Hell & Earth into Heaven. Accompanied by the woman of color (Sojourner Nkrumah), whose "Freedom Train" has broken down at Hellsgate & which she guards presently, how do the people of color cross the borderland into Heaven & create access for their race? This question inflames the RIOT IN HEAVEN. Order from Africana Legacy Press, 808 Lexington Ave., Brooklyn, NY 11221. 718-574-9452.** ***Publisher Provided Annotation.

Riot in the Cities. Journal of Urban Law Editors. Ed. by Michael C. Moran & Richard A. Chikota. LC 74-76132. 411p. 1975. 45.00 (*0-8386-7443-7*) Fairleigh Dickinson.

RIOT Manual. Carman. Date not set. pap. text ed. 4.99 (*0-917143-46-9*) Sparrow TN.

Riot, Rebellion, & Revolution: Rural Social Conflict in Mexico. Ed. by Friedrich Katz. 594p. 1989. pap. text ed. 24.95 (*0-691-02265-8*) Princeton U Pr.

R

Riot, Rout, & Tumult: Readings in American Social & Political Violence. Ed. by Roger Lane & John J. Turner, Jr. LC 77-84752. (Contributions in American History Ser.: No. 69). 399p. 1978. text ed. 49.95 (*0-8371-9845-3*, LRR/, Greenwood Pr) Greenwood.

Rioters & Citizens: Mass Protest in Imperial Japan. Michael Lewis. 1990. 50.00 (*0-520-06642-1*) U CA Pr.

Rioting in America. Paul A. Gilje. (Interdisciplinary Studies in History). 248p. 1996. 35.00 (*0-253-32988-4*) Ind U Pr.

Riotous Assembly. Tom Sharpe. LC 86-28702. 256p. 1987. pap. 10.95 (*0-87113-143-9*, Atlntc Mnthly) Grove-Atltic.

***Riotous Rhymes for Children of All Ages.** Carole Scutt. (Illus.). 47p. (J). (gr. k-6). 1996. 15.95 (*1-887024-15-8*) Bisel Co.

Riots. Philip Steele. LC 92-24195. (Past & Present Ser.). (Illus.). 48p. (YA). (gr. 6 up). 1993. lib. bdg. 12.95 (*0-02-786883-4*, Mac Bks Young Read) S&S Childrens.

Riots & Community Politics in England & Wales, 1790-1810. John Bohstedt. (Illus.). 320p. 1983. 39.95 (*0-674-77120-6*) HUP.

Riots & Pogroms. Ed. by Paul R. Brass. 320p. (C). 1996. 40.00 (*0-8147-1274-6*) NYU Pr.

Riots & Pogroms. Ed. by Paul R. Brass. (C). 1998. pap. 18.50 (*0-8147-1282-7*) NYU Pr.

Riots in New Brunswick: Orange Nativism & Social Violence in the 1840s. Scott W. See. (Social History of Canada Ser.). 288p. 1993. 50.00 (*0-8020-2944-2*); pap. 19.95 (*0-8020-7770-6*) U of Toronto Pr.

Riots in the Cities: Popular Politics & the Urban Poor in Latin America, 1765-1910. Ed. by Silvia M. Arrom & Servando Ortoll. LC 95-25920. (Latin American Silhouettes Ser.). 241p. 1996. 45.00 (*0-8420-2580-4*); pap. 16.95 (*0-8420-2581-2*) Scholarly Res Inc.

Riots, Republicanism, & Citizenship: New York City & Rio de Janeiro City During the Consolidation of the Republican Order. rev. ed. Marco A. Pamplona. LC 95-39434. (Studies in African American History & Culture). (Illus.). 224p. 1996. text ed. 52.00 (*0-8153-2364-6*) Garland.

R.I.P. A Poem. E. S. Miller. Ed. by Gloria V. Hickok. 22p. (Orig.). 1994. pap. 3.50 (*1-884235-04-2*) Helicon Nine Eds.

RIP: Five Stories of the Supernatural. Douglas A. Menville. LC 75-1539. (Supernatural & Occult Fiction Ser.). (Illus.). 1976. lib. bdg. 26.95 (*0-405-08425-0*) Ayer.

RIP: Mining the Subconscious Artifact. James P. Beyor. LC 96-83419. (Illus.). 288p. 1996. per. 19.95 (*0-9651228-0-8*) C T Publns.
A NEW-IMPORTANT STUDY. Embossed Cover, Full index, Bibliography, Illustrated. (Fine paperback). * The RIP is an ardent study involving a philosophical dilemma--the AGREEMENT PROCESSES & what eventually becomes "Perfect Hypocrisy." * ARTISTICALLY PREPARED, the RIP (Reciprocity in Paradox) carefully frames each comprehensive chapter with separate & serious ideas which both affect & become--through belief, the subconscious Mind in MASTER BLAME. * Each chapter boldly focuses upon specific uncensored words, with ART, to represent mankind's symbolic ESSENCE, bringing to Light of Question such subjects as: Belief (Man's crutch), Conscript meaning (intention), Noun/Verb inversion (Future Tense progression), Mental Impasse (Last reason held for reason used), Memory Deficit (think processing), TRUTH paradox (Blame loop synthesis) & much more. * THE IDEA of thinking is not merely remembering to remember. * ROTE-LEARNED memory is, to the agreement process, second Voice--subconscious implant & Psycho mover to an inversive altered state. * Very few people actually THINK--to doubt-down, to feel & find the interrogative to resolve: fear. "If this were the case, the idea of the Human Condition would not exist!" * The RIP identifies any idea which becomes Conscript meaning for Truth, for which the WILL is completely absent, given then to note duty & made both lethal & paradoxically suicidal. "When you READ the RIP, you will become an avid thinker--& enjoy it. Fear will be a friend & your enemies all imaginary." ORDER DIRECT--& SAVE: WRITE TO US AT: ORDER DIRECT SAVING, C-T PUBLICATIONS, P.O. BOX 1070, BUCHANAN, VA 24066. FAX - 24 HOUR SERVICE: 540-254-2870, PHONE - ORDER DIRECT: 540-254-1842. ***Publisher Provided Annotation.***

Rip & Run. Thurman Hoskins. 192p. (Orig.). 1989. mass mkt. 2.95 (*0-87067-200-2*) Holloway.

Rip City: A Quarter Century with the Portland Trail Blazers. limited ed. Steve Cameron. 240p. 1994. 75.00 (*0-87833-090-9*) Taylor Pub.

Rip Cord. William H. Lovejoy. 288p. (Orig.). 1992. mass mkt. 3.99 (*0-380-76447-4*) Avon.

Rip Ford's Texas. John S. Ford. Ed. by Stephen B. Oates. (Personal Narratives of the West Ser.). 573p. 1987. reprint ed. 34.95 (*0-292-77033-2*); reprint ed. pap. 17.95 (*0-292-77034-0*) U of Tex Pr.

Rip in Time. (Illus.). 8.95 (*0-685-70822-5*) Fantagor Pr.

Rip in Time. Bruce Jones & Richard Corben. (Illus.). 112p. (Orig.). 1990. pap. 8.95 (*0-9623841-1-9*) Fantagor Pr.

***Rip-Off.** Jim Thompson. 1998. pap. write for info. (*0-375-70034-X*, Vin) Random.

Rip-Off Book. Victor Santoro. LC 84-81631. 200p. (Orig.). 1984. pap. 14.95 (*0-915179-18-0*) Loompanics.

Rip-Off Tip-Offs: Winning the Auto Repair Game. Robert B. Sikorsky. (Illus.). 154p. 1990. 16.95 (*0-8306-9572-9*, 3572); pap. 9.95 (*0-8306-3572-6*) McGraw-Hill Prof.

Rip-Off U: The Annual Theft & Exploitation of Major College Revenue Producing Student-Athletes. Dick DeVenzio. 256p. 1986. 15.95 (*0-910305-01-3*) Fool Court.

Rip-offs, Cons, & Swindles: Money for Nothing. M. Allen Henderson. LC 92-15881. 192p. 1992. pap. 9.95 (*0-942637-68-2*) Barricade Bks.

***Rip-Roaring High-Flying Mother's Day Fair!** Judy Bradbury. (Illus.). 48p. (J). (gr. k-2). 1997. text ed. 14.95 (*0-07-007041-5*) McGraw.

Rip-Roaring Reads for Reluctant Teen Readers. Gale W. Sherman & Bette D. Ammon. (Illus.). ix, 164p. 1993. pap. text ed. 22.50 (*1-56308-094-X*) Libs Unl.

Rip-Roaring Russell. Johanna Hurwitz. LC 83-1019. (Illus.). 96p. (J). (ps-1). 1983. 16.00 (*0-688-02347-9*, Morrow Junior) Morrow.

Rip-Roaring Russell. Johanna Hurwitz. (Illus.). 96p. (J). (gr. 2-5). 1989. pap. 3.99 (*0-14-032939-0*, Puffin) Puffin Bks.

***Rip-Roaring Russell.** Johanna Hurwitz. (J). 1997. pap. 3.99 (*0-14-038729-3*, Puffin) Puffin Bks.

Rip-Roaring Russell: A Study Guide. Laurie Diamond. Ed. by Joyce Friedland & Rikki Kessler. (Novel-Ties Ser.). 20p. (YA). (gr. 9-12). 1990. pap. text ed. 15.95 (*0-88122-405-7*) Lrn Links.

Rip, Strip & Row: A Builder's Guide to the Cosine Wherry. Brown et al. LC 85-51141. 1985. pap. 19.95 (*0-917436-02-4*) Tamal Vista.

Rip Van Winkle. (Derrydale Fairytale Library). (Illus.). (J). (ps-3). 1985. 1.98 (*0-517-28806-0*) Random Hse Value.

Rip Van Winkle. George Bristow. (Earlier American Music Ser.: No. 25). 297p. 1990. 49.50 (*0-306-76124-6*) Da Capo.

Rip Van Winkle. Charlotte B. Chorpenning. 55p. 1938. pap. 3.45 (*0-87129-050-2*, R45) Dramatic Pub.

Rip Van Winkle. Washington Irving. 1976. 17.95 (*0-8488-1382-0*) Amereon Ltd.

Rip Van Winkle. Washington Irving & Jeffrey Busch. (Classics Illustrated Ser.). (Illus.). 52p. (YA). pap. 4.95 (*1-57209-009-X*) Classics Int Ent.

Rip Van Winkle. Washington Irving. (Illus.). 64p. (YA). (gr. 6 up). 1993. 21.95 (*1-56846-082-1*) Creative Ed.

Rip Van Winkle. Washington Irving. LC 92-9843. (Illus.). 128p. (J). (gr. 1). 1992. pap. 19.00 (*0-8037-1264-2*) Dial Bks Young.

Rip Van Winkle. Washington Irving. (Illus.). (J). (ps-3). 1988. 14.95 (*0-316-37578-0*) Little.

Rip Van Winkle. Washington Irving. (Illus.). (J). (ps-3). 1991. mass mkt. 5.95 (*0-316-37584-5*) Little.

Rip Van Winkle. Washington Irving. LC 87-60720. (Books of Wonder). (Illus.). 110p. (J). (ps up). 1987. 20.00 (*0-688-07459-6*, Morrow Junior) Morrow.

Rip Van Winkle. Washington Irving. (J). 1995. 21.95 (*0-15-200927-2*) HarBrace.

Rip Van Winkle. Washington Irving. LC 94-48134. (J). (gr. 3-5). 1995. 19.95 incl. audio (*0-689-80193-9*, Rabbit) S&S Childrens.

Rip Van Winkle. Illus. & Adapted by Thomas Locker. LC 87-24448. 32p. (J). (ps up). 1988. lib. bdg. 15.89 (*0-8037-0521-2*) Dial Bks Young.

***Rip Van Winkle.** Ed. & Intro. by Walter J. Meserve. (On Stage, America! Ser.). 47p. 1996. spiral bd. 3.95 (*0-937657-28-X*) Feedbk Theabks & Prospero.

Rip Van Winkle. Washington Irving. 73p. 1983. reprint ed. lib. bdg. 16.95 (*0-89966-411-3*) Buccaneer Bks.

Rip Van Winkle: The Mountain Top Edition. rev. ed. Washington Irving. Ed. by Donald T. Oakes. LC 89-62869. (Illus.). 92p. (J). (gr. 9). 1989. pap. write for info. (*0-9624216-0-X*) MTH Soc Inc.

Rip Van Winkle - Wake up, Rip Van Winkle. Washington Irving. 1994. pap. text ed. 4.95 (*0-8114-2222-4*) Raintree Steck-V.

Rip Van Winkle & Other Selected Stories. Washington Irving. 224p. 1993. pap. 2.50 (*0-8125-2332-6*) Tor Bks.

Rip Van Winkle & Other Stories. Washington Irving. 208p. (J). 1996. pap. 3.99 (*0-14-036771-3*) Puffin Bks.

Rip Van Winkle & the Legend of Sleepy Hollow. 2nd ed. Haskell S. Springer. (Illus.). 152p. 1980. 19.95 (*0-912882-42-5*) Sleepy Hollow.

Rip Van Winkle, As Played by Joseph Jefferson. Joseph Jefferson. (BCL1-PS American Literature Ser.). 199p. 1992. reprint ed. lib. bdg. 69.00 (*0-7812-6759-5*) Rprt Serv.

Rip Van Winkle Coloring Book. Washington Irving. (Illus.). (J). 1983. pap. 2.95 (*0-486-24479-2*) Dover.

Rip Van Winkle: or The Works. 1986. pap. 5.95 (*0-88145-044-8*) Broadway Play.

Riparian Ecosystem Recovery in Arid Lands: Strategies & References. Mark K. Briggs. LC 96-9957. (Illus.). 159p. 1996. 45.00 (*0-8165-1642-1*); pap. 19.95 (*0-8165-1644-8*) U of Ariz Pr.

Riparian Forests in California. Ed. by Anne Sands. LC 80-53162. (Illus.). 122p. 1980. reprint ed. pap. 5.00 (*0-931876-41-9*, 4101) ANR Pubns CA.

Riparian Landscapes. George P. Malanson. LC 92-30617. (Studies in Ecology). (Illus.). 296p. (C). 1993. text ed. 62.95 (*0-521-38431-1*) Cambridge U Pr.

Riparian Landscapes. George P. Malanson. (Cambridge Studies in Ecology). (Illus.). 306p. 1996. pap. text ed. 28.95 (*0-521-56683-5*) Cambridge U Pr.

Riparian Road Guide: Managing Roads to Enhance Riparian Areas. Ed. by Rachel Reeder. (Illus.). 32p. (Orig.). 1994. pap. 9.95 (*0-614-14309-8*) Terrene Inst.

Ripe Breadfruit. Armine Von Tempski. LC 92-33054. 384p. 1993. reprint ed. pap. 14.95 (*0-918024-98-6*) Ox Bow.

Ripe Conditions. Claudia Allen. 1994. 5.25 (*0-87129-485-0*, R56) Dramatic Pub.

***Ripe for Plucking.** Alan Shulman. 35.00 (*0-614-25503-1*, 1914S) Am String Tchrs.

Ripe for Resolution: Conflict & Intervention in Africa. I. William Zartman. (Illus.). 320p. (C). 1989. pap. text ed. 18.95 (*0-19-505931-X*) OUP.

Ripe for Revenge. Janie Bolitho. LC 94-37176. 1995. 18.95 (*0-312-11881-3*) St Martin.

Ripe for Revenge. Janie Bolitho. 1996. mass mkt. 4.99 (*0-373-26220-5*, 1-26220-3, Wrldwide Lib) Harlequin Bks.

Ripe Harvest: Educating Migrant Children. Ed. by Arnold B. Cheyney. LC 73-158927. 256p. 1972. 13.95 (*0-87024-206-7*) U of Miami Pr.

Ripe Life: Sermons on the Fruit of the Spirit. C. Thomas Hilton. LC 92-41993. (Protestant Pulpit Exchange Ser.). 96p. (Orig.). 1993. pap. 8.95 (*0-687-38004-9*) Abingdon.

Ripe Mangoes: Miracle Missionary Stories from Bangladesh. 2nd ed. Jay Walsh. (Illus.). 126p. (Orig.). 1991. reprint ed. pap. text ed. 8.95 (*0-87227-060-2*) ABWE Pubng.

Ripening. Edouard Glissant. Tr. by Michael Dash from FRE. (Caribbean Writers Ser.). 195p. (Orig.). (C). 1986. pap. 10.95 (*0-435-98222-2*, 98222) Heinemann.

Ripening. Richard Hague. LC 83-19414. 102p. 1984. 22.50 (*0-8142-0354-X*) Ohio St U Pr.

Ripening: An Almanac of Lesbian Lore & Vision, Vol. 1. Lee Lanning & Nett Hart. 160p. 1992. reprint ed. pap. 8.95 (*0-9615605-2-5*) Word Weavers.

Ripening: Selected Work. 2nd ed. Meridel Le Sueur. Ed. by Elaine Hedges. LC 86-18308. (Illus.). 312p. (C). 1990. pap. 10.95 (*0-935312-41-2*) Feminist Pr.

Ripening Harvest: Mission Strategy for Mainland Chinese Intellectuals in North America. Tsu-Kung Chuang. Ed. by W. Lee Troup. 167p. (Orig.). Date not set. pap. 7.95 (*1-882324-14-5*) Ambssdrs Christ.

***Ripening of Pinstripes.** Rodney Torreson. 106p. (Orig.). 1997. pap. 10.00 (*1-885266-37-5*) Story Line.

Ripening Seed. Colette. 128p. 1996. pap. 9.95 (*0-14-018321-3*, Penguin Classics) Viking Penguin.

Ripening Vine. large type ed. Ellen Clare. 280p. 1995. 25.99 (*0-7505-0886-8*, Pub. by Magna Print Bks UK) Ulverscroft.

Ripken: Cal on Cal. Cal Ripken Jr. Ed. by Mark Vancil. 1995. 39.95 (*1-56530-194-3*) Summit TX.

Ripley under Gound. Patricia Highsmith. LC 92-5351. 1992. pap. 12.00 (*0-679-74230-1*, Vin) Random.

Ripley under Ground. large type ed. Patricia Highsmith. 416p. 1990. 19.95 (*1-85089-304-7*, Pub. by ISIS UK) Transaction Pubs.

Ripley Under Water. Patricia Highsmith. 1993. pap. 12.00 (*0-679-74809-1*, Vin) Random.

Ripley's Believe It or Not: Great & Strange Works of Man. Howard Zimmerman. 128p. (Orig.). 1993. pap. 3.50 (*0-8125-1287-1*) Tor Bks.

Ripley's Believe It or Not: Odd Places. Howard Zimmerman. 1991. pap. 3.50 (*0-8125-1285-5*) Tor Bks.

Ripley's Believe It or Not: Reptiles, Lizards & Prehistoric Beasts. Howard Zimmerman. 128p. 1993. pap. 3.50 (*0-8125-1290-1*) Tor Bks.

Ripley's Believe It or Not: Strange Coincidences. Howard Zimmerman. 1992. pap. 3.50 (*0-8125-1286-3*) Tor Bks.

Ripley's Believe It or Not: Weird Inventions & Discoveries. Howard Zimmerman. 1991. pap. 3.50 (*0-8125-1284-7*) Tor Bks.

Ripley's Believe It Or Not: Wild Animals. Ripley Entertainment Inc. 1992. pap. 3.50 (*0-8125-1289-8*) Tor Bks.

Ripley's Game. 376p. 1991. 22.95 (*1-85089-423-X*, Pub. by ISIS UK) Transaction Pubs.

Ripley's Game. Patricia Highsmith. LC 93-1695. (Vintage Crime - Black Lizard Ser.). 1993. pap. 11.00 (*0-679-74568-8*, Vin) Random.

Ripley's Giant Believe It or Not! Lowell Thomas. 1988. 9.99 (*0-517-49466-3*) Random Hse Value.

Ripoff: A Report on Moral Collapse & Corruption in America. Steve Allen. 1979. 9.95 (*0-8184-0249-0*) Carol Pub Group.

Ripon Cathedral: Its History & Architecture. Bill Forster et al. 1993. pap. 36.00 (*1-85072-119-X*, Pub. by W Sessions UK) St Mut.

Ripon College, a History. Robert Ashley & George H. Miller. (Illus.). 304p. 1992. 18.51 (*0-929331-04-4*) Ripon Coll Pr.

Riposo. Raffaelo Borghini. (Illus.). 648p. 1969. reprint ed. 160.00 (*0-318-71582-1*) G Olms Pubs.

Ripped: The Sensible Way to Achieve Ultimate Muscularity. Clarence Bass. LC 80-81446. (Illus.). 104p. 1980. pap. 11.95 (*0-9609714-0-8*) Clarence Bass.

Ripped-Out Seam. Rebecca Seiferle. LC 93-9982. 192p. (Orig.). 1993. pap. 12.95 (*1-878818-22-8*) Sheep Meadow.

Ripped Three: The Recipes, the Routines & the Reasons. Clarence Bass. LC 80-81446. (Illus.). 195p. 1986. pap. 14.95 (*0-9609714-3-2*) Clarence Bass.

Ripped Two. Clarence Bass. LC 80-81446. (Illus.). 179p. 1982. pap. 14.95 (*0-9609714-1-6*) Clarence Bass.

Ripper. D. E. Athkins. 176p. (YA). (gr. 7-9). 1992. 3.25 (*0-590-45349-1*, Point) Scholastic Inc.

Ripper. Michael Slade. 400p. (Orig.). 1994. pap. 4.99 (*0-451-17702-9*, Sig) NAL-Dutton.

Ripper & the Royals. M. Fairclough. 279p. 1991. pap. 14.95 (*0-7156-2444-X*, Pub. by Duckworth UK) Focus Pub-R Pullins.

Ripping Day Picnic. Duquetteke. 1999. pap. 3.95 (*0-14-054251-5*) NAL-Dutton.

Ripping Yarns. Michael Palin. 1991. pap. 17.95 (*0-413-63980-0*) Routledge Chapman & Hall.

Ripple. Mary Sloan. (Orig.). 1986. pap. 6.00 (*0-912449-22-5*) Floating Island.

Ripple: A Novel about Sexual Invasion. William Zinn. 1987. 16.95 (*0-88191-056-2*) Freundlich.

Ripple from the Storm. Doris Lessing. 272p. 1995. lib. bdg. 35.00 (*0-8095-9171-5*) Borgo Pr.

Ripple From the Storm: A Novel. Doris Lessing. LC 95-31488. (Children of Violence Ser.). 272p. 1995. pap. 13.00 (*0-06-097664-0*, PL) HarpC.

Ripple in Entropy. Paul J. Payack. 80p. 1973. pap. 2.50 (*0-686-15402-9*) Chthon Pr.

***Ripple of Hope.** Daniel Terris & Barbara Harrison. (J). 1997. pap. 16.99 (*0-525-67506-X*) NAL-Dutton.

Ripple of Hope: White Couple's Struggle for Civil Rights in 60's & 70's. Bernard B. Broussard. 200p. reprint ed. pap. 10.00 (*0-924798-09-2*) Cypress Bks.

Ripples. (Orig.). 1995. pap. 10.00 (*0-9645560-1-4*) R Gooneratne-Cooray.

Ripples. William E. Hazelgrove. LC 91-62677. 198p. (Orig.). 1992. pap. 6.95 (*0-9630052-9-4*) Pantonne Pr.

Ripples along Chico Creek: Perspectives on People & Times. Butte County, California Pen Women Staff. LC 91-73882. (Illus.). 250p. 1992. pap. 22.95 (*0-9631582-2-8*) NL Am Pen Women.

Ripples in the Cosmos: A View Behind the Scenes of the New Cosmology. Michael Rowan-Robinson. LC 93-1590. 1995. text ed. write for info. (*0-7167-4503-8*) W H Freeman.

***Ripples in the Pool.** C. H. Scott. 1996. 25.95 (*1-889149-03-9*) C Scott Pub.

Ripples in the River. Lakshmi. Tr. by Indira Ananthakrishnan. (C). 1992. text ed. 4.00 (*81-7201-045-1*, Pub. by National Sahitya Akademi II) S Asia.

***Ripples of Dissent: Women's Stories of Marriage from the 1890s.** Ed. by Bridget Bennet. 384p. 1997. 45.00 (*0-460-87777-1*, Pub. by J M Dent & Sons UK) Trafalgar.

Ripples of Light. Bernard Williams. 156p. pap. text ed. 4.95 (*0-929292-78-2*) Hannibal Bks.

Ripples on the Water. Judy Miller. 150p. (Orig.). 1990. pap. 7.95 (*0-942341-04-X*) Dawn Pubns TX.

***Rippling Waters.** Ed. by Cynthia Stevens. 1996. 69.95 (*1-57553-152-6*) Watermrk Pr.

Rippon Rides Double. large type ed. Max Brand. LC 96-22227. (Western Ser.). 256p. 1996. 19.95 (*0-7862-0808-2*, Thorndike Lrg Prnt) Thorndike Pr.

Rippon's Medical Mycology. 4th ed. Mcginnis. pap. text ed. write for info. (*0-7216-4684-0*) HarBrace.

Riprap & Cold Mountain Poems. Gary Snyder. 80p. 1990. reprint ed. 19.95 (*0-86547-455-9*, North Pt Pr) FS&G.

Ripshin. Kemp B. Nye. LC 92-33504. 1992. pap. 12.00 (*0-930095-13-8*) Signal Bks.

Ripshin. Kemp B. Nye. LC 93-42266. 1993. 16.00 (*0-930095-17-0*) Signal Bks.

Ripsnort. Todd Colby. 1994. pap. 6.00 (*1-887128-05-0*) Soft Skull Pr.

Ripsnorting Whoppers! Humor from America's Heartland. Rick Sowash. (Illus.). 160p. 1994. 19.95 (*0-911861-08-4*); pap. 11.95 (*0-911861-07-6*) Gabriels Horn.

Ripster: A Coloring Book. Cynthia Alvarez. (Happy House Coloring Ser.). (J). 1996. pap. 0.55 (*0-679-87997-8*, Bullseye Bks) Random Bks Yng Read.

Riptide. Mickey Friedman. 288p. 1995. mass mkt. 4.50 (*0-06-104335-4*, Harp PBks) HarpC.

Riptide. Sam Llewellyn. Ed. by Jane Chelius. 288p. (Orig.). 1994. mass mkt. 5.50 (*0-671-89307-6*) PB.

Riptide. Frances W. Weller. (Illus.). 32p. (J). (ps-3). 1990. 15.95 (*0-399-21675-8*, Philomel Bks) Putnam Pub Group.

Riptide. Frances W. Weller. (Illus.). 32p. (J). (ps-3). 1994. pap. 5.95 (*0-399-22766-0*, Philomel Bks) Putnam Pub Group.

Riptide. Frances W. Weller. (Illus.). 32p. (J). (ps-3). 1996. pap. 5.95 (*0-698-11386-1*, Paperstar) Putnam Pub Group.

Riptide. large type ed. Sam Llewellyn. (Charnwood Ser.). 416p. (Orig.). 1994. 27.99 (*0-7089-8754-0*, Charnwood) Ulverscroft.

Riquezas de Su Gracia. Nahum Rosario. 151p. (Orig.). (SPA.). 1994. pap. 8.00 (*0-9634761-4-9*) Pub Maranatha.

Rire: Essai sur la Signification du Comique. 6th ed. Henri L. Bergson. (FRE.). 1991. pap. 15.95 (*0-7859-3017-5*) Fr & Eur.

Rire de Laura. Francoise Mallet-Joris. (FRE.). 1987. pap. 12.95 (*0-7859-3392-1*) Fr & Eur.

Rire de Sara. Renee Massip. (FRE.). 1975. pap. 10.95 (*0-7859-4044-8*) Fr & Eur.

Rires et Pleurs; Poesies, 2 pts. Oswald Durand. (B. E. Ser.: No. 3). (FRE.). 1896. 60.00 (*0-8115-2954-1*) Periodicals Srv.

RIS A Bhruthaich: Somhairle MacGill-eain, the Criticism & Prose Writing of Sorley Maclean. Ed. by Acair Ltd. Staff. 1985. 90.00 (*0-86152-041-6*, Pub. by Acair Ltd UK) St Mut.

Risa de la Medusa. Helene Cixous. 208p. (SPA.). 1995. pap. 14.95 (*0-614-16494-X*) U of PR Pr.

***Risa Santa y la Bencicion de Toronta.** J. Beverly. (SPA.). 9.95 (*0-8297-0508-2*) Life Pubs Intl.

Risa Sheppard's Fitness Formula for a Firm & Flat Stomach. Risa Sheppard & Diane Foglesong-Bos. (Illus.). 24p. (Orig.). 1987. pap. 3.95 (*0-939939-00-2*) Multi Fit Pubns.

An Asterisk (*) at the beginning of an entry indicates that the title is appearing in BIP for the first time.

***Risala: Treatise on the Foundations of Islamic Jurisprudence.** Al-Shafii. 368p. 1996. 40.00 (0-614-21208-1, 1082) Kazi Pubns.

***Risalat al Gufran: The Letter of Forgiveness by Abu 'Ala al Ma'arri.** (Arab Translations Ser.: Vol. 148). (Illus.). 150p. (Orig.). 1997. pap. 6.50 (0-940307-53-7) Wormhoudt.

Risale-i Mi'mariyye: An Early-Seventeenth Century Ottoman Treatise on Architecture. Howard Crane. (Muquarnas Supplements Studies in Islamic Architecture Ser.: Vol. 1). (Illus.). x, 126p. 1987. 85.75 (90-04-07846-0) E J Brill.

RISC - the MIPS-R3000 Family: Architecture, System Components, Compilers, Tools, Applications. R. J. Bruess. (Illus.). 340p. 1991. 68.00 (3-8009-4103-1, VCH) Wiley.

***RISC Architectures.** Heudin. (Illus.). 261p. (Orig.). pap. text ed. 46.50 (0-412-45340-1, Chap & Hall NY) Chapman & Hall.

RISC Architectures. Richard K. Miller & Terri C. Walker. LC 88-81639. (Survey on Technology & Markets Ser.: No. 87). 50p. 1989. pap. text ed. 200.00 (1-55865-086-5) Future Tech Surveys.

RISC Systems & Applications. Daniel Tabak. LC 95-16403. 370p. 1996. text ed. 69.95 (0-471-96027-6) Wiley.

Rise & Awakening of Depressed Classes in India. J. R. Kamble. 327p. 1979. 25.95 (0-318-36818-8) Asia Bk Corp.

Rise & Be Healed. Peter McCall & Maryanne Lacy. 239p. (Orig.). 1992. pap. 15.00 (0-936269-01-4) Hse of Peace.

Rise & Consequences of the Manorial-Serf Economy in East Central Europe. Jerzy Topolski. (Collected Studies: CS 470). 300p. 1994. 94.95 (0-86078-463-0, Pub. by Variorum UK) Ashgate Pub Co.

Rise & Crisis of Psychoanalysis in America, Vol. II: Freud & the Americans. Nathan G. Hale, Jr. 528p. 1995. 30.00 (0-19-504637-4) OUP.

Rise & Crisis of Psychoanalysis in the United States: Freud & the Americans, 1917-1985. Nathan G. Hale, Jr. 476p. 30.00 (0-615-00403-2) OUP.

Rise & Decline of a Dialect: A Study in the Revival of Modern Hebrew. Aaron Bar-Adon. LC 74-80121. (Janua Linguarum, Ser. Practica: No. 197). 116p. (Orig.). 1975. pap. text ed. 36.95 (90-279-3206-9) Mouton.

Rise & Decline of Buddhism in India. Kanai Lal Hazra. 462p. (C). 1995. 44.00 (81-215-0651-4, Pub. by Munshiram Manoharial II) S Asia.

Rise & Decline of Holland's Economy: Merchant Capitalism & the Labour Market. Jan L. Van Zanden. LC 93-2708. 256p. (C). 1993. text ed. 69.95 (0-7190-3806-5, Pub. by Manchester Univ Pr UK) St Martin.

Rise & Decline of International Communism. Geoffrey Stern. 288p. 1990. pap. 25.00 (1-85278-045-2); text ed. 75.00 (1-85278-042-8) E Elgar.

Rise & Decline of Jacksonian Democracy. Glyndon G. Van Deusen. LC 78-11435. (Anvil Ser.). 270p. 1979. reprint ed. pap. 13.50 (0-88275-784-9) Krieger.

Rise & Decline of Militia. Date not set. write for info. (0-945636-92-X) Susquehanna U Pr.

Rise & Decline of Nations: Economic Growth, Stagflation, & Social Rigidities. Mancur Olson. LC 82-40163. 287p. 1984. reprint ed. pap. 15.00 (0-300-03079-7, Y-487) Yale U Pr.

Rise & Decline of the American Cut Nail Industry: A Study of the Interrelationships of Technology, Business Organization, & Management Techniques. Amos J. Loveday, Jr. LC 83-5542. (Contributions in Economics & Economic History Ser.: No. 53). (Illus.). xx, 160p. 1983. text ed. 47.95 (0-313-23918-5, LAC/) Greenwood.

***Rise & Decline of the Asian Century: False Starts on the Path to the Global Millenium.** Christopher Lingle. (Illus.). 224p. 1997. text ed. 59.95 (1-85972-669-0, Pub. by Ashgate UK) Ashgate Pub Co.

Rise & Decline of the British Motor Industry. Roy Church. (New Studies in Economic & Social History: No. 24). 150p. (C). 1995. text ed. 34.95 (0-521-55283-4); pap. text ed. 10.95 (0-521-55770-4) Cambridge U Pr.

Rise & Decline of the English Working Classes, 1918-1990: A Social History. Eric Hopkins. LC 90-27819. 303p. 1991. text ed. 45.00 (0-312-06156-0) St Martin.

Rise & Decline of the Great Atlantic & Pacific Tea Company. William I. Walsh. (Illus.). 256p. 1986. 17.95 (0-8184-0382-9) Carol Pub Group.

Rise & Decline of the Medici Bank: 1397-1494. Raymond A. De Roover. LC 63-11417. (Studies in Business History: No. 21). (Illus.). 522p. 1963. 30.00 (0-674-77145-1) HUP.

Rise & Decline of the Scholastic Quaestio Disputata: With Special Emphasis on Its Use in the Teaching of Medicine & Science. Brian Lawn. LC 92-42729. (Education & Society in the Middle Ages & Renaissance Ser.: No. 2). 176p. 1993. 64.25 (90-04-09740-6) E J Brill.

Rise & Decline of the Wheat Growing Industry in Wisconsin. John G. Thompson. LC 72-2868. (Use & Abuse of America's Natural Resources Ser.). 254p. 1972. reprint ed. 21.95 (0-405-04536-0) Ayer.

Rise & Decline of the Zairian State. Crawford Young & Thomas Turner. LC 84-40204. (Illus.). 472p. 1985. text ed. 37.50 (0-299-10110-X) U of Wis Pr.

Rise & Decline of U. S. Merchant Shipping in the Twentieth Century. Rene De La Pedraja Toman. LC 92-17754. (Twayne's Evolution of American Business Ser.: No. 8). 200p. (C). 1992. pap. 14.95 (0-8057-9827-7, Twayne); text ed. 26.95 (0-8057-9826-9, Twayne) Scribnrs Ref.

Rise & Decline of Urban Industries in Italy & the Low Countries: Late Middle Ages - Early Modern Times. Ed. by H. Van der Wee. (Studies in Social & Economic History: No. 1). 400p. (Orig.). 1988. pap. 67.50 (90-6186-283-3, Pub. by Leuven Univ BE) Coronet Bks.

Rise & Demise. Christopher Chase-Dunn. LC 96-52141. (New Perspectives in Sociology Ser.). (C). 1997. text ed. 60.00 (0-8133-1005-9) Westview.

Rise & Demise: Comparing World Systems. Christopher K. Chase-Dunn & Thomas D. Hall. LC 96-52141. (New Perspectives in Sociology Ser.). (C). 1997. pap. text ed. 22.00 (0-8133-1006-7) Westview.

Rise & Demise of Commodity Agreements: An Investigation into the Breakdown of International Commodity Agreements. Marcelo Raffaelli. 192p. 1994. 135.00 (1-85573-179-7, Pub. by Woodhead Pubng UK) Am Educ Systs.

Rise & Development of Military Music. Henry G. Farmer. LC 79-107801. (Select Bibliographies Reprint Ser.). 1977. 18.95 (0-8369-5204-9) Ayer.

Rise & Development of Military Music. Henry G. Farmer. 156p. 1990. reprint ed. lib. bdg. 59.00 (0-7812-9118-6) Rprt Serv.

Rise & Development of Opera. Joseph Goddard. 210p. 1991. reprint ed. lib. bdg. 79.00 (0-7812-9333-2) Rprt Serv.

Rise & Development of the Gerrymander. Elmer C. Griffith. LC 73-19149. (Politics & People Ser.). 124p. 1974. reprint ed. 13.95 (0-405-05872-1) Ayer.

Rise & Development of Western Civilization, 3 vols., 1. 2nd ed. John L. Stipp & C. Warren Hollister. LC 76-171915. reprint ed. pap. 160.00 (0-317-10555-8, 2013057) Bks Demand.

Rise & Development of Western Civilization, 3 vols., 2. 2nd ed. John L. Stipp & C. Warren Hollister. LC 76-171915. reprint ed. pap. 128.80 (0-317-10556-6) Bks Demand.

Rise & Development of Western Civilization, 3 vols., 3. 2nd ed. John L. Stipp & C. Warren Hollister. LC 76-171915. reprint ed. pap. 159.00 (0-317-10557-4) Bks Demand.

Rise & Dine: Savory Secrets from America's Bed & Breakfast Inns. Marcy Claman. (Illus.). 360p. (Orig.). 1996. pap. 14.95 (1-896511-05-8) Callawind.

Rise & Dine Canada: Savory Secrets from Canada's Bed & Breakfast Inns. Marcy Claman. (Illus.). 320p. (Orig.). 1997. pap. 14.95 (1-896511-06-6) Callawind.

Rise & Expansion of the British Dominion in India. 5th ed. Alfred C. Lyall. (Illus.). reprint ed. text ed. 28.50 (0-685-13409-1) Coronet Bks.

Rise & Extension of Submarine Telegraphy. Willouby Smith. LC 74-4695. (Telecommunications Ser.). (Illus.). 410p. 1974. reprint ed. 35.95 (0-405-06058-0) Ayer.

Rise & Fall of a Frontier Entrepreneur: Benjamin Rathbun, Master Builder & Architect. Roger Whitman. Ed. by Scott Eberle & David A. Gerber. (Illus.). (C). 1996. pap. 17.95 (0-8156-0337-1, WHBRP); text ed. 39.95 (0-8156-2694-0, WHBR) Syracuse U Pr.

***Risc & Fall of a Violent Crime Wave: Crack Cocaine & the Social Construction of a Crime Problem.** Henry H. Brownstein. (C). 1996. pap. text ed. 16.50 (0-911577-36-X) Harrow & Heston.

Rise & Fall of American Lutheran Pietism: The Rejection of an Activist Heritage. Paul P. Kuenning. LC 88-20933. 304p. (C). 1988. 34.95 (0-86554-306-2, MUP/H268) Mercer Univ Pr.

Rise & Fall of American Sport: Mudville's Revenge. Ted Vincent. LC 93-31948. xi, 374p. 1994. pap. 12.95 (0-8032-9613-4, Bison Books) U of Nebr Pr.

Rise & Fall of an American Army: U. S. Ground Forces in Vietnam, 1965-1973. Shelby L. Stanton. 480p. 1995. pap. 17.95 (0-89141-576-9) Presidio Pr.

Rise & Fall of an Urban School System: Detroit, 1907-81. Jeffrey Mirel. 450p. (C). 1992. text ed. 44.50 (0-472-10118-8) U of Mich Pr.

Rise & Fall of Anarchy in America. George N. McLean. LC 72-885. (American History & Americana Ser.: No. 47). 1973. reprint ed. lib. bdg. 75.00 (0-8383-1426-0) M S G Haskell Hse.

Rise & Fall of Anne Boleyn. Retha M. Warnicke. (Illus.). 338p. (C). 1989. text ed. 44.95 (0-521-37000-0) Cambridge U Pr.

Rise & Fall of Anne Boleyn. Retha M. Warnicke. (Canto Book Ser.). (Illus.). 338p. (C). 1991. pap. text ed. 12.95 (0-521-40677-3) Cambridge U Pr.

Rise & Fall of Anti-Americanism: A Century of French Perception. Ed. by Denis Lacorne et al. 280p. 1990. text ed. 45.00 (0-312-04206-X) St Martin.

Rise & Fall of Antichrist. George E. Vandeman. (Anchor Ser.). 80p. 1985. pap. 0.47 (0-8163-0634-6) Pacific Pr Pub Assn.

Rise & Fall of Athens: Nine Greek Lives. Plutarch. Tr. by Ian S. Kilvert. (Classics Ser.). 320p. 1960. pap. 11.95 (0-14-044102-6, Penguin Classics) Viking Penguin.

***Rise & Fall of Black Power.** 125p. (Orig.). 1997. mass mkt. 4.99 (1-55197-610-2, Pub. by Comnwlth Pub CN) Partners Pubs Grp.

Rise & Fall of British Coastal Resorts: Cultural & Economic Perspectives. Allan M. Williams. LC 96-361. (Tourism, Leisure & Recreation Ser.). (Illus.). 192p. (C). 1996. text ed. 79.95 (1-85567-388-6, Pub. by Pntr Pubs UK) Bks Intl VA.

***Rise & Fall of British Empire.** James. Date not set. pap. 19.95 (0-312-16985-X) St Martin.

Rise & Fall of British India: Imperialism as Inequality. K. De Schweintz, Jr. 250p. (C). 1983. pap. text ed. 14.95 (0-415-04505-3, NO. 3496) Routledge Chapman & Hall.

***Rise & Fall of British Liberalism, 1776-1988.** Alan Sykes. LC 97-25080. 1997. write for info. (0-582-06041-9, Pub. by Longman UK) Longman.

***Rise & Fall of British Liberalism, 1776-1988.** ALan Sykes. LC 97-25080. 1997. write for info. (0-582-06057-5, Pub. by Longman UK) Longman.

Rise & Fall of British Naval Mastery. Paul M. Kennedy. LC 87-1785. (Illus.). 436p. (C). 1986. pap. 25.00 (0-948660-01-5, Pub. by Ashfield Pr UK) Humanities.

Rise & Fall of California's Radical Prison Movement. Eric Cummins. LC 93-17831. (Illus.). 352p. (C). 1993. 47.50 (0-8047-2231-5); pap. 17.95 (0-8047-2232-3) Stanford U Pr.

Rise & Fall of Capitalism. Y. S. Brenner. 320p. 1991. text ed. 80.00 (1-85278-527-6) E Elgar.

Rise & Fall of Catholic Religious Orders: A Social Movement Perspective. Patricia Wittberg. LC 94-1068. (SUNY Series in Religion, Culture, & Society). 423p. 1994. text ed. 74.50 (0-7914-2229-1); pap. text ed. 24.95 (0-7914-2230-5) State U NY Pr.

Rise & Fall of Cesar Birotteau. Honore De Balzac. Tr. by Francis T. Furey. (Illus.). 449p. 1989. pap. 8.95 (0-88184-448-9) Carroll & Graf.

Rise & Fall of Childhood. C. John Sommerville. LC 89-40515. 1990. pap. 11.96 (0-679-72829-5, Vin) Random.

Rise & Fall of Childhood. Charles J. Sommerville. LC 82-758. (Sage Library of Social Research: No. 140). 255p. reprint ed. pap. 72.70 (0-8357-4858-8, 2037790) Bks Demand.

Rise & Fall of Civilization: An Inquiry into the Relationship Between Economic Development & Civilization. Shepard B. Clough. LC 77-25973. (Illus.). 291p. 1978. reprint ed. text ed. 38.50 (0-313-20092-0, CLRI, Greenwood Pr) Greenwood.

***Rise & Fall of Culture History.** R. Lee Lyman et al. (Illus.). 263p. (C). 1997. 44.50 (0-306-45537-4, Plenum Pr); pap. 24.50 (0-306-45538-2, Plenum Pr) Plenum.

Rise & Fall of Democracy in Early America, 1630-1789: The Legacy for Contemporary Politics. Joshua Miller. 128p. 1991. 25.00 (0-271-00744-3) Pa St U Pr.

Rise & Fall of Development Theory. Colin T. Leys. LC 95-39293. 1996. pap. text ed. 14.95 (0-253-21016-X) Ind U Pr.

Rise & Fall of Development Theory. Colin T. Leys. LC 95-39293. (C). 1996. 35.00 (0-253-33083-1) Ind U Pr.

Rise & Fall of Diapirs During Thin-Skinned Extension. B. C. Vendeville & M. P. Jackson. (Illus.). 60p. 1992. pap. 4.50 (0-317-05176-8, RI 209) Bur Econ Geology.

Rise & Fall of Economic Justice & Other Essays. C. B. Macpherson. 176p. 1987. reprint ed. pap. 15.95 (0-19-285186-1) OUP.

***Rise & Fall of Economic Liberalism: The Making of the Economic Gulag.** rev. ed. Frederic F. Clairmont. 356p. 1996. pap. 15.00 (0-945257-85-6) Apex Pr.

Rise & Fall of Elites: An Application of Theoretical Sociology. Vilfredo Pareto. 120p. (C). 1991. pap. 21.95 (0-88738-872-8) Transaction Pubs.

***Rise & Fall of English: Reconstructing English as a Discipline.** Robert E. Scholes. LC 97-21686. 1998. write for info. (0-300-07151-5) Yale U Pr.

***Rise & Fall of Gay Culture.** Daniel Harris. LC 96-47822. 1997. 24.95 (0-7868-6165-7) Hyperion.

Rise & Fall of Gorbachev. Dimitry Mikheyev. 178p. (Orig.). (C). 1992. pap. text ed. 12.95 (1-55813-041-1) Hudson Instit IN.

Rise & Fall of Great Cities: Aspects of Urbanization in the Western World. Ed. by Richard Lawton. 185p. 1993. text ed. 47.95 (0-471-94704-0) Wiley.

Rise & Fall of Ilsa: (The Female Lady Giant) Jackie L. High. Ed. by Rodolfo Hillen. (Jaclyn Fairy Tales Ser.: No. 1). (Illus.). 26p. (J). (ps-3). 1991. 8.95 (1-880605-00-7) J Laverne Mus.

Rise & Fall of Infrastructures: Dynamics of Evolution & Technological Change in Transport. A. Grubler. (Contributions to Economics Ser.). (Illus.). viii, 305p. 1990. 77.95 (0-387-91374-2) Spr-Verlag.

Rise & Fall of Jesse James. Robertus Love. LC 89-24965. xxiv, 446p. (YA). 1990. reprint ed. pap. 15.00 (0-8032-7932-9, Bison Books) U of Nebr Pr.

***Rise & Fall of Jewish Nationalism.** Doron Mendels. LC 97-13245. 1997. pap. write for info. (0-8028-4329-8) Eerdmans.

Rise & Fall of Latin Humanism in Early-Modern Russia: Pagan Authors, Ukrainians, & the Resiliency of Muscovy. Max J. Okenfuss. LC 95-15028. (Studies in Intellectual History: Vol. 64). (Illus.). 312p. 1995. 95.50 (90-04-10331-7) E J Brill.

Rise & Fall of Leftist Radicalism in America. Edward Walter. LC 92-13241. 200p. 1992. text ed. 47.95 (0-275-94276-7, C4276, Praeger Pubs) Greenwood.

Rise & Fall of Liberal Government in Victorian Britain. Jonathan Parry. 1996. pap. text ed. 20.00 (0-300-06718-6) Yale U Pr.

Rise & Fall of Little Voice. Jim Cartwright. 96p. (C). 1992. pap. 9.95 (0-413-67130-5, A0653, Pub. by Methuen UK) Heinemann.

***Rise & Fall of Managed Care.** Linda L. Miles. Ed. by Virginia McCullough. 96p. 1997. pap. 12.95 (0-9658409-0-5) Link Pub VA.

Rise & Fall of Marvellous Melbourne. Graeme Davison. 320p. (Orig.). 1993. pap. 24.95 (0-522-84191-0, Pub. by Melbourne Univ Pr AT) Paul & Co Pubs.

Rise & Fall of Merry England: The English Ritual Year, 1400-1700. Ronald Hutton. 390p. 1994. 39.95 (0-19-820363-2) OUP.

Rise & Fall of Merry England: The Ritual Year 1400-1700. Ronald Hutton. 384p. 1996. reprint ed. pap. 15.95 (0-19-285327-9) OUP.

Rise & Fall of National Security Decisionmaking in the Former U. S. S. R. Implications for Russia & the Commonwealth. Harry Gelman. LC 92-17312. 1992. pap. 7.50 (0-8330-1255-X, R-4200-A) Rand Corp.

Rise & Fall of New France, 2 vols. George M. Wrong. (BCL1 - History - Canada Ser.). 1991. reprint ed. lib. bdg. 150.00 (0-7812-6355-7) Rprt Serv.

Rise & Fall of New Sweden: Governor Johan Risingh's Journal in Its Historical Context, 1654-1655. Stellan Dahlgren & Hans Norman. (Acta Bibliothecae R. Universitatis Upsaliensis Ser.: Vol. XXVII). (Illus.). 303p. 1988. 81.00 (91-554-2137-7, Pub. by Uppsala Univ Acta Univ Uppsaliensis SW) Coronet Bks.

***Rise & Fall of Nimrod.** Dudley Cates. LC 97-67139. 72p. (Orig.). 1997. pap. 10.95 (1-57197-068-1) Pentland Pr.

Rise & Fall of Nineteenth Century Idealsim. Holbrook Jackson. 1969. pap. 2.45 (0-8065-0016-6, Citadel Pr) Carol Pub Group.

Rise & Fall of Nuclearism: Fear & Faith As Determinants of the Arms Race. Sheldon Ungar. 240p. 1992. 32.50 (0-271-00840-7); pap. 14.95 (0-271-00841-5) Pa St U Pr.

***Rise & Fall of Palestine: A Personal Account of the Intifada.** Norman G. Finklestein. 1996. pap. 18.95 (0-614-20720-7) U of Minn Pr.

Rise & Fall of Palestine: A Personal Account of the Intifada Years. Norman G. Finkelstein. 192p. (C). 1996. text ed. 47.95 (0-8166-2858-0); pap. text ed. 18.95 (0-8166-2859-9) U of Minn Pr.

Rise & Fall of Patrice Lumumba. Thomas N. Kanza. 385p. 1979. pap. text ed. 24.95 (0-87073-901-8) Schenkman Bks Inc.

Rise & Fall of Philanthropy in East Africa. Robert G. Gregory. 224p. (C). 1991. text ed. 34.95 (1-56000-007-4) Transaction Pubs.

Rise & Fall of Political Parties in the United States, 1789-1989: The Congressional Roll Call Record. Pref. by Joel H. Silbey. LC 90-28967. (Congress of the United States, 1789-1989 Ser.: Vol. 3). 495p. 1991. 100.00 (0-926019-30-9) Carlson Pub.

Rise & Fall of Popular Music. Donald Clarke. 640p. 1996. pap. 19.95 (0-312-14200-5) St Martin.

Rise & Fall of Revolutionary England: An Essay on the Fabrication of Seventeenth-Century History. Alastair MacLachlan. LC 95-31667. (British History in Perspective Ser.). 352p. 1996. text ed. 39.95 (0-312-12841-X) St Martin.

Rise & Fall of Slavery in America. Louis Filler. 165p. (C). 1981. pap. text ed. 12.95 (0-89198-123-3); lib. bdg. 19.95 (0-89198-122-5) Ozer.

Rise & Fall of South African Peasantry. Colin Bundy. LC 79-62841. (Perspectives on Southern Africa Ser.: No. 28). 1979. 55.00 (0-520-03754-5) U CA Pr.

Rise & Fall of Sparrows: A Collection of North American Haiku. Ed. by Alexis Rotella. LC 89-81932. (Orig.). 1990. pap. 8.95 (0-9623497-2-0) Los Hombres.

***Rise & Fall of State Socialism: Industrial Society & the Socialist State.** David S. Lane. LC 96-42467. (C). 1996. text ed. 49.95 (0-7456-0742-X, Pub. by Polity Pr UK); pap. text ed. 19.95 (0-7456-0743-8, Pub. by Polity Pr UK) Blackwell Pubs.

Rise & Fall of Strategic Planning. Henry Mintzberg. 288p. 1994. 32.95 (0-02-921605-2, Free Press) Free Pr.

Rise & Fall of Strategic Planning. Henry Mintzberg. LC 93-39492. 1993. pap. write for info. (0-13-781824-6) P-H Gen Ref & Trav.

Rise & Fall of Structural Marxism: Louis Althusser & His Influence. Ten Benton. Ed. by Anthony Giddens. LC 84-4812. (Theoretical Traditions in the Social Sciences Ser.). 251p. 1984. text ed. 35.00 (0-312-68375-8) St Martin.

Rise & Fall of T. D. Lysenko. Zhores A. Medvedev. LC 79-77519. 304p. reprint ed. pap. 86.70 (0-317-26082-0, 2023770) Bks Demand.

Rise & Fall of the American Left. John P. Diggins. (Illus.). 288p. 1992. 22.95 (0-393-03075-X) Norton.

Rise & Fall of the American Left. John P. Diggins. 432p. 1992. pap. 13.95 (0-393-30917-7) Norton.

Rise & Fall of the Anabaptists. Ernest Belfort Bax. 1972. 59.95 (0-8490-0958-8) Gordon Pr.

Rise & Fall of the British Empire. Lawrence James. LC 95-38774. 720p. 1995. 35.00 (0-312-14039-8) St Martin.

Rise & Fall of the Choctaw Republic. 2nd ed. Angie Debo. LC 69-7973. (Civilization of the American Indian Ser.: No. 6). (Illus.). 1975. pap. 15.95 (0-8061-1247-6) U of Okla Pr.

***Rise & Fall of the Cigarette: A Cultural History of Smoking in the U. S.** Allan Brandt. 1998. pap. 18.00 (0-465-07048-5) Basic.

***Rise & Fall of the Cigarette: A Social & Cultural History of Smoking in the U. S.** Allan Brandt. 1997. 25.00 (0-465-07047-7) Basic.

Rise & Fall of the City of Mahagany & the Seven Deadly Sins of the Petty Bourgeoisie. Bertolt Brecht. Ed. by Ralph Manheim. Tr. by W. H. Auden & Chester Kallman from GER. LC 94-10421. 144p. 1996. pap. 8.95 (1-55970-279-6) Arcade Pub Inc.

Rise & Fall of the Cleveland Mafia: Corn Sugar & Blood. Rick Porrello. LC 95-707. 240p. 1995. 22.00 (1-56980-058-8) Barricade Bks.

Rise & Fall of the Communist Party of Burma (CPB) Bertil Lintner. (Southeast Asia Program Ser.: No. 6). (Illus.). 124p. (Orig.). 1990. pap. 12.00 (0-87727-123-2) Cornell SE Asia.

Rise & Fall of the Communist Revolution. Warren H. Carroll. (Illus.). 852p. 1995. 34.95 (0-931888-60-3); pap. 24.95 (0-931888-59-X) Christendom Pr.

Rise & Fall of the Confederate Government, 2 vols. Jefferson Davis. 1990. pap. write for info. (0-306-80420-4) Da Capo.

Rise & Fall of the Confederate Government. abr. ed. Jefferson Davis. 1990. 22.50 (0-8446-0074-1) Peter Smith.

Rise & Fall of the Confederate Government. Jefferson Davis. 1992. reprint ed. lib. bdg. 49.95 (0-89968-282-0, Lghtyr Pr) Buccaneer Bks.

An Asterisk (*) at the beginning of an entry indicates that the title is appearing in BIP for the first time.

Rise & Fall of the Confederate Government, Vol. 1. Jefferson Davis. (Illus.). 696p. 1990. pap. 17.95 (*0-306-80418-2*) Da Capo.

***Rise & Fall of the Confederate Government, Vol. I.** 2nd deluxe unabridged ed. Jefferson Davis. (Illus.). 760p. 1997. reprint ed. 87.50 (*0-931709-08-3*) B Coats.

***Rise & Fall of the Confederate Government, Vol. I.** 2nd unabridged ed. Jefferson Davis. (Illus.). 760p. 1997. reprint ed. lib. bdg. 44.75 (*0-931709-05-9*) B Coats.

Rise & Fall of the Confederate Government, Vol. 2. Jefferson Davis. (Illus.). 636p. 1990. pap. 17.95 (*0-306-80419-0*) Da Capo.

***Rise & Fall of the Confederate Government, Vol. II.** 2nd deluxe unabridged ed. Jefferson Davis. (Illus.). 880p. 1997. reprint ed. 87.50 (*0-931709-09-1*) B Coats.

***Rise & Fall of the Confederate Government, Vol. II.** 2nd unabridged ed. Jefferson Davis. (Illus.). 880p. 1997. reprint ed. lib. bdg. 44.75 (*0-931709-06-7*) B Coats.

***Rise & Fall of the Confederate Government, Vols. I & II.** 2nd deluxe unabridged ed. Jefferson Davis. 1640p. 1997. reprint ed. 175.00 (*0-931709-10-5*) B Coats.

***Rise & Fall of the Confederate Government, Vols. I & II.** 2nd unabridged ed. Jefferson Davis. 1640p. 1997. reprint ed. 89.50 (*0-931709-07-5*) B Coats.

Rise & Fall of the Dragon King. Lynn Abbey. 1996. pap. 5.99 (*0-7869-0476-3*) TSR Inc.

Rise & Fall of the East India Company: A Sociological Appraisal. Ramkrishna Mukherjee. LC 73-90082. 461p. reprint ed. pap. 131.40 (*0-7837-3919-2*, 2043767) Bks Demand.

Rise & Fall of the Elites: An Application of Theoretical Sociology. Vilfredo Pareto. Ed. by Lewis A. Coser & Walter W. Powell. LC 79-7011. (Perennial Works in Sociology). 1980. reprint ed. lib. bdg. 19.95 (*0-405-12110-5*) Ayer.

Rise & Fall of the Ethnic Revival: Perspectives on Language & Ethnicity. Joshua A. Fishman. (Contributions to the Sociology of Language Ser.: No. 37). xvi, 531p. 1985. 123.10 (*3-11-011260-4*); pap. 38.95 (*0-685-12395-2*) Mouton.

Rise & Fall of the "Fifth Force" Discovery, Pursuit, & Justification in Modern Physics. Allan Franklin. LC 92-43551. 1993. write for info. (*1-56396-119-9*) Am Inst Physics.

Rise & Fall of the French Revolution. Ed. by Timothy C. W. Blanning. (Studies in European History from the Journal of Modern History). 476p. 1996. pap. 22.50 (*0-226-05692-9*); lib. bdg. 42.00 (*0-226-05691-0*) U Ch Pr.

Rise & Fall of the Grand Alliance, 1941-1945. Ed. by Ann Lane & Howard Temperley. LC 95-13886. 1996. text ed. 65.00 (*0-312-12674-3*) St Martin.

Rise & "Fall" of the Great American Novel. Lawrence Buell. (12th James Russell Wiggins Lecture in the History of the Book in American Culture Ser.). 23p. 1995. pap. 6.00 (*0-944026-62-1*) Am Antiquarian.

Rise & Fall of the Great Cities: Aspects of Urbanization in the Western World. Ed. by Richard Lawton. LC 00-89. 185p. 1992. text ed. 43.95 (*0-470-21896-7*) Halsted Pr.

Rise & Fall of the Great Powers: Economic Change & Military Conflict from 1500 to 2000. Paul M. Kennedy. LC 87-9690. 480p. 1987. 24.95 (*0-394-54674-1*) Random.

Rise & Fall of the Great Powers: Economic Change & Military Conflict from 1500 to 2000. Paul M. Kennedy. 1988. pap. 16.00 (*0-679-72019-7*, Vin) Random.

Rise & Fall of the Grenvilles: The Dukes of Buckingham & Chandos, 1710-1921. John Beckett. LC 93-11675. 1994. text ed. 79.95 (*0-7190-3756-5*, Pub. by Manchester Univ Pr UK); text ed. 29.95 (*0-7190-3757-3*, Pub. by Manchester Univ Pr UK) St Martin.

Rise & Fall of the Horror Film. David Soren. (Illus.). 103p. (C). 1995. pap. 10.00 (*1-887664-00-9*) Midnght Marquee Pr.

Rise & Fall of the Imperial Guptas. Ashvini Agrawal. (C). 1989. 26.00 (*81-208-0592-5*, Pub. by Motilal Banarsidass II) S Asia.

Rise & Fall of the Jewish Gangster in America. rev. ed. Albert Fried. 1994. pap. 16.50 (*0-231-09683-6*) Col U Pr.

***Rise & Fall of the Kingdom: Draw Your Way Through the Bible.** Dan Peters. (Picturethis! Ser.: No. 3). (Illus.). 60p. 1997. ring bd. write for info. (*1-890598-09-7*) PictureThis.

Rise & Fall of the Kushana Empire. B. N. Mukherjee. (C). 1988. 96.00 (*0-8364-2393-3*, Pub. by Firma KLM II) S Asia.

Rise & Fall of the Labour Left. Patrick Seyd. LC 87-16710. 256p. 1988. text ed. 35.00 (*0-312-01298-5*) St Martin.

Rise & Fall of the Man of Letters: English Literary Life since 1800. rev. ed. John Gross. 372p. 1992. pap. text ed. 14.95 (*1-56663-000-2*, Elephant Paperbacks) I R Dee.

Rise & Fall of the Mustache. Robert J. Burdette. LC 71-91074. (American Humorists Ser.). 1878. reprint ed. lib. bdg. 19.50 (*0-8398-0179-3*) Irvington.

Rise & Fall of the Mustache & Other Hawk - Eyetems. Robert J. Burdette. LC 88-23013. (Iowa Heritage Collection). (Illus.). 328p. 1988. reprint ed. pap. 9.95 (*0-8138-0138-9*) Iowa St U Pr.

***Rise & Fall of the New Deal Order.** Peter Friedlander. Date not set. 19.95 (*0-465-07032-9*); pap. 15.00 (*0-465-07015-9*) Basic.

Rise & Fall of the New Deal Order, 1930-1980. Ed. by Seve Fraser & Gary Gerstle. 336p. 1989. pap. text ed. 16.95 (*0-691-00607-5*) Princeton U Pr.

Rise & Fall of the New Deal Order, 1930-1980. Ed. by Steve Fraser & Gary Gerstle. LC 88-39842. 337p. reprint ed. pap. 96.10 (*0-8357-7890-8*, 2036309) Bks Demand.

Rise & Fall of the Nicaraguan Revolution. Mary-Alice Waters. 324p. (Orig.). 1994. pap. 14.00 (*0-87348-750-8*) Pathfinder NY.

Rise & Fall of the People's Colleges: The Westfield Normal School, 1839 to 1914. Robert T. Brown. (Illus.). 170p. 1988. 10.00 (*0-685-44692-1*) WSC Inst MA Studies.

Rise & Fall of the Philippine Republic see Filipinos Fight for Freedom

Rise & Fall of the Plantation Complex: Essays in Atlantic History. Philip D. Curtin. (Cambridge Studies in Comparative World History). (Illus.). 224p. (C). 1990. text ed. 54.95 (*0-521-37475-8*); pap. text ed. 15.95 (*0-521-37616-5*) Cambridge U Pr.

***Rise & Fall of the Plantation Complex: Essays in Atlantic History.** 2nd ed. Philip D. Curtin. (Studies in Comparative World History). (Illus.). 234p. (C). 1997. write for info. (*0-521-62076-7*) Cambridge U Pr.

***Rise & Fall of the Plantation Complex: Essays in Atlantic History.** 2nd ed. Philip D. Curtin. (Studies in Comparative World History). (Illus.). 234p. (C). 1997. pap. write for info. (*0-521-62943-8*) Cambridge U Pr.

***Rise & Fall of the Political Press in Britain Vol. 2: The Twentieth Century.** Stephen E. Koss. LC 81-1707. 736p. 1984. reprint ed. pap. 180.00 (*0-608-02803-7*, 2063870) Bks Demand.

***Rise & Fall of the Powhatan Empire: Indians in Seventeenth-Century Virginia.** James Axtell. (Foundations of America Ser.). (Illus.). 42p. 1995. pap. 9.95 (*0-87935-153-5*) Colonial Williamsburg.

Rise & Fall of the Romanovs. Anatole G. Mazour. (Anvil Ser.). 190p. (Orig.). 1960. reprint ed. pap. 11.50 (*0-685-07020-4*) Krieger.

Rise & Fall of the Rural Communist Party, 1927-1939. Daniel Thorniley. 300p. 1988. text ed. 49.95 (*0-312-01360-4*) St Martin.

Rise & Fall of the Saturday Globe. Ralph Frasca. LC 89-40761. (Illus.). 208p. 1992. 36.50 (*0-945636-16-4*) Susquehanna U Pr.

Rise & Fall of the Second Empire, 1852-1871. Alain Plessis. Tr. by Jonathan Mandelbaum. (Cambridge History of Modern France Ser.: No. 3). (Illus.). 210p. 1988. pap. text ed. 18.95 (*0-521-35856-6*) Cambridge U Pr.

***Rise & Fall of the Shah.** Amin Saikal. LC 80-7462. (Illus.). 294p. 1980. reprint ed. pap. 83.80 (*0-608-02585-2*, 2063231) Bks Demand.

Rise & Fall of the Soviet Empire. Stephen Dalziel. (Illus.). 160p. 1993. 14.98 (*0-8317-7368-5*) Smithmark.

***Rise & Fall of the Soviet Empire.** Pearson. LC 96-52562. 1997. text ed. 55.00 (*0-312-17405-5*) St Martin.

***Rise & Fall of the Soviet Empire.** Pearson. LC 96-52562. 1997. text ed. 19.95 (*0-312-17407-1*) St Martin.

Rise & Fall of the Soviet Politburo. James R. Ozinga et al. LC 91-29623. 256p. 1992. text ed. 39.95 (*0-312-04784-3*) St Martin.

Rise & Fall of the Soviet Threat. Alan Wolfe. LC 83-51285. 145p. 1984. 25.00 (*0-89608-207-5*); pap. 9.00 (*0-89608-206-7*) South End Pr.

Rise & Fall of the Soviet Union. Michael G. Kort. (Illus.). 144p. (YA). (gr. 9-12). 1992. lib. bdg. 22.70 (*0-531-11040-0*) Watts.

Rise & Fall of the Soviet Union: A Selected Bibliography of Sources in English. Ed. by Abraham J. Edelheit. LC 92-24470. (Bibliographies & Indexes in World History Ser.: No. 27). 448p. 1992. text ed. 75.00 (*0-313-28625-6*, ERF) Greenwood.

Rise & Fall of the Sportswoman Vol. 180: Women's Health, Fitness, & Athletics, 1860-1940. Gregory K. Stanley. (American University Studies: Ser. IX). 168p. (C). 1996. text ed. 35.95 (*0-8204-2882-5*) P Lang Pubng.

***Rise & Fall of the Suburban Dream: 1945 to the Present.** Elizabeth Ewen. 352p. 1997. 23.00 (*0-465-07045-0*) Basic.

***Rise & Fall of the Suburban Dream: 1945 to the Present.** Elizabeth Ewen. 1998. pap. 15.00 (*0-465-07013-2*) Basic.

Rise & Fall of the Third Party. William B. Hesseltine. 1992. 14.50 (*0-8446-1237-5*) Peter Smith.

Rise & Fall of the Third Reich. William L. Shirer. 1264p. 1990. pap. 16.00 (*0-671-72868-7*) S&S Trade.

Rise & Fall of the Third Reich. William L. Shirer. 1991. reprint ed. lib. bdg. 45.95 (*1-56849-087-9*) Buccaneer Bks.

Rise & Fall of the Third Reich: A History of Nazi Germany. William L. Shirer. 1987. 17.95 (*0-671-08912-9*) S&S Trade.

Rise & Fall of the Third Reich: A History of Nazi Germany. abr. ed. William L. Shirer. (Illus.). 256p. 1994. 19.99 (*0-517-10294-3*) Random Hse Value.

Rise & Fall of the Third Reich: A History of Nazi Germany. 30th ed. William L. Shirer. 1600p. 1991. mass mkt. 7.99 (*0-449-21977-1*, Crest) Fawcett.

Rise & Fall of the Toronto Typographical Union, 1831 - 1972: A Case Study of Foreign Domination. Sally F. Zerker. 407p. reprint ed. pap. 116.00 (*0-685-15862-4*, 2026377) Bks Demand.

Rise & Fall of the Toronto Typographical Union, 1832-1972: A Case Study in Foreign Domination. Sally F. Zerker. 416p. 1982. pap. 17.95 (*0-8020-6431-0*) U of Toronto Pr.

Rise & Fall of the Victorian Servant. Pamela Horn. (Illus.). 224p. 1989. 30.00 (*0-86299-819-0*, Pub. by Sutton Pubng UK); pap. 13.00 (*0-86299-296-6*, Pub. by Sutton Pubng UK) Bks Intl VA.

Rise & Fall of the White Republic: Class Politics & Mass Culture in Nineteenth Century America. Alexander Saxton. 480p. (C). 1991. pap. text ed. 23.00 (*0-86091-986-2*, A4496, Pub. by Vrso UK) Norton.

***Rise & Fall of the Zulu Nation.** John Laband. 1997. 39.95 (*1-85409-421-1*, Pub. by Arms & Armour UK) Sterling.

Rise & Fall of Third Leg. Jon Longhi. 160p. (Orig.). 1994. pap. 9.95 (*0-916397-27-0*) Manic D Pr.

Rise & fall of UNESCO. S. Nihal Singh. LC 87-51509. 150p. (C). 1988. 25.00 (*0-913215-30-9*) Riverdale Co.

Rise & Fall of Weimar Democracy. Hans Mommsen. Ed. by Larry E. Jones. Tr. by Elborg Forster & Larry E. Jones from GER. LC 95-8902. 608p. (GER.). (C). 1996. text ed. 65.00 (*0-8078-2249-3*) U of NC Pr.

Rise & Fall Soviet Union. Tatyana Nestorova. 176p. 1993. per. 31.44 (*0-8403-8467-X*) Kendall-Hunt.

Rise & Fulfilment of British Rule in India. Edward J. Thompson & Geoffrey T. Garratt. LC 70-137299. reprint ed. 49.50 (*0-404-06395-0*) AMS Pr.

Rise & Growth of American Politics. 2nd ed. Henry J. Ford. LC 67-23377. (Law, Politics & History Ser.). 1967. reprint ed. lib. bdg. 35.00 (*0-306-70946-5*) Da Capo.

Rise & Growth of the Anglican Schism. Nicolas Sander. Tr. by David Lewis from LAT. LC 88-50849. 528p. 1988. reprint ed. pap. 20.00 (*0-89555-347-3*) TAN Bks Pubs.

Rise & Growth of the Colonial Port Cities in Asia. Ed. by Dilip K. Basu. LC 85-11095. (Monographs: No. 25). (Illus.). 332p. (Orig.). 1985. lib. bdg. 56.00 (*0-8191-4761-3*) U Pr of Amer.

Rise & Organisation of the Achaemenid Empire: The Eastern Iranian Evidence. W. J. Vogelsang. LC 92-22967. (Studies in the History of the Ancient Near East: Vol. 3). (Illus.). xii, 344p. 1992. 115.00 (*90-04-09682-5*) E J Brill.

Rise & Progress of Assyriology. Ernest A. Budge. LC 73-18849. (Illus.). reprint ed. 37.50 (*0-404-11340-0*) AMS Pr.

Rise & Progress of Negro Colleges in Georgia, 1865-1949. Willard Range. LC 51-14571. (University of Georgia Phelps-Stokes Fellowship Studies: No. 15). 264p. reprint ed. pap. 75.30 (*0-318-34878-0*, 2031088) Bks Demand.

Rise & Progress of Revolution. Alexander Addison. 1979. lib. bdg. 59.95 (*0-8490-3000-5*) Gordon Pr.

Rise & Progress of the English Constitution. 16th ed. Edward Creasy. xii, 400p. 1986. reprint ed. lib. bdg. 37.50 (*0-8377-0450-2*) Rothman.

Rise & Progress of the Kingdoms of Light & Darkness. Lorenzo D. Blackson. LC 72-78568. (Illus.). 288p. reprint ed. lib. bdg. 29.50 (*0-8398-0166-1*) Irvington.

Rise & Progress of the People Called Quakers. William Penn. (C). 1988. 75.00 (*0-913408-32-8*, Pub. by W Sessions UK) St Mut.

Rise & Progress of the Standard Oil Company. Gilbert H. Montague. LC 73-2525. (Big Business; Economic Power in a Free Society Ser.). 1973. reprint ed. 15.95 (*0-405-05104-2*) Ayer.

Rise & Repression of Radical Labor, U. S. A., Eighteen Seventy-Seven to Nineteen Eighteen. Daniel R. Fusfeld. (Illus.). (Orig.). 1979. pap. text ed. 4.95 (*0-88286-051-8*) C H Kerr.

Rise & Rise of Daniel Rocket. Peter Parnell. 1984. pap. 5.25 (*0-8222-0956-X*) Dramatists Play.

***Rise & Rise of David Geffen.** Stephen Singular. LC 97-20553. 1997. write for info. (*1-55972-430-7*) Carol Pub Group.

Rise & Rise of Road Transport, 1700-1900. Theo Barker & Dorian Gerhold. (New Studies in Economic & Social History: No. 21). 94p. (C). 1995. text ed. 34.95 (*0-521-55280-X*) Cambridge U Pr.

Rise & Rise of Road Transport, 1700-1900. Theo Barker & Dorian Gerhold. (New Studies in Economic & Social History: No. 21). 94p. (C). 1996. pap. text ed. 10.95 (*0-521-55773-9*) Cambridge U Pr.

Rise & Rule of Tamerlane. Beatrice F. Manz. (Studies in Islamic Civilization). (Illus.). 250p. (C). 1989. text ed. 69.95 (*0-521-34595-2*) Cambridge U Pr.

Rise & Rule of Tamerlane. Beatrice F. Manz. (Studies in Islamic Civilization). (Illus.). 238p. (C). 1991. pap. text ed. 20.95 (*0-521-40614-5*) Cambridge U Pr.

Rise & Shine. Alma Barkman. (Quiet Time Books for Women). (Orig.). 1987. pap. 4.99 (*0-8024-7387-3*) Moody.

Rise & Shine. Raffi. (J). (ps-3). 1996. 16.00 (*0-517-70939-2*); lib. bdg. 17.99 (*0-517-70940-6*) Crown Bks Yng Read.

Rise & Shine. Jolene Thompson. 100p. 1989. pap. text ed. 6.50 (*1-56770-214-7*) S Scheewe Pubns.

Rise & Shine: Sesame Street. Constance Allen. (J). (ps-3). 1996. pap. text ed. 3.95 (*0-307-10035-9*, Golden Pr) Western Pub.

Rise & Shine see Bride: Renewing Our Passion for the Church

Rise & Shine - Block Book. Snapshot Staff. 22p. (J). 1996. 3.95 (*0-7894-0624-1*) DK Pub Inc.

***Rise & Shine Bunny.** Susan Talkington. (Illus.). (J). 1997. 3.95 (*1-57719-114-5*) GT Pubng Corp.

Rise & Shine, Mariko-Chan! Chiyoko Tomioka. (Illus.). 32p. (J). (ps-1). 1992. pap. 3.95 (*0-590-45507-9*) Scholastic Inc.

Rise Corrupt & Coming Fall of the House of Saud. Said K. Aburish. 326p. 1996. pap. 15.95 (*0-312-16119-0*) St Martin.

Rise, Corruption & Coming Fall of the House of Saud. Said K. Aburish. (Illus.). 336p. 1995. 24.95 (*0-312-12541-0*) St Martin.

***Rise, Corruption & Coming Fall of the House of Saud.** Said K. Aburish. (Illus.). 326p. 1996. pap. 15.95 (*0-614-19279-X*) St Martin.

Rise, Decline & Fall of the Roman Religion. James B. Hannay. 251p. 1972. reprint ed. spiral bd. 14.00 (*0-7873-0369-0*) Hlth Research.

***Rise, Decline, & Renewal of Silicon Valley's High Technology Industry.** rev. ed. Dan M. Khanna. LC 96-49746. (Garland Studies on Industrial Productivity). (Illus.). 195p. 1997. text ed. 52.00 (*0-8153-2724-2*) Garland.

***Rise, Fall & Replacement of Industry-Wide Bargaining in the Basic Steel.** Garth L. Mangum et al. LC 96-41492. (Labor & Human Resources Ser.). 228p. (C). (gr. 13). 1996. text ed. 62.95 (*1-56324-982-0*); pap. text ed. 21.95 (*1-56324-983-9*) M E Sharpe.

Rise Fall of Liberal Government in Victorian Britain. Jonathan Parry. LC 93-5937. 392p. 1994. 45.00 (*0-300-05779-2*) Yale U Pr.

Rise from Want: A Peasant Family in the Machine Age. James C. Davis. LC 86-19228. (Illus.). 180p. 1986. text ed. 35.50 (*0-8122-8034-2*) U of Pa Pr.

***Rise from Want: A Peasant Family in the Machine Age.** James C. Davis. LC 86-19228. 183p. pap. 52.20 (*0-608-04821-6*, 2065478) Bks Demand.

RISE Manual & Self-Study Guide. Rick Flinders et al. LC 92-38499. 1992. write for info. (*0-9634762-0-3*) Rise Inst.

***Rise N Shine: Catholic Education & the African-American Community.** Charles A. Conwell et al. Ed. by Mary A. Chineworth. 90p. (Orig.). 1996. pap. 10.00 (*1-55833-177-8*) Natl Cath Educ.

Rise 'N Unite-The Black Man's Back. Khalid A. Al-Mansour. 985p. (Orig.). (C). 1995. pap. 29.95 (*1-883136-16-4*) First Afr Arabian.
RISE 'N UNITE, THE BLACK MAN'S BACK represents a literary accomplishment. The book's treatment of logic & reason is totally understandable & enjoyable. According to African American author 17 books, Dr. Khalid Abdullah Tariq Al-Mansour insists that the anchor to life & death has everything to do with the framework & competence for systematic reasoning. By using logic, the impossible becomes possible; self confidence & esteem flourish; global uncertainty becomes global brotherhood, peace, stability; political corruption becomes political & economic prosperity. The author successfully teaches the classes & masses alike how to reason correctly. In the process, the book examines marriage, comparative religion, the new world order, holistic medicine, solutions to crime, drugs, family abuse, the American school system, illegitimate political leadership, economic empowerment, music, television, movies, traditional values, Afrocentric perspectives, law & order & the prospects for 21st-century prosperity. Full of surprises, suspense & excitement, RISE uses everyday analyses to penetrate & dislodge forever barriers to the systematic study of logic. You can't afford to miss it! RISE is also available to individuals with Visa, Mastercard, Money Order or Check. 343 Sansome St., Suite 975, San Francisco, CA 94104-1316; 1-800-WORLD HI. ***Publisher Provided Annotation.***

Rise of a Gay & Lesbian Movement. Barry D. Adam. (Social Movements Past & Present Ser.). 200p. 1987. 24.95 (*0-8057-9714-9*, Twayne) Scribnrs Ref.

Rise of a Gay and Lesbian Movement. rev. ed. Barry D. Adam. LC 94-34364. (Social Movements Past & Present Ser.). 1995. 27.95 (*0-8057-3863-0*, Twayne); pap. 15.95 (*0-8057-3864-9*, Twayne) Scribnrs Ref.

Rise of a Merchant Prince Vol. 2: Serpentwar Saga. Raymond E. Feist. (Serpentwar Sage Ser.: Vol. 2). 448p. 1996. mass mkt. 6.50 (*0-380-72087-6*) Avon.

Rise of a New World Economic Power: Postwar Taiwan. Y. Dolly Hwang. LC 90-25219. (Contributions in Economics & Economic History Ser.: No. 121). 176p. 1991. text ed. 49.95 (*0-313-26518-6*, HWR/, Greenwood Pr) Greenwood.

Rise of a Party-State in Kenya: From Harambee! to Nyayo! Jennifer A. Widner. (C). 1992. 50.00 (*0-520-07624-9*) U CA Pr.

Rise of a Refugee God: Hong Kong's Wong Tai Sin. Graeme Lang & Lars Ragvald. LC 92-47422. 1993. pap. write for info. (*0-19-585744-5*) OUP.

Rise of a Refugee God: Hong Kong's Wong Tai Sin. Graeme Lang & Lars Ragvald. LC 92-47422. 224p. 1993. 65.00 (*0-19-585755-0*) OUP.

Rise of a Third Party: A Study in Crisis Politics. enl. ed. Maurice Pinard. LC 75-329930. 331p. reprint ed. pap. 94.40 (*0-7837-1146-8*, 2041675) Bks Demand.

***Rise of a University Teaching Hospital: A Leadership Perspective: The University of Iowa Hospitals & Clinics.** Samuel Levey. LC 96-36389. 618p. 1996. 48.00 (*1-56793-048-4*) Health Admin Pr.

Rise of American Air Power: The Creation of Armageddon. Michael S. Sherry. LC 86-19003. (Illus.). 435p. 1987. 20.00 (*0-300-03600-0*) Yale U Pr.

Rise of American Air Power: The Creation of Armageddon. Michael S. Sherry. LC 86-19003. 435p. (C). 1989. reprint ed. pap. 18.00 (*0-300-04414-3*) Yale U Pr.

Rise of American Civilization. Charles A. Beard. (History - United States Ser.). 824p. 1993. reprint ed. lib. bdg. 119.00 (*0-7812-4848-5*) Rprt Serv.

Rise of American Influence in Asia & the Pacific. Lawrence H. Battistini. LC 74-12576. 241p. 1974. reprint ed. text ed. 59.75 (*0-8371-7728-6*, BAAI, Greenwood Pr) Greenwood.

Rise of American Nationality 1811-1819. K. W. Babcock. LC 68-24970. (American History & Americana Ser.: No. 47). 1969. reprint ed. lib. bdg. 49.95 (*0-8383-0910-0*) M S G Haskell Hse.

Rise of American Philosophy: Cambridge, Massachusetts, 1868-1938. Bruce Kuklick. LC 76-49912. 707p. reprint ed. pap. 180.00 (0-8357-8310-3, 2033791) Bks Demand.

Rise of American Research Universities. Hugh D. Graham & Nancy Diamond. LC 96-30432. 296p. 1997. text ed. 39.95 (0-8018-5425-3) Johns Hopkins.

Rise of an American Business Corporation, Vol. 71. Richard S. Tedlow. (Fundamentals of Pure & Applied Economics Ser.). 71, xp. 1991. pap. text ed. 39.00 (3-7186-5088-6, Harwood Acad Pubs) Gordon & Breach.

Rise of Ancient Israel. Hershel Shanks et al. LC 92-53232. (Illus.). 166p. (C). 1992. text ed. 18.95 (1-880317-07-9, 7H42); pap. text ed. 11.95 (1-880317-05-2, 7H41) Biblical Arch Soc.

Rise of Ancient Israel, Set. LC 92-53232. 1992. audio 32.95 (1-880317-28-1) Biblical Arch Soc.

Rise of Anglo-American Friendship: A Study in World Politics, 1989-1906. Lionel M. Gelber. (History - United States Ser.). 292p. 1993. reprint ed. lib. bdg. 79.00 (0-7812-4864-7) Rprt Serv.

Rise of Anthropological Theory: A History of Theories of Culture. Marvin Harris. LC 68-17392. (C). 1968. text ed. 70.50 (0-690-70322-8) Addson-Wesley Educ.

Rise of Antichrist. Salem Kirban. 201p. 1995. pap. 6.99 (0-912582-29-4) AMG Pubs.

Rise of Architectural History. David Watkin. 136p. 1980. 16.95 (0-89860-040-5) Eastview.

Rise of Babylon: Sign of the End Times. Charles H. Dyer & Angela E. Hunt. (Illus.). 236p. 1991. pap. 8.99 (0-8423-5618-5) Tyndale.

***Rise of Baptist Republicanism.** Oran P. Smith. LC 97-4780. 1997. 38.50 (0-8147-8073-3) NYU Pr.

***Rise of Big Business.** Ed. by Mark Casson. (Origins of Business Economics Ser.). 2400p. (C). 1997. text ed. 35.00 (0-415-15087-6) Routledge.

Rise of Big Business. Ed. by Barry E. Supple. (International Library of Critical Writings in Business History: Vol. 5). 672p. 1992. 200.00 (1-85278-571-3) E Elgar.

Rise of Big Business & the Beginnings of Antitrust & Railroad Regulation, 1870-1900. Intro. by Robert F. Himmelberg. LC 93-47937. (Business & Government in America since 1870 Ser.: Vol. 1). 448p. 1994. text ed. 75.00 (0-8153-1403-5) Garland.

Rise of Big Business, 1865-1920. 2nd ed. Glenn Porter. Ed. by John H. Franklin & A. S. Eisenstadt. (American History Ser.). (Illus.). 120p. 1992. pap. text ed. write for info. (0-88295-882-8) Harlan Davidson.

***Rise of Big Government in the United States.** Harold G. Vatter & John F. Walker. LC 96-40286. 256p. (C). (gr. 13). 1997. text ed. 64.95 (0-7656-0066-8); pap. text ed. 24.95 (0-7656-0067-6) M E Sharpe.

***Rise of Birds: 225 Million Years of Evolution.** Sankar Chatterjee. LC 97-9474. 1998. write for info. (0-8018-5615-9) Johns Hopkins.

Rise of Brandenburg-Prussia to 1786. Sidney B. Fay & Klaus Epstein. LC 81-8334. (European Problem Studies). 156p. (C). 1981. reprint ed. pap. text ed. 11.50 (0-89874-377-X) Krieger.

Rise of Brandenburg-Prussian. Margaret Shennan. LC 95-7166. (Lancaster Pamphlets Ser.). 96p. (C). 1997. pap. 9.95 (0-415-12938-9) Routledge.

Rise of British West Africa. Claude George. 468p. 1968. 45.00 (0-7146-1667-2, Pub. by F Cass Pubs UK) Intl Spec Bk.

Rise of Candidate-Centered Politics: Presidential Elections of the 1980s. Martin P. Wattenberg. LC 90-36471. (Illus.). 186p. 1991. 29.00 (0-674-77130-3, WATRIS) HUP.

Rise of Candidate-Centered Politics: Presidential Elections of the 1980s. Martin P. Wattenberg. (Illus.). 200p. 1992. pap. 13.95 (0-674-77131-1) HUP.

***Rise of Capitalism on the Pampas: The Estancias of Buenos Aires, 1785-1870.** Samuel Amaral. (Latin American Studies: Vol. 83). (Illus.). 400p. (C). 1997. text ed. 59.95 (0-521-57248-7) Cambridge U Pr.

Rise of China: How Economic Reform Is Creating a New Superpower. William H. Overholdt. 1994. pap. 14.00 (0-393-31245-3) Norton.

Rise of China: How Economic Reform Is Creating a New Superpower. William H. Overholt. LC 93-4634. 1993. 25.00 (0-393-03533-6) Norton.

Rise of Chinese Military Power, 1895-1912. Ralph L. Powell. LC 55-6247. 393p. reprint ed. pap. 112.10 (0-317-08480-1, 2000276) Bks Demand.

Rise of Christian Democracy in Europe. Stathis N. Kalyvas. LC 96-5600. (Wilder House Series in Politics, History, & Culture). (Illus.). 312p. 1996. 45.00 (0-8014-3241-3); pap. 19.95 (0-8014-8320-4) Cornell U Pr.

Rise of Christian Europe. Hugh R. Trevor-Roper. (Library of World Civilization). (Illus.). 216p. (Orig.). (C). 1989. pap. text ed. 9.95 (0-393-95802-7) Norton.

Rise of Christianity. W. H. Frend. LC 83-48909. (Illus.). 1026p. 1984. pap. 34.00 (0-8006-1931-5, 1-1931, Fortress Pr) Augsburg Fortress.

***Rise of Christianity.** Rodney Stark. LC 97-5535. 1997. pap. text ed. 14.00 (0-06-067701-5) Harper SF.

Rise of Christianity: A Sociologist Reconsiders History. Rodney Stark. 288p. 1996. text ed. 24.95 (0-691-02749-8) Princeton U Pr.

Rise of Cities. Time-Life Books Editors. (Time Frame Ser.). (Illus.). 176p. 1991. write for info. (0-8094-6487-X); lib. bdg. write for info. (0-8094-6488-8) Time-Life.

Rise of Civilization in India & Pakistan. Bridget Allchin & Raymond Allchin. LC 82-1262. (World Archaeology Ser.). (Illus.). 352p. 1982. pap. text ed. 38.95 (0-521-28550-X) Cambridge U Pr.

Rise of Collectivism see British Political Tradition

Rise of Colleges: Institutions of Learning in Islam & the West. George Makdisi. 377p. 1982. 50.00 (0-85224-375-8, Pub. by Edinburgh U Pr UK) Col U Pr.

Rise of Commercial Banking Series, 60 bks. Ed. by Stuart Bruchey & Vincent P. Carosso. 1981. lib. bdg. 794.00 (0-405-13626-9) Ayer.

Rise of Common Man: Eighteen Thirty to Eighteen Fifty. Carl R. Fish. LC 83-8561. (Illus.). xix, 391p. 1983. reprint ed. text ed. 65.00 (0-313-24065-5, FIRI, Greenwood Pr) Greenwood.

Rise of Confucian Ritualism in Late Imperial China: Ethics, Classics, & Lineage Discourse. Kai-Wing Chow. LC 93-16633. xii, 344p. (C). 1994. 45.00 (0-8047-2173-4) Stanford U Pr.

***Rise of Confucian Ritualism in Late Imperial China: Ethics, Classics & Lineage Discourse.** Kai-Wing Chow. 1996. pap. text ed. 19.95 (0-8047-2791-0) Stanford U Pr.

Rise of Consumer Society in Britain, 1880-1980. John Benson. LC 93-41571. (Themes in British Social History Ser.). (C). 1994. text ed. 56.50 (0-582-07289-1, Pub. by Longman UK) Longman.

Rise of Consumer Society in Britain, 1880-1980. John Benson. LC 93-41571. (Themes in British Social History Ser.). (C). 1995. pap. text ed. 25.50 (0-582-07288-3, Pub. by Longman UK) Longman.

Rise of Cotton Mills in the South. 2nd ed. Intro. by Broadus Mitchell. LC 68-8128. (American Scene Ser.). 1968. reprint ed. lib. bdg. 37.50 (0-306-71141-9) Da Capo.

Rise of Cotton Mills in the South. Broadus Mitchell. LC 78-63974. (Johns Hopkins University. Studies in the Social Sciences. Thirtieth Ser. 1912: 2). reprint ed. 37.50 (0-404-61219-9) AMS Pr.

Rise of David Duke. Tyler Bridges. (Illus.). 308p. 1994. 24.95 (0-87805-678-5) U Pr of Miss.

Rise of David Duke. Tyler Bridges. (Illus.). 320p. 1995. pap. 15.95 (0-87805-684-X) U Pr of Miss.

Rise of David Levinsky. Abraham Cahan. 1976. pap. text ed. 15.00 (0-06-131912-0, TB1912, Torch) HarpC.

Rise of David Levinsky. Abraham Cahan. Ed. & Intro. by Jules Chametzky. 544p. 1993. pap. 12.95 (0-14-018687-5, Penguin Classics) Viking Penguin.

Rise of Devon Seaside Resorts. Travis. (Exeter Maritime Studies). (Illus.). 256p. 1993. text ed. 49.95 (0-85989-392-8, Pub. by Univ Exeter Pr UK) Northwestern U Pr.

Rise of Early Modern Science: Islam, China, & the West. Toby E. Huff. LC 92-36531. (Illus.). 350p. (C). 1993. 65.00 (0-521-43496-3) Cambridge U Pr.

Rise of Early Modern Science: Islam, China, & the West. Toby E. Huff. (Illus.). 420p. (C). 1995. pap. text ed. 18.95 (0-521-49833-3) Cambridge U Pr.

***Rise of East Asia: Critical Visions of the Pacific Century.** Mark T. Berger & Douglas A. Borer. LC 96-43154. 344p. (C). 1997. pap. write for info. (0-415-16168-1); text ed. write for info. (0-415-16167-3) Routledge.

Rise of Ecclesiastical Control in Quebec. Walter A. Riddell. (Columbia University. Studies in the Social Sciences: No. 174). reprint ed. 22.50 (0-404-51174-0) AMS Pr.

Rise of Egyptian Communism, 1939-1970. Selma Botman. LC 88-4916. (Contemporary Issues in the Middle East Ser.). 168p. 1988. text ed. 42.50 (0-8156-2443-3) Syracuse U Pr.

Rise of Elevators. Eric A. Radford. (Orig.). 1996. mass mkt. 4.99 (1-55197-127-5, Pub. by Comnwlth Pub CN) Partners Pubs Grp.

Rise of Embryology. Arthur W. Meyer. LC 40-3220. (Illus.). 115p. reprint ed. pap. 30.00 (0-318-39758-7, 2033132) Bks Demand.

***Rise of Endymion.** Dan Simmons. LC 97-5658. 1997. 23.95 (0-553-10652-X, Spectra) Bantam.

Rise of English Culture. Ed. by E. Johnson. 1984. lib. bdg. 90.00 (0-8490-3238-5) Gordon Pr.

Rise of Eurasiansim. Milan Hauner. 60p. 1996. pap. text ed. 12.95 (1-899658-19-X, Pub. by Royal Inst Intl Affairs UK) Brookings.

Rise of Eurocentrism: Anatomy of Interpretation. Vassilis Lambropoulos. 480p. 1992. text ed. 45.00 (0-691-06949-2) Princeton U Pr.

Rise of European Liberalism. Harold J. Laski. LC 96-20337. 320p. (Orig.). 1996. pap. text ed. 22.95 (1-56000-845-8) Transaction Pubs.

Rise of European Liberalism: An Essay in Interpretation. Harold J. Laski. LC 83-45444. reprint ed. 31.50 (0-404-20152-0) AMS Pr.

Rise of European Music, 1380-1500. Reinhard Strohm. (Illus.). 700p. (C). 1994. text ed. 95.00 (0-521-41745-7) Cambridge U Pr.

Rise of European Regionalism. Christopher T. Harvie. LC 93-13819. (Historical Connections Ser.). 96p. (C). 1994. pap. 11.95 (0-415-09523-9, B2472) Routledge.

Rise of Experimentation in American Psychology. Jill G. Morawski. LC 87-18154. 256p. (C). 1988. text ed. 30.00 (0-300-04153-5) Yale U Pr.

Rise of Fallen Angels: Victory over the Adversary Through Spiritual Renewal. Mark I. Bubeck. 1995. pap. 11.99 (0-8024-7189-7) Moody.

Rise of Fascism. 2nd ed. Francis L. Carsten. LC 80-51592. 1980. pap. 15.95 (0-520-04643-9) U CA Pr.

Rise of Fernando Cortes. H. R. Wagner. (Cortes Society Ser.: Vol. 3). 1944. 70.00 (0-527-19733-5) Periodicals Srv.

Rise of Financial Capitalism: International Capital Markets in the Age of Reason. Larry Neal. (Studies in Monetary & Financial History). (Illus.). 288p. (C). 1991. text ed. 54.95 (0-521-38205-X) Cambridge U Pr.

Rise of Financial Capitalism: International Capital Markets in the Age of Reason. Larry Neal. (Studies in Monetary & Financial History). (Illus.). 288p. (C). 1993. pap. text ed. 17.95 (0-521-45738-6) Cambridge U Pr.

Rise of Fishes: 500 Million Years of Evolution. John A. Long. LC 94-24692. (Illus.). 224p. 1995. text ed. 65.00 (0-8018-4992-6) Johns Hopkins.

Rise of Fishes: 500 Million Years of Evolution. John A. Long. (Illus.). 224p. 1996. reprint ed. pap. text ed. 34.95 (0-8018-5438-5) Johns Hopkins.

Rise of Free Trade. Cheryl Schonhardt-Bailey. LC 96-22601. 1696p. (C). 1997. text ed. write for info. (0-415-14031-5) Routledge.

Rise of French Liberal Thought: A Study of Political Ideas from Bayle to Condorcet. 2nd ed. Kingsley Martin. Ed. by J. P. Mayer. LC 80-11662. xviii, 316p. 1980. reprint ed. text ed. 59.75 (0-313-22368-8, MARF, Greenwood Pr) Greenwood.

Rise of Functional Categories. Elly Van Gelderen. LC 93-33219. (Linguistik Aktuell (LA) Ser.: No. 9). x, 224p. 1993. 59.00 (1-55619-227-4) Benjamins North Am.

Rise of General Bonaparte. Spenser Wilkinson. (Modern Revivals in Military History Ser.). 192p. 1992. 61.95 (0-7512-0039-5, Pub. by Gregg Revivals UK) Ashgate Pub Co.

Rise of Grammatical Categories: Cognition & Language Change in Africa. Bernd Heine. (Hans Wolff Memorial Lecture Ser.). 22p. 1986. pap. text ed. 5.00 (0-941934-49-7) Indiana Africa.

Rise of Guardian Democracy: The Supreme Court's Role in Voting Rights Disputes, 1845-1969. Ward E. Elliott. LC 73-90611. (Harvard Political Studies). 410p. reprint ed. pap. 116.90 (0-7837-3841-2, 2043663) Bks Demand.

Rise of Historical Sociology. Dennis Smith. 244p. (C). 1991. 59.95 (0-87722-919-8); pap. 19.95 (0-87722-920-1) Temple U Pr.

Rise of Hotel Chains in the United States, 1896-1980. Paul L. Ingram. LC 96-25078. (Garland Studies in Entrepreneurship). 163p. 1996. text ed. 47.00 (0-8153-2649-1) Garland.

Rise of Humane Value. Marcus Z. Yo. 1995. 18.95 (0-533-11271-0) Vantage.

Rise of Humanism in Classical Islam & the Christian West. George Makdisi. 448p. 1990. 80.00 (0-85224-630-7, Pub. by Edinburgh U Pr UK) Col U Pr.

***Rise of Humanism in Classical Islam & the Christian West.** George Makdisi. 450p. 1996. 49.50 (0-614-21238-3, 1083) Kazi Pubns.

Rise of Independent Study: The Politics & the Philosophy of an Educational Innovation, 1970-1987. Derek Robbins. 160p. 1988. 95.00 (0-335-15848-X, Open Univ Pr) Taylor & Francis.

Rise of Informal Logic: Essays on Argumentation, Critical Thinking, Reasoning & Culture. Ralph H. Johnson & J. Anthony Blair. (Studies in Critical Thinking & Informal Logic: Vol. 2). 302p. 1996. 48.65 (0-916475-26-3) Vale Pr.

Rise of Instrumental Music & Concert Series in Paris, 1828-1871. Jeffrey Cooper. LC 83-1062. (Studies in Musicology: No. 65). (Illus.). 401p. reprint ed. pap. 114.30 (0-8357-1403-9, 2070479) Bks Demand.

Rise of Intelligence & Culture. SETI Institute Staff. (Life in the Universe Ser.). xxvii, 277p. (J). (gr. 5-6). 1995. pap. text ed. 26.00 (1-56308-326-4); trans. 25.00 (1-56308-414-7, A264) Teacher Ideas Pr.

Rise of Intelligence & Culture, Classroom kit: book, transparencies & poster. SETI Institute Staff. (Life in the Universe Ser.). (J). (gr. 5-6). 1995. trans. 50.00 (1-56308-415-5, B264) Teacher Ideas Pr.

Rise of Islam. John Child. LC 94-37633. (Biographical History Ser.). (Illus.). 64p. (YA). (gr. 5 up). 1995. lib. bdg. 17.95 (0-87226-116-6) P Bedrick Bks.

Rise of Islam. Richard Tames. LC 95-20616. (History Ser.). (Illus.). (J). 1996. lib. bdg. write for info. (1-57572-010-8) Rigby Interact Libr.

Rise of Islam & the Bengal Frontier, 1204-1760. Richard M. Eaton. LC 92-34002. (Comparative Studies on Muslim Societies: No. 17). 1993. 50.00 (0-520-08077-7) U CA Pr.

Rise of Islam & the Bengal Frontier, 1204-1760. Richard M. Eaton. LC 92-34002. (Comparative Studies on Muslim Societies: Vol. 17). (Illus.). 388p. (C). 1996. pap. 18.95 (0-520-20507-3) U CA Pr.

Rise of Islamic Fundamentalism: Sunnis & Shias. 1991. lib. bdg. 79.95 (0-8490-4622-X) Gordon Pr.

Rise of Italian Fascism, 1918-1922. A. Rossi. 1975. 300.00 (0-87968-435-6) Gordon Pr.

Rise of Japan & the Pacific Rim. Stewart Ross. LC 95-17257. (Causes & Consequences Ser.). 80p. (YA). (gr. 7 up). 1995. lib. bdg. 27.11 (0-8172-4054-3) Raintree Steck-V.

Rise of Labour: The British Labour Party 1890-1979. Keith Laybourn. 192p. 1991. 34.95 (0-7131-6600-2, A3045, Pub. by E Arnold UK) Routledge Chapman & Hall.

Rise of Landscape Painting in France: Corot to Monet. Kermit S. Champa. (Illus.). 232p. 1992. pap. 29.95 (0-8109-2520-6) Abrams.

Rise of Life: The First Three & a Half Billion Years. John Reater. 1990. 14.99 (0-517-05173-7) Random Hse Value.

Rise of Life on Earth. Joyce Carol Oates. LC 90-48706. 144p. 1991. 16.95 (0-8112-1171-1) New Directions.

Rise of Life on Earth. Joyce Carol Oates. LC 90-48706. 144p. 1992. pap. 9.95 (0-8112-1213-0, NDP746) New Directions.

Rise of Local School Supervision in Massachusetts. Henry Suzzallo. LC 70-89241. (American Education: Its Men, Institutions, & Ideas. Series 1). 1970. reprint ed. 15.95 (0-405-01478-3) Ayer.

Rise of Local School Supervision in Massachusetts (the School Committee, 1635-1827) Henry Suzzallo. LC 70-177735. (Columbia University. Teachers College. Contributions to Education Ser.: No. 3). reprint ed. 37.50 (0-404-55003-7) AMS Pr.

Rise of Los Angeles As an American Bibliographical Center. Kevin Starr. (Coulter Lecture 1988 Ser.). 37p. 1989. pap. text ed. 5.95 (0-929722-26-4) CA State Library Fndtn.

Rise of Magic in Early Medieval Europe. Valerie I. Flint. 406p. 1991. text ed. 65.00 (0-691-03165-7) Princeton U Pr.

Rise of Magic in Early Medieval Europe. Valerie I. Flint. 472p. (C). 1991. pap. text ed. 18.95 (0-691-00110-3) Princeton U Pr.

Rise of Man. Harold S. Cober. LC 95-1101. 1995. pap. 5.99 (1-877633-28-3) Luthers.

Rise of Managerial Computing: The Best of the Center for Information Systems Research. John F. Rockart & Christine V. Bullen. 350p. 1986. text ed. 45.00 (0-87094-757-5) Irwin Prof Pubng.

Rise of Marginal Voices: Gender Balance in the Workplace. Anne Statham. LC 96-9244. 400p. 1996. pap. text ed. 42.00 (0-7618-0445-5); lib. bdg. 62.00 (0-7618-0444-7) U Pr of Amer.

Rise of Market Culture: The Textile Trade & French Society, 1750-1900. William M. Reddy. (Illus.). 352p. 1984. 75.00 (0-521-25653-4) Cambridge U Pr.

Rise of Market Culture: The Textile Trade & French Society, 1750-1900. William M. Reddy. (Illus.). 352p. 1987. pap. 19.95 (0-521-34779-3) Cambridge U Pr.

Rise of Merchant Banking. Stanley Chapman. (Illus.). 240p. (C). 1984. text ed. 42.95 (0-04-332094-5) Routledge Chapman & Hall.

Rise of Merchant Banking. Stanley D. Chapman. (Modern Revivals in Economic & Social History Ser.). 235p. 1992. 61.95 (0-7512-0077-8, Pub. by Gregg Revivals UK) Ashgate Pub Co.

Rise of Merchant Empires: Long Distance Trade in the Early Modern World, 1350-1750. Ed. by James D. Tracy. (Studies in Comparative Early Modern History). 400p. (C). 1990. text ed. 23.95 (0-521-38210-6) Cambridge U Pr.

Rise of Merchant Empires: Long Distance Trade in the Early Modern World, 1350-1750. Ed. by James D. Tracy. (Studies in Comparative Early Modern History). 460p. (C). 1993. pap. text ed. 23.95 (0-521-45735-1) Cambridge U Pr.

Rise of Meso Government in Europe. Ed. by L. J. Sharpe. (Modern Politics Ser.: Vol. 32). (Illus.). 320p. (C). 1993. text ed. 65.00 (0-8039-8776-5) Sage.

Rise of Modern America: A History of the American People, 1890-1945. George D. Moss. LC 94-36595. 400p. 1994. pap. text ed. 32.00 (0-13-181587-3) P-H.

Rise of Modern Business in Great Britain, the United States, & Japan. Mansel G. Blackford. LC 87-10022. (Illus.). xiv, 176p. 1988. 29.95 (0-8078-1760-0); pap. 13.95 (0-8078-4202-8) U of NC Pr.

Rise of Modern China. Dorothy Morrison. 1988. pap. text ed. 13.98 (0-05-004183-5, 78260) Longman.

Rise of Modern China. 5th ed. Immanuel C. Hsu. (Illus.). 976p. (C). 1995. text ed. 44.95 (0-19-508720-8) OUP.

Rise of Modern Diplomacy, 1450-1919. M. S. Anderson. LC 92-34237. (C). 1993. text ed. 70.95 (0-582-21232-4) Longman.

Rise of Modern Diplomacy, 1450-1919. M. S. Anderson. LC 92-34237. (C). 1994. pap. text ed. 33.50 (0-582-21237-5) Longman.

Rise of Modern Industry. J. L. Hammond & Barbara Hammond. LC 74-30150. (World History Ser.: No. 48). 1974. lib. bdg. 75.00 (0-8383-1795-2) M S G Haskell Hse.

Rise of Modern Japan. William G. Beasley. 300p. 1990. text ed. 14.95 (0-312-04077-6) St Martin.

Rise of Modern Japan, 2 Vols. Duus. (C). Date not set. pap. 24.76 (0-395-74604-3) HM.

Rise of Modern Japan. Peter Duus. LC 75-33416. (Illus.). 304p. (C). 1976. text ed. 45.16 (0-395-20665-0) HM.

Rise of Modern Judaism: An Intellectual History of German Jewry 1650-1942. Heinz M. Graupe. LC 77-9059. 344p. 1979. lib. bdg. 32.50 (0-88275-395-9) Krieger.

Rise of Modern Judaism: An Intellectual History of German Jewry 1650-1942. Heinz M. Graupe. LC 77-9059. 344p. 1983. pap. text ed. 21.50 (0-89874-562-4) Krieger.

Rise of Modern Judicial Review: From Judicial Interpretation to Judge-Made Law. rev. ed. Christopher Wolfe. 1994. 58.50 (0-8476-7887-3) Littlefield.

Rise of Modern Mythology, Sixteen Hundred Eighty to Eighteen Hundred Sixty. Burton Feldman & Robert D. Richardson. LC 71-135005. 591p. reprint ed. pap. 168.50 (0-685-16265-6, 2056249) Bks Demand.

Rise of Modern Philosophy: The Tension Between the New & Traditional Philosophies. Ed. by Tom Sorell. LC 92-24022. 368p. (C). 1993. 75.00 (0-19-823953-X, Clarendon Pr) OUP.

Rise of Modern Philosophy: The Tension Between the New & Traditional Philosophies from Machiavelli to Leibniz. Ed. by Tom Sorell. 368p. 1995. pap. 23.00 (0-19-823605-0) OUP.

Rise of Modern Police & the European State System from Metternich to the Second World War. Hsi-Huey Liang. 448p. (C). 1992. text ed. 69.95 (0-521-43022-4) Cambridge U Pr.

Rise of Moralism. C. FitzSimons Allison. LC 84-61194. 262p. (Orig.). 1984. reprint ed. pap. 9.95 (0-8192-1353-5) Morehouse Pub.

Rise of Moscow's Power. Henryk Paszkiewicz. 1984. text ed. 80.00 (0-88033-036-8, 145) Col U Pr.

Rise of Multinationals in Continental Europe. Ed. by Geoffrey Jones & Harm G. Schroeter. (New Business History Ser.). 240p. 1993. 85.00 (1-85278-544-6) E Elgar.

Rise of Musical Classics in Eighteenth-Century England: A Study in Canon, Ritual, & Ideology. William Weber. LC 92-10567. 288p. 1992. 69.00 (0-19-816287-1, Clarendon Pr) OUP.

R

An Asterisk (*) at the beginning of an entry indicates that the title is appearing in BIP for the first time.

*Rise of Musical Classics in Eighteenth-Century England: A Study in Canon, Ritual, & Ideology.** William Weber. 288p. 1996. reprint ed. pap. 24.95 (0-19-816607-9) OUP.

Rise of National Socialism & the Working Classes in Weimar Germany. Ed. by Conan Fischer. LC 95-51054. 1996. 45.00 (1-57181-915-0) Berghahn Bks.

Rise of Nationalism in Central Africa: The Making of Malawi & Zambia, 1873-1964. Robert I. Rotberg. LC 65-19829. (Center for International Affairs Ser.). (Illus.). 362p. 1965. pap. 13.95 (0-674-77191-5, HP39) HUP.

Rise of Nations in the Soviet Union: American Foreign Policy & the Disintegration of the U. S. S. R. Ed. by Michael Mandelbaum. LC 91-418. 128p. 1991. reprint ed. pap. 36.50 (0-608-02002-8, 2062658) Bks Demand.

Rise of Neo-Kantianism: German Academic Philosophy Between Idealism & Positivism. Klaus C. Kohnke. Tr. by R. J. Hollingdale. (Ideas in Context Ser.: No. 20). (Illus.). 336p. (C). 1991. text ed. 69.95 (0-521-37336-0) Cambridge U Pr.

Rise of Neoconservatism. John Ehrman. LC 94-28386. 1995. 35.00 (0-300-06025-4) Yale U Pr.

Rise of Neoconservatism: Intellectuals & Foreign Affairs, 1945-1994. John Ehrman. 1996. pap. 14.00 (0-300-06870-0) Yale U Pr.

Rise of New York Port, 1815-1860. Robert G. Albion. LC 83-27190. 499p. 1984. reprint ed. text ed. 45.00 (0-930350-58-8); reprint ed. pap. text ed. 18.95 (0-930350-59-6) NE U Pr.

Rise of Normative Christianity. Arland J. Hultgren. LC 93-14307. 1994. 18.00 (0-8006-2645-1, Fortress Pr) Augsburg Fortress.

Rise of Organized Labor: Workers, Employers, & the Public Interest. James R. Giese. (Public Issues Ser.). (Illus.). 68p. (Orig.). 1989. teacher ed. 2.00 (0-89994-336-5); pap. 3.50 (0-89994-333-0) Soc Sci Ed.

Rise of Pennsylvania Protectionism. Malcolm R. Eiselen. LC 73-18438. (Perspectives in American History Ser.: No. 8). 287p. 1974. reprint ed. lib. bdg. 39.50 (0-87991-342-8) Porcupine Pr.

Rise of Photography Eighteen Fifty to Eighteen Eighty: The Age of Collodion. Helmut Gernsheim. LC 87-51303. (Illus.). 250p. 1989. 65.00 (0-500-97349-0) Thames Hudson.

Rise of Political Anti-Semitism in Germany & Austria. rev. ed. Peter Pulzer. LC 88-15062. 384p. 1988. pap. 17.95 (0-674-77166-4) HUP.

*Rise of Political Economy As a Science: Methodology & the Classical Economists.** Deborah A. Redman. LC 97-22275. (Illus.). 470p. 1997. 55.00 (0-262-18179-7) MIT Pr.

Rise of Portuguese Power in India 1497-1550. Richard S. Whiteway. LC 76-407549. xvi, 357p. 1967. reprint ed. 45.00 (0-678-07258-2) Kelley.

Rise of Pragmatic Thought in the Nineteenth & Twentieth Century, Vol. II. (Pragmatics: Handbook of Pragmatic Thought Ser.). 484p. 1987. 79.95 (3-7873-0644-7) Transaction Pubs.

Rise of Professional Society: England since 1880. Harold Perkin. 480p. 1989. 49.95 (0-415-00890-5) Routledge.

Rise of Professional Society: England since 1880. Harold Perkin. 480p. (C). 1990. pap. 19.95 (0-415-04975-X) Routledge.

Rise of Protestant Evangelism in Ecuador, 1895-1990. Alvin M. Goffin. LC 93-36886. (Illus.). 208p. (C). 1994. lib. bdg. 39.95 (0-8130-1260-0) U Press Fla.

Rise of Public Science: Rhetoric, Technology, & Natural Philosophy in Newtonian Britain. Larry Stewart. (Illus.). 400p. (C). 1992. text ed. 74.95 (0-521-41700-7) Cambridge U Pr.

Rise of Public Woman. Glenna Matthews. (Illus.). 316p. 1994. reprint ed. pap. 11.95 (0-19-509045-4) OUP.

Rise of Public Woman: Woman's Power & Woman's Place in the United States, 1630-1970. Glenna Matthews. (Illus.). 320p. 1992. 27.50 (0-19-505460-1) OUP.

Rise of Radical Egalitarianism. Aaron Wildavsky. 266p. (Orig.). (C). 1991. 54.95 (1-879383-01-2); pap. 24.95 (1-879383-00-4) Am Univ Pr.

Rise of Religious Liberty in America: A History. Sanford H. Cobb. LC 68-27517. 541p. 1968. reprint ed. 71.00 (0-8154-0051-9) Cooper Sq.

Rise of Respectable Society: A Social History of Victorian Britain, 1830-1900. F. M. Thompson. LC 88-14802. 384p. 1988. 42.50 (0-674-77285-7) HUP.

Rise of Respectable Society: A Social History of Victorian Britain, 1830-1900. F. M. Thompson. 384p. 1990. pap. 15.95 (0-674-77286-5) HUP.

*Rise of Richelieu.** Francis Bergin. LC 97-4354. 1998. pap. write for info. (0-7190-5238-6, Pub. by Manchester Univ Pr UK) St Martin.

Rise of Robert Dodsley: Creating the New Age of Print. Harry M. Solomon. 1996. 39.95 (0-8093-1651-X) S Ill U Pr.

Rise of Romance. Eugene Vinaver. (Illus.). 188p. 1984. 50.00 (0-85991-158-6) Boydell & Brewer.

Rise of Rome to 220 B. C. Ed. by F. W. Walbank et al. (Cambridge Ancient History Ser.: Vol. 7 Pt. 2). 600p. 1990. text ed. 125.00 (0-521-23446-8) Cambridge U Pr.

Rise of Russia & the Fall of the Soviet Empire. John B. Dunlop. 394p. 1993. pap. text ed. 17.95 (0-691-00173-1) Princeton U Pr.

Rise of Scientific Philosophy. Hans Reichenbach. 1951. pap. 13.00 (0-520-01055-8) U CA Pr.

Rise of Selfishness in America. James L. Collier. 320p. 1991. 30.00 (0-19-505277-3) OUP.

Rise of Settler Power in Southern Rhodesia (Zimbabwe) 1898-1923. James A. Mutambirwa. LC 78-75181. 248p. 1970. 34.50 (0-8386-2267-4) Fairleigh Dickinson.

Rise of Silas Lapham. William Dean Howells. (Airmont Classics Ser.). (J). (gr. 11 up). 1968. mass mkt. 2.95 (0-8049-0165-1, CL-165) Airmont.

Rise of Silas Lapham. William Dean Howells. Ed. by Edwin H. Cady. LC 57-14612. (YA). (gr. 9 up). 1957. pap. 11.56 (0-395-05126-6, RivEd) HM.

Rise of Silas Lapham. William Dean Howells. (YA). (gr. 9). 1963. pap. 5.95 (0-451-52496-9, CE1850, Sig Classics) NAL-Dutton.

Rise of Silas Lapham. William Dean Howells. (American Library). 352p. 1983. pap. 10.95 (0-14-039030-8, Penguin Classics) Viking Penguin.

Rise of Silas Lapham. William Dean Howells. Ed. by Don L. Cook. (Critical Editions Ser.). (C). 1982. pap. text ed. 14.95 (0-393-09165-1) Norton.

Rise of Silas Lapham. William Dean Howells. Ed. & Intro. by John W. Crowley. (World's Classics Ser.). 448p. 1996. pap. 8.95 (0-19-282355-8) OUP.

Rise of Silas Lapham. rev. ed. William Dean Howells. Ed. by Robert J. Dixson. (American Classics Ser.: No. 8). 1988. pap. text ed. 5.75 (0-13-024589-5, 18127); audio 65.00 (0-13-024761-8, 58231) Prentice ESL.

Rise of Silas Lapham. William Dean Howells. reprint ed. lib. bdg. 25.95 (0-89190-456-5, Rivercity Pr) Amereon Ltd.

Rise of Silas Lapham. William Dean Howells. 1990. reprint ed. lib. bdg. 21.95 (0-89968-528-5) Buccaneer Bks.

Rise of Silas Lapham. William Dean Howells. 1992. reprint ed. lib. bdg. 21.95 (0-89968-261-8, Lghtyr Pr) Buccaneer Bks.

Rise of Silas Lapham. William Dean Howells. (Notable American Authors Ser.). 1992. reprint ed. lib. bdg. 75.00 (0-7812-3237-6) Rprt Serv.

Rise of Silas Lapham Notes. Pat Keating. (Orig.). 1982. pap. 4.50 (0-8220-1147-6) Cliffs.

*Rise of Silicon Valley.** James Williams. 1993. pap. 5.00 (0-935089-16-0) CA History Ctr.

Rise of Sinclair Lewis, 1920-1930. James M. Hutchisson. LC 95-15482. (Series in the History of the Book). (Illus.). 288p. 1996. 29.50 (0-271-01503-9) Pa St U Pr.

Rise of Social Theory. Johan Heibron. LC 94-40152. (Contradictions of Modernity Ser.: Vol. 3). 1995. text ed. 49.95 (0-8166-2712-6); pap. text ed. 19.95 (0-8166-2713-4) U of Minn Pr.

*Rise of Socialism in Britain.** Keith Laybourn. 224p. 1997. pap. 22.95 (0-7509-1341-X, Pub. by Sutton Pubng UK) Bks Intl VA.

Rise of Solidarity. Tim Sharman. LC 86-20276. (Flashpoints Ser.). (Illus.). 78p. (YA). (gr. 7 up). 1987. 18.60 (0-86592-030-3); 13.95 (0-685-58242-6) Rourke Corp.

Rise of Sports in New Orleans, 1850-1900. Dale A. Somers. LC 72-181359. 336p. 1972. pap. 95.80 (0-7837-8508-9, 2049316) Bks Demand.

Rise of Statistical Thinking, 1820-1900. Theodore M. Porter. 352p. 1986. reprint ed. pap. text ed. 19.95 (0-691-02409-X) Princeton U Pr.

Rise of Supernatural Fiction, 1762-1800. Emma Clery. (Studies in Romanticism: No. 12). 240p. (C). 1995. text ed. 54.95 (0-521-45316-X) Cambridge U Pr.

Rise of Surgery: From Empiric Craft to Scientific Discipline. Owen H. Wangensteen & Sarah D. Wangensteen. LC 77-87933. (Illus.). xv, 785p. 1978. 50.00 (0-8166-0829-6) Midewiwin.

Rise of the Accounting Profession, 2 vols., 1. John L. Carey. LC 75-7181. 405p. reprint ed. 115.50 (0-685-16192-7, 2027591) Bks Demand.

Rise of the Accounting Profession, 2 vols., 2. John L. Carey. LC 75-7181. reprint ed. 140.30 (0-685-16193-5) Bks Demand.

Rise of the American Electrochemicals Industry, 1880-1910: Studies in the American Technological Environment. Martha M. Trescott. LC 80-23469. (Contributions in Economics & Economic History Ser.: No. 38). (Illus.). 424p. 1981. text ed. 75.00 (0-313-20766-6, TRI/) Greenwood.

Rise of the Anglo-German Antagonism, 1860-1914. Paul M. Kennedy. LC 87-21455. 624p. (C). 1987. pap. 25.00 (0-948660-06-6, Pub. by Ashfield Pr UK) Humanities.

Rise of the Anti-Mission Baptists: Sources & Leaders, 1800-1840. Byron C. Lambert. Ed. by Edwin S. Gaustad. LC 79-52573. (Baptist Tradition Ser.). 1980. lib. bdg. 42.95 (0-405-12441-4) Ayer.

Rise of the Antichrist. Gordon Lindsay. (Revelation Ser.: Vol. 9). 1962. 1.95 (0-89985-042-1) Christ for the Nations.

Rise of the Atlantic Economies. Ralph Davis. Ed. by Charles Wilson. (World Economic History Ser.). 340p. 1973. pap. 17.95 (0-8014-9143-6) Cornell U Pr.

Rise of the Authoritarian State in Peripheral Societies. Clive Y. Thomas. LC 84-16490. 288p. 1984. 27.00 (0-85345-657-7); pap. 16.00 (0-85345-658-5) Monthly Rev.

Rise of the Baltic Question. Walther Kirchner. LC 77-100237. 283p. 1970. reprint ed. text ed. 59.75 (0-8371-3009-3, KIBQ, Greenwood Pr) Greenwood.

Rise of the Barristers: A Social History of the English Bar, 1590-1640. Wilfrid R. Prest. (Oxford Studies in Social History). 440p. 1987. 90.00 (0-19-821764-1) OUP.

Rise of the Black Magus in Western Art. Paul H. Kaplan. Ed. by Linda Seidel. LC 85-8461. (Studies in the Fine Arts: Iconography: No. 10). 344p. reprint ed. 95.00 (0-8357-1667-8, 2070471) Bks Demand.

Rise of the Bourgeoisie, Demise of Empire: Ottoman Westernization & Social Change. Fatma M. Gocek. (Illus.). 232p. 1996. text ed. 45.00 (0-19-509925-7) OUP.

Rise of the British Coal Industry, 2 Vols. John U. Nef. LC 71-37902. (Select Bibliographies Reprint Ser.). 1977. reprint ed. 89.95 (0-8369-6740-2) Ayer.

Rise of the British Coal Industry, 2 vols. John U. Nef. (Illus.). 1966. reprint ed. 95.00 (0-7146-1346-0, BHA-01346, Pub. by F Cass Pubs UK) Intl Spec Bk.

Rise of the British Presidency. Michael Foley. LC 92-37304. (C). 1993. text ed. 79.95 (0-7190-3621-6, Pub. by Manchester Univ Pr UK); text ed. 27.95 (0-7190-4010-8, Pub. by Manchester Univ Pr UK) St Martin.

Rise of the British Provincial Financial Centre. Andrew Leyshon et al. (Progress in Planning Ser.: PRPL 31). 80p. 1990. pap. 38.50 (0-08-037384-4, Pergamon Pr) Elsevier.

Rise of the Castle. M. W. Thompson. (Illus.). 232p. (C). 1991. 49.95 (0-521-37544-4) Cambridge U Pr.

Rise of the Celts. Henri H. Hubert. LC 66-23521. (Illus.). 1934. 35.00 (0-8196-0183-7) Biblo.

Rise of the Chinese Communist Party, 1928-1938: Volume Two of the Autobiography of Chang Kuo-t'ao. Chang Kuo-t'ao. LC 76-141997. viii, 628p. 1971. 40.00 (0-7006-0088-4) U Pr of KS.

*Rise of the Chinese Economy: The Middle Kingdom Emerges.** Greg Mastel. LC 96-53292. 288p. (C). (gr. 13). 1997. text ed. 62.95 (0-7656-0017-X); pap. text ed. 24.95 (0-7656-0018-8) M E Sharpe.

Rise of the Chinese Republic: From the Last Emperor to Deng Xiaoping. Edwin P. Hoyt. (Quality Paperbacks Ser.). (Illus.). xii, 355p. 1991. reprint ed. pap. 13.95 (0-306-80426-3) Da Capo.

Rise of the Church see Anatolia: Land, Men & Gods in Asia Minor

*Rise of the Church of the Nazarene.** 104p. 1985. pap. 6.99 (0-8341-0141-6) Nazarene.

Rise of the Cinema in Great Britain. John Barnes. 272p. 1987. 29.95 (0-900873-51-5, Pub. by Bishopsgte Pr UK) Intl Spec Bk.

Rise of the Common Man, 1830-1850. Carl R. Fish. (BCL1 - U. S. History Ser.). 391p. 1991. reprint ed. lib. bdg. 89.00 (0-7812-6121-X) Rprt Serv.

Rise of the Common Man, 1830-1854. Carl R. Fish. LC 75-41093. reprint ed. write for info. (0-404-14748-8) AMS Pr.

Rise of the Community Builders: The American Real Estate Industry & Urban Land Planning. Marc A. Weiss. (History of Urban Life Ser.). 240p. 1987. text ed. 45.00 (0-231-06504-3) Col U Pr.

Rise of the Community Builders: The American Real Estate Industry & Urban Land Planning. Marc A. Weiss. (History of Urban Life Ser.). 240p. 1989. pap. text ed. 16.50 (0-231-06505-1) Col U Pr.

Rise of the Corporate Commonwealth: United States Business & Public Policy in the 20th Century. Louis P. Galambos & Joseph Pratt. LC 87-47784. 304p. 1989. pap. 17.00 (0-465-07028-0) Basic.

Rise of the Corporate Economy. Leslie Hannah. 288p. (C). 1983. pap. text ed. 12.95 (0-416-34860-2, NO. 4045) Routledge Chapman & Hall.

Rise of the Corporate Economy: The British Experience. Leslie Hannah. LC 76-17228. 255p. reprint ed. pap. 72.70 (0-317-42336-3, 2025816) Bks Demand.

Rise of the Dutch Republic see Writings of John Lothrop Motley

Rise of the English Actress. Sandra L. Richards. LC 91-37873. 352p. 1993. text ed. 39.95 (0-312-07578-2) St Martin.

Rise of the English Street Ballad 1550-1650. Natascha Wurzbach. Tr. by Gayna Walls. (European Studies in English Literature). 400p. (C). 1990. text ed. 80.00 (0-521-32061-5) Cambridge U Pr.

Rise of the Entrepreneurial State: State & Local Economic Development Policy in the United States. Peter K. Eisinger. LC 88-40184. (Badger Reprint Edition Ser.). 336p. (C). 1997. reprint ed. pap. 17.50 (0-299-11874-6) U of Wis Pr.

Rise of the European Economy: An Economic History of Continental Europe from Fifteenth Hundred to Seventeen Fifty. Hermann Kellenbenz. LC 76-7487. 350p. 1976. 37.95 (0-8419-0273-9) Holmes & Meier.

Rise of the European Powers, Sixteen Seventy-Nine to Seventeen Ninety-Three. Jeremy Black. (Illus.). 224p. 1995. text ed. 16.95 (0-7131-6537-5, A4340, Pub. by E Arnld UK) St Martin.

Rise of the Expert Company: How Visionary Companies Are Using Artificial Intelligence to Achieve Higher Productivity & Profits. Edward A. Feigenbaum et al. 256p. 1988. 19.95 (0-8129-1731-6, Times Bks) Random.

Rise of the Feudal Monarchies. Sidney Painter. 147p. 1951. 9.95 (0-8014-9851-1) Cornell U Pr.

Rise of the French Novel. Martin Turnell. LC 77-26792. 1978. pap. 8.95 (0-8112-0716-1, NDP474) New Directions.

Rise of the Goddess in the Hindu Tradition. Tracy Pintchman. LC 93-40617. 288p. (FRE.). (C). 1994. pap. text ed. 19.95 (0-7914-2112-0) State U NY Pr.

Rise of the Goddess in the Hindu Tradition. Tracy Pintchman. LC 93-40617. 288p. (FRE.). (C). 1994. text ed. 59.50 (0-7914-2111-2) State U NY Pr.

Rise of the Gospel Blues: The Music of Thomas Andrew Dorsey in the Urban Church. Michael W. Harris. (Illus.). 354p. 1994. pap. 12.95 (0-19-509057-8) OUP.

Rise of the Gothic Novel. Maggie Kilgour. 336p. (C). 1995. pap. 17.95 (0-415-08182-3, C0205) Routledge.

Rise of the Great Powers: The Great Powers & European States Systems, 1648-1815. Derek Mckay & H. M. Scott. (C). 1983. text ed. write for info. (0-318-56830-6) Longman.

Rise of the Great Powers: The Great Powers & European States Systems, 1648-1815. Derek Mckay & H. M. Scott. LC 82-159. (C). 1991. pap. text ed. 31.95 (0-582-48554-1, 73299) Longman.

Rise of the Greek Socialist Party. Michalis Spourdalakis. 352p. (C). 1988. lib. bdg. 59.50 (0-415-00499-3) Routledge.

Rise of the Gunbelt: The Military Remapping of Industrial America. Ann R. Markusen et al. (Illus.). 360p. 1991. 48.00 (0-19-506648-0) OUP.

Rise of the Habsburg Empire. Victor S. Mamatey. 192p. 1994. pap. 11.50 (0-89464-920-5) Krieger.

Rise of the House of Gorkha: A Study in the Unification of Nepal, 1768-1816. Ed. by Ludwig F. Stiller. 388p. (C). 1975. 30.00 (0-89771-069-X, Pub. by Ratna Pustak Bhandar) St Mut.

Rise of the House of Gorkha: A Study in the Unification of Nepal 1768-1816. Ludwig F. Stiller. 1975. 20.00 (0-7855-0264-5, Pub. by Ratna Pustak Bhandar) St Mut.

Rise of the House of Rothschild. E. Corti. 1973. 300.00 (0-87968-170-5) Gordon Pr.

Rise of the Imperial Self: America's Culture Wars in Augustinian Perspective. Ronald W. Dworkin. LC 96-2178. (C). 1996. pap. text ed. 23.95 (0-8476-8219-6); lib. bdg. 59.50 (0-8476-8218-8) Rowman.

Rise of the Indo-Afghan Empire, c. 1710-1780. Jos J. Gommans. LC 94-33783. (Indological Library Ser.: 8). 1994. 77.00 (90-04-10109-8) E J Brill.

Rise of the Irish Trade Unions. rev. ed. Andrew Boyd. 160p. 1985. reprint ed. pap. 9.95 (0-900068-21-3, Pub. by Anvil Bks Ltd IE) Irish Bks Media.

Rise of the Ironclads. George F. Amadon. LC 88-60845. (Illus.). 80p. 1988. pap. 9.95 (0-933126-90-5) Pictorial Hist.

Rise of the Islamic Empire & the Threat to the West. Anthony J. Dennis. (Illus.). 180p. (C). 1996. text ed. 39.95 (1-55605-268-5); pap. text ed. 19.95 (1-55605-267-7) Wyndham Hall.

Rise of the Japanese Corporate System: The Inside View of a MITI Official. Koji Matsumoto. (Japanese Studies). 220p. (C). 1991. text ed. 89.95 (0-7103-0407-2, A5593) Routledge Chapman & Hall.

Rise of the Japanese Corporate System: The Inside View of a MITI Official. Koji Matsumoto. (Japanese Studies Ser.). 280p. 1994. pap. 25.50 (0-7103-0488-9) Routledge Chapman & Hall.

Rise of the Jew in the Western World. Uriah Z. Engelman. LC 73-2194. (Jewish People; History, Religion, Literature Ser.). 1973. reprint ed. 24.95 (0-405-05260-X) Ayer.

*Rise of the Korean Economy.** 2nd ed. Byung N. Song. (Illus.). 300p. 1997. pap. 18.95 (0-19-590049-9) OUP.

Rise of the Labor Movement in Ceylon. Visakha Jayawardena. LC 77-185465. 398p. reprint ed. pap. 113.50 (0-317-42174-3, 2026205) Bks Demand.

Rise of the Labor Party. 2nd ed. Adelman. (C). 1986. pap. text ed. 13.50 (0-582-35488-9) Addison-Wesley.

Rise of the Labour Movement. Geoffrey Morris. 128p. (C). 1986. 45.00 (0-317-89992-9) St Mut.

Rise of the Labour Party, 1880-1945. 3rd ed. Paul Adelman. (Seminar Studies in History). (C). 1996. pap. text ed. 11.50 (0-582-29210-7, Pub. by Longman UK) Longman.

Rise of the Labour Party 1893-1931. Gordon Phillips. LC 91-28658. (Lancaster Pamphlets Ser.). 96p. (C). 1992. pap. text ed. 10.95 (0-415-04051-5, A7303) Routledge.

Rise of the Latin American Labor Movement. Ben G. Burnett & Moises P. Troncoso. 1960. 12.95 (0-8084-0406-7); pap. 19.95 (0-685-53856-7) NCUP.

Rise of the London Money Market: 1640-1826. W. R. Bisschop. 256p. 1968. reprint ed. 37.50 (0-7146-1206-5, Pub. by F Cass Pubs UK) Intl Spec Bk.

Rise of the Lone Star: The Making of Texas. Andreas V. Reichstein. Tr. by Jeanne R. Willson. LC 89-30386. (Illus.). 328p. 1989. 36.95 (0-89096-318-5) Tex A&M Univ Pr.

Rise of the Marginal Utility School. Richard S. Howey. 288p. 1989. text ed. 47.50 (0-231-07152-3); pap. text ed. 18.00 (0-231-07153-1) Col U Pr.

Rise of the Meritocracy. Michael Young. LC 93-5471. 196p. 1993. reprint ed. pap. text ed. 21.95 (1-56000-704-4) Transaction Pubs.

Rise of the Midwestern Meat Packing Industry. Margaret Walsh. LC 82-40184. 192p. 1982. 20.00 (0-8131-1473-X) U Pr of Ky.

Rise of the Missionary Spirit in America 1790-1815. Oliver W. Elsbree. LC 79-13028. (Perspectives in American History Ser.: No. 55). 187p. 1980. reprint ed. 35.00 (0-87991-376-2) Porcupine Pr.

Rise of the Modern Educational System: Structural Change & Social Reproduction, 1870-1920. Ed. by Detlef Muller et al. 280p. 1990. pap. text ed. 22.95 (0-521-36685-2) Cambridge U Pr.

Rise of the Modern German Novel: Crisis & Charisma. Russell A. Berman. LC 85-24770. (Central Asian Studies). 352p. 1986. 39.95 (0-674-77165-6) HUP.

*Rise of the National Guard: The Evolution of the American Militia, 1865-1920.** Jerry Cooper. LC 97-7630. 296p. 1997. text ed. 45.00 (0-8032-1486-3) U of Nebr Pr.

Rise of the National Trade Union: The Development & Significance of Its Structure, Governing Institutions, & Economic Policies. 2nd ed. Lloyd Ulman. LC 66-5206. (Wertheim Publications in Industrial Relations). (Illus.). 658p. 1955. 37.50 (0-674-77280-6) HUP.

Rise of the Nazis. Conan Fischer. LC 94-23920. (New Frontiers in History Ser.). 1995. text ed. 16.95 (0-7190-3503-1, Pub. by Manchester Univ Pr UK) St Martin.

Rise of the Network Society: The Information Age: Economy, Society & Culture. Manuel Castells. (Illus.). 480p. (C). 1996. 69.95 (1-55786-616-3); pap. 25.95 (1-55786-617-1) Blackwell Pubs.

Rise of the New Physics, Vol. 1. 2nd ed. A. D'Abro. (Illus.). 994p. (C). 1950. pap. 7.95 (0-486-20003-5) Dover.

Rise of the New Physics, Vol. 2. 2nd ed. A. D'Abro. (Illus.). 982p. (C). 1950. pap. 7.95 (0-486-20004-3) Dover.

An Asterisk (*) at the beginning of an entry indicates that the title is appearing in BIP for the first time.

Rise of the New York Intellectuals: Partisan Review & Its Circle. Terry A. Cooney. LC 86-40049. (History of American Thought & Culture Ser.). 352p. 1986. 25.00 (0-299-10710-8) U of Wis Pr.

Rise of the New York Skyscraper: 1865-1913. Sarah B. Landau & Carl W. Condit. (Illus.). 465p. 1996. 50.00 (0-300-06444-6) Yale U Pr.

Rise of the Novel: Studies in Defoe, Richardson & Fielding. Ian Watt. 1957. pap. 14.95 (0-520-01318-2) U CA Pr.

Rise of the Paris Red Belt. Tyler Stovall. 1990. 42.50 (0-520-06320-1) U CA Pr.

Rise of the Penitentiary: Prisons & Punishment in Early America. Adam J. Hirsch. 288p. (C). 1992. text ed. 37.50 (0-300-04297-3) Yale U Pr.

Rise of the Phoenix: Universal Government by Nature's Laws. Christopher Hills. Ed. by Ann Ray & Deborah Rozman. LC 76-53176. (Illus.). 1002p. (Orig.). 1979. pap. 39.95 (0-916438-04-X) Dr Hills Technol.

Rise of the Professions in Twentieth-Century Mexico: University Graduates & Occupational Change since 1929. David E. Lorey. LC 92-15245. (Cycles & Trends Research Ser.: Vol. 2). 1992. pap. 17.95 (0-87903-254-5) UCLA Lat Am Ctr.

Rise of the Professions in Twentieth-Century Mexico: University Graduates & Occupational Change Since 1929. 2nd ed. David E. Lorey. (Cycles & Trends Research Ser.: Vol. 2). 1994. pap. 21.95 (0-87903-257-X) UCLA Lat Am Ctr.

Rise of the Public Library in California. Ray E. Held. LC 73-12719. 217p. reprint ed. pap. 61.90 (0-317-27845-2, 2024218) Bks Demand.

Rise of the Revolutionary Party in the English House of Commons, 1603-1629. William M. Mitchell. LC 75-31471. 209p. 1976. reprint ed. text ed. 55.00 (0-8371-8535-1, MIRR, Greenwood Pr) Greenwood.

Rise of the Right. rev. ed. William A. Rusher. 256p. (C). 1993. pap. text ed. 14.95 (0-9627841-2-5) Natl Review.

Rise of the Roman Empire. Obye Polybius. Tr. by Ian Scott-Kilvert. 576p. 1980. pap. 11.95 (0-14-044362-2, Penguin Classics) Viking Penguin.

Rise of the Roman Jurists: Studies in Cicero's Pro Caecina. Bruce W. Frier. LC 84-42886. 342p. reprint ed. pap. 97.50 (0-7837-1426-2, 2041781) Bks Demand.

Rise of the Russian Democrats: The Causes & Consequences of the Elite Revolution. Judith Devlin. LC 94-48417. (Studies of Communism in Transition). 304p. 1995. 80.00 (1-85898-251-0) E Elgar.

***Rise of the Russian Novel: Carnival, Stylization & Mockery of the West.** David W. Gasperetti. LC 97-11768. 1997. write for info. (0-87580-230-3) N Ill U Pr.

Rise of the Rustbelt. Ed. by Philip Cooke. 1995. text ed. 59.95 (0-312-12943-2) St Martin.

Rise of the Sixties: American & European Art in the Era of Dissent. Thomas Crow. (The Perspectives Ser.). (Illus.). 176p. 1996. 16.95 (0-8109-2731-4) Abrams.

Rise of the Social Gospel in American Protestantism, 1865-1895. Charles H. Hopkins. LC 75-41141. (BCL Ser.: Vol. II). 368p. reprint ed. 37.50 (0-404-14771-2) AMS Pr.

Rise of the Spanish American Republics As Told in the Lives of Their Liberators. William S. Robertson. 1976. lib. bdg. 59.95 (0-8490-2527-3) Gordon Pr.

Rise of the Standard Model: A History of Particle Physics from 1964 to 1979. Ed. by Laurie M. Brown et al. (Illus.). 672p. (C). 1997. text ed. 80.00 (0-521-57082-4); pap. text ed. 34.95 (0-521-57816-7) Cambridge U Pr.

Rise of the Student Estate in Britain. Eric Ashby & Mary Anderson. 196p. 1970. 22.00 (0-674-77290-3) HUP.

Rise of the Sunbelt Cities. Ed. by David C. Perry & Alfred J. Watkins. LC 77-93698. (Urban Affairs Annual Reviews Ser.: No. 14). 309p. reprint ed. pap. 88.10 (0-8357-8504-1, 2034783) Bks Demand.

Rise of the Swiss Republic. 2nd ed. William D. McCracken. LC 75-130235. reprint ed. 57.50 (0-404-04109-4) AMS Pr.

Rise of the Therapeutic State. Andrew J. Polsky. 296p. 1991. text ed. 45.00 (0-691-07878-5); pap. text ed. 17.95 (0-691-00084-0) Princeton U Pr.

Rise of the United Association: National Unionism in the Pipe Trades 1884-1924. Martin Segal. LC 79-101012. (Wertheim Publications in Industrial Relations). 258p. 1969. 16.50 (0-674-77300-4) HUP.

Rise of the Urban South. Lawrence H. Larsen. LC 84-25596. 232p. 1985. 25.00 (0-8131-1538-8) U Pr of Ky.

Rise of the Wave Theory of Light. Jed Z. Buchwald. LC 88-18647. (Illus.). 498p. 1989. lib. bdg. 90.00 (0-226-07884-1) U Ch Pr.

Rise of the Wave Theory of Light. Jed Z. Buchwald. LC 88-18647. (Illus.). 504p. 1989. pap. text ed. 29.95 (0-226-07886-8) U Ch Pr.

Rise of the Welfare Monarchy. Frank Prochaska. LC 95-12271. 1996. 35.00 (0-300-06453-5) Yale U Pr.

Rise of the Welsh Republic. Derrick Hearne. 1989. 20.00 (0-317-52163-2, Pub. by Y Lolfa UK) St Mut.

Rise of the West: A History of the Human Community. William H. McNeill. 860p. 1991. pap. 22.95 (0-226-56141-0) U Ch Pr.

Rise of the Western World: A New Economic History. D. C. North & R. P. Thomas. LC 73-77258. (Illus.). 192p. 1976. pap. text ed. 16.95 (0-521-29099-6) Cambridge U Pr.

Rise of the Wheat State: A History of Kansas Agriculture, 1861-1986. Ed. by George E. Ham & Robin Higham. (Illus.). 216p. 1987. pap. 15.00 (0-89745-083-3) Sunflower U Pr.

Rise of Theodore Roosevelt. Edmund Morris. 896p. 1986. pap. 16.00 (0-345-33902-9, Ballantine Trade) Ballantine.

Rise of Turkish Nationalism, 1876-1908. David Kushner. 126p. 1977. 37.50 (0-7146-3075-6, Pub. by F Cass Pubs UK) Intl Spec Bk.

Rise of U. S. Grant. Arthur L. Conger. LC 74-137371. (Select Bibliographies Reprint Ser.). (Illus.). 1977. 36.95 (0-8369-5572-2) Ayer.

Rise of U. S. Grant. Arthur L. Conger. (Illus.). 432p. 1996. reprint ed. pap. 15.95 (0-306-80693-2) Da Capo.

Rise of Universities. Charles H. Haskins. 118p. 1957. pap. 8.95 (0-8014-9015-4) Cornell U Pr.

Rise of Universities. Charles H. Haskins. 1976. 250.00 (0-87968-379-1) Gordon Pr.

Rise of Urban America, 57 vols. Ed. by Richard C. Wade. 1970. reprint ed. 1,539.50 (0-405-02430-4) Ayer.

Rise of V. P. Singh & the 1989 & 1990 Elections. Surindar Suri. (Illus.). vii, 216p. 1990. text ed. 27.50 (81-220-0185-8, Pub. by Konark Pubs Pvt Ltd II) Advent Bks Div.

Rise of Warren Gamaliel Harding, 1865-1920. rev. ed. Randolph C. Downes. LC 68-31421. 744p. 1970. pap. 180.00 (0-608-00915-6, 2061709) Bks Demand.

***Rise of Western Christendom: Triumph & Diversity Adzoo-1000.** rev. ed. Peter Brown. Ed. by Jacques Le Goff. LC 95-11589. (Making of Europe Ser.). xii, 353p. 1997. pap. 22.95 (1-57718-092-5) Blackwell Pubs.

Rise of Western Christendom: Triumph & Diversity 200-1000 AD. Peter Brown. LC 95-11589. (Making of Europe Ser.). (Illus.). 320p. (C). 1995. 59.95 (1-55786-136-6) Blackwell Pubs.

Rise of Western Rationalism: Max Weber's Developmental History. Wolfgang Schluchter. Tr. by Guenther Roth from GER. LC 81-2763. 300p. 1981. pap. 15.00 (0-520-05464-4) U CA Pr.

Rise of World Lutheranism: An American Perspective. E. Clifford Nelson. LC 80-2376. 445p. reprint ed. pap. 126.90 (0-317-55549-9, 2029618) Bks Demand.

Rise the Euphrates Sampler. Carol Edgarian. 1994. write for info. (0-394-00570-8) Random.

Rise to Follow. Albert Spalding. 1988. reprint ed. lib. bdg. 75.00 (0-7812-0209-4) Rprt Serv.

Rise to Follow: An Autobiography. Albert Spalding. LC 77-5563. (Music Reprint Ser.). 1977. reprint ed. lib. bdg. 39.50 (0-306-77421-6) Da Capo.

Rise to Globalism. 4th ed. Stephen E. Ambrose. 368p. (Orig.). 1985. pap. 7.95 (0-14-022622-2, Penguin Bks) Viking Penguin.

Rise to Globalism: American Foreign Policy Since 1938. 5th rev. ed. Stephen E. Ambrose. 416p. 1988. pap. 8.95 (0-14-022826-8, Penguin Bks) Viking Penguin.

Rise to Globalism: American Foreign Policy Since 1938. 6th rev. ed. Stephen E. Ambrose. 400p. 1991. pap. 10.00 (0-14-014770-5) Viking Penguin.

Rise to Globalism: American Foreign Policy since 1938. 7th rev. ed. Stephen E. Ambrose. 448p. 1993. pap. 14.95 (0-14-017536-9, Penguin Bks) Viking Penguin.

***Rise to Globalism: American Foreign Policy since 1938.** 8th rev. ed. Stephen E. Ambrose. 1997. pap. 14.95 (0-14-026831-6) Viking Penguin.

Rise to Power of the Chinese Communist Party: Documents & Analysis. Ed. by Anthony J. Saich. LC 94-30009. 1504p. (C). (gr. 13). 1995. text ed. 195.00 (1-56324-154-4, East Gate Bk) M E Sharpe.

Rise to Power of the Chinese Communist Party: Documents & Analysis. Ed. by Anthony J. Saich. LC 94-30009. 1504p. (C). 1996. pap. text ed. 45.00 (1-56324-155-2, East Gate Bk) M E Sharpe.

Rise to Shine. Hans Van Blyenburgh. LC 93-93821. (Orig.). 1993. pap. 19.95 (0-9636009-0-7) H Blyenburgh.

Rise up & Read Music: Techniques of Sight-Singing. Jeanne C. Frolick. Ed. by Rick Modlin. (Illus.). 128p. (Orig.). 1994. pap. write for info. (0-915531-39-9) OR Catholic.

Rise up & Sing! 1991. 6.99 (0-8341-9164-4, MB-629) Lillenas.

Rise up My Love. large type ed. Nan Maynard. (General Ser.). 400p. 1993. 25.99 (0-7089-2789-0) Ulverscroft.

***Rise up, O Church.** Date not set. pap. 1.35 (0-8341-9158-X) Lillenas.

Rise up Singing: Mostly Words & Chord Symbols Only. 1992. otabind 17.95 (0-7935-2882-8, 00746394) H Leonard.

Rise up Singing: The Group Singing Songbook. rev. ed. Ed. by Peter Blood. (Illus.). 288p. reprint ed. pap. 17.95 (0-9626704-9-9) Sing Out.

Rise up Singing: The Group Singing Songbook. rev. ed. Ed. by Peter Blood. (Illus.). 288p. 1988. reprint ed. spiral bd. 17.95 (0-9626704-7-2) Sing Out.

Rise up Singing: The Group Singing Songbook. rev. ed. Ed. by Peter Blood. (Illus.). 288p. 1988. reprint ed. lib. bdg. 39.95 (0-9626704-8-0) Sing Out.

Rise Up, Women! The Militant Campaign of the Women's Social & Political Union, 1903-1914. Andrew Rosen. (Modern Revivals in History Ser.). 340p. 1993. 61.95 (0-7512-0173-1, Pub. by Gregg Revivals UK) Ashgate Pub Co.

Risen. Elizabeth Ditchburn & Heather Grove. (Wraith Ser.). (Illus.). 72p. (Orig.). (YA). 1996. suppl. ed., pap. 12.00 (1-56504-663-3, 6302) White Wolf.

***Risen: A Novel of Death, Resurrection.** Susan B. Smith. LC 97-71093. 350p. (Orig.). 1997. pap. 12.99 (1-884369-54-5, Parable Pubns) McDougal Pubng.

Risen: A Worship Sequence for Easter Sunday. Des. by Bruce Greer. 1994. audio 19.99 (0-614-01689-4, MU-2259D) Lillenas.

Risen: A Worship Sequence for Easter Sunday. Des. by Bruce Greer. 1994. suppl. ed. 60.00 (0-614-01690-8, OR-2259) Lillenas.

Risen: A Worship Sequence for Easter Sunday. Des. by Bruce Greer. 1994. 2.99 (0-8341-9285-3, AC-2004) Lillenas.

Risen Adam: D. H. Lawrence's Revisionist Typology. Virginia Hyde. (Illus.). 280p. 1992. text ed. 32.50 (0-271-00776-1) Pa St U Pr.

Risen Christ in Eastertime: Essays on the Gospel Narratives of the Resurrection. Raymond E. Brown. 96p. (Orig.). 1991. pap. 4.95 (0-8146-2014-0) Liturgical Pr.

Risen from the Ashes: A Story of the Jewish Displaced Persons in the Aftermath of World War II, Being a Sequel to Survivors. Jacob Biber. LC 87-851. (Studies in Judaica & the Holocaust: No. 5). 170p. 1990. pap. 21.00 (0-89370-472-5); lib. bdg. 31.00 (0-89370-372-9) Borgo Pr.

***Risen from the Sea.** Sonesh Chainani. 51p. (Orig.). 1997. mass mkt. 5.99 (1-55197-861-X, Pub. by Comnwlth Pub CN) Partners Pubs Grp.

Risen Indeed: A Christian Philosophy of Resurrection. Stephen T. Davis. LC 93-13847. 232p. (Orig.). 1993. pap. text ed. 17.00 (0-8028-0126-9) Eerdmans.

Risen Indeed: Lessons of Faith from the U. S. S. R. Michael Boudeaux. 113p. (Orig.). 1983. pap. text ed. 8.95 (0-88141-021-7) St Vladimirs.

Risen Life: Healing a Broken World. Joseph G. Donders. LC 90-47168. 127p. 1990. reprint ed. pap. 36.20 (0-7837-9848-2, 2060577) Bks Demand.

***Risen Lord: The Jesus of History As the Christ of Faith.** Margaret Barker. (Scottish Journal of Theology Current Issues in Theology Ser.). 176p. 1996. pap. 23.95 (0-567-08537-6, Pub. by T & T Clark UK) Bks Intl VA.

***Risen Lord: The Jesus of History As the Christ of Faith.** Margaret Barker. LC 96-35849. 1996. pap. 20.00 (1-56338-191-5) TPI PA.

Risen Sons: Flannery O'Connor's Vision of History. John F. Desmond. LC 86-30828. (Illus.). 144p. 1987. 20.00 (0-8203-0945-1) U of Ga Pr.

***Riser Two Hearts.** Date not set. write for info. (0-399-21216-7) Putnam Pub Group.

Risers, Arctic Design Criteria, Equipment Reliability in Hydrocarbon Processing: A Workbook for Engineers, Presented at 37th Petroleum Mechanical Engineering Workshop & Conference, September 13-15, 1981, Dallas, Texas. American Society of Mechanical Engineers Staff. Ed. by Thomas J. Kozik. LC 81-186405. 250p. reprint ed. pap. 71.30 (0-317-29899-2, 2019351) Bks Demand.

Rises a Moral Man. B. J. Smith. 205p. 1987. 14.95 (0-920806-88-0, Pub. by Penumbra Pr CN) U of Toronto Pr.

Rishon Transliterated Hagada: The Complete Hebrew Text with English Translation & Transliteration in Linear Format. Tr. by Sholomo Arno & Moshe Borisute. (Illus.). 116p. (Orig.). 1995. pap. text ed. write for info. (1-880880-08-3) Israeli Trad.

Rishonim: Biographical Sketches of the Prominent Early Rabbinic Sages & Leaders from the Tenth-Fifteenth Centuries. Shmuel Teich. Ed. & Intro. by Hersh Goldwurm. (ArtScroll History Ser.). (Illus.). 224p. (J). (gr. 7-8). 1982. 19.99 (0-89906-452-3) Mesorah Pubns.

Rishonim: Biographical Sketches of the Prominent Early Rabbinic Sages & Leaders from the Tenth-Fifteenth Centuries. Shmuel Teich. Ed. & Intro. by Hersh Goldwurm. (ArtScroll History Ser.). (Illus.). 224p. (YA). (gr. 7-8). 1982. pap. 16.99 (0-89906-453-1) Mesorah Pubns.

Risho's Registry. Ray Risho. 130p. (Orig.). 1985. pap. 5.00 (0-939872-03-X) MRP.

Rishukyo: The Sino-Japanese Tantric Prajnaparamita in 150 Verses. Tr. by Ian Astley-Kristensen. (C). 1991. 57.00 (0-9515424-2-7, Pub. by SOAS) S Asia.

Risibles Amours. Milan Kundera. (FRE.). 1986. pap. 10.95 (0-8288-3701-5) Fr & Eur.

Rising. Edgar White. 224p. 1988. 18.95 (0-7145-2878-1) M Boyars Pubs.

***Rising.** Wright. 14.80 (0-687-60974-7) Abingdon.

***Rising: Flight Engineer.** James Doohan & S. M. Stirling. (Flight Engineer Ser.: Bk. 1). 384p. 1997. mass mkt. 6.99 (0-671-87849-2) Baen Bks.

Rising: Flight Engineer, Bk. I. James Doohan & S. M. Stirling. 384p. 1996. 21.00 (0-671-87758-5) Baen Bks.

Rising: Living the Mysteries of Lent, Easter, & Pentecost. Wendy M. Wright. 192p. 1995. pap. 9.95 (0-8358-0716-9) Upper Room Bks.

Rising Above: A Guide to Overcoming Obstacles & Finding Happiness. Jerry Wilde. LC 95-42422. 201p. pap. 14.95 (0-89390-345-0) Resource Pubns.

Rising above Color. Ed. by Philip H. Lotz. LC 78-152190. (Essay Index Reprints - Creative Personalities Ser.: Vol. 5). 1977. reprint ed. 15.95 (0-8369-2605-6) Ayer.

Rising above It All: A Tribute to the Rowan Slaves of Federal Hill. Ida M. Corley Roberts. Ed. by William Strode. (Illus.). 184p. 1994. 14.95 (1-56469-022-9) Harmony Hse Pub.

Rising above Shame: Healing Family Wounds to Self Esteem. Stanley D. Wilson. LC 91-19449. 1991. pap. 12.95 (1-877872-02-4) Launch Pr.

Rising above Strife. Nancy I. Witte. 1983. pap. 6.25 (0-89137-424-8) Quality Pubns.

Rising American Empire. Richard W. Van Alstyne. 240p. 1974. reprint ed. pap. 9.95 (0-393-00750-2) Norton.

Rising & Falling. Margot Farrington. 94p. 1985. pap. 5.00 (0-942292-09-X) Warthog Pr.

Rising Fawn & the Fire Mystery. Marilou Awiakta. Ed. by Roger R. Easson. LC 83-13824. (Child's Christmas in Memphis Ser.: Vol. 1). (Illus.). 48p. (Orig.). (J). (gr. 5 up). 1984. pap. 11.95 (0-918518-29-6) Iris Pr.

Rising from History: U. S. Catholic Theology Looks to the Future. Ed. by Robert J. Daly. LC 87-2011. (College Theology Society Publications, 1988: Vol. 30). 234p. (Orig.). (C). 1987. lib. bdg. 44.00 (0-8191-6155-1) U Pr of Amer.

Rising from the Bottom: How to Move from Loneliness & Fear to Personal & Global Love. Ted Cox. LC 92-72194. 200p. (Orig.). 1992. pap. 10.00 (1-879560-12-7) Harbor Hse West.

Rising from the Plains. John McPhee. 224p. 1986. 23.00 (0-374-25082-0) FS&G.

Rising from the Plains. John McPhee. 224p. 1987. pap. 10.00 (0-374-52065-8) FS&G.

Rising from the Ruins. Daniel J. Peters. 1995. 24.00 (0-615-00090-8) Random.

***Rising from the Ruins: Reason, Being, & the Good after Auschwitz.** Garth J. Gillan. 116p. (C). 1998. text ed. 44.50 (0-7914-3733-7) State U NY Pr.

***Rising from the Ruins: Reason, Being, & the Good after Auschwitz.** Garth J. Gillan. 116p. (C). 1998. pap. text ed. 14.95 (0-7914-3734-5) State U NY Pr.

Rising Germanophobia: The Chief Obstacle to Current World War II Revisionism. Michael F. Conners. (Revisionist Historiography Ser.). 1980. lib. bdg. 59.95 (0-686-59416-9) Revisionist Pr.

Rising Glory of America. Hugh H. Brackenridge. (Works of Hugh Henry Brackenridge). 1989. reprint ed. lib. bdg. 79.00 (0-7812-2043-2) Rprt Serv.

Rising Glory of America, 1760-1820. rev. ed. Ed. by Gordon S. Wood. 1990. pap. text ed. 16.95 (1-55553-090-7) NE U Pr.

***Rising in Consciousness.** Joel S. Goldsmith. (San Francisco Lecture Ser.). 1997. 19.95 (1-889051-05-5, I Lvl) Acrpls Bks CO.

Rising in Love: Opening Your Heart in All Your Relationships. Alan Cohen. LC 96-24369. 160p. 1996. reprint ed. pap. 10.95 (1-56170-340-0) Hay House.

Rising in the East? The Regeneration of East London. Ed. by Tim Butler & Michael Rustin. 320p. 1996. pap. 25.00 (0-85315-844-4, Pub. by Lawrence & Wishart UK) NYU Pr.

Rising in Western Upper Canada, 1837-8: The Duncombe Revolt & After. Colin Read. LC 82-168779. 339p. reprint ed. pap. 96.70 (0-8357-6366-8, 2035720) Bks Demand.

Rising of a New Moon: A Century of Tabwa Art. Evan M. Maurer & Allen F. Roberts. (Illus.). 288p. (Orig.). (C). 1986. pap. 39.95 (0-912303-32-8) Michigan Mus.

Rising of Agricultural Laborers: 1830-(1831?) LC 72-2542. (British Labour Struggles Before 1850 Ser.). 1974. 26.95 (0-405-04434-8) Ayer.

Rising of the Flesh. Karla Andersdatter. 96p. (Orig.). 1983. pap. 5.95 (0-911051-00-7) In Between.

Rising of the Moon. William Martin. 544p. 1995. mass mkt. 5.99 (0-446-36418-5) Warner Bks.

***Rising of the Moon.** unabridged ed. Augusta Gregory. LC 96-46109. 55p. (Orig.). 1996. pap. 6.00 (0-88734-368-6) Players Pr.

Rising of the Red Shawls: A Revolt in Madagascar 1895-1899. Stephen Ellis. (African Studies: No. 43). 230p. 1985. text ed. 80.00 (0-521-26287-9) Cambridge U Pr.

Rising of the Women. Meredith Tax. LC 80-8087. 332p. 1981. pap. 10.00 (0-85345-549-X) Monthly Rev.

Rising Passion. large type ed. Lynsey Stevens. 1991. reprint ed. lib. bdg. 18.95 (0-263-12557-2, Pub. by Mills & Boon UK) Thorndike Pr.

***Rising Phoenix.** Kyle Mills. mass mkt. 5.99 (0-06-101249-1, Harp PBks) HarpC.

***Rising Phoenix.** Kyle Mills. LC 97-20633. 1997. 24.00 (0-06-101248-3) HarpC.

Rising Public Voice: Women in Politics Worldwide. Ed. & Intro. by Alida Brill. LC 95-13894. (Illus.). 294p. 1995. 35.00 (1-55861-110-X); pap. 17.95 (1-55861-111-8) Feminist Pr.

Rising Sign: Your Astrological Mask. Jeanne Avery. LC 77-16894. (Illus.). 480p. 1982. pap. 12.95 (0-385-13278-6, Dolp) Doubleday.

Rising Sign Problem. Willner. 163p. 1992. 15.00 (0-86690-409-3) Am Fed Astrologers.

Rising Signs. Carolyn R. Dodson. LC 82-71708. 120p. 1979. 11.00 (0-86690-034-9, D2405-014) Am Fed Astrologers.

Rising Son: The Antecedents & Advancement of the Colored Race. William W. Brown. LC 79-79008. (Black Heritage Library Collection). 1977. 41.95 (0-8369-8519-2) Ayer.

Rising Song of African American Women. Barbara Omolade. LC 94-4752. 288p. (C). (gr. 13). 1994. text ed. 62.95 (0-415-90760-8) Routledge.

Rising Song of African American Women. Barbara Omolade. 288p. (gr. 13). 1994. pap. 17.95 (0-415-90761-6, Pub. by Tavistock UK) Routledge Chapman & Hall.

Rising Sons & Daughters: Life Among Japan's New Young. Steven Wardell. LC 94-181. 315p. (Orig.). 1994. 22.95 (0-9639230-8-0, HQ799.J3W37); pap. 13.95 (0-9639230-9-9) Plympton Pr.

Rising Star. Julia Kent. 352p. 1992. mass mkt. 4.99 (1-55817-648-9, Pinncle Kensgtn) Kensgtn Pub Corp.

***Rising Star: Dandyism, Gender, & Performance in the Fin de Siecle.** Rhonda K. Garelick. LC 97-21429. 1998. write for info. (0-691-01205-9) Princeton U Pr.

Rising Stars. Nachshon Walls. 80p. (Orig.). 1996. pap. write for info. (1-57502-226-5, P0894) Morris Pubng.

Rising Stars & Fast Fades: Successes & Failure of Fast-Growth Companies. Keith W. Schlit. 242p. 22.95 (0-02-927892-9, Free Press) Free Pr.

Rising Storm. G. Richard Holt. 352p. (Orig.). 1993. pap. 14.95 (0-89896-272-2) Larksdale.

Rising Storm. Bert H. Wallace. LC 95-68077. 117p. 1995. 17.95 (1-57197-000-2) Pentland Pr.

Rising Storm: An Analysis of the Growing Conflict Over the Political Dilemma of Roman Catholics in America. Hiram W. Evans. Ed. by Gerald Grob. LC 76-46075. (Anti-Movements in America Ser.). 1977. lib. bdg. 30.95 (0-405-09948-7) Ayer.

Rising Sun. Michael Crichton. 355p. 1992. 22.00 (0-394-58942-4) Knopf.

***Rising Sun.** Michael Crichton. 1997. pap. 12.00 (0-345-41896-4) Ballantine.

Rising Sun. Michael Crichton. 384p. 1993. mass mkt. 6.99 (*0-345-38037-1*) Ballantine.

Rising Sun. Elizabeth H. Vincent. 68p. 1992. pap. 6.95 (*0-8059-3357-3*) Dorrance.

Rising Sun: Maine Commemorates the Bicentennial of the United States Constitution. Vincent McKeeside et al. 74p. (Orig.). 1988. pap. 5.00 (*0-9621238-0-3*) Maine Commn.

Rising Sun in the Pacific, 1931-April 1942 see History of the United States Naval Operations in World War Two

Rising Tension in Eastern Europe & the Former Soviet Union. Ed. by David Carlton et al. LC 95-47704. (Illus.). 216p. 1996. 59.95 (*1-85521-666-3*, Pub. by Dartmth Pub UK) Ashgate Pub Co.

Rising Tide: Global Warming & World Sea Levels. Natural Resources Defense Council Staff & Lynne T. Edgerton. LC 90-5376. 136p. 1991. 29.95 (*1-55963-068-X*); pap. 17.95 (*1-55963-067-1*) Island Pr.

***Rising Tide: New Churches for the New Millennium.** Raymond W. Hurn. 184p. (Orig.). 1996. pap. 12.99 (*0-8341-1598-0*) Beacon Hill.

***Rising Tide: The Great Mississippi Flood of 1927 & How It Changed America.** John M. Barry. LC 96-40077. 1997. 27.50 (*0-684-81046-8*) S&S Trade.

Rising Tide of Change. Michael Burghley & Nancy Burghley. (Illus.). 69p. (Orig.). 1986. pap. 5.95 (*0-935427-12-0*) Foundation Hse.

Rising Tide of Color. Lothrop Stoddard. 1984. lib. bdg. 250.00 (*0-87700-598-2*) Revisionist Pr.

Rising Tide of Color. T. Lothrop Stoddard. 320p. 1986. pap. 9.50 (*0-906879-70-1*, Noontide Pr) Legion Survival.

Rising Tide of Color Against White World Supremacy. Lothrop Stoddard. 1994. lib. bdg. 255.95 (*0-8490-8941-7*) Gordon Pr.

Rising Tide of Cultural Pluralism: The Nation-State at Bay? Ed. by Crawford Young. LC 93-7103. (Illus.). 318p. (Orig.). (C). 1993. pap. 17.95 (*0-299-13884-4*); lib. bdg. 49.50 (*0-299-13880-1*) U of Wis Pr.

Rising Tide of Suicide: A Guide to Prevention, Intervention & Postvention. L. Richard Batzler. LC 85-82029. 200p. (Orig.). 1988. pap. 10.00 (*0-935710-08-6*) Hid Valley MD.

***Rising Tides.** Emilie Richards. 1997. mass mkt. 5.99 (*1-55166-273-6*, 1-66273-3, Mira Bks) Harlequin Bks.

***Rising to Sea Level.** Rayford E. Hammond. 454p. (Orig.). 1998. mass mkt. 9.99 (*1-889501-27-1*, Appaloosa) Sovereign.

***Rising to the Call: Healing Ourselves & Helping Others.** Jacquelyn Small & Mary Yovino. LC 96-72566. 256p. (Orig.). 1997. pap. 16.95 (*0-87516-704-7*) DeVorss.

***Rising to the Challenge of the National Science Education Standards: The Processes of Science Inquiry.** Karen L. Ostlund & Sheryl A. Mercier. (Illus.). 90p. (J). (gr. 4-8). 1996. teacher ed., pap. text ed. 20.00 (*0-9658768-0-2*) S & K Assocs.

***Rising to the Occasion.** Melanie Mills. 1997. mass mkt. 5.99 (*0-373-80511-X*, Harlequin) Harlequin Bks.

Rising to the Occasion: A Practical Companion for the Occasionally Perplexed. Edith Hazard & Wallace Pinfold. LC 92-44994. 224p. 1993. 14.95 (*1-56512-029-9*) Algonquin Bks.

Rising Trend of Government Employment. Solomon Fabricant. (Occasional Papers: No. 29). 34p. 1949. reprint ed. 20.00 (*0-87014-344-1*) Natl Bur Econ Res.

***Rising Trends in Asthma - Symposium No. 206, Vol. 206.** CIBA Foundation Symposium Staff & Stephen T. Holgate. LC 96-40339. (CIBA Foundation Symposium Ser.). 1997. text ed. write for info. (*0-471-97012-3*) Wiley.

Rising Up: Life Stories of Belizean Women. Henderson & Houghton. 1994. per. 16.95 (*0-920813-78-X*, Pub. by Sister Vision CN) LPC InBook.

***Rising Voices: A Guide to Young Writers' Resources.** 2nd rev. ed. 48p. (J). (gr. k-12). 1997. pap. 8.00 (*0-913734-60-8*) Poets & Writers.

Rising Voices: Writings of Young Native Americans. Arlene Hirschfelder & Beverly R. Singer. 144p. 1993. mass mkt. 4.99 (*0-8041-1167-7*) Ivy Books.

Rising Voices: Writings of Young Native Americans. Ed. by Arlene B. Hirschfelder & Beverly R. Singer. LC 91-32083. 128p. (YA). (gr. 7 up). 1992. lib. bdg. 14.00 (*0-684-19207-1*, C Scribner Sons Young) S&S Childrens.

Rising Wind. Walter F. White. LC 78-138684. 155p. 1971. reprint ed. text ed. 38.50 (*0-8371-5520-7*, WRW&, Greenwood Pr) Greenwood.

Rising Wind: A Novel. Dick Couch. LC 95-49583. 352p. 1996. 24.95 (*1-55750-133-5*) Naval Inst Pr.

Rising Wind: Black Americans & U. S. Foreign Affairs, 1935-1960. Brenda G. Plummer. LC 95-36068. (Illus.). 328p. (C). 1996. pap. text ed. 17.95 (*0-8078-4575-2*); lib. bdg. 39.95 (*0-8078-2272-8*) U of NC Pr.

***Rising with Christ: Catholic Women's Voices Across the World.** Thoralf Thielen. Ed. by Kevin Koch. 132p. (Orig.). 1997. pap. 8.95 (*1-879175-20-7*) Fortkamp.

Rising Zodiacal Sign: It's Meaning & Prognostics. Coulson Turnbull. 81p. 1991. pap. 10.00 (*0-89540-188-6*, SB-188, Sun Bks) Sun Pub.

Rising Zodiacal Sign: Its Meaning & Prognostics. Coulson Turnbull. 50p. 1996. pap. 9.95 (*1-56459-827-6*) Kessinger Pub.

Rising Zodiacal Sign: Its Meaning & Prognostics. Coulson Turnbull. 61p. 1986. reprint ed. spiral bd. 10.00 (*0-7873-1058-1*) Hlth Research.

Risings. Frances L. Hardy. (Illus.). 56p. (Orig.). 1994. pap. 6.00 (*0-9638611-0-7*) Vision Unltd.

Risings. Peter Armstrong. 53p. 8800. reprint ed. pap. 11.95 (*1-870612-00-0*, Pub. by Enitha Pr UK) Dufour.

Risings: An Anthology. David Axelrod et al. Ed. by Jeanne Voege. (Illus.). 48p. 1991. pap. text ed. 6.00 (*0-9616160-5-9*) Bench Pr NY.

Risis in Ancient India. Chandra B. Pandey. 265p. 1987. 26.00 (*0-8364-2022-5*, Pub. by Sundeep II) S Asia.

Risk. Ed. by Edward J. Burger. 178p. 1993. pap. text ed. 17.95 (*0-472-08222-1*) U of Mich Pr.

Risk. Louis Eeckhoudt & Christian Gollier. 1995. pap. 43.00 (*0-13-342825-7*) P-H.

Risk. Dick Francis. 1994. mass mkt. 5.99 (*0-449-22239-X*, Crest) Fawcett.

Risk. Doris Parmett. 336p. (Orig.). 1994. mass mkt. 4.99 (*0-515-11333-6*) Jove Pubns.

Risk. large type ed. Dick Francis. 1979. 12.00 (*0-7089-0309-6*) Ulverscroft.

Risk. Dick Francis. 1994. reprint ed. lib. bdg. 37.95 (*1-56849-281-2*) Buccaneer Bks.

Risk: A Philosophical Introduction to the Theory of Risk Evaluation & Management. Nicholas Rescher. LC 82-21970. (Nicholas Rescher Ser.). 218p. (Orig.). 1983. pap. text ed. 23.00 (*0-8191-2270-X*) U Pr of Amer.

Risk: A Sociological Theory. Niklas Luhmann. (Communication & Social Order Ser.). 249p. 1993. lib. bdg. 49.95 (*0-202-30443-4*) Aldine de Gruyter.

Risk! An Exploration into the Lives of Athletes on the Edge. 2nd ed. Steve Boga. (Illus.). 173p. (Orig.). 1988. pap. 9.95 (*1-55643-042-6*) North Atlantic.

Risk: Derivitive Securities. Bob Tamarkin. 1996. write for info. (*0-8129-2674-9*, Times Bks) Random.

Risk: Forty Golden Rules for Risk Investing. Donald A. Schaberg. Ed. by Jack Schaberg & James H. Soltow. 144p. 1985. 19.95 (*0-9614050-0-7*) Probe Co.

Risk: Man-Made Hazards to Man. M. G. Cooper. (C). 1985. 135.00 (*0-685-33711-1*, Pub. by Witherby & Co UK) St Mut.

Risk: The Policy Implications of Risk Compensation & Plural Rationalities. John Adams. LC 95-88. 1995. 65.00 (*1-85728-067-9*, Pub. by UCL Pr UK); pap. write for info. (*1-85728-068-7*, Pub. by UCL Pr UK) Taylor & Francis.

Risk - Paradise Lost or Gained? A Holistic Approach to the Environment. Ed. by Otto-Peter Obermeier & Mathias Schuez. LC 95-35638. (Illus.). 396p. (C). 1995. text ed. 29.95 (*0-89876-230-8*) Gardner Pr.

Risk a Thousand, Make a Million? How to Trade Stock Index Futures. Mark K. McConnell. (Illus.). 34p. (Orig.). 1989. pap. 6.95 (*0-9622816-0-3*) Capital Growth.

Risk Acceptability According to the Social Sciences. Mary Douglas. LC 85-60758. (Social Research Perspectives: Occasional Reports on Current Topics Ser.). 160p. (Orig.). 1986. pap. text ed. 9.95 (*0-87154-211-0*) Russell Sage.

Risk Adjustment for Measuring Health Care Outcomes. Ed. by Lisa I. Iezzoni. LC 94-7005. 418p. 1994. pap. 38.00 (*1-56793-014-X*, 0944) Health Admin Pr.

***Risk Adjustment for Measuring Healthcare Outcomes.** 2nd ed. Lisa I. Iezzoni. LC 97-21. 1997. write for info. (*1-56793-054-9*) Health Admin Pr.

Risk Analysis. G. C. Dickson. 170p. (C). 1987. pap. 200.00 (*0-948691-78-6*, Pub. by Witherby & Co UK) St Mut.

Risk Analysis. G. C. Dickson. 170p. (C). 1990. 210.00 (*1-85609-014-0*, Pub. by Witherby & Co UK) St Mut.

Risk Analysis: A Guide to Principles & Methods for Analyzing Health & Environmental Risks. 1992. lib. bdg. 250.00 (*0-8490-5572-5*) Gordon Pr.

Risk Analysis: A Guide to Principles & Methods for Analyzing Health & Environmental Risks. John Cohrrsen. 400p. (Orig.). 1989. pap. 17.50 (*0-934213-20-8*, PB89-137772) Natl Tech Info.

Risk Analysis: A Quantitative Guide to Monte Carlo Simulation Modelling. David Vose. 200p. 1996. text ed. 65.00 (*0-471-95803-4*) Wiley.

Risk Analysis: Prospects & Opportunities. Ed. by Constantine Zervos et al. (Advances in Risk Analysis Ser.: Vol. 8). (Illus.). 780p. 1992. 175.00 (*0-306-44113-6*, Plenum Pr) Plenum.

Risk Analysis & Its Applications. David B. Hertz & Howard Thomas. LC 81-16382. 346p. reprint ed. pap. 98.70 (*0-8357-4958-4*, 2037890) Bks Demand.

Risk Analysis & Management of Natural & Man-Made Hazards. Ed. by Yacov Y. Haimes & Eugene Z. Stakhiv. 364p. 1989. 35.00 (*0-87262-688-1*) Am Soc Civil Eng.

***Risk Analysis & Reduction in the Chemical Process.** Santamaria. (Illus.). 416p. 1997. text ed. write for info. (*0-7514-0374-1*, Pub. by Blackie Acad & Prof UK) Routledge Chapman & Hall.

Risk Analysis & Scientific Method: Methodological & Ethical Problems with Evaluating Societal Hazards. Kristin S. Shrader-Frechette. 236p. 1985. lib. bdg. 97.00 (*90-277-1836-9*) Kluwer Ac.

Risk Analysis & the Security Survey. James F. Broder. 235p. 1984. reprint ed. 34.95 (*0-7506-9430-0*) Buttrwrth-Heinemann.

Risk Analysis As a Method of Comparing Safety & Environmental Hazards from Different Field Concepts. J. A. Cumming. 1989. 125.00 (*90-6314-533-0*, Pub. by Lorne & MacLean Marine) St Mut.

Risk Analysis As a Method of Comparing Safety & Environmental Hazards from Different Field Concepts. Ed. by J. A. Cumming. (C). 1989. 95.00 (*0-89771-734-1*, Pub. by Lorne & MacLean Marine) St Mut.

Risk Analysis for Large Projects: Models, Methods, & Cases. Dale F. Cooper & Chris B. Chapman. LC 86-15968. 260p. 1987. text ed. 125.00 (*0-471-91247-6*) Wiley.

***Risk Analysis for Process Plant, Pipelines & Transport.** Ed. by Taylor. (Illus.). 464p. 1994. text ed. 157.95 (*0-419-19090-2*, E & FN Spon) Routledge Chapman & Hall.

Risk Analysis Guide: Exposure Questionnaire for Risk Managers. 75p. 1990. 50.00 (*0-937802-27-1*) RMSP.

Risk Analysis Guide to Insurance & Employee Benefits. A. E. Pfaffle & Sal Nicosia. LC 77-10973. 71p. reprint ed. pap. 25.00 (*0-317-26314-5*, 2055752) Bks Demand.

Risk Analysis in Nuclear Waste Management. Ed. by A. Saltelli et al. (C). 1989. lib. bdg. 198.00 (*0-7923-0476-4*) Kluwer Ac.

Risk Analysis in Project Appraisal. Louis Y. Pouliquen. LC 79-120739. (World Bank Staff Occasional Papers: No. 11). 95p. (Orig.). reprint ed. pap. 27.10 (*0-7837-0342-2*, 2040661) Bks Demand.

Risk Analysis in Project Management. John Raftery. LC 93-32191. 1993. write for info. (*0-419-18420-1*, E & FN Spon) Routledge Chapman & Hall.

Risk Analysis in the Private Sector. Ed. by Chris Shipple & Vincent T. Covello. (Advances in Risk Analysis Ser.: Vol. 3). 516p. 1985. 115.00 (*0-306-41924-6*, Plenum Pr) Plenum.

Risk & Bank Expansion into Nonbanking Businesses. rev. ed. Eek-June Chung. LC 94-42202. (Financial Sector of the American Economy Ser.). 145p. 1995. text ed. 49.00 (*0-8153-1974-6*) Garland.

Risk & Blame: Essays in Cultural Theory. Mary Douglas. 336p. (C). 1994. pap. 18.95 (*0-415-11999-5*, Routledge NY) Routledge.

***Risk & Business Cycles: New & Old Austrian Perspectives.** Tylor Cowen. LC 97-13794. (Foundations of the Modern Economy Ser.). 1997. write for info. (*0-415-16919-4*) Routledge.

Risk & Capital: Proceedings of the 2nd Summer Workshop on Risk & Capital Held at the University of Ulm, West Germany, June 20-24, 1983. Ed. by G. Bamberg & A. Spremann. (Lecture Notes in Economics & Mathematical Systems Ser.: Vol. 227). 320p. 1984. 41.00 (*0-387-12923-5*) Spr-Verlag.

Risk & Consent to Risk in Medicine. Ed. by R. D. Mann. (Illus.). 234p. 1989. 65.00 (*1-85070-263-2*) Prthnon Pub.

Risk & Culture: An Essay on the Selection of Technological & Environmental Dangers. Mary Douglas & Aaron B. Wildavsky. LC 81-16318. 224p. 1982. pap. 14.95 (*0-520-05063-0*) U CA Pr.

Risk & Failure in English Business 1700-1800. Julian Hoppit. 232p. 1987. text ed. 54.95 (*0-521-32624-9*) Cambridge U Pr.

Risk & Human Rationality. Richard C. Jeffrey. (Working Papers on Risk & Rationality). 1988. 2.50 (*0-318-33323-6*, RR7) IPPP.

Risk & Innovation: The Role & Importance of Small, High-Tech Companies in the U. S. Economy. National Academy of Engineering Staff. 104p. (Orig.). 1995. pap. text ed. 20.00 (*0-309-05376-5*) Natl Acad Pr.

Risk & Insurance. Jack Rudman. (Dantes Subject Standardized Tests Ser.: No. Dantes-51). pap. 23.95 (*0-8373-6651-8*) Nat Learn.

Risk & Insurance. 6th ed. Athearn. Date not set. text ed. 63.00 (*0-314-64063-0*); teacher ed., pap. text ed. write for info. (*0-314-65224-8*) West Pub.

Risk & Insurance. 7th ed. Mark R. Greene & James S. Trieschmann. 768p. (C). 1988. text ed. write for info. (*0-538-06550-8*, F55) S-W Pub.

Risk & Insurance. 8th ed. Mark Greene et al. (C). 1991. text ed. write for info. (*0-538-81117-X*, FF65HA) S-W Pub.

Risk & Insurance Management Guide for Medical Group Organizations. Aaron Liberman. 1988. 24.00 (*0-933948-14-X*) Med Group Mgmt.

***Risk & Misfortune: A Social Construction of Accidents.** Judith Green. LC 96-53425. (Health, Risk & Society Ser.). 240p. 1997. 65.00 (*1-85728-560-3*, Pub. by UCL Pr UK); pap. 26.95 (*1-85728-561-1*, Pub. by UCL Pr UK) Taylor & Francis.

***Risk & Our Pedagogical Relation to Children: On the Playground & Beyond.** Stephen J. Smith. LC 97-17264. (Early Childhood Education Ser.). 1998. text ed. 59.50 (*0-7914-3593-8*) State Univ of New York.

***Risk & Our Pedagogical Relation to Children: On the Playground & Beyond.** Stephen J. Smith. LC 97-17264. (Early Childhood Education Ser.). 1998. pap. text ed. 19.95 (*0-7914-3594-6*) State Univ of New York.

Risk & Prevention of Arterial Lipidoses. P. Schwandt. 194p. 1990. 22.50 (*0-87527-232-0*) Green.

Risk & Progression Factors in Carcinogenesis, Vol. 143. Ed. by H. K. Muller-Hermelink et al. LC 96-12853. (Recent Results in Cancer Research Ser.: Vol. 143). 392p. 1996. 157.00 (*3-540-60953-9*) Spr-Verlag.

Risk & Protective Factors in the Development of Psychopathology. Ed. by Jon Rolf et al. (Illus.). 560p. (C). 1990. text ed. 74.95 (*0-521-35099-9*) Cambridge U Pr.

Risk & Protective Factors in the Development of Psychopathology. Ed. by Jon Rolf et al. (Illus.). 576p. (C). 1993. pap. text ed. 26.95 (*0-521-43972-8*) Cambridge U Pr.

Risk & Rationality: Philosophical Foundations for Populist Reforms. Kristin S. Shrader-Frechette. LC 91-3294. 272p. 1991. 45.00 (*0-520-07287-1*); pap. 17.00 (*0-520-07289-8*) U CA Pr.

Risk & Recovery: AIDS, HIV, & Alcohol: A Handbook for Providers. Marcia Quackenbush et al. LC 92-26635. 256p. 1995. pap. 16.95 (*0-89087-690-8*) Celestial Arts.

***Risk & Redemption: Surviving the Network News Wars.** Arthur Kent. (Illus.). 308p. 1997. 26.00 (*976-8056-08-8*, Pub. by Interstellar VB) Skywrtr Comm Inc.

Risk & Reliability in Ground Engineering. Ed. by B. O. Skipp. 308p. 1994. 96.00 (*0-7844-1986-8*) Am Soc Civil Eng.

***Risk & Resilience in Childhood: An Ecological Perspective.** Ed. by Mark W. Fraser. LC 96-6538. 320p. (Orig.). (C). 1997. pap. text ed. 35.95 (*0-87101-274-X*, 274X) Natl Assn Soc Wkrs.

Risk & Responsibility. William Leiss & Christina Chociolko. 424p. 1994. 55.00 (*0-7735-1177-6*, Pub. by McGill CN); pap. 22.95 (*0-7735-1194-6*, Pub. by McGill CN) U of Toronto Pr.

***Risk & Reward: A "How-to" Guide to Choosing an MSO.** David W. Hilgers et al. (Illus.). 130p. 1997. pap. 49.00 (*0-9640262-6-0*) TX Med Assn.

Risk & Reward: How Investors Helped Create America's Industries & What You Should Know About Venture Capital Today. Thomas M. Doerflinger & Jack L. Rivkin. LC 86-10107. 288p. 1987. 19.95 (*0-394-54929-5*) Random.

Risk & Rhetoric in Religion: Whitehead's Theory of Language & the Discourse of Faith. Lyman T. Lundeen. LC 71-171501. 288p. reprint ed. pap. 82.10 (*0-685-15360-6*, 2026868) Bks Demand.

Risk & Safety Assessment Vol. 296: Where Is the Balance? Ed. by E. D. Jones & F. L. Cho. (Proceedings of the 1995 ASME/JSME Pressure Vessels & Piping Conference Ser.: PVP-Vol. 296). 576p. 1995. 150.00 (*0-7918-1327-4*, H00959) ASME.

Risk & Safety Assessments Vol. 320-5: Building Viable Solutions - 1995. Ed. by E. D. Jones & F. L. Cho. (1995 International Mechanical Engineering Congress & Exposition Ser.: PVP-Vol. 320/SERA-Vol. 5). 380p. 1995. 100.00 (*0-7918-1732-6*, H01014) ASME.

Risk & Society: Studies of Risk Generation & Reactions to Risks. Lennart Sjoberg. (Risks & Hazards Ser.: No. 3). 320p. (C). 1987. text ed. 39.95 (*0-04-604001-3*) Routledge Chapman & Hall.

Risk & Society: The Interaction of Science, Technology & Public Policy. Ed. by Marvin Waterstone. (Technology, Risk & Society Ser.: No. 6). 204p. 1992. lib. bdg. 129.50 (*0-7923-1370-4*, Pub. by Klwr Acad Pubs NE) Kluwer Ac.

Risk & Survival in Ancient Greece: Reconstructing the Rural Domestic Economy. Thomas W. Gallant. LC 90-70905. 283p. 1991. 45.00 (*0-8047-1857-1*) Stanford U Pr.

Risk & Technological Innovation: American Manufacturing Methods During the Nineteenth Century. Wolfgang P. Strassmann. LC 81-4252. x, 249p. 1981. reprint ed. text ed. 59.75 (*0-313-23083-8*, STRIT, Greenwood Pr) Greenwood.

Risk & Tenure in Arid Lands: The Political Ecology of Development in the Senegal River Basin. Ed. by Thomas K. Park. LC 93-9691. (Monographs on Arid Lands Development). 383p. 1993. 33.50 (*0-8165-1374-0*) U of Ariz Pr.

Risk & the Business Environment. A. Gordon. 166p. (C). 1987. pap. 200.00 (*0-948691-79-4*, Pub. by Witherby & Co UK) St Mut.

Risk & the Business Environment. Alan Gordon. 166p. (C). 1992. 195.00 (*1-85609-034-5*, Pub. by Witherby & Co UK) St Mut.

Risk & Uncertainty in Economics: Essays in Honour of James L. Ford. Ed. by David G. Dickinson et al. 240p. 1995. 80.00 (*1-85278-736-8*) E Elgar.

Risk Approach in Health Care with Special Reference to Maternal & Child Health, including Family Planning. E. M. Backett et al. (Public Health Papers: No. 76). 121p. 1984. pap. text ed. 11.00 (*92-4-130076-0*, 1110076) World Health.

Risk Assessment: A Glance at the Non-Technical Aspects. (State Legislative Reports: Vol. 19, No. 18). 7p. 1994. 5.00 (*1-55516-386-6*, 7302-1918) Natl Conf State Legis.

Risk Assessment: A Practitioner's Guide to Predicting Harmful Behaviour. Bryony Moore. 250p. 1996. 65.00 (*1-871177-83-9*, Pub. by Whiting & Birch UK); pap. 25.00 (*1-871177-84-7*, Pub. by Whiting & Birch UK) Paul & Co Pubs.

Risk Assessment: Principles & Applications for Hazardous Waste & Related Sites. Peter K. LaGoy. LC 94-2510. (Illus.). 244p. 1994. 48.00 (*0-8155-1349-6*) Noyes.

Risk Assessment - Environmental Fate Methodologies. Calabrese. 192p. 1992. 79.95 (*0-87371-711-2*) CRC Pr.

Risk Assessment & Communication: Techniques for Managing the Transport of Nuclear Spent Fuel & High-Level Radioactive Waste. Rebecca L. Shafer. (State Legislative Reports: Vol. 17, No. 12). 6p. 1992. 5.00 (*1-55516-285-1*, 7302-1712) Natl Conf State Legis.

Risk Assessment & Communication Related to Water Resources: Bibliography January 1985-December 1993. Ed. by Joe Makuch & Bonnie Emmert. 30p. (Orig.). (C). 1995. pap. text ed. 20.00 (*0-7881-2199-5*) DIANE Pub.

Risk Assessment & Decision Making Using Test Results: The Carcinogenicity Prediction & Battery Selection Approach. J. Pet-Edwards et al. (Illus.). 220p. 1989. 69.50 (*0-306-43067-3*, Plenum Pr) Plenum.

Risk Assessment & Management. Ed. by Lester B. Lave. LC 87-21288. (Advances in Risk Analysis Ser.: Vol. 5). (Illus.). 752p. 1987. 155.00 (*0-306-42683-8*, Plenum Pr) Plenum.

Risk Assessment & Management Handbook: For Environmental, Health, & Safety Professionals. Robin Pitblado et al. 1996. text ed. 89.50 (*0-07-035987-3*) McGraw.

Risk Assessment & Regulatory Policy. A. W. Hayes. 84p. 1986. text ed. 96.00 (*2-88124-421-1*) Gordon & Breach.

Risk Assessment & Risk Management. Ed. by Paul Slovic & Howard C. Kunreuther. LC 95-71933. (Annals of the American Academy of Political & Social Science Ser.: Vol. 545). 1996. 28.00 (*0-7619-0297-X*); pap. 18.00 (*0-7619-0298-8*) Am Acad Pol Soc Sci.

Risk Assessment & Risk Management for the Chemical Process Industry. Stone & Webster Engineering Corp. Staff. Ed. by Harris Greenberg et al. 1991. text ed. 83.95 (*0-442-23438-4*) Van Nos Reinhold.

An Asterisk (*) at the beginning of an entry indicates that the title is appearing in BIP for the first time.

Risk Assessment & Risk Management of Industrial & Envrionmental Chemicals. Ed. by Richard Cothera et al. (Advances in Modern Envrionmental Toxicology Ser.: Vol. 15). (Illus.). 246p. 1988. 65.00 (*0-911131-16-7*) Princeton Sci Pubs.

Risk Assessment at Hazardous Waste Sites. Ed. by F. A. Long & Glenn E. Schweitzer. LC 82-16376. (Symposium Ser.: No. 204). 129p. 1982. lib. bdg. 38.95 (*0-8412-0747-X*) Am Chemical.

***Risk Assessment at Hazardous Waste Sites.** Ed. by Franklin A. Long & Glenn E. Schweitzer. LC 82-16376. (ACS Symposium Ser.: No. 204). (Illus.). 139p. 1982. reprint ed. pap. 39.70 (*0-608-03217-4*, 2063736) Bks Demand.

Risk Assessment for Deliberate Releases. W. Klingmuller. (Illus.). 215p. 1988. 63.95 (*0-387-18930-0*) Spr-Verlag.

Risk Assessment for Groundwater Pollution Control. Ed. by William F. McTernan & Edward Kaplan. LC 90-20924. 368p. 1990. pap. text ed. 33.00 (*0-87262-784-5*) Am Soc Civil Eng.

Risk Assessment in Chemical Carcinogenesis. Dietrich Schmahl. (Sitzungsberichte der Heidelberger Akademie der Wissenschaften Ser., Mathematisch-Naturwissenschaftliche Klasse, Jahrgang 1991: Suppl. 1). (Illus.). 180p. 1991. 39.95 (*0-387-54149-7*) Spr-Verlag.

Risk Assessment in Conservation Biology. M. Burgman et al. (Population & Community Biology Ser.). 256p. (gr. 13). 1993. text ed. 66.95 (*0-412-35030-0*, A9451) Chapman & Hall.

Risk Assessment in Setting National Priorities. Ed. by J. J. Bonin & D. E. Stevenson. (Advances in Risk Analysis Ser.: Vol. 7). (Illus.). 698p. 1989. 155.00 (*0-306-43246-3*, Plenum Pr) Plenum.

Risk Assessment in the Chemical Process Industries. Kaplan & Kazarian. 1991. write for info. (*0-8493-6967-3*, TK, CRC Reprint) Franklin.

Risk Assessment in the Process Industries. 2nd ed. Ed. by Robin Turney & Robin Pitblado. 160p. 1996. pap. 45.00 (*0-85295-323-2*, 53232) Gulf Pub.

Risk Assessment Kit. Fowler. Date not set. pap. text ed. 49.00 (*0-15-601976-0*) Profess Pubns.

Risk Assessment Methodologies for Toxic Air Pollutants. Environmental Protection Agency Staff. 278p. 1995. pap. text ed. 79.00 (*0-86587-445-X*) Gov Insts.

Risk Assessment Methods: Approaches for Assessing Health & Environmental Risks. Vincent T. Covello & Miley W. Merkhoher. (Illus.). 330p. (C). 1994. 59.50 (*0-306-44382-1*, Plenum Pr) Plenum.

Risk Assessment of Chemicals: An Introduction. C. J. Van Leeuwen. Ed. by J. L. Hermens. 392p. (C). 1995. lib. bdg. 94.00 (*0-7923-3740-9*) Kluwer Ac.

Risk Assessment of Chemicals in the Environment. Richardson. 1988. 187.00 (*0-85186-118-0*) CRC Pr.

Risk Assessment of Environmental & Human Health Hazards: Textbook of Case Studies. Ed. by Dennis J. Paustenbach. LC 87-35056. 1155p. 1989. text ed. 195.00 (*0-471-84998-7*) Wiley.

Risk Assessment of Essential Elements. Ed. by Charles O. Abernathy et al. LC 94-75706. (Illus.). 320p. 1994. 45.00 (*0-944398-21-9*) ILSI.

***Risk Assessment of Hazardous Chemical Systems in Developing Countries.** Compiled by Kirk R. Smith et al. LC 88-146867. (East-West Environment & Policy Institute, Occasional Paper Ser.: Vol. 5). 150p. 1988. reprint ed. pap. 42.80 (*0-608-03573-4*, 2064396) Bks Demand.

Risk Assessment of N-Nitroso Compounds for Human Health. Dietrich Schmahl. (Journal: Oncology: Vol. 37, No. 4). (Illus.). 120p. 1980. pap. 49.00 (*3-8055-1137-X*) S Karger.

Risk Assessment of Prenatally-Induced Adverse Health Effects. Diether Neubert et al. LC 92-26482. 1992. 125.00 (*0-387-55890-X*) Spr-Verlag.

Risk Assessment/Management Issues in the Environmental Planning of Mines. Ed. by Dirk J. Van Zyl et al. LC 92-64477. (Illus.). 207p. (Orig.). 1992. pap. 55.00 (*0-87335-115-0*, 115-0) SMM&E Inc.

Risk at Delivery. Ed. by G. P. Mandruzzato. (Contributions to Gynecology & Obstetrics Ser.: Vol. 3). (Illus.). 1977. 39.25 (*3-8055-2421-8*) S Karger.

Risk Aversion, Insurance, & the Future. Mark R. Greene. LC 70-633854. (Sesquicentennial Insurance Ser.: No. 2). 1971. 7.50 (*0-685-00048-6*) Ind U Busn Res.

Risk Based Capital: An Economic Overview. J. David Cummins et al. 1992. pap. text ed. 7.50 (*1-887271-08-2*) Alliance Am Insurers.

Risk Based Capital Charges for Municipal Bonds. Robert Godfrey. LC 90-44319. (Contemporary Studies in Economic & Financial Analysis: Vol. 68). 221p. 1990. 73.25 (*1-55938-243-0*) Jai Pr.

Risk-Based Contributions to Private Health Insurance, Vol. 12. Ed. by Mark C. Hornbrook. (Advances in Health Economics & Health Services Research Ser.). 268p. 1991. 73.25 (*1-55938-241-4*) Jai Pr.

Risk-Based Decision Making in Water Resources. Ed. by Yacov Y. Haimes & Eugene Z. Stakhiv. LC 90-48908. 344p. 1990. pap. text ed. 32.00 (*0-87262-782-9*) Am Soc Civil Eng.

Risk-Based Decision Making in Water Resources: Proceedings of the Seventh Conference, October 8-13, 1995, Santa Barbara, California, Vol. II. Yacov Y. Haimes & David A. Moser. LC 96-18517. 1996. 44.00 (*0-7844-0168-3*) Am Soc Civil Eng.

Risk-Based Decision Making in Water Resources V. Ed. by Yacov Y. Haimes et al. 400p. 1992. pap. text ed. 36.00 (*0-87262-899-X*) Am Soc Civil Eng.

Risk-Based Decision Making in Water Resources VI. Ed. by Yacov Y. Haimes et al. 392p. 1994. text ed. 36.00 (*0-7844-0032-6*) Am Soc Civil Eng.

Risk-Based Inspection: Developments of Guidelines, Vol. 2: Light Water Reactor (LWR) Nuclear Power Plant Components. LC 92-54327. 156p. 1993. pap. 100.00 (*0-7918-0658-8*, I00321) ASME.

Risk-Based Internal Auditing for Depository Institutions: Practices & Techniques. William T. Thornhill. 1991. text ed. 55.00 (*1-55520-145-8*) Irwin Prof Pubng.

Risk-Based Management. Richard B. Jones. 300p. 1995. 55.00 (*0-88415-785-7*) Gulf Pub.

Risk-Based Payments under Public Programs, Vol. 10. Ed. by Richard M. Scheffler et al. (Advances in Health Economics & Health Services Research Ser.). 376p. 1989. 73.25 (*0-89232-976-9*) Jai Pr.

Risk-Benefit Analysis: The Microwave Case. Ed. by N. H. Steneck. (Illus.). 1982. 10.00 (*0-911302-44-1*) San Francisco Pr.

Risk-Benefit Analysis for the Use & Approval of Thrombolytic, Antiarrhythmic, & Hypolipidemic Agents. Ed. by Joel Morganroth & E. Neil Moore. (C). 1989. lib. bdg. 120.00 (*0-7923-0294-X*) Kluwer Ac.

Risk-Benefit Assessments & Societal Cost of Nuclear & Other Energy Sources. Ed. by R. A. Karam & L. E. Weaver. 120p. 1983. pap. 48.00 (*0-08-030543-1*, Pergamon Pr) Elsevier.

Risk Business. Michael Blakstad. 144p. (C). 1979. pap. text ed. 50.00 (*0-85072-098-2*) St Mut.

Risk Business. Ron Phillips. (C). 1989. 35.00 (*1-871058-05-8*, Pub. by Dragonheart Pr UK) St Mut.

Risk by Choice: Regulating Health & Safety in the Workplace. W. Kip Viscusi. (Illus.). 216p. 1983. 29.00 (*0-674-77302-0*) HUP.

Risk Calc: Calculating Bounds on Point Estimates. Scott Ferson & Rudiger Kuhn. (Illus.). 49p. (C). 1994. pap. text ed. 395.00 (*1-884977-20-0*); pap. text ed. 795.00 incl. disk (*1-884977-21-9*) Applied Biomath.

Risk, Capital Costs & Project Financing Decisions. Frans G. Derkinderen & Roy L. Crum. (Nijenrode Studies in Business: Vol. 6). 288p. 1980. lib. bdg. 92.00 (*0-89838-046-4*) Kluwer Ac.

Risk Class Evaluation. 10p. 1985. 40.00 (*0-939050-38-2*) Credit Res NYS.

Risk Classification in Life Insurance. J. David Cummins et al. (S. S. Huebner International Ser.). 1983. lib. bdg. 78.00 (*0-89838-114-2*) Huebner Foun Insur.

Risk Classification in Life Insurance (Netherlands) Witherby & Co. Ltd. Staff. (C). 1982. 355.00 (*0-685-33712-X*, Pub. by Witherby & Co UK) St Mut.

Risk Communication: A Handbook for Communicating Environmental, Safety, & Health Risks. Regina E. Lundgren. LC 93-31903. 186p. (C). 1994. pap. text ed. 29.95 (*0-935470-76-X*) Battelle.

***Risk Communication about Chemicals in Your Community: A Manual for Local Officials.** Susan G. Hadden & Barry V. Bales. 68p. 1996. reprint ed. pap. 20.00 (*0-7881-3163-X*) DIANE Pub.

Risk, Communication, & Decision Making in Genetic Counseling. Ed. by Charles J. Epstein. LC 79-5120. (Alan R. Liss Ser.: Vol. 15, No. 5c). 1979. 43.00 (*0-685-03297-3*) March of Dimes.

Risk Control for Churches. M. Douglas Clark. LC 81-86316. (Illus.). ring bd. 39.50 (*0-88061-007-7*) Intl Loss Cntrl.

Risk, Decision Making & Bargaining. Compiled by Richard Schwindt. LC 95-61171. (Business Administration Reading Lists & Course Outlines Ser.: Vol. 13). (Illus.). 208p. (C). 1995. pap. text ed. 24.00 (*0-88024-173-X*) Eno River Pr.

Risk Decision Making in Transport Operations. Ed. by W. Janssen & I. D. Brown. (Ergonomics Ser.: Vol. 31, No. 4). 283p. 1988. pap. 42.00 (*0-85066-916-2*) Taylor & Francis.

***Risk, Economy & Safety, Failure Minimisation & Analysis-Failures 1996: Proceedings of the Second International Symposium, Pilanesberg, South Africa, 22-26 July 1996.** R. K. Penny. 388p. 1996. 95.00 (*90-5410-823-1*, Pub. by A A Balkema NE) Ashgate Pub Co.

Risk Elements in Consumer Installment Financing. David Durand. (Financial Research Program II: Studies in Consumer Installment Financing: No. 8). 128p. 1941. reprint ed. 33.30 (*0-87014-124-4*); reprint ed. mic. film 20.00 (*0-685-61219-8*) Natl Bur Econ Res.

Risk, Environment & Modernity: Towards a New Ecology. Scott Lash & Brian Wynne. (Theory, Culture & Society Ser.). 256p. 1995. 65.00 (*0-8039-7937-1*); pap. 21.95 (*0-8039-7938-X*) Sage.

Risk Estimates for Radiation Protection. Intro. by Charles B. Meinhold. LC 93-44242. (Report Ser.: No. 115). 148p. (Orig.). 1993. pap. text ed. 35.00 (*0-929600-34-7*) NCRP Pubns.

Risk Evaluation & Management. Vincent T. Covello et al. (Contemporary Issues in Risk Analysis Ser.: Advances in Risk Analysis Ser. vol. 1). 556p. 1986. 130.00 (*0-306-41978-5*, Plenum Pr) Plenum.

Risk Evaluation for Sludge-Borne Elements to Wildlife Food Chains. David K. Woodyard & Jonathan B. Haufler. LC 90-26736. (Environment: Problems & Solutions Ser.). 205p. 1991. text ed. 15.00 (*0-8240-9797-1*) Garland.

***Risk Factor Love.** Henriksson. 1997. 50.00 (*1-85489-090-5*) Paul & Co Pubs.

Risk Factors for Adverse Drug Reactions: Epidemiological Approaches. R. Hoigne et al. (Agents & Actions Supplements Ser.: No. 29). 150p. 1990. 42.50 (*0-8176-2372-8*) Birkhauser.

Risk Factors for Cancer in the Workplace. Jack Siemiatycki. (Illus.). 176p. 1991. 133.00 (*0-8493-5018-2*, RC268) CRC Pr.

Risk Factors for Cardiovascular Disease in Non-Smokers. Ed. by D. F. Weetman & D. Wood. (Illus.). x, 150p. 1993. 128.75 (*3-8055-5682-9*) S Karger.

Risk Factors for Cataract Development. Ed. by Otto Hockwin et al. (Developments in Ophthalmology Ser.: Vol. 17). (Illus.). xi, 217p. 1989. 148.00 (*3-8055-4906-7*) S Karger.

Risk Factors for Youth Suicide. Ed. by Lucy Davidson & Markku Linnoila. (Death Education, Aging & Health Care Ser.). 275p. 1990. 57.95 (*1-56032-138-5*) Hemisp Pub.

Risk Factors in Infancy, Vol. 7. Ed. by Alice S. Honig. (Special Aspects of Education Ser.: Vol. 7). 176, xp. 1986. text ed. 117.00 (*0-677-21420-0*); pap. text ed. 28.00 (*0-677-21430-8*) Gordon & Breach.

Risk Financing. Ed. by Alan Gordon. 180p. (C). 1992. 205.00 (*1-85609-001-9*, Pub. by Witherby & Co UK) St Mut.

Risk Financing: A Guide Insurance Cash Flow. 1983. 210.00 (*1-886813-16-7*) Intl Risk Mgt.

Risk-Free Advertising: How to Come Close to It. Victor Wademan. LC 77-8083. (Wiley-Interscience Publications). (Illus.). 157p. reprint ed. pap. 44.80 (*0-7837-3478-6*, 2057811) Bks Demand.

Risk-Free Business Re-Engineering: How to Re-Engineer Your Organization Using Business Event Partitioning to Achieve Ultimate Customer Satisfaction. Brian Dickinson. (Business Re-Engineering Methodology Ser.). (Illus.). 296p. Date not set. text ed. 39.95 (*0-9629276-2-7*); pap. text ed. 29.95 (*0-9629276-1-9*) LCI Pr.

Risk, Information & Insurance. Ed. by Henri Louberge. (C). 1990. lib. bdg. 79.00 (*0-7923-9041-5*, Pub. by Graham & Trotman UK) Kluwer Ac.

Risk, Insurance, Reinsurance: Lexicon. Henri Sommer. 396p. (ENG & FRE.). 1981. 75.00 (*0-8288-0968-2*, M 6354) Fr & Eur.

Risk Insurance Reinsurance Lexicon: Francais - English - American. 3rd ed. Jacques Lesobre et al. 375p. (ENG & FRE.). 1993. pap. 150.00 (*0-7859-1079-4*, 290218945X) Fr & Eur.

Risk It! Empowering Young People to Become Positive Risk Takers in the Classroom & in Life. Cathy Newton. Ed. by Anna Quinn. (Illus.). 192p. (Orig.). 1996. pap. text ed. write for info. (*0-86530-346-0*, IP 346-0) Incentive Pubns.

Risk It-Express! Expression in Creative Practice. Carol H. Bitcon. (Horizon Ser.: No. 8). 56p. (Orig.). (C). 1989. pap. text ed. 12.00 (*0-918812-63-1*, ST 200) MMB Music.

Risk Makers, Risk Takers, Risk Breakers: Reducing the Risks for Young Literacy Learners. Ed. by JoBeth Allen & Jana M. Mason. LC 88-27400. 351p. (Orig.). (C). 1989. pap. 25.00 (*0-435-08483-6*, 08483) Heinemann.

Risk Management. Robert N. Charette. 320p. 1989. text ed. write for info. (*0-07-010719-X*) McGraw.

Risk Management. Neil Crockford. 86p. (C). 1992. 80.00 (*1-85609-024-8*, Pub. by Witherby & Co UK) St Mut.

Risk Management. Robert De Heer. LC 94-28023. 128p. 1994. pap. text ed. write for info. (*0-7931-1155-2*, 152019-01, Real Estate Ed) Dearborn Finan.

Risk Management. Charles Errington. 400p. 1991. 450.00 (*1-85564-114-3*, Pub. by Euromoney UK) Am Educ Systs.

Risk Management. Aaron Liberman & Michael J Woodruff. LC 92-44149. (Creative Pastoral Care & Counseling Ser.). 96p. 1993. 11.00 (*0-8006-2758-X*, 1-2758, Fortress Pr) Augsburg Fortress.

Risk Management. Meyer. (FP - Risk Management Ser.). Date not set. pap. 58.95 (*0-538-86415-X*) S-W Pub.

Risk Management. Schleifer. (Cti to Southwestern Ser.). 1995. pap. 15.00 (*1-56527-276-5*) Course Tech.

Risk Management. Emmett J. Vaughan. LC 96-26882. 812p. 1996. text ed. 68.95 (*0-471-10759-X*) Wiley.

Risk Management. Ed. by Charlotte Weisman. LC 86-721. (Special Collection from the Journal of Commercial Bank Lending). (Illus.). 112p. 1986. pap. text ed. 45.00 (*0-936742-28-3*) Robt Morris Assocs.

Risk Management. 7th ed. S. Travis Pritchett. Date not set. teacher ed., pap. text ed. write for info. (*0-314-06445-1*) West Pub.

Risk Management: Challenges & Solutions. George G. Parker & William Beaver. 1995. text ed. write for info. (*0-07-048588-7*) McGraw.

Risk Management: Computers, Fraud & Insurance. P. M. Ardis & Michael J. Comer. (C). 1986. 240.00 (*0-685-33710-3*, Pub. by Witherby & Co UK) St Mut.

Risk Management: Computers, Fraud & Insurance. Patrick M. Ardis & Michael J. Comer. 576p. 1986. text ed. 37.50 (*0-07-084926-9*) McGraw.

Risk Management: Expanding Horizons, Boston, MA June 8-10, 1992. 352p. 1994. 45.00 (*0-89448-176-2*, 700180) Am Nuclear Soc.

Risk Management: Expanding Horizons in Nuclear Power & Other Industries. Ed. by Ronald A. Knief. 288p. 1991. 66.95 (*1-56032-231-4*) Hemisp Pub.

Risk Management: Health & Safety in Primary Care. N. Higson. LC 96-13133. 128p. 1996. pap. text ed. 37.50 (*0-7506-3064-7*) Buttrwrth-Heinemann.

Risk Management: Practical Ideas & Applications. 2nd ed. Edward W. Siver. 56p. (Orig.). (C). 1991. pap. 9.95 (*0-937802-29-8*) RMSP.

Risk Management: Strategies for Managing Volunteer Programs. Sarah Henson & Bruce Larson. Ed. by Nancy Macduff. 128p. (C). 1988. pap. 25.00 (*0-945795-04-1*) MBA Pub.

Risk Management: Text with Cases. 2nd ed. Serbein Greene & Oscar N. Serbein. LC 82-23115. (C). 1983. teacher ed. write for info. (*0-8359-6737-9*, Reston) P-H.

Risk Management - Professional Liability. 131p. 1990. 90.00 (*0-685-38789-5*, 974) Am Consul Eng.

Risk Management & Construction. Roger Flanagan & George Norman. LC 93-20446. 1993. pap. 54.95 (*0-632-02816-5*, Pub. by Blckwell Sci Pubns UK) Blackwell Sci.

Risk Management & Insurance. W. Sonnenreich. 1994. pap. text ed. write for info. (*0-07-912124-1*) McGraw.

***Risk Management & Insurance.** 2nd ed. James S. Trieschman. LC 97-20809. (Miscellaneous/Catalogs Ser.). 1998. text ed. 130.50 (*0-538-87096-6*) S-W Pub.

Risk Management & Insurance. 6th ed. C. Arthur Williams. (C). 1989. 300.00 (*0-685-33709-X*, Pub. by Witherby & Co UK) St Mut.

Risk Management & Insurance. 7th ed. S. Travis Pritchett et al. LC 95-45304. 750p. (C). 1996. text ed. 63.75 (*0-314-06427-3*) West Pub.

Risk Management & Insurance. 7th ed. C. Arthur Williams et al. LC 94-40588. 1995. text ed. 44.50 (*0-07-070584-4*) McGraw.

***Risk Management & Insurance.** 8th ed. C. Arthur Williams et al. LC 97-25980. 1997. write for info. (*0-07-070630-1*) McGraw.

Risk Management & Insurance. 9th ed. Sandra G. Gustavson & James S. Treischmann. LC 94-15758. 832p. 1995. text ed. 85.95 (*0-538-83920-1*) S-W Pub.

Risk Management & Insurance Audit Techniques. rev. ed. Dwight E. Levick. 952p. ring bd. 169.00 (*0-923240-17-9*) Stndrd Publishing.

Risk Management & Insurance for Commercial Bankers. Douglas M. Temple. Ed. by Sarah A. Burke. LC 88-9153. 108p. (Orig.). 1988. pap. text ed. 29.00 (*0-936742-51-8*, 33171) Robt Morris Assocs.

Risk Management & Insurance for Equipment Lessors. Harry F. Brooks. 260p. 1988. pap. text ed. 110.00 (*0-912413-02-6*) Am Assn Equip Lessors.

***Risk Management & Liability Issues.** Chris E. Stout. LC 96-95356. 150p. 1997. 65.00 (*1-890056-04-9*, 1994-56049) Grayson Pub.

Risk Management & Political Culture. Sheila Jasanoff. LC 86-6443. (Social Science Perspectives Ser.). 112p. 1986. pap. 9.95 (*0-87154-408-3*) Russell Sage.

Risk Management & Total Quality Management: Making the Connection. Eric D. Joseph & David Meyers. 86p. (Orig.). 1994. pap. text ed. 35.00 (*0-916499-51-0*) Care Educ Grp.

Risk Management Excellence: Developing & Organising a Superior Approach. 1993. 395.00 (*0-85058-773-5*) Economist Intell.

***Risk Management for Hazardous Chemicals, 2 vols.** Jeffrey W. Vincoli. LC 96-35282. 3136p. 1996. 295.00 (*1-56670-200-3*) Lewis Pubs.

Risk Management for Newspapers. rev. ed. Risk Management Committee Staff. 40p. 1989. pap. 49.95 (*1-877888-10-9*) Intl Newspaper.

Risk Management for Park, Recreation & Leisure Services. 2nd ed. James A. Peterson & Bruce B. Hronek. 152p. (Orig.). 1992. pap. text ed. 24.95 (*0-915611-57-0*) Sagamore Pub.

Risk Management for Schools. 1988. pap. 20.00 (*0-934338-67-1*) NAIS.

Risk Management for Software Projects. Alex Down et al. LC 93-28798. (IBM McGraw-Hill Ser.). 1994. text ed. 45.00 (*0-07-707816-0*) McGraw.

Risk Management for the Department Head: An Integrated Approach. Meridith B. Cox. (Illus.). 200p. (Orig.). (C). 1991. spiral bd. 55.00 (*0-912665-37-8*); ring bd. 75.00 (*0-912665-30-0*) Cox Pubns.

Risk Management Glossary. 82p. 1985. 10.00 (*0-937802-20-4*) RMSP.

***Risk Management Handbook.** 35p. (Orig.). 1996. pap. text ed. 29.95 (*1-57743-005-0*, 82913) NAUI.

***Risk Management Handbook.** John C. Chicken. 554p. 1996. pap. 99.00 (*0-412-62750-7*) Chapman & Hall.

***Risk Management Handbook.** rev. ed. 40p. 1997. pap. text ed. 9.95 (*1-57743-012-3*, 12908) NAUI.

***Risk Management Handbook.** 2nd rev. ed. American Society for Healthcare Risk Management Staff. Ed. by Roberta Carroll. LC 97-10917. (Illus.). 450p. 1997. text ed. 95.00 (*1-55648-185-3*, 178159) AHPI.

***Risk Management Handbook: Protecting You & Your Practice from Legal Action.** Maryann Ricardo. 250p. 1995. reprint ed. ring bd. 49.95 (*1-57066-033-6*, ME057) Practice Mgmt Info.

Risk Management in a TQM Environment. Peter Absolon & Alex Down. (C). 1994. 150.00 (*0-946655-90-1*, Pub. by Stanley Thornes UK) Trans-Atl Phila.

Risk Management in Aquaculture. Lindsay Laird & Chris Kennedy. Date not set. pap. text ed. 45.00 (*0-471-96629-0*) Wiley.

***Risk Management in Banking.** Joel Bessis. LC 97-25521. 1997. write for info. (*0-471-97465-X*); pap. write for info. (*0-471-97466-8*) Wiley.

Risk Management in Business. 15p. 1987. 3.95 (*0-937802-26-3*) RMSP.

Risk Management in Dentistry. J. B. Matthews. (Illus.). 256p. 1995. pap. text ed. 37.50 (*0-7236-1011-8*) Buttrwrth-Heinemann.

Risk Management in Developing Countries. Stijn Claessens. LC 93-34713. (Technical Paper Ser.: No. 235). 87p. 1993. 7.95 (*0-8213-2668-6*, 12668) World Bank.

Risk Management in Developing Countries. J. O. Irukwu. 225p. 1991. 135.00 (*1-85609-021-3*, Pub. by Witherby & Co UK) St Mut.

Risk Management in Financial Institutions: Risk Management in Financial Institutions. Dimitris N. Chorafas. 370p. 1990. boxed 150.00 (*0-406-16390-1*, UK) MICHIE.

Risk Management in Financial Services. OECD Staff. 104p. (Orig.). 1992. pap. 24.00 (*92-64-13727-0*) OECD.

An Asterisk (*) at the beginning of an entry indicates that the title is appearing in BIP for the first time.

R

***Risk Management in Health Care Institutions.** Allen D. Spiegel. LC 96-39658. 1997. 38.00 (0-7637-0257-9) Jones & Bartlett.

***Risk Management in Project Finance & Implementation.** Henri L. Beenhakker. LC 97-8856. 1997. text ed. write for info. (1-56720-106-7, Quorum Bks) Greenwood.

Risk Management in Schools: A Guide to Minimizing Liability. Jacqueline K. Minor & Vern B. Minor. 96p. 1991. ring bd. 49.95 (0-8039-6006-9, D1478) Corwin Pr.

Risk Management in Therapeutic Recreation: A Component of Quality Assurance. Judy Voelkl. LC 88-50287. 1988. 9.95 (0-910251-23-1) Venture Pub PA.

Risk Management in Volatile Financial Markets. Ed. by Franco Bruni et al. LC 96-16268. (Financial & Monetary Policy Studies: Vol. 32). 1996. lib. bdg. 130.00 (0-7923-4053-1) Kluwer Ac.

***Risk Management Instruments for Pulp & Paper Producers & Consumers.** David W. Cox et al. (Illus.). 132p. (Orig.). 1996. pap. 40.00 (0-9656081-0-7) United Media.

Risk Management Manual. Merritt Company Staff. 1995. ring bd. 397.00 (0-930868-02-1) Merritt Pub.

Risk Management Manual: A Guide to Safety, Loss Control & Malpractice Prevention for Hospitals. 147p. 1977. pap. 15.00 (0-318-14061-6) Fed Am Health Systs.

Risk Management Manual for Motor Carriers. American Trucking Associations National Accounting & Finance Council et al. 460p. 1986. ring bd. 175.00 (0-88711-078-9) Am Trucking Assns.

Risk Management of Chemicals in the Environment. Ed. by H. M. Seip & A. B. Heiberg. (NATO - Challenges of Modern Society Ser.: Vol. 12). (Illus.). 240p. 1988. 79.50 (0-306-43081-9, Plenum Pr) Plenum.

Risk Management Portfolio. 95th ed. Fowler. 1995. pap. 429.00 (0-15-601895-0) HB Legal.

Risk Management Process. George L. Head. 72p. 1982. 5.00 (0-937802-02-6) RMSP.

Risk Management Process. George L. Head. LC 84-60439. 88p. (SPA.). 1984. 10.00 (0-937802-18-2) RMSP.

***Risk Management Processes for Software Engineering Models.** Marian Myerson. LC 96-35955. 1996. 69.00 (0-89006-635-3) Artech Hse.

***Risk Management Strategies Applied to Environmental Cleanup in Central & Eastern Europe.** 300p. 1997. lib. bdg. 56.00 (981-02-2875-9) World Scientific Pub.

Risk Management Techniques in Perinatal & Neonatal Practice. Ed. by Steven M. Donn & Charles W. Fisher. LC 96-12740. (Illus.). 720p. 1996. 115.00 (0-87993-640-1) Futura Pub.

Risk Manager's Desk Reference. Barbara J. Youngberg. 540p. 1994. 140.00 (0-8342-0506-8, 20506) Aspen Pub.

Risk Markers for Oral Diseases, Vol. 1: Dental Caries: Markers of High & Low Risk Groups & Individuals. Ed. by N. W. Johnson. 488p. (C). 1991. text ed. 135.00 (0-521-37563-0) Cambridge U Pr.

Risk Markers for Oral Diseases, Vol. 2: Oral Cancer: Detection of Patients & Lesions at Risk. Ed. by N. W. Johnson. (Illus.). 400p. (C). 1991. text ed. 135.00 (0-521-37421-9) Cambridge U Pr.

Risk Markers for Oral Diseases, Vol. 3: Periodontal Diseases: Markers of Disease Susceptibility & Activity. Ed. by N. W. Johnson. (Illus.). 464p. (C). 1991. text ed. 135.00 (0-521-38566-0) Cambridge U Pr.

Risk-Needs Assessment & Parole Outcome in Massachusetts: An Evaluation Study. Richard Lunden. (Illus.). 65p. (Orig.). (C). 1993. pap. text ed. 25.00 (1-56806-902-2) DIANE Pub.

***Risk of Being: What It Means to Be Good & Bad.** Michael Gelven. LC 96-49104. 1997. 32.50 (0-271-01707-4) Pa St U Pr.

***Risk of Being: What It Means to Be Good & Bad.** Michael Gelven. LC 96-49104. 1997. pap. 17.95 (0-271-01708-2) Pa St U Pr.

Risk of Economic Crisis. Ed. by Martin Feldstein. LC 91-11736. (National Bureau of Economic Research Conference Report Ser.). (Illus.). 208p. 1991. pap. 14.95 (0-226-24091-6) U Ch Pr.

Risk of Heaven. Bob Berger. 352p. 1996. mass mkt. 4.99 (0-440-22052-1) Dell.

***Risk of His Music.** Peter Welther. 208p. (Orig.). 1997. pap. 12.95 (1-55597-253-5) Graywolf.

***Risk of Loving.** Jane Peart. 1997. mass mkt. 4.50 (0-373-87003-5, 1-87003-9) Harlequin Bks.

Risk of Murder: A Dr. Risk Mystery. Bob Berger. 288p. 1995. mass mkt. 4.99 (0-440-22051-3) Dell.

Risk, Organizations, & Society. Ed. by Martin Shubik. (Studies in Risk & Uncertainty). 256p. 1991. lib. bdg. 81.00 (0-7923-9118-7) Kluwer Ac.

Risk Pool. Richard Russo. 1994. pap. 14.00 (0-679-75383-4, Vin) Random.

Risk Portfolio Management & Capital Markets. Ed. by T. E. Cooke et al. 224p. 1992. text ed. 69.95 (0-312-06890-5) St Martin.

Risk Professionals. Thomas Dietz & Robert Rycroft. LC 87-19992. (Social Research Perspectives). 176p. 1988. pap. 9.95 (0-87154-214-5) Russell Sage.

Risk Profiles in Clinical Nephrology. Ed. by G. Buccianti. (Contributions to Nephrology Ser.: Vol. 37). (Illus.). x, 202p. 1984. pap. 72.00 (3-8055-3739-5) S Karger.

Risk Proofing Your Family. Don Joy & Robbie Joy. 57p. 1993. ring bd. 69.95 (0-917851-72-2) Bristol Hse.

Risk-Proofing Your Family. Donald M. Joy. LC 94-42719. (Illus.). (Orig.). 1995. pap. 10.95 (0-87808-763-X, WCL763X) William Carey Lib.

Risk Quantitation & Regulatory Policy. Ed. by David G. Hoel et al. (Banbury Reports: No. 19). 368p. 1985. 67.00 (0-87969-219-7) Cold Spring Harbor.

***Risk Ranking Technique in Decision Making.** John C. Chicken & Michael R. Hayns. 136p. 1989. 41.50 (0-08-037212-0, Pergamon Pr) Elsevier.

***Risk Reduction: Chemicals & Energy into the 21st Century.** Ed. by Mervyn Richardson. 664p. 1997. 199.00 (0-7484-0398-1, Pub. by Tay Francis Ltd UK) Taylor & Francis.

Risk Reduction Engineering Laboratory: 20th Annual Research Symposium, Abstract Proceedings. (Illus.). 242p. (Orig.). (C). 1994. pap. text ed. 60.00 (0-7881-0876-X) DIANE Pub.

Risk, Resilience, & Prevention: Promoting the Well-Being of All Children. Ed. by Rune J. Simeonsson. LC 94-8828. 384p. 1994. pap. 34.00 (1-55766-166-9) P H Brookes.

Risk Retention Act: Bane or Blessing? 104p. 1989. pap. 30.00 (0-614-05735-3) Charter Prop Underwriters Soc.

Risk Retention & Purchasing Group Handbook. 100p. 1995. ring bd. 50.00 (0-89382-312-0) Nat Assn Insurance.

Risk Retention & Purchasing Group Handbook. 1996. ring bd. 50.00 (0-89382-382-1, RIS-BB95) Nat Assn Insurance.

Risk Retention Group Directory & Guide, 1995. Karen Cutts. 160p. (C). 1995. pap. text ed. 185.00 (0-9625840-5-3) Insure Commns.

Risk, Science, & Politics: Regulating Toxic Substances in Canada & the United States. Kathryn Harrison & George Hoberg. 248p. 1994. 55.00 (0-7735-1236-5, Pub. by McGill CN); pap. 18.95 (0-7735-1251-9, Pub. by McGill CN) U of Toronto Pr.

Risk-Sensitive Optimal Control. Peter R. Whittle. LC 89-28165. 246p. 1990. text ed. 135.00 (0-471-92622-1) Wiley.

Risk Sharing in Pref. Provid. Arange. Pamela Taulbee. 1995. 55.00 (1-56925-029-4, RISK) Capitol Publns.

Risk Society: Towards a New Modernity. Ulrick Beck. Tr. by Mark Ritter. (Theory, Culture & Society Ser.: Vol. 17). (Illus.). 304p. 1992. 65.00 (0-8039-8345-X); pap. 24.95 (0-8039-8346-8) Sage.

Risk, Strategy & Management. Ed. by Richard A. Bettis & Howard Thomas. LC 90-4522. (Strategic Management, Policy & Planning Ser.). 215p. 1990. 73.25 (0-89232-801-0) Jai Pr.

Risk-Takers: Alcohol, Drugs, Sex & Youth. Martin A. Plant & Moira Plant. LC 91-41467. 208p. (C). (gr. 13). 1992. text ed. 85.00 (0-415-03538-4, A7514) Routledge.

***Risk Taking.** Arthur Levitt & M. Finn. Date not set. write for info. (0-688-06960-6) Morrow.

Risk Taking: A Guide for Decision Makers. Herbert S. Kindler. Ed. by Michale G. Crisp. LC 89-81247. (Fifty-Minute Ser.). (Illus.). 88p. (Orig.). 1990. pap. 10.95 (0-931961-76-9) Crisp Pubns.

Risk Taking: A Managerial Perspective. Zur B. Shapira. (Illus.). 160p. 1994. 24.95 (0-87154-766-X) Russell Sage.

Risk Taking: A Study in Cognition & Personality. Nathan Kogan & Michael A. Wallach. LC 83-12584. x, 278p. 1983. reprint ed. text ed. 59.75 (0-313-23250-4, KORT, Greenwood Pr) Greenwood.

Risk-Taking: Fifty Ways to Turn Risks into Rewards. Marlene Caroselli & David Harris. (Self-Study Sourcebook Ser.). xii, 148p. (Orig.). 1993. pap. 15.95 (1-878542-32-X, 13-0003) SkillPath Pubns.

Risk Taking: Performing Your Best During Critical Times. Marie Dalloway. (Illus.). 62p. 1993. pap. 14.95 (0-9634933-3-7) Optimal Perf.

***Risk Taking & Decisionmaking: Foreign Military Intervention Decisions.** Yaacov Vertzberger. LC 97-5623. 1997. write for info. (0-8047-2747-3) Stanford U Pr.

Risk-Taking Behavior. Ed. by Frank Yates. LC 91-21229. (Studies in Human Perform). 345p. 1994. pap. text ed. 60.00 (0-471-95140-4) Wiley.

Risk Taking for Personal Growth: A Step-by-Step Workbook. Joseph Ilardo. LC 92-53739. 204p. (Orig.). 1992. pap. 17.95 (1-879237-19-9) New Harbinger.

***Risk-Taking in International Politics: Prospect Theory in American Foreign Policy.** Rose McDermott. LC 97-21113. 1998. write for info. (0-472-10867-0) U of Mich Pr.

Risk-Taking in Learning, K-3. Robert D. Young. 80p. 1991. pap. 9.95 (0-8106-0354-3) NEA.

Risk the Journey: Answering God's Call to Proclaim. Bill J. Leonard. Ed. by Judith Edwards. 130p. (Orig.). 1995. pap. 4.95 (1-56309-122-4) Womans Mission Union.

Risk to Be Healed: The Heart of Personal & Relationship Growth. Barry Vissell & Joyce Vissell. (Illus.). 181p. 1989. pap. 9.95 (0-9612720-2-3) Ramira Pub.

Risk to be Healed: The Heart of Personal & Relationship Growth. Barry Vissell & Joyce Vissell. 181p. (C). 1989. reprint ed. lib. bdg. 29.00 (0-8095-6113-1) Borgo Pr.

Risk Trends of U. S. Multinational & Domestic Firms. Mehmet Y. Geyikdagi. LC 82-10155. 172p. 1982. text ed. 42.95 (0-275-90800-3, C0800, Praeger Pubs) Greenwood.

Risk Versus Risk: Tradeoffs in Protecting Health & the Environment. Ed. by John D. Graham & Jonathan B. Wiener. LC 95-10457. (Illus.). 320p. (C). 1995. text ed. 39.95 (0-674-77304-7) HUP.

***Risk vs. Risk: Tradeoffs in Protecting Health & the Enviorment.** John Graham. 1997. pap. text ed. 18.95 (0-674-77307-1) HUP.

Risk Watch: The Odds of Life. fac. ed. John Urquhart & Klaus Heilmann. LC 84-4046. 232p. 1984. reprint ed. pap. 66.20 (0-7837-8144-X, 2047952) Bks Demand.

Risk Your Life Arcade. Ken McMurtry. (Choose Your Own Nightmare Ser.: No. 6). (Illus.). 96p. (Orig.). (J). (gr. 3-7). 1995. pap. 3.50 (0-553-48234-3, Choose) BDD Bks Young Read.

Risk Your Life Arcade. enl. large type ed. Ken McMurtry. LC 95-39817. (Choose Your Own Nightmare Ser.: No. 6). (Illus.). 96p. (J). (gr. 4 up). 1996. lib. bdg. 15.93 (0-8368-1515-7) Gareth Stevens Inc.

Risking. David Viscott. 1990. pap. 6.50 (0-671-72401-0) PB.

Risking a Nation: U. S. Japanese Trade Failure & the Need for Political, Social, & Economic Reformation. Jerome B. McKinney. LC 95-23283. 426p. (Orig.). (C). 1995. pap. text ed. 34.50 (0-7618-0038-7); lib. bdg. 62.50 (0-7618-0037-9) U Pr of Amer.

Risking a Somersault in the Air: Conversations with Nicaraguan Writers. Margaret Randall. Ed. by Floyce Alexander. Tr. by Christina Mills from SPA. LC 86-10052. (Illus.). 220p. 1990. reprint ed. pap. 9.95 (0-915306-92-1) Curbstone.

Risking Change: Endings & Beginnings. William F. Sturner. 163p. (Orig.). 1987. pap. 14.95 (0-943456-20-7) Bearly Ltd.

Risking Christ for Christ's Sake: Towards an Ecumenical Theology of Pluralism. Madathilparampil M. Thomas. LC 87-159065. 130p. reprint ed. pap. 37.10 (0-7837-5994-0, 2045804) Bks Demand.

***Risking Contact: Readings to Challenge Our Thinking.** Royce Adams. (C). 1997. teacher ed., text ed. 11.96 (0-669-39329-0); pap. text ed. 27.96 (0-669-39327-4) HM College Div.

Risking Dispute Resolution. 2nd ed. Riskin. (American Casebook Ser.). Date not set. text ed. write for info. (0-314-07211-X) West Pub.

Risking Elizabeth. Walter McCloskey. LC 96-44984. 1997. 21.00 (0-684-82434-5) S&S Trade.

Risking Enchantment: Coleridge's Symbolic World of Faery. Jeanie Watson. LC 89-49169. 249p. 1990. reprint ed. pap. 71.00 (0-7837-8902-5, 2049613) Bks Demand.

Risking Faith: Personal Answers for Weary Skeptics. John Guest. (John Guest Accelerated Growth Ser.). 176p. (C). 1993. pap. 9.99 (0-8010-3854-5) Baker Bks.

Risking Free Trade: The Politics of Free Trade in Britain, Canada, Mexico, & the United States. LC 96-25208. (Pitt Series in Political Science). 1996. 49.95 (0-8229-3932-0) U of Pittsburgh Pr.

Risking Free Trade: The Politics of Free Trade in Britain, Canada, Mexico, & the United States. Michael Lusztig. LC 96-25208. (Pitt Series in Political Science). 1996. pap. 22.95 (0-8229-5589-X) U of Pittsburgh Pr.

Risking Hope: Fragile Faith in the Healing Process. expanded ed. Kathleen O. Chesto. LC 96-64498. (Illus.). 128p. (C). 1996. pap. 8.95 (1-55612-322-1, LL1322) Sheed & Ward MO.

Risking It. Jeanette Mines. 160p. (YA). 1988. pap. 2.75 (0-380-75401-0, Flare) Avon.

Risking Peace: Why We Sat in the Road. Jackie Cabasso & Susan Moon. (Illus.). 80p. (Orig.). 1985. pap. 7.00 (0-931416-03-5) Open Books.

Risking Who One Is: Encounters With Contemporary Art & Literature. Rubin Suleiman. LC 93-38741. 1994. text ed. 27.50 (0-674-77301-2) HUP.

Risking Who One Is: Encounters with Contemporary Art & Literature. Susan R. Suleiman. (Illus.). 288p. 1996. pap. 15.95 (0-674-77306-3) HUP.

Risks. Barbara Cummings & Jo-Ann Power. 480p. 1993. mass mkt. 4.99 (1-55817-747-7, Pinncle Kensgtn) Kensgtn Pub Corp.

Risks: Reading Corporate Signals. Haig J. Boyadjian & James F. Warren. LC 86-15661. 392p. 1992. pap. text ed. 65.00 (0-471-93178-0) Wiley.

Risks & Hazards You Cannot Afford. Jacques Melek. (Illus.). (Orig.). 1984. pap. 8.95 (0-685-08399-3, Sunrise Pubns) J Melek.

Risks & Opportunities. Valerie Brown et al. 354p. 1995. pap. 27.95 (1-85383-236-7, Pub. by Erthscan Pubns UK) Island Pr.

Risks & Payoffs of Being Alive: An Introduction to Holistic Therapy. Peter H. Grant. 1979. pap. 4.95 (0-8065-0688-1, Citadel Pr) Carol Pub Group.

Risks & Responsibilities. David Bowker et al. (Patchwork Ser.: No. 3). (Illus.). 12p. 1993. pap. 18.00 (1-873791-45-3) Taylor & Francis.

Risks & Rewards: A Memoir. Julia M. Walsh & Anne C. Carson. LC 96-17593. (Illus.). 214p. 1996. pap. 17.95 (0-939009-98-6) EPM Pubns.

***Risks & Rewards: A Memoir.** Julia M. Walsh & Anne C. Carson. (Illus.). 214p. 27.95 (0-939009-99-4) EPM Pubns.

***Risks & Rewards of Brownfield Redevelopment.** James G. Wright. pap. 14.00 (1-55844-130-1) Lincoln Inst Land.

Risks & the Risk Debate: Searching for Common Ground "the First Step": Evaluating Risk Throughout the Nuclear Weapons Complex. (Illus.). 645p. (Orig.). (C). 1995. pap. text ed. 60.00 (0-7881-2600-8) DIANE Pub.

Risks & Wrongs. Jules L. Coleman. (Cambridge Studies in Philosophy & Law). 504p. (C). 1992. text ed. 69.95 (0-521-32950-7); pap. text ed. 21.95 (0-521-42861-0) Cambridge U Pr.

***Risks Associated with Ionising Radiations.** ICRP Staff. (International Commission on Radiological Protection Ser.: Vol. 22). 126p. 1992. 65.00 (0-08-041840-6, Pergamon Pr) Elsevier.

Risks, Costs & Lives Saved: Getting Better Results from Regulation. Ed. by Robert W. Hahn. 192p. 1996. 29.95 (0-19-521174-X) OUP.

Risks, Dangers, & Rewards in the Nova Scotia Offshore Fishery. Marian Binkley. 1995. 39.95 (0-7735-1313-2, Pub. by McGill CN) U of Toronto Pr.

Risks from Radon in Homes. Institute of Radiation Protection Staff. (Handbook Ser.: No. 5). (C). 1990. 108.00 (0-948237-04-X, Pub. by H&H Sci Cnslts UK) St Mut.

Risks in International Bank Lending. Study Group Staff. (Reports). 76p. 1982. pap. write for info. (1-56708-059-6) Grp of Thirty.

Risks in Labor & Delivery & Pediatrics. Meridith B. Cox. (Risk Management Ser.). (C). 1997. wbk. ed., pap. text ed. 20.00 (0-912665-25-4) Cox Pubns.

Risks in O. R. & Post-Op Care. Meridith B. Cox. (Risk Management Ser.). (Orig.). (C). 1997. wbk. ed., pap. text ed. 25.00 (0-912665-26-2) Cox Pubns.

Risks of Carcinogenesis from Urethane Exposure. Andrew G. Salmon & Lauren Zeise. (Illus.). 240p. 1991. 105.00 (0-8493-5587-7, R) CRC Pr.

Risks of Knowing: Developmental Impediments to School Learning. Karen Zelan. LC 90-29300. (Perspectives in Developmental Psychology Ser.). (Illus.). 328p. 1991. 49.50 (0-306-43759-7, Plenum Pr) Plenum.

Risks of Labour. Ed. by John W. Crawford. LC 84-25653. (Wiley Series on Perinatal Practice: No. 2). (Illus.). 226p. reprint ed. pap. 64.50 (0-8357-4548-1, 2037447) Bks Demand.

Risks of RO - Episode 1: The Beginning of No End. Louisia Fuller. Ed. by Potice Wimberly & Dianne Andrews. 110p. (Orig.). 1988. pap. 5.95 (0-945779-00-3) Ethnic Role Model.

Risks of RO - Episode 2: The African's Honored Guest. Louisia Fuller. Ed. by Potice Wimberly et al. 110p. (Orig.). 1988. pap. 5.95 (0-945779-01-1) Ethnic Role Model.

Risks of RO - Episode 3: The Bronze Frenchman. Louisia Fuller. Ed. by Potice Wimberly & Donna Jones. Tr. by Georgette Delinois. 110p. (Orig.). 1988. pap. 5.95 (0-945779-02-X) Ethnic Role Model.

Risks of RO - Episode 4: Child's Play. Louisia Avery. Ed. by Potice Wimberly & Dianne Andrews. 110p. (Orig.). (J). 1988. pap. text ed. 5.95 (0-945779-03-8) Ethnic Role Model.

Risks of Unintentional Nuclear War. Daniel Frei & Christian Catrina. LC 82-16333. 288p. (C). 1983. pap. text ed. 19.50 (0-86598-106-X) Rowman.

***Risks to Students in School.** (Illus.). 203p. 1996. reprint ed. pap. 40.00 (0-7881-3340-3) DIANE Pub.

***Risks Worth Taking: Poetry & Art from a Decade of Imprisonment.** Timothy Blunk. (Illus.). 90p. (Orig.). 1997. pap. text ed. 14.95 (0-9657912-0-3) Puffin Found.

Risks Worth Taking: The Odyssey of a Foreign Correspondent. Bernard S. Redmont. 264p. (C). 1992. pap. text ed. 29.50 (0-8191-8852-2); lib. bdg. 57.00 (0-8191-8797-6) U Pr of Amer.

Risky Assignment. Judy Baer. (Live from Brentwood High Ser.: No. 1). 160p. (YA). (gr. 7-10). 1994. mass mkt. 4.99 (1-55661-386-5) Bethany Hse.

Risky Business. Michael Hogan. 5.00 (0-686-15296-4) Great Raven Pr.

Risky Business. M. J. Rodgers. (Intrigue Ser.: No. 185). 1992. pap. 2.89 (0-373-22185-1, 1-22185-2) Harlequin Bks.

Risky Business: An Insider's Account of the Collapse of Lloyd's of London. Elizabeth Luessenhop & Martin Mayer. 320p. 1995. 25.00 (0-684-19739-1) S&S Trade.

Risky Business: Church Hiring & Volunteer Recruitment. Lynn R. Buzzard & Susan M. Edwards. 280p. (Orig.). 1994. pap. text ed. 19.95 (1-886569-00-2) J W Edwards.

Risky Business: Communicating Issues of Science, Risk & Public Policy. Ed. by Lee Wilkins & Philip C. Patterson. LC 90-47523. (Contributions to the Study of Mass Media & Communications Ser.: No. 27). 256p. 1991. text ed. 55.00 (0-313-26601-8, WYL/, Greenwood Pr) Greenwood.

Risky Business: Genetic Testing & Exclusionary Practices in the Hazardous Workplace. Elaine Draper. (Studies in Philosophy & Public Policy). 304p. (C). 1991. pap. text ed. 20.95 (0-521-42248-5) Cambridge U Pr.

Risky Business: Managing Employee Violence in the Workplace. Lynne F. McClure. LC 96-4070. 224p. 1996. 39.95 (0-7890-0075-X); pap. 19.95 (0-7890-0100-4) Haworth Pr.

Risky Business: PAC Decisionmaking & Strategy in 1992. Ed. by Robert Biersack et al. LC 94-18902. (American Political Institutions & Public Policy Ser.). (Illus.). 328p. (gr. 13). 1994. text ed. 62.95 (1-56324-294-X); pap. text ed. 25.95 (1-56324-295-8) M E Sharpe.

Risky Business: The Community Impact of Catholic Health Care Expansion. Cynthia Gibson. 7p. (Orig.). 1995. pap. text ed. 2.00 (0-915365-29-4) Cath Free Choice.

Risky Business? Youth, Enterprise & Policy for the 1990s. Robert MacDonald & Frank Coffield. 224p. 1991. 80.00 (1-85000-897-3, Falmer Pr); pap. 31.00 (1-85000-898-1, Falmer Pr) Taylor & Francis.

Risky Friends. Julie A. Peters. 144p. (J). (gr. 5-8). 1993. pap. 2.99 (0-87406-646-8) Willowisp Pr.

***Risky Games.** Olga Bicos. 416p. 1997. mass mkt. 5.99 (0-8217-5679-6, Zebra Kensgtn) Kensgtn Pub Corp.

Risky Living: The Key to Inner Healing. Jamie Buckingham. LC 76-12033. 192p. 1976. pap. 7.95 (0-88270-177-0) Bridge-Logos.

***Risky Prescription: Sports & Health.** Sandy Stiefer. LC 96-48340. 1996. write for info. (0-8225-3304-9) Lerner Group.

Risky Proposition. Cassie Miles. (Temptation Ser.: No 394). 1992. mass mkt. 2.99 (0-373-25494-6, 1-25494-5) Harlequin Bks.

Risky Rivers: The Economics & Politics of Floodplain Farming in Amazonia. Michael Chibnik. (Arizona Studies in Human Ecology). (Illus.). 267p. 1994. 26.95 (0-8165-1482-8) U of Ariz Pr.

Risky Rogue. Pat Cody. 272p. 1995. mass mkt. 3.99 (0-06-108369-0, Harp PBks) HarpC.

***Risky Sex: Gay Men & HIV Prevention.** Dwayne Turner. LC 96-40290. (Between Men - Between Women Ser.). 1997. 45.00 (0-231-10574-6) Col U Pr.

***Risky Sex: Gay Men & HIV Prevention.** Dwayne Turner. LC 96-40290. (Between Men - Between Women Ser.). 1997. pap. 16.50 (0-231-10575-4) Col U Pr.

Risky Sexual Behaviors among African-Americans. Ernest H. Johnson. LC 92-28483. 192p. 1993. text ed. 59.95 (0-275-94162-0, C4162, Praeger Pubs) Greenwood.

An Asterisk (*) at the beginning of an entry indicates that the title is appearing in BIP for the first time.

Risky Times: How to Be AIDS-Smart & Stay Healthy. Jeanne Blake. LC 89-40728. (Illus.). 196p. (Orig.). 1990. pap. 5.95 (0-89480-656-4, 1656) Workman Pub.
Risley: Family History. E. H. Risley. (Illus.). 318p. 1990. reprint ed. pap. 51.00 (0-8328-1619-1); reprint ed. lib. bdg. 59.00 (0-8328-1618-3) Higginson Bk Co.
Riso: The Undiscovered Rice Dishes of Northern Italy. Gioietta Vitale & Lisa Lawley. 160p. 1992. 16.00 (0-517-58856-0, Crown) Crown Pub Group.
Risotti: Risottos & Other Appetizers. Anna Del Conte. LC 93-13330. (Illus.). 1993. 14.00 (0-671-87030-0) S&S Trade.
Risotto. Judith Barrett & Norma Wasserman. 336p. 1989. pap. 12.95 (0-02-030395-5) Macmillan.
Risotto. Kristine Kidd. Ed. by Jill Fox. (Williams-Sonoma Pasta Collection). (Illus.). 128p. 1996. 18.95 (1-875137-08-4) Weldon Owen.
Risotto. Ed. by Chuck Williams. LC 95-31194. (Williams-Sonoma Pasta Collection). (Illus.). 128p. 1996. 18.95 (0-7835-0315-6) Time-Life.
***Risotto Risotti.** Judith Barrett. 1996. 25.00 (0-614-19371-0) Macmillan.
***Risottos, Paellas & Other Rice Specialties.** Raquel B. Agranoff. (Illus.). 176p. (Orig.). 1997. pap. 8.95 (1-55867-166-8, Nitty Gritty Ckbks) Bristol Pub Ent CA.
Risque Rhymes Naughty Poetry. Morgan Lowe. 1994. pap. 20.00 (0-685-72626-6) Moonlite Pubng.
Riss im Raum. Matthias Flugge. 344p. 1994. pap. text ed. 44.00 (3-364-00323-8) Gordon & Breach.
Ristras. Sue Dremann. (Illus.). 8p. (Orig.). (gr. 6-12). 1993. pap. 2.25 (0-933421-35-4) Redwood Seed.
Rita & Frits Markus Collection of European Ceramics & Enamels. Vivian S. Hawes et al. Ed. by D. Margaret Jupe. LC 83-63520. (Illus.). 288p. 1984. pap. 17.95 (0-87846-238-4) Mus Fine Arts Boston.
Rita & Los Angeles. Leo Romero. LC 95-1032. 144p. (Orig.). 1995. pap. 13.00 (0-927534-44-4) Biling Rev-Pr.
Rita & Tim Hildebrandt Fantasy Cookbook. Rita Hildebrandt & Timothy Hildebrandt. LC 82-17798. (Illus.). 208p. 1983. write for info. (0-672-52703-0) Macmillan.
Rita De Casia - Dios Hablara Esta Noche. Francisco Mascaro. 134p. (Orig.). (SPA.). 1991. pap. text ed. 10.00 (0-917049-55-1) Saeta.
***Rita Greer's Vegetarian Cookbook: Healthy Eating the Price-Wise Way.** Rita Greer. 1997. pap. 9.95 (0-285-63344-9, Pub. by Souvenir UK) IPG Chicago.
Rita Hayworth: Her Story. Barbara Leaming. write for info. (0-318-62112-6) Viking Penguin.
***Rita MacNeil - Joyful Sounds: A Seasonal Collection.** Ed. by Michael Lefferts. 96p. (Orig.). (C). 1996. pap. text ed. 19.95 (0-7692-0692-1, CCC122) Warner Brothers.
***Rita MacNeil Songbook.** 96p. (Orig.). (YA). 1997. pap. text ed. 19.95 (0-7692-0165-2, CCC126) Warner Brothers.
Rita Mae Brown. Carol M. Ward. (Twayne's United States Authors Ser.). 160p. 1993. 22.95 (0-8057-4000-7, Twayne) Scribnrs Ref.
Rita Mae Brown. Carol M. Ward. 1995. pap. 14.95 (0-8057-9230-9, Twayne) Scribnrs Ref.
Rita Moreno: Puerto Rican Singer & Actress. Susan Suntree. (Hispanics of Achievement Ser.). (Illus.). 112p. (YA). (gr. 5 up). 1992. lib. bdg. 19.95 (0-7910-1247-6) Chelsea Hse.
***Rita Moreno: Puerto Rican Singer & Actress.** Susan Suntree. (Hispanics of Achievement Ser.). (Illus.). 112p. (J). (gr. 4-7). 1992. pap. 8.95 (0-7910-1274-3) Chelsea Hse.
Rita of Cascia: Priceless Pearl of Umbria. Vittorio Peri. Ed. by John E. Rotelle. Tr. by Matthew J. O'Connell. (Illus.). 174p. 1995. 21.95 (0-941491-90-0); pap. 15.95 (0-941491-89-7) Augustinian Pr.
Rita, Sue & Bob Too with the Arbor & Shirley. Andrea Dunbar. (Methuen New Theatrescripts Ser.). 103p. (C). 1988. pap. 8.95 (0-413-18340-8, A0244) Heinemann.
Rita-The Saint of the Impossible. Jo Lemoine. Tr. by Florestine Audette from FRE. LC 92-34919. 128p. (Orig.). 1992. pap. 5.95 (0-8198-6422-6) Pauline Bks.
Rita, the Weekend Rat. Sonia Levitin. (Illus.). 144p. (Orig.). (J). (gr. 3-7). 1980. pap. 1.95 (0-590-30378-3) Scholastic Inc.
***Rita Will: An Autobiography.** Rita Mae Brown. 480p. 1997. 23.95 (0-553-09973-6) Bantam.
***Rita Wolff Paint.** 1986. pap. 24.95 (0-312-68464-9) St Martin.
Rita Wolff Paintings. Ed. by Academy Editions Staff & Demetri Porphyrios. (Illus.). 96p. 1986. 29.95 (0-312-68463-0); pap. 24.95 (0-685-13216-1) St Martin.
Ritalin: Theory & Patient Management. Laurence L. Greenhill & Betty B. Osman. 338p. 1991. 158.00 (0-913113-53-0) M Liebert.
Ritalin-Free Child: Managing Hyperactivity & Attention Deficits Without Drugs. Diana Hunter. Ed. by Joseph Pappas. LC 95-47004. 155p. (Orig.). 1995. pap. 12.95 (0-9628336-8-1, Womens Pubns) Consumer Press.
Ritalin-Free Kids: Safe & Effective Homeopathic Medicine for ADD & Other Behavioral & Learning Problems. Judyth Reichenberg-Ullman & Robert Ullman. 320p. 1996. pap. 15.00 (0-7615-0719-1) Prima Pub.
Rita's Story. Rita Klaus. LC 93-84601. (Orig.). 1993. pap. 9.95 (1-55725-056-1) Paraclete MA.
Ritchie Blackmore Anthology. (Illus.). 240p. 1988. pap. 21.95 (0-8256-1208-X, AM72471) Music Sales.
Ritchie Blackmore Rock Score. (Illus.). 80p. 1987. pap. 15.95 (0-8256-1114-8, AM67067) Music Sales.
Ritchie County Cemeteries: Through 1993. Ritchie Co. Historical Society Staff. 860p. 1995. 40.00 (0-87012-538-9) McClain.
Ritchie Valens, The First Latino Rocker. Beverly Mendheim. LC 87-71700. 176p. 1987. pap. 15.00 (0-916950-79-4) Biling Rev-Pr.
Rite. Gregory Douglas. (Orig.). 1979. mass mkt. 2.50 (0-89083-529-2, Zebra Kensgtn) Kensgtn Pub Corp.
***Rite & Reason: Explanation of Jewish Laws & Practices.** Shemuel P. Gelbard. LC 97-12194. 1997. write for info. (0-87306-795-9) Feldheim.
Rite Easy from A to Z. Lafayette Robinson. Tr. by Inez Gonzalez. (Illus.). 48p. (ENG & SPA.). (J). (gr. 1-3). 1993. lib. bdg. write for info. (0-9621081-0-3) Educ Graphics.
Rite for the Beautification of All Beings. John Brandi. LC 83-4774. (Illus.). 17p. (Orig.). 1983. pap. 7.50 (0-915124-65-3, Toothpaste) Coffee Hse.
Rite of Baptism. 32p. 1962. pap. 0.95 (0-8146-0568-0) Liturgical Pr.
***Rite of Baptism Booklet.** 64p. 1982. pap. 1.50 (0-89942-080-X, 80/04) Catholic Bk Pub.
Rite of Baptism for Children. 144p. 1983. text ed. 9.25 (0-89942-136-9, 136/22) Catholic Bk Pub.
Rite of Baptism for Children. St. Paul Publications Staff. (C). 1988. 20.00 (0-85439-038-3, Pub. by St Paul Pubns UK) St Mut.
Rite of Baptism for Children. Veritas Publications Staff. 122p. 1989. pap. 22.00 (1-85390-197-0, Pub. by Veritas IE) St Mut.
Rite of Betrothal & Crowning. Tr. by Vladimir Borichevsky from RUS. 32p. (Orig.). 1992. pap. 0.75 (1-878997-27-0) St Tikhons Pr.
Rite of Brotherhood. Cherith Baldry. Ed. by Sue Reck. (Saga of the Six Worlds Ser.). 160p. (YA). (gr. 8-12). 1994. pap. 4.99 (0-7814-0094-5, Chariot Bks) Chariot Victor.
Rite of Christian Initiation of Adults. International Commission on English in the Liturgy Staff & NCCB Committee on the Liturgy Staff. 396p. 1988. 17.95 (1-55586-213-6) US Catholic.
Rite of Christian Initiation of Adults. National Conference of Catholic Bishops. Ed. by International Commission on English in the Liturgy Staff. 404p. 1988. 19.95 (0-89942-355-8, 355-22); student ed., pap. 8.95 (0-89942-358-2, 358-04) Catholic Bk Pub.
Rite of Christian Initiation of Adults. Veritas Publications Staff. 288p. 1989. 60.00 (0-86217-292-6, Pub. by Veritas IE) St Mut.
Rite of Christian Initiation of Adults: Ritual Edition. 375p. 1988. 15.00 (0-930467-93-0, H-RCIA) Liturgy Tr Pubns.
Rite of Christian Initiation of Adults: Ritual Edition. 378p. 1988. 28.95 (0-8146-1592-9) Liturgical Pr.
Rite of Christian Initiation of Adults: Study Edition. 375p. 1988. pap. 12.00 (0-930467-94-9, P-RCIA) Liturgy Tr Pubns.
Rite of Christian Initiation of Adults: Study Edition. 378p. 1988. pap. 16.95 (0-8146-1593-7) Liturgical Pr.
Rite of Christian Initiation of Adults: Study Edition. NCCB, International Commission on English in the Liturgy Staff & NCCB, Bishops' Committee on the Liturgy Staff. 396p. 1988. 7.95 (1-55586-214-4) US Catholic.
Rite of Confirmation. 64p. pap. 1.25 (0-8146-1492-2) Liturgical Pr.
Rite of Confirmation. St. Paul Publications Staff. (C). 1988. 35.00 (0-85439-084-7, Pub. by St Paul Pubns UK) St Mut.
Rite of Confirmation: Altar Edition. Tr. by International Commission on English in the Liturgy Staff. 89p. (Orig.). (C). 1977. pap. 9.95 (1-55586-490-2) US Catholic.
Rite of Confirmation: Moments When Faith Is Strengthened. Peter R. Monkres & R. Kenneth Ostermiller. LC 94-39954. 104p. (Orig.). 1995. pap. 9.95 (0-8298-1020-X) Pilgrim OH.
Rite of Funerals see Order of Christian Funerals
Rite of Holy Communion & Worship of the Eucharist Outside Mass. 1973. 9.75 (0-89942-648-4, 648/22) Catholic Bk Pub.
Rite of Holy Mass & Prayerbook. St. Paul Publications Staff. (C). 1988. 39.00 (0-85439-035-9, Pub. by St Paul Pubns UK) St Mut.
Rite of Holy Matrimony. Tr. by Isaac E. Lambertsen from SLA. 16p. (Orig.). 1991. pap. 2.00 (0-912927-46-1, D008) St John Kronstadt.
Rite of Marriage. large type ed. 1973. text ed. 9.25 (0-89942-238-1, 238/22) Catholic Bk Pub.
Rite of Passage. Richard A. Wright. LC 93-2473. 128p. (YA). (gr. 7 up). 1994. lib. bdg. 13.89 (0-06-023420-2) HarpC Child Bks.
Rite of Passage. Richard A. Wright. LC 93-2473. (Trophy Bk.). 160p. (YA). (gr. 7 up). 1996. pap. 4.50 (0-06-447111-X, Trophy) HarpC Child Bks.
Rite of Passage: How to Teach Your Son about Sex & Manhood. E. James Wilder. Orig. Title: Just Between Father & Son. 210p. 1994. pap. 10.99 (0-89283-873-6, Vine Bks) Servant.
Rite of Penance. large type ed. 160p. 1973. 11.50 (0-89942-528-3, 528/22) Catholic Bk Pub.
Rite of Penance. rev. ed. Secretariat for the Liturgy National Conference of Catholic Bishops Staff. (Study Text Ser.: No. 4). 56p. 1989. pap. 6.95 (1-55586-305-1) US Catholic.
Rite of Redemption: An Interpretation of the Films of Ingmar Bergman. rev. ed. Arthur Gibson. Ed. by Lorine M. Getz. LC 95-13962. Orig. Title: The Rite of Redemption in the Films of Ingmar Bergman. 176p. 1995. 79.95 (0-7734-8892-8) E Mellen.
Rite of Redemption in the Films of Ingmar Bergman: The Rite, The Virgin Spring, Hour of the Wolf, Shame, Passion of Anna, The Touch, Cries & Whispers. Arthur Gibson. LC 92-46050. 436p. 1993. text ed. 109.95 (0-7734-9205-4) E Mellen.
Rite of Redemption in the Films of Ingmar Bergman see Rite of Redemption: An Interpretation of the Films of Ingmar Bergman
Rite of Religious Profession: The Roman Ritual. Sacred Congregation for Divine Worship Staff. Tr. by International Commission on English in the Liturgy Staff from LAT. 140p. (Orig.). 1989. pap. 11.95 (1-55586-273-X) US Catholic.
Rite of War. Stan Windass. 128p. 1986. pap. 10.95 (0-08-033605-1, Pergamon Pr) Elsevier.
Rites: A Guatemalan Boyhood. Victor Perera. LC 94-13776. 216p. 1994. reprint ed. pap. 12.95 (1-56279-065-X) Mercury Hse Inc.
Rites & Ceremonies of the Greek Church in Russia. John G. King. LC 73-126673. reprint ed. 34.50 (0-404-03692-9) AMS Pr.
Rites & Choruses: Three Books of Poems. Mark Dunster. 1980. pap. 4.00 (0-89642-059-0) Linden Pubs.
Rites & Meditations. Paul Murray. 55p. 8200. pap. 10.95 (0-85105-393-9, Pub. by Colin Smythe Ltd UK) Dufour.
Rites & Passages: The Experience of American Whaling, 1830-1870. Margaret S. Creighton. (Illus.). 520p. (C). 1995. text ed. 59.95 (0-521-43336-3); pap. text ed. 18.95 (0-521-48448-0) Cambridge U Pr.
Rites & Symbols of Initiation: The Mysteries of Birth & Rebirth. Mircea Eliade. Tr. by Willard R. Trask from FRE. LC 93-3049. Orig. Title: Birth & Rebirth. xiv, 175p. 1994. reprint ed. pap. 17.50 (0-88214-358-1) Spring Pubns.
Rites & Witnesses. Rolando Hinojosa. LC 82-71655. 120p. (Orig.). 1982. pap. 8.50 (0-934770-19-0) Arte Publico.
Rites for a Plebian Statue. Pritish Nandy. text ed. 4.80 (0-89253-655-1) Ind-US Inc.
***Rites of Alienation.** Douglas Fetherling. 104p. 1988. pap. 12.95 (0-919627-94-3, Pub. by Quarry Pr CN) LPC InBook.
Rites of Assent. Sacvan Bercovitch. 384p. (C). (gr. 13). 1992. pap. 16.95 (0-415-90015-8, 1187); text ed. 62.95 (0-415-90014-X, 1182) Routledge.
Rites of Assent: Two Novellas. Abd A. Qasim. Tr. by Peter Theroux from EGY. (Border Lines Ser.). 160p. (Orig.). (C). 1995. pap. text ed. 14.95 (1-56639-354-X); lib. bdg. 49.95 (1-56639-353-1) Temple U Pr.
***Rites of Autumn: A Falconer's Journey Across the American West.** Dan O'Brien. LC 96-30496. 1997. pap. 12.95 (1-55821-457-7) Lyons & Burford.
Rites of Burial. Tom Jackman. 1992. mass mkt. 4.99 (1-55817-611-X, Pinncle Kensgtn) Kensgtn Pub Corp.
Rites of Christian Initiation. Michel Dujarier. 244p. 1982. pap. 10.80 (0-8215-9328-5) Sadlier.
Rites of Conquest: A History of Michigan's Native Peoples. Charles E. Cleland. (Illus.). 320p. (C). 1992. pap. 18.95 (0-472-06447-9) U of Mich Pr.
Rites of Eastern Christendom, 2 vols, Set. Archdale A. King. LC 70-142246. reprint ed. 125.00 (0-404-03677-5) AMS Pr.
Rites of Eleusis. Aleister Crowley. Ed. by Anthony Naylor. (Illus.). 1990. text ed. 77.00 (1-872736-02-5, Pub. by Mandrake Pr UK) Holmes Pub.
Rites of Execution: Capital Punishment & the Transformation of America Culture, 1776-1865. Louis P. Masur. (Illus.). 224p. 1991. reprint ed. pap. 17.95 (0-19-506663-4) OUP.
Rites of Fall: High School Football in Texas. Geoff Winningham & Al Reinert. (Illus.). 176p. 1979. 24.95 (0-292-77020-0); pap. 14.95 (0-292-77021-9) U of Tex Pr.
Rites of First Blood. Karen D. Wolman. 320p. (Orig.). 1995. pap. 10.95 (1-882587-08-1) Paradigm San Diego.
***Rites of Justice: The Sacraments & Liturgy As Ethical Imperatives.** Megan McKenna. LC 96-49914. 192p. (Orig.). 1997. pap. 13.00 (1-57075-108-0) Orbis Bks.
Rites of Labor: Brotherhoods of Compagnonnage in Old & New Regime France. Cynthia M. Truant. (Illus.). 408p. 1995. 45.00 (0-8014-2769-X); pap. 19.95 (0-8014-8240-2) Cornell U Pr.
Rites of Modernization: Symbols & Social Aspects of Indonesian Proletarian Drama. James Peacock. LC 68-15931. (Symbolic Anthropology Ser.). (Illus.). xxvi, 332p. (C). 1987. pap. text ed. 19.50 (0-226-65131-2) U Ch Pr.
Rites of Odin. Ed Fitch. LC 89-2490. (Teutonic Magick Ser.). (Illus.). 360p. (Orig.). 1990. pap. 14.95 (0-87542-224-1) Llewellyn Pubns.
Rites of Passage. Dewhirst. 192p. (C). 1996. pap. text ed. 21.00 (0-13-442534-0) P-H.
Rites of Passage. Ed. by Jean Holm & John W. Bowker. LC 94-13744. (Themes in Religious Studies). 1994. 45.00 (1-85567-102-6); pap. 16.95 (1-85567-103-4) St Martin.
Rites of Passage. Arnold Van Gennep. Tr. by Monika B. Vizedon & Gabrielle L. Caffee. LC 59-14321. 223p. 1961. pap. text ed. 9.95 (0-226-84849-3, P64) U Ch Pr.
Rites of Passage: A Guide to the Jewish Life Cycle. Ronald H. Isaacs. LC 92-33982. 1992. 12.95 (0-88125-422-3) Ktav.
Rites of Passage: A Memoir of the Sixties in Seattle. Walt Crowley. (Illus.). 352p. (C). 1995. 22.95 (0-295-97492-3) U of Wash Pr.
***Rites of Passage: A Memoir of the Sixties in Seattle.** Walt Crowley. (Illus.). 352p. 1997. pap. 16.95 (0-295-97493-1) U of Wash Pr.
Rites of Passage: An Aspect of Rai Culture. S. Toba. (C). 1992. 35.00 (0-7855-0211-4, Pub. by Ratna Pustak Bhandar) St Mut.
Rites of Passage: Art for the End of the Century. Stuart Morgan & Frances Morris. (Illus.). 136p. 1996. pap. 40.00 (1-85437-156-8, Pub. by Tate Gallery UK) U of Wash Pr.
Rites of Passage: Emigrant Voyages to Australia in the Nineteenth Century. Helen R. Woolcock. 350p. 1986. 52.50 (0-422-60240-X, 1041, Pub. by Tavistock UK) Routledge Chapman & Hall.
***Rites of Passage: Odyssey of a Grunt.** Robert B. Peterson & Joni Peterson. Ed. by J. Allen Kirsch. (Illus.). 396p. 1997. 25.00 (1-878569-48-1); pap. 14.95 (1-878569-45-7) Badger Bks Inc.
Rites of Passage: Stories about Growing up by Black Writers from Around the World. Ed. by Tonya Bolden. LC 93-31304. 240p. (YA). (gr. 5 up). 1994. 16.95 (1-56282-688-3) Hyprn Child.
Rites of Passage: Stories about Growing up by Black Writers from Around the World. Illus. by Floyd Cooper. LC 93-31304. 240p. (YA). (gr. 5 up). 1995. pap. 7.95 (0-7868-1076-9) Hyprn Ppbks.
Rites of Passage: The Pagan Wheel of Life. Pauline Campanelli. LC 94-30677. (Illus.). 288p. 1994. pap. 14.95 (0-87542-119-9) Llewellyn Pubns.
Rites of Passage at One-Hundred-Thousand Dollars Plus: The Insider's Guide to Absolutely Everything about Executive Job-Changing. John Lucht. LC 87-50459. 560p. 1988. 29.95 (0-942785-07-X) H Holt & Co.
Rites of Passage at One Hundred Thousand Dollars Plus: The Insider's Lifetime Guide to Executive Job-Changing & Faster Career Progress. rev. ed. Rev. by John Lucht. 640p. 1993. 29.95 (0-942785-21-5) H Holt & Co.
Rites of Passage in America: Traditions of the Life Cycle. 6.80 (0-614-14841-3) Balch Inst Ethnic Studies.
Rites of Passage in America: Traditions of the Life Cycle. Balch IES Staff. LC 92-72033. (Illus.). 70p. 1992. 8.50 (0-937437-10-7) Balch IES Pr.
Rites of Passage of Jean Genet: The Art & Aesthetics of Risk Taking. Gene A. Plunka. LC 91-55363. 360p. 1992. 45.00 (0-8386-3461-3) Fairleigh Dickinson.
Rites of People: Exploring the Ritual Character of Human Experience. rev. ed. Gerard A. Pottebaum. (Orig.). 1992. pap. text ed. 7.95 (0-912405-94-5) Pastoral Pr.
Rites of Possession. Charlotte Lamb. (Presents Ser.: No. 1345). 1991. pap. 2.75 (0-373-11345-5) Harlequin Bks.
Rites of Possession. large type ed. Charlotte Lamb. 1990. reprint ed. lib. bdg. 18.95 (0-263-12270-0, Pub. by Mills & Boon UK) Thorndike Pr.
Rites of Religious Profession: Pastoral Introduction & Complete Text. Edward Foley. 215p. (Orig.). 1989. pap. 10.00 (0-929650-01-8, RRPROF) Liturgy Tr Pubns.
Rites of Rulers: Ritual in Industrial Society-the Soviet Case. Christel Lane. LC 80-41747. (Illus.). 338p. 1981. 79.95 (0-521-22608-2) Cambridge U Pr.
Rites of Sodom. Jack Spender. 1988. mass mkt. 4.95 (1-56201-001-8, 26) Blue Moon Bks.
Rites of Spring: The Great War & the Birth of the Modern Age. Modris Eksteins. 416p. 1990. pap. 14.95 (0-385-41202-9, Anchor NY) Doubleday.
Rites of Strangers. Phyllis Janowitz. LC 78-16729. (Virginia Commonwealth University Series for Contemporary Poetry). 80p. reprint ed. pap. 25.00 (0-7837-3566-9, 2043424) Bks Demand.
Rites of the Catholic Church, Vol. 1. 3rd rev. ed. 1118p. 1992. pap. 29.95 (0-8146-6015-0, Pueblo Bks) Liturgical Pr.
Rites of the Catholic Church, Vol. 2. 2nd rev. ed. 496p. 1992. pap. 19.95 (0-8146-6037-1, Pueblo Bks) Liturgical Pr.
Ritmo. Rueda. Ed. by Palenque. (Exeter Hispanic Text Ser.: No. 53). 150p. (SPA.). Date not set. pap. text ed. 21.95 (0-85989-401-0, Pub. by Univ Exeter Pr UK) Northwestern U Pr.
Rito De la Iniciacion Cristiana De Adultos. Ed. by Bishops' Committee on the Liturgy Staff & United States Catholic Conference of Bishops Staff. 364p. 1991. 34.95 (0-929650-54-9, S/RCIA); pap. 12.95 (0-929650-75-1, SSRCIA) Liturgy Tr Pubns.
Rito de la Iniciacion Cristiana de Adultos. NCCB Staff. 384p. (SPA.). Study ed. student ed. 12.95 (1-55586-509-7) US Catholic.
Rito de la Iniciacion Cristiana de Adultos. NCCB Staff. 384p. (SPA.). 1981. Ritual ed. 34.95 (1-55586-435-X) US Catholic.
Rito de la Iniciacion Cristiana de Adultos: Ritual Edition. 416p. (SPA.). 1991. 34.95 (0-8146-2084-1) Liturgical Pr.
Rito de la Iniciacion Cristiana de Adultos: Study Edition. 416p. (SPA.). 1993. pap. 12.95 (0-8146-2223-2) Liturgical Pr.
***Rito del Matrimonio.** 94p. (Orig.). (SPA.). 1996. pap. 39.95 (0-89243-936-X) Liguori Pubns.
***Rito, Simbolo e Historia en la Piramide de Akapana, Tiwanaku: Un Analisis de Ceramica Ceremonial Prehispanica.** Sonia A. Mujica. 248p. 1995. pap. 15.00 (1-877812-43-9, UC002) UPLAAP.
Ritorno Di Pulcinella de Padova: Libretto by Andrea Passaro Music by Vincenzo Fioravanti First Performance Naples, Teatro Nuovo Spora Toledo, 27 December 1837. Vincenzo Fioravanti. LC 89-753855. (Italian Opera 1810-1840 Ser.: Vol. 7). 264p. 1990. text ed. 30.00 (0-8240-6556-5) Garland.
Ritos de Iniciacion: Tres Nouvelas Cortas de Hispanoamerica. Grinor Rojo & Cynthia Steele. LC 85-80939. 224p. (SPA.). (C). 1985. text ed. 27.56 (0-395-38125-8) HM.
Ritschl in Retrospect: History, Community & Science. Ed. by Darrell H. Jodock. LC 95-1016. 224p. 1995. pap. 26.00 (0-8006-2606-0, Fortress Pr) Augsburg Fortress.
***Rittenhouse Cookbook: A Year of Heart-Healthy Recipes.** Jim Coleman. LC 97-15249. (Illus.). 160p. (Orig.). 1997. 29.95 (0-89815-864-8) Ten Speed Pr.
***Rittenhouse Cookbook: A Year of Heart-Healthy Recipes.** Jim Coleman. LC 97-15249. (Illus.). 160p. (Orig.). 1997. pap. 19.95 (0-89815-929-6) Ten Speed Pr.

R

R

Rittenhouse Mill & the Beginnings of Papermaking in America. James Green. 32p. (Orig.). 1990. pap. 3.00 (0-685-56524-6) Lib Co Phila.

Rittenhouse Square. Arthur R. Solmssen. LC 68-17265. 313p. 1968. 20.00 (0-940846-03-9) Hastings Bks.

Ritter Galmy see Saemtliche Werke

Ritterburg. (Meyers Kleine Kinderbibliothek Ser.). 1992. 13.25 (3-411-08511-8, Pub. by Bibliogr Inst Brockhaus GW) Langenscheidt.

Ritterlich und Lobwirdig Rayss. Ludovico De Varthema. LC 92-23009. 1992. 55.00 (0-8201-1477-4) Schol Facsimiles.

*Rittners Field Guide to the Web Business & Finance Resources. Don Rittner. 1996. pap. text ed. 19.95 (0-937666-51-3) MNS Pub.

*Rittners Field Guide to the Web Environmental Resources. Don Rittner. 1997. pap. text ed. 19.95 (0-937666-52-1) MNS Pub.

Rittner's Field Guide to Usenet. Don Rittner. LC 96-51251. (Illus.). 132p. (Orig.). 1996. pap. 19.95 (0-937666-50-5) MNS Pub.

*Rittners Field Guide to Web: Medical & Public Health Resources. Don Rittner. 1997. pap. text ed. 19.95 (0-937666-53-X) MNS Pub.

Ritual. William Heffernan. 352p. 1990. pap. 5.99 (0-451-16397-4, Sig) NAL-Dutton.

Ritual. Theodor Reik. 1976. pap. 24.95 (0-8236-8269-2, 025840) Intl Univs Pr.

*Ritual. Malidoma P. Some. 1997. pap. 12.95 (0-14-019558-0) Viking Penguin.

*Ritual: Perspectives & Dimensions. Catherine Bell. LC 96-23945. 432p. 1997. 55.00 (0-19-511051-X); pap. 19.95 (0-19-511052-8) OUP.

Ritual Abuse: What It Is, Why It Happens, & How to Help. Margaret Smith. LC 92-56420. 192p. 1993. Acid-free paper. pap. 13.00 (0-06-250214-X) Harper SF.

Ritual & Belief: Chinese Jade & Related Arts, Vol. 3. Sam Bernstein. (Illus.). 108p. 1994. 65.00 (0-9638932-0-3) S Bernstein & Co.

Ritual & Desire: Catullus 61 & 62 & Other Ancient Documents on Wedding & Marriage. Ole Thomsen. 324p. (C). 1992. text ed. 27.00 (87-7288-288-3, Pub. by Aarhus Univ Pr DK) David Brown.

Ritual & Devotion: An Introduction. Sangharakshita. 125p. (Orig.). 1996. pap. 13.95 (0-904766-87-X) Windhorse Pubns.

*Ritual & el Dia de Los Muertos: A Day of the Dead Curriculum Handbook for Teachers. Bea C. Hocker. 22p. 1988. 8.50 (0-614-24044-1) Mexican Museum.

Ritual & Ethnic Identity: A Comparative Study of the Social Meaning of Liturgical Ritual in Synagogues. Jack N. Lightstone et al. viii, 224p. (C). 1995. text ed. 34.95 (0-88920-247-8) Wilfrid Laurier.

Ritual & Experiment in Modern Poetry. Jacob Korg. 1995. text ed. 39.95 (0-312-12453-8) St Martin.

Ritual & Knowledge among the Baktaman of New Guinea. Fredrik Barth. LC 74-19572. (Illus.). 296p. reprint ed. pap. 84.40 (0-317-11336-4, 2021979) Bks Demand.

Ritual & Myth: Robertson, Smith, Frazer, Hooke, & Harrison. Robert A. Segal. LC 95-36270. (Theories of Myth Ser.: Vol. 5). 424p. 1995. text ed. 70.00 (0-8153-2259-3) Garland.

*Ritual & Myth in Odawa Revitalization: Reclaiming a Sovereign Place. Melissa A. Pflug. 1998. write for info. (0-8061-3007-5) U of Okla Pr.

Ritual & Pastoral Care. Elaine Ramshaw. LC 85-45487. (Theology & Pastoral Care Ser.). 128p. 1987. pap. 12.00 (0-8006-1738-X, 1-1738, Fortress Pr) Augsburg Fortress.

Ritual & Pathos: The Theater of O'Neill. Leonard Chabrowe. (Illus.). 226p. 1976. 32.50 (0-8387-1575-3) Bucknell U Pr.

Ritual & Reconciliation. Ed. by Blair G. Meeks. (Liturgy Ser.). (Illus.). 120p. (Orig.). 1991. pap. 10.95 (0-918208-55-6) Liturgical Conf.

Ritual & Record: Sports Records & Quantification in Pre-Modern Societies. Ed. by John M. Carter & Arnd Kruger. LC 89-78452. (Contributions to the Study of World History Ser.: No. 17). 192p. 1990. text ed. 55.00 (0-313-25699-3, CSE/, Greenwood Pr) Greenwood.

Ritual & Relationships in the Valley of the Sun: The Ketengban of Irian Jaya. Andrew Sims & Anne Sims. LC 92-61811. (International Museum of Cultures Publications: No. 30). xii, 162p. 1992. pap. 12.00 (0-88312-271-5); fiche 12.00 (0-88312-584-6) Summer Instit Ling.

Ritual & Religion among Muslims in India. Ed. by Imtiaz Ahmad. 1982. 20.00 (0-8364-0852-7, Pub. by Manohar II) S Asia.

Ritual & Scripture in Chinese Popular Religion: Five Studies. Ed. by David Johnson. LC 93-44401. (Publications of the Chinese Popular Culture Project: No. 3). 1994. pap. 15.00 (0-9624327-3-3) Chinese Popular.

*Ritual & Semiotics. Ed. by J. Ralph Lindgren & Jay Knaak. (Critic of Institutions Ser.: No. 14). 240p. (C). 1997. text ed. 46.95 (0-8204-2805-1) P Lang Pubng.

Ritual & Speculation in Early Tantrism: Studies in Honor of Andre Padoux. Ed. by Teun Goudriaan. LC 91-10169. (Series in Tantric Studies). 288p. (C). 1992. text ed. 59.50 (0-7914-0897-3); pap. text ed. 19.95 (0-7914-0898-1) State U NY Pr.

Ritual & Spontaneity in the Psychoanalytic Process. Irwin Z. Hoffman. 1998. write for info. (0-88163-172-8) Analytic Pr.

Ritual & Symbol: Essays on Lamaism & Chinese Symbolism. Ferdinand D. Lessing. (Asian Folklore & Social Life Monographs: No. 91). (ENG & GER.). 1976. 20.00 (0-89986-305-1) Oriental Bk Store.

Ritual & Symbol in Transitional Zaramo Society with Special Reference to Women. Marja-Liisa Swantz. (Scandinavian Institute of African Studies). (Illus.). 452p. (Orig.). 1970. reprint ed. pap. text ed. 65.00 (91-7106-253-X, Pub. by Nordisk Afrikainstitutet SW) Coronet Bks.

Ritual Art & Knowledge: Aesthetic Theory & Zoroastrian Ritual. Ron G. Williams & James W. Boyd. LC 92-30865. (Studies in Comparative Religion). (Illus.). 215p. (C). 1993. text ed. 39.95 (0-87249-857-3) U of SC Pr.

Ritual Bath. Faye Kellerman. 288p. 1987. mass mkt. 5.99 (0-449-21373-0, Crest) Fawcett.

Ritual, Belief & Kinship in Sulawesi. Ed. by Marilyn Gregerson. LC 93-86498. (International Museum of Cultures Publications: No. 31). 199p. (Orig.). 1994. pap. 25.00 (0-88312-621-4); fiche 16.00 (1-55671-998-1) Summer Instit Ling.

Ritual Body Art: Drawing the Spirit. Charles Arnold. (Illus.). 160p. (Orig.). 1997. pap. 14.95 (0-919345-74-3) Phoenix WA.

Ritual Book of Magic. Compiled by Clifford Bias. 194p. 1981. pap. 6.95 (0-87728-532-2) Weiser.

Ritual Brotherhood in Renaissance Florence. Ronald F. Weissman. LC 81-17536. (Population & Social Structure: Advances in Historical Demography Ser.). 1981. text ed. 65.00 (0-12-744480-7) Acad Pr.

Ritual Child Abuse: Discovery, Diagnosis, & Treatment. Pamela S. Hudson. (Illus.). 100p. (Orig.). 1991. pap. text ed. 14.95 (0-88247-867-2) R & E Pubs.

Ritual Child Abuse: How & Where to Find Facts & Get Help. Robert D. Reed & Danek S. Kaus. Ed. by Diane Parker. LC 92-53759. (Abuse Ser.). 48p. 1992. pap. 4.50 (0-88247-949-0) R & E Pubs.

Ritual Cosmos: The Sanctification of Life in African Religions. Evan M. Zuesse. LC 79-13454. 256p. 1985. reprint ed. pap. 14.95 (0-8214-0814-3) Ohio U Pr.

Ritual Crime Conduct Beyond the Law. Bob Nations, Jr. 144p. 1991. student ed. 19.95 (0-914513-14-1) Haughton.

Ritual Criticism: Case Studies in Its Practice, Essays on Its Theory. Ronald L. Grimes. (Studies in Comparative Religion). 283p. (C). 1990. text ed. 34.95 (0-87249-692-9) U of SC Pr.

*Ritual Death. Brad Reynolds. (A Father Mark Townsend Mystery Ser.). 256p. (Orig.). 1997. mass mkt. 5.50 (0-380-78401-7) Avon.

Ritual Dinners in Early Historic Sardis. Crawford H. Greenewalt. LC 76-24474. (University of California Publications: Classical Studies: No. 17). (Illus.). 144p. reprint ed. pap. 41.10 (0-685-20474-X, 2029873) Bks Demand.

Ritual, Finance, Politics: Athenian Democratic Accounts Presented to David Lewis. Ed. by Robin Osborne & Simon Hornblower. (Illus.). 416p. 1995. text ed. 79.00 (0-19-814992-1) OUP.

Ritual for Laypersons: Rites for Holy Communion & the Pastoral Care of the Sick & Dying. 176p. (Orig.). Date not set. pap. 14.95 (0-8146-2150-3) Liturgical Pr.

*Ritual Function & Significance of Grasses in the Religion of the Veda. J. Gonda. (Verhandelingen der Koninklijke Nederlandse Akademie van Wetenschappen, Afd. Letterkunde, Nieuwe Reeks Ser.: No. 132). 260p. 1986. pap. text ed. 100.00 (0-444-85634-X) Elsevier.

Ritual Ground: Bent's Old Fort, World Formation, & the Annexation of the Southwest. Douglas C. Comer. (Illus.). 328p. 1996. 45.00 (0-520-20429-8); pap. 16.95 (0-520-20774-2) U CA Pr.

Ritual Healing in Suburban America. Meredith B. Mcguire & Debra Kantor. 335p. (C). 1988. text ed. 45.00 (0-8135-1312-X); pap. text ed. 16.95 (0-8135-1313-8) Rutgers U Pr.

Ritual, History & Power: Selected Papers in Anthropology. Maurice Bloch. LC 88-36611. (London School of Economics Monographs on Social Anthropology: Vol. 58). 288p. (C). 1989. pap. 22.50 (0-485-19658-1, Pub. by Athlone Pr UK); text ed. 70.00 (0-485-19558-5, Pub. by Athlone Pr UK) Humanities.

Ritual Human Sacrifice in Mesoamerica: A Conference at Dumbarton Oaks, October 13 & 14, 1979. Ed. by Elizabeth H. Boone. LC 83-14059. (Illus.). 256p. 1984. 20.00 (0-88402-120-3) Dumbarton Oaks.

Ritual Humor in Highland Chiapas. Victoria R. Bricker. LC 73-6501. (Texas Pan American Ser. & Texas Press Sourcebooks: No. 12). (Illus.). 293p. 1973. pap. 8.95 (0-292-77029-4) U of Tex Pr.

Ritual Humor in Highland Chiapas. Victoria R. Bricker. LC 73-6501. (Texas Pan-American Ser.). 293p. 1973. reprint ed. pap. 83.60 (0-8357-7728-6, 2036085) Bks Demand.

Ritual Illumination: Poems. William C. McDonald. Ed. by Patricia Schultz. LC 90-41266. (Mellen Poetry Ser.: Vol. 12). 72p. 1990. lib. bdg. 24.95 (0-88946-836-2) E Mellen.

*Ritual in Early Modern Europe. Edward Muir. (New Approaches to European History Ser.: Vol. 11). (Illus.). 304p. (C). 1997. text ed. 54.95 (0-521-40169-0) Cambridge U Pr.

*Ritual in Early Modern Europe. Edward Muir. (New Approaches to European History Ser.: Vol. 11). (Illus.). 304p. (C). 1997. pap. text ed. 17.95 (0-521-40967-5) Cambridge U Pr.

Ritual in Family Living. James H. Bossard & Eleanor S. Boll. LC 75-45454. 228p. 1976. reprint ed. text ed. 35.00 (0-8371-8678-1, BORF, Greenwood Pr) Greenwood.

Ritual in the Dark. 2nd ed. Colin Wilson. 416p. 1993. reprint ed. pap. 12.95 (0-914171-63-1) Ronin Pub.

Ritual, Initiation & Secrets in Sufi Circles. 48p. 1980. pap. 7.00 (0-86304-002-0, Pub. by Octagon Pr UK) ISHK.

Ritual Irony: Poetry & Sacrifice in Euripides. Helene P. Foley. LC 84-17470. 288p. (C). 1985. 39.95 (0-8014-1692-2) Cornell U Pr.

Ritual Kinship Vol. 2: Ideological & Structural Integration of the Compadrazgo System in Rural Tlaxcala. Hugo G. Nutini & Betty Bell. LC 79-3225. 520p. 1980. reprint ed. pap. 148.20 (0-7837-9296-4, 2060035) Bks Demand.

Ritual Legislation in the Victorian Church of England: Antecedents & Passage of the Public Worship Regulation Act, 1874. Gary W. Graber. LC 93-24043. 204p. 1993. text ed. 89.95 (0-7734-2216-1) E Mellen.

Ritual Magic: What It Is & How to Do It. Donald Tyson. LC 92-13332. (Llewellyn's Practical Magic Ser.). (Illus.). 282p. 1992. pap. 12.95 (0-87542-835-5) Llewellyn Pubns.

Ritual Magic Course: Practical 11 Lesson Magic Course, 11 lessons, Set. Darren Fox. Ed. & Intro. by Thor Templar. (Illus.). 435p. 1994. 275.00 (1-57179-042-X) Intern Guild ASRS.

*Ritual Magic of the Golden Dawn. Francis King. LC 97-1117. 288p. 1997. pap. 14.95 (0-89281-617-1, Destiny Bks) Inner Tradit.

Ritual Masks: Deceptions & Revelations. Henry Pernet. Ed. by Frederick M. Denny. LC 91-45396. (Studies in Comparative Religion). (Illus.). 211p. 1992. text ed. 29.95 (0-87249-793-3) U of SC Pr.

Ritual Music. Edward Foley. 218p. (Orig.). 1995. pap. text ed. 14.95 (1-56929-057-1) Pastoral Pr.

Ritual of Battle: Krishna in the Mahabharata. Alf Hiltebeitel. LC 89-35594. (SUNY Series in Hindu Studies). 368p. 1990. text ed. 59.50 (0-7914-0249-5); pap. text ed. 19.95 (0-7914-0250-9) State U NY Pr.

Ritual of Eternity: Ancient Egypt Unveiled. Joanna Sanneh. LC 91-90105. 296p. (Orig.). 1992. pap. 18.95 (9983-85-002-8) Nocturnal Sun.

Ritual of Interpretation: The Fine Arts As Literature in Ruskin, Rossetti, & Pater. Richard L. Stein. LC 74-34540. (Illus.). 328p. reprint ed. pap. 93.50 (0-7837-3830-7, 2043651) Bks Demand.

Ritual of Music. Ed. by Doris H. Cooley. 1968. pap. text ed. 1.00 (0-88053-318-8, S-79) Macoy Pub.

Ritual of New Creation: Jewish Tradition & Contemporary Literature. Norman Finkelstein. LC 91-27776. (SUNY Series in Modern Jewish Literature & Culture). 174p. (C). 1992. text ed. 64.50 (0-7914-1089-7); pap. text ed. 21.95 (0-7914-1090-0) State U NY Pr.

*Ritual of Pennsylvania: Ancient York Masonry. 76p. 1996. pap. 19.95 (1-56459-985-X) Kessinger Pub.

Ritual of the Knights of the Ancient Essenic Order. C. J. Weatherby. 52p. 1993. pap. 12.95 (1-56459-318-5) Kessinger Pub.

*Ritual of the Mask. unabridged ed. Jono Ohlgren. (Illus.). 95p. (Orig.). 1997. pap. 17.00 (0-9655445-0-8) Zone Thirty-Three.

Ritual of the Mystery of the Judgement of the Soul: From an Ancient Egyptian Papyrus. Ed. & Tr. by M. W. Blackden. 1986. pap. 6.95 (0-916411-58-3) Holmes Pub.

Ritual of the Original Rose of Seven Seals. 1994. pap. 5.00 (1-56459-473-4) Kessinger Pub.

Ritual of the Secular Franciscan Order. 35p. 1993. pap. 5.95 (1-885057-07-5) C E Hugenberger.

Ritual Passage, Sacred Journey: The Form, Process, & Organization of Religious Movement. Richard P. Werbner. LC 88-29298. (Series in Ethnographic Inquiry: No. 14). (Illus.). 300p. (C). 1989. text ed. 39.00 (0-87474-976-X) Smithsonian.

Ritual Passages & Narrative Structures. Langdon Elsbree. LC 90-5961. (American University Studies: Comparative Literature: Ser. III, Vol. 38). 192p. (C). 1991. text ed. 39.95 (0-8204-1335-6) P Lang Pubng.

*Ritual, Performance, Media. Felicia Hughes-Freeland & Association of Social Anthropologists of the Commonwealth Staff. LC 97-12264. (ASA Monographs). 256p. (C). 1998. pap. write for info. (0-415-16338-2); text ed. write for info. (0-415-16337-4) Routledge.

Ritual Poetry & the Politics of Death in Early Japan. Gary L. Ebersole. 350p. 1989. text ed. 55.00 (0-691-07338-4); pap. text ed. 17.95 (0-691-01929-0) Princeton U Pr.

Ritual, Politics & Power. David I. Kertzer. 235p. (C). 1989. reprint ed. pap. 14.00 (0-300-04362-7) Yale U Pr.

Ritual, Politics, & the City in Fatimid Cairo. Paula Sanders. LC 93-22317. (SUNY Series in Medieval Middle East History). 231p. (C). 1994. text ed. 59.50 (0-7914-1781-6); pap. text ed. 19.95 (0-7914-1782-4) State U NY Pr.

Ritual, Power & Economy: Upland-Lowland Contrasts in Mainland Southeast Asia. Ed. by Susan D. Russell. (Occasional Papers: No. 14). 143p. (Orig.). (C). 1989. pap. 11.00 (1-877979-14-7) SE Asia.

*Ritual, Power & the Body: Historical Perspectives on the Representation of Greek Women. Ed. by C. Nadia Seremetakis. LC 93-84825. 206p. (Orig.). 1993. pap. text ed. 12.00 (0-918618-54-1) Pella Pub.

*Ritual Practices to Gain Power: Adjurations in the Hekhalot Literature, Jewish Amulets, & Greek Revelatory Adjurations. Rebecca M. Lesses. (Harvard Theological Studies: Vol. 44). 320p. (Orig.). 1997. pap. 22.00 (1-56338-219-9) TPI PA.

Ritual Process: Structure & Anti-Structure. Victor W. Turner. (Illus.). 230p. 1969. reprint ed. pap. text ed. 14.95 (0-202-01190-9) Aldine de Gruyter.

Ritual, Religion, & the Sacred. Ed. by Orest A. Ranum & Robert Forster. Tr. by Elborg Forster & Patricia M. Ranum from FRE. LC 81-48184. (Selections from the Annales, Economies, Societies, Civilizations Ser.: No. 7). (Illus.). 256p. (C). 1982. pap. text ed. 14.95 (0-8018-2778-7) Johns Hopkins.

Ritual Sex. Ed. by David A. Clark & Tristan Taormino. (Orig.). 1996. mass mkt. 6.95 (1-56333-391-0, Rhinoceros) Masquerade.

*Ritual Sins. Anne Stuart. 1997. pap. 6.99 (0-451-19252-4, Sig) NAL-Dutton.

*Ritual Slaughter. Sharon Drache. 166p. 1989. pap. 12.95 (0-919627-27-7, Pub. by Quarry Pr CN) LPC InBook.

Ritual, State, & History in South Asia: Essays in Honour of J. C. Heesterman. Dirk H. Kolff & Marianne S. Oort. LC 92-15094. (Memoirs of the Kern Institute Ser.: No. 5). (Illus.). xi, 843p. 1992. 249.25 (90-04-09467-9) E J Brill.

Ritual Systems of Ancient Black Civilizations Vol. 1: Introduction to Meditation. Ra Un Nefer Amen I. 66p. spiral bd., pap. 15.00 (1-877662-00-3) Kamit Pubns.

Ritual Systems of Ancient Black Civilizations Vol. 2: Auset, Mother of the Living. Ra Un Nefer Amen I. 42p. spiral bd., pap. 15.00 incl. audio (1-877662-01-1) Kamit Pubns.

Ritual Systems of Ancient Black Civilizations Vol. 3: The Opening of the Way. Ra Un Nefer Amen I. 40p. spiral bd., pap. 13.00 incl. audio (1-877662-02-X) Kamit Pubns.

Ritual Systems of Ancient Black Civilizations, Vol. 1: Introduction to Meditation. Ra Un Nefer Amen I. 51p. (Orig.). 1988. pap. 14.95 (0-317-93993-9) Kamit Pubns.

Ritual Theory, Ritual Practice. Catherine Bell. 288p. 1992. pap. 18.95 (0-19-507613-3) OUP.

*Ritual Treatment of Human & Animal Remains. Ed. by Sue Anderson & Katherine Boyle. (Illus.). 72p. 1996. pap. 14.95 (1-900188-20-1, Pub. by Oxbow Bks UK) David Brown.

Ritual Year: Winter, Christmas & Other Seasons (Poems) Arnold Kenseth. 1993. pap. 14.00 (0-941895-12-2) Amherst Wri Art.

*Rituales Practico Con Velos. Ray Buckland. Ed. & Tr. by Edgar Rojas from ENG. (Illus.). 216p. (Orig.). (SPA.). 1988. pap. 6.95 (1-56718-096-5) Llewellyn Pubns.

Ritualised Friendship & the Greek State. Gabriel Herman. LC 86-4211. (Illus.). 200p. 1987. text ed. 59.95 (0-521-32541-2) Cambridge U Pr.

Ritualization of Mormon History & Other Essays. Davis Bitton. LC 93-28931. 208p. (C). 1994. text ed. 25.95 (0-252-02079-0) U of Ill Pr.

Ritualized Homosexuality in Melanesia. Ed. by Gilbert H. Herdt. LC 83-18015. (Studies in Melanesian Anthropology: No. 2). (Illus.). 300p. 1984. 47.50 (0-520-05037-1) U CA Pr.

Ritualized Homosexuality in Melanesia. Ed. by Gilbert H. Herdt. (Studies in Melanesian Anthropology: No. 2). (C). 1993. pap. 16.95 (0-520-08096-3) U CA Pr.

*Ritualizing Women: Patterns of Feminine Spirituality. Leslie A. Northup. 144p. (Orig.). 1997. pap. 13.95 (0-8298-1213-X) Pilgrim OH.

Rituals. Craig Hickman. 145p. (Orig.). 1994. pap. 12.95 (0-9644145-0-3) Parfait de Cocoa.

Rituals. Cees Nooteboom. Tr. by Adrienne Dixon. 160p. 1996. pap. 11.00 (0-15-600394-5, Harvest Bks) HarBrace.

Rituals. Kyle Stone. (Orig.). 1994. mass mkt. 4.95 (1-56333-168-3, Badboy) Masquerade.

Rituals: A Novel. Cees Nooteboom. Tr. by Adrienne Dixon from DUT. LC 82-17278. vi, 145p. 1983. 16.95 (0-8071-1081-7) La State U Pr.

Rituals & Ceremonies in Popular Culture. Ed. by Ray B. Browne. LC 80-83188. 1981. 22.95 (0-87972-160-X); pap. 14.95 (0-87972-161-8) Bowling Green Univ Popular Press.

Rituals & Icebreakers: Practical Tools for Forming Community. Kathleen O. Chesto. 110p. (Orig.). 1995. pap. 8.95 (1-55612-757-X) Sheed & Ward MO.

Rituals & Power: The Roman Imperial Cult in Asia Minor. S. R. Price. (Illus.). 316p. 1985. pap. text ed. 24.95 (0-521-31268-X) Cambridge U Pr.

Rituals & Spells of Santeria. Migene Gonzalez-Wippler. 134p. 1986. pap. 6.95 (0-942272-07-2) Original Pubns.

Rituals for a New Age-Alternative Weddings, Funerals, Holidays, Etc. (1987) see Rituals Resource Book: Alternative Weddings, Funerals, Holidays & Other Rites of Passage

Rituals for Everyday Living: Special Ways of Marking Important Events in Your Life. Lorna St. Aubyn. 112p. 1995. pap. 12.95 (0-7499-1355-X, Pub. by Piatkus Bks UK) London Brdge.

Rituals for Home & Parish: Healing & Celebrating Our Families. Jack Rathschmidt & Gaynell B. Cronin. 160p. 1996. pap. 17.95 (0-8091-3650-3, 3650-3) Paulist Pr.

Rituals for Our Times: Celebrating, Healing, & Changing Our Lives & Our Relationships. Evan Imber-Black & Janine Roberts. LC 92-52589. (Illus.). 352p. 1993. reprint ed. pap. 13.00 (0-06-092210-9, PL) HarpC.

Rituals for Resurrection: Celebrating Life & Death. Linda J. Vogel. 144p. (Orig.). 1996. pap. 9.95 (0-8358-0782-7, UR782) Upper Room Bks.

Rituals for the Bath. Kathy Corey & Lynne Blackman. (Illus.). 96p. 1995. 14.95 (0-446-91092-9) Warner Bks.

Rituals Fratres Lucis. 50p. 1993. pap. 12.95 (1-56459-363-0) Kessinger Pub.

Rituals in Babism & Baha'ism. Denis MacEoin. (Pembroke Persian Papers). 192p. 1995. text ed. 59.50 (1-85043-654-1, Pub. by I B Tauris UK) St Martin.

Rituals in Families & Family Therapy. Ed. by Evan Imber-Black et al. 1988. 34.95 (0-393-70064-X) Norton.

Rituals in Psychotherapy: Transition & Continuity. Onno Van der Hart. Tr. by Angie Pleit-Kuiper from DUT. 220p. 1982. text ed. 27.50 (0-8290-0537-4) Irvington.

Rituals in Psychotherapy: Transition & Continuity. Onno Van der Hart. Tr. by Angie Pleit-Kuiper from DUT. 220p. (C). 1986. reprint ed. pap. text ed. 14.95 (0-8290-1925-1) Irvington.

Rituals of Childhood: Jewish Culture & Acculturation in the Middle Ages. Ivan G. Marcus. LC 95-24663. 191p. 1996. 25.00 (0-300-05998-1) Yale U Pr.

Rituals of Conflict: Religion, Politics, & Public Policy in Israel. Ira Sharkansky. LC 96-36342. 175p. 1996. 49.95 (1-55587-678-1, 876781) Lynne Rienner.

An Asterisk (*) at the beginning of an entry indicates that the title is appearing in BIP for the first time.

Rituals of Dinner: The Origins, Evolution, Eccentricities, & Meaning of Table Manners. Margaret Visser. 416p. 1992. pap. 15.95 (*0-14-017079-0*, Penguin Bks) Viking Penguin.

Rituals of Dis-Integration: Romance & Madness in the Victorian Psychomythic Tale. Edwin F. Block, Jr. LC 93-2310. (Origins of Modernism Ser.). 264p. 1993. text ed. 42.00 (*0-8153-1083-8*, H1650) Garland.

Rituals of Healing. Dossey Achterberg. 384p. 1994. pap. 14.95 (*0-553-37347-1*) Bantam.

Rituals of Marginality: Politics, Process, & Culture & Change in Central Urban Mexico, 1969-1974. Carlos G. Velez-Ibanez. (Illus.). 310p. 1991. pap. 16.00 (*0-520-07421-1*) U CA Pr.

***Rituals of National Loyalty: An Anthropology of the State & the Village Scout Movement in Thailand.** Katherine A. Bowie. LC 96-38184. 1997. write for info. (*0-231-10390-5*); pap. write for info. (*0-231-10391-3*) Col U Pr.

Rituals of Renewal: Spiritual Transformation Through Native American Tradition. Leroy L. Bear & David Peat. 1996. pap. 14.95 (*0-8065-1773-5*, Citadel Pr) Carol Pub Group.

Rituals of Retribution: Capital Punishment in Germany, 1600-1987. Richard J. Evans. (Illus.). 1048p. (C). 1996. 65.00 (*0-19-821968-7*) OUP.

Rituals of Royalty: Power & Ceremonial in Traditional Societies. Ed. by David Cannadine & Simon Price. (Past & Present Publications). (Illus.). 349p. 1987. text ed. 59.95 (*0-521-33513-2*) Cambridge U Pr.

Rituals of Royalty: Power & Ceremonial in Traditional Societies. Ed. by David Cannadine & Simon Price. (Past & Present Publications). (Illus.). 369p. (C). 1993. pap. text ed. 19.95 (*0-521-42891-2*) Cambridge U Pr.

Rituals of Rule, Rituals of Resistance: Public Celebrations & Popular Culture in Mexico. Ed. by William H. Beezley et al. LC 94-884. (Latin American Silhouettes Ser.). (Illus.). 404p. 1994. 55.00 (*0-8420-2416-6*); pap. 17.95 (*0-8420-2417-4*) Scholarly Res Inc.

Rituals of Self-Revelation: Shishosetsu As Literary Genre & Socio-Cultural Phenomenon. Irmela Hijiya-K. (Harvard East Asian Monographs: No. 159). 450p. Date not set. pap. 42.00 (*0-674-77319-5*) HUP.

Rituals of Survival: A Woman's Portfolio. Nicholasa Mohr. LC 84-72300. 120p. (Orig.). (C). 1985. pap. 8.50 (*0-934770-39-5*) Arte Publico.

Rituals of the Diviner. Ivan Starr. LC 80-53522. (Bibliotheca Mesopotamica Ser.: Vol. 12). 150p. 1983. pap. 28.00 (*0-89003-064-2*) Undena Pubns.

Rituals of the First Four Grades Societatis Rosicruciana. Charles E. Meyer. 1993. pap. 9.95 (*1-56459-364-9*) Kessinger Pub.

Rituals of the Imagination. Tom Moore. 64p. 1984. pap. 8.00 (*0-911005-03-X*) Dallas Inst Pubns.

Rituals of the Swedenborgian Rite of Freemasonry. 91p. 1993. pap. 16.95 (*1-56459-362-2*) Kessinger Pub.

Rituals Resource Book: Alternative Weddings, Funerals, Holidays & Other Rites of Passage. 2nd rev. ed. Susan M. Mumm. Orig. Title: Rituals for a New Age-Alternative Weddings, Funerals, Holidays, Etc. (1987). 285p. 1995. pap. 21.95 (*0-9619645-1-0*) A Yul Pub & Dist.

Rituel De l'Ordre Martiniste & L'Esthetique de Saint-Martin, Vol. II. Teder, pseud. & Zigmund Czerny. Ed. by Robert Amadou. iv, 111p. reprint ed. write for info. (*0-318-71423-X*) G Olms Pubs.

Riu Riu Chiu Vol. 3: Spanish Christmas Carols of the 16th Century, A Cappella. 8p. 1986. pap. 1.25 (*0-7935-5478-0*) H Leonard.

Rivage de Barbarie. Norman Mailer. (FRE.). 1977. pap. 11. 95 (*0-7859-4084-7*) Fr & Eur.

Rivage des Syrtes. Julien Gracq. 328p. (FRE.). 1991. reprint ed. pap. write for info. (*0-7859-4597-0*) Fr & Eur.

Rivages: Hotels of Character & Charm in Paris. 1996. pap. 13.50 (*0-614-12781-5*) Fodors Travel.

Rivages: Hotels of Character and Charm in Portugal. 1996. pap. 12.00 (*0-614-12782-3*) Fodors Travel.

Rivages: Hotels of Character & Charm in Spain. Fodors Staff. (Fodor's Rivages Ser.). (Illus.). 276p. 1996. pap. 15.00 (*0-679-03314-9*) Fodors Travel.

***Rival.** Kristine K. Rusch. 1997. mass mkt. 5.99 (*0-553-56896-5*, Spectra) Bantam.

Rival Ambassadors at the Court of Queen Mary. E. Harris Harbison. LC 73-107805. (Select Bibliographies Reprint Ser.). 1977. 31.95 (*0-8369-5182-4*) Ayer.

Rival Ambassadors at the Court of Queen Mary. E. Harris Harbison. 1982. reprint ed. lib. bdg. 28.00 (*0-8290-0821-7*) Irvington.

Rival Attractions. Penny Jordan. (Presents Ser.: No. 418). 1991. pap. 2.79 (*0-373-11418-4*) Harlequin Bks.

Rival Capitalists: International Competitiveness in the United States, Japan, & Western Europe. Jeffrey A. Hart. LC 92-52757. (Cornell Studies in Political Economy). (Illus.). 328p. 1993. pap. 16.95 (*0-8014-9949-6*) Cornell U Pr.

Rival Creation. large type ed. Marika Cobbold. (General Ser.). 455p. 1996. pap. 21.95 (*0-7862-0615-2*, Thorndike Lrg Prnt) Thorndike Pr.

Rival Empires of Trade in the Orient, 1600-1800. Holden Furber. LC 76-7337. (Europe & the World in the Age of Expansion Ser.: No. 2). 430p. reprint ed. pap. 122.60 (*0-7837-2956-1*, 2057498) Bks Demand.

Rival Heavens. Keith Althaus. (Provincetown Poets Ser.: No. 1). (Illus.). 64p. 1993. 35.00 (*0-944854-07-9*); pap. 10.00 (*0-944854-06-0*) Provincetown Arts.

***Rival Hypothesis.** 2nd ed. Ed. by Huck. (C). 1998. text ed. write for info. (*0-321-01259-3*) Addson-Wesley Educ.

Rival of the Yosemite: The Canon of the South Fork of King's River, California. John Muir. Ed. by William R. Jones. (Illus.). 24p. 1977. reprint ed. pap. 2.95 (*0-89646-010-X*) Vistabooks.

Rival Playwrights: Marlowe, Jonson, Shakespeare. James Shapiro. 203p. 1991. text ed. 37.50 (*0-231-07540-5*) Col U Pr.

***Rival Queens.** Nathaniel Lee. Ed. by P. F. Vernon. LC 72-91330. (Regents Restoration Drama Ser.). 140p. pap. 39. 90 (*0-608-04823-2*, 2065480) Bks Demand.

***Rival Roommates.** Melissa Lowell. (Silver Blades Ser.: No. 21). (J). 1997. pap. 3.50 (*0-553-48511-3*) BDD Bks Young Read.

Rival Roommates. Christie Wells. LC 88-16954. (Cranberry Cousins Ser.). 128p. (J). (gr. 5-8). 1989. pap. text ed. 2.95 (*0-8167-1497-5*) Troll Communs.

Rival States, Rival Firms: Competition for World Market Shares. John M. Stopford & Susan Strange. (Studies in International Relations: No. 18). (Illus.). 328p. (C). 1991. text ed. 59.95 (*0-521-41022-3*); pap. text ed. 19.95 (*0-521-42386-4*) Cambridge U Pr.

Rival Views of Market Society & Other Recent Essays. Albert O. Hirschman. LC 92-10871. 197p. 1992. pap. text ed. 12.95 (*0-674-77303-9*) HUP.

Rivalitaet zwischen Engeln und Menschen: Untersuchungen zur rabbinischen Engelvorstellung. Peter Schaefer. (Studia Judaica: Vol. 8). xiv, 280p. (C). 1975. 102.35 (*3-11-004632-6*) De Gruyter.

Rivalry: In Business, Science, among Nations. Reuven Brenner. (Illus.). 246p. 1987. text ed. 49.95 (*0-521-33187-0*) Cambridge U Pr.

Rivalry: In Business, Science, among Nations. Reuven Brenner. (Illus.). 256p. (C). 1990. pap. 17.95 (*0-521-38584-9*) Cambridge U Pr.

***Rivalry & Revolution in South & East Asia.** Partha S. Ghosh. LC 96-40481. 350p. 1997. text ed. 63.95 (*1-85521-912-3*, Pub. by Dartmth Pub UK) Ashgate Pub Co.

Rivalry & Tribute: Society & Ritual in a Telegu Village in South India. Bruce E. Tapper. (C). 1987. 44.00 (*81-7075-003-2*, Pub. by Hindustan IA) S Asia.

Rivalry of Genius: Jewish & Christian Biblical Interpretation in Late Antiquity. Marc Hirshman. LC 95-5271. (SUNY Series in Judaica: Hermeneutics, Mysticism, & Religion). 179p. 1995. text ed. 49.50 (*0-7914-2727-7*); pap. text ed. 16.95 (*0-7914-2728-5*) State U NY Pr.

Rivalry of Scandinavian & Native Synonyms, in Middle English Especially "Taken" & "Nimen" With an Excursus on "Nema" & "Tuka" in Old Scandinavian. A. Rynell. (Lund Studies in English: Vol. 13). 1974. reprint ed. pap. 50.00 (*0-8115-0556-1*) Periodicals Srv.

Rivalry of the United States & Great Britain over Latin America. James F. Rippy. (BCL1 - U. S. History Ser.). 322p. 1991. reprint ed. lib. bdg. 89.00 (*0-7812-6047-7*) Rprt Serv.

Rivals. Jilly Cooper. 720p. 1989. mass mkt. 8.99 (*0-552-13264-0*) Bantam.

Rivals. Janet Dailey. 448p. 1990. mass mkt. 6.99 (*0-449-14613-8*, GM) Fawcett.

Rivals. Nancy J. Hopper. 128p. 1987. pap. 2.95 (*0-380-70271-1*, Flare) Avon.

Rivals. Richard B. Sheridan. Ed. by Alan S. Downer. (Crofts Classics Ser.). 128p. 1953. pap. text ed. write for info. (*0-88295-091-6*) Harlan Davidson.

Rivals. Richard B. Sheridan. Ed. by J. A. Lavin. (New Mermaid Ser.). (C). 1980. pap. text ed. 6.95 (*0-393-90044-4*) Norton.

Rivals. Richard B. Sheridan. 22.95 (*0-8488-1162-3*) Amereon Ltd.

Rivals. Richard B. Sheridan. Ed. by C. J. Price. 140p. 1969. pap. 10.95 (*0-19-831908-8*) OUP.

Rivals. Richard B. Sheridan. 1994. pap. text ed. 6.00 (*1-85459-099-5*, Pub. by N Hern Bks UK) Theatre Comm.

***Rivals: An 1890s Colorado Comedy of Manners.** Joel G. Fink. (Illus.). 93p. 1992. pap. 7.50 (*0-87081-264-5*) Univ Pr Colo.

Rivals: William Gwin, David Broderick & the Birth of California. Arthur Quinn. LC 94-20495. (Library of the American West). 1994. 25.00 (*0-517-59573-7*, Crown) Crown Pub Group.

***Rivals: William Gwin, David Broderick, & the Birth of California.** Arthur Quinn. LC 97-17728. 336p. 1997. pap. 16.00 (*0-8032-8851-4*, Bison Books) U of Nebr Pr.

Rivals & Tracy's Ambition. Gerald Griffin. LC 79-8278. reprint ed. 44.50 (*0-404-61892-8*) AMS Pr.

Rivals Beyond Trade: America vs. Japan in Global Competition. Dennis J. Encarnation. LC 91-57900. (Cornell Studies in Political Economy). 240p. 1993. pap. 14.95 (*0-8014-8122-8*) Cornell U Pr.

Rivals Earls. Elizabeth Kidd. 224p. 1996. pap. 5.50 (*0-451-18818-7*, Sig) NAL-Dutton.

Rivals for Power: Presidential - Congressional Relations. Ed. by James A. Thurber. LC 95-48372. 267p. 1996. pap. 24.95 (*1-56802-152-6*) Congr Quarterly.

Rivals in Love. large type ed. Rebecca Bennett. (Linford Romance Library). 320p. 1995. pap. 15.99 (*0-7089-7672-7*, Linford) Ulverscroft.

Rivals in the Ring. Alison Hart. (Riding Academy Ser.). (J). 1996. pap. 3.99 (*0-679-88119-0*) Random Bks Yng Read.

Rivals in the Ring. Alison Hart. (Riding Academy Ser.: No. 14). (J). 1997. pap. 16.00 (*0-679-88199-9*, Bullseye Bks) Random Bks Yng Read.

Rivals of Esthedil. Jonathan Tweet. (Primal Order Ser.). 1994. pap. 12.00 (*1-880992-03-5*) Wizards Coast.

Rivals of Rockwell. Dorye Roettger. 1992. 14.99 (*0-517-06688-2*) Random Hse Value.

Rivals of Sherlock Holmes. Alan K. Russell. 1993. 8.98 (*1-55521-974-8*) Bk Sales Inc.

Rivals of Weird Tales. Robert Weinberg. 1990. 9.99 (*0-517-69331-3*) Random Hse Value.

Rivayat-i Hemit-i Asawahistan: A Study in Zoroastrian Law. Nezhat Safa-Isfahani. (Harvard Iranian Ser.: No. 2). 355p. (C). 1980. pap. 25.00 (*0-674-77305-5*) HUP.

Rive Gauche. Sydney St. James. (Orig.). 1995. mass mkt. 5.95 (*1-56333-317-1*) Masquerade.

Riven. Mark Dunster. 11p. (Orig.). 1995. pap. 4.00 (*0-89642-264-X*) Linden Pubs.

Riven Doggeries. James Tate. LC 78-27837. (American Poetry Ser.: Vol. 18). 1979. pap. 7.95 (*0-912946-64-4*) Ecco Pr.

***Riven Home: Narrative Rivalry in the American Renaissance.** Ken Egan, Jr. LC 96-52298. 224p. 1997. 35.00 (*1-57591-004-7*) Susquehanna U Pr.

Riven Realm. Nigel Tranter. 352p. 1985. 16.95 (*0-8253-0260-9*) Beaufort Bks NY.

Riven Unauthorized Game Secrets. Rick Barba. 256p. 1997. per., pap. 19.99 (*0-7615-0830-9*) Prima Pub.

Riven Unities: Authority & Experience, Self & Other in Milton's Poetry. Ed. by Wendy Furman et al. LC 69-12335. (Milton Studies: Vol. XXVIII). 272p. (C). 1992. 49.95 (*0-8229-3718-2*) U of Pittsburgh Pr.

Rivendell, the House of Elrond. Terry K. Amthor. 36p. (Orig.). (YA). (gr. 10-12). 1987. pap. 7.00 (*0-915795-87-6*, 8080) Iron Crown Ent Inc.

River. Ed. & Illus. by Laura Bour. LC 92-41415. (First Discovery Bks.). (J). 1993. 11.95 (*0-590-47128-7*) Scholastic Inc.

***River.** Judith Fitzgerald. 64p. 1995. pap. 12.00 (*1-55022-259-7*, Pub. by ECW Press CN) Genl Dist Srvs.

River. Judith Heide Gilliland. (J). (ps-3). 1993. 14.95 (*0-395-55963-4*, Clarion Bks) HM.

River. Ma Jaya Sati Bhagavati. 102p. 16.95 (*0-9640469-0-3*) Jaya Commns.

River. Gary Paulsen. 144p. (J). 1991. 15.95 (*0-385-30388-2*) Doubleday.

River. Gary Paulsen. 144p. (YA). 1993. pap. 4.99 (*0-440-40753-2*) Dell.

River. Bill Staines. Date not set. pap. write for info. (*0-14-055534-X*) Viking Penguin.

River. Patti Tana. (Illus.). 20p. (Orig.). (C). 1990. pap. 5.00 (*1-878173-00-6*) Birnham Wood.

River. Henry David Thoreau. Ed. by Dudley C. Lunt. (Masterworks of Literature Ser.). (Illus.). 1963. pap. 14. 95 (*0-8084-0262-5*) NCUP.

River. Roderick Thorp. 1996. mass mkt. 5.99 (*0-8041-1535-4*) Ivy Books.

River: A Haiku Sequence. Phyllis Walsh. 32p. 1993. 8.00 (*0-9629902-1-3*) Hummngbrd WI.

River: One Man's Journey Down the Colorado. Colin Fletcher. LC 96-13220. 1997. 30.00 (*0-394-57421-4*) Knopf.

***River: Reflections on the Times of Our Lives.** Donald X. Burt. LC 97-24743. 1998. write for info. (*0-8146-2477-4*) Liturgical Pr.

River Adventure. Patricia G. Morgan. LC 87-3485. (Let's Take a Trip Ser.). (Illus.). 32p. (J). (gr. 3-6). 1988. lib. bdg. 11.50 (*0-8167-1171-2*) Troll Communs.

River Adventure. Beth A. Wise. (Kidosaurs Ser.). (Illus.). 24p. (J). (ps-2). 1995. pap. 2.95 (*1-56293-536-4*) McClanahan Bk.

River & Bridge. Meena Alexander. 112p. 1996. pap. text ed. 11.95 (*0-920661-56-4*, Pub. by TSAR CN) LPC InBook.

River & Delta Morphology. Richard J. Russell. LC 67-29343. (Louisiana State University Studies, Coastal Studies Ser.: No. 20). 63p. reprint ed. pap. 25.00 (*0-317-29938-7*, 2051688) Bks Demand.

***River & I.** John G. Neihardt. LC 97-2250. (Illus.). xix, 325p. 1997. pap. 16.95 (*0-8032-8372-5*, Bison Books) U of Nebr Pr.

River & I. John G. Neihardt. LC 92-15792. (Landmark Edition Ser.). (Illus.). xix, 325p. 1992. reprint ed. text ed. 50.00 (*0-8032-3335-3*) U of Nebr Pr.

River & Lake Basin Development. (Natural Resources-Water Ser.: No. 20). 496p. 1990. 49.00 (*92-1-104339-5*, 90.II.A.10) UN.

River & Lake Ice Engineering. Ed. by George D. Ashton. (Illus.). 504p. 1986. 58.00 (*0-918334-59-4*) WRP.

River & Reservoir Yield. T. A. McMahon & R. G. Mein. 375p. 1987. text ed. 38.00 (*0-918334-61-6*) WRP.

River & Stream. April P. Sayre. LC 95-34458. (Exploring Earth's Biomes Ser.). (Illus.). 80p. (J). (gr. 5-8). 1996. lib. bdg. 16.98 (*0-8050-4088-9*) TFC Bks NY.

***River & the Gaunlet.** S. L. Marshall. Date not set. write for info. (*0-688-05028-X*) Morrow.

River & the Gauntlet. 14th ed. Samuel L. Marshall. (Combat Arms Ser.). 400p. 1987. reprint ed. 32.50 (*0-89839-097-4*) Battery Pr.

***River & the Lake.** Joanne Page. 88p. 1993. pap. 12.95 (*1-55082-090-7*, Pub. by Quarry Pr CN) LPC InBook.

River & the Mountains: Reading in Sullivan County History. David M. Gold. LC 94-78098. (Illus.). xiii, 446p. pap. 27.50 (*0-9636097-1-8*) Marielle Pr.

River & the Rain: The Lord's Prayer. Bijou Le Tord. (Illus.). 32p. (J). (gr. 1-2). 1996. reprint ed. mass mkt. 5.99 (*0-440-41215-3*, Picture Yearling) BDD Bks Young Read.

River & the Train. Edwin Brock. LC 78-27463. 1979. 7.95 (*0-8112-0722-6*); pap. 3.75 (*0-8112-0723-4*, NDP478) New Directions.

River As Metaphor: Poems. Nixeon C. Handy. LC 92-127306. (Illus.). 56p. (Orig.). 1991. pap. 9.95 (*1-880222-08-6*) Red Apple Pub.

River at Green Knowe. Lucy M. Boston. 176p. (J). (gr. 4-7). 1989. pap. 4.00 (*0-15-267450-0*, Odyssey) HarBrace.

River at Risk. Pierre Coran. (Child's World Library). (Illus.). 32p. (J). (gr. k-5). 1991. lib. bdg. 18.50 (*0-89565-747-3*) Childs World.

***River at Sundown.** Murray. LC 97-13321. 1997. 22.95 (*0-312-86124-9*) St Martin.

River at the Center of the World: A Journey up the Yangtze & Back in Chinese Time. Simon Winchester. (Illus.). 448p. 1996. 27.50 (*0-8050-3888-4*) H Holt & Co.

River at the Door: Unusual Experiences in Remote Areas. Allen Anthony. (Illus.). 143p. (Orig.). 1987. pap. 11.95 (*0-9625865-0-1*) River Microstudies.

River at Wolf. Jean Valentine. LC 92-8795. 72p. (Orig.). (C). 1992. pap. 9.95 (*0-914086-95-2*) Alicejamesbooks.

River Bank & Other Stories from The Wind in the Willows. abr. ed. Kenneth Grahame. Ed. & Illus. by Inga Moore. 96p. (J). (gr. 3 up). 1996. 19.99 (*0-7636-0059-8*) Candlewick Pr.

River Basin Development: Proceedings of the National Symposium on River Basin Development, Dacca, Bangladesh, 4-10 Dec. 1981. Ed. by Munir Zaman et al. (Water Resources Ser.: Vol. 4). (Illus.). 239p. 1983. 85. 00 (*0-907567-56-8*, Tycooly Pub); pap. 45.00 (*0-907567-57-6*, Tycooly Pub) Weidner & Sons.

River Basin Management for Sustainable Development. 302p. 1996. pap. 218.75 (*0-08-042881-9*, Pergamon Pr) Elsevier.

River Basin Management V: Proceedings of the Conference Held in Rovaniemi, Finland, 31 July-4 August 1989. Ed. by H. Laikari. (Advances in Water Pollution Control Ser.: Vol. 9). (Illus.). 438p. 1989. 126.00 (*0-08-037379-8*, Pergamon Pr) Elsevier.

River Basin Planning: Theory & Practice. Ed. by Suranjit K. Saha & Christopher J. Barrow. LC 81-193399. (Illus.). 373p. reprint ed. pap. 106.40 (*0-8357-3083-2*, 2039340) Bks Demand.

River Basin Planning & Management. Mahmoud A. Abu-Zeid & Asit K. Biswas. (Water Resources Management Ser.: Vol. 4). (Illus.). 248p. 1996. 24.95 (*0-19-563755-0*) OUP.

River Basin Survey Papers, No. 25. Frank Roberts, Jr. (Bureau of American Ethnology Bulletins Ser.). 447p. 1995. lib. bdg. 109.00 (*0-7812-4182-0*) Rprt Serv.

River Basin Surveys Papers, No. 7. (Bureau of American Ethnology Bulletins Ser.). 190p. 1995. lib. bdg. 79.00 (*0-7812-4158-8*) Rprt Serv.

River Basin Surveys Papers, No. 8. (Bureau of American Ethnology Bulletins Ser.). 258p. 1995. lib. bdg. 89.00 (*0-7812-4166-9*) Rprt Serv.

River Basin Surveys Papers, Nos. 1-6. (Bureau of American Ethnology Bulletins Ser.). 336p. 1995. lib. bdg. 99.00 (*0-7812-4154-5*) Rprt Serv.

River Basin Surveys Papers, Nos. 9-14. Frank Roberts, Jr. (Bureau of American Ethnology Bulletins Ser.). 392p. 1995. lib. bdg. write for info. (*0-7812-4169-3*) Rprt Serv.

River Basin Surveys Papers, Nos. 15-20. Frank Roberts, Jr. (Bureau of American Ethnology Bulletins Ser.). 337p. 1995. lib. bdg. 99.00 (*0-7812-4176-6*) Rprt Serv.

River Basin Surveys Papers, Nos. 21-24. Frank Roberts, Jr. (Bureau of American Ethnology Bulletins Ser.). 337p. 1995. lib. bdg. 99.00 (*0-7812-4179-0*) Rprt Serv.

River Basin Surveys Papers, Nos. 26-32. Frank Roberts, Jr. (Bureau of American Ethnology Bulletins Ser.). 344p. 1995. lib. bdg. 99.00 (*0-7812-4185-5*) Rprt Serv.

River Basin Surveys Papers, Nos. 33-38. Frank Roberts, Jr. (Bureau of American Ethnology Bulletins Ser.). 405p. 1995. lib. bdg. 109.00 (*0-7812-4189-8*) Rprt Serv.

River Bend. Joan C. New. LC 92-82885. (Orig.). 1993. pap. 8.50 (*0-933598-44-0*) NC Wesleyan Pr.

River Bend. deluxe limited ed. Joan C. New. LC 92-82885. (Orig.). 1993. pap. 17.00 (*0-933598-45-9*) NC Wesleyan Pr.

River Between. Ford Ainsworth. (Illus.). 68p. (Orig.). 1991. pap. 4.00 (*0-88680-348-9*) I E Clark.

River Between. Ngugi Wa Thiong'o. (African Writers Ser.). 152p. (C). 1965. pap. 10.95 (*0-435-90548-1*, 90548) Heinemann.

River Between. Louis Forgione. LC 74-17927. (Italian American Experience Ser.). 262p. 1975. reprint ed. 20. 95 (*0-405-06400-4*) Ayer.

River Between, Fifty-Fifty: Two Novellas. Donner Spencer. 208p. (Orig.). 1993. pap. 12.50 (*0-9635679-0-X*) River Rock.

***River Beyond the World.** Janet Peery. Date not set. pap. 13.00 (*0-312-16986-8*) St Martin.

River Beyond the World: A Novel. Janet Peery. 286p. 1996. 24.00 (*0-312-14719-8*) St Martin.

River Biota: Selected Extracts from the Rivers Handbook. Ed. by Peter Calow & Geoffrey E. Petts. LC 96-6929. 1996. 49.95 (*0-86542-716-X*) Blackwell Sci.

River Birch (Betula nigra L.) Communities of Southeastern Ohio. Larry D. Cribben & Irwin A. Ungar. (Biological Notes Ser.: No. 8). 1974. 3.00 (*0-86727-076-4*) Ohio Bio Survey.

***River Boat Echoes: Batteaux in Virginia.** Ed. by Minnie L. McGehee. (Illus.). viii, 77p. (Orig.). 1995. pap. 12.00 (*1-888838-02-7*) VA Canals & Navigat.

River Book: Cincinnati & the Ohio. 2nd ed. Ed. by Joyce V. Cauffield et al. LC 81-83675. (Illus.). 228p. (gr. 7-12). 1982. reprint ed. 29.95 (*0-9608200-0-0*) Prog Cincinnati.

River Boy. Claire N. White. (Illus.). 48p. 1988. 30.00 (*0-930126-24-6*) Typographeum.

River Called Titash. Adwaita Mallabarman. Tr. & Afterword by Kalpana Bardhan. LC 92-46698. 1993. 45. 00 (*0-520-38040-1*); pap. 15.00 (*0-520-08050-5*) U CA Pr.

River Cam & Lower Ouse. Wilson Ltd. Staff & Imray L. Norie. (C). 1984. 25.00 (*0-85288-115-0*, Pub. by Imray Laurie Norie & Wilson UK) St Mut.

***River Capital: An Illustrated History of Baton Rouge.** Mark T. Carleton. LC 96-78831. (Illus.). 274p. 1996. 39. 95 (*0-9654754-0-9*) Am Historical Pr.

River Channel Changes. Ed. by Kenneth J. Gregory. LC 77-4342. (Illus.). 466p. reprint ed. pap. 132.90 (*0-8357-8515-7*, 2034812) Bks Demand.

River Channel Restoration: Guiding Principles for Sustainable Projects. Ed. by Andrew Brookes & F. Douglas Shields. 1996. write for info. (*0-471-96139-6*) Wiley.

River City Rides: Mountain Biking in West-Central Colorado. Toby Gadd & Alix Craig. 64p. 1993. pap. 8.95 (*0-9639842-0-9*) Prune Prints.

River, Coastal & Shoreline Protection: Erosion Control Using Riprap & Armourstone. Ed. by Colin R. Thorne et al. LC 94-28299. 690p. 1995. text ed. 380.00 (*0-471-94235-9*) Wiley.

River Column. Henry Brackenbury. (Victorian War Ser.: No. 2). (Illus.). 291p. reprint ed. 34.95 (*0-89839-184-9*) Battery Pr.

River Conservation & Management. Ed. by P. J. Boon et al. LC 91-2797. 470p. 1992. text ed. 285.00 (*0-471-92946-8*) Wiley.

River Conservation Directory. (Illus.). 186p. (Orig.). (C). 1995. pap. text ed. 35.00 (*0-7881-1629-0*) DIANE Pub.

River Crossings: Voices of the Diaspora. Ed. by C. Jerome Woods. 170p. (Orig.). (YA). (gr. 6-12). 14.95 (*0-9640477-0-5*) Intl Black Writ.

River Cutters. rev. ed. Jeferey S. Kaufmann et al. Ed. by Kay Fairwell. (Great Explorations in Math & Science (GEMS) Ser.). (Illus.). 84p. (J). (gr. 6-9). 1992. reprint ed. teacher ed., pap. 16.00 (*0-912511-67-2*) Lawrence Science.

***River Danger.** Thomas J. Dygard. (J). Date not set. write for info. (*0-688-14852-2*, Morrow Junior) Morrow.

River Day. Jane Mason. LC 93-26573. (Illus.). 32p. (J). (gr. k-3). 1994. lib. bdg. 14.95 (*0-02-762869-8*, Mac Bks Young Read) S&S Childrens.

River Dogs. Robert Olmstead. LC 97-1749. 1997. pap. 12.00 (*0-8050-5120-1*) H Holt & Co.

River Dragon. Darcy Pattison. LC 90-49931. (Illus.). 32p. (J). (gr. k up). 1991. 13.95 (*0-688-10426-6*) Lothrop.

***River Dragon.** Darcy Pattison. (Illus.). 32p. (J). 3.98 (*0-8317-3071-4*) Smithmark.

***River Dragon Has Come! The Three Gorges Dam & the Fate of China's Yangtze River & Its People.** Dai Qing. Ed. by John G. Thibodeau & Philip Williams. Tr. by Ming Yi. 232p. (C). (gr. 13). 1998. 39.95 (*0-7656-0205-9*) M E Sharpe.

River Dream. Allen Say. (Illus.). 32p. (J). (gr. k-3). 1988. 14.95 (*0-395-48294-1*) HM.

River Dream. Allen Say. (Illus.). 32p. (J). (gr. k-3). 1993. pap. 5.95 (*0-395-65749-0*) HM.

***River Dream.** Allen Say. (J). (gr. 4). 1995. 7.56 (*0-395-73248-4*) HM.

***River Dream.** large type ed. Allen Say. 46p. (J). (gr. 4). 11.50 (*0-614-20616-2*, L-38183-00 APHB) Am Printing Hse.

River Dwellers: Poems on the Settling of the Ohio River. Jeffrey Hillard. LC 92-72994. 72p. 1992. pap. 6.95 (*0-9633551-0-4*) Cinc Writers Proj.

River Eternal. Lance Kinseth. Date not set. pap. 6.95 (*0-14-011479-3*, Viking) Viking Penguin.

River Fishing: A Happy World. rev. ed. Dan D. Gapen, Sr. (Illus.). 354p. 1992. reprint ed. text ed. 21.95 (*0-932985-08-4*) Whitewater Pubns.

River Flows. Christie E. Hoffman. (Orig.). 1996. pap. 10.95 (*0-533-11723-2*) Vantage.

River Flows: The Life of Robert Lardin Fulton. Barbara Richnak. LC 83-51605. (Illus.). 210p. (Orig.). 1984. pap. 9.95 (*0-915933-00-4*) Comstock NV Pub Co.

River Flows & Channel Forms. G. Petts & P. Calow. (Illus.). 272p. (Orig.). 1996. pap. text ed. 39.95 (*0-86542-920-0*) Blackwell Sci.

River Flows Backward. Kathlyn Gay & Ben E. Barnes. Ed. by Sylvia Ashton. LC 74-76645. 1975. 24.95 (*0-87949-027-6*) Ashley Bks.

River Foss - Its History & Natural History. M. G. Fife & P. J. Walls. (C). 1989. pap. 21.00 (*0-900657-17-0*, Pub. by W Sessions UK) St Mut.

***River Gathering: Life in God's Waiting Room.** L. Adelia Duggins. LC 97-71361. 272p. (Orig.). 1997. pap. 6.95 (*1-56167-355-2*) Am Literary Pr.

River Geomorphology. Ed. by Edward J. Hickin. (International Association of Geomorphologists Publication: Vol. 2). 255p. 1995. text ed. 115.00 (*0-471-95531-0*) Wiley.

River George. George W. Lee. LC 73-18590. reprint ed. 36.00 (*0-404-11401-6*) AMS Pr.

River Ghost. George W. Williams. 54p. 1995. pap. 9.00 (*0-9632825-3-0*) Tigermoon Ent.

River Girl. Wendy Cope. (Illus.). 64p. (YA). (gr. 7 up). 1991. pap. 7.95 (*0-571-16136-7*) Faber & Faber.

River God. Wilbur Smith. 662p. (Orig.). 1994. pap. 19.95 (*0-330-33197-3*) Trans-Atl Phila.

River God Vol. 1. Wilbur Smith. 1995. pap. 6.99 (*0-312-95446-8*) St Martin.

River Goddess. Vijay Singh. (Tales of Heaven & Earth Ser.). (Illus.). 40p. (J). (gr. 5 up). 1997. lib. bdg. 14.95 (*0-88682-825-2*) Creative Ed.

River Gods & Spotted Devils. 2nd ed. Ed. by John Culler & Chuck Wechsler. (Illus.). 284p. 1991. 12.95 (*0-929822-00-5*) LiveOak Pr.

***River Gods of Greece.** Brewster. Date not set. text ed. write for info. (*1-86064-207-1*, Pub. by I B Tauris UK) St Martin.

River Guide to Canyonlands National Park & Vicinity. Michael R. Kelsey. (Illus.). 256p. (Orig.). 1991. pap. 11.95 (*0-944510-07-8*) Kelsey Pub.

River Guide to Desolation & Gray Canyons on the Green River, Utah. Thomas G. Rampton. LC 92-97528. (Illus.). 72p. (Orig.). 1992. pap. 9.95 (*0-9634799-0-3*) Blacktail Ent.

River Guide to the Rio Grande, 4 vols. Ed. by John R. Pearson. (Illus.). 72p. (Orig.). 1982. pap. 10.00 (*0-912001-08-9*) Big Bend.

River Guide to the Rio Grande, 4 vols., General Information. Ed. by John R. Pearson. (Illus.). 72p. (Orig.). 1982. 1.00 (*0-912001-04-6*) Big Bend.

River Guide to the Rio Grande, 4 vols., Vol. 1: Colorado & Santa Elena Canyons. Ed. by John R. Pearson. (Illus.). 72p. (Orig.). 1982. Vol. 1, Colorado & Santa Elena Canyons. pap. 3.00 (*0-912001-05-4*) Big Bend.

River Guide to the Rio Grande, 4 vols., Vol. 2: Mariscal & Boquillas Canyons. Ed. by John R. Pearson. (Illus.). 72p. (Orig.). 1982. Vol. 2, Mariscal & Boquillas Canyons. pap. 3.00 (*0-912001-06-2*) Big Bend.

River Guide to the Rio Grande, 4 vols., Vol. 3: The Lower Canyons. Ed. by John R. Pearson. (Illus.). 72p. (Orig.). 1982. Vol. 3, The Lower Canyons. pap. 4.50 (*0-912001-07-0*) Big Bend.

River Guide to Writing, 2 Vols. Hunt. (C). Date not set. text ed. write for info. (*0-395-71714-0*) HM.

***River Guides of the Miramichi.** Wayne Curtis. (Illus.). 120p. 1997. pap. 12.95 (*0-86492-224-8*, Pub. by Goose Ln Edits CN) Genl Dist Srvs.

River Hill Soliloquy. large type ed. Clarence Mitchell. (Illus.). 379p. 1989. 25.99 (*0-7089-1946-4*) Ulverscroft.

River Horseman. David Williams. 217p. (Orig.). 1981. pap. 9.95 (*0-88784-086-8*, Pub. by Hse of Anansi Pr CN) Genl Dist Srvs.

River Hydraulics. LC 96-13765. (Technical Engineering & Design Guides As Adapted from the U. S. Army Corps of Engineers Ser.: No. 18). 150p. 1996. 44.00 (*0-7844-0159-4*) Am Soc Civil Eng.

River Ice Jams. Ed. by Spyros Beltaos. 390p. 1996. boxed 58.00 (*0-918334-87-X*, RIJ) WRP.

***River in Springtime: My Story of Li Yu in Myth & Poetry.** Susan W. Dolling. (Illus.). 72p. 1997. pap. 16.00 (*0-9655255-0-3*) Pucks Gold Proj.

River in Time. David L. Ruggeri. 224p. 1995. mass mkt. 4.99 (*1-896329-48-9*, Pub. by Comnwlth Pub CN) Partners Pubs Grp.

River Intakes & Diversion Dams. Ed. by E. Razvan. (Developments in Civil Engineering Ser.: No. 25). 510p. 1989. 217.00 (*0-444-87315-5*) Elsevier.

River Is Down. large type ed. Lucy Walker. 448p. 1988. 25.99 (*0-7089-1891-3*) Ulverscroft.

River Is Here: Receiving & Sustaining the Blessing of Revival. Melinda Fish. LC 96-3436. (Illus.). 192p. (gr. 10). 1996. pap. 9.99 (*0-8007-9245-9*) Chosen Bks.

River Is Home & Angel City: A Patrick Smith Reader. Patrick Smith. LC 88-37479. 416p. 1989. reprint ed. 17.95 (*0-910923-64-7*) Pineapple Pr.

River Is Us. William Stokes. LC 93-10917. 1993. 16.95 (*1-55971-214-7*) NorthWord.

***River Journal.** Clint McKnight. 45p. (Orig.). 1995. pap. 3.95 (*0-9651504-0-2*, 11719) Dinosaur Nature.

River Ki. Sawako Ariyoshi. Tr. by Mildred Tahara from JPN. LC 79-66240. 248p. 1982. pap. 10.00 (*0-87011-514-6*) Kodansha.

River Kwai Railway: The Story of the Burma-Siam Railroad. Clifford Kinvig. (Illus.). 236p. 1992. 25.00 (*0-08-037344-5*, Pub. by Brasseys UK) Brasseys Inc.

River L'Abbe Mission: A French Colonial Church for the Cahokia Illini on Monks Mound. John A. Walthall & Elizabeth D. Benchley. Ed. by Thomas Emerson & Evelyn Moore. (Studies in Illinois Archaeology: No. 2). (Illus.). 99p. (Orig.). (C). 1987. pap. text ed. write for info. (*0-942579-01-1*) IHPA.

River Lady. Jude Deveraux. Ed. by Linda Marrow. 1991. mass mkt. 6.99 (*0-671-73978-6*) PB.

River Life. Barbara Taylor. LC 92-52822. (Look Closer Ser.). (Illus.). 32p. (J). (gr. 1-4). 1992. 9.95 (*1-56458-130-6*) DK Pub Inc.

River Lost. Lynn E. Bragg. (Illus.). (Orig.). (J). (gr. 2-8). 1995. pap. 12.95 (*0-88839-383-0*) Hancock House.

***River Lost.** Blaine Harden. Date not set. pap. 13.00 (*0-393-31690-4*) Norton.

River Lost: The Life & Death of the Columbia. Blaine Harden. LC 95-38618. 320p. 1996. 25.00 (*0-393-03936-6*) Norton.

River Magic. Martha Hix. 384p. 1995. mass mkt. 4.99 (*0-8217-4863-7*, Zebra Kensgtn) Kensgtn Pub Corp.

***River Management: The Australisian Experience.** S. O. Brizga & B. L. Finlayson. text ed. 80.00 (*0-471-96976-1*) Wiley.

River Meandering. Ed. by G. A. Parker. (Water Resources Monograph Ser.: Vol. 12). 496p. 1989. pap. 26.00 (*0-87590-316-9*) Am Geophysical.

River Meandering: Proceedings of the Rivers '83 Conference Sponsored by the Waterway, Port, Coastal & Ocean Division in Cooperation with the International Association for Hydraulic Research. Ed. by Charles M. Elliott. 1036p. 1984. 75.00 (*0-317-59718-3*, 393-3) Am Soc Civil Eng.

River Mechanics. M. Selim Yalin. LC 92-32241. 235p. 1992. 78.00 (*0-08-040190-2*, Pergamon Pr) Elsevier.

River Medway. Howard Biggs. 160p. 1990. pap. 24.00 (*0-86138-005-3*, Pub. by T Dalton UK) St Mut.

River Menace. deluxe limited ed. Charles Stein. 16p. 1979. 7.50 (*0-930794-12-5*) Station Hill Pr.

River Menace. limited ed. Charles Stein. 16p. 1979. pap. 2.50 (*0-930794-75-3*) Station Hill Pr.

River Mersey. Ron Freethy. 184p. 1990. pap. 24.00 (*0-86138-035-5*, Pub. by T Dalton UK) St Mut.

River Mist & Other Stories. Kunikida Doppo. Tr. by David G. Chibbett. 176p. (C). 1983. text ed. 29.00 (*0-904404-40-4*, Pub. by Curzon Press UK) UH Pr.

River Mixing. J. C. Rutherford. LC 93-33033. 347p. 1994. text ed. 105.00 (*0-471-94282-0*) Wiley.

River Moon. Carol Finch. 1996. mass mkt. 4.99 (*0-8217-5327-4*, Zebra Kensgtn) Kensgtn Pub Corp.

River Morphology: A Guide for Geoscientists & Engineers. J. Mangelsdorf et al. (Springer Series in Physical Environment: Vol. 7). (Illus.). 264p. 1990. 150.95 (*0-387-51108-3*) Spr-Verlag.

***River My Friend.** William Bell. (Illus.). 32p. (J). (ps-4). 1996. 15.95 (*1-55143-084-3*) Orca Bk Pubs.

River Navigation in England: 1600-1750. 2nd ed. Thomas S. Willan. 163p. 1964. 35.00 (*0-7146-1383-5*, Pub. by F Cass Pubs UK) Intl Spec Bk.

River Never Sleeps. R. Haig-Brown. 360p. 1991. pap. 18.95 (*1-55821-116-0*) Lyons & Burford.

River Night. Christopher Munford. 50p. (Orig.). 1989. pap. 3.00 (*0-945085-09-5*) Sub Rosa.

River Nile: Geology, Hydrology, & Utilization. Rushdi Said. LC 93-28862. 332p. 1993. 157.00 (*0-08-041886-4*, Pergamon Pr) Elsevier.

River No More: The Colorado River & the West. Philip L. Fradkin. LC 95-49015. (Illus.). 372p. (C). 1996. pap. 14.95 (*0-520-20564-2*) U CA Pr.

River No More: The Colorado River & the West. Philip L. Fradkin. LC 83-18053. (Illus.). 360p. 1984. reprint ed. pap. 17.95 (*0-8165-0823-2*) U of Ariz Pr.

River Notes: The Dance of Herons. Barry H. Lopez. LC 79-17192. 1979. 6.95 (*0-8362-6106-2*) Andrews & McMeel.

River Notes: The Dance of the Herons. Barry H. Lopez. 96p. 1990. pap. 9.00 (*0-380-52514-3*) Avon.

River Oaks Mall Simulation. 4th ed. Jones. (TA - Typing/Keyboarding Ser.). 1997. pap. 15.95 (*0-538-65088-5*) S-W Pub.

River of Bears. Tom Walker. LC 92-35354. (Illus.). 160p. 1993. 35.00 (*0-89658-178-0*) Voyageur Pr.

River of Beaver, Stream of Gold. Ellen Carney. 156p. (Orig.). 1994. pap. 12.50 (*0-9636479-1-1*) Traildust Pub.

***River of Birds: An Original Bi-Lingual Musical.** Michael W. Schaefer. 26p. 1996. pap. 5.50 (*0-87129-718-3*, R03) Dramatic Pub.

River of Blessings: Essays in Honor of Paul Baxter. Ed. by David Brokensha. LC 94-3061. (Foreign & Comparative Studies, African Ser.: Vol. 44). 1994. write for info. (*0-915984-69-5*) Maxwell Schl Citizen.

River of Blood: The Genesis of a Martyr Cult in Southern Malawi, c. A. D. 1600. J. Matthew Schoffeleers. LC 92-50258. (Illus.). 340p. (Orig.). (C). 1992. pap. 24.95 (*0-299-13324-9*); lib. bdg. 50.00 (*0-299-13320-6*) U of Wis Pr.

River of Champions. Mary H. Schofield. 158p. (Orig.). (YA). 1995. pap. 10.00 (*0-9645173-0-2*) Four Dir Pub.

***River of Change: Prehistory of the Middle Little Colorado River Valley.** Ed. by E. Charles Adams. (Archaeological Ser.: Vol. 185). (Illus.). 342p. 1996. 24.95 (*1-889747-50-5*) Ariz St Mus.

River of Compassion. Bede Griffiths. (Wellspring Bks.). 224p. (Orig.). pap. 11.95 (*0-916349-08-X*) Amity Hse Inc.

River of Compassion: A Christian Commentary on the Bhagavad Gita. Bede Griffiths. 328p. 1994. reprint ed. pap. text ed. 14.95 (*0-8264-0769-2*) Continuum.

River of Dancing Gods. Jack L. Chalker. 1986. mass mkt. 5.99 (*0-345-34501-0*, Del Rey) Ballantine.

***River of Dawn: Unofficial Strategy Guide.** Edward Carmien. 240p. 1997. per. 19.99 (*0-7615-1052-4*) Prima Pub.

***River of Death.** Judd Cole. (Cheyenne Ser.: Vol. 21). 176p. (Orig.). 1997. mass mkt. 3.99 (*0-8439-4206-1*) Dorchester Pub Co.

River of Dreams. Gay Courter. 592p. 1985. pap. 5.99 (*0-451-16454-7*, Sig) NAL-Dutton.

River of Dreams & Other Top Recorded Hits. 64p. 1993. pap. 7.95 (*0-7935-2798-8*, 00311635) H Leonard.

***River of Dust.** Alexander Jablokov. 1997. mass mkt. 5.99 (*0-380-77863-7*) Avon.

River of Dust. Alexander Jablokov. LC 95-34872. 1996. 22.00 (*0-688-14605-8*) Morrow.

River of Earth. James Still. LC 77-92928. 256p. 1978. reprint ed. pap. 15.95 (*0-8131-1372-5*) U Pr of Ky.

River of Eternity. Philip Jose Farmer. 1983. 17.00 (*0-932096-28-X*) Phantasia Pr.

***River of Fire.** Mary J. Putney. 1996. pap. 6.99 (*0-451-18864-0*, Sig) NAL-Dutton.

River of Fire. Alexandre A. Kalomiros. 34p. 1995. reprint ed. pap. 3.00 (*0-913026-82-4*) St Nectarios.

River of Fortune: The Passion. Arthur Moore. (Orig.). 1979. mass mkt. 2.50 (*0-89083-561-6*, Zebra Kensgtn) Kensgtn Pub Corp.

***River of God.** (Shatterzone Ser.). 4.95 (*0-87431-225-6*, 21101) West End Games.

River of Gold: Precolumbian Treasures from Sitio Conte. Ed. by Pamela Hearne & Robert J. Sharer. LC 92-26815. (Illus.). 132p. 1992. pap. 24.95 (*0-934718-91-1*) U PA Mus Pubns.

River of Heaven. Garrett Hongo. LC 87-40485. 88p. 1988. 16.95 (*0-394-56843-5*); pap. 16.00 (*0-394-75785-8*) Knopf.

River of Hidden Dreams. Connie M. Fowler. 320p. 1995. pap. 12.00 (*0-449-98363-3*) Fawcett.

River of Hidden Dreams. large type ed. Connie May Fowler. LC 93-48313. 305p. 1994. reprint ed. lib. bdg. 23.95 (*0-8161-5954-8*, GK Hall) Thorndike Pr.

River of History. Gloria Bird. 32p. (Orig.). 1996. pap. 7.00 (*0-932264-13-1*) Trask Hse Bks.

River of Joy. Jack Metzler. 280p. (Orig.). 1993. pap. 8.95 (*1-56043-658-1*) Destiny Image.

***River of Life.** Francis Frangipane. 144p. 1996. mass mkt. 4.99 (*0-88368-453-5*) Whitaker Hse.

***River of Life.** Joseph A. Quintavella. 221p. (Orig.). 1997. mass mkt. 4.99 (*1-55197-805-9*, Pub. by Comnwlth Pub CN) Partners Pubs Grp.

River of Life. Mary J. Steinkamp. (Illus.). 208p. (Orig.). 1995. pap. 9.95 (*1-883928-14-1*) Longwood.

***River of Life: A Guide to Your Spiritual Journey.** Ruth White. 160p. (Orig.). 1997. pap. 9.95 (*1-57863-002-9*) Weiser.

River of Life: Poems for Main Events in Our Journey. George A. Doyle. 64p. 1995. pap. 7.95 (*0-8059-3608-4*) Dorrance.

River of Life, & Other Stories. Alexander I. Kuprin. LC 75-75781. (Short Story Index Reprint Ser.). 1977. 20.95 (*0-8369-3006-1*) Ayer.

River of Life, Channel of Death. Keith Petersen. LC 94-69720. 250p. (Orig.). 1995. pap. 20.00 (*1-881090-17-5*) Confluence Pr.

River of Light. Brenda Peterson. LC 86-81783. 303p. 1986. pap. 8.00 (*0-915308-89-4*) Graywolf.

River of Light: Spirituality, Judaism, Consciousness. 2nd rev. ed. Lawrence Kushner. 180p. 1990. reprint ed. pap. 14.95 (*1-879045-03-6*) Jewish Lights.

River of Lost Dreams: Navigation on the Rio Grande. Pat Kelley. LC 86-4340. (Illus.). 161p. 1986. reprint ed. pap. 45.90 (*0-7837-8893-2*, 2049604) Bks Demand.

River of Lost Opportunities: The Civil War on the James River 1861-1862. Ed Bearss. (Virginia Civil War Battles & Leaders Ser.). (Illus.). 202p. 1995. 19.95 (*1-56190-078-8*) H E Howard.

River of Love. F. Rosanne Bittner. (Savage Destiny Ser.: No. 3). 1990. mass mkt. 4.50 (*0-8217-3005-3*, Zebra Kensgtn) Kensgtn Pub Corp.

River of Love. F. Rosanne Bittner. 1996. pap. 5.99 (*0-8217-5396-7*); mass mkt. 5.99 (*0-8217-5344-4*, Zebra Kensgtn) Kensgtn Pub Corp.

River of Miracles. G. R. Schoepfer. Ed. by Virginia B. Schoepfer. (Illus.). (J). (gr. 1-11). 1978. pap. text ed. 2.75 (*0-931436-01-X*) G R Schoepfer.

***River of Mirrors: The Fantastic Art of Judson Huss.** Judson Huss. (Illus.). 96p. (Orig.). 1996. pap. 24.95 (*1-883398-17-7*) Morpheus Intl.

River of Mountains: A Canoe Journey down the Hudson. Peter Lourie. (Illus.). 342p. 1995. 29.95 (*0-8156-0315-0*) Syracuse U Pr.

River of No Return. Cort Conley & John Carrey. LC 78-52373. 1978. pap. 11.95 (*0-9603566-2-2*) Backeddy Bks.

River of No Return. Wesley Ellis. (Lone Star Ser.: No. 135). 1993. pap. 3.99 (*0-515-11239-9*) Jove Pubns.

***River of No Return.** Edward Packard. (Choose Your Own Adventure Ser.: No. 179). (J). 1997. pap. 3.50 (*0-553-56755-1*) BDD Bks Young Read.

***River of No Return.** Cleveland Sellers. Date not set. write for info. (*0-688-05016-6*) Morrow.

River of No Return: The Autobiography of a Black Militant & the Life & Death of SNCC. Cleveland Sellers & Robert Terrell. LC 90-12847. 290p. 1990. pap. 17.95 (*0-87805-474-X*) U Pr of Miss.

River of Now & Then: Margaret Laurence's The Diviners. Susan J. Warwick. (Canadian Fiction Studies: No. 17). 87p. (C). 1993. pap. text ed. 14.95 (*1-55022-109-4*, Pub. by ECW Press CN) Genl Dist Srvs.

***River of Our Return.** Gladys Smith. 208p. 1997. 20.00 (*0-06-101143-6*) HarpC.

***River of Our Return.** Gladys Smith. mass mkt. write for info. (*0-06-101144-4*, Harp PBks) HarpC.

River of Promise, River of Peril: The Politics of Managing the Missouri River. John E. Thorson. LC 94-36065. (Development of Western Resources Ser.). (Illus.). 284p. 1994. 29.95 (*0-7006-0648-3*) U Pr of KS.

***River of Red Gold.** Naida West. LC 96-96943. (Illus.). 614p. (Orig.). Date not set. pap. 18.49 (*0-9653487-2-5*) Bridge Hse.

River of Red Wine. Jack Micheline. 60p. 1986. reprint ed. pap. 6.95 (*0-934953-04-X*) Water Row Pr.

River of Secrets. Saskia Hope. (Black Lace Ser.). 1996. pap. 5.95 (*0-352-32925-4*, Pub. by Virgin Pub UK) London Brdge.

River of Sky. Karen Harper. 448p. 1995. mass mkt. 5.99 (*0-451-18490-4*, Sig) NAL-Dutton.

River of Sky. large type ed. Karen Harper. LC 94-29369. 1995. 22.95 (*0-7862-0322-6*) Thorndike Pr.

***River of Snake.** Chris McLeod. 1996. pap. 16.95 (*1-86368-168-X*, Pub. by Fremantle Arts AT) Intl Spec Bk.

***River of Sorrow: Environment & Social Control in Riparian North India, 1770-1994.** Christopher V. Hill. LC 97-15850. (Monograph & Occasional Paper Series ;). 1997. write for info. (*0-924304-36-7*) Assn Asian Studies.

River of Sorrows: Life History of the Maidu-Nisenan Indians. Richard Burrill. LC 88-25528. (Illus.). 219p. (Orig.). 1988. pap. 8.95 (*0-87961-187-1*) Naturegraph.

River of Stars: Selected Poems of Yosano Akiko. Akiko Yosano et al. LC 96-25654. 160p. 1997. pap. 11.00 (*1-57062-146-2*) Shambhala Pubns.

River of Tears. Maud Emery. 96p. 1992. pap. 9.95 (*0-88839-276-1*) Hancock House.

River of Tears: The Politics of Black Women's Health. Ed. by Delores P. Aldridge & LaFrancis Rodgers-Rose. 174p. (Orig.). (C). 1993. pap. text ed. 13.95 (*0-934185-01-8*) Traces Inst.

River of the Carolinas: The Santee. Henry Savage. LC 68-15799. 445p. reprint ed. pap. 126.90 (*0-7837-0281-7*, 2040602) Bks Demand.

River of the Mother of God & Other Essays by Aldo Leopold. Aldo Leopold. Ed. by Susan L. Flader & J. Baird Callicott. LC 90-45491. 400p. 1991. 18.75 (*0-299-12760-5*) U of Wis Pr.

River of the West: The Adventures of Joe Meek, Vol. I: The Mountain Years. Frances F. Victor. Ed. by Winfred Blevins. LC 83-11399. (Classics of the Fur Trade Ser.). (Illus.). 292p. 1983. reprint ed. 24.95 (*0-87842-164-5*); reprint ed. pap. 12.00 (*0-87842-165-3*) Mountain Pr.

River of the West: The Adventures of Joe Meek, Vol. II: The Oregon Years. Frances F. Victor. Ed. by Lee Nash. LC 83-11399. (Classics of the Fur Trade Ser.). (Illus.). 384p. 1985. reprint ed. 24.95 (*0-87842-178-5*); reprint ed. pap. 12.00 (*0-87842-179-3*) Mountain Pr.

An Asterisk (*) at the beginning of an entry indicates that the title is appearing in BIP for the first time.

***River of Time.** Swain. LC 97-19586. 1997. 22.95 (0-312-16989-2) St Martin.

***River of Time: Fergus Falls 125th Anniversary Anthology.** Ed. by Jolie L. Sasseville. 88p. (Orig.). 1997. pap. 11.95 (0-9658782-0-1) Otter Trail Cty.

River of Tomorrow. Dorothy Garlock. 384p. 1988. mass mkt. 5.99 (0-445-20366-8) Warner Bks.

River of Traps: A Village Life. William DeBuys & Alex Harris. (Illus.). 238p. (C). 1996. reprint ed. pap. 24.95 (0-8263-1680-8) U of NM Pr.

River of Used to Be: Reflections of an Ozarks Editor. Jim Hamilton. Ed. by W. C. Jameson. LC 93-86563. 148p. (Orig.). 1994. pap. 9.95 (0-9630829-3-0) Seven Oaks Pub.

River of Wealth, River of Sorrow: The Central Zaire Basin in the Era of the Slave & Ivory Trade, 1500 to 1891. Robert W. Harms. LC 81-1702. 163p. reprint ed. pap. 46.50 (0-7837-3334-8, 2080496) Bks Demand.

***River of West.** Clark. LC 97-20839. 1997. pap. 15.00 (0-312-16987-6) St Martin.

River of Years: Looking Back on My Life As a Methodist Minister. Sam Nader. 208p. (Orig.). 1995. pap. 9.95 (0-925854-14-X) Defiant Pr.

***River of Youth.** Evan Skolnick. (Disney's Enchanting Stories Ser.). 1997. pap. text ed. 4.50 (1-57840-078-3) Acclaim Bks.

River Otters. Lynn M. Stone. LC 94-46895. (Wild Animals of the Woods Ser.). (J). (gr. 2-6). 1995. write for info. (1-57103-096-4) Rourke Pr.

River Out of Eden: A Darwinian View of Life. Richard Dawkins. 176p. 1996. pap. 10.00 (0-465-06990-8) HarpC.

***River Phoenix: A Short Life.** 2nd ed. Brian J. Robb. 1997. pap. text ed. 16.95 (0-85965-214-9, Pub. by Plexus UK) Publishers Group.

River Phoenix Album. Penelope Dening. (Illus.). 80p. 1996. pap. 16.95 (1-56025-130-1) Thunders Mouth.

River Pigs & Cayuses: Oral Histories from the Pacific Northwest. Ron Strickland. LC 84-48239. (Illus.). 224p. (Orig.). 1984. pap. 11.95 (0-938530-29-1) Lexikos.

River Plan-Form Movement in an Alluvial Plain. Khin Ni Ni Thein. (Illus.). 320p. (C). 1994. pap. text ed. 40.00 (90-5410-401-5, Pub. by A A Balkema NE) Ashgate Pub Co.

River Plants of Western Europe: The Macrophytic Vegetation of Watercourses of the European Economic Community. S. M. Haslam. 650p. 1987. text ed. 170.00 (0-521-26427-8) Cambridge U Pr.

River Poems. Ed. by Stephanie Strickland & Anneliese Wagner. 56p. (Orig.). 1992. pap. 8.00 (0-9624178-1-5, HVWC) Slapering Hol.

River Pollution: An Ecological Perspective. S. M. Haslam. (Illus.). 256p. 1992. pap. text ed. 30.95 (1-85293-218-X, Pub. by Pinter Pubs Ltd UK) CRC Pr.

River Pollution: An Ecological Perspective. S. M. Haslam. (Illus.). 256p. 1992. 49.95 (1-85293-073-X, CRC Reprint) Franklin.

River Pollution: An Ecological Perspective. S. M. Haslam. 256p. (C). 1991. text ed. 460.00 (0-89771-633-7, Pub. by Intl Bk Distr II) St Mut.

River Pollution: An Ecological Perspective. S.M. Haslam. LC 90-326. 253p. 1994. pap. text ed. 45.00 (0-471-94634-6) Wiley.

River Predators: Muskie & Northern Pike. Dan D. Gapen, Sr. (Illus.). 130p. (Orig.). 1990. pap. text ed. 7.95 (0-932985-07-6) Whitewater Pubns.

River Projects & Conservation: A Manual for Holistic Appraisal. Ed. by John L. Gardiner. LC 90-40747. 236p. 1991. pap. text ed. 225.00 (0-471-92643-4) Wiley.

River Quality: Dynamics & Restoration. Antonius Laenen & David A. Dunnette. LC 96-22308. 1996. write for info. (1-56670-138-4) Lewis Pubs.

River-Quality Assessments: Proceedings of a Symposium Held in Tucson, Arizona, November 2-3, 1977. Ed. by Phillip E. Greeson. LC 79-87721. 199p. reprint ed. pap. 56.80 (0-317-11245-7, 2017814) Bks Demand.

River Quest. John Vornholt. 1995. pap. 3.99 (0-679-86982-4) Random.

***River Radar Manual.** rev. ed. W. D. Kline. (Illus.). 120p. 1997. pap. text ed. 24.95 (0-9647051-3-3) One River Pr.

River Radar Manual: A Concise Text to Use in Obtaining Your River or Inland. W. D. Kline. (Radar Observer Endorsement Ser.). 113p. 1995. spiral bd. 24.95 (0-9647051-0-9) One River Pr.

River, Rain, or Ruin: Intermittent Prehistoric Land Use along the Middle Little Colorado River. Carla R. Van West. (Statistical Research Technical Ser.: No. 53). (Illus.). 350p. (Orig.). (C). 1994. per., pap. text ed. 25.00 (1-879442-46-9) Stats Res.

***River Ran Between Them.** James A. Welch. 1996. mass mkt. 4.99 (1-55197-032-5, Pub. by Comnwlth Pub CN) Partners Pubs Grp.

River Ran Out of Eden. James V. Marshall. 124p. (J). 1987. pap. 3.95 (0-88741-026-X) Sundance Pub.

River Ran Red: Homestead, Eighteen Ninety-Two. Ed. by Dave Demarest, Jr. LC 91-50935. (Illus.). 244p. 1992. 49.95 (0-8229-3710-7); pap. 19.95 (0-8229-5478-8) U of Pittsburgh Pr.

River Ran Wild: An Environmental History. Lynne Cherry. (Gulliver Green Book Ser.). 40p. (J). (gr. 1-5). 1992. 15.00 (0-15-200542-0, Gulliver Bks) HarBrace.

***River Ran Wild: An Environmental History.** Lynne Cherry. (J). (gr. 4). 1995. 7.56 (0-395-73240-9) HM.

***River Ran Wild: An Environmental History.** large type ed. Lynne Cherry. 54p. (J). (gr. 4). 13.50 (0-614-20617-0, L-38211-00 APHB) Am Printing Hse.

***River Rats.** Franklin Dixon. (J). 1997. mass mkt. 3.99 (0-671-56123-5, Archway) PB.

River Rats. Caroline Stevermer. 176p. (YA). (gr. 7 up). 1992. 17.00 (0-15-200895-0, J Yolen Bks) HarBrace.

River Rats. Caroline Stevermer. (J). 1996. pap. 6.00 (0-15-201411-X, Magic Carpet) HarBrace.

***River Rat's Guide to the Thousand Islands.** Shawn Thompson. 1996. pap. text ed. 15.00 (1-55046-173-7) Genl Dist Srvs.

***River Rattler: Guidebook to the San Juan River.** Don Baars. (River Runner's Guides Ser.: Vol. 4). (Illus.). 96p. (Orig.). (J). (gr. 4-9). 1995. pap. 9.95 (0-9616591-4-9) Canon Pubs.

River Remembers: A History of Tumwater, 1845-1995. Ed. by Gayle Palmer. LC 95-2619. 1995. pap. write for info. (0-89865-930-2) Donning Co.

***River Rescue: A Manual for Whitewater Safety.** 3rd rev. ed. Les Bechdel & Slim Ray. LC 96-53448. (Illus.). 336p. 1997. pap. 16.95 (1-878239-55-4) AMC Books.

River Resource Management in the Grand Canyon. National Research Council Glen Canyon Environmental Studies Review Committee. 226p. (Orig.). 1996. pap. text ed. 35.00 (0-309-05448-6) Natl Acad Pr.

River Restoration. G. Petts & P. Calow. (Illus.). 240p. (Orig.). 1996. pap. text ed. 39.95 (0-86542-919-7) Blackwell Sci.

River Returns. Craig Denton. LC 93-72956. 64p. (Orig.). 1993. pap. 7.98 (0-9638655-0-1) Footfalls Pr.

River Ribble. Ron Freethy. 192p. (C). 1994. pap. 24.00 (0-86138-058-4, Pub. by T Dalton UK) St Mut.

River Road. Michael Gottlieb. 66p. 1996. pap. 10.00 (0-937013-60-9) Potes Poets.

River Road: A Story of Abraham Lincoln. Meridel Le Sueur. 1991. 14.95 (0-930100-37-9) Holy Cow.

***River Road: A Story of Abraham Lincoln.** Meridel Le Sueur. 1998. pap. text ed. 10.95 (0-930100-77-8) Holy Cow.

River Road Recipe II. Junior League Staff. 1976. 15.95 (0-9613026-5-8) Jr League Baton Rouge Inc.

River Road Recipes I. Junior League Staff. 1959. 15.95 (0-9613026-3-1) Jr League Baton Rouge Inc.

River Road Recipes III: A Healthy Collection. Junior League of Baton Rouge, Inc. Staff. (River Road Recipes Cookbooks Ser.). (Illus.). 288p. 1994. 17.95 (0-9613026-4-X) Jr League Baton Rouge Inc.

River Rock: A Climber's Guide to Mississippi Palisades State Park. Bill Collett & Gary Taylor. (Illus.). (Orig.). 1991. pap. text ed. 9.25 (0-9619571-2-3) Granite Wl.

River Rogues! Natchez Pirates, Playboys, & the Rest of the Cock-o-the-Walk Crowd under-the-Hill & along the Trace. Carole Marsh. (Carole Marsh Mississippi Bks.). (J). 1994. pap. 19.95 (0-7933-7323-9); lib. bdg. 29.95 (0-7933-7584-3) Gallopade Pub Group.

River Root: A Suzygy for the Bicentennial of These States. William Everson. 1976. pap. 2.50 (0-685-79269-2) Oyez.

River Root: A Suzygy for the Bicentennial of These States. deluxe limited ed. William Everson. 1976. 50.00 (0-685-79268-4) Oyez.

River-Root: A Syzygy. rev. ed. William Everson. LC 90-83690. 64p. (Orig.). 1990. pap. 14.95 (0-913089-12-5) Broken Moon.

River Run Red. Dodge Tyler. (Dan'l Boone Ser.: No. 1). (Orig.). 1996. mass mkt., pap. text ed. 4.99 (0-8439-3947-8) Dorchester Pub Co.

River Runner's Guide to the History of the Grand Canyon. Kim Crumbo. LC 81-84310. (Illus.). 96p. (Orig.). 1981. pap. 9.95 (0-933472-61-7) Johnson Bks.

River Runners' Guide to Utah & Adjacent Areas. Gary C. Nichols. LC 86-1688. (Bonneville Bks.). (Illus.). 130p. (Orig.). 1986. pap. 14.95 (0-87480-254-7) U of Utah Pr.

River Runners of the Grand Canyon. David Lavender. LC 85-70524. (Illus.). 134p. 1995. pap. 19.95 (0-938216-23-6, 30163) GCA.

River Runner's Recipes. Pat McCairen. 127p. (Orig.). 1994. pap. 12.95 (0-89732-109-X) Menasha Ridge.

***River Running.** Iron Crown Enterprises Staff. 1992. 12.00 (1-55806-159-2) Iron Crown Ent Inc.

River Runs Backward: Flavors & Reflections of Florida's First Coast. 288p. 1995. 19.95 (0-9609338-1-6) Jun League Jackson.

River Runs Through It. Norman Maclean. (Illus.). vi, 168p. 1989. 24.95 (0-226-50060-8) U Ch Pr.

River Runs Through It & Other Stories. Norman Maclean. LC 75-20895. 218p. 1976. 17.95 (0-226-50055-1) U Ch Pr.

River Runs Through It & Other Stories. Norman Maclean. LC 75-20895. 232p. 1979. pap. 9.95 (0-226-50057-8, P821) U Ch Pr.

River Runs Through It & Other Stories. Norman MacLean. Ed. by Sally Peters. 256p. 1992. reprint ed. mass mkt. 6.99 (0-671-77697-5) PB.

River Salmon Fishing. Bill Stinson. (Illus.). 147p. 1995. pap. 14.95 (0-936608-46-3) F Amato Pubns.

***River Scene: Ecology & Cultural Heritage.** Sylvia Haslam. (Illus.). 350p. (C). 1997. text ed. 95.00 (0-521-57410-2) Cambridge U Pr.

River Sedimentation, Vol. III. Hsieh W. Shen. LC 31-25158. (Illus.). 1822p. 1986. 60.50 (0-937099-07-4) U MS Ctr Comput Hydrosci.

River Seen Right: A Fly Fisherman's North Umpqua. Michael Baughman. (Illus.). 144p. 1995. 25.00 (1-55821-421-6) Lyons & Burford.

***River Seine Cruising Guide.** Derek Bowskill. (Illus.). (C). 1996. pap. 24.95 (0-85288-289-0) Bluewater Bks.

River Serpent & Other Poems. Arthur Gregor. LC 94-24548. 98p. 1994. pap. text ed. 10.95 (1-878818-36-8) Sheep Meadow.

River Severn. Keith Kissack. 160p. 1990. pap. 24.00 (0-86138-004-5, Pub. by T Dalton UK) St Mut.

River Sorrow. Craig Holden. 432p. 1995. mass mkt. 5.99 (0-440-21730-X, Island Bks) Dell.

River Sorrow. large type ed. Craig Holden. 1994. lib. bdg. 24.95 (0-7838-1168-3, GK Hall) Thorndike Pr.

River Sprite. Kate Kingsley. (Historical Ser.). 1994. mass mkt. 3.99 (0-373-28818-2, 1-28818-2) Harlequin Bks.

River Stallion. Jake Logan. (Slocum Ser.: No. 197). 192p. (Orig.). 1995. mass mkt. 3.99 (0-515-11654-8) Jove Pubns.

River Stops Here: The Story of One Man Who Fought to Save His Valley. Ted Simon. 1994. 23.00 (0-679-42822-4) Random.

River Stories: Tales from Bo Rockerville. Monte Smith. 292p. 1996. pap. 14.95 (1-886694-01-X) Pahsimeroi Pr.

River Stour: An East Anglian River & Its People. Russell Edwards. 192p. (C). 1990. pap. 24.00 (0-900963-34-4, Pub. by T Dalton UK) St Mut.

River Street: A Novella & Stories. Phil Condon. LC 94-10530. 240p. (Orig.). 1994. 22.50 (0-87074-372-4); pap. 10.95 (0-87074-373-2) SMU Press.

River Sutra. Gita Mehta. LC 92-35779. 304p. 1993. 20.00 (0-385-47007-X, N A Talese) Doubleday.

River Sutra. Gita Mehta. 1994. pap. 12.00 (0-679-75247-1, Vin) Random.

River Syndicate & Other Stories. Charles E. Carryl. LC 70-106258. (Short Story Index Reprint Ser.). 1977. 20.95 (0-8369-3295-1) Ayer.

***River Tales of Idaho.** Darcy Williamson. Ed. by Wayne Cornell. LC 97-12072. (Illus.). 300p. (Orig.). 1997. pap. 17.95 (0-87004-378-1) Caxton.

River Tay & Its People. Graham Ogilvy. (Illus.). 224p. 1994. 34.95 (1-85158-406-4, Pub. by Mnstream UK) Trafalgar.

River Tees. R. Woodhouse. 112p. 1990. pap. 30.00 (0-86138-091-6, Pub. by T Dalton UK) St Mut.

River Teeth: Stories & Writings. David J. Ducan. 272p. 1996. reprint ed. pap. 10.95 (0-553-37827-9, Bantam Trade Bks) Bantam.

River Thames. Andrew Duncan. (C). 1989. 50.00 (1-85368-054-0, Pub. by New Holland Pubs UK) St Mut.

River That Carries Me. Mary Dorcey. 90p. 9600. pap. 14.95 (1-897648-62-6, Pub. by Salmon Poetry IE) Dufour.

River That Flows Uphill: A Journey from the Big Bang to the Big Brain. William H. Calvin. LC 87-381. (Illus.). 544p. 1987. reprint ed. pap. 18.00 (0-87156-719-9) Sierra.

River That Gave Gifts. Margo Humphrey. LC 78-61980. (Illus.). (J). (gr. 2-9). 1987. 14.95 (0-89239-027-1) Childrens Book Pr.

River That Gave Gifts. Raintree Staff. 1992. 24.26 (0-8172-6727-1) Raintree Steck-V.

River That Went to the Sky: Twelve Tales of African Stories Tellers. Ed. by Mary Medlicott. LC 94-44607. (J). (gr. 2 up). 1995. 16.95 (1-85697-608-4, Kingfisher LKC) LKC.

River, the Kettle, & the Bird: A Torah Guide to a Successful Marriage. Aharon Felsman. 1987. 16.95 (0-87306-440-2) Feldheim.

River Through Rivertown. Merrill C. Gilfillan. 1982. pap. 7.50 (0-935724-08-7) Figures.

River Through the Ages. Philip Steele. LC 91-33279. (Through the Ages Ser.). (Illus.). 32p. (J). (gr. 3-6). 1993. lib. bdg. 13.95 (0-8167-2735-X) Troll Communs.

River Through the Ages. Philip Steele. LC 91-33279. (Through the Ages Ser.). (Illus.). 32p. (J). (gr. 3-6). 1997. pap. 4.95 (0-8167-2736-8) Troll Communs.

River Through Time. James A. Crutchfield. (Illus.). 142p. 1995. pap. text ed. 16.95 (0-9640392-8-1) Cool Springs Pr.

River Through Time: The Course of Western Civilization. Charles W. Hollister. LC 74-14972. 584p. reprint ed. pap. 166.50 (0-317-28075-9, 2055765) Bks Demand.

***River Thunder.** Will Hobbs. LC 96-53152. 1997. mass mkt. 15.95 (0-385-32316-6) Doubleday.

River Time. Janet Lembke. 192p. 1989. 16.95 (1-55821-035-0) Lyons & Burford.

River Time: The Cosmic Waters. Dibinga W. Said. (Unity of Thought in Kaffric, Kushanic, Ani & Kemetic Civilizations Ser.: No. 002, Pt. I). 50p. (Orig.). (C). 1995. text ed. 5.00 (0-943324-73-4) Omenana.

***River Tips & Tree Trunks.** Steven H. Semken. LC 96-94009. 112p. (Orig.). 1996. pap. 14.95 (1-888160-63-2) Ice Cube.

River to Cross. Laurie Paige. (Special Edition Ser.). 1994. mass mkt. 3.50 (0-373-09910-X, 1-09910-0) Harlequin Bks.

River to Pickle Beach. Doris Betts. 1996. pap. 12.00 (0-684-81860-4, Scribners PB Fict) S&S Trade.

River to Rim: A Guide to Place Names along the Colorado River in Grand Canyon from Lake Powell to Lake Mead. Nancy J. Brian. LC 92-90263. (Illus.). 176p. (Orig.). 1992. pap. 14.95 (1-881438-00-7) Earthquest.

River to River Trail Guide in Southern Illinois. John O'Dell. (Illus.). 52p. 1995. pap. 19.95 (0-9646435-0-2) River to River Trl Soc.

River Too Far: The Past & Future of the Arid West. Ed. by Joseph Finkhouse & Mark Crawford. (Illus.). 192p. 1991. pap. 16.95 (0-87417-177-6) U of Nev Pr.

River Town. Thomas Keneally. 324p. 1995. 24.00 (0-385-47696-5, N A Talese) Doubleday.

River Town. Thomas Keneally. 1996. pap. 12.95 (0-452-27655-1, Plume) NAL-Dutton.

River Town. large type ed. Thomas Keneally. LC 95-22931. (Large Print Bks.). 1995. 24.95 (1-56895-264-3, Compass) Wheeler Pub.

River Towns in the Great West: The Structure of Provincial Urbanization in the American Midwest, 1820-1870. Timothy R. Mahoney. (Illus.). 331p. (C). 1990. text ed. 54.95 (0-521-36130-3) Cambridge U Pr.

River Towns of Connecticut: A Study of Wethersfield, Hartford & Windsor. Charles M. Andrews. LC 78-63790. (Johns Hopkins University. Studies in the Social Sciences. Thirtieth Ser. 1912: 7-9). reprint ed. 37.50 (0-404-61055-2) AMS Pr.

River Towns of Connecticut: A Study of Wethersfield, Hartford, & Windsor. Charles M. Andrews. 126p. 1995. reprint ed. pap. 19.50 (0-8328-4459-4) Higginson Bk Co.

River Training Techniques: Fundamentals, Design & Applications. B. Przedwojski et al. (Illus.). 648p. (C). 1995. text ed. 145.00 (90-5410-196-2, Pub. by A A Balkema NE) Ashgate Pub Co.

River Underground: Selected Poems. Jean Tardieu. 192p. 9100. pap. 17.95 (1-85224-099-7, Pub. by Bloodaxe Bks UK) Dufour.

River Unvexed: A History & Tour Guide to the Campaign for the Mississippi River. Jim Miles. LC 93-35025. 596p. 1994. pap. 24.95 (1-55853-210-2) Rutledge Hill Pr.

River Valley Recipes. Rock River Valley Girl Scout Council Staff. LC 88-24663. 1987. 12.50 (0-87197-242-5) Favorite Recipes.

River Voices. John Van Peenen & Dirk Van Peenen. (Illus.). 105p. (Orig.). 1991. pap. 2.95 (1-879365-00-6) Goatfoot Pr.

***River Voices: Poets of Butte, Shasta, Tehama, & Trinity Counties, California.** Patricia Wellingham-Jones et al. 97p. (Orig.). 1997. pap. 7.95 (0-939221-13-6) Wellingham-Jones.

River Volga & Its Life. Ed. by D. Mordukhai-Boltovskoi. (Monographiae Biologicae: No. 33). 1979. lib. bdg. 175.00 (90-6193-084-7) Kluwer Ac.

River Walleye: "How to Fish" Dan D. Gapen, Sr. (Illus.). 128p. (Orig.). 1987. pap. text ed. 7.95 (0-932985-04-1) Whitewater Pubns.

River Water Quality Monitoring. L. W. Canter. (Illus.). 192p. 1985. 106.00 (0-87371-011-8, L011) Lewis Pubs.

River Went Out of Eden. Chana B. Cox. (Illus.). 208p. (Orig.). 1992. 24.95 (0-938530-57-7); pap. 14.95 (0-938530-56-9) Lexikos.

***River Where Blood is Born.** Sandra Jackson-Opoku. LC 97-16504. 1997. 23.00 (0-345-39514-X) Ballantine.

River Why. David J. Duncan. LC 82-5508. 320p. (Orig.). 1983. 22.00 (0-87156-321-5) Sierra.

River Why. Forbes Duncan. 304p. (Orig.). 1985. pap. 11.95 (0-553-34486-2) Bantam.

River with No Bridge. Sue Sumii. Tr. by Susan Wilkinson. LC 89-51715. 384p. 1990. 19.95 (0-8048-1590-9) C E Tuttle.

River Within. Karen R. Schultz. 196p. 1993. pap. 12.95 (0-9636082-5-8) Inner Space.

***River Without End.** Pamela Jekel. 448p. 1997. 22.95 (1-57566-172-1, Knsington) Kensgtn Pub Corp.

River Writing: An Eno Journal. James Applewhite. (Contemporary Poets Ser.). 60p. 1988. pap. 9.95 (0-691-01442-6); text ed. 24.95 (0-691-06726-0) Princeton U Pr.

River Wye. Keith Kissack. (Illus.). 144p. 1994. pap. 25.00 (0-86138-040-1, Pub. by T Dalton UK) St Mut.

***Rivera.** Andrea Kettenmann. 1997. pap. text ed. 9.99 (3-8228-8560-6) Taschen Amer.

***Rivera at the Center of the World: A Journey up the Yangtze & Back in Chinese Time.** Simon Winchester. 1997. pap. text ed. 14.95 (0-8050-5508-8) H Holt & Co.

Riverbank Stories: The Tale of Anabelle Hedgehog. Stephen R. Lawhead. (Riverbank Stories Ser.: Bk. 3). 112p. (J). 1994. pap. 3.50 (0-380-72200-3, Camelot) Avon.

Riverbank Stories: The Tale of Jeremy Vole. Stephen R. Lawhead. 112p. (J). (gr. 4). 1993. pap. 3.50 (0-380-72198-8, Camelot) Avon.

Riverbank Stories: The Tale of Timothy Mallard. Stephen R. Lawhead. 112p. (J). (gr. 4). 1993. pap. 3.50 (0-380-72199-6, Camelot) Avon.

Riverbed of Memory. Daisy Zamora. Tr. by Barbara Paschke from SPA. (Pocket Poets Ser.: No. 49). 120p. (Orig.). 1993. pap. 7.95 (0-87286-273-9) City Lights.

Riverbend. Marcia Martin. 384p. (Orig.). 1994. pap. 4.99 (0-451-18053-4, Onyx) NAL-Dutton.

Riverbend. Vicki May. 105p. 1984. 4.95 (0-89697-131-7) Intl Univ Pr.

Riverboat, No. 1. Douglas Hirt. 304p. (Orig.). 1995. pap. text ed. 4.99 (0-515-11566-5) Jove Pubns.

Riverboat Gambler. Alan Spetner. 280p. (Orig.). 1996. pap. 9.95 (0-9649857-0-5) Hard Ten.

Riverboat Gamblers of History, Vol. I. Leslie C. Swanson. (Illus.). 56p. (YA). 1990. per. 5.00 (0-911466-09-6) Swanson.

***Riverboy.** Billy C. Clark. Ed. by Tracey Besmark. LC 97-25377. (Illus.). 160p. 1997. reprint ed. pap. 9.95 (0-945084-65-X) J Stuart Found.

Riverby. John Burroughs. (Works of John Burroughs). 1989. reprint ed. lib. bdg. 79.00 (0-7812-2186-2) Rprt Serv.

Riverdale School Eighteen Eighty-Eight to Nineteen Eighty-Eight. Helen W. Bledsoe. LC 88-70297. (Illus.). 176p. 1988. pap. 17.00 (0-8323-0462-X) Binford Mort.

***Riverdance: The Story.** Sam Smyth. (Illus.). 120p. 1997. 29.95 (0-233-99058-5, Pub. by A Deutsch UK) Trafalgar.

RiverFeast: Still Celebrating Cincinnati. Junior League of Cincinnati Staff. (Illus.). 360p. 1990. 15.95 (0-9607078-1-6) Jr Lea Cincinnati.

Riverhouse Stories: How Pubah S. Queen & Lazy LaRue Save the World. Andrea Carlisle. LC 86-20783. 144p. (Orig.). 1993. reprint ed. pap. 8.95 (0-933377-24-X) Eighth Mount Pr.

Riveries: A Poetry for Earth: An Anthology. Ed. by Walt Franklin. 44p. 1991. 5.00 (0-945251-04-1) Great Elm.

Riverine: A Brown-Water Sailor in the Delta, 1967. Don Sheppard. Ed. by Eric Tobias. 384p. 1994. reprint ed. mass mkt. 5.99 (0-671-79691-7) PB.

***Riverkeepers.** Cronin. 1997. 25.00 (0-684-83908-3) S&S Trade.

R

R

*__Riverkeepers: Two Activists Fight to Reclaim Our Environment As a Basic Human Right.__ John Cronin & Robert F. Kennedy, Jr. 1997. 26.00 (*0-614-28265-9*) Scribnrs Ref.

Riverman: Ted Bundy & I Hunt for the Green River Killer. Robert D. Keppel. 1995. pap. 6.99 (*0-671-86763-6*, PB Trade Paper) PB.

Riverman: The Story of Bus Hatch. Roy Webb. Ed. by Mike Brown & Tom Schmid. (Illus.). 158p. (Orig.). 1989. pap. 5.97 (*0-685-30059-5*); 7.96 (*0-685-30060-9*) Labyrinth WY.

Rivermen. Gail Stewart. (Wild West in American History Ser.). (Illus.). 32p. (J). (gr. 3-8). 1990. 13.50 (*0-685-58652-9*); lib. bdg. 18.00 (*0-86625-409-9*) Rourke Corp.

Rivermen: A Romantic Iconography of the River & the Source. Frederic S. Colwell. 232p. (C). 1989. text ed. 49.95 (*0-7735-0711-6*, Pub. by McGill CN) U of Toronto Pr.

Rivermouth Romance. Thomas B. Aldrich. (Works of Thomas Bailey Aldrich). 1989. reprint ed. lib. bdg. 79.00 (*0-7812-1674-5*) Rprt Serv.

Riverrun. S. P. Somtow. 272p. (Orig.). 1991. mass mkt. 3.99 (*0-380-75925-X*) Avon.

Riverrun Trilogy. S. P. Somtow. (Illus.). 1996. reprint ed. pap. 14.99 (*1-56504-943-8*, Borealis) White Wolf.

Rivers. Donna Bailey. LC 89-26132. (Facts about...Ser.). (Illus.). 48p. (J). (gr. 2-5). 1990. lib. bdg. 21.36 (*0-8114-2510-X*) Raintree Steck-V.

Rivers. Illus. by Philip Corke. (Butterfly Bks.). 32p. (J). (gr. 3-5). 1985. 8.95 (*0-86685-452-5*) Intl Bk Ctr.

Rivers. Randy Frahm. LC 93-46804. (Images Ser.). (Illus.). 32p. (J). (gr. 4 up). 1997. lib. bdg. 16.95 (*0-88682-708-6*) Creative Ed.

*__Rivers.__ Terry J. Jennings. LC 97-16676. (Our Restless Earth Ser.). (J). 1998. write for info. (*0-382-39943-9*); pap. write for info. (*0-382-39944-7*) Silver Burdett Pr.

Rivers. Neil Morris. LC 96-642. (World's Top Ten Ser.). (Illus.). (J). 1997. lib. bdg. 21.40 (*0-8172-4338-0*) Raintree Steck-V.

Rivers. Andres L. Ruiz. (Sequences of Earth & Space Ser.). (Illus.). 32p. (J). 1996. 12.95 (*0-8069-9310-3*) Sterling.

Rivers. Richard Stephen. LC 89-20303. (Our Planet Ser.). (Illus.). 32p. (J). (gr. 4-6). 1990. lib. bdg. 12.95 (*0-8167-1975-6*) Troll Communs.

Rivers. Richard Stephen. LC 89-20303. (Our Planet Ser.). (Illus.). 32p. (J). (gr. 4-6). 1996. pap. 4.95 (*0-8167-1976-4*) Troll Communs.

Rivers: Form & Process in Alluvial Channels. Keith Richards. 272p. 1982. pap. 27.50 (*0-416-74910-0*, NO. 3739) Routledge Chapman & Hall.

Rivers Amazon. Alex Shoumatoff. LC 78-8585. 256p. 1986. pap. 9.00 (*0-87156-771-7*) Sierra.

Rivers & Lakes. Norman S. Barrett & Jenny Mulherin. LC 84-5713. (Picture Library). (Illus.). 32p. (J). (gr. 3-5). 1990. lib. bdg. 20.00 (*0-531-10840-6*) Watts.

Rivers & Lakes. Martyn Bramwell. (Earth Science Library). (Illus.). 32p. (J). (gr. 5-8). 1994. lib. bdg. 18.60 (*0-531-14305-8*) Watts.

*__Rivers & Lakes.__ Rose Pipes. LC 97-9069. (World Habitats Ser.). (J). 1998. write for info. (*0-8172-5002-6*) Raintree Steck-V.

Rivers & Lakes. Helena Ramsay. LC 96-20095. (Step-by-Step Geography Ser.). (J). 1997. lib. bdg. 17.00 (*0-516-20237-5*) Childrens.

Rivers & Lakes. Theodore Rowland-Entwistle. (Our World Ser.). (Illus.). 48p. (J). (gr. 5-8). 1987. lib. bdg. 12.95 (*0-382-09499-9*) Silver Burdett Pr.

Rivers & Mountains. John Ashbery. LC 76-46176. (American Poetry Ser.: Vol. 12). 1977. reprint ed. pap. 9.95 (*0-88001-190-4*) Ecco Pr.

Rivers & Mountains Far From the World: The Rachelle R. Holden Collection, A Personal Commentary. limited ed. Rachelle R. Holden. Ed. by Hugh Moss. LC 94-962345. (Illus.). 416p. 1994. 175.00 (*0-9642462-0-1*) R R Holden.

Rivers & Oceans: Geography Facts & Experiments. Barbara Taylor. LC 92-28421. (Young Discoverers Ser.). (Illus.). 32p. (J). (gr. 1-4). 1993. pap. 6.95 (*1-85697-939-3*, Kingfisher LKC); lib. bdg. 13.90 (*1-85697-630-0*, Kingfisher LKC) LKC.

Rivers & Rapids: A Very Complete Canoeing, Rafting & Fishing Guide to the Streams & Rivers of Texas, Arkansas & Oklahoma, Vol. 8. Ben M. Nolen & Robert E. Narramore. (Illus.). 144p. (Orig.). 1992. pap. 13.95 (*0-9632403-8-2*) Rivers & Rapids.

Rivers & Regions of Early South Carolina: Articles from the South Carolina Historical & Genealogical Magazine. Henry A. Smith & Alexander Moore. LC 87-26623. (Historical Writings of Henry A. M. Smith: Vol. 3). (Illus.). 384p. 1988. 25.00 (*0-87152-426-0*) Reprint.

Rivers & Seas. (Play & Discover Ser.). 32p. (J). (ps-2). 1997. pap. 3.95 (*0-8069-4237-1*) Sterling.

Rivers & Seas. Claire Llewellyn & Anthony Lewis. LC 95-17382. (Why Do We Have? Ser.). (Illus.). (J). 1995. pap. 4.95 (*0-8120-9396-8*) Barron.

Rivers & Seas. Claire Llewellyn. LC 95-17382. (Why Do We Have? Ser.). (Illus.). (J). 1995. 9.95 (*0-8120-6525-5*) Barron.

Rivers & Valleys. Philip Sauvain. LC 95-17369. (Geography Detective Ser.). (Illus.). (J). 1996. write for info. (*0-87614-996-4*, Carolrhoda) Lerner Group.

Rivers at Risk: The Concerned Citizen's Guide to Hydropower. John D. Echeverria et al. LC 89-19831. 214p. (Orig.). 1989. 29.95 (*0-933280-83-1*); pap. 17.95 (*0-933280-82-3*) Island Pr.

River's Call. Lenora H. Nazworth. 1993. 17.95 (*0-8034-8994-3*) Bouregy.

Rivers Chelmer & Blackwater. Stan Jarvis. 144p. 1994. pap. 30.00 (*0-86138-083-5*, Pub. by T Dalton UK) St Mut.

*__Rivers Curriculum Guide - Chemistry.__ Virginia Bryan et al. Ed. by Catherine Anderson & Christine Freeman. (Rivers Curriculum Project Ser.). (Illus.). 238p. (Orig.). (YA). (gr. 9-12). 1996. pap. 23.95 (*0-201-49367-5*, 30617) Seymour Pubns.

*__Rivers Curriculum Guide - Geography.__ Bob Ashley et al. Ed. by Catherine Anderson & Christine Freeman. (Rivers Curriculum Project Ser.). (Illus.). 230p. (Orig.). 1996. teacher ed., pap. 23.95 (*0-201-49368-3*, 30616) Seymour Pubns.

River's Daughter. Vella Munn. 416p. (Orig.). 1993. mass mkt. 4.99 (*0-8125-1930-2*) Tor Bks.

Rivers Delivers. Marion R. Ravenel. (Illus.). 1995. 19.95 (*0-941711-24-2*) Wyrick & Co.

River's Handbook: Hydrological & Ecological Processes, Vol. 1. P. Calow & G. E. Petts. (Illus.). 544p. 1992. 195.00 (*0-632-02832-7*) Blackwell Sci.

River's in My Blood: Riverboat Pilots Tell Their Stories. Jane Curry. LC 82-11068. 318p. 1983. reprint ed. pap. 90.70 (*0-608-01845-7*, 2062495) Bks Demand.

*__Rivers in the Desert.__ Connie Haskin. Ed. by Carrie Neumann & Ginny Ballor. 40p. (Orig.). 1996. pap. 3.00 (*1-882294-11-4*) Green Gate.

Rivers in the Desert. Margaret L. Davis. LC 92-54718. (Illus.). 320p. 1994. reprint ed. pap. 14.00 (*0-06-092194-3*, PL) HarpC.

Rivers in Which Men Drown. Bill Herron. (Voices in the Wind Ser.: No. 5). 64p. 1984. pap. 5.00 (*0-938392-08-5*) Homeward Pr.

River's Life. Richard Manning. 1996. pap. 14.95 (*0-8050-4793-X*) H Holt & Co.

River's Life. Richard Manning. 1997. 25.00 (*0-8050-4792-1*) H Holt & Co.

*__Rivers Must Run.__ Paul Kending. Ed. by J. Allen Kirsch. 210p. (Orig.). (YA). 1997. pap. 12.95 (*1-878569-46-5*) Badger Bks Inc.

*__Rivers of a Dream: A Compilation of Lifechanging & Inspirational Poetry.__ Paula Dalling. Ed. & Illus. by Wanda Sims. (Orig.). (YA). 1997. pap. text ed. 3.99 (*0-9640854-1-0*) M J Beth.

*__Rivers of America - Rivers of the Eastern Shore.__ Hulbert Footner. Date not set. lib. bdg. 26.95 (*0-8488-1977-2*) Amereon Ltd.

*__Rivers of America - The Arkansas.__ Clyde B. Davis. Date not set. lib. bdg. 25.95 (*0-8488-1970-5*) Amereon Ltd.

*__Rivers of America - The Brandywine.__ Henry S. Canby. Date not set. lib. bdg. 23.95 (*0-8488-1962-4*) Amereon Ltd.

*__Rivers of America - The Chicago.__ Harry Hansen. lib. bdg. 26.95 (*0-8488-1980-2*) Amereon Ltd.

*__Rivers of America - The Colorado.__ Frank Waters. lib. bdg. 27.95 (*0-8488-2078-9*) Amereon Ltd.

*__Rivers of America - The Columbia.__ Stewart H. Holbrook. lib. bdg. 27.95 (*0-8488-1986-1*) Amereon Ltd.

*__Rivers of America - The Cumberland.__ James McCague. lib. bdg. 21.95 (*0-8488-2005-3*) Amereon Ltd.

*__Rivers of America - The Delaware.__ Harry E. Wildes. lib. bdg. 27.95 (*0-8488-2082-7*) Amereon Ltd.

*__Rivers of America - The James.__ Blair Niles. lib. bdg. 25.95 (*0-8488-2008-8*) Amereon Ltd.

*__Rivers of America - The Merrimack.__ Raymond P. Holden. lib. bdg. 24.95 (*0-8488-1987-X*) Amereon Ltd.

*__Rivers of America - The Missouri.__ Stanley Vestal. lib. bdg. 26.95 (*0-8488-2039-8*) Amereon Ltd.

*__Rivers of America - The Potomac.__ Frederick Gutheim. lib. bdg. 28.95 (*0-8488-1979-9*) Amereon Ltd.

*__Rivers of America - The Sacramento River of Gold.__ Julian Dana. Date not set. lib. bdg. 23.95 (*0-8488-1968-3*) Amereon Ltd.

*__Rivers of America - The Shenandoah.__ Julia Davis. Date not set. lib. bdg. 26.95 (*0-8488-1971-3*) Amereon Ltd.

*__Rivers of America - The St. Johns.__ Hanna Cabell & A. J. Branch. Date not set. lib. bdg. 24.95 (*0-8488-1960-8*) Amereon Ltd.

*__Rivers of America - The Tennessee.__ Donald Davidson. Date not set. lib. bdg. 25.95 (*0-8488-1969-1*) Amereon Ltd.

*__Rivers of America - The Wabash.__ William E. Wilson. lib. bdg. 25.95 (*0-8488-2084-3*) Amereon Ltd.

Rivers of an Unknown Land: A Guide to the Best Whitewater Rivers of the Former Soviet Union. Vladimir Gavrilov. 1996. pap. text ed. 19.95 (*0-07-023180-X*) McGraw-Hill Prof.

Rivers of Babylon. Robert Liddell. 288p. 9600. 30.00 (*0-7206-0929-1*) Dufour.

Rivers of Blood: A Comparative Study of Government Massacres. Brenda K. Uekert. LC 95-6946. 256p. 1995. text ed. 59.95 (*0-275-95165-0*, Praeger Pubs) Greenwood.

Rivers of Change: Essays on Early Agriculture in Eastern North America. Bruce D. Smith. LC 91-30324. (Illus.). 320p. (C). 1992. text ed. 49.95 (*1-56098-162-8*) Smithsonian.

Rivers of China. Alma De Groen. 69p. (Orig.). 1990. pap. 5.00 (*0-87129-013-8*, R43) Dramatic Pub.

Rivers of Costa Rica: A Canoeing, Kayaking, & Rafting Guide. Michael W. Mayfield & Rafael E. Gallo. LC 88-22783. (Illus.). 123p. 1988. pap. 10.95 (*0-89732-083-2*) Menasha Ridge.

Rivers of Damascus & Other Stories. Donn B. Byrne, pseud. LC 72-106253. (Short Story Index Reprint Ser.). 1977. 20.95 (*0-8369-3290-0*) Ayer.

Rivers of Diamonds: An Alluvial History of the Lower Vaal Basin, South Africa. David M. Helgren. LC 79-17790. (University of Chicago, Department of Geography, Research Paper Ser.: No. 185). 412p. 1979. reprint ed. pap. 117.50 (*0-608-02248-9*, 2062889) Bks Demand.

*__Rivers of Discord.__ Shapland. LC 96-3334. 1997. text ed. write for info. (*0-312-16522-6*) St Martin.

Rivers of Dreams: Fly Fishing Stories. Ed. by Robert Lyon. 192p. (Orig.). 1992. pap. 9.95 (*0-920501-74-5*) Orca Bk Pubs.

Rivers of Eden: The Struggle for Water & the Quest for Peace in the Middle East. Daniel J. Hillel. (Illus.). 352p. 1994. 30.00 (*0-19-508068-8*) OUP.

Rivers of Empire: Water, Aridity, & the Growth of the American West. Donald Worster. LC 91-46685. 416p. 1992. pap. 16.95 (*0-19-507806-3*) OUP.

Rivers of Energy: Harnessing the Hydropower Potential. Daniel Deudney. 1981. pap. write for info. (*0-916468-43-7*) Worldwatch Inst.

Rivers of Eros. Cyrus Colter. (Prairie State Bks.). 248p. 1991. reprint ed. 9.95 (*0-252-06089-X*) U of Ill Pr.

Rivers of Fear: The Great California Flood of 1986. Ed. by Bob Teets & Shelby Young. (Illus.). 128p. 1987. pap. 12.95 (*0-938467-00-X*) CR Pubns.

*__Rivers of Fire: The Conflict over Water in the Middle East.__ Arnon Soffer. Tr. by Mory Rosovesky & Nina Copaken from HEB. (Illus.). 256p. 1997. 62.50 (*0-8476-8510-1*) Rowman.

*__Rivers of Fire: The Conflict over Water in the Middle East.__ Arnon Soffer. Tr. by Mory Rosovesky & Nina Copaken from HEB. (Illus.). 256p. 1997. pap. 23.95 (*0-8476-8511-X*) Rowman.

Rivers of Florida. Ed. by Hermann Remmert et al. (Ecological Studies: Vol. 83). (Illus.). 240p. 1990. 95.95 (*0-387-97363-X*) Spr-Verlag.

Rivers of Gold: A Novel of the California Gold Rush. J. L. Reasoner. 352p. (Orig.). 1995. mass mkt. 5.50 (*0-515-11524-X*) Jove Pubns.

Rivers of History: Life on the Coosa, Tallapoosa, Cahaba & Alabama. Harvey H. Jackson, III. LC 94-32334. (Illus.). 320p. (Orig.). 1995. pap. 29.95 (*0-8173-0771-0*) U of Ala Pr.

Rivers of Indiana. Richard S. Simons. LC 84-47745. (Illus.). 239p. 1985. reprint ed. pap. 68.20 (*0-7837-9667-6*, 2059301) Bks Demand.

Rivers of Judah. Catherine Farnes. LC 95-42661. (Orig.). (YA). 1996. pap. 6.49 (*0-89084-864-5*, 094045) Bob Jones Univ Pr.

Rivers of Life: or Sources & Streams of the Faiths of Man in All Lands Showing the Evolution of Faiths from the Rudest Symbolisms to the Latest Spiritual Developments. J. G. Forlong. (Illus.). 1300p. 1992. reprint ed. pap. 150.00 (*1-56459-291-X*) Kessinger Pub.

*__Rivers of Living Water.__ Mary Blue. LC 96-90341. (Orig.). 1996. pap. 11.95 (*0-533-12006-3*) Vantage.

*__Rivers of Living Water.__ John Osteen. Date not set. mass mkt. 2.99 (*0-912631-08-2*) J O Pubns.

*__Rivers of Mars: Searching for Cosmic Origins of Life.__ Piers Bizony. (Illus.). 192p. (Orig.). 1997. pap. 14.95 (*1-85410-495-0*, Pub. by Aurum Pr UK) London Brdge.

Rivers of Memory. Harry Middleton. LC 92-38119. 110p. 1993. 18.95 (*0-87108-835-5*) Pruett.

*__Rivers of Mirrors: The Fantastic Art of Judson Huss.__ limited ed. Judson Huss. 84p. 1997. lthr. 95.00 (*1-883398-21-5*) Morpheus Intl.

*__Rivers of Oil: The Founding of the North-American Petroleum Industry.__ Hope Morritt. (Illus.). 254p. 1993. pap. 19.95 (*1-55082-088-5*, Pub. by Quarry Pr CN) LPC InBook.

Rivers of Pennsylvania. Tim Palmer. LC 79-15378. (Keystone Bks.). (Illus.). 208p. 1980. pap. 14.50 (*0-271-00246-8*) Pa St U Pr.

*__Rivers of Red Ink: A Common Sense Guide to Saving Taxpayers Money & Restoring Northwest Salmon.__ Friends of the Earth. 14p. (Orig.). 1996. pap. 7.00 (*0-913890-89-8*) Friends of Earth.

*__Rivers of Revival.__ Elmer L. Towns & Neil T. Anderson. LC 97-19967. 1997. write for info. (*0-8307-1934-2*); trans. write for info. (*0-8307-1935-0*) Regal.

Rivers of Salt. Shirley Kaufman. LC 92-45859. 96p. (Orig.). 1993. pap. 11.00 (*1-55659-055-5*) Copper Canyon.

*__Rivers of Sand: A Video Guide.__ Joy Foundation Staff. 96p. 1997. per., pap. text ed. 12.95 (*0-7872-3495-8*); vhs 21.95 (*0-7872-3494-X*) Kendall-Hunt.

Rivers of the Black Moon. Andrew Goliszek. 1996. mass mkt. 5.99 (*0-8125-5179-6*) Tor Bks.

*__Rivers of the Heart.__ George Debord. 1989. pap. 9.95 (*0-944627-33-1*) Sand River Pr.

Rivers of the Pacific Northwest. William Dickey. 1969. pap. 8.00 (*0-685-20658-0*) Twowindows Pr.

*__Rivers of the United States, 6 vols.__ Ruth Patrick. text ed. 595.00 (*0-471-11501-0*) Wiley.

Rivers of the United States: Mississippi Drainage, Vol. 4. Ruth Patrick. 1996. 89.00 (*0-471-30347-X*) Wiley.

Rivers of the United States: Pollution & Environmental Management, Vol. 6. Ruth Patrick. 1997. 89.00 (*0-471-30349-6*) Wiley.

Rivers of the United States: Rivers of the East & Southeast, Vol. 3. Ruth Patrick. LC 93-27583. 928p. 1996. text ed. 125.00 (*0-471-30346-1*) Wiley.

Rivers of the United States: Rivers of the West & Southwest, Vol. 5. Ruth Patrick. 1995. 89.00 (*0-471-30348-8*) Wiley.

Rivers of the United States Vol. 1: Estuaries, Vol. 1. Ruth Patrick. 848p. 1994. text ed. 125.00 (*0-471-30345-3*) Wiley.

Rivers of the United States Vol. 2: Chemical & Physical Characteristics, Vol. 2. Ruth Patrick. 224p. 1995. text ed. 125.00 (*0-471-10752-2*) Wiley.

Rivers of the West: A Guide to the Geology & History. William Orr & Elizabeth L. Orr. LC 85-61228. (Illus.). 342p. (Orig.). 1985. 14.95 (*0-9606502-1-0*) W&E Orr.

Rivers of Time. L. Sprague De Camp. 272p. (Orig.). 1993. mass mkt. 4.99 (*0-671-72195-X*) Baen Bks.

Rivers of Time: A Graphic Chronology of Man. Michael J. Ray. 280p. (C). write for info. (*0-936283-01-7*) U Temecula Pr.

*__Rivers of Wales.__ R. Hutton. (Illus.). 1996. pap. 9.95 (*0-86243-373-8*, Pub. by Y Lifa UK) Intl Spec Bk.

Rivers, Ponds & Lakes. Nicola Barber. (Illus.). 44p. (J). (gr. 5-8). 1996. 19.95 (*0-237-51323-4*, Pub. by Evans Bros Ltd UK) Trafalgar.

Rivers, Ponds, & Lakes. Anita Ganeri. LC 91-5039. (Ecology Watch Ser.). (Illus.). 48p. (J). (gr. 5 up). 1992. lib. bdg. 13.95 (*0-87518-497-9*, Dillon Silver Burdett) Silver Burdett Pr.

Rivers, Railways, & Roads: A History of Henderson County. Robert P. Sutton. (Illus.). 1988. 40.00 (*0-9620376-0-5*) Henderson County Hist Soc.

Rivers Running Free: A Century of Women's Canoeing Adventures. Ed. by Judith Niemi & Barbara Wieser. LC 92-23108. (Adventura Bks.). (Illus.). 304p. 1997. pap. 16.95 (*1-878067-90-7*) Seal Pr WA.

Rivers Rushing to the Sea. Cook. (Heartsong ser.). 176p. 1994. pap. text ed. 4.95 (*1-55748-502-X*) Barbour & Co.

Rivers, Stories, Houses, Dreams. Madelon Sprengnether. 1983. pap. 4.00 (*0-89823-045-4*) New Rivers Pr.

Rivers to Skyscrapers: Ethics in Modern American Literature. Ed. by Mark G. Newton. LC 91-60154. 146p. 1991. pap. 12.95 (*0-945759-02-9*) St Leo Col Pr.

River's Way. John Merrill. 36p. 1986. 45.00 (*0-907496-41-5*, Pub. by JNM Pubns UK) St Mut.

River's Way: The Process Science of the Dreambody. Arnold Mindell. 176p. 1989. 10.95 (*0-14-019124-0*, Arkana); pap. 9.95 (*0-14-019274-3*, Penguin Bks) Viking Penguin.

Rivers West. Louis L'Amour. 160p. (Orig.). 1983. 3.99 (*0-553-25436-7*) Bantam.

Riverside. Miriam P. Ryan. 341p. 1994. 15.95 (*0-9645678-0-6*) Vincent Pub.

Riverside. limited ed. Morty Sklar. (Outstanding Author Ser.: No. 1). 13p. 1974. 6.00 (*0-930370-00-7*) Spirit That Moves.

Riverside: The Heritage, the People, the Vision. Ruth Austen. (Illus.). 152p. 1996. 39.00 (*1-885352-24-7*) Community Comm.

Riverside Anthology Literature: Exams, 2 Vols. Hunt. (C). Date not set. text ed. write for info. (*0-395-57273-8*) HM.

Riverside Anthology Literature: Exams, 3 Vols. Hunt. (C). 1996. text ed. 41.16 (*0-395-76071-2*) HM.

Riverside Anthology of Children's Literature, 6 Vols. 6th ed. Judith Saltman et al. LC 84-81344. 1312p. (C). 1984. text ed. 57.96 (*0-395-35773-X*) HM.

*__Riverside Anthology of Literature, 3 Vols.__ Ed. by Douglas D. Hunt. (C). 1997. teacher ed., text ed. 11.96 (*0-395-76072-0*) HM.

Riverside Anthology of Literature, 2 Vols. 2nd ed. Douglas D. Hunt. (C). 1990. text ed. 41.16 (*0-395-47285-7*) HM Soft Schl Col Div.

*__Riverside Anthology of Literature, 3 Vols.__ 3rd ed. Ed. by Douglas D. Hunt. 1728p. (C). 1996. text ed. 41.16 (*0-395-76070-4*) HM.

*__Riverside Anthology of Literature: Student Paper Packet, 3 Vols.__ 3rd ed. Ed. by Douglas D. Hunt. (C). 1997. text ed. 3.16 (*0-395-76073-9*) HM.

Riverside Chaucer, 3 Vols. 3rd ed. Ed. by Larry D. Benson & Geoffrey Chaucer. LC 86-81304. (C). 1986. text ed. 63.96 (*0-395-29031-7*) HM.

Riverside Counselor's Stories: Vernacular Fiction of Late Heian Japan. Tr. by Robert L. Backus from JPN. LC 84-40446. 272p. 1985. 39.50 (*0-8047-1260-3*) Stanford U Pr.

*__Riverside County Street Guide & Directory: 1998 Edition.__ Thomas Bros. Maps Staff. 240p. 1997. pap. 16.95 (*0-88130-893-5*) Thomas Bros Maps.

*__Riverside Drive.__ Van Wormer. 1998. mass mkt. 5.99 (*1-55166-303-1*) Harlequin Bks.

Riverside Drive. Laura Van Wormer. 1989. mass mkt. 5.95 (*0-312-91572-1*) St Martin.

Riverside Guide to Writing, 2 Vols. Hunt. (C). 1994. text ed. 34.76 (*0-395-68623-7*) HM.

*__Riverside Guide to Writing, 2 Vols.__ 2nd ed. Douglas D. Hunt. 576p. (C). 1994. pap. text ed. 29.96 (*0-395-70962-8*) HM.

*__Riverside Guide to Writing, 2 Vols.__ 2nd ed. Douglas D. Hunt. (C). 1995. teacher ed., text ed. 11.96 (*0-395-72337-X*) HM.

*__Riverside Guide to Writing: Instructor's Support Package, 2 Vols.__ 2nd ed. Douglas D. Hunt. (C). 1995. text ed. 11.96 (*0-395-72339-6*) HM.

Riverside Handbook. Lynn Beene & William J. Vande Kopple. (C). 1991. text ed. 29.96 (*0-395-52372-9*) HM.

*__Riverside Handbook.__ Lynn Beene & William V. Kopple. (C). 1992. teacher ed., text ed. 3.96 (*0-395-59962-8*) HM.

Riverside Handbook. Lynn Beene. (C). 1992. teacher ed., text ed. 24.76 (*0-395-59961-X*) HM.

Riverside Killer. C. Keers & D. St. Pierre. 320p. (Orig.). 1996. mass mkt. 5.99 (*0-7860-0345-6*, Pinncle Kensgtn) Kensgtn Pub Corp.

*__Riverside Milton.__ Flannagan. (C). Date not set. text ed. 41.16 (*0-395-80999-1*) HM.

Riverside Paper Corporation 1893-1993. Ruth L. Friedman. 1994. write for info. (*0-9638996-0-0*); pap. write for info. (*0-9638996-1-9*) Riverside Paper.

Riverside Reader. Joseph F. Trimmer & Maxine C. Hairston. LC 80-82759. 544p. (C). 1982. teacher ed. 2.00 (*0-685-02305-2*) HM.

Riverside Reader, 5 Vols. Joseph F. Trimmer. (C). 1995. pap. 26.76 (*0-395-72972-6*) HM.

Riverside Reader, 4 Vols. Joseph F. Trimmer. (J). 1992. pap. 26.76 (*0-395-61962-9*) HM.

Riverside Reader, 5 Vols. Joseph F. Trimmer. (C). 1995. suppl. ed., teacher ed., pap. 11.96 (*0-395-72974-2*) HM.

Riverside Reader, 2 vols. 2nd ed. Joseph F. Trimmer & Maxine C. Hairston. (C). 1986. teacher ed. 2.36 (*0-318-32575-6*) HM.

An Asterisk (*) at the beginning of an entry indicates that the title is appearing in BIP for the first time.

Riverside Reader: Exams, 5 Vols. Joseph F. Trimmer. (C). 1995. pap. 26.76 (*0-395-72973-4*) HM.
Riverside Reading Oral Language Development System: Changing Time. Houghton Mifflin Company Staff. 1988. pap. 41.20 (*0-8292-7759-5*) HM.
Riverside Reading Oral Language Development System: Defining Time. Riverside Reading Staff. 1988. pap. 31.80 (*0-8292-7758-7*) HM.
Riverside Reading Oral Language Development System: Story Time. Riverside Reading Staff. 1989. teacher ed., pap. 31.80 (*0-8292-8026-X*) HM.
Riverside Remembered. Wallace N. Briggs. LC 92-16397. (Illus.). 248p. (C). 1992. 19.95 (*0-8131-1807-7*) U Pr of Ky.
Riverside Shakespeare, 2 Vols. Evans. (C). 1996. text ed. 59.16 (*0-395-75490-9*) HM.
Riverside Shakespeare. William Shakespeare. Ed. by Charles H. Shattuck et al. 1728p. (C). 1974. text ed. 59.16 (*0-395-04402-2*) HM.
***Riverside Shakespeare, 2 Vols.** 2nd ed. Ed. by Evans. 1997. 135.00 (*0-395-85822-4*) HM.
Riverside Webster's Dictionary, Vol. II. abr. ed. Houghton Mifflin Company Staff. 864p. 1996. reprint ed. pap. 5.99 (*0-425-15418-1*) Berkley Pub.
Riverside Webster's II Dictionary. Berkley Staff. 1996. pap. 5.99 (*0-425-15489-0*) Berkley Pub.
Riverside/Orange Counties Street Guide & Directory: 1997 Edition. (Illus.). 384p. 1996. pap. 27.95 (*0-88130-831-5*) Thomas Bros Maps.
***Riverside/Orange Counties Street Guide & Directory: 1998 Edition.** Thomas Bros. Maps Staff. 384p. 1997. pap. 27.95 (*0-88130-894-3*) Thomas Bros Maps.
***Riverside/San Diego Counties Street Guide & Directory: 1998 Edition.** Thomas Bros. Maps Staff. 472p. 1997. pap. 27.95 (*0-88130-895-1*) Thomas Bros Maps.
***Riversong.** 475p. 1997. write for info. (*0-7814-0300-6*, Victor Bks) Chariot Victor.
Riversong. Craig Lesley. 320p. 1993. pap. 11.95 (*0-385-31277-6*, Delta) Dell.
Riversong Lodge Cookbook: World-Class Cooking in the Alaskan Bush. Kirsten Dixon. LC 93-17711. (Illus.). 272p. 1993. 22.95 (*0-88240-431-8*); pap. 14.95 (*0-88240-397-4*) Alaska Northwest.
***Riversong Recipes.** Pat Crocker. (Illus.). 144p. 1997. pap. 14.95 (*0-9697079-6-7*, Pub. by Moulin Pub CN) Genl Dist Srvs.
Riversongs. fac. ed. Michael Anania. LC 78-12900. 95p. 1978. pap. 27.10 (*0-7837-7606-3*, 2047359) Bks Demand.
Riversongs. Poems. Michael Anania. LC 78-12900. 87p. 1978. 14.95 (*0-252-00717-4*) U of Ill Pr.
Riverton Heights Reservoir, Seattle, Washington. (PCI Journal Reprints Ser.). 14p. 1981. pap. 12.00 (*0-686-40145-X*, JR241) P-PCI.
***Riverview Murders.** Michael Raleigh. LC 97-7586. 1997. 21.95 (*0-312-15641-3*) St Martin.
Riverview, Tape 23. Colleen Neuman. 1993. pap. 3.00 (*0-87129-286-6*, R53) Dramatic Pub.
Riverwalk: History Underfoot. Bernard A. Drew. 24p. 1995. pap. 5.00 (*0-941583-23-6*) Attic Rev Pr.
Riverwalking: Reflections on Moving Water. Kathleen D. Moore. LC 96-11364. 1996. pap. 12.00 (*0-15-600461-5*, Harvest Bks) HarBrace.
Riverwalking: Reflections on Moving Water. Kathleen D. Moore. 176p. 1995. 19.95 (*1-55821-408-9*) Lyons & Burford.
Riverworld War. Philip Jose Farmer. 112p. 1980. 6.95 (*0-933180-13-6*) Ellis Pr.
Rivethead: Tales from the Assembly Line. Ben Hamper. LC 89-40469. 1992. reprint ed. pap. 10.99 (*0-446-39400-9*) Warner Bks.
Riveting & Rationing in Dixie: Alabama Women & the Second World War. Mary M. Thomas. LC 86-16068. (Illus.). 160p. 1987. text ed. 19.95 (*0-8173-0329-4*) U of Ala Pr.
Riviera Off Season & On. Doris Lehman. LC 96-27796. 256p. 1996. pap. 14.95 (*0-312-14726-0*) St Martin.
Rivington Street. Meredith Tax. 416p. 1990. mass mkt. 4.95 (*0-380-70907-4*) Avon.
Rivista. Antonio Carrara & Nancy Levy-Konesky. (Illus.). 220p. (C). 1994. text ed. 24.50 (*0-03-033382-2*) HB Coll Pubs.
Rivky's Great Idea. Tamar Kamins. (B. Y. Times Kid Sisters Ser.: No. 3). 107p. (J). (gr. 4-7). Date not set. pap. 7.95 (*1-56871-004-6*) Feldheim.
Rivulets of Poetry. Lynne S. Chaplin. (Orig.). 1996. pap. write for info. (*1-57553-165-8*) Watermrk Pr.
Rivulets of Prose. Walt Whitman. Ed. by Carolyn Wells. LC 78-88037. (Essay Index Reprint Ser.). 1977. 22.95 (*0-8369-1163-6*) Ayer.
Riyad-us-Salihin, 2 pts., Pt. I. Abu Zakariya An Nawawi. (ARA & ENG.). 20.00 (*0-935782-69-9*) Kazi Pubns.
Riyad-us-Salihin, 2 pts., Pt. II. Abu Zakariya An Nawawi. (ARA & ENG.). 20.00 (*0-933511-38-8*) Kazi Pubns.
Riyad-us-Salihin, 2 pts., Set. Abu Zakariya An Nawawi. (ARA & ENG.). 49.00 (*1-56744-347-8*) Kazi Pubns.
Riyadh. Anthony Guise. 1990. 50.00 (*0-86685-474-6*, Pub. by Stacey Intl UK) Intl Bk Ctr.
Riyadh: The Old City from Its Origins until the 1950s. William Facey. 384p. (C). 1995. 90.00 (*0-907151-32-9*, Pub. by IMMEL Pubng UK) St Mut.
Riyadh Album. Stacey International Staff. 1983. text ed. 45.00 (*0-86685-642-0*) Intl Bk Ctr.
Riyah al-Taghyir. Jawdat Said. (Majalis Bir Ajam Ser.). 264p. (Orig.). (ARA.). 1995. pap. 3.95 (*1-57547-220-1*) Dar Al-Fikr.
***Rizal-Pastells Correspondence.** Ed. by Raul J. Bonoan. 240p. 1997. pap. text ed. 16.00 (*971-550-124-9*, Pub. by Ateneo de Manila Univ Pr PH) UH Pr.
***Rizzi: Plains Myths.** Glenn Obrien. 1997. 95.00 (*0-936598-05-0*) J Szoke Graphics.
Rizzo's Bike Sale. Illus. by Rick Brown. (Muppet Picture Readers Ser.). 32p. (Orig.). (J). (ps-1). 1996. pap. 3.95 (*0-448-41554-2*, G&D) Putnam Pub Group.
***Rizzo's Razzamatazz Activity Book, Vol. 3.** Windy Just. (Muppet Pent Activity Ser.). (Illus.). 48p. (J). (gr. 1 up). 1997. pap. 3.95 (*0-8431-7870-1*) Price Stern Sloan.
RJR Nabisco Holdings Corp. A Report on the Company's Environmental Policies & Practices. (Illus.). 20p. (C). 1994. reprint ed. pap. text ed. 250.00 (*0-7881-0947-2*, Coun on Econ) DIANE Pub.
Rjurik Highlands. Anthony Pryor. 1996. 20.00 (*0-7869-0395-3*) TSR Inc.
RKO: The Biggest Little Major of Them All. Betty Lasky. (Illus.). 240p. 1984. pap. 9.95 (*0-13-781444-5*) P-H.
RKO: The Biggest Little Major of Them All. Betty Lasky. LC 88-64132. 256p. 1989. pap. 16.95 (*0-915677-41-5*) Roundtable Pub.
RKO Features: A Complete Filmography of the Feature Films Released or Produced by RKO Radio Pictures, 1929-1960. James L. Neibaur. LC 92-56669. (Illus.). 332p. 1994. lib. bdg. 49.95 (*0-89950-787-5*) McFarland & Co.
RKO Radio Pictures of 1931-1935. Ed. by R. Gordon. 1976. lib. bdg. 100.95 (*0-8490-2528-1*) Gordon Pr.
RKO Story. R. B. Jewell. 320p. 1984. 19.95 (*0-517-54656-6*) Random Hse Value.
RLG Military Operations & Activities in the Laotian Panhandle. Soutchay Vongsavanh. 120p. 1989. reprint ed. pap. 15.00 (*0-923135-05-7*) Dalley Bk Service.
RLISP '88: An Evolutionary Approach to Program Design. J. Marti. (Computer Science Ser.). 250p. 1993. text ed. 61.00 (*981-02-1479-0*) World Scientific Pub.
RL's Dream. Walter Mosley. 272p. 1996. pap. 12.00 (*0-671-88428-X*) PB.
RMF Job Search. Jim Clayton. 180p. (C). 1996. pap. text ed., spiral bd. 18.84 (*0-7872-2080-9*) Kendall-Hunt.
***RMI: Remote Method Invocation.** Troy Downing. 1997. pap. 39.99 (*0-7645-8043-4*) IDG Bks.
RMI Base Book Series: Breast Cancer. Ed. by Margaret Dion-Marovitz & Deborah L. Mitchell. (Illus.). 110p. (Orig.). 1992. pap. 40.00 (*1-881367-01-0*) Reliance Med.
RMI Review of Breast Cancer Research, 1992. Ed. by Margaret Dion-Marovitz & Deborah L. Mitchell. (Illus.). 200p. (Orig.). 1992. pap. 50.00 (*1-881367-02-9*) Reliance Med.
***RMI Specification & Tutorial.** Jim Waldo. (C). 1997. pap. text ed. write for info. (*0-201-92489-7*) Addison-Wesley.
RMM: The Second Oldest Profession. Robert M. Miller. LC 90-85392. (Illus.). 664p. 1990. 49.00 (*0-939674-35-1*) Am Vet Pubns.
RMM Strikes Again. Robert M. Miller. LC 84-72573. (Illus.). 192p. 1984. 25.50 (*0-939674-16-5*) Am Vet Pubns.
RMS Dictionary of Light Microscopy. Royal Microscopy Society, Nomenclature Committee Staff. (Royal Microscopy Society Microscopy Handbooks Ser.: No. 15). (Illus.). 152p. 1989. 35.00 (*0-19-856421-X*); pap. 16.95 (*0-19-856413-9*) OUP.
RN: Memoirs of Richard Nixon. Richard M. Nixon. (Richard Nixon Library). 1990. pap. 23.00 (*0-671-70741-8*, Touchstone Bks) S&S Trade.
RN & WPL Encyclopedia 1996. Ed. by Andrew Grabois et al. 1996. pap. 249.95 (*0-87228-090-X*) Salesmans.
***RN Core Competencies.** Julia Fulton. 174p. 1996. spiral bd. 130.00 (*1-879575-76-0*) Acad Med Sys.
RN First Assistant: An Expanded Perioperative Nursing Role. 2nd ed. Ed. by Jane C. Rothrock. LC 92-48997. 416p. 1993. text ed. 42.95 (*0-397-55014-6*) Lppncott-Raven.
RN Magazine's NCLEX-RN Review, 1991. Alice Stein. 1990. pap. 29.95 (*0-8273-4646-8*) Delmar.
RN Magazine's NDR - Ninety-One. 2nd ed. George R. Spratto et al. 1991. pap. 25.95 (*0-8273-4737-5*) Delmar.
RN Magazine's NDR-Ninety-Five. George R. Spratto & Adrienne L. Woods. 1395p. 1995. pap. 26.95 (*0-8273-6548-9*) Delmar.
RN Magazine's NDR-Ninety-Four Nurse's Drug Reference. George R. Spratto & Adrienne L. Woods. 1290p. 1994. pap. 25.95 (*0-8273-5711-7*) Delmar.
RN Magazines NDR 1994 - Display Dump. George R. Spratto. (Professional Reference - Nursing Ser.). 1994. 259.50 (*0-8273-6202-1*) Delmar.
RN Magazines' NDR-'93 (Nurses Drug Reference) George R. Spratto & Adrienne L. Woods. 1993. text ed. 25.95 (*0-8273-5284-0*) Delmar.
RN Magazine's Nurses' Drug Reference, '92. George R. Spratto & Adrienne L. Woods. 1992. pap. 25.95 (*0-8273-4844-4*) Delmar.
RN Magazine's the Nurse's Drug Handbook. 7th ed. Suzanne Loebl et al. LC 93-36203. 1420p. 1994. pap. 36.95 (*0-8273-5710-9*) Delmar.
RN NCLEX Review Cards. 2nd ed. Brenda Goodner. 1993. boxed 29.95 (*0-944132-82-0*) Skidmore Roth Pub.
RNA: Catalysis, Splicing, Evolution. Ed. by M. Belfort & D. A. Shub. 236p. 1990. reprint ed. 181.25 (*0-444-81210-5*) Elsevier.
RNA: Structure, Biosynthesis, & Function. Ed. by Dieter Soll & T. L. RajBhandary. LC 94-21051. (Illus.). 600p. 1994. 99.00 (*1-55581-073-X*) Am Soc Microbio.
RNA Editing: The Alteration of Protein Coding Sequences of RNA. Ed. by Rob Benne. LC 93-6500. (Series in Molecular Biology). 200p. 1993. 50.00 (*0-13-782558-7*, Pub. by Tavistock-E Horwood UK) Routledge Chapman & Hall.
RNA Genetics, Vol. I. Ed. by Esteban Domingo et al. 240p. 1988. 131.00 (*0-8493-6666-6*, QR395, CRC Reprint) Franklin.
RNA Genetics, Vol. II. Ed. by Esteban Domingo et al. 240p. 1988. 148.00 (*0-8493-6667-4*, QR395, CRC Reprint) Franklin.
RNA Genetics, Vol. III. Ed. by Esteban Domingo et al. 272p. 1988. 154.00 (*0-8493-6668-2*, QR395, CRC Reprint) Franklin.
RNA Isolation & Analysis. P. Jones et al. 224p. 1994. pap. 52.50 (*1-872748-37-6*, Pub. by Bios Scientific UK) Coronet Bks.
***RNA Isolation & Characterization Protocols.** Ed. by Ralph Rapley & David L. Manning. (Methods in Molecular Biology Ser.: Vol. 86). (Illus.). 300p. 1997. 99.50 (*0-89603-494-1*); spiral bd. 69.50 (*0-89603-393-7*) Humana.
RNA Methodologies: A Laboratory Guide for Isolation & Characterization. Ed. by Robert E. Farrell, Jr. (Illus.). 319p. 1993. pap. 49.95 (*0-12-249700-7*) Acad Pr.
RNA Phages. Ed. by Norton D. Zinder. LC 75-4319. (Cold Spring Harbor Monograph Ser.). 454p. 1975. reprint ed. pap. 129.40 (*0-608-01803-1*, 2062456) Bks Demand.
RNA Polymerase. Ed. by R. Losick & M. Chamberlin. LC 76-17182. (Cold Spring Harbor Monograph Ser.). 909p. reprint ed. pap. 180.00 (*0-7837-6443-X*, 2046443) Bks Demand.
RNA Polymerase III Transcription. Robert J. White. (Molecular Biology Intelligence Unit Ser.). 160p. 1994. 89.95 (*1-57059-046-X*, LN9046) R G Landes.
RNA Processing: A Practical Approach, Vol. I. Ed. by Stephen J. Higgins & B. David Hames. (Practical Approach Ser.: Vol. 135). (Illus.). 240p. 1994. 75.00 (*0-19-963344-4*, IRL Pr); pap. 45.00 (*0-19-963343-6*, IRL Pr) OUP.
RNA Processing: A Practical Approach, Vol. II. Ed. by Stephen J. Higgins & B. David Hames. (Practical Approach Ser.: Vol. 136). (Illus.). 288p. 1994. 75.00 (*0-19-963471-8*, IRL Pr); pap. 45.00 (*0-19-963470-X*, IRL Pr) OUP.
RNA Processing: A Practical Approach, Vols. I & II. Ed. by Stephen J. Higgins & B. David Hames. (Practical Approach Ser.: Vols. 135 & 136). (Illus.). 528p. 1994. 130.00 (*0-19-963473-4*, IRL Pr); pap. 85.00 (*0-19-963472-6*, IRL Pr) OUP.
RNA-Protein Interactions: Frontiers in Molecular Biology. Ed. by K. Nagai & I. Mattaj. (Frontiers in Molecular Biology Ser.). (Illus.). 272p. 1995. text ed. 105.00 (*0-19-963505-6*, IRL Pr); pap. text ed. 55.00 (*0-19-963504-8*, IRL Pr) OUP.
RNA Tumor Viruses. 2nd ed. Ed. by Robin A. Weiss et al. LC 83-26227. (Molecular Biology of Tumor Viruses Ser.: No. 10C). 1245p. reprint ed. pap. 180.00 (*0-7837-6444-8*, 2046444) Bks Demand.
RNA Tumor Viruses, No. 1: Text, Vol. 1. Ed. by Robin A. Weiss et al. LC 83-26227. (Monographs: No. 10C). 1292p. 1984. pap. text ed. 67.00 (*0-87969-166-2*) Cold Spring Harbor.
RNA Tumor Viruses, Oncogenes, Human Cancer & AIDS: On Frontiers of Understanding. Ed. by Philip Furmanski et al. (Developments in Oncology Ser.). 1985. lib. bdg. 109.50 (*0-89838-703-5*) Kluwer Ac.
RNA World. Ed. by Raymond F. Gesteland & John F. Atkins. LC 93-2840. (Monographs: Vol. 24). 632p. 1993. 95.00 (*0-87969-380-0*); pap. 45.00 (*0-87969-456-4*) Cold Spring Harbor.
***RN&WPL Encyclopedia 1997.** Salesman's Guide Staff. 1997. 259.95 (*0-87228-102-7*) Salesmans.
RNT Careers in Teaching Handbook. Recruiting New Teachers, Inc. Staff. (Illus.). 104p. 1993. 9.95 (*1-884139-02-7*) Recruit New Tchrs.
Ro-Ro Market. G. P. Wild (International) Ltd. Staff. (Lloyd's Business Intelligence Centre Ser.). 151p. 1994. pap. 590.00 (*1-85044-581-8*) LLP.
Ro-Ro Shore & Ship Ramp Characteristics: An ICHCA Survey. ICHCA Staff. 330p. (C). 1978. 350.00 (*0-906297-00-1*, Pub. by ICHCA UK) St Mut.
Roach & Company - Pirates & Other Stories. Hector Fuller. LC 78-113662. (Short Story Index Reprint Ser.). 1977. 18.95 (*0-8369-3391-5*) Ayer.
Roach Killer. Jacques Tardi. Tr. by Jean-Marc Lofficier from FRE. 64p. 1992. pap. 11.95 (*1-56163-054-3*, Comics Lit) NBM.
Roach Motel. Molly Cook. 13p. (J). (ps-3). 1996. pap. text ed. 1.95 (*1-56763-170-3*) Ozark Pub.
Roach Relief. Nile Hawking. (Illus.). 32p. (Orig.). 1996. pap. 16.95 (*0-9652220-0-4*) TSM Intl.
Roach, Roberts, Ridgeway & Allied Families. M. R. Fair. 258p. 1991. reprint ed. pap. 41.50 (*0-8328-1938-7*); reprint ed. lib. bdg. 51.50 (*0-8328-1937-9*) Higginson Bk Co.
Roaches Have No King. Daniel E. Weiss. Ed. by Ira Silverberg. (Orig.). 1994. pap. 11.99 (*1-85242-326-9*, High Risk Bks) Serpents Tail.
***Roaches' Revenge.** Allen B. Ury. (Crawlers Ser.: No. 2). 1997. mass mkt. 4.99 (*0-8125-4357-2*) Tor Bks.
***Road.** Craig Krull. (Illus.). 56p. 1996. per. 25.00 (*0-9640494-1-4*) J Fee Photo.
Road. James C. Liu. 509p. 1994. pap. write for info. (*0-9631789-8-9*) Evan Formosan.
Road. Jack London. (Illus.). 320p. 1991. pap. 9.95 (*0-932458-46-7*) Star Rover.
Road. Jack London. 150p. 1993. 17.95 (*1-56723-073-3*) Yestermorrow.
Road. Jack London. 18.95 (*0-8488-0880-0*) Yestermorrow.
***Road.** Jim Nave. LC 96-79549. 84p. 1997. pap. 14.95 (*1-885221-52-5*) BookPartners.
Road. Wole Soyinka. (Three Crowns Bks.). 1965. pap. 9.95 (*0-19-911084-0*) OUP.
Road. rev. ed. John Cartwright. (Methuen Modern Plays Ser.). 84p. (C). 1990. reprint ed. pap. 9.95 (*0-413-62390-4*, A0410, Pub. by Methuen UK) Heinemann.
Road. Jack London. (American Biography Ser.). 224p. 1991. reprint ed. lib. bdg. 69.00 (*0-7812-8250-0*) Rprt Serv.
Road: Indian Tribes & Political Liberty. Russel L. Barsh & James Y. Henderson. LC 77-91777. 1979. pap. 13.00 (*0-520-04636-6*) U CA Pr.
***Road Accidents - Great Britain, 1995.** 129p. 1996. pap. 30.00 (*0-11-551849-5*, HM18495, Pub. by Stationery Ofc UK) Bernan Associates.
Road Accidents- Great Britain 1994. 129p. 1995. pap. text ed. 25.00 (*0-11-551734-0*, HM17340, Pub. by Stationery Ofc UK) Bernan Associates.
Road Aces, 5 novels in ea. set, Set 1. (Illus.). (J). (gr. 2-7). 1985. Set. pap. 17.00 (*0-87879-490-5*) High Noon Bks.
Road Aces, 5 novels in ea. set, Set 2. (Illus.). (J). (gr. 2-7). 1985. pap. 17.00 (*0-87879-496-4*) High Noon Bks.
Road Ahead. Bill Gates. 1995. pap. 22.95 (*0-670-85913-3*, Viking) Viking Penguin.
***Road Ahead.** Bill Gates. 1996. pap. 7.50 (*0-14-025727-6*) Viking Penguin.
Road Ahead. Bill Gates. 288p. 1995. pap. 29.95 incl. cd-rom (*0-670-77289-5*, Viking) Viking Penguin.
Road Ahead. Peter M. Rinearson et al. 320p. 1996. pap. 15.95 (*0-14-026040-4*) Viking Penguin.
Road Ahead. large type ed. Bill Gates. 256p. 1993. 23.95 (*1-85695-170-7*, Pub. by ISIS UK) Transaction Pubs.
Road Ahead. large type ed. Peter M. Rinearson et al. 1996. 25.95 (*1-56895-306-2*) Wheeler Pub.
Road Ahead: A Stroke Recovery Guide. 2nd ed. Ed. by Thelma Edwards. (Illus.). 185p. 1992. reprint ed. pap. text ed. 14.50 (*0-9624876-1-9*) Natl Stroke Assn.
Road Ahead: A Stroke Recovery Guide. 3rd ed. Ed. by Thelam Edwards. 1995. write for info. (*0-614-17653-0*) Natl Stroke Assn.
Road Ahead: A Stroke Recovery Guide. 3rd ed. Ed. by Thelma Edwards. (Illus.). 1995. pap. text ed. write for info. (*0-614-17435-X*) Natl Stroke Assn.
Road Ahead: An Agenda for Canada in the 1990s. Philippe G. Deane. 208p. 1990. 24.95 (*0-7737-2401-X*) Genl Dist Srvs.
Road Ahead: U. S. - Indo Strategic Dialogue. Ed. by Jasjit Singh. (C). 1994. text ed. 32.00 (*1-897829-95-7*, Pub. by Lancer International II) S Asia.
Road & Airport Pavement Response Monitoring Systems. Ed. by Vincent C. Janoo & Robert A. Eaton. LC 92-6799. 440p. 1992. pap. text ed. 40.00 (*0-87262-890-6*) Am Soc Civil Eng.
Road & Paving Materials - Vehicle-Pavement Systems see 1997 Annual Book of ASTM Standards: Construction, Section 4
***Road & the Miles: A Homage to Dundee.** Jim Crumley. (Illus.). 192p. 1996. 29.95 (*1-85158-787-X*, Pub. by Mnstream UK) Trafalgar.
Road & the Truth: The Editing of John's Gospel. Scott G. Sinclair. LC 94-12239. 128p. 1994. pap. 12.95 (*0-941037-31-2*) BIBAL Pr.
***Road Atlas.** Rand McNally Staff. 1997. pap. text ed. 13.95 (*0-528-83917-9*) Rand McNally.
***Road Atlas.** Jon Scieszka. Date not set. pap. 14.95 (*0-670-86809-4*) Viking Penguin.
Road Atlas America 1997. (Illus.). 96p. 1996. pap. 5.95 (*0-8437-2719-5*, 2719-5) Hammond Inc.
Road Atlas & Travel Guide, 1997. deluxe ed. Rand McNally Staff. 176p. 1996. pap. text ed. 7.95 (*0-528-81529-6*) Rand McNally.
***Road Atlas & Trip Planner of Europe 1997.** Universal Staff. 1997. pap. text ed. 17.95 (*0-7625-0335-1*) Universal Map Enterprises Inc.
Road Atlas & Trip Planner, 1997. Rand McNally Staff. 95p. 1996. pap. text ed. 5.95 (*0-528-81560-1*) Rand McNally.
Road Atlas & Vacation Guide 1997. (Illus.). 48p. 1996. pap. 2.95 (*0-8437-2723-3*, 2723-3) Hammond Inc.
***Road Atlas Deluxe Laminated 1997.** Universal Staff. 1996. pap. text ed. 59.95 (*0-7625-0244-4*) Universal Map Enterprises Inc.
***Road Atlas of Australia.** Globetrotter Staff. 1997. pap. text ed. 12.95 (*1-85368-781-2*) Globe Pequot.
***Road Atlas of Britain 1997.** Universal Staff. 1997. pap. text ed. 17.95 (*0-7625-0334-3*) Universal Map Enterprises Inc.
Road Atlas 1996: Bilingual Edition "Atlas de Carreteras" 1995. pap. text ed. 9.95 (*0-528-81491-5*) Rand McNally.
Road Atlas 1997. Rand McNally Staff. 144p. 1996. pap. text ed. 9.95 (*0-528-81517-2*) Rand McNally.
***Road Atlas 1997: Deluxe.** Rand McNally Staff. 144p. 1996. pap. 13.95 (*0-528-81558-X*) Rand McNally.
Road Atlas 1997, Gift Edition. Rand McNally Staff. 1996. pap. text ed. 13.95 (*0-528-81559-8*) Rand McNally.
***Road Back.** Penelope Parker. LC 96-90231. 1996. 12.95 (*0-533-11963-4*) Vantage.
***Road Back.** Eric M. Remarque. 1998. pap. write for info. (*0-449-91246-9*) Fawcett.
Road Back: A POW's Return to Santo Tomas. Dorothy D. Thompson. 160p. 1996. 28.95 (*0-89672-362-3*) Tex Tech Univ Pr.
Road Back: A Report on Alcoholics Anonymous. Joseph Kessel. LC 78-9948. 244p. 1979. reprint ed. text ed. 55.00 (*0-313-21097-7*, KERB, Greenwood Pr) Greenwood.
Road Back: By a Liberal in Opposition. J. W. Pickersgill. 255p. 1986. 30.00 (*0-8020-2598-6*) U of Toronto Pr.
Road Back: Living with a Physical Disability. Harriet Sirof. LC 92-43581. (Open Door Bks.). 160p. (YA). (gr. 6 up). 1993. lib. bdg. 13.95 (*0-02-782885-9*, New Dscvry Bks) Silver Burdett Pr.
Road Back: Rebuilding Survivors Lives. Eva Kahn-Minden. 108p. 1992. pap. 9.95 (*965-229-067-X*, Pub. by Gefen Pub Hse IS) Gefen Bks.
Road Back Home. Sierra Rydell. (Special Edition Ser.: No. 1044). 1996. mass mkt. 3.99 (*0-373-24044-9*, 1-24044-9) Silhouette.
Road Back Home: Tales of Appalachia. Denvil Mullins. 194p. (Orig.). 1996. pap. 9.95 (*1-57072-040-1*) Overmountain Pr.

R

Road Back to Health: Coping with the Emotional Aspects of Cancer. rev. ed. Neil A. Fiore. LC 90-2160. 240p. 1995. reprint ed. pap. 9.95 (0-89087-617-7) Celestial Arts.

*Road Back to Paris. A. J. Liebling. 1997. 17.50 (0-679-60248-8, Modern Lib) Random.

Road Belong Cargo: A Study of the Cargo Movement in the Southern Madang District New Guinea. Peter Lawrence. (Illus.). 293p. (C). 1989. reprint ed. pap. text ed. 12.50 (0-88133-458-8) Waveland Pr.

Road Best Traveled: Knowing God's Will for Your Life. Ray Pritchard. LC 95-15381. 224p. (Orig.). 1995. pap. 10.99 (0-89107-851-7) Crossway Bks.

*Road Best Traveled: Through the Bible in 365 Devotions. G. A. Barbee. 1996. 8.95 (1-55673-994-X) CSS OH.

Road Beyond Loss: 3 Cycles of Poems & an Epilogue. Anesa Miller. (Illus.). 64p. (Orig.). 1995. per. 7.00 (0-9647642-0-2) Mem Fnd Lost Chldrn.

Road Beyond the Open Door, Pt. 1. Stanley R. Smith. Ed. by Amanda J. Christopher. 146p. 1988. spiral bd. 14.95 (0-943439-00-0) Chris-Johns Pr.

*Road Bike Asheville, North Carolina: Favorite Rides of the Blue Ridge Bicycle Club. Blue Ridge Bicycle Club Staff. (Illus.). 96p. (Orig.). 1997. pap. 9.95 (1-889596-00-0) WMC Pubng.

*Road Bike the Smokies: 16 Great Rides in North Carolina's Great Smoky Mountains. Jim Parham. (Illus.). 96p. (Orig.). 1997. pap. 9.95 (1-889596-02-7) WMC Pubng.

Road Builders. Patricia Armentrout & David Armentrout. LC 95-3976. (Heavy Equipment Ser.). (J). (gr. 2-6). 1995. write for info. (1-55916-136-1) Rourke Bk Co.

Road Builders. B. G. Hennessy. (Illus.). 32p. (J). (ps-2). 1994. pap. 14.99 (0-670-83390-8) Viking Child Bks.

Road Builders. B.G. Hennessy. (Illus.). 32p. (J). 1996. pap. 4.99 (0-14-054276-0) NAL-Dutton.

Road-Building Materials in Texas. J. P. Nash et al. (Bulletin Ser.: BULL 1839). (Illus.). 159p. 1918. pap. 0.50 (0-686-29341-X) Bur Econ Geology.

Road by the River. Djohariah Toor. 240p. 1994. pap. 10.95 (0-312-10454-5) St Martin.

Road Car Inspector. Jack Rudman. (Career Examination Ser.: C-676). 1994. pap. 23.95 (0-8373-0676-0) Nat Learn.

*Road Construction Ahead. Fred Levine. LC 94-35519. (Illus.). (J). 1995. lib. bdg. write for info. (0-06-025428-9) Harper SF.

Road Construction Ahead. Fred Levine. LC 94-35519. (J). 1995. 12.95 (0-06-025427-0) HarpC Child Bks.

Road Construction Equipment. Robert Genat. (Enthusiast Color Ser.). (Illus.). 96p. 1995. pap. 12.95 (0-7603-0040-2) Motorbooks Intl.

*Road Dawg. Grady Mathews & Mike Ives. Date not set. write for info. (0-688-09572-0) Morrow.

Road Design Handbook. 3rd ed. G. Robert Lecklider & John W. Lund. (Illus.). 151p. (C). 1976. pap. text ed. 12.00 (0-9619389-0-0) J W Lund.

Road Deterioration & Maintenance Effects: Models for Planning & Management. William D. Paterson. LC 87-22177. (Highway Design & Maintenance Standards Ser.). 352p. (Orig.). 1988. pap. text ed. 32.95 (0-8018-3590-9) Johns Hopkins.

Road Deterioration in Developing Countries. (Policy Study Ser.). (Illus.). 72p. 1988. 9.95 (0-8213-1039-9, 11039) World Bank.

Road Deterioration in Developing Countries & Low-Volume Road Engineering. (Research Record Ser.: No. 1128). 94p. 1987. 13.00 (0-309-04505-3) Transport Res Bd.

Road Drawings. Bob Dylan. 1994. 30.00 (0-679-41788-5) Random.

Road Ends at Tahola. Richard Hugo. 1978. pap. 3.00 (0-918366-07-0) Slow Loris.

Road Ends at Tahola. deluxe ed. Richard Hugo. 1978. pap. 10.00 (0-918366-08-9) Slow Loris.

Road Fever: A High-Speed Travelogue. Tim Cahill. 256p. 1991. 17.95 (0-394-57656-X) Random.

Road Fever: A High-Speed Travelogue. Tim Cahill. 1992. 10.00 (0-685-51847-7, Vin); pap. 12.00 (0-394-75837-4, Vin) Random.

Road Forks. Dennis Trudell. Ed. by Robert Bixby. 30p. 1994. pap. text ed. 6.00 (1-882983-13-0) March Street Pr.

Road Form & Townscape. 2nd ed. Jim McCluskey. (Illus.). 344p. 1992. 99.95 (0-7506-1245-2) Buttrwrth-Heinemann.

Road from Coorain. Jill Ker Conway. LC 89-40547. 256p. 1990. pap. 11.00 (0-679-72436-2, Vin) Random.

Road from Coorain: An Autobiography. Jill Ker Conway. 1989. 25.00 (0-394-57456-7) Knopf.

Road from Coorain: Recollections of a Harsh & Beautiful Journey into Adulthood. large type ed. Jill Ker Conway. (General Ser.). 394p. 1991. lib. bdg. 21.95 (0-8161-5204-7, GK Hall) Thorndike Pr.

*Road from Damascus: The Impact of Paul's Conversion on His Life, Thought, & Ministry. Richard N. Longenecker. LC 97-7870. (McMaster New Testament Studies). 1997. 25.00 (0-8028-4191-0) Eerdmans.

Road from Decadence: From Brothel to Cloister - Selected Letters of J. K. Huysmans. J. K. Huysmans. Ed. & Tr. by Barbara Beaumont from FRE. 273p. 1989. text ed. 58.50 (0-8142-0492-9) Ohio St U Pr.

Road from Home: The Story of an Armenian Girl. David Kherdian. LC 78-72511. 256p. (YA). (gr. 7 up). 1979. lib. bdg. 15.93 (0-688-84205-4) Greenwillow.

Road from Home: The Story of an Armenian Girl. David Kherdian. LC 78-72511. 256p. (YA). (gr. 6 up). 1995. pap. 4.95 (0-688-14425-X) Morrow.

*Road from Home Cookbook: A Collection of Old-Fashioned Recipes, Many Adapted to Present Day Low-Fat, Low-Cholesterol, & Vegetarian Tastes. Martha B. Allison et al. Ed. by Bonnie B. Lindgren. (Illus.). 110p. (Orig.). 1996. pap. 12.95 (0-9655826-0-4, 1891-96) MCB Partnership. Do you crave the taste of old-fashioned food, but don't want all the fat? Then try the recipes in the ROAD FROM HOME COOKBOOK, recently published by two sisters who have adapted their traditional cooking methods to low fat & vegetarian tastes of families in the 90s. Many of the over 200 recipes have tips on how to cut the fat, without sacrificing taste. The book contains stories of the sisters' childhood, complete with pen & ink illustrations. The book is dedicated to their mother. MCB Partnership, 3716 Farwell, Amarillo, TX 79105. $12.95 plus $2.00 postage & handling. *Publisher Provided Annotation.*

Road from Isolation: The Campaign of the American Committee for Non-Participation in Japanese Aggression, 1938-1941. Donald J. Friedman. LC 68-4047. (East Asian Monographs: No. 25). 131p. (Orig.). 1968. pap. 11.00 (0-674-77370-5) HUP.

Road from Los Alamos: Collected Essays of Hans A. Bethe. Hans Bethe. (Masters of Modern Physics Ser.). 192p. 1991. 24.95 (0-88318-707-8) Am Inst Physics.

Road from Monticello: A Study of the Virginia Slavery Debate of 1832. Joseph C. Robert. LC 70-109912. (Duke University. Trinity College Historical Society. Historical Papers: No. 24). reprint ed. 30.00 (0-404-51774-9) AMS Pr.

Road from Paradise: Prospects for Democracy in Eastern Europe. Stjepan G. Mestrovic et al. LC 92-32442. 224p. 1993. 28.00 (0-8131-1827-1) U Pr of Ky.

Road from Rio: Sustainable Development & the Non-Governmental Movements in the Third World. Julie Fisher. LC 92-35339. 280p. 1993. text ed. 59.95 (0-275-94535-9, C4535, Praeger Pubs) Greenwood.

Road from Rio: Sustainable Development & the Nongovernmental Movement in the Third World. Julie Fisher. LC 92-35339. 264p. 1993. pap. text ed. 22.95 (0-275-94715-7, Praeger Pubs) Greenwood.

Road from Serfdom. Robert J. Skidelsky. 224p. 1996. pap. 26.95 (0-7139-9122-4, A Lane) Viking Penguin.

*Road from Serfdom. Robert J. Skidelsky. 1997. pap. 12.95 (0-14-024219-8) Viking Penguin.

Road from Singapore. large type ed. Diana Norman. 1974. 25.99 (0-85456-287-7) Ulverscroft.

Road from the Past. Ina Caro. 352p. 1996. pap. 15.00 (0-15-600363-5) HarBrace.

Road Guide: Arches National Park. Arches National Park Intrepretive Staff. Ed. by Peter Anderson. (Illus.). 32p. 1992. 2.00 (0-937407-03-8) Canyonlands.

*Road Guide Natural Bridges National Monument. Jim Dougan & Ann E. Lundberg. Ed. by Jeanne Treadway. (Illus.). 32p. (Orig.). 1996. pap. 2.00 (0-937407-05-4) Canyonlands.

Road Guide to Backcountry Dirt Roads of Big Bend National Park. Ed. by John R. Pearson. (Illus.). 40p. (Orig.). 1980. pap. 1.25 (0-912001-01-1) Big Bend.

Road Guide to Crater Lake National Park. Robert Decker & Barbara Decker. (Illus.). 48p. (Orig.). 1988. pap. 4.50 (0-9621019-2-3) Double Mariposa.

Road Guide to Death Valley. Barbara Decker & Robert Decker. (Illus.). 48p. (Orig.). 1989. pap. 4.50 (0-9621019-3-1) Double Mariposa.

Road Guide to Haleakala & the Hana Highway. Robert Decker & Barbara Decker. (Illus.). 48p. (Orig.). 1990. pap. 4.50 (0-9621019-4-X) Double Mariposa.

Road Guide to Hawaii Volcanoes National Park. Barbara Decker & Robert Decker. (Illus.). 48p. 1986. pap. 4.50 (0-9621019-0-7) Double Mariposa.

Road Guide to Hawaii Volcanoes National Park. 2nd rev. ed. Barbara Decker & Robert Decker. (Illus.). 48p. 1987. reprint ed. pap. 4.50 (0-9621019-1-5) Double Mariposa.

Road Guide to Paved & Improved Dirt Roads of Big Bend National Park. Ed. by John R. Pearson. (Illus.). 48p. (Orig.). 1980. pap. 1.25 (0-912001-02-X) Big Bend.

Road Guide to the Geology of Big Bend National Park. Kerri Nelson. (Illus.). 76p. (Orig.). 1995. spiral bd. 6.95 (0-912001-15-1) Big Bend.

Road Hog. Jan Pienkowski. (Pienkowski Pop-up Sound Ser.). (Illus.). 10p. (J). (ps up). 1993. 13.99 (0-8431-3586-7) Price Stern Sloan.

Road Hogs (for TMNT) Erick Wujcik. Ed. by Alex Marciniszyn. (After the Bomb Ser.: Bk. 2). (Illus.). 48p. (YA). (gr. 8 up). 1986. pap. 7.95 (0-916211-20-7, 505) Palladium Bks.

Road Home. Joel Rosenberg. LC 94-27301. 272p. 1995. 21.95 (0-451-45433-2, ROC) NAL-Dutton.

Road Home. Joel Rosenberg. 320p. 1995. mass mkt. 5.99 (0-451-45450-2, ROC) NAL-Dutton.

*Road Home. Eliza Thomas. LC 96-53975. 196p. 1997. 16.95 (1-56512-169-4, 72169) Algonquin Bks.

Road Home. Ellen E. White. LC 94-32173. 464p. (J). (gr. 7-9). 1995. 15.95 (0-590-46737-9) Scholastic Inc.

*Road Home: A Photographic Journey. Jon Farrar. (Illus.). 132p. 1995. 24.95 (0-9625959-3-4) NE Game & Parks.

Road I Came: Some Recollections & Reflections Concerning Changes in American Life & Manner Since 1890. Paul J. Smith. LC 60-11328. 476p. reprint ed. pap. 135.70 (0-685-15253-7, 2027150) Bks Demand.

Road in the Dark. Mary Griffith. LC 85-875. 1986. pap. 13.95 (0-87949-257-0) Ashley Bks.

Road Infrastructure Rehabilitation & Safety Strategies in Central & Eastern Europe. OECD Staff. (Road Transport Research Ser.). 188p. (Orig.). 1995. pap. 37.00 (92-64-14579-6, Pub. by Org for Econ FR) OECD.

Road into the Open. Arthur Schnitzler. Tr. by Roger Byers. LC 91-31559. 314p. (C). 1992. 48.00 (0-520-07575-7); pap. 14.00 (0-520-07774-1) U CA Pr.

Road Is For Walking. John R. Terry. 120p. 1988. pap. 4.95 (0-933704-40-2) Dawn Pr.

*Road Kill. Kinky Friedman. LC 97-10201. 1997. 23.00 (0-684-80378-X) S&S Trade.

*Road Kill. Thomas Hughes. 1998. 6.99 (0-679-88668-0) Random Bks Yng Read.

Road Kill. Larry Johnson. Ed. by Doug Tabb. (Champions Ser.). (Illus.). 32p. (Orig.). (YA). (gr. 12). 1991. pap. 7.00 (1-55806-117-7, 415) Iron Crown Ent Inc.

Road Kill Cooking - Redneck Style, Vol. II: And More Tails from the Fast Lane. Jeff Eberbaugh. (Illus.). 52p. 1992. spiral bd. 7.95 (0-9629996-1-X) Rd Kill Cookbks.

Road Kill Cooking Gourmet Style, Vol. I. rev. ed. Jeff Eberbaugh. (Illus.). 96p. 1994. pap. 7.95 (1-886950-00-8) United Cutlery.

Road Kill Cooking Redneck Style, Vol. II. rev. ed. Jeff Eberbaugh. (Illus.). 96p. 1994. pap. 7.95 (1-886950-01-6) United Cutlery.

*Road Less Graveled. Brent Holmes. (Illus.). 128p. (Orig.). 1997. pap. 9.95 (0-942407-34-2) Father & Son.

*Road Less Traveled. Peck. 1998. pap. 15.00 (0-684-84728-0) S&S Trade.

Road Less Traveled: A New Psychology of Love, Traditional Values & Spiritual Growth. M. Scott Peck. 322p. 1980. pap. 12.00 (0-671-25067-1, Touchstone Bks) S&S Trade.

Road Less Traveled: A New Psychology of Love, Traditional Values & Spiritual Growth. M. Scott Peck. 322p. 1988. pap. 14.00 (0-671-67300-9, Touchstone Bks) S&S Trade.

Road Less Traveled: A New Psychology of Love, Traditional Values & Spiritual Growth. large type ed. M. Scott Peck. 448p. 1985. pap. 16.95 (0-8027-2498-1) Walker & Co.

Road Less Traveled: A New Psychology of Love, Traditional Values & Spiritual Growth. M. Scott Peck. 1993. reprint ed. lib. bdg. 28.95 (1-56849-158-1, Touchstone Bks) S&S Trade.

*Road Less Traveled & Beyond. M. Scott Peck. 1998. pap. 13.00 (0-684-83561-4) S&S Trade.

Road Less Traveled & Beyond: Spiritual Growth in an Age of Anxiety. M. Scott Peck. LC 96-43391. 1997. 23.00 (0-684-81314-9) S&S Trade.

*Road Less Traveled & Beyond: Spiritual Growth in an Age of Anxiety. large type ed. M. Scott Peck. LC 96-44451. 463p. 1997. 26.95 (0-7862-0943-7, Thorndike Lrg Prnt) Thorndike Pr.

*Road Less Traveled & Beyond: Spiritual Growth in an Age of Anxiety. large type ed. M. Scott Peck. 1997. pap. 24.95 (0-7862-0944-5) Thorndike Pr.

Road Magic, Pt. 1. Susan Foss. Ed. by Jim Erickson. LC 93-77696. (True Adventure Ser.). (Illus.). 341p. (Orig.). 1993. pap. 12.50 (1-883557-01-1) S Foss.

Road Magic, Pt. 2. Susan Foss. Ed. by Jim Erickson. LC 93-77696. (True Adventure Ser.). (Illus.). 302p. (Orig.). 1994. pap. 12.50 (1-883557-03-8) S Foss.

Road Maintenance & Regravelling Using Labour-Bated Methods (ROMAR) Handbook. Claes-Axel Anderssen et al. (Orig.). 1996. pap. 24.95 (1-85339-348-7, Pub. by Intermed Tech UK) Women Ink.

Road Maintenance & Regravelling Using Labour-Based Methods (ROMAR) Workbook. Claes-Axel Anderssen et al. (Orig.). 1996. pap. 18.95 (1-85339-349-5, Pub. by Intermed Tech UK) Women Ink.

Road Maintenance & Rehabilitation: Funding & Allocation Strategies. OECD Staff. 159p. (Orig.). 1994. pap. 36.00 (92-64-14277-0) OECD.

Road Maintenance Initiative: Building Capacity for Policy Reform: Report on the Policy Seminars. Steve Carapetis et al. (EDI Seminar Ser.: Vol. 1). 96p. 1991. English ed. 7.95 (0-8213-1859-4, 11859) World Bank.

Road Maintenance Management Systems in Developing Countries. OECD Staff. 208p. (Orig.). 1995. pap. 49.00 (92-64-14300-9) OECD.

Road Mangler Deluxe. Phil Kaufman & Colin White. Ed. by Laurie Boucke. LC 94-124384. (Illus.). 368p. (Orig.). 1993. pap. 12.95 (0-9625006-5-8) White-Boucke.

Road Map for Federal Acquisition (FAR) Reform. Debra Van Opstal. LC 95-13776. (CSIS Report Ser.). 74p. (C). 1995. pap. text ed. 19.95 (0-89206-320-3) CSI Studies.

*Road Map of Head & Neck Anatomy. Rumy Hilloowala. (Illus.). 115p. (Orig.). (C). 1996. pap. text ed. 21.95 (0-943025-85-0) Cummngs & Hath.

Road Map to an American Renaissance. John M. Humphrey. 1993. 16.95 (0-533-10539-0) Vantage.

Road Map to Recovery. Cynthia F. Driskell. 1994. 10.00 (0-533-10758-X) Vantage.

Road Map to Repeatable Success: Using QFD to Implement Change. Barbara A. Bicknell & Kris D. Bicknell. LC 94-17627. (Systems Engineering Ser.). 368p. 1994. 61.95 (0-8493-8019-7) CRC Pr.

Road Map to Success: A Unique Development Guide for Small Arts Groups. 173p. 1988. pap. 14.95 (0-685-54650-0, 6800, ACA Bks) Am Council Arts.

Road Map to Your Job Search: A Complete Guide to Finding & Keeping a Job. Godfred T. Ansah. Ed. by Richard McGinnis. LC 95-94458. (Illus.). 210p. 1995. 24.95 (0-9646559-0-X) G T Ansah.

Road-Maps to Prosperity: Essays on Growth & Development. Andres Solimano. (C). 1996. 49.50 (0-472-10729-1) U of Mich Pr.

Road Maps to Success Series, 12 bks. 1993. pap. 15.00 (0-318-72969-5) Corwin Pr.

Road Monitoring for Maintenance Management: Road Transport Research, 2 vols., Set. OECD Staff. 204p. (Orig.). 1990. pap. 22.95 (92-64-13309-7) OECD.

*Road More Traveled. Brookes. Date not set. pap. 10.00 (0-8050-5367-0) H Holt & Co.

*Road More Traveled. Brookes. 1998. 20.00 (0-8050-5366-2) H Holt & Co.

Road Most Traveled: Releasing the Power of Contentment in Your Life. Robert Jeffress. 192p. 1996. pap. 11.99 (0-8054-6266-X, 4262-66) Broadman.

*Road Movie. Godfrey Hamilton. 50p. (Orig.). 1996. pap. 13.95 (1-85459-301-3, Pub. by N Hern Bks UK) Theatre Comm.

*Road Movie Book. Steven Cohan & Ina R. Hark. LC 97-8924. 368p. 1997. pap. write for info. (0-415-14937-1) Routledge.

*Road Movie Book. Steven Cohan & Ina R. Hark. LC 97-8924. 368p. (C). 1997. text ed. write for info. (0-415-14936-3) Routledge.

Road Movies. Lee Ranaldo. 1994. pap. 6.00 (1-887128-07-7) Soft Skull Pr.

Road News from Tibet. R. Langlais. 227p. 1995. 42.95 (0-387-56965-0) Spr-Verlag.

Road Noise & Sentiments. Moustache Pete. (Illus.). 65p. (Orig.). 1987. pap. 6.95 (0-939303-03-5) Educ Lrn Syst.

Road North: One Woman's Adventure Driving the Alaska Highway 1947-1948. Iris Woolcock. Ed. by Edward Bovy. (Illus.). 160p. (Orig.). 1990. pap. 11.95 (0-936425-10-5) Greatland Graphics.

Road Not Taken: A Selection of Robert Frost's Poems. Robert Frost. Ed. by Louis Untermeyer. LC 51-9831. 320p. 1951. 25.00 (0-8050-0529-3) H Holt & Co.

Road Not Taken: A Selection of Robert Frost's Poems. Robert Frost. Ed. by Louis Untermeyer. LC 85-8397. 320p. 1985. reprint ed. pap. 12.95 (0-8050-0528-5, Owl) H Holt & Co.

Road Not Taken: An Introduction to Robert Frost. Robert Frost. LC 51-9831. (Illus.). (J). (gr. 9 up). 1951. 16.95 (0-03-027150-9, Bks Young Read) H Holt & Co.

Road Not Taken: An Introduction to Robert Frost. Robert Frost. LC 51-9831. (Illus.). (J). (gr. 9 up). 1985. pap. 8.95 (0-03-000073-4, Bks Young Read) H Holt & Co.

Road Not Taken: Early Arab-Israeli Negotiations. Itamar Rabinovich. 272p. 1991. 25.00 (0-19-506066-0) OUP.

Road Not Taken & Other Poems. Robert Frost. LC 92-31553. (Thrift Editions Ser.). Orig. Title: Mountain Interval. 64p. 1993. reprint ed. pap. 1.00 (0-486-27550-7) Dover.

Road of Dreams: A Two-Year Bicycling & Hiking Adventure Around the World. Bruce B. Junek. LC 91-73331. (Illus.). 288p. (Orig.). 1991. pap. 12.95 (0-9630448-1-8) Images of the Wrld.

Road of Inquiry: Charles Pierce's Pragmatic Realism. Peter Skagestad. LC 80-25278. 261p. 1981. text ed. 54.00 (0-231-05004-6) Col U Pr.

Road of Life. Ed. by Blaire Meyer et al. (Illus.). 70p. (Orig.). 1987. pap. 5.00 (0-9615214-1-4) Barton Cty Comm.

Road of Life & Death: A Ritual Drama of the American Indians. P. Radin. (Mythos: The Princeton - Bollingen Series in World Mythology). 368p. 1991. pap. text ed. 17.95 (0-691-01916-9) Princeton U Pr.

Road of Stars to Santiago. Edward R. Stanton. LC 93-39521. 208p. 1994. pap. 24.95 (0-8131-1871-9) U Pr of Ky.

Road of the Sun. Emilie. 32p. 1987. 20.00 (0-7223-2143-0, Pub. by A H S Ltd UK) St Mut.

Road of the Sun: Travels of the Zodiac King in Near Eastern & European Myth. D. August Hunt. LC 86-80967. (Illus.). 118p. (Orig.). 1987. pap. 20.00 (0-911437-40-1) Labyrinthos.

Road on Which We Came - Po'i Pentun Tammen Kimmappeh: A History of the Western Shoshone. Steven J. Crum. LC 93-39441. (Illus.). 248p. 1994. 29.95 (0-87480-434-5) U of Utah Pr.

Road on Which We Came - Po'i Pentun Tammen Kimmappeh: A History of the Western Shoshone. Steven J. Crum. 248p. (C). 1996. reprint ed. pap. 19.95 (0-87480-509-0) U of Utah Pr.

Road Past Altamont. Gabrielle Roy. Tr. by Joyce Marshall. LC 93-14195. vi, 147p. 1993. pap. 7.95 (0-8032-8948-0, Bison Books) U of Nebr Pr.

*Road Past Altamont. Gabrielle Roy. 1996. pap. text ed. 6.95 (0-7710-9856-1) McCland & Stewart.

Road Past the View. Anita Barrows. (QRL Poetry Bks.: Vol. XXXI). 1992. 20.00 (0-614-06446-5) Quarterly Rev.

Road Pirates. Franklin W. Dixon. Ed. by Anne Greenberg. (Hardy Boys Casefiles Ser.: No. 74). 160p. (Orig.). (YA). (gr. 6 up). 1993. mass mkt. 3.99 (0-671-73110-6, Archway) PB.

Road Pricing: Theory, Empirical Assessment & Policy. Ed. by Borge Johansson & Lars-Goran Mattsson. (Transportation Research, Economics & Policy Ser.: Vol. 3). 248p. (C). 1994. lib. bdg. 81.50 (0-7923-3134-6) Kluwer Ac.

Road Project Appraisal for Developing Countries. John W. Dickey & Leon H. Miller. LC 83-10270. (Illus.). 293p. reprint ed. pap. 83.60 (0-8357-3519-2, 2034222) Bks Demand.

*Road Racers & Their Training. Joe Henderson. 200p. (Orig.). 1995. pap. 15.00 (0-911521-44-5) Tafnews.

Road Racing Technique & Training. Bernard Hinault & Claude Genzling. Ed. by Barbara George. Tr. by Veronica Brelsford & Georges Herzog from FRE. LC 87-82146. 208p. 1988. 17.95 (0-941950-13-1) Vitesse Pr.

*Road Rage! Tony White. 128p. (Orig.). 1997. pap. 12.95 (1-898928-25-8, Pub. by S T Pubng UK) AK Pr Dist.

*Road Rage. large type ed. Ruth Rendell. LC 97-11737. (Large Print Ser.). 1997. pap. 25.00 (0-679-77443-2) Random.

Road Rally Handbook: The Complete Guide to Competing in Time-Speed-Distance Road Rallies. Clint Goss. (Illus.). 368p. 1993. pap. 34.95 (0-9632401-0-2) Rally Am.

An Asterisk (*) at the beginning of an entry indicates that the title is appearing in BIP for the first time.

Road Retaken: Women Reenter the Academy. Ed. by Irene Thompson & Audrey Roberts. vi, 152p. 1985. pap. 19.75 (*0-87352-341-5*, B817P); lib. bdg. 37.50 (*0-87352-340-7*, B817C) Modern Lang.

Road Roller Saves the Day. Jill Barnes & Junkichi Kanabe. Ed. by Caroline Rubin. Tr. by Japan Foreign Rights Centre Staff from JPN. LC 90-3841. (Dragonfly Tales Ser.). (Illus.). 40p. (J). (gr. k-3). 1990. lib. bdg. 15.93 (*0-944483-81-X*) Garrett Ed Corp.

Road Rollers. Derek Rayner. 1989. pap. 25.00 (*0-7478-0153-3*, Pub. by Shire UK) St Mut.

***Road Rules Book 2.** MTV Staff. 1997. pap. 18.00 (*0-671-01536-2*, MTV Bks) PB.

***Road Runners & Sandwich Terns: Exploring Birds with Children.** Suzanne Samson. (Illus.). 32p. (J). (gr. 1-5). 1997. pap. 9.95 (*1-57098-129-9*) R Rinehart.

Road Safety: Research & Practice. Ed. by Hugh Foot et al. LC 81-191962. 244p. 1981. text ed. 55.00 (*0-275-90625-6*, C0625, Praeger Pubs) Greenwood.

Road Safety Education for Young Children & Teenagers: Fourth Joint ECMT - Council of Europe Conference. OECD Staff. 250p. (Orig.). 1994. pap. 42.00 (*92-821-1195-4*) OECD.

***Road Scholar: An Investigative Journal for the College-Bound Student.** Risa Nye. (Illus.). 90p. (Orig.). (YA). (gr. 10-12). 1996. pap. 10.00 (*0-9657203-0-6*) No Flak.

Road Scholar: Coast to Coast Late in the Century. Andrei Codrescu. LC 92-38416. (Illus.). 224p. 1993. 19.95 (*1-56282-878-9*) Hyperion.

Road Scholars: The Story of Twenty-Eight Kids Who Decided to Take a Hike for Their Health. Robert Sweetgall & Dorith E. Peleg. (Illus.). 64p. (Orig.). (YA). 1989. pap. 6.00 (*0-939041-07-3*) Creative Walking.

Road School. Jim Marousis et al. 1995. pap. 14.95 (*0-933025-36-X*) Blue Bird Pub.

Road Show. Murray Schisgal. 1987. pap. 5.25 (*0-8222-0957-8*) Dramatists Play.

Road Show: A Handbook for Successful Booking & Touring in the Performing Arts. Rena Shagan. LC 84-20491. (Illus.). 268p. (Orig.). (C). 1985. pap. 15.95 (*0-915400-48-0*, 6850, ACA Bks) Am Council Arts.

Road Sign Games. Thomson C. Murray. 1993. pap. 3.95 (*0-87131-750-8*) M Evans.

Road Signs for Success. Jim Whitt. 208p. 1993. pap. 12.95 (*0-9636719-0-1*) J Whitt.

Road Song. Natalie Kusz. 256p. 1990. 18.95 (*0-374-25121-5*) FS&G.

Road Song. large type ed. Natalie Kusz. 395p. 1991. reprint ed. lib. bdg. 20.95 (*1-56054-138-5*) Thorndike Pr.

Road Song: A Memoir. Natalie Kusz. LC 91-55156. 272p. 1991. reprint ed. pap. 12.00 (*0-06-097425-7*, PL) HarpC.

Road Stories & Recipes: The World's First Rock'n'Roll Cookbook. Nix. 1998. 15.00 (*0-02-864625-8*) Schirmer Bks.

Road Stories & Recipes: The World's First Rock'n'Roll Cookbook. Don Nix. LC 96-27474. 1997. 25.00 (*0-02-864621-5*) Macmillan.

Road Strengthening in Central & Eastern European Countries. OECD Staff. (Road Transport Research Ser.). 150p. (Orig.). 1993. pap. text ed. 27.00 (*92-64-13988-5*, 77-93-03-1) OECD.

***Road Swing: One Fan's Journey into the Soul of American Sports.** Steve Rushin. 256p. 1997. 22.95 (*0-385-48229-9*, Anchor NY) Doubleday.

Road Taken: The New Hampshire Library Association, 1889-1989. Ed. by Shirley G. Adamovich. LC 89-30525. (Illus.). 120p. 1989. 17.50 (*0-914659-40-5*, 30525) Phoenix Pub.

Road That Bends. Ruby M. Ayres. 1975. lib. bdg. 15.80 (*0-89966-004-5*) Buccaneer Bks.

Road That Is Not a Road & the Open City, Ritoque, Chile. Ann M. Pendleton-Jullian. (Graham Foundation/MIT Press Series in Contemporary Discourse). (Illus.). 304p. (C). 1996. pap. 17.50 (*0-262-66099-7*) MIT Pr.

Road Through Kurdistan. Archibald M. Hamilton. LC 70-180345. reprint ed. 42.50 (*0-404-56275-2*) AMS Pr.

Road Through Miyama. Leila Philip. 1989. 17.95 (*0-394-57818-X*) Random.

Road Through Miyama. Leila Philip. LC 90-50149. (Vintage Departures Ser.). 288p. 1991. pap. 9.95 (*0-679-72501-6*, Vin) Random.

Road Through the Ages. Philip Steele. LC 91-35878. (Through the Ages Ser.). (Illus.). 32p. (J). (gr. 3-6). 1993. lib. bdg. 13.95 (*0-8167-2737-6*) Troll Communs.

Road Through the Ages. Philip Steele. LC 91-35878. (Through the Ages Ser.). (Illus.). 32p. (J). (gr. 3-6). 1997. pap. 4.95 (*0-8167-2738-4*) Troll Communs.

Road Through the Isles. John Sharkey & Keith Payne. 256p. 1986. text ed. 34.95 (*0-7045-0498-7*, Pub. by Gower UK) Ashgate Pub Co.

Road Through the Rain Forest: Living Anthropology in Highland Papua New Guinea. David M. Hayano. (Illus.). 164p. (Orig.). (C). 1990. pap. text ed. 10.50 (*0-88133-505-3*) Waveland Pr.

Road Through the Wilderness: The Story of the Transcontinental Railway. David Burke. (Illus.). 296p. 39.95 (*0-86840-140-4*, Pub. by New South Wales Univ Pr AT) Intl Spec Bk.

Road to a Championship. Clelia Kruel. (Illus.). 131p. (Orig.). 1996. 25.00 (*0-945402-02-3*) Kruel Pubns.

Road to a Free Economy: Shifting From a Socialist System the Example of Hungary. Janos Kornai. 160p. (Orig.). (C). 1991. pap. text ed. 9.95 (*0-393-30691-7*) Norton.

Road to American Wines & Vines. Pamela Stovall. 1990. pap. 9.95 (*0-671-66899-4*, Fireside) S&S Trade.

Road to Appomattox. Bell I. Wiley. LC 56-13465. (Illus.). 152p. 1994. pap. 9.95 (*0-8071-1911-3*) La State U Pr.

Road to Appomattox: A Sourcebook on the Civil War. Ed. by Carter Smith. LC 92-16546. (American Albums from the Collections of the Library of Congress). (Illus.). 96p. (J). (gr. 5-8). 1993. pap. 8.95 (*1-56294-881-4*); lib. bdg. 19.90 (*1-56294-264-6*) Millbrook Pr.

Road to Armageddon: The Martial Spirit in English Popular Literature, 1870-1914. Cecil D. Eby. LC 87-9212. ix, 280p. (C). 1988. text ed. 35.95 (*0-8223-0775-8*) Duke.

Road to Athletic Scholarship: What Every Student-Athlete, Parent & Coach Needs to Know. Kim McQuilken. LC 96-19530. 210p. (C). 1996. 35.00 (*0-8147-5530-5*); pap. 12.95 (*0-8147-5546-1*) NYU Pr.

Road to Auschwitz: Fragments of a Life. Hedi Fried. Ed. & Tr. by Michael Meyer. LC 96-8536. 190p. 1996. pap. 10.00 (*0-8032-6893-9*, Bison Books) U of Nebr Pr.

Road to Avalon. Joan Wolf. 432p. 1989. pap. 4.50 (*0-451-40138-7*, Onyx) NAL-Dutton.

***Road to Ballybunion.** John Degarmo. 1997. 29.95 (*1-56352-433-3*) Longstreet Pr Inc.

Road to Bellapais: The Turkish Cypriot Exodus to Northern Cyprus. Pierre Oberling. (Brooklyn College Studies on Society in Change). 256p. 1982. text ed. 48.00 (*0-88033-000-7*) East Eur Monographs.

***Road to Bendour.** large type ed. Joyce Eaglestone. (Linford Romance Large Print Ser.). 384p. 1997. pap. 16.99 (*0-7089-7982-3*, Linford) Ulverscroft.

Road to Biomechanics: Selected Papers. Yuan-Cheng B. Fung. LC 97-12963. 1860p. 1997. text ed. 190.00 (*981-02-2063-4*) World Scientific Pub.

Road to Birth Game. Julie Burns & Frank Bialosiewicz. (Technical Notes Ser.: No. 24). (Illus.). 33p. (Orig.). 1983. pap. text ed. 2.00 (*0-932288-71-5*) Ctr Intl Ed U of MA.

***Road to Bloody Sunday: Cultures in Conflict.** 2nd rev. ed. Rayond McClean. (Illus.). 174p. 1997. pap. 11.95 (*0-946451-37-0*, Pub. by Guildhall Pr IE) Irish Bks Media.

Road to Bloody Sunday: Father Gapon & the Petersburg Massacre of 1905. Walter Sablinsky. LC 75-30206. (Studies of the Russian Institute, Columbia University & Harvard Series in Ukrainian Studies). 432p. 1976. pap. text ed. 22.95 (*0-691-10204-X*) Princeton U Pr.

Road to Botany Bay: An Exploration of Landscape & History. Paul Carter. LC 87-46076. 1988. 22.95 (*0-394-57035-9*) Knopf.

Road to Box Office: The Seven Film Comedies of Bing Crosby, Bob Hope & Dorothy Lamour 1940-1662. Randall G. Mielke. LC 96-52179. (Illus.). 171p. 1997. lib. bdg. 34.50 (*0-7864-0162-1*) McFarland & Co.

Road to Brightcity. Mairtin O'Cadhain. 112p. 8100. pap. 10.95 (*0-905169-47-6*, Pub. by Poolbeg Pr IE) Dufour.

Road to Bristoe Station Campaigning with Lee & Meade, August 1-October 20, 1863. William D. Henderson. (Illus.). 259p. 1987. 19.95 (*0-930919-45-9*) H E Howard.

Road to Buenos Aires. Albert Londres. 260p. 1974. lib. bdg. 59.95 (*0-8490-0959-6*) Gordon Pr.

Road to Calvary. Alfred J. Garrotto. 30p. (Orig.). 1995. spiral bd. 6.00 (*1-885587-09-0*) Bridge Lrn Systs.

Road to Camlann: The Death of King Arthur. Rosemary Sutcliff. 144p. (J). (gr. 7 up). 1994. pap. 3.99 (*0-14-037147-8*) Puffin Bks.

Road to Camp David: U. S. Negotiating Strategy Towards the Arab-Israeli Conflict. Thomas Parker. (American University Studies: Political Science: Ser. X, Vol. 9). 175p. (C). 1989. text ed. 39.00 (*0-8204-0495-0*) P Lang Pubng.

Road to Canaan. Pernet Patterson. 1977. 17.95 (*0-8369-9193-1*, 9062) Ayer.

Road to Canterbury: A Modern Pilgrimage. Shirley Du Boulay. LC 95-22775. (Illus.). 256p. 1995. reprint ed. pap. 14.95 (*0-8192-1645-3*) Morehouse Pub.

Road to Capitalism: Economic Transformation in Eastern Europe & the Former Soviet Union. Ed. by David Kennett & Marc Lieberman. 382p. (Orig.). (C). 1993. pap. text ed. 20.00 (*0-03-096374-5*) Dryden Pr.

Road to Chaos: The Destruction of the United States Constitution. McClelland C. Smith. 112p. 1996. pap. 11.00 (*0-8059-3855-9*) Dorrance.

Road to Chlifa. Michele Marineau. Tr. by Susan Ouriou. 144p. (YA). (gr. 9 up). 1992. pap. 8.95 (*0-88995-129-2*, Pub. by Red Deer CN) Orca Bk Pubs.

Road to Chumba. Leoda Buckwalter. LC 94-71563. 188p. (Orig.). (YA). 1994. pap. 7.95 (*0-916035-60-3*) Evangel Indiana.

Road to Cibola. Carl O. Sauer. LC 76-43819. (Ibero-Americana Ser.: No. 3). reprint ed. 34.50 (*0-404-15669-X*) AMS Pr.

Road to College, 1997. Kaplan. Date not set. pap. 29.95 incl. disk (*0-684-83390-5*) S&S Trade.

Road to College, 1997. Kaplan. 1996. pap. 20.00 (*0-684-83389-1*) S&S Trade.

***Road to College 1998.** Kaplan Staff. 1997. pap. 22.95 incl. cd-rom (*0-684-84166-5*) S&S Trade.

Road to Confederation: The Emergence of Canada, 1863-1867. Donald G. Creighton. LC 75-27652. (Illus.). 489p. 1976. reprint ed. text ed. 35.00 (*0-8371-8435-5*, CRRC, Greenwood Pr) Greenwood.

Road to Confrontation: American Policy Toward China & Korea, 1947-1950. William W. Stueck. LC 80-11818. 336p. reprint ed. pap. 95.80 (*0-8357-4402-7*, 2037222) Bks Demand.

Road to Corinth: Playscript. Alan L. Steinberg. (Orig.). 1984. pap. 5.00 (*0-88734-211-6*) Players Pr.

Road to Creative Sales: Power Selling Secrets for the '90s. Jones Baber & Elaine Thomas. LC 93-93939. (Illus.). 117p. (Orig.). 1993. pap. 9.95 (*0-9636855-0-3*) E Thomas & Assocs.

***Road to Damascus.** Lucas. Date not set. text ed. 39.50 (*1-86064-152-0*, Pub. by I B Tauris UK) St Martin.

Road to Damascus. Wyatt T. Walker. 163p. 1985. 10.00 (*0-937644-03-X*) M L King Pr.

Road to Damietta. Scott O'Dell. 240p. (J). 1987. mass mkt. 4.50 (*0-449-70233-2*, Juniper) Fawcett.

Road to Daulis: Psychoanalysis, Psychology & Classical Mythology. Robert Eisner. 284p. 1987. 42.50 (*0-8156-0210-3*) Syracuse U Pr.

Road to Daybreak. Henri J. Nouwen. 240p. 1990. pap. 11.00 (*0-385-41607-5*) Doubleday.

***Road to Deschapelles: The Story of Hopital Albert Schweitzer.** Gwen G. Mellon. 1997. 40.00 (*0-8264-1055-3*) Continuum.

Road to Disappearance: A History of the Creek Indians. Angie Debo. LC 42-1342. (Civilization of the American Indian Ser.). (Orig.). 1979. pap. 17.95 (*0-8061-1532-7*) U of Okla Pr.

Road to Disillusion: From Critical Marxism to Post-Communism in Eastern Europe. Ed. by Raymond C. Taras. LC 90-27828. 216p. (C). (gr. 13). 1992. text ed. 72.95 (*0-87332-790-X*); pap. text ed. 30.95 (*0-87332-791-8*) M E Sharpe.

Road to Disunion, Vol. One: Secessionists at Bay, 1776-1854. (Illus.). 656p. 1991. reprint ed. pap. 21.95 (*0-19-507259-6*) OUP.

Road to Disunion, Vol. 1: Secessionists at Bay, 1776-1854. William W. Freehling. (Illus.). 656p. 1990. 30.00 (*0-19-505814-3*) OUP.

Road to Divorce: England 1530-1987. Lawrence Stone. (Illus.). 496p. 1990. 35.00 (*0-19-822651-9*) OUP.

Road to Divorce: England 1530-1987. Lawrence Stone. (Illus.). 496p. 1995. pap. 17.95 (*0-19-285307-4*) OUP.

Road to East Slope: The Development of Su Shi's Poetic Voice. Michael A. Fuller. 400p. 1990. 47.50 (*0-8047-1587-4*) Stanford U Pr.

Road to Economic Recovery: Report of the Twentieth Century Fund Task Force on International Debt. (Orig.). 1989. pap. 9.95 (*0-87078-227-4*); text ed. 18.95 (*0-87078-228-2*) TCFP-PPP.

Road to Ehvenor. Joel Rosenberg. (Guardians of the Flame Ser.). 320p. (Orig.). 1992. pap. 5.50 (*0-451-45191-0*, ROC) NAL-Dutton.

Road to El-Aguzein. M. V. Seton-Williams. (Illus.). 220p. 1988. text ed. 32.50 (*0-7103-0286-X*) Routledge Chapman & Hall.

***Road to El Dorado.** Ed. by Len Appiano. 450p. 1997. pap. 19.95 (*0-9620286-1-4*) Suthrn Trails Pub.

Road to Emancipation. David C. Klingaman. 1996. write for info. (*0-201-48318-1*) Addison-Wesley.

Road to Emancipation. Sten Nadolny. Date not set. pap. 29.95 (*0-670-86754-3*) Viking Penguin.

Road to Emmaus: A New Model for Catechesis. Dominic F. Ashkar. LC 93-17566. 208p. (Orig.). (C). 1993. pap. text ed. 14.95 (*0-89390-266-7*) Resource Pubns.

Road to Emmaus: Daily Encounters with the Risen Christ. Joseph W. Houle et al. (Illus.). 416p. (Orig.). 1989. pap. 12.95 (*0-9624901-0-5*) Emmaus Pr.

Road to Emmaus: Reading Luke's Gospel. Jan Wojcik. LC 88-27313. 180p. 1989. 21.50 (*1-55753-000-9*) Purdue U Pr.

Road to Equality: Evolution & Social Reality. Seymour W. Itzkoff. LC 92-12113. 240p. 1992. text ed. 39.95 (*0-275-94400-X*, C4400, Praeger Pubs) Greenwood.

Road to Equality: American Women Since 1962 see Young Oxford History of Women in the United States

Road to Europe. Ferdinand Oyono. Tr. by Richard Bjornson from FRE. LC 86-51301. 120p. (Orig.). 1989. 24.00 (*0-89410-590-6*, Three Contnts); pap. 10.00 (*0-89410-591-4*, Three Contnts) Lynne Rienner.

Road to Europe: History, Institutions & Prospects of European Integration 1945-1993. David W. Lewis. 488p. 1993. pap. 29.95 (*0-8204-2113-8*) P Lang Pubng.

Road to Europe: The Past & Future of European Integration, 1945-1993. David W. Lewis. LC 91-16050. 488p. (C). 1993. text ed. 69.95 (*0-8204-1640-1*) P Lang Pubng.

Road to Excellence: The Acquisition of Expert Performance in the Arts & Sciences, Sports, & Games. Ed. by K. Anders Ericsson. 384p. 1996. 69.95 (*0-8058-2231-3*); pap. text ed. 22.50 (*0-8058-2232-1*) L Erlbaum Assocs.

***Road to Exile.** Didier Nebot. Tr. by Henri M. Moyal from FRE. Orig. Title: Le Chemin de L'Exil. 312p. (Orig.). 1997. pap. 18.50 (*1-881283-16-X*) Alef Design.

Road to Extinction: Problems of Categorizing the Status of Taxa Threatened with Extinction - Proceedings of a Symposium Held by the Species Survival Commission of IUCN in Madrid, November, 1984. Richard Fitter & Maisie S. Fitter. (International Union for the Conservation of Nature & Natural Resources: A Belhaven Press Book Ser.). (Illus.). 132p. 1987. pap. 15.00 (*2-88032-929-9*, Pub. by IUCN SZ) Island Pr.

***Road to Financial Integration: Private Capital Flows to Developing Economies.** LC 97-11785. (Policy Research Reports). 300p. 1997. 40.00 (*0-19-521116-2*, 61116) World Bank.

Road to Fitzgerald & Beyond. rev. ed. Phil Dickie. 1989. pap. 16.95 (*0-7022-2244-5*, Pub. by Univ Queensland Pr AT) Intl Spec Bk.

Road to France: The Transportation of Troops & Military Supplies, 1917-1918, 2 vols. in one. Benedict Crowell & Robert F. Wilson. LC 74-75238. (United States in World War I Ser.). (Illus.). xv, 675p. 1974. reprint ed. lib. bdg. 66.95 (*0-89198-100-4*) Ozer.

Road to Freedom. Lev S. Pinsker. LC 70-162734. 142p. 1975. reprint ed. text ed. 45.00 (*0-8371-6195-9*, PIRF, Greenwood Pr) Greenwood.

***Road to Freedom: A Fresh Start.** Regina Smith. (Open Door Bks.). 39p. (Orig.). 1996. pap. 2.95 (*1-56212-205-3*, 1740-1270) CRC Pubns.

***Road to Freedom: A Long Walk.** Regina Smith. (Open Door Bks.). 39p. (Orig.). 1996. pap. 2.95 (*1-56212-206-1*, 1740-1280) CRC Pubns.

***Road to Freedom: A New Home.** Regina Smith. (Open Door Bks.). 44p. (Orig.). 1996. pap. 2.95 (*1-56212-207-X*, 1740-1290) CRC Pubns.

Road to Freedom: A Sociological Study on the Abolition of Scavenging in India. Bindeshwar Pathak. (C). 1991. 34.00 (*81-208-0704-9*, Pub. by Motilal Banarsidass II) S Asia.

***Road to Freedom: A Tough Time.** Regina Smith. (Open Door Bks.). 37p. (Orig.). 1996. pap. 2.95 (*1-56212-204-5*, 1740-1260) CRC Pubns.

Road to Freedom: Photographs & Memorabilia from the 1916 Rising & Afterwards. Michael Kenny. (Treasures of the National Museum of Ireland Ser.). (Illus.). 48p. (Orig.). 1995. pap. 7.95 (*0-946172-35-8*, Pub. by Town Hse IE) R Rinehart.

Road to Freedom: Poems & Prose Poems. Geo Milev. Tr. by Ewald Osers. LC 87-82775. (Illus.). 66p. 1990. reprint ed. pap. 16.95 (*0-948259-45-0*, Pub. by Forest Bks UK) Dufour.

Road to Freedom: Revealing Sidelights. Ram Chandra. 362p. 1980. 29.95 (*0-685-05885-9*) Asia Bk Corp.

***Road to Freedom: The Story of Exodus.** Regina Smith. (Open Door Bks.). 96p. (Orig.). 1996. teacher ed., pap. 12.00 (*1-56212-203-7*, 1740-1250) CRC Pubns.

Road to Freedom, 1750-1783. Stuart A. Kallen. Ed. by Rosemary Walner. LC 90-82611. (Building of a Nation Ser.). (Illus.). 64p. (J). (gr. 4). 1990. lib. bdg. 13.98 (*0-939179-88-1*) Abdo & Dghtrs.

Road to Full Employment. Sean Glynn & Alan Booth. 220p. (C). 1987. text ed. 60.00 (*0-04-330360-9*); pap. text ed. 17.95 (*0-04-330361-7*) Routledge Chapman & Hall.

Road to Full Employment. Dewey B. Larson. LC 75-44558. 1976. 11.00 (*0-913138-06-1*) North Pacific.

Road to Full Employment: An Essay on Regulation, Deregulation, Enterprise Zones & the Productibility of Jobs. Anton J. Butter. 108p. (Orig.). 1982. pap. 21.00 (*90-6032-239-8*, Pub. by B R Gruener NE) Benjamins North Am.

Road to Gandolfo. Robert Ludlum. 320p. 1992. mass mkt. 7.50 (*0-553-27109-1*) Bantam.

Road to Glory: Confederate General Richard S. Ewell. 2nd ed. Samuel J. Martin. LC 91-58045. 420p. 1991. 29.95 (*1-878208-07-1*); pap. 24.95 (*1-878208-42-X*) Guild Pr IN.

Road to Gold. William H. LaBarge. 336p. 1993. mass mkt. 5.99 (*0-06-104139-4*, Harp PBks) HarpC.

Road to Graduate School. 272p. 1996. pap. 19.95 (*0-385-31623-2*) Doubleday.

Road to Greenham Common: Feminism & Anti-Militarism in Britain Since 1820. Jill Liddington. (Syracuse Studies on Peace & Conflict Resolution). (Illus.). 360p. (C). 1991. reprint ed. text ed. 42.50 (*0-8156-2539-1*); reprint ed. pap. text ed. 16.95 (*0-8156-2540-5*) Syracuse U Pr.

Road to Gretna. Carola Dunn. (Regency Romance Ser.: No. 173). 1992. mass mkt. 2.99 (*0-373-31173-7*, 1-31173-7) Harlequin Bks.

Road to Ground Zero. Roger Lipe. 126p. (Orig.). 1993. pap. 6.99 (*1-56043-755-3*) Destiny Image.

Road to Guilford Courthouse: The British Campaign to Regain the Carolinas, 1780-81. John Buchanan. LC 96-9575. 400p. 1997. text ed. 30.00 (*0-471-16402-X*) Wiley.

Road to Harmony...Day-by-Day. Kay E. Meyer. (Illus.). 398p. (Orig.). 1993. 17.00 (*0-9637023-0-0*) Grp Avatar.

Road to Healing: The Twelve Step & the Serenity Prayer. Raymond Guterman. 80p. 1994. pap. write for info. (*1-885904-03-7*) Focus Pubng.

Road to Health Care Reform: Designing a System that Works. J.C. Merrill. 323p. (C). 1994. 29.95 (*0-306-44770-3*, Plenum Pr) Plenum.

***Road to Heaven, Bk. 1.** Paul Carroll. 230p. (Orig.). 1997. pap. 9.00 (*1-57502-455-1*, PO1369) Morris Pubng.

***Road to Heaven, Bk. 2.** Paul Carroll. 230p. (Orig.). 1997. pap. 9.00 (*1-57502-456-X*, PO1370) Morris Pubng.

Road to Heaven: Encounters with Chinese Hermits. Bill Porter. LC 92-42339. (Illus.). 256p. (Orig.). 1993. pap. 14.00 (*1-56279-041-2*) Mercury Hse Inc.

Road to Heaven: The Biblical Doctrine of Holiness. W. Ralph Thompson & Robert Wood. 80p. 1992. pap. 3.95 (*0-89367-177-0*) Light & Life Comm.

Road to Hell. Larry Incollingo & Bob Hammel. 175p. 1987. pap. 8.95 (*0-9619795-0-X*) Reunion Bks.

***Road to Hell.** Robert Weinberg. 1997. mass mkt. 5.99 (*0-614-27810-4*) White Wolf CA.

Road to Hell: A Study of the Conception of the Dead in Old Norse Literature. Hilda R. Ellis. LC 68-23286. (Illus.). 208p. 1968. reprint ed. text ed. 35.00 (*0-8371-0070-4*, ELRH, Greenwood Pr) Greenwood.

***Road to Hell: The Ravaging Effects of Foreing Aid International Charity.** Michael Maren. LC 96-41168. 304p. 1997. 25.00 (*0-684-82800-6*) Free Pr.

Road to Hell: The True Story of George Jackson, Stephen Bingham, & the San Quentin Massacre. Paul Liberatore. 288p. 1996. 23.00 (*0-87113-647-3*, Atlntc Mnthly) Grove-Atltic.

***Road to Immunity.** Bock. 1997. pap. 14.00 (*0-671-54507-8*, PB Trade Paper) PB.

Road to India: Guide to the Overland Routes to India. John Prendergast. (Illus.). 1978. 19.50 (*0-7195-3396-1*) Transatl Arts.

Road to Intervention: March - November 1918. Michael Kettle. 512p. (C). 1988. lib. bdg. 49.95 (*0-415-00371-7*) Routledge.

Road to Isandhlwana: Col. Anthony Durnford in Natal & Zululand, 1873-1879. R. W. Droogleever. 192p. 1992. 37.50 (*1-85367-118-5*, 5578) Stackpole.

Road to ISO 1400. Roy F. Weston, Inc. Staff. LC 95-51289. 64p. 1996. per. 13.95 (*0-7863-0866-4*) Irwin Prof Pubng.

R

Road to Jaramillo: Critical Years of the Revolution in Earth Science. William Glen. LC 80-51647. (Illus.). xvi, 459p. 1982. 59.50 (0-8047-1119-4) Stanford U Pr.

***Road to Java.** Marshall. (Itcp-Uk Computer Science Ser.). 1997. pap. 21.99 (1-85032-307-0) ITCP.

Road to Joy: Letters to New & Old Friends. Thomas Merton. Ed. by Robert E. Daggy. 672p. 1989. 27.95 (0-374-25123-1) FS&G.

Road to Joy: The Letters of Thomas Merton to New & Old Friends. Selected by Robert E. Daggy. LC 92-33540. 1993. pap. 15.95 (0-15-677818-1) HarBrace.

Road to Judgment: From Custom to Court in Medieval Ireland & Wales. Robin C. Stacey. LC 93-47677. (Middle Ages Ser.). (Illus.). 368p. (C). 1994. text ed. 48. 95 (0-8122-3216-X) U of Pa Pr.

Road to Justice. Alfred Denning. (Legal Reprint Ser.). viii, 118p. 1988. reprint ed. lib. bdg. 22.50 (0-8377-2034-6) Rothman.

***Road to Ka-Larry.** Dr.Seuss. 1998. lib. bdg. write for info. (0-679-98836-X) Random Bks Yng Read.

Road to Kadesh: A Historical Interpretation of the Battle Reliefs of King Sety I at Karnak. 2nd rev. ed. William J. Murnane. LC 90-63725. (Studies in Ancient Oriental Civilization: No. 42). (Illus.). 157p. (C). 1990. pap. 25.00 (0-918986-67-2) Orient Inst.

***Road to Kalamata: A Congo Mercenary's Personal Memoir.** Mike Hoare. 1997. 21.95 (0-85052-288-9, Pub. by L Cooper Bks UK) Trans-Atl Phila.

Road to Kathmandu. P. A. Raj. 1994. pap. 30.00 (0-7855-0478-8, Pub. by Ratna Pustak Bhandar) St Mut.

Road to Kilimanjaro: An American Family in Maasailand. rev. ed. Ruth T. Shaffer. 250p. 1992. reprint ed. pap. text ed. write for info. (0-9634036-0-5) Africa Inland.

Road to Komatsubara: A Classical Reading of the Renga Hyakuin. Steven D. Carter. LC 87-15713. (East Asian Monographs: No. 124). 311p. 1988. 28.00 (0-674-77385-3) HUP.

Road to Lagoa Santa. Henrik Stangerup. Tr. by Barbara Bluestone from DAN. 288p. 1984. 14.95 (0-7145-2797-1) M Boyars Pubs.

Road to Lagoa Santa. Henrik Stangerup. Tr. by Barbara Bluestone from DAN. 288p. 1996. reprint ed. pap. 14.95 (0-7145-3016-6) M Boyars Pubs.

Road to Law School. 256p. 1996. pap. 19.95 (0-385-31626-7) Doubleday.

***Road to Liberty (Victory Road) Map.** 1992. 10.95 (2-06-700265-1, 105) Michelin.

Road to Life: The Rescue Operation of Jewish Refugees on the Hungarian-Romanian Border 1936-1944. Moshe C. Weinberger. (Illus.). 189p. (Orig.). (C). 1994. pap. 17.95 (0-88400-175-X) Shengold.

Road to Lonergan's Method in Theology: The Ordering of Theological Ideas. Craig S. Boly. 294p. (C). 1991. lib. bdg. 52.50 (0-8191-7741-5) U Pr of Amer.

Road to Los Angeles. John Fante. LC 85-15098. 167p. 1995. reprint ed. 20.00 (0-87685-650-4); reprint ed. pap. 11.00 (0-87685-649-0) Black Sparrow.

Road to Louisiana: The Saint-Dominigue Refugees, 1792-1809. Ed. by Glenn R. Conrad. Tr. by David Cheramie. 306p. 1992. 20.00 (0-940984-76-8) U of SW LA Ctr LA Studies.

Road to Love Canal: Managing Industrial Waste before EPA. Carig E. Colten & Peter N. Skinner. LC 95-15399. (Illus.). 240p. (Orig.). 1996. text ed. 35.00 (0-292-71182-4) U of Tex Pr.

Road to Love Canal: Managing Industrial Waste before EPA. Craig E. Colten & Peter N. Skinner. LC 95-15399. (Orig.). 1996. pap. 14.95 (0-292-71183-2) U of Tex Pr.

Road to Madiun No. 69: The Indonesian Communist Uprising of 1948. Elizabeth A. Swift. 128p. (Orig.). (C). 1989. pap. text ed. 9.00 (0-87763-035-6) Cornell Mod Indo.

Road to Madness: The Transition of H. P. Lovecraft. H. P. Lovecraft. LC 96-294. 384p. 1996. pap. 10.00 (0-345-38422-9) Ballantine.

Road to Madrid: Developing a Western Consensus on Human Rights. Ed. by Aspen Institute Staff. 104p. 1980. pap. text ed. 13.50 (0-8191-5900-X, Aspen Inst for Humanistic Studies) U Pr of Amer.

Road to Mass Democracy: Original Intent & the Seventeenth Amendment. C. H. Hoebeke. LC 95-16442. 224p. 1995. 34.95 (1-56000-217-4) Transaction Pubs.

Road to Mecca. Muhammad Asad. 380p. (Orig.). 1981. 14. 95 (0-317-52460-7) New Era Publns MI.

***Road to Mecca.** Muhammad Asad. 374p. 1996. 15.95 (0-614-21476-9, 1087) Kazi Pubns.

Road to Mecca. Athol Fugard. LC 88-2110. 80p. 1988. 14. 95 (0-930452-78-X); pap. 7.95 (0-930452-79-8) Theatre Comm.

Road to Mecca. Muhammad Asad. (Illus.). 375p. 1954. reprint ed. 25.00 (0-939660-13-X, Pub. by Dar Al-Andalus SP) Threshold VT.

Road to Medical School. 304p. 1996. pap. 19.95 (0-385-31629-1) Doubleday.

Road to Memphis. Mildred D. Taylor. Ed. by Phyllis J. Fogelman. LC 88-33654. (Illus.). 240p. (YA). (gr. 7 up). 1990. pap. 15.00 (0-8037-0340-6) Dial Bks Young.

Road to Memphis. Mildred D. Taylor. 304p. (J). (gr. 5-9). 1992. pap. 4.50 (0-14-036077-8, Puffin) Puffin Bks.

***Road to Mexico.** Lawrence Taylor. LC 97-4578. (Illus.). 1997. 45.00 (0-8165-1723-1); pap. 19.95 (0-8165-1725-8) U of Ariz Pr.

Road to Miklagard. Henry Treece. LC 57-12280. (Illus.). (J). (gr. 6-10). 1957. 24.95 (0-87599-118-1) S G Phillips.

Road to Mobocracy: Popular Disorder in New York City, 1763-1834. Paul A. Gilje. LC 86-30852. (Illus.). xviii, 316p. (C). 1987. 39.95 (0-8078-1743-0); pap. 16.95 (0-8078-4198-6) U of NC Pr.

Road to Modern Music. Paul Emerich. 1960. pap. 4.00 (0-318-19426-0, 61037-940) Peer-Southrn.

Road to Monetary Union in Europe. Tommaso Padoa-Schioppa. 280p. 1995. 55.00 (0-19-828843-3) OUP.

Road to Music. Nicolas Slonimsky. LC 79-14882. (Music Reprint Ser.). 1979. reprint ed. lib. bdg. 27.50 (0-306-79566-3) Da Capo.

Road to Naka-Ima: A Man's Journey to a New Civilization. Stuart A. Bernstein. (Sounds of a New Order Ser.). 240p. (Orig.). 1995. pap. 19.00 (0-9648834-0-6) Cassiquiare.

Road to Nazareth: Through Palestine Today. John Gibbons. LC 77-180339. reprint ed. 42.50 (0-404-56264-7) AMS Pr.

***Road to New Beginning: A History of Tyro United Methodist Church Lexington, North Carolina.** Allen Rice. (Illus.). 112p. 1997. write for info. (1-57736-054-0) Providence Hse.

Road to Nineteen Eighty-Four. Willis Hall. write for info. (0-671-62031-2) S&S Trade.

***Road to Nineteen Eighty-Four.** Willis Hall. write for info. (0-671-61790-7) S&S Trade.

Road to Nirvana. Arthur Kopit. 96p. 1991. pap. 9.95 (0-374-52308-8, Noonday) FS&G.

Road to Normalcy: The Presidential Campaign & Election of 1920. Wesley M. Bagby. LC 78-64237. (Johns Hopkins University. Studies in the Social Sciences. Thirtieth Ser. 1912: 1). reprint ed. 45.00 (0-404-61342-X) AMS Pr.

Road to Normalcy: The Presidential Campaign & the Election of 1920. Wesley M. Bagby. (Johns Hopkins University Studies in Historical & Political Science: Ser. 80, No. 1). reprint ed. pap. 52.00 (0-317-39641-2, 2023108) Bks Demand.

***Road to Notown.** Michael Foley. 342p. 9700. pap. 15.95 (0-85640-576-0, Pub. by Blackstaff Pr IE) Dufour.

Road to Nowhere. Christopher Pike. Ed. by Pat MacDonald. 224p. (Orig.). (YA). (gr. 9 up). 1993. pap. 3.99 (0-671-74508-5, Archway) PB.

Road to Nowhere: The Genesis of President Clinton's Plan for Health Security. Jacob S. Hacker. LC 96-8083. (Studies in American Politics). 239p. 1997. text ed. 39. 95 (0-691-04423-6) Princeton U Pr.

Road to Nowhere see Heinemann Guided Readers

Road to Nunavut: The Progress of the Eastern Arctic Inuit since the Second World War. R. Quinn Duffy. 376p. 1988. 19.95 (0-7735-0619-5, Pub. by McGill CN) U of Toronto Pr.

Road to Ogdensburg: The Queen's St. Lawrence Conferences on Canadian-American Affairs, 1935-1941. Ed. by Frederick W. Gibson & Jonathan G. Rossie. LC 92-56860. (Canadian Ser.: No. 4). (C). 1993. 35.00 (0-87013-329-2) Mich St U Pr.

Road to Olmutz: The Political Career of Joseph Maria Von Radowitz. Warren B. Morris. 1975. lib. bdg. 250.00 (0-87700-230-4) Revisionist Pr.

Road to Omaha. Robert Ludlum. 608p. 1993. mass mkt. 7.50 (0-553-56044-1) Bantam.

Road to Omaha. Robert Ludlum. 1994. 6.99 (0-517-11695-2) Random Hse Value.

Road to Omaha. large type ed. Robert Ludlum. 1992. 26.00 (0-679-41016-3) Random Hse Lrg Prnt.

Road to OPEC: United States Relations with Venezuela, 1919-1976. Stephen G. Rabe. (Texas Pan American Ser.). 272p. (C). 1982. text ed. 27.50 (0-292-76020-5) U of Tex Pr.

***Road to Open & Healthy Schools: A Handbook for Change, Elementary & Middle School Edition.** Wayne K. Hoy & C. John Tarter. (Illus.). 136p. 1996. 54.95 (0-8039-6540-0); pap. 24.95 (0-8039-6417-X) Corwin Pr.

***Road to Open & Healthy Schools: A Handbook for Change, Middle & Secondary School Edition.** Wayne K. Hoy & C. John Tarter. (Illus.). 136p. 1996. 54.95 (0-8039-6564-8); pap. 24.95 (0-8039-6565-6) Corwin Pr.

Road to Optimism Vol. 1: Change Your Language, Change Your Life. J. Mitchell Perry & Richard E. Griggs. Ed. by Fred Norman. (Illus.). 208p. 1997. 25.00 (0-922530-02-5) Manfit Pubns.

Road to Oregon. William J. Ghent. LC 77-111787. (BCL Ser.: I). (Illus.). reprint ed. 41.50 (0-404-02717-2) AMS Pr.

Road to Oregon: A Chronicle of the Great Emigrant Trail. William J. Ghent. 1988. reprint ed. lib. bdg. 49.00 (0-7812-0199-3) Rprt Serv.

Road to Oregon: A Chronicle of the Great Emigrant Trail. William J. Ghent. (Illus.). 1971. reprint ed. 19.00 (0-403-00987-1) Scholarly.

Road to Oregon: A Chronicle of the Great Emigrant Trail. William J. Ghent. (BCL1 - United States Local History Ser.). 274p. 1991. reprint ed. lib. bdg. 79.00 (0-7812-6323-9) Rprt Serv.

Road to Oxiana. Robert Byron, Jr. (Illus.). 292p. 1982. pap. 13.95 (0-19-503067-2) OUP.

Road to Oz. L. Frank Baum. LC 79-88480. 272p. (J). 1986. mass mkt. 4.95 (0-345-33467-1, Del Rey) Ballantine.

Road to Oz. L. Frank Baum. 1990. 18.75 (0-8446-6250-X) Peter Smith.

Road to Oz. L. Frank Baum. 160p. (J). (gr. 5 up). 1993. pap. 2.99 (0-14-035121-3, Puffin) Puffin Bks.

Road to Oz. L. Frank Baum. 20.95 (0-8488-0788-X) Amereon Ltd.

Road to Oz. L. Frank Baum. 272p. 1986. reprint ed. pap. 5.95 (0-486-25208-6) Dover.

Road to Oz. L. Frank Baum. LC 90-48349. (Books of Wonder). (Illus.). 272p. (J). 1991. reprint ed. 16.95 (0-688-09997-1, Morrow Junior) Morrow.

Road to Paradise. Eleanor McKinney. 1995. 16.95 (0-533-11503-5) Vantage.

Road to Paradise Island. Victoria Holt. 1986. mass mkt. 5.99 (0-449-20888-5, Crest) Fawcett.

***Road to Parnassus: Homage to Peter Russell on His Seventy-Fifth Birthday.** Ed. by James Hogg. 599p. 1996. pap. 29.95 (3-7052-0030-5, Pub. by Univ of Salzburg AT) Intl Spec Bk.

Road to Peace. James J. Daly. LC 78-107691. (Essay Index Reprint Ser.). 1977. 19.95 (0-8369-1495-3) Ayer.

Road to Pearl Harbor: The Coming of the War Between the United States & Japan. Herbert Feis. 368p. reprint ed. pap. 104.90 (0-7837-3874-9, 2043716) Bks Demand.

***Road to Perl.** Farmer. (ITCP-UK Computer Science Ser.). 1997. pap. 19.99 (1-85032-309-7) ITCP.

Road to Post-Communism: Independent Political Movements in the Former Soviet Union. Geoffrey A. Hosking et al. LC 92-14811. 288p. 1992. 59.00 (1-85567-080-1); pap. 19.75 (1-85567-081-X) St Martin.

Road to Power: Herut Party in Israel. Yonathan Shapiro. LC 90-9887. (SUNY Series in Israeli Studies). 208p. (C). 1991. text ed. 64.50 (0-7914-0606-7); pap. text ed. 21.95 (0-7914-0607-5) State U NY Pr.

Road to Power: Political Reflections on Growing into the Revolution. Karl Kautsky. Ed. by John H. Kautsky. Tr. by Raymond Meyer. LC 95-25257. 264p. (C). 1996. pap. 15.00 (0-391-03956-3) Humanities.

Road to Power: Political Reflections on Growing into the Revolution. Karl Kautsky. Ed. by John H. Kautsky. Tr. by Raymond Meyer. LC 95-25257. 264p. (C). 1996. text ed. 49.95 (0-391-03955-5) Humanities.

Road to Power: The Trans-Siberian Railroad & the Colonization of Asian Russia, 1850-1917. Steven G. Marks. LC 90-55734. (Illus.). 272p. 1991. 35.00 (0-8014-2533-6) Cornell U Pr.

Road to QS-9000. Guy A. Hale. LC 96-18118. 56p. 1996. per. 13.95 (0-7863-0884-2) Irwin Prof Pubng.

Road to Radicalism: Further Reflections of a Frustrated Feminist. Elayne Clift. 188p. (Orig.). 1994. pap. 14.95 (0-9634827-1-8) OGN Pubns.

Road to Randomness in Physical Systems. E. M. Engel et al. Ed. by Stephen E. Fienberg et al. (Lecture Notes in Statistics Ser.: Vol. 71). ix, 155p. 1992. 43.95 (0-387-97740-6) Spr-Verlag.

Road to Readability: Basics of Writing & Editing. Digby Whitman. 72p. (Orig.). 1984. pap. text ed. 11.95 (0-931368-17-0) Ragan Comm.

Road to Real Wealth: Genuine Success Stories from the Subscribers of the Real Estate Digest. Steve Bobbitt. 1988. pap. write for info. (0-318-64321-9) Real Estate Digest.

Road to Realism: The Early Years 1837-1886 of William Dean Howells. Edwin H. Cady. LC 86-4633. 293p. 1986. reprint ed. text ed. 69.50 (0-313-25206-8, CARO, Greenwood Pr) Greenwood.

Road to Reality: The Spiritual Path for Everyone. Ed. by Iris M. Turner. 124p. 1986. 35.00 (0-7212-0732-4, Pub. by Regency Press UK) St Mut.

Road to Rebellion: Class Formation & Kansas Populism 1865-1900. Scott G. McNall. (Illus.). xviii, 372p. 1988. lib. bdg. 60.00 (0-226-56126-7) U Ch Pr.

Road to Rebellion: Class Formation & Kansas Populism 1865-1900. Scott G. McNall. (Illus.). xviii, 372p. 1988. pap. text ed. 24.00 (0-226-56127-5) U Ch Pr.

Road to Recovery. large type ed. Frances Crowne. 268p. 1992. 25.99 (0-7505-0389-0) Ulverscroft.

Road to Recovery: Bridges Between the Bible & the Twelve Steps. Dennis C. Morreim. LC 89-49091. 144p. (Orig.). 1990. pap. 7.99 (0-8066-2456-6, 9-2456) Augsburg Fortress.

***Road to Redemption.** Burton L. Visotzky. 1998. write for info. (0-609-60145-8, Crown) Crown Pub Group.

Road to Redemption: Southern Politics, 1869-1879. Michael Perman. LC 83-12498. (Fred W. Morrison Series in Southern Studies). xiv, 353p. 1985. text ed. 45. 00 (0-8078-1526-8); pap. text ed. 14.95 (0-8078-4141-2) U of NC Pr.

Road to Redemption: The Jews of the Yemen 1900-1950. Tudor Parfitt. (Series in Jewish Studies: Vol. 17). 1996. 100.75 (90-04-10544-1) E J Brill.

Road to Reform: The Future of Health Care in America. Eli Ginzberg. 180p. 1994. 24.95 (0-02-911715-1, Free Press) Free Pr.

Road to Reno: A History of Divorce in the United States. Nelson M. Blake. LC 77-11070. 269p. 1977. reprint ed. text ed. 66.50 (0-8371-9797-X, BLRR, Greenwood Pr) Greenwood.

Road to Repentance. Marvin Gorman. 224p. (Orig.). 1996. pap. 9.99 (1-56043-269-1) Destiny Image.

Road to Respectability: James A. Garfield & His World, 1844-1852. Booraem V. Hendrik. LC 86-50895. (Illus.). 304p. 1988. 40.00 (0-8387-5135-0) Bucknell U Pr.

Road to Revolution: Benjamin Franklin in England 1765-1775. Cecil B. Currey. (Illus.). 1990. 14.50 (0-8446-1931-0) Peter Smith.

Road to Revolution: Scotland under Charles I, 1625-37. Maurice Lee, Jr. LC 84-8750. 276p. 1985. text ed. 29.95 (0-252-01136-8) U of Ill Pr.

Road to Revolution, German Marxism & World War 1. John W. Mishark. 15.00 (0-685-16805-0) Moira.

Road to Revolution in Spain: The Coal Miners of Asturias, 1860-1934. Adrian Shubert. LC 86-24998. (Working Class in European History Ser.). (Illus.). 200p. 1987. text ed. 24.95 (0-252-01368-9) U of Ill Pr.

Road to Romance & Ruin: Teen Films & Youth Culture. Jon Lewis. 192p. (C). 1992. pap. 16.95 (0-415-90427-7, A5776, Routledge NY) Routledge.

Road to Romanian Independence. Frederick Kellogg. LC 94-38654. (Illus.). 281p. 1995. 32.95 (1-55753-065-3) Purdue U Pr.

Road to Rome. Russell R. Standish & Colin D. Standish. 261p. (Orig.). 1992. pap. 7.95 (0-923309-03-9) Hartland Pubns.

Road to Rome: An Artist's Year in Italy. Marlene McLoughlin. LC 94-27239. 120p. 1995. 16.95 (0-8118-0577-8) Chronicle Bks.

Road to Ruin. Margaret E. Porter. (Signet Regency Romance Ser.). 224p. 1992. pap. 3.99 (0-451-17508-5, Sig) NAL-Dutton.

Road to Ruin. Margaret E. Porter. 224p. 1991. 18.95 (0-8027-1129-4) Walker & Co.

Road to Ruin. Thomas Holcroft. Ed. by Ruth I. Aldrich. LC 68-18245. 156p. 1968. reprint ed. pap. 44.50 (0-608-02375-2, 2063017) Bks Demand.

Road to Ruin. Thomas Holcroft. LC 91-18552. 112p. 1991. reprint ed. 40.00 (1-85477-072-1, Pub. by Woodstock Bks UK) Cassell.

***Road to Ruin: 22 Unneeded New Highway Projects That Would Waste $10 Billion, Harm Our Communities & Hurt the Environment.** Taxpayers for Common Sense Staff. 32p. 1996. pap. 10.00 (1-888415-03-7) Taxpyrs Common Sense.

Road to Rustenburg: The Church Looking Forward to a New South Africa. Ed. by Louw Alberts & Frank Chikane. LC 92-119117. (Illus.). 294p. 1991. reprint ed. pap. 83.80 (0-7837-6727-7, 2046355) Bks Demand.

Road to Salem. Ed. by Adelaide L. Fries. LC 93-26532. (Illus.). 316p. 1993. reprint ed. pap. 9.95 (0-89587-106-8) Blair.

Road to Salvation. A. A. Maududi. pap. 3.00 (0-933511-42-6) Kazi Pubns.

Road to Sampo & Other Korean Short Stories. Cho Se-Hui et al. Ed. by UNESCO, Korean National Commission. Tr. by B. McHale & Sol Ji-Mun from KOR. (Modern Korean Short Stories Ser.: No. 9). viii, 237p. 1983. 20.00 (0-89209-210-6) Pace Intl Res.

Road to San Giovanni. Italo Calvino. Tr. by Tim Parks. LC 93-3356. (ENG.). 1993. 19.00 (0-679-41523-8) Pantheon.

Road to San Giovanni. Italo Calvino. 1994. pap. 11.00 (0-679-74348-0, Vin) Random.

Road to San Giovanni. Italo Calvino. 1995. 21.50 (0-8446-6873-7) Peter Smith.

Road to San Jacinto. J. Frank Davis. 1993. reprint ed. lib. bdg. 75.00 (0-7812-5964-9) Rprt Serv.

Road to San Jacinto. James Davis. (BCL1-PS American Literature Ser.). 334p. 1993. reprint ed. lib. bdg. 89.00 (0-7812-6955-5) Rprt Serv.

Road to San Jacinto: Texas Becomes a Republic. Ed. by Mary D. Wade. (Perspectives on History Ser.: Vol. 26). (Illus.). 64p. (Orig.). 1997. pap. 5.95 (1-878668-62-5) Disc Enter Ltd.

Road to Santa Fe: The Journal & Diaries of George Champlin Sibley. Ed. by Kate L. Gregg. LC 94-45893. 293p. 1995. reprint ed. pap. 16.95 (0-8263-1567-4) U of NM Pr.

Road to Santiago: A Pilgrimage, Past & Present. Douglas H. Armstrong. LC 94-181267. (American University Studies, Series XXI, Regional Studies: Vol. 13). 1997. write for info. (0-8204-2542-7) P Lang Pubng.

Road to School-to-Work: (School Implementation Resource Guide) AIT Staff. 128p. (Orig.). 1995. pap. text ed. write for info. (0-7842-0771-2) Agency Instr Tech.

Road to School-to-Work: Facilitator's Guide. AIT Staff. 32p. (Orig.). 1995. pap. text ed. write for info. (0-7842-0778-X) Agency Instr Tech.

Road to School-to-Work School Implementation Resource Guide. AIT Staff. 136p. (Orig.). 1995. pap. text ed. write for info. (0-7842-0777-1) Agency Instr Tech.

Road to Science Fiction Vol. 3: From Heinlein to Here, Vol. 3. Harlan Ellison et al. Ed. by James Gunn. 1996. pap. 14.99 (1-56504-821-0, 11089, Borealis) White Wolf.

***Road to Science Fiction Vol. 4: From Here to Forever.** Frank Herbert et al. Ed. by James Gunn. 1997. pap. 14. 99 (1-56504-822-9, 11030) White Wolf.

Road to Sedan. Richard Holmes. (Royal Historical Society: Studies in History: No. 41). 280p. 1984. 63.00 (0-901050-95-4) Boydell & Brewer.

***Road to Self-Employment: A Practical Guide to Microbusiness Development, 5 vols., Vol. 1. Gerri P. Norington. Ed. by Linda C. Puig. (Rose Program Ser.). (Illus.). xvi, 220p. 1997. pap. 24. 95 (1-890499-00-5, WBTC) Womens Busn Trning. THE ROAD TO SELF-EMPLOYMENT, A PRACTICAL GUIDE TO MICROBUSINESS DEVELOPMENT is the most comprehensive book on the market today that lets one know what to expect from & how to prepare for microbusiness development. Set apart from other books by the author's holistic approach, this visually attractive book deals with personal growth as a tool for business success. Using a conversational tone, Ms. Norington, a business development specialist since 1968, walks the reader through the maze of business operations including the developmental phases. This treasure focuses on all aspects of business development while creating a "safe" environment for the reader top learn & grow. Questions like: What steps can be taken to increase the chance of success; how to market on a small budget; why is a business plan needed & how to write a comprehensive one; pricing & working SMART, are all addressed. This easy-to-understand book is truly the practical guide to running an effective & profitable business & provides lots of tips on how to make business work for the reader. $24.95 plus shipping & handling, quantity discounts available. WBTC, P.O. Box 126305, San Diego, CA 92112-**

An Asterisk (*) at the beginning of an entry indicates that the title is appearing in BIP for the first time.

6305. 619-239-9282, FAX: 619-238-5205. ***Publisher Provided Annotation.***

Road to Self-Rule: A Study in Colonial Evolution. William M. Macmillan. LC 77-140365. (Select Bibliographies Reprint Ser.). 1977. reprint ed. 21.95 (*0-8369-5608-7*) Ayer.

Road to Seneca Falls: A Story about Elizabeth Cady Stanton. Gwenyth Swain. LC 96-7387. (Carolrhoda Creative Minds Bks.). (Illus.). (J). 1996. 5.95 (*0-87614-947-6*, Carolrhoda) Lerner Group.

Road to Seneca Falls: A Story about Elizabeth Cady Stanton. Gwenyth Swain. 1996. pap. text ed. 5.95 (*1-57505-025-0*, Carolrhoda) Lerner Group.

Road to Serfdom. Friedrich A. Hayek. 1994. lib. bdg. 24.95 (*1-56849-376-2*) Buccaneer Bks.

Road to Serfdom. Friedrich A. Hayek. 320p. 1994. 25.00 (*0-226-32059-6*) U Ch Pr.

Road to Serfdom. Friedrich A. Hayek. 320p. 1994. pap. 10.95 (*0-226-32061-8*) U Ch Pr.

Road to Shiloh. (Civil War Ser.). (Illus.). 176p. 1983. 18.95 (*0-8094-4716-9*); lib. bdg. 25.93 (*0-8094-4717-7*) Time-Life.

Road to Shiloh: Poems since 1984. Jon Dressel. 115p. 1994. pap. 27.00 (*1-85902-185-9*) St Mut.

Road to Sifat. Jon T. Murphree. 208p. (Orig.). 1990. pap. text ed. write for info. (*0-932281-06-0*) Quill Pubns GA.

Road to Silence: An Irish Spiritual Oddyssey. Sean Dunne. 79p. (Orig.). 1994. pap. 9.95 (*1-874597-12-X*, Pub. by New Island Bks IE) Irish Bks Media.

***Road to Somewhere.** Tana Rieff. (Illus.). 1992. mass mkt. 5.55 (*0-8224-7154-X*) Fearon Teach Aids.

Road to Stonewall. Byrne R.S. Fone. (Twayne's Literature & Society Ser.). (Illus.). 275p. 1994. pap. 16.95 (*0-8057-4534-3*, Twayne) Scribnrs Ref.

Road to Stonewall. Byrne R.S. Fone. (Twayne's Literature & Society Ser.: No. 14). (Illus.). 275p. 1994. 27.95 (*0-8057-8856-5*, Twayne) Scribnrs Ref.

Road to Stratford. Michael O'Donovan. 1988. reprint ed. lib. bdg. 39.00 (*0-7812-0091-1*) Rprt Serv.

Road to Stratford. Michael O'Donovan. reprint ed. 29.00 (*0-403-04239-9*) Somerset Pub.

Road to Success: An Orientation Process for Catholic School Teachers. Jim Brennan. (Illus.). 52p. (Orig.). 1995. pap. 9.00 (*1-55833-149-2*) Natl Cath Educ.

Road to Success Is Always under Construction. Kathleen F. Russell & Larry C. Wall. 160p. 1992. pap. 6.95 (*0-9635176-0-0*) Walrus Prods.

Road to Tamazunchale. Ron Arias. LC 86-70700. (Chicano Classics - Clasicos Chicanos Ser.: No. 3). (Illus.). 134p. 1987. pap. 10.00 (*0-916950-70-0*) Biling Rev-Pr.

Road to Tamazunchale. Ron Arias. 112p. 1992. pap. 8.95 (*0-385-42012-9*, Anchor NY) Doubleday.

Road to Testimony. J. R. Roberts. (Gunsmith Ser.: No. 130). 192p. (Orig.). 1992. mass mkt. 3.99 (*0-515-10957-6*) Jove Pubns.

Road to the Aisle. James Martin. 1993. pap. 22.00 (*0-7152-0375-4*, Pub. by St Andrew UK) St Mut.

Road to the Baldrige Award: Quest for Total Quality. Robert Haavind. Ed. by Electronic Business magazine, staff. (Electronic Business Ser.). 256p. 1992. 47.95 (*0-7506-9262-6*) Buttrwrth-Heinemann.

Road to the City. N. Ginzburg. 1990. 16.95 (*0-8050-0855-1*) H Holt & Co.

Road to the City: Two Novellas. Natalia Ginzburg. Tr. by Frances Frenaye from ITA. 152p. 1990. 16.95 (*1-55970-052-1*) Arcade Pub Inc.

Road to the Coast. large type ed. John Harris. 1977. 25.99 (*0-85456-531-0*) Ulverscroft.

Road to the Graveyard. Horton Foote. 1988. pap. 5.25 (*0-8222-0959-4*) Dramatists Play.

Road to the Heart. Frithjof Schuon. LC 95-1460. (Library of Traditional Wisdom). 103p. (Orig.). 1995. pap. 10.00 (*0-941532-20-8*) Wrld Wisdom Bks.

***Road to the Information Society: New Technologies for Education & Training, EUR 16675.** Dumort Alain & Wolf Paprotte. 267p. 1996. pap. 45.00 (*92-827-7890-8*, CD-NA-16671-ENC, Pub. by Europ Com UK) Bernan Associates.

Road to the Isle. Megan Davidson. 384p. 1995. mass mkt. 4.99 (*0-8217-0131-2*, Zebra Kensgtn) Kensgtn Pub Corp.

***Road to the Khyber: An Accidental Journey up the Grand Trunk Road.** Anthony Weller. LC 97-25270. 1997. 22.95 (*1-56924-751-X*) Marlowe & Co.

***Road to the Killing Fields: The Cambodian War of 1970-1975.** Wilfred P. Deac. LC 97-13661. (Military History Ser.: Vol. 53). (Illus.). 320p. (C). 1997. text ed. 34.95 (*0-89096-750-4*) Tex A&M Univ Pr.

Road to the Kingdom. Luther Sanders. (Illus.). 110p. (Orig.). 1992. write for info. (*0-9632093-0-2*) My Fathers Busn.

Road to the Military Courthouse. 2nd ed. 19p. 1981. pap. 1.50 (*0-685-07160-X*, 515-0007) Amer Bar Assn.

Road to the Never Land: Reassessment of Sir J. M. Barrie's Dramatic Art. Ron Jack. (Illus.). 250p. 1991. text ed. 50.00 (*0-08-037742-4*, Pub. by Aberdeen U Pr) Macmillan.

Road to the Open. Arthur Schnitzler. Tr. by Horace Samuel from GER. 416p. 1991. reprint ed. pap. 14.95 (*0-8101-0996-4*) Northwestern U Pr.

Road to the River. large type ed. Antony Trew. 400p. 1994. 25.99 (*0-7089-3087-5*) Ulverscroft.

Road to the Road to the Isles. Picton Publishing Staff. (C). 1987. 25.00 (*0-317-90415-9*, Pub. by Picton UK) St Mut.

Road to the Somme: Men of the Ulster Division Tell Their Story. Philip Orr. LC 87-18228. (Illus.). 248p. 9200. pap. 29.00 (*0-85640-390-3*, Pub. by Blackstaff Pr IE) Dufour.

Road to the Stars. Houghton Mifflin Company Staff. (Literature Experience 1993 Ser.). (J). (gr. 8). 1992. pap. 9.84 (*0-395-61874-6*) HM.

***Road to the Sundance: My Journey into Native Spirituality.** 240p. 1997. pap. 11.95 (*0-7868-8244-1*) Hyperion.

Road to the Sundance: My Road into Native Spirituality. Manny Twofeathers. 240p. 1996. 21.95 (*0-7868-6215-7*) Hyperion.

***Road to the Super Bowl.** Bob Ryan. LC 97-10425. 1997. pap. text ed. 12.95 (*1-57028-136-X*) Masters Pr IN.

Road to the Top: A Systematic Approach to Training Distance Runners. Joe I. Vigil. Ed. by Doug Lindsey. (Illus.). 264p. 1995. 29.95 (*0-614-11363-6*); pap. 17.95 (*1-880047-34-9*) Creative Des.

Road to the Top: A Systematic Approach to Training Distance Runners. Joe I. Vigil. Ed. by Doug Lindsey. (Illus.). 264p. (C). 1995. text ed. 29.95 (*0-614-10630-3*) Creative Des.

***Road to the White House.** 1992. 29.95 (*0-923763-48-1*) Mayfair Games.

Road to the White House since Television. John Splaine. 226p. 1995. pap. 9.95 (*1-881846-06-7*) C-Span.

Road to the White House 1996. Stephen J. Wayne. 336p. (Orig.). 1995. pap. text ed. 15.50 (*0-312-10593-2*) St Martin.

Road to the World's End. Sigurd Hoel. Tr. by Sverre Lyngstad from NOR. 360p. (Orig.). (YA). 1995. pap. 13.95 (*1-55713-210-0*) Sun & Moon CA.

***Road to the 707: The Inside Story of Designing the 707.** William H. Cook. 288p. 1991. pap. 18.00 (*0-9629605-0-0*) TYC Pub.

Road to Torreon: Photographs of New Mexico Villages & Love Songs & Other Writings. Photos by Cavalliere Ketchum. (Illus.). 108p. 1995. boxed, pap. 59.95 incl. disk (*0-8263-1614-X*) U of NM Pr.

Road to Total Freedom. Roy Wallis. LC 76-27273. 1977. text ed. 52.00 (*0-231-04200-0*) Col U Pr.

***Road to Ubar.** Clapp. 1998. 24.00 (*0-395-87596-X*) HM.

Road to Underfall. Mike Jefferies. 384p. 1990. mass mkt. 5.99 (*0-06-100019-1*, Harp PBks) HarpC.

Road to Understanding. Eleanor H. Porter. 23.95 (*0-8488-0306-X*) Amereon Ltd.

Road to Understanding. Eleanor H. Porter. 1976. lib. bdg. 16.75 (*0-89968-108-5*, Lghtyr Pr) Buccaneer Bks.

Road to Understanding: More Than Dreamt of in Your Philosophy. Joseph M. Bochenski. Tr. by Gerard M. Verschuuren from GER. 144p. 1996. pap. 13.95 (*1-886670-06-4*) Genesis Publ.

Road to Vichy, 1918-1938. rev. ed. Yves R. Simon. Tr. by James A. Corbett & George J. McMorrow. 246p. (C). 1988. reprint ed. pap. text ed. 22.00 (*0-8191-6796-7*) U Pr of Amer.

Road to Virginia City: The Diary of James Knox Polk Miller. James K. Miller. LC 60-8750. (American Exploration & Travel Ser.: Vol. 30). (Illus.). 176p. 1989. pap. 9.95 (*0-8061-2163-7*) U of Okla Pr.

Road to Virtue: Resolutions for Daily Living. Michael L. Loren. 208p. (Orig.). 1996. pap. 7.50 (*0-380-78316-9*) Avon.

Road to War: France & Vietnam 1944-1947. Martin Shipway. LC 96-24310. (Contemporary France Ser.: Vol. 2). 256p. 1996. 49.95 (*1-57181-894-4*) Berghahn Bks.

Road to War: Origins of World War II. Richard Overy. 416p. 1990. 24.95 (*0-394-58260-8*) Random.

Road to Waterloo: The British Army & the Struggle Against Revolutionary & Napoleonic France, 1793-1815. Ed. by Alan Guy. (Illus.). 249p. (C). 1991. 34.00 (*0-86299-919-7*, Pub. by Sutton Pubng UK) Bks Intl VA.

Road to Wealth: How to Improve Your Investing, Saving & Spending Skills for Worry-Free Living & Retirement. W. James Ludlow. LC 93-90503. 144p. (Orig.). 1994. pap. 16.95 (*0-9635781-0-3*) Applewood Pub.

Road to Wellville. 6.98 (*0-8317-9280-9*) Smithmark.

Road to Wellville. T. Coraghessan Boyle. (Contemporary American Fiction Ser.). 480p. 1994. pap. 10.95 (*0-14-016718-8*, Penguin Bks) Viking Penguin.

Road to Wembley. Kim Chapin. LC 93-50815. (J). (gr. 4-7). 1994. 16.00 (*0-374-34849-9*) FS&G.

Road to West 43rd Street. Nash K. Burger & Pearl A. McHaney. (Illus.). 192p. 1995. 25.00 (*0-87805-793-5*) U Pr of Miss.

Road to Westminster: How to Select & Train a Purebred Dog & Prepare It for the Show Ring. Robert B. Freeman & Toni C. Freeman. (Illus.). 176p. (Orig.). 1990. pap. 8.95 (*1-55870-169-9*, Betrwy Bks) F & W Pubns Inc.

***Road to White House.** rev. ed. Wayne. 1997. pap. 24.95 (*0-312-15710-X*) St Martin.

Road to White House 1996. Wayne. 1996. pap. 25.95 (*0-312-13836-9*) St Martin.

***Road to White House, 2000.** Wayne. Date not set. pap. text ed. write for info. (*0-312-16742-3*) St Martin.

***Road to Wigan Pier.** unabridged ed. 157p. 1997. reprint ed. pap. 14.95 (*1-57002-055-8*) Univ Publng Hse.

Road to Wigan Pier. George Orwell. LC 58-10888. 232p. 1972. reprint ed. pap. 11.00 (*0-15-676750-3*, Harvest Bks) HarBrace.

***Road to X Window Programming with Motify.** Marshall. (ITCP-UK Computer Science Ser.). 1997. pap. 24.95 (*1-85032-317-8*) ITCP.

Road to Xanadu: A Study in the Ways of the Imagination. John L. Lowes. (BCL1-PR English Literature Ser.). 639p. 1992. reprint ed. lib. bdg. 109.00 (*0-7812-7501-6*) Rprt Serv.

Road to Yesterday. Lucy Maud Montgomery. 416p. (YA). 1993. mass mkt. 4.99 (*0-553-56068-9*) Bantam.

Road to You: Callings & How We Fulfill Them. Robert J. Furey. LC 96-40978. 155p. (Orig.). 1997. pap. 7.95 (*0-8189-0762-2*) Alba.

Road Traffic: A Guide to Part 1 of the 1991 Act. Peter S. Wallis. 72p. 1991. 33.00 (*1-85190-144-2*, Pub. by Tolley Pubng UK) St Mut.

***Road Traffic Accidents in Developing Countries.** (Technical Report Ser.: No. 703). 36p. 1984. pap. text ed. 5.00 (*92-4-120703-5*) World Health.

***Road Traffic Law.** 2nd ed. Martin Hannibal & Stephen Hardy. (Cavendish Practice Notes Ser.). 1996. pap. 32.00 (*1-85941-299-8*, Pub. by Cavendish UK) Gaunt.

Road Traffic Law: A Practical Guide. L. Dobbs et al. (Waterlow Criminal Law Guides Ser.). (Illus.). 288p. 1990. pap. 60.00 (*0-08-036916-2*, Waterlow) Macmillan.

Road Traffic Legislation: Padverkeerwetgewing. W. E. Cooper. 1990. write for info. (*0-7021-2430-3*, Pub. by Juta SA) Gaunt.

Road Traffic Noise see Progress in Planning

Road Traffic Offenders & Crime Policy. Laszlo Viski. 204p. (C). 1982. 60.00 (*963-05-2841-X*, Pub. by Akad Kiado HU) St Mut.

Road Traffic Statutes. L. Dobbs et al. (Waterlow Criminal Law Guide Ser.). 1990. pap. 70.00 (*0-08-040132-5*, Waterlow) Macmillan.

Road Transport. W. E. Cooper. 400p. 1985. ring bd. 52.00 (*0-7021-1652-1*, Pub. by Juta SA) Gaunt.

Road Transport Before the Railway. Ed. by Dorian Gerhold. LC 96-26139. (Studies in Transport History). 240p. 1996. 67.95 (*1-85928-298-9*, Pub. by Scolar Pr UK) Ashgate Pub Co.

Road Transport Before the Railways: Russell's London Flying Waggons. Dorian Gerhold. (Illus.). 320p. (C). 1993. text ed. 69.95 (*0-521-41950-6*) Cambridge U Pr.

Road Transport Research Outlook: 25th Anniversary. OECD Staff. 100p. (Orig.). 1993. pap. 19.00 (*92-64-13900-1*) OECD.

Road Travel & Transport in Gloucestershire: 1722-1822. Ed. by Nicholas Herbert. (Illus.). 160p. 1993. pap. text ed. 15.00 (*0-86299-235-4*, Pub. by Sutton Pubng UK) Bks Intl VA.

***Road Trip.** Chronicle Books Staff. 1997. spiral bd. 16.95 (*0-8118-1601-X*) Chronicle Bks.

Road Trip. Prod. by Chrysler Corporation Staff. (Illus.). 160p. (Orig.). 1994. pap. 13.95 (*0-312-11137-1*) St Martin.

Road Trip. Carol R. McGrath et al. 80p. 1993. pap. text ed. 12.95 (*0-944459-71-4*) ECS Lrn Systs.

Road Trip: A Travel Activity Book. Holly Kowitt. 32p. (J). (ps-3). 1994. pap. 1.95 (*0-590-48105-3*) Scholastic Inc.

Road Trip: An Interpersonal Adventure. Rebecca B. Rubin & Randi J. Nevins. 164p. (Orig.). (C). 1988. pap. text ed. 11.95 (*0-88133-328-X*) Waveland Pr.

Road Trip: Photographs, 1980-1989. Aaron Siskind. Ed. by David Featherstone. LC 89-84293. (Untitled Ser.: No. 49). (Illus.). 60p. 1989. pap. 18.95 (*0-933286-53-8*) Frnds Photography.

Road Trip U. S. A. A Cross-Country Celebration of America's Two-Lane Highways. Jamie Jensen. (Moon Travel Handbooks Ser.). (Illus.). 800p. (Orig.). 1996. pap. 22.50 (*1-56691-036-6*) Moon Trvl Hdbks.

Road Trip U. S. A. The Road Traveler's Complete Guide to America's Best Scenic Drives. William C. Herow. LC 94-67023. (Illus.). 296p. (Orig.). 1994. pap. 18.95 (*1-885464-24-X*, 1011) Roundabout.

Road Trips, Head Trips, & Other Car-Crazed Writings: An Anthology. Ed. by Jean Lindamood. 272p. 1996. 22.00 (*0-87113-654-6*, Atlntc Mnthly) Grove-Atltic.

Road Unseen. Peter Jenkins & Barbara Jenkins. 256p. 1987. mass mkt. 5.99 (*0-449-21212-2*, Crest) Fawcett.

Road Upward. David Schneider. 64p. 1993. reprint ed. lib. bdg. 69.00 (*0-7812-5253-9*) Rprt Serv.

Road User Protection: Selected Papers from the 8th International Conference on Accident & Traffic Medicine, Aarhus, Denmark, 10-13 June 1980. Ed. by Ronald Somers. 70p. 1981. pap. 35.00 (*0-08-028099-4*, Pergamon Pr) Elsevier.

***Road Vehicle Aerodynamic Design.** R. H. Barnard. (C). 1996. pap. text ed. write for info. (*0-582-24522-2*, Pub. by Longman UK) Longman.

***Road Vehicle Automation II: Towards Systems Integration: ROVA '95 International: Proceedings of the 2nd International Conference, Held at Vehicle Systems Research Centre, School of Engineering, Bolton Institute, Bolton, U. K., 11th-13th September, 1995.** Christopher O. Nwagboso. LC 96-31746. 1996. write for info. (*0-471-96726-2*) Wiley.

Road Vehicle Fuel Economy. HMSO Staff. (TRL State of the Art Review Ser.: No. 3). 190p. 1992. pap. 45.00 (*0-11-551097-4*, HM10974, Pub. by Stationery Ofc UK) Bernan Associates.

Road Vehicle Performance, Vol. 7. G. G. Lucas. (Transportation Studies: Vol. 7). 202p. 1986. text ed. 128.00 (*0-677-21400-6*) Gordon & Breach.

Road Warrior: How to Drive, Survive & Win in Today's Traffic. Dan Hales. 1991. pap. 5.95 (*0-9627973-1-6*) Challex Bks.

Road Warriors. Carin G. Baker. (Karate Club Ser.: No. 3). 144p. (J). (gr. 3-7). 1992. pap. 3.99 (*0-14-036076-X*, Puffin) Puffin Bks.

Road Warriors: Dreams & Nightmares Along the Information Highway. Daniel Burstein & David Kline. 400p. 1995. pap. 24.95 (*0-525-93726-9*, Dutton) NAL-Dutton.

Road Warriors: Dreams & Nightmares Along the Information Highway. Daniel Burstein & David Kline. 480p. 1996. pap. 13.95 (*0-452-27105-3*, Plume) NAL-Dutton.

Road Wars. James Axler. 1994. mass mkt. 4.99 (*0-373-62523-5*, 1-62523-5) Harlequin Bks.

Road We Do Not Know: A Novel of Custer at the Little Bighorn. Frederick J. Chiaventone. LC 96-26015. 288p. 1996. 24.00 (*0-684-83056-6*) S&S Trade.

Road Weather Information Systems, Vol. 1: Research Report. Cyrus Ulberg et al. 219p. (Orig.). (C). 1993. pap. text ed. 15.00 (*0-309-05273-4*, SHRP-H-350) SHRP.

Road Weather Information Systems, Vol. 2: Implementation Guide. S. Edward Boselly, III et al. 82p. (Orig.). (C). 1993. pap. text ed. 10.00 (*0-309-05274-2*, SHRP-H-351) SHRP.

Road Wet, the Wind Close: Celtic Ireland. James C. Roy. LC 85-31100. 220p. 8600. reprint ed. 30.00 (*0-8023-1281-0*) Dufour.

Road Wet, the Wind Close: Celtic Ireland. James C. Roy. LC 85-31100. (Illus.). 220p. 9500. reprint ed. pap. 17.95 (*0-8023-1283-7*) Dufour.

Road Work: A New Highway Pricing & Investment Policy. Clifford M. Winston et al. 130p. 1989. 32.95 (*0-8157-9470-3*); pap. 12.95 (*0-8157-9471-1*) Brookings.

***Road Work: The Ultimate RVing Adventure.** Arline Chandler. Ed. by Rena Copperman. (Illus.). 256p. (Orig.). 1997. pap. 14.95 (*0-9657975-0-3*) Flying Horse.

Roadblock to Reform: ERISA Implications for State Health Care Initiatives. Patricia A. Butler. Ed. by Karen Glass. 94p. (Orig.). 1994. pap. text ed. 20.00 (*1-55877-185-9*) Natl Governor.

Roadcraft - The Police Driver's Handbook. HMSO Staff. 190p. 1994. pap. 20.00 (*0-11-340858-7*, HM08587, Pub. by Stationery Ofc UK) Bernan Associates.

***Roadframes: The American Highway Narrative.** Kris Lackey. LC 96-49443. 168p. 1997. text ed. 30.00 (*0-8032-2924-0*) U of Nebr Pr.

Roadhaze. Brody James. 320p. 1995. mass mkt. 5.99 (*1-896329-47-0*, Pub. by Comnwlth Pub CN) Partners Pubs Grp.

Roadkill. Richard Sanford. 216p. 1995. 19.95 (*1-885173-05-9*) Write Way.

***RoadMap: How to Understand, Diagnose & Transform Organizations.** N. Dean Mayer. 132p. (Orig.). 1997. pap. 8.95 (*0-9641635-2-7*) NDMA Pubng.

***Roadmap: Realizing Organizational Alignment Through the Design of Measures, Actions & Performance.** Mark B. Jacobs et al. (Illus.). 107p. 1996. wbk. ed. 39.95 (*1-890071-01-3*) Milestone Press.

Roadmap for Milspec Reform: Integrating Commercial & Military Manufacturing. Debra Van Opstal. (CSIS Report Ser.). 55p. (Orig.). 1993. pap. text ed. 9.95 (*0-89206-225-8*) CSI Studies.

***Roadmap for Quality Transformation In Education: A Guide for Local Education Reform Leaders.** M. Andrew Frazier. 1997. 39.95 (*1-57444-139-6*) St Lucie Pr.

***Roadmap for Results: Trade Policy, Technology & American Competitiveness.** i, 62p. (Orig.). 1993. wbk. ed., pap. 25.00 (*1-889866-07-5*) Coun on Competitiveness.

***Roadmap for Results: Trade Policy, Technology & American Competitiveness.** (Illus.). ii, 187p. (Orig.). 1993. pap. 40.00 (*1-889866-08-3*) Coun on Competitiveness.

***Roadmap to D.C. Probate.** Anna C. Aldridge. 170p. 1997. 34.95 (*0-9656135-0-X*) Washington Law Pub.

Roadmap to Resolution. Larry Molinaro. 20p. 1995. pap. text ed. write for info. (*0-9646852-6-4*) Wildlife Habitat.

***Roadmap to Restructuring: Charting the Course of Change in American Education.** 2nd ed. David T. Conley. LC 97-8610. xvi, 571p. 1997. 34.95 (*0-86552-136-0*); pap. 23.95 (*0-86552-137-9*) U of Oreg ERIC.

Roadmap to Riches: The Workbook for the Lazy Man's Way to Riches. Richard G. Nixon. 143p. 1993. student ed. 10.00 (*1-884337-14-7*) F P Pubng.

Roadmap to Success 2000: A Guide to Business - Education Partnering. 52p. (Orig.). (C). 1993. pap. text ed. 50.00 (*1-56806-522-1*) DIANE Pub.

***Roadmaps of Packaging Technology.** rev. ed. Eric Bogatin. 580p. 1997. 850.00 (*1-877750-61-1*) ICE Corp.

Roadmarks. Roger Zelazny. 1986. mass mkt. 4.99 (*0-345-34515-0*, Del Rey) Ballantine.

Roadmarks. Roger Zelazny. LC 79-2280. 185p. 1979. 25.00 (*0-345-28530-1*) Ultramarine Pub.

Roadrunner. Wyman Meinzer. LC 92-33693. (Illus.). 128p. 1993. 37.50 (*0-89672-243-0*); pap. 19.95 (*0-89672-244-9*) Tex Tech Univ Pr.

Roadrunner (& His Cuckoo Cousin) Virginia Douglas. LC 84-982. 48p. 1984. pap. 5.95 (*0-87961-147-2*) Naturegraph.

Roadrunner Kitsap - Mason - Thurston County Street Atlas. Karen Jones. (Illus.). 185p. 1994. 38.95 (*0-9622357-9-2*) Roadrunner Maps.

Roadrunner Kitsap - Mason County Street Atlas. Karen Jones. (Illus.). 125p. 1994. 25.95 (*1-884957-00-5*) Roadrunner Maps.

Roadrunner Kitsap County Street Atlas: 1994 Edition. Karen Jones. (Illus.). 70p. 1994. 15.95 (*0-9622357-8-4*) Roadrunner Maps.

Roadrunner Kitsap County Street Atlas with Mason County Included: 1993 Edition. Mark Jones & Karen Jones. (Illus.). 118p. (Orig.). 25.95 (*0-9622357-5-X*) Roadrunner Maps.

Roadrunner Kitsap County Street Atlas 1993 Edition. rev. ed. Mark Jones & Karen Jones. (Illus.). 64p. 15.95 (*0-9622357-3-3*) Roadrunner Maps.

Roadrunner Kitsap County: 1996 Edition. rev. ed. Karen Jones. (Illus.). 64p. (C). 1995. 18.95 (*1-884957-01-3*) Roadrunner Maps.

Roadrunner Kitsap-Mason County Street Atlas: 1996 Edition. rev. ed. Karen Jones. (Illus.). 114p. (C). 1995. 28.95 (*1-884957-04-8*) Roadrunner Maps.

Roadrunner Kitsop, Mason, Thurston County Street Atlas: 1996 Edition. rev. ed. Karen Jones. (Illus.). 177p. (C). Date not set. 36.95 (*1-884957-06-4*) Roadrunner Maps.

R

Roadrunner Mason County Street Atlas. Mark Jones & Karen Jones. (Illus.). (Orig.). 15.95 (*0-9622357-4-1*) Roadrunner Maps.

Roadrunner Mason County Street Atlas: 1996 Edition. rev. ed. Karen Jones. (Illus.). 50p. (C). 1995. 18.95 (*1-884957-03-X*) Roadrunner Maps.

Roadrunner, Thurston County Street Atlas: 1993-94 Edition. rev. ed. Karen Jones. (Mapbook Ser.). (Illus.). 63p. 1993. 15.95 (*0-9622357-6-8*) Roadrunner Maps.

Roadrunner Thurston County Street Atlas: 1996 Edition. rev. ed. Karen Jones. 63p. (C). 1995. 18.95 (*1-884957-02-1*) Roadrunner Maps.

Roadrunner, Thurston-Mason County Street Atlas. rev. ed. Karen Jones. (Illus.). 123p. 1993. 25.95 (*0-9622357-7-6*) Roadrunner Maps.

Roadrunner Thurston-Mason Street Atlas: 1996 Edition. rev. ed. Karen Jones. (Illus.). 113p. (C). 1995. 28.95 (*1-884957-05-6*) Roadrunner Maps.

Roads. Philip Sauvain. Ed. by Rebecca Stefoff. LC 90-40359. (How We Build Ser.). (Illus.). 48p. (J). (gr. 4-7). 1990. lib. bdg. 17.26 (*0-944483-77-1*) Garrett Ed Corp.

Roads: A History. Madge Jenison. 1948. 7.50 (*0-910664-49-8*) Gotham.

*__Roads & Airfields in Cold Regions: A State of the Practice Report.__ Wilbur H. Haas et al. Ed. by Ted S. Vinson & James W. Rooney. LC 96-31477. (Technical Council on Cold Regions Engineering Monographs). 332p. 1996. 35.00 (*0-7844-0191-8*) Am Soc Civil Eng.

*__Roads & Crossroads.__ Arie Johnson-Stovall. Ed. by Noel H. Kaylor, Jr. (National Texts Ser.: No. 1). 200p. 1997. pap. 15.95 (*0-9641511-6-2*) Assn Text Study.

Roads & Highways: Soil Stabilization with Cement & Lime. (TRL State of the Art Review Ser.). 162p. 1994. pap. 85.00 (*0-11-551171-7*, HM11717, Pub. by Stationery Ofc UK) Bernan Associates.

Roads & Highways of Ancient Israel. David A. Dorsey. LC 89-32589. (Illus.). 288p. 1991. text ed. 49.95 (*0-8018-3898-3*) Johns Hopkins.

Roads & Rivals: The Political Uses of Access in the Borderlands of Asia. Mahnaz Z. Ispahani. LC 88-47932. (Illus.). 256p. 1989. 39.95 (*0-8014-2220-5*) Cornell U Pr.

Roads & Tunnels. Michael Pollard. LC 96-6958. (Superstructures Ser.). (J). 1996. lib. bdg. 24.26 (*0-8172-4332-1*) Raintree Steck-V.

Roads Are Down. Vanessa Spence. (Caribbean Writers Ser.). 128p. 1993. pap. 9.95 (*0-435-98930-8*, 98930) Heinemann.

Roads Are Not Enough: New Perspectives on Rural Transport Planning in Developing Countries. Jonathan Dawson & Ian Barwell. (Illus.). 80p. (Orig.). 1993. pap. 18.95 (*1-85339-191-3*, Pub. by Intermed Tech UK) Women Ink.

Roads Between the Worlds: The Eternal Champion, Vol. 6. Michael Moorcock. (Illus.). 1996. 21.99 (*1-56504-181-X*, 12507, Borealis) White Wolf.

Roads Dreamed Clear Afternoons - An Anthology of the Poetry of Antonio Machado. Carl W. Cobb. LC 93-61669. 220p. (C). 1994. 40.00 (*0-938972-23-5*) Spanish Lit Pubns.

Roads from Bethlehem: Christmas Literature from Writers Ancient & Modern. Ed. by Pegram Johnson, III & Edna M. Troiano. LC 93-18699. (Illus.). 352p. 1993. text ed. 20.00 (*0-664-22030-4*) Westminster John Knox.

*__Roads from Past to Future.__ Afterword by Arthur L. Stinchcombe. LC 97-21729. (Illus.). 1997. 62.50 (*0-8476-8409-1*); pap. 19.95 (*0-8476-8410-5*) Rowman.

*__Roads from the Bottom: A Survival Journal for America's Black Community.__ C. K. Chiplin. LC 96-28990. 1996. write for info. (*0-937552-73-9*) Quail Ridge.

*__Roads Home.__ Rowell Hoff. 150p. (Orig.). 1997. pap. 15.99 (*0-85398-417-4*) G Ronald Pub.

Roads Home: Seven Paths to Midlife Wisdom. Kathryn D. Cramer. LC 94-46145. 1995. 22.00 (*0-688-12352-X*) Morrow.

*__Roads Home: Seven Pathways to Midlife Wisdom.__ Kathryn D. Cramer. (Illus.). 368p. 1997. reprint ed. pap. 12.00 (*0-688-15122-1*, Quill) Morrow.

Roads in a Market Economy. Grabiel Roth. 292p. 1996. 76.95 (*0-291-39814-6*, Pub. by Avebury Technical UK) Ashgate Pub Co.

Roads in Central Oxfordshire. M. Breakell. (C). 1988. 29.00 (*0-685-30245-8*, Pub. by Oxford Polytechnic UK) St Mut.

Roads in the Sky. Richard O. Clemmer. (C). 1995. pap. text ed. 24.00 (*0-8133-2511-0*) Westview.

Roads I've Traveled. Illus. by Victoria Sheridan. 112p. (Orig.). 1994. pap. 7.95 (*1-56626-068-X*) Country Rds.

Roads Jesus Traveled. Thomas A. Pilgrim. 1991. pap. 8.25 (*1-55673-383-6*, 9201) CSS OH.

Roads Less Travelled. Carol Beaman & Dena Phillips. (Illus.). 85p. (YA). (gr. 8 up). 1994. 19.95 (*1-882935-13-6*) Westphalia.

Roads of Arkansas. William H. Burdett. (Illus.). 124p. 1990. pap. 13.95 (*0-940672-53-7*) Shearer Pub.

Roads of Chinese Childhood: Learning & Identification in Angang. Charles Stafford. (Cambridge Studies in Social & Cultural Anthropology: No. 97). (Illus.). 240p. (C). 1995. text ed. 54.95 (*0-521-46574-5*) Cambridge U Pr.

Roads of Colorado. Ed. by Shearer Publishing Cartographic Department Staff. (Illus.). 176p. 1996. 16.95 (*0-940672-59-6*) Shearer Pub.

Roads of Home: Lanes & Legends of New Jersey. Henry C. Beck. 301p. 1983. reprint ed. pap. 15.95 (*0-8135-1018-X*) Rutgers U Pr.

Roads of Melody. Carrie Jacobs-Bond. Ed. by Annette K. Baxter. LC 79-8776. (Signal Lives Ser.). (Illus.). 1980. reprint ed. lib. bdg. 30.95 (*0-405-12825-8*) Ayer.

Roads of New Mexico. Ed. by William H. Burdett. (Illus.). 128p. 1990. pap. 14.95 (*0-940672-52-9*) Shearer Pub.

Roads of North Carolina. Ed. by William H. Burdett. (Illus.). 80p. 1989. pap. 12.95 (*0-940672-48-0*) Shearer Pub.

*__Roads of Oklahoma.__ Shearer Publishing Staff. (Illus.). 148p. 1997. pap. 16.95 (*0-940672-67-7*) Shearer Pub.

Roads of Texas. 3rd ed. (Illus.). 176p. 1995. pap. 14.95 (*0-940672-64-2*) Shearer Pub.

Roads of Wyoming. Ed. by Shearer Publishing Cartographic Department Staff. (Illus.). 128p. 16.95 (*0-940672-57-X*) Shearer Pub.

Roads, Rails & Waterways: The Army Engineers & Early Transportation. Forest G. Hill. LC 77-14558. 248p. 1978. reprint ed. text ed. 55.00 (*0-8371-9839-9*, HIRW, Greenwood Pr) Greenwood.

Roads Take Us Home. Lee S. Hill. LC 96-11639. (Building Block Bks.). (J). 1996. lib. bdg. write for info. (*1-57505-022-6*, Carolrhoda) Lerner Group.

Roads Taken: A Country Lawyer Looks Back. Kermit R. Mason. Ed. & Intro. by Carl B. Taylor. 152p. 1986. 12.95 (*0-9605948-2-5*) C B Taylor.

Roads Taken: Travels Through America's Literary Landscapes. Fred Setterberg. LC 92-38775. (Literary Roads Ser.). 182p. (Orig.). 1995. pap. 14.95 (*1-56656-183-3*) Interlink Pub.

Roads Taken: Travels Through America's Literary Landscapes. Fred Setterberg. LC 92-38775. (Associated Writing Programs Award for Creative Nonfiction Ser.). 192p. (Orig.). 1993. 24.95 (*0-8203-1517-6*) U of Ga Pr.

Roads They Made, Women in Illinois History. Adade M. Wheeler & Marlene S. Wortman. LC 76-42591. (Illus.). 1977. lib. bdg. 22.95 (*0-88286-020-8*) C H Kerr.

Roads Through the Summer. Brian H. Johnson. Ed. by Malcolm Johnson. LC 84-81933. 100p. (Orig.). 1985. pap. 7.95 (*0-930639-00-6*) Harker Van Pelt.

Roads to a New America. David C. Coyle. LC 77-103649. (Select Bibliographies Reprint Ser.). 1977. 35.95 (*0-8369-5149-2*) Ayer.

Roads to Antietam. John W. Schildt. 220p. (Orig.). Date not set. 24.95 (*1-57249-044-6*) White Mane Pub.

Roads to Be Taken: The Intellectual Odyssey of Charles H. Sandage. Charles H. Sandage. 415p. (Orig.). (C). 1993. pap. 16.00 (*0-9636457-0-6*) Graceland Coll.

Roads to Castles see California

Roads to Center Place: A Cultural Atlas of Chaco Canyon & the Anasazi. Kathryn Gabriel. LC 91-12348. (Illus.). 304p. (Orig.). 1991. pap. 13.95 (*1-55566-079-7*) Johnson Bks.

Roads to Commensurability. David A. Pearce. (Synthese Library: No. 187). 260p. 1987. lib. bdg. 115.50 (*90-277-2414-8*, Pub. by Klwr Acad Pubs NE) Kluwer Ac.

Roads to Dawn Lake. John O. Simon. 1968. pap. 2.00 (*0-685-29877-9*) Oyez.

Roads to Dominion: Bright-Wing Movements & Political Power in the United States. Sara Diamond. LC 95-12887. (Critical Perspectives Ser.). 425p. 1995. pap. text ed. 19.95 (*0-89862-864-4*) Guilford Pr.

Roads to Dominion: Right-Wing Movements & Political Power in the United States. Sara Diamond. LC 95-12887. (Critical Perspectives Ser.). 425p. 1995. lib. bdg. 44.00 (*0-89862-862-8*) Guilford Pr.

*__Roads to Freedom: Freedom, Autonomy & Culture in Western Society.__ Hans T. Blokland. 272p. (C). 1997. text ed. 74.95 (*0-415-15000-0*) Routledge.

Roads to Freedom: Socialism, Anarchism & Syndication. Bertrand Russell. (Unwin Paperbacks Ser.). 1966. pap. 9.95 (*0-04-335033-X*) Routledge Chapman & Hall.

Roads to Geometry. Edward C. Wallace & Stephen F. West. 400p. 1991. text ed. 75.00 (*0-13-781725-8*) P-H.

*__Roads to Geometry.__ 2nd ed. Wallace & West. 1997. text ed. 75.00 (*0-13-181652-7*) P-H.

Roads to Glory. Richard Aldington. (Short Story Index Reprint Ser.). 1977. 20.95 (*0-8369-3666-3*) Ayer.

Roads to Home: Three Related One Act Plays. Horton Foote. 1982. pap. 5.25 (*0-8222-0958-6*) Dramatists Play.

Roads to Liberation from Oflag 64. 2nd ed. Clarence R. Meltesen. LC 90-91707. (Illus.). 535p. 1990. 20.00 (*0-9627005-0-9*) C R Meltesen.

Roads to Medical Management: Physician Executives' Career Decisions. Wesley Curry. 110p. 1988. pap. 24.95 (*0-9605218-6-0*) Am Coll Phys Execs.

Roads to Nowhere: A Child of Lebanon. Mansour Labaky. Tr. by Allen Annelyse. LC 87-32305. 96p. 1988. pap. 4.95 (*0-932506-61-5*) St Bedes Pubns.

*__Roads to Oblivion: Triumphs & Tragedies of British Car Makers 1946-56.__ Christopher Balfour. (Illus.). 208p. 1997. 39.95 (*1-870979-82-6*, Pub. by Bay View Bks UK) Motorbooks Intl.

Roads to Oriskany: A Saga about the Settlement & Defense of New York's Mohawk Valley During the 1700's. Gil Herkimer. (Illus.). 271p. (Orig.). 1996. pap. 18.95 (*0-9651170-0-6*) Alfa Pubs.

Roads to Paradise: Reading the Lives of the Early Saints. Alison G. Elliott. LC 86-40384. 262p. 1987. reprint ed. pap. 74.70 (*0-608-02299-3*, 2062940) Bks Demand.

Roads to Rails: Revolution in British Transport. Elisabeth R. Fairman. LC 92-60281. (Illus.). 30p. (Orig.). 1992. pap. 9.95 (*0-930606-68-X*) Yale Ctr Brit Art.

Roads to Reading Disability: When Poor Readers Become "Learning Disabled" Louise C. Spear-Swerling. LC 95-19900. (Renewing American Schools Ser.). (C). 1997. pap. text ed. 24.00 (*0-8133-8757-4*) Westview.

Roads to Reason: Transportation Administration & Rationing in Colombia. Richard I. Hartwig. LC 83-3676. (Illus.). 296p. 1983. 30.95 (*0-8229-3806-5*) U of Pittsburgh Pr.

Roads to Remember - The Insider's Guide to New Brunswick. Colleen Thompson. 304p. 1994. pap. 12.95 (*0-86492-160-8*, Pub. by Goose Ln Edits CN) Genl Dist Srvs.

Roads to Ride: A Bicyclists' Topographic Guide to Alameda, Contra Costa, & Marin Counties California Bicycling Guides, No. 1. Grant Petersen et al. 1991. reprint ed. lib. bdg. 27.00 (*0-8095-4969-7*) Borgo Pr.

Roads to Rome: The Antebellum Protestant Encounter with Catholicism. Jenny Franchot. LC 93-25760. (New Historicism Ser.: No. 28). (C). 1994. 55.00 (*0-520-07818-7*); pap. 18.00 (*0-520-08606-6*) U CA Pr.

Roads to Santiago: Detours & Riddles in the Lands & History of Spain. Cees Nooteboom. Tr. by Ina Rilke. (Illus.). 352p. 1997. 25.00 (*0-15-100197-9*) HarBrace.

*__Roads to Sata.__ A. Booth. 1996. pap. 15.95 (*0-8348-0246-5*) Weatherhill.

Roads to Sata. large type ed. Alan Booth. (Non-Fiction Ser.). 608p. 1992. 25.99 (*0-7089-2654-1*) Ulverscroft.

*__Roads to Sata: A 2000-Mile Walk Through Japan.__ Alan Booth. 304p. 1997. pap. 14.00 (*1-56836-187-4*, Kodansha Globe) Kodansha.

Roads to Sata Two Thousand Mile Walk... Alan Booth. 1986. pap. 14.95 (*0-8348-0200-7*) Weatherhill.

Roads to Social Peace. Edward A. Ross. LC 79-117830. (Essay Index Reprint Ser.). 1977. 17.95 (*0-8369-1679-4*) Ayer.

Roads to Success. unabridged ed. Joseph A. Boyd, Jr. 299p. (Orig.). 1995. pap. write for info. (*1-888781-02-5*) J A Boyd.

Roads to the Future: Steps to English Proficiency, Vol. 3. T. Robert Purcell. (Illus.). 114p. (C). 1989. text ed. write for info. (*0-318-65772-4*) English Tutors.

Roads to the Future: Strategic Plan for Educational Options in the 21st Century, Final Report. California Department of Education Staff. 156p. 1994. pap. 11.00 (*0-8011-1118-8*) Calif Education.

Roads to the Isles: A Guidebook to Scotland's Far West: Morar, Moidart, Morvern Ardnamurchan. Tom Atkinson. 128p. 1989. pap. text ed. 29.00 (*0-946487-01-4*, Pub. by Luath Pr UK) St Mut.

Roads to the Learning Society. Ed. by Lois Lamdin. 180p. (C). 1991. text ed. 25.00 (*0-9628073-1-1*) CAEL.

Roads to the Palace. Michael Rosenak. LC 95-17226. (Faith & Culture in Contemporary Education Ser.). 288p. (C). 1995. 45.00 (*1-57181-058-7*) Berghahn Bks.

*__Roads to the Unconcious: A Manual for Understanding Road Drawings.__ Michael Hanes. Date not set. spiral bd. 27.95 (*1-885473-13-3*) Wood NBarnes.

Roads to Today's Portugal. Ed. by Nelson H. Vieira. LC 83-83071. (Illus.). 157p. (Orig.). 1983. pap. 8.00 (*0-943722-11-X*) Gavea-Brown.

Roadside America: The Automobile in Design & Culture. Ed. by Jan Jennings. LC 90-32517. (Illus.). 250p. 1990. 39.95 (*0-8138-0131-1*) Iowa St U Pr.

Roadside Bicycle Repair: The Simple Guide to Fixing Your Bike. 3rd ed. Robert Van Der Plas. (Illus.). 96p. (Orig.). 1995. pap. 7.95 (*0-933201-67-2*) Motorbooks Intl.

Roadside Design Guide. (Design Ser.). (C). 1996. pap. text ed. 67.00 (*1-56051-031-5*, RSDG-2) AASHTO.

Roadside Flowers of Oklahoma, Vol. 1. Doyle McCoy. (Illus.). 116p. 1976. reprint ed. pap. 10.00 (*0-9619985-2-0*) McCoy Pub Co.

Roadside Flowers of Oklahoma, Vol. 2. Doyle McCoy. (Illus.). 60p. 1978. reprint ed. pap. 5.00 (*0-9619985-3-9*) McCoy Pub Co.

Roadside Geology of Alaska. Cathy Connor & Daniel O'Haire. LC 88-1651. (Roadside Geology Ser.). (Illus.). 256p. 1988. pap. 15.00 (*0-87842-213-7*) Mountain Pr.

Roadside Geology of Arizona. Halka Chronic. LC 83-2233. (Roadside Geology Ser.). 335p. 1983. pap. 15.00 (*0-87842-147-5*) Mountain Pr.

Roadside Geology of Colorado. Halka Chronic. LC 79-11148. (Roadside Geology Ser.). (Illus.). 336p. 1980. pap. 15.00 (*0-87842-105-X*) Mountain Pr.

Roadside Geology of Hawaii. Richard W. Hazlett & Donald W. Hyndman. LC 96-31763. (Roadside Geology Ser.). (Illus.). 432p. (Orig.). 1996. pap. 24.00 (*0-87842-344-3*) Mountain Pr.

Roadside Geology of Idaho. David Alt & Donald W. Hyndman. LC 89-36471. (Roadside Geology Ser.). (Illus.). 408p. 1989. pap. 15.00 (*0-87842-219-6*) Mountain Pr.

Roadside Geology of Louisiana. Darwin R. Spearing. (Roadside Geology Ser.). 1995. pap. 15.00 (*0-87842-324-9*) Mountain Pr.

Roadside Geology of Montana. David Alt & Donald W. Hyndman. LC 86-17954. (Roadside Geology Ser.). (Illus.). 440p. 1986. pap. 15.00 (*0-87842-202-1*) Mountain Pr.

Roadside Geology of New Mexico. Halka Chronic. Ed. by David Alt & Donald W. Hyndman. LC 86-21748. (Roadside Geology Ser.). (Illus.). 260p. (Orig.). 1987. pap. 14.00 (*0-87842-209-9*) Mountain Pr.

Roadside Geology of New York. Bradford B. Van Diver. LC 85-13871. (Roadside Geology Ser.). (Illus.). 411p. 1985. pap. 15.00 (*0-87842-180-7*) Mountain Pr.

Roadside Geology of Northern California. David Alt & Donald W. Hyndman. LC 74-81834. (Roadside Geology Ser.). (Illus.). 256p. 1975. pap. 15.00 (*0-87842-055-X*) Mountain Pr.

Roadside Geology of Oregon. David Alt & Donald W. Hyndman. LC 77-25841. (Roadside Geology Ser.). (Illus.). 284p. 1978. pap. 14.00 (*0-87842-063-0*) Mountain Pr.

Roadside Geology of Pennsylvania. Bradford B. Van Diver. LC 90-5515. (Roadside Geology Ser.). 352p. 1990. pap. 15.00 (*0-87842-227-7*) Mountain Pr.

Roadside Geology of South Dakota. John P. Gries. (Roadside Geology Ser.). (Illus.). 432p. (Orig.). 1996. pap. 20.00 (*0-87842-338-9*) Mountain Pr.

Roadside Geology of Texas. Darwin R. Spearing. (Roadside Geology Ser.). (Illus.). 432p. 1991. pap. 16.00 (*0-87842-265-X*) Mountain Pr.

Roadside Geology of the Eastern Sierra Region. (Mono Lake Committee Field Guide Ser.). (Illus.). 50p. 1982. pap. text ed. 3.95 (*0-939716-05-4*) Mono Lake Comm.

Roadside Geology of the Yellowstone Country. William J. Fritz. LC 85-4934. (Roadside Geology Ser.). (Illus.). 160p. (Orig.). 1985. pap. 10.00 (*0-87842-170-X*) Mountain Pr.

Roadside Geology of U. S. Interstate 80 Between Salt Lake City & San Francisco. W. Kenneth Hamblin et al. 51p. 1975. pap. 5.00 (*0-913312-43-6*) Am Geol.

Roadside Geology of Utah. Halka Chronic. LC 89-48790. (Roadside Geology Ser.). 325p. 1990. pap. 15.00 (*0-87842-228-5*) Mountain Pr.

Roadside Geology of Vermont & New Hampshire. Bradford B. Van Diver. Ed. by David Alt & Donald W. Hyndman. LC 87-3897. (Roadside Geology Ser.). (Illus.). 240p. (Orig.). 1987. pap. 10.00 (*0-87842-203-X*) Mountain Pr.

Roadside Geology of Virginia. Keith Frye. Ed. by David Alt & Donald W. Hyndman. LC 86-8755. (Roadside Geology Ser.). (Illus.). 256p. (Orig.). (J). 1986. pap. 12.00 (*0-87842-199-8*) Mountain Pr.

Roadside Geology of Washington. David Alt & Donald W. Hyndman. LC 84-8409. (Roadside Geology Ser.). (Illus.). 320p. (Orig.). 1984. pap. 15.00 (*0-87842-160-2*) Mountain Pr.

Roadside Geology of Wyoming. David R. Lageson & Darwin Spearing. Ed. by David Alt & Donald W. Hyndman. LC 88-1650. (Roadside Geology Ser.). (Illus.). 288p. (Orig.). 1988. pap. 14.00 (*0-87842-216-1*) Mountain Pr.

Roadside Guide to Rocky Mountain National Park: History, Natural History, Geology, & Archaeology. Beatrice E. Willard & Susan Q. Foster. LC 89-85046. (Illus.). 336p. 1989. pap. 12.95 (*1-55566-027-4*) Johnson Bks.

Roadside Guide to the Colorado Mountains: Interstate 25 Skylines. Joe Milligan. LC 95-71149. (Peakfinders Ser.: Vol. 1). (Illus.). 112p. (Orig.). 1996. pap. 16.95 (*0-9647522-0-4*) Westcliffe Pubs.

Roadside Guide to the Geology of Newberry Volcano. 2nd ed. Robert A. Jensen. (Illus.). 155p. 1995. pap. 12.95 (*0-9646287-0-8*) CenOreGeoPub.

Roadside Guide to the Geology of the Great Smoky Mountains National Park. Harry L. Moore. LC 87-18796. (Illus.). 192p. 1988. pap. 11.95 (*0-87049-558-5*) U of Tenn Pr.

Roadside History of Arizona. Marshall Trimble. LC 85-28521. (Roadside History Ser.). (Illus.). 496p. (Orig.). 1987. 24.95 (*0-87842-197-1*); pap. 18.00 (*0-87842-198-X*) Mountain Pr.

Roadside History of Arkansas. Alan C. Paulson. (Roadside History Ser.). (Illus.). 480p. 1996. 30.00 (*0-87842-334-6*); pap. 18.00 (*0-87842-335-4*) Mountain Pr.

Roadside History of California. Ruth Pittman. Ed. by Dan Greer. (Roadside History Ser.). (Illus.). 496p. 1995. 30.00 (*0-87842-317-6*); pap. 18.00 (*0-87842-318-4*) Mountain Pr.

Roadside History of Colorado. rev. ed. James McTighe. LC 89-84757. (Illus.). 378p. (Orig.). 1989. pap. 13.95 (*1-55566-054-1*) Johnson Bks.

Roadside History of Idaho. Betty Derig. 1995. 30.00 (*0-87842-327-3*) Mountain Pr.

Roadside History of Idaho. Betty Derig. (Illus.). 384p. 1995. pap. text ed. 18.00 (*0-87842-328-1*) Mountain Pr.

*__Roadside History of Nebraska.__ Candy Moulton. LC 97-22949. 1997. 30.00 (*0-87842-348-6*); pap. text ed. 18.00 (*0-87842-347-8*) Mountain Pr.

Roadside History of New Mexico. Francis L. Fugate & Roberta B. Fugate. LC 89-32930. (Roadside History Ser.). 483p. 1989. 24.95 (*0-87842-248-X*); pap. 16.00 (*0-87842-242-0*) Mountain Pr.

Roadside History of Oregon. Bill Gulick. (Roadside History Ser.). (Illus.). 452p. 1991. 24.95 (*0-87842-253-6*); pap. 16.00 (*0-87842-252-8*) Mountain Pr.

Roadside History of South Dakota. Linda Hasselstrom. 480p. 1994. 25.00 (*0-87842-236-6*); pap. 16.00 (*0-87842-262-5*) Mountain Pr.

Roadside History of Texas. Leon C. Metz. Ed. by Daniel Greer. (Roadside History Ser.). (Illus.). 489p. 1993. 30.00 (*0-87842-293-5*); pap. 18.00 (*0-87842-294-3*) Mountain Pr.

Roadside History of Vermont. Peter S. Jennison. LC 89-3434. (Roadside History Ser.). 271p. 1989. 24.95 (*0-87842-246-3*); pap. 15.00 (*0-87842-232-3*) Mountain Pr.

Roadside History of Wyoming. Candy Moulton. Ed. by Dan Greer. (Roadside History Ser.). (Illus.). 480p. 1995. 30.00 (*0-87842-315-X*); pap. 18.00 (*0-87842-316-8*) Mountain Pr.

Roadside History of Yellowstone Park. Winfred Blevins. (Roadside History Ser.). 116p. 1989. pap. 8.00 (*0-87842-223-4*) Mountain Pr.

Roadside Kansas: A Traveler's Guide to Its Geology & Landmarks. Rex Buchanan & James R. McCauley. LC 87-2013. (Illus.). xiv, 370p. 1987. 25.00 (*0-7006-0323-9*); pap. 9.95 (*0-7006-0322-0*) U Pr of KS.

Roadside Markers in West Virginia. Ed. & Compiled by Charles S. Adams. 90p. 1995. pap. 14.95 (*1-888256-03-6*) CS Adams.

Roadside Meetings. Hamlin Garland. (Collected Works of Hamlin Garland). 1988. reprint ed. lib. bdg. 59.00 (*0-7812-1252-9*) Rprt Serv.

Roadside Meetings see Collected Works of Hamlin Garland

Roadside New Jersey. Peter Genovese. LC 93-31172. (Illus.). 268p. (Orig.). 1994. pap. 18.95 (*0-8135-2061-4*) Rutgers U Pr.

Roadside Noise Abatement. OECD Staff. (Road Transport Research Ser.). 170p. (Orig.). 1995. pap. 50.00 (*92-64-14578-8*, Pub. by Org for Econ FR) OECD.

An Asterisk (*) at the beginning of an entry indicates that the title is appearing in BIP for the first time.

Roadside Plants & Flowers: A Traveler's Guide to the Midwest & Great Lakes Area. Marian S. Edsall. LC 84-40148. (North Coast Bks.). (Illus.). 158p. 1985. pap. 14.95 (0-299-09704-8) U of Wis Pr.

Roadside Plants of Northern New Mexico. Gail D. Tierney & Phyllis Hughes. LC 80-82718. (Illus.). 174p. 1983. pap. 9.95 (0-89016-061-9) Lightning Tree.

Roadside Plants of Southern California. Thomas J. Belzer. LC 83-8082. (Illus.). 158p. 1984. pap. 14.00 (0-87842-158-0) Mountain Pr.

Roadside Prey. Alva Busch. 320p. 1996. mass mkt. 5.99 (0-7860-0221-2, Pinncle Kensgtn) Kensgtn Pub Corp.

Roadside Revelations. Boykin M. Woodruff, Sr. 108p. 1994. write for info. (0-9641645-0-7) Revelations.

Roadside Romance: A Lovers Guide to Americas Favorite Lovers Lanes Honeymoon Hideaways, & Places to Propose & Rekindle the Flames of Passion. Robyn Nash. LC 95-19921. (Illus.). 176p. 1996. pap. 12.95 (0-8065-1716-6, Citadel Pr) Carol Pub Group.

Roadside Safety. (Research Record Ser.: No. 1065). 105p. 1986. 14.40 (0-309-04059-0) Transport Res Bd.

Roadside Safety Design for Small Vehicles. (National Cooperative Highway Research Program Report Ser.: No. 318). 70p. 1989. 10.00 (0-309-04615-7) Transport Res Bd.

Roadside Safety Features. (Research Record Ser.: No. 1133). 57p. 1987. 9.00 (0-309-04512-6) Transport Res Bd.

Roadside Safety Features. (Research Record Ser.: No. 1198). 116p. 1988. 15.50 (0-309-04772-2) Transport Res Bd.

Roadside Safety Features & Landscape & Environmental Design (TRR 1419) Ed. by Susan Brown. (Transportation Research Record Ser.). (Illus.). 140p. 1994. pap. text ed. 29.00 (0-309-05567-9) Natl Res Coun.

Roadside Safety 1990. (Transportation Research Record Ser.: No. 1258). 115p. 1990. 21.00 (0-309-05007-3) Transport Res Bd.

Roadside Sobriety Tests: A Police Officer's Guide to Making Drunk Driving Arrests Stand up in Court. James Whitmore. LC 87-17890. 86p. 1991. reprint ed. pap. 9.95 (0-935878-07-6) Calibre Pr.

***Roadside Stands & Farmers' Markets: A Travel Guide to Westcoast Produce.** Sandra Fuller & Annette Gierke. (Illus.). 350p. 1997. per. 14.95 (0-9658650-0-2) Creekside Publng.

Roadside Trees & Shrubs of Oklahoma. Doyle McCoy. LC 80-5944. (Illus.). 180p. 1981. pap. 12.95 (0-8061-1556-4) U of Okla Pr.

Roadside Wild Fruits of Oklahoma. Doyle McCoy. LC 79-6705. (Illus.). 96p. 1980. pap. 12.95 (0-8061-1626-9) U of Okla Pr.

***Roadside Wildflowers: Flashguides.** Roger T. Peterson. 1997. pap. 7.95 (0-395-82995-X) HM.

Roadside Wildflowers Northwest. Underhill. 1981. pap. 5.95 (0-88839-108-0) Hancock House.

Roadside Wildflowers of the Southern Great Plains. Craig C. Freeman & Eileen K. Schofield. (Illus.). viii, 280p. 1991. 29.95 (0-7006-0447-2); pap. 17.95 (0-7006-0448-0) U Pr of KS.

Roadsigns. Gary Hines. 16p. 1978. pap. 2.00 (0-913719-27-7) High-Coo Pr.

Roadwalkers: A Novel. Shirley A. Grau. LC 93-37262. 1994. 22.00 (0-679-43233-7) Knopf.

Roadway Defects & Tort Liability. John C. Glennon. LC 96-15339. 524p. 1996. 99.00 (0-913875-17-1, 5171) Lawyers & Judges.

Roadway Drivage Techniques in the Coal Mines of the European Community. Commission of the European Communities Staff. 392p. 1984. pap. text ed. 108.00 (0-86010-575-X) G & T Inc.

Roadway Lighting ANSI Approved. rev. ed. Roadway Committee. (Recommended Practices Ser.). (Illus.). 53p. 1993. pap. 28.00 (0-87995-013-7, RP-8-83) Illum Eng.

***Roadway Lighting Equipment (C136) 1994 Edition.** 90.00 (1-55937-417-9, SH17236) IEEE Standards.

Roadway Lighting Maintenance Guide. (Design Guides Ser.). (Illus.). 21p. 1993. pap. 25.00 (0-87995-095-1, DG-4-93) Illum Eng.

Roadway Sign Lighting. Roadway Committee. (Recommended Practices Ser.). (Illus.). 7p. 1989. pap. 25.00 (0-87995-054-4, RP-19-89) Illum Eng.

Roadways: The History of Swindon's Street Names. Peter Sheldon & Richard Tomkins. 112p. (C). 1987. 39.00 (0-317-90467-1, Pub. by Picton UK) St Mut.

Roadways: The History of Swindon's Street Names. Peter Sheldon & Richard Tomkins. 112p. (C). 1990. pap. 22.00 (0-902633-62-7, Pub. by Picton UK) St Mut.

Roadways & Airport Pavements. American Concrete Institute Staff. LC 75-10374. (American Concrete Institute Publication Ser.: SP-51). (Illus.). 291p. reprint ed. pap. 83.00 (0-317-10031-9, 2017593) Bks Demand.

Roadways to Success. Robert Sherfield. 308p. 1996. pap. 27.00 (0-205-18788-9) Allyn.

Roadwork. (Looney Tunes Bks.). (Illus.). (J). 1997. 5.99 (0-8289-0986-5) Penguin.

Roadwork Theory & Practice. 3rd ed. Arthur Wignall et al. (Illus.). 288p. 1991. 59.95 (0-7506-0291-0) Buttrwrth-Heinemann.

Roadworks. Linda McCartney. 1995. 50.00 (0-614-96888-7) Little.

Roadworks. Linda McCartney. (Illus.). 176p. 1994. 55.00 (0-8212-2172-8) Bulfinch Pr.

Roald Dahl. Roald Dahl. Date not set. pap. 9.99 (0-517-14880-3) Random Hse Value.

Roald Dahl. Christopher Meeks. LC 92-42286. (J). (gr. 3-7). 1993. 14.60 (0-86593-259-X); 10.95 (0-685-66357-4) Rourke Corp.

Roald Dahl. Jeremy Treglown. 1994. 25.00 (0-374-25130-4) FS&G.

Roald Dahl. M. West. (Twayne's English Authors Ser.). 150p. 1992. 22.95 (0-8057-7019-4, Twayne) Scribnrs Ref.

Roald Dahl: A Biography. Jeremy Treglown. 336p. 1995. pap. 13.00 (0-15-600199-3, Harvest Bks) HarBrace.

Roald Dahl: Charlie & the Chocolate Factory, Charlie & the Great Glass Elevator & The BFG, 3 bks., Set. Roald Dahl. (J). 1989. pap. 11.95 (0-685-30573-2) Viking Child Bks.

Roald Dahl: Favorite Authors. Caroline Nakajima. (Favorite Authors Ser.). (Illus.). 1994. 11.95 (1-55734-453-1) Tchr Create Mat.

Roald Dahl: From The Gremlins to the Chocolate Factory. enl. rev. ed. Alan Warren. Ed. by Dale Salwak. LC 93-12020. (Milford Series: Popular Writers of Today: Vol. 57). 128p. 1994. pap. 17.00 (0-8095-3001-5) Borgo Pr.

Roald Dahl: From The Gremlins to the Chocolate Factory. 2nd enl. rev. ed. Alan Warren. Ed. by Dale Salwak. LC 93-12020. (Milford Series: Popular Writers of Today: Vol. 57). 128p. 1994. lib. bdg. 27.00 (0-8095-2001-X) Borgo Pr.

Roald Dahl in the Classroom. Thomas J. Palumbo. 176p. teacher ed. 14.99 (0-86653-744-9, GA1459) Good Apple.

***Roald Dahl Quiz Book: Over 300 Questions to Challenge Dahl Fans Everywhere.** Richard Maher & Sylvia Bond. 1997. pap. 3.99 (0-14-038477-4) Puffin Bks.

***Roald Dahl Treasury.** Roald Dahl. (Illus.). (J). 1997. write for info. (0-614-29321-9) Viking Penguin.

Roald Dahl's Book of Ghost Stories. Ed. by Roald Dahl. 235p. (J). (gr. 5 up). 1983. 19.00 (0-374-25131-2) FS&G.

Roald Dahl's Book of Ghost Stories. Ed. by Roald Dahl. 240p. (YA). (gr. 5 up). 1984. pap. 12.00 (0-374-51868-8) FS&G.

Roald Dahl's Charlie & the Chocolate Factory, 4 vols., Set. (J). 1988. boxed 8.70 (0-685-42774-9) Bantam.

Roald Dahl's Revolting Recipes. Roald Dahl & Felicity Dahl. (Illus.). 64p. (J). 1994. pap. 15.99 (0-670-85836-6) Viking Child Bks.

Roald Dahl's Tales of the Unexpected. Roald Dahl. 1979. pap. 7.95 (0-394-74081-5, V-81, Vin) Random.

Roal'd I Flora. Platova Viktoriia. LC 92-42337. 206p. (Orig.). (RUS.). 1993. pap. 12.00 (1-55779-052-3) Hermitage.

Roaming about Universe. Osman Turkay. LC 96-68133. 80p. (Orig.). 1996. pap. 11.95 (1-57197-022-3) Pentland Pr.

Roan Mountain: A Passage of Time. Jennifer Wilson. LC 91-9787. (Illus.). 162p. 1991. pap. 9.95 (0-89587-082-7) Blair.

Roane County, West Virginia Families. William H. Bishop. 704p. reprint ed. pap. 21.50 (0-614-10016-X, 9039) Clearfield Co.

Roanoke: Story of County & City. Writers Program, Virginia Staff. LC 73-3658. (American Guide Ser.). 1942. reprint ed. 18.50 (0-404-57958-2) AMS Pr.

Roanoke: The Abandoned Colony. Karen O. Kupperman. LC 83-24419. 200p. (C). 1984. pap. 14.95 (0-8476-7339-1) Rowman.

Roanoke: The Lost Colony. Angela E. Hunt. LC 95-37575. (Keepers of the Ring Ser.: Vol. 1). 1996. pap. 11.99 (0-8423-2012-1) Tyndale.

Roanoke County Marriages, Eighteen Thirty-Eight to Eighteen Fifty. John Vogt & T. William Kethley, Jr. (Virginia Historic Marriage Register Ser.). (Illus.). viii, 54p. (Orig.). 1984. pap. 5.00 (0-935931-15-5) Borgo Pr.

Roanoke County Marriages, Eighteen Thirty-Eight to Eighteen Fifty. John Vogt & T. William Kethley, Jr. (Virginia Historic Marriage Register Ser.). viii, 54p. (Orig.). (C). 1984. reprint ed. lib. bdg. 25.00 (0-8095-8229-5) Borgo Pr.

Roanoke Hundred. Inglis Fletcher. (Albemarle Ser.). 501p. reprint ed. lib. bdg. 30.95 (0-89244-007-4, Queens House) Amereon Ltd.

Roanoke Hundred. Inglis Fletcher. 1990. reprint ed. lib. bdg. 26.95 (0-89968-507-2) Buccaneer Bks.

Roanoke Island: The Beginnings of English America. David Stick. LC 83-7014. (Illus.). xiii, 266p. 1983. pap. 9.95 (0-8078-4110-2) U of NC Pr.

***Roanoke Rapids: The First Hundred Years, 1897-1997.** Ed. by Robert B. Robinson. LC 97-9929. 1997. 39.95 (1-55618-160-4) Brunswick Pub.

Roanoke, VA. Historical Briefs, Inc. Staff. Ed. by Thomas Antonucci & Michael Antonucci. 200p. 1992. pap. 14.95 (0-89677-044-3) Hist Briefs.

Roanoke Valley's African American Heritage: A Pictorial History. Reginald Shareef. LC 96-19032. 1996. write for info. (0-89865-962-0) Donning Co.

Roanoke Voyages 1584-1590. David B. Quinn. 1990. pap. 14.95 (0-486-26513-7) Dover.

Roanoke Voyages, 1584-1590: Documents to Illustrate the English Voyages to North American under. David B. Quinn. 1990. pap. 14.95 (0-486-26512-9) Dover.

***Roar!, Vol. 1.** Grossman. (Illus.). (J). 1997. 2.95 (0-7868-4076-5) Disney Pr.

Roar! Art Collective. Traudi Allen. 164p. 1995. text ed. 39.95 (976-8097-82-5) Gordon & Breach.

Roar! The Paper Tiger Television Guide to Media Activism. Paper Tiger Television Collective Staff. Ed. by Daniel Marcus. (Illus.). 67p. (Orig.). (C). 1991. pap. 10.00 (0-9630999-3-0) Paper Tiger TV.

Roar & More. Karla Kuskin. LC 56-8138. (Trophy Picture Bk.). (Illus.). 32p. (J). (ps-3). 1977. pap. 1.95 (0-06-443019-7, Trophy) HarpC Child Bks.

Roar & More. rev. ed. Karla Kuskin. LC 89-15650. (Trophy Picture Bk.). (Illus.). 48p. (J). (ps-1). 1990. pap. 4.95 (0-06-443244-0, Trophy); lib. bdg. 14.89 (0-06-023619-1) HarpC Child Bks.

***Roar in the Night: A. D. 64.** Brian Brown & Andres Melrose. (Story Keepers A.D.64: Bk. 7). 64p. (J). 1997. pap. 3.99 (0-310-20344-9) Zondervan.

***Roar in the Night: A. D. 64.** Brian Brown & Andrew Melrose. (Storykeepers Easy Reader Ser.: Vol. 7). 32p. (J). 1997. pap. 3.99 (0-310-20346-5) Zondervan.

Roar of Silence: Healing Powers of Breath, Tone & Music. Don Campbell. LC 89-40173. (Illus.). 174p. (Orig.). 1989. pap. 9.95 (0-8356-0645-7, Quest) Theos Pub Hse.

Roar of the Crowd. James J. Corbett. LC 76-6330. (Irish Americans Ser.). 1976. reprint ed. 29.95 (0-405-09326-8) Ayer.

Roar of Thunder Whisper of Wind: A Portrait of Michigan Waterfalls. Photos by C. J. Elfont. (Illus.). 127p. 1994. reprint ed. 40.00 (1-882376-03-X); reprint ed. pap. 24.95 (1-882376-02-1) Thunder Bay Pr.

Roar, the Silence, the Grandeur. John Reymann. LC 90-70461. 85p. (Orig.). 1991. pap. 7.00 (1-56002-118-7) Aegina Pr.

Roarasaurus. John Patience. (Pop-up Ser.). (Illus.). 12p. (J). (ps up). 1994. 14.95 (0-8431-3686-3) Price Stern Sloan.

Roarin' Twenties: A History of the 312th Bombardment Group - U. S. Army Air Force World War II. Russell L. Sturzebecker. LC 76-6652. (Illus.). 301p. 1994. 20.00 (0-9600466-1-5) Sturzebecker.

Roaring at the Dawn: Journeys in Wild Africa. Brian Jackman. (Illus.). 184p. 1996. 34.95 (1-85310-570-8, Pub. by Swan Hill UK) Voyageur Pr.

Roaring Back: A Story of Transformation & Renewal at the Southern Pacific Railroad. Steve George. 256p. (C). 1995. 60.00 (0-939246-69-4) Wiley.

Roaring Billy. Dee Shulman. (Illus.). 32p. (J). (ps). 1992. 15.95 (0-370-31585-5, Pub. by Bodley Head UK) Trafalgar.

Roaring Boy. Edward Marston. LC 95-8568. 272p. 1995. 21.95 (0-312-13155-0) St Martin.

Roaring Boy. Edward Marston. 1996. mass mkt. 5.99 (0-449-22431-7) Fawcett.

Roaring Boy. large type ed. Edward Marston. LC 95-8568. 555p. 1995. 23.95 (0-7838-1491-7) Thorndike Pr.

Roaring Cargo: Politically Incorrect Poems. Ralph L. Jones, Jr. (Illus.). 52p. (Orig.). 1994. pap. 7.00 (0-9640747-3-7) Wolf-Wise Pr.

Roaring Days: Rossland's Mines & the History of British Columbia. Jeremy Mouat. (Illus.). 256p. 1996. pap. 25.95 (0-7748-0519-6, Pub. by U BC Pr) U of Wash Pr.

***Roaring Girl.** Greg Hollingshead. LC 96-42265. 208p. 1997. 21.95 (0-399-14222-3, Putnam) Putnam Pub Group.

Roaring Girl. Thomas Middleton & Thomas Dekker. Ed. by Paul Mulholland. (Revels Plays Ser.). 1990. text ed. 24.95 (0-7190-1630-4, Pub. by Manchester Univ Pr UK) St Martin.

***Roaring Girl.** 2nd ed. Elizabeth Cook. (C). Date not set. pap. text ed. write for info. (0-393-90085-1) Norton.

Roaring Girl. Thomas Middleton & Thomas Dekker. LC 71-133654. (Tudor Facsimile Texts. Old English Plays Ser.: No. 130). reprint ed. 59.50 (0-404-53430-9) AMS Pr.

Roaring Lambs: A Gentle Plan to Radically Change Your World. Bob Briner. 192p. 1995. pap. 10.99 (0-310-59111-2) Zondervan.

Roaring Lion. Robert Peterson & Martha Peterson. 1989. pap. 4.95 (9971-972-80-8) OMF Bks.

Roaring Queen. Wyndham Lewis. 1973. 10.00 (0-87140-576-8) Liveright.

Roaring Races. Giulio Schmidt et al. Tr. by Pietro Castiglioni. (Illus.). 192p. 1988. 39.95 (88-7672-006-5, 3-AQ-0058) Auto Quarterly.

Roaring Reptiles. D. M. Souza. (J). (gr. 1-4). 1992. lib. bdg. 14.96 (0-87614-710-4, Carolrhoda) Lerner Group.

Roaring River Mystery. Franklin W. Dixon. Ed. by Betty Schwartz. (Hardy Boys Ser.: No. 80). (Orig.). (J). (gr. 3-7). 1991. pap. 3.50 (0-671-73004-5) S&S Trade.

Roaring Roadsters: Track Roadsters from 1924-1956. Don Radbruch. (Illus.). 200p. 1994. pap. 22.95 (1-884089-06-2) CarTech.

***Roaring Rockets.** Tony Mitton. LC 97-5423. (Illus.). 24p. (J). (ps-k). 1997. 8.95 (0-7534-5106-9) LKC.

Roaring Silence. Michael Clarke. pap. 13.95 (1-874250-30-8, 93163) Talman.

Roaring Silence: A Biography of John Cage. David Revill. (Illus.). 272p. 1992. 27.95 (1-55970-166-8) Arcade Pub Inc.

Roaring Silence: John Cage: a Life. David Revill. 384p. 1993. pap. 14.95 (1-55970-220-6) Arcade Pub Inc.

Roaring Stream: A New Zen Reader. Ed. by Nelson Foster & Jack Shoemaker. LC 96-5151. (Companions Ser.). 384p. 1996. 27.50 (0-88001-344-3) Ecco Pr.

Roaring Stream: A New Zen Reader. Ed. by Nelson Foster & Jack Shoemaker. LC 96-5151. (Ecco Companions Ser.). 400p. 1997. pap. 18.00 (0-88001-511-X) Ecco Pr.

Roaring Through the Twenties in Beaverhead County, MT. rev. ed. Sally Garrett & Edith H. Palmer. 52p. 1996. pap. text ed. 4.00 (1-885916-00-0) Unconvntl Pr.

***Roaring Twenties.** David Pietrusza. (World History Ser.). (Illus.). (J). (gr. 4-12). 1997. lib. bdg. 17.96 (1-56006-309-2) Lucent Bks.

Roaring Twenties. Conrad R. Stein. (Cornerstones of Freedom Ser.). (J). (gr. 3-6). 1994. pap. 4.95 (0-516-46675-5) Childrens.

Roaring Twenties. R. Conrad Stein. LC 93-37029. (Cornerstones of Freedom Ser.). (Illus.). 32p. (J). (gr. 3-6). 1994. lib. bdg. 18.00 (0-516-06675-7) Childrens.

***Roaring Twenties: 1920-1930.** (This Fabulous Century Ser.). (Illus.). 288p. 24.95 (0-8094-8212-6) Time-Life.

Roaring Twenties & the Depression. (C. C. Publications Social Studies). (Illus.). 64p. 7.30 (0-574-51771-5) SRA.

Roaring Twenties Cookbook. Bruce Carlson. (Illus.). 224p. 1993. spiral bd. 11.95 (1-878488-86-4) Hearts N Tummies.

Roaring U 50's...Union Pacific's Twin Diesels. Harold Keekley. LC 78-51508. (Great Railroading Ser.). 1978. pap. 10.95 (0-916160-06-8) G R Cockle.

***Roarke: The Adventurer.** Joann Ross. (Temptation Ser.: No. 638). 1997. mass mkt. 3.50 (0-373-25738-4, 1-25738-5) Harlequin Bks.

Roarke's Folly. Claire Delacroix. (Historical Ser.). 1994. mass mkt. 3.99 (0-373-28850-6, 1-28850-5) Harlequin Bks.

Roarke's Kingdom. Sandra Marton. (Presents Ser.). 1993. mass mkt. 2.99 (0-373-11574-1, 1-11574-0) Harlequin Bks.

***Roarke's Wife.** Beverly Barton. 1997. mass mkt. 3.99 (0-373-07807-2, 1-07807-0) Silhouette.

Roark's Formulas for Stress & Strain. 6th ed. Warren C. Young. 800p. 1989. text ed. 79.95 (0-07-072541-1) McGraw.

Roarr: Calder's Circus. Maira Kalman. 32p. 1992. 15.00 (0-87427-079-0) Whitney Mus.

Roas'nears, Rabbit Toback'r, 'n Rosebud Salve. Faye Brown. (Illus.). 238p. (Orig.). 1992. pap. 9.95 (0-943487-39-0) Sevgo Pr.

Roast Beef in April: An Autobiographical Sketch of the '30's & '40's. Bob Higgins. Ed. by Doug Flaming. 165p. (Orig.). (YA). (gr. 7-10). 1993. pap. 9.99 (0-9637936-2-4) Deerlick Ent.

Roast Beef, Medium: The Business Adventures of Emma McChesney. Edna Ferber. LC 70-169550. (Short Story Index Reprint Ser.). (Illus.). 1977. reprint ed. 20.95 (0-8369-4012-1) Ayer.

Roast Chicken & Other Stories. Simon Hopkinson & Lindsey Bareham. (Illus.). 240p. 1995. 29.95 (0-09-177034-3, Pub. by Ebury Pr UK) Trafalgar.

Roast Chicken & Other Stories. Simon Hopkinson. (Illus.). 224p. 1996. pap. 17.95 (0-09-181274-7, Pub. by Ebury Pr UK) Trafalgar.

Roast Leviathan. Louis Untermeyer. LC 74-29528. (Modern Jewish Experience Ser.). 1975. reprint ed. 21.95 (0-405-06752-6) Ayer.

Roast Pan, the Cat & the Rat. Lula M. Neal. (Illus.). (Orig.). (J). (gr. k-3). 1996. pap. 6.95 (0-533-11742-9) Vantage.

Roast Pig & Other Essays. large type ed. Charles Lamb. (YA). (gr. 10 up). reprint ed. 10.00 (0-318-65692-2) NAVH.

Roasted Chestnuts. Michael Dudley. 24p. 1979. pap. 3.50 (0-913719-10-2) High-Coo Pr.

Roasting. Kathy Gunst. LC 94-44742. (Illus.). 272p. 1995. pap. 16.00 (0-02-051340-2) Macmillan.

Roasting: A Simple Art. Barbara Kafka. LC 95-18259. 372p. 1995. 26.00 (0-688-13135-2) Morrow.

Roasting the Swan of Avon: Shakespeare's Redoubtable Enemies & Dubious Friends. Bruce R. Smith. (Folger Shakespeare Library Ser.). (Illus.). 80p. 1994. pap. 14.95 (0-295-97364-1) U of Wash Pr.

***Roasts & Toasts: Snappy One-Liners for Every Occasion.** Gene Perret & Terry P. Martin. LC 96-37008. 1997. 5.95 (0-8069-9444-4) Sterling.

***Rob & Keep/Hide & Seek.** Roger H. Small. 210p. (Orig.). 1997. mass mkt. 4.99 (1-55197-799-0, Pub. by Comnwlth Pub CN) Partners Pubs Grp.

***Rob & Smith's Operative Surgery: Orthopaedics.** 4th ed. Ed. by Bentley & Greer. (Rob & Smith's Operative Surgery Ser.). (Illus.). 1285p. (Orig.). (C). (gr. 13 up). 1993. pap. text ed. 110.95 (0-412-53790-7, Chap & Hall NY) Chapman & Hall.

Rob & Smith's Operative Surgery: Pediatric Surgery. 5th ed. Ed. by Lewis Spitz & Arnold G. Coran. LC 94-68719. 912p. (gr. 13). 1995. text ed. 275.00 (0-412-59110-3) Chapman & Hall.

Rob & Smith's Operative Surgery: Surgery of the Upper Gastrointestinal Tract. 5th ed. G. G. Jamieson. 640p. (gr. 13). 1994. text ed. 205.95 (0-412-53550-5) Chapman & Hall.

***Rob & Smith's Operative Surgery: Vascular Surgery.** 5th ed. Jamieson & Yao. (Rob & Smith's Operative Surgery Ser.). (Illus.). 696p. 1994. text ed. 205.95 (0-412-58630-4, Chap & Hall NY) Chapman & Hall.

Rob Krier. Rob Krier. (Architectural Monographs: No. 30). (Illus.). 144p. 1993. 55.00 (1-85490-204-0); pap. 38.00 (1-85490-205-9) Academy Ed UK.

Rob Krier on Architecture. Rob Krier. (Academy Architecture Ser.). (Illus.). 96p. 1982. 25.00 (0-312-68541-6); pap. 19.95 (0-312-68542-4) St Martin.

Rob Mallet-Stevens: Architecture, Furniture, Interior Design. Ed. by Jean-Francois Pinchon. (Illus.). 160p. 1991. 35.00 (0-262-16116-8) MIT Pr.

Rob of the Bowl. John P. Kennedy. Ed. by William S. Osborne. (Masterworks of Literature Ser.). 1965. 18.95 (0-8084-0263-3); pap. 12.95 (0-8084-0264-1) NCUP.

***Rob Parr's Post-Pregnancy Workout.** Rob Parr & David Rubnitsky. 208p. 1997. pap. 13.00 (0-425-15607-9, Berkley Trade) Berkley Pub.

***Rob Parr's Post Pregnancy Workout.** David Rudnitsky. (Orig.). 1997. pap. 13.00 (0-614-20757-6) Berkley Pub.

Rob-Pat Act, 1. Oppenheim. 1971. 47.00 (0-316-65090-0) Little.

Rob-Pat Act, 2. Oppenheim. 1971. 47.00 (0-316-65091-9) Little.

Rob-Pat Act, 3. Oppenheim. 1971. 47.00 (0-316-65092-7) Little.

Rob-Pat Act, 4. Oppenheim. 1971. 47.00 (0-316-65093-5) Little.

Rob Roy. Walter Scott. 1995. 20.00 (0-679-44362-2) Knopf.

Rob Roy. Walter Scott. 512p. 1995. pap. 8.95 (0-14-043554-9, Penguin Classics) Viking Penguin.

Rob Roy. Walter Scott. (Signet Classics Ser.). 1995. mass mkt. 5.95 (0-451-52623-6, Sig Classics) NAL-Dutton.

***Rob Roy.** Walter Scott. lib. bdg. 30.95 (0-8488-2027-4) Amereon Ltd.

Rob Roy. rev. ed. Walter Scott. Ed. by John Sutherland. 480p. 1995. pap. 7.95 (0-460-87594-9, Everyman's Classic Lib) C E Tuttle.

R

Rob Stene's Dream, a Poem. Ed. by William Motherwell. LC 70-173003. (Maitland Club, Glasgow. Publications: No. 52). reprint ed. 37.50 (*0-404-53033-8*) AMS Pr.

Rob Wellington Quigley: Buildings & Projects. Magali S. Larson. LC 95-43747. (Illus.). 224p. 1996. 60.00 (*0-8478-1945-0*) Rizzoli Intl.

Rob Wellington Quigley: Buildings & Projects. Magali S. Larson. LC 95-43747. (Illus.). 224p. 1996. pap. 40.00 (*0-8478-1946-9*) Rizzoli Intl.

***Robak's Witch: A Dan Robak Mystery.** Joe L. Hensley. 1997. 21.95 (*0-312-15642-1*) St Martin.

Robbe-Grillet: Dans le Labyrinthe. Ed. by David Meakin. (Bristol French Texts Ser.). 144p. (FRE.). 1992. 14.95 (*0-631-13019-5*, Pub. by Blckwell Pubs UK) Focus Pub-R Pullins.

Robbe-Grillet & Modernity: Science, Sexuality, & Subversion. Raylene L. Ramsay. LC 92-12415. (University of Florida Humanities Monographs: No. 66). (Illus.). 336p. 1992. lib. bdg. 49.95 (*0-8130-1145-0*) U Press Fla.

Robbe-Grillet & the Fantastic: A Collection of Essays. Ed. by Virginia Harger-Grinling. LC 93-14462. (Contributions to the Study of Science Fiction & Fantasy Ser.: No. 59). 168p. 1994. text ed. 49.95 (*0-313-28539-X*, Greenwood Pr) Greenwood.

***Robbed of Humanity: Lives of Guatemalan Street Children.** Nancy L. Tierney. 280p. (Orig.). 1997. pap. 16.00 (*0-9630180-5-1*) Pangaea Pub.

Robben Ford Blues Guitar Collection. 19.95 (*0-7935-4454-8*, 00690042) H Leonard.

Robben Island. D. M. Zwelonke. (African Writers Ser.). 151p. (C). 1973. pap. 8.95 (*0-435-90128-1*, 90128) Heinemann.

Robben Island, Hell-Hole: Reminiscences of a Political Prisoner in South Africa. Moses Dlamini. LC 84-72593. 202p. (C). 1985. pap. 8.95 (*0-86543-009-8*); text ed. 25.95 (*0-86543-008-X*) Africa World.

***Robber & Me.** Josef Holub. 1997. 16.95 (*0-8050-5599-1*) H Holt & Co.

Robber Baby: Stories from the Greek Myths. Anne Rockwell. LC 90-39560. (Illus.). 80p. (J). (gr. k up). 1994. 18.00 (*0-688-09740-5*); lib. bdg. 17.93 (*0-688-09741-3*) Greenwillow.

Robber Barons. Matthew Josephson. LC 34-4665. 474p. 1962. pap. 15.00 (*0-15-676790-2*, Harvest Bks) HarBrace.

Robber Barons: The Great American Capitalists, 1861-1901. Matthew Josephson. 30.95 (*0-8488-0091-5*) Amereon Ltd.

Robber Bride. Margaret Atwood. 544p. 1994. mass mkt. 6.99 (*0-7704-2616-6*) Bantam.

Robber Bride. Margaret Atwood. 544p. 1995. mass mkt. 6.50 (*0-553-56905-8*) Bantam.

Robber Bride. Margaret Atwood. 480p. 1993. 23.50 (*0-385-26008-3*, N A Talese) Doubleday.

Robber Bridegroom. Eudora Welty. (Illus.). 1987. 19.95 (*0-15-178318-7*) HarBrace.

Robber Bridegroom. Eudora Welty. LC 78-6660. 185p. 1978. reprint ed. pap. 9.00 (*0-15-676807-0*, Harvest Bks) HarBrace.

Robber in the House. Jessica Treat. LC 93-17101. (Coffee to Go: Short Short Stories Ser.). 128p. (Orig.). 1993. pap. 10.95 (*1-56689-007-1*) Coffee Hse.

Robbers. Peter Whalley. 192p. 1989. pap. 2.95 (*0-380-70615-6*) Avon.

Robbers. Peter Whalley. 1987. 16.95 (*0-8027-0997-4*) Walker & Co.

Robbers. J. Friedrich Von Schiller. LC 89-206183. 248p. 1989. reprint ed. 48.00 (*1-85477-004-7*, Pub. by Woodstock Bks UK) Cassell.

Robbers & Wallenstein. J. Friedrich Von Schiller. (Classics Ser.). 480p. 1980. pap. 12.95 (*0-14-044368-1*, Penguin Classics) Viking Penguin.

Robbers Five...or Is It Six? Maria Van Eeden. (Count Me in Bks.). (Illus.). 24p. (Orig.). (J). (ps-1). 1994. pap. 4.95 (*1-55037-363-3*, Pub. by Annick CN) Firefly Bks Ltd.

***Robbers in the Hills.** Carolyn Swift. Date not set. pap. 5.95 (*0-900068-61-2*) Dufour.

***Robbers in the House.** Carolyn Swift. Date not set. pap. 6.95 (*0-947962-41-7*) Dufour.

***Robbers in the Theatre.** Carolyn Swift. Date not set. pap. 5.95 (*0-900068-88-4*) Dufour.

***Robbers in the Town.** Carolyn Swift. Date not set. pap. 5.95 (*0-900068-68-X*) Dufour.

Robbers on TV. Carolyn Swift. 160p. (J). (ps-8). 1989. pap. 6.95 (*1-85371-033-4*, Pub. by Poolbeg Pr IE) Dufour.

Robbers, Rogues & Ruffians: True Tales of the Wild West. Howard Bryan. LC 91-72481. (Illus.). 320p. 1991. 22.95 (*0-940666-04-9*); pap. 14.95 (*0-940666-23-5*) Clear Light.

Robbers' Roost. Zane Grey. 368p. 1991. mass mkt. 3.99 (*0-06-100280-1*, Harp PBks) HarpC.

***Robbers' Roost.** large type ed. Zane Grey. LC 96-53968. 1997. lib. bdg. 18.95 (*1-57490-057-9*, Sagebrush LP West) T T Beeler.

Robbers Roost Recollections. Pearl Baker. (Western Experience Ser.). (Illus.). 204p. 1991. pap. 14.95 (*0-87421-154-9*) Utah St U Pr.

Robber's Wine. Ellen Hart. Date not set. pap. write for info. (*0-345-40494-7*) Ballantine.

Robber's Wine: A Jane Lawless Mystery. Ellen Hart. LC 96-2692. 304p. 1996. 21.95 (*1-878067-80-X*) Seal Pr WA.

Robbery. (Read with Me Key Words to Reading Ser.: No. 9010-15). (Illus.). (J). (ps-2). 1990. 3.50 (*0-7214-1328-5*, Ladybrd); teacher ed. 3.95 (*0-317-04038-3*, Ladybrd) Penguin.

Robbery at the Diamond Dog Diner. Eileen Christelow. LC 86-2682. (Illus.). 32p. (J). (ps-3). 1988. pap. 6.95 (*0-89919-722-1*, Clarion Bks) HM.

Robbery at the Mall. Francine Pascal. (Sweet Valley Twins & Friends Ser.: No. 81). 144p. (J). (gr. 4-7). 1994. pap. 3.50 (*0-553-48116-9*) Bantam.

***Robbery Diamond Dog.** Christlelo. (J). 1986. pap. 8.95 incl. audio (*0-89919-894-5*) Ticknor & Flds Bks Yng Read.

Robbery-Related Assaults on Police: An Empirical Analysis of National Incidents. Kenneth Meyer et al. 1979. 1.00 (*1-55614-109-2*) U of SD Gov Res Bur.

Robbie. Isaac Asimov. (Creative Short Stories Ser.). 40p. (J). (gr. 5). 1989. 13.95 (*0-88682-231-9*) Creative Ed.

Robbie. David Cookson. (C). 1989. text ed. 40.00 (*0-948929-18-9*) St Mut.

Robbie & the Raggedy Scarecrow. Katy D. Oana. LC 77-18349. (Sound Ser.). (Illus.). 32p. (J). (gr. 2-4). 1978. lib. bdg. 9.95 (*0-87783-154-8*) Oddo.

Robbie & the Raggedy Scarecrow. Katy D. Oana. LC 77-18349. (Illus.). (J). (gr. k-2). 1978. lib. bdg. 5.95 (*0-89508-065-6*) Rainbow Bks.

Robbie Conal: Unauthorized History: Portraits of Power. Robbie Conal. LC 93-7042. (Illus.). 56p. 1990. 22.00 (*0-614-06474-0*) RAM Publications.

***Robbie Rabbit.** John Lasne. (Littlebook Ser.). (Illus.). 18p. (J). (gr. k-4). 1996. 5.95 (*0-9642815-4-6*) Natl Fmly Prtnship.

Robbie Rabbit & the Little Ones. Julie Sykes. (Illus.). 24p. (J). (ps). 1996. 12.95 (*1-888444-01-0*) Little Tiger.

***Robbie Rabbit & the Little Ones.** Julie Sykes. 1997. pap. text ed. 4.95 (*1-888444-11-8*) Little Tiger.

Robbie Raccoon Paper Doll. Judy M. Johnson. (Illus.). (J). (gr. k-3). 1992. pap. 1.00 (*0-486-27208-7*) Dover.

Robbie Robertson: Includes Greatest Hits of The Band. (Recorded Versions - Guitar Ser.). (Illus.). 112p. 1991. pap. 19.95 (*0-7935-0318-3*, 00660060) H Leonard.

Robbie Taggart, Highland Sailor. Michael R. Phillips & Judith Pella. LC 87-29913. (Highland Collection Ser.: Vol. 2). 384p. (Orig.). 1987. pap. 9.99 (*0-87123-919-1*) Bethany Hse.

Robbing the Mother: Women in Faulkner. Deborah Clarke. LC 93-33642. 224p. 1994. text ed. 30.00 (*0-87805-592-4*) U Pr of Miss.

Robbins. D. W. Robbins. 221p. 1991. reprint ed. pap. 34.50 (*0-8328-2028-8*); reprint ed. lib. bdg. 44.50 (*0-8328-2027-X*) Higginson Bk Co.

Robbins Clinical Pathology. Laposata. Date not set. text ed. write for info. (*0-7216-7027-X*) HarBrace.

Robbins E. Cahill: Recollections of Work in State Politics, Government, Taxation, Gaming Control, Clark County Administration, & the Nevada Resort Association, 4 vols. Ed. by Mary E. Glass. 1585p. 1977. lib. bdg. 233.00 (*1-56475-157-0*) U NV Oral Hist.

Robbins E. Cahill: Recollections of Work in State Politics, Government, Taxation, Gaming Control, Clark County Administration, & the Nevada Resort Association, Pt. 1. Ed. by Mary E. Glass. 1977. Pt. I. fiche write for info. (*1-56475-158-9*) U NV Oral Hist.

Robbins E. Cahill: Recollections of Work in State Politics, Government, Taxation, Gaming Control, Clark County Administration, & the Nevada Resort Association, Pt. I. Ed. by Mary E. Glass. 428p. 1977. lib. bdg. 61.00 (*1-56475-153-8*) U NV Oral Hist.

Robbins E. Cahill: Recollections of Work in State Politics, Government, Taxation, Gaming Control, Clark County Administration, & the Nevada Resort Association, Pt. II. Ed. by Mary E. Glass. 316p. 1977. lib. bdg. 50.00 (*1-56475-154-6*); fiche write for info. (*1-56475-159-7*) U NV Oral Hist.

Robbins E. Cahill: Recollections of Work in State Politics, Government, Taxation, Gaming Control, Clark County Administration, & the Nevada Resort Association, Pt. III. Ed. by Mary E. Glass. 445p. 1977. lib. bdg. 63.00 (*1-56475-155-4*); fiche write for info. (*1-56475-160-0*) U NV Oral Hist.

Robbins E. Cahill: Recollections of Work in State Politics, Government, Taxation, Gaming Control, Clark County Administration, & the Nevada Resort Association, Pt. IV. Ed. by Mary E. Glass. 396p. 1977. lib. bdg. 58.00 (*1-56475-156-2*) U NV Oral Hist.

Robbins E. Cahill: Recollections of Work in State Politics, Government, Taxation, Gaming Control, Clark County Administration, & the Nevada Resort Association, Vols. I-IV. Ed. by Mary E. Glass. 1977. fiche write for info. (*1-56475-162-7*) U NV Oral Hist.

Robbins Pathologic Basis of Disease. 5th ed. Ramzi S. Cotran et al. LC 94-2629. 1994. text ed. 72.00 (*0-7216-5032-5*) Saunders.

Robbut: A Tale of Tails. Robert Lawson. LC 89-32367. (Illus.). 94p. (J). (gr. 2-6). 1989. reprint ed. lib. bdg. 17.50 (*0-208-02236-8*, Linnet Bks) Shoe String.

Robby Really Transforms: A Story About Grown-ups Helping Children. Matthew R. Galvin. LC 87-34883. (Illus.). 48p. (J). (ps-6). 1988. 16.95 (*0-945354-05-3*); pap. 8.95 (*0-945354-02-9*) Magination Pr.

Robby's Revelry. Carleton J. Robertson. Ed. by Sidney Vernon. (Illus.). (Orig.). pap. 7.00 (*0-943150-12-4*) Rovern Pr.

Robe. Lloyd C. Douglas. 1942. 24.95 (*0-395-07635-8*) HM.

Robe. Lloyd C. Douglas. 1986. pap. 14.95 (*0-395-40799-0*); pap. 9.95 (*0-395-40299-9*) HM.

Robe. large type ed. Lloyd C. Douglas. LC 95-8707. 889p. 1995. lib. bdg. 21.95 (*0-7838-1362-7*, GK Hall) Thorndike Pr.

Robe & Plough: Monasticism & Economic Interest in Early Medieval Sri Lanka. R. A. Gunawardana. LC 78-26090. (Monographs: No. 35). xii, 377p. 1979. pap. 15.00 (*0-8165-0648-5*) Assn Asian Studies.

Robe & Sword: The Regrouping of the French Aristocracy After Louis XIV. Franklin L. Ford. LC 52-12261. (Historical Studies: No. 64). (Illus.). 292p. 1953. 20.00 (*0-674-77415-9*) HUP.

Robe et le Couteau see Programmed French Readers

Robe Mauve de Valentine. Francoise Sagan. pap. 8.95 (*0-685-23934-9*) Fr & Eur.

Robe of Light: The Persian Years of the Supreme Prophet Baha'u'llah, 1817-1853. David S. Ruhe. (Illus.). 233p. 1994. 24.95 (*0-85398-355-0*) G Ronald Pub.

Robe Pretexte. Francois Mauriac. pap. 9.95 (*0-685-34301-4*) Fr & Eur.

***Robed in Light.** Illus. by National Geographic Staff & Jack Hamm. 111p. (Orig.). 1989. pap. write for info. (*0-614-29607-2*) R A Lectures.

Robed in Light. Alexandria Uriel, pseud. (Illus.). 111p. (Orig.). (C). 1990. 10.00 (*0-9624130-0-3*); pap. text ed. 10.00 (*0-685-28886-2*) R A Lectures.

Robene & Makyne, & the Testament of Cresseid. Robert Henryson. Ed. by George Chalmers. LC 79-144423. (Bannatyne Club, Edinburgh. Publications: No. 6). reprint ed. 27.50 (*0-404-52707-8*) AMS Pr.

Robert: Line by Line, 4 vols., Set. National Association of Parliamentarians Staff. (Orig.). 1995. pap. 60.00 (*1-884048-13-7*) Natl Assn Parliamentarians.

Robert A. Hall, Jr. & American Structuralism. Marcel Danesi. (Edward Sapir Monograph Ser. in Language, Culture & Cognition: No. 15). viii, 92p. (Orig.). 1987. pap. 18.00 (*0-933104-25-1*) Jupiter Pr.

Robert A. Heinlein. Thomas D. Clareson. Ed. by Roger C. Schlobin. (Milford Ser.: Popular Writers of Today). pap. write for info. (*1-55742-131-5*); lib. bdg. write for info. (*1-55742-130-7*) Borgo Pr.

Robert A. Heinlein. Leon Stover. (United States Authors Ser.: No. 522). 168p. 1987. 21.95 (*0-8057-7509-9*, Twayne) Scribnrs Ref.

Robert A. Heinlein: Stranger in His Own Land. 2nd rev. ed. George E. Slusser. LC 77-5657. (Milford Series: Popular Writers of Today: Vol. 1). 64p. 1977. pap. 13.00 (*0-89370-210-2*); lib. bdg. 23.00 (*0-89370-110-6*) Borgo Pr.

***Robert A. Heinlein Cyclopedia: A Complete Guide to the People, Places & Things in the Fiction of Robert A. Heinlein.** Nancy B. Downing. LC 87-714. (Borgo Literary Guide Ser.). 1989. 24.95 (*0-89370-814-3*); pap. 14.95 (*0-89370-914-X*) Borgo Pr.

Robert A. M. Stern. Eric Kudalis. (Architects Ser.). (Illus.). 48p. (J). (gr. 3-9). 1995. lib. bdg. 17.80 (*1-56065-312-4*) Capstone Pr.

Robert A. M. Stern: Buildings. Robert A. Stern. LC 96-22035. (Illus.). 448p. 1996. 75.00 (*1-885254-41-5*) Monacelli Pr.

Robert A. M. Stern, Buildings & Projects, 1987- 1992. Intro. by Vincent Scully. LC 92-18367. (Illus.). 384p. 1992. pap. 40.00 (*0-8478-1619-2*) Rizzoli Intl.

Robert A. Ring: Recollections of Life in California, Nevada Gaming, & Reno & Lake Tahoe Business & Civic Affairs. Intro. by Mary E. Glass. 179p. 1985. lib. bdg. 36.50 (*1-56475-131-7*); fiche write for info. (*1-56475-132-5*) U NV Oral Hist.

Robert A. Woods: Champion of Democracy. Eleanor H. Woods. LC 70-150206. (Select Bibliographies Reprint Ser.). 1977. reprint ed. 25.95 (*0-8369-5719-9*) Ayer.

Robert Adam: Drawings & Imagination. Alan A. Tait. LC 92-47466. (Studies in the History of Architecture). (Illus.). 234p. (C). 1994. text ed. 85.00 (*0-521-43315-0*) Cambridge U Pr.

Robert Adamson: Selected Poems 1970-1989. Robert Adamson. 269p. 1990. pap. 19.95 (*0-7022-2323-9*, Pub. by Univ Queensland Pr AT) Intl Spec Bk.

Robert Altman: Hollywood Survivor. Daniel O'Brien. 144p. 1996. pap. text ed. 16.95 (*0-8264-0933-4*) Continuum.

Robert Altman: Hollywood Survivor, Vol. 1. Daniel O'Brien. LC 94-41864. 144p. 1995. 19.95 (*0-8264-0791-9*) Continuum.

Robert Altman: Jumping Off the Cliff. Patrick McGilligan. 1991. pap. 14.95 (*0-312-05505-6*) St Martin.

Robert Altman's America. Helene Keyssar. (Illus.). 400p. 1991. 55.00 (*0-19-504869-5*) OUP.

***Robert Am Stern: Selected Works.** St. Martin's Press Staff. (Architectural Monographs: No. 17). 1992. pap. 38.00 (*0-312-07246-5*) St Martin.

Robert & Collins du Management Commercial Financier Economique Juridique: Fran-Ang-Fran. Robert. 1044p. (ENG & FRE.). 1994. 150.00 (*0-7859-9202-2*) Fr & Eur.

Robert & Collins Senior: Dictionnaire Francais-Anglais, Anglais-Francais. Collins Staff. 2016p. (ENG & FRE.). 1993. 95.00 (*0-7859-8061-X*, 2850362271) Fr & Eur.

Robert & Elizabeth Browning. Robert Browning & Elizabeth Barrett Browning. (Poets Ser.). 146p. 1993. 5.95 (*0-7117-0442-2*, Pub. by Jarrold Pub UK) Seven Hills Bk.

Robert & Jane Meyerhoff Collection, 1958 to 1995. Mark Rosenthal. LC 95-47555. 1996. pap. write for info. (*0-89468-221-0*) Natl Gallery Art.

Robert & Signorelly. French-Italian. Jean Robert. 3008p. (FRE & ITA.). 1981. 175.00 (*0-8288-4675-8*, M9403) Fr & Eur.

Robert & the Balloon Machine. Benjamin Darling. (Illus.). 32p. (J). 1991. 11.95 (*0-88138-120-9*, Green Tiger S&S) S&S Childrens.

Robert & Van Dale Dictionnaire Francais-Neerlandais, Neerlandais-Francais. Paul Bogaards. 1400p. 1994. 125.00 (*0-7859-9201-4*) Fr & Eur.

Robert Anson Heinlein StormTrooping Guru: A Working Bibliography. Gordon Benson, Jr. & Phil Stephensen-Payne. (Galactic Central Bibliographies Ser.: No. 42). ix, 100p. (C). 1993. lib. bdg. 29.00 (*0-8095-4741-4*) Borgo Pr.

***Robert Arneson: Self Reflections.** Janet C. Bishop et al. LC 96-51834. 1997. write for info. (*0-918471-39-7*) San Fran MOMA.

Robert B. Parker: A New Collection of Three Complete Spencer Novels. Robert B. Parker. 1996. 13.99 (*0-517-14891-9*) Random Hse Value.

Robert Bacon: Life & Letters. James B. Scott. LC 75-2669. (Wall Street & the Security Market Ser.). (Illus.). 1975. reprint ed. 45.95 (*0-405-07232-5*) Ayer.

Robert Baden Powell: The Man Who Created the International Scouting Movement That Gives Young People Opportunities to Excel. Julia Courtney. LC 90-30229. (People Who Have Helped the World Ser.). (Illus.). 64p. (J). (gr. 5-6). 1990. lib. bdg. 23.93 (*0-8368-0214-4*) Gareth Stevens Inc.

Robert Baillie & the Second Scots Reformation. F. N. McCoy. LC 73-76110. 256p. reprint ed. pap. 73.00 (*0-318-34900-0*, 2031307) Bks Demand.

Robert Bakewell & the Longhorn Breed of Cattle. Pat Stanley. 157p. 1995. 29.95 (*0-85236-305-2*, Pub. by Farming Pr UK) Diamond Farm Bk.

Robert Baldridge, His Antecedents & Some of His Descendants. Chester C. Kennedy. (Illus.). 185p. 1994. 34.95 (*1-56869-029-0*) Oldbuck Pr.

Robert Ballard. Bob Italia. Ed. by Rosemary Walner. LC 90-82623. (Explorers of the Past & Present Ser.). (Illus.). 32p. (J). (gr. 4). 1990. lib. bdg. 11.96 (*0-939179-95-4*) Abdo & Dghtrs.

Robert Barnwell Rhett: Father of Secession. Laura A. White. 1913. 14.50 (*0-8446-1477-7*) Peter Smith.

Robert Barry: Come On. (Illus.). 144p. 1987. pap. 30.00 (*90-72191-01-3*, Pub. by Imschoot BE) Dist Art Pubs.

Robert Beauchamp: An American Expressionist. April Kingsley. Ed. by Thomas E. Piche, Jr. LC 84-82511. 100p. (Orig.). 1984. pap. 16.95 (*0-914407-02-3*) Everson Mus.

Robert Bellarmine: Spiritual Writings. Ed. by Patrick Donelly & Ronald J. Teske. (Classics of Western Spirituality Ser.). 1989. 19.95 (*0-8091-0389-3*); pap. 14.95 (*0-8091-2875-6*) Paulist Pr.

Robert Benchley: An Annotated Bibliography. Gordon E. Ernst, Jr. LC 95-6293. (Bibliographies & Indexes in Popular Culture Ser.: No. 6). 312p. 1995. text ed. 65.00 (*0-313-29321-X*, Greenwood Pr) Greenwood.

Robert Benchley Omnibus. Robert Benchley. 26.95 (*0-8488-0069-9*) Amereon Ltd.

Robert Blackburn Workshop. Alternative Museum Staff. LC 88-71297. (Orig.). 1988. pap. 6.00 (*0-932075-18-5*) Alternative Mus.

Robert Bloch. Randall D. Larson. Ed. by Roger C. Schlobin. LC 86-5751. (Starmont Reader's Guide Ser.: Vol. 37). iv, 148p. 1986. pap. 19.00 (*0-930261-58-5*); lib. bdg. 29.00 (*0-930261-59-3*) Borgo Pr.

***Robert Bloch.** Mainhardt. Date not set. pap. 16.95 (*0-312-86385-3*) St Martin.

Robert Bloch: Appreciations of. Ed. by Richard Matheson. 1995. 24.95 (*0-614-08649-3*) Tor Bks.

Robert Bloch: Appreciations of the Master: A Collection of Tributes to & Fiction by Robert Bloch. Richard Matheson. Ed. by Ricia Mainhardt. 320p. 1995. 24.95 (*0-312-85976-7*) Tor Bks.

Robert Bloch Companion. Ed. by Randall D. Larson. LC 89-26126. (Starmont Studies in Literary Criticism: No. 32). iv, 157p. (Orig.). 1989. pap. 21.00 (*1-55742-146-3*); lib. bdg. 29.00 (*1-55742-147-1*) Borgo Pr.

Robert Bloch Tribute Anthology. Ed. by Richard Matheson. 1995. 24.95 (*0-614-03859-6*) Tor Bks.

Robert Bly: A Primary & Secondary Bibliography. William H. Roberson. Ed. by Barbara Lee. LC 86-939. (Author Bibliographies Ser.: No. 75). 419p. 1986. 39.50 (*0-8108-1879-5*) Scarecrow.

Robert Bly: An Introduction to the Poetry. Howard Nelson. Ed. by John Unterecker. LC 83-14481. (Columbia Introductions to Twentieth-Century American Poetry Ser.). 1984. text ed. 33.00 (*0-231-05310-X*) Col U Pr.

Robert Bly: The Poet & His Critics. William V. Davis. (LCENG Ser.). xii, 120p. 1994. 52.95 (*1-879751-79-8*) Camden Hse.

Robert Bolling Woos Anne Miller: Courtship & Love in Colonial Virginia, 1760. Ed. by J. A. Lemay. (Illus.). 208p. 1990. text ed. 29.50 (*0-8139-1259-8*) U Pr of Va.

Robert Boyle: A Free Enquiry into the Vulgarly Received Notion of Nature. Robert Boyle. Ed. by Edward B. Davis & Michael Hunter. (Texts in the History of Philosophy Ser.). 260p. (C). 1996. text ed. 54.95 (*0-521-56100-0*); pap. text ed. 18.95 (*0-521-56796-3*) Cambridge U Pr.

***Robert Boyle: A Study in Science & Christian Belief.** R. Hooykaas. LC 97-3491. 156p. 1997. 36.50 (*0-7618-0708-X*) U Pr of Amer.

Robert Boyle: By Himself & His Friends. Ed. by Michael Hunter. 400p. 1995. 75.00 (*1-85196-085-6*, Pub. by Pickering & Chatto UK) Ashgate Pub Co.

Robert Boyle: Trailblazer of Science. John H. Tiner. (Sower Ser.). (Illus.). (J). (gr. 3-6). 1989. pap. 7.99 (*0-88062-155-9*) Mott Media.

***Robert Boyle & the Limits of Reason.** Jan W. Wojcik. 288p. (C). 1997. text ed. 59.95 (*0-521-56029-2*) Cambridge U Pr.

Robert Boyle on Natural Philosophy: An Essay with Selections from His Writings by Marie Boas Hall. Robert Boyle. LC 80-12187. (Illus.). ix, 406p. 1980. reprint ed. text ed. 45.50 (*0-313-22394-7*, BOON, Greenwood Pr) Greenwood.

Robert Boyle Reconsidered. Ed. by Michael Hunter. 350p. (C). 1994. text ed. 54.95 (*0-521-44205-2*) Cambridge U Pr.

Robert Boyle's Experiments in Pneumatics. Ed. by James B. Conant. (Harvard Case Histories in Experimental Science Ser.: Case 1). (Illus.). 72p. reprint ed. pap. 25.00 (*0-317-08773-8*, 2022240) Bks Demand.

Robert Bridges. F. E. Young. LC 70-129196. (English Biography Ser.: No. 31). 1970. reprint ed. lib. bdg. 58.95 (*0-8383-1161-X*) M S G Haskell Hse.

Robert Bridges: A Biography. Catherine Phillips. (Illus.). 384p. 1992. 65.00 (*0-19-212251-7*) OUP.

An Asterisk (*) at the beginning of an entry indicates that the title is appearing in BIP for the first time.

Robert Bridges: An Annotated Bibliography, 1873-1988. Ed. by Lee T. Hamilton. LC 88-40577. 248p. 1991. 44.50 (0-87413-364-5) U Delaware Pr.

Robert Brown & the Vancouver Island Exploring Expedition. Ed. by John Hayman. (Pioneers of British Columbia Ser.). (Illus.). 228p. 1989. pap. 15.95 (0-7748-0395-9, Pub. by U BC Pr) U of Wash Pr.

Robert Browning. Joseph Bristow. 1991. text ed. 49.95 (0-312-06774-7) St Martin.

***Robert Browning.** Robert Browning. Ed. by Adam Roberts. (The Oxford Authors). 864p. 1997. pap. 19.95 (0-19-282372-8) OUP.

***Robert Browning.** Robert Browning. Ed. by Adam Roberts. (The Oxford Authors Ser.). 704p. 1997. 70.00 (0-19-254203-6) OUP.

Robert Browning. Edward Dowden. 1972. 59.95 (0-8490-0960-X) Gordon Pr.

Robert Browning. Robert B. Pearsall. (English Authors Ser.: No. 168). 200p. 1974. 22.95 (0-8057-1065-5, Twayne) Scribnrs Ref.

Robert Browning. A. Skemp. LC 73-21961. (Studies in Browning: No. 4). 1974. lib. bdg. 75.00 (0-8383-1813-4) M S G Haskell Hse.

Robert Browning. John Woolford & Daniel Karlin. (Studies in 18th & 19th Century Literature Ser.). 352p. (C). 1996. pap. text ed. 21.50 (0-582-09613-8, Pub. by Longman UK) Longman.

Robert Browning. Charles H. Herford. LC 72-130253. (Studies in Browning: No. 4). 1970. reprint ed. lib. bdg. 52.95 (0-8383-1143-1) M S G Haskell Hse.

Robert Browning: Collection of Critical Essays. Harold Bloom & Adrienne Munich. 1979. pap. text ed. 7.95 (0-13-781476-3) P-H.

Robert Browning: Selected Poetry & Prose. Aidan Day. (English Texts Ser.). 192p. (C). 1991. pap. text ed. 15.95 (0-415-00952-9, A5368) Routledge.

Robert Browning: The Later Poetry. Nandita Sinha. 1993. text ed. 30.00 (81-85218-72-2, Pub. by Prestige II) Advent Bks Div.

Robert Browning: The Poems, 2 vols., Vol. 1. Robert Browning. Ed. by John Pettigrew. LC 80-53976. (English Poets Ser.). 121p. reprint ed. pap. 180.00 (0-7837-3541-3, 2057720) Bks Demand.

Robert Browning: The Poems, 2 vols., Vol. 2. Robert Browning. Ed. by John Pettigrew. LC 80-53976. (English Poets Ser.). 1156p. reprint ed. pap. 180.00 (0-7837-3542-1, 2057720) Bks Demand.

Robert Browning: The Poet & the Man. F. Sim. LC 72-3196. (Studies in Browning: No. 4). 1972. reprint ed. lib. bdg. 75.00 (0-8383-1538-0) M S G Haskell Hse.

Robert Browning see Victorian Poets: Critical Heritage

Robert Browning see Modern Critical Views Series

Robert Browning & Twentieth-Century Criticism. Patricia O'Neill. (LCENG Ser.). x, 158p. (C). 1995. 54.95 (1-879751-92-5) Camden Hse.

Robert Browning as a Religious Poet: An Annotated Bibliography of the Criticism. Vincent P. Anderson. LC 82-50407. 325p. 1984. 25.00 (0-87875-221-8) Whitston Pub.

Robert Browning, How to Know Him. William L. Phelps. (BCL1-PR English Literature Ser.). 381p. 1992. reprint ed. lib. bdg. 89.00 (0-7812-7466-4) Rprt Serv.

Robert Browning Personalia. E. Gosse. LC 73-17095. (Studies in Browning: No. 4). 1974. lib. bdg. 75.00 (0-8383-1728-6) M S G Haskell Hse.

Robert Browning Revisited. Roberts. LC 96-3324. 1996. 24.95 (0-8057-4590-4, Twayne) Scribnrs Ref.

Robert Browning, Selected Poems. LC 93-44693. 1994. 7.99 (0-517-10155-6, Pub. by Gramercy) Random Hse Value.

Robert Browning's Asolando: The Indian Summer of a Poet. Richard S. Kennedy. LC 93-14358. (Illus.). 168p. 1993. text ed. 27.50 (0-8262-0917-3) U of Mo Pr.

Robert Browning's Poetry. Robert Browning. Ed. by James M. Loucks. (Critical Editions Ser.). (C). 1979. pap. text ed. 17.95 (0-393-09092-2) Norton.

Robert Browning's Rondures Brave. Michael Bright. 250p. (Orig.). (C). 1995. text ed. 34.95 (0-8214-1125-X) Ohio U Pr.

Robert Bruce & the Community of the Realm of Scotland. rev. ed. Geoffrey W. Barrow. (Illus.). 448p. 1988. pap. 30.00 (0-85224-604-8, Pub. by Edinburgh U Pr UK) Col U Pr.

Robert Bruce, King of Scots. Agnes M. Mackenzie. LC 78-128880. (Select Bibliographies Reprint Ser.). 1977. reprint ed. 24.95 (0-8369-5500-5) Ayer.

Robert Buchanan. Harriett Jay. LC 72-130237. reprint ed. 29.50 (0-404-03555-8) AMS Pr.

Robert Burns. Raymond Bentman & Robert Burns. (English Authors Ser.: No. 452). 160p. 1987. 22.95 (0-8057-6952-8, Twayne) Scribnrs Ref.

Robert Burns. Robert Burns. (Poets Ser.). 146p. 1993. 5.95 (0-7117-0401-5, Pub. by Jarrold Pub UK) Seven Hills Bk.

Robert Burns. Picton Publishing Staff. 240p. (C). 1987. 35.00 (0-317-90413-2, Pub. by Picton UK) St Mut.

Robert Burns. limited ed. Picton Publishing Staff. 240p. (C). 1987. 333.00 (0-317-90414-0, Pub. by Picton UK) St Mut.

Robert Burns. Harriot Curtis. (Works of Harriot Curtis Ser.). 1990. reprint ed. lib. bdg. 79.00 (0-7812-2469-1) Rprt Serv.

Robert Burns. Thomas F. Henderson. LC 73-144556. (Illus.). reprint ed. 37.50 (0-404-08514-8) AMS Pr.

Robert Burns. John C. Shairp. Ed. by John Morley. (English Men of Letters Ser.). reprint ed. lib. bdg. 27.50 (0-404-51727-7) AMS Pr.

Robert Burns: His Life & Genius. Andrew Dakers. LC 72-3378. (English Literature Ser.: No. 33). 1972. reprint ed. lib. bdg. 75.00 (0-8383-1507-0) M S G Haskell Hse.

Robert Burns: The Man & His Work. Hans Hecht. 316p. 1988. 70.00 (0-907526-04-7, Pub. by Alloway Pub UK) St Mut.

Robert Burns: The Man & His Work. Hans Hecht. (C). 1989. pap. text ed. 35.00 (0-907526-51-9, Pub. by Alloway Pub UK) St Mut.

Robert Burns: The Poet's Progress. Ed. by Nicolas Barker et al. LC 95-71919. (Illus.). 64p. (Orig.). 1995. pap. 12.50 (0-939084-28-7) R Mus & Lib.

***Robert Burns: The Scottish Bard.** Chelsea House Publishing Staff. (Illustrated Poetry Anthology Ser.). 1997. 17.95 (1-86019-286-6) Chelsea Hse.

Robert Burns: The Tinder Heart. Hugh Douglas. LC 96-42553. (Illus.). 288p. 1996. 31.95 (0-7509-1213-8, Pub. by Sutton Pubng UK) Bks Intl VA.

Robert Burns see 18th Century Literature Critical Heritage

***Robert Burns & Cultural Authority.** Ed. by Robert Crawford. LC 96-61362. 335p. 1997. 29.95 (0-87745-578-3) U of Iowa Pr.

Robert Burns & His Rhyming Friends. John D. Ross. LC 77-144478. reprint ed. 29.50 (0-404-08538-5) AMS Pr.

Robert Burns & the Common People. William Stewart. LC 74-169187. (English Literature Ser.: No. 33). (C). 1971. reprint ed. lib. bdg. 49.95 (0-8383-1333-7) M S G Haskell Hse.

Robert Burns & the Medical Profession. W. Findlay. 1972. 59.95 (0-8490-0961-8) Gordon Pr.

Robert Burns & the Riddell Family. J. Maxwell Wood. LC 73-21743. (English Biography Ser.: No. 31). 1974. lib. bdg. 52.95 (0-8383-1802-9) M S G Haskell Hse.

Robert Burns, Farmer. Gavin Sprott. (Illus.). 60p. 1993. pap. 3.95 (0-948636-18-1, 6181, Pub. by Ashmolean Mus UK) A Schwartz & Co.

Robert Burns, Sein Leben. J. Veitch. (C). 1988. 30.00 (0-907526-38-1, Pub. by Alloway Pub UK) St Mut.

***Robert Burns Select.** Robert Burns. (Illus.). 124p. (Orig.). 1996. pap. 7.00 (0-9634992-8-9) R Clifton.

Robert Burns the Exciseman. Graham Smith. (C). 1988. pap. 50.00 (0-685-33838-X, Pub. by Alloway Pub UK) St Mut.

Robert Burns the Exciseman. Graham Smith. (C). 1989. pap. text ed. 35.00 (0-907526-43-8, Pub. by Alloway Pub UK) St Mut.

Robert Burns, the Poet. David Daiches. (C). 1994. pap. 39.95 (0-85411-060-7, Pub. by Saltire Soc) St Mut.

Robert Burns Woodward & the Art of Organic Synthesis: To Accompany an Exhibit by the Beckman Center for the History of Chemistry. Mary E. Bowden & Theodor Benfey. (BCHOC Publication: No. 9). (Illus.). 48p. (Orig.). 1992. pap. 6.00 (0-941901-08-4) Chem Heritage Fnd.

Robert Burton & the Anatomy of Melancholy: An Annotated Bibliography of Primary & Secondary Sources. Compiled by Joey Conn. LC 88-24639. (Bibliographies & Indexes in World Literature Ser.: No. 15). 117p. 1988. text ed. 49.95 (0-313-26047-8, CNB/) Greenwood.

Robert Burton, Philosophaster. Ed. & Tr. by Connie McQuillen. (Medieval & Renaissance Texts & Studies: Vol. 103). 240p. 1993. 25.00 (0-86698-123-3, MR103) MRTS.

***Robert C. Bailey: An Oral History.** Contrib. by Dianne Bridgman. (Illus.). xiv, 210p. (Orig.). 1996. pap. write for info. (1-889320-02-1) WA St Oral Hist.

Robert C. Byrd Conference on the Administrative Process, 4th Annual (1992) 329p. 1992. pap. text ed. 45.00 (1-56986-022-X) Federal Bar.

Robert C. Hinckley & the Recreation of the First Operation under Ether. Richard J. Wolfe. (Illus.). 182p. 1993. 20.00 (0-614-03129-X) F A Countway.

Robert C. May Photography Collection. Van D. Coke & Jonathan Greene. LC 95-60170. (Illus.). 120p. 1995. 12.00 (1-882007-09-3) Univ KY Art Mus.

Robert Cantwell. Merrill Lewis. LC 85-70130. (Western Writers Ser.: No. 70). (Illus.). 54p. (Orig.). 1985. pap. 4.95 (0-88430-044-7) Boise St U W Writ Ser.

Robert Capa: A Biography. Richard Whelan. LC 93-46814. (Illus.). vi, 368p. 1994. pap. 14.00 (0-8032-9760-2, Bison Books) U of Nebr Pr.

Robert Capa: Photographs. Cornell Capa. (Illus.). 192p. 1996. 50.00 (0-89381-675-2) Aperture.

Robert Carter of Nomini Hall: A Virginia Tobacco Planter of the 18th Century. Louis Morton. LC 83-45824. 1983. reprint ed. 31.00 (0-404-20187-3) AMS Pr.

Robert Cartmell: A Twenty-Five Year Retrospective. Contrib. by Tammis Groft & Leonard Kastle. LC 96-60220. (Illus.). 35p. 1996. pap. 10.00 (0-910763-13-5) U Albany Art Mus.

Robert Cecil, First Earl of Salisbury, 1563-1612: Servant of Two Sovereigns. Alan Haynes. (Illus.). 208p. 8900. 40.00 (0-7206-0716-7, Pub. by P Owen Ltd UK) Dufour.

Robert Challe: Intimations of the Enlightenment. Lawrence J. Forno. LC 77-139993. 199p. 1975. 29.50 (0-8386-7846-7) Fairleigh Dickinson.

Robert Chapman. Robert L. Peterson. LC 95-33954. 1996. text ed. 16.99 (0-87213-691-4) Loizeaux.

Robert Chester's "Love's Martyr, Or Rosalins Complaint" 1601 & Its Supplement "Diverse Poeticall Essaies" on the Turtle & Phoenix by Shakespeare, Ben Jonson, George Chapman, John Marston, Etc... see Letter on Shakespeare's Authorship of the Two Noble Kinsmen

Robert Chester's Redation of Euclid's Elements, the So-Called Adelard II Version, 2 vols. Ed. by H. L. Busard & M. Folkerts. (Science Networks Ser.: Vols. 8 & 9). (Illus.). 960p. 1992. 322.00 (0-8176-2728-6) Birkhauser.

Robert Church: Entrepreneur. Cookie Lommel. (Black American Ser.). (Illus.). 208p. (YA). 1995. mass mkt. 4.95 (0-87067-789-6) Holloway.

Robert Clarke - To "B" or Not to "B" A Film Actor's Odyssey. Robert Clarke & Tom Weaver. (Illus.). 256p. 1996. pap. 20.00 (1-887664-02-5) Midnght Marquee Pr.

Robert Clive & Imperialism: Mini-Play & Activities. Lawrence Stevens. (World History Ser.). (YA). (gr. 7 up). 1981. 6.50 (0-89550-343-3) Stevens & Shea.

Robert Cochran's U. S. Revenue Cutter South Carolina, 1793-1798. Florence Kern. 1979. 3.95 (0-913377-08-2) Alised.

Robert Coe, Puritan, His Ancestry & Descendants, 1340-1910. J. G. Bartlett. (Illus.). 664p. 1989. reprint ed. pap. 94.50 (0-8328-0409-6); reprint ed. lib. bdg. 102.50 (0-8328-0408-8) Higginson Bk Co.

Robert Coles. Hilligoss. LC 96-54699. 1996. 22.95 (0-8057-4014-7) Macmillan.

Robert Coles: An Intimate Biographical Interview. Robert Coles. Ed. by Bruce Baird-Middleton. (C). 1988. pap. text ed. 59.95 incl. vhs (0-674-77525-2) HUP.

Robert Coles Omnibus. Robert Coles. LC 92-38346. 782p. (Orig.). 1993. pap. 25.95 (0-87745-411-6) U of Iowa Pr.

Robert Cole's World: Agriculture & Society in Early Maryland. Lois G. Carr et al. LC 90-26168. (Illus.). xxii, 384p. (C). 1991. 49.95 (0-8078-1985-9); pap. 19.95 (0-8078-4341-5) U of NC Pr.

Robert Colescott: Another Judgment. Kenneth Baker. Ed. by Henry Barendse. (Illus.). 34p. 1985. 7.50 (0-915427-04-4) Spirit Sq Ctr.

Robert Coover: A Study of the Short Fiction. Thomas E. Kennedy. (Twayne's Studies in Short Fiction). 150p. 1992. 23.95 (0-8057-8347-4, Twayne) Scribnrs Ref.

Robert Coover: The Universal Fictionmaking Process. Lois Gordon. LC 82-10337. (Crosscurrents-Modern Critiques, New Ser.). 192p. 1983. 16.95 (0-8093-1092-9) S Ill U Pr.

Robert Coover's Fictions. Jackson I. Cope. LC 86-45445. 168p. 1986. text ed. 30.00 (0-8018-3365-5) Johns Hopkins.

Robert Copland: Poems. Ed. by Mary C. Erler. (Illus.). 272p. 1993. 60.00 (0-8020-5796-9) U of Toronto Pr.

Robert Cottingham: A Print Retrospective 1972-1986. John Arthur. LC 86-61945. (Illus.). 72p. (Orig.). 1986. pap. text ed. 21.95 (0-934306-07-9) Springfield.

Robert Cottingham: Rolling Stock Series: Works on Paper. Ed. by Kim Eagels-Smith & Philip Eliasoph. (Illus.). 20p. (Orig.). (C). 1991. pap. write for info. (0-941576-16-7) Harcourts Contemporary.

Robert Coverdale's Struggle. Horatio Alger, Jr. (Works of Horatio Alger Jr.). 1989. reprint ed. lib. bdg. 79.00 (0-7812-1714-8) Rprt Serv.

Robert Crayhon's Nutrition Made Simple: A Comprehensive Guide to the Latest Findings in Optimal Nutrition. Robert Crayhon. LC 95-43216. 320p. 1996. pap. 12.95 (0-87131-796-6) M Evans.

Robert Creeley: An Inventory, 1945-1970. Frwd. by Mary Novik & Robert Creeley. LC 72-96943. (Serif Series: Bibliographies & Checklists: No. 28). 228p. reprint ed. pap. 65.00 (0-8357-5578-9, 2035205) Bks Demand.

Robert Creeley: The Poet's Workshop. Ed. by Carroll F. Terrell. LC 83-61521. (Poet's Workshop Ser.). 384p. 1984. 25.00 (0-915032-75-9); pap. 15.95 (0-915032-76-7) Natl Poet Foun.

Robert Creeley & the Genius of the American Common Place: Together with the Poet's Own Autobiography. Tom Clark. LC 93-793. (Illus.). 160p. 1993. 19.95 (0-8112-1250-5) New Directions.

Robert Creeley's Life & Work: A Sense of Increment. Ed. by John Wilson. 1988. 39.50 (0-472-09374-6); pap. 16.95 (0-472-06374-X) U of Mich Pr.

Robert Crowther's Incredible Animal Alphabet. Robert Crowther. LC 94-10566. (J). (gr. k-3). 1995. 14.95 (1-56402-427-X) Candlewick Pr.

Robert Crowther's Pop-up Olympics: Amazing Facts & Record Breakers. Robert Crowther. (Illus.). 12p. (J). (gr. 3-8). 1996. 19.99 (1-56402-801-1) Candlewick Pr.

Robert Cumming: Cone of Vision. Hugh M. Davies & Lynda Forsha. LC 92-62592. (Illus.). 83p. 1993. pap. 20.00 (0-934418-40-3) Mus Contemp Art.

Robert Cumming: Photographic Works 1969-1980. 180p. 1995. pap. 35.00 (2-908257-15-7, Pub. by F R A C FR) Dist Art Pubs.

Robert Curthose, Duke of Normandy. Charles W. David. LC 78-63356. (Crusades & Military Orders Ser.: Second Series). (Illus.). 296p. reprint ed. 49.50 (0-404-17007-2) AMS Pr.

Robert D. FitzGerald. Robert D. Fitzgerald. Ed. by Julian Croft. LC 85-32300. (UQP Australian Authors Ser.). 239p. (Orig.). 1987. pap. text ed. 14.95 (0-7022-1917-7, Pub. by Univ Queensland Pr AT) Intl Spec Bk.

Robert D. Murphy: A Register of His Papers in the Hoover Institution Archives. Compiled by Grace M. Hawes. (Bibliographical Ser.: No. B73). 83p. 1989. pap. 14.95 (0-8179-2732-8) Hoover Inst Pr.

Robert D'Aujourd'Hui. Robert. 1716p. (FRE.). 1994. 89.95 (0-7859-9203-0) Fr & Eur.

Robert Davidson: Eagle of the Dawn. Ian M. Thom et al. LC 93-30. (Illus.). 192p. 1993. 50.00 (0-295-97283-1) U of Wash Pr.

Robert De Blois's Floris et Lyriope. Paul Barrette. LC 68-6610. 152p. 1983. reprint ed. lib. bdg. 35.00 (0-89370-767-8) Borgo Pr.

Robert De Boron: The Grail Trilogy: Joseph, Merlin, & Perceval, 2 vols. Ed. by George T. Diller. (Library of Medieval Literature: Vol. MLA73). 1500p. 165.00 (0-8240-5099-1) Garland.

Robert de Cotte & the Perfection of Architecture in Eighteenth-Century France. Robert Neuman. LC 93-30046. 266p. 1994. 55.00 (0-226-57437-7) U Ch Pr.

Robert De Handlo. Ed. by Luther Dittmer. (Musical Theorists in Translation Ser.: Vol. 2). 1961. pap. 19.00 (0-912024-22-4) Inst Mediaeval Mus.

Robert de Poche: Langue Francaise & Noms Propres. Robert. 928p. (FRE.). 1995. 24.95 (0-7859-9194-8) Fr & Eur.

Robert de Torigni - Chronicle of Robert of Torigni see Chronicles of the Reigns of Stephen, Henry II & Richard I

***Robert DeNiro.** Elfreda Powell. (Superstars of Film Ser.). (Illus.). 48p. (YA). (gr. 7 up). 1997. lib. bdg. 15.95 (0-7910-4645-1) Chelsea Hse.

***Robert DeNiro & the Fireman.** Bill Cosgrove. 80p. 1997. 13.95 (1-887750-63-0) Rutledge Bks.

Robert des Jeunes. Josette Rey-Debove. 1292p. (FRE.). 1991. 95.00 (0-7859-9223-5) Fr & Eur.

Robert des Sports: Dictionaire de la Langue des Sports. Georges Petiot. 583p. (FRE.). 1990. 69.95 (0-7859-9226-X) Fr & Eur.

Robert Dictionnaire de Citations du Monde Entier. Florence Montreynaud & Jeanne Matignon. 794p. (FRE.). 1989. 75.00 (0-8288-9466-3) Fr & Eur.

Robert Dictionnaire de Proverbs et Dictions. Florence Montreynaud. 750p. (FRE.). 1989. pap. 28.95 (0-7859-8059-8, 2850361046) Fr & Eur.

Robert Dictionnaire des Anglicismes. Josette Rey-Debove. 1150p. (FRE.). 1988. 69.95 (0-7859-7121-1, 2850360279) Fr & Eur.

Robert Dictionnaire des Anglicismes. 7th ed. P. Conso. 352p. (FRE.). 1985. pap. 49.95 (0-7859-4815-5) Fr & Eur.

Robert Dictionnaire des Mots Contemporains. Pierre Merle. 232p. (FRE.). 1989. pap. 14.95 (0-7859-4759-0, M2320) Fr & Eur.

Robert Dictionnaire des Synonymes. Henri Bertaud du Chazaud. 800p. (FRE.). 1992. 75.00 (0-8288-9431-0, 285036035X) Fr & Eur.

Robert Dinwiddie: His Career in American Colonial Government & Westward Expansion. Louis K. Koontz. LC 76-140362. (Select Bibliographies Reprint Ser.). 1977. reprint ed. 24.95 (0-8369-5605-2) Ayer.

Robert Doisneau: A Photographer's Life. Peter Hamilton. (Illus.). 368p. 1995. 75.00 (0-7892-0020-1) Abbeville Pr.

Robert Drew & the Development of Cinema Verite in America. P. J. O'Connell. LC 91-39992. 312p. (C). 1992. 34.95 (0-8093-1779-6) S Ill U Pr.

Robert Duchesnay: The Dymaxion Dwelling Machine, an Exhibition of Photographs, Paintings, & Sculpture by Robert Duchesnay. Novelene G. Ross. (Illus.). 12p. (Orig.). 1992. pap. write for info. (0-939324-47-4) Wichita Art Mus.

Robert Duncan. Mark A. Johnson. (United States Authors Ser.). (Illus.). 144p. 1988. text ed. 23.95 (0-8057-7511-0, Twayne) Scribnrs Ref.

Robert Duncan: A Descriptive Bibliography. Robert Bertholf. LC 84-16740. (Illus.). 492p. 1986. 65.00 (0-87685-620-2) Black Sparrow.

Robert Duncan: Scales of the Marvelous. Ed. by Robert J. Bertholf & Ian W. Reid. LC 79-19861. (Insights Ser.). 1979. pap. 5.95 (0-8112-0735-8, NDP487) New Directions.

Robert Duncan in San Francisco. Michael Rumaker. 84p. (Orig.). 1996. pap. 8.95 (0-912516-13-5) Grey Fox.

Robert Duvall. Judith Slawson. 1986. pap. 3.95 (0-312-90422-3) St Martin.

Robert E. Howard. Roger C. Schlobin. LC 85-17161. (Starmont Reader's Guide Ser.: Vol. 35). vi, 156p. (Orig.). 1987. pap. 21.00 (0-930261-27-5); lib. bdg. 31.00 (0-930261-28-3) Borgo Pr.

Robert E. Lee. Keith Brandt. LC 84-2687. (Illus.). 32p. (J). (gr. 3-6). 1985. pap. text ed. 3.50 (0-8167-0279-9) Troll Communs.

***Robert E. Lee.** Warren Brown. (World Leaders - Past & Present Ser.). (Illus.). (YA). (gr. 5 up). 1982. pap. 8.95 (0-7910-0698-0) Chelsea Hse.

Robert E. Lee. Warren Brown. (World Leaders - Past & Present Ser.). (Illus.). (YA). (gr. 5 up). 1992. lib. bdg. 19.95 (1-55546-814-4) Chelsea Hse.

Robert E. Lee. William P. Trent. 1972. 34.95 (0-8490-0962-6) Gordon Pr.

Robert E. Lee. rev. ed. Dan Zadra. (We the People Ser.). (J). (gr. 2-4). 1988. lib. bdg. 14.95 (0-88682-192-4) Creative Ed.

Robert E. Lee. Henry A. White. LC 69-14148. 467p. 1969. reprint ed. text ed. 35.00 (0-8371-1864-6, WHRL, Greenwood Pr) Greenwood.

Robert E. Lee, 1. Douglas S. Freeman. (Hudson River Editions Ser.). 672p. 1977. 60.00 (0-684-15482-X) S&S Trade.

Robert E. Lee, Vol. 2. Douglas S. Freeman. (Hudson River Editions Ser.). 640p. 1977. 60.00 (0-684-15483-8) S&S Trade.

Robert E. Lee, Vol. 3. Douglas S. Freeman. (Hudson River Editions Ser.). 576p. 1977. 55.00 (0-684-15484-6) S&S Trade.

Robert E. Lee, Vol. 4. Douglas S. Freeman. (Hudson River Editions Ser.). 616p. 1977. 60.00 (0-684-15485-4) S&S Trade.

Robert E. Lee: A Biography. Emory M. Thomas. (Illus.). 576p. 1995. 30.00 (0-393-03730-4) Norton.

***Robert E. Lee: A Biography.** Emory M. Thomas. (Illus.). 480p. 1997. pap. 14.95 (0-393-31631-9) Norton.

Robert E Lee: A Hero for Young Americans. Patricia Buchanan. LC 90-70314. 142p. (J). (gr. 5-8). 1990. pap. 6.95 (1-55523-334-1) Winston-Derek.

***Robert E. Lee: A Life Portrait.** David Eicher. LC 97-22165. (Illus.). 240p. 1997. 29.95 (0-87833-950-7) Taylor Pub.

Robert E. Lee: A Portrait. Margaret Sanborn. LC 95-14833. 622p. 1996. 27.95 (0-943972-29-9) Homestead WY.

Robert E. Lee: Brave Leader. Rae Bains. LC 85-1092. (Illus.). 48p. (J). (gr. 4-6). 1986. pap. 3.95 (0-8167-0546-1) Troll Communs.

Robert E. Lee: Defender of the South. Marian G. Cannon. LC 93-415. (First Bks.). (Illus.). 64p. (J). (gr. 4-6). 1993. lib. bdg. 21.00 (0-531-20120-1) Watts.

R

An Asterisk (*) at the beginning of an entry indicates that the title is appearing in BIP for the first time.

R

Robert E. Lee: Gallant Christian Soldier. Lee Roddy. (Sower Ser.). (Illus.). (J). (gr. 3-6). 1977. pap. 7.99 (*0-915134-40-3*) Mott Media.

***Robert E. Lee: Southern Hero of the Civil War.** Mona Kerby. LC 96-31432. (Historical American Biographies Ser.). 128p. (YA). (gr. 6 up). 1997. lib. bdg. 18.95 (*0-89490-782-4*) Enslow Pubs.

Robert E. Lee: The Soldier. Frederick Maurice. LC 70-37898. (Select Bibliographies Reprint Ser.). 1977. reprint ed. 35.95 (*0-8369-6736-4*) Ayer.

Robert E. Lee: Young Confederate. Helen A. Monsell. LC 86-10736. (Childhood of Famous Americans Ser.). (Illus.). 192p. (J). (gr. 2-6). 1986. reprint ed. pap. 4.95 (*0-02-042020-X*) Macmillan.

Robert E. Lee & the Rise of the South. Cathy E. Dubowski. (History of the Civil War Ser.). (Illus.). 160p. (YA). (gr. 5 up). 1990. pap. 7.95 (*0-382-24051-0*) Silver Burdett Pr.

Robert E. Lee & the Southern Confederacy. Henry White. LC 68-25004. (American Biography Ser.: No. 32). 1969. reprint ed. lib. bdg. 75.00 (*0-8383-0259-9*) M S G Haskell Hse.

Robert E. Lee & the Southern Confederacy, 1807- 1870. Henry A. White. (History - United States Ser.). 467p. 1992. reprint ed. lib. bdg. 99.00 (*0-7812-6178-3*) Rprt Serv.

Robert E. Lee & the Thirty Fifth Star. Tim McKinney. LC 93-84769. (Illus.). 152p. 1993. pap. 11.95 (*0-929521-75-7*) Pictorial Hist.

Robert E. Lee: Civil War Hero see Junior World Biographies

***Robert E. Lee Family Cooking & Housekeeping Book.** Anne C. Zimmer. LC 97-14383. 296p. (C). (gr. 13). 1997. 24.95 (*0-8078-2369-4*) U of NC Pr.

Robert E. Lee: Hero of the South see Discovery Biographies

Robert E. Lee Reader. Stanley F. Horn. 1994. 12.98 (*0-8317-2441-2*) Smithmark.

Robert E. Park: Biography of a Sociologist. Winifred Raushenbush. LC 77-88063. 220p. reprint ed. pap. 62.70 (*0-317-55491-3*, 2052212) Bks Demand.

Robert E. Peary & the Fight for the North Pole. Madelyn K. Anderson. (Illus.). 160p. (YA). (gr. 9-12). 1992. lib. bdg. 22.70 (*0-531-13004-5*) Watts.

Robert E. Sherwood: Film Critic. Robert E. Sherwood. (Illus.). 359p. 1973. 250.00 (*0-685-32337-4*) Revisionist Pr.

Robert Earl Keen Songbook. 64p. 1995. pap. 14.95 (*0-7935-4431-9*, 00306029) H Leonard.

Robert Elsmere. Ward. Ed. & Intro. by Clyde D. Ryals. LC 67-12116. (Bison Book Ser.). 682p. 1967. reprint ed. pap. 180.00 (*0-608-02373-6*, 2063015) Bks Demand.

Robert Elsmere. Mary A. Ward. (BCL1-PR English Literature Ser.). 604p. 1992. reprint ed. lib. bdg. 109.00 (*0-7812-7541-5*) Rprt Serv.

Robert et Collins Super Senior/French-English/English-French, 2 vols. Ed. by Robert. 2712p. (ENG & FRE.). 1995. 175.00 (*0-7859-9221-9*) Fr & Eur.

Robert et Elizabeth Browning. Andre Maurois. pap. 17.50 (*0-685-36958-7*) Fr & Eur.

Robert Eyres Landor: A Biographical & Critical Sketch, 2 Vols. Eric Partridge. Bd. with Selections from Robert Landor. LC 78-117909. LC 78-117909. (Select Bibliographies Reprint Ser.). 1977. reprint ed. 26.95 (*0-8369-5362-2*) Ayer.

Robert F. Kennedy. Daniel J. Petrillo. (World Leaders - Past & Present Ser.). (Illus.). 112p. (Orig.). (YA). (gr. 5 up). 1989. lib. bdg. 19.95 (*1-55546-840-3*) Chelsea Hse.

***Robert F. Kennedy: Promise for the Future.** Arlene Schulman. LC 97-20610. (Makers of America Ser.). 1997. write for info. (*0-8160-3674-8*) Facts on File.

Robert F. Kennedy Assassination: New Revelations on the Conspiracy & Cover-Up. Philip H. Melanson. 1994. pap. 14.95 (*1-56171-102-0*, S P I Bks) Sure Seller.

Robert F. Kennedy Assassination: New Revelations on the Conspiracy & Cover-Up. Philip H. Melanson. 1994. pap. 5.99 (*1-56171-324-4*, S P I Bks) Sure Seller.

Robert F. Kennedy Assassination: New Revelations on the Conspiracy & Cover-Up, 1968-1991. Philip H. Melanson. 1991. 19.95 (*1-56171-036-9*) Sure Seller.

Robert F. Wagner Labor Archives, New York University: The Papers of the Jewish Labor Committee. Ed. by Arieh Lebowitz & Gail Malmgreen. LC 89-16915. (Archives of the Holocaust Ser.: Vol. 14). 528p. 1993. text ed. 125.00 (*0-8240-5496-2*) Garland.

***Robert Falcon Scott.** Ken Derby. (YA). (gr. 5 up). 1997. pap. 6.99 (*0-614-28976-9*) Royal Fireworks.

Robert Falconer. George MacDonald. 1990. 33.50 (*0-940652-52-8*) Sunrise Bks.

Robert Falconer. George MacDonald. (George MacDonald Original Works: Series VI). 417p. 1995. reprint ed. 18.00 (*1-881084-39-6*) Johannesen.

Robert Feke, Colonial Portrait Painter. Henry W. Foote. LC 72-75357. (Library of American Art). 1969. reprint ed. lib. bdg. 37.50 (*0-306-71319-5*) Da Capo.

Robert Fergusson. Allan H. MacLaine. LC 65-18225. (Twayne's English Authors Ser.). 178p. (C). 1965. lib. bdg. 17.95 (*0-8057-1192-9*) Irvington.

Robert Fergusson: Scots Poems. Ed. by Alexander Law. 70p. 1986. 20.00 (*0-85411-022-4*, Pub. by Saltire Soc) St Mut.

Robert Finch & His Works. Susan Gingell. (Canadian Author Studies). 37p. (C). 1990. pap. text ed. 9.95 (*1-55022-022-5*, Pub. by ECW Press CN) Genl Dist Srvs.

Robert Flaherty & Hans Richter. Herman G. Weinberg. (Film Ser.). 1979. lib. bdg. 250.00 (*0-8490-3001-3*) Gordon Pr.

Robert Florey: The French Expressionist. Brian Taves. LC 86-17919. (Filmmakers Ser.: No. 14). (Illus.). 438p. 1987. 42.50 (*0-8108-1929-5*) Scarecrow.

Robert Fludd: Hermetic Philosopher & Surveyor of Two Worlds. Joscelyn Godwin. LC 90-46704. (Illus.). 173p. (Orig.). 1991. reprint ed. pap. 17.00 (*0-933999-69-0*) Phanes Pr.

Robert Fludd & His Philosophicall Key. Robert Fludd. (Illus.). 156p. 1979. 45.00 (*0-88202-037-4*) Watson Pub Intl.

Robert Fludd & the End of the Renaissance. William Huffman. 288p. 1989. 49.50 (*0-415-00129-3*) Routledge.

Robert Francis: Collected Poems, 1936-1976. Robert Francis. LC 76-8753. 304p. 1985. pap. 17.95 (*0-87023-510-9*) U of Mass Pr.

Robert Francis Kennedy: The Biography of a Compulsive Politician. Allen Roberts. 1984. 19.95 (*0-8283-1890-5*) Branden Pub Co.

Robert Francis Weatherbee. Munro Leaf. LC 87-26046. (Illus.). 75p. (J). (ps-3). 1988. reprint ed. lib. bdg. 16.00 (*0-208-02211-2*, Linnet Bks) Shoe String.

Robert Frank. Pantheon Photo Library Staff. (American Photographers of the Depression). 1985. write for info. (*0-318-59517-6*) Pantheon.

Robert Frank: An Exhibition of Photography & Films 1945-1977. Intro. by Philip Brookman. (Illus.). 18p. (Orig.). 1978. pap. 8.00 (*0-939982-02-1*) Sesnon Art Gall.

Robert Frank: Moving Out. Text by Sarah Greenough et al. (Illus.). 320p. 75.00 (*1-881616-26-6*, D2005) Dist Art Pubs.

Robert Frank: Moving Out. Sarah Greenough. LC 94-20187. 335p. 1994. pap. 35.00 (*0-89468-172-9*) Natl Gallery Art.

Robert Frank: Photographs. LC 85-43182. 192p. 1986. 25.00 (*0-394-55143-5*) Pantheon.

Robert Frank: The Americans. Robert Frank. 1993. pap. 26.50 (*1-881616-12-6*, Pub. by Scalo Pubs) Dist Art Pubs.

Robert Frank: The Lines of My Hand. Robert Frank. (Illus.). 156p. reprint ed. 39.95 (*1-881616-00-2*) Dist Art Pubs.

Robert Fripp: From King Crimson to Guitar Craft. Eric Tamm. 231p. (Orig.). 1991. pap. 13.95 (*0-571-12912-9*) Faber & Faber.

***Robert Frost.** Meyers. 1997. pap. 15.00 (*0-395-85603-5*) HM.

Robert Frost. Intro. by Peter Porter & Geoffrey Moore. (Great Poets Ser.). (Illus.). 1988. 10.00 (*0-517-56289-8*, C P Pubs) Crown Pub Group.

Robert Frost. rev. ed. Philip L. Gerber. (United States Authors Ser.: No. 107). 224p. (C). 1982. 21.95 (*0-8057-7348-7*, Twayne) Scribnrs Ref.

Robert Frost. Lawrance R. Thompson. LC 59-63268. (University of Minnesota Pamphlets on American Writers Ser.: No. 2). 46p. reprint ed. pap. 25.00 (*0-317-29464-4*, 2055927) Bks Demand.

Robert Frost: A Biography. Jeffrey Meyers. LC 95-45647. (Illus.). 424p. 1996. 30.00 (*0-395-72809-6*) HM.

Robert Frost: A Biography. Jay Parini. 1996. 28.95 (*0-8050-3181-2*) H Holt & Co.

Robert Frost: A Biography. R. H. Winnick & Lawrence R. Thompson. Ed. by Edward C. Lathem. LC 80-28337. (Illus.). 560p. 1982. 25.00 (*0-03-050921-1*) H Holt & Co.

Robert Frost: A Collection of Critical Essays. Ed. by James M. Cox. 1962. 12.95 (*0-13-331512-6*, Spectrum IN) Macmillan Gen Ref.

Robert Frost: A Descriptive Catalogue of Books & Manuscripts in the Clifton Waller Barrett Library, University of Virginia. Clifton Waller Barrett Library Staff & Joan S. Crane. LC 73-89904. 316p. reprint ed. pap. 90.10 (*0-8357-2730-0*, 2039840) Bks Demand.

Robert Frost: A Reference Guide, 1974-1990. Peter Van Egmond. (Reference Guides to Literature Ser.). 150p. 1991. 40.00 (*0-8161-7271-4*, Hall Reference) Macmillan.

Robert Frost: A Study in Sensibility & Good Sense. Gorham B. Munson. LC 72-10857. (Studies in Poetry: No. 38). 1969. reprint ed. lib. bdg. 75.00 (*0-8383-0788-4*) M S G Haskell Hse.

Robert Frost: An Anthology of Recent Criticism. Ed. by Manorama B. Trikha. (New Orientations Ser.). 220p. 1990. text ed. 30.00 (*81-85433-01-1*, Pub. by Pencraft International II) Advent Bks Div.

Robert Frost: Poetry for Young People. Ed. by Gary D. Schmidt. LC 94-11161. (Illus.). 48p. (J). 1994. 14.95 (*0-8069-0633-2*) Sterling.

Robert Frost: Seasons. Robert Frost. (Illus.). 120p. 1996. reprint ed. 12.98 (*1-56731-103-2*, MJF Bks) Fine Comms.

Robert Frost: The Work of Knowing. Richard Poirier. LC 89-60362. 384p. 1990. 47.50 (*0-8047-1741-9*); pap. 15.95 (*0-8047-1742-7*) Stanford U Pr.

Robert Frost see Modern Critical Views Series

Robert Frost among His Poems: A Literary Companion to the Poet's Own Biographical Contexts & Associations. Jeffrey S. Cramer. LC 95-39536. 304p. 1996. lib. bdg. 38.50 (*0-7864-0079-X*) McFarland & Co.

Robert Frost & a Poetics of Appetite. Katherine Kearns. (Cambridge Studies in American Literature & Culture: No. 77). 288p. (C). 1994. text ed. 65.00 (*0-521-44485-3*) Cambridge U Pr.

***Robert Frost & His Printers.** Joseph Blumenthal. 112p. 1985. 45.00 (*0-614-24482-X*, 18950) Oak Knoll.

Robert Frost & His Printers. Joseph Blumenthal. 85.00 (*0-935072-06-3*) W T Taylor.

Robert Frost & New England: The Poet As Regionalist. John C. Kemp. LC 78-70301. 291p. reprint ed. pap. 83.00 (*0-8357-3520-6*, 2052295) Bks Demand.

Robert Frost & Sidney Cox: Forty Years of Friendship. Robert Frost. Ed. by William R. Evans. LC 80-54464. 315p. reprint ed. pap. 89.80 (*0-8357-6513-X*, 2035884) Bks Demand.

***Robert Frost & the Challenge of Darwin.** Robert Faggen. LC 97-4481. (C). 1997. 44.50 (*0-472-10782-8*) U of Mich Pr.

Robert Frost & the New England Renaissance. George Monteiro. LC 88-5479. 192p. 1988. 21.00 (*0-8131-1649-X*) U Pr of Ky.

Robert Frost & Wade Van Dore: The Life of the Hired Man. Wade Van Dore. (Illus.). 291p. 1987. pap. 21.00 (*0-932429-01-7*) Univ Monographs.

Robert Frost Handbook. James L. Potter. LC 79-9145. 1980. text ed. 30.00 (*0-271-00230-1*) Pa St U Pr.

Robert Frost Himself. Stanley Burnshaw. LC 86-20793. (Illus.). 1986. 19.95 (*0-8076-1164-6*) Braziller.

Robert Frost Himself. Stanley Burnshaw. LC 86-20793. (Illus.). 342p. 1989. pap. 12.95 (*0-8076-1234-0*) Braziller.

Robert Frost Poetry & Prose. Edward C. Lathem. LC 74-188990. 496p. 1984. pap. 14.95 (*0-8050-0245-6*, Owl) H Holt & Co.

Robert Frost Speaks. Daniel Smyth. 158p. 29.95 (*0-8290-0203-0*) Irvington.

Robert Frost's Imagery & the Poetic Consciousness. Dennis Vail. (Graduate Studies: No. 12). 83p. (Orig.). 1976. pap. 8.00 (*0-89672-022-5*) Tex Tech Univ Pr.

Robert Frost's Poems. Robert Frost. mass mkt. 5.50 (*0-671-49617-4*, WSP) PB.

Robert Frost's Star in a Stone Boat: A Grammar of Belief. Ed Ingebretsen. LC 94-29284. 1995. 64.95 (*1-883255-73-2*); pap. 44.95 (*1-883255-72-4*) Intl Scholars.

Robert Fulghum: All I Really Need to Know I Learned in Kindergarten, & It Was on Fire When I Lay down on It Uh-Oh, 3 vols., Set. Robert Fulghum. 1993. boxed, pap. 17.93 (*0-8041-1199-5*) Ivy Books.

Robert Fulton. Elaine Landau. LC 90-47865. (First Bks.). (Illus.). 64p. (J). (gr. 4-6). 1991. lib. bdg. 21.00 (*0-531-20016-7*) Watts.

Robert Fulton & the "Clermont" Alice Sutcliffe. 397p. 1993. reprint ed. lib. bdg. 89.00 (*0-7812-5222-9*) Rprt Serv.

Robert Fulton, Engineer & Artist. Henry W. Dickinson. LC 77-148879. (Select Bibliographies Reprint Ser.). 1977. reprint ed. 29.95 (*0-8369-5649-4*) Ayer.

***Robert G. Fowler Pictorial History.** Marla S. Burden. (Illus.). 130p. Date not set. pap. 18.00 (*0-87505-369-6*) Borden.

Robert G. Ingersoll: A Checklist. Gordon Stein. LC 78-626234. (Serif Series: Bibliographies & Checklists: No. 9). 158p. reprint ed. pap. 45.10 (*0-8357-5579-7*, 2035206) Bks Demand.

Robert G. Ingersoll: A Life. Frank Smith. 417p. (C). 1989. 34.95 (*0-87975-588-1*) Prometheus Bks.

Robert Gardner's Challenging Science Experiments. Robert Gardner. LC 92-21116. (Illus.). 176p. (YA). (gr. 9-12). 1993. pap. 6.95 (*0-531-15671-0*); lib. bdg. 22.70 (*0-531-11090-7*) Watts.

Robert Gardner's Favorite Science Experiments. Robert Gardner. LC 92-17579. (Illus.). 128p. (J). (gr. 5-8). 1992. lib. bdg. 20.00 (*0-531-11038-9*) Watts.

Robert Gober: In the Dance Hall of the Dead. Dave Hickey. Ed. by Karen Marta. LC 93-70736. (Illus.). 64p. 1994. 25.00 (*0-944521-25-8*) Dia Ctr Arts.

Robert Goldstein & "The Spirit of '76" Robert Goldstein. LC 93-13397. (Filmmakers Ser.: No. 34). (Illus.). 274p. 1993. 32.50 (*0-8108-2674-7*) Scarecrow.

Robert Gordy - Robert Warrens: Painted Faces - Painted Fantasies. Ed. by Audrey Hammill. LC 88-70589. (Illus.). 40p. (Orig.). 1988. pap. 12.00 (*0-944564-01-1*) Alex Mus.

Robert Gover: A Descriptive Bibliography. Michael Hargraves. 120p. 1988. text ed. 42.95 (*0-313-27676-5*) Greenwood.

Robert Graham: The Duke Ellington Memorial in Progress. Joan Didion & Peter Fusco. LC 88-8214. (Illus.). 108p. (Orig.). 1988. pap. 14.95 (*0-87587-149-6*) LA Co Art Mus.

Robert Graves. George Stade. LC 67-16890. (Columbia Essays on Modern Writers Ser.: No. 25). (Orig.). (C). 1967. pap. text ed. 10.00 (*0-231-02907-1*) Col U Pr.

Robert Graves: Peace-Weaver. James S Mehoke. (Studies in English Literature: No. 63). 168p. 1975. pap. text ed. 53.85 (*90-279-3194-1*) Mouton.

Robert Graves: The Lasting Poetic Achievement. D. N. Carter. LC 88-29245. 256p. (C). 1989. lib. bdg. 44.00 (*0-389-20818-3*) B&N Imports.

Robert Graves & the Hebrew Myths: A Collaboration. Raphael Patai. LC 91-20963. (Jewish Folklore & Anthropology Ser.). (Illus.). 468p. 1992. 49.95 (*0-8143-2114-3*) Wayne St U Pr.

Robert Graves & the White Goddess. John B. Vickery. LC 70-183363. 155p. reprint ed. 44.20 (*0-8357-9713-9*, 2011899) Bks Demand.

Robert Graves & the White Goddess 1940-1985. Richard P. Graves. (Illus.). 618p. 1996. 45.00 (*0-297-81534-2*, Weidenfeld); pap. 24.95 (*0-297-81767-1*, Weidenfeld) Trafalgar.

Robert Graves Manuscripts & Letters at Southern Illinois University: An Inventory. John W. Presley. LC 75-8383. vii, 261p. 1976. 18.00 (*0-87875-075-4*) Whitston Pub.

Robert Greene. Robert Greene & Jerry Saltz. Ed. by John Cheim. (Illus.). 56p. (Orig.). 1992. pap. 30.00 (*0-944680-40-2*) R Miller Gal.

Robert Greene: New Paintings. (Illus.). 52p. 1988. pap. 20.00 (*0-944680-03-8*) R Miller Gal.

Robert Gregory, 1881-1918. Ed. by Colin Smythe. (Illus.). 40p. 8100. pap. 9.95 (*0-86140-108-5*, Pub. by Colin Smythe Ltd UK) Dufour.

Robert Grieve: Paintings, Drawings & Collage. David Ellis. (Illus.). 160p. 1995. text ed. 75.00 (*976-641-011-9*, Pub. by Craftsman Hse VB) Gordon & Breach.

Robert Grilley: A Retrospective. Howard D. Spencer. LC 87-50792. (Illus.). 28p. 1987. pap. 7.00 (*0-939324-30-X*) Wichita Art Mus.

Robert Grosseteste: On the Six Days of Creation: A Translation of the Hexaemeron. Robert Grosseteste. Tr. by C. F. Martin. (Auctores Britannici Medii Aevi; British Academy: Vol. VI, No. 2). (Illus.). 384p. 1997. text ed. 55.00 (*0-19-726150-7*) OUP.

Robert Grosseteste, Bishop of Lincoln: A Contribution to the Religious, Political & Intellectual History of the Thirteenth Century. F. S. Stevenson. (Medieval Studies Ser.). reprint ed. lib. bdg. 39.50 (*0-697-00018-4*) Irvington.

Robert Grosseteste, Exegete & Philosopher. James McEvoy. LC 94-5847. (Collected Studies: No. CS 446). 205p. 1994. 84.95 (*0-86078-433-9*, Pub. by Variorum UK) Ashgate Pub Co.

***Robert Guthrie - The PKU Story: Crusade Against Mental Retardation.** Jean H. Koch. LC 97-2457. (Illus.). 288p. 1997. 20.00 (*0-932727-91-3*) Hope Pub Hse.

Robert H. Goddard. Karin C. Farley. (Pioneers in Change Ser.). (Illus.). 144p. (J). (gr. 5-9). 1992. pap. 6.95 (*0-382-24177-0*); lib. bdg. 13.95 (*0-382-24171-1*) Silver Burdett Pr.

Robert H. Lowie, Ethnologist: A Personal Record. Robert H. Lowie. LC 59-8762. (Illus.). 311p. reprint ed. pap. 64.50 (*0-685-20504-5*, 2029955) Bks Demand.

Robert H. Montgomery: A Pioneer Leader of American Accounting. Alfred R. Roberts. LC 75-31805. (Research Monograph: No. 63). 358p. 1975. spiral bd. 35.00 (*0-88406-095-0*) GA St U Busn Pr.

Robert H. Schuller: The Inspirational Writings. Robert H. Schuller. 1993. 12.98 (*0-88486-078-7*) Arrowood Pr.

Robert H. Schuller Tells You How to Be an Extraordinary Person in an Ordinary World. Robert H. Schuller. 192p. 1986. mass mkt. 4.50 (*0-515-08577-4*) Jove Pubns.

Robert Half on Hiring. Robert Half. LC 85-29771. 256p. 1986. pap. 10.95 (*0-452-25811-1*, Plume) NAL-Dutton.

Robert Half's Success Guide for Accountants. 167p. 1990. pap. 9.95 (*0-685-33067-2*) P-H.

Robert Half's Success Guide for Accountants. Robert Half. 1990. pap. 9.95 (*0-13-781535-2*) P-H.

***Robert Half's Success Guide for Accountants.** 2nd ed. Robert Half. 192p. 44.95 (*0-13-781568-9*) P-H.

Robert Hall Diaries: Vol. I, 1947-1953. Ed. by Alex Cairncross. 326p. 1989. text ed. 90.00 (*0-04-445273-X*) Routledge Chapman & Hall.

Robert Hardin & Descendants. Shirley T. Berg. 300p. (Orig.). 1996. pap. 20.00 (*1-57798-002-6*, 0026) BerryPatch.

Robert Harley: Speaker, Secretary of State & Premier Minister. Brian Hill. LC 87-37186. (C). 1988. text ed. 42.50 (*0-300-04284-1*) Yale U Pr.

Robert Harlow & His Works. Louis K. MacKendrick. (Canadian Author Studies). 57p. (C). 1989. pap. text ed. 9.95 (*0-920763-90-1*, Pub. by ECW Press CN) Genl Dist Srvs.

Robert Hart & China's Early Modernization: His Journals, 1863-1866. Richard J. Smith et al. (East Asian Monographs: No. 155). 582p. (C). 1991. 35.00 (*0-674-77530-9*) HUP.

Robert Hayden: A Critical Analysis of His Poetry. Pontheolla T. Williams. LC 86-6932. 264p. 1987. text ed. 21.95 (*0-252-01289-5*) U of Ill Pr.

Robert Heinecken: 1984, a Case Study in Finding an Appropriate TV Newswoman (A CBS Docudrama in Words & Pictures) Robert Heinecken. LC 86-91872. (Illus.). 1985. pap. 26.00 (*0-614-06476-7*) RAM Publications.

Robert Helm: 1981-1993. Marti Mayo. (Illus.). 144p. 1995. pap. 25.00 (*0-295-97452-4*) U of Wash Pr.

Robert Helm, 1981-1993. Marti Mayo. LC 93-74800. 128p. 1995. pap. 25.00 (*0-941193-09-8*) U Houst Sarah.

Robert Henri: His Life & Art. Bennard B. Perlman. 1991. pap. 11.95 (*0-486-26722-9*) Dover.

Robert Henri & Five of His Pupils: Loan Exhibition of Paintings, April 5, to June 1, 1946. Century Association, New York Staff. LC 74-160918. (Biography Index Reprint Ser.). 1977. reprint ed. 18.95 (*0-8369-8081-6*) Ayer.

Robert Henri & His Circle. William I. Homer. LC 87-81951. (Illus.). 308p. 1988. reprint ed. lib. bdg. 50.00 (*0-87817-326-9*) Hacker.

Robert Henryson. Marshall W. Stearns. LC 73-182718. reprint ed. 20.00 (*0-404-06225-3*) AMS Pr.

Robert Henryson: Selected Poems. Ed. by David Murison. 58p. 1989. 29.00 (*0-85411-010-0*, Pub. by Saltire Soc) St Mut.

Robert Henryson & William Dunbar. Douglas Gray. Ed. by M. C. Seymour. (Authors of the Middle Ages Ser.). 64p. Date not set. pap. 17.95 (*0-86078-424-X*, Pub. by Variorum UK) Ashgate Pub Co.

***Robert Henryson (1425?-1508?) Selected Poems.** Ed. by W. R. Barron. pap. write for info. (*0-85635-301-9*, Pub. by Carcanet Pr UK) Paul & Co Pubs.

Robert Henryson's Tragic Vision. Steven R. McKenna. LC 93-18358. (American University Studies, IV, English Language & Literature: Vol. 171). 221p. (C). 1994. text ed. 39.95 (*0-8204-2265-7*) P Lang Pubng.

Robert Herrick. Roger B. Rollin. (Twayne's English Authors Ser.: No. 34). 180p. 1992. 22.95 (*0-8057-7012-7*, Twayne) Scribnrs Ref.

***Robert Herrick (1591-1674) Selected Poems.** Ed. by David Jesson-Dibley. pap. write for info. (*0-85635-320-5*, Pub. by Carcanet Pr UK) Paul & Co Pubs.

Robert Herrick's Hesperides & the Epigram Book Tradition. Ann B. Coiro. LC 87-22827. 280p. 1988. text ed. 42.50 (*0-8018-3571-2*) Johns Hopkins.

Robert Hooke: New Studies. Ed. by Michael Hunter & Simon Schaffer. (Illus.). 320p. (C). 1990. 79.00 (*0-85115-523-5*) Boydell & Brewer.

Robert Hope-Jones. David H. Fox. (Illus.). xiii, 285p. 1992. 27.00 (*0-913499-09-9*) Organ Hist Soc.

An Asterisk (*) at the beginning of an entry indicates that the title is appearing in BIP for the first time.

Robert Hovda: The "Amen Corner" Robert W. Hovda. Ed. by John F. Baldovin. LC 94-7254. 264p. (Orig.). 1994. pap. text ed. 15.95 (*0-8146-6150-5*, Pueblo Bks) Liturgical Pr.

Robert Hudson: A Survey. Graham W. Beal et al. LC 85-8239. (Illus.). 80p. 1985. pap. 14.95 (*0-918471-02-8*) San Fran MOMA.

Robert Hunter, Sixteen Sixty-Six to Seventeen Thirty-Four: New York's Augustan Statesman. Mary L. Lustig. LC 83-4750. (New York State Bks.). (Illus.). 312p. 1983. text ed. 42.50 (*0-8156-2296-1*) Syracuse U Pr.

Robert Hutchings Goddard. Suzanne M. Coil. (Makers of Modern Science Ser.). (Illus.). 144p. (YA). (gr. 7-12). 1992. lib. bdg. 17.95 (*0-8160-2591-6*) Facts on File.

Robert Indiana. Carl J. Weinhardt, Jr. (Illus.). 240p. 1990. 75.00 (*0-8109-1116-7*) Abrams.

Robert Indiana: Catalogue Raisonne of Prints. (Illus.). 96p. 1992. 60.00 (*0-9629512-0-X*); pap. 35.00 (*0-9629512-1-8*) S Sheehan Gallery.

Robert Ingersoll. David D. Anderson. LC 71-183736. (Twayne's United States Authors Ser.). 137p. (C). 1972. lib. bdg. 17.95 (*0-8290-1703-8*) Irvington.

Robert Irwin. Ed. by Russell Ferguson. LC 93-3337. (Illus.). 1993. write for info. (*0-914357-30-1*) Los Angeles Mus Contemp.

Robert J. Aumann: Collected Papers. Robert J. Aumann. LC 96-6332. (Illus.). 720p. 1997. 65.00 (*0-262-01154-9*) MIT Pr.

Robert J. Aumann Vol. 2: Collected Papers. Robert J. Aumann. LC 96-6332. (Illus.). 672p. 1997. 65.00 (*0-262-01155-7*) MIT Pr.

Robert J. Freedman Collection. (Illus.). 76p. 1973. 2.00 (*0-916746-46-1*) Springfield Lib & Mus.

Robert Johnson. Samuel B. Charters. (Illus.). 88p. 1973. pap. 12.95 (*0-8256-0059-6*, OK62745, Oak) Music Sales.

Robert Johnson: At the Crossroads with Notes & Tablature. R. Johnson. 128p. 1992. otabind 19.95 (*0-7935-1093-7*, 00694799) H Leonard.

Robert Kehlmann - Painting with Glass: A Retrospective. Susanne K. Frantz et al. (Illus.). 48p. (Orig.). 1996. pap. 12.95 (*1-886091-12-9*) Hearst Art Gal.

Robert Kennedy. Hilty. 1966. 26.95 (*0-8057-7796-2*, Twayne) Scribnrs Ref.

Robert Kennedy. Hilty. 1997. pap. 14.95 (*0-8057-7797-0*, Twayne) Scribnrs Ref.

***Robert Kennedy: Brother Protector.** James W. Hilty. LC 97-16908. 1997. write for info. (*1-56639-566-6*) Temple U Pr.

Robert Kennedy: The Final Years. Brian Dooley. 196p. 1996. text ed. 35.00 (*0-312-16130-1*) St Martin.

***Robert Kennedy & His Time.** Arthur M. Schlesinger. 1996. pap. 15.00 (*0-345-41061-0*) Ballantine.

Robert Kennedy & His Times. Arthur M. Schlesinger, Jr. (Illus.). 1072p. 1985. mass mkt. 6.95 (*0-345-32547-8*) Ballantine.

Robert Keyser. Frank Zadlo. (Illus.). (Orig.). 1987. pap. 7.00 (*0-939351-02-1*) Temple U Tyler Gal.

***Robert Kilwardby O. P. De Ortu Scientiarum.** A. G. Judy. (Auctores Britannici Medii Aevi Ser.: Vol. IV). 1976. 19.98 (*0-85672-126-3*) David Brown.

Robert Kilwardby O. P. On Time & Imagination: Introduction & Translation. Robert Kilwardby. Ed. by Alexander Broadie. (Auctores Britannici Medii Aevi British Academy Ser.: Vol. IX, Pt. 2). 192p. (C). 1993. 39.95 (*0-19-726121-3*, 6329) OUP.

Robert Kilwardby O. P., on Time & Imagination: De Tempore, De Spiritu Fantastico. Ed. by Osmund Lewry. (Auctores Britannici Medii Aevi IX). 224p. 1987. 175.00 (*0-19-726054-3*) OUP.

Robert Knightley, Alfrede or Right Reinthron'd: A Translation of William Drury's Aluredus sive Alfredus. Ed. by Albert H. Tricomi. (Medieval & Renaissance Texts & Studies: Vol. 99). 170p. 1993. 30.00 (*0-86698-113-6*, MR99) MRTS.

Robert-Koch-Symposium 1993 on "Progress in Tuberculosis Research" Ed. by Martin E. Mielke et al. (Immunobiology Ser.: No. 191/4-5). (Illus.). v, 282p. (Orig.). 1994. pap. 90.00 (*3-437-11644-4*, Pub. by G Fischer Verlag GW) Lubrecht & Cramer.

Robert Kroetsch & His Works (Fiction) Peter Thomas. (Canadian Author Studies). 52p. (C). 1989. pap. text ed. 9.95 (*0-920763-88-X*, Pub. by ECW Press CN) Genl Dist Srvs.

Robert Kroetsch & His Works (Poetry) Ann Munton. (Canadian Author Studies). 118p. (C). 1992. pap. text ed. 9.95 (*1-55022-072-1*, Pub. by ECW Press CN) Genl Dist Srvs.

Robert Kushner. Janet Kardon & Donald Kuspit. 64p. (Orig.). 1987. pap. 18.00 (*0-88454-043-X*) U of Pa Contemp Art.

***Robert Kushner: Gardens of Earthly Delight.** Alexandra Anderson-Spivy & Holland Cotter. LC 97-2590. (Illus.). 180p. 1997. 50.00 (*1-55595-121-X*) Hudson Hills.

Robert Kushner: Paintings. Raymond Olivero. (Illus.). 15p. 1989. pap. 1.00 (*0-939324-41-5*) Wichita Art Mus.

Robert L. Cooper: A Cattle Trader. Delores J. Cabezut-Ortiz. (Illus.). 50p. 1989. 19.00 (*0-685-26990-6*); text ed. 25.00 (*0-685-26991-4*) D J Cabezut-Ortiz.

Robert L. Robb's Bible Heritage Cookbook: A Gourmet Guide to Cooking with the Bible. Robert L. Robb. LC 78-59914. (Illus.). 14.95 (*0-917182-08-1*) Triumph Pub.

Robert L. Vann of the Pittsburgh Courier: Politics & Black Journalism. Andrew Buni. LC 73-7700. 432p. 1974. 29.95 (*0-8229-3274-1*) U of Pittsburgh Pr.

Robert Laneham's Letters see Rogues & Vagabonds of Shakespeare's Youth, Described by John Awdeley in His Fraternitye Vacabondes 1561-1573; Thomas Harman in His Caveat for Common Cursetors, 1567-1573; & in the Groundworke of Conny-Catching, 1552

Robert Lansing: An Interpretive Biography. Thomas H. Hartig. 1981. 55.95 (*0-405-14085-1*) Ayer.

Robert Lansing & American Neutrality, 1914-1917. Daniel M. Smith. LC 79-126610. (American Scene, Comments & Commentators Ser.). (Illus.). 254p. 1972. reprint ed. lib. bdg. 32.50 (*0-306-70057-3*) Da Capo.

Robert Laurent & American Figurative Sculpture, 1910-1960: Selections from the John N. Stern Collection & The David & Alfred Smart Museum of Art. David & Alfred Smart Museum of Art Staff. Tr. by Richard A. Born. (Illus.). 64p. (Orig.). 1994. pap. text ed. write for info. (*0-935573-15-1*) D & A Smart Museum.

Robert Lawson. Schmidt. LC 97-21000. 1997. 22.95 (*0-8057-4585-8*, Twayne) Scribnrs Ref.

Robert Lawson: A Minister's Fortunes, a Story of New England. Horatio Alger, Jr. (Gold Signature Ser.). (Illus.). 120p. 1987. 20.00 (*0-317-59461-3*) G K Westgard.

***Robert Lee Huber: A Collector Creates.** Walter Liedtke et al. (Illus.). 120p. 1996. write for info. (*0-9636759-2-3*) East Carolin Mus.

Robert Lehman Collection Vol. 10: Italian Majolica. Jorg Rasmussen. 304p. (C). 1989. text ed. 110.00 (*0-691-04073-7*) Princeton U Pr.

Robert Lehman Collection at the Metropolitan Museum of Art: American Drawings & Watercolors, Vol. 8. Carol Clark. (Illus.). 268p. 1992. text ed. 95.00 (*0-691-03208-4*) Princeton U Pr.

Robert Lehman Lectures on Contemporary Art. Stephen Bann et al. Ed. by Karen Kelly. Tr. by Brice Marden et al. LC 93-73430. (Lectures Ser.: No. 1). (Illus.). 112p. (Orig.). 1996. pap. 12.95 (*0-944521-75-4*) Dia Ctr Arts.

Robert Leroy Platzman Memorial. H. Hering. 428p. 1976. pap. 69.00 (*0-08-019957-7*, Pergamon Pr) Elsevier.

Robert Leslie Bellem's Dan Turner, Hollywood Detective. Ed. by John Wooley. LC 82-73982. 1983. 17.95 (*0-87972-231-2*); pap. 11.95 (*0-87972-232-0*) Bowling Green Univ Popular Press.

Robert Lewis Stevenson: Teller of Tales. Beverly Gherman. (J). 1996. 16.00 (*0-689-31985-1*, S&S Bks Young Read) S&S Childrens.

Robert Ley: Hitler's Labor Leader. Ronald Smelser. (Illus.). 338p. 1988. 19.95 (*0-85496-161-5*) Berg Pubs.

Robert Lives with His Grandparents. Martha W. Hickman. LC 95-3122. (Albert Whitman Concept Bks.). (Illus.). 32p. (J). (gr. k-4). 1995. lib. bdg. 14.95 (*0-8075-7084-2*) A Whitman.

Robert Longo. Howard Fox et al. LC 89-45427. (Illus.). 208p. 1990. pap. 29.95 (*0-8478-1105-0*) Rizzoli Intl.

Robert Louis Stevenson. Irving S. Saposnik. (English Authors Ser.: No. 167). 168p. 1974. 22.95 (*0-8057-1517-7*, Twayne) Scribnrs Ref.

Robert Louis Stevenson. Sidney Dark. LC 76-173849. (English Literature Ser.: No. 33). 1971. reprint ed. lib. bdg. 75.00 (*0-8383-1343-4*) M S G Haskell Hse.

Robert Louis Stevenson: A Biography. Frank McLynn. 1994. 30.00 (*0-679-41284-0*) Random.

Robert Louis Stevenson: Author of A Child's Garden of Verses. Carol Greene. (Rookie Biographies Ser.). (Illus.). 48p. (J). (gr. k-3). 1994. pap. 4.95 (*0-516-44265-1*); lib. bdg. 18.30 (*0-516-04265-3*) Childrens.

Robert Louis Stevenson: Catalogue of Collections in the Department of Rare Books. Compiled by A. D. Wainwright. LC 75-163868. (Illus.). 142p. 1971. 20.00 (*0-87811-017-8*) Princeton Lib.

***Robert Louis Stevenson: Finding Treasure Island.** Angelica S. Carpenter & Jean Shirley. LC 96-48274. (J). 1997. write for info. (*0-8225-4955-7*, Lerner Publctns) Lerner Group.

***Robert Louis Stevenson: Great British & Irish Short Stories I.** Illus. by James McConnell. LC 94-75357. (Classic Short Stories Ser.). 80p. 1994. pap. 5.95 (*0-7854-0641-7*, 40047) Am Guidance.

Robert Louis Stevenson: Interviews & Recollections. Ed. by R. C. Terry. LC 95-60601. (Illus.). 256p. 1995. text ed. 24.95 (*0-87745-512-0*) U of Iowa Pr.

Robert Louis Stevenson: Life, Literature & the Silver Screen. Scott A. Nollen. LC 94-17785. (Illus.). 480p. 1994. lib. bdg. 55.00 (*0-89950-788-3*) McFarland & Co.

***Robert Louis Stevenson: Poet & Teller of Tales.** Bryan Bevan. (Illus.). 208p. 1993. pap. 17.95 (*0-948695-29-3*, Pub. by Rubicon Pr UK) David Brown.

Robert Louis Stevenson: Poet & Teller of Tales. Bryan Bevan. 192p. 1993. text ed. 39.95 (*0-312-10302-6*) St Martin.

***Robert Louis Stevenson: Teller of Tales.** Beverly Gherman. (J). (gr. 3-7). Date not set. 16.00 (*0-614-19206-4*, Atheneum Bks Young) S&S Childrens.

Robert Louis Stevenson: The Complete Shorter Fiction. Ed. by Peter Stoneley. 680p. 1991. 28.95 (*0-88184-741-0*) Carroll & Graf.

Robert Louis Stevenson: The Complete Shorter Fiction. Peter Stoneley. 680p. 1993. pap. 14.95 (*0-7867-0022-X*) Carroll & Graf.

Robert Louis Stevenson: The Critical Heritage. Paul Maixner. (Critical Heritage Ser.). 556p. 1981. 53.00 (*0-7100-0505-9*, RKP) Routledge.

Robert Louis Stevenson: The Frail Warrior. Jean M. Carre. Tr. by Eleanor Hard from FRE. LC 78-165619. (Select Bibliographies Reprint Ser.). 1977. reprint ed. 20.95 (*0-8369-5926-4*) Ayer.

Robert Louis Stevenson: Young Storyteller. Francene Sabin. LC 91-3924. (Illus.). 48p. (J). (gr. 4-6). 1992. lib. bdg. 12.95 (*0-8167-2507-1*) Troll Communs.

Robert Louis Stevenson: Young Storyteller. Francene Sabin. LC 91-3924. (Illus.). 48p. (J). (gr. 4-6). 1997. pap. 3.95 (*0-8167-2508-X*) Troll Communs.

Robert Louis Stevenson see Later 19th Century Novelists: Critical Heritage

Robert Louis Stevenson & Other Poems, 1895. Richard LaGallienne. 1996. 48.00 (*1-85477-151-5*, Pub. by Woodstock Bks UK) Cassell.

Robert Louis Stevenson & the Appearance of Modernism: A Future Feeling. Alan Sandison. 432p. 1996. text ed. 59.95 (*0-312-15968-4*) St Martin.

Robert Louis Stevenson & 'The Beach of Falesa' A Study in Victorian Publishing with the Original Text. Barry Menikoff. LC 82-61072. (Illus.). 216p. 1984. 35.00 (*0-8047-1162-3*) Stanford U Pr.

Robert Louis Stevenson & the Fiction of Adventure. Robert Kiely. LC 64-21788. 311p. reprint ed. pap. 88.70 (*0-7837-4114-6*, 2057937) Bks Demand.

Robert Louis Stevenson-Appointment on Moloka'i. Aldyth Morris. LC 94-48702. (Illus.). 60p. 1995. pap. 8.95 (*0-8248-1671-4*) UH Pr.

Robert Louis Stevenson Chronology. J. R. Hammond. 1997. text ed. 45.00 (*0-312-16267-7*) St Martin.

Robert Louis Stevenson Companion. Hammond. 1984. 25.00 (*0-02-913790-X*) Mac Lib Ref.

Robert Louis Stevenson, His Work & His Personality, 2 vols. J. A. Stewart. 1992. reprint ed. lib. bdg. 75.00 (*0-7812-5094-3*) Rprt Serv.

Robert Louis Stevenson's Attitude to Life. John F. Genung. 1972. 59.95 (*0-8490-0963-4*) Gordon Pr.

Robert Louis Stevenson's Selected Essays. Ed. by George Scott-Moncrieff. LC 87-37672. 246p. 1987. pap. 7.95 (*0-89526-781-0*) Regnery Pub.

Robert Lowe & Education. David W. Sylvester. LC 73-82446. (Cambridge Texts & Studies in the History of Education). 250p. reprint ed. pap. 71.30 (*0-317-20811-X*, 2024535) Bks Demand.

Robert Lowell. Jay Martin. LC 73-629878. (University of Minnesota Pamphlets on American Writers Ser.: No. 92). 48p. (Orig.). reprint ed. pap. 25.00 (*0-7837-2876-X*, 2057579) Bks Demand.

Robert Lowell: A Biography. Ian Hamilton. LC 82-40121. 576p. 1983. 19.95 (*0-394-50965-X*, Vin) Random.

Robert Lowell: An Introduction to the Poetry. Mark Rudman. LC 83-2091. 224p. 1983. text ed. 39.50 (*0-231-04672-3*) Col U Pr.

Robert Lowell: Essays on the Poetry. Ed. by Steven G. Axelrod et al. (Cambridge Studies in American Literature & Culture: No. 29). (Illus.). 320p. 1989. pap. text ed. 24.95 (*0-521-37803-6*) Cambridge U Pr.

Robert Lowell: Interviews & Memoirs. Ed. by Jeffrey Meyers. 300p. 1988. 37.50 (*0-472-10089-0*) U of Mich Pr.

Robert Lowell: Nihilist as Hero. Vereen M. Bell. 264p. 1983. 32.00 (*0-674-77585-6*) HUP.

Robert Lowell see Modern Critical Views Series

Robert Lowell & "Life Studies" Revising the Self. Terri Witek. LC 93-27832. 136p. 1993. text ed. 24.95 (*0-8262-0923-8*) U of Mo Pr.

Robert Lowell & the Sublime. Henry Hart. LC 94-38430. 260p. 1995. text ed. 37.50 (*0-8156-2610-X*); pap. text ed. 17.95 (*0-8156-2658-4*) Syracuse U Pr.

Robert Lowell Papers at the Houghton Library, Harvard University: A Guide to the Collection. Compiled by Patrick K. Miehe. LC 90-45082. (Bibliographies & Indexes in American Literature Ser.: No. 12). 240p. 1990. text ed. 85.00 (*0-313-27692-7*, HLW, Greenwood Pr) Greenwood.

Robert Lowell, the Poet & His Critics. Norma Procopiow. LC 84-467. (Poet & His Critics Ser.). 352p. reprint ed. pap. 100.40 (*0-685-16242-7*, 2027726) Bks Demand.

Robert Lowell's Language of the Self. Katharine Wallingford. LC 87-37210. xiii, 179p. (C). 1988. text ed. 32.50 (*0-8078-1799-6*) U of NC Pr.

Robert Lowell's Life & Work: Damaged Grandeur. Richard Tillinghast. LC 95-13706. (Poets on Poetry Ser.). 1995. pap. 13.95 (*0-472-06570-X*) U of Mich Pr.

Robert Lowell's Life & Work: Damaged Grandeur. Richard Tillinghast. LC 95-13706. (Poets on Poetry Ser.). 1995. text ed. 39.50 (*0-472-09570-6*) U of Mich Pr.

Robert Lowell's Poems: A Selection. Robert Lowell. Ed. by Jonathan Raban. 192p. 1974. pap. 10.95 (*0-571-10182-8*) Faber & Faber.

Robert Lowth: The Major Works, 8 vols., Set. 2nd ed. Ed. by University of Tubingen & David Reibel. (English Grammarians 1750 - 1850 ser.). 3500p. (C). (gr. 13 up). 1995. text ed. 925.00 (*0-415-12207-4*, Routledge NY) Routledge.

Robert Ludlum. Gina Macdonald. LC 96-50289. (Critical Companions to Popular Contemporary Writers Ser.). 1997. text ed. 29.95 (*0-313-29971-4*, Greenwood Pr) Greenwood.

Robert Ludlum: Four Complete Novels. Robert Ludlum. 1996. 15.99 (*0-517-14923-0*) Random Hse Value.

Robert M. Ellis - A Painter's Space: Paintings & Works on Paper 1951-1990. Contrib. by James Moore. (Illus.). 29p. (Orig.). 1990. pap. 10.50 (*0-944282-10-5*) UNM Art Mus.

Robert M. Gagne & M. David Merrill: In Conversation. David G. Twitchell. LC 91-11524. (Illus.). 60p. 1991. pap. 24.95 (*0-87778-235-0*) Educ Tech Pubns.

Robert M. Gorrell: University Growing Up: Rambling Reminiscences of an English Professor & Administrator, 1945-1980. Intro. by Kathryn M. Totton. 475p. 1983. lib. bdg. 66.50 (*1-56475-230-5*); fiche write for info. (*1-56475-231-3*) U NV Oral Hist.

Robert M. Hutchins: Portrait of an Educator. Mary A. Dzuback. (Centennial Publication Ser.). (Illus.). 404p. 1991. 24.95 (*0-226-17710-6*) U Ch Pr.

Robert M. La Follette & the Insurgent Spirit. David P. Thelen. LC 85-40844. 224p. 1986. reprint ed. pap. text ed. 12.95 (*0-299-10644-6*) U of Wis Pr.

Robert M. La Follette, Sr. Voice of Conscience. Carl R. Burgchardt. LC 91-32194. (Great American Orators: Critical Studies, Speeches & Sources: No. 14). 256p. 1992. text ed. 49.95 (*0-313-25842-2*, BUR/, Greenwood Pr) Greenwood.

Robert M. Trueblood, CPA: The Consummate Professional. R. Eugene Bryson, Jr. LC 76-48284. (Research Monograph: No. 75). 302p. 1977. spiral bd. 35.00 (*0-88406-112-4*) GA St U Busn Pr.

Robert M. Utley: Bibliographic Checklist. Intro. by Lawrence Frost. 1985. pap. 11.95 (*0-8488-0004-4*, J M C & Co) Amereon Ltd.

***Robert Maillart: Builder, Designer, & Artist.** David P. Billington. (Illus.). 368p. 1997. text ed. 60.00 (*0-521-57132-4*) Cambridge U Pr.

Robert Maillart & the Art of Reinforced Concrete. David P. Billington. (Illus.). 151p. 1991. 70.00 (*0-262-02310-5*) MIT Pr.

Robert Maillart's Bridges: The Art of Engineering. David P. Billington. LC 78-70279. (Illus.). 168p. 1979. pap. text ed. 25.00 (*0-691-02421-9*) Princeton U Pr.

Robert Makes a Graph see Math Set

Robert Mangold: New Paintings. David Carrier. (Illus.). 42p. (Orig.). 1995. pap. write for info. (*1-878283-54-5*) PaceWildenstein.

***Robert Mangold: New Paintings.** Alexander Van Grevenstein. (Illus.). 56p. (Orig.). 1997. pap. write for info. (*1-878283-68-5*) PaceWildenstein.

Robert Mangold Recent Paintings & Drawings. John Yau. LC 94-65714. (Illus.). 42p. (Orig.). 1994. pap. write for info. (*1-878283-41-3*) PaceWildenstein.

Robert Mannyng of Brunne: The Chronicle. Geoffrey Chaucer & Robert Mannyng. Ed. by Idelle Sullens et al. LC 86-60780. (Medieval & Renaissance Texts & Studies: Vol. 153). (Illus.). 920p. 1996. 60.00 (*0-86698-137-3*, MR153) MRTS.

Robert Mapplethorpe. Richard Marshall & Robert Mapplethorpe. (Illus.). 1990. pap. 39.95 (*0-8212-1786-0*) Bulfinch Pr.

Robert Mapplethorpe: Certain People. Photos by Robert Mapplethorpe. (Illus.). 132p. 1985. 100.00 (*0-942642-14-7*) Twelvetrees Pr.

Robert Mapplethorpe: Photographs. Mario Amaya. (Illus.). 16p. 1978. pap. 3.50 (*0-940744-19-8*) Chrysler Museum.

Robert Mapplethorpe: The Perfect Moment. Janet Kardon et al. 1991. pap. 35.00 (*0-88454-046-4*) U of Pa Contemp Art.

Robert Mason: Broadgate Paintings & Drawings, 1989-1990. Richard Burdett & Richard Cork. (Illus.). 63p. (Orig.). 1990. pap. 18.95 (*1-873175-00-0*) Yale Ctr Brit Art.

Robert Mayer & the Conservation of Energy. Kenneth L. Caneva. LC 92-25400. (Illus.). 496p. (C). 1993. text ed. 55.00 (*0-691-08758-X*) Princeton U Pr.

Robert Maynard Hutchins: A Memoir. Milton Mayer. Ed. by John H. Hicks. LC 92-16512. 1993. 35.00 (*0-520-07091-7*) U CA Pr.

Robert Mcalmon. Lorusso. 1997. 23.95 (*0-8057-4527-0*, Twayne) Scribnrs Ref.

Robert McAlmon, Expatriate Publisher & Writer. Robert E. Knoll. LC 57-62784. 110p. reprint ed. pap. 31.40 (*0-685-23688-9*, 2032125) Bks Demand.

Robert McChesney: An American Painter. unabridged ed. Ed. by Mary Fuller. LC 95-73110. (Illus.). 128p. (Orig.). 1996. pap. 30.00 (*0-9650835-9-4*) Sonoma Mtn.

Robert McCloskey. Gary D. Schmidt. (United States Authors Ser.: No. 558). 200p. 1990. 21.95 (*0-8057-7546-3*, Twayne) Scribnrs Ref.

Robert McCloskey Connection. Will C. Howell. (J). (gr. 1-3). 1990. pap. 10.99 (*0-8224-5829-2*) Fearon Teach Aids.

Robert McNamara: Soldier of the American Century. Deborah Shapley. (Illus.). 480p. Date not set. write for info. (*0-688-03971-5*) Morrow.

Robert Menzies: A Life, Vol. I 1894-1943. A. W. Martin. 456p. 1993. 39.95 (*0-522-84442-1*, Pub. by Melbourne Univ Pr AT) Paul & Co Pubs.

Robert Menzies: A Life 1894-1943, Vol. 1. A. W. Martin. 456p. 1996. pap. 24.95 (*0-522-84711-0*, Pub. by Melbourne Univ Pr AT) Paul & Co Pubs.

Robert Merton. Clark & Celia Modgil. 1990. 145.00 (*1-85000-550-8*, Falmer Pr) Taylor & Francis.

Robert Merton: Consensus & Controversy, 3 vols. Ed. by Jon Clark et al. (Falmer International Master-Minds Challenged Ser.). 1990. 300.00 (*1-85000-792-6*, Falmer Pr) Taylor & Francis.

Robert Merton: Consensus & Controversy. Ed. by Jon Clark et al. 520p. 1990. pap. 55.00 (*1-85000-982-1*, Falmer Pr) Taylor & Francis.

Robert Methodique. Josette Rey-Debove. 1617p. (FRE.). 1982. 95.00 (*0-7859-9212-X*) Fr & Eur.

***Robert Micro.** Alain Rey. (FRE.). 1995. 49.95 (*0-7859-9309-6*) Fr & Eur.

Robert Micro: Dictionnaire du Bon Usage & des Difficultes (Nouvelle Edition) Alain Rey. 1472p. (FRE.). 1992. 59.95 (*0-7859-9187-5*) Fr & Eur.

Robert Micro Poche Langue Francaise. Alain Rey. 1510p. (FRE.). 1993. 34.95 (*0-7859-9189-1*) Fr & Eur.

Robert Micro Poche Noms Propres. Alain Rey. 1120p. (FRE.). 1994. 34.95 (*0-7859-9200-6*) Fr & Eur.

Robert Mills's Courthouses & Jails. Gene Wadell & Rhodri W. Liscombe. (Illus.). 143p. 1982. 30.00 (*0-89308-249-X*) Southern Hist Pr.

***Robert Mini: Langue Francaise et Noms Propres.** Ed. by Dictionnaires Robert. 928p. (FRE.). 1995. 34.95 (*0-7859-9310-X*) Fr & Eur.

Robert Mitchum: A Bio-Bibliography. Jerry Roberts. LC 92-23784. (Bio-Bibliographies in the Performing Arts Ser.: No. 32). 448p. 1992. text ed. 49.95 (*0-313-27547-5*, RRM, Greenwood Pr) Greenwood.

Robert Mondavi of the Napa Valley. Cyril Ray. 192p. 1986. pap. 12.95 (*0-446-38322-8*) Warner Bks.

Robert Montgomery Bird. Curtis Dahl. (Twayne's United States Authors Ser.). (C). 1963. lib. bdg. 17.95 (*0-317-38184-9*) Irvington.

R

Robert Montgomery Bird. Curtis Dahl. (Twayne's United States Authors Ser.). 1963. pap. 13.95 (*0-8084-0267-6*, T31) NCUP.

Robert Morris: Land Speculator 1790-1801. Barbara A. Chernow. LC 77-14762. (Dissertations in American Economic History Ser.). 1978. 30.95 (*0-405-11029-4*) Ayer.

Robert Morris: Selected Works, 1970-1980. Text by Marti Mayo. (Illus.). 60p. 1981. pap. 8.00 (*0-936080-06-X*) Cont Arts Museum.

Robert Morris: The Mind-Body Problem. Rosalind Krauss. 1994. 60.00 (*0-89207-117-6*) S R Guggenheim.

Robert Morrison. unabridged ed. Phyllis Matthewman. 71p. 1995. reprint ed. pap. 5.99 (*0-88019-343-3*) Schmul Pub Co.

Robert Morrison: The Scholar & the Man, & Illustrated Catalogue of the Exhibition Held at the University of Hong Kong, September 4-18, 1957, to Commemorate the 150th Anniversary of Robert Morrison's Arrival in China. Lindsay Ride. LC 58-2866. 83p. 1957. reprint ed. pap. 25.00 (*0-608-01383-8*, 2062144) Bks Demand.

Robert Morton: The Collected Works. Robert Morton. Ed. by Allan Atlas. (Masters & Monuments of the Renaissance Ser.: Vol. 2). xxxvi, 105p. 1982. pap. 50.00 (*0-8450-7302-8*) Broude.

Robert Moses: Single-Minded Genius. Ed. by Joann P. Krieg. (Long Island Studies). (Illus.). 1989. lib. bdg. 30.00 (*1-55787-040-3*, NY71044) Hrt of the Lakes.

Robert Moskowitz - Recent Paintings & Pastels, Judith Shea - Recent Sculpture. Katy Kline. (Illus.). 44p. (Orig.). 1985. pap. 4.00 (*0-938437-11-9*) MIT List Visual Arts.

Robert Motherwell. Dore Ashton & Jack Flam. LC 83-3859. (Illus.). 156p. 1983. 55.00 (*0-89659-387-8*); pap. 39.95 (*0-89659-388-6*) Abbeville Pr.

Robert Motherwell. Contrib. by Dore Ashton. LC 92-70856. (Illus.). 32p. 1992. pap. 15.00 (*1-879173-08-5*) Locks Gallery.

Robert Motherwell: New & Revised. H. Horvard Arnason & Barbaralee Diamonstein. (Illus.). 252p. 1982. 95.00 (*0-8109-1333-X*) Abrams.

Robert Motherwell: Paintings. (Illus.). 160p. 1989. pap. 10.00 (*0-9623799-9-9*) Locks Gallery.

Robert Motherwell: The Formative Years. Robert S. Mattison. Ed. by Stephen C. Foster. LC 87-10742. (Studies in the Fine Arts: The Avant-Garde: No. 56). (Illus.). 256p. reprint ed. pap. 73.00 (*0-8357-1810-7*, 2070741) Bks Demand.

Robert Motherwell: What Art Holds. Mary A. Caws. LC 95-20819. (Interpretations in Art Ser.). (Illus.). 215p. 1996. 34.50 (*0-231-09644-5*) Col U Pr.

Robert Motherwell on Paper: Drawings, Prints, Collages. Ed. by David Rosand. LC 96-19574. (Illus.). 208p. 1997. 60.00 (*0-8109-4294-1*) Abrams.

Robert Mugabe - Zimbawe. Richard Worth. (In Focus Biographies Ser.). (Illus.). 128p. (J). 1990. lib. bdg. 13.95 (*0-671-68987-8*, Julian Messner) Silver Burdett Pr.

Robert Mugabe - Zimbawe. Richard Worth. (In Focus Biographies Ser.). (Illus.). 128p. (YA). 1990. pap. 7.95 (*0-671-70684-5*, Julian Messner) Silver Burdett Pr.

***Robert Murase.** Spacemaker Press Staff. Date not set. pap. 19.95 (*0-688-15364-X*) Morrow.

***Robert Murase: Stone & Water.** Michael Leccese. (Land Marks Ser.). 1997. pap. text ed. 19.95 (*1-888931-04-3*) Watsn-Guptill.

Robert Murray McCheyne. A. Smellie. 9.99 (*1-85792-184-4*, Pub. by Christian Focus UK) Spring Arbor Dist.

Robert Musil & the Culture of Vienna. Hannah Hickman. (C). 1991. pap. 16.95 (*0-8126-9156-3*) Open Court.

Robert Musil & the Tradition of the German Novelle. Kathleen O'Connor. (Studies in Austrian Literature, Culture, & Thought). 192p. 1992. 28.00 (*0-929497-45-7*) Ariadne CA.

Robert Musil, Master of the Hovering Life: A Study of the Major Fiction. Frederick G. Peters. LC 78-5158. 286p. 1978. text ed. 55.50 (*0-231-04476-3*) Col U Pr.

Robert Musil's "Nachlass zu Lebzeiten" Gudrun Brokoph-Mauch. (New Yorker Studien zur Neueren Deutschen Literaturgeschichte Ser.: Band 4). 246p. (Orig.). (C). 1984. pap. text ed. 24.35 (*0-8204-0174-9*) P Lang Pubng.

Robert, My Father. Sheridan Morley. (Illus.). 240p. 1994. 34.95 (*0-297-81329-3*) Trafalgar.

Robert Nadeau's Guide to Boston Restaurants: Not Including Locke-Ober, Cafe Budapest or The Ritz. Mark Zanger. LC 78-50749. 1978. pap. 3.95 (*0-930922-00-X*) World Food.

Robert Nathaniel's Tree. RaRa S. Schlitt. (Illus.). 36p. (J). (gr. k up). 1993. 14.95 (*0-9630017-3-6*) Light-Bearer.

Robert Needham Cust, 1821-1909: A Personal Biography. Peter Penner. LC 86-23821. (Studies in British History: Vol. 5). (Illus.). 360p. 1987. lib. bdg. 99.95 (*0-88946-456-1*) E Mellen.

Robert Nozick: Property, Justice, & the Minimal State. Jonathan Wolff. LC 90-70906. 176p. 1991. 37.50 (*0-8047-1855-5*); pap. 11.95 (*0-8047-1856-3*) Stanford U Pr.

Robert O. Anderson: Oil Man-Environmentalist & His Leading Role in the International Environmentalist Movement. Jack Raymond. 64p. (Orig.). (C). 1988. pap. text ed. 10.50 (*0-8191-7043-7*, Aspen Inst for Humanistic Studies) U Pr of Amer.

Robert O. Anderson Building. Earl A. Powell, III et al. LC 86-20862. (Illus.). 96p. (Orig.). 1986. pap. 14.95 (*0-87587-132-1*) LA Co Art Mus.

Robert of Brunne's Handlyng Synne, Pts. 1-2. Robert Mannyng. Ed. by Frederic J. Furnivall. (EETS, OS Ser.: No. 119, 123). 1974. reprint ed. 70.00 (*0-527-00117-1*) Periodicals Srv.

Robert of Normandy. large type ed. Mary Lomer. 490p. 1992. 25.99 (*0-7505-0308-4*) Ulverscroft.

Robert Oliver & Mercantile Bookkeeping in the Early Nineteenth Century. Stuart Bruchey. LC 75-18460. (History of Accounting Ser.). 1979. 17.95 (*0-405-07544-8*) Ayer.

Robert Oliver, Merchant of Baltimore, 1783-1819. Stuart Bruchey. Ed. by Vincent P. Carosso. LC 78-18954. (Small Business Enterprise in America Ser.). 1979. reprint ed. lib. bdg. 35.95 (*0-405-11458-3*) Ayer.

Robert Oppenheimer: Dark Prince. Jack Rummel. (Makers of Modern Science Ser.). (Illus.). 144p. (YA). (gr. 7-12). 1992. lib. bdg. 17.95 (*0-8160-2598-3*) Facts on File.

Robert Oppenheimer: Letters & Recollections. Robert Oppenheimer. Ed. by Alice K. Smith & Charles Weiner. LC 80-10106. (Harvard Paperbacks Ser.). 387p. 1980. text ed. 37.50 (*0-674-77605-4*) HUP.

Robert Oppenheimer: Letters & Recollections. Robert Oppenheimer. Ed. by Alice K. Smith & Charles Weiner. LC 80-10106. (Harvard Paperbacks Ser.). 387p. 1981. pap. text ed. 12.50 (*0-674-77606-2*) HUP.

Robert Oppenheimer: Letters & Recollections. Ed. by Alice K. Smith & Charles Weiner. (Stanford Nuclear Age Ser.). (Illus.). 400p. 1995. pap. 14.95 (*0-8047-2620-5*) Stanford U Pr.

Robert Owen, 2 vols. Frank Podmore. LC 78-156295. (World History Ser.: No. 48). 1971. lib. bdg. 150.00 (*0-8383-1265-9*) M S G Haskell Hse.

Robert Owen, 2 vols. in 1. Frank Podmore. LC 68-9762. 1968. reprint ed. 65.00 (*0-678-00417-X*) Kelley.

Robert Owen: A Chronology. V. Munoz. Tr. by W. Scott Johnson. (Libertarian & Anarchist Chronology Ser.). 1979. lib. bdg. 59.95 (*0-8490-3054-4*) Gordon Pr.

Robert Owen: Prophet of the Poor. Ed. by Sidney Pollard & John Salt. LC 70-156269. 318p. 1975. 40.00 (*0-8387-7952-2*) Bucknell U Pr.

***Robert Owen: Schooling the Innocents.** John Siraj-Blatchford. 1996. pap. 14.95 (*1-900219-00-X*, Pub. by Drake Intl Serv UK) Intl Spec Bk.

Robert Owen & His Social Philosophy. William L. Sargant. LC 78-134409. reprint ed. 42.50 (*0-404-08455-9*) AMS Pr.

Robert Owen & the Owenites in Britain & America: The Quest for the New Moral World. J. F. Harrison. (Modern Revivals in Economic & Social History Ser.). 440p. (C). 1993. text ed. 76.95 (*0-7512-0290-8*, Pub. by Gregg Revivals UK) Ashgate Pub Co.

Robert Owen at New Lanark: 1824-1838. LC 72-2543. (British Labour Struggles Before 1850 Ser.). 1974. 20.95 (*0-405-04435-6*) Ayer.

Robert Owen of New Lanark. Margaret I. Cole. LC 75-77254. vii, 231p. 1969. reprint ed. 35.00 (*0-678-00565-6*) Kelley.

Robert Owen's Millennial Gazette, Set, Nos. 1-16. Robert Owen. LC 74-134408. reprint ed. Set. 115.00 (*0-404-08454-0*) AMS Pr.

Robert Peary & Matthew Henson at the North Pole. William E. Molett. (Illus.). xiii, 123p. 1996. 19.95 (*0-9651653-0-2*) Ky Color Pub.

Robert Peary & the Quest for the North Pole. Christopher Dwyer. Ed. by William H. Goetzmann. (World Explorers Ser.). (Illus.). 112p. (YA). (gr. 5 up). 1992. lib. bdg. 19.95 (*0-7910-1316-2*) Chelsea Hse.

Robert Peers & the Department of Adult Education. G. F. Brown. (C). 1981. 30.00 (*0-902030-59-0*, Pub. by Univ Nottingham UK) St Mut.

Robert Peers & the Dept. of Adult Education. G. F. Brown. 20p. (C). 1981. text ed. 30.00 (*0-685-22134-2*, Pub. by Univ Nottingham UK) St Mut.

Robert Penn Warren. Charles H. Bohner. (Twayne's United States Authors Ser.). 1964. pap. 13.95 (*0-8084-0268-4*, T69) NCUP.

Robert Penn Warren. rev. ed. Charles Bohner. (United States Authors Ser.). 176p. (C). 1981. 22.95 (*0-8057-7345-2*, Twayne) Scribnrs Ref.

Robert Penn Warren. Paul West. LC 64-64451. (University of Minnesota Pamphlets on American Writers Ser.: No. 44). 48p. (Orig.). reprint ed. pap. 25.00 (*0-7837-2855-7*, 2057600) Bks Demand.

Robert Penn Warren: A Biography. Joseph L. Blotner. LC 96-17269. (Illus.). 585p. 1997. 35.00 (*0-394-56957-1*) Random.

Robert Penn Warren: A Collection of Critical Essays. Ed. by John L. Longley. LC 78-25757. 259p. 1979. reprint ed. text ed. 35.00 (*0-313-20807-7*, LORW, Greenwood Pr) Greenwood.

Robert Penn Warren: A Descriptive Bibliography, 1922-1979. James A. Grimshaw, Jr. LC 81-3003. (Illus.). 494p. 1981. text ed. 40.00 (*0-8139-0891-4*) U Pr of Va.

Robert Penn Warren: A Study of the Short Fiction. Joseph R. Millichap. LC 92-14380. (Twayne's Studies in Short Fiction: No. 39). 150p. 1992. 23.95 (*0-8057-8346-6*, Twayne) Scribnrs Ref.

Robert Penn Warren: Critical Perspectives. Ed. by Neil Nakadate. LC 79-57569. 336p. 1981. 35.00 (*0-8131-1425-X*) U Pr of Ky.

Robert Penn Warren: The Dark & Bloody Ground. Leonard Casper. LC 71-90479. 212p. 1969. reprint ed. text ed. 55.00 (*0-8371-2131-0*, CAPW, Greenwood Pr) Greenwood.

Robert Penn Warren & American Idealism. John Burt. LC 87-14742. 256p. (C). 1988. text ed. 32.50 (*0-300-04067-9*) Yale U Pr.

Robert Penn Warren & the American Imagination. Hugh M. Ruppersburg. LC 89-20451. 216p. 1990. 35.00 (*0-8203-1215-0*) U of Ga Pr.

Robert Penn Warren Reader. Robert Penn Warren. LC 86-17850. 528p. 1987. 22.50 (*0-394-55896-0*) Random.

Robert Penn Warren's Brother to Dragons: A Discussion. fac. ed. Ed. by James A. Grimshaw, Jr. LC 82-16207. (Southern Literary Studies). 323p. 1983. reprint ed. pap. 92.10 (*0-7837-7922-4*, 2047678) Bks Demand.

Robert Penn Warren's Modernist Spirituality. Robert S. Koppelman. 216p. 1995. text ed. 32.50 (*0-8262-0996-3*) U of Mo Pr.

Robert Persons: The Biography of an Elizabethan Jesuit, 1546-1610. Francis Edwards. (Original Studies Composed in English: Series III, Vol. 10). (Illus.). vii, 413p. (Orig.). 1995. 42.95 (*1-880810-10-7*); pap. 32.95 (*1-880810-11-5*) Inst Jesuit.

Robert Plumb. Georgia Coopersmith. 1985. pap. text ed. 5.00 (*0-942746-09-0*) SUNYP R Gibson.

Robert Podesta's One Million Dollar No Joke Italian's Success System. Robert Podesta. 10.00 (*0-686-23143-0*) Wave Spray.

Robert Potter, Founder of the Texas Navy. Ernest Fischer. LC 75-33771. 320p. 1976. 19.95 (*0-88289-080-8*) Pelican.

Robert Pour Tous. Robert. 1277p. 1994. 49.95 (*0-7859-8751-7*); 59.95 (*0-7859-9191-3*) Fr & Eur.

***Robert Quebecois d'Aujourd'hui.** Robert. 343p. (FRE.). 1992. 95.00 (*0-7859-9355-X*) Fr & Eur.

Robert R. Churches of Memphis: A Father & Son Who Achieved in Spite of Race. Annette E. Church & Roberta Church. (Illus.). 322p. 1974. 15.00 (*0-937130-13-3*) Burkes Bk Store.

Robert Rahway Zakanitch. Christina M. Strassfield & Arthur C. Danto. (Illus.). 16p. (Orig.). 1995. pap. 5.00 (*0-614-14072-2*) Guild Hall.

***Robert Rauschenberg.** Bernice Rose. (Illus.). 64p. (Orig.). 1996. pap. write for info. (*1-878283-65-0*) PaceWildenstein.

***Robert Rauschenberg: Haywire.** Catherine Craft & Billy Kluver. (Illus.). 120p. 1997. 39.95 (*3-7757-0686-0*) Dist Art Pubs.

Robert Rauschenberg: Works from the Salvage Ser. Mark Ormond. LC 85-60057. (Illus.). 20p. 1985. pap. 3.00 (*0-916758-17-6*) Ringling Mus Art.

Robert Rauschenberg, Work from Four Series: A Sesquicentennial Exhibition. Text by Linda L. Cathcart. (Illus.). 86p. 1985. pap. 22.95 (*0-936080-15-9*) Cont Arts Museum.

Robert Redford. Michael Feeny-Callan. Date not set. pap. write for info. (*0-679-45055-6*) Random.

***Robert Rodriguez.** Barbara Marvis. LC 97-20752. (Real Life Reader Biographies Ser.). (Illus.). 24p. (J). (gr. k-4). 1997. lib. bdg. 15.95 (*1-883845-48-3*) M Lane Pubs.

***Robert Rose Book of Classic Desserts.** Robert Rose. 1997. pap. text ed. 17.95 (*1-896503-11-X*, Pub. by R Rose CN) Firefly Bks Ltd.

***Robert Rose Book of Classic Pasta.** Robert Rose. 1997. pap. text ed. 17.95 (*1-896503-03-9*) Firefly Bks Ltd.

Robert Ross, Friend of Friends: Letters to Robert Ross, Art Critic & Writer. Ed. by Margery Ross. LC 79-8074. reprint ed. 34.50 (*0-404-18384-0*) AMS Pr.

Robert Ruark's Africa. Robert C. Ruark. Ed. by Michael McIntosh. LC 90-86286. (Illus.). 256p. 1991. 32.00 (*0-924357-20-7*, 11420-A) Countrysport Pr.

Robert Runcie: An Assessment. Adrian Hastings. LC 90-19523. 280p. (C). 1991. 15.00 (*0-334-02507-9*) TPI PA.

***Robert Runcie: The Reluctant Archbishop.** Humphrey Carpenter. (Illus.). 404p. 1997. pap. 13.95 (*0-340-66004-X*, Pub. by H & S UK) Trafalgar.

Robert Russa Moton Vol. 1: Successor to Booker T. Washington & a Strong Black Presence from 1916 until 1940, "The Early Years" Robert L. Clayton. 50p. (Orig.). 1988. pap. 9.50 (*0-910363-05-6*) EBONICS.

Robert Russell Bennet: A Bio-Bibliography. George J. Ferencz & Robert R. Bennet. LC 90-45080. (Bio-Bibliographies in Music Ser.: No. 29). 232p. 1990. text ed. 47.95 (*0-313-26472-4*, FRB, Greenwood Pr) Greenwood.

Robert Russett: A Retrospective Survey. Herman Mhire et al. (Illus.). 84p. (Orig.). 1989. pap. 20.00 (*0-936819-05-7*) USL Art Museum.

Robert Russin: A Wyoming Master. Robin Russin & Robert Russin. 48p. 1991. write for info. (*0-9630869-0-1*) U of WY Art Mus.

Robert Ryan: A Biography & Critical Filmography. Franklin Jarlett. LC 89-42725. (Illus.). 320p. 1990. lib. bdg. 38.50 (*0-89950-430-2*) McFarland & Co.

Robert Ryman. Richard Storr. (Illus.). 326p. 1993. 49.50 (*0-8109-3771-9*) Abrams.

Robert S. Duncanson: Nineteenth Century Black Romantic Painter. James D. Parks. (YA). 1990. 12.95 (*0-87498-011-9*) Assoc Pubs DC.

Robert S. Kerr: The Senate Years. Anne H. Morgan. LC 76-62514. (Illus.). 1980. pap. 14.95 (*0-8061-1635-8*) U of Okla Pr.

Robert S. Roeschlaub: Architect of the Emerging West, 1843-1923. Francine Haber et al. viii, 168p. 1988. pap. text ed. 29.95 (*0-942576-31-4*) CO Hist Soc.

***Robert Sabuda's Counting Pop-Up.** Robert Sabuda. (J). 1997. write for info. (*0-614-29301-4*, Litl Simon S&S) S&S Childrens.

Robert Schuller: Your Positive Plan for Love & Happiness. Robert Schuller. 624p. 1996. 14.98 (*0-88486-152-X*, Inspirational Pr) Arrowood Pr.

Robert Schumann. Frederick Niecks. LC 74-24167. (Dent's International Library of Books on Music). reprint ed. 39.50 (*0-404-13065-8*) AMS Pr.

***Robert Schumann: Herald of a "New Poetic Age"** John Daverio. (Illus.). 624p. 1997. 45.00 (*0-19-509180-9*) OUP.

Robert Schumann und das Tonkunstler-Bild der Romantiker. Christina E. Brantner. (Studies in Modern German Literature: Vol. 32). 246p. 1989. text ed. 43.95 (*0-8204-0973-1*) P Lang Pubng.

Robert Schumann, Words & Music: The Vocal Compositions. Dietrich Fischer-Dieskau. Tr. by Reinhard G. Pauly from GER. LC 88-10411. (Illus.). 232p. 1988. 28.95 (*0-931340-06-3*, Amadeus Pr) Timber.

Robert Scott in the Antarctic. Philip Sauvain. LC 93-18209. (Great Twentieth Century Expeditions Ser.). (Illus.). 32p. (J). (gr. 4-6). 1993. lib. bdg. 13.95 (*0-87518-532-0*, Dillon Silver Burdett) Silver Burdett Pr.

Robert Shaw: More Than a Life. Karen Carmean & Georg Gaston. (Illus.). 350p. 1994. 22.95 (*1-56833-021-9*) Madison Bks UPA.

Robert Shaw: The Price of Success. John French. (Illus.). 288p. 1993. 35.00 (*1-85459-126-6*, Pub. by N Hern Bks UK) Theatre Comm.

Robert Silverberg. Thomas D. Clareson. Ed. by Roger C. Schlobin. LC 83-542. (Starmont Reader's Guide Ser.: Vol. 18). 96p. (Orig.). 1983. pap. 17.00 (*0-916732-47-9*); lib. bdg. 27.00 (*0-916732-48-7*) Borgo Pr.

Robert Silverberg's Many Trapdoors: Critical Essays on His Science Fiction. Ed. by Charles L. Elkins & Martin H. Greenberg. LC 92-10679. (Contributions to the Study of Science Fiction & Fantasy Ser.: No. 53). 168p. 1992. text ed. 49.95 (*0-313-26308-6*, ECS/, Greenwood Pr) Greenwood.

Robert Silverberg's Worlds of Wonder. Ed. by Robert Silverberg. 368p. 1989. 12.95 (*0-446-39012-7*) Warner Bks.

Robert Slade's Guide to Computer Viruses: How to Avoid Them, How to Get Rid of Them & How to Get Help. Robert Slade. LC 94-21645. 1994. 29.00 (*0-387-94311-0*) Spr-Verlag.

Robert Slade's Guide to Computer Viruses: How to Avoid Them, How to Get Rid of Them, & How to Get Help. 2nd ed. R. Slade. LC 95-49098. (Illus.). 540p. 1996. pap. text ed. 39.95 (*0-387-94663-2*) Spr-Verlag.

***Robert Smithson: Slideworks.** Carlo Frua & Vicki Goldberg. (Illus.). 200p. 1997. pap. 40.00 (*88-900163-1-0*) Dist Art Pubs.

Robert Smithson: The Collected Writings. Robert Smithson. Ed. by Jack Flam. LC 95-34773. (Documents of Twentieth Century Art Ser.). (Illus.). 385p. 1996. pap. 24.95 (*0-520-20385-2*) U CA Pr.

Robert Smithson Unearthed: Drawings, Collages, Writings. Eugenie Tsai. (Columbia Studies on Art: No. 4). (Illus.). 224p. (C). 1992. pap. text ed. 27.50 (*0-231-07259-7*) Col U Pr.

Robert Smythson & the Elizabethan Country House. Mark Girouard. LC 83-50004. (Illus.). 328p. 1985. pap. 25.00 (*0-300-02389-8*) Yale U Pr.

Robert South (1634-1716) An Introduction to His Life & Sermons. Gerard Reedy. (Studies in Eighteenth-Century English Literature & Thought: No. 12). (Illus.). 200p. (C). 1992. text ed. 57.95 (*0-521-40164-X*) Cambridge U Pr.

Robert Southey. Ernest Bernhardt-Kabisch. Ed. by Sylvia E. Bowman. (Twayne's English Authors Ser.). 200p. (C). 1977. lib. bdg. 17.95 (*0-8057-6692-8*) Irvington.

***Robert Southey: A Life.** Mark Storey. (Illus.). 384p. 1997. text ed. 39.95 (*0-19-811246-7*) OUP.

Robert Southey: The Critical Heritage. Ed. by Lionel Madden. 1972. 69.50 (*0-7100-7375-5*, RKP) Routledge.

Robert Southey see Romantics: Critical Heritage

Robert Southwell. F. W. Brownlow. (Twayne's English Authors Ser.: No. 516). 1996. 24.95 (*0-8057-7806-3*, Twayne) Scribnrs Ref.

Robert Southwell, the Writer (1935) Pierre Janelle. LC 72-162495. 347p. 1971. reprint ed. 15.00 (*0-911858-18-0*) Appel.

Robert Spencer: Earl of Sunderland 1641-1702. John Kenyon. (Modern Revivals in History Ser.). 396p. 1992. 61.95 (*0-7512-0055-7*, Pub. by Gregg Revivals UK) Ashgate Pub Co.

Robert Sperry: A Retrospective. Matthew Kangas & LaMar Harrington. LC 85-72955. 1985. pap. 7.95 (*0-942342-06-2*) Bellevue Art.

Robert Stacy-Judd: Maya Architecture, the Creation of a New Style. David Gebhard. (Illus.). 176p. 1993. pap. 30.00 (*0-88496-351-9*) Capra Pr.

Robert Stacy-Judd: Maya Architecture, the Creation of a New Style. David Gebhard. (Illus.). 176p. (C). 1993. reprint ed. lib. bdg. 53.00 (*0-8095-4117-3*) Borgo Pr.

Robert Stafford of Cumberland Island: Growth of a Planter. Mary R. Bullard. LC 95-15470. 368p. (C). 1995. pap. 19.95 (*0-8203-1738-1*) U of Ga Pr.

Robert Starer Album for Piano. Robert Starer. 240p. 1992. otabind 20.95 (*0-7935-1565-3*, 00120864) H Leonard.

Robert Stead & His Works. Eric Thompson. (Canadian Author Studies). 62p. (C). 1988. pap. text ed. 9.95 (*0-920763-77-4*, Pub. by ECW Press CN) Genl Dist Srvs.

***Robert Steinberg, Collected Papers.** Robert Steinberg & Jean P. Serre. LC 96-51039. (Collected Works Ser.: Vol. 7). 1997. 79.00 (*0-8218-0576-2*, CWORKS/7) Am Math.

Robert Stephenson. D. J. Smith. 1989. pap. 25.00 (*0-85263-186-3*, Pub. by Shire UK) St Mut.

Robert Stern. (Architectural Monographs). (Illus.). 144p. (Orig.). 1992. 55.00 (*1-85490-011-0*); pap. 38.00 (*1-85490-008-0*) Academy Ed UK.

Robert Stern. Vincent Scully & David Dunster. (Academy Editions Ser.). (Illus.). 80p. 1981. pap. 14.95 (*0-312-68753-2*) St Martin.

Robert Stern: An Architectural Monograph. David Dunster et al. (Illus.). 124p. 35.00 (*0-312-68754-0*); pap. 24.95 (*0-312-68755-9*) St Martin.

Robert Stern: Architectural Monograph, Vol. 17. Architectural Monograph Staff. 1992. 55.00 (*0-312-07147-7*) St Martin.

Robert Stewart Hyer, the Man I Knew. Ray H. Brown. (Illus.). 1957. 10.00 (*0-685-05005-X*) A Jones.

Robert Stiffler's Gardening in Southern Virginia & Northeastern North Carolina. Robert Stiffler. Ed. by Aimee C. Batten. (Illus.). 192p. (Orig.). 1995. pap. 16.95 (*0-9648308-0-9*) VA Pilot.

An Asterisk (*) at the beginning of an entry indicates that the title is appearing in BIP for the first time.

***Robert Stivers: Photographs.** A. D. Coleman. 112p. 1997. 65.00 (0-9657280-0-5) Dist Art Pubs.

Robert Stone. Robert Solotaroff. (Twayne's United States Authors Ser.). 272p. 1993. 23.95 (0-8057-4011-2, Twayne) Scribnrs Ref.

Robert Stone: A Bibliography, 1960-1992. Ken Lopez & Bev Chaney. LC 92-25363. (Illus.). 120p. 1992. 40.00 (0-9632898-0-2) Numinous Pr.

Robert Stone: A Bibliography, 1960-1992. limited ed. Ken Lopez & Bev Chaney. LC 92-25363. (Illus.). 120p. 1992. 125.00 (0-9632898-1-0) Numinous Pr.

Robert Stone to Louis Zukofsky see Library of Literary Criticism

Robert Surtees & Early Victorian Society. Norman Gash. 380p. (C). 1993. 75.00 (0-19-820429-9, 32) OUP.

Robert T. Sheen His-Story. Robert T. Sheen. LC 91-91265. (Illus.). 326p. (Orig.). 1991. pap. 14.95 (0-9631491-0-5) R T Sheen.

Robert the Bruce: King of Scots. Ronald M. Scott. 272p. 1996. pap. 12.95 (0-7867-0329-6) Carroll & Graf.

Robert the Bruce & the Struggle for Scottish Independence. Herbert E. Maxwell. LC 73-14456. (Heroes of the Nations Ser.). reprint ed. 37.50 (0-404-58274-5) AMS Pr.

Robert the Rose Horse. Joan Heilbroner. LC 62-9218. (Illus.). 72p. (J). (gr. 1-2). 1962. lib. bdg. 9.99 (0-394-90025-1) Beginner.

Robert the Rose Horse. Joan Heilbroner. LC 62-9218. (Illus.). 72p. (J). (gr. 1-2). 1966. 7.99 (0-394-80025-7) Beginner.

Robert Therrien, Vol. 1. Contrib. by Julia B. Turrell. LC 83-62370. (Illus.). 72p. (Orig.). 1984. pap. 10.00 (0-914357-02-6) Los Angeles Mus Contemp.

Robert Thornton & the London Thornton Manuscript: British Library: MS Additional 31042. John J. Thompson. (Manuscript Studies: Vol. II). 155p. 1987. 90.00 (0-85991-190-X) Boydell & Brewer.

Robert Tolf's South Florida Restaurants. Robert W. Tolf. 240p. (Orig.). 1994. pap. 8.95 (0-915067-06-4) Buchan Pubns.

Robert Troup: A Quest for Security in a Turbulent New Nation, 1775-1832. Wendell E. Tripp. 1981. 38.95 (0-405-14074-6) Ayer.

Robert W. Richardson's Narrow Gauge News. Robert W. Richardson. LC 70-102682. (Colorado Rail Annual Ser.: No. 21). (Illus.). 303p. 1994. 44.95 (0-918654-21-1) CO RR Mus.

Robert W. Service, Best Tales of the Yukon. LC 83-3128. 160p. (Orig.). 1983. pap. 8.95 (0-89471-201-2) Running Pr.

Robert Wakefield, On the Three Languages. 1524, Vol. 68. Ed. & Tr. by G. Lloyd Jones. 272p. 1989. 30.00 (0-86698-077-6, MR68) MRTS.

***Robert Walser.** (Review of Contemporary Fiction Ser.: Vol. 12, No. 1). 1992. pap. 8.00 (1-56478-119-4) Dalkey Arch.

Robert Walser Rediscovered: Stories, Fairy-Tale Plays, & Critical Response Including the Anti-Fairy Tales, Cinderella & Snowwhite. Robert Walser. Tr. by Walter Arndt. LC 84-40585. 237p. 1985. reprint ed. pap. 67.60 (0-608-02314-0, 2062955) Bks Demand.

Robert Ward: A Bio-Bibliography. Kenneth Kreitner. LC 88-24658. (Bio-Bibliographies in Music Ser.: No. 17). 182p. 1988. text ed. 49.95 (0-313-25701-9, KRT/, Greenwood Pr) Greenwood.

Robert Werling: A Way of Seeing. LC 95-83498. (Illus.). 126p. 1996. 70.00 (0-9650664-0-1) Berman Publng.

Robert Werling: A Way of Seeing. deluxe limited ed. LC 96-83083. (Illus.). 126p. 1996. 400.00 (0-9650664-1-X) Berman Publng.

Robert William Addison: A Retrospective Exhibition. Norton, R. W., Art Gallery Staff. LC 73-155783. (Contemporary Realists Ser.). (Illus.). 1971. pap. 1.00 (0-9600182-2-0) Norton Art.

Robert Wilson. Franco Bertoni. (Illus.). 240p. Date not set. 60.00 (1-56898-091-4) Princeton Arch.

Robert Wilson of Blount County, Tennessee, 1750-1826: Some of His Descendants & Related Families Including Gould, Cook, Brooks, Huson, Shearer, Stribling. Ed. & Intro. by Mary W. Kelsey. (Illus.). 299p. 1987. 40.00 (0-918464-78-1) Kelsey-Seybold Found.

Robert Wilson's Civil Wars: Drawings, Models & Documentation. Al Nodal & Sheila L. De Bretteville. Ed. by Andrea P. Belloli. LC 84-6117. (Illus.). 61p. 1984. 15.00 (0-930209-00-1) Otis Gallery.

***Robert Wilson's Production Site Watermill.** Robert Wilson. 1997. 49.95 (3-9520497-6-X, Pub. by Memory Loss Eds SZ) Dist Art Pubs.

Robert Wilson's Vision. Trevor Fairbrother. (Illus.). 144p. 1991. 45.00 incl. audio compact disk (0-8109-3959-2) Abrams.

Robert Wise: A Bio-Bibliography. Frank Thompson. LC 94-39512. (Bio-Bibliographies in the Performing Arts Ser.: Vol. 62). 184p. 1995. text ed. 57.95 (0-313-27812-1, Greenwood Pr) Greenwood.

Robert Wise on His Films: From Editing Room to Director's Chair. Sergio Leemann. LC 95-10963. (Illus.). 224p. (Orig.). 1995. pap. 24.95 (1-879505-24-X) Silman James Pr.

***Robert Worth Bingham & the Southern Mystique: From the Old South to the New South & Beyond.** William E. Ellis. LC 97-6779. 1997. write for info. (0-87338-578-0) Kent St U Pr.

Robert Y. Hayne & His Times. Theodore D. Jervey. LC 73-104330. (American Scene Ser.). (Illus.). 1970. reprint ed. lib. bdg. 65.00 (0-306-71870-7) Da Capo.

Robert Zakanitch. Janet Kardon. (Illus.). 1981. pap. 12.00 (0-88454-025-1) U of Pa Contemp Art.

***Roberta, a Most Remarkable Fulbright.** Dorothy D. Stuck & Nan Snow. LC 96-31043. 1997. 38.00 (1-55728-460-1) U of Ark Pr.

Roberta Flack - Oasis. Ed. by Milton Okun. pap. 12.95 (0-89524-428-4) Cherry Lane.

Roberte Ce Soir & The Revocation of the Edict of Nantes. Pierre Klossowski. Tr. by Austryn Wainhouse from FRE. 216p. 1989. reprint ed. pap. 10.95 (0-7145-2739-4) M Boyars Pubs.

Robert...Experiences Distilled. Robert D. Wuraftic. LC 86-90133. (Illus.). 84p. (Orig.). pap. write for info. (0-9616959-0-0) R D Wuraftic.

Roberti Grosseteste Episcopi Quondam Lincolniensis Epistolae. Ed. by Henry R. Luard. (Rolls Ser.: No. 25). 1974. reprint ed. 70.00 (0-8115-1041-7) Periodicals Srv.

Roberto. Andrew L. Traynor. LC 96-90112. (Orig.). 1996. pap. 15.95 (0-533-11911-1) Vantage.

Roberto Arlt: La Estrategia de Su Ficcion. Aden W. Hayes. (Monagrafias A Ser.: Vol. LXXXIII). 142p. (Orig.). (SPA.). (C). 1981. 25.00 (0-7293-0116-8, Pub. by Tamesis Bks Ltd UK) Boydell & Brewer.

Roberto Arlt y la Rebelion Alienada. Beatriz Pastor. LC 80-70560. 128p. (SPA.). 1980. pap. 8.00 (0-935318-05-4) Edins Hispamerica.

Roberto Burle Marx: The Unnatural Art of the Garden. William H. Adams. (Illus.). 80p. 1991. pap. 22.50 (0-87070-197-5, 0-8109-6096-6) Mus of Modern Art.

***Roberto Clemente.** (Hispanos Notables Ser.). (Illus.). 128p. (SPA.). (YA). (gr. 5 up). pap. 8.95 (0-7910-3115-2) Chelsea Hse.

Roberto Clemente. (Hispanos Notables Ser.). (Illus.). 128p. (SPA.). (YA). (gr. 5 up). 1995. lib. bdg. 19.95 (0-7910-3105-5) Chelsea Hse.

Roberto Clemente. Peter C. Bjarkman. (Baseball Legends Ser.). (Illus.). 64p. (J). (gr. 3 up). 1991. lib. bdg. 14.95 (0-7910-1171-2) Chelsea Hse.

Roberto Clemente. Louis Sabin. (J). pap. 3.50 (0-8167-3068-7) Troll Communs.

Roberto Clemente: Baseball Great. Norman L. Macht. LC 93-26178. (Junior Hispanics of Achievement Ser.). (Illus.). 80p. (J). (gr. 3-6). 1993. pap. 4.95 (0-7910-2541-1); lib. bdg. 15.95 (0-7910-1764-8) Chelsea Hse.

***Roberto Clemente: Baseball Hall of Famer.** Maritza Romero. LC 97-4231. (Great Hispanics of Our Time Ser.). (J). 1997. write for info. (0-8239-5083-2, PowerKids) Rosen Group.

Roberto Clemente: Baseball Legend. Alan West. LC 92-33505. (Hispanic Heritage Ser.). (Illus.). 32p. (J). (gr. 2-4). 1993. pap. 4.95 (1-56294-811-3); lib. bdg. 14.90 (1-56294-367-7) Millbrook Pr.

Roberto Clemente: Baseball Superstar. Carol Greene. LC 91-12664. (Rookie Biographies Ser.). (Illus.). 48p. (J). (gr. k-3). 1991. pap. 4.95 (0-516-44222-8); lib. bdg. 18.30 (0-516-04222-X) Childrens.

Roberto Clemente: Puerto Rican Baseball Player. Thomas W. Gilbert. (Hispanics of Achievement Ser.). (Illus.). 112p. (YA). (gr. 5 up). 1991. lib. bdg. 19.95 (0-7910-1240-9) Chelsea Hse.

Roberto Clemente: Puerto Rican Baseball Player. Tom W. Gilbert. (Hispanics of Achievement Ser.). (Illus.). (YA). (gr. 5 up). 1993. pap. 8.95 (0-7910-1267-0) Chelsea Hse.

***Roberto Clemente: Young Ball Player.** LC 96-37326. (Childhood of Famous Americans Ser.). (J). 1997. pap. 4.99 (0-689-81364-3, Aladdin Paperbacks) S&S Childrens.

Roberto Clemente: Young Baseball Hero. Louis Sabin. LC 91-17851. (Illus.). 48p. (J). (gr. 4-6). 1992. lib. bdg. 12.95 (0-8167-2509-8) Troll Communs.

Roberto Clemente: Young Baseball Hero. Louis Sabin. LC 91-17851. (Illus.). 48p. (J). (gr. 4-6). 1996. pap. 3.95 (0-8167-2510-1) Troll Communs.

Roberto Clemente, Athlete & Hero. Diana Perez. (Illus.). (J). (gr. 1-4). 1994. pap. 6.35 (0-8136-5273-1); lib. bdg. 17.50 (0-8136-5267-7) Modern Curr.

Roberto Clemente, Atleta y Heroe. Diana Perez. (Illus.). (SPA.). (J). (gr. 1-4). 1994. pap. 6.35 (0-8136-5301-0) Modern Curr.

Roberto Goes Fishing. Raquel P. Zaldivar. (Illus.). 32p. (J). (gr. 1-3). 1992. 12.95 (1-880507-00-5) Lectorum Pubns.

Roberto Innocenti: The Spirit of Illustration. Steven L. Brezzo. LC 96-6176. (Illus.). Date not set. write for info. (0-88397-119-4) Art Srvc Intl.

Roberto Marquez: Sojourns in the Labyrinth, a Survey of Paintings, 1984-1994. Edward U. Sullivan. Ed. by D. D. Yares & Joanne Stuhr. Tr. by Wayne H. Finke. (Illus.). 112p. (Orig.). 1994. pap. 30.00 (0-911611-00-2) Tucson Mus Art.

***Roberto Matta: Paintings & Drawings 1937-1959.** Martica Sawin. (Illus.). 65p. (Orig.). 1997. pap. 25.00 (0-9639399-0-4) Latin Am Mstrs.

Roberto Rossellini. Peter Brunette. LC 95-10239. (Illus.). 425p. (C). 1996. pap. 16.95 (0-520-20053-5) U CA Pr.

Roberto Rossellini: A Guide to References & Resources. Patrizio Rossi. 1988. 55.00 (0-8161-7911-5, Hall Reference) Macmillan.

Roberto Rossellini: The War Trilogy. Roberto Rossellini. LC 82-49232. (Cinema Classics Ser.). 487p. 1985. lib. bdg. 16.00 (0-8240-5776-7) Garland.

Roberto Stagno e Gemma Bellincioni Intimi, 2 Vols. Bianca Stagno Bellincioni & Gemma Bellincioni. Ed. by Andrew Farkas. LC 76-29969. (Opera Biographies Ser.). (Illus.). (ITA.). 1977. reprint ed. lib. bdg. 31.95 (0-405-09708-5) Ayer.

Roberts Birds of Southern Africa. Gordon L. Maclean. 600p. (C). 1988. 275.00 (1-85368-037-0, Pub. by New Holland Pubs UK) St Mut.

Roberts' Dictionary of Industrial Relations. rev. ed. Harold S. Roberts. 615p. reprint ed. pap. 175.30 (0-685-15905-1, 2026798) Bks Demand.

Robert's Dictionary of Industrial Relations. 4th ed. University of Hawaii at Manoa, Industrial Relations Center Staff. LC 93-23280. 894p. 1993. 85.00 (0-87179-777-1, 0777) BNA Books.

Roberts' Guide for Butlers & Household Staff. Robert Roberts. LC 93-19131. 180p. 1988. reprint ed. pap. 8.95 (1-55709-120-X) Applewood.

Robert's Handbook of Normal Clinical Values. 64p. write for info. (0-9601862-2-0) Goal Getters.

Roberts' Illustrated Millwork Catalog: A Sourcebook of Turn-of-the-Century Architectural Woodwork. E. L. Roberts & Co., Staff. (Illus.). 416p. 1988. reprint ed. pap. 13.95 (0-486-25697-9) Dover.

Roberts in India: The Military Papers of Field Marshall Lord Roberts, 1876-1893. Ed. by Brian Robson. LC 93-26403. (Publications of the Army Records Society: Vol. 9). 1993. 80.00 (0-7509-0401-1, Pub. by Sutton Pubng UK) Bks Intl VA.

Robert's of Charleston at Home. Robert Dickson. Ed. by Beverly Colman. 58p. 1992. pap. 7.95 (0-685-60201-X) Roberts Charleston.

Roberts on Competition-Antitrust: Canada & the United States. Roberts. 552p. 1992. 153.00 (0-409-80890-3) MICHIE.

***Roberts' Practical Guide to Common Medical Emergencies.** LC 96-40889. 320p. 1997. pap. text ed. 39.95 (0-397-51838-2) Lppncott-Raven.

Robert's Robot. (Illus.). (J). (ps-2). 1991. pap. 5.10 (0-8136-5645-1); lib. bdg. 7.95 (0-8136-5145-X) Modern Curr.

Robert's Rule Order. Longmeadow. 1994. write for info. (0-517-11917-X) Random Hse Value.

Robert's Rules of Disorder: A Guide to Mismanagement. Robert Maidment. 112p. 1990. 7.95 (0-88289-111-1) Pelican.

***Roberts' Rules of Lesbian Break-Ups.** Shelly Roberts. LC 97-238. (Roberts' Rules Ser.: Vol. 2). 175p. (Orig.). 1997. pap. 5.95 (1-883523-19-2) Spinsters Ink.

Roberts' Rules of Lesbian Living. Shelly Roberts. 192p. (Orig.). 1996. pap. 5.95 (1-883523-09-5) Spinsters Ink.

Robert's Rules of Order. Will Eisner. 240p. (Orig.). 1986. mass mkt. 4.99 (0-553-22598-7) Bantam.

Robert's Rules of Order. Henry M. Robert. 192p. (C). 1993. mass mkt. 4.99 (0-8007-8610-6, Spire) Revell.

Robert's Rules of Order. Henry M. Robert. Ed. by Rachel Vixman. 1986. mass mkt. 4.50 (0-515-09032-8) Jove Pubns.

Robert's Rules of Order. rev. ed. Henry M. Robert, III et al. 1981. 16.95 (0-673-15472-6, ScottFrsmn) Addson-Wesley Educ.

Robert's Rules of Order. rev. ed. Henry M. Robert. 1989. mass mkt. 4.50 (0-425-11690-5) Berkley Pub.

Robert's Rules of Order. rev. ed. Henry M. Robert. 160p. 1993. pap. 8.95 (0-425-13928-X, Berkley Trade) Berkley Pub.

Robert's Rules of Order. 9th ed. Ed. by Henry M. Robert, III & William J. Evans. LC 89-10220. 706p. 1991. pap. 15.00 (0-06-276051-3, Harper Ref) HarpC.

Robert's Rules of Order. Henry M. Robert. 1993. reprint ed. lib. bdg. 21.95 (1-56849-216-2) Buccaneer Bks.

Robert's Rules of Order: Classic Man. Henry M. Roberts. 1988. 5.99 (0-517-25920-6) Random Hse Value.

Robert's Rules of Order: Modern Edition. Henry M. Robert. 155p. 1996. 8.97 (1-55748-884-3) Barbour & Co.

Robert's Rules of Order Revised. Henry M. Robert. 1971. reprint ed. pap. 5.95 (0-688-05306-8, Quill) Morrow.

Robert's Tall Friend: A Story of the Fire Island Lighthouse. Vivian Farrell. LC 87-35246. (Illus.). 64p. (J). (gr. 4-7). 1988. 11.50 (0-9619832-0-5) Island-Metro Pubns.

***Robert's Tall Friend: A Story of the Fire Island Lighthouse.** Vivian Farrell. Ed. by Jean Wood. (Illus.). 64p. (J). (gr. 3-6). 1997. text ed. 24.00 (0-9657524-1-0) T Logan Pubns.

***Robert's Tall Friend: A Story of the Fire Island Lighthouse.** Vivian Farrell. Ed. by Jean Wood. (Illus.). 64p. (J). (gr. 3-6). 1997. pap. text ed. 16.00 (0-9657524-7-X) T Logan Pubns.

Roberts' Ultimate Encyclopedia of Hull Pottery. Brenda Roberts. LC 91-68348. (Illus.). 340p. 1992. 41.95 (0-9632136-0-1) Cntry Side Antiques.

Roberts v. U. S. Jaycees, 1984: Women's Rights. Susan D. Gold. LC 95-32361. (Supreme Court Desisions Ser.). (Illus.). 96p. (J). (gr. 7-10). 1995. lib. bdg. 15.98 (0-8050-4238-5) TFC Bks NY.

Robertses of Northern New England. Thomas A. Jacobsen. (Illus.). 412p. (Orig.). 1995. pap. text ed. 30.00 (0-7884-0242-0) Heritage Bk.

Robertson: The Pulpit & the Power. Arthur F. Ide. LC 87-28998. 323p. (Orig.). 1988. pap. 10.00 (0-910309-46-9, 5289) Am Atheist.

Robertson County, Tennessee, Court Minutes, 1796-1807. Carol Wells. vi, 266p. (Orig.). 1993. pap. text ed. 22.00 (1-55613-734-6) Heritage Bk.

Robertson County Texas Eighteen Sixty Census. Mary Collie-Cooper. 72p. (Orig.). 1985. spiral bd. 6.50 (0-943553-02-4) Collie-Cooper Ent.

Robertson Davies. Judith S. Grant. 1998. pap. 15.95 (0-14-011452-1, Viking) Viking Penguin.

Robertson Davies: Man of Myth. Judith S. Grant. (Illus.). 816p. 1995. pap. 35.00 (0-670-82557-3, Viking) Viking Penguin.

Robertson Davies & His Works. John Mills. (Canadian Author Studies). 58p. (C). 1985. pap. text ed. 9.95 (0-920802-65-6, Pub. by ECW Press CN) Genl Dist Srvs.

Robertson on Economic Policy. Dennis H. Robertson. Ed. by S. R. Dennison & John R. Presley. LC 91-44082. 240p. 1992. text ed. 69.95 (0-312-07913-3) St Martin.

Robertson, Purcell, & Related Families. Laura P. Robertson. (Illus.). 242p. 1993. reprint ed. pap. 38.00 (0-8328-3395-9); reprint ed. lib. bdg. 48.00 (0-8328-3394-0) Higginson Bk Co.

Robertsonian Economics: An Examination of the Work of Sir D. H. Robertson on Industry Fluctuation. John R. Presley. LC 78-25958. 320p. 1979. 45.00 (0-8419-0471-5) Holmes & Meier.

Robertson's Practical English-Thai Dictionary. Ed. by Richard G. Robertson. LC 79-87787. 320p. (ENG & THA.). 1969. pap. 14.95 (0-8048-0706-X) C E Tuttle.

Robes of Elegance: Japanese Kimonos of the Sixteenth through Twentieth Centuries. Ishimura Hayao & Maruyama Nobuhiko. Tr. by Haruko Ward from JPN. LC 87-62987. (Illus.). xiv, 246p. (C). 1988. 24.95 (0-88259-955-0) NCMA.

Robes of Power: Totem Poles on Cloth. Doreen Jensen & Polly Sargent. 96p. 1987. pap. 18.95 (0-7748-0264-2, Pub. by U BC Pr) U of Wash Pr.

Robes of Splendor: Native North American Painted Buffalo Hides. Richard W. West. (Illus.). 144p. 1993. 40.00 (1-56584-116-6) New Press NY.

Robes of Splendor: Native North American Painted Buffalo Hides. Richard W. West et al. (Illus.). 144p. 1995. pap. 20.00 (1-56584-117-4) New Press NY.

Robes of the Realm: 300 Years of Ceremonial Dress. Una Campbell. (Illus.). 112p. 1989. 42.50 (0-948397-61-6, Pub. by M OMara Books UK) Trans-Atl Phila.

Robeson: Labor's Forgotten Champion. Charles H. Wright. LC 74-79061. 200p. 1975. 7.95 (0-913642-06-1) Balamp Pub.

Robeson County, North Carolina Marriage Bonds & Certificates, 1799-1868. Francis T. Ingmire. 98p. 1994. pap. 15.00 (0-8095-8677-0); lib. bdg. 39.00 (0-8095-8079-9) Borgo Pr.

Robeson Street. Fanny Howe. LC 85-73075. 72p. (C). 1985. 6.95 (0-914086-58-8); pap. 9.95 (0-914086-59-6) Alicejamesbooks.

Robespierre. Romain Rolland. 318p. (FRE.). 1939. pap. 15.95 (0-7859-5463-5) Fr & Eur.

Robespierre. Otto Scott. Vol. 2. reprint ed. write for info. (0-318-65558-6) Fndtn Amer Ed.

Robespierre: A Study. Hilaire Belloc. LC 72-8441. (Select Bibliographies Reprint Ser.). 1977. reprint ed. 28.95 (0-8369-6964-2) Ayer.

Robespierre: A Study in Deterioration. R. S. Ward. 1972. 69.95 (0-8490-0964-2) Gordon Pr.

Robespierre: The Reign of Terror. rev. ed. Otto Scott. 272p. 1989. reprint ed. pap. 10.95 (0-9623842-0-8, Southron Pr) Fndtn Amer Ed.

Robey, Roby, Robie: The Family History from Early England to America. William G. Robey, Jr. 1078p. (Orig.). 1994. pap. text ed. 80.00 (0-7884-0032-0) Heritage Bk.

***Robi Dobi: The Marvelous Adventures of an Indian Elephant.** Madhur Jaffrey. LC 96-28977. (Illus.). 1997. pap. 14.99 (0-8037-2193-5) Dial Bks Young.

Robidous in North America: Three Hundred Fifty Years (1643-1993) Clyde M. Rabideau. 608p. 1993. 20.00 (0-9636684-0-4) C Rabideau.

Robie House of Frank Lloyd Wright. Joseph Connors. LC 83-4891. (Illus.). 96p. 1984. pap. 16.95 (0-226-11542-9) U Ch Pr.

***Robin.** Delores Bainbridge. Ed. by Eva Petoskey. (Illus.). 36p. (J). (gr. 1-8). 1997. 20.00 (0-9657888-0-6) First Amer Prev Ctr.

***Robin: A Hero Is Born.** Alan Grant. LC 97-5047. 1997. pap. text ed. 3.50 (0-316-17693-1) Little.

Robin: A Hero Reborn. C. Dixon & A. Grant. Ed. by Dan Raspler & Dennis O'Neil. (Illus.). 192p. 1991. pap. 4.95 (1-56389-029-1) DC Comics.

Robin & the Kestrel. Mercedes Lackey. (Bardic Voices Ser.: Bk. 2). 432p. (Orig.). 1994. mass mkt. 5.99 (0-671-87628-7) Baen Bks.

Robin & the Kestrel Bk. II: Bardic Voices, Bk. II. Mercedes Lackey. LC 93-11286. (Bardic Voices Ser.: Bk. 2). 432p. 1993. 20.00 (0-671-72183-6) Baen Bks.

Robin & the King. Parke Godwin. 400p. 1994. reprint ed. mass mkt. 5.50 (0-380-70996-1, AvoNova) Avon.

Robin at Hickory Street. Dana M. Rau. (Smithsonian's Backyard Ser.). (Illus.). 32p. (J). (ps-3). 1995. 15.95 (1-56899-168-1); 4.95 (1-56899-169-X); 19.95 incl. audio (1-56899-172-X) Soundprints.

Robin at Hickory Street, Incl. toy. Dana M. Rau. (Smithsonian's Backyard Ser.). (Illus.). 32p. (J). (ps-3). 1995. 32.95 (1-56899-170-3); 12.95 (1-56899-171-1) Soundprints.

Robin Boyd: A Life. Geoffrey Serle. (The Miegunyah Press Ser.: No. 2). 288p. 1996. 45.00 (0-522-84669-6, Pub. by Melbourne Univ Pr AT) Paul & Co Pubs.

Robin Cook: A Critical Companion. Lorena L. Stookey. LC 96-5804. (Critical Companions to Popular Contemporary Writers Ser.). 224p. 1996. text ed. 29.95 (0-313-29578-6, Greenwood Pr) Greenwood.

Robin Cook - Three Complete Novels: Harmful Intent; Vital Signs; Blindsight. Robin Cook. LC 94-5134. 800p. 1994. 11.98 (0-399-13964-8, Putnam) Putnam Pub Group.

Robin des Bois. Guy Des Cars. 304p. (FRE.). 1978. 6.95 (0-686-55645-3, 2277128589) Fr & Eur.

Robin Drake, a Robot. (Illus.). (J). (ps-2). 1991. pap. 5.10 (0-8136-5665-6); lib. bdg. 7.95 (0-8136-5165-4) Modern Curr.

Robin Goodfellow. Aurand Harris & William Shakespeare. (J). 1977. 5.00 (0-87602-190-9) Anchorage.

***Robin Hatches Her Plan, Incl. doll.** Gordon Henderson. (Illus.). 32p. (J). 1995. pap. 30.00 (1-890414-02-6) Bow Tie.

***Robin Hood.** (Nelson Readers Ser.). (J). Date not set. pap. text ed. write for info. (0-17-557050-7) Addison-Wesley.

Robin Hood. (Children's Classics Ser.). (Illus.). (J). 1992. write for info. (0-89434-125-1) Ferguson.

Robin Hood. (FRE.). (J). (gr. 3-8). 9.95 (0-685-28453-0) Fr & Eur.

R

Robin Hood. (Classics Ser.). 96p. (J). 1994. 7.98 (*1-57082-051-1*) Mouse Works.

Robin Hood. (Illustrated Classics Ser.). (J). 1988. 2.98 (*0-671-09223-5*) S&S Trade.

Robin Hood. 56p. (J). (gr. 2-4). 1996. pap. 2.99 (*0-7214-5652-9*, Ladybrd) Penguin.

Robin Hood. Tony Allan. (Library of Fantasy & Adventure). (Illus.). (J). (gr. 4 up). 1996. pap. 9.95 (*0-7460-2063-5*, Usborne) EDC.

Robin Hood. Tony Allan. (Library of Fantasy & Adventure). (Illus.). 96p. (J). (gr. 4 up). 1996. lib. bdg. 17.95 (*0-88110-790-5*, Usborne) EDC.

Robin Hood. Donald Brice. (Learning & Coloring Bks.). (Illus.). 28p. (Orig.). (J). (gr. k up). 1991. pap. 3.95 (*1-878452-04-5*, Lrning & Coloring Bks) Tory Corner Editions.

Robin Hood. Paul Creswick. LC 84-10662. (Illus.). 362p. 1984. lib. bdg. 28.00 (*0-684-18162-2*, C Scribner Sons Young) S&S Childrens.

Robin Hood. Illus. by Domenick D'Andrea. LC 90-23078. (Bullseye Step into Classics Ser.). 96p. (Orig.). (J). (gr. 2-6). 1991. pap. 3.99 (*0-679-81045-5*) Random Bks Yng Read.

Robin Hood. Mark Dunster. 34p. (Orig.). 1988. pap. 5.00 (*0-89642-166-X*) Linden Pubs.

Robin Hood. Illus. & Retold by Margaret Early. 32p. (J). (ps-3). 1996. 17.95 (*0-8109-4428-6*) Abrams.

***Robin Hood.** Roger L. Green. 1997. pap. 10.95 (*0-14-086502-0*) Viking Penguin.

Robin Hood. Illus. & Retold by Carol Heyer. LC 93-18591. 32p. (J). (ps-3). 1993. 14.95 (*0-8249-8634-2*, Ideals Child); lib. bdg. 15.00 (*0-8249-8648-2*, Ideals Child) Hambleton-Hill.

Robin Hood. Adapted by Ronald Kidd. (Golden Sound Story Book Bks.). 20p. (J). (ps up). 1992. write for info. (*0-307-74703-4*, 64703) Western Pub.

Robin Hood. Elaine Kirn. (Regents Illustrated Classics Ser.). 62p. (gr. 7-12). 1987. pap. text ed. 4.50 (*0-13-781923-4*, 29406) Prentice ESL.

Robin Hood. Illus. by John Lawrence. 240p. (J). (gr. 4-7). 1995. 15.95 (*0-8050-3397-1*) H Holt & Co.

***Robin Hood.** Robin McKinley. (J). Date not set. lib. bdg. 99.98 (*0-688-07179-1*) Greenwillow.

***Robin Hood.** Mouse Works Staff. 1997. 7.98 (*1-57082-756-7*) Mouse Works.

Robin Hood. James Norris. (J). (gr. 1-9). 1952. 5.00 (*0-87602-191-7*) Anchorage.

Robin Hood. Eugene Pawczuk. Ed. by Mary Pronk. (Traditional Fairy Tales Ser.). (Illus.). 32p. (Orig.). (J). (gr. 1-6). 1992. pap. 5.95 (*0-88625-264-4*); lib. bdg. 15.55 (*0-88625-266-0*) Durkin Hayes Pub.

***Robin Hood.** Retold by Neil Philip. (Eyewitness Classics Ser.). (YA). (gr. 3 up). 1997. 14.95 (*0-614-28707-3*) DK Pub Inc.

Robin Hood. Contrib. by Cathryn Pisarski & Phil Smith. (Illus.). 28p. (Orig.). (J). (gr. 1 up). 1988. pap. 3.50 (*0-88680-308-X*); 7.50 (*0-88680-309-8*) I E Clark.

Robin Hood. Martin Powell. 114p. (Orig.). 1991. pap. 9.95 (*0-944735-94-0*) Malibu Comics Ent.

Robin Hood. Howard Pyle. (Illustrated Landoll Classics Ser.). (Illus.). 224p. (J). (ps-6). Date not set. pap. text ed. 3.95 (*1-56987-397-6*) Landoll.

Robin Hood. Louis Rhead. (Children's Classics Ser.). 1988. 12.99 (*0-517-67129-8*) Random Hse Value.

Robin Hood. Adapted by A. L. Singer. LC 91-73806. (Junior Novel Ser.). (Illus.). 64p. (Orig.). (J). (gr. 2-6). 1992. pap. 3.50 (*1-56282-138-5*) Disney Pr.

Robin Hood. Philip Smith. (J). (gr. 5-7). 1993. pap. 1.00 (*0-486-27573-6*) Dover.

Robin Hood. Graham Staplehurst. Ed. by Peter C. Fenlon & S. Coleman Charlton. (Rolemaster Game Adventure Ser.). (Illus.). 160p. (Orig.). (YA). (gr. 10-12). 1987. pap. 15.00 (*0-915795-28-0*, 1010) Iron Crown Ent Inc.

Robin Hood. N. R. Stinnet. (Classic Story Bks.). (J). 1994. 4.98 (*0-8317-1648-7*) Smithmark.

***Robin Hood.** Hudson Talbott. (J). Date not set. write for info. (*0-688-13353-3*, Morrow Junior) Morrow.

Robin Hood. abr. ed. Howard Pyle. (Illustrated Classics Ser.). (Illus.). 128p. (Orig.). (J). 1991. pap. 2.95 (*1-56156-028-6*) Kidsbks.

Robin Hood. rev. ed. James C. Holt. (Illus.). 1989. pap. 14.95 (*0-500-27541-6*) Thames Hudson.

Robin Hood. LC 76-133729. (Tudor Facsimile Texts. Old English Plays Ser.: No. 29). reprint ed. 49.50 (*0-404-53329-9*) AMS Pr.

Robin Hood. Roger L. Green. 1990. reprint ed. lib. bdg. 21.95 (*0-89966-689-2*) Buccaneer Bks.

Robin Hood: A Collection of All the Ancient Poems, Songs & Ballads, 2 vols. 1973. 200.00 (*0-8490-0965-0*) Gordon Pr.

Robin Hood: A Complete Study of the English Outlaw. Stephen Knight. (Illus.). 256p. 1994. pap. 22.95 (*0-631-19486-X*) Blackwell Pubs.

***Robin Hood: Collection of Ancient Poems, 2 vols.** Ed. by Joseph Ritson & Thomas Bewick. (IRTP Library of Folklore & Popular Culture). (Illus.). 600p. (C). 1997. text ed. 95.00 (*0-415-15383-2*) Routledge.

Robin Hood: His Life & Legend. Bernard Miles. LC 79-64615. (Illus.). 128p. (J). (gr. 4 up). 12.95 (*1-56288-412-3*) Checkerboard.

***Robin Hood: The Boy Who Became a Legend.** Kathryn Lasky. LC 97-11769. (J). 1998. write for info. (*0-590-25933-4*, Blue Sky Press) Scholastic Inc.

Robin Hood - The Sheriff Speaks. Alvin Granowsky. 1995. pap. text ed. 4.95 (*0-8114-2219-4*) Raintree Steck-V.

Robin Hood & His Merry Men. Jane Curry. (J). 1994. 13.95 (*0-689-50609-0*, McElderry) S&S Childrens.

Robin Hood & Little John. Barbara Cohen. LC 94-9944. (Illus.). 32p. (J). (ps-3). 1995. 15.95 (*0-399-22732-6*, Philomel Bks) Putnam Pub Group.

***Robin Hood & Other Outlaw Tales.** Stephen T. Knight & Thomas H. Ohlgren. LC 97-21475. (Teams Middle English Texts Ser.). 1997. write for info. (*1-879288-92-3*) Medieval Inst.

Robin Hood in Gotham: Adapted from an English Folktale. Papa Joe. (Step into a Story Bk.). 16p. (Orig.). 1996. pap. 3.50 (*1-889238-02-3*) Papa Joes.

Robin Hood in the Greenwood. Jane L. Curry. (Illus.). 53p. (J). (gr. 2-6). 1995. 15.00 (*0-689-80147-5*, McElderry) S&S Childrens.

Robin Hood of Sherwood Forest. Brenda H. McGee. Ed. by J. Friedland & R. Kessler. (Novel-Ties Ser.). 1993. student ed., pap. text ed. 15.95 (*0-88122-909-1*) Lrn Links.

Robin Hood of Sherwood Forest. Ann McGovern. 128p. (J). (gr. 4-6). 1991. pap. 3.50 (*0-590-45441-2*) Scholastic Inc.

Robin Hood Stories. Ed. by William A. Kottmeyer et al. (Everyreader Ser.). 1962. pap. 7.96 (*0-07-033731-4*) McGraw.

Robin Hood, The Adventures Of. E. Charles Vivian. (Airmont Classics Ser.). (Illus.). (J). (gr. 5 up). 1965. mass mkt. 2.50 (*0-8049-0067-1*, CL-67) Airmont.

***Robin Hood/King Arthur's Knights.** Smithmark Staff. (Classic Library Collection). 1996. 12.98 (*0-7651-9983-1*) Smithmark.

Robin Hood's England. Stephen M. Davis. (Guide Ser.). (Illus.). 150p. (Orig.). 1991. pap. 9.95 (*0-9628576-0-2*) Timetraveler.

Robin Hyman's Dictionary of Quotations. 520p. 1988. 19.95 (*0-8442-5449-5*, Natl Textbk) NTC Pub Grp.

Robin Hyman's Dictionary of Quotations. 520p. 1993. pap. 14.95 (*0-8442-5448-7*, Natl Textbk) NTC Pub Grp.

Robin in the Middle. Francine Pascal. (Sweet Valley Kids Ser.: No. 40). 80p. (J). (gr. 1-3). 1993. pap. 3.50 (*0-553-48014-6*) Bantam.

***Robin Kahn: Reveries of a Spinster, Found Poems.** Robin Kahn. (Illus.). 60p. 1997. pap. 12.95 (*1-881616-93-2*) Dist Art Pubs.

Robin Leach's Healthy Lifestyles Cookbook: Menus & Recipes from the Rich, Famous & Fascinating. Robin Leach & Mardee H. Regan. (Illus.). 250p. 1995. pap. 27.95 (*0-670-85730-0*, Viking Studio) Studio Bks.

Robin MacNaughton's Sun Sign Personality Guide. Robin MacNaughton. 512p. 1983. mass mkt. 7.50 (*0-553-27380-9*) Bantam.

Robin of Sherwood. Michael Morpurgo. (Illus.). (J). 1996. 22.00 (*0-15-201315-6*) HarBrace.

Robin on His Own. Johnniece M. Wilson. 160p. (J). (gr. 4-6). 1992. pap. 2.95 (*0-590-41809-2*, Apple Paperbacks) Scholastic Inc.

***Robin Red Breast.** Illus. by Carl Morton. (J). (gr. k-1). 1992. write for info. (*1-57842-096-2*) Delmas Creat.

Robin-Robin: A Journal. Mary N. Balcomb. LC 95-22236. 80p. 1995. pap. 19.95 (*1-887532-05-6*) Cody Pub.

Robin-Robin: A Journal. limited ed. Mary N. Balcomb. LC 95-22236. 80p. 1995. boxed 125.00 (*1-887532-06-4*) Cody Pub.

***Robin Tanner & the Old Stile Press.** limited ed. Frances McDowall & Nicolas McDowall. 120p. 1993. pap. 200.00 (*0-907664-35-0*, Pub. by Old Stiles UK) St Mut.

***Robin Williams Scrapbook.** Stephen J. Spignesi. LC 97-8682. 224p. 1997. pap. 19.95 (*0-8065-1891-X*, Citadel Pr) Carol Pub Group.

Robin Winters Think Tank. Wim Bereem et al. 60p. 1986. pap. 15.00 (*0-910663-45-9*) ICA Inc.

***Robin with the Red Hat.** Sukhdev K. Dosanjh. (Orig.). (J). (ps-4). 1997. pap. 6.95 (*0-533-12227-9*) Vantage.

Robin Yount: The Legend Lives On. Milwaukee Brewers Baseball Club, Publicity Dept. Staff. (Illus.). 80p. 19.00 (*0-9634967-0-0*) Milwauk BBC.

***Robinhound Crusoe.** Caroline Leavitt. (Adventures of Wishbone Ser.: Vol. 4). (Illus.). 144p. (Orig.). (J). (gr. 3-6). 1997. mass mkt. 3.99 (*1-57064-271-0*, Big Red) Lyrick Pub.

Robins. Chris Mead. (Illus.). 128p. text ed. 19.95 (*0-905483-36-7*, Pub. by Whittet Bks UK) Diamond Farm Bk.

Robin's Country. Monica Furlong. LC 94-19716. (J). 1995. lib. bdg. write for info. (*0-679-94332-3*) Knopf.

Robin's Diary. Claire Labine & Judith Pinsker. (Illus.). 168p. (Orig.). 1995. pap. 9.95 (*0-8019-8775-X*) Chilton.

Robins in Your Backyard. Nancy C. Willis. (Illus.). 32p. (J). (ps-3). 1997. 15.95 (*1-887813-21-7*) Cucumber Island.

Robin's Lunch & Other Poems for Children. Vera E. Johansen. LC 94-90418. (Illus.). (J). 1995. 7.95 (*0-533-11241-9*) Vantage.

***Robins Nest.** Pam Jarrell. (Little Book Ser.). (Illus.). 8p. (Orig.). (J). (ps-k). 1997. pap. text ed. 10.95 (*1-57332-048-X*) HighReach Lrning.

***Robins Nest.** large type ed. Pam Jarrell. (Big Book Ser.). (Illus.). 8p. (Orig.). (J). (ps-k). 1997. pap. text ed. 10.95 (*1-57332-049-8*) HighReach Lrning.

Robin's Play & Learn Book: Creative Activities for Preschoolers. Patricia C. Gallagher. (Illus.). 100p. (Orig.). 1987. pap. 9.95 (*0-943135-10-9*) Gallagher Jordan.

Robin's Song. large type ed. Mary Mackie. (Linford Romance Library). 304p. 1996. pap. 15.99 (*0-7089-7898-3*, Linford) Ulverscroft.

Robinson. Jules Supervielle. 192p. (FRE.). 1948. pap. 10.95 (*0-7859-1591-5*, 207026145X) Fr & Eur.

Robinson: Descendants of Rev. William Robinson. Bertha S. Taylor. (Illus.). 71p. 1992. reprint ed. pap. 14.00 (*0-8328-2403-8*); reprint ed. lib. bdg. 24.00 (*0-8328-2402-X*) Higginson Bk Co.

Robinson Crusoe. 352p. (YA). 1989. pap. 2.50 (*0-8125-0482-8*) Tor Bks.

Robinson Crusoe. 1993. 5.25 (*0-19-585336-9*) OUP.

Robinson Crusoe. 1993. pap. 5.25 (*0-19-422720-0*) OUP.

***Robinson Crusoe.** (Classics Illustrated Study Guides Ser.). (Illus.). (Orig.). 1997. mass mkt. write for info. (*1-57840-043-0*) Acclaim Bks.

Robinson Crusoe. Charlotte B. Chorpenning. (J). (gr. 1-9). 1952. 5.00 (*0-87602-192-5*) Anchorage.

Robinson Crusoe. Joseph Conrad. 288p. 1982. 3.95 (*0-553-21373-3*, Bantam Classics) Bantam.

***Robinson Crusoe.** Defoe. (York Notes Ser.). 1992. pap. text ed. write for info. (*0-582-78111-6*, Pub. by Longman UK) Longman.

Robinson Crusoe. Daniel Defoe. LC 90-46733. (Classics Ser.). (Orig.). (YA). (gr. 6 up). 1963. mass mkt. 2.25 (*0-8049-0022-1*, CL-22) Airmont.

Robinson Crusoe. Daniel Defoe. LC 90-46733. 256p. (Orig.). 1992. 15.00 (*0-679-40585-2*) Knopf.

Robinson Crusoe. Daniel Defoe. LC 90-46733. (Orig.). (J). 1993. 13.95 (*0-679-42819-4*, Everymans Lib) Knopf.

Robinson Crusoe. Daniel Defoe. LC 90-46733. (Orig.). 24.95 (*0-88411-594-1*) Amereon Ltd.

Robinson Crusoe. Daniel Defoe. Ed. by John Man. LC 90-46733. 336p. (Orig.). 1994. pap. text ed. 4.50 (*0-460-87439-X*, Everyman's Classic Lib) C E Tuttle.

Robinson Crusoe. Daniel Defoe et al. LC 90-46733. (Classics Illustrated Ser.). (Illus.). 52p. (Orig.). (YA). pap. 4.95 (*1-57209-021-9*) Classics Int Ent.

Robinson Crusoe. Daniel Defoe. LC 90-46733. (Orig.). (SPA.). 9.95 (*84-241-5636-6*) E Torres & Sons.

Robinson Crusoe. Daniel Defoe. LC 90-46733. (Children's Classics Ser.). (Illus.). (Orig.). (J). 1992. write for info. (*0-89434-126-X*) Ferguson.

Robinson Crusoe. Daniel Defoe. (Illus.). (Orig.). 1991. pap. 3.95 (*0-425-12664-1*) First Classics.

Robinson Crusoe. Daniel Defoe. LC 90-46733. 320p. (Orig.). (J). (gr. 6). 1961. mass mkt. 5.95 (*0-451-52236-2*, Sig Classics) NAL-Dutton.

Robinson Crusoe. Daniel Defoe. Ed. by John N. Fago. LC 90-46733. (Now Age Illustrated IV Ser.). (Illus.). (Orig.). (J). (gr. 4-12). 1978. student ed. 1.25 (*0-88301-344-4*); pap. text ed. 2.95 (*0-88301-320-7*) Pendulum Pr.

Robinson Crusoe. Daniel Defoe. LC 90-46733. (Classics Ser.). (Orig.). 1987. pap. 3.50 (*0-14-035072-1*, Puffin) Puffin Bks.

Robinson Crusoe. Daniel Defoe. LC 90-46733. (Children's Classics Ser.). (Orig.). (J). 1990. 12.99 (*0-517-01757-1*) Random Hse Value.

Robinson Crusoe. Daniel Defoe. LC 90-46733. 368p. (Orig.). (J). (gr. 7-9). 1990. pap. 4.50 (*0-590-43285-0*) Scholastic Inc.

Robinson Crusoe. Daniel Defoe. LC 83-14022. (Illus.). 368p. (Orig.). 1983. lib. bdg. 26.00 (*0-684-17946-6*, C Scribner Sons Young) S&S Childrens.

Robinson Crusoe. Daniel Defoe. LC 90-46733. (Orig.). 1997. pap. 2.95 (*0-89375-414-5*) Troll Communs.

Robinson Crusoe. Daniel Defoe. Ed. & Intro. by Angus Ross. LC 90-46733. (English Library). 320p. (Orig.). (YA). (gr. 9 up). 1966. pap. 6.95 (*0-14-043007-5*, Penguin Classics) Viking Penguin.

Robinson Crusoe. Daniel Defoe. (Young Reader's Christian Library). (Illus.). 224p. (J). (gr. 3 up). 1990. pap. text ed. 1.39 (*1-55748-118-0*) Barbour & Co.

Robinson Crusoe. Daniel Defoe. 1999. pap. 9.95 (*0-14-043597-2*) Viking Penguin.

Robinson Crusoe. Daniel DeFoe. LC 84-52575. (Courage Literary Classics Ser.). 296p. (Orig.). 1995. 5.98 (*1-56138-652-9*) Courage Bks.

***Robinson Crusoe, 2 vols.** Daniel Defoe. 20.00 (*0-614-30538-1*) NAVH.

***Robinson Crusoe.** Ladybird Staff & Daniel Defoe. 1997. pap. 3.50 (*0-7214-5797-5*, Ladybrd) Penguin.

Robinson Crusoe. Madge Miller. (J). (gr. 1-9). 1954. 5.00 (*0-87602-193-3*) Anchorage.

Robinson Crusoe. Van Gool Studio Staff. (Classic Ser.). (Illus.). 64p. (J). (ps-1). 1995. 4.98 (*0-8317-1665-7*) Smithmark.

Robinson Crusoe. abr. ed. Daniel Defoe. LC 95-36752. (Children's Thrift Classics Ser.). (Illus.). 96p. (Orig.). (J). 1995. pap. write for info. (*0-486-28816-1*) Dover.

Robinson Crusoe. abr. ed. Daniel Defoe. (Classics Ser.). 288p. (YA). (gr. 5 up). 1995. pap. 3.99 (*0-14-036722-5*) Puffin Bks.

Robinson Crusoe. large type ed. Daniel Defoe. LC 90-46733. (Isis Clear Type Classic Ser.). 358p. (Orig.). 1992. 24.95 (*1-85089-459-0*, Pub. by ISIS UK) Transaction Pubs.

Robinson Crusoe. Daniel Defoe. LC 90-46733. (Orig.). 1982. reprint ed. lib. bdg. 23.95 (*0-89966-403-2*) Buccaneer Bks.

Robinson Crusoe. Daniel Defoe. Ed. by Edward W. Dolch et al. LC 90-46733. 128p. (Orig.). (J). (gr. k-3). 1988. reprint ed. pap. 2.99 (*0-590-41841-6*) Scholastic Inc.

Robinson Crusoe, Vol I. Defoe. (FRE.). 1996. pap. 7.95 (*2-87714-319-8*, Pub. by Bookking Intl FR) Distribks Inc.

Robinson Crusoe, Vol. II. Defoe. (FRE.). 1996. pap. 7.95 (*2-87714-320-1*, Pub. by Bookking Intl FR) Distribks Inc.

Robinson Crusoe: A Bibliographical Checklist of English Language Editions (1719-1979) Robert W. Lovett & Charles C. Lovett. LC 87-28952. (Bibliographies & Indexes in World Literature Ser.: No. 30). 352p. 1991. text ed. 59.95 (*0-313-27695-1*, LRS/, Greenwood Pr) Greenwood.

Robinson Crusoe: An Authoritative Text, Backgrounds & Sources, Criticism. 2nd ed. Daniel Defoe. Ed. by Michael Shinagel. LC 93-12217. (Critical Editions Ser.). (C). 1993. pap. text ed. 9.95 (*0-393-96452-3*) Norton.

Robinson Crusoe: Illustrated Christian Classics. Daniel Defoe. 160p. 1996. pap. text ed. 1.99 (*1-55748-902-5*) Barbour & Co.

Robinson Crusoe: Island Myths & the Novel. Michael Seidel. Ed. by Robert Lecker. (Twayne's Masterwork Studies). 152p. 1991. 23.95 (*0-8057-8074-2*, MWS 64, Twayne); pap. 13.95 (*0-8057-8120-X*, MWS 64, Twayne) Scribnrs Ref.

***Robinson Crusoe: Movie Tie-In Art.** Daniel Defoe. 1996. mass mkt. 4.99 (*0-8125-5763-8*) Tor Bks.

Robinson Crusoe: Myths & Metamorphoses. Ed. by Lieve Spaas & Brian Stimpson. 300p. 1996. text ed. 59.95 (*0-312-12928-9*) St Martin.

***Robinson Crusoe: Tie-In Art.** Daniel Defoe. 1996. mass mkt. 4.99 (*0-8125-5736-0*) Tor Bks.

Robinson Crusoe see Major Literary Characters

Robinson Crusoe & Its Printing, 1719-1731. Henry C. Hutchins. LC 25-11861. reprint ed. 27.50 (*0-404-03463-2*) AMS Pr.

Robinson Crusoe Notes. Cynthia C. McGowan. (Orig.). 1976. pap. text ed. 3.95 (*0-8220-1150-6*) Cliffs.

***Robinson Crusoe of York, Mariner.** Daniel Defoe. LC 97-3248. (Classic Collection). 1997. 14.99 (*1-56179-557-7*) Focus Family.

***Robinson Crusoe Readalong.** Daniel Defoe. (Illustrated Classics Collection 4). 64p. 1994. pap. 14.95 incl. audio (*0-7854-0770-7*, 40517) Am Guidance.

Robinson Crusoe Story. Martin Green. LC 90-30687. 200p. 1991. lib. bdg. 30.00 (*0-271-00705-2*) Pa St U Pr.

Robinson Crusoe USN: The Adventures of George Tweed, RM1, on Japanese-Held Guam. 2nd rev. ed. George R. Tweed et al. Ed. & Pref. by D. Turner Givens. LC 94-67627. (Illus.). 319p. pap. 24.95 (*0-9642071-0-9*) Pacfc Res Inst.

***Robinson Crusoe's Remarkable Discovery: Brain & the Impress of Culture.** Leslie Brothers. LC 97-13482. (Illus.). 224p. 1997. 25.00 (*0-19-510103-0*) OUP.

Robinson Crusoe's Return. Douglas A. Menville. LC 75-46298. (Supernatural & Occult Fiction Ser.). 1976. reprint ed. lib. bdg. 17.95 (*0-405-08158-8*) Ayer.

Robinson Jeffers. Robert J. Brophy. LC 75-29982. (Western Writers Ser.: No. 19). (Illus.). 50p. (Orig.). 1975. pap. 4.95 (*0-88430-018-8*) Boise St U W Writ Ser.

Robinson Jeffers. Frederic I. Carpenter. (Twayne's United States Authors Ser.). 1962. pap. 13.95 (*0-8084-0269-2*, T22) NCUP.

Robinson Jeffers: Fragments of an Older Fury. Antoninus. 1970. 7.50 (*0-685-04672-9*) Oyez.

Robinson Jeffers: Poet of California. enl. rev. ed. James Karman. 200p. (Orig.). reprint ed. pap. 12.00 (*0-934257-58-2*) Story Line.

Robinson Jeffers: Poet of Inhumanism. Arthur B. Coffin. LC 74-121767. 324p. 1971. 32.50 (*0-299-05840-9*) U of Wis Pr.

Robinson Jeffers: Poet of Inhumanism. Arthur B. Coffin. LC 74-121767. 324p. reprint ed. pap. 92.40 (*0-7837-7022-7*, 2046837) Bks Demand.

Robinson Jeffers: The Dimensions of a Poet. Intro. by Robert J. Brophy. (Illus.). (C). 1994. pap. 16.95 (*0-8232-1566-0*); text ed. 27.00 (*0-8232-1565-2*) Fordham.

Robinson Jeffers: The Man & His Work. Lawrence C. Powell. 1973. lib. bdg. 59.95 (*0-8490-0966-9*) Gordon Pr.

Robinson Jeffers: The Man & His Work. Lawrence C. Powell. LC 68-54176. (American Biography Ser.: No. 32). (Illus.). 1969. reprint ed. lib. bdg. 75.00 (*0-8383-0675-6*) M S G Haskell Hse.

Robinson Jeffers & a Galaxy of Writers: Essays in Honor of William H. Nolte. Ed. by William B. Thesing. LC 95-4335. 232p. 1995. text ed. 29.95 (*1-57003-043-X*) U of SC Pr.

Robinson Jeffers & the Critics, 1912-1983: A Bibliography of Secondary Sources with Selective Annotations. Jeanetta Boswell. LC 86-17862. (Author Bibliographies Ser.). 184p. 1986. 20.00 (*0-8108-1914-7*) Scarecrow.

Robinson on North Carolina Corporation Law. Russell M. Robinson, II. 850p. 1990. 95.00 (*0-87473-657-9*) MICHIE.

***Robinson on North Carolina Corporation Law.** 5th ed. Russell M. Robinson, II. 1000p. 1995. 95.00 (*1-55834-287-7*, 66660-11) MICHIE.

Robinson-Patman Act: Federal Regulation of Price Differences. Richard A. Posner. LC 76-383361. (AEI Studies: No. 131). 63p. reprint ed. pap. 25.00 (*0-8357-4528-7*, 2037405) Bks Demand.

Robinson-Patman Act: Policy & Law, 2 vols., Vol. 1. 178p. 1980. pap. 20.00 (*0-89707-025-9*, 503-0031-01) Amer Bar Assn.

Robinson-Patman Act: Policy & Law, 2 vols., Vol. 2. 1983. pap. 20.00 (*0-685-29679-2*, 503-0048-01) Amer Bar Assn.

Robinson-Patman Act & Effective Competition. John S. McGee. Ed. by Stuart Bruchey & Vincent P. Carosso. LC 78-18968. (Small Business Enterprise in America Ser.). (Illus.). 1979. lib. bdg. 56.95 (*0-405-11472-9*) Ayer.

***Robinson, the Pleasant History of an Unusual Cat.** Walter Anderson. 1996. pap. 16.95 (*0-87805-948-2*) U Pr of Miss.

***Robinson. Thomas Robinson & His Descendants.** rev. ed. Thomas H. Robinson. 233p. 1996. reprint ed. pap. 36.00 (*0-8328-5332-1*); reprint ed. lib. bdg. 46.00 (*0-8328-5331-3*) Higginson Bk Co.

Robinson und Struwwelpeter. 176p. 1991. 64.00 (*3-487-09624-2*) G Olms Pubs.

Robinsonade Tradition in Robert Michael Ballantyne's "The Coral Island" & William Golding's "The Lord of the Flies" Karin Siegl. LC 96-17249. 86p. 1996. text ed. 49.95 (*0-7734-4210-3*) E Mellen.

Robocop I. Bob Harras et al. 48p. 1990. 4.95 (*0-87135-665-1*) Marvel Entmnt.

Robocop Two: The Movie. Alan Grant et al. (Illus.). 64p. 1990. 4.95 (*0-87135-666-X*) Marvel Entmnt.

An Asterisk (*) at the beginning of an entry indicates that the title is appearing in BIP for the first time.

Robot Adept. Piers Anthony. 1989. mass mkt. 5.99 (*0-441-73118-X*) Ace Bks.

Robot Analysis & Control. Jean-Jacques E. Slotine & Haruhiko Asada. LC 85-1579. 288p. 1986. text ed. 89.95 (*0-471-83029-1*) Wiley.

Robot Applications. Karl Wojcikiewicz & Ron Johnson. LC 84-12757. (Illus.). 600p. 1984. 99.95 (*0-87119-055-9*); teacher ed. 9.95 (*0-87119-108-3*); pap. text ed. 19.95 (*0-317-14618-1*); 10.95 (*0-87119-056-7*) Heathkit-Zenith Ed.

Robot Applications Design Manual. Jon Hoshizaki & Emily Bopp. LC 90-36150. 342p. 1990. text ed. 89.95 (*0-471-50691-5*) Wiley.

***Robot Blues.** Margaret Weis & Don Perrin. 1996. pap. 6.99 (*0-451-45581-9*, ROC) NAL-Dutton.

Robot Builder's Bonanza: 99 Inexpensive Robotics Projects. Gordon McComb. pap. 17.95 (*0-8306-2800-2*) McGraw.

Robot Builders Bonanza: 99 Inexpensive Robotics Projects. Gordon McComb. 1987. pap. text ed. 18.95 (*0-07-157146-9*) McGraw.

Robot Calibration. Ed. by R. Bernhardt & S. L. Albright. LC 93-8755. 324p. (gr. 13). 1993. text ed. 104.95 (*0-412-49140-0*) Chapman & Hall.

Robot City, No. 1. write for info. (*0-87135-883-2*) Marvel Entmnt.

Robot City, No. 2. write for info. (*0-87135-884-0*) Marvel Entmnt.

Robot City, No. 3. write for info. (*0-87135-885-9*) Marvel Entmnt.

***Robot Colonies.** LC 97-6002. 1997. lib. bdg. 110.00 (*0-7923-9904-8*) Kluwer Ac.

Robot Comics. Donald D. Spencer. LC 92-3966. 96p. 1992. pap. 9.95 (*0-89218-235-0*) Camelot Pub.

***Robot Control.** I. Troch et al. (IFAC Symposia Ser.: Vol. 9207). 582p. 1992. 197.75 (*0-08-041276-9*, Pergamon Pr) Elsevier.

Robot Control: Dynamics, Motion Planning, & Analysis. Ed. by Frank L. Lewis & Chaouki T. Abdallah. LC 92-5764. (Illus.). 552p. (C). 1992. text ed. 89.95 (*0-7803-0404-7*, PC0299-8) Inst Electrical.

Robot Control: The Task Function Approach. Claude Samson et al. (Oxford Engineering Science Ser.: No. 22). (Illus.). 384p. 1991. 115.00 (*0-19-853805-7*) OUP.

Robot Control 1994 (SYROCO '94) A Postscript Volume from the IFAC Symposium, Capri, Italy, 19-21 September 1994. F. Nicolo. Ed. by L. Sciavicco & C. Bonivento. LC 95-5963. 942p. 1995. pap. 120.50 (*0-08-042227-6*, Pergamon Pr) Elsevier.

Robot Dreams. Isaac Asimov. 1990. mass mkt. 5.99 (*0-441-73154-6*) Ace Bks.

Robot Dynamics & Control. Mark W. Spong. LC 88-22724. 336p. 1989. Net. text ed. 545.00 (*0-471-61243-X*) Wiley.

Robot Evolution: The Development of Anthrobotics. Mark E. Rosheim. 423p. 1994. text ed. 59.95 (*0-471-02622-0*) Wiley.

Robot Exhibit: History, Fantasy & Reality. (Illus.). 64p. 1984. 9.00 (*0-88321-052-5*) Am Craft.

Robot Grippers. Ed. by D. T. Pham & W. B. Heginbotham. (International Trends in Manufacturing Technology Ser.). 360p. 1986. 126.95 (*0-387-16004-3*) Spr-Verlag.

Robot Hands & the Mechanics of Manipulation. Matthew T. Mason & J. Kenneth Salisbury. (Artificial Intelligence Ser.). (Illus.). 275p. 1985. 39.95 (*0-262-13205-2*) MIT Pr.

Robot Hobby: The Complete Manual for Individuals & Clubs. John W. Gutmann. (Illus.). 320p. (Orig.). (J). (gr. 5-12). 1992. pap. 29.95 (*0-9634272-4-5*); text ed. 36.95 (*0-9634272-5-3*) Machine Pr.

Robot Jox. Robert Thurston. 1989. pap. 3.50 (*0-380-75444-4*) Avon.

Robot Kinematics: Symbolic Automation & Numerical Synthesis. C. Y. Ho & Jen Sriwattanathamma. Ed. by George W. Zobrist. LC 89-17753. (Computer Engineering & Computer Science Ser.). 336p. 1990. text ed. 78.50 (*0-89391-574-2*) Ablex Pub.

Robot King. Brian Selznick. LC 94-43808. (Laura Geringer Bk.). (Illus.). 80p. (J). (gr. k up). 1995. 13.95 (*0-06-024493-3*); lib. bdg. 13.89 (*0-06-024494-1*) HarpC Child Bks.

Robot Markets: Increased Plant Automation Translates to 10 Percent Annual Growth. Market Intelligence Staff. 277p. 1993. 1,895.00 (*1-56753-472-4*) Frost & Sullivan.

Robot Motion: Planning & Control. Michael Brady et al. (Artificial Intelligence Ser.). (Illus.). 585p. 1983. 52.50 (*0-262-02182-X*) MIT Pr.

Robot Motion Planning. Jean-Claude Latombe. (International Series in Engineering & Computer Science, VLSI, Computer Architecture, & Digital Screen Processing). 672p. 1990. lib. bdg. 135.50 (*0-7923-9129-2*) Kluwer Ac.

Robot Motion Planning. Jean-Claude Latombe. 672p. (C). 1991. pap. text ed. 93.00 (*0-7923-9206-X*) Kluwer Ac.

Robot Novels. Isaac Asimov. 656p. 1988. pap. 14.95 (*0-345-33119-2*, Del Rey) Ballantine.

Robot Novels, 2 vols. in 1. Isaac Asimov. 416p. 1971. 10.98 (*1-56865-030-2*, GuildAmerica) Dblday Direct.

Robot Pedagogics: The Mathematical Analysis & Elementary Control of a Model Manipulator. E. T. Hammerand. LC 93-25251. (Computer Engineering & Computer Science Ser.). 552p. 1997. 79.50 (*1-56750-081-1*) Ablex Pub.

Robot Ping-Pong Player: Experiment in Real-Time Intelligent Control. Russell L. Anderson. (Artificial Intelligence Ser.). 312p. 1988. 39.95 (*0-262-01101-8*) MIT Pr.

Robot Psychiatrist. Joseph L. Palotta. 603p. 1981. pap. 29.95 (*0-9604852-0-1*) Revelation Hse.

Robot Reliability & Safety. B. S. Dhillon. (Illus.). 280p. 1991. 99.95 (*0-387-97535-7*) Spr-Verlag.

***Robot Revolt.** Fisk. (Sky Bks.). 1991. pap. text ed. write for info. (*0-582-05803-1*, Pub. by Longman UK) Longman.

Robot Rover Visual Navigation. Hans P. Moravec. LC 81-7512. (Computer Science: Artificial Intelligence Ser.: No. 3). (Illus.). 169p. reprint ed. pap. 48.20 (*0-685-20337-9*, 2070023) Bks Demand.

Robot Sensors: Tactile & Non-Vision, Vol. 2. Ed. by A. Pugh. (International Trends in Manufacturing Technology Ser.). 350p. 1986. 118.95 (*0-387-16126-0*) Spr-Verlag.

Robot Sensors: Vision, Vol. 1. Ed. by A. Pugh. (International Trends in Manufacturing Technology Ser.). 300p. 1986. 111.95 (*0-387-16125-2*) Spr-Verlag.

***Robot Shaping: An Experiment in Behavior Engineering.** Marco Dorigo & Marco Colombetti. LC 97-16342. 1997. write for info. (*0-262-04164-2*) MIT Pr.

Robot Standards Workshop: Proceedings. U. S. Department of Commerce, National Bureau of Standards Staff & Navy Manufacturing Technology Program Staff. 180p. (Orig.). 1985. pap. 32.00 (*0-317-39398-7*) Robot Inst Am.

Robot Tactile Sensing. Russell. 270p. 1990. boxed 40.00 (*0-13-781592-1*) P-H.

Robot Technology: Logic & Programming, Vol. 5. Michel Parent & Claude Laurgeau. (Illus.). 192p. (C). 1985. text ed. 66.00 (*0-13-782178-6*) P-H.

Robot Technology: Theory, Design & Applications. Anthony C. McDonald. (Illus.). 384p. 1986. text ed. 32.95 (*0-685-12427-4*, Reston) P-H.

Robot Technology & Applications. Ed. by K. Rathmill et al. (Illus.). 203p. 1985. 69.00 (*0-387-13960-5*) Spr-Verlag.

Robot Technology & Applications. Ed. by Ulrich Rembold. (Manufacturing Engineering & Materials Processing Ser.: Vol. 34). 696p. 1990. 210.00 (*0-8247-8206-2*) Dekker.

Robot That Helped to Make a President. annot. rev. ed. Charles Hamilton. (Illus.). 63p. 1995. reprint ed. 75.00 (*0-9646829-0-7*) Recollect NJ.

Robot Trouble. Bruce Coville. Ed. by Pat MacDonald. (A. I. Gang Ser.). 224p. 1995. mass mkt. 3.99 (*0-671-89252-5*, Minstrel Bks) PB.

Robot Vision. Berthold K. Horn. (Press Series in Electrical Engineering & Computer Science Ser.). (Illus.). 464p. 1986. 60.00 (*0-262-08159-8*) MIT Pr.

Robot Vision. Berthold K. Horn. 1986. text ed. write for info. (*0-07-030349-5*) McGraw.

Robot Visions. Isaac Asimov. 1991. 6.99 (*0-451-45064-7*, ROC) NAL-Dutton.

Robot Wrist Actuators. Mark E. Rosheim. LC 88-22762. 271p. 1989. text ed. 89.95 (*0-471-61595-1*) Wiley.

Robotech: New World Order: Robotech Sourcebook. Kevin Siembieda. (Illus.). 112p. (Orig.). 1995. pap. 11.95 (*0-916211-84-3*, 562) Palladium Bks.

Robotech: Zentraedi Breakout. D. Christian et al. Ed. by Alex Marciniszyn et al. (Robotech RPG Adventures Ser.). (Illus.). 64p. (Orig.). (YA). (gr. 8 up). 1994. pap. 9.95 (*0-916211-67-3*, 561) Palladium Bks.

Robotech Art 1. limited rev. ed. Kay Reynolds. Tr. by Ardith Carlton from JPN. LC 85-16291. (Illus.). 264p. (Orig.). 40.00 (*0-89865-462-9*, Starblaze) Donning Co.

Robotech Art 2. Kay Reynolds. (Illus.). 120p. 1987. pap. 12.95 (*0-89865-517-X*, Starblaze) Donning Co.

Robotech Art 3. limited ed. Carl Macek. Ed. by Kay Reynolds. (Robotech Ser.). (Illus.). 120p. (Orig.). 1988. 40.00 (*0-89865-576-5*, Starblaze) Donning Co.

Robotech Genesis, No. 1. Jack McKinney. 214p. 1987. mass mkt. 5.99 (*0-345-34133-3*, Del Rey) Ballantine.

Robotech II - The Sentinels Vol. 2: The Marriage of Rick Hunter & Lisa Hayes. Tom Mason & Chris Ulm. (Illus.). 124p. 1991. 19.95 (*0-944735-76-2*) Malibu Comics Ent.

Robotech II, the Sentinels: Operation Tirol, Vol. 3. Chris Ulm. 1992. pap. 9.95 (*1-56398-033-9*) Malibu Comics Ent.

Robotech II, the Sentinels: Script Book, Vol. 2. Tom Mason. 1992. pap. 9.95 (*1-56398-036-3*) Malibu Comics Ent.

Robotech II, the Sentinels: The Complete Robotech Handbook. Dan Danko. 1992. pap. 14.95 (*1-56398-034-7*) Malibu Comics Ent.

Robotech II the Sentinels, Vol. 1: Scriptbook. Ed. by Tom Mason. 113p. 1991. pap. 9.95 (*1-56398-021-5*) Malibu Comics Ent.

Robotech Role-Playing Game. Kevin Siembieda. Ed. by Alex Marciniszyn. (Illus.). 112p. (Orig.). (YA). (gr. 8 up). 1986. pap. 11.95 (*0-916211-21-5*, 550) Palladium Bks.

Robotech Strike Force: Robotech Sourcebook. Kevin Siembieda. (Robotech RPG Ser.). (Illus.). 112p. (Orig.). 1995. pap. 11.95 (*0-916211-85-1*, 563) Palladium Bks.

Robotech Three-in-One: Battlehymn; Force of Arms; Doomsday. Jack McKinney. 512p. 1994. reprint ed. mass mkt. 5.99 (*0-345-39145-4*, Del Rey) Ballantine.

Robotech Two, Vol. 1: The Sentinels, Graphic Novel. Tom Mason & Chris Ulm. (Illus.). 128p. 1990. 19.95 (*0-944735-28-2*) Malibu Comics Ent.

Robotech 2 - The Sentinels: A New Beginning. Tom Mason & Chris Ulm. 129p. (Orig.). 1991. pap. 9.95 (*0-944735-83-5*) Malibu Comics Ent.

Robotech 3-in-1: Southern Cross; Metal Fire; The Final Nightmare. Jack McKinney. 480p. 1995. mass mkt. 5.99 (*0-345-39184-5*, Del Rey) Ballantine.

RoboTech 3-in-1 Vols. 1-3: Genesis; Battle Cry; Homecoming, 3 vols. Jack McKinney. 496p. (Orig.). 1994. mass mkt. 5.99 (*0-345-38900-X*, Del Rey) Ballantine.

Robotic Applications in India. Ed. by Amitabha Bhattacharyya. (C). 1989. 80.00 (*0-89771-386-9*, Pub. by Current Dist II) St Mut.

Robotic Applications in Non-Industrial Environments. Richard K. Miller & Terri C. Walker. 311p. 1991. 285.00 (*0-89671-119-6*) SEAI Tech Pubns.

Robotic Deburring Handbook. L. Gillespie. LC 87-61789. 130p. 1987. 37.00 (*0-87263-297-0*) SME.

***Robotic Exploration Close to the Sun: Scientific Basis.** Ed. by Shadia R. Habbal. 1997. text ed. 90.00 (*1-56396-618-2*) Am Inst Physics.

Robotic Object Recognition Using Vision & Touch. Peter K. Allen. (C). 1987. lib. bdg. 69.50 (*0-89838-245-9*) Kluwer Ac.

Robotic Observatories. Ed. by Michael F. Bode. (Wiley-Praxis Series in Astronomy & Astrophysics). 200p. 1995. text ed. 47.95 (*0-471-95690-2*) Wiley.

Robotic Simulation. Daniel L. Ryan. LC 93-17598. 336p. 1993. 74.95 (*0-8493-4468-9*, TJ211) CRC Pr.

Robotic Systems: Advanced Techniques & Applications. Ed. by Spyros G. Tzafestas. LC 92-12521. (Microprocessor Based & Intelligent Systems Engineering Ser.: Vol. 10). 656p. (C). 1992. lib. bdg. 243.00 (*0-7923-1749-1*) Kluwer Ac.

Robotic Systems & Advanced Manufacturing Technology: Proceedings of the IFIP TC5 - WG5.3 International Conference on CAD-CAM & Advanced Manufacturing Technology, Jerusalem, Israel, 11-14 Dec., 1989. Ed. by Gideon Halevi et al. 358p. 1990. 133.75 (*0-444-88828-4*, North Holland) Elsevier.

Robotic Technology. Ed. by A. Pugh. (Control Engineering Ser.: No. 23). 168p. 1983. boxed 79.00 (*0-86341-004-9*, CE 023) Inst Elect Eng.

Robotic Telescopes: Current Capabilities, Present Developments, & Future Prospects for Automated Astronomy. Ed. by Gregory W. Henry & Joel A. Eaton. (ASP Conference Series Proceedings: Vol. 79). 270p. 1995. 44.00 (*0-937707-98-8*) Astron Soc Pacific.

Robotic Telescopes in the 1990s. Ed. by A. Filipenko. (ASP Conference Series Proceedings: Vol. 34). 367p. 1992. 28.00 (*0-937707-53-8*) Astron Soc Pacific.

Robotic, Vision & AI Applications in Agriculture. Richard K. Miller & Terri C. Walker. LC 88-81667. (Survey on Technology & Markets Ser.: No. 76). 50p. 1989. pap. text ed. 200.00 (*1-55865-075-X*) Future Tech Surveys.

Robotic Welding. Ed. by J. D. Lane. (International Trends in Manufacturing Technology Ser.). (Illus.). 380p. 1987. 97.95 (*0-387-16676-9*) Spr-Verlag.

Robotics. Ed. by R. Brockett. LC 90-1220. (Proceedings of Symposia in Applied Mathematics Ser.: Vol. 41). 196p. 1990. 53.00 (*0-8218-0163-5*, PSAPM/41) Am Math.

Robotics. DST Staff. (C). 1988. 47.50 (*81-204-0349-5*, Pub. by Oxford IBH II) S Asia.

Robotics. Alan Gomersall & P. R. Farmer. (Illus.). 200p. 1985. 100.95 (*0-387-15010-2*) Spr-Verlag.

Robotics. T. Potter et al. (Introductions Ser.). (Illus.). 48p. (J). (gr. 6 up). 1983. pap. 6.95 (*0-7460-1466-X*); lib. bdg. 14.95 (*0-88110-661-5*) EDC.

Robotics. Ellen Thro. (Science Sourcebooks Ser.). (Illus.). 128p. (YA). (gr. 7 up). 1993. lib. bdg. 17.95 (*0-8160-2628-9*) Facts on File.

Robotics. Time-Life Books Editors. 1986. 21.27 (*0-8094-5696-6*) Time-Life.

Robotics. Andrew Vowles. (Hayes Technology Ser.). (Illus.). 32p. (J). (gr. 5-9). 1985. pap. 5.95 (*0-88625-113-3*) Durkin Hayes Pub.

Robotics. rev. ed. (Understanding Computers Ser.). (Illus.). 128p. 1991. 19.93 (*0-8094-7582-0*); lib. bdg. 25.93 (*0-8094-7583-9*) Time-Life.

Robotics: An Introduction. 2nd ed. Douglas R. Malcolm. (Electronics Technology Ser.). 1988. text ed. 57.50 (*0-8273-3913-5*) Delmar.

Robotics: An Introduction. 2nd ed. Douglas R. Malcolm. 1988. 50.25 (*0-534-91474-8*) PWS Pubs.

Robotics: Basic Analysis & Design. William A. Wolovich. 256p. (C). 1987. text ed. 61.25 (*0-03-006119-9*); Instr.'s manual. teacher ed. write for info. (*0-03-006123-7*) SCP.

Robotics: Control, Sensing, Vision & Intelligence. K. S. Fu et al. (CAD-CAM Robotics & Computer Vision Ser.). 672p. (C). 1987. text ed. write for info. (*0-07-022625-3*) McGraw.

Robotics: Introduction, Programming, & Projects. James Fuller. 476p. (C). 1991. text ed. 81.00 (*0-675-21078-X*, Merrill Coll) P-H.

Robotics: Kinematics, Dynamics & Controls: Proceedings of the 23rd Biennial Mechanisms Conference, Minneapolis, MN, 1994. Twenty-Third Biennial Mechanisms Conference Staff. 510p. 1994. pap. 90.00 (*0-7918-1286-3*) ASME.

Robotics: Manipulation & Planning. Zexiang Li & Richard M. Murray. 480p. 1994. 64.95 (*0-8493-7981-4*, TJ211) CRC Pr.

Robotics & AI: Sensing, Reasoning, Planning, Manipulation, Mobility. D. T. Pham. (Machine Tools & Manufacture Ser.: Vol. 28). 111p. 1988. 63.00 (*0-08-036627-9*, Pergamon Pr) Elsevier.

Robotics & Automated Systems. Hoekstra. (Electronics Technology Ser.). 1986. teacher ed. 52.95 (*0-538-33650-1*); teacher ed. 14.00 (*0-538-33651-X*) S-W Pub.

Robotics & Automation: Proceedings, IASTED Symposium, Lugano, Switzerland, June 22-24, 1983. Ed. by M. H. Hamza. 173p. 1983. 60.00 (*0-88986-049-1*, 055) Acta Pr.

Robotics & Automation: Proceedings, IASTED Symposium, Lugano, Switzerland, June 22-24, 1983. Ed. by M. H. Hamza. 267p. 1985. 80.00 (*0-88986-077-7*, 092) Acta Pr.

Robotics & Automation: Proceedings IASTED Symposium, Lugano, Switzerland, June 29-July 1, 1987. Ed. by M. H. Hamza. 139p. 1987. 55.00 (*0-88986-122-6*, 118) Acta Pr.

Robotics & Automation: Proceedings IASTED Symposium, Santa Barbara, U. S. A., May 27-29, 1987. Ed. by M. H. Hamza. 171p. 1987. 67.00 (*0-88986-116-1*, 128) Acta Pr.

Robotics & Automation: Proceedings of IASTED Symposium, Santa Barbara, U. S. A., May 25-27, 1988. Ed. by M. H. Hamza. 185p. 1988. 77.00 (*0-88986-101-3*, 143) Acta Pr.

Robotics & Automation '84: Proceedings, IASTED Symposium, New Orleans, U. S. A., November 12-14, 1984. Ed. by M. H. Hamza. 127p. 1984. 50.00 (*0-88986-069-6*, 082) Acta Pr.

Robotics & Automation, '94 International Conference, 4 vols. LC 90-640158. 3816p. 1994. pap. text ed. 340.00 (*0-8186-5330-2*, 5330) IEEE Comp Soc.

Robotics & Factories of the Future. Ed. by S. N. Dwivedi. 650p. 1985. 135.95 (*0-387-15015-3*) Spr-Verlag.

Robotics & Factories of the Future, 3 vols. Ed. by B. Prasad. 1180p. 1989. 256.95 (*0-387-51135-0*) Spr-Verlag.

Robotics & Factories of the Future, Vol. 1. Ed. by B. Prasad. (Illus.). 468p. 1989. 120.95 (*0-387-51132-6*) Spr-Verlag.

Robotics & Factories of the Future, Vol. 2. Ed. by B. Prasad. (Illus.). 312p. 1989. 79.95 (*0-387-51133-4*) Spr-Verlag.

Robotics & Factories of the Future, Vol. 3. Ed. by B. Prasad. (Illus.). 400p. 1989. 107.95 (*0-387-51134-2*) Spr-Verlag.

Robotics & Factories of the Future '87. Ed. by R. Radharamanan. (Illus.). xvii, 878p. 1988. 150.95 (*0-387-50025-1*) Spr-Verlag.

Robotics & Flexible Manufacturing Systems: Selected Papers from the IMACS World Congress, 13th, Dublin, Ireland, July 1991, & the IMACS Conference on Modelling & Control of Technological Systems, Lille, France, May 1991. rev. ed. Ed. by Jean-Claude Gentina & Spyros G. Tzafestas. LC 92-21008. 436p. 1992. 181.50 (*0-444-89705-4*) Elsevier.

Robotics & Flexible Manufacturing Technologies: Assessment, Impacts & Forecast. Robert U. Ayres et al. LC 85-15312. (Illus.). 443p. 1986. 48.00 (*0-8155-1043-8*) Noyes.

Robotics & Foreign Affairs: Developments & Economic Effects of Automated Technology Throughout the World. 1986. lib. bdg. 79.95 (*0-8490-3750-6*) Gordon Pr.

Robotics & Industrial Electronics. Heath Company Staff. (Illus.). 730p. (C). 1983. teacher ed. 9.95 (*0-87119-096-6*); student ed. 14.95 (*0-87119-095-8*); pap. text ed. 29.95 (*0-87119-094-X*, EB-1801) Heathkit-Zenith Ed.

Robotics & Intelligent Machines in Agriculture. LC 83-73657. 160p. 1984. pap. 27.50 (*0-916150-60-7*, PO484) Am Soc Ag Eng.

Robotics & Manipulators: Theory & Practice. Ed. by A. Morecki. 36p. 1983. pap. 10.00 (*0-08-030530-X*, 11, Pergamon Pr) Elsevier.

Robotics & Manufacturing, Vol. 2. Ed. by M. Jamshidi et al. 1112p. 1988. 189.00 (*0-7918-0006-7*, 800067) ASME Pr.

Robotics & Manufacturing, Vol. 3. Ed. by M. Jamshidi & M. Saif. 1026p. 1990. 189.00 (*0-7918-0016-4*, 800164) ASME Pr.

Robotics & Manufacturing, Vol. 4. Mo Shahinpoor. 1032p. 1992. 189.00 (*0-7918-0030-X*, 80030X) ASME Pr.

Robotics & Manufacturing: Recent Trends in Research, Education & Applications, Vol. 5. Ed. by Mohammad Jamshidi. 1032p. 1994. 189.00 (*0-7918-0044-X*, 80044X) ASME Pr.

***Robotics & Manufacturing; Recent Trends in Research, Education, & Applicationx Vol. 6: Proceedings, 6th International Symposium on Robotics & Manufacturing (ISRAM'96), Montpellier, France, 1996.** Ed. by Mohammad Jamshidi et al. LC 88-8138. (ASME Press Ser.). 885p. 1997. pap. 189.00 (*0-7918-0047-4*, TS191) ASME Pr.

Robotics & Manufacturing '89: Proceedings of IASTED Symposium, Santa Barbara, California, U. S. A., November 13-15, 1989. Ed. by M. H. Hamza. 286p. 1989. 90.00 (*0-88986-131-5*, 145) Acta Pr.

Robotics & Remote Handling in Hostile Environments Topical Meeting, Gatlinburg, TN, April 23-27, 1984. 470p. 1984. 47.50 (*0-89448-114-2*, 700090) Am Nuclear Soc.

Robotics Applications for Industry: A Practical Guide. L. L. Toepperwein et al. LC 83-13109. 326p. 1984. 45.00 (*0-8155-0962-6*) Noyes.

Robotics, Applied Mathematics & Computational Aspects: Based on the Proceedings of a Conference on Robotics, Applied Mathematics & Computational Aspects. Institute of Mathematics & Its Applications Staff. Ed. by Kevin Warwick. LC 92-35010. (Institute of Mathematics & Its Applications Conference Series, New Ser.: New Series 41). (Illus.). 614p. 1993. 155.00 (*0-19-853649-6*) OUP.

Robotics-Automated Systems Technology Curriculum Planning Guide. Center for Occupational Research & Development Staff. (Robotics-Automated Systems Technology Ser.). 74p. (C). 1985. pap. text ed. 20.00 (*1-55502-176-X*) CORD Commns.

Robotics-Automated Systems Technology State-of-the-Art Report. Center for Occupational Research & Development Staff. (Robotics-Automated Systems Technology Ser.). 100p. (C). 1985. pap. text ed. 20.00 (*1-55502-149-2*) CORD Commns.

Robotics-Automated Systems Technology Task Analysis. Center for Occupational Research & Development Staff. (Robotics-Automated Systems Technology Ser.). (Illus.). 206p. (C). 1985. pap. text ed. 22.00 (*1-55502-175-1*) CORD Commns.

R

Robotics, Components & Instruments see IFAC '96: 13th World Congress Proceedings

Robotics Design & Maintenance. Anthony C. McDonald. (C). 1986. teacher ed. write for info. (*0-8359-6689-5*, Reston) P-H.

Robotics Explained. James Hanneman. (Series 880). (Orig.). 1983. student ed., pap. 6.00 (*0-8064-0363-2*, 880); audio, vhs 289.00 (*0-8064-0364-0*) Bergwall.

Robotics for Challenging Environments: Proceedings of the ASCE Specialty Conference. Ed. by Laura A. Demsetz & Paul R. Klarer. LC 93-50192. 1994. 41.00 (*0-87262-913-9*) Am Soc Civil Eng.

Robotics for Challenging Environments: Proceedings of the RCE II, the Second Conference, Albuquerque, New Mexico, June 1-6, 1996. Conference on Robotics for Challenging Environments Staff & American Society of Civil Engineers Staff. Ed. by Laura Demsetz. LC 96-8474. 1996. 37.00 (*0-7844-0178-0*) Am Soc Civil Eng.

Robotics for the Welding Engineer. N. A. Kennedy. (Illus.). 38p. 1988. pap. 69.95 (*0-614-07592-0*, Pub. by Woodhead Pubng UK) Am Educ Systs.

Robotics Illustrated Dictionary: French-English-German-Russian. S. M. Paley. (Illus.). 347p. (ENG, FRE, GER & RUS.). 1993. 85.00 (*0-7859-8827-0*) Fr & Eur.

Robotics Illustrated Dictionary French-English-German-Russian. S. M. Paley. (Illus.). 347p. (ENG, FRE & GER.). 1993. 98.00 (*2-85608-052-9*, Pub. by La Maison Du Dict FR) IBD Ltd.

Robotics in Alpe-Adria Region: Proceedings of the Second International Workshop (RAA '93), June 1993, Austria. Ed. by Peter Kopacek. LC 94-1451. (Schriftenreihe der wissenschaftlichen Landesakademie fur Niederosterreich Ser.). (Illus.). x, 230p. 1995. 40.00 (*0-387-82545-2*) Spr-Verlag.

Robotics in Civil Engineering. M. Skibniewski. LC 88-72283. (Topics in Engineering Ser.: Vol. 3). 220p. 1987. 66.00 (*0-931215-64-1*) Computational Mech MA.

Robotics in Education: An Information Guide. Veronica S. Pantelidis. LC 91-24541. 449p. 1991. 47.50 (*0-8108-2466-3*) Scarecrow.

***Robotics in Meat, Fish & Poultry Processing.** Ed. by Khodabandehloo. (Illus.). 232p. text ed. 145.95 (*0-7514-0087-4*, Pub. by Blackie Acad & Prof UK) Routledge Chapman & Hall.

Robotics in Service. Joseph F. Engelberger. 250p. 1989. 39.95 (*0-262-05042-0*) MIT Pr.

Robotics Industry: Profiles & Outlooks. 1986. lib. bdg. 250.00 (*0-8490-3757-3*) Gordon Pr.

Robotics Markets: A State of the Industry Report. (Illus.). 250p. 1987. ring bd. 1,950.00 (*0-317-65753-4*) Busn Trend.

Robotics, Mechatronics & Manufacturing Systems: Transactions of the IMACS-SICE International Symposium, Kobe, Japan, 16-20 September, 1992. Ed. by Toshi Takamori & Kazuo Tsuchiya. LC 93-18964. 976p. 1993. pap. 255.75 (*0-444-89700-3*, North Holland) Elsevier.

Robotics, Nineteen Sixty to Nineteen Eighty-Three: An Annotated Bibliography. Andrew Garoogian. LC 84-1763. (CompuBibs Ser.: No. 1). 119p. (C). 1984. pap. 16.50 (*0-914791-03-6*) Vantage Info.

Robotics Research: The Fifth International Symposium. Hirofumi Miura & Suguru Arimoto. Ed. by Brady et al. (Artificial Intelligence Ser.). 500p. 1990. 70.00 (*0-262-13253-2*) MIT Pr.

Robotics Research: The First International Symposium. Ed. by Michael Brady & Richard P. Paul. LC 83-25592. (Artificial Intelligence Ser.). (Illus.). 600p. 1984. 95.00 (*0-262-02207-9*) MIT Pr.

Robotics Research: The Second International Symposium. Ed. by Hideo Hanafusa & Hirochika Inoue. (Artificial Intelligence Ser.). (Illus.). 500p. 1985. 70.00 (*0-262-08151-2*) MIT Pr.

Robotics Research: The Seventh International Symposium. Ed. by Georges Giralt & Gerhard Hirzinger. 645p. 1996. 149.50 (*3-540-76043-1*) Spr-Verlag.

Robotics Research & Advanced Application: Presented at the Winter Annual Meeting of ASME, Phoenix, Arizona, November 14-19,1982. American Society of Mechanical Engineers Staff. Ed. by Wayne J. Book. LC 82-73173. 293p. reprint ed. pap. 83.60 (*0-317-26618-7*, 2024184) Bks Demand.

Robotics Review One. Tomas Lozano-Perez et al. Ed. by Oussama Khatib & John J. Craig. 200p. 1989. 44.00 (*0-262-11135-7*) MIT Pr.

Robotics Review Two. Ed. by Oussama Khatib et al. (Illus.). 384p. 1992. 60.00 (*0-262-11171-3*) MIT Pr.

Robotics Science. Ed. by Michael Brady. (System Development Foundation, Benchmark Ser.). (Illus.). 632p. 1989. 60.00 (*0-262-02284-2*) MIT Pr.

Robotics Sourcebook & Dictionary. David F. Tver & Roger W. Bolz. LC 83-135. 304p. 1983. 34.95 (*0-8311-1152-6*) Indus Pr.

Robotics Technical Directory, 1986. Ed. by William M. Rowe. LC 86-204600. (Illus.). 178p. reprint ed. pap. 50.80 (*0-8357-2999-0*, 2039268) Bks Demand.

Robotics Technology. James W. Masterson et al. (Illus.). 320p. (Orig.). (C). 1996. pap. text ed. 35.96 (*1-56637-046-9*) Goodheart.

Robotics Technology. Charles J. Spiteri. 352p. (C). 1990. text ed. 52.00 (*0-03-020858-0*) SCP.

***Robotix Teacher's Guide: The Science of Robotics.** Sally Palow. (Illus.). 188p. 1997. ring bd. 69.00 (*1-890647-25-X*) Lrning Curve.

Robotnik: A Short History of the Struggle for Worker Self Management & Free Trade Unions in Poland, 1944-1981. David R. Stefanic. 180p. 1992. text ed. 31.50 (*0-88033-235-2*) Col U Pr.

Robots. Time Life Staff. (How Things Work Ser.). 1990. 19.93 (*0-8094-7866-8*); lib. bdg. 25.93 (*0-8094-7867-6*) Time-Life.

Robots: A Gentle Introduction. Bettie C. Hall & Ernest Hall. write for info. (*0-318-58219-8*) P-H.

Robots: Here They Come! Janet Riehecky. LC 90-30634. (Discovery World Ser.). (Illus.). 32p. (J). (ps-2). 1990. lib. bdg. 21.36 (*0-89565-577-2*) Childs World.

Robots: Machines in Man's Image. Isaac Asimov & Karen A. Frenkel. (Illus.). 160p. 1985. 21.95 (*0-317-39396-0*) Robot Inst Am.

Robots: Your High-Tech World. Gloria Skurzynski. LC 89-70805. (Illus.). 64p. (J). (gr. 4 up). 1990. lib. bdg. 16.95 (*0-02-782917-0*, Bradbury S&S) S&S Childrens.

Robots - What They Are, What They Do. Fredericka Berger. LC 91-14128. (Illus.). 48p. (J). (gr. 1 up). 1992. 14.00 (*0-688-09863-0*); lib. bdg. 13.93 (*0-688-09864-9*) Greenwillow.

Robots & Biological Systems: Towards a New Bionics? Ed. by P. Dario et al. (NATO ASI Series F: Computer & Systems Sciences, Special Programme AET: Vol. 102). xii, 796p. 1993. 215.95 (*0-387-56158-7*) Spr-Verlag.

Robots & Empire. Isaac Asimov. 512p. 1986. mass mkt. 5.99 (*0-345-32894-9*, Del Rey) Ballantine.

Robots & Gardens: Science Fantasy Poems. Al Montes. 48p. 1985. 4.00 (*0-918476-14-3*) Cornerstone Pr.

Robots & Manipulator Systems: Papers, 2 pts., Pt. 1. Conference on Remotely Manned Systems, 2nd, June 1975. Ed. by E. Heer. LC 77-73105. 336p. 1977. pap. 35.00 (*0-08-021727-3*) Elsevier.

Robots & Manipulator Systems: Papers, 2 pts., Pt. 2. Conference on Remotely Manned Systems, 2nd, June 1975. Ed. by E. Heer. LC 77-73105. 336p. 1977. pap. 35.00 (*0-08-022681-7*, Pergamon Pr) Elsevier.

Robots & Manufacturing Automation. 2nd ed. C. Ray Asfahl. LC 91-32355. 512p. (C). 1992. Net. text ed. 54.50 (*0-471-55391-3*) Wiley.

Robots, Androids, & Animatrons: Twelve Incredible Projects You Can Build. John Iovine. 1997. pap. text ed. 19.95 (*0-07-032804-8*) McGraw.

Robot's Dilemma: The Frame Problem in Artificial Intelligence. Ed. by Zenon W. Pylyshyn. LC 86-10801. (Theoretical Issues in Cognitive Science Ser.: Vol. 4). 168p. 1987. text ed. 73.25 (*0-89391-371-5*) Ablex Pub.

Robot's Dilemma Revisited. D. Dennett et al. Ed. by Kenneth Ford & Zenon W. Pylyshyn. (Illus.). 250p. 1996. pap. 39.50 (*1-56750-143-5*) Ablex Pub.

Robot's Dilemma Revisited. D. Dennett et al. Ed. by Kenneth Ford & Zenon W. Pylyshyn. (Illus.). 250p. 1996. text ed. 78.50 (*1-56750-142-7*) Ablex Pub.

Robots for Shearing Sheep: Shear Magic. James P. Trevelyan. (Illus.). 480p. 1992. 79.00 (*0-19-856252-7*) OUP.

Robots Fourteen: Conference Proceedings. Intro. by Fred Z. Sitkins. (Illus.). 419p. 1990. pap. text ed. 60.00 (*0-87263-390-X*) SME.

Robots in Inspection. Ed. by J. Lee. 170p. 1987. 28.00 (*0-87263-286-5*) SME.

Robots in Manufacturing: Key to International Competitiveness. Jack Baranson. LC 83-81240. 168p. 1983. 32.50 (*0-912338-39-3*); fiche 16.50 (*0-912338-40-7*) Lomond.

Robots of Dawn. Isaac Asimov. 448p. 1994. mass mkt. 6.99 (*0-553-29949-2*, Spectra) Bantam.

Robots of Dawn, Vol. 3. Isaac Asimov. 416p. 1984. mass mkt. 5.95 (*0-345-31571-5*, Del Rey) Ballantine.

Robots or Men: French Workman's Experience in American Industry. Hyacinth Dubreuil. Ed. by Leon Stein. LC 77-70491. 1977. reprint ed. lib. bdg. 26.95 (*0-405-10163-5*) Ayer.

Robots' Rebellion: The Story of the Spiritual Renaissance, Vol. 1. 4th ed. David Icke. 366p. (Orig.). 1994. pap. 15.95 (*1-85860-022-7*, Pub. by Gateway Books UK) ACCESS Pubs Network.

Robot's Revenge. Franklin W. Dixon. Ed. by Ellen Winkler. (Hardy Boys Casefiles Ser.: No. 123). 160p. (Orig.). (J). (gr. 3-6). 1993. pap. 3.99 (*0-671-79313-6*, Minstrel Bks) PB.

Robots 12 & Vision '88: Conference Proceedings, June 5-9, 1988, Detroit, MI, Vol. 2. Robots 12 & Vision '88 Conference (1988: Detroit, MI) Staff. LC 88-61194. (Illus.). 806p. reprint ed. pap. 180.00 (*0-8357-6501-6*, 2035872) Bks Demand.

Robsart Affair. Jennette F. Letton & Francis Letton. reprint ed. lib. bdg. 22.95 (*0-89190-237-6*, Rivercity Pr) Amereon Ltd.

Robsart Affair. Jennette F. Letton. 268p. 1976. reprint ed. lib. bdg. 22.95 (*0-89244-015-5*, Queens House) Amereon Ltd.

Robson Rhodes: Personal Financial Planning Manual 1994-95. 10th ed. Robson Rhodes Financial Services Ltd., Personal Financial Planning Department Staff. 1994. pap. 29.95 (*0-406-03597-0*) MICHIE.

Robur le Conquerant. Jules Verne. (Illus.). 185p. (FRE.). 1976. pap. 10.95 (*0-7859-1468-4*, 2253012734); pap. 3.95 (*0-686-55947-9*) Fr & Eur.

Robust Adaptive Control. Petros A. Ioannou. LC 95-24811. 1995. text ed. 73.00 (*0-13-439100-4*) P-H.

Robust Adaptive Control: Proceedings of the IFAC Workshop, Newcastle, Australia, 22-24 August 1988. Ed. by G. C. Goodwin. (IFAC Publication). (Illus.). 273p. 1989. 155.00 (*0-08-036620-1*, 1102; 1301, Pergamon Pr) Elsevier.

***Robust & Adaptive Matching Procedure for Automatic Modelling of Terrain Relief.** Luisa M. Oereira. (Illus.). 204p. (Orig.). 1996. pap. 67.50 (*90-407-1385-5*, Pub. by Delft U Pr NE) Coronet Bks.

Robust & Insensitive Design of Multivariable Feedback Systems: Multimodel Design. Irmfried Hartmann et al. (Advances in Control Systems & Signal Processing Ser.: Vol. 6). (Illus.). xii, 166p. 1986. pap. 38.00 (*3-528-08960-1*, Pub. by Vieweg & Sohn GW) Informatica.

Robust & Nonlinear Time Series Analysis. 2nd ed. Ed. by J. Franke et al. (Lecture Notes in Statistics Ser.: Vol. 26). ix, 286p. 1984. pap. 36.00 (*0-387-96102-X*) Spr-Verlag.

Robust & Optimal Control. Kemin Zhou et al. LC 95-30311. 1995. text ed. 89.33 (*0-13-456567-3*) P-H.

Robust Asymptotic Statistics. Helmut Rieder. LC 94-1070. (Series in Statistics). 416p. 1994. 59.95 (*0-387-94262-9*) Spr-Verlag.

Robust Control. Peter Dorato. LC 87-12448. 528p. 1987. 89.95 (*0-87942-233-5*, PCO2204) Inst Electrical.

Robust Control: Proceedings of a Workshop Held in Tokyo, Japan, 24-25 June, 1991. Ed. by S. Hosoe. LC 92-34065. (Lecture Notes in Control & Information Sciences Ser.). 1992. 63.95 (*0-387-55961-2*) Spr-Verlag.

Robust Control: Systems with Uncertain Physical Parameters. Jurgen Ackermann et al. LC 93-27559. (Communications & Control Engineering Ser.). 1997. 109.00 (*0-387-19843-1*) Spr-Verlag.

Robust Control: The Parametric Approach. S. P. Bhattacharyya et al. LC 95-2313. (Information & System Sciences Ser.). (C). 1995. text ed. 75.00 (*0-13-781576-X*) P-H.

Robust Control Design. Banyasz. (IFAC Postprint Ser.). 1997. pap. text ed. write for info. (*0-08-042606-9*, Pergamon Pr) Elsevier.

Robust Control Design: A Polynomial Approach. Theodore E. Djaferis. 288p. (C). 1995. lib. bdg. 125.00 (*0-7923-9617-0*) Kluwer Ac.

Robust Control for Unstructured Perturbations: An Introduction. P. Dorato et al. Ed. by M. Thoma & A. Wyner. (Lecture Notes in Control & Information Sciences Ser.: Vol. 168). vi, 118p. 1992. 43.95 (*0-387-54920-X*) Spr-Verlag.

Robust Control II: Stochastic Systems see IFAC '96: 13th World Congress Proceedings

Robust Control of Infinite Dimensional Systems: Frequency Domain Methods. Ciprian Foias et al. (Lecture Notes in Control & Information Sciences Ser.: Vol. 209). 218p. 1996. pap. 54.00 (*3-540-19994-2*) Spr-Verlag.

Robust Control of Linear Dynamical Systems. P. C. Chandrasekharan. (Illus.). 384p. 1996. boxed 89.00 (*0-12-167885-7*) Acad Pr.

Robust Control of Linear Systems & Nonlinear Control. M. A. Kaashoek et al. (Progress in Systems & Control Theory Ser.: Vol. 4). 622p. 1990. 137.50 (*0-8176-3470-3*) Birkhauser.

Robust Control System Design. Tsui. LC 96-18121. (Electrical Engineering & Electronics Ser.: Vol. 97). 336p. 1996. 125.00 (*0-8247-9739-6*) Dekker.

Robust Control Theory. Ed. by Bruce A. Francis & Pramod P. Khargonekar. LC 94-46704. (IMA Volumes in Mathematics & Its Applications Ser.: Vol. 66). (Illus.). 224p. 1995. 53.95 (*0-387-94443-5*) Spr-Verlag.

***Robust Control Theory in Hilbert Space.** A. Feintuch. LC 97-22857. (Applied Mathematical Sciences Ser.: Vol. 130). (Illus.). 240p. 1997. 59.95 (*0-387-98291-4*) Spr-Verlag.

Robust Control via Variable Structure & Lyapunov Techniques, Vol. 217. Franco Garofalo & Luigi Glielmo. LC 96-26596. (Lecture Notes in Control & Information Sciences Ser.). 307p. 1996. 63.00 (*3-540-76067-9*) Spr-Verlag.

Robust Design: Key Points for World Class. John Terninko. (Illus.). 57p. (Orig.). 1989. pap. text ed. 4.50 (*1-882382-00-5*) Respons Mgmt.

***Robust Design & Analysis for Quality Engineering.** S. H. Park. 320p. 1996. 64.95 (*0-412-55620-0*, Chap & Hall NY) Chapman & Hall.

***Robust Discrete Optimization & Its Applications.** Panos Kouvelis. LC 96-43291. (Nonconvex Optimization & Its Applications Ser.). 376p. (C). 1996. lib. bdg. 175.00 (*0-7923-4291-7*) Kluwer Ac.

***Robust Engineering Design for Circuits & Systems.** write for info. (*0-340-66277-8*, Pub. by E Arnold UK) Routledge Chapman & Hall.

Robust Estimates of Location: Survey & Advances. D. F. Andrews et al. LC 72-39019. 376p. 1972. pap. 19.95 (*0-691-08116-6*) Princeton U Pr.

***Robust Estimates of Location: Survey & Advances.** David F. Andrews et al. LC 72-39019. 383p. 1972. reprint ed. pap. 109.20 (*0-608-02871-1*, 2063935) Bks Demand.

Robust Estimation & Testing. Robert G. Staudte & Simon J. Sheather. LC 89-36770. (Probability & Mathematical Statistics Ser.). 376p. 1990. text ed. 119.00 (*0-471-85547-2*) Wiley.

***Robust Flight Control, Vol. 224.** Jean-Fran C. Magni et al. LC 97-1194. (Lecture Notes in Control & Information Sciences Ser.). 1997. pap. 88.00 (*3-540-76151-9*) Spr-Verlag.

Robust Industrial Control: Optimal Design Approach for Polynomial Systems. Michael J. Grimble. LC 93-8357. (International Systems & Control Engineering Ser.). 576p. 1994. text ed. 78.00 (*0-13-655283-8*) P-H.

Robust Inference. Tiku et al. (Statistics: Textbooks & Monographs: Vol. 71). 336p. 1986. 125.00 (*0-8247-7532-5*) Dekker.

Robust Linear Control. Michael Green & David J. Limebeer. LC 93-39100. 1994. text ed. 89.33 (*0-13-102278-4*) P-H Gen Ref & Trav.

Robust Methods & Asymptotic Theory in Nonlinear Econometrics. H. J. Bierens. (Lecture Notes in Economics & Mathematical Systems Ser.: Vol. 192). (Illus.). 198p. 1981. 35.00 (*0-387-10838-6*) Spr-Verlag.

Robust Model Reference Adaptive Systems: Dynamics & Modification Update Laws. F. M. Salam & S. Bai. 250p. 1997. text ed. 61.00 (*981-02-1155-4*) World Scientific Pub.

Robust Multivariable Flight Control. Richard Adams et al. LC 94-3683. (Advances in Industrial Control Ser.). 1994. 65.95 (*0-387-19906-3*) Spr-Verlag.

Robust Nonlinear Control Design: State-Space & Lyapunov Techniques. R. A. Freeman & Petar V. Kokotovic. LC 96-19920. 272p. 1996. 64.50 (*0-8176-3930-6*) Spr-Verlag.

Robust Nonlinear Control Design: State-Space & Lyapunov Techniques. Randy A. Freeman & Petar Kokotovi. LC 96-19920. 1996. write for info. (*3-7643-3930-6*, Pub. by Birkhauser Vlg SZ) Birkhauser.

Robust Organization: Transforming Your Company Using Adaptive Design. William A. Stimson. 235p. 1996. text ed. 35.00 (*0-7863-0859-1*) Irwin.

***Robust Planning & Analysis of Experiments.** LC 97-19018. 1997. pap. write for info. (*0-387-98223-X*) Spr-Verlag.

Robust Process Control. Manfred Morari & Evanghelos Zafiriou. 512p. 1988. text ed. 57.00 (*0-13-782153-0*) P-H.

Robust Regression: Analysis & Applications. Lawrence & Arthur. (Statistics: Textbooks & Monographs: Vol. 108). 312p. 1989. 125.00 (*0-8247-8129-5*) Dekker.

Robust Regression & Outlier Detection. Peter J. Rousseeuw & Annick M. Leroy. LC 87-8234. (Probability & Mathematical Statistics Ser.). 329p. 1987. text ed. 96.95 (*0-471-85233-3*) Wiley.

Robust Reliability in the Mechanical Science. Yakov Ben-Haim. LC 96-13060. 233p. 1996. 74.95 (*3-540-61058-8*) Spr-Verlag.

Robust Sales Management. Harvard Business School Press Staff. 1991. pap. text ed. 19.95 (*0-07-103341-6*) McGraw.

Robust Stability & Convexity: An Introduction. Jacob Kogan. (Lecture Notes in Control & Information Sciences: 201). 1994. write for info. (*0-387-19919-5*) Spr-Verlag.

Robust Stability & Convexity: An Introduction. Jacob Kogan. (Lecture Notes in Control & Information Sciences: 201). 1995. 41.00 (*3-540-19919-5*) Spr-Verlag.

Robust Stabilization Against Structured Perurbations. S. P. Bhattacharyya. (Lecture Notes in Control & Information Sciences Ser.: Vol. 99). ix, 172p. 1987. 37.95 (*0-387-18056-7*) Spr-Verlag.

Robust Stabilization in the Gap-Topology. L. C. Habets. (Lecture Notes in Control & Information Sciences Ser.: Vol. 150). ix, 126p. 1991. 31.95 (*0-387-53466-0*) Spr-Verlag.

Robust Statistical Methods. J. J. Rey. (Lecture Notes in Mathematics Ser.: Vol. 690). 1978. 18.95 (*0-387-09091-6*) Spr-Verlag.

***Robust Statistical Procedures.** 2nd ed. Peter J. Huber. LC 96-36142. (CBMS-NSF Regional Conference Series in Applied Mathematics: No. 68). 70p. 1996. pap. 18.50 (*0-89871-379-X*, CB68) Soc Indus-Appl Math.

Robust Statistical Procedures: Asympotics & Interrelations. Jana Jureckova & Pranab Kumar. LC 95-17912. (Wiley Series in Probability & Statistics). 448p. 1996. text ed. 64.95 (*0-471-82221-3*, Wiley-Interscience) Wiley.

Robust Statistics. Peter J. Huber. LC 80-18627. (Probability & Mathematical Statistics Ser.). 308p. 1981. text ed. 110.00 (*0-471-41805-6*) Wiley.

Robust Statistics: The Approach Based on Influence Functions. Frank R. Hampel et al. LC 85-9428. (Probability & Mathematical Statistics Ser.). 502p. 1986. text ed. 127.00 (*0-471-82921-8*) Wiley.

Robust Statistics, Data Analysis, & Computer Intensive Methods: In Honor of Peter Huber's 60th Birthday. Ed. by Helmut Rieder. LC 95-49239. (Lecture Notes in Statistics Ser.: Vol. 109). 429p. 1995. 49.95 (*0-387-94660-8*) Spr-Verlag.

Robust Tracking Control of Robot Manipulators. Zhihua Qu & Darren M. Dawson. 256p. 1995. 79.95 (*0-7803-1065-9*, PC4218) Inst Electrical.

Robust Unionism: Innovations in the Labor Movement. Arthur B. Shostak. 384p. 1991. pap. 19.95 (*0-87546-170-0*, ILR Press) Cornell U Pr.

Robustness in Automatic Speech Recognition: Fundamentals & Applications. Jean-Claude Junqua & Jean-Paul Haton. (International Series in Engineering & Computer Science, Natural Language Processing & Machine Translation). 440p. (C). 1995. lib. bdg. 130.00 (*0-7923-9646-4*) Kluwer Ac.

Robustness in Identification & Control. Ed. by M. Milanese et al. (Applied Information Technology Ser.). (Illus.). 350p. 1989. 85.00 (*0-306-43251-X*, Plenum Pr) Plenum.

***Robustness in Statistical Pattern Recognition.** Yurij Kharin. LC 96-42117. (Mathematics & Its Applications Ser.). 320p. (C). 1996. lib. bdg. 156.00 (*0-7923-4267-4*) Kluwer Ac.

***Robustness of Analytical Chemical Methods & Pharmaceutical Technological Products.** M. W. B. Hendricks et al. LC 96-46758. (Data Handling In Science & Technology Ser.). 360p. 1996. 243.75 (*0-444-89709-7*) Elsevier.

Robustness of Dynamic Systems with Parameter Uncertainties. Ed. by M. Mansour et al. LC 92-27728. (Monte Verita Ser.). ix, 315p. 1992. 87.00 (*0-8176-2791-X*) Birkhauser.

Robustness of Statistical Methods & Nonparametric Statistics. Ed. by Dieter Rasch & Moti L. Tiku. 1986. lib. bdg. 136.00 (*90-277-2076-2*) Kluwer Ac.

Roby: Pedigree of Roby of Castle Donington, County Leicester. H. J. Roby. 69p. 1993. reprint ed. pap. 14.00 (*0-8328-3741-5*); reprint ed. lib. bdg. 24.00 (*0-8328-3740-7*) Higginson Bk Co.

Robyna Neilson Ketchum Collection of Bells. Nicholas Renouf & Richard T. Rephann. (Illus.). 28p. (Orig.). 1975. pap. 3.00 (*0-929530-00-4*) Yale U Coll Musical Instruments.

Robyn's Book. (J). 1986. pap. 2.95 (*0-590-42536-6*) Scholastic Inc.

An Asterisk (*) at the beginning of an entry indicates that the title is appearing in BIP for the first time.

Roc & a Hard Place. Piers Anthony. 320p. 1995. 23.95 (*0-312-85392-0*) Tor Bks.

***Roc & a Hard Place.** Piers Anthony. 1996. mass mkt. 5.99 (*0-614-20532-8*) Tor Bks.

Rocannon's World. Ursula K. Le Guin. LC 76-47250. 136p. 1977. 25.00 (*0-06-012568-3*) Ultramarine Pub.

Rocas Alijos: Scientific Results from the Cordell Expeditions. Ed. by Robert W. Schmieder. LC 96-15904. (Monographiae Biologicae: Vol. 75). 1996. lib. bdg. 248.00 (*0-7923-4056-6*) Kluwer Ac.

Rocas y Minerales. Eyewitness Staff. (Eyewitness Bks.). (SPA.). (J). 1997. 19.99 (*84-372-3722-X*) Random.

Rocco & His Brothers. Sam Rohdie. (BFI Film Classics Ser.). (Illus.). 80p. 1993. pap. 9.95 (*0-85170-340-2*, Pub. by British Film Inst UK) Ind U Pr.

***Roce de un Ala de Angel - Bursh of an Angel's Wing.** Sheed. 203p. (SPA.). 1995. write for info. (*1-56063-902-4*) Editorial Unilit.

***Roch Carrier: La Guerre - C'est Moi!** P. Roch-Carrier. Ed. by G. Snaith. (Bristol Classical Press French Texts Ser.). 128p. (FRE.). (C). 1997. pap. text ed. 18.95 (*1-85399-481-2*, Pub. by Duckworth UK) Focus Pub-R Pullins.

Rochdale: The Runaway College. David Sharpe. 297p. (Orig.). 1987. pap. 15.95 (*0-88784-155-4*, Pub. by Hse of Anansi Pr CN) Genl Dist Srvs.

Roche Collection of Traditional Irish Music. Francis Roche. 1983. pap. 19.95 (*0-8256-0292-0*, Oak) Music Sales.

Roche Edition, 2 vols., 1. Earley. 1980. 8.88 (*0-316-20316-5*) Little.

Roche Edition, 2 vols., 2. Earley. 1980. 8.87 (*0-316-20317-3*) Little.

Roche Lexikon Medizin. 3rd ed. Hoffmann-La Roche. 1849p. (GER.). 1993. 85.00 (*0-7859-8421-6*, 3541112131) Fr & Eur.

Roche Problem: And Its Significance for Double-Star Astronomy. Zdenek Kopal. (C). 1989. lib. bdg. 118.00 (*0-7923-0129-3*) Kluwer Ac.

Rochelle & the Atlantic Economy During the Eighteenth Century. John G. Clark. LC 80-29275. (Illus.). 302p. reprint ed. pap. 86.10 (*0-8357-6607-1*, 2035252) Bks Demand.

***Rochelle City Plan.** (Grafocarte Maps Ser.). 1996. 8.95 (*2-7416-0088-0*, 80088) Michelin.

***Rochelle/Royan/Bordeaux Map.** 1996. 6.95 (*2-06-700071-3*, 71) Michelin.

***Roches.** Ed. by Carol Cuellar. 100p. (Orig.). (C). 1981. pap. text ed. 9.95 (*0-7692-0923-8*, VF0900) Warner Brothers.

Rochester: A Brief History. Blake McKelvey. 110p. 1984. lib. bdg. 59.95 (*0-88946-026-4*) E Mellen.

***Rochester: A Story Historical.** Jenny M. Parker. (Illus.). 412p. 1997. reprint ed. lib. bdg. 44.50 (*0-8328-6214-2*) Higginson Bk Co.

Rochester: City of the Prairie. Harriet W. Hodgson. 114p. 1994. pap. 16.95 (*0-89781-478-9*) Am Historical Pr.

Rochester: Portrait of a Restoration Poet. Vivian De Sola Pinto. LC 73-175707. (Select Bibliographies Reprint Ser.). 1977. reprint ed. 23.95 (*0-8369-6622-8*) Ayer.

Rochester: The Critical Heritage. Ed. by David Farley-Hills. 1978. 69.50 (*0-7100-7157-4*, RKP) Routledge.

Rochester: The Poems in Context. Marianne Thormahlen. LC 92-34379. 372p. (C). 1993. text ed. 59.95 (*0-521-44042-4*) Cambridge U Pr.

Rochester Conference, 1963 see Data Acquisition & Processing in Biology & Medicine: Proceedings

Rochester Conference, 1964 see Data Acquisition & Processing in Biology & Medicine: Proceedings

Rochester Dine-a-Mate. 256p. 1994. pap. 20.00 (*1-57393-006-7*) Dine-A-Mate.

***Rochester Dine-a-Mate Book.** 256p. 1996. pap. text ed. 25.00 (*1-57393-061-X*) Dine-A-Mate.

Rochester Forth Applications Conference, 1984: Proceedings. Ed. by Diane D. Ranocchia. 1984. pap. 25.00 (*0-914593-05-6*) Inst Appl Forth.

Rochester Forth Conference on Automated Instruments, 1991: Proceedings. Ed. by Chris Kasmark. 144p. 1991. pap. 30.00 (*0-914593-11-0*) Inst Appl Forth.

Rochester Forth Conference on Biomedical Applications, 1992: Proceedings. Ed. by Chris Kasmark. 118p. 1992. pap. 30.00 (*0-914593-12-9*) Inst Appl Forth.

Rochester Forth Conference on Embedded Systems, 1990: Proceedings. Ed. by Thomas Hess. 176p. 1990. pap. 30.00 (*0-914593-10-2*) Inst Appl Forth.

Rochester Forth Conference on Emerging Technology, 1995: Proceedings. Ed. by Lawrence P. Forsley. 144p. 1996. pap. 30.00 (*0-914593-15-3*) Inst Appl Forth.

Rochester Forth Conference on Industrial Automation, 1989: Proceedings. Ed. by Thomas Hess. 143p. 1989. pap. 25.00 (*0-914593-09-9*) Inst Appl Forth.

Rochester Forth Conference on Process Control, 1993: Proceedings. Ed. by Lawrence P. Forsley. 138p. 1993. pap. 30.00 (*0-914593-13-7*) Inst Appl Forth.

Rochester Forth Conference on Programming Environments, 1988: Proceedings of the Rochester Forth Conference. Ed. by Lawrence P. Forsley. 256p. 1988. pap. 25.00 (*0-914593-08-0*) Inst Appl Forth.

Rochester Forth Conference on Rapid Prototyping, 1994: Proceedings. Ed. by Lawrence P. Forsley. 123p. 1994. pap. 30.00 (*0-914593-14-5*) Inst Appl Forth.

Rochester Institute of Technology: Industrial Development & Educational Innovation in a American City. Dane R. Gordon. LC 82-6389. (Illus.). 450p. 1982. lib. bdg. 109.95 (*0-88946-150-3*) E Mellen.

Rochester Manual - Practical Patient Care: Medicine, Surgery, Pediatrics, OB-Gyn & Psychiatry. Karl A. Illig & Wendy C. Husser. (Illus.). 690p. Date not set. text ed. write for info. (*1-886128-07-3*) Laennec Pub.

Rochester, NH. Rochester Historical Society Staff. (Images of America Ser.). 1996. pap. 16.99 (*0-7524-0454-7*, Arcdia) Chalford.

Rochester, NY. (Streetfinder Ser.). (Illus.). 1995. pap. 12.95 (*0-528-91367-0*) Rand McNally.

Rochester on the Genesee: The Growth of a City. 2nd ed. Blake McKelvey. LC 93-12303. (New York Classics Ser.). (Illus.). 330p. (C). 1993. pap. text ed. 17.95 (*0-8156-2596-0*) Syracuse U Pr.

***Rochester's Best Places: The Indispensable Guide to Rochester's Best Restaurants, Nightlife, Museums & Shopping.** Francis R. Basile. (Illus.). 160p. 1997. pap. 12.95 (*0-9656691-0-6*) Backhouse Pr.

Rochester's Wife. D. E. Stevenson. 335p. 1976. lib. bdg. 25.95 (*0-89966-164-5*) Buccaneer Bks.

Rochestrivia: An Illuminating Look at Rochester. Peter Dobrovitz. (Illus.). 226p. (Orig.). 1984. pap. 9.95 (*0-930249-00-3*) Big Kids Pub.

Rocheworld. Robert L. Forward. 480p. 1990. mass mkt. 5.99 (*0-671-69869-9*) Baen Bks.

ROCI: Rauschenberg Overseas Culture Interchange. Jack Cowart et al. (Illus.). 199p. 1995. 65.00 (*3-7913-1147-6*, Pub. by Prestel GW) te Neues.

Rock. Daniel A. Birchmore. LC 95-20585. (Illus.). 32p. (J). (ps-3). 1997. 14.95 (*1-887813-03-9*) Cucumber Island.

Rock. Robert Doherty & Mayer. 384p. 1996. mass mkt. 5.99 (*0-440-22072-6*) Dell.

Rock. Mark Dunster. (Rin Ser.: Part 48). 1977. pap. 4.00 (*0-89642-008-6*) Linden Pubs.

Rock: A History of Alcatraz, the Fort - The Prison. Pierre Odier. (Illus.). 260p. 1982. 17.00 (*0-9611632-0-8*) Odier CA.

Rock: Making Musical Choices. Richard Peck. 174p. (Orig.). 1985. pap. 7.95 (*0-89084-297-3*, 025288) Bob Jones Univ Pr.

Rock: The True Story of Alcatraz. Lori Haskins. LC 96-11407. (Step into Reading Ser.: Step 4). (Illus.). (J). 1996. pap. 3.99 (*0-679-88120-4*); lib. bdg. 11.99 (*0-679-98120-9*) Random.

Rock: Tools & Technique. 2nd ed. Michael Benge & Duane Raleigh. LC 95-61192. (Illus.). 128p. (Orig.). 1997. reprint ed. pap. text ed. 11.95 (*1-887216-01-4*, 97004) Elk Mtn Pr.

Rock: Travelling to Uluru. Barry Hill. 304p. 1995. pap. 17.95 (*1-86373-712-X*) IPG Chicago.

Rock-a-By Baby. Taylor. LC 96-19519. 192p. (C). 1996. text ed. 65.00 (*0-415-91291-1*, Routledge NY) Routledge.

Rock-a-By Baby. Verta Taylor. LC 96-19519. 192p. (C). 1996. pap. 18.95 (*0-415-91292-X*, Routledge NY) Routledge.

Rock a Bye. expanded rev. ed. Grady-Sue L. Saxon. (Illus.). 1994. 15.00 (*0-9647959-0-6*) G S L Saxon.

Rock-a-Bye Babies. Anna Ross. (Sesame Street Baby Board Bks.). (Illus.). 12p. (J). (ps). 1994. 4.99 (*0-679-84740-5*) Random Bks Yng Read.

Rock-A-Bye Baby. Illus. by Wendy Straw. (Lullaby Book Ser.). 12p. (J). (ps). 1996. 3.99 (*0-88705-916-3*, Wshng Well Bks) Joshua Morris.

Rock-a-bye Baby Books & Cradle Set. Sam Williams. (Illus.). 10p. (J). (ps). 1992. pap. 19.95 (*0-525-44925-6*) Dutton Child Bks.

Rock a Bye Christmas (Christian Mother Goose) Marjorie Decker. 1991. 5.99 (*0-529-07082-0*, RD3) World Publng.

Rock-a-Bye Christmas Combos. Marjorie Decker. 1992. 15.99 incl. audio (*0-529-07467-2*, RD5) World Publng.

Rock-a-Bye Lambie Pie. Michel Bernstein. (Illus.). 32p. 1994. 6.95 (*0-8362-4727-2*) Andrews & McMeel.

Rock-a-Bye Prayers (Christian Mother Goose) Marjorie Decker. (J). 1990. kivar 7.99 (*0-529-06843-5*, RDZ) World Publng.

Rock-a-Bye Stories of Jesus (Christian Mother Goose) Marjorie Decker. (J). (ps-3). 1993. 5.99 (*0-529-10003-7*, RD6) World Publng.

Rock-a-Bye Whale. Florence P. Strange. LC 77-83196. (Illus.). (J). (gr. k-4). 1977. 11.95 (*0-931644-00-3*) Manzanita Pr.

Rock-a-Doodle-Doo. David B. Zaslow & Lawson F. Inada. (Shakin' Loose with Mother Goose Ser.: No. 2). (Illus.). 32p. (Orig.). (J). (ps-8). 1986. pap. 7.95 (*0-89411-005-5*) Kids Matter.

***Rock Addresses: Rock & Roll Hall of Fame & Museum.** 80p. 1996. 14.95 (*1-55550-686-0*) Universe.

Rock Against the Wind: African-American Poems & Letter of Love & Passion. Ed. by Lindsay Patterson. LC 95-30268. 224p. (Orig.). 1996. pap. 12.00 (*0-399-51982-3*, Perigee Bks) Berkley Pub.

Rock Albums of the Seventies: A Critical Guide. Robert Christgau. (Quality Paperbacks Ser.). Orig. Title: Christgau's Record Guide: Rock Albums of the 70's. 480p. 1990. reprint ed. pap. 15.95 (*0-306-80409-3*) Da Capo.

Rock Alteration as a Guide to Ore East Tintic District, Utah. Thomas S. Lovering & W. M. Stoll. LC 50-6493. (Economic Geology, Monograph Ser.: No. 1). 102p. reprint ed. pap. 29.10 (*0-317-27607-7*, 2014764) Bks Demand.

Rock & a Hard Place. Peter David. Ed. by Dave Stern. (Star Trek: The Next Generation Ser.: No. 10). 256p. 1991. mass mkt. 5.50 (*0-671-74142-X*) PB.

Rock & a Hard Place. Anthony G. Johnson. Date not set. pap. write for info. (*0-452-27208-4*, Plume) NAL-Dutton.

***Rock & A Hard Place, Vol. 1.** Piers Anthony. 1996. mass mkt. 5.99 (*0-8125-3486-7*) Tor Bks.

Rock & a Hard Place: A Contemporary Play about the Christ Viewed Through the Eyes of Simon Peter. Lee E. Shackleford & Robert Montgomery. 1994. pap. 8.99 (*0-8341-9101-6*, MP-750) Lillenas.

Rock & a Hard Place: One Boy's Triumphant Story. Anthony G. Johnson. 304p. 1994. pap. 4.99 (*0-451-18185-9*) NAL-Dutton.

Rock & Blues Guitar Pocketbook. pap. 0.95 (*0-87166-554-9*, 93710) Mel Bay.

Rock & Hawk: A Selection of Shorter Poems by Robinson Jeffers. Robinson Jeffers. Ed. by Robert Hass. LC 87-9612. 336p. 1987. 19.95 (*0-394-55769-7*) Random.

***Rock & Heavy Metal Drums, Bk. 1.** Dave Zubraski. 56p. 1997. 19.95 incl. cd-rom (*0-7119-3747-8*, AM 91525) Omnibus NY.

***Rock & Heavy Metal Drums, Bk. 2.** Dave Zubraski. 56p. 1997. 19.95 (*0-7119-3748-6*, AM 91526) Omnibus NY.

Rock & Metal Techniques. (Four Bass Superchops Ser.). 1992. pap. 12.95 incl. audio (*0-7935-1027-9*, 00660302) H Leonard.

Rock & Metal Techniques. (Four Bass Superchops Ser.). 1992. pap. 14.95 incl. audio compact disk (*0-7935-1028-7*, 00660303) H Leonard.

Rock & Mineral Analysis. Wesley M. Johnson & John A. Maxwell. LC 88-13724. 506p. (C). 1989. reprint ed. lib. bdg. 89.50 (*0-89464-341-X*) Krieger.

Rock & Minerals. Steve Parker. LC 93-12643. (Eyewitness Explorers Ser.). (Illus.). 64p. (J). (gr. 3 up). 1993. 9.95 (*1-56458-394-5*) DK Pub Inc.

Rock & Pop: Day by Day. Frank Laufenberg. 320p. 1994. lib. bdg. 43.00 (*0-8095-7619-8*) Borgo Pr.

Rock & Popular Music: Politics, Policies, Institutions. Ed. by Tony Bennett et al. LC 93-20233. (Culture Ser.). 1993. pap. write for info. (*0-415-06362-0*) Routledge.

Rock & Popular Music: Politics, Policies, Institutions. Ed. by Tony Bennett et al. LC 93-20233. (Culture Ser.). 320p. (C). 1993. pap. 17.95 (*0-415-06369-8*) Routledge.

Rock & Popular Music: Politics, Policies, Instruments. Ed. by Tony Bennett & Simon Frith. 320p. (C). (gr. 13 up). 1993. text ed. 62.95 (*0-415-06368-X*, Routledge NY) Routledge.

***Rock & Roll.** Paul Williams. Date not set. pap. write for info. (*0-688-08919-4*) Morrow.

Rock & Roll: A Social History. Paul Friedlander. LC 95-37864. (Illus.). 341p. (C). 1995. pap. text ed. 24.00 (*0-8133-2725-3*) Westview.

Rock & Roll: An Unruly History. Robert Palmer. LC 95-13367. (Illus.). 336p. 1995. 40.00 (*0-517-70050-6*, Harmony) Crown Pub Group.

Rock & Roll: Art & Anti-Art. Nathan Rubin. 252p. (C). 1995. per. 28.81 (*0-8403-8666-4*) Kendall-Hunt.

Rock & Roll: Its History & Stylistic Development. 2nd ed. Joe Stuessy. LC 93-19894. 432p. (C). 1994. pap. text ed. 41.33 (*0-13-782608-7*) P-H.

Rock & Roll: The One Hundred Best Singles. Paul Williams. 224p. 1993. pap. 10.95 (*0-88184-966-9*) Carroll & Graf.

***Rock & Roll: The 100 Best Singles.** Paul Williams. 10.95 (*0-7867-0966-9*) Carroll & Graf.

Rock & Roll Almanac. Mark Bego. 288p. 1996. 12.95 (*0-02-860432-6*) Macmillan Info.

Rock & Roll Birthday Book. Ed. by Randy Rucker & Linda Rucker. 144p. (Orig.). 1991. pap. 9.95 (*0-944445-03-9*) Musi-Key.

***Rock & Roll Call: The History & Mystery Behind Rock Names.** Dean M. Boland. (Illus.). 400p. (Orig.). 1997. pap. 6.95 (*0-9646452-9-7*) Dowling Pr.

Rock & Roll Classics. 72p. 1992. pap. 12.95 (*0-7935-1140-2*, 00699332) H Leonard.

Rock & Roll Collectibles. Greg Moore. LC 93-91812. 112p. 1993. pap. 22.95 (*0-9639495-0-0*) G Moore Pubng.

Rock & Roll Diner: Popular American Cooking, Classic Rock & Roll Music. Sharon O'Connor. LC 96-76188. (Sharon O'Connor's Menus & Music Ser.). 248p. 1996. 24.95 incl. audio compact disk (*1-883914-12-4*); boxed, pap. 28.00 incl. audio compact disk (*1-883914-13-2*); boxed, pap. 25.00 incl. audio (*1-883914-14-0*) Menus & Music.

Rock & Roll Flyer. Robert Rufe. 96p. 1990. pap. text ed. 8.00 (*0-9627196-0-9*) Aremar Pubns.

Rock & Roll Great Britain. Fodor's Travel Staff. 1997. pap. 18.00 (*0-679-03118-9*) Fodors Travel.

***Rock & Roll Guitar Sourcebook.** Ed. by Aaron Stang. 180p. (Orig.). 1996. pap. text ed. 19.95 (*1-57623-495-9*, GF9519) Warner Brothers.

Rock & Roll Hall Fame & Muse. Date not set. pap. 19.95 (*0-7893-0048-6*) Universe.

Rock & Roll Movie Encyclopedia of the 1950s. Mark T. McGee. LC 89-43657. (Illus.). 224p. 1990. lib. bdg. 32.50 (*0-89950-500-7*) McFarland & Co.

***Rock & Roll Rainforest.** Pamela Platt. 110p. (J). 1996. pap. 10.95 (*0-7022-2773-0*, Pub. by Univ Queensland Pr AT) Intl Spec Bk.

Rock & Roll Recall. Michael Budds & Marian M Ohman. 1993. 33.00 (*0-536-58337-4*) Ginn Pr.

Rock & Roll Revealed: The Outrageous Lives of Rock's Biggest Stars. Maryanne Melloan. (Illus.). 120p. 1993. 14.98 (*0-8317-5159-2*) Smithmark.

Rock & Roll Saxophone. John Laughter. 64p. 1989. pap. text ed. 17.95 incl. audio (*0-931759-36-6*) Centerstream Pub.

Rock & Roll Story. Charles T. Brown. (Illus.). 128p. 1986. 13.50 (*0-13-782227-8*) P-H.

Rock & Roll Waltz. (Ballroom Dance Ser.). 1986. lib. bdg. 59.95 (*0-8490-3290-3*) Gordon Pr.

Rock & Roll Waltz. (Ballroom Dance Ser.). 1985. lib. bdg. 60.00 (*0-87700-782-9*) Revisionist Pr.

Rock & Roll Years. 1990. 29.99 (*0-517-02638-4*) Random Hse Value.

Rock & Roses: Selected Essays Written by Some of the Best Climbers in the World. Ed. by Mike Vause. (Illus.). 144p. (Orig.). 1990. pap. 11.95 (*1-879415-01-1*) Mtn n Air Bks.

***Rock & Royalty.** Gianni Versace et al. (Illus.). 272p. 1997. 75.00 (*0-7892-0177-1*) Abbeville Pr.

Rock & Soil Mechanics. Derski. (Developments in Geotechnical Engineering Ser.: Vol. 48). 1989. 266.25 (*0-444-98950-1*) Elsevier.

Rock & Soil Rheology. 1988. 50.95 (*0-387-18841-X*) Spr-Verlag.

Rock & the Pop Narcotic. 2nd rev. ed. Joe Carducci. (Illus.). 532p. 1995. pap. 18.00 (*1-880985-11-X*) Two Thirteen Sixty-one.

Rock & Wall Paintings of Sri Lanka. Senake Bandaranayake. (C). 1986. 145.00 (*0-8364-2281-3*, Pub. by Navrang) S Asia.

***Rock & Water.** Richard Kell. 96p. 9300. pap. 11.95 (*1-873790-34-1*) Dufour.

***Rock & Water.** Aonghas MacNeacail. 1990. 12.00 (*0-7486-6065-8*, Pub. by Polygon UK) Subterranean Co.

Rock & Water Garden Expert. D. G. Hessayon. (Expert Ser.). (Illus.). 128p. 1993. pap. 12.95 (*0-903505-38-X*, Pub. by Expert Bks UK) Sterling.

Rock & Woodstock. P. Smart & T. P. Moynihan. LC 94-67756. (Illus.). 192p. 1994. pap. 13.00 (*0-935796-54-1*) Purple Mnt Pr.

Rock Around the Bloc: A History of Rock Music in Eastern Europe & the Soviet Union, 1954-1988. Timothy W. Ryback. (Illus.). 304p. 1990. 25.00 (*0-19-505633-7*) OUP.

***Rock Around the Classics: Innovative Ways of Playing Some of the Most Popular Classical Songs Ever.** Dave Celentano. (Illus.). 80p. (Orig.). 1996. pap. text ed. 19.95 incl. audio compact disk (*1-57424-039-0*) Centerstream Pub.

***Rock Art.** PBC International Staff. 1993. pap. 24.95 (*0-688-13022-4*) Morrow.

Rock Art: A Collection of CDs, Albums & Posters. Spencer Drate. LC 93-4834. (Illus.). 1994. pap. 27.50 (*0-86636-277-0*) PBC Intl Inc.

Rock Art & Cultural Resource Management. Georgia Lee. LC 91-33681. (Illus.). 72p. (Orig.). (C). 1991. pap. text ed. 6.95 (*0-937523-04-6*) Wormwood Pr.

Rock Art & Prehistory. Ed. by Paul Bahn & Andree Rosenfeld. (Illus.). 144p. 1991. pap. 27.00 (*0-946897-32-8*, Pub. by Oxbow Bks UK) David Brown.

***Rock Art & the Prehistory of Atlantic Europe: Signing the Land.** Richard Bradley. LC 96-51119. 296p. (C). 1997. pap. write for info. (*0-415-16536-9*); text ed. write for info. (*0-415-16535-0*) Routledge.

***Rock Art in Kumaon Himalaya.** Yashodhar Mathpal. (Illus.). xxii, 92p. 1995. 52.00 (*81-7305-057-0*, Pub. by Aryan Bks Intl II) Nataraj Bks.

Rock Art in the Old World. Ed. by Michel Lorblanchet. (C). 1992. 78.00 (*0-685-66244-6*, Pub. by UBS Pubs Dist II) S Asia.

Rock Art of Africa. Carson I. Ritchie. LC 76-24614. (Illus.). 157p. 1978. 25.00 (*0-87982-024-1*) Art Alliance.

Rock Art of Africa. Carson I. Ritchie. 25.00 (*0-8453-1753-9*, Cornwall Bks) Assoc Univ Prs.

Rock Art of Bandelier National Monument. Arthur H. Rohn et al. LC 88-4736. (Illus.). 170p. 1989. pap. 32.50 (*0-8263-1052-4*) U of NM Pr.

Rock Art of Easter Island: Symbols of Power, Prayers to the Gods. Georgia Lee. LC 92-47034. (UCLA Institute of Archaeology Publications: No. 17). (Illus.). 225p. (C). 1992. 35.00 (*0-917956-74-5*) UCLA Arch.

Rock Art of Kentucky. Fred E. Coy, Jr. LC 96-20466. (Illus.). 176p. 1997. 34.95 (*0-8131-1986-3*) U Pr of Ky.

Rock Art of Owens Valley, California. fac. ed. Jay C. VonWerlhof. (Reports of the University of California Archaeological Survey: No. 65). (Illus.). 136p. 1965. reprint ed. pap. 12.10 (*1-55567-379-1*) Coyote Press.

Rock Art of Texas Indians. W. W. Newcomb. 1996. pap. text ed. 34.95 (*0-292-74326-2*) U of Tex Pr.

Rock Art of Texas Indians. Forrest Kirkland & W. W. Newcomb, Jr. (Illus.). 253p. 1996. reprint ed. pap. 34.95 (*0-292-75326-8*) U of Tex Pr.

Rock Art of the American Indian. 5th ed. Campbell Grant. LC 92-11467. (Illus.). 208p. 1981. reprint ed. pap. 14.95 (*0-89646-084-3*) Vistabooks.

Rock Art of the American Southwest. Scott Thybony. 1994. 29.50 (*1-55868-163-9*) Gr Arts Ctr Pub.

***Rock Art of the Dreamtime.** Josephine Flood. 1997. pap. 26.50 (*0-207-18908-0*) HarpC.

***Rock Art of the Dreamtime.** Josephine Flood. (Illus.). 328p. 1997. pap. 26.50 (*0-207-18903-X*) HarperColl Wrld.

Rock Art of the Western Canyon. Jane Day. 1988. pap. 10.95 (*0-916278-66-2*) Denver Mus Natl Hist.

Rock Art of Utah: A Study from the Donald Scott Collection. rev. ed. Polly Schaafsma. LC 93-2052. (Illus.). 208p. 1993. reprint ed. pap. 19.95 (*0-87480-435-3*) U of Utah Pr.

***Rock Art Studies: News of the World I.** Ed. by Paul G. Bahn & Angelo Fossati. (Oxbow Monographs in Archaeology: No. 72). (Illus.). 229p. 1996. pap. 45.00 (*1-900188-21-X*, Pub. by Oxbow Bks UK) David Brown.

***Rock Art Studies: The Post-Stylistic Era: or Where Do We Go from Here?** Ed. by Michel Lorblanchet & Paul Bahn. (Oxbow Monographs in Archaeology: No. 35). (Illus.). 220p. 1994. pap. 35.00 (*0-946897-63-8*, Pub. by Oxbow Bks UK) David Brown.

***Rock Art Studies in the Americas.** Ed. by Jack Steinbring. (Oxbow Monographs in Archaeology: No. 45). (Illus.). 192p. 1995. pap. 35.00 (*0-946897-76-X*, Pub. by Oxbow Bks UK) David Brown.

Rock Art Symbols of the Southwest: Southwestern Rock Art Symbols. Rick Harris. (Illus.). 32p. 1995. pap. 1.25 (*0-935810-58-7*) Primer Pubs.

Rock at Great Depth: Rock Mechanics & Rock Physics at Great Depth - Proceedings of an International Symposium, Pau, 28 - 31 August 1989, 3 vols. Ed. by Vincent Maury & D. Fourmaintraux. (Illus.). 1620p. (C). 1989. text ed. 250.00 (*90-6191-975-4*, Pub. by A A Balkema NE) Ashgate Pub Co.

R

Rock Ballads. 160p. 1994. otabind 14.95 (*0-7935-3317-1*, 00311673) H Leonard.

Rock Band Handbook: Everything You Need to Know to Get a Band Together & Take It on the Road. Kathryn Lineberger. LC 96-11444. 160p. 1996. pap. 10.00 (*0-399-52237-9*) Berkley Pub.

***Rock Bass Handbook.** Dan Gutt. 1993. 9.95 incl. audio compact disk (*0-7866-2708-5*, 94366BCD) Mel Bay.

***Rock Bass Lines, Bk. 3.** Ed. by Aaron Stang. 52p. (Orig.). (C). 1987. pap. text ed. 8.95 (*0-7692-0951-3*, IF0296) Warner Brothers.

Rock Bass Technique. Mike Hiland. 1993. 8.95 (*0-87166-846-7*, 94332); audio 9.98 (*0-87166-802-5*, 94332) Mel Bay.

***Rock Bass Technique.** Mike Hiland. 1993. 17.95 incl. audio (*0-7866-0991-5*, 94332P) Mel Bay.

***Rock Beneath Vol. 1: 100 Years Ago in Webster Groves.** Mary J. Mahley & Toni McCoy. (Illus.). 195p. (Orig.). 1996. pap. 29.95 (*0-9654641-0-5*) Century Registry.

Rock Blasting & Explosives Engineering: A Textbook for Students & a Handbook for Scientists & Engineers Covering the Science & Engineering of the Industrial Use of Explosives with Major Emphasis on Rock Blasting. Per A. Persson et al. LC 93-28150. 560p. 1993. 77.00 (*0-8493-8978-X*) CRC Pr.

Rock Bolting-Theory & Application in Mining & Underground Construction: Proceedings of the International Conference, Abisko, Sweden, 28 August 2 September 1983. Ed. by Ove Stephansson. 640p. 1984. text ed. 160.00 (*90-6191-514-7*, Pub. by A A Balkema NE) Ashgate Pub Co.

Rock Bottom: An American Heartland Farm-Town & Family from Settlement Through the Great Depression. John M. Wilkinson. (Illus.). 260p. (Orig.). (C). 1993. pap. 14.50 (*0-9637091-0-0*) J M Wilkinson.

Rock Bottom: Crack Cocaine. 140p. (Orig.). 1996. pap. text ed. 7.50 (*0-9651612-1-8*) Nrthstar Pub.

Rock Bottom: Dark Moments in Music Babylon. Pamela Des Barre. 360p. 1996. 24.95 (*0-312-14853-4*) St Martin.

Rock Breakage by Blasting. M. I. Petrosyan. Ed. by A. K. Ghose. (Illus.). 152p. (C). 1994. text ed. 55.00 (*90-6191-902-9*, Pub. by A A Balkema NE) Ashgate Pub Co.

***Rock Burst.** Bert Russell & Marie Russell. LC 97-9491. (Living the West Ser.). 1998. write for info. (*0-89301-197-5*) U of Idaho Pr.

Rock Burst: Another Bert Russell Book. Bert Russell & Marie Russell. LC 94-77720. (Oral History Ser.: Bk. 4). (Illus.). (Orig.). pap. write for info. (*0-930344-11-1*) Lacon Pubs.

Rock Carvings of Northern Britain. Stan Beckensall. 1989. pap. 25.00 (*0-85263-760-8*, Pub. by Shire UK) St Mut.

Rock Chalk Dreams: Adapted from "Cuddy's Baby" adapted ed. Margaret H. McCarter. (Illus.). 96p. Date not set. pap. 14.95 (*0-9649023-0-3*) Hist Advent Pubng.

Rock Characterization, Testing & Monitoring: ISRM Suggested Methods. Ed. by E. T. Brown. LC 80-49711. 200p. 1981. 97.00 (*0-08-027308-4*, Pub. by Pergamon Repr UK) Franklin.

***Rock Child Novel of Journey.** Blevins. Date not set. 22.95 (*0-312-86400-0*) St Martin.

Rock Chord Guide. Harvey Vinson. LC 70-85514. (Illus.). (Orig.). 1970. pap. 12.95 (*0-8256-2147-X*, AM10612) Music Sales.

Rock Chords for Guitar. 32p. 1986. pap. 6.95 (*0-7935-4850-0*, 00689649) H Leonard.

***Rock City Barns: A Passing Era.** David B. Jenkins. LC 96-96410. (Illus.). 160p. 1996. 39.95 (*0-9652308-0-5*) Free Spirit Pr.

Rock Classes, Vol. 3. T. Tucker. 376p. 1994. pap. text ed. 75.00 (*0-471-94273-1*) Wiley.

Rock Classics: With Notes & Tablature. 104p. 1992. otabind 17.95 (*0-7935-0358-2*, 00694760) H Leonard.

Rock Classification Systems for Engineering Purposes, STP 984. Ed. by Louis Kirkaldie. LC 88-5091. (Special Technical Publication (STP) Ser.). (Illus.). 175p. 1988. text ed. 29.00 (*0-8031-0988-1*, 04-984000-38) ASTM.

Rock Climbing. John Barry. (Illus.). 128p. 1989. pap. 18.95 (*0-8117-2231-7*) Stackpole.

***Rock Climbing.** Larry D. Brimner. LC 96-28943. (First Bk.). (J). 1997. lib. bdg. 21.00 (*0-531-20269-0*) Watts.

***Rock Climbing.** Larry D. Brimner. (First Bks.). 1997. pap. text ed. 6.95 (*0-531-15860-8*) Watts.

Rock Climbing. Bob Italia. LC 94-12496. (Action Sports Library Ser.). 1994. lib. bdg. 14.98 (*1-56239-342-1*) Abdo & Dghtrs.

Rock Climbing. Peter Livesey. (Illus.). 160p. 1990. 21.95 (*0-938567-22-5*) Cloudcap.

Rock Climbing. Bill Lund. LC 96-24724. (Extreme Sports Ser.). 1996. write for info. (*1-56065-429-5*) Capstone Pr.

***Rock Climbing.** Bill Lund. (Extreme Sports Ser.). (Illus.). 48p. (J). (gr. 3-7). 1996. 18.40 (*0-516-20256-1*) Childrens.

Rock Climbing. Phil Watts. LC 95-38817. (Outdoor Pursuits Ser.). (Illus.). 144p. (Orig.). 1996. pap. 13.95 (*0-87322-814-6*, PWAT0814) Human Kinetics.

***Rock Climbing: A Trailside Guide.** Don Mellor. LC 96-52821. (Trailside Series Guide). (Illus.). 192p. 1997. pap. 17.95 (*0-393-31653-X*, Norton Paperbks) Norton.

Rock Climbing Basics. Turlough Johnson. LC 94-38238. (Illus.). 1995. 16.95 (*0-8117-2420-4*) Stackpole.

Rock Climbing Colorado. Stewart Green. LC 95-40241. (Falcon Guide Ser.). (Illus.). 470p. 1995. pap. 21.95 (*1-56044-334-0*) Falcon Pr MT.

***Rock Climbing Guide to Lake Tahoe Basin.** rev. ed. Mike Carville. (Illus.). 1997. pap. write for info. (*1-57540-088-X*) Chockstone Pr.

***Rock Climbing in the Wasatch Range.** 2nd rev. ed. Bret Ruckman & Stuart Ruckman. (Illus.). 1997. pap. write for info. (*1-57540-090-1*) Chockstone Pr.

***Rock Climbing Montana.** Ed. by Randall Green. LC 96-49739. (Falcon Guides Ser.). (Illus.). 304p. (Orig.). 1997. pap. 18.95 (*1-56044-465-7*) Falcon Pr MT.

Rock Climbing New Mexico & Texas. Dennis Jackson. LC 96-38829. (Illus.). 256p. (Orig.). 1996. pap. 22.95 (*1-56044-483-5*) Falcon Pr MT.

Rock Climbing Rocky Mountain National Park: The Crags. Richard Rossiter. (Illus.). 277p. 1996. pap. 20.00 (*0-934641-34-X*) Chockstone Pr.

Rock Climbing Techniques. Steve Ashton. (Illus.). 127p. 1991. pap. 19.95 (*1-85223-228-5*, Pub. by Crowood Pr UK) Trafalgar.

Rock Climbing the South Platte. 2nd rev. ed. Peter Hubbel. (Illus.). (Orig.). 1997. pap. write for info. (*1-57540-008-1*) Chockstone Pr.

***Rock Climbs in the White Mountains of New Hampshire (East Volume)** 3rd ed. Edward R. Webster. 1996. write for info. (*0-9653199-0-3*) Mtn Imagery.

Rock Climbs of Tuolumne Meadows. 3rd ed. Don Reid & Chris Falkenstein. (Illus.). 184p. (Orig.). 1992. pap. 20.00 (*0-934641-47-1*) Chockstone Pr.

Rock Collecting. 2nd ed. Roma Gans. LC 83-46170. (Let's-Read-&-Find-Out Science Bk.). (Illus.). 32p. (J). (gr. k-3). 1984. lib. bdg. 14.89 (*0-690-04266-3*, Crowell Jr Bks) HarpC Child Bks.

Rock Collecting. Roma Gans. LC 83-46170. (Trophy Let's-Read-&-Find-Out Science Bk.). (Illus.). 32p. (J). (ps-3). 1987. reprint ed. pap. 4.95 (*0-06-445063-5*, Trophy) HarpC Child Bks.

Rock Creek Crossings: Six Generations on the Kansas Prairie. Anne Fitzgerald. 72p. 1991. 13.95 (*1-880652-08-0*) Wichita Eagle.

Rock Cried Out. Ellen Douglas. LC 79-87474. (Voices of the South Ser.). 350p. 1994. pap. 11.95 (*0-8071-1931-8*) La State U Pr.

Rock Cycle - Understanding the Earth's Crust. J. R. Blueford. 1992. 22.95 (*1-56638-103-7*) Math Sci Nucleus.

Rock Dreams. Guy Peellaert & Nik Cohn. LC 73-7289. (Illus.). 176p. 1982. 19.95 (*0-394-52870-0*) Knopf.

***Rock Drum Basics: Steps One & Two Combined.** Joe Testa & Mike Finkelstein. (Ultimate Beginner Ser.). 48p. (Orig.). 1996. pap. text ed. 12.95 (*1-57623-561-0*, UBSBK002CD) Warner Brothers.

Rock Engineering Applications. John A. Franklin. 432p. 1991. text ed. 58.00 (*0-07-021889-7*) McGraw.

Rock Engineering for Foundations & Slopes: Proceedings of a Specialty Conference, University of Colorado, Boulder, Colorado, August 15-18, 1976, 2 vols., 1. Conference on Rock Engineering for Foundations & Slopes, University of Colorado. LC 77-368041. reprint ed. pap. 112.30 (*0-317-10584-1*, 2019552) Bks Demand.

Rock Engineering for Foundations & Slopes: Proceedings of a Specialty Conference, University of Colorado, Boulder, Colorado, August 15-18, 1976, 2 vols., 2. Conference on Rock Engineering for Foundations & Slopes, University of Colorado. LC 77-368041. reprint ed. pap. 67.50 (*0-317-10585-X*) Bks Demand.

Rock Engineering Systems: Theory & Practice. John A. Hudson. LC 92-18182. (Ellis Horwood Series in Civil Engineering). 1992. 53.95 (*0-13-782624-9*, Pub. by Tavistock-E Horwood UK) Routledge Chapman & Hall.

Rock Engravings of Southern Africa. Thomas A. Dowson. (Illus.). 140p. 1994. 57.50 (*1-86814-120-9*) Ind U Pr.

Rock Eras: Interpretations of Music & Society, 1954-1984. Jim Curtis. LC 87-72615. 363p. 1987. 34.95 (*0-87972-368-8*); pap. 17.95 (*0-87972-369-6*) Bowling Green Univ Popular Press.

Rock Facts. Fred L. Worth. LC 85-10261. 428p. reprint ed. pap. 122.00 (*0-7837-1363-0*, 2041511) Bks Demand.

Rock Farm. Catherine Bowman. LC 96-17261. (Illus.). 64p. (Orig.). 1996. pap. 12.95 (*0-87905-745-9*) Gibbs Smith Pub.

Rock Fences of the Bluegrass. Carolyn Murray-Wooley & Karl B. Raitz. LC 91-22584. (Illus.). 240p. 1992. 35.00 (*0-8131-1762-3*) U Pr of Ky.

Rock File: Making It in the Music Business. Ed. by Norton York. (Illus.). 304p. 1992. pap. 29.95 (*0-19-816248-0*) OUP.

Rock Finds a Friend. Randall J. Wiethorn. (Illus.). 32p. (J). 1991. pap. 5.95 (*0-88138-110-1*, Green Tiger S&S) S&S Childrens.

Rock Finds a Friend. Randall J. Wiethorn. (J). 1998. 5.95 (*0-671-75289-8*, S&S Bks Young Read) S&S Childrens.

Rock Folk. Michael Lydon. 1990. pap. 9.95 (*0-8065-1206-7*, Citadel Pr) Carol Pub Group.

Rock for Erosion Control. Ed. by Charles H. McElroy & David A. Lienhart. LC 92-44625. (ASTM Special Technical Publication Ser.: No. 1177). (Illus.). 150p. 1993. 46.00 (*0-8031-1489-3*, 04-011770-38) ASTM.

Rock Formation: Music, Technology, & the Production of Culture. Steve Jones. (Foundations of Popular Culture Ser.: Vol. 3). 212p. (C). 1992. text ed. 39.95 (*0-8039-4442-X*); pap. text ed. 17.95 (*0-8039-4443-8*) Sage.

Rock Formations & Unusual Geologic Formations. Jon Erickson. (Changing Earth Ser.). (Illus.). 192p. 1992. lib. bdg. 24.95 (*0-685-57570-5*) Facts on File.

Rock Formations & Unusual Geologic Structures: Exploring the Earth's Surface. Jon Erickson. LC 92-32097. 208p. 1993. 24.95 (*0-8160-2589-4*) Facts on File.

***Rock Forming Minerals, Vol. 1.** Deer. 1986. text ed. write for info. (*0-582-46521-4*, Pub. by Longman UK) Longman.

***Rock-Forming Minerals: Non Silicates, Vol. 5B.** 2nd ed. Deer. 1995. 165.08 (*0-582-30093-2*, Pub. by Longman UK) Longman.

***Rock Forming Minerals in Thin Section.** Pichler & Schmitt-Riegsaf. (Illus.). 240p. (Orig.). 1997. pap. text ed. 34.50 (*0-412-64460-6*, Chap & Hall NY) Chapman & Hall.

Rock Foundation: A Foundational Course for a Strong Christian Life. Lawrence Kennedy. Ed. by Margaret J. Kinney. 80p. 1992. pap. 9.95 (*1-880563-02-9*) FAME Pub.

Rock Foundations. LC 95-49328. (Technical Engineering & Design Guides as Adapted from the U. S. Army Corps of Engineers Ser.: No. 16). 134p. 1996. 36.00 (*0-7844-0136-5*) Am Soc Civil Eng.

Rock Foundations: Proceedings of the International Workshop on Rock Foundations, Tokyo, Japan, 30 September 1995. Ed. by R. Yoshinaka & K. Kikuchi. (Illus.). 600p. (C). 1995. text ed. 120.00 (*90-5410-562-3*, Pub. by A A Balkema NE) Ashgate Pub Co.

Rock Fracture Mechanics. Ed. by H. P. Rossmanith. (CISM International Centre for Mechanical Sciences Ser.: No. 275). 484p. 1983. 72.95 (*0-387-81747-6*) Spr-Verlag.

Rock Fracture Mechanics: Principles, Design, & Applications. Barry N. Whittaker et al. LC 92-21001. (Developments in Geotechnical Engineering Ser.: No. 71). 570p. 1992. 219.75 (*0-444-89684-8*) Elsevier.

Rock Fractures & Fluid Flow: Contemporary Understanding & Applications. National Research Council Staff. 568p. (C). 1996. text ed. 74.95 (*0-309-04996-2*) Natl Acad Pr.

***Rock Fragmentation by Blasting: Proceedings of the 5th International Symposium, FRAGBLAST-5, Montreal, 26-29 August 1996.** B. Mohanty. 472p. 1996. 120.00 (*90-5410-824-X*, Pub. by A A Balkema NE) Ashgate Pub Co.

Rock Fragmentation by Blasting: Proceedings, 4th International Symposium, Vienna, Austria, July 1993. Hans P. Rossmanith. (Illus.). 532p. 1993. text ed. 115.00 (*90-5410-316-7*, Pub. by A A Balkema NE) Ashgate Pub Co.

Rock from Which You Were Hewn. Donal O'Donovan. (Illus.). 224p. (Orig.). 1989. pap. 12.50 (*0-9623863-0-8*) D ODonovan.

Rock Garden & Its Plants: From Grotto to Alpine House. Grahm S. Thomas. LC 89-4268. (Illus.). 245p. 1989. 34.95 (*0-88192-139-4*) Sagapr.

Rock Garden in the South. Elizabeth Lawrence. Ed. by Nancy Goodwin & Allen Lacy. LC 89-49426. 239p. 1990. text ed. 21.95 (*0-8223-0986-6*) Duke.

Rock Garden Month-by-Month. Michael Jefferson-Brown & Michael Upward. (Illus.). 144p. 1996. 24.95 (*0-7153-0232-9*, Pub. by D & C Pub UK) Sterling.

***Rock Garden Plants.** DK Publishing Inc. Staff. LC 96-47941. (Eyewitness Gardens Handbks.). 192p. 1997. 17.95 (*0-7894-1455-4*) DK Pub Inc.

Rock Garden Plants of North America: An Anthology from the Bulletin of the North American Rock Garden Society. North American Rock Gardening Society Staff. Ed. by Jane McGary. LC 95-23104. (Illus.). 520p. 1996. 49.95 (*0-88192-343-5*) Timber.

Rock Gardening: A Guide to Growing Alpines & Other Wildflowers in the American Garden. H. Lincoln Foster. LC 82-16994. (Illus.). 466p. 1982. reprint ed. pap. 24.95 (*0-917304-29-2*) Timber.

Rock Gardens. John Kelly. (Planning & Planting Ser.). (Illus.). 96p. 1996. 12.95 (*0-7063-7489-4*, Pub. by Ward Lock UK) Sterling.

***Rock Gardens.** New York Botanical Garden Staff. (Serious Gardner Ser.). (Illus.). 1997. pap. 23.00 (*0-614-27227-0*, C P Pubs) Crown Pub Group.

Rock Gardens: A Firefly Gardener's Guide. Katherine Ferguson. (Illus.). 96p. 1996. pap. text ed. 10.95 (*1-895565-94-4*, Pub. by Camden Hse CN) Firefly Bks Ltd.

Rock Geochemistry in Mineral Exploration. G. J. Govett. (Handbook of Mineral Exploration Geology Ser.: Vol. 3). 462p. 1983. 228.50 (*0-444-42021-5*) Elsevier.

Rock Glaciers. Ed. by John R. Giardino et al. (Illus.). 416p. 1987. text ed. 65.00 (*0-04-551139-X*) Routledge Chapman & Hall.

Rock Grouting & Diaphragm Wall. J. Verfel. (Developments in Geotechnical Engineering Ser.: No. 55). 532p. 1989. 222.50 (*0-444-98890-4*) Elsevier.

Rock Grows Up: The Pacific Northwest up Close & Personal. Randi S. Goodrich & Michael S. Goodrich. (Illus.). 56p. (Orig.). (J). (gr. 4-6). 1996. pap. 9.95 (*0-9651101-0-9*) GeoQuest Publns.

Rock Guitar. Ed. by Mark Phillips. (Illus.). 93p. (Orig.). 1990. pap. text ed. 10.95 (*0-89524-371-7*) Cherry Lane.

Rock Guitar Chord Finder. pap. 4.95 (*0-7935-1694-3*, 00697240) H Leonard.

Rock Guitar Jams. pap. 12.95 incl. audio (*0-7935-3003-2*, 00696531) H Leonard.

Rock Guitar Jams. pap. 14.95 incl. audio compact disk (*0-7935-3004-0*, 00696532) H Leonard.

Rock Guitar Manuscript Book. 2.50 (*1-56222-148-5*, 94548) Mel Bay.

***Rock Hall: A Narrative History.** Shirley G. Hibbard & Friends of Rock Hall, Inc. Staff. LC 97-17295. 1997. write for info. (*0-486-26420-3*) Dover.

Rock Hard: The Autobiography of a Former Alcatraz Inmate. Leon W. Thompson. Ed. by Eric Tobias. vii, 400p. (Orig.). 1994. pap. 6.99 (*0-671-74363-5*) PB.

***Rock Hardware: 40 Years of Rock Instrumentation.** Ed. by Paul Trynka. (Illus.). 160p. 1996. pap. 24.95 (*0-87930-428-6*) Miller Freeman.

Rock Harp. Tony Glover. 1981. pap. 14.95 (*0-8256-0230-0*, OK63768, Oak) Music Sales.

Rock Hits: Alto Saxophone. 1991. pap. 4.95 (*0-7935-0682-4*, 00847204) H Leonard.

Rock Hits: Flute. 1991. pap. 4.95 (*0-7935-0681-6*, 00847202) H Leonard.

Rock Hits: Trombone. 1991. pap. 4.95 (*0-7935-0684-0*, 00847206) H Leonard.

Rock Hits: Trumpet. 1991. pap. 4.95 (*0-7935-0683-2*, 00847205) H Leonard.

Rock Hits for One, Two, or Three Guitars. 1993. pap. 14.95 incl. audio compact disk (*0-7935-2186-6*, 00697273) H Leonard.

Rock Hits for One, Two, or Three Guitars. 1985. pap. 12.95 incl. audio (*0-7935-2565-9*) H Leonard.

Rock Hudson: A Bio-Bibliography. Brenda S. Royce. LC 94-39511. (Bio-Bibliographies in the Performing Arts Ser.: Vol. 61). 336p. 1995. text ed. 59.95 (*0-313-28672-8*, Greenwood Pr) Greenwood.

Rock Hudson: His Story. Rock Hudson & Sara Davidson. (Illus.). 384p. 1987. mass mkt. 4.50 (*0-380-70292-4*) Avon.

Rock in a Weary Land: The African Methodist Episcopal Church During the Civil War & Reconstruction. fac. ed. Clarence E. Walker. LC 81-11731. 169p. reprint ed. pap. 48.20 (*0-7837-7748-5*, 2047504) Bks Demand.

Rock Inscriptions & Graffiti Project: Catalogue of Inscriptions, 1. Compiled by Michael E. Stone. LC 92-33418. (Society of Biblical Literature Resources for Biblical Study: No. 28-29). 1992. pap. 19.95 (*1-55540-791-9*) Scholars Pr GA.

Rock Inscriptions & Graffiti Project: Catalogue of Inscriptions, 2. Compiled by Michael E. Stone. LC 92-33418. (Society of Biblical Literature Resources for Biblical Study: No. 28-29). 1992. pap. 19.95 (*1-55540-793-5*) Scholars Pr GA.

Rock Inscriptions & Graffiti Project: Catalogue of Inscriptions, Vol. 1. Ed. by Michael E. Stone. LC 92-33418. (Society of Biblical Literature Resources for Biblical Study: No. 28-29). 282p. 1992. 29.95 (*1-55540-790-0*, 06 03 28) Scholars Pr GA.

Rock Inscriptions & Graffiti Project: Catalogue of Inscriptions, Vol. 2. Compiled by Michael E. Stone. LC 92-33418. (Society of Biblical Literature Resources for Biblical Study: No. 28-29). 244p. 1992. 29.95 (*1-55540-792-7*, 06 03 29) Scholars Pr GA.

***Rock Inscriptions & Graffiti Project: Catalogue of Inscriptions Vol. 3: Inscriptions 6001-8500.** Ed. by Michael E. Stone. 248p. 1994. 29.95 (*1-55540-945-8*, 060331); pap. 19.95 (*1-55540-946-6*) Scholars Pr GA.

Rock Island: Historical Indian Archaeology in the Northern Lake Michigan Basin. Ronald J. Mason. LC 85-12661. (MCJA Special Paper Ser.: No. 6). 228p. reprint ed. pap. 65.00 (*0-7837-1341-X*, 2041489) Bks Demand.

Rock Island & Tennessee Pass. Michael Doty et al. LC 70-102682. (Colorado Rail Annual Ser.: No. 17). (Illus.). 264p. 1987. 35.95 (*0-918654-17-3*) CO RR Mus.

Rock Island Color Guide to Freight & Passenger Equipment. Hile et al. (Illus.). 1995. 49.95 (*1-878887-48-3*) Morning NJ.

Rock Island in Color Vol. 1: 1948-1964, Set. Lloyd E. Stagner. (Illus.). 128p. 1994. 49.95 (*1-878887-37-8*) Morning NJ.

Rock Island in Color Vol. 2: 1965-1980, Set. Bill Marvel. (Illus.). 1995. 49.95 (*1-878887-39-4*) Morning NJ.

Rock Island '03. C. S. Ferris. LC 92-90463. (Illus.). 64p. (Orig.). 1992. pap. 12.50 (*0-9634123-0-2*) C S Ferris.

Rock-It: An Exciting Trip Through the History of American Popular Music. Jane Beethoven & Carman Moore. 32p. (Orig.). 1980. wbk. ed. 3.50 (*0-88284-474-1*, 1951); pap. text ed. 4.50 (*0-88284-473-3*, 1950) Alfred Pub.

***Rock Jam Trax for Guitar.** Ralph Agresta. 24p. pap. 9.95 incl. cd-rom (*0-8256-1607-7*) Omnibus NY.

Rock JamTrax. Ralph Agresta. (JamTrax Ser.). (Illus.). 1991. pap. 9.95 (*0-8256-1269-1*, AM75870) Music Sales.

Rock JamTrax for Keyboard. Ralph Agresta. (Illus.). 1993. pap. 9.95 (*0-8256-1268-3*, AM76647) Music Sales.

Rock Jockeys. Gary Paulsen. (Gary Paulsen World of Adventure Ser.). 66p. (J). (gr. 4-6). 1995. pap. 3.50 (*0-440-41026-6*) Dell.

***Rock Jocks Guide to Queen Creek Canyon.** Martin Karabin, Jr. (Illus.). 400p. (Orig.). 1996. pap. 32.00 (*0-9653974-7-5*) MK Prods AZ.

Rock Jocks, Wall Rats, & Hang Dogs: Rock Climbing on the Edge of Reality. John Long. LC 94-6416. 176p. 1994. pap. 11.00 (*0-671-88466-2*, Fireside) S&S Trade.

Rock Joints: Proceedings of a Regional Conference of the International Society of Rock Mechanics, Loen, Norway, 4 - 6 June 1990. Ed. by N. R. Barton & O. Stephansson. (Illus.). 820p. (C). 1990. text ed. 140.00 (*90-6191-109-5*, Pub. by A A Balkema NE) Ashgate Pub Co.

***Rock Journal: Rock & Roll Hall of Fame & Museum.** 80p. 1996. 10.95 (*1-55550-679-8*) Universe.

Rock Junction. John Long. 180p. (Orig.). 1994. pap. 12.95 (*0-934641-68-4*) Chockstone Pr.

Rock Ladies of the '80's. 1990. pap. 4.95 (*0-7935-0208-X*, 00001333) H Leonard.

***Rock Lead Scales for Guitar.** Mike Christiansen. 1993. 9.95 incl. audio compact disk (*0-7866-2684-4*, 96538BCD) Mel Bay.

Rock-Lexikon. S. Schmidt-Joos & B. Graves. 448p. (GER.). 1987. pap. 29.95 (*0-8288-2177-1*, M7603) Fr & Eur.

***Rock Licks for Bass.** Jeff Dedrick. 1993. 9.95 incl. audio compact disk (*0-7866-2690-9*, 96545BCD) Mel Bay.

***Rock Licks for Guitar.** Mike Christiansen. 1993. 9.95 incl. audio compact disk (*0-7866-2682-8*, 96536BCD) Mel Bay.

***Rock Lines for Guitar.** 9.95 incl. audio compact disk (*0-7866-2688-7*, 96542BCD) Mel Bay.

Rock Lives: Profiles & Interviews. Timothy White. (Illus.). 832p. 1991. pap. 16.95 (*0-8050-1861-1*, Owl) H Holt & Co.

Rock Lyrics Quiz Book. Presley Love. LC 93-64589. 1994. write for info. (*0-8065-1527-9*, Citadel Pr) Carol Pub Group.

***Rock Magnetism: Fundamentals & Frontiers.** David J. Dunlop & Ozden Ozdemir. (Cambridge Studies in Magnetism: No. 3). (Illus.). 600p. (C). 1997. text ed. 125.00 (*0-521-32514-5*) Cambridge U Pr.

An Asterisk (*) at the beginning of an entry indicates that the title is appearing in BIP for the first time.

Rock Masses: Modeling of Underground Openings-Probability of Slope Failure-Fracture of Intact Rock: Proceedings of a Symposium Sponsored by the Geotechnical Engineering Division. Ed. by C. H. Dowding. 189p. 1985. 25.00 (*0-87262-446-3*) Am Soc Civil Eng.

Rock Mechanics. Ed. by L. Mueller. (CISM International Centre for Mechanical Sciences Ser.: Vol. 165). (Illus.). 390p. 1982. 65.95 (*0-387-81301-2*) Spr-Verlag.

Rock Mechanics: Caverns & Pressure Shafts: ISRM Symposium, Aachen, 26-28 May 1982, 3 vols. Ed. by W. Wittke. 1390p. (C). 1983. text ed. 445.00 (*90-6191-232-6*, Pub. by A A Balkema NE) Ashgate Pub Co.

Rock Mechanics: For Underground Mining. B. H. Brady & E. T. Brown. (Illus.). 1987. pap. text ed. 49.95 (*0-04-622005-4*) Routledge Chapman & Hall.

***Rock Mechanics: For Underground Mining.** 2nd ed. Brady & Brown. (Illus.). 588p. (Orig.). (C). (gr. 13 up). 1992. pap. text ed. 72.95 (*0-412-47550-2*, Chap & Hall NY) Chapman & Hall.

Rock Mechanics: Key to Energy Production: Proceedings of the 27th U. S. Symposium on Rock Mechanics, the University of Alabama, Tuscaloosa, Alabama, June 23-25, 1986. United States Symposium on Rock Mechanics Staff. Ed. by Howard L. Hartman. LC 86-60959. (Illus.). 1006p. reprint ed. pap. 180.00 (*0-685-24005-3*, 2031590) Bks Demand.

Rock Mechanics: Proceedings of the Thirty-Third U. S. Symposium, Sweeney Convention Center, Santa Fe, NM, 8-10 June 1992. Ed. by J. R. Tillerson & W. R. Wawersik. (Illus.). 1130p. (C). 1992. text ed. 95.00 (*90-5410-045-1*, Pub. by A A Balkema NE) Ashgate Pub Co.

Rock Mechanics: Proceedings of the 28th U. S. Symposium Tucson, Arizona, 29 June - 1 July 1987. Ed. by Ian W. Farmer et al. 1264p. (C). 1987. text ed. 130.00 (*90-6191-699-2*, Pub. by A A Balkema NE) Ashgate Pub Co.

Rock Mechanics: Proceedings of the 35th U. S. Symposium, University of Nevada, Reno, 5-7 June 1995. Ed. by Jaak J. Daemen & Richard A. Schultz. (Illus.). 922p. (C). 1995. text ed. 110.00 (*90-5410-552-6*, Pub. by A A Balkema NE) Ashgate Pub Co.

Rock Mechanics: Proceedings of the 8th International Congress on Rock Mechanics, Tokyo, Japan, 1995, 3 vols., Set. Ed. by T. Fuji. (Illus.). 2000p. (C). Date not set. text ed. 420.00 (*90-5410-573-9*, Pub. by A A Balkema NE) Ashgate Pub Co.

Rock Mechanics: Theory & Applications with Case Histories. W. Wittke. Tr. by R. Sykes from GER. (Illus.). 1096p. 1990. 238.95 (*0-387-52719-2*) Spr-Verlag.

***Rock Mechanics: Tools & Techniques: Proceedings of the 2nd North American Rock Mechanics Symposium, NARMS '96, Montreal, Quebec, 19-21 June 1996, Vol. 2.** Ed. by M. Aubertin et al. (Illus.). 2050p. (C). 1996. text ed. 150.00 (*90-5410-838-X*, Pub. by A A Balkema NE) Ashgate Pub Co.

Rock Mechanics: 5th Congress of the International Society for Rock Mechanics, Proceedings Melbourne, 1983, 3 vols., Set. 2060p. (C). 1987. text ed. 695.00 (*90-6191-236-9*, Pub. by A A Balkema NE) Ashgate Pub Co.

Rock Mechanics: 7th Internationaler Kongress Ueber Felsmechanik - Proceedings of the Seventh International Congress on Rock Mechanics - Comptesrendus 7eme Congres International de Mecanique des Roches, Aachen, Germany, 16-20 September 1991, 3 vols. Ed. by W. Wittke. (Illus.). 1800p. (C). 1991. text ed. 450.00 (*90-5410-012-5*, Pub. by A A Balkema NE) Ashgate Pub Co.

Rock Mechanics Vol. 1: Theoretical Fundamentals. Philippe A. Charlez. (Illus.). 360p. (C). 1991. 150.00 (*2-7108-0585-5*, 9ET12) Gulf Pub.

Rock Mechanics - Theory & Practice: Proceedings of the Symposium, 11th, University of California, Berkeley, 1969. Rock Mechanics Symposium Staff. Ed. by Wilbur H. Somerton. LC 73-103203. (Illus.). 772p. reprint ed. pap. 180.00 (*0-317-10996-0*, 2004326) Bks Demand.

Rock Mechanics & Power Plants: Proceedings of the ISRM Symposium, 12-16 September, 1988, 2 vols. Ed. by M. Romana. 900p. (C). 1988. text ed. 195.00 (*90-6191-827-8*, Pub. by A A Balkema NE) Ashgate Pub Co.

Rock Mechanics & the Design of Structures in Rock. Leonard Obert & Wilbur I. Durall. LC 66-26753. 669p. reprint ed. pap. 180.00 (*0-317-28074-0*, 2055766) Bks Demand.

***Rock Mechanics As a Guide for Efficient Utilization of Natural Resources: Proceedings of the 30th U. S. Symposium, West Virginia 19-22 June 1989.** Ed. by A. Khair & A. Wahab. 998p. 1989. 130.00 (*90-6191-871-5*, Pub. by A A Balkema NE) Ashgate Pub Co.

Rock Mechanics As a Multidisciplinary Science: Proceedings of the 32nd U. S. Symposium on Rock Mechanics, Norman, Oklahoma, 10-12 July 1991. Ed. by Jean-Claude Roegiers. (Illus.). 1236p. (C). 1991. text ed. 135.00 (*90-6191-194-X*, Pub. by A A Balkema NE) Ashgate Pub Co.

Rock Mechanics Contributions & Challenges: Proceedings of the 31st U. S. Symposium on Rock Mechanics, Golden, Colorado, 18 - 20 June 1990. Ed. by W. Hustrulid & G. A. Johnson. (Illus.). 1082p. (C). 1990. text ed. 130.00 (*90-6191-123-0*, Pub. by A A Balkema NE) Ashgate Pub Co.

Rock Mechanics in Engineering Practice. Ed. by Kenneth Stagg & O. C. Zienkiewicz. LC 68-9674. (Illus.). 256p. reprint ed. pap. 73.00 (*0-8357-8521-1*, 2034818) Bks Demand.

Rock Mechanics in Petroleum Engineering: Proceedings-Comptes Rendus-Sitzungsberichte-SPE-ISRM International Conference EUROCK 94, Delft, 29-31 August 1994. SPE-ISRM International Conference EUROCK 94 Staff. (Illus.). 992p. (C). 1994. text ed. 99.00 (*90-5410-502-X*, Pub. by A A Balkema NE) Ashgate Pub Co.

Rock Mechanics in Salt Mining. M. L. Jeremic. (Illus.). 532p. (C). 1994. pap. 55.00 (*90-5410-103-2*, Pub. by A A Balkema NE); text ed. 99.00 (*90-5410-113-X*, Pub. by A A Balkema NE) Ashgate Pub Co.

Rock Mechanics on a Geological Base. R. Pusch. LC 95-3973. (Developments in Geotechnical Engineering Ser.: Vol. 77). 518p. 1995. 215.00 (*0-444-89613-9*) Elsevier.

Rock Mechanics Symposium: Presented at the Winter Annual Meeting of the American Society of Mechanical Engineers, Detroit, Michigan, November 11-15, 1973. Rock Mechanics Symposium Staff. Ed. by D. L. Sikarskie. LC 73-87731. (AMD Ser.: Vol. 3). (Illus.). 134p. reprint ed. pap. 38.20 (*0-8357-2880-3*, 2039117) Bks Demand.

Rock Moon Rock Harmonies & Other Poems. Doug Dahl. 8.95 (*0-533-11195-1*) Vantage.

Rock Movers & Shakers: An A-Z of the People Who Made Rock Happen. enl. rev. ed. Dafyyd Rees & Luke Crampton. (Illus.). 608p. 1991. pap. 19.95 (*0-8230-7609-1*, Billboard Bks) Watsn-Guptill.

Rock Movie Hits. (Piano-Vocal-Guitar Ser.). 192p. 1994. otabind 14.95 (*0-7935-3084-9*, 00311646) H Leonard.

Rock Mr. Blues: The Life & Music of Wynonie Harris. Tony Collins. 180p. 1995. pap. 25.00 (*0-936433-19-1*) Big Nickel.

Rock Music: Culture, Aesthetics, & Sociology. Peter Wicke. 256p. (C). 1990. pap. text ed. 20.95 (*0-521-39914-9*) Cambridge U Pr.

Rock Music: Where From? Where to? M. Basilea Schlink. Tr. by Evan. Sisterhood of Mary Staff. 48p. 1990. pap. 0.75 (*3-87209-634-6*) Evang Sisterhood Mary.

***Rock Music Collection.** Ed. by Carol Cuellar. 352p. (Orig.). (YA). 1996. pap. text ed. 18.95 (*1-57623-621-8*) Warner Brothers.

Rock Music in American Popular Culture: Rock & Roll Resources. B. Lee Cooper & Wayne S. Haney. LC 93-15554. (Illus.). 320p. 1995. pap. 19.95 (*1-56023-853-4*) Harrington Pk.

Rock Music in American Popular Culture: Rock & Roll Resources. B. Lee Cooper & Wayne S. Haney. LC 93-15554. (Illus.). 386p. 1995. lib. bdg. 49.95 (*1-56024-861-0*) Haworth Pr.

***Rock Music in American Popular Culture No. II: More Rock 'N' Roll Resources.** B. Lee Cooper & Wayne S. Haney. LC 96-7919. (Illus.). 404p. (C). 1996. 39.95 (*1-56023-877-1*) Harrington Pk.

***Rock Music in American Popular Culture II: More Rock 'n Roll Resources.** B. Lee Cooper & Wayne S. Haney. 1996. 19.95 (*0-614-20830-0*); 39.95 (*0-614-20831-9*) Haworth Pr.

Rock Music Scholarship: An Interdisciplinary Bibliography. Jeffrey N. Gatten. LC 95-36391. (Music Reference Collection: No. 50). 320p. 1995. text ed. 69.50 (*0-313-29455-0*, Greenwood Pr) Greenwood.

Rock Music Styles: A History. Katherine Charlton. 304p. (C). 1989. per. write for info. (*0-697-03050-4*) Wm C Brown Pubs.

Rock Music Styles: A History. 2nd ed. Katherine Charlton. 336p. (C). 1993. per. write for info. (*0-697-12493-2*) Brown & Benchmark.

Rock Musician. Ed. by Tony Scherman. (Illus.). 288p. (Orig.). 1994. pap. 12.95 (*0-312-09502-3*) St Martin.

Rock My Religion: Writings & Projects, 1965-1990. Dan Graham. Ed. by Brian Wallis. LC 92-36954. (Illus.). 400p. (C). 1993. 37.50 (*0-262-07147-9*) MIT Pr.

Rock My Religion: Writings & Projects 1965-1990. Dan Graham. 352p. 1994. pap. 19.95 (*0-262-57106-4*) MIT Pr.

Rock My Soul. Steve Abel-Yesuto. LC 92-61371. 157p. 1993. pap. 7.95 (*1-55523-563-8*) Winston-Derek.

Rock n' Blues Harmonica: A Beginner's Guide to Jamming. Jon Gindick. 224p. 1996. pap. 29.95 incl. audio (*0-930948-13-0*) Cross Harp.

Rock n' Blues Harmonica: A Beginner's Guide to Jamming. Jon Gindick. (Illus.). 226p. 1996. pap. 14.95 (*0-930948-12-2*, CS 10028) Cross Harp.

Rock 'n Blues Harmonica: Stories, Lessons & Record Index. Jon Gindick. (Illus.). 224p. 1983. pap. 9.95 (*0-930948-02-5*) Cross Harp.

Rock 'n' Pop. C. Klose. 80p. pap. 6.95 (*0-7935-2702-3*, 00290057) H Leonard.

Rock 'N' Pop, Bk. 1. Kolar & Ramal. (Keyboard Beginning Ser.). 1990. 5.95 (*0-685-31453-7*, T723) Hansen Ed Mus.

Rock 'N Road: Rock Climbing Areas of North America. Tim Toura. (Illus.). 470p. (Orig.). 1995. pap. 30.00 (*0-934641-35-8*) Chockstone Pr.

Rock n' Roar Dinosaur. 25p. (J). pap. 14.95 (*0-8256-1372-8*, AM91467) Music Sales.

Rock 'n Roll. (Ultimate Ser.). 296p. 1983. pap. 21.95 (*0-88188-135-X*, 00361411) H Leonard.

Rock 'n' Roll: Easy Piano. (Easy Play Ser.). 48p. 1984. pap. 6.95 (*0-7935-2413-X*, 00240218) H Leonard.

Rock 'n' Roll: Steps, Style, Spirit. Paul Bottomer. 1996. 12.95 (*1-85967-226-4*, Lorenz Bks) Anness Pub.

Rock 'n Roll & Bouncing Rock. (Ballroom Dance Ser.). 1986. lib. bdg. 79.95 (*0-8490-3410-8*) Gordon Pr.

Rock 'n Roll & Bouncing Rock. (Ballroom Dance Ser.). 1985. lib. bdg. 64.50 (*0-87700-802-7*) Revisionist Pr.

Rock 'n Roll Classics. Ed. by Carol Cuellar. (World's Greatest Music Ser.). 180p. (Orig.). (YA). 1996. pap. text ed. 16.95 (*1-57623-337-5*, MF9582) Warner Brothers.

Rock 'n Roll Dancing. Derek Young. (Ballroom Dance Ser.). 1986. lib. bdg. 79.95 (*0-8490-3377-2*) Gordon Pr.

Rock 'n Roll Dancing. Derek Young. (Ballroom Dance Ser.). 1985. lib. bdg. 64.95 (*0-87700-709-8*) Revisionist Pr.

Rock 'n' Roll Favorites: Big Note for Piano. 64p. 1995. pap. 9.95 (*0-7935-4435-1*, 00221831) H Leonard.

Rock 'n' Roll for Easy Piano. (Easy Play Ser.). 136p. 1992. otabind 12.95 (*0-7935-1384-7*, 00222544) H Leonard.

Rock 'n Roll Guitar Case Chord Book. Russ Shipton. (Illus.). 48p. pap. 4.95 (*0-86001-880-6*, AM28689) Music Sales.

***Rock N' Roll Heaven: The Death & Lives of Musical Legends from the Big Bopper to Kurt Cobain.** Nikki Corvette. 192p. 1997. pap. 13.00 (*1-57297-167-3*) Blvd Books.

Rock 'n' Roll Hits: Alto Saxophone. 32p. 1993. pap. 4.95 (*0-7935-2270-6*, 00850255) H Leonard.

Rock 'n' Roll Hits: Clarinet. 32p. 1993. pap. 4.95 (*0-7935-2269-2*, 00850254) H Leonard.

Rock 'n' Roll Hits: Flute. 32p. 1993. pap. 4.95 (*0-7935-2268-4*, 00850253) H Leonard.

Rock 'n' Roll Hits: Trombone. 32p. 1993. pap. 4.95 (*0-7935-2272-2*, 00850257) H Leonard.

Rock 'n' Roll Hits: Trumpet. 32p. 1993. pap. 4.95 (*0-7935-2271-4*, 00850256) H Leonard.

Rock 'n Roll Hits for Piano Vol. 1: Easy-Intermediate. Ed. by Tony Esposito. 32p. (YA). 1995. pap. text ed. 5.95 (*0-89724-691-8*, AF9519) Warner Brothers.

Rock 'n Roll Is Here to Pay: The History & Politics of the Music Industry. Steve Chapple & Reebee Garofalo. LC 77-10488. 372p. 1978. 37.95 (*0-88229-395-8*) Nelson-Hall.

Rock 'n Roll Is Here to Stay. H. J. Lucas. 138p. 1983. 40.00 (*0-901976-82-2*, Pub. by United Writers Pubns UK) St Mut.

Rock n' Roll Journals: Poems by Joe Cardillo. Joe Cardillo. (Illus.). 1989. pap. 6.95 (*0-9624082-0-4*) Stone Buzzard.

Rock-N-Roll Pop Music Quizzes: The Best Rock-N-Pop Music Quiz Book Ever! Vol. 1. Ed. by Joanne C. Walker. 143p. (Orig.). 1995. 12.95 (*0-9647593-0-6*) Jonica Pr.

***Rock 'n' Roll Reader's Guide.** Gary M. Krebs. LC 96-32141. 1997. 21.95 (*0-8230-7602-4*, Billboard Bks) Watsn-Guptill.

Rock 'n Roll Record Breakers. Phillip Jacobs. 1992. 12.98 (*1-55521-776-1*) Bk Sales Inc.

Rock 'n' Roll Renegades. Franklin W. Dixon. Ed. by Ellen Winkler. (Hardy Boys Ser.: No. 116). 160p. (Orig.). (J). (gr. 3-6). 1992. pap. 3.99 (*0-671-73063-0*, Minstrel Bks) PB.

Rock 'n Roll Santa. R. Eugene Jackson. (Illus.). 55p. (Orig.). (J). (gr. 1 up). 1991. pap. 4.50 (*0-88680-346-2*); 15.00 (*0-88680-347-0*) I E Clark.

***Rock-N-Roll Singer's Survival Manual.** Mark Baxter. 248p. 16.95 (*0-614-20088-1*, 00660176) H Leonard.

Rock 'n' Roll Summer: Playing for Love. Todd Strasser. 208p. (YA). 1996. mass mkt. 3.50 (*0-06-106256-1*, Harp PBks) HarpC.

Rock 'n' Roll Summer: The Boys in the Band. Todd Strasser. 208p. (J). 1996. mass mkt. 3.50 (*0-06-106255-3*, Harp PBks) HarpC.

Rock 'n' Roll Through 1969: Discographies of All Performers Who Hit the Charts, Beginning in 1955. John W. Edwards. LC 91-50945. (Illus.). 448p. 1992. lib. bdg. 45.00 (*0-89950-655-0*) McFarland & Co.

Rock 'n' Roll, 1970 Through 1979: Discographies of All Performers Who Hit the Charts. John W. Edwards. LC 92-50887. (Illus.). 656p. 1993. lib. bdg. 49.95 (*0-89950-768-9*) McFarland & Co.

Rock Names: From ABBA to ZZ Top - How Rock Bands Got Their Names. Adam Dolgins. (Illus.). 256p. 1992. pap. 10.95 (*0-8065-1363-2*, Citadel Pr) Carol Pub Group.

Rock Names: From Abba to ZZ Top; How Rock Groups Got Their Names. Rev. by Adam Dolgins. (Illus.). 240p. pap. 10.95 (*0-614-01892-7*, Citadel Pr) Carol Pub Group.

Rock Names: From Abba to ZZ Top; How Rock Groups Got Their Names. rev. ed. Adam Dolgins. LC 95-22309. 1995. pap. 10.95 (*0-8065-1617-8*, Citadel Pr) Carol Pub Group.

Rock N'Dirt Construction Company. Blue Waters Communication Staff. (J). write for info. (*0-679-88146-8*) Random Bks Yng Read.

Rock Observed: Studies in the Literature of Newfoundland. rev. ed. Patrick O'Flaherty. (Illus.). 304p. 1992. 40.00 (*0-8020-2807-1*); pap. 18.95 (*0-8020-7683-1*) U of Toronto Pr.

Rock Observed: Studies in the Literature of Newfoundland. Patrick O'Flaherty. LC 80-475278. 254p. reprint ed. pap. 72.40 (*0-685-15820-9*, 2026370) Bks Demand.

Rock Odyssey: A Chronicle of the Sixties. Ian Whitcomb. LC 94-29685. 384p. 1994. reprint ed. pap. 14.95 (*0-87910-182-2*) Limelight Edns.

Rock of Ages. Walter J. Williams. 288p. 1995. 21.95 (*0-312-85963-5*) Tor Bks.

Rock of Ages. Walter J. Williams. 1995. write for info. (*0-614-08646-9*) Tor Bks.

Rock of Ages, Vol. 1. Walter J. Williams. 1996. mass mkt. 5.99 (*0-8125-1182-7*) Tor Bks.

Rock of Chickamauga. Joseph Altsheler. 25.95 (*0-8488-0071-0*) Amereon Ltd.

Rock of Chickamauga. Joseph A. Altsheler. 1993. reprint ed. lib. bdg. 21.95 (*0-89968-567-6*) Buccaneer Bks.

Rock of Chickamauga: The Life of General George H. Thomas. Freeman Cleaves. LC 85-40939. (Illus.). 340p. (Orig.). 1986. pap. 14.95 (*0-8061-1978-0*) U of Okla Pr.

Rock of Exile: Tristan da Cunha. Derrick M. Booy. 10.00 (*0-8159-6711-X*) Devin.

***Rock of Faith.** 80p. 1988. 5.25 (*0-8341-9595-X*) Lillenas.

Rock of Faith. Contrib. by Mosie Lister. 1988. 5.99 (*0-685-68622-1*, ME-39); audio 10.99 (*0-685-68623-X*, TA-9098C) Lillenas.

Rock of Tanios. Amin Maalouf. Tr. by Dorothy S. Blair from FRE. 256p. 1994. 18.50 (*0-8076-1365-7*) Braziller.

Rock of the Gibraltarians: A History of Gibraltar. Williams G. Jackson. (C). 1988. pap. 75.00 (*0-948466-14-6*, Pub. by Gibraltar Bks UK) St Mut.

Rock of the Wind: A Return to Africa. Denis Hills. LC 83-22468. 205p. (C). 1984. 27.95 (*0-8419-0960-1*, Africana) Holmes & Meier.

***Rock On.** Thomas-Cochran. (What a Wonderful World 2 Ser.). 1992. pap. text ed. write for info. (*0-582-90971-6*, Pub. by Longman UK) Longman.

Rock On! The Great Rock & Roll Activity Book. Chip Lovitt. (J). (gr. 5-7). 1990. pap. 2.50 (*0-590-42973-6*) Scholastic Inc.

Rock on the Wild Side: Gay Male Images in Popular Music of the Rock Era. Wayne Studer. (Illus.). 288p. (Orig.). 1994. pap. 15.95 (*0-943595-46-0*) Leyland Pubns.

Rock One Hundred. 3rd ed. Jim Quinn & Barry Cohen. (Illus.). 1981. pap. text ed. 6.00 (*0-917190-09-2*) Chartmasters.

Rock One Hundred. 3rd ed. Jim Quinn & Barry Cohen. (Illus.). 1982. Suppl., 1982. suppl. ed. write for info. (*0-917190-10-6*) Chartmasters.

Rock One Hundred: An Authoritative Ranking of the Most Popular Songs for Each Year, 1954 Through 1991. 5th deluxe ed. Barry Cohen & Jim Quirin. 280p. 1993. pap. 12.95 (*0-917190-21-1*) Chartmasters.

***Rock Paintings at Hueco Tanks State Historical Park.** Kay Sutherland. (Illus.). 26p. (Orig.). 1996. pap. 7.00 (*0-614-29854-7*) TX Prks & Wldlife.

Rock Paintings of Natal Drakensberg. Ed. by David Lewis-Williams & Thomas A. Dowson. (Illus.). 68p. (Orig.). 1992. pap. 18.95 (*0-86980-869-9*, Pub. by Univ Natal Pr SA) Intl Spec Bk.

Rock Paintings of the Chumash. Campbell Grant. (Modified Reprint Ser.). (Illus.). 208p. 1993. 35.00 (*0-945092-28-8*) EZ Nature.

***Rock Patrol, 6.** Mary C. Reid. LC 97-21039. (Backpack Mystery Ser.). 1997. pap. 3.99 (*1-55661-720-8*) Bethany Hse.

Rock Physics & Phase Relations: A Handbook of Physical Constants. Ed. by T. J. Ahrens. (AGU Reference Shelf Ser.: Vol. 3). 270p. 1995. 45.00 (*0-87590-853-5*) Am Geophysical.

Rock Picture Chords & How to Use Them. (Picture Chords Library: EFS187). (Illus.). 32p. 1978. pap. 7.95 (*0-86001-892-X*, AM21718) Music Sales.

Rock Pictures of Europe. Herbert Kuhn. (Illus.). 5.95 (*0-8079-0113-X*); pap. 2.95 (*0-8079-0114-8*) October.

Rock Pool. Cyril Connolly. LC 81-82928. 160p. 1981. reprint ed. pap. 9.95 (*0-89255-059-7*) Persea Bks.

***Rock, Pop, & Classic Cinema Posters.** Ed. by Bruce Hershenson. (Illus.). 148p. (Orig.). 1996. 75.00 (*1-887893-18-0*); pap. 30.00 (*1-887893-17-2*) B Hershenson.

Rock Rabbit & the Rainbow: A Tribute to Laurens Van der Post. Robert Leibshaw. 214p. 1995. pap. text ed. 15.95 (*3-85630-540-8*, Pub. by Daimon Pubs SZ) Continuum.

Rock, Rap, & Rad: How to Be a Rock Or Rap Star. Frances Lantz. 224p. (Orig.). (YA). 1992. mass mkt. 3.99 (*0-380-76793-7*, Flare) Avon.

Rock Reference Library: Classic Blues - Rock Guitar. Ed. by Aaron Stang. 128p. (Orig.). (YA). 1993. pap. text ed. 12.95 (*0-89898-569-2*, F3372GTX) Warner Brothers.

Rock Reference Library: Hot Metal Guitar. Ed. by Aaron Stang. 96p. (Orig.). (YA). 1993. pap. text ed. 12.95 (*0-89898-566-8*, F3369GTX) Warner Brothers.

Rock Reference Library: Hot Rock Guitar Hits. Ed. by Aaron Stang. 128p. (Orig.). (YA). 1993. pap. text ed. 12.95 (*0-89898-567-6*, F3370GTX) Warner Brothers.

Rock Reference Library-Timeless Rock Guitar. CPP Belwin Staff. 1993. pap. 12.95 (*0-89898-565-X*, F3368GTX) Warner Brothers.

Rock Report. Fletcher A. Brothers. 160p. 1987. pap. 6.95 (*0-914984-13-6*) Starburst.

Rock Revival Songbook: Forty Top Hits from the Early Rock Era. 128p. 1988. pap. 12.95 (*0-88188-943-1*, 00360940) H Leonard.

Rock Rheology. N. Cristescu. (C). 1988. lib. bdg. 188.00 (*90-247-3660-9*) Kluwer Ac.

Rock Rhythm & Rag Bk. 3: Piano Solos. 16p. 1986. pap. 4.95 (*0-7935-5191-9*, 50453060) H Leonard.

***Rock Rhythm & Reels.** Lee Fleming. 1997. pap. text ed. 22.95 (*0-921556-65-9*, Pub. by Gynergy-Ragweed CN) LPC InBook.

***Rock Rhythms for Guitar.** Mike Christiansen. 1993. 9.95 incl. audio compact disk (*0-7866-2681-X*, 96535BCD) Mel Bay.

Rock Rhythms for the Young. Joe Ambrosio. 24p. 1984. pap. 5.95 (*0-938170-06-6*) Wimbledon Music.

Rock Riffs for Bass, EFS206. Tom Wolk. (Illus.). 48p. 1978. pap. 11.95 (*0-8256-2206-9*, AM23508) Music Sales.

Rock Riffs for Guitar, EFS171. Mark Michaels. (Illus.). 48p. 1984. pap. 11.95 (*0-8256-2171-2*, AM22211) Music Sales.

Rock Riffs for Keyboard. Kathy Lombard. (Illus.). 40p. 1988. pap. 9.95 (*0-8256-1191-1*, AM63926) Music Sales.

Rock, Rock, My Baby. Kay Chorao. LC 92-61268. (Chunky Shape Bks.). (Illus.). 22p. (J). (ps). 1993. 3.25 (*0-679-84333-7*) Random Bks Yng Read.

Rock Scale Finder. pap. 4.95 (*0-7935-1692-7*, 00697238) H Leonard.

Rock Scales for Guitar: Tablature. A. Clausen. 16p. 1986. pap. 6.95 (*0-7935-3782-7*, 00699164) H Leonard.

Rock Sculpture for Beginners: The Joy of Carving from Stone. Violet Stage. (Illus.). 48p. 1987. pap. 5.95 (*0-87961-167-7*) Naturegraph.

R

Rock She Wrote: Women Write About Rock, Pop & Rap. Ed. by Evelyn McDonnell & Ann Powers. LC 95-5835. 496p. 1995. pap. 15.95 (*0-385-31250-4*, Delta) Dell.

Rock, Slap & Funk Bass. Dan Gutt. 1993. 14.95 incl. audio compact disk (*0-87166-857-2*, 94346BCD) Mel Bay.

***Rock Slide Mystery.** Sandra L. Zaugg. LC 97-12883. (Shoebox Kids Ser.). (Illus.). (J). 1998. pap. write for info. (*0-8163-1387-3*) Pacific Pr Pub Assn.

***Rock Slope Engineering: Published for the Institution of Mining & Metallurgy.** 3rd ed. E. Hoek & Bray. 360p. (Orig.). 1980. pap. text ed. 54.50 (*0-419-16010-8*, E & FN Spon) Routledge Chapman & Hall.

Rock Slope Stability Analysis. Gian P. Giani. (Illus.). 355p. (C). 1992. text ed. 75.00 (*90-5410-122-9*, Pub. by A A Balkema NE) Ashgate Pub Co.

Rock Slopes: Proceedings of the Asian Regional Symposium, 7-11 December 1992, New Delhi, India. (Illus.). 491p. (C). 1993. text ed. 105.00 (*90-5410-243-8*, Pub. by A A Balkema NE) Ashgate Pub Co.

Rock Solid. Frank Bose. 320p. 1993. mass mkt. 5.99 (*0-515-11076-0*) Jove Pubns.

***Rock Solid Drum Patterns.** Dave Zubraski. 64p. pap. 9.95 incl. cd-rom (*0-7119-4799-6*) Omnibus NY.

Rock-Solid Marriage: Building a Permanent Relationship in a Throw-Away World. Robert Barnes & Rosemary J. Barnes. 256p. 1996. pap. 12.99 (*0-310-20804-1*) Zondervan.

Rock Solos for Guitar. Austin Sicard, Jr. 1993. 9.95 (*0-7866-2685-2*, 96539BCD) Mel Bay.

Rock Songs: A Comprehensive Index, From the 50's to Today. Bruce Pollock. LC 96-31950. 464p. 1997. 80.00 (*0-02-872068-7*) Schirmer Bks.

Rock Spell-a-Story Vol. 2. 32p. (Orig.). 1994. pap. 9.95 (*0-89724-242-4*, PF0890) Warner Brothers.

Rock Sport: Tools, Training, & Techniques for Climbers. John F. Gregory. LC 88-32368. (Illus.). 192p. (Orig.). 1989. pap. 14.95 (*0-8117-2296-1*) Stackpole.

Rock Springs. Richard Ford. 1996. pap. 12.00 (*0-676-51112-0*, Vin) Random.

Rock Springs. Richard C. Ford. (Contemporaries Ser.). 1988. pap. 12.00 (*0-394-75700-9*, Vin) Random.

Rock Star. Jackie Collins. 1990. pap. 6.99 (*0-671-70880-5*) PB.

Rock Star Interviews: Conversations with Leading Performers & Songwriters. Petra Zeitz. LC 92-51105. (Illus.). 331p. 1993. pap. 29.95 (*0-89950-898-7*) McFarland & Co.

Rock Star, Stud, Gigolo. Torrance T. Stephens. 130p. 1992. pap. 7.00 (*1-880861-02-X*) Adin.

Rock Stars - Pop Stars: A Comprehensive Bibliography, 1955-1994. Ed. by Brady J. Leyser & Pol Gosset. LC 94-28691. (Music Reference Collection: No. 43). 328p. 1994. text ed. 59.95 (*0-313-29422-4*) Greenwood.

Rock Star's Girl. Francine Pascal. (Sweet Valley High Ser.: No. 72). 160p. (YA). (gr. 9-12). 1991. 3.25 (*0-553-28841-5*) Bantam.

***Rock Station.** Ger Fitzgibbon. 84p. 1995. pap. 9.95 (*1-898256-05-5*) Dufour.

***Rock Steady Bass.** Phil Mulford. 64p. pap. 9.95 incl. cd-rom (*0-7119-4501-2*) Omnibus NY.

***Rock Studies for Bass: The Bottom Line.** Jeff Dedrick. 1993. 9.95 incl. audio compact disk (*0-7866-2691-7*, 94534BCD) Mel Bay.

***Rock Studies for Drum Set.** James Morton. 1993. 9.95 incl. audio compact disk (*0-7866-2709-3*, 94379BCD) Mel Bay.

Rock Superstars: Easy Guitar Transcriptions Complete with Lessons. (Easy Guitar Recorded Versions Ser.). 104p. (Orig.). 1990. pap. 12.95 (*0-7935-0275-6*, HL00660107) H Leonard.

Rock Support in Mining & Underground Construction: Proceedings of the International Symposium, Sudbury, Ontario, 16-19 June 1992. Ed. by P. K. Kaiser & D. McCreath. (Illus.). 718p. (C). 1992. text ed. 99.00 (*90-5410-044-3*, Pub. by A A Balkema NE) Ashgate Pub Co.

Rock Synthesizer Manual. Geary Yelton. LC 83-62290. (Illus.). 124p. (Orig.). 1983. pap. 15.00 (*0-914283-01-4*) Rock Tech Pubns.

Rock Synthesizer Manual. 2nd rev. ed. Geary Yelton. LC 86-4918. (Illus.). 128p. (Orig.). 1986. pap. 11.95 (*0-914283-25-1*) Rock Tech Pubns.

***Rock Talk.** Jim Driver. 190p. 9400. pap. 12.95 (*1-899344-00-4*) Dufour.

Rock Talk: The Great Rock & Roll Quote Book. Ed. by Joe Kohut & John Kohut. 170p. (Orig.). 1994. pap. 13.95 (*0-571-19839-2*) Faber & Faber.

Rock That Is Higher: Story As Truth. Madeleine L'Engle. LC 92-24204. 296p. 1993. 17.99 (*0-87788-726-8*) Shaw Pubs.

Rock the House. Grover G. Norquist. Ed. by Gordon Jones & Charles Gee. 468p. (Orig.). 1995. 25.00 (*0-06-457860-7*) VYTIS Pub.

Rock the House. rev. unabridged ed. Grover G. Norquist. Ed. by VYTIS Publishing Company Staff. LC 95-60040. (Illus.). 460p. (Orig.). 1995. pap. 9.65 (*0-9645786-0-3*) VYTIS Pub.

Rock, the Primary Text: Developing a Musicology of Rock. Allan F. Moore. LC 92-12471. (Popular Music in Britain Ser.). 1993. 90.00 (*0-335-09787-1*, Open Univ Pr); pap. 29.00 (*0-335-09786-3*, Open Univ Pr) Taylor & Francis.

***Rock This!** Chris Rock. 1997. 19.95 (*0-7868-6289-0*) Hyperion.

***Rock This!** Chris Rock. 1997. 239.40 (*0-7868-7940-8*) Hyperion.

Rock to Yesterday. Lucy Maud Montgomery. 416p. (J). 1993. mass mkt. 4.50 (*0-7704-2551-8*) Bantam.

Rock Tombs of El Hawawish, Vol. 1: The Cemetery of Akhmim. Ed. by Kanawati. 1980. pap. 75.00 (*0-85668-203-9*, Pub. by Aris & Phillips UK) David Brown.

Rock Tombs of El Hawawish, Vol. 2: The Cemetery of Akhmim. Ed. by Kanawati. 1981. pap. 75.00 (*0-85668-207-1*, Pub. by Aris & Phillips UK) David Brown.

Rock Tombs of El Hawawish, Vol. 3: The Cemetery of Akhmim. Ed. by Kanawati. 1982. pap. 75.00 (*0-85668-223-3*, Pub. by Aris & Phillips UK) David Brown.

Rock Tombs of El Hawawish, Vol. 4: The Cemetery of Akhmim. Ed. by Kanawati. 1983. pap. 75.00 (*0-85668-270-5*, Pub. by Aris & Phillips UK) David Brown.

Rock Tombs of El Hawawish, Vol. 5: The Cemetery of Akhmim. Ed. by Kanawati. 1986. pap. 75.00 (*0-85668-359-0*, Pub. by Aris & Phillips UK) David Brown.

Rock Tombs of El Hawawish, Vol. 6: The Cemetery of Akhmim. Ed. by Kanawati. 1987. pap. 75.00 (*0-85668-412-0*, Pub. by Aris & Phillips UK) David Brown.

Rock Tombs of El Hawawish, Vol. 7: The Cemetery of Akhmim. Ed. by Kanawati. 1987. pap. 75.00 (*0-85668-434-1*, Pub. by Aris & Phillips UK) David Brown.

Rock Tombs of El Hawawish, Vol. 8: The Cemetery of Akhmim. Ed. by Kanawati. 1989. pap. 75.00 (*0-85668-451-1*, Pub. by Aris & Phillips UK) David Brown.

Rock Tombs of El Hawawish, Vol. 9: The Cemetery of Akhmim. Ed. by Kanawati. 1990. pap. 75.00 (*0-85668-507-0*, Pub. by Aris & Phillips UK) David Brown.

Rock Tracks. Joel Whitburn. 288p. 1996. pap. 29.95 (*0-7935-5940-5*) H Leonard.

Rock Tracks. Joel Whitburn. (Record Research Ser.). 250p. 1995. pap. 34.95 (*0-89820-114-4*) Record Research.

Rock Trax One. 1985. pap. 12.95 incl. audio (*0-7935-0813-4*) H Leonard.

Rock Trax One. 32p. 1993. pap. 14.95 incl. audio compact disk (*0-7935-2182-3*, 00697271) H Leonard.

Rock Trax Two. 1993. pap. 14.95 incl. audio compact disk (*0-7935-2183-1*, 00697272) H Leonard.

***Rock Tricks for Guitar.** Mike Christiansen. 1993. 9.95 incl. audio compact disk (*0-7866-2683-6*, 96537BCD) Mel Bay.

Rock Type Classification for the NZ Land Resource Inventory. I. H. Lynn & T. F. Crippen. 1991. 30.00 (*0-477-02624-9*, Pub. by Manaaki Whenua NZ) Balogh.

Rock University: A Collection of Short Stories & Poems. Deswin R. Gbala. (Illus.). 51p. (Orig.). (J). (gr. 3-10). Date not set. pap. 8.50 (*0-9650629-2-9*) Coulee Region.

Rock Weathering & Landform Evolution. Ed. by D. A. Robinson & R. B. Williams. LC 94-4636. (British Geomorphological Research Group Symposia Ser.). 400p. 1994. text ed. 115.00 (*0-471-95119-6*) Wiley.

Rock Who's Who: A Complete Guide to the Great Artists & Albums of 30 Years - From Rockabilly to New Wave. Brock Helander. 600p. 1982. write for info. (*0-318-56701-6*); pap. 16.95 (*0-685-05966-9*) Macmillan.

Rock with Jazz Bk. 2: Piano Solos. Stecher & Horo. 16p. 1986. pap. 4.95 (*0-7935-4946-9*, 50452600) H Leonard.

Rock with Jazz Bk. 5: Piano. Stecher & Horo. 16p. 1986. pap. 4.95 (*0-7935-3821-1*, 50452610) H Leonard.

Rock Writing. Mildred Trede. (J). (gr. 6-9). 1994. pap. text ed. 9.97 (*0-937659-93-2*) GCT.

Rockabilly: A Bibliographic Resource Guide. B. Lee Cooper & Wayne S. Haney. LC 90-49760. 372p. 1990. 39.50 (*0-8108-2386-1*) Scarecrow.

Rockabilly: A 40-Year Journey. Billy Poore. (Illus.). 200p. (Orig.). 1995. pap. 19.95 (*0-7935-3706-1*, HL00330020) H Leonard.

Rockabilly Hell. William W. Johnstone. 1995. mass mkt. 5.50 (*0-8217-5108-5*, Zebra Kensgtn) Kensgtn Pub Corp.

Rockabilly Limbo. William W. Johnstone. 288p. 1996. mass mkt. 4.99 (*0-8217-5348-7*, Zebra Kensgtn) Kensgtn Pub Corp.

Rockabilly Rebels. Roy Zimmerman. (Illus.). 144p. (Orig.). 1994. pap. 19.95 (*1-56922-046-8*, 07-4043) Creat Cncpts.

Rockaby & Other Short Pieces. Samuel Beckett. LC 80-8916. 80p. 1981. pap. 10.00 (*0-8021-5138-8*, Grove) Grove-Atltic.

Rockabye Crocodile. Jose Aruego & Ariane Dewey. LC 87-463. (Illus.). 32p. (J). (ps-3). 1988. 16.00 (*0-688-06738-7*) Greenwillow.

Rockabye Crocodile. Jose Aruego & Ariane Dewey. LC 92-24587. 32p. (J). (ps up). 1993. pap. 4.95 (*0-688-12333-3*, Mulberry) Morrow.

Rockabye Farm. Diane J. Hamm. LC 91-19127. (Illus.). 40p. (J). (ps-1). 1992. pap. 15.00 (*0-671-74773-8*, S&S Bks Young Read) S&S Childrens.

Rockabye Rabbit. Kersten Hamilton. (Illus.). 32p. (Orig.). (J). (ps-2). 1995. pap. 5.99 (*1-56790-526-9*, Cool Kids Pr) Bkwrld Press.

Rockbound. Red Robinson & Peggy Hodgins. 232p. 1983. 19.95 (*0-88839-162-5*) Hancock House.

Rockbound. rev. ed. Frank P. Day. 328p. 1989. pap. 12.95 (*0-8020-6723-9*) U of Toronto Pr.

Rockbound. Frank P. Day. LC 73-81763. (Literature of Canada, Poetry & Prose in Reprint Ser.). 324p. reprint ed. pap. 92.40 (*0-317-26917-8*, 2023609) Bks Demand.

Rockbound Coast: Travels in Maine. Christopher Little. 1994. 39.95 (*0-393-03635-9*) Norton.

Rockbridge County: Virginia Publick Claims. Janice L. Abercrombie & Richard Slatten. (Virginia Publick Claims Ser.). ix, 24p. 1991. pap. 5.00 (*0-8095-8680-0*) Borgo Pr.

Rockbridge County: Virginia Publick Claims. Janice L. Abercrombie & Richard Slatten. (Virginia Publick Claims Ser.). ix, 24p. (C). 1991. reprint ed. lib. bdg. 25.00 (*0-8095-8358-5*) Borgo Pr.

Rockbridge County Artists & Artisans. Barbara Crawford & Royster Lyle, Jr. LC 95-18877. (Illus.). 272p. (C). 1995. text ed. 62.50 (*0-8139-1638-0*) U Pr of Va.

Rockbridge County Births, 1853-1877, 2 vols. Dorthie Kirkpatrick & Edwin Kirkpatrick. 735p. (C). 1989. reprint ed. Set. lib. bdg. 54.00 (*0-8095-8141-8*) Borgo Pr.

Rockbridge County Births, 1853-1877, 2 vols., Set. Dorthie Kirkpatrick & Edwin Kirkpatrick. 1989. pap. 24.00 (*0-614-04083-3*) Borgo Pr.

Rockbridge County Marriages, 1778-1850. Dorthie Kirkpatrick & Edwin C. Kirkpatrick. LC 88-36693. (Virginia Historic Marriage Register Ser.). (Illus.). ix, 443p. (Orig.). 1985. pap. 15.00 (*0-935931-16-3*) Borgo Pr.

Rockbridge County Marriages, 1778-1850. Dorthie Kirkpatrick & Edwin C. Kirkpatrick. LC 88-36693. (Virginia Historic Marriage Register Ser.). ix, 443p. (Orig.). (C). 1985. reprint ed. lib. bdg. 39.00 (*0-8095-8230-9*) Borgo Pr.

Rockbridge County, Virginia: Notebook. 235p. 1982. pap. 27.75 (*0-686-37183-6*) A M Coppage.

Rockbridge County, Virginia Death Registers, 1853-1870, 1912-1917. Angela M. Ruley. vi, 504p. 1993. pap. 30.00 (*0-8095-8679-7*); lib. bdg. 60.00 (*0-8095-8172-8*) Borgo Pr.

Rockbursts: Global Experiences. Ed. by Ajoy K. Ghose & H. S. Rao. (Papers Presented at the Fifth Plenary Session of Working Group on Rockbursts of International Bureau of Strata Mechanics, February 1988). (Illus.). 228p. (C). 1990. text ed. 70.00 (*90-6191-140-0*, Pub. by A A Balkema NE) Ashgate Pub Co.

Rockbursts & Seismicity in Mines: Proceedings of the Second International Symposium, Minneapolis, Minnesota, 8-10 June 1988. Ed. by Charles Fairhurst. (Illus.). 456p. (C). 1990. text ed. 130.00 (*90-6191-145-1*, Pub. by A A Balkema NE) Ashgate Pub Co.

Rockbursts & Seismicity in Mines 1993: Proceedings of the 3rd International Symposium, Ontario, Canada, August 1993. Ed. by R. Paul Young. (Illus.). 500p. 1993. text ed. 140.00 (*90-5410-320-5*, Pub. by A A Balkema NE) Ashgate Pub Co.

Rockbursts in Coal Mines & Their Prevention. Gerhard Brauner. (Illus.). 144p. (C). 1994. text ed. 70.00 (*90-5410-158-X*, Pub. by A A Balkema NE) Ashgate Pub Co.

Rockclimber's Log. Kenneth Hukari & Scott Griebel. 1993. 14.95 (*1-884751-01-6*) Wy East LogBk.

Rockefeller & His Times. Clemente Cimmora. 1974. lib. bdg. 59.95 (*0-8490-0967-7*) Gordon Pr.

Rockefeller Collection of American Art at the Fine Arts Museums of San Francisco. Marc Simpson. LC 94-4367. 1994. 50.00 (*0-8109-3774-3*) Abrams.

***Rockefeller Family Home: Kykuit.** Ann R. Roberts. (Illus.). 192p. 1997. 50.00 (*0-7892-0222-0*) Abbeville Pr.

Rockefeller File. Gary Allen. 1994. reprint ed. lib. bdg. 24.95 (*1-56849-368-1*) Buccaneer Bks.

Rockefeller Foundation Archives Series 1.1 (Projects) Series 600 (Asia) & Series 601 (China): Guide to the Scholarly Resources Microfilm Edition. LC 94-16888. 1994. 10.00 (*0-8420-4141-9*) Scholarly Res Inc.

***Rockefeller Genealogy.** Henry O. Rockefeller. (Illus.). 401p. 1996. reprint ed. pap. 61.00 (*0-8328-5394-1*); reprint ed. lib. bdg. 71.00 (*0-8328-5393-3*) Higginson Bk Co.

Rockefeller Gift. large type ed. Pauline G. Winslow. 448p. 1984. 25.99 (*0-7089-1150-1*) Ulverscroft.

Rockefeller Internationalist. Emanuel Josephson. 1979. 250.00 (*0-685-96465-5*) Revisionist Pr.

Rockefeller "Internationalist" The Man Who Misrules the World. Emanuel M. Josephson. 125.00 (*0-685-56223-9*) Chedney.

Rockefeller Medicine Men: Medicine & Capitalism in America. E. Richard Brown. LC 78-65461. (Illus.). 295p. 1979. 17.00 (*0-520-04269-7*) U CA Pr.

Rockefeller Public Number One. Emanuel M. Josephson. 1979. 250.00 (*0-685-96466-3*) Revisionist Pr.

Rockefeller Syndrome. Ferdinand Lundberg. LC 75-23031. 1975. 12.50 (*0-8184-0215-6*) Carol Pub Group.

Rockefeller, Vol. II: Transactions of the Rockefeller Family Assoc. Ed. by Henry O. Rockafellar. (Illus.). 338p. 1992. reprint ed. lib. bdg. 56.50 (*0-8328-2203-5*) Higginson Bk Co.

Rockefeller, Vol. II: Transactions of the Rockefeller Family Assoc. Ed. by Henry O. Rockafeller. (Illus.). 338p. 1992. reprint ed. pap. 46.50 (*0-8328-2204-3*) Higginson Bk Co.

Rockefellers: An American Dynasty. Peter Collier & David Horowitz. (Illus.). 1977. pap. 4.95 (*0-451-13455-9*, Sig) NAL-Dutton.

***Rockenwagner.** Hans Rockenwagner. (Illus.). 176p. 1997. 29.95 (*0-89815-875-3*) Ten Speed Pr.

Rocker: An American Design Tradition. Bernice Steinbaum. LC 92-15145. (Illus.). 160p. 1992. 40.00 (*0-8478-1587-0*) Rizzoli Intl.

Rockers: Kings of the Road. John Stuart. 128p. 1994. per. 14.95 (*0-85965-125-8*, Pub. by Plexus UK) Publishers Group.

Rocket! How a Toy Launched the Space Age. Richard Maurer. LC 94-19243. 64p. (J). 1995. lib. bdg. 17.99 (*0-517-59629-6*) Crown Bks Yng Read.

Rocket Altitude Programs & Data-Mac: (Short Title ALT.M) Jerry Irvine & Chuck Rogers. (C). 1986. pap. text ed. 49.00 (*0-685-57427-X*) CA Rocketry.

Rocket & Artillery Technology. A. P. Artmov. (GER & RUS.). 1982. 65.00 (*0-8288-1909-2*, M15457) Fr & Eur.

Rocket & the Reich: Peenemunde & the Coming of the Ballistic Missile Era. Michael J. Neufeld. 400p. 1996. pap. 15.95 (*0-674-77650-X*) HUP.

Rocket & the Reich: Peenemunde & the Coming of the Ballistic Missile Era. Michael J. Neufield. (Illus.). 350p. 1994. 25.00 (*0-02-922895-6*, Free Press) Free Pr.

***Rocket at Heart.** Rudy Tomjanovich & Falkoff. LC 97-2063. 1997. 23.00 (*0-684-83428-6*) S&S Trade.

Rocket Book. Peter Newell. LC 91-3120. (J). (gr. 4-7). 1992. pap. 3.95 (*0-486-26961-2*) Dover.

Rocket Book. Peter Newell. LC 69-12080. (Illus.). 52p. (J). (gr. k-4). 1969. reprint ed. 14.95 (*0-8048-0505-9*) C E Tuttle.

Rocket Book. Peter Newell. (Illus.). 48p. (J). (gr. 4-7). 1992. reprint ed. pap. 3.95 (*0-685-52838-3*) Dover.

Rocket Book: A Guide to Building & Launching Model Rockets for Teachers & Students 0f the Space Age. Robert L. Cannon & Michael A. Banks. (Illus.). 240p. 1985. 22.95 (*0-13-782251-0*) P-H.

Rocket City. Cathryn Alpert. 1996. pap. 12.00 (*0-614-97771-1*) Vintage NY.

Rocket City. Cathryn Alpert. 1996. pap. 12.00 (*0-679-77016-X*) McKay.

Rocket Countdown: A Lift the Flap Book. Nick Sharratt. LC 95-68110. (Illus.). 12p. (J). (ps up). 1995. 12.95 (*1-56402-622-1*) Candlewick Pr.

***Rocket Divers.** Berres et al. (Deep Sea Adventure Ser.). 10.00 (*0-614-30521-7*) NAVH.

***Rocket Girl.** Caroline Barry. (J). 1996. pap. 7.95 (*1-85594-143-0*, Pub. by Attic Press IE) Intl Spec Bk.

Rocket in My Pocket: The Rhymes & Chants of Young Americans. Carl A. Withers. LC 48-4881. (Illus.). 224p. (J). (gr. 2-4). 1988. pap. 9.95 (*0-8050-0804-7*, Bks Young Read) H Holt & Co.

Rocket in Pocket/Mead. (J). pap. write for info. (*0-590-36224-0*) Scholastic Inc.

Rocket Island. Theodore Taylor. 160p. 1985. pap. 3.50 (*0-380-89674-5*, Flare) Avon.

Rocket Mail: Flights of the World. Max Kronstein. 191p. 20.00 (*0-939429-03-9*) Am Air Mail.

Rocket Man: Elton John from A-Z. Claude Bernardin & Tom Stanton. LC 96-22900. 280p. 1996. pap. text ed. 19.95 (*0-275-95698-9*, Praeger Pubs) Greenwood.

Rocket Man: The Encyclopedia of Elton John. Claude Bernardin & Tom Stanton. LC 95-9938. 280p. 1995. text ed. 39.95 (*0-313-29700-2*, Greenwood Pr) Greenwood.

Rocket Man: The Story of Robert Goddard. Thomas Streissguth. LC 94-22836. 96p. (J). (gr. 3-7). 1995. lib. bdg. 16.13 (*0-87614-863-1*, Carolrhoda) Lerner Group.

Rocket Propulsion Elements. 6th ed. George P. Sutton. LC 00-91. 656p. 1992. text ed. 99.95 (*0-471-52938-9*) Wiley.

Rocket Science: 50 Flying, Flipping, Spinning Gadgets Kids Create Themselves. Jim Wiese. LC 95-2092. 115p. (J). (gr. 3-7). 1995. pap. text ed. 12.95 (*0-471-11357-3*) Wiley.

Rocket Ship Galileo. Robert A. Heinlein. 1986. mass mkt. 4.99 (*0-345-33660-7*, Del Rey) Ballantine.

Rocket to the Moon. Brooks Frederick, pseud. (Redbird Ser.). 118p. 1975. 15.00 (*0-88253-616-8*); pap. text ed. 4.80 (*0-88253-615-X*) Ind-US Inc.

***Rocket to the Moon: A Foldout Playbook.** 1997. 12.95 (*0-316-85341-0*) Little.

Rocket to the Morgue. Anthony Boucher. 176p. 1988. pap. 4.95 (*0-930330-82-X*) Intl Polygonics.

Rocketcon Eighty-Four Proceedings: (Short Title RCON84) Jerry Irvine. (Illus.). 48p. (C). 1984. reprint ed. pap. text ed. 15.00 (*0-912468-17-3*) CA Rocketry.

Rocketed into History: NASA Claims a Paradise. J. Q. Frierson. 220p. 1996. 18.95 (*0-944957-82-X*) Rivercross Pub.

Rocketeer. Adapted by Ron Fontes. (Junior Novel Ser.). (J). (gr. 2-6). 1991. pap. 2.95 (*1-56282-065-6*) Disney Pr.

Rocketeer. Dave Stevens. (Illus.). 72p. 1991. 32.95 (*0-913035-09-2*); pap. 8.95 (*0-913035-06-8*) Eclipse Bks.

Rockets. Mary V. Fox. (Inventors & Inventions Ser.). 64p. (J). (gr. 3-5). 1995. lib. bdg. 17.95 (*0-7614-0063-X*, Benchmark NY) Marshall Cavendish.

Rockets, Level 1. Betsy Buttonwood. (Let Me Read Ser.). (J). 1996. 2.95 (*0-673-36333-3*, GoodYrBooks) Addson-Wesley Educ.

Rockets: An Educational Coloring Book. Spizzirri Publishing Co. Staff. Ed. by Linda Spizzirri. (Illus.). 32p. (J). (gr. 1-8). 1986. pap. 1.99 (*0-86545-072-2*) Spizzirri.

Rockets & Crackers. Alvin Westcott. LC 75-108729. (Illus.). 80p. (J). (gr. 4 up). 1970. lib. bdg. 10.95 (*0-87783-033-9*) Oddo.

Rockets & Crackers. deluxe ed. Alvin Westcott. LC 75-108729. (Illus.). 80p. (J). (gr. 4 up). 1970. pap. 3.94 (*0-87783-105-X*) Oddo.

Rockets & Missiles. John Nicholaus. (Army Library). (Illus.). 48p. (J). (gr. 3-8). 1989. lib. bdg. 18.60 (*0-86592-418-X*); lib. bdg. 13.95 (*0-685-58577-8*) Rourke Corp.

Rockets & Spaceflight. Lynn Myring. (Explainers Ser.). (J). (gr. 2-5). 1982. pap. 4.50 (*0-86020-584-3*, Usborne) EDC.

Rocket's Family Fun Activity Guide & Directory. Steven I. Finkelstein. 250p. (Orig.). (J). (ps-7). 1994. pap. 9.95 (*0-9640527-0-9*) Rocket Pubns.

Rocket's Family Fun Activity Guide & Directory. Steven I. Finkelstein. 250p. (Orig.). (J). (ps-7). 1995. pap. 9.95 (*0-9640527-1-7*) Rocket Pubns.

Rocket's Family Fun Activity Guide & Directory. 3rd rev. ed. Steven I. Finkelstein. 293p. (Orig.). (J). (ps-7). 1995. pap. 12.95 (*0-9640527-2-5*) Rocket Pubns.

***Rocket's Family Fun Activity Guide & Directory, Vol. 4.** 4th rev. ed. Steven Finkelstein. 236p. 1997. pap. 12.95 (*0-9640527-3-3*) Rocket Pubns.

Rockets in Ursa Major. Fred Hoyle & Geoffrey Hoyle. 1991. reprint ed. lib. bdg. 19.95 (*1-56849-078-X*) Buccaneer Bks.

An Asterisk (*) at the beginning of an entry indicates that the title is appearing in BIP for the first time.

Rockets into Space. Frank H. Winter. (Frontiers of Space Ser.). (Illus.). 184p. 1990. text ed. 24.95 (0-674-77660-7) HUP.

Rockets into Space. Frank H. Winter. (Frontiers of Space Ser.). 184p. 1993. pap. text ed. 12.95 (0-674-77661-5) HUP.

Rockets, Missiles & Space Travel. Willy Ley. 1994. reprint ed. lib. bdg. 45.95 (1-56849-302-9) Buccaneer Bks.

Rockets, Missiles, & Spacecraft of the National Air & Space Museum, Smithsonian Institution. Compiled by Gregory P. Kennedy. LC 83-600049. (Illus.). 166p. 1984. pap. 9.95 (0-87474-571-3, KERMP) Smithsonian.

Rockets of the World. 2nd rev. ed. Peter Alway. (Illus.). 384p. 1995. 35.00 (0-9627876-5-5) Saturn Pr MI.

Rockets' Red Glare. Clifford Williams. (Illus.). 40p. 1996. pap. 29.00 (0-934274-25-8) Consumertronics.

Rockets' Red Glare: The Maritime Defense of Baltimore in 1814. Scott S. Sheads. LC 86-40238. (Illus.). 168p. 1986. reprint ed. pap. 47.90 (0-7837-9086-4, 2049836) Bks Demand.

Rockets' Red Glare: When America Goes to War: The Presidents & the People. Richard J. Barnet. 476p. 1990. 24.95 (0-685-32960-7) S&S Trade.

Rockets Wit: Words of Wisdom from the Captivating, Charismatic, Clutch NBA Champs. Andrew K. Mekz. Ed. by Anne E. Broussard. (Orig.). 1994. pap. 5.95 (0-9640033-5-X) Wit Press.

Rockfall Prediction & Control & Landslide Case Histories. LC 92-24222. (Transportation Research Record Ser.: No. 1343). 1992. write for info. (0-309-05206-8) Transport Res Bd.

Rockfill Dams: Finite Element Analysis to Determine Stresses & Deformations in Membrane Type Rockfill Dam. (Illus.). 325p. (C). 1992. text ed. 85.00 (90-6191-949-5, Pub. by A A Balkema NE) Ashgate Pub Co.

Rockfilms: A Viewer's Guide to Three Decades of Musicals, Concerts, Documentaries & Soundtracks 1955-1986. Linda J. Sandahl. LC 86-24347. (Illus.). 239p. 1987. reprint ed. pap. 68.20 (0-7837-6687-4, 2046303) Bks Demand.

Rockfire. large type ed. Catherine Dillon. 1978. 25.99 (0-7089-0170-0) Ulverscroft.

***Rockfish Mesa.** large type ed. Jim Slaughter. (Linford Western ibrary). 272p. 1996. pap. 15.99 (0-7089-7952-1, Linford) Ulverscroft.

Rockfishes of the Genus Sebastes: Their Reproduction & Early Life History. Ed. by George Boehlert & Juro Yamada. (Developments in Environmental Biology of Fishes Ser.). (C). 1991. lib. bdg. 213.50 (0-7923-0962-6) Kluwer Ac.

***Rockford: An Illustrated History.** Jon W. Lundin. LC 96-78830. (Illus.). 220p. 1996. 37.95 (0-9654754-1-7) Am Historical Pr.

Rockford Files: The Green Bottle. Stuart M. Kaminsky. LC 96-17316. 320p. Date not set. 22.95 (0-312-86229-6) Forge Pr.

***Rockford Today: Historical, Descriptive, Biographical.** Rockford Morning Star Staff. (Illus.). 179p. 1997. reprint ed. lib. bdg. 26.50 (0-8328-5792-0) Higginson Bk Co.

Rockford Watch Co. 1882. 1983. pap. 2.00 (0-930476-15-8) Am Clock & Watch.

Rockford Watch Company Serial & Grade Number List with Price Guide. rev. ed. (Illus.). 1976. ring bd. 25.00 (0-913902-11-X) Heart Am Pr.

Rockglaciers: Indicators for the Present & Former Geoecology in High Mountain Environments. Dietrich Barsch. LC 96-13769. (Physical Environment Ser.: Vol. 16). 352p. 1996. 179.95 (3-540-60742-0) Spr-Verlag.

Rockhopper. Errol Broome. 96p. (J). (gr. 4-7). 1995. pap. 6.95 (1-86373-678-6, Pub. by Allen & Unwin Aust Pty AT) IPG Chicago.

***Rockhopper Penguins.** large type ed. Erik Stoops. Ed. by Graphic Arts & Production Staff. (Young Explorer Series II: Vol. 5). (Illus.). 32p. (J). (gr. 3-7). 1997. lib. bdg. 12.95 (1-890475-10-6) Faulkners Pub.

Rockhound & Prospector's Bible: A Reference & Study Guide to Rocks, Minerals, Gemstones & Prospecting. 3rd ed. L. J. Ettinger. (Illus.). 144p. 1993. pap. 9.95 (0-9614840-4-7) Ettinger.

Rockhound & Prospector's Bible: A Reference & Study Guide to Rocks, Minerals, Gemstones & Prospecting. 3rd rev. ed. L. J. Ettinger. (Illus.). 140p. 1987. pap. 9.00 (0-9614840-1-2) Ettinger.

Rockhound Mystery. Mary Duplex. LC 92-32971. 1993. pap. 1.97 (0-8163-1130-7) Pacific Pr Pub Assn.

Rockhounding Arizona: 75 Rock-Hunting Sites Throughout Arizona. Gerry Blair. 176p. 1995. pap. text ed. 12.95 (1-56044-389-8) Falcon Pr MT.

Rockhounding Montana. rev. ed. Robert Feldman. LC 96-2718. (Illus.). 154p. 1996. pap. 12.95 (1-56044-466-5) Falcon Pr MT.

***Rockhounding Texas.** Melinda Crow. (Guide Ser.). 176p. 12.95 (1-56044-502-5) Falcon Pr MT.

Rockhounding Utah. William A. Kappele. LC 96-12047. (Illus.). 180p. (Orig.). 1996. pap. 12.95 (1-56044-446-0) Falcon Pr MT.

Rockhounding Wyoming. Kenneth L. Graham. LC 96-22101. (Illus.). 158p. (Orig.). 1996. pap. 12.95 (1-56044-445-2) Falcon Pr MT.

Rockhound's Guide to California. Gail A. Butler. LC 95-34451. (Falcon Guide Ser.). (Illus.). 190p. 1995. pap. 12.95 (1-56044-347-2) Falcon Pr MT.

Rockhound's Guide to Colorado. William A. Kappele. LC 95-31640. (Falcon Guide Ser.). (Illus.). 203p. 1995. pap. 12.95 (1-56044-331-6) Falcon Pr MT.

Rockhound's Guide to New Mexico. Melinda Crow. LC 95-15049. (Falcon Guide Ser.). (Illus.). 156p. 1995. pap. 12.95 (1-56044-340-5) Falcon Pr MT.

Rockhounds Guide to Texas. Melinda Crow. LC 94-12045. (Rockhound Guides Ser.). (Illus.). 166p. (Orig.). 1994. pap. 12.95 (1-56044-277-8) Falcon Pr MT.

***Rockhound's Handbook.** James R. Mitchell. LC 96-77412. (Illus.). 224p. (Orig.). 1996. pap. 12.95 (0-935182-90-X) Gem Guides Bk.

***Rockhurst Review: A Fine Arts Journal.** Ed. by Patricia C. Miller & John Robertson. 120p. (Orig.). 1997. pap. 6.00 (1-886761-09-4) Rockhurst Col.

Rockhurst Review - 1988: A Fine Arts Journal, Vol. I. Ed. by Robert Cronkleton & Frank Garcia-Ferrer. 79p. 1988. pap. 5.00 (1-886761-00-0) Rockhurst Col.

Rockhurst Review - 1989: A Fine Arts Journal, Vol. II. Ed. by Marc Anderson & Maureen Quillen. 80p. 1989. pap. 5.00 (1-886761-01-9) Rockhurst Col.

Rockhurst Review - 1990: A Fine Arts Journal, Vol. III. Ed. by Michelle L. Dew. 72p. 1990. pap. 5.00 (1-886761-02-7) Rockhurst Col.

Rockhurst Review - 1991: A Fine Arts Journal, Vol. IV. Ed. by Eileen M. O'Connell. 75p. 1991. pap. 5.00 (1-886761-03-5) Rockhurst Col.

Rockhurst Review - 1992: A Fine Arts Journal, Vol. V. Ed. by Todd L. Reding. 50p. 1992. pap. 5.00 (1-886761-04-3) Rockhurst Col.

Rockhurst Review - 1993: A Fine Arts Journal, Vol. VI. Melea L. Seward. 86p. 1993. pap. 5.00 (1-886761-05-1) Rockhurst Col.

Rockhurst Review - 1994: A Fine Arts Journal, Vol. VII. Melea L. Seward. 100p. 1994. pap. 6.00 (1-886761-06-X) Rockhurst Col.

Rockhurst Review - 1995: A Fine Arts Journal, Vol. Ed. by Dawnell Reese & Elizabeth Vondrak. 80p. 1995. pap. 6.00 (1-886761-07-8) Rockhurst Col.

Rockhurst Review - 1996: A Fine Arts Journal, Vol. IX. Melea L. Seward. 100p. 1996. pap. 6.00 (1-886761-08-6) Rockhurst Col.

***Rockies.** David Muench. 1997. 50.00 (1-55868-308-9) Gr Arts Ctr Pub.

***Rockies.** 3rd ed. Fodors Travel Staff. 1997. pap. 18.00 (0-679-03527-3) Fodors Travel.

Rockies: Pillars of a Continent. Scott Thybony. 200p. 1996. 16.00 (0-7922-2940-1) Natl Geog.

Rockies: Pillars of a Continent. deluxe ed. Scott Thybony. LC 95-52391. 1996. write for info. (0-7922-2970-3) Natl Geog.

Rockin. Maurie Kerrigan. LC 87-90645. 28p. (Orig.). 1987. pap. text ed. 9.95 (0-9618920-0-5) M Kerrigan.

Rockin Blues Solos. 17.95 (0-89524-848-4, 02503460) Cherry Lane.

Rockin Christmas - Five String Bass. Brian Emmel. (Illus.). 68p. (YA). (gr. 9-12). 1994. pap. 9.95 (0-931759-89-7) Centerstream Pub.

Rockin Christmas - Guitar. Dave Celentano. (Illus.). 68p. (YA). (gr. 9-12). 1994. pap. 17.95 (0-931759-88-9) Centerstream Pub.

***Rockin' Christmas Sing-a-Long.** Ed. by Carol Cuellar. 64p. (Orig.). (YA). 1996. pap. text ed. 18.95 (1-57623-587-4, MF9640G); pap. text ed. 9.95 (1-57623-586-6, MF9640) Warner Brothers.

Rockin' Country. Ed. by Carol Cuellar. 156p. (Orig.). (YA). 1996. pap. text ed. 14.95 (0-7692-0097-4, MF9609) Warner Brothers.

Rockin' Country Guitar. 19.95 (0-7935-3716-9, 00694959) H Leonard.

Rockin' Elvis: Easy Guitar. 32p. 1995. pap. 9.95 (0-7935-4283-9, 00702004) H Leonard.

Rockin' in Time: A Social History of Rock & Roll. David P. Szatmary. (Illus.). 300p. 1987. pap. 19.50 (0-13-782285-5) P-H.

Rockin' in Time: A Social History of Rock-&-Roll. 3rd ed. David P. Szatmary. LC 95-6979. 1995. pap. text ed. 24.00 (0-13-440678-8) P-H.

***Rockin' Out: Popular Music in the U. S. A.** Reebee Garofalo. LC 96-33424. 450p. 1996. pap. 24.95 (0-205-13703-2) Allyn.

Rockin' Records, 1991. 1991. pap. 29.95 (0-932117-15-5) Jellyroll Prodns.

***Rockin' Records, 1997: 20th Anniversary Edition Buyers-Sellers Reference Book & Price Guide.** 18th rev. ed. Jerry Osborne. 934p. (Orig.). 1996. pap. 42.95 (0-930625-61-7, AT5617) Antique Trader Bks.

***Rockin Records 1998 Edition: Buyers-Sellers Reference Book & Price Guide.** 19th rev. ed. Jerry Osborne. 1008p. (Orig.). 1997. pap. 42.95 (0-930625-81-1, AT5811) Antique Trader Bks.

***Rockin Reptiles.** Stephanie Calmenson. (J). 1999. pap. write for info. (0-688-15633-9, Beech Tree Bks) Morrow.

***Rockin' Reptiles.** Joanna Cole & Stephanie Calmenson. (Illus.). (J). (gr. 1-4). 1997. 15.00 (0-614-28867-3) Morrow.

***Rockin' Reptiles Vol. 2: The Gator Girls.** Stephanie Calmenson & Joanna Cole. (Illus.). 80p. (J). (ps-3). 1997. lib. bdg. 14.93 (0-688-12740-1, 707272) Morrow.

***Rockin' Reptiles Vol. 2: The Gator Girls.** Stephanie Calmenson & Joanna Cole. (Illus.). 80p. (J). 1997. 15.00 (0-688-12739-8) Morrow.

Rockin' Rhythms (with MIDI Disk) Sam Holland. 12p. 1994. pap. text ed. 9.95 incl. disk (0-87487-745-8) Summy-Birchard.

Rockin' the Armory: A Gil Thorp Collection. Jack Berrill. 256p. 1995. pap. 19.95 (0-930099-10-9) Take Five Pubs.

Rockin' the Boat: Mass Music & Mass Movements. Ed. by Reebee Garofalo. 240p. (Orig.). 1992. 40.00 (0-89608-428-0); pap. 16.00 (0-89608-427-2) South End Pr.

Rockin' the Classics & Classicizin' the Rock: A Selectively Annotated Discography. Janell R. Duxbury. LC 84-22419. (Discographies Ser.: No. 14). xix, 188p. 1985. text ed. 49.95 (0-313-24605-X, DUR/, Greenwood Pr) Greenwood.

Rockin' the Classics & Classicizin' the Rock: A Selectively Annotated Discography; First Supplement. Compiled by Janell R. Duxbury. LC 91-7899. (Discographies Ser.: No. 43). 192p. 1991. text ed. 49.95 (0-313-27542-4, DRA, Greenwood Pr) Greenwood.

***Rockin' 50's.** Helander. 1998. pap. 20.00 (0-02-864872-2) S&S Trade.

***Rockin' 60's.** Helander. 1998. pap. 20.00 (0-02-864873-0) S&S Trade.

***Rocking & Rolling.** Philip Steele. LC 97-539. (SuperSmarts Ser.). (Illus.). 24p. (J). 1997. 11.99 (0-7636-0303-1) Candlewick Pr.

Rocking Around the Clock. E. Ann Kaplan. 224p. (C). 1987. pap. 11.95 (0-415-03005-6) Routledge.

Rocking Around the Clock: Music Television, Post Modernism & Consumer Culture. E. Ann Kaplan. (Illus.). 224p. 1987. 29.95 (0-416-33370-2); pap. 11.95 (0-416-33390-7) Routledge Chapman & Hall.

***Rocking Chair Love.** unabridged ed. Kathleen Gibson. LC 96-68080. (Rainbow Readers Ser.). (Illus.). 40p. (Orig.). (J). (ps-3). 1996. pap. 12.50 incl. audio (1-888862-02-5, RR6202) Rainbow Rdrs.

Rocking Chair Rebel. Houghton Mifflin Company Staff. (Literature Experience 1993 Ser.). (J). (gr. 7). 1992. pap. 9.84 (0-395-61852-5) HM.

Rocking Chair Rhapsodies, (An Excerpt from the Tarnish on the Golden Years) Nona K. Carver. (Illus.). 24p. (Orig.). 1994. pap. 7.00 (0-9641195-4-4) Carver Cntry.

***Rocking Horse.** J. David Loeb. (Illus.). 32p. (J). (gr. k-4). 1997. pap. 5.95 (1-885744-08-0) Otter Creek.

Rocking Horse. Lalitha Venkateswaran. (Redbird Ser.). 1975. 8.00 (0-88253-618-4); pap. text ed. 4.80 (0-88253-617-6) Ind-US Inc.

Rocking Horse: Children's Stories. Douglas Young. Ed. by Constance Hunting. (Illus.). 88p. (Orig.). 1982. pap. 5.95 (0-913006-26-2) Puckerbrush.

Rocking-Horse Catholic: A Caryll Houselander Reader. Ed. by Marie A. Mayeski. LC 90-62084. 224p. (Orig.). (C). 1991. pap. 12.95 (1-55612-401-5) Sheed & Ward MO.

Rocking Horse Christmas. Mary P. Osborne. LC 96-1993. (Illus.). (J). 1997. write for info. (0-590-92955-0) Scholastic Inc.

Rocking-Horse Maker: Nine Easy-to-Follow Projects. Anthony Dew. (Illus.). 160p. 1994. 27.95 (0-7153-0086-5, Pub. by D & C Pub UK) Sterling.

***Rocking-Horse Maker: Nine Easy-to-Follow Projects.** Anthony Dew. 1997. pap. text ed. 19.95 (0-7153-0554-9) Sterling.

Rocking Horse Secret. Rumer Godden. (J). (gr. 3-7). 1988. pap. 3.95 (0-317-69650-5, Puffin) Puffin Bks.

Rocking Horse Winner. D. H. Lawrence. (Creative's Classics Ser.). 40p. (J). (gr. 6 up). 1982. lib. bdg. 13.95 (0-87191-893-5) Creative Ed.

Rocking Horses. Ruth Bottomley. 1989. pap. 25.00 (0-7478-0138-X, Pub. by Shire UK) St Mut.

Rocking Horses: Woodwork Projects. Margaret Spencer. (Illus.). 160p. 1991. 39.95 (1-85223-454-7, Pub. by Crowood Pr UK) Trafalgar.

Rocking in Time. David P. Szatmary. 22.00 (0-02-864630-4) S&S Trade.

***Rocking the Ages: The Yankelovich Report on Generational Marketing.** J. Walker Smith & Ann S. Clurman. LC 96-52509. (Illus.). 352p. 1997. 27.50 (0-88730-813-9) Harper Busn.

Rocking the Babies. Linda Raymond. 272p. 1995. pap. 10.95 (0-14-023254-0, Penguin Bks) Viking Penguin.

Rocking the Boat: New Zealand, the United States & the Nuclear-Free Zone Controversy in the 1980s. Paul Landais-Stamp & Paul Rogers. 201p. 1989. 19.95 (0-85496-279-4) Berg Pubs.

Rocking the Boat: Women, Unions, & Change, 1915-1975. Ed. by Brigid O'Farrell & Joyce L. Kornbluh. LC 95-33037. (Illus.). 325p. (C). 1996. text ed. 50.00 (0-8135-2268-4); pap. text ed. 17.95 (0-8135-2269-2) Rutgers U Pr.

Rocking the Classics: English Progressive Rock & the Counterculture. Edward L. Macan. (Illus.). 304p. 1997. 35.00 (0-19-509887-0); pap. 17.95 (0-19-509888-9) OUP.

Rocking the Cradle. Nancy B. Jacobs. 304p. 1996. mass mkt. 5.99 (0-06-100893-1, Harp PBks) HarpC.

Rocking the Cradle of Sexual Politics: What Happened When Women Said Incest. Louise Armstrong. 320p. 1994. 23.00 (0-201-62471-0) Addison-Wesley.

Rocking the Pond: The First Season of the Mighty Ducks of Anaheim. Dean Chadwin. (Illus.). 264p. (Orig.). 1994. pap. 9.95 (0-919591-03-5, Pub. by Polestar Bk Pubs CN) Orca Bk Pubs.

Rocking the Roles: Building a Win-Win Marriage. Robert Lewis & William Hendricks. LC 91-61395. 252p. (Orig.). 1991. pap. 12.00 (0-89109-641-8) NavPress.

Rocking the State: Rock Music & Politics in Eastern Europe & the Soviet Union. Sabrina P. Ramet. 1994. text ed. 75.00 (0-8133-1762-2) Westview.

***Rockingham Connection & the Second Founding of the Whig Party.** W. M. Elofson. 280p. 1996. 49.95 (0-7735-1388-4, Pub. by McGill CN) U of Toronto Pr.

Rockingham County: A Brief History. Lindley S. Butler. (Illus.). xiv, 92p. 1982. pap. 5.00 (0-86526-198-9) NC Archives.

Rockingham County: Virginia Publick Claims. Janice L. Abercrombie & Richard Slatten. (Virginia Publick Claims Ser.). ix, 45p. 1991. pap. 7.00 (0-8095-8683-5) Borgo Pr.

Rockingham County: Virginia Publick Claims. Janice L. Abercrombie & Richard Slatten. (Virginia Publick Claims Ser.). ix, 45p. (C). 1991. reprint ed. lib. bdg. 25.00 (0-8095-8359-3) Borgo Pr.

Rockingham County in the World War, 1917-1918. American Legion, Rockingham Post 27 Staff. 128p. 1993. pap. 10.00 (0-8095-8681-9); lib. bdg. 29.00 (0-8095-8185-X) Borgo Pr.

Rockingham County, NH. M. Thomas. (Images of America Ser.). 1994. pap. 14.99 (0-7524-0005-3, Arcdia) Chalford.

Rockingham County, North Carolina, Deed Abstracts, 1785-1800. Irene B. Webster. 142p. (Orig.). 1983. reprint ed. pap. 18.50 (0-89308-351-8) Southern Hist Pr.

Rockingham County, North Carolina Marriage Bonds & Certificates, 1785-1868. Francis T. Ingmire. 160p. 1994. pap. 18.00 (0-8095-8682-7); lib. bdg. 45.00 (0-8095-8078-0) Borgo Pr.

Rockingham County, North Carolina, Will Abstracts: 1785-1865, Vol. 1. Irene B. Webster. 138p. 1973. pap. 18.50 (0-89308-355-0) Southern Hist Pr.

Rockingham County Virginia Marriages, Seventeen Seventy-Eight to Eighteen Fifty. John Vogt & T. William Kethley, Jr. (Virginia Historic Marriage Register Ser.). (Illus.). ix, 433p. 1984. pap. 15.00 (0-935931-17-1) Borgo Pr.

Rockingham County Virginia Marriages, Seventeen Seventy-Eight to Eighteen Fifty. John Vogt & T. William Kethley, Jr. (Virginia Historic Marriage Register Ser.). ix, 433p. (C). 1984. reprint ed. lib. bdg. 39.00 (0-8095-8231-7) Borgo Pr.

Rockingham Pottery & Porcelain, 1745-1842. Alwyn Cox & Angela Cox. LC 82-25158. (Faber Monographs on Pottery & Porcelain). (Illus.). 240p. 1983. 85.00 (0-571-13049-6) Faber & Faber.

***Rockland County in the 1790s: A Bicentennial Publication of the County of Rockland, 1798-1998.** Jacquetta M. Haley. LC 96-46190. (Illus.). 1997. write for info. (0-911183-42-6) Rockland County Hist.

***Rockland County 1850 Federal Census.** Lee S. Wanamaker. 561p. 1996. lib. bdg. 69.50 (1-56012-145-9) Kinship Rhinebeck.

Rockland, ME. Shore Village Historical Society Staff. (Images of America Ser.). 128p. 1996. pap. 16.99 (0-7524-0246-3, Arcdia) Chalford.

Rockley Fake Book. 336p. 1994. spiral bd. 8.98 (0-7935-3924-2, 00240034) H Leonard.

Rock'n'Roll Babylon. rev. ed. Gary Herman. 224p. 1994. per. 14.95 (0-85965-199-1, Pub. by Plexus UK) Publishers Group.

Rockonomics: The Money Behind the Music. Marc Eliot. (Illus.). 320p. 1993. pap. 12.95 (0-8065-1457-4, Citadel Pr) Carol Pub Group.

Rockpile Areas & Other Specialized Activity Sites on the Gila River Terrace: An Appraisal of Hohokam Auxiliary Agricultural Strategies near Florence, Arizona. Rein Vanderpot. (Statistical Research Technical Ser.: No. 32). (Illus.). 112p. 1992. spiral bd. 12.50 (1-879442-30-2) Stats Res.

Rockport - Fulton. San Antonio Cartographers Staff. 1996. 2.95 (0-671-56303-3) Macmillan.

***Rockport Register, 1904 (Town History & Directory)** Mitchell et al. 94p. 1997. reprint ed. pap. 17.00 (0-8328-5906-0) Higginson Bk Co.

Rockport Walking Program. James M. Rippe & Carol A. Ward. 1989. pap. 12.95 (0-318-42596-3) P-H.

Rocks. (Golden Science Close-up Ser.). (Illus.). 24p. (J). (gr. k-5). 1991. 6.50 (0-307-12852-0, Golden Pr) Western Pub.

Rocks. Terry J. Jennings. Ed. by Rebecca Stefoff. LC 91-18190. (Threads Ser.). (Illus.). 32p. (J). (gr. 3-5). 1991. lib. bdg. 15.93 (1-56074-000-0) Garrett Ed Corp.

Rocks. Judy Tuer. LC 92-30670. (Voyages Ser.). (Illus.). (J). 1993. 2.50 (0-383-03649-6) SRA McGraw.

***Rocks: Everyday Life in Early Sydney 1788-1830.** Grace Karskens. (Illus.). 312p. 1997. 34.95 (0-522-84722-6, Pub. by Melbourne Univ Pr AT) Paul & Co Pubs.

Rocks: The True Story of the Worst Team in Baseball History. Wilt Browning. Ed. by Dot Jackson. LC 92-72178. (Illus.). 180p. 1992. 19.95 (1-878086-14-6) Down Home NC.

***Rocks & Alpine Gardens.** (Pleasures of Gardening Ser.). (Illus.). 128p. 12.98 (0-8317-3628-3) Smithmark.

Rocks & Chairs. Robert Hershon. 1975. pap. 4.00 (0-914610-19-8) Hanging Loose.

Rocks & Deals. Geoffrey Young. 1987. 5.00 (0-935724-27-3) Figures.

Rocks & Fossils. Arthur B. Busbey, 3rd et al. LC 95-47661. (Nature Company Guides Ser.). (Illus.). 288p. 1996. write for info. (0-7835-4803-6) Time-Life.

Rocks & Fossils. B. Cork & M. Bramwell. (Hobby Guides Ser.). (Illus.). 32p. (J). (gr. 5-8). 1983. pap. text ed. 6.95 (0-7460-1975-0) EDC.

Rocks & Fossils. B. Cork & M. Bramwell. (Hobby Guides Ser.). (Illus.). 32p. (J). (gr. 5-8). 1983. lib. bdg. 14.95 (0-88110-159-1) EDC.

Rocks & Fossils. Weldon-Owen. (Nature Company Guide Ser.). 288p. 1996. 29.95 (0-8094-9375-6) Time-Life.

***Rocks & Fossils Kid Kit.** 32p. (J). 1996. pap. 13.95 (0-88110-690-9) EDC.

Rocks & Landforms. John Gerrard. 288p. (C). 1987. text ed. 65.00 (0-04-551112-8); pap. text ed. 24.95 (0-04-551113-6) Routledge Chapman & Hall.

Rocks & Mineral Deposits, Vol. 1. Paul Niggli. Tr. by Robert L. Parker. LC 53-8082. (Geology Texts Ser.). 573p. reprint ed. pap. 163.40 (0-317-29240-4, 2055547) Bks Demand.

Rocks & Minerals. (Discover Ser.). (Illus.). 48p. (J). 1993. 9.98 (1-56173-107-2) Pubns Intl Ltd.

Rocks & Minerals. (Ultimate Sticker Bks.). (Illus.). 20p. (J). (ps-3). 1995. pap. 6.95 (0-7894-0007-3) DK Pub Inc.

Rocks & Minerals. 24p. (J). (gr. 3-9). 1997. pap. 9.99 (0-7214-5678-2, Ladybrd) Penguin.

***Rocks & Minerals.** (Spotters Ser.). (Illus.). 32p. (J). 1997. pap. 4.95 (0-7894-1677-8) DK Pub Inc.

R

Rocks & Minerals. D. J. Arneson. (Nature Fact Book). (Illus.). 32p. (Orig.). (J). 1990. pap. 2.50 (*0-942025-90-3*) Kidsbks.

Rocks & Minerals. Basil Booth. 1993. 6.98 (*1-55521-838-5*) Bk Sales Inc.

***Rocks & Minerals.** Dorling Kindersley Staff. (Eyewitness Explorers Ser.). (Illus.). 64p. (J). 1997. pap. 5.95 (*0-7894-1682-4*) DK Pub Inc.

Rocks & Minerals. Sue Fuller. LC 93-48881. (DK Pockets Ser.). (Illus.). 160p. (YA). (gr. 7 up). 1995. pap. 5.95 (*1-56458-663-4*) DK Pub Inc.

***Rocks & Minerals.** Judi Hechtman & Sandra F. Grove. Ed. by Karen P. Hall. (Explore & Discover Ser.). (Illus.). 32p. (Orig.). (J). (gr. 1-3). 1996. teacher ed., pap. text ed. 5.98 (*1-57471-165-2*, 2823) Creat Teach Pr.

Rocks & Minerals. Keith Lye. LC 92-31817. (What About...? Ser.). (Illus.). 32p. (J). (gr. 2-3). 1992. lib. bdg. write for info. (*0-8114-3411-7*) Raintree Steck-V.

Rocks & Minerals. Keith Lye. (J). (ps-3). 1994. pap. 4.95 (*0-8114-6441-5*) Raintree Steck-V.

Rocks & Minerals. Doris H. Metcalf. (Task Cards Ser.). (Illus.). 88p. (YA). (gr. 7-12). 1989. teacher ed. 16.00 (*0-941008-23-1*) Tops Learning.

Rocks & Minerals. Natural History Museum Staff. LC 87-26514. (Eyewitness Bks.). (Illus.). 64p. (J). (gr. 5 up). 1988. 19.00 (*0-394-89621-1*) Knopf Bks Yng Read.

Rocks & Minerals. Natural History Museum Staff. LC 87-26514. (Eyewitness Bks.). (Illus.). 64p. (J). (gr. 5 up). 1988. lib. bdg. 20.99 (*0-394-99621-6*) Knopf Bks Yng Read.

Rocks & Minerals. Judy Nayer. (At Your Fingertips Ser.). (Illus.). 10p. (J). (ps-3). 1995. bds. 6.95 (*1-56293-547-X*) McClanahan Bk.

Rocks & Minerals. Michael O'Donoghue. (American Nature Guide Ser.). 1992. 9.98 (*0-8317-6964-5*) Smithmark.

Rocks & Minerals. Mary Packard. (J). (gr. 4-7). 1997. pap. 6.95 (*0-8167-3527-1*) Troll Communs.

Rocks & Minerals. Chris Pellant. LC 91-58222. (Eyewitness Handbks.). (Illus.). 300p. 1992. 29.95 (*1-56458-033-4*); pap. 17.95 (*1-56458-061-X*) DK Pub Inc.

Rocks & Minerals. Chris Pellant. (Fact Finders Ser.). (Illus.). 64p. (J). 1990. 7.99 (*0-517-05148-6*) Random Hse Value.

Rocks & Minerals. Illa Podendorf. LC 81-38494. (New True Bks.). (Illus.). 48p. (J). (gr. k-4). 1982. pap. 5.50 (*0-516-41648-0*); lib. bdg. 19.00 (*0-516-01648-2*) Childrens.

Rocks & Minerals. Theodore Rowland-Entwistle & Michael O'Donoghue. LC 93-46148. (Science Nature Guides Ser.). (Illus.). 80p. (J). (gr. 3-6). 1994. 12.95 (*1-85028-263-3*) Thunder Bay CA.

Rocks & Minerals. William Russell. LC 94-507. (From This Earth Ser.). (J). (gr. 3 up). 1994. write for info. (*0-86593-362-6*) Rourke Corp.

Rocks & Minerals. B. Simpson. 310p. 1983. pap. text ed. 24.95 (*0-08-030240-8*, Prgamon Press) Buttrwrth-Heinemann.

Rocks & Minerals. Charles Sorrell. (Golden Field Guide Ser.). (Illus.). 280p. 1974. write for info. (*0-307-47005-9*); pap. 11.95 (*0-307-13661-2*) Western Pub.

Rocks & Minerals. Alan Woolley. (Spotter's Guides Ser.). (Illus.). 64p. (J). (gr. 7 up). 1992. pap. 4.95 (*0-86020-112-0*) EDC.

Rocks & Minerals. Herbert S. Zim & Paul R. Shaffer. (Golden Guide Ser.). (Illus.). 160p. (YA). (gr. 6 up). 1957. pap. 5.50 (*0-307-24499-7*, Golden Pr) Western Pub.

Rocks & Minerals: Earth Science Translated. Alfred De Vito. (Illus.). 125p. 1985. pap. 14.95 (*0-942034-04-X*) Creat Ventures IN.

Rocks & Minerals for Pathfinders: A Basic Youth Enrichment Skill Honor Packet. L. S. Gattis, III. (Illus.). 22p. (Orig.). (J). (gr. 5 up). 1987. teacher ed., pap. 5.00 (*0-936241-29-2*) Cheetah Pub.

Rocks & Minerals of California. 3rd rev. ed. Vinson Brown et al. LC 72-13423. (Illus.). 200p. 1987. pap. 9.95 (*0-911010-58-0*) Naturegraph.

Rocks & Minerals of the World. Ed. by Scott Morris. LC 92-22910. (Using & Understanding Maps Ser.). (Illus.). 48p. (YA). (gr. 5 up). 1993. lib. bdg. 17.95 (*0-7910-1803-2*) Chelsea Hse.

Rocks & Mountains. Claire Llewellyn & Anthony Lewis. 1995. pap. 4.95 (*0-8120-9394-1*) Barron.

Rocks & Mountains. Claire Llewellyn. (Why do We Have? Ser.). 1995. 9.95 (*0-8120-6524-7*) Barron.

Rocks & Rock Minerals. Richard V. Dietrich & Brian J. Skinner. LC 79-12111. 319p. 1979. text ed. 24.50 (*0-471-02934-3*) Wiley.

Rocks & Routes of the North Country, New York. Bradford B. Van Diver. LC 76-46243. (Illus.). 1976. pap. text ed. 6.95 (*0-685-05216-8*) Van Diver.

Rocks & Routes of the North Country, New York. Bradford B. Van Diver. 1976. pap. 8.95 (*0-932052-25-8*) North Country.

Rocks & Shoals: Naval Discipline in the Age of Fighting Sail. James E. Valle. (Bluejacket Bks.). (Illus.). 352p. 1996. pap. 16.95 (*1-55750-879-8*) Naval Inst Pr.

***Rocks & Soil.** Maria Gordon. (Simple Science Ser.). (Illus.). 32p. pap. 18.54 (*0-8172-4504-9*) Raintree Steck-V.

Rocks & Soil: A Thematic Unit. Janet A. Hale. (Thematic Units Ser.). (Illus.). 80p. (Orig.). (gr. 1-3). 1992. student ed. 9.95 (*1-55734-265-2*) Tchr Create Mat.

Rocks & Soil: Hands on Elementary School Science. Linda Poore. 28p. 1994. teacher ed. 35.00 (*1-883410-06-1*) L Poore.

Rocks Are Everywhere. Rice & Cerbu. (Easy Theme Reader Ser.). (Illus.). 16p. (J). (ps-1). 1996. pap. 2.49 (*1-55734-927-4*) Tchr Create Mat.

***Rocks Are Shouting.** Cora E. Cypser. (Illus.). 366p. (Orig.). 1997. write for info. (*0-9625774-2-1*) Kim Pathways.

Rocks Around the World. Stefan Glowacz & Ilu Wiesmeier. (Illus.). 144p. 1996. pap. 25.00 (*0-87156-885-3*) Sierra.

Rocks Begin to Speak. LaVan Martineau. LC 72-85137. (Illus.). 210p. 1973. 19.50 (*0-916122-30-1*) KC Pubns.

Rocks, Erosion, & Weathering: Hands on Elementary School Science. Linda Poore. 31p. 1994. teacher ed. 35.00 (*1-883410-07-X*) L Poore.

***Rocks for Raiders.** Haraldur Karlsson. 180p. (C). 1996. pap. text ed., spiral bd. 20.94 (*0-7872-2852-4*) Kendall-Hunt.

Rocks from Space: Meteorites & Meteorite Hunters. O. Richard Norton. 480p. 1994. pap. 20.00 (*0-87842-302-8*) Mountain Pr.

Rock's Hidden Persuader: The Truth about Back Masking. Dan Peters et al. LC 85-71475. 128p. (YA). 1985. mass mkt. 3.99 (*0-87123-857-8*) Bethany Hse.

Rocks in Her Head. Ed. by Dorchen Forman. (Illus.). 98p. (Orig.). 1987. pap. text ed. 8.00 (*0-918971-3-9*) Siwash Ent.

Rocks, Minerals & Fossils. Keith Lye. (Our World Ser.). (Illus.). 48p. (J). (gr. 5-8). 1991. lib. bdg. 12.95 (*0-382-24226-2*) Silver Burdett Pr.

Rocks, Minerals & Fossils of the World. Chris Pellant. 1990. pap. 19.95 (*0-316-69796-6*) Little.

Rocks, Minerals, Gems, Fossils, & Crystals. Booth. 1995. 15.98 (*0-7858-0242-8*) Bk Sales Inc.

***Rocks of Ages: Being a Celebration & Manifestation of the Historic & Enigmatic Epidermal Icon As Seen by Various Artists.** Ed. by Donald E. Hardy. 120p. 1997. 25.00 (*0-945367-08-2*) Hardy Marks Pubns.

Rocks of Greene County. George H. Chadwick. 1973. pap. 4.00 (*0-910746-06-0*) Hope Farm.

***Rocks, Rails & Trails.** Paul Link & E. Chilton Phoenix. 194p. 1996. reprint ed. pap. text ed. 25.00 (*0-939696-01-0*) Idaho Mus Nat Hist.

Rocks Remain. large type ed. Gavin Maxwell. 1976. 25.99 (*0-85456-404-7*) Ulverscroft.

Rocks, Ridges & Glaciers: A Geologic Tour of the Denali Highway. W. Diel. (Illus.). 82p. 1995. pap. 7.00 (*0-930931-07-6*) Alaska Natural.

Rocks, Rocks Big & Small. Joanne Barkan. Ed. by Bonnie Brook. (First Facts Ser.). (Illus.). 32p. (J). (ps-1). 1990. lib. bdg. 6.95 (*0-671-68656-9*, Silver Pr NJ) Silver Burdett Pr.

Rocks Tell Stories. Sidney Horenstein. LC 92-16562. (Beyond Museum Walls Ser.). (Illus.). 72p. (J). (gr. 4-6). 1993. pap. 6.95 (*1-56294-766-4*); lib. bdg. 17.90 (*1-56294-238-7*) Millbrook Pr.

Rocks to Riches. (Deluxe Sound Story Bks.). (Illus.). 24p. (J). (ps up). 1995. bds. 9.95 (*0-307-74041-2*, Golden Pr) Western Pub.

Rockslides & Avalanches, Pt. 1: Natural Phenomena. B. Voight. (Developments in Geotechnical Engineering Ser.: Vol. 14A). 834p. 1978. 246.25 (*0-444-41507-6*) Elsevier.

Rockspeak: The Language of Rock & Pop. Simon Warner. 320p. 1996. pap. 16.95 (*0-7137-2473-0*, Pub. by Blandford Pr UK) Sterling.

Rockspring. R. G. Vliet. LC 91-52780. (Southwest Life & Letters Ser.). 144p. 1992. reprint ed. pap. 9.95 (*0-87074-334-1*) SMU Press.

Rockwell: The Heritage of North American. Bill Yenne. (Illus.). 224p. 1989. 12.98 (*0-517-67252-9*, Crescent) Random Hse Value.

Rockwell: U. S. Marshal. Richard L. Dewey. 216p. 1987. 15.95 (*0-9616024-2-2*) Paramount Bks.

***Rockwell Dilatometer.** S. P. Rockwell. (Technical Papers). 1925. pap. text ed. 30.00 (*1-55589-321-X*) AGMA.

Rockwell International Corp. A Report on the Company's Environmental Policies & Practices. (Illus.). 50p. (C). 1994. reprint ed. pap. text ed. 250.00 (*0-7881-0909-X*, Coun on Econ) DIANE Pub.

Rockwell Kent. Ed. by Fridolf Johnson. LC 81-47477. (Illus.). 352p. 1982. 60.00 (*0-394-41771-2*) Knopf.

Rockwood. Jonathan D. Smith. LC 91-90551. (Illus.). 136p. (Orig.). 1992. pap. 6.95 (*0-9630323-0-5*) Kilimanjaro Comms.

Rockwood & Green's Fractures in Adults, 2 vols., Set. 4th ed. Ed. by Charles A. Rockwood, Jr. 2405p. 1996. text ed. 295.00 (*0-397-51602-9*) Lppncott-Raven.

Rockwood & Green's Fractures in Adults, 3 vols., Set. 4th ed. Ed. by Charles A. Rockwood, Jr. et al. 4,100p. 1996. text ed. 435.00 (*0-397-51509-X*) Lppncott-Raven.

Rockwood & Green's Fractures in Adults, Vol. 1. 4th ed. Ed. by Charles A. Rockwood, Jr. 1996. write for info. (*0-397-51510-3*) Lppncott-Raven.

Rockwood & Green's Fractures in Adults, Vol. 2. 4th ed. Ed. by Charles A. Rockwood, Jr. 1996. write for info. (*0-397-51511-1*) Lppncott-Raven.

Rockwood Pottery, Bk. 2. Herbert Peck. 1987. 19.95 (*0-943633-00-1*) Cinc Art Gal.

***Rocky & Bullwinkle & Friends.** (Pop-Up Desk Calendars Ser.). (Illus.). 26p. 1996. spiral bd. 14.95 (*1-889412-06-6*) Village Sq.

Rocky & Bullwinkle Book. Louis Chunovic. 224p. 1996. 50.00 (*0-553-10503-5*) Bantam.

Rocky Bobocky, the Pizza Man. Emily Ellison. (Illus.). 32p. (J). 1995. 14.95 (*1-56352-274-8*) Longstreet Pr Inc.

***Rocky Creek Adventure, No. 4.** 208p. (J). 1995. write for info. (*0-7814-0083-X*, Chariot Bks) Chariot Victor.

***Rocky Goes Hunting.** Walter L. Rickard. LC 96-27269. (J). 1997. write for info. (*1-56763-237-8*) Ozark Pub.

***Rocky Goes Hunting.** Walter L. Rickard. LC 96-27269. (J). 1997. pap. write for info. (*1-56763-238-6*) Ozark Pub.

Rocky Horror Picture Show. Bill Henkin. 1979. pap. 18.95 (*0-452-26654-8*, Plume) NAL-Dutton.

Rocky Horror Picture Show. Richard O'Brien. (Illus.). 72p. 1991. pap. 15.95 (*0-7119-2764-2*, AM86101) Music Sales.

Rocky Horror Picture Show Book. Bill Henkin. (Illus.). 1979. pap. 15.95 (*0-8015-9005-1*, Dutton) NAL-Dutton.

Rocky Island & Other Stories. Samuel Wilburforce & Margaret Gatty. LC 82-74324. (Victorian Children's Classics Ser.). 106p. 1982. pap. 5.95 (*0-88270-543-1*) Bridge-Logos.

***Rocky Memories.** April Gap. (Wee Write Bks.: No. 33). (Illus.). 50p. (J). (gr. 3-6). 1997. pap. 8.95 (*1-57635-009-6*) WeWrite.

Rocky Mountain: The Story Behind the Scenery. Michael T. Smithson. LC 86-80495. (Illus.). 48p. (Orig.). 1986. pap. 7.95 (*0-88714-007-6*) KC Pubns.

Rocky Mountain Adventure Collection: The Adventures of a Colorado Mountaineer. T. J. Burr. LC 91-23499. (Illus.). 320p. (Orig.). 1992. pap. 12.95 (*1-56474-003-X*) Fithian Pr.

Rocky Mountain Adventures: The Driver's Guide. Fraser Bridges. 1992. pap. 14.95 (*0-9694136-5-3*) Amer Traveler.

Rocky Mountain Bench: The Territorial Supreme Courts of Colorado, Montana, & Wyoming, 1861-1890. John D. Guice. LC 72-75195. (Yale Western Americana Ser.: No. 23). 234p. reprint ed. pap. 66.70 (*0-317-29580-2*, 2022002) Bks Demand.

Rocky Mountain Berry Book. Bob Krumm. LC 90-81720. (Illus.). 162p. (Orig.). 1991. pap. 9.95 (*1-56044-040-6*) Falcon Pr MT.

Rocky Mountain Birds: Easy Identification. Betty R. Seacrest & Delbert A. McNew. (Illus.). 104p. 1991. pap. 7.95 (*0-937321-01-X*) Avery Pr CO.

Rocky Mountain Boom Town: A History of Durango, Colorado. Duane A. Smith. (Illus.). 234p. 1992. reprint ed. pap. 17.50 (*0-87081-257-2*) Univ Pr Colo.

Rocky Mountain Brave. Bill Cunningham. (Illus.). 240p. (Orig.). 1994. pap. 12.95 (*0-9640890-1-7*) Parchment UT.

Rocky Mountain Carbonate Reservoirs. Ed. by Mark W. Longman et al. (Core Workshop Notes Ser.: No. 7). 482p. 1985. pap. 42.00 (*0-918985-55-2*) SEPM.

Rocky Mountain Christmas: Yuletide Stories of the West. 2nd ed. John H. Monnett. LC 92-16281. (Illus.). 144p. (Orig.). 1992. pap. 14.95 (*0-87108-830-4*) Pruett.

Rocky Mountain Clothes Co., Inc. 5th ed. Frances H. Carpenter. 48p. (C). 1991. per. 20.95 (*0-256-09260-5*, 34-1449-05) Irwin.

Rocky Mountain Company: Cheyenne Winter. Richard S. Wheeler. 1992. mass mkt. 3.99 (*1-55817-599-7*, Pinncle Kensgtn) Kensgtn Pub Corp.

Rocky Mountain Company Fitzhug. Richard S. Wheeler. 1991. mass mkt. 3.95 (*1-55817-489-3*, Pinncle Kensgtn) Kensgtn Pub Corp.

Rocky Mountain Constitution Making, 1850-1912. Gordon M. Bakken. LC 86-12143. 194p. 1987. text ed. 49.95 (*0-313-25538-5*, BKC/, Greenwood Pr) Greenwood.

Rocky Mountain Creative Sourcebook, 1996. Ed. by Joey D. Petelle. (Illus.). 300p. 1996. spiral bd. 50.00 (*1-886295-06-9*) Everest Pubng.

Rocky Mountain Divide: Selling & Saving the West. John B. Wright. LC 93-7705. (Illus.). 288p. (C). 1993. 29.95 (*0-292-79079-1*) U of Tex Pr.

Rocky Mountain Feud. Jon Sharpe. (Canyon O'Grady Ser.: No. 25). 176p. (Orig.). 1993. pap. 3.50 (*0-451-17595-6*, Sig) NAL-Dutton.

Rocky Mountain Flora. 5th ed. William A. Weber. LC 67-15956. (Illus.). 1976. pap. 20.00 (*0-87081-068-5*) Univ Pr Colo.

Rocky Mountain Flower Finder: A Guide to Wildflowers Found below Tree Line in the Rocky Mountains. Janet L. Wingate. (Illus.). 128p. 1991. pap. 3.75 (*0-912550-20-1*) Nature Study.

Rocky Mountain Golf Directory. annuals 144p. 1995. write for info. (*1-887351-00-0*) Pastime CO.

***Rocky Mountain Gourmet: The Complete How-To Guide on Starting Your Own Gourmet Dining Group.** Rand A. Christenson. (Illus.). 75p. (Orig.). 1997. pap. 12.95 (*0-9651602-0-3*) Colo Weight-Away.

***Rocky Mountain Gourmet Cookbook.** Leslie M. DeDominic. (Illus.). 224p. 1997. 24.95 (*1-56044-559-9*) Falcon Pr MT.

Rocky Mountain Home: Spirited Western Hideaways. Elizabeth C. Flood. LC 95-47413. (Illus.). 160p. 1996. 39.95 (*0-87905-704-1*) Gibbs Smith Pub.

Rocky Mountain Journals of William Marshall Anderson: The West in 1834. William M. Anderson. Ed. by Dale L. Morgan & Eleanor T. Harris. LC 66-25064. (Huntington Library Publications). 430p. reprint ed. pap. 122.60 (*0-317-29233-1*, 2055539) Bks Demand.

Rocky Mountain Kettle Cuisine Two. Sheila A. Mills. (Illus.). (Orig.). 1990. pap. 15.95 (*0-9628428-0-X*) Sheilas Good.

Rocky Mountain Life, or: Startling Scenes & Perilous Adventures in the Far West During an Expedition of Three Years. Rufus B. Sage. LC 82-20165. (Illus.). 377p. reprint ed. pap. 107.50 (*0-7837-4648-2*, 2044372) Bks Demand.

Rocky Mountain Man. Charles Potts. LC 77-82730. 148p. 1978. pap. 6.00 (*0-912292-47-4*) Smith.

Rocky Mountain Men: Code of Silence, Silver Lady, Touch the Sky. Linda R. Wisdom et al. 1997. mass mkt. 5.99 (*0-373-20138-9*, 1-20138-3) Harlequin Bks.

Rocky Mountain Mineral Law Institute Proceedings: 1955-1992, 37 vols. mic. film write for info. (*0-318-57456-X*) Rothman.

Rocky Mountain Mineral Law Institute Proceedings: 1955-1992, 38 vols., Set. Bound set incl. Index 1-10. 2,535.00 (*0-8377-9137-5*) Rothman.

Rocky Mountain National Park. Ed. by Jeff Nicholas. (Wish You Were Here Postcard Bks.). (Illus.). 32p. (Orig.). 1995. pap. 4.95 (*0-939365-45-6*) Sierra Pr CA.

Rocky Mountain National Park. Nilsson. 1978. pap. 5.95 (*0-02-499400-6*, Macmillan Coll) P-H.

Rocky Mountain National Park. David Petersen. LC 93-798. (New True Bks.). (Illus.). 48p. (J). (gr. k-4). 1993. lib. bdg. 19.00 (*0-516-01196-0*) Childrens.

Rocky Mountain National Park: A Family Guide. Lisa G. Evans. LC 90-21232. (Illus.). 224p. 1991. pap. 12.95 (*0-89886-263-9*) Mountaineers.

Rocky Mountain National Park: A History. Curt W. Buchholtz. 1983. pap. 17.50 (*0-87081-146-0*) Univ Pr Colo.

Rocky Mountain National Park: A Visual Interpretation. George Wuerthner. Ed. by Nicky Leach & Jeff Nicholas. (Wish You Were Here Postcard Bks.). (Illus.). 64p. (Orig.). 1995. pap. 9.95 (*0-939365-43-X*) Sierra Pr CA.

Rocky Mountain National Park: A Wildlife Watcher's Guide. Todd Wilkinson. LC 93-45668. (Wildlife Watcher's Guide Ser.). (Illus.). 96p. 1994. pap. 11.95 (*1-55971-227-9*) NorthWord.

Rocky Mountain National Park: A 100 Year Perspective. John Fielder & T. A. Barron. (Illus.). 204p. 1995. 70.00 (*1-56579-123-1*) Westcliffe Pubs.

Rocky Mountain National Park: Classic Hikes & Climbs. Gerry Roach. LC 88-16307. (Fulcrum's Guide Ser.). 272p. 1988. pap. 14.95 (*1-55591-033-5*) Fulcrum Pub.

***Rocky Mountain National Park: Jewel of the Rockies.** David Dahms. (Illus.). 60p. (Orig.). 1997. pap. 12.95 (*0-9646359-1-7*) Paragon Pr.

***Rocky Mountain National Park - CO.** (Illus.). 1996. pap. 2.95 (*1-56695-026-0*) Trails Illustrated.

Rocky Mountain National Park, CO. rev. ed. Ed. by Trails Illustrated Staff. (Illus.). 1995. Folded topographical map. 8.99 (*0-925873-00-4*) Trails Illustrated.

Rocky Mountain National Park Dayhiker's Guide: A Scenic Guide to 33 Favorite Hikes Including Longs Peak. Jerome Malitz. LC 92-42538. (Illus.). 144p. (Orig.). 1993. pap. 15.95 (*1-55566-110-6*) Johnson Bks.

Rocky Mountain National Park Natural History Handbook. John Emerick. LC 94-66091. (Illus.). 164p. (Orig.). 1994. pap. 14.95 (*1-879373-80-7*) R Rinehart.

Rocky Mountain National Park Roadguide. Thomas Schmidt. (Illus.). 96p. (Orig.). 1995. pap. 4.95 (*1-881480-03-8*) Free Wheel Trvl.

Rocky Mountain National Park Trail Guide & Journal. Laurie Mendon. LC 94-66661. 225p. 1994. pap. 12.95 (*0-9641329-6-6*) Pinnacle Ventures.

Rocky Mountain Petroleum Directory. 41th rev. ed. Ed. by Paula Jepperson. 550p. 1995. pap. text ed. 79.00 (*0-912553-52-9*) Hart Pubns.

Rocky Mountain Petroleum Directory. 42th ed. Ed. by Paula Jepperson. 500p. 1996. pap. text ed. 79.00 (*0-912553-59-6*) Hart Pubns.

***Rocky Mountain Petroleum Directory.** 43th rev. ed. Kelly Holder. 1997. pap. text ed. 99.00 (*0-912553-67-7*) Hart Pubns.

***Rocky Mountain Proud.** Bill Cunningham. Ed. by Karen S. Arnold. (Illus.). 274p. (Orig.). 1997. pap. 12.95 (*0-9640890-2-5*, RM3) Parchment UT.

Rocky Mountain Rabbit. Becky Woods. LC 90-70093. (Illus.). 86p. (J). (gr. 4-8). 1991. 12.00 (*0-932433-65-0*) Windswept Hse.

Rocky Mountain Railroad Memories - A Quarter Century View. Ed Fulcomer. (Illus.). 64p. 1990. 12.95 (*0-918654-43-2*) CO RR Mus.

Rocky Mountain Railroads of Colorado. William M. Thayer. Ed. by William R. Jones. (Illus.). 56p. 1995. reprint ed. pap. 4.95 (*0-89646-020-7*) Vistabooks.

Rocky Mountain Rancher. Pamela Toth. (Special Edition Ser.). 1995. mass mkt. 3.75 (*0-373-09951-7*, 1-09951-4) Silhouette.

Rocky Mountain Reader. Ray West. (BCL1-PS American Literature Ser.). 436p. 1993. reprint ed. lib. bdg. 99.00 (*0-7812-6932-6*) Rprt Serv.

Rocky Mountain Rendezvous. Fred Gowans. LC 84-27586. (Illus.). 256p. 1985. pap. 14.95 (*0-87905-193-0*) Gibbs Smith Pub.

Rocky Mountain Safari: A Wildlife Discovery Guide. Cathy Illg & Gordon Illg. LC 94-65086. (Illus.). 92p. 1994. pap. 9.95 (*1-879373-79-3*) R Rinehart.

***Rocky Mountain Salvation Company: How the West Was Conned.** Ron Carter. (The Settlement Trilogy Ser.). 1997. 12.95 (*0-9643672-7-0*) Harbour Bks.

Rocky Mountain Section Field Guide. Ed. by S. S. Beus. (DNAG Centennial Field Guides Ser.: No. 2). (Illus.). 489p. 1987. 43.50 (*0-8137-5402-X*) Geol Soc.

Rocky Mountain Sketches. Marj Dunmire. (Illus.). 24p. (Orig.). 1978. pap. 4.95 (*0-942559-00-2*) Pegasus Graphics.

Rocky Mountain Skiing. 2nd ed. Claire Walter. (Illus.). 432p. (Orig.). 1996. pap. 21.95 (*1-55591-330-X*) Fulcrum Pub.

Rocky Mountain Splendor: A Mile by Mile Guide for Rocky Mountain National Park. Doris B. Osterwald. (Illus.). 272p. (Orig.). (YA). 1989. pap. 13.95 (*0-931788-89-7*) Western Guideways.

Rocky Mountain Spotted Fever: History of a Twentieth-Century Disease. Victoria A. Harden. LC 89-48033. (Henry E. Sigerist Series in the History of Medicine). 416p. 1990. text ed. 49.95 (*0-8018-3905-X*) Johns Hopkins.

***Rocky Mountain States.** Jerry C. Dunn & Donald Young. LC 96-40545. (Smithsonian Guides to Historic America Ser.). 1998. write for info. (*1-55670-639-1*) Stewart Tabori & Chang.

An Asterisk (*) at the beginning of an entry indicates that the title is appearing in BIP for the first time.

Rocky Mountain States: Colorado, Wyoming, Idaho, Montana. Jerry C. Dunn, Jr. Ed. by Roger G. Kennedy. LC 89-4607. (Smithsonian Guide to Historic America Ser.). (Illus.). 464p. 1989. 24.95 (*1-55670-103-9*); pap. 18.95 (*1-55670-107-1*) Stewart Tabori & Chang.

Rocky Mountain States: U. S. A. Guide. Wayne Bernhardson et al. (Illus.). 992p. 1995. pap. 21.95 (*0-86442-241-5*) Lonely Planet.

Rocky Mountain Tough. Bill Cunningham. (Illus.). 220p. (Orig.). 1993. pap. 12.95 (*0-9640890-0-9*) Parchment UT.

Rocky Mountain Traveler: A Guide to Locating Rocky Mountain Wildflowers. Panayoti Kelaidis. 1994. pap. 4.95 (*1-55838-148-1*) R H Pub.

Rocky Mountain Traveler: A Travelers Guide to Tracking Dinosaurs in the Western U. S. William D. Panczner. 1994. pap. 5.95 (*1-55838-149-X*) R H Pub.

Rocky Mountain Traveler: A Visitor's Guide to the U. S. Air Force Academy. Donald Anderson. 1994. pap. 4.95 (*1-55838-154-6*) R H Pub.

Rocky Mountain Tree Finder: A Manual for Identifying Rocky Mountain Trees. Tom Watts. (Illus.). 62p. 1972. pap. 3.00 (*0-912550-05-8*) Nature Study.

Rocky Mountain Trout Fishing. Merton D. Leeper. (Illus.). (Orig.). 1991. pap. text ed. 9.95 (*0-9617325-3-9*) ML Pubns.

Rocky Mountain Urban Politics. Ed. by JeDon A. Emenhiser. LC 79-637413. 172p. (Orig.). reprint ed. pap. 49.10 (*0-8357-7909-2*, 2036337) Bks Demand.

Rocky Mountain Walks. Gary Ferguson. LC 92-74515. (Illus.). 304p. (Orig.). 1993. pap. 15.95 (*1-55591-120-X*) Fulcrum Pub.

Rocky Mountain Welcome Book. Sandy Fails. (Illus.). 120p. per. 16.95 (*0-614-04390-5*) Crested Butte Pub.

Rocky Mountain West: Colorado, Wyoming, & Montana, 1859-1915. Duane A. Smith. LC 91-41638. (Histories of the American Frontier Ser.). (Illus.). 304p. 1992. pap. 17.95 (*0-8263-1340-X*) U of NM Pr.

Rocky Mountain West in Eighteen Sixty-Seven. Louis L. Simonin. LC 66-16514. 184p. reprint ed. pap. 52.50 (*0-7837-1842-X*, 2042042) Bks Demand.

***Rocky Mountain Wild Flowers.** A. E. Porsild. 1979. pap. text ed. 11.95 (*0-660-00073-3*) U Ch Pr.

Rocky Mountain Wild Foods Cookbook. Darcy Williamson. LC 95-21282. (Illus.). 250p. (Orig.). 1995. pap. 17.95 (*0-87004-367-6*) Caxton.

Rocky Mountain Wildflowers. Kent Dannen & Donna Dannen. LC 81-7439. (Illus.). 64p. (Orig.). 1981. pap. 5.95 (*0-9606768-0-5*) Tundra Pubns.

Rocky Mountain Wildflowers. A. E. Porsild. 454p. 1987. pap. 9.95 (*0-226-56495-9*) U Ch Pr.

Rocky Mountain Wildflowers. 2nd ed. Ronald Taylor et al. LC 86-61099. (Illus.). 96p. 1986. pap. 7.95 (*0-89886-131-4*) Mountaineers.

Rocky Mountain Wildlife. Don Blood. (Illus.). 126p. 1988. 50.00 (*0-919654-37-1*) Hancock House.

Rocky Mountain Wildlife. David Dahms. 60p. (Orig.). 1995. pap. 11.95 (*0-9646359-0-9*) Paragon Pr.

Rocky Mountain Wildlife of Yellowstone & Grand Teton National Parks. Bill Perry. (Illus.). 68p. 1995. pap. 10. 95 (*0-943972-41-8*) Homestead WY.

Rocky Mountain Wineries: A Travel Guide to the Wayside Vineyards: Colorado, New Mexico, Idaho, Arizona, Utah, & Montana. Linda Collison & Bob Russell. LC 94-18957. (Illus.). 75p. (Orig.). 1994. pap. 16.95 (*0-87108-848-7*) Pruett.

Rocky Mountains. Janis A. Kraulis. 1990. 19.98 (*0-88486-033-7*) Arrowood Pr.

Rocky Mountains: A Young Reader's Journal. Robert Bullock. LC 93-77117. (Illus.). 64p. (Orig.). (J). (gr. k-5). 1994. pap. 8.95 (*0-943972-18-3*) Homestead WY.

Rocky Mountains: Crest of a Continent. Janis A. Kraulis. (Illus.). 200p. (Orig.). 1986. pap. 19.95 (*1-55013-630-5*, Pub. by Key Porter Bks CN) Firefly Bks Ltd.

Rocky Mountains: Der Geologische Aufbau des Kanadischen Felsengebirges. Dietrich H. Roeder. (Illus.). 1967. 99.50 (*3-443-11005-3*) Lubrecht & Cramer.

Rocky Mountains: Wildlife in the High Country. Shin Yoshino. LC 94-18510. (Illus.). 104p. 1995. pap. 14.95 (*0-8118-0897-1*) Chronicle Bks.

Rocky Mountains of Canada North. 7th ed. Robert Kruszyna & William L. Putnam. LC 84-72248. (Illus.). 336p. 1985. pap. 14.50 (*0-930410-19-X*) Amer Alpine Club.

Rocky Mountains of Canada South. 7th ed. Glen W. Boles et al. LC 79-87636. (Illus.). 450p. 1979. pap. 14.50 (*0-930410-08-4*) Amer Alpine Club.

Rocky Mountains Receipts Remedies. rev. ed. Ed. by Jack Benham & Sarah Benham. (Illus.). 60p. (Orig.). 1966. pap. text ed. 2.95 (*0-941026-08-6*) Bear Creek Pub.

Rocky Point. Alice Sharpe. 192p. 1994. 17.95 (*0-8034-9043-7*) Bouregy.

Rocky Point. large type ed. Alice Sharpe. 197p. 1996. 19.95 (*0-7838-1516-6*, GK Hall) Thorndike Pr.

Rocky Point Gringo Guide: A Travel Guide to Puerto Penasco, Mexico. Mary Weil. 190p. 1994. 11.95 (*0-9642264-0-5*) Frontier Trvl.

***Rocky Point Gringo Guide to Puerto Penasco Mexico.** Mary Weil. (Illus.). 320p. (Orig.). 1997. pap. 14.95 (*0-9642264-1-3*) Frontier Trvl.

Rocky Ridge, 4 vols., Set. Roger L. MacBride. (Little House Bks.). (Illus.). (J). (gr. 3-7). 1996. boxed, pap. 18. 00 (*0-06-449628-7*, Trophy) HarpC Child Bks.

Rocky Road. Anne Stuart. 1994. 3.59 (*0-373-45169-5*) Harlequin Bks.

***Rocky Road: The Legendary Life & Times of Billy Rancher.** Bill Reader. (Illus.). x, 240p. (Orig.). 1996. pap. 12.00 (*0-9655377-0-6*) No Fate Pub.

Rocky Road to Dublin. Seumas MacManus. 9.95 (*0-8159-6712-8*) Devin.

Rocky Road to Lesbos. pap. 4.95 (*0-8216-5100-5*, Univ Books) Carol Pub Group.

Rocky Road to Reform: Adjustment, Income Distribution, & Growth in the Developing World. Lance Taylor. LC 92-39611. (Illus.). 450p. (C). 1993. 45.00 (*0-262-20093-7*) MIT Pr.

***Rocky Road to Wisdom: Painstakingly Traveled over a Long Lifespan Through the Maze of Life's Tragi-Comedy.** Maurice M. Clairmont. LC 96-90992. 1997. 12.50 (*0-533-12241-4*) Vantage.

Rocky Shore. John M. Kingsbury. LC 71-122758. (Illus.). 1970. pap. 7.95 (*0-85699-015-9*) Chatham Pr.

Rocky Shores: Exploitation in Chile & South Africa. Ed. by W. Roy Siegfried. LC 93-26020. 1994. 109.95 (*0-387-56808-5*) Spr-Verlag.

Rocky Times in Rocky Mountain National Park: An Unnatural History. Karl Hess, Jr. (Illus.). 240p. 1993. 29.95 (*0-87081-309-9*) Univ Pr Colo.

Rocky Top Bluegrass Banjo. Bill Knopf. 96p. (Orig.). 1995. pap. 14.95 (*1-56922-082-4*, 07-3003) Creat Cncpts.

Rocky Top Saturdays: The Owl Bay Guide to Tennessee Volunteer Tailgating. Lucy Littleton. 128p. 1994. pap. 8.95 (*0-9638568-7-1*) Owl Bay Pubs.

Rocky's Boxing Book. Rocky Graziano & Howard Liss. (Illus.). 96p. 1980. pap. 9.95 (*0-87460-377-3*); lib. bdg. 12.95 (*0-87460-352-8*) Lion Bks.

Rocky's Private Jokes. Rocky Hadzovic. 115p. 1990. pap. 4.95 (*0-9627579-0-X*) K Hadzovic.

Rococo Adventure, Discovering the Art of Belgian Bobbin Lace. Caroline Coffield. (Illus.). 100p. 1988. 14.95 (*0-915113-05-8*) Bizarre Butterfly.

Rococo Age: French Masterpieces of the Eighteenth Century. Eric M. Zafran & Jean-Luc Bordeaux. LC 83-81104. (Illus.). 168p. 1983. pap. 2.50 (*0-939802-19-8*) High Mus Art.

Rococo Interior: Decoration & Social Spaces in Early Eighteenth-Century Paris. Katie Scott. LC 95-11085. 1995. write for info. (*0-300-04582-4*) Yale U Pr.

Rococo Poetry: An Introduction. Patrick Brady. 109p. 1992. pap. text ed. 12.95 (*1-886935-00-9*) New Prdigm Pr.

Rococo to Revolution. Michael Levey. (World of Art Ser.). (Illus.). 252p. 1985. pap. 14.95 (*0-500-20050-5*) Thames Hudson.

Rod & Lightning. Carroll F. Terrell. (Collected Poems Ser.). 130p. (Orig.). 1985. 8.95 (*0-915032-49-X*); pap. 5.00 (*0-915032-37-6*) Natl Poet Foun.

Rod Building & Repair. Len Head. (Illus.). 80p. 1993. pap. 22.95 (*1-85223-719-8*, Pub. by Crowood Pr UK) Trafalgar.

Rod in India. H. S. Thomas. 435p. 1964. pap. 175.00 (*81-7089-069-1*, Pub. by Intl Bk Distr II) St Mut.

Rod Machado's Instrument Pilot's Survival Manual. rev. ed. Rod Machado. 232p. (C). 1992. reprint ed. pap. text ed. 29.95 (*0-9631229-0-8*) Av Speak Bur.

Rod Machado's Private Pilot Handbook: The Ultimate Private Pilot Book. Rod Machado. Ed. by Diane Titterington & Brian Weiss. (Illus.). 572p. (C). 1996. per., pap. text ed. 34.95 (*0-9631229-9-1*) Av Speak Bur.

Rod Milgate. Peter Pinson. (Illus.). 168p. 1996. text ed. 75. 00 (*976-641-065-8*, ECU58, Harwood Acad Pubs) Gordon & Breach.

Rod Morgenstein - Double Bass Drumming. pap. 24.95 incl. audio (*0-89524-691-0*) Cherry Lane.

Rod Morgenstein - Grooving in Styles. pap. 24.95 incl. audio (*0-89524-689-9*) Cherry Lane.

***Rod of an Almond Tree in God's Master Plan.** Peter A. Michas et al. LC 97-60123. 224p. (Orig.). 1997. pap. 12. 00 (*1-57921-007-4*) WinePress Pub.

Rod of Iron: French Counterinsurgency Policy in Aragon During the Peninsular War. Don W. Alexander. LC 84-5561. 260p. (C). 1985. 40.00 (*0-8420-2218-X*) Scholarly Res Inc.

Rod of Mercury. Henry B. Stein. 53p. 1968. reprint ed. spiral bd. 8.00 (*0-7873-1054-9*) Hlth Research.

Rod of Mercury: The Druids & Their Significance. H. H. Stein. 1991. lib. bdg. 79.95 (*0-8490-4550-9*) Gordon Pr.

Rod of Seven Parts. Douglas Niles. 1996. 21.99 (*0-7869-0479-8*) TTH Inc.

Rod of Seven Parts. Skip Williams. (Advanced Dungeons & Dragons Ser.). 1996. 30.00 (*0-7869-0418-6*) TSR Inc.

Rod Powell's Flame Painting Techniques: How to Flame Hot Rods, Trucks & Motorcycles. Rod Powell. Ed. by David Fetherston. LC 96-60749. (Illus.). 128p. 1997. pap. 19.95 (*0-9652005-5-8*, 106) Thaxton Pr.

Rod Serling's Twilight Zone: Twenty-Six Unforgettable Explorations into the Realm of the Supernatural. Walter B. Gibson. 1990. 10.99 (*0-517-41318-3*) Random Hse Value.

Rod Stewart: A Spanner in the Works. 14.95 (*0-7935-5280-X*, 00306053) H Leonard.

Rod Stewart: Storyteller. 256p. 1991. otabind 19.95 (*0-7935-0031-1*, 00490408) H Leonard.

Rod Stewart: The Visual Documentary. John Gray. (Illus.). 96p. pap. 19.95 (*0-7119-2906-8*, OP 46762) Omnibus NY.

Rod Stewart: Unplugged & Seated. 72p. 1994. otabind 16. 95 (*0-7935-3608-1*, 00308245) H Leonard.

Rod Stewart: Vagabond Heart. Geoffrey Giuliano. 262p. 1994. pap. 12.95 (*0-7867-0163-3*) Carroll & Graf.

***Rod Stewart - Blondes Have More Fun.** Ed. by Carol Cuellar. 68p. (Orig.). (C). 1979. pap. text ed. 12.95 (*0-7692-0880-0*, VF0662) Warner Brothers.

Rod Stewart - Vagabond Heart. Ed. by Michael Lefferts. (Piano-Vocal-Guitar Ser.). 80p. (Orig.). (C). 1997. pap. text ed. 17.95 (*0-7935-0907-6*, 00308109) H Leonard.

Rod, the Root & the Flower. Coventry K. Patmore. Ed. by Derek Patmore. LC 68-16966. (Essay Index Reprint Ser.). 1977. 19.95 (*0-8369-0775-2*) Ayer.

***Rod Wooden Smoke & Moby Dick.** Ed. by Franc Chamberlain. (Contemporary Theatre Review). 1997. pap. text ed. 32.00 (*90-5702-022-X*, Harwood Acad Pubs) Gordon & Breach.

Rod, Write On: Pts. I-VIII, 1970-80. Rod Law. (Orig.). (C). text ed. 19.95 (*0-9601730-2-1*); pap. text ed. 12.50 (*0-9601730-3-X*) Rod Law.

Rodale Book of Composting: Easy Methods for Every Gardner. Ed. by Grace Gershuny & Deborah L. Martin. LC 91-27284. 304p. 1992. pap. 14.95 (*0-87857-991-5*, 01-248-1) Rodale Pr Inc.

Rodale's All-New Encyclopedia of Organic Gardening: The Indispensable Resource for Every Gardener. Ed. by Fern M. Bradley & Barbara W. Ellis. LC 91-32088. (Illus.). 704p. 1992. 29.95 (*0-87857-999-0*, 01-432-0) Rodale Pr Inc.

Rodale's All-New Encyclopedia of Organic Gardening: The Indispensable Resource for Every Gardener. Ed. by Fern M. Bradley & Barbara W. Ellis. 704p. 1993. pap. 19.95 (*0-87596-599-7*) Rodale Pr Inc.

Rodale's Basic Natural Foods Cookbook. Charles Gerras. (Illus.). 1994. 16.98 (*1-56731-044-3*, MJF Bks) Fine Comms.

Rodale's Basic Natural Foods Cookbook. Ed. by Charles Gerras. 912p. 1989. pap. 19.00 (*0-671-67338-6*, Fireside) S&S Trade.

Rodale's Book of Practical Formulas. Ed. by Paula D. Bakule. (Illus.). 1994. 12.98 (*1-56731-046-X*, MJF Bks) Fine Comms.

Rodale's Chemical Free Yard & Garden: The Ultimate Authority on Successful Organic Gardening. Fern M. Bradley & Fern Marshall. Date not set. pap. 17.95 (*0-87596-694-2*) Rodale Pr Inc.

Rodale's Color Handbook of Garden Insects. Anna Carr. LC 79-4048. (Illus.). 256p. (C). 1983. pap. 14.95 (*0-87857-460-3*, 01-637-1) Rodale Pr Inc.

***Rodale's Complete Garden Problem Solver: Instant Answers to the Most Common Gardening Questions.** Delilah Smittle et al. LC 97-4795. 1998. write for info. (*0-87596-774-4*) Rodale Pr Inc.

Rodale's Fix It Fast, Fix It Right. Gene Hamilton & Katie Hamilton. (Illus.). 1994. 9.98 (*1-56731-058-3*, MJF Bks) Fine Comms.

Rodale's Flower Garden Problem Solver. Jeff Ball & Liz Ball. (Illus.). 1994. 9.98 (*1-56731-045-1*, MJF Bks) Fine Comms.

Rodale's Flower Garden Problem Solver. Jeff Ball & Liz Ball. Date not set. pap. 14.95 (*0-87596-698-5*) Rodale Pr Inc.

Rodale's Garden Answers. large type ed. Ed. by Fern M. Bradley. 1996. pap. 25.95 (*0-7838-1608-1*, GK Hall) Thorndike Pr.

Rodale's Garden Answers: Vegetables, Fruits, Herbs At-a-Glance Solutions for Every Gardening Problem. large type ed. Ed. by Fern M. Bradley. 1996. 30.95 (*0-7838-1607-3*) G K Hall.

Rodale's Garden Answers-Vegetables, Fruits & Herbs: At-a-Glance Solutions for Every Gardening Problem. Crow Miller. Ed. by Fern M. Bradley. (Illus.). 384p. 1995. 27. 95 (*0-87596-639-X*) Rodale Pr Inc.

Rodale's Garden Problem Solver. Jeff Ball. 1996. pap. 14.95 (*0-87596-699-3*) Rodale Pr Inc.

Rodale's Illustrated Encyclopedia of Gardening & Landscaping Techniques. Rodale Press Inc., Editors. (Illus.). 1995. pap. 17.95 (*0-87596-693-4*) Rodale Pr Inc.

Rodale's Illustrated Encyclopedia of Gardening & Landscaping Techniques. Ed. by Barbara W. Elils. (Illus.). 1995. reprint ed. 14.98 (*1-56731-070-2*, MJF Bks) Fine Comms.

***Rodale's Illustrated Encyclopedia of Herbs.** Ed. by Claire Kowalchik & William H. Hylton. (Illus.). 552p. 1998. pap. 17.95 (*0-87596-964-X*) Rodale Pr Inc.

Rodale's Illustrated Encyclopedia of Herbs. Rodale Press Editors. Ed. by William H. Hylton & Claire Kowalchik. (Illus.). 552p. 1987. 26.95 (*0-87857-699-1*, 01-316-0) Rodale Pr Inc.

Rodale's Illustrated Encyclopedia of Perennials. Ellen Phillips & C. Colston Burrell. LC 92-30109. 533p. 1993. 29.95 (*0-87596-570-9*, 01-690-0) Rodale Pr Inc.

Rodales Landscape Problem Solver. Jeff Ball & Liz Ball. 1995. pap. 14.95 (*0-87596-692-6*) Rodale Pr Inc.

Rodale's Landscape Problem Solver: A Plant by Plant Guide. Jeff Ball & Liz Ball. LC 89-30190. 448p. 1989. 24.95 (*0-87857-802-1*, 01-185-0) Rodale Pr Inc.

***Rodale's No-Fail Flower Garden: How to Plan, Plant, & Grow a Beautiful, Easy-Care Garden.** Ed. by Joan Benjamin & Barbara Ellis. 1997. pap. 15.95 (*0-87596-954-2*) Rodale Pr Inc.

Rodale's No-Fail Flower Garden: How to Plan, Plant & Grow a Beautiful, Easy-Care Garden. Ed. by Barbara Ellis & Joan Benjamin. (Illus.). 384p. 1994. 27.95 (*0-87596-606-3*) Rodale Pr Inc.

***Rodale's No-Fall Flower Garden.** Ed. by Joan Benjamin & Barbara Ellis. 1997. pap. 15.95 (*0-614-27248-3*) Rodale Pr Inc.

Rodale's Pest & Disease Problem Solver: A Chemical-Free Guide to Keeping Your Garden Healthy. Miranda Smith et al. LC 95-30429. 1996. 27.95 (*0-87596-705-1*) Rodale Pr Inc.

Rodale's Sensational Desserts. J. Bingham & Delores Riccio. (Illus.). 288p. 1991. 6.99 (*0-517-66179-9*) Random Hse Value.

Rodale's Visual Encyclopedia of Needlecrafts: Applique, Crochet, Cross-Stitch, Duplicate Stitch... Carolyn Christmas. LC 95-29999. 1996. 27.95 (*0-87596-718-3*) Rodale Pr Inc.

***Rodale's Weekend Gardener: Create a Low-Maintenance Landscape to Enjoy Year-Round.** Erin Hynes. 352p. 1998. 27.95 (*0-87596-803-1*) Rodale Pr Inc.

Rodant Pel Mon: Roaming about the World with Urbici Soler, Sculptor (1890-1953) Paul D. Daniggelis. 152p. 1995. 25.00 (*0-9648062-0-7*) Intl Assn Vis Arts.

Rodant Pelmon: Roaming about the World with Urbici Soler-Sculptor (1890-1953) Paul D. Daniggelis. (Illus.). 152p. 1995. 25.00 (*0-614-13061-1*) Intl Assn Vis Arts.

***Rodchenko: Photography, 1924-1954.** Alexander Lavrentiev. 344p. 1996. 49.95 (*1-57715-002-3*) Knckerbocker.

R

Rodchenko: The Complete Works. T. Khan-Magomedov. (C). 1990. 400.00 (*0-685-34353-7*, Pub. by Collets) St Mut.

Rodchenko, Alexander: Works on Paper 1914-1920. Ed. by David Elliot & Alexander Lavrentiev. (Illus.). 212p. 1995. 95.00 (*0-85667-418-4*) Sothebys Pubns.

Roddis Line. Harvey Huston. LC 78-184838. 1972. 20.00 (*0-9600048-2-3*) Huston.

Rodd's Chemistry of Carbon Compounds. 2nd ed. Ed. by M. F. Ansell. 320p. 1995. suppl. ed. 229.25 (*0-444-82260-7*) Elsevier.

Rodd's Chemistry of Carbon Compounds. 2nd ed. Ed. by M. Sainsbury. 370p. 1995. suppl. ed. 252.00 (*0-444-82229-1*) Elsevier.

Rodd's Chemistry of Carbon Compounds, 3. 2nd ed. Ed. by M. Sainsbury. 382p. 1995. suppl. ed. 261.75 (*0-444-82242-9*) Elsevier.

Rodd's Chemistry of Carbon Compounds, 2 pts. in 1, Suppl. Vol. 1 A & B. Ed. by M. F. Ansell. 268p. 1975. 208.75 (*0-444-40972-6*) Elsevier.

Rodd's Chemistry of Carbon Compounds, 2 pts. in 1, Suppl. Vol. 1 C & D. Ed. by M. F. Ansell. 464p. 1973. 286.00 (*0-444-41072-4*) Elsevier.

Rodd's Chemistry of Carbon Compounds, 2 pts. in 1, Suppl. Vol. 2 A & B. Ed. by M. F. Ansell. 424p. 1974. 286.00 (*0-444-41133-X*) Elsevier.

Rodd's Chemistry of Carbon Compounds, 3 pts. in 1, Suppl. Vol. 2, Pts. C-E. Ed. by M. F. Ansell. 318p. 1974. 226. 00 (*0-444-41135-6*) Elsevier.

Rodd's Chemistry of Carbon Compounds, Suppl. Vol 3F, (Partial) G. 2nd ed. M. F. Ansell. 290p. 1984. 226.00 (*0-444-42269-2*, I-479-83) Elsevier.

Rodd's Chemistry of Carbon Compounds, Suppl. Vols. 3 B & C. Ed. by M. F. Ansell. 358p. 1981. 286.00 (*0-444-42017-7*) Elsevier.

Rodd's Chemistry of Carbon Compounds, Suppl. Vols. 3, Pts. D-F. Ed. by M. F. Ansell. 424p. 1982. 286.00 (*0-444-42088-6*) Elsevier.

Rodd's Chemistry of Carbon Compounds, Vols. 1-3 in 20 pts. 2nd ed. Incl. Vol. 1, Pt. A. Hydrocarbon-Halogen Derivatives. S. Coffey. 570p. 1964. 323.50 (*0-444-40131-8*); Vol. 1, Pt. B. Monohydric Alcohols, Their Ethers & Esters. S. Coffey. 314p. 1965. 252.00 (*0-444-40132-6*); Vol. 1, Pt. C. Monocarbonyl Derivatives of Aliphatic Hydrocarbons, Analogues & Derivatives. S. Coffey. 432p. 1965. 276.75 (*0-444-40133-4*); Vol. 1, Pt. D. Dihydric Alcohols, Their Oxidation Products & Derivatives. S. Coffey. 418p. 1965. 276.75 (*0-444-40134-2*); Vol. 1, Pt. E. Tri & Tetra-hydric Alcohols, Their Oxidation Products & Derivatives. S. Coffey. 488p. 1976. 303.25 (*0-444-40680-8*); Vol. 1, Pt. F. Carbohydrate Chemistry. S. Coffey. 780p. 1968. 434.75 (*0-444-40135-0*); Vol. 1, Pt. G. Enzymes, Macromolecules: Cumulative Index to Vol. 1. S. Coffey. 344p. 1976. 276.75 (*0-444-41447-9*); Vol. 2, Pt. A. Monocarbocyclic Compounds to & Including Five Ring Atoms. S. Coffey. 228p. 1968. 252. 00 (*0-444-40136-9*); Vol. 2, Pt. B. Six & Higher-Membered Monocarbocyclic Compounds. S. Coffey. 464p. 1968. 276.75 (*0-444-40137-7*); Vol. 2, Pt. C. Polycyclic Compounds Excluding Steroids. S. Coffey. 522p. 1969. 323.50 (*0-444-40681-6*); Vol. 2, Pt. D. Steroids. S. Coffey. 500p. 1970. 315.00 (*0-444-40774-X*); Vol. 2, Pt. E. Steroids. S. Coffey. 290p. 1971. 268.75 (*0-444-40775-8*); Vol. 3, Pt. A. Mononucleic Hydrocarbons & Their Halogen Derivatives. E. H. Rodd. Ed. by S. Coffey. 560p. 1971. 357.50 (*0-444-40878-9*); Vol. 3, Pt. B. Benzoquinones & Related Compounds. S. Coffey. 520p. 1974. 357.50 (*0-444-40971-8*); Vol. 3, Pt. C. Nuclear Sub-Benzene Hydrocarbons. S. Coffey. 334p. 1973. 276.75 (*0-444-41092-9*); Vol. 3, Pt. D. Aralkyl Compounds: Their Derivatives & Oxidation Products. S. Coffey. 322p. 1976. 276.75 (*0-444-41209-3*); Vol. 3, Pt. E. Monobenzine Hydrocarbons Derivatives with Functional Groups. E. H. Rodd. Ed. by S. Coffey. 314p. 1975. 276.75 (*0-444-41210-7*); Vol. 3, Pt. F. Polybenzine Hydrocarbons & Their Derivatives. S. Coffey. 416p. 1974. 297.75 (*0-444-41211-5*); Pt. G. Aromatic Compounds with Fused Carbocyclic Ring Systems. , 2 Pts. Ed. by S. Coffey. 344p. 1979. 276.75 (*0-444-41573-4*); Pt. H. Aromatic Compounds with Fused Carbocyclic Ring Systems. , 2 Pts. Ed. by S. Coffey. 660p. 1979. 407.50 (*0-444-41645-5*); write for info. (*0-318-51824-4*) Elsevier.

Rodd's Chemistry of Carbon Compounds: Aromatic Compounds, Pt. A, Vol. 3, Pt. A. 2nd ed. Ed. by M. F. Ansell. 438p. 1983. 286.00 (*0-444-42150-5*) Elsevier.

Rodd's Chemistry of Carbon Compounds Vol. 4, Pt. L: Heterocyclic Compunds, Fused-Ring Heterocycles with Three or More N Atoms. Ed. by S. Coffey. 506p. 1980. 357.50 (*0-444-41768-0*) Elsevier.

Rodd's Chemistry of Carbon Compounds - Volume IV: Heterocyclic Compounds; Part IJ. 2nd ed. M. F. Ansell. 552p. 1989. 511.25 (*0-444-87322-8*) Elsevier.

Rodd's Chemistry of Carbon Compounds-Heterocyclic Compounds Vol. 4, Pt. A: Three, Four & Five-Membered Compounds, Vol. 4A. M. F. Ansell. 540p. 1984. suppl. ed. 383.50 (*0-444-42397-4*) Elsevier.

An Asterisk (*) at the beginning of an entry indicates that the title is appearing in BIP for the first time.

R

Rodd's Chemistry of Carbon Compounds Heterocyclic Compounds, Vol. 4, Pt. D: Five Membered Heterocyclic Compunds with More Than Two Hetero-Atoms in the Ring. Ed. by S. Coffey & M. F. Ansell. 274p. 1986. 281.00 (0-444-42556-X) Elsevier.

Rodd's Chemistry of Carbon Compounds, Vol. 4 - Supplements: Heterocyclic Compounds, Part E: Six-Membered Monoheterocyclic Compounds Containing Oxygen, Sulphur, Selenium, Tellurium, Silicon, Germanium, Tin, Lead or Iodine as the Hetero-atom. 2nd ed. Ed. by M. F. Ansell. 640p. 1990. 466.25 (0-444-88611-7) Elsevier.

Rodd's Chemistry of Carbon Compounds, Vol. 4, Pt. A: Three, Four & Five-Membered Heterocyclic Compounds. S. Coffey. 650p. 1973. 407.50 (0-444-41093-7) Elsevier.

Rodd's Chemistry of Carbon Compounds, Vol. 4, Pt. C: Heterocyclic Compounds; Five-Membered Heterocyclic Compounds with Two Hetero-Atoms in the Ring from Groups V or VI of the Periodic Table. 2nd ed. Ed. by S. Coffey & M. F. Ansell. 594p. 1986. 562.50 (0-444-42555-1) Elsevier.

Rodd's Chemistry of Carbon Compounds, Vol. 4, Pt. E: Heterocyclic Compounds; Six-Membered Monoeterocyclic Compounds. S. Coffey. 522p. 1977. 357.50 (0-444-41363-4) Elsevier.

Rodd's Chemistry of Carbon Compounds, Vol. 4, Pt. G: Six-Membered Heterocyclic Compounds with a Single Nitrogen Atom from Group V of the Periodic Table. Ed. by Coffey. 506p. 1977. 357.50 (0-444-41644-7) Elsevier.

Rodd's Chemistry of Carbon Compounds, Vol. 4, Pt. H: Heterocyclic Compounds. 2nd ed. Ed. by S. Coffey. 536p. 1978. 357.50 (0-444-41575-0) Elsevier.

Rodd's Chemistry of Carbon Compounds, Vol. 4, Pt. J Vol. 4, Pt. I/J: Proteins. S. Coffey. 1989. 460.75 (0-685-84873-6) Elsevier.

Rodd's Chemistry of Carbon Compounds, Vol. 4, Pt. K: Six Membered Heterocyclic Compounds with Two or More Hetero-Atoms. S. Coffey. 552p. 1979. 357.50 (0-444-41647-1) Elsevier.

Rodd's Chemistry of Carbon Compounds, Vol. 4, Pt. L: Heterocyclic Compounds, Fused-Ring Heterocycles with Three or More N Atoms. Ed. by S. Coffey. 506p. 1980. 322.00 (0-444-40664-6) Elsevier.

Rodd's Chemistry of Carbon Compounds, Vol. 4, Pts. B & F. 2nd ed. Incl. Pt. B. Five-Membered Heterocyclic Compounds, Alkaloids, Dyes & Pigments. Ed. by S. Coffey. LC 64-4605. 462p. 1977. 323.50 (0-444-41504-1); Pt. F. Six Membered Heterocyclic Compounds with a Single Atom in the Rind, Pyridine, Polymethyl-Epyridines, Quinoline, Isoquinoline & Their Derivatives. S. Coffey. LC 64-4605. 486p. 1977. 323.50 (0-444-41503-3); LC 64-4605. write for info. (0-318-51825-2) Elsevier.

***Roddy the Rooster.** Eddie Bowman. LC 96-54301. (Illus.). (J). 1997. write for info. (1-56763-326-9); pap. write for info. (1-56763-327-7) Ozark Pub.

Rodeada Esta de Ensueno see Aguilas

Rodeados for Cazadozes de Cabezas: True Story of Frank & Marie Drown's Life with Shuar Indians in Ecuador, South America. Sandra Klaus. Tr. by Eduardo Aparicio. (Illus.). (SPA.). (J). (gr. 2-7). 1996. pap. 10.95 (0-9617490-4-0) Gospel Missionary.

Rodell Revisited: Selected Writings of Fred Rodell. Ed. by Loren Ghiglione et al. LC 93-41512. xli, 265p. 1994. 42. 50 (0-8377-1047-2) Rothman.

Roden Crater. 32p. 1988. 4.95 (0-89734-089-2, PL59-3) Mus Northern Ariz.

Rodent Angel: Poems. Debra Weinstein. LC 95-52194. 96p. (C). 1996. 25.00 (0-8147-9308-8); pap. 12.95 (0-8147-9307-X) NYU Pr.

Rodent Pest Management, 2 vols. Ed. by Ishwar Prakash. 496p. 1988. 271.00 (0-8493-6726-3, SB994, CRC Reprint) Franklin.

Rodent Pest Management in Eastern Africa. Lynwood A. Fiedler. (Plant Production & Protection Papers: 123). 106p. 1994. pap. 12.00 (92-5-103447-8, F34478, Pub. by FAO IT) Bernan Associates.

Rodent Pests & Their Control. Ed. by A. P. Buckle & R. Smith. 416p. 1994. 100.00 (0-85198-820-2) CAB Intl.

Rodent Tumor Moles in Experimental Cancer Therapy. R. F. Kallman. 1987. text ed. 88.00 (0-07-105286-0) McGraw.

Rodents. National Research Council, Committee on Vision Staff. (Laboratory Animal Management Ser.). 190p. (Orig.). (C). 1996. pap. text ed. 24.95 (0-309-04936-9) Natl Acad Pr.

Rodents: A World Survey of Species of Conservation Concern. Ed. by William Z. Lidicker, Jr. (Occasional Papers of the IUCN Species Survival Commission: No. 4). (Illus.). 64p. (Orig.). 1989. pap. 17.00 (2-88032-971-X, Pub. by IUCN SZ) Island Pr.

Rodents & Rabbits: Current Research Issues. Steven M. Niemi. LC 94-65718. 81p. 1994. pap. 30.00 (0-614-06558-5) Scientists Ctr.

Rodents in Indian Agriculture, 2 vols., 1. P. K. Ghosh & Ishwar Prakash. (C). 1992. text ed. 325.00 (0-685-61679-7, Pub. by Scientific Pubs II); text ed. 450. 00 (0-685-63524-4, Pub. by Scientific Pubs II) St Mut.

Rodents in Indian Agriculture, 2 vols., 2. P. K. Ghosh & Ishwar Prakash. (C). 1992. text ed. 100.00 (0-685-61680-0, Pub. by Scientific Pubs II); text ed. 150. 00 (0-685-63525-2, Pub. by Scientific Pubs II) St Mut.

Rodents in Indian Agriculture, 2 vols., Set. P. K. Ghosh & Ishwar Prakash. (C). 1992. text ed. 415.00 (0-685-61678-9, Pub. by Scientific Pubs II) St Mut.

Rodents in Indian Agriculture State of Art. Ishwar Prakash & P. K. Ghosh. Ed. by Jodhpur Cazri. 707p. 1992. pap. 550.00 (81-7233-014-6, Pub. by Scientific Pubs II) St Mut.

Rodents of Southern Africa. De Graaff. 1981. 52.95 (0-409-09829-9) Buttrwrth-Heinemann.

Rodents of Southern Africa. deluxe ed. De Graaff. 1981. write for info. (0-409-09830-2) Buttrwrth-Heinemann.

***Rodents of the World.** David Alderton. 192p. 1996. 27.95 (0-614-25031-5) Facts on File.

Rodeo. Ken Robbins. LC 95-49677. (Illus.). 32p. (J). (gr. k up). 1996. 14.95 (0-8050-3388-2, Bks Young Read) H Holt & Co.

Rodeo. Louise L. Serpa. (Illus.). 96p. 1994. pap. 24.95 (0-89381-585-3) Aperture.

Rodeo. Louise L. Serpa. 88p. pap. text ed. 24.95 (0-89381-650-7) FS&G.

Rodeo. Cheryl W. Bellville. (Photo Bks.). (Illus.). 32p. (J). (ps-5). 1985. reprint ed. pap. 5.95 (0-87614-492-X, Lerner Publctns) Lerner Group.

Rodeo: An Anthropologist Looks at the Wild & the Tame. Elizabeth A. Lawrence. LC 83-18176. (Illus.). xvi, 304p. (C). 1984. reprint ed. pap. text ed. 15.95 (0-226-46955-7) U Ch Pr.

Rodeo, America's Number One Sport. 2nd ed. Thomas A. Bryant. (Illus.). 64p. (J). (gr. 3-5). 1986. reprint ed. pap. 4.00 (0-941875-00-8) Wolverine Distrib.

Rodeo, an Anthropologist Looks at the Wild & the Tame. Elizabeth A. Lawrence. LC 81-3330. (Illus.). 304p. reprint ed. pap. 86.70 (0-8357-8604-8, 2035001) Bks Demand.

Rodeo & the Mimosa Tree. Jennifer Olds. LC 91-74038. 80p. 1991. pap. 9.95 (0-9627501-4-X) Event Horizon.

Rodeo Cartoons from The Buckboard. Walt LaRue. LC 89-91854. (Illus.). x, 135p. 1989. 12.95 (0-9624489-0-7) G Logsdon Bks.

Rodeo Cartoons from The Buckboard. deluxe limited ed. Walt LaRue. LC 89-91854. (Illus.). x, 135p. 1989. Leather bd., numbered & signed collector's ed. 50.00 (0-9624489-1-5) G Logsdon Bks.

Rodeo Clown: Laughs & Danger in the Ring. Keith Greenberg. Ed. by Bruce Glassman. LC 94-39123. (Risky Business Ser.). (Illus.). 32p. (J). (gr. 2-5). 1995. lib. bdg. 14.95 (1-56711-152-1) Blackbirch.

Rodeo Day. Jonelle Toriseva. LC 92-39475. (Illus.). 32p. (J). 1994. lib. bdg. 14.95 (0-02-789405-3, Mac Bks Young Read) S&S Childrens.

Rodeo Drawings of Murray Tinkelman. LC 82-71584. 130p. 1982. pap. 12.50 (0-910158-92-4); text ed. 17.50 (0-910158-91-6) Art Dir.

Rodeo Drive. Barney Leason. 416p. 1988. mass mkt. 3.95 (1-55817-093-6, Pinncle Kensgtn) Kensgtn Pub Corp.

Rodeo Harpsicord. Dennis Lucas. (Sundown Ser.). 22p. 1991. pap. 5.00 (1-879969-01-7) Catskill Reading.

Rodeo History & Legends. Bob Jordan. (Illus.). 258p. 1993. 30.00 (0-9638495-0-6) Rodeo Stuff.

Rodeo in America: Wranglers, Roughstock, & Paydirt. Wayne S. Wooden & Gavin Ehringer. LC 96-16328. (Illus.). 264p. 1996. 24.95 (0-7006-0813-3) U Pr of KS.

Rodeo Nights. Patricia McLinn. (Special Edition Ser.). 1994. mass mkt. 3.50 (0-373-09904-5, 1-09904-3) Harlequin Bks.

Rodeo of John A. Stryker. Ron Tyler. (Illus.). 1978. 20.00 (0-88426-050-X) Encino Pr.

Rodeo Patterns, No. 1. Gene Vinson & Marion Vinson. 36p. 1991. pap. text ed. 3.95 (0-9629174-4-3) Vinson Prodns.

***Rodeo Rhymes & Sagebrush Satire: Cowboy Prose & Poetry.** Steve DeMott. LC 97-90036. (Illus.). 96p. (Orig.). 1997. pap. 7.95 (0-9656669-0-5) Three Lazy D.

Rodeo Rider. Bonnie Bryant. (Saddle Club Ser.: No. 12). 144p. (J). (gr. 4 up). 1990. pap. 3.99 (0-553-15821-X) Bantam.

Rodeo Rider, Vol. 12. large type ed. Bonnie Bryant. LC 95-38629. (Saddle Club Ser.: No. 12). 144p. (J). (gr. 4 up). 1996. lib. bdg. 15.93 (0-8368-1534-3) Gareth Stevens Inc.

***Rodeo Rough Cut, Vol. 3.** Marianne Hering. (Lights, Camera, Action! Mysteries Ser.). (J). 1997. pap. text ed. 4.99 (0-7814-1548-9) Chariot Victor.

***Rodeo Town.** John Bennett. (Illus.). 80p. 1997. pap. 12.00 (0-912824-38-7) Vagabond Pr.

***Rodeoin' A Legend Lives On.** John McQuarrie. 152p. 39. 95 (0-9699761-0-0) Mountain Pr.

Rodeos. James W. Fain. LC 82-23460. (Spanish New True Bks.). (Illus.). 48p. (SPA.). (J). (gr. k-4). 1987. lib. bdg. 18.30 (0-516-31685-0) Childrens.

Rodeos: The Greatest Show on Dirt. Judith Alter. LC 96-12143. (First Books-Performances & Entertainment Ser.). 64p. (J). 1996. lib. bdg. 21.00 (0-531-20245-5) Watts.

***Rodeos: The Greatest Show on Dirt.** Judith Alter. (First Bks.). 64p. (J). 1997. pap. 6.95 (0-531-15816-0) Watts.

Rodeos, Pig Races & Other Cowboy Stories. Ken Adams. 128p. 1994. pap. 9.95 (0-9638828-0-5) Two Bit Pubns.

Roderic O'Conor. Paula Murphy. (Lives of Irish Artists Ser.). (Illus.). 36p. 1995. 7.95 (0-948524-38-3, Pub. by Town Hse IE) R Rinehart.

Roderic O'Conor: A Biography with a Catalogue of His Work. Jonathan Benington. (Illus.). 248p. (C). 1992. 22. 95 (0-7165-2492-9, Pub. by Irish Acad Pr IE) Intl Spec Bk.

Roderick. John Sladek. 210p. 1987. pap. 3.95 (0-88184-325-3) Carroll & Graf.

Roderick at Random. John Sladek. 316p. 1988. pap. 3.95 (0-88184-341-5) Carroll & Graf.

Roderick Hudson. Henry James. 10.25 (0-8446-5700-X) Peter Smith.

Roderick Hudson. Henry James. Ed. & Intro. by Geoffrey Moore. (Classics Ser.). 400p. 1986. pap. 9.95 (0-14-043264-7, Penguin Classics) Viking Penguin.

Roderick Hudson. Henry James. LC 75-158780. (Novels & Tales of Henry James Ser.: Vol. 1). 1971. reprint ed. lib. bdg. 45.00 (0-678-02801-X) Kelley.

Roderick Random. Tobias Smollett. Ed. by David Blewett. 1996. pap. 8.95 (0-14-17285-3) Penguin.

Rodewalt: With Weapons Drawn. Vance Rodewalt. (Illus.). 128p. (Orig.). 1994. pap. 16.95 (1-55059-092-8) Temeron Bks.

Rodgers & Hammerstein. Ethan Mordden. (Illus.). 224p. 1992. 45.00 (0-8109-1567-7) Abrams.

Rodgers & Hammerstein. Ethan Mordden. LC 95-4039. (Illus.). 224p. 1995. pap. 19.98 (0-8109-8144-0) Abrams.

Rodgers & Hammerstein. Richard Rodgers & Oscar Hammerstein. 64p. 1989. pap. 9.95 (0-7935-2115-7, 00240825) H Leonard.

Rodgers & Hammerstein: A Celebration. Ethan Mordden. (Illus.). 224p. 1993. pap. 19.95 (0-8065-1469-8, Citadel Pr) Carol Pub Group.

Rodgers & Hammerstein: The Piano Duet Book for One Piano, Four Hands. Richard Rodgers & Oscar Hammerstein. 56p. 1981. pap. 7.95 (0-7935-0498-8, 00312691) H Leonard.

Rodgers & Hammerstein Children's Songs. 080p. 1981. 12. 95 (0-88188-245-3, 0312350) H Leonard.

Rodgers & Hammerstein Favorites. Richard Rodgers & Oscar Hammerstein. 48p. 1991. pap. 7.95 (0-7935-0608-5, 00290326) H Leonard.

Rodgers & Hammerstein for the Harp. Deborah Friou. 48p. (Orig.). (YA). 1990. pap. 15.95 (0-9628120-0-5) Friou Music.

***Rodgers & Hammerstein Songbook.** Oscar Rogers & Oscar Hammerstein. Date not set. write for info. (0-688-12685-5, Tambourine Bks) Morrow.

***Rodgers & Hammerstein Songbook.** Richard Rogers & Oscar Hammerstein. Date not set. lib. bdg. write for info. (0-688-12686-3, Tambourine Bks) Morrow.

Rodgers & Hammerstein Songbook, Vol. 165. 80p. 1982. per. 8.95 (0-7935-0750-2, 00101895) H Leonard.

Rodgers & Hammerstein Styling of Dick Hyman: Easy Piano Solos. Richard Rodgers & Oscar Hammerstein. 64p. 1993. pap. 10.95 (0-7935-1106-2, 00290352) H Leonard.

Rodgers & Hart. (Piano Solos Ser.). 64p. 1991. pap. 8.95 (0-7935-0447-3, 00009081) H Leonard.

Rodgers & Hart's All Time Favorites. Rodger. 1995. pap. 12.95 (0-89724-945-3, MF9560) Warner Brothers.

Rodgers' Child. J. R. Churgin. LC 90-62549. 1991. 10.50 (0-87212-243-3) Libra.

***Rodgers-Hearne & Related Families.** Bettie T. Cobb. (Illus.). 270p. 1997. 30.00 (0-9606128-6-6) Durant Pub.

Rodin. Claudine Mitchell. (Illus.). 224p. 1997. pap. 14.95 (0-500-20296-6) Thames Hudson.

Rodin. Rainer M. Rilke. LC 74-6405. (Studies in French Literature: No. 45). 1974. lib. bdg. 75.00 (0-8383-1913-0) M S G Haskell Hse.

Rodin. Yvon Taillandier. (CAL Art Ser.). (Illus.). 1988. 14. 95 (0-517-08266-7, Crown) Crown Pub Group.

Rodin. Yvon Taillandier. (Art Library). 1995. pap. 12.00 (0-517-88378-3, Crown) Crown Pub Group.

Rodin. 10th ed. Selected by Ludwig Goldscheider. (Illus.). 128p. 1996. reprint ed. pap. 19.95 (0-7148-3577-3, Pub. by Phaidon Press UK) Chronicle Bks.

Rodin. Bernard Champigneulle. LC 85-51233. (World of Art Ser.). (Illus.). 288p. 1994. reprint ed. pap. 14.95 (0-500-20061-0) Thames Hudson.

Rodin: Eros & Creativity. Ed. by Rainer Crone et al. (Illus.). 236p. 1995. 70.00 (3-7913-1185-9, Pub. by Prestel GW) te Neues.

***Rodin: Eros & Creativity.** Ed. by Rainer Crone & Siegfried Salzmann. LC 97-3599. (Illus.). 236p. 1997. pap. 29.95 (3-7913-1809-8, Pub. by Prestel GW) te Neues.

Rodin: Sculpture & Drawings. Catherine Lampert. LC 86-50765. 256p. 1987. pap. 27.50 (0-300-03832-1) Yale U Pr.

Rodin: The Hand of Genius. Helene Pinet. Tr. by Caroline Palmer. (Discoveries Ser.). (Illus.). 144p. 1992. pap. 12. 95 (0-8109-2888-4) Abrams.

Rodin: The Shape of Genius. Ruth Butler. LC 92-43552. (Illus.). 592p. 1993. 40.00 (0-300-05400-9) Yale U Pr.

Rodin: The Shape of Genius. Ruth Butler. (Illus.). 1996. pap. 20.00 (0-300-06498-5) Yale U Pr.

Rodin: The Shape of Genius. Ruth Butler. (C). 1996. pap. 20.00 (0-614-12572-3) Yale U Pr.

Rodin & Camille Claudel. J. A. Schmoll-Eisenwerth et al. (Pegasus Library). (Illus.). 128p. 1995. 25.00 (3-7913-1382-7, Pub. by Prestel GW) te Neues.

Rodin & His Contemporaries: The Iris & B. Gerald Cantor Collection. Albert E. Elsen & Philip Conisbee. (Illus.). 256p. 1992. 45.00 (1-55859-364-0, Cross Riv Pr) Abbeville Pr.

***Rodin & Michelangelo: A Study in Artistic Inspiration.** Flavio Fergonzi et al. LC 97-6631. 1997. write for info. (0-87633-110-X); pap. write for info. (0-87633-109-6) Phila Mus Art.

Rodin on Art & Artists: With Sixty Illustrations of His Work. 2nd ed. Rodin. (Fine Art Ser.). (Illus.). 160p. 1983. reprint ed. pap. 7.95 (0-486-24487-3) Dover.

Rodina-Russkaja khrestomatija. (Illus.). 416p. 1960. reprint ed. 20.00 (0-685-42885-0) Holy Trinity.

Rodine Arias: For Soprano Canzone di Doretta Ore Dolci e Divine. Giacomo Puccini. 16p. 1992. pap. 5.95 (0-7935-1571-8, 00747029) H Leonard.

Rodman the Boat-Steerer, & Other Stories. Louis Becke. LC 70-125206. (Short Story Index Reprint Ser.). 1977. 21.95 (0-8369-3573-X) Ayer.

Rodman the Keeper: Southern Sketches. Constance F. Woolson. LC 77-137310. reprint ed. 29.50 (0-404-07038-8) AMS Pr.

Rodman the Keeper: Southern Sketches. Constance F. Woolson. (C). 1972. reprint ed. lib. bdg. 14.50 (0-8422-8130-4) Irvington.

Rodman the Keeper: Southern Sketches. Constance F. Woolson. (C). 1986. reprint ed. pap. text ed. 7.95 (0-8290-1926-X) Irvington.

Rodman the Keeper: Southern Sketches. Constance F. Woolson. (BCL1-PS American Literature Ser.). 339p. 1992. reprint ed. lib. bdg. 89.00 (0-7812-6911-3) Rprt Serv.

Rodmoor. John Cowper Powys. LC 73-77361. 1973. 33.95 (0-912568-05-4) Colgate U Pr.

Rodney. David Hannay. LC 72-8678. (American Revolutionary Ser.). reprint ed. lib. bdg. 37.50 (0-8398-0805-4) Irvington.

Rodney Alan Greenblat's Reality & Imagination: Two Taste Treats in One (Exhibition Catalogue) Sanford S. Shaman. (Illus.). 56p. (Orig.). 1987. pap. 12.00 (0-911209-35-2) Palmer Mus Art.

Rodney King & the L.A. Rebellion: Analysis & Commentary by 13 Independent Black Writers. Ras M. Collier et al. 144p. (Orig.). 1992. pap. 10.00 (1-56411-036-2) Untd Bros & Sis.

Rodney Kinsman: The Logical Art of Furniture. Jose Manser. (Illus.). 112p. 1992. 29.95 (1-85702-010-3, Pub. by Fourth Estate UK) Trafalgar.

***Rodney's Inside Story.** Lynne Barasch. (Illus.). 32p. (J). 3.98 (0-8317-6836-3) Smithmark.

Rodo & Ruben Dario. Max Henriquez Urena. 1976. lib. bdg. 59.95 (0-8490-2529-X) Gordon Pr.

Rodogune. Pierre Corneille. 128p. (FRE.). 1985. pap. 8.95 (0-7859-4644-6) Fr & Eur.

Rodogune: The French Text with a Facing English Translation. Pierre Corneille. Ed. & Tr. by William G. Clubb. LC 73-86397. (Regents Continental Drama Ser.). 169p. reprint ed. pap. 48.20 (0-7837-4657-1, 2044381) Bks Demand.

Rodolfo Gonzalez Pacheco: A Chronology. V. Munoz. Tr. by W. Scott Johnson. (Libertarian & Anarchist Chronology Ser.). 1979. lib. bdg. 59.95 (0-8490-3032-3) Gordon Pr.

Rodolfo Machado & Jorge Silvetti: Buildings for Cities. Peter G. Rowe. (Illus.). 96p. 1989. 25.00 (0-614-14663-1) Harvard Univ Graduate Schl of.

***Rodolfo Morales: Juegos y Evocaciones.** Margarita G. Arredondo. 74p. 1996. 22.95 (968-6951-07-5) Mexican Museum.

Rodolphe Bresdin, 2 vols. V. Gelder. 1987. lib. bdg. 468.00 (90-247-1917-8) Kluwer Ac.

Rodomonte's Revenge. Gary Paulsen. 96p. (J). 1994. pap. 3.50 (0-440-41024-X) Dell.

Rodrigo Chronicles: Conversations about America & Race. Richard Delgado. 275p. (C). 1995. 35.00 (0-8147-1863-9) NYU Pr.

Rodrigo Chronicles: Conversations about America & Race. Richard Delgado. 275p. (C). 1996. pap. 18.95 (0-8147-1882-5) NYU Pr.

***Rodrigue Retrospective.** George Rodrigue. Date not set. pap. 75.00 (0-670-86948-1) Viking Penguin.

Rodriques the Interpreter: An Early Jesuit in Japan & China. Michael Cooper. (Illus.). 416p. (Orig.). 1994. pap. 17.95 (0-8348-0319-4) Weatherhill.

Rods, Rods, Rods. Planet Dexter Editors. 1995. pap. 17.50 (0-201-48314-9) Addison-Wesley.

Rodtschenko. A. M. Rodtschenko. 224p. 1992. text ed. 45. 00 (3-364-00273-8) Gordon & Breach.

Rodulfi Tortarii Carmina. Rudolphus Tortarius. Ed. by Marbury B. Ogle & Dorothy M. Schullian. LC 34-3402. (American Academy in Rome. Papers & Monographs: Vol. 8). 560p. reprint ed. pap. 159.60 (0-685-15604-4, 2026724) Bks Demand.

Rodzianko: An Orthodox Journey from Revolution to Millennium 1917-1988. Larry Witham. 262p. (Orig.). (C). 1990. pap. text ed. 29.50 (0-8191-7996-5); lib. bdg. 52.50 (0-8191-7995-7) U Pr of Amer.

Roe-Rowe: The Decendents of William Roe-D1720-VA.'s Son John. Rupert O. Godley. LC 87-90965. (Illus.). 98p. 1987. pap. text ed. 42.00 (0-9619024-0-X) R O Godley.

Roe v. Wade: The Abortion Question. D. J. Herda. LC 93-22403. (Landmark Supreme Court Cases Ser.). (Illus.). 104p. (YA). (gr. 6 up). 1994. lib. bdg. 18.95 (0-89490-459-0) Enslow Pubs.

Roe v. Wade (1973) Abortion. Susan D. Gold. (Supreme Court Decisions Ser.). (Illus.). 96p. (YA). (gr. 6 up). 1994. lib. bdg. 15.98 (0-8050-3659-8) TFC Bks NY.

Roe vs. Wade: The Fight over Life & Liberty. Nancy Tompkins. LC 96-13523. (Historic Supreme Court Cases Ser.). 144p. (J). 1996. lib. bdg. 22.00 (0-531-11286-1) Watts.

Roebling's Delaware. Robert M. Vogel. (Illus.). 52p. 1995. reprint ed. pap. 3.95 (0-915992-71-X) Eastern Acorn.

Roehenstart: A Late Stuart Pretender. George Sherburn. LC 60-8402. 156p. reprint ed. 44.50 (0-8357-9655-8, 2013622) Bks Demand.

Roemer: Man Against the Mob. William F. Roemer, Jr. 416p. 1991. mass mkt. 5.99 (0-8041-0718-1) Ivy Books.

Roemer's Texas. 4th ed. Ferdinand Roemer. Ed. & Tr. by Oswald Mueller from GER. 320p. 1995. 27.95 (1-57168-040-3, Eakin Pr) Sunbelt Media.

Roemische Geschichte, 4. Theodor Mommsen. 121p. (GER.). 1966. pap. text ed. 13.95 (3-487-10124-6) G Olms Pubs.

Roemische Politik & Piraterie im Oestlichen Mittelmeer: Vom 3. Bis 1, Jh. v. Chr. Hartel Pohl. (Untersuchungen zur Antiken Literatur & Geschichte Ser.: Band 42). x, 310p. (GER.). (C). 1993. lib. bdg. 114.70 (3-11-013890-5) De Gruyter.

Roemische Tempel in Syrien: Nach Aufnahmen und Untersuchungen von Mitgliedern der Deutschen Baalbekexpedition, 1901-1904, 2 pts, Pt. 1. Daniel Krencker & Willy Zschietzschmann. (Denkmaeler Antiker Architektur Ser.: Vol. 5). (Illus.). 298p. (GER.). (C). 1978. reprint ed. 253.85 (3-11-004989-9) De Gruyter.

An Asterisk (*) at the beginning of an entry indicates that the title is appearing in BIP for the first time.

Roemische Tempel in Syrien: Nach Aufnahmen und Untersuchungen von Mitgliedern der Deutschen Baalbekexpedition, 1901-1904, 2 pts, Pt. 2. Daniel Krencker & Willy Zschietzschmann. (Denkmaeler Antiker Architektur Ser.: Vol. 5). (Illus.). 298p. (GER.). (C). 1978. reprint ed. 161.55 (3-11-004990-2) De Gruyter.

Roemischen Inschriften von Tarraco, 2 vols. Geza Alfoeldy. (Madrider Forschungen Ser.: Vol. 10). (GER.). (C). 1975. 246.15 (3-11-004403-X) De Gruyter.

Roemischen Skulpturen von Tarraco. Eva M. Koppel. (Madrider Forschungen Ser.: Band 15). (Illus.). xii, 171p. (GER.). 1985. 152.35 (3-11-009728-1) De Gruyter.

Roenigk & Roenigk's Dermatologic Surgery: Principles & Practice. 2nd ed. Ed. by Randall K. Roenigk & Henry H. Roenigk, Jr. LC 95-46848. 1408p. 1996. 175.00 (0-8247-9503-2) Dekker.

Roentgen Appearance of the Hand in Diffuse Disease. Howard L. Steinbach et al. LC 74-83116. 690p. reprint ed. pap. 180.00 (0-685-15289-8, 2026507) Bks Demand.

Roentgen Diagnosis of the Urogenital System. O. Olsson. LC 73-14486. (Encyclopedia of Medical Radiology Ser.: Vol. 13, Pt. 1). (Illus.). 690p. 1974. 300.00 (0-387-06514-8) Spr-Verlag.

Roentgenographic Diagnosis of Renal Mass Lesions. Erich K. Lang. LC 70-125008. (Illus.). 190p. 1971. 10.60 (0-87527-047-6) Green.

Roentgenologist. Jack Rudman. (Career Examination Ser.: C-697). 1994. pap. 39.95 (0-8373-0697-3) Nat Learn.

Roerich Pact & Banner of Peace. Roerich, Nicholas, Museum Staff. 2.00 (0-686-79664-0) Agni Yoga Soc.

Roeser's Audiology Desk Reference: A Guide to the Practice of Audiology. Ed. by Ross J. Roeser. (Illus.). 400p. 1996. pap. 42.50 (0-86577-574-5) Thieme Med Pubs.

Roesone Domain Pack: Birthright: Legacy of Kings Accessory. TSR Inc. Staff. 1995. 6.95 (0-7869-0284-1) TSR Inc.

Roger. Robert C. Wright. LC 94-69399. (Illus.). 100p. (Orig.). 1994. pap. write for info. (0-88100-084-1) Natl Writ Pr.

Roger - An Extraordinary Peace Campaigner. Wild Goose Publications Staff. (C). 1990. text ed. 30.00 (0-947988-38-6, Pub. by Wild Goose Pubns UK) St Mut.

Roger Adams: Scientist & Statesman. Ed. by D. Stanley Tarbell & Ann T. Tarbell. LC 81-17625. 240p. 1981. 15.95 (0-8412-0598-1); pap. 10.95 (0-8412-0711-9) Am Chemical.

*Roger & Gray Italian Cookbook. Ruth Rogers & Rose Gray. 1996. 40.00 (0-676-51948-2) Random.

Roger Ascham. Lawrence V. Ryan. viii, 352p. 1963. 42.50 (0-8047-0149-0) Stanford U Pr.

Roger Ascham. fac. ed. Lawrence V. Ryan. LC 63-10735. 111p. 1963. reprint ed. pap. 30.00 (0-7837-7912-7, 2047668) Bks Demand.

Roger B. Taney: Jacksonian Jurist. Charles W. Smith. LC 72-8802. (American Constitutional & Legal History Ser). 252p. 1973. reprint ed. lib. bdg. 32.50 (0-686-85848-4) Da Capo.

Roger Bacon: Christian Mystic & Alchemist. H. Stanley Redgrove. 1994. pap. 6.95 (1-55818-303-5) Holmes Pub.

Roger Bacon & His Search for a Universal Science. Stewart C. Easton. LC 70-100159. 255p. 1970. reprint ed. text ed. 38.50 (0-8371-3399-8, EARB, Greenwood Pr) Greenwood.

*Roger Bacon & the Origins of Perspectiva in the Middle Ages: A Critical Edition & English Translation of Bacon's Perspectiva with Introduction & Notes. Roger Bacon. Tr. & Intro. by David C. Lindberg. (Illus.). 528p. 1996. 105.00 (0-19-823992-0) OUP.

Roger Bacon, Three Treatments of Universals. Tr. by Thomas S. Maloney. (Medieval & Renaissance Texts & Studies: Vol. 66). 176p. 1989. 24.00 (0-86698-075-X, MR66) MRTS.

Roger Bacon's Letter: Concerning the Marvelous Power of Art & Nature & Concerning the Nullity of Magic Together with Notes & an Account of Bacon's Life & Work. Roger Bacon. Tr. by Tenney L. Davis. 77p. 1992. pap. 5.95 (1-56459-278-2) Kessinger Pub.

Roger Bacon's Letter Concerning the Marvelous Power of Art & of Nature & Concerning the Nullity of Magic. Roger Bacon. Tr. by Tenney L. Davis from LAT. LC 79-8594. 80p. reprint ed. 42.50 (0-404-18495-2) AMS Pr.

*Roger Bergolds Dairy Wine Companion Vol. 1: A Term a Day Wine Calendar. Roger Bergold. Ed. by Ann Winfield. (Illus.). 320p. (Orig.). 1996. 12.95 (1-889841-04-8) Chapel Hill.

Roger Black's Desktop Design Power. Roger Black. 1991. pap. 24.95 (0-679-79018-7) Random.

Roger Blin & Twentieth-Century Playwrights. Odette Aslan. Tr. by Ruby Cohn. (Directors in Perspective Ser.). (Illus.). 220p. 1988. text ed. 69.95 (0-521-22440-3) Cambridge U Pr.

Roger Boyle, First Earl of Orrery. Kathleen M. Lynch. LC 65-17348. 328p. reprint ed. pap. 93.50 (0-317-29904-2, 2021780) Bks Demand.

*Roger C. Parker's Guide to Web Content & Design. Roger C. Parker. 1997. 39.95 (1-55828-553-9) MIS Press.

Roger Caras Dog Book. 3rd ed. Roger Caras. (Illus.). 320p. 1996. 21.95 (0-87131-814-8); pap. 14.95 (0-87131-799-0) M Evans.

*Roger Caras' Treasury of Classic Nature Tales. Roger Caras. 1997. 10.99 (1-57866-009-2) Galahad Bks.

Roger Caras' Treasury of Great Cat Stories. Roger Caras. 1990. 9.98 (0-88365-763-5) Galahad Bks.

Roger Caras' Treasury of Great Dog Stories. Roger Caras. 1990. 9.98 (0-88365-764-3) Galahad Bks.

Roger Caras' Treasury of Great Dog Stories. Intro. by Roger A. Caras. 512p. 1988. pap. 12.50 (0-525-48428-0, 01212-360, Dutton-Truman Talley) NAL-Dutton.

Roger Caras Treasury of Great Fishing Stories. Roger Caras. 1996. 27.00 (0-88486-142-2, Bristol Park Bks) Arrowood Pr.

Roger Caras' Treasury of Great Horse Stories. Roger Caras. 1993. 9.98 (0-88365-840-2) Galahad Bks.

Roger Caras' Treasury of Great Horse Stories. Ed. by Roger Caras. 512p. 1994. pap. 15.95 (0-452-27307-2, Plume-Truman Talley Bks) NAL-Dutton.

Roger Conant: A Founder of Massachusetts. Clifford K. Shipton. (Illus.). 171p. 1991. reprint ed. lib. bdg. 35.00 (0-8328-2895-5) Higginson Bk Co.

Roger Corman: The Best of the Cheap Acts. Mark T. McGee. LC 87-46389. (Illus.). 261p. 1988. lib. bdg. 32.50 (0-89950-330-6) McFarland & Co.

Roger Dawson's Secrets of Power Negotiating. Roger Dawson. LC 94-46691. 256p. 1995. 21.99 (1-56414-153-5) Career Pr Inc.

Roger Dawson's Secrets of Power Negotiating. Roger Dawson. 320p. 1996. pap. 13.99 (1-56414-259-0) Career Pr Inc.

Roger de Piles' Theory of Art. Thomas Puttfarken. LC 85-40467. (Illus.). 148p. 1985. 30.00 (0-300-03356-7) Yale U Pr.

Roger Ebert's Book of Film: From Tolstoy to Tarantino - The Finest Writing from a Century of Film. Ed. by Roger Ebert. LC 96-14271. 512p. 1996. 30.00 (0-393-04000-3) Norton.

Roger Ebert's Video Companion, 1997 Edition. Roger Ebert. 994p. (Orig.). 1996. pap. 17.95 (0-8362-2152-4) Andrews & McMeel.

*Roger Ebert's Video Companion, 1998 Edition: With Pocket Video Guide. Roger Ebert. (Illus.). 994p. (Orig.). 1997. pap. 17.95 (0-8362-3688-2) Andrews & McMeel.

Roger Fenton. Pref. by Richard Pare. (Masters of Photography Ser.: Vol. 4). (Illus.). 96p. 1988. 22.95 (0-89381-270-6); pap. 15.95 (0-89381-271-4) Aperture.

Roger Fenton: Pasha & Bayadere. Gordon Baldwin. LC 96-1755. (Getty Museum Studies on Art Ser.). (Illus.). 122p. (Orig.). 1996. pap. 16.95 (0-89236-367-3, J P Getty Museum) J P Getty Trust.

Roger Fenton, Photographer of the Crimean War: With an Essay on His Life & Work by Helmut & Alison Gernsheim. Roger Fenton. LC 72-9200. (Literature of Photography Ser.). 1976. reprint ed. 18.95 (0-405-04909-9) Ayer.

Roger Friday: Live from the Fifth Grade. Colleen O. McKenna. LC 93-13706. 160p. (YA). (gr. 4-6). 1994. 13.95 (0-590-46684-4) Scholastic Inc.

Roger Fry: A Biography. Virginia Woolf. LC 75-34023. (Illus.). 307p. 1976. reprint ed. pap. 10.95 (0-15-678520-X, Harvest Bks) HarBrace.

Roger Fry & the Beginnings of Formalist Art Criticism. Jacqueline V. Falkenheim. LC 80-23577. (Studies in Fine Arts: Criticism: No. 8). (Illus.). 169p. reprint ed. pap. 48.20 (0-685-20452-9, 2070317) Bks Demand.

Roger Fry Reader. Roger Fry. (Illus.). 456p. 1996. pap. text ed. 19.95 (0-226-26642-7) U Ch Pr.

Roger Fry Reader. Ed. & Intro. by Christopher Reed. 456p. 1996. lib. bdg. 50.00 (0-226-26643-5) U Ch Pr.

*Roger Godwin. Thomas Gifford. Date not set. write for info. (0-688-04718-1) Morrow.

Roger Haines on Controls. Roger W. Haines. (Illus.). 224p. 1990. 36.95 (0-8306-7625-2, 3625, TAB/TPR) TAB Bks.

Roger Haines on Report Writing: A Guide for Engineers. Roger W. Haines. 1990. text ed. 22.95 (0-07-155359-2) McGraw.

*Roger Jennings Database Developers Guide with Visual Basic. Roger Jennings. 1300p. 1997. 59.99 (0-672-31063-5) Sams.

Roger Joseph Boscovich, S.J., F.R.S., 1711-1787: Studies of His Life & Work on the 250th Anniversary of His Birth. Lancelot L. Whyte. LC 63-21822. 234p. reprint ed. pap. 66.70 (0-7837-0479-8, 2040802) Bks Demand.

Roger, Karl, Rick, & Shane Are Friends of Mine. Charles Stetler. 1973. 3.50 (0-917554-16-7) Maelstrom.

Roger L. Crossgrove Three Decades: Works on Paper & Photographs. Intro. by William E. Parker. LC 65-15853. (Illus.). 15p. Date not set. 4.50 (0-614-10429-7) W Benton Mus.

Roger Maris: A Title to Fame. Harvey Rosenfeld. (Illus.). 288p. 1991. 19.95 (0-911007-12-1) Prairie Hse.

Roger Mertin, Records 1976-1978. Roger Mertin. Ed. by Desmarais. LC 78-17219. 46p. 1978. pap. 3.95 (0-932026-02-8) Columbia College Chi.

Roger North's The Musicall Grammarian 1728. Ed. by Mary Chan & Jamie Kassler. (Cambridge Studies in Music). (Illus.). 300p. (C). 1990. text ed. 80.00 (0-521-33131-5) Cambridge U Pr.

Roger of Salisbury: Viceroy of England. Edward J. Kealey. LC 78-92681. 328p. reprint ed. pap. 93.50 (0-7837-4811-6, 2044458) Bks Demand.

Roger of Sicily & the Normans in Lower Italy, 1016-1154. Edmund Curtis. LC 70-180443. (Heroes of the Nations Ser.). reprint ed. 30.00 (0-404-56536-0) AMS Pr.

Roger of Wendover: Chronica Sive Flores Historiarum, 4 vols. Ed. by H. O. Coxe. (English Historical Society Publications: Vol. 12). 1974. reprint ed. 250.00 (0-8115-1537-0) Periodicals Srv.

Roger Sherman & the Independent Oil Men. fac. ed. Chester M. Destler. LC 67-13466. 317p. 1967. reprint ed. pap. 90.40 (0-608-01013-8, 2061871) Bks Demand.

Roger Sherman's Connecticut: Yankee Politics & the American Revolution. Christopher Collier. LC 78-153104. 423p. reprint ed. pap. 120.60 (0-685-23464-9, 2056659) Bks Demand.

Roger Taney: The Dred Scott Legacy. Suzanne Freedman. LC 94-30953. (Justices of the Supreme Court Ser.). (Illus.). 112p. (YA). (gr. 6 up). 1995. lib. bdg. 18.95 (0-89490-560-0) Enslow Pubs.

Roger Tappen's Simply Elegant Cookbook. Roger Tappen. LC 93-72896. 208p. 1993. 14.95 (0-9638143-0-3) Benwood Pubng.

Roger Teglia: Those Were the Days: Dayton, Nevada, Fish & Game Affairs, Agricultural Business, Nevada Politics. Ed. by Mary E. Glass. 276p. 1995. lib. bdg. 47.50 (1-56475-133-3) U NV Oral Hist.

Roger the Puppy. (Illus.). 8p. (J). (ps). 16.99 (1-881445-46-1) Sandvik Pub.

Roger Tory Peterson: The Art & Photography of the World's Foremost Birder. Photos by Roger T. Peterson. LC 94-14288. (Illus.). 208p. 1994. 50.00 (0-8478-1816-0) Rizzoli Intl.

Roger Tory Peterson's ABC of Birds: A Book for Little Birdwatchers. Illus. & Photos by Roger T. Peterson. LC 95-15540. 32p. (J). (gr. 1-3). 1995. 15.95 (0-7893-0009-5) Universe.

Roger Tory Peterson's World of Birds 1997. Peterson. 1996. pap. 12.95 (0-684-81602-4) S&S Trade.

Roger Verge's Entertaining in the French Style. Roger Verge. Ed. by Stephanie Curtis. Tr. by Geoffrey O'Brien from FRE. LC 86-5816. (Illus.). 320p. 1986. 60.00 (0-941434-90-7) Stewart Tabori & Chang.

*Roger Verge's New Entertaining in the French Style. Roger Verge. LC 97-12776. (Illus.). 160p. 1997. 35.00 (1-55670-624-3) Stewart Tabori & Chang.

Roger Verge's Vegetables in the French Style. Edward L. Schneider. LC 94-11420. (Illus.). 256p. 1994. 35.00 (1-885183-04-6) Artisan.

Roger Vieillard. Contrib. by Marc P. Vincent. (Illus.). 48p. (Orig.). 1988. pap. 15.00 (0-944751-01-6) Maxwells Busn.

Roger Waters: Amused to Death. (Illus.). 80p. 1992. pap. 24.95 (0-7119-3220-4, AM90154) Music Sales.

Roger Waters: Pros & Cons of Hitchhiking. (Illus.). 64p. 1984. pap. 14.95 (0-7119-1959-3, AM76480) Music Sales.

Roger Waters: Radio KAOS. (Illus.). 56p. 1987. pap. 14.95 (0-8256-1158-X, AM68040) Music Sales.

Roger White Collection. Roger White. 1987. pap. 25.00 (0-85398-310-0) G Ronald Pub.

Roger Williams. unabridged ed. Mark Ammerman. (Young Reader's Christian Library). (Illus.). 224p. (J). (gr. 3-7). 1996. pap. 1.39 (1-55748-761-8) Barbour & Co.

Roger Williams. Edmund J. Carpenter. LC 72-13. (Select Bibliographies Reprint Ser.). 1977. reprint ed. 19.95 (0-8369-9955-X) Ayer.

Roger Williams: Mini-Play. (U. S. History Ser.). (J). (gr. 5 up). 1982. 6.50 (0-89550-349-2) Stevens & Shea.

Roger Williams: Prophet & Pioneer. Emily Easton. 1988. reprint ed. lib. bdg. 49.00 (0-7812-0207-8) Rprt Serv.

Roger Williams: Prophet & Pioneer. Emily Easton. LC 78-144994. 399p. 1972. reprint ed. 49.00 (0-403-00793-3) Scholarly.

*Roger Williams - Contemporary Piano Solos. Ed. by Carol Cuellar. 76p. (Orig.). (C). 1984. pap. text ed. 11.95 (0-7692-0484-8, TPF0133) Warner Brothers.

Roger Williams' Dream for America, Vol. 129. Donald Skaggs. LC 92-4486. (American University Studies: Vol. IX). 240p. (C). 1994. text ed. 45.95 (0-8204-1870-6) P Lang Pubng.

Roger Williams, God's Apostle of Advocacy: Biography & Rhetoric. L. Raymond Camp. LC 88-26708. (Studies in American Religion: Vol. 36). 240p. 1989. lib. bdg. 89.95 (0-88946-679-3) E Mellen.

Roger Williams, Prophet & Pioneer. Emily Easton. LC 71-102235. (Select Bibliographies Reprint Ser.). 1977. 35.95 (0-8369-5120-4) Ayer.

Roger Williams, Prophet & Pioneer. Emily Easton. (BCL1 - United States Local History Ser.). 399p. 1991. reprint ed. lib. bdg. 89.00 (0-7812-6560-6) Rprt Serv.

Roger Williams, the Pioneer of Religious Liberty. Oscar S. Straus. LC 76-137385. (Select Bibliographies Reprint Ser.). 1977. 23.95 (0-8369-5586-2) Ayer.

Roger Zelany's Amber Seven No-Trump. 320p. 1988. pap. 3.50 (0-8125-6419-7) Tor Bks.

Roger Zelazny. Theodore Krulik. (Recognitions Ser.). 192p. 1986. 19.95 (0-8044-2490-X, F Ungar Bks) Continuum.

Roger Zelazny. Jane M. Lindskold. LC 93-29505. (Twayne's United States Authors Ser.). 192p. 1993. 22.95 (0-8057-3953-X, Twayne) Scribnrs Ref.

Roger Zelazny. Carl B. Yoke. Ed. by Roger C. Schlobin. LC 79-17107. (Starmont Reader's Guide Ser.: Vol. 2). 112p. (Orig.). 1979. pap. 17.00 (0-916732-04-5); lib. bdg. 27.00 (0-916732-13-4) Borgo Pr.

Roger Zelazny & Jane Lindskold's Chronomaster: A Novel. Jane M. Lindskold. 1996. mass mkt., per. 5.99 (0-7615-0422-2) Prima Pub.

Roger Zelazny & Jane Lindskold's Chronomaster: The Official Strategy Guide. Jane Lidskold. 1996. pap. 19.95 (0-7615-0413-3) Prima Pub.

Roger Zelazny Master of Amber: A Working Bibliography. Gordon Benson, Jr. & Phil Stephensen-Payne. (Galactic Central Bibliographies Ser.: No. 38). ix, 65p. (C). 1992. lib. bdg. 25.00 (0-8095-4736-8) Borgo Pr.

Roger Zelazny's Visual Guide to Castle Amber. Roger Zelazny & Neil Randall. (Illus.). 1988. pap. 10.00 (0-380-75566-1) Avon.

Rogerian Perspectives: Collaborative Rhetoric for Oral & Written Communication. Nathaniel Teich. Ed. by Marcia Farr. (Writing Research Ser.). 304p. (C). 1992. pap. 39.50 (0-89391-668-4); text ed. 73.25 (0-89391-667-6) Ablex Pub.

Rogers - Turfler Family: A Search for Ancestors. I. N. Williams. (Illus.). 120p. 1992. reprint ed. pap. 19.00 (0-8328-2717-7); reprint ed. lib. bdg. 29.00 (0-8328-2716-9) Higginson Bk Co.

*Rogers & Gray Italian Country. Ruth Rogers & Rose Gray. 1996. write for info. (0-679-45957-X) Random.

Rogers & Gray Italian Country Cookbook. Ruth Rogers & Rose Gray. 317p. 1996. 40.00 (0-679-45001-7) Fodors Travel.

Rogers Hornsby. Jack Kavanagh. (Baseball Legends Ser.). (Illus.). 64p. (J). (gr. 3 up). 1991. lib. bdg. 15.95 (0-7910-1178-X) Chelsea Hse.

Rogers Hornsby: A Biography. Charles C. Alexander. (Illus.). 384p. 1996. pap. 14.95 (0-8050-4697-6, Owl) H Holt & Co.

Rogers' Rangers. John Dandola. (Learning & Coloring Bks.). (Illus.). 24p. (Orig.). (J). (gr. k-6). 1992. pap. 3.95 (1-878452-08-8, Lrning & Coloring Bks) Tory Corner Editions.

Rogers' Reminiscences of the French War & Memoir of General Stark. Robert Rogers. LC 88-80441. (Illus.). 343p. (Orig.). 1988. pap. 20.00 (0-9620261-3-1) Freedom Historical.

Rogers Ridge (4-SBr-5250) A Fossil Spring Site of the Lake Mojave & Pinto Periods - Phase 2 Test Excavations & Site Evaluation. fac. ed. Dennis Jenkins. (Fort Irwin Archaeology Project, Research Reports: No. 18). (Illus.). 221p. 1985. reprint ed. pap. text ed. 20.00 (1-55567-543-3) Coyote Press.

Rogers Ridge (4-SBr-5250) A Fossil Spring Site of the Lake Mojave & Pinto Periods - Phase 2 Test Excavations & Site Evaluation - Appendices. fac. ed. H. T. Ore et al. (Fort Irwin Archaeology Project, Research Reports: No. 18: Appendices). 60p. 1985. reprint ed. pap. text ed. 5.55 (1-55567-544-1) Coyote Press.

Rogers' Rules for Success: Tips That Will Take You to the Top by One of America's Foremost Public Relations Experts. Henry C. Rogers. 304p. 1986. pap. 8.95 (0-312-68830-X) St Martin.

Roger's Rules of Public Relations. William R. Davis & Judy G. Davis. (Illus.). 100p. (Orig.). 1984. pap. 9.95 (0-915113-01-5) Bizarre Butterfly.

Roger's Twentieth Century Music. Richard Kostelznetz. LC 96-25603. 1996. 25.00 (0-02-864581-2) Schirmer Bks.

Roger's Version. John Updike. 1986. 17.95 (0-394-55435-3) Knopf.

Roger's Version. John Updike. 368p. 1987. mass mkt. 6.99 (0-449-21288-2, Crest) Fawcett.

*Roger's Version. John Updike. 1996. pap. 12.95 (0-449-91218-3) Fawcett.

Roget A to Z: The Classic Thesaurus in Dictionary Form. Ed. by Robert L. Chapman. 768p. 1994. 17.00 (0-06-270058-8, Harper Ref) HarpC.

Roget A to Z: The Classic Thesaurus in Dictionary Form. Ed. by Robert L. Chapman. 1995. pap. 10.00 (0-06-272059-7, Harper Ref) HarpC.

*Roget A-Z. Ed. by Robert Chapman. mass mkt. 5.99 (0-06-100989-X, Harp PBks) HarpC.

Roget's II: The New Thesaurus. 1980. Plain-edged. 10.95 (0-395-29604-8); 12.95 (0-685-02306-0) HM.

Roget's II: The New Thesaurus. rev. ed. Peter M. Roget. 1989. pap. 5.99 (0-425-11769-3) Berkley Pub.

Roget's II: The New Thesaurus. 2nd ed. Houghton Mifflin Company Staff. 1997. mass mkt. 5.99 (0-425-15668-0) Berkley Pub.

Roget's II: The New Thesaurus. 3rd deluxe ed. 1280p. 1995. 18.95 (0-395-73679-X) HM.

Roget's II: The New Thesaurus. 3rd ed. American Heritage Dictionary Editors. LC 94-42879. 1995. 20.00 (0-395-68722-5) HM.

*Roget's II: The New Thesaurus, 4 vols. 3rd large type ed. American Heritage Dictionary Editors. 1306p. 326.50 (0-614-20562-X, L-38172-00 APHB) Am Printing Hse.

Roget's II: The New Thesaurus, 2 Vols., Set. 3rd deluxe ed. 1280p. 1995. 39.95 (0-395-73725-7) HM.

*Roget's II Desk Thesaurus. Roget. 1995. 9.00 (0-395-74447-4) HM.

Roget's II the New Thesaurus see American Heritage Dictionary

Roget's International Thesaurus. Peter M. Roget. 800p. 1994. mass mkt. 4.99 (0-06-100709-9, Harp PBks) HarpC.

Roget's International Thesaurus. 5th ed. Ed. by Robert L. Chapman. LC 92-7615. 1168p. 1992. Indexed. 19.95 (0-06-270014-6, Harper Ref); Plain. 18.95 (0-06-270046-4, Harper Ref) HarpC.

Roget's International Thesaurus. 5th ed. Ed. by Robert L. Chapman. 1328p. 1993. pap. 13.50 (0-06-272037-6, Harper Ref) HarpC.

Roget's International Thesaurus of the Bible Index. Peter M. Roget & A. Colin Day. LC 92-53896. 944p. 1992. 35.00 (0-06-061773-X) Harper SF.

Roget's New American Thesaurus. Peter M. Roget. Date not set. pap. write for info. (0-451-18025-9, Sig) NAL-Dutton.

Roget's Pocket Thesaurus. 192p. 1994. pap. write for info. (1-884907-11-3) Paradise Miami.

Roget's Pocket Thesaurus. Ed. by C. O. Mawson. pap. 3.95 (0-317-56742-X) PB.

Roget's Student Thesaurus. rev. ed. LC 92-54689. (Illus.). 528p. (J). (gr. 4-8). 1994. 15.00 (0-06-275012-7, Harper Ref) HarpC.

Roget's Superthesaurus. Marc McCutcheon. LC 94-34221. 624p. 1995. 22.99 (0-89879-658-X, Wrtrs Digest Bks) F & W Pubns Inc.

*Roget's Thesaurus. (C). Date not set. text ed. 12.76 (0-669-41881-1) HM College Div.

Roget's Thesaurus. 256p. 1992. pap. 5.95 (0-938261-08-8) PSI & Assocs.

Roget's Thesaurus. 256p. 1994. pap. write for info. (1-884907-05-9) Paradise Miami.

Roget's Thesaurus. 1995. write for info. (0-673-46926-3) Addson-Wesley Educ.

Roget's Thesaurus. Random House Staff. (Orig.). 1996. mass mkt. 4.99 (0-345-40094-1) Ballantine.

Roget's Thesaurus. Intro. by Laurence Urdang. 418p. 1987. 49.95 (0-7475-0105-X, 070822-M99348) Gale.

R

***Roget's Thesaurus.** 94th ed. Ed. by Roget. (C). 1994. text ed. 10.95 (0-673-99706-5) Addison-Wesley.

Roget's Thesaurus: Vest-Pocket Edition. LC 87-3799. 272p. 1987. pap. 3.95 (0-395-44296-6) HM.

Roget's Thesaurus of English Words & Phrases. Susan M. Lloyd. 1250p. 1989. 9.95 (0-582-55635-X, TV2782) Longman.

Roget's Twenty-First Century Looseleaf Thesaurus. LC 93-484. pap. 1.95 (0-8407-6831-1) Nelson.

Roget's Twenty-First Century Thesaurus. LC 92-10709. 1992. 1.95 (0-8407-6827-3) Nelson.

Roget's Twenty-First Century Thesaurus in Dictionary Form. Princeton Language Institute Staff. 880p. 1993. mass mkt. 5.99 (0-440-21555-2) Dell.

Roget's Vest Pocket Thesaurus. Rogets Staff. 1995. pap. 2.15 (0-395-74452-0) HM.

Roget's 21st Century Thesaurus. Barbara A. Kiffer. 992p. 1992. 19.95 (0-385-31606-2) Doubleday.

Roget's 21st Century Thesaurus. Ed. by Princeton Language Institute Staff & Barbara A. Kipfer. 880p. 1994. pap. 12.95 (0-385-31255-5, Delta) Dell.

Roggy Lived on Planet Sun. Jim Robinson. 288p. 1992. 22.00 (0-9634367-0-8) Swallows In-Hse.

***Rogowski Reflexive Labor Law.** 1994. pap. text ed. 84.50 (90-6544-588-9) Kluwer Ac.

Rogue. Janet Dailey. 1993. mass mkt. 5.99 (0-671-87512-4) PB.

***Rogue.** Ian Edginton. (Aliens Ser.). (Illus.). 1997. pap. text ed. 16.95 (1-56971-267-0) Dark Horse Comics.

Rogue. Fabio. 416p. (Orig.). 1994. mass mkt. 5.99 (0-380-77047-4) Avon.

Rogue. Howard Mackie. (Illus.). 96p. 1995. pap. 12.95 (0-7851-0140-3) Marvel Entmnt.

Rogue. Lindsay McKenna. (Special Edition Ser.). 1993. mass mkt. 3.50 (0-373-09824-3, 5-09824-9) Silhouette.

Rogue: A River to Run. Florence Arman & Glen Wooldridge. LC 81-52732. (Illus.). 1982. pap. 16.95 (0-9607260-0-4) Wildwood Pr.

Rogue Agent. (Executioner Ser.). 1995. mass mkt. 3.50 (0-373-61199-4, 1-61199-5) Harlequin Bks.

Rogue Agent, No. 1. Jack Drake. 256p. 1991. pap. 2.95 (0-380-75988-8) Avon.

Rogue Agent No. 2: Hard to Kill. Jack Drake. 224p. 1991. pap. 2.95 (0-380-75989-6) Avon.

Rogue Agent No. 3: Blood Money. Jack Drake. 224p. (Orig.). 1991. pap. 2.95 (0-380-76177-7) Avon.

Rogue Agent No. 4: Last Rites. Jack Drake. 192p. (Orig.). 1991. pap. 2.95 (0-380-76178-5) Avon.

Rogue Agent No. 5: Guerrilla War. Jack Drake. 224p. (Orig.). 1991. pap. 3.50 (0-380-76549-7) Avon.

Rogue Agent No. 6: Silent Assassin. Jack Drake. 192p. (Orig.). 1992. mass mkt. 3.99 (0-380-76550-0) Avon.

Rogue & a Pirate. large type ed. Carole Mortimer. (Magna Large Print Ser.). 1994. 25.99 (0-7505-0741-1, Pub. by Magna Print Bks UK) Ulverscroft.

Rogue & the Horse. Robert McGraw. (Illus.). 32p. (Orig.). (J). (ps-3). 1993. pap. 5.95 (0-9633385-0-1) Imagin Pr.

Rogue & the Rich Girl. Christine Pacheco. 1995. mass mkt. 3.25 (0-373-05960-4, 1-05960-9) Silhouette.

Rogue Angel - a Novel of Fra Filippo Lippi. Carol Damioli. Ed. by Adolfo Caso. (Illus.). 248p. 1994. reprint ed. text ed. 21.95 (0-937832-33-2, Dante Press) Branden Pub Co.

Rogue Asteroids & Doomsday Comets: The Search for the Million Megaton Menace that Threatens Life on Earth. Duncan Steel. LC 94-23409. 320p. 1995. text ed. 24.95 (0-471-30824-2) Wiley.

Rogue Cop: A Trilogy. Joe Hikade. 120p. (Orig.). 1996. pap. 15.60 (1-57502-185-4, P0809) Morris Pubng.

Rogue Diamond. large type ed. James B. Lynne. 534p. 1982. 27.99 (0-7089-8044-9) Ulverscroft.

Rogue Mistress. Keith Herber et al. (Stormbringer Roleplaying Game System Ser.). (Illus.). 144p. (Orig.). 1991. pap. text ed. 18.95 (0-933635-73-7, 2111) Chaosium.

Rogue Moon. Algis Budrys. 1993. reprint ed. lib. bdg. 18.95 (0-89968-334-7, Lghtyr Pr) Buccaneer Bks.

Rogue: or the Life of Guzman De Alfarache, 4 vols. Matheo Aleman. Tr. by James Mabbe. (Tudor Translations, Second Ser.: No. 2-5). reprint ed. 230.00 (0-404-51970-9) AMS Pr.

Rogue Primate: An Exploration of Human Domestication. John A. Livingston. LC 95-69270. 236p. 1995. 22.95 (1-57098-058-6) R Rinehart.

Rogue Programs: Viruses, Worms, & Trojan Horses. A. J. Hoffman. 1990. pap. 39.95 (0-442-00454-0) Van Nos Reinhold.

***Rogue Regimes.** Tanter. LC 97-21494. 1997. text ed. 29.95 (0-312-17300-8) St Martin.

Rogue River Feud. Jon Sharpe. (Trailsman Ser.: No. 161). 176p. (Orig.). 1995. mass mkt. 3.99 (0-451-18218-9, Sig) NAL-Dutton.

Rogue River Guide: Kayaking Adventures, & Travels. Kevin K. Tice. (Whitewater Adventures Ser.). (Illus.). 240p. 1995. pap. 15.00 (1-879415-12-7) Mtn n Air Bks.

***Rogue River Indian War & Its Aftermath, 1850-1980.** A. E. Schwartz. LC 96-32767. (Illus.). 368p. 1997. 34.95 (0-8061-2906-9) U of Okla Pr.

Rogue River Rendezvous. Junior Service League of Jackson County Staff. 222p. 1992. 19.95 (0-9632671-0-8) Jr Srv Leag JC.

Rogue River War. A. G. Henry. 43p. 1995. 5.95 (0-87770-573-9) Ye Galleon.

Rogue Saucer. John Vornholt. (Star Trek Next Generation Ser.: No. 39). 1996. mass mkt. 5.99 (0-671-54917-0) PB.

Rogue Squadron. Michael A. Stackpole. (Star Wars X-Wing Ser.: No. 1). 400p. (YA). 1996. mass mkt. 5.99 (0-553-56801-9) Bantam.

Rogue States & Nuclear Outlaws: America's Search for a New Foreign Policy. Michael T. Klare. 1995. 25.00 (0-8090-8243-8) Hill & Wang.

Rogue States & Nuclear Outlaws: America's Search for a New Foreign Policy. Michael T. Klare. 292p. 1996. pap. text ed. 12.00 (0-8090-1587-0) Hill & Wang.

Rogue Trader: How I Brought down Barings Bank & Shook the Financial World. Nick Leeson & Edward Whitley. 288p. 1996. 24.95 (0-316-51856-5) Little.

Rogue Warrior. Richard Marcinko & John Weisman. Ed. by Judith Regan & Paul McCarthy. (Rogue Warrior Ser.). 352p. 1992. 23.00 (0-671-70390-0) PB.

***Rogue Warrior.** Richard Marcinko. 1997. pap. 3.99 (0-671-00982-6) PB.

***Rogue Warriors Strategy for Success.** Richard Marcinko. 1997. 20.00 (0-671-00993-1, PB Hardcover) PB.

Rogue Wave. Susan Dunlap. 272p. 1992. mass mkt. 4.99 (0-440-21197-2) Dell.

Rogue Wave: And Other Sea Stories. Theodore Taylor. LC 96-14585. (J). 1996. 16.00 (0-15-201408-X) HarBrace.

Rogue Who Came to Stay. Arlene James. (Romance Ser.). 1995. pap. 2.99 (0-373-19061-1, 1-19061-0) Silhouette.

Rogue Wildcatter. Dub Hicks. 1994. pap. text ed. 14.95 (1-881116-39-5) Black Forest Pr.

Rogues. Peter Whalley. 192p. 1989. reprint ed. pap. 3.50 (0-380-70616-4) Avon.

Rogues & Heroes from Iowa's Amazing Past. George Mills. (Iowa Heritage Collection Ser.). (Illus.). 252p. 1986. reprint ed. pap. 10.95 (0-8138-1446-4) Iowa St U Pr.

***Rogues & Toads: A Poetry Collection.** Peter M. Leschah. (Illus.). 64p. 1997. pap. 9.95 (0-87839-117-7) North Star.

Rogues & Vagabonds: The Vagrant Underworld in Britain 1815-1985. Lionel Rose. 272p. (C). 1988. lib. bdg. 65.00 (0-415-00275-3) Routledge.

Rogues & Vagabonds of Shakespeare's Youth, Described by John Awdeley in His Fraternitye Vacabondes 1561-1573; Thomas Harman in His Caveat for Common Cursetors, 1567-1573; & in the Groundworke of Conny-Catching, 1552. Ed. by Edward Viles & F. J. Furnivall. Bd. with Robert Laneham's Letters. (New Shakespeare Society, London, Ser. 6: Nos. 7 & 14). 1974. reprint ed. Set pap. 37.00 (0-8115-0246-5) Periodicals Srv.

Rogue's Bride. Paula Roland. 304p. 1990. mass mkt. 3.95 (0-8217-2880-6, Zebra Kensgtn) Kensgtn Pub Corp.

***Rogue's Gallery.** Grant Antrews. 1997. mass mkt. 6.95 (1-56333-522-0, Rhinoceros) Masquerade.

Rogues Gallery. Gary Gygax. 1980. 5.00 (0-394-51548-X) Random.

Rogues Gallery. Peter Haining. 320p. 1996. 12.95 (0-316-34637-3) Little.

***Rogues' Gallery: Profiles of My Eminent Contemporaries.** Frank Scully. 276p. 9172. 19.95 (0-8369-2975-6) Ayer.

Rogue's Heart. Laurie Paige. (Silhouette Romance Ser.). 1994. pap. 2.75 (0-373-19013-1, 5-19013-7) Harlequin Bks.

Rogue's Justice: A Michael Carolina Mystery. Thomas G. Briody. 288p. 1996. 22.95 (0-312-14402-4) St Martin.

Rogue's Lady. Victoria Thompson. 352p. (Orig.). 1988. pap. 3.95 (0-380-75526-2) Avon.

***Rogue's March: John Riley & the St. Patrick's Battalion.** Peter F. Stevens. 336p. 1998. 25.95 (1-57488-145-0) Brasseys Inc.

Rogue's Masquerade. Valerie King. 1993. mass mkt. 3.99 (0-8217-4273-6, Zebra Kensgtn) Kensgtn Pub Corp.

Rogue's Mistress. 1996. pap. 2.99 (0-8217-5488-2) Kensgtn Pub Corp.

Rogue's Mistress. Eugenia Riley. 400p. (Orig.). 1991. mass mkt. 4.50 (0-380-76474-1) Avon.

Rogue's Mistress. large type ed. Jo Goodman. LC 93-46127. 1994. lib. bdg. 20.95 (0-8161-5949-1, GK Hall) Thorndike Pr.

Rogues of San Francisco. Ed. by Bill Lee. (Rogues Ser.: No. 3). 230p. (Orig.). 1993. pap. 11.95 (1-879194-15-5) GLB Pubs.

Rogues of the Borderlands. Jessica M. Ney. (Middle Earth Ser.). (Illus.). 40p. (Orig.). (YA). (gr. 12). 1990. pap. 7.00 (1-55806-083-9, 8014) Iron Crown Ent Inc.

Rogue's Paradise: Crime & Punishment in Antebellum Florida, 1821-1861. James M. Denham. LC 96-24837. 336p. 1997. text ed. 39.95 (0-8173-0847-4) U of Ala Pr.

Rogues, Rebels, & Reformers. Ted R. Gurr. LC 76-17370. 204p. reprint ed. pap. 58.20 (0-317-09470-X, 2021909) Bks Demand.

Rogue's Return. Anita Mills. (Signet Regency Romance Ser.). 224p. 1992. 3.99 (0-451-17258-2) NAL-Dutton.

***Rogue's Return.** Margaret Moore. 1997. pap. 4.99 (0-373-28976-6, 1-28976-8) Harlequin Bks.

Rogue's Revenge. Olivia Fontayne. 208p. (Orig.). 1994. pap. text ed. 3.99 (0-515-11374-3) Jove Pubns.

Rogue's Reward. Jean R. Ewing. (Orig.). 1995. mass mkt. 3.99 (0-8217-5146-8, Zebra Kensgtn) Kensgtn Pub Corp.

Rogues' River: Crime on the River Thames in the Eighteenth Century. Frank Martin. (Illus.). 200p. 1991. 15.00 (0-86025-874-2, Pub. by Ian Henry Pubns UK) Empire Pub Srvs.

Rogues, Royalty & Reporters: The Age of Queen Anne Through Its Newspapers. William B. Ewald, Jr. LC 78-17410. 254p. 1978. reprint ed. text ed. 59.75 (0-313-20506-X, EWRR, Greenwood Pr) Greenwood.

Rogues to Remember. Bill Lee. (Rogues Ser.: No. 1). 168p. (Orig.). 1991. pap. 10.95 (1-879194-00-7) GLB Pubs.

Rogue's Valley. Kathleen Creighton. (Men Made in America Ser.). 1994. mass mkt. 3.59 (0-373-45162-8, 1-45162-4) Silhouette.

***Rogue's Wager: A Michael Carolina Mystery.** Thomas G. Briody. LC 97-19588. (A Michael Carolina Mystery Ser.). 1997. 20.95 (0-312-16990-6) Thomas Dunne Bks.

Rohan Master. Intro. by Millard Meiss & Marcel Thomas. LC 73-77880. (Illus.). 247p. 1973. boxed 100.00 (0-8076-0690-1) Braziller.

Rohm & Haas: History of a Chemical Company. Sheldon Hochheiser. LC 84-25770. (Illus.). 232p. 1986. text ed. 38.95 (0-8122-7940-9) U of Pa Pr.

Rohrbach Genealogy, Vol. III: The Rorabaugh, Rohrbough, Rohrabaugh, Rohrabough, Rohrabaugh, Rorabough & Rhorabaugh Families of America Who Are Descendants of Johann Reinhart Rohrbach Who Emigrated from Germany to America in 1749. Lewis B. Rohrbach. LC 71-118879. 376p. 1982. 45.00 (0-929539-00-1, 1111) Picton Pr.

Rohrbough Family. F. W. Rohrbough. (Illus.). 130p. 1993. reprint ed. pap. 26.00 (0-8328-3743-1); reprint ed. lib. bdg. 36.00 (0-8328-3742-3) Higginson Bk Co.

Rohrig Tarot. Carl-W. Rohrig. 72p. 1995. 19.50 (1-885394-08-X) Bluestar Commun.

***Rohrig-Tarot Book.** Carl W. Rohrig & Francesca Marzano-Fritz. Tr. by Howard Fine from GER. (Illus.). 160p. (Orig.). 1997. pap. 15.95 (1-885394-18-7, 94187) Bluestar Commun.

Rohstoffe des Pflanzenreichs, 7 pts. 5th ed. Incl. Pt. 1. Tanning Materials (Gerbstoffe). 5th ed. H. Endres et al. Ed. by C. Von Regel. (ENG & GER.). 302p. 1962. 52.00 (3-7682-0111-2, Pub. by Cramer GW); Pt. 2. Antibiotiques (Antibiotica). 5th ed. G. Hagemann. (FRE.). 272p. 1964. 62.40 (3-7682-0170-8, Pub. by Cramer GW); Pt. 3. Organic Acids. 5th ed. G. C. Whitting. Ed. by C. Von Regel. 194p. 1964. 44.50 (3-7682-0244-5, Pub. by Cramer GW); Pt. 4. Insecticides. 5th ed. A. J. Fuell. Ed. by C. Von Regel. 224p. 1965. 52.00 (3-7682-0259-3, Pub. by Cramer GW); Pt. 5. Glykoside. 5th ed. L. Zechner. Ed. by C. Von Regel. (GER.). 290p. 1966. 52.00 (3-7682-0298-4, Pub. by Cramer GW); Pt. 6. Staerke. E. Samecl & M. Bling. (Illus.). 1966. 52.00 (3-7682-0186-4); Pt. 7. Aetherische Oele. 5th ed. K. Bournot & M. Weber. Ed. by C. Von Regel. (GER., Illus.). 175p. 1968. 52.00 (3-7682-0562-2, Pub. by Cramer GW); write for info. (0-318-54144-0) Lubrecht & Cramer.

Roi Babar. Laurent De Brunhoff. (FRE.). (J). (gr. 4-6). 1975. 15.95 (0-685-11533-X) Fr & Eur.

Roi, Dame, Valet. Vladimir Nabokov. (FRE.). 1975. pap. 11.95 (0-7859-4045-6) Fr & Eur.

***Roi de Rien.** Raymond Plante. (Novels in the Roman Jeunesse Ser.). 96p. (FRE.). (J). (gr. 4-7). 1996. pap. 7.95 (2-89021-081-2, Pub. by Les Editions CN) Firefly Bks Ltd.

Roi des Aulnes. Michel Tournier. (Folio Ser.: No. 656). 599p. (Orig.). (FRE.). 1970. pap. 12.95 (2-07-036656-1) Schoenhof.

Roi des Aulnes. Michel Tournier. (FRE.). 1975. pap. 15.95 (0-8288-3800-3, M4210) Fr & Eur.

Roi Gilgamesh. Ludmila Zeman. Tr. by Michele Boileau from ENG. LC 91-67565. (Illus.). 24p. (FRE.). (J). (gr. 3 up). 1993. 19.95 (0-88776-288-3) Tundra Bks.

Roi Pecheur. Alphonse Daudet. 78p. (FRE.). 1988. 13.95 (0-7859-1202-9, 2876230321) Fr & Eur.

Roi san Divertissement. Jean Giono. (Chroniques Ser.: No. I). 256p. (FRE.). 1972. pap. 10.95 (0-7859-2283-0, 2070362205) Fr & Eur.

Roi sans Divertissement. Jean Giono. (Folio Ser.: No. 220). 256p. (FRE.). 1972. 8.95 (2-07-036220-5) Schoenhof.

Roi se Meurt. Eugene Ionesco. (Folio Ser.: No. 361). (FRE.). pap. 6.95 (2-07-036361-9) Schoenhof.

Roi Se Meurt. Eugene Ionesco. (FRE.). 1973. pap. 10.95 (0-8288-3694-9, M3584) Fr & Eur.

Roi Vert. Paul-Loup Sulitzer. (FRE.). 1984. pap. 14.95 (0-7859-3120-1) Fr & Eur.

Roi Vert see Green King

Roi's Amuse/The Prince's Play. Tony Harrison & Victor Hugo. 98p. (Orig.). 1996. pap. 10.95 (0-571-17965-7) Faber & Faber.

Rois En Exil. Alphonse Daudet. (FRE.). 1940. pap. 13.95 (0-7859-5493-7) Fr & Eur.

Rois et les Voleurs. Muriel Cerf. 212p. (FRE.). 1977. pap. 10.95 (0-7859-1837-X, 2070368807) Fr & Eur.

Rois Mages. Michel Tournier. (Folio - Junior Ser.: No. 280). (Illus.). 160p. (FRE.). (J). (gr. 5-10). 1978. pap. 7.95 (2-07-033280-2) Schoenhof.

Roissy Express: A Journey Through the Paris Suburbs. LC 93-42235. 330p. (gr. 13). 1994. pap. 19.00 (0-86091-698-7, B4760, Pub. by Vrso UK) Norton.

Roissy Express: A Journey Through the Paris Suburbs. Francois Maspero. Tr. by Paul Jones & David Bellos. LC 93-42235. (Illus.). 330p. (C). (gr. 13). 1994. text ed. 65.00 (0-86091-373-2, B2577, Pub. by Vrso UK) Norton.

Roister Doister: Written before 1553. Nicholas Udall. Ed. by Edward Arber. 1992. reprint ed. pap. 15.00 (0-87556-340-6) Saifer.

***Roithamer's Universe.** Tom Whalen. LC 96-70181. (Illus.). 128p. (Orig.). 1996. pap. 12.00 (0-916620-98-0) Portals Pr.

Rojak's Rule. Steven M. Krauzer. Ed. by Doug Grad. 256p. (Orig.). 1992. mass mkt. 4.99 (0-671-72339-1) PB.

***Rojo.** Karen Bryant-Mole. (Images Ser.). (SPA.). 1996. pap. text ed. 4.95 (0-382-39578-6) Silver Burdett Pr.

Rokeby, A Page in History: The Archives Revisited. Kathryn I. Coughlan. (Illus.). 48p. (Orig.). (C). 1993. pap. 9.95 (0-9637161-0-7) K&D Ltd.

Rol' Cerkvi v Sozdanii Russkogo Gosudarstva: The Role of the Church in the Foundation of Russian Nation. V. I. Alexeev. 310p. 1990. write for info. (0-9616413-7-1) Multilingual.

Rol' Pravoslavnoi Tserkvi V Istorii Rosii: The Role of the Orthodox Church in Russian History. Sergei Pushkarev. LC 85-80831. 125p. (RUS.). 1985. 9.50 (0-911971-13-0) Effect Pub.

Roland. Niccolo Piccinni. Ed. by Gustave Lefevre & Arthur Pougin. (Chefs-d'oeuvre classiques de l'opera francaise Ser.: Vol. 29). (Illus.). 390p. (FRE.). 1970. reprint ed. pap. 40.00 (0-8450-1129-4) Broude.

Roland Allen: Pioneer, Priest & Prophet. Lesslie Newbigin. 248p. 1995. pap. 10.95 (0-88028-157-X, 1305) Forward Movement.

Roland Alpha Juno-One: Getting the Most out of Yours. Lorenz M. Rychner. Ed. by Peter L. Alexander. (Roland Juno Support Ser.). (Illus.). 65p. (C). 1987. pap. text ed. 16.95 (0-939067-11-0) Alexander Pub.

Roland Alpha Juno-Two: Getting the Most out of Yours. Lorenz M. Rychner. Ed. by Peter L. Alexander. (Roland Juno Support Ser.). (Illus.). 65p. (C). 1987. pap. text ed. 16.95 (0-939067-43-9) Alexander Pub.

Roland Barthes. Roland Barthes. LC 94-7545. 1994. pap. 11.00 (0-520-08783-6) U CA Pr.

Roland Barthes. Jonathan Culler. 130p. 1983. 25.00 (0-19-520420-4) OUP.

Roland Barthes. Michael Moriarty. LC 90-72070. (Key Contemporary Thinkers Ser.). 280p. 1992. 42.50 (0-8047-1932-2); pap. 14.95 (0-8047-1933-0) Stanford U Pr.

Roland Barthes. Rick Rylance. 192p. 1994. pap. text ed. 24.95 (0-13-302654-X) P-H.

Roland Barthes: A Bibliography. (Social Theory: A Bibliographic Ser.: No. 34). 72p. (C). 1994. pap. 15.00 (0-937855-67-7) Ref Rsch Serv.

Roland Barthes: A Biography. Louis-Jean Calvet. Tr. by Sarah Wykes from FRE. LC 94-24230. 294p. 1995. text ed. 35.00 (0-253-34987-7) Ind U Pr.

Roland Barthes: A Conservative Estimate. Philip Thody. LC 83-5112. 214p. 1984. pap. text ed. 10.95 (0-226-79513-6) U Ch Pr.

Roland Barthes: Structuralism & After. Annette Lavers. LC 81-13447. 310p. 1982. 37.50 (0-674-77721-2) HUP.

Roland Barthes: The Figures of Writing. Andrew Brown. 320p. 1992. 80.00 (0-19-815171-3) OUP.

***Roland Barthes: The Professor of Desire.** Steven Ungar. LC 83-6836. 226p. 1983. reprint ed. pap. 64.50 (0-608-03366-9, 2064078) Bks Demand.

Roland Barthes on Photography. Nancy Shawcross. (Crosscurrents Ser.). 160p. 1997. lib. bdg. 39.95 (0-8130-1469-7) U Press Fla.

Roland D-50: Sixty-Four New Sounds. Dan Walker. Ed. by Peter L. Alexander. (Roland D-Fifty Support Ser.). (Illus.). 148p. (C). 1987. pap. text ed. 24.95 (0-939067-54-4) Alexander Pub.

Roland D-50 Vol. II: Sound Making & Programming. Dan Walker. Ed. by Peter L. Alexander. (Roland D-Fifty Support Ser.). (Illus.). 250p. (C). 1987. pap. text ed. 27.95 (0-939067-53-6) Alexander Pub.

Roland D10-20 Drum Pattern Handbook. Dan Walker & Jack Verga. Ed. by Peter L. Alexander. (Roland D-Ten-Twenty Support Ser.). (Illus.). 60p. (C). 1988. pap. text ed. 9.98 (0-939067-61-7) Alexander Pub.

Roland D10-20 Operations & Programming Guide. Dan Walker. Ed. by Peter L. Alexander. (Roland D-Ten-Twenty Support Ser.). (Illus.). 251p. (C). 1988. pap. text ed. 27.95 (0-939067-60-9) Alexander Pub.

Roland D110 Programming & Basic Operations. Dan Walker. Ed. by Peter L. Alexander. (Illus.). 189p. (C). 1988. pap. text ed. 24.95 (0-939067-63-3) Alexander Pub.

Roland H. Bainton: An Examination of His Reformation Historiography. Steven Simpler. LC 85-21567. (Texts & Studies in Religion: Vol. 24). 250p. 1985. lib. bdg. 89.95 (0-88946-812-5) E Mellen.

Roland Legend in Nineteenth-Century French Literature. Harry Redman, Jr. LC 90-26581. 264p. 1991. text ed. 32.00 (0-8131-1732-1) U Pr of Ky.

Roland Martin's One Hundred One Bass-Catching Secrets. Roland Martin. Ed. by Tim Tucker. 1988. 19.95 (0-8329-0457-0, Winchester Pr) New Win Pub.

Roland Mathias. Sam Adams. 200p. 1995. pap. 10.95 (0-7083-1285-3, Pub. by Univ Wales Pr UK) Paul & Co Pubs.

Roland-Michel Barrin de la Galissoni Ere, 1693-1756. Lionel A. Groulx. LC 74-22181. (Canadian Biographical Studies: No. 2). 104p. reprint ed. pap. 29.70 (0-317-27037-0, 2023627) Bks Demand.

Roland Poulin: Sculpture. Diana Nemiroff & Donald Kuspit. 160p. 1995. pap. text ed. 29.95 (0-88884-634-7) U Ch Pr.

Roland PR100 Sequencing Handbook. Dan Walker. Ed. by Peter L. Alexander. (Illus.). 108p. (C). 1988. pap. text ed. 17.95 (0-939067-24-2) Alexander Pub.

Roland Reiss Vol. 1: A Seventeen Year Survey. Betty A. Brown. LC 91-73980. (Illus.). 96p. (Orig.). 1991. pap. 24.00 (0-911291-19-9) Fellows Cont Art.

Roland the Minstrel Pig. William Steig. LC 68-14923. (Michael di Capua Bks.). (Illus.). 32p. (J). (ps-3). 1997. 14.95 (0-06-025761-X) HarpC Child Bks.

***Roland the Minstrel Pig.** William Steig. LC 68-14923. (Michael di Capua Bks.). (Illus.). 32p. (J). (ps-3). 1997. lib. bdg. 14.89 (0-06-025762-8) HarpC Child Bks.

***Rolando Hinojosa & the American Dream.** Joyce G. Lee. LC 96-50027. (Texas Writers Ser.: Vol. 5). 192p. 1997. 19.95 (1-57441-023-7) UNTX Pr.

Rolando Hinojosa Reader. Ed. by Jose D. Saldivar. LC 83-72578. 190p. (Orig.). 1985. pap. 11.00 (0-934770-30-1) Arte Publico.

Role & Career Problems of the Chicago Public School Teacher. Howard S. Becker. Ed. by Harriet Zuckerman & Robert K. Merton. LC 79-8974. (Dissertations on Sociology Ser.). 1980. lib. bdg. 31.95 (0-405-12951-3) Ayer.

Role & Competencies of Graduates of Diploma Programs in Nursing. 2nd ed. NLN Council of Diploma Programs Staff. 4p. 1989. 4.95 (0-88737-474-3, 16-1735) Natl League Nurse.

An Asterisk (*) at the beginning of an entry indicates that the title is appearing in BIP for the first time.

Role & Contribution of Small Business Research: Proceedings of the Ninth National Small Firms Policy & Research Conference, 1986. Ed. by Peter Rosa. (Illus.). 256p. 1989. text ed. 68.95 (*0-566-07103-7*, Pub. by Avebury Pub UK) Ashgate Pub Co.

Role & Control of Weapons in the Nineteen Nineties. Frank Barnaby. LC 92-9373. 192p. (C). (gr. 13). 1992. text ed. 69.95 (*0-415-07673-0*, A9751, Routledge NY) Routledge.

Role & Future of Special Collections in Research Libraries: British & American Perspectives. Ed. by Sul H. Lee. LC 93-30716. (Journal of Library Administration: Vol. 19, No. 1). 98p. 1993. lib. bdg. 29.95 (*1-56024-479-8*) Haworth Pr.

Role & Importance of Managing Information for Competitive Positioning in Economic Development. Keith Harman. Ed. by Peter Hernon & Charles R. McClure. (Information Management, Policies & Services Ser.: Vol. 1). 176p. (C). 1989. text ed. 73.25 (*0-89391-584-X*) Ablex Pub.

Role & Responsibility of the Moral Philosopher: Proceedings, Vol. 56. Ed. by John T. Noonan, Jr. et al. LC 81-69068. 214p. 1982. pap. 20.00 (*0-918090-16-4*) Am Cath Philo.

Role & Status of International Humanitarian Volunteers & Organizations: The Right & Duty to Humanitarian Assistance. Yves Beigbeder. 432p. (C). 1991. lib. bdg. 171.00 (*0-7923-1190-6*) Kluwer Ac.

Role & Status of Women in India. R. Ray et al. 167p. 1978. 11.95 (*0-318-37071-9*) Asia Bk Corp.

Role & Status of Women in the Soviet Union. Ed. by Donald R. Brown. LC 68-27326. 151p. reprint ed. pap. 43.10 (*0-317-42025-9*, 2025995) Bks Demand.

Role Change: A Resocialization Perspective. Melvyn L. Fein. LC 89-23038. 212p. 1990. text ed. 55.00 (*0-275-93358-X*, C3358, Praeger Pubs) Greenwood.

Role Conflict among the Working Women. Puspa Sinha. 1987. 24.95 (*0-318-37077-8*) Asia Bk Corp.

Role Conflict among the Working Women. Puspa Sinha. 1987. 17.50 (*0-8364-2257-0*, Pub. by Anmol II) S Asia.

Role Crystal Growth. Niizeki. (Progress in Crystal Growth & Character Ser.). 436p. 1992. 486.50 (*0-08-042045-1*) Elsevier.

Role de l'ecrivain dans le monde d'aujourd'hui see Soixante Ans de Ma Vie Litteraire

Role de Plaisance. Jacques Perret. (FRE.). 1975. pap. 10.95 (*0-7859-4037-5*) Fr & Eur.

Role Delineation for Registered Dietitians & Entry-Level Dietetic Technicians. American Dietetic Association Staff. 311p. 1990. pap. 38.50 (*0-88091-079-8*, 0303) Am Dietetic Assn.

Role Delineation Study for Entry-Level Registered Dietitians, Entry-Level Dietetic Technicians, & Beyond-Entry-Level Registered Dietitians Technical Report, 3 vols. American Dietetic Association Staff. 1989. ring bd. 125.00 (*0-88091-080-1*, 0301); Vol. 1 415 p. 58.00 (*0-318-68899-9*); Vol. 2 180 p. 33.00 (*0-318-68900-6*); Vol. 3 277 p. 46.00 (*0-318-68901-4*) Am Dietetic Assn.

Role Delineation Study of the Entry-Level Athletic Trainer Certification Examination. 3rd ed. NATA Board of Certification Staff. 62p. (C). 1994. pap. text ed. 26.95 (*0-8036-6504-0*) Davis Co.

Role Drama: A Teacher's Handbook. Carole Tarlington & Patrick Verriour. LC 91-26266. 128p. 1991. pap. text ed. 17.50 (*0-435-08599-9*, 08599) Heinemann.

Role du Langage dans les Processus Perceptuals. Alfred Korzybski. 93p. (FRE.). 1951. pap. 4.75 (*0-937298-03-4*) Inst Gen Seman.

Role for Marketing in College Admissions. 128p. 1976. pap. 5.00 (*0-87447-078-1*, 200685) College Bd.

Role for Private Citizens in Historic Preservation. Ann Swanson. (Local History Technical Leaflets Ser.). (Illus.). 14p. (Orig.). 1985. pap. 1.50 (*0-931406-10-2*) Idaho State Soc.

Role Motivation Theories. John B. Miner. LC 92-28816. (People & Organizations Ser.). (Illus.). 304p. (C). 1993. text ed. 49.95 (*0-415-08486-5*, B0012, Routledge NY) Routledge.

Role Motivation Theories. John B. Miner. (People & Organizations Ser.). (Illus.). 376p. (C). 1994. pap. 19.95 (*0-415-11994-4*, C03985) Routledge.

Role of Acacia Species in the Rural Economy of Dry Africa & the Near East. G. E. Wickens & A. G. Seif. (FAO Conversation Guides: Vol. 27). 110p. 1995. pap. 20.00 (*92-5-103651-9*) Food & Agriculture Organization of.

Role of Accounting in the Stock Market Crash of 1929. Gadis J. Dillon. 270p. 1984. Spiral. spiral bd. 35.00 (*0-88406-170-1*, RM96) GA St U Busn Pr.

Role of Acetaldehyde in the Actions of Ethanol: Satellite Symposium to the Sixth International Congress of Pharmacology. Ed. by K. O. Lindros & C. J. Eriksson. (Finnish Foundation for Alcohol Studies: Vol. 23). (Illus.). 1975. pap. 8.00 (*951-9191-23-2*) Rutgers Ctr Alcohol.

Role of Adenosine & Adenine Nucleotides in the Biological System: Metabolism, Release, Transport, Receptors, Transduction Mechanisms & Biological Actions. Ed. by S. Imai & M. Nakazawa. 752p. 1991. 358.25 (*0-444-81361-6*) Elsevier.

Role of Adenosine in Cerebral Metabolism & Blood Flow. Ed. by V. Stefanovich & I. Okyayuz-Baklouti. 141p. 1987. lib. bdg. 96.00 (*90-6764-098-0*, Pub. by VSP NE) Coronet Bks.

***Role of Adult Guidance & Employment Counselling in a Changing Labour Market: Final Report on Eurocounsel.** Glenys Watt. 200p. 1996. pap. 35.00 (*92-827-8279-4*, SY98-96-776-ENC, Pub. by Europ Com UK) Bernan Associates.

Role of African Student Movements in the Political & Social Evolution of Africa 1900-75. UNESCO Staff. (General History of Africa: Studies & Documents: No. 12). 210p. 1994. pap. 14.00 (*92-3-102804-9*, U2804, Pub. by UNESCO FR) Bernan Associates.

Role of Aggression in Human Pathology. Ed. by H. Musaph & P. J. Mettrop. (Psychotherapy & Psychosomatics Journal: Vol. 20, No. 5). (Illus.). 1972. pap. 14.50 (*3-8055-1562-6*) S Karger.

Role of Agriculture in Economic Development. Ed. by Erik Thorbecke. (Universities-National Bureau Conference Ser.: No. 21). 490p. 1970. 127.40 (*0-87014-203-8*) Natl Bur Econ Res.

Role of Agriculture in Economic Development: A Conference of the Universities-National Bureau Committee for Economic Research. Ed. by Erik Thorbecke. LC 78-79876. (Universities-National Bureau Conference Ser.: No. 21). (Illus.). 490p. reprint ed. pap. 139.70 (*0-8357-7582-8*, 2056903) Bks Demand.

Role of Air-Sea Exchange in Geochemical Cycling. Ed. by Patrick Buat-Menard. 1986. lib. bdg. 204.50 (*90-277-2318-4*) Kluwer Ac.

Role of Analytical Procedures in Detecting Management Fraud. Edward Blochet. Ed. by Claire Barth. 73p. (Orig.). 1993. pap. 20.00 (*0-86641-218-2*, 93280) Inst Mgmt Account.

Role of Ancient Israel "Written with the Finger of God" A Swedenborgian Perspective on the History of the Israelites from Abraham to Jesus. William R. Kintner. 1996. 19.95 (*0-533-11740-2*) Vantage.

Role of Animals in Biomedical Research. Ed. by Jeri A. Sechzer. 1983. 40.00 (*0-89766-204-0*); pap. 40.00 (*0-89766-205-9*, VOL. 406) NY Acad Sci.

Role of Antihormones. Ed. by Anthony Howell. (Current Controversies in the Treatment of Breast Cancer Ser.). (Illus.). 182p. (C). 1990. 65.00 (*1-85070-295-0*) Prthnon Pub.

***Role of Apoptosis in Development, Tissue Homeostasis & Malignancy: Death from Inside Out.** Dexter et al. (Illus.). 112p. (C). 1995. text ed. 69.95 (*0-412-63810-X*, Chap & Hall NY) Chapman & Hall.

Role of Aquaculture in World Fisheries: Proceedings of the World Fisheries Congress, Athens, Greece, Theme 6. Ed. by T. G. Heggberget. (Illus.). 1996. lib. bdg. 68.00 (*1-886106-29-0*) Science Pubs.

Role of Architects & Planners in Post-Earthquake Studies: Proceedings of a Colloquium Held February 23-24, 1982 in Berkeley, CA. 24p. 1982. pap. 12.00 (*0-685-14403-8*) Earthquake Eng.

Role of Argument Structure in Grammar: Evidence from Romance. Alex Alsina. 320p. (C). 1996. text ed. 69.95 (*1-57586-035-X*); pap. text ed. 24.95 (*1-57586-034-1*) CSLI.

Role of Armenian Women During the Revolutionary Movement. Sona Zeitlian. (Illus.). 224p. (Orig.). (ARM.). 1992. pap. write for info. (*0-9632833-0-8*) H S Zeitliau.

Role of Art in the Late Anglo-Saxon Church. Richard Gameson. (Oxford Historical Monographs). (Illus.). 340p. 1995. 74.00 (*0-19-820541-4*) OUP.

Role of ASEAN in the Uruguay Round: Opportunities & Constraints. Mohamed Ariff. LC 92-42718. 1993. pap. 6.95 (*1-55815-249-0*) ICS Pr.

Role of Bacterial Antigens in Organ Specific Autoimmunity. Bernice M. Wenzel. 106p. 1990. text ed. 84.00 (*3-7186-5081-9*, Harwood Acad Pubs) Gordon & Breach.

Role of Banks in the Interwar Economy. Ed. by Harold James et al. 275p. (C). 1991. text ed. 69.95 (*0-521-39437-6*) Cambridge U Pr.

Role of Behavior in Evolution. Ed. by Henry C. Plotkin. 240p. 1988. 30.00 (*0-262-16107-9*, Bradford Bks) MIT Pr.

Role of Beta Agonist Therapy in Asthma Mortality. Beasley. 288p. 1993. 195.00 (*0-8493-6761-1*, QR201) CRC Pr.

Role of Biological Control in Pest Management. George Allen & Alejandro Rada. 184p. 1984. reprint ed. pap. 52.50 (*0-608-01994-1*, 2062650) Bks Demand.

Role of Bone in Acid Base Regulation. Ed. by J. Green. (Journal: Mineral & Electrolyte Metabolism: Vol. 20, Nos. 1-2, 1994). (Illus.). 96p. 1994. pap. 81.00 (*3-8055-5963-1*) S Karger.

Role of Brain Dopamine. Ed. by Edward Fluckiger et al. (Basic & Clinical Aspects of Neuroscience Ser.: Vol. 3). (Illus.). 70p. 1989. 27.95 (*0-387-50040-5*) Spr-Verlag.

Role of Business in Society. John Diebold. LC 82-71322. 144p. reprint ed. pap. 41.10 (*0-317-26958-5*, 2023576) Bks Demand.

Role of Calcium in Biological Systems, Vol. I. Ed. by Leopold J. Anghileri & Ann M. Tuffet-Anghileri. 288p. 1982. 163.00 (*0-8493-6280-6*, QP535, CRC Reprint) Franklin.

Role of Calcium in Biological Systems, Vol. II. Ed. by Leopold J. Anghileri & Ann M. Tuffet-Anghileri. 240p. 1982. 138.00 (*0-8493-6281-4*, QP535, CRC Reprint) Franklin.

Role of Calcium in Biological Systems, Vol. III. Ed. by Leopold J. Anghileri & Ann M. Tuffet-Anghileri. 272p. 1982. 153.00 (*0-8493-6282-2*, QP535, CRC Reprint) Franklin.

Role of Calcium in Biological Systems, Vol. IV. Ed. by Leopold J. Anghileri & Ann M. Tuffet-Anghileri. 272p. 1987. 155.00 (*0-8493-6283-0*, QP535, CRC Reprint) Franklin.

Role of Calcium in Biological Systems, Vol. 5. rev. ed. Leopold J. Anghileri. LC 81-155380. 304p. 1990. 153.00 (*0-8493-6284-9*, QP535) Franklin.

Role of Calcium Ions in Drug Action. M. Denborough. (International Encyclopedia of Pharmacology & Therapeutics Ser.: No. 124). (Illus.). 200p. 1987. 210.00 (*0-08-034193-4*, Pergamon Pr) Elsevier.

Role of Capital: Improving Innovations in American Manufacturing During the 1920's. John H. Lorant. LC 75-2588. (Dissertations in American Economic History Ser.). (Illus.). 1975. 34.95 (*0-405-07207-4*) Ayer.

Role of Carriers in Buyer/Supplier Strategic Alliances. Julie J. Gentry. 46p. (C). 1995. pap. text ed. 20.00 (*0-945968-22-1*) Ctr Advanced Purchasing.

Role of Case in Russian Syntax. Carol Neidle. (C). 1988. lib. bdg. 143.50 (*1-55608-042-5*) Kluwer Ac.

Role of Cell Surface Development, Vol. I. Salem S. Rao. 152p. 1987. 88.00 (*0-8493-4688-6*) CRC Pr.

Role of Cell Types in Hepatocarcinogenesis. Alphonse E. Sirica. 368p. 1992. 232.00 (*0-8493-4746-7*, RC280) CRC Pr.

Role of Central Banking in China's Economic Reforms. Carsten Holz. (Cornell East Asia Ser.: No. 59). 236p. (Orig.). (C). 1993. pap. 12.00 (*0-939657-59-7*) Cornell East Asia Pgm.

Role of Central Conceptual Structures in the Development of Children's Thought. Robbie Case & Yukari Okamoto. 225p. 1996. pap. text ed. 19.50 (*0-226-09540-1*) U Ch Pr.

Role of Ceramics in Advanced Electrochemical Systems. Ed. by P. N. Kumta et al. (Ceramic Transactions Ser.: No. 65). (Illus.). 386p. 1996. 90.00 (*1-57498-009-2*, CT065) Am Ceramic.

Role of Chemical Mediators in the Pathophysiology of Acute Illness & Injury. Ed. by Rita McConn. LC 81-40742. (Illus.). 407p. 1982. reprint ed. pap. 116.00 (*0-608-00608-4*, 2061195) Bks Demand.

Role of Chemicals & Radiation in the Etiology of Cancer. Ed. by Eliezer Huberman. LC 85-11886. (Carcinogenesis-a Comprehensive Survey Ser.: No. 10). (Illus.). 560p. 1985. reprint ed. pap. 159.60 (*0-7837-9568-8*, 2060317) Bks Demand.

Role of Chemistry in the Quality of Processed Foods. Owen R. Fennema et al. 366p. 1986. 82.00 (*0-917678-19-2*) Food & Nut Pr.

Role of Ch'i in Mao Tse-Tung's Leadership Style. Lam Lai Sing. LC 93-29019. 336p. 1993. text ed. 99.95 (*0-7734-2224-2*, Mellen Univ Pr) E Mellen.

***Role of Child Care Centers in the Lives of Parents.** Marybeth Shinn et al. 33p. 1990. pap. 10.00 (*0-614-22688-0*, C90-04) Families & Work.

Role of Chiropractic. Leonard W. Rutherford. 324p. (Orig.). 1989. text ed. 30.00 (*0-9625065-1-6*); pap. text ed. 22.50 (*0-9625065-0-8*) Hlth Educ Pub.

***Role of Chromium in Animal Nutrition.** 100p. 1997. pap. 19.00 (*0-309-06354-X*) Natl Acad Pr.

Role of Citrus in Health & Disease. Willard A. Krehl. LC 76-4502. (Illus.). 126p. reprint ed. pap. 36.00 (*0-7837-4901-5*, 2044566) Bks Demand.

Role of Cognates in the Teaching of the Romance Languages. Petra Hammer & Gerald S. Giauque. (American University Studies: Romance Languages & Literature: Ser. II, Vol. 94). 237p. (C). 1989. text ed. 34.50 (*0-8204-0761-5*) P Lang Pubng.

Role of Competition in Economic Transition & Integration. Ed. by Christopher T. Saunders. LC 92-38065. 330p. 1993. text ed. 79.95 (*0-312-09151-6*) St Martin.

Role of Comptroller & Auditor General in Indian Democracy. Sameer C. Mookerjee. (C). 1989. 64.00 (*81-7024-224-X*, Pub. by Ashish II) S Asia.

Role of Computers in Sci-Tech Libraries. Ed. by Ellis Mount. LC 86-7619. (Science & Technology Libraries: Vol. 6, No. 4). 145p. 1986. 29.95 (*0-86656-577-9*) Haworth Pr.

Role of Conceptual Models in Demonstrating Repository Postclosure Safety: Proceedings of an NEA Workshop Paris 16-18 Nov. 1993. OECD. 190p. (Orig.). 1995. pap. 50.00 (*92-64-14429-3*, Pub. by Org for Econ FR) OECD.

Role of Conference Literature in Sci-Tech Libraries. Ed. by Ellis Mount. (Science & Technology Libraries: Vol. 9, No. 2). 146p. 1989. 29.95 (*0-86656-780-1*) Haworth Pr.

***Role of Construction & Marketing in Economic Development: A Framework for Planning.** Pheng. 1995. pap. 24.00 (*0-85406-676-4*, Pub. by R-I-C-S Bks UK) St Mut.

Role of Copper in Lipid Metabolism. Lei. 296p. 1990. 202.00 (*0-8493-5564-8*, QR186) CRC Pr.

Role of Corridors. Ed. by D. Saunders & R. Hobbs. 457p. (C). 1991. text ed. 180.00 (*0-949324-35-3*, Pub. by Surrey Beatty & Sons AT) St Mut.

Role of Counsel at the Grand Jury. Ed. by Lawrence N. Gray. LC 87-60723. 147p. 1987. 20.00 (*0-942954-14-9*) NYS Bar.

Role of Crack Growth in Metal Fatigue. P. L. Pook. 157p. (Orig.). 1983. pap. text ed. 31.50 (*0-904357-63-5*, Pub. by Inst Materials UK) Ashgate Pub Co.

Role of Cyclic AMP in Cell Function. fac. ed. Ed. by Paul Greengard & Erminio Costa. LC 73-84113. (Advances in Biochemical Psychopharmacology Ser.: No. 3). 386p. pap. 110.10 (*0-7837-7193-2*, 2047106) Bks Demand.

Role of Cytokines in Cancer Treatment. Ed. by F. Takaku. (Journal: Oncology: Vol. 51, No. 2, 1994). (Illus.). 96p. 1994. pap. 88.75 (*3-8055-5948-8*) S Karger.

***Role of Cytokines in the Inflammatory Response.** Ed. by S. L. Kunkel. (Journal: Vol. 5, No. 4, 1996). (Illus.). 54p. 1996. pap. 28.00 (*3-8055-6380-9*) S Karger.

Role of Dampers in a Total Fire Protection System. Kenneth J. Schwartz. 1986. pap. 7.50 (*0-318-22361-9*, TR 86-2) Society Fire Protect.

Role of Demand & Supply in the Generation & Diffusion of Technical Change, Vol. 21. Colin G. Thirtle & Vernon W. Ruttan. (Fundamentals of Pure & Applied Economics Ser.: Vol. 21). 174, viiip. 1987. pap. text ed. 50.00 (*3-7186-0384-5*) Gordon & Breach.

Role of Design in International Competitiveness. M. J. Baker & D. O. Ughanwa. 448p. 1989. 87.50 (*0-415-00013-0*, A2516) Routledge.

Role of Design in the Furniture Industry. 4th ed. Lorraine Tierney. LC 95-24847. 77p. (Orig.). 1995. pap. 310.00 (*0-921577-54-0*) AKTRIN.

***Role of Developing Countries in Ground Based Experiments in Support of Space Observations for Global & Regional Studies.** K. Kasturirangan & R. R. Daniel. (Advances in Space Research (RJ) Ser.: Vol. 17). 112p. 1995. 97.75 (*0-08-042652-2*, Pergamon Pr) Elsevier.

***Role of Dietary Supplements for Physically Active People: Current Bibliographies in Medicine: January 1966 Through April 1996.** Kristine M. Scannell et al. 53p. (Orig.). 1996. pap. 25.00 (*0-7881-3347-0*) DIANE Pub.

Role of Diffusion in Catalysis. Charles N. Satterfield & Thomas K. Sherwood. LC 63-16570. (Addison Wesley Series in Chemical Engineering). 125p. reprint ed. pap. 35.70 (*0-317-10680-5*, 2055595) Bks Demand.

Role of Direct & Indirect Taxes in the Federal Revenue System. (Other Conferences Ser.: No. 3). 333p. 1964. reprint ed. 86.60 (*0-87014-469-3*) Natl Bur Econ Res.

Role of Discipline-Based Art Education in America's Schools. Elliot W. Eisner. LC 88-21516. (Illus.). 47p. 1988. pap. 7.50 (*0-89236-146-8*, Getty Educ Inst) J P Getty Trust.

Role of Domestic Courts in International Legal Order. Richard A. Falk. LC 64-16924. xvi, 184p. 1964. 42.00 (*1-57588-358-9*, 306630) W S Hein.

Role of Drugs & Electrolytes in Hormonogenesis. Ed. by K. Fotherby & S. B. Pal. LC 84-7611. (Illus.). xii, 360p. 1984. 138.50 (*3-11-008463-5*) De Gruyter.

Role of Drugs in Community Psychiatry. Ed. by Charles Shagass. (Modern Problems of Pharmacopsychiatry Ser.: Vol. 6). 1971. 28.00 (*3-8055-1200-7*) S Karger.

***Role of Dust in the Formation of Stars.** Ed. by Hans U. Kaufl & Ralf Siebenmorgen. LC 96-29226. (ESO Astrophysics Symposia Ser.). 454p. 1996. 38.00 (*3-540-61462-1*) Spr-Verlag.

Role of Economic Advisors in Developing Countries. Lauchlin Currie. LC 81-6623. (Contributions in Economics & Economic History Ser.: No. 44). (Illus.). 288p. 1981. text ed. 55.00 (*0-313-23064-1*, CUE/, Greenwood Pr) Greenwood.

Role of Economic Theory. Ed. by Philip A. Klein. LC 93-47645. (Recent Economic Thought Ser.). 272p. (C). 1994. lib. bdg. 105.00 (*0-7923-9452-6*) Kluwer Ac.

***Role of Economists in Modern Antitrust.** Fred McChesney & Paul Rubin. text ed. 95.00 (*0-471-97074-3*) Wiley.

Role of Education in Contemporary Africa. Ed. by Charles E. Nnolim. LC 88-9931. 133p. (Orig.). 1988. pap. 9.95 (*0-943852-53-6*) Prof World Peace.

Role of Educators in the Prevention & Treatment of Child Abuse & Neglect. Cynthia C. Tower. 82p. (Orig.). (C). 1995. pap. text ed. 25.00 (*0-7881-1660-6*) DIANE Pub.

Role of Elites & Citizens in Rural Development of India. Ed. by Sharada Rath et al. 198p. (C). 1993. 60.00 (*81-85880-18-2*, Pub. by Print Hse II) St Mut.

Role of Emotions in Social & Personality Development: History, Theory & Research. Carol Magai & Susan H. McFadden. (Emotions, Personality, & Psychotherapy Ser.: Vol. 1). 360p. 1995. 45.00 (*0-306-44866-1*, Plenum Pr) Plenum.

Role of Endorphins & Neuropsychiatry. Ed. by H. M. Emrich. (Modern Problems of Pharmacopsychiatry Ser.: Vol. 17). (Illus.). viii, 292p. 1981. 106.50 (*3-8055-2918-X*) S Karger.

Role of Engineering in Sustainable Development. Ed. by Monica D. Ellis. 1994. 15.00 (*0-87615-030-X*) AAES.

Role of Entrepreneur in Backward Areas. H. Sadhak. (C). 1989. 24.00 (*81-7035-058-1*, Pub. by Daya Pub Hse II) S Asia.

Role of Enzyme Treatment in Pancreatic Disease. Ed. by H. G. Beger et al. (Journal: Digestion: Vol. 54, Suppl. 2, 1993). (Illus.). vi, 54p. 1993. pap. 26.25 (*3-8055-5861-9*) S Karger.

Role of Epidemiology in Regulatory Risk Assessment. Ed. by John D. Graham. LC 95-36824. (International Congress Ser.: Vol. 1092). 166p. 1995. 162.50 (*0-444-82201-1*) Elsevier.

Role of Equalization in Federal Grants. U. S. Advisory Commission on Intergovernmental Relations. LC 77-74926. (American Federalism-the Urban Dimension Ser.). (Illus.). 1978. reprint ed. lib. bdg. 23.95 (*0-405-10475-8*) Ayer.

Role of Ethics in Social Theory: Essays from a Habermasian Perspective. Tony Smith. LC 90-40194. (SUNY Series in Ethical Theory). 246p. 1991. text ed. 64.50 (*0-7914-0652-0*); pap. text ed. 21.95 (*0-7914-0653-9*) State U NY Pr.

Role of European Naval Forces after the Cold War. Created by Gert De Nooy. LC 96-12721. 194p. 1996. pap. 64.00 (*90-411-0227-2*) Kluwer Law Tax Pubs.

Role of Exactions in Controlling Pollution. Frederick D. Stocker. 125p. 1987. pap. 7.50 (*1-55844-045-3*) Lincoln Inst Land.

Role of Exercise in Internal Medicine. Ed. by E. Jokl & D. Brunner. (Medicine & Sport Science Ser.: No. 10). 160p. 1976. 78.50 (*3-8055-2362-9*) S Karger.

Role of Experience in Science: Proceedings of the 1986 Conference of the Academic Internationale de Philosophie des Sciences (Bruxelles) Ed. by Ekhard Scheibe. 200p. (C). 1988. lib. bdg. 77.70 (*3-11-011303-1*) De Gruyter.

R

Role of Extracellular Matrix in Development. Ed. by Robert L. Trelstad. 643p. 1984. text ed. 219.00 (*0-471-83427-0*) Wiley.

Role of Eye Movements in Perceptual Processes. Ed. by Eugene Chekaluk & Keith Llewellyn. LC 92-13138. (Advances in Psychology Ser.: Vol. 88). 348p. 1992. 160.50 (*0-444-89005-X*, North Holland) Elsevier.

***Role of Family Planning & Targeted Credit Programs in Demographic Change in Bangladesh.** Shahidur R. Khandker & Abdul M. Latif. (Discussion Paper Ser.: No. 337). 42p. 1996. 7.95 (*0-8213-3707-6*, 13707) World Bank.

***Role of Farm-Level Diversification in the Adoption of Modern Technology in Brazil, Vol. 104.** Marc Nerlove et al. LC 96-49242. (Research Report ;). 1996. write for info. (*0-89629-107-3*) Intl Food Policy.

Role of Fats in Human Nutrition. J. Podmore. LC 85-5491. 210p. 1985. text ed. 65.00 (*3-527-26219-9*, VCH) Wiley.

Role of Fats in Human Nutrition. 2nd ed. Ed. by A. J. Vergroesen & M. Crawford. 500p. 1989. text ed. 149.00 (*0-12-718051-6*) Acad Pr.

***Role of Federal Courts in U. S. Customs & International Trade Law.** Patrick C. Reed. LC 96-43143. 453p. 1997. lib. bdg. 105.00 (*0-379-21375-3*) Oceana.

Role of Federal Credit Aids in Residential Construction. Leo Grebler. (Occasional Papers: No. 39). 83p. 1953. reprint ed. 21.60 (*0-87014-354-9*); reprint ed. mic. film 20.00 (*0-685-61290-2*) Natl Bur Econ Res.

Role of Federal Military Forces in Domestic Disorders. 1992. lib. bdg. 289.95 (*0-8490-5551-2*) Gordon Pr.

Role of Federal Military Forces in Domestic Disorders, 1789-1878. Robert W. Coakley. (Illus.). 372p. 1996. reprint ed. text ed. 50.00 (*0-7881-2818-3*) DIANE Pub.

Role of Finance in the Transition to Socialism. Stephany Griffith-Jones. LC 81-12844. 208p. 1981. text ed. 46.00 (*0-86598-069-1*) Rowman.

Role of Fine-Scale Magnetic Fields on the Structure of the Solar Atmosphere. Ed. by Egon-Horst Schroter et al. (Illus.). 430p. 1988. 69.95 (*0-521-34281-3*) Cambridge U Pr.

Role of Finite Elements & Boundary Elements in Computational Fluid Mechanics. R. L. Batra. LC 92-13901. 300p. 1996. text ed. 34.95 (*0-470-21860-6*) Halsted Pr.

Role of Fire in Ecological Systems. Ed. by Louis V. Trabaud. (Illus.). viii, 157p. 1987. pap. 42.50 (*90-5103-007-X*, Pub. by SPB Acad Pub NE) Balogh.

Role of Fire in Mediterranean-Type Ecosystems. Ed. by Jose M. Moreno & Walter C. Oechel. LC 93-42622. (Ecological Studies). 1994. 95.95 (*0-387-94215-7*) Spr-Verlag.

***Role of Fish in Enhancing Ricefield Ecology & in Integrated Pest Management.** Ed. by C. R. Dela Cruz. (ICLARM Conference Proceedings Ser.: No. 43). 50p. 1994. write for info. (*971-8709-51-7*, Pub. by ICLARM PH) Intl Spec Bk.

Role of Fisheries in Rural Development. S. Giriappa. (C). 1994. 24.00 (*81-7035-126-X*, Pub. by DK Pubs Dist II) S Asia.

Role of Fluids in Crustal Processes. Geophysics Study Committee, National Research Council Staff. (Studies in Geophysics). 196p. 1990. text ed. 29.95 (*0-309-04037-X*) Natl Acad Pr.

Role of Food Product Development in Implementing Dietary Guidelines. G. E. Livingston et al. 212p. 1982. 50.00 (*0-685-67749-4*) Food & Nut Pr.

***Role of Food Safety in Health & Development.** (Technical Report Ser.: No. 705). 79p. 1984. pap. text ed. 8.00 (*92-4-120705-1*) World Health.

Role of Foreign Languages in American Life see Foreign Language Teachers & Tests

Role of Free Economic Zones in the U. S. S. R. & Eastern Europe. (UNCTC Current Studies A: No. 14). 84p. 10. 00 (*92-1-104334-4*, E.90.II.A.5) UN.

Role of Free Radicals in Biological Systems. Janos Feher. 270p. (C). 1993. 156.00 (*963-05-6501-3*, Pub. by Akad Kiado HU) St Mut.

***Role of Gender in the Expansion of Practice Knowledge: A Criical Approach to Curriculum in Applied Sciences.** Josefina F. Mcdonough & F. Ellen Netting. Ed. by Ann Nichols-Casebolt. (Social-Psychology Reference Ser.). 250p. 1997. text ed. 38.00 (*0-8153-2228-3*) Garland.

***Role of Gene Duplications in Metazoan Evolution.** Lundin. 256p. 1997. text ed. write for info. (*0-412-75520-3*, Chap & Hall NY) Chapman & Hall.

Role of General Government Elected Officials in Criminal Justice. (Illus.). 216p. (Orig.). (C). 1994. pap. text ed. 50.00 (*0-7881-1331-3*) DIANE Pub.

Role of Glia in Neurotoxicity. Ed. by Michael Aschner & Harold K. Kimbelberg. 400p. 1996. 125.00 (*0-8493-4792-0*, 4792) CRC Pr.

***Role of Government & the Private Sector in Fighting Poverty.** George Psacharopoulos & Nguyen X. Nguyen. (Technical Paper Ser.: No. 346). 104p. 1997. 8.95 (*0-8213-3817-X*, 13817) World Bank.

Role of Government in a Market Economy. Ed. by Lowell D. Hill. LC 82-17298. 110p. 1982. reprint ed. pap. 31.40 (*0-608-00107-4*, 2060872) Bks Demand.

***Role of Government in East Asian Economic Development: Comparative Institutional Analysis.** Ed. by Masahiko Aoki et al. (Illus.). 440p. 1997. 85.00 (*0-19-829213-9*) OUP.

Role of Government in Monitoring & Regulating Religion in Public Life. Ed. by Derek Davis. LC 92-74168. 273p. (Orig.). (C). 1993. pap. 9.95 (*0-929182-18-9*); text ed. 24.95 (*0-929182-17-0*) Baylor U J M Dawson.

Role of Government in the Industrialization of Iraq. F. Jalal. 160p. 1972. 39.50 (*0-7146-2586-8*, Pub. by F Cass Pubs UK) Intl Spec Bk.

Role of Government in the Singapore Economy. Florian Von Alten. LC 95-11830. (European University Studies; Ser. 5, Economics & Management: Vol. 1695). 249p. 1995. pap. 39.95 (*3-631-48325-2*) P Lang Pubng.

Role of Governor in Non-Congress States. P. L. Mathur. (C). 1988. 32.00 (*81-7033-050-5*, Pub. by Rawat II) S Asia.

Role of Ground Water Research in Agricultural Policy Development & Implementation: Proceedings of a Conference Sponsored by ARI, May 1990. pap. 25.00 (*0-614-04332-8*) Agri Research Inst.

Role of Gut Bacteria in Human Toxicology & Pharmacology. Ed. by M. Hill. 350p. 1995. 99.00 (*0-7484-0110-5*, Pub. by Tay Francis Ltd UK) Taylor & Francis.

Role of Gut Flora in Toxicity & Cancer. Ed. by I. Rowland. 517p. 1988. text ed. 149.00 (*0-12-599920-8*) Acad Pr.

Role of Health Centres in the Development of Urban Health Systems: Report of a WHO Study Group on Primary Health Care in Urban Areas. (Technical Report Ser.: No. 827). iv, 38p. (ENG, FRE & SPA.). 1992. pap. text ed. 7.00 (*92-4-120827-9*, 1100827) World Health.

Role of Health Insurance in the Health Services Sector. Universities-National Bureau Staff & Richard N. Rosett. LC 76-8856. (Universities-National Bureau Conference Ser.: No. 27). 584p. 1976. reprint ed. 140.50 (*0-87014-272-0*) Natl Bur Econ Res.

Role of Health Insurance in the Health Services Sector: A Conference of the Universities-National Bureau Committee for Economic Research. Ed. by Richard N. Rosett. LC 76-8856. (Universities-National Bureau Conference Ser.: 27). 562p. reprint ed. pap. 160.20 (*0-317-42091-7*, 2052158) Bks Demand.

Role of Heat in the Development of Energy & Mineral Resources in the Northern Basin & Range Province. Ed. by Gordon Eaton. (Special Reports: No. 13). 500p. 1988. 15.00 (*0-934412-13-8*) Geothermal.

Role of High Energy Electrons in the Treatment of Cancer. Ed. by J. M. Vaeth & J. L. Meyer. (Frontiers of Radiation Therapy & Oncology Ser.: Vol. 25). (Illus.). x, 342p. 1991. 282.75 (*3-8055-5235-1*) S Karger.

Role of History As a Social Force. A. E. Afigbo. LC 79-88988. write for info. (*0-88357-013-0*); pap. write for info. (*0-88357-052-1*) NOK Pubs.

Role of Horticulture in Human Well-Being & Social Development. Ed. by Diane Relf. LC 91-19911. (Illus.). 254p. 1992. 49.95 (*0-88192-209-9*) Timber.

***Role of Hospitals in Ambulatory & Domiciliary Medical Care.** (Technical Report Ser.: No. 176). 32p. 1959. pap. text ed. 3.00 (*92-4-120176-2*) World Health.

Role of Human Rights in Foreign Policy. Peter R. Baehr. LC 94-5975. 1994. text ed. 49.95 (*0-312-12173-3*) St Martin.

Role of Hyperparasitism in Biological Control: A Symposium. David Rosen. LC 81-65779. (Illus.). 52p. 1981. pap. 3.00 (*0-931876-47-8*, 4103) ANR Pubns CA.

Role of Ideology in Church Participation. Phillip E. Hammond. Ed. by Harriet Zuckerman & Robert K. Merton. LC 79-9003. (Dissertations on Sociology Ser.). 1980. lib. bdg. 30.95 (*0-405-12972-6*) Ayer.

Role of Ideology in the American Revolution. Ed. by John R. Howe, Jr. LC 76-3777. (Americam Problem Studies). 132p. 1976. reprint ed. pap. 9.50 (*0-88275-406-8*) Krieger.

***Role of IEA Governments in Energy.** IEA Staff. 364p. (Orig.). 1996. pap. 94.00 (*92-64-14890-6*, 61-96-13-1, Pub. by Org for Econ FR) OECD.

Role of IEA Governments in Energy - A Survey: A Survey. OECD Staff. 304p. (Orig.). 1992. pap. 72.00 (*92-64-13740-8*, 61-92-12-1) OECD.

Role of Imagery in Learning. Harry S. Broudy. LC 88-21521. (Occasional Paper Ser.: Vol. 1). 56p. 1988. pap. 10.00 (*0-89236-145-X*, Getty Educ Inst) J P Getty Trust.

***Role of Immune Complexes in Disease: Report of a WHO Scientific Group, 1977.** (Technical Report Ser.: No. 606). 58p. 1977. pap. text ed. 8.00 (*92-4-120606-3*, 1100606) World Health.

Role of Immune Mechanisms in Cardiovascular Disease. H. P. Schultheiss & P. Schwimmbeck. LC 96-27976. 1996. 99.50 (*3-540-61358-7*) Spr-Verlag.

Role of Immunological Factors in Infectious, Allergic, & Autoimmune Processes. Ed. by Roland F. Beers & Edward Basset. LC 75-25109. (Miles International Symposium Ser.: No. 8). (Illus.). 556p. 1976. reprint ed. pap. 158.50 (*0-608-00630-0*, 2061218) Bks Demand.

Role of India in the Emergence of Bangladesh. Sucheta Ghosh. 1984. 18.50 (*0-8364-0780-6*) S Asia.

Role of Infertility in Adoption. C. Brebner et al. (C). 1989. 60.00 (*0-903534-62-2*, Pub. by Brit Ag for Adopt & Fost UK) St Mut.

Role of Inflection in Scandinavian Syntax. Anders Holmberg & Christer Platzack. (Oxford Studies in Comparative Syntax). 272p. 1995. 42.00 (*0-19-506745-2*); pap. 24.00 (*0-19-506746-0*) OUP.

Role of Information in Broadening Education & Employment Opportunities. Lorraine Amico. Ed. by Karen Glass. 51p. (Orig.). 1991. pap. text ed. 15.00 (*1-55877-139-5*) Natl Governor.

Role of Information in the Economy & Society: Proceedings of a Workshop. Ed. by Kirsty Hughes & Nick Moore. 150p. (Orig.). (C). 1994. pap. text ed. 40.00 (*0-7881-0648-1*) DIANE Pub.

Role of Institutional Finance in Agriculture. J. P. Singh. 378p. 1986. 36.00 (*81-7024-029-8*, Pub. by Ashish II) S Asia.

Role of Insulin-Like Growth Factors in the Nervous System. Ed. by Mohan K. Raizada & Derek LeRoith. LC 93-11672. (Annals Ser.: Vol. 692). 348p. 1993. write for info. (*0-89766-789-1*); pap. 95.00 (*0-89766-790-5*) NY Acad Sci.

Role of Integrated Rural Development Projects in Developing Local Institutional Capacity. Diana Conyers et al. (Studies in Technology & Social Change: No. 2). 50p. (Orig.). (C). 1988. pap. 6.00 (*0-945271-02-6*) ISU-CIKARD.

Role of Interest Groups in the European Community. Emil J. Kirchner & Konrad Schwaiger. 192p. 1981. text ed. 59.95 (*0-566-00257-4*, Pub. by Dartmth Pub UK) Ashgate Pub Co.

Role of Interest in Learning & Development. Ed. by K. Ann Renninger et al. 368p. 1992. text ed. 79.95 (*0-8058-0718-7*) L Erlbaum Assocs.

Role of Interfaces on Material Dumping: Proceedings of an International Symposium Held in Conjunction with ASM's Materials Week & TMS-AIME Fall Meeting, 13-17 October 1985, Toronto, Ontario, Canada. Ed. by B. B. Rath & M. S. Misra. LC 86-71998. (Illus.). 131p. reprint ed. pap. 37.40 (*0-318-39723-4*, 2033081) Bks Demand.

Role of Interleukin-2 in the Treatment of Cancer Patients. Ed. by John Wagstaff. LC 93-104. 200p. (C). 1993. lib. bdg. 122.00 (*0-7923-2164-2*) Kluwer Ac.

Role of Internal Auditors in Environmental Issues: CH2M Hill, Commissioned by the Institute of Internal Auditors Research Foundation. Ed. by Lee A. Campbell. 220p. 1993. pap. text ed. 25.00 (*0-89413-284-9*, A863) Inst Inter Aud.

Role of Internal Friction in Dynamic Analysis of Structures. A. I. Tseitlin & A. A. Kusainov. Tr. by N. K. Mehta from RUS. (Russian Translation Ser.: No. 80). (Illus.). 223p. (C). 1991. text ed. 95.00 (*90-6191-959-2*, Pub. by A A Balkema NE) Ashgate Pub Co.

Role of International Companies in Latin American Integration: Autos & Petrochemicals. Jack N. Behrman. LC 79-183711. 185p. 1972. pap. 4.50 (*0-87186-235-2*) Comm Econ Dev.

Role of International Law in the Prevention & Punishment of Economic Crimes with Particular Reference to the Crime of Indigenous Spoilation. Ndiva Kofele-Kale. LC 95-2025. 1995. lib. bdg. 160.00 (*0-7923-3358-6*, Pub. by M Nijhoff NE) Kluwer Ac.

Role of Intonation in Spoken English. Maria Schubiger. 1973. text ed. 1.00 (*0-686-09402-6*) Expression.

***Role of Intraoperative Radiation Therapy in the Treatment of Cancer: 6th International IORT Symposium & 31st San Francisco Cancer Symposium, San Francisco, CA, September 1996.** J. M. Vaeth. LC 97-5478. (Frontiers of Radiation Therapy & Oncology Ser.: Vol. 31, 1997). (Illus.). x, 280p. 1997. 252.25 (*3-8055-6456-2*) S Karger.

Role of Inventories in Business Cycles. Moses Abramovitz. (Occasional Papers: No. 26). 32p. 1948. reprint ed. 20. 00 (*0-87014-341-7*) Natl Bur Econ Res.

Role of ISC's. Anne C. Ward & Robert L. Sandidge. 1996. pap. 27.50 (*1-57654-003-0*, Creative Core) New Orient Media.

Role of It: Practical Issues for the Primary Teacher. Avril Loveless. (Children, Teachers & Learning Ser.). (Illus.). 160p. 1996. 90.00 (*0-304-33214-3*); pap. 19.95 (*0-304-33217-8*) Cassell.

Role of Japan in Asia. Shinichi Ichimura. LC 92-46607. (Occasional Papers: No. 36). 32p. 1993. pap. 9.95 (*1-55815-242-3*) ICS Pr.

Role of Joseph McGarrity in the Struggle for Irish Independence. Marie V. Tarpey. LC 76-6368. (Irish Americans Ser.). 1976. 33.95 (*0-405-09360-8*) Ayer.

***Role of Judges & Lawyers.** Henk J. Snijders. 1992. pap. text ed. 24.00 (*90-6544-636-2*) Kluwer Ac.

Role of Junior & Middle Level Management in TQM. David Bertram. (C). 1994. 150.00 (*0-946655-74-X*, Pub. by Stanley Thornes UK) Trans-Atl Phila.

***Role of Knowledge in Learning & Instruction: A Special Issue of Educational Psychologist, Vol. 31, No. 2, 1996.** Ed. by Patricia A. Alexander. 56p. 1996. pap. 20.00 (*0-8058-9889-1*) L Erlbaum Assocs.

Role of Labour-Intensive Sectors in Japanese Industrialization. 219p. 1991. 40.00 (*92-808-0512-6*) UN.

Role of Language in the Struggle for Power & Legitimacy in Africa. Abiodun Goke-Pariola. LC 93-30579. (African Studies: Vol. 31). 212p. 1993. text ed. 89.95 (*0-7734-9351-4*) E Mellen.

Role of Laser in Gastroenterology: Analysis of Eight Years' Experience. Lisabeth M. Mathus-Vliegen. (Developments in Gastroenterology Ser.). (C). 1989. lib. bdg. 158.50 (*0-7923-0425-X*) Kluwer Ac.

Role of Law Enforcement in the Response to Child Abuse & Neglect. Donna Pence & Charles Wilson. 78p. (Orig.). (C). 1995. pap. text ed. 25.00 (*0-7881-1667-3*) DIANE Pub.

Role of Legumes in the Farming Systems of the Mediterranean Areas. Ed. by A. E. Osman et al. (C). 1990. lib. bdg. 137.50 (*0-7923-0419-5*) Kluwer Ac.

Role of Libraries in the Growth of Knowledge: Proceedings of the 40th Conference of the Graduate Library School, May 18-19, 1978. Chicago University, Graduate Library School Staff. Ed. by Don R. Swanson. LC 79-5467. (University of Chicago Studies in Library Science). 142p. reprint ed. pap. 40.50 (*0-685-15490-4*, 2026746) Bks Demand.

Role of Local Organizations in Development. Matthias Schmale. 272p. 1993. 59.95 (*1-85628-511-1*, Pub. by Avebury Pub UK) Ashgate Pub Co.

Role of Low-Cost Power in Economic Development: A Case Study; Alaska. Gunter Schramm. Ed. by Stuart Bruchey. LC 78-22707. (Energy in the American Economy Ser.). (Illus.). 1979. lib. bdg. 28.95 (*0-405-12009-5*) Ayer.

Role of M. J. P. Koledade (1902-73) in Pioneering Nigerian Education. E. Adeleye Ijagbemi. LC 92-11658. 320p. 1992. lib. bdg. 99.95 (*0-7734-9724-2*) E Mellen.

Role of Magnetic Fields in Physics & Astrophysics, Vol. 257. Ed. by V. Canuto. (Annals Ser.). 226p. 1975. 38.00 (*0-89072-012-6*) NY Acad Sci.

Role of Mail in Decision Making in Congress. Orval Hansen & Ellen Miller. (Congressional Operations Ser.). 80p. (Orig.). 1987. pap. text ed. 12.25 (*0-939715-06-6*) Ctr Politics.

Role of Management Accounting in the Emerging Team Approach to Work. International Federation of Accountants Staff. 38p. (Orig.). 1995. pap. text ed. 10.00 (*1-887464-06-9*) Intl Fed Accts.

Role of Manufacturing Technology in Trade Adjustment Strategies. National Research Council (U. S.), Committee on Biologic Markers of Air-Pollution Damage in Trees Staff. 64p. reprint ed. pap. 25.00 (*0-8357-7685-9*, 2036035) Bks Demand.

Role of Maps in Sci-Tech Libraries. Ed. by Ellis Mount. LC 84-27919. (Science & Technology Libraries: Vol. 5, No. 3). 122p. 1985. text ed. 29.95 (*0-86656-395-4*) Haworth Pr.

Role of Mathematics in Science. M. M. Shiffer & Leon Bowden. (New Mathematical Library: No. 30). 207p. 1984. pap. 10.00 (*0-88385-630-1*, NML-30) Math Assn.

Role of Mathematics in the Rise of Science. Salomon Bochner. LC 66-10550. 396p. reprint ed. pap. 112.90 (*0-8357-7012-5*, 2052287) Bks Demand.

Role of Medicine. Thomas McKeown. LC 79-84025. 180p. 1980. pap. text ed. 16.95 (*0-691-02362-X*) Princeton U Pr.

Role of Medroxyprogesterone in Endocrine-Related Tumors Vol. 3. fac. ed. Ed. by A. Pellegrini et al. LC 80-5550. (Progress in Cancer Research & Therapy Ser.: No. 15). (Illus.). 191p. pap. 54.50 (*0-7837-7150-9*, 2047146) Bks Demand.

Role of Melatonin & Pineal Peptides in Neuroimmunomodulation. Ed. by Russell J. Reiter & F. Fraschini. (NATO ASI Series A, Life Sciences: Vol. 204). (Illus.). 312p. 1991. 105.00 (*0-306-43921-2*, Plenum Pr) Plenum.

Role of Membranes in Lens Ageing & Cataract: Proceedings of the Spring Meeting 1995. Ed. by G. F. Vrensen & T. Libondi. (Journal: Ophthalmic Research Ser.: Vol. 28, Suppl. 1, 1996). (Illus.). xii, 106p. 1996. pap. 36.50 (*3-8055-6304-3*) S Karger.

Role of Mental Health Professionals in the Prevention & Treatment of Child Abuse & Neglect. Anthony J. Urquiza. 73p. (Orig.). (C). 1995. pap. text ed. 25.00 (*0-7881-1664-9*) DIANE Pub.

Role of Mergers in the Growth of Large Firms. John F. Weston & University of California, Bureau of Business & Economic Research Staff. LC 76-2049. (Illus.). 159p. 1976. reprint ed. text ed. 35.00 (*0-8371-8742-7*, WERM, Greenwood Pr) Greenwood.

Role of Metals in Ancient Greek History. Michail Y. Treister. LC 95-44263. (Mnemosyne, Bibliotheca Classica Batava Ser.: Vol. 156). 1996. 159.00 (*90-04-10473-9*) E J Brill.

Role of Micro-Organisms in Non-Infectious Disease. Ed. by R. R. De Vries et al. (Argenteuil Symposia Ser.). (Illus.). 208p. 1990. 81.00 (*0-387-19623-4*) Spr-Verlag.

***Role of Microenvironment in Axonal Regeneration: Influence of Lesion-Induced Changes & Glial Implants on the Regeneration of the Postcommissural Fornix.** C. C. Stichel-Gunkel. LC 97-10368. (Advances in Anatomy, Embryology & Cell Biology Ser.: Vol. 137). (Illus.). vi, 70p. 1997. pap. 59.00 (*3-540-62787-1*) Spr-Verlag.

Role of Microglial Cells & Astrocytes in Pathology. Ed. by J. E. Merrill. (Journal: Vol. 16, No. 3-4, 1994). (Illus.). 124p. 1995. pap. 50.50 (*3-8055-6086-9*) S Karger.

Role of Middleman Transactions in World Trade. Robert M. Lichtenberg. (Occasional Papers: No. 64). 104p. 1959. reprint ed. 27.10 (*0-87014-378-6*); reprint ed. mic. film 20.00 (*0-685-61320-8*) Natl Bur Econ Res.

Role of Minor Elements in Cement Manufacturing & Use. Portland Cement Association Staff. (Illus.). 44p. 1995. 35.00 (*0-89312-131-2*, RD109T) Portland Cement.

Role of Minorities in Freedom Struggle. Asghar A. Engineer. 195p. 1986. 18.00 (*81-202-0164-7*, Pub. by Ajanta II) S Asia.

Role of Money: What It Should Be, Contrasted to What It Has Become. Frederick Soddy. 1976. lib. bdg. 59.95 (*0-8490-2530-3*) Gordon Pr.

Role of Mood in Heidegger's Ontology. Bruce W. Ballard. 154p. (Orig.). (C). 1990. pap. text ed. 20.50 (*0-8191-7979-5*); lib. bdg. 35.50 (*0-8191-7978-7*) U Pr of Amer.

Role of Movement Patterns in Development I. Judith Kestenberg. 138p. (C). 1967. reprint ed. pap. text ed. 17. 95 (*0-932582-05-2*, Pub. by Dance Bks UK) Princeton Bk Co.

Role of Movement Patterns in Development II. Judith Kestenberg & K. Mark Sossin. 164p. 1979. pap. text ed. 17.95 (*0-932582-01-X*, Pub. by Dance Bks UK) Princeton Bk Co.

Role of Multinational Companies in Nation's Economy: A Case Study of Iran. Shahbazzadeh Mohsen. (C). 1994. 42.00 (*81-7018-747-8*, Pub. by BR Pub II) S Asia.

Role of Multinationals in India's Foreign Trade. Usha Saxena. (C). 1987. 34.00 (*81-7024-081-6*, Pub. by Ashish II) S Asia.

An Asterisk (*) at the beginning of an entry indicates that the title is appearing in BIP for the first time.

Role of Music in the New Roman Liturgy. William Herring. LC 75-14548. 1971. pap. 0.50 (*0-915866-01-3*) Am Cath Pr.

Role of Muslim Scientists in the Advancement of Science. Hujjat al-Islan Muhammad Mufatteh. Tr. by Elahe Assair. 48p. (Orig.). 1989. pap. text ed. 3.30 (*1-871031-30-3*) Abjad Bk.

Role of Muslims in the National Movement. Muhammad M. Imam. 306p. (C). 1987. 27.50 (*81-7099-033-5*, Pub. by Mittal II) S Asia.

Role of National Libraries in Developing Countries: With Special Reference to Saudi Arabia. A. Al-Nahari. 174p. 1984. text ed. 70.00 (*0-7201-1696-1*, Mansell Pub) Cassell.

Role of National Saving in the World Economy: Recent Trends & Prospects. Bijan B. Aghevli et al. (Occasional Paper Ser.: No. 67). vii, 64p. 1990. pap. 10.00 (*1-55775-134-X*) Intl Monetary.

Role of Nationalised Banks in the Development of Small Scale Industries. M. A. Hasnat. (C). 1991. text ed. 22.00 (*81-7054-139-5*, Pub. by Classical Pub II) S Asia.

Role of Natural Gas in Environmental Policy. Intro. by Stephen L. MacDonald. LC 92-76046. 120p. (Orig.). 1993. pap. 16.50 (*0-87755-332-7*) Bureau Busn TX.

Role of Natural Gas in Environmental Policy. Ed. by Stephen L. McDonald & Mina Mohammadioun. (Illus.). 63p. (Orig.). (C). 1994. pap. text ed. 30.00 (*0-7881-0274-5*) DIANE Pub.

Role of Neuroplasticity in the Response to Drugs. 1993. lib. bdg. 259.95 (*0-8490-8505-5*) Gordon Pr.

Role of Neurotransmitter Systems in Anxiety Modulation. (Journal: Psychopathology: Vol. 17, Suppl. 3, 1984). (Illus.). iv, 84p. 1984. pap. 22.50 (*3-8055-3983-5*) S Karger.

Role of Neurotransmitters in Brain Injury. Ed. by W. Dalton Dietrich & Mordecai Y. Globus. LC 92-49215. (Illus.). 362p. (C). 1992. 95.00 (*0-306-44255-8*, Plenum Pr) Plenum.

*__Role of NGOs under Authoritarian Political Systems.__ Seamus Cleary. LC 97-5332. (International Political Economy Ser.). 1997. write for info. (*0-312-17464-0*) St Martin.

Role of Nitric Oxide & Sepsis & ARDS. Ed. by M. P. Fink & D. Payen. LC 95-37672. (Update in Intensive Care & Emergency Medicine Ser.: No. 24). 416p. 1995. 147.00 (*3-540-60128-7*) Spr-Verlag.

Role of Nitric Oxide in Physiology & Pathophysiology. Ed. by Hilary Koprowski & H. Maeda. (Currents Topics in Microbiology & Immunology Ser.: Vol. 196). 117p. 1995. 108.95 (*0-387-58214-2*) Spr-Verlag.

Role of Nonliving Organic Matter in the Earth's Carbon Cycle. Richard G. Zepp. (Dahlem Workshop Reports - (PC) Physical Ser.). 346p. 1995. text ed. 125.00 (*0-471-95463-2*) Wiley.

Role of North Carolina State Government in the Development of Minority-Owned Business Enterprises, 1975-1991. 69p. (Orig.). 1992. 500.00 (*0-9633115-1-4*) NC Inst Min Econ Devel.

Role of Nucleation in Boiling & Cavitation: Symposium Presented at Joint Fluids Engineering, Heat Transfer & Lubrication Conference, Detroit, Michigan, May 26-27, 1970. American Society of Mechanical Engineers Staff. 23p. reprint ed. pap. 25.00 (*0-317-09023-2*, 2016877) Bks Demand.

Role of Occupational Therapy with the Elderly (ROTE) Linda J. Davis. Ed. by Martha Kirkland. 436p. (C). 1986. 45.00 (*0-910317-19-4*) Am Occup Therapy.

Role of Opposition Parties in Indian Politics: The Andhra Pradesh Experience. D. Sundar Ram. (C). 1992. 29.50 (*81-7100-412-1*, Pub. by Deep II) S Asia.

Role of Organic Matter in Modern Agriculture. Ed. by Y. Chen & Y. Avnimelech. (Developments in Plant & Soil Sciences Ser.). 1986. lib. bdg. 159.00 (*90-247-3360-X*) Kluwer Ac.

Role of Outside Powers. Ed. by Shahram Chubin. LC 80-28314. (Security in the Persian Gulf Ser.: Vol. 4). 180p. 1982. pap. 19.50 (*0-86598-047-0*) Rowman.

Role of Oxygen in Improving Chemical Processes: Proceedings of the BOC Priestley Conference, Paris, France, 1992. 6th ed. M. Fetizon & W. J. Thomas. 286p. 1993. 126.00 (*0-85186-725-1*) CRC Pr.

Role of Oxygen Radicals in Cardiovascular Disease. Ed. by Antonia L'Abbate. (C). 1988. lib. bdg. 143.50 (*0-89838-407-9*) Kluwer Ac.

Role of Parallel Catamorphic Systems in the Structure of Zola's "Rougon-Maquart" Gabrielle M. Rochecouste. (Romanistische Texte und Studien: Vol. 2). (Illus.). 276p. 1988. 35.10 (*3-487-07964-X*) G Olms Pubs.

Role of Parent Education in Achieving School Readiness. Elizabeth Stief. Ed. by Gerry Feinstein. 40p. (Orig.). 1993. pap. text ed. 15.00 (*1-55877-223-5*) Natl Governor.

*__Role of Parents in School to Work Transition.__ William Rouix. (Education Reform & School-to-Work Transition Ser.). 22p. 1995. teacher ed., pap. text ed. 12.00 (*0-614-24524-9*) Natl Inst Work.

Role of Parliament in a Communist Revolution. Jan Kozak. 44p. 1963. reprint ed. spiral bd. 5.00 (*0-7873-0513-8*) Hlth Research.

Role of Patents in Sci-Tech Libraries. Ed. by Ellis Mount. LC 82-2885. (Science & Technology Libraries: Vol. 2, No. 2). 97p. 1982. pap. text ed. 29.95 (*0-86656-114-5*) Haworth Pr.

Role of Peptides in Neuronal Function. Ed. by Jeffery L. Barker & T. G. Smith, Jr. LC 80-24658. (Illus.). 769p. reprint ed. pap. 180.00 (*0-7837-0962-5*, 2041267) Bks Demand.

*__Role of Pharmacoeconomics in Outcomes Management.__ Ed. by Nelda E. Johnson & David B. Nash. LC 96-35331. 98p. (Orig.). 1996. pap. 35.00 (*1-55648-169-1*, 169111) AHPI.

Role of Pharmacology in Pediatric Oncology. Ed. by L. Massimo et al. (Developments in Oncology Ser.). 1987. lib. bdg. 197.00 (*0-89838-795-7*) Kluwer Ac.

Role of Phonological Coding in Reading Kanji: A Research Report & Some Pedagogical Implications. Sachiko Matsunaga. (Technical Reports: No. 6). 64p. (Orig.). (C). 1995. pap. text ed. 10.00 (*0-8248-1734-6*) Sec Lang Tching.

*__Role of Phonological Structure in Sound Change from Latin to Spanish & Portuguese.__ Kenneth J. Wireback. (American University Studies II: Vol. 215). 152p. (C). 1997. text ed. 33.95 (*0-8204-2765-9*) P Lang Pubng.

Role of Phosphonates in Living Systems. Ed. by Richard L. Hilderbrand. 216p. 1983. 144.00 (*0-8493-5724-1*, QP801) CRC Pr.

Role of Phosphorous in Agriculture. Ed. by F. E. Khasawneh et al. (Illus.). 910p. 1980. 25.00 (*0-89118-062-1*) Am Soc Agron.

Role of Place in Literature. Leonard Lutwack. LC 83-24264. 304p. 1984. 39.95 (*0-8156-2305-4*) Syracuse U Pr.

Role of Platelet-Activating Factor in Immune Disorders, Part 2. Ed. by P. Braquet. (New Trends in Lipid Mediators Research Ser.: Vol. 2). (Illus.). viii, 214p. 1988. 158.50 (*3-8055-4744-7*) S Karger.

Role of Platelets in Blood-Biomaterial Interactions. Ed. by Y. F. Missirlis & J. L. Wautier. LC 93-2728. 1993. lib. bdg. 123.50 (*0-7923-2162-6*) Kluwer Ac.

Role of Police Psychology in Controlling Excessive Force. Ellen M. Scrivner. 52p. (Orig.). (C). 1994. pap. text ed. 25.00 (*0-7881-1434-4*) DIANE Pub.

Role of Politicians in Public Charities. Ellen M. Freeberg & Ellen S. Miller. (Public Policy & Foundations Ser.). 130p. (Orig.). (C). 1987. pap. text ed. 13.75 (*0-939715-07-4*) Ctr Politics.

Role of Politics in Social Change. Charles E. Merriam. LC 83-1490. 149p. 1983. reprint ed. text ed. 49.75 (*0-313-23852-9*, MERO, Greenwood Pr) Greenwood.

*__Role of Postsecondary Education in Workforce Development: Challenges for State Policy.__ Robert A. Wallhaus. 36p. 1996. lib. bdg. 8.00 (*0-614-23675-4*) SHEEO.

Role of Power in Nonviolent Struggle. Gene Sharp. (Monograph Ser.). 19p. 1990. 2.00 (*1-880813-02-5*) A Einstein Inst.

*__Role of Precious Metals in European Economic Development: From the Roman Times to the Eve of the Industrial Revolution.__ S. M. Bozorgnia. (Contributions in Economics and Economic History: Vol. 192). 1997. text ed. write for info. (*0-313-29445-3*, Greenwood Pr) Greenwood.

Role of Prescriptivism in American Linguistics 1820-1970. Glendon F. Drake. x, 130p. 1977. 39.00 (*90-272-0954-5*, SIHOLS 13) Benjamins North Am.

Role of Print on Paper in the Publishing House of the Future. Joost Kist. (Illus.). 23p. (Orig.). 1993. pap. text ed. write for info. (*1-879716-05-4*, I-93-3) Ctr Info Policy.

Role of Private Financial Wealth in a Portfolio Model: A Study of the Effects of Fiscal Deficits on the Real Exchange Rate. Angel Calderon-Madrid. LC 94-45746. 1995. text ed. 75.00 (*0-312-12605-0*) St Martin.

Role of Private Pensions in Maintaining Living Standards in Retirement. Robert Clark. LC 77-87188. 64p. 1977. 3.50 (*0-89068-041-8*) Natl Planning.

Role of Procoagulant Activity in Health & Disease. Levy. 240p. 1993. 169.95 (*0-8493-5566-4*, QP93) CRC Pr.

Role of Procoagulant Activity in Health & Disease. Levy. 1993. 165.00 (*0-317-05735-9*, QR186, CRC Reprint) Franklin.

Role of Prolactin in Human Reproduction. Ed. by M. Mizuno et al. (Illus.). x, 314p. 1988. 207.25 (*3-8055-4786-2*) S Karger.

Role of Proof Loading in Structural Integrity. D. J. Smith & S. J. Garwood. 256p. 1996. 125.00 (*1-85573-093-6*, Pub. by Woodhead Pubng UK) Am Educ Systs.

Role of Proteoglycans & Glycosaminoglycans in Aging. K. Sames. (Interdisciplinary Topics in Gerontology Ser.: Vol. 28). (Illus.). xiv, 140p. 1994. 128.75 (*3-8055-5925-9*) S Karger.

Role of Providence in the Social Order: An Essay in Intellectual History. Jacob Viner. LC 72-184168. (American Philosophical Society, Memoirs Ser.: Vol. 90). 123p. reprint ed. pap. 35.10 (*0-317-29441-5*, 2024290) Bks Demand.

Role of Psychiatry in Medical Education: An Appraisal & a Forecast. Sidney L. Werkman. LC 66-10810. (Commonwealth Fund Publications). (Illus.). 203p. 1966. 22.00 (*0-674-77730-1*) HUP.

Role of Psychoanalysis in Psychiatric Education: Past, Present, & Future. Ed. by Sidney H. Weismann & Robert Thurnblad. (Emotions & Behavior Monographs: No. 7). (C). 1987. 50.00 (*0-8236-5850-3*) Intl Univs Pr.

Role of Psychosocial Factors in the Pathogenesis of Coronary Heart Disease, 1980. Ed. by A. D. Appels & P. Falger. (Journal: Psychotherapy & Psychosomatics: Vol. 34, No. 2-3). (Illus.). iv, 160p. 1981. pap. 33.00 (*3-8055-2286-X*) S Karger.

Role of Public Agencies in Fostering New Technology & Innovation in Building. National Research Council, Committee on Vision Staff. Ed. by Andrew C. Lemer & David R. Dibner. LC 92-62883. 142p. (Orig.). 1993. pap. text ed. 28.00 (*0-309-04783-8*) Natl Res Coun.

*__Role of Public & Private Agents in the Food & Agricultural Sectors of Developing Countries.__ 130p. 1991. 12.00 (*92-5-103001-4*, F0014, Pub. by FAO IT) Bernan Associates.

*__Role of Public Health Officers & General Practitioners in Mental Health Care.__ (Technical Report Ser.: No 235). 54p. 1962. pap. text ed. 3.00 (*92-4-120235-1*) World Health.

Role of Reason in Sankara Vedanta. S. P. Verma. (C). 1992. text ed. 15.00 (*0-8364-2840-4*, Pub. by Manohar II) S Asia.

Role of Receptors in Biology & Medicine: Proceedings of the Ninth Argenteuil Symposium, Brussels, Belgium, 1984. Argenteuil Symposium Staff. Ed. by Antonio M. Gotto, Jr. & Bert W. O'Malley. LC 85-23389. 233p. 1986. reprint ed. pap. 66.50 (*0-608-00375-1*, 2061088) Bks Demand.

Role of Regional Development Agencies in Economic Regeneration. Michael W. Danson et al. (Regional Policy & Development Ser.: Vol. 1). 160p. 1993. 55.00 (*1-85302-067-2*) Taylor & Francis.

Role of Regional Organizations in Context of Climate Change. Ed. by Michael H. Glantz. LC 93-27582. (NATO ASI Series I: Global Environmental Change: Vol. 14). 1993. 131.95 (*0-387-57252-X*) Spr-Verlag.

*__Role of Reliability for Bearings & Gears.__ Charles A. Moyer. (1992 Fall Technical Meeting). 1992. pap. text ed. 30.00 (*1-55589-588-3*) AGMA.

*__Role of Religion & Ethics in the Prevention & Control of Aids: Health Education Through Religion, 6.__ 1992. pap. text ed. 10.00 (*92-9021-153-9*) World Health.

Role of Religion in American Life: An Interpretive Historical Anthology. 2nd ed. Robert R. Mathisen. 368p. (Orig.). (C). 1996. per. 41.94 (*0-8403-9367-9*) Kendall-Hunt.

Role of Religion in Ethnic Self-Identity: A Vietnamese Community. Paul Rutledge. (Illus.). 140p. (Orig.). (C). 1985. lib. bdg. 41.00 (*0-8191-4505-X*) U Pr of Amer.

Role of Religion in the Making of Public Policy. Ed. by James E. Wood, Jr. & Derek Davis. 257p. (Orig.). (C). 1991. pap. 9.95 (*0-929182-16-2*); text ed. 24.95 (*0-929182-15-4*) Baylor U J M Dawson.

Role of Religious Organizations in Social Movements. Ed. by Barbara M. Yarnold. LC 91-7206. 152p. 1991. text ed. 45.00 (*0-275-94017-9*, C4017, Praeger Pubs) Greenwood.

Role of Remnants of Native Vegetation. Ed. by D. Saunders et al. 410p. (C). 1987. text ed. 160.00 (*0-949324-08-6*, Pub. by Surrey Beatty & Sons AT) St Mut.

Role of Research & Information Systems in Decision-Making for the Development of Human Resources for Health: Report of a WHO Study Group. (Technical Report Ser.: No. 802). 53p. (ENG, FRE & SPA.). 1990. pap. text ed. 8.00 (*92-4-120802-3*, 1100802) World Health.

Role of Research in Educational Change. Ed. by Alfred Yates. LC 75-134226. (International Studies in Education: No. 20). 224p. 1971. 17.95 (*0-87015-187-8*) Pacific Bks.

*__Role of Retained Austenite in Carburized Steel Gears.__ R. A. Wilde. (Technical Papers). 1967. pap. text ed. 30.00 (*1-55589-352-X*) AGMA.

Role of RNA & DNA in Brain Function. Ed. by Antonia Giuditta et al. 1986. lib. bdg. 105.50 (*0-89838-814-7*) Kluwer Ac.

Role of Rules in the International Monetary System. Kenneth W. Dam. LC 76-47303. 1976. pap. 1.50 (*0-916770-03-6*) Law & Econ U Miami.

Role of Rural Credit Projects in Reaching the Poor: IFAD's Experience. International Fund for Agricultural Development Staff. 104p. 1986. pap. text ed. 50.00 (*1-85148-000-5*, Tycooly Pub) Weidner & Sons.

*__Role of Rural Finance for Food Security of the Poor in Cameroon.__ Gertrud Schrieder. LC 96-4310. (Development Economics & Policy Ser.: Bd. 6). 300p. 1996. pap. 63.95 (*0-8204-2986-4*, HG2051) P Lang Pubng.

Role of Rural Women in Development. Ed. by Vina Mazumdar. 373p. 1979. 11.95 (*0-318-37072-7*) Asia Bk Corp.

Role of Scent Glands in Pollination: On the Structure & Function of Osmophores. Stefan Vogel. Tr. by J. S. Bhatti from GER. (Illus.). 218p. (C). 1990. text ed. 85.00 (*90-6191-033-1*, Pub. by A A Balkema NE) Ashgate Pub Co.

Role of Science & Technology in Rural & Economic Development in India. Ed. by B. N. Pandey. 1983. text ed. 26.50 (*0-685-14096-2*) Coronet Bks.

Role of Science & Technology in Rural & Economic Development of India. B. N. Pandey. 220p. 1983. 27.95 (*0-318-37334-3*) Asia Bk Corp.

Role of Science in Civilization. Robert B. Lindsay. LC 73-3234. (Illus.). 318p. 1973. reprint ed. text ed. 35.00 (*0-8371-6837-6*, LIRS, Greenwood Pr) Greenwood.

*__Role of Science in the Third Millennium.__ 228p. 1996. lib. bdg. 56.00 (*981-02-2838-4*) World Scientific Pub.

Role of Science in the Uruguay Round & NAFTA Trade Disciplines. (Environment & Trade Ser.: No. 8). 68p. 1995. 10.00 (*92-1-127013-8*, E.95.III.D.64) UN.

Role of Science in Toxic Tort Litigation: Evaluating Causation & Risk. LC 89-46282. 176p. 1989. pap. 39.95 (*0-89707-502-1*, 519-0097) Amer Bar Assn.

Role of Scientific Societies in the Seventeenth Century. Martha Ornstein. LC 74-26282. (History, Philosophy & Sociology of Science Ser.). 1980. reprint ed. 25.95 (*0-405-06609-0*) Ayer.

Role of Scientists in the Professional Development of Science Teachers. National Research Council Staff. 238p. (C). 1996. text ed. 37.95 (*0-309-04999-7*) Natl Acad Pr.

Role of Script Supervision in Film & Television: A Career Guide. Shirley Ulmer & C. R. Sevilla. (Communication Arts Bks.). (Illus.). 288p. 1986. pap. 22.00 (*0-8038-6366-7*) Hastings.

Role of Seed Certification in the Seed Industry. Ed. by M. B. McDonald, Jr. & W. D. Pardee. 46p. 1985. 12.00 (*0-89118-521-6*) Crop Sci Soc Am.

Role of Self-Assessment. H. C. Howlett, 2nd. 4p. 1994. pap. 2.00 (*1-57614-010-5*) TECHSTAR.

Role of Serials in Sci-Tech Libraries. Ed. by Ellis Mount. LC 83-12682. (Science & Technology Libraries: Vol. 4, No. 1). 109p. 1983. text ed. 29.95 (*0-86656-260-5*) Haworth Pr.

Role of Serotonin in Psychiatric Disorders. Ed. by Serena-Lynn Brown & Herman M. Van Praag. LC 90-2285. (Einstein Clinical & Experimental Psychiatry Monograph Ser.: No. 4). (Illus.). 352p. 1991. text ed. 51.95 (*0-87630-589-3*) Brunner-Mazel.

*__Role of Service-Learning in Educational Reform.__ Robert Bhaerman et al. 115p. (Orig.). 1997. pap. text ed. write for info. (*0-937883-17-4*) NSEE.

Role of Sexual Abuse in the Etiology of Borderline Personality Disorder. Ed. by Mary C. Zanarini. LC 95-26270. (Progress in Psychiatry Ser.: No. 52). 259p. 1997. text ed. 40.00 (*0-88048-496-9*, 8496) Am Psychiatric.

Role of Shame in Symptom Formation. Ed. by Helen B. Lewis. 264p. 1987. text ed. 49.95 (*0-89859-600-9*) L Erlbaum Assocs.

Role of Social & Behavioral Sciences in Water Resources, Planning & Management: Conference Proceedings. Ed. by Duane D. Baumann & Yacov Y. Haimes. 424p. 1988. 38.00 (*0-87262-668-7*) Am Soc Civil Eng.

Role of Solar Ultraviolet Radiation in Marine Ecosystems. Ed. by John Calkins. LC 82-3792. (NATO Conference Series IV, Marine Sciences: Vol. 7). 740p. 1982. 135.00 (*0-306-40909-7*, Plenum Pr) Plenum.

Role of Somatostatin & Octreotide in Pancreatic Disease: Proceedings of a Symposium During the EPC Meeting, Ulm, October 1992. Ed. by M. W. Buechler et al. (Journal: Digestion: Vol. 55, Suppl. 1, 1994). (Illus.). vi, 52p. 1994. pap. 25.25 (*3-8055-5950-X*) S Karger.

Role of Spectroscopy in the Acceptance of the Internally Structured Atom. Clifford L. Maeir. Ed. by I. Bernard Cohen. LC 80-2093. (Development of Science Ser.). (Illus.). 1981. lib. bdg. 55.95 (*0-405-13858-X*) Ayer.

Role of Standards in Sci-Tech Libraries. Ed. by Ellis Mount. LC 90-4306. (Science & Technology Libraries: Vol. 10, No. 3). 127p. 1990. text ed. 29.95 (*1-56024-021-0*) Haworth Pr.

*__Role of State Department of Education in Complex School Reform.__ Susan F. Lusi. LC 97-9743. (Series on School Reform). 396p. (C). 1997. text ed. 54.00 (*0-8077-3629-5*); pap. text ed. 24.95 (*0-8077-3628-7*) Tchrs Coll.

Role of State Government in the Nineteenth-Century American Economy, 1820-1902: A Quatative Study. Charles F. Holt. Ed. by Stuart Bruchey. LC 76-39830. (Nineteen Seventy-Seven Dissertations Ser.). (Illus.). 1977. lib. bdg. 34.95 (*0-405-09910-X*) Ayer.

Role of State Library Agencies in the Evolving National Information Network: Proceedings of the Joint Meeting of the Library of Congress Network Advisory Committee & the Chief Officers of State Library Agencies, April 27-29, 1992. LC 92-39542. (Network Planning Papers: No. 23). 1992. pap. 18.00 (*0-8444-0770-4*) Lib Congress.

Role of State Supreme Courts in the New Judicial Federalism. Susan P. Fino. LC 86-19439. (Contributions in Legal Studies: No. 36). (Illus.). 166p. 1987. text ed. 45.00 (*0-313-25437-0*, FRS/, Greenwood Pr) Greenwood.

Role of Student Organizations in Vocational Education. Edward D. Miller. 10p. 1983. 2.25 (*0-318-22195-0*, OC94) Ctr Educ Trng Employ.

Role of Students in Freedom Movement: With Special Reference to Madras Presidency. V. Sankaran Nair. 248p. 1991. text ed. 30.00 (*81-220-0197-1*, Pub. by Konark Pubs Pvt Ltd II) Advent Bks Div.

Role of Subject Knowledge in the Early Years. Ed. by Carol Aubrey. LC 93-32628. 1994. write for info. (*0-7507-0194-3*, Falmer Pr); pap. write for info. (*0-7507-0195-1*, Falmer Pr) Taylor & Francis.

Role of Swine Symbolism in Medieval Culture: Blanc Sanglier. Milo Kearney. LC 91-26821. (Illus.). 385p. 1991. lib. bdg. 99.95 (*0-7734-9682-3*) E Mellen.

Role of Systems Methodology in Social Science Research. Roger Cavallo. (Frontiers in Systems Research Ser.: Vol. 1). 1979. lib. bdg. 61.00 (*0-89838-005-7*) Kluwer Ac.

Role of Tamoxifen in Breast Cancer. Ed. by Stefano Iacobelli et al. LC 82-5393. (Illus.). 136p. 1982. reprint ed. pap. 38.80 (*0-7837-9520-3*, 2060269) Bks Demand.

Role of Tax Reform in Central & Eastern European Economies. 458p. (Orig.). 1991. pap. 68.00 (*92-64-13575-8*) OECD.

Role of Technical Reports in Sci-Tech Libraries. Ed. by Ellis Mount. LC 81-7231. (Science & Technology Libraries: Vol. 1, No. 4). 82p. 1982. pap. 29.95 (*0-917724-74-7*) Haworth Pr.

*__Role of Technology Transfer Projects in the Innovation Process, EUR 17010.__ Ken Guy. 323p. 1996. pap. 60.00 (*92-827-8049-X*, CDNA-17010-ENC, Pub. by Europ Com UK) Bernan Associates.

Role of Telecommunications in Hate Crimes. 1996. lib. bdg. 261.95 (*0-8490-8368-0*) Gordon Pr.

Role of Tennessee in the War Between the States. Nell M. Lee. (Illus.). 72p. 1995. pap. 10.00 (*1-888366-01-X*) Dixie Pr.

Role of the Academic Reference Librarian. Jo B. Whitlatch. LC 90-2702. (New Directions in Information Management Ser.: No. 22). 128p. 1990. text ed. 39.95 (*0-313-26634-4*, WRL/, Greenwood Pr) Greenwood.

Role of the Accountant in Strategic Planning. Crispin Simon. 125p. 1992. 61.95 (*0-566-07364-1*, Pub. by Gower UK) Ashgate Pub Co.

Role of the Aged in Primitive Society. Leo W. Simmons. 1970. 79.50 (*0-614-01811-0*) Elliots Bks.

R

Role of the American Academic Library in International Programs, Vol. 27. Ed. by Bruce D. Bonta & James G. Neal. LC 92-4314. (Foundations in Library & Information Science: Vol. 27). 283p. 1992. 73.25 (*1-55938-383-6*) Jai Pr.

Role of the Americas in History. Leopoldo Zea. 256p. 1991. pap. text ed. 24.00 (*0-8476-7721-4*) Rowman.

Role of the Americas in History. Leopoldo Zea. 256p. (C). 1991. text ed. 58.50 (*0-8476-7720-6*) Rowman.

Role of the Animal Technician: Past, Present & Future. Ed. by Universities Federation for Animal Welfare Staff. 1984. 16.00 (*0-317-43891-3*) St Mut.

Role of the Assembly in Christian Initiation. Catherine Vincie. LC 92-42396. (Forum Essays Ser.). 122p. 1993. pap. 6.00 (*0-929650-70-0*, ASMBLY) Liturgy Tr Pubns.

Role of the Association President: The Role of the Association President, No. 23. rev. ed. Robert T. Dennistoun. (GAP Report Ser.: Vol. 23). 20p. (C). 1996. pap. 17.50 (*0-944715-24-9*) CAI.

Role of the Association Treasurer. Howard Goldklang. (GAP Report Ser.: Vol. 22). (C). 1996. pap. 17.50 (*0-944715-23-0*) CAI.

Role of the Attorney in Financial Planning. John F. Blake. LC 90-11209. 1990. 35.00 (*1-55871-201-1*, TMFP-01) BNA.

Role of the Bacterial Membrane in Chromosome Replication & Partition. Barbara E. Funnell. (Molecular Biology Intelligence Unit Ser.). 156p. 1996. 89.95 (*0-412-10501-2*) R G Landes.

Role of the Bank of England, 1945-1958. John Fforde. 765p. (C). 1992. text ed. 125.00 (*0-521-39139-3*) Cambridge U Pr.

Role of the Board Chairperson. Eugene C. Dorsey. (Nonprofit Governance Ser.: No. 11). 20p. (Orig.). (C). 1993. reprint ed. pap. text ed. 12.00 (*0-925299-17-0*) Natl Ctr Nonprofit.

Role of the Cell Surface in Development, 2 vols. Salem S. Rao. 1987. 229.95 (*0-8493-4687-8*, QH601) CRC Pr.

Role of the Cell Surface in Development, 2 vols., Vol. II. K. V. Rao. LC 86-13684. 144p. 1987. 87.00 (*0-8493-4689-4*, QH601, CRC Reprint) Franklin.

Role of the Cerebellum & Basal Ganglia in Voluntary Movement: Proceedings of the Seventh Tokyo Metropolitan Institute for Neuroscience (TMIN) International Symposium on the Role of the Cerebellum & Basal Ganglia in Voluntary Movement, Tokyo, 17-19 November 1992. Tokyo Metropolitan Institute for Neuroscience. Ed. by Noriichi Mano et al. LC 93-15800. (International Congress Ser.: No. 1024). 302p. 1993. Alk. paper. 187.25 (*0-444-89813-1*, Excerpta Medica) Elsevier.

Role of the Chimpanzee in Research. Ed. by G. Eder et al. (Illus.). xx, 204p. 1994. 198.50 (*3-8055-5850-3*) S Karger.

Role of the Chinese Army. John Gittings. (Royal Institute of International Affairs Ser.). 352p. 1967. 19.95 (*0-19-500160-5*) OUP.

Role of the Chinese Army. John Gittings. LC 80-28560. xix, 331p. 1981. reprint ed. text ed. 65.00 (*0-313-22879-5*, GIRC, Greenwood Pr) Greenwood.

***Role of the Chinese Military in National Security Policymaking.** Michael D. Swaine. LC 96-24777. (Illus.). 109p. (Orig.). 1996. pap. 15.00 (*0-8330-2419-1*, MR-782-OSD) Rand Corp.

Role of the Church in Aging: Implications for Policy & Action. Ed. by Michael C. Hendrickson. LC 85-17564. (Journal of Religion & Aging: Vol. 2, Nos. 1-2). 178p. 1986. text ed. 29.95 (*0-86656-482-9*) Haworth Pr.

Role of the Church in Aging, Vol. III: Programs & Services for Seniors. Michael C. Hendrickson. LC 85-17564. (Journal of Religion & Aging: Vol. 2, No. 4). 80p. (Orig.). 1987. text ed. 29.95 (*0-86656-677-5*) Haworth Pr.

Role of the Church in Aging, Vol. 2: Implications for Practice & Service. Ed. by Michael C. Hendrickson. LC 86-18415. (Journal of Religion & Aging: Vol. 2, No. 3). 105p. 1986. text ed. 29.95 (*0-86656-614-7*) Haworth Pr.

Role of the Civil Engineer in Highway Safety. Ed. by Martha E. Lipinski. 215p. 1983. pap. 25.00 (*0-87262-374-2*) Am Soc Civil Eng.

***Role of the Coincidence Site Lattice in Grain Boundary Engineering.** Valerie Randle. (Illus.). 128p. 1996. 70.00 (*1-86125-006-1*, Pub. by Inst Materials UK) Ashgate Pub Co.

Role of the Community Hospital in the Care of the Dying Patient & Bereaved. Ed. by E. Gerchick et al. 250p. 1976. 39.50 (*0-8422-7278-X*) Irvington.

Role of the Community Hospital in the Care of the Dying Patient, & the Bereaved. Elias Gerchick. 1979. 18.95 (*0-405-12506-2*) Ayer.

Role of the Computer in Economic & Social Research in Latin America. Ed. by Nancy D. Ruggles. (Other Conferences Ser.: No. 8). 409p. 1975. 106.90 (*0-87014-260-7*) Natl Bur Econ Res.

Role of the Cotton Textile Industry in the Economic Development of the American Southeast: 1900-1940. Mary J. Oates. LC 75-4023. (Dissertations in American Economic History Ser.). (Illus.). 1975. 24.95 (*0-405-07211-2*) Ayer.

Role of the Court Interpreter. O. N. Channan. (C). 1982. pap. 30.00 (*0-7219-0920-5*, Pub. by Scientific UK) St Mut.

Role of the Current Account in Asset Market Models of Exchange Rate Determination. Alexander Gross. (European University Institute, Series D (Economy): No. 2). xvi, 391p. 1987. lib. bdg. 126.95 (*3-11-011346-5*) De Gruyter.

Role of the Economist in Government: An International Perspective. Ed. by Joseph A. Pechman. 336p. (C). 1990. text ed. 40.00 (*0-8147-6611-0*) NYU Pr.

Role of the European Court of Justice in the Interpretation of Uniform Law among the Member States of the European Communities. Jurgen Schwarze. 53p. 1988. pap. 17.00 (*3-7890-1554-7*, Pub. by Nomos Verlags GW) Intl Bk Import.

***Role of the Expert Witness in a Court Trial: A Guide for the Expert Witness.** LC 96-85935. (Illus.). xii, 160p. (Orig.). 1996. spiral bd., pap. 19.50 (*0-614-19794-5*) Civil Evidence.

***Role of the Expert Witness in a Court Trial: A Guide for the Expert Witness.** Benjamin J. Cantor. (Illus.). 160p. (Orig.). 1996. spiral bd. 19.50 (*0-9653897-0-7*) Civil Evidence.

***Role of the Family in TBI Rehab.** 2nd rev. ed. Ed. by William H. Burke. (Professional Series on Traumatic Brain Injury: Vol. 19). 56p. 1996. pap. 9.50 (*1-882855-46-9*) HDI Pubs.

Role of the Family in the Development Process. 65p. 1987. 8.50 (*92-1-130113-0*, E.86.IV.7) UN.

Role of the Father in Child Development. 3rd ed. Michael E. Lamb. LC 96-4899. 350p. 1996. text ed. 49.95 (*0-471-11771-4*) Wiley.

Role of the First Language in Foreign Language Learning. Hakan Ringbom. 1987. 69.00 (*0-905028-81-3*); pap. 24.95 (*0-905028-80-5*) Taylor & Francis.

Role of the Forebrain in Sensation & Behavior: Proceedings of the Symposium, Moffett Field, CA, May 26-27, 1989. Ed. by G. Holstege. (Progress in Brain Research Ser.: No. 87). 430p. 1991. 277.25 (*0-444-81181-8*) Elsevier.

Role of the Fund-Financing & Its Interactions with Adjustments & Surveillance. Paul R. Masson & Michael Mussa. (Pamphlet Ser.: No. 50). 1996. pap. write for info. (*1-55775-551-5*) Intl Monetary.

***Role of the Health Sector in Food & Nutrition.** (Technical Report Ser.: No. 667). 92p. 1981. pap. text ed. 6.00 (*92-4-120667-5*) World Health.

Role of the Horse in Man's Culture. Harold Barclay. 398p. 1990. 58.00 (*0-85131-329-9*, Pub. by J A Allen & Co UK) St Mut.

Role of the Immigrant Woman in the U. S. Labor Force 1890-1910. Francesco Cordasco. Ed. by Joan Y. Dickinson. LC 80-852. (American Ethnic Groups Ser.). 1981. lib. bdg. 26.95 (*0-405-13415-0*) Ayer.

Role of the International Financial Centres in Underdeveloped Countries. Xabier Gorostiaga. Tr. by Annette Honeywell from SPA. LC 83-40177. 148p. 1984. text ed. 29.95 (*0-312-68945-4*) St Martin.

Role of the Jewish Underground in American Landing in Algiers: 1940-1942. Gitta Amipaz-Silber. 206p. 1992. 18.95 (*965-229-077-7*, Pub. by Gefen Pub Hse IS) Gefen Bks.

Role of the Job Counselor in the Military Enlistment Process. Beth J. Asch & Lynn A. Karoly. LC 93-36448. 1993. pap. 13.00 (*0-8330-1451-X*, MR-315-P&R) Rand Corp.

Role of the Judge in Contemporary Society (UNICRI) 80p. 1984. 6.00 (*88-7621-826-2*, 84.III.N.2) UN.

Role of the Judiciary in Plural Societies. Neelan Truchelvam & Oki Ombaaka. LC 87-4862. 250p. 1987. text ed. 39.95 (*0-312-00775-2*) St Martin.

Role of the Juvenile Court. Francis X. Hartmann. LC 86-29724. (From Children to Citizens Ser.: Vol. 2). 1987. 105.95 (*0-387-96434-7*) Spr-Verlag.

Role of the Laboratory in Hemolytic Disease of the Newborn. John G. Gorman. LC 73-102711. 241p. reprint ed. pap. 68.70 (*0-685-20932-6*, 2056512) Bks Demand.

***Role of the Laser in Dermatology: An Atlas.** Toshio Ohshiro. LC 96-30947. 1996. text ed. 199.95 (*0-471-96630-4*) Wiley.

Role of the Learning Resource Center in Instruction. Ed. by Margaret Holleman. LC 85-644753. (New Directions for Community Colleges Ser.: No. CC 71). 1990. 19.00 (*1-55542-803-7*) Jossey-Bass.

Role of the Liver in Maintaining Glucose Homeostasis. Alan D. Cherrington et al. (Medical Intelligence Unit Ser.). 118p. 1994. 94.00 (*1-57059-006-0*, LN9006) R G Landes.

Role of the Master in Human Evolution. Parthasarathi Rajagopalachari. 182p. 1994. 10.00 (*0-945242-29-8*) Shri Ram Chandra.

Role of the Media in Controlling Corruption. David Burham. (Criminal Justice Center Monogrpahs). 1978. pap. text ed. 3.00 (*0-318-37486-2*) John Jay Pr.

Role of the Messenger & the Message in the Ancient Near East. John T. Greene. LC 88-30292. (Brown Judaic Studies). 335p. 1989. 68.95 (*1-55540-324-7*, 14 01 69) Scholars Pr GA.

Role of the Military in Politics: A Case Study of Iraq to 1941. Mohammad A. Tarbush. 320p. 1985. pap. 22.50 (*0-7103-0124-3*) Routledge Chapman & Hall.

Role of the Military in Underdeveloped Countries: Papers of a Conference Sponsored by the Rand Corp. at Santa Monica, Calif. in August 1959. Ed. by John J. Johnson. LC 80-25808. viii, 423p. 1981. reprint ed. text ed. 75.00 (*0-313-22784-5*, JORM) Greenwood.

Role of the Minister in Caring for the Dying Patient & the Bereaved. Brian P. O'Connor et al. 18.95 (*0-405-12504-6*) Ayer.

Role of the Modern Corporation in a Free Society. John R. Danley. LC 93-2103. (Soundings: A Series in Ethics, Economics & Business). (C). 1994. text ed. 46.00 (*0-268-01647-X*) U of Notre Dame Pr.

Role of the Modern Quality Manager. Stephen J. Warwood. (C). 1994. 150.00 (*0-946655-73-1*, Pub. by Stanley Thornes UK) Trans-Atl Phila.

Role of the Museum & Art Gallery in Community Education. A. F. Chadwick. 160p. (C). 1980. text ed. 45.00 (*0-685-22163-6*, Pub. by Univ Nottingham UK) St Mut.

Role of the Museum & Art Gallery in Community Education. A. F. Chadwick. (C). 1980. 45.00 (*0-902031-44-9*, Pub. by Univ Nottingham UK) St Mut.

Role of the Mythic West in Some Representative Examples of Classic & Modern American Literature: The Shaping Force of the American Frontier. J. Bakker. LC 91-20378. (Studies in American Literature: Vol. 13). 284p. 1991. lib. bdg. 89.95 (*0-7734-9713-7*) E Mellen.

Role of the Nun in Nineteenth Century America. Mary Ewens. 1978. 40.95 (*0-405-10828-1*) Ayer.

Role of the Nurse in Clinical Medical Education. Norma A. Wylie. LC 87-63229. (Medical Humanities Ser.). (Illus.). 274p. 1988. 18.95 (*0-931369-21-5*) Southern IL Univ Sch.

Role of the Ocean in the 21st Century: Proceedings, the Law of the Sea Institute, Twenty-Seventh Annual Conference, Seoul, Korea, July 13-16, 1993. Korea Ocean Research & Development Institute Staff. Ed. by Seoung-Yong Hong et al. LC 95-23059. 1995. write for info. (*0-911189-30-0*) Law Sea Inst.

Role of the Oceans as a Waste Disposal Option. Ed. by G. Kullenberg. 1986. lib. bdg. 266.50 (*90-277-2209-9*) Kluwer Ac.

Role of the One Hundred & Fifty-Third Regiment, Pennsylvania Volunteers, Infantry, in the Civil War, 1862-1863. Edwin B. Coddington. (Illus.). 37p. (Orig.). 1949. pap. text ed. 4.00 (*1-877701-08-4*) NCH&GS.

Role of the Painting in the Works of Theodor Storm. David L. Dysart. LC 91-29512. (North American Studies in Nineteenth-Century German Literature: Vol. 11). 161p. (C). 1992. text ed. 35.95 (*0-8204-1690-8*) P Lang Pubng.

Role of the Paris Club in Managing Debt Problems. Alexis Rieffel. LC 85-23294. (Essays in International Finance Ser.: No. 161). 48p. 1985. pap. text ed. 8.00 (*0-88165-068-4*) Princeton U Int Finan Econ.

Role of the Physician Executive: Cases & Commentary. Ed. by David A. Kindig & Anthony R. Kovner. LC 92-49823. 268p. (Orig.). (C). 1992. pap. text ed. 31.00 (*0-910701-88-1*, 0922) Health Admin Pr.

Role of the Poet in Early Societies. Morton W. Bloomfield & Charles W. Dunn. (Illus.). 176p. (C). 1992. pap. 25.00 (*0-85991-347-3*) Boydell & Brewer.

Role of the Poet in Early Societies. Morton W. Bloomfield & Charles W. Dunn. (Illus.). 176p. (C). 1992. reprint ed. 71.00 (*0-85991-279-5*) Boydell & Brewer.

***Role of the Preceptor: A Guide for Nurse Educators & Clinicians.** Ed. by Jean P. Flynn. (Illus.). 152p. 1996. write for info. (*0-8261-9460-5*) Springer Pub.

Role of the Prime Minister in France, 1980-91. Robert Elgie. LC 93-1890. 1993. text ed. 65.00 (*0-312-10194-5*) St Martin.

Role of the Principal in Development. Joel M. Konzen. 65p. (Orig.). 1991. pap. 6.60 (*1-55833-063-1*) Natl Cath Educ.

Role of the Private Sector in Manpower Development. Charles A. Myers. LC 72-152912. (Policy Studies in Employment & Welfare: No. 13). 111p. reprint ed. pap. 31.70 (*0-317-19898-X*, 2023134) Bks Demand.

Role of the Prosecutor. J. E. Hall-Williams. 150p. 1988. text ed. 44.95 (*0-566-05723-9*, Pub. by Dartmth Pub UK) Ashgate Pub Co.

Role of the Reader: Explorations in the Semiotics of Texts (Advances in Semiotics Ser.) Umberto Eco. LC 78-18299. (Advances in Semiotics Ser.). (Illus.). 288p. 1979. 29.95 (*0-253-11139-0*) Ind U Pr.

Role of the Reader: Explorations in the Semiotics of Texts (Advances in Semiotics Ser.) Umberto Eco. LC 78-18299. (Advances in Semiotics Ser.). (Illus.). 288p. 1994. pap. 13.95 (*0-253-20318-X*, MB-318) Ind U Pr.

Role of the Reader in Rousseau's "Confessions" Catherine A. Beaudry. LC 91-18783. (Age of Revolution & Romanticism: Interdisciplinary Studies: Vol. 2). 174p. (C). 1992. text ed. 43.95 (*0-8204-1647-9*) P Lang Pubng.

Role of the Registry in Cancer Control. Ed. by D. M. Parkin et al. (IARC Scientific Publications: No. 66). (Illus.). 150p. 1986. 20.00 (*0-19-723066-0*) OUP.

Role of the Republic of China in the International Community. Ed. by Ray S. Cline. LC 91-65990. 98p. (Orig.). (C). 1991. pap. text ed. 10.50 (*0-943057-04-3*) US Global Strat.

Role of the Resident Engineer: Proceedings of a Specialty Conference Sponsored by the Committee on Contract Administration of the Construction Division. Ed. by Robert Del Re & Harold V. McKittrick. 197p. 1985. 17.00 (*0-87262-477-3*) Am Soc Civil Eng.

Role of the Scholarly Disciplines. Richard D. Lambert et al. 43p. pap. 10.95 (*0-915390-25-6*, Pub. by Change Mag) Transaction Pubs.

Role of the SDR in the International Monetary System. Studies by the Research & Treasurer's Depts. International Monetary Fund Staff. (Occasional Paper Ser.: No. 51). 62p. 1987. pap. 7.50 (*0-939934-81-7*) Intl Monetary.

Role of the Secretariat in Multilateral Negotiation: The Case of Maurice Strong & the 1972 UN Conference on the Human Environment. Christian Herter. LC 93-20115. (FPI Case Studies: No. 21). 1993. write for info. (*0-941700-84-4*) JH FPI SAIS.

Role of the State in Development Processes. Ed. by Claude Auroi. LC 92-26250. (EADI Book Ser.: Vol. 15). 1992. 37.50 (*0-7146-3493-X*, Pub. by F Cass Pubs UK) Intl Spec Bk.

Role of the State in Economic Change. Ed. by Ha-Joon Chang & Robert Rowthorn. (WIDER Studies in Development Economics). (Illus.). 320p. 1996. text ed. 74.00 (*0-19-828984-7*) OUP.

Role of the State in Property Taxation. Ed. by H. Clyde Reeves & Scott Ellsworth. LC 82-48536. (Lincoln Institute of Land Policy Book Ser.). 231p. reprint ed. pap. 65.90 (*0-7837-3272-4*, 2043291) Bks Demand.

Role of the State in Taiwan's Development. Ed. by Joel D. Aberbach et al. LC 93-33071. (Taiwan in the Modern World Ser.). 400p. (C). (gr. 13). 1994. text ed. 75.95 (*1-56324-325-3*, East Gate Bk); pap. text ed. 30.95 (*1-56324-326-1*, East Gate Bk) M E Sharpe.

Role of the State Legislatures in the Confederacy. May S. Ringold. LC 66-27607. 149p. reprint ed. pap. 42.50 (*0-318-34872-1*, 2031051) Bks Demand.

Role of the Stratosphere in Global Change. Ed. by Marie-Lise Chanin. LC 93-4662. (NATO ASI Series I: Global Environmental Change: Vol. 8). (Illus.). 560p. 1993. 307.95 (*0-387-56843-3*) Spr-Verlag.

Role of the Sun in Climate Change. Douglas V. Hoyt & Kenneth H. Shatten. (Illus.). 288p. 1997. 60.00 (*0-19-509413-1*); pap. 29.95 (*0-19-509414-X*) OUP.

Role of the Supreme Court in American Government. 1, 976th ed. Archibald S. Cox. LC 75-29958. 125p. 1977. pap. 8.95 (*0-19-519909-X*) OUP.

Role of the Supreme Court in American Government & Politics 1795-1835. Charles G. Haines. LC 73-604. (American Constitutional & Legal History Ser). 698p. 1973. reprint ed. lib. bdg. 79.50 (*0-306-70571-0*) Da Capo.

Role of the Supreme Court in American Government & Politics 1835-1864. Charles G. Haines. LC 73-604. (American Constitutional & Legal History Ser). 544p. 1973. reprint ed. lib. bdg. 59.50 (*0-306-70566-4*) Da Capo.

Role of the Supreme Court with Regard to the Right to Life & Personal Liberty. Nishtha Jaswal. (C). 1991. 62.50 (*81-7024-369-6*, Pub. by Ashish II) S Asia.

Role of the Symbol in French Romantic Poetry. Marion E. Carter. LC 77-94178. (Catholic University of America. Studies in Romance Languages & Literatures: No. 32). reprint ed. 37.50 (*0-404-50332-2*) AMS Pr.

Role of the Teacher in the Nursery School. Joan E. Cass. 97p. 1975. 43.00 (*0-08-018282-8*, Pub. by Pergamon Repr UK) Franklin.

Role of the Thymus in Health & Senescence, Vol. 1: Thymus & Immunity. Ed. by Nate F. Cardarelli. LC 88-39539. 368p. 1989. 172.00 (*0-8493-6909-6*, QP188, CRC Reprint) Franklin.

Role of the Thymus in Health & Senescence, Vol. 1: Thymus & Immunity, II. Ed. by Nate F. Cardarelli. LC 88-39539. 368p. 1989. 197.00 (*0-8493-6910-X*, QP188, CRC Reprint) Franklin.

Role of the Thymus in Tolerance Induction, 4, Vol. 3. Ed. by Marion D. Kendall. (Thymus Update Ser.: Vol. 3). 327p. 1990. text ed. 184.00 (*3-7186-5020-7*, Harwood Acad Pubs) Gordon & Breach.

Role of the Trial in the School Prose of the Weimar Republic. Roy L. Ackermann. (European University Studies: German Language & Literature: Ser. 1, Vol. 488). 138p. 1983. 23.70 (*3-261-04980-4*) P Lang Pubng.

Role of the Trypanosomiases in African Ecology: A Study of the Tsetse Fly Problem. John Ford. LC 76-23168. 582p. reprint ed. pap. 165.90 (*0-317-29955-7*, 2051719) Bks Demand.

Role of the U. N. in Cyprus from 1964-1979. George Kaloudis. LC 90-22167. (American University Studies: History: Ser. IX, Vols. 107). 161p. (C). 1991. text ed. 31.95 (*0-8204-1467-0*) P Lang Pubng.

Role of the United Nations in the Field of Verification. (Disarmament Studies: No. 20). 90p. 1992. 15.00 (*92-1-142174-8*) UN.

Role of the United States in Chinese Civil Conflicts, 1944-1949. Chonghal P. Shaw. LC 90-39500. xiv, 268p. 1992. pap. 16.95 (*1-884445-20-9*) C Schlacks Pub.

Role of the University in Extension Education. Ed. by Munir Bashshur. (Middle East Bks.). 176p. 1982. text ed. 24.95 (*0-8156-6062-6*) Syracuse U Pr.

Role of the University Teaching Hospital: An International Perspective: Report of a Conference. Ed. by Elizabeth F. Purcell. LC 82-83988. 266p. reprint ed. pap. 75.90 (*0-685-15485-8*, 2026696) Bks Demand.

Role of the Unrealizable: A Study in Regulative Ideals. Dorothy Emmet. LC 93-23258. 1994. text ed. 49.95 (*0-312-10660-2*) St Martin.

Role of the Volunteer Director in the Care of the Terminal Patient & the Family. Harriet H. Naylor. 1981. 19.95 (*0-405-13092-9*) Ayer.

Role of the Volunteer in the Care of the Terminal Patient & the Family. Harriet H. Naylor. 1981. 17.95 (*0-405-13091-0*) Ayer.

Role of the World Bank in Agricultural Development in the 1990s. large type ed. Robert L. Pearlberg & Michael Lipton. 56p. 1990. 10.00 (*0-89629-315-7*) Intl Food Policy.

Role of Theory in Language Description. Ed. by William A. Foley. LC 92-46639. (Trends in Linguistics, Studies & Monographs: No. 69). (Illus.). viii, 467p. (C). 1993. lib. bdg. 167.70 (*3-11-013516-7*) Mouton.

Role of Top Management in the Control of Inventory. George W. Plossl & W. Evert Welch. (Illus.). 1978. 35.00 (*0-8359-6697-6*, Reston) P-H.

Role of Topology in Classical & Quantum Physics. G. Morandi. Ed. by W. Beiglbock et al. (Lecture Notes in Physics, New Series, Monographs: Vol. M7). xiv, 239p. (C). 1992. 61.95 (*0-387-55088-7*) Spr-Verlag.

Role of Trade Literature in Sci-Tech Libraries. Ed. by Ellis Mount. LC 90-4806. (Science & Technology Libraries: Vol. 10, No. 4). 135p. 1990. text ed. 29.95 (*1-56024-038-5*) Haworth Pr.

Role of Traditional Folk Media in Rural India. N. Vijaya. (C). 1989. 21.00 (*81-212-0232-9*, Pub. by Gian Publng Hse II) S Asia.

Role of Traditional Medicine in Primary Health Care. Ed. by Ivan Wolffers. 75p. 1991. pap. 24.95 (*90-6256-936-6*, Pub. by VU Univ Pr NE) Paul & Co Pubs.

An Asterisk (*) at the beginning of an entry indicates that the title is appearing in BIP for the first time.

Role of Traditional Rulers in Elective Politics in Nigeria. William C. Reed. (Graduate Student Term Paper Ser.: No. 5). 1982. pap. text ed. 2.00 (*0-941934-41-1*) Indiana Africa.

Role of Translations in Sci-Tech Libraries. Ed. by Ellis Mount. LC 82-23353. (Science & Technology Libraries: Vol. 3, No. 2). 94p. 1983. 29.95 (*0-86656-217-6*) Haworth Pr.

Role of Transportation in the Industrial Revolution: A Comparison of England & France. Rick Szostak. 1991. 49.95 (*0-7735-0840-6*, Pub. by McGill CN) U of Toronto Pr.

Role of Trazodone in Antidepressant Therapy: Safety & Clinical Efficacy. Ed. by B. Silvestrini et al. (Journal: Psychopathology: Vol. 17, Supp. 2). (Illus.). iv, 104p. 1984. pap. 46.50 (*3-8055-3884-7*) S Karger.

Role of Trees in Sustainable Agriculture: Review Papers Presented at the Australian Conference, Albury, Victoria, Australia, October 1991. Ed. by Roslyn T. Prinsley. LC 92-36592. (Forestry Sciences Ser.: Vol. 43). 192p. (C). 1992. lib. bdg. 98.50 (*0-7923-2030-1*) Kluwer Ac.

Role of U. S. Agriculture on Foreign Policy. Ed. by Richard Fraenkel et al. LC 78-19761. 270p. 1979. text ed. 55.00 (*0-275-90353-2*, C0353, Praeger Pubs) Greenwood.

Role of U. S. in a Changing World. Mark Lindemann & William Rose. (Illus.). 192p. (Orig.). (C). 1992. per. 13.95 (*1-56134-110-X*) Dushkin Pub.

Role of Utility Companies in Solar Energy Executive Conference, November 1977. (Solar Energy Ser.). 176p. 1978. 25.00 (*0-910091-41-2*) Inst Gas Tech.

Role of Values in Psychology & Human Development. Ed. by William M. Kurtines et al. LC 91-18870. 304p. 1992. text ed. 70.00 (*0-471-53945-7*) Wiley.

Role of Vascular Endothelial Cells in Hemostasis & Thrombosis. Ed. by J. A. Van Mourik. (Journal: Haemostasis: Vol. 18, Vols. 4-6, 1988). (Illus.). vi, 198p. 1989. 98.50 (*3-8055-4979-2*) S Karger.

Role of Vocational Education in Rural America. Duane G. Jansen. 1988. 4.00 (*0-318-40006-5*, IN 328) Ctr Educ Trng Employ.

Role of Vocational Education in the Development of Students' Academic Skills. 1989. 5.25 (*0-317-03011-6*, IN340) Ctr Educ Trng Employ.

Role of Volcanism in Climate & Evolution. fac. ed. Daniel I. Axelrod. LC 81-80345. (Geological Society of America, Special Paper Ser.: No. 185). (Illus.). 62p. 1981. reprint ed. pap. 25.00 (*0-7837-7940-2*, 2047696) Bks Demand.

Role of Voluntary Organisations. Ed. by V. Chandra Mowli. 104p. 1990. text ed. 18.95 (*81-207-1142-4*, Pub. by Sterling Pubs II) Apt Bks.

Role of Waste Minimization. Domenic Forcella. Ed. by National Governors' Assoc. Staff. (Hazardous Waste Management in the States Ser.). 86p. (Orig.). 1989. pap. text ed. 15.00 (*1-55877-039-9*) Natl Governor.

Role of Water & the Hydrological Cycle in Global Change. Ed. by Howard R. Oliver & Sylvia A. Oliver. (NATO ASI Ser.: Ser. 1, Vol. 31). (Illus.). 480p. 1995. 244.95 (*3-540-59429-9*) Spr-Verlag.

Role of Woman in the Middle Ages. Ed. by Rosemarie T. Morewedge. LC 74-23227. (Illus.). 195p. 1975. text ed. 22.50 (*0-87395-274-X*) State U NY Pr.

Role of Women in Early Christianity. Jean LaPorte. LC 82-8281. (Studies in Women & Religion: Vol. 7). 196p. (C). 1982. lib. bdg. 79.95 (*0-88946-545-2*) E Mellen.

Role of Women in India's Freedom Struggle. V. Rajendra Raju. (C). 1994. text ed. 20.00 (*81-7141-238-6*, Pub. by Discovery Pub Hse II) S Asia.

Role of Women in Ministry Today. H. Wayne House. LC 95-401. 176p. (Orig.). (C). 1995. pap. 12.99 (*0-8010-2006-9*) Baker Bks.

Role of Women in Rebuilding the Russian Economy. Monica S. Fong. LC 93-31979. (Studies of Economics in Transformation Paper: No. 10). 60p. 1993. 6.95 (*0-8213-2626-0*, 12626) World Bank.

Role of Women in Rebuilding the Russian Economy. Monica S. Fong. (Studies of Economies in Transition: No. 10). 66p. (RUS.). 1994. 6.95 (*0-8213-3015-2*, 13015) World Bank.

Role of Women in Rural Development. S. P. Jain & Reddy Jain. 94p. 1979. 7.95 (*0-318-37078-6*) Asia Bk Corp.

Role of Women in the Development of Science & Technology in the Third World. Ed. by A. M. Faruqui et al. 992p. (C). 1991. text ed. 89.00 (*981-02-0100-1*) World Scientific Pub.

Role of Women in the Freedom Movement in Bengal (1919-1947), (Midnapore, Bankura & Purulia District) Niranjan Ghosh. (C). 1988. 23.50 (*0-8364-2428-X*, Pub. by Mukhopadhyaya II) S Asia.

Role of Women in the History of Orissa. Kumudini Barai. (C). 1994. 32.00 (*81-85094-78-0*, Pub. by Punthi Pus II) S Asia.

***Role of 5-Hydroxytryptamine-1 Receptors in the Regulation of Gastrointestinal Motility.** Bernard Coulie. (Acta Biomedica Lovaniensia Ser.: No. 129). (Illus.). 141p. (Orig.). 1996. pap. 42.50 (*90-6186-742-8*, Pub. by Leuven Univ BE) Coronet Bks.

Role Play. 1987. 12.95 (*0-19-437095-X*) OUP.

***Role Play.** Anne Melville. 224p. 1996. 24.00 (*0-7278-5142-X*) Severn Hse.

Role-Play: A Practical Guide. Ed. by Elizabeth Milroy. (Illus.). 150p. 1982. text ed. 22.00 (*0-08-025744-5*, R130, Pergamon Pr); pap. text ed. 17.90 (*0-08-025745-3*, R132, Pergamon Pr) Elsevier.

***Role Play: Theory & Practice.** Krysia M. Yardley-Matwiejczuk. 192p. 1997. 69.95 (*0-8039-8450-2*) Sage.

***Role Play: Theory & Practice.** Krysia M. Yardley-Matwiejczuk. 192p. 1997. pap. 23.95 (*0-8039-8451-0*) Sage.

***Role Play Action-Learning Manual.** (Literacy Linkage Series Manuals). 29p. (Orig.). 1996. pap. 4.00 (*0-932288-98-7*) Ctr Intl Ed U of MA.

Role Play in Language Learning. Carol Livingstone. Ed. by Donn Byrne. (Handbooks for Language Teachers Ser.). (Illus.). 94p. (Orig.). 1983. pap. 13.50 (*0-582-74611-6*) Longman.

Role-Play Practice: German. Willis & Bryant. (GER.). 1986. pap. text ed. 8.97 (*0-582-22443-8*, 78554) Longman.

Role-Play Practice French. Barbara Whelpton. 1985. pap. text ed. 8.97 (*0-582-22444-6*, 70935) Longman.

Role Played by the American Political Scientists in the Supreme Command for the Allied Powers: The Purge Program: Why & How Japan Invaded China & the United States, & Why & How Japan Was Defeated & Occupied. Joseph D. Lowe. LC 90-91738. (Illus.). xii, 201p. 1982. reprint ed. pap. 36.00 (*0-9605506-3-1*) Lowe Pub.

Role Played by the Ch'in Army: With Emphasis on Political & Legal Aspects. Joseph D. Lowe. LC 90-91739. (Illus.). iii, 24p. 1976. reprint ed. pap. 16.00 (*0-9605506-7-4*) Lowe Pub.

Role Playing. Wallace Wohlking & Patricia J. Gill. Ed. by Danny G. Langdon. LC 79-23435. (Instructional Design Library). 136p. 1980. 27.95 (*0-87778-152-4*) Educ Tech Pubns.

Role Playing: A Real Estate Training Tool. Alice McIntyre. Ed. by Dawn M. Gerth. LC 82-83133. (Illus.). 151p. (Orig.). 1982. pap. text ed. 16.00 (*0-913652-43-1*, BK 152) Realtors Natl.

Role Playing: The Principles of Selling. 2nd ed. David Sellars. 120p. (C). 1992. pap. text ed. 23.00 (*0-03-055382-2*) Dryden Pr.

Role Playing & Identity: The Limits of Theatre As Metaphor. Bruce Wilshire. LC 81-47779. (Studies in Phenomenology & Existential Philosophy). 320p. (Orig.). 1982. 31.50 (*0-253-35025-5*) Ind U Pr.

Role Playing & Identity: The Limits of Theatre As Metaphor. Bruce Wilshire. LC 81-47779. (Studies in Phenomenology & Existential Philosophy). 320p. (Orig.). 1991. pap. 9.95 (*0-253-20599-9*, MB-599) Ind U Pr.

Role Portrayal & Stereotyping on Television: An Annotated Bibliography of Studies Relating to Women, Minorities, Aging, Sexual Behavior, Health & Handicaps. Compiled by Nancy Signorielli. LC 85-9823. (Bibliographies & Indexes in Sociology Ser.: No. 5). xix, 214p. 1985. text ed. 59.95 (*0-313-24855-9*, SRP/) Greenwood.

***Role Quests in the Post-Cold War Era: Foreign Policies in Transition.** Ed. by Philippe G. Le Prestre. 336p. 1997. pap. 23.95 (*0-7735-1533-X*, Pub. by McGill CN) U of Toronto Pr.

***Role Quests in the Post-Cold War Era: Foreign Policies in Transition.** Ed. by Philippe G. Le Prestre. 336p. 1997. 55.00 (*0-7735-1532-1*, Pub. by McGill CN) U of Toronto Pr.

Role Relationships of Men & Women: New Testament Teaching. George C. Knight, III. 96p. 1989. pap. 7.99 (*0-87552-302-1*, Pub. by Evangelical Pr) Presby & Reformed.

Role-Set: Problems in Sociological Theory. Robert K. Merton. (Reprint Series in Sociology). (C). 1993. reprint ed. pap. text ed. 1.00 (*0-8290-3696-2*, S-193) Irvington.

Role-Sharing Marriage. Audrey D. Smith & William J. Reid. LC 85-9650. 216p. 1985. text ed. 37.50 (*0-231-06110-2*) Col U Pr.

Role Simulation Manual: A Technique for Resolving Human Conflict. George Borelli. 115p. (C). 1994. pap. text ed. 9.95 (*1-885792-00-X*) Gemini Pubng.

Role Theory: Expectations, Identities & Behaviors. Bruce J. Biddle. 1979. text ed. 66.00 (*0-12-095950-X*) Acad Pr.

Role Theory & Foreign Policy Analysis. Stephen J. Walker. LC 86-29162. xvi, 304p. 1987. text ed. 54.95 (*0-8223-0714-6*) Duke.

Role Theory & Illness. Gerald Gordon. pap. 19.95 (*0-8084-0270-6*) NCUP.

Role Transition to Patient Care Management. Marlent K. Strader et al. LC 94-39826. 1994. pap. text ed. 32.95 (*0-8385-6996-X*) Appleton & Lange.

Role Viruses & the Immune System in Diabetes Mellitus. Ed. by T. Dyrberg. (Current Topics in Microbiology & Immunology Ser.: Vol. 156). (Illus.). 160p. 1990. 95.00 (*0-387-51918-1*) Spr-Verlag.

Rolemaps. Diane Dormant. Ed. by Danny G. Langdon. LC 79-23398. (Instructional Design Library). 128p. 1980. 27.95 (*0-87778-153-2*) Educ Tech Pubns.

***Rolemaster.** 1989. 38.00 (*1-55806-091-X*) Iron Crown Ent Inc.

***Rolemaster Companion.** 1993. 14.00 (*1-55806-185-1*) Iron Crown Ent Inc.

Rolemaster Companion. Mark Colborn. Ed. by S. Coleman Charlton. 96p. (YA). (gr. 10-12). 1986. pap. 12.00 (*0-915795-12-4*, 1500) Iron Crown Ent Inc.

***Rolemaster Companion.** 5th ed. Iron Crown Enterprises Staff. 1991. 14.00 (*1-55806-145-2*) Iron Crown Ent Inc.

***Rolemaster Companion.** 6th ed. Iron Crown Enterprises Staff. 1992. 14.00 (*1-55806-164-9*) Iron Crown Ent Inc.

Rolemaster Companion, No. III. Darrin Anderson et al. Ed. by Coleman Charlton. (Rolemaster Ser.). (Illus.). 96p. (Orig.). (C). 1988. pap. 12.00 (*1-55806-050-2*, 1700) Iron Crown Ent Inc.

Rolemaster Companion, No. IV. Andrew Durston et al. Ed. by Coleman Charlton. (Rolemaster Ser.). (Illus.). 96p. (Orig.). (C). 1990. pap. 13.00 (*1-55806-127-4*, 1800) Iron Crown Ent Inc.

RoleMaster Companion II. Khanna et al. 112p. (Orig.). (YA). (gr. 10-12). 1987. pap. 12.00 (*0-915795-97-3*, 1600) Iron Crown Ent Inc.

Rolemaster Heros & Rogues. Troy Christiansen. Ed. by S. Coleman Charlton. (Rolemaster Ser.). (Illus.). 112p. (Orig.). (C). 1990. pap. 16.00 (*1-55806-141-X*, 1420) Iron Crown Ent Inc.

Roleplaying in Psychotherapy: A Manual. Raymond J. Corsini & Samuel Cardone. LC 65-22488. 219p. 1966. lib. bdg. 28.95 (*0-202-26007-0*) Aldine de Gruyter.

Roles & Relationships: School Boards & Superintendents. American Association of School Administrators Staff. 1994. 3.50 (*0-87652-208-8*, 021-00439) Am Assn Sch Admin.

Roles & Responsibilities in Geoscience Information: Proceedings of the Eighteenth Meeting of the Geoscience Information Society, October 31-November 3, 1983. Geoscience Information Society Staff. Ed. by Unni H. Rowell. (Geoscience Information Society Proceedings Ser.: Vol. 14). 249p. reprint ed. pap. 71.00 (*0-7837-5634-8*, 2045543) Bks Demand.

Roles & Responsibilities in the Primary School: Changing Demands, Changing Practices. Rosemary Webb & Graham Vulliamy. LC 95-34487. 160p. 1996. 79.00 (*0-335-19473-7*, Open Univ Pr); pap. 23.00 (*0-335-19472-9*, Open Univ Pr) Taylor & Francis.

Roles & Rituals for Hindu Women. Ed. by Julia Leslie. LC 91-18883. 256p. 1991. 42.50 (*0-8386-3475-3*) Fairleigh Dickinson.

Roles & Tasks of Community Mental Health Teams. Gerald Wistow & Stephen Brown. (Avebury Studies of Care in the Community). 144p. 1990. text ed. 55.95 (*1-85628-003-9*, Pub. by Avebury Pub UK) Ashgate Pub Co.

Roles for Sociologists in Service Organizations. James E. Trela & Richard O'Toole. LC 74-81674. 91p. reprint ed. pap. 26.00 (*0-685-16418-7*, 2027308) Bks Demand.

Roles in Interpretation. 2nd ed. Judy E. Yordon. 448p. (C). 1988. per. write for info. (*0-697-00498-8*) Brown & Benchmark.

***Roles in Interpretation.** 3rd ed. Yordon. 1993. teacher ed., pap. text ed. 11.88 (*0-697-12940-3*) McGraw.

Roles in Interpretation. 3rd ed. Judy E. Yordon. 496p. (C). 1993. per. write for info. (*0-697-12939-X*) Brown & Benchmark.

***Roles in Interpretation.** 4th ed. Yordon. 1998. pap. text ed. 27.00 (*0-697-32731-0*) McGraw.

Roles in Literacy Learning: A New Perspective. Ed. by Duane R. Tovey & James E. Kerber. LC 85-17691. (Illus.). 188p. reprint ed. pap. 53.60 (*0-7837-4734-9*, 2044542) Bks Demand.

Roles in Ministry. Cindy Bunch. (Created Male & Female Bible Studies). 64p. (Orig.). 1993. wbk. ed., pap. 4.99 (*0-8308-1134-6*, 1134) InterVarsity.

Roles, Mission & Operation of the U. S. General Accounting Office. naturally. 10.00 (*1-57744-004-8*) Nat Acad Public Admin.

Roles, Missions, & Functions of the Armed Forces: Opportunities for Eliminations, Reductions, Consolidations, & Realignments. (Illus.). 79p. (Orig.). (C). 1994. pap. text ed. 30.00 (*0-7881-0258-3*) DIANE Pub.

Roles of Amino Acid Chelates in Animal Nutrition. Ed. by H. DeWayne Ashmead. LC 92-25242. (Illus.). 479p. 1993. 64.00 (*0-8155-1312-7*) Noyes.

***Roles of Government, Industry & Consumers in Solid Waste Management.** (Solid Waste Papers: No. 1). 1996. pap. 5.00 (*1-55516-506-0*, 4652) Natl Conf State Legis.

Roles of Magistrates: Nine Case Studies. Federal Judicial Center Staff & Carroll Seron. (Illus.). xiii, 149p. 1985. write for info. (*0-318-60743-3*) Bates Info Serv.

Roles of Men & Women in Eskimo Culture. Naomi M. Giffen. LC 74-5837. reprint ed. 29.50 (*0-404-11642-6*) AMS Pr.

Roles of Occupational Therapists in Continuity of Care. Ed. by Florence S. Cromwell. LC 85-899. (Occupational Therapy in Health Care Ser.: Vol. 2, No. 1). 159p. 1985. text ed. 39.95 (*0-86656-392-X*); pap. text ed. 19.95 (*0-86656-393-8*) Haworth Pr.

Roles of Organic Matter in Sediment Diagenesis. Ed. by Donald L. Gautier. (Special Publications: No. 38). 203p. 1986. 42.00 (*0-918985-59-5*) SEPM.

***Roles of Organic Matter in Sediment Diagenesis: Based on a Symposium Sponsored by the Society of Economic Paleontologists & Mineralogists.** Ed. by Donald L. Gautier. LC 87-159377. (Society of Economic Paleontologists & Mineralogists Ser.: No. 38). (Illus.). 210p. pap. 59.90 (*0-608-05187-X*, 2065724) Bks Demand.

Roles of Physician Assistants & Nurse Practitioners in Primary Care. Ed. by Marian Osterweis & Stephen Garfinkel. (Orig.). 1993. pap. write for info. (*1-879694-07-7*) AAH Ctrs.

Roles of Reference Librarians: Today & Tomorrow. Kathleen Low. LC 96-12748. (Reference Librarian Ser.: No. 54). 173p. (C). 1996. 39.95 (*1-56024-798-3*) Haworth Pr.

Roles of Sense & Thought in Knowledge. Branab De Kumar. (C). 1992. 16.00 (*81-7074-117-3*, Pub. by KP Bagchi IA) S Asia.

Roles of Teachers & Learners. 1987. 14.95 (*0-19-437133-6*) OUP.

Roles of the Labor Leader. Duane Beeler & Harry Krushenbaum. 131p. (Orig.). 1969. pap. 3.95 (*0-317-12249-5*) Union Rep.

Roles of the Police in Urban Society: Conflicts & Consequences. Norman L. Weiner. LC 76-14958. 1976. pap. text ed. 4.95 (*0-672-61365-4*, Bobbs) Macmillan.

***Roles of the Public Library in Society: The Results of a National Survey (Final Report)** George D'Elia & Eleanor J. Rodger. pap. 29.50 (*0-614-29740-0*) Urban Libraries.

***Roles of the Public Library in Society: The Results of a National Survey (Technical Appendix)** George D'Elia & Eleanor J. Rodger. pap. 10.00 (*0-614-29741-9*) Urban Libraries.

Roles of the United States, Russia, & China in the New World. Ed. by Hafeez Malik. LC 96-2607. 350p. 1997. text ed. 59.95 (*0-312-12896-7*) St Martin.

***Roles of Third World Militaries.** Ed. by Harold Isaacs. (Journal of Third World Studies: Vol. V, No. 1). (Orig.). pap. 11.25 (*0-614-30659-0*) Assn Third Wld.

***Roles of Third World Militaries.** Ed. by Harold Isaacs. (Journal of Third World Studies: Vol. V, No. 1). 282p. 1988. pap. 7.00 (*0-931971-07-1*) Assn Third Wld.

Roles of Women in Muslim Countries. Ed. by Man S. Das. 205p. (C). 1991. 75.00 (*81-85880-00-X*, Pub. by Print Hse II) St Mut.

Rolex Wristwatches: The Best of Times. James M. Dowling & Jeffrey P. Hess. LC 96-9370. (Illus.). 320p. 1996. 125.00 (*0-7643-0011-3*) Schiffer.

Rolf & Edgar. Rosenbluth. (J). 1998. 11.95 (*0-671-75272-3*, S&S Bks Young Read) S&S Childrens.

Rolf & the Rainbow Christmas. Robert F. Wedell. LC 89-91971. (Illus.). 133p. (Orig.). (J). 1989. pap. 5.00 (*0-9625221-1-2*) Milrob Pr.

Rolf Armstrong: The Dream Girls. Ben Stevens. Ed. by Gail Manchur. (Vignettes Ser.). (Illus.). 64p. (Orig.). 1996. pap. 8.95 (*1-888054-03-4*) Collectors Pr.

Rolf Boldrewood. Ed. by Alan Brissenden. (UQP Australian Authors Ser.). 519p. 1979. pap. 16.95 (*0-7022-1277-6*) Intl Spec Bk.

Rolf in the Woods: The Adventures of a Boy Scout with Indian Quonab & Little Dog Skookum. Ernest T. Seton. (Illus.). 436p. (YA). 1994. pap. 24.95 (*1-885529-09-0*) Stevens Pub.

Rolf the Green Ghost. Robert F. Wedell. (Illus.). 69p. (Orig.). (J). (ps-8). 1988. pap. 4.95 (*0-685-30435-3*) Milrob Pr.

Rolfing. Ida P. Rolf. (Illus.). 304p. 1989. pap. 24.95 (*0-89281-335-0*, Heal Arts VT) Inner Tradit.

Rolfing: The Integration of Human Structures. Ida P. Rolf. LC 76-52192. (Illus.). 1977. 27.50 (*0-930422-10-4*) Dennis-Landman.

Rolfing & Physical Reality. Ida P. Rolf. 224p. 1990. pap. 12.95 (*0-89281-380-6*) Inner Tradit.

Roll Along: Poems on Wheels. Ed. by Myra C. Livingston. LC 92-32714. 80p. (J). (gr. 4 up). 1993. lib. bdg. 11.95 (*0-689-50585-X*, McElderry) S&S Childrens.

Roll & Web Defect Terminology. Ed. by R. Duane Smith. (Illus.). 256p. (Orig.). 1995. pap. 73.00 (*0-89852-279-X*, 0101R234) TAPPI.

Roll Around a Point: Aerobatics. Duane Cole. (Illus.). 101p. 1976. pap. 14.95 (*0-911721-28-2*) Aviation.

Roll Away Saloon: Cowboy Tales of the Arizona Strip. Rowland Rider & Deirdre Paulsen. (Western Experience Ser.). 114p. 1985. pap. 12.95 (*0-87421-124-7*) Utah St U Pr.

Roll Away the Stone: An Introduction to Aleister Crowleys Essays on the Psychology of Hashish. Israel Regardie. 249p. 1994. pap. 12.95 (*0-87877-194-8*) Newcastle Pub.

Roll Call. Carol Dixon. LC 95-33242. 270p. (Orig.). 1995. pap. text ed. 8.99 (*1-56722-138-6*) Word Aflame.

Roll Call. Ed. by Julian Whybra. (C). 1989. 100.00 (*1-873058-10-1*, Pub. by Roberts UK) St Mut.

Roll-Call. Arnold Bennett. LC 74-17047. (Collected Works of Arnold Bennett: Vol. 71). 1977. reprint ed. 26.95 (*0-518-19152-4*) Ayer.

Roll Call: Thud: A Photographic Record of the Republic F-105 Thunderchief. John M. Campbell & Michael Hill. (Illus.). 176p. 1996. 59.95 (*0-7643-0062-8*) Schiffer.

Roll Call at Oeyama. Frank Evans. 159p. (C). 1985. pap. 20.00 (*0-86383-129-X*, Pub. by Gomer Pr UK) St Mut.

Roll Call of Death. P. J. Kumar. 1971. 6.95 (*0-87141-033-8*) Manyland.

Roll Call of Mirrors: Selected Poems of Ivan V. Lalic. Ivan V. Lalic. Tr. by Charles Simic from SER. LC 87-21185. (Wesleyan Poetry in Translation Ser.). 80p. 1988. pap. 11.95 (*0-8195-1152-8*, Wesleyan Univ Pr); text ed. 25.00 (*0-8195-2151-5*, Wesleyan Univ Pr) U Pr of New Eng.

Roll Call of the Blessed Ones. Janos Starker. (Illus.). 132p. 1985. 11.95 (*0-911050-60-4*) Occidental.

***Roll Call of the Blessed Ones.** Janos Starker. 136p. 1997. 13.00 (*0-8059-4117-7*) Dorrance.

Roll Call of the Iroquois Chiefs: A Study of a Mnemonic Cane from the Six Nations Reserve. William N. Fenton. LC 76-43704. (Smithsonian Miscellaneous Collections: Vol. 3, No. 15). reprint ed. 37.50 (*0-404-15536-7*) AMS Pr.

Roll Call on the Little Big Horn. John M. Carroll. 1976. 34.95 (*0-8488-0233-0*, J M C & Co) Amereon Ltd.

Roll Call Voting Behavior in the South Dakota Legislature. Alan L. Clem. 1966. 1.00 (*1-55614-110-6*) U of SD Gov Res Bur.

Roll Defect Terminology: A Project of the Winding Committee of the Paper Finishing & Converting Division. Technical Association of the Pulp & Paper Industry Staff. Ed. by William Gilmore. (Illus.). 111p. reprint ed. pap. 31.70 (*0-7837-0496-8*, 2040820) Bks Demand.

Roll down Your Window: Stories of a Forgotten America. Juan Gonzalez. LC 95-20744. 240p. 1995. 25.00 (*0-86091-449-6*, Pub. by Vrso UK) Norton.

Roll 'Em! Action! How to Produce a Motion Picture on a Shoestring Budget. Harry M. Joyner, Jr. LC 92-56656. (Illus.). 191p. 1994. pap. 30.00 (*0-89950-860-X*) McFarland & Co.

Roll Forming: Collected Articles & Technical Papers. Ed. by Amy J. Nickel. (Illus.). 132p. (Orig.). (C). 1994. pap. 34.95 (*1-881113-07-8*) Croydon Grp.

***Roll Forming of Gears at Ford Motor Company.** L. N. De Vos. (Technical Papers). 1968. pap. text ed. 30.00 (*1-55589-443-7*) AGMA.

R

An Asterisk (*) at the beginning of an entry indicates that the title is appearing in BIP for the first time.

R

Roll, Jordan, Roll: The World the Slaves Made. Eugene D. Genovese. 1976. pap. 18.00 (*0-394-71652-3*, Vin) Random.

Roll Me in Your Arms, Vol. 1: "Unprintable" Ozark Folksongs & Folklore. Vance Randolph. Ed. by G. Legman. LC 91-17685. 582p. 1992. 60.00 (*1-55728-231-5*) U of Ark Pr.

Roll Me Over. Ed. by Harry Babad. (Illus.). 144p. 1972. pap. 14.95 (*0-8256-0067-7*, OK62455, Oak) Music Sales.

***Roll Me Over: An Infantryman's World War II.** 1997. mass mkt. 5.99 (*0-8041-1605-9*) Ivy Books.

Roll of Graduates of the University of Aberdeen, 1956-1970: With Supplement 1860-1955. Ed. by W. S. MacDonald. 1982. 70.00 (*0-08-028469-8*, Pergamon Pr) Elsevier.

Roll of Honour South Africa 1939-1945 European, Natives & Coloured. Roberts Staff. (C). 1993. 95.00 (*1-873058-86-1*, Pub. by Roberts UK) St Mut.

Roll of New Hampshire Soldiers at the Battle of Bennington, August 16, 1777. George C. Gilmore. 63p. 1995. reprint ed. pap. 14.00 (*0-614-10004-6*, 9127) Clearfield Co.

Roll of Plate Held by Hugh de Neville, 9 John, 1207-1208 see Memoranda Roll for the 10th Year of the Reign of King John, 1207-1208

Roll of the Dice: NRC's Efforts to Renew Nuclear Reactor Licenses. Critical Mass Energy Project Staff. (Illus.). 54p. (C). 1995. pap. text ed. 40.00 (*0-937188-89-1*) Pub Citizen Inc.

Roll of the Household Expenses of Richard De Swinfield Bishop of Hereford During Part of the Years 1289 & 1290, 2 Vols. Johannes De Kemeseye. Ed. by John Webb. (Camden Society, London. Publications, First Ser.: Nos. 59 & 62). reprint ed. 115.00 (*0-404-50207-5*) AMS Pr.

Roll of the Indian Medical Service, 1615-1930. Ed. by D. G. Crawford. (C). 1987. 336.00 (*0-317-90448-5*, Pub. by Picton UK) St Mut.

Roll of the Proceedings of the King's Council in Ireland for a Portion of the 16th Year of the Reign of Richard II, 1392-1393. Ed. by James Graves. (Rolls Ser.: No. 69). 1974. reprint ed. 70.00 (*0-8115-1137-5*) Periodicals Srv.

Roll of Thunder. Holt. 1989. student ed., pap. 10.00 (*0-03-023434-4*) HR&W Schl Div.

***Roll of Thunder Gift Set, 4 bks.** Mildred D. Taylor. (J). (gr. 5 up). 1996. boxed, pap. 13.99 (*0-14-095334-5*) Puffin Bks.

Roll of Thunder, Hear My Cry. Mildred D. Taylor. LC 76-2287. (Illus.). (J). (gr. 6 up). 1976. pap. 15.99 (*0-8037-7473-7*) Dial Bks Young.

Roll of Thunder, Hear My Cry. Mildred D. Taylor. 276p. (YA). (gr. 5-9). 1991. pap. 4.99 (*0-14-034893-X*) Puffin Bks.

***Roll of Thunder, Hear My Cry.** Mildred D. Taylor. (J). 1997. pap. 4.99 (*0-14-038451-0*) Viking Penguin.

Roll of Thunder, Hear My Cry: A Literature Unit. Michael H. Levin. (Literature Units Ser.). (Illus.). 48p. 1994. student ed. 7.95 (*1-55734-439-6*) Tchr Create Mat.

Roll of Thunder, Hear My Cry: L-I-T Guide. Charlotte Jaffe & Barbara Roberts. (L-I-T Guides: Literature in Teaching Ser.). 1991. Grades 4-8. teacher ed. 8.95 (*0-910857-95-4*) Educ Impress.

Roll of Thunder, Hear My Cry - Study Guide. Gloria Levine. Ed. by Joyce Friedland & Rikki Kessler. (Novel-Ties Ser.). (YA). (gr. 6-10). 1993. pap. text ed. 15.95 (*0-88122-126-0*) Lrn Links.

Roll on Columbia: The Columbia River Collection. Woody Guthrie. Ed. by Bill Murlin. (Illus.). 96p. (Orig.). 1991. pap. 9.95 (*0-9626704-3-X*) Sing Out.

***Roll on, Columbia Bk. 1: To the Pacific.** Bill Gulick. LC 97-7616. 504p. 1997. 27.50 (*0-87081-425-7*) Univ Pr Colo.

Roll on, Little Dogies: Songs & Activities for Young Cowpokes. Meghan Merker. 48p. (J). 1996. 12.95 incl. audio (*0-87905-726-2*) Gibbs Smith Pub.

Roll Over! Mordicai Gerstein. LC 83-18884. (Illus.). 32p. (J). (ps-1). 1988. 12.00 (*0-517-55209-4*) Crown Bks Yng Read.

Roll Over! A Counting Song. Merle Peek. (Illus.). 32p. (J). (ps-2). 1981. 15.00 (*0-395-29438-X*, Clarion Bks) HM.

Roll Over! A Counting Song. Merle Peek. (Illus.). 32p. (J). (ps). 1991. reprint ed. pap. 5.95 (*0-395-58105-2*, Clarion Bks) HM.

Roll Over! A Counting Song. Merle Peek. (Illus.). 32p. (J). (ps). 1991. reprint ed. pap. 8.95 incl. audio (*0-395-60117-7*, Clarion Bks) HM.

Roll over & Play Dead. Joan Hess. 1992. reprint ed. mass mkt. 4.50 (*0-345-37586-6*) Ballantine.

Roll over Beethoven: The Return of Cultural Strife. Stanley Aronowitz. LC 92-56898. 291p. (C). 1993. pap. 17.95 (*0-8195-6262-9*, Wesleyan Univ Pr) U Pr of New Eng.

Roll Over Che Guevara: Travels of a Radical Reporter. Mark Cooper. (Haymarket Ser.). 320p. (C). (gr. 13 up). 1996. pap. 19.00 (*1-85984-065-5*, Pub. by Vrso UK) Norton.

Roll-Over Credits: The System of Adaptable Interest Rates. Paul Einzig. LC 73-87565. 114p. (C). 1974. text ed. 29.95 (*0-312-68950-0*) St Martin.

Roll-Over Relief on Reinvestment. Simon Mckie. 140p. 1993. pap. text ed. 48.00 (*0-406-02800-1*, UK) MICHIE.

Roll Over, Rover. Richard Dommers. 128p. 1996. mass mkt. 5.99 (*0-7860-0317-0*, Pinncle Kensgtn) Kensgtn Pub Corp.

Roll Over Rover. Carolyn A. Wilkins. 20p. (J). (gr. 1-3). 1994. pap. 6.95 (*0-9644947-0-1*) C Aassa Wilkins.

Roll over Rover. Carolyn A. Wilkins. (Illus.). 20p. (Orig.). (J). (gr. 3-5). 1994. pap. 6.95 (*0-9644947-1-X*) C Aassa Wilkins.

***Roll-Ramp - A New Principle for Heavy Duty Linear Actuation.** J. M. Hamilton. (Technical Papers). 1965. pap. text ed. 30.00 (*1-55589-442-9*) AGMA.

Roll River. James Boyd. 1993. reprint ed. lib. bdg. 89.00 (*0-7812-5431-0*) Rprt Serv.

***Roll the Dice: A True Saga of Love, Money & Betrayal.** Darius Guppy. 1996. 27.50 (*1-85782-159-9*, Pub. by Blake Publng UK) Seven Hills Bk.

Roll the Union On: A Pictorial History of the Southern Tenant Farmers' Union. H. L. Mitchell. (Illus.). 96p. (Orig.). 1987. pap. 12.00 (*0-88286-159-X*) C H Kerr.

***Roll with Punches.** Kallen. LC 97-17190. 1997. 21.95 (*0-312-16991-4*) St Martin.

Rollback! Right-Wing Power in U. S. Foreign Policy. Thomas Bodenheimer & Robert Gould. LC 88-29479. 272p. (Orig.). (C). 1989. 30.00 (*0-89608-346-2*); pap. 12.00 (*0-89608-345-4*) South End Pr.

Rolle des Konigs und Seiner Familie nach den Texten von Ugarit. Jehad Aboud. (Forschungen zur Anthropologie und Religionsgeschichte Ser.: No. 27). xi, 217p. 1994. 27.50 (*3-927120-20-0*, Pub. by UGARIT GW) Eisenbrauns.

Rolled Buttercream Icing. Marsha Winbeckler. (Illus.). 24p. (Orig.). 1993. pap. 10.95 (*0-930113-15-2*) Winbeckler.

***Rollei TLR: The History.** Ian Parker. (Illus.). 192p. 1996. 19.95 (*1-874657-00-9*, Pub. by Jersey Photographic UK); 19.95 (*1-874657-01-7*, Pub. by Hove Photo UK) Watsn-Guptill.

***Rollei 6000 Series Users Manual: SLX Through to 6008.** Hove Foto Books Staff. 1997. pap. text ed. 29.95 (*1-874657-02-5*, Pub. by Hove Photo UK) Watsn-Guptill.

Roller: Cad. 1995. 49.00 (*3-540-58779-9*) Spr-Verlag.

Roller Birds of Rampur. Indi Rana. 320p. 1994. mass mkt. 3.99 (*0-449-70434-3*, Juniper) Fawcett.

Roller-Coaster. Michael Gilbert. 256p. 1994. 19.95 (*0-88184-996-0*) Carroll & Graf.

Roller Coaster. Michael Gilbert. 252p. 1995. mass mkt. 4.95 (*0-7867-0220-6*) Carroll & Graf.

Roller Coaster. Kevin O'Malley. LC 94-79123. (Illus.). 24p. (J). (ps up). 1995. 16.00 (*0-688-13971-X*); lib. bdg. 15.93 (*0-688-13972-8*) Lothrop.

Roller Coaster: A Story of Alcoholism & the Family. Don Fitzmahan. LC 88-63798. (Illus.). 36p. (Orig.). (J). (gr. 2-6). 1986. pap. 9.00 (*0-935529-11-X*) Comprehen Health Educ.

Roller Coaster for the Twins! Francine Pascal. (Sweet Valley Kids Ser.: No. 68). 96p. (J). 1996. pap. 3.50 (*0-553-48334-X*) Bantam.

Roller Coaster Kid Finds His Way Home. Dan Jones. 109p. 1992. pap. 9.95 (*0-9633927-1-9*) Mandala B & T.

***Roller Coaster Lover's Companion: A Thrill Seeker's Guide to the World's Best Coasters.** Steven J. Urbanowicz. LC 97-25234. 1997. pap. text ed. 16.95 (*0-8065-1924-X*, Citadel Pr) Carol Pub Group.

Roller Coaster Science: 50 Wet, Wacky, Wild, Dizzy Experiments about Things Kids Like Best. Jim Wiese. 113p. (J). 1994. pap. text ed. 12.95 (*0-471-59404-0*) Wiley.

Roller Coaster Year. Alan Ryan. (C). 1991. text ed. 25.62 (*0-06-045687-6*) Addson-Wesley Educ.

***Roller-Coaster Years: Raising Your Child Through the Maddening Yet Magical Middle School Years.** Charlene C. Giannetti & Margaret Sagarese. LC 96-53468. 336p. 1997. pap. 15.00 (*0-553-06684-6*) Broadway BDD.

Roller Coasters. Gil Chandler. (Cruisin' Ser.). 48p. (J). (gr. 3-4). 1994. lib. bdg. 17.80 (*1-56065-221-7*) Capstone Pr.

***Roller Coasters.** Gil Chandler. (Cruisin' Ser.). (Illus.). 48p. (J). (gr. 3-6). 1995. 18.40 (*0-516-35221-0*) Childrens.

Roller Coasters: An Illustrated Guide to the Rides in the United States & Canada, with a History. Todd H. Throgmorton. LC 92-50939. (Illus.). 159p. 1993. lib. bdg. 29.95 (*0-89950-805-7*) McFarland & Co.

Roller Coasters of America. Todd H. Throgmorton. (Illus.). 160p. 1994. pap. 17.95 (*0-87938-929-X*) Motorbooks Intl.

Roller-Compacted Concrete. LC 94-259. (Technical Engineering & Design Guides as Adapted from the U. S. Army Corps of Engineers Ser.: No. 5). 1994. write for info. (*0-87262-999-6*) Am Soc Civil Eng.

Roller Compacted Concrete: Proceedings of a Symposium Sponsored by the Colorado Section & the Construction Division. Ed. by Kenneth D. Hansen. 142p. 1985. 18.00 (*0-87262-455-2*) Am Soc Civil Eng.

Roller-Compacted Concrete Dams. Kenneth D. Hansen & William G. Reinhardt. (Illus.). 352p. 1991. text ed. 55.00 (*0-07-026072-9*) McGraw.

Roller Compacted Concrete Pavement. 55p. 1987. 22.75 (*0-318-35472-1*, C8BOW6) ACI.

Roller Compacted Concrete Three. Ed. by Kenneth D. Hansen & Francis G. McLean. LC 92-43347. 520p. 1992. pap. text ed. 39.00 (*0-87262-862-0*) Am Soc Civil Eng.

Roller Compacted Concrete Two. Ed. by Kenneth D. Hansen & Leslie K. Guice. (Conference Proceedings Ser.). 504p. 1988. 39.00 (*0-87262-632-6*) Am Soc Civil Eng.

Roller Hockey. Bill Gutman. (Action Sports Ser.). 48p. (J). (gr. 3-4). 1994. lib. bdg. 17.80 (*1-56065-250-0*) Capstone Pr.

***Roller Hockey.** Bill Gutman. (Action Sports Ser.). (Illus.). 48p. (J). (gr. 3-4). 1995. 18.40 (*0-516-35232-6*) Childrens.

Roller Hockey. Cam Millar. LC 95-39403. (Illus.). 96p. (J). 1996. 17.95 (*0-8069-4375-0*) Sterling.

***Roller Hockey.** Cam Millar. (Illus.). 96p. (J). 1997. pap. 12.95 (*0-8069-4376-9*) Sterling.

***Roller Hockey: Skills & Strategies for Winning on Wheels.** Greg Siller. LC 97-7369. (Illus.). 224p. (Orig.). 1997. pap. 17.95 (*1-57028-118-1*) Masters Pr IN.

Roller Hockey FANFOLD. Lorina R. Okamoto, pseud. (Illus.). 2p. 1995. 2.95 (*0-9628248-1-X*) L R Okamoto.

Roller Rink. Tom Baer. 24p. (Orig.). 1994. pap. 3.00 (*1-57141-001-5*) Runaway Spoon.

Roller Skates! Stephanie Calmenson. (Hello Reader! Ser.). 32p. (J). (gr. k-2). 1992. pap. 3.50 (*0-590-45716-0*, Cartwheel) Scholastic Inc.

Roller Skates. Ruth Sawyer. (J). (gr. 5-7). 1988. 18.75 (*0-8446-6343-3*) Peter Smith.

Roller Skates. Ruth Sawyer. (Newbery Library). (Illus.). 184p. (J). (gr. 5-9). 1986. pap. 4.99 (*0-14-030358-8*, Puffin) Puffin Bks.

Roller Skates. Ruth Sawyer. 1936. pap. 15.99 (*0-670-60310-4*) Viking Penguin.

***Roller Skating.** Eileen Kulper. (Action Sports Ser.). (Illus.). 48p. (J). (gr. 3-4). 1991. 18.40 (*0-516-35050-1*) Childrens.

Roller Skating for Gold. David H. Lewis. LC 96-21274. (American Sports History Ser.: No. 5). 232p. 1996. 42.50 (*0-8108-3048-5*) Scarecrow.

Roller Skating Guide. Straus. 1979. pap. 6.95 (*0-02-499410-3*, Macmillan Coll) P-H.

***Roller Test to Determine Pitting Fatigue Strength.** S. Way. (Technical Papers). 1937. pap. text ed. 30.00 (*1-55589-245-0*) AGMA.

***Rollercoaster Ride.** Karen Patterson. 64p. (Orig.). (YA). 1998. mass mkt. 6.99 (*1-889501-31-X*, Homage Pr) Sovereign.

Rollerderby: The Book. Lisa Carver. (Illus.). 220p. (Orig.). 1996. pap. 16.95 (*0-922915-38-5*) Feral Hse.

Rollerskating. Eileen Kulper. (Action Sports Ser.). 48p. (J). (gr. 3-4). 1991. lib. bdg. 17.80 (*1-56065-050-8*) Capstone Pr.

Rolli. Koji Takihara. LC 87-29262. (Illus.). (J). (ps-12). 1991. pap. 14.95 (*0-88708-058-8*, Picture Book Studio) S&S Childrens.

Rollick of Recorders or Other Instruments: Thirteen Popular Colonial Tunes Set for Trio. Herbert Watson. LC 75-12728. 16p. (Orig.). 1975. pap. 4.95 (*0-87935-029-6*) Colonial Williamsburg.

Rollicking Pacific: Selection of Poems. Edward D. Allen. (Shorey Historical Ser.). 118p. reprint ed. pap. 7.95 (*0-8466-0286-5*, S286) Shorey.

Rollicking Shore. E. R. Karr. 1960. 12.95 (*0-8392-1093-0*) Astor-Honor.

Rollie Burns: or An Account of the Ranching Industry on the South Plains. W. C. Holden. LC 85-20799. (Southwest Landmark Ser.: No. 4). 254p. 1985. reprint ed. 15.95 (*0-89096-261-8*) Tex A&M Univ Pr.

Rollin 80's: Drugs, Money, Politics & Reality. John Watts, Jr. (Illus.). 243p. 1995. 22.00 (*0-9644708-0-2*) Watts Pub.

Rolling - In-Line! Larry D. Brimner. LC 93-51255. (First Bks.). 64p. (J). (gr. 4-6). 1994. lib. bdg. 21.00 (*0-531-20171-6*) Watts.

Rolling - In-Line! Larry D. Brimner. LC 93-51255. (First Bks.). (Illus.). 64p. (J). (gr. 4-6). 1996. pap. 6.95 (*0-531-15739-3*) Watts.

***Rolling Along.** Sally Hewitt. LC 97-2154. (It's Science! Ser.). (J). 1997. write for info. (*0-516-20793-8*) Childrens.

Rolling Along. Annie Kubler. (Baby Carriage Ser.). (J). 1991. 6.99 (*0-85953-448-0*) Childs Play.

Rolling & Learning with Tri-Square Dice: Math Games. Thomas Silva. 96p. (J). (gr. k-8). 1992. pap. text ed. 14.95 (*0-9641895-5-0*) Creat Ent MA.

Rolling Around Puget Sound: Thirty-Six Places You Can Skate in Snohomish, King & Pierce Counties. David McCreary. 96p. 1994. pap. write for info. (*0-9642001-0-4*) McCreary Direct.

Rolling Back Government: A Budget Plan to Rebuild America. Ed. by Scott A. Hodge. 292p. 1995. pap. 20.00 (*0-89195-060-5*) Heritage Found.

Rolling Bearing Analysis. 3rd ed. Tedric A. Harris. LC 90-33828. 1013p. 1991. text ed. 175.00 (*0-471-51349-0*) Wiley.

Rolling Bearings for Industrial Robots, Vol. 3. T. Yoda et al. viii, 160p. 1990. text ed. 208.00 (*2-88124-744-X*) Gordon & Breach.

Rolling Bearings Handbook & Troubleshooting Guide. rev. ed. Raymond A. Guyer, Jr. LC 96-15798. Orig. Title: Bearing Failure Analysis System. 1996. 175.00 (*0-8019-8871-3*) Chilton.

Rolling Contact Fatigue Testing of Bearing Steels - STP 771. Ed. by Joseph J. Hoo. 422p. 1982. 43.95 (*0-8031-0712-9*, 04-771000-02) ASTM.

Rolling down the River. large type ed. Donna Alvermann et al. 1995. 9.50 (*0-614-09607-3*, L-34796-00) Am Printing Hse.

Rolling Green: A Century of Tulane Football. Marty Mule. (Illus.). 101p. 1993. 24.95 (*0-9639795-0-7*) Tulane U Athletic.

Rolling Harvey Down the Hill. Jack Prelutsky. LC 79-18236. (Illus.). 32p. (J). (gr. k-3). 1980. 16.00 (*0-688-80258-3*); lib. bdg. 15.93 (*0-688-84258-5*) Greenwillow.

Rolling Harvey Down the Hill. Jack Prelutsky. LC 92-24606. (Illus.). 40p. (J). (gr. 2 up). 1993. reprint ed. pap. 4.95 (*0-688-12270-1*, Mulberry) Morrow.

Rolling Road. Ernest A. Ewart. LC 73-110186. (Short Story Index Reprint Ser.). 1977. 20.95 (*0-8369-3337-0*) Ayer.

Rolling Rose. James Stevenson. LC 90-24169. 24p. (J). (ps up). 1992. lib. bdg. 15.93 (*0-688-10675-7*) Greenwillow.

Rolling Stock. Hubert Moore. 56p. (Orig.). 9100. pap. 14.95 (*1-870612-51-5*, Pub. by Enitha Pr UK) Dufour.

Rolling Stone. Horatio Alger, Jr. (Works of Horatio Alger Jr.). 1989. reprint ed. lib. bdg. 79.00 (*0-685-27556-6*) Rprt Serv.

Rolling Stone: Book of Love, Miniature Edition. Rolling Stone Editors. 128p. 1996. 4.95 (*1-56138-740-1*) Running Pr.

Rolling Stone: Book of Respect; Wisdom from Women in Rock, Miniature Edition. Rolling Stone Editors. 128p. 1996. 4.95 (*1-56138-741-X*) Running Pr.

Rolling Stone Album Guide: Completely New Reviews: Every Essential Album, Every Essential Artist. Ed. by Anthony DeCurtis et al. LC 92-50156. 1992. pap. 20.00 (*0-679-73729-4*) Random.

***Rolling Stone Book of Life: Miniature Edition.** Illus. by Philippe Lardy. 128p. 1997. 4.95 (*0-7624-0154-0*, Running Pr Mini Edtns) Running Pr.

***Rolling Stone Book of Rock Wisdom: Miniature Edition.** Illus. by Philippe Lardy. 128p. 1997. 4.95 (*0-7624-0153-2*, Running Pr Mini Edtns) Running Pr.

Rolling Stone Book of Women in Rock: Trouble Girls. 1997. pap. 25.00 (*0-679-76874-2*) Random.

Rolling Stone Environmental Reader. Ed. by Rolling Stone Editors. LC 92-5175. 268p. (Orig.). 1992. pap. 15.00 (*1-55963-166-X*) Island Pr.

Rolling Stone Environmental Reader. Ed. by Rolling Stones Magazine Staff. LC 92-5175. 268p. (Orig.). 1992. 25.00 (*1-55963-167-8*) Island Pr.

Rolling Stone Film Reader: Best Film Writing from Rolling Stone Magazine. Peter Travers. 1996. pap. 16.00 (*0-671-50111-9*) PB.

Rolling Stone Illustrated History of Rock & Roll: The Definitive History of the Most. Anthony Decurtis. 1992. pap. 25.95 (*0-679-73728-6*) Random.

Rolling Stone Illustrated History of Rock & Roll, 1950-1980. rev. ed. Rolling Stone Editors. (Illus.). 1980. pap. 25.00 (*0-394-51322-3*) Random.

Rolling Stone Illustrated History of Rock & Roll, 1950-1980. rev. ed. Rolling Stone Editors. Ed. by Jim Miller. (Illus.). 1980. pap. 19.95 (*0-394-73938-8*) Random.

***Rolling Stone Images of Rock & Roll.** Rolling Stone Magazine Editors. 1997. pap. text ed. 24.95 (*0-316-75679-2*) Little.

Rolling Stone Images of Rock & Roll. Rolling Stones Editors. 1995. 50.00 (*0-316-75468-4*) Little.

Rolling Stone Index: Twenty-Five Years of Popular Culture, 1967-1991. Compiled by Jeffrey N. Gatten. LC 92-81114. 850p. 1993. lib. bdg. 85.00 (*1-56075-030-8*) Popular Culture.

Rolling Stone Interviews 1967-1980. Rolling Stone Editors. 1989. pap. 15.95 (*0-312-03486-5*) St Martin.

Rolling Stone Jazz Record Guide. Ed. by John Swenson. LC 84-42510. 320p. 1985. pap. 12.00 (*0-394-72643-X*) Random.

Rolling Stone Journalism Awards. Rolling Stone Editors. 160p. 1992. pap. 7.95 (*0-8065-1314-4*, Citadel Pr) Carol Pub Group.

Rolling Stone: or The Adventures of Wanderer. Horatio Alger. 294p. 1974. reprint ed. lib. bdg. 23.95 (*0-88411-806-1*) Amereon Ltd.

Rolling Stone Rock Almanac. Rolling Stone Editors. 1987. pap. 19.95 (*0-02-604490-0*) Macmillan.

Rolling Stones. (Guitar Collection Ser.: Vol. 1). 24.95 (*0-7935-4006-2*, 00690005) H Leonard.

***Rolling Stones.** (Illus.). 80p. 1996. 8.99 (*0-517-16029-3*) Random Hse Value.

Rolling Stones. David Carter. (Illus.). 64p. 1994. write for info. (*1-57215-034-3*) World Pubns.

Rolling Stones. Robert A. Heinlein. 253p. 1985. mass mkt. 5.99 (*0-345-32451-X*, Del Rey) Ballantine.

Rolling Stones. Mark Paytress. (Complete Guides to the Music Of...Ser.). (Illus.). 168p. (Orig.). pap. 7.95 (*0-7119-4303-6*, OP 47737) Omnibus NY.

Rolling Stones. William Ruhlmann. (Illus.). 96p. 1993. 12.98 (*0-8317-7367-7*) Smithmark.

Rolling Stones. Chris Welch. (CD Bks.). (Illus.). 120p. (Orig.). 1995. pap. 7.99 (*1-886894-02-7*, MBS Paperbk) Mus Bk Servs.

Rolling Stones. William S. Porter. 1993. reprint ed. lib. bdg. 75.00 (*0-7812-5894-4*) Rprt Serv.

Rolling Stones, Vol. 2. 24.95 (*0-7935-3994-3*, 00694946) H Leonard.

Rolling Stones: A Visual Documentary. Miles. (Illus.). 160p. pap. 22.95 (*0-7119-3460-6*, OP 47318) Omnibus NY.

Rolling Stones: An Annotated Bibliography. Mary L. Dimmick. LC 78-53599. 173p. reprint ed. pap. 49.40 (*0-8357-4637-2*, 2037568) Bks Demand.

Rolling Stones: Atripped: A Trip Through the Voodoo Lounge Tour 1994-1995. Mark Hayward. (Illus.). 80p. pap. 19.95 (*1-873884-41-9*, VX 04000, Pub. by UFO Books UK) Music Sales.

Rolling Stones: Black & White Blues, 1963. Photos by Gus Coral. Date not set. pap. 14.95 (*0-614-17881-9*) Turner Pub.

Rolling Stones: Black & White Blues, 1963. David Hinckley. LC 94-37539. 1995. 19.95 (*1-57036-150-9*) Turner Pub GA.

***Rolling Stones: CD Interview Book.** (Interview CD Bks.). Date not set. 14.99 (*1-57899-006-8*) Mus Bk Servs.

Rolling Stones: In Their Own Words. rev. ed. David Dalton & Mick Farren. (In Their Own Words Ser.). (Illus.). 144p. (Orig.). pap. 15.95 (*0-86001-541-6*, OP 40401, Pub. by Bobcat Bks UK) Omnibus NY.

***Rolling Stones: It's Only Rock 'N' Roll.** Steve Appleford. 1997. pap. text ed. 20.00 (*0-02-864899-4*) Macmillan.

Rolling Stones: Tear-Out Photo Book. (Photo Bks.). (Illus.). 22p. (Orig.). 1996. pap. 11.95 (*1-870049-50-0*, OB 11012, Pub. by Oliver Bks UK) Music Sales.

Rolling Stones: The Last Tour. Peter Goddard. LC 82-4572. (Illus.). 128p. 1982. pap. 9.95 (*0-8253-0118-1*) Beaufort Bks NY.

Rolling Stones - Singles Collection: The London Years for Guitar. Ed. by Carol Cuellar. 336p. (Orig.). 1991. reprint ed. pap. text ed. 29.95 (*0-89898-739-3*, P08708GTX) Warner Brothers.

An Asterisk (*) at the beginning of an entry indicates that the title is appearing in BIP for the first time.

Rolling Stone's Alt-Rock-a-Rama: An Outrageous Compendium of Fact, Fiction, Trivia & Critiques on Alternative Rock. Rolling Stone Editors. LC 95-23266. 432p. 1996. pap. 14.95 (*0-385-31360-8*, Delta) Dell.

Rolling Stones Anthology. 144p. 1994. otabind 16.95 (*0-7935-3648-0*, 00308248) H Leonard.

***Rolling Stones Chronicle: The First Thirty-Five Years.** 2nd ed. Massimo Bonanno. 1997. pap. text ed. 19.95 (*0-85965-237-8*, Pub. by Plexus UK) Publishers Group.

Rolling Stones Collection: With Notes & Tablature. 128p. 1994. otabind 17.95 (*0-7935-3655-3*, 00702093) H Leonard.

Rolling Stones Greatest Hits, No. 332. 64p. 1991. pap. 7.95 (*0-7935-1185-2*, 00102204) H Leonard.

Rolling Stones in Europe. James Karnbach. (Illus.). 128p. 1983. pap. 9.95 (*0-8253-0152-1*) Beaufort Bks NY.

Rolling Stones Singles Collection: The London Years. 336p. (Orig.). (YA). 1990. boxed 35.00 (*0-89898-580-3*, P0870SMX) Warner Brothers.

Rolling Stones Singles Guitar. CPP Belwin Staff. 1993. pap. 29.95 (*0-89898-639-7*) Warner Brothers.

***Rolling Store.** Angela Johnson. LC 96-42151. (Illus.). 32p. (J). (ps-2). 1997. 15.95 (*0-531-30015-3*); lib. bdg. 16.99 (*0-531-33015-X*) Orchard Bks Watts.

***Rolling the R's.** R. Zamora Linmark. 150p. 1997. pap. 12.95 (*1-885030-03-7*) Dist Art Pubs.

Rolling the R's. R. Zamora Linmark. LC 94-75595. 168p. 1996. 21.00 (*1-885030-04-5*) Kaya Prod.

Rolling the R's. R. Zamora Linmark. LC 94-75595. 168p. 1996. 21.00 (*1-885030-02-9*) Kaya Prod.

Rolling Thunder. Mark Berent. 1989. mass mkt. 5.99 (*0-515-10190-7*) Jove Pubns.

Rolling Thunder. Doug Boyd. 288p. 1976. pap. 12.95 (*0-385-28859-X*, Delta) Dell.

Rolling Thunder. Cassie Edwards. 384p. 1996. mass mkt. 5.99 (*0-451-40665-6*) NAL-Dutton.

Rolling Thunder: A Portrait of North American Railroading. Gary J. Benson. 1991. 49.95 (*0-393-02907-7*) Norton.

Rolling Thunder: January, 1967-November, 1968. James B. Overton. 53p. 1993. reprint ed. pap. 10.00 (*0-923135-71-5*) Dalley Bk Service.

Rolling Thunder: July 1965-December 1966. Wesley R. Melyan & Lee Bonetti. 149p. 1993. reprint ed. pap. 18.50 (*0-923135-70-7*) Dalley Bk Service.

Rolling Thunder: March-June 1965. Sea Checo Team Staff. 83p. 1993. reprint ed. pap. 12.50 (*0-923135-69-3*) Dalley Bk Service.

Rolling Thunder: The Strategic Bombing Campaign, North Vietnam 1965-1968. John T. Smith. (Illus.). 360p. (C). 1995. pap. 29.95 (*1-871187-20-6*) Phalanx Pub.

Rolling Thunder: Turning Junk into Automobile Weaponry. Ryan K. Kephart. (Illus.). 72p. 1992. pap. 12.00 (*0-87364-667-3*) Paladin Pr.

Rolling Thunder: Understanding Policy & Program Failure. James C. Thompson. LC 79-11768. 215p. 1980. reprint ed. pap. 61.30 (*0-7837-9889-X*, 2060615) Bks Demand.

Rolling Thunder: 17 November, 1967. Robert L. Vining. 56p. 1993. reprint ed. pap. 9.50 (*0-923135-72-3*) Dalley Bk Service.

Rolling with Life's Punches: You Can Live Victoriously. Virginia V. Thompson. 88p. 1989. pap. 5.99 (*0-8341-1298-1*) Beacon Hill.

Rolling Years. Agnes Turnbull. 1993. reprint ed. lib. bdg. 89.00 (*0-7812-5845-6*) Rprt Serv.

Rollins College - Then & Now. Photos by Tommy Thompson. (First Edition Ser.). (Illus.). 112p. 1991. 39.95 (*0-916509-90-7*) Harmony Hse Pub.

Rollo & the Wishee. Betsy Brown. 16p. (J). (gr. 1-3). 1995. write for info. (*1-888479-00-0*) Tarpley Pubng.

Rollo & Tweedy & the Ghost at Dougal Castle. Laura J. Allen. LC 89-26921. (I Can Read Bk.). (Illus.). 64p. (J). (gr. k-3). 1992. lib. bdg. 14.89 (*0-06-020107-X*) HarpC Child Bks.

Rollo & Tweedy & the Ghost at Dougal Castle. Laura J. Allen. LC 89-26921. (I Can Read Bk.). (Illus.). 64p. (J). (gr. k-3). 1994. pap. 3.75 (*0-06-444182-2*, Trophy) HarpC Child Bks.

***Rollo & Tweedy & the Ghost at Dougal Castle.** Laura J. Allen. (J). (ps-3). 1996. pap. 7.95 incl. digital audio (*0-694-70053-3*) HarpC.

Rollo May. Abzug. 1996. write for info. (*0-201-40767-1*) Addison-Wesley.

Rollover, Mona Lisa! How Anyone Can Model for Artists. Theresa M. Danna. LC 91-77256. (Illus.). 64p. 1992. pap. 6.95 (*0-9631074-0-2*) T M Danna.

Rolls & Historical Sketch, Tenth S.C. Walker. 31.00 (*0-934085-02-1*, J M C & Co) Amereon Ltd.

Rolls & Lists of Connecticut Men in the Revolution 1775-1783. Connecticut Historical Society Staff. 389p. 1993. reprint ed. pap. 26.00 (*0-7884-0300-1*) Heritage Bk.

Rolls & Register of Bishop Oliver Sutton, 1280-1299, Vol. VIII. Rosalind M. Hill. (Lincoln Record Society Ser.: No. 76). 1986. 39.00 (*0-901503-40-1*) Boydell & Brewer.

Rolls for the Metalworking Industries. Ed. by Robert B. Corbett. LC 89-82593. 357p. 1990. reprint ed. pap. 101.00 (*0-608-00481-2*, 2061300) Bks Demand.

Rolls of Arms of Edward I (1272-1307) Ed. by Gerard J. Brault. LC 96-25817. (Aspilogia, Being Materials of Heraldry Ser.). (Illus.). 960p. 1997. 117.00 (*0-85115-669-X*) Boydell & Brewer.

Rolls of Arms of Edward I (1272-1307), Vol. I. Ed. by Gerard J. Brault. (Society of Antiquaries Ser.: Vol. III). 1997. text ed. 53.00 (*0-85115-677-0*, Boydell Pr) Boydell & Brewer.

Rolls of Arms of Edward I (1272-1307), Vol. II. Ed. by Gerard J. Brault. (Society of Antiquaries Ser.: Vol. III). 1997. text ed. 53.00 (*0-85115-676-2*, Boydell Pr) Boydell & Brewer.

Rolls-Royce. Jonathan Wood. 1989. pap. 25.00 (*0-85263-873-6*, Pub. by Shire UK) St Mut.

Rolls-Royce: Leader in Luxury. Craven. (Car Classics Ser.). (J). 1991. 12.50 (*0-86593-147-X*); lib. bdg. 16.67 (*0-685-59198-0*) Rourke Corp.

Rolls-Royce: The History of the Car. M. Bennett. (Illus.). 160p. 1996. 39.95 (*0-85429-972-6*, Pub. by G T Foulis Ltd) Haynes Pubns.

***Rolls-Royce & Bentley.** Malcolm Bobbett. (Illus.). 160p. 1997. pap. 15.95 (*0-7509-1575-7*, Pub. by A Sutton UK) Motorbooks Intl.

Rolls-Royce & Bentley: A History. Klaus Rossfeldt. (Illus.). 304p. 1991. 150.00 (*0-85429-920-3*) Haynes Pubns.

Rolls-Royce & Bentley: The Crewe Years. Martin Bennett. (Illus.). 384p. 1995. 100.00 (*0-85429-908-4*, Pub. by J H Haynes & Co UK) Motorbooks Intl.

Rolls-Royce & Bentley Collector's Guides 1945-1984: Coachbuilt Cars, Vol. 2. Graham Robson. (Illus.). 144p. 1984. 27.95 (*0-900549-87-4*) Motorbooks Intl.

Rolls-Royce & Bentley Collector's Guides 1965-1985, Vol. 3. Graham Robson. (Illus.). 144p. 1985. 27.95 (*0-900549-99-8*) Motorbooks Intl.

Rolls-Royce Catalogue 1910-11. Ed. by Charles Sykes. (Illus.). 1978. 40.00 (*0-685-31464-2*) Charles River Bks.

Rolls-Royce, Fact & Legend: An Abbreviated History. 3rd rev. ed. C. S. Shoup & T. E. Reich. LC 88-90630. (Illus.). 96p. 1989. pap. 10.00 (*0-9621925-0-3*) Rolls-Royce Owners Club.

Rolls-Royce Heritage. Richard Bird. (Osprey Colour Library). (Illus.). 128p. 1995. pap. 15.95 (*1-85532-410-5*, Pub. by Osprey Pubng Ltd UK) Motorbooks Intl.

Rolls-Royce Shadow & Bentley T-Series. Malcolm Bobbit. (Illus.). 160p. 1996. 41.95 (*1-874105-64-2*, Pub. by Veloce Pub UK) Motorbooks Intl.

Rollwagenbuechlein see Saemtliche Werke

Rolvaag, His Life & Art. Paul Reigstad. LC 70-175804. 182p. 1972. reprint ed. pap. 51.90 (*0-608-02041-9*, 2062694) Bks Demand.

Roly Goes Exploring. Philip Newth. LC 81-5899. (J). (ps-1). 1987. lib. bdg. 13.99 (*0-399-61217-3*, Philomel Bks) Putnam Pub Group.

Roly-Poly Pudding. Beatrix Potter. (J). 1996. 4.99 (*0-517-12325-8*) Random Hse Value.

Roly-Poly Puppies: A Counting Book. Jacqueline Rogers. LC 95-30067. (Story Corner Ser.). (Illus.). 32p. (J). (ps). 1996. 6.95 (*0-590-46665-8*, Cartwheel) Scholastic Inc.

Roly Poly Spider. Jill Sardegna. LC 93-40653. (Illus.). 32p. (J). 1994. 13.95 (*0-590-47119-8*) Scholastic Inc.

Rolypolyology. Michael E. Ross. LC 94-22327. (Backyard Buddies Ser.). (Illus.). 48p. (J). (gr. 1-4). 1995. lib. bdg. 14.96 (*0-87614-862-3*, Carolrhoda) Lerner Group.

ROM Dance: A Range of Motion & Relaxation Program. 2nd ed. Diane Harlowe & Patricia Beadles. (Illus.). 120p. 1992. 149.95 (*1-877950-06-8*) SMH Med Ctr.

ROM Dance: A Range of Motion & Relaxation Program. 2nd rev. ed. Diane Harlowe et al. (Illus.). 120p. 1992. pap. 24.95 (*1-877950-07-6*) SMH Med Ctr.

ROM Dance Instructional Kit. Diane Harlowe & Patricia Beadles. (Illus.). 113p. (Orig.). 1984. pap. 124.95 incl. audio, vhs (*0-685-28070-5*) SMH Med Ctr.

Roma: During Two Invasions. Sandra Brand. LC 92-85455. 237p. 1992. 18.95 (*0-88400-158-X*) Shengold.

Roma: The Gypsy World. S. S. Shashi. 1990. 40.00 (*81-85067-44-9*, Pub. by Sundeep II) S Asia.

Roma Arcaica. Compiled by Soprintendenza Archeologica di Roma. (Illus.). 32p. 1990. pap. 15.00 (*88-7140-025-9*) J P Getty Trust.

***Roma Clandestina de Francisco Delicado y Pietro Aretino.** Louis Imperiale. (Studies on Cervantes & His Times: Vol. 6). 288p. (SPA.). (C). 1997. text ed. 49.95 (*0-8204-3137-0*) P Lang Pubng.

Roma Nela Memoria e Nelle Immaginazioni del Medio Evo. Arturo Graf. xii, 811p. reprint ed. write for info. (*0-318-71586-4*) G Olms Pubs.

Roma Resurgens: Papal Medals from the Age of the Baroque. Nathan T. Whitman & John L. Varriano. (Illus.). 188p. 1983. pap. 15.00 (*0-912303-28-X*) Michigan Mus.

Roma Sacra: Essays on Christian Rome. William F. Barry. LC 68-14896. (Essay Index Reprint Ser.). 1977. 20.95 (*0-8369-0174-6*) Ayer.

Roma (1972) (Computer Poetry Ser.). 1,000.00 (*0-685-75205-4*) Parpaglion.

Romac Report: Restaurant Guide to Philadelphia. Lynne V. Rosen et al. 256p. (Orig.). 1994. pap. 9.95 (*0-9644383-0-5*) Romac Report.

***Romac Report: 1997 Philadelphia Restaurant Guide.** Andrew J. McElfresh. Ed. by Charles W. McElfresh. 224p. Date not set. pap. 9.95 (*0-9644383-8-0*) Romac Report.

Romac Report - New York, Fall - Winter 1995-96, New Restaurants. Joan M. Lang & Katherine Colton. Ed. by Charles W. McElfresh. (Illus.). 96p. 1995. pap. 5.95 (*0-9644383-1-3*) Romac Report.

Romac Report - Philadelphia Restaurants, 1996. J. Lang et al. Ed. by Charles W. McElfresh. 252p. 1995. pap. 9.95 (*0-9644383-2-1*) Romac Report.

Romac Report NYC Spring 1996 New Restaurants. Andrew J. McElfresh. Ed. by Charles W. McElfresh. (Illus.). 128p. Date not set. pap. 5.95 (*0-9644383-5-6*) Romac Report.

Romac Report 1997 NYC Restaurants. Andrew J. Mcelfresh et al. (Illus.). Date not set. pap. 10.95 (*0-9644383-7-2*) Romac Report.

Romagnol: Language & Literature. D. B. Gregor. (Language & Literature Ser.). (Illus.). 1976. pap. 35.00 (*0-902675-12-5*) Oleander Pr.

Romagnolis' Italian Fish Cookbook. Margaret Romagnoli. 1995. pap. 15.95 (*0-8050-2538-3*) H Holt & Co.

Romain: Dictionary of Legal & Commercial Terms, 2 vols. (ENG & GER.). 1984. 260.00 (*0-406-03810-4*) MICHIE.

Romain Gary. David B. Parsell. 1996. 24.95 (*0-8057-4532-7*, Twayne) Scribnrs Ref.

Romain Rolland. Stefan Zweig. LC 70-130266. (Studies in French Literature: No. 45). 1970. reprint ed. lib. bdg. 75.00 (*0-8383-1173-3*) M S G Haskell Hse.

Romain Rolland: One Against All, a Biography. Starr. (Studies in French Literature). 39.50 (*0-685-37079-8*) Fr & Eur.

Romain Rolland: The Man & His Works. Stefan Zweig. LC 74-174836. (Illus.). 1977. reprint ed. lib. bdg. 26.95 (*0-405-09113-3*) Ayer.

Romain Rolland & a World at War. William T. Starr. LC 72-128947. (Northwestern University. Humanities Ser.: No. 31). reprint ed. 32.50 (*0-404-50731-X*) AMS Pr.

Romain Rolland & the Politics of Intellectual Engagement. David J. Fisher. (Illus.). 416p. 1988. 48.00 (*0-520-05787-2*) U CA Pr.

Romain Rolland et le Mouvement Florentin de la Voce. Romain Rolland. (Illus.). 400p. (FRE.). 1966. pap. 14.95 (*0-7859-5464-3*) Fr & Eur.

Romaine Brooks, "Thief of Souls" Romaine Brooks & Adelyn D. Breeskin. LC 79-150515. (Illus.). 144p. reprint ed. pap. 41.10 (*0-317-10220-6*, 2051197) Bks Demand.

Romaji Diary & Sad Toys. Takuboku Ishikawa. Tr. by Sanford Goldstein & Seishi Shinoda from JPN. LC 84-52395. 288p. 1985. pap. 12.95 (*0-8048-1494-5*) C E Tuttle.

Romalos Kai Philhellen: Romanus et Graecorum Studiosus: A Celebration of Aldus Manutius 500 Years after His First Dated Publication. Ed. by David R. Jordan. ix, 140p. 1995. text ed. 25.00 (*0-89241-567-3*) Caratzas.

Romalpa Clauses: Reservation of Title in Sale of Goods Transactions. Berna Collier. xxxiv, 192p. 1989. 44.50 (*0-455-20833-6*, Pub. by Law Bk Co AT) Gaunt.

Roman. Francois Mauriac. pap. 9.50 (*0-685-34302-2*) Fr & Eur.

Roman. Mika Waltari. 1994. lib. bdg. 29.95 (*1-56849-486-6*) Buccaneer Bks.

Roman. Francois Mauriac. LC 75-41191. (FRE.). reprint ed. 27.50 (*0-404-14766-6*) AMS Pr.

Roman Africa. Alexander Graham. LC 70-157369. (Black Heritage Library Collection). 1977. 38.95 (*0-8369-8807-8*) Ayer.

Roman Afternoon: Two Thousand & Nineteen A.D., 3 vols., Vol. 1. Clarence W. Durant. 116p. (Orig.). 1984. pap. 4.80 (*0-915153-03-3*) Gold Star Pr.

Roman Algerien De Langue Francaise: Vers un Espace De Communication Litteraire Decolonise? Charles Bonn. LC 85-172737. 359p. (FRE.). reprint ed. pap. 102.40 (*0-7837-6943-1*, 2046772) Bks Demand.

Roman Alphabet. Arthur Baker. LC 76-44477. (Illus.). 1977. 15.00 (*0-910158-23-1*) Art Dir.

Roman & British Martyrology. Catholic Church Staff. 1980. lib. bdg. 79.95 (*0-8490-3128-1*) Gordon Pr.

Roman & Byzantine Near East: Some Recent Archaeological Research. Ed. by J. H. Humphrey. (JRA Supplementary Ser.: No. 14). (Illus.). 346p. (ENG & FRE.). 1995. 89.50 (*1-887829-14-8*) Jour Roman Arch.

Roman & Byzantine Papers. Barry Baldwin. (London Studies in Classical Philology: Vol. 21). 691p. 1989. 147.00 (*90-5063-017-0*, Pub. by Gieben NE) Benjamins North Am.

Roman & Civil Law & the Development of Anglo-American Jurisprudence in the Nineteenth Century. M. H. Hoeflich. LC 96-5522. 1997. 40.00 (*0-8203-1839-6*) U of Ga Pr.

Roman & European Mythologies. Tr. by Gerald Honigsblum & Wendy Doniger. LC 92-15402. (Illus.). 344p. (ENG & FRE.). 1992. pap. 26.95 (*0-226-06455-7*) U Ch Pr.

Roman & German Humanism 1450-1550. John F. D'Amico. Ed. by Paul F. Grendler. (Collected Studies: No. 413). 368p. 1993. 95.00 (*0-86078-388-X*, Pub. by Variorum UK) Ashgate Pub Co.

Roman & Islamic Water-Lifting Wheels. Thorkild Schioler. (Acta Historica Scientiarum Ser.: No. 28). 201p. (Orig.). 1973. pap. 29.00 (*87-7492-090-1*, Pub. by Odense Universitets Forlag DK) Coronet Bks.

Roman & Moslem Moneys. Alexander Del Mar. 1972. 59.95 (*0-8490-0968-5*) Gordon Pr.

Roman & Neopolitan Schools. Michael Jaffe. (Devonshire Collection of Italian Drawings). (Illus.). 304p. (C). 1994. 125.00 (*0-7148-2934-X*, Pub. by Phaidon Press UK) Chronicle Bks.

Roman & Pre-Roman Glass in the Royal Ontario Museum: A Catalogue. John W. Hayes. 1994. 50.00 (*0-88854-027-2*, Pub. by Royal Ont Mus CN) U of Toronto Pr.

Roman Antiquities, 1. Dionysius of Halicarnassus. (Loeb Classical Library: No. 319, 347, 357, 364, 372, 378, 388). 602p. 1937. 18.95 (*0-674-99352-7*) HUP.

Roman Antiquities, 2. Dionysius of Halicarnassus. (Loeb Classical Library: No. 319, 347, 357, 364, 372, 378, 388). 538p. 1939. 18.95 (*0-674-99382-9*) HUP.

Roman Antiquities, 3. Dionysius of Halicarnassus. (Loeb Classical Library: No. 319, 347, 357, 364, 372, 378, 388). 394p. 1940. 18.95 (*0-674-99394-2*) HUP.

Roman Antiquities, 4. Dionysius of Halicarnassus. (Loeb Classical Library: No. 319, 347, 357, 364, 372, 378, 388). 392p. 1943. 18.95 (*0-674-99401-9*) HUP.

Roman Antiquities, 5. Dionysius of Halicarnassus. (Loeb Classical Library: No. 319, 347, 357, 364, 372, 378, 388). 384p. 1945. 18.95 (*0-674-99410-8*) HUP.

Roman Antiquities, 6. Dionysius of Halicarnassus. (Loeb Classical Library: No. 319, 347, 357, 364, 372, 378, 388). 378p. 1947. 18.95 (*0-674-99416-7*) HUP.

Roman Antiquities, 7. Dionysius of Halicarnassus. (Loeb Classical Library: No. 319, 347, 357, 364, 372, 378, 388). 482p. 1950. 18.95 (*0-674-99427-2*) HUP.

Roman Antiquities, Vols. 1-7. Dionysius of Halicarnassus. No. 319, 347, 357, 364, 372, 378, 388. write for info. (*0-318-53176-3*) HUP.

Roman Arabia. G. W. Bowersock. (Illus.). 256p. 1994. pap. 15.95 (*0-674-77756-5*, BOWROX) HUP.

Roman Arabia. Glen W. Bowersock. (Illus.). 256p. (C). 1983. 29.00 (*0-674-77755-7*) HUP.

Roman Architecture. Frank E. Brown. LC 61-13688. (Great Ages of World Architecture Ser.). (Illus.). 128p. 1961. pap. 10.95 (*0-8076-0331-7*) Braziller.

Roman Architecture. Frank Sear. LC 82-48715. (Illus.). 300p. 1983. 49.95 (*0-8014-1591-8*); pap. 19.95 (*0-8014-9245-9*) Cornell U Pr.

Roman Architecture. M. Thorpe. (Classical World Ser.). pap. 14.95 (*1-85399-421-9*, Pub. by Brstl Class Pr UK) Focus Pub-R Pullins.

***Roman Architecture & Society.** James C. Anderson, Jr. LC 96-48175. (Ancient Society & History Ser.). (Illus.). 474p. 1997. text ed. 39.95 (*0-8018-5546-2*) Johns Hopkins.

***Roman Architecture in the Greek World.** Ed. by F. H. Thompson & Sarah Macready. (Illus.). 124p. 1988. pap. 27.00 (*0-85431-245-5*, Pub. by Soc Antiquaries UK) David Brown.

Roman Aristocrats in Barbarian Gaul: Strategies for Survival in an Age of Transition. Ralph W. Mathisen. LC 92-22725. (Illus.). 293p. 1993. text ed. 35.00 (*0-292-77051-0*) U of Tex Pr.

Roman Army. Peter Hodge. (Aspects of Roman Life Ser.). (Illus.). 48p. (Orig.). (gr. 7-12). 1977. pap. text ed. 9.00 (*0-582-31414-3*, 71974) Longman.

Roman Army. J. Wilkes. (Cambridge Introduction to World History Topic Bks.). (Illus.). 48p. (YA). (gr. 7 up). 1973. pap. text ed. 10.95 (*0-521-07243-3*) Cambridge U Pr.

Roman Army: Caesar to Trajan. Michael Simkins. (Men-at-Arms Ser.: No. 46). (Illus.). 48p. pap. 11.95 (*0-85045-528-6*, 9005, Pub. by Osprey UK) Stackpole.

Roman Army: Hadrian to Constantine. Michael Simkins. (Men-at-Arms Ser.: No. 93). (Illus.). 48p. pap. 11.95 (*0-85045-333-X*, 9029, Pub. by Osprey UK) Stackpole.

Roman Army: Papers, Nineteen Twenty-Nine to Nineteen Eighty-Six. Eric Birley. (Mavors Roman Army Researches Ser.: Vol. IV). 460p. (C). 1988. 134.00 (*90-5063-002-2*, Pub. by Gieben NE) Benjamins North Am.

***Roman Army: Wars of the Empire.** Graham Sumner. Ed. by Tim Newark. LC 97-24405. (History of Uniforms Ser.). (Illus.). 144p. 1997. 31.95 (*1-85753-212-0*, Pub. by Brasseys UK) Brasseys Inc.

Roman Army at War 100 BC - AD 200: 100 BC-AD 200. Adrian Goldsworthy. LC 96-7430. (Oxford Classical Monographs). (Illus.). 328p. 1996. 72.00 (*0-19-815057-1*, Clarendon Pr) OUP.

Roman Army in the East. Contrib. by D. Kennedy et al. (JRA Supplementary Ser.: No. 18). (Illus.). 320p. 1996. lib. bdg. 89.50 (*1-887829-18-0*) Jour Roman Arch.

Roman Army Papers. J. F. Gilliam. (Mavors Roman Army Researches Ser.: Vol. II). 481p. (C). 1986. 127.00 (*90-70265-28-1*, Pub. by Gieben NE) Benjamins North Am.

Roman Army, 31 B.C.-A.D. 337: A Sourcebook. Brian Campbell. LC 93-9032. 288p. (C). 1994. pap. 17.95 (*0-415-07173-9*) Routledge.

***Roman Aromas.** Mary Dobson. (Illus.). 32p. 1997. pap. 7.95 (*0-19-910094-2*) OUP.

Roman Art. Susan Walker. (British Museum Paperbacks Ser.). 72p. (C). 1991. pap. 12.50 (*0-674-77759-X*) HUP.

Roman Art. rev. ed. Donald Strong & Roger Ling. 360p. 1988. pap. 18.95 (*0-317-66049-7*, Penguin Bks) Viking Penguin.

Roman Art. Ed. by Roger Ling et al. (Pelican History of Art Ser.). (Illus.). 406p. (C). 1988. reprint ed. pap. text ed. 25.00 (*0-300-05293-6*) Yale U Pr.

Roman Art: A Modern Survey of the Art of Ancient Rome. George M. Hanfmann. (Illus.). 250p. (C). 1975. reprint ed. pap. text ed. 14.95 (*0-393-09222-4*) Norton.

Roman Art: Romulus to Constantine. Nancy H. Ramage & Andrew Ramage. (Illus.). 304p. 1991. 49.50 (*0-8109-3755-7*) Abrams.

Roman Art: Romulus to Constantine. 2nd ed. Nancy H. Ramage. 320p. (C). 1995. pap. text ed. 52.33 (*0-13-440702-4*) P-H.

Roman Art & Architecture. Mortimer Wheeler. (World of Art Ser.). (Illus.). 252p. 1985. pap. 14.95 (*0-500-20021-1*) Thames Hudson.

Roman Art & Imperial Policy. Niels Hannestad. (Jutland Archaeological Society Publications: Vol. XIX). (Illus.). 486p. 1988. pap. 87.50 (*87-7288-043-0*) Coronet Bks.

Roman Art & Imperial Policy. Niels Hannestad. (Illus.). 488p. (C). 1988. pap. 52.00 (*87-7288-166-6*, Pub. by Aarhus Univ Pr DK) David Brown.

Roman Art in Context: An Anthology. Eve D'Ambra. 256p. 1993. pap. text ed. 29.00 (*0-13-781808-4*) P-H.

Roman Augury & Etruscan Divination. Ed. by W. R. Connor. LC 75-10649. (Ancient Religion & Mythology Ser.). 1979. 18.95 (*0-405-07273-2*) Ayer.

Roman Baroque Sculpture: The Industry of Art. Jennifer Montagu. LC 88-30482. (C). 1989. text ed. 55.00 (*0-300-04392-9*) Yale U Pr.

Roman Baroque Sculpture: The Industry of Art. Jennifer Montagu. (Illus.). 256p. (C). 1993. reprint ed. pap. text ed. 30.00 (*0-300-05366-5*) Yale U Pr.

Roman Bath. Barry W. Cunliffe. LC 72-856399. (Society of Antiquaries of London, Research Committee Reports: No. 24). 364p. reprint ed. pap. 103.80 (*0-317-28840-7*, 2020785) Bks Demand.

Roman Baths in Britain. Tony Rook. 1989. pap. 25.00 (*0-7478-0157-6*, Pub. by Shire UK) St Mut.

***Roman Baths of Lycia: An Architectural Study.** Andrew Farrington. (Illus.). 176p. 1995. 47.00 (*1-898249-04-0*, Pub. by Brit Inst Arch UK) David Brown.

R

R

***Roman Baths of Lycia: An Architectural Study.** Andrew Farrington. (BIAA Monographs: No. 20). (Illus.). 176p. 1995. 47.00 (0-614-22054-8, Pub. by Brit Inst Arch UK) David Brown.

Roman Black-&-White Figural Mosaics. John R. Clarke. LC 78-68553. (College Art Association Monographs: Vol. 35). (Illus.). 172p. 1985. reprint ed. 35.00 (0-271-00401-0) Pa St U Pr.

Roman Blood. Steven W. Saylor. 416p. 1992. mass mkt. 5.99 (0-8041-1039-5) Ivy Books.

Roman Bourgeois. Antoine Furetiere. (Folio Ser.: No. 1277). 306p. (FRE.). 1981. pap. 9.95 (2-07-037277-4) Schoenhof.

Roman Bourgeois. Antoine Furetiere. (FRE.). 1981. pap. 11.95 (0-7859-2443-4, 2070372774) Fr & Eur.

Roman Brick & Tile: An Analytical Survey & Corpus of Surviving Examples. Gerald Brodribb. (Illus.). 176p. 1989. 24.00 (0-86299-363-6, Pub. by Sutton Pubng UK) Bks Intl VA.

Roman Brick Stamps in the Kelsey Museum. John Bodel. (Kelsey Museum of Archaeology Ser.). (Illus.). 1983. pap. text ed. 27.95 (0-472-08039-3) U of Mich Pr.

***Roman Brickstamps: The Thomas Ashby Collection in the American Academy at Rome.** James Anderson. (British School at Rome Archaeological Monographs). (Illus.). 141p. 1991. pap. 81.00 (0-904152-18-9, Pub. by British Schl Rome UK) David Brown.

Roman Bridal Drama. Alan Little. 1978. 6.50 (0-89679-009-6) Moretus Pr.

Roman Bridges. Colin O'Connor. LC 92-30900. (Illus.). 200p. (C). 1994. text ed. 105.00 (0-521-39326-4) Cambridge U Pr.

Roman Britain. S. Hill & S. Ireland. (Classical World Ser.). 100p. 1996. pap. 14.95 (1-85399-140-6, Pub. by Brstl Class Pr UK) Focus Pub-R Pullins.

Roman Britain. T. W. Potter. (Illus.). 72p. 1983. pap. 11.95 (0-674-77766-2) HUP.

***Roman Britain.** T. W. Potter. 1997. pap. text ed. 18.95 (0-674-77767-0) HUP.

Roman Britain. T. W. Potter & Catherine Johns. LC 92-25283. (Exploring the Roman World Ser.). (C). 1993. 40.00 (0-520-08168-4) U CA Pr.

Roman Britain. T. W. Potter. 1983. pap. 9.95 (0-674-77765-4) HUP.

Roman Britain. I. A. Richmond. 1978. mass mkt. 5.95 (0-14-020315-X, Penguin Bks) Viking Penguin.

Roman Britain. Peter Salway. (Oxford History of England Ser.). (Illus.). 858p. 1981. 55.00 (0-19-821717-X) OUP.

Roman Britain. Peter Salway. (Oxford History of England Ser.). (Illus.). 858p. 1984. pap. 24.95 (0-19-285143-8) OUP.

Roman Britain: A Sourcebook. Ed. by Stanley Ireland. 288p. (Orig.). (C). 1996. pap. 18.95 (0-415-13134-0, Routledge NY) Routledge.

Roman Britain: Outpost of the Empire. Howard H. Scullard. LC 78-63042. (Illus.). 192p. 1986. pap. 15.95 (0-500-27405-3) Thames Hudson.

Roman Britain & the English Settlements. R. G. Collingwood & John N. Myres. 515p. 1936. pap. 26.00 (0-8196-1160-3) Biblo.

Roman Building: Materials & Technique. Jean-Pierre Adam. Tr. by Anthony S. Mathews from FRE. LC 94-17349. (Illus.). 364p. 1994. 57.50 (0-253-30124-6) Ind U Pr.

Roman Buildings of the Republic: An Attempt to Date Them from Their Materials. Tenney Frank. LC 25-7064. (American Academy in Rome. Papers & Monographs: Vol. 3). 163p. reprint ed. pap. 46.50 (0-685-15588-9, 2026718) Bks Demand.

Roman-Byzantine Burial Cave in Northern Palestine. Ovid R. Sellers. (American Schools of Oriental Research, Supplement Ser.: Vols. 15-16). 55p. 1953. pap. text ed. 10.00 (0-89757-315-3) Am Sch Orient Res.

Roman Cambridgeshire. David M. Browne. (Cambridge Town, Gown & County Ser.: Vol. 13). (Illus.). 1977. pap. 4.95 (0-900891-09-2) Oleander Pr.

Roman camerounais d'expression Francaise. Claire L. Dehon. LC 89-62177. 371p. (FRE.). 1989. lib. bdg. 37. 95 (0-917786-72-6) Summa Pubns.

Roman Candle. Sidney Sheldon. 1960. pap. 5.25 (0-8222-0960-8) Dramatists Play.

Roman Canon Law in Reformation England. R. H. Helmholz. (Cambridge Studies in English Legal History). 272p. (C). 1990. text ed. 59.95 (0-521-38191-6) Cambridge U Pr.

Roman Capitals Stroke by Stroke: An Arthur Baker Calligraphy Manual. Arthur Baker. (Illus.). 64p. (Orig.). (gr. 6 up). 1983. pap. 3.50 (0-486-24450-4) Dover.

Roman Catholic Beliefs in England: Customary Catholicism & Transformations of Religious Authority. Michael P. Hornsby-Smith. 261p. (C). 1991. text ed. 59.95 (0-521-36327-6) Cambridge U Pr.

***Roman Catholic Church: Its Origins & Nature.** John F. O'Grady. LC 97-22380. 1997. write for info. (0-8091-3740-2) Paulist Pr.

Roman Catholic Church & the Creation of the Modern Irish State, 1878-1886. Emmet J. Larkin. LC 75-7169. (American Philosophical Society, Memoirs Ser.: Vol. 108). 436p. reprint ed. pap. 124.30 (0-317-29437-7, 2024293) Bks Demand.

Roman Catholic Church & the Emergence of the Modern Irish Political System, 1874-1878. Emmet J. Larkin. 618p. 1996. text ed. 74.95 (0-8132-0873-4) Cath U Pr.

Roman Catholic Church & the Home Rule Movement in Ireland, 1870-1874. Emmet J. Larkin. LC 89-36347. xxii, 416p. (C). 1990. 65.00 (0-8078-1886-0) U of NC Pr.

Roman Catholic Church & the North-West School Question: A Study in Church-State Relations in Western Canada, 1875-1905. Manoly R. Lupul. LC 73-89844. 304p. reprint ed. pap. 86.70 (0-8357-3646-6, 2036373) Bks Demand.

Roman Catholic Church in Ireland & the Fall of Parnell, 1888-1891. Emmet J. Larkin. LC 78-22056. xxi, 316p. 1979. 37.50 (0-8078-1352-4) U of NC Pr.

Roman Catholic Church in Latin America. Intro. by Jorge I. Dominguez. LC 93-45525. 424p. 1994. text ed. 72.00 (0-8153-1487-6) Garland.

Roman Catholic Controversy: What Draws & Divides Evangelicals. James R. White. 272p. 1996. pap. text ed. 10.99 (1-55661-819-0) Bethany Hse.

Roman Catholic Diocese. Turner Publishing Company Staff. LC 93-61860. 300p. 1994. 48.00 (1-56311-129-2) Turner Pub KY.

Roman Catholic Exegesis since Divino Afflante Spiritu: Hermeneutical Implications. Robert B. Robinson. LC 88-11432. (Society of Biblical Literature Ser.). 192p. 1988. 18.95 (1-55540-240-2, 06 21 11); pap. 12.95 (1-55540-241-0, 06 21 11) Scholars Pr GA.

Roman Catholic Hierarchy. Thomas E. Watson. (Studies in Populism). 1980. lib. bdg. 69.95 (0-686-68883-X) Revisionist Pr.

Roman Catholic Modernism. Ed. by Bernard M. Reardon. 254p. 1970. 37.50 (0-8047-0750-2) Stanford U Pr.

Roman Catholic Prophecies in the Holy Bible. (Orig.). 1994. pap. write for info. (0-930179-44-7) Johns Enter.

Roman Catholic-Protestant Colloquium, Ecumenical Dialogue at Harvard. Ed. by Samuel H. Miller & G. Ernest Wright. LC 64-19583. 396p. 1964. 35.00 (0-674-23700-5) Belknap Pr.

Roman Catholic Worship: Trent to Today. James F. White. LC 95-17516. 192p. (Orig.). 1995. pap. 11.95 (0-8091-3588-4) Paulist Pr.

***Roman Catholic Writings on Doctrinal Development.** John H. Newman. Tr. & Comment by James Gaffney. LC 97-16289. (Orig.). 1997. pap. 15.95 (1-55612-973-4, LL1973) Sheed & Ward MO.

Roman Catholicism. Loraine Boettner. LC 61-11748. 1962. 12.99 (0-87552-130-4, Pub. by Evangelical Pr) Presby & Reformed.

Roman Catholicism: An Introduction. John T. Carmody & Denise L. Carmody. 521p. (C). 1989. pap. text ed. 30.60 (0-02-319390-5, Macmillan Coll) P-H.

Roman Catholicism: Evangelical Protestants Analyze What Divides & Unites Us. Ed. by John Armstrong. 400p. 1994. text ed. 19.99 (0-8024-7181-1) Moody.

Roman Catholicism: The Search for Relevance. William McSweeney. 1980. text ed. 25.00 (0-312-68969-1) St Martin.

Roman Catholicism: Yesterday & Today. Robert A. Burns. 258p. 1992. pap. 11.95 (0-8294-0711-1) Loyola Pr.

Roman Catholicism & Freemasonry. Dudley Wright. 1977. lib. bdg. 250.00 (0-8490-2531-1) Gordon Pr.

Roman Catholicism & Political Form. Carl Schmitt & G. L. Ulmen. LC 96-24987. (Global Perspectives in History & Politics Ser.). 112p. 1996. text ed. 39.95 (0-313-30105-0) Greenwood.

Roman Catholicism & the American Way of Life. Ed. by Thomas T. McAvoy. LC 72-13177. (Essay Index Reprint Ser.). 1977. reprint ed. 18.95 (0-8369-8167-7) Ayer.

Roman Catholicism & the Right to Work. Edward B. McLean. 186p. (Orig.). (C). 1986. lib. bdg. 46.00 (0-8191-5009-6) U Pr of Amer.

Roman Catholics. Patrick W. Carey. LC 93-20125. (Denominations in America Ser.: No. 6). 400p. 1993. text ed. 59.95 (0-313-25439-7, CRT/, Greenwood Pr) Greenwood.

Roman Catholics & Evangelicals: Agreements & Differences. Norman L. Geisler & Ralph E. MacKenzie. LC 95-18062. 544p. (Orig.). (C). 1995. pap. 24.99 (0-8010-3875-8) Baker Bks.

***Roman Catholics in America.** Patrick W. Carey. LC 93-20125. 208p. 1996. pap. text ed. 17.95 (0-275-95802-7, Praeger Pubs) Greenwood.

Roman Catholics in England: Studies in Social Structure since the Second World War. Michael P. Hornsby-Smith. (Illus.). 288p. 1987. text ed. 59.95 (0-521-30313-3) Cambridge U Pr.

***Roman Cavalry: From the First to the Third Century A. D.** Karen R. Dixon & Pat Southern. 272p. (C). 1997. pap. 24.95 (0-415-17039-7, Routledge NY) Routledge.

Roman Cemeteries on the Territory of Pecs, Sopianae. F. Fulep. (Fontes Archaeological Hungariae Ser.). 64p. (C). 1977. pap. 39.00 (963-05-1079-0, Pub. by Akad Kiado HU) St Mut.

Roman Children's Sarcophagi: Their Decoration and Social Significance. Janet Huskinson. (Oxford Monographs on Classical Archaeology). (Illus.). 160p. (C). 1996. 90.00 (0-19-814086-X) OUP.

Roman Cieslewica - Posters & Collages: Warsaw - Lvov - Cracow - Paris 1956-1993. Christopher D. Kamyszew & Jan Lenica. (Illus.). 48p. (Orig.). 1993. pap. text ed. 10. 00 (1-883123-01-1) Polish Museum Am.

Roman Cinerary Urns in Stockholm Collections. Charlotte Scheffer. (Illus.). 96p. (Orig.). 1987. pap. 72.50 (91-7192-676-3) Coronet Bks.

Roman Circuses: Arenas for Charioteers. John Humphrey. LC 82-40413. 1985. 75.00 (0-520-04921-7) U CA Pr.

Roman Cities: "Les villes romaines" Pierre Grimal. Ed. & Tr. by Michael Woloch from FRE. LC 81-69831. (Illus.). 349p. 1984. pap. 16.95 (0-299-08934-7) U of Wis Pr.

Roman Citizenship & the Athenian Elite: A. D. 96-161: Two Prosopographical Catalogues. Michael Woloch. xviii, 315p. 1989. pap. 74.00 (90-256-0939-2, Pub. by A M Hakkert NE) Benjamins North Am.

Roman Civilization, Vols. I & II. 3rd ed. Naphtali Lewis & Meyer Reinhold. 1990. text ed. 140.00 (0-231-07054-3); pap. text ed. 47.50 (0-231-07055-1) Col U Pr.

Roman Classics Notes. Mary E. Snodgrass. 376p. 1988. pap. 7.95 (0-8220-1152-2) Cliffs.

Roman Coins & Values. David R. Sear. 1979. lib. bdg. 70.00 (0-685-06752-1, Pub. by Seaby UK) S J Durst.

***Roman Coins from 140 Sites in Britain.** Richard Reece. (Illus.). 107p. 1991. pap. 18.00 (1-873132-20-4) David Brown.

Roman Coins from the Mazzini Collection, 2 vols. Dennis J. Kroh. 800p. 1994. 225.00 (0-9638751-3-2) Empire Coins.

Roman Coins from the Mazzini Collection, 2 vols., 2. Dennis J. Kroh. 800p. 1994. write for info. (0-9638751-2-4) Empire Coins.

Roman Coins in the Princeton Library, I. Republic to Commodus. Brooks E. Levy & Pierre C. Bastien. (Editions NR, 1985 Ser.). 191p. 1994. 100.00 (0-685-72019-5) Am Numismatic.

Roman Coins of Alexandria: Quantitative Studies, 2 vols., Set. Erik Christiansen. 550p. (C). 1988. 47.00 (87-7288-158-5, Pub. by Aarhus Univ Pr DK) David Brown.

Roman Colonate: The Theories of Its Origin. Roth Clausing. LC 70-78011. (Columbia University. Studies in the Social Sciences: No. 260). 1969. reprint ed. 37.50 (0-404-51260-7) AMS Pr.

***Roman Colosseum.** Fred Finney. LC 97-10020. (Mystery History of a--Ser.). (J). 1997. lib. bdg. 17.90 (0-7613-0613-7, Copper Beech Bks) Millbrook Pr.

Roman Colosseum. Fiona Macdonald. LC 96-15138. (Inside Story Ser.). (Illus.). 48p. (YA). (gr. 5 up). 1996. lib. bdg. 18.95 (0-87226-275-8) P Bedrick Bks.

***Roman Colosseum.** Don Nardo. LC 97-2839. (Building History Ser.). (Illus.). (J). (gr. 4-12). 1997. lib. bdg. 17.96 (1-56006-429-3) Lucent Bks.

Roman Colosseum: De Amphitheatro Liber, 1584, 2 vols. Justus Lipsius. (Printed Sources of Western Art Ser.). (Illus.). (LAT.). 1981. reprint ed. pap. 55.00 (0-915346-58-3) A Wofsy Fine Arts.

Roman Comedy. David Konstan. LC 82-22112. 184p. 1983. pap. 14.95 (0-8014-9398-6) Cornell U Pr.

Roman Comedy. Kenneth McLeish. (Inside the Ancient World Ser.). 80p. 1983. reprint ed. pap. 14.95 (0-86292-186-4, Pub. by Brstl Class Pr UK) Focus Pub-R Pullins.

Roman Comique. Paul Scarron. 384p. (FRE.). 1981. pap. 12.95 (0-7859-4396-X, 2080703609) Fr & Eur.

Roman Conquest of Italy. Jean-Michel David. Tr. by Antonia Nevill. LC 96-17076. 224p. 1996. pap. 19.95 (0-631-20325-7) Blackwell Pubs.

Roman Conquest of Italy. Jean-Michel David. Tr. by Antonia Nevill. LC 96-17076. 224p. (C). 1996. 54.95 (0-631-20321-4) Blackwell Pubs.

Roman Conquests. Neil Grant. (Wars That Changed the World Ser.: Group 2). (Illus.). 32p. (J). (gr. 3-9). 1991. lib. bdg. 11.95 (1-85435-262-8) Marshall Cavendish.

Roman Conquests. Phil Andros. LC 92-6305. 154p. 1992. reprint ed. pap. 7.95 (1-55583-225-3) Alyson Pubns.

Roman Construction in Italy from Nerva Through the Antonines. Marion E. Blake. Ed. by Doris T. Bishop. LC 72-83463. (American Philosophical Society, Memoirs Ser.: No. 96). 454p. reprint ed. pap. 129.40 (0-7837-1112-3, 2041642) Bks Demand.

Roman Converts. Arnold H. Lunn. LC 67-22102. (Essay Index Reprint Ser.). 1977. 20.95 (0-8369-0636-5) Ayer.

Roman Converts. Arnold H. Lunn. (Essay Index Reprint Ser.). 275p. 1982. reprint ed. lib. bdg. 17.00 (0-8290-0482-3) Irvington.

Roman Copies of Greek Sculpture: The Problem of the Originals. Brunhilde S. Ridgway. (Jerome Lectures: No. 15). 304p. (C). 1984. text ed. 52.50 (0-472-10038-6) U of Mich Pr.

Roman Cordoba. Robert C. Knapp. LC 83-1195. (University of California Publications: No. 30). 172p. 1983. pap. 49. 10 (0-7837-7489-3, 2049211) Bks Demand.

Roman Corinth: An Alternative Model for the Classical City. Donald W. Engels. LC 89-27004. (Illus.). 274p. 1990. 42.50 (0-226-20870-2) U Ch Pr.

Roman Crafts & Industries. Alan McWhirr. 1989. pap. 25. 00 (0-85263-594-X, Pub. by Shire UK) St Mut.

Roman Crete. Sanders. 1982. pap. 69.95 (0-85668-150-4, Pub. by Aris & Phillips UK) David Brown.

Roman Culture & Society: Collected Papers. Elizabeth Rawson. 384p. 1991. 175.00 (0-19-814752-X, 12235) OUP.

Roman Cursive Writing. Henry B. Van Hoesen. LC 34-20123. 332p. reprint ed. pap. 94.70 (0-317-10623-6, 2050380) Bks Demand.

Roman de Fauvel in the Edition of Mesire Chaillou de Pesstain: Facsimile of Paris, Bibliotheque Nationale Manuscript. fac. ed. Chaillou. (Illus.). 1990. lib. bdg. 575.00 (0-8450-0007-1) Broude.

Roman de la Manekine par Philippe de Reimes. Philippe De Remi. LC 74-174193. (Bannatyne Club, Edinburgh. Publications: No. 68). reprint ed. 47.50 (0-404-52788-4) AMS Pr.

Roman de la Momie. Theophile Gautier. Ed. by Boschot. (Class. Garnier Ser.). pap. 24.95 (0-685-34912-8) Fr & Eur.

Roman de la Momie. Theophile Gautier & G. Van Den Bogaert. 186p. (FRE.). 1966. 10.95 (0-8288-9989-4, F63020) Fr & Eur.

Roman de La Momie. Theophile Gautier. 314p. (FRE.). 1986. pap. 11.95 (0-7859-2514-7, 2070377180) Fr & Eur.

Roman de la Momie. unabridged ed. Gautier. (FRE.). pap. 5.95 (2-87714-293-0, Pub. by Bookking Intl FR) Distribks Inc.

Roman de la Monie. Theophile Gautier. Ed. by Boschot. (Coll. Prestige). 49.95 (0-685-34913-6) Fr & Eur.

Roman de la Rose, 5 tomes. Guillaume De Lorris & Jean De Meur. Ed. by E. Langlois. 199.00 (0-685-34019-8) Fr & Eur.

Roman de la Rose. Guillaume De Lorris & Jean De Meun. 293p. 1983. 9.95 (0-8288-7437-9) Fr & Eur.

Roman de la Rose. Guillaume De Lorris. Ed. by Stephen G. Nichols, Jr. LC 67-25114. (Medieval French Literature Ser.). (FRE.). (C). 1967. pap. text ed. 6.95 (0-89197-496-2) Irvington.

Roman De la Rose. Guillaume De Lorris & Jean De Meun. (Folio Ser.: No. 1518). (FRE.). pap. 13.95 (2-07-037518-8) Schoenhof.

***Roman de la Rose.** Ed. by Lorris & Strubel. write for info. (0-7859-9331-2) Fr & Eur.

Roman de la Rose: An Annotated Bibliography. Heather M. Arden. LC 93-15492. (Medieval Bibliographies Ser.: Vol. 8). 416p. 1993. text ed. 20.00 (0-8240-5799-6, H1358) Garland.

Roman de Miraut: Chien de Chasse. Louis Pergaud. (FRE.). 1978. pap. 11.95 (0-7859-4102-9) Fr & Eur.

Roman de Renart. (FRE.). 1986. pap. 10.95 (0-7859-2912-6) Fr & Eur.

Roman de Renart. Jacques Haumont. 203p. 1966. 9.95 (0-8288-7495-6) Fr & Eur.

Roman de Renart, 6 tomes. Ed. by Marlo Roques. 75.00 (0-685-34018-X) Fr & Eur.

Roman de Renart, 3 vols. Ed. by Ernest Martin. 1476p. (C). 1973. reprint ed. 480.75 (3-11-003337-2) De Gruyter.

***Roman de Tristan en Prose.** Ed. by Renee L. Curtis. LC 84-24337. (Arthurian Studies: No. 12). (Illus.). 268p. 1985. 63.00 (0-85991-181-0) Boydell & Brewer.

Roman de Tristan en Prose, Vol. II. Renee L. Curtis. LC 84-24337. (Arthurian Studies: No. XIII: No. XIII). 320p. 1985. text ed. 63.00 (0-85991-182-9) Boydell & Brewer.

Roman Declamation: Selections. Michael Winterbottom. (Bristol Latin Texts Ser.). 120p. 1980. 17.95 (0-906515-10-6, Pub. by Brstl Class Pr UK) Focus Pub-R Pullins.

Roman Defeat, Christian Response, & the Literary Construction of the Jew. David M. Olster. LC 93-42841. (Middle Ages Ser.). 224p. (C). 1994. text ed. 33. 95 (0-8122-3152-X) U of Pa Pr.

Roman des Eles. Raoul De Hodenc. (Utrecht Publications in Comparative Literature: Vol. 17). x, 175p. 1983. 59.00 (90-272-2192-8); pap. 32.95 (90-272-2202-9) Benjamins North Am.

Roman des Romans. Ed. by I. C. LeCompte. (Elliott Monographs: Vol. 14). 1974. reprint ed. 25.00 (0-527-02617-4) Periodicals Srv.

Roman des sept sages de Rome. Mary B. Speer. LC 88-82137. (Edward C. Armstrong Monographs on Medieval Literature: No. 4). 399p. (Orig.). 1989. pap. 24.95 (0-917058-73-9) French Forum.

Roman Dmowski: Party, Tactics, Ideology, Eighteen Ninety-Five to Nineteen Seven. Alvin M. Fountain, 2nd. (East European Monographs: No. 60). 240p. 1980. text ed. 51.00 (0-914710-53-2) East Eur Monographs.

Roman Documents from the Greek East: Senatus Consulta & Epistulae to the Age of Augustus. Robert K. Sherk. LC 68-19442. 408p. reprint ed. pap. 116.30 (0-317-29909-3, 2017565) Bks Demand.

Roman Domestic Buildings. Ed. by Barton. (Exeter Studies in History). (Illus.). 176p. 1995. pap. text ed. 19.95 (0-85989-415-0, Pub. by Univ Exeter Pr UK) Northwestern U Pr.

Roman du Roi Arthur. Xavier De Langlais. 229p. 1965. 19. 95 (0-8288-7418-2) Fr & Eur.

Roman d'un Spahi. Pierre P. Loti-Viaud. (Folio Ser.: No. 2393). (FRE.). pap. 10.95 (2-07-038531-0) Schoenhof.

Roman Eastern Frontier & the Persian Wars, AD 226-363: A Documentary History. Ed. by Michael H. Dodgeon & Samuel N. Lieu. (Illus.). 464p. (C). 1994. pap. 24.95 (0-415-10317-7) Routledge.

Roman Economic Policy in the Erythra Thalassa. Steven E. Sidebotham. (Mnemosyne Ser.: Supplement 91). (Illus.). xiv, 226p. 1986. pap. 60.75 (90-04-07644-1) E J Brill.

***Roman Elegies: And Other Poems & Epigrams.** Johann W. Von Goethe & Michael Hamburger. (Poetica). 118p. 1996. pap. 16.95 (0-85646-274-8, Pub. by Anvil Press UK) Dufour.

Roman Elegies & the Diary. Johann Wolfgang Von Goethe. Tr. by David Luke. 136p. (GER.). 1991. text ed. 55.00 (1-870352-05-X, Pub. by Libris UK); pap. text ed. 19.95 (1-870352-20-3, Pub. by Libris UK) Paul & Co Pubs.

***Roman Eloquence: Rhetoric in Society & Literature.** LC 96-52767. 288p. (C). 1997. text ed. write for info. (0-415-12544-8) Routledge.

***Roman Eloquence: Rhetoric in Society & Literature.** William J. Dominik. LC 96-52767. 288p. (C). 1997. pap. write for info. (0-415-12545-6) Routledge.

Roman Empire. Naphtali Lewis & Meyer Reinhold. (Roman Civilization Ser.: Vol. 2). 736p. 1990. text ed. 75.00 (0-231-07132-9); pap. text ed. 25.00 (0-231-07133-7) Col U Pr.

Roman Empire. James Mason. 1991. pap. text ed. 13.32 (0-582-20736-3) Longman.

Roman Empire. Don Nardo. LC 93-6906. (World History Ser.). 100p. (J). (gr. 6-9). 1994. lib. bdg. 17.96 (1-56006-231-2) Lucent Bks.

***Roman Empire.** Paul Veyne. 1997. pap. text ed. 14.95 (0-674-77771-9) HUP.

Roman Empire. Colin Wells. LC 83-40699. (Illus.). 368p. 1984. 42.50 (0-8047-1237-9); pap. 12.95 (0-8047-1238-7) Stanford U Pr.

An Asterisk (*) at the beginning of an entry indicates that the title is appearing in BIP for the first time.

Roman Empire. Martyn Whittock. LC 95-44430. (Biographical History Ser.). (Illus.). 64p. (YA). (gr. 5 up). 1996. lib. bdg. 17.95 (*0-87226-118-2*) P Bedrick Bks.

Roman Empire. 2nd ed. Colin Wells. LC 95-2270. (Illus.). 368p. (Orig.). (C). 1995. pap. text ed. 14.00 (*0-674-77770-0*) HUP.

Roman Empire. Martin P. Charlesworth. LC 86-29443. (Oxford Paperbacks University Ser.). (Illus.). 155p. 1987. reprint ed. text ed. 52.50 (*0-313-25669-1*, CHAR, Greenwood Pr) Greenwood.

Roman Empire: Augustus to Hadrian. Ed. & Tr. by Robert K. Sherk from GRE. (Translated Documents of Greece & Rome Ser.: No. 6). 304p. 1988. pap. text ed. 23.95 (*0-521-33887-5*) Cambridge U Pr.

Roman Empire: Economy, Society & Culture. Peter Garnsey & Richard P. Saller. LC 86-25029. 232p. 1987. pap. 16.95 (*0-520-06067-9*) U CA Pr.

***Roman Empire: From the Etruscans to the Decline of Roman Empire.** Henri Stierlin. (World Architecture Ser.). 1996. 29.99 (*3-8228-8562-2*) Taschen Amer.

***Roman Empire & Its Germanic Peoples.** Herwig Wolfram. LC 96-39741. 1997. write for info. (*0-520-08511-6*) U CA Pr.

Roman Empire & Its Neighbours. 2nd ed. Ed. by Fergus Millar. LC 81-326. 376p. 1981. 49.50 (*0-8419-0711-0*) Holmes & Meier.

***Roman Emperor of Ammianus.** John F. Matthews. LC 89-45756. 623p. 1989. reprint ed. pap. 177.60 (*0-608-03735-4*, 2064560) Bks Demand.

Roman Empire, Twenty-Seven B.C. Four Hundred Seventy-Six A.D. A Study in Survival. Chester G. Starr, Jr. LC 81-22310. (Illus.). 224p. 1983. pap. 18.95 (*0-19-503130-X*) OUP.

Roman Engineers. L. A. Hamey & J. A. Hamey. 48p. 1981. pap. text ed. 10.95 (*0-521-22511-6*) Cambridge U Pr.

Roman Enigma. Murphy. 1981. 13.95 (*0-02-588250-3*) Macmillan.

Roman Epic. Anthony J. Boyle. LC 92-25458. 240p. (C). (gr. 13). 1993. 74.95 (*0-415-04230-5*, A9949, Routledge NY) Routledge.

Roman Epic. Anthony J. Boyle. 352p. (C). 1996. pap. 22.95 (*0-415-14357-8*) Routledge.

Roman Epistle. Robert A. Brooks. LC 83-21044. 72p. (Orig.). 1984. pap. 8.95 (*0-87233-072-9*) Bauhan.

Roman Experimental. Emile Zola. Ed. by Aime Guedj. pap. 8.95 (*0-7859-2967-3*) Fr & Eur.

Roman Family. Suzanne Dixon. LC 91-25876. (Ancient Society & History Ser.). (Illus.). 232p. 1992. text ed. 48.50 (*0-8018-4199-2*); pap. text ed. 15.95 (*0-8018-4200-X*) Johns Hopkins.

Roman Family: A Bridge to Roman Culture, Values & Literature. Ed. by Charles Lloyd. 191p. (Orig.). 1991. spiral bd. 11.30 (*0-939507-35-8*, B308) Amer Classical.

***Roman Family in Italy: Status, Sentiment, Space.** Beryl Rawson & Paul Weaver. LC 96-45146. (OUP/ Humanities Research Centre of the Australian National University Ser.). (Illus.). 320p. 1997. 75.00 (*0-19-815052-0*) OUP.

Roman Family Life. Peter Hodge. (Aspects of Roman Life Ser.). 64p. (Orig.). (gr. 7-12). 1974. pap. text ed. 9.00 (*0-582-31411-9*, 71971) Longman.

Roman Festivals of the Period of the Republic. W. Warde Fowler. 1977. lib. bdg. 59.95 (*0-8490-2532-X*) Gordon Pr.

Roman Fever & Other Stories. Edith Wharton. LC 64-11254. 1240p. 1981. 35.00 (*0-684-17011-6*) S&S Trade.

***Roman Fever & other Stories.** Edith Wharton. 1997. pap. 10.00 (*0-684-82990-8*, Scribners PB Fict) S&S Trade.

Roman Finds from Exeter. Holbrook & Bidwell. (Illus.). 333p. 1991. text ed. 95.00 (*0-85989-367-7*, Pub. by Univ Exeter Pr UK) Northwestern U Pr.

Roman Fort. Peter Connolly. (Illus.). 32p. (YA). (gr. 6-9). 1991. bds. 20.95 (*0-19-917108-4*) OUP.

Roman Fort. Fiona Macdonald. LC 93-16397. (Inside Story Ser.). (Illus.). 48p. (J). (gr. 5 up). 1993. lib. bdg. 18.95 (*0-87226-370-3*) P Bedrick Bks.

Roman Fort. Fiona Macdonald. LC 93-16397. (Inside Story Ser.). (Illus.). 48p. (YA). (gr. 5 up). 1993. 9.95 (*0-87226-259-6*) P Bedrick Bks.

Roman Forum. Old Vicarage Publications Staff. 104p. (C). 1982. pap. text ed. 34.00 (*0-685-44227-6*, Pub. by Old Vicarage UK) St Mut.

Roman Foundations of Modern Law. Herbert F. Jolowicz. LC 78-5583. xvii, 217p. 1978. reprint ed. text ed. 55.00 (*0-313-20442-X*, JORF, Greenwood Pr) Greenwood.

Roman Francais Depuis Nineteen Hundred. Rene Lalou. 127p. 1966. 9.95 (*0-8288-7413-1*) Fr & Eur.

Roman Funerary Monuments. Ed. by Guntram Koch. LC 89-2207. (Occasional Papers on Antiquities: No. 6). (Illus.). 144p. 1990. pap. 40.00 (*0-89236-151-4*, J P Getty Museum) J P Getty Trust.

Roman Funerary Sculpture: Catalogue of the Collections, the J. Paul Getty Museum. Guntram Koch. LC 88-15425. (Illus.). 144p. 1988. 40.00 (*0-89236-085-2*, J P Getty Museum) J P Getty Trust.

***Roman Gardens: Villas of the Countryside.** Marcello Fagiolo. LC 97-18503. 1997. 60.00 (*1-885254-57-1*) Monacelli Pr.

Roman Gates, Caerleon. D. R. Evans & V. M. Metcalf. (Oxbow Monographs in Archaeology: No. 15). (Illus.). 216p. 1992. pap. 42.00 (*0-946897-36-0*, Pub. by Oxbow Bks UK) David Brown.

Roman Gaul. J. F. Drinkwater. LC 83-45143. (Illus.). 272p. 1983. 42.50 (*0-8014-1642-6*) Cornell U Pr.

Roman Gaul & Germany. Anthony King. 1990. 45.00 (*0-520-06989-7*) U CA Pr.

***Roman Glass: Two Centuries of Art & Invention.** Ed. by Martine Newby & Kenneth Painter. (Illus.). 174p. 1991. pap. 37.50 (*0-85431-255-2*, Pub. by Soc Antiquaries UK) David Brown.

Roman Gloucestershire. Alan McWhirr. (Illus.). 192p. 1993. pap. text ed. 15.00 (*0-904387-60-7*, Pub. by Sutton Pubng UK) Bks Intl VA.

Roman Goddess Ceres. Barbette S. Spaeth. LC 95-13112. (Illus.). 304p. 1995. pap. 19.95 (*0-292-77693-4*); text ed. 40.00 (*0-292-77692-6*) U of Tex Pr.

Roman Government's Response to Crisis, A.D. 235-337. Ramsey MacMullen. LC 76-43324. 320p. reprint ed. pap. 91.20 (*0-8357-8311-1*, 2033810) Bks Demand.

Roman Granaries & Store Buildings. Geoffrey Rickman. LC 76-116843. 397p. reprint ed. pap. 113.20 (*0-317-10131-5*, 2013245) Bks Demand.

Roman Hasford. Douglas C. Jones. 464p. 1996. mass mkt. 5.50 (*0-06-100922-9*) HarpC.

***Roman Hat Mystery.** Ellery Queen. lib. bdg. 21.95 (*0-8488-1871-7*) Amereon Ltd.

Roman Hat Mystery. Ellery Queen. 340p. 1994. reprint ed. 35.00 (*1-883402-19-0*) S&S Trade.

Roman Heritage: Textiles from Egypt & the Eastern Mediterranean, 300-600 A.D. James Trilling. LC 82-50367. (Textile Museum Journal Ser.). (Illus.). 112p. (Orig.). 1982. pap. 17.50 (*0-87405-019-7*) Textile Mus.

Roman Heritage: Textiles from Egypt & the Eastern Mediterranean, 300-600 A.D. James Trilling. LC 82-50367. (Illus.). 112p. (Orig.). 1982. pap. 24.95 (*0-295-96980-6*) U of Wash Pr.

Roman Historical Myths: The Regal Period in Augustan Literature. Matthew Fox. LC 95-19065. (Oxford Classical Monographs). 288p. (C). 1996. 65.00 (*0-19-815020-2*, Clarendon Pr) OUP.

Roman Historique. Gabor Lukacs. (FRE.). 1977. pap. 28.95 (*0-7859-3036-1*) Fr & Eur.

Roman History, 14 vols. Incl. Vol. 1. Bks. 1-2. 14.50 (*0-674-99126-5*); Vol. 2. Bks. 3-4. Livy. 14.50 (*0-674-99148-6*); Vol. 3. Bks. 5-7. Livy. (*0-674-99190-7*); Vol. 4. Bks. 8-10. Livy. (*0-674-99210-5*); Vol. 5. Bks. 21-22. Livy. (*0-674-99256-3*); Vol. 6. Bks. 23-25. Livy. (*0-674-99392-6*); Vol. 7. Bks. 26-27. Livy. (*0-674-99404-3*); Vol. 8. Bks. 28-30. Livy. (*0-674-99419-1*); Vol. 9. Bks. 31-34. Livy. (*0-674-99326-8*); Vol. 10. Bks. 35-37. Livy. (*0-674-99332-2*); Vol. 11. Bks. 37-39. Livy. (*0-674-99346-2*); Vol. 12. Bks. 40-42. Livy. (*0-674-99366-7*); Vol. 13. Bks. 43-45. Livy. (*0-674-99435-3*); Vol. 14. Summaries: Fragments; General Index. Ed. by Livy. (*0-674-99445-0*); (Loeb Classical LibraryNos. 114, 133, 172, 191, 233, 355, 367, 381, 295, 301, 313, 332, 396, 404). write for info. (*0-318-53181-X*) HUP.

Roman History, 3 vols. Marcellinus Ammianus. (Loeb Classical Library: No. 300, 315, 331). write for info. (*0-318-53177-1*) HUP.

Roman History, 4 vols. Appian. No. 2-5. write for info. (*0-318-53178-X*) HUP.

Roman History, 9 vols. Dio Cassius. Incl. Vol. 1. . 482p. 1914. 14.50 (*0-674-99036-6*); Vol. 2. . 528p. 1914. 14.50 (*0-674-99041-2*); Vol. 3. . 528p. 1914. 14.50 (*0-674-99059-5*); Vol. 4. . 508p. 1916. 14.50 (*0-674-99073-0*); Vol. 5. . 534p. 1917. 14.50 (*0-674-99091-9*); Vol. 6. . 498p. 1917. 14.50 (*0-674-99092-7*); Vol. 7. . 456p. 1924. 14.50 (*0-674-99193-1*); Vol. 8. . 488p. 1925. 14.50 (*0-674-99195-8*); Vol. 9. . 578p. 1927. 14.50 (*0-674-99196-6*); (Loeb Classical Library: Nos. 32, 37, 53, 66, 82, 83, 175-177). write for info. (*0-318-53179-8*) HUP.

Roman History. Florus. Bd. with Lives. (Loeb Classical Library: No. 231). 15.50 (*0-674-99254-7*) HUP.

Roman History, 43 Vols. Ed. by James Luce, Jr. 1975. 1,787.00 (*0-405-07177-9*) Ayer.

Roman History, Bks 53.1-55.9. Cassius Dio. Ed. by J. W. Rich. (Classical Texts Ser.). 272p. (C). 1991. text ed. 49.95 (*0-85668-383-3*, Pub. by Aris & Phillips UK); pap. text ed. 24.95 (*0-85668-384-1*, Pub. by Aris & Phillips UK) David Brown.

Roman History, 3 vols., Vol. 1. Marcellinus Ammianus. (Loeb Classical Library: No. 300). 632p. 1935. 18.95 (*0-674-99331-4*) HUP.

Roman History, 4 vols., Vol. 1. Appian. (Loeb Classical Library: No. 1-4). 660p. 1912. Vol. 2. 18.95 (*0-674-99004-8*) HUP.

Roman History, 3 vols., Vol. 2. Marcellinus Ammianus. (Loeb Classical Library: No. 315). 692p. 1940. 18.95 (*0-674-99348-9*) HUP.

Roman History, 4 vols., Vol. 2. Appian. (Loeb Classical Library: No. 1-4). 484p. 1912. Vol. 3. 18.95 (*0-674-99005-6*) HUP.

Roman History, 4 vols., Vol. 3. Appian. (Loeb Classical Library: No. 1-4). 576p. 1913. Vol. 4. 18.95 (*0-674-99006-4*) HUP.

Roman History, 3 vols., Vol. 3, Bks. 27-31. Marcellinus Ammianus. (Loeb Classical Library: No. 300, 315, 331). 612p. 1939. 18.95 (*0-674-99365-9*) HUP.

Roman History, 4 vols., Vol. 4. Appian. (Loeb Classical Library: No. 1-4). 690p. 1913. Vol. 1. 18.95 (*0-674-99002-1*) HUP.

Roman History: The Reign of Augustus. Dio Cassius. Tr. by Ian Scott-Kilvert. 336p. 1987. pap. 12.95 (*0-14-044448-3*, Penguin Classics) Viking Penguin.

***Roman History for Second Year Latin.** Donna Girard. 46p. (Orig.). (YA). (gr. 10). 1996. spiral bd. 6.00 (*0-939507-51-X*, B-0029) Amer Classical.

Roman Holiday: The Catholic Novels of Evelyn Waugh. A. A. De Vitis. LC 71-153314. (BCL Ser. I). reprint ed. 29.50 (*0-404-02119-0*) AMS Pr.

Roman House. Peter Hodge. (Aspects of Roman Life Ser.). (Illus.). 64p. (Orig.). (YA). (gr. 7-12). 1971. pap. text ed. 9.00 (*0-582-20300-7*, 70709) Longman.

Roman Household: A Sourcebook. Jane F. Gardner & Thomas Wiedemann. (Illus.). 240p. (C). 1991. pap. 18.95 (*0-415-04422-7*, A5216) Routledge.

Roman Household: A Sourcebook. Jane F. Gardner & Thomas Wiedemann. (Illus.). 240p. (C). (gr. 13). 1991. text ed. 79.95 (*0-415-04421-9*, A5212) Routledge.

Roman Ideas of Deity in the Last Century Before the Christian Era. William W. Fowler. LC 75-102236. (Select Bibliographies Reprint Ser.). 1977. 21.95 (*0-8369-5121-2*) Ayer.

Roman Images: Selected Papers from the English Institute, 1982. Ed. by Annabel Patterson. LC 83-17560. 208p. 1984. text ed. 31.00 (*0-8018-3127-X*) Johns Hopkins.

Roman Imperial Architecture. J. B. Ward-Perkins. (Pelican History of Art Ser.). (Illus.). 532p. (C). 1981. reprint ed. pap. text ed. 26.50 (*0-300-05292-8*) Yale U Pr.

***Roman Imperial Army of the First & Second Centuries, A. D.** Graham Webster. 1998. pap. write for info. (*0-8061-3000-8*) U of Okla Pr.

Roman Imperial Art in Greece & Asia Minor. Cornelius C. Vermeule. LC 67-20886. (Illus.). 572p. reprint ed. pap. 163.90 (*0-7837-4196-0*, 2059046) Bks Demand.

Roman Imperial Coinage, 11 vols. C. H. Sutherland & R. A. Carson. 1986. 950.00 (*0-685-51530-3*) S J Durst.

Roman Imperial Grand Strategy. Arther Ferrill. (Publications of the Association of Ancient Historians). 84p. (C). 1991. pap. text ed. 16.50 (*0-8191-8446-2*); lib. bdg. 43.00 (*0-8191-8445-4*) U Pr of Amer.

Roman Imperial Money. M. Grant. (Illus.). 1990. reprint ed. lib. bdg. 30.00 (*0-685-46465-2*) S J Durst.

Roman Imperial Money. Michael Grant. (Illus.). 331p. 1954. reprint ed. lib. bdg. 72.50 (*0-685-13379-6*, Pub. by AM Hakkert NE) Coronet Bks.

Roman Imperial Navy: 31 B.C. - A.D. 324. 3rd ed. C. G. Starr. (Illus.). xx, 232p. (C). 1993. text ed. 30.00 (*0-89005-544-0*) Ares.

Roman Imperial Navy, 31 B.C.-A.D. 324. Chester G. Starr, Jr. LC 74-28526. (Cornell Studies in Classical Philology: Vol. 26). (Illus.). 228p. 1975. reprint ed. text ed. 35.00 (*0-8371-7918-1*, STIN, Greenwood Pr) Greenwood.

Roman Imperial Titulature & Chronology, A.D. 235-284. Michael Peachin. xxviii, 515p. 1990. 174.00 (*90-5063-034-0*, Pub. by Gieben NE) Benjamins North Am.

Roman Impromptu see Oeuvres

Roman Inacheve. Louis Aragon. (FRE.). 1978. pap. 14.95 (*0-7859-3462-6*, 2070300110) Fr & Eur.

Roman Inacheve. Louis Aragon. (Poesie Ser.). (FRE.). pap. 9.95 (*2-07-030011-0*) Schoenhof.

***Roman Ingarden's Ontology & Aesthetics.** Jeff Mitscherling. 260p. 1997. 45.00 (*0-7766-0435-X*, Pub. by Univ Ottawa Pr CN); pap. 26.00 (*0-7766-0425-2*, Pub. by Univ Ottawa Pr CN) Paul & Co Pubs.

Roman Inquisition & the Venetian Press, 1540-1605. Paul F. Grendler. LC 76-45900. 400p. 1977. text ed. 70.00 (*0-691-05245-X*) Princeton U Pr.

Roman Inscriptions of Britain, Vol. II, Fascicule 5. R. G. Collingwood & R. P. Wright. (C). 1993. text ed. 70.00 (*0-7509-0319-8*, Pub. by Sutton Pubng UK) Bks Intl VA.

Roman Inscriptions of Britain, Vol. II, Fascicule 3. Shepherd Frere & R. S. Tomlin. (Illus.). 192p. 1991. text ed. 70.00 (*0-86299-935-9*, Pub. by Sutton Pubng UK) Bks Intl VA.

Roman Inscriptions of Britain, Vol. II, Fascicule 4. R. G. Collingwood & R. P. Wright. Ed. by S. S. Frere & R. S. Tomlin. (Illus.). 256p. 1992. 70.00 (*0-7509-0086-5*, Pub. by Sutton Pubng UK) Bks Intl VA.

Roman Inscriptions of Britain, Vol. II: Instrumentum Domesticum. Ed. by R. S. Tomlin & S. S. Frere. (Illus.). 224p. 1994. 70.00 (*0-7509-0536-0*, Pub. by Sutton Pubng UK) Bks Intl VA.

Roman Italy. T. W. Potter. (Exploring the Roman World Ser.: Vol. 1). 240p. 1987. 40.00 (*0-520-06065-2*); pap. 17.00 (*0-520-06975-7*) U CA Pr.

Roman Italy 338BC-AD200. L. S. Ramaiah. LC 96-24878. 256p. 1996. text ed. 49.95 (*0-312-16072-0*) St Martin.

Roman Jakobson: A Bibliography of His Writings. Roman Jakobson. LC 70-180723. (Janua Linguarum, Ser. Minor: No. 134). 60p. 1971. pap. text ed. 36.95 (*90-279-1816-3*) Mouton.

Roman Jakobson: A Complete Bibliography of His Writings. Ed. by Stephen Rudy. xii, 188p. 1990. lib. bdg. 67.70 (*0-89925-068-8*) Mouton.

Roman Jakobson: Life, Language Art. Richard Brandford. LC 93-26943. (Critics of the Twentieth Century Ser.). 192p. (C). 1994. pap. 17.95 (*0-415-07732-X*) Routledge.

Roman Jakobson: Life, Language Art. Richard Brandford. LC 93-26943. (Critics of the Twentieth Century Ser.). 192p. (C). (gr. 13). 1994. text ed. 74.95 (*0-415-07731-1*) Routledge.

Roman Jakobson: What He Taught Us. Ed. by Morris Halle. 94p. (Orig.). 1983. pap. 9.95 (*0-89357-118-0*) Slavica.

Roman Jakobson & Beyond: Language as a System of Signs - The Quest for the Ultimate Invariants in Language. Rodney B. Sangster. (Janua Linguarum, Series Major: No. 109). xiv, 207p. 1982. 53.85 (*90-279-3040-6*) Mouton.

Roman Jakobson Selected Writings, Vol. VIII. Ed. by Stephen Rudy. 685p. (C). 1988. lib. bdg. 242.35 (*0-89925-175-7*) Mouton.

Roman Jakobson's Approach to Language: Phenomenological Structuralism. Elmar Holenstein. LC 76-12368. 223p. reprint ed. pap. 63.60 (*0-317-27825-8*, 2056039) Bks Demand.

Roman Jakobson's Science of Language. Linda R. Waugh. 115p. 1976. pap. 22.00 (*90-316-0112-8*, Pub. by Gruner NE) Benjamins North Am.

Roman Lancaster: Rescue Archaeology in an Historic City 1970-75. David Shotter. (Illus.). 246p. 1993. pap. text ed. 33.00 (*0-907740-10-3*, Pub. by Sutton Pubng UK) Bks Intl VA.

Roman Land Surveyors: An Introduction to the Agrimensores. O. A. Dilke. (Illus.). 260p. 1993. pap. 60.00 (*90-256-1000-5*, Pub. by A M Hakkert NE) Benjamins North Am.

Roman Laughter: The Comedy of Plautus. 2nd ed. Erich Segal. 272p. 1987. pap. 18.95 (*0-19-504166-6*) OUP.

Roman Laughter: The Comedy of Plautus. Erich Segal. LC 68-25618. (Harvard Studies in Comparative Literature: No. 29). 239p. reprint ed. pap. 68.20 (*0-7837-3849-8*, 2043671) Bks Demand.

Roman Law: An Historical Introduction. Hans J. Wolff. 1976. reprint ed. pap. 18.95 (*0-8061-1296-4*) U of Okla Pr.

Roman Law: Origins & Influence. D. G. Crackenell & C. H. Wilson. 200p. (C). 1990. pap. 60.00 (*1-85352-823-4*, Pub. by HLT Pubns UK) St Mut.

Roman Law & Common Law: A Comparison in Outline. W. W. Buckland & Arnold D. McNair. LC 93-79709. 376p. 1994. reprint ed. 85.00 (*1-56169-067-8*) Gaunt.

Roman Law & Comparative Law. Alan Watson. LC 90-36930. 344p. 1991. 50.00 (*0-8203-1260-6*); pap. 25.00 (*0-8203-1261-4*) U of Ga Pr.

Roman Law in a Nutshell: With a Selection of Questions Set at Bar Examinations. 2nd ed. Marston Garsia. LC 93-79692. 134p. 1994. reprint ed. 40.00 (*1-56169-050-3*, Pub. by Sweet & Maxwll UK) Gaunt.

Roman Law in Medieval Europe. Paul Vinogradoff. xvi, 155p. 1994. reprint ed. 45.00 (*1-56169-103-8*) Gaunt.

Roman Law in Modern Practice. James Mackintosh. xii, 202p. 1995. lib. bdg. 32.50 (*0-8377-2477-5*) Rothman.

Roman Law in the Modern World, 3 vols. Charles P. Sherman. 1312p. 1993. reprint ed. lib. bdg. 175.00 (*0-8377-1173-8*) Rothman.

Roman Law in the Modern World, 3 vols., Set. 2nd ed. Charles P. Sherman. 1994. 275.00 (*1-56169-097-X*) Gaunt.

***Roman Law in the Modern World, 3 vols., Set.** 2nd ed. Charles P. Sherman. 1994. reprint ed. 225.00 (*0-614-19462-8*) Gaunt.

***Roman Law in the Modern World, Vol. 1.** 2nd ed. Charles P. Sherman. 418p. 1994. reprint ed. write for info. (*0-614-19463-6*) Gaunt.

***Roman Law in the Modern World, Vol. 2.** 2nd ed. Charles P. Sherman. 498p. 1994. reprint ed. write for info. (*0-614-19464-4*) Gaunt.

***Roman Law in the Modern World, Vol. 3.** 2nd ed. Charles P. Sherman. x, 320p. 1994. reprint ed. write for info. (*0-614-19465-2*) Gaunt.

Roman Law of Damage to Property: A Commentary on the Title of the Digest Ad Legem Aquiliam IX.2 with an Introduction to the Study of the Corpus Iuris Civilis. Erwin Grueber. LC 93-79706. 318p. reprint ed. 75.00 (*1-56169-064-3*) Gaunt.

Roman Law of Sale: With Modern Illustrations Digest XVIII.1 & XIX.1 Translated with Notes & References to Cases & the Sale of Goods Act. 2nd enl. ed. James Mackintosh. LC 93-79722. (Illus.). 313p. 1994. reprint ed. 75.00 (*1-56169-080-5*) Gaunt.

Roman Law of Sale: With Notes & References to Cases & the Sale of Goods Bill. James Mackintosh. LC 93-79721. (Illus.). 292p. 1994. reprint ed. 70.00 (*1-56169-079-1*) Gaunt.

Roman Law of Slavery. William W. Buckland. LC 70-94318. (BCL Ser. I). reprint ed. 41.50 (*0-404-00140-8*) AMS Pr.

Roman Law of Slavery: The Condition of the Slave in Private Law from Augustus to Justinian. W. W. Buckland. xvi, 736p. 1994. reprint ed. 110.00 (*1-56169-098-8*) Gaunt.

Roman Law of Slavery: The Condition of the Slave in Private Law from Augustus to Justinian. William W. Buckland. 749p. reprint ed. pap. 180.00 (*0-317-26066-9*, 2024426) Bks Demand.

Roman Law of Testaments, Codicils & Gifts in the Event of Death (Mortis Causa Donationes) Mosees A. Dropsie. LC 96-26114. xii, 198p. 1996. reprint ed. lib. bdg. 37.50 (*0-8377-2042-7*) Rothman.

Roman Law Pleading: An Outline of Its Historical Growth & General Principles. Henry R. Danner. 63p. 1983. reprint ed. lib. bdg. 15.00 (*0-8377-0519-3*) Rothman.

Roman Law Tradition. Ed. by A. D. Lewis & D. J. Ibbetson. 248p. (C). 1994. text ed. 59.95 (*0-521-44199-4*) Cambridge U Pr.

Roman Laws & Charters. Ernest G. Hardy. LC 75-7320. (Roman History Ser.). 1975. reprint ed. 25.95 (*0-405-07084-5*) Ayer.

Roman Legions. H. M. Parker. 286p. 1980. reprint ed. pap. 20.00 (*0-89005-356-1*) Ares.

Roman Legions: Recreated in Colour Photographs. Daniel Peterson. (Europa Militaria Ser.: No. 2). (Illus.). 96p. 1992. pap. 19.95 (*1-872004-06-7*, Pub. by Windrow & Green UK) Motorbooks Intl.

Roman-Letter Swordguard Postmarks of Japan. Charles A. Swenson. LC 94-74119. (Illus.). 325p. (Orig.). 1995. lib. bdg. 60.00 (*1-886343-01-2*) C A L Swenson.

Roman-Letter Swordguard Postmarks of Japan. Charles A. Swenson. LC 94-74119. (Illus.). 325p. (Orig.). 1995. pap. 45.00 (*1-886343-00-4*) C A L Swenson.

Roman Letters: History from a Personal Point of View. Ed. by Finley Hooper & Matthew Schwartz. LC 90-12142. (Classical Studies: Pedagogy Ser.). (Illus.). 338p. (C). 1991. pap. text ed. 19.95 (*0-8143-2023-6*) Wayne St U Pr.

***Roman Life.** Mary Johnson. (J). 1976. write for info. (*0-688-05548-6*) Lothrop.

Roman Life & Manners under the Early Empire, 4 Vols., Set. Ludwig Friedlander. Ed. by Moses Finley. LC 79-4973. (Ancient Economic History Ser.). 1979. reprint ed. lib. bdg. 176.95 (*0-405-12359-0*) Ayer.

R

Roman Life & Manners under the Early Empire, 4 Vols., Vol. 1. Ludwig Friedlander. Ed. by Moses Finley. LC 79-4973. (Ancient Economic History Ser.). 1979. reprint ed. lib. bdg. 44.95 (0-405-12360-4) Ayer.

Roman Life & Manners under the Early Empire, 4 Vols., Vol. 2. Ludwig Friedlander. Ed. by Moses Finley. LC 79-4973. (Ancient Economic History Ser.). 1979. reprint ed. lib. bdg. 44.95 (0-405-12361-2) Ayer.

Roman Life & Manners under the Early Empire, 4 Vols., Vol. 3. Ludwig Friedlander. Ed. by Moses Finley. LC 79-4973. (Ancient Economic History Ser.). 1979. reprint ed. lib. bdg. 44.95 (0-405-12486-4) Ayer.

Roman Life & Manners under the Early Empire, 4 Vols., Vol. 4. Ludwig Friedlander. Ed. by Moses Finley. LC 79-4973. (Ancient Economic History Ser.). 1979. reprint ed. lib. bdg. 44.95 (0-405-12487-2) Ayer.

Roman Life in the Days of Cicero. Alfred J. Church. LC 61-24994. (YA). (gr. 7-11). 1968. 28.00 (0-8196-0105-5) Biblo.

Roman Literary Culture: From Cicero to Apuleius. Elaine Fantham. LC 95-37599. (Ancient Society & History Ser.). 352p. (C). 1996. text ed. 39.95 (0-8018-5204-8) Johns Hopkins.

Roman Literature & Society. R. M. Ogilvie. 304p. 1980. mass mkt. 6.95 (0-14-022081-X, Penguin Bks) Viking Penguin.

Roman Marble Quarries in Southern Euboea & the Associated Road System. Doris Vanhove. 1995. 122.50 (90-04-10484-4) E J Brill.

Roman Marriage. Stephanie Howard. (Romance Ser.). 1993. pap. 2.89 (0-373-03247-1, 1-03247-3) Harlequin Bks.

Roman Marriage: Iusti Coniuges from the Time of Cicero to the Time of Ulpian. Susan M. Treggiari. 600p. 1993. reprint ed. pap. 32.00 (0-19-814939-5) OUP.

Roman Medallions. Jocelyn M. Toynbee. (Numismatic Studies: No. 5). (Illus.). 332p. reprint ed. pap. 94.70 (0-7837-6998-9, 2046811) Bks Demand.

Roman Middle Class in the Republican Period. Herbert Hill. LC 79-136867. 226p. 1974. reprint ed. text ed. 35.00 (0-8371-5303-4, HIRM, Greenwood Pr) Greenwood.

Roman Military Equipment. M. C. Bishop & J. C. Coulston. 1989. pap. 25.00 (0-7478-0005-7, Pub. by Shire UK) St Mut.

***Roman Military Equipment: Experiment & Reality.** Ed. by C. Van Driel-Murray. (Journal of Roman Military Equipment Studies: Vol. 6). (Illus.). 150p. 1997. pap. 40.00 (1-900188-24-4, Pub. by Oxbow Bks UK) David Brown.

Roman Military Tombstones. Alastair Scott Anderson. 1989. pap. 25.00 (0-85263-571-0, Pub. by Shire UK) St Mut.

Roman Mind at Work. Paul L. MacKendrick. LC 80-13022. (Anvil Ser.). 192p. 1980. reprint ed. pap. text ed. 9.50 (0-89874-200-5) Krieger.

Roman Mines in Europe. Oliver Davies. Ed. by Moses Finley. LC 79-4966. (Ancient Economic History Ser.). (Illus.). 1979. reprint ed. lib. bdg. 44.95 (0-405-12354-X) Ayer.

Roman Money. B. Kennett. (Illus.). 16p. 1975. pap. 2.00 (0-916710-18-1) Obol Intl.

***Roman Monody, Cantata & Opera from the Circles around Cardinal Montalto, 2 vols.** John W. Hill. (Illus.). 512p. 1997. 150.00 (0-19-816613-3) OUP.

Roman Mornings. James Lees-Milne. 148p. (Orig.). 1992. pap. 14.95 (1-56131-011-5) New Amsterdam Bks.

Roman Mossaics, or Studies in Rome & It's Neighbourhood. Hugh P. Macmillan. 1977. 18.95 (0-8369-7322-4, 8115) Ayer.

Roman Mother. Suzanne Dixon. LC 87-30027. (Illus.). 288p. 1988. 37.95 (0-8061-2125-4) U of Okla Pr.

Roman Myths. Jane F. Gardner. (Legendary Past Ser.). (Illus.). 80p. (Orig.). (C). 1994. pap. 9.95 (0-292-72768-2) U of Tex Pr.

Roman Nature: The Thought of Pliny the Elder. Mary Beagon. (Classical Monographs). 320p. 1992. 65.00 (0-19-814726-0) OUP.

Roman Near East: 31 B. C.-A. D. 337. Fergus G. Millar. (Illus.). 617p. 1995. pap. text ed. 19.95 (0-674-77886-3, MILROX) HUP.

Roman Near East, 31 B. C. - A. D. 337. Fergus Millar. LC 93-18174. 617p. 1993. 47.50 (0-674-77885-5) HUP.

Roman News. Andrew Langley & Philip De Souza. Ed. by Anton Powell & Philip Steele. LC 96-3584. (Illus.). 32p. (J). (gr. 4-9). 1996. 15.99 (0-7636-0055-5) Candlewick Pr.

Roman Nose: A History of the Park. M. C. Weber. 150p. 1993. pap. 11.95 (0-9637373-0-9) Oak Haven Bks.

Roman Novel. P. Walsh. (Classical Paperbacks Ser.). 286p. 1995. pap. 26.95 (1-85399-450-2, Pub. by Brstl Class Pr UK) Focus Pub-R Pullins.

Roman Numerals. David A. Adler. LC 77-2270. (Crowell Young Math Bk.). (Illus.). 40p. (J). (gr. 1-4). 1977. lib. bdg. 14.89 (0-690-01302-7, Crowell Jr Bks) HarpC Child Bks.

Roman Numerals I to MM: Numerabilia Romana Uno Ad Duo Mila. Arthur Geisert. LC 95-36247. (Illus.). 32p. (J). 1996. 15.95 (0-395-74519-5) HM.

Roman Oratorio 1770-1800: The Repertory at Santa Maria in Vallicella. Joyce L. Johnson. LC 86-6901. (Studies in Musicology: No. 91). 346p. reprint ed. pap. 98.70 (0-8357-1692-9, 2070606) Bks Demand.

Roman Origins of Our Calendar. Van L. Johnson. 80p. 5.00 (0-939507-11-0, B406) Amer Classical.

***Roman Ostia Revisited.** Ed. by Amanda Claridge & Anna Gallina-Zevi. (Illus.). 1996. 75.00 (0-614-21813-6, Pub. by British Schl Rome UK) David Brown.

Roman Painting. Roger Ling. (Illus.). 236p. (C). 1991. text ed. 95.00 (0-521-30614-0); pap. text ed. 34.95 (0-521-31595-6) Cambridge U Pr.

Roman Palace. Wood. (J). 13.95 (0-7136-3812-5, 93339, Pub. by A&C Black UK) Talman.

Roman Papers, Vol. III. Ronald Syme. Ed. by Anthony R. Birley. 704p. 1984. 95.00 (0-19-814839-9) OUP.

Roman Papers, Vol. IV. Ronald Syme. Ed. by Anthony R. Birley. 448p. 1988. 115.00 (0-19-814873-9) OUP.

Roman Papers, Vol. VI. Ronald Syme. Ed. by Anthony R. Birley. (Illus.). 488p. 1991. 125.00 (0-19-814494-6, 5953) OUP.

Roman People. Sarah Howarth. (People & Places Ser.). (Illus.). 48p. (J). (gr. 4-6). 1995. lib. bdg. 16.40 (1-56294-650-1) Millbrook Pr.

Roman People. Robert B. Kebric. LC 91-44297. 276p. (C). 1993. pap. text ed. 20.95 (0-87484-915-2, 915) Mayfield Pub.

Roman People. 2nd rev. ed. Robert B. Kebric. LC 96-18443. (Illus.). 312p. (C). 1996. pap. text ed. 20.95 (1-55934-644-2, 1644) Mayfield Pub.

Roman Perspective Painting. Alan Little. 1976. 6.50 (0-686-75219-8) Moretus Pr.

Roman Pines at Berkeley. Hugh O'Donnell. 51p. 9000. pap. 9.95 (0-948339-36-5, Pub. by Salmon Pubng IE) Dufour.

Roman Places. Sarah Howarth. LC 94-32663. (People & Places Ser.). 48p. (J). (gr. 4-6). 1995. lib. bdg. 16.40 (1-56294-651-X) Millbrook Pr.

Roman Plays: Julius Caesar, Antony & Cleopatra, Coriolanus see Narrative & Dramatic Sources of Shakespeare

Roman Poems: Bilingual Edition. Pier P. Pasolini. Tr. by Lawrence Ferlinghetti & Francesca Valente. (Pocket Poets Ser.: No. 41). (Illus.). 96p. (Orig.). (ENG & ITA.). 1986. pap. 7.95 (0-87286-187-2) City Lights.

Roman Poetry: From the Republic to the Silver Age. Tr. & Intro. by Dorothea Wender. LC 79-28219. 160p. (C). 1990. pap. 10.95 (0-8093-1694-3) S Ill U Pr.

Roman Poetry & Propaganda in the Age of Augustus. Ed. by A. Powell. 181p. 1992. 58.95 (1-85399-230-5, Pub. by Brstl Class Pr UK) Focus Pub-R Pullins.

***Roman Poets: Everymans's Library Pocket Poets.** Peter Washington. 1997. 12.50 (0-375-40071-0, Everymans Lib) Knopf.

Roman Poets of the Augustan Age: Horace & the Elegiac Poets. William Y. Sellar. xviii, 362p. 1892. reprint ed. pap. 24.00 (0-8196-0165-9) Biblo.

Roman Poets of the Augustan Age: Virgil (1908), Bk. 2. 3rd ed. William Y. Sellar. xiv, 423p. reprint ed. pap. 28.00 (0-8196-0162-4) Biblo.

Roman Poets of the Augustean Age, 2 vols. William Y. Sellar. xxxviii, 815p. (GER.). write for info. (0-318-70460-9); Vol. I: Virgil. write for info. (0-318-70461-7); Vol. II: Horace & the Elegiac Poets. write for info. (0-318-70462-5) G Olms Pubs.

Roman Poets of the Early Empire. Xenophon. Ed. by A. J. Boyle & J. P. Sullivan. 480p. 1992. pap. 10.95 (0-14-044544-7, Penguin Classics) Viking Penguin.

Roman Poets of the Republic. William Y. Sellar. LC 65-23490. 474p. 1990. reprint ed. pap. 24.00 (0-8196-0160-8) Biblo.

Roman Polanski. Virginia W. Wexman. (Filmmakers Ser.). 168p. 1985. 23.95 (0-8057-9296-1, Twayne) Scribnrs Ref.

Roman Policy in Epirus & Acarnania in the Age of the Roman Conquest of Greece. Stewart I. Oost. LC 75-7333. (Roman History Ser.). 1975. reprint ed. 12.95 (0-405-07050-0) Ayer.

Roman Political Ideas & Practice. Frank E. Adcock. (Jerome Lectures). 1964. pap. 12.95 (0-472-06088-0, 88, Ann Arbor Bks) U of Mich Pr.

Roman Political Life, 90 B.C. - A.D. 69. Ed. by Wiseman. 88p. 1985. pap. text ed. 11.95 (0-85989-225-5, Pub. by Univ Exeter Pr UK) Northwestern U Pr.

Roman Politics: 220-150 B.C. Howard H. Scullard. LC 81-13434. (Illus.). xvi, 325p. 1982. reprint ed. text ed. 55.00 (0-313-23296-2, SCRP, Greenwood Pr) Greenwood.

Roman Pompeii. Laurence. 176p. 1996. pap. text ed. 16.95 (0-415-13816-7) Routledge.

Roman Pompeii: Space & Society. Ray Laurence. LC 93-42553. (Illus.). 176p. (C). (gr. 13). 1994. 49.95 (0-415-09502-6, B4672, Routledge NY) Routledge.

***Roman Pompeii: Space & Society.** Ray Laurence. 176p. (C). 1996. pap. 16.95 (0-415-14103-6) Routledge.

Roman Port & Fishery of Cosa: A Center of Ancient Trade. Anna M. McCann et al. LC 85-42693. (Illus.). 750p. 1985. text ed. 195.00 (0-691-03581-4) Princeton U Pr.

Roman Portrait Sculpture (217-260 A. D.). The Transformation of an Artistic Tradition. B. Wood. (Columbia Studies in the Classical Tradition: No. 12). (Illus.). xiv, 150p. 1986. 58.50 (90-04-07282-9) E J Brill.

***Roman Portraits.** Moses S. Slaughter. 128p. Date not set. 15.95 (0-8369-1212-8) Ayer.

Roman Portraits: Illustrium Imagines, 1517. Andrea Fulvio. (Printed Sources of Western Art Ser.). (Illus.). 236p. (LAT.). 1981. reprint ed. boxed 45.00 (0-915346-57-5) A Wofsy Fine Arts.

Roman Portraits in Context. Maxwell L. Anderson & Leila Nista. (Illus.). 96p. 1995. pap. text ed. 24.95 (88-7813-138-5) U of Pa Pr.

Roman Portraiture: Images of Character & Virtue in the Late Republic & Early Principate. Intro. by John Pollini. (Illus.). 44p. (Orig.). (C). 1990. pap. 15.00 (0-945192-04-5) USC Fisher Gallery.

Roman Portugal, 3 vols. De Alarcao. 1992. 250.00 (0-85668-290-X, Pub. by Aris & Phillips UK); pap. 125.00 (0-85668-393-0, Pub. by Aris & Phillips UK) David Brown.

Roman Portugal, Vol. 1: Introduction. De Alarcao. 1982. 49.95 (0-85668-444-9, Pub. by Aris & Phillips UK); pap. 49.95 (0-85668-289-6, Pub. by Aris & Phillips UK) David Brown.

Roman Portugal, Vol. 2: Fas 1 Gazetteer Porto Braganca & Viseu. De Alarcao. 1987. pap. 35.00 (0-85668-390-6, Pub. by Aris & Phillips UK) David Brown.

Roman Portugal, Vol. 2: Fas 2 Gazetteer Coimbra & Lisboa. De Alarcao. 1987. pap. 35.00 (0-85668-391-4, Pub. by Aris & Phillips UK) David Brown.

Roman Portugal, Vol. 2: Fas 3 Gazetteer Evora Faro & Lagos. De Alarcao. 1987. pap. 35.00 (0-85668-392-2, Pub. by Aris & Phillips UK) David Brown.

***Roman Potters' Kilns of Colchester.** M. R. Hull. (Illus.). 324p. 1963. 25.00 (0-85431-199-8, Pub. by Soc Antiquaries UK) David Brown.

Roman Pottery. Kevin Greene. 1992. pap. 11.00 (0-520-08031-9) U CA Pr.

Roman Pottery in the Royal Ontario Museum: A Cagalogue. John W. Hayes. 1994. 30.00 (0-88854-172-4, Pub. by Royal Ont Mus CN) U of Toronto Pr.

Roman Pottery of Kent. R. J. Pollard. (Illus.). 296p. 1993. text ed. 66.00 (0-906746-12-4, Pub. by Sutton Pubng UK) Bks Intl VA.

Roman Private Law: Founded on the 'Institutes' of Gaius & Justinian. R. W. Leage. LC 93-79711. 450p. 1994. reprint ed. 95.00 (1-56169-069-4, Pub. by Juta SA) Gaunt.

Roman Private Law: Founded on the Institutes' of Gaius & Justinian. 2nd ed. C. H. Ziegler & R. W. Leage. LC 93-79712. 476p. 1994. reprint ed. 105.00 (1-56169-070-8) Gaunt.

Roman Private Law in the Times of Cicero & of the Antonines, 2 vols. Henry J. Roby. 1977. lib. bdg. 195.00 (0-8490-2533-8) Gordon Pr.

Roman Provincial Administration. W. T. Arnold. 298p. 1974. pap. 20.00 (0-89005-027-9) Ares.

Roman Provincial Administration. J. Richardson. (Inside the Ancient World Ser.). 88p. 1984. reprint ed. 13.95 (0-86292-128-7, Pub. by Brstl Class Pr UK) Focus Pub-R Pullins.

Roman Provincial Capital & Its Hinterland: The Survey of the Territory of Tarragona, Spain, 1985-1990. J. M. Carrete et al. (JRA Supplementary Ser.: No. 15). (Illus.). 312p. 1995. 89.50 (1-887829-15-6) Jour Roman Arch.

Roman Public Buildings. Ed. by Barton. 190p. 1989. pap. text ed. 19.95 (0-85989-239-5, Pub. by Univ Exeter Pr UK) Northwestern U Pr.

Roman Quarry & Other Sequences. David Jones. LC 81-52307. 283p. 1981. pap. 14.95 (0-935296-24-7) Sheep Meadow.

Roman Question. Noel Blakiston. LC 79-91770. 360p. 1980. 40.00 (0-89453-150-6) Scholarly Res Inc.

Roman Questions of Plutarch. Plutarch. Ed. by Herbert J. Rose. LC 75-14267. (Ancient Religion & Mythology Ser.). 1976. reprint ed. 19.95 (0-405-07272-4) Ayer.

***Roman Reader, Vol. 1.** Atchity. 1996. pap. 16.95 (0-8050-3949-X) St Martin.

Roman Realities. Finley Hooper. LC 78-15237. (Illus.). 584p. (C). 1978. pap. 17.95 (0-8143-1594-1) Wayne St U Pr.

Roman Reformer & Inventor. E. M. Thompson. 1996. pap. 25.00 (0-89005-559-9) Ares.

Roman Reformer & Inventor: Being a New Text of the Treatise De rebus bellicis. E. A. Thompson. Ed. by Moses Finley. LC 79-5008. (Ancient Economic History Ser.). (Illus.). 1979. reprint ed. lib. bdg. 17.95 (0-405-12396-5) Ayer.

Roman Regionaliste aux Etats-Unis, 1913-1940. Harry Bernard. (BCL1-PS American Literature Ser.). 387p. 1993. reprint ed. lib. bdg. 89.00 (0-7812-6589-4) Rprt Serv.

Roman Religion. Michael Massey. Ed. by Peter Hodge. (Aspects of Roman Life Ser.). 48p. (Orig.). (gr. 7-12). 1979. pap. text ed. 9.00 (0-582-21573-0, 70846) Longman.

Roman Religion & Roman Empire: Five Essays. Robert E. Palmer. LC 73-89289. (Haney Foundation Ser.: No. 15). 303p. reprint ed. 86.40 (0-685-07759-4, 2055281) Bks Demand.

***Roman Remains: John Izard Middleton's Visual Souvenirs of 1820-1823, with Addition Views in Italy, France, & Switzerland.** Ed. by Charles R. Mack & Lynn Robertson. LC 97-4726. (Illus.). 175p. 1997. 39.95 (1-57003-169-X) U of SC Pr.

Roman Remains of Southern France. Bromwich. 272p. 1996. pap. 18.95 (0-415-13817-5) Routledge.

Roman Remains of Southern France: A Guide Book. James Bromwich. LC 92-14820. (Illus.). 208p. (C). (gr. 13). 1993. text ed. 69.95 (0-415-00837-9, A7934) Routledge.

***Roman Remains of Southern France: Guide Book.** James Bromwich. (Illus.). 368p. (C). 1996. pap. 18.95 (0-415-14358-6, Routledge NY) Routledge.

Roman Replies & CLSA Advisory Opinions, 1990. Ed. by William A. Schumacher & Lynn Jarrell. 130p. (Orig.). 1990. pap. 6.25 (0-943616-47-6) Canon Law Soc.

Roman Replies & CLSA Advisory Opinions, 1991. Ed. by Lynn Jarrell & Kevin W. Vann. 130p. (Orig.). 1991. pap. 7.50 (0-943616-51-4) Canon Law Soc.

Roman Replies & CLSA Advisory Opinions, 1992. Ed. by Kevin W. Vann & Lynn Jarrell. 145p. (Orig.). 1992. pap. 7.50 (0-943616-58-1) Canon Law Soc.

Roman Replies & CLSA Advisory Opinions, 1993. Ed. by Kevin W. Vann & James I. Donlon. 89p. (Orig.). 1993. pap. 5.00 (0-943616-62-X) Canon Law Soc.

Roman Replies & CLSA Advisory Opinions 1994. Ed. by Kevin W. Vann & James I. Donlon. 162p. 1994. pap. 8.00 (0-943616-64-6) Canon Law Soc.

Roman Replies & CLSA Advisory Opinions, 1995. Ed. by Kevin W. Vann & James I. Donlon. 112p. 1995. pap. 5.50 (0-943616-69-7) Canon Law Soc.

***Roman Replies & CLSA Advisory Opinions 1996.** Ed. by Kevin W. Vann & James I. Donlon. 126p. (Orig.). 1996. pap. text ed. 12.00 (0-943616-75-1) Canon Law Soc.

Roman Republic. Don Nardo. LC 93-6905. (World History Ser.). 100p. (J). (gr. 6-9). 1994. lib. bdg. 17.96 (1-56006-230-4) Lucent Bks.

Roman Republic. 2nd ed. Michael Crawford. LC 93-1102. 252p. 1993. pap. 13.95 (0-674-77927-4) HUP.

Roman Republic, 3 vols. William E. Heitland. LC 69-13930. 1970. reprint ed. text ed. 145.00 (0-8371-2077-2, HERO, Greenwood Pr) Greenwood.

Roman Republic, 3 vols., 3. William E. Heitland. 1970. reprint ed. lib. bdg. 22.70 (0-685-02008-8, HERC, Greenwood Pr) Greenwood.

Roman Republic, 3 vols., Vol. 2. William E. Heitland. LC 69-13930. 1970. reprint ed. text ed. 65.00 (0-8371-2078-0, HERB, Greenwood Pr) Greenwood.

Roman Republic, Vol. 3. William E. Heitland. LC 69-13930. 1970. text ed. 65.00 (0-8371-2079-9, Greenwood Pr) Greenwood.

Roman Republic & the Principate of Augustus. Naphtali Lewis & Meyer Reinhold. (Roman Civilization Ser.: Vol. 1). (Illus.). 696p. 1990. text ed. 75.00 (0-231-07130-2); pap. text ed. 25.00 (0-231-07131-0) Col U Pr.

Roman Republican Coinage. Michael Crawford. LC 77-164450. (Illus.). 750p. 1975. text ed. 300.00 (0-521-07492-4) Cambridge U Pr.

Roman Revolution. Ronald Syme. (Oxford Paperbacks Ser.). 580p. 1960. pap. 19.95 (0-19-881001-6) OUP.

Roman Rhetoric: Revolution & the Greek Influence. Richard Enos. (Illus.). 132p. (Orig.). (C). 1995. pap. text ed. 10.95 (0-88133-830-3) Waveland Pr.

Roman Rhetorical Schools As Preparation for the Courts Under the Early Empire. Edilbert P. Parks. LC 78-64198. (Johns Hopkins University. Studies in the Social Sciences. Thirtieth Ser. 1912: 2). reprint ed. 32.50 (0-404-61304-7) AMS Pr.

Roman Rite in Orthodoxy, Part I: Additional Testimonies, Pt. II. Chrysostomos H. Stratman & Apostolos Makrakis. 62p. 1957. pap. 3.95 (0-938366-38-6) Orthodox Chr.

Roman Road. Gwendoline Keats. LC 71-157782. (Short Story Index Reprint Ser.). 1977. reprint ed. 19.95 (0-8369-3894-1) Ayer.

Roman Roi. Albert Camus. (FRE.). 1985. pap. 19.95 (0-7859-2699-2) Fr & Eur.

Roman Rule in Asia Minor to the End of the Third Century After Christ, 2 Vols. David Magie. LC 75-7328. (Roman History Ser.). 1975. reprint ed. 121.95 (0-405-07098-5) Ayer.

Roman Rule in Asia Minor to the End of the Third Century After Christ, 2 Vols., Vol. 1. David Magie. LC 75-7328. (Roman History Ser.). 1975. reprint ed. 60.95 (0-405-07099-3) Ayer.

Roman Rule in Asia Minor to the End of the Third Century After Christ, 2 Vols., Vol. 2. David Magie. LC 75-7328. (Roman History Ser.). 1975. reprint ed. 60.95 (0-405-07100-0) Ayer.

Roman Rulers & Rebels. P. Gordon & B. Stillman. 1972. 11.64 (0-88334-048-8, 76058) Longman.

Roman Sarcophagi in The Metropolitan Museum of Art. Anna M. McCann. LC 77-28089. (Illus.). 152p. 1978. 25.00 (0-87099-173-6) Metro Mus Art.

Roman Satire. 2nd ed. M. Coffey. (Bristol Classical Paperbacks Ser.). 312p. 1989. pap. 26.95 (1-85399-046-9, Pub. by Brstl Class Pr UK) Focus Pub-R Pullins.

***Roman Satirists & Their Masks.** S. Braund. (BCP Classical World Ser.). 96p. (Orig.). 1996. pap. text ed. 14.95 (1-85399-139-2, Pub. by Brstl Class Pr UK) Focus Pub-R Pullins.

***Roman Satirists in Seventeenth-Century England.** William Kupersmith. LC 85-1103. 205p. 1985. reprint ed. pap. 58.50 (0-608-02675-1, 2063328) Bks Demand.

Roman Science: Origins, Development, & Influence to the Later Middle Ages. William H. Stahl. LC 78-5597. 308p. 1978. reprint ed. text ed. 75.00 (0-313-20473-X, STRO, Greenwood Pr) Greenwood.

Roman Sculpture. Diana E. Kleiner. (Publications in the History of Art). (Illus.). 496p. (C). 1992. text ed. 65.00 (0-300-04631-6) Yale U Pr.

Roman Sculpture. Diana E. Kleiner. (Illus.). 489p. 1994. pap. 32.50 (0-300-05948-5) Yale U Pr.

Roman Sculpture from Augustus to Constantine. Eugenie Strong. LC 76-116362. (Illus.). 1971. lib. bdg. 30.00 (0-87817-053-7) Hacker.

Roman Sculpture from Augustus to Constantine. Eugene S. Strong. LC 79-88825. (Art Histories Collection). 1979. reprint ed. 36.95 (0-405-02230-1) Ayer.

***Roman Sexualities.** Judith P. Hallett. 1997. pap. text ed. 19.95 (0-691-01178-8) Princeton U Pr.

***Roman Sexualities.** Judith P. Hallett & Marilyn B. Skinner. LC 97-12684. 1998. write for info. (0-691-01179-6) Princeton U Pr.

***Roman Shakespeare: Warriors, Wounds & Women.** Coppelia Kahn. LC 96-31834. (Feminist Readings of Shakespeare Ser.). 224p. (C). 1997. pap. write for info. (0-415-05451-6); text ed. write for info. (0-415-05450-8) Routledge.

Roman Silver Coins. Incl. Vol. I. Republic. lib. bdg. 35.00 (0-686-45272-0); Vol. II. Tiberius to Commodus. lib. bdg. 35.00 (0-686-45273-9); write for info. (0-318-57013-0, Pub. by Seaby UK) S J Durst.

Roman Singer. Francis M. Crawford. (Works of Francis Marion Crawford Ser.). 1990. reprint ed. lib. bdg. 79.00 (0-7812-2543-4) Rprt Serv.

***Roman Slave Law.** Alan Watson. LC 86-21351. 183p. 1987. reprint ed. pap. 52.20 (0-608-03665-X, 2064491) Bks Demand.

***Roman Small Towns in Eastern England & Beyond.** Ed. by A. E. Brown. (Oxbow Monographs in Archaeology: No. 52). (Illus.). 208p. 1995. pap. 48.00 (0-946897-90-5, Pub. by Oxbow Bks UK) David Brown.

An Asterisk (*) at the beginning of an entry indicates that the title is appearing in BIP for the first time.

Roman Social Habitat: Studies of Housing at Pompeii & Herculaneum. Andrew Wallace-Hadrill. LC 93-17828. 272p. 1994. text ed. 59.50 (*0-691-06987-5*) Princeton U Pr.

Roman Social Relations, 50 B. C to A. D. 284. Ramsay MacMullen. LC 73-86909. 317p. 1981. pap. 14.00 (*0-300-02702-8*, Y-392) Yale U Pr.

Roman Society. D. Taylor. (Inside the Ancient World Ser.). pap. 14.95 (*0-17-438503-X*) Focus Pub-R Pullins.

Roman Society: A Social, Economic, & Cultural History. 2nd ed. Henry C. Boren. (Civilization & Society Ser.). 338p. (C). 1992. pap. text ed. 24.76 (*0-669-17801-2*) HM College Div.

Roman Society & Roman Law in the New Testament. A. N. Sherwin-White. 224p. 1992. reprint ed. pap. 14.99 (*0-8010-8148-3*) Baker Bks.

Roman Society from Nero to Marcus Aurelius. S. Dill. 1973. 300.00 (*0-87968-059-8*) Gordon Pr.

Roman Society in the Last Century of Western Empire. S. Dill. 1973. 300.00 (*0-87968-060-1*) Gordon Pr.

Roman Soldier. Giovanni Caselli. LC 86-4366. (Everyday Life of Ser.). (Illus.). 32p. (J). (gr. 3-6). 1991. lib. bdg. 12.95 (*0-87226-106-9*) P Bedrick Bks.

Roman Soldier. G. R. Watson. LC 69-11153. (Aspects of Greek & Roman Life Ser.). (Illus.). 256p. (C). 1985. pap. 15.95 (*0-8014-9312-9*) Cornell U Pr.

***Roman Soldiers Don't Wear Watches: 501 Film Flubs-Memorable Movie Mistakes.** Bill Givens. LC 96-46056. 1996. pap. text ed. 9.95 (*0-8065-1829-4*, Citadel Pr) Carol Pub Group.

Roman Sonnets. G. G. Belli. Tr. by Harold Norse. LC 60-9955. 1960. pap. 10.00 (*0-912330-72-4*) Jargon Soc.

Roman Sources of Christian Art. Emerson H. Swift. LC 73-100181. (Illus.). 248p. 1970. reprint ed. 38.50 (*0-8371-3430-7*, SWCA, Greenwood Pr) Greenwood.

Roman Spain. S. J. Keay. (Exploring the Roman World Ser.: Vol. 2). (Illus.). 240p. 1988. 40.00 (*0-520-06380-5*) U CA Pr.

Roman Spain: Conquest & Assimilation. Leonard A. Curchin. (Illus.). 240p. 1991. 49.95 (*0-415-06451-1*, A6147) Routledge.

Roman Spain: Conquest & Assimilation. Leonard A. Curchin. (Illus.). 260p. (C). 1991. text ed. 59.95 (*0-415-02365-3*, Routledge NY) Routledge.

Roman Sport & Entertainment. David A. Buchanan. Ed. by Peter Hodge. (Aspects of Roman Life Ser.). (Illus.). 64p. (Orig.). (gr. 7-12). 1976. pap. text ed. 9.00 (*0-582-31415-1*, 71975) Longman.

Roman Spring. Sandra Marton. 1994. mass mkt. 2.99 (*0-373-11660-8*, 1-11660-7) Harlequin Bks.

Roman Spring of Mrs. Stone. Tennessee Williams. 1994. reprint ed. lib. bdg. 27.95 (*1-56849-360-6*) Buccaneer Bks.

Roman Spring of Mrs. Stone. Tennessee Williams. LC 50-9067. (Bibelot Ser.). 128p. 1993. reprint ed. pap. 6.00 (*0-8112-1249-1*, NDP770) New Directions.

Roman Stoicism. Edward V. Arnold. LC 76-169750. (Select Bibliographies Reprint Ser.). 1977. reprint ed. 39.95 (*0-8369-5970-1*) Ayer.

Roman Stoicism. Edward V. Arnold. LC 76-169750. 468p. reprint ed. 26.50 (*0-8290-0494-7*) Irvington.

Roman Stopa: Die Schnalze Ihre Natur Entwicklung und Ursprung. (Bibliotheca Nostratica Ser.: Vol. 7). 213p. 1986. 26.00 (*0-931922-25-9*) Eurolingua.

Roman System of Provincial Administration: To the Accession of Constantine the Great. 3rd ed. William T. Arnold. Ed. by E. S. Bouchier. LC 79-179501. (Select Bibliographies Reprint Ser.). 1977. reprint ed. 34.95 (*0-8369-6630-9*) Ayer.

Roman System of Provincial Administration to the Accession of Constantine the Great. William T. Arnold. 288p. reprint ed. lib. bdg. 59.00 (*0-7812-0730-4*) Rprt Serv.

***Roman Temple at Wanborough.** Ed. by M. G. O'Connell & Joanna Bird. (Surrey Archaeological Collections: Vol. 82, 1994). 235p. 1994. pap. 27.00 incl. mic. form (*0-946897-82-4*, Pub. by Oxbow Bks UK) David Brown.

Roman Theater & Society: E. Togo Salmon Papers, Vol. I. Ed. by William J. Slater. LC 96-10300. (C). 1995. 42.50 (*0-472-10721-6*) U of Mich Pr.

Roman Theatre & Its Audience. Richard C. Beacham. (Illus.). 276p. (C). 1992. 35.00 (*0-674-77913-4*) HUP.

Roman Theatre & its Audience. Richard C. Beacham. (Illus.). 288p. 1996. pap. 16.95 (*0-674-77914-2*) HUP.

Roman Times. Jan Chisholm. (First History Ser.). (Illus.). 24p. (J). (gr. 3-6). 1982. pap. 4.50 (*0-86020-619-X*); lib. bdg. 12.95 (*0-88110-105-2*) EDC.

***Roman Town.** Hazel Martell. (Metropolis). (Illus.). (J). 1998. write for info. (*0-531-14467-4*) Watts.

Roman Towns. Peter Hodge. (Aspects of Roman Life Ser.). (Illus.). 48p. (Orig.). (gr. 7-12). 1977. pap. text ed. 9.00 (*0-582-20301-5*, 70710) Longman.

Roman Transliteration of Part 29 of the Holy Qur'an (Arabic Text, Translation & Transliteration) Abdullah Y. Ali. Ed. & Intro. by Ali R. Abuza'kuk. 128p. (Orig.). 1996. pap. text ed. 3.00 (*1-881963-57-8*) Al-Saadawi Pubns.

Roman Transliteration of the Holy Quran. Abdullah Yusuf Ali. 800p. (C). 1991. text ed. 19.95 (*1-56744-371-0*) Kazi Pubns.

***Roman Transliteration of the 28th Part of the Qur An: With Arabic Text.** Abdullah Yusuf Ali & Ali R. Abuza'Kuk. LC 96-40482. 1997. write for info. (*1-881963-61-6*) Al-Saadawi Pubns.

***Roman Transliteration of the 30th Part of the Holy Qur'an: Arabic Text, Translation & Transliteration.** Abdullah Y. Ali. Ed. by Ali R. Abuza'kuk. 128p. (Orig.). 1996. pap. text ed. 2.50 (*1-881963-56-X*) Al-Saadawi Pubns.

Roman Tree. Wayne S. Griffin. LC 92-72489. 1995. 14.95 (*0-8158-0487-3*) Chris Mass.

***Roman Urbanism: Beyond the Consumer City.** Ed. by Helen Parkins. 272p. (C). 1997. text ed. 65.00 (*0-415-11771-2*) Routledge.

Roman Villa: Inside Story. Jacqueline Morley & John James. LC 92-15279. (Illus.). 48p. (J). (gr. 5 up). 1992. lib. bdg. 18.95 (*0-87226-360-6*) P Bedrick Bks.

Roman Villa at Lullingstone, Kent: The Site, Vol. 1. G. W. Meates. (Illus.). 222p. 1993. text ed. 40.00 (*0-85033-341-5*, Pub. by Sutton Pubng UK) Bks Intl VA.

Roman Villa at Lullingstone, Kent: The Wall Paintings & Finds, Vol. 2. G. W. Meates. (Illus.). 368p. 1993. text ed. 86.00 (*0-906746-09-4*, Pub. by Sutton Pubng UK) Bks Intl VA.

***Roman Villas: A Study in Social Structure.** J. T. Smith. LC 97-248. 464p. (C). 1997. text ed. write for info. (*0-415-16719-1*) Routledge.

Roman Voting Assemblies: From the Hannibalic War to the Dictatorship of Caesar. Lily R. Taylor. 200p. 1990. pap. 17.95 (*0-472-08125-X*) U of Mich Pr.

***Roman War Machine.** John Peddie. (Medieval Military Library). (Illus.). 169p. Date not set. pap. 16.95 (*0-938289-85-3*, Combined Bks) Combined Pub.

Roman Water Law. Translated from the Pandects of Justinian. Eugene F. Ware. 160p. 1985. reprint ed. lib. bdg. 22.50 (*0-8377-1336-6*) Rothman.

Roman Way. Edith Hamilton. 1994. lib. bdg. 21.95 (*1-56849-503-X*) Buccaneer Bks.

Roman Way. Edith Hamilton. LC 93-8329. 1993. pap. 8.95 (*0-393-31078-7*) Norton.

Roman West & the Byzantine East. Bishop Chrysostomos & Hieromonk Auxentios. 57p. (Orig.). 1988. pap. 5.00 (*0-911165-12-6*) Ctr Trad Orthodox.

Roman Women, Their History & Habits. John P. Balsdon. LC 75-8718. (Illus.). 351p. 1975. reprint ed. text ed. 59.75 (*0-8371-8040-6*, BAROW, Greenwood Pr) Greenwood.

Roman World, 2 vols. Ed. by John Wacher. LC 85-24476. 872p. 1987. 225.00 (*0-7100-9975-4*, RKP) Routledge.

Roman World. Victor Chapot. 444p. reprint ed. 25.00 (*0-8196-0367-8*) Biblo.

Roman World: From Republic to Empire. Peter Mantin & Richard Pulley. (Cambridge History Programme Ser.). (Illus.). 80p. (YA). (gr. 6 up). 1993. pap. text ed. 12.95 (*0-521-40608-0*) Cambridge U Pr.

***Roman World Foundation Course: Pompey & Caesar.** 72p. 1986. pap. text ed. 11.95 (*0-521-28699-9*) Cambridge U Pr.

Roman World of Dio Chrysostom. C. P. Jones. LC 78-5869. (Loeb Classical Monographs). 216p. 1978. 34.50 (*0-674-77915-0*) HUP.

***Roman World 44BC 180AD.** Martin Goodman. (Routledge History of the Ancient World). (Illus.). 416p. (C). 1997. pap. 18.95 (*0-415-04970-9*); text ed. 65.00 (*0-415-04969-5*) Routledge.

Roman York from A.D. 71. Herman Ramm. (C). 1989. 45.00 (*1-85072-084-3*, Pub. by W Sessions UK) St Mut.

Roman York from AD 71: A Pictorial Guide with Map & Suggested Roman Walk. Herman Ramm. (C). 1990. 35.00 (*1-85072-001-0*, Pub. by W Sessions UK) St Mut.

***Romance.** Barbara L. Ascher. 320p. Date not set. 24.00 (*0-06-017442-0*) HarpC.

Romance. Rosetta Brooks et al. Ed. by Henry Barendse et al. LC 87-81971. 35p. (Orig.). 1987. 7.50 (*0-915427-07-9*) Spirit Sq Ctr.

***Romance.** Marion Chesney. 1998. mass mkt. write for info. (*0-449-28776-9*, Crest) Fawcett.

Romance. Joseph Conrad & Ford Madox Ford. 558p. 1985. pap. 8.95 (*0-88184-166-8*) Carroll & Graf.

Romance. Ed McBain. 352p. 1996. mass mkt. 6.50 (*0-446-60280-9*) Warner Bks.

Romance. Illus. by Norman Rockwell. 40p. 1993. 6.95 (*0-8362-4709-4*) Andrews & McMeel.

Romance. Ann Sansom. 80p. 9600. pap. 14.95 (*1-85224-285-X*, Pub. by Bloodaxe Bks UK) Dufour.

***Romance, Vol. 5.** Marion Chesney. LC 96-51553. (Daughters of Mannerling Ser.). 1997. 20.95 (*0-312-15202-7*) St Martin.

Romance: A Tradition Lost. rev. ed. Alexandra Allison. 90p. (Orig.). 1990. pap. 29.99 (*1-878235-01-X*) Taylor Pub MI.

Romance: Generic Transformation from Chretien de Troyes to Cervantes. Ed. by Kevin Brownlee & Marina S. Brownlee. LC 84-40581. 303p. 1985. reprint ed. pap. 86.40 (*0-608-02304-3*, 2062945) Bks Demand.

Romance al Divin Martir, Juda Creyente Don Lope de Vera y Alarcon Martirizado en Valladolid por la Inquisicion. Antonio E. Gomez. Ed. & Tr. by Timothy Oelman from SPA. LC 83-49348. (Illus.). 216p. 1986. 42.50 (*0-8386-3219-X*) Fairleigh Dickinson.

Romance & Capitalism at the Movies. Joan J. Hall. LC 84-72767. 1985. 15.95 (*0-914086-54-5*); pap. 9.95 (*0-914086-55-3*) Alicejamesbooks.

Romance & Folklore National Railroads. Bill Yenne. (Illus.). 160p. 1995. 14.98 (*0-8317-7746-X*) Smithmark.

Romance & History of California. Myrtle Garrison. 1992. reprint ed. lib. bdg. 75.00 (*0-7812-5036-6*) Rprt Serv.

Romance & Love Divination - Business & Financial Divination. D. A. Shanelec. (Illus.). 130p. 1987. 9.95 (*0-914833-02-2*) Kapala Corp.

Romance & Love Stories. LC 95-36154. 1995. write for info. (*0-8444-0893-X*) Lib Congress.

Romance & Psychological Realism in William Godwin's Novels. Dean T. Hughes. Ed. by Devendra P. Varma. LC 79-8459. (Gothic Studies & Dissertations). 1980. lib. bdg. 23.95 (*0-405-12673-5*) Ayer.

Romance & Realism: A Study in English Bourgeois Literature. Christopher Caudwell. Ed. by Samuel Hynes. LC 78-120752. 148p. 1970. reprint ed. pap. 42.20 (*0-7837-8578-X*, 2049393) Bks Demand.

***Romance & Realism in Modern France, Vol. 7.** Date not set. write for info. (*0-8369-4798-3*) Ayer.

Romance & Realism in Southern Politics. fac. ed. Thomas H. Williams. LC 61-9798. (Eugenia Dorothy Blount Lamar Memorial Lectures: Vol. 1960). 96p. 1960. reprint ed. pap. 27.40 (*0-7837-7759-0*, 2047515) Bks Demand.

Romance & Revolution: Shelley & the Politics of a Genre. David Duff. LC 93-34648. (Studies in Romanticism: No. 7). (Illus.). 272p. (C). 1994. text ed. 59.95 (*0-521-45018-7*) Cambridge U Pr.

Romance & Rise of the American Tropics. Samuel Crowther. Ed. by Stuart Bruchey & Eleanor Bruchey. LC 76-4999. (American Business Abroad Ser.). (Illus.). 1976. reprint ed. lib. bdg. 47.95 (*0-405-09268-7*) Ayer.

***Romance & Sexuality: Leader's Guide, 2.** Concordia Publishing House Staff. 1996. pap. 5.75 (*0-570-09637-5*) Concordia.

***Romance & Sexuality: Study Guide, 2.** Concordia Publishing House Staff. 1996. pap. 4.75 (*0-570-09636-7*) Concordia.

Romance & the Erotics of Property: Mass Market Fiction for Women. Jan Cohn. LC 87-27401. vii, 181p. (C). 1988. text ed. 35.95 (*0-8223-0799-5*) Duke.

Romance & the "Yellow Peril" Race, Sex, & Discursive Strategies in Hollywood Fiction. Gina Marchetti. LC 92-10878. 1993. 40.00 (*0-520-07974-4*); pap. 14.00 (*0-520-08495-0*) U CA Pr.

***Romance & Tragedy: A Study of Classic & Romantic Elements in the Great Tragedies of European Literature.** Prosser H. Frye. LC 61-10518. 386p. 1980. reprint ed. pap. 110.10 (*0-608-02735-9*, 2063400) Bks Demand.

Romance & Tragedy of Banking: Problems & Incidents of Government Supervision of National Banks. Thomas P. Kane & Vincent Corosso. Ed. by Stuart Bruchey. LC 80-1153. (Rise of Commercial Banking Ser.). (Illus.). 1981. reprint ed. lib. bdg. 55.95 (*0-405-13659-5*) Ayer.

Romance at Perristone. large type ed. Cora Mayne. 1990. 25.99 (*0-7089-2127-2*) Ulverscroft.

Romance at St. Elna. large type ed. Della Foster. (Linford Romance Library). 308p. 1984. pap. 15.99 (*0-7089-6040-5*) Ulverscroft.

***Romance Begins in the Kitchen: Romantic Italian Recipes & Their Complementary Wines.** Dawn Bause et al. LC 97-70185. (Illus.). 128p. 1997. pap. 12.95 (*0-9656889-0-9*) Bause Hse.

Romance Cycle of Charlemagne & His Peers. Jessie L. Weston. 1977. lib. bdg. 59.95 (*0-8490-2534-6*) Gordon Pr.

Romance Cycle of Charlemagne & His Peers. Jessie L. Weston. LC 77-139173. (Popular Studies in Mythology, Romance & Folklore: No. 10). reprint ed. 27.50 (*0-404-53510-0*) AMS Pr.

Romance de Carnaval. Maria J. Santiago. (Romance Real Ser.). 192p. 1981. pap. 1.50 (*0-88025-000-3*) Roca Pub.

Romance de la Guardia Civil Espanola (Ballad of the Spanish Civil Guard) Federico Garcia Lorca. Tr. by A. L. Lloyd. (Illus.). (ENG & SPA.). 1962. 50.00 (*0-317-61299-9*) Dufour.

Romance de los Mayores. Marina Easley. LC 91-77114. (Coleccion Hispanica - Literaria). 73p. (SPA.). 1992. pap. 9.95 (*0-89729-631-1*) Ediciones.

***Romance en el Matrimonio - Holding on to Romance.** Wright. 252p. (SPA.). 1994. write for info. (*1-56063-706-4*) Editorial Unilit.

Romance Epic: Essays on a Medieval Literary Genre. Ed. by Hans-Erich Keller. (Studies in Medieval Culture: No. 24). 1988. pap. 15.95 (*0-918720-86-9*); boxed 32.95 (*0-918720-85-0*) Medieval Inst.

***Romance Fiction: A Handbook for Readers, Writers, & Librarians.** Kristin Ramsdell. 350p. 1997. lib. bdg. 40.00 (*1-56308-335-3*) Libs Unl.

Romance for Shawnee. Laura E. Williams. 1994. 17.95 (*0-8034-9081-X*, 094511) Bouregy.

Romance, Gender, & Religion in a Vietnamese-American Community: Tales of God & Beautiful Women. Ed. by Jesse W. Nash & Elizabeth T. Nguyen. LC 94-16411. 192p. 1995. text ed. 79.95 (*0-7734-9087-6*) E Mellen.

***Romance God's Way.** Eric Ludy & Leslie Ludy. Ed. by Marlene Bagnull. (Illus.). 130p. (Orig.). 1997. pap. write for info. (*0-9656251-0-9*) Makarios.

Romance in America: Studies in Cooper, Poe, Hawthorne, Melville, & James. Joel Porte. LC 69-17795. 247p. reprint ed. pap. 70.40 (*0-685-23379-0*, 2032492) Bks Demand.

Romance in G Minor. Bess S. Aldrich. 25.95 (*0-8488-0066-4*) Amereon Ltd.

Romance in Glenmore Street. large type ed. Ivy Preston. (Romance Ser.). 1991. 25.99 (*0-7089-2467-0*) Ulverscroft.

***Romance in HPSG.** Ed. by Sergio Balari & Luca Dini. LC 96-50436. (Lecture Notes Ser.). 425p. (C). 1997. 69.95 (*1-57586-083-X*); pap. 27.95 (*1-57586-082-1*) CSLI.

Romance in Medieval England. Ed. by Maldwyn Mills et al. 236p. (C). 1991. 71.00 (*0-85991-326-0*) Boydell & Brewer.

Romance in Norway. large type ed. Cora Mayne. (Linford Romance Library). 255p. 1984. pap. 15.99 (*0-7089-6019-7*, Trailtree Bookshop) Ulverscroft.

Romance in the Making: Chretien de Troyes & the Earliest French. Foster E. Guyer. 1954. pap. 15.95 (*0-913298-35-2*) S F Vanni.

Romance in the Oil Fields of Texas. Ocee McRae. 182p. 1990. 6.95 (*0-911724-01-X*, 962) Lunan-Ferguson.

Romance, Inc. Jocelyn Raines. 1996. mass mkt. 5.99 (*0-671-89953-8*) PB.

Romance Is a Wonderful Thing. Ellen E. White. 192p. 1983. pap. 2.95 (*0-380-83907-5*, Flare) Avon.

Romance Jumble: Puzzles for Lovers. (Jumble Ser.). (Illus.). 192p. (Orig.). 1996. pap. 9.95 (*1-57243-146-6*) Triumph Bks.

***Romance Languages.** Ed. by Martin Harris & Nigel Vincent. (Language Family Descriptions Ser.). (Illus.). 512p. 1998. 100.00 (*0-415-16417-6*) Routledge.

Romance Languages. Rebecca Posner. (Cambridge Language Surveys Ser.). 400p. (C). 1996. text ed. 69.95 (*0-521-23654-1*) Cambridge U Pr.

Romance Languages. Rebecca Posner. (Cambridge Language Surveys Ser.). 400p. (C). 1996. pap. text ed. 24.95 (*0-521-28139-3*) Cambridge U Pr.

Romance Languages. Ed. by Martin Harris & Nigel Vincent. (Illus.). 512p. 1990. reprint ed. pap. 23.00 (*0-19-520829-3*) OUP.

Romance Languages: A Linguistic Introduction. Raphael Posner. 1990. 24.75 (*0-8446-0853-X*) Peter Smith.

Romance Languages & Modern Linguistic Theory: Selected Papers from the Twentieth Linguistic Symposium on Romance Languages, University of Ottawa, April 10-14, 1990. Ed. by Paul Hirschbuehler & Konrad Koerner. LC 92-25813. (Current Issues in Linguistic Theory Ser.: No. 91). viii, 416p. 1992. 100.00 (*1-55619-148-0*) Benjamins North Am.

Romance Linguistics: The Portuguese Context. Donaldo P. Macedo & Dale A. Koike. LC 92-19868. 216p. 1992. text ed. 45.00 (*0-89789-297-6*, H297, Bergin & Garvey) Greenwood.

Romance of a Great Singer: Memoir of Mario. Cecilia M. Pearse & Frank Hird. Ed. by Andrew Farkas. LC 76-29961. (Opera Biographies Ser.). (Illus.). 1977. reprint ed. lib. bdg. 28.95 (*0-405-09701-8*) Ayer.

Romance of a Lifetime. Carole Mortimer. (Presents Ser.: No. 468). 1992. pap. 2.89 (*0-373-11468-0*, 1-11468-5) Harlequin Bks.

Romance of Adventure: The Genre of Historical Adventure in the Movies. Brian Taves. LC 93-19458. (Studies in Popular Culture). (Illus.). 288p. 1993. 40.00 (*0-87805-597-5*); pap. 16.95 (*0-87805-598-3*) U Pr of Miss.

Romance of American Psychology: Political Culture in the Age of Experts. Ellen Herman. LC 94-26930. 1995. 35.00 (*0-520-08598-1*) U CA Pr.

Romance of American Psychology: Political Culture in the Age of Experts. Ellen Herman. (Illus.). 512p. 1996. pap. text ed. 16.95 (*0-520-20703-3*) U CA Pr.

Romance of an Eastern Capital. Birt Bradley. (Illus.). 360p. 1986. reprint ed. 26.00 (*0-8364-1751-8*, Pub. by Chanakya II) S Asia.

Romance of Arthur: An Anthology of Medieval Texts in Translation. expanded ed. James J. Wilhelm. LC 93-44265. 592p. 1994. text ed. 65.00 (*0-8153-0727-6*, H1267) Garland.

Romance of Arthur: An Anthology of Medieval Texts in Translation. expanded ed. James J. Wilhelm. LC 93-44265. (Reference Library of the Humanities: Vol. 1267). 592p. 1994. pap. text ed. 19.95 (*0-8153-1511-2*) Garland.

Romance of Arthur III: An Anthology. Ed. by James J. Wilhelm. LC 88-11027. (Illus.). 268p. 1988. pap. text ed. 16.95 (*0-8240-4107-0*) Garland.

Romance of Atlantis. Taylor Caldwell & Jess Stearn. 272p. 1980. pap. 2.95 (*0-449-23787-7*, Crest) Fawcett.

Romance of Atlantis. Taylor Caldwell. 1976. 22.95 (*0-8488-0443-0*) Amereon Ltd.

Romance of Balboa Park. 4th ed. Florence Christman. (Illus.). 136p. 1985. pap. 9.50 (*0-918740-03-7*) San Diego Hist.

Romance of Billy-Goat Hill. Alice H. Rice. 27.95 (*0-8488-1136-4*) Amereon Ltd.

Romance of Blonde of Oxford & Jehan of Dammartin. Philippe De Remi. Ed. by M. Le-Roux De Lincy. (Camden Society, London. Publications, First Ser.: No. 72). reprint ed. 55.00 (*0-404-50172-9*) AMS Pr.

Romance of Book Collecting. J. Slater. 1976. lib. bdg. 59.95 (*0-8490-2535-4*) Gordon Pr.

Romance of British Colonial Style. Tricia Foley. LC 92-30330. 1993. 35.00 (*0-517-58425-5*, C P Pubs) Crown Pub Group.

Romance of Caerbhall & Fearbhlaidh. James E. Doan. 1984. 17.95 (*0-685-20031-0*, Pub. by Colin Smythe Ltd UK) Dufour.

***Romance of California Vineyard.** Chappellet. Date not set. 19.95 (*0-7893-0114-8*) Universe.

Romance of Coin Collecting. Edward C. Rochette. (Illus.). 184p. (Orig.). 1991. pap. text ed. 12.95 (*0-943161-28-2*) Bowers & Merena.

Romance of Country Inns. Elizabeth Bond. 1996. 15.98 (*0-8317-7560-2*) Smithmark.

Romance of Country Inns: A Decorating Book for Your Home. Gail Greco. LC 93-11708. (Illus.). 288p. (YA). (gr. 10 up). 1993. 29.25 (*1-55853-175-0*) Rutledge Hill Pr.

Romance of Crime. Gareth Roberts. (Dr. Who Missing Adventures Ser.). (Illus.). 1995. mass mkt. 5.95 (*0-426-20435-2*, Pub. by Virgin Pub UK) London Brdge.

Romance of Davis Mountains & Big Bend Country. Carlysle G. Raht. 1993. reprint ed. lib. bdg. 75.00 (*0-7812-5896-0*) Rprt Serv.

***Romance of Desire: Emerson's Commitment to Incompletion.** Susan L. Field. LC 97-21640. 1997. write for info. (*0-8386-3738-8*) Fairleigh Dickinson.

Romance of Dollard. Mary Catherwood. LC 75-137725. (American Fiction Reprint Ser.). 1977. 20.95 (*0-8369-7024-1*) Ayer.

Romance of Dolls & Teddy Bears. Ho Phi Le. (Illus.). 176p. 1992. 39.95 (*0-87588-390-7*) Hobby Hse.

Romance of Double Wedding Ring Quilts. Robert Bishop. (Illus.). 80p. 1989. pap. 29.95 (*0-525-24753-X*, Dutton) NAL-Dutton.

Romance of Emare. Ed. by Edith Rickert. (EETS, ES Ser.: Vol. 99). 1974. reprint ed. 40.00 (*0-8115-3407-3*) Periodicals Srv.

An Asterisk (*) at the beginning of an entry indicates that the title is appearing in BIP for the first time.

R

***Romance of Engines.** Takashi Suzuki. LC 96-52945. 212p. 1997. 35.00 (*1-56091-911-6*, R-188) Soc Auto Engineers.

Romance of Flamenca. Ed. & Tr. by E. D. Blodgett from PRO. LC 95-12161. (Library of Medieval Literature: Vol. 101A). Orig. Title: Flamenca. (Illus.). 504p. 1995. text ed. 95.00 (*0-8240-5169-6*) Garland.

Romance of Forgotten Men. John T. Faris. LC 68-58787. (Essay Index Reprint Ser.). 1977. 26.95 (*0-8369-1033-8*) Ayer.

Romance of Forgotten Men. John T. Faris. 1993. reprint ed. lib. bdg. 89.00 (*0-7812-5450-7*) Rprt Serv.

Romance of God. Harold J. Green. 128p. 1994. pap. 9.95 (*0-9640962-1-8*) Ariel Pr IA.

Romance of Golden Star. George Griffith. Ed. by R. Reginald & Douglas Melville. LC 77-84234. (Lost Race & Adult Fantasy Ser.). (Illus.). 1978. reprint ed. lib. bdg. 26.95 (*0-405-10982-2*) Ayer.

Romance of Greeting Cards: An Historical Account of the Origin, Evolution, & Development. Ernest D. Chase. (Illus.). 1998. reprint ed. 54.00 (*1-55888-219-7*) Omnigraphics Inc.

Romance of Guy of Warwick the Second of 15th Century Version, Set, Vols. I & II. J. Zupitza. (EETS Extra Ser.: Vol. 25). 1966. reprint ed. 40.00 (*0-19-722568-3*, Pub. by EETS UK) Boydell & Brewer.

Romance of His Life, & Other Romances. Mary Cholmondeley. LC 70-37540. (Short Story Index Reprint Ser.). 1977. reprint ed. 19.95 (*0-8369-4099-7*) Ayer.

Romance of History. Herbert G. Smith. LC 72-5733. (Essay Index Reprint Ser.). 1977. reprint ed. 23.95 (*0-8369-7285-6*) Ayer.

***Romance of History: Essays in Honor of Lawrence S. Kaplan.** Ed. by Scott L. Bills & E. Timothy Smith. LC 96-27660. 1997. 35.00 (*0-87338-563-2*) Kent St U Pr.

Romance of Indian Life. Mary Eastman. LC 77-104445. (Illus.). 298p. reprint ed. lib. bdg. 29.00 (*0-8398-0451-2*) Irvington.

Romance of Indian Life. Mary Eastman. (Illus.). 298p. (C). 1986. reprint ed. pap. text ed. 8.95 (*0-8290-1927-8*) Irvington.

Romance of Jehan De Paris - Le Romant De Jehan De Paris. Tr. by Guy R. Mermier from FRO. LC 92-45566. (Studies in French Literature: Vol. 15). 120p. 1993. text ed. 59.95 (*0-7734-9225-9*) E Mellen.

***Romance of K'tut Tantri & Indonesia.** Timothy Lindsey. (Illus.). 312p. 1997. 60.00 (*983-56-0018-X*) OUP.

Romance of London's Underground. W. J. Passingham. LC 72-80705. (Illus.). 1972. reprint ed. 36.95 (*0-405-08839-6*) Ayer.

Romance of Lust. 537p. 1996. pap. 11.95 (*1-56201-003-4*, 116) Blue Moon Bks.

Romance of Lust. 432p. 1995. mass mkt. 5.95 (*0-7867-0231-1*) Carroll & Graf.

Romance of Merlin: An Anthology. Ed. by Peter Goodrich. LC 90-43703. 417p. 1990. pap. text ed. 20.95 (*0-8240-7042-9*) Garland.

Romance of Michigan's Past. Larry B. Massie. (Illus.). 272p. (Orig.). 1991. pap. 10.95 (*0-9626408-1-6*) Priscilla Pr.

Romance of Missionary Heroism, 1. John C. Lambert. 1979. pap. 4.99 (*0-88019-103-1*) Schmul Pub Co.

Romance of Missionary Heroism, 2. John C. Lambert. 1979. pap. 4.99 (*0-88019-104-X*) Schmul Pub Co.

Romance of My Life: Theodore Roosevelt's Speeches in Dakota. James R. Vivian. (Illus.). 272p. 1989. 19.95 (*0-911007-10-5*) Prairie Hse.

Romance of Names. Janet C. Hannah. 100p. (Orig.). 1991. 60.00 (*1-56216-004-4*); pap. 30.00 (*1-56216-005-2*) Systems Co.

Romance of Names. 2nd ed. Janet C. Hannah. (Illus.). 204p. (Orig.). 1993. 70.00 (*1-56216-211-X*); pap. 40.00 (*1-56216-212-8*) Systems Co.

Romance of Navigation. W. B. Whall. LC 72-83272. (Illus.). 1972. reprint ed. 24.95 (*0-405-09061-7*) Ayer.

Romance of Old Philadelphia. John T. Faris. 1993. reprint ed. lib. bdg. 89.00 (*0-7812-5451-5*) Rprt Serv.

Romance of Origins: Language & Sexual Difference in Middle English Literature. Gayle Margherita. LC 94-12610. 256p. (Orig.). (C). 1994. text ed. 36.95 (*0-8122-3217-8*); pap. text ed. 15.95 (*0-8122-1502-8*) U of Pa Pr.

***Romance of Patchwork Quilt.** Carrie A. Hall & Kretsinger. (Illus.). pap. 7.95 (*0-486-25792-4*) Dover.

Romance of Paula Vaughan. 1993. 19.95 (*0-942237-19-6*) Leisure AR.

Romance of Perfume. F. S. Clifford. 1977. lib. bdg. 250.00 (*0-8490-2536-2*) Gordon Pr.

Romance of Perlesvaus. Jessie L. Weston. Ed. by Janet Grayson. 188p. (C). 1988. pap. 30.00 (*0-85991-378-3*) Boydell & Brewer.

Romance of Perlesvaus. Jessie L. Weston. Ed. by Janet Grayson. 188p. (C). 1992. 50.00 (*0-85991-344-9*) Boydell & Brewer.

Romance of Preaching. James W. Angell. LC 95-13429. 1995. 6.95 (*0-7880-0574-X*) CSS OH.

Romance of Proctology. Charles E. Blanchard. LC 75-23684. reprint ed. 49.50 (*0-404-13297-5*) AMS Pr.

Romance of Publishing: An Agent Recalls Thirty-Three Years with Authors & Editors. Alex Jackinson. LC 85-41059. 232p. 1987. 16.95 (*0-8453-4797-7*, Cornwall Bks) Assoc Univ Prs.

Romance of Real Life: Charles Brockden Brown & the Origins of American Culture. Steven Watts. LC 93-11601. 1994. text ed. 35.95 (*0-8018-4686-2*) Johns Hopkins.

Romance of Reason: An Adventure in the Thought of Thomas Aquinas. Montague Brown. 177p. (Orig.). 1993. pap. 12.95 (*0-932506-96-8*) St Bedes Pubns.

Romance of Redemption. R. Edward Miller. 213p. (Orig.). (YA). (gr. 10). 1990. pap. 8.95 (*0-945818-09-2*) Peniel Pubns.

Romance of Redemption: Studies in the Book of Ruth. M. R. De Haan. 184p. 1996. pap. 9.99 (*0-8254-2480-1*) Kregel.

Romance of Reunion: Northerners & the South, 1865-1900. Nina Silber. LC 93-18626. (Civil War America Ser.). (Illus.). xiv, 258p. 1993. 37.50 (*0-8078-2116-0*) U of NC Pr.

***Romance of Reunion: Northerners & the South, 1865-1900.** Nina Silber. 272p. (C). 1997. pap. 14.95 (*0-8078-4685-6*) U of NC Pr.

Romance of Reynard the Fox. Ed. & Tr. by Roy Owen. (World's Classics Ser.). 304p. 1994. pap. 9.95 (*0-19-282801-0*) OUP.

Romance of Rice. Denton S. Harewood. LC 95-79907. (Illus.). 100p. (Orig.). 1996. pap. 24.95 (*0-934789-02-9*) Hands-On Pub Co.

***Romance of Risk: Why Teenagers Do the Things They Do.** Lynn E. Ponton. LC 97-12138. 1997. write for info. (*0-465-07075-2*) Basic.

Romance of Romans. Noah W. Hutchings. 470p. (Orig.). 1990. pap. 9.95 (*0-9624517-4-6*); pap. 9.95 (*0-9624517-3-8*) Hearthstone OK.

***Romance of Sex.** Block. 1997. pap. text ed. 12.95 (*0-13-644635-3*) P-H.

***Romance of Shells.** Louise Barnaby & Lyon. Date not set. write for info. (*0-688-05622-9*) Morrow.

Romance of Sir Degrevant. Ed. by L. F. Casson. (EETS Original Ser.: Vol. 221). 1970. reprint ed. 30.00 (*0-19-722221-8*, Pub. by EETS UK) Boydell & Brewer.

Romance of Sorcery. Sax Rohmer. 1976. reprint ed. lib. bdg. 24.95 (*0-89190-808-0*, Rivercity Pr) Amereon Ltd.

Romance of Steel: Story of a Thousand Millionaires. Herbert N. Casson. LC 72-179510. (Select Bibliographies Reprint Ser.). 1977. reprint ed. 41.95 (*0-8369-6639-2*) Ayer.

Romance of the American Living Room. Peter Plate. 192p. (Orig.). 1994. pap. 18.00 (*0-7486-6166-2*, Pub. by Polygon UK) Subterranean Co.

Romance of the American Theatre. Mary C. Crawford. LC 70-144957. 1971. reprint ed. 59.00 (*0-403-00909-X*) Scholarly.

Romance of the Bells: The California Missions in Art. Jean Stern et al. LC 95-76027. (Illus.). 128p. 1995. 35.00 (*0-9635468-5-6*); pap. 17.50 (*0-9635468-6-4*) Irvine Mus.

Romance of the Book. deluxe ed. Baldwin et al. Ed. by Marshall Brooks. LC 95-76146. 192p. (Orig.). 1995. 75.00 (*0-913559-32-6*) Birch Brook Pr.

Romance of the Book. limited ed. Baldwin et al. Ed. by Marshall Brooks. LC 95-76146. (Illus.). 200p. (Orig.). 1995. pap. 18.00 (*0-913559-28-8*) Birch Brook Pr.

Romance of the Castle. Raoul J. Fajardo. 156p. (Orig.). 1986. pap. 15.00 (*0-940774-02-X*) Pulsante Assn News.

Romance of the Chevelere Assigne. Beatrix Chanson Degeste. Ed. by Lord Aldenham. (EETS, ES Ser.: No. 6). 1974. reprint ed. pap. 30.00 (*0-527-00221-6*) Periodicals Srv.

Romance of the Chordal Guitar. Bucky Pizzarelli. 5.95 (*1-56222-946-X*, 95105); audio 9.98 (*1-56222-982-6*, 95105C) Mel Bay.

***Romance of the Chordal Guitar.** Bucky Pizzarelli. 14.95 incl. audio (*0-7866-1208-8*, 95105P) Mel Bay.

Romance of the Commonplace. Gelett Burgess. LC 68-57308. (Essay Index Reprint Ser.). 1977. 21.95 (*0-8369-0103-7*) Ayer.

Romance of the Desert. Silvana P. Batista. Ed. & Tr. by Manuel Araujo. LC 96-85047. (Illus.). viii, 154p. (Orig.). 1996. per., pap. 12.95 (*0-9651694-9-9*) Company of Words Pubng.

Romance of the English Stage, 2 vols. Percy H. Fitzgerald. LC 72-6956. (Essay Index Reprint Ser.). 1977. reprint ed. 39.95 (*0-8369-7256-2*) Ayer.

Romance of the Episcopal Church in West Tennessee. Ellen Davies-Rodgers. 1964. 12.00 (*0-685-84991-0*) Plantation.

Romance of the Floridas. Michael Kenny. LC 70-120573. (Illus.). reprint ed. 20.00 (*0-404-03656-2*) AMS Pr.

Romance of the Floridas: The Finding & the Founding. Michael Kenny. (Illus.). 1971. reprint ed. 13.00 (*0-403-00767-4*) Scholarly.

Romance of the Forest. Ann Radcliffe. Ed. & Intro. by Chloe Chard. (World's Classics Ser.). 427p. 1986. pap. 8.95 (*0-19-281712-4*) OUP.

***Romance of the Forest.** Ann Radcliffe. lib. bdg. 27.95 (*0-8488-2023-1*) Amereon Ltd.

Romance of the Forest: Interspersed with Some Pieces of Poetry, 3 Vols. Ann Radcliffe. LC 73-22770. 794p. 1979. reprint ed. 94.95 (*0-405-06020-3*) Ayer.

Romance of the Fungus World: An Account of Fungus Life in Its Numerous Guises, Both Real & Legendary. R. T. Rolfe & F. W. Rolfe. LC 74-81401. (Illus.). 352p. 1974. reprint ed. pap. 6.95 (*0-486-23105-4*) Dover.

Romance of the Harem. Anna Leonowens. (Victorian Literature & Culture Ser.). (Illus.). 368p. 1991. pap. 14.95 (*0-8139-1328-4*); text ed. 35.00 (*0-8139-1327-6*) U Pr of Va.

Romance of the Kiss. Illus. by Susan Zulauf. (Charming Petites Ser.). 80p. 1996. 4.95 (*0-88088-793-1*) Peter Pauper.

Romance of the Law Merchant: Being an Introduction to the Study of International & Commercial Law with Some Account of the Commerce & Fairs of the Middle Ages. Wyndham A. Bewes. (Legal Reprint Ser.). ix, 148p. 1986. reprint ed. lib. bdg. 22.50 (*0-8377-1940-2*) Rothman.

Romance of the Law Merchant: Being an Introduction to the Study of International & Commercial Law with Some Account of the Commerce & Fairs of the Middle Ages. Wyndham A. Bewes. LC 88-80855. 148p. 1988. reprint ed. 40.00 (*0-912004-65-7*, Pub. by Sweet & Maxwll UK) Gaunt.

Romance of the Milky Way & Other Studies & Stories. Lafcadio Hearn. LC 77-75779. (Short Story Index Reprint Ser.). 1977. 15.95 (*0-8369-3004-5*) Ayer.

Romance of the Mission. Elmo Baca. LC 95-45343. (Illus.). 128p. 1996. 37.95 (*0-87905-740-8*) Gibbs Smith Pub.

Romance of the National Parks. Harlean James. LC 72-2847. (Use & Abuse of America's Natural Resources Ser.). (Illus.). 258p. 1972. reprint ed. 26.95 (*0-405-04513-1*) Ayer.

Romance of the Piano. Eric Blom. LC 69-15608. (Music Ser.). (Illus.). 1969. reprint ed. 32.50 (*0-306-71060-9*) Da Capo.

Romance of the Rails, 2 Vols. Agnes C. Laut. LC 75-37891. (Select Bibliographies Reprint Ser.). 1977. reprint ed. 48.95 (*0-8369-6728-3*) Ayer.

Romance of the Republic. Lydia Maria Child. LC 76-83926. (Black Heritage Library Collection). 1977. 24.95 (*0-8369-8540-0*) Ayer.

***Romance of the Republic.** Lydia Maria Child. Ed. & Intro. by Dana D. Nelson. LC 97-10443. 464p. 1997. pap. 19.95 (*0-8131-0928-0*) U Pr of Ky.

Romance of the River Plate, 2 vols., Set. W. H. Koebel. (Latin America Ser.). 1979. lib. bdg. 200.00 (*0-8490-3002-1*) Gordon Pr.

Romance of the Road: The Literature of the American Highway. Ronald Primeau. LC 96-6221. 171p. 1996. 34.95 (*0-87972-697-0*); pap. 17.95 (*0-87972-698-9*) Bowling Green Univ Popular Press.

Romance of the Rose. Heather Arden. (World Authors Ser.: No. 791). 144p. 1987. 23.95 (*0-8057-6645-6*, Twayne) Scribnrs Ref.

Romance of the Rose. Guillaume De Lorris & Jean De Meun. Tr. by Frances Horgan. (Illus.). 384p. 1994. pap. 13.95 (*0-19-282689-1*) OUP.

Romance of the Rose. 3rd ed. Guillaume De Lorris & Jean De Meun. Tr. by Charles Dahlberg from FRE. LC 95-11748. 510p. 1909. pap. text ed. 18.95 (*0-691-04456-2*) Princeton U Pr.

Romance of the Rose, 3 Vols. Guillaume De Lorris & J. Clopinel. Tr. by Frederick S. Ellis. LC 74-154119. reprint ed. 155.00 (*0-404-09640-9*) AMS Pr.

***Romance of the Rose: An Anthology of Verse & Prose.** Books Lorenz. (Illus.). 64p. 1997. 9.95 (*1-85967-333-3*, Lorenz Bks) Anness Pub.

Romance of the Rose & Its Medieval Readers: Interpretation, Reception, Manuscript Transmission. Silvia Huot. (Studies in Medieval Literature: No. 16). (Illus.). 420p. (C). 1993. text ed. 69.95 (*0-521-41713-9*) Cambridge U Pr.

Romance of the Rose; Or Guillaume de Dole: The Late Medieval Resistance to the Renaissance. Jean Renart. Ed. by Patricia Terry & Nancy V. Durling. Tr. by Nancy V. Durling from FRE. LC 93-16414. (Middle Ages Ser.). 136p. (Orig.). (C). 1993. text ed. 26.95 (*0-8122-3111-2*) U of Pa Pr.

Romance of the Rothschilds. Ignatius Balla. 1981. lib. bdg. 250.00 (*0-87700-280-0*) Revisionist Pr.

***Romance of the Stars.** Bessie Leo. (Being a Series of Astrological Stories). 201p. 1997. pap. 18.00 (*0-89540-344-7*, Sun Bks) Sun Pub.

Romance of the Three Kingdoms. Kuan-Chung Lo. Tr. by C. H. Brewitt-Taylor. 1280p. 1990. pap. 39.95 (*0-8048-1649-2*) C E Tuttle.

Romance of the Three Kingdoms, Set, Vols. 1-2. Lou Guan Zhong. 1276p. 1985. reprint ed. text ed. 34.50 (*981-218-043-5*) Heian Intl.

Romance of the Three Kingdoms, Vol. 1. Lou Guan Zhong. 623p. 1985. reprint ed. text ed. 17.25 (*9971-947-94-3*) Heian Intl.

Romance of the Three Kingdoms Vol. IV: Wall of Fire: The Official Strategy Guide. Bill Kunkel. 1995. pap. text ed. 19.95 (*0-7615-0224-6*) Prima Pub.

Romance of the Word: One Man's Love Affair with Theology. Robert F. Capon. 380p. (Orig.). 1995. pap. 20.00 (*0-8028-4084-1*) Eerdmans.

Romance of Trade: A Commercial & Economic Survey. Adam W. Kirkaldy. 1977. 59.95 (*0-8490-2537-0*) Gordon Pr.

Romance of Tristan. Beroul. Tr. by Alan S. Fredrick. (Classics Ser.). 176p. 1978. pap. 9.95 (*0-14-044230-8*, Penguin Classics) Viking Penguin.

Romance of Tristan. Tr. by Renee L. Curtis. LC 93-41829. (World's Classics Ser.). 384p. 1994. pap. 7.95 (*0-19-282792-8*) OUP.

Romance of Tristan & Iseult. Joseph Bedier. 1965. pap. 5.56 (*0-394-70271-9*, Vin) Random.

Romance of Tristan & Iseult. Joseph Bedier. 208p. 1994. pap. 10.00 (*0-679-75016-9*, Vin) Random.

Romance of Tristan & Isolt. Tr. by Norman B. Spector from FRE. 91p. 1985. pap. 12.95 (*0-8101-0767-8*) Northwestern U Pr.

Romance of Two Worlds. Marie Corelli. 1986. 15.95 (*0-87505-333-5*) Borden.

Romance of Two Worlds. Marie Corelli. 870p. 1996. pap. 24.95 (*1-56459-763-6*) Kessinger Pub.

Romance of Two Worlds. 3rd ed. Marie Corelli. LC 85-81601. 320p. 1986. reprint ed. pap. 12.95 (*0-8334-0018-5*, Spir Lit Lib) Garber Comm.

Romance of Two Worlds. Marie Corelli. 370p. 1971. reprint ed. spiral bd. 10.50 (*0-7873-0207-4*) Hlth Research.

Romance of William Morris. Carole Silver. LC 82-2278. xviii, 233p. (C). 1983. pap. 19.95 (*0-8214-0706-6*) Ohio U Pr.

Romance of William of Palerne. Guillaume De Palerne. Ed. by Walter W. Skeat. (EETS, ES Ser.: No. 1). 1974. reprint ed. 54.00 (*0-527-00211-9*) Periodicals Srv.

***Romance of Wine.** Ben Gale. LC 97-19651. 1997. write for info. (*965-229-172-2*) Gefen Bks.

Romance of Wisconsin Place. rev. ed. Robert Gard & L. G. Jorden. LC 68-29817. 201p. 1979. reprint ed. pap. 4.95 (*0-686-28112-8*) Milwaukee Sentinel.

Romance of World Trade. Alfred P. Dennis. 1977. lib. bdg. 59.95 (*0-8490-2538-9*) Gordon Pr.

Romance of Yder. Ed. by Alison Adams. (Arthurian Studies: No. VIII). 267p. 1983. 63.00 (*0-85991-133-0*) Boydell & Brewer.

Romance on a Shoestring: Cheap Dates in & Around Seattle & Puget Sound from Bellingham to Tacoma. 2nd ed. Colleen S. Cramer. Ed. by Ted Fry. LC 92-61650. 176p. 1995. pap. 9.95 (*0-9632481-2-X*) Shoestring.

Romance on Lizard Island. large type ed. Cora Mayne. (Linford Romance Library). 215p. 1984. pap. 15.99 (*0-7089-6021-9*) Ulverscroft.

Romance on the Confederate Coast: A Pictorial History of the Ships, Plantations, Mansions, Friends, & Enemies of George Trenholm, "the Real Rhett Butler" Date not set. 29.95 (*0-614-16775-2*) Narwhal Pr.

Romance on the Confederate Coast: A Pictorial History of the Ships, Plantations, Mansions, Friends, & Enemies of George Trenholm, "the Real Rhett Butler" Date not set. pap. 19.95 (*0-614-16776-0*) Narwhal Pr.

Romance on the Menu. Tracy Sinclair. (Special Edition Ser.). 1993. mass mkt. 3.50 (*0-373-09821-9*, 5-09821-5) Silhouette.

Romance on the Run: Five Minutes of Quality Sex for Busy Couples. Tara R. Madden. 96p. 1995. pap. 10.00 (*0-8217-4885-8*, Zebra Kensgtn) Kensgtn Pub Corp.

Romance on Your Hands: Palmistry for Lovers. Spencer Grendahl. LC 94-40406. (Illus.). 208p. 1995. pap. 12.95 (*1-56718-337-9*) Llewellyn Pubns.

Romance, Poetry & Surgical Sleep: Literature Influences Medicine. E. M. Papper. LC 94-24189. (Contributions in Medical Studies: Vol. 42). 176p. 1995. text ed. 55.00 (*0-313-29405-4*, Greenwood Pr) Greenwood.

Romance Reader. Pearl Abraham. LC 95-964. 304p. (YA). 1996. pap. 12.00 (*1-57322-548-7*, Riverhd Trade) Berkley Pub.

Romance Reader. Pearl Abraham. LC 95-964. 304p. (YA). 1995. 21.95 (*1-57322-015-9*, Riverhead Books) Putnam Pub Group.

Romance Reader's Handbook. Compiled by Melinda Helfer et al. 353p. 1989. pap. 12.95 (*0-940338-25-4*) Romantic Times.

Romance Revisited. Ed. by Lynne Pearce & Jackie Stacey. (Illus.). 310p. (C). 1995. 45.00 (*0-8147-6630-7*); pap. 16.00 (*0-8147-6631-5*) NYU Pr.

Romance Revolution: Erotic Novels for Women & the Quest for a New Sexual Identity. Carol Thurston. LC 86-30759. (Illus.). 272p. (C). 1987. text ed. 27.95 (*0-252-01247-X*) U of Ill Pr.

Romance Rhythm & Revolution: New & Selected Poetry. 2nd ed. Rob Penny. 100p. (YA). (gr. 9-12). 1993. reprint ed. pap. text ed. 9.95 (*0-685-60180-3*) Magnolia PA.

Romance Rhythm & Revolution: Selected Poetry of Rob Penny. Rob Penny. 200p. 1990. 15.95 (*0-929917-00-6*) Magnolia PA.

Romance, Romance. 1994. pap. 14.95 (*1-57007-012-1*, XW1640) Astor Bks.

***Romance, Romance: Vocal Selections.** Ed. by Carol Cuellar. 60p. (Orig.). (C). 1988. pap. text ed. 14.95 (*0-7692-0542-9*, VF1496) Warner Brothers.

***Romance Sampler.** 1993. pap. write for info. (*0-515-11204-6*) Berkley Pub.

***Romance Sampler.** 1994. write for info. (*0-425-14603-0*) Berkley Pub.

***Romance Slip.** Mouse Works Staff. (J). 1997. 31.92 (*1-57082-708-7*) Mouse Works.

Romance Thing. Anne Waldman. LC 86-73203. 80p. (Orig.). 1987. pap. 8.50 (*0-917453-11-5*) Bamberger.

Romance Thing. deluxe limited ed. Anne Waldman. LC 86-73203. 80p. (Orig.). 1987. Signed Ltd. ed. pap. 25.00 (*0-917453-12-3*) Bamberger.

Romance Tradition in Urdu. Frances W. Pritchett. 1991. text ed. 37.50 (*0-231-07164-7*) Col U Pr.

Romance under the Wing. Katie Goode. (Illus.). 9.95 (*0-614-13182-0*, 21-38057) EAA Aviation.

Romance, Vision & Satire: English Alliterative Poems of the Fourteenth Century. Jessie L. Weston. (BCL1-PR English Literature Ser.). 336p. 1992. reprint ed. lib. bdg. 89.00 (*0-7812-7136-3*) Rprt Serv.

Romance Vocabulary in Latin: Vocabulario de Romance en Latin. A. Nebrija. 200p. (LAT & SPA.). 1981. pap. 45.00 (*0-8288-1617-4*, S39785) Fr & Eur.

Romance with Realism: The Art of Jean-Baptiste Carpeaux. Jennifer G. Lovett. LC 89-60886. (Illus.). 48p. 1989. pap. 12.95 (*0-931102-26-X*) S & F Clark Art.

Romance Writer's Pink Pages: The Insider's Guide to Getting Your Romance Novel Published. Eve Paludan. 272p. (Orig.). 1993. pap. 12.95 (*1-55958-349-5*) Prima Pub.

Romance Writer's Pink Pages, 1995-1996: The Insider's Guide to Getting Your Romance Novel. Eve Paludan. 1994. pap. 12.95 (*1-55958-581-1*) Prima Pub.

Romance Writer's Pink Pages, 1996-1997. Eva Paludan. 1995. pap. text ed. 14.95 (*0-7615-0168-1*) Prima Pub.

Romance Writer's Sourcebook: Where to Sell Your Manuscripts. Ed. by David Borcherding. 464p. 1996. 19.99 (*0-89879-726-8*, Wrtrs Digest Bks) F & W Pubns Inc.

Romance Writings. Mary W. Montagu. Ed. by Isobel Grundy. LC 95-25046. 304p. (C). 1996. 70.00 (*0-19-818319-4*, Clarendon Pr) OUP.

Romance 101: Lessons in Love. Gregory J. Godek. (Illus.). 320p. 1993. pap. 12.95 (0-9629803-8-2, Casablanca) Sourcebks.

Romanceiro: choix de vieux chants portugais. T. J. Boudet De Puymaigre. LC 78-20109. (Collection de contes et de chansons populaires: No. 2). reprint ed. 21.50 (0-404-60352-1) AMS Pr.

Romancero Aux Etoiles. Jacques S. Alexis. (Imaginaire Ser.). 271p. (FRE.). 1988. pap. 12.95 (2-07-071229-X) Schoenhof.

Romancero de la Conquista. Ester M. Feliciano. (Coleccion Ninos y Letras). (Illus.). 71p. 1985. pap. 8.00 (0-8477-3533-8) U of PR Pr.

Romancero Del Cid. Anonimo. 214p. (SPA.). 1966. 5.50 (0-8288-7021-7) Fr & Eur.

Romancero Gitano. Federico Garcia Lorca. Ed. by Emilio De Miquel. (Nueva Austral Ser.: Vol. 156). (SPA.). 1991. pap. text ed. 24.95 (84-239-1956-0) Elliots Bks.

Romancero Gitano. Federico Garcia Lorca. LC 87-38262. (Spanish Texts Ser.). 160p. 1988. text ed. 18.95 (0-7190-1724-6, Pub. by Manchester Univ Pr UK) St Martin.

Romancero Gitano. Federico Garcia Lorca. 96p. 1996. pap. 9.95 (0-14-025583-4, Viking) Viking Penguin.

Romancero Gitano. Federico Garcia Lorca. 176p. 1993. pap. 12.95 (0-7859-9792-X) Fr & Eur.

Romancero Tradicional de Costa Rica. Ed. by Michele Cruz-Saenz. 138p. 1986. pap. 12.50 (0-936388-23-4) Juan de la Cuesta.

Romancero Viejo y Tradicional. Manuel A. Ezquerra. 404p. (SPA.). 1971. 11.95 (0-8288-7055-1, S7492) Fr & Eur.

Romances, No. 46. Duque De Rivas. 245p. (SPA.). write for info. (0-8288-8582-6) Fr & Eur.

Romances & Ballads of Ireland. Hercules Ellis. 1980. lib. bdg. 79.95 (0-8490-3172-9) Gordon Pr.

Romances & Epics of the Northern Ancestors: Norse, Celt & Teuton. W. Wagner. 1977. lib. bdg. 59.95 (0-8490-2539-7) Gordon Pr.

Romances & Narrative, 16 vols. Daniel Defoe. Ed. by George Aitken. (Illus.). reprint ed. write for info. (0-404-07910-5) AMS Pr.

Romances Del Alma. Ram-Mar, pseud. LC 93-74228. (Coleccion Espejo de Paciencia). 112p. (Orig.). (SPA.). 1993. pap. 9.95 (0-89729-714-8) Ediciones.

Romances Hispanicos Contenidos en el Ingenioso Hidalgo Don Quijote de la Mancha. Jorge A. Silveira. Ed. by Editorial Arcos, Inc., Staff. LC 87-83312. (Coleccion Interdisciplinar: No. 1). (Illus.). 216p. (SPA.). 1987. 20.00 (0-937509-02-7) Edit Arcos.

Romances I. Duque De Rivas. 276p. (SPA.). 1966. 12.50 (0-8288-7116-7) Fr & Eur.

Romances II. Duque De Rivas. 279p. (SPA.). 1965. 12.50 (0-8288-7117-5) Fr & Eur.

***Romances (La Poesia del Amor)** Salvador Castillo. LC 95-92257. 202p. (SPA.). Date not set. write for info. (0-9644410-1-2) Salvador Castillo.

Romances of Alexander. Dennis M. Kratz. LC 90-23378. (Library of Medieval Literature). 240p. 1991. text ed. 15.00 (0-8240-4631-5) Garland.

Romances of Chivalry in the Spanish Golden Age. Daniel Eisenberg. Ed. by Thomas Lathrop et al. (Documentacion Cervantina Ser.: No. 3). 182p. 1982. pap. 10.50 (0-936388-12-9) Juan de la Cuesta.

Romances of Chretien de Troyes: A Symposium. Ed. by Douglas Kelly. LC 85-70103. (Edward C. Armstrong Monographs on Medieval Literature: No. 3). 353p. (Orig.). 1985. pap. 24.95 (0-917058-59-3) French Forum.

Romances of Guy of Warwick, from the Auchinleck MS & the Caius MS, Set, Vols. I, II & III. J. Zupitza. (EETS Extra Ser.: Vol. 42). 1966. reprint ed. 40.00 (0-19-722571-3, Pub. by EETS UK) Boydell & Brewer.

Romances of Old France. Richard Le Gallienne. LC 75-81271. (Short Story Index Reprint Ser.). 1977. 20.95 (0-8369-3023-1) Ayer.

Romances of Roguery: The Picaresque Novel in Spain. F. W. Chandler. 1977. lib. bdg. 59.95 (0-8490-2540-0) Gordon Pr.

Romances of the East. Conte D. Gobineau. LC 73-6282. (Middle East Ser.). 1973. reprint ed. 26.95 (0-405-05340-1) Ayer.

Romances of the Republic: Women, the Family, & Violence in the Literature of the Early American Nation. Shirley Samuels. (Illus.). 208p. (C). 1996. 39.95 (0-19-507988-4) OUP.

Romances of William Morris. Amanda Hodgson. 221p. 1987. text ed. 69.95 (0-521-32075-5) Cambridge U Pr.

Romances Tradicionales de Castilla y Leon. Joaquin Diaz & Luis Diaz Viana. (Spanish Ser.: No. 7). iv, 160p. 1982. 12.50 (0-942260-22-8) Hispanic Seminary.

Romancier et Ses Personnages. Francois Mauriac. Bd. with Education des Filles. (FRE.). 1990. Set pap. 10.95 (0-7859-3230-5, 2266033859) Fr & Eur.

Romanciers & Conteurs du 19e Siecle. Ed. by Jean Sareil & Jacqueline Sareil. 429p. (YA). (gr. 12 up). 1974. pap. text ed. 6.75 (0-88345-207-3, 18134) Prentice ESL.

Romanciers du XVII Siecle: Sorel Scarron, Furetiere, Mme. de La Fayette. deluxe ed. A. Adam. (Pleiade Ser.). 1512p. (FRE.). 72.95 (2-07-010479-6) Schoenhof.

Romanciers du XVIII Siecle: Memoires du Comte de Gramont, Gil Blas de Santillane, Manon Lescaut, Etc., Vol. 1. deluxe ed. (Pleiade Ser.). 1572p. (FRE.). 83.95 (2-07-010480-X) Schoenhof.

Romancing: A Human Imperative & Human Rights Criterion. Anastasios Zavales. 105p. (Orig.). (C). 1995. pap. text ed. 39.95 (1-884090-05-2) Ecumenics Intl.

Romancing Annie. Nikki Rivers. 1997. mass mkt. 3.75 (0-373-16664-8, 1-16664-4) Silhouette.

***Romancing Antiquity: German Critique of the Enlightenment from Weber to Habermas.** George E. McCarthy. LC 97-1989. 320p. 1997. 72.00 (0-8476-8528-4) Rowman.

***Romancing Antiquity: German Critique of the Enlightenment from Weber to Habermas.** George E. McCarthy. LC 97-1989. 320p. 1997. pap. 27.95 (0-8476-8529-2) Rowman.

Romancing Cody. Rena McKay. (Silhouette Romance Ser.). 1994. pap. 2.75 (0-373-19004-2) Harlequin Bks.

Romancing Cody. Rena McKay. (Romance Ser.). 1994. pap. 2.75 (0-373-91004-5, 5-91004-7) Silhouette.

Romancing Minnesota: Intimate Places to Stay & Dine. Mike Link & Kate Crowley. (Orig.). 1995. pap. 12.95 (1-57025-043-X) Pfeifer-Hamilton.

Romancing Nevada's Past: Ghost Towns & Historic Sites of Eureka, Lander, & White Pine Counties. Shawn Hall. LC 93-22777. (Illus.). 240p. 1993. pap. 16.95 (0-87417-228-4) U of Nev Pr.

Romancing of Rome. Illus. by Michael J. Page & Andrew Scheinman. LC 94-75890. xiii, 34p. 1994. pap. write for info. (1-883015-03-0) Krannert Art.

Romancing Rhetorics: Social Expressivist Perspectives on the Teaching of Writing. Sherrie Gradin. LC 94-26169. 188p. 1995. text ed. 37.50 (0-86709-349-8, 0349) Boynton Cook Pubs.

Romancing the Bean: Essentials for Creating Vegetarian Bean Dishes. Joanne Saltzman. LC 93-1828. (Illus.). 184p. 1993. pap. 12.95 (0-915811-48-0) H J Kramer Inc.

***Romancing the Book: A Study of Literary Elements.** Anne D. Jordan. (Tall Literary Companion Ser.). (Illus.). 112p. (Orig.). 1997. pap. 13.95 (1-890429-03-1) Essmont Pub.

Romancing the Business Loan: Getting Your Bank to Say "Yes" in the 90's. Gary Goldstick. 254p. pap. 19.95 (0-02-912398-4, Free Press) Free Pr.

Romancing the Dream. Heidi Johanna. 176p. 1992. pap. 8.95 (0-9628938-0-3) Rising NY.

***Romancing the Goddess: Three Middle English Romances about Women.** Marijane Osborn & Geoffrey Chaucer. LC 97-4702. (ENG & ENM.). 1997. text ed. 46.95 (0-252-02350-1); pap. text ed. 19.95 (0-252-06655-3) U of Ill Pr.

Romancing the Grail: Genre, Science, & Quest in Wolfram's "Parzival" Arthur Groos. 264p. 1995. 37.50 (0-8014-3068-2) Cornell U Pr.

***Romancing the Holy: Gateways to Christian Experience.** Debra K. Farrington. LC 96-36905. 180p. 1997. pap. 13.95 (0-8245-1648-6) Crossroad NY.

Romancing the Home: How to Have a Marriage That Sizzles. Ed Young. LC 93-4579. 240p. 1993. 16.99 (0-8054-6086-1, 4260-86) Broadman.

Romancing the Home: How to Have a Marriage That Sizzles. Ed Young. 240p. 1994. pap. 10.99 (0-8054-6159-0, 4261-59) Broadman.

Romancing the Horsehide: Baseball Poems on Players & the Game. Gene Carney. LC 92-42356. (Illus.). 127p. 1993. lib. bdg. 18.95 (0-89950-838-3) McFarland & Co.

Romancing the Mountain: Two Tales of Marin Trails. Marilyn Pinnow. 224p. (Orig.). 1994. pap. 12.00 (0-9643293-0-1) F I D Ent.

Romancing the Nephites. Becky Paget. LC 92-70860. 1993. pap. 7.95 (1-55503-552-3, 29004780) Covenant Comms.

Romancing the Net: A "Tell All" Guide to Love Online. Richard Booth & Marshal Jung. 1996. 19.95 (0-7615-0322-6) Prima Pub.

Romancing the Past: The Rise of Vernacular Prose Historiography in Thirteenth-Century France. Gabrielle M. Spiegel. (New Historicism: Studies in Cultural Poetics: No. 23). (C). 1993. 50.00 (0-520-07710-5) U CA Pr.

Romancing the Past: The Rise of Vernacular Prose Historiography in Thirteenth-Century France. Gabrielle M. Spiegel. (New Historicism: Studies in Cultural Poetics: Vol. 23). 440p. 1995. pap. 16.00 (0-520-08935-9) U CA Pr.

Romancing the Personals: How to Find Your Partner in the Classifieds. Peggi Ridgway. LC 96-90124. (Illus.). 112p. 1996. pap. 9.95 (0-9635836-1-1) Wordpictures.

Romancing the Postmodern. Diane Elam. LC 91-33915. 224p. (C). 1992. pap. 18.95 (0-415-07987-X, Routledge NY) Routledge.

Romancing the Postmodern: Romance, History & the Figure of Woman. Diane Elam. LC 91-33915. 240p. (C). (gr. 13). 1992. text ed. 79.95 (0-415-05732-9, A7394) Routledge.

Romancing the Real: Folklore & Ethnographic Representation in North Africa. Sabra J. Webber. (Publications of the American Folklore Society, Bibliographical & Special Ser.). 320p. (C). 1991. text ed. 31.95 (0-8122-8236-1) U of Pa Pr.

***Romancing the Shadow.** C. Zweig & S. Wolf. LC 97-19716. 1997. 27.00 (0-345-41739-9) Ballantine.

***Romancing the Shadow: A Guide to Finding Gold in the Dark Side.** Connie Zweig & Steve Wolf. 1996. 24.00 (0-06-251428-8) Harper SF.

***Romancing the Shadow: A Guide to Finding Gold in the Dark Side.** Connie Zweig. pap. 13.00 (0-06-251429-6) HarpC.

***Romancing the Southland: The Romantic & Unusual in Southern California.** 2nd rev. ed. Robert Badal. 720p. (Orig.). 1997. pap. 24.95 (1-880396-51-3, JP9651-3) Jalmar Pr.

***Romancing the Stones.** Janis Flores. (Weddings by DeWilde Ser.). 1997. 4.50 (0-373-82547-1, 1-82547-0) Harlequin Bks.

Romancing Your Future: How to Leverage Time. Philip Stills. 208p. 1994. pap. write for info. (0-9644551-0-2) P Stills Bus Bks.

Romancing Your Future - How to Leverage Time see Get a Life: How to Leave That Dead-End Job Behind & Create Your Perfect Future - Today!

***Romancing Your Marriage.** 11.85 (0-8307-1226-7) Regal.

***Romancing Your Wind.** Cicely. (Illus.). 117p. (Orig.). 1996. pap. 9.95 (0-9654770-0-2) Empowermnt Pr.

Romane Hugo Loetschers im Spannungsfeld von Fremde und Vertrautheit, Vol. 72. Romey Sabalius. (Studies in Modern German Literature). 224p. (GER.). (C). 1995. 48.95 (0-8204-2670-9) P Lang Pubng.

***Romane und Erzahlungen, 3 bande.** Alexis. (GER.). 1996. write for info. (3-487-10102-5) G Olms Pubs.

***Romane und Erzahlungen, Bd. 4.** (Fruhe Frauenliteratur in Deutschland Ser.). viii, 656p. (GER.). 1996. reprint ed. write for info. (3-487-10162-9) G Olms Pubs.

Romanee Conti. Richard Olney. (Illus.). 208p. 1995. 35.00 (0-8478-1927-2) Rizzoli Intl.

Romanesque. George Zarnecki. (History of Art & Architecture Ser.). 196p. 1989. pap. 13.95 (0-87663-759-4) Universe.

Romanesque Architectural Criticism: A Pre-History. Tina W. Bizzarro. (Illus.). 288p. (C). 1992. text ed. 80.00 (0-521-41017-7) Cambridge U Pr.

Romanesque Architecture: A Bibliography. Martin Davies. LC 93-820. (Illus.). 340p. 1993. 90.00 (0-8161-1826-4, Hall Reference) Macmillan.

Romanesque Art. Andreas Petzold. LC 94-37842. (The Perspectives Ser.). (Illus.). 176p. 1995. 16.95 (0-8109-2744-6) Abrams.

Romanesque Art. Andreas Petzold. 176p. 1995. pap. text ed. 15.60 (0-13-433517-1) P-H.

Romanesque Art. Meyer Schapiro. LC 76-11842. (Selected Papers of Meyer Schapiro Ser.: Vol. 1). (Illus.). 368p. 1993. pap. 19.95 (0-8076-1294-4) Braziller.

Romanesque Bible Illumination. Walter Cahn. LC 82-71593. (Illus.). 308p. 1982. 125.00 (0-8014-1446-6) Cornell U Pr.

Romanesque Frieze & Its Spectator: The Lincoln Symposium Papers. Ed. by Deborah Kahn. 232p. 1992. text ed. 95.00 (1-872501-70-2) Gordon & Breach.

Romanesque Manuscripts. Walter Cahn. (Survey of Manuscripts Illuminated in France Ser.: Vol. 1). (Illus.). 224p. 1996. text ed. 200.00 (1-872501-60-5, Pub. by Harvey Miller UK) Gordon & Breach.

Romanesque Sculpture: The Revival of Monumental Stone Sculpture in the Eleventh & the Twelfth Centuries. M. F. Hearn. LC 80-14383. (Illus.). 240p. (C). 1985. pap. 29.95 (0-8014-9304-8) Cornell U Pr.

Romanesque Sculpture in Campania: Patrons, Programs, & Style. Dorothy F. Glass. (Illus.). 336p. 1992. 49.50 (0-271-00713-3) Pa St U Pr.

Romanesque Sculpture in Saintonge. Elizabeth L. Mendell. (Illus.). 1940. 150.00 (0-685-89780-X) Elliots Bks.

Romanesque Wall Painting in Central France: The Politics of Narrative. Marcia Kupfer. LC 92-24013. (Publications in the History of Art). (Illus.). 384p. (C). 1993. text ed. 60.00 (0-300-05720-2) Yale U Pr.

Romanesque Wooden Doors of Auvergne. Walter Cahn. LC 74-15391. (College Art Association Monographs: Vol. 30). (Illus.). 225p. 1985. reprint ed. 35.00 (0-271-00400-2) Pa St U Pr.

Romanesques. Edmond Rostand. 3.95 (0-686-55337-3) Fr & Eur.

Romani in Contact: The History, Structure & Sociology of a Language. Ed. by Yaron Matras & International Conference on Romani Linguistics Staff. LC 95-15437. (Current Issues in Linguistic Theory Ser.: No. 126). xvii, 208p. 1995. lib. bdg. 55.00 (1-55619-580-X) Benjamins North Am.

Romani Sociolinguistics. Ed. by Ian F. Hancock. (International Journal of the Sociology of Language Ser.: No. 19). 1979. pap. text ed. 60.00 (90-279-7817-4) Mouton.

Romania. (Illus.). 1995. 170.00 (1-85564-438-X, Pub. by Euromoney UK) Am Educ Systs.

Romania. Ed. by Arunas Alisauskas. (C). 1995. 50.00 (0-929851-36-6) Am Assn Coll Registrars.

Romania. Betty B. Carran. LC 87-35423. (Enchantment of the World Ser.). (Illus.). 124p. (J). (gr. 5-9). 1988. lib. bdg. 30.00 (0-516-02703-4) Childrens.

Romania. Andrea Deletant & Dennis Deletant. (World Bibliographical Ser.: No. 59). 236p. 1987. lib. bdg. 38.00 (1-85109-002-9, Pub. by Clio Pr UK) ABC-CLIO.

***Romania.** Jerry Morton. (Illus.). 112p. (Orig.). 1996. pap. 24.95 (0-9655400-3-0) J Lee Pr.

Romania. Mark Sanborne. LC 95-23517. (Nations in Transition Ser.). (Illus.). 160p. (YA). 1996. 17.95 (0-8160-3089-8) Facts on File.

Romania. Gershon Shafir. (Marxist Regimes Ser.). 250p. 1985. text ed. 49.00 (0-86187-438-2); pap. text ed. 17.50 (0-86187-439-0) St Martin.

Romania: A Case of "Dynastic" Communism. Ed. by James Finn. LC 88-34002. (Perspectives on Freedom Ser.: No. 11). (Illus.). 119p. (C). 1989. 27.25 (0-932088-35-X); pap. 12.50 (0-932088-34-1) Freedom Hse.

Romania: A Workshop Report on the Educational System & Guide to the Academic Placement of Students in Educational Institutions in the United States. Margery Ismail et al. LC 95-25843. (PIER World Education Ser.). 1995. 50.00 (0-929851-75-7) Am Assn Coll Registrars.

Romania: Ethnic Hungarians in Post-Ceausescu Romania: Struggling for Ethnic Identity. Human Rights Watch Helsinki Staff. 152p. (Orig.). 1993. pap. 10.00 (1-56432-115-0) Hum Rts Watch.

Romania: Forty Years: 1944-1984. Ed. by Vladimir Georgescu. LC 85-6401. (Washington Papers: Vol. XXIII, No. 115). 112p. 1985. text ed. 45.00 (0-275-90213-7, C0213, Praeger Pubs); pap. text ed. 11.95 (0-275-91644-8, B1644, Praeger Pubs) Greenwood.

Romania: Human Rights Violations in the Eighties. 1987. 4.00 (0-86210-127-1) Amnesty Intl USA.

Romania: In Pictures. Lerner Publications, Department of Geography Staff. LC 92-32861. (Visual Geography Ser.). (J). 1993. lib. bdg. 19.95 (0-8225-1894-5, Lerner Publctns) Lerner Group.

***Romania: Out of the Grey.** 96p. 1996. 6.75 (0-8341-1614-6) Nazarene.

Romania: The Entangled Revolution. Nestor Ratesh. Ed. by Walter Laqueur. LC 91-18244. (Washington Papers: No. 152). 208p. 1991. text ed. 45.00 (0-275-94145-0, C4145); pap. text ed. 12.95 (0-275-94144-2, B4244) CSI Studies.

Romania: The Penal Code of the Romanian Socialist Republic. Tr. by Simone-Marie Kleckner from RUM. (American Series of Foreign Penal Codes: Vol. 20). xvi, 143p. 1976. text ed. 17.50 (0-8377-0040-X) Rothman.

Romania: The Source Book 1993-94. (Illus.). 148p. 1993. pap. 30.00 (0-9638370-0-1) Cosmos MD.

Romania see Cultures of the World - Group 8

Romania After Ceausescu. Tom Gallagher. 240p. 1996. pap. 29.50 (0-7486-0613-0, Pub. by Edinburgh U Pr UK) Col U Pr.

Romania & the Great Powers, 1933-1940. Dov B. Lungu. LC 89-1553. 294p. 1989. text ed. 54.95 (0-8223-0915-7) Duke.

Romania & the Turks (c.1300-c.1500) Elizabeth A. Zachariadou. (Collected Studies: No. CS211). (Illus.). 304p. (C). 1985. reprint ed. lib. bdg. 89.95 (0-86078-159-3, Pub. by Variorum UK) Ashgate Pub Co.

Romania Between East & West. Ed. by Stephen Fischer-Galati & Radu R. Florescu. (East European Monographs: No. 103). 414p. 1982. text ed. 54.00 (0-914710-97-4) East Eur Monographs.

Romania Germanica: Sprach-und Siedlungsgeschichte der Germanen auf dem Boden des alten Roemerreiches. Ernst Gamillscheg. Incl. Vol. 1. Zu den aeltesten Beruehrungen zwischen Roemern und Germanen: Die Franken. 2nd rev. ed. (Illus.). xvi, 474p. 1970. 170.00 (3-11-002680-5); (GER.). write for info. (0-318-51641-1) De Gruyter.

***Romania in Transition.** Ed. by Stan Lavinia. LC 96-36537. (Illus.). 240p. 1997. text ed. 67.95 (1-85521-886-0, Pub. by Dartmth Pub UK) Ashgate Pub Co.

Romania in Turmoil. Martin Rady. 256p. 1992. text ed. 22.50 (1-85043-500-6, Pub. by I B Tauris UK) St Martin.

Romania vs. the United States: Diplomacy of the Absurd, 1985-1989. Roger Kirk & Mircea Raceanu. 320p. 1994. text ed. 55.00 (0-312-12059-1) St Martin.

Romanian: A Complete Course for Beginners. Dennis Deletant & Yvonne Alexandrescu. (Teach Yourself Ser.). 428p. (ROM.). pap. 24.95 incl. audio (0-8442-3870-8, Teach Yourslf) NTC Pub Grp.

Romanian: A Complete Course for Beginners. Dennis Deletant & Yvonne Alexandrescu. (Teach Yourself Ser.). 428p. (ROM.). 1994. pap. 14.95 (0-8442-3820-1, Teach Yourslf) NTC Pub Grp.

Romanian & East German Policies in the Third World: Comparing the Strategies of Ceausescu & Honecker. Thomas P. Barnett. LC 92-3380. 200p. 1992. text ed. 55.00 (0-275-94117-5, C4117, Praeger Pubs) Greenwood.

Romanian Army of World War II. M. Axworthy. (Men-at-Arms Ser.: No. 246). (Illus.). 48p. pap. 11.95 (1-85532-169-6, 9209, Pub. by Osprey UK) Stackpole.

Romanian Cassandra: Ion Antonescu & the Struggle for Reform, 1916-1941. Larry L. Watts. 320p. (C). 1993. text ed. 47.50 (0-88033-255-7, 358) Col U Pr.

Romanian Cassette Pack. Berlitz Editors. (Cassette Pack Ser.). (Illus.). 192p. 1994. audio 15.95 (2-8315-1108-9) Berlitz.

Romanian Continuity in Roman Dacia: Linguistic Evidence. Virgiliu Stefanescu-Draganesti. 90p. 1986. write for info. (0-937019-04-6); pap. 15.00 (0-937019-05-4) Romanian Hist.

Romanian Conversation Guide. Mihai Miroiu. (Language Bks.). 200p. (C). 1989. pap. 9.95 (0-87052-803-3) Hippocrene Bks.

Romanian Economic Reform Program. Dimitrios Demekas & Mohsin S. Khan. LC 91-4066. (Occasional Paper Ser.: No. 89). v, 36p. 1991. 15.00 (1-55775-190-0) Intl Monetary.

Romanian Economy in the Twentieth Century. David Turnock. 320p. 1986. text ed. 39.95 (0-312-69164-5) St Martin.

Romanian-English - English-Romanian Dictionary. 751p. (ENG & RUM.). 1991. reprint ed. 41.00 (0-88431-075-2) IBD Ltd.

Romanian-English Dictionary & Grammar for the Mathematical Sciences. Ed. by S. H. Gould & P. E. Obreanu. 51p. (ENG & RUM.). 1978. reprint ed. pap. 19.00 (0-8218-0038-8, ROMA) Am Math.

Romanian-English, English-Romanian Dictionary. Mihai Miroiu. 800p. (Orig.). 1996. pap. 17.95 (0-7818-0444-2) Hippocrene Bks.

Romanian Fairy Tales. Karen Reynolds-Strauss & Adrian Gligor. (Illus.). 85p. (Orig.). (J). (ps-6). 1992. pap. text ed. 11.95 (0-9634797-0-9) K Strauss & A Gligor.

Romanian Folk Music Texts. Bartok. (Rumanian Folk Music Ser: Vol. 3). 1967. lib. bdg. 185.00 (90-247-0625-4) Kluwer Ac.

Romanian Foreign Policy & the United Nations. Robert Weiner. LC 84-2149. 208p. 1984. 37.95 (0-275-91290-6, C1290, Praeger Pubs) Greenwood.

Romanian Foreign Policy since 1965: The Political & Military Limits of Autonomy. Aurel Braun. LC 78-9516. (Praeger Special Studies). 1978. text ed. 59.95 (0-275-90287-0, C0287, Praeger Pubs) Greenwood.

Romanian History Eighteen Forty-Eight to Nineteen Eighteen: Essays from the First Dutch-Romanian Colloquium of Historians Utrecht 1977. Ed. by Albert P. Van Goudoever. (Historische Studies: No. XXXVI). 159p. (Orig.). 1979. pap. 23.00 (90-01-39022-6, Pub. by Boumas Boekhuis NE) Benjamins North Am.

An Asterisk (*) at the beginning of an entry indicates that the title is appearing in BIP for the first time.

R

Romanian Icons on Glass. Juliana Dancu & Dumitru Dancu. Tr. by Georgeta Ciocaltea. LC 82-10846. (Romanian Traditions & Customs Ser.). (Illus.). 179p. reprint ed. pap. 51.10 (*0-7837-3577-4*, 2043436) Bks Demand.

Romanian-Macedonian, Macedonian-Romanian Dictionary: Romansko-Wakedonski I Makedonsko-Romanski Ronick, 2 vols. 2341p. 1986. 24.95 (*0-8288-1750-2*, F78700) Fr & Eur.

Romanian Military Doctrine: Past & Present. Ilie Ceausescu. 246p. 1988. text ed. 58.00 (*0-88033-135-6*) East Eur Monographs.

Romanian Nationalism: The Legionary Movement. Alexander . Ronnett. Tr. by Uasile C. Barsan from RUM. LC 74-3350. 93p. reprint ed. pap. 26.60 (*0-8357-9431-8*, 2015062) Bks Demand.

Romanian Novel. Sorin Parvu. 320p. 1994. text ed. 46.50 (*0-88033-226-3*) Col U Pr.

***Romanian Patericon: Saints of the Romanian Orthodox Church.** Ioanichie Balan. Tr. by Brigid McCarthy. LC 95-72085. (Illus.). 504p. (RUM.). 1996. pap. 20.00 (*0-938635-97-2*) St Herman Pr.

Romanian Phrase Book. Berlitz Editors. (Phrase Bk.). 192p. 1994. pap. 6.95 (*2-8315-0933-5*) Berlitz.

Romanian Phrasebook. (Hugo's Language Courses Ser.). 128p. (Orig.). 1993. pap. 4.95 (*0-85285-192-8*) Hunter NJ.

Romanian Politics in the Ceausescu Era. Daniel N. Nelson. 236p. 1988. text ed. 116.00 (*2-88124-261-8*) Gordon & Breach.

Romanian Public Law. H. B. Jacobini. 182p. 1987. text ed. 46.00 (*0-88033-119-4*, 223) East Eur Monographs.

Romanian Textbook. Alexandra Roceric. LC 89-85238. 356p. 1990. 48.00 (*0-931745-57-8*) Dunwoody Pr.

Romanian Traditions & Customs. Adrian Gligor & Karen Strauss. (Illus.). 32p. (Orig.). (J). (ps-4). 1993. pap. 11.95 (*0-9634797-1-7*) K Strauss & A Gligor.

Romanian Travel Pack. (Hugo's Language Courses Ser.). 128p. 1993. 14.95 incl. audio (*0-85285-193-6*) Hunter NJ.

Romanians: A History. Vlad Georgescu. Tr. by Alexandra Bley-Vroman from RUM. (Illus.). 356p. 1991. 60.00 (*0-8142-0511-9*) Ohio St U Pr.

Romanians in America & Canada: A Guide to Information Sources. Ed. by Vladimir Wertsman. LC 80-191. (Information Guide Ser.: Vol. 5). 184p. 1980. 68.00 (*0-8103-1417-7*) Gale.

Romanians, 1774-1866. Keith Hitchins. (Illus.). 352p. (C). 1996. 49.95 (*0-19-820591-0*, Clarendon Pr) OUP.

Romania's Communist Takeover: The Radescu Government. Dinu C. Giurescu. LC 94-70331. 201p. 1994. 31.00 (*0-88033-285-9*) East Eur Monographs.

Romania's Diplomatic Relations with Yugoslavia in the Interwar Period 1919-1941. Eugene Boia. 450p. (C). 1993. text ed. 66.00 (*0-88033-253-0*, 356) Col U Pr.

Romanico en Espana. I. G. Bango Torviro. (Illus.). 416p. (SPA.). 1993. 295.00 (*84-239-5295-9*) Elliots Bks.

***Romanies/Gypsies.** Marta Osorio. 1997. pap. text ed. 7.95 (*84-207-3103-X*) Lectorum Pubns.

Romaniote Penitential Poetry. Ed. by Leon J. Weinberger. 208p. (HEB.). 1980. pap. text ed. 19.50 (*0-8173-0047-3*) U of Ala Pr.

***Romanische Zentralbauten in Oberitalien Vorlaufer und Anverwandte.** Manuel Kling. (Studien Zur Kunstgeschichte Ser.: Vol. 95). 386p. (GER.). 1995. write for info. (*3-487-09979-9*) G Olms Pubs.

Romanisches Etymologisches Woerterbuch. 5th ed. Wilhelm Meyer-Luebke. 1204p. (GER & ITA.). 1992. 395.00 (*0-8288-6419-5*, M-7604) Fr & Eur.

Romanism: The Relentless Roman Catholic Assault on the Gospel of Jesus Christ! Robert M. Zins. LC 95-60418. 285p. 1995. pap. 8.95 (*0-9637141-4-7*) White Hrse.

Romanism & the Reformation. H. Grattan Guinness. 217p. 1995. reprint ed. pap. 12.95 (*0-923309-31-4*) Hartland Pubns.

Romanism & Truth. G. G. Coulton. 1977. lib. bdg. 59.95 (*0-8490-2541-9*) Gordon Pr.

Romanist: 1980-81, No. 4-5. Ed. by John C. Moran et al. 1982. 10.00 (*0-318-20641-2*) F M Crawford.

Romanist: 1982-84, No. 6-8. Ed. by John C. Moran et al. 1986. 10.00 (*0-318-20642-0*) F M Crawford.

Romanistische Texte und Studien, Vol. 1: Le 'Egloghe Viscontee' Di Alligretti. Diego Rossi. write for info. (*0-318-71469-8*) G Olms Pubs.

Romanistische Texte und Studien, Vol. 3: Due Epistole Di Giovanni Conversini Da Ravenna. Diego Rossi. write for info. (*0-318-71470-1*) G Olms Pubs.

Romanization of Africa Proconsularis. Thomas R. Broughton. LC 78-64276. (Johns Hopkins University. Studies in the Social Sciences. Thirtieth Ser. 1912: 5). reprint ed. 37.50 (*0-404-61377-2*) AMS Pr.

Romanization of Britain: An Essay in Archaeological Interpretation. Martin Millett. 252p. (C). 1990. text ed. 75.00 (*0-521-36084-6*) Cambridge U Pr.

Romanization of Britain: An Essay in Archaeological Interpretation. Martin Millett. (Illus.). 252p. (C). 1992. pap. text ed. 25.95 (*0-521-42864-5*) Cambridge U Pr.

Romanization of Roman Britain. Francis J. Haverfield. LC 78-12798. (Illus.). 91p. 1979. reprint ed. text ed. 45.00 (*0-313-21148-5*, HARM, Greenwood Pr) Greenwood.

***Romanized Hebrew-English/English-Hebrew Compact Dictionary.** 157p. (Orig.). (ENG & HEB.). 1997. pap. 7.95 (*0-7818-0568-6*) Hippocrene Bks.

Romano-British Cavemen. K. Branigan & M. J. Dearne. (Oxbow Monographs in Archaeology: No. 19). (Illus.). 120p. 1992. pap. 18.00 (*0-946897-43-3*, Pub. by Oxbow Bks UK) David Brown.

Romano-British Villa at Castle Copse, Great Bedwyn. Ed. by Eric Hostetter & Thomas N. Howe. LC 94-47082. 704p. 1995. 39.95 (*0-253-32802-0*) Ind U Pr.

Romano-British Wall Painting. Roger Ling. 1989. pap. 25.00 (*0-85263-715-2*, Pub. by Shire UK) St Mut.

Romano-Byzantine Armies Fourth-Ninth Century. David Nicolle. (Men-at-Arms Ser.: No. 247). (Illus.). 48p. pap. 11.95 (*1-85532-224-2*, 9218, Pub. by Osprey UK) Stackpole.

***Romano Guardini: A Precursor of Vatican II.** Robert A. Krieg. LC 97-22854. 268p. (C). Date not set. write for info. (*0-268-01661-5*) U of Notre Dame Pr.

Romano Guardini: Proclaiming the Sacred in a Modern World. Robert A. Krieg et al. 119p. (Orig.). 1995. pap. 15.00 (*1-56854-106-6*, GUARD) Liturgy Tr Pubns.

***Romanoff - Prince of Rogues: The Life & Times of a Hollywood Icon.** Jane Pejsa. LC 97-93326. Date not set. 22.95 (*0-9612776-8-8*) Kenwood Pub.

Romanos. Evis L. Carballosa. 352p. (SPA.). 1994. pap. 11.99 (*0-8254-1105-X*, Edit Portavoz) Kregel.

Romanos. Charles Erdman. (SPA.). 1993. pap. 5.95 (*0-939125-21-8*) Evangelical Lit.

Romanos: Cuaderno del Alumno. Merle Den Bleyker. (SPA.). 1984. 3.00 (*1-55955-100-3*) CRC Wrld Lit.

Romanos: Manual del Maestro. Merle Den Bleyker. (SPA.). 1984. 3.00 (*1-55955-101-1*) CRC Wrld Lit.

Romanos: Versiculo por Versiculo. William R. Newell. Orig. Title: Romans: Verse by Verse. 464p. (SPA.). 1984. pap. 12.99 (*0-8254-1507-1*, Edit Portavoz) Kregel.

Romanos, Bosquejo Explicativo. 2nd ed. David Steele. 178p. (SPA.). 1976. pap. 7.50 (*0-939125-41-2*) Evangelical Lit.

Romanos, First & Second Corintios (Version Popular) Romans, First & Second Corinthians in Spanish. 218p. (SPA.). write for info. (*0-614-00647-3*, 5026) LBW.

Romanov Connection: A Novel. William M. Green. 320p. 1984. 16.95 (*0-8253-0221-8*) Beaufort Bks NY.

Romanov Legacy. Zoia Belyakova. 1995. pap. 44.95 (*0-670-86339-4*, Viking) Viking Penguin.

***Romanovs.** Robert K. Massie. Date not set. 3.99 (*0-517-17590-8*) Random Hse Value.

Romanovs: Autocrats of All the Russias. W. Bruce Lincoln. LC 80-39902. (Illus.). 864p. 1983. pap. 18.95 (*0-385-27908-6*, Dial Pr) Dell.

***Romanovs: Love, Power & Tragedy.** (Illus.). 321p. 69.95 (*0-9521644-0-X*, Pub. by Leppi Pubns UK) BookWorld Dist.

Romanovs: The Final Chapter. Robert K. Massie. (Illus.). 320p. 1996. pap. 12.95 (*0-345-40640-0*) Ballantine Trade.

Romanovs: The Final Chapter. Robert K. Massie. (Illus.). 308p. 1995. 25.00 (*0-394-58048-6*) Random.

Romanov's Russian - English, English - Russian Dictionary. 3rd ed. A. C. Romanov & E. Wedel. 509p. (ENG & RUS.). 1992. 29.95 (*0-7859-1083-2*, 5850540113) Fr & Eur.

Romans. (Life Application Bible Study Guide Ser.). 96p. 1989. New Intl Version Text. 5.99 (*0-8423-2718-5*, 02-2718-5) Tyndale.

Romans. (History of Britain Ser.: No. F895-1). (Illus.). (YA). (gr. 5 up). 1990. pap. 3.95 (*1-85543-006-1*, Ladybrd) Penguin.

Romans. Paul J. Achtemeier. LC 84-47796. (Interpretation: A Bible Commentary for Teaching & Preaching Ser.). 240p. 1985. 24.00 (*0-8042-3137-0*, John Knox) Westminster John Knox.

Romans. William Barclay. 240p. 1993. pap. 24.00 (*0-7152-0277-4*, Pub. by St Andrew UK) St Mut.

Romans. Reginald H. Barrow. (Orig.). (YA). (gr. 9 up). 1975. mass mkt. 5.95 (*0-14-020196-3*, Penguin Bks) Viking Penguin.

Romans. Reginald H. Barrow. 1975. pap. 11.95 (*0-14-013502-2*, Viking) Viking Penguin.

Romans. David L. Bartlett. Ed. by Patrick D. Miller. LC 95-10453. (Westminster Bible Companion Ser.). 160p. (Orig.). 1995. pap. 15.00 (*0-664-25254-0*) Westminster John Knox.

Romans. Bruce B. Barton et al. LC 92-26510. (Life Application Bible Commentary Ser.). 320p. 1992. 14.99 (*0-8423-2818-1*) Tyndale.

Romans. Bruce B. Barton & David R. Veerman. (Life Application Bible Commentary Ser.). 320p. 1992. pap. 14.99 (*0-8423-2890-4*) Tyndale.

Romans. Nicola Baxter. (Craft Topics Ser.). (Illus.). 32p. (J). (gr. 4-6). 1992. lib. bdg. 19.10 (*0-531-14143-8*) Watts.

Romans. Matthew W. Black. (New Century Bible Ser.). 191p. 1973. 7.50 (*0-551-00447-9*) Attic Pr.

Romans. D. Briscoe. (Communicator's Commentary Ser.: Vol. 6). 1991. pap. 14.99 (*0-8499-3322-6*) Word Pub.

Romans. D. Stuart Briscoe. (Communicator's Commentary Ser.: Vol. 6). 264p. 1982. 22.99 (*0-8499-0159-6*) Word Pub.

Romans. John C. Brunt. LC 95-42653. (Abundant Life Bible Amplifier Ser.). 1996. pap. 12.99 (*0-8163-1295-8*) Pacif Pr.

Romans. John C. Brunt. LC 95-42653. (Abundant Life Bible Amplifier Ser.). 1996. 17.99 (*0-8163-1296-6*) Pacif Pr.

***Romans.** Roy Burrell. (Rebuilding the Past). (Illus.). 112p. (J). 1997. pap. 14.95 (*0-19-917102-5*) OUP.

Romans. Louis-Ferdinand Celine. Ed. by Henri Godard. 1981. lib. bdg. 125.00 (*0-7859-3875-3*) Fr & Eur.

Romans. Louis-Ferdinand Celine. Ed. by Henri Godard. 1988. lib. bdg. 140.00 (*0-7859-3885-0*) Fr & Eur.

Romans. Peter Chrisp. LC 93-29441. (Journey into Civilization Ser.). (Illus.). 32p. (J). (gr. 3-7). 1994. pap. 7.95 (*0-7910-2731-7*); lib. bdg. 15.95 (*0-7910-2707-4*) Chelsea Hse.

Romans. Jacqueline Dineen. LC 91-511. (Worlds of the Past Ser.). (Illus.). 64p. (YA). (gr. 6 up). 1992. lib. bdg. 14.95 (*0-02-730651-8*, Mac Bks Young Read) S&S Childrens.

Romans. James R. Edwards. (New International Biblical Commentary Ser.). 320p. 1992. pap. 9.95 (*0-943575-34-6*) Hendrickson MA.

Romans. I. Fielding. (FRE.). 1964. 99.50 (*0-8288-3446-6*, F1950) Fr & Eur.

Romans. Andrea Giardina. Tr. by Lydia G. Cochrane. 404p. (C). 1993. pap. text ed. 19.50 (*0-226-29050-6*); lib. bdg. 60.50 (*0-226-29049-2*) U Ch Pr.

Romans. Willam M. Greathouse. Ed. by Willard H. Taylor. (Bible Exposition Ser.: Vol. 6). 223p. 1975. 13.99 (*0-8341-0317-6*) Beacon Hill.

Romans. Everett F. Harrison. Ed. by Frank E. Gaebelein. (Expositor's Bible Commentary Ser.: Vol. 7). 188p. 1995. pap. 12.99 (*0-310-20109-8*) Zondervan.

Romans. John Haywood. (Spotlights Ser.). (J). (gr. 3-5). 1996. 9.95 (*0-614-15689-0*) OUP.

Romans. John Haywood. (Spotlights Ser.). (Illus.). 46p. (J). 1996. pap. 9.95 (*0-19-521240-1*) OUP.

Romans. William Hendriksen. LC 82-71911. 534p. (C). 1982. 29.99 (*0-8010-4265-8*) Baker Bks.

Romans. Sally Hewitt. LC 94-42246. (Footsteps in Time Ser.). (Illus.). 24p. (J). (ps-3). 1995. lib. bdg. 15.00 (*0-516-08058-X*) Childrens.

***Romans.** H. A. Ironside. LC 97-20364. 1997. pap. write for info. (*0-87213-423-7*) Loizeaux.

Romans. Henry A. Ironside. 176p. 1928. 12.99 (*0-87213-386-9*) Loizeaux.

Romans. Ralph Jackson et al. (Illus.). (J). (gr. 2-6). pap. 3.95 (*0-7141-1282-8*, Pub. by Brit Mus UK) Parkwest Pubns.

Romans. Edgar C. James. (Survey of the Scriptures Study Guides Ser.). 1995. pap. 8.99 (*1-56570-005-8*) Meridian MI.

Romans. Irving L. Jensen. (Bible Self-Study Ser.). 112p. (Orig.). 1970. pap. 6.99 (*0-8024-4453-9*) Moody.

***Romans.** Robert Jewett. (Genesis to Revelation Ser.). 1997. pap. text ed. 4.95 (*0-687-06233-0*) Abingdon.

Romans. Andre Malraux. Incl. Conquerants. 1947. (*0-318-63593-3*); Condition Humaine. 1947. (*0-318-63594-1*); Espoir. 1947. (*0-318-63595-X*); 1947. write for info. (*0-318-63592-5*) Fr & Eur.

Romans. M. Wojciech Maly. 1989. pap. 21.00 (*0-86217-009-5*, Pub. by Veritas IE) St Mut.

Romans. A. Marks & Graham I. Tingay. (Illustrated World History Ser.). (Illus.). 96p. (YA). 1990. pap. 10.95 (*0-7460-0340-4*); lib. bdg. 18.95 (*0-88110-439-6*) EDC.

Romans. Robert Morgan. (New Testament Guides Ser.). 164p. pap. 9.95 (*1-85075-739-9*) CUP Services.

Romans. Robert H. Mounce. LC 95-17311. (New American Commentary: Vol. 27). 304p. 1995. 27.99 (*0-8054-0127-X*) Broadman.

***Romans.** John Murray. 1997. 30.00 (*0-8028-4341-7*) Eerdmans.

Romans. Navigator Staff. (LifeChange Ser.). 213p. (Orig.). 1987. pap. 7.00 (*0-89109-073-8*) NavPress.

Romans. Pamela Odijk. (Ancient World Ser.). (Illus.). 48p. (J). (gr. 5-8). 1989. 7.95 (*0-382-24260-2*); teacher ed. 4.50 (*0-382-24275-0*); lib. bdg. 14.95 (*0-382-09885-4*) Silver Burdett Pr.

Romans. Robert Rogland. 1988. student ed., pap. 6.99 (*0-87552-403-6*, Pub. by Evangelical Pr) Presby & Reformed.

Romans. Jennifer Ruby. (People in Costume Ser.). 48p. (J). (gr. 5-8). 1995. 19.95 (*0-7134-7621-4*, Pub. by Batsford UK) Trafalgar.

Romans. R. C. Sproul. (Focus on the Bible Commentary Ser.). 11.99 (*1-85792-077-5*, Pub. by Christian Focus UK) Spring Arbor Dist.

Romans. Lester Sumrall. 127p. (C). 1988. pap. text ed. 10.00 (*0-937580-16-3*) LeSEA Pub Co.

Romans. abr. ed. Charles Hodge. LC 93-49651. (Classic Commentaries Ser.). 392p. 1994. pap. 17.99 (*0-89107-724-3*) Crossway Bks.

Romans. deluxe ed. Guy De Maupassant. (Pleiade Ser.). (FRE.). 1959. 93.95 (*2-07-011118-0*) Schoenhof.

Romans. deluxe ed. Andre Gide. (Pleiade Ser.). (FRE.). 80.95 (*2-07-010225-4*) Schoenhof.

Romans. deluxe ed. Andre Malraux. 864p. (FRE.). 1978. 110.00 (*0-7859-1621-0*, 2070103293) Fr & Eur.

Romans. rev. ed. F. F. Bruce. Ed. by Leon Morris. (Tyndale New Testament Commentaries Ser.). 288p. 1985. pap. 13.00 (*0-8028-0062-9*) Eerdmans.

Romans. Geoffrey B. Wilson. 254p. (Orig.). 1984. reprint ed. pap. 7.99 (*0-85151-238-0*) Banner of Truth.

Romans, 2 tomes, 1. deluxe ed. Stendhal. Ed. by Martineau. (Pleiade Ser.). (FRE.). 1952. 77.95 (*2-07-010535-0*) Schoenhof.

Romans, 2 tomes, 2. deluxe ed. Stendhal. Ed. by Martineau. (Pleiade Ser.). (FRE.). 1952. 71.95 (*2-07-010536-9*) Schoenhof.

Romans, Vol. 1. Henry De Montherlant. (FRE.). 1960. lib. bdg. 110.00 (*0-8288-3568-3*, F115180) Fr & Eur.

Romans, Vol. 1. J. Vernon McGee. LC 90-41340. (Thru the Bible Commentary Ser.: Vol. 42). 1995. pap. 8.99 (*0-7852-1046-6*) Nelson.

Romans, 3 tomes, Vol. I: Voyage au Bout de la Nuit. deluxe ed. Louis-Ferdinand Celine. (Pleiade Ser.). (FRE.). 83.95 (*2-07-011000-1*) Schoenhof.

Romans, Vol. 2. Louis-Ferdinand Celine. Ed. by J. Godard. (FRE.). 1974. lib. bdg. 110.00 (*0-7859-3827-3*) Fr & Eur.

Romans, Vol. 2. Henry De Montherlant. (FRE.). 1982. lib. bdg. 125.00 (*0-8288-3569-1*, M12083) Fr & Eur.

Romans, Vol. 2. J. Vernon McGee. LC 90-41340. (Thru the Bible Commentary Ser.: Vol. 42). 1995. pap. 8.99 (*0-7852-1047-4*) Nelson.

Romans, 3 tomes, Vol. II: D'un Chateau l'Autre. deluxe ed. Louis-Ferdinand Celine. (Pleiade Ser.). (FRE.). 71.95 (*0-685-37272-3*) Schoenhof.

Romans, 3 tomes, Vol. III. deluxe ed. Louis-Ferdinand Celine. (Pleiade Ser.). (FRE.). 89.95 (*2-07-011155-5*) Schoenhof.

Romans, Vol. 6. Brendan Byrne. Ed. by Daniel J. Harrington. (Sacra Pagina Ser.: Vol. 6). 576p. (Orig.). 1996. 29.95 (*0-8146-5808-3*, M Glazier) Liturgical Pr.

Romans: A Bible Commentary in the Wesleyan Tradition. Clarence L. Bence. Ed. by David Higle. (Bible Commentary in the Wesleyan Tradition Ser.). 247p. 1996. 24.95 (*0-89827-157-6*, BK975) Wesleyan Pub Hse.

Romans: A New Translation with Introduction & Commentary. Joseph A. Fitzmyer. LC 92-29702. (Anchor Bible Ser.: Vol. 33). 800p. 1993. 40.00 (*0-385-23317-5*) Doubleday.

Romans: A Reasoned Faith...a Reasonable Faith. rev. ed. Marilyn Kunz & Catherine Schell. (Neighborhood Bible Studies). 84p. 1994. pap. 4.99 (*1-880266-07-5*) Neighborhood Bible.

***Romans: Alive in Christ.** (God's Word for Today Ser.). 1996. pap. 4.99 (*0-570-09596-4*, 20-2660) Concordia.

Romans: An Existential Interpretation. 2nd ed. James Park. LC 83-8852. 96p. 1991. pap. text ed. 10.50 (*0-89231-200-9*) Existential Bks.

***Romans: An Expositional Commentary, 4 vols.** James M. Boice. 2080p. 1995. 110.96 (*0-8010-1109-4*) Baker Bks.

Romans: An Introduction. Antony Kamm. LC 95-1996. 232p. (gr. 13). 1995. pap. 15.95 (*0-415-12040-3*) Routledge.

Romans: An Introduction. Antony Kamm. LC 95-1996. 232p. (C). (gr. 13). 1995. text ed. 49.95 (*0-415-12039-X*) Routledge.

Romans: An Introduction to Their History & Civilization. Karl Christ. Tr. by Christopher Holme from GER. LC 83-40483. (Illus.). 275p. (C). 1984. pap. 15.95 (*0-520-05634-5*) U CA Pr.

Romans: Avec: Erec et Enide, Vol. 1. Chretien de Troyes & Marlo Roques. 288p. (FRE.). 1973. pap. 15.00 (*0-7859-5365-5*) Fr & Eur.

Romans: Cliges, Vol. 2. Chretien de Troyes & Alexandre Micha. 256p. (FRE.). 1982. pap. 24.95 (*0-7859-5366-3*) Fr & Eur.

Romans: Critical & Exegetical Commentary. William Sanday & Arthur C. Headlam. Ed. by Samuel R. Driver et al. (International Critical Commentary Ser.). 568p. 1902. 39.95 (*0-567-05026-2*, Pub. by T & T Clark UK) Bks Intl VA.

Romans: Critical & Exegetical Commentary, 2 vols., Vol. I. Charles E. Cranfield. Ed. by John A. Emerton. (International Critical Commentary Ser.). 472p. 1975. 49.95 (*0-567-05040-8*, Pub. by T & T Clark UK) Bks Intl VA.

Romans: Critical & Exegetical Commentary, 2 vols., Vol. II. Charles E. Cranfield. Ed. by John A. Emerton. (International Critical Commentary Ser.). 496p. 1979. 49.95 (*0-567-05041-6*, Pub. by T & T Clark UK) Bks Intl VA.

Romans: D'un Chateau l'Autre; Nord; Rigodon, Tome 2. deluxe ed. Louis-Ferdinand Celine. (Pleiade Ser.). 1272p. (FRE.). 1974. 71.95 (*2-07-010797-3*) Schoenhof.

***Romans: Geneva Series of Commentaries.** Robert Haldane. 729p. 1996. reprint ed. 31.99 (*0-85151-708-0*) Banner of Truth.

Romans: Getting It All Together. Joel Kok. (Revelation Series for Adults). 63p. 1995. student ed., pap. text ed. 4.50 (*0-933140-04-5*) CRC Pubns.

Romans: God's Good News for the World. John Stott. 432p. 1995. 19.99 (*0-8308-1692-5*, 1692) InterVarsity.

Romans: Interpretive Outline. David H. Steele & Curtis C. Thomas. LC 63-21694. (Illus.). 1963. pap. 8.99 (*0-87552-443-5*, Pub. by Evangelical Pr) Presby & Reformed.

Romans: Joseph Andrews, Jonathan Wild, Tom Jones. I. Fielding. 1640p. 82.95 (*0-686-56510-X*) Fr & Eur.

Romans: Le Chevalier au Lion, Yvain, Vol. 4. Chretien de Troyes & Marlo Roques. 266p. (FRE.). 1982. pap. 24.95 (*0-7859-5368-X*) Fr & Eur.

Romans: Le Chevalier de la Charrette, Vol. 3. Chretien de Troyes & Marlo Roques. 244p. (FRE.). 1982. pap. 24.95 (*0-7859-5367-1*) Fr & Eur.

Romans: Les Souffrances du jeune Werther, Les Affinites Electives, Wilhelm Meister. Johann Wolfgang Von Goethe. 1424p. 39.95 (*0-686-56515-0*) Fr & Eur.

Romans: Life in the Empire. Charles Guittard. Tr. by Mary K. LaRose from FRE. LC 92-9467. (Peoples of the Past Ser.). (Illus.). 64p. (J). (gr. 4-6). 1992. lib. bdg. 16.90 (*1-56294-200-X*) Millbrook Pr.

Romans: Life in the Empire. Charles Guittard. (Peoples of the Past Ser.). (Illus.). 64p. (J). (gr. 4-6). 1996. 7.95 (*0-7613-0097-X*) Millbrook Pr.

Romans: Moll Flanders, Mme. Veal, Memoires d'un Canalier, Vie du Capitaine Singleton, Etc., Vol. 2. Daniel Defoe. 1760p. 1970. 105.00 (*0-686-56494-4*, F77001) Fr & Eur.

Romans: Notre-Dame de Paris & Les Travailleurs de la Mer. Victor Hugo. 1768p. 45.00 (*0-686-56530-4*) Fr & Eur.

Romans: Righteousness from Heaven. R. Kent Hughes. LC 90-49412. (Preaching the Word Ser.). 352p. 1991. 19.99 (*0-89107-524-0*) Crossway Bks.

Romans: Robinson Crusoe, Journal de l'Annee de la Peste, Jean Gow, Jean Sheppard, Etc., Vol. 1. Daniel Defoe. 1376p. 85.00 (*0-686-56493-6*, F77000) Fr & Eur.

Romans: Seeing the World Through God's Eyes. Marshall Shelley. (Great Books of the Bible). 64p. 1995. 4.99 (*0-310-49821-X*) Zondervan.

Romans: The Christian Story. James Reapsome. (Fisherman Bible Studyguide Ser.). 96p. 1989. pap. 4.99 (*0-87788-734-9*) Shaw Pubs.

Romans: The Gift of Righteousness. Jack Kuhatschek. (LifeGuide Bible Studies). 96p. (Orig.). 1986. wbk. ed., pap. 4.99 (*0-8308-1008-0*, 1008) InterVarsity.

***Romans: The Good News According to Paul.** Daniel J. Harrington. (Spiritual Commentaries Ser.). 152p. 1997. pap. 9.95 (*1-56548-096-1*) New City.

An Asterisk (*) at the beginning of an entry indicates that the title is appearing in BIP for the first time.

Romans: The Gospel According to Paul. Arden E. Gilmer. LC 85-72274. 1985. pap. 4.50 (*0-934970-05-X*) Brethren Church.

Romans: The Gospel for All. Keith L. Brooks. (Teach Yourself the Bible Ser.). 1962. pap. 5.99 (*0-8024-7372-5*) Moody.

Romans: The Righteousness of God. Adolf Schlatter. Tr. by Siegfried Sschatzmann from GER. LC 95-2443. 340p. (ENG & GER.). 1995. 29.95 (*0-943575-89-3*) Hendrickson MA.

Romans: Verse-by-Verse. William R. Newell. 576p. 1994. pap. 18.99 (*0-8254-3326-6*) Kregel.

Romans: Werther, les Affinities. Johann Wolfgang von Goethe. (FRE.). 1976. 95.00 (*0-8288-3490-3*, M5099) Fr & Eur.

Romans: Where Life Begins. Roy L. Laurin. LC 88-12130. (Life Commentary Ser.). 540p. 1988. pap. 16.99 (*0-8254-3130-1*) Kregel.

Romans Vol. 1: An Expositional Commentary: Justification by Faith (Romans 1-4) James M. Boice. LC 91-7204. 512p. (Orig.). 1991. text ed. 29.99 (*0-8010-1002-0*) Baker Bks.

Romans Vol. 1: The Freedom Letter, 2 Vols., Vol. 1. rev. ed. Alan F. Johnson. (Everyman's Bible Commentary Ser.). (C). 1984. pap. 9.99 (*0-8024-0446-4*) Moody.

Romans Vol. 2: An Expositional Commentary: The Reign of Grace (Romans 5-8) James M. Boice. LC 91-7204. 536p. (C). 1992. 29.99 (*0-8010-1003-9*) Baker Bks.

Romans Vol. 2: The Freedom Letter, 2 Vols., Vol. 2. rev. ed. Alan F. Johnson. (Everyman's Bible Commentary Ser.). 1985. pap. 9.99 (*0-8024-2079-6*) Moody.

Romans Vol. 3: An Expositional Commentary: God & History (Romans 9-11) James M. Boice. LC 91-7204. 544p. (C). 1993. 29.99 (*0-8010-1058-6*) Baker Bks.

Romans Vol. 4: An Expositional Commentary: The New Humanity (Romans 12-16) James M. Boice. LC 91-7204. 512p. (C). 1995. 29.99 (*0-8010-1039-X*) Baker Bks.

Romans see Commentaries on the New Testament

Romans see Bible Class Commentaries

Romans - Recits, Contes et Nouvelles. A. Marivaux. (FRE.). 1949. lib. bdg. 85.00 (*0-8288-3553-5*, F48100) Fr & Eur.

Romans - Recits et Soties: Oeuvres Lyrique. Andre Gide. (FRE.). 1959. 110.00 (*0-685-48736-9*, F102450) Fr & Eur.

Romans - 2 Corinthians. Ed. by Albert F. Harper & W. T. Purkiser. (Bible Commentary Ser.: Vol. 8). 655p. 1968. 29.99 (*0-8341-0307-9*) Beacon Hill.

Romans Abandonnes. Stendhal, pseud. Ed. by Crouzet. (Bibliotheque 10-18 Ser.). pap. 4.50 (*0-685-35017-7*) Fr & Eur.

Romans & Barbarians: The Decline of the Western Empire. E. A. Thompson. 344p. (C). 1982. 25.00 (*0-299-08700-X*) U of Wis Pr.

Romans & Blacks. Lloyd A. Thompson. LC 88-40549. (Oklahoma Series in Classical Culture: Vol. 2). 256p. 1989. 39.95 (*0-8061-2201-3*) U of Okla Pr.

Romans & Crete. G. W. Harrison. (Illus.). xv, 469p. 1993. pap. 94.00 (*90-256-1012-9*, Pub. by A M Hakkert NE) Benjamins North Am.

Romans & Galatians. University of Navarre, Theological Faculty Staff. (Navarre Bible Ser.). pap. 14.95 (*0-614-16417-6*, Pub. by Four Cts Pr IE) Intl Spec Bk.

Romans & Pompeii. Philip Steele. (Hidden Worlds Ser.). (Illus.). 32p. (J). (gr. 6 up). 1994. lib. bdg. 13.95 (*0-87518-538-X*, Dillon Silver Burdett) Silver Burdett Pr.

Romans & the Apologetic Tradition: The Purpose, Genre & Audience of Paul's Letter. Anthony J. Guerra. (Society for New Testament Studies Monographs: No. 81). 218p. (C). 1995. text ed. 59.95 (*0-521-47126-5*) Cambridge U Pr.

Romans & Their Empire. John Badcock & Graham I. Tingay. (History Matters Ser.). (Illus.). 75p. (Orig.). (J). (gr. 6-8). 9100. pap. 17.95 (*0-7487-1186-4*) Dufour.

Romans & Their Empire. Trevor Cairns. LC 69-11026. (Cambridge Introduction to World History Topic Bks.: Bk. 2). (Illus.). 96p. (YA). (gr. 7 up). 1970. pap. text ed. 17.95 (*0-521-07227-1*) Cambridge U Pr.

Romans & Their Gods in the Age of Augustus. R. M. Ogilvie. (Ancient Culture & Society Ser.). (Illus.). (C). 1970. pap. text ed. 10.95 (*0-393-00543-7*) Norton.

***Romans & Thessalonians: Torrance Edition.** John Calvin. (Calvin's New Testament Commentaries Ser.: Vol. 8). pap. 20.00 (*0-8028-0808-5*) Eerdmans.

***Romans Berlinois de Clara Viebig (1860-1952) Vol. 19: Contribution a l'Etude du Naturalisme Tardif en Allemagne.** Michel Durand. (Etudes & Documents Ser.: Serie 3). 428p. (FRE.). 1993. 55.80 (*3-906750-84-1*) P Lang Pubng.

Romans Complets, 3 vols. Victor Hugo. (Illus.). 1970. 19.95 (*0-685-73328-9*) Fr & Eur.

Romans Complets, Vol. 3. Victor Hugo. (FRE.). 1970. lib. bdg. 49.95 (*0-7859-3934-2*) Fr & Eur.

Romans Complets: Les Miserables, Vol. 2. Victor Hugo. (FRE.). 1970. pap. 49.95 (*0-7859-3933-4*) Fr & Eur.

Romans, Contes et Melanges, 2 vols. Francois-Marie De Voltaire. pap. 4.95 (*0-685-73329-7*) Fr & Eur.

Romans De la Table Ronde... Chretien de Troyes. (FRE.). 1975. pap. 11.95 (*0-7859-1809-4*, 2070366960) Fr & Eur.

Romans de la Table Ronde: Erec et Enide, Cliges, Lancelot, Yvain (MO) Chretien De Troyes. (Folio Ser.: No. 696). (FRE.). pap. 10.95 (*2-07-036696-0*) Schoenhof.

Romans de Robert Pinget: Une Ecriture des Possibles. Michele Praeger & Alain Robbe-Grillet. LC 86-80313. (French Forum Monographs: No. 65). 165p. 1986. pap. 12.95 (*0-917058-66-6*) French Forum.

Romans Debate. expanded rev. ed. Ed. by Karl P. Donfried. LC 91-13252. 416p. 1991. 19.95 (*0-943575-42-7*) Hendrickson MA.

Romans et Contes. Francois-Marie De Voltaire. Ed. by Groos. 1933. write for info. (*0-318-63596-8*) Fr & Eur.

Romans et Contes. Francois-Marie De Voltaire. Ed. by Frederic Deloffre. (FRE.). 1979. lib. bdg. 110.00 (*0-7859-3849-4*) Fr & Eur.

Romans et Contes. Francois-Marie De Voltaire. 512p. (FRE.). 1992. pap. 11.95 (*0-7859-1638-5*, 2070384829) Fr & Eur.

Romans et Contes. deluxe ed. Voltaire. Ed. by Groos. (Pleiade Ser.). (FRE.). 1933. 71.95 (*2-07-010961-5*) Schoenhof.

Romans et Contes, Vol 1: Zadig et Autres Contes. Voltaire. 512p. (FRE.). 1992. pap. 11.95 (*0-7859-1637-7*, 2070384810) Fr & Eur.

Romans et Nouvelles. Marie-Madeleine De La Fayette. 468p. 1967. 27.50 (*0-7859-0689-4*) Fr & Eur.

Romans et Nouvelles, 2 tomes. Prosper Merimee. Ed. by Parturier. (Coll. Prestige). 69.90 (*0-685-34944-6*) Fr & Eur.

Romans et Nouvelles. Stendhal. 4.95 (*0-686-55080-3*) Fr & Eur.

Romans et Nouvelles. Stendhal. Ed. by Del Litto. (Livre de Poche Classique Ser.). pap. 9.95 (*0-685-35018-5*) Fr & Eur.

Romans et Nouvelles, 2 Vols., 1. Stendahl, pseud. Ed. by Louis Martineau & Henri Martineau. 1948. lib. bdg. 120.00 (*0-7859-3794-3*) Fr & Eur.

Romans et Nouvelles, 2 Vols., 2. Stendahl, pseud. Ed. by Louis Martineau & Henri Martineau. 1948. lib. bdg. 110.00 (*0-7859-3795-1*) Fr & Eur.

Romans et Nouvelles: Armance, Le Rouge et le Noir, Lucien Leuwen, Vol. 1. Stendhal. 1600p. 42.95 (*0-686-56572-X*) Fr & Eur.

Romans et Nouvelles: Avec: La Princesse de Cleves, La Comtesse de Tende, La Princesse de Montpensier, Zaide. Marie-Madeleine De La Fayette. Ed. by Emile Magne. (Illus.). 488p. (FRE.). 1961. pap. 24.95 (*0-7859-1496-X*, 2705001638) Fr & Eur.

Romans et Nouvelles: Charles IX; Mateo Falcone; Vision de Charles IX; Enlevement de la Redoute; Tamango; Federico, 2 tomes. Prosper Merimee. Ed. by Parturier. 318p. (FRE.). 1969. pap. 29.95 (*0-7859-4875-9*, F68021) Fr & Eur.

Romans et Nouvelles: La Chartreuse de Parme, Chroniques Italiennes, Lamiel, Romans et Nouvelles, Vol. 2. Stendhal. 1488p. 41.50 (*0-686-56573-8*) Fr & Eur.

Romans et Nouvelles Complets, Vol. 1. Ivan S. Turgenev. (FRE.). 1981. lib. bdg. 95.00 (*0-8288-3578-0*, F53130) Fr & Eur.

Romans et Nouvelles Complets, Vol. 2. Ivan S. Turgenev. (FRE.). 1982. lib. bdg. 99.50 (*0-8288-3579-9*, F75640) Fr & Eur.

Romans et Nouvelles Complets, Vol. 3. Ivan S. Turgenev. (FRE.). 1986. lib. bdg. 135.00 (*0-8288-3580-2*, F29974) Fr & Eur.

Romans et Oeuvres De Fiction Non Theatrales, 1. Henry De Montherlant. (Pleiade Ser.). 1960. 72.95 (*0-685-11538-0*) Fr & Eur.

Romans et Oeuvres De Fiction Non Theatrales, 2. Henry De Montherlant. (Pleiade Ser.). 1960. 64.95 (*0-685-01762-1*) Fr & Eur.

Romans: Fact & Fiction. Robin Place. (Illus.). 32p. (J). 1989. text ed. 15.95 (*0-521-33267-2*); pap. text ed. 10.95 (*0-521-33787-9*) Cambridge U Pr.

Romans, First & Second Corinthians (New International Version) large type ed. write for info. (*0-318-68665-1*, 5025) LBW.

Romans Grecs et Latins: Les Metamorphoses (Apulee), Daphnis et Chloe (Longus), etc. 1584p. 42.95 (*0-686-56558-4*) Fr & Eur.

Romans' Guide to Rome. Jaffe. 4.95 (*0-8065-0329-7*, Citadel Pr) Carol Pub Group.

Romans in Britain. Howard Brenton. 103p. (C). 1988. pap. 9.95 (*0-685-63034-X*, A0246) Heinemann.

Romans in Britain. Cottia Howard & Penny Liddiard. (Primary History Ser.). (Illus.). 48p. (C). 1996. pap. text ed. 6.95 (*0-521-55805-0*) Cambridge U Pr.

Romans in Central Europe. Herbert Schutz. LC 84-52245. (Illus.). 200p. 1985. 37.00 (*0-300-03200-5*) Yale U Pr.

***Romans in Northern Campania: Settlement & Land-Use Around the Massico & the Garigliano Basin.** Paul Arthur. (British School at Rome Archaeological Monographs). (Illus.). 137p. 1991. pap. 54.00 (*0-904152-15-4*, Pub. by British Schl Rome UK) David Brown.

Romans in Scotland. Gordon Maxwell. 250p. (C). 1989. 90.00 (*0-901824-76-3*, Pub. by Mercat Pr Bks UK) St Mut.

Romans in Spain. John S. Richardson. (History of Spain Ser.). (Illus.). 360p. (C). Date not set. 74.95 (*0-631-17706-X*) Blackwell Pubs.

Romans in Spain, 217 B.C.-A.D. 117. C. H. Sutherland. LC 82-15846. (Illus.). xi, 264p. 1982. reprint ed. text ed. 65.00 (*0-313-23745-X*, SURS, Greenwood Pr) Greenwood.

Romans, Nouvelles, Oeuvres Diverses. Boris Vian. (FRE.). 1991. pap. 56.95 (*0-7859-3161-9*, 2253055123) Fr & Eur.

Romans of Partenay or of Lusignen. Cauldrette. Ed. by Walter W. Skeat. (EETS, OS Ser.: No. 22). 1974. reprint ed. 50.00 (*0-527-00022-1*) Periodicals Srv.

Romans on the Riviera & the Rhone. W. H. Hall. 230p. 1974. 20.00 (*0-89005-022-8*) Ares.

Romans Outlined & Summarized. Alva J. McClain. 1979. pap. 3.50 (*0-88469-015-6*) BMH Bks.

Romans Picaresques Espagnols. 1124p. 41.50 (*0-686-56559-2*) Fr & Eur.

Romans Picaresques Espagnols. Maurice Molho. Ed. by M. Molho. 1120p. (FRE.). 1968. lib. bdg. 95.00 (*0-7859-3786-2*, 2070104842) Fr & Eur.

Romans Pop-Up. Andy Hall & Maggie Hall. (Tarquin Pop-up Ser.). (Illus.). 32p. (Orig.). (J). (gr. 3 up). 1985. pap. 7.95 (*0-906212-29-4*, Pub. by Tarquin UK) Parkwest Pubns.

Romans Realized. Don DeWelt. LC 72-1068. (Bible Study Textbook Ser.). (Illus.). 270p. (C). 1959. 13.99 (*0-89900-037-1*) College Pr Pub.

Romans, Recits, Contes et Nouvelles. Pierre C. De Marivaux. Ed. by Marcel Arland. (Bibliotheque de la Pleiade Ser.). 74.95 (*0-685-34042-2*) Fr & Eur.

Romans, Recits, Contes et Nouvelles: Avec: La Vie de Marianne. Pierre C. De Marivaux. 1192p. 1950. 85.00 (*0-8288-9608-9*, F48100) Fr & Eur.

Romans, Recits et Soties: Oeuvres Lyriques. Andre Gide. (Bibliotheque de la Pleiade Ser.). 1959. 110.00 (*0-8288-9773-5*, F102450) Fr & Eur.

Romans Road of Grace. Doug Huffman. 1980. pap. 2.99 (*1-56632-008-9*) Revival Lit.

Romans Speak for Themselves. Gilbert Lawall. 1989. teacher ed. 7.50 (*0-8013-0269-2*, 78040) Longman.

Romans Speak for Themselves, Bk. I. Gilbert Lawall. 1988. pap. text ed. 7.80 (*0-8013-0267-6*, 75919) Longman.

Romans Speak for Themselves, Bk. II. Gilbert Lawall. 1987. pap. text ed. 7.80 (*0-8013-0268-4*, 78041) Longman.

Romans, the Gospel of God's Grace. Alva J. McClain. 1979. 12.99 (*0-88469-080-6*) BMH Bks.

Romans to Revelations. Gordon Jones. LC 96-1096. (New Sermon Outlines Ser.). 112p. 1996. pap. 7.99 (*0-87213-453-9*) Loizeaux.

Romans: Verse by Verse see Romanos: Versiculo por Versiculo

Romans, Vol. 1: Crusoe, Etc. Daniel Defoe. (FRE.). 1939. 85.00 (*0-8288-3473-3*, F77000) Fr & Eur.

Romans, Vol. 2: Moll Flanders, Etc. Daniel Defoe. (FRE.). 1970. 105.00 (*0-8288-3474-1*, F77001) Fr & Eur.

Roman's World. Frank G. Moore. LC 65-23486. (Illus.). 502p. (J). (gr. 7 up). 1936. 30.00 (*0-8196-0155-1*) Biblo.

Romans 1-8. James D. Dunn. (Biblical Commentary Ser.: Vol. 38a). 1988. 29.99 (*0-8499-0237-1*) Word Pub.

Romans 1-8. John J. MacArthur, Jr. (MacArthur New Testament Commentary Ser.). 1991. 21.99 (*0-8024-0767-6*) Moody.

***Romans 8: Verses One to Four.** Thomas Jacomb. 381p. 1996. reprint ed. 24.99 (*0-85151-707-2*) Banner of Truth.

***Romans 9-11: A Reader-Response Analysis.** John G. Lodge. LC 96-41546. (University of South Florida International Studies in Formative Christianity & Judaism). 243p. 1996. 84.95 (*0-7885-0312-X*, 242506) Scholars Pr GA.

Romans 9-16. James D. Dunn. (Biblical Commentary Ser.: Vol. 38B). 1988. 29.99 (*0-8499-0252-5*) Word Pub.

Romans 9-16. John MacArthur, Jr. (MacArthur New Testament Commentary Ser.). 1994. text ed. 21.99 (*0-8024-0768-4*) Moody.

RoManSy Nine: Proceedings of the Ninth CISM-IFToMM Symposium on Theory & Practice of Robots & Manipulators, Udine, Italy, Sept. 1-4, 1992. Ed. by A. Morecki et al. (Lecture Notes in Control & Information Sciences Ser.: Vol. 187). (Illus.). xxxi, 438p. 1993. 104.95 (*0-387-19834-2*) Spr-Verlag.

Romantic. Aram Saroyan. 224p. 1989. text ed. 16.95 (*0-685-67673-0*) Blackberry Bks.

Romantic Affinities: German Authors & Carlyle - A Study in the History of Ideas. E. M. Vida. 256p. 1993. 45.00 (*0-8020-5012-3*) U of Toronto Pr.

Romantic Age in Britain. Ed. by Boris Ford. (Cultural History of Britain Ser.). (Illus.). 336p. (C). 1992. pap. text ed. 24.95 (*0-521-42886-6*) Cambridge U Pr.

Romantic & Victorian: Studies in Memory of William H. Marshall. Paul W. Elledge & Richard L. Hoffman. LC 79-124099. 366p. 1975. 40.00 (*0-8386-7742-8*) Fairleigh Dickinson.

Romantic Androgyny: The Women Within. Diane L. Hoeveler. LC 89-71135. (Illus.). 272p. 1991. lib. bdg. 35.00 (*0-271-00704-4*) Pa St U Pr.

Romantic Applique. Yvonne Overton. (Illus.). 96p. 1995. pap. 12.95 (*0-614-07136-4*, Pub. by S Milner AT) Sterling.

Romantic Applique. Yvonne Overton. (Illus.). 72p. 1995. pap. 14.95 (*1-86351-140-7*, Pub. by S Milner AT) Sterling.

Romantic Art. William Vaughn. (World of Art Ser.). (Illus.). 288p. 1985. 19.95 (*0-500-18160-8*) Thames Hudson.

***Romantic Art of Confession: De Quincey, De Musset, Sand, Lamb, Hogg, & Others.** Susan M. Levin. (COMPLIT Ser.). 240p. 1998. 54.00 (*1-57113-189-2*) Camden Hse.

Romantic Art of Theodor von Holst, 1810-44. Max Browne. (Illus.). 112p. (C). 1994. pap. 32.50 (*0-85331-661-9*, Pub. by Lund Humphries UK) Antique Collect.

Romantic at Heart & Other Faults. Andre Farkas. 1980. pap. 3.00 (*0-916696-11-1*) Cross Country.

Romantic at-Home Dinners: Sneaky Strategies for Couples with Kids. Nan Booth & Gary Fischler. LC 93-33634. 160p. (Orig.). 1994. pap. 9.95 (*0-918420-19-9*) Brighton Pubns.

Romantic Atlanta. Susan Murphy. (Romantic Guide Ser.). (Illus.). 296p. (Orig.). 1993. pap. 10.95 (*1-879244-45-4*) Windom Bks.

Romantic Ballads & One Waltz, Vol. 82. rev. ed. 64p. Date not set. pap. 7.95 (*0-7935-4796-2*, 00100565) H Leonard.

Romantic Ballet as Seen by Theophile Gautier. Theophile Gautier. LC 79-7764. (Dance Ser.). (Illus.). 1980. reprint ed. lib. bdg. 18.95 (*0-8369-9292-X*) Ayer.

Romantic Ballet in England: Its Development, Fulfilment, & Decline. Ivor F. Guest. LC 77-172138. (Illus.). 202p. reprint ed. pap. 57.60 (*0-685-23377-4*, 2032490) Bks Demand.

Romantic Bards & British Reviewers: A Selected Edition of the Contemporary Reviews of the Works of Wordsworth, Coleridge, Byron, Keats, & Shelley. John O. Hayden. LC 71-125670. 453p. reprint ed. pap. 129.20 (*0-7837-6461-8*, 2046465) Bks Demand.

Romantic Biography of the Age of Elizabeth: Or, Sketches of Life from the Bye-Ways of History, 2vols. Ed. by William C. Taylor. LC 72-14121. (Essay Index Reprint Ser.). 1977. reprint ed. 51.95 (*0-518-10027-8*) Ayer.

Romantic Body: Love & Sexuality in Keats, Wordsworth, & Blake. Jean H. Hagstrum. LC 85-7485. (Hodges Lectures). (Illus.). 196p. 1986. text ed. 23.00 (*0-87049-482-1*) U of Tenn Pr.

Romantic California Getaways. Larry Fox & Barbara Radin-Fox. LC 91-24758. 272p. 1992. pap. text ed. 12.95 (*0-471-53999-6*) Wiley.

Romantic Castles of Scotland, Bk. 1. (Illus.). 32p. 1993. pap. 3.95 (*0-7117-0150-4*) Seven Hills Bk.

Romantic Castles of Scotland, Bk. 2. (Illus.). 32p. 1993. pap. 3.95 (*0-7117-0185-7*) Seven Hills Bk.

Romantic Castles of Scotland, Bk. 3. (Illus.). 32p. 1993. pap. 3.95 (*0-7117-0303-5*) Seven Hills Bk.

Romantic Child: From Runge to Sendak. Robert Rosenblum. (Walter Neurath Memorial Lecture). (Illus.). 1989. 12.95 (*0-500-55020-4*) Thames Hudson.

Romantic Comedians. Ellen Glasgow. 288p. (C). 1995. pap. 14.95 (*0-8139-1615-1*) U Pr of Va.

Romantic Comedians. Ellen A. Glasgow. Ed. by Elizabeth Hardwick. LC 76-51668. (Rediscovered Fiction by American Women Ser.). 1977. reprint ed. lib. bdg. 33.95 (*0-405-10047-7*) Ayer.

Romantic Comedy. David G. James. LC 80-18323. reprint ed. 20.00 (*0-404-14011-4*) AMS Pr.

Romantic Composers. Daniel G. Mason. LC 73-119654. reprint ed. 29.50 (*0-404-04223-6*) AMS Pr.

Romantic Composers. Daniel G. Mason. LC 69-13990. 353p. 1970. reprint ed. text ed. 65.00 (*0-8371-4096-X*, MARC, Greenwood Pr) Greenwood.

Romantic Composers. Daniel G. Mason. 353p. 1990. reprint ed. lib. bdg. 79.00 (*0-7812-9040-6*) Rprt Serv.

***Romantic Confusions of the Good: Beauty As Truth, Truth Beauty.** Marion Montgomery. LC 96-36051. 288p. 1996. pap. 23.95 (*0-8476-8394-X*) Rowman.

***Romantic Confusions of the Good: Beauty As Truth, Truth Beauty.** Marion Montgomery. LC 96-36051. 288p. 1996. 62.50 (*0-8476-8393-1*) Rowman.

Romantic Contraries: Freedom vs. Destiny. fac. ed. Peter L. Thorslev. LC 83-17114. 235p. 1984. pap. 67.00 (*0-7837-7722-1*, 2080193) Bks Demand.

Romantic Correspondence: Women, Politics & the Fiction of Letters. Mary A. Favret. (Cambridge Studies in Romanticism: No. 1). (Illus.). 284p. (C). 1993. 59.95 (*0-521-41096-7*) Cambridge U Pr.

Romantic Critical Essays. Ed. by David Bromwich. (Cambridge English Prose Texts Ser.). 350p. 1988. pap. 18.95 (*0-521-28672-7*) Cambridge U Pr.

***Romantic Dates: Ways to Woo & Wow the One You Love.** Greg Godek. LC 96-52863. 128p. (Orig.). 1997. pap. 6.95 (*1-57071-153-4*, Casablanca) Sourcebks.

Romantic Days & Nights in Boston: Intimate Escapes in the Hub. Patricia Harris & David Lyon. LC 96-44129. (Romantic Cities Ser.). (Illus.). 240p. 1997. pap. 14.95 (*1-56440-876-0*) Globe Pequot.

Romantic Days & Nights in Chicago: Intimate Escapes in the Windy City. Susan Figliulo. LC 96-44136. (Romantic Cities Ser.). (Illus.). 240p. 1997. pap. 14.95 (*1-56440-972-4*) Globe Pequot.

***Romantic Days & Nights in Los Angeles: Intimate Escapes in the City of Angels.** Stephen Dolainski. (Romantic Cities Ser.). (Illus.). 288p. 1997. pap. 14.95 (*0-7627-0128-5*) Globe Pequot.

***Romantic Days & Nights in Montreal: Intimate Escapes in the Paris of North America.** Linda Kay. LC 97-19935. (Romantic Cities Ser.). (Illus.). 256p. (Orig.). 1997. pap. 14.95 (*0-7627-0038-6*) Globe Pequot.

***Romantic Days & Nights in New Orleans: Intimate Escapes in the Big Easy.** Constance Snow. LC 97-24501. (Romantic Cities Ser.). (Illus.). 288p. 1997. pap. 14.95 (*0-7627-0121-8*) Globe Pequot.

Romantic Days & Nights in New York City: Intimate Escapes in the Big Apple. Pamela Thomas. LC 96-36878. (Romantic Cities Ser.). (Illus.). 240p. (Orig.). 1997. pap. 14.95 (*1-56440-970-8*) Globe Pequot.

Romantic Days & Nights in San Francisco. Donna Peck. LC 96-28009. (Romantic Cities Ser.). 240p. 1996. pap. 14.95 (*1-56440-875-2*) Globe Pequot.

***Romantic Days & Nights in Seattle: Intimate Escapes in the Emerald City.** Jo Brown. LC 97-14378. (Romantic Cities Ser.). (Illus.). 275p. (Orig.). 1997. pap. 14.95 (*0-7627-0037-8*) Globe Pequot.

Romantic Decatur. Charles L. Lewis. LC 79-164614. (Select Bibliographies Reprint Ser.). 1977. reprint ed. 23.95 (*0-8369-5898-5*) Ayer.

Romantic Dialogue: Communication in Dating & Marriage. Michael J. Beatty. 160p. (C). 1986. pap. text ed. 14.95 (*0-89582-146-X*) Morton Pub.

Romantic Discourse & Political Modernity: Wordsworth, the Intellectual & Cultural Critique. Richard Bourke. LC 92-47355. 272p. 1993. text ed. 39.95 (*0-312-09630-5*) St Martin.

Romantic Doctor Rydon. large type ed. Anne Durham. (Linford Romance Library). 272p. 1987. pap. 8.95 (*0-7089-6446-X*, Linford) Ulverscroft.

Romantic Drama. Ed. by Gerald Gillespie. LC 93-34838. (Comparative History of Literatures in European Languages Ser.: No. 9). xvi, 516p. 1994. lib. bdg. 150.00 (*1-55619-600-8*) Benjamins North Am.

Romantic Dramas of Garcia Gutierrez. Nicholson B. Adams. 1976. lib. bdg. 59.95 (*0-8490-2542-7*) Gordon Pr.

Romantic Dramas of Garcia Gutierrez. Nicholson B. Adams. 149p. 1922. 1.00 (*0-318-14303-8*) Hispanic Inst.

Romantic Dream: Wordsworth & the Poetics of the Unconscious. Douglas Wilson. LC 92-25123. xx, 200p. (C). 1993. text ed. 37.50 (*0-8032-4761-3*) U of Nebr Pr.

Romantic Duets. 96p. 1986. pap. 9.95 (*0-7935-1240-9*, 50504300) H Leonard.

Romantic Encounter. Betty A. Neels. (Romance Ser.). 1993. pap. 2.89 (*0-373-03249-8*, 1-03249-9) Harlequin Bks.

Romantic Encounter. Lindsay Welsh. (Orig.). 1995. mass mkt. 5.95 (*1-56333-359-7*, Rosebud) Masquerade.

Romantic Encounter. large type ed. Betty A. Neels. 1993. reprint ed. lib. bdg. 18.95 (*0-263-13184-X*, Pub. by Mills & Boon UK) Thorndike Pr.

Romantic Enlightenment. Geoffrey Clive. LC 72-8238. 219p. 1973. reprint ed. text ed. 55.00 (*0-8371-6544-X*, CLRE, Greenwood Pr) Greenwood.

Romantic Era. Friedman-Fairfax & Sony Music Staff. (Life, Times & Music Book/CD Ser.). 1995. pap. 16.98 incl. audio compact disk (*1-56799-001-0*, Friedman-Fairfax) M Friedman Pub Grp Inc.

Romantic Era see Source Readings in Music History

Romantic Ethic & the Spirit of Modern Consumerism. Colin Campbell. 320p. 1989. pap. 26.95 (*0-631-16941-5*) Blackwell Pubs.

Romantic Fairy Tale: Seeds of Surrealism. Marianne Thalmann. Tr. by Mary B. Corcoran. LC 64-17439. 143p. reprint ed. pap. 40.80 (*0-317-26227-0*, 2055656) Bks Demand.

Romantic Fallacies. Richard Hoffpauir. (American University Studies: English Language & Literature: Ser. IV, Vol. 31). 189p. 1986. text ed. 30.50 (*0-8204-0257-5*) P Lang Pubng.

***Romantic Fantasies: And Other Sexy Ways of Expressing Your Love.** Greg Godek. LC 96-52852. 128p. (Orig.). 1997. pap. 6.95 (*1-57071-154-2*) Sourcebks.

Romantic Fantastic. Tobin Siebers. LC 83-20999. 195p. 1984. 35.00 (*0-8014-1671-X*) Cornell U Pr.

Romantic Feminism in Hindi Novels Written by Women. Indu P. Pandey. 1989. 21.50 (*81-85313-00-8*, Pub. by Usha II) S Asia.

Romantic Florals with Sculpey III. Donna Kato. (Illus.). 20p. (Orig.). 1994. pap. 6.95 (*1-885669-00-3*) Prairie Crft.

Romantic Flower. Silvio Cadelo. Ed. by Bernd Metz. Tr. by Tom Leighton from FRE. (Illus.). 49p. (Orig.). 1990. pap. 9.95 (*0-87416-088-X*) Catalan Communs.

Romantic Foundations of the American Renaissance. Leon Chai. LC 87-5428. 456p. (C). 1987. pap. 17.95 (*0-8014-9715-9*) Cornell U Pr.

Romantic Fragment Poem: A Critique of a Form. Marjorie Levinson. LC 85-28927. x, 268p. 1986. 37.50 (*0-8078-1684-1*) U of NC Pr.

***Romantic Garden.** (Garden Journal Ser.). 1998. 12.95 (*1-56799-612-4*, Friedman-Fairfax) M Friedman Pub Grp Inc.

Romantic Garden. Graham Rose. 168p. 1988. pap. 19.95 (*0-14-025143-X*, Viking) Viking Penguin.

Romantic Generation. Charles Rosen. LC 94-46239. (Illus.). 723p. 1995. 39.95 (*0-674-77933-9*, ROSROM) HUP.

Romantic Generation of Modern Chinese Writers. Leo O. Lee. LC 73-75058. (Harvard East Asian Ser.: No. 71). (Illus.). 379p. reprint ed. pap. 109.20 (*0-7837-4166-9*, 2059014) Bks Demand.

Romantic Genesis of the Modern Novel. Charles Schug. LC 78-26484. (Critical Essays in Modern Literature Ser.). 279p. reprint ed. pap. 79.60 (*0-7837-2148-X*, 2042434) Bks Demand.

Romantic Germany. (Panorama Bks.). (Illus.). (ENG & FRE.). 3.95 (*0-685-11540-2*) Fr & Eur.

Romantic Getaways in the Pacific Northwest & Western Canada. Larry Fox & Barbara Radin-Fox. LC 92-7197. 256p. 1992. pap. text ed. 12.95 (*0-471-53997-X*) Wiley.

Romantic Guitar. Frederick M. Noad. (Illus.). 128p. 1974. pap. 16.95 (*0-8256-2415-0*, AM38993) Music Sales.

Romantic Hawaiian Getaways. Larry Fox & Barbara Radin-Fox. LC 91-287. 224p. 1991. pap. text ed. 12.95 (*0-471-52538-3*) Wiley.

Romantic Hearts: A Personal Logbook for Romance Readers. Peggy Jaegly. 630p. 1992. pap. text ed. 16.95 (*0-9630622-0-4*) Rose NJ.

Romantic Hearts: A Personal Reference for Romance Readers. 1,995th ed. Peggy J. Jaegly. LC 95-12406. 928p. 1995. 59.00 (*0-8108-3002-7*) Scarecrow.

***Romantic Hearts: A Personal Reference for Romance Readers.** 3rd ed. Peggy J. Jaegly. LC 96-37378. 928p. 1997. pap. 27.95 (*1-57886-000-8*) Scarecrow Trade.

Romantic Heritage of Marxism: A Study of East German Love Poetry. Boria Sax. (Studies in Modern German Literature: Vol. 15). 199p. (C). 1987. text ed. 34.00 (*0-8204-0487-X*) P Lang Pubng.

Romantic Heroic Ideal. James D. Wilson. LC 82-58. 237p. 1982. reprint ed. pap. 67.60 (*0-608-00873-7*, 2061667) Bks Demand.

***Romantic Hideaways.** Thomas Kinkade. (Lighted Path Collection). (Illus.). 48p. (Orig.). 1997. 16.99 (*1-56507-541-2*) Harvest Hse.

Romantic Hits for Piano Vol. 1: Easy-Intermediate. Ed. by Tony Esposito. 32p. (YA). 1995. pap. text ed. 5.95 (*0-89724-690-X*, AF9518) Warner Brothers.

Romantic Homage to Greece & Spain. Leo Bronstein. (Illus.). 290p. 1991. 30.00 (*0-933858-24-8*) Kennebec River.

Romantic Homage to Greece & Spain: My Fable, Their Art. Leo Bronstein. LC 93-9949. (Illus.). 317p. (C). 1993. text ed. 79.95 (*1-56000-117-8*) Transaction Pubs.

Romantic Horizons: Aspects of the Sublime in English Poetry & Painting, 1770-1850. James B. Twitchell. LC 83-3679. (Illus.). 248p. 1983. text ed. 32.50 (*0-8262-0411-2*) U of Mo Pr.

Romantic Houses. Ed. by Andreas Papadakis. (Architectural Design Ser.: No. 34). (Illus.). 96p. (Orig.). 1981. pap. 15.00 (*0-85670-754-6*) Academy Ed UK.

Romantic Identities: Varieties of Subjectivity, 1774-1830. Andrea K. Henderson. (Studies in Romanticism: No. 20). (Illus.). 193p. (C). 1996. text ed. 44.95 (*0-521-48164-3*) Cambridge U Pr.

Romantic Ideology: A Critical Investigation. Jerome J. McGann. LC 82-17494. 184p. (C). 1985. pap. text ed. 10.95 (*0-226-55850-9*) U Ch Pr.

Romantic Ideology Unmasked: The Mentally Constructed Tyrannies in Dramas of William Wordsworth, Lord Byron, Percy Shelley, & Joanna Baillie. Marjean D. Purinton. LC 93-41730. 1994. 36.50 (*0-87413-499-4*) U Delaware Pr.

Romantic Imagination. C. M. Bowra. (Oxford Paperbacks Ser.). 318p. 1976. pap. 17.95 (*0-19-281006-5*) OUP.

***Romantic Imagination.** Hill. 1997. text ed. 17.95 (*0-333-21235-5*, Pub. by Macm UK) St Martin.

Romantic Imagination in the Works of Gustavo Adolfo Becquer. B. Brant Bynum. LC 92-56386. (Studies in the Romance Languages & Literatures: No. 246). 150p. (C). 1993. pap. text ed. 22.50 (*0-8078-9250-5*) U of NC Pr.

Romantic Impulse in Victorian Fiction. Donald D. Stone. LC 79-27736. 404p. 1980. 36.50 (*0-674-77932-0*) HUP.

Romantic Indian: Sentimental Views from Nineteenth-Century American Literature, 4 vols. LC 80-19248. 1981. 200.00 (*0-8201-1356-5*) Schol Facsimiles.

Romantic Influences: Contemporary, Victorian, Modern. John B. Beer. LC 93-29451. 256p. 1993. text ed. 49.95 (*0-312-10639-4*) St Martin.

Romantic Interior. Clive Wainwright. 1989. text ed. 67.50 (*0-300-04225-6*) Yale U Pr.

Romantic Interludes: A Sensuous Lover's Guide. 3rd ed. Kenneth R. Stubbs. 192p. 1996. pap. 12.95 (*0-939263-14-9*) Secret Garden.

Romantic Irony: A Comparative History of Literatures in European Languages, Vol. 8. Ed. by Fredrick Garber. (Comparative History of Literatures in European Languages Ser.: Vol. 8). 395p. (C). 1988. lib. bdg. 75.00 (*963-05-4844-5*, Pub. by Akadem Kiado HU) Benjamins North Am.

Romantic Irony in French Literature: From Diderot to Beckett. Lloyd Bishop. LC 89-35563. 256p. 1990. 29.95 (*0-8265-1233-X*) Vanderbilt U Pr.

Romantic Irony of Semiotics: Friedrich Schlegel & the Crisis of Representation. Marike Finlay. (Approaches to Semiotics Ser.). 293p. (C). 1988. text ed. 119.25 (*0-89925-330-X*) Mouton.

Romantic Journey. Stephanie Howard. (Romance Ser.: No. 195). 1992. pap. 2.89 (*0-373-03195-5*, 1-03195-4) Harlequin Bks.

Romantic Journey. Andrea Sinclair. 1994. 17.95 (*0-8034-9076-3*, 094424) Bouregy.

Romantic Keepsakes: Exquisite Heirlooms to Create, Give & Treasure. Lucinda Ganderton & Debbie Patterson. (Illus.). 160p. 1995. 27.95 (*0-8069-0801-7*) Sterling.

Romantic L. A. Susan Murphy. (Romantic Guide Ser.). (Illus.). 296p. (Orig.). 1994. pap. 10.95 (*1-879244-49-7*) Windom Bks.

Romantic Lady. Sylvia Thorpe. 224p. 1980. pap. 1.75 (*0-449-50057-8*, Coventry) Fawcett.

Romantic Landscape Vision: Constable & Wordsworth. Karl Kroeber. LC 74-5905. (Illus.). 156p. 1975. 27.50 (*0-299-06710-6*) U of Wis Pr.

Romantic Legacy. Charles Larmore. 120p. 1996. 20.00 (*0-231-10134-1*) Col U Pr.

Romantic Legacy. large type ed. Cora Mayne. (Linford Romance Library). 304p. 1984. pap. 15.99 (*0-7089-6008-1*) Ulverscroft.

Romantic Legends of Spain. Gustavo A. Becquer. Tr. by Cornelia F. Bates & Katharine L. Bates. LC 78-169539. (Short Story Index Reprint Ser.). 1977. reprint ed. 22.95 (*0-8369-4000-8*) Ayer.

Romantic Life of Shelley & the Sequel. Francis Gribble. LC 72-3624. (Studies in Shelley: No. 25). 1972. reprint ed. lib. bdg. 58.95 (*0-8383-1566-6*) M S G Haskell Hse.

Romantic Lives of Louise Mack. Nancy Phelan. 1991. pap. 19.95 (*0-7022-2361-1*, Pub. by Univ Queensland Pr AT) Intl Spec Bk.

Romantic Longings: Love in America. Steven Seidman. 256p. (C). 1993. pap. 17.95 (*0-415-90828-0*, Routledge NY) Routledge.

Romantic Love. Susan S. Hendrick & Clyde Hendrick. (Series on Close Relationships: Vol. 1). 160p. (C). 1992. text ed. 38.00 (*0-8039-3670-2*); pap. text ed. 16.95 (*0-8039-3671-0*) Sage.

Romantic Love: A Philosophical Inquiry. Dwight Van de Vate, Jr. LC 81-47171. 176p. (C). 1981. 28.50 (*0-271-00288-3*) Pa St U Pr.

***Romantic Love & Sexual Behavior: Perspectives from the Social Sciences.** Ed. by Victor C. De Munck. 1998. text ed. write for info. (*0-275-95726-8*, Praeger Pubs) Greenwood.

Romantic Manifesto. Ayn Rand. 1971. pap. 5.99 (*0-451-14916-5*, AE2374, Sig) NAL-Dutton.

Romantic Manifesto. Ayn Rand. 1993. pap. write for info. (*0-451-17399-6*, Sig) NAL-Dutton.

Romantic Manifesto: An Anthology. Larry H. Peer. (American University Studies: Comparative Literature: Ser. III, Vol. 23). 156p. (C). 1988. text ed. 36.50 (*0-318-37856-6*) P Lang Pubng.

Romantic Masquerade. Lois Stewart. 1990. mass mkt. 3.95 (*0-8217-3221-8*, Zebra Kensgtn) Kensgtn Pub Corp.

***Romantic Massage.** R. J. Nikola. LC 97-21597. 1997. write for info. (*0-8069-9973-X*) Sterling.

Romantic Massage. Anne K. Rush. 1991. pap. 14.00 (*0-380-75985-3*) Avon.

***Romantic Masters.** Ed. by Dale Tucker. 32p. (Orig.). (C). 1996. pap. text ed. 7.95 (*1-57623-716-8*, EL96116) Warner Brothers.

Romantic Medicine & John Keats. Hermione De Almeida. 432p. 1990. 58.00 (*0-19-506307-4*) OUP.

Romantic Melody. Pamela Fudge. (Rainbow Romances Ser.: No. 895). 160p. 1994. 14.95 (*0-7090-4949-8*, Hale-Parkwest) Parkwest Pubns.

***Romantic Melody.** large type ed. Pamela Fudge. (Linford Romance Library). 240p. 1996. pap. 15.99 (*0-7089-7920-3*) Ulverscroft.

Romantic Miami. Donna Sweeny. (Romantic Guide Ser.). (Illus.). 256p. (Orig.). 1993. pap. 10.95 (*1-879244-43-8*) Windom Bks.

***Romantic Mischief: The Playful Side of Love.** Greg Godek. 128p. (Orig.). 1997. pap. 6.95 (*1-57071-151-8*, Casablanca) Sourcebks.

Romantic Mother: Narcissistic Patterns in Romantic Poetry. Barbara A. Schapiro. LC 82-14023. 160p. 1983. pap. 45.60 (*0-7837-7455-9*, 2049177) Bks Demand.

Romantic Motives: Essays on Anthropological Sensibility. Ed. by George W. Stocking, Jr. LC 89-40268. (History of Anthropology Ser.: Vol. 6). (Illus.). 294p. (C). 1989. text ed. 27.50 (*0-299-12360-X*) U of Wis Pr.

Romantic Motives: Essays on Anthropological Sensibility. Ed. by George W. Stocking. LC 89-40268. (History of Anthropology Ser.: Vol. 6). (Illus.). 294p. 1996. pap. 14.95 (*0-299-12364-2*) U of Wis Pr.

Romantic Movement. Maurice Cranston. (Making of Europe Ser.). 194p. 1994. 45.95 (*0-631-17399-4*) Blackwell Pubs.

Romantic Movement. Maurice Cranston. (Making of Europe Ser.). 194p. 1994. pap. 20.95 (*0-631-19471-1*) Blackwell Pubs.

Romantic Movement. Alain De Botton. 336p. 1996. pap. 13.00 (*0-312-14403-2*, Picador USA) St Martin.

Romantic Movement. Alan Menhennet. (Literary History of Germany Ser.: Vol. 6). 276p. 1981. 58.50 (*0-389-20104-9*, N6878) B&N Imports.

Romantic Movement: A Selective & Critical Bibliography for 1987. Ed. by David V. Erdman. 451p. (C). 1988. lib. bdg. 60.00 (*0-933951-22-1*) Locust Hill Pr.

Romantic Movement: A Selective & Critical Bibliography for 1988. Ed. by David V. Erdman. 464p. (C). 1989. lib. bdg. 60.00 (*0-933951-34-5*) Locust Hill Pr.

Romantic Movement: A Selective & Critical Bibliography for 1989. Ed. by David V. Erdman. 526p. 1990. lib. bdg. 60.00 (*0-933951-37-X*) Locust Hill Pr.

Romantic Movement: A Selective & Critical Bibliography for 1990. Ed. by David V. Erdman. 473p. (C). 1991. lib. bdg. 60.00 (*0-933951-47-7*) Locust Hill Pr.

Romantic Movement: A Selective & Critical Bibliography for 1991. Ed. by David V. Erdman. 534p. (C). 1992. lib. bdg. 60.00 (*0-933951-49-3*) Locust Hill Pr.

Romantic Movement: A Selective & Critical Bibliography for 1992. David V. Erdman. 530p. (C). 1993. lib. bdg. 60.00 (*0-933951-51-5*) Locust Hill Pr.

Romantic Movement: A Selective & Critical Bibliography for 1993. Ed. by David V. Erdman. 544p. (C). 1994. lib. bdg. 60.00 (*0-933951-62-0*) Locust Hill Pr.

Romantic Movement: A Selective & Critical Bibliography for 1994. Ed. by David V. Erdman. 424p. 1995. lib. bdg. 60.00 (*0-933951-65-5*) Locust Hill Pr.

***Romantic Movement: A Selective & Critical Bibliography for 1995.** Ed. by David V. Erdman & Peter Lundman. 488p. (C). 1996. lib. bdg. 60.00 (*0-933951-72-8*) Locust Hill Pr.

Romantic Movement: Sex, Shopping & the Novel. Alain de Botton. (Illus.). 326p. 1995. 23.00 (*0-312-13159-3*) St Martin.

Romantic Movement & Methodism: A Study of English Romanticism & the Evangelical Revival. Frederick C. Gill. 189p. (C). 1966. reprint ed. text ed. 75.00 (*0-8383-0660-8*) M S G Haskell Hse.

Romantic Movement Bibliography, 1936-1970: A Master Cumulation from ELH, Philological Quarterly & English Language Notes, 7 Vols, Set. Ed. by A. C. Elkins & Lorne Forstner. LC 77-172773. (Cumulated Bibliography Ser.: No. 3). 1973. 290.00 (*0-87650-025-4*) Pierian.

Romantic Movement in English Poetry. Arthur Symons. LC 74-90371. 356p. (C). 1969. reprint ed. 75.00 (*0-87753-038-6*) Phaeton.

Romantic Movement in English Poetry. Arthur Symons. (BCL1-PR English Literature Ser.). 344p. 1992. reprint ed. pap. text ed. 69.00 (*0-685-52727-1*); reprint ed. lib. bdg. 89.00 (*0-7812-7091-X*) Rprt Serv.

Romantic Music. Leon Plantinga. LC 83-42653. (Introduction to Music History Ser.). (Illus.). (C). 1985. text ed. 33.95 (*0-393-95196-0*) Norton.

Romantic Music: A Concise History from Schubert to Sibelius. Arnold Whittall. LC 86-71617. (World of Art Ser.). (Illus.). 1987. pap. 14.95 (*0-500-20215-X*) Thames Hudson.

Romantic Music: Sound & Syntax. Leonard G. Ratner. 348p. 1992. 45.00 (*0-02-872065-2*) Schirmer Bks.

Romantic Naiad. Naiad Press Authors Staff. Ed. by Katherine V. Forrest & Barbara Grier. 352p. 1993. pap. 14.95 (*1-56280-054-X*) Naiad Pr.

Romantic Nationalism & Liberalism: Joachim Lelewel & the Polish National Idea. Joan S. Skurnowicz. (East European Monographs: No. 83). 202p. 1981. text ed. 57.00 (*0-914710-77-X*) East Eur Monographs.

Romantic Needlepoint: 20 Needlepoint Designs Inspired by Love, Vol. 1. Candace Bahouth. 1996. 29.95 (*0-8212-2238-4*) Bulfinch Pr.

Romantic New England Getaways. Andrea Brox. Ed. by Beverly J. Wood. LC 93-5825. (Illus.). 348p. 1993. pap. 15.95 (*0-9636123-0-1*) Pleasant St Pr.

Romantic New Orleans. Deirdre Stanforth. LC 86-2472. (Illus.). 136p. 1986. reprint ed. pap. 11.95 (*0-88289-496-X*) Pelican.

Romantic New York. Susan Murphy. (Romantic Guide Ser.). (Illus.). 296p. (Orig.). 1994. pap. 10.95 (*1-879244-48-9*) Windom Bks.

***Romantic New York City.** William King & Jimmy Hahn. 180p. 1997. pap. 14.95 (*0-9634403-3-0*) Magellan Pr.

Romantic Notions: To Show the Love You Feel. deluxe ed. Lisa T. Bergren. 160p. 1993. pap. 5.99 (*0-88070-652-X*, Multnomah Bks) Multnomah Pubs.

Romantic Novel in England. Robert Kiely. LC 79-186677. 282p. reprint ed. pap. 81.80 (*0-7837-4160-X*, 2059008) Bks Demand.

Romantic Novellas. Heinrich Von Kleist & Jean Paul. Ed. by Frank G. Ryder & Robert M. Browning. (German Library: Vol. 34). 320p. 1985. 29.50 (*0-8264-0294-1*); pap. text ed. 16.95 (*0-8264-0295-X*) Continuum.

Romantic Oil Painting Made Easy. Robert Hagan. 1996. 29.95 (*0-646-25893-1*, Wrtrs Digest Bks) F & W Pubns Inc.

Romantic Old West Christmas. Murray W. Nabors. (Orig.). 1993. pap. write for info. (*0-9639523-3-1*) Associates CO.

Romantic Opera & Literary Form. Peter Conrad. (Quantum Bks.: No. 9). (Illus.). 185p. 1977. pap. 14.00 (*0-520-04508-4*) U CA Pr.

Romantic Opus n' Bill. Berkeley Breathed. LC 94-925. (Illus.). 1994. mass mkt. 1.40 (*0-316-10879-0*) Little.

Romantic Orpheus: Profiles of Clemens Brentano. John F. Fetzer. LC 72-85527. 325p. reprint ed. pap. 92.70 (*0-685-44490-2*, 2031504) Bks Demand.

Romantic Outlaws, Beloved Prisons: The Unconscious Meanings of Crime & Punishment. Martha G. Duncan. 288p. (C). 1996. 29.95 (*0-8147-1880-9*) NYU Pr.

Romantic Paintings in America. James T. Soby & Dorothy C. Miller. LC 73-86430. (Museum of Modern Art Publications in Reprint). (Illus.). 1969. reprint ed. 18.95 (*0-405-01550-X*) Ayer.

Romantic Paradox: An Essay on the Poetry of Wordsworth. Colin C. Clarke. LC 78-10859. 101p. 1979. reprint ed. text ed. 52.50 (*0-313-20758-5*, CLPA, Greenwood Pr) Greenwood.

Romantic Parodies, 1797-1831. Ed. by David A. Kent & Dale R. Ewen. LC 91-55380. 416p. 1992. 59.50 (*0-8386-3458-3*) Fairleigh Dickinson.

***Romantic Passion: A Universal Experience?** William Jankowiak. 1997. pap. text ed. 17.00 (*0-231-09687-9*) Col U Pr.

***Romantic Passion: A Universal Experience?** Ed. by William Jankowiak. 1997. pap. 17.00 (*0-614-27657-8*) Col U Pr.

Romantic Passion: The Universal Experience? Ed. by William Jankowiak. LC 95-6954. 1995. 27.50 (*0-231-09686-0*) Col U Pr.

Romantic Period, Vol. 5. Ed. by David B. Pirie. (Penguin History of Literature Ser.). 448p. 1994. pap. 12.95 (*0-14-017755-8*, Penguin Bks) Viking Penguin.

Romantic Pilgrim. Beryl Shill. (Rainbow Romances Ser.: No. 885). 160p. 1994. 14.95 (*0-7090-4941-2*, Hale-Parkwest) Parkwest Pubns.

Romantic Pilgrim. large type ed. Beryl Shill. (Linford Romance Library). 240p. 1995. pap. 15.99 (*0-7089-7670-0*, Linford) Ulverscroft.

Romantic Places on the Westside. 3rd rev. ed. Bob Lewis. (Illus.). 80p. 1996. pap. 4.95 (*0-9650931-3-1*) B Lewis.

Romantic Poetry. Mary Y. Sampson et al. Ed. by Mary Bertschmann. (Port Authority Poetry Review Ser.). (Illus.). 100p. (Orig.). 1988. pap. 6.00 (*0-935505-04-0*) Bank St Pr.

Romantic Poetry: Recent Revisionary Criticism. Ed. by Karl Kroeber & Gene W. Ruoff. LC 93-17229. 450p. (C). 1993. text ed. 48.00 (*0-8135-2009-6*); pap. text ed. 17.00 (*0-8135-2010-X*) Rutgers U Pr.

Romantic Poetry & Prose. Ed. by Harold Bloom & Lionel Trilling. (Anthology of English Literature Ser.). (Illus.). 830p. 1973. pap. 25.00 (*0-19-501615-7*) OUP.

Romantic Poetry by Women: A Bibliography, 1770-1835. J. R. De J. Jackson. LC 92-35190. 520p. (C). 1993. 75.00 (*0-19-811239-4*, 14309, Clarendon Pr) OUP.

Romantic Poetry on the European Continent: An English Language Anthology, Vol. I. Ed. by Miroslav J. Hanak. LC 83-1169. 624p. (Orig.). (C). 1983. pap. text ed. 36.00 (*0-8191-3059-1*) U Pr of Amer.

Romantic Poets: Byron, Keats, Shelley, Wordsworth. Percy Bysshe Shelley et al. (Illus.). 224p. 1996. 14.95 (*1-85410-232-X*, Pub. by Aurum Pr UK) London Brdge.

Romantic Poets & Prose Writers. Richard H. Fogle. LC 66-29743. (Goldentree Bibliographies Series in Language & Literature). (C). 1967. pap. text ed. write for info. (*0-88295-513-6*) Harlan Davidson.

Romantic Pops: Early Intermediate Piano Solos. 20p. 1992. pap. 5.95 (*0-7935-1591-2*, 00290380) H Leonard.

Romantic Potency: The Paradox of Desire. Laura Claridge. LC 91-55556. 288p. 1992. 45.00 (*0-8014-2696-0*); pap. 15.95 (*0-8014-8016-7*) Cornell U Pr.

Romantic Predicament. Geoffrey Thurley. LC 83-15995. 240p. 1984. text ed. 29.95 (*0-312-69182-3*) St Martin.

Romantic Presences. Jeffrey C. Robinson. LC 95-11043. 1995. write for info. (*0-88268-198-2*) Station Hill Pr.

Romantic Prison: The French Tradition. Victor H. Brombert. LC 77-85532. 250p. 1978. reprint ed. pap. 71.30 (*0-7837-9492-4*, 2060236) Bks Demand.

Romantic Quest. Hoxie N. Fairchild. (BCL1-PR English Literature Ser.). 444p. 1992. reprint ed. lib. bdg. 99.00 (*0-7812-7050-2*) Rprt Serv.

***Romantic Questions: Growing Closer Through Intimate Conversation.** Greg Godek. LC 96-50431. 128p. (Orig.). 1997. pap. 6.95 (*1-57071-152-6*, Casablanca) Sourcebks.

***Romantic Quilt Block Designs.** Jodie Davis & Linda H. Schiffer. LC 96-38477. (Foundation Piecing Library). 1997. write for info. (*1-56799-443-1*, Friedman-Fairfax) M Friedman Pub Grp Inc.

Romantic Rascals. Charles J. Finger. LC 71-90637. (Essay Index Reprint Ser.). 1977. 23.95 (0-8369-1259-4) Ayer.

Romantic Rebels: Essays on Shelley & His Circle. Ed. by Kenneth N. Cameron. LC 72-97087. (Carl H. Pforzheimer Library). 330p. 1973. 25.50 (0-674-77937-1) HUP.

Romantic Recollections. Lydia Kyasht. Ed. by Erica Beale. LC 77-27057. (Series in Dance). (Illus.). 1978. reprint ed. lib. bdg. 29.50 (0-306-77572-7) Da Capo.

***Romantic Reformation: Religious Politics in English Literature 1789-1824.** Robert M. Ryan. (Studies in Romanticism: Vol. 24). 323p. (C). 1997. text ed. 59.95 (0-521-57008-5) Cambridge U Pr.

Romantic Relationships: A Psychologist Answers Frequently Asked Questions. Paul R. Robbins. LC 96-24583. 211p. 1996. pap. 22.95 (0-7864-0192-3) McFarland & Co.

Romantic Rendezvous: Twenty-Four Great Times Just Waiting to Happen. Lynn H. Fife. Ed. by Janet Lafferty. 150p. (Orig.). 1993. pap. 12.95 (1-882947-00-2) Evergreen Tech.

Romantic Reviewers, 1802-1824. John O. Hayden. LC 68-16694. 340p. reprint ed. pap. 96.90 (0-317-26507-5, 2024045) Bks Demand.

Romantic Revisions. Ed. by Robert Brinkley & Keith Hanley. (Illus.). 364p. (C). 1992. text ed. 80.00 (0-521-38074-X) Cambridge U Pr.

Romantic Revival - Setting the Record Straight. Frank Cooper & Jesse F. Knight. Ed. by Roberto Villegas. LC 79-50797. (YA). (gr. 7 up). 1980. pap. 2.95 (0-930962-02-8) Villegas Pub.

***Romantic Revival in England, Vol. 13.** John W. Cunliffe. Date not set. write for info. (0-8369-4804-1) Ayer.

Romantic Revolutionary: A Biography of John Reed. Robert A. Rosenstone. 464p. 1990. pap. text ed. 12.95 (0-674-77938-X) HUP.

Romantic Revolutions: Criticism & Theory. Ed. by Kenneth R. Johnston et al. LC 89-45355. 448p. 1990. 40.00 (0-253-33132-3); pap. 9.95 (0-253-20562-X, MB-562) Ind U Pr.

Romantic Rhapsody: Quotes from the Heart. Peggy Schaffer. Ed. by Patrick Caton. 168p. (Orig.). 1996. pap. 5.95 (1-56245-239-8) Great Quotations.

Romantic Rose. Photos by Murray Alcosser. LC 95-13263. 1995. 12.99 (0-517-14702-5) Random.

Romantic San Diego. Ken Christensen. 120p. (Orig.). 1989. pap. text ed. 5.95 (0-685-29966-X) KC Design.

Romantic Santa Fe. Hallie Love. (Romantic Guide Ser.). (Illus.). 296p. (Orig.). 1993. pap. 10.95 (1-879244-46-2) Windom Bks.

Romantic School & Other Essays. Heinrich Heine. Ed. by Volkmar Sander. (German Library: Vol. 33). 320p. 1985. 29.50 (0-8264-0290-9); pap. text ed. 16.95 (0-8264-0291-7) Continuum.

Romantic Scotland. Charles MacLean. (Country Ser.). (Illus.). 160p. 1995. pap. 17.95 (0-297-83396-0, Pub. by Orion Bks UK) Trafalgar.

***Romantic Silk Ribbon Embroidery.** Mary J. Hiney. 128p. 1997. 27.95 (0-8069-8143-1, Chapelle) Sterling.

Romantic Spain: Voices from Within, Views from Without. Gabriel H. Lovett. (American University Studies: Romance Languages & Literature: Ser. II, Vol. 74). 247p. (C). 1989. text ed. 43.95 (0-8204-0605-8) P Lang Pubng.

Romantic Spirit. Mary J. Kay. (Romance Bibliography Ser.). (Orig.). 1982. pap. 8.95 (0-9610996-0-7) MJK Ent.

Romantic Spirit: German Drawings, 1780-1850, from the German Democratic Republic. Peter Betthausen et al. (Illus.). 276p. 1989. 60.00 (0-19-520715-7) OUP.

Romantic Spirit: 1983-1984 Update. Mary J. Kay. (Orig.). 1984. pap. 5.95 (0-9610996-1-5) MJK Ent.

Romantic Spirit in German Art: 1790-1990. Robert Rosenblum et al. LC 94-60293. (Illus.). 400p. 1994. 75.00 (0-500-23693-3) Thames Hudson.

Romantic Stages: Set & Costume Design in Victorian England. Alicia Finkel. LC 96-639. (Illus.). 215p. 1996. lib. bdg. 38.50 (0-7864-0234-2) McFarland & Co.

***Romantic Stories of the Legal Profession.** Francillon. iv, 324p. 1996. reprint ed. lib. bdg. 42.50 (0-8377-2578-X) Rothman.

Romantic Sublime: Studies in the Structure & Psychology of Transcendence. Thomas Weiskel. LC 75-36932. (Illus.). 236p. reprint ed. 67.30 (0-8357-9283-8, 2019109) Bks Demand.

Romantic Syndrome: Toward a New Method in Cultural Anthropology & History of Ideas. W. T. Jones. (International Scholars Forum Ser.: No. 14). 294p. 1974. pap. text ed. 64.50 (90-247-0382-4, Pub. by M Nijhoff NE) Kluwer Ac.

Romantic Texts & Contexts. Donald H. Reiman. 408p. 1988. text ed. 39.95 (0-8262-0649-2) U of Mo Pr.

Romantic Theatre: An International Symposium. Ed. by Richard A. Cave. LC 86-26492. 144p. (C). 1987. 45.00 (0-389-20697-0) B&N Imports.

***Romantic Theatricality: Gender, Poetry, & Spectatorship.** Judith Pascoe. LC 96-34905. (Illus.). 272p. 1996. 39.95 (0-8014-3304-5) Cornell U Pr.

Romantic Theory of Poetry: An Examination in the Light of Croce's Aesthetic. Annie E. Dodds. LC 75-28996. reprint ed. 44.50 (0-404-14007-6) AMS Pr.

***Romantic Theory of the Novel: Genre & Reflection in Cervantes, Melville, Flaubert, Joyce, & Kafka.** Piotr Parlej. LC 97-9301. (Horizons in Theory & American Culture Ser.). 344p. 1997. text ed. 50.00 (0-8071-2141-X) La State U Pr.

Romantic Times. 24p. 1.25 (0-940338-00-9) Romantic Times.

Romantic to Modern Literature: Essays & Ideas of Culture 1750-1900. John Lucas. LC 82-6842. 240p. (C). 1982. text ed. 58.50 (0-389-20311-4, N7148) B&N Imports.

***Romantic Tomato.** Virginia B. Elliott. Ed. by David F. Elliott. 112p. (Orig.). 1997. pap. 9.95 (1-883782-02-3) Best Image.

Romantic Tradition. Ed. by Gerald Chapple et al. (Illus.). 532p. (C). 1991. lib. bdg. 64.50 (0-8191-8165-X) U Pr of Amer.

Romantic Tradition in American Literature, 33 bks. Ed. by Harold Bloom. 1972. reprint ed. 891.00 (0-405-04620-0) Ayer.

Romantic Triumph. Thomas S. Omond. LC 74-38364. (Select Bibliographies Reprint Ser.). 1977. reprint ed. 25.95 (0-8369-6781-X) Ayer.

Romantic Tutu Construction. Kathryn K. Conrad. (Illus.). 34p. 1979. pap. text ed. 20.00 (0-9646987-1-4) K K Angleman.

Romantic Unconscious. David Punter. 208p. (C). 1990. text ed. 32.00 (0-8147-6612-9) NYU Pr.

Romantic Understanding: Education During the Middle School Years. Kieran Egan. 304p. (C). 1990. pap. 17.95 (0-415-90348-3, A4776, Routledge NY) Routledge.

Romantic Vagrancy: Wordsworth & the Simulation of Freedom. Celeste Langan. (Cambridge Studies in Romanticism: No. 15). (Illus.). 302p. (C). 1995. text ed. 59.95 (0-521-47507-4) Cambridge U Pr.

***Romantic Valentines - A Price Guide.** Dan Campanelli & Pauline Campanelli. (Illus.). 160p. (Orig.). 1996. pap. 14.95 (0-89538-078-1) L-W Inc.

Romantic Ventriloquists: Wordsworth, Coleridge, Keats, Shelley, Byron. rev. ed. Edward E. Bostetter. LC 63-10795. 372p. 1975. reprint ed. pap. 10.00 (0-295-95318-7) U of Wash Pr.

Romantic Verse Narrative: The History of a Genre. Hermann Fischer. Tr. by Sue Bollans. (European Studies in English Literature). 304p. (C). 1991. text ed. 69.95 (0-521-30964-6) Cambridge U Pr.

Romantic View of Poetry. Joseph W. Beach. 1990. 14.50 (0-8446-1061-5) Peter Smith.

Romantic View of Poetry. Joseph W. Beach. 1988. reprint ed. lib. bdg. 29.00 (0-7812-0048-2) Rprt Serv.

Romantic View of Poetry. Joseph W. Beach. reprint ed. 39.00 (0-403-03886-3) Somerset Pub.

Romantic Virtuoso. Morse Peckham. LC 94-26406. 270p. 1995. 39.95 (0-8195-5280-1, Wesleyan Univ Pr) U Pr of New Eng.

Romantic Vision: The Novels of George Sand. Robert Godwin-Jones. LC 95-69365. 332p. 1995. lib. bdg. 43.95 (1-883479-06-1) Summa Pubns.

Romantic Vision & the Novel. Jay Clayton. LC 86-12918. 264p. 1987. text ed. 64.95 (0-521-32776-8) Cambridge U Pr.

Romantic Vision, Ethical Context: Novalis & Aritistic Autonomy. Geza Von Molnar & Jochen Schulte-Sasse. LC 86-11229. (Theory & History of Literature Ser.: Vol. 39). 288p. (Orig.). 1991. pap. 15.95 (0-8166-1497-0) U of Minn Pr.

***Romantic Vision of Alex la Guma & Other Critical Essays.** Cecil Abrahams. 1997. pap. 18.95 (0-86543-579-0) Africa World.

Romantic Vision of Caspar David Friedrich: Paintings & Drawings from the U.S.S.R. Ed. by Sabine Rewald. (Illus.). 120p. 1991. 22.50 (0-8109-6402-3) Abrams.

***Romantic Wedding Destinations: Getaways in Hawaii.** 3rd large type rev. ed. Jackie Carrington. LC 97-70261. (Illus.). 44p. 1997. spiral bd. 14.95 (1-888759-13-5) Innovanna Pub Co Inc.

***Romantic Wedding Destinations: Getaways in the Caribbean.** 3rd large type rev. ed. Jackie Carrington. LC 97-70260. (Illus.). 76p. 1997. spiral bd. 19.95 (1-888759-14-3) Innovanna Pub Co Inc.

Romantic Wedding Destinations: Guide to Wedding & Honeymoon Getaways Around the World. 2nd rev. ed. Jackie Carrington. LC 96-76479. (Illus.). 154p. 1996. pap. 24.95 (1-888759-11-9) Innovanna Pub Co Inc.

***Romantic Wedding Destinations: Guide to Wedding & Honeymoon Getaways Around the World.** 3rd large type rev. ed. Jackie Carrington. LC 97-70259. (Illus.). 206p. 1997. pap. 24.95 (1-888759-12-7) Innovanna Pub Co Inc.

Romantic Weekend Getaways: The Mid-Atlantic States. 2nd ed. Larry Fox & Barbara Radin-Fox. 224p. 1993. pap. text ed. 14.95 (0-471-58500-9) Wiley.

***Romantic Weekend Getaways: The Mid-Atlantic States.** 3rd ed. Larry Fox & Barbara Radin-Fox. LC 97-21269. 272p. 1997. pap. 15.95 (0-471-17828-4) Wiley.

***Romantic Weekends: New York.** Irvina Lew. (Romantic Weekends Ser.). (Illus.). 224p. (Orig.). 1997. pap. 14.95 (1-55650-771-2) Hunter NJ.

***Romantic Weekends: San Francisco Bay Area.** Robert White & Phyllis White. (Romantic Weekends Ser.). 250p. (Orig.). 1997. pap. 14.95 (1-55650-774-7) Hunter NJ.

***Romantic Weekends: Southern California.** Louann W. Murray. (Romantic Weekends Ser.). 275p. (Orig.). 1997. pap. 15.95 (1-55650-773-9) Hunter NJ.

Romantic Weekends: Virginia, Washington, D. C., & Maryland. Norman P. Renouf & Kathy Renouf. 304p. 1995. pap. 14.95 (1-55650-702-X) Hunter NJ.

***Romantic Women Poets: An Anthology.** Duncan Wu. 672p. Date not set. 79.95 (0-631-20329-X) Blackwell Pubs.

***Romantic Women Poets: An Anthology.** Duncan Wu. 672p. Date not set. pap. 34.95 (0-631-20330-3) Blackwell Pubs.

Romantic Women Writers: Voices & Countervoices. Ed. by Paula R. Feldman & Theresa M. Kelley. LC 94-39710. (Illus.). 336p. 1995. pap. 19.95 (0-87451-724-9) U Pr of New Eng.

Romantic World of Music. William Armstrong. LC 71-90602. (Essay Index Reprint Ser.). 1977. 21.95 (0-8369-1271-3) Ayer.

***Romantic Writing & Pedestrian Travel.** Robin Jarvis. LC 97-5874. 1997. write for info. (0-312-17531-0) St Martin.

***Romantic Writings.** Stephen Bygrave. 352p. (C). 1996. pap. 19.95 (0-415-13578-8) Routledge.

Romantic Writings: An Introductory Anthology. Ed. by Stephen Bygrave. LC 96-7542. (Approaching Literature Ser.). 352p. (C). 1996. text ed. 65.00 (0-415-13577-X) Routledge.

Romantica: On Peace & Romance. Frederick D. Harper. 124p. (Orig.). (gr. 7 up). 1988. pap. 10.95 (0-935392-07-6) Douglass Pubs.

***Romantically Tole Bavemmalerei.** Sherry Gall. 61p. 1994. pap. 9.50 (1-56770-311-9) S Scheewe Pubns.

Romanticas: Women Writers & Subjectivity in Spain, 1835-1850. Susan Kirkpatrick. 1989. 50.00 (0-520-06370-8) U CA Pr.

Romanticism. Intro. by Cynthia Chase. LC 92-14309. (Critical Readers Ser.). 272p. (C). 1992. pap. text ed. 18.25 (0-685-72519-7, 79348) Longman.

Romanticism. Cynthia Chase. (C). 1993. pap. text ed. 24.50 (0-582-04799-4, Pub. by Longman UK) Longman.

Romanticism. Cynthia Chase. (C). 1992. text ed. 57.50 (0-582-05000-6) Addison-Wesley.

Romanticism. Aiden Day. LC 95-8288. (New Critical Idiom Ser.). 217p. (C). 1995. pap. 9.95 (0-415-08378-8); text ed. write for info. (0-415-12266-X) Routledge.

Romanticism. Hugh Honour. LC 78-2146. (Icon Editions Ser.). (Illus.). 1979. pap. text ed. 16.00 (0-06-430089-7, IN-89, Icon Edns) HarpC.

Romanticism. 2nd ed. Lilian R. Furst. (Critical Idiom Ser.). (C). 1976. pap. 8.50 (0-416-83920-7, NO. 2209) Routledge Chapman & Hall.

Romanticism: A Critical Reader. Duncan Wu. (Illus.). 384p. 1995. pap. 29.95 (0-631-19504-1) Blackwell Pubs.

***Romanticism: An Anthology.** 2nd ed. Ed. by Duncan Wu. (Anthologies Ser.). 1152p. 1994. pap. 34.95 (0-631-20481-4) Blackwell Pubs.

Romanticism: Critical Essays. James Barbour & Thomas Quick. LC 85-20649. 354p. 1985. pap. text ed. 18.95 (0-8240-9349-6) Garland.

Romanticism: Critical Essays. James Barbour & Thomas Quirk. LC 85-20649. 354p. 1986. text ed. 35.00 (0-8240-9348-8) Garland.

Romanticism: Points of View. 2nd ed. Ed. by Robert Gleckner & Gerald Enscoe. LC 75-4682. (Waynebooks Ser.: No. 40). 352p. 1975. reprint ed. pap. text ed. 17.95 (0-8143-1543-7) Wayne St U Pr.

Romanticism & Anthony Trollope: A Study in the Continuities of Nineteenth Century Literary Thought. L. J. Swingle. 288p. 1990. text ed. 42.50 (0-472-10189-7) U of Mich Pr.

Romanticism & Art. rev. ed. William Vaughan. LC 93-61831. (World of Art Ser.). (Illus.). 288p. 1994. pap. 14.95 (0-500-20275-3) Thames Hudson.

Romanticism & Beyond: A Festschrift for John F. Fetzer. Ed. by Clifford A. Bernd et al. (California Studies in German & European Romanticism & in the Age of Goethe: Vol. 2). 296p. (C). 1996. 55.95 (0-8204-3006-4) P Lang Pubng.

Romanticism & Children's Literature in Nineteenth-Century England. Ed. by James H. McGavran, Jr. LC 90-36157. 256p. 1991. 35.00 (0-8203-1289-4) U of Ga Pr.

Romanticism & Consciousness. Ed. by Harold Bloom. (Orig.). (C). 1970. pap. text ed. 10.95 (0-393-09954-7) Norton.

Romanticism & Contemporary Criticism. Ed. by Morris Eaves & Michael Fischer. LC 85-19472. (Illus.). 256p. (C). 1986. 39.95 (0-8014-1795-3) Cornell U Pr.

Romanticism & Contemporary Criticism: The Gauss Seminar & Other Papers. Paul De Man. Ed. by E. S. Burt et al. 232p. 1993. text ed. 35.95 (0-8018-4460-6) Johns Hopkins.

***Romanticism & Contemporary Criticsm: The Gauss Seminar & Other Papers.** De Man Paul Staff. Ed. by E. S. Burt et al. 224p. (C). 1996. reprint ed. pap. text ed. 14.95 (0-8018-4461-4) Johns Hopkins.

Romanticism & Evolution: The Nineteenth Century, an Anthology. Ed. by Bruce Wilshire. 320p. (Orig.). 1985. reprint ed. pap. text ed. 24.50 (0-8191-4383-9) U Pr of Amer.

Romanticism & Feminism. Ed. by Anne K. Mellor. LC 87-45406. 244p. 1988. 39.95 (0-253-35083-2); pap. 13.95 (0-253-20462-3, MB-462) Ind U Pr.

Romanticism & Gender. Anne K. Mellor. LC 92-22902. 256p. (C). 1992. pap. 18.95 (0-415-90664-4, A7604, Routledge NY) Routledge.

Romanticism & Ideology. Morse Peckham. 400p. 1985. lib. bdg. 32.50 (0-913283-05-5) Penkevill.

Romanticism & Ideology. Morse Peckham. LC 94-45308. 329p. 1995. pap. 19.95 (0-8195-6285-8, Wesleyan Univ Pr) U Pr of New Eng.

Romanticism & Language. Ed. by Arden Reed. LC 84-45146. 320p. 1984. pap. 16.95 (0-8014-9891-0) Cornell U Pr.

Romanticism & Religion. Stephen Prickett. LC 75-2254. 320p. 1976. text ed. 80.00 (0-521-21072-0) Cambridge U Pr.

Romanticism & Revolt. J. R. Talmon. (Library of World Civilization). (Illus.). (C). 1979. pap. text ed. 9.95 (0-393-95081-6) Norton.

Romanticism & the Androgynous Sublime. Warren Stevenson. LC 95-43311. (Illus.). 160p. (C). 1996. 29.50 (0-8386-3668-3) Fairleigh Dickinson.

Romanticism & the Forms of Ruin: Wordsworth, Coleridge & Modalities of Fragmentation. Thomas McFarland. LC 80-7546. 432p. 1981. text ed. 69.50 (0-691-06437-7) Princeton U Pr.

***Romanticism & the Forms of Ruin: Wordsworth, Coleridge, & Modalities of Fragmentation.** Thomas McFarland. LC 80-7546. 467p. 1981. reprint ed. pap. 133.10 (0-608-02513-5, 2063157) Bks Demand.

Romanticism & the Gothic Revival. Agnes Addison. 204p. 1967. reprint ed. 45.00 (0-87752-000-3) Gordian.

Romanticism & the Heritage of Rousseau. Thomas McFarland. 320p. 1995. 55.00 (0-19-818287-2) OUP.

Romanticism & the Rise of History. Stephen Bann. LC 94-12814. (Twayne's Studies in Intellectual & Cultural History). (Illus.). 204p. 1994. 24.95 (0-8057-8618-X, Twayne); pap. 15.95 (0-8057-8619-8, Twayne) Scribnrs Ref.

Romanticism & the Romantic School in Germany. Robert M. Wernaer. LC 68-681. (Studies in German Literature: No. 13). 1969. reprint ed. lib. bdg. 75.00 (0-8383-0685-3) M S G Haskell Hse.

***Romanticism & the Self-Conscious Poem.** Michael O'Neill. 256p. 1997. 65.00 (0-19-812285-3) OUP.

Romanticism in National Context. Ed. by Roy Porter & Mikulas Teich. 382p. 1988. text ed. 69.95 (0-521-32605-2); pap. text ed. 23.95 (0-521-33913-8) Cambridge U Pr.

Romanticism in Puerto Rican Literature. Cesario Rosa-Nieves. (Puerto Rico Ser.). 1979. lib. bdg. 59.95 (0-8490-3003-X) Gordon Pr.

Romanticism in Science: Science in Europe, 1790-1840. Ed. by Stefano Poggi et al. LC 93-1728. (Boston Studies in the Philosophy of Science). 264p. 1994. lib. bdg. 123.50 (0-7923-2336-X, Pub. by Klwr Acad Pubs NE) Kluwer Ac.

Romanticism, Modernism, Postmodernism. Ed. by Harry R. Garvin. LC 79-50103. (Bucknell Review Ser.: Vol. 25, No. 2). 192p. 1980. 22.00 (0-8387-5004-4) Bucknell U Pr.

Romanticism, Nationalism, & the Revolt Against Theory. David Simpson. LC 92-27447. 254p. (C). 1993. pap. text ed. 16.95 (0-226-75946-6) U Ch Pr.

Romanticism, Nationalism, & the Revolt Against Theory. David Simpson. LC 92-27447. 254p. (C). 1993. lib. bdg. 46.50 (0-226-75945-8) U Ch Pr.

Romanticism, Pragmatism, and Deconstruction. Kathleen M. Wheeler. LC 92-46235. 304p. 1993. pap. 27.95 (0-631-18964-5) Blackwell Pubs.

Romanticism, Race, & Imperial Culture, 1780-1834. Ed. by Alan Richardson & Sonia Hofkosh. LC 95-48392. (Illus.). 400p. 1996. text ed. 39.95 (0-253-33212-5) Ind U Pr.

***Romanticism, Radicalism & the Press.** Stephen C. Behrendt. LC 96-51736. 1997. pap. write for info. (0-8143-2568-8) Wayne State Univ Ctr for.

Romanticism Reconsidered: Selected Papers from the English Institute. Ed. by Northrop Frye. LC 63-18020. 141p. reprint ed. pap. 40.20 (0-685-15559-5, 2026709) Bks Demand.

Romanticism Reconsidered see English Institute Essays

Romanticism, Writing, & Sexual Difference: Essays on The Prelude. Mary Jacobus. (Illus.). 328p. 1990. 60.00 (0-19-812969-6) OUP.

Romanticism, Writing, & Sexual Difference: Essays on the Prelude. Mary Jacobus. (Illus.). 328p. 1995. reprint ed. pap. 24.00 (0-19-818330-5) OUP.

Romanticisme Francais. Philippe Van Tieghem. 126p. 9.95 (0-8288-7415-8) Fr & Eur.

Romanticismo y Modernidad, 2 vols. Esteban Tollinchi. 157p. 1989. pap. 30.00 (0-8477-2827-7) U of PR Pr.

Romantics: Critical Heritage, 7 vols., Set. Incl. John Keats. Ed. by Matthews. 448p. (C). 1996. text ed. 130.00 (0-415-13447-1); Vol. 1. Samuel Taylor Coleridge. 688p. (C). 1996. text ed. 150.00 (0-415-13442-0); William Blake. Bentley, Jr. 314p. (C). 1996. text ed. 120.00 (0-415-13441-2); Vol. 2. Samuel Taylor Coleridge. 276p. (C). 1996. text ed. 130.00 (0-415-13443-9); Robert Southey. Ed. by Madden. 512p. (C). 1996. text ed. 150.00 (0-415-13444-7); Lord Byron. Ed. by Rutherford. 531p. (C). 1996. text ed. 150.00 (0-415-13445-5); Percy Bysshe Shelley. Ed. by Barcus. 448p. (C). 1996. text ed. 130.00 (0-415-13446-3); 3217p. (C). 1996. Set boxed, text ed. 769.00 (0-415-13440-4) Routledge.

***Romantics: England in a Revolutionary Age.** E. P. Thompson. 1997. 25.00 (1-56584-360-6) New Press NY.

***Romantics: England in a Revolutionary Age.** E. P. Thompson. 1997. 25.00 (0-614-27829-5) New Press NY.

Romantics: Symphonie Fantastique. Text by Alan Rich. (Play by Play Ser.). 1996. 25.00 (0-614-96872-0) Harper SF.

Romantics: The Context of English Literature. Stephen Prickett. 270p. 1981. text ed. 37.50 (0-8419-0723-4); pap. text ed. 19.50 (0-8419-0724-2) Holmes & Meier.

***Romantics: Women Novelists.** Intro. by Peter Garside. 3060p. (C). 1995. text ed. 995.00 (0-415-11351-2) Routledge.

Romantics: Women Poets of the Romantic Period 1770 - 1830, 12 vols., Set. Ed. by Carolin Franklin. 4182p. (C). (gr. 13 up). 1996. boxed, text ed. 995.00 (0-415-13266-5, Routledge NY) Routledge.

Romantics - Play by Play: Symphonie Fantastique, Opus 14, Orchestre Revolutionnaire Et... Alan Rich. LC 96-15447. 160p. 1996. 25.00 (0-06-263559-X) Harper SF.

Romantics & Us: Essays on Literature & Culture. Ed. by Gene W. Ruoff. 275p. (Orig.). (C). 1990. pap. 16.95 (0-8135-1499-1); text ed. 45.00 (0-8135-1498-3) Rutgers U Pr.

Romantics Anonymous: Under the Mistletoe. Lauryn Chandler. (Romance Ser.). 1993. pap. 2.75 (0-373-08981-3, 5-08981-8) Silhouette.

Romantics, Gangsters & Other Marginals. Torrance T. Stephens. 81p. 1991. pap. 7.00 (1-880861-00-3) Adin.

Romantics, Rebels, & Reactionaries: English Literature & Its Background, 1760 to 1830. Marilyn Butler. (Opus Ser.). 220p. 1985. pap. 19.95 (0-19-289132-4) OUP.

An Asterisk (*) at the beginning of an entry indicates that the title is appearing in BIP for the first time.

R

***Romantics, Reformers, Reactionaries: Russian Conservative Thought & Politics in the Reign of Alexander I.** Alexander M. Martin. LC 96-53558. 1997. 35.00 (*0-87580-226-5*) N Ill U Pr.

Romantics to Rodin: French Nineteenth-Century Sculpture from American Collections. H. W. Janson & Peter Fuseo. 1980. pap. 11.95 (*0-8076-0953-6*) Braziller.

Romantiques Allemand, Vol. 2. Alf. (FRE.). 1977. 59.95 (*0-8288-5636-2*, M6119) Fr & Eur.

Romantiques Allemand Vol. 1: Anthology of German Literature of the Nineteenth Century, 2 vols., Vol. 1. (Pleiade Ser.). 1977. 135.00 (*0-7859-6511-4*) Fr & Eur.

Romantiques Allemand Vol. 2: Anthology of German Literature of the Nineteenth Century, 2 vols., Vol. 2. (Pleiade Ser.). 1977. 135.00 (*0-7859-6510-6*) Fr & Eur.

Romantiques Allemands, Vol. 1. Juan Alfaro Perez. 478p. (ENG & SPA.). 1976. pap. 115.00 (*0-8288-5614-1*, S50094) Fr & Eur.

Romantiques Allemands: Brentano, von Arnim, Grimm, Chamisso, Morike, Buchner, etc., Vol. 2. 1792p. 48.95 (*0-686-56561-4*) Fr & Eur.

Romantiques Allemands: Jean-Paul, Novalis, E. T. A. Hoffman, H. von Kleist, etc., Vol. 1. 1648p. 42.95 (*0-686-56560-6*) Fr & Eur.

Romantische Poesie. Raimund Belgardt. 1970. text ed. 61.55 (*90-279-1248-3*) Mouton.

Romantische Schule. Rudolf Haym. LC 72-168953. reprint ed. 67.50 (*0-404-03166-8*) AMS Pr.

Romantisicm & the Anglican Newman. David Goslee. 371p. (C). 1995. text ed. 44.95 (*0-8214-1126-8*) Ohio U Pr.

Romantisme Aux Encheres: Ducange, Pixerecourt, Hugo. Marie-Pierre Le Hir. LC 92-3694. (Purdue University Monographs in Romance Languages: Vol. 42). viii, 225p. 1992. 65.00 (*1-55619-312-2*); pap. 27.95 (*1-55619-313-0*) Benjamins North Am.

Romantist: 1977, No. 1. Ed. by John C. Moran & Don Herron. 1977. 10.00 (*0-317-01472-2*) F M Crawford.

Romantist: 1985-86, No. 9-10. Ed. by John C. Moran et al. 1988. 10.00 (*0-317-01473-0*) F M Crawford.

Romanwerk von Ingeborg Drewitz. Gerhild B. Rogers. (Studies in Modern German Literature: Vol. 26). 246p. (C). 1989. text ed. 37.00 (*0-8204-0715-1*) P Lang Pubng.

Romany Herbal Remedies. Gipsy Petulengro & Walter F. Starkie. 1972. reprint ed. pap. 5.95 (*0-87877-016-X*, H-16) Newcastle Pub.

Romany Justice. H. Chalk. (C). 1989. 50.00 (*0-7223-2288-7*, Pub. by A H S Ltd UK) St Mut.

Romany of the Snows. Gilbert Parker. LC 79-94741. (Short Story Index Reprint Ser.). 1977. 19.95 (*0-8369-3121-1*) Ayer.

Romany Remedies & Recipes. Gipsy Petulengro. 47p. 1971. reprint ed. spiral bd. 6.00 (*0-7873-0669-X*) Hlth Research.

Romanza: The California Architecture of Frank Lloyd Wright. David Gebhard. (Illus.). 132p. 1988. 29.95 (*0-87701-379-9*) Chronicle Bks.

Romanza see California Architecture of Frank Lloyd Wright

Romare Bearden: Artist. Kevin Brown. Ed. by Nathan I. Huggins. (Black Americans of Achievement Ser.). (Illus.). 144p. (YA). (gr. 5 up). 1993. lib. bdg. 19.95 (*0-7910-1119-4*) Chelsea Hse.

Romare Bearden: His Life & Art. Myron Schwartzman. (Illus.). 320p. 1990. 65.00 (*0-8109-3108-7*) Abrams.

Romare Bearden in Black & White. Gail Gelburd & Thelma Golden. (Illus.). 96p. 1996. pap. 19.95 (*0-8109-6823-1*) Abrams.

Rombo y Otros Momentos. Sarah Baquedano. LC 83-82850. (Coleccion Caniqui). 309p. (SPA.). 1984. pap. 9.95 (*0-89729-345-2*) Ediciones.

Rome. (DK Action Packs Ser.). (Illus.). 16p. (J). (gr. 3 up). 1995. pap. 16.95 (*1-56458-896-3*, 5-70551) DK Pub Inc.

Rome. (Panorama Bks.). (Illus.). (FRE.). 3.95 (*0-685-11541-0*) Fr & Eur.

Rome. (Baedeker's Ser.). (Illus.). 1991. pap. 17.00 (*0-13-094814-4*, P-H Travel) P-H Gen Ref & Trav.

Rome. (Citypacks Ser.). 1996. 10.00 (*0-614-12780-7*) Fodors Travel.

***Rome.** LC 96-54633. (Cities of the World Ser.). (J). 1997. write for info. (*0-516-20465-3*) Childrens.

Rome. John Agnew. (World Cities Ser.). 224p. 1994. text ed. 49.95 (*0-470-21992-0*) Halsted Pr.

Rome. John Agnew. LC 94-44396. (World Cities Ser.). 189p. 1995. text ed. 70.00 (*0-471-94886-1*) Wiley.

Rome. Ros Belford & Rodney Palmer. LC 92-53473. (Eyewitness Travel Guides Ser.). (Illus.). 432p. 1993. pap. 24.95 (*1-56458-186-1*) DK Pub Inc.

Rome. Berlitz Editors. (Pocket Guides Ser.). (Illus.). 144p. 1994. pap. 7.95 (*2-8315-1451-7*) Berlitz.

Rome. Enzo Cucchi. Ed. by Danilo Eccher & Achile Bonito Oliva. (Special Editions for Bibliofiles Ser.). (Illus.). 160p. 1993. 175.00 (*84-343-0660-3*) Elliots Bks.

Rome. Paul Duncan. (Illustrated Travel Guides from Thomas Cook Ser.). (Illus.). 192p. (Orig.). 1994. pap. 12.95 (*0-8442-9077-7*, Passport Bks) NTC Pub Grp.

Rome. G. W. Edwards. 1972. 59.95 (*0-8490-0969-3*) Gordon Pr.

Rome. Saviour Pirotta. LC 92-19685. (Holy Cities Ser.). (Illus.). 48p. (YA). (gr. 5 up). 1993. lib. bdg. 13.95 (*0-87518-570-3*, Dillon Silver Burdett) Silver Burdett Pr.

***Rome.** St. Martin's Press Staff. (Let's Go Ser.). 1997. pap. 14.99 (*0-312-16901-9*) St Martin.

Rome. Nelles Verlag. (Nelles Guides Ser.). 1994. pap. 14.95 (*3-88618-391-2*, Pub. by Nelles Verlag GW) Seven Hills Bk.

Rome. Emile Zola. Tr. by Ernest A. Vizetelly. LC 93-26291. (Pocket Classics Ser.). (ENG & FRE.). 1993. 9.00 (*0-7509-0451-8*, Pub. by Sutton Pubng UK) Bks Intl VA.

Rome. 2nd ed. Dana Facaros & Michael Pauls. LC 92-28246. (Cadogan City Guides Ser.). (Illus.). 464p. 1993. pap. 14.95 (*1-56440-131-6*) Globe Pequot.

***Rome.** 3rd ed. Dana Facaros. (Cadogan Guides). 1997. pap. text ed. 17.95 (*1-86011-028-2*, Pub. by Cadogan Books UK) Macmillan.

Rome. Mikhail I. Rostovtzeff. Ed. by Elias J. Bickerman. Tr. by J. D. Duff. 368p. 1960. reprint ed. pap. 19.95 (*0-19-500224-5*) OUP.

Rome, Pt. 1. Ed. by Anne Schnoebelen. LC 86-755546. (Solo Motets from the Seventeenth Century Ser.: Vol. 8). 368p. 1988. text ed. 45.00 (*0-8240-0643-7*) Garland.

Rome, Pt. 3. Ed. by Anne Schnoebelen. LC 86-755546. (Solo Motets from the Seventeenth Century Ser.: Vol. 10). 256p. 1989. text ed. 35.00 (*0-8240-0645-3*) Garland.

***Rome: A New Look.** Reg Butler. (City Breaks Ser.). 1997. pap. 6.95 (*1-872876-53-6*, Pub. by Settle Pr UK) Assoc Pubs Grp.

Rome: Crusade or Crucible? 2nd ed. O. Talmadge Spence. (Charismatic Ser.: Vol. 2). 217p. (C). 1981. reprint ed. pap. 8.95 (*1-882542-01-0*) Fndtns NC.

Rome: Danger to Pedestrians. Rafael Alberti. Tr. by Swann & Scheer. (QRL Poetry Bks.: Vol. XXV). (SPA.). 1984. 20.00 (*0-614-06409-0*) Quarterly Rev.

Rome: Echoes of Imperial Glory. Ed. by Dale Brown. LC 93-37766. (Lost Civilizations Ser.). (Illus.). 168p. 1994. 19.95 (*0-8094-9016-1*); lib. bdg. 25.93 (*0-8094-9017-X*) Time-Life.

Rome: Its People, Life & Customs. U. Paoli. 1996. pap. 26.95 (*1-85399-121-X*, Pub. by Brstl Class Pr UK) Focus Pub-R Pullins.

Rome: Profile of a City, 312-1308. Richard Krautheimer. LC 78-70304. (Illus.). 408p. 1980. pap. text ed. 35.00 (*0-691-00319-X*) Princeton U Pr.

Rome: The Biography of a City. Christopher Hibbert. (Nonfiction Ser.). 400p. 1988. pap. 24.95 (*0-14-007078-8*, Penguin Bks) Viking Penguin.

Rome: The Book of Foundations. Michel Serres. Tr. by Felicia McCarren from FRE. 296p. 1991. 37.50 (*0-8047-1867-9*) Stanford U Pr.

***Rome: The Travel Notebook.** Pascale Loiseau. 104p. 1997. 14.95 (*2-911141-02-4*, Pub. by Les Edtns Pascale FR) Assoc Pubs Grp.

Rome a Mobile Home. Jerry Estrin. LC 93-85179. (Roof Bks.). 81p. (Orig.). 1993. pap. 9.95 (*0-937804-51-7*) Segue NYC.

Rome Access. (Access Ser.). 1986. pap. 10.95 (*0-685-12111-9*) P-H.

Rome Access. Richard S. Wurman. (Access Travel Guides Ser.). (Illus.). 136p. (Orig.). 1986. pap. 14.95 (*0-671-62578-0*, Access NY) HarpC.

Rome Access. 4th ed. Richard S. Wurman. (Access Travel Guides Ser.). 176p. 1995. pap. 18.50 (*0-06-277150-7*, Harper Ref) HarpC.

Rome-Amsterdam: Two Growing Cities in Seventeenth Century Europe. Ed. by P. J. Van Kessel & E. M. Schulte. (C). 1996. text ed. 62.50 (*90-5356-222-2*, Pub. by Amsterdam U Pr NE) U of Mich Pr.

Rome & Baetica: Urbanization in Southern Spain c. 50 B.C. - A.D. 150. A. T. Fear. (Oxford Classical Monographs). (Illus.). 304p. (C). 1996. 70.00 (*0-19-815027-X*) OUP.

Rome & Canterbury. D. MacLeod. 5.99 (*0-906731-88-7*, Pub. by Christian Focus UK) Spring Arbor Dist.

Rome & Constantinople: Essays in the Dialogue of Love. Ed. by Robert Barringer. 86p. (Orig.). 1985. pap. 2.00 (*0-917651-05-7*) Holy Cross Orthodox.

Rome & Environs. Old Vicarage Publications Staff. 240p. (C). 1982. pap. text ed. 45.00 (*0-685-22067-2*, Pub. by Old Vicarage UK) St Mut.

Rome & Her Empire: An Illustrated History. Barry Cunliffe. (Illus.). 320p. 1994. 67.50 (*0-09-473500-X*, Pub. by Constable Pubs UK) Trans-Atl Phila.

Rome & Her Kings: Extracts from Livy I. Ed. by W. D. Lowe & C. E. Freeman. (Textbook Ser.). 110p. 1981. pap. text ed. 11.00 (*0-86516-000-7*) Bolchazy-Carducci.

Rome & India: The Ancient Sea Trade. Ed. by Vimala Begley & Richard D. DePuma. LC 91-6579. (Studies in Classics). (Illus.). 248p. (C). 1992. 40.00 (*0-299-12640-4*) U of Wis Pr.

Rome & Italy. Titus Livy. Tr. & Anno. by Betty Radice. 400p. (Orig.). 1982. pap. 9.95 (*0-14-044388-6*, Penguin Classics) Viking Penguin.

Rome & Its Empire. Stephen Johnson. LC 88-32336. 240p. (C). (gr. 13). 1989. text ed. 49.95 (*0-415-03267-9*) Routledge.

Rome & Its Story. St. Clair Baddeley & L. D. Gordon. 1977. lib. bdg. 59.95 (*0-8490-2543-5*) Gordon Pr.

Rome & Jerusalem. Moses Hess. 177p. 1994. pap. 10.00 (*0-9642465-0-3*) Jewish Radical.

Rome & Pompeii: Archaeological Rambles. Gaston Boissier. Tr. by D. Havelock Fisher. LC 77-39193. (Select Bibliographies Reprint Ser.). (Illus.). 435p. reprint ed. lib. bdg. 28.00 (*0-8290-0505-6*) Irvington.

Rome & Pompeii: Archeological Rambles. Gaston Boissier. Tr. by D. Havelock Fisher. LC 77-39193. (Select Bibliographies Reprint Ser.). (Illus.). 1977. 31.95 (*0-8369-6795-X*) Ayer.

Rome & Reform, 2 vols. Thomas L. Kington-Oliphant. LC 76-118541. reprint ed. lib. bdg. 66.00 (*0-8290-1928-6*) Irvington.

Rome & Reform, Vol. 1. Thomas L. Kington-Oliphant. (C). 1989. reprint ed. pap. text ed. 14.00 (*0-8290-2470-0*) Irvington.

Rome & Romans. Heather Amery & P. Vanage. (Time Travelers Bks.). (J). (gr. 4-9). 1976. pap. 6.95 (*0-86020-070-1*, Usborne); lib. bdg. 14.95 (*0-88110-101-X*, Usborne) EDC.

***Rome & the African Church in the Time of Augustine.** J. E. Merdinger. LC 96-20999. 1997. write for info. (*0-300-04017-2*) Yale U Pr.

Rome & the Ancient World. Mike Corbishley. (Illustrated History of the World Ser.). (Illus.). 80p. (J). (gr. 2-6). 1993. 17.95 (*0-8160-2786-2*) Facts on File.

Rome & the Anglicans: Historical & Doctrinal Aspects of Anglican-Roman Catholic Relations. J. C. Aveling et al. Ed. by Wolfgang Haase. 301p. 1982. 126.95 (*3-11-008267-5*) De Gruyter.

Rome & the Arabs: A Prolegomenon to the Study of Byzantium & the Arabs. Irfan Shahid. LC 83-8930. (Illus.). 228p. 1984. 15.00 (*0-88402-115-7*) Dumbarton Oaks.

Rome & the Counter-Reformation in Scandinania Vol. 2: (1583-1622) Until the Establishment of the S. Congregatiode Propaganda Fide in 1622. Oskar Garstein. 626p. 1980. 70.00 (*82-00-06165-5*) Scandnvan Univ Pr.

Rome & the Counter-Reformation in Scandinavia: Jesuit Educational Strategy, Vol. 3. Oskar Garstein. 462p. 1992. write for info. (*82-00-21565-2*) Scandnvan Univ Pr.

Rome & the Counter-Reformation in Scandinavia: Jesuit Educational Strategy, 1553-1622. Oskar Garstein. LC 64-1040. (SHCT Ser.: No. 46). iii, 462p. 1991. 156.50 (*90-04-09393-1*) E J Brill.

Rome & the Counter-Reformation in Scandinavia: The Age of Gustavus Adolphus & Queen Christina of Sweden, Vol. 4. Oskar Garstein. 833p. 1992. write for info. (*82-00-21566-0*) Scandnvan Univ Pr.

Rome & the Counter-Reformation in Scandinavia, 1622-1656: The Age of Gustavus Adolphus & Queen Christina of Sweden. Oskar Garstein. LC 64-1040. (SHCT Ser.: No. 47). xviii, 833p. 1991. 213.50 (*90-04-09395-8*) E J Brill.

Rome & the Eastern Churches: A Study in Schism. Aidan Nichols. 240p. (Orig.). 1992. pap. text ed. 19.95 (*0-8146-5019-8*, M Glazier) Liturgical Pr.

Rome & the Germans As Seen in Coinage. Thomas S. Burns & Bernhard H. Overbeck. (Illus.). 88p. (Orig.). 1987. pap. text ed. 10.00 (*0-9619281-0-7*) Burns & Overbeck.

Rome & the Greek East to the Death of Augustine. Robert K. Sherk. LC 83-1833. (Translated Documents of Greece & Rome Ser.: No. 4). 224p. 1984. text ed. 65.00 (*0-521-24995-3*); pap. text ed. 22.95 (*0-521-27123-1*) Cambridge U Pr.

Rome & the Mediterranean. Titus Livy. Tr. by Henry Bettenson. (Classics Ser.). 704p. 1976. pap. 12.95 (*0-14-044318-5*, Penguin Classics) Viking Penguin.

Rome & the Mediterranean to 133 B. C. 2nd ed. Ed. by A. C. Astin et al. (Cambridge Ancient History Ser.: Vol. 8). 650p. 1990. text ed. 110.00 (*0-521-23448-4*) Cambridge U Pr.

Rome & the New Republic: Conflict & Community in Philadelphia Catholicism Between the Revolution & the Civil War. Dale B. Light. LC 95-16520. (Notre Dame Studies in American Catholicism: Vol. 14). (C). 1996. text ed. 48.95 (*0-268-01652-6*) U of Notre Dame Pr.

Rome & the Provinces: Studies in the Transformation of Art & Architecture in the Mediterranean World. Charles B. McClendon et al. LC 86-18234. (Illus.). 83p. (Orig.). 1986. pap. 13.00 (*0-89467-043-3*) Yale Art Gallery.

Rome & the Unification of Italy. Arthur Keaveney. 226p. 1987. lib. bdg. 45.00 (*0-7099-3121-2*, Pub. by Croom Helm UK) Routledge Chapman & Hall.

Rome & the Western Greeks, 350 BC-AD 200: Conquest & Acculturation in Southern Italy. Kathryn Lomas. LC 92-40807. 272p. (C). (gr. 13). 1993. text ed. 62.95 (*0-415-05022-7*, Routledge NY) Routledge.

Rome Antics. David Macaulay. 1997. 18.00 (*0-395-82279-3*) HM.

***Rome as Female.** Fraschetti. 1996. pap. text ed. 16.95 (*0-226-26094-1*); lib. bdg. 35.00 (*0-226-26093-3*) U Ch Pr.

Rome before Avignon: A Social History of Thirteenth-Century Rome. Robert Brentano. (Illus.). 357p. 1991. pap. 18.00 (*0-520-06952-8*) U CA Pr.

Rome, Conservatoria di Musica Santa Cecilia MS A-400. Ed. by Alexander Silbiger. (Seventeenth-Century Keyboard Music Ser.). 175p. 1988. text ed. 25.00 (*0-8240-8012-2*) Garland.

Rome, Constantinople, Moscow: Historical & Theological Studies. 3,457th ed. John Meyendorff. 208p. 1996. pap. 10.95 (*0-88141-134-5*) St Vladimirs.

Rome Express. Arthur Griffiths. LC 75-35443. (Literature of Mystery & Detection Ser.). 1976. reprint ed. 21.95 (*0-405-07874-9*) Ayer.

Rome Green Guide. Ed. by Michelin Travel Publications, Staff. 1995. per. 18.00 (*2-06-153901-7*, 1539) Michelin.

Rome Green Guide. 2nd ed. Michelin Staff. 1992. pap. 18.95 (*0-7859-9158-1*) Fr & Eur.

Rome Green Guide English Edition. Michelin Staff. pap. 17.95 (*0-7859-7199-8*, 2067015591) Fr & Eur.

Rome Guide. Doug Morris. (Illus.). 288p. (Orig.). 1996. pap. 13.95 (*1-883323-42-8*) Open Rd Pub.

Rome Haul. Walter D. Edmonds. Ed. by Frank Bergmann. (New York Classics Ser.). 362p. 1987. pap. 14.95 (*0-8156-0213-8*) Syracuse U Pr.

Rome in Africa. rev. ed. Susan Raven. LC 92-13208. (Illus.). 304p. (C). 1993. pap. 18.95 (*0-415-08150-5*, A9619, Routledge NY) Routledge.

Rome in Africa. rev. ed. Susan Raven. LC 92-13208. (Illus.). 304p. (C). (gr. 13). 1993. text ed. 74.95 (*0-415-08261-7*, A9615, Routledge NY) Routledge.

Rome in Canada: The Vatican & Canadian Affairs in the Late Victorian Age. Robert Perin. 300p. 1990. text ed. 45.00 (*0-8020-5854-X*); pap. text ed. 20.95 (*0-8020-6762-X*) U of Toronto Pr.

Rome in the Age of Enlightenment: The Post-Tridentine Syndrome & the Ancient Regime. Hanns Gross. (Studies in Early Modern History). (Illus.). 400p. (C). 1990. text ed. 69.95 (*0-521-37211-9*) Cambridge U Pr.

Rome in the Augustan Age. Henry T. Rowell. (Centers of Civilization Ser.: Vol. 5). 258p. 1971. pap. 12.95 (*0-8061-0956-4*) U of Okla Pr.

Rome in the Dark Ages. Peter Llewellyn. (Illus.). 324p. 1996. pap. 28.50 (*0-09-473370-8*, Pub. by Constable Pubs UK) Trans-Atl Phila.

Rome in the Fourth Century A.D. An Annotated Bibliography with Historical Overview. Alden M. Rollins. LC 91-52762. 358p. 1991. lib. bdg. 65.00 (*0-89950-624-0*) McFarland & Co.

Rome in Your Pocket Guide. Michelin Travel Publications, Staff. (In Your Pocket Guides Ser.). (Orig.). 1996. per. 9.95 (*2-06-650601-X*, 6506) Michelin.

Rome, la Grece et les Monarchies Hellenistiques au IIIe Siecle avant J. - C. - (273-205) Maurice Holleaux. iv, 386p. 1969. reprint ed. write for info. (*0-318-70761-6*) G Olms Pubs.

Rome, N. Y., Our City & Its People. 2nd rev. ed. Daniel E. Wager. Ed. by Arthur Pierce. LC 95-83833. (Illus.). 266p. 1997. 35.00 (*0-9646900-1-2*) Berry Hill NY.

Rome, Naples et Florence. Stendhal, pseud. (Folio Ser.: No. 1845). (FRE.). pap. 10.95 (*2-07-037845-4*) Schoenhof.

Rome, Naples et Florence, 3 vols. Stendhal. 100.00 (*0-686-55081-1*) Fr & Eur.

Rome, Naples et Florence Eighteen Seventeen. Stendhal. 263p. 1964. 24.95 (*0-8288-7443-3*) Fr & Eur.

Rome of Alexander VII, 1655-1667. Richard Krautheimer. LC 84-26553. (Illus.). 214p. 1985. pap. text ed. 19.95 (*0-691-00277-0*) Princeton U Pr.

Rome Papers: The Baths of Trajan Decius, Iside e Serapide Nel Palazzo, a Late Domus on the Palatine, & Nero's Golden House. L. La Follette et al. (JRA Supplementary Ser.: No. 11). (Illus.). 254p. 1994. 89.50 (*1-887829-11-3*) Jour Roman Arch.

***Rome Pocket Guide.** Berlitz Editors. 144p. 1998. pap. 8.95 (*2-8315-6370-4*) Berlitz.

Rome Reborn: The Vatican Library & Renaissance Culture. Ed. by Anthony Grafton. LC 92-33013. 1993. write for info. (*0-8444-0767-4*) Lib Congress.

Rome Reborn: The Vatican Library & Renaissance Culture. Ed. by Anthony Grafton. (Illus.). 352p. (C). 1993. pap. text ed. 65.00 (*0-300-05442-4*) Yale U Pr.

***Rome Street Map with Index.** 1997. 12.95 (*2-06-700038-1*, 38) Michelin.

Rome Studio. Barbara Gladstone et al. (Illus.). 84p. (Orig.). 1993. pap. 20.00 (*0-933519-25-7*) D W Bell Gallery.

Rome Sweet Home: Our Journey to Catholicism. Scott Hahn & Kimberly Hahn. LC 93-79336. 210p. 1993. pap. 10.95 (*0-89870-478-2*) Ignatius Pr.

Rome, the Law-Giver. Joseph Declareuil. Tr. by Edward A. Parker. LC 73-98752. xvi, 400p. 1970. reprint ed. text ed. 45.00 (*0-8371-2796-3*, DERL, Greenwood Pr) Greenwood.

Rome the Sorceress, La Sorciere de Rome. Andre Frenaud. Tr. by Keith Bosley from FRE. LC 96-164127. 128p. 9600. pap. 18.95 (*1-85224-318-X*, Pub. by Bloodaxe Bks UK) Dufour.

Rome, the Sweet Tempestuous Life. Paul E. Hoffman. 224p. 1982. 14.95 (*0-685-04739-3*) St Martin.

Rome 360 Degrees. Boccazzi-Varotto. LC 97-3971. 1997. pap. write for info. (*0-679-44286-3*) Random Hse Value.

Rome up Close. (Handbooks of the World Ser.). 1995. pap. 12.95 (*0-8442-9476-4*, Passport Bks) NTC Pub Grp.

Rome Walking Guide. rev. ed. Jeanne B. Oelerich. (Illus.). 16p. 1994. pap. 9.95 (*1-882546-04-0*) Just Marvelous.

Rome, 1954 see General Assembly Proceedings

Romeinsrechtelijke Grondslagen van het Nederlands Privaatrecht. R. Feenstra. 1993. reprint ed. 54.25 (*90-04-09284-6*) E J Brill.

Romeo. Shane De-Rolf. (J). 1997. write for info. (*0-679-88332-0*, Bullseye Bks) Random Bks Yng Read.

Romeo. Mark Dunster. 30p. (Orig.). 1995. pap. 5.00 (*0-89642-254-2*) Linden Pubs.

Romeo: A Novel. Elise Title. LC 95-24114. 488p. 1996. 21.95 (*0-553-09710-5*, Bantam Trade Bks) Bantam.

Romeo & Juliet. LC 96-16129. (Shorter Shakespeare Ser.). 1996. 9.95 (*0-02-861228-0*) Macmillan.

***Romeo & Juliet.** (J). 1996. mass mkt. 4.99 (*0-440-22712-7*) BDD Bks Young Read.

Romeo & Juliet. Arden. 1985. pap. 8.95 (*0-416-17860-X*) Routledge Chapman & Hall.

***Romeo & Juliet.** Ed. by Flower. 1993. text ed. write for info. (*0-582-24591-5*, Pub. by Longman UK) Longman.

***Romeo & Juliet.** Roma Gill. (Oxford School Shakespeare Ser.). (C). 1994. text ed. 10.72 (*0-669-40347-4*) HM College Div.

***Romeo & Juliet.** Sasha Roberts. (Writers & Their Work Ser.). 96p. (Orig.). 1996. pap. 15.00 (*0-7463-0812-4*, Pub. by Nrthcote House UK) U Pr of Miss.

Romeo & Juliet. Ed. by A. L. Rowse. LC 84-5086. (Contemporary Shakespeare Ser.: Vol. I). 140p. (C). 1984. pap. text ed. 4.00 (*0-8191-3903-3*) U Pr of Amer.

***Romeo & Juliet.** William Shakespeare. (Illustrated Classics Shakespeare Collection). 64p. 1994. pap. 4.95 (*0-7854-0811-8*, 40615) Am Guidance.

***Romeo & Juliet.** William Shakespeare. LC 95-77832. 32p. (YA). (gr. 6-12). 1995. pap. 3.95 (*0-7854-1129-1*, 40204) Am Guidance.

Romeo & Juliet. William Shakespeare. (Classics Ser.). 208p. 1988. pap. 3.95 (*0-553-21305-9*, Bantam Classics) Bantam.

Romeo & Juliet. William Shakespeare. (Shakespeare Made Easy Ser.). 288p. (gr. 9-12). 1985. pap. 6.95 (*0-8120-3572-0*) Barron.

An Asterisk (*) at the beginning of an entry indicates that the title is appearing in BIP for the first time.

Romeo & Juliet. William Shakespeare. Ed. by Maynard Mack & Robert W. Boynton. (Shakespeare Ser.). 159p. (YA). (gr. 6 up). 1990. pap. text ed. 7.50 (*0-86709-035-9*, 0035) Boynton Cook Pubs.
Romeo & Juliet. William Shakespeare. Ed. by G. Blakemore Evans. (New Cambridge Shakespeare Ser.). (Illus.). 263p. 1984. text ed. 39.95 (*0-521-22223-0*); pap. text ed. 10.95 (*0-521-29405-3*) Cambridge U Pr.
Romeo & Juliet. William Shakespeare. Ed. by Rex Gibson. (Cambridge School Shakespeare Ser.). (Illus.). 224p. (YA). 1992. pap. text ed. 7.95 (*0-521-39574-7*) Cambridge U Pr.
Romeo & Juliet. William Shakespeare. Ed. by John F. Andrews. (Everyman Shakespeare Ser.). 260p. 1993. pap. 3.95 (*0-460-87177-3*, Everyman's Classic Lib) C E Tuttle.
Romeo & Juliet. William Shakespeare. 1900. pap. text ed. 2.95 (*0-582-52729-5*) Longman.
Romeo & Juliet. William Shakespeare. Ed. by Richard Adams. (Study Texts Ser.). 1988. pap. text ed. 4.29 (*0-582-33192-7*, 72070) Longman.
Romeo & Juliet. William Shakespeare. Ed. by Roy Blatchford. (Literature Ser.). 1993. pap. 5.95 (*0-582-08836-4*, TG7665) Longman.
Romeo & Juliet. William Shakespeare. 256p. 1995. pap. 7.95 (*0-8442-5747-8*) NTC Pub Grp.
Romeo & Juliet. William Shakespeare. Ed. by Joseph Bryant. pap. 2.75 (*0-451-52060-2*, L1040, Sig Classics) NAL-Dutton.
Romeo & Juliet. William Shakespeare. Ed. by R. E. Houghton. (New Clarendon Shakespeare Ser.). (Illus.). 192p. 1975. 7.95 (*0-19-831923-1*) OUP.
Romeo & Juliet. William Shakespeare. (BBC Television Plays Ser.). 1978. pap. 4.95 (*0-563-17615-6*, Pub. by BBC UK) Parkwest Pubns.
Romeo & Juliet. William SHakespeare. Ed. by Paul Werstine & Barbara Mowat. (New Folger Library). 304p. 1992. pap. 3.99 (*0-671-72285-9*, Folger Lib) PB.
Romeo & Juliet. William Shakespeare. LC 79-24465. (Short Classics Ser.). (Illus.). 48p. (J). (gr. 4 up). 1983. lib. bdg. 24.26 (*0-8172-1653-7*) Raintree Steck-V.
Romeo & Juliet. William Shakespeare. (Illustrated Shakespeare Ser.). (Illus.). 128p. 1990. 9.99 (*0-517-05057-9*) Random Hse Value.
Romeo & Juliet. William Shakespeare. Ed. by Diane Davidson. LC 83-12309. (Shakespeare on Stage Ser.: Vol. 3). (Illus.). 129p. (YA). (gr. 8-12). 1983. pap. 6.95 (*0-934048-06-1*) Swan Books.
Romeo & Juliet. William Shakespeare. Ed. by Neil King. (Illustrated Shakespeare Ser.). (Illus.). 112p. 1995. pap. 17.95 (*0-85950-843-9*, Pub. by Stanley Thornes UK) Trans-Atl Phila.
Romeo & Juliet. William Shakespeare. Ed. by John E. Hankins. (Pelican Shakespeare Ser.). 154p. 1960. pap. 3.95 (*0-14-071419-7*, Pelican Bks) Viking Penguin.
Romeo & Juliet. William Shakespeare. Ed. by T. J. Spencer. 304p. 1981. pap. 5.50 (*0-14-070701-8*, Penguin Bks) Viking Penguin.
***Romeo & Juliet.** William Shakespeare. (English Ser.). (C). Date not set. pap. 9.95 (*0-17-443533-9*) Wadsworth Pub.
***Romeo & Juliet.** William Shakespeare. (English Ser.). (C). 1997. pap. 9.95 (*0-17-443471-5*) Wadsworth Pub.
Romeo & Juliet. William Shakespeare. (Signet Classics Ser.). 1964. mass mkt. 3.95 (*0-451-52438-1*, Sig Classics) NAL-Dutton.
Romeo & Juliet. William Shakespeare. Date not set. write for info. (*0-517-15126-X*) Random Hse Value.
Romeo & Juliet. William Shakespeare. (Wishbone Classics Ser.: No. 3). 128p. 1996. mass mkt. 3.99 (*0-06-106415-7*, Harp PBks) HarpC.
Romeo & Juliet. William Shakespeare. (J). 1995. pap. text ed. 4.95 (*0-8114-6838-0*) Raintree Steck-V.
Romeo & Juliet. Cedric P. Watts. (Twayne's New Critical Introduction to Shakespeare Ser.: No. 12). 134p. (C). 1991. 24.95 (*0-8057-8724-0*, Twayne); pap. 13.95 (*0-8057-8725-9*, Twayne) Scribnrs Ref.
Romeo & Juliet. large type ed. William Shakespeare. 1991. pap. 24.95 (*0-7089-4502-3*, Trail West Pubs) Ulverscroft.
Romeo & Juliet. rev. ed. William Shakespeare. Ed. by Joseph Bryant. 248p. 1989. pap. 2.75 (*0-451-52136-6*, Sig Classics) NAL-Dutton.
Romeo & Juliet. rev. ed. William Shakespeare. Ed. by Roma Gill. (Oxford School Shakespeare Ser.). (Illus.). 168p. (YA). (gr. 9-11). 1993. pap. 7.50 (*0-19-831972-X*) OUP.
***Romeo & Juliet.** 3rd ed. William Shakespeare. (English Ser.). (C). Date not set. text ed. 45.00 (*0-17-443566-5*) Wadsworth Pub.
Romeo & Juliet. William Shakespeare. LC 92-38288. (Thrift Editions Ser.). 96p. 1993. reprint ed. pap. 1.00 (*0-486-27557-4*) Dover.
Romeo & Juliet: A Play Packet to Accompany Elementary, My Dear Shakespeare. Barbara Engen & Joy Campbell. (Illus.). 1989. reprint ed. teacher ed. 8.95 (*0-922947-02-3*) Mkt Masters.
Romeo & Juliet: And Other Stories. Adnan Sarhan. 64p. 1989. pap. 5.00 (*1-884328-05-9*) Sufi Fnd Amer.
***Romeo & Juliet: Complete Study Edition.** Ed. by Sidney Lamb. 1996. pap. text ed. 6.95 (*0-8220-1438-6*) Cliffs.
Romeo & Juliet: Complete Study Guide. Sidney Lamb. 1965. pap. 6.95 (*0-8220-1437-8*) Cliffs.
Romeo And Juliet: Critical Essays. John Andrews. Ed. by Philip C. Kolin. LC 93-16203. (Shakespeare Criticism Ser.: Vol. 10). 440p. 1993. text ed. 25.00 (*0-8240-4795-8*) Garland.
Romeo & Juliet: Granville Barker's Prefaces to Shakespeare. Granville Barker. 93p. 1995. pap. 6.95 (*0-435-08656-1*, 08656) Heinemann.
Romeo & Juliet: HBJ Shakespeare 1989. William Shakespeare. Ed. by Roy. 1989. student ed., pap. 12.00 (*0-7747-1269-4*) HB Schl Dept.
Romeo & Juliet: Original Text & Modern Verse. Alan Durband & William Shakespeare. (Shakespeare Made Easy Ser.). (Orig.). 1995. pap. 16.95 (*0-7487-0255-5*, Pub. by Stanley Thornes UK) Trans-Atl Phila.
Romeo & Juliet: Parallel Texts of the First 2 Quartos; Quarto 1, 1597 & Quarto 2, 1599. Ed. by P. A. Daniel. Incl. Reprint of Quarto 1, 1597. 1974. reprint ed. (*0-318-59044-1*); Reprint of Q. 2, 1599. 1974. reprint ed. (*0-318-59045-X*); Revised Edition Quarto 2, 1599. 1974. reprint ed. (*0-318-59046-8*); (New Shakespeare Society, London, Ser. 2: Nos. 1-4). 1974. pap. 60.00 (*0-8115-0233-3*) Periodicals Srv.
Romeo & Juliet: Plainspoken. Susan Solomon & Greta B. Lipson. Ed. by Greta B. Lipson. (Illus.). 256p. (J). (gr. 7-12). 1985. 17.99 (*0-86653-283-8*, GA 659) Good Apple.
Romeo & Juliet: Shakespeare Made Easy. William Shakespeare. Ed. by John Hort & Leela Hort. 52p. 1992. pap. 6.00 (*0-948662-02-6*, Pub. by Kabet Pr UK) Empire Pub Srvs.
Romeo & Juliet - Original Text of Masuccio, Da Porto, Bandello, Shakespeare. Masuccio et al. Tr. by Percy Pinkerton & Maurice Jonas from ITA. 212p. 1992. 19.95 (*0-937832-32-4*) Dante U Am.
Romeo & Juliet - Study Guide. Mary Peitz. Ed. by Joyce Friedland & Rikki Kessler. (Novel-Ties Ser.). (YA). (gr. 9-12). 1993. pap. text ed. 15.95 (*0-88122-127-9*) Lrn Links.
Romeo & Juliet - Together (& Alive!) at Last. Avi. LC 87-7680. 128p. (J). (gr. 6-8). 1987. 15.95 (*0-531-05721-6*); lib. bdg. 16.99 (*0-531-08321-7*) Orchard Bks Watts.
Romeo & Juliet - Together (& Alive) at Last. Avi. 128p. (J). 1988. pap. 4.50 (*0-380-70525-7*, Camelot) Avon.
Romeo & Juliet - with a Happy Ending, Vol. 1. rev. ed. Frank J. Guida. (Shakespeare for Children Ser.). (Illus.). 20p. (J). 1991. lib. bdg. write for info. (*1-878476-00-9*) Rockmasters Intl.
Romeo & Juliet & West Side Story. Ed. by Norris Houghton. 256p. (YA). (gr. 7 up). 1965. mass mkt. 5.50 (*0-440-97483-6*, LLL BDD) BDD Bks Young Read.
Romeo & Juliet for Young People. William Shakespeare. Ed. by Diane Davidson. LC 86-5958. (Shakespeare for Young People Ser.: Vol. 2). (Illus.). 64p. (J). (gr. 5-8). 1986. pap. 5.95 (*0-934048-19-3*) Swan Books.
Romeo & Juliet Notes. Gary Carey. (Cliffs Notes Ser.). 1979. pap. 4.50 (*0-8220-0074-1*) Cliffs.
***Romeo & Juliet Readalong.** William Shakespeare. (Illustrated Classics Shakespeare Collection). 64p. 1994. pap. 14.95 incl. audio (*0-7854-0827-4*, 40617) Am Guidance.
Romeo & Juliet (Shakespeare) Linnea. (Book Notes Ser.). (C). 1984. pap. 3.50 (*0-8120-3440-6*) Barron.
Romeo & 2 Juliets. Francine Pascal. (Sweet Valley Twins Ser.: No. 84). 144p. (J). (gr. 4-7). 1995. pap. 3.50 (*0-553-48105-3*) Bantam.
Romeo et Juliette see Nouvelles Pieces Noires
Romeo et Juliette, Macbeth. William Shakespeare. (FRE.). 1985. pap. 15.95 (*0-7859-4232-7*) Fr & Eur.
***Romeo in the Rain, Bk. 30.** Kasey Michaels. (Born in the U. S. A. Ser.). 1997. 4.50 (*0-373-47180-7*, 1-47180-4) Harlequin Bks.
Romero: A Life. rev. ed. James Brockman. LC 89-15989. Orig. Title: The Word Remains. 290p. 1989. pap. 15.50 (*0-88344-652-9*) Orbis Bks.
Rome's Challenge. Catholic Mirror Staff. LC 95-70520. 32p. 1995. pap. 0.99 (*1-57258-052-6*) Teach Servs.
Rome's Desert Frontier from the Air. David Kennedy & Derrick Riley. (Illus.). 256p. (C). 1990. text ed. 50.00 (*0-292-77045-6*) U of Tex Pr.
Rome's Enemies: Germanics & Dacians. Peter Wilcox. (Men-at-Arms Ser.: No. 129). (Illus.). 48p. pap. 11.95 (*0-85045-473-5*, 9061, Pub. by Osprey UK) Stackpole.
Rome's Enemies, Vol. 2: Gallic & British Celts. Peter Wilcox. (Men-at-Arms Ser.: No. 158). (Illus.). 48p. pap. 11.95 (*0-85045-606-1*, 9090, Pub. by Osprey UK) Stackpole.
Rome's Enemies, Vol. 3: Parthians & Sassanids. Peter Wilcox. (Men-at-Arms Ser.: No. 175). (Illus.). 48p. pap. 11.95 (*0-85045-688-6*, 9107, Pub. by Osprey UK) Stackpole.
Rome's Enemies, Vol. 4: Spanish Armies 218 BC-19 BC. Rafael Trevino. (Men-at-Arms Ser.: No. 180). (Illus.). 48p. pap. 11.95 (*0-85045-701-7*, 9112, Pub. by Osprey UK) Stackpole.
Rome's Enemies, Vol. 5: The Desert Frontier. David Nicolle. (Men-at-Arms Ser.: No. 243). (Illus.). 48p. pap. 11.95 (*1-85532-166-1*, 9203, Pub. by Osprey UK) Stackpole.
Rome's Fall & After. Walter Goffart. 381p. 1981. boxed 60.00 (*1-85285-001-9*) Hambledon Press.
Rome's Responsibility for the Assassination of Abraham Lincoln. Thomas M. Harris. 78p. 1993. pap. 12.95 (*0-9636975-2-8*) Laymen Relig Lib.
Rome's Ruin by Lead Poison. S. Colum Gilfillan & Clair C. Patterson. LC 84-51627. (Illus.). 248p. 1990. 15.95 (*0-930887-02-6*) Wenzel Pr.
Romeus & Iuliet. Arthur Brooke. Ed. by P. A. Daniel. Bd. with Rhomeo & Julietta. (New Shakespeare Society, London, Ser.: Ser. 3, No. 1). 1974. reprint ed. Set pap. 35.00 (*0-8115-0237-6*) Periodicals Srv.
Romewalks: Five Ultimate Walking Tours of Rome. rev. ed. Anya M. Shetterly. (Illus.). 256p. 1994. pap. 14.95 (*0-8050-2054-3*) H Holt & Co.
Romie & Rudolph: An Intimate History Told in Letters of Friendship, Family, Courtship & Marriage. R. M. Reid, Jr. 226p. 1995. pap. 20.00 (*0-9648967-0-2*) M Reid Pubns.
Romin-Englez Dictionar. Jean Anouilh. (FRE.). 1973. pap. 10.95 (*0-7859-3603-3*, M2956) Fr & Eur.
Romische Agrargeschichte. Max M. Weber. Ed. by Moses Finley. LC 79-5013. (Ancient Economic History Ser.). (GER.). 1979. reprint ed. lib. bdg. 25.95 (*0-405-12405-8*) Ayer.
Romische Annalistik. Karl W. Nitzsch. xii, 355p. 1974. reprint ed. write for info. (*3-487-05190-7*) G Olms Pubs.
Romische Forschungen, 2 vols. Theodor Mommsen. viii, 952p. 1962. reprint ed. write for info. (*0-318-71178-8*) G Olms Pubs.
Romische Heeresgeschichte: Beitrage 1962-1985. Geza Alfoldy. (Mavors Roman Army Researches Ser.: Vol. III). 587p. (GER.). (C). 1987. 134.00 (*90-70265-48-6*, Pub. by Gieben NE) Benjamins North Am.
Romische Ikonographie, 4 vols. Johann J. Bernoulli. xlviii, 1284p. 1969. reprint ed. 465.00 (*0-318-71075-7*) G Olms Pubs.
Romische Militargeschichte Von Gallienus bis zum Beginn der Byzantinischen Themenverfassung. Robert Grosse. LC 75-7319. (Roman History Ser.). (GER.). 1975. reprint ed. 29.95 (*0-405-07083-7*) Ayer.
Romische Mythologie, Bd. 1. Ludwig Preller. xii, 455p. 1978. write for info. (*3-296-15111-7*) G Olms Pubs.
Romische Mythologie: Roman Mythology. Ludwig Preller. Ed. by Kees W. Bolle. LC 77-79154. (Mythology Ser.). (GER.). 1978. reprint ed. lib. bdg. 58.95 (*0-405-10563-0*) Ayer.
Romische Namengebung. Bruno Doer. 230p. 1974. reprint ed. write for info. (*3-487-05159-1*) G Olms Pubs.
Romische Namengebung: Ein Historischer Versuch. Bruno Doer. LC 75-7317. (Roman History Ser.). (GER.). 1975. reprint ed. 18.95 (*0-405-07081-0*) Ayer.
Romische Staatsverwaltung, 3 Vols. Joachim Marquardt. LC 75-7329. (Roman History Ser.). 1975. reprint ed. 121.95 (*0-405-07101-9*) Ayer.
Romische Staatsverwaltung, 3 Vols., Vol. 1. Joachim Marquardt. LC 75-7329. (Roman History Ser.). 1972. reprint ed. 32.95 (*0-405-08997-X*) Ayer.
Romische Staatsverwaltung, 3 Vols., Vol. 2. Joachim Marquardt. LC 75-7329. (Roman History Ser.). 1975. reprint ed. 40.95 (*0-405-07103-5*) Ayer.
Romische Staatsverwaltung, 3 Vols., Vol. 3. Joachim Marquardt. LC 75-7329. (Roman History Ser.). 1975. reprint ed. 40.95 (*0-405-07104-3*) Ayer.
***Romische Tradition und Englische Politik.** Christiane Kunst. (Spudasmata Ser.: Vol. 55). x, 232p. (GER.). 1994. write for info. (*3-487-09001-5*) G Olms Pubs.
Romische Tragodie Im Zeitalter der Republik. Otto Ribbeck. viii, 692p. 1968. reprint ed. write for info. (*0-318-71213-X*) G Olms Pubs.
Romischen Grabaltare der Kaiserzeit. Walter Altmann. LC 75-10626. (Ancient Religion & Mythology Ser.). (Illus.). (GER.). 1976. reprint ed. 22.95 (*0-405-07002-0*) Ayer.
Romischen Medaillone Im Berliner Munzkabinett. Heinrich Dressel. xvi, 485p. 1973. Textband, xvi, 485p. write for info. (*3-296-12601-5*); Tafelband. write for info. (*3-296-12602-3*) G Olms Pubs.
Romiscche Alterthumer, 3 vols. Ludwig Lange. xxxvi, 2366p. 1974. reprint ed. write for info. (*3-487-05235-0*) G Olms Pubs.
Romissche Metrik. Friedrich Crusius. vi, 148p. (GER.). 1989. reprint ed. 20.00 (*3-487-07532-6*) G Olms Pubs.
Romisscshe Mythologie, Bd. 2. Ludwig Preller. xi, 490p. 1978. write for info. (*3-296-15112-5*) G Olms Pubs.
***Rommel: Battles & Campaigns.** Kenneth Macksey. LC 97-10973. 1997. pap. write for info. (*0-306-80786-6*) Da Capo.
Rommel: In His Own Words. Ed. by John Pimlott. (Illus.). 192p. 1994. 29.95 (*1-85367-185-1*, 5439) Stackpole.
Rommel: The Desert Fox. Desmond Young. LC 86-25366. (Illus.). 264p. 1987. reprint ed. pap. 12.00 (*0-688-06771-9*, Quill) Morrow.
Rommel & the Rebel. Lawrence Wells. LC 85-6974. 434p. 1992. reprint ed. pap. 14.95 (*0-916242-65-X*) Yoknapatawpha.
Rommel & the Secret War in North Africa 1941-1943: Secret Intelligence in the North African Campaign. Janusz Piekalkiewicz. Tr. by Fred Clemens from GER. LC 91-62740. (Illus.). 240p. 1992. 29.95 (*0-88740-340-9*) Schiffer.
Rommel in the Desert-Victories & Defeat of the Afrika Korps 1941-1943. Volkmar Kuhn. LC 90-62985. (Illus.). 224p. 1991. 35.00 (*0-88740-292-5*) Schiffer.
Rommel Papers. Intro. by Basil H. Liddell-Hart. (Quality Paperbacks Ser.). (Illus.). xxx, 544p. 1982. reprint ed. pap. 16.95 (*0-306-80157-4*) Da Capo.
Rommel the Desert Fox. Desmond Young. 27.95 (*0-8488-0869-X*) Amereon Ltd.
Rommel's Army in Africa. Dal McGuirk. (Illus.). 194p. 1993. 29.95 (*0-87938-835-8*) Motorbooks Intl.
Rommel's North African Campaign: September 1940-November 1942. Jack Greene & Alessandro Massignani. (Illus.). 272p. 1994. 22.95 (*0-938289-34-9*, 7326) Combined Pub.
Romney Dealer Text: How to Make Money Buying & Selling Old Cameras. Edward H. Romney. 84p. 1977. pap. text ed. 24.00 (*1-886996-59-8*) Hillcrst Pub.
Romney Marsh: Evolution, Occupation, Reclamation. Ed. by Jill Eddison. (Illus.). 208p. 1988. pap. 45.00 (*0-947816-24-0*, Pub. by Oxford Univ Comm Arch UK) David Brown.
***Romney Marsh: The Debatable Ground.** Ed. by Jill Eddison & Mark Gardiner. (Oxford University Committee for Archaeology Monograph Ser.: No. 41). (Illus.). 174p. 1995. pap. 40.00 (*0-947816-41-0*, Pub. by Oxford Univ Comm Arch UK) David Brown.
Romola. George Eliot. Ed. by Andrew Brown. LC 92-14326. 774p. 1993. 160.00 (*0-19-812594-1*, Clarendon Pr) OUP.
Romola. George Eliot. Ed. by Andrew Sanders. (English Library). 736p. 1980. pap. 8.95 (*0-14-043139-X*, Penguin Classics) Viking Penguin.
***Romola.** George Eliot. 1997. pap. 10.95 (*0-14-043470-4*) Viking Penguin.
Romola. George Eliot. (World's Classics Ser.). 656p. 1994. pap. 7.95 (*0-19-282964-5*) OUP.
Romp in Green Heat. large type ed. Alan Sewart. (Linford Mystery Library). 336p. 1994. pap. 15.99 (*0-7089-7571-2*, Linford) Ulverscroft.
Romp Through the Bible. William R. Phillippe. LC 88-11830. 192p. (Orig.). 1987. 20.00 (*0-940473-01-1*); pap. 9.95 (*0-940473-02-X*) Wm Caxton.
***Rompamos el Silenco.** E. Wilson. (SPA.). 5.95 (*0-8297-0304-7*) Life Pubs Intl.
Rompiendo Ataduras. Victor Ricardo. 28p. 1992. pap. 1.15 (*1-885630-01-8*) HLM Producciones.
Rompiendo Cadenas. Juan G. Gonzalez. LC 89-83580. (Coleccion Caniqui). 150p. (Orig.). (SPA.). 1990. pap. 15.00 (*0-89729-529-3*) Ediciones.
Rompiendo la Maldicion. Nicky Cruz. 259p. (SPA.). 6.99 (*1-56063-404-9*, 550130) Editorial Unilit.
***Rompiendo las Cadenas.** Neal Anderson. (SPA.). (J). 1995. write for info. (*0-614-27134-7*) Editorial Unilit.
***Rompiendo las Cadenas.** Neal T. Anderson. 167p. (SPA.). 1994. pap. write for info. (*1-56063-468-5*) Editorial Unilit.
***Rompiendo las Cadenas.** Neil T. Anderson & Dave Park. Date not set. write for info. (*1-56063-519-3*) Editorial Unilit.
***Rompiendo las Cadenas - Bondage Breaker: Ed. Jovenes - The Youth Edition.** Anderson. (SPA.). 1995. write for info. (*0-614-24403-X*) Editorial Unilit.
***Romps: Poems from Hollywood.** Mark Dunster. 17p. (Orig.). (YA). (gr. 9-12). 1997. pap. 5.00 (*0-89642-346-8*) Linden Pubs.
Romualdo Pacheco: Governor of California. Anthony Ramirez, Jr. (Illus.). 1974. 5.00 (*0-911302-26-3*, PS3-6) San Francisco Pr.
Romualdo Pacheco: Illustrious Californio. 2nd ed. Ronald Gemini & Richard Hitchman. (Illus.). 160p. (Orig.). 1990. pap. 12.95 (*0-939919-27-3*) Bear Flag Bks.
Romualdo Pacheco's California! The Mexican-American Who Won. Loren Nicholson. (California Heritage Ser.: No. 2). (Illus.). 112p. (Orig.). (YA). (gr. 10-12). 1991. pap. text ed. 12.95 (*0-9623233-2-2*) CA HPA.
***Romulan Bird-of-Prey.** Ruth Wickings. (Star Trek Make Your Own Starship Ser.). (J). 1997. 5.99 (*0-689-81591-3*) S&S Childrens.
Romulan Prize. Simon Hawke. Ed. by Dave Stern. (Star Trek: The Next Generation Ser.: No. 26). 288p. (Orig.). 1993. mass mkt. 5.50 (*0-671-79746-8*) PB.
Romulan Stratagem. Robert Greenberger. (Star Trek: The Next Generation Ser.: No. 35). 1995. mass mkt. 5.99 (*0-671-87997-9*) PB.
Romulan Way. Diane Duane. (Star Trek Ser.: No. 35). 1991. mass mkt. 4.99 (*0-671-74357-0*) PB.
Romulo Betancourt & the Transformation of Venezuela. Robert J. Alexander. LC 81-14684. 600p. (C). 1982. 49.95 (*0-87855-450-5*) Transaction Pubs.
Romulus. adapted ed. Friedrich Durrenmatt. 1963. pap. 5.25 (*0-8222-0961-6*) Dramatists Play.
Romulus & Remus. Rockwell. 1997. pap. 3.99 (*0-689-81290-6*) S&S Childrens.
Romulus & Remus. Rockwell. LC 96-25565. (J). 1997. 15.00 (*0-689-81291-4*) S&S Childrens.
Romulus Linney, Seventeen Short Plays. Romulus Linney. LC 92-27781. (Contemporary Playwrights Ser.). 276p. 1994. pap. 16.95 (*1-880399-21-0*) Smith & Kraus.
Romulus Remembered. Clarence Graveldling. LC 89-28130. (Illus.). 160p. (Orig.). 1990. pap. 12.95 (*1-55787-061-6*, NY75035) Hrt of the Lakes.
Romy. Catherine Hermary-Vielle. 256p. (FRE.). 1988. pap. 10.95 (*0-7859-2558-9*, 2070380424) Fr & Eur.
***Ron Arad.** (Illus.). 128p. 1997. pap. 23.50 (*2-906571-59-8*) Dist Art Pubs.
Ron Bacardi y Compania, S. A., Administration Building (Cuba) & Other Buildings & Projects. Ed. by Franz Schulze & George E. Danforth. LC 86-9980. (Mies Van Der Rohe Archive Series: An Illustrated Catalog of the Mies Van Der Rohe Drawing in the Museum of Modern Art, Pt. II, 1938-1967, the American Work: Vol. 17). (Illus.). 480p. 1993. text ed. 300.00 (*0-8153-0118-9*) Garland.
Ron Bacardi y Compania, S. A., Administration Building (Mexico) & Other Buildings & Projects. Ed. by Franz Schulze & George E. Danforth. LC 86-9980. (Mies Van Der Rohe Archive Series: An Illustrated Catalog of the Mies Van Der Rohe Drawing in the Museum of Modern Art, Pt. II, 1938-1967, the American Work: Vol. 18). (Illus.). 496p. 1993. text ed. 300.00 (*0-8153-0119-7*) Garland.
Ron Bauer's Easy DOS It! 5th rev. ed. Ron Bauer. Ed. by Ann Trottier. (Easy Way Ser.: Vol. 1). (Illus.). 160p. 1992. pap. 14.95 (*0-942019-10-5*) Easy Way Pr.
Ron Cooper. Jay Belloli. (Illus.). 24p. 1973. 6.00 (*0-686-99822-7*) Mus Contemp Art.
Ron Kovic: The Paralyzed U. S. Marine Who Became an Antiwar Activist. Nathaniel Moss. LC 93-16373. (Great Achievers). (Illus.). (YA). (gr. 5 up). 1994. lib. bdg. 19.95 (*0-7910-2076-2*) Chelsea Hse.
Ron Nagle: A Survey Exhibition. Michael McTwigan. LC 93-79949. 84p. 1993. pap. 25.00 (*0-9638030-0-X*) Mills Art Gal.
Ron Nagle: A Survey Exhibition 1958-1993. Michael McTwigan. (Illus.). 84p. 1994. pap. 30.00 (*0-295-97370-6*) U of Wash Pr.
Ron O'Brien's Diving for Gold. Ron O'Brien. LC 91-28668. (Illus.). 200p. 1992. pap. 19.95 (*0-88011-448-7*, POBR0448) Human Kinetics.
Ron Ransom Carves an Amish Family, Plain & Simple. Ron Ransom. LC 95-34653. (Schiffer Book for Woodcarvers). (Illus.). 64p. (gr. 10). 1996. pap. 12.95 (*0-88740-893-1*) Schiffer.

R

Ron Ransom Carves Athletic Santa Mini-Cheers: Step-by-Step Instructions Plus Patterns for 5 Original Santas. Jeffrey B. Snyder. LC 95-7003. (Book for Woodcarvers). (Illus.). 64p. (Orig.). 1995. pap. 12.95 (*0-88740-825-7*) Schiffer.

Ron Ransom Carves More Angels. Photos & Text by Jeffrey B. Snyder. LC 95-37211. (Illus.). 64p. (YA). (gr. 10). 1996. pap. 12.95 (*0-88740-892-3*) Schiffer.

***Ron Ranson on Skies: Techniques in Watercolor & Other Media.** Ron Ranson. 160p. 1997. 27.95 (*0-289-80152-4*, Pub. by Studio Vista Bks UK) Sterling.

Ron Rood's Vermont: A Nature Guide. Ronald Rood. LC 88-9856. (Illus.). 224p. (Orig.). 1988. pap. 10.95 (*0-933050-56-9*) New Eng Pr VT.

Ron Rooney & the Million Dollar Comic. Susan Schade. LC 95-32721. (Stepping Stone Bks.). (Illus.). (J). 1996. pap. 3.99 (*0-679-87385-6*) Random Bks Yng Read.

Ron Rooney & the Million Dollar Comic. Susan Schade. LC 95-32721. (Stepping Stone Bks.). (Illus.). (J). 1996. lib. bdg. 11.99 (*0-679-97385-0*) Random Bks Yng Read.

Ron Santo: For Love of Ivy, an Autobiography. Ron Santo & Randy Minkoff. (Illus.). 224p. 1993. 20.00 (*0-929387-92-9*) Bonus Books.

Ron Santo: For Love of Ivy, an Autobiography. Ron Santo & Randy Minkoff. (Illus.). 230p. 1994. pap. 9.95 (*1-56625-005-6*) Bonus Books.

***Ron Schara's Minnesota Fishing Guide 1997.** Ron Schara et al. 1997. 6.95 (*0-9647179-2-1*) Star MN.

Ron Schara's Twin Cities Fishing Guide. Ron Schara. LC 81-22555. (Illus.). 120p. 1982. pap. 6.95 (*0-932272-08-8*) Minneapolis Tribune.

Ron Truffle: His Life & Bump Out. Barry Dickins. 140p. (C). 1990. 30.00 (*0-947087-10-9*, Pub. by Pascoe Pub AT) St Mut.

Ron Yablon Graphic Archives: Nature. Ron Yablon. 1990. pap. 24.50 (*0-910158-50-9*) Art Dir.

Ron Yablon Graphic Archives: People. Ron Yablon. 1990. pap. 24.50 (*0-910158-51-7*) Art Dir.

Ron Yablon Graphic Archives: Things. Ron Yablon. 1990. pap. 24.50 (*0-910158-52-5*) Art Dir.

Ron Yablon Graphic Archives: Typography. Ron Yablon. 1990. pap. 24.50 (*0-910158-53-3*) Art Dir.

Rona the Distant Island. Michael Robson. 179p. (C). 1992. text ed. 75.00 (*0-86152-867-0*, Pub. by Acair Ltd UK); pap. text ed. 39.00 (*0-86152-823-9*, Pub. by Acair Ltd UK) St Mut.

Ronald Allen Leax - Leon Shulman: Two Massachusetts Artists. (Illus.). 24p. 1976. 2.00 (*0-916746-47-X*) Springfield Lib & Mus.

***Ronald Colman: A Bio-Bibliography.** Sam Frank. Vol. 74. 336p. 1997. text ed. 65.00 (*0-313-26433-3*, Greenwood Pr) Greenwood.

Ronald Colman, Gentleman of the Cinema. R. Dixon Smith. LC 90-53524. (Illus.). 336p. 1991. lib. bdg. 38.50 (*0-89950-581-3*) McFarland & Co.

Ronald Davis: Dodecagons, 1968-69. Barbara Rose. (Illus.). 32p. (Orig.). 1989. pap. 15.00 (*0-924008-03-2*) Blum Helman.

Ronald Dworkin. Stephen Guest. LC 91-75060. (Jurists: Profiles in Legal Theory Ser.). 320p. (C). 1992. 45.00 (*0-8047-1997-7*); pap. 16.95 (*0-8047-2019-3*) Stanford U Pr.

Ronald Dworkin & Contemporary Jurisprudence. M. Cohen. pap. 28.95 (*0-7156-1817-2*, Pub. by Duckworth UK) Focus Pub-R Pullins.

Ronald Dworkin & Contemporary Jurisprudence. Ed. by Marshall Cohen. LC 83-11091. (Philosophy & Society Ser.). 316p. (C). 1984. text ed. 59.50 (*0-8476-7124-0*) Rowman.

Ronald Dworkin on Law As Integrity: Rights As Principles of Adjudication. Paul Gaffney. LC 96-505. 232p. 1996. 89.95 (*0-7734-2268-4*, Mellen Univ Pr) E Mellen.

Ronald Firbank: An Annotated Bibliography of Secondary Materials, 1905-1995. Steven Moore. LC 96-15667. (Bibliography Ser.: No. 3). 160p. (Orig.). 1996. pap. 30.00 (*1-56478-133-X*) Dalkey Arch.

Ronald H. Coase. Steven G. Medema. LC 93-37501. 1994. text ed. 65.00 (*0-312-12039-7*, Pub. by Macm UK) St Martin.

Ronald Harwood Plays, No. 2. Ronald Harwood. 224p. (Orig.). 1995. pap. 13.95 (*0-571-17401-9*) Faber & Faber.

Ronald McDonald House of New York City Cookbook. Volunteers of the Ronald McDonald House of New York. LC 94-5416. 1994. write for info. (*0-9642366-0-5*) Gryphon Three.

Ronald McNair: Astronaut. Nathan I. Huggins & Corinne J. Naden. (Black Americans of Achievement Ser.). (Illus.). 112p. (YA). (gr. 5 up). 1991. lib. bdg. 19.95 (*0-7910-1133-X*) Chelsea Hse.

Ronald McNair: Astronaut. Corinne J. Naden. Ed. by Nathan I. Huggins. (Black Americans of Achievement Ser.). (Illus.). (YA). (gr. 5 up). 1993. pap. 8.95 (*0-7910-1158-5*) Chelsea Hse.

Ronald McNair: Astronaut. Dena Shaw. (Junior Black Americans of Achievement Ser.). (Illus.). 80p. (J). (gr. 3-6). 1993. lib. bdg. 15.95 (*0-7910-2110-6*) Chelsea Hse.

Ronald McNair: Astronaut. Dena Shaw. (Junior Black Americans of Achievement Ser.). (Illus.). 80p. (J). (gr. 3-6). 1994. pap. 4.95 (*0-7910-2116-5*) Chelsea Hse.

***Ronald Morgan.** Patricia R. Giff. Date not set. pap. 11.99 (*0-670-87493-0*); pap. 11.99 (*0-670-87494-9*) Viking Penguin.

Ronald Morgan Goes to Bat. Patricia R. Giff. (Illus.). 32p. (J). (ps-3). 1990. pap. 4.99 (*0-14-050669-1*, Puffin) Puffin Bks.

Ronald Morgan Goes to Bat. Patricia R. Giff. (Illus.). 32p. (J). (gr. k-4). 1988. pap. 10.95 (*0-670-81457-1*) Viking Child Bks.

Ronald Morgan Goes to Camp. Patricia R. Giff. (Illus.). 26p. (J). 1995. pap. 13.99 (*0-670-86195-2*) Viking Penguin.

***Ronald Morgan Goes to Camp.** Patricia R. Giff & Susanna Natti. 1997. pap. 4.99 (*0-14-055647-8*) Viking Penguin.

Ronald Prather: Laboratory Manual for Data Structures: To Accompany Horowitz & Sahni Fundamentals of Data Structure. 3rd ed. Ronald E. Prather. (Illus.). (C). 1995. write for info. (*0-7167-8236-7*) W H Freeman.

Ronald Reagan. 1995. 20.00 (*0-00-225126-4*, HarpT) HarpC.

Ronald Reagan. annuals (YA). 1996. pap. write for info. (*0-934551-04-9*) Starlog Pr.

Ronald Reagan. John Devaney. (Presidential Biography Ser.). (Illus.). (YA). (gr. 7 up). 1990. 13.95 (*0-8027-6931-4*); lib. bdg. 14.85 (*0-8027-6932-2*) Walker & Co.

***Ronald Reagan.** Dsouza. 1997. 24.00 (*0-684-84428-1*) S&S Trade.

***Ronald Reagan.** Karen Judson. LC 96-36482. (United States Presidents Ser.). (Illus.). 112p. (YA). (gr. 5 up). 1997. lib. bdg. 18.95 (*0-89490-835-9*) Enslow Pubs.

Ronald Reagan. Zachary Kent. LC 89-33746. (Encyclopedia of Presidents Ser.). (Illus.). 100p. (J). (gr. 3 up). 1989. lib. bdg. 22.00 (*0-516-01373-4*) Childrens.

Ronald Reagan. Rebecca Larsen. (Impact Biographies Ser.). (Illus.). 112p. (YA). (gr. 7-12). 1994. lib. bdg. 22.70 (*0-531-11191-1*) Watts.

Ronald Reagan. Random House Value Publishing Staff. 1997. 20.00 (*0-517-20078-3*) Random Hse Value.

Ronald Reagan. rev. ed. George Sullivan. 1985. 14.98 (*0-671-74537-9*) PB.

***Ronald Reagan: A Biography.** William E. Pemberton. 1997. 62.95 (*1-56324-302-4*); pap. 21.95 (*1-56324-303-2*) M E Sharpe.

Ronald Reagan: A Remarkable Life. Jim Cardigan. (Illus.). 128p. 1995. pap. 12.95 (*0-8362-0449-2*) Andrews & McMeel.

Ronald Reagan: His First Career, a Bibliography of the Movie Years. Ed. by Arthur F. McClure et al. LC 88-7198. (Studies in American History: Vol. 1). 240p. 1988. lib. bdg. 89.95 (*0-88946-098-1*) E Mellen.

Ronald Reagan: The Great Communicator. Kurt Ritter & David Henry. LC 91-28148. (Great American Orators: Critical Studies, Speeches & Sources Ser.: No. 13). 248p. 1992. text ed. 49.95 (*0-313-26069-9*, HRR/, Greenwood Pr) Greenwood.

Ronald Reagan & the American Presidency. David Mervin. 1990. 48.50 (*0-582-03487-6*, Pub. by Longman UK) Longman.

Ronald Reagan & the Public Lands: America's Conservation Debate, 1979-1984. C. Brant Short. LC 88-32639. (Environmental History Ser.: No. 10). 192p. 1989. 29.95 (*0-89096-382-7*); pap. 16.95 (*0-89096-411-4*) Tex A&M Univ Pr.

Ronald Reagan in Hollywood: Movies & Politics. Steven Vaughn. (Cambridge Studies in the History of Mass Communications). (Illus.). 384p. (C). 1994. text ed. 27.95 (*0-521-44080-7*) Cambridge U Pr.

Ronald Reagan in Movie America. Jules Feiffer. 1988. pap. 7.95 (*0-8362-1829-9*) Andrews & McMeel.

Ronald Reagan-Paper Dolls in Full Color. Tom Tierney. (J). 1984. pap. 3.95 (*0-486-24628-0*) Dover.

Ronald Reagan Talks to America. Ronald Reagan. 1985. 12.95 (*0-8159-6719-5*) Devin.

Ronald Reagan Talks to America. 2nd rev. ed. Ronald Reagan. LC 68-26085. 226p. 1982. 12.95 (*0-8159-5222-8*) Devin.

Ronald Reagan the Movie, & Other Episodes in Political Demonology. Michael P. Rogin. 480p. (C). 1987. pap. 16.95 (*0-520-06469-0*) U CA Pr.

Ronald Reagan's America, Set. Ed. by Eric J. Schmertz et al. LC 96-5785. (Contributions in Political Science Ser.: No. 377). 852p. 1997. text ed. 145.00 (*0-313-30116-6*, Greenwood Pr) Greenwood.

Ronald Reagan's America, Vol. 1. Ed. by Eric J. Schmertz et al. LC 96-5785. (Contributions in Political Science Ser.: No. 377). 424p. 1997. text ed. 145.00 (*0-313-30117-4*, Greenwood Pr) Greenwood.

Ronald Reagan's America, Vol. 2. Ed. by Eric J. Schmertz et al. LC 96-5785. (Contributions in Political Science Ser.: No. 377). 472p. 1997. text ed. 145.00 (*0-313-30118-2*, Greenwood Pr) Greenwood.

***Ronald Reagan's Crusade.** Norman E. Wymbs. Ed. by Charles G. Gee. (Illus.). 365p. 1997. text ed. 25.00 (*1-889936-00-6*) Skyline Pubs Inc.

Ronald Reagan's Crusade. Norman E. Wymbs. Ed. by Charles G. Gee. (Illus.). 300p. 1995. 25.00 (*0-9645786-1-1*) VYTIS Pub.

Ronald Reagan's Weekly Radio Addresses: The President Speaks to America, Vol. I. Compiled by Fred L. Israel. LC 87-9461. 274p. 1987. 14.95 (*0-8420-2282-1*) Scholarly Res Inc.

Ronald Rosensweig Alpha Chi Sigma Award Winner: A Special Issue of the Journal Chemical Engineering Communications. Ed. by R. Ananth. 342p. 1988. pap. text ed. 587.00 (*2-88124-281-2*) Gordon & Breach.

Ronald Ross: Malariologist & Polymath, a Biography. E. R. Nye & M. E. Gibson. LC 96-8835. 1996. text ed. 59.95 (*0-312-16296-0*) St Martin.

Ronald Searle's Non-Sexist Dictionary. Ronald Searle. (Illus.). 64p. 1989. reprint ed. pap. 7.95 (*0-89815-322-0*) Ten Speed Pr.

Ronald Stevenson: A Musical Biography. Malcolm MacDonald. 1990. 21.95 (*0-912483-62-8*) Pro-Am Music.

Ronald W. Reagan: Fortieth President of the United States. Neal E. Robbins. Ed. by Richard G. Young. LC 89-39955. (Presidents of the United States Ser.). (Illus.). 128p. (J). (gr. 5-9). 1990. lib. bdg. 17.26 (*0-944483-66-6*) Garrett Ed Corp.

Ronald's Report Card. (Illus.). (J). (ps-2). 1991. pap. 5.10 (*0-8136-5664-8*); lib. bdg. 7.95 (*0-8136-5164-6*) Modern Curr.

Ronay Guide: Arts & Crafts Shown in the Carolinas, 1997. Ed. by Bill Ronay & Camille Ronay. 1996. pap. 8.95 (*1-56736-048-3*) A Step Ahead.

***Ronay Guide: Arts & Crafts Shown in Virginia, 1997.** Ed. by Bill Ronay & Camille Ronay. 1996. pap. 8.95 (*1-56736-058-0*) A Step Ahead.

***Ronay Guide: Arts & Crafts Shows in Georgia.** 6th rev. ed. Ed. by Camille Ronay & W. R. Ronay. 60p. 1996. pap. 8.95 (*0-614-29570-X*) A Step Ahead.

***Ronay Guide: Arts & Crafts Shows in Georgia, 1997.** Ed. by Bill Ronay & Camille Ronay. 1996. pap. 8.95 (*1-56736-055-6*) A Step Ahead.

***Ronay Guide: Arts & Crafts Shows in the Carolinas.** rev. ed. Ed. by Camille Ronay & W. R. Ronay. 60p. 1996. pap. 8.95 (*0-614-29572-6*) A Step Ahead.

***Ronay Guide: Arts & Crafts Shows in Virginia.** rev. ed. Ed. by Camille Ronay & W. R. Ronay. 60p. 1996. pap. 8.95 (*0-614-29571-8*) A Step Ahead.

Ronayne's Hand-Book of Freemasonry: With Appendix, Revised, Enlarged, Complete (1917) Edmond Ronayne. 282p. 1996. pap. 19.95 (*1-56459-745-8*) Kessinger Pub.

Ronde de Nuit. Patrick Modiano. (Folio Ser.: No. 835). 152p. (FRE.). 1976. pap. 6.95 (*2-07-036835-1*) Schoenhof.

Ronde de Nuit. Patrick Modiano. (FRE.). 1976. pap. 8.95 (*0-7859-2887-1*) Fr & Eur.

Ronde et Autres Faits Divers. J. M. Le Clezio. (FRE.). 1990. pap. 10.95 (*0-8288-3708-2*) Fr & Eur.

Ronde et Autres Faits Divers. J. M. Le Clezio. (Folio Ser.: No. 2148). (FRE.). pap. 8.95 (*2-07-038237-0*) Schoenhof.

Rondeaux. Laura Moriarty. LC 90-61555. (Roof Bks.). 88p. (Orig.). 1990. pap. text ed. 8.00 (*0-937804-39-8*) Segue NYC.

Rondo. Kazimierz Brandys. Tr. by Jaroslaw Anders. 265p. 1989. 19.95 (*0-374-25200-9*) FS&G.

Rondo Flute & Piano. write for info. (*0-7935-3838-6*, 50482256) H Leonard.

Rondo for Flute & Piano. 12p. pap. 6.95 (*0-7935-5286-9*, 50482556) H Leonard.

***Rondos: Poems from Hollywood.** Mark Dunster. 19p. (Orig.). 1997. pap. 5.00 (*0-89642-366-2*) Linden Pubs.

Rondo's Toy Dinosaurs. Clements. (J). 1997. 3.99 (*0-689-81305-8*) S&S Childrens.

Rondout: A Hudson River Port. Bob Steuding. LC 95-42766. (Illus.). 208p. (Orig.). 1995. pap. 24.00 (*0-935796-70-3*) Purple Mnt Pr.

***Rongorongo: The Easter Island Script.** Steven R. Fischer. (Illus.). 540p. 1997. 115.00 (*0-19-823710-3*) OUP.

Roni Horn: Inner Geography. LC 94-2475. 1994. pap. 19.95 (*0-912298-67-7*) Baltimore Mus.

Roni Horn: Rare Spellings: Selected Drawings 1985-1992. (Illus.). 144p. 1995. 60.00 (*3-928762-09-5*) Dist Art Pubs.

Roni Horn: To Place: Bluff Life. deluxe limited ed. 1991. boxed 250.00 (*0-317-04284-X*) Dist Art Pubs.

Roni Horn: To Place: Folds. Roni Horn. (Illus.). 70p. 1991. 35.00 (*0-941862-21-6*) Metron Pr.

Roni Horn, Gurgles, Sucks, Echoes. Roni Horn. 1995. pap. 25.00 (*1-880146-10-X*) M Marks.

Ronia, the Robber's Daughter. Astrid Lindgren. (J). (gr. 3-7). 1993. 18.25 (*0-8446-6649-1*) Peter Smith.

Ronia, the Robber's Daughter. Astrid Lindgren. (Illus.). 176p. (J). (gr. 4-7). 1985. pap. 4.99 (*0-14-031720-1*, Puffin) Puffin Bks.

Ronicky Doone. Max Brand. 256p. 1995. mass mkt., pap. text ed. 3.99 (*0-8439-3738-6*) Dorchester Pub Co.

Ronicky Doone: A Western Story. large type ed. Max Brand. LC 93-13225. 1993. 19.95 (*0-8161-5713-8*) Thorndike Pr.

Ronicky Doone's Reward. Max Brand. 224p. 1995. mass mkt., pap. text ed. 3.99 (*0-8439-3779-3*) Dorchester Pub Co.

Ronicky Doone's Reward. large type ed. Max Brand. LC 94-15062. 326p. 1995. lib. bdg. 20.95 (*0-8161-5999-8*, GK Hall) Thorndike Pr.

Ronicky Doone's Treasure. Max Brand. 256p. 1995. mass mkt., pap. text ed. 3.99 (*0-8439-3748-3*) Dorchester Pub Co.

Ronicky Doone's Treasure. large type ed. Max Brand. LC 94-13482. 261p. 1994. lib. bdg. 20.95 (*0-8161-5998-X*, GK Hall) Thorndike Pr.

Ronin. Frank Miller. Ed. by Barry Marx. (Illus.). 302p. 1987. pap. 14.95 (*0-930289-21-8*) DC Comics.

Ronin. Frank Miller. 302p. 1987. pap. 12.95 (*0-446-38674-X*) Warner Bks.

***Ronin: A Novel.** W. Jennings. 1996. pap. 14.95 (*0-8048-1672-7*) C E Tuttle.

***Ronin: Darkness & Light, Vol. 2.** D. A. Heeley. LC 97-14408. 1997. pap. text ed. 14.95 (*1-56718-356-5*) Llewellyn Pubns.

Roni's Dream Boy. Janet Quin-Harkin. LC 93-50680. (Boyfriend Club Ser.: No. 2). (Illus.). 176p. (J). (gr. 3-6). 1997. pap. 2.95 (*0-8167-3415-1*) Troll Communs.

Roni's Two-Boy Trouble. Janet Quin-Harkin. LC 94-27321. (Boyfriend Club Ser.). 176p. (J). (gr. 3-6). 1994. pap. 2.95 (*0-8167-3419-4*, Rainbow NJ) Troll Communs.

***Ronnie Cutrone.** Walter Guadagnini. 1997. pap. 19.95 (*88-8158-031-4*, Pub. by Charta IT) Dist Art Pubs.

Ronnie Gilbert on Mother Jones: Face to Face with the Most Dangerous Woman in America. Ronnie Gilbert. (Illus.). 150p. (Orig.). (C). 1993. reprint ed. lib. bdg. 29.00 (*0-8095-5875-0*) Borgo Pr.

Ronnie Goose Rhymes for Grown-Ups. Milton Loventhal & Jennifer McDowell. LC 84-60716. (Mother Goose Rhymes for Grown-ups Ser.). 1984. 10.95 (*0-930142-07-1*) Merlin Pr.

Ronnie Hawkins: Last of the Good Ol' Boys. Ronnie Hawkins & Peter Goddard. (Illus.). 314p. 1990. pap. 14.95 (*0-7737-5388-5*) Genl Dist Srvs.

Ronnie the Rabbit. (Frog Pond Ser.). (Illus.). (J). (ps-1). 2.98 (*0-517-46986-3*) Random Hse Value.

***Ron's Jog.** Illus. by Toni D. Stewart. 13p. (Orig.). (J). (gr. k-2). 1997. pap. 2.25 (*1-889658-05-7*) New Canaan Pub.

Ronsard. Jean Joubert. (Maison D'Ecrivain Collection). (Illus.). (FRE.). 1995. 49.95 (*2-86808-038-3*) Intl Scholars.

Ronsard: Selected Poems. Ed. by C. Scollen-Jimack. (French Texts Ser.). (FRE.). pap. 16.95 (*1-85399-455-3*, Pub. by Brstl Class Pr UK) Focus Pub-R Pullins.

Ronsard et Montaigne: Ecrivains Engages? Michel Dassonville. LC 88-82136. (French Forum Monographs: No. 71). 128p. (Orig.). 1989. pap. 12.95 (*0-917058-72-0*) French Forum.

Ronsard Poete de l'Amour, 3 tomes. Incl. Tome I. Cassandre. Desonay. 21.50 (*0-685-34201-8*); Tome II. De Marie a Genevre. Ed. by Desonay. 21.50 (*0-685-34202-6*); Tome III. Du Poete de la Cour au Chantre d'Helene. Desonay. 23.95 (*0-685-34203-4*); (Academie Royale de Belgique Ser.). write for info. (*0-318-52252-7*) Fr & Eur.

Ronsard's Hymnes: A Literary & Iconographical Study. Philip Ford. LC 96-4062. (Medieval & Renaissance Texts & Studies: No. 157). (Illus.). 352p. 1997. 30.00 (*0-86698-197-7*, MR157) MRTS.

Ronsard's Successful Epic Venture: The Epyllion. Bruce R. Leslie. LC 78-52838. (French Forum Monographs: No. 11). 137p. (Orig.). 1979. pap. 9.95 (*0-917058-10-0*) French Forum.

Ronstadt's Financials. Robert C. Ronstadt et al. 250p. 1988. 99.00 (*0-930204-24-7*) Lord Pub.

Ronstadt's Financials Professional Planning & Budgeting Software & Documentation. R. Lord. 50p. (Orig.). 1989. pap. 99.00 (*0-930204-20-4*) Lord Pub.

***Rontgen Centennial, X-Rays Today in Natural & Life Sicences.** 740p. 1997. text ed. 91.00 (*981-02-3085-0*) World Scientific Pub.

***Roo Plays Baseball.** Steve Turner. (Illus.). 32p. (Orig.). (J). (gr. 3-8). 1996. pap. 6.99 (*1-57532-025-8*) Press-Tige Pub.

***Roo Rat's Tale.** J. Bruce Monson. LC 95-90990. (Illus.). 64p. (Orig.). (J). 1997. pap. 16.95 (*1-56002-638-3*, Univ Edtns) Aegina Pr.

***Roof & Siding Essentials.** Cowles Creative Pub. Staff. (Black & Decker Quick Steps Ser.). (Illus.). 80p. (Orig.). 1997. pap. 9.95 (*0-86573-649-9*) Cowles Creative.

Roof Collapse at Antioch High School. (PCI Journal Reprints Ser.). 25p. 1981. pap. 14.00 (*0-686-40144-1*, JR240) P-PCI.

Roof Coverings & Roof Deck Constructions. National Fire Protection Association Staff. 1992. 16.75 (*0-317-63329-5*, 203-92) Natl Fire Prot.

***Roof Framer's Bible: The Complete Pocket Reference to Roof Framing.** 2nd rev. ed. Barry D. Mussell. LC 94-96225. (Illus.). 230p. (C). 1996. 18.95 (*0-9643354-1-7*) M E I.

Roof Framing. Charley G. Chadwick et al. Ed. by Lois G. Harrington. (Basic Carpentry Skills Ser.). (Illus.). 24p. (Orig.). 1991. teacher ed. 3.00 (*0-89606-292-9*, 703TK); pap. text ed. 10.00 (*0-89606-287-2*, 703) Am Assn Voc Materials.

Roof Framing. Marshal Gross. 1989. pap. 22.00 (*0-910460-40-X*) Craftsman.

Roof Garden Design & Implementation. Theodore Osmundson. 1985. text ed. write for info. (*0-442-27297-9*) Van Nos Reinhold.

Roof Gardens: History, Design & Construction. Theodore Osmundson. 320p. 1997. 75.00 (*0-393-73012-3*) Norton.

***Roof Gardens, Balconies & Terraces.** David Stevens. LC 96-71420. (Illus.). 160p. 1997. 35.00 (*0-8478-2015-7*) Rizzoli Intl.

Roof Gardens of Broadway Theatres, 1883-1942. Stephen B. Johnson. Ed. by Oscar G. Brockett. LC 85-17822. (Theater & Dramatic Studies: No. 31). 242p. reprint ed. 72.20 (*0-8357-1693-7*, 2070456) Bks Demand.

Roof of Stone. Franz Schneider. LC 83-629. 88p. (Orig.). 1983. pap. 4.95 (*0-911723-00-5*) Temporal.

***Roof of the Americas: From Alaska to Cape Horn.** John Warburton-Lee. (High Adventure Ser.). (Illus.). 192p. 1997. 29.95 (*0-8117-1475-6*) Stackpole.

Roof of the World. Mohamed Amin. 1992. 45.00 (*1-869828-05-4*, Pub. by Moonstone Bks UK) St Mut.

Roof of the World: Being the Narrative of a Journey over the High Plateau of Tibet to the Russian Frontier & the Oxus Sources on Pamir. T. E. Gordon. (C). 1994. reprint ed. text ed. 34.00 (*81-7305-049-X*, Pub. by Aryan Bks Intl II) S Asia.

Roof over Your Head: A Housing Programme for Labour. Labour Housing Group Staff. Ed. by Jane Darke. 128p. (Orig.). 1992. pap. 33.50 (*0-85124-531-5*, Pub. by Spokesman Bks UK) Coronet Bks.

Roof Slates & Other Poems of Pierre Reverdy. Tr. by Mary Ann Caws & Patricia Terry from FRE. LC 80-26806. 293p. 1981. pap. text ed. 16.95 (*0-930350-52-9*) NE U Pr.

Roof Tile of Tempyo. Yasushi Inoue. 140p. 1982. pap. 22.50 (*0-86008-307-1*) Col U Pr.

Roof-Top Heliport Construction & Protection. National Fire Protection Association Staff. 1990. 16.75 (*0-317-63436-4*, 418-90) Natl Fire Prot.

Roofed Theaters of Classical Antiquity. George C. Izenour. (Illus.). 216p. (C). 1992. text ed. 130.00 (*0-300-04685-5*) Yale U Pr.

Roofer. Jack Rudman. (Career Examination Ser.: C-677). 1994. pap. 23.95 (*0-8373-0677-9*) Nat Learn.

Roofers Handbook. William E. Johnson. LC 76-5875. (Illus.). 250p. 1976. pap. 19.00 (*0-910460-17-5*) Craftsman.

An Asterisk (*) at the beginning of an entry indicates that the title is appearing in BIP for the first time.

***Roofing.** (Laxton's Trade Price Bks.). 288p. 1996. pap. write for info. (*0-7506-2979-7*, Pub. by Laxtons UK) Buttrwrth-Heinemann.

***Roofing.** FHB Editors & Taunton Press Staff. LC 96-48869. (Builder's Library). (Illus.). 112p. 1997. 24.95 (*1-56158-211-5*, 070339) Taunton.

Roofing, Level 1. National Center for Construction Education & Research Staff. (Wheels of Learning Ser.). 1996. teacher ed., pap. text ed. 50.00 (*0-13-265554-3*) P-H.

Roofing, Level 1. National Center for Construction Education & Research Staff. (Wheels of Learning Ser.). 1996. student ed., pap. text ed. 50.00 (*0-13-266461-5*) P-H.

Roofing, Level 2. National Center for Construction Education & Research Staff. (Wheels of Learning Ser.). 1996. teacher ed., pap. text ed. 80.00 (*0-13-265562-4*) P-H.

Roofing, Level 2. National Center for Construction Education & Research Staff. (Wheels of Learning Ser.). 1996. student ed., pap. text ed. 80.00 (*0-13-265943-3*) P-H.

Roofing, Level 3. National Center for Construction Education & Research Staff. (Wheels Ser.). 1996. teacher ed., pap. text ed. 80.00 (*0-13-265570-5*) P-H.

Roofing, Level 3. National Center for Construction Education & Research Staff. (Wheels of Learning Ser.). 1996. student ed., pap. text ed. 80.00 (*0-13-265950-6*) P-H.

Roofing, Level 4. National Center for Construction Education & Research Staff. (Wheels Ser.). 1996. teacher ed., pap. text ed. 55.00 (*0-13-265588-8*) P-H.

Roofing, Level 4. National Center for Construction Education & Research Staff. (Wheels of Learning Ser.). 1996. student ed., pap. text ed. 50.00 (*0-13-265968-9*) P-H.

Roofing: Asphalt & Wood Shingling, Workbook & Testbook. California Department of Education Staff. (Apprenticeship Instructional Materials Ser.). (Illus.). 80p. 1982. pap. 5.25 (*0-8011-0601-X*) Calif Education.

Roofing: Built-up Roofing, Workbook & Testbook. California Department of Education Staff. (Apprenticeship Instructional Materials Ser.). (Illus.). 94p. 1981. pap. 5.25 (*0-8011-0604-4*) Calif Education.

Roofing: Cold-Applied Roofing Systems & Waterproofing & Dampproofing, Workbook & Testbook. California Department of Education Staff. (Apprenticeship Instructional Materials Ser.). (Illus.). 80p. 1982. pap. 5.25 (*0-8011-0607-9*) Calif Education.

Roofing: Common Roofing & Waterproofing Materials & Equipment, Workbook & Testbook. California Department of Education Staff. (Apprenticeship Instructional Materials Ser.). (Illus.). 64p. 1993. pap. 8.00 (*0-8011-1105-6*) Calif Education.

Roofing: Design Criteria, Options, Selection. Robert D. Herbert, III. (Illus.). 240p. (C). 1989. 62.95 (*0-87629-104-3*, 67253) ACMDG Co.

Roofing: Entering the Roofing & Waterproofing Industry, Workbook & Tests. California Department of Education Staff. (Apprenticeship Instructional Materials Ser.). (Illus.). 96p. 1991. pap. 6.50 (*0-8011-0971-X*) Calif Education.

Roofing: First-Aid Training, Workbook & Testbook. California Department of Education Staff. (Apprenticeship Instructional Materials Ser.). (Illus.). 72p. 1982. pap. 5.25 (*0-8011-0616-8*) Calif Education.

Roofing: Level 1. Ed. by National Center for Construction Staff. 1996. pap. text ed. 50.00 (*0-13-462664-8*) P-H.

Roofing: Level 1. Ed. by National Center for Construction Staff. 1996. teacher ed., pap. text ed. 50.00 (*0-13-462672-9*) P-H.

Roofing: Level 2. Ed. by National Center for Construction Staff. 1996. pap. text ed. 80.00 (*0-13-462680-X*) P-H.

Roofing: Level 2. Ed. by National Center for Construction Staff. 1996. teacher ed., pap. text ed. 80.00 (*0-13-462698-2*) P-H.

Roofing: Level 3. Ed. by National Center for Construction Staff. 1996. pap. text ed. 80.00 (*0-13-462706-7*) P-H.

Roofing: Level 3. Ed. by National Center for Construction Staff. 1996. teacher ed., pap. text ed. 80.00 (*0-13-462714-8*) P-H.

Roofing: Level 4. Ed. by National Center for Construction Staff. 1996. pap. text ed. 50.00 (*0-13-462722-9*) P-H.

Roofing: Level 4. Ed. by National Center for Construction Staff. 1996. teacher ed., pap. text ed. 55.00 (*0-13-462730-X*) P-H.

Roofing: Maintenance Repair, & Roofing, Workbook & Testbook. California Department of Education Staff. (Apprenticeship Instructional Materials Ser.). (Illus.). 72p. 1983. pap. 5.25 (*0-8011-0619-2*) Calif Education.

Roofing: Plans & Specifications, Workbook & Testbook. California Department of Education Staff. (Apprenticeship Instructional Materials Ser.). (Illus.). 56p. 1983. pap. 5.25 (*0-8011-0622-2*) Calif Education.

Roofing: Rigid Roofing, Workbook & Testbook. California Department of Education Staff. (Apprenticeship Instructional Materials Ser.). (Illus.). 88p. 1980. pap. 5.25 (*0-8011-0625-7*) Calif Education.

Roofing: Single-Ply Roofing & Waterproofing Workbook & Tests. California Department of Education Staff. (Apprenticeship Instructional Materials Ser.). (Illus.). 88p. 1987. pap. 6.25 (*0-8011-0661-3*) Calif Education.

Roofing: The Best of Fine Homebuilding. LC 96-5432. (Illus.). 112p. 1996. pap. 14.95 (*1-56158-141-0*) Taunton.

Roofing & Siding. (Fix-It-Yourself Ser.). (Illus.). 144p. 1989. 17.27 (*0-8094-6240-0*); lib. bdg. 23.27 (*0-8094-6241-9*) Time-Life.

Roofing & Siding: Residential, Commercial & Industrial Markets. 130p. 1995. 1,995.00 (*0-945235-25-9*) Lead Edge Reports.

Roofing Ceremony & The Silver Lake. August Strindberg. Tr. by David M. Paul & Margareta Paul from SWE. LC 86-30898. (Modern Scandinavian Literature in Translation Ser.). viii, 118p. 1987. text ed. 16.95 (*0-8032-4171-2*) U of Nebr Pr.

Roofing Construction & Estimating. Daniel Atcheson. (Illus.). 432p. (Orig.). 1995. pap. 35.00 (*1-57218-007-2*) Craftsman.

***Roofing Contractors - System Performance Information 1996.** Dean T. Kashiwagi et al. 182p. 1996. lib. bdg. 20.00 (*1-889857-02-5*) Perform Based Studies.

***Roofing Contractors - System Performance Information 1997.** Dean T. Kashiwagi & Jamie Conner. Date not set. lib. bdg. 25.00 (*1-889857-03-3*) Perform Based Studies.

Roofing Handbook. Robert Scharff & Roofer Magazine Editors. 1995. text ed. 49.95 (*0-07-057123-6*) McGraw.

Roofing Industry. Ed. by Peter Allen. 314p. 1982. pap. 295.00 (*0-931634-23-7*) FIND-SVP.

***Roofing Materials & Systems Directory 1997.** (C). 1997. pap. text ed. 18.00 (*0-7629-0095-4*) Underwrtrs Labs.

***Roofing Materials & Systems 1996.** (C). 1996. pap. text ed. 17.00 (*1-55989-953-0*) Underwrtrs Labs.

Roofing Research & Standards Development. Ed. by Richard A. Critchell. (Special Technical Publication Ser.: No. 959). (Illus.). 126p. 1987. text ed. 26.00 (*0-8031-0956-3*, 04-959000-10) ASTM.

Roofing Research & Standards Development. 3rd ed. Ed. by Thomas J. Wallace & Walter J. Rossiter, Jr. LC 94-13348. (Special Technical Publication (STP) Ser.: Vol. 1224). (Illus.). 195p. 1994. 51.00 (*0-8031-1883-X*, 04-012240-57) ASTM.

Roofing Research & Standards Development, Vol. 2: STP 1088. Ed. by J. Wallace & Walter J. Rossiter. LC 87-31938. (Special Technical Publication Ser.). (Illus.). 236p. 1990. text ed. 37.00 (*0-8031-1393-5*, 04-010880-57) ASTM.

Roofing Simplified. Donald R. Brann. LC 81-65487. 176p. 1983. pap. 7.95 (*0-87733-896-5*) Easi-Bild.

Roofing Simplified. rev. ed. Donald R. Brann. LC 71-99939. 1977. lib. bdg. 5.95 (*0-87733-096-4*) Easi-Bild.

Roofing Simplified. Donald R. Brann. LC 71-99939. 1979. reprint ed. pap. 7.95 (*0-87733-696-2*) Easi-Bild.

Roofing Systems: Materials & Applications. John A. Watson. (Illus.). 1979. text ed. 46.00 (*0-8359-6687-9*, Reston) P-H.

Roofing Systems - STP 603. Ed. by D. E. Brotherson. 148p. 1987. pap. 21.00 (*0-8031-0559-2*, 04-603000-10) ASTM.

Roofing Technology Conference, 9th: Proceedings. Ed. by Walter J. Rossiter, Jr. 98p. 1989. 28.00 (*0-934809-05-4*) Natl Roofing Cont.

Roofing the Right Way. 2nd ed. Steven Bolt. (Illus.). 240p. 1990. pap. 14.95 (*0-8306-3387-1*) McGraw-Hill Prof.

Roofing the Right Way. 2nd ed. Steven Bolt. (Illus.). 240p. 1990. 24.95 (*0-8306-7387-3*, 3387) TAB Bks.

Roofing the Right Way. 3rd ed. Steven Bolt. LC 96-41056. (Illus.). 368p. 1997. text ed. 34.95 (*0-07-006649-3*); pap. text ed. 24.95 (*0-07-006650-7*) McGraw.

Roofing the Right Way: A Step-by-Step Guide for the Homeowner. Steven Bolt. (Illus.). 192p. 1986. 19.95 (*0-8306-0367-0*, 2667); pap. 11.95 (*0-8306-0467-7*) McGraw-Hill Prof.

Roofing, Waterproofing, & Bituminous Materials see 1997 Annual Book of ASTM Standards: Construction, Section 4

Roofs & Rails. Gavin Ehringer. Ed. by Gary Vorhes. (Illus.). (Orig.). 1995. pap. 14.95 (*0-911647-31-7*) Western Horseman.

Roofs & Siding. (Home Repair & Improvement Ser.). (Illus.). 136p. 1977. 14.60 (*0-8094-2390-1*); lib. bdg. 20.60 (*0-8094-2391-X*) Time-Life.

Roofs & Siding. Time-Life Books Editors. (Home Repair & Improvement Ser.). (Illus.). 128p. 1996. write for info. (*0-7835-3904-5*) Time-Life.

Roofs, Voices, Roads. Reginald Gibbons. (QRL Poetry Bks.: Vol. XX). 1978. 20.00 (*0-614-06370-1*) Quarterly Rev.

Rooftop Astronomer: A Story about Maria Mitchell. Stephanie S. McPherson. (Illus.). 32p. (J). (gr. 3-6). 1990. lib. bdg. 14.21 (*0-87614-410-5*, Carolrhoda) Lerner Group.

Rooftop Mystery. Joan M. Lexau. LC 68-16821. (Harper I Can Read Mystery Bk.). (Illus.). 64p. (J). (gr. k-3). 1968. lib. bdg. 14.89 (*0-06-023865-8*) HarpC Child Bks.

Rooftop Piper. David Hernandez. 90p. 1991. pap. 7.95 (*0-9624287-3-6*) Tia Chucha Pr.

Rooftop Secrets & Other Stories of Anti-Semitism. Sherry H. Blumberg. LC 86-1362. (Illus.). 144p. (Orig.). (J). (gr. 7-9). 1987. teacher ed., pap. 5.00 (*0-8074-0326-1*, 201441) UAHC.

Rooftop Secrets & Other Stories of Anti-Semitism. Lawrence Bush. LC 86-1362. (Illus.). 144p. (Orig.). (J). (gr. 7-9). 1986. pap. text ed. 7.95 (*0-8074-0314-8*, 121720) UAHC.

Rooftops. Terence Brennan. 1989. pap. 3.95 (*0-380-75755-9*) Avon.

Rook. Graham Masterton. 256p. 1996. 24.00 (*0-7278-4991-3*) Severn Hse.

Rook-Shoot. large type ed. Margaret Duffy. (Dales Mystery Ser.). 392p. 1993. pap. 17.99 (*1-85389-399-4*, Medcom-Trainex) Ulverscroft.

Rookery Blues. Jon Hassler. 496p. 1996. pap. 12.00 (*0-345-40641-9*) Ballantine.

Rookery Blues. J. Massler. Date not set. pap. write for info. (*0-345-40627-3*) Ballantine.

Rookery Blues: A Novel. Jon Hassler. 496p. 1995. 23.00 (*0-345-39356-2*) Ballantine.

Rookie. Leonard Lesourd. 1996. 18.99 (*0-345-40504-8*) Ballantine.

***Rookie.** rev. ed. Jerry B. Jenkins. LC 96-50946. 384p. 1997. pap. 12.99 (*1-57673-045-X*, Multnomah Bks) Multnomah Pubs.

Rookie: The Story of a Season. Jerome Walton & Jim Langford. LC 89-49283. (Illus.). 176p. 1990. pap. 8.95 (*0-912083-44-1*) Diamond Communications.

Rookie: When Michael Jordan Came to the Minor Leagues. Jim Patton. 256p. 1995. 23.00 (*0-201-40959-3*) Addison-Wesley.

***Rookie Arrives.** Thomas Dygard. (J). Date not set. lib. bdg. write for info. (*0-688-07599-1*, Morrow Junior) Morrow.

Rookie Arrives. Thomas J. Dygard. 176p. (J). (gr. 5-9). 1989. pap. 4.99 (*0-14-034112-9*, Puffin) Puffin Bks.

Rookie Card Collector. Wayne Menicucci. (Illus.). 42p. (Orig.). 1987. pap. 4.95 (*0-942755-57-X*) Diamond M Bks.

Rookie Coaches Gymnastics Guide. American Coaching Effectiveness Program Staff. LC 92-5412. (Illus.). 80p. 1992. pap. 9.95 (*0-87322-390-X*, ACEP0408) Human Kinetics.

***Rookie Coaches Ski Racing Guide.** American Coaching Effectiveness Program Staff. LC 93-11877. (Illus.). 73p. 1994. reprint ed. pap. 25.00 (*0-608-04280-3*, 2065059) Bks Demand.

Rookie Coaches Swimming Guide. American Sport Education Program Staff & John Leonard. LC 94-27661. (Illus.). 80p. (Orig.). 1994. pap. 9.95 (*0-87322-645-3*, ACEP0410) Human Kinetics.

Rookie Coaches Tennis Guide. American Coaching Effectiveness Program Staff. LC 90-22335. (Illus.). 80p. (Orig.). 1991. pap. 8.95 (*0-88011-420-7*, ACEP0403) Human Kinetics.

Rookie Coaches Wrestling Guide. American Coaching Effectiveness Program Staff & U. S. A. Wrestling Staff. LC 91-20203. 72p. 1992. pap. 9.95 (*0-88011-421-5*, ACEP0402) Human Kinetics.

Rookie Cookie Cookbook: Everyday Recipes for Kids. Betty Debnam. (Illus.). 128p. (Orig.). (J). 1989. pap. 7.95 (*0-8362-4206-8*) Andrews & McMeel.

Rookie Dad. Pepper Adams. (Romance Ser.: No. 862). 1992. pap. 2.69 (*0-373-08862-0*, 5-08862-0) Silhouette.

Rookie Days of a Soldier. Fred J. Sasse. (Illus.). 304p. 1924. 15.00 (*0-685-25915-3*) Piper.

Rookie of the Year. John R. Tunis. 240p. (J). (gr. 3-7). 1990. pap. 4.00 (*0-15-268880-3*, Odyssey) HarBrace.

Rookie of the Year. John R. Tunis. 240p. (J). (gr. 3-7). 1990. 15.00 (*0-15-268881-1*) HarBrace.

Rookie Quarterback. Jackson V. Scholz. LC 92-43375. 224p. (J). (gr. 6 up). 1993. pap. 4.95 (*0-688-12644-8*, Morrow Junior) Morrow.

Rookie Summer. Bill Gutman. (YA). (gr. 7-12). 1988. pap. 4.25 (*0-89872-300-0*) Turman Pub.

Rookies. Doug Marx. (Baseball Heroes Ser.). (J). 1991. 12.50 (*0-86593-132-1*); lib. bdg. 16.67 (*0-685-66097-4*) Rourke Corp.

***Rookie's Guide to Money Management: How to Keep Score of Your Finances.** Princeton Review Publishing Staff. 1997. pap. 12.00 (*0-679-77882-9*) Random.

Rookies of the Year: New Kids Who Took the Field. David Craft. LC 94-27732. 80p. 1995. 11.98 (*1-56799-143-2*, MetroBooks) M Friedman Pub Grp Inc.

Rookledge's International Typefinder. Christopher Perfect & Gordon Rookledge. 284p. 1991. pap. 34.95 (*1-55921-052-4*) Moyer Bell.

Rookwood: A Romance, 3 vols. in 2. William H. Ainsworth. LC 79-8225. (Illus.). reprint ed. 84.50 (*0-404-61758-1*) AMS Pr.

***Rookwood - A Price Guide.** 2nd rev. ed. (Illus.). 261p. 1995. pap. 19.95 (*0-89538-022-6*) L-W Inc.

Rookwood II. Riley Humler. (Illus.). 212p. (Orig.). 1992. pap. 35.00 (*0-943633-04-4*) Cinc Art Gal.

***Rookwood III.** Ed. by Riley Humler. (Illus.). 212p. 1993. pap. 40.00 (*0-943633-05-2*) Cinc Art Gal.

Rookwood Pottery: The Glaze Lines. Anita J. Ellis. LC 95-16801. (Illus.). 240p. 1995. 69.95 (*0-88740-838-9*) Schiffer.

Rookwood Pottery Potpourri. Virginia R. Cummins. (Illus.). 136p. (Orig.). 1991. reprint ed. pap. 26.00 (*0-943633-03-6*) Cinc Art Gal.

***Rookwood V & Keramics 1995.** Ed. by Riley Humler. (Illus.). 174p. 1995. pap. 45.00 (*0-943633-08-7*) Cinc Art Gal.

***Rookwood VI & Keramics 1996.** Ed. by Riley Humler. (Illus.). 188p. 1996. pap. 45.00 (*0-943633-09-5*) Cinc Art Gal.

***Rookwood VII & Keramics 1997.** Ed. by Riley Humler. (Illus.). 212p. (Orig.). 1997. pap. 45.00 (*0-943633-10-9*) Cinc Art Gal.

Room. Lisa W. Peters. LC 92-39807. (Illus.). (J). 1994. pap. 15.99 (*0-8037-1431-9*); pap. 14.89 (*0-8037-1432-7*) Dial Bks Young.

Room. Hubert Selby. 1989. 19.95 (*0-7145-0888-8*) M Boyars Pubs.

Room - Raum. Linda Mussmann. Tr. by Tarcisi Schelbert & Hedwig Rappolt from ENG. LC 81-51013. 107p. (Orig.). 1981. pap. 6.00 (*0-939858-00-2*) T S L Pr.

Room Air Conditioner Energy Efficiency Slide Rule. 1985. 5.00 (*0-317-03098-1*) Consumer Energy Coun.

Room Air Distribution: Design & Evaluation. G. E. Whittle. (C). 1986. 110.00 (*0-86022-138-5*, Pub. by Build Servs Info Assn UK) St Mut.

Room Air Movement with Ceiling Mounted Diffusers. M. J. Holmes. (C). 1975. 75.00 (*0-86022-019-2*, Pub. by Build Servs Info Assn UK) St Mut.

Room at the Mark: A History of the Development of Yachts, Yacht Clubs, Yacht Racing & the Racing Rules. Robert C. MacArthur. (Illus.). 340p. 1990. 40.00 (*0-915953-03-X*) Yacht Owners.

Room at the Top. John Braine. 22.95 (*0-8488-0921-1*) Amereon Ltd.

Room at the Top. large type ed. John Braine. 288p. 1996. 24.95 (*1-85695-357-2*, Pub. by ISIS UK) Transaction Pubs.

Room at the Top. John Braine. 1993. reprint ed. lib. bdg. 18.95 (*1-56849-187-5*) Buccaneer Bks.

***Room Behaviour.** Rob Kovitz. (Illus.). 256p. 1997. pap. 19.99 (*1-895837-44-8*, Pub. by Insomniac Pr CN) Login Pubs Consort.

Room Called Remember: Uncollected Pieces. Frederick Buechner. 190p. 1992. reprint ed. pap. 12.00 (*0-06-061185-5*) Harper SF.

Room Care for Hotels & Motels. Bruce H. Axler. 1974. pap. 3.95 (*0-672-96125-3*, Bobbs) Macmillan.

Room Enough: Housing & Open Space in the Bay Area (May 1983) 1983. write for info. (*0-9605262-2-6*) Greenbelt.

Room Finishing: A Step by Step Guide. Ray McReynolds & Elaine McReynolds. (How-to Ser.). 48p. (Orig.). 1991. Canadian Edition. pap. 4.95 (*0-88908-957-4*) Self-Counsel Pr.

Room for a Stepdaddy. Jean T. Cook. LC 95-3128. (Albert Whitman Concept Bks.). (Illus.). (J). (ps-2). 1995. lib. bdg. 14.95 (*0-8075-7106-7*) A Whitman.

Room for a Stranger. Ann Turnbull. LC 95-40889. 128p. (J). (gr. 5-9). 1996. 15.99 (*1-56402-868-2*) Candlewick Pr.

Room for God? A Worship Challenge for a Church-Growth & Marketing Era. Robert Wenz. LC 93-32051. (Illus.). 208p. (Orig.). (C). 1994. pap. 11.99 (*0-8010-9729-0*) Baker Bks.

Room for Loving, Room for Learning: Finding the Space You Need in Your Family Child Care Home. Hazel Osborn. LC 94-2503. 109p. 1994. pap. 11.95 (*0-934140-98-7*, 1090) Redleaf Pr.

Room for Maneuver: Reading (the) Oppositional (in) Narrative. Ross Chambers. 312p. 1991. pap. text ed. 17.95 (*0-226-10076-6*) U Ch Pr.

Room for Maneuvre. E. J. Clay & B. B. Schaffer. LC 84-5631. 210p. 1985. 32.50 (*0-8386-3243-2*) Fairleigh Dickinson.

Room for Rent. W. A. Avery. 1994. 12.95 (*0-533-10949-3*) Vantage.

Room for the Dead. Noel Hynd. 1994. 18.95 (*0-8217-4583-2*, Zebra Kensgtn) Kensgtn Pub Corp.

Room for the Dead. Noel Hynd. 416p. 1995. mass mkt. 5.99 (*0-7860-0089-9*, Pinncle Kensgtn); mass mkt. 5.99 (*0-8217-0089-8*, Zebra Kensgtn) Kensgtn Pub Corp.

Room Fourteen: A Social Language Program, 3 bks., Set. Carolyn C. Wilson. (Illus.). (J). (gr. 1-5). 1993. student ed., teacher ed. 59.95 (*1-55999-255-7*) LinguiSystems.

Room Full of Children: How to Observe & Evaluate a Preschool Program. Carol H. Schlank & Barbara Metzger. (Illus.). 1977. 3.00 (*0-9613271-0-3*) RAEYC.

Room Full of Women. Elisabeth Nonas. 256p. 1990. pap. 9.95 (*0-941483-69-X*) Naiad Pr.

Room Groups. David P. Weikart et al. (Program Guidebook Ser.). 56p. 1994. pap. 10.95 (*0-929816-86-2*) High-Scope.

Room In-Between. Ana M. Delgado. Ed. by Yvette E. Miller. Tr. by Sylvia E. Lipp from SPA. LC 95-9455. (Discoveries Ser.). 96p. 1995. pap. 12.95 (*0-935480-76-5*) Lat Am Lit Rev Pr.

***Room in Context: Design Without Boundaries.** Katherine F. Benzel. LC 97-14909. 1997. text ed. 49.95 (*0-07-005956-X*) McGraw.

Room in the Attic. Gabrielle Charbonnet. (Princess Ser.: No. 2). 128p. (J). (gr. 3-7). 1995. pap. 3.50 (*0-590-22288-0*) Scholastic Inc.

Room in the Inn: Ways Your Congregation Can Help Homeless People. Charles F. Strobel. 112p. (Orig.). 1992. pap. 2.39 (*0-687-36588-0*) Abingdon.

***Room of Her Own: Women's Personal Spaces.** Chris Madden. 1997. 30.00 (*0-517-59939-2*, C P Pubs) Crown Pub Group.

Room of Mirrors. Nomi Joval. (Concept Books Ser.). (Illus.). 16p. (J). (gr. k-4). 1991. lib. bdg. 13.95 (*1-879567-06-7*, Valeria Bks) Wonder Well.

Room of One's Own. Virginia Woolf. Ed. by Jenifer Smith. (Literature Ser.). 160p. (C). 1996. pap. 6.95 (*0-521-48590-8*) Cambridge U Pr.

Room of One's Own. Virginia Woolf. 1989. pap. 7.00 (*0-15-678733-4*) HarBrace.

Room of Ones' Own. Virginia Woolf. 17.95 (*0-8488-1227-1*) Amereon Ltd.

Room of One's Own. Virginia Woolf. 1994. reprint ed. lib. bdg. 27.95 (*1-56849-366-5*) Buccaneer Bks.

Room of One's Own: Modern Classic Ser. Virginia Woolf. 1991. 15.95 (*0-15-178733-6*) HarBrace.

Room of One's Own: Women Writers & the Politics of Creativity. Ellen B. Rosenman. (Twayne's Masterwork Studies: No. 151). 124p. 1994. 23.95 (*0-8057-8374-1*, Twayne) Scribnrs Ref.

Room of One's Own: Women Writers & the Politics of Creativity. Ellen B. Rosenman. (Twayne's Masterwork Studies: No. 151). 124p. 1994. pap. 13.95 (*0-8057-8594-9*, Twayne) Scribnrs Ref.

Room of One's Own Revisited. Teresa Susskind. 1977. pap. 7.50 (*0-911302-30-1*) San Francisco Pr.

Room Service. Alan Boretz. 1944. pap. 5.25 (*0-8222-0962-4*) Dramatists Play.

Room Service: A Step-by-Step Guide to Accessorizing Your Home. Charlotte Moss. LC 94-16052. (Illus.). 1995. pap. 29.95 (*0-670-84799-2*, Viking Studio) Studio Bks.

Room Temperature. Nicholson Baker. LC 90-55705. 128p. 1991. pap. 10.00 (*0-679-73440-6*, Vin) Random.

Room Temperature Tunable Color Center Lasers. T. T. Basiev & S. B. Mirov. LC 92-41423. (Laser Science & Technology Ser.). 1994. pap. text ed. 85.00 (*3-7186-5349-4*) Gordon & Breach.

R

Room Themes. Joy Evans & Jo E. Moore. (Illus.). 48p. (J). (gr. k-6). 1988. teacher ed., pap. 5.95 (1-55799-121-9, EMC 177) Evan-Moor Corp.

***Room 13.** Henry Garfield. LC 96-47862. 1997. 23.95 (0-312-15203-5) Thomas Dunne Bks.

Room to Breathe. David Clewell. LC 76-42865. 1976. pap. 7.50 (0-915316-29-3) Pentagram.

Room to Breathe. deluxe limited ed. David Clewell. LC 76-42865. 1976. 15.00 (0-915316-30-7) Pentagram.

Room to Grow: The Physical Environment for Infants & Toddlers. Barbara P. Garner. (Bright Ideas Ser.). (Illus.). 21p. (C). 1993. pap. 3.00 (0-942388-15-1) So Early Chldhood Assn.

Room to Grow - How to Create Quality Early Childhood Environments. rev. ed. Linda Ard & Mabel Pitts. Ed. by Louise Parks. (Illus.). 242p. (C). Date not set. 22.00 (0-9640108-1-X) TX Assoc Educ.

***Room to Roam: Tales of a Montana Veterinarian.** R. W. Gustafson. (Illus.). 80p. (Orig.). 1996. pap. 9.95 (1-56044-497-5) Falcon Pr MT.

Room to Write: Daily Invitations to a Writer's Life. Bonni Goldberg. LC 95-36134. 240p. (Orig.). 1996. pap. 12.95 (0-87477-825-5, Tarcher Putnam) Putnam Pub Group.

Room Where Summer Ends. Peter Cooley. LC 79-51605. (Poetry Ser.). 1979. 16.95 (0-915604-27-2); pap. 11.95 (0-915604-28-0) Carnegie-Mellon.

Room with a Clue. Kate Kingsbury. 208p. mass mkt. 5.50 (0-425-14326-0) Berkley Pub.

Room with a Different View: First Through Third Graders Build Community & Create Curriculum. Jill Ostrow. (Illus.). 168p. (Orig.). (C). 1995. pap. text ed. 20.00 (1-57110-009-1) Stenhse Pubs.

Room with a View. E. M. Forster. 224p. 1988. mass mkt. 5.95 (0-553-21323-7, Bantam Classics) Bantam.

Room with a View. E. M. Forster. LC 89-40096. 248p. 1989. pap. 10.00 (0-679-72476-1, Vin) Random.

Room with a View. E. M. Forster. 1976. 22.95 (0-8488-0491-0) Amereon Ltd.

***Room with a View.** PBC International Staff. 1993. 39.95 (0-688-12632-4) Morrow.

Room with a View. large type ed. E. M. Forster. (Large Print Ser.). 345p. 1993. reprint ed. lib. bdg. 24.00 (0-939495-42-2) North Bks.

Room with a View. unabridged ed. E. M. Forster. (Thrift Editions Ser.). 160p. 1995. pap. text ed. 2.00 (0-486-28467-0) Dover.

Room with a View. E. M. Forster. 246p. 1987. reprint ed. lib. bdg. 25.95 (0-89966-607-8) Buccaneer Bks.

Room with a View & Howards End. E. M. Forster. LC 93-15340. 560p. 1993. 18.00 (0-679-60069-8) Random.

***Room with No Doors.** Kate Orman. (New Adventures Ser.). 256p. (Orig.). 1997. mass mkt. 5.95 (0-426-20500-6, Pub. by Virgin Pub UK) London Brdge.

Room with Twenty-Three Qualities: Joseph Kosuth in Dialogue with 23 Students. Joseph Kosuth. (Illus.). 144p. 1992. 35.00 (3-89322-366-5, Pub. by Edition Cantz GW) Dist Art Pubs.

Room Without Walls. Bo Carpelan. 143p. 8700. pap. 16.95 (0-948259-08-6) Dufour.

Room Without Walls: Selected Poems. Bo Carpelan. Tr. & Intro. by Anne Born. 143p. 1987. pap. 14.95 (0-318-39997-0) Dufour.

Room Without Walls: Selected Poems. Ernst Meister. Ed. by Georg M. Gugelberger. Orig. Title: Wandloser Raum. 64p. 1981. pap. 4.00 (0-88031-057-X) Invisible-Red Hill.

***Room 109: The Promise of a Portfolio Classroom.** Richard B. Kent. LC 97-15865. 1997. write for info. (0-86709-429-X) Boynton Cook Pubs.

Room 23: Playscript. Richard A. Booth. LC 88-93073. (Illus.). 41p. (Orig.). 1989. pap. 6.00 (0-88734-218-3) Players Pr.

Roomate: Thriller Edition. Francine Pascal. (Sweet Valley University Ser.: No. 6). 288p. (YA). (gr. 9 up). 1996. mass mkt. 4.50 (0-553-57010-2, Sweet Valley) BDD Bks Young Read.

***Roomate's Secret.** Paul Little. 1997. pap. 8.95 (1-56333-557-3) Masquerade.

Roomers: A One-Act Comedy. Jerome McDonough. 36p. 1983. pap. 3.25 (0-88680-165-6) I E Clark.

Roomful of Flowers. Paul Bott. (Illus.). 144p. 1992. 34.95 (0-8109-3763-8) Abrams.

Roomful of Hovings & Other Profiles. John McPhee. LC 68-23746. 250p. 1969. 19.95 (0-374-25208-4) FS&G.

Roomful of Hovings & Other Profiles. John McPhee. LC 68-23746. 256p. 1979. pap. 11.00 (0-374-51501-8) FS&G.

***Roomful of Roses.** Palmer. 1997. mass mkt. 5.50 (1-55166-418-6) Harlequin Bks.

Roomful of Roses. Edith Sommer. 1956. pap. 5.25 (0-8222-0963-2) Dramatists Play.

Roomies: Tales from the Worlds of TV News & Sports. Don Farmer & Skip Caray. LC 94-77588. (Illus.). 176p. 1994. 18.95 (1-56352-176-8) Longstreet Pr Inc.

Roominghouse Madrigals: Early Selected Poems 1946-1966. Charles Bukowski. LC 88-10426. 260p. 1996. reprint ed. 25.00 (0-87685-733-0); reprint ed. pap. 14.00 (0-87685-732-2) Black Sparrow.

Roommate. Diane Hoh. (Nightmare Hall Ser.: No. 2). 176p. (YA). (gr. 7-9). 1993. pap. 3.50 (0-590-47136-8) Scholastic Inc.

Roommate Connection. Suzanne M. Hagopian. LC 85-3460. 192p. 1986. 17.95 (0-13-782961-2, Busn) P-H.

Roommates. 1995. pap. 5.99 (0-8217-5243-X) NAL-Dutton.

Roommates. Kathryn O. Galbraith. 48p. (J). (gr. 1-4). 1991. pap. 2.99 (0-380-71357-8, Camelot) Avon.

Roommates. Kathryn O. Galbraith. LC 89-33434. (Illus.). 48p. (J). (gr. 1-4). 1990. lib. bdg. 14.00 (0-689-50487-X, McElderry) S&S Childrens.

Roommates. Mary Orr. 1989. pap. 3.25 (0-8222-0964-0) Dramatists Play.

***Roommates.** Stone. LC 97-23468. 1997. 20.00 (0-7862-1207-1) Mac Lib Ref.

Roommates. Katherine Stone. 1987. mass mkt. 4.95 (0-8217-3355-9, Zebra Kensgtn) Kensgtn Pub Corp.

Roommates. Katherine Stone. 1996. mass mkt. 6.99 (0-8217-5206-5, Zebra Kensgtn) Kensgtn Pub Corp.

***Roommates.** large type ed. Katherine Stone. LC 96-31683. (Large Print Bks.). 1996. 24.95 (1-56895-356-9, Compass) Wheeler Pub.

Roommates: My Grandfather's Story. Max Apple. 224p. 1994. 19.95 (0-446-51826-3) Warner Bks.

Roommates: My Grandfather's Story. Max Apple. 256p. 1995. mass mkt. 5.99 (0-446-60200-0) Warner Bks.

Roommates: My Grandfather's Story. large type ed. Max Apple. LC 94-39795. 1995. pap. 19.95 (0-7862-0366-8) Thorndike Pr.

Roommates Vol. 1: Human Biography. Brenda Lee. Ed. by Hired Pen. (Illus.). 200p. (Orig.). 1997. pap. 21.00 (0-9649571-3-2) Princess Lee.

Roommates Again. Kathryn O. Galbraith. LC 93-8709. (Illus.). 48p. (J). 1994. text ed. 13.00 (0-689-50597-3, McElderry) S&S Childrens.

Roommates & Rachel. Kathryn O. Galbraith. LC 90-34768. (Illus.). 48p. (J). (gr. 1-4). 1991. lib. bdg. 14.00 (0-689-50520-5, McElderry) S&S Childrens.

Roommates & Rachel. Kathryn O. Galbraith. 48p. (J). (gr. 1). 1993. reprint ed. pap. 3.50 (0-380-71762-X, Camelot Young) Avon.

Roommates from Hell: True Tales from the Tormented. Michelle Weathers & Julia Miller. LC 94-9507. 1994. pap. 7.95 (0-452-27116-9, Plume) NAL-Dutton.

Rooms, Airy Rooms. Adam Fisher. (Illus.). 36p. 1988. 12.00 (0-89304-760-0); pap. 6.00 (0-89304-761-9) Writers Ink Pr.

Rooms by Design. Gerd Hatje & Herbert Weisskamp. (Illus.). 208p. 1989. 49.50 (0-8109-1598-7) Abrams.

Rooms by the Sea. Mary A. Samyn. LC 94-29383. (Wick Poetry Chapbook Ser.: No. 4). 50p. (Orig.). 1994. pap. 4.75 (0-87338-514-4) Kent St U Pr.

Rooms in the House of Stone. Michael Dorris. LC 93-16147. (Thistle Series of Chapbooks). 74p. 1993. pap. 4.95 (0-915943-70-0) Milkweed Ed.

Rooms of Our Own: More Stories for Young Feminists. Ed. by Margaret Crane. (Illus.). 192p. (YA). (gr. 8 up). 1996. 15.95 (0-8050-1616-3, Bks Young Read) H Holt & Co.

Rooms of the Heart. Donna Hill. 1990. pap. 4.25 (1-878634-00-3) Odyssey Bks.

Rooms of the Soul: A Novel Told in Hasidic Tales. Howard Schwartz. (Illus.). 208p. 1984. pap. 7.95 (0-940646-11-0) Rossel Bks.

Rooms Overhead. Betsy Sholl. LC 86-70727. 72p. (C). 1986. 6.95 (0-914086-66-9); pap. 9.95 (0-914086-67-7) Alicejamesbooks.

Rooms to Grow: Creating Rooms & Furniture for Children. Jane Cornell. Ed. by Kimberly Kerrigone. LC 92-74444. 128p. 1993. pap. 9.95 (1-880029-16-2) Creative Homeowner.

Rooms to Grow: Natural Language Arts in the Middle School. Tom Liner & Deborah Butler. LC 93-74700. (Illus.). 456p. (C). 1995. per. 27.95 (0-89089-577-5) Carolina Acad Pr.

Rooms We Make Our Own. Toni Mirosevich. LC 96-34564. 112p. (Orig.). 1996. pap. 9.95 (1-56341-080-X); lib. bdg. 20.95 (1-56341-081-8) Firebrand Bks.

Rooms, Which Were People. Mary Cross. (OSU Press - The Journal Award in Poetry Ser.). 64p. 1990. 21.50 (0-8142-0532-1); pap. 11.95 (0-8142-0533-X) Ohio St U Pr.

***Rooms with a View.** PBC International Staff. 1995. pap. 29.95 (0-688-14677-5) Morrow.

Rooms with a View: Two Decades of Outstanding American Interior Design. Chris C. Madden & Kips B. Showhouse. LC 92-35193. 1993. 45.00 (0-86636-190-1) PBC Intl Inc.

Rooms with a View: Two Decades of Outstanding American Interior Design from the Kips Bay. Chris C. Madden. 192p. 1995. pap. 39.95 (0-86636-289-4) PBC Intl Inc.

Roomscapes: The Decorative Architecture of Renzo Mongiardino. Renzo Mongiardino. LC 93-10435. (Illus.). 208p. 1993. 60.00 (0-8478-1553-6) Rizzoli Intl.

Rooney's Guide to the Dissection of the Horse. 6th ed. Wolfgang O. Sack. (Illus.). 203p. (C). 1991. pap. 19.50 (0-9601152-3-4) Veterinary Textbks.

Roosevelt. Edmund O'Connor. Ed. by Malcolm Yapp & Margaret Killingray. (World History Program Ser.). (Illus.). 32p. (YA). (gr. 6-11). 1980. reprint ed. pap. text ed. 4.72 (0-89908-100-2) Greenhaven.

Roosevelt: From Munich to Pearl Harbor. Basil Rauch. LC 74-34446. (FDR & the Era of the New Deal Ser.). 527p. 1975. reprint ed. lib. bdg. 45.00 (0-306-70739-X) Da Capo.

***Roosevelt: Soldier of Freedom.** James M. Burns. (Leaders of Our Time Ser.). (Illus.). 640p. 1996. reprint ed. 14.98 (1-56852-091-3, Konecky & Konecky) W S Konecky Assocs.

Roosevelt: The Party Leader, 1932-1945. Sean J. Savage. 240p. 1991. text ed. 25.00 (0-8131-1755-0) U Pr of Ky.

Roosevelt: The Soldier of Freedom, 1940-1945. James M. Burns. 1973. pap. 19.95 (0-15-678875-6, Harvest Bks) HarBrace.

Roosevelt- & Then? Stanley High. LC 78-165643. (Select Bibliographies Reprint Ser.). 1977. reprint ed. 23.95 (0-8369-5952-3) Ayer.

Roosevelt & Churchill: Their Secret Wartime Correspondence. Francis Loewenheim et al. (Quality Paperbacks Ser.). (Illus.). 840p. 1990. reprint ed. pap. 17.95 (0-306-80390-9) Da Capo.

Roosevelt & De Gaulle: Allies in Conflict: A Personal Memoir. Raoul Aglion. (Illus.). 400p. 1988. text ed. 29.95 (0-02-901540-5, Free Press) Free Pr.

Roosevelt & His America. Bernard Fay. 1972. 59.95 (0-8490-0970-7) Gordon Pr.

Roosevelt & Hitler: Prelude to War. Robert E. Herzstein. 500p. 1994. pap. text ed. 16.95 (0-471-03341-3) Wiley.

Roosevelt & Romanism: Catholics & American Diplomacy, 1937-1945. George Q. Flynn. LC 75-35343. (Contributions in American History Ser.: No. 47). 272p. 1976. text ed. 55.00 (0-8371-8581-5, FRR/, Greenwood Pr) Greenwood.

Roosevelt & the Caribbean. Howard C. Hill. (History - United States Ser.). 232p. 1992. reprint ed. lib. bdg. 79.00 (0-7812-6218-6) Rprt Serv.

Roosevelt & the French. Mario Rossi. LC 93-12973. 224p. 1993. text ed. 59.95 (0-275-94613-4, C4613, Praeger Pubs) Greenwood.

Roosevelt & the Isolationists, 1932-45. Wayne S. Cole. LC 82-8624. 710p. reprint ed. pap. 180.00 (0-7837-4654-7, 2044378) Bks Demand.

Roosevelt & the Magic Box. Richard Rogers & Frank Sparacino. (Illus.). 24p. (J). 1994. lib. bdg. 11.95 (0-9642564-9-5) Bookbuddy.

***Roosevelt & the Munich Crisis: A Study of Political Decision-Making.** Barbara Farnham. LC 96-27218. (Princeton Studies in International History & Politics). 328p. 1997. text ed. 39.50 (0-691-02611-4) Princeton U Pr.

***Roosevelt & the New Deal.** Adam Woog. (World History Ser.). (Illus.). (J). (gr. 4-12). 1997. lib. bdg. 17.96 (1-56006-324-6) Lucent Bks.

Roosevelt & the Russians: The Yalta Conference. Edward R. Stettinius. Ed. by Walter Johnson. LC 75-100179. (Illus.). 367p. 1970. reprint ed. text ed. 35.00 (0-8371-2976-1, STRR, Greenwood Pr) Greenwood.

Roosevelt & the Russo-Japanese War. Tyler Dennett. 1958. 14.50 (0-8446-1150-6) Peter Smith.

Roosevelt Bears: Their Travels & Adventures. Seymour Eaton. (Illus.). 192p. (J). (gr. 1 up). 1979. reprint ed. pap. 5.95 (0-486-23819-9) Dover.

Roosevelt Community Development Study. Ed. by Mark D. Elson et al. (Anthropological Papers: No. 14). (Illus.). (Orig.). 1995. pap. 70.00 (1-886398-15-1) Desert Archaeol.

Roosevelt Community Development Study. James P. Holmlund et al. (Anthropological Papers: No. 13). (Illus.). 774p. (Orig.). 1994. pap. 60.00 (1-886398-11-9) Desert Archaeol.

Roosevelt Community Development Study: Introduction & Small Sites, No. 1. Mark D. Elson & Deborah L. Swartz. (Anthropological Papers: No. 13). (Illus.). 302p. (Orig.). 1994. pap. 60.00 (1-886398-12-7) Desert Archaeol.

Roosevelt Community Development Study: Meddler Point, Griffin Wash & Pyramid Point Sites, No. 2. James P. Holmlund et al. (Anthropological Papers: No. 13). (Illus.). 472p. (Orig.). 1994. pap. 60.00 (1-886398-13-5) Desert Archaeol.

Roosevelt Community Development Study: New Perspectives on Tonto Basin Prehistory. Ed. by Mark D. Elson et al. (Anthropological Papers: No. 15). (Illus.). (Orig.). 1995. pap. 35.00 (1-886398-19-4) Desert Archaeol.

Roosevelt Community Development Study Vol. 1: Stone & Shell Artifacts. Ed. by Mark D. Elson & Jeffery J. Clark. (Anthropological Papers: No. 14). (Illus.). (Orig.). 1995. pap. write for info. (1-886398-16-X) Desert Archaeol.

Roosevelt Community Development Study Vol. 2: Ceramic Chronology, Technology, & Economics. Ed. by James M. Heidke & Miriam T. Stark. (Anthropological Papers: No. 14). (Illus.). (Orig.). 1995. pap. 35.00 (1-886398-17-8) Desert Archaeol.

Roosevelt Community Development Study Vol. 3: Paleobotanical & Osteological Analyses. Ed. by Mark D. Elson & Jeffery J. Clark. (Anthropological Papers: No. 14). (Illus.). (Orig.). 1995. pap. write for info. (1-886398-18-6) Desert Archaeol.

Roosevelt Confronts Hitler: America's Entry into World War II. Patrick J. Hearden. LC 86-23688. 1987. pap. 14.00 (0-87580-538-8) N Ill U Pr.

Roosevelt, de Gaulle & the Posts: Franco-American War Relations Viewed Through Their Effects on the French Postal System, 1942-1944. D. M. Giangreco. LC 86-72122. (Illus.). 192p. (Orig.). 1986. pap. 9.95 (0-9616684-0-7) J V Bush.

Roosevelt Dime, No. 1: 1946-1964. 1988. 2.20 (0-307-09029-9) Western Pub.

Roosevelt Dimes: 1965 to Date. 2.20 (0-307-09034-5, Golden Pr) Western Pub.

Roosevelt Field - World's Premier Airport. Joshua Stoff & William Camp. (Illus.). 140p. 1993. pap. text ed. 22.95 (0-943691-06-0) Aviation Heritage.

Roosevelt Foreign-Policy Establishment & the "Good Neighbor" The United States & Argentina, 1941-1945. Randall B. Woods. LC 78-10435. xiv, 278p. 1979. 29.95 (0-7006-0188-0) U Pr of KS.

Roosevelt Leadership Nineteen Thirty-three to Nineteen Fourty-Five. Edgar E. Robinson. LC 75-146154. (American Scene Ser.). 1972. reprint ed. lib. bdg. 49.50 (0-306-70202-9) Da Capo.

***Roosevelt Lectures of Paul Shorey 1913-14.** Ed. by Ward W. Briggs & E. Christian Kopff. Tr. & Anno. by Edgar C. Reinke. xxxii, 416p. 1995. write for info. (3-487-09982-9) G Olms Pubs.

Roosevelt Legacy & the Kent Case. Tyler Kent. 1983. lib. bdg. 79.95 (0-87700-467-6) Revisionist Pr.

Roosevelt Lion & the Fox. James M. Burns. 1963. pap. 20.00 (0-15-678870-5) HarBrace.

Roosevelt-Litvinov Agreements: The American View. Donald G. Bishop. LC 65-15852. 1965. 45.00 (0-8156-2077-2) Syracuse U Pr.

Roosevelt Myth. 1992. lib. bdg. 79.75 (0-8490-5410-9) Gordon Pr.

Roosevelt Presence: A Biography of F. D. R. Patrick J. Maney. (Twayne's Twentieth-Century American Biography Ser.). 250p. (C). 1992. pap. 14.95 (0-8057-9825-0, Twayne) Scribnrs Ref.

Roosevelt Presence: A Biography of F. D. R. Patrick J. Maney. (Twayne's Twentieth-Century American Biography Ser.). 250p. (C). 1993. 26.95 (0-8057-7758-X, Twayne) Scribnrs Ref.

Roosevelt Presidency: Four Intimate Perspectives of FDR. Ed. by Kenneth W. Thompson. LC 82-17479. (Portraits of American Presidents Ser.: Vol. I). 100p. 1983. pap. text ed. 12.50 (0-8191-2828-7); lib. bdg. 40.50 (0-8191-2827-9) U Pr of Amer.

Roosevelt Red Record & Its Background. Elizabeth Dilling. 439p. 1986. 25.00 (0-317-52985-4, Noontide Pr) Legion Survival.

Roosevelt Red Record & Its Background. Elizabeth Dilling. 1985. lib. bdg. 79.95 (0-87700-654-7) Revisionist Pr.

Roosevelt Research: Collections for the Study of Theodore, Franklin & Eleanor. DeeGee Lester. LC 92-10072. (Bibliographies & Indexes in American History Ser.: No. 23). 224p. 1992. text ed. 59.95 (0-313-27204-2, LRC/, Greenwood Pr) Greenwood.

Roosevelt Revolution. Mario Einaudi. LC 77-24020. 372p. 1977. reprint ed. text ed. 35.00 (0-8371-9740-6, EIRR, Greenwood Pr) Greenwood.

Roosevelt Revolution, First Phase. Ernest K. Lindley. LC 74-637. (FDR & the Era of the New Deal Ser.). 328p. 1974. reprint ed. lib. bdg. 39.50 (0-306-70651-2) Da Capo.

Roosevelt Rural Sites Study Vol. 2: Prehistoric Rural Settlements in the Tonto Basin, 3 vols., Set. Richard Ciolek-Torrello et al. (Statistical Research Technical Ser.: No. 28). (Illus.). 750p. (Orig.). 1994. per. 35.00 (1-879442-42-6) Stats Res.

Roosevelt Rural Sites Study Vol. 3: Changing Land Use in the Tonto Basin, 3 vols., Set. Richard Ciolek-Torrello & John R. Welch. (Statistical Research Technical Ser.: No. 28). (Illus.). 692p. (Orig.). 1994. per. 35.00 (1-879442-43-4) Stats Res.

Roosevelt Rural Sites Study, Vol. 1: Research Design, 3 vols., Set. Richard S. Ciolek-Torrello et al. (Statistical Research Technical Ser.: No. 28). (Illus.). 75p. 1991. reprint ed. spiral bd. 7.50 (1-879442-26-4) Stats Res.

Roosevelt Versus Hitler: The Trade War Between the United States & Nazi Germany. 1991. lib. bdg. 79.95 (0-8490-4466-9) Gordon Pr.

***Roosevelt Women.** Betty Caroli. 288p. 1998. 28.00 (0-465-07133-3) Basic.

Roosevelt Years of Depression & War see U. S. History - Two

Roosevelts: An American Saga. Peter Collier & David Horowitz. (Illus.). 544p. 1994. 27.50 (0-671-65225-7) S&S Trade.

Roosevelts: An American Saga. Peter Collier & David Horowitz. 1995. pap. 15.00 (0-684-80140-X, Touchstone Bks) S&S Trade.

Roosevelt's Blues: African-American Blues & Gospel Songs on FDR. Guido Van Rijn. LC 96-24693. (American Made Music Ser.). (Illus.). 200p. 1996. 45.00 (0-87805-937-7); pap. 18.00 (0-87805-938-5) U Pr of Miss.

***Roosevelt's Children.** Edward D. Phillips. LC 96-909799. (Orig.). 1997. pap. 14.95 (0-533-12168-X) Vantage.

Roosevelt's Communist Manifesto. Emanuel M. Josephson. 1979. 250.00 (0-685-96467-1) Revisionist Pr.

Roosevelt's Communist Manifesto: Incorporating a Reprint of the Science of Government Founded on -Natural Law by Clinton Roosevelt. Emanuel M. Josephson. (Illus.). 1976. reprint ed. 75.00 (0-685-66410-4) Chedney.

Roosevelt's Farmer: Claude R. Wickard in the New Deal. Dean Albertson. LC 74-23430. (FDR & the Era of the New Deal Ser.). 1975. reprint ed. lib. bdg. 49.50 (0-306-70702-0) Da Capo.

Roosevelt's Road to Russia. George N. Crocker. LC 74-26540. (FDR & the Era of the New Deal Ser.). (Illus.). xvii, 312p. 1975. reprint ed. lib. bdg. 39.50 (0-306-70714-4) Da Capo.

***Roosevelt's War.** David Irving. Date not set. write for info. (0-688-10666-8) Morrow.

Roosevelt's Warrior: Harold L. Ickes & the New Deal. Jeanne N. Clarke. LC 95-44493. (Illus.). 423p. (C). 1996. text ed. 39.95 (0-8018-5094-0) Johns Hopkins.

Rooster. A. Fine. 1993. 10.99 (0-89906-418-3); 7.99 (0-89906-419-1) Mesorah Pubns.

Rooster. Kwok Man-Ho. LC 93-48006. (Chinese Horoscopes Library). (Illus.). 48p. 1994. pap. 8.95 (1-56458-609-X) DK Pub Inc.

Rooster & the Two Gold Coins: A Hungarian Folk Tale. Tr. & Adapted by Judit Bodnar. LC 94-14827. (J). Date not set. write for info. (0-688-11439-3); lib. bdg. write for info. (0-688-11440-7) Lothrop.

Rooster & the Weather Vane. Sharon Peters. LC 86-30838. (Illus.). 32p. (J). (gr. k-2). 1988. lib. bdg. 9.79 (0-8167-0980-7) Troll Communs.

Rooster & the Weather Vane. Sharon Peters. LC 86-30838. (Illus.). 32p. (J). (gr. k-2). 1997. pap. 2.50 (0-8167-0981-5) Troll Communs.

Rooster & Uncle's Wedding. 95th ed. HB Staff. (J). (gr. 2). 1995. lib. bdg. 8.00 (0-15-305201-5) HB Coll Pubs.

Rooster Crows. Ragnhild Scamell. LC 93-31348. (Illus.). (J). 1994. 15.00 (0-688-13290-1, Tambourine Bks); lib. bdg. 14.93 (0-688-13291-X, Tambourine Bks) Morrow.

Rooster Crows: A Book of American Rhymes & Jingles. Maud Petersham & Miska Petersham. LC 46-446. (Illus.). 64p. (J). (ps-2). 1969. lib. bdg. 14.95 (0-02-773100-6, Mac Bks Young Read) S&S Childrens.

An Asterisk (*) at the beginning of an entry indicates that the title is appearing in BIP for the first time.

R

Rooster Crows: A Book of American Rhymes & Jingles. Maud Petersham & Miska Petersham. LC 87-1138. (Illus.). 64p. (J). (ps-3). 1987. reprint ed. pap. 6.95 (*0-689-71153-0*, Aladdin Paperbacks) S&S Childrens.

Rooster Strut on the Suwannee & Two Short Stories. Grace E. Moses. LC 88-3458. 149p. 1988. 13.75 (*0-930950-15-1*); pap. 8.75 (*0-930950-16-X*) Nopoly Pr.

Rooster Who Lost His Crow. Wendy C. Lewison. LC 93-28059. (Illus.). (J). 1995. pap. 14.99 (*0-8037-1545-5*) Dial Bks Young.

Rooster Who Understood Japanese. Yoshiko Uchida. (J). 10.95 (*0-684-14672-X*) JACP Inc.

Roosters. Milcha Sanchez-Scott. 1988. pap. 5.25 (*0-8222-0965-9*) Dramatists Play.

*__Roosters at the Fort.__ Craig Kulchak. (Illus.). 130p. 1997. 29.00 (*0-614-30369-9*) Walkabout Pr.

*__Roosters at the Fort.__ limited ed. Craig Kulchak. (Illus.). 130p. 1997. lthr. 49.00 (*0-9655833-1-7*) Walkabout Pr.

*__Rooster's Egg.__ Patricia J. Williams. 1997. pap. text ed. 14.00 (*0-674-77943-6*) HUP.

Rooster's Egg: On the Persistence of Prejudice. Patricia J. Williams. LC 95-9562. 262p. (C). 1995. 22.00 (*0-674-77942-8*) HUP.

Rooster's Gift. Pam Conrad. LC 93-14490. (Laura Geringer Bk.). (Illus.). 40p. (J). (ps-3). 1996. 15.95 (*0-06-023603-5*); lib. bdg. 14.89 (*0-06-023604-3*) HarpC Child Bks.

*__Rooster's Off to See the World.__ Carle. (J). 1997. pap. 12.95 (*0-689-81772-X*) S&S Childrens.

Rooster's Off to See the World. Eric Carle. LC 86-25509. (Illus.). 28p. (J). (ps up). 1991. pap. 16.00 (*0-88708-042-1*, Picture Book Studio) S&S Childrens.

Rooster's Off to See the World. Eric Carle. LC 91-15246. (Pixies Miniature Reprint Ser.). (Illus.). 28p. (J). (gr. k up). 1992. reprint ed. pap. 4.95 (*0-88708-178-9*, Picture Book Studio) S&S Childrens.

Root: The Marines in Beirut, August 1982-February 1984. Eric Hammel. LC 93-5604. (Illus.). 496p. 1993. reprint ed. pap. 17.95 (*0-935553-05-3*) Pacifica Pr.

Root-a-Toot-Toot. Bernice Myers. (Whole-Language Big Bks.). (Illus.). 16p. (Orig.). (J). (ps-2). 1994. pap. 14.95 (*1-56784-066-3*) Newbridge Comms.

Root-a-Toot-Toot. Anne Rockwell. LC 90-46747. (Illus.). 24p. (J). (ps-1). 1991. lib. bdg. 12.95 (*0-02-777272-1*, Mac Bks Young Read) S&S Childrens.

Root Activity Patterns of Some Tree Crops. (Technical Reports: No. 170). (Illus.). 154p. 1975. pap. 35.00 (*92-0-115175-6*, IDC170, Pub. by IAEA AU) Bernan Associates.

*__Root & Branch.__ Joseph A. Pipa. 140p. Date not set. pap. write for info. (*1-871676-16-9*, Pub. by Christian Focus UK) Spring Arbor Dist.

Root & Its Modification in Primitive Indo-European. Benjamin I. Schwartz. (LD Ser.: No. 40). 1947. pap. 25.00 (*0-527-00786-2*) Periodicals Srv.

Root & Shoot Growth of Shortleaf & Loblolly Pines in Relation to Certain Environmental Conditions. John F. Reed. LC 40-13430. (Duke University, School of Forestry Bulletin Ser.: No. 4). 54p. reprint ed. pap. 25.00 (*0-7837-6052-3*, 2045865) Bks Demand.

Root & Sky: Poetry from the Plays of Christopher Fry. deluxe limited ed. Ed. & Illus. by Charles E. Wadsworth. 1975. boxed 550.00 (*0-930954-17-3*) Tidal Pr.

*__Root & Tuber Crops, Plantains & Bananas in Developing Countries: Challenges & Opportunities.__ 90p. 1988. 9.00 (*92-5-102669-6*, F3222, Pub. by FAO IT) Bernan Associates.

Root Atlas of Lympho-Graphy. 1975. lib. bdg. 129.50 (*90-207-0479-6*) Kluwer Ac.

*__Root Awakenings: Vocabulary Development Using Classical Word Roots.__ Craig Sirles. 191p. (Orig.). 1997. pap. text ed. 14.95 (*0-87563-581-4*) Stipes.

Root Beer Advertising & Collectibles. Tom Morrison. LC 92-60625. (Illus.). 128p. 1992. pap. 24.95 (*0-88740-421-9*) Schiffer.

*__Root Beer Book: A Celebration of America's Best-Loved Soft Drink.__ Laura E. Quarantiello. LC 97-3954. (Illus.). 100p. (Orig.). 1997. pap. 14.95 (*0-936653-78-7*) Tiare Pubns.

Root Beer Lady: The Dorothy Molter Story. Bob Cary. LC 92-61331. (Illus.). 192p. (Orig.). 1993. pap. 12.95 (*0-938586-68-8*) Pfeifer-Hamilton.

*__Root Bending Fatigue Strength of Acetal Spur Gears: A Design Approach to Allow for Load Sharing.__ Henri Yelle & D. J. Burns. (Technical Papers). 1981. pap. text ed. 30.00 (*1-55589-191-8*) AGMA.

Root Book: How to Plant Wildflowers. Norma Phillips. LC 83-91289. (Illus.). 118p. (Orig.). (C). 1983. spiral bd. 9.50 (*0-9622758-0-8*) Little Bridge.

Root-Bound & Other Sketches. Rose Cooke. LC 68-23719. (Americans in Fiction Ser.). (Illus.). 264p. reprint ed. pap. text ed. 6.95 (*0-89197-924-7*); reprint ed. lib. bdg. 24.00 (*0-8398-0275-7*) Irvington.

Root Canal Cover-up. 2nd ed. George E. Meinig. Ed. by Charlene Koonce & Mark Lovendale. LC 93-72133. (Illus.). 257p. 1994. pap. 19.95 (*0-945196-14-8*) Bion Pub.

Root Canal Cover-Up: Dentist to the Stars Discovers Hidden Truth ... Tells What to Do! 4th ed. George E. Meinig. Ed. by Charlene Koonce & Mark Lovendale. LC 93-72133. (Illus.). 257p. 1996. pap. 19.95 (*0-945196-19-9*) Bion Pub.

Root Cause Analysis: A Tool for Total Quality Management. Paul F. Wilson et al. LC 92-20670. 216p. 1992. 45.00 (*0-87389-163-5*, H0701) ASQC Qual Pr.

*__Root Cause Analysis (RCA)__ Tromp & Warner. 92p. (C). 1997. per. 12.95 (*0-7872-3902-X*) Kendall-Hunt.

Root Cellar. Janet Lunn. 230p. (YA). (gr. 7 up). 1985. pap. 3.99 (*0-14-031835-6*, Puffin) Puffin Bks.

Root Cellar. Janet Lunn. 240p. (J). (gr. 5-9). 1996. pap. 4.99 (*0-14-038036-1*) Puffin Bks.

Root Cellar. Janet Lunn. LC 83-3246. 256p. (YA). (gr. 5 up). 1983. lib. bdg. 17.00 (*0-684-17855-9*, C Scribner Sons Young) S&S Childrens.

Root Cellaring: Natural Cold Storage of Fruits & Vegetables. 2nd ed. Mike Bubel & Nancy Bubel. Ed. by Pam Art. LC 91-55012. (Illus.). 320p. 1991. 21.95 (*0-88266-740-8*, Garden Way Pub); pap. 14.95 (*0-88266-703-3*, Garden Way Pub) Storey Comm Inc.

Root Clustering in Parameter Space. S. Gutman. (Lecture Notes in Control & Information Sciences Ser.: Vol. 141). (Illus.). viii, 153p. 1990. 37.95 (*0-387-52361-8*) Spr-Verlag.

Root Crop Processing: Food Cycle Technology Sourcebooks. UNIFEM Staff. 76p. (Orig.). 1993. pap. 13.50 (*1-85339-138-7*, Pub. by Intermed Tech UK) Women Ink.

Root Crops see NGA Garden Library

Root-Determinatives in Semitic Speech. Solomon T. Hurwitz. LC 14-7725. (Columbia University. Contributions to Oriental History & Philology Ser.: No. 6). reprint ed. 27.50 (*0-404-50536-8*) AMS Pr.

Root Development & Function: Effects of the Physical Environment. Ed. by P. J. Gregory et al. (Society for Experimental Biology Seminar Ser.: No. 30). (Illus.). 224p. 1987. 65.00 (*0-521-32931-0*) Cambridge U Pr.

Root Genealogical Records, 1600-1870, Comprising the History of the Root & Roots Family in America. J. P. Root. 533p. 1989. reprint ed. pap. 80.00 (*0-8328-1031-2*); reprint ed. lib. bdg. 88.00 (*0-8328-1030-4*) Higginson Bk Co.

Root Growth: Proceedings. Easter School in Agricultural Science (14th 1967, University of Nottingham) Staff. Ed. by W. J. Whittington. 462p. reprint ed. pap. 131.70 (*0-317-42111-5*, 2025755) Bks Demand.

Root Is Man. Dwight Macdonald. 187p. Date not set. 7.00 (*1-57027-017-1*) Autonomedia.

*__Root, Leaf, Bud & Berry: A Collection of Plants from Central Pennsylvania.__ Harrison H. Arnold & Rae D. Chambers. (Illus.). 176p. (Orig.). 1993. pap. 10.00 (*1-887315-07-1*) Centre Cty Hist Soc.

Root Location of Fruit-Trees & Its Agrotechnical Consequences. J. Tamasi. 198p. (C). 1986. 72.00 (*963-05-4180-7*, Pub. by Akad Kiado HU) St Mut.

Root Metaphor: The Live Thought of Stephen C. Pepper. Ed. by Arthur Efron & John Herold. LC 79-92716. (Paunch Ser.: Nos. 53-54). 224p. 1980. pap. 10.00 (*0-9602478-4-X*) Paunch.

*__Root of All Evil.__ Dewi Anggraeni. 140p. 1987. pap. 14.95 (*0-9587718-0-4*, Pub. by Indra Pub AT) Intl Spec Bk.

*__Root of All Evil.__ David A. Farrow. LC 97-5845. 306p. 1997. 23.95 (*0-941711-36-6*) Wyrick & Co.

Root of All Evil. Dell Shannon. 208p. 1993. pap. 3.95 (*0-88184-978-2*) Carroll & Graf.

*__Root of All Evil: The Protestant Clergy & the Economic Mind of the Old South.__ Kenneth M. Startup. LC 97-14084. 232p. 1997. text ed. 48.00 (*0-8203-1905-8*) U of Ga Pr.

Root of All Good - Essene Reflections: The Link of Basic Health, Religion, Spirituality in Anceint, Traditional & Modern Beliefs. Ruth A. Maniscalco. LC 97-60776. 168p. (Orig.). 1997. pap. 19.95 (*0-9658581-9-7*) Essene Found. These are the Letters & Lessons which were designed for teaching the Essene beliefs & the Essene Way of Life to students of the Health & Ministerial Programs of The First Christians' Essene Church, a predenominational interfaith church; they were never meant for public consumption, but because of requests & demands by those who have read the manuscript, it is, therefore, being published. It is not casual reading but requires quiet reflection & meditation on its concentrated & power-packed contents. Ancient Essene Wisdom, from the writers of the Dead Sea Scrolls, & modern science blend to provide fundamental information to: maintain or restore health & emotional balance; improve thoughts & creativity; impart powerful spiritual guidance; & promote beneficial lifestyle changes; all designed for tremendous potential evolutionary growth. The words alone can not effect these changes, but making this information a part of one's being & living it, can. This is presented in a step-by-step manner to provide deep insight & connect us all with the collective consciousness of the ancient Essene Master & Prophets. To order: Essene Foundation, Inc., 399 Compass Road, Oceanside, CA 92054-4641. 760-433-0220.** ***Publisher Provided Annotation.

Root of All Religion. Alvin B. Kuhn. 1993. pap. 9.95 (*1-56459-376-2*) Kessinger Pub.

Root of Bitterness: Documents of the Social History of American Women. 2nd ed. Ed. by Nancy F. Cott et al. LC 95-44965. 448p. (C). 1996. text ed. 45.00 (*1-55553-255-1*); pap. text ed. 15.95 (*1-55553-256-X*) NE U Pr.

Root of Chaos. Douglas Soderberg. 1986. pap. 3.25 (*0-8222-0966-7*) Dramatists Play.

Root of Chinese Chi Kung. 3rd ed. Jwing-Ming Yang. (Illus.). 288p. 1989. pap. 19.95 (*0-940871-07-6*, B011) YMAA Pubn.

*__Root of Chinese Qigong: Secrets of Healing, Longevity & Enlightenment.__ rev. ed. Jwing-Ming Yang. (Qigong - In Depth Ser.). (Illus.). 320p. 1997. pap. 24.95 (*1-886969-50-7*, BO11R) YMAA Pubn.

*__Root of Deception.__ Asen. 1997. mass mkt. 5.99 (*0-553-57516-3*, Crimeline) Bantam.

Root of His Evil. large type ed. James McCain. LC 93-697. (Large Print Bks.). 256p. 1993. pap. 17.95 (*0-8161-5715-4*, GK Hall) Thorndike Pr.

Root of Jesse. David E. Manley. (Illus.). 288p. (Orig.). 1997. pap. 14.95 (*0-89407-090-8*) Strawberry Hill.

Root of Rejection. Joyce Meyer. 112p. 1994. pap. 7.99 (*0-89274-738-2*, HH-738) Harrison Hse.

Root of Righteousness. A. W. Tozer. 160p. (C). pap. text ed. 5.95 (*0-87509-375-2*) Omega Pubns OR.

Root of the Matter. Ed. by Hugh R. Sheppard. LC 67-26784. (Essay Index Reprint Ser.). 1977. 20.95 (*0-8369-0874-0*) Ayer.

Root of the World. Roger Bacon. 1984. reprint ed. pap. 3.95 (*0-916411-42-7*) Holmes Pub.

Root Parasitic Nematodes: Family Hoplolaimidae. E. L. Krall. LC 88-18118. (Illus.). xx, 580p. 1990. 135.50 (*90-04-08923-3*) E J Brill.

Root Planing & Scaling. Wasserman. (Illus.). 160p. 1986. text ed. 92.00 (*0-86715-177-3*, 1773) Quint Pub Co.

Root Song. Cid Corman. 96p. (Orig.). 1986. pap. 7.50 (*0-937013-15-3*) Potes Poets.

Root Vitality & the Decline of Red Spruce. P. M. Wargo et al. LC 92-39258. (Contributiones Biologiae Arborum Ser.: Vol. 4). (Illus.). 144p. 1993. 44.50 (*0-8176-2779-0*) Birkhauser.

Rootabaga Stories, Pt. 1. Carl Sandburg. LC 89-26773. (Illus.). 176p. (J). 1990. pap. 7.00 (*0-15-269065-4*, Odyssey) HarBrace.

Rootabaga Stories, Pt. 2. Carl Sandburg. (Illus.). 158p. (J). 1989. 20.00 (*0-15-269062-X*) HarBrace.

Rootabaga Stories, Pt. 2. Carl Sandburg. LC 89-26773. (Illus.). 158p. 1990. pap. 6.00 (*0-15-269063-8*, Odyssey) HarBrace.

Rooted Against the Wind: Personal Essays. Gloria Wade-Gayles. LC 96-12167. 216p. 1996. 20.00 (*0-8070-0938-5*) Beacon Pr.

*__Rooted Against the Wind: Personal Essays.__ Gloria Wade-Gayles. LC 96-12167. 208p. 1997. reprint ed. pap. 12.00 (*0-8070-0939-3*) Beacon Pr.

*__Rooted in Dust: Surviving Drought & Depression in Southwestern Kansas.__ Pamela Riney-Kehrberg. (Illus.). 264p. 1997. reprint ed. pap. 14.95 (*0-7006-0839-7*) U Pr of KS.

Rooted in Dust: Surviving Drought & Depression in Southwestern Kansas. Pamela Riney-Kehrberg. LC 94-11032. (Rural America Ser.). (Illus.). 264p. 1997. reprint ed. 29.95 (*0-7006-0644-0*) U Pr of KS.

Rooted in Remembering. James Cobb et al. 1989. pap. 7.60 (*1-55673-133-7*, 9858) CSS OH.

Rooted in Resources: Iron County, 1893-1993. Catherine Techtmann. Ed. by Michael J. Goc. (Illus.). 160p. 1993. 24.95 (*0-938627-18-X*) New Past Pr.

Rooted in Spirit: The Heart of Chinese Medicine. Claude Larre. Tr. by Elisabeth R. De la Vallee from CHI. LC 93-33271. 224p. 1992. pap. 19.95 (*0-88268-120-6*); pap. 19.95 (*0-88268-114-1*) Station Hill Pr.

Rooted in the Earth. Sandra Lindow. Ed. by Eugenia Moore & Esther M. Leiper. (Illus.). 32p. (Orig.). (YA). (gr. 9 up). 1989. pap. 3.95 (*0-9617284-8-5*) Sand & Silk.

Rooted in the Land: Essays on Community & Place. Ed. by William Vitek & Wes Jackson. LC 96-12670. 336p. 1996. 35.00 (*0-300-06541-8*) Yale U Pr.

Rooted in the Land: Essays on Community & Place. Ed. by William Vitek & Wes Jackson. 336p. 1996. pap. text ed. 17.00 (*0-300-06961-8*) Yale U Pr.

Rooted in the Sky: A Faith to Cope with Cancer. Betty G. Ulrich. 112p. (Orig.). 1989. pap. 9.00 (*0-8170-1147-1*) Judson.

*__Rooted in the Spirit: Exploring Inspirational Gardens.__ Maureen Gilmer. LC 96-53544. (Illus.). 192p. 1997. 32.00 (*0-87833-938-8*) Taylor Pub.

Rooted in Volcanic Ashes: Collection of Poems (1983-1986) rev. ed. Bahman Sholevar. LC 84-70285. (Literature-Poetry Ser.). 110p. 1987. pap. 6.95 (*0-911323-08-2*) Concourse Pr.

Rooted Sorrow: Dying in Early Modern England. Bettie A. Doebler. LC 94-2935. 1994. 43.50 (*0-8386-3543-1*) Fairleigh Dickinson.

Rooter Remembers. Joann Oppenheim. 1999. pap. 3.99 (*0-14-054091-1*) NAL-Dutton.

Rootes Brothers: Story of a Motoring Empire. John Bullock. (Illus.). 256p. 1994. 34.95 (*1-85260-454-9*, Pub. by J H Haynes & Co UK) Motorbooks Intl.

Rootes Commercial Vehicles: The Anatomy of the Commercial Motor Vehicle. Les Geary. LC 94-22817. 1995. pap. 30.00 (*0-88734-630-8*) Players Pr.

Rootie Kazootie. Lawrence Naumoff. 288p. 1996. pap. 12.00 (*0-15-600336-8*) HarBrace.

Rootin' Tootin' Bugle Boy. Patricia R. Giff. (Lincoln Lions Band Ser.: No. 4). 80p. (J). (ps-3). 1993. mass mkt. 3.25 (*0-440-40757-5*) Dell.

*__Rooting Democracy: Growing the Society We Want.__ Moira Rayner. 304p. 1997. pap. 17.95 (*1-86448-132-3*, Pub. by Allen Unwin AT) Paul & Co Pubs.

*__Roots.__ pap. 19.95 (*0-89524-997-9*) H Leonard.

Roots. Alex Haley. 1994. lib. bdg. 39.95 (*1-56849-471-8*) Buccaneer Bks.

Roots. Alex Haley. 736p. (gr. 7 up). 1980. mass mkt. 7.99 (*0-440-17464-3*) Dell.

Roots. Alex Haley. LC 72-76164. 320p. 1976. 25.00 (*0-385-03787-2*) Doubleday.

Roots. Kamau Brathwaite. 300p. (C). 1993. reprint ed. text ed. 39.50 (*0-472-09544-7*); reprint ed. pap. text ed. 16.95 (*0-472-06544-0*) U of Mich Pr.

Roots: A Vegetarian Bounty. Kathleen Mayes & Sandra Gottfried. LC 94-48213. (Illus.). 208p. (Orig.). 1995. pap. 14.95 (*0-88007-206-7*) Woodbridge Pr.

Roots: An Asian American Reader. Ed. by Amy Tachiki et al. (Illus.). (C). 1971. pap. 11.95 (*0-934052-06-9*) UCLA Asian Am Studies Ctr.

Roots: An Underground Botany. Douglas Elliott. LC 75-46234. (Illus.). 160p. 1976. pap. 14.95 (*0-85699-132-5*) Chatham Pr.

Roots: Foundation Quarter Horse Bloodlines. Andrea L. Mattson. (Illus.). 160p. 1992. pap. 16.95 (*1-879984-78-4*) Premier KS.

Roots: The Miniature Wirehaired Dachsund. deluxe ed. Peter A. Kartye. 152p. 1995. 25.00 (*0-614-04532-0*) Donald R Hoflin.

Roots & Blossoms: An Anthology of 13 African American Plays African & Caribbean Plays with a Critical Introduction & Bibliographies. Illus. by Shirley W. Reid. 620p. (Orig.). (C). 1991. pap. 21.00 (*0-911557-03-2*) Bedford Publishers.

Roots & Boots: From Crypto-Jew in New Spain to Community Leader in the American Southwest. Floyd S. Fierman. 1987. 25.00 (*0-88125-114-3*) Ktav.

Roots & Branches. Robert Duncan. LC 64-24233. 1969. reprint ed. pap. 4.95 (*0-8112-0034-5*, NDP275) New Directions.

Roots & Branches: A Legacy of Multicultural Music for Children. Patricia S. Campbell et al. LC 94-39274. (Illus.). 153p. (Orig.). 1994. pap. 24.95 incl. audio (*0-937203-52-1*); pap. 29.95 incl. audio compact disk (*0-937203-55-6*) World Music Pr.

Roots & Branches: Contemporary Essays by West Coast Writers. Ed. by Howard Junker. LC 91-9961. (Illus.). 304p. (Orig.). 1991. pap. 10.95 (*1-56279-014-5*) Mercury Hse Inc.

Roots & Branches: Germanic Epic - Romanic Legend. Robert L. Surles. (American University Studies: Germanic Languages & Literature: Ser. I, Vol. 58). 247p. (C). 1987. text ed. 38.50 (*0-8204-0493-4*) P Lang Pubng.

Roots & Branches: Grounding Religion in Human Experience. rev. ed. Kenneth R. Overberg. LC 91-61103. 160p. (C). 1991. pap. 10.95 (*1-55612-457-0*, LL1457) Sheed & Ward MO.

Roots & Branches: The Religious Heritage of Washington State. David M. Buerge & Junius Rochester. (Illus.). 280p. (Orig.). 1988. pap. 12.95 (*0-9619863-0-1*) CCGS.

Roots & Branches of Christian Beliefs. 100p. (Orig.). 1995. pap. write for info. (*0-9644642-0-9*) Providence MD.

Roots & Causes of the War, Nineteen Fourteen-Nineteen Eighteen, 2 vols. John S. Ewart. 1972. 200.00 (*0-8490-0972-3*) Gordon Pr.

Roots & Development of Cobra Art. Eleanor Flomenhaft. (Illus.). 192p. 1985. 55.00 (*0-933535-00-7*) FA Mus LI.

Roots & Fruits. Jamie S. Lash. 1980. reprint ed. pap. 2.95 (*0-915775-04-2*) Love Song Mess Assn.

Roots & Heritage of Hempstead Town. Ed. by Natalie A. Naylor. (Illus.). 256p. 1994. lib. bdg. 25.00 (*1-55787-124-8*, NY71063) Hrt of the Lakes.

Roots & Heritage of Hempstead Town. Ed. by Natalie A. Naylor. (Illus.). 256p. 1994. pap. 15.00 (*1-55787-109-4*, NY71064) Heart of the Lakes.

Roots & New Frontiers in Social Group Work. Ed. by Marcos Leiderman et al. LC 88-529. (Social Work with Groups Supplement Ser.: No. 3). 252p. 1989. text ed. 49.95 (*0-86656-727-5*) Haworth Pr.

Roots & Reaches of United Nations Actions & Decisions. Moses Moskowitz. LC 80-51741. 220p. 1980. lib. bdg. 68.50 (*90-286-0140-6*) Kluwer Ac.

Roots & Recipes: Six Generations of Heartland Cookery. Vern Berry & Connie K. Heckert. LC 93-44949. (Illus.). 224p. 1996. 15.95 (*1-56554-041-7*) Pelican.

Roots & Rhythm Guide to Rock: Over 3,000 Annotated Entries on LPs, Cassettes, & CDs. Roots & Rhythm Mail Order Staff et al. LC 93-8143. (Illus.). 400p. 1993. pap. 16.95 (*1-55652-154-5*) A cappella Bks.

Roots & Shadows. S. Deshpande. 216p. 1983. pap. 4.95 (*0-86131-287-2*, Pub. by Orient Longman Ltd I) Apt Bks.

*__Roots & Wings.__ 124p. 1995. pap. 12.95 (*0-9653016-0-5*) Bennett Publng.

Roots & Wings. Jakub Herzig & Lena Allen-Shore. LC 82-60602. 152p. 1982. 18.95 (*0-88400-087-7*); pap. 10.95 (*0-88400-085-0*) Shengold.

Roots & Wings. Elaine M. Ward. LC 83-1593. (Illus.). 17p. 1983. reprint ed. pap. 25.00 (*0-608-00237-2*, 2060739) Bks Demand.

Roots & Wings: Affirming Culture in Early Childhood Settings. Stacey L. York. LC 91-2812. (Illus.). 208p. 1991. pap. 24.95 (*0-934140-63-4*, 1706) Redleaf Pr.

Roots & Wings: Discovering & Developing Family Strengths. Karen L. Allen & Gary G. Allen. LC 92-31646. 152p. (Orig.). 1992. pap. 10.95 (*0-8298-0928-7*) Pilgrim OH.

Roots & Wings: Dreamers & Doers of the Christian Family Movement. Rose M. Lucey. 135p. (Orig.). (C). 1987. pap. 7.95 (*0-89390-113-X*) Resource Pubns.

Roots & Wings: For the Graduate. rev. ed. James W. Angell. 11.85 (*0-687-36582-1*) Abingdon.

Roots & Wings: Notes on Growing a Family. Terry Kellogg & Marvel E. Harrison. (Illus.). 56p. 1991. 12.95 (*1-880257-01-7*) BRAT Pub.

Roots & Wings: Poems to My Daughter. Roger Desmarais. LC 95-26686. 1996. pap. text ed. 7.95 (*0-88396-423-6*) Blue Mtn Pr CO.

*__Roots & Wings: The Family Record of Benjamin Hamrick.__ Leslie W. Hamrick, Jr. LC 97-72920. (Illus.). 432p. 1997. 40.00 (*0-929915-20-8*) Headline Bks.

*__Roots & Wings...a Scrapbook of Time: Cannon Falls, Minnesota.__ Connie Bickman. (Illus.). 448p. (Orig.). 1996. pap. 50.00 (*1-889644-13-7*) Yatra Publns.

An Asterisk (*) at the beginning of an entry indicates that the title is appearing in BIP for the first time.

R

Roots Branches Leaves: Hardwick Edition. Milton W. Hardwick. (Illus.). 330p. 1991. lib. bdg. 40.00 (*0-9616067-0-3*) M W Hardwick.

Roots, Deep & Strong: Great Men & Women of the Church. Mary Penrose. LC 94-39477. 224p. (Orig.). (C). 1995. pap. 12.95 (*0-8091-3538-8*) Paulist Pr.

Roots, Feathers & Blooms: 4-Block Quilts Their History & Patterns, Bk. 1. Linda G. Carlson. 1995. pap. 16.95 (*0-89145-825-5*) Collector Bks.

Roots, Flowers & Fruits. Kamaldeen A. Ibraheem. 44p. 1977. pap. 2.00 (*0-916418-08-1*) Lotus.

Roots for Revolt. Darol B. Rasmussen. LC 94-90174. 300p. 1996. 17.95 (*0-533-11117-X*) Vantage.

Roots Illustrated: How to Bring Your Family Tree to Life. Anne P. Dee. 128p. 1993. pap. 12.50 (*0-937448-00-1*) Juneberry Pr.

Roots in a Parched Ground. Horton Foote. 1962. pap. 5.25 (*0-8222-0967-5*) Dramatists Play.

Roots in a Parched Ground, Convicts, Lily Dale, & the Widow Claire. Horton Foote. LC 87-35058. 352p. 1988. pap. 12.95 (*0-8021-3081-X*, Grove) Grove-Atltic.

Roots in Adobe. Dorothy L. Pillsbury. LC 59-13409. 240p. 1983. reprint ed. pap. 8.95 (*0-89016-071-6*) Lightning Tree.

Roots in Concrete. Esther G. Mock. LC 90-84996. 1992. 15.95 (*0-8158-0466-0*) Chris Mass.

Roots in Print: A Multicultural Exhibit of Small Press Books on Ethnic History, Culture, Customs & Neighborhoods: An Exhibition, May 15-June 25, 1992, at the Small Press Center. annot. ed. Ed. by Paula Matta. 208p. (Orig.). 1992. pap. 6.00 (*0-9622769-3-6*) Small Pr Ctr.

*__Roots in the Air.__ Michael Hamburger. 104p. 1991. pap. 17.95 (*0-85646-243-8*, Pub. by Anvil Press UK) Dufour.

Roots in the Air: New & Selected Poems. Shirley Kaufman. 225p. 1996. pap. 15.00 (*1-55659-111-X*) Copper Canyon.

Roots in the Mid-West. Ed. by Nita Neblock. (Illus.). 79p. 1991. pap. 5.00 (*0-913233-22-6*) AFRA.

Roots in the Outfield. Jane Zirpoli. LC 87-33900. (J). (gr. 3-7). 1988. 13.95 (*0-395-45184-1*) HM.

Roots in the Void: Baul Songs of Bengal. Dasgupta Alokeranjan. 1983. 5.00 (*0-8364-0972-8*, Pub. by KP Bagchi IA) S Asia.

Roots in Water. Richard Nelson. 1991. pap. 5.95 (*0-88145-093-6*) Broadway Play.

Roots, Nutrient & Water Influx, & Plant Growth. Ed. by S. A. Barber & D. R. Bouldin. 136p. 1984. 16.00 (*0-89118-082-6*) Am Soc Agron.

Roots of a Thousand Embraces. Juan F. Herrerra. 64p. (Orig.). 1994. pap. 7.00 (*0-916397-28-9*) Manic D Pr.

Roots of Acehnese Rebellion, 1989-1992. Tim Kell. (Indonesia Project Ser.: No. 74). (Illus.). 93p. (Orig.). 1995. pap. 10.00 (*0-87763-040-2*, CMIP-74) Cornell Mod Indo.

Roots of Action & Idea. Edward Emanual. 128p. (C). 1995. per., pap. text ed. 14.43 (*0-7872-0950-3*) Kendall-Hunt.

Roots of African American Drama: An Anthology of Early Plays, 1858-1938. Ed. by Leo Hamalian & James V. Hatch. LC 90-12002. (African American Life Ser.). 456p. (Orig.). (C). 1992. pap. 17.95 (*0-8143-2142-9*) Wayne St U Pr.

Roots of America: A Anthology of Documents Relating to American History in the West Sussex Record Office. Ed. by Kim C. Leslie. 114p. 1976. 75.00 (*0-686-75544-8*) St Mut.

Roots of American Bureaucracy, 1830-1900. Wilson E. Nelson. 224p. 1982. 34.50 (*0-674-77945-2*) HUP.

Roots of American Civilization: A History of American Colonial Life. 2nd ed. Curtis P. Nettels. LC 63-8707. (Illus.). reprint ed. write for info. (*0-89197-386-9*); reprint ed. pap. text ed. write for info. (*0-89197-925-5*) Irvington.

Roots of American Communism. Theodore Draper. 504p. 1989. reprint ed. pap. text ed. 11.95 (*0-929587-00-6*, Elephant Paperbacks) I R Dee.

Roots of American Order. Russell Kirk. LC 90-43184. 400p. 1992. pap. 14.95 (*0-89526-755-1*) Regnery Pub.

Roots of American Psychology: Historical Influences & Implications for the Future, Vol. 291. Ed. by R. W. Rieber & Kurt Salzinger. (Annals Ser.). 394p. 1977. 22.00 (*0-89072-037-1*) NY Acad Sci.

Roots of American Racism: Essays on Early American Perceptions & Policies. Alden T. Vaughan. LC 94-9766. (Illus.). 416p. 1995. pap. 19.95 (*0-19-508687-2*) OUP.

Roots of American Society. Waters. (Arab Translation Ser.). 20.00 (*0-06-016796-3*, HarpT) HarpC.

Roots of Anti-Semitism. Ernest L. Abel. LC 73-8286. 264p. 1975. 35.00 (*0-8386-1406-X*) Fairleigh Dickinson.

Roots of Antisemitism in South Africa. Milton Shain. LC 93-33137. (Reconsiderations in Southern African History Ser.). 272p. (C). 1994. text ed. 45.00 (*0-8139-1487-6*); pap. text ed. 17.50 (*0-8139-1488-4*) U Pr of Va.

Roots of Appeasement: The British Weekly Press & Nazi Germany During the 1930s. Benny Morris. 1991. text ed. 45.00 (*0-7146-3417-4*, Pub. by F Cass Pubs UK) Intl Spec Bk.

Roots of Architectural Invention: Site, Enclosure, Materials. David Leatherbarrow. LC 92-38508. (RES Monographs on Anthropology & Aesthetics). (Illus.). 272p. (C). 1993. 70.00 (*0-521-44265-6*) Cambridge U Pr.

Roots of Artifice: On the Origin & Development of Literary Creativity. Jay Harris & Jean Harris. LC 80-23061. 320p. 1981. 42.95 (*0-89885-004-5*) Human Sci Pr.

Roots of Backpropagation: From Ordered Derivatives to Neural Networks & Political Forecasting. Paul J. Werbos. 319p. 1994. text ed. 74.95 (*0-471-59897-6*) Wiley.

Roots of Behaviourism, 6 vols., Set. Ed. by Robert H. Wozniak. 2488p. (C). 1993. text ed. 580.00 (*0-415-10165-4*, Routledge NY) Routledge.

Roots of Black Music: The Vocal, Instrumental & Dance Heritage of Africa & Black America. Ashenafi Kebede. 178p. 1995. pap. text ed. 16.95 (*0-86543-285-6*) Africa World.

*__Roots of Black Music: The Vocal, Instrumental & Dance Heritage of Africa & Black America.__ Ashenafi Kebede. 178p. 1996. 49.95 (*0-86543-284-8*) Africa World.

Roots of Blitzkrieg: Hans von Seeckt & German Military Reform. James S. Corum. LC 92-5178. (Modern War Studies). (Illus.). xviii, 276p. 1992. 29.95 (*0-7006-0541-X*); pap. 14.95 (*0-7006-0628-9*) U Pr of KS.

Roots of Capitalism. John Chamberlain. LC 76-58035. 1977. reprint ed. 10.00 (*0-913966-23-1*) Liberty Fund.

Roots of Character. Wendell Smith. (Illus.). (J). 1987. teacher ed. 37.95 (*0-914936-90-5*) BT Pub.

Roots of Chicano Politics, 1600-1940. Juan Gomez-Quinones. LC 93-31940. 553p. 1994. 42.50 (*0-8263-1471-6*); pap. 16.95 (*0-8263-1431-7*) U of NM Pr.

Roots of Christian Anti-Semitism. Malcolm Hay. 356p. 10.00 (*0-686-95112-3*) ADL.

*__Roots of Christian Mysticism: Text & Commentary.__ Olivier Clement. 1996. pap. text ed. 19.95 (*0-904287-44-0*) New City.

Roots of Christian Mysticism: Text & Commentary. 3rd ed. Olivier Clement. Tr. by Theodore Berkeley from FRE. LC 94-32957. 392p. 1995. pap. 19.95 (*1-56548-029-5*) New City.

Roots of Communal Politics: The Cawnpur Riot Commission Report. Ed. by N. G. Barrier. LC 76-6253. 1976. reprint ed. 16.00 (*0-88386-609-9*) S Asia.

Roots of Conflict: British Armed Forces & Colonial Americans, 1677-1763. Douglas E. Leach. LC 85-24492. xv, 232p. (C). 1989. reprint ed. pap. 16.95 (*0-8078-4258-3*) U of NC Pr.

Roots of Consciousness. D. Trinidad Hunt. write for info. (*1-881904-03-2*) Elan Pr HI.

*__Roots of Consciousness.__ Jeffrey Mishlove. 1997. pap. text ed. 19.95 (*1-56924-747-1*) Marlowe & Co.

Roots of Consciousness. enl. ed. David C. McClelland. (Illus.). text ed. write for info. (*0-8290-0124-7*) Irvington.

Roots of Consciousness. rev. ed. Jeffrey Mishlove. LC 92-72319. (Illus.). 416p. 1995. pap. 26.95 (*0-933031-70-X*) Coun Oak Bks.

Roots of Contemporary American Architecture. Lewis Mumford. LC 75-171490. 1972. reprint ed. pap. text ed. 11.95 (*0-486-22072-9*) Dover.

Roots of Country: The Legends Look Back. Robert K. Oermann. LC 95-42484. 1996. pap. 24.95 (*1-57036-228-9*) Turner Pub GA.

*__Roots of Country: The Story of Country Music.__ Peter O. Bekker. LC 96-29063. 1996. write for info. (*1-56799-376-1*, Friedman-Fairfax) M Friedman Pub Grp Inc.

*__Roots of Country: The Story of Country Music, 4 cass., Set.__ (Illus.). 144p. 1996. 69.95 incl. audio compact disk (*1-56799-380-X*, Friedman-Fairfax) M Friedman Pub Grp Inc.

Roots of Country Guitar: With Notes & Tablature. 120p. 1994. otabind 19.95 (*0-7935-2696-5*, 00694897) H Leonard.

Roots of Crime: A Bio-Physical Approach to Crime Prevention & Rehabilitation. Thomas O. Marsh. 208p. 1984. reprint ed. pap. text ed. 14.95 (*0-8290-1570-1*) Irvington.

Roots of Crime: Selected Papers on Psychoanalysis, Vol. 2. Edward Glover. 1960. pap. 24.95 (*0-8236-8270-6*, 025860) Intl Univs Pr.

Roots of Crisis: Interpreting Contemporary Indian Society. Satish Saberwal. LC 96-4408. 176p. 1996. 27.50 (*0-8039-9285-8*) Sage.

Roots of Crisis in Southern Africa. Ann Seidman. (Impact Audit Ser.: No. 4). 208p. (Orig.). (C). 1985. pap. 6.95 (*0-910281-03-3*) Oxfam Am.

Roots of Crisis in Southern Africa. 2nd ed. Ann Seidman. LC 85-72995. 225p. (C). 1990. 29.95 (*0-86543-025-X*); pap. 9.95 (*0-86543-026-8*) Africa World.

Roots of Delinquency: Infancy, Adolescence & Crime. Michael Wadsworth. LC 79-10065. 150p. 1979. text ed. 44.00 (*0-06-497305-0*, N6726) B&N Imports.

Roots of Democracy: American Thought & Culture, 1760-1800. Robert E. Shalhope. (American Thought & Culture Ser.). 208p. 1989. 26.95 (*0-8057-9051-9*, Twayne); pap. 15.95 (*0-8057-9056-X*, Twayne) Scribnrs Ref.

Roots of Dependency: Subsistance, Environment, & Social Change among the Choctaws, Pawnees, & Navajos. Richard White. LC 82-11146. (Illus.). xix, 433p. 1983. reprint ed. pap. text ed. 16.00 (*0-8032-9724-6*, Bison Books) U of Nebr Pr.

Roots of Disease. Stan Malstrom. (Tree of Knowledge Ser.: No. 1). 26p. pap. 3.95 (*0-913923-34-6*) Woodland UT.

Roots of Disunity: A Look at Canadian Political Culture. 2nd ed. David Bell. (Studies in Canadian Politics). 272p. 1992. 18.95 (*0-19-540858-6*) OUP.

*__Roots of Education.__ 2nd ed. Rudolf Steiner. (Foundations of Waldorf Education Ser.). 128p. 1997. pap. 12.95 (*0-88010-415-5*, 1982) Anthroposophic.

Roots of Egyptian Christianity. Ed. by Birger A. Pearson & James E. Goehring. LC 85-47736. (Studies in Antiquity & Christianity). 336p. 1986. pap. 24.00 (*0-8006-2706-7*, 1-2706, Fortress Pr) Augsburg Fortress.

Roots of Ethics: Science, Religion, & Values. Ed. by Daniel Callahan & H. Tristram Engelhardt, Jr. (Hastings Center Series in Ethics). 464p. 1981. 60.00 (*0-306-40796-5*, Plenum Pr) Plenum.

Roots of Ethnicity: The Origins of the Acholi of Uganda Before 1800. Ronald R. Atkinson. LC 94-12548. (Ethnohistory Ser.). (Illus.). 344p. (C). 1994. text ed. 34.95 (*0-8122-3248-8*) U of Pa Pr.

Roots of Evil. Kay Mitchell. (WWL Mystery Ser.). 1995. pap. 3.99 (*0-373-26162-4*, 1-26162-7) Harlequin Bks.

Roots of Evil: A Social History of Crime & Punishment. Christopher Hibbert. LC 77-18940. 524p. 1978. reprint ed. text ed. 35.00 (*0-313-20198-6*, HIRE, Greenwood Pr) Greenwood.

Roots of Evil: The Origins of Genocide & Other Group Violence. Ervin Staub. (Illus.). 352p. (C). 1989. text ed. 42.95 (*0-521-35407-2*) Cambridge U Pr.

Roots of Evil: The Origins of Genocide & Other Group Violence. Ervin Staub. (Illus.). 336p. (C). 1992. pap. text ed. 19.95 (*0-521-42214-0*) Cambridge U Pr.

Roots of Failure: United States Policy in the Third World. Melvin Gurtov & Ray Maghroori. LC 84-10718. (Contributions in Political Science Ser.: No. 108). (Illus.). ix, 224p. 1984. text ed. 55.00 (*0-313-24561-4*, GUR/, Greenwood Pr) Greenwood.

Roots of Faith: An Anthology of Early Christian Spirituality to Contemplate & Treasure. Ed. by Robert Van de Weyer. (Illus.). 128p. (Orig.). 1997. 20.00 (*0-8028-3751-4*) Eerdmans.

Roots of Futility. Norman A. Polansky et al. LC 72-5894. (Jossey-Bass Behavioral Science Ser.). 286p. reprint ed. pap. 81.60 (*0-685-16139-0*, 2027766) Bks Demand.

Roots of German Nationalism. Louis L. Snyder. LC 77-74437. (Illus.). 319p. reprint ed. pap. 91.00 (*0-8357-6691-8*, 2056871) Bks Demand.

Roots of Ghana Methodism. Francis L. Bartels. LC 64-21525. 382p. reprint ed. pap. 108.90 (*0-317-08427-5*, 2050799) Bks Demand.

Roots of Healing: A Woman's Book of Herbs. Deb Soule. 320p. 1994. pap. 12.95 (*0-8065-1578-3*, Citadel Pr) Carol Pub Group.

*__Roots of Healing: The New Medicine.__ R. Andrew Weil et al. Ed. by Michael Toms. LC 96-49306. 200p. (Orig.). 1997. pap. 12.95 (*1-56170-422-9*, 891) Hay House.

*__Roots of Healing Are in the Earth: A Journey into Medical Anthropology.__ William Evans. (Illus.). 209p. 1997. 39.95 (*0-9619258-3-3*) Clearwtr Pools Pub Co.

*__Roots of Healing Are in the Earth: A Journey into Medical Anthropology.__ William Evans. (Illus.). 209p. 1997. pap. 14.95 (*0-9619258-4-1*) Clearwtr Pools Pub Co.

Roots of Horror in the Fiction of H.P. Lovecraft. Barton L. Armand. (Illus.). 1977. 45.00 (*0-911499-04-0*, Dragon Pr) Ultramarine Pub.

Roots of Human Rights. Edward W. O'Rourke. (Synthesis Ser.). 117p. 1981. pap. 1.00 (*0-8199-0373-6*, Frncscn Herld) Franciscan Pr.

Roots of Identity: Language & Literacy in Mexico. Linda King. LC 93-33888. xiv, 193p. 1994. 45.00 (*0-8047-2121-1*) Stanford U Pr.

*__Roots of Inner Peace: Finding Fresh Courage & Strength in the Face of Fear & Worry.__ Don Hawkins. 192p. 1996. pap. 10.99 (*0-8254-2870-X*) Kregel.

Roots of Insurgency: Mexican Regions, 1750-1824. Brian R. Hamnett. (Cambridge Latin American Studies: No. 59). (Illus.). 334p. 1986. text ed. 80.00 (*0-521-32148-4*) Cambridge U Pr.

Roots of International Style Architecture. Lawrence Wodehouse. LC 91-16782. (Illus.). 304p. 1991. lib. bdg. 7.50 (*0-933951-46-9*) Locust Hill Pr.

Roots of Isolationism: Congressional Voting & Presidential Leadership in Foreign Policy. Leroy N. Rieselbach. (Orig.). (C). 1966. write for info. (*0-672-51169-X*, Bobbs) Macmillan.

Roots of Jamaican Culture. Mervyn C. Alleyne. 196p. 1989. text ed. 29.95 (*0-7453-0245-9*); pap. text ed. 15.95 (*0-7453-0369-2*) Routledge Chapman & Hall.

Roots of Justice: Crime & Punishment in Alameda County, California, 1870-1910. Lawrence M. Friedman & Robert V. Percival. LC 80-29036. (Studies in Legal History). xvi, 335p. 1981. 39.95 (*0-8078-1476-8*) U of NC Pr.

Roots of King Tutankhamun. Arthur Wallace & Audrey Ford. (Illus.). 16p. 1980. pap. 1.95 (*0-686-32534-6*) LL Co.

Roots of Language Set, 3 bks., Set. Joan Robinson. (J). (gr. 4-9). 28.99 (*1-56417-729-7*, FE0005) Fearon Teach Aids.

Roots of Lesbian & Gay Oppression: A Marxist View. Bob McCubbin. 1993. pap. 7.95 (*0-89567-116-6*) World View Forum.

Roots of Liberty: Magna Carta, Ancient Constitution, & the Anglo-American Tradition of Rule of Law. Intro. by Ellis Sandoz. 384p. 1993. text ed. 44.95 (*0-8262-0867-3*) U of Mo Pr.

Roots of Lo Mexicano: Self & Society in Mexican Thought, 1900-1934. Henry C. Schmidt. LC 77-99280. 212p. 1978. 29.95 (*0-89096-048-8*) Tex A&M Univ Pr.

Roots of Lyric: Primitive Poetry & Modern Poetics. Andrew Welsh. LC 77-72141. (Illus.). 296p. reprint ed. pap. 84.40 (*0-8357-6549-0*, 2035913) Bks Demand.

Roots of Marketing Strategy: An Original Anthology. Ed. by Larry J. Rosenberg & Henry Assael. LC 78-289. (Century of Marketing Ser.). 1979. lib. bdg. 47.95 (*0-405-11189-4*) Ayer.

Roots of Maryland Democracy, 1753-1776. David C. Skaggs. LC 72-833. (Contributions in American History Ser.: No. 30). (Illus.). 253p. 1973. text ed. 55.00 (*0-8371-6402-8*, SMD/, Greenwood Pr) Greenwood.

Roots of Mexican Labor Migration. Alexander Monto. LC 93-25058. 272p. 1994. text ed. 62.95 (*0-275-94630-4*, C4630, Praeger Pubs) Greenwood.

Roots of Modern Biochemistry: Fritz Lipmann's Squiggle & Its Consequences. Ed. by Horst Kleinkauf et al. 988p. (C). 1988. 344.65 (*3-11-011585-9*) De Gruyter.

Roots of Modern Egypt: A Study of the Regimes of Ali Bey al-Kabir & Muhammad Bey Abu al-Dhahab, 1760-1775. Daniel Crecelius. LC 81-65972. (Middle Eastern History Studies: No. 6). 300p. (C). 1982. 30.00 (*0-88297-029-1*) Bibliotheca.

*__Roots of Modern Environmentalism.__ D. M. Pepper. (Natural Environment Problems & Management Ser.). (C). 1987. pap. 19.95 (*0-415-03972-X*) Routledge.

Roots of Modern Environmentalism. David Pepper. LC 84-19867. 246p. 1986. pap. text ed. 19.95 (*0-685-30336-5*, Pub. by Croom Helm UK) Routledge Chapman & Hall.

Roots of Modern Gerontology & Geriatrics: An Original Anthology. Ed. by Gerald J. Gruman & Robert J. Kastenbaum. LC 78-22184. (Aging & Old Age Ser.). 1979. lib. bdg. 31.95 (*0-405-11801-5*) Ayer.

Roots of Modern Mormonism. Mark P. Leone. LC 78-25965. 259p. 1979. 23.95 (*0-674-77970-3*) HUP.

Roots of Modern Social Psychology (1872-1954) Robert M. Farr. (Illus.). 208p. (C). 1996. 54.95 (*0-631-15251-2*); pap. 21.95 (*0-631-19447-9*) Blackwell Pubs.

Roots of Molecular Medicine. Huemer. 1995. pap. text ed. write for info. (*0-7167-1762-X*) W H Freeman.

Roots of National Socialism 1783-1933. Rohan D. Butler. LC 78-63657. (Studies in Fascism: Ideology & Practice). 312p. reprint ed. 41.50 (*0-404-16917-1*) AMS Pr.

Roots of Negro Racial Consciousness. Stephen H. Bronz. 1964. 10.00 (*0-87212-019-8*) Libra.

Roots of NLP. Robert Dilts. LC 83-61048. 1983. 22.00 (*0-916990-12-5*) META Pubns.

Roots of North Indian Shi'ism in Iran & Iraq: Religion & State in Awadh, 1722-1859. J. R. Cole. (Comparative Studies on Muslim Societies: No. 6). 352p. (C). 1988. 47.50 (*0-520-05641-8*) U CA Pr.

Roots of Open Education in America: Reminiscences & Reflections on the Ways Americans Have Educated Themselves, in & Out of Schools. Ed. by Ruth Dropkin & Arthur Tobier. LC 76-53146. (Illus.). 1976. pap. 5.00 (*0-918374-01-4*) City Coll Wk.

Roots of Oppression: The American Indian Question. Steve Talbot. LC 81-654. 240p. (Orig.). (C). 1981. pap. 5.25 (*0-7178-0583-2*) Intl Pubs Co.

Roots of Organic Development. Ed. by Jean-Roger Desmurs & Serge Ratton. LC 96-5960. (Industrial Chemistry Library: No. 8). 578p. 1996. text ed. 324.25 (*0-444-82434-0*) Elsevier.

Roots of Our Common Faith: Faith in the Scriptures & in the Early Church. Ed. by Hans-Georg Link. (Faith & Order Paper Ser.: No. 119). (Illus.). 143p. reprint ed. pap. 40.80 (*0-7837-6002-7*, 2045812) Bks Demand.

*__Roots of Parliamentary Democracy in India: Montagu Chelmsford Reforms, 1917-1923.__ Philip Woods. (C). 1996. 36.00 (*81-7001-108-6*, Pub. by Chanakya II) S Asia.

Roots of Peace, Seeds of Hope: A Journey for Peacemakers. Maggie S. Davis. LC 93-80449. (Illus.). 60p. (J). 1993. pap. 10.00 (*0-9638813-0-2*) Heartsong Bks.

Roots of Pendle Hill. Carol R. Murphy. LC 78-1768. (Orig.). 1979. pap. 3.00 (*0-87574-223-8*) Pendle Hill.

Roots of Perception: Individual Differences in Information Processing Within & Beyond Awareness. Ed. by U. Hentschel et al. (Advances in Psychology Ser.: No. 38). 476p. 1986. 175.75 (*0-444-70075-7*, North Holland) Elsevier.

Roots of Phonics: A Historical Introduction. Miriam Balmuth. LC 92-35885. 251p. 1992. pap. 23.00 (*0-912752-32-7*) York Pr.

Roots of Political Philosophy: Ten Forgotten Socratic Dialogues. Ed. by Thomas L. Pangle. LC 87-47550. 424p. (C). 1987. 49.95 (*0-8014-1986-7*); pap. 18.95 (*0-8014-9465-6*) Cornell U Pr.

Roots of Postmodernism. William V. Dunning. LC 94-5936. 336p. 1994. pap. text ed. 35.80 (*0-13-097387-4*) P-H.

Roots of Power: One Hundred Fifty Years of British Trade Union - a Personal View. Mark Stephens. 260p. (C). 1986. 65.00 (*0-907590-06-3*) St Mut.

Roots of Prejudice. Walter F. Zeltmann. LC 93-93974. 93p. (YA). 1993. 24.90 (*0-9622705-4-7*) Yellow Hook Pr.

Roots of Prosocial Behavior in Children. Nancy Eisenberg. Ed. by Paul H. Mussen. (Cambridge Studies in Social & Emotional Development). (Illus.). 208p. (C). 1989. pap. text ed. 17.95 (*0-521-33771-2*) Cambridge U Pr.

Roots of Prosocial Behavior in Children. Nancy Eisenberg. Ed. by Paul H. Mussen. (Cambridge Studies in Social & Emotional Development). (Illus.). 195p. (C). 1989. text ed. 44.95 (*0-521-33190-0*) Cambridge U Pr.

Roots of Psychotherapy. Carl A. Whitaker & Thomas P. Malone. LC 80-24437. (Brunner Mazel Classics in Psychoanalysis & Psychotherapy: No. 9). 272p. 1981. reprint ed. text ed. 39.95 (*0-87630-265-7*) Brunner-Mazel.

Roots of Realism. Ed. by Benjamin Frankel. (Cass Series on Security). (Orig.). (C). 1996. text ed. 45.00 (*0-7146-4669-5*, Pub. by F Cass Pubs UK); pap. text ed. 20.00 (*0-7146-4203-7*, Pub. by F Cass Pubs UK) Intl Spec Bk.

Roots of Rebellion. Clarence A. Weber. LC 79-111802. 142p. 1971. 7.65 (*0-87527-085-9*) Green.

*__Roots of Rebellion.__ Anne S. Williams. Date not set. write for info. (*0-688-03505-1*) Morrow.

Roots of Rebellion: Land & Hunger in Central America. Tom Barry. LC 87-4519. 220p. (Orig.). 1987. 25.00 (*0-89608-288-1*); pap. 12.00 (*0-89608-287-3*) South End Pr.

Roots of Rebellion: Land & Hunger in Central America. Tom Barry. LC 87-4519. (Illus.). 234p. 1987. reprint ed. pap. 66.70 (*0-7837-9239-5*, 2049990) Bks Demand.

Roots of Rebellion: Workers' Politics & Organizations in St. Petersburg & Moscow, 1900-1914. Victoria E. Bonnell. LC 83-1084. 528p. (C). 1983. pap. 16.00 (*0-520-05114-9*) U CA Pr.

An Asterisk (*) at the beginning of an entry indicates that the title is appearing in BIP for the first time.

*__Roots of Red Clydeside 1910-1914.__ W. Kenefick & A. McIvor. 180p. 1996. pap. 30.00 (*0-85976-434-6*, Pub. by J Donald UK) St Mut.

Roots of Reference. Willard V. Quine. LC 73-86488. (Paul Carus Lectures: Vol. 14). 163p. 1973. pap. 17.95 (*0-8126-9101-6*) Open Court.

Roots of Relational Ethics: Responsibility in Origin & Maturity in H. Richard Niebuhr. R. Melvin Keiser. LC 95-26370. (AAR Reflection & Theory in the Study of Religion Ser.: No. 9). 270p. (C). 1996. 39.95 (*0-7885-0211-5*, 011009); pap. 24.95 (*0-7885-0212-3*, 011009) Scholars Pr GA.

Roots of Renewal in Myth & Madness: The Meaning of Psychotic Episodes. John W. Perry. LC 76-19500. (Jossey-Bass Behavioral Science Ser.). 268p. reprint ed. pap. 76.40 (*0-317-42373-8*, 2052164) Bks Demand.

Roots of Resistance: The Nonviolent Ethic of Martin Luther King Jr. William D. Watley. 160p. 1985. 17.00 (*0-8170-1092-0*) Judson.

Roots of Revolution: An Interpretive History of Modern Iran. Nikki R. Keddie & Yann Richard. LC 81-40438. (Illus.). 316p. (C). 1981. pap. 17.00 (*0-300-02611-0*, YF-24) Yale U Pr.

Roots of Revolution: Radical Thought in Cuba. Sheldon B. Liss. LC 86-7109. xxvi, 269p. 1987. text ed. 30.00 (*0-8032-2873-2*); pap. text ed. 15.00 (*0-8032-7920-5*, Bison Books) U of Nebr Pr.

Roots of Robert Johnson. Stefan Grossman & Woody Mann. 10.95 (*1-56222-921-4*, 95074); audio 10.98 (*1-56222-908-7*, 95074C) Mel Bay.

*__Roots of Robert Johnson.__ Stefan Grossman & Woody Mann. 19.95 incl. audio compact disk (*0-7866-2776-X*, 95074BCD) Mel Bay.

Roots of Rock, Vol. 2: The Fifties. Stuart A. Kallen. Ed. by Bob Italia. LC 89-84914. (History of Rock n' Roll Ser.). (Illus.). 48p. (J). (gr. 4). 1989. lib. bdg. 12.94 (*0-939179-73-3*) Abdo & Dghtrs.

Roots of Rural Capitalism: Western Massachusetts, 1780-1860. Christopher Clark. LC 89-46177. (Illus.). 352p. 1990. 42.50 (*0-8014-2422-4*) Cornell U Pr.

Roots of Rural Capitalism: Western Massachusetts, 1780-1860. Christopher Clark. LC 89-46177. (Illus.). 352p. 1992. pap. 16.95 (*0-8014-9693-4*) Cornell U Pr.

Roots of Russia: Paving the Way. Ed. by N. Maslova & T. Pleshakova. 157p. (C). 1995. lib. bdg. 59.00 (*1-56072-210-X*) Nova Sci Pubs.

Roots of Russian Communism: A Social & Historical Study of Russian Social Democracy 1898-1907. David Lane. LC 74-15196. 1975. pap. text ed. 14.95 (*0-271-01178-5*) Pa St U Pr.

Roots of Russian Through Chekhov: A Study in Word-Formation. Margaret I. Gibson. LC 81-43705. 236p. (Orig.). (C). 1982. pap. text ed. 25.00 (*0-8191-2682-9*) U Pr of Amer.

Roots of Salsa: A History of Cuban Music. Cristobal Diaz Ayala. LC 95-24021. (Contributions to the Study of Music & Dance Ser.: Vol. 37). 296p. 1996. text ed. 59.95 (*0-313-29804-1*, Greenwood Pr) Greenwood.

Roots of Separatism in Palestine: British Economic Policy, 1920-1929. Ed. by Barbara J. Smith. (Contemporary Issues in the Middle East Ser.). 400p. 1992. text ed. 39.95 (*0-8156-2578-2*) Syracuse U Pr.

Roots of Social Knowledge. Charles H. Cooley. (Reprint Series in Social Sciences). (C). 1993. reprint ed. pap. text ed. 1.90 (*0-8290-2690-8*, S-50) Irvington.

Roots of Solidarity: A Political Sociology of Poland's Working Class Democratization. Roman Laba. (Illus.). 267p. 1991. text ed. 37.50 (*0-691-07862-9*) Princeton U Pr.

Roots of Southern Distinctiveness: Tobacco & Society in Danville, Virginia, 1780-1865. Frederick F. Siegel. LC 86-19356. xvi, 206p. 1987. text ed. 32.50 (*0-8078-1727-9*) U of NC Pr.

Roots of Southern Populism: Yeoman Farmers & the Transformation of the Georgia Upcountry, 1850-1890. Steven Hahn. 320p. 1985. pap. 19.95 (*0-19-503508-9*) OUP.

Roots of Southern Writing: Essays on the Literature of the American South. Clarence H. Holman. LC 74-184774. 250p. reprint ed. pap. 71.30 (*0-318-34881-0*, 2031175) Bks Demand.

Roots of St. Francis. Raphael Brown. 216p. 1982. 9.50 (*0-8199-0824-X*, Frncscn Herld) Franciscan Pr.

Roots of State Intervention in the Brazilian Economy. Gustavo M. Gomes. LC 85-31174. 394p. 1986. text ed. 65.00 (*0-275-92144-1*, C2144, Praeger Pubs) Greenwood.

Roots of Strategy, Bk. 2. LC 86-23195. (Illus.). 560p. (Orig.). 1987. pap. 14.95 (*0-8117-2260-0*) Stackpole.

Roots of Strategy: A Collection of Classics. Raphael T. Phillips. LC 82-11890. 448p. 1982. reprint ed. text ed. 48.50 (*0-313-23657-7*, PHRS, Greenwood Pr) Greenwood.

Roots of Strategy: The Five Greatest Military Classics of All Time-Complete in One Volume. Ed. by Thomas R. Phillips. LC 84-26826. 448p. 1985. pap. 14.95 (*0-8117-2194-9*) Stackpole.

Roots of Strategy, Bk. 3: Von Leeb's "Defense," von Freytag-Loringhoven's "The Power of Personality in War," Erfurth's "Surprise" Ritter Von Leeb, Hugo Von Freytag-Loringhoven, & Waldemar Erfurth. Ritter Von Leeb et al. Tr. by Daniel Vilfroy et al. from GER. LC 84-26685. (Illus.). 554p. 1991. reprint ed. pap. 16.95 (*0-8117-3060-3*) Stackpole.

Roots of Street Style. Zenshu Takamura. (Illus.). 208p. 1997. pap. text ed. 39.95 (*4-7661-0895-7*, Pub. by Graphic Sha JA) Bks Nippan.

Roots of Success: Why Children Follow in Their Parents' Career Footsteps. David N. Laband & Bernard F. Lentz. LC 84-26309. 192p. 1985. text ed. 45.00 (*0-275-90132-7*, C0132, Praeger Pubs) Greenwood.

Roots of Survival: Native American Storytelling & the Sacred. Joseph Bruchac. 272p. 1996. 24.95 (*1-55591-145-5*) Fulcrum Pub.

*__Roots of Swing & Big Bands.__ Warner Brothers Staff. 1996. pap. text ed. 16.95 (*1-57623-675-7*, MF9647) Warner Brothers.

Roots of Tadicalism: Jews, Christians, & the Left. Stanley Rothman & S. Lichter. 505p. 1996. pap. text ed. 26.95 (*1-56000-889-X*) Transaction Pubs.

Roots of the Blues. Samuel B. Charters. 15.00 (*0-7145-2705-X*) M Boyars Pubs.

Roots of the Blues: An African Search. Samuel B. Charters. (Illus.). 151p. 1991. reprint ed. pap. 10.95 (*0-306-80445-X*) Da Capo.

Roots of the Catholic Tradition. Thomas P. Rausch. (Theology & Life Ser.: Vol. 16). 247p. 1986. pap. 14.95 (*0-8146-5538-6*) Liturgical Pr.

Roots of the Conflicts in Indochina: With Chronology of Laos History, & Major Successive Political Events in Laos from 1316 Through 1975. William K. Bouarouy. (Illus.). 201p. 1992. text ed. 35.00 (*0-9646220-0-9*) Asian-Am Res Ctr.

Roots of the Earthman. Dan Smith. (Illus.). 116p. 1981. pap. 7.00 (*0-932642-63-2*) Unarius Acad Sci.

Roots of the European Tradition: Proceedings of the Groningen 1987 Achaemenid History Workshop. Ed. by Heleen Sancisi-Weerdenburg & Jan W. Drijvers. (Achaemenid History Ser.: Vol. 5). xii, 170p. 1990. text ed. 73.50 (*90-6258-405-5*, Pub. by Netherlands Inst NE) Eisenbrauns.

*__Roots of the Human Condition.__ Frithjof Schuon. 136p. (Orig.). 1996. pap. 12.00 (*0-614-21239-1*, 1391); pap. 12.00 (*0-614-21680-X*, 1391) Kazi Pubns.

Roots of the Human Condition. Frithjof Schuon. LC 90-23459. (Library of Traditional Wisdom). 109p. (Orig.). (C). 1991. pap. 12.00 (*0-941532-11-9*) Wrld Wisdom Bks.

Roots of the Modern Christian Tradition. Ed. by E. R. Elder. 1984. 10.95 (*0-87907-855-3*) Cistercian Pubns.

Roots of the Paradoxism. Florin Vasiliu. Ed. by R. Muller. Tr. by Rodica Stefanescu from ROM. 100p. (Orig.). 1993. pap. text ed. 11.95 (*1-879585-36-7*) Erhus Univ Pr.

Roots of the Public Sector Fiscal Crisis. Max B. Sawicky. 1992. 10.00 (*0-944826-43-1*) Economic Policy Inst.

Roots of the Radical Theology. John C. Cooper. 174p. (C). 1988. reprint ed. pap. text ed. 22.50 (*0-8191-7115-8*) U Pr of Amer.

Roots of the Republic: American Founding Documents Interpreted. Ed. by Stephen L. Schechter. 472p. 1990. 35.95 (*0-945612-20-6*); pap. text ed. 19.95 (*0-945612-19-2*) Madison Hse.

*__Roots of the Republic: The Grolier Library of the Founders of America, 6 vols.__ (Illus.). 960p. (YA). (gr. 7-12). 1996. lib. bdg. 159.00 (*0-7172-7608-2*) Grolier Educ.

Roots of the Russian Language. George Z. Patrick. 248p. 1994. pap. 16.95 (*0-8442-4267-5*, Natl Textbk) NTC Pub Grp.

Roots of the Self: Unraveling the Mystery of Who We Are. Robert E. Ornstein & Ted Dewan. LC 92-56116. 240p. (Orig.). 1994. pap. 12.00 (*0-06-250789-3*) ISHK.

Roots of the Transplanted, 2 vols. Ed. by Dirk Hoerder et al. 876p. 1994. 135.00 (*0-88033-288-3*) East Eur Monographs.

Roots of the Western Tradition: A Short History of the Ancient World. 5th ed. Warren C. Hollister. 1991. pap. text ed. write for info. (*0-07-029607-3*) McGraw.

Roots of the Western Tradition: A Short History of the Ancient World. 6th ed. C. Warren Hollister. LC 95-5469. 1996. pap. text ed. 18.75 (*0-07-029659-6*) McGraw.

Roots of Thinking. Maxine Sheets-Johnstone. 408p. 1990. pap. 22.95 (*0-87722-769-1*) Temple U Pr.

Roots of Ticasuk: An Eskimo Woman's Family Story. Emily I. Brown. LC 81-3458. (Illus.). 120p. (Orig.). 1981. pap. 9.95 (*0-88240-117-3*) Alaska Northwest.

Roots of Time: A Portrait of African Life & Culture. Margo Jefferson & Elliott P. Skinner. LC 90-80149. (J). 1990. pap. 7.95 (*0-86543-169-8*) Africa World.

*__Roots of Time: A Portrait of African Life & Culture.__ Margo Jefferson & Elliott P. Skinner. (Young Readers Ser.). (Illus.). (J). 1996. 19.95 (*0-86543-168-X*) Africa World.

Roots of Tragedy: The United States & the Struggle for Asia, 1945-1953. Lisle A. Rose. LC 75-35354. (Contributions in American History Ser.: No. 48). 352p. 1976. text ed. 55.00 (*0-8371-8592-0*, RRT/, Greenwood Pr) Greenwood.

*__Roots of United States Foreign Policy Toward Apartheid South Africa, 1969-1985.__ Kema Irogbe. LC 97-17415. 336p. 1997. text ed. 99.95 (*0-7734-2294-3*, Mellen Univ Pr) E Mellen.

Roots of Violence. Vincent P. Miceli. LC 88-70610. 1989. 19.95 (*0-8158-0449-0*) Chris Mass.

*__Roots of Violence.__ Cornell West. 256p. 1997. 23.00 (*0-465-07082-5*) Basic.

*__Roots of Violence.__ Cornell West. 256p. 1997. pap. 12.00 (*0-465-07083-3*) Basic.

Roots of Violence in Black Philadelphia, 1860-1900. Roger Lane. (Illus.). 224p. 1986. 35.00 (*0-674-77990-8*) HUP.

Roots of Violence in Black Philadelphia, 1860-1900. Roger Lane. 224p. 1989. reprint ed. pap. 14.95 (*0-674-77978-9*) HUP.

Roots of Walden & the Tree of Life. Gordon V. Boudreau. LC 90-12297. 256p. (C). 1990. 29.95 (*0-8265-1235-6*) Vanderbilt U Pr.

Roots of War. Melvin Konner. Date not set. pap. 22.00 (*0-670-82937-4*) Viking Penguin.

Roots of Western Civilization, 2 vols. Wesley D. Camp. Incl. Vol. 1. From Ancient Times to 1715. 1983. pap. text ed. (*0-07-554669-8*); Vol. 2. From the Enlightenment to the 1980's. 1983. pap. text ed. (*0-07-554670-1*); (Illus.). (C). 1983. pap. text ed. write for info. (*0-318-57752-6*) McGraw.

Roots of Western Civilization: A Multicultural Resource, 12 vols., Set. (Illus.). 144 ea.p. 1994. 289.00 (*0-7172-7324-5*) Grolier Educ.

Roots of Whitman's Grass. T. R. Rajasekharaiah. LC 76-85762. 522p. 1975. 50.00 (*0-8386-7493-3*) Fairleigh Dickinson.

Roots of William Powell Lear. Institute of Family Research Staff. (Illus.). 87p. reprint ed. pap. 25.00 (*0-317-09100-X*, 2051627) Bks Demand.

Roots of Wisdom. Helen B. Mitchell. (Philosophy Ser.). 1996. student ed., pap. 17.95 (*0-534-23091-1*) Wadsworth Pub.

Roots of Wisdom: A Multicultural Reader. 4th ed. Helen B. Mitchell. LC 96-8978. (Philosophy Ser.). 368p. (C). 1997. pap. 21.95 (*0-534-23089-X*) Wadsworth Pub.

Roots of Wisdom: Speaking the Language of Philosophy. Helen B. Mitchell. LC 95-9385. 524p. (C). 1996. text ed. 46.95 (*0-534-23088-1*) Wadsworth Pub.

Roots of Wisdom: The Oldest Proverbs of Israel & Other Peoples, GER. Claus Westermann. Tr. by J. Daryl Charles. Orig. Title: Wurzeln der Weisheit. 208p. (Orig.). 1994. pap. 20.00 (*0-664-25559-0*) Westminster John Knox.

*__Roots on the Prairie: Tracing Your Illinois Ancestors.__ Patricia A. Hamilton. LC 96-29903. 1996. pap. 5.00 (*0-943788-10-2*) McLean County.

Roots, Radicals & Quadratic Equations. rev. ed. Mervin L. Keedy & Marvin L. Bittinger. (Algebra, a Modern Introduction Ser.). (gr. 7-9). 1981. pap. text ed. write for info. (*0-201-03988-5*) Addison-Wesley.

Roots, Renewal & the Brethren. 2nd ed. Nathan D. Smith. LC 86-7136. 152p. (Orig.). 1986. pap. 12.95 (*0-932727-08-5*); text ed. 17.95 (*0-932727-09-3*) Hope Pub Hse.

Roots-Routes. Richard Burns. (Illus.). 44p. (Orig.). 1982. pap. 8.00 (*0-914946-32-3*) Cleveland St Univ Poetry Ctr.

Roots Schmoots: Journeys among Jews. Howard Jacobson. 502p. 1994. 23.95 (*0-87951-521-X*) Overlook Pr.

Roots Schmoots: Journeys Among Jews. Howard Jacobson. 502p. 1995. pap. 14.95 (*0-87951-605-4*) Overlook Pr.

Roots to Power: A Manual for Grassroots Organizing. Lee Staples. LC 84-3405. 234p. 1984. pap. text ed. 22.95 (*0-275-91800-9*, B1800, Praeger Pubs) Greenwood.

*__Roots, Tubers, Plantains & Bananas in Human Nutrition.__ (Food & Nutrition Ser.: No. 24). 198p. 1990. 30.00 (*92-5-102862-1*, F8621, Pub. by FAO IT) Bernan Associates.

Roots, Verb Forms & Primary Derivatives of the Sanskrit Language. William D. Whitney. (American Oriental Ser.: Vol. 30). xiii, 250p. 1945. 16.00 (*0-940490-30-7*) Am Orient Soc.

Roots, Verb Forms & Primary Derivatives of the Sanskrit Language. William D. Whitney. (C). 1991. reprint ed. 12.50 (*81-208-0484-8*, Pub. by Motilal Banarsidass II) S Asia.

Rootstocks for Florida Citrus: Rootstock Selection, the First Step to Success. 2nd ed. (Illus.). 100p. 1993. pap. text ed. 8.00 (*0-916287-07-6*, SP42) Univ Fla Food.

Rootstocks for Fruit Crops. Ed. by Roy C. Rom & Robert F. Carlson. LC 86-15730. 494p. 1987. text ed. 110.00 (*0-471-80551-3*) Wiley.

Rootwork & Voodoo in Mental Health. Faheem C. Ashanti. LC 87-71941. 280p. 1987. lib. bdg. 43.50 (*0-911325-04-2*) Tone Bks Inc.

Rootworker. Glenda Dumas. 256p. (Orig.). 1992. mass mkt. 3.50 (*0-87067-387-4*) Holloway.

Rootworker. Glenda Dumas. (Orig.). 1983. pap. 1.95 (*0-87067-711-X*, BH711) Viking Penguin.

Ropa Con Ajuste Perfecto: Singer Biblioteca De Costura. Singer. (SPA.). 17.95 (*0-86573-229-9*) Cowles Creative.

Ropa del Bebe. Neil Ricklen. (SPA.). (J). 1995. bds. 4.95 (*0-689-80436-9*, Atheneum Bks Young) S&S Childrens.

Ropa Fina Tecnicas De Alta Costura: Singer Biblioteca De Costura. Singer. (SPA.). 17.95 (*0-86573-223-X*) Cowles Creative.

Ropa Para Deportistas: Singer Biblioteca De Costura. Singer. (SPA.). 1994. 17.95 (*0-86573-227-2*) Cowles Creative.

Ropa para Ninos - Sewing for Children. Singer. (Singer Biblioteca de Costura Ser.). 1992. 17.95 (*0-86573-272-8*) Cowles Creative.

Rope see Anthology of Roman Drama

Rope see Little Carthaginian

Rope above, the Bed Below. Jason Fury. (Orig.). 1994. mass mkt. 4.95 (*1-56333-269-8*, Badboy) Masquerade.

Rope & Faggot: Biography of Judge Lynch. Walter F. White. LC 69-18545. (American Negro: His History & Literature. Series 2). 1978. reprint ed. 30.95 (*0-405-01907-6*) Ayer.

Rope & Other Plays. Plautus. Tr. by E. F. Watling. Incl. Ghost. 1964. pap. (*0-318-55085-7*); Three-Dollar Day. 1964. pap. (*0-318-55086-5*); Amphitryon. 1964. pap. (*0-318-55087-3*); (Classics Ser.). 288p. 1964. pap. 9.95 (*0-14-044136-0*, Penguin Classics) Viking Penguin.

*__Rope & Rhymes.__ Klutz Editors. (J). (gr. 1 up). 1997. 9.95 (*1-57054-140-X*) Klutz Pr.

Rope-Dancer: Short Stories. M. J. Fitzgerald. LC 86-26159. 158p. 1987. 15.95 (*0-394-55921-5*) Random.

Rope Dances. David Porush. LC 78-68135. 127p. 1979. 15.95 (*0-914590-50-2*); pap. 6.95 (*0-914590-51-0*) Fiction Coll.

Rope Drawings by Patrick Ireland: An Exhibition. Edit Deak. (Illus.). 32p. 1977. pap. 3.00 (*0-934418-04-7*) Mus Contemp Art.

Rope for Dr. Webster. limited ed. James G. Cozzens. 1976. boxed 55.00 (*0-89723-010-8*) Bruccoli.

Rope of Sand: The AFL-CIO Committee on Political Education, 1955-1967. Alan Draper. LC 88-11773. 176p. 1988. text ed. 45.00 (*0-275-93045-9*, C3045, Praeger Pubs) Greenwood.

Rope Rescue Manual. Frank. 1992. 24.95 (*0-9618337-1-8*) California Mountain Co Ltd.

*__Rope Rescue Manual.__ 2nd ed. James A. Frank & Jerrold B. Smith. 178p. 1992. 23.00 (*0-9618337-0-X*) California Mountain Co Ltd.

Rope Splicing. Percy W. Blandford. (C). 1987. 45.00 (*0-85174-268-8*, Pub. by Brwn Son Ferg) St Mut.

Rope, the Chair, & the Needle: Capital Punishment in Texas, 1923-1990. James W. Marquart et al. LC 93-15717. (Illus.). 328p. (C). 1994. 27.95 (*0-292-75158-3*) U of Tex Pr.

*__Rope Trick.__ (FunFax Horror Ser.). (Illus.). 144p. (J). (gr. 3-9). 1996. pap. 2.95 (*0-7894-1156-3*) DK Pub Inc.

Ropeless Jumping: The Conversion of a Jogger. Bruce McBogg. (Illus.). 71p. 1981. 3.45 (*0-686-32863-9*) B McBogg.

Ropemakers of Plymouth: A History of the Plymouth Cordage Company, 1824-1949. Samuel E. Morison. LC 75-41772. (Companies & Men: Business Enterprises in America Ser.). (Illus.). 1976. reprint ed. 23.95 (*0-405-08086-7*) Ayer.

Roper's North Carolina Business Resource Guide. Jess R. McLamb. 120p. (Orig.). 1997. pap. text ed. 16.95 (*0-9645096-1-X*) Roper Grp.

Ropers of Sterling & Rutland. E. Roper. (Illus.). 473p. 1989. reprint ed. pap. 71.00 (*0-8328-1033-9*); reprint ed. lib. bdg. 79.00 (*0-8328-1032-0*) Higginson Bk Co.

Ropes Course Manual. WOA, Inc. Staff. 128p. 1994. pap. text ed., spiral bd. 28.50 (*0-7872-0019-0*) Kendall-Hunt.

Ropes to Skip & the Ropes to Know: Studies in Organizational Behavior. 4th ed. R. Richard Ritti. 312p. 1993. Net. pap. text ed. 19.50 (*0-471-58593-9*) Wiley.

*__Ropes to Skip & the Ropes to Know: Studies in Organizational Behavior.__ 5th ed. R. Richard Ritti. LC 97-41. (Management Ser.). 1997. pap. write for info. (*0-471-13304-3*) Wiley.

*__Ropework: Knots, Ropes, Cordage & Slings for Climbers.__ Duane Raleigh. LC 97-22467. 1998. write for info. (*0-8117-2871-4*) Stackpole.

Ropics: The Next Jump Forward in Fitness. Ken M. Solis. LC 90-24893. (Illus.). 152p. (Orig.). 1992. pap. 12.95 (*0-88011-444-4*, PSOL0444) Human Kinetics.

Roping: Trick & Fancy Rope Spinning. Chester Byers. 89p. 1986. pap. 7.95 (*0-918222-95-8*) Applewood.

Roping Can be Hazardous to Your Health: More Stories by Curt Brummett. Curt Brummett. 96p. 1991. pap. 6.95 (*0-87483-146-6*) August Hse.

Roping Colors. John Speirs. (S-t-r-e-t-c-h a String Bks.). (J). (ps-3). 1996. 6.95 (*0-307-17681-9*, Golden Pr) Western Pub.

Roping Lions in the Grand Canyon. Zane Grey. 1976. 20.95 (*0-8488-1027-9*) Amereon Ltd.

Roping Lions in the Grand Canyon. Zane Grey. 1996. mass mkt. 4.99 (*0-8125-6353-0*) Tor Bks.

Roping the Wind: A Personal History of Cowboys & the Land. Lyman Hafen. 1995. pap. 14.95 (*0-87421-188-3*) Utah St U Pr.

Roquelaure Reader: A Companion to Anne Rice's Erotica. Katherine Ramsland. LC 95-34847. 240p. 1996. pap. 12.95 (*0-452-27510-5*, Plume) NAL-Dutton.

Ror. Mark Dunster. (Rin Ser.: Pt. 50). 50p. (Orig.). 1981. pap. 4.00 (*0-89642-080-9*) Linden Pubs.

*__Rorgo Fretellus de Nazareth et Sa Description de la Terre Sainte.__ P. C. Boeren. 108p. pap. 56.25 (*0-7204-8492-8*) Elsevier.

Rork Vol. 3: The Graveyard of Cathedrals & Starlight. Andreas. 96p. 1996. pap. 12.95 (*1-56163-150-7*) NBM.

Rork No. 1: Fragments. Andreas. Tr. by Bell & Jean-Marc Lofficier from FRE. 54p. 1991. pap. 9.95 (*1-56163-016-0*) NBM.

Rork, No. 2: Passages. Andreas. Tr. by Jean-Marc Lofficier. 1991. pap. 9.95 (*1-56163-028-4*) NBM.

Rorke's Drift: The Zulu War, 1879. James W. Bancroft. (Illus.). 176p. 1994. 40.00 (*1-885119-09-7*) Sarpedon.

Rorke's Drift 1879. Ian Knight. (Campaign Ser.). (Illus.). 96p. 1995. pap. 14.95 (*1-85532-506-3*, Pub. by Osprey UK) Stackpole.

Rororo Musikhandbuch, 2 vols. Heinrich Lindlar. (GER.). 1976. pap. 35.00 (*0-8288-5753-9*, M7605) Fr & Eur.

Rorschach: A Comprehensive System, 3 vols., Vol. 3. 3rd ed. John E. Exner. 1560p. 1996. text ed. 215.00 (*0-471-11987-3*) Wiley.

Rorschach: A Developmental Perspective. Martin Leichtman. 368p. 1996. text ed. 45.00 (*0-88163-138-8*) Analytic Pr.

Rorschach Assessment of Children & Adolescents: A Comprehensive System, Vol. 3. 2nd ed. John E. Exner. (Series on Personality Processes). 430p. 1994. text ed. 80.00 (*0-471-55927-X*) Wiley.

Rorschach - A Comprehensive System Interpretation: Assessment of Personality & Psychopathology, Vol. 2. 2nd ed. John E. Exner. LC 90-13160. (Personality Processes Ser.). 476p. 1991. text ed. 80.00 (*0-471-85080-2*) Wiley.

Rorschach - a Comprehensive System Vol. 1: Basic Foundations. 3rd ed. John E. Exner. LC 93-9878. (Series on Personality Processes). 672p. 1993. text ed. 80.00 (*0-471-55902-4*) Wiley.

Rorschach Assessment of Aggressive & Psychopathic Personalities. Carl B. Gacono & J. Reid Meloy. (SPA Monographs Ser.). 432p. 1994. text ed. 39.95 (*0-8058-0980-5*) L Erlbaum Assocs.

Rorschach Responses in Old Age. rev. ed. Janet L. Rodell et al. 242p. 1995. pap. 40.00 (*1-56821-490-1*) Aronson.

R

Rorschach Study of Child Development. Nettie H. Ledwith. LC 75-26632. 336p. 1975. reprint ed. text ed. 59.75 (*0-8371-8365-0*, LERS, Greenwood Pr) Greenwood.

Rorschach Technique: An Introductory Manual. Bruno Klopfer & Helen H. Davidson. (Illus.). 245p. (C). 1962. text ed. 40.00 (*0-15-577873-0*) HB Coll Pubs.

Rorschach Technique: Content, Interpretation, & Application. 2nd ed. Edward Aronow et al. 1994. text ed. 54.50 (*0-205-14912-X*, Longwood Div) Allyn.

Rorschach Test. Franz Wright. LC 94-68941. (Poetry Ser.). 80p. 1995. pap. 11.95 (*0-88748-209-0*) Carnegie-Mellon.

***Rorschach Test: Theory & Practice.** Rajendra K. Misra et al. LC 96-28316. 295p. 1996. 32.00 (*0-8039-9328-5*) Sage.

Rorschach Test Scoring. Alvin G. Burstein & Sandra Loucks. LC 66-56615. 300p. 1989. 78.95 (*0-89116-771-4*); pap. 39.95 (*0-89116-780-3*) Hemisp Pub.

Rorschach Workbook. rev. ed. Lucille H. Blum et al. LC 74-10227. 193p. (Orig.). 1975. spiral bd. 30.00 (*0-8236-5901-1*) Intl Univs Pr.

Rorschachiana. Ed. by Irving B. Weiner. (Yearbook of the International Rorschach Society Ser.: Vol. 18). (Illus.). 151p. 1993. text ed. 34.00 (*0-88937-114-8*) Hogrefe & Huber Pubs.

***Rorschachiana.** Ed. by Irving B. Weiner. (Yearbook of the International Rorschach Society Ser.: Vol. 22). 200p. 1997. text ed. 38.00 (*0-88937-180-6*) Hogrefe & Huber Pubs.

Rorschachiana: Yearbook of the International Rorschach Society, Vol. 19. Ed. by Irving B. Weiner. (Illus.). 176p. 1994. text ed. 36.00 (*0-88937-128-8*) Hogrefe & Huber Pubs.

Rorschachiana: Yearbook of the International Rorschach Society, Vol. 20. Ed. by Irving B. Weiner. (Illus.). 216p. 1995. text ed. 38.00 (*0-88937-141-5*) Hogrefe & Huber Pubs.

Rorschachiana: Yearbook of the International Rorschach Society, Vol. 21. Ed. by Irving B. Weiner. (Yearbook of the International Rorschach Society Ser.: Vol. 21). (Illus.). 200p. 1996. text ed. 38.00 (*0-88937-160-1*) Hogrefe & Huber Pubs.

Rorstrand Porcelain: Art Nouveau Masterpieces. Bengt Nystrom. (Illus.). 192p. 1996. 80.00 (*1-55859-844-8*) Abbeville Pr.

Rorty & Pragmatism: The Philosopher Responds to His Critics. Ed. by Herman J. Saatkamp, Jr. LC 94-47580. (Vanderbilt Library of American Philosophy). 304p. 1995. 24.95 (*0-8265-1263-1*) Vanderbilt U Pr.

Rorty's Humanistic Pragmatism: Philosophy Democratized. Konstantin Kolenda. 160p. 1990. lib. bdg. 34.75 (*0-8130-0970-7*) U Press Fla.

***Rosa.** Peter Greenaway. 1994. pap. text ed. 22.50 (*2-906571-30-X*, Pub. by Editions Dis Voir FR) Dist Art Pubs.

Rosa. Marjorie E. Haines. LC 95-12592. (Open Door Books Ser.). 1995. 3.95 (*1-56212-102-2*) CRC Pubns.

***Rosa.** Knut Hamsun. (Sun & Moon Classics Ser.: Vol. 113). 1997. pap. 12.95 (*1-55713-359-X*) Sun & Moon CA.

Rosa. large type ed. Valerie Kershaw. (Linford Mystery Library). 336p. 1994. pap. 15.99 (*0-7089-7565-8*, Linford) Ulverscroft.

Rosa: A Biography of Rosa Townsend. Beryl Hackner. pap. 24.95 (*1-875560-38-6*, Pub. by Univ of West Aust Pr AT) Intl Spec Bk.

Rosa: The Life of an Italian Immigrant. Marie H. Ets. LC 70-110658. 266p. reprint ed. pap. 75.90 (*0-317-39688-9*, 2055862) Bks Demand.

Rosa & Her Singing Grandfather. Leon Rosselson. LC 95-10320. (Illus.). 73p. (J). (gr. k-3). 1996. 12.95 (*0-399-22733-4*, Philomel Bks) Putnam Pub Group.

***Rosa Bonheur: The Artist's (Auto)biography.** Anna Klumpke. Tr. by Gretchen Van Slyke. LC 97-20701. (C). 1997. 39.50 (*0-472-10825-5*) U of Mich Pr.

Rosa Decidua. Aleister Crowley. 1993. pap. 5.95 (*1-55818-251-9*) Holmes Pub.

Rosa Fielding: Victim of Lust. 192p. 1983. reprint ed. pap. 3.95 (*0-88184-053-X*) Carroll & Graf.

Rosa Gallica. Suzanne Verrier. LC 95-70491. (Illus.). 150p. (Orig.). 1996. pap. 29.50 (*0-913643-12-2*) Capabilitys.

Rosa Lee: A Mother & Her Family in Urban America. Leon Dash. LC 96-19403. (Illus.). 224p. 1996. 23.00 (*0-465-07092-2*) Basic.

***Rosa Lee: A Mother & Her Family in Urban America.** Leon Dash. LC 97-11543. 1997. pap. 12.95 (*0-452-27896-1*) NAL-Dutton.

Rosa Lemberg Story. Tr. by Eva H. Erickson. 1993. write for info. (*0-9633780-3-1*) Tyomies Soc.

Rosa Luxemberg & Emma Goldman No. 43: A Bibliography. Ed. by Joan Nordquist. (Social Theory: A Bibliographic Ser.: No. 43). (Orig.). 1996. pap. 15.00 (*0-937855-85-5*) Ref Rsch Serv.

Rosa Luxemburg. Wendy Forrest. (In Her Time Ser.). (Illus.). 64p. (YA). (gr. 6-10). 1991. 15.95 (*0-237-60040-4*, Pub. by Evans Bros Ltd UK) Trafalgar.

Rosa Luxemburg. Paul Frolich. 1972. 59.95 (*0-8490-0973-1*) Gordon Pr.

Rosa Luxemburg: A Life for the International. Richard Abraham. LC 89-31671. (Women's Ser.). 185p. 1989. 19.95 (*0-85496-182-8*) Berg Pubs.

***Rosa Luxemburg: A Revolutionary of Our Time.** Stephen E. Bronner. 1997. pap. 14.95 (*0-271-01685-X*) Pa St U Pr.

Rosa Luxemburg: Her Life & Work. Paul Froelich. Tr. by Johanna Hoornweg. LC 72-81776. 352p. reprint ed. pap. 100.40 (*0-8357-3521-4*, 2034349) Bks Demand.

Rosa Luxemburg & the Noble Dream: Studies in Modern European History. Donald E. Shepardson. (Studies in Modern European History: Vol. 17). 171p. (C). 1996. pap. text ed. 43.95 (*0-8204-2739-X*, HX274) P Lang Pubng.

Rosa Luxemburg Speaks. Ed. by Mary-Alice Waters. LC 90-70745. 473p. 1970. reprint ed. pap. 22.95 (*0-87348-146-1*); reprint ed. lib. bdg. 60.00 (*0-87348-589-0*) Pathfinder NY.

Rosa Luxemburg, Women's Liberation, & Marx's Philosophy of Revolution. 2nd ed. Raya Dunayevskaya. 276p. 1991. text ed. 32.50 (*0-252-01838-9*); pap. text ed. 12.95 (*0-252-06189-6*) U of Ill Pr.

Rosa May: The Search for a Mining Camp Legend. rev. ed. George Williams, III. Ed. by Bill Dalton. LC 82-11154. (Prostitutes Ser.). (Illus.). 240p. 1986. 20.95 (*0-935174-21-4*); pap. 10.95 (*0-935174-07-9*) Tree by River.

Rosa Mecanica. Lourdes Vazquez. 96p. (SPA.). 1991. pap. 6.95 (*0-929157-14-1*) Ediciones Huracan.

Rosa Montero's Odyssey. Alma Amell. 126p. (Orig.). (C). 1994. lib. bdg. 37.00 (*0-8191-9353-4*) U Pr of Amer.

***Rosa Moves to Town.** Barbro Lindgren. (J). 1997. 15.95 (*0-88899-288-2*) Firefly Bks Ltd.

***Rosa Mundi.** Theo Dorgan. 74p. 9700. pap. 13.95 (*1-897648-64-2*, Pub. by Salmon Pubng IE) Dufour.

Rosa Mundi, & Other Stories. Ethel M. Dell. LC 79-121535. (Short Story Index Reprint Ser.). 1977. 24.95 (*0-8369-3491-1*) Ayer.

Rosa Parks. Did You Know Publishings Staff. LC 92-71756. 32p. (J). 1992. 11.99 (*0-9633151-0-2*) Did You Know Pub.

Rosa Parks. Eloise Greenfield. LC 95-35497. (Trophy Chapter Bk.). (Illus.). 64p. (J). (gr. 2-4). 1995. pap. 3.95 (*0-06-442025-6*, Trophy) HarpC Child Bks.

Rosa Parks. Eloise Greenfield. LC 95-35497. (Illus.). 64p. (J). (gr. 2-4). 1996. lib. bdg. 13.89 (*0-06-027110-8*) HarpC Child Bks.

***Rosa Parks.** Gini Holland. (J). 1997. pap. text ed. 5.95 (*0-8172-6885-5*) Raintree Steck-V.

Rosa Parks. Gini Holland. LC 96-23015. (First Biographies Ser.). (J). 1997. lib. bdg. 21.40 (*0-8172-4451-4*) Raintree Steck-V.

Rosa Parks: Civil Rights Leader. Mary Hull. Ed. by Nathan I. Huggins. LC 93-17699. (Black Americans of Achievement Ser.). (Illus.). (J). (gr. 5 up). 1994. pap. 8.95 (*0-7910-1910-1*) Chelsea Hse.

Rosa Parks: Civil Rights Leader. Mary Hull. Ed. by Nathan I. Huggins. LC 93-17699. (Black Americans of Achievement Ser.). (Illus.). 144p. (YA). (gr. 5 up). 1994. lib. bdg. 19.95 (*0-7910-1881-4*) Chelsea Hse.

Rosa Parks: Fight for Freedom. Keith Brandt. LC 91-34939. (Illus.). 48p. (J). (gr. 4-6). 1993. pap. 3.95 (*0-8167-2832-1*); lib. bdg. 12.95 (*0-8167-2831-3*) Troll Communs.

Rosa Parks: Hero of Our Time. Garnet N. Jackson. LC 92-28583. (Illus.). (J). 1992. pap. 5.25 (*0-8136-5705-9*) Modern Curr.

Rosa Parks: Hero of Our Time. Garnet N. Jackson. LC 92-28583. (Illus.). (J). (gr. 1-4). 1992. lib. bdg. 10.55 (*0-8136-5232-4*) Modern Curr.

Rosa Parks: Mother to a Movement. Rosa Parks. LC 89-1124. (Illus.). 200p. (J). 1992. pap. 17.00 (*0-8037-0673-1*) Dial Bks Young.

Rosa Parks: The Movement Organizes. Kai J. Friese. Ed. by Richard Gallin. (History of the Civil Rights Movement Ser.). (Illus.). 128p. (J). (gr. 5 up). 1990. lib. bdg. 12.95 (*0-382-09927-3*) Silver Burdett Pr.

Rosa Parks: The Movement Organizes. Kai J. Friese. Ed. by Richard Gallin. (History of the Civil Rights Movement Ser.). (Illus.). 128p. (YA). (gr. 5 up). 1990. pap. 7.95 (*0-382-24065-0*) Silver Burdett Pr.

Rosa Parks & the Montgomery Bus Boycott. Teresa Celsi. (Gateway Civil Rights Ser.). (Illus.). 32p. (J). (gr. 2-4). 1991. pap. 5.95 (*1-878841-34-3*); lib. bdg. 15.40 (*1-878841-14-9*) Millbrook Pr.

***Rosa Perfecta - A Perfect Rose.** Metsy Hingle. (SPA.). 1997. pap. 3.50 (*0-373-35191-7*, 1-35191-5) Harlequin Bks.

***Rosa Ponselle: A Centenary Biography.** James A. Drake. LC 96-28709. (Opera Biography Ser.). 540p. 1997. 39.95 (*1-57467-019-0*, Amadeus Pr) Timber.

***Rosa Ponselle: American Diva.** Mary J. Phillips-Matz. LC 97-19825. (Illus.). 320p. 1997. 29.95 (*1-55553-317-5*) NE U Pr.

***Rosa Raye: Crime Reporter.** Sue Kerman. (Longman Originals Ser.). 1996. pap. text ed. 7.00 (*0-582-08139-4*, Pub. by Longman UK) Longman.

Rosa Rugosa. Suzanne Verrier. LC 91-72462. (Illus.). 90p. (Orig.). 1991. pap. 22.95 (*0-913643-07-6*) Capabilitys.

Rosa Separada. 4th ed. Pablo Neruda. 112p. (SPA.). 1990. pap. 16.95 (*0-7859-5001-X*) Fr & Eur.

***Rosabeth Moss Kanter on the Frontiers of Management.** Rosabeth M. Kanter. LC 97-2747. (Review Book Ser.). 320p. 1997. 29.95 (*0-87584-802-8*, HBS Pr) Harvard Busn.

Rosacruz de Oro. Jan Van Rijckenborgh. 76p. (SPA.). 1988. 13.00 (*84-300-8341-3*) Rosycross Pr.

Rosaire Biblique (French) Christianica Staff. (Illus.). (FRE.). 1988. 8.95 (*0-911346-12-0*) Christianica.

Rosalba. large type ed. Sheila Bishop. 416p. (Orig.). 1994. 25.99 (*0-7089-3128-6*) Ulverscroft.

Rosalba's Journal & Other Papers. Austin Dobson. LC 71-111827. (Essay Index Reprint Ser.). 1977. 23.95 (*0-8369-1605-0*) Ayer.

***Rosalee.** Thomas Sharp. 1996. mass mkt. 4.99 (*1-55197-608-0*, Pub. by Comnwlth Pub CN) Partners Pubs Grp.

Rosalee Pritchett. Carlton Molette & Barbara Molette. 1972. pap. 3.25 (*0-8222-0968-3*) Dramatists Play.

Rosalia de Castro & the Galician Revival. Shelly Stevens. 1986. 45.00 (*0-7293-0250-4*, Pub. by Tamesis Bks Ltd UK) Boydell & Brewer.

Rosalie. large type ed. Patricia Hemstock. LC 95-36129. (Romance Ser.). 288p. 1996. pap. 17.95 (*0-7838-1543-3*, GK Hall) Thorndike Pr.

Rosalie of Grand Traverse Bay. Donna Winters. Ed. by Pamela Q. Chambers. LC 95-83814. (Great Lakes Romances Ser.). 352p. (Orig.). 1996. pap. 10.95 (*0-923048-84-7*) Bigwater Pub.

***Rosalie S'En Va-T-En Guerre.** Ginette Anfousse. (Novels in the Roman Jeunesse Ser.). 96p. (FRE.). (J). (gr. 4-7). 1996. pap. 7.95 (*2-89021-093-6*, Pub. by Les Editions CN) Firefly Bks Ltd.

Rosalie, Sylvia & Melanie. Felix Pirani. (I Love to Read Collection). (Illus.). 48p. (J). (ps-1). 1992. lib. bdg. 12.79 (*0-89565-888-7*) Childs World.

***Rosalie Whyel Museum of Doll Art.** Rosalie Whyel & Susan Hedrick. (Illus.). 80p. 1996. pap. 12.95 (*0-614-23813-7*, C4677) Hobby Hse.

Rosalie's Battle. Ginette Anfousse. Tr. by Linda Gaboriau. 96p. (J). (gr. 2-6). 1996. mass mkt. 3.50 (*0-440-41076-2*, YB BDD) BDD Bks Young Read.

***Rosalie's Battles.** Ginette Anfousse. Tr. by Linda Gaboriau. (Rosalie Ser.). (Illus.). 96p. (J). pap. 5.95 (*0-921556-50-0*, Pub. by Gynergy-Ragweed CN) LPC InBook.

Rosalie's Big Dream. Ginette Anfousse. 96p. (J). 1996. pap. 3.50 (*0-440-41079-7*) Dell.

***Rosalie's Big Dream.** Ginette Anfousse. (Rosalie Ser.). (Illus.). 96p. (J). pap. 5.95 (*0-921556-52-7*, Pub. by Gynergy-Ragweed CN) LPC InBook.

Rosalie's Catastrophy. Marisol Sarrazin. 96p. (J). 1996. pap. 3.50 (*0-440-41073-8*) Dell.

Rosalind. James M. Barrie. Ed. by William-Alan Landes. LC 93-15725. 1993. pap. 5.00 (*0-88734-331-7*) Players Pr.

Rosalind: A Family Romance. Myra Goldberg. LC 95-2274. 304p. 1996. 22.95 (*0-944072-59-3*) Zoland Bks.

Rosalind see Major Literary Characters

Rosalind & Helen: A Modern Eclogue with Other Poems. Percy Bysshe Shelley. Ed. by H. Buxton Forman. LC 74-30294. (Shelley Society, Second Ser.: No. 17). reprint ed. 29.50 (*0-404-11512-8*) AMS Pr.

Rosalind Franklin & DNA. Anne Sayre. (Illus.). 1978. pap. 9.95 (*0-393-00868-1*) Norton.

***Rosaline Lace.** Ghislaine Eamans-Moors. (Illus.). 144p. 1997. 39.95 (*0-7134-7603-6*, Pub. by Batsford UK) Trafalgar.

Rosalynde, Being the Original of Shakespeare's As You Like It. Thomas Lodge. Ed. by W. W. Greg. LC 75-128890. (Select Bibliographies Reprint Ser.). 1977. reprint ed. 18.95 (*0-8369-5510-2*) Ayer.

***Rosalynn Carter: Steel Magnolia.** Ruth Turk. LC 96-50025. (First Bk.). (J). 1997. write for info. (*0-531-20312-3*) Watts.

Rosamond Lehmann. Diana E. Lestourgeon. LC 64-8331. (Twayne's English Authors Ser.). 157p. (C). 1965. lib. bdg. 17.95 (*0-8290-1723-2*) Irvington.

Rosamond Lehmann. Judy Simons. LC 91-34149. (Modern Novelists Ser.). 160p. 1992. text ed. 39.95 (*0-312-07208-2*) St Martin.

Rosamond Lehmann: A Thirties Writer. Ruth Siegel. (American University Studies: English Language & Literature: Ser. IV, Vol. 98). 194p. (C). 1989. text ed. 35.50 (*0-8204-1046-2*) P Lang Pubng.

Rosamund. Janice Johnson. LC 92-44115. (Illus.). (J). (gr. 5 up). 1994. pap. 15.00 (*0-671-79329-2*, S&S Bks Young Read) S&S Childrens.

Rosamund Gray. Charles Lamb. LC 91-16915. 146p. 1991. reprint ed. 43.00 (*1-85477-075-6*, Pub. by Woodstock Bks UK) Cassell.

***Rosamunda's Revenge.** Emma Craig. 368p. (Orig.). 1997. mass mkt. 5.50 (*0-505-52213-6*, Love Spell) Dorchester Pub Co.

Rosamunde Pilcher, No. 2. Rosamunde Pilcher. 1990. boxed 19.80 (*0-440-36020-X*) Dell.

Rosamunde Pilcher, No. 3. Rosamunde Pilcher. 1990. boxed 19.80 (*0-440-36021-8*) Dell.

Rosamunde Pilcher, 3 vols., Set. Rosamunde Pilcher. 1991. pap. 19.97 (*0-312-92620-0*) St Martin.

Rosamunde Pilcher, 3 vols., Set. Rosamunde Pilcher. 1992. pap. 20.97 (*0-312-92893-9*) St Martin.

Rosanna of the Amish. rev. ed. Joseph W. Yoder. 256p. 1973. pap. 5.99 (*0-8361-1714-X*) Herald Pr.

Rosanna of the Amish: Centennial Edition. 3rd ed. Joseph W. Yoder. (Illus.). 320p. 1995. pap. 9.99 (*0-8361-9018-1*) Herald Pr.

Rosanne Somerson - Earthly Delights: Peter Joseph Gallery, New York. Photos by Michael Galatis & Adam Reich. LC 92-63364. 1993. write for info. (*1-881658-04-X*) P J Gallery.

Rosano Sculptures. Aureleo Rosano. LC 83-90393. (Illus.). 120p. 1984. 38.00 (*0-914817-00-0*) Rose Pubns AZ.

Rosario: La Oraciaon de Unino. 1995. pap. 1.95 (*0-8091-6626-7*) Paulist Pr.

Rosario Biblico. Christianica Staff. (Illus.). (POR.). 1995. 8.95 (*0-911346-14-7*) Christianica.

Rosario Biblico (Italian) 1988 Edition. Christianica Staff. (Illus.). (ITA.). 1988. 8.95 (*0-911346-11-2*) Christianica.

Rosario Biblico (Spanish) Christianica Staff. (Illus.). (SPA.). 1980. 8.95 (*0-911346-04-X*) Christianica.

Rosario Castellanos Reader. Rosario Castellanos. Tr. by Maureen Ahern from SPA. (Texas Pan American Ser.). 400p. 1988. 34.95 (*0-292-77039-1*); pap. 17.95 (*0-292-77036-7*) U of Tex Pr.

Rosario Ferre, a Search for Identity: The Prose of Rosario Ferre. Suzanne S. Hintz. LC 94-41326. (Wor(l)ds of Change Ser.: Vol. 12). 288p. (C). 1995. text ed. 48.95 (*0-8204-2691-1*) P Lang Pubng.

Rosario Mistico con Oracion de la Misa Mistica. Luke Zimmer. 20p. (Orig.). (SPA.). 1996. pap. 1.00 (*1-882972-68-6*) Queenship Pub.

Rosario y el Dinosaurio: Big Book. Ina Cumpiano. (Que Maravilla! Ser.: Level 1). (Illus.). 24p. (Orig.). (SPA.). (J). (gr. 1-3). 1992. pap. text ed. 29.95 (*1-56334-168-9*) Hampton-Brown.

Rosario y el Dinosaurio: Small Book. Ina Cumpiano. (Que Maravilla! Ser.: Level 1). (Illus.). 24p. (Orig.). (SPA.). (J). (gr. 1-3). 1992. pap. text ed. 6.00 (*1-56334-170-0*) Hampton-Brown.

Rosario Yesterdays. Christopher M. Peacock. LC 85-51170. (Illus.). 72p. (Orig.). 1985. pap. 9.98 (*0-9614970-0-9*) Rosario Prod.

Rosarum Monographia: Or a Botanical History of Roses. John Lindley. (Old Roses Ser.). (Illus.). 1979. reprint ed. text ed. 27.50 (*0-930576-17-9*) E M Coleman Ent.

***Rosary.** (Illus.). 32p. (Orig.). (J). (ps-3). 1985. pap. 0.99 (*0-89942-671-9*, 671/00) Catholic Bk Pub.

Rosary. St. Paul Publications Staff. 1993. 19.00 (*0-85439-444-3*, Pub. by St Paul Pubns UK) St Mut.

Rosary. Mary F. Windeatt. (Catholic Story Coloring Bks.). (Illus.). 32p. (J). (gr. 1-5). 1993. reprint ed. student ed. 3.00 (*0-89555-379-1*) TAN Bks Pubs.

***Rosary: "The Little Summa"** 2nd rev. ed. Robert Feeney. (Illus.). 142p. 1997. pap. 8.95 (*0-9622347-4-5*) Aquinas Pr.

Rosary: A Child's Prayer (Coloring Book) Homer T. Martinez, Jr. (Illus.). 32p. (Orig.). (J). 1995. pap. 1.95 (*0-8091-6622-4*) Paulist Pr.

Rosary: A Gospel Prayer. J. Patrick Gaffney. 1991. 2.95 (*0-910984-56-5*) Montfort Pubns.

Rosary: A Gospel Prayer. Wilfrid J. Harrington. LC 75-44676. (Illus.). 160p. 1976. pap. 3.95 (*0-8189-1129-8*, Pub. by Alba Bks AT) Alba.

***Rosary: A Way into Prayer.** Anne Vail. 112p. 1997. pap. 11.95 (*1-85311-160-0*, Pub. by Canterbury Press Norwich UK) Morehouse Pub.

Rosary: Great Weapon of the Twentieth Century. Louis M. De Montfort & Antonio R. Marin. Ed. by Foundation for a Christian Civilization, Inc. Staff. LC 87-70850. (Illus.). 96p. (Orig.). 1987. pap. 13.95 (*1-877905-07-0*) Am Soc Defense TFP.

Rosary: Prayer for All Seasons. Joanna Hastings. 232p. (Orig.). 1993. pap. 11.95 (*0-8146-2134-1*) Liturgical Pr.

Rosary: The Life of Jesus & Mary. Bob Lord & Penny Lord. 192p. 1993. 12.95 (*0-926143-12-3*) Journeys Faith.

Rosary - "The Little Summa" Reflections from St. Thomas Aquinas Vatican II & Pope John Paul II. Robert Feeney. LC 91-74016. 118p. (Orig.). 1991. pap. 8.95 (*0-9622347-1-0*) Aquinas Pr.

Rosary & Devotion to Mary. Andrew J. Gerakas. LC 88-11319. 75p. 1988. pap. 5.95 (*0-8198-6417-X*) Pauline Bks.

Rosary & the Crisis of Faith: Fatima & World Peace. 51p. 1995. pap. 2.00 (*0-89555-306-6*) TAN Bks Pubs.

Rosary Companion. Michael Scanlan. 51p. 1993. pap. 2.95 (*0-940535-59-9*) Franciscan U Pr.

Rosary for Children. Louis M. Savary. (J). (ps-3). Date not set. pap. text ed. 1.25 (*0-88271-158-X*) Regina Pr.

Rosary in Action. John S. Johnson. 1977. reprint ed. pap. 9.00 (*0-89555-023-7*) TAN Bks Pubs.

Rosary in the Steps of the Gospel. rev. ed. Jean Guilmard. 52p. 1994. pap. 4.95 (*0-87061-209-3*, 6928) Chr Classics.

Rosary, Mat, & Molo: A Study in the Spiritual Epic of Omar Seku Tal. Oumarou Watta. LC 92-22229. (American University Studies: Theology & Religion: Ser. VII, Vol. 135). 218p. 1992. 4.95 (*0-8204-1891-9*) P Lang Pubng.

Rosary Murders. William X. Kienzle. 304p. 1989. mass mkt. 5.99 (*0-345-35668-3*) Ballantine.

Rosary Novenas. 1.80 (*0-685-42007-8*, Benzger Pub) Glencoe.

Rosary Novenas. C. Lacy. 1974. pap. write for info. (*0-02-645810-1*) Macmillan.

Rosary of Evil. Eli Siegel. 25p. 1964. pap. 3.00 (*0-911492-04-6*) Aesthetic Realism.

Rosary of Our Lady. Romano Guardini. Tr. by H. Von Schuecking. LC 94-28899. 160p. 1994. 11.95 (*0-918477-23-9*) Sophia Inst Pr.

Rosary Psalms. Peter Huyck. 64p. 1994. pap. 40.00 (*0-85439-489-3*, Pub. by St Paul Pubns UK) St Mut.

***Rosas de Invierno.** M. Heavilin. (SPA.). 1.50 (*0-8297-0295-4*) Life Pubs Intl.

Rosas de Otono - Pepa Doncel. J. Benavente. 163p. (SPA.). 1968. 9.95 (*0-8288-7029-2*, S8761) Fr & Eur.

Rosas, Diablos y Sonrisas. La Sonrisa de Eros. Juan Perucho. (Nueva Austral Ser.: Vol. 137). (SPA.). 1991. pap. text ed. 24.95 (*84-239-1937-4*) Elliots Bks.

Rosa's Diary. Rita Benson. LC 93-28972. (Voyages Ser.). (Illus.). (J). 1994. 4.25 (*0-383-03772-7*) SRA McGraw.

Rosata. Holly Keller. LC 94-21916. (Illus.). 32p. (J). (ps up). 1995. 15.00 (*0-688-05320-3*); lib. bdg. 14.93 (*0-688-05321-1*) Greenwillow.

Rosato's Plastics Encyclopedia & Dictionary. 2nd ed. Dominick V. Rosato. 884p. (C). 1992. text ed. 148.00 (*1-56990-088-4*) Hanser-Gardner.

Rosaura a las Diez. Marco Denevi. Ed. by Donald A. Yates. (Illus.). 219p. (SPA.). 1964. pap. text ed. 30.67 (*0-13-783234-6*) P-H.

***Roscarrock.** Gloria Cook. 384p. 1997. pap. 11.95 (*0-7472-5396-X*, Pub. by Headline UK) Trafalgar.

Roscius Anglicanus. John Downes. Ed. by Montague Summers. LC 68-20220. 1972. reprint ed. 24.95 (*0-405-08464-1*) Ayer.

Roscius Anglicanus: or An Historical Review of the Stage. John Downes. LC 92-22031. (Augustan Reprints Ser.: No. 134). 1969. reprint ed. 14.50 (*0-404-70134-5*, PN2592) AMS Pr.

Roscoe: Generations - Regeneration. Lorle Porter. (Illus.). 442p. 1991. 18.95 (*1-880443-05-8*) Roscoe Village.

An Asterisk (*) at the beginning of an entry indicates that the title is appearing in BIP for the first time.

Roscoe "Fatty" Arbuckle: A Bio-Bibliography. Robert Young, Jr. LC 94-3033. (Bio-Bibliographies in the Performing Arts Ser.: No. 53). 328p. 1994. text ed. 59.95 (0-313-26537-2, Greenwood Pr) Greenwood.

Roscoe "Fatty" Arbuckle: A Biography of the Silent Film Comedian, 1887-1933. Stuart Oderman. LC 92-56674. (Illus.). 255p. 1994. lib. bdg. 29.95 (0-89950-872-3) McFarland & Co.

Roscoe I. Jeri B. Borowitz. 159p. 1995. 7.50 (0-9645624-0-5) Clinton Pub.

Roscoe Pound: Philosopher of Law. David Wigdor. LC 72-852. (Contributions in American History Ser.: No. 33). 356p. 1974. text ed. 38.50 (0-8371-6419-2, WIP/, Greenwood Pr) Greenwood.

*Roscoe Pound & Karl Llewellyn: Searching for an American Jurisprudence. N. E. Hull. LC 97-2975. 1996. 34.95 (0-226-36043-1) U Ch Pr.

Roscoe Pucannon at Lodge Vol. 3: First Two Blurred: How I Spent All My Life up till Now Trying to Survive Being Born. B. W. Coile. LC 90-86217. (Illus.). 128p. (Orig.). 1991. pap. 8.95 (0-9628749-0-6) B W Coile.

Roscoe Turner: Aviation's Master Showman. Carroll V. Glines. Ed. by Von Hardesty. LC 94-24956. (Aviation Ser.). (Illus.). 368p. 1995. 29.95 (1-56098-456-2) Smithsonian.

Roscoe Village Recipes see Eliza Johnson's Kitchen Book

Roscoe's Leap. Gillian Cross. LC 87-45328. 160p. (YA). (gr. 7 up). 1987. 15.95 (0-8234-0669-5) Holiday.

Roscommon Before the Famine: The Parishes of Kiltoom & Cam, 1749-1845. William Gacquin. 64p. 1996. pap. 9.95 (0-7165-2597-6, Pub. by Irish Acad Pr IE) Intl Spec Bk.

*Rose. Ariel Books Staff. 1996. 3.95 (0-8362-1011-5, Arie Bks) Andrews & McMeel.

Rose. Glenda S. Kachelmeier. Ed. by Sheila S. Darst. LC 83-80689. 267p. 1983. 7.95 (0-89896-003-7) Larksdale.

Rose. Jill M. Landis. 1990. mass mkt. 5.99 (0-515-10346-2) Jove Pubns.

Rose. Li-Young Lee. 71p. 1986. pap. 10.00 (0-918526-53-1) BOA Edns.

*Rose. Kathleen Leverich. LC 96-38907. (Flower Girls Ser.: Vol. 4). (Illus.). 96p. (J). (gr. 1-4). 1997. pap. 3.95 (0-06-442020-5, Trophy) HarpC Child Bks.

Rose. Ann Reilly. (Illus.). 152p. 1989. 22.99 (0-517-68830-1) Random Hse Value.

Rose. Martin C. Smith. LC 95-37914. 364p. 1996. 25.00 (0-679-42661-2) Random.

*Rose. Martin C. Smith. 1997. pap. 12.50 (0-345-39044-X) Ballantine.

Rose. large type ed. Martin C. Smith. LC 95-50061. 1996. pap. 25.00 (0-679-75878-X) Random.

Rose. H. B. Ellwanger. (Old Roses Ser.). 1979. reprint ed. text ed. 19.50 (0-930576-15-2) E M Coleman Ent.

Rose. Leigh Greenwood. (Seven Brides Ser.). 448p. 1996. reprint ed. mass mkt. 5.99 (0-8439-4019-0) Dorchester Pub Co.

Rose. Charles Harness. 1993. reprint ed. lib. bdg. 18.95 (0-89968-341-X, Lghtyr Pr) Buccaneer Bks.

Rose: A Novel. large type ed. Martin Cruz Smith. 588p. 1996. pap. 25.00 (0-7838-1681-2, GK Hall) Thorndike Pr.

Rose: An Encyclopedia of North American Roses, Rosarians, & Rose Lore. Sean McCann. LC 93-9589. (Illus.). 224p. 1993. 24.95 (0-8117-1490-X) Stackpole.

Rose: Once upon a Dream: Based on Beauty & the Beast. Jennifer Baker. (J). 1996. mass mkt. 3.99 (0-590-25948-2) Scholastic Inc.

Rose: The Life & Times of Rose Fitzgerald Kennedy. Charles Higham. (Illus.). 454p. 1995. 23.00 (0-615-00723-6); 23.00 (0-671-89026-3) PB.

Rose: The Life & Times of Rose Fitzgerald Kennedy. Charles Higham. 1996. mass mkt., pap. 6.99 (0-671-89027-1) PB.

Rose-a-Down Dilly. Judi Beckley & Randy West. (Illus.). 32p. (Orig.). 1981. pap. 4.95 (0-942478-01-0) Photopia Pr.

Rose Amateur's Guide. Thomas Rivers. (Old Roses Ser.). 1979. 15.00 (0-685-01528-9) E M Coleman Ent.

Rose & a Wedding Vow: (This Time, Forever) Andrea Edwards. (Special Edition Ser.). 1995. pap. 3.75 (0-373-09944-4, 1-09944-9) Silhouette.

Rose & Black's Clinical Patterns in Nephrology. Jeffrey S. Stoff. 597p. 1995. text ed. 99.95 (0-316-75652-0) Lppncott-Raven.

Rose & Ciriaco Herrera: Life in Eureka, 1920s-1950s. Intro. by R. T. King. (Illus.). 108p. 1988. lib. bdg. 37.50 (1-56475-331-X); fiche write for info. (1-56475-332-8) U NV Oral Hist.

*Rose & Dorothy. unabridged ed. Roslyn Schwartz. (Illus.). 32p. (J). (gr. k-2). 1990. pap. 4.95 (1-55074-065-2, Pub. by Kids Can Pr CN) Genl Dist Srvs.

Rose and her Rat see Rosie's Birthday Rat

Rose & Lotus: Narrative of Desire in France & China. Tonglin Lu. LC 90-9599. 201p. (C). 1991. text ed. 64.50 (0-7914-0463-3); pap. text ed. 21.95 (0-7914-0464-1) State U NY Pr.

Rose & Nefr Dance Manual. Rosanore of Redthorn. (Illus.). 136p. (C). 1989. pap. text ed. 20.00 (1-877934-03-8) Rose & Nefr Pr.

Rose & Sebastian. Cynthia Zarin. LC 95-16367. (Illus.). 1997. 16.00 (0-395-75920-X) HM.

Rose & the Clematis: As Good Companions. John Howells. 120p. 1996. 39.50 (1-870673-19-0, Pub. by Garden Art Pr UK) Antique Collect.

Rose & the Key. Le-Fanu J. Sheridan. (Pocket Classics Ser.). 400p. 1994. pap. write for info. (0-7509-0670-7, Pub. by Sutton Pubng UK) Bks Intl VA.

Rose & the Key. Sheridan LeFanu & Norman Donaldson. (Mystery Ser.). 448p. 1983. reprint ed. pap. 7.95 (0-486-24377-X) Dover.

Rose & the Key, 3 vols, 1. Joseph S. Le Fanu. Ed. by Devendra P. Varma. LC 76-5275. (Collected Works). 1977. reprint ed. 29.95 (0-405-09230-X) Ayer.

Rose & the Key, 3 vols, Set. Joseph S. Le Fanu. Ed. by Devendra P. Varma. LC 76-5275. (Collected Works). 1977. reprint ed. 87.95 (0-405-09229-6) Ayer.

Rose & the Key, 3 vols, Vol. 2. Joseph S. Le Fanu. Ed. by Devendra P. Varma. LC 76-5275. (Collected Works). 1977. reprint ed. 29.95 (0-405-09231-8) Ayer.

Rose & the Key, 3 vols, Vol. 3. Joseph S. Le Fanu. Ed. by Devendra P. Varma. LC 76-5275. (Collected Works). 1977. reprint ed. 29.95 (0-405-09232-6) Ayer.

Rose & the Pickle. Adrienne Golday. LC 84-51030. (Illus.). 9.95 (0-930509-00-5) Wisdom Bk Pubs.

Rose & the Sword. Alice Gebhardt. 32p. (Orig.). 1989. pap. 5.00 (0-914598-90-2) Padre Prods.

Rose & the Yew Tree. large type ed. Mary Westmacott. 1978. 25.99 (0-7089-0180-8) Ulverscroft.

Rose & Twenty-Five Popular Classics. (Coates Big Note Arrangements Ser.). 112p. (Orig.). 1996. pap. 12.95 (0-89724-025-1, PF0873) Warner Brothers.

Rose & 29 Soft Rock Classics. Ed. by Carol Cuellar. 1994. pap. 14.95 (0-89724-227-0, VF1376) Astor Bks.

*Rose & 49 Top Professional Touch Hits. 2nd ed. Ed. by Carol Cuellar. 196p. (Orig.). (YA). 1997. reprint ed. pap. text ed. 16.95 (1-57623-980-2, PF0826A) Warner Brothers.

Rose & 50 Soft Rock Classics. Ed. by Carol Cuellar. 1994. pap. 16.95 (0-89724-229-7, VF2092) Astor Bks.

Rose at la Vie Revee. Peg Sutherland. (OR Ser.). (FRE.). 1994. pap. 4.50 (0-373-38163-8, 1-38163-1) Harlequin Bks.

Rose at Midnight. Anne Stuart. 400p. (Orig.). 1993. mass mkt. 4.50 (0-380-76740-6) Avon.

*Rose Beyond the Wall. Kristi Holl. (Illus.). (J). (gr. 7-10). 1997. reprint ed. pap. 6.99 (0-88092-425-X) Royal Fireworks.

Rose Bib Crisis, Vol. 1. 1975. text ed. 125.00 (0-8371-8011-2, RBCRR1, Greenwood Pr) Greenwood.

Rose Bib Crisis, Vol. 2. 1975. text ed. 125.00 (0-8371-8012-0, RBCRR2, Greenwood Pr) Greenwood.

Rose Bib Crisis, Vol. 3. 1975. text ed. 125.00 (0-8371-8013-9, RBCRR3, Greenwood Pr) Greenwood.

Rose Bible. Rayford C. Reddell. LC 92-40231. 1994. 50.00 (0-517-58821-8, Harmony) Crown Pub Group.

Rose Blanche. Roberto Innocenti. Ed. by Christophe Gallaz. LC 95-45378. (J). 1996. 17.00 (0-15-200918-3) HarBrace.

Rose Blanche. Roberto Innocenti. Ed. by Christophe Gallaz. LC 95-45378. (J). 1996. pap. 8.00 (0-15-200917-5) HarBrace.

Rose Blanche: Based on the Original Idea of Roberto Innocenti. Roberto Innocenti & Christophe Gallaz. Tr. by Martha Coventry from FRE. LC 85-70219. (Illus.). 32p. (J). (gr. 6 up). 1986. lib. bdg. 16.95 (0-87191-994-X) Creative Ed.

Rose, Blanche & Violet, 3 vols. in 2, Set. George H. Lewes. LC 79-8153. reprint ed. 84.50 (0-404-61975-4) AMS Pr.

Rose Bloom, Vol. 1. Alcott. 1996. 17.95 (0-316-03782-6) Little.

Rose Book: Cerithous. Michael T. Bucci & Cerithous. (Illus.). 116p. (Orig.). 1995. pap. 12.50 (0-9630824-1-8) M T Grp.

Rose, Both Red & White. large type ed. Betty King. 432p. 1995. 25.99 (0-7089-3377-7) Ulverscroft.

Rose Bowl. Paul Deegan. (Great Moments in Sports Ser.). (J). (gr. 5 up). 1992. lib. bdg. 14.95 (0-88682-534-2) Creative Ed.

Rose Bowl. large type ed. Judy Gardiner. 457p. 1994. 25.99 (0-7505-0597-4, Pub. by Magna Print Bks UK) Ulverscroft.

Rose Bowl, 1902-1929: Game-by-Game History of Collegiate Football's Foremost Event, from Its Advent Through Its Golden Era. John C. Hibner. LC 92-56650. (Illus.). 216p. 1993. lib. bdg. 35.00 (0-89950-775-1) McFarland & Co.

Rose by Another Name: A Survey of Literary Flora from Shakespeare to Eco. Robert F. Fleissner. LC 89-12804. (Locust Hill Literary Studies: No. 5). (Illus.). 164p. (C). 1989. lib. bdg. 24.00 (0-933951-33-7) Locust Hill Pr.

Rose by Any Other Name. David Zaslow. (Illus.). 96p. (Orig.). (J). 1980. pap. 4.95 (0-89411-002-0) Kids Matter.

*Rose Ceremony. Sivananda Radha. Ed. by David Forsee. (Illus.). 73p. (Orig.). (C). 1997. pap. 9.95 (0-931454-86-7) Timeless Bks.

Rose-Colored Glasses: Melanie Adjusts to Poor Vision. Linda R. Leggett & Linda G. Andrews. LC 79-12501. (Illus.). 32p. (J). (gr. 3 up). 1979. 16.95 (0-87705-408-8) Human Sci Pr.

Rose Cookbook: Featuring Pink Ribbon Recipes. Suzanne Laverdiere & Ibenthal. 256p. 1996. write for info. (0-9647648-0-6) The Rose.

*Rose Cottage. Mary Stewart. 1997. write for info. (0-688-15584-7) Morrow.

Rose Cottingham. Netta Syrett. LC 77-16345. 399p. 1978. reprint ed. pap. 9.00 (0-915864-19-3) Academy Chi Pubs.

Rose Cross & the Age of Reason: Eighteenth-Century Rosicrucianism in Central Europe & Its Relationship to the Enlightenment. Christopher McIntosh. LC 91-44752. (Brill's Studies in Intellectual History: Vol. 29). (Illus.). 200p. 1992. 77.00 (90-04-09502-0) E J Brill.

Rose Cross College: A Resume of the Teachings & Proceedings of the Rose Cross College During Its Session Held in the Month of October 1916. Ed. by R. Swinburne Clymer. 247p. 1970. reprint ed. spiral bd. 10.00 (0-7873-0184-1) Hlth Research.

Rose Cross College (1917) R. Swinburne Clymer. 216p. 1996. pap. 18.95 (1-56459-662-1) Kessinger Pub.

Rose Cross Order: A Short History of the Rose Cross Order in America (1916) R. Swinburne Clymer. 208p. 1996. pap. 18.95 (1-56459-664-8) Kessinger Pub.

Rose Cross Order: History Repeats Itself. R. Swinburne Clymer. 232p. 1970. reprint ed. spiral bd. 10.00 (0-7873-0180-9) Hlth Research.

Rose Crossing. Nicholas Jose. LC 96-3577. 288p. 1996. 22.95 (0-87951-673-9) Overlook Pr.

*Rose Crossing. Nicholas Jose. 280p. 1997. pap. 13.95 (0-87951-797-2) Overlook Pr.

Rose Culture: A Source Guide. 1991. lib. bdg. 75.00 (0-8490-4887-7) Gordon Pr.

*Rose Daughter. Robin McKinley. LC 96-48783. 320p. (YA). (gr. 5 up). 1997. 15.00 (0-688-15439-5) Greenwillow.

Rose de Java. Joseph Kessel. 224p. (FRE.). 1972. pap. 10.95 (0-7859-2273-3, 2070361748) Fr & Eur.

Rose des Vents: 32 Rhumbs pour Charles Fournier. Michel Butor. (Coll. Le Chemin). pap. 9.95 (0-685-37258-8) Fr & Eur.

Rose Driftwood. Adams. 1993. 20.00 (0-8212-2030-6) Bulfinch Pr.

Rose Elliot's Vegetarian Christmas: Over 150 Recipes for the Festive Season. Rose Elliot. (Illus.). 160p. 1995. pap. 12.00 (0-7225-2852-3, Pub. by HarperCollins UK) Harper SF.

*Rose Engagement. expanded ed. Richard E. Brown & Beverly A. Brown. 205p. (Orig.). (C). 1996. pap. text ed. 12.00 (0-9654000-2-6) Kent Info Srvcs.

*Rose Engagement. unabridged ed. Richard E. Brown & Beverly A. Brown. 203p. (Orig.). 1996. pap. 12.00 (0-9654000-1-8) Kent Info Srvcs.

Rose et le Rosaire. Paul Claudel. 272p. (FRE.). 1947. 10.95 (0-7859-1122-7, 2070215121) Fr & Eur.

Rose et le Vert, Mina de Vanghel, et Autres Nouvelles. Stendhal, pseud. (FRE.). 1982. pap. 16.95 (0-7859-2900-2) Fr & Eur.

Rose Expert. D. G. Hessayon. (Expert Ser.). (Illus.). 128p. (Orig.). 1995. pap. 12.95 (0-903505-25-8, Pub. by Expert Bks UK) Sterling.

*Rose Faces the Music. Nina Alexander. Ed. by Susan Korman. (Magic Attic Club Ser.). (Illus.). 72p. (J). (gr. 2 up). 1997. 12.95 (1-57513-108-0) Magic Attic.

Rose Faces the Music see Magic Attic Club Series

Rose for a Homely Hero. J. Leon McClaire. 120p. 1995. pap. 10.00 (0-8059-3772-2) Dorrance.

Rose for Abby. Donna Guthrie. LC 88-10577. (Illus.). (J). (gr. 2 up). 1988. 12.95 (0-687-36586-4) Abingdon.

Rose for Barbie. (J). 1996. 9.98 (1-57082-381-2) Mouse Works.

Rose for Barbie. Funworks Staff. (J). 1996. 9.98 (1-57082-334-0) Mouse Works.

*Rose for Emily. William Faulkner & Joseph Robinette. 35p. (J). (gr. 6-8). 1983. pap. 3.00 (0-87129-721-3, R33) Dramatic Pub.

Rose for Her Grave. Rule. 1996. mass mkt. 6.99 (0-671-53798-9) PB.

Rose for Her Grave & Other True Cases. Ann Rule. (Ann Rule's Crime Files Ser.: Vol. 1). 1993. mass mkt. 6.50 (0-671-79353-5) PB.

Rose for Lady Edwina. Melinda Pryce. 1990. mass mkt. 3.95 (1-55817-368-4, Pinncle Kensgtn) Kensgtn Pub Corp.

Rose for Maggie. Kathleen Korbel. 1996. mass mkt. 3.99 (0-373-60078-X, 1-60078-2) Harlequin Bks.

Rose for Maggie. Kathleen Korbel. (Intimate Moments Ser.: No. 396). 1991. mass mkt. 3.25 (0-373-07396-8) Silhouette.

Rose for Pinkerton. Steven Kellogg. LC 81-65848. (Pied Piper Bks.). (Illus.). 32p. (J). (ps-3). 1981. pap. 14.99 (0-8037-7502-4); lib. bdg. 12.89 (0-8037-7503-2) Dial Bks Young.

Rose for Pinkerton. Steven Kellogg. 1992. pap. 5.99 (0-14-054696-0) NAL-Dutton.

Rose for Tomorrow: Biography of Frederick C. Schreiber. Ed. by Jerome D. Schein. (Illus.). 148p. 1981. text ed. 10.00 (0-913072-46-X) Natl Assn Deaf.

Rose for Your Pocket. Thich Nhat Hanh. Tr. by Elin Sand from FRE. 14p. (Orig.). 1987. pap. 3.50 (0-938077-08-2) Parallax Pr.

Rose from Brier. Amy Carmichael. 1992. mass mkt. 6.95 (0-87508-077-4) Chr Lit.

Rose from My Garden: My Memories of Camille. Ilsa Hart. Ed. by Linda Hopkins. 98p. (Orig.). 1994. pap. text ed. write for info. (0-9631271-2-8) Hopkins Intl.

Rose Galbraith. large type ed. Grace L. Hill. LC 92-15079. 386p. 1992. reprint ed. lib. bdg. 20.95 (1-56054-367-1) Thorndike Pr.

Rose Galbraith, No. 22. Grace L. Hill. (Grace Livingston Hill Ser.: Vol. 22). 288p. 1995. pap. 4.99 (0-8423-5726-2) Tyndale.

*Rose Garden. (Garden Journal Ser.). 1998. 12.95 (1-56799-613-2, Friedman-Fairfax) M Friedman Pub Grp Inc.

*Rose Garden. Courage Books Staff. 1997. 6.98 (0-7624-0127-3) Courage Bks.

*Rose Garden. Nevit O. Ergin. 1997. pap. text ed. 9.95 (1-887991-04-2) Echo Pubns CA.

*Rose Garden. Kristjana Gunnars. 192p. 1996. pap. 9.95 (0-88995-150-0, Pub. by Red Deer CN) Orca Bk Pubs.

Rose Garden: Sadi. Tr. by Edward Eastwick. 1979. 25.00 (0-900860-65-0, Pub. by Octagon Pr UK) ISHK.

Rose Garden Memories. (Little Ribbons of Love Ser.). (Illus.). Date not set. 4.99 (1-57051-121-7) Brownlow Pub Co.

Rose Gardening. Traditional Home Staff. (Better Homes & Gardens Ser.). (Illus.). 224p. 1995. 29.95 (0-696-01981-7) Meredith Bks.

*Rose Gardening on the Prairies. George W. Shewchuk. 1992. pap. text ed. 15.95 (0-88864-140-0) Univ of Alberta Pr.

*Rose Gardens. Warren Schultz. LC 96-31567. (For Your Garden Ser.). 72p. 1996. pap. 12.95 (1-56799-398-2, Friedman-Fairfax) M Friedman Pub Grp Inc.

Rose Gardens of England. Michael Gibson. (Illus.). 160p. 1992. 34.95 (0-8464-1538-0) Beekman Pubs.

Rose Genealogy, Including Descendants of Israel Rose, Pioneer of Washington & Oregon, with Additions & Corrections. J. A. Nunamaker. (Illus.). 71p. 1993. reprint ed. pap. 16.00 (0-8328-3779-2); reprint ed. lib. bdg. 26.00 (0-8328-3778-4) Higginson Bk Co.

*Rose-Geranium. Eilean Chuilleanain. 44p. 8100. pap. 11.95 (0-904011-24-0) Dufour.

Rose Hawthrone Lathrop: Selected Writings. Rose H. Lathrop. LC 93-14622. (Sources of American Spirituality Ser.). 256p. 1993. 24.95 (0-8091-0463-6) Paulist Pr.

Rose Hills, a Place to Remember. Maureen R. Michelson. Ed. by Dessie L. Maze & Sandy V. Durko. LC 89-90901. 112p. 1989. 60.00 (0-9622358-1-4) Rose Hills Pubns.

Rose Hills, a Place to Remember. limited ed. Maureen R. Michelson. Ed. by Dessie L. Maze & Sandy V. Durko. LC 89-90901. 112p. 1989. Limited edition. 200.00 (0-9622358-0-6) Rose Hills Pubns.

Rose Horse. Deborah L. Rose. LC 94-19629. (Illus.). 80p. (J). (gr. 3-7). 1995. 16.00 (0-15-200068-2, HB Juv Bks) HarBrace.

*Rose I Am. Sharon Woodworth. 49p. 1997. pap. 8.00 (0-8059-4213-0) Dorrance.

Rose in Bloom. Louisa May Alcott. (Illus.). (J). (gr. 7 up). 1976. 19.95 (0-316-03098-8) Little.

Rose in Bloom. Louisa May Alcott. (Puffin Classics Ser.). 326p. (YA). (gr. 5 up). 1995. pap. 3.99 (0-14-037451-5) Puffin Bks.

Rose in Bloom. Louisa May Alcott. (Works of Louisa May Alcott). 1989. reprint ed. lib. bdg. 79.00 (0-7812-1634-6) Rprt Serv.

Rose in Bloom: A Sequel to Eight Cousins. Louisa May Alcott. LC 95-19929. 256p. (YA). (gr. 5 up). 1995. 8.95 (0-316-03089-9) Little.

Rose in My Garden. Arnold Lobel. LC 83-14097. (Illus.). 40p. (J). (gr. k-3). 1984. 16.00 (0-688-02586-2); lib. bdg. 15.93 (0-688-02587-0) Greenwillow.

Rose in My Garden. Arnold Lobel. LC 92-24588. (Illus.). 40p. (J). (ps up). 1993. reprint ed. pap. 4.95 (0-688-12265-5, Mulberry) Morrow.

*Rose in Splendor. 1987. 3.95 (0-446-73451-9) Warner Bks.

*Rose in Stained Glass. Nancy B. Burrell. 1997. mass mkt. 4.99 (1-55197-402-9, Pub. by Comnwlth Pub CN) Partners Pubs Grp.

Rose in the Heather. large type ed. Suzanne Ebel. 308p. 1980. 25.99 (0-7089-0510-2) Ulverscroft.

*Rose in Winter. Kathleen Woodiwiss. Date not set. write for info. (0-688-12501-8) Morrow.

Rose in Winter. Kathleen E. Woodiwiss. 576p. 1983. reprint ed. mass mkt. 6.99 (0-380-84400-1) Avon.

Rose Jar: The Autobiography of Edna Meudt. Edna Meudt. (Illus.). 352p. 1990. 17.50 (0-944133-07-X) Nrth Cntry Pr.

Rose Kennedy: The Best and Worst of Their Lives and Times. Barbara Gibson & Ted Schwarz. 352p. 1995. 22.50 (1-55972-299-1, Birch Ln Pr) Carol Pub Group.

Rose Kennedy see Library of Biography

*Rose Kennedy & Her Family: The Best & Worst of Their Lives & Times. Barbara Gibson & Ted Schwarz. 336p. 1997. mass mkt. 6.99 (0-8065-8010-0, Citadel Stars) Carol Pub Group.

Rose Kohn Goldsen Papers: A Descriptive Guide. Matthew N. Lyons. (Illus.). 32p. 1992. pap. text ed. write for info. (0-935995-02-1) Cornell Manu.

Rose Lover's Address Book. Helen Exley. (Mini Address Bks.). (Illus.). 64p. 1995. 7.50 (1-85015-539-9) Exley Giftbooks.

Rose Madder. Stephen King. 420p. 1995. pap. 25.95 (0-670-85869-2, Viking) Viking Penguin.

Rose Madder. Stephen King. 1996. mass mkt. 7.50 (0-451-18636-2, Sig) NAL-Dutton.

Rose Madder. Stephen King. 1996. mass mkt. 7.50 (0-451-18876-4, Sig) NAL-Dutton.

Rose Madder. large type ed. Stephen King. 1995. 27.95 (1-56895-261-9, Compass) Wheeler Pub.

Rose Manual. Robert Buist. LC 78-9704. 1978. reprint ed. text ed. 12.50 (0-930576-10-1) E M Coleman Ent.

Rose Marie Reid: An Extraordinary Life Story. Carole R. Burr & Roger K. Peterson. LC 95-15844. 1995. 15.95 (1-55503-810-7, 01111906) Covenant Comms.

Rose Meets Mr. Wintergarten. Bob Graham. LC 91-71824. (Illus.). 32p. (J). (ps up). 1992. 14.95 (1-56402-039-8) Candlewick Pr.

Rose Meets Mr. Wintergarten. Bob Graham. LC 91-71824. (Illus.). 32p. (J). (ps up). 1994. pap. 5.99 (1-56402-395-8) Candlewick Pr.

Rose Mellie Rose. Marie Redonnet. Tr. by Jordan Stump. LC 94-1313. (European Women Writers Ser.). vii, 123p. 1994. pap. 10.00 (0-8032-8952-9, Bison Books) U of Nebr Pr.

*Rose Mystique. Selma Hudson. Ed. by Patrick Caton. LC 97-71657. 168p. 1997. pap. 5.95 (1-56245-302-5) Great Quotations.

Rose of Blacksword. Rexanne Becnel. 448p. 1992. mass mkt. 5.99 (0-440-20910-2) Dell.

Rose of Consciousness. Lois P. Seeley. LC 94-92324. (Illus.). 89p. 1994. 10.00 (0-9643385-0-5) L P Seeley.

Rose of Dutcher's Coolly. Hamlin Garland. LC 74-90103. reprint ed. 27.50 (0-404-02685-0) AMS Pr.

Rose of Dutcher's Coolly. Hamlin Garland. Ed. by Donald Pizer. LC 79-82509. (Bison Book Ser.). 438p. reprint ed. pap. 124.90 (0-7837-1898-5, 2042102) Bks Demand.

Rose of Dutcher's Cooly. Hamlin Garland. (Collected Works of Hamlin Garland). 1988. reprint ed. lib. bdg. 59.00 (0-7812-1223-5) Rprt Serv.

An Asterisk (*) at the beginning of an entry indicates that the title is appearing in BIP for the first time.

R

Rose of Dutcher's Cooly see Collected Works of Hamlin Garland

***Rose of Five Petals: A Path for the Christian Mystic.** Betsy Serafin. LC 97-3915. 192p. (Orig.). 1997. pap. 12.95 (0-8245-1650-8) Crossroad NY.

Rose of Jericho. large type ed. Rosemary Friedman. 1990. 25.99 (0-7089-2207-4) Ulverscroft.

Rose of Jericho, & Other Stories. Tage Aurell. Tr. by Martin S. Allwood & Kathrine Aurell from SWE. LC 68-14036. (Nordic Translation Ser.). 151p. 1968. reprint ed. pap. 43.10 (0-608-01928-3, 2062583) Bks Demand.

Rose of Mother-of-Pearl. Grozdana Olujic. Tr. by Jascha Kessler. LC 83-18254. (Illus.). 19p. (Orig.). (CRO & SER.). (J). (gr. 4 up). 1983. pap. 6.00 (0-915124-90-4, Toothpaste) Coffee Hse.

Rose of Old Virginia: A Romance of the Old South & the War Between the States. Charles E. Clarkson. 59p. 1927. 6.00 (0-937130-11-7) Burkes Bk Store.

Rose of Prophet, No. 2. Margaret Weis. 384p. 1989. mass mkt. 6.50 (0-553-27902-5, Spectra) Bantam.

Rose of Prophet, No. 3. Margaret Weis. 416p. 1989. mass mkt. 5.99 (0-553-28143-7, Spectra) Bantam.

Rose of Rapture. Rebecca. 1984. pap. 6.95 (0-446-37613-2) Warner Bks.

Rose of Ravenscrag. Patricia Phillips. 368p. (Orig.). 1996. mass mkt., pap. text ed. 4.99 (0-8439-3905-2) Dorchester Pub Co.

***Rose of Sonora.** Rosetta M. Moore & Carol L. Rochette. 306p. (Orig.). 1997. mass mkt. 4.99 (1-55197-668-4, Pub. by Comnwlth Pub CN) Partners Pubs Grp.

***Rose of the World.** Daniil Andreev et al. (Esalen-Lindisfarne Library of Russian Philosophy). 320p. (Orig.). 1997. pap. 19.95 (0-940262-83-5, 2040) Lindisfarne Bks.

Rose of Thorns. Deborah L. Reeves. 393p. (Orig.). 1996. pap. 6.99 (0-9652862-0-7) Weikel Publishing.

Rose of Tibet. Lionel Davidson. 1996. mass mkt. 6.50 (0-312-95833-1) Tor Bks.

Rose of Yesterday. Francis M. Crawford. (Works of Francis Marion Crawford Ser.). 1990. reprint ed. lib. bdg. 79.00 (0-7812-2548-5) Rprt Serv.

Rose Oil. Julia Lawless. 1996. pap. 7.00 (0-7225-3173-7) Harper SF.

Rose O'Neal Greenhow & the Blockade Runners. George Johnson, Jr. (Illus.). 128p. 1996. 25.00 (0-9649826-0-9) G Johnson.

Rose O'Neill: The Collector's & Dealer's Price & Identification Guide. 3rd rev. ed. Denis C. Jackson. (Illus.). 52p. (Orig.). 1997. pap. 7.95 (1-888687-04-5) Illust Collectors.

Rose Penski. Roz Perry. 192p. 1989. pap. 8.95 (0-941483-37-1) Naiad Pr.

Rose Petals. (Little Treasures Ser.). (Illus.). 96p. 1996. 4.99 (1-57051-123-3) Brownlow Pub Co.

Rose Pour Morrison. Christiane Rochefort. 1966. 18.95 (0-686-55230-X) Fr & Eur.

***Rose Program: Beyond the Business Basics.** Gerri P. Norington. (Illus.). 1998. boxed 25.00 (1-890499-04-8, KMN) Womens Busn Trning.

***Rose Program Instructor's Manual: Beyond the Business Basics.** Gerri P. Norington. Ed. by Jane Onstott. (Illus.). 1998. teacher ed. 24.95 (1-890499-01-3, KMN) Womens Busn Trning.

***Rose Program Visual Aids: Beyond the Business Basics.** Gerri P. Norington. Ed. by Karen Hurst-Warren. (Illus.). 200p. 1998. teacher ed. 125.00 (1-890499-03-X, KMN) Womens Busn Trning.

***Rose Program Workbook: Beyond the Business Basics.** Gerri P. Norington. Ed. by Jane Onstott. (Illus.). 1998. wbk. ed. 19.95 (1-890499-02-1, KMN) Womens Busn Trning.

Rose Quilts: The Portable Wrap-Around Method. Betty Cossey & Lucille Harrington. LC 93-21684. (Illus.). 1994. pap. 24.95 (1-884209-99-8) Small Change.

***Rose Rabbi.** Daniel Stern. LC 97-17835. (Library of Modern Jewish Literature). 140p. 1997. pap. 14.95 (0-8156-0512-9) Syracuse U Pr.

Rose Recipes from Olden Times. Eleanor S. Rohde. (Illus.). 95p. 1973. reprint ed. pap. 2.95 (0-486-22957-2) Dover.

Rose Red. Flora M. Speer. 400p. (Orig.). 1996. mass mkt. 5.99 (0-505-52139-3, Love Spell) Dorchester Pub Co.

Rose Red & Snow White: A Grimms Fairy Tale. Illus. & Retold by Ruth Sanderson. LC 95-14518. 1997. 15.95 (0-316-77094-9) Bulfinch Pr.

Rose Reisman Brings Home Light Pasta. Rose Reisman. (Illus.). 256p. 1995. 27.95 (1-896503-06-3); pap. 16.95 (1-896503-04-7) Firefly Bks Ltd.

Rose Reisman's Enlighted Home Cooking. Rose Reisman. (Illus.). 256p. (Orig.). 1996. pap. 18.95 (1-896503-16-0, Pub. by R Rose CN) Firefly Bks Ltd.

Rose Remembered. Michael Phillips. LC 94-4351. (Secret of the Rose Ser.: Vol. 2). 576p. 1994. pap. 11.99 (0-8423-5929-X) Tyndale.

Rose Rent. Ellis Peters. 1988. mass mkt. 4.95 (0-449-21495-8, Crest) Fawcett.

***Rose Rent.** Ellis Peters. 240p. 1997. mass mkt. 5.99 (0-446-40533-7, Mysterious Paperbk) Warner Bks.

Rose Revived. Forde. 352p. 1996. 23.95 (0-312-14040-1) St Martin.

***Rose Revived.** large type ed. Katie Fforde. (Ulverscroft Large Print Ser.). 688p. 1997. 27.50 (0-7089-3644-X) Ulverscroft.

Rose, Rose, Where Are You? large type ed. R. Ellerbeck. 1981. 25.99 (0-7089-0596-X) Ulverscroft.

Rose Round. Meriol Trevor. LC 95-78062. (Young Adult Bookshelf Ser.). 211p. (YA). (gr. 6-12). 1995. reprint ed. pap. 11.95 (1-883937-09-4, 09-4) Bethlehem ND.

Rose Scott: Vision & Revision in Feminism 1880-1925. Judith Allen. (Illus.). 306p. 1994. 55.00 (0-19-554846-9) OUP.

Rose Sea. S. M. Stirling & Holly Lisle. 384p. (Orig.). 1994. mass mkt. 5.99 (0-671-87620-1) Baen Bks.

Rose Tattoo. Tennessee Williams. 1951. pap. 5.25 (0-8222-0971-3) Dramatists Play.

Rose Tattoo see Three by Tennessee Williams

Rose Tattoo see Best American Plays: Fourth Series, 1952-1957

Rose Terry Cooke: Am Anthology in Memoriam (1827-1892) Ed. by M. A. Myers. LC 92-82713. 202p. (Orig.). 1992. pap. text ed. 24.95 (1-879183-17-X) Bristol Banner.

Rose That Refused to Bloom. Veronica F. DiPippo & Dan Levy. 19p. (Orig.). (J). (gr. k-5). 1993. pap. 3.50 (1-57514-158-2, 0037) Encore Perform Pub.

Rose Theatre. Christine Eccles. 288p. (C). 1991. pap. 15.95 (0-87830-107-0, Thtre Arts Bks) Routledge.

Rose Theatre. Gilbert Sorrentino. LC 87-71643. 160p. 1987. 20.00 (0-916583-23-6) Dalkey Arch.

Rose to Remember. Michael Phillips. (Secret of the Rose Ser.). 1995. 16.99 (0-8423-5960-5) Tyndale.

Rose Township Cemeteries, Oakland County, Michigan. Ed. by Joan Pate. 72p. 1987. pap. 5.00 (1-879766-09-4) OCG Society.

Rose Township Eighteen Thirty-Seven - Nineteen Eighty-Seven. Rose Township Historical Society Staff. LC 86-63912. (Illus.). 141p. 1987. 15.00 (0-9617648-0-5) Rose Twsp Hist Soc.

Rose Tree. write for info. (0-318-63153-9) Viking Penguin.

Rose Tree. John Broderick. (Fiction Ser.). 192p. 1985. 14.95 (0-7145-2824-2) M Boyars Pubs.

***Rose Virginie Pelletier: The Woman & Her Legacy.** Jane T. McVeigh. LC 96-53027. 232p. 1997. text ed. 39.50 (0-7618-0690-3) U Pr of Amer.

Rose War Files, Vol. I: Abstracts of Rose Land Bounty Records. Christine Rose. 210p. 1987. pap. 13.50 (0-929626-00-1) Rose Family Assn.

Rose, Where Did You Get That Red: Teaching Great Poetry to Children. Kenneth Koch. LC 73-17480. 355p. 1990. pap. 12.00 (0-679-72471-0, Vin) Random.

Rose Will Grow Anywhere: Renewing Your Confidence that God Works All Things Together for Good. David A. Redding. LC 95-23221. 208p. 1996. pap. 9.99 (0-8054-5392-X, 4253-92) Broadman.

Rose Window. large type ed. Lizanne Carlyle. 256p. 1992. pap. 15.99 (0-7089-7140-7, Trailtree Bookshop) Ulverscroft.

***Rose Window & Other Verses from New Poems: An Illustrated Selection.** Rainer M. Rilke. (Illus.). 1997. 22.95 (0-8212-2364-X) Bulfinch Pr.

Rose Without a Thorn. large type ed. Jean Plaidy. 1994. 23.95 (1-56895-161-2) Wheeler Pub.

Rose, 1989. Robert Mapplethorpe. 1992. 30.00 (0-8212-1945-6) Bulfinch Pr.

Roseanna. Roscoe Howells. 285p. (C). 1991. 40.00 (0-86383-774-3, Pub. by Gomer Pr UK) St Mut.

Roseanna. Maj Sjowall & Per Wahloo. Tr. by Lois Roth from SWE. LC 92-50692. (Vintage Crime - Black Lizard Ser.). 1993. pap. 10.00 (0-679-74598-X, Vin) Random.

Roseanne. Roseanne Barr. 1990. pap. 5.95 (0-00-003853-9, Harp PBks) HarpC.

***Roseanne.** Ann Gaines. (Overcoming Adversity Ser.). (YA). (gr. 7 up). 1997. lib. bdg. 19.95 (0-7910-4706-7) Chelsea Hse.

***Roseanne.** Ann Gaines. (Overcoming Adversity Ser.). (YA). (gr. 7 up). 1997. pap. 8.95 (0-7910-4707-5) Chelsea Hse.

Roseanne. Robert Italia. Ed. by Rosemary Wallner. LC 91-73035. (Reaching for the Stars Ser.). (J). 1991. lib. bdg. 13.98 (1-56239-058-9) Abdo & Dghtrs.

Roseanne: My Life As a Woman. Roseanne Barr. 256p. 1990. mass mkt. 5.99 (0-06-109903-1, PL) HarpC.

Roseanne Arnold: Comedy's Queen Bee. Katherine E. Krohn. LC 92-42653. (Achievers Ser.). (J). (gr. 4-9). 1993. lib. bdg. 17.50 (0-8225-0520-7, Lerner Publctns) Lerner Group.

Roseanne Arnold: Comedy's Queen Bee. Katherine E. Krohn. (J). (gr. 4-9). 1993. pap. 4.95 (0-8225-9644-X, Lerner Publctns) Lerner Group.

Roseate Spoonbill. Robert P. Allen. (Illus.). 1990. 7.50 (0-8446-1528-5) Peter Smith.

***Rosebeth Moss Kanter on the Frontiers of Management.** Harvard Business School Press Staff. 1997. text ed. 29.95 (0-07-105053-1) McGraw.

Rosebloom. Harvey Perr. 1972. pap. 5.25 (0-8222-0969-1) Dramatists Play.

Rosebud. Faye Adams. Ed. by Linda Marrow. 320p. (Orig.). 1994. mass mkt. 5.50 (0-671-88298-8) PB.

Rosebud. Jenny Holzer et al. (Illus.). 102p. 25.00 (90-72893-15-8) Dist Art Pubs.

Rosebud. David Thomson. 1997. pap. 15.00 (0-679-77283-9) McKay.

Rosebud. Debbie Woolard. (Illus.). 20p. (J). 1997. pap. 6.95 (1-57532-056-8) Press-Tige Pub.

Rosebud. deluxe ed. Gerard Malanga. (Illus.). 40p. 1975. 25.00 (0-915778-15-7) Penmaen Pr.

Rosebud. large type ed. Joan Hemingway & Paul Bonnecarrere. 433p. 1981. 25.99 (0-7089-0725-3) Ulverscroft.

Rosebud: The Story of Orson Welles. David Thomson. 463p. 1996. 30.00 (0-614-95706-0) Knopf.

Rosebud: The Story of Orson Wells. David Thomson. LC 95-44216. 448p. 1996. 30.00 (0-679-41834-2) Knopf.

Rosebud Bursts. Randy Brooks. 40p. 1979. pap. 3.50 (0-913719-67-6) High-Coo Pr.

Rosebud I Remember. Jacob Verduin. LC 93-92784. (Illus.). 176p. 15.95 (1-56002-373-2, Univ Edtns) Aegina Pr.

Rosebud Reader. 1995. mass mkt. 5.95 (1-56333-319-8, Rosebud) Masquerade.

Rosebud Sutra. Valentina Cilescu. (Orig.). 1994. mass mkt. 4.95 (1-56333-242-6, Rosebud) Masquerade.

***Rosebud, with Fangs.** Beverly Keller. (J). Date not set. pap. write for info. (0-688-15493-X, Beech Tree Bks) Morrow.

Rosebush Witch. Vivian W. Owens. LC 96-83179. (Illus.). 112p. (Orig.). (J). (gr. 3-9). 1996. pap. 8.95 (0-9623839-4-5) Eschar Pubns.

Rosedale: The Eighteenth-Century Country Estate of General Uriah Forrest Cleveland Park, Washington, D. C. LC 89-60733. (Illus.). 95p. (C). 1989. 10.95 (0-9623591-0-6) L Mann-Kenney.

Rosedale Hoax. Rachel Wyatt. (Anansi Fiction Ser.: No. 37). 136p. (Orig.). 1977. pap. 8.95 (0-88784-061-2, Pub. by Hse of Anansi Pr CN) Genl Dist Srvs.

Rosegger's Religion. Henry C. Sorg. LC 78-140029. (Catholic University Studies in German: No. 11). 1970. reprint ed. 37.50 (0-404-50231-8) AMS Pr.

Rosehaven. Catherine Coulter. LC 96-6494. 384p. 1996. 21.95 (0-399-14143-X, Putnam) Putnam Pub Group.

Rosehaven. Lila Peiffer. LC 93-43512. 1994. 10.99 (0-7852-8227-0) Nelson.

***Rosehaven.** large type ed. Catherine Coulter. LC 96-49134. (Large Print Bks.). 1997. 26.95 (1-56895-405-0) Wheeler Pub.

***Rosehaven.** Catherine Coulter. 384p. 1997. reprint ed. mass mkt. 6.99 (0-515-12088-X) Jove Pubns.

Roseland Park Cemetery (Military Sections) Ed. by Joan Pate. 59p. (Orig.). 1993. pap. text ed. 5.00 (1-879766-19-1) OCG Society.

Roseland Peabody. (Ballroom Dance Ser.). 1985. lib. bdg. 250.00 (0-87700-771-3) Revisionist Pr.

Rosellen Brown Reader: Selected Poetry & Prose. Rosellen Brown. LC 91-50808. (Bread Loaf Series of Contemporary Writers). 309p. 1992. pap. 18.95 (0-87451-645-5) U Pr of New Eng.

***Rosellini: Immigrants' Son & Progressive Governor.** Payton Smith. (Illus.). 288p. 1997. 24.95 (0-295-97595-4) U of Wash Pr.

Roselynde. Roberta Gellis. (Roselynde Chronicles Ser.). 512p. 1994. reprint ed. mass mkt., pap. text ed. 5.99 (0-8439-3559-6) Dorchester Pub Co.

Rosemaling: Design Collection, No. II. Helen E. Blanck. (Illus.). 27p. 1991. pap. 12.95 (0-941016-67-6) Penfield.

Rosemarie Parse: Health As Human Becoming. Sheila Bunting. LC 92-49481. (Notes on Nursing Theories Ser.: Vol. 5). (Illus.). 60p. (C). 1992. 21.50 (0-8039-4795-X); pap. 9.50 (0-8039-4549-3) Sage.

Rosemarie Trockel. (Illus.). 126p. 1992. 50.00 (3-909158-63-3, Pub. by Wiese Verlag SZ) Dist Art Pubs.

Rosemarie Trockel. Ed. by Sidra Stich et al. (Illus.). 144p. 1995. 50.00 (3-7913-1144-1, Pub. by Prestel GW) te Neues.

***Rosemarie Trockel: Herde, Catalogue Raisonnee.** Mario Diacono & Wilfred Dickhoff. (Illus.). 88p. (C). 1997. 70.00 (3-932189-00-0) Dist Art Pubs.

Rosemary. Jedediah V. Huntington. (Notable American Authors Ser.). 1992. reprint ed. lib. bdg. 75.00 (0-7812-3294-5) Rprt Serv.

***Rosemary: A Book of Recipes.** (Illus.). 64p. 1997. 12.95 (1-85967-489-5, Lorenz Bks) Anness Pub.

Rosemary Cottage. large type ed. Pat Lacey. 1990. pap. 15.99 (0-7089-6930-5) Ulverscroft.

***Rosemary for Remembrance: A Novel.** Yvonne West. 192p. 1997. 19.95 (1-56474-202-4) Fithian Pr.

***Rosemary Haughton: Witness to Hope.** Eilish Ryan. LC 97-20332. 1997. write for info. (1-55612-860-6) Sheed & Ward MO.

Rosemary Lane. J. D. Hall & Leslie Brandt. (Orig.). 1993. mass mkt. 4.95 (1-56333-078-4) Masquerade.

***Rosemary Oil.** Lawless. 1997. pap. 7.00 (0-7225-3349-7) Thorsons SF.

Rosemary Remembered. Susan W. Albert. LC 95-15062. 304p. 1995. text ed. 19.95 (0-425-14937-4, Prime Crime) Berkley Pub.

Rosemary Remembered. Susan W. Albert. 1996. mass mkt. 5.99 (0-425-15405-X) Berkley Pub.

Rosemary Tree. Elizabeth Goudge. 381p. 1979. reprint ed. lib. bdg. 16.95 (0-89966-107-6) Buccaneer Bks.

Rosemary Verey's English Country Gardens. Rosemary Verey. (Illus.). 192p. 1996. 36.00 (0-8050-5080-9) H Holt & Co.

Rosemary Verey's Garden Diary. Rosemary Verey. 1992. 14.95 (0-316-89979-8) Little.

Rosemary Verey's Good Planting Plans. Rosemary Verey. 1993. 40.00 (0-316-89982-8) Little.

Rosemary Verey's Making of a Garden. Rosemary Verey. (Illus.). 192p. 1995. 45.00 (0-8050-3956-2) H Holt & Co.

Rosemary Verey's Making of a Garden. Rosemary Verey. 1995. 45.00 (0-614-15491-X) H Holt & Co.

Rosemary's Baby. Ira Levin. 1991. lib. bdg. 21.95 (1-56849-065-8) Buccaneer Bks.

***Rosemary's Baby.** Ira Levin. 1997. mass mkt. 6.99 (0-451-19400-4, Sig) NAL-Dutton.

***Rosemary's Purgatory.** Rosemary Kaminski. Ed. by Frank Beaumont. (Orig.). 1997. pap. 5.00 (0-9659029-1-9, 627) Cavalier Comns.

Rosemonde E. & Emile Kuntz Collection: A Catalogue of the Manuscripts & Printed Ephemera. Ed. by Guillermo Nanez-Falcon. LC 81-13168. 1981. pap. 20.00 (0-9603212-3-3) Tulane Univ.

Rosemont: The History & Archaeology of Post-1880 Sites in the Rosemont Area, Santa Rita Mountains, Arizona see ANAMAX-Rosemont Project

Rosemoore. Arthur Canaugh. 384p. 1989. mass mkt. 4.95 (0-380-70484-6) Avon.

Rosen: Sexuality TBA. Rosen. 1986. write for info. (0-07-556315-0) McGraw.

Rosen by Any Other Name. Israel Horovitz. 1987. pap. 5.25 (0-8222-0970-5) Dramatists Play.

Rosen Method of Movement. Marion Rosen & Susan Brenner. LC 91-35742. 97p. (Orig.). 1991. pap. 12.95 (1-55643-117-1) North Atlantic.

Rosen Photo Guide to a Career in Magic. Randall Williams. (Careers in Depth Ser.). (Illus.). (YA). (gr. 7-12). 1988. lib. bdg. 12.95 (0-8239-0817-8) Rosen Group.

Rosen Photo Guide to a Career in the Circus. Cynthia Laslo. (Illus.). (YA). (gr. 7-12). 1988. lib. bdg. 12.95 (0-8239-0819-4) Rosen Group.

Rosenbach Abroad: In Pursuit of Books in Private Collections. Leslie A. Morris. (Illus.). 64p. 1988. pap. 12.50 (0-939084-22-8) R Mus & Lib.

Rosenbach Redux: Further Book Adventures in England & Ireland. Leslie A. Morris. (Illus.). 111p. 1989. pap. 15.00 (0-939084-25-2) R Mus & Lib.

***Rosenberg File.** 2nd ed. Ronald Radosh & Joyce Milton. 1997. pap. 18.00 (0-300-07205-8) Yale U Pr.

Rosenberg Letters: A Complete Edition of the Prison Correspondence of Julius & Ethel Rosenberg. Ed. by Michael Meeropol. LC 93-40860. 792p. 1994. text ed. 35.00 (0-8240-5948-4, H1184) Garland.

Rosencrantz & Guildenstern Are Dead. Tom Stoppard. LC 67-30108. 126p. 1988. pap. 8.95 (0-8021-3275-8, Grove) Grove-Atltic.

Rosendorf Quartet: A Novel. Nathan Shaham. LC 91-6482. 357p. 1993. pap. 12.00 (0-8021-3316-9, Grove) Grove-Atltic.

Rosenkavalier. Richard Strauss. Ed. by Nicholas John. (English National Opera Guide Series: No. 8). (Illus.). (Orig.). 1982. pap. 9.95 (0-7145-4268-7) Riverrun NY.

Rosenkrans: Family in Europe & America. A. Rosenkrans. (Illus.). 333p. 1990. reprint ed. pap. 52.50 (0-8328-1621-3); reprint ed. lib. bdg. 60.50 (0-8328-1620-5) Higginson Bk Co.

Rosenol, 2 vols. in 1. Joseph F. Von Hammer-Purgstall. (Volkskundliche Quellen Ser.: No. III). xxxii, 659p. 1971. reprint ed. write for info. (3-487-04023-9) G Olms Pubs.

***Rosen's Management of Labor: Physician's Judgment & Patient Care.** 2nd ed. Ralph W. Hale & Mortimer G. Rosen. LC 97-3650. 1997. write for info. (0-412-13811-5) Chapman & Hall.

Rosenstock-Huessy Papers, Vol. 1. Eugen Rosenstock-Huessy. 1981. pap. 25.00 (0-912148-15-2) Argo Bks.

***Rosenthal Collection of Printed Books with Manuscript Annotations: A Catalog of 242 Editions Mostly Before 1600 Annotated by Contemporary or Near-Contemporary Readers.** Bernard M. Rosenthal. Ed. by Robert G. Babcock. (Illus.). 392p. 1997. 50.00 (0-8457-3131-9) Yale U Lib.

Rosenwald & Rosenbach: Two Philadelphia Bookmen. Seymour Adelman. (Illus.). 40p. 1983. pap. 10.00 (0-939084-15-5, U Pr of Va) R Mus & Lib.

Rosepath Motif: An Approach to Weaving Design. Margaret B. Windeknecht. LC 87-90542. (Illus.). 64p. (Orig.). 1987. pap. 9.95 (0-9618797-0-X) T G Windeknecht.

Roses. LC 95-43904. (Eyewitness Handbks.). (Illus.). 160p. 1996. pap. 17.95 (0-7894-0607-1) DK Pub Inc.

***Roses.** (Derek Fell's Handy Garden Guides Ser.). (Illus.). 192p. 1996. pap. 12.95 (1-56799-375-3, Friedman-Fairfax) M Friedman Pub Grp Inc.

Roses. Suzanne F. Bales. LC 92-43069. (Burpee American Gardening Ser.). (Illus.). 1994. pap. 9.00 (0-671-85044-X) P-H.

Roses. Otto Bunemann. 160p. 1994. pap. 13.95 (0-8120-1818-4) Barron.

Roses. Derek Fell. (American Garden Association's Garden Guides Ser.). (Illus.). 192p. 1993. 9.98 (0-8317-6938-6) Smithmark.

Roses. Ed. by Wolfgang Hageney. (Express Art Ser.). (Illus.). 96p. (Orig.). 1993. pap. 11.95 (88-7070-174-3) Belvedere USA.

Roses. Halina Heitz. (Mini Fact Finders Ser.). 64p. 1991. pap. 4.95 (0-8120-4450-9) Barron.

Roses. Peter Murray. LC 95-1747. (Nature Bks.). (Illus.). 32p. (J). (gr. 2-6). 1995. lib. bdg. 22.79 (1-56766-192-0) Childs World.

Roses. Roger Phillips & Martyn E. Rix. LC 87-43216. (Illus.). 224p. 1988. pap. 27.50 (0-394-75867-6) Random.

Roses. John F. Prevost. (J). 1996. lib. bdg. 13.98 (1-56239-610-2) Abdo & Dghtrs.

Roses. Ellis Rawnsley. (Illus.). 48p. 1984. 20.00 (0-88014-070-4) Mosaic Pr OH.

Roses. David Squire. (Illus.). 112p. 1995. write for info. (1-57215-028-9) World Pubns.

Roses. David S. Stump. (Plants & Gardens Ser.). (Illus.). 1990. per., pap. 7.95 (0-945352-13-1) Bklyn Botanic.

Roses. Time-Life Books Editors. Ed. by Janet Cave. LC 95-40912. (Complete Gardener Ser.). (Illus.). 160p. 1996. write for info. (0-7835-4109-0) Time-Life.

Roses. rev. ed. Gertrude Jekyll & Edward Mawley. LC 82-16337. (Jekyll Garden Bks.). Orig. Title: Roses for English Gardens. (Illus.). 301p. 1983. reprint ed. 25.95 (0-88143-001-3) Ayer.

Roses. rev. ed. Gertrude Jekyll & Edward Mawley. LC 82-16337. (Jekyll Garden Bks.). Orig. Title: Roses for English Gardens. (Illus.). 301p. 1984. reprint ed. pap. 10.95 (0-88143-057-9) Ayer.

Roses: A Celebration in Words & Paintings. Helen Exley. (Words & Paintings Ser.). (Illus.). 60p. 1993. 8.00 (1-85015-283-7) Exley Giftbooks.

Roses: A Kew Gardening Guide. David Welch. (Illus.). 124p. 1992. 19.95 (0-88192-219-6) Timber.

Roses: Four One-Act Plays. Hermann Sudermann. Tr. by Grace Frank. LC 79-50031. (One-Act Plays in Reprint Ser.). (GER.). 1979. reprint ed. 20.00 (0-8486-2055-0) Roth Pub Inc.

An Asterisk (*) at the beginning of an entry indicates that the title is appearing in BIP for the first time.

Roses: From Dreams to Reality. Herb Swim. Ed. by Lorraine A. Stump. (Illus.). 188p. 1988. 26.95 (*0-937594-14-8*) Stump Pub.

Roses: Inspirations for Natural Gifts, Country Crafts & Decorative Displays. Gilly Love. 128p. 1996. 19.95 (*1-85967-211-6*, Lorenz Bks) Anness Pub.

***Roses: 20 Practical Inspirations.** Joanne Rippin. (Design Motifs Ser.). (Illus.). 64p. 1997. 9.95 (*1-85967-345-7*, Lorenz Bks) Anness Pub.

***Roses after Rain.** Cassie Edwards. 448p. 1997. mass mkt. 5.50 (*0-505-52219-5*, Love Spell) Dorchester Pub Co.

Roses After Rain. Deirdre Purcell. 1996. pap. 5.99 (*0-451-18630-3*, Sig) NAL-Dutton.

Roses & Floral Bouquets. Lola Ades. (How to Draw & Paint Ser.). (Illus.). 32p. (Orig.). 1989. pap. 6.95 (*0-929261-88-7*, HT214) W Foster Pub.

Roses & How to Paint Them. D. M. Campana. (Illus.). 9.95 (*0-939608-40-5*) Campana Art.

***Roses & Other Flower Designs.** Lindsay P. Butterfield. LC 96-36599. (Illus.). 48p. 1996. pap. 5.95 (*0-486-29417-X*) Dover.

Roses & Other Flowers. Lola Ades. (How to Draw & Paint Ser.). (Illus.). 32p. (Orig.). 1989. pap. 6.95 (*0-929261-19-4*, HT130) W Foster Pub.

Roses & Thorns: A Synopsis of Life Between Two Worlds. Aneeta B. Chakrabarty. 297p. (Orig.). 1993. pap. 9.99 (*0-9637198-0-7*) Chakra Pubns.

Roses & Thorns: Poetry & Prose. Phyllis R. Beaumonte. LC 93-74871. (Illus.). 67p. (Orig.). 1994. pap. text ed. 8.95 (*0-9640059-0-5*) P R Beaumonte.

Roses & Thorns: The Second Blooming of the Hundred Flowers in Chinese Fiction, 1979-80. Perry Link. LC 83-9147. (Illus.). 300p. (C). 1984. pap. 15.00 (*0-520-04980-2*) U CA Pr.

Roses Are Dead: Divorce Means Never Having to Say I Love You. Joyce McWilliams. (Illus.). 110p. (Orig.). 1991. pap. 6.95 (*0-9630605-0-3*) PrimRose CA.

Roses are Difficult Here. W. O. Mitchell. 304p. 1991. mass mkt. 7.50 (*0-7704-2523-2*) Bantam.

Roses Are Pink, Your Feet Really Stink. Diane DeGroat. LC 94-43774. (Illus.). (J). 1996. lib. bdg. 14.93 (*0-688-13605-2*, Morrow Junior) Morrow.

Roses Are Pink, Your Feet Really Stink. Diane DeGroat. LC 94-43774. (Illus.). (J). (gr. k up). 1996. 15.00 (*0-688-13604-4*, Morrow Junior) Morrow.

***Roses Are Pink, Your Feet Really Stink.** Diane Degroat. 1997. pap. 4.95 (*0-688-15220-1*, Mulberry) Morrow.

Roses Are Red - & White. Jack Witt. LC 96-13563. 1996. 20.00 (*1-883911-08-7*) Brandylane.

Roses Are Red, Violets Are Blue, My Cat's in Heat & I'm Thinking of You. Ruth Hayes. (Illus.). (Orig.). 1990. pap. 4.95 (*0-941104-48-6*) Real Comet.

Roses at Dawn. Laura Jordan. (Lucky in Love Ser.: No. 13). 320p. 1992. mass mkt. 3.99 (*0-8217-4011-3*, Zebra Kensgtn) Kensgtn Pub Corp.

***Roses at Midnight.** Alexa Smart. 320p. 1997. mass mkt. 5.50 (*0-7860-0432-0*, Pinncle Kensgtn) Kensgtn Pub Corp.

Roses Charted Designs. Ed. by Lindberg Press Staff. (Illus.). 32p. (Orig.). 1987. pap. 3.50 (*0-486-25523-9*) Dover.

Rose's Christmas Cookies. Rose L. Beranbaum. LC 90-6505. (Illus.). 118p. 1990. 25.00 (*0-688-10136-4*) Morrow.

Roses de Septembre. Andre Maurois. 123.50 (*0-685-36968-4*) Fr & Eur.

***Roses for Christmas.** 1997. mass mkt. 3.99 (*0-373-83340-7*) Harlequin Bks.

***Roses for Dummies.** Lance Walheim. (Illus.). 384p. 1997. pap. 16.99 (*0-7645-5031-4*) IDG Bks.

Roses for English Gardens. Gertrude Jekyll. 1994. 29.50 (*1-85149-214-3*) Antique Collect.

Roses for English Gardens see Roses

***Roses for Gita.** Rachna Gilmore. 24p. (J). (ps-3). 1996. mass mkt. 5.95 (*0-929005-85-6*, Pub. by Second Story Pr CN) LPC InBook.

***Roses for Gita.** Rachna Gilmore. (Illus.). 24p. (J). (ps-3). 1996. 12.95 (*0-929005-86-4*, Pub. by Second Story Pr CN) LPC InBook.

Roses for Harriet. Patricia Oliver. (Regency Romance Ser.). 224p. (Orig.). 1995. mass mkt. 3.99 (*0-451-18093-3*, Sig) NAL-Dutton.

Roses for Mama. Janette Oke. 224p. (Orig.). 1991. pap. 8.99 (*1-55661-185-4*) Bethany Hse.

Roses for Mama. large type ed. Janette Oke. 224p. (Orig.). 1991. pap. 10.99 (*1-55661-199-4*) Bethany Hse.

Roses for Northern Gardeners. David Harrap. 1993. pap. text ed. 4.95 (*1-55105-031-5*) Lone Pine.

***Roses for Remembrance/Best Is Yet to Be.** large type ed. Patience Strong. (Magna Large Print Ser.). 128p. 1996. 25.99 (*0-7505-1045-5*, Pub. by Magna Print Bks UK) Ulverscroft.

***Roses for Sarah.** Anne Philips. 1996. mass mkt. 4.99 (*1-55197-125-9*, Pub. by Comnwlth Pub CN) Partners Pubs Grp.

Roses for Today. Ed. by Peter Harkness. (Illus.). 72p. (Orig.). 1995. pap. 6.95 (*0-903001-67-5*) J Markham & Assocs.

***Roses Forever.** Richard E. Ainsworth. (Illus.). 152p. (Orig.). 1996. pap. 7.99 (*0-9655298-0-0*) R E Ainsworth.

Roses, Gardener's Collection. Better Homes & Gardens Editors. (Better Homes & Gardens Ser.). (Illus.). 64p. 1995. pap. 4.95 (*0-696-02575-2*) Meredith Bks.

Roses Have Thorns. Naum L. Ware. 186p. 1994. pap. 16.95 (*1-884699-00-6*) N Bu Pubs.

Roses Have Thorns. large type ed. M. Stephenson. (Linford Romance Library). 1989. pap. 15.99 (*0-7089-6796-5*) Ulverscroft.

Roses in a Desert Garden. Hallie Beck. Ed. by Judy Harper. (Illus.). 150p. 1996. 14.95 (*0-9625961-1-6*) PHG AZ.

Roses in December. P. Kirpal. 1990. 100.00 (*81-209-0792-2*, Pub. by Pitambar Pub II) St Mut.

Roses in December. Esther S. Myers. (Illus.). 164p. 1979. 13.00 (*0-931068-01-0*) Purcells.

***Roses in December.** Susan Paul. 1996. mass mkt. 4.99 (*1-55197-640-4*) Commonwealth Pr.

Roses in December. Catherine Tedesco. 68p. 1993. 12.99 (*0-925037-17-6*) Great Lks Poetry.

Roses in December: Finding Strength Within Grief. Marilyn W. Heaveilin. 1993. pap. 8.99 (*0-8407-6952-0*) Nelson.

Roses in December: My Memory Book. Nancy R. Edwards. (Illus.). 74p. 1989. 14.95 (*0-9613287-3-8*) Strawberry GA.

Roses in December: Prose & Verse. Clarine C. Gren Fell. (Illus.). 136p. (Orig.). reprint ed. pap. 8.50 (*0-9612766-1-4*) Gren Fell Read Ctr.

Roses in December: The Last Forty Years. Rose M. Brauer. LC 94-79032. (Illus.). 243p. 1994. pap. 15.00 (*0-9643204-1-X*) Gregory Pubs.
This book is a sequel to Mrs. Brauer's book MY NORTH DAKOTA PRAIRIE CHILDHOOD. It recounts how her family kept their courage & faith during a succession of traumatic events, shared by many but relived by few. A recent quote from an Historian/Theologian: "Like its predecessor, this sequel is a disarming, open, unpretentious human chronicle, not only of Mrs. Brauer's life but of the lives of many of us. She brings to remembrance much of what we had forgotten, disproving the quip, 'Nostalgia isn't what it used to be.'" MY NORTH DAKOTA PRAIRIE CHILDHOOD, ISBN 0-9643204-0-1, 138 pages, $15.00, now in its FIFTH PRINTING. This book is about daily life during the years of the "Great Depression," & how country folks survived. Letters from readers recall their experiences from those early years & how this book brings them to the realization that our past shapes us as adults. Readers' quotes: "History with a human face is what happens down on the farm. Garrison Keillor has proved that to us. The Leininger family made history every day. Read this book & have your own humanity enriched." "You are blessed with a superbly vivid memory matched with wit, color & charm in every chapter. Your book is a slice of Americana, served up with grace & gusto." Both books in larger print. ORDER from GREGORY PUBLISHERS, Wachesaw Plantation East, 4566 Painted Fern Court, Nurrells Inlet, SC 29576. 800-451-0115. Also: Bookmen Inc., c/o John Kudrie, 525 N. 3rd St., Minneapolis, MN 55401; 612-341-3333; FAX 612-341-3065. 40% discount from Gregory Publishers. ***Publisher Provided Annotation.***

Roses in December: Women My Husband Married: The Caress & the Hurt: Prose & Verse, 3 bks., Set. Clarine C. Gren Fell. (Illus.). reprint ed. pap. 20.00 (*0-685-60006-8*) Gren Fell Read Ctr.

Roses in Porcelain by Jean du Tilleux. Norton, R. W., Art Gallery Staff. LC 73-81397. (Illus.). 16p. 1973. pap. 3.50 (*0-913060-02-X*) Norton Art.

Roses in the Mirror: Translated Poems of Julia De Burgos. Julia De Burgos. Ed. & Tr. by Carmen D. Lucca from SPA. 140p. (Orig.). (C). 1992. pap. 8.00 (*0-9623968-1-8*) Poets Refuge.

Roses in the Night. Kay Gregory. (Romance Ser.). 1995. mass mkt. 2.99 (*0-373-03358-3*, 1-03358-8) Harlequin Bks.

Rose's Last Summer. Margaret Millar. 223p. 1985. pap. 4.95 (*0-930330-26-9*) Intl Polygonics.

Roses Love Garlic: Secrets of Companion Planting with Flowers. Louise Riotte. LC 83-1464. (Illus.). 240p. (Orig.). 1983. pap. 11.95 (*0-88266-331-3*, Garden Way Pub) Storey Comm Inc.

***Rose's Magic Touch.** Laura Williams. Ed. by Susan Korman. (Magic Attic Club Ser.). (Illus.). 72p. (J). (gr. 2 up). 1997. 12.95 (*1-57513-106-4*) Magic Attic.

Rose's Magic Touch see Magic Attic Club Series

Roses of Sharron. Sharron Maline. 70p. (Orig.). 1995. pap. 5.95 (*1-57502-071-8*) Morris Pubng.

Roses of Yesterday & Today. Will Tillotson. Ed. by Dorothy Stemler. (Illus.). 88p. 1980. reprint ed. pap. 5.95 (*0-936736-03-8*) Sweetbrier.

Roses on a Broken Fence. Mildred F. Hobbs. 96p. 1995. pap. text ed. 9.95 (*1-881576-57-4*) Providence Hse.

***Roses on Baker Street.** (Illus.). 48p. (Orig.). 1997. pap. 6.49 (*0-89084-934-X*) Bob Jones Univ Pr.

Roses on the Trail. Paul Lamb. 135p. (Orig.). 1995. pap. text ed. 10.00 (*0-9639719-3-X*) Lambs Fold Ranch.

***Roses Red - Crayon Blue, Vol. 2.** Ed. by Dianne M. Henderson & Lana Wegeng. 66p. 1996. pap. write for info. (*1-889463-09-4*) Golden Apple.

Roses Red, Violets Blue: Why Flowers Have Colors. Sylvia A. Johnson. (Discovery! Ser.). (Illus.). 64p. (J). (gr. 5 up). 1991. lib. bdg. 23.95 (*0-8225-1594-6*, Lerner Publctns) Lerner Group.

Roses Round the Door. large type ed. Doreen Tovey. 1993. 45.00 (*0-7066-1013-X*, Pub. by Remploy Pr CN) St Mut.

***Rose's Smile: Farizad of the Arabian Nights.** David Kherdian & Arabian Nights Staff. LC 96-52539. (Illus.). (J). 1997. 15.95 (*0-8050-3912-0*) H Holt & Co.

Rose's Story: Rose, A Survivor of Our Social Services. LC 91-33602. 136p. 1991. 10.95 (*0-87304-244-1*) Families Intl.

***Roses to Rodeos: 77 Year History of the Inter-Mountain Fair 1919-1995.** Glorianne Weigand. (Illus.). 141p. (Orig.). 1996. pap. 15.00 (*0-9644141-2-0*) One-Hund-One Ranch.

Roses under the Sun: A Guide for Growing Roses in Florida. large type ed. Ted Stevens. Ed. by LaVerne Stevens. LC 94-70608. (Illus.). 104p. 1994. Laminated, perfect bdg. per., pap. 8.50 (*0-9630441-2-5*) B&B Pr.

Roses Uses: Uses for the Rose. rev. ed. Recycling Consortium Staff. 1992. ring bd. 19.95 (*0-317-04798-1*) Prosperity & Profits.

***Roses with Prickly Thorns.** Ronda Faircloth. 160p. 1996. 15.00 (*0-8059-3982-2*) Dorrance.

Roses, 1988. Robert Mapplethorpe. 1993. 30.00 (*0-8212-2011-X*) Bulfinch Pr.

Rosetree. Sabra Loomis. LC 88-31561. 72p. (Orig.). 1989. pap. 9.95 (*0-914086-85-5*) Alicejamesbooks.

Rosetta Stone. Ed. by Carol Andrews. (Illus.). 1989. 14.95 (*0-8109-1572-3*) Abrams.

Rosetta Stone. E. A. Budge. 352p. 1989. pap. 8.95 (*0-486-26163-8*) Dover.

Rosetta Stone. Wallis Budge. 27p. 1986. pap. 7.50 (*0-89005-331-6*) Ares.

Rosetta Stone see Decrees of Memphis & Canopus

Rosetta Stone in the British Museum. Ernest A. Budge. LC 73-16549. (Illus.). reprint ed. 32.50 (*0-404-11362-1*) AMS Pr.

Rosette & the Muddy River. Diane C. Leger & Pamela Cambiazo. (Illus.). 32p. (Orig.). (J). (gr. 1-4). 1991. pap. 4.95 (*0-920501-65-6*) Orca Bk Pubs.

Rosetti's Portrait Drawings of Elizabeth Siddall: Catalogue of the Drawings & Watercolours. Virginia Surtees. (Illus.). 64p. 1991. text ed. 25.95 (*0-85967-885-7*, Pub. by Scolar Pr UK) Ashgate Pub Co.

Rosewood Casket. Sharyn McCrumb. 320p. 1996. pap. 23.95 (*0-525-94011-1*) NAL-Dutton.

Rosewood Casket. Sharyn McCrumb. 1997. mass mkt. 6.99 (*0-451-18471-8*, Sig) NAL-Dutton.

Rosewood Casket. large type ed. Sharyn McCrumb. 435p. 1996. lib. bdg. 25.95 (*0-7838-1826-2*, GK Hall) Thorndike Pr.

***Rosewood Casket, She Walks These Hills, Hangman's Beautiful Daugther.** Sharyn McCrumb. 1997. mass mkt. 251.64 (*0-451-93400-8*, Sig) NAL-Dutton.

Rosey Grier's All-American Heroes: Multicultural Success Stories. Roosevelt R. Grier. 1993. pap. 9.95 (*0-942361-63-6*) MasterMedia Pub.

***Rosey the Baby Killer & Other Stories.** Bill Shields. 1997. pap. text ed. 10.00 (*1-880985-54-3*) Two Thirteen Sixty-one.

Rosey...the Imperfect Angel. Sandra L. Peckinpah. LC 90-63058. (Imperfect Angels Ser.). (Illus.). 32p. (J). (ps-4). 1991. 15.95 (*0-9627806-0-X*) Dasan Prodns.

Rosh Hashana - Ashkenaz: Zichron Reuven see Machzor

Rosh Hashanah, 1 vol. (ENG & HEB.). 15.00 (*0-910218-56-0*) Bennet Pub.

Rosh Hashanah. Y. Ganz. (ArtScroll Youth Holiday Ser.). (YA). 1990. 8.99 (*0-89906-976-2*) Mesorah Pubns.

Rosh Hashanah. Norma Simon. (Festival Series of Picture Storybooks). (Illus.). (J). (ps). 1961. spiral bd. 4.50 (*0-8381-0700-1*) USCJE.

Rosh Hashanah. Philip Goodman. LC 74-105069. (Holiday Anthologies Ser.). (Illus.). 380p. 1992. reprint ed. pap. text ed. 15.95 (*0-8276-0408-4*) JPS Phila.

Rosh Hashanah: A Holiday Funtext. Judy Bin-Nun & Franne Einhorn. (Illus.). (J). (gr. 1-3). 1978. pap. 5.00 (*0-8074-0230-3*, 101300) UAHC.

Rosh Hashanah: Its Significance, Laws, & Prayers. Hersh Goldwurm & Avie Gold. (ArtScroll Mesorah Ser.). 128p. 1983. 17.99 (*0-89906-195-8*); pap. 14.99 (*0-89906-196-6*) Mesorah Pubns.

Rosh Hashanah - A Family Service. Judith Z. Abrams. LC 90-4855. (Illus.). 32p. (Orig.). (J). (ps-4). 1990. pap. 3.95 (*0-929371-16-X*) Kar-Ben.

Rosh Hashanah & the Messianic Kingdom to Come: A Messianic Jewish Interpretation of the Feast of Trumpets. 2nd ed. Joseph Good. 197p. (C). 1991. reprint ed. pap. text ed. 10.00 (*0-9624858-0-2*) Hatikva Ministries.

Rosh HaShanah & the Messianic Kingdom to Come: A Messianic Jewish Interpretation of the Feast of Trumpets. Joseph Good. Ed. by Deborah Herzberg. 197p. (Orig.). (C). 1989. reprint ed. pap. text ed. 7.00 (*0-685-29811-6*) Hatikva Ministries.

Rosh Hashanah Sefard: Zichron Moshe see Machzor

Rosh Hashanah Walk. Carol Levin. LC 87-3106. (Illus.). (J). (ps-3). 1987. 4.95 (*0-930494-70-9*) Kar-Ben.

Rosh Hashanah-Yom Kippur-Soccos see Festivals in Halachah

Rosh Hashanah Yom Kippur Survival Kit. Shimon Apisdorf. (Illus.). 112p. 1995. 14.95 (*1-881927-06-7*) Leviathan OH.

***Rosh Hashanah Yom Kippur Survival Kit.** Shimon Apisdorf. 1997. 14.95 (*1-881927-14-8*) Leviathan OH.

Rosh Hodesh Table: Foods at the New Moon. Judith Y. Solomon. LC 95-77510. 150p. (Orig.). 1995. pap. 8.95 (*0-930395-23-9*) Biblio NY.

Rosh Yeshiva: The Story of Rav Chaim Shmulevitz, the "Stutchiner" Reuven Grossman. Tr. by Yaakov M. Rapoport from HEB. (Illus.). 240p. 1988. 14.95 (*0-944070-03-5*); pap. 11.95 (*0-944070-05-1*) Targum Pr.

Rosicrucian Brotherhood. Alexander Wilder. 1992. pap. 4.95 (*1-55818-165-2*, Sure Fire) Holmes Pub.

Rosicrucian Child Training Collection. Max Heindel & Rosicrucian Fellowship Staff. (Illus.). 1429p. 1990. reprint ed. pap. text ed. 25.00 (*0-911274-26-X*) Rosicrucian.

Rosicrucian Christianity Lectures. 4th ed. Max Heindel. Ed. by Rosicrucian Fellowship Staff. 374p. (C). 1985. reprint ed. pap. text ed. 16.00 (*0-911274-84-7*) Rosicrucian.

Rosicrucian Cosmo-Conception: Mystic Christianity. Max Heindel. Ed. by Rosicrucian Fellowship Staff. (Illus.). 717p. (C). 1988. reprint ed. text ed. 20.00 (*0-911274-02-2*); reprint ed. pap. text ed. 12.00 (*0-911274-34-0*) Rosicrucian.

Rosicrucian Cross Unveiled. John Heydon. Ed. by J. D. Holmes. 1993. pap. 5.95 (*1-55818-285-3*, Sure Fire) Holmes Pub.

Rosicrucian Emblems of Daniel Cramer. Daniel Cramer. Tr. by Fiona Tait from LAT. LC 90-47420. (Magnum Opus Hermetic Sourceworks Ser.: No. 4). (Illus.). 84p. (Orig.). 1991. 27.00 (*0-933999-87-9*); pap. 15.00 (*0-933999-88-7*) Phanes Pr.

Rosicrucian Enlightenment. Frances A. Yates. 320p. (C). 1986. pap. 13.95 (*0-415-10912-4*) Routledge.

***Rosicrucian Enlightenment.** rev. ed. Ed. & Intro. by Ralph White. 256p. 1997. pap. write for info. (*0-940262-84-3*, 2039) Lindisfarne Bks.

Rosicrucian Esotericism. Rudolf Steiner. Tr. by Dorothy S. Osmond from GER. 122p. 1978. 14.00 (*0-910142-78-5*) Anthroposophic.

Rosicrucian Fraternity in America, 2 vols. R. Swinburne Clymer. 1935. 75.00 (*0-686-10446-3*) Philos Pub.

Rosicrucian Fundamentals: A Synthesis of Religion, Science, & Philosophy. F. R. Khei. 413p. 1996. pap. 29.95 (*1-56459-634-6*) Kessinger Pub.

Rosicrucian Manual. Abet. 131p. 1974. reprint ed. spiral bd. 14.00 (*0-7873-0015-2*) Hlth Research.

Rosicrucian Mysteries. 9th ed. Max Heindel. Ed. by Rosicrucian Fellowship Staff. 207p. (C). 1987. reprint ed. pap. 8.00 (*0-911274-86-3*) Rosicrucian.

Rosicrucian Notebook: The Secret Sciences Used by Members of the Order. Willy Schrodter. LC 92-20656. 312p. (Orig.). 1992. pap. 19.95 (*0-87728-757-0*) Weiser.

Rosicrucian Philosophy in Questions & Answers, Vol. I. 3rd ed. Max Heindel. Ed. by Rosicrucian Fellowship Staff. (Illus.). 417p. (C). 1978. reprint ed. pap. 8.00 (*0-911274-89-8*) Rosicrucian.

Rosicrucian Philosophy in Questions & Answers, Vol. II. Max Heindel. Ed. by Rosicrucian Fellowship Staff. 589p. (C). 1990. reprint ed. pap. text ed. 8.00 (*0-911274-90-1*) Rosicrucian.

Rosicrucian Primer: Ancient Landmarks of the Rosicrucians. John Heydon et al. Ed. by J. D. Holmes. 128p. (Orig.). 1994. pap. 17.95 (*1-55818-277-2*) Holmes Pub.

Rosicrucian Principles for the Home & Business. H. Spencer Lewis. LC 54-21694. 241p. 1929. pap. 12.95 (*0-912057-54-8*, 502030) RO AMORC.

Rosicrucian Symbology. F. R. Khei. 67p. 1972. reprint ed. spiral bd. 14.00 (*0-7873-0490-5*) Hlth Research.

Rosicrucian Symbology: A Treatise Wherein the Discerning Ones Will Find the Elements of Constructive Symbology & Certain Other Things. F. R. Khei. 69p. 1996. pap. 12.95 (*1-56459-842-X*) Kessinger Pub.

Rosicrucian Symbols. Franz Hartman. 1983. 3.95 (*0-916411-15-X*, Sure Fire) Holmes Pub.

Rosicrucian Thoughts on the Ever-Burning Lamps of the Ancients. W. W. Westcott. 1986. reprint ed. pap. 2.95 (*0-916411-56-7*, Sure Fire) Holmes Pub.

Rosicrucian "Three Treasures" The Curious Prophecies of Paracelsus. Lewis Biddulph. 1994. pap. 6.95 (*1-55818-309-4*, Sure Fire) Holmes Pub.

Rosicrucianism & Modern Initiation: Mystery Centres of the Middle Ages. 3rd ed. Rudolf Steiner. Tr. by Mary Adams. 98p. 1982. pap. 12.95 (*0-85440-381-7*, Pub. by Steiner Book Centre CN) Anthroposophic.

Rosicrucians. 4th ed. Hargrave Jennings. 426p. 1966. reprint ed. spiral bd. 17.50 (*0-7873-0469-7*) Hlth Research.

Rosicrucians: Past & Present, At Home & Abroad. William W. Westcott. 1989. reprint ed. pap. 3.95 (*1-55818-121-0*) Holmes Pub.

***Rosicrucians: The History, Mythology, & Rituals of an Occult Order.** Christopher McIntosh. LC 97-8592. (Illus.). 192p. (Orig.). 1997. 22.95 (*0-87728-893-3*) Weiser.

Rosicrucians: Their Rites & Mysteries. 4th ed. Hargrave Jennings. LC 75-36845. (Occult Ser.). (Illus.). 1976. reprint ed. 40.95 (*0-405-07957-5*) Ayer.

Rosicrucians: Their Rites & Mysteries. Hargrave Jennings. 339p. 1992. reprint ed. pap. 24.95 (*1-56459-118-2*) Kessinger Pub.

Rosicrucians & Magister Christoph Schlegel. Manly P. Hall. 15.95 (*0-89314-422-3*) Philos Res.

Rosicrucians in Russia. B. Telepnef. 1993. reprint ed. pap. 5.95 (*1-55818-236-5*) Holmes Pub.

Rosicrucians, Past & Present, at Home & Abroad. W. Wynn Westcott. 71p. 1996. pap. 12.95 (*1-56459-756-3*) Kessinger Pub.

Rosicrucians, Past & Present, at Home & Abroad. W. Wynn Westcott. 64p. 1966. reprint ed. spiral bd. 5.50 (*0-7873-0955-9*) Hlth Research.

***Rosie.** Anne Lamott. 1997. pap. 11.95 (*0-14-026479-5*) Viking Penguin.

Rosie. Anne Lamott. LC 88-34553. 288p. 1989. reprint ed. pap. 9.95 (*0-86547-390-0*, North Pt Pr) FS&G.

Rosie: My Rufous Hummingbird. Arnette Heidcamp. 1995. 16.00 (*0-517-70076-X*, Crown) Crown Pub Group.

***Rosie: Rosie O'Donnell's Biography.** James R. Parish. LC 96-6561. (Illus.). 288p. 1997. 23.00 (*0-7867-0410-1*) Carroll & Graf.

R

Rosie: Selected Works by Rosemary Richmond. Rosemary Richmond. 180p. (Orig.). 1995. pap. 10.95 (*0-9646037-2-1*) Rosehill Pr IL.

Rosie: The Oldest Horse in St. Augustine. Miriam Gilbert. LC 67-30409. (Illus.). (ENG, FRE & SPA.). (J). (gr. k-6). 1974. pap. 5.95 (*0-87208-007-2*) Shoeless Pub.

Rosie: The Shopping Cart Lady. Chia Martin. (Illus.). 32p. (J). (gr. k-2). 1996. 15.95 (*0-934252-51-3*) Hohm Pr.

Rosie, a Visiting Dog's Story. Stephanie Calmenson. LC 93-21243. (Illus.). (J). (gr. k up). 1994. 15.95 (*0-395-65477-7*, Clarion Bks) HM.

Rosie & Michael. Judith Viorst. LC 74-75571. (Illus.). 40p. (J). (gr. 1-4). 1974. lib. bdg. 15.00 (*0-689-30439-0*, Atheneum Bks Young) S&S Childrens.

Rosie & Michael. 2nd ed. Judith Viorst. LC 86-13969. (Illus.). 40p. (J). (gr. 1-4). 1988. pap. 3.95 (*0-689-71272-3*, Aladdin Paperbacks) S&S Childrens.

Rosie & the Bear Flag. Harry Knill. (J). (gr. 1-9). 1992. pap. 3.95 (*0-88388-055-5*) Bellerophon Bks.

Rosie & the Dance of the Dinosaurs. Betty R. Wright. LC 89-2083. 112p. (J). (gr. 3-7). 1989. 15.95 (*0-8234-0782-9*) Holiday.

Rosie & the Poor Rabbits. Maryann MacDonald. LC 92-42766. (Illus.). 32p. (J). (ps-2). 1994. lib. bdg. 13.95 (*0-689-31832-4*, Atheneum Bks Young) S&S Childrens.

Rosie & the Rustlers. Roy Gerrard. 32p. (J). (ps up). pap. 4.95 (*0-374-46339-5*) FS&G.

Rosie & the Rustlers. Roy Gerrard. 32p. (J). (ps up). 1989. 15.00 (*0-374-36345-5*) FS&G.

***Rosie Backstage.** unabridged ed. Amanda Lewis & Tim Wynne-Jones. (Illus.). 96p. (J). (gr. 3-7). 1994. 16.95 (*1-55074-209-4*, Pub. by Kids Can Pr CN) Genl Dist Srvs.

***Rosie Backstage.** unabridged ed. Amanda Lewis & Tim Wynne-Jones. (Illus.). 96p. (J). (gr. 3-7). 1994. pap. 10.95 (*1-55074-148-9*, Pub. by Kids Can Pr CN) Genl Dist Srvs.

Rosie Goes Exploring. Zita Newcome. (Illus.). 32p. (J). (ps). 1992. 11.95 (*1-85681-170-0*, Pub. by J MacRae UK) Trafalgar.

Rosie No-Name & the Forest of Forgetting. Gareth Owen. LC 96-11217. 112p. (J). (gr. 4-7). 1996. 15.95 (*0-8234-1266-0*) Holiday.

***Rosie O'Donnell.** (Women of Achievement Ser.). (Illus.). (YA). (gr. 7 up). 1997. lib. bdg. 19.95 (*0-7910-4710-5*) Chelsea Hse.

***Rosie O'Donnell.** (Women of Achievement Ser.). (Illus.). (YA). (gr. 7 up). 1997. pap. 8.95 (*0-7910-4711-3*) Chelsea Hse.

***Rosie O'Donnell: Her True Story.** George Mair. LC 97-178. 288p. 1997. 22.50 (*1-55972-416-1*, Birch Ln Pr) Carol Pub Group.

***Rosie O'Donnell Story.** Bill Adler. Date not set. write for info. (*0-688-15315-1*) Morrow.

Rosie Posie Has a Bath. Joan Haines. (Illus.). 16p. (J). (ps-1). 1985. pap. 2.65 (*0-936652-02-0*, Ed Concern Pubns) Two Ems.

Rosie Posie Makes Friends. Joan Haines. (Illus.). 16p. (Orig.). (J). (ps-1). 1985. pap. 2.65 (*0-936652-01-2*, Ed Concern Pubns) Two Ems.

Rosie Pugh & the Great Clothes War. Caroline Castle. LC 94-44716. (Illus.). 128p. (J). 1995. pap. 3.50 (*0-8120-9181-7*) Barron.

***Rosie Rabbit At the Sea Shore.** Yee. (J). 1998. pap. 6.99 (*0-689-81840-8*) S&S Childrens.

***Rosie Rabbit Goes to Playschool.** Patrick Yee. (J). 1997. 6.99 (*0-689-81361-9*, Atheneum S&S) S&S Trade.

***Rosie Rabbit Visits the Farm.** Yee. (J). 1998. pap. 6.99 (*0-689-81841-6*) S&S Childrens.

***Rosie Rabbit's Birthday Party: Lift-The-Flap.** Patrick Yee. (J). 1997. 6.99 (*0-689-81362-7*, Atheneum S&S) S&S Trade.

Rosie Rabbit's Easter. Harriet Ziefert. (Happy Holiday Sticker Bks.). (Illus.). 10p. (J). (ps-1). 1997. 7.99 (*1-56402-974-3*) Candlewick Pr.

Rosie Rabbit's Valentine's Day. Harriet Ziefert. (Happy Holiday Sticker Bks.). (Illus.). 10p. (J). (ps-1). 1996. 7.99 (*1-56402-887-9*) Candlewick Pr.

Rosie the Courageous Crybaby. Fannie S. Jefferson. (Illus.). 224p. (Orig.). 1993. pap. 16.95 (*0-9636463-0-3*) F S A Jefferson.

Rosie the Riveter. 1988. pap. 12.95 (*0-452-01024-1*, Mer) NAL-Dutton.

***Rosie the Riveter.** Penny Colman. 1998. pap. 9.99 (*0-517-88567-0*) Crown Pub Group.

Rosie the Riveter: Women Working on the Home Front in World War II. Penny Colman. LC 94-3614. 128p. (J). 1995. lib. bdg. 20.99 (*0-517-59791-8*) Crown Bks Yng Read.

Rosie the Riveter: Women Working on the Home Front in World War II. Penny Colman. LC 94-3614. (Illus.). 128p. (J). (gr. 4 up). 1995. 19.00 (*0-517-59790-X*) Crown Bks Yng Read.

Rosie the Riveter Revisited: Women, the War & Social Change. Sherna B. Gluck. Ed. by Donald A. Ritchie. (Oral History Ser.). 296p. 1987. 22.95 (*0-8057-9022-5*, Twayne) Scribnrs Ref.

Rosie the Riveter Revisited: Women, the War, & Social Change. Sherna B. Gluck. LC 87-30685. (Illus.). 304p. 1988. pap. 8.95 (*0-452-00911-1*, Mer) NAL-Dutton.

Rosie, the Rosedown Rabbit: A Storybook to Color. Poppy Sundeen. Ed. & Illus. by Joanne West. 26p. (Orig.). (J). 1988. pap. text ed. 5.95 (*0-929317-00-9*) Rosedown Plantation.

Rosie the Talking Parrot Learns about Friendship & Love. Deborah Baur. (Illus.). 32p. (J). (gr. k-3). 1996. 8.00 (*0-8059-3862-1*) Dorrance.

Rosie Wells Enterprises' Official Price Guide for Precious Moments Applause Dolls. Patty Merritt & Rosie Wells. 88p. (Orig.). 1995. pap. 9.95 (*1-886812-04-7*) R Wells.

Rosie Wells Enterprises' Official Secondary Market Price Guide for Cherished Teddies. Rosie Wells. 1995. pap. 11.95 (*1-886812-06-3*) R Wells.

Rosie Wells Enterprises Secondary Market Price Guide for the Cherished Teddies Collection. 2nd ed. 128p. 1996. pap. 12.95 (*1-886812-09-8*) R Wells.

Rosiebelle Lee Wildcat Tennessee. Raymond Andrews. LC 87-21160. (Brown Thrasher Bks.). (Illus.). 290p. 1988. reprint ed. pap. 11.95 (*0-8203-0994-X*) U of Ga Pr.

Rosier de Madame Husson. Guy De Maupassant & Pierre Cogny. (FRE.). 1976. 10.95 (*0-8288-9625-9*, F67790) Fr & Eur.

Rosier de Madame Husson. Guy De Maupassant. (Folio Ser.: No. 2153). (FRE.). pap. 8.95 (*2-07-038243-5*) Schoenhof.

Rosie's Baby Tooth. Maryann MacDonald. LC 90-35923. (Illus.). 32p. (J). (ps-2). 1991. lib. bdg. 12.95 (*0-689-31626-7*, Atheneum Bks Young) S&S Childrens.

***Rosie's Bakery All Butter, Fresh Cream, Sugar-Packed, No Holds Barred Baking Book.** Judy Rosenberg. 1991. pap. text ed. 13.95 (*0-89480-723-4*) Workman Pub.

Rosie's Bakery All Butter, Fresh Cream, Sugar-Packed, No-Holds-Barred Baking Book. rev. ed. Judy Rosenberg. LC 91-50380. (Illus.). 256p. (Orig.). 1996. pap. 13.95 (*0-7611-0633-2*, 10633) Workman Pub.

Rosie's Bakery Chocolate-Packed, Jam Filled, Butter-Rich Cookie Book. Judy Rosenberg. LC 96-43823. (Illus.). 1996. 23.95 (*0-7611-0625-1*); pap. 12.95 (*1-56305-506-6*, 3506) Workman Pub.

Rosie's Ballet Slippers. Susan Hampshire. LC 95-31713. (Illus.). 32p. (J). (ps-2). 1996. 14.95 (*0-06-026466-7*) HarpC Child Bks.

Rosie's Bingo Directory: Chicago. Rosalie T. Edelstein. 96p. 1995. pap. 6.95 (*0-9648101-0-7*) Boo Boo Pr.

Rosie's Birthday Rat. Linda Glaser. LC 95-21363. Orig. Title: Rose and her Rat. (Illus.). 48p. (J). (gr. k-4). 1996. pap. 3.99 (*0-440-41113-0*, Picture Yearling) BDD Bks Young Read.

Rosie's Birthday Rat. Linda Glaser. LC 95-21363. Orig. Title: Rose and her Rat. (Illus.). 48p. (J). (gr. k-4). 1996. 13.95 (*0-385-32172-4*) Delacorte.

Rosie's Day Out. Sue Camm. (Read to Me Ser.). 10p. (J). (ps). 1994. bds. 3.98 (*1-85854-138-7*) Brimax Bks.

Rosie's Fiddle. Phyllis Root. LC 93-37430. (Illus.). 32p. (J). (ps up). 1997. 16.00 (*0-688-12852-1*); lib. bdg. 15.93 (*0-688-12853-X*) Lothrop.

Rosie's Fishing Trip. Amy Hest. LC 93-28543. (Illus.). 32p. (J). (ps up). 1994. 13.95 (*1-56402-296-X*) Candlewick Pr.

Rosie's Fishing Trip. Amy Hest. LC 93-28543. (Illus.). 32p. (J). (ps up). 1996. reprint ed. pap. 4.99 (*1-56402-849-6*) Candlewick Pr.

Rosie's Nutcracker Dreams. Patricia R. Giff. LC 96-15254. (Ballet Slippers Ser.: Vol. 2). (Illus.). 64p. (J). (gr. 2-6). 1996. pap. 13.99 (*0-670-86865-5*, Viking) Viking Penguin.

***Rosie's Nutcracker Dreams.** Patricia R. Giff. 1997. pap. 3.99 (*0-14-038576-2*) Viking Penguin.

***Rosie's Place.** Andrea Cleghorn. (Illus.). 184p. 1997. 23.95 (*0-9641089-9-2*) VanderWyk & Burnham.

***Rosie's Place.** Andrea Cleghorn. (Illus.). 184p. 1997. pap. write for info. (*1-889242-00-4*) VanderWyk & Burnham.

Rosie's Posies. Marcy D. Ramsey. (Illus.). 32p. (J). (ps-3). 1995. bds. 14.95 (*0-87033-472-7*, Tidewtr Pubs) Cornell Maritime.

Rosie's Red String. Harriet Ziefert. (J). 1996. 14.95 (*0-7894-0586-5*) DK Pub Inc.

Rosie's Roses: An Accounting Practice Set. B. G. Burns. 75p. 1993. pap. 15.00 (*0-409-30843-9*, Austral) MICHIE.

Rosie's Secondary Market Price Guide for Enesco's Precious Moments Collection. 14th ed. Ed. by Rosie Wells. 236p. (Orig.). 1996. pap. 21.95 (*1-886812-07-1*) R Wells.

***Rosie's Secondary Market Price Guide for Hallmark Ornaments.** 11th ed. Ed. by Rosie Wells. 352p. 1996. pap. 21.95 (*1-886812-12-8*) R Wells.

***Rosie's Secondary Market Price Guide Precious Moments by Enesco.** 15th anniversary ed. Ed. by Rosie Wells. 264p. (Orig.). 1997. pap. 21.95 (*1-886812-14-4*) R Wells.

***Rosie's Secondary Market Price Guide to Boyds Bears & Friends.** Ed. by Rosie Wells. (Illus.). 96p. (Orig.). 1996. pap. 11.95 (*1-886812-13-6*) R Wells.

Rosie's Story. Martine Gogoll. LC 94-28975. (Illus.). 24p. (Orig.). (J). (ps-4). 1994. pap. 4.95 (*1-879531-62-3*) Mondo Pubng.

Rosie's Tiger. Anna Myers. LC 94-50814. (J). 1994. 14.95 (*0-8027-8305-8*) Walker & Co.

***Rosie's Two Left Feet.** (Ready Readers Stage 2 Ser.). (Illus.). 32p. (J). (gr. 2-4). 1995. pap. write for info. (*1-56144-751-X*, Honey Bear Bks) Modern Pub NYC.

Rosie's Walk. Hutchins. 1997. 6.99 (*0-689-81317-1*) S&S Childrens.

Rosie's Walk. Pat Hutchins. (Big Bks.). (J). (ps-3). 1992. 19.95 (*0-590-71809-6*) Scholastic Inc.

Rosie's Walk. Pat Hutchins. LC 68-12090. (Illus.). 32p. (J). (ps-1). 1968. lib. bdg. 16.00 (*0-02-745850-4*, Mac Bks Young Read) S&S Childrens.

Rosie's Walk. Pat Hutchins. LC 87-17550. (Illus.). 32p. (J). 1971. reprint ed. pap. 5.99 (*0-02-043750-1*) Macmillan.

Rosina's Choice. Pamela Edgar. 288p. 1995. 22.00 (*0-7278-4817-8*) Severn Hse.

Rosita's Block Party. (Golden Story Book 'n' Tape Ser.). (Illus.). 24p. (J). (ps-3). 1995. write for info. incl. audio (*0-307-14294-9*, 14294) Western Pub.

Rosita's Calico Cat: Sesame Street. Emily Thompson. (Sesame Street Words - Palabras Ser.). (Illus.). 24p. (J). (ps-3). 1994. pap. 2.25 (*0-307-13127-0*, Golden Pr) Western Pub.

Rosita's Christmas Wish. Mary-Ann S. Bruni. LC 85-52040. (Texas Ser.). (Illus.). 48p. (J). (gr. k-8). 1985. 13.95 (*0-935857-00-1*); write for info. (*0-935857-09-5*); pap. write for info. (*0-935857-01-X*); pap. write for info. (*0-935857-10-9*) Texart.

Rosita's Christmas Wish. limited ed. Mary-Ann S. Bruni. LC 85-52040. (Texas Ser.). (Illus.). 48p. (J). (gr. k-8). 1985. 125.00 (*0-935857-03-6*) Texart.

Rosita's New Friends. Allison Davis. (Sesame Street Words - Palabras Ser.). (Illus.). 24p. (J). 1994. write for info. (*0-307-13129-7*) Western Pub.

Rosita's Surprise. Allison Davis. (Sesame Street Words - Palabras Ser.). (Illus.). 24p. (J). (ps-3). 1994. 2.25 (*0-307-13128-9*, Golden Books) Western Pub.

Roslindale, MA. Anthony Sammarco. (Images of America Ser.). 1997. pap. 16.99 (*0-7524-0424-5*, Arcdia) Chalford.

***Rosmersholm.** Henrik Ibsen. Ed. by William-Alan Landes. 72p. (Orig.). 1997. pap. write for info. (*0-88734-726-6*) Players Pr.

Rosmersholm see Ibsen: Plays Three

Rosmersholm see Master Builder & Other Plays

Rosmersholm see Eight Plays

***Ross: A Boy Who Lived till Spring.** Carol Horvath. 112p. 1997. pap. 12.00 (*0-8059-4114-2*) Dorrance.

Ross: Drafting & Negotiating Commercial Leases - Supplement. 4th ed. Elizabeth McKibbin et al. Ed. by Murray J. Ross. 84p. 1996. pap. 143.00 (*0-406-01026-9*, UK) MICHIE.

Ross & Cromarty: An Illustrated Architectural Guide. Elizabeth Beaton. (Illus.). 112p. (C). 1992. pap. 35.00 (*1-873190-04-2*, Pub. by Rutland Pr UK) St Mut.

Ross & Wilson: Anatomy & Physiology in Health & Illness. 7th ed. Kathleen J. Wilson. (Illus.). 412p. 1990. pap. text ed. 37.95 (*0-443-04243-8*) Churchill.

Ross & Wilson Anatomy & Physiology in Health & Illness. 8th ed. Kathleen J. Wilson et al. LC 96-25832. 465p. 1996. pap. 32.00 (*0-443-05156-9*) Churchill.

Ross Bleckner. Ross Bleckner & Christina M. Strassfield. (Illus.). 12p. 1993. pap. 4.00 (*0-933793-28-6*) Guild Hall.

Ross Bleckner. Lisa Dennison et al. (Illus.). 250p. 1995. 85.00 (*0-8109-6880-0*) Abrams.

Ross Board Books, 2 Vols. Ross. 1995. bds. 24.00 (*0-15-201274-5*) HarBrace.

Ross Essays Urbanism Colonial. 1984. lib. bdg. 117.50 (*90-247-2925-4*) Kluwer Ac.

Ross Ice Shelf: Glaciology & Geophysics, Papers 3-5. Ed. by C. R. Bentley & D. E. Hayes. (Antarctic Research Ser.: Vol. 42). 72p. 1990. Papers 3, 4, & 5, 1990, 72p. 21.00 (*0-87590-195-6*) Am Geophysical.

Ross Information Processing Assessment: A Cognitive-Linguistic Assessment. Deborah G. Ross. 44p. 1986. 69.00 (*0-88120-379-3*, 2102) PRO-ED.

Ross Is a Gymnast: Valuing & Enhancing Differences in Children. Belinda Gutwein & Ed Gutwein. (Illus.). 36p. (Orig.). (J). (ps-3). 1995. pap. text ed. 4.95 (*0-9646176-0-9*) FGI Motiv Trng.

Ross Lee Finney: A Bio-Bibliography. Susan H. Hitchens. LC 96-21948. 208p. 1996. text ed. 65.00 (*0-313-28671-X*, Greenwood Pr) Greenwood.

Ross MacDonald. Bernard A. Schopen. (Twayne's United States Authors Ser.: No. 557). 160p. (C). 1990. 21.95 (*0-8057-7548-X*, Twayne) Scribnrs Ref.

Ross MacDonald-Kenneth Millar: A Descriptive Bibliography. Matthew J. Bruccoli. LC 83-1398. (Series in Bibliography). (Illus.). 280p. 1983. 100.00 (*0-8229-3482-5*) U of Pittsburgh Pr.

Ross of Silver Ridge. large type ed. Gwen Westwood. 1991. 25.99 (*0-7089-2357-7*) Ulverscroft.

Ross Orogen of the Transantarctic Mountains. Edmund Stump. (Cambridge Studies in New Art History & Criticism). (Illus.). 250p. (C). 1995. text ed. 110.00 (*0-521-43314-2*) Cambridge U Pr.

Ross Perot: An American Maverick Speaks Out. Ed. by Bill Adler, Jr. LC 93-40570. 1994. 10.95 (*0-8065-1500-7*, Citadel Pr) Carol Pub Group.

Ross Perot: Billionaire Politician. Carmen Bredeson. LC 94-27996. (People to Know Ser.). (Illus.). 128p. (YA). (gr. 6 up). 1995. lib. bdg. 18.95 (*0-89490-545-7*) Enslow Pubs.

Ross Perot: Businessman Politician. Aaron Boyd & Michael Causey. (Notable Americans Ser.). (Illus.). 144p. (YA). (gr. 6 up). 1994. lib. bdg. 17.95 (*1-883846-04-8*) M Reynolds.

Ross Perot: In His Own Words. Tony Chiu. 208p. 1992. mass mkt. 4.99 (*0-446-36456-8*) Warner Bks.

***Ross Perot: My Life & the Principles for Success.** Ross Perot. 163p. 1996. 13.99 (*1-56530-237-0*) Summit TX.

Ross Perot & Third-Party Politics. Gerald L. Posner. 320p. 1996. 25.00 (*0-679-44731-8*) Random.

Ross Perot & Third Party Politics. Gerald L. Posner. 1996. 25.00 (*0-614-95759-1*) Random.

Ross Register of Siberian Industry: A Guide to Resources, Factories, Products, Mines, Banks & Stock Exchanges Throughout Siberia. Ed. by Robert E. Ross. LC 94-28437. xii, 168p. 1995. 99.00 (*0-88354-125-4*) N Ross.

Ross Sloan Life Insurance Buyer's Guide: Helping You Watch Your $ Ross Sloan. (Illus.). (Orig.). (C). 1995. pap. 4.95 (*0-9646482-0-2*) ASR Pr.

Ross Test of Higher Cognitive Process. John D. Ross & Catherine H. Ross. 1976. student ed. 22.00 (*0-87879-151-5*); 12.00 (*0-685-74188-5*); 6.00 (*0-685-74189-3*); student ed. 20.00 (*0-87879-152-3*); vinyl bd. 63.00 (*0-685-74187-7*) Acad Therapy.

***Ross und Reiter.** Werner Bohm. (Documenta Hippologica Ser.). (Illus.). 254p. (GER.). 1996. write for info. (*3-487-08373-6*) G Olms Pubs.

Rossby Vortices, Spiral Structures, Solitons: Astrophysics & Plasma Physics in Shallow Water Experiments. Mikhail V. Nezlin & E. N. Snezhkin. Tr. by A. Dobrolavsky & A. Pletnev. LC 93-28898. (Nonlinear Dynamics Ser.). (Illus.). 240p. 1993. 97.95 (*0-387-50115-0*) Spr-Verlag.

Rossel Island: An Ethnological Study. Wallace E. Armstrong. LC 75-32798. reprint ed. 54.00 (*0-404-14101-3*) AMS Pr.

Rossetti. David Rodgers. (Color Library). (Illus.). 128p. (Orig.). 1996. pap. 14.95 (*0-7148-3341-X*, Pub. by Phaidon Press UK) Chronicle Bks.

Rossetti. Arthur C. Benson. (BCL1-PR English Literature Ser.). 238p. 1992. reprint ed. lib. bdg. 79.00 (*0-7812-7630-6*) Rprt Serv.

Rossetti & His Circle. M. Beerbohm. 1972. 250.00 (*0-8490-0974-X*) Gordon Pr.

Rossetti & His Poetry. Frederick S. Boas. LC 75-22072. (English Literature Ser.: No. 33). 1975. lib. bdg. 39.95 (*0-8383-2074-0*) M S G Haskell Hse.

Rossetti & His Poetry. Henrietta O. Boas. LC 74-120979. (Poetry & Life Ser.). reprint ed. 16.00 (*0-404-52504-0*) AMS Pr.

Rossetti Assessment & Intervention with High-Risk Infants & Toddlers. Louis M. Rossetti. 1992. 49.95 incl. audio (*1-55999-215-8*) LinguiSystems.

Rossetti, Dante & Ourselves. Nicolette Gray. LC 74-6406. (Studies in Italian Literature: No. 46). 1974. lib. bdg. 75.00 (*0-8383-1917-3*) M S G Haskell Hse.

Rossetti Family, 1824-1854. R. D. Waller. LC 73-145352. 324p. 1972. reprint ed. 39.00 (*0-403-01261-9*) Scholarly.

Rossetti Infant-Toddler Language Scale: A Measure of Communication & Interaction. Louis M. Rossetti. 80p. (ps). 1990. student ed., spiral bd. 38.00 (*1-55999-121-6*) LinguiSystems.

Rossetti Infant-Toddler Language Scale Kit: A Measure of Communication & Interaction. Louis M. Rossetti. 140p. (ps). 1990. student ed. 54.95 (*1-55999-143-7*) LinguiSystems.

Rossetti Papers, 1862-1870. William M. Rossetti. LC 76-130238. reprint ed. 32.50 (*0-404-05438-2*) AMS Pr.

Rossetti to Sexton: Six Women Poets at Texas. Intro. by Dave Oliphant. (Illus.). 237p. (Orig.). (C). 1992. pap. 20.00 (*0-87959-127-7*) U of Tex H Ransom Ctr.

Rossettis. Elizabeth L. Cary. LC 74-30190. (Studies in the Rossettis: No. 81). 1974. lib. bdg. 75.00 (*0-8383-1943-2*) M S G Haskell Hse.

Rossettis: Brothers & the Brotherhood. limited ed. Illus. by Linda Holmes. (Ellen Clarke Bertrand Library: Vol. 6). 48p. 175.00 (*0-916375-22-6*) Press Alley.

Rossetti's Portraits of Elizabeth Siddal. Virginia Surtees & Jon Whiteley. (Illus.). 64p. 1995. 17.95 (*1-85444-008-X*, 008-X, Pub. by Ashmolean Mus UK) A Schwartz & Co.

Rossignol: An Edition & Translation. Ed. by J. L. Baird & John R. Kane. LC 78-38. 99p. reprint ed. pap. 28.30 (*0-7837-1349-5*, 2041497) Bks Demand.

Rossignol de l'Empereur de Chine. Hans Christian Andersen. (Folio - Cadet Rouge Ser.: No. 179). (Illus.). 56p. (FRE.). (J). (gr. 3-7). 1990. pap. 8.95 (*2-07-031179-1*) Schoenhof.

Rossignol de l'Empereur de Chine. Jean Cocteau & Jiri Trinka. 9.95 (*0-686-54559-1*) Fr & Eur.

Rossiia-Entsiklopedicheski Slovar. Broghaus-Ephron. 874p. reprint ed. 75.00 (*0-317-05089-3*) Szwede Slavic.

Rossiia Glazami Zhenshchin: Literaturnaia Antologiia. A. Akhmatova et al. LC 89-11681. (Illus.). 192p. (Orig.). (RUS.). 1989. pap. 8.50 (*0-938920-94-4*) Hermitage.

***Rossiia Na Dal'Nem Vostoke - Russia in a Far East.** Victor P. Petrov. LC 96-43613. 190p. (Orig.). (RUS.). 1996. pap. 12.00 (*1-55779-090-7*) Hermitage.

Rossiia V Pis'menakh: Tom 1. Aleksei M. Remizov. LC 79-91965. (Illus.). 232p. (RUS.). 1982. reprint ed. pap. 7.95 (*0-89830-013-4*) Russica Pubs.

Rossini. (Dent Master Musicians Ser.). (Illus.). (C). pap. write for info. (*0-19-816490-4*) OUP.

Rossini. Ed. by Pierluigi Alvera & Marco Spada. Tr. by Raymond Rosenthal from ITA. (Portraits of Greatness Ser.). (Illus.). 87p. (ENG & ITA.). 1987. 17.50 (*0-918367-11-5*) Elite.

Rossini. Ed. by Pierluigi Alvera & Marco Spada. Tr. by Raymond Rosenthal from ITA. (Portraits of Greatness Ser.). (Illus.). 87p. 1987. pap. 12.50 (*0-918367-21-2*) Elite.

Rossini. David Mountfield. LC 95-5611. (Compact Companions Ser.). 1995. 17.50 (*0-684-81361-0*) S&S Trade.

Rossini. Nicholas Till. (Illustrated Lives of the Great Composers Ser.). (Illus.). 144p. 1996. 14.95 (*0-7119-0988-1*, OP 44023) Omnibus NY.

Rossini: A Study in Tragi-Comedy. Francis Toye. 1988. reprint ed. lib. bdg. 49.00 (*0-7812-0096-2*) Rprt Serv.

Rossini: A Study in Tragi-Comedy. Francis Toye. LC 77-181281. 269p. 1954. reprint ed. 49.00 (*0-403-01704-1*) Scholarly.

Rossini: The Man & His Music. Francis Toye. 288p. 1987. reprint ed. pap. 7.95 (*0-486-25396-1*) Dover.

***Rossiter Arrangement.** large type ed. Jasmine Cresswell. (Linford Romance Library). 304p. 1996. pap. 15.99 (*0-7089-7901-7*) Ulverscroft.

Rossiter in Pictures. Frank Basile. (Illus.). 170p. 1991. text ed. write for info. (*0-935648-34-8*) Halldin Pub.

Rossiter's Memory. John Levesque. 200p. 1995. lib. bdg. 39.00 (*0-8095-4579-9*) Borgo Pr.

Rossmore Appliances. Ruth Patmore & Elizabeth Ross. 50p. (C). 1972. write for info. (*0-686-66706-9*) Macmillan.

Rosso in Italy: The Italian Career of Rosso Fiorentino. David Franklin. LC 93-47989. (Illus.). (C). 1994. 60.00 (*0-300-05893-4*) Yale U Pr.

***Rosso on Fund Raising: Lessons from a Masters Lifetime Experience.** Henry A. Rosso. 1996. 25.95 (*0-7879-0304-3*) Jossey-Bass.

An Asterisk (*) at the beginning of an entry indicates that the title is appearing in BIP for the first time.

Ross's Adventures of the First Settlers on the Oregon or Columbia River, 1810-13 see Early Western Travels, 1748-1846

Rostand: Cyrano de Bergerac. Rostand. Ed. by C. G. Wooden. (French Texts Ser.). 298p. (FRE.). 1994. pap. 19.95 (1-85399-372-7, Pub. by Brstl Class Pr UK) Focus Pub-R Pullins.

Roster of All Regimental Surgeons & Assistant Surgeons in the Late War. 304p. 1989. reprint ed. 30.00 (0-942211-75-8) Olde Soldier Bks.

Roster of Civilizations & Culture. Alfred L. Kroeber. LC 85-747. 96p. 1985. reprint ed. text ed. 49.75 (0-313-24838-9, KRCI, Greenwood Pr) Greenwood.

***Roster of Confederate Soldiers 1861-1865, 16 vols.** Ed. by Janet B. Hewett. 510p. 1997. 1,000.00 (1-56837-306-6) Broadfoot.

Roster of General Officers of the Confederate Service During the Civil War. John M. Carroll. Date not set. 29.95 (0-8488-0009-5, J M C & Co); pap. 19.95 (0-8488-0043-5, J M C & Co) Amereon Ltd.

Roster of Non-Commissioned Officers of the Tenth U. S. Cavalry. 1897. pap. 12.95 (0-8488-0002-8, J M C & Co) Amereon Ltd.

Roster of Officers & Similar Assigned Persons, Listed by Ranks, in the Hungarian Armed Forces, 3 vols., Set. LC 76-17260. Orig. Title: A M. Kir. honvedseg Csendorseg Tisztjeinek Es Hasonlo Allasuaknak Rangsorolasa. 1340p. 1976. write for info. (0-935484-01-9) Universe Pub Co.

Roster of Officers & Similar Assigned Persons, Listed by Ranks, in the Hungarian Armed Forces, 3 vols., Vol. 3. LC 76-17260. Orig. Title: A M. Kir. honvedseg Csendorseg Tisztjeinek Es Hasonlo Allasuaknak Rangsorolasa. 1340p. 1976. 20.00 (0-686-61485-2) Universe Pub Co.

Roster of Officers & Similar Assigned Persons, Listed by Ranks, in the Hungarian Armed Forces, 3 vols., Vols. 1 & 2. Orig. Title: A M. Kir. honvedseg Csendorseg Tisztjeinek Es Hasonlo Allasuaknak Rangsorolasa. 1340p. 1976. 20.00 (0-318-56303-7) Universe Pub Co.

Roster of Ohio Soldiers in the Mexican War. Jana Broglin. 1991. 25.00 (0-935057-63-3) OH Genealogical.

Roster of Ohio Soldiers in the War of 1812. Ed. by Adjutant General of Ohio. 264p. 1995. reprint ed. pap. text ed. 18.00 (0-7884-0198-X) Heritage Bk.

Roster of Regional Experts & Institutions on Conservation & Efficient Utilization of Energy. 200p. write for info. (92-1-119652-3, E.95.II.F.2) UN.

***Roster of Revolutionary Soldiers in Georgia, Vol. I.** McCall. 294p. 1996. reprint ed. pap. 27.00 (0-614-23494-8, 3501) Clearfield Co.

***Roster of Revolutionary Soldiers in Georgia, Vol. II.** McCall. 215p. 1996. reprint ed. pap. 24.00 (0-614-23495-6, 3502) Clearfield Co.

***Roster of Revolutionary Soldiers in Georgia, Vol. III.** McCall. 463p. 1996. reprint ed. pap. 38.00 (0-614-23496-4, 3503) Clearfield Co.

***Roster of Soldiers & Patriots of the American Revolution Buried in Indiana.** O'Byrne. 407p. 1994. reprint ed. pap. 25.00 (0-614-23559-6, 4260) Clearfield Co.

Roster of South Carolina Patriots in the American Revolution. Bobby G. Moss. LC 82-83584. (Illus.). 1023p. 1994. reprint ed. 50.00 (0-8063-1005-7, 3915) Genealog Pub.

Roster of the Seventh Cavalry Campaigns. Charles K. Mills. 1976. 26.95 (0-8488-0012-5, J M C & Co) Amereon Ltd.

Roster of the Vermont Legislature: 1966-1990. Ed. by Clark H. Bensen. (Illus.). x, 408p. (Orig.). 1989. spiral bd. 65.00 (1-57708-031-9, PMR-VT-90) Polidata.

Rostnikov's Vacation. large type ed. Stuart M. Kaminsky. 304p. 1992. reprint ed. lib. bdg. 20.95 (1-56054-340-X) Thorndike Pr.

***Rostov Oblast: Economy, Industry, Government, Business.** 2nd rev. ed. Russian Information & Business Center, Inc. Staff. (Russian Regional Business Directories Ser.). (Illus.). 200p. 1997. pap. 99.00 (1-57751-409-2) Russ Info & Busn Ctr.

Rostpilze, Uredinales, auf Carex im Ostalpenraum: Ein Neues Artenkonzept. Peter Zwetko. (Bibliotheca Mycologica Ser.: Vol. 153). (Illus.). 222p. (GER.). 1993. pap. 57.60 (3-443-64120-2, Pub. by Cramer-Borntraeger GW) Lubrecht & Cramer.

***Rostro Cambiante de la Politica en Estados Unidos: La Politica Obrera y los Sindicatos.** Jack Barnes. 470p. (SPA.). 1997. pap. 21.95 (0-87348-851-2) Pathfinder NY.

Rostro Cercano: (Antologia Poetica) Maricel Mayor Marsan. LC 86-82717. 62p. (SPA.). 1986. pap. 8.00 (0-935318-12-7) Edins Hispamerica.

***Rostro Inolvidable.** Olga Rosado. (SPA.). Date not set. pap. write for info. (0-89729-837-3) Ediciones.

Rostro y la Mascara. Jose A. Rosado & C. Gomez. 208p. (SPA.). 1995. pap. 12.95 (0-8477-0240-5) U of PR Pr.

Rostropovic in Red Square: A Selection of Love Poems. Peter Pease. LC 95-20575. (Illus.). 80p. 1996. pap. 12.95 (0-7734-2805-4, Mellen Poetry Pr) E Mellen.

Rostros Del Protestantismo Latinoamericano. Jose Miquez Bonino. (Nueva Creacion Ser.). 167p. 1996. pap. 10.00 (0-8028-0934-0, Neuva Creacion) Eerdmans.

Rosty. Cohen. 1998. 22.95 (0-02-874099-8) Free Pr.

Rosty. Cohen. 1998. 22.95 (0-684-82752-2) Free Pr.

***Roswell - Chall Auditory Blending Test: Manual of Instructions.** Jeanne S. Chall & Florence G. Roswell. Ed. by Jen Noon. 5p. (Orig.). (J). (gr. 1-4). 1997. pap. text ed. 3.50 (0-614-30961-1, 2316) Ed Pub Serv.

***Roswell - Chall Diagnostic Reading Test of Word Analysis Skills: Manual of Instruction.** Jeanne S. Chall & Florence G. Roswell. Ed. by Jen Noon. 14p. (Orig.). (J). (gr. 1-4). 1997. pap. text ed. 4.00 (0-614-30963-8, 2318) Ed Pub Serv.

***Roswell - Chall Diagnostic Reading Test of Word Analysis Skills: Technical Supplement.** Jeanne S. Chall & Florence G. Roswell. Ed. by Jen Noon. 16p. (Orig.). (J). (gr. 1-4). 1997. pap. text ed. 3.75 (0-614-30962-X, 2317) Ed Pub Serv.

***Roswell Crewman.** 2nd rev. ed. LC 95-96038. 220p. 1997. reprint ed. pap. 12.95 (0-9649580-1-5) Black Mesa.

***Roswell Files.** Tim Shawcross. 1997. 24.95 (0-7603-0471-8) Motorbooks Intl.

Roswell Garst: A Biography. Harold Lee. LC 83-26452. (Henry A. Wallace Series on Agricultural History & Rural Studies). (Illus.). 351p. reprint ed. pap. 100.10 (0-8357-6756-6, 2035413) Bks Demand.

Roswell Incident. Charles Berlitz. 1990. pap. 5.50 (0-425-12602-1) Berkley Pub.

***Roswell Incident.** Charles Berlitz & William L. Moore. (Illus.). 1997. 6.98 (1-56731-132-6, MJF Bks) Fine Comms.

Roswell Report: A Historical Perspective. Ed. by George M. Eberhart. (Illus.). 152p. 1991. pap. text ed. 12.00 (0-929343-59-X) J A Hynek Ctr UFO.

***Roswell Report: Fact vs. Fiction in the New Mexico Desert.** James McAndrew & Richard L. Weaver. (Illus.). 1995. pap. 52.00 (0-16-048023-X) Off Air Force.

***Roswell Report: Fact vs. Fiction in the New Mexico Desert - A UFO Encounter, 2 vols.** 1997. lib. bdg. 600. 99 (0-8490-6156-3) Gordon Pr.

***Roswell UFO Crash: What They Don't Want You To Know.** Kal K. Korff. LC 97-1555. 1997. 26.95 (1-57392-127-0) Prometheus Bks.

Rosy & Ground Boas. J. Walls. (Illus.). 64p. 1995. pap. text ed. 9.95 (0-7938-0277-6, RE-130) TFH Pubns.

***Rosy Cole: She Grows & Graduates.** Sheila Greenwald. LC 97-9899. (Illus.). 96p. (J). (gr. 2-6). 1997. 14.95 (0-531-30022-6); lib. bdg. 15.99 (0-531-33022-2) Orchard Bks Watts.

Rosy Cole: She Walks in Beauty. Sheila Greenwald. LC 93-40114. (J). (gr. 5 up). 1994. 14.95 (0-316-32743-3) Little.

Rosy Cross: Its Teachings. R. Swinburne Clymer. 287p. 1965. 7.95 (0-932785-43-3) Philos Pub.

Rosy Dock. abr. ed. Jeannie Baker. LC 94-4677. (Illus.). 32p. (J). (ps up). 1995. lib. bdg. 14.93 (0-688-11493-8) Greenwillow.

***Rosy Future of War.** Delmas. LC 97-4177. 1997. 24.00 (0-684-83370-0, Free Press) Free Pr.

Rosy Glasses. Kazuo Ozaki. Tr. by Robert Epp. 150p. (C). 1988. text ed. 29.00 (0-904400-52-8, Pub. by Curzon Press UK) UH Pr.

Rosy Medallions: Selected Work. Camille Roy. Ed. by Patricia Dienstfrey. LC 95-2637. 72p. (Orig.). (C). 1995. pap. text ed. 10.00 (0-932716-35-0) Kelsey St Pr.

Rosy Noses, Freezing Toes. Judy Delton. (Pee Wee Scouts Ser.: No. 13). 96p. (Orig.). (J). 1990. mass mkt. 3.99 (0-440-40384-7, YB BDD) BDD Bks Young Read.

Rosy Thoughts for Cross Cultural Living. Betty J. Williams. (Illus.). 112p. (Orig.). 1990. pap. 9.95 (0-9626728-0-7) BJS Williams.

Rosy's Garden: A Child's Keepsake of Flowers. Satomi Ichikawa & Elizabeth Laird. (Illus.). 48p. (YA). 1990. 16.95 (0-399-21881-5, Philomel Bks) Putnam Pub Group.

Rot at the Top: Dysfunctional Bureaucracy in Academia. Bogdan Mieczkowski. 252p. (Orig.). (C). 1995. pap. text ed. 29.50 (0-8191-9845-5); lib. bdg. 52.50 (0-8191-9844-7) U Pr of Amer.

Rota Veneris. Boncompagno da Signa. Ed. by Josef Purkart. LC 74-18250. 128p. 1975. reprint ed. lib. bdg. 50.00 (0-8201-1137-6) Schol Facsimiles.

Rotaformidae, a New Family of Upper Cretaceous Nassellariina (Radiolaria) from the Great Valley Sequence, California Coast Ranges. E. A. Pessagno, Jr. 34p. 1970. write for info. (0-614-17835-5) Paleo Res.

Rotal Anthology: An Annotated Index of Rotal Decisions from 1971-1988. Augustine Mendonqa. 771p. 1992. 45. 00 (0-943616-59-X) Canon Law Soc.

Rotary Basic Library. David H. Bailey & Louise Gottlieb. Ed. by Willmon L. White & Mark Perlberg. (Illus.). 506p. (JPN.). 1982. 16.75 (0-915062-13-5) Rotary Intl.

Rotary Basic Library, 7 vols. David H. Bailey et al. Ed. by Willmon L. White & Mark Perlberg. (Illus.). 506p. 1987. 16.75 (0-915062-08-9) Rotary Intl.

Rotary Cameras for 16mm Microfilm - Mechanical & Optical Characteristics: ANSI-AIIM MS47-1990. Association for Information & Image Management Staff. 1990. pap. 33.00 (0-89258-207-3, MS47) Assn Inform & Image Mgmt.

Rotary Cement Kiln. 2nd enl. rev. ed. K. Peray. (Illus.). 1986. 85.00 (0-8206-0314-7) Chem Pub.

Rotary Club Murder Mystery. Graham Landrum. 1996. mass mkt. 4.99 (0-312-95796-3) Tor Bks.

***Rotary Crossed Axes Shaving of Spur & Helical Gears.** R. S. Drummond. (Technical Papers). 1935. pap. text ed. 30.00 (1-55589-226-4) AGMA.

Rotary Cutting Companion for Feathered Star Quilts. Marsha R. McCloskey. 24p. 1995. pap. 6.95 (0-9635422-4-9) Feathered Star.

Rotary Diecutting: Dimensional Accuracy Control. Compiled by Corrugated Containers Division, TAPPI, Engineering Committee Staff. LC 92-14356. 1992. 27.00 (0-89852-274-9, 0101R205) TAPPI.

Rotary Engine Design: Analysis & Developments. 140p. 1989. 19.00 (0-89883-695-6, SP768) Soc Auto Engineers.

Rotary in Baton Rouge 1918-1970. M. E. Blankenstein. 15. 00 (1-57980-031-9) Claitors.

Rotary International. L. Levy. 1990. 135.00 (0-7121-1851-9, Pub. by Northcote UK) St Mut.

Rotary, Kelly & Swivel. Ed. by Fernando Albornoz. Tr. by Roberto Quiroga. (Rotary Drilling Ser.: Unit I, Lesson 4). (Illus.). 69p. (Orig.). (SPA.). 1982. pap. text ed. 14.00 (0-88698-032-1, 2.10422) PETEX.

Rotary, Kelly & Swivel: Canadian Metric Edition. 2nd ed. Ed. by Jodie Leecraft. (Rotary Drilling Ser.: Unit I, Lesson 4). (Illus.). 68p. 1981. pap. text ed. 14.00 (0-88698-020-8, 2.10421) PETEX.

Rotary, Kelly, Swivel, Tongs, & Top Drive. L. D. Davis. Ed. by K. R. Bork. (Rotary Drilling Ser.: Unit I, Lesson 4). (Illus.). 164p. (Orig.). (C). 1995. pap. text ed. 15.00 (0-88698-172-7, 2.104101) PETEX.

***Rotary Magic & More: Easy Techniques to Instantly Improve Every Quilt You Make.** Nancy Johnson-Srebro. 224p. 1998. 29.95 (0-87596-783-3) Rodale Pr Inc.

Rotary Power Transmission Design. Ed. by Ken Hurst. LC 94-10056. 1995. pap. text ed. 34.00 (0-07-707852-7) McGraw.

Rotary Pump Standards for Nomenclature, Definitions, Application, & Operation, No. 3.1-3.5. (Hydraulic Institute Ser.: No. 3.1-3.5). 46p. 1994. 59.00 (1-880952-06-8, S111) Hydraulic Inst.

Rotary Pump Test Standard, No. 3.6. (Hydraulic Institute Ser.: No. 3.6). 19p. 1994. 39.00 (1-880952-07-6, S112) Hydraulic Inst.

Rotary Rig & Its Components. Ed. by Fernando Albornoz. Tr. by Vivian Carmona-Agosto. (Rotary Drilling Ser.: Unit I, Lesson 1). (Illus.). 47p. (Orig.). (SPA.). 1980. pap. 14.00 (0-88698-029-1, 2.10132) PETEX.

Rotary Rig & Its Components. 4th ed. K. R. Bork. LC 93-49573. (Rotary Drilling Ser.: Unit 1, Lesson 1). (Illus.). 128p. 1995. pap. text ed. 15.00 (0-88698-166-2, 2.10140) PETEX.

Rotary Riot: Forty Fast & Fabulous Quilts. Nancy J. Martin & Judy D. Hopkins. LC 91-26050. (Illus.). 128p. 1992. pap. 21.95 (0-943574-86-2, B126) That Patchwork.

Rotary Roundup. Judy D. Hopkins et al. LC 93-27838. (Illus.). 96p. (Orig.). 1994. pap. 21.95 (1-56477-028-1, B164) That Patchwork.

Rotary Spokes. Fiona Cooper. 1996. pap. 13.99 (1-85242-507-5) Serpents Tail.

Rotary Tiller Service Manual. 3rd ed. Intertec Publishing Staff. (Illus.). 200p. 1989. pap. text ed. 24.95 (0-87288-353-1, RTS-3) Intertec Pub.

Rotary-Wing Aerodynamics. W. Z. Stepniewski & C. N. Keys. (Engineering Ser.). (Illus.). 236p. 1984. pap. 14.95 (0-486-64647-5) Dover.

Rotary Wing Flight. Ed. by ASA Staff & Nicholas Ean. (Illus.). 120p. 1992. pap. 15.95 (1-56027-118-3, ASA-RW-4) Av Suppl & Acad.

Rotating Electric Machinery & Transformer Technology. 4th ed. Donald V. Richardson & Arthur J. Caisse, Jr. LC 96-1816. 704p. (C). 1996. text ed. 90.00 (0-13-409640-1) P-H.

Rotating Electrical Machinery. 4th ed. Richardson. 1996. lab manual ed., pap. text ed. 35.20 (0-13-409657-6) P-H.

Rotating Electrical Machines & Power Systems. 2nd ed. Patrick & Fardo. (C). 1996. text ed. 79.00 (0-13-268665-1) P-H.

Rotating Electrical Machines & Power Systems. 2nd ed. Dale R. Patrick & Stephen W. Fardo. LC 96-9543. 399p. 1996. 79.00 (0-88173-239-7) Fairmont Pr.

Rotating Fields in General Relativity. Jumal N. Islam. 136p. 1985. 47.95 (0-521-26082-5) Cambridge U Pr.

Rotating Fluids in Engineering in Science. James P. Vanyo. LC 92-46788. 440p. 1993. 94.95 (0-7506-9261-8) Buttrwrth-Heinemann.

Rotating Fluids in Geophysical & Industrial Applications. Ed. by E. J. Hopfinger. (CISM International Centre for Mechanical Sciences Ser.: Vol. 329). (Illus.). vi, 378p. 1992. 106.95 (0-387-82393-X) Spr-Verlag.

Rotating Machinery: Proceedings of the 3rd International Symposia on Transport Phenomena, Dynamics, & Design of Rotating Machinery, 2 pts., Pt. 1. Ed. by Jong H. Kim & W. J. Yang. 750p. 1992. 115.00 (1-56032-156-3) Hemisp Pub.

Rotating Machinery: Proceedings of the 3rd International Symposia on Transport Phenomena, Dynamics, & Design of Rotating Machinery, 2 pts., Pt. 2. Ed. by Jong H. Kim & W. J. Yang. 750p. 1992. 115.00 (1-56032-157-1) Hemisp Pub.

Rotating Machinery: Proceedings of the 3rd International Symposia on Transport Phenomena, Dynamics, & Design of Rotating Machinery, 2 pts., Set. Ed. by Jong H. Kim & W. J. Yang. 1500p. 1992. 214.00 (1-56032-147-4) Hemisp Pub.

Rotating Machinery Explained: DC Motors. Richard Hunter. LC 80-730089. (Orig.). 1980. student ed. 6.00 (0-8064-0315-2, 810); audio, vhs 319.00 (0-8064-0316-0) Bergwall.

Rotating Machinery Explained: Single Phase AC Motors. Richard Hunter. LC 82-730333. (Orig.). 1982. student ed. 7.00 (0-8064-0317-9, 812); audio, vhs 279.00 (0-8064-0318-7) Bergwall.

Rotating Machinery Explained: Three Phase AC Motors. Richard Hunter. (Orig.). 1982. student ed. 7.00 (0-8064-0319-5, 813); audio, vhs 299.00 (0-8064-0320-9) Bergwall.

Rotating Machines & Magnetic Devices. USNA Staff. 256p. (C). 1994. per. 20.84 (0-8403-8496-3) Kendall-Hunt.

***Rotating Mirror Streak & Framing Cameras.** E. A. Igel & M. Kristiansen. LC 97-6011. 1997. pap. write for info. (0-8194-2461-7) SPIE.

Rotating Objects & Relativistic Physics: Proceedings of the El Escarial Summer School on Gravitation & General Relativity 1992. Ed. by F. J. Chinea & Romero Gonzalez. (Lecture Notes in Physics Ser.). 1993. 80.95 (0-387-57364-X); write for info. (3-540-57364-X) Spr-Verlag.

***Rotation: The Twelve Months of Intern Life.** M. Robert Marion. LC 97-4135. 1997. 25.00 (0-06-017263-0) HarpC.

Rotation & Lorentz Groups & Their Representations for Physicists. K. N. Rao. (C). 1988. 35.00 (81-224-0056-6) S Asia.

Rotation & Mixing in Stellar Interiors: Proceedings of the Workshop "Frontiers in Stellar Structure Theory" Held in Honor of Professor Evry Schatzman in Les Houches, France, June 19-25, 1989. Ed. by M. J. Goupil et al. (Lecture Notes in Physics Ser.: Vol. 366). xiii, 183p. 1990. 40.95 (0-387-53059-2) Spr-Verlag.

Rotation Diet. 1996. lib. bdg. 250.99 (0-8490-5916-X) Gordon Pr.

Rotation Diet. Martin Katahn. 272p. 1987. mass mkt. 6.50 (0-553-27667-0) Bantam.

***Rotation Diet Cookbook: A 4-Day Plan for Relieving Allergies.** Jill Carter. LC 97-6977. 144p. 1997. pap. 9.95 (1-85230-965-2) Element MA.

Rotation Manual for Clinical Laboratory Science. Lori Rice-Spearman & Hal S. Larsen. 181p. 1994. pap. 35.00 (0-683-07259-5) Williams & Wilkins.

Rotation Manual for Clinical Laboratory Science. Lori Rice-Spearman & Hal S. Larsen. 1994. write for info. (0-683-04821-X) Williams & Wilkins.

Rotation of Spheres (TCP) in Five Dimensions: A Sphere or Charge (4D) Moves in a Cylinder of (4D) Time. Cosmatom Staff. (C). 1992. pap. text ed. 25.00 (1-874686-07-6, Pub. by Cosmatom UK) St Mut.

Rotation of the Earth: Proceedings of the International Astronomical Union, 48th Symposium, Morioka, Japan, 1971. International Astronomical Union Staff. Ed. by Paul Melchior & S. Yumi. LC 70-188004. 244p. 1972. lib. bdg. 88.00 (90-277-0242-X) Kluwer Ac.

Rotation-Vibration of Polyatomic Molecules: Higher Order Energies & Frequencies of Spectral Transitions. Gilbert Amat et al. LC 71-152569. 447p. reprint ed. pap. 127.40 (0-685-16268-0, 2027115) Bks Demand.

Rotation with Patterns Blocks. Arthur Wiebe. 24p. (J). (gr. 3-9). 1985. student ed. 5.95 (1-878669-31-1, CTA-4767) Crea Tea Assocs.

Rotational Dynamics of Small & Macromolecules. Ed. by T. Dorfmueller & Robert Pecora. (Lecture Notes in Physics Ser.: Vol. 293). 250p. 1987. 34.95 (0-387-18688-3) Spr-Verlag.

Rotational Moulding of Plastics. 2nd ed. Ed. by R. J. Crawford. LC 96-18253. (Polymer Engineering Ser.: Vol. 2). 1996. text ed. 96.00 (0-471-96303-8) Wiley.

Rotational Physics: The Principles of Energy. Myrna M. Milani & Brian R. Smith. LC 85-16305. (Rational Physics Ser.). (Illus.). (Orig.). 1986. pap. 12.00 (0-943290-03-1) Fainshaw Pr.

Rotator Cuff Disorders. Ed. by Wayne Z. Burkhead, Jr. LC 95-14112. 422p. 1995. 129.00 (0-683-01215-0) Williams & Wilkins.

Rotator Cuff Disorders: Evaluation & Treatment. Ed. by J. P. Iannotti. LC 91-33008. 88p. 1991. pap. 35.00 (0-89203-051-8) Amer Acad Ortho Surg.

***Rotator Cuff Repair: A Guide for Patients.** David Collins. (Ortho Ser.). 32p. 1997. pap. text ed. 2.95 (1-885274-52-1) HIN.

Rotatoria. Die Raedertiere Mitteleuropas. Monogonta, 2 vols. 2nd rev. ed. Max Voigt. (Illus.). 673p. (GER.). 1978. lib. bdg. 150.00 (0-685-13284-6) Lubrecht & Cramer.

Rotch: The Rotches (Biography & Genealogy of the Rotch Family of Nantucket & New Bedford, Mass.) J. M. Bullard. (Illus.). 583p. 1991. reprint ed. pap. 89.00 (0-8328-1887-9); reprint ed. lib. bdg. 99.00 (0-8328-1886-0) Higginson Bk Co.

Rote Kapelle. CIA Staff. Ed. by Paul Kesaris. LC 79-51270. 404p. 1979. text ed. 55.00 (0-313-27051-1, U7051, Greenwood Pr) Greenwood.

Rote List 1996 (German Physician's Desk Reference) (GER.). 1996. 195.00 (0-7859-9764-4) Fr & Eur.

Rote Walker. Mark Jarman. LC 81-69799. (Poetry Ser.). 1981. 20.95 (0-915604-64-7) Carnegie-Mellon.

***Rotella.** Renato Barilli. 1997. pap. 29.95 (88-8158-088-8, Pub. by Charta IT) Dist Art Pubs.

***Rotenone Health & Safety Guide.** (Health & Safety Guides Ser.: No. 73). 17p. 1992. pap. text ed. 5.00 (92-4-151073-0, 1860073) World Health.

Roth: The Family of Nicholas Roth, American Settlers from Germany, with Information on Associate Families of Winters, Darnold & Keppler. Steve Roth. (Illus.). 197p. 1993. reprint ed. pap. 29.50 (0-8328-3397-5); reprint ed. lib. bdg. 39.50 (0-8328-3396-7) Higginson Bk Co.

Roth Collection of Natural Products Data: Concise Descriptions & Spectra. Ed. by Lutz Roth & Gabriele Rump. 500p. 1995. 190.00 (3-527-28180-0, VCH) Wiley.

Rothage. Mark Dunster. 23p. (Orig.). 1987. pap. 4.00 (0-89642-154-6) Linden Pubs.

Rothbaum's Guide to the King County Courthouse. Leslie Rothbaum. (Illus.). 152p. (Orig.). 1994. pap. 19.95 (0-89716-515-2) P B Pubng.

Rothenberg Lease-Option Strategy. Ed Rothenberg. (Orig.). 1986. pap. 7.95 (0-9613865-1-7) E Rothenberg.

Rothko Chapel Paintings: Form as Meaning in the American Abstract Sublime. Sheldon Nodelman. (Illus.). 128p. (Orig.). pap. 23.95 (0-292-77054-5) U of Tex Pr.

***Rothko Chapel Paintings: Origins, Structure, Meaning.** Sheldon Nodelman. LC 96-48538. (Illus.). 359p. 65.00 (0-939594-36-6); pap. 34.95 (0-939594-37-4) U of Tex Pr.

R

Rothko Chaptel: An Act of Faith. 2nd ed. Susan J. Barnes. (Illus.). 135p. 1996. pap. 23.09 (*0-945472-02-1*) Rothko Chapel.

Rothman-Simeone the Spine. 4th ed. Herkowitz. 1998. text ed. write for info. (*0-7216-7176-4*) HarBrace.

Roth's American Poetry Annual, 1988. Ed. by Roth Publishing, Inc. Staff. 727p. 1989. 60.00 (*0-89609-285-2*) Roth Pub Inc.

Roth's American Poetry Annual, 1989. Ed. by Roth Publishing, Inc. Staff. 700p. 1990. 60.00 (*0-89609-295-X*) Roth Pub Inc.

Roth's American Poetry Annual, 1990. Ed. by Roth Publishing, Inc. Staff. 735p. 1991. 60.00 (*0-89609-302-6*) Roth Pub Inc.

Roth's Essay Index. Ed. by Roth Publishing, Inc. Staff. LC 88-62954. 494p. 1989. 49.95 (*0-89609-286-0*, Poetry Index Pr) Roth Pub Inc.

Roth's Essay Index, Second Cumulative Supplement, Phases VI-X. Roth Publishing, Inc. Staff. (Corefiche Ser.). 478p. (Orig.). 1993. pap. text ed. 49.95 (*0-89609-326-3*) Roth Pub Inc.

Roth's Index to Great American & English Essays. Roth Publishing, Inc. Staff. 87p. 1988. pap. text ed. 29.95 (*0-89609-293-3*) Roth Pub Inc.

Roth's Index to Literary Criticism. rev. ed. 139p. 1991. pap. text ed. 19.95 (*0-89609-319-0*) Roth Pub Inc.

Roth's Index to Short Stories. 2nd ed. 110p. 1991. pap. text ed. 19.95 (*0-89609-317-4*) Roth Pub Inc.

***Rothsay, Minnesota School Based Enterprises Case Study Report.** Anne M. Rogers & Susan Hubbard. (Cross Case Report & Case Studies). 50p. 1995. teacher ed., text ed. 20.00 (*0-614-24534-6*); teacher ed., pap. text ed. 10.00 (*0-614-24535-4*) Natl Inst Work.

Rothschild Canticles: Art & Mysticism in Flanders & the Rhineland Circa 1300. Jeffrey F. Hamburger. 480p. (C). 1991. text ed. 65.00 (*0-300-04308-2*) Yale U Pr.

Rothschild Gardens. Miriam Rothschild et al. 192p. 1997. 35.00 (*0-8109-3790-5*, Abradale Pr) Abrams.

Rothschild Library: A Catalogue of the Collection of Eighteenth-Century Printed Books & Manuscripts Formed by Lord Rothschild, 2 vols. (Illus.). 1993. reprint ed. 250.00 (*1-882860-11-X*); reprint ed. 750.00 (*1-882860-12-8*) J Cummins Bksell.

Rothschild Mahzor. Schmelzer et al. 1983. pap. 25.00 (*0-87334-017-5*) Ktav.

Rothschild Money Trust. George W. Armstrong. 1988. lib. bdg. 250.00 (*0-87700-370-X*) Revisionist Pr.

***Rothschild Short Stories.** Michael Rothschild. 1999. pap. write for info. (*0-670-81375-3*) Viking Penguin.

***Rothschilds.** Niall Ferguson. 1998. pap. 29.95 (*0-670-85768-8*) Viking Penguin.

Rothschilds: A European Family. Ed. by Georg Heuberger. (Illus.). 232p. 1994. 45.00 (*0-85115-371-2*) Boydell & Brewer.

Rothschilds: A Family Portrait. Frederic Morton. 304p. 1991. reprint ed. pap. 12.95 (*0-02-023002-8*) Macmillan.

Rothschilds: Essays on the History of a European Family. Ed. by Georg Heuberger. (Illus.). 420p. 1994. 63.00 (*0-85115-595-2*) Boydell & Brewer.

Rothschilds: Financial Rulers of Nations. John Reeves. 1975. 300.00 (*0-87968-193-4*) Gordon Pr.

Rothschilds: Five Men of Frankfurt. M. E. Ravage. 1973. reprint ed. lib. bdg. 300.00 (*0-8490-0975-8*) Gordon Pr.

Rothschilds Battle Rockefellers: The Bankers World Power Struggle. C Baker. 1982. lib. bdg. 69.00 (*0-87700-435-8*) Revisionist Pr.

Rothschild's Fiddle, & Other Stories. Anton P. Chekhov. LC 72-121528. (Short Story Index Reprint Ser.). 1977. 18.95 (*0-8369-3484-9*) Ayer.

Rothschild's Fiddle & Other Stories. Anton P. Chekhov. 1976. 22.95 (*0-8488-0182-2*) Amereon Ltd.

Rothschilds of Nordstetten: Their History & Genealogy. Charles B. Bernstein. (Illus.). 280p. 1989. pap. 30.00 (*0-9622737-0-8*) C B Bernstein.

Rothstein on Reference: ...With Some Help From Friends. Ed. by Charles Bunge & Bill Katz. LC 89-19886. (Reference Librarian Ser.: Nos. 25 & 26). (Illus.). 646p. 1989. text ed. 59.95 (*0-86656-840-9*) Haworth Pr.

Rotifer & Microalgae Culture Systems: Proceedings of a U. S.-Asia Workshop. Ed. by Wendy Fulks & Kevan L. Main. (C). 1991. pap. text ed. write for info. (*0-9617016-2-5*) Oceanic Inst.

Rotifer Fauna of Wisconsin. H. K. Harring & F. J. Myers. (Illus.). 1973. reprint ed. 130.00 (*3-7682-0820-6*) Lubrecht & Cramer.

Rotifer Symposium, No. IV. Ed. by L. May et al. (C). 1987. lib. bdg. 267.00 (*90-6193-645-4*) Kluwer Ac.

Rotifer Symposium, No. V. Terry W. Snell. (Developments in Hydrobiology Ser.). (C). 1990. lib. bdg. 299.00 (*0-7923-0413-6*) Kluwer Ac.

Rotifer Symposium VI: Proceedings of the Sixth International Rotifer Symposium, Held in Banyoles, Spain, June 3-8, 1991. Ed. by J. J. Gilbert et al. LC 92-46547. (Developments in Hydrobiology Ser.: No. 83). 600p. (C). 1993. reprint ed. lib. bdg. 333.50 (*0-7923-2125-1*) Kluwer Ac.

Rotifera VII: Proceedings of the Seventh Rotifer Symposium, Held in Mikolajki, Poland, June 6-11, 1994, Vol. 109. Ed. by J. Ejsmont-Karabin & R. M. Pontin. LC 95-24706. (Developments in Hydrobiology Ser.). 420p. (C). 1996. lib. bdg. 262.50 (*0-7923-3692-5*) Kluwer Ac.

***Rotimi Fani-Kayode & Alex Hirst: Photographs.** Rotimi Fani-Kayode. 1997. pap. text ed. 69.50 (*2-909571-17-3*, Pub. by Revue Noire FR) Dist Art Pubs.

Rotisser 97. Glen Waggoner. 1997. pap. 15.95 (*0-316-91749-4*) Little.

Rotisserie Baseball: Playing for Fun & Playing for Blood, Vol. 1. John C. Benson & Randall Baron. 200p. 1996. pap. 12.95 (*0-910791-86-4*) Diamond Lib.

Rotisserie Baseball: Playing for Fun & Playing for Blood, Vol. 2. John C. Benson & Randall Baron. 200p. 1996. pap. 12.95 (*0-910791-87-2*) Diamond Lib.

Rotisserie Baseball A to Z - 1993. John Bensen. 1993. pap. 15.95 (*1-880876-35-3*) Diamond Lib.

Rotisserie Baseball Analyst, 1992. John C. Benson. 320p. 1991. pap. 22.95 (*1-880876-33-7*) Diamond Lib.

Rotisserie Baseball Annual 1993. John Bensen. 1993. pap. 22.95 (*1-880876-36-1*) Diamond Lib.

Rotisserie Baseball Annual 1994. John Benson. 1994. pap. 22.95 (*1-880876-50-7*) Diamond Lib.

Rotisserie Baseball Annual 1995. John Benson. 1994. pap. 22.95 (*1-880876-16-7*) Diamond Lib.

Rotisserie Baseball Annual 1996. John Benson. 1995. pap. 22.95 (*1-880876-04-3*) Diamond Lib.

***Rotisserie Baseball Annual 1997.** 8th ed. John C. Benson. 336p. 1996. pap. 22.95 (*1-880876-09-4*) Diamond Lib.

Rotisserie de la Reine Pedauque. Anatole France. (Coll. Bleue). 256p. (FRE.). 1959. pap. 10.95 (*0-8288-9764-6*, F101361) Fr & Eur.

Rotisserie de la Reine Pedauque. Anatole France. (Folio Ser.: No. 2098). (FRE.). pap. 10.95 (*2-07-038186-2*) Schoenhof.

Rotisserie de la Reine Pedauque. Anatole France. 256p. 1959. 9.95 (*0-686-55876-6*) Fr & Eur.

Rotisserie de la Reine Pedauque. Anatole France. 308p. (FRE.). 1989. pap. 11.95 (*0-7859-2577-5*, 2070381862) Fr & Eur.

Rotisserie de la reine Pedauque. Anatole France. LC 75-41103. reprint ed. 27.50 (*0-404-14788-7*) AMS Pr.

Rotisserie League Baseball. 6th ed. 1992. write for info. (*0-318-69135-3*) Bantam.

Rotisserie League Baseball: The Offical Rule Book & Draft Day Guide 1994. Ed. by Glen Waggoner. 1994. pap. 14.95 (*0-316-91712-5*) Little.

Rotisserie League Baseball: The Official Rule Book & Draft-Day Guide, 1995, Vol. 1. Glen Waggoner. 1995. pap. 14.95 (*0-316-91714-1*) Little.

Rotisserie League Baseball: The Official Rule Book & Draft-Day Guide 1996 Edition. Glen Waggoner. (Illus.). 1996. pap. 15.95 (*0-316-91771-0*) Little.

Rotodynamic Pump Design. R. K. Turton. (Illus.). 160p. (C). 1994. text ed. 54.95 (*0-521-30502-0*) Cambridge U Pr.

Rotonda: The Vision & the Reality, A Short History of a Florida Development. Jack Alexander. (Illus.). 224p. 1995. 14.95 (*1-881539-07-5*) Tabby Hse Bks.

Rotor Dynamical Instability: Presented at the Applied Mechanics, Bioengineering, & Fluids Engineering Conference, Houston, Texas, June 20-22, 1983. Ed. by Maurice L. Adams. LC 83-71215. (AMD Ser.: Vol. 55). 106p. pap. 30.30 (*0-7837-0203-5*, 2040499) Bks Demand.

Rotor Magazine. Helicopter Assn. International Staff. 48p. 1995. write for info. (*0-614-04282-8*) Helicopter Assn Intl.

Rotordynamics of Turbomachinery. John M. Vance. LC 87-34055. 388p. 1988. text ed. 99.95 (*0-471-80258-1*) Wiley.

***Rotordynamics Prediction in Engineering.** M. Lalanne & Guy Ferraris. LC 97-22472. 1997. write for info. (*0-471-97288-6*) Wiley.

Rotordynamics Prediction in Engineering. Michel LaLanne et al. 198p. 1990. text ed. 82.95 (*0-471-92633-7*) Wiley.

Rotordynamics Two Problems in Turbomachinery. Ed. by N. F. Rieger. (CISM International Centre for Mechanical Sciences Ser.: Vol. 297). (Illus.). viii, 586p. 1989. 111.95 (*0-387-82091-4*) Spr-Verlag.

Rotordynamics, 1992: Proceedings of the International Conference on Rotating Machine Dynamics Hotel Des Bains, Venice, 28-30 April 1992. Ed. by M. J. Goodwin. (Illus.). 456p. 1993. 163.95 (*0-387-19754-0*) Spr-Verlag.

Rotraut Uecker Klein. Klaus Ottmann. (Illus.). 32p. (Orig.). (C). 1989. pap. 12.00 (*0-929687-02-7*) E & C Zilkha Gal.

Rotten: No Irish, No Blacks, No Dogs. John Lydon. 1995. pap. 14.00 (*0-312-11883-X*) St Martin.

***Rotten Apples.** Natasha Cooper. (Worldwide Library Mystery: No. 244). 1997. mass mkt. 4.99 (*0-373-26244-2*, 1-26244-3, Wrldwide Lib) Harlequin Bks.

Rotten Apples. Natasha Cooper. LC 95-1734. 288p. 1995. 21.95 (*0-312-13161-5*) St Martin.

Rotten Chicken: A Modern Fable. 2nd rev. ed. L. Ursa Solomon. (Illus.). 34p. (J). 1989. reprint ed. spiral bd. 11.00 (*0-9615756-3-8*) Henchanted Bks.

Rotten Heart of Europe: The Dirty War for Europe's Money. Bernard Connolly. 416p. 1996. 27.95 (*0-571-17520-1*) Faber & Faber.

Rotten Island. William Steig. LC 70-86945. (Illus.). 32p. (J). (gr. 2 up). 1985. 15.95 (*0-87923-526-8*) Godine.

***Rotten Island.** William Steig. (Illus.). 32p. (J). (gr. 2 up). 1996. pap. 6.95 (*1-895565-16-2*) Firefly Bks Ltd.

Rotten Island. William Steig. LC 84-4075. (Illus.). 32p. (J). (gr. k-5). 1985. pap. 7.95 (*0-87923-960-3*) Godine.

Rotten Lies. Charlotte Elkins & Aaron Elkins. 240p. 1995. 19.95 (*0-89296-598-3*) Mysterious Pr.

Rotten Lies. Charlotte Elkins & Aaron Elkins. 224p. 1997. mass mkt. 5.99 (*0-446-40452-7*, Mysterious Paperbk) Warner Bks.

Rotten Ralph. Jack Gantos. LC 75-34101. (Illus.). 48p. (J). (gr. k-3). 1976. 14.95 (*0-395-24276-2*); pap. 4.50 (*0-685-02307-9*) HM.

Rotten Ralph. Jack Gantos. (Book & Cassette Favorites Ser.). (Illus.). (J). 1988. Incl. cass. pap. 8.95 (*0-395-48873-7*) HM.

Rotten Ralph. Jack Gantos. (Illus.). (J). (gr. k-3). 1980. reprint ed. pap. 5.95 (*0-395-29202-6*, Sandpiper) HM.

Rotten Ralph's Rotten Christmas. Jack Gantos. LC 84-664. (Illus.). 32p. (J). (ps-3). 1984. 13.95 (*0-395-35380-7*) HM.

Rotten Ralph's Rotten Christmas. Jack Gantos. LC 84-664. (Illus.). 32p. (J). (ps-3). 1987. pap. 4.95 (*0-395-45685-1*) HM.

Rotten Ralph's Rotten Romance. Jack Gantos. LC 95-43098. (Illus.). 32p. (J). (ps-3). 1997. 14.95 (*0-395-73978-0*) HM.

Rotten Ralph's Show & Tell. Jack Gantos. (Illus.). 32p. (J). (ps-3). 1989. 15.00 (*0-395-44312-1*) HM.

Rotten Ralph's Show & Tell. Jack Gantos. (Illus.). 32p. (J). (gr. k-3). 1991. pap. 6.95 (*0-395-60285-8*, Sandpiper) HM.

Rotten Ralph's Trick or Treat. Jack Gantos. LC 86-7276. (Illus.). 32p. (J). (gr. k-3). 1986. 15.00 (*0-395-38943-7*) HM.

Rotten Ralph's Trick or Treat. Jack Gantos. (Illus.). 32p. (J). (gr. k-3). 1988. pap. 6.95 (*0-395-48655-6*, Sandpiper) HM.

Rotten Reggie. Marsha Marquardt. 12p. (J). (gr. 1). 1990. pap. text ed. 3.00 (*1-882225-00-7*) Tott Pubns.

Rotten Rejections. Ed. by Andre Bernard. 1990. 12.50 (*0-916366-57-X*) Pushcart Pr.

Rotten Reviews: A Literary Companion. Ed. by Bill Henderson. 112p. 1986. 12.50 (*0-916366-40-5*) Pushcart Pr.

Rotten Reviews II: A Literary Companion. Ed. by Bill Henderson. (Illus.). 1987. 12.95 (*0-916366-46-4*) Pushcart Pr.

***Rotten Romans.** Terry Deary. (J). 1997. pap. text ed. 3.99 (*0-590-03152-X*); mass mkt. 3.99 (*0-590-73893-3*) Scholastic Inc.

***Rotten Teeth.** Laura Simms. LC 97-2528. (Illus.). (J). 1998. write for info. (*0-395-82850-3*) HM.

Rotten to the Core. Julia Martin. (Twenty-Three Hundred AD Ser.). (Illus.). 64p. (Orig.). (YA). 1990. pap. 8.00 (*1-55878-059-9*) Game Designers.

Rotten to the Core: Crime, Sex & Corruption in Johnny Appleseed's Hometown. Martin D. Yant. 162p. 1994. pap. 10.95 (*0-9642780-0-6*) Public Eye Pubns.

Rotten Way to Be Wounded: The Tragicomedy of the Sun Also Rises. Wolfgang E. Rudat. LC 90-5903. (American University Studies: American Literature: Ser. XXIV, Vol. 21). 214p. (C). 1990. text ed. 38.95 (*0-8204-1282-1*) P Lang Pubng.

***Rotterdam/Apeldoorn/Maastricht Map.** 1996. 8.95 (*2-06-700211-2*, 211) Michelin.

Rotting Hill. Ed. by Paul Edwards. LC 85-22834. 355p. (Orig.). 1986. reprint ed. pap. 14.00 (*0-87685-646-6*) Black Sparrow.

Rottweiler. Jean Forster. (Owner's Guide to a Happy, Healthy Pet Ser.). (Illus.). 160p. 1995. 12.95 (*0-87605-379-7*) Howell Bk.

Rottweiler. Richard F. Stratton. (Illus.). 224p. 1985. 24.95 (*0-86622-732-6*, PS-820) TFH Pubns.

Rottweiler. Charlotte Wilcox. LC 96-26563. (Learning about Dogs Ser.). 1996. write for info. (*1-56065-395-7*) Capstone Pr.

***Rottweiler.** Charlotte Wilcox. (Learning about Dogs Ser.). (Illus.). 48p. (J). (gr. 3-7). 1996. 18.40 (*0-516-20247-2*) Childrens.

Rottweiler: An International Study of the Breed. Dagmar Hodinar. (Illus.). 347p. (Orig.). 1986. pap. 25.95 (*0-932375-00-6*) Von Palisaden Pubns.

Rottweiler Champions, 1948-1981. Jan L. Freund. (Illus.). 118p. 1983. 36.95 (*0-940808-24-2*) Camino E E & Bk.

Rottweiler Champions, 1982-1986. Camino E. E. & Bk. Co. Staff. (Illus.). 128p. 1987. pap. 28.95 (*0-940808-53-6*) Camino E E & Bk.

Rottweiler Champions, 1987-1993. Camino E. E. & Bk. Co. Staff. (Illus.). 160p. 1998. pap. text ed. 32.95 (*1-55893-025-6*) Camino E E & Bk.

Rottweiler, New. Jim Pettengell. (Illus.). 224p. 1994. 29.95 (*0-7938-0080-3*, TS202) TFH Pubns.

Rottweiler Today. Larry Elsden & Judy Elsden. (Illus.). 192p. 1992. pap. 25.95 (*0-87605-294-4*) Howell Bk.

***Rottweilers.** Robert Hutchinson. LC 97-23663. 1997. write for info. (*1-56313-900-6*) BrownTrout Pubs Inc.

Rottweilers: A Complete Pet Owner's Manual. Kerry V. Kern. 64p. 1991. pap. 6.95 (*0-8120-4483-5*) Barron.

***Rottweilers: AKC Rank # 2.** Anna K. Nicholas. (Illus.). 1996. 9.95 (*0-7938-2323-4*, KW-116S) TFH Pubns.

***Rottweillers.** Ariel Books Staff. 1996. 4.95 (*0-8362-1521-4*, Arie Bks) Andrews & McMeel.

***Rotuli Parliamentorum.** H. Richardson. (Camden Third Ser.). 63.00 (*0-86193-051-7*) David Brown.

Rotuman Grammar & Dictionary. Clerk M. Churchward. LC 75-32808. reprint ed. 42.50 (*0-404-14112-9*) AMS Pr.

Rotunda Music in Eighteenth-Century Dublin. Brian Boydell. (Illus.). 224p. 1992. 14.95 (*0-7165-2487-2*, Pub. by Irish Acad Pr IE) Intl Spec Bk.

Rouault's Complete Graphic Work, 2 Vols., Vol. 1. Francois Chapon & Isabelle Rouault. (Illus.). 340p. (ENG & FRE.). 1978. 1,500.00 (*0-915346-86-9*) A Wofsy Fine Arts.

Rouault's Complete Paintings, 2 vols., Set. Isabelle Rouault. (Illus.). (ENG & FRE.). 1988. 1,500.00 (*1-55660-031-3*) A Wofsy Fine Arts.

Rouault's Illustrated Books: Catalogue Raisonne. Francois Chapon. (Illus.). 1993. 125.00 (*1-55660-246-4*) A Wofsy Fine Arts.

Roubiliac & the Eighteenth Century Monument. David Bindman. 1995. 65.00 (*0-300-06333-4*) Yale U Pr.

Roubles in Words, Kopeks in Figures: And Other Stories. Vasily Shukshin. Tr. by Natasha Ward & David Iliffe from RUS. 210p. 1994. pap. 12.95 (*0-7145-2959-1*) M Boyars Pubs.

Roubles in Words, Kopeks in Figures & Other Stories. Vasily Shuksin. Tr. by Natasha Ward & David Iliffe from RUS. 224p. 1985. 14.95 (*0-7145-2813-7*) M Boyars Pubs.

Rouch: History of the Roush Family in America, from Its Founding by John Adam Rausch in 1736 to the Present (1928) L. L. Roush. (Illus.). 738p. 1995. reprint ed. pap. 109.00 (*0-8328-4828-X*); reprint ed. lib. bdg. 119.00 (*0-8328-4827-1*) Higginson Bk Co.

Roucou. Jacques Perret. (FRE.). 1984. pap. 11.95 (*0-7859-4202-5*) Fr & Eur.

***Rouen City Plan.** (Grafocarte Maps Ser.). 1995. 8.95 (*2-7416-0035-X*, 80035) Michelin.

Rouen-Edinburgh-York: Early Sixteenth Century Printing Connections. Sessions, William Ltd., Staff. 67p. (C). 1983. 85.00 (*0-900657-73-1*, Pub. by W Sessions UK) St Mut.

Rouge: Photographs by Michael Kenna. Michael Kenna. (Illus.). 60p. 1995. 45.00 (*0-9630785-1-8*) RAM Publications.

Rouge Atomique. N. Richard Nash. 1955. pap. 3.25 (*0-8222-0972-1*) Dramatists Play.

***Rouge C'Est Bien Mieux - Red Is Best.** Kathy Stinson. (Picture Bks.). (Illus.). 32p. (FRE.). (J). 1996. pap. 4.95 (*0-920303-71-4*, Pub. by Les Editions CN) Firefly Bks Ltd.

Rouge et le Noir. Stendhal, pseud. 1972. pap. 12.95 (*0-7859-3070-1*) Fr & Eur.

Rouge et le Noir, 2 vols. Stendhal & Beatrice Didier. pap. 4.50 (*0-685-73330-0*) Fr & Eur.

Rouge et le Noir. Stendhal. Ed. by Henri Martineau. (FRE.). 1990. pap. 10.95 (*0-7859-1484-6*, 2266033530) Fr & Eur.

Rouge et le Noir. Stendhal. (Folio Ser.: No. 17). (FRE.). pap. 10.95 (*2-07-036017-2*) Schoenhof.

Rouge et le Noir. unabridged ed. Stendhal. (FRE.). pap. 7.95 (*2-87714-145-4*, Pub. by Bookking Intl FR) Distribks Inc.

Rouge et le Noir, 2 tomes, Set. Stendhal, pseud. 150.00 (*0-685-35027-4*) Fr & Eur.

Rough & Ready. Leslie D. Guccione. (Desire Ser.: No. 713). 1992. pap. 2.89 (*0-373-05713-X*, 5-05713-8) Harlequin Bks.

Rough & Ready. E. J. Hunter. (White Squaw Ser.: No. 24). 1992. mass mkt. 3.50 (*0-8217-3721-X*, Zebra Kensgtn) Kensgtn Pub Corp.

Rough & Ready. Horatio Alger, Jr. (Works of Horatio Alger Jr.). 1989. reprint ed. lib. bdg. 79.00 (*0-685-27557-4*) Rprt Serv.

Rough & Ready Cowboys. A. S. Gintzler. LC 93-32343. 48p. (J). 1996. pap. 4.95 (*1-56261-232-8*) John Muir.

Rough & Ready Homesteaders. A. S. Gintzler. LC 93-32342. 48p. (J). 1996. pap. 4.95 (*1-56261-233-6*) John Muir.

Rough & Ready Loggers. A. S. Gintzler. LC 94-20758. 48p. 1996. pap. 4.95 (*1-56261-234-4*) John Muir.

Rough & Ready Outlaws & Lawmen. A. S. Gintzler. LC 94-4039. 48p. 1996. pap. 4.95 (*1-56261-235-2*) John Muir.

Rough & Ready Prospectors. A. S. Gintzler. LC 93-36415. 48p. 1996. pap. 4.95 (*1-56261-236-0*) John Muir.

Rough & Ready Railroaders. A. S. Gintzler. LC 93-46317. 48p. 1996. pap. 4.95 (*1-56261-237-9*) John Muir.

Rough & Rowdy Ways: The Life & Hard Times of Edward Anderson. Patrick Bennett. LC 88-1151. (Tarleton State University Southwestern Studies in the Humanities: No. 4). (Illus.). 208p. 1988. 19.95 (*0-89096-352-5*) Tex A&M Univ Pr.

Rough & Smooth Collies. Stella Clark. (Illus.). 160p. 1993. 24.95 (*0-948955-82-1*, Pub. by Ringpr Bks UK) Seven Hills Bk.

Rough & Tender. Selina MacPherson. 384p. 1991. pap. 3.95 (*0-380-76322-2*) Avon.

Rough Australia. Rough Guides Staff. 1995. pap. 19.95 (*1-85828-141-5*) NAL-Dutton.

Rough Beast. Gary Goshgarian. 296p. (YA). 1995. pap. 21.95 (*1-55611-464-8*) D I Fine.

***Rough Beast.** Gary Goshgarian. 304p. 1997. reprint ed. mass mkt. 4.99 (*0-8439-4152-9*) Dorchester Pub Co.

Rough Beast: A Novel by the Author of Murder at the Red October. Anthony Olcott. 320p. 1992. text ed. 20.00 (*0-684-19406-6*) S&S Trade.

Rough Carpentry Illustrated. Elizabeth Williams & Robert Williams. (Illus.). 1991. 21.95 (*0-8306-5319-8*) McGraw-Hill Prof.

Rough Carpentry Illustrated. 2nd ed. Elizabeth Williams & Robert Williams. LC 93-12802. (Illus.). 1993. 24.95 (*0-8306-4408-3*); pap. 14.95 (*0-8306-4409-1*) McGraw-Hill Prof.

Rough Collies: An Owner's Companion. Hazel Hunt. (Illus.). 256p. 1996. 39.95 (*1-85223-289-7*, Pub. by Crowood Pr UK) Trafalgar.

***Rough Corsica.** 2nd ed. Theo Taylor. 1997. pap. 16.95 (*1-85828-227-6*) Viking Penguin.

Rough Crossing & On the Razzle. Tom Stoppard. 190p. (Orig.). 1991. 18.95 (*0-571-16400-5*); pap. 10.95 (*0-571-16401-3*) Faber & Faber.

Rough Cut. Stan Cutler. 336p. (Orig.). 1994. pap. 4.99 (*0-451-18253-7*) NAL-Dutton.

Rough Cuts. Grymes. 1996. pap. 5.99 (*0-517-88615-4*) Random Hse Value.

Rough Cuts & Kindling. Dale Pendell. 40p. 1986. 5.00 (*1-882623-03-7*) Exiled-Am Pr.

Rough Cyprus, No. 2. 2nd ed. Marc Dubin. (Illus.). 368p. 1996. pap. 16.95 (*1-85828-182-2*) NAL-Dutton.

Rough Drafts Activity Book. 4th ed. Cain. 1995. pap. text ed. 9.40 (*0-13-438441-5*) P-H.

Rough England, No. 2. (Rough Guide Ser.). (Illus.). 752p. 1996. pap. 17.95 (*1-85828-160-1*, Penguin Bks) Viking Penguin.

An Asterisk (*) at the beginning of an entry indicates that the title is appearing in BIP for the first time.

R

Rough-Face Girl. Rafe Martin. (Illus.). 32p. (J). (ps-3). 1992. lib. bdg. 15.95 (*0-399-21859-9*, Putnam) Putnam Pub Group.

Rough Field. 5th rev. ed. John Montague & Thomas D. Redshaw. LC 89-40526. (Illus.). 100p. 1989. pap. 7.95 (*0-916390-42-X*) Wake Forest.

***Rough First Time through Europe 2.** Louis Casabianca. 1997. pap. 9.95 (*1-85828-270-5*) Viking Penguin.

Rough Framing Carpentry. Mark Currie. (Illus.). 256p. (Orig.). 1993. pap. 26.50 (*0-934041-86-5*) Craftsman.

***Rough Green Snakes: Basic Care.** (Herpetological Library). 5.00 (*0-614-29988-8*) Serpents Tale.

Rough Guide Specials to Able to Travel. 1994. pap. 19.95 (*1-85828-110-5*, Penguin Bks) Viking Penguin.

Rough Guide Specials to Women Travel, No. 17. 1994. pap. 12.95 (*1-85828-071-0*, Penguin Bks) Viking Penguin.

Rough Guide to Amsterdam. 1994. pap. 13.95 (*1-85828-086-9*, Penguin Bks) Viking Penguin.

Rough Guide to Andalucia. (Illus.). 256p. 1994. pap. 14.95 (*1-85828-094-X*, Penguin Bks) Viking Penguin.

***Rough Guide to Andalucia.** Rough Guides Publishing Staff. (Rough Guide Ser.). 1997. pap. text ed. 16.95 (*1-85828-219-5*) Viking Penguin.

***Rough Guide to Australia.** 3rd ed. Rough Guides Staff. 1997. pap. 21.95 (*1-85828-220-9*) Viking Penguin.

Rough Guide to Bali. 1996. pap. 14.95 (*0-614-12856-0*, Penguin Bks) Viking Penguin.

Rough Guide to Barcelona & Catalunya. 2nd ed. Jules Brown. (Rough Guide Ser.). (Illus.). 416p. 1994. pap. 13.95 (*1-85828-106-7*, Penguin Bks) Viking Penguin.

Rough Guide to Berlin. 1994. pap. 13.99 (*1-85828-033-8*, Penguin Bks) Viking Penguin.

Rough Guide to Berlin. 4th ed. (Rough Guide Ser.). (Illus.). 432p. (Orig.). 1995. pap. 14.95 (*1-85828-129-6*, Penguin Bks) Viking Penguin.

Rough Guide to Brazil. 2nd ed. David Cleary et al. (Rough Guide Ser.). (Illus.). 640p. 1994. pap. 15.95 (*1-85828-102-4*, Penguin Bks) Viking Penguin.

Rough Guide to Britain: A Traveling Guide to England, Scotland, & Wales. (Illus.). 912p. 1996. pap. 19.95 (*1-85828-208-X*, Penguin Bks) Viking Penguin.

Rough Guide to Brittany & Normandy. 1994. pap. 14.95 (*1-85828-019-2*, Penguin Bks) Viking Penguin.

Rough Guide to Brittany & Normandy. 4th ed. (Rough Guide Ser.). (Illus.). 352p. (Orig.). 1995. pap. 14.95 (*1-85828-126-1*, Penguin Bks) Viking Penguin.

Rough Guide to Bulgaria. 2nd ed. Jonathan Bousfield & Dan Richardson. 384p. 1996. pap. 16.95 (*1-85828-183-0*, Penguin Bks) Viking Penguin.

Rough Guide to California. 3rd ed. Deborah Bosley et al. (Illus.). 608p. 1994. 14.95 (*1-85828-090-7*, Penguin Bks) Viking Penguin.

Rough Guide to California, No. 4. 4th ed. Bosley et al. 640p. 1996. pap. 16.95 (*1-85828-181-4*) Viking Penguin.

Rough Guide to Canada. 1994. pap. 14.95 (*1-85828-001-X*, Penguin Bks) Viking Penguin.

Rough Guide to Canada. 2nd ed. (Rough Guide Ser.). (Illus.). 672p. (Orig.). 1995. pap. 14.95 (*1-85828-130-X*, Penguin Bks) Viking Penguin.

Rough Guide to Classical Music on CD: A Companion to the Composers, Performers, & Recordings. (Rough Guide Ser.). (Illus.). 512p. (Orig.). 1994. pap. 19.95 (*1-85828-113-X*, Penguin Bks) Viking Penguin.

***Rough Guide to Corfu.** Rough Guides Staff. 1997. pap. 14.95 (*1-85828-226-8*) Viking Penguin.

Rough Guide to Corsica. Theo Taylor. (Illus.). 256p. 1994. pap. 14.95 (*1-85828-089-3*, Penguin Bks) Viking Penguin.

Rough Guide to Crete. 1994. pap. 14.95 (*1-85828-049-4*, Penguin Bks) Viking Penguin.

Rough Guide to Cyprus. 1994. pap. 13.99 (*1-85828-032-X*, Penguin Bks) Viking Penguin.

Rough Guide to Czech. 224p. (Orig.). 1995. pap. 5.00 (*1-85828-148-2*, Penguin Bks) Viking Penguin.

Rough Guide to Czech & Slovak Republics. 3rd ed. 1994. pap. 16.95 (*1-85828-029-X*, Penguin Bks) Viking Penguin.

Rough Guide to Egypt. 3rd ed. Richardson. 1996. pap. 17.95 (*1-85828-188-1*, Penguin Bks) Viking Penguin.

Rough Guide to Europe. 1994. pap. 18.95 (*1-85828-077-X*, Penguin Bks) Viking Penguin.

***Rough Guide to Europe 98.** Rough Guides Staff. 1997. pap. 21.95 (*1-85828-289-6*) Viking Penguin.

***Rough Guide to European Football.** Rough Guides Staff. 1997. pap. 19.95 (*1-85828-256-X*) Viking Penguin.

Rough Guide to Florida. 1994. pap. 14.95 (*1-85828-074-5*, Penguin Bks) Viking Penguin.

Rough Guide to Florida. Mick Sinclair. 1996. pap. 16.95 (*1-85828-184-9*, Penguin Bks) Viking Penguin.

Rough Guide to France. 1994. pap. 16.95 (*1-85828-050-8*, Penguin Bks) Viking Penguin.

Rough Guide to French. 224p. (Orig.). 1995. pap. 5.00 (*1-85828-144-X*, Penguin Bks) Viking Penguin.

Rough Guide to Germany. 3rd ed. (Rough Guide Ser.). (Illus.). 1024p. (Orig.). 1995. pap. 19.95 (*1-85828-128-8*, Penguin Bks) Viking Penguin.

***Rough Guide to Goa.** Mark Ellingham & John Fisher. (Illus.). 288p. 1997. 15.95 (*1-85828-275-6*, Penguin Bks) Viking Penguin.

Rough Guide to Goa. 2nd ed. Mark Ellingham & John Fisher. (Illus.). 176p. 1995. pap. 14.95 (*1-85828-156-3*, Penguin Bks) Viking Penguin.

Rough Guide to Greece. 1994. pap. 16.95 (*1-85828-020-6*, Penguin Bks) Viking Penguin.

Rough Guide to Greek. 224p. (Orig.). 1995. pap. 5.00 (*1-85828-145-8*, Penguin Bks) Viking Penguin.

Rough Guide to Guatemala & Belize. 1994. pap. 14.95 (*1-85828-045-1*, Penguin Bks) Viking Penguin.

Rough Guide to Guatemala & Belize. Eltringham. (Orig.). 1996. pap. 16.95 (*1-85828-189-X*, Penguin Bks) Viking Penguin.

Rough Guide to Hawaii. 1996. pap. 16.95 (*0-614-12857-9*, Penguin Bks) Viking Penguin.

***Rough Guide to Hawaii.** Greg Ward. (Rough Guide Ser.). 1996. pap. 16.95 (*1-85828-206-3*) Viking Penguin.

Rough Guide to Holland, Belgium & Luxembourg. 1994. pap. 15.95 (*1-85828-087-7*, Penguin Bks) Viking Penguin.

Rough Guide to Hong Kong. 1994. pap. 13.95 (*1-85828-066-4*, Penguin Bks) Viking Penguin.

Rough Guide to Hong Kong. Jules Brown. 1996. pap. 14.95 (*1-85828-187-3*, Penguin Bks) Viking Penguin.

Rough Guide to Hungary. 1994. pap. 13.95 (*1-85828-021-4*, Penguin Bks) Viking Penguin.

Rough Guide to Hungary. 3rd ed. (Rough Guide Ser.). (Illus.). 416p. (Orig.). 1995. pap. 14.95 (*1-85828-123-7*, Penguin Bks) Viking Penguin.

Rough Guide to India. David Abram et al. (Rough Guide Ser.). (Illus.). 1072p. 1994. pap. 22.95 (*1-85828-104-0*, Penguin Bks) Viking Penguin.

***Rough Guide to India.** 2nd ed. David Abram. (Rough Guide Ser.). 1997. pap. 23.95 (*1-85828-200-4*, Penguin Bks) Viking Penguin.

Rough Guide to Ireland. 4th ed. Greenwood & Hawkins. (Illus.). 640p. 1996. pap. 17.95 (*1-85828-179-2*) Viking Penguin.

***Rough Guide to Israel.** Rough Guides Staff. 1998. pap. 16.95 (*1-85828-248-9*) Viking Penguin.

Rough Guide to Italian. (Rough Guide Phrasebks.). 224p. (Orig.). 1995. pap. 5.00 (*1-85828-143-1*, Penguin Bks) Viking Penguin.

Rough Guide to Italy, No. 3. Belford & Dunford. (Illus.). 1056p. 1996. pap. 19.95 (*1-85828-167-9*) Viking Penguin.

Rough Guide to Jazz: The Essential Companion to Artists & Albums. Ian Carr et al. 912p. (Orig.). 1995. pap. 24.95 (*1-85828-137-7*, Penguin Bks) Viking Penguin.

Rough Guide to Kenya. 1994. pap. 15.95 (*1-85828-043-5*, Penguin Bks) Viking Penguin.

Rough Guide to Kenya. 5th ed. Richard Trillo. 1996. pap. 18.95 (*1-85828-192-X*, Penguin Bks) Viking Penguin.

Rough Guide to Malaysia, Singapore & Brunei. Charles De Ledesma et al. (Rough Guide Ser.). (Illus.). 512p. (Orig.). 1994. pap. 16.95 (*1-85828-103-2*, Penguin Bks) Viking Penguin.

Rough Guide to Mallorca & Menorca. Phil Lee. 1996. pap. 14.95 (*1-85828-165-2*) Viking Penguin.

Rough Guide to Mexican Spanish Phrasebook. Lexus. 224p. 1996. pap. 5.00 (*1-85828-176-8*) NAL-Dutton.

Rough Guide to Mexico. 1995. pap. 16.95 (*1-85828-044-3*, Penguin Bks) Viking Penguin.

Rough Guide to Morocco. 1994. pap. 16.95 (*1-85828-040-0*, Penguin Bks) Viking Penguin.

Rough Guide to Moscow. (Rough Guide Ser.). (Illus.). 320p. 1995. pap. 14.95 (*1-85828-118-0*, Penguin Bks) Viking Penguin.

Rough Guide to Nepal. 1994. pap. 13.95 (*1-85828-046-X*, Penguin Bks) Viking Penguin.

Rough Guide to Nepal. 3rd ed. 1996. pap. 17.95 (*1-85828-190-3*, Penguin Bks) Viking Penguin.

Rough Guide to New York. Date not set. pap. 13.95 (*1-85828-073-7*, Penguin Bks) Viking Penguin.

Rough Guide to New York. Jack Holland. 1987. pap. 11.95 (*0-7102-0671-2*, RKP) Routledge.

***Rough Guide to New Zealand.** Rough Guides Staff. 1997. pap. 18.95 (*1-85828-233-0*) Viking Penguin.

Rough Guide to Opera. Matthew Boyden. (Rough Guide Ser.). (Illus.). 608p. 1997. pap. 24.95 (*1-85828-138-5*) Viking Penguin.

Rough Guide to Paris. 1994. pap. 12.95 (*1-85828-038-9*, Penguin Bks) Viking Penguin.

Rough Guide to Peru. 1996. pap. 17.95 (*0-614-12858-7*, Penguin Bks) Viking Penguin.

***Rough Guide to Peru.** 3rd ed. Dilwyn Jenkins. (Rough Guide Ser.). (Orig.). 1996. pap. 17.95 (*1-85828-142-3*, Penguin Bks) Viking Penguin.

Rough Guide to Poland. 1994. pap. 16.95 (*1-85828-034-6*, Penguin Bks) Viking Penguin.

Rough Guide to Poland. Salter & McLachland. 640p. 1996. pap. 17.95 (*1-85828-168-7*) Viking Penguin.

Rough Guide to Polish. Lexus. (Rough Guide Ser.). 224p. 1996. pap. 5.00 (*1-85828-174-1*, Penguin Bks) Viking Penguin.

Rough Guide to Portugal. 1994. 15.95 (*1-85828-084-2*, Penguin Bks) Viking Penguin.

Rough Guide to Portugal, No. 7. 7th ed. Ellingham & Fisher. 512p. 1996. pap. 16.95 (*1-85828-180-6*) Viking Penguin.

Rough Guide to Portuguese. Lexus. (Rough Guide Ser.). 224p. 1996. pap. 5.00 (*1-85828-175-X*, Penguin Bks) Viking Penguin.

Rough Guide to Prague. 1994. pap. 14.95 (*1-85828-015-X*, Penguin Bks) Viking Penguin.

Rough Guide to Prague. 2nd ed. (Rough Guides Travel Guide Ser.). 352p. 1995. pap. 14.95 (*1-85828-122-9*, Penguin Bks) Viking Penguin.

Rough Guide to Provence & Cote D'Azur. 1994. pap. 14.95 (*1-85828-023-0*, Penguin Bks) Viking Penguin.

Rough Guide to Provence & the Cote d'Azur. 3rd ed. (Rough Guides Travel Guide Ser.). 448p. 1996. pap. 16.95 (*1-85828-127-X*, Penguin Bks) Viking Penguin.

Rough Guide to Rhodes & the Eastern Aegean. Marc Dubin. (Illus.). 272p. 1996. pap. 14.95 (*1-85828-120-2*, Penguin Bks) Viking Penguin.

***Rough Guide to Rock.** Ed. by Mark Ellingham. 1996. pap. 26.95 (*0-614-20803-3*) Viking Penguin.

Rough Guide to Romania. (Rough Guide Ser.). (Illus.). 352p. (Orig.). 1995. pap. 15.95 (*1-85828-097-4*, Penguin Bks) Viking Penguin.

Rough Guide to San Francisco. 1994. pap. 13.95 (*1-85828-082-6*, Penguin Bks) Viking Penguin.

Rough Guide to San Francisco. D. Bosley & Jamie Jensen. (Illus.). 336p. 1996. pap. 14.95 (*1-85828-185-7*) NAL-Dutton.

Rough Guide to Scandinavia. 1994. pap. 16.99 (*1-85828-039-7*, Penguin Bks) Viking Penguin.

Rough Guide to Sicily. 3rd ed. Jules Brown & Robert Andrews. (Illus.). 384p. 1996. pap. 16.95 (*1-85828-178-4*, Penguin Bks) Viking Penguin.

Rough Guide to Singapore. (Illus.). 192p. 1995. pap. 14.95 (*1-85828-135-0*, Penguin Bks) Viking Penguin.

***Rough Guide to South Africa.** Rough Guides Staff. 1997. pap. 16.95 (*1-85828-238-1*) Viking Penguin.

Rough Guide to Spain. 1994. pap. 16.95 (*1-85828-081-8*, Penguin Bks) Viking Penguin.

Rough Guide to Spanish. (Rough Guide Phrasebks.). 224p. (Orig.). 1995. pap. 5.00 (*1-85828-147-4*, Penguin Bks) Viking Penguin.

Rough Guide to St. Petersburg. 1994. pap. 14.95 (*1-85828-030-3*, Penguin Bks) Viking Penguin.

Rough Guide to St. Petersburg. 2nd ed. (Rough Guide Ser.). (Illus.). 400p. (Orig.). 1995. pap. 14.95 (*1-85828-133-4*, Penguin Bks) Viking Penguin.

Rough Guide to Thai Phrasebook. Lexus. 224p. 1996. pap. 5.00 (*1-85828-177-6*) NAL-Dutton.

Rough Guide to Thailand. 1994. pap. 15.95 (*1-85828-016-8*, Penguin Bks) Viking Penguin.

Rough Guide to Thailand. 2nd ed. Paul Gray & Lucy Ridout. 528p. 1995. pap. 17.95 (*1-85828-140-7*, Penguin Bks) Viking Penguin.

Rough Guide to the Big Island of Hawaii. (Illus.). 176p. 1995. pap. 12.95 (*1-85828-158-X*, Penguin Bks) Viking Penguin.

Rough Guide to the Czech & Slovak Republics. 3rd ed. (Rough Guides Travel Guide Ser.). 480p. 1996. pap. 16.95 (*1-85828-121-0*, Penguin Bks) Viking Penguin.

Rough Guide to the Greek Islands. Mark Ellingham. 1995. pap. 14.95 (*1-85828-163-6*) Viking Penguin.

***Rough Guide to the Internet & the World Wide Web: Version 2.** Angus J. Kennedy. (Rough Guide Ser.). 320p. 1996. pap. 8.00 (*1-85828-216-0*) Viking Penguin.

***Rough Guide to the Internet 3.0.** Angus J. Kennedy. 1997. pap. 8.95 (*1-85828-288-8*) Viking Penguin.

Rough Guide to the Pacific Northwest. Tim Jepson & Phil Lee. (Illus.). 448p. 1994. pap. 14.95 (*1-85828-092-3*, Penguin Bks) Viking Penguin.

Rough Guide to the Pyrenees. 2nd ed. (Illus.). 416p. 1994. pap. 15.95 (*1-85828-093-1*, Penguin Bks) Viking Penguin.

Rough Guide to the U. K. Nick Gillot. (Illus.). 128p. (Orig.). 1994. pap. 12.00 (*0-937279-47-1*, CP3281) R Talsorian.

Rough Guide to the U. S. A. Samantha Cook et al. 1996. pap. 19.95 (*0-614-97945-5*, Penguin Bks) Viking Penguin.

***Rough Guide to the U. S. A.** Greg Ward. 1997. pap. 16.95 (*1-85828-239-X*) Viking Penguin.

Rough Guide to Tunisia. 1994. pap. 15.95 (*1-85828-065-6*, Penguin Bks) Viking Penguin.

Rough Guide to Tunisia. Peter Morris & Daniel Jacobs. (Illus.). 448p. 1995. pap. 17.95 (*1-85828-139-3*, Penguin Bks) Viking Penguin.

Rough Guide to Turkey. 3rd ed. (Illus.). 800p. 1994. pap. 16.95 (*1-85828-088-5*, Penguin Bks) Viking Penguin.

Rough Guide to Turkish. Lexus. (Rough Guide Ser.). 224p. 1996. pap. 5.00 (*1-85828-173-3*, Penguin Bks) Viking Penguin.

Rough Guide to Tuscany & Umbria. 2nd ed. Jonathan Buckley et al. (Illus.). 576p. 1994. pap. 15.95 (*1-85828-091-5*, Penguin Bks) Viking Penguin.

Rough Guide to Venice. 1994. pap. 13.99 (*1-85828-036-2*, Penguin Bks) Viking Penguin.

Rough Guide to Vietnam. 1996. pap. 15.95 (*0-614-12859-5*, Penguin Bks) Viking Penguin.

***Rough Guide to Vietnam.** Jan Dodd. (Rough Guide Ser.). (Orig.). 1996. pap. 15.95 (*1-85828-191-1*, Penguin Bks) Viking Penguin.

Rough Guide to Vietnam. Lexus. (Rough Guide Ser.). 224p. 1996. pap. 5.00 (*1-85828-172-5*, Penguin Bks) Viking Penguin.

Rough Guide to Wales. Mike Parker & Paul Whitfield. (Rough Guides Ser.). (Illus.). 288p. (Orig.). 1994. pap. 14.95 (*1-85828-096-6*, Penguin Bks) Viking Penguin.

Rough Guide to West Africa. Jim Hudgens & Richard Trillo. (Rough Guide Ser.). (Illus.). 1296p. (Orig.). 1995. pap. 24.95 (*1-85828-101-6*, Penguin Bks) Viking Penguin.

Rough Guide to World Music: Salsa to Soukous, Cajun to Calypso. (Rough Guide Ser.). (Illus.). 560p. (Orig.). 1994. pap. 22.95 (*1-85828-017-6*, Penguin Bks) Viking Penguin.

Rough Guide to Zimbabwe & Botswana. 1994. pap. 16.95 (*1-85828-041-9*, Penguin Bks) Viking Penguin.

Rough Guide to Zimbabwe & Botswana. Pinchuck. 1996. pap. 18.95 (*1-85828-186-5*, Penguin Bks) Viking Penguin.

Rough in Brutal Print: The Legal Sources of Browning's "Red Cotton Night-Cap Country" Mark Siegchrist. LC 81-3993. 197p. 1981. 42.00 (*0-8142-0327-2*) Ohio St U Pr.

Rough Israel. Eber & O'Sullivan. 1999. pap. 16.95 (*1-85828-042-7*) NAL-Dutton.

***Rough Jamaica.** Thomas. 1997. pap. 16.95 (*1-85828-230-6*) Viking Penguin.

***Rough Justice.** Cadman. 1992. pap. text ed. write for info. (*0-340-52420-0*) Addison-Wesley.

Rough Justice. Ken Gross. 1992. mass mkt. 4.99 (*0-8125-0728-2*) Tor Bks.

Rough Justice. Ernest Haycox. 1976. 20.95 (*0-89190-978-8*) Amereon Ltd.

***Rough Justice.** Lisa Scottoline. LC 97-5810. 1997. write for info. (*0-06-018746-8*) HarpC.

Rough Justice. Claire Youmans. Ed. by Beth Heyn. LC 96-67602. (Janet Schilling Mystery Ser.). 256p. (Orig.). 1996. pap. 10.99 (*1-883061-10-5*) Rising NY.

Rough Justice: Essays on Crime in English Literature. Ed. by Martin L. Friedland. 264p. 1991. 50.00 (*0-8020-5906-6*); pap. 18.95 (*0-8020-6849-9*) U of Toronto Pr.

Rough Landings. Ted McNulty. 84p. 9200. pap. 12.95 (*0-948339-88-8*, Pub. by Salmon Pubng IE) Dufour.

Rough Magic. Joyce Johnson. (Rainbow Romances Ser.). 160p. 1994. 14.95 (*0-7090-4923-4*, 914, Hale-Parkwest) Parkwest Pubns.

Rough Magic. large type ed. Joyce Johnson. (Linford Romance Library). 256p. 1995. pap. 15.99 (*0-7089-7787-1*, Linford) Ulverscroft.

Rough Med Europe. Dunford Buckley. Date not set. pap. 17.95 (*1-85828-085-0*) NAL-Dutton.

***Rough Meditations.** Bradley S. Klein. 268p. 1997. 24.95 (*1-886947-17-1*) Sleeping Bear Software.

***Rough Mix: An Unapologetic Look at the Music Business & How It Got That Way, a Lifetime in the World of Rock, Pop & Country, As Told by One of the Industry's Most Powerful Players.** Jimmy Bowen & Jim Jerome. LC 96-51007. 1997. 25.00 (*0-684-80764-5*, S&S) S&S Trade.

Rough Music. Deborah Digges. 80p. 1995. 20.00 (*0-679-44176-X*) Random.

***Rough Music.** Deborah Digges. 1997. pap. 14.00 (*0-679-76597-2*) Knopf.

Rough Music. large type ed. Barbara Bennett. 428p. 1981. 25.99 (*0-7089-0719-9*) Ulverscroft.

***Rough News - Daring Views: 1950s' Pioneer Gay Press.** Jim Kepner. LC 97-16940. 432p. 1997. lib. bdg. 49.95 (*0-7890-0140-3*) Haworth Pr.

***Rough News - Daring Views: 1950s' Pioneer Gay Press.** Jim Kepner. 432p. 1997. pap. 24.95 (*1-56023-896-8*) Harrington Pk.

Rough Night at the North Pole. Craig Alpaugh. 36p. 1989. pap. 3.00 (*0-87129-607-1*, R40) Dramatic Pub.

***Rough Norway 1.** Rough Guide Staff. 1997. pap. 17.95 (*1-85828-234-9*) Viking Penguin.

Rough Notes from Buck Creek I. rev. ed. Harvey Jackins et al. LC 78-68934. 1979. pap. 15.00 (*0-911214-52-6*) Rational Isl.

Rough Notes from Calvinwood I. 2nd rev. ed. Harvey Jackins et al. 137p. 1993. pap. 7.00 (*0-913937-71-1*) Rational Isl.

Rough Notes from Liberation I & II. Harvey Jackins et al. LC 76-9553. 260p. 1976. 15.00 (*0-911214-46-1*); pap. 10.00 (*0-911214-42-9*) Rational Isl.

***Rough Notes of Seven Campaigns in Portugal, Spain, France & America During the Years 1809-1815.** John S. Cooper. 1996. 29.95 (*1-873376-65-0*) Howell Pr VA.

Rough Notes of Seven Campaigns in Portugal, Spain, France & America During the Years 1809-1815. John S. Cooper. 1996. 29.95 (*1-885119-35-6*) Sarpedon.

Rough Passage. R. D. Graham. 258p. (Orig.). 1985. pap. 9.00 (*0-246-12311-7*, Pub. by Granada UK) Academy Chi Pubs.

Rough Pulpwood Operating in Northwestern Maine, 1935-1940. C. Max Hilton. 1992. pap. 12.50 (*0-89101-000-9*) U Maine Pr.

Rough Red. large type ed. Martin Sylvester. 1991. 25.99 (*0-7089-2354-2*) Ulverscroft.

***Rough Reggae 1.** Barrow. 1997. pap. 19.95 (*1-85828-247-0*) Viking Penguin.

Rough Ride. John Francome. 336p. 1995. mass mkt. 4.99 (*0-06-104286-2*, Harp PBks) HarpC.

Rough Rider. Jack Cummings. 192p. 1988. 17.95 (*0-8027-4089-8*) Walker & Co.

Rough Rider. Jack Cummings. 1991. mass mkt. 3.50 (*1-55817-481-8*, Pinnacle Kensgtn) Kensgtn Pub Corp.

Rough Rider. large type ed. Jack Cummings. LC 93-21818. 1993. Alk. paper. pap. 15.95 (*1-56054-437-6*) Thorndike Pr.

Rough Rider. large type ed. Gilbert Morris. LC 96-20904. 458p. 1996. lib. bdg. 22.95 (*0-7838-1853-X*, GK Hall) Thorndike Pr.

Rough Rider, Vol. 18. Gilbert Morris. LC 95-45280. (House of Winslow Ser.). 304p. (Orig.). 1995. pap. 9.99 (*1-55661-394-6*) Bethany Hse.

***Rough Rider: Buckey O'Neill of Arizona.** Dale L. Walker. (Illus.). 224p. 1997. pap. 12.95 (*0-8032-9796-3*, Bison Books) U of Nebr Pr.

Rough Riders. Heatley. 1976. 19.95 (*0-8488-0889-4*) Amereon Ltd.

***Rough Riders.** Theodore Roosevelt & Richard Bak. LC 97-14743. (Illus.). 256p. 1997. 29.95 (*0-87833-982-5*) Taylor Pub.

Rough Riders. Theodore Roosevelt. (Illus.). 384p. 1971. reprint ed. 26.95 (*0-87928-018-2*) Corner Hse.

Rough Riders. Theodore Roosevelt. (Quality Paperbacks Ser.). (Illus.). 296p. 1990. reprint ed. pap. 13.95 (*0-306-80405-0*) Da Capo.

Rough Riding. Franklin W. Dixon. Ed. by Anne Greenberg. (Hardy Boys Casefiles Ser.: No. 68). 160p. (Orig.). (J). (gr. 6 up). 1992. pap. 3.75 (*0-671-73104-1*, Archway) PB.

***Rough Riding Reformer: Theofore Roosevelt.** Gary L. Blackwood. LC 96-53087. (Benchmark Biographies Ser.: No. 2). (Illus.). 48p. (YA). (gr. 3 up). 1998. lib. bdg. 14.95 (*0-7614-0520-8*, Benchmark NY) Marshall Cavendish.

Rough Road Home: A True & Moving Story of One Woman's Courage under Adversity. Melissa Mather. LC 86-19774. 256p. 1986. reprint ed. 14.95 (*0-8397-7236-X*) Eriksson.

Rough Road Home: Stories by North Carolina Writers. Intro. by Robert Gingher. LC 92-53705. xviii, 332p. (C). 1992. 27.50 (*0-8078-2064-4*); pap. 15.95 (*0-8078-4397-0*) U of NC Pr.

Rough Road to Glory. Arlow W. Anderson. LC 88-62780. 271p. 1990. 44.50 (0-944190-02-2) Balch IES Pr.

Rough Road to Renaissance: Urban Revitalization in America, 1940-1985. Jon C. Teaford. LC 89-49001. (Creating the North American Landscape Ser.). (Illus.). 400p. 1990. text ed. 65.00 (0-8018-3971-8); pap. text ed. 16.95 (0-8018-4134-8) Johns Hopkins.

***Rough Rock.** 1996. pap. 26.95 (1-85828-201-2) Viking Penguin.

Rough Route to Rodd County. large type ed. Marshall Grover. (Linford Western Library). 1991. pap. 15.99 (0-7089-7013-3) Ulverscroft.

***Rough Scandinavia.** Sinclair Brow. 1997. pap. 20.95 (1-85828-236-5) Viking Penguin.

***Rough Sets & Data Mining: Analysis of Imprecise Data.** Ed. by T. Y. Lin. LC 96-27716. 448p. (C). 1996. lib. bdg. 140.00 (0-7923-9807-6) Kluwer Ac.

Rough Sets, Fuzzy Sets & Knowledge Discovery. Ed. by Wojciech P. Ziarko & C. J. Van Rijsbergen. 476p. 1994. 78.95 (0-387-19885-7) Spr-Verlag.

Rough Shaking. George MacDonald. (George MacDonald Original Works: Series I). (Illus.). 384p. 1992. reprint ed. 16.00 (1-881084-04-3) Johannesen.

Rough Shooting. Mike Swan. (Illus.). 240p. 1992. 31.95 (1-85310-178-8, Pub. by Swan Hill UK) Voyageur Pr.

Rough-Shooting Dog. Charles Fergus. (Illus.). 224p. 1991. 22.95 (1-55821-128-4) Lyons & Burford.

***Rough Side of the Mountain.** D. Geraldine Lawson. (Illus.). 136p. (Orig.). 1997. pap. 8.00 (1-56002-611-1, Univ Edtns) Aegina Pr.

Rough Side of War: The Civil War Journal of Chesley A. Mosman, 1st Lieutenant, Company D, 59th Illinois Volunteer Infantry Regiment, 1862-1866. Chesley A. Mosman. (Illus.). 448p. 1987. 25.00 (0-940591-06-5) Basin Pub.

Rough Sketch Beginning. James Berry. LC 95-15471. (Illus.). 32p. (J). (gr. 4 up). 1996. 18.00 (0-15-200112-3) HarBrace.

Rough Sketches: Political Cartoons by Joel Pett, Lexington Herald-Leader. Joel W. Pett. (Illus.). 164p. (Orig.). 1989. pap. write for info. (0-318-65564-0) Lex Herald-Leader.

***Rough Spain 7.** Fishcer. 1997. pap. 18.95 (1-85828-240-3) Viking Penguin.

Rough Stuff. G. H. Stone. LC 88-11904. (Three Investigators Crimebusters Ser.). 144p. (J). (gr. 5 up). 1989. pap. 2.95 (0-394-80178-4) Knopf Bks Yng Read.

***Rough Sweden 1.** Rough Guide Staff. 1997. pap. 17.95 (1-85828-241-1) Viking Penguin.

Rough, Tough, & Rowdy. William H. Hooks. Date not set. pap. 3.95 (0-14-054094-6) NAL-Dutton.

Rough Trade. Red J. Arobateau. (Orig.). 1996. mass mkt. 6.50 (1-56333-470-4, Rosebud) Masquerade.

Rough Trade. Ed. by John W. Dagion. (True Revelations & Strange Happenings Ser.: Vol. 7). 160p. (Orig.). 1996. pap. 14.95 (0-943595-58-4) Leyland Pubns.

Rough Trade. Cole Riley. 320p. (Orig.). 1987. mass mkt. 3.50 (0-87067-835-3) Holloway.

Rough Trades. Charles Bernstein. (Sun & Moon Classics Ser.: No. 14). 112p. 1989. pap. 10.95 (1-55713-080-9) Sun & Moon CA.

Rough Translations: Stories by Molly Giles. Molly Giles. LC 84-16363. (Flannery O'Connor Award for Short Fiction Ser.). 144p. 1993. pap. 12.95 (0-8203-1574-5) U of Ga Pr.

***Rough Treatment.** Harvey. 1997. pap. 6.95 (0-8050-5496-0) H Holt & Co.

Rough Treatment. John Harvey. 304p. 1991. mass mkt. 3.99 (0-380-71171-0) Avon.

***Rough Turkey 3.** Ayliffe. 1997. pap. 18.95 (1-85828-242-X) Viking Penguin.

***Rough Vienna 1.** Rough Guides Staff. 1997. pap. 14.95 (1-85828-244-6) Viking Penguin.

Rough Water. Sally Gunning. Ed. by Jane Chelius. 320p. (Orig.). 1994. mass mkt. 5.50 (0-671-87137-4) PB.

Rough Water Man: Elwyn Blake's Colorado River Expeditions. Richard E. Westwood. LC 92-1233. (Illus.). 288p. (C). 1992. 27.95 (0-87417-188-1) U of Nev Pr.

Rough Water Power Boating. Mark A. Robinson. 268p. (C). 1990. 90.00 (0-7316-4701-7, Pub. by Pascoe Pub AT) St Mut.

Rough Ways in Prayer. Paul Wallis. 1991. pap. 6.95 (0-687-86115-2) Abingdon.

***Rough Ways in Prayer: How Can I Pray When I Feel Spiritually Dead?** Paul Wallis. 144p. 1995. pap. 5.95 (0-687-86112-8) Abingdon.

Rough Weather Makes Good Timber: Carolinians Recall. Patsy M. Ginns & J. L. Osborne. LC 76-20765. 204p. reprint ed. pap. 58.20 (0-7837-2073-4, 2042347) Bks Demand.

Roughage for Dairy Cows. Marshall E. McCullough. Ed. by Elvira B. Kau. (Illus.). 40p. (C). 1989. pap. text ed. 3.00 (0-932147-08-9) Hoard & Sons Co.

***Roughcut: Poems.** Date not set. 12.95 (0-252-06615-4) U of Ill Pr.

Roughened Roundnesses. Barriss Mills. 1976. 10.00 (0-685-79208-0); pap. 5.00 (0-685-79209-9) Elizabeth Pr.

Roughing It. D. L. Carey. (Distress Call 911 Ser.: No. 6). (YA). (gr. 7 up). 1996. mass mkt. 3.99 (0-671-00096-9) PB.

Roughing It. Mark Twain. (Airmont Classics Ser.). (Illus.). (J). (gr. 8 up). 1967. mass mkt. 2.95 (0-8049-0134-1, CL-134) Airmont.

Roughing It. Mark Twain. 26.95 (0-8488-1495-9) Amereon Ltd.

Roughing It. Mark Twain. (Illus.). 592p. 1988. pap. 9.95 (0-87052-708-8) Hippocrene Bks.

Roughing It. Mark Twain. (YA). (gr. 10). 1962. pap. 5.95 (0-451-52407-1, CE1829, Sig Classics) NAL-Dutton.

Roughing It. Mark Twain. (Iowa-California Edition of the Works of Mark Twain: No. 2). 1972. pap. 14.95 (0-520-02478-8) U CA Pr.

Roughing It. Mark Twain. Ed. by Harriet E. Smith et al. LC 93-23042. (Iowa-California Edition of the Works of Mark Twain). (Illus.). 1993. 65.00 (0-520-08498-5) U CA Pr.

Roughing It. Mark Twain. Ed. & Intro. by Hamlin Hill. (American Library). 592p. 1981. pap. 10.95 (0-14-039010-3, Penguin Classics) Viking Penguin.

Roughing It. Mark Twain, pseud. Ed. by Harriet E. Smith et al. LC 95-30007. (Mark Twain Library: Vol. 8). (Illus.). 885p. (C). 1996. 45.00 (0-520-20558-8); pap. 16.95 (0-520-20559-6) U CA Pr.

Roughing It. Mark Twain. 448p. 1986. reprint ed. lib. bdg. 25.95 (0-89966-524-1) Buccaneer Bks.

Roughing It, 2 vols., 1. Samuel L. Clemens. (Works of Mark Twain). 1988. reprint ed. lib. bdg. 79.00 (0-7812-1112-3) Rprt Serv.

Roughing It, 2 vols., 2. Samuel L. Clemens. (Works of Mark Twain). 1988. reprint ed. lib. bdg. 79.00 (0-7812-1113-1) Rprt Serv.

Roughing It, 2 vols., Set. Mark Twain, pseud. (Works of Mark Twain). 1988. reprint ed. lib. bdg. 99.00 (0-317-90239-3) Rprt Serv.

Roughing It Easy. rev. ed. Dian Thomas. LC 94-9876. 256p. 1994. pap. 14.99 (0-9621257-3-3) D Thomas Co.

Roughing It Elegantly: A Practical Guide to Canoe Camping. 2nd ed. Patricia J. Bell. LC 93-74305. 250p. (Orig.). 1994. pap. 14.95 (0-9618227-0-8) Cats-paw MN.

***Roughing It in the Bush.** Susanna Moodie. 1996. pap. text ed. 8.95 (0-7710-9975-4) McCland & Stewart.

***Roughing It (1872)** Shelley F. Fishkin. (Oxford Mark Twain). 704p. 1997. lib. bdg. 25.00 (0-19-511401-9) OUP.

Roughneck. Alexandra Sellers. (Intimate Moments Ser.). 1996. mass mkt. 3.75 (0-373-07689-4, 1-07689-2) Silhouette.

***Roughneck.** Jim Thompson. 1998. pap. write for info. (0-375-70033-1, Vin) Random.

Roughnecks. D. R. Bulla. 327p. (Orig.). 1994. 8.95 (0-9643895-0-9) DRB-ROUGHNECK.

***Roughnecks.** Thomas Cochran. LC 96-43939. (J). 1997. write for info. (0-15-201433-0) HarBrace.

Roughnecks, Drillers, & Tool Pushers: Thirty-three Years in the Oil Fields. Gerald Lynch. (Personal Narratives of the West Ser.). (Illus.). 278p. 1987. 24.95 (0-292-71553-6) U of Tex Pr.

Roughnecks, Drillers, & Tool Pushers: Thirty-Three Years in the Oil Fields. Gerald Lynch. LC 87-13857. (Personal Narratives of the West Ser.). (Illus.). 278p. 1991. reprint ed. pap. 12.95 (0-292-77052-9) U of Tex Pr.

Roughshod. Gary D. Trump. Ed. by Ann Cross. LC 89-51598. 298p. (Orig.). 1990. pap. 5.95 (0-9622856-9-2) Tag Bks.

Roughshod. large type ed. Norman A. Fox. LC 92-32524. (General Ser.). 1993. lib. bdg. 19.95 (0-8161-5642-5, GK Hall) Thorndike Pr.

Roughshooter's Dog. Michael Brander. (Illus.). 198p. 1991. 22.95 (0-948253-38-X, Pub. by Sportsmans Pr UK) Trafalgar.

***Roughstock.** Laura Crum. 224p. Date not set. 20.95 (0-312-15643-X) St Martin.

Rougon-Macquart, 5 tomes, 1. deluxe ed. Emile Zola. Ed. by Mitterand & Armand Lanoux. (Pleiade Ser.). (FRE.). 1968. 84.95 (2-07-010589-X) Schoenhof.

Rougon-Macquart, 5 tomes, 2. deluxe ed. Emile Zola. Ed. by Mitterand & Armand Lanoux. (Pleiade Ser.). (FRE.). 1968. 75.95 (2-07-010590-3) Schoenhof.

Rougon-Macquart, 5 tomes, 3. deluxe ed. Emile Zola. Ed. by Mitterand & Armand Lanoux. (Pleiade Ser.). (FRE.). 1968. 84.95 (2-07-010591-1) Schoenhof.

Rougon-Macquart, 5 tomes, 4. deluxe ed. Emile Zola. Ed. by Mitterand & Armand Lanoux. (Pleiade Ser.). (FRE.). 1968. 85.95 (2-07-010592-X) Schoenhof.

Rougon-Macquart, 5 tomes, 5. deluxe ed. Emile Zola. Ed. by Mitterand & Armand Lanoux. (Pleiade Ser.). (FRE.). 1968. 84.95 (2-07-010593-8) Schoenhof.

Rougon-Macquart, Vol. 1. Emile Zola. Ed. by Armand Lanoux. (FRE.). 1960. lib. bdg. 130.00 (0-7859-3923-7) Fr & Eur.

Rougon-Macquart, Vol. 2. Emile Zola. Ed. by Rene Lanoux. 1961. 130.00 (0-7859-3806-0) Fr & Eur.

Rougon-Macquart, Vol. 3. Emile Zola. Ed. by Armand Lanoux. (FRE.). 1964. lib. bdg. 130.00 (0-7859-3807-9) Fr & Eur.

Rougon-Macquart, Vol. 4. Emile Zola. Ed. by Armand Lanoux. (FRE.). 1966. lib. bdg. 130.00 (0-7859-3924-5) Fr & Eur.

Rougon-Macquart, Vol. 5. Emile Zola. (FRE.). 1967. lib. bdg. 130.00 (0-7859-3808-7) Fr & Eur.

Rougue's Heart. Laurie Paige. 1994. pap. 2.75 (0-373-91013-4, 5-91013-8) Harlequin Bks.

Roulades: Poems from Hollywood. Mark Dunster. 27p. (Orig.). 1989. pap. 4.00 (0-89642-167-8) Linden Pubs.

***Roulault.** Ed. by Jose M. Faerna. (Great Modern Masters Ser.). (Illus.). 64p. 1997. pap. 11.98 (0-8109-4697-1) Abrams.

Roulette. Tony Korfman. (Playing to Win Ser.). 99p. (Orig.). 1985. pap. text ed. 2.50 (0-934047-05-7) Gaming Bks Intl.

Roulette see Fortunes

Roulette for the Casual Gambler. Jack Short. Ed. by Lissa Poincenot et al. LC 96-83148. 70p. (Orig.). 1996. pap. 25.00 (0-9640976-1-3) Cnslt Pubns.

Roulette for the Weekend Gambler: How to Get in, Make Your Hit & Get Out a Winner. J. R. Miller. 86p. 1995. spiral bd. 7.95 (0-9636500-2-5) Flying M Grp.

Roulette System Tester. Erick St. Germain. (System Tester Ser.). 305p. (Orig.). 1995. pap. 24.95 (0-9640595-8-4) Zumma Pubng.

Roumain Sans Peine: Roumanian for French Speakers. Assimil Staff. (FRE & RUM.). 28.95 (0-8288-4399-6, M6666); audio 125.00 (0-685-53048-5) Fr & Eur.

Roumanian Bird & Beast Stories, Rendered into English. M. Gaster. (Folk-Lore Society, London Monographs: Vol. 75A). 1974. reprint ed. pap. 40.00 (0-8115-0534-0) Periodicals Srv.

Roumanian Folktales Retold from the Original. Ed. by Jacob Segall. 1977. lib. bdg. 59.95 (0-8490-2544-3) Gordon Pr.

Roumanian Handbook. Norman L. Forter & Demeter B. Rostovsky. LC 77-135805. (Eastern Europe Collection). 1971. reprint ed. 24.95 (0-405-02747-8) Ayer.

Roumanian Stories. Tr. by Lucy M. Byng from RUM. LC 73-169543. (Short Story Index Reprint Ser.). 1977. reprint ed. 20.95 (0-8369-4004-0) Ayer.

Roumeli: Travels in Northern Greece. Patrick L. Fermor. (Travel Library). 366p. 1984. pap. 7.95 (0-14-009504-7, Penguin Bks) Viking Penguin.

Round - Rounds Genealogy: Descendants of John Round of Swansen MA. N. R. Nichols. (Illus.). 259p. reprint ed. pap. 39.00 (0-8328-1671-X); reprint ed. lib. bdg. 49.00 (0-8328-1670-1) Higginson Bk Co.

Round about a Pound a Week. large type ed. Maud P. Reeves. 256p. 1993. 22.95 (1-85695-030-1, Pub. by ISIS UK) Transaction Pubs.

Round about Middle Thames: Glimpses of Rural Victorian Life. (Illus.). 192p. 1992. 16.00 (0-86299-032-7, Pub. by Sutton Pubng UK) Bks Intl VA.

Round about Midnight: A Portrait of Miles Davis. 2nd ed. Eric Nisenson. (Illus.). 300p. 1996. pap. 13.95 (0-306-80684-3) Da Capo.

Round & about the Dunes. Norma Schaeffer & Kay Franklin. (Illus.). 256p. 1984. pap. 6.00 (0-9613419-0-4) Dunes.

Round & Round: A Triptych. Poems. Dabney Stuart. LC 75-27664. x, 70p. 1977. pap. 6.95 (0-8071-0281-4) La State U Pr.

Round & Round Again. Nancy Van Laan. LC 93-45918. (Illus.). 32p. (J). (ps-3). 1994. 13.95 (0-7868-0009-7) Hyprn Child.

Round & Round the Garden. Illus. by Moira Kemp. 12p. (J). (ps). 1992. pap. 2.50 (0-525-67395-4, Lodestar Bks) Dutton Child Bks.

Round & Round the Garden. Anne Shufflebotham. LC 91-12964. (J). (gr. 4 up). 1991. 5.99 (0-85953-426-X) Childs Play.

Round & Round the Money Goes: What Money Is & How We Use It. Melvin Berger & Gilda Berger. LC 93-14770. (Discovery Readers Ser.). (Illus.). 48p. (J). (gr. k-4). 1993. per., pap. 4.50 (0-8249-8598-2, Ideals Child); lib. bdg. 12.00 (0-8249-8640-7, Ideals Child) Hambleton-Hill.

Round & Round the Seasons Go. Rozanne L. Williams. (Emergent Reader Big Bks.). (Illus.). 16p. (Orig.). (J). (gr. k-2). 1995. pap. 11.98 (1-57471-018-4) Creat Teach Pr.

Round & Round the Seasons Go, Level II. Rozanne L. Williams. (Emergent Reader Science Ser.). 16p. 1994. 2.49 (0-916119-40-8, 3530) Creat Teach Pr.

Round & Round with Kahlil Gibran. Jim W. Miller. LC 90-30378. 10p. (Orig.). 1990. pap. 4.00 (0-926487-05-1) Rowan Mtn Pr.

***Round Ball to Rimfire: A History of Civil War Small Arms Ammunition.** (Illus.). 344p. 1997. 40.00 (1-57747-015-X) Thomas Publications.

***Round Book: Rounds Kids Love to Sing.** Margaret R. MacDonald & Winifred Jaeger. (Illus.). 128p. (J). (gr. 1-4). 1997. pap. 16.50 (0-208-02472-7, Linnet Bks); lib. bdg. 22.50 (0-208-02441-7, Linnet Bks) Shoe String.

Round Buildings, Square Buildings & Buildings That Wiggle Like a Fish. Phillip M. Isaacson. LC 87-16967. (Illus.). 128p. (J). (gr. 5 up). 1988. 22.00 (0-394-89382-4) Knopf Bks Yng Read.

Round Buildings, Square Buildings & Buildings That Wiggle Like a Fish. Phillip M. Isaacson. LC 87-16967. (Illus.). 128p. (J). (gr. 5 up). 1990. pap. 13.00 (0-679-80649-0) Knopf Bks Yng Read.

Round Burns Grave. enl. ed. John D. Ross. LC 70-144479. reprint ed. 34.50 (0-404-08539-3) AMS Pr.

Round Dance Book: A Century of Waltzing. Lloyd Shaw. (Ballroom Dance Ser.). 1986. lib. bdg. 79.95 (0-8490-3339-X) Gordon Pr.

Round Dance Book: A Century of Waltzing. Lloyd Shaw. (Ballroom Dance Ser.). 1985. lib. bdg. 79.95 (0-87700-661-X) Revisionist Pr.

***Round Dozen.** Elizabeth Cadell. 1997. pap. 21.95 (0-7862-0846-5) Thorndike Pr.

Round Fittings Used Today Including Methods & Techniques of Fabricating Round Work. 4th ed. Richard S. Budzik. LC 71-182388. (Illus.). (C). 1988. 29.95 (0-912914-39-4) Practical Pubns.

Round Garden: Plans for a Small Intensive Vegetable Garden for Year Round Production in the Tropics. Franklin W. Martin & Ruth M. Ruberte. (Studies in Tropical Agriculture). 1980. lib. bdg. 59.95 (0-8490-3073-0) Gordon Pr.

Round in Circles: Poltergeists, Pranksters, & the Secret History of the Cropwatchers. Jim Schnabel. LC 94-26225. (Illus.). 295p. (C). 1994. 24.95 (0-87975-934-8) Prometheus Bks.

Round Indiana: Round Barns in the Hoosier State. John T. Hanou. LC 91-46904. (Illus.). 144p. 1993. 29.95 (1-55753-022-X); pap. 19.95 (1-55753-037-8) Purdue U Pr.

Round Kanchenjunga. Douglas Freshfield. 1979. 60.00 (0-7855-0320-X, Pub. by Ratna Pustak Bhandar) St Mut.

Round Kangchenjunga. D. Freshfield. (Illus.). 373p. (C). 1979. reprint ed. 130.00 (0-89771-107-6) St Mut.

***Round Lake Erie: A Bicyclist's Tour Guide.** Harvey Botzman. (Great Lakes Bicycle Touring Ser.). (Illus.). 156p. 1996. pap. 20.00 (1-889602-06-X); lib. bdg. 20.00 (1-889602-05-1); spiral bd. 20.00 (1-889602-07-8) Cyclotour Guide.

***Round Lake Huron: A Bicyclist's Tour Guide.** Harvey Botzman. (Great Lakes Bicycle Touring Ser.). (Illus.). 200p. (Orig.). 1997. pap. 20.00 (1-889602-11-6) Cyclotour Guide.

***Round Lake Huron: A Bicyclist's Tour Guide.** Harvey Botzman. (Great Lakes Bicycle Touring Ser.). (Illus.). 200p. 1997. spiral bd. 20.00 (1-889602-12-4) Cyclotour Guide.

***Round Lake Michigan: A Bicyclist's Tour Guide.** Harvey Botzman. (Great Lakes Bicycle Touring Ser.). (Illus.). 200p. (Orig.). 1997. pap. 20.00 (1-889602-13-2) Cyclotour Guide.

***Round Lake Michigan: A Bicyclist's Tour Guide.** Harvey Botzman. (Great Lakes Bicycle Touring Ser.). (Illus.). 200p. 1997. spiral bd. 20.00 (1-889602-14-0) Cyclotour Guide.

***Round Lake Ontario: A Bicyclist's Tour Guide.** Harvey Botzman. LC 95-92677. (Great Lakes Bicycle Touring Ser.). (Illus.). 152p. 1995. pap. 20.00 (1-889602-03-5); lib. bdg. 20.00 (1-889602-02-7); spiral bd. 20.00 (1-889602-04-3) Cyclotour Guide.

Round Midnight: The Life & Times of Thelonius Monk. Gourse. LC 97-10509. 1997. 27.00 (0-02-864656-8) Mac Lib Ref.

Round Midnight Sextet. Monk & Hanighe. 1995. pap. text ed. 20.00 (0-7935-4819-5, 00000690) H Leonard.

***Round Mt. Hood in Easy Stages.** Sonia Buist. 120p. (Orig.). 1997. pap. 9.95 (0-9643836-1-6) Lolits Pr.

Round My Way: Authority & Double-Consciousness in Three Urban High School Writers. Eli C. Goldblatt. LC 95-3284. (Series in Composition, Literacy, & Culture). 1995. 49.95 (0-8229-3879-0); pap. 19.95 (0-8229-5563-6) U of Pittsburgh Pr.

Round Oak: A Good Thing from Doe-Wah-Jack. rev. ed. Leland M. Haines. (Illus.). 272p. 1994. pap. 18.00 (0-9616910-4-2) L M Haines.

Round of Golf. Tommy Armour. (Illus.). 160p. 1993. pap. 13.95 (1-55821-217-5) Lyons & Burford.

Round of Golf Courses. Patric Dickinson. pap. 12.95 (0-7136-3238-0, 91926, Pub. by A&C Black UK) Talman.

***Round of Rounds for the 52 Weeks of the Year: Wir Singen Durch die Jahresrunde, Kanons fur die 52 Wochen.** Anna R. Meuss. 96p. (J). 1990. pap. write for info. (0-904693-26-0, Pub. by Temple Ldge Pub UK) Anthroposophic.

Round River: From the Journals of Aldo Leopold. Ed. by Luna B. Leopold. (Illus.). 286p. (C). 1972. reprint ed. pap. 9.95 (0-19-501563-0) OUP.

Round River from the Journals Aldo Leopold. Illus. by Mary Shafer. 208p. 1991. 19.95 (1-55971-084-5) NorthWord.

Round Robin Quilts: Friendship Quilts of the 90s & Beyond. Paat Magaret & Donna I. Slusser. Ed. by Barbara Weiland. LC 94-21147. (Illus.). 112p. (Orig.). 1994. pap. 22.95 (1-56477-065-6, B185) That Patchwork.

***Round Rock.** Michelle Huneven. LC 97-5831. 1997. 24.00 (0-679-45437-3) Knopf.

***Round Rock.** Michelle Huneven. 1998. pap. write for info. (0-679-77616-8, Vin) Random.

Round Structures of Aboriginal Middle America. Harry E. Pollock. LC 77-11514. (Carnegie Institution of Washington. Publications: No. 471). reprint ed. 37.50 (0-404-16274-6) AMS Pr.

Round Table. William C. Hazlitt & Leigh Hunt. LC 91-30186. 524p. 1991. reprint ed. 65.00 (1-85477-070-5, Pub. by Woodstock Bks UK) Cassell.

Round Table Discussion on Bioscience Society. Ed. by J. J. Cherfas et al. (Schering Foundation Workshop Ser.: Vol. 2). 96p. 1991. 54.95 (0-387-55032-1) Spr-Verlag.

Round Table Movement & Imperial Union. John E. Kendle. LC 73-81758. (Illus.). 348p. reprint ed. pap. 99.20 (0-8357-3522-2, 2034047) Bks Demand.

Round Table on Comparison of Dietary Recommendation in Different European Countries see European Nutrition Conference: Proceedings, 2nd, Munich, 1976

Round Table on Law & Semiotics (8th 1993) Penn State in Reading, Conscience, Consensus, & Crossroads in Law. Ed. by Roberta Kevelson. (Semiotics & the Human Sciences Ser.: Vol. 8). 416p. (C). 1995. text ed. 64.95 (0-8204-2511-7) P Lang Pubng.

Round the Bend. Nevil Shute. 1977. reprint ed. lib. bdg. 26.95 (0-89244-053-8) Queens Hse-Focus Serv.

Round the Christmas Tree. Ed. by Sarah Corrin & Stephen Corrin. (J). (gr. 3-7). reprint ed. pap. 3.95 (0-317-62263-3, Puffin) Puffin Bks.

Round the Circle: Key Experiences in Movement for Children Ages 3 to 5. Phyllis S. Weilkart. LC 87-8453. (Illus.). 125p. 1987. pap. 19.95 (0-931114-39-X) High-Scope.

Round the Fire: Stories. Arthur Conan Doyle. 256p. (Orig.). 1991. reprint ed. pap. 9.95 (0-87701-883-9) Chronicle Bks.

***Round the Glory Manger: Christmas Spirituals.** Thea Bowman. 72p. 7.95 (0-8198-6428-5) Pauline Bks.

Round the Horn Before the Mast. Basil Lubbock. (C). 1987. 102.00 (0-85174-506-7, Pub. by Brwn Son Ferg) St Mut.

Round the Levee. Ed. by Stith Thompson. LC 75-11936. (Texas Folklore Society Publications: No. 1). 112p. 1975. reprint ed. 11.95 (0-87074-115-2) UNTX Pr.

An Asterisk (*) at the beginning of an entry indicates that the title is appearing in BIP for the first time.

R

Round the Moon. Jules Verne. (Airmont Classics Ser.). (J). (gr. 7 up). 1968. mass mkt. 1.50 (*0-8049-0182-1*, CL-182) Airmont.

*__Round the Moon.__ Jules Verne. lib. bdg. 22.95 (*0-8488-2045-2*) Amereon Ltd.

Round the Mountain Activity Book, Unit 2. (Networks Ser.). 1991. 3.90 (*0-88106-711-3*, N124) Charlesbridge Pub.

Round the Mountain Anthology, N121. (Networks Ser.). 1991. 7.45 (*0-88106-710-5*, N121) Charlesbridge Pub.

Round the Red Lamp. Arthur Conan Doyle. LC 77-101802. (Short Story Index Reprint Ser.). 1977. 18.95 (*0-8369-3190-4*) Ayer.

Round the Roses: Portland Past Perspectives. Karl T. Klooster. (Illus.). 272p. (Orig.). 1987. pap. 15.95 (*0-9619847-0-8*) K T Klooster.

Round the Roses, No. Two: More Portland Past Perspectives. Karl T. Klooster. (Illus.). 288p. (Orig.). 1992. pap. 17.95 (*0-9619847-1-6*) K T Klooster.

Round the World Cookbook. Anne Millard. (Illus.). 48p. (J). 1993. pap. 8.95 (*0-7460-0966-6*, Usborne) EDC.

Round the World Cookbook: Recipes & Party Ideas. Favorite Recipes Press Staff & Great American Opportunities Staff. LC 92-44405. 1993. write for info. (*0-87197-362-6*) Favorite Recipes.

Round-the-World Cooking at the Natural Gourmet. Debra Stark. LC 93-48569. reprint ed. pap. 17.95 (*0-87983-625-3*) Keats.

Round-The-World Flights. 2nd ed. Cv Glines. 1990. pap. 17.95 (*0-8306-3393-6*) McGraw-Hill Prof.

Round the World Folktale Mini-Books: 13 Easy-to-Make Books to Promote Literacy & Cultural... Maria Fleming. 1995. pap. text ed. 9.95 (*0-590-49793-6*) Scholastic Inc.

Round the World in Eighty Days. (Fiction Ser.). (YA). 1993. pap. text ed. 6.50 (*0-582-09671-5*, 79826) Longman.

Round the World Songbook. Kate Elliott & Emma Danes. (Songbooks Ser.). (Illus.). (J). (ps up). 1996. pap. 9.95 (*0-7460-1758-8*, Usborne); lib. bdg. 17.95 (*0-88110-826-X*, Usborne) EDC.

Round the World Voyage of Hieromonk Gideon, 1803-1809. Ed. by Richard A. Pierce. Tr. by Lydia T. Black from RUS. (Alaska History Ser.: No. 32). (Illus.). 1989. 29.00 (*0-919642-20-9*) Limestone Pr.

Round the Year with the World's Religions. Royston Pike. (Illus.). 208p. 1993. reprint ed. lib. bdg. 40.00 (*1-55888-996-5*) Omnigraphics Inc.

Round Tower. Catherine Cookson. 336p. (Orig.). 1994. mass mkt. 7.99 (*0-552-14075-9*) Bantam.

Round Towers of Ireland. George L. Barrow. (Illus.). 232p. 1979. 35.00 (*0-8159-6726-8*) Devin.

Round Trip. Ann Jonas. LC 82-12026. (Illus.). 32p. (J). (gr. k-3). 1983. 16.00 (*0-688-01772-X*); lib. bdg. 15.93 (*0-688-01781-9*) Greenwillow.

Round Trip. Ann Jonas. LC 82-12026. (Illus.). 32p. (J). (ps up). 1990. pap. 3.95 (*0-688-09986-6*, Mulberry) Morrow.

Round Trip. Ann Jonas. (Illus.). (J). (gr. k-3). 1992. pap. 15.95 incl. audio (*0-87499-268-0*) Live Oak Media.

Round Trip. Ann Jonas. (Illus.). (J). (gr. k-3). 1992. 22.95 incl. audio (*0-87499-269-9*) Live Oak Media.

Round Trip, 4 bks., Set. Ann Jonas. (Illus.). (J). (gr. k-3). 1992. pap. 29.95 incl. audio (*0-87499-270-2*) Live Oak Media.

Round Trip Home. Elizabeth Kouhi. 64p. 1984. 6.95 (*0-920806-57-0*, Pub. by Penumbra Pr CN) U of Toronto Pr.

Round-Trip to America: The Immigrants Return to Europe, 1880-1930. Mark Wyman. LC 93-18180. (Illus.). 272p. 1993. 37.50 (*0-8014-2875-0*) Cornell U Pr.

Round-Trip to America: The Immigrants Return to Europe, 1880-1930. Mark Wyman. (Illus.). 280p. 1996. pap. 14.95 (*0-8014-8112-0*) Cornell U Pr.

Round Trip to Byzantium. Harry Barba. LC 84-80153. 379p. (Orig.). 1985. pap. 9.95 (*0-911906-29-0*); lib. bdg. 17.95 (*0-911906-28-2*) Harian Creative Bks.

Round-Up. large type ed. Clarence E. Mulford. Date not set. reprint ed. lib. bdg. 24.95 (*0-88411-238-1*, Aeonian Pr) Amereon Ltd.

Round-Up: A Pictorial History of Western Movie & Television Stars Through the Years. Ed. by Donald R. Key. LC 93-74258. (Illus.). 320p. 1995. 35.00 (*0-944019-12-9*) Empire NC.

Round-Up see Hopalong Cassidy Series

*__Round up the Sin Gang!__ Patricia Holland. (J). pap. 49.95 (*0-614-18226-3*, R100) Let Us Tch Kids.

Round Up the Usual Suspects: The Making of Casablanca - Bogart, Bergman, & World War II. Aljean Harmetz. (Illus.). 416p. 1993. pap. 12.95 (*1-56282-761-8*) Hyperion.

Round Valley Indians of California: An Unpublished Chapter in Acculturation in Seven (or Eight) American Indian Tribes. LC 77-622988. (University of California, Archaeological Research Facility Contributions Ser.: No. 31). 141p. reprint ed. pap. 40.20 (*0-317-26283-1*, 2024262) Bks Demand.

Round We Go! Elizabeth Gilpatrick. 48p. (Orig.). 1991. pap. 6.95 (*0-88284-491-1*, 7993) Alfred Pub.

Roundabout. large type ed. Diana Raymond. 368p. 1996. 25.99 (*0-7089-3403-X*) Ulverscroft.

Roundabout - The Physics of Rotation in the Everyday World: A Scientific American Reader. Jearl Walker. LC 85-4358. (Illus.). 70p. (C). 1995. text ed. write for info. (*0-7167-1725-5*) W H Freeman.

*__Rounders 3.__ Max Evans. LC 97-23476. 1997. write for info. (*0-87081-455-9*) Univ Pr Colo.

Rounding Ballast Key. George E. Murphy. 1987. 5.00 (*0-935331-01-8*) Ampersand RI.

Rounding Errors in Algebraic Processes. James H. Wilkinson. LC 94-7412. (Illus.). 161p. 1994. reprint ed. pap. 6.95 (*0-486-67999-3*) Dover.

*__Rounding Third.__ Donald A. Blackwell. Ed. by Pamela S. Rodriguez & Michelle Rothkopf. (Illus.). 32p. (Orig.). 1997. pap. write for info. (*0-9650332-1-X*) D A Blackwell.

Rounds. Arnett Gosisgi-Carroll. (Review Chapbook Ser.: No. 20: Native American (Cherokee) Poetry 3). 32p. 1982. 15.00 (*0-89304-844-5*, CCC148); pap. 5.00 (*0-89304-819-4*) Cross-Cultrl NY.

Rounds & Canons for Reading, Recreation & Performance - Cello. Contrib. by William Starr. 56p. 1996. pap. text ed. 7.95 (*0-87487-982-5*) Summy-Birchard.

Rounds & Canons for Reading, Recreation & Performance - Viola. Contrib. by William Starr. 56p. 1996. pap. text ed. 7.95 (*0-87487-981-7*) Summy-Birchard.

Rounds & Canons for Reading, Recreation & Performance - Violin. William Starr. 56p. 1995. pap. text ed. 7.95 (*0-87487-980-9*) Summy-Birchard.

*__Rounds & Canons for Reading, Recreation, & Performance Piano, Vol. 1.__ William Starr & Connie Starr. 40p. 1996. pap. text ed. 7.95 (*0-87487-983-3*) Summy-Birchard.

*__Rounds & Canons for Reading, Recreation, & Performance Piano, Vol. 2.__ William Starr & Connie Starr. 52p. 1996. pap. text ed. 7.95 (*0-87487-984-1*) Summy-Birchard.

Rounds, Catches & Canons of England: A Collection of Specimens of the Sixteenth, Seventeenth, & Eighteenth Centuries Adopted to Modern Use. Edward F. Rimbault. LC 76-21067. (Music Reprint Ser.). 208p. 1976. 35.00 (*0-306-70823-X*) Da Capo.

Rounds for Children. (Illus.). 64p. 1986. pap. 8.95 (*0-8256-2442-8*, AM60260) Music Sales.

Rounds Re-Sounding: Circular Music for Voices & Instruments: An Eight-Century Reference. Compiled by Gloria T. Delamar. LC 85-43576. 347p. 1987. lib. bdg. 58.50 (*0-89950-203-2*) McFarland & Co.

Roundtable Conference on International Law Problems in Asia. Vincent Shepherd. LC 74-15225. 669p. reprint ed. pap. 180.00 (*0-317-09593-5*, 2017731) Bks Demand.

Roundtable in Poictesme. James-Branch Cabell. 1973. 250.00 (*0-87968-234-5*) Gordon Pr.

*__Roundtable Learning: Building Understanding Through Enhanced MI Strategies.__ LC 96-52122. 1997. write for info. (*1-56976-061-6*) Zephyr Pr AZ.

Roundtable on Mass Deacidification. Association of Research Libraries Staff. 115p. 1992. pap. 20.00 (*0-918006-21-X*) ARL.

Roundtable Pulpit: Where Leadership & Preaching Meet. John S. McClure. LC 95-3956. 144p. 1995. pap. 14.95 (*0-687-01142-6*) Abingdon.

Roundtable Talks & the Breakdown of Communism. Jon Elster. 216p. 1996. 39.95 (*0-226-20628-9*) U Ch Pr.

Roundup, Vol. 3. Rick Steber. (Heart of the West Ser.). (Illus.). 162p. 1996. lib. bdg. 29.95 (*0-945134-30-4*) Bonanza Pub.

Roundup, Vol. 3. Rick Steber. (Heart of the West Ser.). (Illus.). 162p. 1996. pap. 17.50 (*0-945134-31-2*) Bonanza Pub.

Roundup: A Nebraska Reader. Line Drawings by Elmer Jacobs. Virginia Faulkner. LC 57-8597. 509p. reprint ed. pap. 145.10 (*0-685-15567-6*, 2026751) Bks Demand.

Roundup of Cowboy Humor. Ed. by Ted Stone. 192p. 1995. pap. 14.95 (*0-88995-141-1*, Pub. by Red Deer CN) Orca Bk Pubs.

Roundup on the Pecos. Ed. by Elvis E. Fleming & Minor S. Huffman. LC 78-51726. (Illus.). 465p. 1978. text ed. 45.00 (*0-961531O-1-0*) Hist Soc SE NM.

Roundup on the Pecos. deluxe ed. Ed. by Elvis E. Fleming & Minor S. Huffman. LC 78-51726. (Illus.). 465p. 1978. boxed 75.00 (*0-9615310-0-2*) Hist Soc SE NM.

Roupes Valley: A History of the Pioneer Settlement of Roupes Valley Located in Tuscaloosa & Jefferson Counties, Alabama. rev. ed. James H. Walker. (Illus.). 144p. (C). 1993. reprint ed. text ed. write for info. (*0-9633197-1-X*) Instant Heirloom.

Rourke Dinosaur Dictionary. J. Hincks. (Dinosaur Dictionary Ser.). (Illus.). 96p. (J). (gr. k-8). 1987. lib. bdg. 26.60 (*0-86592-049-4*) Rourke Corp.

Rouse a Sleeping Cat. Dan Crawford. 256p. (Orig.). 1993. mass mkt. 4.99 (*0-441-73553-3*) Ace Bks.

Rousing Minds to Life: Teaching, Learning, & Schooling in Social Context. Roland G. Tharp & Ronald G. Gallimore. (Illus.). 336p. (C). 1989. text ed. 59.95 (*0-521-36234-2*) Cambridge U Pr.

Rousing Minds to Life: Teaching, Learning, & Schooling in Social Context. Roland G. Tharp & Ronald G. Gallimore. (Illus.). 336p. (C). 1991. pap. text ed. 19.95 (*0-521-40603-X*) Cambridge U Pr.

*__Rousing the Nation: Radical Culture in Depression America.__ Laura Browder. (Illus.). 256p. 1998. 29.95 (*1-55849-125-2*) U of Mass Pr.

Rousseau. Doreen Ehrlich. (Illus.). 112p. 1995. 14.98 (*0-8317-7166-6*) Smithmark.

*__Rousseau.__ Cornelia Stabenow. 1994. pap. text ed. 8.99 (*3-8228-0552-1*) Taschen Amer.

Rousseau. Robert Wokler. (Past Masters Ser.). 144p. 1995. pap. 8.95 (*0-19-287640-6*) OUP.

Rousseau: "Confessions" Peter France. (Landmarks of World Literature Ser.). 128p. 1986. pap. text ed. 11.95 (*0-521-31500-X*) Cambridge U Pr.

Rousseau: Dreamer of Democracy. James Miller. LC 83-17396. (Illus.). 274p. (C). 1995. reprint ed. pap. text ed. 12.95 (*0-300-03518-7*) Hackett Pub.

Rousseau: Political Writings. Ed. by Frederick M. Watkins. LC 86-7749. 376p. 1986. reprint ed. pap. text ed. 16.50 (*0-299-11094-X*) U of Wis Pr.

Rousseau: Totalitarian or Liberal? John W. Chapman. LC 68-54260. (Columbia University. Studies in the Social Sciences: No. 589). reprint ed. 20.00 (*0-404-51589-4*) AMS Pr.

Rousseau & Education According to Nature. T. Davidson. 1972. 59.95 (*0-8490-0976-6*) Gordon Pr.

Rousseau & Education According to Nature. Thomas Davidson. LC 70-136373. reprint ed. 32.50 (*0-404-01977-3*) AMS Pr.

Rousseau & Education According to Nature. Thomas Davidson. (Notable American Authors Ser.). 1992. reprint ed. lib. bdg. 75.00 (*0-7812-2622-8*) Rprt Serv.

Rousseau & Education According to Nature. Thomas Davidson. LC 70-108469. 1970. reprint ed. 15.00 (*0-403-00427-6*) Scholarly.

Rousseau & His Era. John V. Morley. 700p. 1996. pap. 49.95 (*1-56459-578-1*) Kessinger Pub.

Rousseau & Liberty. Ed. by Robert Wokler. LC 94-41731. 1995. text ed. 79.95 (*0-7190-3510-4*, Pub. by Manchester Univ Pr UK) St Martin.

Rousseau & Liberty. Robert Wokler. 1995. text ed. 24.95 (*0-7190-4721-8*, Pub. by Manchester Univ Pr UK) St Martin.

Rousseau & Revolution. Will Durant & Ariel Durant. (Story of Civilization Ser.: Vol. 10). (Illus.). 1140p. 1967. 35.00 (*0-671-63058-X*) S&S Trade.

Rousseau & Revolution, Vol. X. Will Durant & Ariel Durant. (Story of Civilization Ser.: Vol. 10). (Illus.). 1994. 17.98 (*1-56731-021-4*, MJF Bks) Fine Comms.

Rousseau & Romanticism. Irving Babbitt. 426p. (C). 1991. pap. 24.95 (*0-88738-888-4*) Transaction Pubs.

Rousseau & Romanticism. Irving Babbitt. LC 75-28989. (BCL Ser.: No. II). 1976. reprint ed. 49.50 (*0-404-14000-9*) AMS Pr.

Rousseau & the Republic of Virtue: The Language of Politics in the French Revolution. Carol Blum. 1989. pap. 15.95 (*0-8014-9557-1*) Cornell U Pr.

*__Rousseau & the Wicked.__ Bill Griffiths. 1996. 11.00 (*0-9521256-3-3*, Pub. by Invisible Bks UK) SPD-Small Pr Dist.

*__Rousseau Art Activity Pack.__ Mila Boutan. (Art Activity Packs Ser.). (Illus.). (J). (ps-3). 1997. pap. 9.95 (*0-8118-1691-5*, 706777T) Chronicle Bks.

Rousseau Dictionary. N. J. Dent. 260p. 1992. pap. 22.95 (*0-631-17569-5*) Blackwell Pubs.

Rousseau in Deutschland: Neue Beitraege Zur Erforschung Seiner Rezeption. Ed. by Herbert Jaumann. 338p. (GER.). (C). 1994. lib. bdg. 130.80 (*3-11-014078-0*) De Gruyter.

*__Rousseau in Geneva: From the First Discourse to the Social Contract, 1749-1762.__ Helena Rosenblatt. (Ideas in Context Ser.: No. 46). 350p. 1997. 59.95 (*0-521-57004-2*) Cambridge U Pr.

Rousseau in the Spanish World Before 1833: A Study in Franco-Spanish Literary Relations. Jefferson R. Spell. LC 76-93257. 325p. (C). 1969. reprint ed. 50.00 (*0-87752-104-2*) Gordian.

Rousseau, Judge of Jean-Jacques: Dialogues. Jean-Jacques Rousseau. Ed. by Roger D. Masters et al. Tr. by Christopher Kelly et al. LC 89-40234. (Collected Writings of Rousseau: Vol. 1). (Illus.). 309p. 1990. 45.00 (*0-87451-495-9*) U Pr of New Eng.

Rousseau, Nature, & History. Asher Horowitz. 274p. 1992. 40.00 (*0-8020-5681-4*); pap. 19.95 (*0-8020-7381-6*) U of Toronto Pr.

Rousseau on International Relations. Jean-Jacques Rousseau. Ed. by Stanley Hoffman & David P. Fidler. 296p. 1991. 55.00 (*0-19-827321-5*) OUP.

Rousseau: Still Voyages see Art for Children

Rousseau's Art of Persuasion in "La Nouvelle Heloise" Santo L. Arico. 212p. (Orig.). (C). 1994. pap. text ed. 28.50 (*0-8191-9618-5*); lib. bdg. 51.00 (*0-8191-9617-7*) U Pr of Amer.

Rousseau's Exemplary Life: The Confessions As Political Philosphy. Christopher Kelly. LC 86-32961. 288p. (C). 1987. 39.95 (*0-8014-1936-0*) Cornell U Pr.

Rousseau's First & Second Discourses. Roger D. Masters & Anthony Masters. 1969. write for info. (*0-318-63175-X*) St Martin.

Rousseau's Legacy: Emergence & Eclipse of the Writer in France. Dennis Porter. (Illus.). 336p. 1995. 45.00 (*0-19-509107-8*) OUP.

Rousseau's Occasional Autobiographies. Susan Jackson. 280p. 1992. 42.50 (*0-8142-0565-8*) Ohio St U Pr.

Rousseau's Political Writings. Jean-Jacques Rousseau. Ed. by Alan Ritter. Tr. by Julia C. Bondanella. LC 87-24056. (Critical Editions Ser.). (C). 1987. pap. text ed. 10.95 (*0-393-95651-2*) Norton.

Rousseau's Socratic Aemilian Myths: A Literary Collation of "Emile" & the "Social Contract" Madeline B. Ellis. LC 76-28197. 433p. 1977. 40.00 (*0-8142-0223-3*) Ohio St U Pr.

Rousseau's Theory of Literature: The Poetics of Art & Nature. James F. Hamilton. LC 78-74002. 219p. 1979. 16.95 (*0-917786-09-2*) Summa Pubns.

*__Roustabout: A Novel.__ Michelle Chalfoun. 240p. 1997. pap. 12.50 (*0-06-092799-2*, PL) HarpC.

Route. 2nd ed. J. K. Huymans. Ed. by Pierre Cogny. (Conversion Trilogy Ser.: Vol. 1). (Illus.). 408p. (FRE.). 1995. 74.95 (*2-86808-007-3*) Intl Scholars.

Route Across the Rocky Mountains. Overton Johnson. Ed. by William H. Winter. LC 77-87648. (American Scene Ser.). (Illus.). 200p. 1972. reprint ed. lib. bdg. 29.50 (*0-306-71780-8*) Da Capo.

Route Across the Rocky Mountains. Overton Johnson et al. 166p. 1982. reprint ed. 14.95 (*0-87770-269-1*) Ye Galleon.

Route & Other Poems. James R. Scrimgeour. Ed. by Robert D. Sutherland. 90p. (Orig.). 1996. pap. write for info. (*0-936044-07-1*) Pikestaff Pr.

Route & Resorts of the Chesapeake & Ohio Railway. Ed. by Jim Singleton. (Illus.). 82p. 1992. reprint ed. pap. 9.95 (*1-881413-05-5*) Thomas In-Prints.

Route Au Tabac. Erskine Caldwell. 256p. (FRE.). 1973. pap. 10.95 (*0-7859-1753-5*, 2070364380) Fr & Eur.

Route Choice: Wayfinding in Transport Networks. Piet H. Bovy & Eliahu Stern. (C). 1990. lib. bdg. 141.50 (*0-7923-0812-3*) Kluwer Ac.

Route Choice & Signal Control: The Potential for Integrated Route Guidance. Ton Van Vuren & Dirck Van Vliet. (Institute of Transport Studies). 240p. 1992. 68.95 (*1-85628-289-9*, Pub. by Avebury Pub UK) Ashgate Pub Co.

Route Guidance & In-Car Communications Systems. OECD Staff. (Road Transport Research Ser.). 104p. (Orig.). 1988. pap. 16.50 (*92-64-13046-2*) OECD.

*__Route Guidance & In-Car Communications Systems.__ OECD Staff. (Road Transport Research Ser.). 104p. (Orig.). 1988. pap. 16.50 (*92-64-23046-7*) OECD.

Route Location & Design. 5th ed. Thomas F. Hickerson. (Illus.). 1967. text ed. write for info. (*0-07-028680-9*) McGraw.

*__Route Maps in Gene Technology.__ Matthew R. Walker. LC 96-31611. (Illus.). 336p. (Orig.). (C). 1997. pap. text ed. 39.95 (*0-632-03792-X*) Blackwell Sci.

Route National. Goodman & Stephens. (Secondary French Ser.). 1993. teacher ed., pap. 33.95 (*0-17-439594-9*) Heinle & Heinle.

Route National, Bk. 2. Goodman & Stephens. (Secondary French Ser.). 1993. teacher ed., pap. 34.95 (*0-17-439601-5*) Heinle & Heinle.

Route National: Level Two. Goodman & Stephens. (Secondary French Ser.). 1993. student ed., pap. 23.95 (*0-17-439505-1*) Heinle & Heinle.

Route National, Level 1. Goodman-Stephens et al. 1993. pap. 23.95 (*0-17-439500-0*) Heinle & Heinle.

Route Nationale: Stage 3. Goodman. (Secondary French Ser.). 1995. student ed., pap. 24.95 (*0-17-439510-8*) Heinle & Heinle.

Route Ninety-Three: A Rocky Flats Fable. Dennis S. Smith. LC 95-80453. 311p. (Orig.). 1995. pap. 5.95 (*1-888087-01-3*) Aardvark Pr CO.

*__Route Ninety-Three: A Rocky Flats Fable.__ 2nd ed. Dennis S. Smith. 311p. (Orig.). 1997. pap. 6.95 (*1-888087-02-1*) Aardvark Pr CO.

Route of the Erie Limited. Dirkes & John Krause. (Illus.). 48p. 1989. pap. 7.95 (*0-911868-11-9*, C11) Carstens Pubns.

Route of the Mayas. Gallimard Editions Staff. LC 94-8389. (Knopf Guides Ser.). (Illus.). 424p. (YA). 1995. pap. 25.00 (*0-679-75569-1*) Knopf.

Route of the Orange Limited. William R. Gordon. LC 86-12042. (Illus.). 100p. 1986. reprint ed. pap. 5.95 (*0-932334-80-6*, NY75038) Hrt of the Lakes.

Route Planning Issues for Low Observable Aircraft & Cruise Missiles: Implications for the Intelligence Community. Myron Hura & Gary W. McLeod. LC 93-7687. 1993. pap. 13.00 (*0-8330-1368-8*, MR-187-AF) Rand Corp.

*__Route Planning Map of France.__ 1997. 8.95 (*2-06-700911-7*, 911) Michelin.

Route Sixty-Six: The Highway & Its People. Quinta Scott & Susan C. Kelly. LC 88-40208. (Illus.). 210p. 1990. pap. 19.95 (*0-8061-2291-9*) U of Okla Pr.

Route Sixty-Six: The Mother Road. Michael Wallis. 1990. 35.00 (*0-312-04049-0*) St Martin.

Route Sixty-Six: The Mother Road. Michael Wallis. (Illus.). 256p. 1992. pap. 19.95 (*0-312-08285-1*) St Martin.

Route 66 - A Guidebook to the Mother Road. 2nd ed. Bob Moore & Patrick Grauwels. (Illus.). 140p. 1997. spiral bd. 21.95 (*0-9641457-0-7*) Inovative Pubng.
Travelers along America's Main Street are a diverse group with one common goal: they want to find & experience the places & the people of the Mother Road. ROUTE 66 - A GUIDEBOOK TO THE MOTHER ROAD will take them to where the road exists as no other book has ever done. Lavishly illustrated with over 200 pictures, this 100-page, large-format guidebook is designed for the traveler who is seeking Route 66 as it exists today. Three years of research & actual driving of the highway produced the exclusive mile-by-mile detail available nowhere else. An exclusive feature is the inclusion of 20 beautiful RoadStamps (tm) that allow the traveler to personalize their copy of the book as a lasting memory of that Route 66 Trip. Uniquely designed for use in the car, ROUTE 66 - A GUIDEBOOK TO THE MOTHER ROAD can be read with ease while traveling or comfortably seated in the armchair at home. Increase your sales with ROUTE 66 - A GUIDEBOOK TO THE MOTHER ROAD. A sure-fire on-sight seller to the Route 66 traveler & those interested in the greatest highway in the United States. ***Publisher Provided Annotation.***

Route Sixty Six Across New Mexico: A Wanderer's Guide. Jill Schneider. LC 91-12599. (Coyote Bks.). (Illus.). 212p. 1991. pap. 14.95 (*0-8263-1280-2*) U of NM Pr.

Route Sixty-Six Revisited, a Wanderer's Guide to New Mexico: Albuquerque to the Arizona Border. K. Hilleson. LC 87-92204. (Wanderer's Guide Ser.: Vol. 2). (Illus.). 127p. (Orig.). 1988. pap. 9.95 (*0-9615195-4-1*) Nakii Ent.

Route 66 Traveler's Guide & Roadside Companion. rev. ed. Tom Snyder. LC 95-8863. (Illus.). 112p. 1995. pap. 10.95 (*0-312-13162-3*) St Martin.

An Asterisk (*) at the beginning of an entry indicates that the title is appearing in BIP for the first time.

Route Step March: Edwin M Stanton's Special Military Units & the Prosecution of the War, 1862-1865. Robert G. Mangrum. 237p. 1980. 37.95 (*0-89126-091-9*) MA-AH Pub.

Route Surveying & Design. 5th ed. Carl F. Meyer & David W. Gibson. (Illus.). (C). 1979. text ed. 72.95 (*0-7002-2524-2*) Addson-Wesley Educ.

Route Three Englewood. Kenton Forrest. (Illus.). 24p. 1980. pap. text ed. 8.50 (*0-932497-02-0*) Tramway Pr.

Route to Food Self-Sufficiency in Mexico: Interactions with the U. S. Food System. Cassio Luiselli. (Monographs: No. 17). 64p. (Orig.). (C). 1985. pap. 7.50 (*0-935391-68-1*, MN-17) UCSD Ctr US-Mex.

Route Tournante. Kjell Espmark. Tr. by Joan Tate from SWE. LC 93-71944. 64p. 1994. pap. 14.95 (*1-85610-027-8*, Pub. by Forest Bks UK) Dufour.

Route Two. deluxe ed. Michael Dorris & Louise Erdrich. 40p. 1990. 50.00 (*0-935716-54-8*) Lord John.

Route '66: The Five Year Diary of a Journey Across America. David Wilde. (Sun Also Sets Ser.). (Illus.). 140p. (Orig.). 1991. 19.95 (*0-9625472-1-2*); pap. 12.95 (*0-9625472-3-9*) Wilde Pub.

Route 66 Cookbook. Marian Clark. (Illus.). 237p. 1995. 24.95 (*0-933031-80-7*) Coun Oak Bks.

Route 66 Cookbook. Marian Clark. (Illus.). 237p. 1995. pap. 17.95 (*1-57178-020-3*) Coun Oak Bks.

Route 66 Postcards: Greetings from the Mother Road. Michael Wallis & Suzanne Wallis. (Illus.). 64p. 1993. pap. 9.95 (*0-312-09904-5*) St Martin.

Route 66 Remembered. Michael K. Witzel. (Illus.). 192p. 1996. 29.95 (*0-7603-0114-X*) Motorbooks Intl.

Routed. Jeffrey Sweet. 1982. pap. 3.25 (*0-8222-0973-X*) Dramatists Play.

Router. Bruce Hunter. LC 81-730633. (Orig.). 1982. student ed. 5.00 (*0-8064-0269-5*, 706); audio, vhs 219.00 (*0-8064-0270-9*) Bergwall.

Router Basics. Patrick Spielman. LC 90-40301. (Basics Ser.). (Illus.). 128p. (Orig.). 1990. pap. 10.95 (*0-8069-7222-X*) Sterling.

Router Handbook. Patricia Spielman. (Sterling Publishing Co. Ser.). 1983. pap. 12.95 (*0-8273-5389-8*) Delmar.

Router Jigs & Techniques. Patrick Spielman. LC 87-33674. (Illus.). 383p. (Orig.). 1988. pap. 17.95 (*0-8069-6694-7*) Sterling.

***Router Joinery.** Gary Rogowski. LC 97-6238. (Illus.). 192p. 1997. 24.95 (*1-56158-174-7*, 070299) Taunton.

Router Magic: Jigs, Fixtures, & Tricks to Unleash Your Router's FULL Potential. Bill Hylton. 1996. 27.95 (*0-87596-711-6*) St Martin.

***Router Projects.** Spielman. Date not set. write for info. (*0-8069-0483-6*) Sterling.

Router Table Book. Ernie Conover. LC 94-24591. (Illus.). 128p. 1994. pap. 19.95 (*1-56158-084-8*) Taunton.

Router Techniques: A Woodworker's Guide. Kevin Harris. (Illus.). 128p. 1995. 34.95 (*1-85223-832-1*, Pub. by Crowood UK) Trafalgar.

***Routers.** Scott Ballew. Ed. by Mike Loukides. (Illus.). 1997. pap. write for info. (*1-56592-342-1*) OReilly & Assocs.

Routes. John Okas. LC 93-27528. 225p. 1994. 24.00 (*1-877946-43-5*) Permanent Pr.

***Routes: Travel & Translation in the Late Twentieth Century.** James Clifford. LC 96-38454. 1997. write for info. (*0-674-77960-6*); pap. write for info. (*0-674-77961-4*) HUP.

***Routes: Travel & Translation in the Late Twentieth Century.** James Clifford. 1997. 39.95 (*0-614-27418-4*) HUP.

***Routes: Travel & Translation in the Late Twentieth Century.** James Clifford. 1997. pap. 14.95 (*0-614-27419-2*) HUP.

Routes de Pekin. Paul-Loup Sulitzer. 1991. pap. 18.95 (*0-7859-3423-5*) Fr & Eur.

Routes into the Mainstream: Career Choices of Women & Minorities. Sue E. Berryman. 1988. 2.75 (*0-318-40008-1*, OC 124) Ctr Educ Trng Employ.

***Routes of Resistance: Travellers & Second-Level Schooling.** Mairin Kenny. (Illus.). 326p. 1997. text ed. 59.95 (*1-85972-628-3*, Pub. by Ashgate UK) Ashgate Pub Co.

Routes of the Valkyries. John Pickering. 94p. (C). 1987. 49.00 (*0-902633-43-0*, Pub. by Picton UK) St Mut.

Routes to Hospital: A Sociological Analysis of the Paths to Psychiatric Hospitalization. Roger Manktelow. LC 94-9576. 1994. 51.95 (*1-85628-492-1*, Pub. by Avebury Pub UK) Ashgate Pub Co.

***Routes to Slavery: Direction, Ethnicity, & Mortality in the Transatlantic Slave Trade.** Ed. by David Eltis & David Richardson. LC 97-11887. 152p. (C). 1997. text ed. 35.00 (*0-7146-4820-5*, Pub. by F Cass Pubs UK); pap. text ed. 18.50 (*0-7146-4390-4*, Pub. by F Cass Pubs UK) Intl Spec Bk.

Routiers Guide to Britain & N. Ireland 1994: Quality & Value Food & Accommodation. 432p. 1994. pap. text ed. 20.00 (*0-7509-0546-8*, Pub. by Sutton Pubng UK) Bks Intl VA.

Routiers Guide to France 1994: Quality & Value Food & Accommodation. 288p. 1994. pap. 18.00 (*0-7509-0547-6*, Pub. by Sutton Pubng UK) Bks Intl VA.

Routine Activity & Rational Choice. Ed. by Ronald V. Clarke & Marcus Felson. (Advances in Criminological Theory Ser.: Vol. 5). 418p. (C). 1993. text ed. 49.95 (*1-56000-087-2*) Transaction Pubs.

Routine Circumcision: The Tragic Myth. N Carter. 1982. lib. bdg. 59.75 (*0-87700-398-X*) Revisionist Pr.

Routine Circumcision: The Tragic Myth. Nicholas Carter. 1979. pap. 6.00 (*0-911038-26-4*, Noontide Pr) Legion Survival.

Routine Drilling Operations. (Drilling Technology Ser.: Segment II). (Illus.). 224p. 1983. 40.00 (*0-88698-144-1*, 2.01210) PETEX.

Routine Investigation. large type ed. Hartley Howard. 309p. 1980. 25.99 (*0-7089-0491-2*) Ulverscroft.

Routine Justice: Processing Cases in Women's Court. Marcia J. Lipetz. (New Observations Ser.). 128p. 1983. 32.95 (*0-87855-483-1*) Transaction Pubs.

Routine Surveillance for Radionuclides in Air & Water. (Illus.). 64p. 1968. pap. text ed. 8.00 (*92-4-156005-3*, 1150136) World Health.

Routine Ultrasonography. Quarashi M. Ali. 1993. pap. 16.95 (*0-533-10260-X*) Vantage.

***Routine Urinalysis & Collection, Transportation, & Preservation of Urine Specimens: Approved Guideline (1995)** Contrib. by Helen M. Free. 1995. 95.00 (*1-56238-282-9*, GP16-A) Natl Comm Clin Lab Stds.

Routinen und Rituale in der Altagskommunikation: Lehrerhandreichungen see Deutsch Aktiv Neu, Level 1B

Routinen und Rituale in der Altagskommunikation: Lehrerhandreichungen see Deutsch Konkret, Level 1

Routinen und Rituale in der Altagskommunikation: Lehrerhandreichungen see Deutsch Konkret, Level 2

Routinen und Rituale in der Altagskommunikation: Lehrerhandreichungen see Deutsch Konkret, Level 3

Routinen und Rituale in der Altagskommunikation: Lehrerhandreichungen see Deutsch Aktiv Neu, Level 1C

Routines. Lawrence Ferlinghetti. LC 64-23652. (Orig.). 1964. pap. 1.00 (*0-8112-0044-2*, NDP187) New Directions.

Routing & Dimensioning for Circuit-Switched Networks. Ambrose Bierce. (Illus.). (C). 1990. text ed. 69.95 (*0-201-12792-X*) Addison-Wesley.

Routing & Scheduling. Bodin. (Computers & Operations Research). 1983. pap. 47.00 (*0-08-030227-0*, Pergamon Pr) Elsevier.

Routing & Shaping. LC 93-18854. (Art of Woodworking Ser.). 144p. 1993. 19.95 (*0-8094-9937-1*); lib. bdg. write for info. (*0-8094-9938-X*) Time-Life.

Routing & Shaping. Nick Engler. LC 91-27328. (Illus.). 128p. 1992. 19.95 (*0-87596-107-X*, 14-318-0) Rodale Pr Inc.

Routing & Shaping. Nick Engler. (Workshop Companion Ser.). 1996. pap. 12.95 (*0-87596-610-1*) Rodale Pr Inc.

Routing in Communications Networks. Martha Steenstrup. (C). 1995. text ed. 54.00 (*0-13-010752-2*) P-H.

Routing in the Internet. Christian Huitema. (C). 1995. text ed. 49.00 (*0-13-132192-7*) P-H.

Routing in the Third Dimension: From VLSI Chips to MCMs. Naveed A. Sherwani et al. LC 94-44113. 376p. 1995. 79.95 (*0-615-00568-3*, PC4473) Inst Electrical.

Routing in Today's Internetworks: The Routing Protocols of IP, DECnet, NetWare & AppleTalk. Mark Dickie. (Illus.). 273p. 1994. text ed. 46.95 (*0-442-01811-8*) Van Nos Reinhold.

Routing, Placement, & Partitioning. Ed. by George W. Zobrist. LC 92-15441. (Computer Engineering & Computer Science Ser.). 304p. (C). 1994. text ed. 78.50 (*0-89391-784-2*) Ablex Pub.

Routledge - French-English & English-French Dictionary of Commercial & Financial Terms. Phrases & Practice. 2nd ed. Julius O. Kettridge. (ENG & FRE.). 1972. reprint ed. 50.00 (*0-7100-1671-9*, RKP) Routledge.

Routledge Anthology of Cross-Gendered Verse. Ed. by Alan M. Parker & Mark Willhardt. LC 95-18991. 288p. (gr. 13). 1996. pap. 17.95 (*0-415-11291-5*) Routledge.

Routledge Anthology of Lesbian & Gay Writing: The Seventeenth & Eighteenth Century. Ian McCormick. LC 96-1605. 272p. (C). 1997. pap. write for info. (*0-415-13954-6*); text ed. write for info. (*0-415-13953-8*) Routledge.

***Routledge Anthology of Nineteenth Century Short Stories by Women.** Harriet D. Jump. LC 97-23393. 1998. write for info. (*0-415-16781-7*); pap. write for info. (*0-415-16782-5*) Routledge.

Routledge Anthology of Poets on Poets. David Hopkins. LC 94-19754. 352p. (C). 1994. pap. 18.95 (*0-415-11847-6*, B4786) Routledge.

Routledge Anthology of Twentieth Century Political Theory. LC 96-24599. 500p. 1996. pap. 27.95 (*0-415-91533-3*) Routledge.

Routledge Anthology of Twentieth Century Political Theory. Stephen E. Bronner. LC 96-24599. 500p. (C). 1996. text ed. 74.95 (*0-415-91532-5*) Routledge.

***Routledge Atlas of British History: From 54 B.C. to the Present Day.** 2nd ed. Martin Gilbert. 152p. 1995. pap. write for info. (*0-460-86180-8*) Routledge.

***Routledge Atlas of British History: From 54 B.C. to the Present Day.** 2nd ed. Martin Gilbert. 152p. (C). 1995. text ed. write for info. (*0-460-86179-4*) Routledge.

***Routledge Atlas of Classical History: from 1700 B.C. to A.D. 565.** 5th ed. Michael Grant. 108p. (C). 1995. text ed. write for info. (*0-415-11934-0*) Routledge.

***Routledge Atlas of Classical History: From 1700 B.C. to A.D. 565.** 5th ed. Michael Grant. 108p. 1995. pap. write for info. (*0-415-11935-9*) Routledge.

Routledge Atlas of Jewish History. 5th ed. Gilbert. 148p. (C). 1995. text ed. 39.95 (*0-460-86181-6*) Routledge.

***Routledge Atlas of Russian History: From 800 B. C. to the Present Day.** 2nd ed. Martin Gilbert. 1995. pap. write for info. (*0-460-86176-X*) Routledge.

***Routledge Atlas of Russian History: From 800 B.C. to the Present Day.** 2nd ed. Martin Gilbert. 208p. (C). 1995. text ed. write for info. (*0-460-86175-1*) Routledge.

***Routledge Atlas of the Arab-Israeli Conflict: Complete History of the Struggle & the Efforts to Resolve It.** 6th ed. Martin Gilbert. 1995. pap. write for info. (*0-460-86178-6*) Routledge.

***Routledge Atlas of the Arab-Israeli Conflict: Complete History of the Struggle & the Efforts to Resolve It.** 6th ed. Martin Gilbert. 152p. (C). 1996. text ed. write for info. (*0-415-13630-X*) Routledge.

***Routledge Atlas of the First World War: Complete History.** 3rd ed. Martin Gilbert. 196p. 1995. pap. write for info. (*0-415-11933-2*) Routledge.

***Routledge Atlas of the First World War: Complete History.** 3rd ed. Martin Gilbert. 196p. (C). 1995. text ed. write for info. (*0-415-11932-4*) Routledge.

***Routledge Atlas of the Holocaust: Complete History.** 2nd ed. Martin Gilbert. 282p. 1995. pap. write for info. (*0-460-86172-7*) Routledge.

***Routledge Atlas of the Holocaust: Complete History.** 2nd ed. Martin Gilbert. 282p. (C). 1995. text ed. write for info. (*0-460-86171-9*) Routledge.

Routledge Dictionary of Economics. Donald Rutherford. 552p. (C). 1995. pap. 18.95 (*0-415-12291-0*, C0460) Routledge.

Routledge Dictionary of Language & Linguistics. Gregory Trauth & Hadumod Bussmann. (Illus.). 544p. (C). (gr. 13). 1996. text ed. 99.00 (*0-415-02225-8*, B4344) Routledge.

Routledge Dictionary of Twentieth Century Political Thinkers. Ed. by Bob Benewick & Phil Green. 464p. (C). (gr. 13). 1992. text ed. 74.95 (*0-415-04371-9*, B0142) Routledge.

***Routledge Dictionary of Twentieth Century Political Thinkers.** 2nd ed. Robert Benewick & Philip Green. LC 97-11585. 1997. pap. write for info. (*0-415-09623-5*) Routledge.

***Routledge Dictionary of Twentieth Century Political Thinkers.** 2nd ed. Robert Benewick & Philip Green. LC 97-11585. 280p. (C). 1998. text ed. write for info. (*0-415-15881-8*) Routledge.

***Routledge Encyclopedia of Philosophy, 10 vols.** Ed. by Edward Craig. 6400p. (C). 1998. text ed. 2,995.00 (*0-415-07310-3*) Routledge.

***Routledge Encyclopedia of Philosophy, 10 vols.** Ed. by Edward Craig. 8136p. (C). 1998. text ed., pap. 3,495.00 incl. cd-rom (*0-415-16917-8*) Routledge.

Routledge French Technical Dictionary - Dictionnaire Technique Anglais, 2 vols., Set. (Specialist Dictionaries Ser.). 1760p. (ENG & FRE.). (C). (gr. 13). 1994. 275.00 (*0-415-05670-5*, B4346) Routledge.

Routledge French Technical Dictionary - Dictionnaire Technique Anglais Vol. 1: French-English. (Specialist Dictionaries Ser.). 880p. (ENG & FRE.). (C). (gr. 13). 1994. 150.00 (*0-415-11224-9*, B4350) Routledge.

Routledge French Technical Dictionary - Dictionnaire Technique Anglais Vol. 2: English-French. (Specialist Dictionaries Ser.). 880p. (ENG & FRE.). (C). (gr. 13). 1994. 150.00 (*0-415-11225-7*, B4354) Routledge.

***Routledge German Dictionary of Construction & Civil Engineering.** Ed. by Junge. LC 96-39328. 370p. (C). 1997. 130.00 (*0-415-11242-7*) Routledge.

***Routledge German Dictionary of Construction Engineering.** 1996. 145.00 incl. audio compact disk (*0-415-14028-5*) Routledge.

Routledge German Technical Dictionary: Universal-Worterbuch der Technik, Vol. 1. (Specialist Dictionaries Ser.). 832p. (ENG & GER.). (C). (gr. 13). 1995. 150.00 (*0-415-11209-5*, C0474) Routledge.

Routledge German Technical Dictionary: Universal-Worterbuch der Technik, Vol. 2. (Specialist Dictionaries Ser.). 776p. (ENG & GER.). (C). (gr. 13). 1995. 150.00 (*0-415-11210-9*, C0475) Routledge.

***Routledge History of Literature in English: Britain & Ireland.** Ronald Carter & John McRae. LC 96-41221. 512p. (C). 1997. pap. write for info. (*0-415-12343-7*); text ed. write for info. (*0-415-12342-9*) Routledge.

Routledge History of Philosophy Vol. 1: From the Beginning to Plato. Ed. by C. W. Taylor. LC 96-21374. (History of Philosophy Ser.). 368p. (C). 1997. 85.00 (*0-415-06272-1*) Routledge.

Routledge History of Philosophy Vol. 4: The Renaissance & Seventeenth Century Rationalism. Ed. by George H. Parkinson. LC 92-37350. 448p. (C). (gr. 13). 1993. 89.95 (*0-415-05378-1*, B0731, Routledge NY) Routledge.

Routledge History of Philosophy Vol. 5: British Philosophy & the Age of Enlightenment. Ed. by Stuart Brown. LC 95-15815. 440p. (C). (gr. 13). 1995. 89.95 (*0-415-05379-X*) Routledge.

Routledge History of Philosophy Vol. 6: The Age of German Idealism. Ed. by Robert C. Solomon & Kathleen M. Higgins. LC 92-32040. 384p. (C). (gr. 13). 1993. 89.95 (*0-415-05604-7*) Routledge.

Routledge History of Philosophy Vol. 7: The Nineteenth Century. Ed. by C. L. Ten. LC 93-44442. Vol. 7. 496p. 1994. 89.95 (*0-415-06003-6*, B4673, Routledge NY) Routledge.

Routledge History of Philosophy Vol. 10: Philosophy of the English Speaking World in the 20th Century. John Canfield. 400p. (C). 1996. text ed. 85.00 (*0-415-05605-5*, Routledge NY) Routledge.

Routledge Philosophy Guidebook to Heidegger & Being & Time. Stephen Mulhall. LC 95-38893. (Philosophy Guidebooks Ser.). 224p. (C). 1996. pap. 9.95 (*0-415-10093-3*); text ed. 45.00 (*0-415-10092-5*) Routledge.

***Routledge Philosophy Guidebook to Mill on Utilitarianism.** Roger Crisp. (Routledge Philosophy Guidebooks). 256p. (C). 1997. pap. write for info. (*0-415-10978-7*); text ed. write for info. (*0-415-10977-9*) Routledge.

Routledge Philosophy Guidebook to Spinoza & The Ethics. Genevieve Lloyd. LC 96-6392. (Philosophy Guidebooks Ser.). 176p. (C). 1996. pap. 9.95 (*0-415-10782-2*); text ed. 44.95 (*0-415-10781-4*) Routledge.

***Routledge Philosophy Guidebook to Wittgenstein & the Philosophical Investigations.** Marie McGinn & Ludwig Wittgenstein. LC 96-27227. (Philosophy Guidebks.). 192p. (C). 1997. text ed. 49.95 (*0-415-11190-0*) Routledge.

***Routledge Philosophy Guidebook to Wittgenstein & the Philosophical Investigations.** Marie McGinn & Ludwig Wittgenstein. LC 96-27227. (Routledge Philosophy Guidebks.). 192p. (C). 1997. pap. 9.95 (*0-415-11191-9*) Routledge.

Routledge Reader in Caribbean Literature. Compiled by Alison Donnell & Sarah L. Welsh. 560p. (C). 1996. text ed. 74.95 (*0-415-12048-9*) Routledge.

Routledge Reader in Caribbean Literature. Compiled by Alison Donnell & Sarah L. Welsh. 560p. 1996. pap. 22.95 (*0-415-12049-7*) Routledge.

Routledge Rides Alone. Will L. Comfort. 1976. reprint ed. lib. bdg. 24.95 (*0-89190-852-8*, Rivercity Pr) Amereon Ltd.

***Routledge Spanish Technical Dictionary, 2vols.** 1600p. (C). 1997. 270.00 (*0-415-11274-5*) Routledge.

***Routledge Spanish Technical Dictionary Vol. 2: English-Spanish.** 830p. (C). 1997. 135.00 (*0-415-11273-7*, D1375) Routledge.

Routledge Who's Who in Nazi Germany. 2nd ed. Robert S. Wistrich. LC 95-6027. 312p. (C). 1995. pap. 14.95 (*0-415-11888-3*) Routledge.

Routledge Who's Who in Nazi Germany. 2nd ed. Robert S. Wistrich. LC 95-6027. 312p. (C). (gr. 13). 1995. text ed. 35.00 (*0-415-12723-8*) Routledge.

Routledge's German Dictionary of Business, Commerce, & Finance. 1200p. (C). 1997. 120.00 (*0-415-09391-0*) Routledge Chapman & Hall.

***Routt National Forest.** Outdoor Books & Maps Inc. Staff. 62p. 1997. 9.95 (*0-930657-12-8*) Outdr Bks & Maps.

Rouxdolph & the Ornery Ornament. Andy Smith. (Illus.). 32p. (J). (gr. 6-8). 1994. 14.95 (*0-9618564-7-5*) LA Proud Pr.

Rouxdolph & the White Egret. Kirby Ward & Andy Smith. Ed. by Denis Deshon & Eileen Sonnier. (Illus.). 32p. (J). 1995. 14.95 (*0-9618564-8-3*) LA Proud Pr.

Rouxdolph's Louisiana Gumbo & Soup Book. Andy Smith & Andrew M. Smith, Sr. (Illus.). 96p. 1992. pap. 9.95 (*0-9618564-4-0*) LA Proud Pr.

Rova Improvisations. Clark Coolidge. (Sun & Moon Classics Ser.: No. 34). 208p. (Orig.). 1993. pap. 11.95 (*1-55713-149-X*) Sun & Moon CA.

Rove Beetles of the Subtribe Philonthina of America North of Mexico (Coleptera: Staphylinidae) Classification: Phylogeny & Revision, Vol. 3. Ales Smetana. Ed. by Virendra K. Gupta. LC 95-79417. (Memoirs on Entomology, International Ser.: Vol. 3, 1995). (Illus.). 960p. 1995. 125.00 (*1-56665-058-5*) Assoc Pubs FL.

Rover. Aphra A. Behn. 69p. (C). 1995. pap. 9.95 (*0-413-66880-0*, A0680, Pub. by Methuen UK) Heinemann.

Rover. Aphra A. Behn. Ed. by Frederick M. Link. LC 66-20828. xvi, 144p. (C). 1967. pap. text ed. 6.95 (*0-8032-5350-8*, Bison Books) U of Nebr Pr.

Rover. William Congreve. (New Mermaid Ser.). (C). Date not set. pap. text ed. 7.95 (*0-393-90076-2*, Norton Paperbks) Norton.

Rover. Joseph Conrad. Ed. by Andrew Busza & John H. Stape. (World's Classics Ser.). (Illus.). 352p. 1998. pap. 8.95 (*0-19-282623-9*) OUP.

Rover. George Mowat-Brown. 1989. pap. 25.00 (*0-7478-0154-1*, Pub. by Shire UK) St Mut.

Rover: Aphra Behn. Ed. by Anne Russell. 220p. 1994. pap. 9.95 (*1-55111-037-7*) Broadview Pr.

Rover & Coo Coo. Hay. (J). 12.95 (*0-671-75217-0*, S&S Bks Young Read) S&S Childrens.

Rover & Other Plays: The Rover; the Feigned Courtesans; the Lucky Chance; the Emperor of the Moon. Aphra A. Behn. Ed. by Jane Spencer. (World's Classics Ser.). 416p. (C). 1996. pap. 8.95 (*0-19-282248-9*) OUP.

Rover & Other Plays: The Rover; The Feigned Courtesans; The Lucky Chance; The Emperor of the Moon. Aphra A. Behn. Ed. by Jane Spencer. (Oxford Drama Library). 432p. (C). 1996. 74.00 (*0-19-812154-7*) OUP.

Rover Boys at College. Arthur Winfield. 191p. (J). 1981. reprint ed. lib. bdg. 12.95 (*0-89966-330-3*) Buccaneer Bks.

Rover Boys at College. Arthur Winfield. 312p. (J). 1980. reprint ed. lib. bdg. 12.95 (*0-89967-008-3*) Harmony Raine.

Rover Boys at School. Arthur Winfield. 302p. (J). 1980. reprint ed. lib. bdg. 12.95 (*0-89967-009-1*) Harmony Raine.

Rover P5 & P5B: The Complete Story. James Taylor. (Illus.). 200p. 1996. 34.95 (*1-86126-003-2*, Pub. by Crowood UK) Motorbooks Intl.

Rover V-8 Engine. David Hardcastle. (Illus.). 224p. 1990. 36.95 (*0-85429-692-1*, Pub. by G T Foulis Ltd) Haynes Pubns.

Rover V8 Engine. 2nd ed. David Hardcastle. (Illus.). 224p. 1995. 44.95 (*0-85429-961-0*, Pub. by J H Haynes & Co UK) Motorbooks Intl.

Rovering to Success: A Guide for Young Manhood. Lord Baden-Powell. (Illus.). 247p. (Orig.). (YA). 1992. pap. 16.95 (*0-9632054-3-9*) Stevens Pub.

Rovers of the Night Sky. MC Nighthawk, pseud. 214p. pap. 19.95 (*0-947898-01-8*, 5579) Stackpole.

***Rovers Tales.** Lewin. Date not set. write for info. (*0-312-18169-8*) St Martin.

Rovigo & Ruggier Trofeo Canzoni da Suonare a Quattro et a otto (Milan) (1613) Ed. by James Ladewig. LC 88-750072. (Italian Instrumental Music of the Sixteenth & Early Seventeenth Centuries Ser.). 174p. 1988. text ed. 80.00 (*0-8240-4521-1*) Garland.

Rovina di Kasch see Ruin of Kasch

Roving Across Fields: A Conversation with William Stafford. William Stafford. Ed. & Intro. by Thom Tammaro. LC 82-73446. 48p. (Orig.). (C). 1983. pap. 6.95 (*0-935306-15-3*) Barnwood Pr.

An Asterisk (*) at the beginning of an entry indicates that the title is appearing in BIP for the first time.

Roving Editor, Or, Talks with Slaves in the Southern States. James Redpath. Ed. by John R. McKivigan. LC 95-31729. 328p. 1996. 45.00 (0-271-01532-2); pap. 16.95 (0-271-01533-0) Pa St U Pr.

Roving Mind. Isaac Asimov. LC 83-60203. 350p. 1983. pap. 21.95 (0-87975-315-3) Prometheus Bks.

***Roving Mind.** Isaac Asimov. 1997. pap. text ed. 18.95 (1-57392-181-5) Prometheus Bks.

Roving Naturalist: Travel Letters of Theodosius Dobzhansky. Theodosius G. Dobzhansky. Ed. by Bentley Glass. LC 79-55229. (American Philosophical Society, Memoirs Ser.: No. 139). 337p. reprint ed. pap. 96.10 (0-7837-2683-X, 2043060) Bks Demand.

Roving Rosie Reports. LC 90-27867. (Gus Is Gone Ser.). (Illus.). 24p. (J). 1991. pap. 3.95 (1-56288-010-1) Checkerboard.

Rovings in the Pacific, from 1837 to 1849, 2 vols. in 1. Edward Lucatt. LC 75-35203. reprint ed. 110.00 (0-404-14280-X) AMS Pr.

Row Away from the Rocks. George T. Henry. LC 92-90219. (Illus.). 101p. 1992. 42.50 (0-9632742-6-0); pap. 17.95 (0-9632742-0-1) G T Henry.

River lore written & published by a boatman of 38 years with the fun, unusual & accidental happenings of the wonderful people that I have met & worked with. I had the chance to meet & photograph Bob Kennedy, Art Buchwald, Andy Williams, Jim Whitaker, John Glenn & many others. What people say: Don Hatch - Hatch River Expeditions - "The stories we treasure, but the photographs are beyond professionalism - super great. These alone make the book great." Others: "I couldn't put it down. It brought back so many memories of the things that happened or could have happened on our trip." "I never wanted to go on a raft trip before I read the book; now I can't wait." "Wonderful text. I loved it." "After the book, I appreciate God's creation even more." For direct purchase, autographed if desired, send to: Row Away from the Rocks, 2325 Grande Ave., S.E., Cedar Rapids, IA 52403. (319) 363-5389; FAX (319) 362-8391. ***Publisher Provided Annotation.***

Row of Pine. Jeffrey Winke. 16p. 1994. pap. 4.00 (0-685-72958-3) Distant Pr.

***Row, Row, Row Your Boat.** Pippa Goodheart. LC 97-16169. 1998. lib. bdg. 14.99 (0-517-70969-4) Crown Bks Yng Read.

***Row, Row, Row Your Boat.** Stephen Lambert. LC 97-7095. (J). 1997. 16.00 (0-517-70970-8) Crown Bks Yng Read.

Row, Row, Row Your Boat. Robin Muller. (Illus.). 32p. (J). (ps-2). 1995. pap. 4.95 (1-895565-78-2) Firefly Bks Ltd.

Row, Row, Row Your Boat. Oppenheim. 32p. (J). 1993. pap. 3.99 (0-553-37193-2) Bantam.

***Row, Row, Row Your Boat: And Other Play Ryhmes.** Illus. by Steve Augarde. (Playtime Pop-Ups Ser.). 12p. (J). (ps-k). 1997. bds. 6.95 (0-590-88023-3, Cartwheel) Scholastic Inc.

Row, Row, Row Your Class: Using Music As a Springboard for Writing, Exploration & Learning. 48p. 1994. 12.95 (1-877673-22-6, ROW) Cottonwood Pr.

***Row Row Row Your Goat.** Most. (J). 1998. write for info. (0-15-201250-8, HB Juv Bks) HarBrace.

Row the Boat: Jesus Fills the Nets. Mary M. Simon. (Hear Me Read Ser.). (Illus.). 24p. (J). (ps-1). 1990. pap. 2.49 (0-570-04186-4, 56-1645) Concordia.

Row upon Row: Sea Grass Baskets of the South Carolina Lowcountry. 1993. pap. 11.95 (0-87249-956-1) U of SC Pr.

Row upon Row: Sea Grass Baskets of the South Carolina Lowcountry. George D. Terry. (Illus.). 64p. (Orig.). 1986. pap. 10.00 (0-938983-02-4) McKissick.

Row upon Row (Latch-Hooking) large type ed. pap. 13.00 (0-317-01859-0) Cath Guild Blind.

Rowallan. Lord Rowallan. (Illus.). 1977. 24.95 (0-8464-0802-3) Beekman Pubs.

Rowan. Anne McCaffrey. 1991. mass mkt. 6.50 (0-441-73576-2) Ace Bks.

Rowan County, N. C., Abstracts of Deeds, 1753-1785. LC 83-81914. (Illus.). 270p. 1983. 30.00 (0-918470-16-1) J W Linn.

Rowan County, N. C., Tax List 1815. Jo W. Linn. LC 87-92111. (Illus.). 1987. pap. 12.00 (0-918470-18-8) J W Linn.

Rowan County, North Carolina Marriage Bonds & Certificates, 1754-1866, 3 vols., Set. Francis T. Ingmire. 350p. 1994. pap. 45.00 (0-8095-8687-8); lib. bdg. 117.00 (0-8095-8105-1) Borgo Pr.

Rowan County, North Carolina Marriage Bonds & Certificates, 1754-1866, Vol. 1: A-F. Francis T. Ingmire. 1994. pap. 15.00 (0-8095-8684-3); lib. bdg. 39.00 (0-8095-8081-0) Borgo Pr.

Rowan County, North Carolina Marriage Bonds & Certificates, 1754-1866, Vol. 2: G-N. Francis T. Ingmire. 1994. pap. 15.00 (0-8095-8685-1); lib. bdg. 39.00 (0-8095-8082-9) Borgo Pr.

Rowan County, North Carolina Marriage Bonds & Certificates, 1754-1866, Vol. 3: O-Z. Francis T. Ingmire. 1994. pap. 15.00 (0-8095-8686-X); lib. bdg. 39.00 (0-8095-8104-3) Borgo Pr.

Rowan County, North Carolina, Tax Lists 1757-1800: Annotated Transcriptions. Jo W. Linn. LC 95-81908. 458p. 1996. 40.00 (0-918470-24-2) J W Linn.

Rowan County, North Carolina Vacant Land Entries 1778-1789. Richard A. Enochs. LC 88-91217. (Illus.). 280p. (C). 1988. write for info. (0-9620244-0-6) R A Enochs.

Rowan Farm. Margot Benary-Isbert. (YA). (gr. 5-12). 1991. 20.00 (0-8446-6475-8) Peter Smith.

Rowand Anderson. Sam McKinstry. 1991. text ed. 65.00 (0-7486-0252-6, Pub. by Edinburgh U Pr UK) Col U Pr.

Rowantree Crop. Elisabeth Pollack. LC 89-39542. 280p. 1989. 16.95 (0-945980-18-3); pap. 9.95 (0-945980-16-7) Nrth Country Pr.

Rowayton on the Half Shell: The History of a Connecticut Coastal Village. Frank E. Raymond. LC 90-7392. (Illus.). 240p. 1990. 20.00 (0-914659-48-0) Phoenix Pub.

Rowboat to Prague see So Many Heroes

Rowdy & Laughing. B. L. Holmes. LC 87-90460. 88p. (Orig.). 1987. pap. 4.95 (0-941300-06-4) Mother Courage.

Rowdy Richard: A Firsthand Account of the National League Baseball Wars of the 1930's & the Men Who Fought Them. 2nd ed. Dick Bartell & Norman Macht. (Illus.). 388p. 1987. 18.95 (0-938190-97-0) North Atlantic.

Rowdy Tales from Early Alabama: The Humor of John Gorman Barr. Ed. by G. Ward Hubbs. LC 80-19299. (Illus.). 232p. 1989. pap. 17.95 (0-8173-0477-0) U of Ala Pr.

***Rowdy's Raiders.** large type ed. Edwin Derek. (Linford Western Large Print Ser.). 272p. 1997. pap. 16.99 (0-7089-5131-7, Linford) Ulverscroft.

Rowe v. Pacific Quad, Inc. 3rd ed. David B. Oppenheimer. 150p. 1993. pap. 18.95 (1-55681-376-7) Natl Inst Trial Ad.

Rowe v. Pacific Quad, Inc. Teaching Notes. 3rd ed. David B. Oppenheimer. 35p. 1993. teacher ed., pap. 8.95 (1-55681-445-3) Natl Inst Trial Ad.

Rowell Family of New England & Their English Origins 1560-1900: Descendants of Thomas Rowell 1594-1662. William H. Jones. 335p. (Orig.). 1996. pap. 28.00 (0-7884-0421-0, J552) Heritage Bk.

Rowers, the Swimmers & the Drowned. Linda Ashear. (Illus.). 80p. (Orig.). 1996. pap. 5.95 (1-57502-176-5, P0798) Morris Pubng.

Rowhani. Clara W. Whalen. LC 95-72381. 240p. (YA). (gr. 9-12). 1995. 20.95 (1-56167-234-3) Noble Hse MD.

***Rowing.** (Illus.). 80p. (YA). (gr. 6-12). 1993. pap. 2.40 (0-8395-3404-3, 33404) BSA.

Rowing. Silken Laumann et al. (Illus.). 152p. 40.00 (1-55046-083-8, Pub. by Boston Mills Pr CN) Genl Dist Srvs.

Rowing. Rosie Mayglothing. (Skills of the Game Ser.). (Illus.). 144p. pap. text ed. 19.95 (1-85223-753-8, Pub. by Crowood Pr UK) Trafalgar.

Rowing - Olympics. J. David Farmer. (Illus.). 67p. 1984. 10.00 (0-942006-06-2) U of CA Art.

Rowing for the Hell of It: A Manual for Recreational Rowers. Peter Raymond. (Illus.). 154p. 1982. 11.95 (0-89182-048-5) Charles River Bks.

Rowing in Eden. Barbara Rogan. 304p. 1996. 23.00 (0-684-81414-5, S&S) S&S Trade.

Rowing in Eden: Rereading Emily Dickinson. Martha N. Smith. LC 92-6368. (Illus.). 300p. (Orig.). (C). 1992. pap. 15.95 (0-292-77666-7); text ed. 35.00 (0-292-72084-X) U of Tex Pr.

Rowing Machine Workouts. 2nd ed. Charles T. Kuntzleman. 1986. pap. 5.95 (0-8092-4949-9) Contemp Bks.

Rowing the Experience. Bob Stewart. 128p. 1988. 35.00 (0-944738-00-1) Boathouse Row.

Rowing, the Experience. Robert Stewart. (Illus.). 128p. 1991. 35.00 (0-685-60717-8) Broad St Bks.

Rowland Williams: Patriot & Critic. Owain W. Jones. 86p. (C). 1991. 24.00 (0-86383-805-7, Pub. by Gomer Pr UK) St Mut.

Rowlandson Drawings from the Paul Mellon Collection. John Riely & Edmund P. Pillsbury. LC 77-85174. (Illus.). 93p. (Orig.). 1977. pap. 10.00 (0-930606-05-1) Yale Ctr Brit Art.

Rowley & Chatterton in the Shades: or Nugae Antiquae et Novae: A New Elysian Interlude, in Prose & Verse. George Hardinge. LC 92-23721. (Augustan Reprints Ser.: No. 193). 1979. reprint ed. 14.50 (0-404-70193-0, PR3506) AMS Pr.

Rowley Poems. Thomas Chatterton. 1977. 20.95 (0-8369-7105-1, 7939) Ayer.

Rowley Poems. Thomas Chatterton. LC 90-39171. 374p. 1990. reprint ed. 55.00 (1-85477-040-3, Pub. by Woodstock Bks UK) Cassell.

Rowley Poems. Thomas Chatterton. (BCL1-PR English Literature Ser.). 333p. 1992. reprint ed. lib. bdg. 89.00 (0-7812-7331-5) Rprt Serv.

Rowlf's Very First Book of Classic Themes. 24p. 1993. pap. 5.95 (0-7935-1987-X, 00292022) H Leonard.

Rowlf's Very Own First Piano Book. L. Olson. 24p. 1987. pap. 5.95 (0-7935-2431-8, 00240835) H Leonard.

Rowntree & the Marketing Revolution, 1862-1969. Robert Fitzgerald. (Illus.). 750p. (C). 1995. text ed. 150.00 (0-521-43512-9) Cambridge U Pr.

Rowntrees of Riseborough: A Genealogy. C. Brightwen Rowntree & E. M. Sessions. (C). 1986. 118.00 (0-900657-67-7, Pub. by W Sessions UK) St Mut.

Rows of Corn: A True Account of a Parris Island Recruit. Herbert L. Moore, Jr. LC 83-3229. (Illus.). 232p. 1983. 9.95 (0-87844-048-8) Sandlapper Pub Co.

Rox & Rouky. Walt Disney Company Staff. 96p. (FRE.). (J). (gr. k-5). pap. 9.95 (0-7859-8851-3) Fr & Eur.

Roxa. William B. Patrick. 1989. 20.00 (0-918526-68-X); pap. 12.50 (0-918526-69-8) BOA Edns.

Roxaboxen. Alice Mclerran. (J). (ps-3). 1991. 16.00 (0-688-07592-4) Lothrop.

Roxaboxen. Alice McLerran. (Picture Puffins Ser.). (Illus.). 32p. (J). (ps-3). 1992. pap. 5.99 (0-14-054475-5) Lothrop.

Roxaboxen. Alice McLerran. (J). (ps-3). 1991. lib. bdg. 15.93 (0-688-07593-2) Lothrop.

Roxaboxen. large type ed. Alice McLerran. (Illus.). 1993. 9.50 (0-614-09852-1, L-34095-00) Am Printing Hse.

Roxana. Daniel Defoe. Ed. by Jane Jack. (World's Classics Paperback Ser.). 362p. 1982. pap. 7.95 (0-19-281563-6) OUP.

Roxana. Daniel Defoe. Ed. by David Blewett. 416p. 1982. pap. 10.95 (0-14-043149-7, Penguin Classics) Viking Penguin.

Roxana: The Fortunate Mistress. Daniel Defoe. Ed. & Intro. by John Mullan. (World's Classics Ser.). (Illus.). 400p. 1996. pap. 8.95 (0-19-282459-7) OUP.

Roxana's Children: The Biography of a Nineteenth-Century Vermont Family. Lynn A. Bonfield & Mary C. Morrison. LC 95-2417. (Illus.). 288p. 1995. pap. 19.95 (0-87023-981-3); text ed. 50.00 (0-87023-972-4) U of Mass Pr.

Roxanna Mennella, in Search of a Song, Vol. 6. Richard A. Spiegel. 40p. (Orig.). (J). (gr. 4-7). 1984. pap. 2.00 (0-934830-32-0) Ten Penny.

Roxanna Mennella, in Search of a Song: Inner Clockwork, Vol. 8. Roxanna Mennella. Ed. by Barbara Fisher. (Illus.). 10p. (Orig.). (J). (gr. 5-9). 1985. pap. 2.00 (0-934830-36-3) Ten Penny.

Roxanne Bookman: Live at Five. Cathy Warren. (J). 1997. pap. 2.95 (0-8167-1839-3) Troll Communs.

Roxanne, Does Your Husband Travel? The Corporate Wife: for Bitters or Wurst. Georgina R. Doyle. 196p. 1985. pap. write for info. (0-931515-07-6) Triumph Pr.

RoxBurghe Ballads, 8 vols., Set. Ed. by W. Chappell & J. W. Ebsworth. reprint ed. 935.00 (0-404-50840-5) AMS Pr.

Roxburgh's Common Skin Diseases. 16th ed. R. M. Marks. (Illus.). 296p. (gr. 13). 1994. pap. text ed. 52.95 (0-412-41130-X) Chapman & Hall.

Roxbury Dictionary of Criminal Justice: Key Terms & Leading Court Cases. Dean J. Champion. LC 96-8392. 350p. (Orig.). (C). 1997. pap. text ed. 19.95 (0-935732-84-5) Roxbury Pub Co.

***Roxbury, MA.** Anthony Sammarco. (Images of America Ser.). 1997. pap. 16.99 (0-7524-0542-X, Arcdia) Chalford.

Roxene. Wendy Stephenson. 70p. (Orig.). 1983. pap. 5.95 (0-920490-28-X) Temeron Bks.

Roxette - Five of the Best. Ed. by Milton Okun. pap. 6.95 (0-89524-540-X) Cherry Lane.

Roxette - Joyride. Ed. by Milton Okun. pap. 14.95 (0-89524-673-2) Cherry Lane.

Roxette - Look Sharp. Ed. by Milton Okun. pap. 14.95 (0-89524-473-X) Cherry Lane.

Roxette - Tourism. Ed. by Milton Okun. pap. 16.95 (0-89524-729-1) Cherry Lane.

Roxette for Easy Piano. Ed. by Milton Oku. 48p. (YA). pap. 9.95 (0-89524-889-1, 02505509) Cherry Lane.

Roxey's Choice: A Novel. Virginia Havens. LC 94-13091. 1994. pap. 9.95 (1-55503-712-7) Covenant Comms.

Roxie & the Red Rose Mystery. Hilda Stahl. LC 92-4851. (Best Friends Ser.: Vol. 5). 160p. (YA). (gr. 4-7). 1992. pap. 4.99 (0-89107-681-6) Crossway Bks.

Roxie Raker. large type ed. Ray Hogan. 1994. pap. 14.95 (1-85389-464-8, Dales) Ulverscroft.

Roxie's Mall Madness. Hilda Stahl. LC 93-22575. (Best Friends Ser.: Vol. 15). 160p. (Orig.). (YA). (gr. 6-9). 1993. pap. 4.99 (0-89107-753-7) Crossway Bks.

Roxie's Mirage: Featuring the Original Boys & Girls from the Hood. Rachel Slaughter. 65p. (YA). (gr. 8-12). 1994. pap. 9.50 (0-9639858-0-9) Fruits for Knowldge.

Roxy. Edward Eggleston. LC 68-20010. (Americans in Fiction Ser.). (Illus.). 432p. reprint ed. pap. text ed. 6.95 (0-89197-926-3); reprint ed. lib. bdg. 32.00 (0-8398-0455-5) Irvington.

Roxy. Edward Eggleston. (Collected Works of Edward Eggleston). 1988. reprint ed. lib. bdg. 59.00 (0-7812-1177-8) Rprt Serv.

Roxy see Collected Works of Edward Eggleston

***Roxy & the Rich Man.** Elizabeth Bevarly. (Desire Ser.). 1997. 3.50 (0-373-76053-1, 1-76053-7) Silhouette.

***Roxy's Gift.** Susan B. Pickford. (Illus.). 16p. (Orig.). (YA). (gr. 4-8). 1997. pap. 4.50 (1-889664-06-5) SBP.

Roy A. Cheville: Explorer of Spiritual Frontiers. Henry K. Inouye, Jr. LC 96-14673. (Makers of Church Thought Ser.). 171p. (Orig.). Date not set. pap. text ed. 12.00 (0-8309-0744-0) Herald Hse.

Roy Acuff: The Smokey Mountain Boy. 2nd ed. Elizabeth Schlappi. LC 92-31931. (Illus.). 320p. 1992. pap. 14.95 (0-88289-932-5) Pelican.

Roy Adaptation Model: The Definitive Statement. Carrista Roy & Heather A. Andrews. (Illus.). 472p. (C). 1991. pap. text ed. 33.95 (0-8385-2272-6, A2272-1) Appleton & Lange.

Roy Area, Pierce County Washington: An Historical Overview. Compiled by Janet N. Baccus. (Illus.). 426p. 1995. pap. text ed. 46.40 (0-9629578-5-2) Intl Long WA.

Roy Bean: Law West of the Pecos. Charles L. Sonnichsen. (Illus.). 14.95 (0-8159-6715-2) Devin.

Roy Bean: Law West of the Pecos. Charles L. Sonnichsen. LC 91-15426. (Illus.). xvi, 207p. 1991. reprint ed. pap. 10.95 (0-8032-9204-X, Bison Books) U of Nebr Pr.

***Roy Bedicheck Family Letters.** Compiled by Jane G. Bedicheck. (Illus.). 352p. 1998. 32.50 (1-57441-032-6) UNTX Pr.

Roy Blakely on the Mohawk Trail. Percy K. Fitzhugh. LC 74-15738. (Popular Culture in America Ser.). 222p. 1975. reprint ed. 23.95 (0-405-06373-3) Ayer.

Roy Blount, Jr. Jerry E. Brown. (Twayne's United States Authors Ser.: No. 567). 176p. 1990. 21.95 (0-8057-7609-5, Twayne) Scribnrs Ref.

Roy Blount's Book of Southern Humor. Ed. by Roy Blount, Jr. LC 94-18611. 1994. 27.50 (0-393-03695-2) Norton.

Roy Campanella. James Tackach. (Baseball Legends Ser.). (Illus.). 64p. (J). (gr. 3 up). 1991. lib. bdg. 15.95 (0-7910-1170-4) Chelsea Hse.

Roy Campanella: Major-League Champion. Carol Greene. LC 93-37878. (Rookie Biographies Ser.). (Illus.). 48p. (J). (gr. k-3). 1994. lib. bdg. 18.30 (0-516-04261-0) Childrens.

Roy Campanella: Major-League Champion. Carol Greene. LC 93-37878. (Rookie Biographies Ser.). (Illus.). 48p. (J). (gr. k-3). 1994. pap. 4.95 (0-516-44261-9) Childrens.

Roy Campanella: The Baseball Star Who Became Paralyzed in a Car Accident see Great Achievers: Lives of the Physically Challenged

Roy Campbell. John F. Povey. LC 77-1358. (Twayne's World Authors Ser.). 233p. (C). 1977. lib. bdg. 17.95 (0-8057-6277-9) Irvington.

Roy Cheville: The Graceland College Years. Malcolm L. Ritchie. (Illus.). 356p. (Orig.). 1995. pap. 10.50 (0-9636457-1-4) Graceland Coll.

***Roy Clark Sing & Strum Guitar: 3 Easy Ways to Play Today!** 196p. (Orig.). 1995. pap. text ed. write for info. (1-890281-18-2, JT112) J T Pubns.

Roy, Comintern & Marxism in India. Kiran S. Maitra. (C). 1991. 22.00 (81-85169-24-1, Pub. by Naya Prokash IA) S Asia.

Roy De Carava, a Retrospective. Peter Galassi. (Illus.). 280p. 1996. 60.00 (0-87070-127-4, 0-8109-6156-3); pap. 29.95 (0-87070-126-6) Mus of Modern Art.

Roy de Maistre: The English Years 1930-1968. Heather Johnson. 140p. 1995. text ed. 90.00 (976-8097-51-5) Gordon & Breach.

Roy DeCarava: A Retrospective. Peter Galassi. (Illus.). 280p. 1996. 60.00 (0-8109-6156-3) Abrams.

Roy Fuller: A Bibliography. Steven E. Smith. 228p. 1996. text ed. 68.95 (1-85928-172-9, Pub. by Scolar Pr UK) Ashgate Pub Co.

Roy Fuller: Writer & Society. Neil Powell. 320p. 1996. 45.00 (1-85754-133-2, Pub. by Carcanet Pr UK) Paul & Co Pubs.

Roy Harris: A Bio-Bibliography. Dan Stehman. LC 91-21554. (Bio-Bibliographies in Music Ser.: No. 40). 488p. 1991. text ed. 75.00 (0-313-25079-0, SRH, Greenwood Pr) Greenwood.

***Roy High School Case Study Report.** Ivan Charner & Susan Hubbard. (Cross Case Report & Case Studies). 50p. 1995. teacher ed., text ed. 20.00 (0-614-24532-X); teacher ed., pap. text ed. 10.00 (0-614-24533-8) Natl Inst Work.

Roy Hopp Hymnary. Roy Hopp. 44p. 1990. pap. 4.50 (0-9622553-3-5, 125-020) Selah Pub Co.

Roy Houck Buffalo Man. Dale Lewis. 148p. text ed. 20.00 (0-614-07280-8) Buffalo Pr.

Roy Jenkins: A Biography. John L. Campbell. LC 83-10927. (Illus.). 280p. 1983. text ed. 29.95 (0-312-69460-1) St Martin.

Roy Lacaster Travels in China: A Plantsman's Paradise. Roy Lancaster. (Illus.). 520p. 1989. 79.50 (1-85149-175-9) Antique Collect.

Roy Lancaster Travel in China: A Plantsman Paradise. Roy Lancaster. 1989. 79.50 (1-85149-019-1) Antique Collect.

Roy Lichtenstein. Lawrence Alloway. LC 83-2788. (Modern Masters Ser.). (Illus.). 128p. 1983. 32.95 (0-89659-330-4); pap. 22.95 (0-89659-331-2) Abbeville Pr.

Roy Lichtenstein. Diane Waldman. LC 92-36643. (Rizzoli Art Ser.). (Illus.). 24p. (Orig.). 1993. pap. 7.95 (0-8478-1666-4) Rizzoli Intl.

Roy Lichtenstein. Diane Waldman. (Orig.). 1993. 59.95 (0-89207-108-7) S R Guggenheim.

Roy Lichtenstein. Diane Waldman. 1994. 75.00 (0-8109-6875-4) Abrams.

Roy Lichtenstein: Pop Paintings 1961-1969. Schirmer's Visual Library Staff. (Illus.). 1994. pap. 14.95 (0-393-31258-5, Norton Paperbks) Norton.

Roy Lichtenstein: The Modern Work, 1965-1970. Elisabeth Sussman. (Illus.). 1978. 4.00 (0-910663-16-5) ICA Inc.

Roy Lichtenstein Bronze Sculpture 1976-1989. Frederic Tuten. 92p. 1989. write for info. (0-318-65123-8) Sixtyfive Thompson.

Roy Lichtenstein Ceramic Sculpture. Constance W. Glenn. (Illus.). 64p. (Orig.). 1977. pap. 50.00 (0-936270-05-5) CA St U LB Art.

Roy Orbison Greatest Hits, No. 309. 96p. 1991. otabind 9.95 (0-7935-0793-6, 00102185) H Leonard.

Roy Orbison LPs, Vol. 6. CPP Belwin Staff. 1988. pap. 13.95 (0-89898-618-4, TPF0146) Warner Brothers.

Roy Poper's Guide to the Brasswind Methods of James Stamp. Roy Poper. 32p. (C). 1995. pap. 9.80 (0-9630856-4-6) Balquhidder.

Roy Raccoon. Dave Sargent & Pat L. Sargent. LC 96-1499. (Animal Pride Ser.: No. 1). (Illus.). 35p. (J). 1996. 12.95 (1-56763-077-4) Ozark Pub.

Roy Raccoon. Dave Sargent & Pat L. Sargent. (Animal Pride Ser.: No. 1). (Illus.). 35p. (J). (gr. 2-8). 1996. pap. 2.95 (1-56763-005-7) Ozark Pub.

Roy Rogers: A Biography, Radio History, Television Career Chronicle, Discography, Filmography, Comicography, Merchandising & Advertising History, Collectibles Description, Bibliography & Index. Robert W. Phillips. LC 94-31152. (Illus.). 446p. 1995. lib. bdg. 55.00 (0-89950-937-1) McFarland & Co.

Roy Rogers Book: A Reference-Trivia-Scrapbook. David Rothel. LC 87-8183. 224p. 1987. pap. 25.00 (0-944019-00-5) Empire NC.

R

Roy Rogers King Cowboys LTD. Morris Poll. 75.00 (*0-685-69283-3*, HarpT) HarpC.

Roy Stryker: U. S. A., 1943-1950, The Standard Oil (New Jersey) Photography Project. Steven W. Plattner. (Illus.). 144p. 1983. 27.95 (*0-292-77028-6*) U of Tex Pr.

Royal Abbey of Saint-Denis from Its Beginnings to the Death of Suger 475-1151. Sumner M. Crosby. LC 85-26464. 570p. 1987. text ed. 75.00 (*0-300-03143-2*); 75.00 (*0-300-03896-8*) Yale U Pr.

Royal Affair. Luis Santeiro. 1995. pap. 5.25 (*0-8222-1491-1*) Dramatists Play.

***Royal Air Force: A Pocket Guide.** Charles Heyman. (Illus.). 139p. (Orig.). 1994. pap. 10.95 (*0-85052-416-4*, Pub. by L Cooper Bks UK) Trans-Atl Phila.

***Royal Air Force at War: Memories & Personal Experiences: 1039 to the Present Day.** Martin Bowman. (Illus.). 192p. 1997. 42.95 (*1-85260-540-5*) Haynes Pubns.

***Royal Air Force in the Great War.** British Air Historical Branch Staff. (Great War Ser.: No. 52). 504p. 1996. reprint ed. 39.95 (*0-89839-251-9*) Battery Pr.

Royal Air Force of World War Two in Color. Roger Freeman. (Illus.). 300p. 1993. 35.00 (*0-933424-58-2*) Specialty Pr.

Royal Air Force 1935-45. Andrew Cormack. (Men-at-Arms Ser.: No. 225). (Illus.). 48p. pap. 11.95 (*0-85045-966-4*, 9183, Pub. by Osprey UK) Stackpole.

***Royal Air Force, 1939-1945.** Chaz Bowyer. 1997. pap. text ed. 16.95 (*0-85052-528-4*, Pub. by L Cooper Bks UK) Trans-Atl Phila.

Royal Albert Hall. John R. Thackrah. 192p. (C). 1988. 60.00 (*0-86138-012-6*, Pub. by T Dalton UK) St Mut.

Royal American Shows: World's Largest Midway, a Pictorial History. Bob Golosack & Fred Heatley. (Illus.). 106p. 1996. pap. 33.95 (*1-880545-03-9*) Midway Mus.

***Royal & Ancient Golfer's Handbook: A Comprehensive & Authoritative Reference Book to the Golfing World.** Ed. by Michael Williams. (Illus.). 912p. 1997. 87.50 (*0-333-65891-4*, Pub. by Macmlln UK) Trans-Atl Phila.

Royal & Other Historical Letters Illustrative of the Reign of Henry III, from the Originals in the Public Record Office, 2 vols., Set. Ed. by Walter W. Shirley. Incl. Vol. 1. Twelve Sixteen to Twelve Thirty-Five. 1974. (*0-8115-1045-X*); Vol. 2. Twelve Thirty-Six to Twelve Seventy-One. 1974. (*0-8115-1046-8*); (Rolls Ser.: No. 27). 1974. reprint ed. 140.00 (*0-685-10000-6*) Periodicals Srv.

Royal & Republican Rome. Tyler Whittle. (History in Pictures Ser.: Bk. 3). (Illus.). 60p. 1972. 12.95 (*0-8464-1185-7*) Beekman Pubs.

***Royal & Republican Sovereignty in Early Modern Europe: Essays in Memory of Ragnhild Hatton.** Ed. by Robert Oresko et al. 540p. 1997. text ed. 95.00 (*0-521-41910-7*) Cambridge U Pr.

Royal Anthropological Institute Film Library Catalogue, Vol. 1. Ed. by James Woodburn. 100p. reprint ed. pap. 28.50 (*0-7837-6666-1*, 2046278) Bks Demand.

Royal Aquarium: Failure of a Victorian Compromise. John M. Munro. 1971. 10.00 (*0-8156-6033-2*, Am U Beirut) Syracuse U Pr.

Royal Arch: Its Hidden Meaning. George H. Steinmetz. (Illus.). 145p. 1996. reprint ed. 9.50 (*0-88053-046-4*, M-302) Macoy Pub.

Royal Arms Apartments Business Project. 5th ed. Rosenberg & Swinney. (BB - Record Keeping I Ser.). 1985. pap. 5.95 (*0-538-11292-1*) S-W Pub.

Royal Art of Benin: The Perls Collection. Kate Ezra. (Illus.). 344p. 1992. 39.95 (*0-8109-6414-7*) Abrams.

Royal Art of Benin: The Perls Collection. Kate Ezra. (Illus.). 344p. 1992. pap. 29.95 (*0-87099-633-9*) Metro Mus Art.

***Royal Arts of Africa: The Majesty of Form.** Susanne P. Blier. LC 97-25456. (Perspectives Ser.). 1998. pap. write for info. (*0-8109-2705-5*) Abrams.

***Royal Assassin.** Robin Hobb. (Farseer Ser.: No. 2). 704p. 1997. mass mkt. 6.50 (*0-553-57341-1*) Bantam.

Royal Australian Navy in World War II. Ed. by David Stevens. (Illus.). 240p. 1997. 34.95 (*1-86448-035-1*, Pub. by Allen Unwin AT) Paul & Co Pubs.

Royal Ballet. Katherine S. Walker & Sarah Woodcock. (Quality Paperbacks Ser.). (Illus.). 144p. 1982. reprint ed. pap. 10.95 (*0-306-80176-0*) Da Capo.

Royal Bardia National Park. B. N. Upreti. 1994. pap. 25.00 (*0-7855-0479-6*, Pub. by Ratna Pustak Bhandar) St Mut.

Royal Bastards of Medieval England. Chris Given-Wilson & Alice Curteis. 195p. (C). 1988. pap. text ed. 14.95 (*0-415-02826-4*) Routledge.

Royal Bavarian Castles. J. H. Spronge. 1976. lib. bdg. 250.00 (*0-8490-2545-1*) Gordon Pr.

Royal Bayreuth: A Collector's Guide. Mary J. McCaslin. (Illus.). 150p. 1994. 42.95 (*0-915410-97-4*); pap. 34.95 (*0-915410-96-6*) Antique Pubns.

Royal Beasts & Other Works. William Empson. LC 87-51312. 201p. 1988. pap. 14.95 (*0-87745-196-6*); text ed. 32.95 (*0-87745-195-8*) U of Iowa Pr.

***Royal Blood.** Barry Davies. 256p. 1997. 23.95 (*1-85227-624-X*, Pub. by Virgin Pub UK) London Brdge.

Royal Blood: Fifty Years of Classic Thoroughbreds. Illus. & Intro. by Richard S. Reeves. 284p. 1994. text ed. 75.00 (*0-939049-63-5*) Blood-Horse.

Royal Blood: Fifty Years of Classic Thoroughbreds. Richard S. Reeves & Jim Bolus. (Illus.). 288p. 1995. 75.00 (*0-8212-2207-4*) Bulfinch Pr.

***Royal Blue: A Novel.** Christina Oxenberg. LC 96-52207. 1997. 22.00 (*0-684-80093-4*, Scribners PB Fict) S&S Trade.

***Royal Book of Oz.** Ruth P. Thomson. (Illus.). 312p. (YA). (gr. 3 up). 1997. reprint ed. 27.95 (*0-929605-67-5*) Books Wonder.

Royal Botanic Gardens Kew Day Book. 1992. 14.99 (*1-85145-635-X*, Pavilion Bks) Viking Penguin.

Royal Botanic Gardens Kew Postcard Book: Dog Rose. 1992. pap. text ed. 7.99 (*1-85145-616-3*, Pavilion Bks) Viking Penguin.

Royal Botanic Gardens Kew Visitor's Book. 1992. 16.99 (*1-85145-610-4*, Pavilion Bks) Viking Penguin.

Royal Botanical Expedition to the Nuevo Reyno de Granada: Mutis & His Contemporaries. Marta F. De Rueda. Ed. by Benjamin Boyington & Gabrielle Sanders. (Illus.). 20p. (Orig.). pap. text ed. write for info. (*1-883592-09-7*) Perm Mission.

Royal Broomstick. Heather Amery. (Castle Tales Ser.). (Illus.). 16p. (J). (ps up). 1996. pap. 4.50 (*0-7460-2512-2*, Usborne); lib. bdg. 12.95 (*0-88110-867-7*, Usborne) EDC.

Royal Buggy Garden. Freeda Lapos-Massey. (Illus.). 29p. (J). (gr. 3-6). 1994. lib. bdg. 13.75 (*1-886272-00-X*) Bugsy-n-Doc.

Royal Canadian Air Force at War 1939-1945. Larry Milberry & Hugh Halliday. (Illus.). 480p. 1996. 65.00 (*0-921022-04-2*, Zenith Aviation) Howell Pr VA.

Royal Canadian Air Force Exercise Plans for Physical Fitness. RCAF Staff. 1990. mass mkt. 5.50 (*0-671-72755-9*) PB.

Royal Canadian Air Force Exercise Plans for Physical Fitness. Royal Canadian Air Force Staff. 80p. 1978. pap. 7.00 (*0-671-24651-8*) S&S Trade.

Royal Canadian Airforce Association. Turner Publishing Company Staff. LC 90-71734. 112p. 1991. 48.00 (*0-685-50320-8*) Turner Pub KY.

Royal Canadian Mounted Police. Robin May & David Ross. (Men-at-Arms Ser.: No. 197). (Illus.). 48p. pap. 11.95 (*0-85045-834-X*, 9130, Pub. by Osprey UK) Stackpole.

Royal Cars. James D. McLintock. 1989. pap. 25.00 (*0-7478-0167-3*, Pub. by Shire UK) St Mut.

Royal Cat. Garrison Allen. 1996. mass mkt. 4.99 (*1-57566-045-8*) Kensgtn Pub Corp.

Royal Chaos. Dan McGirt. 240p. 1990. pap. 3.95 (*0-451-45014-0*) NAL-Dutton.

***Royal Child.** Cheryl P. Salem. 93p. 1996. pap. 6.99 (*0-89274-931-8*, HH931) Harrison Hse.

Royal Childhoods. Charles Carlton. (Illus.). 192p. (C). 1986. 29.95 (*0-7102-0185-0*, RKP) Routledge.

Royal Childhoods. Charles Carlton. 192p. (C). 1990. pap. text ed. 22.95 (*0-415-00779-8*) Routledge.

Royal Children. Ingrid Seward. 1995. mass mkt. 5.99 (*0-312-95375-5*) Tor Bks.

Royal Chitwan National Park: Wildlife Sanctuary of Nepal. Hemanta R. Mishra & Margaret Jefferies. (Illus.). 192p. 1991. pap. 18.95 (*0-89886-266-3*) Mountaineers.

Royal City. Les Savage, Jr. Ed. by Richard C. Weaver. (Orig.). 1988. reprint ed. pap. 0.40 (*0-941108-01-5*) Friends Palace Pr.

Royal City of Susa: Ancient Near Eastern Treasures from the Louvre. Ed. by Prudence O. Harper et al. LC 92-28330. (Illus.). 336p. 1992. 25.00 (*0-87099-651-7*, 0-8109-6422-8) Metro Mus Art.

Royal City of Susa: Ancient Near Eastern Treasures in the Louvre. Ed. by Prudence O. Harper et al. (Illus.). 336p. 1993. 60.00 (*0-8109-6422-8*) Abrams.

Royal Clocks: British Monarchy & Its Timekeepers 1300-1900. Cedric Jagger. (Illus.). 340p. 1983. pap. 57.50 (*0-7090-2661-7*) Trans-Atl Phila.

Royal Collection at the National Gallery Day Book. 1992. 14.99 (*1-85145-620-1*, Pavilion Bks) Viking Penguin.

Royal College of General Practitioners: The First 25 Years. John Fry et al. (Illus.). 350p. 1982. text ed. 29.00 (*0-85200-360-9*) Kluwer Ac.

Royal Commandments. F. R. Havergal. pap. 5.99 (*0-87377-043-9*) GAM Pubns.

Royal Commentaries of the Incas & General History of Peru. Garcilaso De La Vega. Tr. by Harold V. Livvermore. LC 65-13518. (Texas Pan-American Ser.). reprint ed. pap. 160.00 (*0-685-73712-8*) Bks Demand.

Royal Commentaries of the Incas & General History of Peru, Pt. I. Garcilaso De la Vega. Tr. by Harold V. Livermore. (Texas Pan American Ser.). (Illus.). 740p. 1987. reprint ed. pap. 19.95 (*0-292-77038-3*) U of Tex Pr.

Royal Commentaries of the Incas & General History of Peru, Pts. 1 & 2. Garcilaso De La Vega. Tr. by Harold V. Livermore. LC 65-13518. (Texas Pan-American Ser.). reprint ed. pap. 160.00 (*0-685-73711-X*, 2025129) Bks Demand.

Royal Commission on Environmental Pollution, 18th Report: Transport & the Environment. HMSO Staff. 176p. 1994. pap. 55.00 (*0-10-126742-8*, HM267428, Pub. by Stationery Ofc UK) Bernan Associates.

Royal Commission on the Losses & Services of the American Loyalists 1783-1785. Daniel P. Coke. Ed. by Hugh E. Egerton. LC 79-90166. (Mass Violence in America Ser.). 1969. reprint ed. 27.95 (*0-405-01308-6*) Ayer.

Royal Company of Printers & Booksellers of Spain: 1763-1794. Diana M. Thomas. LC 82-50405. 182p. 1982. 18.50 (*0-87875-237-4*) Whitston Pub.

Royal Conflict: Sir John Conroy & the Young Victoria. Katherine Hudson. (Illus.). 256p. 1995. 45.00 (*0-340-60749-1*, Pub. by Hodder & Stoughton Ltd UK) Trafalgar.

Royal Cookery Book. Jules Gouffe. (Illus.). 1977. reprint ed. 21.00 (*0-85409-809-7*) Charles River Bks.

Royal Copenhagen. H. V. Winstone. (Illus.). 160p. 1989. boxed 49.95 (*0-905743-37-7*, Pub. by Stacey Intl UK) Intl Bk Ctr.

Royal Copley: Identification & Price Guide. Mike Schneider. LC 94-41367. (Illus.). 144p. 1994. 29.95 (*0-88740-739-0*) Schiffer.

Royal Correspondence in the Hellenistic Period. H. B. Welles. (Illus.). 510p. 1974. 50.00 (*0-89005-019-8*) Ares.

Royal County of Berkshire: Official Guide. 104p. 1987. pap. 50.00 (*0-317-61995-0*) St Mut.

Royal Courtship. large type ed. West. (Dales Large Print Ser.). 1995. pap. 17.99 (*1-85389-587-3*, Dales) Ulverscroft.

Royal Crescent in Bath: A Fragment of English Life. William Lowndes. 96p. 1988. 60.00 (*0-905459-34-2*, Pub. by Redcliffe Pr Ltd) St Mut.

Royal Cricket of Japan: An Original Fantasy. James Lash. Ed. by Darwin R. Payne & Christian H. Moe. 44p. 1971. pap. 2.95 (*0-8093-0554-2*) S Ill U Pr.

Royal Crown Derby. 3rd ed. John Twitchett & Betty Bailey. (Illus.). 272p. 1988. 69.50 (*1-85149-057-4*) Antique Collect.

Royal Demesne in English Constitutional History, 1066-1272. Robert S. Hoyt. LC 68-23299. xii, 253p. 1968. reprint ed. text ed. 35.00 (*0-8371-0109-3*, HORD, Greenwood Pr) Greenwood.

Royal Designers on Design. Design Council Staff. 200p. 1987. 80.00 (*0-85072-167-9*) St Mut.

Royal Disclosure: Problematics of Representation in French Classical Tragedy. Harriet Stone. LC 87-62170. 176p. 1988. lib. bdg. 23.95 (*0-917786-57-2*) Summa Pubns.

Royal Dockyards. Phillip MacDougall. 1989. pap. 35.00 (*0-7478-0033-2*, Pub. by Shire UK) St Mut.

Royal Doulton Bunnykins Collectors Book. Louise Irvine. (Illus.). 96p. 1993. pap. 26.95 (*0-903685-32-9*, Pub. by R Dennis UK) Antique Collect.

Royal Doulton Figures: Third Edition, Produced at Burlem, Staffordshire 1892-1994. Desmond Eyles. (Illus.). 408p. 1991. 115.00 (*0-903685-35-3*, Pub. by R Dennis UK) Antique Collect.

Royal Doulton Limited Edition Loving-Cups & Jugs. (Illus.). 32p. pap. 17.95 (*0-903685-09-4*, Pub. by R Dennis UK) Antique Collect.

Royal Doulton Series Ware, Vol. I. Louise Irvine. (Illus.). 112p. 1980. 24.95 (*0-903685-07-8*, Pub. by R Dennis UK) Antique Collect.

Royal Doulton Series Ware, Vol. II. Louise Irvine. (Illus.). 144p. 1984. 24.95 (*0-903685-14-0*, Pub. by R Dennis UK) Antique Collect.

Royal Doulton Series Ware, Vol. III. Louise Irvine. (Illus.). 1986. 24.95 (*0-903685-17-5*, Pub. by R Dennis UK) Antique Collect.

Royal Doulton Series Ware, Vol. IV. Louise Irvine. (Illus.). 242p. 1988. 29.95 (*0-903685-21-3*, Pub. by R Dennis UK) Antique Collect.

Royal Dress: The Image & the Reality, 1580 to the Present. Valerie Cumming. 225p. 1989. 49.95 (*0-8419-1267-X*) Holmes & Meier.

Royal Drum: An Ashanti Tale. Mary D. Lake. 24p. (J). (gr. 1-5). 1996. 13.95 (*1-57255-140-2*) Mondo Pubng.

Royal Drum: An Ashanti Tale. Illus. by Carol O'Malia. LC 95-33612. (J). 1996. write for info. (*1-57255-125-9*) Mondo Pubng.

Royal Dynasties in Ancient Israel. Tomoo Ishida. (C). 1977. 91.55 (*3-11-006519-3*) De Gruyter.

Royal Eggplant. Beatrice Ford. Ed. by Dorothy B. Duthie. (Vegetable Stories for Warren Ser.). (Illus.). (J). 1991. pap. write for info. (*1-880172-52-6*) Storyteller.

Royal Elizabeths: The Romance of Five Princesses, 1464-1840. Elsie Thornton-Cook. LC 67-23274. (Essay Index Reprint Ser.). 1977. reprint ed. 18.95 (*0-8369-0938-0*) Ayer.

Royal Escapade. Judy Delton. LC 95-18359. (Lottery Luck Ser.: Bk. 7). (Illus.). 96p. (Orig.). (J). (gr. 2-5). 1996. pap. 3.95 (*0-7868-1024-6*) Hyprn Ppbks.

Royal Facts of Life: Biology & Politics in Sixteenth-Century Europe. Mark Hansen. LC 80-12557. 354p. 1980. lib. bdg. 30.00 (*0-8108-1297-5*) Scarecrow.

***Royal Families of Medieval Scandinavia, Flanders, & Kiev.** Anna M. Dahlquist & Rupert Alen. LC 96-80004. 248p. (Orig.). 1997. pap. 12.99 (*0-9641261-2-5*) Kings River.

Royal Family. Josie Stewart & Lynn Salem. (Illus.). 8p. (J). (gr. k-1). 1995. pap. 3.50 (*1-880612-37-2*) Seedling Pubns.

Royal Family: Finding Your Identity & Purpose in the Kingdom of God. John N. Prassas. LC 93-90361. (Orig.). 1993. pap. 11.95 (*0-9636999-0-3*) ABBA Pr.

Royal Family at Home & Abroad. Trevor Hall. (Illus.). 248p. 1991. 19.99 (*0-517-00146-2*) Random Hse Value.

***Royal Family of Thailand: The Descendants of King Chulalongkorn.** Jeffrey Finestone. (Illus.). 688p. 1996. 85.00 (*0-904568-88-1*, Pub. by New Cavendish UK) Pincushion Pr.

Royal Family of the Columbia. Alberta B. Fogdall. (Illus.). 330p. 1978. 19.95 (*0-87770-168-7*) Ye Galleon.

Royal Family of the Columbia: Dr. John McLoughlin & His Family. 2nd ed. Alberta B. Fogdall. LC 78-17170. (Illus.). 1982. 16.95 (*0-8323-0413-1*) Binford Mort.

Royal Family Paper Dolls. Bellerophon Staff. (J). (gr. 1-9). 1992. pap. 4.95 (*0-88388-097-0*) Bellerophon Bks.

Royal Family, Royal Lovers: King James of England & Scotland. David M. Bergeron. (Illus.). 240p. 1991. text ed. 32.50 (*0-8262-0783-9*) U of Mo Pr.

Royal Festival Hall. (Architecture in Detail Ser.). (Illus.). 60p. 1993. pap. 29.95 (*0-7148-2773-8*, Pub. by Phaidon Press UK) Chronicle Bks.

Royal Flash. George M. Fraser. 1985. pap. 11.95 (*0-452-26112-0*, Plume) NAL-Dutton.

Royal Flash. George M. Fraser. 1989. mass mkt. 6.95 (*0-452-25676-3*) NAL-Dutton.

Royal Flush. large type ed. Margaret E. Irwin. (Shadows of the Crown Ser.). 1974. 25.99 (*0-85456-617-1*) Ulverscroft.

Royal Flying Corps: (Military Wing) 256p. (C). 1987. 105.00 (*0-948251-29-8*, Pub. by Picton UK) St Mut.

Royal Flying Corps: (Military Wing) Honours & Awards. Picton Publishing (Chippenham) Ltd. Staff. (C). 1987. 75.00 (*0-685-39335-6*, Pub. by Picton UK) St Mut.

Royal Flying Corps-Boy Service, 1917. John Ross. 192p. (C). 1990. 45.00 (*0-7212-0830-4*, Pub. by Regency Press UK) St Mut.

Royal Forests of England. Raymond Grant. 224p. 1991. 48.00 (*0-86299-781-X*, Pub. by Sutton Pubng UK) Bks Intl VA.

Royal Fort Frontenac. Richard A. Preston. LC 58-3089. (Champlain Society Publications, Ontario Ser.: No. 2). 547p. reprint ed. pap. 155.90 (*0-7837-2050-5*, 2042325) Bks Demand.

Royal French State, 1460-1610: Louis XI-Henri IV, 1460-1610. Emmanuel Le Roy Ladurie. Tr. by Juliet Vale from FRE. (History of France Ser.). (Illus.). 384p. 1994. 56.95 (*0-631-17027-8*) Blackwell Pubs.

Royal Funding of the Parisian Academie Royale des Sciences During the 1690s. Alice Stroup. LC 86-71785. (Transactions Ser.: Vol. 77, Pt. 4). 167p. (Orig.). (C). 1987. pap. 15.00 (*0-87169-774-2*, T774-STA) Am Philos.

Royal Gardens. Roy Strong. Ed. by Bill Grose. LC 92-22698. (Illus.). 168p. 1993. 40.00 (*0-671-79594-5*) PB.

Royal Gentleman. Albion W. Tourgee. LC 67-29281. (Illus.). 467p. reprint ed. lib. bdg. 49.50 (*0-8398-1970-6*) Irvington.

Royal Glens. Robert Smith. 136p. (C). 1992. text ed. 36.00 (*0-685-65183-5*, Pub. by J Donald UK) St Mut.

Royal Gloucestershire Hussars: A Photographic History of the Royal Gloucestershire Yeomanry Cavalry. Rollo Clifford. (Illus.). 192p. 1991. 25.00 (*0-86299-982-0*, Pub. by Sutton Pubng UK) Bks Intl VA.

Royal Government in Colonial Brazil: With Special Reference to the Administration of the Marquis of Lavradio, Viceroy, 1769-1779. Dauril Alden. LC 68-26064. (Illus.). 583p. reprint ed. pap. 166.20 (*0-685-20494-4*, 2029942) Bks Demand.

Royal Government in Virginia, 1624-1775. Percy S. Flippin. LC 76-168047. (Columbia University. Studies in the Social Sciences: No. 194). reprint ed. 37.50 (*0-404-51194-5*) AMS Pr.

Royal Governors of Georgia, 1754-1775. William W. Abbot. LC 59-9568. (Illus.). 208p. reprint ed. pap. 59.30 (*0-8357-3910-4*, 2036644) Bks Demand.

Royal Greek Portrait Coins. Edward T. Newell. LC 88-73216. (Illus.). 110p. 1990. pap. 12.00 (*0-942666-60-7*) S J Durst.

Royal Harlot. Lucy Gordon. 1994. 3.99 (*0-373-28819-0*) Harlequin Bks.

Royal Heritage: The Story of Britain's Royal Builders & Collectors. H. Wheldon. (Illus.). 360p. 1981. pap. 16.95 (*0-563-17974-0*, Pub. by BBC UK) Parkwest Pubns.

Royal Highness. Thomas Mann. Tr. by A. Cecil Curtis. 360p. 1992. 30.00 (*0-520-07674-5*); pap. 14.00 (*0-520-07673-7*) U CA Pr.

Royal Historical Society Annual Bibliography of British & Irish History: Publications of 1983. Ed. by Geoffrey R. Elton. LC 81-641280. 208p. 1984. text ed. 35.00 (*0-312-69472-5*) St Martin.

Royal Historical Society Annual Bibliography of British & Irish History: Publications of 1989. Ed. by Barbara English & J. J. Palmer. 254p. 1991. 85.00 (*0-19-820186-9*) OUP.

Royal Historical Society Annual Bibliography of British & Irish History: Publications of 1990. Ed. by Barbara English & J. J. Palmer. 188p. 1991. 79.00 (*0-685-53257-7*) OUP.

Royal Historical Society Annual Bibliography of British & Irish History: Publications of 1991. Ed. by Barbara English & J. J. Palmer. 328p. 1992. 75.00 (*0-19-820391-8*) OUP.

Royal Historical Society Annual Bibliography of British & Irish History: Publications of 1992. Ed. by Barbara English & J. J. Palmer. 324p. (C). 1993. 69.00 (*0-19-820461-2*, 1937) OUP.

Royal Historical Society Annual Bibliography of British & Irish History: Publications of 1993. Ed. by Barbara English & J. J. Palmer. 330p. 1994. 69.00 (*0-19-820488-4*) OUP.

Royal Historical Society Annual Bibliography of British & Irish History: Publications of 1994. Ed. by Barbara B. English & J. J. Palmer. 304p. 1995. 68.00 (*0-19-820489-2*) OUP.

***Royal Historical Society Annual Bibliography of British & Irish History Publications of 1995.** Ed. by Austin Gee. 290p. 1996. 85.00 (*0-19-820490-6*) OUP.

Royal Historical Society Transactions. (Royal Historical Society Transactions Ser.). 267p. 1995. text ed. 34.95 (*0-521-55170-6*) Cambridge U Pr.

Royal Historical Society Transactions, Vol. 1, 1991, Sixth Series. (Royal Historical Society Transactions Ser.). 272p. 1995. text ed. 34.95 (*0-521-55171-4*) Cambridge U Pr.

Royal Historical Society Transactions, Vol. 3, 1993, Sixth Series. (Royal Historical Society Transactions Ser.). 311p. 1995. 34.95 (*0-521-55169-2*) Cambridge U Pr.

Royal Historical Society Transactions, Vol. 4, 1994, Sixth Series. (Royal Historical Society Transactions Ser.). 306p. (C). 1995. text ed. 34.95 (*0-521-55168-4*) Cambridge U Pr.

Royal Historical Society Transactions, Vol. 5, 1995. Royal Historical Society Staff. (Royal Historical Society Transactions Ser.: No. 6). 300p. (C). 1996. text ed. 34.95 (*0-521-55200-1*) Cambridge U Pr.

Royal Historical Society Transactions, Vol. 40, 1990, Fifth Series. 417p. 1995. 34.95 (*0-521-55172-2*) Cambridge U Pr.

Royal Homes in Gloucestershire: Highgrove, Gatcombe Park, Nether Lypiatt. rev. ed. Geoffrey Sanders & David Verey. (Illus.). 128p. 1992. reprint ed. 30.00 (*0-7509-0078-4*, Pub. by Sutton Pubng UK) Bks Intl VA.

An Asterisk (*) at the beginning of an entry indicates that the title is appearing in BIP for the first time.

Royal Horse & Rider. Walter Liedtke. 336p. 1989. 65.00 (*0-89835-267-3*) Abaris Bks.
Royal Horse of Europe. Sylvia Loch. 256p. 1990. 110.00 (*0-85131-422-8*, Pub. by J A Allen & Co UK) St Mut.
Royal Horticultural Society Plant & Garden Record Book. Royal Horticultural Society Staff. 1993. 18.00 (*0-517-59402-1*, Crown Arts & Letters) Crown Pub Group.
Royal Horticultural Society's Five-Year Gardener's Record Book. Patty Eddy. 1992. 16.00 (*0-517-58910-9*, Ebury Pr Stationery) Crown Pub Group.
Royal Hours of Nativity: Complete Texts & Music. Timothy Clader. Tr. by Laurence Campbell & Isaac E. Lambertsen from SLA. 57p. 1996. pap. 12.00 (*0-912927-66-6*, D032) St John Kronstadt.
Royal Hunt. D. R. Popescu. Tr. by J. E. Cottrell & M. Bogdan from RUM. LC 85-4985. Orig. Title: Vinatoarea Regala. 187p. 1985. 30.00 (*0-8142-0386-8*) Ohio St U Pr.
***Royal Hunt of the Sun.** Shaffer. 1991. pap. text ed. write for info. (*0-582-06014-1*, Pub. by Longman UK) Longman.
Royal Hunter: Art of the Sasanian Empire. Prudence O. Harper. LC 77-13082. (Illus.). 1978. 19.95 (*0-87848-050-1*) Asia Soc.
Royal Image: Illustrations of the "Grandes Chroniques de France," 1274-1422. Anne D. Hedeman. (California Studies in the History of Art: No. 28). (Illus.). 365p. 1991. 85.00 (*0-520-07069-0*) U CA Pr.
***Royal Imagery in Medieval Georgia.** Antony Eastmond. LC 96-18791. Date not set. 55.00 (*0-271-01628-0*) Pa St U Pr.
Royal India. Katherine H. Diver. LC 76-142620. (Essay Index Reprint Ser.). 1977. 24.95 (*0-8369-2152-6*) Ayer.
Royal India. Maud Diver. (Essay Index Reprint Ser.). (Illus.). 288p. reprint ed. lib. bdg. 21.00 (*0-8290-0780-6*) Irvington.
Royal Inscriptions on Clay Cones from Ashur Now in Istanbul. Veysel Donbaz & A. Kirk Grayson. 144p. 1984. 50.00 (*0-8020-5650-4*) U of Toronto Pr.
Royal Insignia: Orders of Chivalry from the Royal Collection. Stephen Patterson. (Illus.). 216p. 1996. 75.00 (*1-85894-025-7*, Pub. by Merrell Holberton Pubs UK) U of Wash Pr.
***Royal Institute of British Architects: A Guide to the Manuscripts & Archives.** Angela Mace & Royal Institute of British Architects Staff. LC 97-6588. 1997. write for info. (*0-7201-2195-7*, Mansell Pub) Cassell.
Royal Institute of International Affairs: Problem of International Investment. 371p. 1965. 35.00 (*0-7146-1247-2*, Pub. by F Cass Pubs UK) Intl Spec Bk.
Royal Institution: Its Founder & First Professors. Bence Jones. LC 74-26270. (History, Philosophy & Sociology of Science Ser.). 1975. reprint ed. 37.95 (*0-405-06598-1*) Ayer.
Royal Intrigue: Crisis at the Court of Charles VI, 1392-1420. R. C. Famiglietti. LC 85-48004. (Studies in the Middle Ages: No. 9). 1986. 39.50 (*0-404-61439-6*) AMS Pr.
Royal Invitation. Julia Fenton. 384p. (Orig.). 1995. mass mkt. 5.99 (*0-515-11548-7*) Jove Pubns.
Royal Jelly Miracle. John B. Lust. 1981. pap. 1.95 (*0-87904-023-8*) Lust.
Royal King & Loyal Subject: A Woman Skilled with Kindness: Two Historical Plays on the Life & Reign of Queen Elizabeth: The Golden & Silver Ages: An Apology for Actors see Thomas Heywood, Dramatic Works, with a Life & Remarks on His Writing by J. P. Collier
Royal Kingdoms of Ghana, Mali, & Soghay: Life in Medieval Africa. Patricia McKissack. (Illus.). 160p. (J). (gr. 5-9). 1994. 15.95 (*0-8050-1670-8*, Bks Young Read) H Holt & Co.
Royal Kingdoms of Ghana, Mali & Songhay: Life in Medieval Africa. Patricia McKissack & Fredrick McKissack. (Illus.). (J). (gr. 5-9). 1995. pap. 7.95 (*0-8050-4259-8*) H Holt & Co.
***Royal Landscape: The Royal Gardens & Parks of Windsor.** Jane Roberts. LC 97-15718. 1997. 125.00 (*0-300-07079-9*) Yale U Pr.
Royal Lao Army & U. S. Army Advice & Support. Oudone Sananikone. 180p. 1988. reprint ed. pap. 20.00 (*0-923135-04-9*) Dalley Bk Service.
Royal Laotian Air Force, 1954-1970. John C. Pratt. 184p. 1993. reprint ed. pap. 20.00 (*0-923135-50-2*) Dalley Bk Service.
Royal Letters, Charters, & Tracts. Bannatyne Club Staff. LC 78-174971. (Bannatyne Club, Edinburgh. Publications: No. 119). reprint ed. 62.50 (*0-404-52878-3*) AMS Pr.
Royal Letters, Charters, & Tracts. Ed. by David Laing. LC 70-171639. (Bannatyne Club, Edinburgh. Publications: No. 114). reprint ed. 42.50 (*0-404-52869-4*) AMS Pr.
Royal Life in Manasollasa. P. Arundhati. (C). 1995. 62.00 (*81-85067-89-9*, Pub. by Sundeep II) S Asia.
Royal Line of France: The Story of the Kings & Queens of France. Elsie Thornton-Cook. LC 67-26789. (Essay Index Reprint Ser.). 1977. 23.95 (*0-8369-0939-9*) Ayer.
Royal Mail: The Post Office since 1840. M. J. Daunton. (Illus.). 388p. (C). 1985. text ed. 45.00 (*0-485-11280-9*, Pub. by Athlone Pr UK) Humanities.
Royal Mail Case: Rex vs. Lord Kylsant, & Another. Ed. by Collin Brooks & Richard P. Brief. LC 80-1475. (Dimensions of Accounting Theory & Practice Ser.). 1980. reprint ed. lib. bdg. 35.95 (*0-405-13505-X*) Ayer.
***Royal Mail Case: Rex vs. Lord Kylsant, & Another.** Ed. by Collin Brooks. (Notable British Trials Ser.). xiii, 276p. 1995. reprint ed. 86.00 (*1-56169-178-X*) Gaunt.
Royal Marines since 1956. William Fowler. (Men-at-Arms Ser.: No. 156). (Illus.). 48p. pap. 11.95 (*0-85045-568-5*, 9088, Pub. by Osprey UK) Stackpole.
Royal Marines 1939-1993. Nickolas Van Der Bijl. (Elite Ser.). (Illus.). 64p. 1995. pap. 12.95 (*1-85532-388-5*, Pub. by Osprey UK) Stackpole.
Royal Marsden Hospital Manual of Clinical Nursing Procedures. 3rd ed. A. P. Pritchard & Jane Mallett. (Illus.). 560p. 1992. pap. 34.95 (*0-632-03387-8*) Blackwell Sci.
Royal Marsden Hospital Manual of Multidisciplinary Standards of Care. Joanna M. Luthert & Lorraine Robinson. (Illus.). 256p. 1993. pap. 26.95 (*0-632-03386-X*) Blackwell Sci.
Royal Marsden NHS Trust Manual of Clinical Nursing Procedures. 4th ed. Jane Mallett & Christopher Bailey. LC 96-19076. 662p. 1996. pap. 34.95 (*0-632-04068-8*) Blackwell Sci.
Royal Marys, Princess Mary & Her Predecessors. Elsie Thornton-Cook. LC 67-23275. (Essay Index Reprint Ser.). 1977. 21.95 (*0-8369-0940-2*) Ayer.
Royal Masonic Cyclopaedia. Kenneth R. Mackenzie. 790p. 1994. pap. 49.95 (*1-56459-420-3*) Kessinger Pub.
Royal Matron's Treasury of Addresses & Ceremonies. Geraldine B. Maxwell. pap. 2.00 (*0-88053-319-6*, S-295) Wilson Pub.
Royal Mews. Mary Stewart-Wilson. (Illus.). 192p. 1993. 34.95 (*0-370-31345-3*, Pub. by Bodley Head UK) Trafalgar.
Royal Mile: Scotland's Most Romantic Way. Jim Crumley. (Illus.). 96p. (C). 1989. 70.00 (*0-948473-14-2*) St Mut.
***Royal Mummies in the Egyptian Museum.** Salima Ikram. 1997. pap. text ed. 14.95 (*977-424-431-1*, Pub. by Am Univ Cairo Pr UA) Col U Pr.
Royal Mummies of Deir el-Bahri. Gaston C. Maspero & Emile Brugsch. Ed. by Nicholas Reeves. Tr. by G. Raggett. (Illus.). 162p. 1993. 49.95 (*0-7103-0392-0*, A5045) Routledge Chapman & Hall.
Royal Murder. large type ed. Elliott Roosevelt. LC 94-40019. 1995. 22.95 (*1-56895-171-X*) Wheeler Pub.
***Royal Nap.** Charles Black. (J). 1997. pap. 4.99 (*0-14-055470-X*) Viking Penguin.
Royal Nap. Charles C. Black. LC 94-30728. (Illus.). 32p. (J). (ps-3). 1995. pap. 14.99 (*0-670-85863-3*) Viking Child Bks.
Royal Navy. Robert Wilkinson-Latham. (Men-at-Arms Ser.: No. 65). (Illus.). 48p. pap. 11.95 (*0-85045-248-1*, 9169, Pub. by Osprey UK) Stackpole.
Royal Navy: A History from the Earliest Times, 7 vols., Set. Ed. by William L. Clowes. reprint ed. 535.00 (*0-404-01640-5*) AMS Pr.
Royal Navy: A History from the Earliest Times to 1900, Vol. 1. William L. Clowes. (Illus.). 620p. 1996. pap. 29.95 (*1-86176-010-8*) Naval Inst Pr.
Royal Navy: A History from the Earliest Times to 1900, Vol. 2. William L. Clowes. (Illus.). 620p. 1996. pap. 29.95 (*1-86176-011-6*) Naval Inst Pr.
Royal Navy: A History from the Earliest Times to 1900, Vol. 3. William L. Clowes. (Illus.). 620p. 1996. pap. 29.95 (*1-86176-012-4*) Naval Inst Pr.
***Royal Navy: A History from the Earliest Times to 1900, Vol. 4.** William L. Clowes. (Illus.). 640p. 1997. pap. 29.95 (*1-86176-013-2*) Naval Inst Pr.
***Royal Navy: A History from the Earliest Times to 1900, Vol. 5.** William L. Clowes. (Illus.). 648p. 1997. pap. 29.95 (*1-86176-014-0*) Naval Inst Pr.
***Royal Navy: A History from the Earliest Times to 1900, Vol. 6.** William L. Clowes. (Illus.). 624p. 1997. pap. 29.95 (*1-86176-015-9*) Naval Inst Pr.
***Royal Navy: A History from the Earliest Times to 1900, Vol. 7.** William L. Clowes. (Illus.). 648p. 1997. pap. 29.95 (*1-86176-017-5*) Naval Inst Pr.
Royal Navy: An Illustrated History. Anthony J. Watts. (Illus.). 256p. 1995. 29.95 (*1-55750-730-9*) Naval Inst Pr.
Royal Navy: An Illustrated Social History, 1870-1982. John Wells. LC 94-3173. (Illus.). 320p. 1994. 44.00 (*0-7509-0524-7*, Pub. by Sutton Pubng UK) Bks Intl VA.
***Royal Navy: An Illustrated Social History 1870-1982.** John Wells. (Illus.). 320p. 1996. pap. 22.95 (*0-7509-0833-5*, Pub. by Sutton Pubng UK) Bks Intl VA.
Royal Navy & the Slave Trade. Raymond Howell. LC 87-9608. 224p. 1987. text ed. 39.95 (*0-312-00854-6*) St Martin.
Royal Navy at Gibraltar. Tito Benady. (C). 1988. text ed. 105.00 (*0-907771-49-1*, Pub. by Gibraltar Bks UK) St Mut.
Royal Navy at Malta, Vol. 1: The Victorian Era. Maritime Books Staff. (C). 1986. text ed. 190.00 (*0-907771-43-2*, Pub. by Maritime Bks UK) St Mut.
Royal Navy at Malta, Vol. 2: 1907-39. 1989. pap. 81.00 (*0-907771-48-3*, Pub. by Maritime Bks UK) St Mut.
Royal Navy at Portland since Eighteen Forty-Five. Maritime Books Staff. (C). 1986. text ed. 100.00 (*0-907771-29-7*, Pub. by Maritime Bks UK) St Mut.
Royal Navy in American Waters, 1775-1783. David Syrett. 300p. 1989. text ed. 61.95 (*0-85967-806-7*, Pub. by Scolar Pr UK) Ashgate Pub Co.
Royal Navy in Focus, 1920-29. 1989. pap. 24.00 (*0-907771-46-7*, Pub. by Maritime Bks UK) St Mut.
Royal Navy in Focus, 1930-39. Maritime Books Staff. (C). 1986. text ed. 60.00 (*0-907771-04-1*, Pub. by Maritime Bks UK) St Mut.
Royal Navy in Focus, 1940-49. Maritime Books Staff. (C). 1986. text ed. 60.00 (*0-907771-11-4*, Pub. by Maritime Bks UK) St Mut.
Royal Navy in Focus, 1950-59. Maritime Books Staff. (C). 1986. text ed. 50.00 (*0-907771-22-X*, Pub. by Maritime Bks UK) St Mut.
Royal Navy in Focus, 1960-69. Maritime Books Staff. (C). 1986. text ed. 50.00 (*0-907771-33-5*, Pub. by Maritime Bks UK) St Mut.
Royal Navy in Lincolnshire. E. C. Coleman. 82p. (C). 1989. text ed. 65.00 (*0-902662-99-6*, Pub. by R K Pubns UK) St Mut.
Royal Navy in the Mediterranean, 1915-1918. Paul G. Halpern. 580p. 1987. text ed. 77.95 (*0-566-05488-4*, Pub. by Scolar Pr UK) Ashgate Pub Co.
Royal Navy in the River Plate, 1806-1807. Ed. by John D. Grainger. LC 95-49047. (Navy Records Ser.: Vol. 135). 500p. 1996. 99.95 (*1-85928-292-X*, Pub. by Scolar Pr UK) Ashgate Pub Co.
Royal Navy on the Danube. Charles Fryer. (East European Monographs: No. 232). 228p. 1988. text ed. 49.50 (*0-88033-129-1*) East Eur Monographs.
Royal Navy, Rum, Rumour & a Pinch of Salt. E. T. Ashton. (C). 1987. 95.00 (*0-685-45081-3*, Pub. by Brwn Son Ferg) St Mut.
***Royal Nepal: A Political History.** Ram Rahul. 1996. 14.00 (*81-259-0070-5*, Pub. by Vikas II) S Asia.
Royal New Zealand Air Force. J. M. Ross. (Official History Ser.: No. 2). (Illus.). 400p. 1993. reprint ed. 49.95 (*0-89839-187-3*) Battery Pr.
Royal Observatory, Cape of Good Hope, 1820-1831: The Founding of a Colonial Observatory: Incorporating a Biography of Fearon Fallows. Brian Warner. LC 95-17562. (C). 1995. lib. bdg. 119.00 (*0-7923-3527-9*) Kluwer Ac.
Royal Occasions: Watercolours & Drawings. John Castle. (Illus.). 174p. 1992. 67.50 (*1-85479-019-6*, Pub. by M OMara Books UK) Trans-Atl Phila.
***Royal Palaces of India.** George Michell. Date not set. pap. 39.95 (*0-500-27964-0*) Thames Hudson.
Royal Palaces of Tudor England: Architecture & Court Life, 1460-1547. Simon Thurley. (Illus.). 280p. 1993. 55.00 (*0-300-05420-3*) Yale U Pr.
Royal Pardon. John Arden & Margaretta D'Arcy. 109p. (C). 1988. pap. 8.95 (*0-413-33410-4*, A0249, Pub. by Methuen UK) Heinemann.
Royal Passion. Jennifer Blake. 384p. (Orig.). 1991. mass mkt. 5.99 (*0-449-14790-8*, GM) Fawcett.
Royal Passion: Louis XIV As Patron of Architecture. Robert W. Berger. (Illus.). 248p. (C). 1994. text ed. 55.00 (*0-521-44029-7*) Cambridge U Pr.
***Royal Passion: Louis XIV As Patron of Architecture.** Robert W. Berger. (Illus.). 224p. 1997. pap. text ed. 22.95 (*0-521-58644-5*) Cambridge U Pr.
Royal Path: A Layman's Look at the Tarot. Patricia H. Sisson. Ed. by Beryl O. Lumpkin. LC 89-83887. (Illus.). 80p. (Orig.). 1989. pap. 7.95 (*0-9622568-1-1*) Earthside Pubns.
Royal Patronage of Indian Music. Gowri Kuppuswamy & M. Hariharan. 1985. 36.00 (*0-8364-1488-8*, Pub. by Sundeep Prakashan II) S Asia.
***Royal Penguins.** large type ed. Erik Stoops. Ed. by Graphic Arts & Production Staff. (Young Explorer Series II: Vol. 6). (Illus.). 32p. (J). (gr. 3-7). 1997. lib. bdg. 12.95 (*1-890475-11-4*) Faulkners Pub.
Royal Persons: Patriarchal Monarchy & the Feminine Principle. Patricia Springborg. 256p. (C). 1990. text ed. 79.95 (*0-04-445376-0*) Routledge Chapman & Hall.
Royal Pharmacopoeia Society of Great Britain: 1841-1991. Ed. by Holloway. 1991. 91.00 (*0-85369-244-0*, Pub. by Pharmaceutical Pr UK) Rittenhouse.
Royal Portraits in Sculpture & Coins: Pyrrhos & the Successors of Alexander the Great, Vol. 5. Blanche R. Brown. LC 94-13113. (Hermeneutics of Art Ser.: Vol. 5). 192p. (C). 1995. 45.95 (*0-8204-2577-X*) P Lang Pubng.
Royal Prerogative. H. V. Evatt. xviii, 282p. 1987. 83.00 (*0-455-20756-9*, Pub. by Law Bk Co AT) Gaunt.
Royal Priesthood. Basilea M. Schlink. 1971. pap. 0.95 (*3-87209-654-0*) Evang Sisterhood Mary.
Royal Priesthood: A Theology of Ordained Ministry. rev. ed. Thomas F. Torrance. 128p. 1993. pap. text ed. 19.95 (*0-567-29222-3*, Pub. by T & T Clark UK) Bks Intl VA.
Royal Priesthood: Essays Ecclesiological & Ecumenical. John H. Yoder. Ed. & Intro. by Michael G. Cartwright. 400p. 1994. pap. 23.00 (*0-8028-0707-0*) Eerdmans.
Royal Protomedicato: The Regulation of the Medical Profession in the Spanish Empire. John T. Lanning. Ed. by John J. TePaske. LC 85-4611. v, 485p. (C). 1985. 48.00 (*0-8223-0651-4*) Duke.
Royal Quest. Mary Lide. 1988. pap. 12.95 (*0-446-38791-6*) Warner Bks.
Royal Raven. Hans Wilhelm. 32p. (J). 1996. 15.95 (*0-590-54337-7*, Cartwheel) Scholastic Inc.
Royal Rebel: A Psychological Portrait of Crown Prince Rudolf of Austria-Hungary. John T. Salvendy. LC 87-25317. (Illus.). 278p. (Orig.). (C). 1988. lib. bdg. 45.00 (*0-8191-6675-8*) U Pr of Amer.
Royal Recipes. Michele Brown. (Illus.). 160p. 1995. 19.95 (*1-85793-691-4*, Pub. by Pavilion UK) Trafalgar.
Royal Recipes from the Cajun Country. Glenna Uhler. 1980. pap. 6.95 (*0-87511-125-4*) Claitors.
Royal Republicans: The French Naval Dynasties Between the World Wars. Ronald C. Hood, III. LC 84-21331. (Illus.). 221p. 1985. text ed. 32.50 (*0-8071-1211-9*) La State U Pr.
Royal Resident. Marcus Lehmann. 1981. 8.95 (*0-87306-256-6*) Feldheim.
Royal Rewards: A Tribute to Fathers. Grace D. Jessen. (Illus.). 28p. (YA). 1986. reprint ed. pap. 1.79 (*0-88290-019-6*) Horizon Utah.
Royal Road. Stephan A. Hoeller. LC 75-4244. (Illus.). 119p. (Orig.). 1975. pap. 6.95 (*0-8356-0465-9*, Quest) Theos Pub Hse.
Royal Road. George Fathman. 252p. 1977. reprint ed. spiral bd. 12.50 (*0-7873-1053-0*) Hlth Research.
Royal Road: A Study of Sacred Numbers & Symbols. George Fatham. 256p. 1996. pap. 21.00 (*1-56459-710-5*) Kessinger Pub.

Royal Road to Reality: Anatomy of Spirituality, 1. Barbara M. Muhl. (Anatomy of Spirituality Ser.: Vol. 1). 352p. (Orig.). 1994. pap. 24.95 (*1-880863-01-4*) Christus Pub.

Married for forty-six years to Edward Muhl (Vice President in Charge of Production at Universal Pictures, until his retirement in 1973) the author found life as the wife of a motion picture executive unfulfilling. With her husband's understanding, & seeking personal growth, she went to UCLA to study opera & languages, becoming fluent in Spanish, German & Italian. Later she graduated summa cum laude form California State University, Northridge, in French Language & Literature, going on to receive her Master's degree. Though she believed herself to be embarked on an operatic career, in 1958 she met her spiritual teacher, Joel Goldsmith, author of THE INFINITE WAY, & her life was turned in a new direction. In 1962, under his instruction, she began her teaching ministry which has continued until the present time. Her work has resulted in hundreds of healings & changed lives. Mrs. Muhl refers to her teaching as the "how to" which complements the "what" of Mr. Goldsmith. The present book is a textbook of Infinite Way Principles & Practices, & provides step-by-step methods for achieving "freedom from the human struggle." To order write, phone, or FAX: Christus Publishing, 802649, Santa Carita, CA 91380-2649. U.S.A. Order line: 805-296-7836, FAX: 805-296-2182.
Publisher Provided Annotation.

R

Royal Road to Romance. Richard Halliburton. LC 75-92301. 399p. 1969. reprint ed. text ed. 35.00 (*0-8371-2412-3*, HARR, Greenwood Pr) Greenwood.
***Royal Roads: Spanish Trails in North America.** LC 96-37369. (American Trails Ser.). (J). 1997. lib. bdg. 27.11 (*0-8172-4074-8*) Raintree Steck-V.
Royal Romance Paper Dolls. Peggy DeRosemond. (J). (gr. 8-12). 1984. pap. 4.00 (*0-914510-14-2*) Evergreen.
Royal Route to Heaven: Studies in First Corinthians. Alan Redpath. (Alan Redpath Library). 248p. 1993. reprint ed. pap. 11.99 (*0-8007-5491-3*) Revell.
***Royal Russia.** Townend. Date not set. 25.00 (*0-312-17936-7*) St Martin.
Royal Saints of Anglo-Saxon England: A Study of West Saxon & East Anglian Cults. Susan J. Ridyard. (Cambridge Studies in Medieval Life & Thought: No. 9). 376p. 1989. text ed. 80.00 (*0-521-30772-4*) Cambridge U Pr.
Royal Scandals: True Tales of Sex, Lust & Greed. Diane Osen. LC 94-34641. 120p. 1995. 16.98 (*1-56799-161-0*, MetroBooks) M Friedman Pub Grp Inc.
Royal Scots in the Gulf: First Battalion Royal Scots on Operation GRANBY 1990-1991. Laurie Milner. (Illus.). 256p. 1994. 42.50 (*0-85052-273-0*, Pub. by L Cooper Bks UK) Trans-Atl Phila.
Royal Secret. I. Edward Clark. (Illus.). 363p. 1995. pap. 27.95 (*1-56459-494-7*) Kessinger Pub.
Royal Seduction. Jennifer Blake. 416p. 1985. mass mkt. 5.95 (*0-449-12979-9*, GM) Fawcett.
Royal Service. Stephen P. Barry. 288p. 1984. pap. 3.95 (*0-380-67397-5*) Avon.
Royal Shakespeare Company's Centenary Production of Henry V. Sally Beauman. 1976. 11.00 (*0-08-020874-6*, Pergamon Pr) Elsevier.
Royal Society of British Artists: 1824-1893. Antique Collector's Club Staff. 620p. 1975. 89.50 (*0-902028-35-9*) Antique Collect.
Royal Society of Chemistry: The First 150 Years. Whiffen. 1995. 30.00 (*0-85186-294-2*) CRC Pr.
Royal Society, Sixteen Sixty to Nineteen Forty: A History of Its Administration under Its Charters. Henry G. Lyons. LC 69-10124. (Illus.). 354p. 1968. reprint ed. text ed. 35.00 (*0-8371-0155-7*, LYRS, Greenwood Pr) Greenwood.
Royal Song of Saraha: A Study in the History of Buddhist Thought. Herbert V. Guenther. 214p. reprint ed. 25.00 (*957-638-087-1*, PRE014, Pub. by SMC Pub CC); reprint ed. pap. 18.00 (*0-318-69528-6*, Pub. by SMC Pub CC) Oriental Bk Store.
Royal Stars of the States. 2nd rev. ed. Ed. by Sandra L. Hatch. (Illus.). 192p. 1995. 19.95 (*1-882138-15-5*) Hse White Birches.
Royal Stars of the States: Fifty Fabulous Quilts with Complete Instructions. Ed. by Sandra L. Hatch. (Illus.). 184p. 1988. 14.95 (*1-882138-00-7*) Hse White Birches.
Royal Street, a Novel of Old New Orleans. Walter A. Roberts. LC 73-18605. reprint ed. 42.50 (*0-404-11415-6*) AMS Pr.
Royal Style Wars. rev. ed. Lesley Ebbetts. (Illus.). 128p. 1989. 9.99 (*0-517-69239-2*) Random Hse Value.
Royal Succession in Capetian France: Studies on Familial Order & the State. Andrew W. Lewis. LC 81-6360. (Historical Studies: No. 100). (Illus.). 374p. 1982. 37.00 (*0-674-77985-1*) HUP.
***Royal Switch.** Duchess of York. (Illus.). 176p. (J). (gr. 2-6). 1997. pap. 4.99 (*0-440-41213-7*) BDD Bks Young Read.
Royal Switch. H. R. H. the Duchess of York. LC 95-52437. 112p. (J). 1996. 14.95 (*0-385-32177-5*) Delacorte.
Royal Tapestry. Christopher Howkins. 96p. 1987. 50.00 (*0-9509105-1-1*) St Mut.
Royal Three Quarters of the Town of Charlotte Amalie: A Study of Architectural Details & Forms That Have Endured from 1837. Edith de Jongh. (Illus.). 158p. (Orig.). 1988. pap. 15.95 (*0-926330-02-0*) Mapes Monde.

R

Royal Throne: The Future of the Monarchy. Elizabeth Longford. 195p. 1995. 21.95 (*1-85695-141-3*, Pub. by ISIS UK) Transaction Pubs.

Royal Tombs of Sipan. Walter Alva & Christopher B. Donnan. LC 93-26536. 234p. 1993. pap. 35.00 (*0-930741-30-7*) UCLA Fowler Mus.

Royal Tour of France by Charles IX & Catherine de' Medici: Festivals & Entries, 1564-6. Ed. by Victor E. Graham & W. McAllister Johnson. LC 78-4841. 482p. reprint ed. pap. 137.40 (*0-685-15919-1*, 2056124) Bks Demand.

Royal Tours of the British Empire, 1860-1927. John Fabb. (Illus.). 128p. 1989. 39.95 (*0-7134-5205-6*, Pub. by Batsford UK) Trafalgar.

Royal Treasure: Muslim Communities under the Crown of Aragon in the Fourteenth Century. John Boswell. LC 77-76303. 542p. reprint ed. pap. 154.50 (*0-8357-8762-1*, 2033676) Bks Demand.

Royal Treasuries of the Spanish Empire in America, 4 vols., Vol. I: Peru. John J. TePaske et al. LC 82-2457. 563p. 1982. text ed. 59.95 (*0-8223-0530-5*) Duke.

Royal Treasuries of the Spanish Empire in America, 4 vols., Vol. II: Upper Peru (Bolivia) John J. TePaske et al. LC 82-2457. 422p. 1982. text ed. 53.00 (*0-8223-0531-3*) Duke.

Royal Treasuries of the Spanish Empire in America, 4 vols., Vol. III: Chile & Rio de la Plata. John J. TePaske et al. LC 82-2457. 406p. 1982. text ed. 53.00 (*0-8223-0532-1*) Duke.

Royal Treasuries of the Spanish Empire in America, 4 vols., Vol. 4: Mexico. John J. TePaske et al. LC 82-2457. 532p. 1982. pap. 32.00 (*0-8223-0814-2*) Duke.

Royal Treasuries of the Spanish Empire in America, Vol. 4: Eighteenth-Century Ecuador. Ed. by Alvaro Jara & John J. TePaske. LC 82-2457. 192p. 1991. text ed. 36.00 (*0-8223-1042-2*) Duke.

***Royal Treatment: How You Can Take Home the Pleasures of the World's Great Luxury Spas.** Steve Capellini. LC 97-3174. (Illus.). 224p. 1997. pap. 14.95 (*0-440-50776-6*, Delta) Dell.

Royal Vic: The Story of Montreal's Royal Victoria Hospital, 1894-1994. Neville Terry. (Illus.). 288p. 1994. 49.95 (*0-7735-1170-9*, Pub. by McGill CN) U of Toronto Pr.

Royal Visit. Rebecca Baldwin. 208p. (Orig.). 1996. mass mkt. 4.50 (*0-06-108365-8*) HarpC.

***Royal Visit.** Rebecca Baldwin. (Candlelights Ser.). 191p. 1997. 18.95 (*0-7862-1089-3*) Thorndike Pr.

Royal Voyage. Laurie Lisle. Date not set. pap. write for info. (*0-670-81366-4*) Viking Penguin.

Royal Voyage. Laurie Lisle. 1999. pap. write for info. (*0-14-009479-2*, Viking) Viking Penguin.

Royal Watercolour Society, Vol. 1: The First Fifty Years, 1805-1855. 300p. 1992. 89.50 (*1-85149-099-X*) Antique Collect.

Royal Way of the Cross. Archbishop Fenelon. Ed. by Hal M. Helms. LC 80-67874. (Living Library). 166p. 1982. pap. 9.95 (*0-941478-00-9*) Paraclete MA.

Royal Weddings. 1996. mass mkt. 5.99 (*0-373-20129-X*, 1-20129-2) Harlequin Bks.

Royal Women of Amarna. James Allen et al. (Illus.). 144p. 1996. 45.00 (*0-8109-6504-6*) Abrams.

***Royal Women of Amarna: Images of Beauty from Ancient Egypt.** Dorothea Arnold & Metropolitan Museum of Art Staff. LC 96-34517. 1996. 45.00 (*0-87099-816-1*); pap. 29.95 (*0-87099-818-8*) Metro Mus Art.

***Royal Writs Addressed to John Buchingham, Bishop of Lincoln, 1363-1398: Lincoln Register 12B: A Calendar.** Ed. by A. K. McHardy. 256p. 1997. 53.00 (*0-901503-63-0*, Lincoln Record Soc); 53.00 (*0-907239-58-7*, Canterbury & York Soc) Boydell & Brewer.

Royal Year: Present-Day Portrait of the Royal Family. Tim Graham. LC 94-19663. (Illus.). 1994. 12.99 (*0-517-12066-6*) Crescent.

Royal Year 1993. Tim Graham. 1994. 20.00 (*0-671-88216-3*) S&S Trade.

***Royalism & Poetry in the English Civil Wars: The Drawn Sword.** James Loxley. LC 97-11644. (Early Modern Literature in History Ser.). 1997. write for info. (*0-312-17608-2*) St Martin.

Royalist & Realist: The Life & Work of Sir Joseph Edgar Boehm. Mark Stocker. LC 87-28413. (Outstanding Theses in the Fine Arts Ser.). 768p. 1988. text ed. 48.00 (*0-8240-0093-5*) Garland.

Royalist Political Thought During the French Revolution. James L. Osen. LC 94-25056. (Contributions to the Study of World History Ser.: Vol. 47). 168p. 1995. text ed. 57.95 (*0-313-29441-0*, Greenwood Pr) Greenwood.

Royalist Volunteer: Un Voluntario Realista. Benito Perez Galdos. Tr. by Lila W. Guzman from SPA. LC 93-29746. 488p. 1993. 109.95 (*0-7734-9360-3*) E Mellen.

Royalist's Notebook: The Commonplace Book of Sir John Oglander. John Oglander. Ed. by Francis Bamford. LC 72-174427. (Illus.). 1972. reprint ed. 19.95 (*0-405-08827-2*) Ayer.

Royall Drummes & Martiall Musick. Tabourot. (Illus.). 179p. 1993. pap. 22.00 (*1-881428-02-8*) Tactus Pr.

***Royall Drummes & Martiall Musick.** 2nd ed. Tabourot Staff. (Illus.). 1997. pap. write for info. (*1-881428-10-9*) Tactus Pr.

Royall Tyler. George T. Tanselle. LC 67-12103. (Illus.). 303p. reprint ed. pap. 86.40 (*0-7837-3846-3*, 2043668) Bks Demand.

***Royals.** Kitty Kelley. 1997. 27.00 (*0-446-51712-7*) Warner Bks.

***Royalscope Fe-As-Ko.** Randall B. Platt. LC 96-54506. 300p. 1997. 21.95 (*0-945774-35-4*, PS3566.L293R68) Catbird Pr.

***Royalty: The Royalty of Queen Victoria's African-American Grandson.** Yaphet Kotto. (Illus.). 415p. 1997. 24.95 (*0-9655950-1-3*) Cauldwell-Bissell.

Royalty & Their Jewels. Jack Laverick. Ed. by Mark Laverick. LC 93-84490. (Illus.). 120p. (Orig.). 1993. per. 18.95 (*1-884054-99-4*) Printers Shopper.

Royalty for Commoners: The Complete Known Lineage of John of Gaunt, Son of Edward III, King of England, & Queen Philippa. 2nd rev. ed. Roderick W. Stuart. 277p. 1995. 30.00 (*0-8063-1344-7*, 5655) Genealog Pub.

***Royalty in Medieval India.** Khaliq A. Nizami. 1996. 29.50 (*81-215-0733-2*, Pub. by M Manoharial II) Coronet Bks.

Royalty of the Pulpit. Edgar D. Jones. LC 79-134105. (Essay Index Reprint Ser.). 1977. 30.95 (*0-8369-1979-3*) Ayer.

Royalty Without a Future. Alvin Jones. 252p. (Orig.). 1994. pap. 9.95 (*1-56043-769-3*) Destiny Image.

***Royan/Marennes City Plan.** (Grafocarte Maps Ser.). 1996. 8.95 (*2-7416-0095-3*, 80095) Michelin.

Royaume De Ce Monde. Alejo Carpentier. 192p. (FRE.). 1980. pap. 10.95 (*0-7859-1927-9*, 2070372480) Fr & Eur.

Royaume de Navarre a la Fin du Moyen Age: Gouvernement et Societe. Beatrice Leroy. (Collected Studies: No. CS 335). 320p. (FRE.). 1991. text ed. 94.95 (*0-86078-284-0*, Pub. by Variorum UK) Ashgate Pub Co.

***Royce Aller Hardy: Reminiscence & a Short Autobiography.** Ed. & Intro. by Mary E. Glass. (Illus.). 46p. 1965. lib. bdg. 24.50 (*1-56475-011-6*) U NV Oral Hist.

***Royce Aller Hardy: Reminiscence & a Short Autobiography.** Ed. & Intro. by Mary E. Glass. (Illus.). 1965. fiche write for info. (*1-56475-012-4*) U NV Oral Hist.

Royce's Mature Ethics. Frank M. Oppenheim. LC 92-53531. (C). 1993. text ed. 42.50 (*0-268-01642-9*) U of Notre Dame Pr.

Royce's Mature Philosophy of Religion. Frank M. Oppenheim. LC 87-12458. 432p. 1987. text ed. 40.50 (*0-268-01633-X*) U of Notre Dame Pr.

Royce's Metaphysics. Gabriel Marcel. LC 56-11854. 200p. reprint ed. pap. 57.00 (*0-317-08060-1*, 2055292) Bks Demand.

Royce's Metaphysics. Gabriel Marcel. Tr. by Virginia Ringer & Gordon Ringer from GER. LC 74-33746. 180p. 1975. reprint ed. text ed. 49.75 (*0-8371-7978-5*, MARO, Greenwood Pr) Greenwood.

Royce's Powerboating Illustrated. Patrick M. Royce. (Illus.). 416p. 1992. 12.95 (*0-930030-67-2*) ProStar Pubns.

Royce's Sailing Illustrated: The Sailors Bible since '56. rev. ed. Patrick M. Royce. (Sailing Illustrated Series: The Best of Royce). (Illus.). 368p. (C). 1993. pap. text ed. write for info. (*0-911284-00-1*) Royce Pubns.

Royce's Sailing Illustrated Course: Sailors Helping Sailors. Patrick M. Royce. (Sailing Illustrated Series: The Best of Royce). (Illus.). 96p. (Orig.). (C). 1993. pap. text ed. write for info. (*0-911284-01-X*) Royce Pubns.

Royce's Voyage Down Under: A Journey of the Mind. Frank M. Oppenheim. LC 79-4007. 136p. reprint ed. pap. 38.80 (*0-7837-5786-7*, 2045452) Bks Demand.

Roycroft Art Metal. rev. ed. Kevin McConnell. LC 89-63420. (Illus.). 144p. 1994. pap. 16.95 (*0-88740-694-7*) Schiffer.

Roycroft Collectibles: Including Collector Items Related to Elbert Hubbard, Founder of the Roycroft Shops. Charles F. Hamilton. (Illus.). 152p. 1992. 24.95 (*1-881099-00-8*) SPS Pubns.

Roycroft Furniture. Ed. by Stephen Gray. (Mission Furniture Catalogues Ser.: No. 3). 52p. 1981. pap. 7.95 (*0-940326-03-5*) Turn of Cent.

Roycroft Furniture Catalog, 1906. Roycrofters Staff. LC 93-49373. Orig. Title: A Catalog of Roycrofters Furniture & Other Things. (Illus.). 64p. 1994. reprint ed. pap. 5.95 (*0-486-28113-2*) Dover.

Roycroft Shops 1894-1915. Lynette I. Rhodes. (Illus.). 20p. 1975. pap. 8.95 (*0-9616623-8-7*) Erie Art Mus.

Royden Brown's Bee Hive Product Bible: Wonderous Products from One of Nature's Most Productive Creatures. Royden Brown. LC 93-3222. 256p. pap. 9.95 (*0-89529-521-0*) Avery Pub.

Royer-Collard. Gabriel Remond. Ed. by J. P. Mayer. LC 78-67377. (European Political Thought Ser.). (FRE.). 1980. reprint ed. lib. bdg. 17.95 (*0-405-11727-2*) Ayer.

Royers' Round Top Cafe: A Relational Odessey. Karen Royer & Bud Royer. 176p. text ed. write for info. (*0-9647729-0-6*) Royers Domain.

Roylake Ruby. large type ed. Cora Mayne. 1991. 25.99 (*0-7089-2373-9*) Ulverscroft.

Royles III: The Princes Royal. Virginia Coffman. 1994. 22.00 (*0-7278-4608-6*) Severn Hse.

Royles IV: Heir to a Throne. Virginia Coffman. (Royles Ser.: Bk. 4). 320p. 1995. 22.00 (*0-7278-4825-9*) Severn Hse.

Roy's Feasts from Hawaii. Roy Yamaguchi. (Illus.). 240p. (Orig.). 1995. text ed. 27.95 (*0-89815-637-8*) Ten Speed Pr.

Roy's Rot: Rules of Thumb to Wit & Wisdom. Roy T. Maloney. LC 85-7015. (Illus.). 1985. pap. 12.95 (*0-913257-01-X*) Dropzone Pr.

Roy's Rules: Guidelines for Solid Business Success & a Great Life. Roy M. Jacobson & Herbert J. Henderson. LC 93-74658. 207p. 1994. pap. 14.95 (*0-9640244-1-1*) Busn Focus.

***Roz & Ozzie.** Johanna Hurwitz. (J). Date not set. lib. bdg. write for info. (*0-688-10946-2*, Morrow Junior) Morrow.

Roz & Ozzie. Johanna Hurwitz. LC 91-42338. (Illus.). 128p. (J). (gr. 2 up). 1992. 13.00 (*0-688-10945-4*, Morrow Junior) Morrow.

Roz & Ozzie. Johanna Hurwitz. LC 91-42338. 128p. (J). (gr. 2 up). 1995. pap. 4.95 (*0-688-14424-1*) Morrow.

Rozan with Personnel. Kamala Masihlall. (Illus.). 16p. (J). (gr. k-3). 1993. pap. 9.95 (*1-895583-60-8*) MAYA Pubs.

Rozenie ou Les Moscovites. Charles-Henri D'Estaing. LC 93-73005. (East European Monographs: No. 383). 154p. 1994. 24.00 (*0-88033-280-8*) East Eur Monographs.

Rozhdestvo Khristovo. M. Skaballanovitch. 195p. reprint ed. pap. 7.00 (*0-317-29162-9*) Holy Trinity.

Rozhdestvo Presvjatia Bogoroditsi. M. Skaballanovitch. 134p. reprint ed. pap. 5.00 (*0-317-29149-1*) Holy Trinity.

***RPA, NIDDK Meeting - Selected Presentations 1995: Joint Annual Meeting of Renal Physicians Association & National Institute of Diabetes, Digestive & Kidney Diseases, Washington, May 1995.** Ed. by T. A. Golper & M. J. Scherbenske. (Journal: Blood Purification: Vol. 14, No. 4, 1996). (Illus.). 62p. 1996. pap. 44.50 (*3-8055-6371-X*) S Karger.

***RPC for NT.** Guy R. Eddon. 428p. pap. 39.95 (*0-87930-450-2*) Miller Freeman.

RPG: Programming Language for Today. Doris B. Cable. 528p. (C). 1992. per. 60.95 (*0-697-11475-9*) Bus & Educ Tech.

RPG Companion. Ronald Wartow & BradyGAMES Staff. (Illus.). 400p. (Orig.). 1995. 24.99 (*1-56686-340-6*) Brady Pub.

RPG Error Handling Technique: Bulletproofing Your Applications. Russell Popeil. (Illus.). 164p. (Orig.). 1995. pap. 39.00 (*1-882419-38-3*) Duke Commns Intl.

RPG Game Collection. Petra Schlunk. 256p. 1996. per., pap. 22.99 (*0-7615-0713-2*) Prima Pub.

RPG II & RPG III Programming. Dennis Van Tassel. 397p. (Orig.). (C). 1986. teacher ed. write for info. (*0-938188-33-X*); pap. text ed. 27.95 (*0-938188-26-7*) Mitchell Pub.

RPG II Programming. 2nd ed. Douglas D. Minkema & Gerald L. Carter. (RPG II Programming-Advanced Topics Ser.). 1977. pap. text ed. 17.50 (*0-9610582-2-6*) Apollo Com.

RPG II Programming Advanced Topics. Douglas D. Minkema & Mark T. Pasquini. (RPG II Programming-Advanced Topics Ser.). 187p. 1977. pap. text ed. 14.50 (*0-9610582-3-4*) Apollo Com.

RPG II Programming Advanced Topics Teacher's Guide. Douglas D. Minkema & Mark T. Pasquini. 210p. (gr. 9-12). text ed. 55.00 (*0-9610582-6-9*) Apollo Com.

RPG II Programming Teacher's Guide. Douglas D. Minkema & Gerald L. Carter. 175p. text ed. 55.00 (*0-9610582-5-0*) Apollo Com.

RPG II, RPG III, & RPG-400. Gary B. Shelly et al. 656p. 1990. pap. 41.00 (*0-87835-246-5*) Course Tech.

RPG II with Business Applications. Stanley E. Myers. (Illus.). 1979. teacher ed. write for info. (*0-8359-6304-7*, Reston); text ed. write for info. (*0-8359-6303-9*, Reston) P-H.

RPG IV by Example. George Farr & Shailan Topiwala. (By Example Ser.). (Illus.). 600p. (Orig.). 1996. pap. 99.00 (*1-884322-26-3*) Duke Commns Intl.

RPG IV by Example. George Farr & Shailan Topiwala. (By Example Ser.). 500p. (Orig.). 1996. pap. 79.00 (*1-882419-34-0*, Duke Pr) Duke Commns Intl.

RPG IV Jump Start: Moving Ahead with the New RPG. Bryan Meyers. LC 95-6510. 193p. (Orig.). 1995. pap. 39.95 (*1-882419-17-0*) Duke Commns Intl.

***RPG IV Jump Start: Moving Ahead with the New RPG.** 2nd rev. ed. Byran Meyers. LC 96-51286. 214p. 1997. pap. 39.95 (*1-882419-67-7*, Duke Pr) Duke Commns Intl.

***RPG IV Programming on the AS/400.** Myers. (C). 1997. pap. text ed. 67.00 (*0-13-460411-3*) P-H.

RPG on the IBM AS-400: A Guide for Programmers & Managers. W. J. Tomlinson. 288p. 1992. spiral bd. 72.50 (*1-85058-287-4*, Pub. by Sigma Press UK) Coronet Bks.

RPG Two, RPG Three & RPG - 400 with Business Applications. 2nd ed. Stanley E. Myers. 896p. 1991. pap. text ed. 62.00 (*0-13-783077-7*, 260301) P-H.

RPG 2 & RPG 3: Structured Programming. 2nd ed. Nancy B. Stern. LC 90-23834. 685p. 1991. Net. pap. text ed. 43.50 (*0-471-52196-5*) Wiley.

RPG-400 Interactive Template Technique. Carson A. Soule. (Programming Technique Ser.). (Illus.). 256p. (Orig.). 1994. pap. 129.00 (*1-884322-25-5*) Duke Commns Intl.

RPG-400 Programming on the AS-400. Stanley E. Myers & Candice E. Myers. LC 94-25819. (C). 1995. pap. text ed. 68.00 (*0-13-096736-X*) P-H.

RPG/400 Interactive Template Technique. Carson A. Soule. (Illus.). 258p. (Orig.). 1994. pap. 89.00 (*1-882419-48-0*) Duke Commns Intl.

RPL Dosimetry: Radiophotoluminescence in Health Physics. Ed. by J. A. Perry. (Medical Science Ser.). (Illus.). 192p. 1987. 96.00 (*0-85274-272-X*) IOP Pub.

RPM Unlimited: A Business Machines Practice Set. 2nd ed. Dorothy L. Albertson. (Illus.). (gr. 9-12). 1980. 14.56 (*0-07-000955-4*) McGraw.

***RPR Test Material.** Carolee Freer. 45p. (C). Date not set. teacher ed. 25.00 (*0-9618340-7-2*) Prof Educ Dist.

RR & Bentley Collector Guide, Vol. 1. Graham Robson. (Collector's Guide Ser.). (Illus.). 144p. 1984. 27.95 (*0-900549-86-6*, Pub. by Motor Racing UK) Motorbooks Intl.

***RR of Nineties I.** Myungkark Park. (Illus.). 100p. (Orig.). 1996. pap. write for info. (*1-877974-24-2*) Prompter Pubns.

***RR of Nineties II.** Myungkark Park. 100p. (Orig.). 1994. pap. write for info. (*1-877974-25-0*) Prompter Pubns.

R.R.A.S. Field List of the Birds of Nevada. rev. ed. Compiled by Carolyn K. Titus. 8p. 1996. pap. 2.00 (*0-9635550-2-2*) Red Rock Audubon.

RREL Hazardous Waste Research Symposium: Abstract Proceedings, 19th Annual. (Illus.). 255p. (Orig.). (C). 1993. pap. text ed. 75.00 (*1-56806-601-5*) DIANE Pub.

RRL Hot Country Guitar. CPP Belwin Staff. 1993. pap. 12.95 (*0-89898-568-4*, F3714GTX) Warner Brothers.

RRSP Answer Book. Gail Vaz-Oxlade. 112p. 1993. pap. 9.95 (*0-7737-5561-6*) Genl Dist Srvs.

RS Ophiuchi Light Curves 1890-1995: AAVSO Monograph 7. Janet A. Mattei et al. (Illus.). 39p. 1996. pap. text ed. 10.00 (*1-878174-13-4*) Am Assn Var Star.

RS Opiuchi (1985) & the Recurrent Nova Phenomenon. Ed. by M. F. Bode. 270p. 1986. lib. bdg. 98.00 (*90-6764-074-3*, Pub. by VSP NE) Coronet Bks.

R.S. Thomas: Conceding & Absence. Shepherd. 1996. text ed. 49.95 (*0-312-16098-4*) St Martin.

RS-232 Card: Serial Communications Reference. Specialized Systems Consultants, Inc. Staff. (Illus.). 8p. (Orig.). (C). 1990. pap. 3.00 (*0-916151-42-5*) Specialized Sys.

RS-232 Simplified: Connecting, Interfacing & Troubleshooting Peripheral Devices. Byron W. Putman. (Illus.). 264p. (C). 1986. 21.40 (*0-13-783499-3*) P-H.

RSFSR, Russian Soviet Federated Socialist Republic, 2 vols. Thomas Fitzsimmons. LC 74-12008. (Country Survey Ser.). (Illus.). 681p. 1974. reprint ed. text ed. 75.00 (*0-8371-7668-9*, FIRS) Greenwood.

RSFSR, Russian Soviet Federated Socialist Republic, 2 vols., 1. Thomas Fitzsimmons. LC 74-12008. (Country Survey Ser.). (Illus.). 681p. 1974. reprint ed. text ed. 45.00 (*0-8371-7703-0*, FIRT) Greenwood.

RSFSR, Russian Soviet Federated Socialist Republic, 2 vols., Vol. 2. Thomas Fitzsimmons. LC 74-12008. (Country Survey Ser.). (Illus.). 681p. 1974. reprint ed. text ed. 45.00 (*0-8371-7704-9*, FIRW) Greenwood.

RSL Market Timing Method. Humphrey E. Lloyd. 1990. 50.00 (*0-930233-45-X*) Windsor.

RSNA, 1992: Selected Scientific Exhibits. Radiological Society of North America-RadioGraphics Staff. 1994. vdisk 500.00 (*1-56815-024-5*, 10024) Mosby Yr Bk.

RSPB Guide to Birdwatching. Peter Conder. (Illus.). 1979. 12.50 (*0-600-31423-5*) Transatl Arts.

RSRM '87: Advances in Remote Sensing Retrieval Methods. Ed. by Adarsh Deepak et al. LC 89-36947. (Illus.). 519p. 1988. 78.00 (*0-937194-13-1*) A Deepak Pub.

RSS: Myth & Reality. D. N. Mishra. 218p. 1980. 19.95 (*0-7069-1020-6*) Asia Bk Corp.

RSS & Hindu Nationalism. K. Jayaprasad. (C). 1991. 36.00 (*81-7100-353-2*, Pub. by Deep II) S Asia.

***RSTA: Reconnaissance, Surveillance, & Target Acquisition for the Unmanned Ground Vehicle.** Ed. by DARPA Staff. 456p. 1997. pap. 54.95 (*1-55860-451-0*) Morgan Kaufmann.

RSVP: Invitation a Ecrire. Michel Beaujour & Nancy F. Regalado. 253p. (Orig.). (FRE.). (C). 1965. pap. text ed. 16.00 (*0-15-577920-6*) HB Coll Pubs.

***RSVP: The College Reading, Study, & Vocabulary Program, 5 Vols.** 5th ed. James F. Shepherd. 384p. (C). 1995. pap. text ed. 31.56 (*0-395-74777-5*) HM.

RSVP: The Directory of Illustration & Design. Richard Lebenson & Kathleen Creighton. (Illus.). 320p. (Orig.). 1992. pap. 21.00 (*1-878118-01-3*) RSVP NY.

RSVP: The Golden Rules for Entertaining. Raechel Donahue. Ed. by Colby Allerton. 160p. pap. 5.99 (*1-881649-65-2*) Genl Pub Grp.

RSVP, No. 19: The Directory of Illustration & Design. Ed. by Richard Lebenson & Kathleen Creighton. (Illus.). 304p. 1994. pap. 21.00 (*1-878118-03-X*) RSVP NY.

RSVP Twenty: The Directory of Illustration & Design. Ed. by Richard Lebenson & Kathleen Creighton. 320p. 1995. pap. 24.00 (*1-878118-04-8*) RSVP NY.

RSVP16: The Directory of Illustration & Design. Ed. by Richard Lebenson & Kathleen Creighton. (Illus.). 320p. (Orig.). 1991. pap. 20.00 (*1-878118-00-5*) RSVP NY.

RSVP18: The Directory of Illustration & Design. Ed. by Richard Lebenson & Kathleen Creighton. (Directory of Illustration & Design Ser.). (Illus.). 304p. 1993. pap. 21.00 (*1-878118-02-1*) RSVP NY.

RSVP21: The Directory of Illustration & Design. Ed. by Richard Lebenson & Kathleen Creighton. (Illus.). 308p. 1996. pap. 24.00 (*1-878118-05-6*) RSVP NY.

***RSVP22: The Directory of Illustration & Design.** Ed. by Richard Lebenson & Kathleen Creighton. (Illus.). 304p. (Orig.). 1997. pap. 21.00 (*1-878118-06-4*) RSVP NY.

RT: A Readers Theater Ministry. Todd V. Lewis. 1987. 8.99 (*0-685-68712-0*, MP-641) Lillenas.

RT 2: Two Scripts for Readers Theater. Todd V. Lewis. 1989. 8.99 (*0-685-68698-1*, MP-657) Lillenas.

RTD Vol. 9: Proceedings of the 1995 IEEE/ASME Jt Railroad Conference. 172p. 1995. 80.00 (*0-7918-1217-0*, 100380) ASME.

Rte 2, Titus, Ohio. David D. Anderson. Ed. by Carol Spelius & Wayne Spelius. 219p. (Orig.). 1993. pap. 7.95 (*0-941363-26-0*) Lake Shore Pub.

RTKL Associates. RTKL Staff. (Process Architecture Ser.: No. 111). (Illus.). 155p. 1993. pap. 44.95 (*4-89331-111-5*, Pub. by Process Archit JA) Bks Nippan.

RTI-2 Design & Philosophy. John G. Barnes. 176p. 1976. text ed. 87.95 (*0-471-25596-3*, Pub. by Wiley Heyden) Wiley.

RTL-2 Design & Philosophy. John G. Barnes. LC 77-363518. (Heyden International Topics in Science Ser.). (Illus.). 176p. reprint ed. pap. 50.20 (*0-685-23439-8*, 2032692) Bks Demand.

Rtu. Gurani Anjali. LC 85-50207. (Illus.). 200p. (Orig.). 1989. pap. 14.95 (*0-933989-00-8*) Vajra Print & Pub.

Rtu: Meditational Poems. abr. ed. Gurani Anjali. LC 95-10322. (Illus.). 120p. 1995. pap. 7.95 (*0-933989-05-9*) Vajra Print & Pub.

An Asterisk (*) at the beginning of an entry indicates that the title is appearing in BIP for the first time.

Rtusamhara Angita Surabhi: Musical Rendition of Rtusamhara. Sushma Kulshreshtha. (C). 1992. 54.00 (81-85133-66-2, Pub. by Eastern Bk Linkers II) S Asia.

Rtusamhara with New Commentary by Vyankatacharya Upadhye. Kalidasa. Tr. by M. R. Kale. 1986. reprint ed. 5.50 (81-208-0031-1, Pub. by Motilal Banarsidass II) S Asia.

Ru Four Hundred Eighty-Six: The Pill That Could End the Abortion Wars & Why American Women Don't Have It. Lawrence Lader. 1991. 16.30 (0-201-57069-6) Addison-Wesley.

RUA-TV? Heidegger & the Televisual. Ed. by Tony Fry. 128p. (C). 1993. 29.95 (0-253-32562-5); pap. 13.95 (0-909952-21-3) Ind U Pr.

Ruah: 1996, Vol. 6. annuals 6th ed. 40p. (Orig.). 1996. pap. 10.00 (1-883734-00-2) Power of Poetry.

***Ruah: 1997.** Ed. by C. J. Rene & Gregory Thielen. (Ruah: Vol. VII). (Orig.). 1997. pap. 10.00 (1-883734-07-X) Power of Poetry.

Ruah, 1991, Vol. 1. Intro. by Armando P. Ibanez. 38p. (Orig.). 1991. pap. 7.00 (1-883734-02-9) Power of Poetry.

Ruah, 1992, Vol. 2. Intro. by Armando P. Ibanez. 44p. 1992. pap. 7.00 (1-883734-03-7) Power of Poetry.

Ruah, 1993, Vol. 3. Ed. by Chris Renz. 44p. 1993. pap. 7.00 (1-883734-04-5) Power of Poetry.

Ruah 1994, Vol. 4. Ed. by Anne L. Bourdon. 48p. 1994. write for info. (1-883734-05-3) Power of Poetry.

Ruah 1995, Vol. 5. Ed. by C. J. Renz. 28p. 1995. write for info. (1-883734-06-1) Power of Poetry.

Rub-a-Dub-Dub. Illus. by Page E. O'Rourke. (So Tall Board Bks.). 189p. (J). (ps-1). 1993. bds. 4.95 (0-448-40521-0, G&D) Putnam Pub Group.

***Rub-a-Dub-Dub.** Annalisa Suid. (Illus.). 80p. (Orig.). (J). (ps-k). 1996. pap. 9.95 (1-878279-88-2, 2017) Monday Morning Bks.

Rub a Dub Dub & Other Splashy Rhymes. Illus. by Anthea Sieveking. (Nursery Rhyme Board Bks.). 12p. (J). (ps-3). 1991. bds. 5.95 (0-8120-6219-1) Barron.

Rub-a-Dub-Dub Seven Dwarfs & a Tub Bath Book. Walt Disney Staff. (J). (ps). 1993. 5.98 (0-453-03099-8) NAL-Dutton.

Rub-a-dub-dub-What's in the Tub? Big Book. Mary Blocksma. (Just One More Big Bks.). 24p. (J). (ps-2). 1987. pap. 32.40 (0-516-49505-4) Childrens.

Rub-a-Dub Suds. Sharon Peters. LC 86-30856. (Illus.). 32p. (J). (gr. k-2). 1997. pap. 2.50 (0-8167-0985-8) Troll Communs.

Rub of Cultures in Modern Turkey: Literary Views of Education. Frank A. Stone. (Uralic & Altaic Ser.: No. 123). 184p. 1973. pap. text ed. 93.10 (90-279-2702-2) Mouton.

Rub of Cultures in Modern Turkey: Literary Views of Education. Frank A. Stone. LC 73-620167. (Uralic & Altaic Ser.: Vol. 123). 184p. 1973. pap. text ed. 19.00 (0-87750-179-3) Res Inst Inner Asian Studies.

***Rub of the Green.** Bill Hallberg. 1998. pap. write for info. (0-345-41749-6) Ballantine.

Rubaiyat. Mark Dunster. 14p. (Orig.). 1992. pap. 4.00 (0-89642-214-3) Linden Pubs.

Rubaiyat. Nazim Hikmet. Tr. by Randy Blasing & Mutlu Konuk from TUR. LC 85-15151. 50p. (Orig.). 1985. pap. 6.95 (0-914278-48-7) Copper Beech.

Rubaiyat Is-Cykx. Ray Buttigieg. (MLT.). 1978. pap. 3.99 (0-932436-00-5) Cykx.

Rubaiyat of a Persian Kitten. Oliver Herford. LC 92-38393. (Illus.). 80p. 1993. 14.95 (0-8478-1707-5) Rizzoli Intl.

Rubaiyat of Baba Tahir Oryan of Hamadan. Baba T. Oryan. Tr. & Intro. by Mehdi K. Nakosteen. (Illus.). 60p. (PER.). (C). 1988. text ed. 20.00 (0-936347-42-2) Iran Bks.

Rubaiyat of Omar Khayyam. 128p. 1983. 8.95 (0-312-69527-6) St Martin.

Rubaiyat of Omar Khayyam. Edward Fitzgerald. (Illus.). 112p. 1985. pap. 8.95 (0-685-09898-2) Beaufort Bks NY.

Rubaiyat of Omar Khayyam. Edward FitzGerald. 64p. 1990. pap. 1.00 (0-486-26467-X) Dover.

Rubaiyat of Omar Khayyam. Omar Khayyam. Tr. by Edward Fitzgerald. (Airmont Classics Ser.). (Illus.). (J). (gr. 9 up). 1969. mass mkt. 1.95 (0-8049-0204-6, CL-204) Airmont.

Rubaiyat of Omar Khayyam. Omar Khayyam. Tr. by Edward Fitzgerald. (Illus.). 1996. pap. 3.95 (0-8283-1452-7, 12, Intl Pocket Lib) Branden Pub Co.

Rubaiyat of Omar Khayyam. Omar Khayyam. 1995. 7.98 (0-8317-1582-0) Smithmark.

Rubaiyat of Omar Khayyam. Omar Khayyam. Tr. by Peter Avery & John Heath-Stubbs. 120p. 1981. pap. 8.95 (0-14-044384-3, Penguin Classics) Viking Penguin.

Rubaiyat of Omar Khayyam. Omar Khayyam. Tr. by Edward FitzGerald. 112p. 1989. pap. 8.95 (0-14-058606-7, Penguin Classics) Viking Penguin.

Rubaiyat of Omar Khayyam. Omar Khayyam. Tr. by Peter Avery & John Heath-Stubbs. 128p. 1984. pap. 11.95 (0-14-005954-7, Penguin Bks) Viking Penguin.

Ruba'iyat of Omar Khayyam. Omar Khayyam. Tr. by Ahmad Saidi & Seyyed H. Nasr from PER. LC 91-20526. 304p. (Orig.). 1991. 25.00 (0-89581-897-3) Asian Humanities.

Ruba'iyat of Omar Khayyam. Ahmad Saidi & Omar Khayyam. Tr. by Seyyed H. Nasr from PER. LC 91-20526. 304p. (Orig.). 1992. pap. 14.95 (0-89581-898-1) Asian Humanities.

Rubaiyat of Omar Khayyam: A Critical Edition. Edward Fitzgerald & Omar Khayyam. Ed. by Christopher Decker. LC 96-24529. (Victorian Literature & Culture Ser.). 352p. 1997. text ed. 42.50 (0-8139-1689-5) U Pr of Va.

Rubaiyat of Omar Khayyam Explained. Paramahansa Yogananda. Ed. by J. Donald Walters. 376p. 1994. 19.95 (1-56589-675-0) Crystal Clarity.

Rubaiyat of Omar Khayyam in English Verse. Edward Fitzgerald. (Illus.). (ARA, ENG & PER.). 1976. 125.00 (0-86685-430-4, KET4304) Intl Bk Ctr.

Ruban au Cou d'Olympia. Michel Leiris. (Imaginaire Ser.). (FRE.). pap. 14.95 (2-07-071702-X) Schoenhof.

Rubato Jitter. John Sullivan. 1994. 5.00 (0-932593-20-8) Black Bear.

Rubbed Stones: Collected Poems, 1960-1990. Rochelle Owens. 108p. (Orig.). 1994. pap. 8.00 (0-9641837-0-6) Texture Pr.

Rubber-Ball Games of the Americas. Theodore Stern. LC 84-45518. (American Ethnological Society Monographs: No. 17). 1988. reprint ed. 22.50 (0-404-62916-4) AMS Pr.

Rubber-Band Banjos & a Java Jive Bass: Projects & Activities on the Science of Music & Sound. Alex Sabbeth. LC 96-22144. (J). 1997. pap. text ed. 12.95 (0-471-15675-2) Wiley.

Rubber Band Runner Champion. Rita Friedman & Elaine Weimann. (Fables from the Letter People Ser.). (Illus.). 30p. (J). (ps-1). 1989. lib. bdg. 12.95 (0-89796-017-3) New Dimens Educ.

Rubber Band Shape-up Program: How to Firm, Strengthen & Shape-up Your Body, Fast! Kyle P. Zook & Sandy J. Zook. LC 87-90500. (Illus.). 194p. (Orig.). (C). 1987. pap. 11.95 (0-941141-07-1, 711-Z) S&B Ent Intl.

Rubber Bullets: Power & Conscience in Modern Israel. Yaron Ezrahi. LC 96-16862. 320p. 1996. 25.00 (0-374-25279-3) FS&G.

Rubber Chicken Book: A Fine Collection of Bad Skits, Goofball Stunts, Front Yard Acrobatics & Really Dumb Jokes. Ed. by Klutz Press Staff. (Illus.). 66p. (J). (gr. 2-8). 1995. spiral bd. 9.95 (1-57054-021-7) Klutz Pr.

Rubber Chickens for the Soul: 50 1/2 Tales to Rekindle Your Heartburn. Bad Dog Press Editors. (Illus.). 96p. (Orig.). 1995. pap. 7.00 (1-887317-03-1) Bad Dog Pr.

Rubber Compounding: Principles, Materials, & Techniques. 2nd ed. Barlow. 304p. 1993. 175.00 (0-8247-8968-7) Dekker.

Rubber Dam in Clinical Practice. J. S. Reid et al. (Illus.). 108p. 1991. pap. text ed. 34.00 (1-85097-011-4) Quint Pub Co.

Rubber Dinosaurs & Wooden Elephants: Essays on Literature, Film & History. L. Sprague De Camp. LC 95-5348. (I. O. Evans Studies in the Philosophy & Criticism of Literature: No. 26). 144p. 1996. pap. 19.00 (0-89370-454-7); lib. bdg. 29.00 (0-89370-354-0) Borgo Pr.

Rubber Duckie & Other Songs: Late Elementary Piano Solos. 32p. 1994. pap. 4.95 (0-7935-2405-9, 00290428) H Leonard.

Rubber Duckies Don't Say Quack! Anna Ross. (Sesame Street Baby Board Bks.). (Illus.). 12p. (J). (ps). 1994. 4.99 (0-679-84741-3) Random Bks Yng Read.

Rubber Gun Wars. Morgan Moore. LC 95-94830. 400p. 1995. write for info. (0-9648414-0-1) Morgan Creek.

Rubber in Offshore Engineering: Proceedings of a Conference Held in London from April 13 to April 15, 1983. fac. ed. Ed. by A. Stevenson. LC 84-235096. (Illus.). 358p. 1984. reprint ed. pap. 102.10 (0-7837-8007-9, 2047763) Bks Demand.

***Rubber Industry: Evaluation of Carcinogenic Risks to Humans.** (IARC Monographs: No. 28). 486p. 1982. text ed. 84.00 (92-832-1528-1) World Health.

***Rubber Insulated Wire & Cable for the Transmission & Distribution of Electrical Energy.** 6th ed. 39.00 (0-614-18697-8, S-19-81) Insulated Cable.

Rubber Legs & White Tail-Hairs. Patrick F. McManus. 216p. 1988. pap. 8.95 (0-8050-0912-4, Owl) H Holt & Co.

Rubber Man. Frank Kubic. LC 95-72977. 18p. (J). (gr. 3-10). 1996. pap. 4.25 (0-9636320-7-8) Nuggets Wisdom.

Rubber-Modified Thermoset Resins. Ed. by C. Keith Riew & John K. Gillham. LC 84-21566. (Advances in Chemistry Ser.: No. 208). 374p. 1984. lib. bdg. 96.95 (0-8412-0828-X) Am Chemical.

Rubber-Modified Thermoset Resins: Based on a Symposium Sponsored by the Division of Polymeric Materials Science & Engineering at the 186th Meeting of the American Chemical Society, Washington, DC, August 28-September 2, 1983. Ed. by C. Keith Riew & John K. Gillham. LC 84-21566. (Advances in Chemistry Ser.: No. 208). 384p. reprint ed. pap. 109.50 (0-7837-1962-0, 2052440) Bks Demand.

Rubber, Natural & Synthetic - General Test Methods - Carbon Black see 1997 Annual Book of ASTM Standards: Rubber, Section 9

Rubber Powered Model Airplanes: Comprehensive Building & Flying Basics Plus Advanced Design-Your-Own Instructions. Don Ross. LC 88-13066. (Illus.). 168p. (Orig.). 1988. pap. 13.95 (0-938716-19-0) Markowski Intl.

Rubber Processing: Technology, Materials, Principles. James L. White. LC 93-48549. (C). 1994. text ed. write for info. (1-56990-165-1) Hanser-Gardner.

Rubber Processing & Production Organization. Philip K. Freakley. 472p. 1985. 125.00 (0-306-41745-6, Plenum Pr) Plenum.

Rubber Products, Industrial - Specifications & Related Test Methods, Gaskets, Tires see 1997 Annual Book of ASTM Standards: Rubber, Section 9

Rubber Products Manufacturing Technology. Ed. by Bhowmick et al. 936p. 1994. 250.00 (0-8247-9112-6) Dekker.

Rubber Soul: Rubber Stamps & Correspondence Art. Sandra M. Posey. (Illus.). 72p. 1996. 32.50 (0-87805-902-4); pap. 16.95 (0-87805-903-2) U Pr of Miss.

Rubber Soul: With Notes & Tablature. 88p. 1994. otabind 19.95 (0-7935-3162-4, 00694914) H Leonard.

Rubber Stamp Art. Susan N. James. (Funstations Ser.). (Illus.). 48p. (YA). (gr. 3 up). 1996. 21.95 (0-8431-3991-9) Price Stern Sloan.

Rubber Stamp Bones & Book Set. Reader's Digest Editors. (Illus.). 24p. (J). 1995. 9.99 (0-89577-804-1) RD Assn.

Rubber Stamp Bugs & Book Set. Reader's Digest Editors. (Illus.). 24p. (J). 1995. 9.99 (0-89577-818-1) RD Assn.

Rubber Stamp Sourcebook: A Guide to Images, Projects & Resources. David Ward. LC 94-90242. (Illus.). 352p. (Orig.). 1995. pap. 19.95 (0-9641445-0-6) Cornucopia WA.

Rubber Stamping. 1995. 12.98 (0-7858-0358-0) Bk Sales Inc.

Rubber Stamping: Beyond the Basics. Michele Abel. 184p. 1994. pap. 16.95 (0-9630756-1-6) Creative MN.

Rubber, Tea & Cacao with Special Sections on Coffee, Spices & Tobacco. W. A. Maclaren. 1980. lib. bdg. 75.00 (0-8490-3110-9) Gordon Pr.

Rubber Technology. 3rd ed. Ed. by C. Hepburn. (Illus.). 624p. 1990. write for info. (0-7506-1078-6) Buttrwrth-Heinemann.

Rubber Technology. 3rd ed. Maurice Morton. (Illus.). 1987. text ed. 62.95 (0-442-26422-4) Chapman & Hall.

Rubber Technology & Manufacture. 2nd ed. Ed. by C. M. Blow & C. Hepburn. (Illus.). 624p. 1982. pap. 72.95 (0-408-00587-4) Buttrwrth-Heinemann.

Rubber Technology Handbook. Werner Hofmann. 600p. 1988. 78.00 (0-02-947931-2, Free Press) Free Pr.

Rubber Technology Handbook. Werner Hofmann. 644p. (C). 1989. text ed. 79.95 (1-56990-038-8); text ed. 79.95 (1-56990-145-7) Hanser-Gardner.

Rubber Toughened Engineering Plastics. A. A. Collyer. 384p. (gr. 13). 1994. text ed. 157.95 (0-412-58380-1) Chapman & Hall.

Rubber Tree: Memoir of a Vietnamese Woman Who Was an Anti-French Guerrilla, a Publisher & a Peace Activist. Nguyen T. Mai. Ed. by Monique Senderowicz. LC 94-2055. (Illus.). 272p. 1994. lib. bdg. 29.95 (0-89950-954-1) McFarland & Co.

Rubber Up! Edward King. 1996. pap. 4.95 (0-304-33409-X, Pub. by Cassell Pubng UK) LPC InBook.

Rubberbit Roundup. Elaine Weimann & Rita Friedman. (Read to Me Bks.). (Illus.). 30p. (J). (ps-1). 1986. lib. bdg. 12.50 (0-89796-998-7) New Dimens Educ.

Rubberlike Elasticity: A Molecular Primer. James E. Mark & Burak Erman. LC 88-5518. 196p. 1988. text ed. 99.95 (0-471-61499-8) Wiley.

Rubbers & Yanks Three Detroit Zero Top of the Seventh: Two Plays. Jonathan Reynolds. 1976. pap. 5.25 (0-8222-0974-8) Dramatists Play.

Rubbers As an Engineering Material: How to Design Rubber Components. Khairi Nagdi. 280p. (C). 1992. text ed. 89.95 (1-56990-067-1) Hanser-Gardner.

Rubbers Bros. Comics, Vol. 1, No. 1. Peter A. Mozeleski. Ed. by Paul M. Mozeleski & Rosie Dominguez. Tr. by Margarita Pagan. (Illus.). 16p. (YA). (gr. 6-12). 1990. pap. 1.75 (1-880058-01-4); pap. 1.75 (1-880058-13-8) Rubbers Bros Comics.

Rubbers Bros. Comics, Vol. 1, No. 2. Peter A. Mozeleski. Ed. by Paul M. Mozeleski & Rosie Dominguez. Tr. by Margarita Pagan. (Illus.). 16p. (YA). (gr. 6-12). 1991. pap. 1.75 (1-880058-02-2); pap. 1.75 (1-880058-14-6) Rubbers Bros Comics.

Rubbers Bros. Comics, Vol. 1, No. 3. Peter A. Mozeleski. Ed. by Paul M. Mozeleski & Rosie Dominguez. Tr. by Margarita Pagan. (Illus.). 16p. 1992. English. pap. text ed. 1.75 (1-880058-03-0); Spanish. pap. text ed. 1.75 (1-880058-15-4) Rubbers Bros Comics.

Rubbers Bros. Comics, Vol. 1, No. 4. Peter A. Mozeleski. Ed. by Paul M. Mozeleski & Rosie Dominguez. Tr. by Guadalupe Castalanas. (Illus.). 16p. 1992. pap. text ed. 1.50 (0-685-74434-5) Rubbers Bros Comics.

Rubbers Bros. Comics, Vol. 1, No. 4. Peter A. Mozeleski. Ed. by Paul M. Mozeleski & Rosie Dominguez. Tr. by Guadalupe Castalanas. (Illus.). 16p. (SPA.). (YA). (gr. 6-12). 1992. pap. text ed. 1.75 (1-880058-16-2) Rubbers Bros Comics.

Rubbers Bros. Comics, Vol 1, Nos. 1-6. Peter A. Mozeleski. Ed. by Paul M. Mozeleski & Rosie Dominguez. (Illus.). (YA). (gr. 6-12). 1992. pap. 1.75 (1-880058-00-6) Rubbers Bros Comics.

***Rubbers Bros. Comics Vol. 1, No. 7: AIDS Prevention Publications.** 2nd large type ed. Peter A. Mozeleski. Ed. by Paul M. Mozeleski. (Illus.). 16p. (SPA.). (YA). (gr. 6-12). 1996. pap. 1.75 (1-880058-07-3) Rubbers Bros Comics.

Rubbers Bros. Comics, When AIDS Strikes, AIDS World Newsletter: AIDS Talk Seminars, Activity. Peter A. Mozeleski. Ed. by Paul M. Mozeleski & Rosie Dominguez. (SPA.). 1991. pap. 1.75 (0-614-95896-2) Rubbers Bros Comics.

Rubbers Bros. Comics, When AIDS Strikes, AIDS World Newsletter: AIDS Talk Seminars, Comic. Peter A. Mozeleski. Ed. by Paul M. Mozeleski & Rosie Dominguez. (SPA.). 1991. pap. 1.75 (0-614-95895-4); pap. 1.75 (1-880058-05-7); pap. 1.75 (1-880058-17-0) Rubbers Bros Comics.

Rubbery Materials & Their Compounds. J. A. Brydson. 458p. 1989. 163.50 (1-85166-215-4) Elsevier.

Rubbing Shoulders. Harry Y. Greeley. LC 90-71970. (Illus.). 361p. (Orig.). 1991. pap. 12.95 (1-56002-031-8) Aegina Pr.

Rubbing Torsos. John Latta. LC 79-465. 93p. 1979. 4.50 (0-87886-101-7, Greenfld Rev Pr) Greenfld Rev Lit.

Rubbish! The Archaeology of Garbage. William Rathje & Cullen Murphy. LC 91-50452. (Illus.). 256p. 1993. pap. 13.00 (0-06-092228-1, PL) HarpC.

***Rubbish on Our Plates.** Fabien Perucca & Gerard Pouradier. 192p. 1997. pap. 14.95 (1-85375-223-1, Pub. by Orion Bks UK) Trafalgar.

***Rube.** J. Huddleston. 180p. (Orig.). 1997. mass mkt. 10.95 (1-57532-110-6) Press-Tige Pub.

***Rubel Collection: Sun Pictures Catalogue 8.** Larry J. Schaaf. (Illus.). 80p. (Orig.). 1997. pap. 40.00 incl. cd-rom (0-9621096-7-3) H P Kraus Jr.

Rubel on Karl Marx: Five Essays. Maximilien Rubel. Ed. by Joseph O'Malley & Keith Algozin. LC 80-21734. 272p. 1981. 59.95 (0-521-23839-0) Cambridge U Pr.

Rubella Virus see Polyoma Virus

Ruben Blades: Panamanian Lawyer & Entertainer. Betty Marton. (Hispanics of Achievement Ser.). (Illus.). (YA). (gr. 5 up). 1992. lib. bdg. 19.95 (0-7910-1235-2) Chelsea Hse.

***Ruben Blades: Salsa Singer & Actor.** Barbara Cruz. LC 97-13031. (Hispanic Biographies Ser.). (Illus.). (YA). (gr. 6 up). 1997. lib. bdg. 18.95 (0-89490-893-6) Enslow Pubs.

Ruben Dario: A Centennial Celebration. George D. Schade. (Illus.). 51p. 1967. 5.00 (0-87959-129-3) U of Tex H Ransom Ctr.

Ruben Dario & the Pythagorean Tradition. Raymond Skyrme. LC 75-11675. (Latin American Monographs: Ser. 2, No. 15). 116p. reprint ed. pap. 33.10 (0-7837-4969-4, 2044635) Bks Demand.

Ruben Dario & the Romantic Search for Unity: The Modernist Recourse to Esoteric Tradition. Cathy L. Jrade. (Texas Pan American Ser.). 192p. (C). 1983. text ed. 19.95 (0-292-75075-7) U of Tex Pr.

Ruben Dario bajo el Signo del Cisne. Iris M. Zavala. LC 89-5383. 153p. (Orig.). 1989. pap. text ed. 8.95 (0-8477-3637-7) U of PR Pr.

Ruben Dario in New York. E. G. Fay. 1972. 59.95 (0-8490-0977-4) Gordon Pr.

Ruben Dario y "El Cojo Ilustrado" G. Moser & H. C. Woodbridge. 69p. 1.00 (0-318-22350-3) Hispanic Inst.

Rubens. Gerhard Gruitrooy. 1993. 4.99 (0-7852-8306-4) Nelson.

Rubens. Vera Razdolskaya. (Masters of World Painting Ser.). (C). 1983. text ed. 60.00 (0-569-08768-6, Pub. by Collets) St Mut.

Rubens. Charles Scribner, III. (Masters of Art Ser.). (Illus.). 128p. 1989. 22.95 (0-8109-1569-3) Abrams.

Rubens: A Double Life. Marie-Anne Lescourret. Tr. by Elfreda Powell from FRE. (Illus.). 304p. 1993. text ed. 27.50 (1-56663-015-0) I R Dee.

Rubens: The Artist As Collector. Jeffrey M. Muller. (Illus.). 330p. 1989. text ed. 85.00 (0-691-04064-8); pap. text ed. 29.95 (0-691-00298-3) Princeton U Pr.

Rubens: The Garden of Love as Conversatie a la Mode. Elise Goodman. LC 91-42976. (Studies in the Art of the Low Countries (OCULI): No. 4). (Illus.). x, 199p. 1992. 76.00 (1-55619-269-X) Benjamins North Am.

Rubens & Rembrandt in Their Century. Felice Stampfle. LC 79-9113. (Illus.). 151p. 1979. pap. 29.95 (0-87598-069-4) Pierpont Morgan.

Rubens & the Poetics of Landscape. Lisa Vergara. LC 81-11385. (Illus.). 223p. reprint ed. pap. 63.60 (0-7837-3331-3, 2057738) Bks Demand.

Rubens & the Roman Circle: Studies of the First Decade. Frances Huemer. LC 95-50298. (Studies in the Ranaissance: No. 5). (Illus.). 312p. 1996. text ed. 75.00 (0-8153-2282-8, H1970) Garland.

Rubens' Copies after the Antique Vol. 1: Introduction, Vol. 23. Marjon Van Der Meulen. 1995. text ed. 98.00 (1-872501-56-7) Gordon & Breach.

Rubens' Copies after the Antique Vol. 2: Catalogue, Vol. 23. Marjon Van Der Meulen. 1995. text ed. 98.00 (1-872501-61-3) Gordon & Breach.

Rubens' Copies after the Antique Vol. 3: Plates with 575 Illustrations, Vol. 23. Marjon Van Der Meulen. (Illus.). 1995. text ed. 98.00 (1-872501-66-4) Gordon & Breach.

Rubens Drawings. Peter P. Rubens. 1989. pap. 4.95 (0-486-25963-3) Dover.

Ruben's Landscapes: Making & Meaning. Christopher Brown. (Illus.). 128p. 1996. 27.50 (0-300-06947-2) Yale U Pr.

Ruben's Self-Portrait in Focus. David Jaffe. 63p. (C). 1990. 38.00 (0-86439-065-3, Pub. by Boolarong Pubns AT) St Mut.

***Rubens' Subjects from History, 2 vols., Pt. XIII.** Elizabeth McGrath. (Illus.). 752p. 225.00 (0-905203-69-0, Pub. by Harvey Miller UK) Gordon & Breach.

Rubens to Rhubarb: The Ringling Museum Cookbook. (Illus.). 224p. 1995. 16.95 (0-916758-35-4) Ringling Mus Art.

Rubes. Leigh Rubin. 160p. (Orig.). 1988. pap. 4.95 (0-399-51488-0) Rubes Pubns.

Rubezahl - Marchen. unabridged ed. Musaus. (World Classic Literature Ser.). (GER.). pap. 5.95 (3-89507-036-X, Pub. by Bookking Intl FR) Distribks Inc.

***Rubia Muy Especial - A Very Special Blonde Girl, Vol. 421.** Susan Napier. (Harlequin Bianca Ser.). (SPA.). 1997. mass mkt. 3.50 (0-373-33421-4, 1-33421-8) Harlequin Bks.

Rubicon. Gail Kopf. LC 93-7431. 1993. 8.99 (0-8407-7800-7) Nelson.

Rubicon. S. Phillip Miles. (Illus.). 40p. 1994. pap. 7.95 (1-884778-03-8) Old Mountain.

***Rubicon: The Love Story of Emily Dickinson's Brother, Austin, & Mabel Todd, the Woman Who Saved Emily's Poetry.** Candace E. Ridington. LC 97-6883. 496p. (Orig.). 1997. pap. 19.95 (0-9656773-1-1) Arlngton Pr.

Rubicon - 5th Dimension of Biology. A. Campbell. 319p. 1994. 49.95 (0-7156-2499-7, Pub. by Duckworth UK) Focus Pub-R Pullins.

***Rubicon Beach.** Steve Erickson. LC 97-1503. 1997. pap. 12.00 (0-8050-5071-X, Owl) H Holt & Co.

R

Rubicon Dictionary of Positive, Motivational, Life-Affirming & Inspirational Quotations. John Cook. 445p. 19.95 (0-9630359-3-2) Rubicon Pr.

Rubicon One: A Novel. Dennis Jones. 256p. 1983. 14.95 (0-8253-0156-4) Beaufort Bks NY.

Rubidium. 1973. 250.00 (0-387-93181-3) Spr-Verlag.

Rubies & Rebels: Jewish Female Identity in Contemporary British Art. Ed. by Monica Bohm-Duchen. (Illus.). 96p. 1996. pap. 29.95 (0-85331-703-8, Pub. by Lund Humphries UK) Antique Collect.

Rubies & Sapphires. rev. ed. Fred Ward. Ed. by Charlotte Ward. (Fred Ward Gem Book Ser.). 64p. 1995. pap. 14.95 (0-9633723-0-0) Gem Bk Pubs.

Rubies & Sapphires. 2nd rev. ed. Fred Ward. Ed. by Charlotte Ward. (Fred Ward Gem Book Ser.). (Illus.). 64p. 1995. pap. 14.95 (0-9633723-7-8) Gem Bk Pubs.

Rubies in the Sand see Myth of Medicine

Rubik's Cubic Compendium. Erno Rubik et al. (Recreations in Mathematics Ser.). 200p. 1988. 29.95 (0-19-853202-4) OUP.

Rubin & Sugarman: Law, Economy & Society - Essays in the History of English Law. Ed. by G. R. Rubin & David Sugarman. 1984. 78.00 (0-86205-085-5); pap. 58.00 (0-86205-098-7) MICHIE.

Rubinstein: A Life. Harvey Sachs. LC 95-13539. (Illus.). 448p. 1995. 27.50 (0-8021-1579-9, Grove) Grove-Atltic.

Rubinstein Complex: Of the Nimzo Indian Defense. Leon Pliester. Ed. by Jonathan Berry. (Illus.). 376p. (Orig.). 1995. pap. 24.95 (1-879479-25-7) ICE WA.

Rubinstein Variation: Nimzo-Indian Defense. Tim Taylor. (Illus.). 76p. (Orig.). 1984. pap. 6.00 (0-931462-30-4) Chess Ent.

Rubinstein's Chess Masterpieces. Akiba Rubinstein. Ed. by Hans Kmoch. Tr. by Barnie F. Winkelman. 1941. pap. 5.95 (0-486-20617-3) Dover.

Ruble Problem: A Competitive Solution. Annelise G. Anderson. LC 92-17681. (Essays in Public Policy Ser.: No. 31). 20p. 1992. pap. text ed. 5.00 (0-8179-5362-0) Hoover Inst Pr.

Rubouts: Mob Murders in America. Richard Monaco & Lionel Bascom. 200p. (Orig.). 1991. mass mkt. 4.50 (0-380-75938-1) Avon.

Rubs of the Green: Golf's Triumphs & Tragedies. Webster Evans. (Illus.). 1970. 12.00 (0-7207-0251-8) Transatl Arts.

Ruby. V. C. Andrews. Ed. by Linda Marrow. 448p. (Orig.). 1994. mass mkt. 6.99 (0-671-75934-5) PB.

Ruby. Barbara Emberley. 1990. 14.95 (0-316-88859-1) Little.

Ruby. Michael Emberley. (J). (ps-3). 1992. mass mkt. 5.95 (0-316-23660-8) Little.

Ruby. Rosa Guy. 192p. (YA). 1992. mass mkt. 3.99 (0-440-21130-1) Dell.

***Ruby.** Ruth Langan. 1997. mass mkt. 4.99 (0-373-28984-7, 1-28984-2) Harlequin Bks.

Ruby. Ann Maxwell. 384p. 1997. mass mkt. 5.50 (0-06-104269-2, Harp PBks) HarpC.

Ruby. Roberta Stalberg & Christina Skye. 544p. 1992. mass mkt. 5.50 (0-440-20864-5) Dell.

Ruby. Colin Thompson. (J). 1994. write for info. (0-318-72538-X) Knopf.

Ruby. large type ed. V. C. Andrews. (Orig.). 1994. 25.95 (1-56895-074-8) Wheeler Pub.

Ruby. large type ed. Pamela Bennetts. 352p. 1994. 25.99 (0-7089-3071-9) Ulverscroft.

Ruby: An Ordinary Woman. Ed. by Bonnie Glaser & Ann Worster. (Illus.). 272p. 1995. 24.95 (0-571-19858-9) Faber & Faber.

***Ruby & Other Lives: Poems by Sharon Negri.** Sharon Negri. Ed. by R. D. Baker. (Poetry Chapbook Ser.). (Illus.). 28p. (Orig.). 1996. pap. 4.00 (1-887641-11-4) Argonne Hotel Pr.

Ruby & Sapphire. Richard W. Hughes. 512p. 1997. 98.00 (0-9645097-6-8) RWH Pub.

Ruby & Sapphire Buying Guide: How to Spot Value & Ripoffs. 2nd ed. Renee Newman. LC 93-9054. (Illus.). 204p. (C). 1994. pap. 19.95 (0-929975-21-9) Intl Jewelry Pubns.

Ruby Cover-Up. Seth Kantor. 1980. mass mkt. 3.99 (0-8217-3920-4, Zebra Kensgtn) Kensgtn Pub Corp.

Ruby Glass of the Twentieth Century. Naomi L. Over. Ed. by Tom Klopp. (Illus.). 128p. (Orig.). 1990. 29.95 (0-915410-67-2, 3085HB); pap. 21.95 (0-915410-68-0, 3084SB) Antique Pubns.

Ruby in the Rough. Robert H. Ruby. LC 76-40031. 1976. 11.95 (0-88289-099-9) Pelican.

Ruby in the Smoke. Philip Pullman. LC 86-20983. 208p. (YA). (gr. 7 up). 1987. lib. bdg. 11.99 (0-394-98826-4) Knopf Bks Yng Read.

Ruby in the Smoke. Philip Pullman. LC 86-20983. 240p. (YA). (gr. 7 up). 1988. reprint ed. pap. 4.99 (0-394-89589-4) Knopf Bks Yng Read.

Ruby Knight. David Eddings. (Elenium Ser.: Bk. 2). 384p. 1991. mass mkt. 5.99 (0-345-37352-9, Del Rey) Ballantine.

Ruby Knight-O.M. David Eddings. 1991. mass mkt. 5.95 (0-345-37240-9, Del Rey) Ballantine.

Ruby Mae Has Something to Say. David Small. LC 91-33785. (Illus.). 40p. (J). (ps-4). 1992. 12.00 (0-517-58248-1) Crown Bks Yng Read.

Ruby, Mono Ve, Mono Hace: Ruby the Copycat. Peggy Rathman. 32p. (J). (ps-k). 1995. pap. 4.95 (0-590-50211-5) Scholastic Inc.

Ruby Necklace. Martha Kirkland. 224p. 1996. mass mkt. 4.99 (0-451-18720-2, Sig) NAL-Dutton.

Ruby of Cochin: An Indian Jewish Woman Remembers. Ruby Daniels & Barbara Johnson. 1995. 29.95 (0-8276-0539-0) JPS Phila.

***Ruby Princess Runs Away.** Jahnna N. Malcolm. (Jewel Kingdom Ser.: No. 1). (Illus.). (J). (gr. 1-4). 1997. pap. text ed. 3.99 (0-590-21283-4) Scholastic Inc.

***Ruby Red.** William P. Fox. 375p. 1997. reprint ed. pap. 14.00 (0-9642949-2-3) Orloff Pr.

Ruby-Red Clue. William F. Love. Orig. Title: The Fundamentals of Murder. 288p. 1992. pap. 4.99 (0-451-40329-0, Onyx) NAL-Dutton.

***Ruby Ridge: Report of the Subcommittee on Terrorism, Technology & Government Information of the Senate Committee on the Judiciary.** 154p. (Orig.). 1996. pap. 30.00 (0-7881-2976-7) DIANE Pub.

Ruby Slippers, Golden Tears. Ed. by Ellen Datlow & Terri Windling. 432p. 1995. 22.00 (0-688-14363-6) Morrow.

***Ruby Slippers, Golden Tears.** Ed. by Ellen Datlow & Terri Windling. 432p. 1996. mass mkt. 5.99 (0-380-77872-6, AvoNova) Avon.

Ruby Slippers of Oz: The Pursuit, Power & Passion of the World's Most Famous Shoes. Rhys Thomas. 200p. (Orig.). 1989. pap. 14.95 (0-942139-09-7) Tale Weaver.

***Ruby Tear.** Rebecca Brand. LC 96-29342. 1997. 22.95 (0-312-86165-6) Forge NYC.

Ruby Tears of Edgecliff Manor. Elizabeth Carroll. 1992. mass mkt. 3.99 (0-8217-3665-5, Zebra Kensgtn) Kensgtn Pub Corp.

Ruby the Copycat. Peggy Rathmann. 32p. (J). 1991. 14.95 (0-590-43747-X, Scholastic Hardcover) Scholastic Inc.

Ruby the Copycat. Peggy Rathmann. 32p. (J). (ps-3). 1993. pap. 4.95 (0-590-47423-5) Scholastic Inc.

***Ruby the Copycat.** Peggy Rathmann. (J). 1997. 9.95 (0-590-76715-1) Scholastic Inc.

Ruby Thoughts. Gro Warling. 96p. 1993. pap. 6.95 (1-879244-80-2) Windom Bks.

Ruby-Throated Hummingbirds. James E. Gerholdt. LC 95-48185. (J). 1997. lib. bdg. 13.98 (1-56239-586-6) Abdo & Dghtrs.

***Ruby Throne: Realm of Light.** Deborah Chester. 400p. 1997. mass mkt. 6.99 (0-441-00480-6) Ace Bks.

Rubycat of Waldo Japussy. Waldo Japussy. 1998. pap. 9.95 (0-89804-831-1, Enthea Pr) Ariel GA.

Rubyfruit Jungle. Rita Mae Brown. 256p. 1983. mass mkt. 6.50 (0-553-27886-X, Bantam Classics) Bantam.

Rubyfruit Mountain: A Stonewall Riots Collection. Andrea Natalie. (Illus.). 84p. (Orig.). 1993. pap. 9.95 (0-939416-74-3) Cleis Pr.

Ruby's Low-Fat Soul-Food Cookbook. Ruby Banks-Payne. 208p. 1996. pap. 12.95 (0-8092-3153-0) Contemp Bks.

Ruby's Storm. Amy Hest. LC 92-31242. (Illus.). 32p. (J). (ps-2). 1994. lib. bdg. 14.95 (0-02-743160-6, Four Winds Pr) S&S Childrens.

Ruch & the Upper Applegate Valley: An Oregon Documentary. enl. ed. John Black & Marguerite Black. Ed. by Bert Webber. LC 89-19917. (Illus.). 240p. (Orig.). 1994. pap. 12.95 (0-936738-39-1) Webb Research.

***Ruckblick: Texte und Bilder Nach 1945.** Andreas Lixl-Purcell. 305p. (GER.). (C). 1994. pap. text ed. 32.36 (0-395-69904-5) HM.

Rucker: Genealogy of the Rucker Family, with Bush Genealogy. L. B. Rucker. 148p. 1995. reprint ed. pap. 24.00 (0-8328-4830-1); reprint ed. lib. bdg. 34.00 (0-8328-4829-8) Higginson Bk Co.

Ruckers: A Harpsichord & Virginal Building Tradition. Grant O'Brien. (Cambridge Musical Texts & Monographs). (Illus.). 360p. (C). 1990. text ed. 130.00 (0-521-36565-1) Cambridge U Pr.

Rucker's Personal Guide to Successful Money Making Opportunities & Credit Information. Edward W. Rucker. LC 86-90451. 245p. 1987. pap. 29.95 (0-9614352-1-6) Edw Rucker Ent.

***Ruckstellungen als Problem der Wirtschaftlichen Betrachtungsweise.** Angelika Thies. xviii, 312p. (GER.). 1996. 57.95 (3-631-30550-8) P Lang Pubng.

***Ruckus along the Rivers.** Barbara Barton. (Illus.). 110p. 1996. pap. 4.95 (0-943639-28-X) Anchor Pub Co.

Ruckus at Gila Wells: Larry & Stretch. large type ed. Marshall Grover. (Linford Western Library). 272p. 1993. pap. 15.99 (0-7089-7365-5, Linford) Ulverscroft.

Rudder: Divine Canons of the Seven Decumenical & of Local Synods. Agapius et al. Ed. by Orthodox Christian Educational Society Staff & Apostolos Makrakis. Tr. by Denver Cummings. Orig. Title: Pedalion. 1097p. (C). 1957. 79.95 (0-938366-00-9) Orthodox Chr.

Rudder Grangers Abroad, & Other Stories. Frank R. Stockton. LC 79-90592. (Short Story Index Reprint Ser.). 1977. 18.95 (0-8369-3075-4) Ayer.

Rudder, Stick & Throttle: Research & Reminiscences on Flying in Nebraska. Robert E. Adwers. (Illus.). x, 550p. (Orig.). 1993. pap. 25.00 (0-9631699-4-7) Making Hist.

Ruddigore. (Vocal Score Ser.). 224p. 1986. pap. 14.95 (0-88188-727-7, 50337830) H Leonard.

Ruddlemoor. E. V. Thompson. 640p. 1996. pap. 10.95 (0-7472-4822-2, Pub. by Headline UK) Trafalgar.

***Ruddlemoor.** large type ed. E. V. Thompson. (Charnwood Large Print Ser.). 784p. 1996. 27.99 (0-7089-8898-9) Ulverscroft.

Ruddy Ducks & Other Stifftails: Their Behavior & Biology. Paul A. Johnsgard & Montserrat Carbonell. LC 95-42400. (Animal Natural History Ser.: Vol. 1). (Illus.). 328p. 1996. 44.95 (0-8061-2799-6) U of Okla Pr.

Rude & Barbarous Kingdom: Russia in the Accounts of Sixteenth-Century English Voyagers. Ed. by Lloyd E. Berry & Robert O. Crummey. LC 68-16059. 405p. reprint ed. pap. 115.50 (0-317-27784-7, 2015353) Bks Demand.

Rude Assignment. Wyndham Lewis. Ed. by Toby Foshay. LC 84-16837. (Illus.). 315p. (Orig.). 1984. 25.00 (0-87685-604-0); pap. 14.00 (0-87685-603-2) Black Sparrow.

Rude Astronauts: Real & Imagined Stories. Allen Steele. LC 93-16413. 266p. 1993. pap. 15.00 (1-882968-00-X) Old Earth Bks.

Rude Astronauts: Real & Imagined Stories. deluxe limited ed. Allen Steele. LC 93-16413. 266p. 1993. 85.00 (1-882968-01-8) Old Earth Bks.

Rude Awakening. Durnell Christian. (Illus.). 112p. 1996. pap. 12.95 (0-939767-25-2) D McMillan.

***Rude Awakening.** Pamela Kyle. (Black Lace Ser.). 300p. 1996. mass mkt. 5.95 (0-352-33036-8, Pub. by Virgin Pub UK) London Brdge.

Rude Awakening: A First-Hand Account of Western Society's Reaction to Zen Satori. 2nd ed. Wogen Jeng. (Illus.). 31p. 1993. text ed. 49.00 (1-883496-03-9) P S Melvil Pr.

Rude Awakenings. Bob Rosenthal. LC 81-21943. 1981. pap. 3.50 (0-916328-16-3) Yellow Pr.

Rude Awakenings: What the Homeless Crisis Tells Us. Richard W. White, Jr. 330p. 1992. 29.95 (1-55815-158-3) ICS Pr.

Rude Awakenings: Zen, the Kyoto School, & the Question of Nationalism. Ed. by James W. Heisig & John C. Maraldo. LC 94-49174. (Nanzan Library of Asian Religion & Culture). 390p. (C). 1995. text ed. 40.00 (0-8248-1735-4) UH Pr.

Rude Awakenings: Zen, the Kyoto School, & the Questions of Nationalism. Ed. by James W. Heisig & John C. Maraldo. LC 94-49174. (Nanzan Library of Asian Religion & Culture). 390p. (C). 1995. pap. text ed. 19.95 (0-8248-1746-X) UH Pr.

Rude Computers, Angry People: Learning to Live with Computers. Daniel J. Schuster. LC 92-700561. (Illus.). 124p. (Orig.). 1992. pap. 11.95 (0-9632026-3-4) Info Hse.

***Rude Gal.** Sheri T. Campbell. 1997. pap. 9.95 (1-874509-32-8, Pub. by X Pr UK) LPC InBook.

***Rude Giants.** Wood. 1997. pap. write for info. (0-15-201596-5) HarBrace.

Rude Giants. Audrey Wood. LC 91-13015. (Illus.). 32p. (J). (ps-2). 1993. 14.00 (0-15-269412-9, HB Juv Bks) HarBrace.

Rude Girls & Dangerous Women: Cartoons by Jennifer Camper. Jennifer Camper. (Illus.). 96p. (Orig.). 1994. pap. 8.95 (0-9632526-5-8) Laugh Lines.

***Rude Girls & Good Girls.** Thom. Date not set. text ed. 59.50 (1-86064-198-9, Pub. by I B Tauris UK) St Martin.

Rude Gross Jokes, Vol. XI. Julius Alvin. 1991. mass mkt. 3.50 (0-8217-3616-7, Zebra Kensgtn) Kensgtn Pub Corp.

Rude Hiver. Raymond Queneau. (Imaginaire Ser.). 174p. (FRE.). 1977. 11.95 (2-07-029648-2) Schoenhof.

***Rude Is...by Tammy & Andrew Jackson.** Bo Jackson. 72p. 1996. pap. 7.95 (0-8059-4044-8) Dorrance.

Rude Mechanicals. Ed Graczyk. (J). (gr. 4-12). 1970. 5.00 (0-87602-194-1) Anchorage.

Rude Noises. Martha Meek. 1995. 3.00 (0-941127-16-8) Dacotah Terr Pr.

***Rude Osolnik: A Life Turning Wood.** Jane Kessler & Dick Burrows. (Illus.). 144p. 1997. 40.00 (1-889937-05-3) Crescent Hill Bks.

***Rude Osolnik: A Life Turning Wood.** limited ed. Jane Kessler & Dick Burrows. (Illus.). 144p. 1997. boxed 225.00 (1-889937-04-5) Crescent Hill Bks.

Rude Pursuits & Rugged Peaks: Schoolcraft's Ozark Journal, 1818-19. Contrib. & Intro. by Milton D. Rafferty. (Illus.). 1996. 26.00 (1-55728-412-1) U of Ark Pr.

***Rude Roger.** (Little Monsters Ser.). (J). 1997. write for info. (0-614-21784-9, Pub. by Splash UK) Assoc Pubs Grp.

Rude, Rowdy Rumors, No. 2. Elizabeth Levy. LC 93-46792. (Illus.). 96p. (J). (gr. 2-5). 1994. 13.00 (0-06-023462-8); lib. bdg. 12.89 (0-06-023463-6) HarpC Child Bks.

Rude Rowdy Rumors: Starring Brian & Pea Brain. Elizabeth Levy. LC 93-46792. (Trophy Chapter Bk.). (Illus.). 96p. (J). (gr. 2-5). 1995. pap. 3.95 (0-06-442002-7, Trophy) HarpC Child Bks.

Rudelstein Affair. Michael Marsh. LC 80-29323. 205p. 1981. 9.95 (0-918056-02-0) Ariadne Pr.

Rudeness & Civility: Manners in Nineteenth-Century Urban America. John F. Kasson. (American Century Ser.). (Illus.). 320p. 1991. pap. 14.00 (0-374-52299-5, Noonday) FS&G.

Rudeness & Civility: Manners in Nineteenth-Century Urban America. John F. Kasson. 1990. 22.95 (0-8090-3470-0) Hill & Wang.

Rudens. Plautus. Ed. & Intro. by H. C. Fay. (College Classical Ser.). v, 221p. (C). 1983. reprint ed. pap. text ed. 17.50 (0-89241-386-7) Caratzas.

Rudens, Curculio, Casina. Plautus. Tr. by Christopher Stace. LC 81-6086. (Translations from Greek & Roman Authors Ser.). (Illus.). 160p. 1982. pap. 12.95 (0-521-28046-X) Cambridge U Pr.

Rudi: Entering Infinity. Swami Rudrananda. Ed. by Cheryl B. Rosen. LC 92-45648. 210p. 1994. pap. 16.95 (0-915801-41-8) Rudra Pr.

Rudi: Fourteen Years with My Teacher. John Mann. Ed. by Diane Asay. 243p. (Orig.). 1987. pap. 14.95 (0-915801-04-3) Rudra Pr.

Rudi in His Own Words. Swami Rudrananda. LC 90-20083. 197p. (Orig.). 1990. pap. 14.95 (0-915801-20-5) Rudra Pr.

Rudian Dichoso: Pedro de Urdemalas. Miguel de Cervantes Saavedra. 392p. 1986. pap. 12.95 (0-7859-5162-8) Fr & Eur.

Rudimenta Musices see Monuments of Music & Music Literature in Facsimile

Rudimental Divine Science. Mary Baker Eddy. 1908. pap. 5.00 (0-87952-059-0) Eddy Wrtngs M B Eddy.

Rudimental Divine Science. Mary M. Eddy. (Notable American Authors Ser.). 1992. reprint ed. lib. bdg. 75.00 (0-7812-2754-2) Rprt Serv.

Rudimental Divine Science: No & Yes. Mary Baker Eddy. 1976. lib. bdg. 69.95 (0-8490-2546-X) Gordon Pr.

Rudimental Divine Science & Other Writings on Christian Science. Mary B. Eddy. 252p. (C). 1992. reprint ed. pap. 10.95 (0-930227-20-4) Bookmark CA.

Rudimentary Treatise on Well-Digging, Boring & Pumpwork, 1849. John G. Swindell. (Illus.). 88p. 1983. reprint ed. pap. text ed. 17.50 (0-87556-703-7) Saifer.

***Rudiments of America's Christian History & Government: Student Handbook.** 2nd rev. ed. Rosalie J. Slater & Verna M. Hall. (Illus.). 112p. 1994. pap. 13.00 (0-912498-14-5, RUDVA) F A C E.

Rudiments of Architecture: 1814 see Works of Asher Benjamin: Boston, 1806-1843

Rudiments of Ballroom Dancing. V. Barton. (Ballroom Dance Ser.). 1986. lib. bdg. 79.95 (0-8490-3261-X) Gordon Pr.

Rudiments of Ballroom Dancing. V. Varton. (Ballroom Dance Ser.). 1985. lib. bdg. 76.00 (0-87700-853-1) Revisionist Pr.

Rudiments of Militarie Dicipline. LC 70-25967. (English Experience Ser.: No. 105). 14p. 1969. reprint ed. 20.00 (90-221-0105-3) Walter J Johnson.

Rudiments of Music. 2nd ed. Ottman & Frank D. Mainous. 1987. pap. text ed. 52.00 (0-13-783671-6) P-H.

Rudiments of Music. 2nd ed. Robert W. Ottman & Frank D. Mainous. (Illus.). 320p. (C). 1987. write for info. (0-318-61355-7) P-H.

Rudiments of Music. 3rd ed. Robert W. Ottman & Frank D. Mainous. LC 94-41687. 326p. 1995. pap. text ed. 43.67 (0-13-706740-2) P-H.

Rudiments of Plane Affine Geometry. Peter Scherk & R. Lingenberg. LC 75-11705. (Mathematical Expositions Ser.: No. 20). 122p. reprint ed. pap. 34.80 (0-685-16073-4, 2056135) Bks Demand.

Rudiments of Ramsey Theory. Ronald L. Graham. LC 80-29667. (CBMS Regional Conference Series in Mathematics: No. 45). 65p. 1981. reprint ed. pap. 15.00 (0-8218-1696-9, CBMS/45) Am Math.

Rudiments of Ranching. Edward D. Sethness. (Illus.). 175p. (Orig.). (C). 1988. write for info. (0-318-63701-4) Edsco Enterprises.

Rudiments of Runelore. Stephen Pollington. 96p. 1995. pap. 12.95 (1-898281-16-5) Paul & Co Pubs.

Rudin. Ivan S. Turgenev. (Classics Ser.). 192p. 1975. pap. 10.95 (0-14-044304-5, Penguin Classics) Viking Penguin.

Rudists of Jamaica see Palaeontographica Americana: Vol. 7

***Rudman's Cigar Buying Guide: Selecting & Savoring the Perfect Cigar for Any Occasion.** Theo Rudman. 225p. 1997. pap. 12.95 (1-57243-233-0) Triumph Bks.

***Rudman's Complete Guide to Cigars: How to Find, Select & Smoke Them.** rev. ed. Theo Rudman. 366p. 1997. pap. 14.95 (1-57243-245-4) Triumph Bks.

Rudo Ensayo: A Description of Sonora & Arizona in 1764. Juan Nentvig. Tr. by Alberto F. Pradeau & Robert R. Rasmussen. LC 79-20420. 188p. 1980. reprint ed. pap. 53.60 (0-608-02353-1, 2062994) Bks Demand.

***Rudolf.** Elizabeth Maslen et al. LC 96-9840. (Writings from an Unbound Europe). 128p. 1996. 39.95 (0-8101-1417-8); pap. 14.95 (0-8101-1418-6) Northwestern U Pr.

***Rudolf Arnheim: Revealing Vision.** Ed. by Kent Kleinman & Leslie Van Duzer. (C). 1997. 29.95 (0-472-10859-X) U of Mich Pr.

Rudolf Bahro, Critical Responses. International Congress for & about Rudolf Bahro Staff. Ed. by Ulf Wolter. LC 80-15954. 245p. 1980. reprint ed. pap. 69.90 (0-7837-9935-7, 2060662) Bks Demand.

Rudolf Bultman: Interpreting Faith for the Modern Era. Ed. by Roger Johnson. LC 91-14237. (Making of Modern Theology Ser.). 352p. 1991. pap. 18.00 (0-8006-3402-0, 1-3402) Augsburg Fortress.

Rudolf Carnap, Logical Empiricist: Materials & Perspectives. Ed. by Jaakko Hintikka. (Synthese Library: No. 73). 468p. 1975. lib. bdg. 152.00 (90-277-0583-6) Kluwer Ac.

Rudolf Hess: Prisoner of Peace. 1984. lib. bdg. 250.00 (0-87700-611-3) Revisionist Pr.

Rudolf Hess: Prisoner of Peace. Rudolf Hess. Ed. by George Pile. Tr. by Meyrick Booth. LC 82-83959. (Illus.). 151p. 1982. reprint ed. pap. 8.95 (0-939484-02-1) Legion Survival.

Rudolf Hess, Deputy Fuhrer: A Psychological Study. David M. Moriarty. (Illus.). 325p. (Orig.). (C). 1996. pap. 35.00 (0-87527-489-7) Green.

Rudolf Hilferding: Theory & Politics of Democratic Socialism. F. Peter Wagner. LC 95-22986. 224p. (C). 1996. text ed. 45.00 (0-391-03920-2) Humanities.

***Rudolf II & Prague: The Court & the City.** Ed. by Eliska Fucikova. LC 97-60327. (Illus.). 784p. 1997. 75.00 (0-500-23737-9) Thames Hudson.

Rudolf L. Baumfeld Collection of Landscape Drawings & Prints. Norman Katkov et al. LC 89-23550. (Illus.). 219p. (Orig.). 1989. 50.00 (0-943739-13-6); pap. 29.95 (0-943739-12-8) F S Wight Art.

***Rudolf Nureyev.** Diane Solway. Date not set. write for info. (0-688-12873-4) Morrow.

Rudolf Otto: An Introduction to His Philosophical Theology. Philip C. Almond. LC 83-19865. (Studies in Religion). 182p. reprint ed. pap. 51.90 (0-7837-2450-0, 2042599) Bks Demand.

***Rudolf Otto & the Concept of Holiness.** Melissa Raphael. LC 97-489. 200p. 1997. 55.00 (0-19-826932-3) OUP.

Rudolf Scheffler. Peter H. Falk. (Illus.). 48p. 1989. pap. 12.00 (0-932087-06-X) Sound View Pr.

Rudolf Scheffler (1884-1973) Peter H. Falk. (Illus.). 48p. (Orig.). 1989. pap. 10.00 (1-880897-16-4) Lyme Hist.

***Rudolf Steiner: Aspects of His Spiritual World-View.** Roy Wilkinson. (Anthroposophy Ser.). (Illus.). 96p. 1994. pap. write for info. (0-904693-63-5, Vol. 3, Pub. by Temple Ldge Pub UK) Anthroposophic.

***Rudolf Steiner: Aspects of His Spiritual World-View, Vol. 1.** Roy Wilkinson. (Anthroposophy Ser.). (Illus.). 96p. 1993. pap. write for info. (0-904693-47-3, Pub. by Temple Ldge Pub UK) Anthroposophic.

An Asterisk (*) at the beginning of an entry indicates that the title is appearing in BIP for the first time.

***Rudolf Steiner: Aspects of His Spiritual World-View, Vol. 2.** Roy Wilkinson. (Anthroposophy Ser.). (Illus.). 96p. 1993. pap. write for info. (*0-904693-51-1*, Pub. by Temple Ldge Pub UK) Anthroposophic.

Rudolf Steiner: His Life & Work, an Illustrated Biography. Gilbert Childs. (Rudolf Steiner's Ideas in Practice Ser.). (Illus.). 111p. (Orig.). 1994. pap. 9.95 (*0-88010-391-4*) Anthroposophic.

Rudolf Steiner: Life, Work, Inner Path & Social Initiatives. Rudi Lissau. 192p. 1987. pap. 14.95 (*1-869890-06-X*, 1230, Pub. by Hawthorn Press UK) Anthroposophic.

Rudolf Steiner: Scientist of the Invisible. A. P. Shepherd. 224p. 1987. pap. 10.95 (*0-89281-174-9*) Inner Tradit.

Rudolf Steiner & Holistic Medicine. Francis X. King. LC 87-12290. 224p. (Orig.). 1987. pap. 10.95 (*0-89254-015-X*) Nicolas-Hays.

Rudolf Steiner & Initiation. Paul E. Schiller. 143p. 1990. pap. 5.95 (*0-910142-96-3*, 418) Anthroposophic.

***Rudolf Steiner & the Founding of the New Mysteries.** 2nd expanded rev. ed. Sergei O. Prokofieff. Tr. by Paul King & Simon B. De Lange from RUS. (Illus.). 480p. 1994. write for info. (*0-904693-61-9*, Pub. by Temple Ldge Pub UK) Anthroposophic.

Rudolf Steiner Education: The Waldorf Schools. rev. ed. Francis Edmunds. 139p. 1987. pap. 15.95 (*0-85440-596-8*, Steinerbks) Anthroposophic.

Rudolf Steiner Education & the Developing Child. Willi Aeppli. Tr. by Angelika V. Ritscher from GER. 200p. 1987. pap. 12.95 (*0-88010-164-4*) Anthroposophic.

Rudolf Steiner on Education: A Compendium. Roy Wilkinson. (Learning Resources Ser.). (Illus.). 159p. (Orig.). 1993. pap. 12.95 (*1-869890-51-5*, Pub. by Hawthorn Press UK) Anthroposophic.

Rudolf Steiner on Nutrition & Stimulants. Rudolf Steiner. Tr. by K. Castelliz & B. Saunders-Davies from GER. 238p. (C). 1991. pap. text ed. 13.50 (*0-938250-29-9*) Bio-Dynamic Farm.

Rudolf Steiner's New Approach to Color on the Ceiling of the First Goetheanum. D. J. Van Bemmelen. (Illus.). 1980. pap. 18.95 (*0-916786-44-7*, Saint George Pubns) R Steiner Col Pubns.

Rudolf Steiner's Sculpture in Dornach. Ake Fant et al. Tr. by Erik Westerberg. (Illus.). 85p. (GER.). 1975. 16.95 (*0-85440-301-9*, Steinerbks) Anthroposophic.

Rudolf Virchow: The Scientist As Citizen. Byron A. Boyd. LC 91-12024. (Modern European History Outstanding Studies & Dissertations). 286p. 1991. text ed. 20.00 (*0-8153-0412-9*) Garland.

***Rudolf von Ems.** Deutschen Akademie der Wissenschaften Staff & Willehalm Von Orlens. (Deutsche Texte des Mittelalters Ser.: Band II). xliii, 278p. (GER.). 1967. write for info. (*3-296-17210-6*, Pub. by Weidmann GW) Lubrecht & Cramer.

***Rudolf von Ems: Der Gute Gerhard.** M. Haupt. xvi, 224p. (GER.). 1988. 68.00 (*3-615-00039-0*, Pub. by Weidmann GW) Lubrecht & Cramer.

***Rudolf von Ems: Wilhelm von Orlens: Studien zur Ausstattung und zur Ikonographie einer Illustrierten Deutschen Epenhandschrift des 13. Jahrhunderts am Beispiel des Cgm 63 der Bayerischen Staatsbibliothek Munchen.** Erika Weigele-Ismael. (Europaische Hochschulschriften, Reihe 28: Bd. 285). 365p. (GER.). 1997. 76.95 (*3-631-30202-9*) P Lang Pubng.

***Rudolfs von Ems Weltchronik.** Deutschen Akademie der Wissenschaften Staff. (Deutsche Texte des Mittelalters Ser.: Band XX). xxxvii, 634p. (GER.). 1967. write for info. (*3-296-17220-3*, Pub. by Weidmann GW) Lubrecht & Cramer.

***Rudolpf Stainer's Research into Karma & the Mission of the Anthroposophical Society.** Sergei O. Prokofieff. Tr. by Richard Michell. 48p. 1995. pap. write for info. (*0-904693-69-4*, Pub. by Temple Ldge Pub UK) Anthroposophic.

Rudolph Ackerman & the Repository of Arts: In Search of the Picturesque. Margaret Smith. (Illus.). 8p. (Orig.). 1995. pap. 3.00 (*0-914630-16-4*) Houghton Lib.

Rudolph Ganz: A Musical Pioneer. Jeanne C. Collester. LC 94-9688. 1994. 29.50 (*0-8108-2883-9*) Scarecrow.

Rudolph J. Nunnemacher Collection of Projectile Arms, 2 pts., 1. Milwaukee Public Museum Staff. Ed. by John Metschl. Bd. with Pt. 1. Long Arms. Ed. by Milwaukee Public Museum et al.; Pt. 2. Short Arms. Ed. by Milwaukee Public Museum et al. LC 74-111395. (Illus.). 1970. reprint ed. Set text ed. 75.00 (*0-8371-4627-5*, MPMO, Greenwood Pr) Greenwood.

Rudolph J. Nunnemacher Collection of Projectile Arms, 2 pts., Vol. 2. Milwaukee Public Museum Staff. Ed. by John Metschl. Bd. with Pt. 1. Long Arms. Ed. by Milwaukee Public Museum et al.; Pt. 2. Short Arms. Ed. by Milwaukee Public Museum et al. LC 74-111395. (Illus.). 1970. reprint ed. Set text ed. 75.00 (*0-8371-4628-3*, MPMP, Greenwood Pr) Greenwood.

Rudolph J. Nunnemacher Collection of Projectile Arms, 2 pts., Vol. 9. Milwaukee Public Museum Staff. Ed. by John Metschl. Bd. with Pt. 1. Long Arms. Ed. by Milwaukee Public Museum et al.; Pt. 2. Short Arms. Ed. by Milwaukee Public Museum et al. LC 74-111395. (Illus.). 1970. reprint ed. Set text ed. 125.00 (*0-8371-4626-7*, MPMN, Greenwood Pr) Greenwood.

***Rudolph Pseudomonas Syringes.** Rudolph. LC 97-19457. 1997. text ed. write for info. (*0-7923-4601-7*) Kluwer Ac.

Rudolph Reconsidered. Alba Roberto De. 1997. 65.00 (*0-8230-4612-5*) Watsn-Guptill.

Rudolph Red Nosed Reindeer. (Illus.). (J). (ps-3). pap. 1.59 (*0-307-08461-2*, Golden Books) Western Pub.

Rudolph Shines Again. 1986. 17.70 (*0-8136-6023-8*) Modern Curr.

Rudolph Steiner Goetheanum, Dornach. Wolfgang Pehnt. 95p. 1993. 45.00 (*0-685-67851-2*, Pub. by Ernst & Sohn GW) Wiley.

Rudolph the Red-Nosed Reindeer. (J). 1986. 17.70 (*0-8136-6022-X*) Modern Curr.

Rudolph the Red-Nosed Reindeer. (Golden Story Book 'n' Tape Ser.). (Illus.). 24p. (J). (ps-3). audio write for info. (*0-307-14191-8*, 14191-00, Golden Books) Western Pub.

Rudolph the Red Nosed Reindeer. (Illus.). (J). (ps-3). pap. 1.59 (*0-307-07109-X*, Golden Books) Western Pub.

Rudolph the Red Nosed Reindeer. (Illus.). (J). (ps-3). 1.59 (*0-307-01118-6*, Golden Books) Western Pub.

Rudolph the Red-Nosed Reindeer. (Little Golden Books Holiday Favorites Ser.). (Illus.). 24p. (J). (ps-2). 1995. bds. 1.49 (*0-307-02071-1*, Golden Pr) Western Pub.

***Rudolph the Red-Nosed Reindeer.** Golden Books Staff. (Illus.). (J). 1997. pap. text ed. 2.29 (*0-307-08372-1*, Golden Books) Western Pub.

Rudolph the Red Nosed Reindeer. Robert May. LC 91-156221. (J). (ps-3). 1990. 9.95 (*1-55709-139-0*) Applewood.

Rudolph the Red-Nosed Reindeer. Robert L. May. 32p. 1993. spiral bd. 5.95 incl. audio (*1-55709-137-4*) Applewood.

Rudolph the Red-Nosed Reindeer. Robert L. May. LC 94-20997. (Illus.). 32p. (J). (ps-3). 1994. 9.95 (*1-55709-294-X*) Applewood.

Rudolph the Red-Nosed Reindeer. Robert L. May. (Illus.). 14p. (J). (ps-3). 1993. 3.95 (*0-307-12396-0*, Golden Books) Western Pub.

Rudolph the Red-Nosed Reindeer. Illus. by Christopher Santoro. LC 86-62550. (Night Light Bks.). 14p. (J). (ps-1). 1987. 5.95 (*0-394-88923-1*) Random Bks Yng Read.

Rudolph the Red-Nosed Reindeer. Illus. by Richard Scarry. (Big Golden Bks.). 24p. (J). (ps-3). 1985. reprint ed. 3.50 (*0-307-10203-3*, Golden Books) Western Pub.

Rudolph Virchow: Doctor, Statesman, Anthropologist & Virchow-Bibliographie 1843-1901, 2 vols. in 1. Erwin H. Ackerknecht. Ed. by J. Schwalbe & I. Bernard Cohen. LC 80-2112. (Development of Science Ser.). (Illus.). 1981. reprint ed. lib. bdg. 49.95 (*0-405-13832-6*) Ayer.

Rudolph Wurlitzer, American Novelist & Screenwriter. David Seed. LC 91-36889. 192p. 1991. lib. bdg. 79.95 (*0-7734-9643-2*) E Mellen.

Rudolph's Adventure. Carolyn Quattrocki. (Favorite Christmas Tales Ser.). (Illus.). 24p. (J). (ps-4). 1992. lib. bdg. 10.95 (*1-56674-025-8*, HTS Bks) Forest Hse.

***Rudolph's Fund Pediatrics.** 2nd ed. Rudolph & Kamei. 1997. pap. text ed. 39.95 (*0-8385-8236-2*) P-H.

Rudolph's Fundamentals of Pediatrics. Abraham M. Rudolph & Robert Kamei. (Illus.). 650p. 1994. pap. text ed. 39.95 (*0-8385-8233-8*, A8233-7) Appleton & Lange.

Rudolph's Pediatrics. 20th ed. Abraham M. Rudolph. (Illus.). (C). 1995. text ed. 110.00 (*0-8385-8492-6*, A8492-9) Appleton & Lange.

Rudolph's Second Christmas. Robert L. May. LC 92-18416. (Illus.). (J). (ps-3). 1992. 9.95 (*1-55709-192-7*) Applewood.

Rudy Vallee Discography, No. 15. Compiled by Larry F. Kiner. LC 84-22491. (Discographies Ser.). xxi, 190p. 1985. text ed. 49.95 (*0-313-24512-6*, KIR/, Greenwood Pr) Greenwood.

Rudy Visits the North. Aubrey Lang. LC 91-75423. (Illus.). 40p. (J). (ps-2). 1992. lib. bdg. 14.89 (*1-56282-208-X*) Hyprn Child.

***Rudy Visits the North.** large type ed. Aubrey Lang. (Illus.). 40p. (J). (gr. k-4). 1992. 13.95 (*0-920534-73-2*, Pub. by Hyperion Pr Ltd CN) Sterling.

Rudy Wiebe & His Works. Susan Whaley. (Canadian Author Studies). 61p. (C). 1987. pap. text ed. 9.95 (*0-920763-26-X*, Pub. by ECW Press CN) Genl Dist Srvs.

Rudyard Kipling. (Illus.). 700p. (J). 8.98 (*0-517-34798-9*) Random Hse Value.

Rudyard Kipling. Hilton Brown. LC 74-7017. (English Literature Ser.: No. 33). 1974. lib. bdg. 49.95 (*0-8383-1853-3*) M S G Haskell Hse.

Rudyard Kipling. Rupert Croft-Cooke. LC 74-7100. (English Biography Ser.: No. 31). 1974. lib. bdg. 75.00 (*0-8383-1856-8*) M S G Haskell Hse.

***Rudyard Kipling.** Ed. by Roger L. Green. (Critical Heritage Ser.). 428p. (C). 1997. text ed. 35.00 (*0-415-15909-1*) Routledge.

Rudyard Kipling. James Harrison. (English Authors Ser.: No. 339). 192p. (C). 1982. 22.95 (*0-8057-6825-4*, Twayne) Scribnrs Ref.

Rudyard Kipling. Rudyard Kipling. (Poets Ser.). 146p. 1993. 5.95 (*0-7117-0400-7*, Pub. by Jarrold Pub UK) Seven Hills Bk.

Rudyard Kipling. Richard LeGallienne. LC 73-21739. (English Literature Ser.: No. 33). 1974. lib. bdg. 49.95 (*0-8383-1838-X*) M S G Haskell Hse.

Rudyard Kipling. J. Palmer. LC 73-21706. (English Literature Ser.: No. 33). 1974. lib. bdg. 49.95 (*0-8383-1830-4*) M S G Haskell Hse.

Rudyard Kipling. deluxe ed. Date not set. write for info. (*0-517-20041-4*) Random Hse Value.

Rudyard Kipling: A Bibliographical Catalogue. James M. Stewart. Ed. by A. W. Yeats. LC 60-339. reprint ed. pap. 160.00 (*0-685-15456-4*, 2626548) Bks Demand.

Rudyard Kipling: A Study in Short Fiction. Helen P. Bauer. LC 94-6829. (Twayne's Studies in Short Fiction: No. 58). 192p. 1994. 23.95 (*0-8057-8345-8*, Twayne) Scribnrs Ref.

Rudyard Kipling: Author of the Jungle Books. Carol Greene. LC 94-11940. (Rookie Biographies Ser.). 48p. (J). (gr. k-3). 1994. pap. 4.95 (*0-516-44266-X*); lib. bdg. 18.30 (*0-516-04266-1*) Childrens.

***Rudyard Kipling: Great British & Irish Short Stories I.** Illus. by James McConnell. LC 94-75353. (Classic Short Stories Ser.). 80p. 1994. pap. 5.95 (*0-7854-0638-7*, 40043) Am Guidance.

Rudyard Kipling: Selected Stories. Rudyard Kipling. 346p. 1987. pap. 8.95 (*0-460-87220-6*, Everyman's Classic Lib) C E Tuttle.

Rudyard Kipling: The Complete Verse: New Edition. Rev. by James Fenwick. 704p. 1996. pap. 19.95 (*1-85626-179-4*, C Kyle) Trafalgar.

***Rudyard Kipling: Victorian Balladeer.** Chelsea House Publishing Staff. (Illustrated Poetry Anthology Ser.). 1997. 17.95 (*1-86019-202-5*) Chelsea Hse.

Rudyard Kipling & the Fiction of Adolescence. Robert F. Moss. LC 81-14561. 256p. 1982. text ed. 29.95 (*0-312-69549-7*) St Martin.

Rudyard Kipling in New England. Howard C. Rice. LC 72-6747. (English Biography Ser.: No. 31). 39p. 1972. reprint ed. lib. bdg. 50.95 (*0-8383-1635-2*) M S G Haskell Hse.

Rudyard Kipling to Rider Haggard. Morton Cohen. LC 68-22229. 196p. 1975. 18.00 (*0-8386-6881-X*) Fairleigh Dickinson.

Rudyard Kipling's Vermont Feud. Frederick F. Van De Water. LC 74-1100. (English Literature Ser.: No. 33). 1974. lib. bdg. 59.95 (*0-8383-2024-4*) M S G Haskell Hse.

Rudyard Kipling's Vermont Feud. Frederick F. Van De Water. LC 81-69854. (Illus.). 112p. reprint ed. pap. 5.95 (*0-914960-37-7*) Academy Bks.

***Rudy's Incredible Plant.** Kathe Levenson. (J). Date not set. write for info. (*0-688-03799-2*); lib. bdg. write for info. (*0-688-03800-X*) Lothrop.

***Rudy's Lessons for Yang Champions: Choices & Challenges.** Rudy Ruettiger et al. (Illus.). 195p. (Orig.). (J). (gr. 4-6). 1997. pap. 14.95 (*0-9658119-0-5*) Rudy Intl.

Rue aux Trois Poussins. Georges Simenon. (FRE.). 1992. pap. 11.95 (*0-7859-3260-7*, 2266052993) Fr & Eur.

Rue Cases-Negres see Black Shack Alley

Rue des Boutiques Obscures. Patrick Modiano. (FRE.). 1982. pap. 10.95 (*0-7859-2899-5*) Fr & Eur.

Rue des Boutiques Obscures. Patrick Modiano. (Folio Ser.: No. 1358). 250p. (FRE.). 1982. pap. 8.95 (*2-07-037358-4*) Schoenhof.

Rue des Ravissantes, et Neuf Autres Scenarios. Boris Vian. (FRE.). 1992. pap. 16.95 (*0-7859-3203-8*, 2264017368) Fr & Eur.

Rue du Havre. Paul Guimard. 160p. (FRE.). 1982. pap. 10.95 (*0-7859-2267-9*, 2070361276) Fr & Eur.

Rue du Retour. Abdellatif Laabi. Tr. by Jacqueline Kaye from FRE. LC 88-63241. 250p. (Orig.). 1989. 17.95 (*0-930523-64-4*); pap. 9.95 (*0-930523-65-2*) Readers Intl.

Rue Morgue Avenue. Boyle. 1995. 20.00 (*1-883402-42-5*) S&S Trade.

Rue Ordener, Rue Labat. Sarah Kofman. Tr. & Intro. by Ann Smock. LC 95-52462. (Stages Ser.: Vol. 7). xiii, 87p. (C). 1996. pap. 10.00 (*0-8032-7780-6*, Bison Books); text ed. 25.00 (*0-8032-2731-0*) U of Nebr Pr.

Rue Prevail Sextet. A. Farmer. 1995. pap. text ed. 20.00 (*0-7935-4838-1*) H Leonard.

Rue Sans Nom. Marcel Ayme. (FRE.). 1979. pap. 10.95 (*0-7859-1898-1*, 2070371255) Fr & Eur.

Rue Traversiere, et Autres Recits Sur Reve. N. Bonnefoy. (FRE.). 1992. pap. 16.95 (*0-7859-2829-4*) Fr & Eur.

Rueda en el Tejado - The Wheel on the School. Meindart Dejong. 1996. pap. text ed. 9.75 (*84-279-3217-0*) Lectorum Pubns.

***Rueful Death.** Susan W. Albert. 1997. mass mkt. 5.99 (*0-614-27730-2*, Prime Crime) Berkley Pub.

***Rueful Death.** Susan W. Albert. 288p. 1997. reprint ed. mass mkt. 5.99 (*0-425-15941-8*, Prime Crime) Berkley Pub.

Rueful Death: A China Bayles Mystery. Susan W. Albert. LC 95-26165. 320p. 1996. 21.95 (*0-425-15469-6*) Berkley Pub.

Ruettner, J. R. Festschrift. Ed. by H. J. Leu. (Journal: Experimental Cell Biology: Vol. 56, No. 4, 1988). (Illus.). 60p. 1988. pap. 32.00 (*3-8055-4923-7*) S Karger.

Ruff: New Kid Two for One Offer. 1995. 29.50 (*1-57135-026-8*) Living Bks.

Ruff Vol. 2: Individuality in a Gregarious Wading Bird. Johan G. Van Rhijn. 224p. 1991. text ed. 37.00 (*0-85661-062-3*, 784662, Pub. by Poyser UK) Acad Pr.

Ruff Country. Budge Ruffner. (Illus.). 198p. 1994. pap. 14.95 (*0-9624499-3-8*) Prickly AZ.

Ruff Tales: High Octane Stories from the Ruff Creek General Store. Joe McHugh. LC 87-92243. (Illus.). 144p. 1988. 11.95 (*0-9619943-0-4*) Catalpa Pr.

Ruffed Grouse. Ed. by Sally Atwater & Judith Schnell. LC 89-4636. (Wildlife Ser.). (Illus.). 384p. 1989. 59.95 (*0-8117-1650-3*) Stackpole.

Ruffed Grouse. Gordon Gullion. (Illus.). 144p. 1989. 19.95 (*1-55971-012-8*) NorthWord.

Ruffian. Jane Schwartz. (Orig.). 1994. mass mkt. 5.99 (*0-345-38602-7*) Ballantine.

***Ruffians.** Tim Green. 288p. 4.98 (*0-7651-0130-0*) Smithmark.

Ruffians Vol. 1. Tim Green. 1994. mass mkt. 5.99 (*0-312-95388-7*) St Martin.

Ruffian's Wage: Intelligence & Espionage in the Reign of Charles the Second, 1660-1685. Alan Marshall. LC 93-44477. (Cambridge Studies in Early Modern British History). (Illus.). 352p. (C). 1994. text ed. 59.95 (*0-521-43180-8*) Cambridge U Pr.

Ruffle, Coo & Hoo Doo. Randy Houk. (Humane Society of the U. S. Animal Tales Ser.). (Illus.). 32p. (J). (gr. 1-5). 1993. 12.95 (*1-882728-02-5*) Benefactory.

***Ruffle, Coo, & Hoo Doo.** Randy Houk. (Illus.). 32p. (J). (gr. 1-5). 1993. pap. 9.95 incl. audio (*1-882728-48-3*) Benefactory.

Ruffle, Coo & Hoo Doo, Incl. plush animal. Randy Houk. (Illus.). 32p. (J). (gr. 1-5). 1993. 34.95 incl. audio (*1-882728-17-3*) Benefactory.

***Ruffle, Coo, & Hoo Doo, Incl. plush animal.** Randy Houk. (Illus.). 32p. (J). (gr. 1-5). 1993. 29.95 (*1-882728-14-9*); pap. 19.95 incl. audio (*1-882728-38-6*); pap. 14.95 (*1-882728-43-2*) Benefactory.

Ruffled Feathers. Taylor McCafferty. Ed. by Jane Chelius. 224p. (Orig.). 1992. mass mkt. 4.50 (*0-671-72803-2*) PB.

Ruffles & Bows: The Complete Guide to Sewing for Baby Girls. Kathy Sandmann. (Illus.). 96p. (Orig.). 1985. pap. text ed. 7.95 (*0-937679-00-3*) Sewing Sampler.

Ruffles & Flourishes. Liz Carpenter. LC 92-34545. (Illus.). 388p. 1993. reprint ed. pap. 11.95 (*0-89096-548-X*) Tex A&M Univ Pr.

Ruffles on My Longjohns. Isabel Edwards. 298p. 1988. pap. 17.95 (*0-88839-102-1*) Hancock House.

***Ruffles on My Longjohns.** large type ed. Isabel Edwards. (Ulverscroft Large Print Ser.). 576p. 1997. 27.50 (*0-7089-3752-7*) Ulverscroft.

Ruffly Speaking. large type ed. Susan Conant. LC 94-28127. 410p. 1994. lib. bdg. 20.95 (*0-7862-0313-7*) Thorndike Pr.

Ruffly Speaking: A Dog Lover's Mystery. Susan Conant. 304p. 1994. mass mkt. 5.99 (*0-553-29484-9*) Bantam.

Ruffo: My Parabola. Titta Ruffo. (Great Voices Ser.: Vol. 1). (Illus.). 490p. 1995. 38.00 (*1-880909-39-1*) Baskerville.

Ruff's Bone. Noyes. 1994. 23.75 (*1-57135-107-8*) Living Bks.

Rufian Dichoso. Miguel de Cervantes Saavedra. 125p. (SPA.). 1977. 7.95 (*0-8288-7058-6*) Fr & Eur.

Rufin von Aquileia, De Ieiunio I, II, Zwei Predigten uber das Fasten nach Basileios von Kaisareia. Heinrich Marti. LC 89-35687. (Supplements to Vigiliae Christianae Ser.: Vol. 6). xxxiii, 56p. (GER.). 1989. 34.50 (*90-04-08897-0*) E J Brill.

Rufino Tamayo: Myth & Magic. Octavio Paz. Tr. by Rachel Phillips from SPA. LC 79-63734. (Illus.). (Orig.). 1979. pap. 12.95 (*0-89207-019-6*) S R Guggenheim.

Rufinus: A Commentary of the Apostles' Creed. Ed. by W. J. Burghardt et al. LC 78-62468. (Ancient Christian Writers Ser.: No. 20). 167p. 1955. 14.95 (*0-8091-0257-9*) Paulist Pr.

Rufus. Grace Chetwin. (Illus.). 32p. (J). (ps-k). 1996. boxed 15.95 incl. audio (*0-9649349-0-6*) Feral Press.

Rufus. Rutherford G. Montgomery. LC 78-150819. (Illus.). (Orig.). (J). (gr. 4-8). 1973. 4.95 (*0-87004-227-0*) Caxton.

Rufus. Tomi Ungerer. (SPA.). (J). 8.50 (*84-204-3706-9*) Santillana.

Rufus. 2nd ed. Ronald Fair. LC 79-88743. 58p. (YA). (gr. 7-12). 1980. reprint ed. per. 4.00 (*0-916418-21-9*) Lotus.

Rufus: A Dog's Tale. Karl Pruter. 42p. 1994. lib. bdg. 23.00 (*0-8095-6605-2*) Borgo Pr.

Rufus & Christopher & the Box of Laughter. Hastings. LC 77-190270. (Rufus & Christopher Ser.). (Illus.). 32p. (J). (gr. 2-4). 1972. lib. bdg. 9.95 (*0-87783-060-6*); audio 7.94 (*0-87783-196-3*) Oddo.

Rufus & Christopher & the Box of Laughter. deluxe ed. Hastings. LC 77-190270. (Rufus & Christopher Ser.). (Illus.). 32p. (J). (gr. 2-4). 1972. pap. 3.94 (*0-87783-106-8*) Oddo.

Rufus & Christopher & the Magic Bubble. Hastings. LC 73-87799. (Rufus & Christopher Ser.). (Illus.). 32p. (J). (gr. k-2). 1974. lib. bdg. 9.95 (*0-87783-127-0*); audio 7.94 (*0-87783-197-1*) Oddo.

Rufus & Christopher & the Magic Bubble. deluxe ed. Hastings. LC 73-87799. (Rufus & Christopher Ser.). (Illus.). 32p. (J). (gr. k-2). 1974. pap. 3.94 (*0-87783-128-9*) Oddo.

Rufus & Christopher in the Land of Lies. Hastings. LC 70-190271. (Rufus & Christopher Ser.). (Illus.). 32p. (J). (gr. 2-4). 1972. lib. bdg. 9.95 (*0-87783-061-4*); audio 7.94 (*0-87783-198-X*) Oddo.

Rufus & Christopher in the Land of Lies. deluxe ed. Hastings. LC 70-190271. (Rufus & Christopher Ser.). (Illus.). 32p. (J). (gr. 2-4). 1972. pap. 3.94 (*0-87783-107-6*) Oddo.

Rufus & Christopher Series, 3 vols. Hastings. (Illus.). (J). (gr. 2-4). audio 23.82 (*0-87783-234-X*) Oddo.

Rufus & Christopher Series, 3 vols., Set. Hastings. (Illus.). (J). (gr. 2-4). lib. bdg. 29.95 (*0-87783-168-8*) Oddo.

Rufus & Christopher Series, 3 vols., Set. deluxe ed. Hastings. (Illus.). (J). (gr. 2-4). pap. 11.82 (*0-87783-169-6*) Oddo.

Rufus & Rachel. unabridged ed. Joseph A. Boyd, Jr. (Illus.). 156p. (Orig.). (J). (gr. k-6). 1991. pap. write for info. (*1-888781-03-3*) J A Boyd.

Rufus & Rose. Horatio Alger, Jr. (Works of Horatio Alger Jr.). 1989. reprint ed. lib. bdg. 79.00 (*0-685-27561-2*) Rprt Serv.

***Rufus & the Nitwits, Vol. 1.** large type ed. Melody Singer. (Illus.). 67p. (J). (gr. 4-6). 1996. 16.00 (*0-9655349-0-1*) Rufus Pr.

Rufus Jones, Master Quaker. David Hinshaw. LC 74-133522. (Select Bibliographies Reprint Ser.). 1977. reprint ed. 23.95 (*0-8369-5554-4*) Ayer.

Rufus King, American Federalist. Robert Ernst. LC 68-15747. 466p. reprint ed. pap. 132.90 (*0-8357-3921-X*, 2036656) Bks Demand.

Rufus W. Adams: The Historic Adams Ranch. Intro. by Kathryn M. Totton. 246p. 1982. lib. bdg. 43.50 (*1-56475-214-3*); fiche write for info. (*1-56475-215-1*) U NV Oral Hist.

Rufus Woods, the Columbia River, & the Building of Modern Washington. Robert E. Ficken. (Illus.). 316p. 1995. pap. 25.00 (*0-87422-122-6*) Wash St U Pr.

Rufus's Big Day. Jane L. Wilson. LC 96-10309. (Illus.). 29p. (J). 1996. 12.95 (*1-56763-094-4*); pap. 3.45 (*1-56763-095-2*) Ozark Pub.

R

R

Rug & Carpet Cleaning: A Comprehensive Technical Guide for Training & Professional Certification. 3rd rev. ed. William R. Griffin et al. Ed. by Gary Kanter. (Illus.). 283p. 1988. pap. 23.00 (0-944352-06-5) Cleaning Cons.
Rug Before My Time: Memoirs of Pecker the Cat. Pecker The Cat. (Illus.). 32p. (J). 1982. pap. 1.25 (0-9604894-1-X) Borf Bks.
Rug Hook Book: Techniques, Projects & Patterns for This Easy. Ed. by Thom Boswell. (Illus.). 144p. 1994. pap. 16.95 (0-8069-8359-0) Sterling.
Rug Merchants of Chaos & Other Plays. Ronald Ribman. LC 92-2568. 240p. 1992. 24.95 (1-55936-050-X); pap. 12.95 (1-55936-049-6) Theatre Comm.
Rug Weaver's Source Book. Ed. by Linda C. Ligon. LC 84-82358. (Illus.). 176p. 1986. pap. 20.00 (0-934026-16-5) Interweave.
Rug Weaving Techniques: Beyond the Basics. Peter Collingwood. (Illus.). 160p. 1991. pap. 29.95 (0-934026-62-9) Interweave.
***Rugby.** LC 97-18823. (Know the Sport Ser.). (Illus.). 48p. 1997. pap. 5.95 (0-8117-2837-4) Stackpole.
Rugby: A Player's Guide to the Laws. Derek Robinson. 192p. 1996. pap. 10.00 (0-00-218700-0) HarpC.
Rugby: Body & Soul. Bill Samuel. 155p. (C). 1986. text ed. 49.00 (0-86383-289-X, Pub. by Gomer Pr UK) St Mut.
***Rugby: Steps to Success.** Tony Biscombe & Peter Drewett. (Illus.). (Orig.). 1997. pap. 16.95 (0-88011-509-2, PBIS0509) Human Kinetics.
Rugby: The All Black's Way. J. J. Stewart. (Illus.). 168p. 1992. pap. 24.95 (1-85223-629-9, Pub. by Crowood Pr UK) Trafalgar.
Rugby & Rosie. Nan Rossiter. (J). 1997. pap. 14.99 (0-525-45484-5) NAL-Dutton.
Rugby Disunion: The Making of Three World Cups. Derek Wyatt. (Illus.). 256p. 1996. 39.95 (0-85493-241-0, Pub. by V Gollancz UK) Trafalgar.
***Rugby Disunion: The Making of Three World Cups.** Derek Wyatt. (Illus.). 224p. 1997. pap. 15.95 (0-575-60015-2, Pub. by V Gollancz UK) Trafalgar.
Rugby for Three-Quarters. Peter Johnson. pap. 18.95 (0-7136-3782-X, 92984, Pub. by A&C Black UK) Talman.
Rugby Lesson Plans for Three-Quarters. Peter Johnson. pap. 17.95 (0-7136-4041-3, 93302, Pub. by A&C Black UK) Talman.
Rugby Tactics. Peter Winder. (Illus.). 128p. 1992. pap. 19.95 (0-7136-3449-9, Pub. by A&C Black UK) Talman.
Rugby, Tennessee. Thomas Hughes. LC 74-31275. (American Utopian Adventure Ser.). x, 168p. 1975. reprint ed. lib. bdg. 29.50 (0-87991-018-6) Porcupine Pr.
Rugby Training. Barrie Corless et al. (Illus.). 128p. 1996. pap. 19.95 (1-85223-897-6, Pub. by Crowood Pr UK) Trafalgar.
Rugby Training. Winder. pap. 19.95 (0-7136-3267-4, 92254, Pub. by A&C Black UK) Talman.
***Rugby Union.** Peter Johnson. (Crowood Sports Guide Ser.). (Illus.). 128p. 1997. pap. 22.95 (1-86126-028-8, Pub. by Crowood Pr UK) Trafalgar.
Rugby World Cup '95: In Association with Scottish Life. Ed. by Ian Robertson. (Illus.). 192p. 1995. 35.00 (0-340-64953-4, Pub. by H & S UK) Trafalgar.
Ruger. R. L. Wilson. 1996. 65.00 (0-684-80367-4) S&S Trade.
Ruger 10-22. William Workman. LC 93-80098. (Illus.). 320p. 1994. pap. 19.95 (0-87341-277-X, RT01) Krause Pubns.
Ruger 1022 Exotic Weapons System. rev. ed. (Exotic Weapons Systems Ser.). (Illus.). 96p. 1989. pap. 16.00 (0-87364-514-6) Paladin Pr.
Ruger .22 Automatic Pistol: Standard-Mark I-Mark II Series. Duncan Long. (Illus.). 168p. 1988. pap. 12.00 (0-87364-488-3) Paladin Pr.
Rugg: The Descendents of John Rugg. E. R. Rugg. 580p. 1990. reprint ed. pap. 86.00 (0-8328-1623-X); reprint ed. lib. bdg. 94.00 (0-8328-1622-1) Higginson Bk Co.
Rugged & Sublime: The Civil War in Arkansas. Ed. by Mark K. Christ. (Illus.). 192p. 1994. 25.00 (1-55728-356-7); pap. 16.00 (1-55728-357-5) U of Ark Pr.
Rugged Flanks of Caucasus, 2 Vols. John F. Baddeley. LC 73-6267. (Middle East Ser.). 1973. reprint ed. 60.95 (0-405-05321-5) Ayer.
Rugged Hills, Gentle Folk: My Friends & Neighbors in the Big Pine Valley. William J. Weber. Ed. by Nick Pabst. LC 94-69754. 148p. 1995. 14.95 (0-89821-134-4, 19963) Reiman Pubns.
Rugged Individualism Reconsidered: Essays in Psychological Anthropology. Francis L. Hsu. LC 82-13687. 482p. (C). 1983. text ed. 42.50 (0-87049-370-1); pap. text ed. 19.95 (0-87049-371-X) U of Tenn Pr.
Rugged Justice: The Ninth Circuit Court of Appeals & the American West, 1891-1941. David C. Frederick. LC 93-1309. 1994. 40.00 (0-520-08381-4) U CA Pr.
***Rugged Southern Appalachia.** Willard Mounts. Ed. by Beatrice Brandhorst. LC 96-80009. (Illus.). 192p. (Orig.). 1997. per., pap. 14.95 (0-9630038-2-8) Ginwill Pub.
Rugged Terrain: A True Story of Life Survival. 2nd rev. ed. Jose B. Viloria, Jr. Ed. by Jonathan Briones & Noel T. Castorillo. (Illus.). 500p. (Orig.). 1995. 17.99 (0-9623298-4-3); pap. 24.95 (0-9623298-3-5) SGV Pub Co.
Rugged Vessels. Patricia Turnbull. 42p. 1992. pap. 8.00 (0-9635523-0-9) Archipelago.
***Rugged Walker.** Patricia Kirk. (Illus.). 200p. (Orig.). 1997. pap. 15.95 (0-88011-689-7, PKIR0689) Human Kinetics.
Rugged Years on the Alaska Frontier. Emil Goulet. (American Autobiography Ser.). 304p. 1995. reprint ed. lib. bdg. 89.00 (0-7812-8536-4) Rprt Serv.
Rugging Room Coloring Book: A Collection of Designs for Hooked Rugs from the Rugging Room. (Illus.). 1990. pap. write for info. (0-9611554-5-0) Rugging Rm.
Ruggles Family of England & America. E. Stoddard Ruggles. (Illus.). 232p. 1995. reprint ed. pap. 36.00 (0-8328-4942-1); reprint ed. lib. bdg. 46.00 (0-8328-4941-3) Higginson Bk Co.
Ruggles of New York: A Life of Samuel B. Ruggles. Daniel G. Thompson. LC 76-76651. (Columbia University. Studies in the Social Sciences: No. 524). reprint ed. 21.00 (0-404-51524-X) AMS Pr.
Ruggles' Regiment: The 122nd New York Volunteers in the American Civil War. David B. Swinfen. LC 81-69940. 176p. reprint ed. pap. 50.20 (0-7837-0381-3, 2040701) Bks Demand.
Rugg's Recommendations on the Colleges. 12th ed. Frederick E. Rugg. LC 89-62896. 144p. 1995. pap. 18.95 (1-883062-06-3) Ruggs Recommend.
Rugg's Recommendations on the Colleges. 13th ed. Frederick E. Rugg. LC 89-62896. 148p. 1996. 18.95 (1-883062-09-8) Ruggs Recommend.
Rugg's Recommendations on the Colleges. 14th rev. ed. Frederick E. Rugg. LC 89-62896. 156p. (YA). (gr. 11-12). 1997. pap. 19.95 (1-883062-14-4) Ruggs Recommend.
***Rugg's Recommendations on the Colleges.** 15th rev. ed. Frederick E. Rugg. 172p. (YA). (gr. 11-12). 1998. 19.95 (1-883062-22-5) Ruggs Recommend.
Rugrats. Wigand. LC 96-24132. (Ready-to-Read Ser.: No. 1). (J). 1997. 3.99 (0-689-81259-0) S&S Childrens.
Rugrats. Wigand. LC 96-24130. (Ready-to-Read Ser.: No. 2). (J). 1997. 3.99 (0-689-81260-4) S&S Childrens.
Rugrats, No. 1. St. Pierre. 1997. pap. 3.25 (0-689-81274-4) S&S Childrens.
Rugrats, No. 2. St. Pierre. 1997. pap. 3.25 (0-689-81275-2) S&S Childrens.
***Rugrats & Rawhide.** Peggy Moreland. 1997. pap. 3.99 (0-373-24084-8, 1-24084-5) Silhouette.
***Rugrats Book of Chanukah.** Sarah Willson. (J). 1997. pap. text ed. 6.99 (0-689-81676-6, Aladdin Paperbacks) S&S Childrens.
***Rugs & Carpets: Techniques, Traditions & Designs.** Andrew Middleton. (Illus.). 192p. 1996. 30.00 (1-85732-634-2, Pub. by Reed Illust Books UK) Antique Collect.
Rugs & Carpets from Central Asia. Elena Tsariova. (Allen Lane Bk.). (Illus.). 1984. 25.00 (0-7139-1504-8) Viking Penguin.
***Rugs & Carpets of the World.** I. Bennett. 1996. 29.98 (0-7858-0201-0) Bk Sales Inc.
Rugs & Posts: The Story of Navajo Weaving & the Role of the Indian Trader. H. L. James. LC 88-61473. (Illus.). 160p. 1988. pap. 19.95 (0-88740-134-1) Schiffer.
Rugs of Teec Nos Pos: Jewels of the Navajo Loom. Ruth K. Belikove. LC 94-7094. (Illus.). 48p. (Orig.). (C). 1994. pap. 22.50 (0-9633710-1-0) Adobe Gallery.
Rugs of the Caucasus: Structure & Design. Peter F. Stone. LC 84-80392. (Illus.). 188p. 1984. 32.50 (0-940582-01-5) Greenleaf Co.
Rugs to Riches: An Insider's Guide to Buying Oriental Rugs. Caroline Bosly. (Illus.). 1985. pap. 17.00 (0-394-73957-4) Pantheon.
Ruhela Chieftaincies: The Rise & Fall of Ruhela Power in India in the Eighteenth Century. Iqbal Husain. (Illus.). 256p. (C). 1994. 17.95 (0-19-563068-8, 14342) OUP.
Ruhleben: A Prison Camp Society. Frwd. by John D. Ketchum & Robert B. MacLeod. LC 65-1938. (Illus.). 431p. reprint ed. pap. 122.90 (0-317-09620-6, 2014269) Bks Demand.
Ruhmann & Beasley Family Roots: A Revised Edition of Ruhmann Roots, Limbs & Branches. rev. ed. Dorothy B. Ruhmann. LC 93-87095. (Illus.). 405p. 1993. pap. 49.95 (0-9638818-0-9) Ruhmann Pr.
Ruhr. (Panorama Bks.). (Illus.). (FRE.). 3.95 (0-685-11549-6) Fr & Eur.
Ruhr-Lorraine Industrial Problem. Guy Greer. (Brookings Institution Reprint Ser.). reprint ed. lib. bdg. 37.00 (0-697-00156-3) Irvington.
Rui Barbosa, Brazilian Crusader. C. W. Turner. 1977. lib. bdg. 34.95 (0-8490-2547-8) Gordon Pr.
Ruidoso Country. Frank Mangan & Judy Mangan. LC 94-20105. (Illus.). 192p. 1994. 39.95 (0-930208-33-1) Mangan Books TX.
Ruin. Beppe Fenoglio. Tr. by John Shepley from ITA. LC 92-80362. 94p. 1992. 25.95 (0-910395-83-7) Marlboro Pr.
Ruin. Beppe Fenoglio. Tr. by John Shepley from ITA. LC 92-80362. 94p. 1994. pap. 9.95 (0-910395-84-5) Marlboro Pr.
Ruin. Michael O'Brien. 32p. 1986. pap. 5.00 (1-886044-02-3) Cairn Editions.
***Ruin & Restitution: Reinterpreting Romanticism in Spain.** Philip W. Silver. LC 97-4823. 208p. 1997. 29.95 (0-8265-1289-5) Vanderbilt U Pr.
Ruin Creek. large type ed. David Payne. LC 93-45632. 1994. lib. bdg. 23.95 (0-8161-5948-3, GK Hall) Thorndike Pr.
Ruin Creek Vol. 1. David Payne. 1994. mass mkt. 5.50 (0-312-95389-5) St Martin.
Ruin from the Air. Gordon Thomas. 23.95 (0-8488-1204-2) Amereon Ltd.
***Ruin from the Air.** Gordon Thomas. 25.95 (1-56723-093-8) Yestermorrow.
Ruin Islanders: Early Thule Culture Pioneers in the Eastern High Arctic. Karen M. McCullough. (Merury Ser.: No. 141). (Illus.). 368p. 1989. pap. 29.95 (0-660-10793-7, Pub. by Can Mus Civil CN) U of Wash Pr.
Ruin of Antichrist. John Bunyan. pap. 1.99 (0-87377-986-X) GAM Pubns.
Ruin of Kasch. Roberto Calasso. Tr. by William Weaver & Stephen Sartorelli from ITA. LC 94-5383. Orig. Title: Rovina di Kasch. 400p. 1996. pap. text ed. 24.95 (0-674-78026-4) Belknap Pr.
Ruin of Kasch. Roberto Calasso. Tr. by William Weaver & Stephen Sartarelli. Orig. Title: Rovina di Kasch. 400p. 1996. pap. 14.95 (0-674-78029-9) HUP.
Ruin of Representation in Modernist Art & Texts. Jo A. Isaak. LC 86-19289. (Studies in the Fine Arts - Art Theory: No. 13). 180p. reprint ed. pap. 51.30 (0-8357-1895-6, 2070659) Bks Demand.
Ruin Probability. Soren Asmussen. (Advanced Series on Statistical & Applied Probability). 250p. 1997. text ed. 38.00 (981-02-2293-9) World Scientific Pub.
Ruin Redemption. W. F. Bell. pap. 6.00 (0-87377-122-2) GAM Pubns.
Ruin the Sacred Truths: Poetry & Belief from the Bible to the Present. Harold Bloom. LC 88-21651. (Charles Eliot Norton Lectures). 204p. 1989. 32.00 (0-674-78027-2) HUP.
Ruin the Sacred Truths: Poetry & Belief from the Bible to the Present. Harold Bloom. (Charles Eliot Norton Lectures). 204p. (C). 1989. pap. text ed. 9.95 (0-674-78028-0) HUP.
Ruined by Reading: A Life in Books. Lynne Sharon Schwartz. LC 95-43482. 128p. 1996. 18.00 (0-8070-7082-3) Beacon Pr.
***Ruined by Reading: A Life in Books.** Lynne Sharon Schwartz. 1997. pap. text ed. 10.00 (0-8070-7083-1) Beacon Pr.
***Ruined Cities.** Vern Rutsala. LC 86-72300. (Poetry Ser.). 72p. (C). 1987. pap. 11.95 (0-88748-041-1) Carnegie-Mellon.
Ruined Cities of Ceylon. H. W. Cave. (Illus.). 136p. 1986. reprint ed. 44.00 (0-8364-1745-3, Pub. by Chanakya II) S Asia.
Ruined Cities of Iraq. S. Lloyd. (Illus.). 72p. 1980. pap. 15.00 (0-89005-375-8) Ares.
Ruined Cities of Mashonaland. James T. Bent. LC 70-161256. (Black Heritage Library Collection). 1977. reprint ed. 32.95 (0-8369-8528-1) Ayer.
Ruined City. Nevil Shute. 23.95 (0-8488-1166-6) Amereon Ltd.
Ruined Cottage & The Pedlar. William Wordsworth. Ed. by James Butler. LC 78-58066. (Cornell Wordsworth Ser.). (Illus.). 512p. 1978. 80.00 (0-8014-1153-X) Cornell U Pr.
Ruined Eden of the Present: Hawthorne, Melville, & Poe: Critical Essays in Honor of Darrel Abel. Ed. by G. R. Thompson & Virgil L. Lokke. LC 80-80816. (Illus.). 408p. 1981. 15.75 (0-911198-60-1) Purdue U Pr.
Ruined House. Mick Manning. LC 93-21295. (Illus.). 32p. (J). (gr. k-4). 1996. reprint ed. pap. 5.99 (1-56402-936-0) Candlewick Pr.
Ruined Map: A Novel. Kobo Abe. Tr. by E. Dale Saunders from JPN. LC 92-16918. 320p. 1993. reprint ed. pap. 13.00 (4-7700-1635-2) Kodansha.
Ruined Pages: Selected Poems. Padraic Fiacc. Ed. by Gerald Dawe & Aodan Mac Poilin. 171p. 9400. pap. 15.95 (0-85640-529-9, Pub. by Blackstaff Pr IE) Dufour.
***Ruins.** Kevin J. Anderson. 1997. mass mkt. 5.99 (0-06-105736-3, HarperPrism) HarpC.
***Ruins.** limited ed. Kevin Anderson. 304p. 1996. mass mkt. 50.00 (0-06-105273-6, HarperPrism) HarpC.
Ruins along the River: Montezuma Castle, Tuzigoot & Montezuma Well National Monuments. Carle Hodge. Ed. by T. J. Priehs & Carolyn Dodson. LC 86-61462. (Illus.). 48p. (Orig.). 1986. pap. 4.95 (0-911408-68-1) SW Pks Mnmts.
Ruins & Empire: The Evolution of a Theme in Augustan & Romantic Literature. Laurence Goldstein. LC 76-50889. 286p. reprint ed. pap. 81.60 (0-317-26643-8, 2025438) Bks Demand.
Ruins & Excavations of Ancient Rome. Rodolfo Lanciani. LC 67-29706. (Illus.). 1972. reprint ed. 52.95 (0-405-08729-2, Pub. by Blom Pubns UK) Ayer.
Ruins & the Law of Nature: Meditation on the Revolutions of Empires. C. F. Volney. 226p. 1987. reprint ed. spiral bd. 21.00 (0-7873-0911-7) Hlth Research.
Ruins at Kiatuthlanna, Eastern Arizona. Frank Roberts, Jr. (Bureau of American Ethnology Bulletins Ser.). 195p. 1995. lib. bdg. 79.00 (0-7812-4100-6) Rprt Serv.
***Ruins of Athens.** Peter Liotta. 68p. (Orig.). 1998. pap. 14.95 (1-882329-08-2) Garden St Pr.
Ruins of Civility. James Bradberry. 256p. 1996. 21.95 (0-312-14041-X) St Martin.
Ruins of Desert Cathay. M. Aurel Stein. (C). 1990. 68.50 (81-85418-85-3, Pub. by Low Price II) S Asia.
Ruins of Desert Cathay: Personal Narrative of Explorations in Central Asia & Westernmost China, 2 vols., 1. M. Aurel Stein. 1376p. 1987. reprint ed. pap. 15.95 (0-486-25351-1) Dover.
Ruins of Desert Cathay: Personal Narrative of Explorations in Central Asia & Westernmost China, 2 vols., 2. M. Aurel Stein. 1376p. 1987. reprint ed. pap. 15.95 (0-486-25404-6) Dover.
Ruins of Desert Cathay: Personal Narrative of Explorations in Central Asia & Westernmost China, 3 Vols., Set. M. Aurel Stein. LC 68-56900. (Illus.). 1972. reprint ed. 87.95 (0-405-08996-1) Ayer.
Ruins of Desert Cathay: Personal Narrative of Explorations in Central Asia & Westernmost China, 3 Vols., Vol. 1. M. Aurel Stein. LC 68-56900. (Illus.). 1968. reprint ed. 32.95 (0-685-00514-3) Ayer.
Ruins of Desert Cathay: Personal Narrative of Explorations in Central Asia & Westernmost China, 3 Vols., Vol. 2. M. Aurel Stein. LC 68-56900. (Illus.). 1972. reprint ed. 32.95 (0-405-08998-8) Ayer.
Ruins of Desert Cathay: Personal Narrative of Explorations in Central Asia & Westernmost China, 3 Vols., Vol. 3. M. Aurel Stein. LC 68-56900. (Illus.). 1972. reprint ed. 32.95 (0-405-08999-6) Ayer.
Ruins of Empires. C. F. Volney. (African Heritage Classical Research Studies). 225p. reprint ed. 15.00 (0-938818-62-7) ECA Assoc.
Ruins of Empires: or Meditation on the Revolution of Empires & the Law of Nature. C. F. Volney. LC 90-82691. 225p. 1990. reprint ed. pap. 11.95 (0-933121-52-0) Black Classic.
Ruins of Montarek: Spatial Visualization. Glenda Lappan et al. (Connected Mathematics Ser.). (Illus.). 1996. teacher ed. 16.50 (1-57232-161-X, 21456) Seymour Pubns.
Ruins of Montarek: Spatial Visualization. Glenda Lappan et al. (Connected Mathematics Ser.). (Illus.). (J). (gr. 6). 1996. wbk. ed. 5.95 (1-57232-160-1, 21455) Seymour Pubns.
***Ruins of Montarek: Spatial Visualization.** rev. ed. Glenda Lappan et al. Ed. by Catherine Anderson et al. (Connected Mathematics Ser.). (Illus.). 85p. (YA). (gr. 6 up). 1997. student ed., pap. text ed. 5.95 (1-57232-622-0, 45817) Seymour Pubns.
***Ruins of Montarek: Spatial Visualization.** rev. ed. Glenda Lappan et al. Ed. by Catherine Anderson et al. (Connected Mathematics Ser.). (Illus.). 166p. (YA). (gr. 6 up). 1997. teacher ed., pap. text ed. 16.50 (1-57232-623-9, 45818) Seymour Pubns.
***Ruins of Paris.** Jacques Reda. Tr. by Mark Treharne from FRE. (Topographics Ser.). 144p. 1997. pap. 18.95 (0-948462-93-0, Pub. by Reaktion Bks UK) Consort Bk Sales.
Ruins of Providence: Local Pieces. Keith Waldrop. LC 83-15119. 53p. (Orig.). 1983. pap. 5.00 (0-914278-41-X) Copper Beech.
Ruins of Ranghar. Mike Carr. 1983. 1.95 (0-394-72315-5) Random.
Ruins of Rome: A Guide to the Classical Antiquities. C. Wade Meade. LC 80-81128. (Illus.). 1980. 21.95 (0-936638-00-1); pap. 16.95 (0-936638-01-X) Palatine Pubns.
Ruins of the Morning. S. C. Saha. 8.00 (0-89253-729-9); text ed. 4.00 (0-89253-730-2) Ind-US Inc.
Ruins of the Saga Time. Erlingsson Thorsteinn. LC 76-43951. (Viking Society for Northern Research, Extra Ser.: No. 2). (Illus.). 120p. reprint ed. 39.50 (0-404-60022-0) AMS Pr.
Ruins of the Southwest. Ed. by Jeff Nicholas. (Wish You Were Here Postcard Bks.). (Illus.). 32p. 1993. pap. 4.95 (0-939365-23-5) Sierra Pr CA.
Ruins of Undermountain. Ed Greenwood. 1991. 25.00 (1-56076-061-3) TSR Inc.
Ruins of Undermountain II. TSR Inc. Staff. (Illus.). 1994. 25.00 (1-56076-821-5) TSR Inc.
Ruins of Zhentil Keep. 1995. 25.00 (0-7869-0109-8) TSR Inc.
Ruins Official Strategy Guide. Brady Games Staff. 1996. 19.99 (1-56686-496-8) Brady Pub.
Ruins or Meditation of the Revolutions of Empires, Vol. 1. C. F. Volney. 152p. 1990. pap. text ed. 7.50 (0-916157-23-7) African Islam Miss Pubns.
Ruins or Meditation of the Revolutions of Empires, Vol. 2. C. F. Volney. Ed. by Al I. Obaba. 138p. 1990. pap. text ed. 7.50 (0-916157-33-4) African Islam Miss Pubns.
Ruins or Meditations on the Revolutions of Empires & the Law of Nature (1890) C. F. Volney. 248p. 1996. pap. 19.95 (1-56459-785-7) Kessinger Pub.
Rukovodstvo k Izucheniju Svijashchennago Pisanija Vjetkhago Zavjeta, 3 vols. Archpriest Michael Kheraskov & D. Athanasiev. 942p. reprint ed. pap. text ed. 32.00 (0-317-29295-1) Holy Trinity.
Rukovodstvo k Izuchjeniju Svjashchennago Pisanija Novago Zavjeta-Tchetvjerojevangelija. Archbishop Averky Taushev. 345p. 1974. pap. text ed. 12.00 (0-317-29299-4) Holy Trinity.
Rukovodstvo po Gomiletikje. Archbishop Averky Taushev. 110p. 1961. pap. text ed. 5.00 (0-317-30276-0) Holy Trinity.
Rule & End in Morals. John H. Muirhead. LC 74-99665. (Select Bibliographies Reprint Ser.). 1977. 19.95 (0-8369-5094-1) Ayer.
Rule & Exercises of Holy Dying: Means & Instruments of Preparing Ourselves & Others Respectively for a Blessed Death. Jeremy Taylor. Ed. by Robert J. Kastenbaum & Thomas Thirlwall. LC 76-19590. (Death & Dying Ser.). 1977. reprint ed. lib. bdg. 28.95 (0-405-09585-6) Ayer.
Rule & Exercises of Holy Living & the Rule & Exercises of Holy Dying. Jeremy Taylor. LC 82-80478. (Treasures from the Spiritual Classics Ser.). 64p. 1982. reprint ed. pap. 3.95 (0-8192-1309-8) Morehouse Pub.
Rule & Order: Dutch Planning Doctrine in the Twentieth Century. Andreas Faludi & Arnold Van der Valk. LC 93-38215. 288p. (C). 1994. lib. bdg. 120.00 (0-7923-2619-9) Kluwer Ac.
Rule & Regulations of Brahmanical Asceticism. Patrick Olivelle. LC 94-36124. (SUNY Series in Religious Studies). 458p. 1994. pap. text ed. 18.95 (0-7914-2284-4) State U NY Pr.
Rule & Regulations of Brahmanical Asceticism. Patrick Olivelle. LC 94-36124. (SUNY Series in Religious Studies). 458p. 1994. text ed. 57.50 (0-7914-2283-6) State U NY Pr.
Rule & Testament of St. Clare & Constitutions of the Poor Clares. 134p. 1987. 7.50 (0-8199-0907-6, Frncscn Herld) Franciscan Pr.
Rule & the Model: On the Theory of Architecture & Urbanism. Francoise Choay. (Illus.). 400p. (C). Date not set. 40.00 (0-262-03226-0) MIT Pr.
***Rule-Based Programming.** Thaddeus J. Kowalski & Leon S. Levy. LC 96-31374. (Kluwer International Series in Engineering & Computer Science: Vol. 369). 328p. (C). 1996. lib. bdg. 125.00 (0-7923-9769-X) Kluwer Ac.
Rule-Based Programming with OPS5. Thomas Cooper & Nancy Wogrin. 349p. (C). 1988. text ed. 49.95 (0-934613-51-6) Morgan Kaufmann.

An Asterisk (*) at the beginning of an entry indicates that the title is appearing in BIP for the first time.

R

Rule Book. Diagram Group Staff. 1987. pap. 14.95 (*0-312-00677-2*) St Martin.

Rule Breaker. Cassie Miles. (Intrigue Ser.). 1996. mass mkt. 3.75 (*0-373-22381-1*, 1-22381-7) Harlequin Bks.

Rule Britannia: Women, Empire, & Victorian Writing. Deirdre David. (Illus.). 256p. 1996. 37.50 (*0-8014-3170-0*); pap. 15.95 (*0-8014-8277-1*) Cornell U Pr.

Rule by Records: Land Registration & Village Customs in Early British Panjab. Richard S. Smith. (Illus.). 488p. 1996. text ed. 39.95 (*0-19-563673-2*) OUP.

Rule Eleven in Transition: The Report of the Third Circuit Task Force on Federal Rule of Civil Procedure 11. Stephen B. Burbank. LC 89-80411. 216p. (Orig.). 1989. pap. 20.00 (*0-938870-41-6*) Am Judicature.

Rule Eleven Sanctions in Civil Litigation (1992) 177p. 1992. pap. text ed. 25.00 (*1-56986-014-9*) Federal Bar.

***Rule-Following & Realism.** LC 96-51880. 1997. write for info. (*0-674-78031-0*) HUP.

Rule for a New Brother. H. Van der Looy. (Illus.). 94p. 1987. pap. 4.95 (*0-87243-165-7*) Templegate.

Rule Generalization Second Optionality in Language Change. Keyser & O'Neil. (Studies in Generative Grammar: No. 23). 153p. 1985. pap. 38.50 (*90-6765-127-3*) Mouton.

Rule Golden & Double Meaning. Damon Knight. 1991. pap. 3.95 (*0-8125-1294-4*) Tor Bks.

Rule-Governed Behavior: Cognition, Contingencies, & Instructional Control. Ed. by S. C. Hayes. LC 89-35845. (Applied Clinical Psychology Ser.). (Illus.). 412p. 1989. 65.00 (*0-306-43172-6*, Plenum Pr) Plenum.

Rule-Governed Linguistic Behavior. Raymond D. Gumb. (Janua Linguarum, Ser. Minor: No. 141). 139p. 1972. pap. text ed. 24.65 (*90-279-2316-7*) Mouton.

Rule Induction in Knowledge Engineering Data Analysis & Case. Akeel Al-Attar & Thamir Hassan. (Artificial Intelligence Ser.). 200p. 1991. write for info. (*0-13-783101-3*, 270601) P-H.

Rule-Making Authority in the English Supreme Court. xiv, 321p. 1993. reprint ed. 38.50 (*0-8377-2547-X*) Rothman.

Rule of Art: Literature & Painting in the Renaissance. Clark Hulse. LC 89-39546. (Illus.). 232p. 1990. 39.00 (*0-226-36052-0*) U Ch Pr.

Rule of Benedict. Joan Chittister. 180p. (C). 1993. text ed. 45.00 (*0-85439-428-1*, Pub. by St Paul Pubns UK) St Mut.

Rule of Benedict: A Guide to Christian Living. George Holzherr. Tr. by Placid Murray. 352p. 1994. pap. 30.00 (*1-85182-121-X*, Pub. by Four Cts Pr IE) Intl Spec Bk.

Rule of Benedict: Insights for the Ages. Joan Chittister. (Spiritual Legacy Ser.). 192p. 1992. pap. 12.95 (*0-8245-2503-5*) Crossroad NY.

Rule of Darkness: British Literature & Imperialism, 1830-1914. Patrick Brantlinger. LC 87-47823. 328p. 1990. reprint ed. pap. 15.95 (*0-8014-9767-1*) Cornell U Pr.

Rule of Five (How to Conduct Successful Meetings) Ervin Smith. (Management the Key Ser.). (Illus.). vii, 88p. (Orig.). 1996. pap. write for info. (*0-9652721-0-9*) E-S Cnslts.

***Rule of Four: Four Essays on the Principle of Quaternity.** Robert L. Berner. (Studies on Themes & Motifs in Literature: Vol. 21). 168p. (C). 1996. text ed. 39.95 (*0-8204-2840-X*) P Lang Pubng.

Rule of Gold. Norma M. Bracy. (Illus.). 20p. (J). (ps-12). 1983. pap. text ed. 2.50 (*0-915783-00-2*) Book Binder.

Rule of Law. K. K. Beck. 1996. write for info. (*0-614-14425-6*) Warner Bks.

Rule of Law: Foundation of Constitutional Democracy. Geoffrey D. Walker. (C). 1988. 69.95 (*0-522-84347-6*, Pub. by Melbourne Univ Pr AT) Paul & Co Pubs.

Rule of Law: Nomos XXXVI. Ed. by Ian Shapiro. LC 93-30298. (American Society of Political & Legal Philosophy Ser.: Vol. 36). 360p. (C). 1994. text ed. 36.00 (*0-8147-7983-2*) NYU Pr.

Rule of Law: Nomos XXXVI. Ed. by Ian Shapiro. (American Society of Political & Legal Philosophy Ser.). 360p. (C). 1995. pap. 19.50 (*0-8147-8024-5*) NYU Pr.

Rule of Law & Conditions on Foreign Aid to Turkey. write for info. (*0-941882-03-9*) Amer Hellenic Inst.

***Rule of Law & Economic Reform in Russia.** Jeffrey Sachs & Katerina Pistor. LC 96-52474. (John M. Olin Critical Issues Ser.). (C). 1997. pap. text ed. 24.00 (*0-8133-3314-8*) Westview.

***Rule of Law & Economic Reform in Russia.** Jeffrey Sachs & Katherina Pistor. LC 96-52474. (John M. Olin Critical Issues Ser.). 1997. text ed. 70.00 (*0-8133-3313-X*) Westview.

Rule of Law & the Role of Psychiatry. Justine W. Polier. LC 68-12900. (Isaac Ray Award Lectures: No. 1966). 192p. reprint ed. pap. 54.80 (*0-8357-8312-X*, 2034124) Bks Demand.

Rule of Law As a Channel of Right or Power? 2nd ed. Vigdor Schreibman. LC 89-1836. (Essays on the Impact of the Constitution & Legal System on American Life & Government Ser.: No. 1). (Illus.). 162p. (Orig.). 1990. pap. 30.00 (*0-942539-16-8*); pap. 20.00 (*0-942539-17-6*) Amicas Pubns.

Rule of Law in a Penal Colony: Law & Politics in Early New South Wales. David Neal. (Studies in Australian History). 224p. (C). 1992. text ed. 64.95 (*0-521-37264-X*) Cambridge U Pr.

Rule of Law in a State of Emergency. Subrata R. Chaudhury. (C). 1989. 980.00 (*0-685-36534-4*) St Mut.

***Rule of Law in the Arab World: Courts in Egypt & the Gulf.** Nathan J. Brown. (Middle East Studies: Vol. 6). 300p. (C). 1997. text ed. 59.95 (*0-521-59026-4*) Cambridge U Pr.

Rule of Law Under Siege: Selected Essays of Franz L. Neumann & Otto Kirchheimer. Ed. by William E. Scheuerman. (Weimer & Now Ser.: No. 9). (Illus.). 280p. (C). 1996. 40.00 (*0-520-20379-8*) U CA Pr.

***Rule of Life.** Society of St. John the Evangelist Staff. LC 97-19605. 1997. pap. 12.95 (*1-56101-132-0*) Cowley Pubns.

Rule of Metaphor: Multi-Disciplinary Studies of the Creation of Meaning in Language. Paul Ricoeur. Tr. by Robert Czerny. 1977. pap. 22.50 (*0-8020-6447-7*) U of Toronto Pr.

Rule of Metaphor: Multi-Disciplinary Studies of the Creation of Meaning in Language. Paul Ricoeur. Tr. by Robert Czerny et al. LC 77-5514. 394p. reprint ed. pap. 112.30 (*0-8357-8313-8*, 2034022) Bks Demand.

Rule of Money: Gender, Class, & Exchange Economics in the Fiction of Henry James. Peggy McCormack. LC 89-20489. (Studies in Modern Literature: No. 116). 132p. (C). reprint ed. 37.40 (*0-8357-2059-4*, 2070743) Bks Demand.

Rule of Prayer, Rule of Faith: Essays in Honor of Aidan Kavanagh, O. S. B. Ed. by Nathan D. Mitchell & John F. Baldovin. 376p. (Orig.). 1996. pap. 34.95 (*0-8146-6158-0*, Pueblo Bks) Liturgical Pr.

Rule of Property for Bengal: An Essay on the Idea of Permanent Settlement. Amartya K. Sen. LC 95-43034. 264p. 1996. text ed. 49.95 (*0-8223-1761-3*); pap. text ed. 17.95 (*0-8223-1771-0*) Duke.

Rule of Property for Bengal: An Essay on the Idea of Permanent Settlement. 2nd ed. Amartya K. Sen. 22p. 1982. text ed. 22.50 (*0-86131-289-9*, Pub. by Orient Longman Ltd II) Apt Bks.

Rule of Reason: The Philosophy of C. S. Peirce. Ed. by Jacqueline Brunning & Paul Forster. (Toronto Studies in Philosophy). 352p. 1996. 80.00 (*0-8020-0829-1*); pap. 24.95 (*0-8020-7819-2*) U of Toronto Pr.

Rule of Saint Augustine: An Essay in Understanding. Sister Agatha Mary. 352p. 1992. 27.95 (*0-941491-48-X*) Augustinian Pr.

Rule of Saint Benedict. Esther De Waal. Tr. by Abbot Parry. 118p. (Orig.). 1990. pap. 9.95 (*0-85244-168-1*, Pub. by Gracewing UK) Morehouse Pub.

Rule of St. Ailbhe. Ailbhe. 1990. reprint ed. pap. 1.50 (*0-89981-111-6*) Eastern Orthodox.

Rule of St. Benedict. Tr. by Anthony C. Meisel & M. L. Del Mastro. LC 74-33611. 120p. 1975. pap. 5.50 (*0-385-00948-8*, Image Bks) Doubleday.

Rule of St. Benedict: A Doctrinal & Spiritual Commentary. Adalbert De Vogue. Tr. by John B. Hasbrouck from FRE. (Cistercian Studies: No. 54). 1983. pap. 25.00 (*0-87907-845-6*) Cistercian Pubns.

Rule of St. Cormac: Irish Monastic Rules, Vol. III. St. Cormac, Bishop of Munster. pap. 1.50 (*0-89981-077-2*) Eastern Orthodox.

Rule of St. Pachomius. Pachomius. Tr. by E. A. Budge from COP. 1975. reprint ed. pap. 2.95 (*0-89981-078-0*) Eastern Orthodox.

Rule of the Bone. Russell Banks. 1996. pap. 10.00 (*0-614-97779-7*, PL) HarpC.

Rule of the Many: Fundamental Issues in Democratic Theory. Thomas Christiano. LC 96-8404. (Focus Ser.). (C). 1996. text ed. 54.00 (*0-8133-1454-2*) Westview.

Rule of the Many: Fundamental Issues in Democratic Theory. Thomas Christiano. LC 96-8404. (Focus Ser.). (C). 1996. pap. text ed. 23.00 (*0-8133-1455-0*) Westview.

***Rule of the Master: Regula Magistri.** Luke Eberle. LC 77-3986. (Cistercian Studies: No. 6). 1977. pap. 10.95 (*0-87907-906-1*) Cistercian Pubns.

Rule of the Road: An International Guide to History & Practice. Peter Kincaid. LC 86-354. 249p. 1986. text ed. 47.95 (*0-313-25249-1*, KRU/, Greenwood Pr) Greenwood.

Rule of the Secular Franciscan Order: With a Catechism & Instructions. 186p. 1980. pap. 7.50 (*0-8199-0810-X*, Frncscn Herld) Franciscan Pr.

Rule of the Taewon'gun, 1864-1873: Restoration in Yi Korea. Choe Ching Young. LC 73-183975. (East Asian Monographs: No. 45). 196p. 1972. pap. 14.00 (*0-674-78030-2*) HUP.

***Rule of the Templars.** J. M. Upton-Ward. (Studies in the History of Medieval Religion). 208p. (Orig.). 1997. pap. 30.00 (*0-85115-701-7*, Boydell Pr) Boydell & Brewer.

Rule of the Templars: The French Text of the Rule of the Order of Knights Templar. J. M. Upton-Ward. (Studies in the History of Medieval Religion). 208p. (C). 1992. 59.00 (*0-85115-315-1*) Boydell & Brewer.

Rule of Three. Elizabeth Garrett. 64p. (Orig.). 9100. pap. 14.95 (*1-85224-162-4*, Pub. by Bloodaxe Bks UK) Dufour.

***Rule of Thumb, or Death in the Family: A Mystery Without Plot, Character, or Action.** Paul Hruban. LC 96-90849. 268p. (Orig.). 1996. pap. 49.95 (*0-9655751-0-1*) Echo Books.

***Rule of Thumb, or Death in the Family: A Mystery Without Plot, Character, or Action.** Paul Hruban. LC 96-90849. 268p. (Orig.). 1997. pap. 14.95 (*0-9655751-1-X*, Shady Bks) Echo Books.

Rule of Two: Observations on Close Relationship. Ann Woodin. LC 84-60490. (Illus.). 136p. 1984. 25.00 (*0-917041-01-1*) Oracle Pr AZ.

***Rule Six.** Paul Weissman. Date not set. write for info. (*0-688-05100-6*) Morrow.

Rule Statutes & Customs of the Hospitallers, 1099-1310. Knights of Malta Staff. LC 78-63347. (Crusades & Military Orders Ser.: Second Series). 272p. reprint ed. 39.50 (*0-404-16246-0*) AMS Pr.

***Rule, the Bible, & the Council: The Library of the Benedictine Abbey at Praglia.** Diana Gisolfi & Staale Sinding-Larsen. (Illus.). 330p. 1997. 55.00 (*0-295-97661-6*) U of Wash Pr.

Rulebook for Arguments. 2nd ed. Anthony Weston. LC 92-26328. 112p. (C). 1992. pap. text ed. 4.95 (*0-87220-156-2*); lib. bdg. 24.95 (*0-87220-157-0*) Hackett Pub.

Rulemaking: How Government Agencies Write Law & Make Policy. Cornelius W. Kerwin. LC 93-46944. 321p. 1994. pap. 23.95 (*0-87187-673-6*) Congr Quarterly.

Rulemaking: How Government Agencies Write Law & Make Policy. Cornelius W. Kerwin. LC 93-46944. 321p. 1994. 36.95 (*0-87187-993-X*) Congr Quarterly.

***Ruler As Philosopher.** H. Daiber. (Mededelingen der Koninklijke Nederlandse Akademie van Wetenschappen, Afd. Letterkunde Ser.: No. 49(4)). 1986. pap. text ed. 13.75 (*0-444-85657-9*) Elsevier.

Ruler of the Nativity. Alexander Volguine. LC 74-90427. (French Astrology Ser.). write for info. (*0-88231-076-3*) ASI Pubs Inc.

***Ruler of the Range.** large type ed. Peter Dawson. LC 97-330. (Western Ser.). 252p. 1997. 18.95 (*0-7862-1077-X*, Thorndike Lrg Prnt) Thorndike Pr.

Ruler, Townsmen, & Bazaars: North Indian Society in the Age of British Expansion 1770-1870. C. A. Bayly. (Oxford India Paperbacks Ser.). 532p. 1994. pap. 14.95 (*0-19-562876-4*) OUP.

Rulers & Nobles in Fifteenth-Century Muscovy. Gustave Alef. (Collected Studies: No. CS172). 354p. (C). 1983. reprint ed. lib. bdg. 109.95 (*0-86078-120-8*, Pub. by Variorum UK) Ashgate Pub Co.

***Rulers & Ruled: An Introduction to Classical Political Theory.** Irving M. Zeitlin. 256p. 1996. 50.00 (*0-8020-0894-1*); pap. 16.95 (*0-8020-7877-X*) U of Toronto Pr.

Rulers & Ruled in Late Medieval England: Essays Presented to Gerald Harriss. Ed. by Rowena E. Archer & Simon Walker. LC 95-49415. 1995. boxed 65.00 (*1-85285-133-3*) Hambledon Press.

Rulers & Subjects: Government & People in Russia 1801-1991. John Gooding. 288p. 1996. text ed. 22.95 (*0-340-61405-6*, Pub. by E Arnld UK) St Martin.

Rulers & Subjects: Government & People in Russia 1801-1991. John Gooding. 288p. 1996. text ed. 59.95 (*0-340-66288-3*, Pub. by E Arnld UK) St Martin.

Rulers from the Steppe: State Formation on the Inner Eurasian Periphery. Ed. by Daniel Marks. Tr. by Mary F. Zirin. LC 90-84794. (Ethnographics Monographs). (Illus.). 328p. (Orig.). (C). 1991. pap. 12.00 (*1-878986-01-5*) Ethnogphics Pr.

Ruler's Imperative: Strategies for Political Survival in Asia & Africa. W. Howard Wriggins. LC 73-90431. (Southern Asian Institute Publications). 1969. text ed. 49.50 (*0-231-03314-1*) Col U Pr.

Rulers, Nomads and Christians in Roman North Africa. Brent Shaw. (Collected Studies: Vol. 497). 352p. 1995. 89.95 (*0-86078-490-8*, Pub. by Variorum UK) Ashgate Pub Co.

Rulers of Babylonia: From the Second Dynasty of Isin to the End of Assyrian Domination (1157-612 BC) Grant Frame. (Royal Inscriptions of Mesopotamia Ser.). 376p. 1995. 150.00 (*0-8020-0724-4*) U of Toronto Pr.

Rulers of British Africa, 1870-1914. Lewis H. Gann & Peter Duignan. LC 77-92945. (Illus.). xiv, 406p. 1978. 55.00 (*0-8047-0981-5*) Stanford U Pr.

***Rulers of Darkness, Vol. 1.** Spruill. 1997. pap. write for info. (*0-312-95668-1*) St Martin.

Rulers of German Africa, 1884-1914. Lewis H. Gann & Peter Duignan. LC 76-54100. (Illus.). xviii, 286p. 1977. 45.00 (*0-8047-0938-6*) Stanford U Pr.

Rulers of Mecca. Gerald De Gaury. LC 78-63458. (Pilgrimages Ser.). (Illus.). 1982. reprint ed. 44.00 (*0-404-16517-6*) AMS Pr.

Rulers of Reality & the Ruled Races: The Struggle of Black Ministers to Bring Afro- Americans to Full Citizenship in America. Joseph R. Washington. LC 90-5570. (Studies in American Religion: Vol. 49). 672p. 1990. lib. bdg. 129.95 (*0-88946-696-3*) E Mellen.

Rulers of Roman Britain: Kings, Queens, Governors & Emperors from Julius Caesar to Agricola. David Braund. LC 95-52388. 232p. (C). 1996. text ed. 59.95 (*0-415-00804-2*) Routledge.

Rulers of Russia. Denis Fahey. 1986. pap. 5.50 (*0-317-52999-4*, Noontide Pr) Legion Survival.

Rulers of Russia: Jewish Bolshevism & Jewish Influence in the Soviet Government. Dennis Fahey. 1980. lib. bdg. 250.00 (*0-8490-3098-6*) Gordon Pr.

Rulers of the Lakes. Joseph A. Altsheler. 25.95 (*0-8488-0906-8*) Amereon Ltd.

Rulers of the Lakes. Joseph A. Altsheler. 1993. reprint ed. lib. bdg. 21.95 (*0-89968-565-X*) Buccaneer Bks.

Rulers of the Mediterranean. Richard H. Davis. LC 76-38788. (Essay Index Reprint Ser.). 1977. reprint ed. 26.95 (*0-8369-2645-5*) Ayer.

Rulers of the South. Francis M. Crawford. (Works of Francis Marion Crawford Ser.). 1990. reprint ed. lib. bdg. 79.00 (*0-7812-2566-3*) Rprt Serv.

Rulers of the South, 2 vols., Set. Francis M. Crawford. 1972. 250.00 (*0-8490-0979-0*) Gordon Pr.

Rulers of Tikal: An Historical Reconstruction & Field Guide to the Stelae. Genevieve Michel. (Illus.). 148p. (Orig.). (C). 1989. pap. 13.00 (*0-9626221-1-7*) Vista Pubns FL.

Rulership of Heaven. Wim Malgo. 9.95 (*0-937422-28-2*); pap. 6.95 (*0-937422-27-4*) Midnight Call.

Rules. Ellen Fein & Sherrie Schneider. Date not set. pap. 5.99 (*0-614-17420-1*) Warner Bks.

Rules: A Systematic Study. Joan S. Ganz. (Janua Linguarum, Ser. Minor: No. 96). (Illus.). 144p. (Orig.). 1972. pap. text ed. 41.35 (*90-279-1853-8*) Mouton.

RULES: Remediating Unintelligible Linguistic Expressions of Speech. Jane C. Webb & Barbara Duckett. (Illus.). 200p. (J). (ps-3). 1994. teacher ed. 43.95 (*0-937857-51-3*, 1557) Speech Bin.

***Rules: Time-Tested Secrets for Capturing the Heart of Mr. Right.** Ellen Fein & Sherrie Schneider. 192p. 1997. 15.95 (*0-446-52291-0*) Warner Bks.

Rules: Time Tested Secrets to Capturing the Heart of Mr. Right. Ellen Fein & Sherrie Schneider. 192p. 1996. mass mkt. 5.99 (*0-446-60274-4*) Warner Bks.

Rules & Choice in Economics. Victor J. Vanberg. (Economics As Social Theory Ser.). (Illus.). 352p. (Orig.). (C). 1994. pap. 22.95 (*0-415-09479-8*, B4351) Routledge.

Rules & Choice in Economics. Victor J. Vanberg. (Economics As Social Theory Ser.). 336p. (Orig.). (C). (gr. 13). 1994. text ed. 79.95 (*0-415-06873-8*, B4347) Routledge.

Rules & Conventions: Literature, Philosophy, Social Theory. Ed. by Mette Hjort. (Parallax: Re-Visions of Culture & Society Ser.). 368p. 1992. text ed. 49.95 (*0-8018-4394-4*); pap. text ed. 16.95 (*0-8018-4395-2*) Johns Hopkins.

Rules & Discretion in International Economic Policy. Manuel Guitian. LC 92-12943. (Occasional Paper Ser.: No. 97). v, 52p. 1992. pap. 15.00 (*1-55775-237-0*) Intl Monetary.

Rules & Examples of Perspective. Andrea Pozzo. LC 69-13450. (Illus.). 1972. reprint ed. 38.95 (*0-405-08861-2*, Pub. by Blom Pubns UK) Ayer.

***Rules & Government.** Robert Baldwin. (Oxford Socio-Legal Studies). 352p. 1997. pap. 32.00 (*0-19-826489-5*) OUP.

Rules & Government: Non-Statutory Rules & Administrative Law. Robert Baldwin. (Oxford Socio-Legal Studies). 300p. 1995. 59.00 (*0-19-825909-3*) OUP.

Rules & Institutions. Nicholas Rowe. 224p. 1989. text ed. 47.50 (*0-472-10155-2*) U of Mich Pr.

Rules & Mysteries of Brother Solomon. Sandol Stoddard. 48p. (Orig.). 1987. pap. 2.95 (*0-8091-6560-0*) Paulist Pr.

Rules & Precepts of the Jesuit Missions of Northwestern New Spain. Charles W. Polzer. LC 75-8456. 141p. 1976. pap. 12.95 (*0-8165-0488-1*) U of Ariz Pr.

Rules & Racial Equality. Edwin Dorn. LC 79-64228. 1979. 35.00 (*0-300-02362-6*) Yale U Pr.

***Rules & Regulations for Building Services Contractors in France.** BSRIA Staff. 1995. pap. 250.00 (*0-86022-427-9*, Pub. by Build Servs Info Assn UK) St Mut.

***Rules & Regulations for Building Services Contractors in Germany.** BSRIA Staff. 1995. pap. 250.00 (*0-86022-428-7*, Pub. by Build Servs Info Assn UK) St Mut.

Rules & Regulations for Prevention & Control of Environmental Pollution by Radioactive Materials. (Illus.). 31p. (Orig.). (C). 1993. pap. text ed. 20.00 (*1-56806-762-3*) DIANE Pub.

***Rules & Regulations of the Securities & Exchange Commission: Red Box Service.** Ed. by Bowne Publishing Division Staff & Susan Hood. 2500p. 1997. 250.00 (*1-885100-04-3*, R-1) Bowne Pubng.

***Rules & Regulators.** Julia Black. (Oxford Socio-Legal Studies). 304p. 1997. 70.00 (*0-19-826294-9*) OUP.

Rules & Representations. Noam Chomsky. LC 79-26145. (Woodbridge Lectures Ser.: No. 11). 1982. pap. text ed. 18.00 (*0-231-04827-0*) Col U Pr.

Rules & Resolutions, 1990 Edition. 72p. 1990. pap. text ed. 13.00 (*0-8309-0582-0*) Herald Hse.

Rules & Rights in the Middle East: Democracy, Law, & Society. Ed. by Ellis Goldberg & Resat Kasaba. LC 93-4679. (Jackson School Publications in International Studies). 304p. 1993. 35.00 (*0-295-97286-6*); pap. 17.50 (*0-295-97287-4*) U of Wash Pr.

Rules & Techniques of Bourre: A Cajun Card Game. Preston Guidry. Ed. & Illus. by Benny Graeff. 1988. pap. 4.95 (*0-317-91204-6*) Natl Cajun Bourre.

Rules & the Summa. Robertus De Handlo & Johannes Hanboys. Ed. & Tr. by Peter M. Lefferts. LC 90-415133. (Greek & Latin Music Theory Ser.). (Illus.). x, 403p. 1990. text ed. 40.00 (*0-8032-7934-5*) U of Nebr Pr.

***Rules Are Flexible.** Rosanne Donahue. 177p. (Orig.). 1997. mass mkt. 4.99 (*1-55237-138-7*, Pub. by Comnwlth Pub CN) Partners Pubs Grp.

Rules Are No Game: The Strategy of Communication. Anthony Wilden. (Illus.). 368p. 1987. 27.50 (*0-7100-9868-5*, 98685, RKP) Routledge.

***Rules Book: 1997-2000 Racing Rules.** 6th rev. ed. Eric Twiname. (Illus.). 208p. 1997. pap. 14.95 (*1-57409-033-X*) Sheridan.

Rules Book & Update Service. Ed. by Marc G. Perlin. 1990. 102.10 (*0-318-18709-4*) Lawyers Weekly.

***Rules Dating Journal.** Ellen Fein & Sherrie Schneider. 1997. 11.50 (*0-614-30493-8*) Warner Bks.

***Rules Dating Journal: More Rules to Live & Love By.** Ellen Fein. 1997. 12.00 (*0-446-52314-3*) Warner Bks.

Rules, Decisions, & Inequality in Egalitarian Societies. James G. Flanagan & Steve Rayner. 200p. 1988. text ed. 59.95 (*0-566-05762-X*, Pub. by Avebury Pub UK) Ashgate Pub Co.

Rules, Exceptions, & Social Order. Robert B. Edgerton. LC 84-28134. 1985. 50.00 (*0-520-05481-4*) U CA Pr.

Rules for a Pious Life. Platon. 1994. pap. 0.50 (*0-89981-153-1*) Eastern Orthodox.

Rules for Automatic Sprinkler Installations. Fire Protection Association Staff. (C). 1992. 295.00 (*0-902167-32-4*, Pub. by Fire Protect Assn UK) St Mut.

***Rules for Cats.** Michael Cader. (J). 1997. pap. 11.95 (*0-525-94362-5*) Dutton Child Bks.

***Rules for Cats.** Leigh A. Jasheway. LC 96-51689. 96p. (Orig.). 1997. pap. 6.95 (*0-8362-3291-7*) Andrews & McMeel.

Rules for Determining Income & Expenses As Domestic or Foreign. (Cahiers de Droit Fiscal International Ser.: Vol. LXVb). 690p. 1980. pap. 110.50 (*90-200-0604-5*) Kluwer Law Tax Pubs.

***Rules for Discerning the Spirits: In the "Spiritual Exercises" of St. Ignatius of Loyola.** Ludovic-Marie Barrielle. 60p. 1992. reprint ed. pap. 4.25 (*0-935952-77-2*) Angelus Pr.

***Rules for Dogs.** Leigh A. Jasheway. LC 96-51662. 96p. (Orig.). 1997. pap. 6.95 (*0-8362-3292-5*) Andrews & McMeel.

Rules for Free International Trade in Services. Ed. by Daniel Friedmann & Ernst-Joachim Mestmacker. 383p. 1990. 89.00 (*3-7890-1947-X*, Pub. by Nomos Verlags GW) Intl Bk Import.

Rules for Inboard, Inboard Endurance & Unlimited Racing, 1989. Ed. by Renee M. Olejnik & Marie Masters. 98p. 1990. 10.00 (*0-318-41009-5*) Am Power Boat.

***Rules for Medical Terminology.** 2nd ed. Lois Mack. 256p. (C). 1996. pap. text ed. 34.59 (*0-7872-2844-3*) Kendall-Hunt.

Rules for Offshore Racing, 1989. Ed. by Renee M. Olejnik & Marie Masters. 62p. 1990. 10.00 (*0-318-41010-9*) Am Power Boat.

Rules for Prayer. William O. Paulsell. LC 93-4387. 160p. 1993. pap. 9.95 (*0-8091-3410-1*) Paulist Pr.

Rules for Radicals. Saul Alinsky. 1989. pap. 10.00 (*0-679-72113-4*, Vin) Random.

Rules for Reaching Consensus: A Modern Approach to the Age-Old Process of Making Decisions. Steven Saint & James Lawson. LC 94-4486. 96p. 1994. pap. 9.95 (*0-89384-256-7*, Pfffr & Co) Jossey-Bass.

Rules for Reasoning. Ed. by Richard E. Nisbett. LC 92-39042. 424p. 1993. pap. 34.50 (*0-8058-1257-1*); text ed. 89.95 (*0-8058-1256-3*) L Erlbaum Assocs.

Rules for Regulating Intervention under a Managed Float. Marsha R. Shelburn. LC 84-25287. (Studies in International Finance: No. 55). 56p. 1984. pap. text ed. 11.00 (*0-88165-227-X*) Princeton U Int Finan Econ.

Rules for Rulers: The Politics of Advice. Arnold J. Meltsner. 208p. 1990. 24.95 (*0-87722-685-7*) Temple U Pr.

***Rules for Sex on Wedding Night.** Herbert I. Kavet. (Illus.). 64p. (Orig.). 1997. pap. 5.99 (*1-889647-12-8*) Boston Am.

Rules for Spiritual Initiation. Zachary F. Lansdowne. LC 90-38635. 194p. (Orig.). 1990. pap. 7.95 (*0-87728-707-4*) Weiser.

Rules for Sports Played in the U. S. Army. Intro. by Tom Heski. (Guidon Monographs). 1891. 12.00 (*0-685-10883-X*, J M C & Co) Amereon Ltd.

Rules for Sports Played, U. S. Army. Carroll. 1976. pap. 12.00 (*0-19-875220-2*, J M C & Co) Amereon Ltd.

Rules for Stock Outboard, PRO Outboard, Modified Outboard, & Outboard Performance Craft, 1989. Ed. by Renee M. Olejnik & Marie Masters. 86p. 1990. 5.00 (*0-318-41011-7*) Am Power Boat.

***Rules for Success.** Mamie McCullough. 160p. Date not set. pap. 5.99 (*1-57757-012-X*) Honor Bks OK.

Rules for the Spiritual Life. Jose G. Trevino. Tr. by Benjamin Hunt. 187p. 1995. reprint ed. text ed. 15.95 (*0-912141-28-X*) Roman Cath Bks.

Rules for the Traditional Family. Nicholas Puiia. 114p. (Orig.). 1988. pap. 2.00 (*0-8294-0604-2*) Loyola Pr.

Rules for Writers. Hacker. 1995. teacher ed., pap. text ed. 5.00 (*0-312-13812-1*) St Martin.

Rules for Writers. 3rd ed. Hacker. 1997. pap. text ed. 12.50 (*0-312-14849-6*) St Martin.

Rules For Writers. 3rd ed. Diana Hacker. 1995. pap. text ed. 11.50 (*0-312-11966-6*) St Martin.

Rules for Writing: Development Exercises. 3rd ed. Hacker. 1995. pap. text ed. 6.00 (*0-312-13678-1*) St Martin.

Rules for Writing: Development Exercises & Answers. 3rd ed. Hacker. 1995. suppl. ed., pap. text ed. 5.00 (*0-312-13716-8*) St Martin.

Rules for Young Friends. Gregg Harris. 32p. 1989. pap. text ed., pap. 10.95 (*0-923463-64-X*) Noble Pub Assocs.

Rules, Games, & Common-Pool Resources. Elinor Ostrom et al. LC 93-44406. 370p. (C). 1994. text ed. 59.50 (*0-472-09546-3*); pap. text ed. 21.95 (*0-472-06546-7*) U of Mich Pr.

Rules Governing Medicinal Products in the European Community, Addendum No. 2, May 1992, Vols. 1-5: Guidelines on the Quality Safety... Human Use. 200p. 1992. pap. 35.00 (*92-826-4550-9*, CO-75-92-558-EN-C, Pub. by Europ Com UK) Bernan Associates.

Rules Governing Medicinal Products in the European Community Rev. 11-1992: Rules Governing Veterinary Medicinal Products in the E. C., Vol. 5A. 1993. pap. 35.00 (*92-826-5174-6*, CO-77-92-384ENC, Pub. by Europ Com UK) Bernan Associates.

Rules Governing Medicinal Products in the European Community, Vol. 3: Addendum, July 1990 - Guidelines on the Quality, Safety & Efficacy...Human Use. 200p. 1990. pap. 30.00 (*92-826-0421-7*, CB-59-90-936-EN-C, Pub. by Commiss Europ Commun BE) Bernan Associates.

Rules Governing Medicinal Products in the European Community, Vol. 4: Good Manufacturing Practice for Medicinal Products. 200p. 1992. pap. 30.00 (*92-826-3180-X*, CO-71-91-760-EN-C, Pub. by Europ Com UK) Bernan Associates.

***Rules II: More Rules to Live & Love By.** Ellen Fein & Sherrie Schneider. 1997. 15.00 (*0-446-52265-1*) Warner Bks.

Rules in Database Systems: Proceedings of the 1st International Workshop on Rules in Database Systems, Edinburgh, Scotland, 30 August-1 September 1993. Ed. by Norman W. Paton & M. Howard Williams. LC 93-27566. (Workshops in Computing Ser.). 1994. 84.95 (*0-387-19846-6*) Spr-Verlag.

Rules in Database Systems: Proceedings Second International Workshop, RIDS '95, Glyfada, Athens, Greece, September 1995. Ed. by Timos Sellis. (Lecture Notes in Computer Science Ser.: Vol. 985). 373p. 1995. pap. 62.00 (*3-540-60365-4*) Spr-Verlag.

Rules in Practice, 1993-96. Bryan Willis. 80p. (C). 1993. text ed. 59.00 (*0-906754-87-9*, Pub. by Fernhurst Bks UK) St Mut.

Rules in the Making: A Statistical Analysis. Wesley A. Magat et al. LC 85-43555. 182p. 1986. text ed. 22.50 (*0-915707-24-1*) Resources Future.

Rules, Norms, & Decisions: On the Conditions of Practical & Legal Reasoning in International Relations & Domestic Affairs. Friedrich V. Kratochwil. (Studies in International Relations: No. 2). (Illus.). 333p. (C). 1991. pap. text ed. 19.95 (*0-521-40971-3*) Cambridge U Pr.

Rules Notebook. Barbara A. Wilson. (Wilson Reading System Ser.). 32p. 1988. teacher ed. 8.00 (*1-56778-005-9*) Wilson Lang Trning.

Rules of Art: Genesis & Structure of the Literary Field. Pierre Bourdieu. Tr. by Susan Emanuel from FRE. LC 94-74140. (Meridian: Crossing Aesthetics Ser.). 288p. 1995. 49.50 (*0-8047-2568-3*) Stanford U Pr.

Rules of Art: Genesis & Structure of the Literary Field. Pierre Bourdieu. Tr. by Susan Emanuel. LC 94-74140. (Meridian Ser.: Crossing Aesthetics). 288p. 1995. pap. 15.95 (*0-8047-2627-2*) Stanford Univ Committee on Linguistics.

Rules of Attraction. Bret Easton Ellis. 288p. 1988. pap. 11. 95 (*0-14-011228-6*, Penguin Bks) Viking Penguin.

***Rules of Attraction.** Bret Easton Ellis. 1997. pap. write for info. (*0-679-78148-X*, Vin) Random.

Rules of Baseball. David Nemec. (Illus.). 272p. 1994. pap. 16.95 (*1-55821-280-9*) Lyons & Burford.

Rules of Chaos. Stephen Vizinczey. 1995. pap. 14.95 (*0-226-85892-8*) U Ch Pr.

Rules of Chaos. Stephen Vizinczey. 1996. 25.00 (*0-226-85890-1*) U Ch Pr.

Rules of Christian Decorum & Civility. John B. De La Salle. Ed. by Gregory Wright. Tr. by Richard Arnandez. LC 90-60706. 176p. 1990. 23.00 (*0-944808-04-2*); pap. 15.00 (*0-944808-05-0*) Lasallian Pubns.

***Rules of Civility.** Richard Brookhiser. LC 96-6521. 1997. 18.95 (*0-684-83723-4*, Free Press) Free Pr.

Rules of Composition of the Talmud of Babylonia. Jacob Neusner. 280p. 1991. 59.95 (*1-55540-539-8*) Scholars Pr GA.

Rules of Contract Law. Knapp. 1993. 14.50 (*0-316-49932-3*) Little.

Rules of Criminal Procedure, 4 vols. Robert M. Cipes. Ed. by Marvin Waxner & Michael Eisenstein. 1965. Updates. ring bd. write for info. (*0-8205-1201-X*) Bender.

Rules of Criminal Procedure for U. S. District Courts. 70p. (Orig.). (C). 1993. pap. text ed. 20.00 (*1-56806-198-6*) DIANE Pub.

Rules of Decoration see Decoration

Rules of Descent: Studies in the Sociology of Parentage. Guy E. Swanson. (Anthropological Papers: No. 39). 1969. pap. 1.00 (*0-932206-37-9*) U Mich Mus Anthro.

***Rules of Disorder.** Peter Marsh & Elizabeth Rosser. (Social Worlds of Childhood Ser.). 150p. (C). 1980. pap. text ed. 22.95 (*0-415-11948-0*, Routledge NY) Routledge.

Rules of Encounter: Designing Convention for Automated Negotiation among Computers. Jeffrey S. Rosenschein & Gilad Zlotkin. (Artificial Intelligence Ser.). (Illus.). 225p. 1994. 35.00 (*0-262-18159-2*) MIT Pr.

Rules of Engagement. Lis Harris. 1996. pap. 11.00 (*0-684-82527-9*) S&S Trade.

Rules of Engagement. P. H. Liotta. (CSU Poetry Ser.: No. XXXIV). 137p. (Orig.). 1991. 15.00 (*0-914946-88-9*); pap. 10.00 (*0-914946-89-7*) Cleveland St Univ Poetry Ctr.

Rules of Engagement. Peter Morwood. (Star Trek Ser.: No. 48). 288p. 1990. pap. 4.50 (*0-685-28839-0*) PB.

Rules of Engagement. Norwood. (Star Trek Ser.: No. 48). 1990. pap. 4.99 (*0-671-66129-9*) PB.

***Rules of Engagement.** Nicola Thorne. 256p. 1996. 24.00 (*0-7278-5118-7*) Severn Hse.

Rules of Engagement. Joe Weber. 384p. 1992. mass mkt. 5.99 (*0-515-10990-8*) Jove Pubns.

Rules of Engagement: Four Couples & American Marriages Today. Lis Harris. LC 95-457. 256p. 1995. 23.00 (*0-684-80826-9*, S&S) S&S Trade.

***Rules of Etiquette for Very Young Ladies, Incl. doll.** Marybeth Barba. 10p. (J). 1996. pap. 19.90 (*1-890414-10-7*) Bow Tie.

Rules of Evidence. George T. Felkenes. (Criminal Justice Ser.). 1974. pap. 23.95 (*0-8273-1425-6*) Delmar.

Rules of Evidence. Jay Brandon & Bill Grose. Ed. by Dana Isaacson. 352p. 1992. reprint ed. pap. 6.50 (*0-671-79389-6*) PB.

Rules of Golf. (Illus.). 36p. pap. 2.95 (*0-8362-8730-4*) Andrews & McMeel.

Rules of Golf Applied. Cliff Schrock. (Spalding Sports Library). (Illus.). (Orig.). 1995. pap. 16.95 (*1-57028-033-9*) Masters Pr IN.

Rules of Golf Explained & Illustrated. Thom Watson & Frank Hannigan. LC 79-4758. (Illus.). 1984. 14.95 (*0-685-42318-2*) Random.

Rules of Golf Illustrated & Explained. Tom Watson & Frank Hannigan. 16.95 (*0-686-30836-0*); pap. 9.95 (*0-686-30837-9*) US Golf Assn.

Rules of Golf Through 1999. Tom Watson & Frank Hannigan. 192p. 1996. pap. 16.00 (*0-671-00314-3*) PB.

Rules of HAJJ. Ayatullah Al-Khu'i. Tr. by Shaikh Muhammad Sarwar from ARA. 50p. 1981. pap. 2.00 (*0-941724-02-6*) Islamic Seminary.

Rules of Hope. James R. Averill et al. (Recent Research in Psychology Ser.). vii, 134p. 1990. 44.95 (*0-387-97219-6*) Spr-Verlag.

Rules of Insanity: Moral Responsibility & the Mentally Ill. Carl Elliott. LC 95-34254. 143p. (C). 1996. text ed. 54. 50 (*0-7914-2951-2*); pap. text ed. 17.95 (*0-7914-2952-0*) State U NY Pr.

Rules of Neighborhood Poker According to Hoyle. Stewart Wolpin. (Illus.). 288p. (Orig.). 1990. pap. 6.95 (*0-942257-19-7*) New Chapter Pr.

Rules of North Carolina: 1994 Edition. annot. ed. pap. 37. 50 (*1-55834-046-7*) MICHIE.

Rules of Order. rev. ed. Roberts. 1999. 18.95 (*0-395-53309-0*) HM.

Rules of Order: An Authoritative, Simplified Guide to Parliamentary Procedure. James E. Davis. LC 92-895. (Illus.). 180p. 1992. 24.95 (*1-55652-150-2*) Chicago Review.

***Rules of Order & Procedure Parliamentary Law.** Howard W. Pollock. Ed. by Richard Garstang. 63p. (Orig.). 1996. pap. 9.00 (*0-9653617-0-5*) H W Pollock.

Rules of Origin in International Trade: A Comparative Study. Ed. by Edwin A. Vermulst et al. (Studies In International Trade Policy). 400p. 1993. text ed. 69.50 (*0-472-10411-X*) U of Mich Pr.

Rules of Prey. John Sandford. 1990. mass mkt. 6.99 (*0-425-12163-1*) Berkley Pub.

Rules of Procedure for the Board of County Commissioners. 3rd ed. Joseph S. Ferrell. (C). 1995. pap. text ed. 7.00 (*1-56011-236-0*, 94.24) Institute Government.

Rules of Procedure of the Committee on the Elimination of Racial Discrimination. 209p. 1985. 15.50 (*92-1-054001-8*, 85.XIV.11) UN.

Rules of Procedure of the Economic & Social Council. 50p. Date not set. pap. 5.00 (*92-1-100489-6*, E.92.I.22) UN.

***Rules of Public Engagement.** Daniel Yankelovich & John Immerwahr. 24p. (Orig.). 1993. pap. 6.50 (*1-889483-23-0*) Public Agenda.

Rules of Seduction. Daniel L. Magida. 432p. 1994. pap. 10. 00 (*0-449-90852-6*, Columbine) Fawcett.

***Rules of Soccer.** Barbara Bonney. LC 97-8101. (Play It Like a Pro Ser.). (J). 1997. write for info. (*1-57103-140-5*) Rourke Pr.

Rules of Social Interaction Workbook. M. J. Bienvenu & Betty Colonomos. (Introduction to American Deaf Culture Ser.). 76p. 1992. pap. text ed. 7.95 (*1-881133-00-1*) Sign Media.

Rules of Sociological Method. Emile Durkheim. 1982. pap. 16.95 (*0-02-907940-3*, Free Press) Free Pr.

Rules of Speed Chess. Kristan Lawson. LC 92-73541. (Illus.). 56p. (Orig.). 1992. pap. 5.95 (*0-9634205-7-7*) J Roger Pr.

Rules of Tennis & Cases & Decisions. rev. ed. (Illus.). 28p. 1991. 0.85 (*0-938822-84-5*) USTA.

Rules of the Antenna Game. 2nd ed. Ted Hart. Ed. by Jack L. Stone. (Illus.). 1989. pap. 6.95 (*0-685-28858-7*) Franklin-Belle.

Rules of the Aztec Language: Classical Nahuatl Grammar. Arthur J. Anderson. LC 72-88553. 124p. reprint ed. pap. 35.40 (*0-8357-6850-3*, 2035545) Bks Demand.

Rules of the Communist Party of the Soviet Union. Ed. by Graeme Gill. LC 87-4815. 272p. (gr. 13). 1988. text ed. 72.95 (*0-87332-434-X*) M E Sharpe.

Rules of the Game. Nora Roberts. (NR Flowers Ser.: No. 18). 1992. mass mkt. 3.59 (*0-373-51018-7*, 5-51018-5) Harlequin Bks.

Rules of the Game: Buying Real Estate in Costa Rica. Bill Baker. 139p. 1994. 29.00 (*1-885557-01-9*) Intl Mrkting.

Rules of the Game: Culture Defining Gender. Judith A. Barter & Anne Mochon. (Illus.). 32p. (Orig.). 1986. pap. text ed. 1.00 (*0-914337-08-4*) Mead Art Mus.

Rules of the Game: Ethics in College Sport. Ed. by Richard E. Lapchick & John B. Slaughter. LC 94-28029. (American Council on Education - Oryx Press Series on Higher Education). 272p. 1989. reprint ed. text ed. 19.95 (*0-89774-831-X*) Oryx Pr.

Rules of the Game: Global Business Protocol. Leaptrott & Company Staff & Nan Leaptrott. LC 95-38856. (Organizational Behavior Ser.). 280p. 1996. 32.95 (*0-538-85455-3*) S-W Pub.

Rules of the Game: International Money & Exchange Rates. Ronald I. McKinnon. LC 95-36690. (Illus.). 528p. 1996. 55.00 (*0-262-13318-0*) MIT Pr.

***Rules of the Game: Jutland & British Naval Command.** Andrew Gordon. (Illus.). 708p. 1997. 48.95 (*1-55750-718-X*) Naval Inst Pr.

Rules of the Game: Simple Truths Learned from Little League. Kurt Hohenstein. 240p. 1996. 12.99 (*0-7852-7504-5*) Nelson.

Rules of the Game: Struggles in Black Recreation & Social Welfare Policy in South Africa. Alan G. Cobley. LC 96-23337. (Contributions in Afro-American & African Studies: No. 182). 192p. 1997. text ed. 59.95 (*0-313-30108-5*, Greenwood Pr) Greenwood.

Rules of the Game: The Complete Illustrated Encyclopedia of all the Sports of the World. Diagram Group Staff. 1994. pap. 15.95 (*0-312-11940-2*) St Martin.

Rules of the Game - Beyond the Pale: Memoirs of Sir Oswald Mosley & Family. Nicholas Mosley. LC 90-14042. (Illus.). 600p. 1991. 27.50 (*0-916583-75-9*) Dalkey Arch.

Rules of the Game in Paris. Nathan C. Leites. Tr. by Derek Coltman. LC 69-19276. 365p. reprint ed. pap. 104.10 (*0-317-26519-9*, 2024055) Bks Demand.

***Rules of the Game in the Global Economy: Policy Regimes for International Business.** Lee E. Preston. LC 97-1578. 280p. (C). 1997. pap. text ed. 50.00 (*0-7923-9888-2*) Kluwer Ac.

Rules of the Game in the Global Economy: Policy Regimes for International Business. Lee H. Preston. 320p. (C). 1992. lib. bdg. 127.50 (*0-7923-9225-6*) Kluwer Ac.

***Rules of the Game in the Global Economy: Policy Regimes for International Business.** 2nd ed. Lee E. Preston. LC 97-1578. 280p. (C). 1997. lib. bdg. 125.00 (*0-7923-9887-4*) Kluwer Ac.

***Rules of the Game of Baseball.** Godin, Seth, Productions Staff. (Cader Flip Ser.). 1997. pap. text ed. 3.95 (*0-8362-3303-4*, Cader Bks) Andrews & McMeel.

***Rules of the Game of Bridge.** Godin, Seth, Productions Staff. (Cader Flip Ser.). 1997. pap. text ed. 3.95 (*0-8362-2563-5*, Cader Bks) Andrews & McMeel.

***Rules of the Game of Golf.** Godin, Seth, Productions Staff. (Cader Flip Ser.). 1997. pap. text ed. 3.95 (*0-8362-2564-3*, Cader Bks) Andrews & McMeel.

***Rules of the Game of Poker.** Godin, Seth, Productions Staff. (Cader Flip Ser.). 1997. pap. text ed. 3.95 (*0-8362-2562-7*, Cader Bks) Andrews & McMeel.

Rules of the Game Resource Guide. Leaptrott & Company Staff. (GC - Principles of Management Ser.). 1996. text ed. 19.95 (*0-538-86199-1*) S-W Pub.

***Rules of the Green: A History of the Rules of Golf.** Kenneth G. Chapman. (Illus.). 240p. 1997. 34.95 (*1-57243-173-3*); lib. bdg. 50.00 (*1-57243-210-1*) Triumph Bks.

Rules of the Hunt. Victor O'Reilly. 512p. (Orig.). 1995. mass mkt. 6.99 (*0-425-15097-6*) Berkley Pub.

Rules of the Italian Political Game. Franco D. Marengo. 144p. 1981. text ed. 53.95 (*0-566-00301-5*, Pub. by Dartmth Pub UK) Ashgate Pub Co.

Rules of the Legal Profession - Cases & Materials on the Legal Profession. Robert F. Cochran, Jr. & Teresa S. Collett. (American Casebook Ser.). 375p. (C). 1996. text ed. write for info. (*0-314-09884-4*) West Pub.

Rules of the Mind. John R. Anderson. 336p. 1993. pap. 27. 50 (*0-8058-1200-8*); text ed. 69.95 (*0-8058-1199-0*) L Erlbaum Assocs.

Rules of the Net: Online Operating Instructions for Human Beings. Thomas Mandel & Gerard Van Der Leun. 288p. 1996. pap. 12.00 (*0-7868-8135-6*) Hyperion.

***Rules of the Radio Ratings Game.** Robert E. Balon. 130p. 1988. pap. 24.95 (*0-8058-1048-X*) L Erlbaum Assocs.

Rules of the Road. Contractors' Service Center, Inc. Staff. 372p. 1990. 29.95 (*0-9627309-0-4*) Contractor's Srvc Ctr.

Rules of the Road. rev. ed. Contractors' Service Center, Inc., Staff. 372p. 1991. 29.95 (*0-9627309-1-2*) Contractor's Srvc Ctr.

Rules of the Road for Registered Representatives: A Guide to Securities Compliance. Thomas R. Keyes & David S. Miller. 250p. 1991. pap. 19.95 (*0-13-770314-7*) NY Inst Finance.

Rules of the Road for Registered Representatives, 1989-90. Thomas R. Keyes & David S. Miller. 156p. 1989. pap. 24.50 (*0-9624115-0-7*) Keyes Pub.

Rules of the Road for the Information Superhighway: Electronic Communications & the Law. Ed. by Legal Research Network Staff. 747p. (C). 1995. text ed. write for info. (*0-314-06663-2*) West Pub.

Rules of the Road Toads. John M. Williams. LC 93-61007. (Illus.). 24p. (J). 1993. lib. bdg. 7.95 (*1-883084-03-2*) Wonder Bks.

Rules of the U. S. Courts in New York: Federal Rules of Appellate Procedure. 2nd ed. Clerks of the Federal Courts in New York. LC 65-16452. (Federal Court Rules Ser.). 1978. ring bd. 145.00 (*0-87632-070-1*) Clark Boardman Callaghan.

Rules of Thumb. R. H. Hayward. (C). 1991. 75.00 (*0-86022-213-6*, Pub. by Build Servs Info Assn UK) St Mut.

***Rules of Thumb.** N. L. Pavey. 1995. pap. 250.00 (*0-86022-419-8*, Pub. by Build Servs Info Assn UK) St Mut.

Rules of Thumb, Vol. 1. Tom Parker. 1983. pap. 9.95 (*0-395-34642-8*) HM.

Rules of Thumb: A Guide for Writers. 2nd ed. Jay Silverman. 1993. pap. text ed. write for info. (*0-07-057582-7*) McGraw.

Rules of Thumb: A Guide for Writers. 2nd ed. Jay Silverman. 1993. pap. text ed. write for info. (*0-07-057611-4*) McGraw.

Rules of Thumb: A Guide for Writers. 3rd ed. Jay Silverman et al. LC 95-10037. (Illus.). 1996. pap. text ed. write for info. (*0-07-057640-8*) McGraw.

Rules of Thumb: A Guide for Writers. 3rd ed. Jay Silverman et al. LC 95-10037. (Illus.). 1995. write for info. (*0-07-057647-5*) McGraw.

Rules of Thumb: A Guide for Writers - Good Measures: a Practice Book. 2nd ed. Jay Silverman et al. 1993. pap. text ed. write for info. (*0-07-057583-5*) McGraw.

Rules of Thumb for Chemical Engineers. Carl Branan. 368p. 1994. 79.00 (*0-88415-162-X*) Gulf Pub.

***Rules of Thumb for Chemical Engineers.** 2nd ed. Carl Branan. 1999. pap. 79.00 (*0-88415-788-1*, 5788) Gulf Pub.

***Rules of Thumb for Home Building, Improvement & Repair.** Katie Hamilton & Gene Hamilton. LC 96-46906. pap. text ed. write for info. (*0-471-30983-4*) Wiley.

***Rules of Thumb for Home Building, Improvement & Repair.** Katie Hamilton & Gene Hamilton. I C 96-46906. 1997. text ed. write for info. (*0-471-30984-2*) Wiley.

Rules of Thumb for Mechanical Engineers. E. Pope et al. 400p. 1996. 79.00 (*0-88415-790-3*, 5790) Gulf Pub.

Rules of Thumb for Scientists & Engineers. David J. Fisher. 256p. 1990. 28.95 (*0-87201-786-9*) Gulf Pub.

Rules of Thumb Practice Book: A Guide for Writers, Good Measures. 3rd ed. Jay Silverman et al. 1995. pap. text ed. write for info. (*0-07-057645-9*) McGraw.

***Rules of Thumb-U. K./France.** P. Compton & N. L. Pavey. 1995. pap. 250.00 (*0-86022-420-1*, Pub. by Build Servs Info Assn UK) St Mut.

RULES Phonological Evaluation. Jane C. Webb & Barbara Duckett. (Illus.). 140p. (J). (ps-3). 1990. text ed. 54.95 (*0-937857-12-2*, 1577) Speech Bin.

Rules, Reputation & Macroeconomic Policy Coordination. David Currie & Paul Levine. LC 92-30613. (Illus.). 448p. (C). 1993. text ed. 69.95 (*0-521-44196-X*) Cambridge U Pr.

Rules That Babies Look By: The Organization of Newborn Visual Activity. Marshall M. Haith. LC 80-10601. (Child Psychology Ser.). (Illus.). 159p. 1980. text ed. 29.95 (*0-89859-033-7*) L Erlbaum Assocs.

Rules vs. Relationships: The Ethnography of Legal Discourse. John M. Conley & William M. O'Barr. LC 89-20497. (Language & Legal Discourse Ser.). 236p. 1990. pap. text ed. 17.95 (*0-226-11491-0*); lib. bdg. 41.00 (*0-226-11490-2*) U Ch Pr.

Rules Without Meaning: Essays on Ritual, Mantras & the Science of Man. Frits Staal. (Toronto Studies in Religion: Vol. 4). 492p. (C). 1989. text ed. 99.95 (*0-8204-0553-1*) P Lang Pubng.

Rules Without Meaning: Essays on Ritual, Mantras & the Science of Man. Frits Staal. (Toronto Studies in Religion: Vol. 4). 490p. 1993. pap. 39.95 (*0-8204-2418-8*) P Lang Pubng.

Ruling & Reigning in the Nineties. Charles E. Winburn, Jr. 1989. pap. 7.95 (*0-88144-143-0*) RCP Inc OH.

Ruling Britannia: A Political History of Britain 1688-1988. Glyn Williams. 1989. 68.95 (*0-582-48485-5*, Pub. by Longman UK) Longman.

Ruling Brittania: Political History of Britain, 1688-1988. Glyn Williams & John Ramsden. (Illus.). 544p. (C). 1989. pap. text ed. 37.50 (*0-582-49073-1*, 78503) Longman.

Ruling Chiefs of Hawaii. rev. ed. Samuel M. Kamakau. Tr. by Mary K. Pukui et al. from HAW. (Illus.). 513p. 1992. 39.95 (*0-87336-015-X*); pap. 24.95 (*0-87336-014-1*) Kamehameha Schools.

Ruling Class. Gaetano Mosca. Ed. by Arthur Livingston. Tr. by Hannah D. Kahn from ITA. LC 80-17230. xli, 514p. 1980. reprint ed. text ed. 45.50 (*0-313-22617-2*, MORU, Greenwood Pr) Greenwood.

Ruling Class: A Study of British Finance Capital. Sam Aaronovitch. LC 78-23485. 192p. 1979. reprint ed. text ed. 49.75 (*0-313-20764-X*, AARC, Greenwood Pr) Greenwood.

Ruling Class: Inside the Imperial Congress. Eric Felten. LC 92-36247. 256p. 1993. 24.00 (*0-89526-506-0*) Regnery Pub.

Ruling Class in Italy Before 1900. Vilfredo Pareto. LC 73-20130. 143p. 1975. reprint ed. 30.00 (*0-86527-176-3*) Fertig.

Ruling Class of Judaea: The Origins of the Jewish Revolt Against Rome AD 66-70. Martin Goodman. 272p. 1987. text ed. 69.95 (*0-521-33401-2*) Cambridge U Pr.

Ruling Class of Judaea: The Origins of the Jewish Revolt Against Rome AD 66-70. Martin Goodman. 288p. (C). 1993. pap. text ed. 21.95 (*0-521-44782-8*) Cambridge U Pr.

Ruling Communist Parties & Their Status under Law. Ed. by D. A. Loeber. 1986. lib. bdg. 235.00 (*90-247-3209-3*) Kluwer Ac.

Ruling Elites of Rajasthan: A Changing Profile. C. L. Sharma. 153p. (C). 1993. 48.00 (*81-85880-13-1*, Pub. by Print Hse II) St Mut.

***Ruling Families of Arabia: Documentary Records of the Dynasties of Saudi Arabia, Jordan, Kuwait, Bahrain, Qatar, UAE & Oman, 12 vols.** Ed. by A. De L. Rush. (Illus.). 7500p. 1991. reprint ed. lib. bdg. 2,795.00 (*1-85207-310-1*, Pub. by Archive Editions UK) N Ross.

Ruling Illusions: Philosophy & the Social Order. Anthony Skillen. (Modern Revivals in Philosophy Ser.). 190p. 1993. 50.95 (*0-7512-0200-2*, Pub. by Gregg Revivals UK) Ashgate Pub Co.

Ruling Lines. Carl Japikse & Robert R. Leichtman. 1990. pap. 7.95 (*0-89804-091-4*) Ariel GA.

Ruling Passion. Reginald Hill. 320p. 1990. mass mkt. 4.99 (*0-440-16889-9*) Dell.

Ruling Passion: British Colonial Allegory & the Paradox of Homosexual Desire. Christopher Lane. LC 95-6484. 344p. 1995. text ed. 49.95 (*0-8223-1677-3*); pap. text ed. 16.95 (*0-8223-1689-7*) Duke.

Ruling Passion: Tales of Nature & Human Nature. Henry Van Dyke. LC 71-38725. (Short Story Index Reprint Ser.). (Illus.). 1977. reprint ed. 23.95 (*0-8369-4138-1*) Ayer.

Ruling Passions: Sexual Violence, Reputation & the Law. Sue Lees. LC 96-19876. 192p. 1996. 79.95 (*0-335-19614-4*, Open Univ Pr); pap. 23.95 (*0-335-19613-6*, Open Univ Pr) Taylor & Francis.

***Ruling Race.** James Oakes. Date not set. pap. 14.95 (*0-393-31705-6*) Norton.

***Ruling Russia: Politics & Administration in the Age of Absolutism, 1762-1796.** John P. LeDonne. LC 84-2168. (Studies of the Harriman Institute). 427p. 1984. reprint ed. pap. 121.70 (*0-608-03332-4*, 2064044) Bks Demand.

Ruling the Roost: What's Bigger Than Tobacco, More Dangerous Than Mining, & Foul to Eat? Ed. by Bob Hall & Eric Bates. (Illus.). 64p. (Orig.). 1989. pap. 5.00 (*0-943810-41-8*) Southern Exposure.

Ruling the Waves: The Political Economy of International Shipping. Alan W. Cafruny. LC 86-30889. (Studies in International Political Economy: Vol. 17). 356p. 1987. 55.00 (*0-520-05968-9*) U CA Pr.

***Ruling Well: Leadership in Our Church Today.** Curtis Redmon. (Practical Church Ser.). 129p. (Orig.). 1996. pap. text ed. 7.95 (*1-881685-05-5*) LUA Stand Minist.

Rulings of the Night: An Ethnography of Nepalese Shaman Oral Texts. Gregory G. Maskarinec. LC 94-23024. (Illus.). 1995. 65.50 (*0-299-14490-9*); pap. 22.95 (*0-299-14494-1*) U of Wis Pr.

***Rullion Green 1983.** T. F. Watkins. 81p. 1984. pap. 7.50 (*0-614-21836-5*) David Brown.

***Rullion Green 1984.** T. F. Watkins. 100p. 1984. pap. 7.50 (*0-614-21838-1*) David Brown.

***Rullion Green 1985.** T. F. Watkins & J. Murray. 41p. 1990. pap. 7.50 (*0-614-21846-2*) David Brown.

Rum-A-Tum-Tum. Angela S. Medearis. LC 94-9929. (Illus.). 32p. (J). (ps-3). 1997. lib. bdg. 16.95 (*0-8234-1143-5*) Holiday.

Rum Across the Border: The Prohibition Era in Northern New York. Allan S. Everest. (New York State Bks.). (Illus.). 172p. (Orig.). 1992. reprint ed. pap. 9.95 (*0-8156-2547-2*) Syracuse U Pr.

Rum & Coke. Keith Reddin. 1986. pap. 5.95 (*0-88145-042-1*) Broadway Play.

Rum & Razors. Jessica Fletcher & Donald Bain. (Murder, She Wrote Mystery Ser.). 304p. (Orig.). 1995. mass mkt., pap. 4.99 (*0-451-18383-5*) NAL-Dutton.

Rum & Razors. large type ed. Jessica Fletcher & Donald Bain. LC 95-17172. (Murder, She Wrote). (Orig.). 1995. pap. 22.95 (*1-56895-219-8*) Wheeler Pub.

***Rum & Reggae.** Jonathan Runge. Date not set. pap. 3.99 (*0-517-17832-X*) Random Hse Value.

Rum & Reggae: What's Hot & What's Not in the Caribbean. Jonathan Runge. LC 87-29938. (Illus.). 224p. 1988. pap. 10.95 (*0-312-01509-7*) St Martin.

Rum & the American Revolution, 2 vols., Set. John J. McCusker. (Outstanding Studies in Early American History). 1396p. 1989. reprint ed. 75.00 (*0-8240-6191-8*) Garland.

Rum Gully Tales from Tuck'em Inn. Pratt Gasque. LC 89-20438. (Illus.). 148p. (YA). (gr. 6 up). 1990. 14.95 (*0-87844-094-1*) Sandlapper Pub Co.

Rum Punch. Elmore Leonard. 304p. 1992. 21.00 (*0-385-30143-X*) Delacorte.

Rum Punch. Elmore Leonard. 368p. 1993. mass mkt. 6.50 (*0-440-21415-7*) Dell.

Rum Punch. large type ed. Elmore Leonard. LC 93-35521. (General Ser.). 1994. pap. 18.95 (*0-8161-5807-X*, GK Hall) Thorndike Pr.

Rum Punch in the Caribbean. P. L. Berg. LC 95-90269. 1996. 18.95 (*0-533-11516-7*) Vantage.

Rum Rebellion: A Study of the Overthrow of Governor Bligh by John Macarthur & the New South Wales Corps, Including the John Murtagh Macrossan Memorial Lectures Delivered at the University of Queensland, June, 1937. Herbert V. Evatt. 1977. 19.95 (*0-8369-7109-4*, 7943) Ayer.

Rum, Religion, & Votes: Nineteen Twenty-Eight Re-Examined. Ruth C. Silva. LC 80-24997. (Illus.). 76p. 1981. text ed. 49.75 (*0-313-22768-3*, SIRR, Greenwood Pr) Greenwood.

***Rum Runners.** Frank Anderson. Date not set. pap. 5.95 (*0-919433-22-7*) Lone Pine.

***Rum State: Alcohol & State Policy in Australia.** Milton Lewis. 232p. 24.95 (*0-644-22024-4*, Pub. by Aust Gov Pub AT) Aubrey Bks.

Rum-Tum-Tum: Mississippi Recipes for a Festive Southern Christmas. Joy Price. (Illus.). 48p. (Orig.). 1985. reprint ed. pap. 5.00 (*0-945301-01-4*) Druid Pr.

Rumana's New Clothes. Khurshid Hasan & Rachel Warner. (Duets Ser.). (Illus.). 25p. (J). (gr. 2-4). 1991. 15.95 (*0-237-60160-5*, Pub. by Evans Bros Ltd UK) Trafalgar.

Rumania. Romulus Seisanu. 116p. 1987. write for info. (*0-937019-06-2*); pap. 15.00 (*0-937019-07-0*) Romanian Hist.

Rumania: A Bibliographic Guide. Stephen Fischer-Galati. LC 63-60076. (Bibliographic Guides Ser.). 1978. reprint ed. 12.95 (*0-405-00057-X*) Ayer.

Rumania: Political Problems of an Agrarian State. Henry L. Roberts. 1951. 89.50 (*0-685-45660-9*) Elliots Bks.

Rumania: Political Problems of an Agrarian State. Henry L. Roberts. LC 69-13629. (Illus.). xiv, 414p. (C). 1969. reprint ed. lib. bdg. 45.00 (*0-208-00651-6*, Archon Bks) Shoe String.

Rumanian. Graham Mallinson. (Descriptive Grammars Ser.). 384p. 1986. 72.50 (*0-7099-3537-4*, Pub. by Croom Helm UK) Routledge Chapman & Hall.

Rumanian-English Dictionary. Serban Andronescu. 42.50 (*0-87557-063-1*) Saphrograph.

Rumanian-English Dictionary. Serban Andronescu. 252p. (ENG & RUM.). 1993. reprint ed. lib. bdg. 35.00 (*0-8288-2630-7*) Fr & Eur.

Rumanian Folk Music, 5 vols., Set. Bartok. 1987. lib. bdg. 94.00 (*90-247-0622-X*) Kluwer Ac.

Rumanian-Hungarian Concise Dictionary. F. Bakos. 835p. 1991. 50.00 (*963-05-5877-7*, Pub. by Akad Kiado HU) St Mut.

Rumanian National Movement in Transylvania, 1780-1849. Keith Hitchins. LC 69-12724. (Historical Monographs: No. 61). 327p. 1969. 25.00 (*0-674-78035-3*) HUP.

Rumanian Verb System. Alphonse Juilland & P. M. Edwards. LC 66-15853. (Janua Linguarum, Ser. Practica: No. 28). (Orig.). 1971. pap. text ed. 18.50 (*90-279-1605-5*) Mouton.

Rumba. Earl Atkinson. (Ballroom Dance Ser.). 1986. lib. bdg. 250.00 (*0-8490-3631-3*) Gordon Pr.

Rumba: Dance & Social Change in Contemporary Cuba. Yvonne Daniel. LC 94-34363. (Blacks in the Diaspora Ser.). (Illus.). 224p. 1995. 29.95 (*0-253-31605-7*); pap. 12.95 (*0-253-20948-X*) Ind U Pr.

Rumba Combinations. Earl Atkinson. (Ballroom Dance Ser.). 1983. lib. bdg. 250.00 (*0-87700-477-3*) Revisionist Pr.

Rumba Incesante Hacia la Nada. Omar A. Garcia-Obregon. 96p. (Orig.). (SPA.). 1993. pap. write for info. (*1-56167-109-6*) Am Literary Pr.

Rumba Is My Life. Xavier Cugat. (Ballroom Dance Ser.). 1986. lib. bdg. 250.00 (*0-8490-3262-8*) Gordon Pr.

Rumba Is My Life. Xavier Cugat. (Ballroom Dance Ser.). 1985. lib. bdg. 250.00 (*0-87700-848-5*) Revisionist Pr.

Rumba Is My Life: American Autobiography. Xavier Cugat. 210p. 1995. lib. bdg. 79.00 (*0-7812-8493-7*) Rprt Serv.

Rumba Made Easy. (Ballroom Dance Ser.). 1985. lib. bdg. 77.95 (*0-87700-670-9*) Revisionist Pr.

Rumble Fish. S. E. Hinton. 112p. (J). (gr. k up). 1989. mass mkt. 3.99 (*0-440-97534-4*, LLL BDD) BDD Bks Young Read.

Rumble Fish. S. E. Hinton. 112p. (YA). (gr. 7 up). 1975. 13.95 (*0-385-28675-9*) Delacorte.

Rumble Fish - Study Guide. Cheryl Gluzband. Ed. by Joyce Friedland & Rikki Kessler. (Novel-Ties Ser.). (YA). (gr. 6-9). 1993. pap. text ed. 15.95 (*0-88122-128-7*) Lrn Links.

***Rumble in the Jungle.** Giles Andreae. LC 96-34423. (Illus.). (J). 1997. 14.95 (*1-888444-08-8*) Little Tiger.

***Rumble in the Jungle.** Britta Teckentrup. (J). 1997. pap. 14.99 (*0-670-87473-6*) Viking Penguin.

Rumble Rumble: Jesus Feeds the Crowd. M. Simon. 24p. 1990. pap. text ed. 2.49 (*0-570-04179-1*, 56-1638) Concordia.

Rumble Thumble Boom! Anna G. Hines. LC 91-31808. (Illus.). 24p. (J). (ps-4). 1992. lib. bdg. 13.93 (*0-688-10912-8*) Greenwillow.

Rumbling Volcano: Islamic Fundamentalism in Egypt. Nabeel T. Jabbour. 320p. (Orig.). 1993. pap. 11.95 (*0-87808-241-7*, WCL241-7) William Carey Lib.

Rumbling Wine Barrels. Bruno Buti. 356p. 1995. 19.95 (*0-9648960-0-1*) B Buti.

Rumbly Tumbly Glittery Gritty Place. Mary L. Ray. LC 92-20084. (Illus.). 32p. (J). (ps-3). 1993. 14.00 (*0-15-292861-8*, HB Juv Bks) HarBrace.

Rumbo. Joaquin Delgado-Sanchez. LC 85-81208. (Coleccion Caniqui). 118p. (Orig.). (SPA.). 1986. pap. 9.95 (*0-89729-381-9*) Ediciones.

***Rumbo Al Infierno.** Luis Torres. (SPA.). 0.95 (*0-8297-1242-9*) Life Pubs Intl.

Rumbo al Punto Cierto. Rosario Rexach. 1979. pap. 7.50 (*84-499-2644-0*) Edit Mensaje.

Rumbuli. Frida Michelson. Tr. by Wolf Goodman from RUS. 224p. 1983. reprint ed. pap. 5.95 (*0-686-99459-0*) ADL.

Rumen Protozoa. A. G. Williams & G. S. Coleman. (Contemporary Bioscience Ser.). (Illus.). 464p. 1991. 212.95 (*0-387-97548-9*) Spr-Verlag.

Rumer Godden. Rosenthal. 1996. 24.95 (*0-8057-7930-2*, Hall Reference) Macmillan.

***Rumi: Divan-i Kebir.** Jalal A. Rumi. Tr. by Nevit O. Ergin. 418p. 1996. pap. 25.00 (*0-614-21336-3*, 1376) Kazi Pubns.

***Rumi: Fountain of Fire.** 2nd ed. Nader Khalili. 143p. (Orig.). 1996. reprint ed. pap. 11.95 (*1-889625-03-5*) Cal-Earth.

***Rumi: In the Arms of the Beloved.** Tr. by Jonathan Star. LC 97-13844. 208p. 1997. 19.95 (*0-87477-894-8*, Tarcher Putnam) Putnam Pub Group.

Rumi: Poet & Mystic. Reynold A. Nicholson. 190p. 1995. pap. 11.95 (*1-85168-096-9*) Onewrld Pubns.

Rumi: The Persian Mystic. F. Hadland Davis. 107p. (Orig.). (C). 1985. pap. text ed. 4.50 (*1-56744-372-9*) Kazi Pubns.

Rumi & Sufism. 2nd ed. Eva De Vitray-Meyerovitch. Tr. by Simone Fattal. (World of Islam Ser.). (Illus.). 167p. (Orig.). (FRE.). 1989. reprint ed. pap. 12.95 (*0-942996-08-9*) Post Apollo Pr.

***Rumi Daylight: A Daybook of Spiritual Guidance.** Jalal A. Rumi. Tr. by Camille Helminski & Kabir Helminski. 224p. 1996. 19.00 (*0-614-21335-5*, 1091) Kazi Pubns.

Rumi Speaks Through Sufi Tales. K. Khosla. 252p. (C). 1996. pap. text ed. 19.95 (*1-56744-516-0*) Kazi Pubns.

Rumic Theatre. Rumiko Takahashi. 1996. pap. 15.95 (*1-56931-054-8*) Viz Commns Inc.

Rumic World. Rumiko Takahashi. Ed. by Seiji Horibuchi. Tr. by Satoru Fujii from JPN. (Illus.). 150p. (Orig.). pap. 14.95 (*0-929279-83-2*) Viz Commns Inc.

***Rumic World Trilogy, Vol. 1.** Rumiko Takahashi. 1996. pap. text ed. 15.95 (*1-56931-126-9*, Viz Comics) Viz Commns Inc.

***Rumic World Trilogy, Vol. 2.** Rumiko Takahashi. 1997. pap. text ed. 15.95 (*1-56931-194-3*, Viz Comics) Viz Commns Inc.

***Rumic World Trilogy, Vol. 3.** Rumiko Takahashi. 1997. pap. text ed. 15.95 (*1-56931-206-0*, Viz Comics) Viz Commns Inc.

Ruminant Animal: Digestive Physiology & Nutrition. 2nd ed. David C. Church. (Illus.). 576p. 1987. text ed. 50.00 (*0-13-783754-2*) P-H.

Ruminant Animal: Digestive Physiology & Nutrition. Ed. by D. C. Church. (Illus.). 564p. (C). 1993. reprint ed. text ed. 47.95 (*0-88133-740-4*) Waveland Pr.

Ruminant Pestivirus Infections: Virology, Pathogenesis, & Perspectives of Prophylaxis. Ed. by B. Liess et al. (Archives of Virology Ser.: Supplementum 3). (Illus.). viii, 271p. 1993. 175.00 (*0-387-82279-8*) Spr-Verlag.

Ruminant Urogenital Surgery. C. F. Hofmeyr. LC 86-34266. (Illus.). 182p. 1987. reprint ed. pap. 51.90 (*0-608-00082-5*, 2060845) Bks Demand.

Ruminations. Arthur S. McDowall. LC 68-22925. (Essay Index Reprint Ser.). 1977. 17.95 (*0-8369-0646-2*) Ayer.

***Ruminations.** Oguchi H. Nkwocha. LC 88-90126. 1997. 7.95 (*0-533-08006-1*) Vantage.

Ruminations. William Steig. LC 84-45423. (Illus.). 160p. 1984. 20.00 (*0-374-25283-1*) FS&G.

Ruminations: Poetry, Images & Memories. Clarinda Rose-Turner. (Illus.). 30p. (Orig.). 1989. pap. 4.00 (*0-924120-02-9*) Intl Oil Work.

Ruminations in C++ Reflections on a Decade of C++ Programming. Andrew Koenig. LC 96-20161. (C). 1997. pap. text ed. 27.95 (*0-201-42339-1*) Addison-Wesley.

Ruminations in Search of Destiny-a Philosophy of Pattern. R. Ashbridge Yarnall. 1994. 20.00 (*0-533-11125-0*) Vantage.

Ruminative Thoughts: Advances in Social Cognition, Vol. 9. Ed. by Robert S. Wyer, Jr. 224p. 1996. pap. 19.95 (*0-8058-1816-2*); text ed. 49.95 (*0-8058-1815-4*) L Erlbaum Assocs.

Ruminator: A Collection of Thoughts & Suggestions on Contrary Thinking. Humphrey B. Neill. LC 92-82739. 128p. (C). 1992. reprint ed. pap. 12.00 (*0-87034-105-7*) Fraser Pub Co.

Rumi's Sufism. K. Khosla. 256p. (C). 1996. pap. text ed. 14.95 (*1-56744-515-2*) Kazi Pubns.

Rummage Sale: A Fun Book of Shapes & Colors. Neil Morris. (Fun Books of Learning). (Illus.). 32p. (J). (ps-2). 1991. lib. bdg. 13.50 (*0-87614-676-0*, Carolrhoda) Lerner Group.

Rummage Sale: A Fun Book of Shapes & Colors. Neil Morris. (J). (ps). 1992. pap. 6.95 (*0-87614-575-6*, Carolrhoda) Lerner Group.

Rummager's Handbook: Finding, Buying, Cleaning, Fixing, Using & Selling Secondhand Treasures. R. S. McClurg. LC 94-47930. 160p. 1995. pap. 12.95 (*0-88266-894-3*, Storey Pub) Storey Comm Inc.

Rummies: A Novel. Peter Benchley. 1989. 18.95 (*0-394-57667-5*) Random.

Rumor. Carol Gorman. LC 93-37774. (I Witness Ser.). (Illus.). 96p. (Orig.). (J). (gr. 4-7). 1994. pap. 4.99 (*0-570-04631-9*, 12-3212) Concordia.

***Rumor about Julia.** Stephanie Sinclair. (Love Stories Ser.: No. 23). 192p. (Orig.). (YA). (gr. 7 up). 1997. mass mkt. 3.99 (*0-553-49218-7*) BDD Bks Young Read.

***Rumor & Revenge.** Jim Boulden & Joan Boulden. Ed. by Joann Farness. (Illus.). 24p. (Orig.). (J). (gr. 5-8). 1996. pap. 5.95 (*1-878076-81-7*) Boulden Pub.

Rumor Has It. Charles Dickinson. 240p. 1992. pap. 9.00 (*0-380-71346-2*) Avon.

***Rumor Has It.** Connie Keenan. LC 97-93465. 192p. 1997. lib. bdg. 17.95 (*0-8034-9234-0*, Avalon Bks) Bouregy.

Rumor in the Marketplace: The Social Psychology of Commercial Hearsay. Frederick W. Koenig. LC 84-12379. 224p. 1985. text ed. 49.95 (*0-86569-117-7*, Auburn Hse) Greenwood.

Rumor of Angels. Peter L. Berger. 208p. 1990. pap. 11.95 (*0-385-41592-3*) Doubleday.

Rumor of Bones. Beverly Connor. LC 96-31985. 254p. 1996. 20.95 (*1-888952-08-3*) Cumberland Hse.

Rumor of Distant Tribes. Eugene Jeffers. 255p. 1994. pap. 16.95 (*0-918056-06-3*) Ariadne Pr.

Rumor of Revolt: The "Great Negro Plot" in Colonial New York. T. J. Davis. LC 90-34785. 336p. (C). 1990. reprint ed. pap. 17.95 (*0-87023-725-X*) U of Mass Pr.

Rumor of War. Philip Caputo. 352p. 1987. mass mkt. 6.99 (*0-345-33122-2*) Ballantine.

Rumor of War. Philip Caputo. LC 96-19314. 1996. 0.85 (*0-8050-4965-7*) H Holt & Co.

Rumor of War. Philip Caputo. 384p. 1996. pap. 11.95 (*0-8050-4695-X*) H Holt & Co.

***Rumor of War.** large type ed. Philip Caputo. (Niagara Large Print Ser.). 512p. 1997. 29.50 (*0-7089-5864-8*) Ulverscroft.

Rumor Transmissable Ad Infinitum in Either Direction. Raymond Federman. (Illus.). 320p. 1976. pap. 5.00 (*0-915066-20-3*) Assembling Pr.

Rumor Verified: Poems, 1979-1980. Robert Penn Warren. 91p. 1981. 9.95 (*0-394-52136-6*); pap. 5.95 (*0-394-74960-X*) Random.

***Rumores de Mi Bohio.** Oscar Perez Moro. (SPA.). pap. 7.95 (*0-89729-066-6*) Ediciones.

Rumors. Sara Fitzgerald. 368p. (Orig.). 1992. mass mkt. 4.99 (*0-446-36197-6*) Warner Bks.

Rumors. Fran C. Goodman. 190p. 1995. 10.95 (*0-9643473-3-4*) Francie PR.

Rumors: Uses, Interpretations & Images. Jean-Noel Kapferer. 163p. 1990. 39.95 (*0-88738-325-4*) Transaction Pubs.

Rumors & Stones: A Journey. Wayne Karlin. 214p. (Orig.). 1996. 19.95 (*1-880684-42-X*) Curbstone.

Rumors at the Rink. Melissa Lowell. (Silver Blades Ser.: No. 8). (J). (gr. 4-7). 1995. pap. 3.50 (*0-553-48293-9*) Bantam.

Rumors from the Cauldron: Selected Essays, Reviews, & Reportage. Valerie Miner. 318p. (C). 1991. text ed. 42.50 (*0-472-09472-6*); pap. text ed. 14.95 (*0-472-06472-X*) U of Mich Pr.

Rumors from the Lost World: A Collection of Stories. Alan Davis. (Minnesota Voices Project Ser.: Vol. 54). 136p. (Orig.). 1993. pap. 9.95 (*0-89823-142-6*) New Rivers Pr.

Rumors of Change: Essays of Five Decades. Ihab Hassan. LC 95-2966. 232p. (C). 1995. pap. 24.95 (*0-8173-0830-X*); text ed. 49.95 (*0-8173-0802-4*) U of Ala Pr.

Rumors of Existence: Newly Discovered, Supposedly Extinct, & Unconfirmed Inhabitants of the Animal Kingdom. Matthew A. Bille. (Illus.). 192p. (Orig.). 1995. pap. 12.95 (*0-88839-335-0*) Hancock House.

Rumors of No Law: Poems from Berkeley 1968-1977. Peter D. Scott. LC 80-17862. (Orig.). 1981. pap. 4.50 (*0-914476-88-2*) Thorp Springs.

Rumors of Peace. Ella Leffland. LC 78-20209. 400p. 1985. pap. 13.00 (*0-06-091301-0*, PL 1301, PL) HarpC.

Rumors of Separate Worlds. Robert Coles. LC 89-32838. (Illus.). 90p. 1989. 19.95 (*0-87745-258-X*); pap. 11.95 (*0-87745-260-1*) U of Iowa Pr.

Rumors of War. Kenneth Copeland. 13p. 1991. pap. 1.00 (*0-88114-832-6*) K Copeland Pubns.

***Rumors of War.** Dean Hughes. LC 96-45548. 1997. write for info. (*1-57345-199-1*) Deseret Bk.

Rumors, Race, & Riots. Terry A. Knopf. LC 73-85098. (Social Policy Ser.). 390p. 1975. text ed. 39.95 (*0-87855-063-1*) Transaction Pubs.

R

R

Rumour of Calcutta: Tourism, Charity & the Poverty of Representation. John Hutnyk. 240p. (C). 1996. 65.00 (1-85649-407-1, Pub. by Zed Bks Ltd UK) Humanities.

Rumour of Calcutta: Tourism, Charity & the Poverty of Representation. John Hutnyk. 240p. (C). 1996. pap. 22.50 (1-85649-408-X, Pub. by Zed Bks Ltd UK) Humanities.

Rumour of the Flesh & Soul. Modhusudan Sanyal. (Writers Workshop Redbird Ser.). 1975. 8.00 (0-88253-620-6); pap. text ed. 4.00 (0-88253-619-2) Ind-US Inc.

***Rumpah!** Frank W. Lewis. 300p. pap. 14.95 (0-614-25162-1) Western Tales.

Rumpelstiltskin. (Ladybird Stories Ser.). (Illus.). (ARA.). (J). (gr. 4-6). 1987. 3.95 (0-86685-265-4) Intl Bk Ctr.

Rumpelstiltskin. (J). 1996. pap. 1.25 (0-8167-0565-8) Troll Communs.

Rumpelstiltskin. (Little Landoll Fairytale Ser.). 32p. (J). (ps-3). Date not set. text ed. 1.29 (1-56987-229-5) Landoll.

Rumpelstiltskin. (Favorite Fairy Tale Classics Ser.). 24p. (J). (ps-3). Date not set. text ed. 3.50 (1-56987-209-0) Landoll.

Rumpelstiltskin. (Spanish Fairytale Little Landoll Ser.). 32p. (SPA.). (J). (ps-3). Date not set. text ed. write for info. (1-56987-251-1) Landoll.

Rumpelstiltskin. Berthe Amoss. (Illus.). 10p. (J). (ps-7). 1989. pap. 2.95 (0-922589-03-8) More than Card.

Rumpelstiltskin. Nicola Baxter. (Favorite Tales Ser.). (Illus.). 28p. (J). 1994. 2.99 (0-7214-5456-9, Ladybrd) Penguin.

Rumpelstiltskin. Charlotte B. Chorpenning. (J). (gr. 1-7). 1944. 5.00 (0-87602-195-X) Anchorage.

Rumpelstiltskin. Fred Crump, Jr. (Illus.). 44p. (J). (gr. k-2). 1991. pap. 6.95 (1-55523-409-7) Winston-Derek.

Rumpelstiltskin. Bren Dubay. 22p. (J). (gr. 2-7). 1989. pap. 3.00 (1-57514-259-7, 1050) Encore Perform Pub.

Rumpelstiltskin. Paul Galdone. LC 84-12741. (Illus.). 32p. (J). (ps-3). 1985. 14.95 (0-89919-266-1, Clarion Bks) HM.

Rumpelstiltskin. Paul Galdone. (Illus.). 1990. pap. 5.95 (0-395-52599-3, Clarion Bks) HM.

Rumpelstiltskin. Paul Galdone. 1994. pap. 8.95 (0-395-69175-3) HM.

***Rumpelstiltskin.** Marie-Louise Gay. 1997. 15.95 (0-88899-279-3, Pub. by Groundwood-Douglas & McIntyre CN) Firefly Bks Ltd.

Rumpelstiltskin. Jacob W. Grimm & Wilhelm K. Grimm. (Illus.). 32p. (J). (ps-3). 1992. 6.95 (0-8362-4922-4) Andrews & McMeel.

Rumpelstiltskin. Jacob W. Grimm & Wilhelm K. Grimm. LC 86-4482. (Illus.). 40p. (J). (gr. k up). 1986. pap. 15.99 (0-525-44265-0) Dutton Child Bks.

Rumpelstiltskin. Jacob W. Grimm & Wilhelm K. Grimm. (J). pap. 3.95 (0-8167-3344-9) Troll Communs.

Rumpelstiltskin. Jacob W. Grimm & Wilhelm K. Grimm. LC 78-18079. (Illus.). 32p. (J). (gr. k-3). 1979. pap. 3.95 (0-89375-118-9) Troll Communs.

Rumpelstiltskin. Jacob W. Grimm. (Illus.). 48p. (J). 1996. pap. 5.99 (0-14-055864-0) Viking Penguin.

Rumpelstiltskin. Jacob W. Grimm & Wilhelm K. Grimm. (Golden Sound Story Bks.). (Illus.). 20p. (J). (ps-3). 1992. write for info. (0-307-74711-5, 64711, Golden Books) Western Pub.

Rumpelstiltskin. Ed McBain. 1992. mass mkt. 4.99 (0-446-40167-6, Mysterious Paperbk) Warner Bks.

Rumpelstiltskin. Ed McBain. 240p. 1994. mass mkt. 5.99 (0-446-60130-6) Warner Bks.

***Rumpelstiltskin.** Martha Mutz. (J). 1997. pap. 16.00 (1-889397-31-8) Curiosity Canyon.

Rumpelstiltskin. Christopher Noel. LC 92-4592. (We All Have Tales Ser.). (Illus.). 40p. (J). (gr. k up). 1993. 19.95 incl. audio (0-88708-280-7, Rabbit); 14.95 (0-88708-279-3, Rabbit) S&S Childrens.

Rumpelstiltskin. Illus. by Helen Roy. LC 95-8420. (J). 1995. pap. write for info. (1-57255-001-5) Mondo Pubng.

Rumpelstiltskin. Illus. by Helen Roy. LC 95-8420. 24p. (J). (ps-4). 1995. 13.95 (1-57255-000-7) Mondo Pubng.

Rumpelstiltskin. Illus. by Peter Sis. (J). (ps up). 1995. 19.95 incl. audio (0-689-80061-4) S&S Trade.

***Rumpelstiltskin.** Swan. Date not set. pap. text ed. write for info. (0-582-02567-2, Pub. by Longman UK) Longman.

Rumpelstiltskin. rev. ed. D. Nomathande Dixon. LC 93-72071. (Illus.). 32p. (J). (ps-2). 1995. pap. 9.95 (1-882171-01-2) Confetti Ent.

Rumpelstiltskin: A Fairy Tale. Jacob W. Grimm. 1996. pap. text ed. 6.95 (1-55858-617-2) North-South Bks NYC.

Rumpelstiltskin: A Participation Play (Playscript) Moses Goldberg. (J). (gr. k-3). 1987. pap. 5.00 (0-87602-269-7) Anchorage.

Rumpelstiltskin: Director's Guide. rev. ed. William-Alan Landes. LC 89-43683. (Wondrawhopper Ser.). 52p. (J). (gr. 3-12). 1985. teacher ed., pap. 30.00 (0-88734-005-9) Players Pr.

Rumpelstiltskin: Music & Lyrics. rev. ed. William-Alan Landes & Jeff Rizzo. (Wondrawhopper Ser.). (J). (gr. 3-12). 1985. pap. text ed. 15.00 (0-88734-004-0) Players Pr.

Rumpelstiltskin: Playscript. rev. ed. William-Alan Landes. LC 89-43683. (Wondrawhopper Ser.). 52p. (J). (gr. 3-12). 1985. pap. 6.00 (0-88734-104-7) Players Pr.

Rumpelstiltskin - Musical. Robert Johanson & Albert Evans. 1995. 5.00 (0-87129-524-5, R02) Dramatic Pub.

Rumpelstiltskin Deal Is a Deal. Granowskay. 1994. pap. 4.95 (0-8114-2213-5) Raintree Steck-V.

Rumpelstiltskin Is My Name. Contrib. by R. Eugene Jackson. 52p. (J). (gr. k up). 1978. pap. 3.50 (0-88680-166-4) I E Clark.

Rumpelstiltskin's Daughter. Diane Stanley. LC 96-14834. (J). 1997. lib. bdg. 14.93 (0-688-14328-8, Morrow Junior) Morrow.

Rumpelstiltskin's Daughter. Diane Stanley. LC 96-14834. (Illus.). (J). 1997. 15.00 (0-688-14327-X, Morrow Junior) Morrow.

Rumpf und Extremitaeten see Atlas der Plastischen Chirurgie

Rumpole a la Carte. 256p. 1993. pap. 10.00 (0-14-017981-X, Penguin Bks) Viking Penguin.

Rumpole a la Carte. John Mortimer. 256p. 1991. reprint ed. pap. 10.95 (0-14-015609-7, Penguin Bks) Viking Penguin.

Rumpole & the Age of Miracles. John Mortimer. (Orig.). 1989. pap. 9.95 (0-14-013116-7, Penguin Bks) Viking Penguin.

Rumpole & the Age of Miracles. large type ed. John Mortimer. 1995. pap. 19.95 (0-7838-1188-8, GK Hall) Thorndike Pr.

Rumpole & the Angel of Death. John Mortimer. 1995. 22.95 (0-614-96276-5, Viking) Viking Penguin.

Rumpole & the Angel of Death. John Mortimer. 256p. 1996. pap. 22.95 (0-670-86451-X, Viking) Viking Penguin.

***Rumpole & the Angel of Death.** John Mortimer. 1997. pap. 9.95 (0-14-026314-4) Viking Penguin.

Rumpole & the Angel of Death. large type ed. John Mortimer. 426p. 1996. lib. bdg. 22.95 (0-7838-1794-0, GK Hall) Thorndike Pr.

Rumpole & the Golden Thread. John Mortimer. 1984. pap. 9.95 (0-14-025014-X, Penguin Classics) Viking Penguin.

Rumpole for the Defence. John Mortimer. (Crime Monthly Ser.). 192p. 1984. mass mkt. 5.95 (0-14-006060-X, Penguin Bks) Viking Penguin.

***Rumpole for the Defense.** John Mortimer. 1984. pap. 9.95 (0-14-025013-1) Viking Penguin.

***Rumpole of the Bailey.** John Mortimer. 1980. pap. 9.95 (0-14-025012-3) Viking Penguin.

Rumpole on Trial. large type ed. John Mortimer. LC 93-7198. 1993. lib. bdg. 21.95 (1-56054-727-8) Thorndike Pr.

Rumpole on Trial. John Mortimer. 256p. 1993. reprint ed. pap. 10.00 (0-14-017510-5, Penguin Bks) Viking Penguin.

Rumpole 2. John Mortimer. 1996. audio 16.99 (0-553-47439-1) Bantam.

Rumpole's Last Case. John Mortimer. 288p. 1988. pap. 3.95 (0-14-010447-X, Penguin Bks) Viking Penguin.

Rumpoles Last Case. John Mortimer. 1990. pap. 9.95 (0-14-012695-3, Penguin Bks) Viking Penguin.

Rumpole's Return. John Mortimer. 160p. 1982. pap. 6.00 (0-14-005571-1, Penguin Bks); pap. 9.95 (0-14-024698-3, Penguin Classics) Viking Penguin.

Rumrunner: The Life & Times of Johnny Schnarr. Marion Parker & Robert Tyrrell. 224p. (Orig.). 1993. pap. 10.95 (0-920501-94-X) Orca Bk Pubs.

***Rumrunning & the Roaring Twenties: Prohibition on the Michigan-Ontario Waterway.** Philip P. Mason. LC 95-4610. (Illus.). 186p. 1995. 29.95 (0-8143-2583-1, Great Lks Bks) Wayne St U Pr.

Rums of the Eastern Caribbean. Edward Hamilton. (Illus.). 208p. (Orig.). 1995. pap. 20.00 (0-9647653-0-6) Tafia Pubng.

Rumson, NJ. Randall Gabrielan. (Images of America Ser.). 128p. 1996. pap. 16.99 (0-7524-0290-0, Arcdia) Chalford.

Rumunsko-Cesky-Rumunsky Slovnik. Felix-Krecan-Blaha. 460p. (CZE & RUM.). 1980. 19.95 (0-8288-1699-9, M14019) Fr & Eur.

Run a Golden Mile. large type ed. Cyril A. Joyce. (Linford Mystery Library). 1991. pap. 15.99 (0-7089-7030-3) Ulverscroft.

Run According to Hawkeye. JoAnn Phillips. (Illus.). 24p. (Orig.). (J). 1993. pap. 9.95 (0-9638403-0-4) Cherokee Strip.

Run & Not Be Weary - Chinese Edition. Dwight L. Carlson. Tr. by J. Y. Liu. 231p. (CHI.). 1993. pap. 6.50 (1-56582-041-X) Christ Renew Min.

Run-&-Shoot Football: The Now Attack. Glenn Ellison. 194p. 1984. 19.95 (0-13-783879-4, Parker Publishing Co) P-H.

***Run Away Home.** Pat McKissack. LC 96-43673. (J). 1997. write for info. (0-590-46751-4) Scholastic Inc.

Run Away Home: A Novel. Jennie Hansen. Ed. by Darla H. Isackson. 200p. (Orig.). 1993. pap. 9.95 (1-55503-567-1) Covenant Comms.

***Run Away to War.** Emeline H. Malpas. 288p. (Orig.). 1997. pap. 12.95 (1-884570-72-0) Research Triangle.

Run Baby Run: The Story of a Gang-Lord Turned Crusader. Nicky Cruz & Jamie Buckingham. LC 68-23446. 239p. 1988. pap. 7.95 (0-88270-630-6) Bridge-Logos.

Run, Bambi, Run. Kris Radish. 408p. 1992. pap. 5.50 (0-451-40351-7, Onyx) NAL-Dutton.

Run, Bambi, Run: The Beautiful Ex-Cop Convicted of Murder Who Escaped to Freedom & Won America's Heart. Kris Radish. (Illus.). 1992. 18.95 (1-55972-103-0, Birch Ln Pr) Carol Pub Group.

Run Before the Wind. Stuart Woods. 320p. 1988. mass mkt. 6.50 (0-380-70507-9) Avon.

Run, Billy, Run. Matt Christopher. (J). (gr. 3-6). 1988. mass mkt. 3.95 (0-316-13993-9) Little.

Run, Chelsea, Run, Vol. 3. 2nd ed. Al Tarvin. Ed. by Bobbi Haycox & CJH Enterprises Staff. (Chelsea Ser.: Vol. 5). 260p. 1996. pap. 12.95 (0-9643250-3-9) CJH Ent.

Run Children Run: Tiny Warns Children about the Dangers of Drugs. Jeannette N. Hafford. (Tiny's Books for Children Ser.). (Illus.). (J). (ps-8). 1989. pap. text ed. write for info. (0-9616549-2-9) Tinys Self Help Bks.

Run, Computer, Run: The Mythology of Educational Innovation. Anthony G. Oettinger. LC 71-78522. (Illus.). 323p. reprint ed. pap. 92.10 (0-7837-5940-1, 2045739) Bks Demand.

Run, Don't Walk. Elizabeth Kontoyiannaki. (Illus.). (J). (gr. k-3). pap. 13.95 (1-56606-016-8) Bradley Mann.

***Run down Fired up & Teed Off.** John Parker. 80p. 1993. 6.95 (0-915297-11-6) Cedarwinds.

Run, Ducky, Run. Lael J. Littke. LC 95-48820. (Bee There Ser.: Bk. 6). 168p. (Orig.). (J). (gr. 3-7). 1996. pap. 6.95 (1-57345-134-7) Deseret Bk.

***Run East: Flight from the Holocaust.** Jack Pomerantz & Lyric W. Winik. LC 96-51240. 1997. 26.95 (0-252-02325-0) U of Ill Pr.

Run, Eunice: A Story of Childhood in the 1890s, Clarke County, Alabama. Kathleen W. Schad. LC 90-82162. 144p. (Orig.). (YA). (gr. 5-12). 1990. pap. 8.95 (0-9618941-1-3) Ana Pubns.

Run Far, Run Fast. Walt Morey. (Walt Morey Adventure Library). (YA). (gr. 4-9). 1989. reprint ed. pap. 7.95 (0-936085-16-9) Blue Heron OR.

Run Farther Run Faster. Joe Henderson. 1979. pap. 5.95 (0-02-499420-0, Macmillan Coll) P-H.

Run Fast: How to Train for a Five-K or 10-K Race. Hal Higdon. LC 91-42426. 224p. (Orig.). 1992. pap. 14.95 (0-87596-103-7, 12-251-1) Rodale Pr Inc.

Run, Fool, Run. large type ed. Frank Gruber. (Mystery Library). 320p. 1995. pap. 15.99 (0-7089-7646-8, Linford) Ulverscroft.

***Run for Daniel.** William B. Keller. 150p. (Orig.). 1997. mass mkt. 4.99 (1-55197-466-5, Pub. by Comnwlth Pub CN) Partners Pubs Grp.

Run for Stars & Echoes of Thunder. Harlan Ellison et al. 1991. pap. 3.95 (0-8125-1180-8) Tor Bks.

Run for the Elbertas. James Still. LC 80-51019. 160p. 1980. 16.00 (0-8131-1414-4); pap. 10.95 (0-8131-0151-4) U Pr of Ky.

***Run for the Money.** Fred L. Schroder. 224p. (Orig.). 1997. mass mkt. 4.99 (1-55197-990-X, Pub. by Comnwlth Pub CN) Partners Pubs Grp.

Run for Your Life. Phil Arnot & Elvira Monroe. 1977. pap. 3.95 (0-933174-01-2) Wide World-Tetra.

Run for Your Life. Ann Brahms. 352p. 1993. mass mkt. 4.50 (0-8217-4193-4, Zebra Kensgtn) Kensgtn Pub Corp.

Run for Your Life. Marilyn Levy. LC 95-24379. 224p. (J). (gr. 5-9). 1996. 14.95 (0-395-74520-9) HM.

***Run for Your Life.** Marilyn Levy. 224p. (Orig.). (J). (gr. 3-7). 1997. pap. 5.95 (0-698-11608-9, Paperstar) Putnam Pub Group.

***Run Forever Bk. 2.** Booth. (J). (gr. 4). 1990. pap. text ed. 36.25 (0-03-927202-8) HR&W Schl Div.

Run Gently Run Long. Joe Henderson. 1979. pap. 5.95 (0-02-499430-8, Macmillan Coll) P-H.

Run Jane Run: A True Story of Murder & Courage. Jane Wells. 304p. 1996. 22.95 (0-88282-140-7) New Horizon NJ.

Run, Little Leather Boy. Larry Townsend. (Orig.). 1993. mass mkt. 4.95 (1-56333-143-8, Badboy) Masquerade.

Run Log: Diary & Guide for the Runner. Nate Foster & Tim Houts. (SportsLog Ser.). (Illus.). 176p. 1995. spiral bd. 9.95 (1-57028-055-X) Masters Pr IN.

Run Man Run. Chester Himes. 192p. 1995. pap. 8.95 (0-7867-0209-5) Carroll & Graf.

Run, Naomi, Run. Pauline M. Shook. 320p. 1995. 20.95 (1-886591-01-6); pap. 13.95 (1-886591-02-4) Cabinet Crest Bks.

Run No More. Larry Townsend. 1993. mass mkt. 4.95 (1-56333-152-7, Badboy) Masquerade.

Run, Nurse, Run. large type ed. Jean Carew. (Linford Mystery Library). 272p. 1996. pap. 15.99 (0-7089-7852-5, Linford) Ulverscroft.

***Run of His Life.** Jeffrey Toobin. 1996. 25.00 (0-614-21931-0) Random.

Run of His Life: The People v. O. J. Simpson. Jeffrey Toobin. 466p. 1996. 25.00 (0-679-44170-0) McKay.

***Run of His Life: The People vs. O. J. Simpson.** Jeffery Toobin. LC 97-5462. 1997. pap. 12.95 (0-684-84278-5, Touchstone Bks) S&S Trade.

Run of the Country. Shane Connaughton. LC 92-43886. 1993. pap. 10.95 (0-312-08883-3) St Martin.

Run of the Country: A Novel. Shane Connaughton. 1995. pap. 12.00 (0-312-13599-8, Picador USA) St Martin.

Run of the House: Poems. Wyatt Prunty. LC 92-43034. (Poetry & Fiction Ser.). 68p. 1993. pap. 12.95 (0-8018-4626-9); text ed. 30.00 (0-8018-4625-0) Johns Hopkins.

Run, Rabbit, Run. Rabbit Maranville. 120p. (Orig.). 1991. pap. 9.95 (1-55643-081-7) North Atlantic.

Run, Rabbit, Run: The Hilarious & Mostly True Tales of Rabbit Maranville. Walter R. Maranville. 1991. pap. 9.95 (0-910137-44-7) Soc Am Baseball Res.

Run River. Joan Didion. 1961. 18.95 (0-8392-1094-9) Astor-Honor.

Run River. Joan Didion. 1994. pap. 13.00 (0-679-75250-1, Vin) Random.

Run, River, Run: A Naturalist's Journey down One of the Great Rivers of the West. Ann Zwinger. LC 84-8640. (Illus.). 317p. 1984. reprint ed. pap. 17.95 (0-8165-0885-2) U of Ariz Pr.

Run Roadrunner. Bevan Clair. LC 80-82912. (J). (ps-6). 1980. pap. 1.50 (0-686-30719-4) B A Scott.

Run! Run! JoAnn Vandine. 8p. (J). (ps-1). 1995. pap. 2.95 (1-57255-042-2) Mondo Pubng.

Run, Run, As Fast As You Can. Mary P. Osborne. 1995. 18.00 (0-8446-6829-X) Peter Smith.

Run Run Run: The Lives of Abbie Hoffman. Jack Hoffman & Daniel Simon. (Illus.). 336p. 1996. pap. 14.95 (0-87477-811-5, Tarcher Putnam) Putnam Pub Group.

Run Run Run: The Lives of Abbie Hoffman. Jack Joffman & Daniel Simon. 336p. 1994. 22.95 (0-87477-760-7, Tarcher Putnam) Putnam Pub Group.

***Run, Run, Run, Little Book.** Pals. (J). 1996. ring bd. 4.33 (0-201-85311-6) Addison-Wesley.

Run Sailing Races Right! United States Sailing Association Staff & Training Committee of U.S. Sailing. Ed. by Race Management Committee Staff. (Illus.). 22p. 1995. pap. text ed. 10.00 (1-882502-26-4) US Sail Assn.

Run, Sara, Run. large type ed. Anne Worboys. 400p. 1984. 25.99 (0-7089-1122-6) Ulverscroft.

Run School Run. Roland S. Barth. LC 79-25686. (Illus.). 304p. 1980. 32.00 (0-674-78036-1) HUP.

Run School Run. Roland S. Barth. 304p. 1985. pap. 14.95 (0-674-78037-X) HUP.

Run, Shelley, Run. Gertrude Samuels. (J). (gr. 7). 1975. pap. 2.50 (0-451-13987-9, AE2746, Sig) NAL-Dutton.

Run Silent, Run Deep. Edward L. Beach. 432p. 1988. mass mkt. 3.95 (0-8217-2408-8, Zebra Kensgtn) Kensgtn Pub Corp.

Run Silent, Run Deep. Edward L. Beach. LC 85-21801. (Classics of Naval Literature Ser.). 304p. 1986. reprint ed. 32.95 (0-87021-557-4) Naval Inst Pr.

Run So Fast. Sandra Woody. Ed. by Cheryle Sytsma. LC 90-63615. (Illus.). 25p. (Orig.). (J). (gr. k-5). 1991. pap. write for info. (1-879068-05-2) Ray-Ma Natsal.

Run Swift, Run Free. Tom McCaughren. 191p. (J). (ps-8). 1987. 14.95 (0-86327-111-1); pap. 7.95 (0-685-25877-7) Dufour.

Run Swift Run Free. Tom McCaughren. 1987. pap. 9.95 (0-86327-106-5) Dufour.

Run That Sucker at Six! The Second Morgan Calabrese Collection. N. Leigh Dunlap. 1989. pap. 6.95 (0-312-02951-9) St Martin.

***Run the Greatest Race: Be a Disciple Who Makes a Difference.** Greg Spalding. (Illus.). 110p. (Orig.). 1996. pap. 20.00 (0-9649311-3-3) City of Champns.

Run, Thief Run! Joe Manchester. 1964. pap. 3.00 (0-8222-0977-2) Dramatists Play.

Run to Death. Patrick Quentin. LC 91-70602. 192p. 1991. reprint ed. pap. 5.95 (1-55882-095-7, Lib Crime Classics) Intl Polygonics.

Run to Glory! William Sears. LC 89-3297. (Illus.). 380p. (YA). (gr. 8-12). 1989. pap. 9.95 (0-87961-195-2) Naturegraph.

Run to Gold Rock. large type ed. Peter Dawson. LC 92-44605. (General Ser.). 1993. lib. bdg. 20.95 (0-8161-5733-2, GK Hall) Thorndike Pr.

Run to Morning. Jack Higgins. 1991. pap. 6.50 (0-671-72774-5) PB.

***Run to the Battle.** Roberts Liardon. 1996. pap. 7.99 (1-880089-70-X) Albury Pub.

Run to the Battle. rev. ed. Roberts Liardon. 137p. 1989. pap. 7.00 (1-879993-06-6) Embassy Pub.

Run to the Lee. Kenneth F. Brooks, Jr. LC 87-46314. (Maryland Paperback Bookshelf Ser.). 192p. 1988. reprint ed. pap. 8.95 (0-8018-3677-8) Johns Hopkins.

Run to the Mountain: The Story of a Vocation. Thomas Merton. Ed. by Patrick Hart. LC 94-43414. (Journals of Thomas Merton: Vol. 1). 1996. pap. 15.00 (0-06-065475-9) Harper SF.

Run to the Mountain/Day of the Buzzard, 2 bks. in 1. Theodore V. Olsen. 368p. 1996. reprint ed. mass mkt. 4.99 (0-8439-4059-X, Leisure Bks) Dorchester Pub Co.

Run to the Rainbow. Margaret Hillert. (Illus.). (J). (ps). 1981. pap. 5.10 (0-8136-5565-X, TK2362); lib. bdg. 7.95 (0-8136-5065-8, TK2361) Modern Curr.

Run to Win: Devotions & Chapel Talks for Athletes, Coaches & Sports Fans. Mike Rohrbach & Denny Rydberg. 142p. (Orig.). (YA). (gr. 6 up). 1993. pap. 8.95 (1-887002-05-7) Cross Trng.

Run Today's Race. Oswald Chambers. 1968. pap. 4.95 (0-87508-125-8) Chr Lit.

Run with the Horseman. Ferrol Sams. (Contemporary American Fiction Ser.). 432p. 1984. pap. 12.95 (0-14-007274-8, Penguin Bks) Viking Penguin.

Run with the Horsemen. Ferrol Sams. LC 81-22671. 422p. 1982. 25.95 (0-931948-32-0) Peachtree Pubs.

Run with the Horsemen & the Whisper of the River, Set. Ferrol Sams. 1991. Boxed set. 50.00 (1-56145-040-5) Peachtree Pubs.

Run with the Horses. Eugene H. Peterson. LC 83-13005. 213p. (Orig.). 1983. pap. 11.99 (0-87784-905-6, 905) InterVarsity.

Run with the Hunted. Charles Bukowski. Ed. by John Martin. LC 92-53353. 400p. 1994. reprint ed. pap. 14.00 (0-06-092458-6, PL) HarpC.

Run with the Hunted: A Charles Bukowski Reader. Charles Bukowski. Ed. by John Martin. LC 92-53353. 497p. (C). 1993. 15.00 (0-87685-980-5) Black Sparrow.

***Run with the Torch: The Church of the Nazarene in El Salvador.** 96p. 1995. 6.25 (0-8341-1532-8) Nazarene.

Run with the Vision. Bob Sjogren et al. LC 95-7498. 288p. 1995. pap. 10.99 (1-55661-321-0) Bethany Hse.

Run with the Vision. Lester Sumrall. 183p. (Orig.). 1986. pap. text ed. 6.00 (0-937580-46-5) LeSEA Pub Co.

Run with the Vision. Lester Sumrall. 184p. (Orig.). 1995. mass mkt. 3.99 (0-88368-363-6) Whitaker Hse.

Run with the Winners: How to Develop a Championship Lifestyle from Hebrews 11. Warren W. Wiersbe. LC 94-37815. 160p. 1995. pap. 9.99 (0-8254-3997-3) Kregel.

Run with Your Dreams. Maureen A. Burns. (Illus.). 60p. 1982. pap. 10.00 (0-9613084-0-0) Empey Ent.

Run, Yell & Tell! A Safety Book for Children. Carol Watson. (Illus.). 32p. (J). (ps-2). 1993. 4.95 (0-9641123-0-2); 4.95 (0-9641123-1-0) Missing Chldrn.

Run Your Car on Sunshine: Using Solar Energy for a Solar Powered Car. James N. Blake. LC 80-82734. (Illus.). 64p. 1981. pap. 2.95 (0-915216-65-5) Marathon Intl Bk.

Runa. J. Allison James. LC 92-13936. 144p. (J). (gr. 5-9). 1993. lib. bdg. 13.95 (0-689-31708-5, Atheneum Bks Young) S&S Childrens.

Runabout. Pamela Morsi. 304p. (Orig.). 1994. mass mkt. 4.99 (0-515-11305-0) Jove Pubns.

Runabout. large type ed. Pamela Morsi. LC 94-32215. 400p. 1994. pap. 18.95 (0-7838-1126-8, GK Hall) Thorndike Pr.

Runabout Renovation: How to Find & Fix up an Old Fiberglass Speedboat. Jim Anderson. (Illus.). 160p. 1992. pap. 14.95 (0-87742-295-8) Intl Marine.

An Asterisk (*) at the beginning of an entry indicates that the title is appearing in BIP for the first time.

Runabout Renovation: How to Find & Fix up an Old Fiberglass Speedboat. Jim Anderson. 1992. pap. text ed. 16.95 (*0-07-158008-5*) McGraw.

***Runabouts (Propellers & Jet Drives) Owner's Manual.** TAL Marketing Services Staff. (Illus.). 91p. (Orig.). 1996. pap. 6.95 (*1-887960-00-7*, 596-207F) TotalConcepts.

Runagates Club. John Buchan. (Pocket Classics Ser.). 192p. 1996. pap. 10.95 (*0-7509-1159-X*, Pub. by Sutton Pubng UK) Bks Intl VA.

Runamay Bride. Carolyn Keene. Ed. by Rush Ashby. (Nancy Drew Files Ser.: No. 96). 160p. (Orig.). (YA). (gr. 6 up). 1994. mass mkt. 3.99 (*0-671-79488-4*, Archway) PB.

Runamok: A Novel about the Realties of Small Business. Tom Park. (Pacesetter Bks.). 256p. 1996. text ed. 19.95 (*1-56079-662-6*, Petersons Pacesetter) Petersons.

***Runamuck Recipes, Reminiscences & Ramblin's.** William H. Hammer & George A. Gadotti. Ed. by Rick W. Biggs. (Illus.). xiv, 104p. (Orig.). 1996. pap. 18.95 (*0-9656766-0-9*) Oregon Trail Grp.

***Runaway.** 174p. (Orig.). 1996. pap. 12.95 (*1-889455-00-8*) Flagg Mtn Pr.

Runaway. Mary C. Blew. LC 88-62764. 201p. 1990. pap. 10.00 (*0-917652-77-0*) Confluence Pr.

Runaway. A. Brown. (Freestyle Ser.). 1995. 4.99 (*1-85792-101-1*, Pub. by Christian Focus UK) Spring Arbor Dist.

Runaway. Heather X. Graham. 512p. 1995. mass mkt. 5.99 (*0-440-21688-5*) Dell.

***Runaway.** Terry Kay. 448p. 1997. write for info. (*0-688-15033-0*) Morrow.

Runaway. Francine Pascal. (Sweet Valley High Ser.: No. 21). 176p. (Orig.). (YA). 1985. pap. 3.99 (*0-553-27566-6*) Bantam.

Runaway. Patricia M. St. John. (Patricia St. John Bks.). 1985. mass mkt. 5.99 (*0-8024-9159-6*) Moody.

Runaway. Maureen C. Wartski. 1997. mass mkt. 4.50 (*0-449-70458-0*) Fawcett.

Runaway. large type ed. Heather X. Graham. 1994. pap. 21. 95 (*1-56895-080-2*) Wheeler Pub.

Runaway. large type ed. Bret Rey. (Linford Western Library). 256p. 1992. pap. 15.99 (*0-7089-7151-2*, Traitree Bookshop) Ulverscroft.

***Runaway.** 6th ed. Nissan Mindel. (Illus.). 1969. reprint ed. pap. 1.00 (*0-8266-0325-4*) Kehot Pubn Soc.

Runaway: Musical. Ed Graczyk. (J). (gr. 7-12). 1973. 5.00 (*0-87602-196-8*) Anchorage.

Runaway: Stories by Gordon Hoban. Gordon Hoban. LC 88-92497. 224p. (Orig.). 1989. pap. 13.95 (*0-944204-05-8*) Omniun.

Runaway see Ride the Wild River

Runaway Adolescents: A Family Systems Perspective. rev. ed. Brenda K. Melson. LC 95-25280. (Children of Poverty Ser.). 132p. 1995. text ed. 42.00 (*0-8153-2334-4*) Garland.

Runaway America: U. S. Jobs & Factories on the Move. Harry Browne & Beth Sims. 149p. 1993. 11.95 (*0-911213-43-0*) Interhemisp Res Ctr.

Runaway Angel. Misty Taggart. LC 94-45098. (Angel Academy Ser.: Vol. 6). (Illus.). (J). 1995. pap. 3.99 (*0-8499-5085-6*) Word Pub.

Runaway Balloon, Rescue in the Trinity River, Apartment Inferno! Deborah Morris. (Real Kids, Real Adventures Ser.: Vol. 3). (J). (gr. 3-10). 1995. pap. 4.99 (*0-8054-4053-4*, 4240-53) Broadman.

Runaway Bear. Chester D. Freeman & John E. McGuire. LC 93-16893. (Illus.). 32p. (J). (gr. k-3). 1993. 14.95 (*0-88289-956-2*) Pelican.

Runaway Bride. Pamela Caldwell. 1998. pap. 4.99 (*0-8217-5352-5*) Kensgtn Pub Corp.

***Runaway Bride.** Pamela Caldwell. 1997. mass mkt. 4.99 (*0-8217-5728-8*) Kensgtn Pub Corp.

Runaway Bride. Deborah Gordon. 400p. (Orig.). 1994. mass mkt. 4.99 (*0-380-77758-4*) Avon.

Runaway Bride. Sheila Walsh. 1983. pap. 3.99 (*0-451-13888-0*, Sig) NAL-Dutton.

Runaway Bride. large type ed. Jane A. Hodge. 1980. 12.00 (*0-7089-0440-8*) Ulverscroft.

Runaway Bride: (In Name Only) Jacqueline Diamond. (American Romance Ser.). 1995. mass mkt. 3.50 (*0-373-16583-8*, 1-16583-6) Harlequin Bks.

Runaway Brides. Debbie Macomber et al. 1996. pap. 5.99 (*0-373-20124-9*, 1-20124-3) Harlequin Bks.

Runaway Buggy. Carol Duerksen & Maynard Knepp. (Jonas Ser.: Bk. 1). (Illus.). 144p. (Orig.). 1995. pap. 9.95 (*0-9648525-0-0*) Willowsprng.

***Runaway Bunny.** Margaret W. Brown. (Illus.). (J). pap. 7.95 incl. audio (*0-89845-995-8*) HarperAudio.

Runaway Bunny. Margaret Wise Brown. LC 94-13860. (Illus.). 40p. (J). (ps-2). 1942. lib. bdg. 12.89 (*0-06-020766-3*) HarpC Child Bks.

Runaway Bunny. Margaret Wise Brown. LC 94-13860. (Illus.). 40p. (J). (ps-2). 1942. 13.00 (*0-06-020765-5*) HarpC Child Bks.

Runaway Bunny. Margaret Wise Brown. LC 94-13860. (Trophy Picture Bk.). (Illus.). 40p. (J). (ps-2). 1977. pap. 3.95 (*0-06-443018-9*, Trophy) HarpC Child Bks.

Runaway Bunny. Margaret Wise Brown. LC 94-13860. (Illus.). (J). (gr. k-3). 1985. 22.95 incl. audio (*0-941078-78-7*); pap. 15.95 incl. audio (*0-941078-76-0*) Live Oak Media.

Runaway Bunny, 4 bks., Set. Margaret Wise Brown. LC 94-13860. (Illus.). (J). (gr. k-3). 1985. student ed., pap. 31. 95 incl. audio (*0-941078-77-9*) Live Oak Media.

Runaway Bunny Board Book. Margaret Wise Brown. LC 71-183168. (Illus.). 32p. (J). (ps-2). 1991. pap. 6.95 (*0-06-107429-2*) HarpC Child Bks.

Runaway Bus! Eric Weiner. (Cliffhangers Ser.). 1996. pap. text ed. 3.99 (*0-425-15380-0*) Berkley Pub.

Runaway Children: How & Where to Find Facts & Get Help. Robert D. Reed & Danek S. Kaus. Ed. by Diane Parker. LC 92-53768. (Abuse Ser.). 48p. 1993. pap. 4.50 (*0-88247-937-7*) R & E Pubs.

Runaway Christmas Toy. Linda Hayward. (Pictureback Shapes Ser.). (Illus.). 24p. (Orig.). (J). (ps-2). 1994. pap. 3.25 (*0-679-86173-4*) Random Bks Yng Read.

Runaway Clown. Lois W. Johnson. (Adventures of the Northwoods Ser.: Vol. 8). 160p. (Orig.). (J). (gr. 3-8). 1993. pap. 5.99 (*1-55661-240-0*) Bethany Hse.

Runaway Convention or Proving a Preposterous Negative. Aaron Wildavsky. (Orig.). 1983. pap. 2.50 (*0-685-08895-2*) Natl Taxpayers Union Found.

Runaway Coordinator. Jack Rudman. (Career Examination Ser.: C-3467). 1994. pap. 29.95 (*0-8373-3467-5*) Nat Learn.

***Runaway Cowboy.** Edwin L. Skipworth. Ed. by Donald H. Keller. LC 96-93114. (Illus.). 160p. (Orig.). 1997. pap. 9.95 (*0-9656523-0-0*) Skip-Don.

Runaway Duchess. Patricia Oliver. (Regency Romance Ser.). 224p. 1993. pap. 3.99 (*0-451-17730-4*, Sig) NAL-Dutton.

Runaway Elephant Calf. E. R. Davidar & Jagadish Joshi. (Illus.). 24p. (Orig.). (J). (gr. k-3). 1980. pap. 2.75 (*0-89744-216-4*, Pub. by Childrens Bk Trust II) Auromere.

Runaway Flight. Susan S. Saba. (Illus.). 40p. (J). (gr. 1-3). 1996. 7.95 (*0-533-11066-1*) Vantage.

***Runaway Fred.** Rosemary Debnam. (Blue Bananas Ser.). (J). 1997. pap. 4.99 (*0-7497-2681-4*) Dell.

Runaway from Love. Jessica Steele. (Romance Ser.: No. 203). 1992. pap. 2.89 (*0-373-03203-X*, 1-03203-6) Harlequin Bks.

Runaway Hamster. Francine Pascal. (Sweet Valley Kids Ser.: No. 2). 80p. (J). (ps-3). 1989. pap. 3.50 (*0-553-15759-0*, Skylark BDD) BDD Bks Young Read.

Runaway Heart. Jane Peart. LC 94-20318. (Westward Dreams Ser.: Vol. 1). 256p. 1994. pap. 9.99 (*0-310-41271-4*) Zondervan.

Runaway Hearts. Shanna Swendson. 192p. 1994. 17.95 (*0-8034-9054-2*) Bouregy.

Runaway Hill. large type ed. Marina Oliver. (Historical Romance Ser.). 288p. 1992. 25.99 (*0-7089-2592-8*) Ulverscroft.

Runaway Homeless Youth: FY 1985 Annual Report to the Congress. U. S. Dept. of Health & Human Services Editorial Staff. 60p. 1986. write for info. (*0-318-61581-9*) US HHS.

Runaway Honeymoon. Ruth J. Dale. 1997. mass mkt. 3.25 (*0-373-03441-5*, 1-03441-2) Silhouette.

***Runaway Honeymoon.** large type ed. Ruth J. Dale. 1997. mass mkt. 3.25 (*0-373-15687-1*) Harlequin Bks.

Runaway Horses. Yukio Mishima & Gallagher. LC 89-40560. (Vintage International Ser.). 1990. pap. 14.00 (*0-679-72240-8*, Vin) Random.

Runaway in Oz. John R. Neill. (Illus.). 242p. (J). (gr. 3 up). 1995. 24.95 (*0-929605-39-X*) Books Wonder.

***Runaway Jury.** John Grisham. 560p. 1997. mass mkt. 7.99 (*0-440-22147-1*, Island Bks); mass mkt. 10.99 (*0-440-22441-1*) Dell.

Runaway Jury. John Grisham. 402p. 1996. 26.95 (*0-385-47294-3*) Doubleday.

***Runaway Jury.** John Grisham. 1997. mass mkt. write for info. (*0-440-78693-2*) Dell.

***Runaway Jury.** John Grisham. 1997. mass mkt. write for info. (*0-440-78694-0*) Dell.

Runaway Jury. large type ed. John Grisham. 656p. 1996. 30.95 (*0-385-48015-6*) Doubleday.

Runaway Jury. limited ed. John Grisham. 416p. 1996. 250. 00 (*0-385-48016-4*) Doubleday.

Runaway Kids: Jack & Jill in the Volcano. Curtis Williams. (Illus.). 99p. (Orig.). 1990. 24.81 (*1-878382-53-5*); pap. 5.65 (*1-878382-55-1*); lib. bdg. 9.57 (*1-878382-54-3*) Book Gallery.

Runaway Kids: Jack & Jill in the Volcano. limited ed. Curtis Williams. (Illus.). 99p. (Orig.). 1990. pap. 29.99 (*1-878382-51-9*) Book Gallery.

Runaway Learning Machine: Growing up Dyslexic. James J. Bauer. LC 92-71009. 96p. (Orig.). (C). 1992. pap. text ed. 6.95 (*0-932796-43-5*) Ed Media Corp.

Runaway Magic. Deborah Gordon. 384p. (Orig.). 1996. mass mkt. 5.99 (*0-380-78452-1*) Avon.

Runaway Magic. Elaine Pageler. Ed. by Betty L. Kratoville. (Meridian Bks.). (Illus.). 64p. (J). (gr. 3-9). 1989. lib. bdg. 4.95 (*0-87879-652-5*) High Noon Bks.

Runaway Me: A Survivor's Story. Evan K. Cutler. 384p. 1994. pap. 14.95 (*1-884607-15-2*) Blooming Pr.

Runaway Mittens. Jean Rogers. LC 87-12024. (Illus.). 24p. (J). (ps-3). 1988. lib. bdg. 15.93 (*0-688-07054-X*) Greenwillow.

Runaway Molly Midnight, the Artist's Cat. Nadja Maril. LC 80-17097. (Illus.). 40p. (J). (gr. k up). 1980. 12.95 (*0-916144-62-3*) Stemmer Hse.

***Runaway Monkey.** Lynn Salem. (Illus.). 8p. (Orig.). (J). (gr. k-1). 1997. pap. 3.50 (*1-880612-62-3*) Seedling Pubns.

Runaway Opposites. Richard Wilbur. LC 94-13188. (Illus.). 32p. (J). (ps up). 1995. 15.00 (*0-15-258722-5*) HarBrace.

Runaway Parents: A Parable of Problem Parents. John Bibee. LC 91-22762. (Spirit Flyer Ser.: Bk. 6). (Illus.). 204p. (Orig.). (J). (gr. 3-8). 1991. pap. 6.99 (*0-8308-1205-9*, 1205) InterVarsity.

Runaway Pony. Jeanne Betancourt. (Pony Pals Ser.: No. 7). (J). 1995. pap. 2.99 (*0-590-54338-5*) Scholastic Inc.

***Runaway Pony.** Susannah Leigh. (Sandy Lane Stables Ser.). (Illus.). 96p. (Orig.). (J). (gr. 4-8). 1997. pap. 3.95 (*0-7460-2482-7*, Usborne) EDC.

***Runaway Pony.** Susannah Leigh. (Sandy Lane Stables Ser.). (Illus.). 96p. (J). (gr. 4-8). 1997. lib. bdg. 11.95 (*0-88110-942-8*, Usborne) EDC.

Runaway Presents: Playscript. Judith Martin & Donald Ashwander. 16p. (Orig.). (J). (ps up). 1977. 4.00 (*0-87602-197-6*) Anchorage.

Runaway Princess. Milly Howard. Ed. by Laurie Garner. (Pennant Ser.). (Illus.). 116p. (Orig.). (J). 1988. pap. 6.49 (*0-89084-465-8*, 043273) Bob Jones Univ Pr.

Runaway Ralph. (J). 1923. pap. 3.25 (*0-440-77519-1*) Dell.

Runaway Ralph. Beverly Cleary. 176p. (J). 1991. pap. 4.50 (*0-380-70953-8*, Camelot) Avon.

Runaway Ralph. Beverly Cleary. LC 77-95786. (Illus.). (J). (gr. 3-7). 1970. 16.00 (*0-688-21701-X*, Morrow Junior); lib. bdg. 15.93 (*0-688-31701-4*, Morrow Junior) Morrow.

Runaway Religious in Medieval England, c. 1240-1540. F. Donald Logan. (Studies in Medieval Life & Thought: No. 32). 320p. (C). 1996. text ed. 59.95 (*0-521-47502-3*) Cambridge U Pr.

Runaway Rescue. Paul Hutchens. (Sugar Creek Gang Ser.: Vol. 28). 96p. (J). (gr. 3-7). 1973. mass mkt., pap. 3.99 (*0-8024-4828-3*) Moody.

Runaway Riceball. Hiriko C. Quackenbush. Ed. by Ogawa & Tazawa. (Kodansha's Nihongo Folktales Ser.). (Illus.). 32p. (J). 1993. pap. 7.00 (*4-7700-1762-6*) Kodansha.

Runaway Robot. pap. 1.95 (*0-590-02261-X*) Scholastic Inc.

Runaway Row. Lindsay Grater. (Illus.). 24p. (J). (ps-3). 1992. pap. 5.95 (*1-55037-210-6*, Pub. by Annick CN) Firefly Bks Ltd.

***Runaway Roy.** Gail Herman. (J). Date not set. pap. 3.95 (*0-448-41602-6*) Putnam Pub Group.

Runaway Rusty: And Other Dog & Cat Stories. Highlights Staff. LC 94-72485. (Illus.). 96p. (J). (gr. 2-5). 1995. 2.95 (*1-56397-444-4*) Boyds Mills Pr.

***Runaway School Bus.** Deborah Morris. (Real Kids Real Adventures Ser.: No. 4). 112p. 1997. mass mkt. 3.99 (*0-425-16086-6*) Berkley Pub.

Runaway Servants, Convicts, & Apprentices Advertised in the Pennsylvania Gazette, 1728-1796. Farley Grubb. 198p. 1992. 25.00 (*0-8063-1365-X*, 2415) Genealog Pub.

Runaway Sister. large type ed. Ann Jennings. (Romance Ser.). 352p. 1994. pap. 15.99 (*0-7089-7534-8*) Ulverscroft.

Runaway Slave Advertisements: A Documentary History from the 1730s to 1790, 4 vols. Lathan A. Windley. LC 83-1486. (Documentary Reference Collections). 1983. text ed. 265.00 (*0-313-23025-0*, WRS/) Greenwood.

Runaway Slave Advertisements: A Documentary History from the 1730s to 1790, 4 vols., 1. Lathan A. Windley. LC 83-1486. (Documentary Reference Collections). 1983. text ed. 85.00 (*0-313-23911-8*, WRS/01) Greenwood.

Runaway Slave Advertisements: A Documentary History from the 1730s to 1790, 4 vols., Vol. 2. Lathan A. Windley. LC 83-1486. (Documentary Reference Collections). 1983. text ed. 85.00 (*0-313-23912-6*, WRS/ 02) Greenwood.

Runaway Slave Advertisements: A Documentary History from the 1730s to 1790, 4 vols., Vol. 3. Lathan A. Windley. LC 83-1486. (Documentary Reference Collections). 1983. text ed. 95.00 (*0-313-23945-2*, WRS/ 03) Greenwood.

Runaway Slave Advertisements: A Documentary History from the 1730s to 1790, 4 vols., Vol. 4. Lathan A. Windley. LC 83-1486. (Documentary Reference Collections). 1983. text ed. 65.00 (*0-313-23946-0*, WRS/ 04) Greenwood.

***Runaway Soul.** Brodkey. LC 97-23052. 1997. 16.00 (*0-8050-5503-7*) H Holt & Co.

Runaway Soul. Harold Brodkey. 835p. 1991. 30.00 (*0-374-25286-6*) FS&G.

Runaway Stallion. Walt Morey. (Walt Morey Adventure Library). 176p. (YA). (gr. 4-8). 1989. reprint ed. pap. 6.95 (*0-936085-12-6*) Blue Heron OR.

Runaway Tail. (J). 1996. 5.98 (*1-57082-345-6*) Mouse Works.

Runaway Thanksgiving: A Story about the Meaning of Thanksgiving. Louise Mandrell & Ace Collins. (Illus.). 32p. (J). (gr. 1-4). 1992. 12.95 (*1-56530-011-4*) Summit TX.

Runaway Time. Deborah Gordon. 416p. (Orig.). 1995. mass mkt. 5.50 (*0-380-77759-2*) Avon.

Runaway to Freedom. Barbara Smucker. LC 77-11834. (Trophy Bk.). (Illus.). 160p. (J). (gr. 4-8). 1979. pap. 3.95 (*0-06-440106-5*, Trophy) HarpC Child Bks.

Runaway to Freedom. Barbara Smucker. (J). (gr. 4-8). 1992. 18.00 (*0-8446-6585-1*) Peter Smith.

Runaway Tractor. H. Amery. (Farmyard Tales Ser.). (Illus.). 16p. (J). (ps). 1989. 3.95 (*0-7460-0472-9*, Usborne) EDC.

***Runaway Train.** Benedict Blathwayt. 32p. (J). (gr. 1-4). 1997. pap. 9.95 (*0-09-938571-6*, Pub. by Red Fox UK) Trafalgar.

Runaway Valentines. Lisa Trumbauer. LC 93-14181. (Illus.). (J). (gr. k-2). 1993. pap. 2.95 (*0-8167-3264-7*) Troll Communs.

***Runaway Wedding.** Ruth J. Dale. 1997. 20.95 (*0-263-14929-3*) Thorndike Pr.

Runaway Who Stayed Home. Joseph A. Gagliardi. 256p. (Orig.). 1992. pap. 12.00 (*1-884690-10-6*) Owl Press.

Runaway Wife. large type ed. Charlotte Lamb. 1990. reprint ed. lib. bdg. 18.95 (*0-263-12078-3*, Pub. by Mills & Boon UK) Thorndike Pr.

***Runaway with Words: Poems from Florida's Youth Shelters.** Ed. by Joann Gardner. 180p. (Orig.). 1996. pap. 14.95 (*0-938078-47-X*) Anhinga Pr.

Runaway Women Elopements & Other Miscreant Deeds As Advertised in the Pennsylvania Gazette, 1728-1789. Judith A. Meier. 113p. 1993. pap. 10.95 (*1-55856-119-6*) Closson Pr.

***Runaway Youth: Stress, Social Support, & Adjustment.** Jon Bradley. LC 96-37894. (Children of Poverty Ser.). 152p. 1997. text ed. 40.00 (*0-8153-2798-6*) Garland.

Runaways. Beverley B. Ashwill. LC 87-72441. (Illus.). 48p. (J). (gr. 4-8). 1988. 12.95 (*0-941381-02-1*); pap. 5.95 (*0-941381-01-3*) BJO Enterprises.

Runaways. Marian Bray. (Reba Novel Ser.: Vol. 2). 144p. 1992. pap. 5.99 (*0-310-54361-4*) Zondervan.

Runaways. Jay Christopher. 72p. (YA). 1980. pap. 5.00 (*0-87129-666-7*, R25) Dramatic Pub.

Runaways. Andrew J. Fenady. 192p. 1994. 19.95 (*0-8027-4145-2*) Walker & Co.

Runaways. Keith E. Greenberg. LC 95-8074. (In My Shoes Ser.). (Illus.). 40p. (J). (gr. 6-8). 1995. lib. bdg. 18.95 (*0-8225-2557-7*, Lerner Publctns) Lerner Group.

Runaways. Ed. by John Patrick. (Orig.). 1996. pap. 14.95 (*1-877978-79-5*, STARbks Pr) Woldt.

***Runaways: A Musical Play for Children.** Ed. by Michael Lefferts. 48p. (Orig.). (C). 1997. pap. text ed. 7.95 (*0-7692-0836-3*, 00312358) Warner Brothers.

Runaways: In Their Own Words, Vol. 1. Jeffrey Artenstein. 1990. 16.95 (*0-312-93132-8*) St Martin.

Runaways: In Their Own Words: Kids Talking about Living... Jeffrey Artenstein. 128p. 1995. mass mkt. 3.99 (*0-8125-1354-1*) Tor Bks.

Runaways, Deserters & Notorious Villains from Rhode Island Newspapers Vol. 1: The Providence Gazette, 1762-1800. Maureen A. Taylor. LC 94-74032. 189p. 1995. 29.50 (*0-89725-218-7*, 1595) Picton Pr.

Runaways, Illegal Aliens in Their Own Land: Implications for Service. Dorothy Miller. LC 79-11682. (Praeger Special Studies). 224p. 1980. text ed. 55.00 (*0-275-90525-X*, C0525, Praeger Pubs) Greenwood.

Runaways in Texas: A Statistical Estimate, 1985. Contrib. by Lodis Rhodes. (Special Project Report). 33p. 1985. pap. 5.00 (*0-89940-852-4*) LBJ Sch Pub Aff.

Runaway's Revenge: John Newton. Dave Jackson & Neta Jackson. LC 95-43622. (Trailblazer Bks.: No. 18). (Illus.). 144p. (Orig.). (J). (gr. 3-8). 1995. pap. 5.99 (*1-55661-471-3*) Bethany Hse.

***Runbo Al Exito: Una Guia para Juntas Directivas de Organizaciones Sin Fines Delurro.** Alex H. Sanchez et al. Ed. by Ana Baron. (Illus.). 200p. Date not set. write for info. (*1-886765-07-3*) Nature VA.

Rundbauten im Kerameikos, Vol. 12. Wolf Koenigs et al. (Kerameikos Ser.). (Illus.). (C). 1979. 92.35 (*3-11-007210-6*) De Gruyter.

Rundfunkkompetenz & Rundfunkfreiheit: Eine Untersuchung uber das Verhaltnis des Rundfunkhoheit der Lander zu den Gesetzgebungszustandigkeiten des Bundes. Karin Gabriel-Brautigam. (Law & Economics of International Telecommunications Ser.). 189p. (GER.). 1990. 62.00 (*3-7890-1882-1*, Pub. by Nomos Verlags GW) Intl Bk Import.

Rune: A Survey. Karl Kempton. (Light & Dust Bks.). (Illus.). 80p. (Orig.). 1992. pap. 7.00 (*0-87924-068-7*) Membrane Pr.

Rune Cards. Tony Linsell. 30p. 19.95 (*0-9516209-7-5*, Pub. by Anglo-Saxon Bks UK) Paul & Co Pubs.

***Rune Dice Divination: Reading Fortunes Doing Magic & Making Charms.** Donald Tyson. LC 97-21570. (Illus.). 288p. (Orig.). 1997. pap. 17.95 (*1-56718-748-X*) Llewellyn Pubns.

Rune Journey: Pathway to Yggdraszl. Robert Blanchard. Ed. by Thorguard Templar. (Illus.). 112p. 1994. 25.00 (*1-57179-030-6*) Intern Guild ASRS.

Rune Magic. Nigel Pennick. 240p. 1993. pap. 17.00 (*1-85538-105-2*) Thorsons SF.

Rune Magic. Donald Tyson. LC 87-45741. (Practical Magick Ser.). (Illus.). 224p. (Orig.). 1988. pap. 12.95 (*0-87542-826-6*) Llewellyn Pubns.

Rune Magick. Keith Morgan. (Orig.). 1995. pap. 7.95 (*1-872189-55-5*, Pub. by Mandrake Pr UK) Holmes Pub.

Rune Magick Northumbrian. IGOOS Staff. (Illus.). 98p. 1994. 29.95 (*1-57179-031-4*) Intern Guild ASRS.

Rune Might: Secret Practices of the German Rune Magicians. Edred Thorsson. LC 89-35506. (Teutonic Magick Ser.). (Illus.). 176p. (Orig.). 1989. pap. 9.95 (*0-87542-778-2*) Llewellyn Pubns.

Rune Mysteries. Nigel Jackson & Silver Ravenwolf. LC 96-20697. (Illus.). 288p. 1996. pap. 29.95 (*1-56718-364-6*) Llewellyn Pubns.

Rune of Salt Air. Jill McGrath. Ed. by Shirley Warren. (Illus.). 36p. 1991. pap. 5.00 (*1-877801-16-X*) Still Waters.

Rune Play. Ed. by Ralph H. Blum. LC 90-36874. 226p. 1991. pap. 12.95 (*0-312-05150-6*, Thomas Dunne Bks) St Martin.

Rune Poem: Wisdom's Fulfillment, Prophecy's Reach. Tr. & Anno. by Jim Paul. LC 95-17625. 96p. (ANG.). 1996. 14.95 (*0-8118-1136-0*) Chronicle Bks.

Rune Power. Kenneth Meadows. 208p. 1996. pap. 15.95 (*1-85230-706-4*) Element MA.

Rune Power: Runic Power Course 18 Lessons, Set. IGOOS Staff. Ed. by Thorguard Templar. 220p. 1994. 216.00 (*1-57179-026-8*) Intern Guild ASRS.

Rune Rhythms: A Divination System for Women. Sue Ware & Diane Carson. 1995. 44.00 (*0-9647257-0-3*); 74. 00 (*0-9647257-1-1*) Earth Gypsy.

Rune Stones for the New Ages: The Lost 13 Runes. 2nd ed. Ronald G. Kaufmann. LC 87-200714. (Illus.). 172p. (Orig.). 1991. pap. 12.95 (*0-685-51161-8*) Heridonius.

Rune-6: Figures of Speech. Karl Kempton. 27p. (Orig.). 1993. pap. 5.00 (*0-926935-89-5*) Runaway Spoon.

Rune-7: Poem, a Mapping. Karl Kempton. 30p. (Orig.). 1993. pap. 5.00 (*0-926935-90-9*) Runaway Spoon.

***Runecards.** Blum. LC 97-14666. 1997. 29.95 (*0-312-16992-2*) St Martin.

Runelore: A Handbook of Esoteric Runology. Edred Thorsson. LC 86-24719. (Illus.). 186p. 1987. pap. 10.95 (*0-87728-667-1*) Weiser.

Runemaker. Tiina Nunnally. LC 96-28795. 210p. (Orig.). 1996. pap. 12.00 (*0-940242-77-X*) Fjord Pr.

R

Runequest: Deluxe. Greg Stafford. Ed. by Sandy Peterson. (Illus.). 96p. (YA). (gr. 8 up). 1989. 29.95 (0-911605-51-7) Avalon Hill.

Runes. David V. Barrett. LC 95-11679. (The Predictions Library). (Illus.). 64p. 1995. 8.95 (0-7894-0310-2, 6-70516) DK Pub Inc.

Runes. R. I. Page. (Reading the Past Ser.: Vol. 4). 64p. 1987. pap. 11.00 (0-520-06114-4) U CA Pr.

Runes: An Introduction. Ralph W. Elliott. LC 80-26090. (Illus.). xvi, 124p. 1981. reprint ed. text ed. 47.50 (0-313-22870-1, ELRU, Greenwood Pr) Greenwood.

Runes & Riddles: The Empire of Elwolf. F. J. Carradine. (Illus.). 378p. (Orig.). (YA). (gr. 7-12). 1993. pap. 7.00 (0-88092-074-2) Royal Fireworks.

Runes & Runic Inscriptions: Collected Essays on Anglo-Saxon & Viking Runes. R. I. Page. (Illus.). 360p. 1995. 89.00 (0-85115-387-9) Boydell & Brewer.

Runes Are Cast. R. P. Back. 1981. 30.00 (0-7223-1368-3, Pub. by A H S Ltd UK) St Mut.

Runes for Beginners. Kristyna Arcarti. (Headway Guide for Beginners Ser.). (Illus.). 112p. 1995. pap. 11.95 (0-340-62081-1, Pub. by Headway UK) Trafalgar.

Runes for Today's Woman. Cassandra Eason. 160p. 1995. pap. 7.95 (0-572-01813-4, Pub. by Foulsham UK) Assoc Pubs Grp.

Runes in Ten Minutes. R. T. Kaser. 432p. (Orig.). 1995. pap. 12.00 (0-380-77605-7) Avon.

Runes of Autumn. Larry Elmore & Robert Elmore. 1996. pap. 5.99 (0-7869-0504-2) TSR Inc.

***Runes of the North.** Sigurd F. Olson. LC 97-22170. (Fesler-Lampert Minnesota Heritage Book Ser.). 1997. write for info. (0-8166-2994-3) U of Minn Pr.

Runes of the North. Sigurd F. Olson. 1963. 24.00 (0-394-44348-9) Knopf.

Runestone. Don Coldsmith. 544p. 1995. reprint ed. mass mkt., pap. 5.99 (0-553-57280-6, Bantam Domain) Bantam.

Runeweaving: Meditations with the Runes. Maia C. Shamayyim. (Illus.). 61p. 1985. spiral bd. 12.95 (1-888420-12-X) Johannine Grove.

Rungless Ladder: Harriet Beecher Stowe & New England Puritanism. Charles H. Foster. LC 54-10987. 298p. reprint ed. pap. 85.00 (0-317-42198-0, 2026198) Bks Demand.

Rungs of the Ladder. Thakazhi S. Pillai. Tr. by C. Paul Verghese from MAL. 423p. 1976. pap. 3.50 (0-86578-146-X) Ind-US Inc.

Runic & Mediterranean Epigraphy. Richard L. Morris. (NOWELE Ser.: Suppl. Vol. 4). 178p. (Orig.). 1988. pap. 42.50 (87-7492-683-7, Pub. by Odense Universitets Forlag DK) Coronet Bks.

Runic Astrology. Nigel Pennick. (Illus.). 270p. (Orig.). 1995. pap. 22.95 (1-898307-45-8, Pub. by Capall Bann Pubng UK) Holmes Pub.

Runic Meaning in Texas Cattle Brands: Plays of the Organic Theatre. 2nd rev. ed. Bob Burleson. LC 94-61670. (Illus.). 541p. 1995. 24.95 (0-913699-89-6); pap. 16.95 (0-913699-88-8) Worksworth.

Runic Records of the Norsemen in America. O. G. Landsverk. (Library of Scandinavian Literature). 1974. lib. bdg. 39.50 (0-8057-5457-1) Irvington.

Runic States: The Shamanic Perception of Quantum Realities. Kevin Steffen. 192p. 1996. pap. 12.50 (1-57353-108-1) Eschaton Prods.

Runic Workbook: Understanding & Using the Power. Tony Willis. (Illus.). 192p. 1996. pap. 14.95 (0-8069-8170-9) Sterling.

RUniform Coding for Fire Protection. National Fire Protection Association Staff. 113p. 1990. 26.50 (0-317-63509-3, 901-90) Natl Fire Prot.

Runische Schriftkultur in Kontinental-Skandin-Avischer und-Angelsaesischer Wechselbeziehung. Ed. by Klaus Duewel. (Ergaenzungsbaende zum Reallexikon der Germanischen Altertumskunde: Bd. 10). 417p. (GER.). (C). 1994. lib. bdg. 167.70 (3-11-014328-3) De Gruyter.

Runkle Family, Being an Account of the Runkles in Europe & Their Descendants in America. Ben V. Fisher. (Illus.). 366p. 1989. reprint ed. pap. 55.50 (0-8328-1037-1); reprint ed. lib. bdg. 63.50 (0-8328-1036-3) Higginson Bk Co.

Runkles: A Manual of Wit & Wisdom for All Ages. William J. Stewart. LC 86-90405. (Illus.). 96p. (Orig.). 1986. pap. 5.95 (0-9615440-0-7) W J Stewart.

Runner. Edgar R. Chasteen. LC 79-53673. (Illus.). 177p. 1980. 12.95 (0-934864-00-4) Amity Bks MO.

Runner. Brian Swann. LC 79-9366. (Illus.). (Orig.). 1979. pap. 12.50 (0-914140-07-8) Carpenter Pr.

Runner. Cynthia Voigt. (Tillerman Ser.). 224p. (YA). (gr. 5 up). 1987. mass mkt. 3.95 (0-449-70294-4, Juniper) Fawcett.

Runner. Cynthia Voigt. 192p. (J). (gr. 7-9). 1994. pap. 4.50 (0-590-48380-3) Scholastic Inc.

Runner. Cynthia Voigt. LC 84-21663. 192p. (YA). (gr. 8 up). 1985. lib. bdg. 15.95 (0-689-31069-2, Atheneum Bks Young) S&S Childrens.

Runner in the Sun. D'Arcy McNickle. LC 87-5986. (Zia Bks.). (Illus.). 260p. (J). 1987. reprint ed. pap. 12.95 (0-8263-0974-7) U of NM Pr.

Runner Mack. Barry Beckham. LC 83-6140. (Howard University Press Library of Contemporary Literature). 213p. 1984. pap. 14.95 (0-88258-116-3) Howard U Pr.

Runner Stumbles. Milan Stitt. 1976. pap. 5.25 (0-8222-0975-6) Dramatists Play.

***Runner-Up Bride.** Lisa Bingham. (Love & Laughter Ser.: No. 22). 1997. mass mkt. 3.50 (0-373-44022-7, 1-44022-1) Harlequin Bks.

Runners. Gerald Hausman. LC 84-2487. 40p. (Orig.). 1984. 10.00 (0-86534-052-8); pap. 6.95 (0-86534-022-6) Sunstone Pr.

Runners after Forty. Runner's World Editors. 1980. pap. 4.95 (0-02-499690-4, Macmillan Coll) P-H.

***Runners & Other Dreamers.** John L. Parker, Jr. 211p. (Orig.). 1988. pap. 12.95 (0-915297-24-8) Cedarwinds.

***Runners & Riders.** Georgina Brown. (Black Lace Ser.). 300p. 1996. mass mkt. 5.95 (0-352-33117-8, Pub. by Virgin Pub UK) London Brdge.

Runners & Soft Targets. Stephen Poliakoff. 112p. (C). 1988. pap. 8.95 (0-413-54150-9, A0251, Pub. by Methuen UK) Heinemann.

Runner's Bible. Marc Bloom. LC 82-46075. (Outdoor Bible Ser.). (Illus.). 144p. 1986. pap. 12.95 (0-385-18874-9) Doubleday.

Runners Bible. Nora Holm. 1996. 16.95 (0-933062-33-8) R H Sommer.

Runners' Book of Training Secrets: More Than 50 Elite Runners Share Their Best Tips & Techniques for: Speed Training, Distance Running, Racing Strategies, Injury Protection... Ken Sparks & Dave Kuehls. 1996. pap. 15.95 (0-87596-307-2) Rodale Pr Inc.

***Runners' Coach.** Roy Benson. 128p. 1994. 12.95 (0-915297-13-2) Cedarwinds.

Runners Diet. rev. ed. Worldworld Staff. 1980. pap. 3.95 (0-02-499450-2, Macmillan Coll) P-H.

Runner's Easylog: An Easy Way for Runners to Plan, Organize, & Assess Their Training & Performance. Marty Kaufman. LC 91-90957. 160p. (Orig.). 1991. pap. 12.95 (0-9629427-3-1) Textrific.

Runner's Foot Doctor. Steven I. Subotnick. 1979. pap. 4.95 (0-02-499700-5, Macmillan Coll) P-H.

Runner's Guide to Boulder County. Vici DeHaan. LC 81-71143. (Illus.). 200p. 1982. pap. 7.95 (0-941388-01-8) Am Trend Pub.

Runners Guide to Cross Country-Skiing. 2nd ed. Dick Mansfield. LC 89-17754. (Illus.). 160p. 1990. pap. 10.95 (0-937921-49-1) Acorn Pub.

Runner's Handbook. Bob Glover & Jack Shepherd. 192p. 1985. pap. 12.95 (0-14-046713-0, Penguin Bks) Viking Penguin.

Runner's Handbook: The Bestselling Classic Fitness Guide for Beginner & Intermediate Runners. Bob Glover et al. LC 95-25847. 701p. 1996. pap. 17.95 (0-14-046930-3, Penguin Bks) Viking Penguin.

Runner's Heart. Chuck Cornelius. (Illus.). 138p. (Orig.). 1996. pap. 14.95 (0-9651241-1-8) C E Cornelius.

Runner's Literary Companion. Ed. by Garth Battista. 336p. 1996. pap. 12.95 (0-14-025353-X) Viking Penguin.

Runner's Literary Companion: Great Stories & Poems About Running. Ed. by Garth Battista. 352p. 1994. 23.00 (1-55821-335-X) Lyons & Burford.

Runners Log Two Thousand. Michael Nathan & Jeff Galloway. (Illus.). 80p. (Orig.). 1988. spiral bd. write for info. (0-318-63185-7) Nathan & Co.

Runner's Outdoor Sports Photography. McQuilkin. (Illus.). 1982. 9.95 (0-02-499580-0, Macmillan Coll) P-H.

Runner's Repair Manual. Murray F. Weisenfeld. 192p. 1981. pap. 9.95 (0-312-69597-7) St Martin.

Runners, Sliders, Bouncers, Climbers: A Pop-up Look at Animals in Motion. Nick Bantock & Stacie Strong. (Illus.). 15p. (J). (gr. 1-5). 1992. 14.95 (1-56282-219-5) Hyprn Child.

***Runner's Training Diary: For Fitness Runners & Competitive Racers.** Bob Glover & Shelly-Lynn F. Glover. LC 96-49050. 1997. pap. 9.95 (0-14-046991-5) Penguin.

Runners Training Guide. Runner's World Editors. 1978. pap. 3.95 (0-02-499440-5, Macmillan Coll) P-H.

Runner's Triathlon Training Book. Hosiery. 1983. pap. 6.95 (0-02-499630-0, Macmillan Coll) P-H.

Runner's Weight Control Book. Bruce Nash. 1982. pap. 9.95 (0-02-499640-8, Macmillan Coll) P-H.

Runner's Weight Control Book. Bruce Nash. 1984. 9.95 (0-02-499650-5, Macmillan Coll) P-H.

***Runner's World Complete Book of Running: Everything You Need to Know to Run for Fun, Fitness & Competition.** Ed. by Amby Burfoot. LC 96-53296. 1997. 24.95 (0-87596-354-4, Daybrk) Rodale Pr Inc.

Runners World Training Diary. Runnersworld Staff. 172p. 1995. 8.95 (0-02-860820-8) Macmillan.

Runner's World Yoga Book see Runner's Yoga Book: A Balanced Approach to Fitness

Runner's Yoga Book: A Balanced Approach to Fitness. rev. ed. Jean Couch. LC 90-70758. Orig. Title: Runner's World Yoga Book. (Illus.). 207p. 1990. reprint ed. pap. 19.95 (0-9627138-1-3) Rodmell Pr.

Runnery Granary. Nancy Farmer. LC 95-961. (Illus.). 32p. (J). (gr. k up). 1996. 15.00 (0-688-14187-0); lib. bdg. 14.93 (0-688-14188-9) Greenwillow.

***Runnin' Crazy: A Portrait of the Genesee River.** Ruth Rosenberg-Naparsteck & Edward P. Curtis. LC 96-38421. 1997. write for info. (0-89865-978-7) Donning Co.

Runnin' down Some Lines: The Language & Culture of Black Teenagers. Edith A. Folb. LC 79-26708. 284p. reprint ed. pap. 81.00 (0-7837-3832-3, 2043653) Bks Demand.

Runnin' with the Big Dogs: A Guide to Bartending. Steven Shafer & Wade Miller. Ed. by Linda Stone et al. 97p. 1992. 11.99 (0-9632884-0-7) Paradise Pub.

Running. Ace Collins. (You Can Do It! Ser.). (Illus.). 96p. (J). (ps up). 1993. pap. 12.95 (1-56530-092-0) Summit TX.

Running. Herbert I. Kavet. 64p. 1993. 8.95 (0-88032-361-2) Ivory Tower Pub.

Running. Jeff Savage. LC 93-37943. (J). 1995. lib. bdg. 15.95 (0-89686-855-9, Crstwood Hse) Silver Burdett Pr.

Running. Jeff Savage. LC 93-37943. (Working Out Ser.). (Illus.). (J). (gr. 5 up). 1995. pap. 7.95 (0-382-24948-8, Crstwood Hse) Silver Burdett Pr.

Running: Fitness & Injuries - a Self-Help Guide. Vivian Grisogono. (Illus.). 256p. 1995. pap. 24.95 (0-7195-5064-5, Pub. by John Murray UK) Trafalgar.

Running: Index of Modern Information. Walt E. Weldome. LC 88-47998. 150p. 1989. 37.50 (1-55914-080-1); pap. 34.50 (1-55914-081-X) ABBE Pubs Assn.

Running: The Consequences. Richard C. Crandall. LC 85-43574. 300p. 1986. lib. bdg. 32.50 (0-89950-201-6) McFarland & Co.

***Running a Meeting That Works.** 2nd ed. Robert F. Miller & Marilyn Pincus. LC 96-46273. (Barron's Business Success Ser.). 1997. pap. 6.95 (0-8120-9823-4) Barron.

Running a One-Person Business. rev. ed. Claude Whitmyer & Salli Rasberry. LC 93-50577. 224p. 1994. pap. 14.00 (0-89815-598-3) Ten Speed Pr.

Running a Parent-Child Workshop: A How-to-Do-It Manual for Librarians. Kathy East. LC 94-46345. (How-to-Do-It Manuals Ser.: Vol. 49). (Illus.). 150p. 1995. pap. 32.50 (1-55570-182-5) Neal-Schuman.

Running a Parent/Child Workshop: A-How-to-Do-It Manual for Librarians. Sandra Feinberg & Kathleen Deerr. (How-to-Do-It Manuals Ser.: Vol. 46). 175p. (Orig.). 1995. pap. 32.50 (1-55570-189-2) Neal-Schuman.

***Running a Perfect BBS.** 2nd ed. Mark Chambers. 608p. 1995. pap. 49.99 (0-7897-0664-4) Que.

Running a Perfect Business Web Site. 1998. 34.99 (0-7897-0672-5) Que.

Running a Perfect Internet Site. Que Development Group Staff. (Illus.). 900p. (Orig.). 1996. 49.99 (0-7897-0255-X) Que.

Running a Perfect Internet Site with LINUX. Que Development Group Staff. (Illus.). 500p. (Orig.). 1996. 49.99 (0-7897-0514-1) Que.

Running a Perfect Intranet. Que Development Group Staff. 608p. 1996. pap. text ed. 49.99 incl. cd-rom (0-7897-0823-X) Que.

Running a Perfect Web Site. Que Development Group Staff. (Illus.). 456p. (Orig.). 1995. 39.99 (0-7897-0210-X) Que.

***Running a Perfect Web Site.** 2nd ed. Steve Wynkoop. 744p. 1996. 49.99 (0-7897-0944-9) Mac Comp Pub.

Running a Perfect Web Site with UNIX. 2nd ed. David Chandler. 560p. 1996. pap. text ed. 49.99 incl. cd-rom (0-7897-0745-4) Que.

Running a Perfect Web Site with Windows NT. David Chandler. 720p. 1996. pap. text ed. 49.99 incl. cd-rom (0-7897-0763-2) Que.

Running a Professional Corporation. Ronald A. Anderson. 7.50 (0-914770-02-0) Littoral Develop.

***Running a Public Relations Consultancy.** Peter Hehir. (PR in Practice Ser.). 1997. pap. 16.95 (0-7494-1998-9) Kogan Page Ltd.

***Running a Ring of Spies: Spycraft & Black Operations in the Real World of Espionage.** Jefferson Mack. 216p. 1996. pap. 20.00 (0-87364-902-8) Paladin Pr.

Running a School Library Media Center: A How-to-Do-It Manual for Librarians. Barbara L. Stein & Risa W. Brown. (How-to-Do-It Ser.). 160p. 1992. 35.00 (1-55570-100-0) Neal-Schuman.

Running a Shop. Ed. by Gary Jones. 320p. 1991. pap. 36.00 (0-273-03515-0) St Mut.

Running a Stable As a Business. Janet W. MacDonald. 112p. 1984. pap. 20.00 (0-87556-544-1) Saifer.

Running a Stables as a Business. Janet W. Macdonald. 112p. (C). 1990. pap. 21.00 (0-685-68110-6, Pub. by J A Allen & Co UK) St Mut.

Running a Successful Franchise. Kirk Shivell. 1993. text ed. 29.95 (0-07-056987-8) McGraw.

Running a Successful Graphic Design Business. Nat Bukar. LC 91-72286. 116p. (Orig.). 1991. text ed. 12.95 (0-88108-091-8); pap. text ed. 10.95 (0-88108-092-6) Art Dir.

Running a Summer Sports Day Camp. Barry Kipnes. 46p. (Orig.). 1987. pap. 8.95 (0-932741-09-6) Championship Bks & Vid Prodns.

Running a Tack Shop As a Business. Janet W. Macdonald. 112p. (C). 1990. pap. 21.00 (0-85131-425-2, Pub. by J A Allen & Co UK) St Mut.

***Running a Team for Disabled Children & Their Families.** 150p. 1994. text ed. 44.95 (0-901260-99-1) Cambridge U Pr.

Running a Team for Disabled Children & Their Families. Martin F. Robards. (Clinics in Developmental Medicine Ser.: No. 130). (Illus.). 150p. (C). 1994. 44.95 (0-521-45517-0) Cambridge U Pr.

Running a Thousand Miles for Freedom: Or, the Escape of William & Ellen Craft from Slavery. William Craft. LC 77-89417. (Black Heritage Library Collection). 1977. 22.95 (0-8369-8549-4) Ayer.

Running Accompaniments. Henry W. Nevinson. 1972. 69.95 (0-8490-0980-4) Gordon Pr.

Running Again in Hollywood Cemetery. Ron Smith. LC 88-2628. 77p. (Orig.). 1988. pap. 10.95 (0-8130-0881-6) U Press Fla.

***Running Aground & Getting Afloat.** Joachim Schult. 1996. pap. text ed. 18.50 (0-07-057868-0) McGraw.

Running Aground & Getting Afloat. Joachim Schult. (Illus.). 112p. 1994. pap. 18.50 (0-7136-3896-6) Sheridan.

Running Amok. Michael D. Schneider. (Illus.). iv, 96p. (Orig.). 1996. pap. write for info. (0-9651850-0-1) MDS & Assocs.

Running Amok: A Historical Inquiry. John C. Spores. LC 88-5253. (Monographs in International Studies, Asia: No. 82). 190p. 1988. pap. text ed. 13.00 (0-89680-140-3, Ohio U Ctr Intl) Ohio U Pr.

Running an Effective Help Desk: Planning, Implementing, Advertising, Improving, Outsourcing. Barbara Czegel. 400p. 1994. pap. text ed. 34.95 (0-471-02544-5) Wiley.

Running an Effective Sales Office. Patrick Forsythe. Date not set. pap. text ed. 35.95 (0-471-96262-7) Wiley.

Running an Effective Training Session. Patrick Forsyth. 142p. 1992. 48.95 (0-566-07320-X, Pub. by Gower UK) Ashgate Pub Co.

***Running & Growing Your Business: Kiplinger's Comprehensive Guide for the Small & Growing Business.** Andrew Sherman. LC 97-6700. 1997. 25.00 (0-8129-2860-1, Times Bks) Random.

Running & Maintenance of Marine Machinery. 2nd rev. ed. Ed. by J. Cowley. 250p. 1992. 80.00 (0-907206-42-5) Info Today Inc.

Running & Racing after Thirty-Five. Allan Lawrence. 1990. pap. 14.95 (0-316-51675-9) Little.

Running & Stamping Book. Neil Cameron. 96p. (C). 1995. pap. 19.95 (0-86819-410-7) Aubrey Bks.

Running & Stamping Book. Neil Cameron. 96p. 1995. pap. 9.95 (0-435-08681-2, 08681) Heinemann.

Running Applied Psychology Experiments. John Leach. (Open Guides to Psychology Ser.). 160p. 1991. pap. 29.00 (0-335-09482-1, Open Univ Pr) Taylor & Francis.

Running as a Woman: Gender & Power in American Politics. Witt et al. 1995. pap. 14.95 (0-02-874069-6) S&S Trade.

Running As a Woman: Gender & Power in American Politics. Linda Witt et al. 300p. 1993. 24.95 (0-02-920315-5, Free Press) Free Pr.

***Running As Therapy: An Integrated Approach.** Ed. by Michael L. Sachs & Gary W. Buffone. LC 97-16480. (Master Works Ser.). 360p. 1997. pap. text ed. 35.00 (0-7657-0093-X) Aronson.

Running Away. Charlotte V. Allen. 1996. mass mkt. 5.50 (1-55166-150-0, 1-66150-3, Mira Bks) Harlequin Bks.

Running Away. Sheryl Prenzlau. (B. Y. Times Kid Sisters Ser.: No. 5). (Illus.). 120p. (Orig.). (J). (gr. 2-6). 1993. pap. 6.95 (1-56871-018-6) Targum Pr.

Running Away see Life Issues - Group 3

Running Away from Home. Nigel Gray. LC 95-38217. (Illus.). 32p. (J). 1996. 16.00 (0-517-70923-6, Crown) Crown Pub Group.

Running Backs. Doug Marx. LC 92-8764. (Football Heroes Ser.). (J). 1992. 17.26 (0-86593-151-8); lib. bdg. 12.95 (0-685-59321-5) Rourke Corp.

Running Back...to God. Cookie Jackson. (Illus.). 112p. (Orig.). 1993. pap. 6.95 (0-9622413-5-0) WinePress Pub.

Running Backwards: Selected Poems. Barbara A. Holland. 251p. 1983. pap. 8.00 (0-942292-01-4) Warthog Pr.

Running Bear: Grandson of Red Snake. George McMullen. 96p. (Orig.). 1996. pap. 10.95 (1-57174-037-6) Hampton Roads Pub Co.

***Running Bible.** John Stanton & Melissa Stanton. (Illus.). 292p. (Orig.). 1997. pap. write for info. (1-55105-096-X) Lone Pine.

Running City Hall: Municipal Administration in America. 2nd ed. David L. Martin. LC 89-37627. 224p. 1990. pap. text ed. 17.95 (0-8173-0465-7) U of Ala Pr.

Running Conventions, Conferences, & Meetings. Robert W. Lord. LC 80-69704. 104p. reprint ed. pap. 29.70 (0-317-20407-6, 2023503) Bks Demand.

***Running Databases on the Internet with Cold Fusion 3.** John Burke. 1997. text ed. 49.95 (0-07-913092-5) McGraw.

Running Dead. Robert Coram. 336p. (Orig.). 1993. pap. 5.99 (0-451-17556-5, Sig) NAL-Dutton.

Running Dog. Don DeLillo. (Vintage Contemporaries Ser.). 1989. pap. 13.00 (0-679-72294-7, Vin) Random.

Running Dogs of Loyalty: Honest Reflections on a Magical Zoo. Gale R. Walker. 54p. (Orig.). 1995. pap. 9.95 (0-9647972-0-8) G R Walker.

Running DOS Games. Brian Howard. 1996. pap. text ed. 19.95 incl. cd-rom (1-55755-322-X) Abacus MI.

Running Duck. large type ed. Paula Gosling. 369p. 1981. 25.99 (0-7089-0618-4) Ulverscroft.

Running Eagle: Woman Warrior of the Blackfeet. 2nd ed. James W. Schultz. (Indian Culture Ser.). 25p. (J). (gr. 4 up). 1996. reprint ed. pap. 3.95 (0-89992-138-8) Coun India Ed.

Running Effective Meetings. Barbara J. Streibel et al. (Illus.). 150p. (Orig.). 1993. student ed., teacher ed. 425.00 (0-9622264-5-9) Joiner Assoc.

Running Fiercely Toward a High Thin Sound. Judith Katz. LC 92-28085. 188p. (Orig.). 1992. pap. 10.95 (1-56341-019-2); lib. bdg. 22.95 (1-56341-020-6) Firebrand Bks.

Running Fix. Tony Gibbs. 1990. 18.95 (0-394-57580-6) Random.

Running Foot Doctor. Steven I. Subotnick. 1979. pap. 6.95 (0-02-499710-2, Macmillan Coll) P-H.

***Running for Cover.** Pat Van Wie. 240p. 1997. mass mkt. 3.50 (0-553-44617-7) Bantam.

Running for Freedom: Black Politics in White America. 2nd ed. Steven F. Lawson. LC 96-25931. 1996. pap. text ed. write for info. (0-07-036801-5) McGraw.

Running for Freedom: Civil Rights & Black Politics in America. Steven F. Lawson. 1991. pap. text ed. write for info. (0-07-556975-2) McGraw.

Running for Freedom: Slave Runaways in North Carolina, 1775 to 1840. Freddie L. Parker. LC 92-38603. (Studies in African American History & Culture). 264p. 1993. text ed. 64.00 (0-8153-1005-6) Garland.

Running for Her Life. Francine Pascal. (Sweet Valley University Ser.: No. 5). 288p. (YA). 1996. mass mkt. 4.50 (0-553-57009-9) Bantam.

Running for Lifelong Fitness: A Scientific & Personal Guide. Robert N. Girandola. (Illus.). 128p. 1987. 14.50 (0-13-783937-5) P-H.

Running for Office: The Political Education of Campaigners. Marjorie R. Hershey. LC 84-17609. (Chatham House Series on Change in American Politics). 320p. reprint ed. pap. 91.20 (0-7837-2601-5, 2042765) Bks Demand.

Running for Our Lives. Glennette T. Turner. LC 93-28430. (Illus.). 208p. (J). (gr. 3-7). 1994. 16.95 (0-8234-1121-4) Holiday.

An Asterisk (*) at the beginning of an entry indicates that the title is appearing in BIP for the first time.

Running for President: The Candidates & Their Images, 2 vols. Ed. by Arthur M. Schlesinger, Jr. et al. LC 93-46386. 1994. reprint ed. 175.00 (*0-13-303371-6*) S&S Trade.

Running for President: The Candidates & Their Images, Vol. 1, 1789-1896. Ed. by Arthur M. Schlesinger, Jr. et al. LC 93-46386. 1995. reprint ed. 95.00 (*0-13-303355-4*) S&S Trade.

Running for President: The Candidates & Their Images, Vol. 2, 1900-1992. Ed. by Arthur M. Schlesinger, Jr. et al. LC 93-46386. 1995. reprint ed. 95.00 (*0-13-303363-5*) S&S Trade.

Running for Ribbons. J. Grubbs et al. 32p. (J). (gr. 1-5). 1984. pap. 28.00 (*1-56611-224-9*); lib. bdg. 32.00 (*1-56611-001-7*) Jones.

Running for Shelter: A Laura Principal Mystery. Michelle Spring. 288p. 1996. 21.00 (*0-671-87093-9*) PB.

***Running for Shelter: A Laura Principal Mystery.** Michelle Spring. 1997. mass mkt. 5.99 (*0-671-87094-7*) PB.

Running for the Exit. H. W. Wright. LC 79-12275. (Illus.). 160p. (Orig.). 1981. 6.95 (*0-89407-035-5*) Strawberry Hill.

Running for Their Lives: Physical & Sexual Abuse of Runaway Adolescents. Scott Brown et al. LC 95-7515. (Children of Poverty Ser.). (Illus.). 120p. 1995. text ed. 35.00 (*0-8153-2058-2*) Garland.

Running Foxes. large type ed. Joyce Stranger. 1995. 25.99 (*0-7089-3302-5*) Ulverscroft.

Running Free: Poems. Sebastian Temple. LC 94-31971. 176p. (C). 1995. 19.95 (*0-930887-26-3*) Wenzel Pr.

Running from Police on a Peoria Friday Night: A Politically Incorrect Epic. Ralph L. Jones, Jr. 512p. 1996. 24.95 (*0-9640747-7-X*) Wolf-Wise Pr.

Running from Safety. Richard Bach. 1994. pap. 22.95 (*1-55927-308-9*) St Martin.

Running from Safety. Richard Bach. 368p. 1995. reprint ed. pap. 11.95 (*0-385-31528-7*, Delta) Dell.

Running from Safety: An Adventure of the Spirit. large type ed. Richard Bach. LC 95-2008. (Large Print Bks.). 1995. 23.95 (*1-56895-174-4*) Wheeler Pub.

Running from the Hunter: The Life & Works of Charles Beaumont. Lee Prosser. LC 95-5346. (Milford Ser. : Popular Writers of Today: No. 68). 136p. 1996. pap. 19.00 (*0-89370-291-9*) Borgo Pr.

Running from the Hunter: The Life & Works of Charles Beaumont. Lee Prosser. LC 95-5346. (Milford Ser. : Popular Writers of Today: Vol. 68). 136p. 1996. lib. bdg. 29.00 (*0-89370-191-2*) Borgo Pr.

Running from the Law. Lisa Scottoline. LC 95-24319. 320p. (J). 1995. 20.00 (*0-06-017659-8*, HarpT) HarpC.

Running from the Law. Lisa Scottoline. 256p. 1996. mass mkt. 5.99 (*0-06-109411-0*) HarpC.

Running from the Law. large type ed. Lisa Scottoline. LC 96-11052. 1996. 24.95 (*1-56895-319-4*) Wheeler Pub.

***Running Girl: The Diary of Ebonee Rose.** Sharon B. Mathis. LC 96-29066. (J). 1997. write for info. (*0-15-200674-5*) HarBrace.

Running Gun. Robert Macleod. 1980. pap. 1.75 (*0-449-14302-3*, GM) Fawcett.

Running High/Looking Good. W. C. Osborne. LC 95-62051. (Illus.). 270p. 1995. 27.95 (*0-9643126-3-8*) Woodburner Pr.

Running Home: An Across-Iowa Journal. Paddy Blackman & Jennifer Figge. (Illus.). 126p. (Orig.). 1989. pap. text ed. 8.95 (*0-9625942-0-2*) Bawden Printing.

Running Horse Inn. Jane W. Clark. LC 95-94641. 192p. 1995. 17.95 (*0-8034-9122-0*) Bouregy.

Running Hot: Structure & Stress in Ambulance Work. Donald L. Metz. 252p. 1984. reprint ed. lib. bdg. 20.00 (*0-8191-4069-4*) U Pr of Amer.

***Running in & Around Boston.** Greg Wilmore. (Illus.). 128p. (Orig.). 1997. pap. 9.95 (*0-9655870-0-2*) Ouizel Bks.

Running in Circles: How to Find Freedom from Addictive Behavior. Gary S. Shogren & Edward T. Welch. LC 95-92. (Strategic Christian Living Ser.). 112p. (Orig.). (gr. 10). 1995. pap. 7.99 (*0-8010-8387-7*) Baker Bks.

Running in Place: A Campaign Journal. Bruce E. Altschuler. LC 95-21336. 1996. 18.95 (*0-8304-1439-8*) Nelson-Hall.

Running in Place: How American Families Are Faring in a Changing Economy & an Individualistic Society. Nicholas Zill & Christine W. Nord. LC 94-11581. 1994. write for info. (*0-932359-04-3*) Child Trends.

Running in Place: How Bill Clinton Disappointed America. Richard Reeves. (Illus.). 128p. (Orig.). 1996. pap. 8.95 (*0-8362-1091-3*) Andrews & McMeel.

Running in Place: Scenes from the South of France. Nicholas Delbanco. LC 88-27031. 1990. pap. 9.95 (*0-87113-362-8*, Atlntc Mnthly) Grove-Atltic.

Running in the Family. Michael Ondaatje. LC 93-10494. 1993. pap. 10.00 (*0-679-74669-2*, Vin) Random.

***Running in the Family.** Michael Ondaatje. 1997. audio 18.00 (*0-679-44912-4*) Random.

Running in the Red: The Political Dynamics of Urban Fiscal Stress. Irene S. Rubin. LC 81-9329. 171p. (C). 1983. text ed. 64.50 (*0-87395-564-1*); pap. text ed. 21.95 (*0-87395-565-X*) State U NY Pr.

Running Injuries. Gary N. Guten. Ed. by Richard Lampert. (Illus.). 304p. 1997. text ed. 55.00 (*0-7216-6843-7*) Saunders.

Running Injuries: How to Prevent & Overcome Them. 2nd ed. Timothy D. Noakes & Stephen Granger. (Illus.). 176p. 1996. pap. 19.95 (*0-19-571384-2*) OUP.

Running Injury Free: How to Prevent, Treat & Recover from Dozens of Painful Problems. Joe Ellis & Joe Henderson. (Illus.). 288p. (Orig.). 1994. pap. 14.95 (*0-87596-221-1*) Rodale Pr Inc.

Running into Trouble. Carolyn Keene. (Nancy Drew Files Ser.: 115). (YA). (gr. 6 up). 1996. pap. 3.99 (*0-671-50358-8*) S&S Trade.

Running Iron Ranch Cook Book. Kathy Weber. LC 90-91536. (Illus.). 185p. (Orig.). 1989. pap. 9.95 (*1-878438-00-X*) Ranch House Pr.

Running Lights. Henry Carlile. LC 80-67971. 66p. (C). 1981. 9.00 (*0-937872-00-8*); pap. 5.00 (*0-937872-01-6*) Dragon Gate.

Running Linux. 2nd rev. ed. Matt Welsh & Lar Kaufman. (Illus.). 650p. (Orig.). 1996. pap. 29.95 (*1-56592-151-8*) OReilly & Assocs.

***Running Log Book.** F. Stop Fitzgerald. (Illus.). 100p. (Orig.). 1997. pap. 9.95 (*1-56025-148-4*) Thunders Mouth.

Running Log Two Thousand. 1988. pap. 6.95 (*0-9620706-0-2*) Nathan & Co.

Running Loose. Chris Crutcher. 192p. (YA). (gr. 7 up). 1986. pap. 3.50 (*0-440-97570-0*, LLL BDD) BDD Bks Young Read.

Running Loose. Chris Crutcher. LC 82-20935. 160p. (YA). (gr. 10 up). 1983. 17.95 (*0-688-02002-X*) Greenwillow.

Running Man. Richard Bachman, pseud. 1982. reprint ed. pap. 4.99 (*0-451-15122-4*, Sig) NAL-Dutton.

Running Mates. Stacie Johnson. (Young Adults Ser.). 160p. (YA). 1994. pap. 3.50 (*0-553-56564-8*) Bantam.

Running Microsoft Access for Windows 95: In-Depth Reference & Inside Tips from THE Software Experts. John L. Viescas. (Running Ser.). 944p. 1996. pap. 39.95 incl. cd-rom (*1-55615-886-6*) Microsoft.

Running Microsoft Access 2 for Windows. 2nd ed. John L. Viescas. (Running Ser.). 944p. 1993. pap. 39.95 incl. disk (*1-55615-592-1*) Microsoft.

Running Microsoft Access 97. John L. Viescas. LC 96-37065. 1997. pap. text ed. 39.95 incl. disk (*1-57231-323-4*) Microsoft.

Running Microsoft Excel for Windows 95: In-Depth Reference & Inside Tips from THE Software Experts. Mark Dodge et al. (Running Ser.). 1200p. 1995. pap. 29.95 (*1-55615-831-9*) Microsoft.

Running Microsoft Excel 5 for Windows. 4th ed. Cobb Group Staff. (Running Ser.). 1184p. 1994. pap. 29.95 (*1-55615-585-9*) Microsoft.

Running Microsoft Excel 97. Mark Dodge et al. LC 96-39339. 1996. pap. text ed. 39.95 incl. disk (*1-57231-321-8*) Microsoft.

***Running Microsoft FrontPage.** pap. 34.99 (*1-57231-645-4*) Microsoft.

***Running Microsoft FrontPage 97.** Jim Buyens. 34.99 (*1-57231-426-5*) Microsoft.

***Running Microsoft Internet Information Server 3.0.** Leon Braginski & Powell. 1997. pap. text ed. 39.99 incl. cd-rom (*1-57231-585-7*) Microsoft.

Running Microsoft Office for Windows 95: In-Depth Reference & Inside Tips from THE Software Experts. Michael Halvorson & Michael Young. (Running Ser.). 1088p. 1996. pap. 39.95 (*1-55615-897-1*) Microsoft.

Running Microsoft Office 97. Michael Halvorson & Michael Young. LC 96-44022. 1996. pap. text ed. 39.95 incl. disk (*1-57231-322-6*) Microsoft.

***Running Microsoft Outlook 97.** Russell Borland. LC 97-14337. 416p. 1997. 29.99 incl. cd-rom (*1-57231-608-X*) Microsoft.

Running Microsoft PowerPoint for Windows 95: In-Depth Reference & Inside Tips from THE Software Experts. Stephen W. Sagman. (Running Ser.). 512p. 1995. pap. 24.95 (*1-55615-852-1*) Microsoft.

Running Microsoft Powerpoint 4 for Windows. Stephen W. Sagman. (Running Ser.). 496p. 1994. pap. 24.95 (*1-55615-639-1*) Microsoft.

Running Microsoft Powerpoint 97. Stephen W. Sagman. LC 96-40954. 1996. pap. text ed. 29.95 incl. disk (*1-57231-324-2*) Microsoft.

Running Microsoft Windows NT Server 4.0. Charlie Russel & Sharon Crawford. 1996. pap. text ed. 39.95 (*1-57231-333-1*) Microsoft.

Running Microsoft Windows 95: In-Depth Reference & Inside Tips from THE Software Experts. Craig Stinson. (Running Ser.). 832p. 1995. pap. 39.95 incl. cd-rom (*1-55615-674-X*) Microsoft.

Running Microsoft Word for Windows 95: In-Depth Reference & Inside Tips from THE Software Experts. Russell Borland. (Running Ser.). 1056p. 1995. pap. 29.95 (*1-55615-848-3*) Microsoft.

Running Microsoft Word 97. Russell Borland. LC 96-40186. 1997. pap. text ed. 39.95 incl. disk (*1-57231-320-X*) Microsoft.

Running Microsoft Works for Windows 95: In-Depth Reference & Inside Tips from THE Software Experts. Neil J. Salkind & JoAnne Woodcock. (Running Ser.). 592p. 1995. 24.95 (*1-55615-883-1*) Microsoft.

Running Microsoft Works 3 for Windows: The Microsoft Guide to Mastering the Power & Features of Works for Windows. JoAnne Woodcock & Neil J. Salkind. (Running Ser.). 608p. 1994. pap. 24.95 (*1-55615-584-0*) Microsoft.

Running MS-DOS: Version 6.22. 7th ed. Van Wolverton. LC 93-12270. (Running Ser.). 704p. (Orig.). 1994. pap. 19.95 (*1-55615-633-2*) Microsoft.

Running MS-DOS QBasic. Michael Halvorson & David Rygmyr. (Running Ser.). 496p. 1991. pap. 22.95 (*1-55615-340-6*) Microsoft.

Running near the End of the World. Walter Pavlich. LC 91-31623. (Edwin Ford Piper Poetry Award Ser.). 100p. (Orig.). 1992. pap. 10.95 (*0-87745-358-6*) U of Iowa Pr.

Running Novell's Personal NetWare: PC Networking for Workgroups. Martin Jost & Lee Purcell. LC 93-40078. 313p. 1994. pap. 24.95 (*0-201-62635-7*) Addison-Wesley.

Running on Empty. Jack Heifner. 1987. pap. 5.25 (*0-8222-0976-4*) Dramatists Play.

Running on Empty. Ellen S. Stern. 384p. 1992. pap. 9.95 (*0-553-35149-4*) Bantam.

Running on Empty: Refilling Your Spirit at the Low Points of Life. Jill Briscoe. 180p. 1995. pap. 8.99 (*0-87788-739-X*) Shaw Pubs.

Running on Empty: The Complete Guide to Chronic Fatigue Syndrome. 2nd ed. Katrina Berne. LC 95-44914. (Illus.). 336p. 1995. 24.95 (*0-89793-192-0*); pap. 14.95 (*0-89793-191-2*) Hunter Hse.

Running on Empty & Looking for the Next Exit: How Smart Women Learn to Cope with Everyday Life. Annie Chapman. LC 95-39285. 176p. (Orig.). 1995. pap. 8.99 (*1-55661-587-6*) Bethany Hse.

Running on Empty in the Fast Lane: Redefining Success. Curt Dodd. 137p. 1990. pap. 7.99 (*0-89636-260-4*, AC 211, LifeJourney) Chariot Victor.

Running on the Bias. William C. Tremmel. LC 93-29558. 64p. 1993. pap. 12.95 (*0-7734-2781-3*, Mellen Poetry Pr) E Mellen.

Running on the March Wind: Other Dreams & References. Keeshig-Tobias. 1995. per. 13.95 (*0-920813-48-8*, Pub. by Sister Vision CN) LPC InBook.

***Running on the Record: Civil War-Era Politics in New Hampshire.** Lex Renda. LC 96-37995. 1997. 32.50 (*0-8139-1722-0*) U Pr of Va.

Running Out of Time. Margaret P. Haddix. LC 95-8459. 184p. (J). (gr. 3-7). 1995. 16.00 (*0-689-80084-3*, S&S Bks Young Read) S&S Childrens.

Running Out of Time. Maddix. 1997. pap. 3.99 (*0-689-81236-1*) S&S Childrens.

Running Patterns. Randall R. Freisinger. LC 85-25273. 1985. pap. 7.00 (*0-9613984-1-8*) Flume Pr.

Running Press Book Buddy. Penny Dann. (Little Book Buddies Ser.). (Illus.). 9p. (J). (ps up). 1996. 14.95 (*1-56138-655-3*, Running Pr Mini Edtns) Running Pr.

Running Press Cyclopedia: The Portable Visual Encyclopedia. Diagram Group Staff. (Illus.). 638p. 1995. pap. 8.95 (*1-56138-661-8*) Running Pr.

Running Register: Recording the State of the English Colledges in All Forraine Parts. Lewis Owen. LC 68-54654. (English Experience Ser.: No. 19). 118p. 1968. reprint ed. 20.00 (*90-221-0019-7*) Walter J Johnson.

***Running Revolution.** Joe Henderson. 205p. 1980. 6.95 (*0-915297-16-7*) Cedarwinds.

Running Risks. Larry Laudan. 240p. 1994. pap. text ed. 12.95 (*0-471-31034-4*) Wiley.

Running Scared. Thomas J. Dygard. 192p. (J). (gr. 5 up). 1992. pap. 3.99 (*0-14-034914-6*, Puffin) Puffin Bks.

Running Scared. Gregory McDonald. 1964. 12.95 (*0-8392-1095-7*) Astor-Honor.

***Running Scared.** Lawrence Walsh & Suella Walsh. (J). (gr. 5-7). 1997. pap. 5.99 (*0-614-28970-X*) Royal Fireworks.

***Running Scared: How Athletics Lost Its Innocence.** Steven Downes & Duncan Mackay. (Illus.). 224p. 1997. 29.95 (*1-85158-855-8*, Pub. by Mnstream UK) Trafalgar.

Running Scared: Masculinity & the Representation of the Male Body. Peter Lehman. LC 92-46733. (Illus.). 256p. 1993. 39.95 (*1-56639-099-0*) Temple U Pr.

Running Scared: Masculinity & the Representation of the Male Body. Peter Lehman. (C). 1994. pap. text ed. 18.95 (*1-56639-222-5*) Temple U Pr.

Running Scared: The Dangerous Life & Treacherous Times of Las Vegas Casino King Steve Wynn. abr. ed. John L. Smith. Ed. by William Hinton. LC 95-15251. 352p. 1995. 24.00 (*1-56980-039-1*) Barricade Bks.

***Running Scared: The Victory of Campaigning over Governing in America.** Anthony King. 1997. 24.00 (*0-614-20399-6*, Free Press) Free Pr.

Running Shoe Book. Cavanagh. 1980. pap. 11.95 (*0-02-499730-7*, Macmillan Coll) P-H.

Running Skills. S. Peach. (Superskills Ser.). (Illus.). 48p. (YA). (gr. 6-10). 1988. pap. 5.95 (*0-7460-0165-7*) EDC.

Running Starts - Teens. 368p. 1991. spiral bd. 6.50 (*1-879127-04-0*) Lighten Up Enter.

Running the Amazon. Joe Kane. 1989. 19.95 (*0-394-55331-4*) Knopf.

Running the Amazon. Joe Kane. LC 89-40610. (Vintage Departures Ser.). 1990. pap. 13.00 (*0-679-72902-X*, Vin) Random.

Running the Amazon. Joe Kane. LC 94-72783. (Adventure Library: Vol. 3). (Illus.). 344p. 1995. reprint ed. lib. bdg. 25.00 (*1-885283-02-4*) Advent Library.

Running the American Corporation. Ed. by William R. Dill. LC 78-16922. 1978. 10.95 (*0-13-783894-8*); pap. 4.95 (*0-13-783886-7*) Am Assembly.

Running the American Corporation. American Assembly Staff. LC 78-16922. (Spectrum Book Ser.). 196p. reprint ed. pap. 55.90 (*0-685-23644-7*, 2027982) Bks Demand.

Running the Blockade: A Personal Narrative of Adventures, Risks, & Escapes During the American Civil War. Thomas E. Taylor. (Classics of Naval Literature Ser.). (Illus.). 224p. 1994. 32.95 (*1-55750-804-6*) Naval Inst Pr.

Running the Blockade: A Personal Narrative of Adventures, Risks, & Escapes During the American Civil War. Thomas E. Taylor. LC 79-154163. (Select Bibliographies Reprint Ser.). 1977. reprint ed. 28.95 (*0-8369-5779-2*) Ayer.

Running the Lydiard War. Arthur Lydiard. 1978. 12.95 (*0-02-499720-X*, Macmillan Coll) P-H.

Running the Palestine Blockade: The Last Voyage of the Paducah. Rudolph W. Patzert. LC 93-28122. 244p. 1994. 29.95 (*1-55750-679-5*) Naval Inst Pr.

Running the Road to ABC. Denize Lauture. LC 95-38290. (Illus.). 32p. (J). (gr. 1-5). 1996. 16.00 (*0-689-80507-1*, S&S Bks Young Read) S&S Childrens.

Running the Show: Twenty-One Years of London Weekend Television. David Docherty. 208p. (C). 1990. 60.00 (*1-85283-103-0*, Pub. by Boxtree Ltd UK) St Mut.

Running the Trans America Footrace: Trials & Triumphs of Life on the Road. Barry Lewis. (Illus.). 160p. 1994. pap. 14.95 (*0-8117-2582-0*) Stackpole.

Running Things. 1989. pap. 4.95 (*0-451-62871-3*, Ment) NAL-Dutton.

Running Things: The Art of Making Things Happen. Philip B. Crosby. 254p. 1986. text ed. 27.95 (*0-07-014513-X*) McGraw.

Running Things: The Art of Making Things Happen. Philip B. Crosby. 256p. 1989. pap. 4.95 (*0-451-62689-3*, Ment) NAL-Dutton.

***Running Through the Tall Grass: A Novel.** Thomas Givon. LC 97-2033. 304p. 1997. 23.00 (*0-06-039200-2*, ReganBooks) HarpC.

Running Through the Thickets. Adam N. Gladefly. 1991. 13.95 (*0-533-09255-8*) Vantage.

Running Through the Thistles: Terminating a Ministerial Relationship with a Parish. Roy M. Oswald. pap. 6.95 (*1-56699-004-1*) Alban Inst.

Running Tide. large type ed. Audrey Curling. 384p. 1987. 25.99 (*0-7089-1582-5*) Ulverscroft.

***Running Tide.** large type ed. Connie Monk. (Large Print Ser.). 624p. 1996. 25.99 (*0-7089-3594-X*) Ulverscroft.

Running Tide. large type ed. Cynthia S. Roberts. (Romance Suspense Ser.). 624p. 1989. 25.99 (*0-7089-1998-7*) Ulverscroft.

Running to Keep Fit. Brian Mitchell. 96p. 1980. pap. 2.95 (*0-679-12428-4*) McKay.

***Running to Paradise: Yeat's Poetic Art.** M. L. Rosenthal. LC 96-52763. (Illus.). 384p. 1997. reprint ed. pap. 18.95 (*0-19-511391-8*) OUP.

Running to Safety: International Edition. Richard Bach. 288p. 1995. mass mkt. 6.99 (*0-440-29543-2*) Dell.

Running to the Shrouds: 19th-Century Sea Stories. Konstantin Stanyukovich. Tr. by N. Parsons. LC 86-81346. 100p. 8600. pap. 16.95 (*0-948259-06-X*) Dufour.

Running to the Top. Clayton. 1983. pap. 5.95 (*0-02-499740-4*, Macmillan Coll) P-H.

Running to the Top of the Mountain. John F. Durkin & Joe Newton. (Illus.). 350p. (Orig.). (YA). (gr. 9-12). 1988. pap. text ed. 24.95 (*0-9621313-0-X*) J & J Win Edge.

Running to Win! A Positive Biblical Approach to Rewards & Inheritance. G. Harry Leafe. 108p. (Orig.). 1992. pap. 5.00 (*0-9635128-0-3*) Scriptel Pubs.

Running Toward Your Giant. Jesse Duplantis. (Mini-Bks.). 16p. 1993. pap. 0.75 (*0-89274-644-0*, HH-644) Harrison Hse.

***Running Towards a New Life.** Marcus Cumberlege. Date not set. 14.95 (*0-900977-72-8*, Pub. by Anvil Press UK) Dufour.

***Running Trax: Computerized Running Training Programs.** J. Gerry Purdy. 127p. (Orig.). 1996. spiral bd., pap. 17.50 (*0-911521-48-8*) Tafnews.

Running Twice As Hard: The Disadvantage Schools Program in Australia. Ed. by R. W. Connell et al. 299p. 1992. pap. 57.00 (*0-7300-1364-2*, ESA842, Pub. by Deakin Univ AT) St Mut.

Running UNIX So It Doesn't Run You. Don Crabb. 1993. pap. 29.95 (*1-56276-061-0*, Ziff-Davis Pr) Que.

Running, Walking & Jumping: The Science of Locomotion. A. J. Dagg. 143p. 1977. pap. 18.00 (*0-85109-530-5*) Taylor & Francis.

Running West. James Houston. 1992. mass mkt. 4.99 (*0-8217-3505-5*, Zebra Kensgtn) Kensgtn Pub Corp.

Running West. James Houston. 1996. pap. text ed. 14.00 (*1-57566-044-X*) Kensgtn Pub Corp.

Running Wild. Thomas J. Dygard. 208p. (YA). (gr. 7 up). 1996. 15.00 (*0-688-14853-0*, Morrow Junior) Morrow.

***Running Wild.** Alison Fraser. 1996. 20.95 (*0-263-14820-3*, Pub. by Mills & Boon UK) Thorndike Pr.

***Running Wild: Dispelling the Myths of the African Wild Dog.** John McNutt & Lesley P. Boggs. (Illus.). 150p. 1996. 45.00 (*1-56098-717-0*) Smithsonian.

***Running Wild: Extraordinary Adventures from the Spiritual World of Running.** 2nd ed. John Annerino. 1997. pap. text ed. 13.95 (*1-56025-175-1*) Thunders Mouth.

Running Wild: New Chinese Writers. Ed. by David Wang & Jeanne Tai. LC 93-37041. 1994. pap. 16.00 (*0-231-09649-6*) Col U Pr.

Running Wild: New Chinese Writers. Ed. by David Wang & Jeanne Tai. LC 93-37041. 264p. 1994. 49.50 (*0-231-09648-8*) Col U Pr.

Running Windows Applications in OS/2: A Power User's Guide. Ayodele Anise et al. 400p. 1995. pap. text ed. 34.95 (*0-471-13124-5*) Wiley.

Running Windows on LANtastic. Michael S. Montgomery. 1993. pap. 22.95 (*0-8306-4447-4*, Windcrest) TAB Bks.

Running with Bill. Stephen Dunning. (Illus.). 22p. (Orig.). 1985. pap. 10.00 (*0-9608802-2-4*) Years Pr.

Running with Bonnie & Clyde: The Ten Fast Years of Ralph Fults. John N. Phillips. LC 95-42771. (Illus.). 416p. 1996. 27.95 (*0-8061-2810-0*) U of Okla Pr.

Running with Man's Best Friend. Davia A. Gallup. LC 85-52454. (Illus.). 128p. (Orig.). 1986. pap. 7.95 (*0-931866-25-1*) Alpine Pubns.

Running with Mr. Search for Love. Martin Taragano. 138p. (Orig.). 1995. pap. 13.95 (*0-9647920-4-4*) Loanshark Pr.

Running with the Angels: The Gifts of AIDS. Bobbie Stasey. Ed. by Ed Dziczek. LC 94-8913. (Illus.). 350p. 1994. pap. 14.95 (*0-9635589-8-6*) Elysian Hills.

***Running with the Demon.** Terry Brooks. LC 97-9381. 1997. 24.00 (*0-345-37962-4*, Del Rey) Ballantine.

Running with the Devil: Power, Gender, & Madness in Heavy Metal Music. Robert Walser. LC 92-56911. (Music - Culture Ser.). (Illus.). 242p. 1993. pap. 16.95 (*0-8195-6260-2*, Wesleyan Univ Pr) U Pr of New Eng.

Running with the Dolphins & Other Tybee Tales. Michael Elliott. LC 95-5840. 192p. 1995. pap. 12.95 (*1-57312-006-5*) Smyth & Helwys.

Running with the Krays: My Life in London's Gangland. Billy Webb. (Illus.). 208p. 1994. 29.95 (*1-85158-558-3*, Pub. by Mnstream UK) Trafalgar.

R

*Running with the Krays: My Life in London's Gangland. Billy Webb. (Illus.). 224p. 1996. pap. 15.95 (1-85158-769-1, Pub. by Mnstream UK) Trafalgar.

Running with the Legends. Michael Sandrock. LC 96-3790. 568p. 1996. pap. 19.95 (0-87322-493-0, PSAN0493) Human Kinetics.

Running with the Whole Body: A 30-Day Program for Running Faster with Less Effort. Jack Heggie. LC 96-24591. (Illus.). 190p. (Orig.). 1996. pap. 12.95 (1-55643-226-7) North Atlantic.

*Running Woman. Patricia Carlon. LC 97-16842. 1998. write for info. (1-56947-110-X) Soho Press.

*Running Your Best. Timothy D. Noakes & Stephen Granger. Date not set. write for info. (0-19-570956-X) OUP.

Running Your Business with Quattro Pro for Windows. Marina McInnis. 300p. 1993. pap. 34.95 (1-883327-42-3) TitleWave Pr.

Running Your Indexing Business. 1995. write for info. (0-936547-32-4) Am Soc Index.

*Running Your Own Boarding Kennels. 2nd ed. Sheila Zabawa. (Working for Yourself Ser.). 1992. pap. 14.95 (0-7494-0595-3) Kogan Page Ltd.

*Running Your Own Catering Company. 2nd ed. Judy Ridgway. (Working for Yourself Ser.). 1992. pap. 14.95 (0-7494-0830-8) Kogan Page Ltd.

Running Your Own Guest House. W. Wright. (C). 1989. 85.00 (0-09-161741-3, Pub. by S Thornes Pubs UK) St Mut.

*Running Your Own Photographic Business. 2nd ed. J. Rose & L. Hankin. (Working for Yourself Ser.). 1989. pap. 14.95 (1-85091-998-4) Kogan Page Ltd.

Running Your Own Photographic Business. 2nd ed. John Rose & Linda Hankin. 145p. (Orig.). 1992. pap. 27.95 (0-8464-1378-7) Beekman Pubs.

Running Your Own Private Residential or Nursing Home. Colin M. Barron. 148p. 1990. 29.95 (1-85302-062-1) Taylor & Francis.

Running Your Own Rock & Roll Band. William Henderson. 250p. 1996. 18.00 (0-02-864611-8) Macmillan.

Running Your Remodeling Business. Harry Hardenbrook & Harold Hammerman. 272p. (Orig.). 1988. pap. 21.00 (0-934041-37-7) Craftsman.

Runoff Elections in the United States. Charles S. Bullock, III & Loch K. Johnson. LC 92-53626. (Thornton H. Brooks Series in American Law & Society). xxii, 206p. (C). 1992. 34.95 (0-8078-2053-9) U of NC Pr.

Runoff, Infiltration, & Subsurface Flow of Water in Aris & Semi-Arid Regions. Ed. by Arie S. Issar & Sol D. Resnick. (Water Science & Technology Library: Vol. 21). 1996. lib. bdg. 97.00 (0-7923-4034-5) Kluwer Ac.

Runpoem. Eugene Combs. LC 92-21595. 68p. 1992. pap. 12.95 (0-7734-9523-1, Mellen Poetry Pr) E Mellen.

Runs & Patterns in Probability: Selected Papers. Ed. by Anant P. Godole & Stavros G. Papastavridis. LC 94-13377. (Mathematics & Its Applications Ser.: Vol. 283). 360p. (C). 1994. lib. bdg. 155.00 (0-7923-2834-5) Kluwer Ac.

Runs, Hits, & an Era: The Pacific Coast League, 1903-58. Paul J. Zingg & Mark D. Medeiros. (Illus.). 150p. 1994. 19.95 (0-252-06402-X); text ed. 44.95 (0-252-02117-7) U of Ill Pr.

Runs with Horses. Brian Burks. LC 95-8460. 128p. (J). (gr. 7 up). 1995. 11.00 (0-15-200264-2, HB Juv Bks) HarBrace.

Runs with Horses. Brian Burks. LC 95-8460. 128p. (YA). (gr. 7 up). 1995. pap. 5.00 (0-15-200994-9, HB Juv Bks) HarBrace.

Runt Pig Principle: A Fundamental Approach to Solving Problems & Creating Value. Clifford D. Cooper. LC 92-81924. 184p. (Orig.). 1992. pap. 12.95 (0-9633046-0-7) Alliance Prog.

*Runton Werewolf. large type ed. Ritchie Perry. (J). 1997. 16.95 (0-7451-6908-2, Galaxy Child Lrg Print) Chivers N Amer.

Runaway from Innocence. Jay P. Mitchell. LC 92-60807. 256p. 1993. 10.95 (1-55523-536-0) Winston-Derek.

*Runway: Reflections on the Ten Commandments. Robert G. Tuttle. LC 96-38668. 82p. (Orig.). 1997. pap. 8.75 (0-7880-0388-7) CSS OH.

Runway at Eland Springs. Rebecca Beguin. LC 87-60528. 240p. (Orig.). 1987. pap. 7.95 (0-934678-10-3) New Victoria Pubs.

Runway Towards Orion: The True Adventures of a Red Cross Girl on a B-29 Air Base in World War II India. Mary T. Sargent. (Illus.). 240p. (Orig.). 1984. pap. 10.95 (0-931515-01-7) Triumph Pr.

Runway Wedding. Ruth J. Dale. (Romance Ser.). 1996. mass mkt. 3.25 (0-373-03413-X, 1-03413-1) Harlequin Bks.

Runzheimer Meal-Lodging Cost Index: Primary & Secondary U. S. Locations. 200p. 1995. 300.00 (0-614-08359-1) Runzheimer International.

Ruodlieb. Ed. by Grocock. (Classical Texts Ser.). 1985. 49.95 (0-85668-292-6, Pub. by Aris & Phillips UK); pap. 24.95 (0-85668-293-4, Pub. by Aris & Phillips UK) David Brown.

Ruodlieb. Ed. & Intro. by C. W. Grocock. (BC-AP Classical Ser.). 240p. (Orig.). (ENG & LAT.). 1986. 49.00 (0-86516-098-8) Bolchazy-Carducci.

Ruodlieb: The Earliest Courtly Novel after 1050. Ed. & Tr. by Edwin H. Zeydel. LC 59-63490. (North Carolina. University. Studies in the Germanic Languages & Literatures: NO. 23). 1959. 27.00 (0-404-50923-1) AMS Pr.

Rupa-Ikshana: Development of Indian Art & Culture. Ed. by Sudha Bose. (C). 1991. 59.50 (81-85067-74-0, Pub. by Sundeep Prakashan II) S Asia.

Rupert & the Blackberries. (Rupert Board Bks.). (Illus.). 24p. (J). (ps-3). Date not set. bds. 4.95 (1-56987-417-4) Landoll.

Rupert & the Blackberries. (Rupert Storybooks Ser.). 24p. (J). (ps-6). Date not set. text ed. 4.95 (1-56987-364-X) Landoll.

Rupert & the Fun Fair. (Rupert Board Bks.). (Illus.). 24p. (J). (ps-3). Date not set. bds. 4.95 (1-56987-418-2) Landoll.

Rupert & the Fun Fair. (Rupert Storybooks Ser.). 24p. (J). (ps-6). Date not set. text ed. 4.95 (1-56987-365-8) Landoll.

Rupert & the Mysterious Island. (Rupert Board Bks.). (Illus.). 24p. (J). (ps-3). Date not set. bds. 4.95 (1-56987-416-6) Landoll.

Rupert & the Mysterious Island. (Rupert Storybooks Ser.). 24p. (J). (ps-6). Date not set. text ed. 4.95 (1-56987-362-3) Landoll.

Rupert & the Royal Hiccups: And Other Silly Stories. Highlights for Children Editors. LC 93-70408. 96p. (Orig.). (J). (gr. 2-5). 1994. pap. 2.95 (1-56397-267-0) Boyds Mills Pr.

Rupert & the Seven Sleepers. (Rupert Storybooks Ser.). 24p. (J). (ps-6). Date not set. text ed. 4.95 (1-56987-363-1) Landoll.

Rupert & the Snow Dragon. (Rupert Board Bks.). (Illus.). 24p. (J). (ps-3). Date not set. bds. 4.95 (1-56987-415-8) Landoll.

Rupert Annual No. 55: 70th Anniversary Issue. James Henderson. (Illus.). 100p. 1990. 13.50 (0-85079-206-1) Scholium Intl.

Rupert Brooke. Rupert Brooke. (Pocket Poet Ser.). 1968. pap. 3.95 (0-8023-9042-0) Dufour.

Rupert Brooke. William E. Laskowski, Jr. LC 93-40510. (Twayne's English Authors Ser.: No. 504). 1994. 22.95 (0-8057-7025-9, Twayne) Scribnrs Ref.

Rupert Brooke & the Intellectual Imagination. Walter J. De La Mare. LC 72-3166. (English Literature Ser.: No. 33). 1972. reprint ed. lib. bdg. 75.00 (0-8383-1515-1) M S G Haskell Hse.

Rupert Brooke in Canada. Sandra Martin & Roger Hall. 154p. 1978. 14.95 (0-88778-184-5) Genl Dist Srvs.

*Rupert Garcia. 38p. 1985. 10.95 (0-614-24046-8) Mexican Museum.

Rupert Garcia: Aspects of Resistance. Alternative Museum Staff. LC 93-73974. 1993. pap. text ed. 15.00 (0-932075-39-8) Alternative Mus.

Rupert Garcia: Prints & Posters 1967-1990. Fine Arts Museums of San Francisco Staff. (Illus.). 64p. 1991. pap. text ed. 17.95 (0-88401-069-4) Fine Arts Mus.

*Rupert Hughes: A Hollywood Legend. James O. Keum. (Illus.). 400p. 1997. 24.95 (0-938817-49-3) Pomegranate Pr.

Rupert Murdoch: Ringmaster of the Information Circus. William Shawcross. (Illus.). 626p. 1993. pap. 22.50 (0-330-32975-8, Pub. by Pan Books UK) Trans-Atl Phila.

Rupert of Deutz. John H. Van Engen. LC 82-40089. (Publications of the UCLA Center for Medieval & Renaissance Studies: No. 18). (Illus.). 417p. reprint ed. pap. 118.90 (0-7837-4686-5, 2044433) Bks Demand.

Rupert of Hentzau (Sequel) Anthony Hope. 1976. 22.95 (0-8488-1040-6) Amereon Ltd.

Rupert of Hentzau (Sequel to Prisoner of Zenda) Anthony Hope. 1987. lib. bdg. 25.95 (0-89966-227-7) Buccaneer Bks.

Rupert, Polly & Daisy. Jody Silver. LC 83-24979. (Illus.). 48p. (J). (ps-3). 1984. 5.95 (0-8193-1124-3) Parents.

Rupert, Polly, & Daisy. Jody Silver. LC 94-16227. (Parents Magazine Whole Language Library). (Illus.). (J). (gr. 1 up). lib. bdg. 17.27 (0-8368-0994-7) Gareth Stevens Inc.

Rupert the Devil. large type ed. Jeanne Montague. (Dales Large Print Ser.). 1995. pap. 17.99 (1-85389-575-X, Dales) Ulverscroft.

Rupert the Duck. Dan Slottje. LC 94-8926. (Illus.). 48p. (J). (ps up). 1994. 14.95 (1-885108-00-1) Armstrong CT.

Ruperts Amition. Horatio Alger, Jr. (Works of Horatio Alger Jr.). 1989. reprint ed. lib. bdg. 79.00 (0-685-27560-4) Rprt Serv.

Rupert's Birthday & Other Monologues. Ken Jenkins. 1985. pap. 5.25 (0-8222-0978-0) Dramatists Play.

Ruprecht on End-User Computing, Lecture 3. Ruprecht. (KU - Office Procedures Ser.). 1992. 177.95 (0-538-70788-7) S-W Pub.

Rupture Ductility of Creep Resistant Steels. A. Strang. 1991. pap. 80.00 (0-901716-04-9, Pub. by Inst Materials UK) Ashgate Pub Co.

Ruptured Cerebral Aneurysm. rev. ed. Oliver D. Grin & Dorothy L. Bouwman. Ed. by Carol E. Roberts. (Patient Education Ser.). (Illus.). 26p. 1989. pap. text ed. 4.00 (0-929689-36-4) Ludann Co.

Ruptured Decade, 1938-1948. Milan J. Halla. 1976. 26.95 (0-8488-0336-1) Amereon Ltd.

Ruptured Heart...a Caretaker's Journey. Suzanne. Ed. by Carolyn S. Zagury. LC 94-61760. 120p. (Orig.). 1995. pap. 10.95 (1-880254-21-2) Vista.

Ruptures of Major Earthquakes & Active Deformation in Mongolia. I. Baijinnyam et al. (Memoir Ser.: No. 181). 1993. 18.75 (0-8137-1181-9) Geol Soc.

Rupturierte Bauaortenaneurysma: Klinisches Expertengespraech Ueber Anaesthesie und Chirurgie, Hamburg, January 1993. Ed. by H. Imig. (Illus.). viii, 70p. 1993. pap. 33.25 (3-8055-5826-0) S Karger.

Rural Acreage: Finding the Right Place. James R. Harris. (Illus.). 86p. (C). 1994. lib. bdg. 14.95 (0-9637037-0-6) J Harris.

Rural Action. Ed. by Paul Henderson & David Francis. (Community Development Foundation Ser.). 178p. (C). 1994. pap. text ed. 24.95 (0-7453-0789-2) Westview.

Rural Action: A Collection of Community Work Case Studies. Ed. by Paul Henderson & David Francis. LC 93-26326. 178p. 1994. 21.95 (0-7453-0733-7); pap. write for info. (0-7453-0732-9) Westview.

Rural Ain't Necessarily Country. Jack M. Holland. (Illus.). 208p. (Orig.). 1985. pap. 5.95 (0-935777-03-2) Country Pub.

Rural Aint Necessarily Country, Vol. II. Jack M. Holland. (Illus.). 200p. (Orig.). 1990. pap. text ed. 6.95 (0-685-45269-7) Country Pub.

Rural America: A Pictorial Folk Memory. Mary A. Shafer. (Illus.). 144p. 1995. 29.95 (1-57223-021-5, 0215) Idyll Arbor.

Rural America: A Tribute to Will. William F. Silhan. LC 91-38998. 80p. (Orig.). 1992. pap. 8.95 (1-56474-015-3) Fithian Pr.

Rural America: Prints from the Collection of Steven Schmidt. Bill North et al. (Illus.). (Orig.). 1993. pap. 11.95 (0-913689-37-8) Spencer Muse Art.

Rural America a Century Ago. 160p. 1976. pap. 12.95 (0-916150-06-2, HO776) Am Soc Ag Eng.

Rural America at the Crossroads. 1993. lib. bdg. 255.95 (0-8490-9011-3) Gordon Pr.

Rural America in the Information Age: Telecommunications Policy for Rural Development. Edwin B. Parker et al. 186p. (Orig.). (C). 1989. pap. text ed. 19.50 (0-8191-7494-7, Aspen Inst for Humanistic Studies); lib. bdg. 38.50 (0-8191-7493-9, Aspen Inst for Humanistic Studies) U Pr of Amer.

Rural & Agrarian Social Structure of Nepal. Sohan R. Yadav. (C). 1992. 28.50 (81-7169-174-9, Pub. by Commonwealth II) S Asia.

Rural & Agricultural Development in Ukbekistan. Paul Craumer. (Former Soviet-South Papers). 60p. (C). 1995. pap. 12.95 (1-899658-02-5) Brookings.

Rural & Agricultural Glossary for the NW Provinces & Oudh. William Crooke. (C). 1989. reprint ed. 28.50 (81-85326-00-2, Pub. by Usha II) S Asia.

Rural & Farming Systems Analysis: European Perspectives. Ed. by J. B. Dent & M. J. McGregor. 384p. 1994. 100.00 (0-85198-914-4) CAB Intl.

Rural & Small Town America: The Population of the United States in the 1980's. Glenn V. Fuguitt et al. LC 89-10067. (Census Monograph Ser.). 512p. 1989. 55.00 (0-87154-272-2) Russell Sage.

Rural & Tribal Development Practices in India. Ed. by Pradip K. Bhowmick. 212p. (C). 1994. 60.00 (81-85880-25-5, Pub. by Print Hse II) St Mut.

Rural & Urban Aged. Maninder S. Randhawa. (C). 1991. 28.00 (81-85135-55-X, Pub. by Natl Bk Org II) S Asia.

Rural & Urban Aspects of Early Medieval Northwest Europe. Adriaan Verhulst. (Collected Studies: No. CS385). 352p. 1992. 98.95 (0-86078-344-8, Pub. by Variorum UK) Ashgate Pub Co.

Rural & Urban Economies. Joel M. Halpern. (Laos Project Papers: No. 19). 87p. 1990. pap. 10.50 (0-923135-20-0) Dalley Bk Service.

Rural & Urban House Types in North America. Steven Holl. (Pamphlet Architecture Ser.: No. 9). (Illus.). 60p. 1982. pap. 10.95 (0-910413-15-0) Princeton Arch.

Rural & Urban Patterns: An Exploration of How Older Adults Use In-Home Care. Janette K. Newhouse. LC 94-22166. (Studies on the Elderly in America). (Illus.). 256p. 1995. text ed. 69.00 (0-8153-1631-3) Garland.

Rural Architecture in the Chinese Taste. William Halfpenny & John Halfpenny. LC 68-58993. (Illus.). 1972. reprint ed. 18.95 (0-405-08591-5, Pub. by Blom Pubns UK) Ayer.

Rural Architecture of Northern New Mexico & Southern Colorado. Myrtle Stedman. LC 88-30116. (Illus.). 96p. (Orig.). 1989. pap. 10.95 (0-86534-001-3) Sunstone Pr.

Rural Arts Collaborations. Ed. by Amry Altman & John Caddy. (Illus.). 193p. (Orig.). 1994. pap. 10.00 (0-927663-22-8) COMPAS.

Rural Australia & New Zealand: Some Observations of Current Trends. Edmund D. Brunner. LC 75-30123. (Institute of Pacific Relations Ser.). reprint ed. 34.50 (0-404-59513-8) AMS Pr.

Rural Banking. J. P. Singh et al. (C). 1988. 26.00 (81-7024-193-6, Pub. by Ashish II) S Asia.

Rural Banking in Nigeria. Ed. by Adeniyi Osuntogun & Wole Adewunmi. LC 82-176. (Illus.). 144p. reprint ed. pap. 41.10 (0-8357-2964-8, 2039226) Bks Demand.

*Rural Banking Nigeria. Osuntogun & Adewunm. 1983. pap. text ed. write for info. (0-582-64419-4, Pub. by Longman UK) Longman.

Rural Banks & Rural Credit. V. Balamohan Das. (C). 1991. 46.00 (81-7141-120-7) S Asia.

Rural Black Heritage Between Chicago & Detroit, 1850-1929: A Photograph Album & Random Thoughts. 3rd ed. Benjamin C. Wilson. LC 84-62334. 1991. reprint ed. pap. 7.95 (0-932826-19-9) New Issues MI.

Rural Blacksmith, Rural Businessman: Making & Selling Metal Goods in Malawi. Val Rea & Mike Martin. (Orig.). 1991. pap. 42.95 (1-85339-094-1, Pub. by Intermed Tech UK) Women Ink.

Rural Building Course: Basic Knowledge, 4 vols. S, Vol. 2. 184p. (Orig.). 1995. pap. 20.95 (1-85339-315-0, Pub. by Intermed Tech UK) Women Ink.

Rural Building Course: Construction, Vol. 3. 302p. (Orig.). 1995. pap. 28.50 (1-85339-320-7, Pub. by Intermed Tech UK) Women Ink.

Rural Building Course: Drawing Book, Vol. 4. (Illus.). 126p. (Orig.). 1995. pap. 18.95 (0-614-17099-0, Pub. by Intermed Tech UK) Women Ink.

Rural Building Course Vol. 1: Reference, 4 vols. 244p. (Orig.). 1995. pap. 24.95 (1-85339-310-X, Pub. by Intermed Tech UK) Women Ink.

Rural by Design: Maintaining Small Town Character. Randall Arendt. LC 93-71517. (Illus.). 441p. (Orig.). 1994. lib. bdg. 86.00 (0-918286-86-7) Planners Pr.

Rural Canada: Structure & Change. Satadal Dasgupta. LC 87-21644. (Canadian Studies: Vol. 3). 232p. 1987. lib. bdg. 89.95 (0-88946-196-1) E Mellen.

Rural Carpenter's World: The Craft in a Nineteenth-Century New York Township. Wayne Franklin. LC 89-20613. (American Land & Life Ser.). (Illus.). 312p. 1990. text ed. 37.95 (0-87745-277-6) U of Iowa Pr.

Rural Carrier (U.S.P.S.) Jack Rudman. (Career Examination Ser.: C-678). 1994. pap. 19.95 (0-8373-0678-7) Nat Learn.

Rural Change & Royal Finances in Spain at the End of the Old Regime. Richard Herr. (C). 1988. 89.00 (0-520-05948-4) U CA Pr.

Rural Change in Machakos, Kenya: A Historical Geography Perspective. Marilyn Silberfein. LC 89-32248. (Illus.). 210p. (C). 1989. lib. bdg. 49.00 (0-8191-7470-X) U Pr of Amer.

Rural Change in South Asia. Gilbert Etienne. (C). 1995. 37.50 (0-7069-8756-X, Pub. by Vikas II) S Asia.

Rural Change in the Third World: Pakistan & the Aga Khan Rural Support Program. Mahmood H. Khan & Shoaib S. Khan. LC 91-25445. (Contributions in Economics & Economic History Ser.: No. 129). 200p. 1992. text ed. 55.00 (0-313-28011-8, KRG, Greenwood Pr) Greenwood.

Rural Children in Selected Counties of North Carolina. United States Children's Bureau Staff. Ed. by Francis S. Bradley & Margaretta A. Williamson. LC 76-78778. (Illus.). 118p. 1969. reprint ed. text ed. 45.00 (0-8371-1399-7, RCN&) Greenwood.

Rural China in Transition: Non-Agricultural Development in Rural Jiangsu, 1978-1990. Samuel P. Ho. LC 93-48891. (Studies in Contemporary China). (Illus.). 350p. 1994. 69.00 (0-19-828823-9, Old Oregon Bk Store) OUP.

Rural Church in America: A Century of Writings, a Bibliography. Gary A. Goreham. LC 89-39156. 288p. 1990. text ed. 42.00 (0-8240-3439-2, 1160) Garland.

Rural Communities: Legacy & Change. Cornelia B. Flora et al. 334p. (C). 1992. pap. text ed. 24.00 (0-8133-1477-1) Westview.

Rural Communities: Legacy & Change. Jan L. Flora et al. LC 92-32593. 220p. (C). 1992. student ed., pap. text ed. 16.50 (0-8133-1478-X) Westview.

Rural Communities, Alcohol, Tobacco & Other Drugs: A Resource Guide. 1995. lib. bdg. 251.95 (0-8490-6796-0) Gordon Pr.

Rural Communities in Advanced Industrial Society: Development & Developers. Ted K. Bradshaw & Edward J. Blakely. LC 78-19736. 202p. 1979. text ed. 49.95 (0-275-90333-8, C0333, Praeger Pubs) Greenwood.

Rural Communities in the Medieval West. Leopold Genicot. LC 89-37340. (Symposia in Comparative History Ser.). (Illus.). 200p. 1990. text ed. 32.00 (0-8018-3870-3) Johns Hopkins.

Rural Communities Under Stress: Peasant Farmers & the State in Africa. Jonathan Barker. (African Society Today Ser.). (Illus.). 240p. (C). 1990. pap. text ed. 20.95 (0-521-31358-9) Cambridge U Pr.

Rural Community Development: A Comprehensive Model for Programs, Policy, & Research. Stephen J. Fitzsimmons & Abby J. Freedman. LC 80-69664. (Illus.). 544p. 1981. text ed. 40.00 (0-89011-556-7) Abt Bks.

Rural Community Economic Development. Ed. by Norman L. Walzer. LC 91-23637. 216p. 1991. text ed. 59.95 (0-275-93942-1, C3942, Praeger Pubs) Greenwood.

Rural Community in the Appalachian South. rev. ed. Patricia D. Beaver. 182p. (C). 1992. reprint ed. pap. text ed. 10.50 (0-88133-656-4) Waveland Pr.

Rural Community Studies in Europe: Trends, Selected & Annotated Bibliographies, Analyses, Vol. I. Ed. by Jean-Louis Durand-Drouhin & Lili-Marie Szwengrub. LC 80-41523. (Publications of the Vienna Centre). (Illus.). 342p. 1981. 149.00 (0-08-021384-7, Pub. by Pergamon Repr UK) Franklin.

*Rural Congregational Studies: A Guide for Good Shepherds. Shannon Jung & Mary Agria. 192p. 1997. pap. 16.95 (0-687-03139-7) Abingdon.

*Rural Context of Giant Clam Mariculture in Solomon Islands: An Anthropological Study. E. Hviding. (ICLARM Technical Reports: No. 39). 93p. 1993. per. write for info. (971-8709-39-8, Pub. by ICLARM PH) Intl Spec Bk.

Rural Cooperatives in Socialist Utopia: Thirty Years of Moshav Development in Israel. Gideon Kressel. Ed. by Moshe M. Schwartz et al. LC 95-11276. 288p. 1995. text ed. 62.95 (0-275-95309-2, Praeger Pubs) Greenwood.

Rural Credit: Issues for the 90s. Surjeet Singh. (C). 1991. 17.50 (81-204-0646-X, Pub. by Oxford IBH II) S Asia.

Rural Credit: Lessons for Rural Bankers & Policy Makers. K. P. Padmanabhan. 160p. 1989. text ed. 45.00 (0-312-03175-0) St Martin.

Rural Crime Control. Bruce Smith. LC 74-3851. (Criminal Justice in America Ser.). 1974. reprint ed. 26.95 (0-405-06182-X) Ayer.

Rural Crime in the Eighteenth Century. B. J. Davey. 167p. 1995. pap. 18.95 (0-85958-618-9, Pub. by Univ of Hull Pr UK) Paul & Co Pubs.

Rural Crime Prevention in South Dakota. Donald C. Dahlin. LC 84-621635. (Special Project Ser.: No. 47). (Illus.). viii, 193p. 1982. write for info. (1-55614-111-4) U of SD Gov Res Bur.

Rural Crime Survey. Raymond H. Teske, Jr. 22p. 1980. 1.50 (0-318-02510-8) S Houston Employ.

Rural Criminal Justice: Conditions, Constraints, & Challenges. Ed. by Thomas D. McDonald et al. 254p. (Orig.). (C). 1995. pap. text ed. 14.95 (1-879215-29-2) Sheffield WI.

An Asterisk (*) at the beginning of an entry indicates that the title is appearing in BIP for the first time.

Rural Delivery: Real Photo Postcards from Central Pennsylvania 1905-1935. Jody Blake & Jeannette Lasansky. Ed. by Jean M. Ruhl. LC 96-4372. 136p. (Orig.). 1996. 40.00 (*0-917127-09-9*); pap. 25.00 (*0-917127-10-2*) Oral Traditions.

Rural Delivery: Real Photo Postcards from Central Pennsylvania, 1905-1935. Jody Blake & Jeannette Lasansky. (Illus.). 136p. 1996. 40.00 (*0-271-01625-6*); pap. 25.00 (*0-271-01626-4*) Pa St U Pr.

Rural Democracy: Family Farmers & Politics in Western Washington, 1890-1925. Marilyn P. Watkins. (Illus.). 264p. 1996. 42.50 (*0-8014-3073-9*) Cornell U Pr.

Rural Development. Sung Hwan Ban et al. (East Asian Monographs: No. 89). 493p. 1980. 25.00 (*0-674-78042-6*) HUP.

Rural Development: An Annotated Bibliography of ILO Publications & Documents, 1983-1990. Evelyn Schaad. (International Labour Bibliography Ser.: No. 7). iii, 338p. (Orig.). 1991. pap. 31.50 (*92-2-106451-4*) Intl Labour Office.

Rural Development: Institutions & Strategies, India. S. C. Jain. 1985. 24.00 (*0-8364-1492-6*, Pub. by Rawat II) S Asia.

Rural Development: IRDP in Mahendragargh District Haryana. R. K. Khatkar. 1989. 17.00 (*81-85119-53-8*, Pub. by Northern Bk Ctr II) S Asia.

Rural Development: Learning from China. Sartaj Aziz. LC 78-489. 201p. (C). 1978. 39.95 (*0-8419-0371-9*); pap. 19.00 (*0-8419-0372-7*) Holmes & Meier.

Rural Development: Patchwork of Federal Programs Needs to Be Reappraised. John W. Harman. 65p. (Orig.). (C). 1994. pap. text ed. 20.00 (*0-7881-1338-0*) DIANE Pub.

***Rural Development: Patchwork of Federal Water & Sewer Programs Is Difficult to Use.** (Illus.). 44p. (Orig.). (C). 1996. pap. 25.00 (*0-7881-3432-9*) DIANE Pub.

Rural Development: Problems & Practices. Ed. by Henry Buller & Susan Wright. (Illus.). 258p. 1990. text ed. 68.95 (*0-566-07018-9*, Pub. by Avebury Pub UK) Ashgate Pub Co.

Rural Development: Retrospect & Prospect. Gobinda C. Mandal. (C). 1992. text ed. 16.00 (*81-7022-396-2*, Pub. by Concept II) S Asia.

Rural Development: Rural America Faces Many Challenges. 126p. (Orig.). (C). 1993. pap. text ed. 30.00 (*0-7881-0136-6*) DIANE Pub.

***Rural Development: Steps Towards Realizing the Potential of Telecommunications Technologies.** (Illus.). 51p. (Orig.). (C). 1996. pap. 25.00 (*0-7881-3405-1*) DIANE Pub.

Rural Development & Human Rights in South East Asia: Report of a Seminar in Penang, December 1981. Seminar on Human Rights & Development in the Rural Areas of South East Asia (1981: Pinang, Pulau Pinang). LC 83-941121. 262p. reprint ed. pap. 74.70 (*0-685-16183-8*, 2027732) Bks Demand.

Rural Development & Local Organization in Asia: East Asia, Vol. II. Ed. by Norman T. Uphoff. 360p. 1982. 13.00 (*0-86731-121-5*) Cornell CIS RDC.

Rural Development & Local Organization in Asia: South East Asia, Vol. III. Ed. by Norman T. Uphoff. (RDC Bks.). 399p. 1983. 13.00 (*0-86731-122-3*) Cornell CIS RDC.

Rural Development & Planning in Zimbabwe. N. D. Mutizwa-Mangiza & A. H. Helmsing. 491p. 1991. text ed. 85.95 (*1-85628-142-6*, Pub. by Avebury Pub UK) Ashgate Pub Co.

Rural Development & Planning Perspective. K. Munirathnak Naidu. 1993. 40.00 (*0-685-65107-X*, Pub. by Reliance Pub Hse II) Apt Bks.

Rural Development & Population: Institutions & Policy - A Supplement to Population & Development Review, Vol. 15, 1989. Ed. by Geoffrey McNicholl & Mead Cain. (Population & Development Review Supplements Ser.: No. 1). 376p. 1991. 29.95 (*0-19-506847-5*); pap. 12.00 (*0-19-506849-1*) OUP.

Rural Development & Social Legislation. Raj Singh. 118p. 1986. 11.00 (*81-202-0155-8*, Pub. by Ajanta II) S Asia.

Rural Development & the State: Contradictions & Dilemmas in Developing Countries. Ed. by David A. Lea & D. P. Chaudhri. 338p. 1984. pap. 22.50 (*0-416-31320-5*, NO. 3955) Routledge Chapman & Hall.

Rural Development & Urban Bound Migration in Mexico. Arthur L. Silvers. LC 80-8024. (Resources for the Future Research Paper: Paper R-17). (Illus.). 160p. (Orig.). 1980. pap. text ed. 11.00 (*0-8018-2493-1*) Johns Hopkins.

Rural Development & Women in Africa. (WEP Study Ser.). v, 156p. 1989. pap. 18.00 (*92-2-103633-2*) Intl Labour Office.

Rural Development in Action: (A Case Study of Coastal Areas) S. Giriappa. (C). 1993. 24.00 (*81-7035-113-8*, Pub. by Daya Pub Hse II) S Asia.

Rural Development in Asia: Case Studies on Programme Implementation. Ed. by G. Shabbir Cheema. (Illus.). 268p. 1986. text ed. 30.00 (*0-86590-794-3*, Pub. by Sterling Pubs II) Apt Bks.

Rural Development in China: Prospect & Retrospect. Hsiao-Tung Fei. 252p. 1989. pap. text ed. 13.50 (*0-226-23960-8*); lib. bdg. 30.00 (*0-226-23959-4*) U Ch Pr.

Rural Development in India. Vinod K. Lawania. (C). 1992. 15.00 (*81-7024-468-4*, Pub. by Ashish II) S Asia.

Rural Development in India: A Public Policy Approach. 2nd ed. Shriram Maheshwari. LC 94-34877. 280p. 1995. text ed. 24.95 (*0-8039-9209-2*) Sage.

Rural Development in India: A Study of Industry, Business & Service Sector. R. T. Tewari. (C). 1988. 14.00 (*81-7024-173-1*, Pub. by Ashish II) S Asia.

Rural Development in Ireland: A Challenge for the 1990s. Ed. by Michael Murray & John Greer. 278p. 1993. 68.95 (*1-85628-408-5*, Pub. by Avebury Pub UK) Ashgate Pub Co.

Rural Development in North-East India. P. D. Saikia. (C). 1989. 20.00 (*81-7018-551-3*, Pub. by BR Pub II) S Asia.

Rural Development in South Korea: A Sociopolitical Analysis. William W. Boyer & Byong Man Ahn. LC 90-50708. (Illus.). 160p. 1992. 32.50 (*0-87413-431-5*) U Delaware Pr.

Rural Development in the Caribbean. Ed. by P. I. Gomes. LC 85-14357. 272p. (Orig.). 1985. text ed. 14.95 (*0-312-69599-3*) St Martin.

Rural Development in the Third World. Chris Dixon. 144p. (C). 1990. pap. 13.95 (*0-415-01597-9*, A4135) Routledge.

Rural Development in the United States: Connecting Theory, Practice, & Possibilities. William A. Galston & Karen J. Baehler. 304p. (C). 1995. pap. text ed. 32.00 (*1-55963-326-3*) Island Pr.

Rural Development in White Nile Province, Sudan: A Study of Interaction Between Man & Natural Resources. 142p. 1986. 15.00 (*92-808-0579-7*, E.86.III.A.5) UN.

Rural Development Issues of the Nineties: Perspectives from the Social Sciences (A Centennial Preview of Outreach Activities) Ed. by Thomas T. Williams et al. (Professional Agricultural Workers Conference Proceedings, 1988 Ser.). 210p. (Orig.). (C). 1989. 19.95 (*0-9625021-0-3*) Tuskegee U Schl Agr Home Econ.

Rural Development Participation: Concepts & Measures for Project Design, Implementation & Evaluation. John M. Cohen & John M. Uphoff. (Monograph: No. 2). 317p. (Orig.). (C). 1977. pap. text ed. 14.25 (*0-86731-001-4*) Cornell CIS RDC.

Rural Development-Planning in India. B. C. Chattopadhaya. 1979. text ed. 52.50 (*0-685-14097-0*) Coronet Bks.

Rural Development Problems in Nigeria. Ed. by Toyin Falola & S. A. Olanrewaju. 120p. 1992. 68.95 (*1-85628-240-6*, Pub. by Avebury Pub UK) Ashgate Pub Co.

Rural Development Research: A Foundation for Policy. Thomas D. Rowley et al. LC 95-22979. (Contributions in Economics & Economic History Ser.: Vol. 170). 264p. 1996. text ed. 65.00 (*0-313-29726-6*, Greenwood Pr) Greenwood.

Rural Development Strategies. Ed. by David W. Sears & J. Norman Reid. 304p. 1995. 31.95 (*0-8304-1339-1*) Nelson-Hall.

Rural Development Strategies & Public Policy. Ed. by David Sears & Norman Reid. (Orig.). 1992. pap. 15.00 (*0-944285-24-4*) Pol Studies.

Rural Development Strategies for Southcentral Nebraska. Jack J. Ruff. 176p. (Orig.). 1982. pap. 11.50 (*1-55719-035-6*) U NE CPAR.

Rural Developoment & Local Organization in Asia: Introlduction & South Asia, Vol. I. Ed. by Norman T. Uphoff. (RDC Bks.). 560p. 1982. 15.00 (*0-86731-120-7*) Cornell CIS RDC.

Rural Discontent in 19th Century Britain. J. P. Dunbabin. LC 73-94070. 320p. (C). 1975. 39.95 (*0-8419-0146-5*) Holmes & Meier.

Rural Drug Abuse: Prevalence, Relation to Crime, & Programs. (Illus.). 72p. (Orig.). (C). 1994. pap. text ed. 25.00 (*0-7881-0308-3*) DIANE Pub.

Rural Ecology. C. Mumtamayee. (C). 1989. 34.00 (*81-7024-231-2*, Pub. by Ashish II) S Asia.

Rural Economic Modelling: An Input-Output Approach. Ed. by P. Midmore & L. Harrison-Mayfield. 128p. 1996. 50.00 (*0-85199-112-2*, Pub. by CAB Intntl UK) OUP.

Rural Economy in New England at the Beginning of the 19th Century. Percy W. Bidwell. LC 68-55480. (Reprints of Economic Classics Ser.). (Illus.). 159p. 1972. reprint ed. 35.00 (*0-678-00815-9*) Kelley.

Rural Economy of England. Joan Thirsk. 430p. (C). 1984. pap. 20.00 (*0-907628-29-X*); text ed. 60.00 (*0-907628-28-1*) Hambledon Press.

***Rural Economy of Guangdong, 1870-1937: A Study of the Agrarian Crisis & Its Origins in Southernmost China.** A. Lin. LC 97-13959. 1997. write for info. (*0-312-17594-9*) St Martin.

Rural Economy of India. A. N. Sadhu & Amarjit Singh. 380p. 1982. 34.95 (*0-318-36611-8*) Asia Bk Corp.

Rural Economy of Pre-Liberation China: Trade Expansion & Peasant Livelihood in Jiangsu & Guangdong, 1870-1937. David Faure. (South-East Asian Historical Monographs). (Illus.). 304p. 1990. 35.00 (*0-19-582707-4*) OUP.

Rural Economy of the West of England: Including Devonshire, & Parts of Somersetshire, Dorsetshire & Cornwall, 2 vols., Vols. 1 - 2. William Marshall. LC 78-85333. 1970. reprint ed. 95.00 (*0-678-05564-5*) Kelley.

Rural Economy Through Transportation. K. Munirathna Naidu. 130p. 1991. text ed. 25.00 (*0-685-40676-8*, Pub. by Reliance Pub Hse II) Apt Bks.

Rural Elderly: An Annotated Bibliography of Social Science Research. Compiled by John A. Krout. LC 83-10881. xiii, 123p. 1983. text ed. 47.95 (*0-313-23509-0*, KEL/, Greenwood Pr) Greenwood.

Rural Electric & Supply Cooperatives Were My Concern. Walter G. Schmidt. LC 86-91678. 250p. 1987. 12.95 (*0-940533-00-6*) Wl Pan Pr.

Rural Electric Power Conference, 1995. IEEE (Industry Applications Society) Staff. LC 83-641006. 190p. 1995. pap. text ed. write for info. (*0-7803-2043-3*); lib. bdg. write for info. (*0-7803-2044-1*, 95CH3477-7); fiche write for info. (*0-7803-2045-X*) Inst Electrical.

Rural Electrification: REA Borrowers' Investments in Cable & Satellite Television Services. (Illus.). 51p. (Orig.). (C). 1994. pap. text ed. 30.00 (*0-7881-1392-5*) DIANE Pub.

Rural Electrification in Africa. AFREPREN Staff. Ed. by V. Ranganathan. LC 92-28908. 240p. (C). 1992. text ed. 55.00 (*1-85649-111-0*, Pub. by Zed Bks Ltd UK) Humanities.

Rural Elite & Community Work. G. Naryanana Reddy. 1986. 31.00 (*81-85076-03-0*, Pub. by Chugh Pubns II) S Asia.

Rural Elite, Entrepreneurship & Social Change. Ram S. Singh. 1986. 30.00 (*81-7033-008-4*, Pub. by Rawat II) S Asia.

Rural Elites in India. S. Sharma. 267p. 1979. 19.95 (*0-318-36856-0*) Asia Bk Corp.

Rural Emergency Medical Services. 1990. lib. bdg. 75.00 (*0-8490-4026-4*) Gordon Pr.

***Rural Employment: An International Perspective.** Ed. by R. D. Bollman & J. Bryden. LC 97-8471. 480p. 1997. 100.00 (*0-85199-198-X*, Pub. by CAB Intntl UK) OUP.

Rural Employment & Manpower Problems in China. Curtis Ullerich. LC 78-63607. 130p. reprint ed. pap. 37.10 (*0-317-29621-3*, 2021861) Bks Demand.

Rural Employment Programmes: Longitudinal Analysis. Prodipto Roy et al. 1990. text ed. 25.00 (*0-7069-5297-9*, Pub. by Vikas II) S Asia.

Rural Energy. N. Somasekhara. 125p. 1986. text ed. 22.50 (*81-207-0121-6*, Pub. by Sterling Pubs II) Apt Bks.

Rural Energy: Consumption, Problems & Prospects. D. R. Veena. (C). 1988. 44.00 (*81-7024-208-8*, Pub. by Ashish II) S Asia.

Rural Energy Alternatives in the Hilly Areas: (Social Forestry & Biogas Systems) Pradeep Monga & T. N. Lakhanpal. (International Bioscience Monographs: Vol. XX). (Illus.). 225p. 1988. 39.00 (*1-55528-155-9*, Messers Today & Tomorrow) Scholarly Pubns.

***Rural Energy & Development: Improving Energy Supplies for Two Billion People.** (Development in Practice Ser.). 132p. 1996. 11.95 (*0-8213-3806-4*, 13806) World Bank.

Rural Energy Crisis: A Diagnostic Analysis. Hemlata Rao. 1990. 32.50 (*81-7024-275-4*, Pub. by Ashish II) S Asia.

Rural Energy Development in China. Robert P. Taylor. LC 81-48250. 274p. 1982. 15.00 (*0-8018-2822-8*) Resources Future.

***Rural England: A Nation Committed to a Living Countryside - White Paper.** (Command Papers: No. 3016). 146p. 1995. pap. 40.00 (*0-10-130162-6*, HM01626, Pub. by Stationery Ofc UK) Bernan Associates.

Rural England, Ten Eighty-Six to Eleven Thirty-Five: A Study of Social & Agrarian Conditions. Reginald V. Lennard. LC 80-2222. reprint ed. 49.50 (*0-404-18767-6*) AMS Pr.

Rural Enterprise: Shifting Perspectives on Small-Scale Production. Ed. by Sarah Whatmore et al. 164p. (Orig.). 1991. 69.00 (*0-8464-4334-1*) Beekman Pubs.

***Rural Enterprise: Shifting Perspectives on Small-Scale Production.** Ed. by Sarah Whatmore et al. (Critical Perspectives on Rural Change Ser.). 142p. (Orig.). 1995. text ed. 68.95 (*0-471-95929-4*, GE11) Wiley.

Rural Enterprise in Kenya: Development & Spatial Organization of the Nonfarm Sector. Donald B. Freeman & Glen B. Norcliffe. LC 85-1037. (University of Chicago, Department of Geography, Research Paper Ser.: No. 214). 198p. 1985. reprint ed. pap. 56.50 (*0-608-02256-X*, 2062897) Bks Demand.

Rural Enterprise, Vol. 3: Shifting Perspectives on Small-Scale Production. 224p. (C). 1991. 110.00 (*1-85346-113-X*, Pub. by D Fulton Pubs UK) St Mut.

Rural Environmental Planning for Sustainable Communities. Frederic O. Sargent et al. LC 91-2620. 254p. 1991. 39.95 (*1-55963-025-6*); pap. 26.95 (*1-55963-024-8*) Island Pr.

Rural Essays. Andrew J. Downing. Ed. by George W. Curtis. LC 69-13713. (Architecture & Decorative Art Ser.). 640p. 1975. reprint ed. lib. bdg. 69.50 (*0-306-71035-8*) Da Capo.

***Rural Europe.** write for info. (*0-340-59699-6*, Pub. by E Arnold UK) Routledge Chapman & Hall.

Rural Europe: Identity & Change. Keith Hoggart et al. LC 95-4832. 256p. 1996. pap. text ed. 29.95 (*0-470-23571-3*) Halsted Pr.

Rural Evangelism: Catching the Vision. Kevin E. Ruffcorn. LC 93-36830. 128p. 1994. pap. 10.99 (*0-8066-2642-9*, 9-2642) Augsburg Fortress.

Rural, Exceptional, at Risk. Doris Helge. (Exceptional Children at Risk Ser.). 48p. 1991. pap. text ed. 9.75 (*0-86586-216-8*, P359) Coun Exc Child.

Rural Exodus & Squatter Settlements in the Third World: Case of Iran. Abol H. Danesh. LC 87-10627. (Illus.). 184p. (Orig.). (C). 1987. pap. text ed. 22.50 (*0-8191-6444-5*); lib. bdg. 43.50 (*0-8191-6443-7*) U Pr of Amer.

Rural Families in Soviet Georgia: A Case Study in Ratcha Province. Tamara Dragadze. 250p. (C). 1988. text ed. 69.50 (*0-415-00619-8*) Routledge.

Rural Families on Relief. C. C. Zimmerman & N. L. Whetten. LC 70-165606. (FDR & the Era of the New Deal Ser.). 1971. reprint ed. lib. bdg. 22.50 (*0-306-70349-1*) Da Capo.

***Rural Finance for Food Security of the Poor: Implications for Research & Policy.** Manfred Zeller & International Food Policy Research Institute Staff. LC 97-7361. (Food Policy Review Ser.). 1997. write for info. (*0-89629-503-6*) Intl Food Policy.

Rural Financial Institutions. B. M. Desai et al. (C). 1989. 17.50 (*81-204-0389-4*, Pub. by Oxford IBH II) S Asia.

Rural Firefighting Operations, Bk. I: The First No-Nonsense Guide to Small Community Fire Protection. Larry Davis. (Illus.). 1986. pap. text ed. 24.95 (*0-9615990-0-6*) Intl Soc Fire Serv.

Rural Firefighting Operations, Bk. II: The Encyclopedia of Water Supplies & Water Delivery Techniques. Larry Davis. (Illus.). 375p. 1986. pap. text ed. 24.95 (*0-9615990-1-4*) Intl Soc Fire Serv.

Rural Growth in Western States: Economic & Environmental Issues. Larry Morandi & Justin Worthley. 40p. 1995. 10.00 (*1-55516-402-1*, 4341) Natl Conf State Legis.

Rural Guatemala, 1760-1940. David McCreery. LC 93-27405. xii, 450p. 1994. 49.50 (*0-8047-2318-4*) Stanford U Pr.

***Rural Guatemala, 1760-1940.** David Mccreery. 1996. pap. text ed. 18.95 (*0-8047-2792-9*) Stanford U Pr.

***Rural Harmony.** Jean Carter. (Illus.). 296p. 1997. 21.00 (*0-8059-4009-X*) Dorrance.

Rural Hausa: A Village & a Setting. Polly Hill. LC 75-161287. 384p. 1972. text ed. 80.00 (*0-521-08242-0*) Cambridge U Pr.

Rural Health. N. D. Kamble. 1985. 19.00 (*0-8364-1327-X*, Pub. by Ashish II) S Asia.

***Rural Health & Aging Research: Theory, Methods & Practical Applications.** NC Rural Aging Program Staff. Ed. by Wilbert M. Gesler et al. (Society & Aging Ser.). 248p. Date not set. write for info. (*0-89503-183-3*) Baywood Pub.

Rural Health Care: Innovation in a Changing Environment. Ed. by LaVonne A. Straub & Norman L. Walzer. LC 92-11921. 240p. 1992. text ed. 55.00 (*0-275-94315-1*, C4315, Praeger Pubs) Greenwood.

***Rural Health Challenges in the 1990s: Strategies from the Hospital-Based Rural Health Care Program.** Karin Gillespie. Ed. by Victoria D. Weisfeld. 176p. (Orig.). 1996. write for info. (*0-942054-10-5*) R W Johnson Found.

Rural Health Nursing. Ed. by Patricia F. Winstead-Fry et al. 424p. 1991. 32.95 (*0-88737-524-3*) Natl League Nurse.

Rural Health Organization: Social Networks & Regionalization. Edward W. Hassinger. LC 82-15323. (Illus.). 204p. 1982. reprint ed. pap. 58.20 (*0-608-00030-2*, 2060796) Bks Demand.

Rural Health Services: A Management Perspective. Ed. by Joyce E. Beaulieu & David E. Berry. 350p. 1994. pap. 39.00 (*1-56793-018-2*, 0948) Health Admin Pr.

Rural Health Services: Organization, Delivery, & Use. Ed. by Edward W. Hassinger & Larry R. Whiting. LC 75-45496. (Illus.). 316p. 1976. reprint ed. pap. 90.10 (*0-608-00069-8*, 2060835) Bks Demand.

Rural Home Modifications: Urban & Rural Survival. CWL. (Security & Survival Ser.). (Illus.). 60p. (Orig.). 1985. pap. 25.00 (*0-939856-48-4*) Tech Group.

***Rural Home Techniques Series 1: Labour-Saving Ideas: Laundry, Water, Transport.** (Economic & Social Development Papers: No. 5, Pt. 2). 84p. 1981. 13.00 (*92-5-000969-0*, Pub. by FAO IT) Bernan Associates.

Rural Hospital: Its Structure & Organization. R. F. Bridgman. (Monograph Ser.: No. 21). (Illus.). 162p. (ENG & FRE.). 1955. pap. text ed. 20.00 (*92-4-140021-8*, 1140021) World Health.

Rural Hospitals in Evolution: State Policy Issues & Initiatives. Stephen Phillips & John Luehrs. Ed. by Karen Glass. 40p. (Orig.). 1989. pap. text ed. 20.00 (*1-55877-067-4*) Natl Governor.

Rural Hours. Susan F. Cooper. 380p. 1995. pap. 14.95 (*0-8156-0317-7*) Syracuse U Pr.

Rural Households in Emerging Societies: Technology & Change in Sub-Saharan Africa. Ed. by Margaret Haswell & Diana Hunt. 275p. 1991. 49.95 (*0-85496-730-3*) Berg Pubs.

Rural Housing: Recent Research & Policy Issues. Mark Shucksmith et al. (Illus.). 224p. 1987. pap. text ed. 24.00 (*0-08-034529-8*, Pub. by Aberdeen U Pr) Macmillan.

Rural Hunterdon: An Agricultural History. Hubert G. Schmidt. LC 77-139149. (Illus.). 331p. 1972. reprint ed. text ed. 69.50 (*0-8371-5765-X*, SCRH, Greenwood Pr) Greenwood.

Rural Images: Estate Maps in the Old & New Worlds. Ed. by David Buisseret. LC 95-30609. (Kenneth Nebenzahl, Jr., Lectures in the History of Cartography Ser.). 208p. 1996. 55.00 (*0-226-07990-2*) U Ch Pr.

Rural India: Land, Power & Society under British Rule. Ed. by Peter Robb. (Oxford India Paperbacks Ser.). 324p. 1993. pap. 15.95 (*0-19-563186-2*) OUP.

Rural Indian Social Relations: A Study of Southern Andhra Pradesh. Wendy K. Olsen. 368p. (C). 1996. 35.00 (*0-19-563641-4*) OUP.

Rural Indonesia: Socio-Economic Development in a Changing Environment. Erik Thorbecke & Theodore Van Der Pluijm. (Studies in Rural Poverty: An International Fund for Agricultural Development Ser.). 240p. (C). 1992. 50.00 (*0-8147-8197-7*) NYU Pr.

Rural Industrialization in China. Jon Sigurdson. (East Asian Monographs: No. 73). 350p. 1977. 26.00 (*0-674-78072-8*) HUP.

Rural Industrialisation & Regional Development. Mohan Lal. 168p. 1987. 21.00 (*0-8364-2031-4*, Pub. by Deep II) S Asia.

Rural Industrialisation in India. R. V. Rao. 1987. reprint ed. 10.50 (*0-8364-2258-9*, Pub. by Concept II) S Asia.

Rural Industrialization: Problems & Potentials. North Central Regional Center for Rural Development Staff. LC 73-20027. 163p. reprint ed. pap. 46.50 (*0-317-55353-4*, 2029164) Bks Demand.

Rural Industrialization Challenges & Perspectives. Ed. by T. M. Dak. 1989. 31.00 (*81-85119-46-5*, Pub. by Northern Bk Ctr II) S Asia.

Rural Industrialization in India. S. Y. Thakur. 156p. 1985. text ed. 25.00 (*0-86590-727-7*, Pub. by Sterling Pubs II) Apt Bks.

Rural Industrialization in Third World Countries. R. P. Misra. 332p. 1986. text ed. 35.00 (*0-86590-795-1*, Pub. by Sterling Pubs II) Apt Bks.

Rural Information Systems: New Directions in Data Collection & Retrieval. Rueben C. Buse. LC 92-13228. 468p. 1992. text ed. 49.95 (*0-8138-0932-0*) Iowa St U Pr.

Rural Infrastructure, the Settlement System, & Development of the Regional Economy in Southern India. Sudhir Wanmali. LC 92-28423. (Research Report Ser.: Vol. 91). 1992. write for info. (*0-89629-094-8*) Intl Food Policy.

Rural Innovations in Agriculture. Mohammad Salim. 1986. 38.50 (*81-85076-09-X*, Pub. by Chugh Pubns II) S Asia.

Rural Intelligent Vehicle Highway System (IVHS) Proceedings: 1993 National Conference for Rural IVHS. 134p. 1993. pap. 10.00 (*1-884508-00-6*) CO Dept Transport.

***Rural Ireland, Real Ireland?** Ed. by Jacqueline Genet. (Irish Literary Studies: No. 49). 248p. 1996. text ed. 49.95 (*0-86140-385-1*) OUP.

Rural Japan: Radiance of the Ordinary. Linda Butler. LC 91-17090. (Illus.). 144p. 1992. pap. 24.95 (*1-56098-141-5*) Smithsonian.

Rural Land Degradation in Australia. Ed. by Arthur Conacher & Jeannettel Conacher. (Meridian). (Illus.). 192p. (C). 1995. pap. text ed. 26.95 (*0-19-553436-0*) OUP.

Rural Land Use in Asia & the Pacific. 391p. 1993. pap. 15.00 (*92-833-2134-0*, APO1340, Pub. by Asian Prod Organ JA) Bernan Associates.

Rural Land-Use Planning in Developed Nations. Ed. by Paul J. Cloke. 256p. 1989. text ed. 55.00 (*0-04-711025-2*) Routledge Chapman & Hall.

Rural Land-Use Planning in the Western United States: Techniques for the Protection of Important Landscapes. Heather Kinkade. LC 92-20415. (CPL Bibliographies Ser.: No. 283). 1992. 10.00 (*0-86602-283-X*, Sage Prdcls Pr) Sage.

Rural Landowners of Barbour County, Alabama. Marie H. Godfrey. 164p. 1990. reprint ed. pap. 20.00 (*0-89308-670-3*, AL 23) Southern Hist Pr.

Rural Landscape: Abstracts of Papers Presented at the Annual Meeting of CELA, October 23-27, 1982. Council of Educators in Landscape Architecture Staff. 127p. reprint ed. pap. 36.20 (*0-317-29834-8*, 2019634) Bks Demand.

Rural Leadership among Scheduled Castes. D. R. Singh. 238p. 1986. 30.00 (*0-8364-1643-0*, Pub. by Chugh Pubns II) S Asia.

Rural Leadership in India. V. Lalini. 1991. 28.50 (*81-212-0333-3*, Pub. by Gian Publng Hse II) S Asia.

Rural Legal Services from the Pit to the Pendulum. 193p. 1981. 15.75 (*0-317-03741-2*, 31,684) NCLS Inc.

Rural Libraries & Internetworking: Proceedings of the Internetworking Rural Libraries Institute Held in May 1994 at the University of Wisconsin, Milwaukee. Ed. by Judith J. Senkewitch et al. LC 94-46652. 223p. 1995. 29.50 (*0-8108-2988-6*) Scarecrow.

Rural Life: Guide to Local Records. Peter Edwards. (Illus.). 176p. 1993. 45.00 (*0-7134-6787-8*, Pub. by Batsford UK) Trafalgar.

Rural Life in Eighteenth-Century English Poetry. John Goodridge. (Studies in Eighteenth-Century English Literature & Thought: No. 27). 262p. (C). 1996. text ed. 59.95 (*0-521-43381-9*) Cambridge U Pr.

Rural Life in Northern Ireland: Five Regional Studies Made for the Northern Ireland Council of Social Service, Inc. John M. Mogey. LC 77-87692. reprint ed. 38.00 (*0-404-16488-9*) AMS Pr.

Rural Life in Texas. Ike Whitely. Ed. by Phillip A. Sperry. (Illus.). 91p. 1993. reprint ed. 24.95 (*1-56869-016-9*); reprint ed. pap. 14.95 (*1-56869-017-7*) Oldbuck Pr.

Rural Life in Victorian England. G. E. Mingay. (Illus.). 224p. (C). 1991. text ed. 34.00 (*0-86299-539-6*, Pub. by Sutton Pubng UK) Bks Intl VA.

Rural Life in Wessex 1500-1900. J. H. Bettey. (Illus.). 160p. 1989. pap. 14.00 (*0-86299-425-X*, Pub. by Sutton Pubng UK) Bks Intl VA.

Rural Life Prayers, Blessings & Liturgies. Illus. by Chuck Trapkus. 68p. 1996. 8.00 (*1-877739-00-6*) NCRLC.

Rural Lighting: A Guide for Development Workers. Modibo Dicko et al. (Illus.). 120p. (Orig.). 1993. pap. 28.50 (*1-85339-200-6*, Pub. by Intermed Tech UK) Women Ink.

Rural Livelihoods: Crises & Responses. Ed. by Ben Crow et al. 368p. 1992. 69.00 (*0-19-877334-X*); pap. 21.00 (*0-19-877335-8*) OUP.

Rural Living Handbook: An Illustrated Guide to Practical Country Skills. Mother Earth News Editors. 1989. pap. write for info. (*0-671-65794-1*, Fireside) S&S Trade.

Rural Local Government in India. S. Bhatnagar. 278p. 1978. 16.95 (*0-318-36617-7*) Asia Bk Corp.

Rural Malay Women in Tradition & Transition. Heather Strange. LC 81-5140. 288p. 1981. text ed. 49.95 (*0-275-90724-4*, C0724, Praeger Pubs) Greenwood.

Rural Marketing in India. Shamim Ahmad. (C). 1991. text ed. 19.00 (*81-7024-407-2*, Pub. by Ashish II) S Asia.

Rural Markets & Development. H. M. Saxena. (C). 1988. 24.00 (*81-7033-054-8*, Pub. by Rawat II) S Asia.

Rural Markets & Trade in East Africa: A Study of the Functions & Development of Exchange Institutions in Ankole, Uganda. Charles M. Good. LC 72-128466. (University of Chicago, Department of Geography, Research Paper Ser.: No. 128). (Illus.). 271p. reprint ed. pap. 77.30 (*0-7837-0403-8*, 2040724) Bks Demand.

Rural Middle East: Peasant Lives & Modes of Production. Ed. by Kathy Glavanis & Pandeli Glavanis. LC 89-9032. 288p. (C). 1990. pap. 19.95 (*0-86232-771-7*, Pub. by Zed Bks Ltd UK); text ed. 55.00 (*0-86232-770-9*, Pub. by Zed Bks Ltd UK) Humanities.

Rural Middlemen: Network of Patronage. H. C. Srivastava & M. K. Chaturvedi. 1986. 19.00 (*81-7024-042-5*, Pub. by Ashish II) S Asia.

Rural Migrants in An Urban Setting. P. S. Majumdar & Ila Majumdar. 176p. (C). 1978. text ed. 32.95 (*0-87855-330-4*) Transaction Pubs.

Rural Migration in the United States. C. E. Lively & Conrad Taeuber. LC 71-165601. (Research Monographs: Vol. 19). 1971. reprint ed. 25.00 (*0-306-70351-3*) Da Capo.

Rural Muslims in Transition. Sarfarazuddin Ahmad. (C). 1991. 26.50 (*81-7169-170-6*, Pub. by Commonwealth II) S Asia.

Rural New York. Elmer O. Fippin. 381p. 1993. reprint ed. lib. bdg. 89.00 (*0-7812-5231-8*) Rprt Serv.

Rural Non-Farm Economy: A WEP Study. Ashwani Saith. Ed. by International Labour Office Staff. v, 121p. (Orig.). 1992. pap. 18.00 (*92-2-107750-0*) Intl Labour Office.

Rural Nursing, Vol. 1. Angeline Bushy. (Illus.). 404p. 1991. text ed. 58.00 (*0-8039-3834-9*); pap. text ed. 28.00 (*0-8039-3835-7*) Sage.

Rural Nursing, Vol. 2. Angeline Bushy. (Illus.). 358p. 1991. text ed. 52.00 (*0-8039-4240-0*); pap. text ed. 25.00 (*0-8039-4241-9*) Sage.

Rural Oasis: History of Windham, New Hampshire, 1883-1975 see History of Windham in New Hampshire, 1719-1883

Rural One-Room Schools of Mid-America. Leslie C. Swanson. (Illus.). 1976. 4.00 (*0-911466-23-1*) Swanson.

Rural Parish. Anna Gebhard. (American Autobiography Ser.). 121p. 1995. reprint ed. lib. bdg. 69.00 (*0-7812-8527-5*) Rprt Serv.

Rural Pennsylvania Clothing. 2nd ed. Ellen Gehret. LC 73-18534. (Illus.). 307p. 1993. pap. 30.00 (*0-87387-064-6*) Shumway.

Rural Performance Benchmarks System: Policymaker's Guide & User's Manual. Corporation for Enterprise Development Staff. 124p. 1993. spiral bd. 35.00 (*1-883187-03-6*) Corp Ent Dev.

Rural Planning & Development in the United States. Mark B. Lapping et al. LC 89-2231. 342p. 1989. pap. text ed. 21.95 (*0-89862-517-3*); lib. bdg. 47.95 (*0-89862-384-7*) Guilford Pr.

Rural Policy. Ed. by William Browne & Don Hadwiger. (Orig.). (C). 1982. pap. 15.00 (*0-918592-55-0*) Pol Studies.

Rural Policy for the EEC? H. Clout. (EEC Ser.). 227p. 1984. pap. text ed. 12.95 (*0-416-34550-6*, 9105) Routledge Chapman & Hall.

Rural Politics: Policies for Agriculture, Forestry, & the Environment. Michael Winter. LC 95-38688. 360p. (C). 1996. text ed. 69.95 (*0-415-08175-0*) Routledge.

Rural Politics: Policies for Agriculture, Forestry, & the Environment. Michael Winter. LC 95-38688. 360p. (C). 1997. pap. 22.95 (*0-415-08176-9*) Routledge.

Rural Politics & Social Change in the Middle East. LC 77-180485. (Studies in Development: No. 5). 512p. reprint ed. pap. 146.00 (*0-317-10061-0*, 2050046) Bks Demand.

Rural Politics in Northern Ireland: Policy Networks & Agricultural Development since Partition. Alan Greer. 200p. 1996. 55.95 (*1-85972-064-1*, Pub. by Avebury Pub UK) Ashgate Pub Co.

Rural Poor in the Great Depression: Three Studies. LC 70-137177. (Poverty U. S. A. Historical Record Ser.). 1971. reprint ed. 46.95 (*0-405-03133-5*) Ayer.

Rural Population Growth in New England. A. E. Luloff & Thomas E. Steahr. 92p. 1987. pap. 5.00 (*0-9609010-2-7*) NE Regional Ctr.

Rural Poverty: Problems & Prospects. A. C. Nambiar. (Illus.). xiv, 134p. (C). 1992. 18.00 (*81-7024-510-9*, Pub. by Ashish Pub Hse II) Nataraj Bks.

Rural Poverty: Special Causes & Policy Reforms. Gregory R. Weiher. LC 88-35817. (Studies in Social Welfare Policies & Programs: No. 12). 190p. 1989. text ed. 47.95 (*0-313-26630-1*, RRR/, Greenwood Pr) Greenwood.

Rural Poverty - Issues & Options. J. L. Bajaj. 252p. (C). 1985. 190.00 (*81-85009-11-2*, Pub. by Print Hse II) St Mut.

Rural Poverty Alleviation: International Development Perspectives. Ed. by Joseph Mullen. 200p. 1995. 59.95 (*1-85628-864-1*, Pub. by Avebury Pub UK) Ashgate Pub Co.

Rural Poverty Alleviation: Policies & Trends. (Economic & Social Development Papers: No. 113). 81p. 1993. pap. 10.00 (*92-5-103211-4*, F32114, Pub. by FAO IT) Bernan Associates.

Rural Poverty & Agrarian Reform. Steve Jones et al. 390p. 1986. 32.50 (*0-907108-45-8*, Pub. by Allied II) S Asia.

Rural Poverty & Economic Change in India. Ed. by V. R. Dutta. 167p. 1992. text ed. 25.00 (*0-685-37817-9*, Pub. by Radiant Pubs II) S Asia.

Rural Poverty & Environmental Degradation in Haiti. Anthony V. Catanese. Ed. by Dennis Conway. (Series on Environment & Development). 40p. (Orig.). 1991. pap. 1.75 (*1-881157-07-5*) In Ctr Global.

Rural Poverty & Public Policy in the United States. Ed. by Aruna N. Michie. (Orig.). 1986. pap. 15.00 (*0-918592-93-3*) Pol Studies.

Rural Poverty & the Policy Crisis. Ed. by Robert O. Coppedge & Carlton G. Davis. LC 76-53751. (Illus.). 232p. 1977. reprint ed. pap. 66.20 (*0-608-00060-4*, 2060826) Bks Demand.

Rural Poverty & the Urban Crisis: A Strategy for Regional Development. Niles M. Hansen. LC 78-10260. (Illus.). 352p. 1979. reprint ed. text ed. 75.00 (*0-313-21079-9*, HARP, Greenwood Pr) Greenwood.

Rural Poverty & Unemployment. Bepin Behari. 304p. 1990. text ed. 50.00 (*0-7069-4954-4*, Pub. by Vikas II) S Asia.

Rural Poverty in America. Cynthia M. Duncan. LC 91-18655. 328p. 1992. text ed. 59.95 (*0-86569-013-8*, T013, Auburn Hse); pap. text ed. 22.95 (*0-86569-014-6*, R014, Auburn Hse) Greenwood.

Rural Poverty in Asia: Priority Issues & Policy Options. Ed. by M. G. Quibria. (Illus.). 352p. 1994. 75.00 (*0-19-586003-9*) OUP.

Rural Poverty in Developing Asia, Vol. II. 774p. 1996. pap. 25.00 (*971-561-047-1*, Pub. by Asian Devel Bank PH) Paul & Co Pubs.

Rural Poverty in India. Sibnath Bhattacharya. (C). 1989. 42.50 (*81-7024-254-1*, Pub. by Ashish II) S Asia.

Rural Poverty in India. B. C. Mehta. 1993. 23.00 (*81-7022-432-2*, Pub. by Concept II) S Asia.

Rural Poverty in South Asia. Ed. by T. N. Srinivasan & Pranab K. Bardhan. (Illus.). 565p. 1988. text ed. 72.00 (*0-231-06224-9*) Col U Pr.

Rural Power Sources. R. Hill & N. M. Pearsall. (C). 1983. 125.00 (*0-685-33078-8*, Pub. by Interntl Solar Energy Soc UK) St Mut.

Rural Power Sources (C32) R. Hill & N. M. Pearsall. 210p. (C). 1983. 105.00 (*0-685-30219-9*, Pub. by Interntl Solar Energy Soc UK) St Mut.

Rural Process-Pattern Relationships: Nomadization, Sedentarization, & Settlement Fixation. David Grossman. LC 91-23138. 232p. 1992. text ed. 59.95 (*0-275-94084-5*, C4084, Praeger Pubs) Greenwood.

Rural Property in Transition. (Monographs). 1985. 6.00 (*0-911780-82-3*) Appraisal Inst.

Rural Property Planning: Risk Management. Mike Krause. 144p. 1995. pap. 47.95 (*0-7506-8917-X*) Buttrwrth-Heinemann.

Rural Psychology. Ed. by Alan W. Childs & Gary B. Melton. 458p. 1983. 75.00 (*0-306-41045-1*, Plenum Pr) Plenum.

Rural Public Administration: Problems & Prospects. Jim Seroka. LC 85-27253. (Contributions in Political Science Ser.). 217p. 1986. text ed. 55.00 (*0-313-25246-7*, SRL/, Greenwood Pr) Greenwood.

Rural Public Management. OECD Staff. 86p. (Orig.). 1986. pap. 10.00 (*92-64-12858-1*) OECD.

Rural Public Welfare: Selected Records. Grace Browning. LC 75-17209. (Social Problems & Social Policy Ser.). 1976. reprint ed. 47.95 (*0-405-07481-6*) Ayer.

***Rural Radicals.** Catherine Stock. 1997. pap. 12.95 (*0-14-026847-2*) Viking Penguin.

Rural Radicals: Righteous Rage in the American Grain. Catherine M. Stock. (Illus.). 240p. 1996. 25.00 (*0-8014-3294-4*); pap. write for info. (*0-8014-8365-4*) Cornell U Pr.

Rural Reconstruction, Ecosystem & Forestry. Pramod Singh. 271p. (C). 1993. 90.00 (*81-85880-05-0*, Pub. by Print Hse II) St Mut.

Rural Reform & Peasant Income in China: The Impact of China's Post-Mao Rural Reforms in Selected Regions. Zhu Ling. LC 90-44603. 130p. 1991. text ed. 65.00 (*0-312-05325-8*) St Martin.

Rural Reform in Mexico: The View from the Comarca Lagunera. Jose L. Solis-Gonzalez. (Transformation of Rural Mexico Ser.: No. 4). (C). 1994. pap. 8.00 (*1-878367-22-6*, DP-04) UCSD Ctr US-Mex.

Rural Regional Planning: Towards an Operational Theory. D. Conyers. 66p. 1984. pap. 22.00 (*0-08-032351-0*, Pergamon Pr) Elsevier.

Rural Reminiscences: The Agony of Survival. Kenneth Hassebrock. LC 90-33656. (Illus.). 232p. 1990. text ed. 23.95 (*0-8138-0284-9*) Iowa St U Pr.

Rural Rescue & Emergency Care. Ed. by Robert Worsing. 368p. 1993. pap. 32.00 (*0-89203-075-5*) Amer Acad Ortho Surg.

Rural Residences. Alexander J. Davis. (Architecture & Decorative Art Ser.). 1980. reprint ed. 110.00 (*0-306-71165-6*) Da Capo.

Rural Resource Management: Problem Solving for the Long Term. Sandra E. Miller et al. LC 93-38131. (Illus.). 340p. (C). 1994. pap. text ed. 24.95 (*0-8138-0686-0*) Iowa St U Pr.

Rural Restructuring: Global Processes & Their Responses. Terry Marsden et al. (Critical Perspectives on Rural Change Ser.: Vol. 1). 224p. (C). 1990. text ed. 66.00 (*0-389-20947-3*) B&N Imports.

***Rural Restructuring: Global Processes & Their Responses.** Ed. by Terry Marsden et al. (Critical Perspectives on Rural Change Ser.). 197p. 1995. text ed. 88.00 (*0-471-95927-8*, GE11) Wiley.

Rural Restructuring, Vol. 1: Global Processes & Their Responses. 208p. (C). 1990. 95.00 (*1-85346-111-3*, Pub. by D Fulton Pubs UK) St Mut.

Rural Revolution in France: The Peasantry in the Twentieth Century. Gordon Wright. (Illus.). xi, 271p. 1964. 42.50 (*0-8047-0190-3*) Stanford U Pr.

Rural Revolution in South China: Peasants & the Making of History in Haifeng County, 1570-1930. Robert B. Marks. LC 83-16980. (Illus.). 368p. 1984. 32.50 (*0-299-09530-4*) U of Wis Pr.

Rural Rites. large type ed. Mullen. (Dales Large Print Ser.). 1995. pap. 17.99 (*1-85389-593-8*, Dales) Ulverscroft.

***Rural Road Condition Survey Guide.** Curt A. Beckemeyer. (Illus.). 79p. (Orig.). (C). 1996. pap. 30.00 (*0-7881-3147-8*) DIANE Pub.

Rural Roads in Sub-Saharan Africa: Lessons from World Bank Experience. John D. Riverson et al. (Technical Paper Ser.). 62p. 1991. pap. 6.95 (*0-8213-1869-1*, 11869); pap. 6.95 (*0-8213-2064-5*, 12064) World Bank.

Rural Routes: Essays on Living in Rural Minnesota. Edith Rylander. LC 93-4854. 1993. pap. 9.95 (*0-87839-079-0*) North Star.

Rural Russia: Economic, Social, & Moral Crisis. L. N. Denisova. (Illus.). 207p. (C). 1995. 69.00 (*1-56072-212-6*) Nova Sci Pubs.

Rural Russia under the New Regime. Viktor Danilov. Tr. & Intro. by Orlando Figes. LC 88-2778. (Second World Ser.). 352p. 1988. 18.95 (*0-253-35075-1*) Ind U Pr.

Rural Russia under the Old Regime: A History of the Landlord-Peasant World & a Prologue to the Peasant Revolution of 1917. Geroid T. Robinson. (C). 1967. pap. 15.00 (*0-520-01075-2*) U CA Pr.

Rural Sanitation in the Tropics. M. Watson. 1976. lib. bdg. 69.95 (*0-8490-2548-6*) Gordon Pr.

Rural Scenes & National Representation: Britain, 1815-1850. Elizabeth K. Helsinger. LC 96-14314. (Literature in History Ser.). 320p. 1997. text ed. 45.00 (*0-691-02146-5*) Princeton U Pr.

Rural Schools of Stoddard County. Glynda J. Bates & Shelby Spears. LC 95-79279. (Illus.). 240p. (Orig.). 1995. pap. text ed. 21.95 (*0-934426-65-1*) NAPSAC Reprods.

Rural Scotland During the War. David T. Jones et al. (Economic & Social History of the World War Ser.). 1926. 95.00 (*0-317-27576-3*) Elliots Bks.

Rural Scotland Today: The Best of Both Worlds? Mark Shucksmith et al. 532p. 1996. 84.95 (*1-85972-367-5*, Pub. by Avebury Pub UK) Ashgate Pub Co.

Rural Settlement in Britain. Brian K. Roberts. LC 76-30000. (Studies in Historical Geography). (Illus.). 221p. (C). 1977. 32.50 (*0-208-01621-X*, Archon Bks) Shoe String.

Rural Settlement Structure & African Development. Ed. by Marilyn Silberfein. 256p. (C). 1997. text ed. 54.00 (*0-8133-8657-8*) Westview.

Rural Small-Scale Industries & Employment in Africa & Asia: A Review of Problemes & Policies. Ed. by E. Chuta & S. V. Sethuraman. x, 160p. (Orig.). 1983. pap. 22.50 (*92-2-103513-1*) Intl Labour Office.

Rural Small-Scale Industry in the People's Republic of China. Ed. by Dwight G. Perkins. LC 76-20015. 1977. pap. 13.00 (*0-520-04401-0*) U CA Pr.

Rural Social & Community Work in the U. S. & U. K. A Cross-Cultural Perspective. Emilia E. Martinez-Brawley. LC 81-23464. 304p. 1982. text ed. 49.95 (*0-275-90855-0*, C0855, Praeger Pubs) Greenwood.

Rural Social Organization in a Spanish-American Culture Area. Sigurd Johansen. LC 48-45369. 146p. 1982. reprint ed. lib. bdg. 35.00 (*0-89370-730-9*) Borgo Pr.

***Rural Social Systems & Their Demographic Responses: Implications for Theory & Public Policy.** Ed. by Nan Johnson & Ching-Li Wang. LC 96-39877. (Illus.). 240p. 1997. 25.95 (*0-87013-470-1*) Mich St U Pr.

Rural Social Transformation. Sheo K. Lal. (C). 1992. text ed. 32.00 (*81-7033-159-5*, Pub. by Rawat II) S Asia.

Rural Social Trends. Edmund de S. Brunner & John H. Kolb. LC 70-98825. 386p. 1970. reprint ed. text ed. 35.00 (*0-8371-2889-7*, BRRS, Greenwood Pr) Greenwood.

Rural Social Welfare: An Annotated Bibliography for Educators & Practitioners. Dennis L. Poole. LC 80-28691. 334p. 1981. text ed. 55.00 (*0-275-90704-X*, C0704, Praeger Pubs) Greenwood.

Rural Social Work Practice. O. William Farley. 256p. (C). 1982. 35.00 (*0-02-910480-7*, Free Press) Free Pr.

Rural Society. Irwin T. Sanders. (Illus.). 192p. 1977. pap. text ed. 12.95 (*0-13-784439-5*) P-H.

Rural Society: Landowners, Peasants & Labourers, 1500-1750. Ed. by Christopher Clay. 479p. (C). 1990. pap. text ed. 34.95 (*0-521-36883-9*) Cambridge U Pr.

Rural Society after the Black Death: Essex, 1350-1525. Larry Poos. (Studies in Population, Economy & Society in Past Time: No. 18). (Illus.). 336p. (C). 1991. text ed. 69.95 (*0-521-38260-2*) Cambridge U Pr.

***Rural Society & Cotton in Colonial Zaire.** Osumaka Likaka. LC 96-36690. (Illus.). 192p. 1997. 47.95 (*0-299-15330-4*); pap. 19.95 (*0-299-15334-7*) U of Wis Pr.

Rural Society & Environment in America. Carlson & William R. Lassey. (Agricultural Sciences Ser.). (Illus.). 448p. (C). 1981. text ed. write for info. (*0-07-009959-6*) McGraw.

Rural Society & French Politics. Michael Burns. LC 84-3253. (Illus.). 264p. 1984. text ed. 49.50 (*0-691-05423-1*) Princeton U Pr.

Rural Society & the Search for Order in Early Modern Germany. Thomas Robisheaux. (Illus.). 352p. (C). 1989. text ed. 74.95 (*0-521-35626-1*) Cambridge U Pr.

Rural Society in France. Orest A. Ranum & Robert Forster. Tr. by Elborg Forster & Patricia M. Ranum from FRE. LC 76-47373. (Selections from the Annales, Economics, Societies, Civilizations Ser.: Vol. 3). (Illus.). 1977. pap. 14.95 (*0-8018-1917-2*) Johns Hopkins.

Rural Society in Medieval France: The Gatine of Poitou in the Eleventh & Twelfth Centuries. George T. Beech. LC 78-64241. (Johns Hopkins University. Studies in the Social Sciences. Thirtieth Ser. 1912: 1). reprint ed. 32.50 (*0-404-61346-2*) AMS Pr.

Rural Sociology: A Bibliography of Bibliographies. Judy Berndt. LC 85-26070. 185p. 1986. 20.00 (*0-8108-1860-4*) Scarecrow.

Rural Sociology & the Environment. Donald R. Field, Jr. & William R. Burch. LC 88-15483. (Contributions in Sociology Ser.: No. 74). 155p. 1988. text ed. 45.00 (*0-313-26365-5*, FRY/, Greenwood Pr) Greenwood.

Rural Sociology & the Environment. Donald R. Field & William R. Burch, Jr. 135p. 1991. pap. 15.00 (*0-941042-11-1*, Social Ecology Resources Inc) Soc Ecology Pr.

An Asterisk (*) at the beginning of an entry indicates that the title is appearing in BIP for the first time.

R

Rural Sociology of the Advanced Societies: Critical Perspectives. Ed. by Frederick H. Buttel & Howard Newby. LC 79-5177. 538p. 1980. pap. text ed. 29.00 (*0-916672-34-4*) Rowman.

Rural Sports: A Poem. John B. Jones. (Notable American Authors Ser.). 1992. reprint ed. lib. bdg. 75.00 (*0-7812-3514-6*) Rprt Serv.

Rural State? Limits to Planning in Rural Society. Paul J. Cloke & Jo Little. (Illus.). 304p. 1990. 75.00 (*0-19-823287-X*) OUP.

***Rural Sustainable Development in America.** Ed. by Ivonne Audirac. LC 96-34519. 500p. 1997. text ed. 59.95 (*0-471-15233-1*) Wiley.

Rural Texas. William Bizzell. 1993. reprint ed. lib. bdg. 75.00 (*0-7812-5917-7*) Rprt Serv.

Rural Tradition: A Study of the Non-Fiction Prose Writers of the English Countryside. W. J. Keith. LC 73-81754. 324p. reprint ed. pap. 92.40 (*0-317-39690-0*, 2055820) Bks Demand.

Rural Transformation in Asia. Ed. by Jan Breman. 560p. 1991. 21.00 (*0-19-562519-6*) OUP.

Rural Transformation in Central Europe. Nigel Swain. (Central European University Press Bk.). (Illus.). 272p. 1997. 82.00 (*1-85866-048-3*); pap. 24.95 (*1-85866-049-1*) OUP.

Rural Transformation in Tropical Africa. Ed. by Douglas Rimmer. LC 89-212560. (Illus.). 187p. 1988. reprint ed. pap. 53.30 (*0-608-00190-2*, 2060973) Bks Demand.

Rural Transformation Seen from Below: Regional & Local Perspectives from Western Mexico. Sergio Zendejas & Pieter De Vries. (Transformation of Rural Mexico Ser.). 128p. 1995. pap. 12.00 (*0-614-07596-3*) UCSD Ctr US-Mex.

Rural Transformations Seen from Below: Regional & Local Perspectives from Western Mexico. Ed. by Sergio Zendejas & Pieter De Vries. (Transformations of Rural Mexico Ser.: No. 8). 85p. 1995. pap. 12.00 (*1-878367-27-7*, DP-08) UCSD Ctr US-Mex.

Rural Transport: Energy & Environment Technology Source Book. Unifem Staff. (Energy & Environment Technology Source Book Ser.). 80p. (Orig.). 1996. pap. 15.50 (*1-85339-345-2*, Pub. by Intermed Tech UK) Women Ink.

Rural Transport & Planning: A Bibliography with Abstracts. D. Banister. 456p. 1985. text ed. 100.00 (*0-7201-1692-9*, Mansell Pub) Cassell.

Rural Transport Services: A Guide to Their Planning & Implementation. Henril Beenhakker et al. 380p. (Orig.). 1989. pap. 30.50 (*1-85339-032-1*, Pub. by Intermed Tech UK) Women Ink.

Rural Trends in Depression Years: A Survey of Village-Centered Agricultural Communities, 1930-1936. Edmund D. Brunner & Irving Lorge. LC 75-137157. (Poverty U. S. A. Historical Record Ser.). 1977. reprint ed. 29.95 (*0-405-03095-9*) Ayer.

Rural U. S. A. Persistence & Change. Ed. by Thomas R. Ford. LC 77-27286. 263p. 1978. reprint ed. pap. 75.00 (*0-608-00167-8*, 2060949) Bks Demand.

Rural University: The Jawaja Experiment in Educational Innovation. Ravi J. Mattai. 1985. 27.50 (*0-8364-1406-3*, Pub. by Popular Prakashan II) S Asia.

Rural-Urban Fringe: Perspectives in Urban Geography. C. S. Yadav. 355p. (C). 1987. 56.00 (*81-7022-032-7*, Pub. by Concept II) S Asia.

Rural-Urban Migration: A Study of Socio-Economic Implications. Ajit S. Bhatia. (C). 1992. text ed. 22.00 (*81-7100-443-1*, Pub. by Deep II) S Asia.

***Rural-Urban Migration & Its Impact on Economic Development in China.** Wenbao Qian. 192p. 1996. text ed. 55.95 (*1-85972-456-6*, Pub. by Avebury Pub UK) Ashgate Pub Co.

Rural Versus Urban Political Power: The Nature & Consequences of Unbalanced Representation. Gordon E. Baker. LC 78-12263. 70p. 1979. reprint ed. text ed. 38.50 (*0-313-21223-6*, BARV, Greenwood Pr) Greenwood.

Rural Village in a Changing World: A Community Study. Jeanne Ewing. 560p. (Orig.). pap. 49.95 (*1-884690-03-3*) Owl Press.

Rural Violence in Bihar. Bindeshway Pathak. (C). 1993. 18.00 (*81-7022-474-8*, Pub. by Concept II) S Asia.

Rural vs. Urban Poverty. Gregory R. Weiher. (Orig.). 1988. pap. 15.00 (*0-944285-05-8*) Pol Studies.

Rural Vulnerability to Famine in Ethiopia: 1958-77. Mesfin W. Mariam. 208p. (Orig.). 1986. pap. 20.95 (*0-946688-03-6*, Pub. by Intermed Tech UK) Women Ink.

***Rural Wales Community & Marginalization.** Paul Clarke et al. 200p. 1997. pap. 25.00 (*0-7083-1365-5*, Pub. by Univ Wales Pr UK) Paul & Co Pubs.

Rural Water Resource Utilization & Planning: A Geographical Approach in Varanasi District. Ram Bilas. (C). 1988. 24.00 (*81-7022-027-0*, Pub. by Concept II) S Asia.

***Rural Water Supplies.** (Euro Reports & Studies Ser.: No. 87). 66p. 1983. pap. text ed. 7.00 (*92-890-1253-6*) World Health.

Rural Water Supply & Sanitation. 3rd ed. Forrest B. Wright. LC 75-14110. 320p. 1977. 37.50 (*0-88275-334-7*) Krieger.

***Rural Wisdom: Time-Honored Values of the Midwest.** Photos by Steve Apps. LC 97-1138. (Illus.). 128p. (Orig.). 1997. pap. 14.95 (*0-942495-63-2*) Amherst Pr.

Rural Women: A System Approach for Income Generation. Ed. by Shashi Kumar. (C). 1995. 20.00 (*81-241-0311-9*, Pub. by Har-Anand Pubns II) S Asia.

Rural Women: An Annotated Bibliography Prepared from the CAB Abstracts Database. 271p. 1992. pap. 77.00 (*0-85198-829-6*) CAB Intl.

Rural Women: Unequal Partners in Development. Martha F. Loutfi. (WEP Study Ser.). (Illus.). 80p. 1987. pap. 13.50 (*92-2-102389-3*) Intl Labour Office.

Rural Women & Development. V. Shobha. 1987. 35.00 (*0-8364-2259-7*, Pub. by Mittal II) S Asia.

Rural Women at Work: Strategies for Development in South Asia. Ruth B. Dixon. LC 78-5825. 227p. 1978. 18.50 (*0-8018-2124-X*) Resources Future.

Rural Women in Education: A Study in Underachievement. Prem L. Sharma. vii, 95p. 1988. text ed. 15.95 (*81-207-0785-0*, Pub. by Sterling Pubs II) Apt Bks.

Rural Women in India: A Socio-Economic Profile. I. Awasthi. 482p. 1982. 39.95 (*0-318-37073-5*) Asia Bk Corp.

Rural Women Teachers in the United States: A Sourcebook. Andrea Wyman. LC 96-11847. 184p. 1996. 35.00 (*0-8108-3156-2*) Scarecrow.

Rural Worker Adjustment to Urban Life: As Assessment of the Research. Varden Fuller. LC 79-629117. (Policy Papers in Human Resources & Industrial Relations Ser.: No. 15). (Orig.). (C). 1970. pap. text ed. 5.00 (*0-87736-115-0*) U of Mich Inst Labor.

Rural Workers' Organisations in Fiji. 41p. 1982. 10.80 (*92-2-103004-0*) Intl Labour Office.

Rural Workforce: Non-Agricultural Occupations in America. Clifton D. Bryant et al. LC 84-28410. 288p. (C). 1985. text ed. 49.95 (*0-89789-076-0*, Bergin & Garvey) Greenwood.

Rural Workplace Literacy: Community College Partnerships. Ed. by Lynn Barnett. 1991. pap. 5.00 (*0-87117-247-X*, 1336) Am Assn Comm Coll.

Rural Worlds Lost: The American South 1920-1960. Jack T. Kirby. LC 86-10253. (Illus.). xvi, 390p. 1986. pap. text ed. 18.95 (*0-8071-1360-3*) La State U Pr.

Rural York County, ME. A. Swenson. (Images of America Ser.). 1995. pap. 16.99 (*0-7524-0089-4*, Arcdia) Chalford.

Rural Youth: Their Situation & Prospects. Bruce L. Melvin. LC 71-165687. (Research Monographs: Vol. 15). 1971. reprint ed. lib. bdg. 22.50 (*0-306-70347-5*) Da Capo.

Rural Youth in Urban India. P. K. Gandhi. 1983. 26.00 (*0-8364-1062-9*) S Asia.

Rural Youth on Relief. Bruce L. Melvin. LC 74-37899. (Select Bibliographies Reprint Ser.). 1977. reprint ed. 20.95 (*0-8369-6737-2*) Ayer.

Rural Youth on Relief. Bruce L. Melvin. LC 78-165686. (Research Monographs: Vol. 11). 1971. reprint ed. lib. bdg. 19.50 (*0-306-70343-2*) Da Capo.

Ruralists: Art & Design Profile Twenty-Three. Ed. by Nicola Kearton & Christopher Martin. (Art & Design Ser.: No. 23). (Illus.). 96p. (Orig.). 1990. pap. 21.95 (*1-85490-123-0*) Academy Ed UK.

***Ruralists: Art & Design 23.** Christopher Martin. 1992. pap. 26.95 (*0-312-07264-3*) St Martin.

RUS. 5th ed. (Agni Yoga Ser.). 1980. 12.00 (*0-933574-04-5*) Agni Yoga Soc.

Rus. see Flight & Bliss

Rusalka. C. J. Cherryh. 352p. 1990. mass mkt. 5.99 (*0-345-36934-3*, Del Rey) Ballantine.

Ruses for War. 1996. lib. bdg. 251.99 (*0-8490-6935-1*) Gordon Pr.

Ruses for War: American Interventionism Since World War II. John Quigley. LC 92-19288. 310p. (C). 1992. 27.95 (*0-87975-767-1*) Prometheus Bks.

Rush. Michael Arkush. 1993. mass mkt. 4.99 (*0-380-77539-5*) Avon.

Rush. Ed. by Aaron Stang. (Bass Superstars Ser.). 80p. (Orig.). 1994. pap. 14.95 (*0-89724-192-4*, IF0198) Warner Brothers.

Rush. Ed. by Aaron Stang & Colgan Bryan. (Guitar Anthology Ser.). 224p. (YA). 1995. pap. 24.95 (*0-89724-935-6*, PG9530) Warner Brothers.

***Rush: Reader's Edition.** Kimberly Wozencraft. 1996. pap. write for info. (*0-679-72993-3*) Random.

***Rush: Test for Echo.** Ed. by Aaron Stang. (Illus.). 120p. (Orig.). 1997. pap. text ed. 21.95 (*1-57623-571-8*, PG9658) Warner Brothers.

***Rush - A Show of Hands.** Ed. by Carol Cuellar. 120p. (Orig.). (C). 1989. pap. text ed. 16.95 (*0-7692-0925-4*, VF1522) Warner Brothers.

Rush - Chronicles. Ed. by Carol Cuellar. 196p. (Orig.). 1994. pap. 22.95 (*0-89724-349-8*, VF1682) Warner Brothers.

***Rush - Complete.** Ed. by Carol Cuellar. 436p. (Orig.). (C). 1983. pap. text ed. 29.95 (*0-7692-0551-8*, VF1060) Warner Brothers.

***Rush - Complete, Vol. 2.** Ed. by Carol Cuellar. 276p. (Orig.). (C). 1995. pap. text ed. 22.95 (*0-7692-0506-2*, VF1285) Warner Brothers.

***Rush - Deluxe Anthology.** Ed. by Carol Cuellar. 210p. (Orig.). (C). 1981. pap. text ed. 17.95 (*0-7692-0550-X*, VF0901) Warner Brothers.

***Rush - Hold Your Fire.** Ed. by Carol Cuellar. 96p. (Orig.). (C). 1987. pap. text ed. 12.95 (*0-7692-0479-1*, VF1424) Warner Brothers.

***Rush - Moving Pictures.** Ed. by Carol Cuellar. 60p. (Orig.). (C). 1981. pap. text ed. 12.95 (*0-7692-0477-5*, VF0872) Warner Brothers.

***Rush - Permanent Waves.** Ed. by Carol Cuellar. 60p. (Orig.). (C). 1980. pap. text ed. 12.95 (*0-7692-0924-6*, VF0766) Warner Brothers.

***Rush - Presto.** Ed. by Carol Cuellar. 100p. (Orig.). (C). 1990. pap. text ed. 16.95 (*0-7692-0475-9*, VF1622) Warner Brothers.

***Rush - Retrospective.** Ed. by Carol Cuellar. 260p. (Orig.). (C). 1988. pap. text ed. 16.95 (*0-7692-0544-5*, VF1475) Warner Brothers.

Rush Hour. Kevin Fitzpatrick. LC 96-76209. 84p. (Orig.). 1996. pap. 9.00 (*0-935697-08-X*) Midwest Villages.

Rush Hour. Christine Loomis. LC 94-47192. (Illus.). 32p. (J). (ps-3). 1996. 15.95 (*0-395-69129-X*) HM.

Rush Hour: Talk Radio, Politics, & the Rise of Rush Limbaugh. Philip Seib. Ed. by Mike Towle. 320p. 1994. 22.95 (*1-56530-100-5*) Summit TX.

Rush Limbaugh & the Bible. Daniel J. Evearitt. 1996. pap. 9.99 (*0-88965-110-8*, Pub. by Horizon Books CN) Chr Pubns.

Rush Limbaugh in Night School. Charlie Varon. 1997. pap. 5.25 (*0-8222-1534-9*) Dramatists Play.

Rush Limbaugh Is a Big Fat Idiot. Al Franken. 1996. mass mkt. 6.99 (*0-440-22330-X*) Dell.

Rush Limbaugh Is a Big Fat Idiot: And Other Observations. Al Franken. LC 95-43454. 240p. 1996. 21.95 (*0-385-31474-4*) Delacorte.

Rush Limbaugh Is a Big Fat Idiot: And Other Observations. large type ed. Al Franken. 410p. 1996. 24.95 (*0-7862-0721-3*, Thorndike Lrg Prnt) Thorndike Pr.

Rush Limbaugh Story. Paul D. Colford. 320p. 1994. mass mkt. 5.99 (*0-312-95272-4*) St Martin.

Rush of Eagle Wings. Richard C. Folta. LC 82-6810. 1990. 13.95 (*0-87949-219-8*) Ashley Bks.

***Rush Review of Surgery.** 3rd ed. Deziel. 1998. pap. text ed. write for info. (*0-7216-7581-6*) Saunders.

***Rush Rhees on Religion & Philosophy.** Ed. by D. Z. Phillips. 416p. (C). 1997. text ed. 69.95 (*0-521-56410-7*) Cambridge U Pr.

Rush That Never Ended: A History of Australian Mining. 4th ed. Geoffrey Blainey. 404p. 1993. pap. 29.95 (*0-522-84557-6*, Pub. by Melbourne Univ Pr AT) Paul & Co Pubs.

Rush to Be Rich: A History of the Colony of Victoria 1883-89. Geoffrey Serle. 402p. 1994. pap. 24.95 (*0-522-84059-0*, Pub. by Melbourne Univ Pr AT) Paul & Co Pubs.

Rush to Burn: Solving America's Garbage Crisis? Newsday Staff. LC 89-1939. (Illus.). 269p. (Orig.). 1989. 25.00 (*1-55963-001-9*); pap. 15.95 (*1-55963-000-0*) Island Pr.

Rush to Development: Economic Change & Class Struggle in South Korea. Martin Hart-Landsberg. 352p. (C). 1993. text ed. 38.00 (*0-85345-856-1*); pap. text ed. 22.00 (*0-85345-857-X*) Monthly Rev.

Rush to German Unity. Konrad H. Jarausch. LC 93-625. 304p. 1994. 42.00 (*0-19-507275-8*); pap. 16.95 (*0-19-508577-9*) OUP.

Rush to Judgement. Irving Greenfield. 384p. (Orig.). 1995. pap. 4.99 (*0-451-18088-7*, Sig) NAL-Dutton.

Rush to Judgment. Mark Lane. 512p. 1992. pap. 13.95 (*1-56025-043-7*) Thunders Mouth.

Rush to Judgment: A Special Report on the Anti-Muslim Stereotyping, Harrassment & Hate Crimes Following the Bombing of Oklahoma City's Murrah Federal Building - April 19, 1995. (Illus.). 34p. (Orig.). (C). 1995. pap. text ed. 25.00 (*0-7881-2575-3*) DIANE Pub.

Rush to Policy: Analytic Techniques in Public Sector Decisions. Peter W. House & Roger D. Shull. 380p. 1987. 39.95 (*0-88738-134-0*) Transaction Pubs.

Rush to the Alps. Paul P. Bernard. (East European Monographs: No. 37). 228p. 1978. text ed. 46.00 (*0-914710-30-3*) East Eur Monographs.

Rush to the Lake. Forrest Gander. LC 87-72606. 72p. (Orig.). (C). 1988. 6.95 (*0-914086-78-2*); pap. 9.95 (*0-914086-79-0*) Alicejamesbooks.

Rush to Union: Understanding the European Federal Bargain. David McKay. (Illus.). 200p. 1996. 55.00 (*0-19-828058-0*) OUP.

Rush to Us. Howard King & Geoffrey Morris. 352p. 1994. mass mkt. 5.99 (*0-7860-0082-1*, Pinncle Kensgtn) Kensgtn Pub Corp.

Rush University Review of Surgery. 2nd ed. Steven G. Economou et al. LC 93-6622. (Illus.). 512p. 1993. pap. text ed. 39.95 (*0-7216-3780-9*) Saunders.

Rush Visions: The Official Biography. Bill Banasiewicz. (Illus.). 96p. pap. 19.95 (*0-7119-1162-2*, OP 44387) Omnibus NY.

***Rush Week.** Stephanie Prince. (Sorority Sisters Ser.: No. 1). (J). 1997. pap. 4.50 (*0-06-106507-2*) HarpC Child Bks.

Rush 929. Gerald A. Browne. 1998. pap. 23.95 (*1-55611-509-1*) D I Fine.

Rushdie Affair: The Novel, the Ayatollah, & the West. Daniel Pipes. 224p. 1990. 18.95 (*1-55972-025-5*, Birch Ln Pr) Carol Pub Group.

Rushdie File. Ed. by Sara Maitland & Lisa Appignanesi. (Contemporary Issues in the Middle East Ser.). (Illus.). 256p. 1990. pap. 16.95 (*0-8156-0248-0*) Syracuse U Pr.

Rushdie Letters: Freedom to Speak, Freedom to Write. Ed. by Steve MacDonogh. LC 92-45585. (Stages Ser.). 190p. (C). 1993. pap. 9.95 (*0-8032-8198-6*, Bison Books); text ed. 25.00 (*0-8032-3174-1*) U of Nebr Pr.

***Rushes.** John Rechy. 224p. 1997. reprint ed. pap. 12.00 (*0-8021-3497-1*, Grove) Grove-Atltic.

***Rushford & Rushford People.** Helen J. Gilbert. (Illus.). 572p. 1997. reprint ed. lib. bdg. 59.00 (*0-8328-6216-9*) Higginson Bk Co.

Rushing to Deceive: Disagreements with Rush Limbaugh. Ernest Ndukwe. LC 95-976890. 140p. 1995. pap. 9.95 (*1-885487-14-2*) Brownell & Carroll.

Rushing to Eva: A Pilgrimage in Search of the Great Mother. 3rd ed. Mary M. Leue. (Illus.). 337p. 1992. reprint ed. pap. 12.95 (*1-878115-04-9*) Dwn-To-Erth Bks.

Rushing to Paradise. J. G. Ballard. 240p. 1996. pap. 12.00 (*0-312-13415-0*, Picador USA) St Martin.

Rushing to Paradise: A Novel. J. G. Ballard. 240p. 1995. 21.00 (*0-312-13164-X*) St Martin.

Rushman. Carlos Toth. 80p. 1992. pap. text ed. 9.95 (*1-881116-15-8*) Black Forest Pr.

Rushton & His Times in American Canoeing. Atwood Manley. (Illus.). 224p. 1968. pap. 16.95 (*0-8156-0141-7*) Syracuse U Pr.

Rushtons Rowboats & Canoes: The 1903 Catalog in Perspective. Ed. by William Crowley. 80p. 1993. reprint ed. pap. 9.95 (*0-910020-42-6*) Adirondack Mus.

Rusi & Brassey's Defence Yearbook 1983. 93th ed. Royal United Services Institute Staff. (Brassey's Defence Yearbook Ser.). 400p. 1983. 60.50 (*0-08-028346-2*, Pergamon Pr); pap. 24.50 (*0-08-028347-0*, Pergamon Pr) Elsevier.

Rusi & Brassey's Defence Yearbook 1985. 95th ed. Royal United Services Institute Staff. (Brassey's Defence Yearbook Ser.). 388p. 1985. 46.00 (*0-08-031168-7*, Pergamon Pr); pap. 20.50 (*0-08-031169-5*, Pergamon Pr) Elsevier.

RUSI & Brassey's Defence Yearbook, 1990. 100th ed. RUSI Staff. 450p. 1990. 56.00 (*0-08-037336-4*, Pergamon Pr); pap. 15.25 (*0-08-037338-0*, Pergamon Pr) Elsevier.

RUSI-Brassey's Defence Yearbook. 94th ed. Royal United Services Institute Staff. (Brassey's Defence Yearbook Ser.). 350p. 1984. 60.50 (*0-08-030552-0*, Pergamon Pr); pap. 19.25 (*0-08-031176-8*, Pergamon Pr) Elsevier.

RUSI-Brassey's Defence Yearbook 1974-75. 85th ed. Royal United Services Institute Staff. (Brassey's Defence Yearbook Ser.). (Illus.). 338p. 1974. 30.50 (*0-08-027000-X*, Pergamon Pr) Elsevier.

RUSI-Brassey's Defence Yearbook 1975-76. 86th ed. Royal United Services Institute Staff. (Brassey's Defence Yearbook Ser.). 418p. 1975. 30.50 (*0-08-027001-8*, Pergamon Pr) Elsevier.

RUSI-Brassey's Defence Yearbook 1976-77. 87th ed. Royal United Services Institute Staff. (Brassey's Defence Yearbook Ser.). 377p. 28.00 (*0-317-66873-0*, Pergamon Pr) Elsevier.

RUSI-Brassey's Defence Yearbook 1977-78. 88th ed. Royal United Services Institute Staff. (Brassey's Defence Yearbook Ser.). 430p. 1977. 30.50 (*0-08-027003-4*, Pergamon Pr) Elsevier.

RUSI-Brassey's Defence Yearbook 1978-79. 89th ed. Royal United Services Institute Staff. (Brassey's Defence Yearbook Ser.). 365p. 1978. 44.00 (*0-08-027004-2*, Pergamon Pr) Elsevier.

RUSI-Brassey's Defence Yearbook 1979-80. 90th ed. Royal United Services Institute Staff. (Brassey's Defence Yearbook Ser.). 355p. 1979. 44.00 (*0-08-027005-0*, Pergamon Pr) Elsevier.

RUSI-Brassey's Defence Yearbook 1981. 91th ed. Royal United Services Institute Staff. 376p. 1980. 55.00 (*0-08-027006-9*, Pergamon Pr) Elsevier.

Rusi-Brassey's Defence Yearbook 1982. 92th ed. Royal United Services Institute Staff. 365p. 1981. 48.50 (*0-08-027039-5*, Pergamon Pr); pap. 30.50 (*0-08-027040-9*, Pergamon Pr) Elsevier.

RUSI-Brassey's Defence Yearbook 1986. 96th ed. Royal United Services Institute Staff. 350p. 1986. 48.50 (*0-08-031210-1*, Pergamon Pr); pap. 24.00 (*0-08-031220-9*, Pergamon Pr) Elsevier.

RUSI-Brassey's Defence Yearbook 1987. 97th ed. Royal United Services Institute Staff. 350p. 1987. 50.00 (*0-08-033607-8*, Pergamon Pr); pap. 24.00 (*0-08-033608-6*, Pergamon Pr) Elsevier.

RUSI-Brassey's Defence Yearbook 1988. 98th ed. Royal United Services Institute Staff. (Brassey's Defence Yearbook Ser.). 350p. 1988. 61.00 (*0-08-035815-2*, Pergamon Pr); pap. 33.00 (*0-08-035816-0*, Pergamon Pr) Elsevier.

RUSI-Brassey's Defence Yearbook 1989. RUSI Staff. LC 75-641843. (Brassey's Defence Yearbook Ser.). 361p. 1988. 63.00 (*0-08-036698-8*, Pergamon Pr) Elsevier.

Rusk County, Texas. Historical Commission & Virginia Knapp. (Illus.). 398p. 1992. 60.00 (*0-88107-197-8*) Curtis Media.

Rusk Family of Harrison County, Indiana. Daniel E. Anderson. LC 91-70985. (Illus.). 215p. (Orig.). 1991. pap. 35.00 (*0-9614527-1-4*) Dan Anderson.

Ruskin: A Study in Personality. Arthur C. Benson. (BCL1-PR English Literature Ser.). 323p. 1992. reprint ed. lib. bdg. 89.00 (*0-7812-7637-3*) Rprt Serv.

Ruskin: A Study of Personality. A. Benson. 1972. 59.95 (*0-8490-0981-2*) Gordon Pr.

Ruskin: Rossetti: Pre-Raphaelitism, Papers 1854-62. William M. Rossetti. LC 73-127453. reprint ed. 36.00 (*0-404-05437-4*) AMS Pr.

Ruskin: The Critical Heritage. J. L. Bradley. LC 83-11102. (Critical Heritage Ser.). 416p. 1984. 69.50 (*0-7100-9286-5*, RKP) Routledge.

Ruskin: The Genesis of Invention. Sheila Emerson. LC 92-45708. (Illus.). 272p. (C). 1994. text ed. 59.95 (*0-521-41807-0*) Cambridge U Pr.

Ruskin: Unto This Last. Y. Yarker. 1990. 29.00 (*0-7121-0144-6*, Pub. by Northcote UK) St Mut.

Ruskin & Environment: The Storm Cloud of the Nineteenth Century. Ed. by Michael Wheeler. LC 94-24564. 1995. text ed. 69.95 (*0-7190-4377-8*) St Martin.

Ruskin & Italy. Alexander Bradley. LC 87-24376. 138p. 1991. 39.00 (*0-8357-1854-9*) Univ Rochester Pr.

Ruskin & Jewel Caves: A Brief History. William E. Anchors, Jr. 94p. 1989. pap. 4.95 (*1-880417-01-4*) Star Tech.

Ruskin & Others on Byron. Raymond W. Chambers. LC 78-100737. (English Literature Ser.: No. 33). 1970. reprint ed. pap. 39.95 (*0-8383-0012-X*) M S G Haskell Hse.

Ruskin & Oxford: The Art of Education. Robert Hewison. LC 96-1247. 1996. pap. write for info. (*0-19-817404-7*, Clarendon Pr) OUP.

Ruskin & Oxford: The Art of Education. Robert Hewison. (Illus.). 188p. 1996. text ed. 65.00 (*0-19-817403-9*) OUP.

R

Ruskin & the Art of the Beholder. Elizabeth K. Helsinger. LC 81-13428. (Illus.). 424p. 1982. 42.50 (*0-674-78082-5*) HUP.

Ruskin As Literary Critic. John Ruskin. (BCL1-PR English Literature Ser.). 291p. 1992. reprint ed. lib. bdg. 79.00 (*0-7812-7633-0*) Rprt Serv.

Ruskin as Literary Critic: Selections. John Ruskin. Ed. by A. H. Ball. LC 69-14066. 291p. 1969. reprint ed. text ed. 59.75 (*0-8371-1149-8*, RULC, Greenwood Pr) Greenwood.

Ruskin Bond Children's Omnibus. 1995. pap. 14.00 (*81-7167-288-4*, Pub. by Rupa II) S Asia.

Ruskin Chronology. Bradley. 1997. text ed. 49.95 (*0-312-16159-X*) St Martin.

Ruskin Family Letters: The Correspondence of John James Ruskin, His Wife, & Their Son, John, 1801-1843, 2 vols. John J. Ruskin. Ed. by Van A. Burd. Incl. Vol. 1. 1801 to 1837. 1973. (*0-318-51449-4*); Vol. 2. 1837 to 1843. 1973. (*0-318-51450-8*); Vol. 1. 1801 to 1837. 1973. (*0-318-51449-4*); Vol. 2. 1837 to 1843. 1973. (*0-318-51450-8*); (Illus.). 792p. 1973. 100.00 (*0-8014-0725-7*) Cornell U Pr.

Ruskin on Architecture: His Thought & Influence. Kristine O. Garrigan. LC 73-2045. 237p. reprint ed. pap. 67.60 (*0-7837-1658-3*, 2041955) Bks Demand.

Ruskin Pottery: The Pottery of Edward Richard Taylor & William Howson Taylor 1898-1935. Paul Atterbury. (Illus.). 160p. 1993. 95.00 (*0-9520933-0-8*, Pub. by R Dennis UK) Antique Collect.

Ruskinian Gothic: The Architecture of Deane & Woodard, 1845-1861. Eve Blau. LC 81-7302. 313p. 1982. reprint ed. pap. 89.30 (*0-7837-9300-6*, 2060039) Bks Demand.

Ruskin's Drawings in the Ashmolean Museum. Nicholas Perry. (Illus.). 79p. 1995. pap. 17.95 (*0-907849-74-1*, 741P, Pub. by Ashmolean Mus UK); text ed. 19.95 (*1-85444-039-X*, 741, Woodstocker Bks) A Schwartz & Co.

Ruskin's Landscape of Beatitude. David A. Downes. LC 83-48767. (American University Studies: English Language & Literature: Ser. IV, Vol. 4). 247p. (C). 1984. pap. text ed. 24.75 (*0-8204-0049-1*) P Lang Pubng.

Ruskin's Letters from Venice Eighteen Forty-One to Eighteen Fifty-Two. John Ruskin. Ed. by John L. Bradley. LC 78-6260. (Yale Studies in English: Vol. 129). 330p. 1978. reprint ed. text ed. 38.50 (*0-313-20456-X*, RULE, Greenwood Pr) Greenwood.

Ruskin's Maze: Mastery & Madness in His Art. Jay Fellows. LC 81-47124. 320p. reprint ed. pap. 91.20 (*0-8357-6931-3*, 2037990) Bks Demand.

Ruskin's Myths. Dinah Birch. (Oxford English Monographs). 224p. 1988. 70.00 (*0-19-812872-X*) OUP.

Ruskin's Poetic Argument: The Design of the Major Works. Paul L. Sawyer. LC 84-45801. 320p. (C). 1985. 45.00 (*0-8014-1739-2*) Cornell U Pr.

Rusky. James H. Weidner. 104p. 1980. pap. 3.95 (*90-70176-19-X*, Tycooly Pub) Weidner & Sons.

Ruslan & Ludmilla: A Novel in Verse. Aleksandr Pushkin & Nancy Dargel. 1994. 14.95 (*0-930267-39-7*) Bergh Pub.

Rusling Family. J. F. Rusling. (Illus.). 160p. 1991. reprint ed. pap. 24.00 (*0-8328-1889-5*); reprint ed. lib. bdg. 34.00 (*0-8328-1888-7*) Higginson Bk Co.

Russ Meyer - the Life & Films: A Biography & a Comprehensive, Illustrated & Annotated Filmography & Bibliography. David K. Frasier. LC 89-43688. (Illus.). 252p. 1990. lib. bdg. 55.00 (*0-89950-475-2*) McFarland & Co.

Russe sans Peine. Albert O. Cherel. 24.95 (*0-685-11550-X*); Three cassettes. audio 125.00 (*0-685-01763-X*) Fr & Eur.

Russe Sans Peine: Russian for French Speakers. Assimil Staff. (FRE & RUS.). 28.95 (*0-8288-4361-9*, F50690); audio 125.00 (*0-685-53029-9*) Fr & Eur.

Russell. A.C. Grayling. (Past Masters Ser.). 128p. 1996. pap. 7.95 (*0-19-287683-X*) OUP.

Russell. C. W. Kilmister. LC 84-18050. 1985. text ed. 32.50 (*0-312-69613-2*) St Martin.

Russell. Mark Sainsbury. (Arguments of the Philosophers Ser.). 1979. pap. 15.95 (*0-7102-0536-8*, RKP) Routledge.

Russell: William Russell & Descendants, & the Russell Family of Virginia. Anna R. Des Cognets & Louis Des Cognets, Jr. (Illus.). 319p. 1993. reprint ed. pap. 46.50 (*0-8328-2975-7*); reprint ed. lib. bdg. 56.50 (*0-8328-2974-9*) Higginson Bk Co.

Russell, Alexandra & John. enl. rev. ed. Joseph R. Simonetta. 192p. 1989. pap. 10.00 (*0-941594-02-5*) Glbl Visions.

Russell & Analytic Philosophy. Ed. by A. D. Irvine & G. A. Wedeking. (Studies in Philosophy). 329p. 1993. 115.00 (*0-8020-2875-6*) U of Toronto Pr.

Russell & Elisa. Johanna Hurwitz. (J). (gr. 4 up). 1990. pap. 3.99 (*0-14-034406-3*, Puffin) Puffin Bks.

Russell & Elisa. Johanna Hurwitz. LC 88-37578. (Illus.). 96p. (J). (gr. k up). 1989. 15.00 (*0-688-08792-2*, Morrow Junior) Morrow.

Russell & Jones Clock Co. 1890. 1988. pap. 6.00 (*0-930476-19-0*) Am Clock & Watch.

Russell Baker's Book of American Humor. Ed. by Russell Baker. 608p. 1993. 30.00 (*0-393-03592-1*) Norton.

Russell Banks. Niemi. LC 96-50231. 1997. 22.95 (*0-8057-4018-X*, Twayne) Scribnrs Ref.

Russell Chatham. Etel Adnan et al. (Illus.). 61p. 1984. pap. 14.95 (*0-916947-00-9*) Winn Bks.

Russell Chatham. deluxe limited ed. Etel Adnan et al. (Illus.). 61p. 1984. 175.00 (*0-916947-01-7*) Winn Bks.

Russell Chatham: One Hundred Paintings. Jim Harrison et al. LC 90-80684. (Illus.). 144p. 1990. pap. 24.95 (*0-944439-24-1*) Clark City Pr.

Russell Cowles: American Autobiography. Russell Cowles. 53p. 1995. lib. bdg. 69.00 (*0-7812-8490-2*) Rprt Serv.

***Russell Forester: Unauthorized Autobiography.** Michael Zakian & Alain J. Cohen. (Illus.). 90p. 1997. 35.00 (*1-889195-09-X*); pap. 25.00 (*1-889195-08-1*) Smart Art Pr.

Russell Graders Photo Archive. Ed. by P. A. Letourneau. LC 93-80438. (Photo Archive Ser.). (Illus.). 144p. 1993. pap. text ed. 29.95 (*1-882256-11-5*) Iconografix.

Russell Grant's Astrology Kit. Russell Grant. (Illus.). 128p. 1995. 22.95 (*0-86369-851-4*, Pub. by Virgin Pub UK) London Brdge.

Russell Grant's Illustrated Dream Dictionary. Russell Grant. 144p. 1995. 19.95 (*1-85227-523-5*, Pub. by Virgin Pub UK) London Brdge.

Russell, Idealism, & the Emergence of Analytic Philosophy. Peter Hylton. 440p. 1993. reprint ed. pap. 32.00 (*0-19-824018-X*) OUP.

Russell Kirk: A Bibliography. Ed. by Charles Brown. LC 82-182871. (Illus.). 172p. 1981. 7.50 (*0-916699-05-6*) CMU Clarke Hist Lib.

Russell Lee's FSA Photographs of Chamisal & Penasco, New Mexico. Ed. by William Wroth. LC 85-71305. (New Deal & Folk Culture Ser.). (Illus.). 152p. (Orig.). 1995. pap. 15.95 (*0-941270-23-8*) Ancient City Pr.

Russell on Crime, 2 vols., Set. 12th ed. J. W. Turner. (Legal Reprint Ser.). 1986. reprint ed. 120.00 (*0-421-35560-3*) Rothman.

Russell Periodic Chart of the Elements I. 1991. write for info. (*1-879605-27-9*) U Sci & Philos.

Russell Periodic Chart of the Elements I, II, 2 vols., Set. 1991. write for info. (*1-879605-29-5*) U Sci & Philos.

Russell Periodic Chart of the Elements II. 1991. write for info. (*1-879605-28-7*) U Sci & Philos.

Russell Rides Again. Johanna Hurwitz. LC 85-7287. (Illus.). 96p. (J). (ps-2). 1985. 16.00 (*0-688-04628-2*, Morrow Junior); lib. bdg. 15.93 (*0-688-04629-0*, Morrow Junior) Morrow.

Russell Sage. Paul Sarnoff. (Illus.). 1965. 17.95 (*0-8392-1142-2*) Astor-Honor.

Russell Sprouts. Johanna Hurwitz. (Illus.). 80p. (J). (gr. 2-5). 1989. pap. 3.99 (*0-14-032942-0*, Puffin) Puffin Bks.

Russell Sprouts. Johanna Hurwitz. LC 87-5494. (Illus.). 80p. (J). (ps-2). 1987. 16.00 (*0-688-07165-1*, Morrow Junior) Morrow.

Russell Wright: American Designer. William Hennessey. (Illus.). 96p. (Orig.). 1983. pap. 15.95 (*0-262-58066-7*) MIT Pr.

Russellism - The Latest Blasphemy: Millions-Now-Living-Will-Never-Die-Ism. F. Mellows. 23p. 1988. reprint ed. pap. 1.95 (*1-883858-50-X*) Witness CA.

Russellism Unveiled. O. C. Lambert. 1940. pap. 3.50 (*0-88027-090-X*) Firm Foun Pub.

Russell's Civil War Photographs: 115 Historic Prints. Andrew J. Russell. (Illus.). 120p. 1982. pap. 9.95 (*0-486-24283-8*) North South Trader.

Russell's Hell vs. the Bible Hell. John H. Mosemann. 15p. 1988. reprint ed. pap. 0.95 (*1-883858-54-2*) Witness CA.

Russell's Magazine, Set, Vols. 1-6. reprint ed. Set. lib. bdg. 405.00 (*0-404-19547-4*) AMS Pr.

***Russells of New England & Their Immigrant Ancestors: Featuring the Russell, Poore, Cooley, Clough, Arms, Childs, & MacIntyre Families.** Franklin H. White. 300p. 1997. 40.00 (*0-614-29577-7*) WHE OH.

***Russell's Soil Conditions & Plant Growth.** 11th ed. Ed. by Alan Wild. 1988. 107.66 (*0-582-44677-5*, Pub. by Longman UK) Longman.

Russell's Standard Fashions 1915-1918. Phil Livoni. LC 96-10939. (Illus.). reprint ed. pap. 11.95 (*0-486-29122-7*) Dover.

Russell's Union Pacific Railroad Photographs. Andrew J. Russell. (Illus.). 96p. 1995. pap. text ed. 9.95 (*0-486-28633-9*) Dover.

***Russell's Union Pacific Railroad Photographs.** Andrew J. Russell. (Illus.). 96p. 1997. reprint ed. pap. text ed. 11.95 (*0-486-29667-9*) Dover.

Russet Coat: A Study of Robert Burns Poetry. Christina Keith. LC 70-130263. (Studies in Poetry: No. 38). 1970. reprint ed. lib. bdg. 75.00 (*0-8383-1170-9*) M S G Haskell Hse.

Russia. (Insight Guides, Windows on the World Ser.). (Illus.). 350p. 1993. pap. 22.95 (*0-395-66167-6*) HM.

Russia. (Insider's Guides Ser.). (Illus.). 224p. 1993. pap. 17.95 (*1-55650-558-2*) Hunter NJ.

***Russia.** LC 96-45133. (Globe-Trotter's Club Ser.). (J). 1997. lib. bdg. write for info. (*1-57505-101-X*, Carolrhoda) Lerner Group.

***Russia.** (Major World Nations Ser.). (Illus.). 120p. (YA). (gr. 5 up). 1997. lib. bdg. 19.95 (*0-7910-4750-4*) Chelsea Hse.

Russia. Edward Acton. (Present & the Past Ser.). 342p. (C). 1986. pap. text ed. 24.75 (*0-685-73796-9*, 73577) Longman.

Russia. Arnaldo Alberti. 1995. 12.98 (*0-8317-1576-6*) Smithmark.

Russia. Helen Arnold. LC 95-8100. (Postcards from Ser.). (J). 1995. lib. bdg. 21.40 (*0-8172-4006-3*) Raintree Steck-V.

Russia. Helen Arnold. (Postcards From Ser.). (J). 1996. pap. text ed. 4.95 (*0-8172-4227-9*) Raintree Steck-V.

***Russia.** Clare Boast. LC 97-16745. (Next Stop! Ser.). (J). 1997. write for info. (*1-57572-569-X*) Rigby Interact Libr.

Russia. Chantal Deltenre & Maximilien Dauber. (Tintin's Travel Diaries Ser.). (Illus.). 76p. (YA). (gr. 5 up). 1995. 11.95 (*0-8120-6491-7*); pap. 6.95 (*0-8120-9162-0*) Barron.

***Russia.** Kim B. Fader. (Overview Series). (Illus.). (J). (gr. 4-12). 1997. lib. bdg. 17.96 (*1-56006-521-4*) Lucent Bks.

Russia. David Flint. LC 92-43190. (On the Map Ser.). (Illus.). 32p. (J). (gr. 3-4). 1992. lib. bdg. 22.83 (*0-8114-2941-5*) Raintree Steck-V.

***Russia.** Grolier Educational Staff. LC 97-19378. (Fiesta! Ser.). 1997. write for info. (*0-7172-9113-8*) Grolier Educ.

Russia. Robert G. Kaiser. 576p. (gr. 10 up). 1984. mass mkt. 5.95 (*0-671-50324-3*, WSP) PB.

Russia. David C. King. LC 94-45832. (Dropping in On Ser.). (J). (gr. 2-6). 1995. write for info. (*1-55916-086-1*) Rourke Bk Co.

Russia. Michael G. Kort. LC 95-12200. (Nations in Transition Ser.). 160p. (YA). (gr. 7 up). 1995. 17.95 (*0-8160-3061-8*) Facts on File.

Russia. Hyman Kublin. 1989. pap. 17.60 (*0-395-47083-8*) HM.

Russia. Hyman Kublin. 1989. teacher ed., pap. 3.68 (*0-395-53617-0*) HM.

Russia. Ed. by Lerner Geography Department Staff. (Then & Now Ser.). (Illus.). 64p. (YA). (gr. 5 up). 1992. lib. bdg. 22.95 (*0-8225-2805-3*, Lerner Publctns) Lerner Group.

***Russia.** William Lychack. LC 96-31126. (Games People Play Ser.). 64p. 1996. lib. bdg. 22.00 (*0-516-04441-9*) Childrens.

Russia. Penelope Perrin. LC 93-30422. (Discovering Science Ser.). (Illus.). 32p. (J). (gr. 4 up). 1994. lib. bdg. 13.95 (*0-89686-775-7*, Crstwood Hse) Silver Burdett Pr.

***Russia.** John Sallnow & Tatyana Saiko. LC 96-32783. (Country Fact Files Ser.). (J). 1997. lib. bdg. 24.26 (*0-8172-4625-8*) Raintree Steck-V.

Russia. Jenny Vaughn. LC 89-26121. (Where We Live Ser.). (Illus.). 32p. (J). (gr. 2-5). 1990. pap. 3.95 (*0-8114-7180-2*); lib. bdg. 21.40 (*0-8114-2549-5*) Raintree Steck-V.

***Russia.** Harlinah Whyte. LC 97-7879. (Festivals of the World Ser.). (J). 1997. write for info. (*0-8368-1936-5*) Gareth Stevens Inc.

Russia. 2nd ed. Edward Acton. LC 94-11457. (Present & Past Ser.). 416p. (C). 1995. text ed. 53.95 (*0-582-08915-8*, 77000, Pub. by Longman UK); pap. text ed. 30.50 (*0-582-08922-0*, 76999, Pub. by Longman UK) Longman.

***Russia.** 4th ed. McClellan. LC 97-14284. 1997. pap. text ed. 40.00 (*0-13-646613-3*) P-H.

Russia. Theophile Gautier. LC 77-115550. (Russia Observed, Series I). 1970. reprint ed. 56.95 (*0-405-03028-2*) Ayer.

Russia. Donald Wallace. LC 73-112349. reprint ed. 72.50 (*0-404-06809-X*) AMS Pr.

Russia: A Chronicle of Three Journeys in the Aftermath of the Revolution. Nikos Kazantzakis. Tr. by Michael Antonakes & Thanasis Maskaleris from GRE. LC 88-38224. (Illus.). 208p. 1989. 18.95 (*0-88739-072-2*) Creat Arts Bk.

Russia: A Concise History. rev. ed. Ronald Hingley. LC 90-72013. (Illus.). 224p. 1991. pap. 15.95 (*0-500-27627-7*) Thames Hudson.

***Russia: A History.** Ed. by Gregory Freeze. (Illus.). 448p. 1998. 49.95 (*0-19-215899-6*) OUP.

Russia: A Novel. David E. Kaun. LC 94-27514. 320p. 1995. 24.95 (*1-56474-119-2*); pap. 12.95 (*1-56474-112-5*) Fithian Pr.

Russia: A Portrait. Lev Poliakov. (Illus.). 1991. 50.00 (*0-374-25290-4*) FS&G.

Russia: A Return to Imperialism? Ed. by Uri Ra'anan & Kate Martin. 199p. 1996. text ed. 45.00 (*0-312-12927-0*) St Martin.

Russia: A Social History. Dimitry S. Mirsky. Ed. by C. G. Seligman. LC 83-26517. (Illus.). 312p. 1984. text ed. 69.50 (*0-313-24296-8*, MRUS, Greenwood Pr) Greenwood.

Russia: Broken Idols, Solemn Dreams. David K. Shipler. (Nonfiction Ser.). 416p. 1984. pap. 7.95 (*0-14-007408-2*, Penguin Bks) Viking Penguin.

Russia: Broken Idols, Solemn Dreams. rev. ed. David K. Shipler. (Illus.). 1989. 22.50 (*0-8129-1788-X*, Times Bks) Random.

Russia: Building Democracy. John Bradley. LC 95-20811. (Topics in the News Ser.). 32p. (J). (gr. 6-8). 1995. 22.83 (*0-8172-4177-9*) Raintree Steck-V.

Russia: Business Promotion & Support, 1996. 2nd rev. ed. (Russian Business Library: No. 20). (Illus.). 250p. 1996. pap. 99.00 (*1-57751-001-1*) Russ Info & Busn Ctr.

***Russia: Chronicles of Change.** Lucian Perkins. (Illus.). 24p. (Orig.). 1996. pap. text ed. 8.00 (*1-887040-19-6*) SE Mus Photo.

Russia: Creating Private Enterprise & Efficient Markets. Ed. by Ira W. Lieberman et al. LC 94-49067. (Studies of Economies in Transformation: No. 15). 266p. 1995. 15.95 (*0-8213-3187-6*, 13187) World Bank.

***Russia: Empire & Nation.** Geoffrey A. Hosking. LC 97-5069. 1997. 27.95 (*0-674-78118-X*) HUP.

***Russia: Essential Guide for Business.** John Mattock. 1997. pap. text ed. 14.95 (*0-7494-1964-4*, Kogan Pg Educ) Stylus Pub VA.

***Russia: Forest Policy During Transition.** (Country Study Ser.). 296p. 1997. 17.95 (*0-614-28624-7*, 13896) World Bank.

Russia: Joint Ventures in Moscow. 2nd rev. ed. (Russian Business Library). 300p. 1996. pap. 99.00 (*1-57751-008-9*) Russ Info & Busn Ctr.

***Russia: Joint-Ventures in Moscow.** 2nd rev. ed. Russian Information & Business Center, Inc. Staff. (Russian Business Library). 400p. 1997. pap. 99.00 (*1-57751-314-2*) Russ Info & Busn Ctr.

Russia: Joint Ventures in Russian Regions. 2nd rev. ed. (Russian Business Library). 300p. 1996. pap. 99.00 (*1-57751-009-7*) Russ Info & Busn Ctr.

***Russia: Joint-Ventures in Russian Regions.** 2nd rev. ed. Russian Information & Business Center, Inc. Staff. (Russian Business Library). 400p. 1997. pap. 99.00 (*1-57751-315-0*) Russ Info & Busn Ctr.

Russia: Land of Opportunity? Stephen R. Sestanovich. (Global Business White Paper Ser.). 1994. 20.00 (*0-614-13871-X*) CSI Studies.

Russia: On the Eve of War & Revolution. Donald M. Wallace. Ed. by Cyril E. Black. LC 83-43100. 542p. 1984. reprint ed. pap. text ed. 24.95 (*0-691-00774-8*) Princeton U Pr.

Russia: People to People. Ed. by Jim Haynes. 1996. pap. 11.95 (*0-939010-45-3*) Zephyr Pr.

Russia: Photographic Journey. Outlet Book Co. Staff. (Illus.). 1992. 14.99 (*0-517-07678-0*) Random Hse Value.

Russia: Political & Economical Development. George Breslauer et al. (Monograph Ser.: Vol. 9). 1995. pap. write for info. (*0-930607-20-1*) Keck Ctr.

Russia: St. Petersburg, Moscow, Kharkoff, Riga, Odessa, the German Provinces on the Baltic, the Steppes, the Crimea & the Interior of the Empire. J. G. Kohl. LC 71-115554. (Russia Observed, Series I). 1970. reprint ed. 29.95 (*0-405-03040-1*) Ayer.

Russia: The Banking System During Transition. LC 93-44834. (Country Study Ser.). 72p. 1994. 6.95 (*0-8213-2718-6*, 12718); 6.95 (*0-8213-2754-2*, 12754) World Bank.

Russia: The Ingush-Ossetian Conflict in the Prigorodnyi Region. Human Rights Watch/Helsinki Staff. 112p. (Orig.). 1996. pap. 10.00 (*1-56432-165-7*) Hum Rts Watch.

Russia: The Present & the Past. Edward Acton. (C). 1986. pap. text ed. 27.95 (*0-582-49323-4*) Addison-Wesley.

Russia: The Roots of Confrontation. Robert V. Daniels. LC 85-27267. (American Foreign Policy Library). (Illus.). 432p. 1985. 37.50 (*0-674-77965-7*) HUP.

Russia: The Roots of Confrontation. Robert V. Daniels. (American Foreign Policy Library). 432p. 1986. pap. 14.95 (*0-674-77966-5*) HUP.

Russia: The Soviet Period & After. 3rd ed. Woodford McClellan. LC 93-5364. 357p. (C). 1993. pap. text ed. 49.33 (*0-13-035965-3*) P-H.

Russia: Then & Now. Laura Young. (Illus.). 150p. (Orig.). 1993. pap. 9.95 (*0-9637841-0-2*) L Young PC.

Russia: Travels & Studies. Annette M. Meakin. LC 72-115565. (Russia Observed Ser.). (Illus.). 1971. reprint ed. 35.95 (*0-405-03086-X*) Ayer.

Russia: Under the Last Tsar. Ed. by Theofanis G. Stavrou. LC 74-79047. (Minnesota Paperbacks Ser.: No. 19). 277p. reprint ed. pap. 79.00 (*0-8357-3335-1*, 2039561) Bks Demand.

***Russia: Why Revolution?** Bucklow & Russell. 1976. pap. text ed. write for info. (*0-582-68238-X*, Pub. by Longman UK) Longman.

***Russia: Why Revolution.** Bucklow & Russell. 1991. pap. text ed. write for info. (*0-582-87039-9*, Pub. by Longman UK) Longman.

Russia No. 1: Yesterday, Today, Tomorrow. The Results of Essay Competition & Survey in Nizhmy, Russia in 1995. Victor Pavlenkov. Ed. by Alexander Babyonishev. 400p. (Orig.). 1996. pap. 12.95 (*0-9637035-4-4*) FC-Izdat.

Russia Vol. 3: Around the World. Betsy Franco. (Illus.). 48p. (J). (gr. 1-3). 1993. pap. text ed. 7.95 (*1-55799-258-4*, EMC 277) Evan-Moor Corp.

Russia see Women in Society - Group 3

Russia see Cultures of the World - Group 8

Russia - U. S. S. R. - Russia: The Drive & Drift of a Superstate. Moshe Lewin. 384p. 1994. 30.00 (*1-56584-123-9*) New Press NY.

Russia - Women - Culture. Ed. by Beth Holgrem & Helena Goscilo. 400p. 1995. 45.00 (*0-253-33019-X*); pap. text ed. 24.95 (*0-253-21044-5*) Ind U Pr.

Russia According to Women. Intro. by Marina Ledkovsky. LC 91-11292. (Illus.). 172p. (Orig.). (C). 1991. pap. text ed. 9.50 (*1-55779-023-X*) Hermitage.

***Russia after Communism.** Anders Aslund. 1997. pap. text ed. 16.95 (*0-87003-151-1*) Carnegie Endow.

Russia after the Coup: Politics & Economics, Perspectives from the Russian Press August 1991 to February 1993, Supplement to the 8th Edition of The U. S. S. R. Today. Ed. by Fred Schulze & Robert Ehlers. 60p. 1993. pap. 12.00 (*0-913601-88-8*) Current Digest.

Russia Against Japan, 1904-1905: A New Look at the Russo-Japanese War. J. N. Westwood. LC 85-22112. 183p. (C). 1986. text ed. 29.50 (*0-88706-191-5*) State U NY Pr.

Russia & a Divided Azerbaijan. Tadeusz Swietochowski. LC 94-48574. 272p. 1995. 32.50 (*0-231-07068-3*) Col U Pr.

Russia & America: A Philosophical Comparison. William J. Gavin & Thomas J. Blakeley. (Sovietica Ser.: No. 38). 1976. lib. bdg. 67.00 (*90-277-0749-9*) Kluwer Ac.

Russia & America: From Rivalry to Reconciliation. Ed. by George Ginsburgs et al. LC 93-15877. 368p. (C). (gr. 13). 1993. text ed. 80.95 (*1-56324-284-2*); pap. text ed. 27.95 (*1-56324-285-0*) M E Sharpe.

Russia & America: The Roots of Economic Divergence. Colin J. White. 272p. 1988. lib. bdg. 39.95 (*0-7099-5246-5*, Pub. by Croom Helm UK) Routledge Chapman & Hall.

Russia & Arabia: Soviet Foreign Policy Toward the Arabian Peninsula. Mark N. Katz. LC 85-45046. 296p. 1986. text ed. 45.00 (*0-8018-2897-X*) Johns Hopkins.

Russia & Asia. Andrei A. Lobanov-Rostovsky. 1951. 20.00 (*0-911586-18-0*) Wahr.

***Russia & Beyond.** Nick Gheissari & Patricia Raine. (Russia & Beyond Ser.). (Illus.). 128p. 1996. 40.00 (*0-9652398-0-2*) Escoaa Images.

Russia & Black Africa Before World War II. Edward Wilson. LC 73-84939. 300p. 1974. 44.95 (*0-8419-0109-0*) Holmes & Meier.

***Russia & Central Asia by Road.** Hazel Barker. 1997. pap. text ed. 18.95 (*1-898323-61-5*, Pub. by Bradt Pubns UK) Globe Pequot.

An Asterisk (*) at the beginning of an entry indicates that the title is appearing in BIP for the first time.

R

Russia & China: Their Diplomatic Relations to 1728. Mark Mancall. LC 74-85077. (Harvard East Asian Ser.: No. 61). 412p. reprint ed. pap. 117.50 (*0-685-20531-2*, 2029993) Bks Demand.

Russia & China on the Eve of a New Millennium. Carl A. Linden. LC 96-33083. 412p. 1996. text ed. 44.95 (*1-56000-291-3*) Transaction Pubs.

Russia & Eastern Europe after Communism: The Search for New Political, Economic & Security Systems. Ed. by Michael Kraus & Ronald D. Liebowitz. 286p. (C). 1996. text ed. 69.95 (*0-8133-8948-8*) Westview.

Russia & Europe: An End to Confrontation? Ed. by Neil Malcolm. LC 93-27883. 1994. 49.00 (*1-85567-161-1*) St Martin.

Russia & Europe: The Emerging Security Agenda. Ed. by Vladimir Baranovsky. (SIPRI Publication). 640p. 1997. 85.00 (*0-19-829201-5*) OUP.

Russia & Europe 1825-1878. Andrei A. Lobanov-Rostovsky. 1954. 20.00 (*0-911586-19-9*) Wahr.

Russia & Germany: A Century of Conflict. Walter Laqueur. 379p. (C). 1990. pap. 21.95 (*0-88738-349-1*) Transaction Pubs.

Russia & Germany in British Policy Toward Europe since 1815. (Prince Albert Studies: Vol. 11). 217p. 1994. 50.00 (*3-598-21411-1*) K G Saur.

Russia & Her Neighbors. John Tomikel & Bonnie Henderson. (Illus.). 160p. 1994. pap. 19.95 (*0-910042-70-5*); lib. bdg. 24.95 (*0-910042-71-3*) Allegheny.

Russia & Italy Against Hitler: The Bolshevik-Fascist Rapproachment of the 1930s. Joseph C. Clarke, III. LC 90-43372. (Contributions to the Study of World History Ser.: No. 21). 232p. 1991. text ed. 55.00 (*0-313-27468-1*, CRY/, Greenwood Pr) Greenwood.

Russia & Its Banking System. (Illus.). 200p. 1995. 170.00 (*1-85564-397-9*, Pub. by Euromoney UK) Am Educ Systs.

Russia & Its Mysterious Market: Getting Started & Doing Business in the New Russian Marketplace, 1992. Ed. by Stanislav Tverdohlebou & Thomas Mullen. 112p. (Orig.). 1991. pap. 24.95 (*0-9631202-0-4*) TradeWinds Pr.

Russia & Japan: An Unresolved Dilemma Between Distant Neighbors. Ed. by Tsuyoshi Hasegawa et al. LC 93-2854. (Research Ser.: No. 87). xii, 456p. (C). 1993. pap. text ed. 26.50 (*0-87725-187-8*) U of Cal IAS.

Russia & Nationalism in Central Asia: The Case of Tadzhikistan. Published in Cooperation with the Institute for Sino-Soviet Studies, the George Washington University. Teresa Rakowska-Harmstone. LC 69-13722. 342p. reprint ed. pap. 97.50 (*0-317-41760-6*, 2025866) Bks Demand.

***Russia & NIS: Beer Production.** Russian Information & Business Center, Inc. Staff. 1997. pap. 99.00 (*1-57751-164-6*) Russ Info & Busn Ctr.

***Russia & NIS Distilling & Wine Production.** Russian Information & Business Center, Inc. Staff. 400p. 1997. pap. 99.00 (*1-57751-163-8*) Russ Info & Busn Ctr.

Russia & Northern Eurasia see Encyclopedia of World Geography

Russia & Ourselves. Vidkun Quisling. Ed. by James K. Warner. (Illus.). 183p. (Orig.). pap. 15.00 (*0-89562-156-8*) Sons Lib.

Russia & the American Revolution. Nikolai Bolkhovitinov. Tr. by C. Jay Smith & George A. Len Sen from RUS. LC 74-42220. 277p. 1976. 29.70 (*0-910512-20-5*) Diplomatic IN.

***Russia & the Arms Trade.** Ed. by Ian Anthony. (Illus.). 400p. 1997. 200.00 (*0-19-829278-3*) OUP.

Russia & the Balkans: Inter-Balkan Rivalries & Russian Foreign Policy, 1908-1914. Andrew Rossos. LC 81-142342. 327p. reprint ed. pap. 93.20 (*0-685-16003-3*, 2026405) Bks Demand.

Russia & the Challenge of Fiscal Federalism. Ed. by Christine I. Wallich. LC 93-47897. (World Bank Regional & Sectorial Studies). 320p. 1994. 18.95 (*0-8213-2683-X*, 12683) World Bank.

Russia & the Challenge of Fiscal Federalism. Christine I. Wallich. (World Bank Ser.). 314p. 1996. 78.95 (*1-85972-225-3*, Pub. by Avebury Pub UK) Ashgate Pub Co.

Russia & the Cholera, Eighteen Twenty-Three to Eighteen Thirty-Two. Roderick E. McGrew. (Illus.). 240p. 1965. 27.50 (*0-299-03710-X*) U of Wis Pr.

Russia & the Commonwealth of Independent States. James Riordan. (Countries Ser.). (Illus.). 48p. (J). (gr. 5 up). 1992. lib. bdg. 14.95 (*0-382-24378-1*) Silver Burdett Pr.

Russia & the Commonwealth of Independent States: Documents, Data, & Analysis. Ed. by Zbigniew Brzezinski & Paige Sullivan. LC 96-18164. 896p. (C). (gr. 13). 1996. text ed. 225.00 (*1-56324-637-6*) M E Sharpe.

Russia & the Commonwealth of Independent States Oil & Gas Industry Guide. Oilfield Publications Limited Staff. 480p. (C). 1993. 3,800.00 (*1-870945-31-X*, Pub. by Oilfield Pubns UK) St Mut.

Russia & the Commonwealth of Independent States Oil & Gas Industry Report. 2nd ed. Oilfield Publications Limited Staff. (Illus.). 550p. 1994. pap. 1,850.00 (*1-870945-58-1*, Pub. by Oilfld Pubns Ltd UK) Am Educ Systs.

Russia & the Formation of the Romanian Empire: 1821 to 1878. Barbara Jelavich. LC 82-23578. (Illus.). 360p. 1984. text ed. 85.00 (*0-521-25318-7*) Cambridge U Pr.

Russia & the Former Soviet Union: A Bibliographic Guide to English Language Publications, 1986-1991. Helen F. Sullivan & Robert H. Burger. xii, 380p. 1994. lib. bdg. 65.00 (*1-56308-046-X*) Libs Unl.

Russia & the Golden Horde: The Mongol Impact on Medieval Russian History. Charles J. Halperin. LC 84-48254. (Illus.). 192p. 1985. 31.50 (*0-253-35033-6*) Ind U Pr.

Russia & the Golden Horde: The Mongol Impact on Medieval Russian History. Charles J. Halperin. LC 84-48254. (Illus.). 192p. 1987. pap. 10.95 (*0-253-20445-3*, MB-445) Ind U Pr.

Russia & the Idea of Europe: A Study in Identity & International Relations. Iver B. Neumann. LC 95-22617. (New International Relations Ser.). 240p. (C). (gr. 13). 1995. text ed. 62.95 (*0-415-11370-9*) Routledge.

Russia & the Idea of Europe: A Study in Identity & International Relations. 906th ed. Iver B. Neumann. LC 95-22617. (New International Relations Ser.). 240p. (C). 1995. pap. 18.95 (*0-415-11371-7*) Routledge.

Russia & the Independent Nations of the Former U. S. S. R. Geofacts & Maps. William A. Dando et al. 112p. (C). 1995. spiral bd. write for info. (*0-697-27754-2*) Wm C Brown Pubs.

Russia & the Independent States. Daniel C. Diller. LC 92-33273. 1992. pap. 32.95 (*0-87187-617-5*) Congr Quarterly.

Russia & the Independent States. Daniel C. Diller. LC 92-33273. 1993. 50.95 (*0-87187-862-3*) Congr Quarterly.

Russia & the Jews see Shield

Russia & the Mongol Yoke: The History of Russian Principalities & the Golden Horde, 1221- 1996. text ed. 59.50 (*1-85043-961-3*, Pub. by I B Tauris UK) St Martin.

Russia & the Near Abroad. John Tomikel & Bonnie Henderson. LC 96-84450. (Illus.). 224p. (Orig.). 1996. pap. 29.95 (*0-910042-76-4*) Allegheny.

Russia & the Negro: Blacks in Russian History & Thought. Allison Blakely. LC 85-5251. (Illus.). 224p. 1987. pap. 14.95 (*0-88258-175-9*) Howard U Pr.

Russia & the New Independent States: The Political & Economic Transitions. Constantine C. Menges. 1996. 300p. (C). 1994. pap. text ed. 27.50 (*0-8191-9551-0*) U Pr of Amer.

Russia & the New States of Eurasia: The Politics of Upheaval. Karen Dawisha & Bruce Parrott. LC 93-20994. 480p. (C). 1994. pap. text ed. 22.95 (*0-521-45895-1*) Cambridge U Pr.

Russia & the New States of Eurasia: The Politics of Upheaval. Karen Dawisha & Bruce Parrott. LC 93-20994. 480p. (C). 1994. text ed. 59.95 (*0-521-45262-7*) Cambridge U Pr.

Russia & the NIS in the World Economy: East-West Investment, Financing & Trade. Ed. by Deborah A. Palmieri. LC 93-48213. 200p. 1994. text ed. 55.00 (*0-275-94531-6*, Praeger Pubs) Greenwood.

Russia & the Post Soviet Scene: A Geographical Perspective. James H. Bater. 1996. text ed. 54.95 (*0-470-23636-1*) Halsted Pr.

Russia & The Post Soviet Scene: A Geographical Perspective. James H. Bater. 1996. pap. text ed. 34.95 (*0-470-23685-X*) Halsted Pr.

Russia & the Republics Legal Materials, 7 vols., Set. Ed. by John N. Hazard & Vratislav Pechota. 6000p. 1992. ring bd. 595.00 (*0-929179-46-3*) Juris Pubng.

***Russia & the Republics Travellers Survival Kit.** Emily Hatchwell & Simon Calder. (Travellers Survival Kit Guides Ser.). 368p. (Orig.). 1997. pap. 17.95 (*1-85458-132-5*, Pub. by Vac Wrk Pubns UK) Seven Hills Bk.

***Russia & the Restored Gospel.** Gary Browning. LC 96-37332. 1997. write for info. (*1-57345-202-5*) Deseret Bk.

Russia & the Road to Appeasement: Cycles of East-West Conflict in War & Peace. George Liska. LC 81-48188. 288p. 1982. text ed. 39.50 (*0-8018-2763-9*) Johns Hopkins.

Russia & the Roots of the Chinese Revolution, 1896-1911. Don C. Price. LC 74-80443. (Harvard East Asian Ser.: No. 79). 318p. reprint ed. pap. 90.70 (*0-7837-3858-7*, 2043680) Bks Demand.

Russia & the Rumanian National Cause, 1858-1859. Barbara Jelavich. xv, 169p. (C). 1974. reprint ed. lib. bdg. 30.00 (*0-208-01430-6*, Archon Bks) Shoe String.

Russia & The Soviet Union. 3rd ed. John M. Thompson. LC 93-41558. (C). 1994. pap. text ed. 23.00 (*0-8133-1964-1*) Westview.

Russia & the Third World in the Post-Soviet Era. Ed. by Mohiaddin Mesbahi. 376p. (C). 1994. pap. text ed. 19.95 (*0-8130-1271-6*); lib. bdg. 49.95 (*0-8130-1270-8*) U Press Fla.

Russia & the U. S. S. R. in the 20th Century. 3rd ed. David MacKenzie & Michael W. Curran. LC 96-44924. (C). 1997. pap. text ed. 49.95 (*0-534-51688-2*) Wadsworth Pub.

***Russia & the U. S. S. R. 1905-91.** Phil Ingram. (Histroy Programme Ser.). (Illus.). 64p. (C). 1997. pap. 11.95 (*0-521-56867-6*) Cambridge U Pr.

Russia & the United States. Nikolai V. Sivachev & Nikolai N. Yakovlev. Tr. by Olga A. Titelbaum. LC 78-10554. (United States in the World: Foreign World Perspectives Ser.). 320p. 1980. pap. text ed. 14.50 (*0-226-76150-9*, P902) U Ch Pr.

Russia & the United States: An Analytical Survey of Archival Documents & Historical Studies. N. N. Bolkhovitinov. Ed. & Tr. by J. Dane Hartgrove. LC 86-27955. 88p. (Orig.). (gr. 13). 1986. text ed. 43.95 (*0-87332-414-5*) M E Sharpe.

Russia & the Weimar Republic. Lionel Kochan. LC 78-17679. 190p. 1978. reprint ed. text ed. 49.75 (*0-313-20503-5*, KORW, Greenwood Pr) Greenwood.

Russia & the West in Iran, 1918-1948: A Study in Big Power Rivalry. George Lenczowski. LC 68-23307. (Illus.). 383p. 1968. reprint ed. 69.50 (*0-8371-0144-1*, LERW, Greenwood Pr) Greenwood.

Russia & the West in the Eighteenth Century. Ed. by A. G. Cross. (Illus.). 371p. 1983. 36.00 (*0-685-07028-X*) Orient Res Partners.

Russia & the World: New Views on Foreign Policy. Ed. by Boris D. Pyadyshen. 352p. 1991. 21.95 (*1-55972-087-5*, Birch Ln Pr) Carol Pub Group.

Russia & the World Economy: Problems of Integration. Alan Smith. LC 92-38841. 272p. (C). 1993. pap. 17.95 (*0-415-08925-5*, B2345, Routledge NY) Routledge.

***Russia & the World since 1917.** Kennedy-Pipe. Date not set. text ed. write for info. (*0-340-65204-7*); text ed. write for info. (*0-340-65205-5*) St Martin.

***Russia & U. S. S. R., 1905-1964.** MacDonald. 1994. pap. text ed. write for info. (*0-582-22672-4*, Pub. by Longman UK) Longman.

Russia & World Order: Strategic Choices & the Laws of Power in History. George Liska. LC 79-22872. 1980. 14.50 (*0-8018-2314-5*) Johns Hopkins.

Russia & World Order: Strategic Choices & the Laws of Power in History. George Liska. LC 79-22872. 208p. reprint ed. pap. 59.30 (*0-317-20468-8*, 2023001) Bks Demand.

Russia As State-Capitalist Society: The Original Historical Analysis. Raya Dunayevskaya. 27p. (Orig.). 1973. pap. 1.00 (*0-914441-23-X*) News & Letters.

Russia at the Barricades: Eyewitness Accounts of the August 1991 Coup. Ed. by Victoria E. Bonnell et al. LC 93-27944. (Illus.). 392p. (gr. 13). 1994. text ed. 65.95 (*1-56324-271-0*); pap. text ed. 26.95 (*1-56324-272-9*) M E Sharpe.

Russia at the Crossroads: The Twenty-Sixth Congress of the CPSU. Ed. by Seweryn Bialer & Thane Gustafson. 256p. 1982. text ed. 55.00 (*0-04-329039-6*) Routledge Chapman & Hall.

Russia at the Twenty-First Century: Politics & Social Changes in the Post-Soviet Era. Steve D. Boilard. 224p. (C). 1997. pap. text ed. 19.00 (*0-15-505317-5*) HB Coll Pubs.

Russia at War. Wallace B. Black & Jean F. Blashfield. (World War II 50th Anniversary Ser.). (Illus.). 48p. (J). (gr. 5-6). 1991. lib. bdg. 12.95 (*0-89686-556-8*, Crstwood Hse) Silver Burdett Pr.

Russia at War. Alexander Werth. 1136p. 1984. pap. 17.95 (*0-88184-084-X*) Carroll & Graf.

Russia Before Peter the Great, 900-1700 see Readings in Russian Civilization

Russia by Rail. Athol Yates. LC 96-17017. (Bradt Guides Ser.). 1996. pap. 18.95 (*0-7627-0008-4*) Globe Pequot.

Russia Changes: The Events of August 1991 & the Russian Constitution. Ed. by A. S. Durgo. (Illus.). 162p. 1992. lib. bdg. 69.00 (*1-56072-079-4*) Nova Sci Pubs.

Russia-China-USA: Redefining the Triangle. Ed. by Alexei D. Voskressenski. LC 94-41593. 247p. (C). 1995. lib. bdg. 69.00 (*1-56072-209-6*) Nova Sci Pubs.

Russia Complex: The British Labour Party & the Soviet Union. Bill Jones. 229p. 1977. 38.00 (*0-8476-6082-6*) Rowman.

Russia, Eurasia & the Global Economy. Peter Rutland. LC 95-34838. (Integrating National Economies: Promise & Pitfalls Ser.). 1997. 34.95 (*0-8157-7648-9*); pap. 14.95 (*0-8157-7647-0*) Brookings.

Russia-Eurasia Facts & Figures Annual (REFFA), Vol. 18. Ed. by Krasniak. Orig. Title: U. S. S. R. Facts & Figures Annual. 1993. 95.00 (*0-87569-172-2*) Academic Intl.

Russia, Eurasian States & Eastern Europe, 1996. 27th ed. M. Wesley Shoemaker. 372p. 1996. pap. 14.50 (*1-887985-01-8*) Stryker-Post.

***Russia First.** Truscott. Date not set. text ed. 39.50 (*1-86064-199-7*, Pub. by I B Tauris UK) St Martin.

Russia from the American Embassy April, 1916 to November, 1918. David R. Francis. LC 78-115537. (Russia Observed, Series I). 1970. reprint ed. 26.95 (*0-405-03026-6*) Ayer.

Russia Gathers Her Jews: The Origins of the "Jewish Question" in Russia, 1772-1825. John Klier. LC 86-2473. 1986. 30.00 (*0-87580-117-X*) N Ill U Pr.

Russia Goes Dry: Alcohol, State & Society. Stephen White. (Illus.). 260p. (C). 1995. text ed. 59.95 (*0-521-55211-7*); pap. text ed. 19.95 (*0-521-55849-2*) Cambridge U Pr.

Russia Goes to the Polls: The Election to the All-Russian Constituent Assembly, 1917. Oliver H. Radkey. LC 89-42884. (Cornell Studies in Soviet History & Society - Studies of the Harriman Institute). 192p. 1989. 35.00 (*0-8014-2360-0*) Cornell U Pr.

Russia House. 1989. audio 16.00 (*0-394-57952-6*) Random.

Russia House. John Le Carre. 1989. 19.95 (*0-394-57789-2*) Knopf.

Russia in Central Asia in Eighteen Eighty-Nine & the Anglo-Russian Question. George N. Curzon. (Illus.). 477p. 1967. 55.00 (*0-7146-1465-3*, Pub. by F Cass Pubs UK) Intl Spec Bk.

Russia in Darkness ... on Education & the Future. Boris S. Gershunsky. LC 92-73153. 103p. (Orig.). (C). 1993. pap. 12.95 (*1-880192-04-7*) Caddo Gap Pr.

Russia in Flux. John Maynard. Ed. by S. Haden Guest. LC 83-45812. reprint ed. 48.50 (*0-404-20173-3*) AMS Pr.

Russia in Flux: The Political & Social Consequences of Reform. Ed. by David Lane. 272p. 1992. 80.00 (*1-85278-680-9*) E Elgar.

Russia in Flux: The Political & Social Consequences of Reform. Ed. by David Lane. 272p. 1993. pap. 30.00 (*1-85278-713-9*) E Elgar.

Russia in My Backyard: The Reading. Rhett S. James. 100p. 1995. pap. 14.00 (*0-9643538-0-6*) Wstrn Profiles.

Russia in North America: Proceedings of the Second International Conference on Russian America August 19-22, 1987, Sitka, Alaska. (Alaska History Ser.: No. 35). (Illus.). 1990. 45.00 (*0-919642-44-6*) Limestone Pr.

Russia in Search of Its Future. Ed. by Amin Saikal & William Maley. 256p. (C). 1995. 49.95 (*0-521-48260-7*) Cambridge U Pr.

Russia in Search of Its Future. Ed. by Amin Saikal & William Maley. 256p. (C). 1995. pap. text ed. 18.95 (*0-521-48387-5*) Cambridge U Pr.

Russia in the Age of Catherine the Great. Isabel De Madariaga. LC 80-21993. 710p. reprint ed. pap. 180.00 (*0-8357-8763-X*, 2033704) Bks Demand.

Russia in the Age of Modernization & Revolution, 1881-1917. Hans Rogger. LC 83-714. (History of Russia Ser.). 323p. (Orig.). (C). 1983. pap. text ed. 30.50 (*0-582-48912-1*, 73395) Longman.

Russia in the Age of Reaction & Reform, 1801-1881. David Saunders. LC 92-7477. (History of Russia Ser.). 400p. (C). 1993. pap. text ed. 33.95 (*0-582-48978-4*) Longman.

Russia in the Era of NEP: Explorations in Soviet Society & Culture. Ed. by Sheila Fitzpatrick et al. LC 90-25044. (Indiana-Michigan Series in Russian & East European Studies). (Illus.). 352p. 1991. 35.00 (*0-253-32224-3*); pap. 13.95 (*0-253-20657-X*, MB-657) Ind U Pr.

Russia in the Pacific: A Missing Nation. Vladimir I. Ivanov. (Illus.). 287p. (C). 1997. lib. bdg. 69.00 (*1-56072-218-5*) Nova Sci Pubs.

***Russia in the Post Soviet Scene.** pap. write for info. (*0-340-60149-3*, Pub. by E Arnold UK) Routledge Chapman & Hall.

***Russia in the Post Soviet Scene.** write for info. (*0-340-67679-5*, Pub. by E Arnold UK) Routledge Chapman & Hall.

Russia in the 20th Century: Catalog of the Bakhmeteff Archives. Columbia University Staff. 1992. 120.00 (*0-8161-1796-9*, Hall Library) G K Hall.

Russia in Transition: Policies, Classes & Inequalities. Ed. by David Lane. 292p. (C). 1996. pap. text ed. 22.50 (*0-582-27566-0*) Longman.

Russia Kingdom Come. Lynn R. Eliason. LC 93-93761. 168p. 1994. pap. 4.00 (*1-56002-297-3*, Univ Edtns) Aegina Pr.

Russia Looks at America: The View to 1917. Robert V. Allen. LC 88-600001. 322p. 1988. 20.00 (*0-8444-0593-0*, 030-001-00128) Lib Congress.

Russia, Mongolia & China, 2 vols. John F. Baddeley. 1976. lib. bdg. 500.00 (*0-8490-2549-4*) Gordon Pr.

Russia: New Freedoms, New Challenges see Exploring Cultures of the World - Group 1

Russia Nineteen Seventeen: The February Revolution. George Katkov. LC 78-31187. (Illus.). 489p. 1979. reprint ed. text ed. 85.00 (*0-313-20932-4*, KARU, Greenwood Pr) Greenwood.

Russia Nineteen Seventeen: The Kornilov Affair: Kerensky & the Breakup of the Russian Army. George Katkov. LC 79-41450. (Illus.). 210p. 1980. text ed. 27.00 (*0-582-49101-0*) Longman.

Russia Observed, 91 Vols. Ed. by Harmon Tupper & Harry W. Nerhood. 1970. reprint ed. 2,445.00 (*0-405-03000-2*) Ayer.

***Russia of the Tsars.** Jim Strickler. LC 97-10876. (World History Ser.). (Illus.). (J). (gr. 4-12). 1997. lib. bdg. 17.96 (*1-56006-295-9*) Lucent Bks.

Russia on Canvas: Ilya Repin. Fan Parker & Stephen J. Parker. LC 79-20577. (Illus.). 196p. 1980. 35.00 (*0-271-00252-2*) Pa St U Pr.

Russia on the Threshold of an Uncertain Future. G. Diligensky. 249p. (C). 1995. lib. bdg. 69.00 (*1-56072-214-2*) Nova Sci Pubs.

Russia: or Miscellaneous Observations on the Past & Present State of That Country & Its Inhabitants. Robert Pinkerton. LC 74-115579. (Russia Observed, Series I). 1970. reprint ed. 28.95 (*0-405-03058-4*) Ayer.

Russia, Poland, & Universal Regeneration: Studies in Russian & Polish Thought of the Romantic Epoch. Andrzej Walicki. LC 90-50972. (C). 1991. text ed. 42.50 (*0-268-01641-0*) U of Notre Dame Pr.

Russia, Pt. I, 1859-1914 see British Documents on Foreign Affairs: Series A: Russia/The Soviet Union

Russia Reborn? The Labor Pains of the New Russia. Parker. 1996. 25.00 (*0-02-874078-5*) Free Pr.

Russia, Ritual, & Reform: The Liturgical Reforms of Nikon in the 17th Century. Paul Meyendorff. 256p. (Orig.). 1991. pap. 14.95 (*0-88141-090-X*) St Vladimirs.

Russia, Siberia & Great Tartary. Philip J. Von Strahlenberg. LC 71-115589. (Russia Observed, Series I). 1970. reprint ed. 25.95 (*0-405-03066-5*) Ayer.

Russia since Nineteen Seventeen. J. N. Westwood. LC 79-27598. 1980. text ed. 32.50 (*0-312-69607-8*) St Martin.

Russia Survival Guide: The Definitive Guide to Doing Business & Traveling in Russia. 7th ed. Paul E. Richardson. 260p. 1997. pap. 18.50 (*1-880100-30-4*) Russian Info Srvs.

Russia, the Atom, & the West. George F. Kennan. LC 74-1557. 116p. 1974. reprint ed. text ed. 48.50 (*0-8371-7394-9*, KERU, Greenwood Pr) Greenwood.

Russia, the Soviet Union & the United States: An Interpretive History. 2nd ed. John L. Gaddis. (America & the World Ser.). 360p. 1990. pap. text ed. write for info. (*0-07-557258-3*) McGraw.

Russia Through Women's Eyes: Autobiographies from Tsarist Russia. Ed. by Toby W. Clyman & Judith Vowles. LC 96-16374. (Illus.). 352p. 1996. 35.00 (*0-300-06753-4*) Yale U Pr.

Russia to the Revolution. Susan Finney & Patricia C. Kindle. (Gifted Learning Ser.). 64p. (J). (gr. 4-8). teacher ed. 8.99 (*0-86653-398-2*, GA1020) Good Apple.

Russia Today: Atlas for Business & Political Decision Makers. (Illus.). 120p. 1996. 149.00 (*0-9646241-4-1*) Russ Info & Busn Ctr.

Russia Transformed. Dimitry Mikheyev. (Hudson Institute Book Ser.). 288p. (Orig.). (C). 1996. pap. 12.95 (*1-55813-054-3*) Hudson Instit IN.

Russia Transformed: Breakthrough to Hope, August 1991. James H. Billington. 202p. 1992. text ed. 24.95 (*0-02-903515-5*, Free Press) Free Pr.

Russia Twenty Years After: Includes Thirty Years after the Russian Revolution. Victor Serge. Tr. by Max Shachtman from FRE. LC 95-49359. (Revolutionary Studies). 350p. (C). 1996. pap. 19.95 (0-391-03855-9) Humanities.

Russia, Ukraine & Belarus: Travel Survival Kit. Richard Nebesky et al. (Illus.). 1200p. 1996. pap. 27.95 (0-86442-320-9) Lonely Planet.

Russia under Bolshevik Regime. Richard Pipes. 1995. pap. 19.00 (0-679-76184-5, Vin) Random.

Russia under Catherine the Great, 2 vols., 1. Paul Dukes. 1978. 12.00 (0-89250-106-5) Orient Res Partners.

Russia under Catherine the Great, 2 vols., 2. Paul Dukes. 1978. 12.00 (0-89250-105-7) Orient Res Partners.

Russia under Catherine the Great, 2 vols., Set. Paul Dukes. 1978. 24.00 (0-89250-104-9) Orient Res Partners.

Russia under Peter the Great. Francois-Marie De Voltaire. Tr. by M. F. Jenkins. LC 81-72050. 340p. 1984. 40.00 (0-8386-3148-7) Fairleigh Dickinson.

Russia under the Old Regime. Pipes. 1984. 21.75 (0-684-14826-9) S&S Trade.

Russia under the Old Regime. Richard Pipes. 1997. pap. 12.95 (0-14-024768-8) Viking Penguin.

Russia under the Old Regime. Richard E. Pipes. LC 74-32564. 360p. 1976. pap. write for info. (0-02-395700-X, Macmillan Coll) P-H.

Russia Versus China & What Next? Yung-Hwan Jo & Ying-Hsien Pi. LC 80-1404. 164p. 1980. lib. bdg. 48.00 (0-8191-1237-2) U Pr of Amer.

Russia, World War III & Armageddon. audio 7.00 (1-884137-77-6) J Van Impe.

***Russia: Yesterday, Today, Tomorrow: Voice of the Young Generation.** Victor Pavlenkov. Ed. by Peter Pappas. (Illus.). 295p. (Orig.). 1997. pap. 12.95 (0-9637035-5-2) FC-Izdat.

Russia, 1472-1917 see West in Russia & China: Religious & Secular Thought in Modern Times

***Russia 1881-1921 from Tsarism to Communism.** McClgan. 1994. pap. text ed. write for info. (0-05-005087-7) Addison-Wesley.

Russia 2010: And What It Means for the West. Daniel H. Yergin. 1995. pap. 13.00 (0-679-75922-0, Vin) Random.

***Russian.** (Rough Guide Phrasebooks Ser.). 272p. 1997. pap. 6.00 (1-85828-251-9, Penguin Bks) Viking Penguin.

Russian. Harrap's Books Limited Staff. (Indispensable Ser.). 128p. 1992. pap. 13.00 (0-13-391129-2, Harraps IN) Macmillan Gen Ref.

Russian. Natalia Lusin. (Master the Basics Ser.). 290p. 1995. pap. 10.95 (0-8120-9164-7) Barron.

Russian. rev. ed. Frank Hill. (LanguageCard Pac Ser.). 1993. Incl. 4 language cards. 4.00 (0-88699-006-8) Travel Sci.

Russian. 3rd ed. Clark. 1982. text ed. 62.95 (0-8384-3551-3) Heinle & Heinle.

Russian. 3rd ed. Clark. (College Russian Ser.). 1982. suppl. ed., pap. 28.95 incl. audio (0-8384-3552-1) Heinle & Heinle.

Russian. 3rd ed. Clark. (College Russian Ser.). 1982. teacher ed., pap. 6.95 (0-8384-3553-X) Heinle & Heinle.

Russian: A Practical Grammar with Exercises. I. M. Pulkina. 582p. (C). 1992. 17.95 (0-8285-4993-1) Firebird NY.

Russian: A Practical Grammar with Exercises. Ed. by I. M. Pulkina & E. Zakhlava-Nekrasova. 584p. (C). 1988. 80.00 (0-569-09174-8, Pub. by Collets) St Mut.

Russian: Stage Two. ACTR Staff. 440p. 1993. per. 48.00 (0-8403-7961-7) Kendall-Hunt.

***Russian - English - German - French Dictionary of Computer Science Basic Terms.** E. K. Maslovskii et al. 393p. (Orig.). (ENG, FRE, GER & RUS.). (C). 1990. pap. 15.95 (0-8285-5290-8) Firebird NY.

***Russian - English Dictionary.** 9th rev. ed. A. M. Taube et al. 624p. (ENG & RUS.). (C). 1993. 16.95 (0-8285-0609-4) Firebird NY.

***Russian - English Dictionary.** 34th rev. ed. O. S. Akhmanova. Ed. by E. A. Wilson. 536p. (ENG & RUS.). 1987. 7.95 (0-8285-0607-8) Firebird NY.

Russian - English Dictionary of Disarmament. T. F. Dmitrichev. (ENG & RUS.). 1990. 125.00 (0-8288-3973-5, F39625) Fr & Eur.

***Russian - English Dictionary of Microbiological Terms.** V. A. Dmitrieva & V. V. Dmitriev. 248p. (ENG & RUS.). (C). 1991. 21.95 (0-8285-5310-6) Firebird NY.

Russian - English Geological Dictionary. American Geological Society Staff. 559p. (ENG & RUS.). 1993. reprint ed. lib. bdg. 49.95 (0-7859-3711-0) Fr & Eur.

***Russian - English Phrasebook.** G. A. Sorokin et al. 312p. (Orig.). (ENG & RUS.). 1986. pap. 4.95 (0-8285-3212-5) Firebird NY.

Russian - English Picture Dictionary. Claudia Schwalm. (Illus.). 89p. (J). (gr. k-6). 1995. 22.95 incl. audio (1-57371-003-2) Cultural Cnnect.

***Russian - English Technical Dictionary of Defects & Disrepair.** N. N. Levinskii & G. A. Mkrtchian. 334p. (ENG & RUS.). (C). 1985. 12.95 (0-8285-5307-6) Firebird NY.

Russian - Italian, Italian - Russian Economic & Commercial Dictionary. Vladimir Kovalev. 702p. (ITA & RUS.). 1993. 125.00 (0-685-63260-1) Fr & Eur.

Russian ABC: Featuring Masterpieces from the Hermitage, St. Petersburg. Florence C. Mayers. (ABC Ser.). (Illus.). 36p. (J). 1992. 12.95 (0-8109-1919-2) Abrams.

Russian Adult Humor: Naughty Tales of Old Russia. Ed. by Aleksandr Afanasiev. Tr. by G. Perkoff from RUS. (Illus.). 118p. (Orig.). 1996. pap. 7.95 (1-57201-022-3) Berkeley Slavic.

Russian Advertising Directory. (Russian Business Library). (Illus.). 300p. (Orig.). 1996. pap. 99.00 (1-57751-013-5) Russ Info & Busn Ctr.

***Russian Advertising Directory.** 2nd rev. ed. Russian Information & Business Center, Inc. Staff. (Russian Business Library). 400p. 1997. pap. 99.00 (1-57751-317-7) Russ Info & Busn Ctr.

Russian Air Force in the Eyes of German Commanders. Walter Schwabedissen. LC 68-22552. (German Air Force in World War 2 Ser.). (Illus.). 1968. reprint ed. 18.95 (0-405-00047-2) Ayer.

Russian Album: Bourgeois Culture at the Turn of the Century. Asuncion Lavrin. 1995. 15.98 (0-8317-1888-9) Smithmark.

Russian, Alexander Pushkin: Tales of Belkin, 3 cassettes, Set. 168p. 1987. pap. 49.50 incl. audio (1-57970-013-6, SRU260) Audio-Forum.

Russian Alphabet & Phonetics. Leon Stilman. LC 51-4951. (Columbia Slavic Studies). 30p. (YA). (gr. 9 up). 1951. pap. text ed. 16.50 (0-231-09922-3) Col U Pr.

Russian America: Seventeen Forty-One to Eighteen Sixty-Seven, a Biographical Dictionary. Richard A. Pierce. (Alaska History Ser.: No. 33). (Illus.). 1990. 45.00 (0-919642-45-4) Limestone Pr.

Russian America: The Great Alaskan Venture 1741-1867. Hector Chevigny. LC 65-12027. 288p. 1992. reprint ed. pap. 9.95 (0-8323-0320-8) Binford Mort.

Russian American Colonies: A Documentary Record, 1798-1867. Ed. by Basil Dmytryshyn et al. (To Siberia & Russian America Ser.: Vol. 3). (Illus.). 650p. 1989. 40.00 (0-87595-150-3) Oregon Hist.

Russian-American Company Correspondence: Communications Sent-1818. Tr. by Richard A. Pierce from RUS. (Alaska History Ser.: No. 25). (Illus.). 1984. 30.00 (0-919642-02-0) Limestone Pr.

Russian-American Dialogue on Cultural Relations, 1776-1914. Ed. by Norman E. Saul et al. LC 96-31075. (Russian-American Dialogues on United States History Ser.: Vol. III). 280p. (C). 1996. 42.50 (0-8262-1097-X) U of Mo Pr.

Russian-American Dialogue on the American Revolution. Ed. by Gordon S. Wood & Louise G. Wood. (Russian-American Dialogues on United States History Ser.: Vol. 2). 304p. (C). 1995. 42.50 (0-8262-1020-1) U of Mo Pr.

Russian-American Feasts. Leda Voropaeff. 1996. 19.95 (0-533-11782-8) Vantage.

***Russian-American Relations & the Sale of Alaska, 1834-1867.** Nikolai N. Bolkhovitinov. Tr. by Richard A. Pierce. (Alaska History Ser.: No. 45). (Illus.). 394p. 1997. 35.00 (1-895901-06-5) Limestone Pr.

Russian-American Seminar on Critical Thinking & the Library: Papers from the Seminar, Moscow, June 1-5, 1992. Ed. by Cerise Oberman & Dennis Kimmage. (Occasional Papers: No. 200/201). 160p. (Orig.). 1995. pap. 15.00 (0-614-15032-9) U of Ill Grad Sch.

Russian Americans. Paul R. Magocsi. Ed. by Sandra Stotsky. LC 95-12599. 110p. (YA). (gr. 7 up). 1995. lib. bdg. 19.95 (0-7910-3367-8) Chelsea Hse.

Russian Americans see Cultures of America - Group 3

Russian & East European Publications in the Libraries of the United States. Melville J. Ruggles & Vaclav Mostecky. LC 73-437. (Illus.). 396p. 1973. reprint ed. text ed. 65.00 (0-8371-6767-1, RURE, Greenwood Pr) Greenwood.

Russian & East European Studies, Vol. 1: Econ. Reform in Poland: The Aftermath of M. Ed. by Steven K. Batalden & Thomas Noonan. 278p. 1991. 73.25 (1-55938-288-0) Jai Pr.

Russian & East European Studies, Vol. 2: On the Heights of Creation: Lyrics by Fedo. Ed. by Steven K. Batalden & Thomas Noonan. 330p. 1993. 73.25 (0-614-09950-1) Jai Pr.

Russian & East European Studies, Vol. 3: Playing Politics: Soviet Sport Diplomacy t. Ed. by Steven K. Batalden & Thomas Noonan. 184p. 1993. 73.25 (1-55938-472-7) Jai Pr.

Russian & East European Studies, Vol. 4. Ed. by Steven K. Batalden & Thomas Noonan. 1996. 73.25 (1-55938-899-4) Jai Pr.

Russian & Eastern European History: Selected Papers from the Second World Congress for Soviet & East European Studies. Ed. by Ralph C. Elwood. 306p. 1984. pap. 12.00 (0-933884-28-1) Berkeley Slavic.

Russian & German Dictionary of Chemistry & Chemical Engineering: Chemie & Chemische Technik. 5th ed. Helmut Gross. 832p. (GER & RUS.). 1987. 150.00 (0-8288-0870-8, F 47440) Fr & Eur.

Russian & German Dictionary of Electrical Engineering: Elektrotechnik-Elektronik. 4th ed. Helmut Gross. 464p. (GER & RUS.). 1982. 95.00 (0-8288-0931-3, M7841) Fr & Eur.

Russian & Japanese Prize Cases, 2 vols. Ed. by C. B. Hurst et al. Vols. 1 & 2. 1972. reprint ed. 90.00 (0-318-56356-8, 300630) W S Hein.

***Russian & Japanese Prize Cases, 2 vols.** Ed. by C. B. Hurst et al. 1972. reprint ed. 90.00 (1-57588-266-3, 300630) W S Hein.

Russian & Japanese Prize Cases, Vol. 1. Ed. by C. B. Hurst et al. LC 72-76352. (International Military Law & History Ser.: Vols. 1 & 2). 382p. 1972. reprint ed. 45.00 (0-930342-43-7, 300630) W S Hein.

Russian & Japanese Prize Cases, Vol. 2. Ed. by C. B. Hurst et al. LC 72-76352. (International Military Law & History Ser.: Vols. 1 & 2). 476p. 1972. reprint ed. 45.00 (0-930342-44-5, 300630) W S Hein.

Russian & Polish Women's Fiction. Ed. & Tr. by Helena Goscilo. LC 84-20915. 360p. 1985. pap. text ed. 20.00 (0-87049-472-4) U of Tenn Pr.

Russian & Serbocroatian Economics Dictionary: Ekonomski Recnik. Milan Bogdanovic. 463p. (RUS & SER.). 1984. 39.95 (0-8288-1281-0, F14121) Fr & Eur.

Russian & Slavic Grammar Studies 1931-1981. Roman Jakobson. Ed. by Linda Wough & Morris Halle. xvi, 160p. 1984. text ed. 49.50 (90-279-3029-5) Mouton.

***Russian & Soviet Economic Performance & Structure.** 6th ed. Gregory Stuart. (C). 1998. text ed. write for info. (0-321-01427-8) Addson-Wesley Educ.

Russian & Soviet Education, 1731-1989: A Multilingual Annotated Bibliography. William W. Brickman & John T. Zepper. LC 91-45874. (Reference Books in International Education: Vol. 9). 556p. 1992. text ed. 89.00 (0-8240-9052-7, SS200) Garland.

Russian & Soviet Music: Essays for Boris Schwarz. Ed. by Malcolm H. Brown. LC 84-50049. (Russian Music Studies: No. 11). (Illus.). 335p. reprint ed. pap. 95.50 (0-8357-1545-0, 2070534) Bks Demand.

***Russian & Soviet Peasantry 1880-1991.** Channon. 1997. pap. text ed. write for info. (0-582-09807-6, Pub. by Longman UK) Longman.

Russian & Soviet Policy in Manchuria & Outer Mongolia, 1911-1931. Peter S. Tang. LC 59-7084. 518p. reprint ed. pap. 147.70 (0-8357-9117-3, 2017935) Bks Demand.

Russian & Soviet Theatre Tradition & the Avantgarde. V. Rudnitsky. (C). 1990. 400.00 (0-685-34352-9, Pub. by Collets) St Mut.

Russian Annexation of Bessarabia. George F. Jewsbury. (East European Monographs: No. 15). 199p. 1976. text ed. 60.00 (0-914710-09-5) East Eur Monographs.

Russian Antisemitism, Pamyat & the Demonology of Zionism. William Korey. (Studies in Antisemitism: Vol. 2). 350p. 1995. text ed. 59.00 (3-7186-5740-6, Harwood Acad Pubs); pap. text ed. 29.00 (3-7186-5742-2, Harwood Acad Pubs) Gordon & Breach.

Russian Apocalypse: Songs & Tales about the Coming of Christianity to Russia. Robert Mann. 151p. (C). 1987. 12.95 (0-87291-172-1) Coronado Pr.

Russian Applied Art: 13th to Early 20th Centuries. Trofimova. 280p. (C). 1982. 138.00 (0-685-34474-6, Pub. by Collets) St Mut.

Russian Applied Art: 13th to Early 20th Centuries. T. Trofimova. (Illus.). 280p. (C). 1982. text ed. 160.00 (0-685-40314-9, Pub. by Collets) St Mut.

Russian Applied Art: 13th to Early 20th Centuries in the Collection of the Vladimir Suzdal Museum Reserve. Trofimova. 280p. (ENG & RUS.). 1982. 83.00 (0-317-57425-6) St Mut.

Russian Approaches to Peacekeeping Operations. (UNDIR Research Papers: No. 28). 182p. Date not set. pap. 32.00 (92-9045-094-0, E.GV.94.0.18) UN.

Russian-Arabic Dictionary. deluxe ed. 1056p. (ARA & RUS.). 1979. 39.95 (0-8288-4834-3, M9073) Fr & Eur.

Russian-Arabic Medical Dictionary. G. T. Arslanian. 622p. (ARA & RUS.). 1983. 49.95 (0-8288-1158-X, M15440) Fr & Eur.

Russian Architecture of the Soviet Period. Aleksei A. Ikonnikov. 398p. (C). 1988. text ed. 100.00 (0-569-08953-0, Pub. by Collets) St Mut.

Russian Arms & Armour: The Armoury of the Moscow Kremlin & the Historical Museum, Moscow. Alexander Sedov & Mikhail Portnov. 208p. 1982. 154.00 (0-317-57428-0) St Mut.

Russian Army & Fleet in the Nineteenth Century: A Handbook of Armaments, Personnel & Policy. L. G. Beskrovny. Ed. by Gordon E. Smith. 405p. 1996. lib. bdg. 50.00 (0-87569-139-0) Academic Intl.

Russian Army & the Japanese War, 2 vols. Alekei N. Kuropatkin. 1976. lib. bdg. 134.95 (0-8490-2550-8) Gordon Pr.

Russian Army in a Time of Troubles. Pavel K. Baev. (Peace Research Institute, Oslo Ser.). 224p. 1996. 75.00 (0-7619-5186-5); pap. 27.95 (0-7619-5187-3) Sage.

Russian Army of the Crimean War, 1854-56. R. Thomas. (Men-at-Arms Ser.: No. 241). (Illus.). 48p. pap. 11.95 (1-85532-161-0, 9199, Pub. by Osprey UK) Stackpole.

Russian Army of the Seven Years War. Angus Konstam. (Illus.). 48p. 1996. pap. 12.95 (1-85532-585-3, Pub. by Osprey UK) Stackpole.

***Russian Army of the Seven Years War No. 2: Cavalry & Artillery.** Angus Konstam. (Men-at-Arms Ser.: No. 298). (Illus.). 48p. 1996. pap. 12.95 (1-85532-587-X, Pub. by Osprey UK) Stackpole.

Russian Army 1794-1814, Vol. 1. Philip J. Haythornthwaite. (Men-at-Arms Ser.: No. 185). (Illus.). 48p. pap. 11.95 (0-85045-737-8, 9117, Pub. by Osprey UK) Stackpole.

Russian Army 1798-1814, Vol. 2: Cavalry 1799-1814. Michael Barthorp. (Men-at-Arms Ser.: No. 189). (Illus.). 48p. pap. 11.95 (0-85045-746-7, 9122, Pub. by Osprey UK) Stackpole.

Russian Art & American Money, 1900-1940. Robert C. Williams. LC 79-16925. (Illus.). 319p. reprint ed. pap. 91.00 (0-7837-3838-2, 2043660) Bks Demand.

Russian Art from Neoclassicism to the Avant-Garde 1800-1917: Painting, Sculpture, Architecture. Dmitri V. Sarabianov. (Illus.). 320p. 1990. 65.00 (0-8109-3750-6) Abrams.

Russian Art Nouveau. B. Borisova. (C). 1990. 650.00 (0-685-34385-5, Pub. by Collets) St Mut.

Russian Art of the Avant-Garde Theory & Criticism, 1902-1934. L. Bowlt. (C). 1990. pap. 160.00 (0-685-34351-0, Pub. by Collets) St Mut.

Russian As We Speak It. S. Khavronina. 237p. 1989. pap. text ed. 6.95 (0-8285-4955-9) Firebird NY.

Russian As We Speak It. S. Khavronina. 236p. (ENG & RUS.). (C). 1989. 60.00 (0-569-09281-7, Pub. by Collets) St Mut.

Russian at a Glance. Thomas Beyer. 1991. pap. 6.95 (0-8120-4299-9) Barron.

Russian Autocracy in Crisis, 1878-1882. Peter A. Zaionchkovsky. (Russian Ser.: Vol. 33). 1979. 40.00 (0-87569-031-9) Academic Intl.

Russian Autocracy under Alexander III. Peter A. Zaionchkovsky. Ed. & Tr. by David R. Jones. (Russian Ser.: Vol. 22). 1976. 40.00 (0-87569-067-X) Academic Intl.

Russian Autocrats from Ivan the Great to the Fall of the Romanov Dynasty: An Annotated Bibliography of English Language Sources to 1985. David R. Egan & Melinda A. Egan. LC 86-26003. 548p. 1987. 49.50 (0-8108-1958-9) Scarecrow.

Russian Avant Garde. Catherine Cooke. 1995. pap. 50.00 (1-85490-390-X) Academy Ed UK.

Russian Avant-Garde. Ed. by Catherine Cooke. (Architectural Design Ser.: No. 47). (Illus.). 96p. (Orig.). 1983. pap. 21.95 (0-85670-832-1) Academy Ed UK.

Russian Avant-Garde: Art & Architecture. Ed. by Catherine Cooke. (Academy Editions Ser.). (Illus.). 96p. 1984. pap. 21.95 (0-312-69612-4) St Martin.

Russian Avant Garde & American Abstract Artists. (Illus.). 69p. 1983. 8.00 (0-930794-84-2) Station Hill Pr.

Russian Avant-Garde Books, 1917-34. Susan Compton. LC 92-22918. (Illus.). 175p. 1992. 29.95 (0-262-03201-5) MIT Pr.

Russian Avant-Garde-Costakis Collection. C. Cooke. (C). 1990. 600.00 (0-685-34349-9, Pub. by Collets) St Mut.

Russian Avantgarde: Art & Architecture. C. Cooke. (C). 1990. pap. 80.00 (0-685-34350-2, Pub. by Collets) St Mut.

Russian Avantgarde: Art & Russian Constructivism. V. Lodder. (C). 1990. 450.00 (0-685-34347-2, Pub. by Collets); pap. 190.00 (0-685-34348-0, Pub. by Collets) St Mut.

Russian Ballet in Western Europe, 1909-1920. W. A. Propert. LC 72-86601. (Illus.). 1972. reprint ed. 36.95 (0-405-08865-5, Pub. by Blom Pubns UK) Ayer.

***Russian Banks & Financial Institutions Directory.** 2nd rev. ed. Russian Information & Business Center, Inc. Staff. (Russian Business Library). 400p. 1997. pap. 99.00 (1-57751-324-X) Russ Info & Busn Ctr.

Russian Banks & Financial Institutions, '96. 2nd rev. ed. (Russian Business Library). (Illus.). 300p. 1996. pap. 149.00 (1-57751-016-X) Russ Info & Busn Ctr.

Russian Bear. Joseph Meek. (Mountain Jack Pike Ser.: No. 7). 1991. mass mkt. 3.50 (1-55817-467-2, Pinncle Kensgtn) Kensgtn Pub Corp.

***Russian Beauty.** Victor Erofeyev. 344p. 3.98 (0-8317-9185-3) Smithmark.

Russian Beauty. Vladimir Nabokov. 1976. 22.95 (0-8488-0838-X) Amereon Ltd.

Russian Bishop's House. NPS Staff. (Illus.). 16p. 1995. pap. 2.95 (0-614-04305-0) Alaska Natural.

Russian Blood. Alex Shoumatoff. 1990. pap. 12.95 (0-679-72578-4, Vin) Random.

Russian Blue Cat. Ingeborg Urcia. 1992. pap. 14.95 (0-9634121-0-8) Elias Holl Pr.

Russian Blue Cats, 2 vols., Set. Stuart A. Kallen. (Cats Ser.). (J). 1998. lib. bdg. 13.98 (1-56239-583-1) Abdo & Dghtrs.

Russian Blues, Faceted & Fancy Beads from the West African Trade, Vol. V. John Picard & Ruth Picard. (Beads from the West African Trade Ser.). (Illus.). 44p. (Orig.). 1989. pap. 15.00 (0-9622884-0-3) Picard African.

Russian Bolshevism & British Labor: 1917-1921. Morton Cowden. 238p. 1984. text ed. 52.50 (0-88033-045-7) East Eur Monographs.

***Russian Book of Life Vol. 2: Youth Version.** Ed. by Vern Peterson. (Book of Life Ser.: Vol. 39). (Illus.). 64p. (Orig.). (ENG & RUS.). (YA). (gr. 7 up). 1997. mass mkt. write for info. (1-890525-02-2) Bk of Life.

***Russian Book of Life Vol. 3: Children's Version.** 2nd rev. ed. Ed. by Vern Peterson. (Book of Life Ser.: Vol. 40). (Illus.). 64p. (ENG & RUS.). (J). (gr. 1-7). 1997. mass mkt. write for info. (1-890525-01-4) Bk of Life.

Russian-Bulgarian Dictionary. Leonidova. 463p. (BUL & RUS.). 1978. 14.95 (0-8288-5269-3, M9101) Fr & Eur.

Russian-Bulgarian Machine-Building Dictionary. Technika. 1981. 75.00 (0-8288-2097-X, F10027) Fr & Eur.

Russian Bureau: A Case Study in Wilsonian Diplomacy. Linda Killen. LC 83-10403. 216p. 1983. 24.00 (0-8131-1495-0) U Pr of Ky.

***Russian Business & Investment Services Directory.** 2nd rev. ed. Russian Information & Business Center, Inc. Staff. (Russian Business Library). 400p. 1997. pap. 99.00 (1-57751-319-3) Russ Info & Busn Ctr.

Russian Business Law Handbook. Ed. by H. Timanova. 207p. (RUS.). 1993. pap. 54.95 (5-85270-053-3) Austin & Winfield.

***Russian Business Relationships.** Hertz. LC 97-12060. 1997. text ed. 69.95 (0-312-17369-5) St Martin.

***Russian Business Survival Guide.** 2nd rev. ed. Russian Information & Business Center, Inc. Staff. (Russian Business Library). 400p. 1997. pap. 99.00 (1-57751-309-6) Russ Info & Busn Ctr.

Russian Business White & Yellow Pages: 25,000 Business Contacts in Russia & Worldwide. Ed. by Igor S. Oleynik. (Illus.). 1200p. (Orig.). (C). 1996. pap. 99.00 (0-9646241-0-9) Russ Info & Busn Ctr.

Russian by Subjects: A Classified Vocabulary. Compiled by Patrick Waddington. 93p. (C). 1992. reprint ed. pap. 13.95 (1-85399-246-1, Pub. by Brstl Class Pr UK) Focus Pub-R Pullins.

Russian Campaign, Eighteen Hundred Twelve. Raymond Montesquiou-Fezensac. LC 70-90563. 159p. reprint ed. pap. 45.40 (0-318-34879-9, 2031091) Bks Demand.

Russian Cassette Pack. Berlitz Editors. (Cassette Pack Ser.). 1993. audio 15.95 (2-8315-1103-8) Berlitz.

Russian-Catalan Dictionary: Diccionari Rus-Catala. Dorota Szmidt. 487p. 1988. write for info. (0-7859-4909-7) Fr & Eur.

Russian Central Asia: Including Kuldja, Bokhara, Khiva & Merv. Henry Lansdell. LC 79-115556. (Russia Observed, Series I). 1970. reprint ed. 70.95 (0-405-03041-X) Ayer.

An Asterisk (*) at the beginning of an entry indicates that the title is appearing in BIP for the first time.

Russian Centralism & Ukrainian Autonomy: Imperial Absorption of the Hetmanate, 1760s-1830s. Zenon E. Kohut. LC 88-42807. (Monograph Ser.). 360p. 1990. 17.00 (*0-916458-17-2*) Harvard Ukrainian.
Russian Century: A History of the Last 100 Years. Brian Moynahan. 1995. pap. 15.00 (*0-679-76436-4*) Random.
Russian Century: Birth of a Nation, 1894-1994. Brian Moynahan. 1994. 45.00 (*0-679-42075-4*) Random.
***Russian Century: Russia's Global Legacy.** Steven Marks. 256p. Date not set. pap. 15.00 (*0-465-07162-7*) Basic.
***Russian Century: Russia's Global Legacy.** Steven Marks. 256p. 1998. 28.00 (*0-465-07161-9*) Basic.
***Russian Charity, Religions & Non-Profit Organizations.** 2nd rev. ed. Russian Information & Business Center, Inc. Staff. (Russian Business Library). 400p. 1997. pap. 99.00 (*1-57751-318-5*) Russ Info & Busn Ctr.
Russian Charity, Religious & Non-Profit Organizations. 2nd rev. ed. (Russian Business Library). 1996. pap. 99.00 (*1-57751-014-3*) Russ Info & Busn Ctr.
Russian Childhood. S. Kovalevskaya. (Illus.). 1978. 64.95 (*0-387-90348-8*) Spr-Verlag.
Russian-Chinese Dictionary of Export & Economics. deluxe ed. 708p. (CHI & RUS.). 1961. 39.95 (*0-8288-6827-1*, M-9068) Fr & Eur.
Russian-Chinese-English Glossary of Education. C. T. Hu & Beatrice Beach. LC 73-108419. (Columbia University, Center for Education in Asia, Publications). 127p. reprint ed. pap. 36.20 (*0-317-41942-0*, 2026023) Bks Demand.
Russian Church & Russian Dissent. Albert F. Heard. LC 70-127907. reprint ed. 42.50 (*0-404-03198-6*) AMS Pr.
Russian Church & the Soviet State, 1917-1950. John S. Curtiss. 1953. 14.50 (*0-8446-1141-7*) Peter Smith.
Russian Church Singing: Orthodox Worship & Hymnography, Vol. I. Johann Von Gardner. LC 79-27480. 146p. 1980. pap. 10.95 (*0-913836-59-1*) St Vladimirs.
Russian Church under the Soviet Regime, Set. Dimitry V. Pospielovsky. LC 84-5336. 533p. 1984. pap. 26.95 (*0-88141-033-0*) St Vladimirs.
Russian Church under the Soviet Regime, Vol. I. Dimitry V. Pospielovsky. LC 84-5336. 248p. 1984. pap. 10.95 (*0-88141-015-2*) St Vladimirs.
Russian Church under the Soviet Regime, Vol. II. Dimitry V. Pospielovsky. LC 84-5336. 285p. 1984. pap. 11.95 (*0-88141-016-0*) St Vladimirs.
Russian City Between Tradition & Modernity: 1850-1900. Daniel R. Brower. 1990. 45.00 (*0-520-06764-9*) U CA Pr.
Russian Civil-Military Relations. Dale R. Herspring. LC 96-11635. 272p. 1997. text ed. 35.00 (*0-253-33225-7*) Ind U Pr.
Russian Civil War. Evan Mawdsley. (Illus.). 320p. (C). 1987. text ed. 55.00 (*0-04-947024-8*); pap. text ed. 18.95 (*0-04-947025-6*) Routledge Chapman & Hall.
Russian Civil War: Documents from the Soviet Archives. V. P. Butt. LC 96-19904. 1997. text ed. 69.95 (*0-312-16337-1*) St Martin.
Russian Civil War Diary: Alexis V. Babine in Saratov, 1917-1922. Ed. by Donald J. Raleigh. LC 88-3967. (Illus.). xxiv, 264p. 1988. text ed. 35.95 (*0-8223-0835-5*) Duke.
Russian Civilization. David A. Law. (Illus.). 490p. (C). 1975. 39.50 (*0-8422-5232-0*); pap. text ed. 12.50 (*0-8422-0529-2*) Irvington.
Russian Classics, Leo Tolstoi: Fables, Tales, Stories, 2 cassettes, Set. 84p. pap. 39.50 incl. audio (*1-57970-011-X*, SRU115) Audio-Forum.
Russian Classics, Nikolai Gogol: The Overcoat, 2 cassettes, Set. 72p. (YA). 1993. pap. 39.50 incl. audio (*1-57970-012-8*, SRU120) Audio-Forum.
Russian Clergy. Jean X. Gagarin. LC 70-131035. reprint ed. 39.50 (*0-404-02666-4*) AMS Pr.
Russian Colonial Expansion to 1917. Ed. by Michael Rywkin. LC 84-71094. (Issue Studies (U. S. S. R. & East Europe): No. 4). xviii, 274p. 1988. 30.00 (*0-7201-1867-0*) Assn Study Nat.
Russian Comedy of Errors: With Other Stories & Sketches of Russian Life. George F. Kennan. LC 72-11847. (Short Story Index Reprint Ser.). 1977. reprint ed. 25.95 (*0-8369-4238-8*) Ayer.
Russian Common Usage Dictionary. 1987. pap. 3.00 (*0-517-51268-8*, Living Language) Crown Pub Group.
Russian Community Guide. 1981. write for info. (*0-935090-07-X*) Almanac Pr.
Russian Community Guide. 1983. write for info. (*0-935090-08-8*) Almanac Pr.
Russian Community Guide. 1989. write for info. (*0-935090-22-3*) Almanac Pr.
Russian Community Reference Guide. 48p. 1980. pap. write for info. (*0-935090-04-5*) Almanac Pr.
Russian Community Reference Guide. 78p. 1984. pap. write for info. (*0-935090-12-6*) Almanac Pr.
Russian Community Reference Guide. 96p. 1985. pap. write for info. (*0-935090-15-0*) Almanac Pr.
Russian Community Reference Guide. 96p. 1987. write for info. (*0-935090-19-3*) Almanac Pr.
Russian Community Reference Guide. 1988. write for info. (*0-935090-20-7*) Almanac Pr.
Russian Composers & Musicians: A Biographical Dictionary. Ed. by Alexandria Vodorsky-Shiraeff. LC 71-76422. (Music Ser.). 1969. reprint ed. lib. bdg. 25.00 (*0-306-71321-7*) Da Capo.
Russian Composition & Conversation. C. R. Buxton. 184p. 1994. pap. 14.95 (*0-8442-4221-7*, Natl Textbk) NTC Pub Grp.
Russian Concept of Work: Suffering, Drama, & Tradition in Pre & Post Revolutionary Russia. Anna F. Leibovich. LC 95-3869. 184p. 1995. text ed. 52.95 (*0-275-95135-9*, Praeger Pubs) Greenwood.
***Russian Conquest of the Caucasus.** J. F. Baddeley. (Illus.). 660p. 1997. reprint ed. 120.00 (*0-7007-0634-8*, Pub. by Curzon Pr UK) Paul & Co Pubs.
Russian Constitutional Experiment: Government & Duma, 1907-1914. Geoffrey A. Hosking. LC 72-87181. (Soviet & East European Studies). 291p. reprint ed. pap. 83.00 (*0-317-28403-7*, 2022456) Bks Demand.
Russian Constructivism & Iakov Chernikhov. Ed. by Catherine Cooke. (Architectural Design Ser.: No. 80). (Illus.). 96p. (Orig.). 1989. pap. 21.95 (*1-85490-019-6*) Academy Ed UK.
Russian Contributions to Inverterbrate Behavior. Ed. by Charles I. Abramson et al. LC 95-40578. 256p. 1996. text ed. 75.00 (*0-275-94525-1*, Praeger Pubs) Greenwood.
Russian Cookbook. Ed. by Sergey Morkovine. (Illus.). 32p. (Orig.). 1994. pap. 4.99 (*0-9643971-2-9*) Isometry.
Russian Cookbook. Kyra Petrovskaya. LC 92-10473. Orig. Title: Kyra's Secrets of Russian Cooking. 224p. 1992. reprint ed. pap. text ed. 5.95 (*0-486-27329-6*) Dover.
***Russian Cooking.** Vladimir Usov. Ed. by Natalya Lozinskaya. Tr. by Irina Avdeyeva from RUS. (Illus.). 207p. (Orig.). 1992. pap. 6.95 (*0-8285-5174-X*) Firebird NY.
Russian Copper Icons & Crosses from the Kunz Collection: Castings of Faith. Ed. by Richard E. Ahlborn & Vera B. Espinola. LC 90-19630. (Illus.). 92p. (Orig.). (C). 1991. pap. text ed. 16.95 (*1-56098-068-0*) Smithsonian.
Russian Corporate Capitalism from Peter the Great to Perestroika. Thomas C. Owen. (Illus.). 272p. 1995. 55.00 (*0-19-509677-0*) OUP.
***Russian Costume: Costume in Russian Culture from the 18th Century to the First Half of the 20th.** R. Kirsanova. (Illus.). 352p. 1995. 69.95 (*1-57292-036-X*) Austin & Winfield.
Russian Course: Pt. 1. Alexander Lipson. (Illus.). ix, 338p. (Orig.). (C). 1981. pap. text ed. 16.95 (*0-89357-080-X*) Slavica.
Russian Course: Pt. 2. Alexander Lipson. (Illus.). 343p. (Orig.). (C). 1981. pap. text ed. 16.95 (*0-89357-081-8*) Slavica.
Russian Course: Pt. 3. Alexander Lipson. (Illus.). iv, 105p. (Orig.). 1981. pap. text ed. 12.95 (*0-89357-082-6*) Slavica.
Russian Course: Teacher's Manual. Steven J. Molinsky. (Illus.). 222p. (Orig.). 1981. pap. 12.95 (*0-89357-083-4*) Slavica.
Russian Critics on the Cinema of Glasnost. Ed. by Michael Brashinsky & Andrew Horton. LC 93-43590. (Studies in Film). (Illus.). 160p. (C). 1994. text ed. 64.95 (*0-521-44475-6*) Cambridge U Pr.
Russian Cubo-Futurism, 1910-1930: A Study in Avant-Gardism. Vahan D. Barooshian. LC 73-81271. (De Proprietatibus Litterarum, Ser. Major: No. 24). 176p. 1974. text ed. 43.85 (*90-279-2659-X*) Mouton.
Russian Cultural Revival: A Critical Anthology of Russian Emigre Literature Before 1939. Ed. & Tr. by Temira Pachmuss. LC 80-20670. 476p. 1981. 45.00 (*0-87049-296-9*); pap. 21.00 (*0-87049-306-X*) U of Tenn Pr.
Russian Culture & Civilization. Lorraine T. Kapitanoff. 272p. (C). 1994. per. 33.54 (*0-8403-5863-6*) Kendall-Hunt.
Russian Culture at the Crossroasds: Paradoxes of Postcommunist Consciousness. Ed. by Dmitri N. Shalin. (C). 1996. pap. text ed. 24.00 (*0-8133-2714-8*) Westview.
Russian Culture at the Crossroasds: Paradoxes of Postcommunist Consciousness. Ed. by Dmitri N. Shalin. (C). 1996. text ed. 65.95 (*0-8133-2713-X*) Westview.
Russian Culture in Transition: Selected Papers of the Working Group for the Study of Contemporary Russian Culture (1990-1991) Lev Anninskii et al. Ed. & Intro. by Gregory Freidin. (Stanford Slavic Studies: Vol. 7). (Illus.). 323p. (Orig.). (ENG & RUS.). (C). 1993. pap. 30.00 (*0-933884-85-0*) Berkeley Slavic.
Russian Culture Keys. 2nd ed. Klara K. Lewis. (In the Shoes of the Traveler Ser.). 1995. audio 12.95 (*1-886821-13-5*) Pavleen.
Russian Currency & Finance: A Currency Board Approach to Finance. Steve H. Janke et al. LC 93-4355. 240p. (C). (gr. 13). 1994. text ed. 62.95 (*0-415-09651-0*, B2434) Routledge.
Russian-Czech Polytechnical Dictionary. V. S. Petrov & S. A. Tulin. 639p. (CZE & RUS.). 1962. 125.00 (*0-8288-6813-1*, M-9074) Fr & Eur.
Russian-Czechoslovakian Dictionary. Vlchek. 896p. (CZE & RUS.). 1974. 29.95 (*0-7859-0788-2*, M-9116) Fr & Eur.
Russian-Dari (Afghani Persian) Teaching Dictionary. Kendajtene. 432p. (RUS.). 1983. 24.95 (*0-8288-1737-5*, F47660) Fr & Eur.
Russian Declension & Conjugation: A Structural Description with Exercises. Maurice I. Levin. x, 159p. 1978. pap. 15.95 (*0-89357-048-6*) Slavica.
Russian Declensions & Conjugations Handbook. Oscar E. Swan. 180p. 1992. pap. 14.95 (*0-88432-695-0*, BRU111) Audio-Forum.
Russian Democracy's Fatal Blunder: The Summer Offensive of 1917. Louise E. Heenan. LC 87-12505. 224p. 1987. text ed. 49.95 (*0-275-92829-2*, C2829, Praeger Pubs) Greenwood.
Russian Design: Traditions & Experiment. Yuri Nasarov & Alexander Lavrentiev. (Illus.). 160p. (Orig.). 1996. pap. 35.00 (*1-85490-426-4*) Academy Ed UK.
Russian Design & the Fine Arts, 1750-1917. Evgenia Kirichenko. 1991. 75.00 (*0-8109-3758-1*) Abrams.
Russian Desk: A Listening & Conversation Course. Cynthia L. Martin et al. x, 136p. (Orig.). (C). 1991. pap. text ed. 12.95 (*0-89357-218-7*) Slavica.
Russian Desk: Instructor's Manual. Cynthia L. Martin et al. vi, 64p. (Orig.). (C). 1991. pap. text ed. 7.95 (*0-89357-219-5*) Slavica.
Russian Desubstantival Derivation: A Paradigmatic View. Richard D. Schupbach. (Studia Linguistica et Philological Ser.: No. 2). 1977. pap. 46.50 (*0-915838-41-9*) Anma Libri.
Russian Diction, Vol. 4. Dahl. 1981. 40.00 (*0-08-023589-1*, Pergamon Pr) Elsevier.
Russian Dictionaries: Selected Bibliography, 1960-1990. Alena Aissing. LC 90-23731. 81p. 1991. 12.95 (*0-912526-52-1*) Lib Res.
Russian Dictionary. (Hugo Pocket Dictionaries Ser.). (Illus.). 640p. (Orig.). 1991. pap. 7.95 (*0-85285-162-6*) Hunter NJ.
***Russian Dictionary: Russian-English, English-Russian.** William Harrison & Svetlana Le Fleming. (Routledge Language Dictionaries Ser.). 580p. (ENG & RUS.). 1981. pap. 16.95 (*0-415-05177-0*) Routledge.
Russian Dilemma. rev. ed. Robert Wesson. LC 85-16742. 206p. 1985. pap. text ed. 13.95 (*0-275-91677-4*, B1677, Praeger Pubs) Greenwood.
Russian Dilemma. 2nd rev. ed. Robert Wesson. LC 85-16742. 206p. 1985. text ed. 49.95 (*0-275-90234-X*, C0234, Praeger Pubs) Greenwood.
Russian Dilemma: A Political & Geopolitical View. Robert G. Wesson. LC 74-1412. 238p. reprint ed. pap. 68.40 (*0-8357-7953-X*, 2057028) Bks Demand.
Russian Diplomatic & Consular Officials in East Asia. Ed. by George A. Lensen. LC 68-26393. (Monuments Nipponica Monograph). 294p. 1968. 15.00 (*0-910512-06-X*) Diplomatic IN.
Russian Discovery of Hawaii. Glynn R. Barratt. (Illus.). 259p. 1987. text ed. 27.50 (*0-915013-08-8*) Editions Ltd.
Russian Doll & Other Stories. Adolfo Bioy Casares. Tr. by Suzanne J. Levine from SPA. LC 92-10432. 128p. 1992. 22.95 (*0-8112-1211-4*); pap. 10.95 (*0-8112-1212-2*, NDP745) New Directions.
Russian Drama from Its Beginnings to the Age of Pushkin. Simon Karlinsky. LC 84-8442. 1985. pap. 16.00 (*0-520-05882-8*) U CA Pr.
Russian Drama of the Revolutionary Period. Robert Russell. 192p. 1987. 50.50 (*0-389-20757-8*) B&N Imports.
Russian Drawings of the Eighteenth Century: Russkii Risunok XVIII Veka. E. I. Gavrilova. 202p. 1983. 89.00 (*0-317-57444-2*) St Mut.
Russian Drinking: Use & Abuse of Alcohol in Pre-Revolutionary Russia. Boris M. Segal. LC 86-620003. (Monograph Ser.: No. 15). xx, 383p. 1987. 29.95 (*0-911290-18-4*); pap. 19.95 (*0-911290-19-2*) Rutgers Ctr Alcohol.
Russian Eagle: A History of Russia from Its Origins to the End of the Romanoff Dynasty. Louise C. Samoiloff. LC 85-18432. 1987. lib. bdg. 250.00 (*0-87700-866-3*) Revisionist Pr.
Russian Ecclestastical Mission in Peking During the Eighteenth Century. Eric Widmer. (East Asian Monographs: No. 69). 272p. 1976. 24.00 (*0-674-78129-5*) HUP.
Russian Ecological & Health Atlas, '96. (Russian Regional & Business Atlases Ser.). (Illus.). 300p. (Orig.). 1996. pap. 95.00 (*1-57751-137-9*) Russ Info & Busn Ctr.
Russian Economic Atlas: Economy, Industrial Development, Market Reforms. (Illus.). 600p. (Orig.). 1996. pap. 149.00 (*0-9646241-2-5*) Russ Info & Busn Ctr.
***Russian Economic Atlas: Geography, Economy, Industry.** 2nd rev. ed. Russian Information & Business Center, Inc. Staff. 1997. pap. 149.00 (*1-57751-174-3*) Russ Info & Busn Ctr.
Russian Economic Development Since the Revolution. Maurice Dobb. (Business Enterprises Reprint Ser.). xii, 415p. 1986. reprint ed. lib. bdg. 45.00 (*0-89941-502-4*, 304380) W S Hein.
Russian Economic History: A Guide to Information Sources. Ed. by Daniel R. Kazmer & Vera Kazmer. LC 73-17588. (Economics Information Guide Ser.: Vol. 4). 536p. 1977. 68.00 (*0-8103-1304-9*) Gale.
Russian Economic History: The Nineteenth Century. Arcadius Kahan. Ed. by Roger Weiss. LC 88-26093. (Illus.). 256p. 1989. pap. text ed. 23.00 (*0-226-42243-7*) U Ch Pr.
Russian Economic Reform. Jim Leitzel. LC 94-24768. 208p. (C). 1995. pap. 18.95 (*0-415-12511-1*, C0438) Routledge.
Russian Economic Reform. Jim Leitzel. LC 94-24768. 208p. (C). (gr. 13). 1995. text ed. 62.95 (*0-415-12510-3*, C0437) Routledge.
Russian Economic Reform: Crossing the Threshold of Structural Change. LC 92-31109. (Country Study Ser.). 406p. 1992. 30.00 (*0-8213-2241-9*, 12241) World Bank.
Russian Economic Reform at Risk. Ed. by Anders Aslund. 224p. 1995. 59.95 (*1-85567-286-3*, Pub. by Pntr Pubs UK) Bks Intl VA.
Russian Economy: From Rags to Riches. Ed. by A. Sizov. LC 94-47470. 237p. 1994. 69.00 (*1-56072-215-0*) Nova Sci Pubs.
Russian Economy: Past, Present & Future. Stuart & Gregory. (C). 1995. text ed. 22.95 (*0-673-99461-9*) Addson-Wesley Educ.
Russian Education: Tradition & Transition. Brian Holmes et al. LC 94-8442. (Reference Books in International Education, Vol. 27, Reference Library of Social Science: Vol. 26). 400p. 1995. text ed. 58.00 (*0-8153-1169-9*, SS906) Garland.
Russian Elementary, Vol I. Nina F. Potapova. Set. 27.50 (*0-87557-070-4*) Saphrograph.
Russian Elementary, Vol. II. Nina F. Potapova. 27.50 (*0-87557-136-0*) Saphrograph.
Russian Elementary Course, 2 Vols, Vol. 1. 3rd ed. Nina F. Potapova. 366p. (C). 1969. text ed. 142.00 (*0-677-20890-1*) Gordon & Breach.
Russian Elite: Inside Spetsnaz & the Airborne Forces. Carey Schofield. LC 93-27482. (Illus.). 256p. 1993. 29.95 (*1-85367-155-X*, 5445) Stackpole.
Russian Emergency & Services Directory, '96. 2nd rev. ed. (Illus.). 300p. 1996. pap. 99.00 (*1-57751-017-8*) Russ Info & Busn Ctr.
***Russian Emergency Services Directory.** 2nd rev. ed. Russian Information & Business Center, Inc. Staff. (Russian Business Library). 400p. 1997. pap. 99.00 (*1-57751-325-8*) Russ Info & Busn Ctr.
Russian Emigre Literature: A Bibliography of Titles Held by the University of California, Berkeley Library. Compiled & Intro. by Allan Urbanic. 329p. (Orig.). (C). 1993. pap. 50.00 (*0-933884-88-5*) Berkeley Slavic.
Russian Empire: Its People, Institutions, & Resources. Franz A. Von Haxthausen. LC 78-115545. (Russia Observed, Series I). 1970. reprint ed. 46.95 (*0-405-03033-9*) Ayer.
Russian Empire & Grand Duchy of Muscovy: A 17th Century French Account. Jacques Margeret. Ed. & Tr. by Chester S. Dunning. LC 82-20126. (Russian & East European Studies: No. 5). 251p. 1983. reprint ed. pap. 71.60 (*0-608-00909-1*, 2061703) Bks Demand.
***Russian Empire & the World, 1700-1917: The Geopolitics of Expansion & Containment.** John P. LeDonne. (Illus.). 400p. (C). 1996. text ed. 45.00 (*0-19-510926-0*); pap. text ed. 22.95 (*0-19-510927-9*) OUP.
Russian Empire in the Eighteenth Century: Tradition & Modernization. Aleksandr B. Kamenskii. Tr. by David Griffiths. LC 97-5683. (The New Russian History Ser.). 320p. (C). (gr. 13). 1997. pap. text ed. 24.95 (*1-56324-575-2*) M E Sharpe.
Russian Empire in the Eighteenth Century: Tradition & Modernization from Peter to Catherine. Aleksandr B. Kamenskii. Tr. by David Griffiths. LC 97-5683. (The New Russian History Ser.). 320p. (C). (gr. 13). 1997. text ed. 65.95 (*1-56324-574-4*) M E Sharpe.
Russian Enamel of the 12th-Early 20th Centuries. N. Kalizina. (Illus.). 260p. (C). 1987. text ed. 125.00 (*0-685-40312-2*, Pub. by Collets) St Mut.
Russian Enamel of the 12th to Early 20th Centuries. N. Kaliazina. 260p. (C). 1987. 115.00 (*0-685-34472-X*, Pub. by Collets) St Mut.
***Russian Enamels.** Anne Odom & William R. Johnston. (Illus.). 208p. 1996. 45.00 (*0-85667-446-X*, Pub. by P Wilson Pubs) Sothebys Pubns.
***Russian Enamels: Kievan Rus to Faberge.** Anne Odom. (Illus.). 208p. 1996. write for info. (*0-911886-45-1*); pap. write for info. (*0-911886-46-X*) Walters Art.
Russian Energy Prices, Taxes & Costs, 1993. OECD Staff. 100p. (Orig.). 1994. pap. 23.00 (*92-64-14158-8*) OECD.
Russian-English - English-Russian Dictionary on Probability, Statistics, & Combinatorics, Vol. 40. K. A. Borokov. viii, 154p. (ENG & RUS.). 1994. pap. 47.50 (*0-89871-316-1*) Soc Indus-Appl Math.
Russian-English Aerospace Dictionary. H. L. Darcy. 407p. 1985. 110.00 (*0-8288-0016-2*, M15472) Fr & Eur.
Russian-English & English-Russian Dictionary. W. Harrison & Svetlana LeFlemming. (Routledge Pocket Dictionaries Ser.). 580p. (Orig.). 1981. pap. 15.95 (*0-7100-0800-7*, RKP) Routledge.
Russian-English & English-Russion Dictionary of Radar & Electronics. Sergey A. Leonov & William F. Barton. LC 93-30104. (ENG & RUS.). 1993. 35.00 (*0-89006-705-8*) Artech Hse.
Russian, English & French Construction Dictionary: Bauwesen. L. Hoffmann. 99p. (ENG, FRE & RUS.). 1984. 29.95 (*0-8288-0890-2*, M15024) Fr & Eur.
Russian, English & German Dictionary of Shipbuilding & Fishing Industry: Schiffbau-Schiffahrt Fischereittechnik: Russisch-English-Deutsch. E. Bensch et al. 784p. (ENG, GER & RUS.). 1981. 125.00 (*0-8288-4677-4*, M12665) Fr & Eur.
Russian-English Atomic Dictionary: Physics, Mathematics, Nucleonics. 2nd rev. ed. Eugene A. Carpovich. LC 57-8256. (ENG & RUS.). 1959. 20.00 (*0-911484-00-0*) Tech Dict.
***Russian English Automotive Dictionary.** Vladimir Kotchine. 380p. (Orig.). (ENG & RUS.). 1996. pap. 49.95 (*0-9653484-0-7*) Allied Translation.
Russian-English Chemical Dictionary. 2nd ed. Eugene A. Carpovich. LC 61-11700. (ENG & RUS.). 1963. 30.00 (*0-911484-03-5*) Tech Dict.
***Russian-English Collocational Dictionary of the Human Body.** Lidija Iordanskaja & Slava Paperno. Ed. by Richard L. Leed. xxx, 418p. 1996. 29.95 (*0-89357-265-9*) Slavica.
***Russian English Comprehensive Dictionary.** Ed. by Oleg P. Benyukh. LC 96-54645. 800p. (ENG & RUS.). 1997. pap. 35.00 (*0-7818-0560-0*) Hippocrene Bks.
Russian-English Comprehensive Dictionary, Vol. 2. Ed. by Oleg Benyukh. LC 96-54645. 800p. (ENG & RUS.). 1996. 60.00 (*0-7818-0506-6*) Hippocrene Bks.
Russian-English Dictionaries with Aids for Translators: A Selected Bibliography. Wojciech Zalewski. LC 81-50870. (Bibliography Ser.: No. 1). 101p. (Orig.). 1981. pap. 12.00 (*0-89830-041-X*) Russica Pubs.
Russian-English Dictionary. A. S. Romanov. pap. 5.99 (*0-671-70924-0*) PB.
Russian-English Dictionary. A. Smirnitskii. 766p. (C). 1989. 95.00 (*0-569-09276-0*, Pub. by Collets) St Mut.
Russian-English Dictionary. A. I. Smirnitsky. 758p. (C). 1991. 25.95 (*0-8285-0608-6*) Firebird NY.
Russian-English Dictionary. A. L. Smirnitsky. 766p. (ENG & RUS.). 1985. 49.95 (*0-8288-1232-2*, M 8874) Fr & Eur.
Russian-English Dictionary. A. M. Taube. 831p. (ENG & RUS.). 1978. 29.95 (*0-8288-5270-7*, M9108) Fr & Eur.

An Asterisk (*) at the beginning of an entry indicates that the title is appearing in BIP for the first time.

Russian-English Dictionary. Ed. by A. M. Taube & R. C. Daglish. 624p. (ENG & RUS.). (C). 1990. 100.00 (*0-569-09285-X*, Pub. by Collets) St Mut.

Russian-English Dictionary. 3rd ed. A. I. Smirnitsky. 42.50 (*0-87557-066-6*) Saphrograph.

Russian-English Dictionary. 13th ed. A. I. Smirnitskii. 766p. (ENG & RUS.). (C). 1990. 110.00 (*0-569-00006-8*, Pub. by Collets) St Mut.

Russian-English Dictionary. 33th ed. O. Akhmanova & E. Wilson. 534p. (C). 1988. 100.00 (*0-569-08924-7*, Pub. by Collets) St Mut.

Russian-English Dictionary of Advertising Terms. 2nd ed. I. S. Sedelnikov. 290p. (ENG & RUS.). 1994. pap. 49.95 (*0-7859-9095-X*) Fr & Eur.

Russian-English Dictionary of Applied Geophysics. 488p. (ENG & RUS.). 1982. 50.00 (*0-8288-0359-5*, M 14398) Fr & Eur.

***Russian-English Dictionary of Contemporary Slang.** 2nd ed. UFO Staff. (ENG & RUS.). 1996. pap. 19.95 (*1-900405-03-2*, Pub. by Drake Intl Serv UK) Intl Spec Bk.

Russian-English Dictionary of Diplomacy. unabridged ed. K. V. Zhuravchenko et al. 736p. (ENG & RUS.). (C). 1995. 45.00 (*0-8285-5004-2*) Firebird NY.

Russian-English Dictionary of Electrotechnology & Applied Sciences. Paul Macura. LC 85-8653. 958p. 1986. reprint ed. lib. bdg. 99.50 (*0-89874-869-0*) Krieger.

Russian-English Dictionary of Helminthology & Plant Nematology. G. I. Pozniak. 108p. (Orig.). (C). 1979. 125.00 (*0-89771-926-3*, Pub. by Collets) St Mut.

Russian-English Dictionary of Mathematics. Oleg F. Efimov. 432p. 1993. 100.00 (*0-8493-4456-5*, QA5) CRC Pr.

Russian-English Dictionary of Science & Technology. 3rd ed. L. I. Callaham. 852p. (ENG & RUS.). 1993. 150.00 (*0-7859-9081-X*) Fr & Eur.

Russian-English Dictionary of Scientific & Technical Usage. B. V. Kuznetsov. 656p. (ENG & RUS.). 1992. 75.00 (*0-7859-1093-X*, 5823400225) Fr & Eur.

Russian-English Dictionary of Scientific & Technical Usage. B. V. Kuznetsov. 656p. (ENG & RUS.). 1992. 95.00 (*0-7859-9085-2*) Fr & Eur.

Russian-English Dictionary of Scientific & Technical Usage. unabridged ed. B. V. Kuznetsov. 656p. (ENG & RUS.). (C). 1992. 21.95 (*0-8285-5086-7*) Firebird NY.

Russian-English Dictionary of Socio-Economic Terms. Rodionova. (ENG & RUS.). 1987. 75.00 (*0-8288-3974-3*, F39311) Fr & Eur.

Russian-English Dictionary of Sports Terms & Phrases. A. V. Gavrilovets. 352p. (ENG & RUS.). (C). 1979. 90.00 (*0-569-08607-8*, Pub. by Collets) St Mut.

Russian-English Dictionary of the Mathematical Sciences. A. J. Lohwater. LC 90-270. 343p. (ENG & RUS.). 1990. reprint ed. pap. 38.00 (*0-8218-0133-3*, REDS) Am Math.

Russian-English Dictionary of Verbal Collocations (REDVC) Ed. by Morton Benson & Evelyn Benson. LC 92-34482. ix, 269p. 1993. 47.00 (*1-55619-483-8*); pap. 22.95 (*1-55619-484-6*) Benjamins North Am.

Russian-English Dictionary (RED) 1994. write for info. (*0-8493-7541-X*) CRC Pr.

Russian-English, English-Russian Concise Dictionary. Oleg Beniukh & Ksana Beniukh. (Concise Dictionaries Ser.). 400p. (Orig.). 1993. pap. 11.95 (*0-7818-0132-X*) Hippocrene Bks.

Russian-English, English-Russian Dictionary of Business & Legal Terms. Shane DeBeer. 800p. (ENG & RUS.). 1996. reprint ed. pap. 35.00 (*0-7818-0505-8*) Hippocrene Bks.

Russian-English English-Russian Dictionary Pocket. S. G. Zaimovsky. 19.50 (*0-87557-069-0*) Saphrograph.

Russian English English Russian Standard Dictionary (With Business Terms) Oleg Beniuykh. 418p. 1997. reprint ed. pap. 18.95 (*0-7818-0280-6*) Hippocrene Bks.

***Russian-English Foreign Trade & Economic Dictionary.** 65.00 (*5-200-01097-7*) Juris Pubng.

Russian-English Foreign Trade & Foreign Economic Dictionary. Zdanopov. 1019p. (ENG & RUS.). 1991. 95.00 (*0-7859-1092-1*, 5200010977) Fr & Eur.

Russian-English Foreign Trade & Foreign Economic Dictionary. I. F. Zhdanova. 1022p. (C). 1991. 29.95 (*0-8285-4997-4*) Firebird NY.

Russian-English Geological Dictionary. 559p. 1983. 24.95 (*0-317-02600-3*) Am Geol.

Russian-English-German French Mathematics Dictionary. Vladimir N. Orlov. 300p. (C). 1987. 90.00 (*0-685-37161-1*, Pub. by Collets) St Mut.

Russian-English Idiom Dictionary. Alexander J. Vitek. Ed. by Harry H. Josselson. LC 72-14076. 337p. reprint ed. pap. 96.10 (*0-7837-3546-4*, 2008982) Bks Demand.

Russian-English Legal Dictionary. Tr. by William E. Butler. 200p. (ENG & RUS.). 1996. 55.00 (*1-898029-20-2*, Pub. by Simmonds & Hill Pubng UK) Gaunt.

Russian-English Mathematical Dictionary: Words & Phrases in Pure & Applied Mathematics with Roots & Accents, Arranged for Easy Reference. Louis M. Milne-Thomson. LC 62-7217. (Mathematics Research Center, United States Army, University of Wisconsin Publication Ser.: No. 7). 205p. reprint ed. pap. 58.50 (*0-317-28131-3*, 2055742) Bks Demand.

Russian-English Medical Dictionary. 2nd rev. ed. I. B. Eliseenkov et al. 647p. (RUS.). 1995. 49.95 (*0-8285-5002-6*) Firebird NY.

Russian-English Medical Dictionary Phrase Book. 3rd ed. V. I. Petrov. 595p. 1993. 95.00 (*0-7859-9075-5*) Fr & Eur.

***Russian-English Medical Dictionary Phrase-Book.** 3rd ed. V. I. Petrov et al. 596p. (C). 1993. reprint ed. 32.95 (*0-8285-5177-4*) Firebird NY.

***Russian-English Medical Dictionary with Definitions.** V. L. Rivkin & N. V. Morozov. 384p. (C). 1996. 37.50 (*0-8285-5120-0*) Firebird NY.

Russian-English Metals & Machines Dictionary. Eugene A. Carpovich. LC 60-12013. (ENG & RUS.). 1960. 20.00 (*0-911484-02-7*) Tech Dict.

Russian-English Oil-Field Dictionary. D. E. Stoliarov. 432p. (ENG & RUS.). 1982. 95.00 (*0-8288-0703-5*, M15452) Fr & Eur.

Russian-English Phrase-Book for Physicists. L. A. Smirnova. 336p. 1968. 49.95 (*0-685-57823-2*, M-9109) Fr & Eur.

Russian-English Phrase Book for Physicists. 2nd ed. L. A. Smirnova. 304p. (ENG & RUS.). 1977. write for info. (*0-7859-9092-5*) Fr & Eur.

Russian-English Phrase Book on Foreign Economic Relations. L. G. Pamukhina. 700p. (ENG & RUS.). 1993. 95.00 (*0-7859-9098-4*) Fr & Eur.

***Russian English Phrase Book on Foreign Economic Relations.** Russki Yazyk. 650p. 55.00 (*5-200-00628-7*) Juris Pubng.

Russian-English Phrase Book on Foreign Economic Relations. unabridged ed. L. G. Pamukhina et al. 654p. (ENG & RUS.). (C). 1993. 27.95 (*0-8285-5094-8*) Firebird NY.

Russian English Phrasebook for Physicists. D. M. Tolstoi & L. A. Smirnova. (ENG & RUS.). 1977. 19.95 (*0-8288-3925-5*, M9109) Fr & Eur.

Russian English Phrasebook on Building & Civil Engineering. V. Y. Fomenko. (ENG & RUS.). 1990. 95.00 (*0-8288-3926-3*, F39886) Fr & Eur.

Russian-English Plastics Dictionary: Reversed From an English-Russian Dictionary by Computer Processing. Ed. by Harry H. Josselson. LC 76-99790. (Autolex Series of Scientific & Technical Dictionaries: No. 1). 316p. reprint ed. 90.10 (*0-685-16256-7*, 2027607) Bks Demand.

Russian-English Polytechnic Dictionary. 3rd ed. B. V. Kuznetsov et al. 723p. (ENG & RUS.). (C). 1995. reprint ed. 65.00 (*0-8285-5080-8*) Firebird NY.

Russian-English Polytechnical Dictionary. B. V. Kuznetsov. 723p. (ENG & RUS.). 1980. 95.00 (*0-8288-0660-8*, M 15529) Fr & Eur.

Russian-English Reference Guide for Studying the Bible. Ernest Clevenger. Tr. by Eugene Salurien. (Parchment Ready Reference Ser.). 36p. (ENG & RUS.). 1992. pap. 1.50 (*0-88428-062-4*) Parchment Pr.

Russian-English Science & Engineering Dictionary. E. A. Carpovich. 676p. (ENG & RUS.). 1988. 250.00 (*0-7859-7145-9*) Fr & Eur.

Russian-English Scientific & Technical Dictionary, 2 vols, Set. M. H. Alford & V. L. Alford. LC 73-88348. (ENG & RUS.). 1970. 637.00 (*0-08-012227-2*, Pub. by Pergamon Repr UK) Franklin.

Russian-English Scientific & Technical Dictionary of Useful Combinations & Expressions. M. G. Zimmerman. (ENG & RUS.). 29.50 (*0-87559-119-1*); 34.50 (*0-87559-140-X*) Shalom.

Russian-English Social Science Dictionary. enl. rev. ed. Ed. by R. E. Smith. 613p. (C). 1990. reprint ed. text ed. 49.95 (*0-8223-1088-0*) Duke.

Russian English Translator's Dictionary. M. G. Zimmerman. 736p. (ENG & RUS.). (C). 1991. text ed. 160.00 (*0-569-14852-9*, Pub. by Collets) St Mut.

Russian-English Translators Dictionary. Mikhail Zimmerman. (ENG & RUS.). 1984. 225.00 (*0-8288-0662-4*, F63851) Fr & Eur.

Russian-English Translators' Dictionary: A Guide to Scientific & Technical Usage. 2nd ed. Mikhail Zimmerman. LC 83-10229. 554p. reprint ed. pap. 157.90 (*0-8357-4252-0*, 2037069) Bks Demand.

Russian-English Translator's Dictionary: A Guide to Scientific & Technical Usage. 3rd ed. Mikhail Zimmerman & Claudia Vedeneeva. LC 92-319. 735p. 1992. text ed. 180.00 (*0-471-93316-3*) Wiley.

Russian-English Veterinary Dictionary. R. Mack. 104p. (Orig.). (C). 1972. 50.00 (*0-89771-927-1*, Pub. by Collets) St Mut.

Russian-English Vocabulary with Grammatical Sketch. Ed. by Gabrielle Rainich & A. H. Kuipers. 66p. (ENG & RUS.). 1990. reprint ed. pap. 17.00 (*0-8218-0037-X*, REV) Am Math.

***Russian-English/English-Russian Compact Dictionary.** 536p. (ENG & RUS.). 1997. pap. 9.95 (*0-7818-0537-6*) Hippocrene Bks.

Russian Engravings of the Late Seventeenth & Eighteenth Centuries: Russkaia Graviur Kontsa XVIII Veka. 1983. 297.00 (*0-317-57445-0*) St Mut.

Russian Enigma. Ante Ciliga. Tr. by Fernand G. Renier et al. from RUS. 588p. 1989. pap. text ed. 15.95 (*0-906133-23-8*) Routledge Chapman & Hall.

Russian Enterprise in Transition. Ed. by Simon Clarke. LC 96-15888. (Management & Industry in Russia Ser.). 416p. 1996. 80.00 (*1-85898-341-X*) E Elgar.

Russian Entrepreneur: Publisher Ivan Sytin of Moscow, 1851-1934. Charles A. Ruud. (Illus.). 304p. (C). 1990. text ed. 49.95 (*0-7735-0773-6*, Pub. by McGill CN) U of Toronto Pr.

Russian Epic Studies. Roman Jakobson & Ernest J. Simmons. LC 50-5215. (American Folklore Society Memoirs Ser.). 1974. reprint ed. 30.00 (*0-527-01094-4*) Periodicals Srv.

***Russian Essays on Shakespeare & His Contemporaries.** A. T. Parfenov & Joseph G. Price. LC 97-18597. 1997. write for info. (*0-87413-619-9*) U Delaware Pr.

Russian Essential. Berlitz Editors. (Essential Ser.). (Illus.). 296p. 1994. pap. 10.95 (*2-8315-1793-1*) Berlitz.

Russian Etiquette & Ethics in Business. Lloyd Donaldson & Drew Wilson. (Etiquette & Ethics Ser.). 200p. 1995. pap. 16.95 (*0-8442-4216-0*, NTC Busn Bks) NTC Pub Grp.

Russian Etymological Dictionary. Terence R. Wade. 272p. 1996. pap. 28.95 (*1-85399-414-6*, Pub. by Brstl Class Pr UK) Focus Pub-R Pullins.

Russian European: Paul Miliukov in Russian Politics. Thomas Riha. LC 68-27582. 391p. reprint ed. pap. 111.50 (*0-317-55789-0*, 2029312) Bks Demand.

Russian Executive Government: Encyclopedic Directory 1996. (Illus.). 500p. (Orig.). 1997. pap. 99.00 (*0-9646241-6-8*) Russ Info & Busn Ctr.

***Russian Executive Government Directory.** Russian Information & Business Center, Inc. Staff. 100p. 1997. pap. 99.00 (*1-57751-168-9*) Russ Info & Busn Ctr.

Russian Experience: Ideas in History. Ed. by N. Maslova & T. Pleshakova. 137p. (C). 1995. lib. bdg. 59.00 (*1-56072-211-8*) Nova Sci Pubs.

Russian Experiment in Art 1863-1922. rev. ed. Camilla Gray. LC 86-50219. (World of Art Ser.). (Illus.). 324p. 1986. reprint ed. pap. 16.95 (*0-500-20207-9*) Thames Hudson.

Russian Experimental Fiction: Resisting Ideology after Utopia. Edith W. Clowes. LC 92-46315. 200p. 1993. text ed. 35.00 (*0-691-03222-X*) Princeton U Pr.

Russian Exploration in Southwest Alaska: The Travel Journal of Petr Korsakovskiy (1818) & Ivan Ya. Vasilev (1829) Petr Korsakovskiy & Ivan V. Vasilev. Tr. by David H. Kraus from RUS. LC 88-51165. (Rasmuson Library Historical Translation Ser.: Vol. IV). (Illus.). 128p. 1989. pap. 15.00 (*0-912006-27-7*) U of Alaska Pr.

***Russian Export-Import & Business Directory.** 2nd rev. ed. Russian Information & Business Center, Inc. Staff. (Russian Business Library). 400p. 1997. pap. 99.00 (*1-57751-300-2*) Russ Info & Busn Ctr.

Russian Export-Import & Trade Directory - 96. 2nd rev. ed. (Russian Business Library: No. 20). (Illus.). 250p. 1996. pap. 99.00 (*1-57751-000-3*) Russ Info & Busn Ctr.

Russian Eyes on American Literature. Ed. by Sergei Chakovsky & M. Thomas Inge. LC 92-19552. 368p. 1992. 42.50 (*0-87805-584-3*) U Pr of Miss.

Russian: Face to Face: Beginning. George W. Morris et al. (RUS.). (YA). 1993. student ed. 13.25 (*0-8442-4307-8*, Natl Textbk) NTC Pub Grp.

Russian: Face to Face: Beginning. George W. Morris et al. (RUS.). (YA). 1994. teacher ed. 41.25 (*0-8442-4302-7*, Natl Textbk) NTC Pub Grp.

Russian: Face to Face: Beginning. George W. Morris et al. (RUS.). (YA). 1994. student ed. 9.25 (*0-8442-4301-9*, Natl Textbk) NTC Pub Grp.

Russian: Face to Face: Beginning. George W. Morris et al. (RUS.). (YA). 1995. text ed. 34.60 (*0-8442-4300-0*, Natl Textbk) NTC Pub Grp.

Russian: Face to Face: Beginning. George W. Morris et al. (RUS.). (YA). 1995. audio 40.00 (*0-8442-4303-5*, Natl Textbk) NTC Pub Grp.

Russian Faces & Voices. ACTR Staff. 444p. 1995. boxed 39.95 (*0-7872-0504-4*) Kendall-Hunt.

Russian Faces & Voices. ACTR Staff. 160p. 1995. per., pap. 10.95 (*0-7872-1423-X*) Kendall-Hunt.

Russian Faces & Voices: Instructor's Manual. ACTR Staff & Corlac. 94p. 1996. per. 12.95 (*0-7872-1425-6*) Kendall-Hunt.

Russian Factory Women: Workplace & Society, 1880-1914. Rose L. Glickman. LC 83-6968. 250p. (C). 1984. 45.00 (*0-520-04810-5*) U CA Pr.

Russian Fairy Tales. Aleksandr Afanasev. LC 44-37884. (Fairy Tale & Folklore Library). 664p. (J). (gr. 6 up). 1976. pap. 18.00 (*0-394-73090-9*) Pantheon.

Russian Fairy Tales. Gillian Avery & Arthur Ransome. 1995. 14.95 (*0-679-43641-3*) Knopf.

Russian Fairy Tales. Illus. by Ivan Bilibin. LC 95-15334. (Everyman's Library of Children's Classics). 1995. write for info. (*0-614-07798-2*, Evrymans Lib Childs) Knopf.

Russian Fairy Tales: Russian Reader with Explanatory Notes. N. N. Kovacheva. (Illus.). 158p. 1987. text ed. 10.95 (*0-8285-4902-8*) Firebird NY.

Russian Far East. Erik Azulay & Allegra Azulay. (Companion Guides Ser.). (Illus.). 311p. (Orig.). 1995. pap. 18.95 (*0-7818-0325-X*) Hippocrene Bks.

***Russian Far East: A Business Reference Guide.** Ed. by Elisa Miller & Soula Stefanopoulos. 275p. 1997. pap. 59.00 (*0-9641286-2-4*) Russian Far East.

Russian Far East: A Business Reference Guide. 2nd ed. Ed. by Elisa B. Miller. 200p. 1995. pap. text ed. 37.50 (*0-9641286-1-6*) Russian Far East.

Russian Far East: A History. John J. Stephan. LC 93-42011. xxv ,p. 1994. 55.00 (*0-8047-2311-7*) Stanford U Pr.

Russian Far East: A History. John J Stephan. LC 93-42011. 516p. (Orig.). 1996. pap. 18.95 (*0-8047-2701-5*) Stanford U Pr.

Russian Far East: An Economic Handbook. Ed. by Pavel A. Minakir & Gregory L. Freeze. Tr. by Gregory L. Freeze from RUS. LC 94-18817. 544p. (gr. 13). 1994. text ed. 181.95 (*1-56324-456-X*) M E Sharpe.

Russian Fare. R. Gorina. pap. 10.00 (*0-87557-106-9*) Saphrograph.

Russian Federation. David Flint. LC 92-5737. (Former Soviet States Ser.). (Illus.). 32p. (J). (gr. 4-6). 1992. lib. bdg. 16.40 (*1-56294-305-7*) Millbrook Pr.

Russian Federation. Karen Jacobsen. LC 93-36996. (New True Bks.). (Illus.). 48p. (J). (gr. k-4). 1994. lib. bdg. 19.00 (*0-516-01060-3*) Childrens.

Russian Federation. Karen Jacobsen. (New True Bks.). (Illus.). 48p. (J). (gr. k-4). 1994. pap. 5.50 (*0-516-41060-1*) Childrens.

Russian Federation: Economic Review. International Monetary Fund Staff. vii, 115p. 1992. pap. 10.00 (*1-55775-256-7*) Intl Monetary.

Russian Federation: Toward Medium-Term Viability. LC 96-16. (Country Study Ser.). 150p. 1996. 9.95 (*0-8213-3567-7*, 13567) World Bank.

Russian Federation in Transition: External Developments. Benedicte V. Christensen. LC 94-5967. (Occasional Paper Ser.: No. 111). vii, 45p. 1994. 15.00 (*1-55775-371-7*) Intl Monetary.

Russian Federation Legislative Survey: June 1990 - December 1992. Ed. by F. J. Feldbrugge. LC 94-41365. (Law Specials Ser.: Vol. 7). 1995. pap. text ed. 58.50 (*0-7923-3243-1*, Pub. by M Nijhoff NE) Kluwer Ac.

Russian Festive Cooking. Susan Ward. 1995. 6.98 (*0-7858-0502-8*) Bk Sales Inc.

***Russian Fighter Aircraft 1920-1941.** Heinz J. Nowarra. 48p. 1997. pap. 9.95 (*0-7643-0294-9*) Schiffer.

Russian-Finnish Dictionary: Venelais-Suomalainen Taskusanakirja. J. Jelisijev. 582p. (FIN & RUS.). 1987. pap. 35.00 (*0-8288-1075-3*, F96840) Fr & Eur.

Russian-Finnish Trade - Business Dictionary: Venalais-Suomalainen Kaupan Sanakirja. M. Pasanen. 341p. (FIN & RUS.). 1985. 250.00 (*0-8288-0834-1*, F17170) Fr & Eur.

Russian Flag over Hawaii: The Mission of Jeffery Tolamy. Darwin Teilhet. 283p. 1986. reprint ed. mass mkt. 5.95 (*0-935180-28-1*) Mutual Pub HI.

Russian Folk Art. Allison Hilton. LC 94-30901. (Indiana-Michigan Series in Russian & East European Studies). 320p. 1995. 39.95 (*0-253-32753-9*) Ind U Pr.

Russian Folk Belief. Linda J. Ivanits. LC 87-32067. 272p. (gr. 13). 1989. 63.95 (*0-87332-422-6*) M E Sharpe.

Russian Folk Belief. Linda J. Ivanits. LC 87-32067. 272p. (gr. 13). 1992. pap. text ed. 22.95 (*0-87332-889-2*) M E Sharpe.

Russian Folk Epics. James O. Bailey. 1997. pap. text ed. write for info. (*0-87332-641-5*) M E Sharpe.

Russian Folk Epics. James O. Bailey, Jr. (C). (gr. 13). 1997. text ed. write for info. (*0-87332-640-7*) M E Sharpe.

Russian Folk Epos in Czech Literature: 1800-1900. William E. Harkins. LC 76-141414. 282p. 1971. reprint ed. text ed. 59.75 (*0-8371-4687-9*, HACL, Greenwood Pr) Greenwood.

Russian Folk Lyrics. Ed. & Tr. by Roberta Reader. LC 92-7155. (Illus.). 208p. 1993. 35.00 (*0-253-34623-1*); pap. text ed. 16.95 (*0-253-20749-5*, MB-749) Ind U Pr.

Russian Folk-Tales. William S. Ralston. Ed. by Richard M. Dorson. LC 77-70619. (International Folklore Ser.). 1977. reprint ed. lib. bdg. 33.95 (*0-405-10122-8*) Ayer.

Russian Folk Theatre. E. Warner. (Slavistic Printings & Reprintings Ser.: No. 104). 1977. 83.10 (*90-279-3325-1*) Mouton.

Russian Folktale - My Mother Is the Most Beautiful Woman in the World. Carol J. Cincereli. (Integrating Literature, Language & the Arts Ser.). 96p. (J). (gr. 1-6). teacher ed. 6.99 (*0-86653-539-X*, GA1162) Good Apple.

***Russian Food & Culture.** Ann L. Burckhardt. (Multicultural Cookbooks Ser.). (Illus.). 48p. (J). (gr. 3-7). 1996. 18.40 (*0-516-20262-6*) Childrens.

Russian for Beginners. Charles Duff & Dmitri Makaroff. 1971. pap. 12.00 (*0-06-463287-3*, EH 287) HarpC.

Russian for Beginners. Y. G. Ovsiyenko. 448p. (C). 1992. 17.95 (*0-8285-4999-0*) Firebird NY.

Russian for Chessplayers. Russell. 1995. pap. 12.95 (*0-938650-44-0*) Thinkers Pr.

Russian for Everybody. Robert L. Baker. 288p. 1984. 49.95 (*0-317-42700-8*, Pub. by Collets) St Mut.

Russian for Everybody. V. G. Kostomarov. (ENG & RUS.). (C). 1987. 49.95 (*0-569-09125-X*, Pub. by Collets) St Mut.

Russian for Everybody: American Edition, Set. 6th ed. R. Baker & E. Stepanova. Ed. by V. G. Kostomarov. 544p. (C). 1992. 25.95 (*0-8285-3001-7*) Firebird NY.

Russian for Everybody: Let's Talk & Read. V. G. Kostomarov. 176p. (C). 1986. 49.95 (*0-317-92482-6*, Pub. by Collets) St Mut.

Russian for Everybody: Let's Talk & Read! 3rd ed. V. G. Kostomarov. 176p. (ENG & RUS.). (C). 1987. 49.95 (*0-685-39376-3*, Pub. by Collets) St Mut.

Russian for Expository Prose, Vol. 1: Introductory Course. Ruth L. Pearce. 413p. (Orig.). (C). 1983. pap. text ed. 18.95 (*0-89357-121-0*) Slavica.

Russian for Expository Prose, Vol. 2: Advanced Course. Ruth L. Pearce. 255p. (Orig.). 1983. pap. text ed. 16.95 (*0-89357-122-9*) Slavica.

Russian for Reading. Patricia M. Arant. 214p. 1981. pap. text ed. 16.95 (*0-89357-086-9*) Slavica.

Russian for Restaurant & Hotels: Russisch fuer das Gaststaetten-und Hotelwesen. 3rd ed. U. Meckert. 184p. (GER & RUS.). 1982. 29.95 (*0-8288-1476-7*, M15241) Fr & Eur.

Russian for Retailers: Russisch fur den Einzelhandel. 5th ed. Diethelm Schulz & Stramel I. Schulz. 132p. (GER & RUS.). 1986. pap. 14.95 (*0-8288-1477-5*, M15240) Fr & Eur.

Russian for Scientists: General Scientific Terminology. V. I. Mitrokhina & Motovilova. 343p. (GER & RUS.). 1981. 49.95 (*0-8288-1561-5*, M13015) Fr & Eur.

Russian for the Business Traveler. Shane R. De Beer. LC 93-31834. (Foreign Language Business Dictionaries Ser.). 600p. (ENG & RUS.). 1994. pap. 11.95 (*0-8120-1784-6*) Barron.

Russian for the Mathematician. S. H. Gould. LC 72-76762. (Illus.). 224p. 1982. 69.95 (*0-387-05811-7*) Spr-Verlag.

Russian for the Scientist & Mathematician. Clive A. Croxton. LC 83-10209. 226p. reprint ed. pap. 64.50 (*0-318-35026-2*, 2030926) Bks Demand.

Russian for Tourists. V. G. Kostomarov. (Illus.). 183p. 1987. pap. 4.95 (*0-8285-0562-4*) Firebird NY.

Russian Foreign Policy: Essays in Historical Perspective. Ivo Lederer. 1962. 97.50 (*0-685-26675-3*) Elliots Bks.

Russian Foreign Policy: From Empire to Nation-State. Nicolai N. Petro & Alvin Z. Rubinstein. LC 96-16348. (C). 1997. text ed. 31.95 (*0-673-99636-0*) Addson-Wesley Educ.

An Asterisk (*) at the beginning of an entry indicates that the title is appearing in BIP for the first time.

Russian Foreign Policy after the Cold War. Leszek Buszynski. LC 96-551. 256p. 1996. text ed. 59.95 (*0-275-95585-0*, Praeger Pubs) Greenwood.

***Russian Foreign Policy & the End of the Cold War.** Mike Bowker. LC 96-39521. 320p. 1997. text ed. 72.95 (*1-85521-461-X*, Pub. by Dartmth Pub UK) Ashgate Pub Co.

Russian Foreign Policy since 1990. Ed. by Peter Shearman. 325p. (C). 1995. text ed. 65.50 (*0-8133-8778-7*) Westview.

Russian Foreign Policy since 1990. Ed. by Peter Shearman. (C). 1995. pap. text ed. 24.00 (*0-8133-2633-8*) Westview.

Russian Foreign Policy Today: The Soviet Legacy & Post-Soviet Beginnings. 5th ed. Ed. by Gordon Livermore. (Current Digest Foreign Policy Readers Ser.). 228p. (Orig.). (C). 1992. pap. 15.00 (*0-913601-64-0*) Current Digest.

Russian Formalism: A Metapoetics. Peter Steiner. LC 84-7708. 278p. 1984. 39.95 (*0-8014-1710-4*); pap. 15.95 (*0-8014-9366-8*) Cornell U Pr.

Russian Formalism: A Retrospective Glance, a Festschrift in Honor of Victor Erlich. Ed. by Robert L. Jackson & Stephen Rudy. LC 85-50188. (Yale Russian & East European Publications: No. 6). 304p. 1985. 20.00 (*0-936586-06-0*) Yale Russian.

Russian Formalism: History-Doctrine. 2nd ed. Victor Erlich. (Slavistic Printings & Reprintings Ser.: No. 4). 1965. text ed. 62.35 (*90-279-0450-2*) Mouton.

Russian Formalism: History-Doctrine. 3rd ed. Victor Erlich. 1981. pap. 19.00 (*0-300-02635-8*, Y-397) Yale U Pr.

Russian Formalism & Anglo-American New Criticism: A Comparative Study. Ewa M. Thompson. (De Proprietatibus Litterarum, Ser. Major: No. 8). 160p. 1971. text ed. 33.85 (*90-279-1845-7*) Mouton.

Russian Formalist Criticism: Four Essays. Tr. by Lee T. Lemon & Marion J. Reis. LC 65-21899. (Regents Critics Ser.). xvii, 143p. 1965. pap. text ed. 10.00 (*0-8032-5460-1*, Bison Books) U of Nebr Pr.

Russian Formalist Film Theory. Herb Eagle. (Michigan Slavic Materials Ser.: No. 19). 1981. pap. 10.00 (*0-930042-42-5*) Mich Slavic Pubns.

Russian Formalist Theory & Its Poetic Ambience. Krystyna Pomorska. 1968. text ed. 55.40 (*3-10-800116-7*) Mouton.

Russian Four: Textbook for Foreign Schools. M. N. Viatiutnev. 190p. (C). 1987. 40.00 (*0-685-24097-5*) St Mut.

Russian-French Dictionary: Dictionnaire Russe-Francais. 11th ed. L. Scerba. (FRE & RUS.). 1983. 69.95 (*0-8288-0790-6*, M6735) Fr & Eur.

Russian-French, French-Russian Legal & Economic Dictionary: Dictionnaire Juridique et Economique Russe-Francais-Russe. Long Doucet. 844p. (FRE & RUS.). 1984. 175.00 (*0-8288-0402-8*, F800) Fr & Eur.

Russian-French Polytechnical Dictionary: Dictionnaire Polytechnique Russe-Francais. L. Vassiliev. 800p. (FRE & RUS.). 1980. 75.00 (*0-8288-2133-X*, M6737) Fr & Eur.

Russian Frontier: The Impact of Borderlands upon the Course of Early Russian History. Joseph L. Wieczynski. LC 75-43753. 120p. reprint ed. pap. 34.20 (*0-8357-3143-X*, 2039406) Bks Demand.

Russian Futurism Through Its Manifestos, 1912-1928. Ed. by Anna Lawton & Herbert Eagle. Tr. by Herbert Eagle. LC 88-47733. 320p. 1988. 49.95 (*0-8014-1883-6*); pap. 17.95 (*0-8014-9492-3*) Cornell U Pr.

Russian Gentleman. Sergei Aksakov. Ed. by Edward Crankshaw. Tr. by J. D. Duff from RUS. (World's Classics Paperback Ser.). 288p. 1982. pap. 11.95 (*0-19-281573-3*) OUP.

Russian-German & German-Russian Dictionary of Librarianship. Ed. by G. Wasikiewitsch. 260p. (C). 1988. 79.00 (*0-685-54138-X*, Pub. by Collets) St Mut.

Russian-German Construction Dictionary: Bauwesen: Russisch-Deutsch. Walter Sturm. 664p. (GER & RUS.). 1985. 95.00 (*0-8288-0888-0*, M5883) Fr & Eur.

Russian-German Dictionary. deluxe ed. 919p. (GER & RUS.). 1960. 19.95 (*0-7859-0789-0*, M-9075) Fr & Eur.

Russian-German Dictionary: Russisch-Deutsches Woerterbuch. 8th ed. O. N. Nikonowa & M. J. Zwilling. 798p. (GER & RUS.). 1982. 75.00 (*0-8288-1239-X*, F60170) Fr & Eur.

Russian-German Dictionary: Russisch-Deutsches Woerterbuch. 14th ed. Hans H. Bielfeldt. 1119p. (GER & RUS.). 1982. 55.00 (*0-8288-0793-0*, F60180) Fr & Eur.

Russian-German Dictionary of Modern Colloquial Russian: Woerterbuch der Modernen Russischen Umgangssprache: Russisch-Deutsch. Soia Koester & Elena Rom. 458p. (GER & RUS.). 1985. 185.00 (*0-8288-0796-5*, M9157) Fr & Eur.

Russian-German Dictionary of Proverbs. J. N. Afon'kin. 287p. (GER & RUS.). 1985. 19.95 (*0-8288-2285-9*, M15188) Fr & Eur.

Russian-German Dictionary of Sporting Terms: Russisch-Deutsches Sportwoerterbuch. 381p. (GER & RUS.). 1987. 75.00 (*0-8288-2349-9*, M1997) Fr & Eur.

Russian-German Economics Dictionaries: Grosses Oekonomisches Woerterbuch Russisch-Deutsch. 3rd ed. Gerhard Mochel. 576p. (GER & RUS.). 1983. 95.00 (*0-8288-0821-X*, M7575) Fr & Eur.

Russian-German Law Directory: Rechtsworterbuch Russisch-Deutsch. H. Engelbert. 640p. (GER & RUS.). 1986. 125.00 (*0-8288-0403-6*, M1983) Fr & Eur.

Russian-German Legal Dictionary: Juristisches Woerterbuch: Russisch-Deutsch. L. Lingen. 608p. (GER & RUS.). 1985. 85.00 (*0-8288-0982-8*, M8601) Fr & Eur.

Russian Girl. Kingsley Amis. 304p. 1995. pap. 10.95 (*0-14-014475-7*, Penguin Bks) Viking Penguin.

Russian Girl. Kingsley Amis. 1995. pap. 10.95 (*0-14-025172-3*, Viking) Viking Penguin.

Russian Girl: Life in an Old Russian Town. Russell Kendall. LC 93-13198. (Illus.). 40p. (J). (ps-4). 1994. 14.95 (*0-590-45789-6*) Scholastic Inc.

Russian Glass of the Seventeenth-Twentieth Centuries. Nina Asharina et al. LC 89-81837. (Illus.). 192p. 1990. pap. 40.00 (*0-87290-123-8*) Corning.

Russian Glass of the 17th-20th Centuries. Corning Museum of Glass Staff. 1991. pap. 40.00 (*0-486-26775-X*) Dover.

Russian Gothic Novel & Its British Antecedents. Mark S. Simpson. 110p. 1986. pap. 14.95 (*0-89357-162-8*) Slavica.

Russian Government & the Massacres. E. P. Semenov. LC 70-97304. (Judaica Ser.). 265p. 1972. reprint ed. text ed. 59.75 (*0-8371-2632-0*, SERG, Greenwood Pr) Greenwood.

Russian Government Guide: 4000 Top Government Officials in Russia. (Illus.). 300p. (Orig.). 1997. pap. 99.00 (*0-9646241-8-4*) Russ Info & Busn Ctr.

***Russian Grammar.** Davidson. (Grammar Card Guides Ser.). (ENG & RUS.). 1964. pap. 3.95 (*0-8120-5072-X*) Barron.

Russian Grammar. Natalia Lusin. 250p. (RUS.). 1992. pap., vinyl bd. 5.95 (*0-8120-4902-0*) Barron.

Russian Grammar in Context. Olga Kagan & Frank Miller. LC 95-8438. 416p. (ENG & RUS.). (C). 1995. pap. text ed. 46.00 (*0-13-474891-3*) P-H.

Russian Grammar in Pictures. K. I. Pekhlivanova. (Illus.). 352p. 1987. text ed. 18.75 (*0-8285-3735-6*) Firebird NY.

Russian Grammar Workbook. Terence R. Wade. (Blackwell Reference Grammars Ser.). 240p. (C). pap. 27.95 (*0-631-19381-2*) Blackwell Pubs.

Russian Gypsy Fortune Telling Cards. Svetlana A. Touchkoff. LC 90-56459. 176p. 1991. 35.00 (*0-06-250876-8*) Harper SF.

Russian Gypsy Tales. Tr. by James Riordan. LC 92-7316. (International Folk Tale Ser.). (Illus.). 160p. 1992. 24.95 (*1-56656-100-0*); pap. 11.95 (*0-940793-97-0*) Interlink Pub.

Russian Hand-Painted Trays. I. Krapivina. (Illus.). 170p. (C). 1986. text ed. 140.00 (*0-685-40311-4*, Pub. by Collets) St Mut.

Russian Health Care Crisis: History, Evaluation, & Recommendations. David E. Powell. (Twentieth Century Fund Bk.). 120p. (C). 1996. pap. 9.95 (*0-87078-373-4*) TCFP-PPP.

Russian Heart: Days of Crisis & Hope. David C. Turnley. (Illus.). 144p. 1992. 40.00 (*0-89381-509-8*) Aperture.

Russian Heraldry & Nobility. D. R. Mandich & Joseph A. Placek. (Illus.). 700p. 1992. 135.00 (*0-9633063-9-1*) Dramco Pubs.

Russian Herbal: Traditional Remedies for Health & Healing. Igor V. Zevin et al. (Illus.). 240p. 1997. pap. 14.95 (*0-89281-549-3*, Heal Arts VT) Inner Tradit.

Russian Hero in Modern Chinese Fiction. Mau-sang Ng. LC 88-2165. (SUNY Series in Chinese Philosophy & Culture). 332p. 1988. text ed. 64.50 (*0-88706-880-4*); pap. text ed. 21.95 (*0-88706-881-2*) State U NY Pr.

Russian Hill: Storm Year. Elihu Blotnick. Ed. by Ariel Fragment. 64p. 1983. pap. 7.25 (*0-915090-17-1*) Calif Street.

***Russian Hill - The Summit 1853-1906: A Neighborhood History.** William Kostura. (Russian Hill History Ser.). (Illus.). 132p. (Orig.). 1997. pap. 17.95 (*0-9656400-0-0*) Aerie Pubns.

Russian History. Neil Heyman. 1992. pap. text ed. 11.95 (*0-07-028649-3*) McGraw.

Russian History. 7th ed. Walther Kirchner. LC 90-56008. (HarperCollins College Outline Ser.). (Illus.). 288p. (Orig.). 1991. pap. 15.00 (*0-06-467117-8*, Harper Ref) HarpC.

Russian History & Culture, Index to Unit 21. 26p. (RUS.). 1990. pap. 20.00 (*0-8357-0928-0*) Univ Microfilms.

Russian History & Culture: A Cumulative Index to Units 1-20. 508p. (RUS.). 1988. 125.00 (*0-8357-0750-4*) Univ Microfilms.

***Russian Hotel Directory.** 2nd rev. ed. Russian Information & Business Center, Inc. Staff. (Russian Business Library). 400p. 1997. pap. 99.00 (*1-57751-320-7*) Russ Info & Busn Ctr.

***Russian Hotels in Regions Directory.** Russian Info & Business Center, U. S. A. Staff. Ed. by Igor S. Oleynik & Natalia Alexeyeva. 300p. 1996. lib. bdg. 99.00 (*1-57751-150-6*) Russ Info & Busn Ctr.

Russian Houses. Elizabeth Gaynor. 1995. 29.95 (*3-8228-9049-9*) Taschen Amer.

Russian Housing in the Modern Age: Design & Social History. Ed. by William C. Brumfield & Blair A. Ruble. (Woodrow Wilson Center Ser.). (Illus.). 300p. (C). 1993. text ed. 110.00 (*0-521-43197-2*) Cambridge U Pr.

Russian-Hungarian & Hungarian Russian Dictionary for Schools. M. Szabo. 680p. 1988. 24.00 (*963-05-4840-2*, Pub. by Akad Kiado HU) St Mut.

Russian-Hungarian Comprehensive Dictionary, 2 vols., Set. 7th ed. L. Hadrovics & Laszlo Galdi. 2224p. (HUN & RUS.). 1986. 150.00 (*0-8288-0524-5*, F102190) Fr & Eur.

Russian-Hungarian Comprehensive Dictionary Vol. 1: A-O; Vol. 2: P-Q, 2 vols., Set. L. Hadrovics & Laszlo Galdi. 2224p. 1989. 120.00 (*963-05-5333-3*, Pub. by Akad Kiado HU) St Mut.

Russian-Hungarian Concise Dictionary. Laszlo Galdi. (HUN & RUS.). 1987. 49.95 (*0-8288-1066-4*, M 8576) Fr & Eur.

Russian-Hungarian Concise Dictionary. Laszlo Galdi. 1120p. (C). 1989. 36.00 (*963-05-5274-4*, Pub. by Akad Kiado HU) St Mut.

Russian-Hungarian Dictionary. Bibikov. 223p. (HUN & RUS.). 1982. 14.95 (*0-8288-1065-6*, F47675) Fr & Eur.

Russian-Hungarian Dictionary of Military Terms. L. Toth. 1148p. 1976. 42.00 (*963-05-1021-9*, Pub. by Akad Kiado HU) St Mut.

Russian-Hungarian Pocket Dictionary. M. Szabo. 542p. 1989. pap. 6.00 (*963-05-5343-0*, Pub. by Akad Kiado HU) St Mut.

Russian-Hungarian-Russian School Dictionary. 14th ed. M. Szabo. 262p. (HUN & RUS.). 1986. 14.95 (*0-8288-1667-0*, M 8603) Fr & Eur.

Russian-Hungarian Technical Dictionary, 2 vols. L. Katona. (HUN & RUS.). 1982. 125.00 (*0-8288-2148-8*, M8610) Fr & Eur.

Russian Hussar: A Story of the Imperial Cavalry, 1911-1920. Vladimer Littauer. LC 93-2299. (Illus.). 301p. (C). 1993. 24.95 (*0-942597-53-2*) White Mane Pub.

***Russian Icon: From Its Origins to the Sixteenth Century.** V. N. Lazarev. LC 97-25470. 404p. 1997. 99.95 (*0-8146-2452-9*) Liturgical Pr.

Russian Icon Painting: Russkaia Ikonopis'. Ot Istokov Do Nachala XVI Veka. V. N. Lazarev. 538p. (ENG & RUS.). 1984. 305.00 (*0-317-57449-3*) St Mut.

Russian Icons. D. Ivanov. (C). 1990. 500.00 (*0-685-34325-1*, Pub. by Collets) St Mut.

Russian Icons from the Humble Collection. Christine Hauice. (Illus.). 44p. (Orig.). (C). 1995. pap. 12.00 (*1-882007-11-5*) Univ KY Art Mus.

Russian Icons in the Santa Barbara Museum of Art. A. Dean McKenzie. LC 82-62426. (Illus.). 54p. (Orig.). 1982. pap. 8.25 (*0-89951-049-3*) Santa Barb Mus Art.

Russian Idea. Nikolai A. Berdiaev. Tr. by Reginald M. French. LC 78-32021. 255p. 1979. reprint ed. text ed. 59.75 (*0-313-20968-5*, BERN, Greenwood Pr) Greenwood.

Russian Idea. Nikolai Berdyaev. Tr. by R. M. French from RUS. Orig. Title: Russkaya Ideya. 280p. 1992. reprint ed. 26.95 (*0-940262-54-1*); reprint ed. pap. 16.95 (*0-940262-49-5*) Lindisfarne Bks.

Russian Idioms. Agnes Arany-Makkai. 1996. pap. text ed. 6.95 (*0-8120-9436-0*) Barron.

***Russian Image of Goethe, Vol. 1.** Andre Von Gronicka. LC 84-28060. 314p. 1968. reprint ed. pap. 89.50 (*0-608-03633-1*, 2064460) Bks Demand.

***Russian Image of Goethe, Vol. 2.** Andre Von Gronicka. LC 84-28060. 280p. 1968. reprint ed. pap. 79.80 (*0-608-03634-X*, 2064460) Bks Demand.

Russian Immigrant. Jerome Davis. LC 69-18770. (American Immigration Collection. Series 1). 1969. reprint ed. 11.95 (*0-405-00518-0*) Ayer.

Russian Impact on Art. Mikhail V. Alpatov. Ed. by Martin L. Wolf. Tr. by Ivy Litvinov. LC 75-90461. 352p. 1969. reprint ed. text ed. 37.50 (*0-8371-2160-4*, ALRA, Greenwood Pr) Greenwood.

Russian Imperial Military Doctrine & Education, 1832-1914. Carl Van Dyke. LC 90-36062. (Contributions in Military Studies: No. 105). 216p. 1990. text ed. 65.00 (*0-313-27249-2*, VDR, Greenwood Pr) Greenwood.

***Russian Imperial Style.** Laura Cerwinske. 1997. 19.99 (*0-517-18705-1*) Random Hse Value.

Russian Imperialism: Development & Crisis. Ariel Cohen. LC 95-43730. 192p. 1996. text ed. 55.00 (*0-275-95337-8*, Praeger Pubs) Greenwood.

Russian Impersonal Expressions Used with Reference to a Person. Friedrich Scholz. (S R P Ser.: No. 258). 1974. text ed. 72.35 (*90-279-2609-3*) Mouton.

***Russian Impressionnists & Post-Impressionnists.** Mikhail Guerman. (Illus.). 208p. 1997. 55.00 (*1-85995-340-9*) Parkstone Pr.

Russian in Exercises. S. Khavronina. 285p. 1989. text ed. 9.95 (*0-8285-4966-4*) Firebird NY.

Russian in Exercises. S. Khavronina & A. Shiroshenskaia. 352p. (C). 1984. 35.00 (*0-317-92379-X*, Pub. by Collets) St Mut.

Russian in Exercises. 6th ed. S. Khavronina. 285p. 1993. 39.95 (*0-7859-9090-9*) Fr & Eur.

***Russian in No Time.** (Now Your Talking in No Time Ser.). (ENG & RUS.). 1991. pap. 13.95 incl. audio (*0-8120-7733-4*) Barron.

Russian in Ten Days. S. Teskova & T. Akishina. 180p. (ENG & RUS.). (C). 1988. pap. 35.00 (*0-685-39374-7*, Pub. by Collets) St Mut.

Russian in Ten Days. S. Treskova. 180p. (Orig.). 1988. pap. text ed. 2.95 (*0-8285-4963-X*) Firebird NY.

Russian in the United States: Market Forces, Strategic Capacity, & the National Interest. A. Ronald Walton et al. (C). 1995. pap. text ed. write for info. (*1-880671-04-2*) NFLC Pubns.

Russian in Three Months. (Hugo's Language Bks.). 224p. 1988. 49.95 incl. audio (*0-85285-129-4*) Hunter NJ.

***Russian in 10 Minutes a Day.** Kristine K. Kershul. (ENG & RUS.). 1997. pap. text ed. 17.95 (*0-944502-47-4*) Bilingual Bks.

Russian in 7 Days. Shirley Baldwin et al. (Language in 7 Days Ser.). 96p. (RUS.). 1995. pap. 12.95 incl. audio (*0-8442-9137-4*, Natl Textbk) NTC Pub Grp.

***Russian Industrialists in an Era of Revolution: The Association of Industry & Trade, 1906-1917.** Ruth A. Roosa. Ed. & Frwd. by Thomas C. Owen. LC 97-8403. 288p. (C). (gr. 13). 1997. text ed. 66.95 (*0-7656-0154-0*) M E Sharpe.

Russian Industry: Automobile Industry. 2nd rev. ed. (Russian & Nis Industrial Directories Ser.). (Illus.). 300p. 1996. pap. 99.00 (*1-57751-107-7*) Russ Info & Busn Ctr.

Russian Industry: Building Materials. 2nd rev. ed. (Russian & Nis Industrial Directories Ser.). (Illus.). 400p. 1996. pap. 99.00 (*1-57751-108-5*) Russ Info & Busn Ctr.

Russian Industry: Chemical, Pharmaceutical & Microbiology Industry. 2nd rev. ed. (Russian & Nis Industrial Directories Ser.). (Illus.). 200p. 1996. pap. 99.00 (*1-57751-109-3*) Russ Info & Busn Ctr.

Russian Industry: Clothing Industry. 2nd rev. ed. (Russian & Nis Industrial Directories Ser.). (Illus.). 600p. 1996. pap. 99.00 (*1-57751-110-7*) Russ Info & Busn Ctr.

Russian Industry: Coal Mining & Peat. 2nd rev. ed. (Russian & Nis Industrial Directories Ser.). (Illus.). 200p. 1996. pap. 99.00 (*1-57751-111-5*) Russ Info & Busn Ctr.

Russian Industry: Consumer Goods, Household & Cultural Goods. 2nd rev. ed. (Russian & Nis Industrial Directories Ser.). (Illus.). 200p. 1996. pap. 99.00 (*1-57751-112-3*) Russ Info & Busn Ctr.

Russian Industry: Electrical Engineering. 2nd rev. ed. (Russian & Nis Industrial Directories Ser.). (Illus.). 250p. 1996. pap. 99.00 (*1-57751-113-1*) Russ Info & Busn Ctr.

Russian Industry: Fishing & Fish Processing. 2nd rev. ed. (Russian & Nis Industrial Directories Ser.). (Illus.). 200p. 1996. pap. 99.00 (*1-57751-114-X*) Russ Info & Busn Ctr.

Russian Industry: Footwear & Tanning Industry. 2nd rev. ed. (Russian & Nis Industrial Directories Ser.). (Illus.). 200p. 1996. pap. 99.00 (*1-57751-116-6*) Russ Info & Busn Ctr.

Russian Industry: Forestry & Timber. 2nd rev. ed. (Russian & Nis Industrial Directories Ser.). (Illus.). 350p. 1996. pap. 99.00 (*1-57751-117-4*) Russ Info & Busn Ctr.

Russian Industry: Gold Mining & Mining Industry. 2nd rev. ed. (Russian & Nis Industrial Directories Ser.). (Illus.). 200p. 1996. pap. 99.00 (*1-57751-125-5*) Russ Info & Busn Ctr.

Russian Industry: High-Tech Products, PC, Research & Design. 2nd ed. (Russian & Nis Industrial Directories Ser.). (Illus.). 250p. 1996. pap. 99.00 (*1-57751-118-2*) Russ Info & Busn Ctr.

Russian Industry: Machine-Building. 2nd rev. ed. (Russian & Nis Industrial Directories Ser.). (Illus.). 400p. 1996. pap. 99.00 (*1-57751-119-0*) Russ Info & Busn Ctr.

Russian Industry: Medical Equipment Industry. 2nd rev. ed. (Russian & Nis Industrial Directories Ser.). (Illus.). 250p. 1996. pap. 99.00 (*1-57751-120-4*) Russ Info & Busn Ctr.

Russian Industry: Metal-Working. 2nd rev. ed. (Russian & Nis Industrial Directories Ser.). (Illus.). 350p. 1996. pap. 99.00 (*1-57751-121-2*) Russ Info & Busn Ctr.

Russian Industry: Mining Industry/Construction Materials. 2nd rev. ed. (Russian & Nis Industrial Directories Ser.). (Illus.). 250p. 1996. pap. 99.00 (*1-57751-122-0*) Russ Info & Busn Ctr.

Russian Industry: Oil & Gas Industry. 2nd rev. ed. (Russian & Nis Industrial Directories Ser.). (Illus.). 200p. 1996. pap. 99.00 (*1-57751-123-9*) Russ Info & Busn Ctr.

Russian Industry: Oil Refining & Gas Processing. 2nd rev. ed. (Russian & Nis Industrial Directories Ser.). (Illus.). 200p. 1996. pap. 99.00 (*1-57751-124-7*) Russ Info & Busn Ctr.

Russian Industry: Power Industry. 2nd rev. ed. (Russian & Nis Industrial Directories Ser.). (Illus.). 300p. 1996. pap. 99.00 (*1-57751-126-3*) Russ Info & Busn Ctr.

Russian Industry: Publishing & Printing. 2nd rev. ed. (Russian & Nis Industrial Directories Ser.). (Illus.). 250p. 1996. pap. 99.00 (*1-57751-127-1*) Russ Info & Busn Ctr.

Russian Industry: Pulp & Paper. 2nd rev. ed. (Russian & Nis Industrial Directories Ser.). (Illus.). 400p. 1996. pap. 99.00 (*1-57751-128-X*) Russ Info & Busn Ctr.

Russian Industry: Radio-Electronics. 2nd rev. ed. (Russian & Nis Industrial Directories Ser.). (Illus.). 200p. 1996. pap. 99.00 (*1-57751-129-8*) Russ Info & Busn Ctr.

Russian Industry: Rubber & Plastic. 2nd rev. ed. (Russian & Nis Industrial Directories Ser.). (Illus.). 250p. 1996. pap. 99.00 (*1-57751-130-1*) Russ Info & Busn Ctr.

Russian Industry: Scrap & Waste Processing. 2nd rev. ed. (Russian & Nis Industrial Directories Ser.). (Illus.). 300p. 1996. pap. 99.00 (*1-57751-131-X*) Russ Info & Busn Ctr.

Russian Industry: Textile Industry. 2nd rev. ed. (Russian & Nis Industrial Directories Ser.). (Illus.). 400p. 1996. pap. 99.00 (*1-57751-132-8*) Russ Info & Busn Ctr.

Russian Industry: Tobacco Industry. 2nd rev. ed. (Russian & Nis Industrial Directories Ser.). (Illus.). 1996. pap. 99.00 (*1-57751-133-6*) Russ Info & Busn Ctr.

Russian Industry: Transport & Civil Engineering. rev. ed. (Russian & Nis Industrial Directories Ser.). (Illus.). 200p. 1996. pap. 99.00 (*1-57751-134-4*) Russ Info & Busn Ctr.

Russian Industry: 1000 Largest Companies. 2nd rev. ed. (Russian & Nis Industrial Directories Ser.). (Illus.). 250p. 1996. pap. 99.00 (*1-57751-106-9*) Russ Info & Busn Ctr.

Russian Industry: 500 Largest Companies. 2nd rev. ed. (Russian & Nis Industrial Directories Ser.). (Illus.). 200p. 1996. pap. 99.00 (*1-57751-105-0*) Russ Info & Busn Ctr.

***Russian Industry-97: Automobile Industry.** 3rd ed. Russian Information & Business Center, Inc. Staff. (Russian Industrial Directories Ser.: Vol. 3). 400p. 1997. pap. 99.00 (*1-57751-252-9*) Russ Info & Busn Ctr.

***Russian Industry-97: Building Materials Industry.** 3rd ed. Russian Information & Business Center, Inc. Staff. (Russian Industrial Directories Ser.: Vol. 4). 400p. 1997. pap. 99.00 (*1-57751-253-7*) Russ Info & Busn Ctr.

***Russian Industry-97: Chemical, Pharmaceutical & Microbiology Industry.** 3rd ed. Russian Information & Business Center, Inc. Staff. (Russian Industrial Directories Ser.: Vol. 5). 400p. 1997. pap. 99.00 (*1-57751-254-5*) Russ Info & Busn Ctr.

An Asterisk (*) at the beginning of an entry indicates that the title is appearing in BIP for the first time.

***Russian Industry-97: Clothing Industry.** 3rd ed. Russian Information & Business Center, Inc. Staff. (Russian Industrial Directories Ser.: Vol. 6). 400p. 1997. pap. 99.00 (*1-57751-255-3*) Russ Info & Busn Ctr.

***Russian Industry-97: Coal Mining & Peat Industry.** 3rd ed. Russian Information & Business Center, Inc. Staff. (Russian Industrial Directories Ser.: Vol. 7). 400p. 1997. pap. 99.00 (*1-57751-256-1*) Russ Info & Busn Ctr.

***Russian Industry-97: Consumer Goods, Household & Cultural Foods.** 3rd ed. Russian Information & Business Center, Inc. Staff. (Russian Industrial Directories Ser.: Vol. 8). 400p. 1997. pap. 99.00 (*1-57751-257-X*) Russ Info & Busn Ctr.

***Russian Industry-97: Defence Industry.** 3rd ed. Russian Information & Business Center, Inc. Staff. (Russian Industrial Directories Ser.: Vol. 28). 400p. 1997. pap. 99.00 (*1-57751-277-4*) Russ Info & Busn Ctr.

***Russian Industry-97: Electrical Engineering.** 3rd ed. Russian Information & Business Center, Inc. Staff. (Russian Industrial Directories Ser.: Vol. 9). 400p. 1997. pap. 99.00 (*1-57751-258-8*) Russ Info & Busn Ctr.

***Russian Industry-97: Fishing & Fish Processing.** 3rd ed. Russian Information & Business Center, Inc. Staff. (Russian Industrial Directories Ser.: Vol. 10). 400p. 1997. pap. 99.00 (*1-57751-259-6*) Russ Info & Busn Ctr.

***Russian Industry-97: Food & Food Processing.** 3rd ed. Russian Information & Business Center, Inc. Staff. (Russian Industrial Directories Ser.: Vol. 11). 400p. 1997. pap. 99.00 (*1-57751-260-X*) Russ Info & Busn Ctr.

***Russian Industry-97: Footwear & Tanning Industry.** 3rd ed. Russian Information & Business Center, Inc. Staff. (Russian Industrial Directories Ser.: Vol. 12). 400p. 1997. pap. 99.00 (*1-57751-261-8*) Russ Info & Busn Ctr.

***Russian Industry-97: Forestry & Timber Industry.** 3rd ed. Russian Information & Business Center, Inc. Staff. (Russian Industrial Directories Ser.: Vol. 13). 400p. 1997. pap. 99.00 (*1-57751-262-6*) Russ Info & Busn Ctr.

***Russian Industry-97: Gold Mining & Mining Industry.** 3rd ed. Russian Information & Business Center, Inc. Staff. (Russian Industrial Directories Ser.: Vol. 14). 400p. 1997. pap. 99.00 (*1-57751-263-4*) Russ Info & Busn Ctr.

***Russian Industry-97: High-Tech Products, PC, Research & Design.** 3rd ed. Russian Information & Business Center, Inc. Staff. (Russian Industrial Directories Ser.: Vol. 15). 400p. 1997. pap. 99.00 (*1-57751-264-2*) Russ Info & Busn Ctr.

***Russian Industry-97: Machine-Building.** 3rd ed. Russian Information & Business Center, Inc. Staff. (Russian Industrial Directories Ser.: Vol. 16). 400p. 1997. pap. 99.00 (*1-57751-269-3*) Russ Info & Busn Ctr.

***Russian Industry-97: Medical Equipment.** 3rd ed. Russian Information & Business Center, Inc. Staff. (Russian Industrial Directories Ser.: Vol. 17). 400p. 1997. pap. 99.00 (*1-57751-266-9*) Russ Info & Busn Ctr.

***Russian-Industry-97: Metal-Working.** 3rd ed. Russian Information & Business Center, Inc. Staff. (Russian Industrial Directories Ser.: Vol. 19). 400p. 1997. pap. 99.00 (*1-57751-268-5*) Russ Info & Busn Ctr.

***Russian-Industry-97: Metallurgy.** 3rd ed. Russian Information & Business Center, Inc. Staff. (Russian Industrial Directories Ser.: Vol. 18). 400p. 1997. pap. 99.00 (*1-57751-267-7*) Russ Info & Busn Ctr.

***Russian Industry-97: Mining (Building Materials)** 3rd ed. Russian Information & Business Center, Inc. Staff. (Russian Industrial Directories Ser.: Vol. 20). 400p. 1997. pap. 99.00 (*0-614-30774-0*) Russ Info & Busn Ctr.

***Russian Industry-97: Oil & Gas Industry.** 3rd ed. Russian Information & Business Center, Inc. Staff. (Russian Industrial Directories Ser.: Vol. 21). 400p. 1997. pap. 99.00 (*1-57751-270-7*) Russ Info & Busn Ctr.

***Russian Industry-97: Oil Refining & Gas Processing.** 3rd ed. Russian Information & Business Center, Inc. Staff. (Russian Industrial Directories Ser.: Vol. 22). 400p. 1997. pap. 99.00 (*1-57751-271-5*) Russ Info & Busn Ctr.

***Russian Industry-97: Power Industry.** 3rd ed. Russian Information & Business Center, Inc. Staff. (Russian Industrial Directories Ser.: Vol. 23). 400p. 1997. pap. 99.00 (*1-57751-272-3*) Russ Info & Busn Ctr.

***Russian Industry-97: Publishing & Printing Industry.** 3rd ed. Russian Information & Business Center, Inc. Staff. (Russian Industrial Directories Ser.: Vol. 25). 400p. 1997. pap. 99.00 (*1-57751-274-X*) Russ Info & Busn Ctr.

***Russian Industry-97: Pulp & Paper Industry.** 3rd ed. Russian Information & Business Center, Inc. Staff. (Russian Industrial Directories Ser.: Vol. 27). 400p. 1997. pap. 99.00 (*1-57751-276-6*) Russ Info & Busn Ctr.

***Russian Industry-97: Radio-Electronic Industry.** 3rd ed. Russian Information & Business Center, Inc. Staff. (Russian Industrial Directories Ser.: Vol. 26). 400p. 1997. pap. 99.00 (*1-57751-275-8*) Russ Info & Busn Ctr.

***Russian Industry-97: Rubber & Plastic Industry.** 3rd ed. Russian Information & Business Center, Inc. Staff. (Russian Industrial Directories Ser.: Vol. 29). 400p. 1997. pap. 99.00 (*1-57751-278-2*) Russ Info & Busn Ctr.

***Russian Industry-97: Scrap & Waste Processing.** 3rd ed. Russian Information & Business Center, Inc. Staff. (Russian Industrial Directories Ser.: Vol. 32). 400p. 1997. pap. 99.00 (*1-57751-282-0*) Russ Info & Busn Ctr.

***Russian Industry-97: Textile Industry.** 3rd ed. Russian Information & Business Center, Inc. Staff. (Russian Industrial Directories Ser.: Vol. 24). 400p. 1997. pap. 99.00 (*1-57751-273-1*) Russ Info & Busn Ctr.

***Russian Industry-97: Tobacco Industry.** 3rd ed. Russian Information & Business Center, Inc. Staff. (Russian Industrial Directories Ser.: Vol. 30). 400p. 1997. pap. 99.00 (*1-57751-279-0*) Russ Info & Busn Ctr.

***Russian Industry-97: Transport & Civil Engineering.** 3rd ed. Russian Information & Business Center, Inc. Staff. (Russian Industrial Directories Ser.: Vol. 31). 400p. 1997. pap. 99.00 (*1-57751-280-4*) Russ Info & Busn Ctr.

***Russian Industry-97: 1000 Largest Companies.** 3rd ed. Russian Information & Business Center, Inc. Staff. (Russian Industrial Directories Ser.: Vol. 2). 400p. 1997. pap. 99.00 (*1-57751-251-0*) Russ Info & Busn Ctr.

***Russian Industry-97: 500 Largest Companies.** 3rd ed. Russian Information & Business Center, Inc. Staff. (Russian Industrial Directories Ser.: Vol. 1). 400p. 1997. pap. 99.00 (*1-57751-250-2*) Russ Info & Busn Ctr.

Russian Instant Help Cards. Klara K. Lewis. (Illus.). (ENG & RUS.). 1995. pap. 14.95 incl. audio (*1-886821-31-3*) Pavleen.

Russian Instant Help Cards: Everyday Expressions, Frequently Asked Questions, Gratitude, Apology, Agreement, Refusal, Regret, Congratulations & Good Wishes, Requests, Wants & Needs, Compliments, Toasts. Klara K. Lewis. (In the Shoes of the Traveler Ser.). (Illus.). (Orig.). (RUS.). 1995. pap. 7.95 (*1-886821-10-0*); pap. 13.95 incl. audio (*1-886821-11-9*) Pavleen.

Russian Intellectual History: An Anthology. Ed. by Marc Raeff. 416p. (C). 1978. reprint ed. pap. 25.00 (*0-391-00905-2*) Humanities.

***Russian Intelligentsia.** Andrei Sinyavsky. 1997. 19.95 (*0-231-10726-9*) Col U Pr.

Russian Intelligentsia: From Torment to Silence. Vladimir Nahirny. LC 82-4796. 192p. 1982. 34.95 (*0-87855-463-7*) Transaction Pubs.

Russian Interpreter. Michele Melaragno. 150p. 1996. pap. text ed. 11.95 (*1-889421-04-9*) Minerva Archit.

Russian Intourist Guide Visits the U. S. A. Russell H. Volkema & Elena Turner. LC 95-90915. 1996. 16.95 (*0-533-11736-4*) Vantage.

Russian Jewish Artists in a Century of Change 1890-1990. Ed. by Susan Tumarkin-Goodman et al. (Illus.). 288p. 1995. text ed. 65.00 (*3-7913-1601-X*, Pub. by Prestel GW) te Neues.

Russian Jewish Experience. Jane M. Leder. LC 95-38544. (Journey Between Two Worlds Ser.). (J). 1996. lib. bdg. write for info. (*0-8225-3401-0*, Lerner Publctns) Lerner Group.

***Russian Jewish Family.** Howard Fast. Date not set. write for info. (*0-688-04738-6*) Morrow.

Russian Jewish Family. Jane M. Leder. (J). 1996. pap. text ed. 8.95 (*0-8225-9744-6*) Lerner Group.

Russian-Jewish Literature & Identity: Jabotinsky, Babel, Grossman, Galich, Roziner, Markish. Alice S. Nakhimovsky. LC 90-15804. (Jewish Studies). 240p. 1991. text ed. 42.00 (*0-8018-4205-0*) Johns Hopkins.

Russian Jewry Reader. Evan R. Chesler. 1976. 18.95 (*0-8488-0694-8*) Amereon Ltd.

Russian Jewry Situation Game see Kadima Kesher Series

***Russian Jews on Three Continents: Emigration & Resettlement.** Ed. by Noah Lewin-Spstein et al. (The Cummings Center Ser.: Vol. 6). 568p. (C). 1997. text ed. 64.50 (*0-7146-4726-8*, Pub. by F Cass Pubs UK); pap. text ed. 29.50 (*0-7146-4276-2*, Pub. by F Cass Pubs UK) Intl Spec Bk.

Russian Joint-Stock Societies: Basic Legislation. Tr. & Intro. by William E. Butler. 175p. 1996. 56.00 (*1-898029-23-7*, Pub. by Simmonds & Hill Pubng UK) Gaunt.

Russian Journal. Andrea Lee. LC 81-40214. 1981. 13.00 (*0-394-51891-8*) Random.

Russian Journal. Andrea Lee. 1984. pap. 7.95 (*0-394-71127-0*, Vin) Random.

Russian Journal. Inge Morath. (Illus.). 128p. 1991. 40.00 (*0-89381-473-3*) Aperture.

Russian Journal: During the August Coup of '91. Joe M. King. LC 92-18799. 1992. 12.95 (*0-86554-416-6*, MUP/P099) Mercer Univ Pr.

***Russian Journal of Aquatic Ecology.** 286p. 1997. 79.95 (*0-614-28284-5*) Intl Scholars.

Russian Journal of Lady Londonderry 1836-37. W. A. Seaman & J. R. Sewell. (Illus.). 185p. 1974. 14.00 (*0-7195-2851-8*) Transatl Arts.

Russian Journalism & Politics, 1861-1881: The Career of Aleksei S. Suvorin. Effie Ambler. LC 72-173671. 239p. reprint ed. pap. 68.20 (*0-685-20905-9*, 2032032) Bks Demand.

Russian Journals of Martha & Catherine Wilmot. Ed. by Marchioness of Londonberry Staff & H. M. Hyde. LC 71-115597. (Russia Observed Ser.). (Illus.). 1971. reprint ed. 29.95 (*0-405-03139-4*) Ayer.

Russian Lace Making. Bridget M. Cook. (Illus.). 144p. 1994. 39.95 (*0-7134-6101-2*, Pub. by Batsford UK) Trafalgar.

Russian Lace Patterns. Bridget Cook & Anna Korableva. (Illus.). 144p. 1996. 39.95 (*0-7134-6792-4*, Pub. by Batsford UK) Trafalgar.

Russian Lacquer Boxes. David Armstrong. (C). 1992. text ed. 110.00 (*0-569-23751-3*, Pub. by Collets) St Mut.

Russian Lacquer, Legends & Fairy Tales. Lucy Maxym. LC 81-51492. (Illus.). 80p. 1981. 35.00 (*0-940202-01-8*) Crnrs of the Wrld.

Russian Lacquer, Legends & Fairy Tales, Vol. II. Lucy Maxym. (Illus.). 80p. 1986. 35.00 (*0-940202-03-4*) Crnrs of the Wrld.

Russian Lacquered Minatures: Fedoskino, Palekh, Mstiora, Kholui. V. Guliayev. (Illus.). 287p. (C). 1989. text ed. 180.00 (*0-685-40310-6*, Pub. by Collets) St Mut.

Russian Lacquered Miniatures, Fedoskino, Palekh, Mstiora, Kholui. V. Guliayev. 287p. (C). 1989. 100.00 (*0-569-09216-7*, Pub. by Collets) St Mut.

Russian Land. Albert R. Williams. LC 73-39405. (Select Bibliographies Reprint Ser.). 1977. reprint ed. 18.95 (*0-8369-9924-X*) Ayer.

Russian Landed Gentry & the Peasant Emancipation of 1861. Terence Emmons. LC 68-29654. 496p. reprint ed. pap. 141.40 (*0-317-20620-6*, 2024574) Bks Demand.

Russian Language Fundamentals: Expanded Foreign Language Card Guides. 1992. pap. 5.95 (*0-8120-6309-0*) Barron.

Russian Language in the Twentieth Century. Bernard Comrie et al. 400p. 1996. 80.00 (*0-19-824066-X*) OUP.

***Russian Law & Legal Services Directory: Justice Departments, Courts, Law Firms, Bar Associations.** Russian Information & Business Center, Inc. Staff. 250p. 1997. pap. 99.00 (*1-57751-166-2*) Russ Info & Busn Ctr.

***Russian Law Books: Books on Russian Law & Private & Public International Law Published in Russia.** Ed. by W. E. Butler & Jolanta Murjas. 250p. 1997. 70.00 (*1-898029-28-8*, Pub. by Simmonds & Hill Pubng UK) Gaunt.

***Russian Law of Treaties.** William E. Butler. 170p. 1997. 55.00 (*1-898029-29-6*, Pub. by Simmonds & Hill Pubng UK) Gaunt.

Russian Learner's Dictionary. Nicholas J. Brown. 256p. 1996. pap. 18.95 (*0-415-13792-6*) Routledge.

Russian Legal Theory. Ed. by W. E. Butler. 500p. (C). 1996. 150.00 (*0-8147-1183-9*) NYU Pr.

***Russian Lessons: A Burned-Out Businesswoman Finds Herself in Postmodernist Moscow.** Carole D. Schweitzer. Ed. by Susan Antonovitz. LC 96-97007. (Illus.). 274p. (Orig.). 1996. pap. 18.00 (*0-9654782-0-3*) Cameron Publns.

Russian Letters of Spiritual Direction 1834-1860. Marcarius Starets of Optina & Staretz Macarius. Tr. by Iulia De Beausorbe from RUS. LC 75-1064. 115p. (Orig.). 1994. pap. 7.95 (*0-913836-23-0*) St Vladimirs.

Russian Levites: Parish Clergy in the Eighteenth Century. Gregory L. Freeze. LC 76-30764. (Russian Research Center Studies: No. 78). 334p. reprint ed. pap. 95.20 (*0-7837-4145-6*, 2057993) Bks Demand.

Russian Liberalism, from Gentry to Intelligentsia. George Fischer. LC 57-13462. (Harvard University, Russian Research Center Studies: No. 30). (Illus.). 256p. reprint ed. pap. 73.00 (*0-317-09570-6*, 2006417) Bks Demand.

Russian Life in Town & Country. Francis H. Palmer. LC 76-115574. (Russia Observed Ser., No. 1). 1970. reprint ed. 19.95 (*0-405-03056-8*) Ayer.

Russian Lindbergh: The Life of Valery Chkalov. Georgiy Baidukov. Tr. by Peter Belov. LC 91-6718. (History of Aviation Ser.). (Illus.). 352p. (C). 1991. reprint ed. pap. text ed. 19.95 (*1-56098-046-X*) Smithsonian.

Russian Listening Comprehension I & II: Sample Packet, No. 89. Richard Robin & Maria D. Lekic. (Illus.). 54p. (Orig.). (RUS.). (C). 1993. pap. text ed. 25.00 incl. audio (*0-87415-174-0*) OSU Foreign Lang.

Russian Listening Comprehension I, Pt. A: News & Public Affairs. 1991. teacher ed., pap. 40.00 incl. audio (*0-87415-176-7*, 71A) OSU Foreign Lang.

Russian Listening Comprehension I, Pt. A: News & Public Affairs. Richard Robin. (Illus.). 315p. (RUS.). 1991. Incl. audiotape. teacher ed., pap. text ed. 27.00 incl. audio (*0-87415-175-9*, 71) OSU Foreign Lang.

Russian Listening Comprehension I, Pt. A: News & Public Affairs, 3 cass., Set. 1991. audio 15.00 (*0-87415-178-3*, 71C); vhs 40.00 (*0-87415-177-5*, 71B) OSU Foreign Lang.

Russian Listening Comprehension I, Pt. B: "The Courier" Maria D. Lekic. (Illus.). 173p. (RUS.). (C). 1992. student ed., pap. 15.00 (*0-87415-179-1*, 72); teacher ed., pap. 35.00 incl. audio (*0-87415-180-5*, 72A); 7.50 (*0-87415-172-4*, 72C); audio 5.00 (*0-87415-181-3*, 72B) OSU Foreign Lang.

Russian Listening Comprehension II, Pt. A. Richard Robin. 97p. (RUS.). (C). 1994. teacher ed., pap. 36.00 incl. audio (*0-87415-183-X*, RUS-73A); Incl. 2 audio tapes. student ed., pap. text ed. 27.00 incl. audio (*0-87415-182-1*, 73) OSU Foreign Lang.

Russian Listening Comprehension II, 2 cass., Set. 1993. audio 10.00 (*0-87415-185-6*, 73C); vhs 25.00 (*0-87415-184-8*, 73B) OSU Foreign Lang.

Russian Listening Comprehension II, Part A, Units 45-49 Scripts. Richard Robin. (OSU Foreign Language Publications: No. 73D). 86p. (Orig.). (RUS.). (C). 1994. pap. text ed. 9.00 (*0-87415-275-5*, 73D) OSU Foreign Lang.

Russian Listening Comprehension II, Pt. B: "An Office Affair" Otterbein College Staff. (RUS.). (C). 1992. student ed., pap. 16.00 (*0-87415-186-4*, 74); teacher ed., pap. 68.50 incl. audio (*0-87415-187-2*, 74A); pap. 9.50 (*0-87415-173-2*, 74C) OSU Foreign Lang.

Russian Listening Comprehension II, Pt. B: "An Office Affair", 2 cass., Set. Otterbein College Staff. (RUS.). (C). 1992. audio 10.00 (*0-87415-188-0*, 74B) OSU Foreign Lang.

Russian Listening Comprehension III, Pt. A. Cynthia L. Martin & Maria D. Lekic. 96p. (RUS.). (C). 1995. teacher ed., pap. 36.00 incl. audio (*0-87415-190-2*, RUS-75A); student ed., pap. text ed. 23.00 (*0-87415-189-9*, RUS-75) OSU Foreign Lang.

Russian Listening Comprehension III, 5 videos, Set. 1994. vhs 50.00 (*0-87415-191-0*, 75B1) OSU Foreign Lang.

Russian Literary Criticism: A Short History. Robert H. Stacy. 288p. (C). 1974. pap. 22.50 (*0-8156-0108-5*) Syracuse U Pr.

Russian Literary Politics & the Pushkin Celebration of 1880. Marcus C. Levitt. LC 88-43237. (Studies of the Harriman Institute). (Illus.). 240p. 1989. 37.50 (*0-8014-2250-7*) Cornell U Pr.

Russian Literature. Piotr A. Kropotkin. LC 67-13334. 340p. 1972. reprint ed. 18.95 (*0-405-08721-7*, Pub. by Blom Pubns UK) Ayer.

Russian Literature: Ideals & Realities. Peter Kropotkin. 385p. (C). 1990. reprint ed. 38.95 (*0-921689-85-3*, Pub. by Black Rose Bks CN); reprint ed. pap. 19.95 (*0-921689-84-5*, Pub. by Black Rose Bks CN) Consort Bk Sales.

Russian Literature & American Critics. Ed. by Kenneth Brostrom. (Papers in Slavic Philology: No. 4). 412p. 1984. pap. 15.00 (*0-930042-58-1*) Mich Slavic Pubns.

Russian Literature & Criticism: Selected Papers from the Second World Congress for Soviet & East European Studies. Ed. by Evelyn Bristol. 254p. 1983. pap. 12.00 (*0-933884-27-3*) Berkeley Slavic.

Russian Literature & Empire: The Conquest of the Caucasus from Pushkin to Tolstoy. Susan Layton. LC 93-47121. (Studies in Russian Literature). 280p. (C). 1995. text ed. 59.95 (*0-521-44443-8*) Cambridge U Pr.

Russian Literature & Modern English Fiction: A Collection of Critical Essays. Ed. by Donald Davie. LC 65-18337. (Patterns of Literary Criticism Ser.). 250p. reprint ed. pap. 71.30 (*0-317-09846-2*, 2020052) Bks Demand.

Russian Literature & Psychoanalysis. Ed. by Daniel Rancour-Laferriere. LC 89-280. (Linguistic & Literary Studies in Eastern Europe: Vol. 31). x, 485p. 1989. 130.00 (*90-272-1536-7*); pap. 32.95 (*90-272-1540-5*) Benjamins North Am.

Russian Literature & the Classics. Ed. by Peter I. Barta et al. (Studies in Russian & European Literature). 1996. text ed. 60.00 (*3-7186-0605-4*); pap. text ed. 25.00 (*3-7186-0606-2*) Gordon & Breach.

Russian Literature from Pushkin to the Present Day. Richard Hare. LC 76-126237. (Select Bibliographies Reprint Ser.). 1977. 18.95 (*0-8369-5463-7*) Ayer.

***Russian Literature in the Age of Pushkin.** 1997. 140.00 (*0-7876-1682-6*, 00157047) Gale.

Russian Literature in the Baltic Between the World Wars. Temira Pachmuss. 448p. 1988. 29.95 (*0-89357-181-4*) Slavica.

Russian Literature of the Twenties: An Anthology. Ed. by Carl R. Proffer et al. 480p. 1987. 39.50 (*0-88233-820-X*); pap. 22.95 (*0-88233-821-8*) Ardis Pubs.

Russian Literature since the Revolution. enl. rev. ed. Edward J. Brown. (Illus.). 424p. 1982. 42.50 (*0-674-78203-8*); pap. 17.95 (*0-674-78204-6*) HUP.

Russian-Lithuanian Dictionary, 4 vols., Set. (LIT & RUS.). 1982. 295.00 (*0-8288-1105-9*, F60900) Fr & Eur.

Russian Local Government During the War & the Union of Zemstvos. Tikhon J. Polner et al. (Economic & Social History of the World War Ser.). 1930. 100.00 (*0-317-27559-3*) Elliots Bks.

***Russian Love Story.** Steven Strasser. Date not set. write for info. (*1-55710-000-4*) Morrow.

Russian Management Revolution: Preparing Managers for the Market Economy. Ed. by Sheila M. Puffer. LC 92-9034. 320p. (gr. 13). 1992. text ed. 79.95 (*1-56324-042-4*); pap. text ed. 30.95 (*1-56324-043-2*) M E Sharpe.

Russian Manual. 1987. pap. 3.00 (*0-517-51267-X*, Living Language) Crown Pub Group.

Russian Martyr. Ivan V. Moiseyev. 1974. 1.95 (*0-89985-107-X*) Christ for the Nations.

Russian Marxists & the Origins of Bolshevism. Leopold H. Haimson. LC 55-10972. (Russian Research Center Studies: No. 19). 260p. reprint ed. pap. 74.10 (*0-317-09492-0*, 2003777) Bks Demand.

***Russian Mass Media Directory.** 2nd rev. ed. Russian Information & Business Center, Inc. Staff. (Russian Business Library). 400p. 1997. pap. 99.00 (*1-57751-316-9*) Russ Info & Busn Ctr.

Russian Mass Media Directory, '96. (Russian Business Library). (Illus.). 300p. (Orig.). 1996. pap. 99.00 (*1-57751-012-7*) Russ Info & Busn Ctr.

Russian Master & Other Stories. Anton P. Chekhov. Tr. by Ronald Hingley from RUS. (World's Classics Ser.). 256p. 1984. pap. 6.95 (*0-19-281680-2*) OUP.

***Russian Medical Services & Recreation Facilities Directory.** 2nd rev. ed. Russian Information & Business Center, Inc. Staff. (Russian Business Library). 400p. 1997. pap. 99.00 (*0-614-30776-7*) Russ Info & Busn Ctr.

Russian Medical Services & Recreation Facilities Directory, '96. (Russian Business Library). 300p. (Orig.). 1996. pap. 99.00 (*1-57751-018-6*) Russ Info & Busn Ctr.

Russian Medicine. William A. Gantt. LC 75-23669. (Clio Medica Ser.: 20). (Illus.). 1978. reprint ed. 40.00 (*0-404-58920-0*) AMS Pr.

Russian Memoirs of John Quincy Adams: His Diary from 1809 to 1814. Ed. by Charles F. Adams, Jr. LC 74-115501. (Russia Observed, Series I). 1970. reprint ed. 29.95 (*0-405-03001-0*) Ayer.

Russian Metaphysical Romanticism: The Poetry of Tiutchev & Boratynskii. Sarah Pratt. LC 82-42863. 272p. 1984. 39.50 (*0-8047-1188-7*) Stanford U Pr.

***Russian Military's Role in Politics.** James H. Brusstar & Ellen Jones. 62p. (Orig.). (C). 1996. pap. 25.00 (*0-7881-3233-4*) DIANE Pub.

Russian Mind since Stalin's Death. Yuri Glazov. (Sovietica Ser.: No. 47). 272p. 1985. pap. text ed. 57.00 (*90-277-1969-1*); lib. bdg. 112.00 (*90-277-1828-8*) Kluwer Ac.

Russian Missions in China & Japan. Charles Hale. 1974. reprint ed. pap. 1.50 (*0-89981-079-9*) Eastern Orthodox.

Russian, Modern. Clayton L. Dawson et al. 1980. pap. text ed. 255.00 incl. audio (*0-88432-056-1*, AFB125) Audio-Forum.

Russian, Modern, 24 cass., Vol. I. Clayton L. Dawson et al. 480p. 1980. pap. text ed. 255.00 incl. audio (*0-88432-044-8*, AFB101) Audio-Forum.

Russian-Modern Greek Dictionary: Dictionnaire Russe-Grec Moderne. 808p. (GRE & RUS.). 1983. 55.00 (*0-8288-0798-1*, F47640) Fr & Eur.

***Russian Modernism: Collections of the Getty Research Institute for the History of Art & the Humanities.** Compiled by David Woodruff & Ljiljana Grubioic. LC 96-34895. (Bibliographies & Dossiers Ser.). (Illus.). 208p. (Orig.). 1997. pap. 35.00 (*0-89236-385-1*, Getty Res Inst) J P Getty Trust.

An Asterisk (*) at the beginning of an entry indicates that the title is appearing in BIP for the first time.

***Russian Modernism: The Transfiguration of the Everyday.** Stephen C. Hutchings. (Studies in Russian Literature). 220p. (C). 1997. text ed. 59.95 (*0-521-58009-9*) Cambridge U Pr.

Russian Mother. Alain Bosquet. Tr. by Barbara Bray from FRE. (French Expressions Ser.). 284p. 1996. 26.00 (*0-8419-1329-3*) Holmes & Meier.

Russian Motion Verbs for Intermediate Students. William J. Mahota. LC 95-48780. 139p. (RUS.). (C). 1996. pap. 17.00 (*0-300-06413-6*) Yale U Pr.

Russian Museum, Leningrad. Compiled by Vladimir A. Leniashin. (C). 1987. 195.00 (*0-685-22621-2*, Pub. by Collets) St Mut.

Russian Museum, Leningrad. N. Novouspensky. 193p. 1975. 40.00 (*0-317-14293-3*, Pub. by Collets) St Mut.

Russian Museum, Leningrad: Paintings of the Twelfth to Early Twentieth Centuries. Izobrazitel'noe Iskusstvo. 1986. 132.00 (*0-317-14295-X*, Pub. by Collets) St Mut.

Russian Mystics. Sergius Bolshakoff. (Cistercian Studies: No. 26). Orig. Title: I Mistici Russi. 303p. 1981. reprint ed. pap. 11.95 (*0-87907-926-6*) Cistercian Pubns.

Russian Narrative & Visual Art: Varieties of Seeing. Ed. by Roger Anderson & Paul Debreczeny. LC 93-34786. (Illus.). 216p. (C). 1994. lib. bdg. 49.95 (*0-8130-1255-4*) U Press Fla.

***Russian Narrative of Art 1901-2000: Towards Historiography of Modern Art Russia.** Bowlt & Misler. 1998. 85.00 (*0-7838-2034-8*) Mac Lib Ref.

Russian National Security & Foreign Policy in Transition. Eugene B. Rumer. LC 94-42678. x, 68p. 1995. pap. text ed. 15.00 (*0-8330-1615-6*, MR-512-AF) Rand Corp.

Russian Nationalism & the Legacy of Empire. Darrell P. Hammer. 200p. 1996. 32.50 (*0-8133-0440-7*) Westview.

Russian Nationalism & Ukraine: The Nationality Policy of the Volunteer Army During the Civil War. Anna M. Procyk. 1995. 39.95 (*1-895571-04-9*) Ukrainian Acad.

Russian Natural Gas Availability. Jonathan Stern. 91p. (C). 1995. pap. 14.95 (*0-905031-92-X*) Brookings.

***Russian Nights.** I. V. Odoevski et al. LC 96-52851. (European Classics Ser.). 1997. write for info. (*0-8101-1520-4*) Northwestern U Pr.

Russian Nights. Vladimir F. Odoevsky. Tr. by Olga Koshansky-Olienikov & Ralph E. Matlaw from RUS. 265p. reprint ed. pap. 14.95 (*0-8101-1087-3*) Northwestern U Pr.

Russian Normative Stress Notation. John G. Nicholson. 176p. 1968. 49.95 (*0-7735-0020-0*, Pub. by McGill CN) U of Toronto Pr.

Russian Normative Stress Notation. John G. Nicholson. LC 67-31404. 187p. reprint ed. pap. 53.30 (*0-7837-6929-6*, 2046758) Bks Demand.

Russian Novel. Eugene M. Vogue. 1972. 250.00 (*0-8490-0982-0*) Gordon Pr.

Russian Novel from Pushkin to Pasternak. Ed. by John Garrard. LC 83-1070. 320p. 1983. 47.50 (*0-300-02935-7*) Yale U Pr.

Russian Novel in English Fiction. Gilbert Phelps. LC 79-158907. 1971. reprint ed. 39.00 (*0-403-01301-1*) Scholarly.

Russian Novelists. E. M. De Vogue. LC 74-28331. (Studies in Russian Literature & Life: No. 100). 1974. lib. bdg. 75.00 (*0-8383-1949-1*) M S G Haskell Hse.

Russian Novelists. Eugene N. De Vogue. Tr. by Jane L. Edmands. LC 72-1328. (Essay Index Reprint Ser.). 1977. reprint ed. 18.95 (*0-8369-2870-9*) Ayer.

Russian Now. Barron Staff. 1996. 18.95 (*0-8120-6633-2*) Barron.

Russian Now! Barron Staff. 1996. wbk. ed., pap. text ed. 6.95 (*0-8120-9453-0*); teacher ed., pap. text ed. 9.95 (*0-8120-9454-9*) Barron.

Russian Now! Grammar Book. Barron Staff. 1996. pap. text ed. 5.95 (*0-8120-9633-9*) Barron.

Russian Nuclear Business Directory. (Illus.). 250p. (Orig.). 1996. pap. 295.00 (*1-57751-033-X*) Russ Info & Busn Ctr.

Russian Officialdom in Crisis: Autocracy & Local Self-Government, 1861-1900. Thomas S. Pearson. (Illus.). 368p. (C). 1989. text ed. 74.95 (*0-521-36127-3*) Cambridge U Pr.

Russian-on-a-Disk. Oscar E. Swan. 60p. (YA). 1992. pap. text ed. 39.95 incl. mac hd (*0-88432-701-9*, SRU300) Audio-Forum.

Russian on Location. Eli Hinkel. (On Location Ser.). 1994. audio 10.95 (*0-8120-8149-8*) Barron.

Russian on the Go, Level 1. Thomas R. Beyer. (On the Go Ser.). 1994. pap. 11.95 incl. audio (*0-8120-8128-5*) Barron.

***Russian on the Go, Level 2.** Beyer. (Languages on the Go Ser.). (ENG & RUS.). 1995. pap. 12.95 (*0-8120-8211-7*) Barron.

Russian on Your Own: Course in Six Parts with Cassettes. 2nd ed. E. Vasilenko & E. Lamm. 1987. text ed. 59.95 (*0-8285-4969-9*) Firebird NY.

Russian on Your Own: Russian-English Vocabulary. Ed. by E. Vasilenko & E. Lamm. 62p. (C). 1987. 35.00 (*0-685-33706-5*, Pub. by Collets) St Mut.

Russian Opera. Martin Cooper. 1988. reprint ed. lib. bdg. 49.00 (*0-7812-0142-X*) Rprt Serv.

Russian Opera. Martin Cooper. LC 77-181127. 65p. 1951. reprint ed. 59.00 (*0-403-01528-6*) Scholarly.

Russian Opera. Rosa H. Newmarch. LC 72-109807. (Illus.). 403p. 1972. reprint ed. text ed. 79.50 (*0-8371-4298-9*, NERO, Greenwood Pr) Greenwood.

Russian Orders, Decorations & Medals. 2nd ed. Robert Werlich. LC 81-171055. (Illus.). 1981. 50.00 (*0-685-90818-6*) Quaker.

Russian Orders, Decorations & Medals Including a Historical Resume & Notes under the Monarchy. C. Hurley. 90p. (C). 1987. 84.00 (*0-317-90442-6*, Pub. by Picton UK) St Mut.

Russian Orders, Decorations & Medals Including Those of Imperial Russia, the Provisional Government, the Civil War & the Soviet Union. Robert Werlich. (Illus.). 1981. lib. bdg. 50.00 (*0-911200-03-7*) Quaker.

***Russian Organized Crime: The New Threat?** Ed. by Phil Williams. LC 96-30098. 280p. 1997. text ed. 42.50 (*0-7146-4763-2*, Pub. by F Cass Pubs UK); pap. text ed. 22.50 (*0-7146-4312-2*, Pub. by F Cass Pubs UK) Intl Spec Bk.

***Russian Origami.** Hull. Date not set. pap. write for info. (*0-312-16993-0*) St Martin.

Russian Orthodox Church Outside Russia: A History & Chronology. Alexey Young. LC 91-36884. (Autocephalous Orthodox Churches Ser.: No. 2). 136p. 1993. pap. 19.00 (*0-8095-3300-6*); lib. bdg. 29.00 (*0-8095-2300-0*) Borgo Pr.

Russian Orthodox Church, 1985-94. Jane Ellis. LC 96-17557. (St. Antony's Ser.). 1996. text ed. 59.95 (*0-312-16227-8*) St Martin.

Russian Orthodox Missions. Eugene Smirnoff. reprint ed. pap. 8.95 (*0-89981-080-2*) Eastern Orthodox.

Russian Overseas Commerce with Great Britain During the Reign of Catherine II. Herbert H. Kaplan. LC 94-78517. (Memoirs Ser.: Vol. 218). (Illus.). 301p. (C). 1996. 40.00 (*0-87169-218-X*, M218-kah) Am Philos.

Russian Painted Shop Signs & Avant-Garde Artists. E. Kovtun & A. Povelikhina. 199p. (C). 1991. 225.00 (*0-89771-821-6*, Pub. by Collets) St Mut.

Russian Painting of the Mid 19th Century. M. N. Shumova. 238p. (RUS.). 1984. 60.00 (*0-317-57342-X*) St Mut.

Russian Painting of the 17th Century. V. G. Briusova. (Illus.). 338p. (RUS.). 1984. 300.00 (*0-317-57433-7*) St Mut.

***Russian Paintings.** Sergei Daniel. 1997. 55.00 (*1-85995-355-7*) Parkstone Pr.

Russian Paintings & Drawings. Larissa Salmina-Haskell. (Illus.). 112p. 1995. 25.00 (*0-907849-95-4*, 989, Pub. by Ashmolean Mus UK) A Schwartz & Co.

Russian Paintings & Drawings. Larissa Salmina-Haskell. (Illus.). 112p. 1995. pap. 17.95 (*0-907849-96-2*, 970, Pub. by Ashmolean Mus UK) A Schwartz & Co.

Russian Parliament: Encyclopedic Directory 1996. (Illus.). 250p. 1996. pap. 99.00 (*0-9646241-5-X*) Russ Info & Busn Ctr.

***Russian Parliament Directory.** 2nd ed. Russian Information & Business Center, Inc. Staff. 250p. 1997. pap. 99.00 (*1-57751-167-0*) Russ Info & Busn Ctr.

***Russian Parliamentary Elections of 1995: The Battle for the Duma.** Open Media Research Institute, Prague Staff et al. LC 96-29822. (Omri Bks.). 224p. (C). (gr. 13). 1997. text ed. 62.95 (*0-7656-0084-6*) M E Sharpe.

Russian-Pashto-Dari Dictionary. K. A. Lebedev. 768p. (PUS & RUS.). 1983. 59.95 (*0-8288-1738-3*, F 47690) Fr & Eur.

Russian Peasant. Howard P. Kennard. LC 77-87519. (Anthropology Ser.). (Illus.). reprint ed. 39.50 (*0-404-16607-5*) AMS Pr.

Russian Peasant Design Motifs for Needleworkers & Craftsmen. V. Stasov. (Pictorial Archive Ser.). (Illus.). 32p. (Orig.). 1976. pap. 2.95 (*0-486-23235-2*) Dover.

Russian Peasant Schools: Officialdom, Village Culture, & Popular Pedagogy, 1861-1914. Ben Eklof. (Illus.). 667p. 1987. pap. 18.95 (*0-520-06957-9*) U CA Pr.

Russian Peasant Women. Ed. by Beatrice Farnsworth & Lynne Viola. (Illus.). 320p. (C). 1992. pap. text ed. 18.95 (*0-19-506694-4*) OUP.

Russian Peasant, 1920 & 1984. Ed. by Robert E. Smith. (Library of Peasant Studies: No. 4). 120p. 1977. 28.50 (*0-7146-3078-0*, Pub. by F Cass Pubs UK) Intl Spec Bk.

Russian Peasants & Soviet Power: A Study of Collectivization. Moshe Lewin. 544p. (C). 1975. reprint ed. pap. text ed. 18.95 (*0-393-00752-9*) Norton.

Russian Penetration of the North Pacific Ocean: A Documentary Record 1700-1797. Ed. by Basil Dmytryshyn et al. (To Siberia & Russian America Ser.). 640p. 1988. 40.00 (*0-87595-149-X*) Oregon Hist.

Russian People: A Reader on their History & their Culture. 3rd ed. Ed. by V. Tschebotarioff Bill. LC 74-17005. 191p. reprint ed. pap. 54.50 (*0-317-42257-X*, 2025784) Bks Demand.

Russian People Speak: Democracy at the Crossroads. Nikolai Popov. 144p. (C). 1994. 28.95 (*0-8156-0300-2*) Syracuse U Pr.

Russian-Persian Dictionary. G. A. Voskanjan. 832p. (PER & RUS.). 1986. 95.00 (*0-8288-1127-X*, F 47890) Fr & Eur.

Russian-Persian Polytechnical Dictionary. 2nd ed. Z. M. Mirzabekian. 720p. (PER & RUS.). 1983. 95.00 (*0-8288-2160-7*, M8890) Fr & Eur.

Russian-Persian Polytechnical Dictionary. 2nd ed. Z. M. Mirzabekian. 720p. (C). 1983. 140.00 (*0-685-46895-X*, Pub. by Collets) St Mut.

Russian Philosophy, 3 vols., 1. James P. Scanlan & Mary-Barbara Zeldin. Ed. by James M. Edie et al. LC 64-10928. 1976. reprint ed. pap. 16.00 (*0-87049-200-4*) U of Tenn Pr.

Russian Philosophy, 3 vols., 2. James P. Scanlan & Mary-Barbara Zeldin. Ed. by James W. Edie et al. LC 64-10928. 1976. reprint ed. pap. 16.00 (*0-87049-715-4*) U of Tenn Pr.

Russian Philosophy, 3 vols., 3. James P. Scanlan & Mary-Barbara Zeldin. Ed. by James M. Edie et al. LC 64-10928. 1976. reprint ed. pap. 16.00 (*0-87049-716-2*) U of Tenn Pr.

Russian Phoenix see Millenium of Faith: Christianity in Russia 988 - 1988

Russian Phrase Book. (Hugo Ser.). (Illus.). 128p. (Orig.). 1991. pap. 4.95 (*0-85285-152-9*) Hunter NJ.

Russian Phrase Book. Berlitz Editors. (Phrase Bk.). 192p. (RUS.). 1992. pap. 6.95 (*2-8315-0910-6*) Berlitz.

***Russian Phrase Book.** Berlitz Editors. 192p. 1997. pap. 7.95 (*2-8315-6238-4*) Berlitz.

Russian Phrasebook. 2nd ed. James Jenkin. (Orig.). (RUS.). 1995. pap. 5.95 (*0-86442-307-1*) Lonely Planet.

Russian Phrasebook & Dictionary. rev. ed. Erika Haber. (Orig.). 1993. digital audio 12.95 (*0-7818-0192-3*) Hippocrene Bks.

Russian Phrasebook & Dictionary. 2nd rev. ed. Erika Haber. 256p. (Orig.). 1993. pap. 9.95 (*0-7818-0190-7*) Hippocrene Bks.

***Russian Physicians in an Era of Reform & Revolution, 1856-1905.** Nancy M. Frieden. LC 81-47128. 397p. 1981. reprint ed. pap. 113.20 (*0-608-03331-6*, 2064043) Bks Demand.

Russian Piano Concerto, Vol. I: The Nineteenth Century. Jeremy Norris. LC 93-11565. (Russian Music Studies). 244p. 1994. 35.00 (*0-253-34112-4*) Ind U Pr.

Russian Piano Music. Dmitry Feofanov. (Carl Fischer's "All Time Favorites" Music Ser.). 152p. (Orig.). 1988. pap. 10.95 (*0-8258-0397-7*, ATF113) Fischer Inc NY.

Russian Picture Alphabet. Klara K. Lewis. (In the Shoes of the Traveler Ser.). (Illus.). (Orig.). (RUS.). 1995. pap. 8.95 (*1-886821-00-3*); pap. 14.95 incl. audio (*1-886821-01-1*); pap. 15.95 incl. audio (*1-886821-24-0*); pap. text ed. 8.95 (*1-886821-18-6*) Pavleen.

Russian Picture Dictionary. Klara K. Lewis. (Illus.). (ENG & RUS.). 1995. pap. 17.95 incl. audio (*1-886821-25-9*) Pavleen.

Russian Picture Dictionary: Things Around Me, Colors, Numbers, Pronouns, Professions, Days of the Week, Family, Fruits, Vegetables, Groceries, Parts of the Body, Weather, Clothing, Living Room, Kitchen, Bedroom, Office, Questions, Animals, Verbs, Time, Etc. Klara K. Lewis. (In the Shoes of the Traveler Ser.). (Illus.). (Orig.). (RUS.). 1995. pap. 13.95 (*1-886821-02-X*); pap. 17.95 incl. audio (*1-886821-03-8*); pap. text ed. 13.95 (*1-886821-17-8*) Pavleen.

Russian Piety. Nicholas Arseniev. 143p. 1964. pap. 8.95 (*0-913836-21-4*) St Vladimirs.

Russian Plays for Young Audiences. Ed. by Miriam Morton. 401p. 1977. 13.95 (*0-932720-62-5*); pap. 9.95 (*0-932720-61-7*) New Plays Inc.

Russian Pluralism, Now Irreversible? Ed. by Uri Ra'anan et al. LC 92-28597. 224p. 1993. text ed. 39.95 (*0-312-08648-2*) St Martin.

Russian Poetics Proceedings of the International Colloquium at UCLA, September 22-26, 1975. Ed. by Thomas Eekman & Dean S. Worth. (UCLA Slavic Studies: Vol. 4). (Illus.). 544p. (RUS.). 1983. 34.95 (*0-89357-101-6*) Slavica.

Russian Poetry. Tr. by Natalia Uspenskaya from RUS. (C). 1989. pap. 30.00 (*1-85072-083-5*, Pub. by W Sessions UK) St Mut.

Russian Poetry: A Personal Anthology. Ed. & Tr. by R. A. Ford. 128p. 1995. lib. bdg. 29.00 (*0-8095-4870-4*) Borgo Pr.

Russian Poetry: A Personal Anthology. Ed. & Tr. by R. A. Ford. 128p. 1987. reprint ed. pap. 9.95 (*0-88962-267-1*) Mosaic.

Russian Poetry: An Anthology in Russian & in English. Tr. by Natalia Uspenskaya. (C). 1991. 30.00 (*0-685-57491-1*, Pub. by W Sessions UK) St Mut.

Russian Poetry: Meter, Rhythm & Rhyme. Barry P. Scherr. LC 84-28045. 475p. 1986. 60.00 (*0-520-05299-4*) U CA Pr.

Russian Poetry: Reader--I. Ed. by S. Knovalov et al. 153p. (C). 1971. reprint ed. pap. 29.95 (*0-8236-5940-2*) Intl Univs Pr.

Russian Poetry: The Modern Period. Ed. by John Glad & Daniel Weissbort. LC 78-8650. (Iowa Translations Ser.). 418p. reprint ed. pap. 119.20 (*0-7837-1247-2*, 2041384) Bks Demand.

Russian Poetry for Children. Elena Sokol. LC 83-6703. (Illus.). 258p. 1984. text ed. 36.00 (*0-87049-406-6*) U of Tenn Pr.

Russian Poetry for Intermediates. rev. ed. Ed. by E. Aitken. (Russian Texts Ser.). (RUS.). 1996. pap. 15.95 (*1-85399-415-4*, Pub. by Brstl Class Pr UK) Focus Pub-R Pullins.

Russian Pogroms...a Child's Story. Riva T. Holtz. 1995. 10.95 (*0-533-11490-X*) Vantage.

Russian Policy Debate on Central Asia. Irina Zviagelskaia. 60p. (C). 1995. pap. 12.95 (*1-899658-01-7*) Brookings.

Russian-Polish Dictionary. Levinskaja. 320p. (POL & RUS.). 1981. 14.95 (*0-8288-0488-5*, F 47670) Fr & Eur.

Russian-Polish Political Dictionary. deluxe ed. B. Dudawaki et al. 726p. (POL & RUS.). 1955. 29.95 (*0-8288-6866-2*, M-9114) Fr & Eur.

Russian-Polish-Russian Pocket Dictionary. 19th ed. I. Mitronowa. 575p. (POL & RUS.). 1980. 9.95 (*0-8288-1632-8*, M9102) Fr & Eur.

***Russian Political Atlas.** Russian Information & Business Center, Inc. Staff. 300p. 1997. pap. 149.00 (*1-57751-171-9*) Russ Info & Busn Ctr.

Russian Political Atlas: Elections, Political Parties, Parliament, Regional Political Profiles. (Illus.). 500p. (Orig.). 1996. pap. 149.00 (*0-9646241-3-3*) Russ Info & Busn Ctr.

***Russian Political Parties, Unions & Membership Organizations.** Russian Info & Business Center, U. S. A. Staff. Ed. by Igor S. Oleynik & Natalia Alexeyeva. 250p. 1996. lib. bdg. 99.00 (*1-57751-147-6*) Russ Info & Busn Ctr.

***Russian Political Parties, Unions & Membership Organizations Directory.** 2nd ed. Russian Information & Business Center, Inc. Staff. (Russian Business Library). 400p. 1997. pap. 99.00 (*1-57751-321-5*) Russ Info & Busn Ctr.

Russian Politics. Kelley. (C). 1997. pap. text ed. write for info. (*0-15-500785-8*) HB Coll Pubs.

***Russian Politics, Vol. 1.** Smith. Date not set. pap. text ed. write for info. (*0-312-11607-1*) St Martin.

Russian Politics: The Struggle for a New Order. Joseph L. Nogee & R. Judson Mitchell. LC 96-14435. 352p. (C). 1996. pap. 28.00 (*0-02-388062-7*, Macmillan Coll) P-H.

***Russian Politics & Society.** 2nd ed. Richard Sakwa. 488p. (C). 1996. pap. 22.95 (*0-415-12160-4*); text ed. 79.95 (*0-415-15483-9*) Routledge.

***Russian Politics in Transition, 3 Vols.** 2nd ed. Joan DeBardeleben. 288p. (C). 1997. text ed. 25.56 (*0-669-41618-5*) HM College Div.

Russian Popular Culture: Entertainment & Society since 1900. Richard Stites. (Soviet Paperbacks Ser.: No. 7). (Illus.). 288p. (C). 1992. text ed. 59.95 (*0-521-36214-8*); pap. text ed. 18.95 (*0-521-36986-X*) Cambridge U Pr.

Russian Population in Alaska & California: Late 18th Century to 1867. Svetlana G. Fedorova. Tr. by R. A. Pierce & A. S. Donnelly from RUS. LC 73-83208. (Alaska History Ser.: No. 4). (Illus.). 1973. 29.00 (*0-919642-53-5*) Limestone Pr.

Russian Portraits. Dorothy Hoobler & Thomas Hoobler. LC 93-38362. (J). 1994. lib. bdg. 27.11 (*0-8114-6380-X*) Raintree Steck-V.

***Russian Presidential Elections of 1996.** Open Media Research Institute, Prague Staff et al. (Omri Bks.). 256p. (C). (gr. 13). 1998. text ed. 62.95 (*0-7656-0085-4*) M E Sharpe.

Russian Press from Brezhnev to Yeltsin: Behind the Paper Curtain. John Murray. LC 93-49830. (Studies in Communism in Transition). 288p. 1994. 80.00 (*1-85278-885-2*) E Elgar.

Russian Primary Chronicle: Laurentian Text. Ed. by Samuel H. Cross. Tr. by O. P. Sherbowitz-Wetzor. LC 53-10264. (Medieval Academy Bks.: No. 60). 1968. reprint ed. 25.00 (*0-910956-34-0*) Medieval Acad.

Russian Primer. Agnes Jacques. 1959. pap. 12.95 (*0-87532-159-3*) Hendricks House.

Russian Propliners & Jetliners. Collin Ballantine. (Illus.). 128p. 1993. pap. 19.95 (*0-87938-831-5*) Motorbooks Intl.

Russian Proprietor & Other Stories. Leo Tolstoy. Tr. by Nathan H. Dole. LC 77-110219. (Short Story Index Reprint Ser.). 1977. 23.95 (*0-8369-3371-0*) Ayer.

Russian Prose: Reader--I. S. Knovalov et al. 1545p. (C). 1945. 29.95 (*0-8236-5960-7*) Intl Univs Pr.

Russian Prose Composition: Annotated Passages for Translation into Russian. F. M. Borras & R. F. Christian. 1964. 4.50 (*0-19-815618-9*) OUP.

Russian Proverbs. Chris Skillen. 60p. 1994. 7.95 (*0-8118-0539-5*) Chronicle Bks.

Russian Proverbs & Sayings. Ed. by Peter Mertvago. 477p. (RUS.). 1996. pap. 35.00 (*0-7818-0424-8*) Hippocrene Bks.

Russian Provisional Government, 1917: Documents, 3 vols., Set. Ed. by Robert P. Browder & Alexander F. Kerensky. 1949p. 1961. 129.50 (*0-8047-0023-0*) Stanford U Pr.

Russian Provisional Government, 1917: Documents, Vol. 1. Ed. by Robert P. Browder & Alexander F. Kerensky. LC 60-9052. (Hoover Institution Publications). 507p. 1961. reprint ed. pap. 30.00 (*0-7837-9059-7*, 2049810) Bks Demand.

Russian Provisional Government, 1917: Documents, Vol. 2. Ed. by Robert P. Browder & Alexander F. Kerensky. LC 60-9052. (Hoover Institution Publications). 742p. 1961. reprint ed. pap. 30.00 (*0-7837-9060-0*, 2049810) Bks Demand.

Russian Provisional Government, 1917: Documents, Vol. 3. Ed. by Robert P. Browder & Alexander F. Kerensky. LC 60-9052. (Hoover Institution Publications). 701p. 1961. reprint ed. pap. 30.00 (*0-7837-9061-9*, 2049810) Bks Demand.

***Russian Psychology: Past, Present & Future.** Ed. by Elena L. Grigorenko et al. 457p. (C). 1996. lib. bdg. 59.00 (*1-56072-389-0*) Nova Sci Pubs.

Russian Publicistic Satire under Glasnost: The Journalistic Feuilleton. Karen L. Ryan-Hayes. LC 93-30736. 212p. 1993. text ed. 89.95 (*0-7734-9348-4*) E Mellen.

Russian Punch Needle Embroidery. Gail Bird. 1981. pap. 3.95 (*0-486-24146-7*) Dover.

Russian Question. Aleksandr I. Solzhenitsyn. 128p. 1995. 15.00 (*0-374-25291-2*) FS&G.

Russian Rambles. Isabel F. Hapgood. LC 77-115542. (Russia Observed, Series I). 1970. reprint ed. 21.95 (*0-405-03031-2*) Ayer.

Russian Reactions to German Air Power in World War II. Klaus Uebe. LC 68-22556. (German Air Force in World War 2 Ser.). (Illus.). 1968. 18.95 (*0-405-00049-9*) Ayer.

Russian Readers for Beginners, Bks. 1 & 2. N. Scorer & J. O. Lewis. 64p. (C). 1986. 50.00 (*0-317-92453-2*, Pub. by Collets) St Mut.

Russian Readers for Beginners, Bks. 3 & 4. N. Scorer & J. O. Lewis. 58p. 1984. 50.00 (*0-569-08787-2*, Pub. by Collets) St Mut.

Russian Readings for Close Analysis. ACTR Staff. 288p. 1993. per. 34.00 (*0-8403-8587-0*) Kendall-Hunt.

Russian Realist Art, the State & Society: The Peredvizhniki & Their Tradition. Elizabeth K. Valkenier. (Studies of the Harriman Institute - A Morningside Book). (Illus.). 272p. 1989. pap. text ed. 18.50 (*0-231-06971-5*) Col U Pr.

Russian Refuge: Religion, Migration, & Settlement on the North American Pacific Rim. Susan W. Hardwick. LC 93-10519. (Geography Research Papers). (Illus.). 242p. 1993. pap. text ed. 20.00 (*0-226-31611-4*); lib. bdg. 41.50 (*0-226-31610-6*) U Ch Pr.

Russian Refugees in France & the United States Between the World Wars. James E. Hassell. LC 91-76294. (Transactions Ser.: Vol. 81, Pt. 7). 100p. 1992. pap. 12.50 (*0-87169-817-X*, T817-HAJ) Am Philos.

Russian Regional Business Directories: Adygey Republic: (Government, Economy, Ecology, Industry, Business) (Russian Regional Business Directories Ser.). (Illus.). 250p. (Orig.). 1996. pap. 99.00 (*1-57751-034-8*) Russ Info & Busn Ctr.

Russian Regional Business Directories: Altay Kray: (Government, Economy, Ecology, Industry, Business) (Russian Regional Business Directories Ser.). (Illus.). 250p. (Orig.). 1996. pap. 99.00 (*1-57751-099-2*) Russ Info & Busn Ctr.

Russian Regional Business Directories: Amur Oblast: (Government, Economy, Ecology, Industry, Business) (Russian Regional Business Directories Ser.). (Illus.). 250p. (Orig.). 1996. pap. 99.00 (*1-57751-050-X*) Russ Info & Busn Ctr.

Russian Regional Business Directories: Arkhangelsk Oblast: (Government, Economy, Ecology, Industry, Business) (Russian Regional Business Directories Ser.). (Illus.). 250p. (Orig.). 1996. pap. 99.00 (*1-57751-051-8*) Russ Info & Busn Ctr.

Russian Regional Business Directories: Astrakhan Oblast: (Government, Economy, Ecology, Industry, Business) (Russian Regional Business Directories Ser.). (Illus.). 250p. (Orig.). 1996. pap. 99.00 (*1-57751-052-6*) Russ Info & Busn Ctr.

Russian Regional Business Directories: Bashkortostan Republic: (Government, Economy, Ecology, Industry, Business) (Russian Regional Business Directories Ser.). (Illus.). 250p. (Orig.). 1996. pap. 99.00 (*1-57751-035-6*) Russ Info & Busn Ctr.

Russian Regional Business Directories: Belgorod Oblast: (Government, Economy, Ecology, Industry, Business) (Russian Regional Business Directories Ser.). (Illus.). 250p. (Orig.). 1996. pap. 99.00 (*1-57751-053-4*) Russ Info & Busn Ctr.

Russian Regional Business Directories: Bryansk Oblast: (Government, Economy, Ecology, Industry, Business) (Russian Regional Business Directories Ser.). (Illus.). 250p. (Orig.). 1996. pap. 99.00 (*1-57751-054-2*) Russ Info & Busn Ctr.

Russian Regional Business Directories: Buryat Republic: (Government, Economy, Ecology, Industry, Business) (Russian Regional Business Directories Ser.). (Illus.). 250p. (Orig.). 1996. pap. 99.00 (*1-57751-036-4*) Russ Info & Busn Ctr.

Russian Regional Business Directories: Chechen Republic: (Government, Economy, Ecology, Industry, Business) (Russian Regional Business Directories Ser.). (Illus.). 250p. (Orig.). 1996. pap. 99.00 (*1-57751-037-2*) Russ Info & Busn Ctr.

Russian Regional Business Directories: Chelyabinsk Oblast: (Government, Economy, Ecology, Industry, Business) (Russian Regional Business Directories Ser.). (Illus.). 250p. (Orig.). 1996. pap. 99.00 (*1-57751-055-0*) Russ Info & Busn Ctr.

Russian Regional Business Directories: Chita Oblast: (Government, Economy, Ecology, Industry, Business) (Russian Regional Business Directories Ser.). (Illus.). 250p. (Orig.). 1996. pap. 99.00 (*1-57751-056-9*) Russ Info & Busn Ctr.

Russian Regional Business Directories: Chuvash Republic: (Government, Economy, Ecology, Industry, Business) (Russian Regional Business Directories Ser.). (Illus.). 250p. (Orig.). 1996. pap. 99.00 (*1-57751-038-0*) Russ Info & Busn Ctr.

Russian Regional Business Directories: Dagestan Republic: (Government, Economy, Ecology, Industry, Business) (Russian Regional Business Directories Ser.). (Illus.). 250p. (Orig.). 1996. pap. 99.00 (*1-57751-039-9*) Russ Info & Busn Ctr.

Russian Regional Business Directories: Gornyi Altay Republic: (Government, Economy, Ecology, Industry, Business) (Russian Regional Business Directories Ser.). (Illus.). 250p. (Orig.). 1996. pap. 99.00 (*1-57751-040-2*) Russ Info & Busn Ctr.

Russian Regional Business Directories: Ingush Republic: (Government, Economy, Ecology, Industry, Business) (Russian Regional Business Directories Ser.). (Illus.). 250p. (Orig.). 1996. pap. 99.00 (*1-57751-041-0*) Russ Info & Busn Ctr.

Russian Regional Business Directories: Irkutsk Oblast: (Government, Economy, Ecology, Industry, Business) (Russian Regional Business Directories Ser.). (Illus.). 250p. (Orig.). 1996. pap. 99.00 (*1-57751-057-7*) Russ Info & Busn Ctr.

Russian Regional Business Directories: Ivanovo Oblast: (Government, Economy, Ecology, Industry, Business) (Russian Regional Business Directories Ser.). (Illus.). 250p. (Orig.). 1996. pap. 99.00 (*1-57751-058-5*) Russ Info & Busn Ctr.

Russian Regional Business Directories: Kabardin-Balkar Republic: (Government, Economy, Ecology, Industry, Business) (Russian Regional Business Directories Ser.). (Illus.). 250p. (Orig.). 1996. pap. 99.00 (*1-57751-042-9*) Russ Info & Busn Ctr.

Russian Regional Business Directories: Kaliningrad Oblast: (Government, Economy, Ecology, Industry, Business) (Russian Regional Business Directories Ser.). (Illus.). 250p. (Orig.). 1996. pap. 99.00 (*1-57751-059-3*) Russ Info & Busn Ctr.

Russian Regional Business Directories: Kalmykia-Khalmg-Tangch Republic: (Government, Economy, Ecology, Industry, Business) (Russian Regional Business Directories Ser.). (Illus.). 250p. (Orig.). 1996. pap. 99.00 (*1-57751-043-7*) Russ Info & Busn Ctr.

Russian Regional Business Directories: Kaluga Oblast: (Government, Economy, Ecology, Industry, Business) (Russian Regional Business Directories Ser.). (Illus.). 250p. (Orig.). 1996. pap. 99.00 (*1-57751-060-7*) Russ Info & Busn Ctr.

Russian Regional Business Directories: Kamchatka Oblast: (Government, Economy, Ecology, Industry, Business) (Russian Regional Business Directories Ser.). (Illus.). 250p. (Orig.). 1996. pap. 99.00 (*1-57751-061-5*) Russ Info & Busn Ctr.

Russian Regional Business Directories: Karachay-Cherkess Republic: (Government, Economy, Ecology, Industry, Business) (Russian Regional Business Directories Ser.). (Illus.). 250p. (Orig.). 1996. pap. 99.00 (*1-57751-044-5*) Russ Info & Busn Ctr.

Russian Regional Business Directories: Karelian Republic: (Government, Economy, Ecology, Industry, Business) (Russian Regional Business Directories Ser.). (Illus.). 250p. (Orig.). 1996. pap. 99.00 (*1-57751-045-3*) Russ Info & Busn Ctr.

Russian Regional Business Directories: Kemerovo Oblast: (Government, Economy, Ecology, Industry, Business) (Russian Regional Business Directories Ser.). (Illus.). 250p. (Orig.). 1996. pap. 99.00 (*1-57751-062-3*) Russ Info & Busn Ctr.

Russian Regional Business Directories: Khabarovsk Kray: (Government, Economy, Ecology, Industry, Business) (Russian Regional Business Directories Ser.). (Illus.). 250p. (Orig.). 1996. pap. 99.00 (*1-57751-100-X*) Russ Info & Busn Ctr.

Russian Regional Business Directories: Khakass Republic: (Government, Economy, Ecology, Industry, Business) (Russian Regional Business Directories Ser.). (Illus.). 250p. (Orig.). 1996. pap. 99.00 (*1-57751-046-1*) Russ Info & Busn Ctr.

Russian Regional Business Directories: Kirov Oblast: (Government, Economy, Ecology, Industry, Business) (Russian Regional Business Directories Ser.). (Illus.). 250p. (Orig.). 1996. pap. 99.00 (*1-57751-063-1*) Russ Info & Busn Ctr.

Russian Regional Business Directories: Komi Mu Republic: (Government, Economy, Ecology, Industry, Business) (Russian Regional Business Directories Ser.). (Illus.). 250p. (Orig.). 1996. pap. 99.00 (*1-57751-047-X*) Russ Info & Busn Ctr.

Russian Regional Business Directories: Kostroma Oblast: (Government, Economy, Ecology, Industry, Business) (Russian Regional Business Directories Ser.). (Illus.). 250p. (Orig.). 1996. pap. 99.00 (*1-57751-064-X*) Russ Info & Busn Ctr.

Russian Regional Business Directories: Krasnodar Kray: (Government, Economy, Ecology, Industry, Business) (Russian Regional Business Directories Ser.). (Illus.). 250p. (Orig.). 1996. pap. 99.00 (*1-57751-101-8*) Russ Info & Busn Ctr.

Russian Regional Business Directories: Krasnoyarsk Kray: (Government, Economy, Ecology, Industry, Business) (Russian Regional Business Directories Ser.). (Illus.). 250p. (Orig.). 1996. pap. 99.00 (*1-57751-102-6*) Russ Info & Busn Ctr.

Russian Regional Business Directories: Kurgan Oblast: (Government, Economy, Ecology, Industry, Business) (Russian Regional Business Directories Ser.). (Illus.). 250p. (Orig.). 1996. pap. 99.00 (*1-57751-065-8*) Russ Info & Busn Ctr.

Russian Regional Business Directories: Kursk Oblast: (Government, Economy, Ecology, Industry, Business) (Russian Regional Business Directories Ser.). (Illus.). 250p. (Orig.). 1996. pap. 99.00 (*1-57751-066-6*) Russ Info & Busn Ctr.

Russian Regional Business Directories: Leningrad Oblast: (Government, Economy, Ecology, Industry, Business) (Russian Regional Business Directories Ser.). (Illus.). 250p. (Orig.). 1996. pap. 99.00 (*1-57751-086-0*) Russ Info & Busn Ctr.

Russian Regional Business Directories: Lipetsk Oblast: (Government, Economy, Ecology, Industry, Business) (Russian Regional Business Directories Ser.). (Illus.). 250p. (Orig.). 1996. pap. 99.00 (*1-57751-067-4*) Russ Info & Busn Ctr.

Russian Regional Business Directories: Magadan Oblast: (Government, Economy, Ecology, Industry, Business) (Russian Regional Business Directories Ser.). (Illus.). 250p. (Orig.). 1996. pap. 99.00 (*1-57751-068-2*) Russ Info & Busn Ctr.

Russian Regional Business Directories: Mordovian Republic: (Government, Economy, Ecology, Industry, Business) (Russian Regional Business Directories Ser.). (Illus.). 250p. (Orig.). 1996. pap. 99.00 (*1-57751-048-8*) Russ Info & Busn Ctr.

Russian Regional Business Directories: Moscow Oblast: (Government, Economy, Ecology, Industry, Business) (Russian Regional Business Directories Ser.). (Illus.). 250p. (Orig.). 1996. pap. 99.00 (*1-57751-069-0*) Russ Info & Busn Ctr.

Russian Regional Business Directories: Murmansk Oblast: (Government, Economy, Ecology, Industry, Business) (Russian Regional Business Directories Ser.). (Illus.). 250p. (Orig.). 1996. pap. 99.00 (*1-57751-070-4*) Russ Info & Busn Ctr.

Russian Regional Business Directories: Nizhniy Novgorod Oblast: (Government, Economy, Ecology, Industry, Business) (Russian Regional Business Directories Ser.). (Illus.). 250p. (Orig.). 1996. pap. 99.00 (*1-57751-071-2*) Russ Info & Busn Ctr.

Russian Regional Business Directories: North Osetian Republic: (Government, Economy, Ecology, Industry, Business) (Russian Regional Business Directories Ser.). (Illus.). 250p. (Orig.). 1996. pap. 99.00 (*1-57751-049-6*) Russ Info & Busn Ctr.

Russian Regional Business Directories: Novgorod Oblast: (Government, Economy, Ecology, Industry, Business) (Russian Regional Business Directories Ser.). (Illus.). 250p. (Orig.). 1996. pap. 99.00 (*1-57751-072-0*) Russ Info & Busn Ctr.

Russian Regional Business Directories: Novosibirsk Oblast: (Government, Economy, Ecology, Industry, Business) (Russian Regional Business Directories Ser.). (Illus.). 250p. (Orig.). 1996. pap. 99.00 (*1-57751-073-9*) Russ Info & Busn Ctr.

Russian Regional Business Directories: Omsk Oblast: (Government, Economy, Ecology, Industry, Business) (Russian Regional Business Directories Ser.). (Illus.). 250p. (Orig.). 1996. pap. 99.00 (*1-57751-074-7*) Russ Info & Busn Ctr.

Russian Regional Business Directories: Orenburg Oblast: (Government, Economy, Ecology, Industry, Business) (Russian Regional Business Directories Ser.). (Illus.). 250p. (Orig.). 1996. pap. 99.00 (*1-57751-075-5*) Russ Info & Busn Ctr.

Russian Regional Business Directories: Oryol Oblast: (Government, Economy, Ecology, Industry, Business) (Russian Regional Business Directories Ser.). (Illus.). 250p. (Orig.). 1996. pap. 99.00 (*1-57751-076-3*) Russ Info & Busn Ctr.

Russian Regional Business Directories: Penza Oblast: (Government, Economy, Ecology, Industry, Business) (Russian Regional Business Directories Ser.). (Illus.). 250p. (Orig.). 1996. pap. 99.00 (*1-57751-077-1*) Russ Info & Busn Ctr.

Russian Regional Business Directories: Perm Oblast: (Government, Economy, Ecology, Industry, Business) (Russian Regional Business Directories Ser.). (Illus.). 250p. (Orig.). 1996. pap. 99.00 (*1-57751-078-X*) Russ Info & Busn Ctr.

Russian Regional Business Directories: Primorskiy Kray: (Government, Economy, Ecology, Industry, Business) (Russian Regional Business Directories Ser.). (Illus.). 250p. (Orig.). 1996. pap. 99.00 (*1-57751-103-4*) Russ Info & Busn Ctr.

Russian Regional Business Directories: Pskov Oblast: (Government, Economy, Ecology, Industry, Business) (Russian Regional Business Directories Ser.). (Illus.). 250p. (Orig.). 1996. pap. 99.00 (*1-57751-079-8*) Russ Info & Busn Ctr.

Russian Regional Business Directories: Rostov Oblast: (Government, Economy, Ecology, Industry, Business) (Russian Regional Business Directories Ser.). (Illus.). 250p. (Orig.). 1996. pap. 99.00 (*1-57751-080-1*) Russ Info & Busn Ctr.

Russian Regional Business Directories: Ryazan Oblast: (Government, Economy, Ecology, Industry, Business) (Russian Regional Business Directories Ser.). (Illus.). 250p. (Orig.). 1996. pap. 99.00 (*1-57751-081-X*) Russ Info & Busn Ctr.

Russian Regional Business Directories: Sakhalin Oblast: (Government, Economy, Ecology, Industry, Business) (Russian Regional Business Directories Ser.). (Illus.). 250p. (Orig.). 1996. pap. 99.00 (*1-57751-082-8*) Russ Info & Busn Ctr.

Russian Regional Business Directories: Samara Oblast: (Government, Economy, Ecology, Industry, Business) (Russian Regional Business Directories Ser.). (Illus.). 250p. (Orig.). 1996. pap. 99.00 (*1-57751-083-6*) Russ Info & Busn Ctr.

Russian Regional Business Directories: Saratov Oblast: (Government, Economy, Ecology, Industry, Business) (Russian Regional Business Directories Ser.). (Illus.). 250p. (Orig.). 1996. pap. 99.00 (*1-57751-084-4*) Russ Info & Busn Ctr.

Russian Regional Business Directories: Smolensk Oblast: (Government, Economy, Ecology, Industry, Business) (Russian Regional Business Directories Ser.). (Illus.). 250p. (Orig.). 1996. pap. 99.00 (*1-57751-085-2*) Russ Info & Busn Ctr.

Russian Regional Business Directories: Stavropol Kray: (Government, Economy, Ecology, Industry, Business) (Russian Regional Business Directories Ser.). (Illus.). 250p. (Orig.). 1996. pap. 99.00 (*1-57751-104-2*) Russ Info & Busn Ctr.

Russian Regional Business Directories: Tambov Oblast: (Government, Economy, Ecology, Industry, Business) (Russian Regional Business Directories Ser.). (Illus.). 250p. (Orig.). 1996. pap. 99.00 (*1-57751-087-9*) Russ Info & Busn Ctr.

Russian Regional Business Directories: Tomsk Oblast: (Government, Economy, Ecology, Industry, Business) (Russian Regional Business Directories Ser.). (Illus.). 250p. (Orig.). 1996. pap. 99.00 (*1-57751-088-7*) Russ Info & Busn Ctr.

Russian Regional Business Directories: Tula Oblast: (Government, Economy, Ecology, Industry, Business) (Russian Regional Business Directories Ser.). (Illus.). 250p. (Orig.). 1996. pap. 99.00 (*1-57751-090-9*) Russ Info & Busn Ctr.

Russian Regional Business Directories: Tver Oblast: (Government, Economy, Ecology, Industry, Business) (Russian Regional Business Directories Ser.). (Illus.). 250p. (Orig.). 1996. pap. 99.00 (*1-57751-091-7*) Russ Info & Busn Ctr.

Russian Regional Business Directories: Tyumen Oblast: (Government, Economy, Ecology, Industry, Business) (Russian Regional Business Directories Ser.). (Illus.). 250p. (Orig.). 1996. pap. 99.00 (*1-57751-092-5*) Russ Info & Busn Ctr.

Russian Regional Business Directories: Ulyanovsk Oblast: (Government, Economy, Ecology, Industry, Business) (Russian Regional Business Directories Ser.). (Illus.). 250p. (Orig.). 1996. pap. 99.00 (*1-57751-093-3*) Russ Info & Busn Ctr.

Russian Regional Business Directories: Vladimir Oblast: (Government, Economy, Ecology, Industry, Business) (Russian Regional Business Directories Ser.). (Illus.). 250p. (Orig.). 1996. pap. 99.00 (*1-57751-094-1*) Russ Info & Busn Ctr.

Russian Regional Business Directories: Volgograd Oblast: (Government, Economy, Ecology, Industry, Business) (Russian Regional Business Directories Ser.). (Illus.). 250p. (Orig.). 1996. pap. 99.00 (*1-57751-089-5*) Russ Info & Busn Ctr.

Russian Regional Business Directories: Vologda Oblast: (Government, Economy, Ecology, Industry, Business) (Russian Regional Business Directories Ser.). (Illus.). 250p. (Orig.). 1996. pap. 99.00 (*1-57751-095-X*) Russ Info & Busn Ctr.

Russian Regional Business Directories: Voronezh Oblast: (Government, Economy, Ecology, Industry, Business) (Russian Regional Business Directories Ser.). (Illus.). 250p. (Orig.). 1996. pap. 99.00 (*1-57751-096-8*) Russ Info & Busn Ctr.

Russian Regional Business Directories: Yaroslavl Oblast: (Government, Economy, Ecology, Industry, Business) (Russian Regional Business Directories Ser.). (Illus.). 250p. (Orig.). 1996. pap. 99.00 (*1-57751-097-6*) Russ Info & Busn Ctr.

Russian Regional Business Directories: Yekaterinburg Oblast: (Government, Economy, Ecology, Industry, Business) (Russian Regional Business Directories Ser.). (Illus.). 250p. (Orig.). 1996. pap. 99.00 (*1-57751-098-4*) Russ Info & Busn Ctr.

***Russian Regional Economic & Business Atlas.** (Illus.). 500p. 1997. 149.00 (*1-57751-160-3*) Russ Info & Busn Ctr.

***Russian Regional Economic & Business Atlas.** 2nd rev. ed. Russian Information & Business Center, Inc. Staff. 600p. 1997. pap. 149.00 (*1-57751-172-7*) Russ Info & Busn Ctr.

Russian Regional Explorer: Geography, Government, Economy, Ecology. Igor S. Oleynik & Oleg Musin. (Illus.). 500p. (C). 1996. audio compact disk, cd-rom 149.00 (*0-9646241-9-2*) Russ Info & Busn Ctr.

Russian Regional Government: Encyclopedic Directory. (Illus.). 500p. (Orig.). 1996. pap. 99.00 (*0-9646241-7-6*) Russ Info & Busn Ctr.

***Russian Regional Government Directory.** Russian Information & Business Center, Inc. Staff. 400p. 1997. pap. 99.00 (*1-57751-170-0*) Russ Info & Busn Ctr.

***Russian Regional Investment & Business Guide.** 2nd rev. ed. Russian Information & Business Center, Inc. Staff. (Russian Business Library). 400p. 1997. pap. 99.00 (*1-57751-308-8*) Russ Info & Busn Ctr.

Russian Regional Investment & Business Guide: Stategic Information & Data for Corporate Executives on Russia. Igor S. Oleynik. 1996. pap. 59.00 (*0-9646241-1-7*) Russ Info & Busn Ctr.

Russian Religious Philosophy. Frederick Copleston. 192p. 1994. 45.00 (*0-85532-630-1*, Pub. by Srch Pr UK) St Mut.

Russian Religious Philosophy: Selected Aspects. Frederick C. Copleston. (C). 1988. text ed. 29.00 (*0-268-01635-6*) U of Notre Dame Pr.

Russian Religious Thought. Ed. by Judith D. Kornblatt & Richard F. Gustafson. LC 96-15084. (Illus.). 276p. 1996. 53.00 (*0-299-15130-1*); 21.95 (*0-299-15134-4*) U of Wis Pr.

Russian Requiem. Roland Merullo. LC 93-22526. 1993. 22.95 (*0-316-56789-2*) Little.

***Russian Research Institutions & Scientists Directory.** 2nd ed. Russian Information & Business Center, Inc. Staff. (Russian Business Library). 400p. 1997. pap. 99.00 (*1-57751-323-1*) Russ Info & Busn Ctr.

Russian Restaurant Menu. Klara K. Lewis. (Illus.). (ENG & RUS.). 1995. pap. 5.95 (*1-886821-29-1*) Pavleen.

Russian Restaurant Menu: Food & Drink Guide for Breakfast, Lunch & Dinner. Klara K. Lewis. (In the Shoes of the Traveler Ser.). (Illus.). (Orig.). (RUS.). 1995. pap. 4.95 (*1-886821-12-7*) Pavleen.

Russian Review Grammar. Marianna Bogojavlensky. xviii, 450p. (Orig.). (C). 1982. pap. text ed. 19.95 (*0-89357-096-6*) Slavica.

***Russian Revolution, 2 vols.** W. H. Chamberlin. 130p. 1992. pap. text ed. 35.00 (*0-691-00816-7*) Princeton U Pr.

Russian Revolution. Philip Clark. (Wars That Changed the World Ser.). (Illus.). 32p. (J). (gr. 3-9). 1988. lib. bdg. 11.95 (*0-86307-935-0*) Marshall Cavendish.

Russian Revolution. John M. Dunn. LC 93-22869. (World History Ser.). 112p. (J). (gr. 6-9). 1994. lib. bdg. 17.96 (*1-56006-234-7*) Lucent Bks.

Russian Revolution. Alan Moorehead. (Illus.). 301p. 1987. pap. 10.95 (*0-88184-331-8*) Carroll & Graf.

Russian Revolution. Ed. by Bertrand M. Patenaude. LC 91-45133. (Articles on Russian & Soviet History, 1500-1991 Ser.: Vol. 5). 334p. 1992. text ed. 20.00 (*0-8153-0562-1*) Garland.

Russian Revolution. Richard E. Pipes. LC 91-50008. 976p. 1991. pap. 23.00 (*0-679-73660-3*, Vin) Random.

Russian Revolution. Beryl Williams. (Historical Association Studies). 96p. (C). 1988. pap. text ed. 11.95 (*0-631-15083-8*) Blackwell Pubs.

Russian Revolution. Susan Willoughby. LC 95-33456. (Rigby Interactive Library--History). (J). 1996. write for info. (*1-57572-008-6*) Rigby Interact Libr.

Russian Revolution. 2nd ed. Sheila Fitzpatrick. LC 93-46676. 224p. 1994. 11.95 (*0-19-289257-6*) OUP.

Russian Revolution. Virgil D. Medlin. LC 79-4332. (European Problem Studies). 218p. 1979. reprint ed. pap. 11.50 (*0-88275-937-X*) Krieger.

***Russian Revolution: 1917-1921.** Ronald I. Kowalski. (Sources in History Ser.). 272p. (C). 1997. pap. 17.95 (*0-415-12438-7*); text ed. 59.95 (*0-415-12437-9*) Routledge.

An Asterisk (*) at the beginning of an entry indicates that the title is appearing in BIP for the first time.

Russian Revolution & Bolshevik Victory: Visions & Revisions. 3rd ed. Ronald G. Suny. LC 89-84256. (Problems in European Civilization Ser.). 495p. (C). 1990. pap. text ed. 21.16 (*0-669-20877-9*) HM College Div.

Russian Revolution, & Leninism or Marxism? Rosa Luxemburg. 1961. pap. 13.95 (*0-472-06057-0*, 57, Ann Arbor Bks) U of Mich Pr.

Russian Revolution, & Leninism or Marxism? Rosa Luxemburg. LC 80-24374. (Ann Arbor Paperbacks for the Study of Communism & Marxism). 109p. 1981. reprint ed. text ed. 38.50 (*0-313-22429-3*, LURR, Greenwood Pr) Greenwood.

Russian Revolution from Lenin to Stalin, 1917-1929. E. H. Carr. 200p. 1980. pap. 33.50 (*0-333-29036-4*, Pub. by Papermac UK) Trans-Atl Phila.

Russian Revolution in Switzerland, 1914-1917. Alfred E. Senn. LC 76-143766. reprint ed. pap. 75.90 (*0-608-01893-7*, 2062545) Bks Demand.

Russian Revolution, Nineteen Seventeen, & Indian Nationalism: Studies of Lajpat Rai, Subhas Chandra Bose, & Rammonohar Lohia. Karuna Kaushik. 1985. 20.00 (*0-8364-1314-8*, Pub. by Chanakya II) S Asia.

Russian Revolution, Nineteen Seventeen to Nineteen Twenty-One, Vol. II: 1918-1921: From the Civil War to the Consolidation of Power. William H. Chamberlin. Ed. by Diane P. Koenker. 612p. 1987. 85.00 (*0-691-05493-2*) Princeton U Pr.

Russian Revolution, Nineteen Seventeen to Nineteen Twenty-One, Vol. 1: 1917-1918: From the Overthrow of the Tsar to the Assumption of Power by the Bolsheviks. William H. Chamberlin. Ed. by Diane P. Koenker. 536p. 1987. pap. 26.95 (*0-691-00814-0*) Princeton U Pr.

***Russian Revolution 1900 to 1927.** 2nd ed. 1996. text ed. 10.95 (*0-333-56036-1*, Pub. by Macm UK) St Martin.

Russian Revolution, 1905-1921: A Bibliographic Guide to Works in English. Compiled by Murray Frame. LC 95-2463. (Bibliographies & Indexes in World History Ser.: No. 40). 328p. 1995. text ed. 79.50 (*0-313-29559-X*, Greenwood Pr) Greenwood.

Russian Revolution 1917-1921: A Short History. James D. White. 304p. 1995. text ed. 18.95 (*0-340-53910-0*, B3583, Pub. by E Arnld UK) St Martin.

Russian Revolutionary Emigres, Eighteen Twenty-Five to Eighteen Seventy. Martin A. Miller. LC 86-2715. (Studies in Historical & Political Science: 104th Series, No. 2). 320p. 1986. text ed. 49.95 (*0-8018-3303-5*) Johns Hopkins.

Russian Revolutionary Intelligentsia. 2nd ed. Philip Pomper. Ed. by Keith Eubank. LC 92-5628. (European History Ser.). 256p. (C). 1993. pap. text ed. write for info. (*0-88295-895-X*) Harlan Davidson.

Russian Revolutionary Movement in the 1880s. Derek C. Offord. (Illus.). 230p. 1986. text ed. 59.95 (*0-521-32723-7*) Cambridge U Pr.

Russian Revolutionary Novel. Richard Freeborn. 302p. 1985. pap. text ed. 28.95 (*0-521-31737-1*) Cambridge U Pr.

Russian Revolutions. Max Weber. Ed. by Gordon C. Wells & Peter Baehr. 300p. 1995. 39.95 (*0-8014-3153-0*) Cornell U Pr.

Russian Revolutions of 1917. John S. Curtiss. LC 82-15180. (Anvil Ser.). 192p. 1982. reprint ed. pap. 11.50 (*0-89874-499-7*) Krieger.

Russian Rightists & the Revolution of Nineteen Hundred Five. Don C. Rawson. LC 94-8850. (Russian, Soviet & Post-Soviet Studies: No. 95). (Illus.). 300p. (C). 1995. text ed. 85.00 (*0-521-46487-0*) Cambridge U Pr.

Russian Rightists & the Revolution of Nineteen Hundred Five. David Richards. LC 94-8850. (Cultural Margins Ser.: No. 2). (Illus.). 300p. (C). 1995. pap. text ed. 29.95 (*0-521-48386-7*) Cambridge U Pr.

Russian-Romanian Aeronautics Dictionary. U. Spajaiv. 335p. (RUM & RUS.). 1964. write for info. (*0-8288-6151-X*) Fr & Eur.

Russian Romantic Criticism: An Anthology. Ed. by Lauren G. Leighton. LC 86-29605. (Contributions to the Study of World Literature Ser.: No. 18). 227p. 1987. text ed. 49.95 (*0-313-25584-9*, LRU/, Greenwood Pr) Greenwood.

Russian Romantic Fiction. John Mersereau, Jr. 270p. 1983. pap. 13.95 (*0-88233-740-8*) Ardis Pubs.

Russian Romantic Prose: An Anthology. Ed. by Carl R. Proffer. (Illus.). 1979. 17.50 (*0-931556-00-7*) Translation Pr.

Russian Root List with a Sketch of Russian Word Formation. 2nd ed. Charles E. Gribble. 62p. (RUS.). (C). 1982. pap. 7.95 (*0-89357-052-4*) Slavica.

Russian Roulette: Among Other Things. Gyeorgos C. Hatonn. (Phoenix Journals). 234p. 1993. pap. 6.00 (*1-56935-026-4*) Phoenix Source.

Russian Roulette: Nuclear Power Reactors in Eastern Europe & the Former Soviet Union. Jim Barnes & Keith Alexander. 76p. (Orig.). 1993. pap. 15.00 (*0-913890-97-9*) Friends of Earth.

Russian Round-the-World Voyages, 1803-1849. Nikolai A. Ivashintsov. Ed. by Richard A. Pierce. Tr. by Glynn R. Barratt from RUS. (Alaska History Ser.: No. 14). (Illus.). 1980. 18.00 (*0-919642-76-4*) Limestone Pr.

Russian-Rumanian Military Dictionary. deluxe ed. 335p. (RUM & RUS.). 1964. 39.95 (*0-8288-6780-1*, M-9079) Fr & Eur.

Russian Samovar. Collets. 223p. (C). 1991. 150.00 (*0-89771-891-7*, Pub. by Collets) St Mut.

***Russian Satellite Conference '93, St. Petersburg, Russia.** 195.00 (*0-614-26541-X*, R93SAT) Info Gatekeepers.

Russian Satiric Comedy. Ed. & Tr. by Laurence Senelick. LC 83-61195. 1983. 38.50 (*0-933826-52-4*); pap. 13.95 (*0-933826-53-2*) PAJ Pubns.

Russian Science Fiction Nineteen Fifty-Six to Nineteen Seventy-Four: A Bibliography. 2nd rev. ed. Darko R. Suvin. 1976. 25.00 (*0-911499-05-9*, Dragon Pr) Ultramarine Pub.

Russian Seapower & "The Eastern Question", 1827-41. John C. Daly. LC 90-62893. (Illus.). 290p. 1991. 41.95 (*1-55750-726-0*) Naval Inst Pr.

Russian Search for Peace, February-October 1917. Rex A. Wade. LC 79-83120. (Illus.). xii, 196p. 1969. 32.50 (*0-8047-0707-3*) Stanford U Pr.

Russian Security After the Cold War: Seven Views from Moscow. Ed. by Teresa P. Johnson & Steven E. Miller. (CSIA Studies in International Security Ser.). 212p. 1994. pap. 15.50 (*0-02-881088-0*) Brasseys Inc.

Russian-Serbocroatian-Russian with Russian Grammar. 710p. (CRO, RUS & SER.). 1981. 29.95 (*0-8288-4676-6*, M9691) Fr & Eur.

Russian-Serbocroatian Scientific-Technical Dictionary: Naucno - Tehnicki Recnik Rusko-Srpskohrvatski. Relja Popic. 812p. (RUS & SER.). 1986. 75.00 (*0-8288-2129-1*, F28341) Fr & Eur.

Russian-Serbocroatian, Serbocroatian-Russian Dictionary & Grammatical Primer: Rusko-Srpskohrvatski i Srpskohrvatsko-Ruski Recenicnik sa Primenjenon Gramatik. Zivan Miloradovic. 611p. (RUS & SER.). 1987. 95.00 (*0-8288-1056-7*, F114894) Fr & Eur.

Russian Serf Girl. (Red Stripe Ser.). 1989. pap. 4.50 (*0-8216-5060-2*, Univ Books) Carol Pub Group.

Russian Shores of the Black Sea: In the Autumn of 1852 with a Voyage Down the Volga, & a Tour Through the Country of the Don Cossacks. Laurence Oliphant. LC 75-115571. (Russia Observed, Series I). 1970. reprint ed. 19.95 (*0-405-03054-1*) Ayer.

***Russian Short Stories.** Harry C. Schweikert. 450p. 1972. 24.95 (*0-8369-4160-8*) Ayer.

Russian Short Stories. Tr. by R. S. Townsend from RUS. 390p. 1992. pap. 7.95 (*0-460-87164-1*, Everyman's Classic Lib) C E Tuttle.

Russian Silhouettes. Anton P. Chekhov. Tr. by Marian Fell. LC 72-142260. (Short Story Index Reprint Ser.). 1977. 23.95 (*0-8369-3744-9*) Ayer.

Russian Silver of the 14th to the Early 20th Centuries: From the Collection of the Moscow Kremlin. S. Ia. Kovarskaia. (Illus.). 250p. 1984. 193.00 (*0-317-57435-3*) St Mut.

Russian Singer. Leif Davidsen. 1991. 19.00 (*0-394-58502-X*) Random.

Russian Sketches: Memoirs. A. Davydoff. 303p. 1985. pap. 85.00 (*0-317-40637-X*) St Mut.

Russian-Slovene Dictionary: Rusko-Slovenski Slovar. Janko Pretner. 995p. (RUS & SLV.). 1986. 59.95 (*0-8288-1139-3*, F114898) Fr & Eur.

Russian Small Arms Manufacture & Export Patterns: "Izhmash" Production Association. Valerii N. Shilin. (Foreign Technology Assessment Ser.). v, 119p. (Orig.). 1994. pap. 55.00 (*1-881874-12-5*) Global Cnslts.

Russian Social Democratic Labour Party, 1898-October, 1917 see Resolutions & Decisions of the Communist Party of the Soviet Union

Russian Society & the Greek Revolution. Theophilus C. Prousis. LC 94-7870. 269p. 1994. lib. bdg. 30.00 (*0-87580-193-5*) N Ill U Pr.

Russian Society in Transition. Ed. by Christopher Williams et al. 312p. 1996. text ed. 62.95 (*1-85521-748-1*, Pub. by Dartmth Pub UK) Ashgate Pub Co.

Russian Society since the Revolution. Ed. by Harrison E. Salisbury. LC 78-19596. (Great Contemporary Issues Ser.). 1980. lib. bdg. 27.95 (*0-405-11526-1*) Ayer.

Russian Sociology. Julius F. Hecker. (Columbia Studies in the Social Sciences: No. 161). 1970. reprint ed. 29.50 (*0-404-51161-9*) AMS Pr.

Russian Sociology: A Contribution to the History of Sociological Thought & Theory. Julius F. Hecker. LC 69-20018. 309p. 1969. reprint ed. 39.50 (*0-678-00487-0*) Kelley.

***Russian Songbook.** Rose N. Rubin & Stillman. pap. 8.95 (*0-486-26118-2*) Dover.

Russian Songs: Text in Romanized Russian, English, & Music. 2nd ed. I. Veriat. 22p. (ENG & RUS.). 1996. pap. 9.95 (*1-882427-14-9*, 314-9) Aspasia Inc.

***Russian Songs & Arias: Phonetic Readings, Word-by-Word Translations, & a Concise Guide to Russian Diction.** Jean Piatak & Regina Aurashou. 206p. (Orig.). (ENG & RUS.). 1991. pap. 34.95 (*1-877761-52-4*) Pst Inc.

Russian-Soviet & Western Psychiatry: A Contemporary Comparative Study. Paul Calloway. (Series in General & Clinical Psychiatry). 288p. 1993. text ed. 60.00 (*0-471-59574-8*) Wiley.

Russian-Soviet Unconventional Wars in the Caucasus, Central Asia, & Afghanistan. Date not set. lib. bdg. 251.99 (*0-8490-5987-9*) Gordon Pr.

Russian, Speak. 188p. (YA). 1990. pap. 29.95 incl. audio (*1-57970-014-4*, SRU100) Audio-Forum.

Russian Spring. Dennis Jones. 368p. 1984. 16.95 (*0-8253-0249-8*) Beaufort Bks NY.

Russian Stage Design: Scenic Innovation, 1900-1930: from the Collection of Mr. & Mrs. Nikita D. Lobanov-Rostovsky. Ed. by John E. Bowlt. viii, 344p. 1982. pap. 15.95 (*1-884445-12-8*) C Schlacks Pub.

***Russian Stage One Vol. 1: Live from Moscow.** 3rd ed. ACTR Staff. 625p. 1996. 45.00 (*0-8403-9964-2*) Kendall-Hunt.

***Russian Stage Two: Grammar Supplement.** ACTR Staff. 134p. 1996. per., pap. text ed. 12.00 (*0-7872-2926-1*) Kendall-Hunt.

***Russian Stage Two: Pak.** ACTR Staff. 134p. 1996. 60.00 (*0-7872-2927-X*) Kendall-Hunt.

Russian Stories - Cuentos Espanoles: A Dual Language Book. Gleb Struve. pap. 7.95 (*0-486-26244-8*) Dover.

Russian Story Book. Richard Wilson. 1976. lib. bdg. 75.00 (*0-8490-2551-6*) Gordon Pr.

Russian Studies of Japan: An Exploratory Survey. E. Stuart Kirby. LC 80-18128. 200p. 1981. text ed. 29.95 (*0-312-69610-8*) St Martin.

Russian Studies, 1941-1958: A Cumulation of the Annual Bibliographies from the Russian Review. Ed. by Thomas Schultheiss. LC 70-172774. (Cumulated Bibliography Ser.: No. 4). 1972. 29.50 (*0-87650-024-6*) Pierian.

Russian-Style Formation Evaluation. Ed. by Bob Harrison. (Illus.). 234p. 1995. 324.00 (*1-897799-20-9*, 229, Pub. by Geol Soc Pub Hse UK) AAPG.

Russian Symbolism & Literary Tradition: Goethe, Novalis, & the Poetics of Vyacheslav Ivanov. Michael Wachtel. LC 94-25682. 256p. 1995. 47.50 (*0-299-14450-X*) U of Wis Pr.

Russian Symphony. Dmitri Shostakovich et al. LC 78-86781. (Essay Index Reprint Ser.). 1977. 20.95 (*0-8369-1192-X*) Ayer.

Russian Symphony - Thoughts about Tchaikovsky: Music Book Index. Dmitri Shostakovich. 271p. 1993. reprint ed. lib. bdg. 79.00 (*0-7812-9627-7*) Rprt Serv.

Russian Syndrome: One Thousand Years of Political Murder. Helene C. D'Encausse. Tr. by Caroline Higgitt from FRE. LC 91-3752. 475p. (C). 1993. 34.95 (*0-8419-1293-9*) Holmes & Meier.

Russian T-34 Battle Tank. Horst Scheibert. Tr. by Edward Force from GER. (Illus.). 48p. 1992. pap. 8.95 (*0-88740-405-7*) Schiffer.

Russian Tales & Legends. Charles Downing. (Oxford Myths & Legends Ser.). (Illus.). 224p. (YA). (gr. 4 up). 1990. pap. 12.95 (*0-19-274144-6*) OUP.

Russian Tales of the Fantastic. Tr. by M. Minto. 214p. 1994. pap. 19.95 (*1-85399-225-9*, Pub. by Brstl Class Pr UK) Focus Pub-R Pullins.

***Russian Talk: Culture & Conversation During Perestroika.** Nancy Ries. LC 97-10136. (Illus.). 1996. 39.95 (*0-8014-3385-1*); pap. 16.95 (*0-8014-8416-2*) Cornell U Pr.

Russian Tarot of St. Petersburg. Cynthia Giles. (Illus.). 256p. 1995. pap. 12.00 (*0-88079-196-9*, BK40) US Games Syst.

Russian Tarot of St. Petersburg, Set, incl. deck. Cynthia Giles. (Illus.). 231p. 1996. pap. 33.00 (*0-88079-426-7*, RTS99) US Games Syst.

Russian Tea Room: A Celebration. Faith S. Gordon. LC 92-31648. (Illus.). 1993. 16.00 (*0-517-58826-9*, C P Pubs) Crown Pub Group.

Russian Teachers & Peasant Revolution: The Politics of Education in 1905. Scott J. Seregny. LC 88-45386. (Indiana-Michigan Series in Russian & East European Studies). (Illus.). 304p. 1989. 12.95 (*0-253-35031-X*) Ind U Pr.

***Russian Telecommunication Directory.** 2nd rev. ed. Russian Information & Business Center, Inc. Staff. (Russian Business Library). 400p. 1997. pap. 99.00 (*1-57751-302-9*) Russ Info & Busn Ctr.

Russian Telecommunication Directory, '96. 2nd rev. ed. (Russian Business Library). (Illus.). 300p. 1996. pap. 149.00 (*1-57751-011-9*) Russ Info & Busn Ctr.

Russian Theatre. 1,930th ed. Rene Fulop-Miller & Joseph Gregor. LC 68-21213. (Illus.). 1972. 53.95 (*0-405-08542-7*, Pub. by Blom Pubns UK) Ayer.

Russian Themes. Ed. by Miriam Kochan & Lionel Kochan. LC 67-106641. (Selections from History Today Ser.: No. 3). (Illus.). 1967. 9.95 (*0-686-85916-2*) Dufour.

Russian Themes. Ed. by Miriam Kochan & Lionel Kochan. LC 67-106641. (Selections from History Today Ser.: No. 3). (Illus.). 6700. pap. 9.95 (*0-05-000991-5*) Dufour.

Russian Theoretical Thought in Music. Gordon D. McQuere. LC 83-9097. (Russian Music Studies: No. 10). (Illus.). 404p. reprint ed. pap. 115.20 (*0-8357-1457-8*, 2070510) Bks Demand.

Russian Think & Talk. Berlitz Editors. (Think & Talk Language Courses Ser.). (Illus.). (RUS.). 1994. audio 185.00 (*2-8315-1675-7*) Berlitz.

Russian Thinkers. Isaiah Berlin. 1992. 20.00 (*0-8446-6604-1*) Peter Smith.

Russian Thinkers. Isaiah Berlin. (Pelican Ser.). 1979. pap. 9.95 (*0-14-022260-X*, Penguin Bks) Viking Penguin.

Russian Thinkers. Isaiah Berlin. 336p. 1979. pap. 12.95 (*0-14-013625-8*, Viking) Viking Penguin.

Russian Thought after Communism: The Recovery of a Philosophical Heritage. Ed. by James P. Scanlan. LC 94-27343. 256p. (gr. 13). 1994. text ed. 65.95 (*1-56324-388-1*) M E Sharpe.

Russian Thought after Communism: The Recovery of a Philosophical Heritage. Ed. by James P. Scanlan. LC 94-27343. 256p. (C). (gr. 13). 1994. pap. text ed. 28.95 (*1-56324-389-X*) M E Sharpe.

***Russian Trade Directory: 1000 Largest Wholesale Companies in Russian Regions.** 2nd ed. Russian Information & Business Center, Inc. Staff. (Russian Business Library). 400p. 1997. pap. 99.00 (*1-57751-301-0*) Russ Info & Busn Ctr.

Russian Trade Directory-96: 100 Largest Wholesale Companies in Russian Regions. 2nd rev. ed. (Russian Business Library: No. 20). (Illus.). 250p. 1996. pap. 99.00 (*1-57751-002-X*) Russ Info & Busn Ctr.

Russian Tradition in Education. Nicholas Hans. LC 73-7104. 196p. 1973. reprint ed. text ed. 35.00 (*0-8371-6914-3*, HART, Greenwood Pr) Greenwood.

Russian Traditional Culture: Religion, Gender, & Customary Law. Ed. & Intro. by Marjorie M. Balzer. LC 92-4775. (Illus.). 332p. (C). (gr. 13). 1992. text ed. 72.95 (*1-56324-039-4*); pap. text ed. 30.95 (*1-56324-040-8*) M E Sharpe.

Russian Tragedy. Alexander Berkman. Ed. by William G. Nowlin, Jr. 1979. 11.25 (*0-932366-03-1*); pap. 4.50 (*0-932366-02-3*) Black Thorn Bks.

Russian Tragedy. Alexander Berkman. 112p. 1976. 14.95 (*0-919618-40-5*, Pub. by Black Rose Bks CN); pap. 6.95 (*0-919618-39-1*, Pub. by Black Rose Bks CN) Consort Bk Sales.

Russian Tragedy. Alexander Berkman. 96p. 1988. reprint ed. pap. 5.95 (*0-948984-00-7*, Pub. by Phoenix Pr UK) AK Pr Dist.

Russian Tragedy: Comprising, the Russian Tragedy, the Russian Revolution & the Communist Party, the Kronstadt Rebellion. Alexander Berkman. 136p. 1976. reprint ed. pap. 38.80 (*0-608-00453-7*, 2061272) Bks Demand.

Russian Tragedy: The Burden of History. Hugh Ragsdale. LC 95-39310. 328p. (C). (gr. 13). 1996. pap. text ed. 23.95 (*1-56324-756-9*) M E Sharpe.

Russian Tragedy: The Burden of History. Hugh Ragsdale. LC 95-39310. 328p. (C). (gr. 13). 1996. text ed. 65.95 (*1-56324-755-0*) M E Sharpe.

Russian Translation Series, 4 vols in 10 parts, Set. Harvard University. Peabody Museum of Archaeology & Ethnology Staff. reprint ed. lib. bdg. 544.50 (*0-404-52640-3*) AMS Pr.

***Russian Transportation Directory.** 2nd rev. ed. Russian Information & Business Center, Inc. Staff. (Russian Business Library). 400p. 1997. pap. 99.00 (*1-57751-303-7*) Russ Info & Busn Ctr.

Russian Transportation Directory, '96. 2nd rev. ed. (Russian Business Library). (Illus.). 300p. 1996. pap. 99.00 (*1-57751-010-0*) Russ Info & Busn Ctr.

Russian Travel Pack. (Hugo Ser.). (Illus.). 128p. (Orig.). 1991. pap. 14.95 incl. audio (*0-85285-155-3*) Hunter NJ.

Russian Travelers to Constantinople in the Fourteenth & Fifteenth Centuries. George P. Majeska. LC 82-24255. (Dumbarton Oaks Studies: Vol. 19). (Illus.). 464p. 1984. 35.00 (*0-88402-101-7*) Dumbarton Oaks.

Russian Travelers to the Christian East from the Twelfth to the Twentieth Century. Theofanis G. Stavrou & Peter R. Weisensel. li, 925p. 1986. 39.95 (*0-89357-157-1*) Slavica.

Russian Triptych. 2nd ed. Yevgeny Lubin. 230p. (ENG.). 1989. write for info. (*0-929924-06-1*); pap. 7.95 (*0-929924-07-X*) RWCPH.

Russian-Ukrainian-Latin Zoological Dictionary. A. P. Markevich. 410p. 1983. 39.95 (*0-8288-2393-6*, M 15541) Fr & Eur.

Russian Unemployment & Enterprise Restructuring: Reviving Dead Souls. Guy Standing. 404p. 1996. text ed. 65.00 (*0-312-16134-4*) St Martin.

Russian Universities & Research Institutions Directory. 2nd rev. ed. (Russian Business Library). (Illus.). 300p. 1996. pap. 99.00 (*1-57751-015-1*) Russ Info & Busn Ctr.

***Russian Universities Directory.** 2nd rev. ed. Russian Information & Business Center, Inc. Staff. (Russian Business Library). 400p. 1997. pap. 99.00 (*1-57751-322-3*) Russ Info & Busn Ctr.

Russian Verb: A Guide to Its Forms & Usage for Advanced Learners. R. Bivon. 202p. (C). 1992. 60.00 (*0-569-09311-2*, Pub. by Collets) St Mut.

Russian Verb: Prepositional & Non-Prepositional Government. V. Andreyeva-Georg. 336p. 1987. text ed. 12.95 (*0-8285-3474-8*) Firebird NY.

Russian Verb Aspects. E. Vasilenko. 228p. 1988. pap. text ed. 7.95 (*0-8285-4940-0*) Firebird NY.

Russian Verb Aspects. E. Vasilenko. 228p. (ENG & RUS.). (C). 1988. 50.00 (*0-685-39368-2*, Pub. by Collets) St Mut.

Russian Verbs. Patricia A. Davis. 322p. 1992. pap. 5.95 (*0-8120-4754-0*) Barron.

Russian Verbs of Motion. Leon Stilman. LC 51-7695. (Columbia Slavic Studies). 78p. 1953. pap. text ed. 17.50 (*0-231-09931-2*) Col U Pr.

Russian Verse Theory: Proceedings of the 1987 Conference at UCLA. Ed. by Barry P. Scherr & Dean S. Worth. (UCLA Slavic Studies: Vol. 18). 514p. 1989. 34.95 (*0-89357-198-9*) Slavica.

Russian Verses. Joseph A. Labadie. (Men & Movements in the History & Philosophy of Anarchism Ser.). 1979. lib. bdg. 59.95 (*0-87700-309-2*) Revisionist Pr.

Russian Version of the Second World War: The History of the War As Taught to Soviet Schoolchildren. Ed. by Graham Lyons. Tr. by Marjorie Vanston from RUS. LC 82-24236. (Illus.). 168p. reprint ed. pap. 47.90 (*0-7837-1572-2*, 2041864) Bks Demand.

Russian Vest Pocket Dictionary. Ed. by Stefan Congrat-Butlar. (RUS.). 1974. 6.99 (*0-394-40068-2*) Random.

Russian-Vietnamese Dictionary, 2 vols. 3rd ed. J. Alikanov. 1352p. (C). 1987. 220.00 (*0-685-46894-1*, Pub. by Collets) St Mut.

Russian View of Honolulu. Glynn R. Barratt. (Illus.). 424p. (C). 1988. text ed. 27.50 (*0-88629-060-0*) Editions Ltd.

Russian View of U. S. Strategy: Its Past - Its Future. 2nd ed. Jonathan S. Lockwood & Kathleen O. Lockwood. 233p. (C). 1992. 34.95 (*1-56000-031-7*) Transaction Pubs.

Russian Views of Pushkin's Eugene Onegin. Tr. by Sona S. Hoisington from RUS. LC 87-45980. 220p. 1988. 14.95 (*0-253-35067-0*) Ind U Pr.

Russian Village Prose: The Radiant Past. Kathleen F. Parthe. 216p. 1992. text ed. 37.50 (*0-691-06889-5*); pap. text ed. 14.95 (*0-691-01534-1*) Princeton U Pr.

Russian Vocabulary. Eli Hinkel. LC 93-30424. 260p. 1994. pap. 6.95 (*0-8120-1554-1*) Barron.

Russian Vocabulary Builder, Seven Verbs a Day. Alex Pronin. (RUS.). 1971. 8.00 (*0-87505-314-9*) Borden.

Russian Vocabulary-Building Dictionary: 10,000 Russian Words in Frequency Order. Nicholas J. Brown. LC 95-37292. 256p. (C). 1996. text ed. 69.95 (*0-415-13791-8*) Routledge.

Russian Volunteers in Hitler's Army. 1991. lib. bdg. 79.95 (*0-8490-4458-8*) Gordon Pr.

R

*__Russian War Photography.__ Koch. Date not set. write for info. (0-312-17052-1) St Martin.

Russian Warriors. Roy R. Braybrook et al. (Osprey Ser.). (Illus.). 128p. 1993. 15.95 (1-85532-293-5) Motorbooks Intl.

Russian Way. Thomas Cook. (Illustrated Travel Guides from Thomas Cook Ser.). 1995. pap. 12.95 (0-8442-4296-9, Passport Bks) NTC Pub Grp.

*__Russian Way: A History of the Russian People.__ Garo Dorian. 304p. 1997. 22.00 (0-8059-4118-5) Dorrance.

Russian Without Toil: Russian for English Speakers. Assimil Staff. (ENG & RUS.). 28.95 (0-8288-4364-3, F38008); audio 125.00 (0-685-53031-0) Fr & Eur.

Russian Women in Politics & Society. Ed. by Wilma Rule & Norma Noonan. LC 96-10766. (Contributions in Women's Studies: Vol. 157). 208p. 1996. text ed. 59.95 (0-313-29363-5, Greenwood Pr) Greenwood.

Russian Women's Shorter Fiction: An Anthology 1935-1860. Ed. by Joe Andrew. 488p. 1996. 95.00 (0-19-815884-X) OUP.

Russian Women's Studies: Essays on Sexism in Soviet Culture. Tatyana Mamonova. (Athene Ser.). (Illus.). 198p. 1988. text ed. 45.00 (0-08-036482-9, Pergamon Pr); pap. text ed. 17.95 (0-08-036481-0, Pergamon Pr) Elsevier.

Russian Women's Studies: Essays on Sexism in the Soviet Culture. Tatyana Mamonova. (Athene Ser.). 198p. (C). 1988. pap. text ed. 18.95 (0-8077-6210-5) Tchrs Coll.

Russian Word-Formation, Corrected Reprint. Charles E. Townsend. xviii, 272p. 1980. pap. 19.95 (0-89357-023-0) Slavica.

Russian Worker: Life & Labor under the Tsarist Regime. Ed. by Victoria E. Bonnell. LC 83-47856. 240p. (C). 1983. pap. 16.00 (0-520-05059-2) U CA Pr.

Russian Worker: Life & Labor under the Tsarist Regime. Ed. by Victoria E. Bonnell. LC 83-47856. (Illus.). 234p. reprint ed. pap. 66.70 (0-7837-4760-8, 2044507) Bks Demand.

Russian Wristwatches: Pocket Watches, Onboard Clocks, & Marine Chronometers. Juri Levenberg. Tr. by Gertraud Hechl. LC 95-34594. (Illus.). 96p. 1995. pap. 19.95 (0-88740-873-7) Schiffer.

Russian Writers on Russian Writers. Ed. by Faith Wigzell. 224p. 1994. 45.95 (0-85496-942-X) Berg Pubs.

Russian? Yes, Please, Vol. 1. (Illus.). 100p. (RUS.). (J). 1996. pap. 12.95 (88-8148-021-2, Pub. by European Lang IT) Distribks Inc.

Russian? Yes, Please, Vol. 2. (Illus.). 100p. (RUS.). (J). 1996. pap. 12.95 (88-8148-022-0, Pub. by European Lang IT) Distribks Inc.

Russian-Yiddish Dictionary. 721p. 1984. 35.00 (0-8288-1776-6) Fr & Eur.

Russian-Yiddish Dictionary. Shapiro. 721p. (RUS & YID.). 1984. 75.00 (0-7859-1095-6) Fr & Eur.

Russian-Yiddish Dictionary. 2nd ed. M. Shapiro. 720p. (C). 1989. 125.00 (0-685-46893-3, Pub. by Collets) St Mut.

Russian Youth: Law, Deviance, & the Pursuit of Freedom. James O. Finckenauer. LC 95-12225. 252p. 1995. 39.95 (1-56000-206-9) Transaction Pubs.

RussianAlive! An Introduction to Russian. 2nd ed. Samuel D. Cioran. (Illus.). 428p. (ENG & RUS.). (C). 1993. reprint ed. pap. text ed. 37.95 (0-87501-102-0) Ardis Pubs.

Russian/English-English/Russian Business Dictionary. Aleksandra Zagorskaya & Nina Petrochenko. LC 95-22028. 624p. (ENG & RUS.). 1996. text ed. 34.95 (0-471-95785-2) Wiley.

*__Russian/German Dictionary of Technical & Applied Sciences.__ 6th ed. Horst Gorner. 1188p. (GER & RUS.). 350.00 (0-7859-9339-8) Fr & Eur.

Russianization of Gil Blas: A Study in Literary Appropriation. Ronald D. LeBlanc. 292p. (Orig.). 1986. pap. 22.95 (0-89357-159-8) Slavica.

Russianness: An Examination of Russian & the West: In Memory of Rufus W. Mathewson. Ed. by Robert L. Belknap. 1989. 29.50 (0-87501-055-5) Ardis Pubs.

*__Russians.__ Robin R. Milner-Gulland. LC 96-51542. (Peoples of Europe Ser.). (Illus.). 304p. 1997. 29.95 (0-631-18805-3) Blackwell Pubs.

Russians. Hedrick Smith. 720p. 1984. mass mkt. 6.99 (0-345-31746-7) Ballantine.

Russians. Hedrick Smith. LC 83-45113. 580p. 1983. 30.00 (0-8129-1086-9, Times Bks) Random.

*__Russians, Vol. 1-5.__ Judith Pella. 1995. pap. text ed. 54.99 (1-55661-795-X) Bethany Hse.

Russians & Their Church. Nicolas Zernov. 196p. 1977. reprint ed. pap. 10.95 (0-913836-36-2) St Vladimirs.

Russians & Their Favorite Books. Klaus Mehnert. LC 83-6108. (Publication Ser.: No. 282). (Illus.). 296p. 1983. 19.95 (0-8179-7821-6) Hoover Inst Pr.

Russians Aren't Coming: New Soviet Policy in Latin America. Ed. by Wayne S. Smith. LC 91-28838. 195p. 1991. lib. bdg. 26.50 (1-55587-270-0) Lynne Rienner.

Russians As the New Minority: Ethnicity & Nationalism in the Soviet Successor States. Jeff Chinn. 8p. (C). 1996. pap. text ed. 23.00 (0-8133-2248-0) Westview.

Russians As the New Minority: Ethnicity & Nationalism in the Soviet Successor States. Jeff Chinn & Robert Kaiser. 1996. text ed. 64.95 (0-8133-2249-9) Westview.

Russians in Ethiopia: An Essay in Futility. Czeslaw Jesman. LC 75-20979. (Illus.). 159p. 1975. reprint ed. text ed. 49.75 (0-8371-8345-6, JERE, Greenwood Pr) Greenwood.

Russians in Focus. Harold J. Berman. LC 71-90610. (Essay Index Reprint Ser.). 1977. 23.95 (0-8369-1391-4) Ayer.

Russians in Germany: A History of the Soviet Zone of Occupation, 1945-1949. Norman M. Naimark. LC 95-7725. (Illus.). 608p. (C). 1995. 35.00 (0-674-78405-7) Belknap Pr.

*__Russians in Germany: A History of the Soviet Zone of Occupation, 1945-1949.__ Norman M. Naimark. 1997. pap. text ed. 17.95 (0-674-78406-5) HUP.

Russians in the Former Soviet Republics. Paul Kolstoe. LC 95-5773. 348p. 1995. 37.50 (0-253-32917-5) Ind U Pr.

Russians on Russian Music, 1830-1880: An Anthology in Translation. Ed. by Stuart Campbell. 376p. (C). 1994. text ed. 69.95 (0-521-40267-0) Cambridge U Pr.

Russian's World: Life & Language. Genevra Gerhart. LC 73-13208. (Illus.). 257p. (Orig.). (C). 1974. pap. text ed. 22.00 (0-15-577983-4) HB Coll Pubs.

Russian's World: Life & Language. 2nd ed. Genevra Gerhart. LC 94-73035. (Illus.). 419p. (Orig.). (C). 1994. pap. 39.25 (0-15-501053-0) HB Coll Pubs.

Russia's Age of Silver: Precious Metal Production & Economic Production & Economic Growth in the Eighteenth Century. Ian Blanchard. 384p. 1989. 79.95 (0-415-00831-X, A3631) Routledge.

*__Russia's Air Power at the Crossroads.__ Benjamin S. Lambeth. LC 96-27099. 1996. pap. 20.00 (0-8330-2426-4, MR-623-AF) Rand Corp.

Russia's Alternative Prose. Robert Porter. 288p. 1994. 45.95 (0-85496-935-7) Berg Pubs.

Russia's American Colony. Ed. by S. Frederick Starr. LC 86-19916. (Publication of the Kennan Institute for Advanced Russian Studies). (Illus.). vi, 430p. 1986. text ed. 49.95 (0-8223-0688-3) Duke.

*__Russia's Arms, Catalog Vol. 3: Navy.__ 592p. 1996. 495.00 (0-614-27164-9, DK189, Zigzag Pub) Digital Visn.

Russia's Attitude Towards Union with Rome: 9th-16th Centuries. Joseph B. Kincevicious. 208p. 1984. reprint ed. 39.95 (0-939738-10-4) Zubal Inc.

Russia's Balkan Entanglements, 1806-1914. Barbara Jelavich. (Illus.). 320p. (C). 1991. text ed. 80.00 (0-521-40126-7) Cambridge U Pr.

Russia's Children: A First Report on Child Welfare in the Soviet Union. Herschel Alt & Edith Alt. LC 75-18353. 240p. 1975. reprint ed. text ed. 55.00 (0-8371-8330-8, ALRC, Greenwood Pr) Greenwood.

Russia's Children, Our Children. Barbara Monahan. LC 95-71903. (Illus.). 144p. 1996. pap. 13.95 (1-57197-011-8) Pentland Pr.

Russia's Choice: An Economic Challenge to the West. Ed. by Mason Gaffney et al. 250p. 1997. pap. text ed. 19.95 (0-85683-143-3, Pub. by Shepheard-Walwyn Pubs UK) Paul & Co Pubs.

*__Russia's Communists at the Crossroads.__ Joan B. Urban & V. D. Solovei. LC 96-53174. 1997. text ed. 58.00 (0-8133-2930-2) Westview.

*__Russia's Communists at the Crossroads.__ Joan B. Urban & V. D. Solovei. LC 96-53174. (C). 1997. pap. text ed. 21.00 (0-8133-2931-0) Westview.

Russia's Conquest of Siberia, 1558-1700, Vol. 1: A Documentary Record. Ed. by Basil Dmytryshyn et al. (To Siberia & Russian America Ser.: Vol. 1). (Illus.). 1986. 40.00 (0-87595-148-1) Oregon Hist.

Russia's Constitutional Revolution: Constitutional Structures, Legal Consciousness, & the Emergence of Constitutionalism from Below, 1985-1995. Robert B. Ahdieh. LC 96-6116. 1997. 30.00 (0-271-01609-4); pap. 14.95 (0-271-01610-8) Pa St U Pr.

Russia's Contribution to Science. Alexander Petrunkevitch. (Connecticut Academy of Arts & Sciences Ser., Trans.: Vol. 23). 1920. pap. 49.50 (0-685-22832-0) Elliots Bks.

Russia's Cotton Workers & the New Economic Policy: Shop Floor Culture & State Policy, 1921-1929. Chris Ward. (Cambridge Russian, Soviet & Post-Soviet Studies: No. 69). (Illus.). 300p. (C). 1990. text ed. 69.95 (0-521-34580-4) Cambridge U Pr.

Russia's Crimean War. John S. Curtiss. LC 76-28915. (Illus.). 617p. reprint ed. pap. 175.90 (0-685-20324-7, 2052235) Bks Demand.

*__Russia's Demographic "Crisis"__ Ed. by Julie DaVanzo. (Illus.). 65p. 1996. pap. text ed. 9.00 (0-8330-2446-9, CF-124-CRES) Rand Corp.

*__Russia's Economic Transformation in the 1990s.__ Anders Aslund. LC 97-19559. 1997. write for info. (1-85567-461-0, Pub. by Pntr Pubs UK); pap. write for info. (1-85567-462-9, Pub. by Pntr Pubs UK) Bks Intl VA.

*__Russia's Error, Vol. 1.__ large type ed. Paul Trinchard. 200p. (Orig.). 1996. pap. 10.00 (1-889168-03-3) Maeta.

Russia's Evolving Foreign Policy, 1992-1994: A Supplement to the 5th Edition of Russian Foreign Policy Today. Ed. by Gordon Livermore. (Foreign Policy Readers Ser.). 120p. 1994. pap. 21.00 (0-913601-65-9) Current Digest.

Russia's First Modern Jews: The Jews of Shklov. David E. Fishman. LC 94-29482. (Reappraisals in Jewish Social & Intellectual History Ser.). 194p. (C). 1994. 40.00 (0-8147-2614-3) NYU Pr.

Russia's First Modern Jews: The Jews of Shklov. David E. Fishman. 194p. (C). 1996. pap. 20.00 (0-8147-2660-7) NYU Pr.

Russia's Future: Consolidation Or Disintegration? Ed. by Douglas W. Blum. LC 94-1305. (C). 1994. pap. text ed. 19.95 (0-8133-2202-2) Westview.

Russia's Future: The Communist Education of Soviet Youth. Kitty Weaver. LC 80-287545. 240p. 1981. text ed. 49.95 (0-275-91705-3, C1705, Praeger Pubs) Greenwood.

Russia's Great Reforms, 1855-1881. Ed. by Ben Eklof et al. LC 93-26586. (Indiana-Michigan Series in Russian & East European Studies). 320p. 1994. 39.95 (0-253-31937-4); pap. 18.95 (0-253-20861-0) Ind U Pr.

Russia's Hawaiian Adventure, Eighteen Fifteen to Eighteen Seventeen. Richard A. Pierce. (Alaska History Ser.: No. 8). (Illus.). 1976. pap. 18.00 (0-919642-69-1) Limestone Pr.

Russia's Hotbeds of Tension. George N. Vachnadze. (Illus.). 257p. 1994. lib. bdg. 69.00 (1-56072-141-3) Nova Sci Pubs.

Russia's Iron Age. William H. Chamberlin. LC 73-115517. (Russia Observed, Series I). 1970. reprint ed. 25.95 (0-405-03013-4) Ayer.

Russia's Japan Expedition of Eighteen Eighty-Five. George A. Lensen. LC 82-9156. (Illus.). xxviii, 208p. 1982. reprint ed. text ed. 55.00 (0-313-23621-6, LERJ, Greenwood Pr) Greenwood.

Russia's Last Capitalists: The Nepmen, 1921-1929 with a New Preface. Alan M. Ball. 243p. 1988. pap. 16.00 (0-520-07174-3) U CA Pr.

Russia's Leading Commercial Banks. Martin McCauley. LC 94-70632. 178p. 69.00 (0-9639807-0-X) CEBIS.

Russia's Missing Middle Class: The Professions in Russian History. Ed. by Harley D. Balzer. LC 95-42117. 352p. (C). (gr. 13-13). 1996. text ed. 74.95 (1-56324-707-0); pap. text ed. 29.95 (1-56324-748-8) M E Sharpe.

Russia's Most Secret Weapon Ignored or Unrecognized by the United States. 1992. lib. bdg. 79.95 (0-8490-8730-9) Gordon Pr.

Russia's Muslim Frontiers: New Directions in Cross-Cultural Analysis. Ed. by Dale F. Eickelman. LC 92-43844. (Indiana Series in Arab & Islamic Studies). 224p. (C). 1993. 31.50 (0-253-31939-0); pap. 13.95 (0-253-20823-8) Ind U Pr.

*__Russia's Noble Ladies: Their Alliances with Europe's Aristocratic Families.__ Timothy F. Boettger. (Illus.). (Orig.). write for info. (0-614-29787-7) T F Boettger.

*__Russia's Orient: Imperial Borderlands & Peoples, 1750-1917.__ Daniel R. Brower & Edward J. Lazzerini. LC 96-39473. (Indiana-Michigan Series in Russian & East European Studies). 1997. write for info. (0-253-33274-5); pap. write for info. (0-253-21113-1) Ind U Pr.

Russia's Parliamentary Elections, 1993 & 1995: And the Russian Constitution of 1993. Ed. by Fred Schulze & Ann C. Bigelow. (Soviet/Russian Domestic Policy Ser.). 52p. (Orig.). 1996. pap. 10.00 (0-913601-80-2) Current Digest.

Russia's Policy Towards India from Stalin to Yeltsin. J. A. Naik. 219p. 1995. pap. 150.00 (81-85880-79-4, Pub. by Print Hse II) St Mut.

*__Russia's Politics of Uncertainty.__ Mary McAuley. (Illus.). 336p. (C). 1997. text ed. 59.95 (0-521-47452-3) Cambridge U Pr.

*__Russia's Politics of Uncertainty.__ Mary McAuley. (Illus.). 336p. (C). 1997. pap. write for info. (0-521-47976-2) Cambridge U Pr.

Russia's Protectorates in Central Asia: Bukhara & Khiva, 1865-1924. Seymour Becker. LC 67-30825. (Russian Research Center Studies: No. 54). (Illus.). 434p. 1968. reprint ed. pap. 123.70 (0-7837-4446-3, 2057976) Bks Demand.

*__Russias Provinces.__ Kirkow. LC 97-8880. 1997. text ed. 65.00 (0-312-17595-7) St Martin.

Russia's Revolutions. Tom Corfe. (Cambridge Introduction to World History Topic Bks.). (Illus.). 64p. (YA). (gr. 7 up). 1989. pap. text ed. 12.95 (0-521-31591-3) Cambridge U Pr.

Russia's Road from Peace to War: Soviet Foreign Relations, Nineteen Seventeen to Nineteen Forty-One. Louis Fischer. LC 78-27750. (Illus.). 499p. 1979. reprint ed. text ed. 99.75 (0-313-20941-3, FIRF, Greenwood Pr) Greenwood.

Russia's Road to Democracy: Parliament, Communism, & Traditional Culture. Victor Sergeyev & Nikolai Biryukov. (Studies of Communism in Transition). 240p. 1993. 80.00 (1-85278-851-8) E Elgar.

Russia's Road to the Cold War: Diplomacy, Strategy, & the Politics of Communism, 1941-1945. Vojtech Mastny. LC 78-13433. 384p. 1980. pap. text ed. 21.00 (0-231-04361-9) Col U Pr.

Russia's Rulers Before the Revolution. Dominic C. Lieven. LC 88-38155. 384p. 1989. text ed. 45.00 (0-300-04371-6) Yale U Pr.

Russia's Rulers under the Old Regime. Dominic C. Lieven. (Illus.). 384p. (C). 1991. reprint ed. pap. text ed. 22.00 (0-300-04937-4) Yale U Pr.

Russia's Second Revolution: The February 1917 Uprising in Petrograd. E. N. Burdzhalov. Ed. & Tr. by Donald J. Raleigh. LC 86-45955. (Indiana-Michigan Series in Russian & East European Studies). (Illus.). 412p. 1987. 18.50 (0-253-35037-9); pap. 6.95 (0-253-20440-2, MB 440) Ind U Pr.

Russia's Security in a Rapidly Changing World. Konstantin Sorokin. 95p. (Orig.). 1994. pap. 10.00 (0-935371-32-X) CFISAC.

*__Russia's Transformation: Snapshots of a Crumbling System.__ Robert V. Daniels. 256p. 1997. 64.00 (0-8476-8708-2) Rowman.

*__Russia's Transformation: Snapshots of a Crumbling System.__ Robert V. Daniels. 256p. (Orig.). 1997. pap. 22.95 (0-8476-8709-0) Rowman.

*__Russia's Transition to Democracy: An Internal Political History.__ G. D. Murrell. 288p. 1996. 69.95 (1-898723-57-5, Pub. by Sussex Acad Pr UK) Intl Spec Bk.

Russia's Underground Press: The Chronicle of Current Events. Mark Hopkins. LC 83-11133. 208p. 1983. text ed. 49.95 (0-275-91008-3, C1008, Praeger Pubs) Greenwood.

*__Russia's War: Blood upon the Snow.__ Richard Overy. 1997. 29.95 (1-57500-051-2) TV Bks.

*__Russia's Western Borderlands, 1710-1870.__ Edward C. Thaden. LC 84-13300. 291p. 1984. reprint ed. pap. 83.00 (0-608-03339-1, 2064051) Bks Demand.

Russia's Women: Accommodation, Resistance, Transformation. Ed. by Barbara E. Clements et al. LC 90-37203. (Illus.). 352p. 1991. 48.00 (0-520-07023-2); pap. 16.00 (0-520-07024-0) U CA Pr.

Russia's Youth & Its Culture: A Nation's Constructors & Constructed. Hilary Pilkington. LC 93-26766. 320p. (C). 1994. pap. 19.95 (0-415-09044-X, Routledge NY) Routledge.

Russia's Youth & Its Culture: A Nation's Constructors & Constructed. Hilary Pilkington. LC 93-26766. 320p. (C). (gr. 13). 1994. text ed. 74.95 (0-415-09043-1, Routledge NY) Routledge.

*__Russia's 1996 Presidential Election: The End of Bipolar Politics, Vol. 442.__ Michael McFaul. LC 97-9350. (Publication Ser.). 1997. pap. write for info. (0-8179-9502-1) Hoover Inst Pr.

*__Russia/U. S. S. R., Vol. 6.__ rev. ed. Lesley Pitman. (World Bibliographical Ser.). 414p. 1994. 86.50 (1-85109-221-8) ABC-CLIO.

Russica Eighty-One: Literaturnyi sbornik. Ed. by Alexander Sumerkin. LC 82-80731. (Illus.). 420p. (RUS.). 1982. 25.00 (0-89830-047-9); pap. 20.00 (0-89830-048-7) Russica Pubs.

*__Russification in the Baltic Provinces & Finland, 1855-1914.__ Michael H. Haltzel et al. Ed. by Edward C. Thaden. LC 80-7557. 511p. 1981. reprint ed. pap. 145.70 (0-608-02512-7, 2063156) Bks Demand.

Russisch-Deutsches Woerterbuch. 11th ed. K. Leyn. 735p. (GER & RUS.). 1991. 105.00 (0-7859-8548-4, 3894511117) Fr & Eur.

Russisch-Deutsches Woerterbuch. 34th ed. A. A. Leping. 514p. (GER & RUS.). 1992. 29.95 (0-7859-8573-5, 5200021472) Fr & Eur.

Russisch-Deutsches Woerterbuch fuer Naturwissenschaftler und Ingenieure. S. Halbauer. 170p. (GER & RUS.). 1971. 24.95 (0-8288-6476-4, M-7607) Fr & Eur.

Russisch-Deutsches Worterbuch der Funkechnik. deluxe ed. P. K. Gorochow. 390p. (GER & RUS.). 1961. 6.95 (0-8288-6828-X) Fr & Eur.

Russisch Elymologisches Woerterbuch, Vol. 1: Russian Etymological Dictionary. Max Vasmer. (GER & RUS.). 1953. 175.00 (0-8288-6879-4, M-7608) Fr & Eur.

Russisch Etymologisches Woerterbuch, Vol. 3. Max Vasmer. (GER & RUS.). 1958. 175.00 (0-8288-6853-0, M-7610) Fr & Eur.

Russisch Etymologisches Woerterbuch, Vol. 2: Russian Etymological Dictionary. Max Vasmer. (GER & RUS.). 1955. 175.00 (0-8288-6867-0, M-7609) Fr & Eur.

Russisch Ohne Muhe: Russian for German Speakers. Assimil Staff. (GER & RUS.). 28.95 (0-8288-4363-5, F49480); audio 125.00 (0-685-53030-2) Fr & Eur.

*__Russisch Ohne Muhe Heute.__ (Illus.). (Orig.). (GER & RUS.). 1997. pap. 75.00 incl. audio (2-7005-1005-4, Pub. by ASSIMIL FR) Distribks Inc.

*__Russische Expressionistische Lyrik 1919-1922.__ Valentin Belentschikow. (GER.). 1996. 63.95 (3-631-30160-X) P Lang Pubng.

*__Russische Volksbilderbogen in Bild und Text - Ein Kultur- und Kunsthistorisches Intermedium.__ Wulfhild Ziel. (GER.). 1996. 42.95 (3-631-30258-4) P Lang Pubng.

*__Russischer Kontruktivismus - Plakatkunst.__ Jelena Barchatowa. Tr. by Erhard Glier from FRE. 216p. (GER.). (C). 1992. 50.00 (3-8170-2024-4, Pub. by Knstvrlag Weingrtn GW) Intl Bk Import.

Russka: The Novel of Russia. Edward Rutherfurd. 1992. mass mkt. 6.99 (0-8041-0972-9) Ivy Books.

Russkaia Armiia Na Chuzhbine: The Russian Army in Exile (1920-1923) V. Davats & N. Lvov. LC 85-62402. 124p. (RUS.). 1985. 9.50 (0-911971-18-1) Effect Pub.

Russkaia Sud'ba: Zapiski Chlena NTS o Grazhdanskoi i Vtoroi Mirovoi Voinakh. Pavel Zhadan. LC 88-62407. 240p. (Orig.). (RUS.). (C). 1989. 15.00 (0-911971-38-6) Effect Pub.

Russkaya Ideya see Russian Idea

*__Russkaya Ruletka - Russian Roullette.__ Gennady Bocharov. LC 94-60801. (Illus.). 144p. (Orig.). 1994. pap. 12.00 (1-885563-01-9) VIA Press MD.

Russkeye Bestizhie Poslovitsi i Pogovorki - Russian Shameless Proverbs & Sayings. 2nd expanded rev. ed. Ed. by Mikhail Armalinsky. 95p. (Orig.). (RUS.). 1995. pap. 6.00 (0-916201-18-X) M I P Co.

Russkie Razgovory: Antologiia Sovremennoi Prozy. Photos by Mikhail Lemkhin. LC 92-17803. (Illus.). 200p. (Orig.). (RUS.). (C). 1992. pap. 10.00 (1-55779-049-3) Hermitage.

Russkie vs. Amerike, XX Vek: Russians in Amerika, XX Century. Victor P. Petrov. LC 91-72887. (Illus.). 240p. (Orig.). (RUS.). 1991. pap. 16.00 (0-911971-67-X) Effect Pub.

Russkii Biograficheskii Slovar' - Russian Biographical Dictionary Vols. V & T, 2 vols., Set. (RUS.). 1991. lib. bdg. 400.00 (0-88354-381-8) N Ross.

Russkii Biograficheskii Slovar' - Russian Biographical Dictionary Vols. V & T, Vol. V. xii, 624p. (RUS.). 1991. lib. bdg. write for info. (0-88354-350-8) N Ross.

Russkii Biograficheskii Slovar' - Russian Biographical Dictionary Vols. V & T, Vol. T. xii, 208p. (RUS.). 1991. lib. bdg. write for info. (0-88354-351-6) N Ross.

Russkii Kalambur: 1200 Kalamburov Starykh i Sovremennykh. Vladimir Z. Sannikov. LC 94-30966. 212p. (Orig.). (RUS.). 1995. pap. 12.00 (1-55779-078-7) Hermitage.

Russkii Triptich: A Novel & Stories. Yevgeny Lubin. 1982. 7.95 (0-685-22656-5) RWCPH.

Russkije Podvizhniki Blagotchestija 19-20 vekev. E. Poseljanin. 908p. reprint ed. 35.00 (0-317-29250-1) Holy Trinity.

*__Russkiy Yazik Delovom Obshcheniy (Russian for Business Communication)__ L. Klobukova et al. 304p. 1997. pap. text ed. 30.00 (0-9643332-4-4) ACTR.

Russkoya-Celo: The Ethnography of a Russian-American Community. Stanford N. Gerber. LC 83-45354. (Immigrant Communities & Ethnic Minorities in the U. S. & Canada Ser.: No. 11). 135p. 1985. 37.50 (0-404-19407-9) AMS Pr.

An Asterisk (*) at the beginning of an entry indicates that the title is appearing in BIP for the first time.

R

Russo: Michele Russo at Marylhurst. Jane VanCleve. (Illus.). 1984. pap. 3.00 (0-914435-12-4) Marylhurst Art.

Russo-American Relations, 1815-1867. Benjamin P. Thomas. LC 78-64136. (Johns Hopkins University. Studies in the Social Sciences. Thirtieth Ser. 1912: 2). reprint ed. 37.50 (0-404-61248-2) AMS Pr.

Russo-American Relations, 1815-1867. Benjamin P. Thomas. LC 70-87709. (American History, Politics & Law Ser.). 1970. reprint ed. lib. bdg. 27.50 (0-306-71681-X) Da Capo.

Russo-Chinese Empire. Alexander Ular. LC 75-32325. (Studies in Chinese History & Civilization). 334p. 1975. reprint ed. text ed. 65.00 (0-313-26968-8, U6968, Greenwood Pr) Greenwood.

Russo-Finnish War. Alan L. Paley. Ed. by D. Steve Rahmas. LC 72-89216. (Events of Our Times Ser.: No. 5). 32p. 1973. lib. bdg. 7.25 (0-87157-705-4) SamHar Pr.

Russo German Campaign 1941-43. Ed. by R. K. Bhonsle. 200p. (C). 1988. 45.00 (81-7002-037-9, Pub. by Himalayan Bks II) St Mut.

Russo-German War: Autumn 1941. Ed. by W. Victor Madeja. (Battle Situation - East Front Ser.). (Illus.). 80p. (Orig.). (GER.). 1988. pap. 12.95 (0-941052-82-6) Valor Pub.

Russo-German War: Autumn 1944 to January 25 1945. Ed. by W. Victor Madeja. (Battle Situation - East Front Ser.). (Illus.). 78p. (Orig.). (GER.). 1987. pap. 18.00 (0-941052-89-3) Valor Pub.

Russo-German War: January 25 Through Spring 1945: The Last 100 Days, No. 35. Ed. by W. Victor Madeja. 80p. (GER.). 1987. pap. 18.00 (0-941052-90-7) Valor Pub.

Russo-German War: Small Unit Actions. Ed. by W. Victor Madeja. (East Front Handbooks Ser.). (Illus.). 192p. pap. 14.00 (0-941052-36-2) Valor Pub.

Russo-German War: Small Unit Actions. Ed. by W. Victor Madeja. 194p. 1986. 14.00 (0-941052-74-5) Valor Pub.

Russo-German War: Summer-Autumn 1942. Ed. by W. Victor Madeja. (Ost-Lage Ser.: No. 29). 80p. 1993. pap. 18.00 (0-941052-79-6) Valor Pub.

Russo-German War: Summer-Fall 1943. Ed. by W. Victor Madeja. (Battle Situation - East Front Ser.). (Illus.). 100p. (Orig.). pap. text ed. 18.00 (0-941052-86-9, 31) Valor Pub.

Russo-German War: Summer 1941. Ed. by W. Victor Madeja. (Battle Situation - East Front Ser.). (Illus.). 138p. (Orig.). (GER.). pap. text ed. 18.00 (0-941052-76-1) Valor Pub.

Russo-German War: Summer 1944. Ed. by W. Victor Madeja. (Battle Situation - East Front Ser.). (Illus.). 80p. (Orig.). (GER.). 1992. pap. text ed. 18.00 (0-941052-88-5) Valor Pub.

Russo-German War: Winter-Spring 1942. Ed. by W. Victor Madeja. (Battle Situation - East Front Ser.). (Illus.). 80p. (Orig.). (GER.). 1993. pap. text ed. 18.00 (0-941052-78-8) Valor Pub.

Russo-German War: Winter-Spring 1943. Ed. by W. Victor Madeja. (Battle Situation - East Front Ser.). (Illus.). 80p. (Orig.). 1994. pap. text ed. 18.00 (0-941052-85-0) Valor Pub.

Russo-German War: Winter-Spring 1944. Ed. by W. Victor Madeja. (Battle Situation - East Front Ser.). (Illus.). 92p. (Orig.). (GER.). 1988. pap. text ed. 18.00 (0-941052-87-7) Valor Pub.

Russo-German War - Balkans: November 1940 - November 1944. Ed. by W. Victor Madeja. (Battle Situation - East Front Ser.). (Illus.). 128p. 1989. pap. 18.00 (0-962052-91-5) Valor Pub.

Russo-German War, 1941-45. Albert Seaton. 656p. 1993. pap. 19.95 (0-89141-491-6) Presidio Pr.

Russo-German War, 1943-45. (East Front Handbooks Ser.). (Illus.). 190p. Date not set. 14.00 (0-941052-65-6) Valor Pub.

Russo-Japanese Alliance of 1916. Peter Berton. (Pew Caes Studies in International Affairs). 50p. (C). 1988. pap. text ed. 3.50 (1-56927-326-X) Geo U Inst Dplmcy.

Russo-Japanese Relations & the Future of the U. S.-Japanese Alliance. Harry Gelman. LC 93-3079. 124p. 1993. pap. 15.00 (0-8330-1333-5, MR-168-AF) Rand Corp.

Russo-Japanese War: A Complete Photographic Record. 1986. lib. bdg. 250.00 (0-8490-3842-1) Gordon Pr.

Russo-Persian Commercial Relations, 1828-1914. Marvin L. Entner. LC 65-64001. (University of Florida Monographs: Social Sciences: No. 28). 87p. reprint ed. pap. 25.00 (0-7837-4991-0, 2044658) Bks Demand.

Russo-Turkish War 1877. Ian Drury. (Men-at-Arms Ser.: No. 277). (Illus.). 48p. 1994. pap. 11.95 (1-85532-371-0, 9249, Pub. by Osprey UK) Stackpole.

Russo Untitled #2. David A. Russo. (J). Date not set. pap. 7.95 (0-689-80550-0) S&S Trade.

Russulae (Russula Monographie) 2nd ed. Julius Schaefer. (Pilze Mitteleuropas Ser.: Vol. 3). (Illus.). 296p. (GER.). 1971. reprint ed. lib. bdg. 120.00 (3-7682-0689-0, Pub. by Cramer GW) Lubrecht & Cramer.

Russules d'Europe et d'Afrique du Nord: With English Translation of the Keys by R. W. G. Dennis. Henri Romagnesi. (Illus.). 1030p. 1985. reprint ed. lib. bdg. 150.00 (3-7682-1316-1) Lubrecht & Cramer.

Rust. Michael Hogan. 1977. 20.00 (0-918824-01-X); pap. 5.00 (0-918824-00-1) Turkey Pr.

Rust: A History of the Clark County Ohio Pioneer Family. Ed. by Wm. L. Griffin. LC 73-88655. 177p. 1973. 10.00 (0-9623047-0-0) W L Griffin.

Rust: How to Keep It from Destroying Your Car. Steven B. Joseph. LC 89-84792. 218p. (Orig.). 1989. pap. 19.95 (0-9623380-4-4) Ward Hill Pr.

Rust in Peace: With Tablature. 136p. 1994. otabind 22.95 (0-7935-3665-0, 00694951) H Leonard.

Rust of Virginia: Genealogical & Biographical Sketches of the Descendants of William Rust, 1654-1940. Ellsworth M. Rust. (Illus.). 462p. 1992. reprint ed. pap. 83.00 (0-8328-2487-9); reprint ed. lib. bdg. 73.00 (0-8328-2486-0) Higginson Bk Co.

Rust on the Razor. Mark R. Zubro. 224p. 1996. 20.95 (0-312-14404-0) St Martin.

***Rust on the Razor.** Mark R. Zubro. 1997. pap. 10.95 (0-312-15644-8) St Martin.

Rusted Childhood Memoirs. Gustave Morin. 17p. (Orig.). 1994. pap. 7.00 (0-926935-96-8) Runaway Spoon.

Rusted Dreams: Hard Times in a Steel Community. David Bensman & Roberta Lynch. 1988. pap. 13.95 (0-520-06302-3) U CA Pr.

Rusted Hauberk: Feudal Ideals of Order & Their Decline. Ed. by Liam O. Purdon & Cindy L. Vitto. (Illus.). 352p. (C). 1994. pap. text ed. 19.95 (0-8130-1282-1); lib. bdg. 49.95 (0-8130-1281-3) U Press Fla.

Rusted Laughter. Vijay N. Shankar. (Writers Workshop Redbird Ser.). 1975. 6.75 (0-88253-622-2); pap. text ed. 4.00 (0-88253-621-4) Ind-US Inc.

Rustic & Rough-Hewn Alphabets: One Hundred Complete Fonts. Dan X. Solo. (Lettering, Calligraphy, Typography Ser.). (Illus.). 112p. (Orig.). 1991. pap. 5.95 (0-486-26716-4) Dover.

Rustic Artistry of Clarence O. Nichols. Ed. by Craig Gilborn. (Illus.). 1987. 9.95 (0-910020-39-6) Adirondack Mus.

Rustic Charms, Vol. 1. Sharon Rachal. 100p. 1987. pap. text ed. 6.50 (1-56770-175-2) S Scheewe Pubns.

Rustic Charms, Vol. 2. Sharon Rachal. 100p. 1988. pap. text ed. 9.50 (1-56770-199-X) S Scheewe Pubns.

Rustic Charms, Vol. 3. Sharon Rachal. 100p. 1990. pap. text ed. 6.50 (1-56770-217-1) S Scheewe Pubns.

Rustic Charms, Vol. 4. Sharon Rachal. 100p. 1991. pap. text ed. 7.50 (1-56770-238-4) S Scheewe Pubns.

***Rustic Charms No. V: Florals.** Sharon Rachal. 96p. 1992. pap. 9.50 (1-56770-261-9) S Scheewe Pubns.

Rustic Construction. rev. ed. W. Ben Hunt. (Illus.). 80p. 1994. pap. 6.95 (0-916638-22-7) Meyerbooks.

Rustic European Breads from Your Bread Machine. Linda W. Eckhardt & Diana C. Butts. LC 94-40186. 352p. 1995. 25.00 (0-385-47777-5) Doubleday.

Rustic Furniture Companion: Traditions, Techniques & Inspirations. Daniel Mack. Ed. by Deborah Morgenthal. LC 95-40314. (Illus.). 144p. 1996. 26.95 (0-937274-97-6) Lark Books.

Rustic Furniture Makers. Ralph R. Kylloe. LC 95-11532. (Illus.). 128p. 1995. 29.95 (0-87905-680-0) Gibbs Smith Pub.

***Rustic Garden Architecture.** Ralph R. Kylloe. LC 96-41831. (Illus.). 144p. 1997. 34.95 (0-87905-795-5) Gibbs Smith Pub.

Rustic Moralist. William R. Inge. 1977. text ed. 18.95 (0-8369-8161-8, 8301) Ayer.

Rustic Sounds & Other Studies in Literature & Natural History. Francis Darwin. LC 69-17572. (Essay Index Reprint Ser.). 1977. 19.95 (0-8369-0069-3) Ayer.

Rustic Sunset: Stories. Yitzak Ben Ner. Tr. by Robert Whitehill from HEB. LC 97-14266. 234p. (Orig.). 1997. 24.00 (0-89410-804-2, Three Contnts); pap. text ed. 12.00 (0-89410-805-0, Three Contnts) Lynne Rienner.

Rustic Traditions. Ralph R. Kylloe. (Illus.). 176p. 1995. pap. 24.95 (0-87905-670-3) Gibbs Smith Pub.

Rustic Vignettes. W. H. Pyne. LC 77-80117. (Orig.). 1977. pap. 6.95 (0-486-23547-5) Dover.

Rusticator's Journal: Essays about Mount Desert Island & Acadia National Park. Ed. by Tammis E. Coffin. (Illus.). 104p. (Orig.). 1993. pap. 14.95 (0-9637694-0-5) Frnds of Acadia.

Rustico di Filippo & the Florentine Lyric Tradition. Joan H. Levin. (American University Studies: Romance Languages & Literature: Ser. II, Vol. 16). 197p. 1986. text ed. 29.50 (0-8204-0150-1) P Lang Pubng.

Rusties, Riddles, & Gee-Haw Whimmy-Diddles. James Still. LC 89-5517. Orig. Title: Way Down Yonder on Troublesome Creek & The Wolfpen Rusties. (Illus.). 112p. 1990. reprint ed. 15.00 (0-8131-1686-4) U Pr of Ky.

Rustification of Urban Youth in China: A Social Experiment. Ed. by Peter J. Seybolt. LC 76-17395. (China Book Project Ser.). 232p. reprint ed. pap. 66.20 (0-685-23746-X, 2032787) Bks Demand.

Rustle in the Grass. Robin Hawdon. 1989. pap. 3.95 (0-8125-0068-7) Tor Bks.

Rustle of Angels: The Truth about Angels in Real-Life Stories & Scripture. Marilynn C. Webber & William D. Webber. 208p. 1994. 16.99 (0-310-40500-9) Zondervan.

Rustle of Language. Roland Barthes. Tr. by Richard Howard. 1989. pap. 13.95 (0-520-06629-4) U CA Pr.

Rustler on the Beach. Frank Mulville. 160p. 1982. 12.95 (0-89182-047-7) Charles River Bks.

Rustlers of Beacon Creek. large type ed. Max Brand. LC 94-45645. 378p. 1995. lib. bdg. 18.95 (0-7862-0395-1) Thorndike Pr.

Rustlers of Panther Gap, Vol. 2. Gilbert Morris. LC 94-7128. (Ozark Adventures Ser.: Vol. 2). (J). (gr. 3-7). 1994. pap. 5.99 (0-8423-4393-8) Tyndale.

Rustlers of Silver River. Zane Grey. 226p. reprint ed. lib. bdg. 21.95 (0-89190-765-3, Rivercity Pr) Amereon Ltd.

Rustlers of West Fork: A Hopalong Cassidy Novel. Louis L'Amour. 288p. 1992. mass mkt. 4.99 (0-553-29539-X) Bantam.

Rustlers of West Fork: A Hopalong Cassidy Novel. large type ed. Louis L'Amour. LC 94-9291. 353p. 1994. pap. 19.95 (0-8161-5798-7) G K Hall.

Rustler's Trail. Doyle Trent. 240p. 1988. mass mkt. 2.95 (0-8217-2263-8, Zebra Kensgtn) Kensgtn Pub Corp.

Rustler's Valley. large type ed. Clarence E. Mulford. Date not set. reprint ed. lib. bdg. 25.95 (0-88411-239-X, Aeonian Pr) Amereon Ltd.

Rustler's Valley see Hopalong Cassidy Series

Rustling of Many Winds. 10.95 (0-318-00147-0) R Basu.

Rustling of Wings: An Angelic Guide to the Twin Cities. 2nd ed. Joan Nyberg. LC 94-90051. (Illus.). 194p. (Orig.). 1994. pap. 15.95 (0-9640578-2-4) Wingtip Pr.

***Rustungs- & Kriegsaltlasten: Offentlich-Rechtliche Verantwortlichkeit & Steuerliche Probleme bei Rustungs- & Kriegsaltlasten des Ersten & Zweiten Weltkriegs.** Volker M. Jorczyk. 268p. (GER.). 1996. 51.95 (3-631-30332-7) P Lang Pubng.

Rusty: How Me & Her Went to Colorado & Everything, Except Not Really. Garbo. 227p. (Orig.). 1992. pap. 10.95 (1-881152-04-9) Big Breakfast.

Rusty Lizard: A Population Study. W. Frank Blair. LC 59-8122. 205p. reprint ed. pap. 58.50 (0-317-29262-5, 2055521) Bks Demand.

***Rusty Needle.** Ivan V. Lalic & Francis R. Jones. 196p. 1997. pap. 18.95 (0-85646-241-1, Pub. by Anvil Press UK) Dufour.

Rusty Person Is Worse than Rusty Iron: Adult Education & the Development of Africa. L. Brown. (Tolley Medal Ser.). 1975. pap. text ed. 1.50 (0-685-76692-6, WPT 6) Syracuse U Cont Ed.

Rusty Wallace Racer. Gerald Martin. (Illus.). 128p. 1994. 49.95 (0-89404-092-8) Aztex.

Rusty Wallace Racer. deluxe limited ed. Gerald Martin. (Illus.). 128p. 1995. boxed 187.50 (0-89404-093-6) Aztex.

Rusty's House. (Tales of Oaktree Wood Ser.). (J). 1989. 2.99 (0-517-69122-1) Random Hse Value.

Rusty's Red Vacation. Kelly A. Asbury. LC 96-21712. 1996. 7.95 (0-8050-4021-8) H Holt & Co.

Rusum Dar Al-Khila Fah (Rules & Regulations of Abbasid Court) Hilal Al-Sabi. Ed. by Elie A. Salem. 1977. 19.95 (0-8156-6046-4, Am U Beirut) Syracuse U Pr.

Rusyns. Ed. by Alexander Bonkalo & Patricia Krafeik. 1990. text ed. 44.00 (0-88033-190-9) Col U Pr.

Rusyns of Slovakia: An Historical Survey. Paul R. Magocsi. LC 93-71875. (East European Monographs: No. CCCLXXXI). 185p. 1994. 30.00 (0-88033-278-6) East Eur Monographs.

Rut: The Spectacular Fall Ritual of North American Horned & Antlered Animals. Ron Spomer. (Illus.). 1996. 35.00 (1-57223-050-9, 0509) Idyll Arbor.

***Rut - Ruth.** Gordon Stowell. (Serie Pescaditos - Little Fish Ser.). 16p. (SPA.). (J). 1989. write for info. (0-945792-99-9) Editorial Unilit.

Rut Buster! Wayne Burleson. (Illus.). 80p. (Orig.). 1994. pap. 14.95 (0-89716-514-4) P B Pubng.

Rut, Rot or Revival. Aiden W. Tozer. LC 91-58261. 180p. 1992. pap. 8.99 (0-87509-474-0) Chr Pubns.

Ruta de Severo Sarduy. Roberto G. Echevarria. (Rama Ser.). 282p. (SPA.). 1987. pap. 18.00 (0-910061-32-7, 1506) Ediciones Norte.

Ruta Maya Driver's Travelog. Mike Nelson. (Mexico by Land Ser.). 150p. (Orig.). 1993. pap. 19.95 (1-878166-08-5) Wanderlust Pubns.

Rutaceae of the Guyana Highland see Memoirs of the New York Botanical Garden: No. 14(3)

Rutan Family Index. James J. Keegan. 173p. (Orig.). 1996. pap. 19.00 (0-7884-0457-1, K112) Heritage Bk.

Rutan Voyager. I. Goold. (Great Adventure Ser.). (Illus.). 32p. (J). (gr. 4 up). 1988. lib. bdg. 17.27 (0-86592-869-X); lib. bdg. 12.95 (0-685-58288-4) Rourke Corp.

Rutgers Law Journal: 1969-1995/96, 27 vols., Set. Bound set. 1,290.00 (0-8377-9138-3) Rothman.

Rutgers Law Review: 1947-1995/96, 48 vols., Set. Bound set. 2,240.00 (0-8377-9139-1) Rothman.

Rutgers Picture Book: An Illustrated History of Student Life in the Changing College & University. Michael Moffatt. (Illus.). 250p. 1985. text ed. 12.50 (0-8135-1091-0) Rutgers U Pr.

Rutgers University - Then & Now. Photos by Tom Sobolik. (First Edition Ser.). (Illus.). 112p. 1992. 39.00 (0-916509-91-5) Harmony Hse Pub.

Rutgers University College of Pharmacy: A Centennial History. Glenn Sonnedecker. LC 90-39149. (Illus.). 175p. (C). 1991. text ed. 35.00 (0-8135-1634-X) Rutgers U Pr.

Ruth. Edward F. Campbell. LC 74-18785. (Anchor Bible Ser.: Vol. 7). (Illus.). 216p. 1975. 29.00 (0-385-05316-9, Anchor NY) Doubleday.

Ruth. Elizabeth C. Gaskell. Ed. by Alan Shelston. (World's Classics Ser.). 500p. 1985. pap. 6.95 (0-19-281669-1) OUP.

Ruth. Robert L. Hubbard. (New International Commentary on the Old Testament Ser.). 331p. 1994. 34.00 (0-8028-2526-5) Eerdmans.

Ruth. Philip Mauro. pap. 9.99 (0-87377-057-9) GAM Pubns.

Ruth. R. H. Munce. 117p. 1971. 3.95 (0-914674-00-5) Freelandia.

Ruth. Robert E. Tourville. 60p. (Orig.). (C). 1984. pap. 3.95 (0-912981-12-1) Hse BonGiovanni.

Ruth. Ellen G. Traylor. (Living Bks.). 278p. (Orig.). 1986. mass mkt. 5.99 (0-8423-5809-9) Tyndale.

Ruth. William Wallis. LC 91-65501. 96p. (Orig.). 1991. 25.00 (0-9627031-1-7) Stone & Scott Pubs.

Ruth. large type ed. Lois Henderson. (Large Print Inspirational Ser.). 1987. pap. 7.95 (0-8027-2609-7) Walker & Co.

Ruth. 2nd ed. Jack M. Sasson. (Biblical Seminar Ser.: Vol. 10). 292p. pap. 19.95 (1-85075-213-3, Pub. by Sheffield Acad UK) CUP Services.

***Ruth: A Commentary.** Kirsten Nielsen. LC 96-41719. (The Old Testament Library). 120p. (Orig.). 1997. 20.00 (0-664-22092-4) Westminster John Knox.

Ruth: A Story of Devotion, Virtue & Love. Paul E. Heaton. 150p. (Orig.). 1995. pap. write for info. (1-57502-078-5) Morris Pubng.

Ruth: A Story of God's Grace. Cyril J. Barber. LC 89-2763. 192p. 1989. 17.99 (0-87213-024-X) Loizeaux.

***Ruth: A Story of God's Love.** Grace T. Cook. (Great Big Bks.). 16p. (J). 1997. pap. text ed. 14.95 (0-687-00007-6) Abingdon.

Ruth: Computer Generated Tools for the Correlated Greek & Hebrew Texts. Raymond Martin. (Computer Bible Ser.: Vol. 30-C). 272p. 1995. pap. 89.95 (0-935106-49-9) Biblical Res Assocs.

Ruth: God's Loving Woman. Janice A. Duseau. 16p. (Orig.). 1989. pap. write for info. (0-318-65838-0) Word Power Pub.

Ruth: Surely There Is a Future. E. John Hamlin. LC 95-44352. (International Theological Commentary Ser.). 94p. 1995. pap. 10.00 (0-8028-4150-3) Eerdmans.

Ruth: The Harvest Girl. C. Mackenzie. (BibleTime Bks.). (J). 1995. 2.99 (0-906731-07-0, Pub. by Christian Focus UK) Spring Arbor Dist.

Ruth see Young Readers Christian Library

***Ruth, a Portrait: The Ruth Bell Graham Story.** Patricia D. Cornwell. LC 96-41961. 1997. 21.95 (0-385-48879-3) Doubleday.

Ruth & Daniel: God's People in an Alien Society. Penelope Stokes. (Fisherman Bible Studyguide Ser.). 64p. (Orig.). 1986. pap. 4.99 (0-87788-735-7) Shaw Pubs.

Ruth & Daniel: God's People in an Alien Society - Chinese Edition. Penelope J. Stokes. Tr. by Hai-In Lee. 64p. (CHI.). 1990. pap. 4.00 (1-56582-006-1) Christ Renew Min.

Ruth & Esther. (LifeChange Ser.). 132p. 1987. pap. 7.00 (0-89109-074-6) NavPress.

Ruth & Esther. Katrina J. Larkin. (Old Testament Guide Ser.). 133p. 1996. pap. 9.95 (1-85075-755-0, Pub. by Sheffield Acad UK) CUP Services.

Ruth & Naomi. (Arch Bks.: No. 21). (Illus.). 24p. 1984. pap. 1.99 (0-570-06188-1, 59-1289) Concordia.

***Ruth & Naomi: Two Aliens.** Ellen Van Wolde. 160p. (Orig.). 1997. pap. 24.00 (0-334-02694-6, SCM Pr) TPI PA.

Ruth & Skitch Henderson's Christmas in the Country: Recipes, Crafts, & Gifts. Ruth Henderson et al. (Illus.). 192p. 1993. pap. 30.00 incl. cd-rom (0-670-84783-6, Viking Studio) Studio Bks.

Ruth Ann Fredenthal: Paintings. Donald Kuspit. (Illus.). 24p. 1995. pap. 15.00 (0-9638945-1-X) Stark Gallery.

Ruth B. McDowell. Ruth B. McDowell. Ed. by Elizabeth Aneloski. LC 96-10010. (Art & Inspirations Ser.: No. 1). (Illus.). 144p. (Orig.). 1996. pap. 29.95 (1-57120-015-0, 10139) C & T Pub.

Ruth Bader Ginsburg. Eleanor H. Ayer. LC 94-17854. (People in Focus Ser.). (J). (gr. 5). 1994. text ed., lib. bdg. 13.95 (0-87518-651-3, Dillon Silver Burdett) Silver Burdett Pr.

Ruth Bader Ginsburg. Eleanor H. Ayer. (People in Focus Ser.). (J). (gr. 5). 1994. pap. 7.95 (0-382-24721-3, Dillon Silver Burdett) Silver Burdett Pr.

Ruth Bader Ginsburg. Christopher Henry. LC 94-978. (First Bks.). 64p. (J). (gr. 4 up). 1994. lib. bdg. 21.00 (0-531-20174-0) Watts.

Ruth Bader Ginsburg. Bob Italia. LC 93-42168. (Supreme Court Justices Ser.). (J). 1994. lib. bdg. 14.98 (1-56239-098-8) Abdo & Dghtrs.

Ruth Bader Ginsburg: Supreme Court Justice. Carmen Bredeson. LC 95-12286. (People to Know Ser.). (Illus.). 128p. (YA). (gr. 6 up). 1995. lib. bdg. 18.95 (0-89490-621-6) Enslow Pubs.

Ruth Bader Ginsburg: Supreme Court Justice. Jack L. Roberts. LC 93-39015. (Gateway Biographies Ser.). (Illus.). 48p. (J). (gr. 2-4). pap. 6.95 (1-56294-744-3) Millbrook Pr.

***Ruth Bell Graham's Collected Poems.** Ruth B. Graham. 224p. Date not set. 16.99 (0-8010-1138-8) Baker Bks.

Ruth Benedict: Stranger in This Land. Margaret M. Caffrey. LC 88-20589. (American Studies). (Illus.). 448p. 1989. 19.95 (0-292-74655-5) U of Tex Pr.

***Ruth Bernhard: Gift of the Commonplace.** Photos by Ruth Bernhard. (Illus.). 1996. 40.00 (0-9630393-4-2) Ctr for Photo.

***Ruth Bernhard: Known & Unknown.** Ilee Kaplan. Ed. by Constance W. Glenn. (Illus.). 62p. (Orig.). 1996. pap. 24.95 (0-936270-35-7) CA St U LB Art.

Ruth Bernhard: The Collection of Ginny Williams. Intro. by Peter C. Bunnell. (Illus.). 50p. 1993. 65.00 (1-881138-04-6); pap. 40.00 (0-685-71951-0) Tallgrass Pr.

Ruth Brown Martin Story: How to Market Yourself & Sell 100 Houses Every Year. Ruth Martin & Walter Brown. LC 94-71237. (Illus.). 160p. (Orig.). 1995. reprint ed. pap. 15.95 (0-923687-31-9) Celo Valley Bks.

***Ruth Crawford: Music for Small Orchestra (1926) & Suite # 2 for 4 Strings & Piano (1929)** 2nd rev. ed. Ruth Crawford. Ed. by Judith Tick & Wayne Schneider. (Music of the U. S. A. - Recent Researches in American Music Ser.: Vol. MUSA1). xxvi, 63p. 1993. pap. 43.20 (0-89579-326-1) A-R Eds.

Ruth Crawford Seeger: A Composer's Search for American Music. Judith Trick. (Illus.). 448p. 1997. 39.95 (0-19-506509-3) OUP.

Ruth, Esther. Frederic Bush. (World Biblical Commentary Ser.: Vol. 9). 450p. 1996. 29.99 (0-8499-0208-8) Word Pub.

Ruth Hall. Fanny Fern. 1997. pap. 10.95 (0-14-018952-1, Viking) Viking Penguin.

***Ruth Hall.** Fanny Fern. 1997. pap. 10.95 (0-14-043640-5) Viking Penguin.

Ruth Hall & Other Writing. Fanny Fern. Ed. by Joyce W. Warren. (American Women Writers Ser.). 400p. (C). 1986. text ed. 40.00 (0-8135-1167-4); pap. text ed. 12.00 (0-8135-1168-2) Rutgers U Pr.

An Asterisk (*) at the beginning of an entry indicates that the title is appearing in BIP for the first time.

R

Ruth Hanna McCormick: A Life in Politics, 1880-1944. Kristie Miller. LC 91-28230. 3533p. 1992. 13.95 (0-8263-1333-7) U of NM Pr.

Ruth Heller Connection. Will C. Howell. 1992. pap. 9.99 (0-8224-1635-2) Fearon Teach Aids.

Ruth in Canaan. Rabbit. (J). 1998. pap. 10.95 (0-689-80232-3, Aladdin Paperbacks) S&S Childrens.

Ruth Laredo Becoming a Musician Book. Ruth Laredo. (Illus.). 72p. 1992. pap. 11.95 (0-913574-99-6, EA00714) Eur-Am Music.

Ruth Law Thrills a Nation. Illus. & Text by Don Brown. LC 92-45701. 32p. (J). (ps-2). 1993. 15.00 (0-395-66404-7) Ticknor & Flds Bks Yng Read.

***Ruth Law Thrills a Nation.** Don Brown. 1995. pap. 5.95 (0-395-73517-3) HM.

Ruth M. Reynolds Papers. Ed. by Evelina L. Antonetty. (Finding Aid Ser.). (Illus.). 29p. (C). reprint ed. pap. text ed. 5.00 (1-878483-24-2) Hunter Coll CEP.

Ruth McEnery Stuart. Hall. 1998. 22.95 (0-8057-4589-0, Twayne) Scribnrs Ref.

Ruth Montgomery: Herald of the New Age. Ruth Montgomery & Joanne Garland. 288p. 1987. mass mkt. 5.99 (0-449-21252-1, Crest) Fawcett.

Ruth Orkin: A Retrospective. Miles Barth. 40p. (Orig.). 1995. pap. 15.00 (0-9646247-0-2) Est R Orkin.

Ruth Page: An Intimate Biography. John J. Martin. LC 76-18427. (Dance Program Ser.: No. 4). (Illus.). 378p. reprint ed. pap. 107.80 (0-7837-0981-1, 2041288) Bks Demand.

Ruth Pitter Collected Poems. Ruth Pitter. 299p. (Orig.). 9000. pap. 22.00 (1-870612-06-X, Pub. by Enitha Pr UK) Dufour.

Ruth Prawar Jhabwala: A Critical Study of Her Fiction. R. G. Agarwal. 160p. 1990. text ed. 18.95 (0-938719-29-7, Envoy Pr) Apt Bks.

Ruth Prawer Jhabvala. Ralph J. Crane. LC 92-11257. (English Authors Ser.: No. 494). 160p. 1992. 23.95 (0-8057-7030-5, Twayne) Scribnrs Ref.

Ruth Prawer Jhabvala. 2nd rev. ed. Vasant A. Shahane. (Indian Writers Ser.: Vol. 11). 206p. 1983. lib. bdg. 12.00 (0-89253-074-X) Ind-US Inc.

Ruth Prawer Jhabvala: Fiction & Film. Jayanti Bailur. (C). 1992. text ed. 12.00 (0-685-63535-X, Pub. by Arnold Pubs II) S Asia.

***Ruth Rabbah: An Analytical Translation.** Jacob Neusner. 209p. 1989. 51.95 (1-55540-397-2) Scholars Pr GA.

Ruth Rendell. Bernheim. Date not set. 22.95 (0-8057-4625-0, Twayne) Scribnrs Ref.

Ruth Rosetta's Memories. Ruth B. Brown. 150p. 1993. pap. text ed. 10.00 (1-881908-06-2) PanPress.

***Ruth Schonthal Ein Kompositorischer Werdegang Im Exil.** Martina Helmig. (Studien und Materialien Zur Musikwissenschaft Ser.: Vol. 10). iv, 384p. (GER.). 1994. write for info. (3-487-09896-2) G Olms Pubs.

Ruth Slonim: Proems & Poems. Ruth Slonim. LC 91-42039. (Washington State University Press Art Ser.). 63p. 1992. 15.95 (0-87422-084-X); pap. 9.95 (0-87422-077-7) Wash St U Pr.

***Ruth Sova's 1997 Positive Affirmation Daily Calendar.** Ruth Sova. Ed. by Ellen Dybdahl. 370p. (Orig.). 1996. pap. 8.95 (1-889959-01-4) D S L Ltd.

Ruth St. Denis: A Biography of the Divine Dancer. Suzanne Shelton. (American Studies: No. 21). (Illus.). 404p. 1990. reprint ed. pap. 14.95 (0-292-77046-4) U of Tex Pr.

Ruth St. Denis: An Unfinished Life. Ruth St. Denis. LC 80-2893. (BCL Ser.: No. II). reprint ed. 42.50 (0-404-18075-2) AMS Pr.

Ruth Suckow. Abigail A. Hamblen. LC 78-52563. (Western Writers Ser.: No. 34). 48p. 1978. pap. 4.95 (0-88430-058-7) Boise St U W Writ Ser.

Ruth Suckow. Leedice M. Kissane. LC 68-24300. (Twayne's United States Authors Ser.). 1969. lib. bdg. 17.95 (0-8057-0712-3) Irvington.

Ruth Suckow Omnibus. Ruth Suckow. LC 88-15059. (Bur Oak Bk.). 328p. (Orig.). 1988. pap. 13.95 (0-87745-207-5) U of Iowa Pr.

Ruth, The Gleaner, & the Boy Samuel. Gordon Lindsay. (Old Testament Ser.: Vol. 17). 1965. 1.95 (0-89985-137-1) Christ for the Nations.

Ruth Weisberg: A Circle of Life. Ann S. Harri & Selma Holo. LC 85-82393. 48p. (Orig.). 1986. pap. 12.00 (0-9602974-3-X) USC Fisher Gallery.

Ruth Weisberg - Mid-Life, 1961-1990. R. Barrett & Mac McCloud. (Artists & Their Work Ser.). (Illus.). 134p. (Orig.). 1990. pap. 29.95 (1-877675-10-5) Midmarch Arts-WAN.

Ruthenium. 1968. 150.00 (0-387-93182-1) Spr-Verlag.

Rutherford & Boltwood: Letters on Radioactivity. Ernest Rutherford & Bertram B. Boltwood. Ed. by Lawrence Badash. LC 78-81411. (Yale Studies in the History of Science & Medicine: No. 4). (Illus.). 402p. reprint ed. pap. 114.60 (0-8357-9490-3, 2016787) Bks Demand.

Rutherford & Son. Githa Sowerby. 1995. pap. (0-413-68950-6) Chapman & Hall.

Rutherford & the Nature of the Atom. E. N. Andrade. (Illus.). 1990. 14.50 (0-8446-2053-X) Peter Smith.

Rutherford B. Hayes. Zachary Kent. LC 88-8679. (Encyclopedia of Presidents Ser.). (Illus.). 100p. (J). (gr. 3 up). 1989. lib. bdg. 22.00 (0-516-01365-3) Childrens.

Rutherford B. Hayes: And His America. Harry Barnard. LC 92-73458. (Signature Ser.). (Illus.). 606p. 1992. reprint ed. 32.50 (0-945707-05-3) Amer Political.

Rutherford B. Hayes: Nineteenth President of the United States. Neal E. Robbins. Ed. by Richard G. Young. LC 88-24565. (Presidents of the United States Ser.). (Illus.). (J). (gr. 5-9). 1989. lib. bdg. 17.26 (0-944483-23-2) Garrett Ed Corp.

***Rutherford B. Hayes: One of the "Good" Colonels.** Ari Hoogenboom. (Civil War Campaigns & Commanders Ser.). (Illus.). 132p. (Orig.). 1997. pap. 12.95 (1-886661-20-0) Ryan Place Pub.

Rutherford B. Hayes: Warrior & President. Ari Hoogenboom. LC 94-5274. (Illus.). 608p. 1995. 45.00 (0-7006-0641-6) U Pr of KS.

Rutherford B. Hayes Show. Ron Wertheimer. 224p. 1986. 11.95 (0-8184-0391-8) Carol Pub Group.

Rutherford Co., TN: County Court Minutes 1811-1815. Carol Wells. 187p. (Orig.). 1994. pap. 18.00 (1-55613-965-9) Heritage Bk.

Rutherford County, North Carolina Marriage Bonds & Certificates, 1799-1867. Francis T. Ingmire. 190p. 1994. pap. 20.00 (0-8095-8688-6); lib. bdg. 49.00 (0-8095-8127-2) Borgo Pr.

Rutherford County, North Carolina, Wills & Miscellaneous Records, 1783-1868. James E. Wooley & Vivian F. Wooley. 184p. 1984. pap. 25.00 (0-89308-413-1) Southern Hist Pr.

Rutherford Mound, Hardin County, Illinois. Melvin L. Fowler. (Scientific Papers: Vol. VII, No. 1). (Illus.). 44p. 1974. pap. 2.00 (0-89792-015-5) Ill St Museum.

Rutherford Racket. Charles P. Windle. 30p. 1988. reprint ed. pap. 1.95 (1-883858-53-4) Witness CA.

Rutherford Uncovered: A Resume of the Reasons that Lay behind Jim Brown's Manifesto. Richard Felix. 34p. 1988. reprint ed. pap. 1.95 (1-883858-49-6) Witness CA.

Rutherford vs. the United States, Vols. 1 & 2. 1503p. (C). 1986. pap. 19.95 (1-883858-32-1); pap. write for info. (1-883858-33-X); pap. write for info. (1-883858-34-8) Witness CA.

***Rutherford Wolf.** Thomas Hischak. 32p. (Orig.). 1997. pap. 5.00 (0-87440-034-1) Bakers Plays.

***Ruthie, Bretheren Girl.** Ruth R. Stokes. 240p. (Orig.). 1996. pap. 14.95 (1-883893-60-7) WinePress Pub.

Ruthie's Four Hearts. Ruth S. Hoien. (J). pap. 3.99 (0-88019-105-8) Schmul Pub Co.

***Ruthie's Gift.** Kimberly B. Bradley. LC 97-19396. (Illus.). (J). 1998. write for info. (0-385-32525-8) Delacorte.

Ruthka: A Diary of War. Ruthka Lieblich. Ed. by Jehoshua Eibeshitz & Anna Eibeshitz. Tr. by Anna Eibeshitz. (Illus.). 170p. 1993. 15.95 (0-932351-42-5); pap. 12.95 (0-932351-43-3) Besad Prodns.

***Ruthless.** Michelle Goodwin. 350p. (Orig.). 1998. mass mkt. 8.99 (1-889501-96-4, Flirtation) Sovereign.

Ruthless Contract. large type ed. Kathryn Ross. 288p. 1996. 21.50 (0-263-14388-0, Pub. by M & B UK) Ulverscroft.

Ruthless Contract (Wedlocked!) Kathryn Ross. 1996. mass mkt. 3.50 (0-373-11807-4, 1-11807-4) Harlequin Bks.

Ruthless Criticism: New Perspectives in U. S. Communications History. Ed. by William Solomon & Robert McChesney. LC 92-36571. (Illus.). 395p. (C). 1993. pap. text ed. 16.95 (0-8166-2170-5) U of Minn Pr.

***Ruthless Economy.** Head. 1999. write for info. (0-395-86559-X) HM.

Ruthless Exploits of Admiral John Winslow: Naval Hero of the Civil War. Paul Ditzel. (True Adventure Stories from the Civil War Ser.). (Illus.). 112p. (Orig.). 1991. pap. 9.95 (0-925165-05-0) Fire Buff Hse.

Ruthless Gun. Ted Lewellen. 160p. 1981. pap. 1.75 (0-449-12796-6, GM) Fawcett.

Ruthless Range - Death Rides a Black Horse. Lewis B. Patten. 320p. 1995. mass mkt., pap. text ed. 4.99 (0-8439-3741-6) Dorchester Pub Co.

***Ruthless Realtor Murders.** Kaufelt. 1997. 22.00 (0-671-51147-5, PB Hardcover) PB.

Ruth's Adventures in Israel. Harriett Ottow. LC 87-51493. 44p. (J). (gr. k-2). 1988. 5.95 (1-55523-133-0) Winston-Derek.

Ruth's Journey: A Survivor's Memoir. Ruth G. Gold. LC 95-6771. (Illus.). 312p. (C). 1996. lib. bdg. 34.95 (0-8130-1400-X) U Press Fla.

***Ruth's Journey: A Survivor's Memoir.** Ruth G. Gold. (Illus.). 312p. 1997. pap. 19.95 (0-8130-1547-2) U Press Fla.

Ruth's Primer of Africa. Ruth N. Cyr. 368p. 1996. 59.00 (1-880836-07-6) Pine Isl Pr.

Ruth's Story Reusable Sticker Book. Laura Kelly. (Little Lamb Mini Activity Bks.). (Illus.). 12p. (J). 1993. pap. 1.49 (0-7847-0026-5, 01526) Standard Pub.

Ruthwell Cross: Papers from the Colloquium Sponsored by the Index of Christian Art, Princeton University, 8 December 1989. Ed. by Brendan Cassidy. LC 92-34870. (Occasional Papers - Index of Christian Art). (Illus.). 220p. 1992. 49.50 (0-691-03211-4); pap. 19.95 (0-691-00038-7) Princeton A & A.

Rutiodon. D. White. (Dinosaur Library). (Illus.). 24p. (J). (gr. 3 up). 1989. 10.95 (0-685-58284-1); lib. bdg. 14.60 (0-86592-522-4) Rourke Corp.

Rutland Betterments - Statistics. R. W. Nimke. LC 89-81530. (Rutland Ser.). (Illus.). 192p. (Orig.). 1989. 35.00 (0-914960-90-3); pap. 25.00 (0-914960-77-6) Academy Bks.

Rutland Boughton & the Glastonbury Festivals. Michael Hurd. LC 92-37066. (Illus.). 438p. (C). 1993. 85.00 (0-19-816316-9, Old Oregon Bk Store) OUP.

Rutland Herald History: Bicentennial Chronicle. Tyler Resch. 1995. write for info. (0-9643308-2-2); lib. bdg. write for info. (0-9643308-3-0) Herald Assn.

Rutland, MA. B. Anderson. (Images of America Ser.). 1997. pap. 16.99 (0-7524-0449-0, Arcdia) Chalford.

Rutland Papers Original Documents Illustrative of the Courts & Times of Henry Seven & Henry Eight. John H. Rutland. Ed. by William Jerden. LC 17-1204. (Camden Society, London. Publications, First Ser.: No. 21). reprint ed. 35.00 (0-404-50121-4) AMS Pr.

Rutland Place. Anne Perry. 1986. mass mkt. 6.99 (0-449-21285-8) Fawcett.

***Rutland Road.** 2nd ed. Jim Shaughnessy. LC 96-51169. (Illus.). 436p. 1997. pap. 32.95 (0-8156-0456-4) Syracuse U Pr.

***Rutland Road.** 2nd ed. Jim Shaughnessy. LC 96-51169. (Illus.). 436p. 1997. 70.00 (0-8156-0469-6) Syracuse U Pr.

Rutland, VT. Historical Briefs, Inc. Staff. Ed. by Thomas Antonucci & Michael Antonucci. 224p. 1992. pap. 13.95 (0-89677-033-8) Hist Briefs.

Rutland Words. C. Wordsworth. (English Dialect Society Publications: No. 64). 1974. reprint ed. pap. 15.00 (0-8115-0484-0) Periodicals Srv.

Rutley's Elements of Minerology. rev. ed. H. H. Read & Colin D. Gribble. 512p. 1988. pap. text ed. 27.95 (0-04-549011-2) Routledge Chapman & Hall.

Rutley's Elements of Minerology. 27th rev. ed. H. H. Read & Colin D. Gribble. 512p. 1988. text ed. 75.00 (0-04-549010-4) Routledge Chapman & Hall.

***Ruts: Gender Roles & Realities.** Anne R. Mahoney et al. 160p. (Orig.). 1996. pap. text ed. 15.95 (0-9630149-1-9) Red Mesa.

Rutters of the Sea: The Sailing Directions of Pierre Garcie. Pierre Garcie. LC 67-17722. (Illus.). 501p. reprint ed. pap. 142.80 (0-317-08232-9, 2022051) Bks Demand.

Rusbroec & His Mysticism. Paul Verdeyen. Tr. by Andre Lefevere. LC 93-47034. (Way of the Christian Mystics Ser.: No. 11). 168p. (Orig.). 1994. pap. text ed. 12.95 (0-8146-5628-5, M Glazier) Liturgical Pr.

Ruwenzori: Mountains of the Moon. Syed Z. Ahmed. 168p. 1993. pap. 22.00 (1-880365-72-3) Prof Pr NC.

Ruxton of the Rockies. George F. Ruxton. Ed. by LeRoy R. Hafen. LC 50-9832. (American Exploration & Travel Ser.: Vol. 13). (Illus.). 344p. 1984. pap. 14.95 (0-8061-1603-X) U of Okla Pr.

Ruy Blas. Victor Hugo. (Univers des Lettres Bordas Ser.). pap. 5.95 (0-685-34921-7) Fr & Eur.

Ruy Blas. Victor Hugo. 192p. (FRE.). 1970. pap. 7.95 (0-7859-0008-X, F64414) Fr & Eur.

Ruy Blas, 2 vols., 1. Victor Hugo. (FRE.). 1971. 10.95 (0-7859-1072-7) Fr & Eur.

Ruy Blas, 2 vols., 2. Victor Hugo. (FRE.). 1971. 30.00 (0-686-54039-5, 2038700613) Fr & Eur.

Ruy Lopez: Winning Chess with 1P-K4. L. W. Barden. 185p. 1963. 13.00 (0-08-013006-2, Pergamon Pr); pap. 8.50 (0-08-009997-1, Pergamon Pr) Elsevier.

***Ruy Lopez Exchange Variation Vol. 2: (C69)** Falchetta. Ed. by S. L. Edritrice. (Illus.). 1996. pap. 18.95 (88-86127-57-X) Thinkers Pr.

Ruysbroeck the Admirable. A. Wautier D'Aygalliers. 372p. 1996. pap. 24.95 (1-56459-558-7) Kessinger Pub.

Ruzbihan Baqli: Mysticism & the Rhetoric of Sainthood in Persian Sufism. Carl W. Ernst. (Jewish Philosophy Ser.: No. 4). 208p. (C). 1996. pap. 25.00 (0-7007-0342-X, Pub. by Curzon Pr UK) Paul & Co Pubs.

RU486: The Pill That Could End the Abortion Wars & Why American Women Don't Have It. Lawrence Lader. 1992. pap. 9.57 (0-201-60819-7) Addison-Wesley.

RU486: The Pill That Could End the Abortion Wars & Why American Women Don't Have It. rev. ed. Lawrence Lader. 1992. 18.95 (0-201-63203-9) Addison-Wesley.

RV - Travel Leisurely Year Round. Rolanda D. Masse. (U. S. A. Guides Ser.). 200p. (Orig.). 1991. pap. 14.95 (0-87052-958-7) Hippocrene Bks.

RV Air Conditioning Preventive Maintenance & Service Manual. Robert L. Cain. (Illus.). 66p. 1991. pap. 12.95 (0-9628736-0-8) Cain Bks.

RV Electrical Systems: Basic Troubleshooting, Repair & Improvement. Bill Moeller & Jan Moeller. LC 94-30072. (Illus.). 288p. 1994. pap. text ed. 19.95 (0-07-042778-X, Ragged Mntn) Intl Marine.

RV Foreign Travel Maps. write for info. (0-318-62951-8) Am Map.

RV Handbook. Bill Estes. LC 90-10926. (Illus.). 352p. (Orig.). 1990. pap. 29.95 (0-934798-28-1, Trailer Life Bks) TL Enterprises.

***RV Handbook.** 2nd rev. ed. Bill Estes. Ed. by Bob Livingston. (Illus.). 400p. (Orig.). 1997. pap. 29.95 (0-934798-44-3) TL Enterprises.

RV Having Fun Yet? Comic Adventures on the Road. Ray Parker. LC 94-65905. (Illus.). 151p. (Orig.). 1995. 12.95 (0-9640924-0-9) Oldfield Pub.

RV Rating Book: 1992-1996 Models: with the Language of RVing. J. D. Gallant & RV Consumer Group Staff. LC 96-11456. (Illus.). 512p. 1996. per. 68.00 (1-884046-62-2) Quill Pubng.

***RV Rating Book 1996-97: With the Language of RVing - Introduction by J.D. Gallant.** 2nd ed. RV Consumer Group Staff & J. D. Gallant. (Orig.). 1997. per. 48.00 (1-884046-63-0) R V Consumer Grp.

***RV Repair & Maintenance.** 3rd rev. ed. Bob Livingston. (Illus.). 400p. 1997. pap. 34.95 (0-934798-45-1) TL Enterprises.

RV Repair & Maintenance Manual. 298p. 1989. 19.95 (0-318-17003-5) RV Indus Assn.

***RVer's Friend: National Diesel & Parking Directory.** 3rd rev. ed. (Illus.). 272p. 1997. pap. 9.95 (1-890141-01-1, RV97) TR Info Pubs.

RVers Guide to Solar Battery Charging. Noel Kirkby. (Illus.). 176p. 1987. pap. 12.95 (0-937948-08-X) aatec Pubns.

***Rver's Travel Log.** Bob Livingston. 1997. pap. text ed. 12.95 (0-934798-49-4) TL Enterprises.

***RVing Alaska! And Canada.** Sharlene G. Minshall. (Illus.). 192p. (Orig.). 1997. pap. 14.95 (0-9643970-1-3) Gypsy Press.

RVing Basics. Bill Moeller & Jan Moeller. (Illus.). 224p. 1995. pap. text ed. 14.95 (0-07-042779-8, Ragged Mntn) Intl Marine.

***RV'ing for Fun & Profit.** Tom Magee & Mary L. Magee. (Illus.). 300p. (Orig.). 1996. pap. 19.95 (1-56559-901-2) HGI Mrktng.

RVing from A-Z. Bill Farlow. 223p. 1995. pap. 14.95 (0-937877-07-7) Cottage Pubns Inc.

RVing in Alaska: Campgrounds & Services. Richard D. Anderson. (Illus.). 208p. (Orig.). 1991. 16.95 (0-9629325-2-3) Billiken Pr.

RVing in Alaska: Campgrounds & Services. rev. ed. Richard D. Anderson. (Illus.). 210p. (Orig.). 1994. 16.95 (0-9629325-3-1) Billiken Pr.

***RVing Made Easy: How to Choose, Operate & Enjoy Your RV.** Joe Kieva & Vicki Kieva. 160p. (Orig.). 1997. pap. 12.95 (0-9655620-0-X) R V Travel.

RVing North America: Silver, Single, & Solo. Sharlene G. Minshall. LC 94-96691. (Illus.). 288p. (Orig.). 1995. pap. 12.95 (0-9643970-0-5) Gypsy Press.

RVing with Dolly. Virgil Gorans. 131p. (Orig.). 1988. pap. 6.95 (0-9620138-0-3) M-V Charters.

RVP Fees, 2 bks., Set. rev. ed. Relative Value Studies, Inc. Staff. 900p. 1995. ring bd. 795.00 incl. disk (0-07-810179-4) Hlthcare Mgmt Grp.

RVP Fees: Primary Care. Relative Value Studies, Inc. Staff. 1994. 99.95 incl. disk (0-07-809883-1) Hlthcare Mgmt Grp.

RVs & Vans. Stephen Burt. (Cruisin' Ser.). (Illus.). 48p. (J). (gr. 3-6). 1992. lib. bdg. 17.80 (1-56065-071-0) Capstone Pr.

***RV's to Riches.** Donald Shaffer. Ed. by Terri Shaffer & Jean Jestus. (Illus.). 126p. (Orig.). 1996. per., pap. 249.00 (0-9655746-1-X) Debon Auto.

***Rwala Bedouin Today.** 2nd rev. ed. William Lancaster. (Illus.). 203p. (C). 1997. pap. text ed. 10.95 (0-88133-943-1) Waveland Pr.

Rwanda. Randall Eegley. (World Bibliographical Ser.). 1993. lib. bdg. 68.50 (1-85109-202-1) ABC-CLIO.

Rwanda. Carl Lawrence. 1995. pap. 9.99 (1-885305-34-6) Multnomah Pubs.

Rwanda. Joseph Sevigny. LC 95-22473. (Country Guide Series Report from the AACRAO-AID Project). 1996. 20.00 (0-929851-57-9) Am Assn Coll Registrars.

***Rwanda: A Country Torn Apart.** Kari Bodnarchuk. LC 96-43424. (World in Conflict Ser.). (J). 1997. lib. bdg. write for info. (0-8225-3557-2, Lerner Publctns) Lerner Group.

Rwanda: An Agenda for International Action. Guy Vassall-Adams. (Oxfam Insights). 64p. (C). 1994. pap. 7.50 (0-85598-299-3, Pub. by Oxfam UK) Humanities.

Rwanda: An Agenda for International Action. Guy Vassall-Adams. (Insight Ser.). (FRE.). 1994. pap. 3.95 (0-85598-311-6, Pub. by Oxfam UK) Humanities.

Rwanda: Fierce Clashes in Central Africa. Keith Greenberg. Ed. by Bruce Glassman. LC 95-51828. (Children in Crisis Ser.). (Illus.). 32p. (J). (gr. 3-7). 1996. lib. bdg. 14.95 (1-56711-185-8) Blackbirch.

Rwanda: Which Way Now? David Waller. (Country Profiles Ser.). (Illus.). 64p. (C). 1993. pap. 9.95 (0-85598-217-9, Pub. by Oxfam UK) Humanities.

***Rwanda - Sexual Violence During the Rwandan Genocide & Its Aftermath: Shattered Lives.** Human Rights Watch, Africa Staff et al. 112p. (Orig.). 1996. pap. 10.00 (1-56432-208-4) Hum Rts Watch.

Rwanda - The Silence. Gilles Peress. 1995. pap. 29.50 (1-881616-38-X, Pub. by Scalo Pubs) Dist Art Pubs.

Rwanda & Genocide in the Twentieth Century. Alain Destexhe. Tr. by Alison Marschner. 140p. (C). 1995. 19.95 (0-8147-1873-6) NYU Pr.

Rwanda Crisis: History of a Genocide. Gerard Prunier. LC 95-18203. 250p. 1995. 29.95 (0-231-10408-1) Col U Pr.

***Rwanda Crisis: History of a Genocide.** Gerard Prunier. 1997. pap. 16.50 (0-231-10409-X) Col U Pr.

***Rwanda, Which Way Now?** David Waller. (Oxfam Country Profiles Ser.). (Illus.). 72p. 1996. pap. 9.95 (0-614-18273-5, Pub. by Oxfam UK) Humanities.

***Rwanda Which Way Now.** David Waller. (Oxfam Country Profiles Ser.). (C). 1996. pap. 9.95 (0-85598-354-X, Pub. by Oxfam UK) Humanities.

RWD Guide: Rear Wheel Drive Interchange Guide. S. H. Friedman. 464p. 1994. pap. 95.00 (0-916966-30-5) Interchange.

RW8 Manual: Tips & Tricks for 8-Way Sequential Freefall Skydiving. Pal Bergan & Audun Wik. 96p. (Orig.). 1990. pap. text ed. 14.95 (0-9607814-6-3) AeroGraphics.

Rx: Charcoal. Agatha Thrash & Calvin L. Thrash. (Illus.). 110p. 1988. pap. 6.95 (0-942658-09-4) NewLife Bks.

Rx: For a Liberated Childbirth. Bev Smucha & Alice Unger. Ed. by Evie Heilbrun. LC 77-80302. 1979. 19.95 (0-87949-098-5) Ashley Bks.

Rx: Handwriting; An Individualized, Prescriptive System for Painless Managing Handwriting Instruction. Jane E. Bluestein. (Illus.). 48p. 1983. pap. 8.95 (0-915817-01-2) ISS Pubns.

RX: Reading & Following the Directions for All Kinds of Medications. Carloyn Simpson. LC 94-702. (Life Skills Library). (Illus.). 48p. (YA). 1994. lib. bdg. 14.95 (0-8239-1696-0) Rosen Group.

Rx: Spiritist As Needed: A Study of a Puerto Rican Community Mental Health Resource. Alan Harwood. LC 87-47599. (Anthropology of Contemporary Issues Ser.). 288p. 1987. pap. 16.95 (0-8014-9470-2) Cornell U Pr.

Rx: Take One Daily at Bedtime. Marjorie G. Mobberley. 64p. (Orig.). 1989. pap. 4.95 (1-877759-04-X) Exodus Pr.

RX & OTC Cough & Cold Products. Ed. by Peter Allen. 206p. 1985. pap. text ed. 2,955.00 (0-931634-51-2) FIND-SVP.

***RX Andromedae Light Curves 1963-1995.** Compiled by Janet A. Mattei et al. (Monograph Ser.: Vol. 9). (Illus.). 76p. (Orig.). 1996. pap. text ed. 10.00 (1-878174-20-7) Am Assn Var Star.

An Asterisk (*) at the beginning of an entry indicates that the title is appearing in BIP for the first time.

RX Executive Diet. Virginia Aronson & Frederick J. Stare. 1986. pap. 9.75 (0-8158-0424-5) Chris Mass.

***Rx Factor: Strategic Creativity in Pharmaceutical Marketing.** Pavan Choudary. LC 97-18645. 1997. write for info. (0-8039-9378-1); pap. write for info. (0-8039-9379-X) Sage.

Rx for Business: A Troubleshooting Guide for Building a High-Performance Organization. Mark G. Brown et al. 1996. pap. 25.00 (0-614-12582-0) Irwin Prof Pubng.

Rx for Business: A Troubleshooting Guide for Building a High Performance Organization. Mark G. Brown et al. LC 96-3990. (Illus.). 250p. 1996. pap. 24.95 (0-7863-0477-4, H0945) ASQC Qual Pr.

Rx for Fine Dining. Ed. by Jayne Fina. 206p. (Orig.). 1989. pap. 14.95 (0-9622715-1-9) FTCTSNCH.

Rx for Hospitals: New Hope for Medicare. Philip Hassen. 1994. 18.95 (0-7737-2700-0) Genl Dist Srvs.

Rx for Living: Take as Needed. Max L. Foreman. 1982. 20.00 (0-8197-0490-3) Bloch.

***Rx for Murder.** Renee B. Horowitz. 1997. mass mkt. 5.50 (0-380-78619-2) Avon.

Rx for Small Business Success: Accounting, Planning, & Recordkeeping Techniques for a Healthy Bottom Line. Jeffrey Slater. (Illus.). 256p. 1981. 18.95 (0-685-03921-8, Spectrum IN) Macmillan Gen Ref.

Rx for the Classroom Blahs. Lynn Embry. (Illus.). 64p. (J). (gr. 4-8). 1983. student ed. 7.99 (0-86653-104-1, GA 462) Good Apple.

***Rx for the Soul: Moments from a Physician's Practice That Brings Inspiration & Encouragement.** David B. Wilhelm. LC 96-40023. 228p. 1997. pap. 10.99 (0-7852-7245-3) Nelson.

RX, Inc. The Small Business Handbook for Building a Healthier Workforce. Howard Rothman. Ed. by Debra J. Lyne. 84p. (Orig.). 1990. pap. 10.00 (0-89154-398-8) Intl Found Employ.

Rx PC: The Anti-Virus Handbook. Janet Endrijonas. (Illus.). 208p. 1992. 39.95 (0-8306-4202-1, 4262, Windcrest); pap. 29.95 (0-8306-4201-3, 4262, Windcrest) TAB Bks.

RX: Prescription for the Boards: A Student-to-Student Guide. Radhika S. Breaden et al. LC 95-45312. 512p. 1995. pap. text ed. 29.95 (0-316-10626-7) Lppncott-Raven.

Rx Shikse: A Trans-Placental Romance. J. P. Ephraim. LC 88-81437. 192p. (Orig.). 1988. pap. 9.95 (0-941404-75-7) New Falcon Pubns.

***RX Shorthand.** Stanley Jablonski. 100p. (Orig.). 1996. pap. text ed. 9.95 (1-56053-167-3) Hanley & Belfus.

RX Television: Enhancing the Preventive Impact of TV. Joyce N. Sprafkin. LC 82-15778. (Prevention in Human Services Ser.: Vol. 2, Nos. 1-2). 139p. 1983. pap. text ed. 29.95 (0-86656-219-2) Haworth Pr.

RX 2000 see Our Medical Future: Breakthroughs in Health & Longevity by the Year 2000 & Beyond

***RX7 Mazda.** J. Yamaguchi. (Illus.). 282p. 29.95 (4-947659-01-7, Pub. by Ring Ltd JA) Motorbooks Intl.

Ry: A Play. Mark Dunster. 1977. 4.00 (0-89642-032-9) Linden Pubs.

RY Sagittarii Light Curves 1892-1990: AAVSO Monograph 5. Janet A. Mattei et al. (Illus.). 22p. 1994. pap. text ed. 10.00 (1-878174-04-5) Am Assn Var Star.

RY Sagittarii Light Curves 1991-1995: AAVSO Monograph 5, Supplement 1. Janet A. Mattei et al. (Illus.). 12p. 1996. pap. text ed. 10.00 (1-878174-18-5) Am Assn Var Star.

Ryan: A Mother's Story of Her Hyperactive-Tourette Syndrome Child. Susan Hughes. LC 89-83295. 160p. (Orig.). 1990. 14.95 (1-878267-25-6); pap. 9.95 (1-878267-26-4) Hope Pr CA.

Ryan & Ryan's Thots That Stick to the Roof of Your Mind. Gary Ryan & Bob Ryan. Ed. by Karen Lindsay. 192p. (Orig.). 1994. pap. text ed. 7.95 (0-9644687-0-0) R&R Creat Adv.

Ryan Blake's Revenge. Clara Wimberly. (Intimate Moments Ser.). 1993. mass mkt. 3.50 (0-373-07521-9, 5-07521-3) Silhouette.

Ryan Family of Breckinridge County, Kentucky. Perry T. Ryan. LC 83-62918. (Illus.). 528p. 1989. reprint ed. 30.00 (0-9625504-0-X) P T Ryan.

Ryan FR-1 Fireball & XF2R-1 Darkshark. Steve Ginter. (Naval Fighters Ser.: No. 28). (Illus.). 74p. 1995. pap. 14.95 (0-942612-28-0) Naval Fighters.

Ryan Law Capsule-Property. Ryan Staff. 1985. pap. text ed. 9.95 (0-15-900134-X) HB Legal.

Ryan Rolant: The Medieval Welsh Version of the Song of Roland. Annalee C. Rejhon. LC 82-20031. (University of California Publications in Entomology: No. 113). 276p. (ENG & WEL.). 1984. pap. 78.70 (0-7837-8422-8, 2049224) Bks Demand.

Ryan White: My Own Story. Ryan White & Ann M. Cunningham. (Illus.). 144p. (J). (gr. 5 up). 1991. pap. 16.95 (0-8037-0977-3) Dial Bks Young.

Ryan White: My Own Story. Ryan White & Ann M. Cunningham. (Illus.). 360p. 1992. pap. 5.99 (0-451-17322-8, Sig) NAL-Dutton.

***Ryan White Care Act: Access to Services by Minorities, Women & Substance Abusers.** (Illus.). 25p. (Orig.). (C). 1996. pap. 20.00 (0-7881-3135-4) DIANE Pub.

Ryanodine Receptors. Ed. by Vincenzo Sorrentino & Mannfred A. Hollinger. LC 95-14214. (CRC Pharmacology & Toxicology). 192p. 1995. 104.95 (0-8493-8543-1, 8543) CRC Pr.

Ryan's Bride. Julie Kistler. (American Romance Ser.). 1995. pap. 3.50 (0-373-16575-7, 1-16575-2) Harlequin Bks.

Ryan's Enchantress. Connie Harwell. 416p. (Orig.). 1993. mass mkt., pap. text ed. 4.99 (0-8439-3436-0) Dorchester Pub Co.

Ryan's Manual of the Law of Income Tax in Australia. 7th ed. G. W. O'Grady & K. J. O'Rourke. xliv, 513p. 1989. 68.00 (0-455-20906-5, Pub. by Law Bk Co AT); pap. 42.50 (0-455-20907-3, Pub. by Law Bk Co AT) Gaunt.

Ryan's Quadrangle. Elizabeth Daish. 256p. 1996. 22.00 (0-7278-4891-7) Severn Hse.

Ryan's Return. Barbara Freethy. 384p. 1996. mass mkt. 5.99 (0-380-78531-5) Avon.

Ryan's Trials. Linda E. Shepherd. LC 93-25995. (YA). (gr. 9-12). 1993. pap. 7.99 (0-8407-9681-1) Nelson.

***Ryazan Oblast: Economy, Industry, Government, Business.** 2nd rev. ed. Russian Information & Business Center, Inc. Staff. (Russian Regional Business Directories Ser.). (Illus.). 200p. 1997. pap. 99.00 (1-57751-410-6) Russ Info & Busn Ctr.

***Ryboe's Best Birthday Ever!** Rebecca Wilson. LC 96-90195. (Illus.). 32p. (Orig.). (J). (ps-3). 1996. pap. text ed. 6.95 (0-9654893-0-2) Beezle Bug.

Rycroft on Analysis Creativity. Charles Rycroft. 192p. (C). 1992. pap. 17.50 (0-8147-7428-8); text ed. 28.00 (0-8147-7427-X) NYU Pr.

Rydberg Atoms. Thomas F. Gallagher. LC 93-37132. (Monographs on Atomic, Molecular, & Chemical Physics: No. 3). (Illus.). 550p. (C). 1994. text ed. 110.00 (0-521-38531-8) Cambridge U Pr.

Rydberg States of Atoms & Molecules. Ed. by R. F. Stebbings & F. B. Dunning. LC 82-1181. (Illus.). 500p. 1983. 135.00 (0-521-24823-X) Cambridge U Pr.

Ryder. 2nd ed. Djuna Barnes. LC 90-2769. (Illus.). 250p. 1990. reprint ed. pap. 11.95 (0-916583-55-4) Dalkey Arch.

***Ryder Gambit Accepted: Blackmar-Diemer Gambit.** Eric Schiller & John Crayton. 81p. (Orig.). 1995. pap. 9.95 (0-945470-57-6) Chess Ent.

RyderFIRST: Facilitating a Turn-Around in Ryder System's Consumer Truck Rental Division. Joyce Elam. (Prentice Hall Case Series for Management Information). 1995. write for info. (0-13-207614-4) P-H.

***Ryder's Wife.** Sharon Sala. 1997. mass mkt. 3.99 (0-373-07817-X, 1-07817-9) Silhouette.

Rye: Production, Chemistry, & Technology. W. Bushuk. LC 76-29382. 181p. 1976. text ed. 89.00 (0-913250-11-2) Am Assn Cereal Chem.

Rye & Rye Beach, NH. W. Varrell. (Images of America Ser.). 1995. pap. 16.99 (0-7524-0218-8, Arcdia) Chalford.

Rye Creek Project: Archaeology in the Upper Tonto Basin. Mark D. Elson & Douglas B. Craig. (Anthropological Papers: No. 11). (Illus.). 1214p. (Orig.). 1992. pap. 50.00 (1-886398-06-2) Desert Archaeol.

Rye Creek Project: Archaeology in the Upper Tonto Basin: Artifact & Specific Analyses, No. 2. Mark D. Elson & Douglas B. Craig. (Anthropological Papers: No. 11). (Illus.). 504p. (Orig.). 1992. pap. 30.00 (1-886398-08-9) Desert Archaeol.

Rye Creek Project: Archaeology in the Upper Tonto Basin: Introduction & Site Descriptions, No. 1. Mark D. Elson & Douglas B. Craig. (Anthropological Papers: No. 11). (Illus.). 362p. (Orig.). 1992. pap. 30.00 (1-886398-07-0) Desert Archaeol.

Rye Creek Project: Archaeology in the Upper Tonto Basin: Synthesis & Conclusions, No. 3. Mark D. Elson & Douglas B. Craig. (Anthropological Papers: No. 11). (Illus.). 348p. (Orig.). 1992. pap. 30.00 (1-886398-09-7) Desert Archaeol.

Rye in the Twenties. Colin Dunne. 1978. 15.95 (0-405-09141-9, 19506) Ayer.

Ryer Avenue Story. Dorothy Uhnak. Date not set. 99.95 (1-56054-866-5) Thorndike Pr.

Ryerson Genealogy: Genealogy & History of the Knickerbocker Family of Ryerson, Ryerse, Ryerss; Also Adriance & Martense Family; All Descendants of Martin & Adrisen Reyersz (Reyerszen) of Amsterdam, Holland. A. L. Holman. (Illus.). 459p. 1993. reprint ed. pap. 69.50 (0-8328-3058-5); reprint ed. lib. bdg. 79.50 (0-8328-3057-7) Higginson Bk Co.

Ryerson's Manhunt. R. C. House. 1994. mass mkt. 3.99 (0-671-87243-5) PB.

***Ryman Remembers: Recipes & Recollections, the Ryman Auditorium.** Favorite Recipes Press Staff. LC 96-33463. 1996. write for info. (0-87197-449-5) Favorite Recipes.

***Rymes of Robyn Hood: An Introduction to the English Outlaw.** rev. ed. R. B. Dobson & J. Taylor. (History Paperbacks Ser.). (Illus.). 368p. 1997. pap. 26.95 (0-7509-1661-3, Pub. by Sutton Pubng UK) Bks Intl VA.

Ryoanji Temple & Other Poems. John M. Steadman. LC 92-44457. 64p. 1993. pap. 9.95 (0-7734-2802-X) E Mellen.

Ryokan: Zen Monk - Poet of Japan. Ryokan. Tr. by Burton Watson from JPN. 126p. 1992. pap. 11.95 (0-231-04415-1) Col U Pr.

***Ryokan - the Japanese Inn.** D. Richie. 1996. 31.95 (4-07-974222-3) Shufu no Tomo-Sha.

***Ryolite: Death Valley's Ghost City of Golden Dreams.** Harold Weight & Lucile Weight. (Illus.). 40p. (Orig.). 1996. pap. 4.25 (1-878900-32-3) DVNH Assn.

***Rypins' Basic Sciences Review.** 17th ed. Harold Rypins & Edward D. Frohlich. LC 96-34954. 848p. 1996. pap. text ed. 34.95 (0-397-51488-3) Lppncott-Raven.

***Rypins' Clinical Sciences Review.** 17th ed. Harold Rypins & Edward D. Frohlich. LC 96-36162. 400p. 1996. pap. text ed. 32.95 (0-397-51544-8) Lppncott-Raven.

***Rypins' Intensive Reviews: Physiology.** Hall & Adair. LC 97-21928. (Illus.). 200p. 1997. pap. text ed. write for info. (0-397-51549-9) Lppncott-Raven.

Rypins' Intensive Reviews: Psychiatry & Behavioral Medicine. Gordon Deckert. LC 96-22473. 144p. 1996. pap. text ed. 19.95 (0-397-51554-5) Lppncott-Raven.

Rypins' Intensive Reviews: Surgery. Ravi Chari. LC 96-18898. 338p. 1996. pap. text ed. 19.95 (0-397-51551-0) Lppncott-Raven.

Rypins' Medical Boards Review, Vol. II: Clinical Sciences. (Illus.). 448p. 1989. text ed. 26.50 (0-397-50907-3) Lppncott-Raven.

***Rypins' Questions & Answers for Basic Sciences Review.** 3rd ed. Edward D. Frohlich. LC 96-43597. 256p. 1996. pap. text ed. 29.95 (0-397-51545-6) Lppncott-Raven.

Rystari Dukha. M. S. Cherepakhov. 78p. 1983. 25.00 (0-685-12140-2) St Mut.

Ryuijie Photographs. Ryuijie. (Illus.). 100p. 1991. 50.00 (0-9627927-0-5); pap. 25.00 (0-9627927-1-3) Freshsilver.

Ryukyuan Culture & Society: Proceedings of the Pacific Science Congress, 10th, Honolulu, 1961. Pacific Science Congress Staff. LC 63-19525. 121p. reprint ed. pap. 34.50 (0-317-08484-4, 2000073) Bks Demand.

***Ryusei-Ha.** K. Yoshimura. 1996. pap. 10.95 (4-07-973352-6); pap. 10.95 (4-07-973369-0) Shufu no Tomo-Sha.

***Ryusei-Ha: Motifs.** K. Yoshimura. 1996. pap. 10.95 (4-07-973346-1) Shufu no Tomo-Sha.

Rywka Rybak: A Survivor of the Holocaust. Rywka Rybak. LC 93-60965. 88p. (Orig.). 1993. pap. 10.95 (0-9638507-0-9) Prologue Pubns.

Ryzhii D'Iavol. Mikhail Dyomin. LC 87-60055. 300p. (Orig.). 1987. pap. 18.00 (0-89830-110-6) Russica Pubs.

Rzoska the Nile. 1976. lib. bdg. 175.00 (90-6193-081-2) Kluwer Ac.

***R2-D2's Missing.** Mouseworks Staff. (J). 1997. 6.98 (1-57082-612-9) Mouse Works.

S

S. Cid Corman. 1976. pap. 8.00 (0-686-63995-2); bds. 16.00 (0-686-63994-4) Elizabeth Pr.

S. John Updike. LC 87-40496. 288p. 1988. 17.95 (0-394-56835-4) Knopf.

S. John Updike. 320p. 1989. mass mkt. 6.99 (0-449-21652-7, Crest) Fawcett.

***S.** John Updike. 1996. pap. 12.00 (0-449-91212-4) Fawcett.

S: An Interactive Environment for Data Analysis & Graphics. Richard A. Becker & John M. Chambers. Ed. by Peter J. Bickel et al. LC 84-3654. (Statistics-Probability Ser.). 576p. (C). (gr. 13). 1984. pap. text ed. 48.95 (0-534-03313-X) Chapman & Hall.

***S: Semainer de Suzanne.** Harry Mathews et al. LC 97-2553. 124p. 1997. pap. 12.95 (1-57129-043-5) Brookline Bks.

S - Car Ninety: Computer Applications to Assist Radiology. Ronald L. Arenson & Richard M. Friedenberg. 774p. 1990. 99.00 (0-88372-005-1) CRC Pr.

S - Z. Roland Barthes. Tr. by Richard Miller. 271p. 1975. pap. 11.95 (0-374-52167-0, Noonday) FS&G.

S. A. T. Math Preparatory Set. Norman Levy & Joan U. Levy. 600p. 1989. pap. text ed. 9.95 (1-55637-085-7) Visual Educ.

S & C Invest. Schneider. 1995. 125.00 (0-316-77445-6) Little.

S & L: Transactions in the Post-Industrial Era. (Illus.). 32p. 1991. pap. 5.00 (0-930495-13-6) San Fran Art Inst.

S & L Debacle: Public Policy Lessons for Bank & Thrift Regulation. Lawrence J. White. (Illus.). 304p. 1991. 30.00 (0-19-506733-9) OUP.

S & L Insurance Mess: How Did It Happen? Edward J. Kane. LC 89-5786. (Illus.). 200p. (Orig.). 1989. pap. text ed. 10.95 (0-87766-468-4); lib. bdg. 29.95 (0-87766-469-2) Urban Inst.

S & Ls of Your State 1989. 1989. 295.00 (0-317-93233-0) Sheshunoff.

***S & M.** Jeffrey De Shell. 231p. (Orig.). 1997. pap. 11.95 (1-57366-024-8) Fiction Coll.

S & M: Studies in Dominance & Submission. rev. ed. Ed. by Thomas S. Weinberg. LC 95-12356. 312p. 1995. pap. 16.95 (0-87975-978-X) Prometheus Bks.

S. Andrea in Mantua: The Building. Eugene J. Johnson. LC 74-30085. (Illus.). 220p. 1975. 55.00 (0-271-01186-6) Pa St U Pr.

S. Aureli Augustini - De Beata Vita: A Translation with an Introduction & Commentary, Vol. 72. Ruth A. Brown. (Patristic Studies). 211p. 1984. reprint ed. 30.00 (0-939738-30-9) Zubal Inc.

S. B. Bl()nk Space. John Dolis. 56p. (Orig.). 1993. pap. 5.00 (0-926935-92-5) Runaway Spoon.

S. B. C. House on the Sand? David O. Beale. 246p. (Orig.). 1985. pap. 8.25 (0-89084-281-7, 025106) Bob Jones Univ Pr.

***"S" Book: Independent Schools & Programs for Individuals with Dyslexia: What Are the Questions?** Jean M. Foss & Diana H. King. (Orton Emeritus Ser.: Pt. 1). 5.00 (0-614-29498-3) Orton Dyslexia.

***"S" Book: Public Schools & Programs for Individuals with Dyslexia: What Are the Questions?** Jean M. Foss & Diane H. King. (Orton Emeritus Ser.: Pt. II). Date not set. 5.00 (0-614-29499-1) Orton Dyslexia.

***S. C. P. Bingo: Bingo Game & Activity Book.** Arden Martenz & Ken Smith. LC 95-81935. (Illus.). 24p. 1996. 10.95 (1-57543-001-0) Mar Co Prods.

S. C. Yuan. Intro. by Brenda Morrison. LC 94-72075. 200p. (Orig.). 1994. write for info. (1-885666-06-3); pap. write for info. (1-885666-07-1) Carmel Art.

S Complete. Marilyn M. Toomey & Paula Carmel. (Illus.). 217p. 1988. vinyl bd. 28.00 (0-923573-08-9) Circuit Pubns.

S Corporation: Planning & Operation. Sydney S. Traum et al. 500p. 165.00 (0-916592-45-6) Panel Pubs.

S Corporation Answer Book. Sydney S. Traum. 330p. 96.00 (1-878375-02-4) Panel Pubs.

S Corporation Desk Book. Michael Schlesinger. 336p. 1988. text ed. 59.95 (0-13-785635-0, Busn) P-H.

S Corporation Desk Book-Supplement. Michael Schlesinger. 144p. 1990. pap. text ed. 32.50 (0-13-788274-2) P-H.

S Corporation Manual. Peter L. Faber & Prentice Hall Editorial Staff. 250p. 1989. 42.50 (0-13-785650-4, Busn) P-H.

S Corporation Manual: A Special Tax Break for Small Business Corporations. Peter L. Faber & Martin E. Holbrook. LC 86-194493. 250p. 1988. 41.50 (0-13-785544-3); ring bd. 306.00 (0-13-785528-1); ring bd. 282.00 (0-685-17616-9) P-H.

S Corporation Tax Practice Manual. Ira Fox. Ed. by Laura B. Kaiser. 488p. 1990. pap. text ed. 99.00 (1-878375-28-8) Panel Pubs.

S Corporation Tax Practice Manual: 1992 Edition. Ira Fox. Ed. by Laura B. Kaiser. 1991. ring bd. 99.00 (1-878375-73-3) Panel Pubs.

S Corporations: Complete Tax Practice & Planning Guide. M. Kevin Bryant. 1000p. 1996. ring bd. 135.00 (1-886035-01-6) Pro Tax & Business.

S Corporations: Federal Taxation. Richard Blau et al. 1989. 130.00 (0-685-44924-6) Clark Boardman Callaghan.

S Corporations: State Law & Taxation, 2 vols., Set. James E. Maule. 1990. 250.00 (0-685-28165-5) Clark Boardman Callaghan.

S Corporations: Tax Choices for Business Planning. Prentice Hall Editorial Staff. 1984. write for info. (0-318-58011-X) P-H.

S-Curve. Richard J. Foster. 1986. 19.45 (0-671-50918-7) S&S Trade.

S. D. I. Negotiations. David W. Felder. 44p. 1996. pap. text ed. 8.95 (0-910959-57-9, B&G 11C) Wellington Pr.

S Devjatogo Bala: Poems. Eugenia Dimer. 1981. 4.00 (0-685-44307-8) RWCPH.

S. E. Asian Special Forces. Kenneth Conboy. (Elite Ser.: No. 33). (Illus.). 64p. pap. 12.95 (1-85532-106-8, 9433, Pub. by Osprey UK) Stackpole.

S. E. Britaines Busse: Or Herring-Fishing Ship, with the States Proclamation Annexed Unto the Same, As Concerning Herring-Fishing. LC 74-80211. (English Experience Ser.: No. 690). 1974. reprint ed. 10.00 (90-221-0690-X) Walter J Johnson.

S. E. E. K. Self-Esteem Enhancement Kit. Stephanie Roth-Nelson. LC 93-29345. 176p. (Orig.). 1993. pap. 14.95 (0-942097-49-1) Ctr Adolescent.

S. E. E. K. Facilitator's Guide: Accompanies the Self-Esteem Enhancement Kit Workbook. Stephanie Roth-Nelson & Nancy Jessop Conway. 123p. (Orig.). 1994. teacher ed., pap. 29.95 (0-942097-48-3) Ctr Adolescent.

S. E. X. Blackjack System. Alan Mandel. LC 86-70882. (Illus.). 224p. (Orig.). 1987. pap. 12.95 (0-9616765-0-7) Bronx Bks.

***S-E-X Word.** Jerry Cooper. 24p. (Orig.). 1996. pap. 3.95 (1-889419-22-2) J Cooper.

***S. F. Comic Strip: Big-Ass Mocha.** Don Asmussen. LC 97-66721. (Illus.). 200p. 1997. write for info. (0-9653524-6-3) Russn Hill Pr.

S. F. W. A. M. Wellman. 160p. 1992. mass mkt. 4.99 (0-446-36291-3) Warner Bks.

S-F 2: A Pictorial History of Science Fiction Films from Roller Ball to Return of the Jedi. Richard Meyers. LC 83-20964. (Illus.). 1984. 19.95 (0-8065-0875-2, Citadel Pr) Carol Pub Group.

S France Pilot Golfe du Lion, Spain to Toulon. Robin Brandon. (Illus.). 339p. 1993. 69.95 (0-85288-163-0) Bluewater Bks.

S France Pilot V 1 Intro & Info. Robin Brandon. (Illus.). 1989. pap. 18.95 (0-85288-136-3, Pub. by Imray Laurie Norie & Wilson UK) Bluewater Bks.

S Gauge Building & Repair Manual. 1989. pap. 3.00 (0-911581-17-0) Heimburger Hse Pub.

S-He. Randy W. Rader. 20p. 1983. pap. 2.00 (0-913719-65-X) High-Coo Pr.

S I Units: A Source Book. G. S. Ramaswamy & V. V. Rao. 1973. text ed. 15.00 (0-07-096575-7) McGraw.

S. J. Perelman: A Critical Study. Steven H. Gale. LC 86-12106. (Contributions to the Study of Popular Culture Ser.: No. 15). 251p. 1987. text ed. 55.00 (0-313-25003-0, GSJ/, Greenwood Pr) Greenwood.

S. J. Perelman: Critical Essays. Ed. by Steven H. Gale. LC 91-21460. (Studies in Humor: Vol. 1). 336p. 1991. text ed. 50.00 (0-8240-3422-8, H1274) Garland.

S. J. V. Chelvanayakam & the Crisis of Ceylon Tamil Nationalism, 1947-1977. A. Jeyaratnam Wilson. LC 93-31628. 1994. text ed. 26.00 (0-8248-1608-0) UH Pr.

S. Klein Directory of Computer Graphics Suppliers: Hardware, Software Systems, Services & Supplies. 5th ed. 224p. 1987. 73.00 (0-317-65576-0) TBC Inc.

S. Klein Directory of Computer Suppliers: Hardware, Software, Systems & Services. Ed. by Malcolm Stiefel. 224p. 1987. 73.00 (0-317-20391-6) TBC Inc.

S. L. Frank: The Life & Work of a Russian Philosopher, 1877-1950. Philip Boobbyer. (Illus.). 290p. (C). 1995. text ed. 45.00 (0-8214-1110-1) Ohio U Pr.

S L R Nineteen Eighty-Three: Sign Language Research. William C. Stokoe. LC 84-52800. 1985. pap. text ed. 20.95 (0-932130-08-9) Linstok Pr.

S. Legend in Applied Probability & Statistics, Vol. 1. V. Shvyrkov. (Illus.). 205p. 1981. write for info. (0-942004-25-6) Throwkoff Pr.

S. Lesniewski's Logic Lecture Notes. Ed. by Jan T. Srzednicki. 196p. (C). 1988. lib. bdg. 167.00 (90-247-3416-9) Kluwer Ac.

S-M: The Last Taboo. Gerald Greene & Caroline Greene. 345p. 1996. pap. 8.95 (1-56201-066-2, North Star Line) Blue Moon Bks.

***S. M. Eisenstein: Writings 1934-47.** Ed. by Richard Taylor. Tr. by William F. Powell. (Selected Works: Vol. III). (Illus.). 424p. 1996. 55.00 (0-85170-530-8, Pub. by British Film Inst UK) Ind U Pr.

S

An Asterisk (*) at the beginning of an entry indicates that the title is appearing in BIP for the first time.

S. M. Eisenstein Vol. II: Towards a Theory of Montage; Selected Works. Richard Taylor. 1994. pap. 29.95 (*0-85170-461-1*, Pub. by British Film Inst UK) Ind U Pr.

S. M. Eisenstein - Selected Works Vol. 1: Writings, 1922-34. S. M. Eisenstein. Ed. & Tr. by Richard Taylor. LC 86-45516. (Illus.). 344p. 1988. 19.95 (*0-253-35042-5*) Ind U Pr.

S. M. Eisenstein - Selected Works Vol. 2: Towards a Theory of Montage, 1937-40. Ed. by S. M. Eisenstein & Michael Glenny. Tr. by Michael Glenny from RUS. LC 86-45516. 300p. 1992. 70.00 (*0-85170-211-2*, Pub. by British Film Inst UK) Ind U Pr.

S, M, L, XL: Small, Medium, Large, Extra Large. Rem Koolhaas & Bruce Mau. Ed. by Jennifer Sigler. LC 94-76578. (Illus.). 1376p. (C). 1996. 75.00 (*1-885254-01-6*) Monacelli Pr.

***S. M.'s Widow, Mau Mau's Daughter: The Autobiography of Wambui Waiyaki Otieno.** Wambui Otieno & Cora A. Presley. 250p. 1997. write for info. (*1-55587-722-2*) Lynne Rienner.

S. N. Behrman: A Research & Production Sourcebook. Robert F. Gross. LC 92-26481. (Modern Dramatists Research & Production Sourcebooks Ser.: No. 3). 224p. 1992. text ed. 59.95 (*0-313-27852-0*, GSX/, Greenwood Pr) Greenwood.

S

S. N. I. C. K. E. R. Same Names in Cities, Kingdoms, Empires & Regions. Marjory Cutler & Maxwell Cutler. LC 94-96433. 296p. (Orig.). 1994. pap. 12.95 (*0-9643131-0-3*) M Lee Ent.

S. O. D. - Speak English or Die. (Play-It-Like-It-Is Guitar Ser.). pap. 14.95 (*0-89524-627-9*) Cherry Lane.

S. O. Davies: A Socialist Faith. Robert Griffiths. 312p. (C). 1983. 25.00 (*0-85088-887-5*, Pub. by Gomer Pr UK) St Mut.

***S. O. H. O. Desk Reference: A Practical A to Z Guide for the Entrepreneurs, Small Office & Home Office.** Peter H. Engel. 1997. 35.00 (*0-06-270144-4*, Harper Ref) HarpC.

S. O. R. Losers. Avi. 96p. (J). (gr. 3-7). 1986. reprint ed. pap. 4.50 (*0-380-69993-1*, Camelot) Avon.

S. O. S. Bobomobile. Jan Wahl. 128p. (J). 1995. 3.99 (*0-8125-2405-5*) Tor Bks.

***S. O. S. Men Against the Sea.** Bernard Edwards. Ed. by Norman Stobart. 206p. 1994. pap. 9.95 (*1-899694-00-5*, Pub. by New Guild UK) Brick Tower.

S. O. S. Rhino. C. A. W. Guggisberg. (Illus.). 1967. 12.50 (*0-8079-0116-4*) October.

S. O. S. (Ship Operational Safety) Manual. OCS Marine Staff. (C). 1989. text ed. 425.00 (*0-906314-09-7*, Pub. by Lorne & MacLean Marine) St Mut.

S. O. S., Ships Operational Safety Manual. (C). 1989. 320.00 (*0-89771-714-7*, Pub. by Lorne & MacLean Marine) St Mut.

***S. O. T. S. Book List, 1992.** Ed. by Lester L. Grabbe. 154p. 1992. pap. 29.00 (*0-905495-11-X*) Scholars Pr GA.

***S. O. T. S. Book List, 1993.** Ed. by Lester L. Grabbe. 176p. 1993. pap. 29.00 (*0-905495-12-8*) Scholars Pr GA.

***S. O. T. S. Book List, 1994.** Ed. by Lester L. Grabbe. 185p. 1994. pap. 29.00 (*0-905495-13-6*) Scholars Pr GA.

***S. O. T. S. Book List, 1995.** Ed. by Lester L. Grabbe. 203p. 1995. pap. 29.00 (*0-905495-18-7*) Scholars Pr GA.

***S. O. T. S. Book List, 1996.** Ed. by Lester L. Grabbe. 187p. 1996. pap. 29.00 (*0-905495-14-4*) Scholars Pr GA.

S. P. Eagle: A Biography of Sam Spiegel. Andrew Sinclair. 256p. 1988. 17.95 (*0-316-79236-5*) Little.

***S. P. Likes A. D.** Catherine Brett. 118p. (YA). pap. 5.95 (*0-88961-142-4*, Pub. by Wmns Pr CN) LPC InBook.

S PeRM K T Harryette Mullen. 48p. (Orig.). 1992. pap. 8.00 (*0-935162-12-7*) Singing Horse.

***S Pota v Ameriko: Voyage to the U. S. A. in 1935.** Gregorij Rozman. (Studia Slovenica Ser.: SP.S. 7). (Illus.). 110p. (Orig.). (SLV.). 1997. pap. 8.00 (*0-614-25686-0*) Studia Slovenica.

S. R. Ranganathan & the West. Ed. by Ravindra N. Sharma. 1993. 27.50 (*81-207-1475-X*, Pub. by Sterling Pubs II) Apt Bks.

S. S. Alibi of a Nation, 1922-1945. Gerald Reitlinger. (Quality Paperbacks Ser.). (Illus.). 534p. 1989. reprint ed. pap. 16.95 (*0-306-80351-8*) Da Capo.

***S. S. Chetverikov's "On Certain Aspects of the Evolutionary Process from the Standpoint of Modern Genetics" (1926)** S. S. Chetverikov. Ed. by Charles D. Mellon. Tr. by Malina Barker from RUS. LC 97-73089. 100p. 1997. pap. 14.95 (*0-9653362-6-3*) Genetics Heritage.

S. S. Consultation Handbook. Joanne S. Hayden. (C). 1988. pap. write for info. (*0-9619427-2-X*) J S Hayden.

S. S. Happiness Crew: Book of Numbers. Eric Hill. LC 83-70386. (Illus.). 1983. 5.95 (*0-317-01758-6*) Determined Prods.

S. S. Happiness Crew Book of Numbers. Eric Hill. (Illus.). 11p. (J). (ps). write for info. (*0-915696-65-7*) Determined Prods.

S. S. Heartbreak. Francine Pascal. (Sweet Valley University Ser.: No. 13). 240p. (YA). (gr. 9-12). 1995. mass mkt. 3.99 (*0-553-56692-X*) Bantam.

***S. S. Leopoldville Disaster, December 24, 1944.** Allan Andrade. LC 97-22938. 1997. write for info. (*1-890309-54-0*) Tern Bk Co.

S-s-s-snakes! Lucille R. Penner. LC 93-46799. (Step into Reading Bks.: Step 2). (Illus.). 48p. (J). (gr. k-2). 1994. pap. 3.99 (*0-679-84777-4*); lib. bdg. 11.99 (*0-679-94777-9*) Random Bks Yng Read.

S. S. San Pedro. James G. Cozzens. LC 67-19206. 85p. 1968. reprint ed. pap. 1.15 (*0-15-684830-9*, Harvest Bks) HarBrace.

***S. S. Savannah.** Braynard. (Illus.). pap. 7.95 (*0-486-25750-9*) Dover.

S. S. United States. William H. Miller. (Illus.). 224p. 1991. 35.00 (*0-393-03030-X*) Norton.

S. T. A. R. Instructor's Guide. Sheila Greeley. 65p. (Orig.). 1992. spiral bd. 15.95 (*0-9622812-0-4*) FAFCTPC.

S. T. A. R. T. Karen Kish & Janet Lanier. (Illus.). 165p. (Orig.). 1995. pap. 19.95 (*0-614-15864-8*) Janelle Pubns.

S-T Alphabook. Karen Sevaly. (Illus.). 128p. (Orig.). (J). (gr. k-4). 1995. teacher ed., pap. 7.95 (*0-943263-30-1*, TF-1810) Teachers Friend Pubns.

S. T. O. P. Guide: The Smokeless Tobacco Outreach Prevention & Cessation Guide. Herbert H. Severson. 100p. 1996. ring bd. 89.00 (*0-9639557-8-0*, Appld Behvr Sci) A R K Co.

S-Ticulation. Mary Zellmer. (Illus.). (J). (ps-4). 1987. 19.00 (*0-930599-24-1*) Thinking Pubns.

S. U. M. Poems, 1978. Ed. by Selwyn Kittredge et al. 40p. (Orig.). 1978. pap. 1.00 (*0-89120-011-8*) From Here.

S-V Forty Viruses. Keerti V. Shah et al. (Illus.). 220p. (C). 1973. text ed. 27.50 (*0-8422-7064-7*) Irvington.

***S. W. A. P. - "Sent with a Prayer" Expressions of Life.** Ed. by Marie Mamaril. (Illus.). 92p. (Orig.). Date not set. pap. text ed. write for info. (*1-889534-05-6*) Jay St Pubs.

S. W. A. T. & Hostage Negotiation. 50p. (Orig.). (C). 1993. pap. text ed. 20.00 (*1-56806-862-X*) DIANE Pub.

S. W. A. T. Tactics. Jeffrie Jacobs. (Illus.). 98p. 1983. pap. 20.00 (*0-87364-265-1*) Paladin Pr.

S. W. A. T. Team Manual. Robert P. Cappel. (Illus.). 150p. 1979. pap. 16.95 (*0-87364-169-8*) Paladin Pr.

S. W. A. T. Training & Employment. Steven Mattoon. (Illus.). 152p. 1987. pap. 20.00 (*0-87364-439-5*) Paladin Pr.

***S W O T Employment Law.** 4th ed. A. E. Holmes. 288p. 1996. pap. 22.00 (*1-85431-586-2*, Pub. by Blackstone Pr UK) Gaunt.

S. Weir Mitchell. Joseph P. Lovering. LC 76-125256. (Twayne's United States Authors Ser.). 1971. pap. text ed. 9.95 (*0-8290-0002-X*); lib. bdg. 17.95 (*0-89197-984-0*) Irvington.

S' Wonderful Gershwin Showstoppers. Warner. 1995. pap. 16.95 (*0-89724-591-1*, MF9510) Warner Brothers.

S-Z. Roland Barthes. 288p. (FRE.). 1976. 29.95 (*0-686-53944-3*, F56510); pap. 16.95 (*0-7859-0670-3*, F56510) Fr & Eur.

S-Z see Soren Kierkegaard's Journals & Papers

S.A. Cunningham & the Confederate Heritage. John A. Simpson. LC 93-9956. (Illus.). 272p. (C). 1994. 35.00 (*0-8203-1570-2*) U of Ga Pr.

Sa Majeste des Mouches. William Golding. 256p. (FRE.). 1983. pap. 11.95 (*0-7859-2476-0*, 2070374807) Fr & Eur.

Sa Shiko: Blue & White Quilt Art of Japan. Kazuko Mende & Beiko Morishige. (Illus.). 120p. 1997. 45.50 (*0-87040-828-3*) Japan Pubns USA.

SA 1921-45: Hitler's Stormtroopers. David Littlejohn. (Men-at-Arms Ser.: No. 220). (Illus.). 48p. 1990. pap. 11.95 (*0-85045-944-3*, 9177, Pub. by Osprey Pubng Ltd UK) Stackpole.

SAA: Applications for PC to Mainframe Connectivity. Peter Coates. 400p. 1992. pap. text ed. 68.00 (*0-13-787854-0*) P-H.

***SAA & Applications Development.** G. Norman. 120p. 1991. 245.00 (*1-85617-125-6*, Pub. by Elsvr Adv Tech UK) Elsevier.

SAA Handbook. Dennis Linnell. (C). 1990. pap. text ed. 24.95 (*0-201-51786-8*) Addison-Wesley.

***Saab.** Eric Dymock. (Illus.). 192p. 1997. 54.95 (*0-85429-981-5*) Haynes Pubns.

Saab 900 Eight Valve Official Service Manual, 1981-1988. 560p. 1992. 49.95 (*0-8376-0310-2*) Bentley.

Saab 900 Sixteen Valve Official Service Manual: 1985-1992 Including 900S, Turbo, Turbo SPG & Convertible. 622p. 1992. 49.95 (*0-8376-0312-9*) Bentley.

SAAB 900, 16 Valve Official Service Manual 1985-1993. Robert Bentley. 1994. pap. 49.95 (*0-8376-0313-7*) Bentley.

***Saadeh's Dictionary.** Khalil Saadeh. (ARA & ENG.). 1996. 65.00 (*0-86685-675-7*) Intl Bk Ctr.

Saadia Anniversary Volume. Ed. by Boaz Cohen & Steven Katz. LC 79-7168. (Jewish Philosophy, Mysticism & History of Ideas Ser.). 1980. reprint ed. lib. bdg. 31.95 (*0-405-12244-6*) Ayer.

Saadia Gaon: Book of Beliefs & Opinions. Tr. by Samuel Rosenblatt. 1989. pap. 25.00 (*0-300-04490-9*) Yale U Pr.

Saadia Gaon Book of Beliefs & Opinions. Tr. by Samuel Rosenblatt. (Judaica Ser.: No. 1). 1948. 65.00 (*0-300-00865-1*) Yale U Pr.

Saadia Gaon, the Earliest Hebrew Grammarian. Solomon L. Skoss. ix, 66p. 1955. 10.00 (*0-685-70564-1*, Ctr Judaic Studies) Eisenbrauns.

Saadiah Gaon: Selected Essays: An Original Anthology. Ed. by Steven Katz. LC 79-7171. (Jewish Philosophy, Mysticism & History of Ideas Ser.). 1980. lib. bdg. 37.95 (*0-405-12230-6*) Ayer.

Saadiah Weissman. Benzion Firer. 140p. (J). (gr. 5-12). 1982. 10.95 (*0-87306-294-9*) Feldheim.

Saadya Studies: In Commemoration of the One Thousandth Anniversary of the Death of R. Saadya Gaon. Ed. by Erwin I. Rosenthal & Steven Katz. LC 79-7170. (Jewish Philosophy, Mysticism & History of Ideas Ser.). 1980. reprint ed. lib. bdg. 28.95 (*0-405-12284-5*) Ayer.

Saama-Veda (Summary) 5.00 (*0-938924-31-1*) Sri Shirdi Sai.

Saami, Reindeer & Gold in Alaska: The Emigration of Saami from Norway to Alaska. Ornulv Vorren. (Illus.). 172p. (Orig.). (C). 1994. pap. text ed. 10.50 (*0-88133-786-2*) Waveland Pr.

Saanich, North Straits Salish: Classified Word List. Timothy Montler. (Mercury Ser.: No. 119). 184p. 1991. pap. 19.95 (*0-660-12908-6*, Pub. by Can Mus Civil CN) U of Wash Pr.

Saanii Dahataal - the Women Are Singing: Poems & Stories. Luci Tapahonso. LC 92-35093. (Sun Tracks Ser.: Vol. 23). 95p. (Orig.). 1993. pap. 10.95 (*0-8165-1361-9*) U of Ariz Pr.

SAARC: Challenges & Opportunities. Nasir A. Naqash. ix, 175p. (C). 1995. 22.00 (*81-7024-611-3*, Pub. by Ashish II) S Asia.

Saarc: Origin, Growth, & Future. E. Sudhakar. (C). 1994. 22.00 (*81-212-0459-3*, Pub. by Gian Publng Hse II) S Asia.

SAARC: Origin, Growth & Future. E. Sudhakar. 1994. pap. 60.00 (*0-7855-0483-4*, Pub. by Ratna Pustak Bhandar) St Mut.

SAARC: Regional Cooperation & Development. Ed. by Debendra K. Das. (C). 1992. 26.00 (*0-8364-2808-0*, Pub. by Deep II) S Asia.

***SAARC: Trade & Development.** P. A. Joy. 1995. 22.00 (*81-7100-701-5*, Pub. by Deep II) S Asia.

SAARC - ASEAN: Prospects & Problems of Interregional Cooperation. Ed. by Bhabani S. Gupta. (C). 1988. 26.00 (*81-7003-095-1*, Pub. by S Asia Pubs II) S Asia.

Saarc from Dhaka to Kathmandu. Shankar M. Singh. 79p. (C). 1987. 65.00 (*0-89771-091-6*, Pub. by Ratna Pustak Bhandar) St Mut.

SAARC from Dhaka to Kathmandu. Shankar M. Singh. 1987. 30.00 (*0-7855-0296-3*, Pub. by Ratna Pustak Bhandar) St Mut.

Saarinen House & Garden: A Total Work of Art. Ed. & Contrib. by Gregory Wittkopp. LC 94-33282. 1995. 45.00 (*0-8109-4462-6*) Abrams.

Saatchi & Saatchi: The Inside Story. Alison Fendley. 240p. 1996. 23.95 (*1-55970-363-6*) Arcade Pub Inc.

Saatchi & Saatchi: The Inside Story. Philip Kleinman. 200p. 1988. 24.95 (*0-8442-3194-0*, NTC Busn Bks) NTC Pub Grp.

Sab. Gertrudis Gomez de Avellaneda. LC 93-30913. (Hispanic Literature Ser.: Vol. 20). 256p. (SPA.). 1993. text ed. 89.95 (*0-7734-9331-X*) E Mellen.

Sab & Autobiography. Gertrudis G. De Avellaneda y Arteaga. Ed. & Tr. by Nina M. Scott from SPA. LC 92-21961. (Texas Pan American Ser.). 185p. (C). 1993. pap. 12.95 (*0-292-70442-9*); text ed. 30.00 (*0-292-77655-1*) U of Tex Pr.

Sabaean Inscriptions from Mahram Bilgis (Marib) Jamme Albert. LC 62-10311. (American Foundation for the Study of Man Ser.: Vol. 3). 557p. reprint ed. pap. 158.80 (*0-317-09904-3*, 2005199) Bks Demand.

Sabaic Dictionary: English-French-Arabic Dictionary. Alfred F. Beeston. 183p. (ARA, ENG & FRE.). 1982. 19.95 (*0-86685-359-6*, LDL3596, Pub. by Librairie du Liban FR) Intl Bk Ctr.

***Sabal Palm: A Native Monarch.** Barbara Oehlbeck. Ed. by Amy Bennett. (Illus.). 100p. 1996. 19.95 (*0-9654019-0-1*) Gulfshore Commun.

Sabana see Abahn

Sabarimalai Pilgrimage & Ayyappan Cultus. Radhika Sekar. (C). 1992. 16.00 (*81-208-1056-2*, Pub. by Motilal Banarsidass II) S Asia.

Sabas, Leader of Palestinian Monasticism: A Comparative Study in Eastern Monasticism, Fourth to Seventh Centuries. Joseph Patrich. LC 93-49099. (Dumbarton Oaks Studies: No. 32). 1995. 50.00 (*0-88402-221-8*) Dumbarton Oaks.

***Sabazius: The Teachings of a Greek Magus.** Douglas Lockhart. LC 97-1807. 304p. 1997. pap. 17.95 (*1-85230-970-9*) Element MA.

Sabbatai Sevi: The Mystical Messiah. Gershom G. Scholem. Tr. by R. Zwi Werblowski from HEB. LC 75-166389. (Bollingen Ser.: Vol. 93). (Illus.). 1040p. 1973. pap. 29.95 (*0-691-01809-X*) Princeton U Pr.

Sabbatai Zevi. Sholem Asch. Tr. by Florence Whyte & George R. Noyes. LC 74-3622. (Illus.). 131p. 1974. reprint ed. text ed. 59.75 (*0-8371-7449-X*, ASSZ, Greenwood Pr) Greenwood.

***Sabbatampel Im Erfurter Dom.** Hans G. Meyer. (Studien Zur Kunstgeschichte Ser.: Bd. 16). 175p. (GER.). 1982. write for info. (*3-487-07294-7*) G Olms Pubs.

Sabbatarianism in the Sixteenth Century: A Page in the History of the Radical Reformation. Daniel Liechty. LC 93-71090. 104p. 1993. pap. 13.99 (*0-943872-99-5*) Andrews Univ Pr.

Sabbath. Samuel H. Dresner. 1970. pap. 2.95 (*0-8381-2114-4*) USCJE.

Sabbath. Abraham J. Heschel. 126p. 1996. pap. 11.00 (*0-374-51267-1*) FS&G.

Sabbath. Abraham Joshua Heschel. 126p. 15.00 (*0-374-25321-8*) FS&G.

Sabbath: A Guide to Its Understanding & Observance. I. Grunfeld. 11.95 (*0-87306-266-3*); pap. 9.95 (*0-87306-099-7*) Feldheim.

Sabbath - Which Day & Why? fac. ed. M. L. Andreasen. LC 95-61755. 256p. 1996. reprint ed. per. 9.95 (*1-57258-053-4*) Teach Servs.

Sabbath among the Ruins: New Poems. Deena Metzger. 120p. 1992. pap. 10.00 (*0-938077-53-8*) Parallax Pr.

Sabbath & Festival Praybook. 9.85 (*0-686-96035-1*) USCJE.

Sabbath & Sectarianism in Seventeenth-Century England. David S. Katz. Ed. by A. J. Vanderjagt. LC 88-2849. (Brill's Studies in Intellectual History: Vol. 10). xiv, 224p. 1988. 85.75 (*90-04-08754-0*) E J Brill.

Sabbath & Synagogue Vol. 122: The Question of Sabbath in Ancient Judaism. Heather A. McKay. 1994. 83.50 (*90-04-10060-1*) E J Brill.

Sabbath & the Lord's Day. H. M. Riggle. 160p. pap. 1.50 (*0-686-29165-4*) Faith Pub Hse.

Sabbath Bread: For Personal Sacred-Searching & Group Faith-Sharing. Georgene L. Wilson. LC 87-62530. 160p. (Orig.). (C). 1987. pap. 9.95 (*0-89390-101-6*) Resource Pubns.

Sabbath Chapter: A Novel of the Apocalypse. Grant Garber. LC 92-23333. 160p. (Orig.). 1993. pap. 9.95 (*1-56474-041-2*) Fithian Pr.

***Sabbath Dinner.** (Illus.). (J). (ps-1). 1995. 29.99 (*1-888074-41-8*) Pckts Lrning.

***Sabbath in Crisis: The Gospel, the Sabbath, the Old & New Covenants.** Dale Ratzlaff. LC 90-91938. (Illus.). 352p. (Orig.). 1995. pap. 14.95 (*0-9627546-0-9*) Life Assurance.

Sabbath in Puritan New England. Alice M. Earle. 335p. 1969. reprint ed. 26.95 (*0-87928-005-0*) Corner Hse.

Sabbath in Puritan New England. Alice M. Earle. LC 89-38500. 335p. 1998. reprint ed. lib. bdg. 27.00 (*1-55888-920-5*) Omnigraphics Inc.

Sabbath in the Classical Kabbalah. Elliot K. Ginsburg. LC 87-26764. (SUNY Series in Judaica: Hermeneutics, Mysticism, & Religion). 341p. (C). 1989. text ed. 59.50 (*0-88706-778-6*); pap. text ed. 19.95 (*0-88706-779-4*) State U NY Pr.

Sabbath-Law of Rabbi Meir. Robert Goldenberg. LC 78-14370. (Brown Judaic Studies: No. 6). 307p. reprint ed. pap. 87.50 (*0-7837-5871-5*, 2045590) Bks Demand.

Sabbath Lion: A Jewish Folktale from Algeria. Howard Schwartz & Barbara Rush. LC 91-63576. (Trophy Picture Bk.). (Illus.). 32p. (J). (gr. k-4). 1996. pap. 4.95 (*0-06-443382-X*, Trophy) HarpC Child Bks.

Sabbath Morn. large type ed. John Wainwright. LC 93-43550. (General Ser.). 1994. lib. bdg. 16.95 (*0-8161-5927-0*, GK Hall) Thorndike Pr.

***Sabbath Peace: A Book of Meditations.** Moshe Braun. 1997. write for info. (*0-7657-9957-X*) Aronson.

***Sabbath Sense: A Spiritual Antidote for the Overworked.** Donna E. Schaper. 128p. (Orig.). 1997. pap. 11.95 (*1-880913-25-9*) Innisfree Pr.

Sabbath Shiurim, I. Miller. 1979. 18.95 (*0-87306-993-5*) Feldheim.

Sabbath Shiurim, II. Miller. 1979. 13.95 (*0-87306-222-1*) Feldheim.

***Sabbath Time.** Edwards. 14.80 (*0-687-61008-7*) Abingdon.

Sabbath Time: Understanding & Practice for Contemporary Christians. Tilden Edwards. LC 92-80947. 144p. 1992. pap. 9.95 (*0-8358-0665-0*) Upper Room Bks.

Sabbath Walk & Other Stories. Alex B. Stone. 39p. (Orig.). 1989. pap. 6.00 (*1-878326-00-7*) East Hall Pr.

Sabbathday Lake Shakers: An Introduction to the Shaker Heritage. 2nd ed. R. Mildred Barker. (Illus.). 26p. 1985. pap. 3.00 (*0-915836-04-1*) United Soc Shakers.

Sabbaths. Wendell Berry. LC 87-60877. 98p. 1987. pap. 9.00 (*0-86547-290-4*, North Pt PR) FS&G.

Sabbaths. Wendell Berry. LC 87-60877. 98p. 1987. 12.95 (*0-86547-289-0*) Gnomon Pr.

Sabbath's Theater. Philip Roth. LC 95-914. 451p. 1995. 24.95 (*0-395-73982-9*) HM.

Sabbath's Theater, Vol. 1. Philip Roth. 1996. pap. 13.00 (*0-679-77259-6*) McKay.

Sabbatical: A Romance. John Barth. 366p. 1996. reprint ed. pap. 12.95 (*1-56478-096-1*) Dalkey Arch.

Sabbatical in Japan. Akhtar Qamber. 1976. 8.00 (*0-89253-819-8*); text ed. 4.00 (*0-89253-820-1*) Ind-US Inc.

***Sabbatical Journey: The Final Year.** Henri J. Nouwen. 1998. 19.95 (*0-8245-1708-3*) Crossroad NY.

Sabbatical Mentor: A Practical Guide to Successful Sabbaticals. Kenneth J. Zahorski. 240p. (C). 1994. pap. text ed. 24.95 (*1-882982-00-2*) Anker Pub.

Sabbatical on Winifrede Hollow. Joseph W. Caldwell. 40p. (Orig.). 1992. pap. 4.95 (*1-881692-03-5*) Trillium WV.

Sabbatical Planning: For Clergy & Congregations. Richard Bullock. pap. 8.25 (*1-56699-019-X*) Alban Inst.

Sabbats: A New Approach to Living the Old Ways. Edain McCoy. LC 94-29602. (Illus.). 368p. 1994. pap. 14.95 (*1-56718-663-7*) Llewellyn Pubns.

***Sabbethai Sofer & His Prayer-Book.** 400p. 1979. text ed. 85.00 (*0-521-21171-9*) Cambridge U Pr.

Sabda: A Study of Bhartrharti's Philosophy of Language. Tandra Patnaik. (C). 1994. text ed. 19.00 (*81-246-0028-7*, Pub. by DK Pubs Dist II) S Asia.

Sabda Ratnakaram: A Dictionary of the Telegu Language. Sitaramacharyulu. 1988. reprint ed. 30.00 (*81-206-0305-2*, Pub. by Asian Educ Servs II) S Asia.

Sabdapramana: Word & Knowledge. Parusottama Bilimoria. 400p. (C). 1988. lib. bdg. 203.00 (*90-277-2675-2*, Pub. by Klwr Acad Pubs NE) Kluwer Ac.

***Sabe UD...Como? Cuando? Donde? Tecnicas de Investigacion.** Mat Dabbah. Ed. by Tiboas Zylberglait. (Illus.). 307p. (Orig.). (SPA.). 1996. pap. 29.95 (*0-945406-06-1*) Magnum Schl.

Sabelotodo: The Bilingual Teacher's Best Friend. Shirleyann Costigan et al. (Illus.). 176p. (Orig.). (ENG & SPA.). 1988. pap. 21.95 (*0-917837-01-0*) Hampton-Brown.

Sabelotodo Entiendelonada & Other Stories. Jim Sagel. LC 88-70704. 139p. (ENG & SPA.). 1988. pap. 12.00 (*0-916950-87-5*) Biling Rev-Pr.

Saber & Scapegoat: J. E. B. Stuart & the Gettysburg Controversy. Mark V. Nesbitt. (Illus.). 272p. 1994. 19.95 (*0-8117-0915-9*) Stackpole.

Saber & Shadow: A New Adventure in the Fifth Millennium. S. M. Stirling & Shirley Meier. 384p. (Orig.). 1992. mass mkt. 4.99 (*0-671-72143-7*) Baen Bks.

Saber Tiger. Yukinobu Hoshino. Ed. by Seiji Horibuchi. (Illus.). 80p. 1991. pap. 12.95 (*0-929279-62-X*) Viz Commns Inc.

Saber Tooth: A Dinosaur World Adventure. Geoffrey T. Williams. (Dinosaur World Ser.). (Illus.). 32p. (J). (gr. k-6). 1988. audio 9.95 (*0-8431-2319-2*) Price Stern Sloan.

Saber-Tooth Curriculum. J. A. Peddiwell. 1959. pap. text ed. 5.95 (*0-07-049151-8*) McGraw.

An Asterisk (*) at the beginning of an entry indicates that the title is appearing in BIP for the first time.

Saber-Toothed Blennies, Tribe Nemophini (Pisces: Blenniidae) William F. Smith-Vaniz. (Monograph: No. 19). (Illus.). 196p. (Orig.). 1976. pap. 10.00 (*0-910006-27-X*) Acad Nat Sci Phila.

Saber-Toothed Cats - Prehistoric Worlds. Querida L. Pearce. (Amazing Science Ser.). (Illus.). 64p. (J). (gr. 4-6). 1991. pap. 5.95 (*0-671-70692-6*, Julian Messner) Silver Burdett Pr.

***Saber-Toothed Poodnoobie.** Bruce Coville. (Space Brat Ser.). (J). 1997. write for info. (*0-614-29160-7*, Minstrel Bks) PB.

***Saber-Toothed Poodnoobie.** Katherine Coville. (Space Brat Ser.: No. 5). (Illus.). (J). (gr. 2 up). 1997. 14.00 (*0-671-00871-4*, Minstrel Bks) PB.

***Saber-Toothed Poodnoobie.** Illus. by Katherine Coville. (Space Brat Ser.: No. 5). (J). (gr. 2 up). 1997. mass mkt. 3.99 (*0-671-00870-6*, Minstrel Bks) PB.

Saber-Toothed Tiger. Laurence Antony. LC 96-4998. (Extinct Species Collection). (Illus.). (J). 1996. lib. bdg. 18.60 (*0-8368-1596-3*) Gareth Stevens Inc.

Saber y Decir: El Manual Para Padres e Hijos Sobre Como Prevenir el Abuso a los Ninos. 2nd ed. Yvette K. Lehman. Tr. by Vivian Chavez & Gloria Costas from ENG. (Illus.). 46p. (J). (ps-4). 1993. student ed. 9.00 (*0-9638555-1-4*) Y K Lehman.

Sabers West. Patrick E. Andrews. 256p. 1988. mass mkt. 2.95 (*0-8217-2436-3*, Zebra Kensgtn) Kensgtn Pub Corp.

Sabertooth: The Rip-Roaring Adventures of a Legendary Game Warden. Terry Hodges. 288p. 1988. text ed. 19.95 (*0-87364-453-0*) Paladin Pr.

Sabertooth: The Rip-Roaring Adventures of a Legendary Game Warden. Terry Hodges. 275p. 1992. reprint ed. 17.95 (*0-9634092-0-4*) T&C Bks.

Sabertooth Mountain. John Vornholt. (Dinotopia Digest Novels Ser.). (J). (gr. 3-7). 1996. pap. 3.99 (*0-614-15730-7*) Random.

Sabian Manual: A Ritual of Living. Marc E. Jones. 309p. 1957. 13.00 (*0-394-40586-2*) Sabian Pub.

Sabian Symbols in Astrology: A Symbol Explained for Each Degree of the Zodiac. Marc E. Jones. (Illus.). 437p. 1993. reprint ed. pap. 18.95 (*0-943358-40-X*) Aurora Press.

***Sabias Que?, Vol. 2.** Bill Vanpatten et al. 1992. lab manual ed., wbk. ed., pap. text ed. write for info. (*0-07-067170-2*) McGraw.

Sabiduria para la Vida Familiar. Charles R. Swindoll. (SPA.). 1988. 6.99 (*1-56063-218-6*, 498467) Editorial Unilit.

***Sabiduria para la Vida Familiar.** Charles R. Swindoll. 354p. (SPA.). 1992. pap. write for info. (*0-614-27135-5*) Editorial Unilit.

Sabine. (Orig.). 1992. mass mkt. 4.95 (*1-56333-046-6*) Masquerade.

Sabine. Daniel Vian. 219p. 1996. mass mkt. 7.95 (*0-8216-5029-7*) Blue Moon Bks.

Sabine County Marriages, Eighteen Seventy-Five to Nineteen Ten. Blanche Toole. LC 82-84531. 150p. (Orig.). 1983. pap. write for info. (*0-911317-08-2*) Ericson Bks.

Sabine Spring. James L. Burke. 200p. 1989. reprint ed. pap. 8.00 (*0-922820-05-8*) Watermrk Pr.

Sabine's Notebook: In Which the Extraordinary Correspondence of Griffin & Sabine Continues. Nick Bantock. (Illus.). 48p. 1992. 17.95 (*0-8118-0180-2*) Chronicle Bks.

Sabinetown - Gateway to Texas. Robert J. Beddoe. (Illus.). 165p. (Orig.). 1991. pap. 8.00 (*1-56002-053-9*) Aegina Pr.

Sabino Canyon: The Life of a Southwestern Oasis. David W. Lazaroff. LC 92-18057. (Illus.). 119p. (Orig.). 1993. pap. 17.95 (*0-8165-1344-9*) U of Ariz Pr.

Sabino's Map: Life in Chimayo's Old Plaza. Don J. Usner. LC 95-16878. (Illus.). 264p. 1995. 29.95 (*0-89013-289-5*) Museum NM Pr.

Sabino's Map: Life in Chimayo's Old Plaza. Don J. Usner. LC 95-16878. (Illus.). 264p. 1996. pap. 19.95 (*0-89013-290-9*) Museum NM Pr.

***Sabio y Prudente: Para el Estudiante, Vol. 2.** Orlando Rodriguez. (Manuel de Exploracion Ser.). 1996. pap. text ed. 4.99 (*0-89922-296-X*); pap. text ed. 3.99 (*0-89922-297-8*) Edit Caribe.

Sabishi: Poems from Japan. David Hassler. LC 94-26870. (Wick Poetry Chapbook Ser.: No. 3). 28p. (Orig.). 1994. pap. 4.75 (*0-87338-513-6*) Kent St U Pr.

Sabiston Essentials of Surgery. 2nd rev. ed. Ed. by David C. Sabiston, Jr. & H. Kim Lyerly. LC 93-33972. 1994. pap. text ed. 41.00 (*0-7216-5019-8*) Saunders.

Sable. Karen Hesse. (J). 1994. 14.95 (*0-8050-2416-6*) H Holt & Co.

Sable & Rosenfeld Cookbook. Myra Sable & Colleen Mathieu. (Illus.). 256p. 1995. pap. 18.95 (*1-895565-73-1*) Firefly Bks Ltd.

Sable Arm: Black Troops in the Union Army, 1861-1865. Dudley T. Cornish. LC 87-50106. (Modern War Studies). (Illus.). xviii, 342p. 1987. reprint ed. pap. 9.95 (*0-7006-0328-X*) U Pr of KS.

Sable Cloud: A Southern Tale with Northern Comments. Nehemiah Adams. LC 78-138329. (Black Heritage Library Collection). 1977. 25.95 (*0-8369-8721-7*) Ayer.

***Sable Doughboys.** Tom Willard. LC 96-44259. (Black Sabre Chronicles: Bk. 2). 1996. 22.95 (*0-312-86040-4*) St Martin.

Sable et Cendre. Bernard Dimey. (FRE.). 1995. 49.95 (*2-86808-068-5*) Intl Scholars.

Sable Island. Bruce Armstrong. (Illus.). 220p. 1995. pap. 14.95 (*0-88780-058-0*) Formac Dist Ltd.

***Sable Scenes: Real Life Stories & Black Family Life & Living in a Southern Town, 1935-1965.** 101p. (Orig.). 1996. pap. 9.95 (*0-9653826-0-5*) AfrAgen.

Sable, Shadow, & Ice. Cheryl J. Franklin. 400p. (Orig.). 1994. mass mkt. 4.99 (*0-88677-609-0*) DAW Bks.

Sable Vif. Pierre Moinot. (FRE.). 1979. pap. 10.95 (*0-7859-4120-7*) Fr & Eur.

Sables d'Olonne to La Gironde. Imray, Laurie, Norie & Wilson Ltd. Staff. (Illus.). (C). 1990. text ed. 60.00 (*0-685-40215-0*, Pub. by Imray Laurie Norie & Wilson UK) St Mut.

Sablier. Maurice Maeterlinck. 224p. (FRE.). 1967. reprint ed. pap. 11.95 (*0-7859-4633-0*) Fr & Eur.

Sabor de la Venganza - Vengeful Bride. Rosalie Ash. (SPA.). 1996. mass mkt. 3.50 (*0-373-33380-3*, 1-33380-6) Harlequin Bks.

Sabor de lo Prohibido: Antologia Personal. Jose A. Almanzar. (Caribbean Collection). 1993. pap. 11.50 (*0-8477-0188-3*) U of PR Pr.

Sabotage. Piet Prins. Tr. by James C. Van Oosterom from DUT. (Shadow Ser.: No. 5). (Illus.). 120p. (Orig.). (J). 1989. pap. 7.20 (*0-921100-08-6*) Inhtce Pubns.

Sabotage: A Study in Industrial Conflict. Geoff Brown. 402p. 1977. 42.50 (*0-85124-158-1*, Pub. by Spokesman Bks UK) Coronet Bks.

***Sabotage: Doom's Day, Bk. 2.** Pierce Askegren & Danny Fingeroth. (Spider-Man & Iron Man Ser.). 1997. mass mkt. write for info. (*1-57297-235-1*) Blvd Books.

Sabotage & Subversion: Stories from the Files of the SOE & OSS. Ian Dear. (Illus.). 240p. 1996. 27.95 (*1-85409-260-X*, Pub. by Arms & Armour UK) Sterling.

Sabotage at Sea. Franklin W. Dixon. Ed. by Ruth Ashby. (Hardy Boys Casefiles Ser.: No. 92). 160p. (Orig.). (YA). (gr. 6 up). 1994. mass mkt. 3.99 (*0-671-79476-0*, Archway) PB.

Sabotage at Sports City. Franklin W. Dixon. Ed. by Ellen Winkler. (Hardy Boys Ser.: No. 115). 160p. (Orig.). (J). (gr. 3-6). 1992. pap. 3.99 (*0-671-73062-2*, Minstrel Bks) PB.

Sabotage Flight. Paul Meyerhoff, 2nd. LC 94-37177. (Illus.). 200p. (Orig.). (J). (gr. 5-9). 1995. pap. 9.95 (*0-931625-24-6*) DIMI Pr.

Sabotage in Air Transport Regulation. Pablo M. De Leon. LC 92-18237. 282p. (C). 1992. lib. bdg. 119.00 (*0-7923-1795-5*) Kluwer Ac.

Sabotage in the American Workplace: Anecdotes of Dissatisfaction, Mischief & Revenge. Ed. by Martin Sprouse. (Illus.). 184p. (Orig.). 1992. pap. 12.00 (*0-9627091-3-1*) Pressure Drop.

Sabotage of the Challenger. James Green & Linda Green. LC 92-91123. 184p. 1994. pap. 9.00 (*1-56002-258-2*, Univ Edtns) Aegina Pr.

Sabotage on the Set. Joan L. Nixon. (Disney Adventures Casebusters Ser.: No. 10). (Illus.). 96p. (J). (gr. 2-6). 1996. pap. 3.95 (*0-7868-4087-0*) Disney Pr.

Sabotaging the World Church. Jack Van Impe. 159p. 1991. pap. 7.00 (*0-934803-83-8*) J Van Impe.

***Saboteurs from the Sea.** large type ed. Henry Chesham. (Linford Mystery Library). 368p. 1996. pap. 15.99 (*0-7089-7931-9*) Ulverscroft.

SABR Presents the Home Run Encyclopedia: The Who, What, & Where of Every Home Run Hit since 1876. Bob McConnell. Ed. by David Vincent. LC 95-33413. 1008p. 1996. 40.00 (*0-02-860816-X*) Macmillan Info.

SABR Review of Books. Ed. by Paul Adomites. (Illus.). 112p. 1987. pap. 6.00 (*0-910137-27-7*) Soc Am Baseball Res.

SABR Review of Books. Ed. by Paul Adomites. (Illus.). 112p. 1988. pap. 6.00 (*0-910137-33-1*) Soc Am Baseball Res.

SABR Review of Books. Ed. by Paul Adomites. (Illus.). 128p. 1989. pap. 7.00 (*0-910137-38-2*) Soc Am Baseball Res.

SABR Review of Books. Ed. by Paul Adomites. (Illus.). 147p. 1990. pap. 7.00 (*0-910137-42-0*) Soc Am Baseball Res.

SABR Review of Books. Ed. by Paul D. Adomites. (Illus.). 112p. 1986. pap. 6.00 (*0-910137-23-4*) Soc Am Baseball Res.

Sabra & Shatila: Inquiry into a Massacre. Amnon Kapeliouk. Ed. by Khalil Jahshan. Tr. by Kalil Jahshan from FRE. 89p. (Orig.). (C). 1983. pap. text ed. 5.95 (*0-937694-63-0*) Assn Arab-Amer U Grads.

Sabra Crossing: An Ecological Adventure on the North Atlantic. Michael L. Frankel. LC 91-77947. 225p. (Orig.). 1992. pap. 14.95 (*1-879269-03-1*) Ctr Marine Cnsrv.

Sabra Field: The Art of Place. Tom Slayton. LC 93-24093. (Illus.). 128p. 1993. 29.95 (*1-881527-22-0*) Chapters Pub.

Sabratha: A Guide for Visitors. Philip Ward. (Libya Past & Present Ser.: Vol. 2). (Illus.). 1966. pap. 12.50 (*0-902675-05-2*) Oleander Pr.

Sabre. McGregor & Gulacy. (Illus.). 1990. pap. 5.95 (*0-913035-65-3*) Eclipse Bks.

SABRE Reservations: Basic & Advanced Training. 2nd ed. Gerald K. Capwell & Barry P. Resnick. LC 92-17416. 1993. pap. 38.95 (*0-538-70619-8*) S-W Pub.

Sabre Squadron. Simon Raven. 240p. 1987. 15.95 (*0-317-46031-5*) Beaufort Bks NY.

Sabres: 26 Seasons in Buffalo's Memorial Auditorium. Ross Brewitt. 1997. 36.00 (*0-87833-125-5*) Taylor Pub.

Sabres: 26 Seasons in Buffalo's Memorial Auditorium. limited ed. Ross Brewitt. 1997. 75.00 (*0-87833-126-3*) Taylor Pub.

***Sabres & Pistols: The Civil War Career of Colonel Harry Gilmor, CSA. Timothy Ackinclose. (Illus.). 288p. 1997. 25.00 (*1-879664-30-5*) Stan Clark Military.**
"Harry Gilmor is one of the more interesting players in the sub-plot of partisan warfare along the upper Potomac. Tim Ackinclose's study of Gilmor is both scholarly & well written. It is a valuable contribution to Civil War literature."--Ted Alexander, Park Historian, Antietam National Battlefield. "Colonel Harry Gilmor has been overlooked too long as the subject of in-depth attention by serious historians. Mr. Ackinclose has now filled the gap with his well-researched biography of a fascinating wartime personality. His comprehensive work immediately sets the standard against which any future Gilmor biography must be measured."--P. James Kurapka, Sons of Confederate Veterans. "Mr. Ackinclose's biography challenges previous assumptions regarding Gilmor's role in the Civil War. Using the partisan's own memoirs as a guide, the author has scrupulously examined every event & detail to reveal the true nature of Harry Gilmor's exploits. This study provides fresh insight into partisan activities during the war & makes for dramatic reading.--David Dixon, Ph.D. "Mr. Ackinclose has vividly brought to life a true hell-for-leather Confederate horse soldier. As the author demonstrates in this thoroughly researched study, Harry Gilmor embodied the 'Cavalry Spirit'."--Michael Phipps. STAN CLARK MILITARY BOOKS, 915 Fairview Avenue, Gettysburg, PA 17325. (717) 337-1728, FAX (717) 337-0581. ***Publisher Provided Annotation.***

Sabres in the Shenandoah: The 21st New York Cavalry 1862-1866. John C. Bonnell, Jr. LC 96-31752. (Illus.). 400p. 1996. 34.95 (*1-57249-012-8*, Burd St Pr) White Mane Pub.

Sabres in the Sun. Charles Whiting. 185p. 1992. 22.95 (*0-7126-3048-1*, Pub. by Century UK) Trafalgar.

Sabres of Paradise. Lesley Blanch. 495p. 1984. pap. 12.95 (*0-88184-042-4*) Carroll & Graf.

Sabretooth. Larry Hama. 96p. 1994. pap. 12.95 (*0-7851-0050-4*) Marvel Entmnt.

Sabretooth Mountain. John Vornholt. 156p. (J). 1996. pap. 3.99 (*0-679-88095-X*) Random.

Sabriel. Garth Nix. LC 96-1295. 304p. (YA). (gr. 7 up). 1996. 15.95 (*0-06-027322-4*); lib. bdg. 15.89 (*0-06-027323-2*) HarpC Child Bks.

***Sabriel.** Garth Nix. LC 96-1295. (Trophy Book Ser.). (YA). (gr. 5 up). 1997. pap. 5.95 (*0-06-447183-7*, Trophy) HarpC Child Bks.

Sabrina. Mary Kingsley. 400p. 1993. mass mkt. 3.99 (*0-8217-4043-1*, Zebra Kensgtn) Kensgtn Pub Corp.

Sabrina. Ransom. (Orig.). (J). 1993. pap. 2.75 (*0-685-66034-6*) Scholastic Inc.

Sabrina Fair. Samuel Taylor. 1955. pap. 5.25 (*0-8222-0979-9*) Dramatists Play.

Sabrina Kane. Will Cook. 288p. 1995. mass mkt., pap. text ed. 4.50 (*0-8439-3827-7*) Dorchester Pub Co.

Sabrina (Movie Tie-in) Deborah Chiel. 1996. mass mkt. 5.99 (*0-671-53751-2*) PB.

Sabrina the Dancer. Roxanne E. Stout. (Illus.). 30p. (Orig.). (J). (gr. 4-5). 1993. pap. 3.00 (*0-88092-048-3*) Royal Fireworks.

Sabrina the Schemer. Karen Rispin. LC 93-39634. (Anika Scott Ser.: Vol. 5). (J). (gr. 3-7). 1994. pap. 4.99 (*0-8423-1296-X*) Tyndale.

***Sabrina the Teenage Witch, 5.** Pocket Books, Staff. (J). 1997. mass mkt. 3.99 (*0-671-01519-2*) PB.

***Sabrina the Teenage Witch, Vol. 1.** Weiss. (J). 1997. pap. 3.99 (*0-671-01433-1*) S&S Trade.

***Sabrina the Teenage Witch: Becoming a Witch.** Shelagh Canning. (J). 1997. pap. text ed. 4.99 (*0-689-81743-6*) S&S Childrens.

***Sabrina The Teenage Witch: Dream Date.** Margo Lundell. (J). 1997. pap. text ed. 4.99 (*0-689-81744-4*) S&S Childrens.

***Sabrina's Gifts: A Fairy Tale about Learning to See with Your Heart.** Debbie Runions. (Illus.). 64p. (Orig.). 1996. pap. 10.00 (*0-9653297-0-4*) Hero Pub TN.

***Sabriya: Damascus Bitter Sweet.** Ulfat Idilbi. Tr. by Peter Clark. LC 96-46045. (Emerging Voices: New International Fiction Ser.). 248p. 1997. 29.95 (*1-56656-219-8*); pap. 12.95 (*1-56656-254-6*) Interlink Pub.

Sabuda - Untitled, No. 2. Robert Sabuda. (J). Date not set. 19.95 (*0-689-81192-6*) S&S Childrens.

Sabuda Untitled, No. 1. Robert Sabuda. (J). 1997. 19.95 (*0-689-81191-8*) S&S Childrens.

Sac & Fox see Indians of North America

Sac & Fox Indians. William T. Hagan. LC 58-6851. (Civilization of the American Indian Ser.: Vol. 48). (Illus.). 320p. 1988. pap. 14.95 (*0-8061-2138-6*) U of Okla Pr.

Sac & Fox Indians. Melissa McDaniel. LC 94-44785. 1995. pap. 7.95 (*0-7910-2034-7*) Chelsea Hse.

Sac & Fox Indians see Junior Library of American Indians

Sac de Couffignal. Dashiell Hammett. 1988p. (FRE.). 1988. pap. 10.95 (*0-7859-2553-8*, 2070379329) Fr & Eur.

Sac Metroscan. S. E. Ansell. 35p. (Orig.). 1994. pap. 10.95 (*0-9640436-0-2*) Quad As Elect.

SAC, the Strategic Air Command. Richard G. Hubler. LC 77-634. 280p. 1977. reprint ed. text ed. 59.75 (*0-8371-9489-X*, HUSAC, Greenwood Pr) Greenwood.

Sacagawea. Jan Gleiter & Kathleen Thompsom. LC 94-43269. (First Biographies Ser.). (Illus.). (J). 1995. lib. bdg. 19.97 (*0-8114-8453-X*) Raintree Steck-V.

***Sacagawea.** Judith St. George. 128p. (J). (gr. 3-6). 1997. 16.95 (*0-399-23161-7*) Putnam Pub Group.

Sacagawea: American Pathfinder. Flora W. Seymour. LC 90-23267. (Childhood of Famous Americans Ser.). (Illus.). 192p. (J). (gr. 3-7). 1991. reprint ed. pap. 4.95 (*0-689-71482-3*, Aladdin Paperbacks) S&S Childrens.

Sacagawea: Native American Hero. William R. Sanford & Carol R. Green. LC 96-269. (Legendary Heroes of the Wild West Ser.). (Illus.). 48p. (J). (gr. 4-10). 1997. lib. bdg. 14.95 (*0-89490-675-5*) Enslow Pubs.

Sacagawea: Northwest Explorer. Dennis B. Fradin. LC 96-16063. (Remarkable Children Ser.). (J). 1997. 15.95 (*0-382-39488-7*, Silver Pr NJ); pap. 5.95 (*0-382-39489-5*, Silver Pr NJ) Silver Burdett Pr.

Sacagawea: Westward with Lewis & Clark. Alana J. White. LC 96-22359. (Native American Biographies Ser.). (Illus.). 128p. (YA). (gr. 6 up). 1997. lib. bdg. 18.95 (*0-89490-867-7*) Enslow Pubs.

Sacagawea of the Lewis & Clark Expedition. Ella E. Clark & Margot Edmonds. LC 78-65466. 1979. pap. 13.95 (*0-520-05060-6*) U CA Pr.

Sacajawea. Harold P. Howard. LC 70-160495. (Illus.). 1979. pap. 12.95 (*0-8061-1578-5*) U of Okla Pr.

Sacajawea. Anna L. Waldo. 1424p. 1984. pap. 7.99 (*0-380-84293-9*) Avon.

Sacajawea: A Native American Heroine. Martha F. Bryant. Ed. & Illus. by Hap Gilliland. (Indian Culture Ser.). 256p. (Orig.). (J). 1989. 21.95 (*0-89992-420-4*); pap. 15.95 (*0-89992-120-5*) Coun India Ed.

Sacajawea: The Journey West. Elaine Raphael & Don Bolognese. LC 93-49002. (Drawing America Ser.). 32p. (J). 1994. 12.95 (*0-590-47898-2*) Scholastic Inc.

Sacajawea & the Journey to the Pacific. Gina Ingoglia. LC 92-52977. (Disney's American Frontier Ser.: Bk. 7). (Illus.). 80p. (J). (gr. 1-4). 1992. pap. 3.50 (*1-56282-262-4*) Disney Pr.

***Sacajawea, Shoshone Trailblazer.** Diane Shaughnessy & Jack Carpenter. LC 97-17642. (Famous Native Americans Ser.). 1997. write for info. (*0-8239-5107-3*, PowerKids) Rosen Group.

Sacajawea, Translator & Guide. Irene N. Hamilton. (Illus.). (J). (gr. 1-4). 1995. pap. 4.95 (*0-8136-5765-2*); lib. bdg. 10.60 (*0-8136-5759-8*) Modern Curr.

Sacajawea, Wilderness Guide. Kate Jassem. LC 78-60118. (Illus.). 48p. (J). (gr. 4-6). 1979. pap. 3.50 (*0-89375-150-2*); lib. bdg. 11.89 (*0-89375-160-X*) Troll Communs.

Sacandaga Story: A Valley of Yesterday. rev. ed. Larry Hart. (Illus.). 95p. 1967. reprint ed. pap. 5.00 (*0-932035-00-0*) Old Dorp Bks.

Sacas. Patricio P. Escobal. (SPA.). 1974. pap. 8.00 (*0-86515-016-8*) Edit Mensaje.

Saccadic Eye Movements in Neurological & Ophthalmological Diagnosis. Otmar Meienberg. (Neurology Ser.: Vol. 29). (Illus.). xii, 115p. 1988. 94.95 (*0-387-18547-X*) Spr-Verlag.

Saccharin: Current Status. Ed. by L. Goldberg & D. M. Conning. (Illus.). 148p. 1985. pap. 83.00 (*0-08-032009-0*, H221, H120, Pub. by PPL UK) Elsevier.

Saccharin from China & Korea: An International Trade Investigation. Brian Walters. (Illus.). 58p. (Orig.). (C). 1995. pap. text ed. 30.00 (*0-7881-2370-X*) DIANE Pub.

Saccharine Disease: Sugar & Its Role in Disease. T. L. Cleave. 5.70 (*0-317-05972-6*) Hypoglycemia Foun.

Saccharomyces. Ed. by Mick F. Tuite & S. G. Oliver. (Biotechnology Handbooks Ser.: Vol. 4). (Illus.). 320p. 1990. 85.00 (*0-306-43634-5*, Plenum Pr) Plenum.

Sacco & Vanzetti. Fernando Quesada. 1976. lib. bdg. 250.00 (*0-8490-0984-7*) Gordon Pr.

Sacco & Vanzetti: Developments & Reconsiderations--1979. pap. 15.00 (*0-685-09591-6*) Boston Public Lib.

Sacco & Vanzetti: The Anarchist Background. Paul Avrich. (Illus.). 267p. 1991. text ed. 42.50 (*0-691-04789-8*) Princeton U Pr.

Sacco & Vanzetti: The Anarchist Background. Paul Avrich. 278p. 1991. pap. text ed. 14.95 (*0-691-02604-1*) Princeton U Pr.

Sacco-Vanzetti Case: A Transcript of the Record of the Trial of Nicola Sacco & Bartolomeo Vanzetti in the Courts of Massachusetts & Subsequent Proceedings, 1920-27, 6 Vols, Set. 2nd ed. Pref. by Paul P. Appel. (Illus.). 6400p. 1969. 500.00 (*0-911858-01-6*) Appel.

Sachets, Potpourri & Incense Recipes. Compiled by Clarence Meyer. (Illus.). 96p. (Orig.). 1986. pap. 3.95 (*0-916638-13-8*) Meyerbooks.

Sachie: Daughter of Hawaii. 2nd ed. Patsy S. Saiki. (Illus.). (Orig.). 1977. reprint ed. pap. 10.00 (*0-934625-01-8*) Kisaku.

Sachiko. Shizue Tomoda. LC 91-4451. 1992. pap. 13.95 (*0-87949-351-8*) Ashley Bks.

Sachiko Means Happiness. Kimiko Sakai. LC 90-2248. (Illus.). 32p. (J). (gr. k-5). 1990. 14.95 (*0-89239-065-4*) Childrens Book Pr.

Sachiko Means Happiness. Kimiko Sakai. (J). (gr. 1-7). 1995. pap. 6.95 (*0-89239-122-7*) Childrens Book Pr.

Sachiko's Wedding. Clive Collins. 1990. 21.95 (*0-7145-2910-9*) M Boyars Pubs.

Sachindex zu Kants Kritik der reinen Vernunft. Ed. by Gottfried Martin & Dieter-Juergen Loewisch. (C). 1967. 29.25 (*3-11-005179-6*) De Gruyter.

Sachitra Guljar Hagar: A Pen Picture of Calcutta in the Late 19th Century. Kedar N. Dutta. Tr. by Satyabrata Dutta. (C). 1990. text ed. 22.00 (*0-8364-2592-8*, Pub. by Firma KLM II) S Asia.

***Sachlich Geordnete Glossare.** (Elias Von Steinmeyer - Eduard Sievers Ser.: Band III). xii, 723p. (GER.). 1968. write for info. (*3-296-20323-0*, Pub. by Weidmann GW) Lubrecht & Cramer.

Sachs Engines, 100-125cc, All Years: 100 & 125cc, All Years. Ed. by Jeff Robinson. (Illus.). 144p. (Orig.). Date not set. pap. 25.95 (*0-89287-025-7*, M427) Intertec Pub.

Sachsisches Schriftsteller-Lexicon. Wilhelm Haan. 391p. 1983. write for info. incl. fiche (*0-318-71911-8*) G Olms Pubs.

Sachsisches Wandermarionettetheater. Olaf Bernstengel. 96p. 1995. pap. text ed. 15.00 (*3-364-00316-5*) Gordon & Breach.

S

S

*Sachstand & Probleme Umweltorientierter Unternehmensfuhrung in der Mittelstandischen Industrie: Ergebnisse & Losungsansatze aus Einer Empirischen Untersuchung. Hans-Jurgen Reichardt. (Illus.). 251p. (GER.). 1996. 51.95 (3-631-30734-9) P Lang Pubng.

Sachwoerterbuch der Literatur: Dictionary of Literature. Gero Von Wilpert. 873p. (GER.). 1974. pap. 45.00 (0-8288-6209-5, M-7616) Fr & Eur.

Sack & Destruction of the City of Columbia, S.C. William G. Simms. Ed. by Alexander S. Salley. LC 78-148898. (Select Bibliographies Reprint Ser.). 1977. reprint ed. 11.95 (0-8369-5661-3) Ayer.

Sack Lunch. Bob Reese. LC 92-12183. (School Days Ser.). (Illus.). 24p. (J). (ps-2). 1992. lib. bdg. 14.00 (0-516-05582-8) Childrens.

Sack of Pizzazz. Julie A. Waterman. 5p. (Orig.). 1982. The Sack of Pizzazz. pap. 1.25 (0-943334-01-2) Carmonelle Pubns.

Sack of Rome. Luigi Guicciardini. Tr. & Intro. by James H. McGregor. LC 92-38776. (Illus.). 197p. (Orig.). 1993. pap. 12.00 (0-934977-32-1) Italica Pr.

Sack of Rome, 1527. Andre Chastel. Tr. by Beth Archer. LC 82-47587. (Illus.). 430p. 1982. text ed. 75.00 (0-691-09947-2) Princeton U Pr.

Sack the Board! The End of a Celtic Dynasty. Allan Caldwell. (Illus.). 174p. 1995. pap. 17.95 (1-85158-682-2, Pub. by Mnstream UK) Trafalgar.

Sackbut Blues: Hugh Le Caine, Pioneer in Electronic Music. Gayle Young. (Illus.). 288p. 1991. 29.95 (0-660-12006-2) U Ch Pr.

Sackcloth & Ashes: Liturgical Reflections for Lenten Weekdays. James A. Griffin. LC 74-44463. 74p. 1976. pap. 4.00 (0-8189-0336-8) Alba.

Sacked: The Darkside of Sports at Louisiana State University. B. Brodhead & Mindy Brodhead. 221p. 1987. 19.95 (0-318-23877-2) Beauregard Pr.

Sacked! What to Do When You Lose Your Job. Dean B. Peskin. LC 79-13522. 191p. reprint ed. pap. 54.50 (0-317-19932-3, 2023575) Bks Demand.

Sackett. Louis L'Amour. 160p. 1984. mass mkt. 3.99 (0-553-27684-0) Bantam.

Sackett Brand. Louis L'Amour. 160p. 1985. pap. 3.99 (0-553-27685-9) Bantam.

*Sackett Brand. large type ed. Louis L'Amour. LC 96-36193. (Western Ser.). 211p. 1997. 23.95 (0-7862-0866-X, Thorndike Lrg Prnt) Thorndike Pr.

Sackett Companion: A Personal Guide to the Sackett Novels. Louis L'Amour. LC 88-47530. 288p. 1988. 19.95 (0-553-05305-1) Bantam.

Sackett Companion: A Personal Guide to the Sackett Novels. Louis L'Amour. 352p. 1992. pap. 10.95 (0-553-37102-9) Bantam.

Sackett, the Family Record (Magazine) The Sackett, Weygant & Mapes Families. C. H. Weygant. 148p. 1994. reprint ed. pap. 25.00 (0-8328-4377-6); reprint ed. lib. bdg. 35.00 (0-8328-4376-8) Higginson Bk Co.

Sackett's Land. Louis L'Amour. 208p. 1984. mass mkt. 3.99 (0-553-27686-7) Bantam.

*Sackett's Land. large type ed. Louis L'Amour. LC 96-41327. 1998. write for info. (0-7862-0871-6) Thorndike Pr.

Sacketts of America, Their Ancestors & Descendants, 1630-1907. C. H. Weygant. (Illus.). 553p. 1989. reprint ed. pap. 83.00 (0-8328-1045-2); reprint ed. lib. bdg. 91.00 (0-8328-1044-4) Higginson Bk Co.

*Sacking of El Dorado. Max Brand. 288p. 1997. reprint ed. mass mkt. 4.50 (0-8439-4335-1, Leisure Bks) Dorchester Pub Co.

Sackville & Neave Property Law: Cases & Materials. 5th ed. M. A. Neave. 1072p. 1994. pap. 133.00 (0-409-30529-4, Austral) MICHIE.

Saco, ME. J. Scully. (Images of America Ser.). 1994. pap. 16.99 (0-7524-0066-5, Arcdia) Chalford.

Sacral Treasure of the Guelphs. Patrick M. De Winter. LC 85-3820. (Illus.). 160p. 1985. pap. 10.00 (0-910386-81-1) Cleveland Mus Art.

Sacralization of Politics in Fascist Italy. Emilio Gentile. Tr. by Keith Botsford. LC 96-5074. (Illus.). 240p. 1996. 49.95 (0-674-78475-8) HUP.

Sacrament. Clive Barker. 464p. 1996. 25.00 (0-06-017949-X) HarpC.

Sacrament. Clive Barker. 1995. 24.00 (0-614-96262-5) HarpC.

*Sacrament. Clive Barker. 1996. pap. 6.99 (0-06-109199-5, Harp PBks) HarpC.

*Sacrament. Clive Barker. 1997. mass mkt. 6.99 (0-614-27744-2, Harp PBks) HarpC.

Sacrament. Jane Blue. (Illus.). 32p. (Orig.). 1986. pap. 4.00 (0-914485-08-3) Trill Pr.

Sacrament of Abortion. Ginette Paris. Tr. by Joanna Mott from FRE. LC 91-46372. 113p. (Orig.). 1992. pap. 12.00 (0-88214-352-2) Spring Pubns.

Sacrament of Christian Life. Mary P. McGinty. 1992. pap. 12.95 (0-88347-270-8) Res Christian Liv.

Sacrament of Civil Disobedience. John Dear. 300p. (Orig.). (C). 1994. pap. 17.95 (1-879175-16-9) Fortkamp.

Sacrament of Confirmation in the Early-Middle Scholastic Period. Kilian F. Lynch. (Theology Ser.). 1xxv, 256p. 1957. pap. 17.00 (1-57659-025-9) Franciscan Inst.

Sacrament of Easter. Roger Greenacre & Jeremy Haselock. 1995. pap. 15.00 (0-8028-4099-X) Eerdmans.

Sacrament of Love: The Nuptial Mystery in the Light of the Orthodox Tradition. Paul Evdokimov. Tr. by Anthony P. Gythiel & Victoria Steadman from FRE. LC 85-2261. 192p. (Orig.). 1985. pap. 11.95 (0-88141-042-X) St Vladimirs.

Sacrament of Marriage in Hindu Society. U. M. Apte. 254p. 1978. 19.95 (0-318-36842-0) Asia Bk Corp.

Sacrament of Matrimony According to the Doctrine & Ritual of the Eastern Orthodox Church. F. Basaroff. Tr. by N. Bjerring from RUS. pap. 1.95 (0-89981-081-0) Eastern Orthodox.

Sacrament of Mercy: A Spiritual & Practical Guide to Confession. Thomas G. Weinandy. LC 96-28250. 240p. (Orig.). 1996. pap. 11.95 (0-8198-6992-9) Pauline Bks.

*Sacrament of Penance in the Teaching of the Last Five Popes. Ed. by John-Peter Pham. 64p. (Orig.). 1996. pap. 4.00 (1-890177-02-4) Midwest Theol.

Sacrament of Reconciliation. Bernard Haring. (C). 1988. 45.00 (0-685-22288-8, Pub. by St Paul Pubns UK) St Mut.

Sacrament of Reconciliation. Bernard Haring. 80p. (C). 1990. 45.00 (0-85439-168-1, Pub. by St Paul Pubns UK) St Mut.

*Sacrament of Reconciliation. Lawrence G. Lovasik. (St. Joseph Picture Bks.). (Illus.). 32p. (J). (gr. 1-4). 1997. pap. 1.25 (0-89942-509-7, 509) Catholic Bk Pub.

Sacrament of Reconciliation: A Theological & Canonical Treatise. Andrew Cuschieri. 366p. (Orig.). (C). 1992. lib. bdg. 65.00 (0-8191-8655-4) U Pr of Amer.

Sacrament of Reconciliation: A Theological & Canonical Treatise. Andrew Cuschieri. 366p. (Orig.). (C). 1992. pap. text ed. 37.50 (0-8191-8656-2) U Pr of Amer.

Sacrament of Salvation. Kevin McNamara. 226p. 1981. 4.95 (0-8199-0806-1, Frncscn Herld) Franciscan Pr.

Sacrament of Salvation: An Introduction to Eucharist Ecclesiology. Paul McPartlan. 160p. 1996. pap. 19.95 (0-567-29299-1, Pub. by T & T Clark UK) Bks Intl VA.

Sacrament of Sexuality. Morton Kelsey & Barbara Kelsey. (Wellspring Bks.). 320p. (Orig.). 1986. pap. 9.95 (0-916349-06-3) Amity Hse Inc.

Sacrament of the Present Moment. Jean-Pierre De Caussade. LC 81-48206. 1989. pap. 12.00 (0-06-061811-6) Harper SF.

*Sacramental Acts: The Love Poems of Kenneth Rexroth. Kenneth Rexroth. 1997. pap. 15.00 (0-614-29390-1); pap. text ed. 15.00 (1-55659-080-6) Copper Canyon.

Sacramental & Occasional Homilies. David Q. Liptak. LC 80-29287. 96p. (Orig.). 1981. pap. 5.95 (0-8189-0408-9) Alba.

Sacramental & Spiritual Communion. Dietrich V. Asten. Ed. by Werner Glas. (Orig.). 1984. pap. 2.95 (0-88010-121-0) Anthroposophic.

Sacramental Cocoa & Other Stories from the Parish of the Poor. Lynn E. Perry. LC 94-43406. 164p. (Orig.). 1995. pap. 13.00 (0-664-25521-3) Westminster John Knox.

Sacramental Commodities: Gift, Text, & the Sublime in De Quincey. Charles J. Rzepka. LC 94-38875. 360p. (C). 1995. pap. text ed. 19.95 (0-87023-962-7); lib. bdg. 55.00 (0-87023-961-9) U of Mass Pr.

Sacramental Guidelines: A Companion to the New Catechism for Religious Educators. Kenan B. Osborne. LC 95-3249. 160p. (Orig.). 1995. pap. 12.95 (0-8091-3565-5) Paulist Pr.

Sacramental Life. 3rd ed. Gregory Williams. (Illus.). 72p. 1986. pap. 3.00 (0-912927-00-3, X000) St John Kronstadt.

Sacramental Magic in a Smalltown Cafe. Peter Reinhart. 1994. 20.00 (0-201-62259-9) Addison-Wesley.

*Sacramental Ministry to a Diverse Generation. Margaret L. Black. LC 97-20331. 1997. write for info. (1-55612-976-9) Sheed & Ward MO.

Sacramental Theology. Herbert Vorgrimler. Tr. by Linda M. Maloney from GER. 344p. (Orig.). 1992. pap. text ed. 24.95 (0-8146-1994-0) Liturgical Pr.

Sacramental Theology: A General Introduction. Kenan B. Osborne. 160p. 1988. pap. 9.95 (0-8091-2945-0) Paulist Pr.

*Sacramentals of the Church. (Saint Joseph Picture Bks.). (Illus.). 1985. pap. 1.25 (0-89942-396-5, 396-00) Catholic Bk Pub.

Sacramentarium Fuldense Saeculi X. Ed. by G. Richter & A. Schonfelder. (Henry Bradshaw Society Publication Ser.: No. CI (101)). 1970. 50.00 (0-907077-19-6) Boydell & Brewer.

Sacramentary. 1163p. 1985. 39.50 (0-89942-022-2, 22/22) Catholic Bk Pub.

Sacramentary. deluxe large type rev. ed. 1985. lthr. 91.00 (0-89942-045-1, 44/13) Catholic Bk Pub.

Sacramentary. large type rev. ed. 1985. text ed. 67.00 (0-89942-044-3, 44-02) Catholic Bk Pub.

Sacramentary. rev. ed. 1182p. 1985. 98.00 (0-8146-1434-5) Liturgical Pr.

*Sacramentary & Lectionary Set. (Masses of the Blessed Virgin Mary Collection: Vol. 1 & 2). 1988. 51.00 (0-89942-028-1, 28/22) Catholic Bk Pub.

Sacramentary of Echternach. Ed. by Yitzhak Hen. (Henry Bradshaw Society Ser.: Vol. 110). 480p. 1997. 63.00 (1-870252-08-X) Boydell & Brewer.

Sacramentary Supplement. 32p. (Orig.). 1994. pap. 3.00 (0-8146-2344-1) Liturgical Pr.

*Sacramentary Supplement. 1988. 4.95 (0-89942-042-7, 42/04) Catholic Bk Pub.

Sacramento: Excursions into Its History & Natural World. William M. Holden. Ed. by Patricia E. Mayer. LC 87-51538. (Illus.). 526p. 1991. reprint ed. pap. 12.95 (0-9619561-0-0) Two Rivers Pub CA.

Sacramento: Then & Now. Steve Mellon & Charlene Noyes. Ed. by J. Bruce Baumann. (Illus.). 128p. 29.95 (1-884850-04-9) Scripps Howard.

Sacramento & the California Delta. Phyllis Zauner. LC 79-55950. (Western Mini-Histories Ser.). (Illus.). 64p. (Orig.). 1979. pap. 7.95 (0-936914-02-5) Zanel Pubns.

Sacramento Bride Book. Deborah Wood. 240p. 1987. pap. 16.95 (0-937533-06-8) TEC Pubns.

*Sacramento, CA. Chip O'Brien. (River Journal Ser.: Vol. IV, No. 2). (Illus.). 48p. 1996. pap. 15.95 (1-57188-051-8) F Amato Pubns.

Sacramento, California. Terry J. Dunnahoo. LC 96-111172. (Places in American History Ser.). (J). 1996. pap. 7.95 (0-382-39334-1, Dillon Silver Burdett); lib. bdg. 14.95 (0-382-39333-3, Dillon Silver Burdett) Silver Burdett Pr.

*Sacramento County Including Portions of Placer & El Dorado Counties: Zip Code Edition, 1998. Thomas Bros. Maps Staff. 154p. 1997. pap. 24.95 (0-88130-897-8) Thomas Bros Maps.

*Sacramento County Including Portions of Placer & El Dorado County Street Guide & Directory: 1998 Edition. Thomas Bros. Maps Staff. 152p. 1997. pap. 16.95 (0-88130-896-X) Thomas Bros Maps.

Sacramento County Street Guide & Directory, Including Portions of Placer & El Dorado Counties: 1997 Edition. (Illus.). 152p. 1996. pap. 16.95 (0-88130-833-1) Thomas Bros Maps.

Sacramento County Street Guide & Directory, Including Portions of Placer & El Dorado Counties - Zip Code Edition: 1997 Edition. (Illus.). 154p. 1996. pap. 27.95 (0-88130-834-X) Thomas Bros Maps.

Sacramento County Street Guide & Directory Including Portions of Placer & El Dorado Counties Census Tract Edition: 1994 Edition. Thomas Bros. Maps Staff. (Illus.). 154p. 1994. pap. 49.95 (0-88130-683-5) Thomas Bros Maps.

Sacramento, D. C. A Political Lampoon. Bill Miller. LC 88-30886. 192p. 1988. 15.95 (0-929473-00-0); pap. 8.95 (0-317-91079-5) Erin Pr Inc.

Sacramento Dine-a-Mate. 288p. 1994. pap. 40.00 (1-57393-007-5) Dine-A-Mate.

*Sacramento Dine-a-Mate Book. 224p. 1996. pap. text ed. 30.00 (1-57393-065-2) Dine-A-Mate.

Sacramento Fifty Miles: Musical. Eleanor Harder & Ray Harder. (J). (gr. 1-7). 1969. 5.00 (0-87602-198-4) Anchorage.

Sacramento Kings. Michael E. Goodman. (NBA Today Ser.). (Illus.). 32p. (J). (gr. 4 up). 1993. lib. bdg. 14.95 (0-88682-540-7) Creative Ed.

*Sacramento Kings. Michael E. Goodman. LC 96-6527. (NBA Today Ser.). (J). 1997. write for info. (0-88682-889-9) Creative Ed.

*Sacramento Kings. Bob Italia. LC 96-39612. (Inside the NBA Ser.). (J). 1997. write for info. (1-56239-772-9) Abdo & Dghtrs.

Sacramento, River of Gold. Julian Dana. Ed. by Constance L. Skinner. LC 72-144963. (Illus.). 1971. reprint ed. 29.00 (0-403-00932-4) Scholarly.

Sacramento Tapestry. Steve Wiegand & Charlie Hayward. (Urban Tapestry Ser.). (Illus.). 240p. 1995. 39.50 (1-881096-10-6) Towery Pub.

Sacramento Valley Symposium & Guidebook. Ed. by Raymond V. Ingersoll & Tor H. Nilsen. (Illus.). 215p. (Orig.). 1990. pap. 18.00 (1-878861-04-2) Pac Section SEPM.

Sacramento Weather Guide: 1990 Edition. Tom Loffman. Ed. & Illus. by Randy Mann. 64p. (Orig.). 1989. pap. 2.95 (0-941687-01-5) Weather Pr.

Sacramento with Kids: A Family Guide to the Greater Sacramento Region. Dierdre W. Honnold. LC 94-60204. (Illus.). 256p. (Orig.). 1994. pap. 9.95 (0-9640370-0-9) Wrdwrights Intl.

Sacramento with Kids: A Family Guide to the Greater Sacramento Region. 2nd ed. Dierdre W. Honnold. Ed. by W. Bachmann. (Illus.). 212p. (Orig.). 1997. pap. 11.95 (0-9640370-4-1) Wrdwrights Intl.

Sacramento 1995: McCormack's Guides. 1995. pap. 8.95 (0-931299-49-7) McCormacks Guides.

Sacramento 1996: McCormack's Guides. 1995. pap. 8.95 (0-931299-58-6) McCormacks Guides.

Sacramento 1997: McCormack's Guides. 1996. pap. 9.95 (0-931299-67-5) McCormacks Guides.

Sacramentos. Maria De La Cruz Aymes. (Illus.). 127p. (Orig.). (SPA.). 1990. pap. text ed. 8.95 (0-89505-798-0) Tabor Pub.

Sacramentos. Gary Teja. (SPA.). 1983. 6.75 (1-55955-102-X) CRC Wrld Lit.

*Sacramento's Memorial Auditorium: Seven Decades of Memories. Paula J. Boghosian et al. (Illus.). 176p. (Orig.). 1997. pap. 24.00 (0-9657354-0-0) Sacramento Heritage.

*Sacramento's Shining Rails: A History of Trolley Transportation in California's Capital. Al Mankoff. Date not set. pap. 19.95 (0-912113-44-8) Railhead Pubns.

*Sacramento/Solano Counties Including Portions of Placer & El Dorado Counties Street Guide & Directory: 1998 Edition. Thomas Bros. Maps Staff. 248p. 1997. pap. 27.95 (0-88130-898-6) Thomas Bros Maps.

Sacramento/Solano Counties Street Guide & Directory Including Portions of Placer & El Dorado Counties: 1997 Edition. (Illus.). 248p. 1996. pap. 27.95 (0-88130-835-8) Thomas Bros Maps.

*Sacraments. (Illus.). 32p. (Orig.). (J). (ps-3). 1988. pap. 0.99 (0-89942-687-5, 687/00) Catholic Bk Pub.

Sacraments. Inos Biffi. LC 93-39150. (My First Catechism Ser.). (Illus.). 29p. (J). 1994. 12.00 (0-8028-3757-3) Eerdmans.

Sacraments. K. Cavanagh. (J). Date not set. pap. text ed. 1.25 (0-88271-210-1) Regina Pr.

Sacraments. C. C. Martindale. (Compact Study Ser.). 23p. (Orig.). 1993. pap. 1.95 (0-935952-92-6) Angelus Pr.

Sacraments: A Way of Life. Joyce Solimini. Ed. by Kieran Sawyer. (Developing Faith Ser.). (Orig.). (YA). (gr. 9-12). 1996. teacher ed., pap. 16.95 (0-87793-588-2); pap. text ed. 5.95 (0-87793-587-4) Ave Maria.

Sacraments: An Exploration into Their Meaning & Practice in RLDS Church. rev. ed. Peter A. Judd. LC 92-28306. 1992. pap. 11.50 (0-8309-0624-X) Herald Hse.

Sacraments: Celebrating the Signs of God's Love. Michael F. Pennock. LC 92-75347. (Friendship in the Lord Ser.). (Illus.). 240p. (Orig.). (YA). (gr. 9-12). 1993. student ed., pap. 10.95 (0-87793-503-3); teacher ed., pap. 13.95 (0-87793-504-1) Ave Maria.

Sacraments: Celebrations of Conversion. Patrick J. Brennan. (Illus.). 32p. 1986. pap. text ed. 2.95 (1-55612-046-X, LL1046) Sheed & Ward MO.

Sacraments: Encountering the Risen Lord. Paul A. Feider. LC 85-73569. 128p. (Orig.). 1986. pap. 4.95 (0-87793-327-8) Ave Maria.

Sacraments: How Catholics Pray. Thomas Richstatter. 144p. 1995. pap. 7.95 (0-86716-176-0) St Anthony Mess Pr.

Sacraments: Readings in Contemporary Theology. Ed. by Michael J. Taylor. LC 80-9534. 274p. (Orig.). 1981. pap. 8.95 (0-8189-0406-2) Alba.

Sacraments: Rites of Passage. William J. O'Malley. 256p. (Orig.). 1995. pap. 10.95 (0-88347-293-7) Res Christian Liv.

Sacraments: The Symbols of Our Faith. Garabed D. Kochakian. (Illus.). 99p. (Orig.). 1983. pap. 5.00 (0-934728-07-0) D O A C.

Sacraments Alive: Their History, Celebration, & Significance. Sandra DeGidio. LC 91-65381. 160p. (Orig.). 1991. pap. 9.95 (0-89622-489-9, C59) Twenty-Third.

Sacraments & Life. Gerald Foley. 24p. 1992. pap. text ed. 2.95 (1-55612-573-9) Sheed & Ward MO.

Sacraments & Sacramentality. rev. ed. Bernard Cooke. LC 93-61190. 256p. 1994. pap. 14.95 (0-89622-588-7) Twenty-Third.

Sacraments & the Salvation Army: Pneumatological Foundations. R. David Rightmire. LC 90-21325. (Studies in Evangelicalism: No. 10). 341p. 1990. 44.00 (0-8108-2396-9) Scarecrow.

Sacraments & Their Celebration. Nicholas Halligan. LC 85-23031. 284p. (Orig.). 1986. pap. 14.95 (0-8189-0489-5) Alba.

*Sacraments As God's Self Giving. James F. White. pap. 13.95 (0-687-36707-7) Abingdon.

Sacraments in Religious Education & Liturgy: An Ecumenical Model. Robert L. Browning & Roy A. Reed. LC 84-27536. 313p. (Orig.). 1985. pap. 18.95 (0-89135-044-6) Religious Educ.

Sacraments in the Christian Life. John McDonald. (C). 1988. 39.00 (0-85439-226-2, Pub. by St Paul Pubns UK) St Mut.

Sacraments of Desire. Linda Gregg. 88p. 1992. 14.95 (1-55597-151-2); pap. 10.00 (1-55597-173-3) Graywolf.

*Sacraments of Initiation. Liam G. Walsh. Date not set. pap. 22.95 (0-225-66499-2, Pub. by Geoffrey Chapman UK) Morehouse Pub.

Sacraments of Life, Life of the Sacraments. Leonardo Boff. 88p. 1987. pap. 7.95 (0-912405-38-4) Pastoral Pr.

Sacraments of Love: A Prayer Journal. Andrew M. Greeley. 238p. 1996. pap. text ed. 14.95 (0-8245-1594-3) Crossroad NY.

Sacraments of Simple Folk. Robert R. Marett. LC 77-27192. (Gifford Lectures: 1932-33). reprint ed. 36.50 (0-404-60488-9) AMS Pr.

Sacre du Printemps: Seven Productions from Nijinsky to Martha Graham. Shelley C. Berg. LC 87-29421. (Theater & Dramatic Studies: No. 48). (Illus.). 217p. reprint ed. pap. 61.90 (0-8357-1842-5, 2070591) Bks Demand.

*Sacred. Dennis Lehane. 1997. 23.00 (0-614-27890-2) Morrow.

*Sacred: A Novel. Dennis Lehane. LC 96-53115. 256p. 1997. write for info. (0-688-14381-4) Morrow.

Sacred: In Life & Art. Philip Sherrard. 162p. (Orig.). 1990. 49.95 (0-903880-41-5, Pub. by Golgonooza Pr UK); pap. 22.95 (0-903880-42-3, Pub. by Golgonooza Pr UK) S Perennis.

Sacred: Ways of Knowledge, Sources of Life. Peggy V. Beck & Anna L. Walters. (Illus.). 384p. 1977. pap. 19.95 (0-912586-24-9) Navajo Coll Pr.

Sacred Acts, Sacred Space, Sacred Time. John Walbridge. (Baha'i Studies: Vol. 1). 322p. (Orig.). 1996. pap. 22.95 (0-85398-406-9) G Ronald Pub.

Sacred Adventures of a Taxi Driver. rev. ed. Ansara Ali. LC 93-8602. (Illus.). 544p. 1993. reprint ed. pap. 16.95 (0-9636170-0-1) Royal Rags.

Sacred Afrikan Spiritual Power from Within: Sacred Afrikan Spiritual Verses. Afrikadzata Deku. LC 91-72660. (Sacred Afrikan Spiritual Poetry Ser.). 50p. 1994. pap. 10.00 (1-56454-002-2) Cont Afrikan.

Sacred & Civil Calendar of the Athenian Year. Jon D. Mikalson. LC 74-25622. 240p. reprint ed. pap. 68.40 (0-8357-2784-X, 2039910) Bks Demand.

*Sacred & Its Scholars: Comparative Methodologies for the Study of Primary Religious Data. Thomas A. Idinopulos & Edward A. Yonan. LC 96-27650. (Studies in the History of Religions). 1996. write for info. (90-04-10623-5) E J Brill.

Sacred & Legendary Art. Anna Jameson. Ed. by Estelle M. Hurll. LC 72-145108. (Illus.). 800p. 1972. reprint ed. 17.50 (0-403-01045-4) Scholarly.

Sacred & Legendary Art, 2 Vols. Anna B. Jameson. LC 71-124594. reprint ed. 135.00 (0-404-03551-5) AMS Pr.

Sacred & Profane. Chaim Grade. LC 97-8196. 312p. 1997. 24.95 (1-56821-963-6) Aronson.

Sacred & Profane. Faye Kellerman. 1988. mass mkt. 5.99 (0-449-21502-4) Fawcett.

Sacred & Profane. Michaels. mass mkt. write for info. (0-312-90057-0) Tor Bks.

Sacred & Profane: Secular & Devotional Interplay in Early Modern British Literature. Ed. by Helen Wilcox et al. 320p. 1995. pap. 30.00 (90-5383-367-6) Paul & Co Pubs.

An Asterisk (*) at the beginning of an entry indicates that the title is appearing in BIP for the first time.

Sacred & Profane Love Machine. Iris Murdoch. 368p. 1984. pap. 11.95 (*0-14-004111-7*, Penguin Bks) Viking Penguin.

Sacred & Profane Memories. Carl Van Vechten. LC 75-156727. (Essay Index Reprint Ser.). 1977. reprint ed. 23.95 (*0-8369-2337-5*) Ayer.

Sacred & Profane Memories. Carl Van Vechten. LC 78-27584. 230p. 1979. reprint ed. text ed. 55.00 (*0-313-20835-2*, VVSP, Greenwood Pr) Greenwood.

Sacred & Propane. Bayla Winters. 52p. (Orig.). 1989. pap. 8.95 (*0-317-93456-2*) Croton Review.

Sacred & Secular. Voyager Company Staff. Date not set. write for info. (*1-55940-703-4*) Voyager NY.

Sacred & Secular: Studies on Augustine & Latin Christianity. R. A. Markus. (Collected Studies: CS 465). 350p. 1994. 92.95 (*0-86078-450-9*, Pub. by Variorum UK) Ashgate Pub Co.

Sacred & Shakespearean Affinities. Charles Swinburne. LC 76-159973. (Studies in Shakespeare: No. 24). 1971. reprint ed. lib. bdg. 62.95 (*0-8383-1263-2*) M S G Haskell Hse.

***Sacred & the Feminine in Ancient Greece.** Sue Blundell & Margaret Williamson. LC 97-25099. 1998. write for info. (*0-415-12662-2*); pap. write for info. (*0-415-12663-0*) Routledge.

Sacred & the Profane. Motter & Steacy. (Illus.). 1990. 25.00 (*0-913035-18-1*); pap. 14.95 (*0-913035-17-3*) Eclipse Bks.

***Sacred & the Profane: Josefa de Obidos of Portugal (1630-1684)** Vitor Serrao et al. LC 97-810. 1997. write for info. (*0-940979-36-5*) Natl Museum Women.

Sacred & the Profane: The Nature of Religion. Willard R. Trask. Tr. by Willard Trask. LC 58-10904. 1968. reprint ed. pap. 9.00 (*0-15-679201-X*, Harvest Bks) HarBrace.

Sacred & the Secular: Bengal Muslim Discourses, 1871-1977. Tazeen M. Mushid. (Illus.). 508p. (C). 1996. 39.95 (*0-19-563701-1*) OUP.

Sacred & the Secular in India's Performing Arts. Ed. by V. Subramaniam. 1983. 21.50 (*0-8364-0974-4*, Pub. by Ashish II) S Asia.

Sacred & the Subversive: Political Witch-Hunts as National Rituals. Albert Bergessen. LC 84-61370. (Society for Scientific Study of Religion Monographs: No. 4). 1984. pap. 5.50 (*0-932566-03-0*) Soc Sci Stud Rel.

***Sacred Animals.** Gordon MacLellan. (Illus.). (Orig.). 1997. pap. 22.95 (*0-614-30731-7*, Pub. by Capall Bann Pubng UK) Holmes Pub.

Sacred Anointing: The Preaching of Dr. Martyn Lloyd-Jones. Tony Sargent. LC 94-15556. 352p. (Orig.). 1994. pap. 13.99 (*0-89107-811-8*) Crossway Bks.

***Sacred Architecture.** Caroline Humphrey & Piers Vitebsky. (Living Wisdom Ser.). 1997. pap. 15.95 (*0-316-38122-5*) Little.

Sacred Architecture. A. Tad Mann. 1993. pap. 24.95 (*1-85230-391-3*) Element MA.

Sacred Art. M. A. Couturier. Tr. by Granger Ryan from FRE. (Illus.). 160p. 1989. 35.00 (*0-292-77639-X*) U of Tex Pr.

Sacred Art: Preaching & Theology in the African American Tradition. Olin P. Moyd. 160p. 1995. pap. 12.00 (*0-8170-1220-6*) Judson.

Sacred Art in East & West: Its Principles & Methods. 2nd ed. Titus Burckhardt. Tr. by Lord Northbourne from FRE. (Illus.). 160p. 1986. pap. 15.95 (*0-900588-11-X*) S Perennis.

***Sacred Art in East & West: Principles & Methods.** Titus Burckhardt. 160p. 1996. pap. 15.95 (*0-614-21587-0*, 1095) Kazi Pubns.

Sacred Art of Dying: How the World Religions Understand Death. Kenneth P. Kramer. 240p. 1988. pap. 13.95 (*0-8091-2942-6*) Paulist Pr.

Sacred Art of Lavrans Nielson. Illus. by Lavrans Nielson. 32p. (Orig.). 1992. pap. 24.95 (*1-55612-461-9*) Sheed & Ward MO.

Sacred Art of the Earth: Ancient & Contemporary Earthworks. Maureen A. Korp. LC 95-46735. (Illus.). 280p. 1996. pap. text ed. 29.95 (*0-8264-0883-4*) Continuum.

Sacred Art of Tibet. rev. ed. Tarthang Tulku. LC 72-96555. (Illus.). 98p. 1988. pap. 12.95 (*0-913546-00-3*) Dharma Pub.

***Sacred Art of Tibet: Sacred Art & Books of Tibet Exhibition, 2 vols., Set.** Pref. by Tarthang Tulku. 410p. 400.00 (*0-89800-278-8*) Dharma Pub.

Sacred Art Sacred Earth: Transformative Art - Birthing a New Myth. Heyoka Merrifield. (Illus.). 144p. (Orig.). (YA). 1994. pap. 19.95 (*0-945122-01-2*) Rain Bird Pubs.

Sacred Arts of Haitian Vodou. Ed. by Donald J. Cosentino. 1995. 99.00 (*0-930741-46-3*); pap. 59.00 (*0-930741-47-1*) UCLA Fowler Mus.

Sacred Athlete: On the Mystical Experience & Dionysios - Its Westernworld Fountainhead. Richard Blum & Alexander Golitsin. 510p. (Orig.). (C). 1991. pap. text ed. 40.00 (*0-8191-8183-8*); lib. bdg. 59.00 (*0-8191-8182-X*) U Pr of Amer.

Sacred Bee in Ancient Times & Folklore. Hilda M. Ransome. 1976. lib. bdg. 250.00 (*0-8490-2552-4*) Gordon Pr.

Sacred Beliefs of the Chitimacha Indians. rev. ed. Faye Stouff & Smithsonian Archives Staff. LC 95-74716. Orig. Title: Sacred Chitimacha Indian Beliefs. (Illus.). 81p. 1995. pap. 9.95 (*1-887875-00-X*) Neshobatek Pr.

Sacred Beliefs of the Chitimacha Indians. rev. ed. Faye Stouff. LC 95-74716. Orig. Title: Sacred Chitimacha Indian Beliefs. (Illus.). 81p. 1995. lib. bdg. 12.95 (*1-887875-01-8*) Neshobatek Pr.

Sacred Biography: Saints & Their Biographers in the Middle Ages. Thomas J. Heffernan. 352p. 1992. reprint ed. pap. 19.95 (*0-19-507907-8*) OUP.

Sacred Biography in the Buddhist Traditions of South & Southeast Asia. Ed. by Juliane Schober. LC 96-21003. (Illus.). 372p. 1997. text ed. 49.00 (*0-8248-1699-4*) UH Pr.

Sacred Bonds of Commerce: Religion, Economy, & Trade Society at Hellenistic Roman Delos. Nicholas K. Rauh. xxiv, 376p. 1994. lib. bdg. 87.00 (*90-5063-156-8*, Pub. by Gieben NE) Benjamins North Am.

Sacred Book of Healing. Gentle Wind Project Staff. 116p. (Orig.). 1996. pap. 25.00 (*0-614-14281-4*) Gentle Wind Proj.

Sacred Book of Healing, Vol 1. LC 96-76397. 116p. (Orig.). (C). 1996. pap. 25.00 (*1-889222-01-1*) Gentle Wind Proj.

Sacred Book of the East: Vedic Hymns, 2 vols, Set. Ed. by Max Muller. 1975. 600.00 (*0-8490-3963-0*) Krishna Pr.

Sacred Books of China, 6 vols, Set. James Legge. 1975. 1,800.00 (*0-317-00108-6*) Krishna Pr.

Sacred Books of China: Text of Taoism, 2 vols, Set. Ed. by Max Muller. 1975. lib. bdg. 600.00 (*0-87968-298-1*) Krishna Pr.

Sacred Books of the East. Epiphanius Wilson. 472p. 1981. pap. 40.00 (*0-89540-099-5*, SB-099) Sun Pub.

Sacred Books of the East. Epiphanius Wilson. 464p. 1986. reprint ed. 25.00 (*0-8364-1764-X*, Pub. by Usha II) S Asia.

Sacred Books of the East, Including Selections from Vedic Hymns, The Zend Avesta, The Dhammapada, The Upanishads, The Koran & The Life of Budha. Epiphanius Wilson. 457p. (C). 1987. reprint ed. 21.00 (*0-8364-2192-2*, Pub. by Usha II) S Asia.

Sacred Books of the Hindus, 47 vols. Ed. by Baman Das Basu. reprint ed. 1,575.50 (*0-404-57800-4*) AMS Pr.

Sacred Books of the Jainas, Vol. 1. 1990. reprint ed. 50.00 (*1-55528-199-0*, Pub. by Today & Tomorrows P & P II) Scholarly Pubns.

Sacred Books of the Jainas, Vol. 2. 1990. reprint ed. 55.00 (*1-55528-237-7*, Pub. by Today & Tomorrows P & P II) Scholarly Pubns.

Sacred Books of the Jainas, Vol. 4. 1990. reprint ed. 29.00 (*1-55528-223-7*, Pub. by Today & Tomorrows P & P II) Scholarly Pubns.

Sacred Books of the Jainas, Vol. 5. 1990. reprint ed. 60.00 (*1-55528-191-5*, Pub. by Today & Tomorrows P & P II) Scholarly Pubns.

Sacred Books of the Jainas, Vol. 6. 1990. reprint ed. 55.00 (*1-55528-235-0*, Pub. by Today & Tomorrows P & P II) Scholarly Pubns.

Sacred Books of the Jainas, Vol. 8. 1990. reprint ed. 45.00 (*1-55528-197-4*, Pub. by Today & Tomorrows P & P II) Scholarly Pubns.

Sacred Books of the Jainas, Vol. 10. 1990. reprint ed. 55.00 (*1-55528-196-6*, Pub. by Today & Tomorrows P & P II) Scholarly Pubns.

Sacred Books of the Jainas, Vol. 11. 1990. reprint ed. 55.00 (*1-55528-198-2*, Pub. by Today & Tomorrows P & P II) Scholarly Pubns.

Sacred Books of the Jainas (Bibliotheca Jainica), 11 vols. Ed. by Sarat C. Ghoshal. reprint ed. 491.50 (*0-404-57700-8*) AMS Pr.

Sacred Bridge. Eric Werner. LC 79-18082. (Music Reprint Ser.). 1979. reprint ed. lib. bdg. 65.00 (*0-306-79581-7*) Da Capo.

Sacred Bridge, Vol. 2. Eric Werner. 1985. 49.50 (*0-88125-052-X*) Ktav.

Sacred Buffalo: The Lakota Way for a New Beginning. James Durham & Virginia Thomas. (Illus.). 200p. (Orig.). 1996. pap. 19.95 (*0-87364-868-4*) Paladin Pr.

Sacred Bull: The Inner Obstacles That Hold You Back at Work & How to Overcome Them. Albert J. Bernstein & Sudney C. Rozen. 269p. 1994. text ed. 22.95 (*0-471-59836-4*) Wiley.

Sacred Bull: The Inner Obstacles That Hold You Back at Work & How to Overcome Them. Albert J. Bernstein et al. 350p. 1996. text ed. 39.95 (*0-471-59851-8*) Wiley.

Sacred Bullock & Other Stories. Mazo De La Roche. LC 76-101798. (Short Story Index Reprint Ser.). 1977. 17.95 (*0-8369-3186-6*) Ayer.

Sacred Bundles of the Sac & Fox Indians. Mark R. Harrington. LC 76-43732. (University of Pennsylvania. Museum Anthropological Publications: Vol. 4, No. 1). (Illus.). 192p. reprint ed. 54.00 (*0-404-15573-1*) AMS Pr.

Sacred Calligraphy of the East. 3rd expanded rev. ed. John Stevens. (Illus.). 224p. (Orig.). 1996. pap. 32.50 (*1-57062-122-5*) Shambhala Pubns.

Sacred Canopy: Elements of a Sociological Theory of Religion. Peter L. Berger. LC 67-19805. 240p. 1990. reprint ed. pap. 10.95 (*0-385-07305-4*, Anchor NY) Doubleday.

Sacred Carols for Men. 2.95 (*0-7935-4044-5*, 50482351) H Leonard.

Sacred Cause: Civil-Military Conflict over Soviet National Security, 1917-1992. Thomas M. Nichols. LC 92-34543. (Cornell Studies in Security Affairs). 280p. 1993. 35.00 (*0-8014-2774-6*) Cornell U Pr.

Sacred Cave: And Other Poems. Hugh Fox. 54p. 1992. pap. 6.95 (*0-9631755-0-5*) Omega Cat Pr.

Sacred Celebrations: A Jewish Holiday Handbook. Kerry M. Olitzky & Ronald H. Isaacs. LC 94-1391. 1994. 19.95 (*0-88125-484-3*); pap. 12.95 (*0-88125-496-7*) Ktav.

Sacred Centre As the Focus of Political Interest: Proceedings of the Symposium Held on the Occasion of the 375th Anniversary of the University of Groningen, 5-8 March 1989. Ed. by Hans Bakker. (Groningen Oriental Studies: Vol. VI). ix, 268p. 1992. pap. 52.00 (*90-6980-036-5*, Pub. by Egbert Forsten NE) Benjamins North Am.

Sacred Chain: The History of the Jews. Norman F. Cantor. 496p. 1995. pap. 15.00 (*0-06-092652-X*, HarpT) HarpC.

Sacred Charity: Confraternities & Social Welfare in Spain, 1400-1700. Maureen Flynn. LC 88-47727. 256p. 1988. 37.50 (*0-8014-2227-2*) Cornell U Pr.

Sacred Chitimacha Indian Beliefs see Sacred Beliefs of the Chitimacha Indians

Sacred Choral Music in Print, 2 vols. 2nd ed. Ed. by Gary S. Eslinger & F. Mark Daugherty. LC 85-15368. (Music in Print Ser.: Vol. 1). 1312p. 1985. lib. bdg. 220.00 (*0-88478-017-1*) Musicdata.

Sacred Choral Music in Print: Arranger Index. 2nd ed. LC 87-5337. (Music-in-Print Ser.: Vol. 1C). 137p. 1987. lib. bdg. 35.00 (*0-88478-019-8*) Musicdata.

Sacred Choral Music in Print: Master Index, 1992. LC 92-43440. 413p. 1993. 95.00 (*0-88478-030-9*) Musicdata.

***Sacred Choral Music in Print: Master Index 1996.** LC 92-43440. (Music-in-Print Ser.: Vol. 1x). 451p. 1996. lib. bdg. 95.00 (*0-88478-040-6*) Musicdata.

Sacred Choral Music in Print: 1988 Supplement. Ed. by Susan H. Simon. LC 88-25247. (Music in Print Ser.: Vol. 1S). 263p. 1988. lib. bdg. 95.00 (*0-88478-022-8*) Musicdata.

Sacred Choral Music in Print: 1992 Supplement. Ed. by F. Mark Daugherty & Susan H. Simon. LC 92-27658. (Music-in-Print Ser.: Vol. 1t). 1992. lib. bdg. 95.00 (*0-88478-029-5*) Musicdata.

***Sacred Choral Music in Print: 1996 Supplement.** Ed. by F. Mark Daugherty. LC 85-15368. (Music-in-Print Ser.: Vol. 1u). 225p. 1996. lib. bdg. 95.00 (*0-88478-039-2*) Musicdata.

Sacred Christmas Classics. 56p. 1994. pap. 8.95 (*0-7935-3319-8*, 00222576) H Leonard.

Sacred Christmas Solos. 56p. 1994. pap. 9.95 (*0-7935-3311-2*, 00292056) H Leonard.

Sacred City of Anuradhapura. Chandra B. Charish. (Illus.). 132p. 1986. reprint ed. 26.00 (*0-8364-1746-1*, Pub. by Abhinav II) S Asia.

Sacred Classics: High Voice. 1992. pap. 14.95 incl. audio (*0-7935-0931-9*, 00747013) H Leonard.

Sacred Classics: Low Voice. 1992. pap. 14.95 incl. audio (*0-7935-0930-0*, 00747014) H Leonard.

Sacred Clowns. Tony Hillerman. 368p. 1994. mass mkt. 6.99 (*0-06-109260-6*) HarpC.

Sacred Clowns. large type ed. Tony Hillerman. LC 93-27831. 1994. pap. 16.95 (*0-7862-0016-2*) Thorndike Pr.

***Sacred Clowns of Wisdom Vol. 1: Star Wheel of the Wisdom Keepers.** Carla R. Byers. (Rainbow of Creation Ser.: Vol. 4). (Illus.). 120p. (Orig.). 1998. wbk. ed., pap. 35.00 (*0-9656124-4-9*) Heyokah Pub.

***Sacred Companies: Organizational Aspects of Religion & Religious Aspects of Organizations.** Ed. by N. J. Demerath, III et al. (Religion in America Ser.). (Illus.). 448p. 1997. 49.95 (*0-19-511322-5*) OUP.

Sacred Complex: On the Psychogenesis of Paradise Lost. William Kerrigan. 360p. (C). 1983. 38.00 (*0-674-78500-2*) HUP.

Sacred Complex of Kathmandu Nepal: Religion of the Himalayan Kingdom. Makhan Jha. (C). Date not set. 28.50 (*81-212-0490-9*, Pub. by Gian Publng Hse II) S Asia.

Sacred Contract. Caroline Myss. 1997. write for info. (*0-517-70392-0*) Random Hse Value.

Sacred Country. Rose Tremain. 352p. 1993. text ed. 21.00 (*0-689-12170-9*, Pub. by Ctrl Bur voor Schimmel NE) Macmillan.

Sacred Country. Rose Tremain. Ed. by Julie Rubenstein. 336p. 1995. pap. 10.00 (*0-671-88609-6*) PB.

Sacred Cow. Diamela Eltit. Tr. by Amanda Hopkinson. (Masks Ser.). 112p. 1995. pap. 12.99 (*1-85242-287-4*) Serpents Tail.

Sacred Cow Makes Gourmet Hamburgers: Ministry Anytime, Anywhere, by Anyone. William M. Easum. LC 95-22446. 192p. 1995. pap. 13.95 (*0-687-00563-9*) Abingdon.

Sacred Cows & Hot Potatoes: Agrarian Myths & Agricultural Policy. William P. Browne et al. 151p. (C). 1992. pap. text ed. 19.95 (*0-8133-8558-X*) Westview.

Sacred Cows in Education. Ed. by Frank Coffield & Richard Goodings. 214p. 1984. pap. 25.00 (*0-85224-484-3*, Pub. by Edinburgh U Pr UK) Col U Pr.

Sacred Cows Make the Best Burgers: Developing Change-Ready People & Organizations. Robert J. Kriegel & David Brandt. 352p. 1996. 22.95 (*0-446-51840-9*) Warner Bks.

Sacred Cows Make the Best Burgers: Developing Change-Ready People & Organizations. Robert J. Kriegel & David Brandt. LC 96-34479. 336p. 1997. pap. 14.99 (*0-446-67260-2*) Warner Bks.

Sacred Cows Make the Best Hamburger. JoAnn Roberts. 99p. 1993. pap. 12.00 (*1-880715-13-9*) Creat Des Srvs.

Sacred Cryhmes: A Few Home Girls Path to Self Awareness. Vivian Gartley-Hindrew. LC 91-61313. 1991. pap. 7.95 (*0-88247-876-1*) R & E Pubs.

Sacred Dance. Maria-Gabriele Wosien. LC 85-52298. (Art & Imagination Ser.). (Illus.). 128p. 1986. pap. 14.95 (*0-500-81006-0*) Thames Hudson.

Sacred Dance of India. Mrinalini Sarabhai. 43p. 1988. 9.95 (*0-318-36312-7*) Asia Bk Corp.

Sacred Dance with Physically & Mentally Handicapped. Ann M. Blessin. Ed. by Doug Adams. 1982. pap. 3.00 (*0-941500-28-4*) Sharing Co.

Sacred Dance with Senior Citizens in Churches, Convalescent Homes, & Retirement Homes. Doug Adams. 1982. pap. 3.00 (*0-941500-27-6*) Sharing Co.

Sacred Deposit: History of 200 Year Old Meeting House. Ronald Jager & Sally Krone. (Illus.). 1989. pap. 8.00 (*0-614-14526-0*) Wash Hist Soc.

Sacred Diary of Adrian Plass. Adrian Plass. 1994. pap. 6.99 (*0-551-01418-0*) Zondervan.

Sacred Dimensions of Women's Experience. Ed. by Elizabeth D. Gray. (Illus.). 256p. 1988. pap. 16.95 (*0-934512-05-1*) Roundtable Pr.

Sacred Dramas of J. S. Bach: A Reference & Textual Interpretation. W. Murray Young. LC 91-52104. 223p. 1994. lib. bdg. 47.50 (*0-89950-812-X*) McFarland & Co.

Sacred Drift: Essays on the Margins of Islam. Peter L. Wilson. 256p. (Orig.). 1993. pap. 13.95 (*0-87286-275-5*) City Lights.

Sacred Dust. David Hill. LC 95-23879. 1995. write for info. (*0-614-08094-0*) Delacorte.

Sacred Dust. David Hill. (Illus.). 400p. 1996. 22.95 (*0-385-31534-1*) Delacorte.

***Sacred Dust.** David Hill. 1997. pap. 11.95 (*0-385-31816-2*) Doubleday.

Sacred Dwelling: A Spirituality of Family Life. rev. ed. Wendy M. Wright. 200p. 1994. pap. 10.95 (*0-939516-24-1*) Forest Peace.

Sacred Dying. Barry N. Kaufman & Samahria L. Kaufman. LC 95-67842. 205p. (Orig.). 1996. pap. 12.95 (*1-887254-03-X*) Epic Century.
"An inspiration. A valuable resource & learning tool. A moving, real account of one family's struggle toward death's transcendence through love."--National Cancer Foundation. In this deeply moving story, Sam Millen & his family confront the ultimate challenge. Mom is dying & no one, least of all Sam is prepared. As Sam, Lisa, Chad & Margaret try to uphold a veil of silence around Margaret's advancing disease, isolation & pain pervade their separate lives. Yet with the help of the author Barry Neil Kaufman's mentoring, guidance & friendship, Sam learns to accept & then embrace what is happening... ultimately teaching his entire family how to go beyond the pain & discover new insights, joy & even laughter. Written by Barry Kaufman, author of HAPPINESS IS A CHOICE & SON-RISE, & his wife Samahria Kaufman, A SACRED DYING provides inspiration to adolescents & adults confronting the death of a parent or loved one, & provides a model for anyone facing similar circumstances. A dramatic & heartwarming true tale. The Kaufmans founded & direct THE OPTION INSTITUTE in Sheffield, Massachusetts, an internationally renowned learning center for individuals, couples, groups & families. To order contact: Associated Publishers Group, 3356 Coffey Lane, Santa Rosa, CA 95403. (707) 542-5400. ***Publisher Provided Annotation.***

S

Sacred Earth. Sherrill Miller. (Illus.). 246p. 1993. 49.50 (*0-8109-3831-6*) Abrams.

Sacred Earth. Brian Molyneaux. 1995. pap. 14.95 (*0-316-90303-5*) Little.

Sacred Earth: The Spiritual Landscape of Native America. Arthur Versluis. 144p. (Orig.). 1991. pap. 12.95 (*0-89281-352-0*) Inner Tradit.

Sacred Echoes. Patricia H. Carlson. 140p. (Orig.). 1995. pap. 11.50 (*0-9645393-4-9*) P H S Carlson.

Sacred Edict of K'ang Hsi. F. W. Baller. LC 79-89636. 1979. 18.00 (*0-915032-25-2*); pap. 12.95 (*0-915032-28-7*) Natl Poet Foun.

Sacred Emblems of the Huichols. Carl Lumholtz & Pablo De la Cruz. Ed. & Intro. by Bruce Finson. LC 95-83907. (Illus.). 60p. Date not set. pap. 20.00 (*0-943907-09-8*) Bruce Finson.

Sacred Encounters: Father De Smet & the Indians of the Rocky Mountain West. Jacqueline Peterson. 1993. 39.95 (*0-8061-2575-6*); pap. 24.95 (*0-8061-2576-4*) U of Okla Pr.

Sacred Enigmas: Literary Religion in the Hebrew Bible. Stephen A. Geller. LC 96-1111. 232p. (C). 1996. text ed. 65.00 (*0-415-12771-8*) Routledge.

Sacred Estrangement: The Rhetoric of Conversion in Modern American Autobiography. Peter A. Dorsey. LC 92-16589. 240p. 1993. 35.00 (*0-271-00902-0*) Pa St U Pr.

Sacred Eyes. 4th ed. L. Robert Keck. 297p. 1995. reprint ed. pap. 15.00 (*0-9646978-0-7*) Synergy Assocs.

Sacred Farce from Medieval Bohemia Mastickar. Jarmila F. Veltrusky. Ed. by Ladislav Matejka. (Michigan Studies in the Humanities: No. 6). (C). 1985. 25.00 (*0-936534-05-2*) Mich Studies Human.

Sacred Favorites. (Easy Piano Ser.). 48p. 1992. pap. 8.95 (*0-7935-1296-4*, 00290364) H Leonard.

***Sacred Feathers: The Reverend Peter Jones (Kahkewaquonaby)** Donald B. Smith. LC 86-24914. (American Indian Lives Ser.). 416p. 1987. reprint ed. pap. 118.60 (*0-608-03365-0*, 2064077) Bks Demand.

***Sacred Fictions: Holy Women & Hagiography in Late Antiquity.** Lynda L. Coon. LC 97-3136. (Middle Ages Ser.). (Illus.). 232p. 1997. text ed. 39.95 (*0-8122-3371-9*) U of Pa Pr.

Sacred Fire. Isi Beller. 416p. 1994. 21.95 (*1-55970-226-5*) Arcade Pub Inc.

Sacred Fire. B. Z. Goldberg. (Illus.). 1958. 7.50 (*0-8216-0146-6*, Univ Bks) Carol Pub Group.

Sacred Fire. B. Z. Goldberg. 285p. 1974. reprint ed. pap. 3.95 (*0-8065-0456-0*, Citadel Pr) Carol Pub Group.

Sacred Fire: Rites of Passage & Rituals of Worship with Angelic Guidance. Tiziana De Rovere. LC 95-17971. (Illus.). 208p. 1995. pap. 14.95 (*0-89087-760-2*) Celestial Arts.

Sacred Fire: The Story of Sex in Religion. B. Z. Goldberg. (Illus.). 401p. 1995. pap. 29.95 (*1-56459-502-1*) Kessinger Pub.

Sacred Fire: Willa Cather's Novel Cycle. Evelyn H. Hively. LC 94-4183. 212p. 1994. lib. bdg. 42.50 (*0-8191-9481-6*) U Pr of Amer.

Sacred Fire of Liberty: James Madison & the Founding of the Federal Republic. Lance Banning. LC 95-14369. (Illus.). 536p. 1995. 35.00 (*0-8014-3152-2*) Cornell U Pr.

Sacred Fires: Berurya, a Daughter, a Wife, but First a Woman. Ronald Brown. 272p. 1995. pap. 24.95 (*965-229-126-9*, Pub. by Gefen Pub Hse IS) Gefen Bks.

Sacred Flame: A Play in Three Acts. W. Somerset Maugham. LC 75-25390. (Works of W. Somerset Maugham). 1977. reprint ed. 23.95 (*0-405-07847-1*) Ayer.

***Sacred Flowers: Creating a Heavenly Garden.** Roni Jay. LC 96-80240. (Illus.). 64p. 1997. 14.95 (*1-885223-54-4*) Beyond Words Pub.

Sacred Footsteps: A Traveler's Guide to Spiritual Places of Italy & France. Melanie MacMitchell. (Illus.). 164p. (Orig.). 1991. pap. 9.95 (*0-9629727-0-3*) Opal Star Pr.

***Sacred Fortress: Byzantine Art & Statecraft in Ravenna.** Otto G. Simson. LC 86-42861. 216p. 1987. reprint ed. pap. 61.60 (*0-608-03754-0*, 2064577) Bks Demand.

Sacred Fount. Henry James. LC 94-20572. (Revived Modern Classic Ser.). 236p. 1995. pap. 10.95 (*0-8112-1279-3*, NDP790) New Directions.

Sacred Fount. Henry James. Ed. & Intro. by John Lyon. 240p. 1995. pap. 10.95 (*0-14-043350-3*, Penguin Classics) Viking Penguin.

Sacred Fragments: Recovering Theology for the Modern Jew. Neil Gillman. 296p. 1992. pap. text ed. 14.95 (*0-8276-0403-3*) JPS Phila.

Sacred Game: Provincialism & Frontier Consciousness in American Literature, 1630-1860. Albert V. Frank. (Cambridge Studies in American Literature & Culture: No. 12). 192p. 1985. text ed. 54.95 (*0-521-30159-9*) Cambridge U Pr.

Sacred Game: The Role of the Sacred in the Genesis of Modern Literary Fiction. Cesareo Bandera. LC 93-6295. (Studies in Romance Literatures). 304p. (C). 1994. 45.00 (*0-271-01301-X*); pap. text ed. 16.95 (*0-271-01302-8*) Pa St U Pr.

***Sacred Games: A History of Christian Worship.** Bernhard Lang. 1997. 40.00 (*0-300-06932-4*) Yale U Pr.

Sacred Geography of the American Mound-Builders. Maureen E. Korp. LC 89-28543. (Native American Studies: Vol. 2). 140p. 1990. lib. bdg. 69.95 (*0-88946-484-7*) E Mellen.

Sacred Geography of the Ancient Greeks: Astrological Symbolism in Art, Architecture, & Landscape. Jean Richer. Tr. by Christine Rhone from FRE. LC 94-11960. (SUNY Series in Western Esoteric Traditions). (Illus.). 319p. (C). 1994. text ed. 74.50 (*0-7914-2023-X*); pap. text ed. 24.95 (*0-7914-2024-8*) State U NY Pr.

Sacred Geometry: Philosophy & Practice. Robert Lawlor. LC 88-51328. (Art & Imagination Ser.). (Illus.). 112p. 1989. reprint ed. pap. 15.95 (*0-500-81030-3*) Thames Hudson.

***Sacred Gifts: Precolumbian Art & Creativity.** Tim Hallman & Lisette Reynolds. 29p. 1995. teacher ed. write for info. (*0-614-24036-0*) Mexican Museum.

Sacred Gifts: Precolumbian Art & Creativity. Jeanette F. Peterson. LC 94-37480. 1994. write for info. (*0-89951-090-6*) Santa Barb Mus Art.

Sacred Ground. Mercedes Lackey. 384p. 1995. 5.99 (*0-8125-1965-5*) Tor Bks.

Sacred Ground. Ron Zeilinger. (Illus.). 152p. (Orig.). 1986. pap. 5.95 (*1-877976-04-0*, 406-0009) Tipi Pr.

Sacred Ground: Americans & Their Battlefields. 2nd ed. Edward T. Linenthal. (Illus.). 320p. 1991. text ed. 29.95 (*0-252-01783-8*) U of Ill Pr.

Sacred Ground: Americans & Their Battlefields. 2nd ed. Edward T. Linenthal. LC 93-23925. (Illus.). 320p. 1993. 19.95 (*0-252-06171-3*) U of Ill Pr.

Sacred Ground: Writings about Home. Ed. by Barbara Bonner. LC 96-34814. 385p. (Orig.). 1996. pap. 17.95 (*1-57131-010-X*) Milkweed Ed.

Sacred Ground to Sacred Space: Visionary Ecology, Perennial Wisdom, Environmental Ritual & Art. Rowena P Kryder. (Illus.). 308p. 1994. pap. 24.95 (*1-879181-20-7*) Bear & Co.

Sacred Grove: Mysteries of the Forest. Yvonne Aburrow. 1994. pap. 22.95 (*1-898307-12-1*) Holmes Pub.

Sacred Groves & Ravaged Gardens: The Fiction of Eudora Welty, Carson McCullers & Flannery O'Connor. Louise H. Westling. LC 84-16434. (Illus.). 231p. 1985. reprint ed. pap. 65.90 (*0-7837-9755-9*, 2060483) Bks Demand.

Sacred Harp. Benjamin F. White. 432p. reprint ed. lib. bdg. 59.00 (*0-685-14778-9*) Rprt Serv.

Sacred Harp: A Tradition & Its Music. Buell E. Cobb, Jr. LC 77-6323. (Brown Thrasher Bks.). 272p. 1988. reprint ed. pap. 14.95 (*0-8203-1022-0*) U of Ga Pr.

Sacred Harvest: Ojibway Wild Rice Gathering. Gordon Regguinti. (We Are Still Here: Native Americans Today Ser.). (Illus.). 48p. (J). (gr. 3-6). 1992. lib. bdg. 19.95 (*0-8225-2650-6*, Lerner Publctns) Lerner Group.

Sacred Harvest: Ojibway Wild Rice Gathering. Gordon Regguinti. (J). (gr. 4-7). 1992. pap. 6.95 (*0-8225-9620-2*, Lerner Publctns) Lerner Group.

***Sacred Heart.** Montecino. 1997. 23.00 (*0-671-01539-7*, PB Hardcover) PB.

***Sacred Heart: An Atlas of the Body Seen Through Invasive Surgery.** Max Aguilera-Hellweg. LC 97-5910. 1997. 50.00 (*0-8212-2377-1*) Little.

Sacred Heart & the Priesthood. Louise M. De La Touche. LC 79-90487. 1981. reprint ed. pap. 9.00 (*0-89555-128-4*) TAN Bks Pubs.

Sacred Heart Church. Tim I. Purdy. (Illus.). 105p. 1995. pap. 10.00 (*0-938373-16-1*) Lahontan Images.

Sacred Heart Home Enthronement Prayers. Robert Scherer & Anne Scherer. 1993. 1.60 (*1-56036-073-9*, 37000) AMI Pr.

Sacred Heart of Christmas. 2nd ed. Flower A. Newhouse. Ed. by Athene Bengtson. LC 78-74956. (Illus.). 93p. 1978. pap. 10.00 (*0-910378-14-2*) Christward.

Sacred Heart of Jesus & the Redemption of the World. Bernard Haring. (C). 1988. 39.00 (*0-85439-225-4*, Pub. by St Paul Pubns UK) St Mut.

Sacred Hearts. Greg Boyd. LC 96-76622. 128p. 1996. pap. 13.00 (*1-57650-049-7*) Hi Jinx Pr.

***Sacred Hearts.** Colleen Curran. LC 90-175668. 1997. pap. text ed. 9.95 (*0-88754-484-3*, Pub. by Playwrights CN Pr CN) Theatre Comm.

Sacred Hearts. W. T. Graves. 192p. (Orig.). 1997. pap. 11.95 (*0-89754-118-9*) Dan River Pr.

Sacred Hearts. Alison Joseph. 256p. 1996. 22.95 (*0-312-14405-9*) St Martin.

***Sacred Hearts: Daily Reflections for Divine Renegades.** Sterling Thompson. LC 96-72360. (Illus.). xii, 264p. (Orig.). 1997. pap. 12.95 (*0-9656128-0-5*) Quantum Mind Pubns.

Sacred Hearts: Poems. Phebe Hanson. LC 85-61269. 48p. 1985. pap. 5.00 (*0-915943-08-5*) Milkweed Ed.

***Sacred Heritage: Influence of Shamanism on Analytical Psychology.** Ed. by Donald Sandner & Steve Wong. LC 97-12520. 320p. 1996. pap. 17.95 (*0-415-91516-3*, Routledge NY) Routledge.

***Sacred Heritage: Influence of Shamanism on Analytical Psychology.** Ed. by Donald Sandner & Steve Wong. LC 97-12520. 288p. (C). 1996. text ed. 69.95 (*0-415-91515-5*, Routledge NY) Routledge.

***Sacred Hindu Symbols.** Gautam Chatterjee. (C). 1996. 28.00 (*81-7017-320-5*, Pub. by Abhinav II) S Asia.

Sacred History & Earth Prophecies. Dinawa. Ed. by Sindja. LC 96-68507. (Illus.). 232p. (Orig.). 1997. pap. 13.95 (*1-886966-07-9*) In Print.

***Sacred History & Sacred Texts: A Symposium in Honour of A. S. van der Woude.** Ed. by J. N. Bremmer & F. Garcia Martinez. (Contributions to Biblical Exegesis & Theology Ser.: Vol. 5). 183p. 1992. pap. 35.75 (*90-390-0015-8*, Pub. by KOK Pharos NE) Eisenbrauns.

***Sacred Honor.** Bennett. 1997. 25.00 (*0-684-84138-X*) S&S Trade.

Sacred Honor: Colin Powell. David Roth. 320p. 1994. mass mkt. 6.50 (*0-06-100849-4*) HarpC.

Sacred Honor: Colin Powell: The Inside Account of His Life & Triumphs. David Roth. (Illus.). 272p. 1993. 14.99 (*0-310-61508-9*) Zondervan.

Sacred Honor: Colin Powell: The Inside Account of His Life & Triumphs. David Roth. LC 92-50708. (Illus.). 272p. 1993. 19.99 (*0-310-60480-X*) Zondervan.

***Sacred Honor: The Moral Thought of America's Founders.** William J. Bennett. 1997. 25.00 (*0-8054-0149-0*) Broadman.

Sacred Honor - Colin Powell: The Inside Account of His Life & Triumphs. David Roth. 256p. 1996. reprint ed. pap. 10.99 (*0-310-20656-1*) Zondervan.

Sacred Hoop. Christopher Sergel & John G. Neihardt. 1995. 3.00 (*0-87129-447-8*, SA8) Dramatic Pub.

Sacred Hoop: A Cycle of Earth Tales. Bill Broder. LC 91-33694. (Illus.). 240p. 1992. reprint ed. pap. 12.00 (*0-87156-583-8*) Sierra.

Sacred Hoop: Recovering the Feminine in American Indian Traditions. Paula G. Allen. LC 92-6332. 336p. 1992. pap. 15.00 (*0-8070-4617-5*) Beacon Pr.

Sacred Hoops: Spiritual Lessons of a Hardwood Warrior. Phil Jackson. LC 95-34543. 224p. 1995. 22.95 (*0-7868-6206-8*) Hyperion.

Sacred Hoops: Spiritual Lessons of a Hardwood Warrior. Phil Jackson. 240p. 1996. pap. 12.95 (*0-7868-8200-X*) Hyperion.

Sacred Hour of Song. Ed. by Mack Harrell. 67p. 1939. pap. 11.95 (*0-8258-0153-2*, 02933) Fischer Inc NY.

Sacred Hub: Living in Your Real Self. Robert Rabbin. 132p. 1996. 16.00 (*0-89594-837-0*) Crossing Pr.

Sacred Hunger. Barry Unsworth. 1993. pap. 12.95 (*0-393-31114-7*) Norton.

Sacred Identity: Exploring a Theology of the Person. Jane Kopas. LC 94-18149. 176p. 1994. pap. 11.95 (*0-8091-3497-7*) Paulist Pr.

Sacred Image East & West. Ed. by Robert G. Ousterhout & Leslie Brubaker. LC 93-43343. (Illinois Byzantine Studies: Vol. 4). 320p. 1994. text ed. 29.95 (*0-252-02096-0*) U of Ill Pr.

Sacred Images: A Vision of Native American Rock Art. Leslie G. Kelen & David Sucec. (Illus.). 112p. (Orig.). 1996. pap. 24.95 (*0-87905-734-3*) Gibbs Smith Pub.

Sacred Images: Studies in Jewish Art from Antiquity to the Middle Ages. Joseph Gutmann. (Collected Studies: No. CS303). (Illus.). 286p. (C). 1989. reprint ed. text ed. 103.95 (*0-86078-251-4*, Pub. by Variorum UK) Ashgate Pub Co.

Sacred in a Secular Age: Toward Revision in the Scientific Study of Religion. Ed. by Philip E. Hammond. LC 84-16470. 380p. 1985. pap. 14.95 (*0-520-05343-5*) U CA Pr.

Sacred in the Simple: Making Mantras Part of Christian Living. Mary L. Kownacki. 32p. 1995. pap. 3.95 (*0-89243-780-4*) Liguori Pubns.

Sacred Influences: Spiritual Action in Human Life. J. G. Bennett. LC 89-60084. 96p. 1989. reprint ed. pap. 10.00 (*0-9621901-0-1*) Bennett Bks.

Sacred Interconnections: Postmodern Spirituality, Political Economy & Art. Ed. by David R. Griffin. LC 89-34234. (SUNY Series in Constructive Postmodern Thought). 227p. 1990. text ed. 59.50 (*0-7914-0231-2*); pap. text ed. 19.95 (*0-7914-0232-0*) State U NY Pr.

Sacred Intimacy. Brenton Yorgason & Margaret Yorgason. LC 89-38391. 72p. 1989. 10.95 (*0-87579-273-1*) Deseret Bk.

***Sacred Journey: A Daily Journal - 1998.** Cheryl Thiele. 270p. 1997. spiral bd. 17.95 (*0-9651701-1-X*) Creative Art Srvs.

Sacred Journey: A Daily Journal for Self-Transformation 1997. Cheryl Thiele. (Illus.). 260p. 1996. spiral bd. 17.95 (*0-9651701-0-1*) Creative Art Srvs.

Sacred Journey: A Memoir of Early Days. Frederick Buechner. LC 91-55089. 128p. 1991. reprint ed. pap. 12.00 (*0-06-061183-9*) Harper SF.

Sacred Journey: Prayers & Songs of Native America. Ed. & Selected by Peg Streep. LC 94-23742. (Illus.). 104p. 1995. 12.95 (*0-8212-2160-4*) Bulfinch Pr.

Sacred Journey: The Jewish Quest for a Perfect World. David M. Elcott. LC 94-43471. 232p. 1996. pap. 24.95 (*1-56821-386-7*) Aronson.

***Sacred Journey: You & Your Higher Self.** 2nd ed. Lazaris. 188p. 1987. reprint ed. pap. 11.95 (*1-55638-080-1*, NPN Pub) Concept Synergy.

Sacred Journey of the Peaceful Warrior. Dan Millman. Ed. by Nancy Carleton. LC 91-11234. 252p. 1991. 19.95 (*0-915811-34-0*); pap. 11.95 (*0-915811-33-2*) H J Kramer Inc.

Sacred Journeys. Jennifer Westwood. LC 96-44803. 1997. 35.00 (*0-8050-4845-6*) H Holt & Co.

Sacred Journeys: A Woman's Book of Daily Prayer. Jan L. Richardson. 448p. 1995. pap. 14.95 (*0-8358-0709-6*) Upper Room Bks.

Sacred Journeys: Conversion & Commitment to Divine Light Mission. James V. Downton, Jr. LC 79-546. (Illus.). 1979. text ed. 49.50 (*0-231-04198-5*) Col U Pr.

Sacred Journeys: The Anthropology of Pilgrimage. Alan E. Morinis. LC 91-36833. (Contributions to the Study of Anthropology Ser.: No. 7). 336p. 1992. text ed. 55.00 (*0-313-27879-2*, MJU/, Greenwood Pr) Greenwood.

Sacred Keeper: A Biography of Patrick Kavanagh. Peter Kavanagh. LC 84-61576. (Irish Art Ser.). 403p. (Orig.). 1986. 25.00 (*0-915032-31-7*); pap. 15.95 (*0-915032-32-5*) Natl Poet Foun.

***Sacred Knowledge.** Shah Waliullah. 105p. 1996. pap. 14.95 (*0-614-21337-1*, 1345) Kazi Pubns.

Sacred Knowledge: The Altaf Al-Quds of Shah Waliullah. Shah Waliullah. Tr. by G. N. Jalbani & David L. Pendlebury. 1982. 22.00 (*0-900860-93-6*, Pub. by Octagon Pr UK) ISHK.

Sacred Kural. 2nd ed. Ed. & Tr. by H. A. Popley. Orig. Title: The Tamil Veda of Tiruvalluvar. 159p. pap. 2.80 (*0-88253-386-X*) Ind-US Inc.

Sacred Kurral of Tiruvalluva Nayanar. G. U. Pope. 448p. 1986. reprint ed. 22.00 (*0-8364-1681-3*, Pub. by Abhinav II) S Asia.

Sacred Lake, 3 bks., Set. L. Marie Swann. (Illus.). (J). (gr. 3-4). 1992. pap. text ed. 25.00 (*1-882156-05-6*) Eye Of The Eagle.

Sacred Lake: A History of the Washo Tribe (Native American) Prior to the Coming of the Europeans. L. Marie Swann. 65p. (J). (gr. 3-4). 1992. reprint ed. pap. text ed. 12.00 (*1-882156-00-5*); reprint ed. lib. bdg. 14.00 (*1-882156-01-3*) Eye Of The Eagle.

Sacred Lake Activity Book: Activities to Accompany Reading "The Sacred Lake" Marie L. Swann. 51p. (J). (gr. 3-4). 1992. reprint ed. student ed. 8.00 (*1-882156-04-8*) Eye Of The Eagle.

Sacred Land, Sacred Sex - Rapture of the Deep: Concerning Deep Ecology & Celebrating Life. Dolores LaChapelle. 384p. (C). 1992. reprint ed. pap. 24.95 (*1-882308-11-5*) Kivaki Pr.

Sacred Land, Sacred View: Navajo Perceptions of the Four Corners Region. Robert S. McPherson. LC 91-33322. (Charles Redd Monographs in Western History Ser.: Vol. 19). (Illus.). viii, 151p. 1992. pap. 8.95 (*1-56085-008-6*, C Redd Ctr Wstrn Studies) Signature Bks.

Sacred Lands of the Southwest. Harvey Lloyd. LC 95-30602. (Illus.). 224p. 1995. 60.00 (*1-885254-11-3*) Monacelli Pr.

Sacred Lands of the Southwest, 4 vols., Set. Harvey Lloyd. LC 95-30602. (Illus.). 224p. 1995. 240.00 (*1-885254-18-0*) Monacelli Pr.

Sacred Landscape. Fredric Lehrman. (Illus.). 128p. 1995. pap. 29.95 (*0-89087-542-1*) Celestial Arts.

Sacred Landscape. deluxe ed. Fredric Lehrman. (Illus.). 128p. 1989. boxed 100.00 (*0-89087-549-9*) Celestial Arts.

Sacred Language: The Nature of Supernatural Discourse in Lakota. William K. Powers. LC 86-40079. (Civilization of the American Indian Ser.: Vol. 179). (Illus.). 264p. 1992. pap. 14.95 (*0-8061-2458-X*) U of Okla Pr.

***Sacred Leaves of Candomble: African Magic, Medicine, & Religion in Brazil.** Robert A. Voeks. LC 96-51297. (Illus.). 256p. 1997. pap. 17.95 (*0-292-78731-6*) U of Tex Pr.

***Sacred Leaves of Candomble: African Magic, Medicine, & Religion in Brazil.** Robert A. Voeks. (Illus.). 256p. 1997. 37.50 (*0-292-78730-8*) U of Tex Pr.

Sacred Lies & Silences: A Psychology of Religious Disguise. Vernon Ruland. LC 93-34712. 168p. (Orig.). 1994. pap. text ed. 10.95 (*0-8146-5847-4*, M Glazier) Liturgical Pr.

Sacred Lips of the Bronx. Douglas Sadownick. LC 95-15236. 1995. pap. 9.95 (*0-312-13165-8*) St Martin.

***Sacred Liturgy: Mediator Dei.** Pope Pius XII. 80p. pap. 2.50 (*0-8198-6924-4*) Pauline Bks.

***Sacred Living: A Daily Guide.** rev. ed. Robin H. Lysne. LC 97-15645. 256p. 1997. 14.95 (*1-57324-099-0*) Conari Press.

Sacred Love Affair. Ma P. Smita. (Illus.). 80p. 1996. pap. 13.00 (*0-8059-3891-5*) Dorrance.

Sacred Magic of the Angels. David Goddard. LC 96-3310. (Illus.). 256p. (Orig.). 1996. pap. 14.95 (*0-87728-862-3*) Weiser.

***Sacred Mandates of Conscience: Interpretations of the Baptist Faith & Message.** Jeff B. Pool. LC 97-11346. 1997. write for info. (*1-57312-165-7*) Smyth & Helwys.

Sacred Marriage: Honoring the God & Goddess Within Each Other. Lira Silbury. LC 94-40819. (Illus.). 278p. 1995. pap. 14.95 (*1-56718-654-8*) Llewellyn Pubns.

Sacred Marriage: Psychic Integration in the Faerie Queene. Benjamin G. Lockerd, Jr. LC 85-48293. (Illus.). 216p. 1987. 35.00 (*0-8387-5106-7*) Bucknell U Pr.

***Sacred Marriage: The Wisdom of the Song of Songs.** Nicholas Ayo. 1997. 29.95 (*0-8264-1030-8*) Continuum.

Sacred Marriage of a Hindu Goddess. William P. Harman. LC 87-46092. (Religion in Asia & Africa Ser.). 248p. reprint ed. pap. 70.70 (*0-7837-3711-4*, 2057889) Bks Demand.

Sacred Mask, Sacred Dance: Evan John Jones & Chas Clifton. E. J. Jones. Ed. by Charles Clifton. LC 96-40945. (Craft Ser.). (Illus.). 224p. (Orig.). 1997. pap. 19.95 (*1-56718-373-5*) Llewellyn Pubns.

Sacred Mirror: A Spiritual Diary. Margery Eyre. 94p. 8000. 10.95 (*0-86140-068-2*, Pub. by Colin Smythe Ltd UK) Dufour.

Sacred Mirrors. Alexander Grey et al. (Illus.). 96p. 1990. 39.95 (*0-89281-257-5*); pap. 29.95 (*0-89281-314-8*) Inner Tradit.

Sacred Moments, Vol. 75. 64p. Date not set. pap. 6.95 (*0-7935-0541-0*, 00100568) H Leonard.

***Sacred Moments: Daily Meditations on the Virtues.** Linda K. Popov. LC 97-17813. (Orig.). 1997. pap. 12.95 (*0-452-27811-2*, Plume) NAL-Dutton.

Sacred Moments: Daily Meditations on the Virtues. Linda K. Popov. 480p. (Orig.). 1996. pap. 14.95 (*0-9646633-0-9*) Virtues Comm.

Sacred Moments: Tales from the Jewish Life Cycle. Ed. by Ronald H. Isaacs & Kerry M. Olitzky. LC 94-18553. 272p. 1995. 25.00 (*1-56821-282-8*) Aronson.

Sacred Monsters. Susan Hudson. write for info. (*0-517-59847-7*) Crown Pub Group.

***Sacred Monsters.** Susan Hudson. 1998. pap. write for info. (*0-517-88696-0*) Crown Pub Group.

Sacred Mountain of Colombia's Kogi Indians. Gerardo Reichel-Dolmatoff. LC 90-2138. (Iconography of Religions Ser.: Vol. IX, Pt. 2). (Illus.). 1990. pap. 43.00 (*90-04-09274-9*) E J Brill.

Sacred Mountain of Tibet: On Pilgrimage to Mount Kailas. Russell Johnson & Kerry Moran. (Illus.). 128p. 1989. 24.95 (*0-89281-325-3*, Park St Pr) Inner Tradit.

Sacred Mountain, Vol. 1: Encounters with the Vietnam Beast, 1979-1984. Edward Tick. LC 89-92376. 119p. (Orig.). 1989. 19.95 (*0-944164-01-3*); pap. 9.95 (*0-944164-00-5*) Moon Bear Pr.

Sacred Mountains in Chinese Art. Kiyohiko Munakata. (Illus.). 208p. (Orig.). 1991. pap. 39.95 (*0-252-06188-8*) U of Ill Pr.

Sacred Mountains of Asia. John Einarsen. 1995. pap. 16.00 (*1-57062-088-1*) Shambhala Pubns.

Sacred Mountains of the World. Edwin Bernbaum. LC 90-8038. 1990. 50.00 (*0-87156-712-1*) Sierra.

Sacred Mountains of the World. Edwin Bernbaum. LC 90-8038. (Illus.). 320p. 1992. reprint ed. pap. 25.00 (*0-87156-508-0*) Sierra.

***Sacred Music from Tudor & Elizabethan England for Guitar.** Richard Turner. (Editiones Classicae Ser.). 1993. pap. 17.95 incl. audio (*0-7866-1113-8*, 94808P) Mel Bay.

Sacred Music of Christmas: Carols for the Twenty-First Century. 2nd rev. ed. Ed. by Genia P. Haddon. (Christian-Feminist Resources Ser.). 56p. 1994. pap. 9.95 (*1-881311-08-2*) Plus Pubns CT.

Sacred Mysteries: Sacramental Principles & Liturgical Practice. Dennis C. Smolarski. LC 94-41024. 224p. (Orig.). 1995. pap. 12.95 (*0-8091-3551-5*) Paulist Pr.

Sacred Mysteries among the Mayas & Quiches: Their Relation to the Sacred Mysteries of Egypt, Greece, Chaldea & India. Augustus LePlongeon. 1991. lib. bdg. 79.95 (*0-8490-4555-X*) Gordon Pr.

Sacred Mysteries among the Mayas & the Quiches. Augustus LePlongeon. 163p. 1976. reprint ed. spiral bd. 12.00 (*0-7873-0554-5*) Hlth Research.

Sacred Myths: Stories of World Religions. Marilyn McFarlane. (Illus.). 19p. (J). (gr. 4 up). 1996. 26.95 (*0-9638327-7-8*) Sibyl Pubns.

Sacred Narrative: Reading in the Theory of Myth. Ed. by Alan Dundes. LC 83-17921. (Illus.). ix, 352p. 1984. pap. 16.00 (*0-520-05192-0*) U CA Pr.

Sacred Narrative: Readings in the Theory of Myth. Ed. by Alan Dundes. LC 83-17921. (Illus.). 362p. reprint ed. pap. 103.20 (*0-7837-4817-5*, 2044464) Bks Demand.

Sacred Orgasms: Teachings from the Heart, Vol. 3. 2nd ed. Kenneth R. Stubbs. (Illus.). 79p. (Orig.). 1992. pap. 18.95 (*0-939263-07-6*) Secret Garden.

***Sacred Origins.** Charles Panati. 1996. pap. write for info. (*0-14-019544-0*) Viking Penguin.

Sacred Origins of Profound Things. Charles Panati. LC 96-14594. (Illus.). 608p. 1996. pap. 14.95 (*0-14-019533-5*) Viking Penguin.

***Sacred Pampering Principles: African American Woman's Guide to Self Care & Inner Renewal.** Debrena J. Gandy. 1997. 22.00 (*0-688-14571-X*) Morrow.

***Sacred Pampering Principles: An African-American Woman's Guide to Self-Care & Inner Renewal.** Debrena J. Gandy. LC 96-27808. 224p. 1997. 22.00 (*0-688-14751-8*) Morrow.

***Sacred Passion: The Art of William Schickel.** Gregory Wolfe. LC 97-20750. 1997. write for info. (*0-268-01758-1*); pap. write for info. (*0-268-01760-3*) U of Notre Dame Pr.

Sacred Path: Spells, Prayers & Power Songs of the American Indians. John Bierhorst. LC 82-14118. 192p. (YA). (gr. 7 up). 1984. pap. 9.75 (*0-688-02647-8*, Morrow Junior) Morrow.

An Asterisk (*) at the beginning of an entry indicates that the title is appearing in BIP for the first time.

Sacred Path Workbook: New Teachings & Tools to Illuminate Your Personal Journey. Jamie Sams. LC 90-56440. (Illus.). 304p. (Orig.). 1991. pap. 16.00 (*0-06-250794-X*) Harper SF.

Sacred Paths: Essays on Wisdom. Georg Feuerstein. Ed. by Paul Cash. (Illus.). 272p. (Orig.). 1991. pap. 14.95 (*0-943914-56-6*) Larson Pubns.

Sacred Paths: Understanding the Religions of the World. 2nd ed. Theodore M. Ludwig. LC 95-40351. (Illus.). 560p. (C). 1995. text ed. 52.67 (*0-02-372175-8*, Macmillan Coll) P-H.

Sacred Paths & Muddy Places: Rediscovering Spirit in Nature. Stephen Altschuler. (Illus.). 242p. (Orig.). 1993. pap. 14.95 (*0-913299-92-8*) Stillpoint.

Sacred Paths of the East. Theodore M. Ludwig. (Illus.). 320p. (C). 1992. pap. text ed. 39.00 (*0-02-372163-4*, Macmillan Coll) P-H.

Sacred Paths of the West. Theodore M. Ludwig. LC 93-5914. (Illus.). 272p. (Orig.). (C). 1994. pap. text ed. 39.00 (*0-02-372181-2*, Macmillan Coll) P-H.

Sacred Pathways: Discover Your Soul's Path to God. Gary L. Thomas. LC 95-38502. 256p. 1996. 14.99 (*0-7852-7959-8*) Nelson.

Sacred Performances: Islam, Sexuality, & Sacrifice. M. E. Combs-Schilling. (Illus.). 390p. 1990. pap. text ed. 17.00 (*0-231-06975-8*) Col U Pr.

Sacred Pipe: Black Elk's Account of the Seven Rites of the Oglala Sioux. Ed. by Joseph E. Brown. LC 53-8810. (Civilization of the American Indian Ser.: No. 36). (Illus.). 176p. 1989. 27.95 (*0-8061-0272-1*); pap. 9.95 (*0-8061-2124-6*) U of Okla Pr.

Sacred Pipe/Black Elk, Holy Man of the Oglala. Brown & Michael F. Steltenkamp. (Illus.). 1996. 9.98 (*1-56731-088-5*, MJF Bks) Fine Comms.

Sacred Place. Ed. by Jean Holm & John W. Bowker. LC 94-13745. (Themes in Religious Studies). 1994. 45.00 (*1-85567-104-2*); pap. 16.95 (*1-85567-105-0*) St Martin.

Sacred Place: Witnessing the Holy in the Physical World. Ed. by W. Scott Olsen & Scott Cairns. 360p. 1996. 49.95 (*0-87480-523-6*); pap. 19.95 (*0-87480-524-4*) U of Utah Pr.

Sacred Place to Dwell: Living with Reverence upon the Earth. Henryk Skolimowski. 160p. 1993. pap. 13.95 (*1-85230-443-X*) Element MA.

Sacred Places. Jane Yolen. LC 92-30323. (Illus.). 40p. (J). (gr. 1-7). 1996. 16.00 (*0-15-269953-8*) HarBrace.

Sacred Places: American Tourist Attractions in the Nineteenth Century. John F. Sears. (Illus.). 256p. 1989. 27.95 (*0-19-505350-8*) OUP.

Sacred Places: How the Living Earth Seeks Our Friendship. James A. Swan. LC 89-33139. (Illus.). 240p. 1990. pap. 16.95 (*0-939680-66-1*) Bear & Co.

***Sacred Places: Science & the Study of Ancient Intangibles.** Brian Fagan. 1998. write for info. (*0-201-95991-7*) Addison-Wesley.

***Sacred Places & Profane Spaces: Essays in the Geographics of Judaism, Christianity & Islam.** Ed. by Jamie Scott. 194p. 1996. 45.00 (*0-614-21681-8*, 1395) Kazi Pubns.

Sacred Places & Profane Spaces: Essays in the Geographics of Judaism, Christianity, & Islam. Ed. by Jamie S. Scott & Paul Simpson-Housley. LC 90-19896. (Contributions to the Study of Religion Ser.: No. 30). 216p. 1991. text ed. 45.00 (*0-313-26329-9*, SCZ/, Greenwood Pr) Greenwood.

***Sacred Places & Profane Spaces: Essays in the Geographics of Judaism, Christiantiy & Islam.** Ed. by Jamie Scott. 194p. 1996. 45.00 (*0-614-21588-9*, 1395) Kazi Pubns.

Sacred Places & the Pilgrimage of Life. Lawrence Hoffman. (Meeting House Essays: Architecture & Art for Liturgy Ser.: No. 1). (Illus.). 58p. 1991. pap. 6.00 (*0-929650-49-2*, SACRED) Liturgy Tr Pubns.

Sacred Places in North America: A Journey into the Medicine Wheel. Courtney Milne. LC 94-44794. (Illus.). 128p. 1995. 27.50 (*1-55670-414-3*) Stewart Tabori & Chang.

Sacred Places of Our World Heritage. Mark Swadling. 272p. 1996. 39.95 (*0-646-22646-0*) Hrper-MacRae.

***Sacred Places Pilgrim Paths.** Robinson. 1997. 14.00 (*0-551-03101-8*, Pub. by Marshall Pickering) Harper SF.

***Sacred Places, Pilgrim Paths: An Anthology of Pilgrimage.** Martin Robinson. 288p. Date not set. pap. 14.00 (*0-551-03051-8*, Pub. by Marshall Pickering) Harper SF.

***Sacred Places, Sacred Spaces: The Geography of Pilgrimages.** Robert H. Stoddard & E. Alan Morinis. LC 96-47392. (Geoscience & Man Ser.). 1997. pap. write for info. (*0-938909-66-5*) Geosci Pubns LSU.

Sacred Plant Medicine: Explorations in Indigenous Herbalism. Stephen H. Buhner. 250p. 1996. 30.00 (*1-57098-085-3*) R Rinehart.

Sacred Plant Medicine: Explorations in Indigenous Herbalism. Stephen H. Buhner. LC 96-67085. 240p. 1996. pap. text ed. 18.95 (*1-57098-091-8*) R Rinehart.

Sacred Pleasure: Sex, Myth & the Politics of the Body-New Paths to Power & Love. Riane Eisler. LC 95-5861. 506p. 1995. 25.00 (*0-06-250293-X*, HarpT) HarpC.

Sacred Pleasure: Sex, Myth & the Politics of the Body-New Paths to Power & Love. Riane Eisler. LC 95-5861. 512p. 1996. pap. 15.00 (*0-06-250283-2*, HarpT) HarpC.

***Sacred Poems & Prayers of Love.** Mary Ford-Grabowsky. LC 97-25051. 1998. write for info. (*0-385-48702-9*) Doubleday.

***Sacred Poems of Tibet.** Thupten J. Geshe. 192p. 1997. 23.00 (*0-06-018693-3*) HarpC.

Sacred Poetry on the Path. Mary R. Doe. (Orig.). 1993. pap. 9.95 (*1-883448-00-X*) Rose Pr Pub.

Sacred Portable Now: The Divine Joy of Living in the Moment. Daniel Singer & Marcella B. Weiner. 128p. 1996. boxed 17.00 (*0-7615-0728-0*) Prima Pub.

Sacred Portal: A Primary Symbol in Ancient Judaic Art. Bernard Goldman. LC 86-10983. (Brown Classics in Judaica Ser.). (Illus.). 260p. (C). 1986. reprint ed. pap. text ed. 29.00 (*0-8191-5269-2*) U Pr of Amer.

Sacred Possessions: Vodou, Santeria, Obeah, & the Caribbean. Ed. by Margarite Fernandez-Olmos & Lizabeth Paravisini-Gebert. LC 96-18145. (Illus.). 325p. (C). 1997. text ed. 50.00 (*0-8135-2360-5*); pap. text ed. 17.95 (*0-8135-2361-3*) Rutgers U Pr.

Sacred Power: A Seeker's Guide to Kundalini. Swami Kripananda. LC 95-79046. (Illus.). 176p. (Orig.). 1995. pap. 9.95 (*0-911307-39-7*) SYDA Found.

Sacred Power in Your Name. Ted Andrews. LC 89-77238. (Practical Guide Ser.). 336p. (Orig.). 1990. pap. 12.95 (*0-87542-012-5*) Llewellyn Pubns.

Sacred Powers. Time-Life Books Editors. (American Indians Ser.). 1995. 19.95 (*0-8094-9739-5*) Time-Life.

***Sacred Practices for Conscious Living.** Nancy J. Napier. 240p. 1997. 25.00 (*0-393-04052-6*) Norton.

Sacred Prayers Drawn from the Psalms of David. Peter M. Vermigli. Ed. by John P. Donnelly & Joseph McLelland. LC 95-44461. (Peter Martyr Vermigli Library: Vol. III). 164p. 1996. 40.00 (*0-940474-36-0*) Sixteenth Cent.

Sacred Prey. Vivian Schilling. Ed. by Shari Lovendahl. LC 93-60833. 245p. 1994. 19.95 (*0-9637846-0-9*, 784605) Truman Pr.

Sacred Prey. Vivian Schilling. 1996. mass mkt. 5.50 (*0-312-95693-2*) Tor Bks.

Sacred Prostitute. Nancy Qualls-Corbett. 214p. 1995. pap. 18.00 (*0-919123-31-7*, Pub. by Inner City CN) BookWorld Dist.

***Sacred Psychotherapy.** Ronald L. Mann. 208p. (Orig.). 1997. pap. 14.95 (*1-57733-016-1*, Pelican Pond) B Dolphin Pub.

Sacred Queens & Women of Consequence: Rank, Gender, & Colonialism in the Hawaiian Islands. Jocelyn Linnekin. (Women & Culture Ser.). (Illus.). 296p. 1990. text ed. 42.50 (*0-472-09423-8*); pap. text ed. 17.95 (*0-472-06423-1*) U of Mich Pr.

Sacred Quest: An Invitation to the Study of Religion. 2nd ed. Lawrence Cunningham & John Kelsay. 224p. (C). 1994. pap. text ed. 25.00 (*0-02-326336-9*, Macmillan Coll) P-H.

Sacred Quest: The Life & Writings of Mary Butts. Ed. & Pref. by Christopher Wagstaff. LC 95-15818. (Illus.). 277p. 1995. 25.00 (*0-929701-45-3*) McPherson & Co.

Sacred Reading: The Ancient Art of Lectio Divina. Michael Casey. LC 95-44569. 160p. (Orig.). 1996. pap. 12.95 (*0-89243-891-6*, Triumph Books) Liguori Pubns.

Sacred Realm: The Emergence of the Synagogue in the Ancient World. Ed. by Steven Fine. (Illus.). 240p. 1996. 60.00 (*0-19-510224-X*); pap. 25.00 (*0-19-510225-8*) OUP.

Sacred Refuge. Ralph Romig. LC 80-14984. 1987. pap. 13.95 (*0-87949-189-2*) Ashley Bks.

Sacred Remains: American Attitudes Toward Death, 1799-1883. Gary Laderman. LC 96-10373. 1996. 28.50 (*0-300-06432-2*) Yale U Pr.

Sacred Remains: Myth, History, & Polity in Belau. Richard J. Parmentier. LC 87-6051. (Illus.). 368p. (Orig.). 1987. lib. bdg. 60.00 (*0-226-64695-5*) U Ch Pr.

Sacred Remains: Myth, History, & Polity in Belau. Richard J. Parmentier. LC 87-6051. (Illus.). 368p. (Orig.). 1988. pap. text ed. 19.50 (*0-226-64696-3*) U Ch Pr.

***Sacred Renaissance Music for Classic Guitar.** Richard Turner. (Editiones Classicae Ser.). 1993. pap. 15.95 incl. audio (*0-7866-1092-1*, 94689P) Mel Bay.

Sacred Revolt: The Muskogees' Struggle for a New World. Joel W. Martin. (Illus.). 224p. 1993. pap. 15.00 (*0-8070-5403-8*) Beacon Pr.

Sacred Rhetoric: The Christian Grand Style in the English Renaissance. Debora K. Shuger. 336p. 1988. text ed. 45.00 (*0-691-06736-8*) Princeton U Pr.

***Sacred Rhetoric: The Christian Grand Style in the English Renaissance.** Debora K. Shuger. LC 87-25755. reprint ed. pap. 85.50 (*0-608-04585-3*, 2065355) Bks Demand.

Sacred Ring: The Pagan Origins of British Folk Festivals & Customs. Michael Howard. 1995. pap. 19.95 (*1-898307-34-2*) Holmes Pub.

Sacred River. Ted Lewin. LC 94-18370. (Illus.). 32p. (J). (gr. 1-5). 1995. 14.95 (*0-395-69846-4*, Clarion Bks) HM.

Sacred River. Leonard A. Strong. LC 74-7049. (Studies in Joyce: No. 96). 1974. lib. bdg. 75.00 (*0-8383-1951-3*) M S G Haskell Hse.

***Sacred Romance: Drawing Closer to the Heart of God.** Brent Curtis & John Eldredge. 228p. 1997. pap. 12.99 (*0-7852-7342-5*, J Thoma Bks) Nelson.

Sacred Rose Tarot. Johanna Sherman. 56p. 1982. pap. 15.00 (*0-88079-012-1*) US Games Syst.

Sacred Round. Thelma Palmer. LC 85-18006. (Illus.). 68p. (Orig.). 1985. pap. 7.95 (*0-9615580-0-8*) Island Pubs WA.

Sacred Round. 2nd ed. Thelma Palmer. (Illus.). 68p. (Orig.). 1988. pap. 7.95 (*0-9615580-3-2*) Island Pubs WA.

***Sacred Rules of Management: How to Get Control of Your Time & Your Work.** Stanley E. Smith. Date not set. pap. write for info. (*0-9641089-8-4*) VanderWyk & Burnham.

***Sacred Rules of Management: How to Get Control of Your Time & Your Work.** Stanley E. Smith. LC 96-51965. 80p. 1997. 17.95 (*0-9641089-7-6*) VanderWyk & Burnham.

Sacred Sacrifice Vol. 150: Ritual Paradigms in Vedic Religion & Early Christianity. Rick F. Talbott. LC 93-35795. (American University Studies: Series IX). 356p. (C). 1995. text ed. 59.95 (*0-8204-2322-X*) P Lang Pubng.

Sacred Sage: How It Heals. pap. text ed. 4.00 (*0-9640229-0-7*) WolfWalker.

Sacred Science: The King of Pharaonic Theocracy. R. A. Schwaller De Lubicz. Tr. by A. VandenBroeck & Andre Vandenbroeck. LC 81-344. (Illus.). 318p. 1982. pap. 18.95 (*0-89281-222-2*) Inner Tradit.

Sacred Science of Numbers. Corinne Heline. 140p. 1981. reprint ed. pap. 7.95 (*0-87516-442-0*) DeVorss.

Sacred Scripture. 2nd ed. 215p. (Orig.). (JPN.). 1994. pap. 5.00 (*0-9636435-5-X*) M A P.

Sacred Scrolls of the Southern Ojibway. Selwyn H. Dewdney. LC 73-90150. (Illus.). 211p. reprint ed. pap. 60.20 (*0-8357-3991-0*, 2036690) Bks Demand.

***Sacred Sculpture of Thailand: The Alexander B. Griswold Collection, the Walters Art Gallery.** Hiram W. Woodward, Jr. (Illus.). 331p. 1997. 60.00 (*0-295-97665-9*) U of Wash Pr.

***Sacred Seasons: A Sourcebook for the Jewish Holidays.** Ronald H. Isaacs. LC 96-33635. 176p. 1997. pap. 20.00 (*0-7657-5963-2*) Aronson.

***Sacred Secrets: The Sanctity of Sex in Jewish Law & Lore.** Gershon Winkler. LC 97-19872. 1998. write for info. (*0-7657-9974-X*) Aronson.

Sacred Self: A Cultural Phenomenology of Charismatic Healing. Thomas J. Csordas. LC 93-34279. 1994. 40.00 (*0-520-08311-3*) U CA Pr.

***Sacred Self: A Cultural Phenomenology of Charismatic Healing.** Thomas J. Csordas. LC 93-34279. (Illus.). 1997. pap. 15.95 (*0-520-20884-6*) U CA Pr.

Sacred Self Workshop. Marianne Williamson. 1995. 19.95 (*1-879323-25-7*) Sound Horizons AV.

***Sacred Seven.** Amy Stout. 272p. (Orig.). 1996. mass mkt. 5.99 (*0-380-78186-7*, AvoNova) Avon.

***Sacred Sex.** Ed. by Robert Adkinson. LC 96-61177. (Sacred Symbols Ser.). (Illus.). 80p. 1997. 10.00 (*0-500-06027-4*) Thames Hudson.

Sacred Sex. John Burns & Twenty-Four Magazine Editors. (Illus.). 94p. spiral bd. 11.95 (*0-914896-39-3*) East Ridge Pr.

Sacred Sex. Twenty-Four Magazine Editors & John Burns. Ed. by Thomas R. White. (Illus.). 150p. (Orig.). 1975. pap. 4.95 (*0-914896-01-6*) East Ridge Pr.

Sacred Sex: Ecstatic Techniques for Empowering Relationships. Jwala, pseud. & Roul Smith. Ed. by Navatana. (Illus.). 144p. (Orig.). 1994. pap. write for info. (*1-885201-00-1*) Mandala CA.

Sacred Sexuality. A. Tad Mann. (Sacred Arts). 1995. pap. 24.95 (*1-85230-658-0*) Element MA.

***Sacred Shadows.** Maxine Schur. LC 97-5037. (J). 1997. pap. 14.99 (*0-8037-2295-8*) Dial Bks Young.

***Sacred Shadows.** Maxine R. Schur. Date not set. pap. 14.99 (*0-8037-1800-4*) Dial Bks Young.

Sacred Sins. Nora Roberts. 304p. (Orig.). 1987. mass mkt. 6.50 (*0-553-26574-1*) Bantam.

Sacred Sites of the West. Bernyce Barlow. LC 96-28359. (Illus.). 240p. (Orig.). 1996. pap. 19.95 (*1-56718-056-6*) Llewellyn Pubns.

***Sacred Sites of the West: A Guide to Mystical Centers.** Ed. by Frank Joseph. 176p. (Orig.). 1997. pap. 14.95 (*0-88839-404-7*) Hancock House.

Sacred Sites, Sacred Places. Ed. by David L. Carmichael et al. LC 93-33400. (One World Archaeology Ser.: No. 23). (Illus.). 336p. (C). 1994. text ed. 62.95 (*0-415-09603-0*, B3584, Routledge NY) Routledge.

***Sacred Skies.** Finn Bevan. LC 97-11694. (Landscapes of Legend Ser.). (J). 1997. write for info. (*0-516-20351-7*) Childrens.

Sacred Sleep: Dreams & the Divine. Scott Cunningham. LC 92-14862. 193p. 1992. pap. 12.95 (*0-89594-564-9*) Crossing Pr.

***Sacred Song: The Art of the Illuminated Choir Book.** LC 96-52994. 1997. write for info. (*0-8076-1422-X*) Braziller.

Sacred Song from the Byzantine Pulpit: Romanos the Melodist. R. J. Schork. LC 95-2375. 248p. 1995. 44.95 (*0-8130-1363-1*) U Press Fla.

Sacred Song of the Hermit Thrush. Tehanetorens. LC 93-945. (Illus.). 64p. (J). (gr. 3 up). 1993. pap. 5.95 (*0-913990-36-1*) Book Pub Co.

Sacred Songs, EFS36. Ed. by Michel Whitehall. (Illus.). 192p. 1940. pap. 14.95 (*0-8256-2036-8*, AM40189) Music Sales.

***Sacred Songs of India.** V. K. Subramanian. 1996. 28.00 (*81-7017-321-3*, Pub. by Abhinav II) S Asia.

Sacred Sorrows: Embracing & Transforming Depression. John E. Nelson & Andrea Nelson. (New Consciousness Reader Ser.). 288p. (Orig.). 1996. pap. 14.95 (*0-87477-822-0*, Tarcher Putnam) Putnam Pub Group.

Sacred Sound: Music in Religious Thought & Practice. Ed. by Joyce L. Irwin. LC 83-15390. (American Academy of Religion, Thematic Studies). 180p. (C). 1984. 34.95 (*0-89130-655-2*, 01 25 01) Scholars Pr GA.

Sacred Sound & Social Change: Liturgical Music in Jewish & Christian Experience. Janet R. Walton. LC 91-51120. (Two Liturgical Traditions Ser.: Vol. 3). (C). 1993. pap. text ed. 23.00 (*0-268-01746-8*) U of Notre Dame Pr.

Sacred Sounds, Vol. 22. 64p. Date not set. pap. 6.95 (*0-7935-0533-X*, 00100570) H Leonard.

Sacred Sounds: Transformation Through Music & Word. Ted Andrews. LC 91-45962. (Practical Guide to Personal Power Ser.). (Illus.). 232p. 1992. pap. 9.95 (*0-87542-018-4*) Llewellyn Pubns.

Sacred Sounds for All Seasons. Gloria Baker. (Illus.). 121p. (Orig.). (C). pap. 14.95 (*1-56516-034-7*) H Leonard.

Sacred Space. Marsha Rowe. 1993. pap. 14.99 (*1-85242-260-2*) Serpents Tail.

Sacred Space: A Feminist Vision of Astrology. Geraldine H. Hanon. LC 90-49791. 208p. (Orig.). 1990. pap. 9.95 (*0-932379-86-9*); lib. bdg. 20.95 (*0-932379-87-7*) Firebrand Bks.

Sacred Space: An Aesthetic for the Liturgical Environment. Dennis McNally. LC 85-51230. 215p. (Orig.). (C). 1990. pap. 14.95 (*0-932269-45-1*); text ed. 34.95 (*1-55605-154-9*) Wyndham Hall.

Sacred Space: An Approach to the Theology of the Epistle to the Hebrews. Marie E. Isaacs. (NT Supplement Ser.: No. 73). 253p. (C). 1992. 60.00 (*1-85075-356-3*, Pub. by Sheffield Acad UK) CUP Services.

Sacred Space: Clearing & Enhancing the Energy of Your Home. Denise Linn. 320p. 1996. pap. 12.00 (*0-345-39769-X*) Ballantine.

Sacred Space: Photographs from the Mississippi Delta. Tom Rankin. LC 93-6973. (Illus.). 96p. 1993. pap. 19.95 (*0-87805-641-6*); text ed. 35.00 (*0-87805-640-8*) U Pr of Miss.

Sacred Space: Shrine, City, Land. Werblowsky R. Zwi. 320p. (C). 1997. 45.00 (*0-8147-4680-2*) NYU Pr.

***Sacred Space & Structural Style: Socio-Religious Ideology in Nineteenth-Century Central Canada.** Vicki Bennett. (Illus.). 328p. 1997. pap. 35.00 (*0-7766-0440-6*, Pub. by Univ Ottawa Pr CN) Paul & Co Pubs.

Sacred Spaces & Other Places: A Guide to Grottos & Sculptural Environments in the Upper Midwest. Lisa Stone & James Zanzi. 200p. 1993. 29.95 (*0-9637817-0-7*); pap. 14.95 (*0-9637817-1-5*) Schl Art Inst.

Sacred Springs. Christa Maxfield. (Orig.). 1997. pap. text ed. 10.95 (*1-57532-072-X*) Press-Tige Pub.

Sacred Stones. Terry John. 1994. pap. 21.00 (*1-86902-127-4*, Pub. by Gomer Pr UK) St Mut.

Sacred Stones. William Sarabande. (First Americans Ser.: No. 5). 608p. 1991. 5.99 (*0-553-29105-X*, Bantam Domain) Bantam.

Sacred Stones. Gershon Winkler. Ed. by Marlene Greenspan. (Illus.). 197p. (YA). (gr. 8 up). 1990. 16.95 (*0-910818-82-7*); pap. 12.95 (*0-910818-89-4*) Judaica Pr.

Sacred Stones, Sacred Places. Marianna Lines. 128p. (C). 1991. text ed. 95.00 (*0-685-49634-1*, Pub. by St Andrew UK) St Mut.

Sacred Stones, Sacred Places. Marianna Lines. (Illus.). 160p. (C). 1992. 65.00 (*0-685-60678-3*, Pub. by St Andrew UK) St Mut.

Sacred Stones, Sacred Places. Marianna Lines. 176p. 1993. 39.90 (*0-7152-0652-4*, Pub. by St Andrew UK) St Mut.

Sacred Stories: A Celebration of the Power of Stories to Transform & Heal. Ed. by Charles Simpkinson & Anne Simpkinson. LC 92-56135. 304p. 1993. pap. 14.00 (*0-06-250852-0*) Harper SF.

Sacred Stories of the Sweet Grass Cree. Leonard Bloomfield. LC 74-7933. reprint ed. 67.50 (*0-404-11821-6*) AMS Pr.

Sacred Strands: How Eight Women Came to Their Ministries. 2nd ed. (Illus.). 152p. 1995. pap. 10.95 (*1-883477-05-0*) Lone Oak MN.

Sacred Survival: The Civil Religion of American Jews. Jonathan S. Woocher. LC 85-45790. (Jewish Political & Social Studies). (Illus.). 254p. (C). 1986. 29.95 (*0-253-35041-7*) Ind U Pr.

Sacred Sword: A Novel about the Inquisition. Mayer Abramowitz. 384p. 1992. 15.95 (*965-229-079-3*) Gefen Bks.

Sacred Symbols of Mu. James Churchward. 1991. lib. bdg. 79.50 (*0-8490-4802-8*) Gordon Pr.

***Sacred Symbols of Mu.** Churchwood. 1996. write for info. (*0-85207-198-1*, Pub. by C W Daniel UK) Natl Bk Netwk.

Sacred Symbols of Mu. James Churchward. (Illus.). 307p. 1988. reprint ed. pap. 15.95 (*0-914732-24-2*) Bro Life Inc.

Sacred Symbols of the Ancients. Florence Campbell & Edith L. Randall. (Illus.). 200p. 1982. reprint ed. spiral bd. 21.95 (*0-87516-487-0*) DeVorss.

Sacred Symbols That Speak, Vol. I. Anthony M. Coniaris. 1986. pap. 9.95 (*0-937032-39-5*) Light&Life Pub Co MN.

Sacred Symbols That Speak, Vol. 2. Anthony M. Coniaris. 1987. pap. 9.95 (*0-937032-49-2*) Light&Life Pub Co MN.

Sacred Symphony: The Chanted Sermon of the Black Preacher. Jon M. Spencer. LC 87-29547. (Contributions in Afro-American & African Studies: No. 111). 160p. 1987. text ed. 45.00 (*0-313-25999-2*, SSX/, Greenwood Pr) Greenwood.

Sacred Tales of India. Dwijendra N. Neggi. (C). 1991. reprint ed. 8.50 (*0-685-48886-1*, Pub. by Asian Educ Servs II) S Asia.

Sacred Tarot: The Ancient Art of Card Reading & the Underlying Spiritual Science. C. C. Zain. LC 94-22401. (Brotherhood of Light Home Study Ser.: Course 6). (Illus.). 344p. 1994. pap. 14.95 (*0-87887-376-7*) Church of Light.

Sacred Tarot Unveiled. Allyson Walsh. (Illus.). 256p. (Orig.). 1994. student ed., pap. 18.95 (*0-9643075-0-2*) Allyson Univ.

Sacred Tears: Sentimentality in Victorian Literature. Fred Kaplan. 176p. 1987. text ed. 35.00 (*0-691-06700-7*) Princeton U Pr.

***Sacred Tensions: Modernity & Religious Transformation in Malaysia.** Raymond L. Lee & Susan E. Ackerman. LC 97-4725. (Studies in Comparative Religion). (Illus.). 190p. 1997. 29.95 (*1-57003-167-3*) U of SC Pr.

Sacred Texts of the World: A Universal Anthology. Ed. by Ninian Smart & Richard Hecht. LC 82-7375. 448p. (C). 1984. pap. 29.95 (*0-8245-0639-1*) Crossroad NY.

Sacred Theory of the Earth. Ed. by Thomas Frick. (Io Ser.: No. 36). (Illus.). 256p. 1985. pap. 12.95 (*0-938190-62-8*) North Atlantic.

Sacred Thread: Hinduism in Continuity & Diversity. John L. Brockington. 222p. 1981. pap. 15.00 (*0-85224-393-6*, Pub. by Edinburgh U Pr UK) Col U Pr.

Sacred Thread: Hinduism in Its Continuity & Diversity. John L. Brockington. (Illus.). 232p. 1996. pap. 17.00 (*0-7486-0830-3*, Pub. by Edinburgh U Pr UK) Col U Pr.

Sacred Thread: Modern Transmission of Hindu Traditions in India & Abroad. Ed. by Raymond B. Williams. LC 92-5733. 337p. 1990. pap. 17.00 (*0-89012-065-X*) Col U Pr.

Sacred Thread: Modern Transmission of Hindu Traditions in India & Abroad. Raymond B. Williams. LC 96-26863. 1996. write for info. (*0-231-10779-X*) Col U Pr.

Sacred Threads: Catholic Spirituality in Australia 1922-1962. Katherine Massam & Pauline Reilly. 290p. 1996. pap. 34.95 (*0-86840-183-8*, Pub. by New South Wales Univ Pr AT) Intl Spec Bk.

Sacred Tibet. Philip Rawson. LC 90-70359. (Art & Imagination Ser.). (Illus.). 96p. 1991. pap. 14.95 (*0-500-81032-X*) Thames Hudson.

Sacred Times. National Jewish Center for Learning & Leadership Staff. (Illus.). 132p. 1992. write for info. (*0-9633329-0-2*) Natl Jew Ctr Lrn & Ldership.

***Sacred Times: A New Approach to Festivals.** William Bloom. 144p. (Orig.). 1990. pap. 11.95 (*0-905249-76-3*, Pub. by Findhorn Pr UK) Words Distrib.

Sacred Tradition in the Orthodox Church. Lazarus Moore. 1984. pap. 3.95 (*0-937032-34-4*) Light&Life Pub Co MN.

Sacred Tree. Judie Bopp et al. LC 89-63193. (Illus.). 88p. 1990. pap. 10.95 (*0-941524-58-2*) Lotus Light.

Sacred Tree: The Tree in Religion & Myth. J. H. Philpot. 1977. lib. bdg. 250.00 (*0-8490-2553-2*) Gordon Pr.

Sacred Trees. Nathaniel Altman. LC 93-28182. (Illus.). 288p. (Orig.). 1994. pap. 16.00 (*0-87156-470-X*) Sierra.

***Sacred Trust.** SHaron Mignery. 320p. 1997. mass mkt. 5.50 (*0-8217-5566-8*, Zebra Kensgtn) Kensgtn Pub Corp.

***Sacred Trust.** Stolper. 14.99 (*0-89906-640-2*) Mesorah Pubns.

Sacred Trust: Ministering to Adult Survivors of Child Sexual Abuse. Dorothy W. Kimble. pap. 13.95 (*1-56699-120-X*, OD100) Alban Inst.

Sacred Trust: Nelson Poynter & the St. Petersburg Times. Robert N. Pierce. (Illus.). 408p. 1993. 39.95 (*0-8130-1234-1*) U Press Fla.

Sacred Trust: Parenting & Guardianship of Children & Creating Healthy Families. 109p. 7.95 (*1-880257-09-2*, SACR) BRAT Pub.

Sacred Trust: The Medieval Church As an Economic Firm. Robert B. Ekelund et al. (Illus.). 224p. 1996. 29.95 (*0-19-510337-8*) OUP.

Sacred Trust Vol. 1: Talmudic Age, Medieval Age, & Sephardic Age, Vol. 1. Eugene Labovitz & Annette Labovitz. LC 94-68316. 303p. 1995. pap. 18.00 (*0-914615-12-2*) I Nathan Pub Co.

Sacred Trust Vol. 2: Silver Age of Poland, Vol. 2. Eugene Labovitz & Annette Labovitz. 200p. 1995. pap. 12.00 (*0-914615-13-0*) I Nathan Pub Co.

Sacred Trust Vol. 3: America-Jewish Experience, Return to Israel Period, Vol. 3. Eugene Labovitz & Annette Labovitz. 240p. 1995. pap. 12.00 (*0-914615-14-9*) I Nathan Pub Co.

Sacred Trusts: Essays on Stewardship & Responsibility. Ed. by Michael Katakis. LC 93-872. (Illus.). 304p. 1993. pap. 17.95 (*1-56279-056-0*) Mercury Hse Inc.

Sacred Truths of the Doctrine & Covenants, Vol. 1. Leaun G. Otten & C. Max Caldwell. LC 82-71971. xi, 355p. 1993. 17.95 (*0-87579-783-0*) Deseret Bk.

Sacred Truths of the Doctrine & Covenants, Vol. 2. Leaun G. Otten & C. Max Caldwell. LC 82-71791. xii, 412p. 1993. 17.95 (*0-87579-784-9*) Deseret Bk.

Sacred Union of Citizens: George Washington's Farewell Address & the American Character. Matthew Spalding & Patrick J. Garrity. 256p. 1996. 27.95 (*0-8476-8261-7*) Rowman.

Sacred Verses for My Afrikan Queens. Afrikadzata Deku. LC 91-72661. (Sacred Afrikan Love Poetry Ser.). 73p. 1994. pap. 13.00 (*1-56454-000-6*) Cont Afrikan.

Sacred Vessel. Rolfe. 189p. 1978. 8.50 (*0-85435-324-0*, Pub. by C W Daniel UK) Natl Bk Netwk.

Sacred Vessel. Mona Rolfe. 140p. 12.95 (*0-8464-4286-8*) Beekman Pubs.

Sacred Vessels: The Cult of the Battleship & the Rise of the U. S. Navy. Robert L. O'Connell. LC 92-25712. 432p. (C). 1993. pap. 15.95 (*0-19-508006-8*) OUP.

Sacred Violence: A Reader's Companion to Cormac McCarthy. Ed. by Wade Hall & Rick Wallach. LC 94-61798. 200p. (Orig.). 1995. pap. 20.00 (*0-87404-233-X*) Tex Western.

Sacred Void. John De August. LC 96-60198. 198p. 1997. pap. 9.95 (*1-55523-798-3*) Winston-Derek.

Sacred Void: Spatial Images of Work & Ritual among the Giriama of Kenya. David Parkin. (Cambridge Studies in Social & Cultural Anthropology: No. 80). (Illus.). 280p. (C). 1991. text ed. 69.95 (*0-521-40466-5*) Cambridge U Pr.

Sacred War: Nationalism & Revolution in a Divided Vietnam. William J. Duiker. LC 94-14473. 1994. pap. text ed. write for info. (*0-07-018030-X*) McGraw.

***Sacred Water.** Leslie M. Silko. (Illus.). 88p. (C). 1994. per. 56.00 (*0-614-01628-2*) Flood Plain.

Sacred Water. 2nd ed. Leslie M. Silko. (Illus.). 88p. (C). 1994. pap. text ed. 24.00 (*0-9636554-4-2*) Flood Plain.

Sacred Wisdom. Gyeorgos C. Hatonn. 214p. (Orig.). 1995. pap. 6.00 (*1-56935-055-8*) Phoenix Source.

Sacred Woman, Sacred Dance: Awakening Spirituality Through Dance & Ritual. Iris J. Stewart. (Illus.). 304p. Date not set. pap. 24.95 (*0-89281-605-8*, Inner Trad) Inner Tradit.

Sacred Wood. A. Eliot. 1961. pap. 15.95 (*0-415-05087-1*) Routledge Chapman & Hall.

Sacred Wood. 7th ed. T. S. Eliot. 171p. 1960. pap. 13.95 (*0-416-67610-3*, NO. 2185) Routledge Chapman & Hall.

Sacred Word & Sacred Text: Scripture in World Religions. Harold G. Coward. LC 87-31321. 232p. 1988. reprint ed. pap. 66.20 (*0-7837-9857-1*, 2060586) Bks Demand.

***Sacred Words: A Selection of Spiritual Writings of All Ages.** Ed. by Paul Ladouceur. 272p. (Orig.). 1996. pap. 14.95 (*1-899171-65-7*, Pub. by Findhorn Pr UK) Words Distrib.

Sacred Words: A Study of Navajo Religion & Prayer. Sam D. Gill. LC 80-659. (Contributions in Intercultural & Comparative Studies: No. 4). (Illus.). xxvi, 257p. 1981. text ed. 55.00 (*0-313-22165-0*, GSW/, Greenwood Pr) Greenwood.

***Sacred World of the Celts: An Illustrated Guide to Celtic Spirituality & Mythology.** Nigel Pennick. LC 97-24736. 1997. write for info. (*0-89281-654-6*) Inner Tradit.

Sacred World of the Christian: Sensed in Faith. Mary A. Wagner. 160p. (Orig.). 1993. pap. text ed. 9.95 (*0-8146-2102-3*) Liturgical Pr.

Sacred Worlds: An Introduction to Geography & Religion. Chris C. Park. LC 93-36709. (Illus.). 336p. (C). 1994. pap. 25.00 (*0-415-09013-X*, A9828) Routledge.

Sacred Worlds: An Introduction to Geography & Religion. Chris C. Park. LC 93-36709. (Illus.). 352p. (C). 1994. text ed. 85.00 (*0-415-09012-1*, A9824) Routledge.

Sacred Writings. Ed. by Jean Holm & John Bowker. LC 94-15113. (Themes in Religious Studies). 1994. 45.00 (*1-85567-106-9*); pap. 16.95 (*1-85567-107-7*) St Martin.

Sacred Yew: Rediscovering the Ancient Tree of Life Through the Work of Allen Meredith. Anand Chetan & Diana Brueton. 256p. 1995. pap. 12.95 (*0-14-019476-2*, Arkana) Viking Penguin.

Sacredness & Authority of the Bible: Quarter 2 Workbook. Bill Patterson. (Growing Christian Disciples Ser.). 96p. (Orig.). 1989. teacher ed. 4.95 (*1-56794-017-X*, C2282T); student ed., pap. 3.95 (*1-56794-016-1*, C2282) Star Bible.

Sacrement of Joy. Christopher H. Cooke. (C). 1994. pap. 24.95 (*0-85305-331-6*, Pub. by J Arthur Ltd UK) St Mut.

Sacri Musicali Affetti, Op. 5. Barbara Strozzi. (Women Composers Ser.). 1987. 25.00 (*0-306-76195-5*) Da Capo.

***Sacrifice.** Clive Barker. 1996. write for info. (*0-614-24245-2*) HarpC.

Sacrifice. George Brown. 470p. 1996. pap. 5.95 (*0-09-933751-7*, Pub. by Arrow Bks UK) Trafalgar.

Sacrifice. John Farris. 384p. 1995. 5.99 (*0-8125-0956-0*) Tor Bks.

Sacrifice. Richard Kinion. 384p. 1995. mass mkt. 4.50 (*0-8217-5047-X*, Zebra Kensgtn) Kensgtn Pub Corp.

***Sacrifice.** Mitchell Smith. 1998. pap. 22.95 (*0-525-93979-2*) NAL-Dutton.

***Sacrifice.** Mitchell Smith. 1997. mass mkt. 6.99 (*0-451-18475-0*, Sig) NAL-Dutton.

Sacrifice. Rabindranath Tagore. 256p. 1985. 6.50 (*0-333-90354-4*) Asia Bk Corp.

Sacrifice. Andrew Vachss. 288p. 1996. pap. 11.00 (*0-679-76410-0*) Random.

***Sacrifice.** Cecilia Woloch. 62p. (Orig.). 1997. pap. 12.95 (*0-9649240-4-8*) Cahuenga Pr.

Sacrifice: Its Nature & Function. Henri Hubert & Marcel Mauss. Tr. by W. D. Halls. LC 64-12260. 174p. 1981. pap. text ed. 18.95 (*0-226-35679-5*) U Ch Pr.

Sacrifice: The First Book of the Fey. Kristine K. Rusch. 672p. 1996. mass mkt. 5.99 (*0-553-56894-9*, Spectra) Bantam.

Sacrifice & Redemption: Durham Essays in Theology. Ed. by S. W. Sykes. (Illus.). 280p. (C). 1991. text ed. 75.00 (*0-521-34033-0*) Cambridge U Pr.

Sacrifice & Sharing in the Philippine Highlands: Religion & Society among the Buid of Mindoro. Thomas Gibson. LC 85-15771. (London School of Economics Monographs on Social Anthropology: No. 57). (Illus.). (C). 1986. text ed. 49.95 (*0-485-19559-3*, Pub. by Athlone Pr UK) Humanities.

Sacrifice at Vicksburg: Letters from the Front. Susan T. Puck. LC 96-49465. 168p. Date not set. 24.95 (*1-57249-047-0*) White Mane Pub.

Sacrifice Consenting. W. Dickey. 60p. 1982. ring bd. 100.00 (*0-931757-10-X*); boxed 17.00 (*0-931757-09-6*) Pterodactyl Pr.

Sacrifice in Africa: A Structuralist Approach. Luc De Heusch. Tr. by Linda O'Brien & Alice Morton. LC 84-48487. (African Systems of Thought Ser.). 240p. 1985. 30.00 (*0-253-35038-7*) Ind U Pr.

Sacrifice in Surrealist Novel: The Impact of Early Theories of Primitive Religion on the Depiction of Violence in Modern Fiction. Alice Letvin. LC 90-23039. (Studies in Comparative Literature). 350p. 1991. reprint ed. 20.00 (*0-8240-5473-3*) Garland.

Sacrifice in the Bible. Roger T. Beckwith & Martin J. Selman. (Tyndale House Studies). 196p. (Orig.). (C). 1995. pap. 17.99 (*0-8010-2044-1*) Baker Bks.

Sacrifice of God: A Holistic Theory of Atonement. John Moses. 1994. pap. 21.95 (*1-85311-056-6*, Pub. by Canterbury Press Norwich UK) Morehouse Pub.

Sacrifice of Guam: 1919-1943. Don A. Farrell. Ed. by Phyllis Koontz. (Pictorial History of Guam Ser.). (Illus.). 260p. 1991. write for info. (*0-930839-02-1*) Micronesian.

Sacrifice of Human Being: British Rule & the Konds of Orissa. Felix Padel. 446p. 1996. text ed. 35.00 (*0-19-563640-6*) OUP.

Sacrifice of Isaac. Neil Gordon. LC 94-35370. 304p. 1995. 22.00 (*0-679-43704-5*) Random.

Sacrifice of Isaac. Neil Gordon. 400p. 1997. mass mkt. 6.50 (*0-553-57635-6*) Bantam.

Sacrifice of Isaac in the Spanish & Sephardic Romanceros. Albert Barugel. (American University Studies: Romance Languages & Literature: Ser. II, Vol. 116). 242p. (C). 1989. text ed. 49.95 (*0-8204-0954-5*) P Lang Pubng.

***Sacrifice of Praise.** 1997. write for info. (*0-614-30432-6*) Ukrain Cath Diocese Parma.

Sacrifice of Tamar. Naomi Ragen. 1994. 24.00 (*0-517-59561-3*, Crown) Crown Pub Group.

Sacrifice of Tamar. Naomi Ragen. 400p. 1995. mass mkt. 5.99 (*0-06-100948-2*, Harp PBks) HarpC.

Sacrifice of the Lilies. limited ed. Virginia Walker. (Illus.). 48p. (Orig.). 1985. pap. 4.95 (*0-9615628-0-3*) Tree Hse Pr.

Sacrifice Play. John Ballem. 256p. 1981. mass mkt. 2.25 (*0-449-14381-3*, GM) Fawcett.

Sacrifice to Attis: A Study of Sex & Civilization. W. A. Brend. 1973. 59.95 (*0-8490-0985-5*) Gordon Pr.

***Sacrifice We Offer.** Power. 39.95 (*0-567-09445-6*, Pub. by T & T Clark UK) Bks Intl VA.

Sacrificed for Honor: Italian Infant Abandonment & the Politics of Reproductive Control. David I. Kertzer. 272p. 1994. pap. 16.00 (*0-8070-5605-7*) Beacon Pr.

Sacrificed Life: Keys to Intimacy with God. Bobby Welch. 1992. pap. 8.99 (*0-8054-1018-X*, 4210-18) Broadman.

***Sacrificed Lives: Kristeva on Women & Violence.** Martha J. Reineke. LC 96-53642. 1997. write for info. (*0-253-33299-0*); lib. bdg. write for info. (*0-253-21128-X*) Ind U Pr.

Sacrificed Wife/Sacrificer's Wife: Women, Ritual, & Hospitality in Ancient India. Stephanie W. Jamison. 360p. (C). 1996. text ed. 58.00 (*0-19-509662-2*); pap. text ed. 24.95 (*0-19-509663-0*) OUP.

Sacrifices: Poems. Susan M. Whitmore. LC 92-27707. 64p. 1993. pap. 12.95 (*0-7734-0018-4*, Mellen Poetry Pr) E Mellen.

Sacrifices & Offerings in Ancient Israel: Studies in Their Social & Political Importance. Gary Anderson. LC 87-20498. (Harvard Semitic Museum Monographs). 174p. 1988. 15.95 (*1-55540-169-4*, 04-00-41) Scholars Pr GA.

Sacrificial Ideas in Greek Christian Writers. Frances M. Young. LC 78-61400. (Patristic Monograph: No. 5). 1979. pap. 10.00 (*0-915646-04-8*) N Amer Patristic Soc.

Sacrificial Lambs. Bill Sholin. 265p. 1994. 30.00 (*0-9641754-0-1*) Mtn View.

Sacrificial Lambs: Who Fought Like Lions. rev. ed. Bill Sholin. (Illus.). 1994. 29.95 (*0-9641754-1-X*) Mtn View.

Sacrificial Lambs Vol. 1: Alcohol's Human Road Kill. Dennis J. McDuffy. LC 96-94232. (Illus.). 224p. (Orig.). 1996. pap. 14.95 (*0-9651625-0-8*) D McDuffy.

Sacrificial Logics: Feminist Theory & the Critique of Identity. Allison Weir. (Thinking Gender Ser.). 224p. (gr. 13). 1995. pap. 16.95 (*0-415-90863-9*, B2952, Routledge NY) Routledge.

Sacrificial Logics: Feminist Theory & the Critique of Identity. Allison Weir. (Thinking Gender Ser.). 224p. (C). (gr. 13). 1996. text ed. 59.95 (*0-415-90862-0*, B2948, Routledge NY) Routledge.

***Sacrificial Mother: Loving Your Children Without Losing Yourself.** Carin Rubenstein. LC 97-12076. 288p. 1998. 22.95 (*0-7868-6262-9*) Hyperion.

Sacrificial Priest: The Sanctuary Message. 3rd rev. ed. Colin D. Standish & Russell R. Standish. (Adventism Ser.: Bk. 3). 270p. 1989. pap. 5.95 (*0-923309-20-9*) Hartland Pubns.

***Sacrificial Smoke - Offerrok.** Jan Fridegard. Tr. & Frwd. by Robert E. Bjork. LC 89-4916. (Modern Scandinavian Literature in Translation Ser.: Vol. 3). 201p. 1991. reprint ed. pap. 57.30 (*0-608-02779-0*, 2063846) Bks Demand.

***Sacrificial Years: A Chronicle of Walt Whitman's Experiences in the Civil War.** Ed. by John H. McElroy. LC 97-17833. (Illus.). 256p. 1997. 29.95 (*1-56792-079-9*) Godine.

Sacrificing Commentary: Reading the End of Literature. Sandor Goodhart. 408p. 1996. text ed. 45.00 (*0-8018-5084-3*) Johns Hopkins.

Sacrificing Independence. Adrian Golding. 392p. 1995. mass mkt. 5.99 (*1-896329-36-5*, Pub. by Comnwlth Pub CN) Partners Pubs Grp.

Sacrificing Our Selves for Love: Why Women Compromise Health & Self-Esteem ... & How to Stop. Jane W. Hyman & Esther R. Rome. (Illus.). 288p. 1996. pap. text ed. 18.95 (*0-89594-743-9*) Crossing Pr.

***Sacrificing the Forest.** Karen O'Brien. (C). 1997. text ed. 48.00 (*0-8133-6905-3*) Westview.

Sacrificio de Alabanza. Carlos Jimenez. (SPA.). 1990. 3.25 (*1-56063-041-8*, 498474) Editorial Unilit.

***Sacrificio de Alabanza.** Carlos Jimenez. 110p. (SPA.). 1991. pap. write for info. (*0-614-27136-3*) Editorial Unilit.

***Sacrificio de la Cruz - The Sacrifice of the Cross.** Avila. 44p. (SPA.). 1996. write for info. (*0-7899-0075-0*) Editorial Unilit.

Sacrificio de la Misa, La Vida de Sante Oria el Martirio de San Lorenzo. Gonzalo De Berceo. Ed. by Brian Dutton. (Monografias A Ser.: Vol. LXXX). 208p. (Orig.). (SPA.). (C). 1981. pap. 45.00 (*0-7293-0099-4*, Pub. by Tamesis Bks Ltd UK) Boydell & Brewer.

Sacrilege: An SPQR Mystery. John M. Roberts. 224p. (Orig.). 1992. mass mkt. 4.50 (*0-380-76627-2*) Avon.

Sacrilege of Alan Kent. Erskine Caldwell. LC 95-12605. (Illus.). 1995. 19.95 (*0-8203-1789-6*) U of Ga Pr.

Sacristan's Manual. 4th rev. ed. Illus. by Lynne Raffo. 55p. (C). 1988. pap. text ed. 4.00 (*1-878268-03-1*) Lit Comm Pubs.

Sacristy Manual. Thomas Ryan. Ed. by David Philippart. LC 93-29863. (Illus.). 278p. 1993. 15.00 (*0-929650-92-1*, SACMNL) Liturgy Tr Pubns.

Sacrorum Emblematum Centuria Una. Andrew Willet. LC 84-5360. 1984. reprint ed. 50.00 (*0-8201-1395-6*) Schol Facsimiles.

Sad. Janine Amos. LC 90-46540. (Feelings Ser.). (Illus.). 32p. (J). (ps-3). 1991. pap. 4.95 (*0-8114-6913-1*); lib. bdg. 21.40 (*0-8172-3780-1*) Raintree Steck-V.

Sad. Sylvia R. Tester. LC 79-26252. (What Does It Mean? Ser.). (Illus.). 32p. (J). (ps-2). 1980. lib. bdg. 18.50 (*0-89565-112-2*) Childs World.

Sad & Terrible Blunder: Generals Terry & Custer at the Little Big Horn - New Discoveries. Roger Darling. LC 90-60075. (Illus.). 310p. 1990. 28.50 (*0-9621488-1-4*) Potomac-Western Pr.

Sad, but O.K. - My Daddy Died Today: A Child's View of Death. Barbara F. Juneau. LC 88-155937. (Illus.). 112p. (Orig.). (J). (gr. 5 up). 1988. pap. 9.95 (*0-931892-19-8*) B Dolphin Pub.

Sad Carnival: 1982. Clark W. Holtzman. 1983. pap. 2.00 (*0-918476-04-6*) Cornerstone Pr.

Sad Clowns & Pale Pierrots: Literature & the Popular Comic Arts in 19th Century France. Louisa E. Jones. LC 83-81596. (French Forum Monographs: No. 48). 296p. (Orig.). 1984. pap. 17.95 (*0-917058-48-8*) French Forum.

Sad Cypress. Agatha Christie. LC 93-31257. 320p. 1994. 24.95 (*0-399-13924-9*, Putnam) Putnam Pub Group.

Sad Days, Glad Days: A Story About Depression. DeWitt Hamilton. LC 94-25540. (Albert Whitman Concept Bks.). (Illus.). (J). (PS up). 1995. lib. bdg. 14.95 (*0-8075-7200-4*) A Whitman.

Sad Days of Light. Peter Balakian. LC 92-74529. (Classic Contemporaries Ser.). 1993. pap. 12.95 (*0-88748-160-4*) Carnegie-Mellon.

***Sad Dumb Beauty of Everything.** William M. Taylor, Jr. 20p. (Orig.). 1997. pap. 4.00 (*0-9654684-7-X*) Big Star.

Sad Earth, Sweet Heaven. Lucy Buck. 1995. 21.95 (*0-934530-07-6*) Buck Pub.

Sad Farewell & Other Poems. J. Terrell Wynne. 16p. (Orig.). 1990. pap. 4.00 (*0-925854-01-8*) Defiant Pr.

Sad Fashions. Richard Peabody. LC 89-85142. 64p. (Orig.). 1990. pap. 7.95 (*0-945144-01-6*) Gut Punch Pr.

Sad Girl Sitting on a Running Board. Michael McFee. LC 91-72899. 80p. (Orig.). 1991. pap. 12.50 (*0-917788-49-4*) Gnomon Pr.

***Sad Little Cottage.** Violet W. Nyson. (Illus.). 32p. (Orig.). (J). (ps-4). 1996. pap. 5.95 (*1-888828-05-6*) Anchor Publng.

Sad Macs, Bombs, & Other Disasters: And What to Do about Them. Ted Landau. LC 92-38361. 1993. pap. 24.95 (*0-201-62207-6*) Addison-Wesley.

Sad Macs, Bombs & Other Disasters: And What to Do about Them. 2nd ed. Ted Landau. LC 95-6088. 896p. 1995. pap. 34.95 (*0-201-40958-5*) Addison-Wesley.

***Sad News, Glad News.** (Nightlights Ser.: No. 4). 32p. (J). 1998. write for info. (*0-7459-3733-0*, Lion) Chariot Victor.

Sad Night: The Story of an Aztec Victory & a Spanish Loss. Sally S. Mathews. LC 92-25119. (Illus.). (J). (gr. 1-4). 1994. 16.95 (*0-395-63035-5*, Clarion Bks) HM.

Sad Paradise. Ed. by James Greene. (C). 1989. 39.00 (*0-86334-067-9*, Pub. by Saltire Soc) St Mut.

Sad Sack. George Baker. LC 83-46010. (Classics of Modern American Humor Ser.). reprint ed. 30.00 (*0-404-19926-7*) AMS Pr.

Sad, Sad William. Gitte Spee. (J). 1996. lib. bdg. 18.60 (*0-8368-1607-2*) Gareth Stevens Inc.

Sad Shepherd. Ben Jonson. Ed. by W. W. Greg. Bd. with Waldron's Continuation. (Material for the Study of the Old English Drama Ser.: No. 1, Vol. 11). 1974. reprint ed. Set pap. (*0-8115-0260-0*) Periodicals Srv.

Sad Song Singing. Thomas B. Dewey. 192p. 1984. pap. 3.50 (*0-88184-067-X*) Carroll & Graf.

Sad Songs in Empty Theatres. Huggy-Bear Ferris. 40p. 1994. 4.00 (*0-614-00731-3*) Venom Pr.

Sad Sontag Plays His Hunch. Wilbur C. Tuttle. 1976. lib. bdg. 10.95 (*0-89968-129-8*, Lghtyr Pr) Buccaneer Bks.

Sad Souls & Great, No. 31. pap. 0.15 (*0-87377-156-7*) GAM Pubns.

Sad State of Freedom. Nazim Hikmet. (C). 1990. 35.00 (*0-906887-40-2*, Pub. by Greville Pr UK) St Mut.

Sad Story of Mary Wanna or How Marijuana Harms You. rev. ed. Peggy Mann. 40p. (J). (gr. 1-6). 1990. pap. 3.95 (*0-318-50073-6*) Woodmere Press.

Sad Story of Veronica Who Played the Violin. David McKee. (Illus.). 32p. (J). (gr. k-4). 1991. 10.95 (*0-916291-37-5*) Kane-Miller Bk.

***Sad Strains of a Gay Waltz: A Novel.** Irene Dische. LC 97-9992. 1997. 23.00 (*0-8050-5357-3*) H Holt & Co.

Sad Underwear & Other Complications: More Poems for Children & Their Parents. Judith Viorst. LC 94-3357. (Illus.). 78p. (J). 1995. text ed. 16.00 (*0-689-31929-0*, Atheneum S&S) S&S Trade.

Sadakichi Hartmann, Critical Modernist: Collected Art Writings. Sadakichi Hartmann. Ed. by Jane C. Weaver. (Lannan Ser.: No. 1). (Illus.). 423p. 1990. 42.50 (*0-520-06767-3*) U CA Pr.

Sadako. Eleanor Coerr. LC 92-41483. (Illus.). 48p. (Orig.). (J). (gr. 1-4). 1993. 17.95 (*0-399-21771-1*, Putnam) Putnam Pub Group.

***Sadako.** Eleanor Coerr. (Illus.). 32p. (Orig.). (J). 1997. pap. 5.95 (*0-698-11588-0*, Paperstar) Putnam Pub Group.

Sadako & the Thousand Paper Cranes. Eleanor Coerr. (Illus.). 64p. (J). (gr. 2-5). 1979. pap. 3.50 (*0-440-47465-5*, YB BDD) BDD Bks Young Read.

Sadako & the Thousand Paper Cranes. Eleanor B. Coerr. LC 76-9872. (Illus.). (J). (gr. 3-5). 1977. 14.95 (*0-399-20520-9*, Putnam) Putnam Pub Group.

Sadako & the Thousand Paper Cranes: A Study Guide. Edna Ritzenberg. (Novel-Ties Ser.). 1984. student ed., teacher ed., pap. text ed. 15.95 (*0-88122-062-0*) Lrn Links.

***Sadako y las Mil Grullas de Papel.** Eleanor Coerr. 1996. pap. text ed. 8.95 (*84-241-3353-6*) Lectorum Pubns.

Sadao Hasegawa. Sadao Hasegawa. 1996. pap. 29.95 (*0-85449-226-7*, Pub. by Gay Mens Pr UK) LPC InBook.

An Asterisk (*) at the beginning of an entry indicates that the title is appearing in BIP for the first time.

Sadar's Keep. Midori Snyder. 1991. pap. 3.95 (*0-8125-0912-9*) Tor Bks.

Sadat: The Man Who Changed Mid-East History. George Sullivan. LC 81-50739. (Illus.). 99p. (YA). (gr. 6 up). 1981. lib. bdg. 9.85 (*0-8027-6435-5*) Walker & Co.

Sadat & After: Struggles for Egypt's Political Soul. Raymond W. Baker. 365p. 1990. 42.00 (*0-674-78497-9*) HUP.

Sadat's Journey. Louise O. Neaderland. (Illus.). 1981. 10.00 (*0-942561-14-7*) Bone Hollow.

SADC Region: Profile of Agricultural Potential. K. Davies. 1993. pap. 25.00 (*0-85954-353-6*, Pub. by Nat Res Inst UK) St Mut.

SADCC: Problems & Prospects for Disengagement & Development in South Africa. Ed. by Samir Amin et al. LC 88-5534. 304p. (C). 1987. pap. 19.95 (*0-86232-749-0*, Pub. by Zed Bks Ltd UK); text ed. 55.00 (*0-86232-748-2*, Pub. by Zed Bks Ltd UK) Humanities.

SADCC - Beyond Transportation: The Challenge of Industrial Cooperation in Southern Africa. Tom Ostergaard. (Scandinavian Institute of African Studies). 136p. (Orig.). 1989. pap. 48.00 (*91-7106-294-7*, Pub. by Umea U Bibl SW) Coronet Bks.

SADCC Political Economy of Development in Southern Africa. Margaret C. Lee. LC 88-50765. 242p. 1989. pap. 16.95 (*1-55523-156-X*) Winston-Derek.

Saddam & Uncle Sam. David W. Felder. (Illus.). 1996. pap. text ed. 8.95 (*0-910959-55-2*, B&G 11A) Wellington Pr.

Saddam Hussein. Jane Claypool. LC 92-46994. (Biographies: World Leaders Ser.). (J). 1993. 19.93 (*0-86625-477-3*); 14.95 (*0-685-67775-3*) Rourke Pubns.

Saddam Hussein. Paul J. Deegan. Ed. by Rosemary Wallner. LC 91-73076. (War in the Gulf Ser.). (J). (gr. 4 up). 1991. lib. bdg. 13.99 (*1-56239-025-2*) Abdo & Dghtrs.

Saddam Hussein: Absolute Ruler of Iraq. Rebecca Stefoff. LC 94-16982. (Illus.). 128p. (YA). (gr. 7 up). 1995. lib. bdg. 16.90 (*1-56294-475-4*) Millbrook Pr.

Saddam Hussein on Current Events in Iraq. Saddam Hussein. Tr. by Khalid Kishtainy. LC 78-323367. 103p. reprint ed. pap. 29.40 (*0-685-20309-3*, 2030347) Bks Demand.

Saddam Hussein's Gulf Wars: Ambivalent Stakes in the Middle East. Miron Rezun. LC 92-4197. 164p. 1992. text ed. 45.00 (*0-275-94324-0*, C4324, Praeger Pubs) Greenwood.

Saddam Speaks on the Gulf Crisis: A Collection of Documents. Ed. by Ofra Bengio. (Contemporary Issues in the Middle East Ser.). 220p. 1992. pap. text ed. 16.95 (*0-8156-7055-9*) Syracuse U Pr.

Saddam's Babylon the Great. Charles R. Taylor. (Illus.). 120p. (Orig.). 1991. pap. 7.95 (*0-937682-13-6*) Today Bible.

Saddam's Iraq: Revolution or Reaction? 2nd ed. Ed. by CARDRI Staff. LC 88-20588. 288p. (C). 1989. pap. 15.00 (*0-86232-821-7*, Pub. by Zed Bks Ltd UK); text ed. 49.95 (*0-86232-820-9*, Pub. by Zed Bks Ltd UK) Humanities.

***Saddam's Word: The Political Discourse in Iraq.** Ofra Bengio. (Studies in Middle Eastern History). 288p. 1997. 49.95 (*0-19-511439-6*) OUP.

Saddest Centaur. Terry Page. (Illus.). 24p. (J). (gr. 2-6). pap. text ed. 4.00 (*1-887864-68-7*); lib. bdg. 7.00 (*1-887864-36-9*) Boo Bks.

Saddest Centaur Coloring Book. Terry Page. (Illus.). 32p. (J). (ps-5). pap. 3.00 (*1-887864-37-7*) Boo Bks.

Saddest Pleasure: A Journey on Two Rivers. Moritz Thomsen. (Memoir Ser.). 304p. (Orig.). (C). 1990. pap. 9.95 (*1-55597-124-5*) Graywolf.

Saddest Time. Norma Simon. (Albert Whitman Concept Bks.). (Illus.). 40p. (J). (gr. 1-4). 1986. pap. 4.95 (*0-8075-7204-7*); lib. bdg. 12.95 (*0-8075-7203-9*) A Whitman.

Saddharma-Pundarika: Lotus of True Law. Tr. by H. Kern. 1972. lib. bdg. 79.95 (*0-87968-530-1*) Krishna Pr.

Saddle. Elwyn H. Edwards. 100p. (C). 1990. 28.00 (*0-85131-526-7*, Pub. by J A Allen & Co UK) St Mut.

Saddle a Whirlwind. Eugene C. Vories. 192p. 1990. 18.95 (*0-8027-4106-1*) Walker & Co.

Saddle & Sirloin Portrait Collection. Dale F. Runnion & June A. Runnion. 118p. 1992. pap. 10.00 (*0-9634756-0-6*) N Am Int Livestock.

Saddle Bag Yarns. Byron Grosfield. 171p. (Orig.). 1988. pap. 7.95 (*0-9613875-1-3*) Wild Horse Pubns.

Saddle Bags. Bonnie Bryant. (Saddle Club Ser.: No. 42). 144p. (J). (gr. 4-7). 1995. pap. 3.50 (*0-553-48260-2*) Bantam.

Saddle Club. Bonnie Bryant. (Saddle Club Ser.: No. 19). 144p. (J). 1992. pap. 3.99 (*0-553-15983-6*) Bantam.

Saddle Club, Bk. 2. B. B. Hiller. (Skylark Ser.). 144p. (Orig.). (J). 1988. pap. 3.50 (*0-553-15611-X*, Skylark BDD) BDD Bks Young Read.

Saddle Club, No. 4. B. B. Hiller. 144p. (Orig.). (YA). 1989. 3.99 (*0-553-15637-3*) Bantam.

Saddle Club, 12 bks., Set. enl. ed. Bonnie Bryant. 1728p. (J). (gr. 4 up). lib. bdg. 191.16 (*0-8368-1554-8*) Gareth Stevens Inc.

Saddle Club, No. 17: Horsenapped! Bonnie Bryant. 144p. (J). 1991. pap. 3.99 (*0-553-15937-2*) Bantam.

Saddle Club, No. 5: Trail Mates. Bonnie Bryant. 144p. (YA). 1989. mass mkt. 3.99 (*0-553-15703-5*) Bantam.

Saddle Club, No. 6: Dude Ranch. Bonnie Bryant. 144p. (YA). 1989. mass mkt. 3.99 (*0-553-15728-0*) Bantam.

Saddle Gals: A Filmography of Female Players in B-Westerns of the Sound Era. Steve Turner & Ed Wyatt. LC 94-62172. (Illus.). 100p. (Orig.). 1995. pap. text ed. 10.00 (*0-944019-19-6*) Empire NC.

Saddle-Man. large type ed. Matt Stuart. LC 93-5222. 1993. lib. bdg. 15.95 (*0-8161-5839-8*, GK Hall) Thorndike Pr.

Saddle Marks. Carter White. Ed. by Sybil White et al. (Illus.). 182p. 1983. 22.40 (*0-9613384-1-5*) C White.

Saddle Road Field Site Guide for Teachers. Faith M. Roelofs. (Exploring the Islands Ser.). 1994. teacher ed. write for info. (*1-882163-33-8*) Moanalua Grdns Fnd.

Saddle Serenaders, Set, incl. CD. Guy Logsdon et al. LC 94-1776. (Illus.). 144p. 1994. pap. 29.95 (*0-87905-604-5*) Gibbs Smith Pub.

Saddle Sojourn: Saddle Road, Big Island. Faith M. Roelofs. (Exploring the Islands: Island of Hawai'i Ser.). 1994. pap. write for info. (*1-882163-29-X*) Moanalua Grdns Fnd.

Saddle Soldiers: The Civil War Correspondence of General William Stokes of the 4th South Carolina Calvary. Lloyd Halliburton. Ed. by Nancy Wooten & Virginia Ingram. LC 93-621. (Illus.). 285p. 1993. 19.95 (*0-87844-115-8*) Sandlapper Pub Co.

***Saddle Sore.** Bonnie Bryant. (Saddle Club Ser.: No. 66). (YA). 1997. pap. 3.99 (*0-553-48421-4*) BDD Bks Young Read.

Saddle the Storm. Harry Whittington. 208p. 1989. pap. 2.95 (*0-380-70731-4*) Avon.

Saddle the Storm. large type ed. Harry Whittington. (Linford Western Library). 1990. pap. 15.99 (*0-7089-6939-9*, Trailtree Bookshop) Ulverscroft.

Saddle the Wind. Pat Tracy. (Historical Ser.). 1995. mass mkt. 4.50 (*0-373-28873-5*, 1-28873-7) Harlequin Bks.

***Saddle Up!** Michi Fujimoto. (Puzzle Place Sticker Activity Bks.). (Illus.). 24p. (J). (ps-1). 1997. pap. 3.50 (*0-8431-7934-1*) Price Stern Sloan.

***Saddle Up! A Guide to Planning the Perfect Horseback Vacation.** Ute Haker. LC 96-48730. 248p. 1997. pap. 14.95 (*1-56261-295-6*) John Muir.

Saddle up & R-I-I-D-E. Jim Ross. (Illus.). 100p. 1990. pap. 6.95 (*0-9617932-2-8*) J A Ross.

Saddle Up (Man of the Month) Mary L. Baxter. (Desire Ser.). 1996. mass mkt. 3.50 (*0-373-05991-4*, 1-05991-4) Silhouette.

Saddleback Sightseeing in California: A Guide to Rental Horses, Trail Rides & Guest Ranches. John A. Greenwald. Ed. by Robin Shepherd. LC 92-53796. (Illus.). 208p. (Orig.). 1992. pap. 12.95 (*0-935182-58-6*) Gem Guides Bk.

Saddlebag Patriot: Service of Lt. Underfoot in the War for Independence. David K. Parsons. 106p. 1992. pap. 10.00 (*1-886303-00-2*) Write to Print.

Saddlebag Salesmen. Elizabeth Van Steenwyk. (First Bks.). (Illus.). 64p. (J). (gr. 4-6). 1995. lib. bdg. 21.00 (*0-531-20214-3*) Watts.

Saddlebags. Shelby Strother. 448p. 1991. 24.95 (*1-878005-27-8*); pap. 12.95 (*1-878005-28-6*) Northmont Pub.

Saddlebags, City Streets & Cyberspace: A History of Preaching in the Churches of Christ. Michael W. Casey. (Illus.). 215p. 1995. pap. 14.95 (*0-89112-017-3*) Abilene Christ U.

Saddlebred - America's Horse of Distinction. Judy F. Oefinger. Ed. by William Strode & William Butler. (Illus.). 160p. 1991. 45.00 (*0-916509-79-6*) Harmony Hse Pub.

***Saddlebred Horse.** (Learning about Horses Ser.). (Illus.). 48p. (J). (gr. 3-7). 1996. 18.40 (*0-516-20083-6*) Childrens.

Saddlebred Horse. Charlotte Wilcox. (Learning about Horses Ser.). 48p. (J). (gr. 3-9). 1996. lib. bdg. 17.80 (*1-56065-364-7*) Capstone Pr.

Saddlebrook Papers: A Reader on Growth Management. 177p. 1985. 10.00 (*0-317-01546-X*) Fla Atlantic.

***Saddlemaker to the Stars: The Leather & Silver Art of Edward H. Bohlin.** James H. Nottage. LC 96-78955. (Illus.). 228p. (Orig.). 1996. 60.00 (*0-295-97605-5*) U of Wash Pr.

***Saddlemaker to the Stars Vol. 1: The Leather & Silver Art of Edward H. Bohlin.** James H. Nottage. LC 96-78955. (Illus.). 228p. (Orig.). 1996. pap. 35.00 (*1-882880-02-1*) G Autry Wstrn.

Saddlemaking. Dusty Johnson. (Illus.). 100p. (Orig.). 1993. pap. text ed. 16.95 (*0-9639164-0-8*); vhs 39.95 (*0-9639164-1-6*) Saddleman Pr.

Saddlemaking in Wyoming: History, Utility & Art. Sharon Kahin. 72p. 1993. write for info. (*0-9630869-1-X*) U of WY Art Mus.

Saddlepoint Approximations. Jens L. Jensen. (Statistical Science Ser.: No. 16). (Illus.). 364p. 1995. 95.00 (*0-19-852295-9*) OUP.

Saddlery. British Horse Society Staff. (British Horse Society Manual of Stable Management Ser.: Bk. 4). (Illus.). 128p. 1988. pap. 15.95 (*1-872082-08-4*) Half Halt Pr.

Saddlery. E. Hartley Edwards. 250p. (C). 1990. pap. 30.00 (*0-85131-540-2*, Pub. by J A Allen & Co UK) St Mut.

Saddlery & Harness Making. Paul N. Hasluck. 160p. (C). 1990. 25.00 (*0-85131-148-2*, Pub. by J A Allen & Co UK) St Mut.

Saddles. Russel H. Beatie. LC 79-6708. (Illus.). 408p. 1981. 69.95 (*0-8061-1584-X*) U of Okla Pr.

Saddles & Spurs: The Pony Express Saga. Mary Lee Settle. LC 55-10776. x, 217p. 1972. reprint ed. pap. 11.00 (*0-8032-5765-1*, Bison Books) U of Nebr Pr.

Saddles, Bits & Spurs: Cowboy Crafters at Work. Wyoming State Museum Staff. Ed. by Barbara Allen. 50p. (Orig.). 1993. pap. 10.00 (*0-943398-18-5*) Wyoming St Mus.

Sade. Maurice Lever. 1994. pap. 15.95 (*0-15-600111-X*) HarBrace.

Sade: A Biography. Maurice Lever. 1993. 35.00 (*0-374-20298-2*) FS&G.

Sade: A Sudden Abyss. Annie Le Brun. Tr. by Camille Naish from FRE. 232p. (Orig.). 1991. pap. 12.95 (*0-87286-250-X*) City Lights.

Sade: His Ethics & Rhetoric. Colette V. Michael. (American University Studies: Romance Languages & Literature: Ser. II, Vol. 106). 249p. (C). 1989. text ed. 37.95 (*0-8204-0884-0*) P Lang Pubng.

Sade & the Narratives of Transgression. Ed. by David B. Allison et al. (Studies in French: No. 52). 270p. (C). 1995. text ed. 59.95 (*0-521-44415-2*) Cambridge U Pr.

Sade et Restif de la Bretonne. Maurice Blanchot. (FRE.). 1986. pap. 23.95 (*0-7859-3308-5*, 2870271948) Fr & Eur.

Sade, Fourier, Loyola. Roland Barthes. (FRE.). 1980. pap. 14.95 (*0-7859-0667-3*, M5801) Fr & Eur.

Sade My Neighbor. Pierre Klossowski. Tr. & Intro. by Alphonso Lingis. (Studies in Phenomenology & Existential Philosophy). 144p. (Orig.). 1991. 39.95 (*0-8101-0957-3*); pap. 12.95 (*0-8101-0958-1*) Northwestern U Pr.

Sade/Fourier/Loyola. Roland Barthes. LC 96-42538. 184p. 1997. reprint ed. pap. 14.95 (*0-8018-5526-8*) Johns Hopkins.

Sadeq Hedayat: An Anthology. Ed. by Ehsan Yarshater. 1979. 30.00 (*0-89158-387-4*) Mazda Pubs.

Sadeq Hedayat: The Life & Legend of an Iranian Writer. Homa Katouzian. 350p. 1992. 49.50 (*1-85043-361-5*, Pub. by I B Tauris UK) St Martin.

Sade's Wife: The Woman Behind the Marquis. Margaret Crosland. 192p. 9600. 35.00 (*0-7206-0958-5*, Pub. by P Owen Ltd UK) Dufour.

Sadguru Dattatreya. Satguru S. Keshavadas. (Illus.). 279p. (Orig.). 1988. pap. 21.00 (*0-942508-18-1*) Vishwa.

Sadguru Speaks. Satguru S. Keshavadas. (Illus.). 96p. (Orig.). 1975. pap. 8.00 (*0-942508-06-8*) Vishwa.

Sadhak's Companion. Svami Kripalvananda. Ed. by Darshana Shakti Ma. Tr. by Gauri Modi from GUJ. Orig. Title: Guru Vachanamrit. (Illus.). (Orig.). 1977. pap. text ed. 2.95 (*0-933116-04-7*) Sanatana.

Sadhana: A Way to God. Anthony DeMello. LC 84-6735. 144p. 1984. pap. 9.95 (*0-385-19614-8*, Image Bks) Doubleday.

Sadhana: A Way to God, Christian Exercises in Eastern Form. Anthony De Mello. LC 78-70521. (Studies on Jesuit Topics Series IV: No. 9). xi, 134p. (C). 1978. pap. 7.95 (*0-912422-46-7*) Inst Jesuit.

***Sadhana, the Inward Path.** Sai B. Sathya. Date not set. pap. 2.50 (*0-614-19076-2*, BW-130) Sathya Sai Bk Ctr.

Sadholal Lectures of Nyaya. Ganganath Jha. (C). 1994. text ed. 20.00 (*81-7030-402-4*, Pub. by Sri Satguru Pubns II) S Asia.

Sadhu: A Study in Mysticism & Practical Religion. rev. ed. Burnett H. Streeter. 264p. (C). 1987. 17.50 (*0-8364-2097-7*, Pub. by Mittal II) S Asia.

Sadhus: India's Mystic Holy Men. Dolf Hartsuiker. (Illus.). 128p. (Orig.). 1993. pap. 19.95 (*0-89281-454-3*) Inner Tradit.

Sadhus: The Holy Men of India. Rajesh Bedi. 1993. 44.95 (*81-7107-021-3*) Mandala Media.

Sadhus of India. M. M. Pickthal. 258p. 19.95 (*0-318-37160-X*) Asia Bk Corp.

Sadhus of India: A Study of Hindu Asceticism. Robert L. Gross. (C). 1992. 44.00 (*81-7033-067-X*, Pub. by Rawat II) S Asia.

Sadie: The True Story of a Western Lady. Soren Roegdke & Kay Busse. LC 94-90087. (True Story Ser.). 268p. (Orig.). 1994. pap. 20.00 (*0-9629242-2-9*) WKB Enterp.

Sadie & the Snowman. Allan Morgan. (Illus.). 32p. (J). (ps-2). 1987. pap. 2.50 (*0-590-41826-2*) Scholastic Inc.

Sadie Brower Neakok, an Inupiaq Woman. Margaret B. Blackman. LC 88-33959. (Illus.). 326p. 1989. 30.00 (*0-295-96813-3*) U of Wash Pr.

Sadie Learns a Lesson. Jane Mathews. (Illus.). 48p. (Orig.). (J). (ps-3). 1989. pap. 9.95 (*1-880812-18-5*) S Ink WA.

Sadie Plays House. Eileen Spinelli. (J). 1998. 3.99 (*0-689-81200-0*) S&S Childrens.

Sadie, Remember. Carol Kline. (Illus.). (Orig.). (J). (gr. k-2). 1993. pap. 4.95 (*0-88741-923-2*) Sundance Pub.

Sadie Rose Adventure Series: Boxed Set, Set. Hilda Stahl. 512p. (J). (gr. 4-7). 1991. pap. 19.96 (*0-89107-635-2*) Crossway Bks.

Sadie Rose & the Champion Sharpshooter. Hilda Stahl. LC 91-14322. (Sadie Rose Adventure Ser.: No. 7). 128p. (J). (gr. 4-7). 1991. pap. 4.99 (*0-89107-630-1*) Crossway Bks.

Sadie Rose & the Cottonwood Creek Orphan. Hilda Stahl. LC 88-71808. (Sadie Rose Adventure Ser.: No. 2). 128p. (J). (gr. 4-7). 1989. pap. 4.99 (*0-89107-513-5*) Crossway Bks.

Sadie Rose & the Dangerous Search. Hilda Stahl. LC 92-37204. (Sadie Rose Adventure Ser.: No. 10). (J). (gr. 4-7). 1993. pap. 4.99 (*0-89107-715-4*) Crossway Bks.

Sadie Rose & the Daring Escape. Hilda Stahl. LC 88-70496. (Sadie Rose Adventure Ser.: No. 1). 144p. (J). (gr. 4-7). 1988. pap. 4.99 (*0-89107-492-9*) Crossway Bks.

Sadie Rose & the Double Secret. Hilda Stahl. LC 89-25423. (Sadie Rose Adventure Ser.: No. 4). 124p. (J). (gr. 4-7). 1990. pap. 4.99 (*0-89107-546-1*) Crossway Bks.

Sadie Rose & the Impossible Birthday Wish. Hilda Stahl. LC 92-13637. (Sadie Rose Adventures Ser.: No. 9). 128p. (J). (gr. 4-7). 1992. pap. 4.99 (*0-89107-685-9*) Crossway Bks.

Sadie Rose & the Mad Fortune Hunters. Hilda Stahl. LC 90-80619. (Sadie Rose Advenures Ser.: No. 5). 128p. (Orig.). (J). (gr. 4-7). 1990. pap. 4.99 (*0-89107-578-X*) Crossway Bks.

Sadie Rose & the Mysterious Stranger. Hilda Stahl. LC 93-4203. (Sadie Rose Adventure Ser.: No. 11). 128p. (Orig.). (J). (gr. 4-7). 1993. pap. 4.99 (*0-89107-747-2*) Crossway Bks.

Sadie Rose & the Outlaw Rustlers. Hilda Stahl. LC 89-50331. (Sadie Rose Adventure Ser.: No. 3). 128p. (J). (gr. 4-7). 1989. pap. 4.99 (*0-89107-528-3*) Crossway Bks.

Sadie Rose & the Phantom Warrior. Hilda Stahl. LC 90-24471. (Sadie Rose Adventure Ser.: No. 8). 128p. (Orig.). (J). (gr. 4-7). 1991. pap. 4.99 (*0-89107-612-3*) Crossway Bks.

Sadie Rose & the Secret Romance. Hilda Stahl. LC 91-41491. (Sadie Rose Adventure Ser.: Vol. 8). 128p. (J). (gr. 4-7). 1992. pap. 4.99 (*0-89107-661-1*) Crossway Bks.

Sadie Starr Presents Beading with Seed Beads Gem Stones & Cabochons, Vol. 1. Sadie Starr. (Illus.). 250p. 1993. 24.95 (*0-9633938-0-4*) Shoot Starr Gal.

Sadie the Shrew. Gisela Buck & Siegfried Buck. (Real Baby Animals Ser.). (Illus.). 24p. (J). (gr. 1 up). 1996. lib. bdg. 17.27 (*0-8368-1504-1*) Gareth Stevens Inc.

Sadie When She Died. Ed McBain. 1973. pap. 3.99 (*0-451-15366-9*, Sig) NAL-Dutton.

Sadisfactions. Paul Nagy. 1977. pap. 5.00 (*0-918406-08-0*) Future Pr.

Sadism: Index of New Information & Research Reference Book. Haynes B. Goyer. 150p. 1996. 44.50 (*0-7883-1162-X*); pap. 47.50 (*0-7883-1163-8*) ABBE Pubs Assn.

Sadist, an Account of the Crimes of a Serial Killer, Together with Peter Kurten, a Study in Sadism. Karl Berg & George Godwin. LC 90-6953. (Criminology, Law Enforcement, & Social Problems Ser.: No. 144). (Illus.). 352p. (C). 1996. 35.00 (*0-87585-144-4*) Patterson Smith.

Sadistic Statistics: An Introduction to Statistics for the Social & Behavioral Sciences. 2nd ed. Gideon Horowitz. (Illus.). 170p. (C). 1981. pap. text ed. 12.95 (*0-89529-135-5*) Avery Pub.

Sadler Bollen Untitled #2. B. Sadler. (J). Date not set. 14.00 (*0-689-80554-3*) S&S Childrens.

Sadler's Wells Ballet: A History & an Appreciation. Mary Clarke. LC 77-563. (Series in Dance). 1977. reprint ed. lib. bdg. 37.50 (*0-306-70863-9*) Da Capo.

Sadler's Wells Royal Ballet "Swan Lake" Barbara Newman. (Illus.). 143p. 1983. 29.95 (*0-903102-72-2*, Pub. by Dance Bks UK) Princeton Bk Co.

***Sadness after Song.** Photos by David L. Givens. (Illus.). 24p. (Orig.). 1997. pap. 25.00 (*0-9655720-3-X*) Anemone Editions.

Sadness & Happiness: Poems. Robert Pinsky. LC 75-3486. (Contemporary Poets Ser.). 740p. 1975. pap. 9.95 (*0-691-01322-5*, 358) Princeton U Pr.

Sadness at Leaving. Erje Ayden. 250p. 1989. pap. 6.00 (*0-936756-57-8*) Autonomedia.

Sadness at Leaving: A Novel of Espionage. Erje Ayden. 110p. (Orig.). 1972. pap. 15.00 (*0-89366-005-1*) Ultramarine Pub.

Sadness at the Private University. Ralph Adamo. LC 77-79216. (Lost Roads Poetry Ser.: No. 3). 1978. pap. 3.00 (*0-918786-05-3*) Lost Roads.

Sadness in Sunshine: The Flood of Estes Park, an Illustrated Journal. Henry F. Pedersen, Jr. (Illus.). 64p. (Orig.). 1995. pap. 8.50 (*0-9641585-3-1*) H F Pedersen.

Sadness of Christ. Thomas More. (Yale University Press Translation Ser.). 184p. 1993. pap. 9.95 (*0-933932-66-9*) Scepter Pubs.

Sadness of Days: Selected & New Poems. Luis O. Salinas. LC 85-73348. 160p. (Orig.). 1987. pap. 8.00 (*0-934770-58-1*) Arte Publico.

Sado: Japan's Island in Exile. Angus Waycott. LC 96-15449. (Illus.). 208p. (Orig.). 1996. pap. 14.95 (*1-880656-21-3*) Stone Bridge Pr.

Sadomasochism: Etiology & Treatment. Suzanne P. Schad-Somers. LC 95-52080. 304p. 1996. pap. 35.00 (*1-56821-789-7*) Aronson.

Sadomasochism: Painful Perversion or Pleasurable Play? Bill Thompson. (Sexual Politics Ser.). 224p. 1994. pap. 15.95 (*0-304-34305-6*, Pub. by Cassell Pubng UK) LPC InBook.

Sadomasochism: Painful Perversion or Pleasurable Play? Bill Thompson. (Sexual Politics Ser.). 224p. 1994. 55.00 (*0-304-34307-2*, Pub. by Cassell Pubng UK) LPC InBook.

Sadomasochism in Everyday Life: The Dynamics of Power & Powerlessness. Lynn S. Chancer. LC 91-32362. 240p. 1992. pap. 16.95 (*0-8135-1808-3*); text ed. 40.00 (*0-8135-1807-5*) Rutgers U Pr.

***Sadomasochism of Everyday Life: Why We Hurt Ourselves & How to Stop.** John M. Ross. LC 96-50196. 1997. 22.00 (*0-684-81049-2*) S&S Trade.

Sadomasochistic Homotext: Readings in Sade, Balzac & Proust. Douglas Saylor. LC 91-43602. (Sexuality & Literature Ser.: Vol. 2). 127p. (C). 1993. text ed. 44.95 (*0-8204-1828-5*) P Lang Pubng.

Sadopaideia. (Orig.). 1993. mass mkt. 5.95 (*1-56201-053-0*) Blue Moon Bks.

Sadtler Guide to Carbon-13 NMR Spectra. LC 82-50006. 1983. 225.00 (*0-8456-0087-7*) Sadtler Res.

Sadtler Guide to Carbon-13 NMR Spectra of Polymers & Resins. LC 88-60354. 1988. 250.00 (*0-8456-0150-4*) Sadtler Res.

Sadtler Guide to NMR Spectra. W. W. Simons & M. Zanger. LC 72-75379. 1972. 160.00 (*0-8456-0001-X*) Sadtler Res.

Sadtler Guide to the NMR Spectra of Polymers. W. W. Simons & M. Zanger. LC 73-90432. 1973. pap. 165.00 (*0-8456-0002-8*) Sadtler Res.

Sadtler Handbook of Infrared Spectra. Sadtler Research Labs, Inc., Staff. (Sadtler Handbooks Ser.). 1978. 295.00 (*0-8456-0034-6*) Sadtler Res.

Sadtler Handbook of Proton NMR Spectra. Sadtler Research Labs, Inc., Staff. (Sadtler Handbooks Ser.). 1978. 295.00 (*0-8456-0035-4*) Sadtler Res.

Sadtler Handbook of Ultraviolet Spectra. Sadtler Research Labs, Inc., Staff. (Sadtler Handbooks Ser.). 1978. 295.00 (*0-8456-0033-8*) Sadtler Res.

Sadtler Spectra Handbook of Esters. LC 80-52850. 1982. IR, LC 80-52850. 195.00 (*0-8456-0078-8*); NMR, LC 82-50009. 195.00 (*0-8456-0079-6*) Sadtler Res.

An Asterisk (*) at the beginning of an entry indicates that the title is appearing in BIP for the first time.

Sadtler Standard Gas Chromatography Retention Index Library, 1. LC 84-50510. 1985. ring bd. write for info. (*0-8456-0105-9*) Sadtler Res.

Sadtler Standard Gas Chromatography Retention Index Library, 2. LC 84-50510. 1986. ring bd. write for info. (*0-8456-0124-5*) Sadtler Res.

Sadtler Standard Gas Chromatography Retention Index Library, 3. LC 84-50510. 1986. ring bd. write for info. (*0-8456-0125-3*) Sadtler Res.

Sadtler Standard Gas Chromatography Retention Index Library, 4. LC 84-50510. 1986. write for info. (*0-8456-0126-1*) Sadtler Res.

Sadtler Standard Gas Chromatography Retention Index Library, 4 vols., Set. LC 84-50510. 1986. 895.00 (*0-8456-0127-X*) Sadtler Res.

Saducismus Triumphatus: Or, Full & Plain Evidence Concerning Witches & Apparitions. Joseph Glanvill. LC 66-60009. 1966. reprint ed. 75.00 (*0-8201-1021-3*) Schol Facsimiles.

Saducismus Triumphatus: or Full & Plain Evidence Concerning Witches & Apparitions. Joseph Glanvill. Ed. by Bernhard Fabian. (Collected Works: Vol. IX). 329p. 1978. reprint ed. 86.45 (*3-487-02695-3*) G Olms Pubs.

Sady. Georgii Ivanov. 78p. (RUS.). (C). 1994. reprint ed. pap. text ed. 9.00 (*1-57201-000-2*) Berkeley Slavic.

***SAE Aerospace Power Systems Conference Proceedings.** 1997. 74.00 (*0-7680-0009-2*) Soc Auto Engineers.

SAE Dictionary of Aerospace Engineering. Ed. by William H. Cubberly. 845p. 1992. 85.00 (*1-56091-286-3*, M-107) Soc Auto Engineers.

SAE Dictionary of Materials & Testing. William H. Cubberly. 408p. 1993. 55.00 (*1-56091-361-4*, M-109) Soc Auto Engineers.

***SAE Fatigue Design Handbook.** 3rd ed. Richard C. Rice & Society of Automotive Engineers Staff. LC 96-39685. 1997. write for info. (*1-56091-917-5*) Soc Auto Engineers.

SAE Manual on Shot Peening. 3rd ed. 52p. 1992. pap. 59.00 (*1-56091-259-6*, HS-84/92) Soc Auto Engineers.

SAE Motor Vehicle, Safety & Environmental Terminology. 345p. 1994. pap. 42.00 (*1-56091-574-9*, HS-215/95) Soc Auto Engineers.

SAE Motorcycle Standards Manual. LC 94-205779. 78p. 1995. pap. 69.00 (*1-56091-395-9*, HS-2500) Soc Auto Engineers.

SAE Vehicle Occupant Restraint Systems & Component Standards Manual, 1996. LC 93-224606. (HS Ser.: No. 13). 264p. 1996. pap. 79.00 (*1-56091-730-X*, HS-13/96) Soc Auto Engineers.

Saechtling International Plastics Handbook: For the Technologies, Engineer & User. 3rd rev. ed. Wilbrand Woebcken et al. 644p. (C). 1995. text ed. 59.95 (*1-56990-182-1*) Hanser-Gardner.

Saeculum: History & Society in the Theology of St. Augustine. Robert A. Markus. LC 71-87136. 264p. reprint ed. pap. 75.30 (*0-318-34820-9*, 2031687) Bks Demand.

Saecvli noni avctoris in Boetii Consolationem Philosophiae Commentarivs. Ed. by Edmund T. Silk. LC 36-7788. (American Academy in Rome. Papers & Monographs: Vol. 9). 411p. reprint ed. pap. 117.20 (*0-685-15605-2*, 2026725) Bks Demand.

Saemmtliche Werke, 8 vols. Johann G. Fichte. (C). 1966. reprint ed. 400.00 (*3-11-005147-8*) De Gruyter.

Saemtliche Briefe: Kritische Studienausgabe in 8 Baenden. Friedrich Wilhelm Nietzsche. Ed. by Giorgio Colli & Mazzino Montinari. 3630p. 1986. pap. 121.55 (*3-11-010963-8*) De Gruyter.

Saemtliche Dramen, 2 vols. Jos Murer. Ed. by Hans-Joachim Adomatis et al. LC 73-78235. (Ausgaben Deutscher Literatur des XV bis XVIII Jahrhunderts Ser.: Reihe Drama 4). (C). 1974. 634.60 (*3-11-003865-X*) De Gruyter.

Saemtliche Dramen, Vol. 2. Sixt Birck. Ed. by M. Brauneck. (Ausgaben Deutscher Literatur des XV bis XVIII Jahrhunderts Ser.). (C). 1976. 361.55 (*3-11-006758-7*) De Gruyter.

Saemtliche Dramen see Ausgewaehlte Werke

Saemtliche Dramenuebertragungen see Ausgewaehlte Werke

Saemtliche Schriften, 4 vols. Alexander Seitz. Ed. by Peter Ukena. Incl. Vol. 1. Medizinische Schriften. iv, 299p. (C). 1970. 196.00 (*3-11-000362-7*); Vol. 2. Politische und theologische schriften, monucleus aureus. iv, 481p. (C). 1975. 315.00 (*3-11-005715-8*); Vol. 3. Tragedi vom Grossen Abentmal. iv, 132p. 1969. 88.15 (*3-11-000356-2*); (Ausgaben Deutscher Literatur des XV bis XVIII Jahrhunderts Ser.). (GER.). (C). write for info. (*0-318-51642-X*) De Gruyter.

Saemtliche Werke. Incl. Vol. 1. Dramatische Dichtungen: Irenaromachia, Perseus. Ed. by Johann Rist et al. (Illus.). iv, 289p. 1967. 193.00 (*3-11-000346-5*); Vol. 2. Dramatische Dichtungen. Ed. by Johann Rist et al. 1972. 304.00 (*3-11-004125-1*); Vol. 4. Epische Dichtungen. Ed. by Johann Rist et al. 1972. 207.00 (*3-11-004124-3*); Vol. 5. Epische Dichtungen. Die Alleredelste Torheit. Die Alleredelste Belustigugh. Ed. by Johann Rist et al. 1974. 274.00 (*3-11-004591-5*); Vol. 6. Epische Dichtungen: Die alleredelste Erfindung, Die alleredelste Zeitverkuerzung. Ed. by Johann Rist et al. 1976. 296.00 (*3-11-006817-6*); Vol. 7. Philosophischer Phoenix, Rettung des Phoenix, Teutsche Hauptsprache, Adelicher Hausvatter. Ed. by Johann Rist et al. 1982. 256.00 (*3-11-008659-X*); (Ausgaben Deutscher Literatur des XV bis XVIII Jahrhunderts Ser.). (GER.). (C). write for info. (*0-318-51643-8*) De Gruyter.

Saemtliche Werke, 14 vols. Incl. Vol. 1. Ritter Galmy. Georg Wickram. Ed. by Hans-Gert Roloff. (Illus.). vi, 338p. 1967. 222.00 (*3-11-000347-3*); Vol. 2. Gabriotto und Reinhart. Georg Wickram. Ed. by Hans-Gert Roloff. vi, 297p. 1967. 281.00 (*3-11-000348-1*); Vol. 3. Knaben Spiegel: Dialog vom ungeratnen Sohn. Georg Wickram. Ed. by Hans-Gert Roloff. (Illus.). iv, 208p. 1968. 137.00 (*3-11-000354-6*); Vol. 4. Von Guten und Boesen Nachbaurn. Georg Wickram. Ed. by Hans-Gert Roloff. (Illus.). iv, 207p. 1969. 137.00 (*3-11-000358-9*); Vol. 5. Goldtfaden. Georg Wickram. Ed. by Hans-Gert Roloff. viii, 294p. 1968. 193.00 (*3-11-000352-X*); Vol. 6. irr reitende Pilger. Ed. by Georg Wickram & Hans-Gert Roloff. 1972. 137.00 (*3-11-003923-0*); Vol. 7. Rollwagenbuechlein. Georg Wickram & Hans-Gert Roloff. 1973. 215.00 (*3-11-004126-X*); Vol. 8. Sieben Hauptlaster. Georg Wickram. Ed. by Hans-Gert Roloff. 1972. 159.00 (*3-11-004002-6*); Vol. 11. Verlorene Sohn. Georg Wickram. Ed. by Hans-Gert Roloff. 1971. 244.00 (*3-11-003736-X*); Vol. 12. Apostelspiel: Knaben Spiegel. Georg Wickram. Ed. by Hans-Gert Roloff. (Illus.). vi, 281p. 1968. 185.00 (*3-11-000349-X*); (Ausgaben Deutscher Literatur des XV bis XVIII Jahrhunderts Ser.). (GER.). (C). write for info. (*0-318-51644-6*) De Gruyter.

Saemtliche Werke, 26 Vols, Set. Georg W. Hegel. Ed. by H. Glockner. 2,786.00 (*3-7728-0171-4*) Adlers Foreign Bks.

Saemtliche Werke: Ausgaben Deutscher Literatur des 15 bis 18 Jahrhunderts. Volker Meid. Incl. Vol. 6. Afrikanische Sofonisbe. 1972. 500.00 (*3-11-003918-4*); Vol. 8. Simson. 1970. 444.00 (*3-11-006364-6*); Vol. 9. Deutscher Helicon. 1971. 393.00 (*3-11-003598-7*); Vol. 11. Sprach-Vebung, Rosen-Mand, Helikonische Hechell, Sendeschreiben a Den Kreutztragenden. 1973. 304.00 (*3-11-004525-7*); (C). write for info. (*0-318-51645-4*) De Gruyter.

Saemtliche Werke: Erster Band, Erster Teil: Lyrik in Zyklen. Daniel Czepko. Ed. by Marian Szyrocki & Hans-Gert Roloff. iv, 381p. (C). 1989. lib. bdg. 242.30 (*3-11-011316-3*) De Gruyter.

Saemtliche Werke: Erster Band, Zweiter Teil: Lyrik in Zyklen. Daniel Czepko. Ed. by Marion Szyrocki & Hans-Gert Roloff. (Ausgaben Deutscher Literatur des XV bis XVIII Jahrhunderts Ser.). iv, 450p. (GER.). (C). 1989. lib. bdg. 288.50 (*3-11-012251-0*) De Gruyter.

Saemtliche Werke: Ibrahim. Incl. Vol. 5, Pt. 1. In. Ed. by Philipp Von Zesen et al. 1977. 411.00 (*3-11-007081-2*); Vol. 5, Pt. 2. . Ed. by Philipp Von Zesen et al. 1977. 460.00 (*3-11-007082-0*); (Ausgaben Deutscher Literatur des XV bis XVIII Jahrhunderts Ser.). (C). 1977. write for info. (*0-318-51636-5*) De Gruyter.

Saemtliche Werke: Kritische Studierausgabe, 15 vols. Friedrich Wilhelm Nietzsche. 8800p. (GER.). 1980. 199.95 (*3-11-008117-2*) De Gruyter.

Saemtliche Werke: Salomon, Vol. 2. Wolfhart Spangenberg. Ed. by M. Bircher-Glueckswechsel & Andras Vizkelety. 420p. (GER.). 1975. 284.60 (*3-11-005883-9*) De Gruyter.

***Saemtliche Werke Bd. II: Vermischte Gedichte, Zweiter Teil: Deutsche Gedichte.** Daniel Czepko. Ed. by Hans-Gert Roloff. (Ausgaben Deutscher Literatur des 15. Bis 18. Jahrhunderts Ser.). 672p. (GER.). (C). 1997. lib. bdg. 435.00 (*3-11-014163-9*) De Gruyter.

***Saemtliche Werke Vol. II: Vermischte Gedichte, Pt. 1: Lateinische Gedichte.** Daniel Czepko. Ed. by Hans-Gert Roloff & Marian Szyrocki. (Ausgaben Deutscher Literatur des XV. bis XVIII. Jahrhunderts Ser.). iv, 821p. (GER.). (C). 1996. lib. bdg. 462.85 (*3-11-014164-7*) De Gruyter.

Saemtliche Werke, Vol. I: Historische Dramen 1. Christian Weise. iv, 629p. (C). 1971. 426.95 (*3-11-001891-8*) De Gruyter.

Saemtliche Werke, Vol. III: Historische Dramen 3. Christian Weise. iv, 433p. (C). 1971. 296.15 (*3-11-003592-8*) De Gruyter.

Saemtliche Werke, Vol. IV: Biblische Dramen I. Christian Weise. LC 71-860995. (Ausgaben Deutscher Literatur des XV bis XVIII Jahrhunderts Ser.). iv, 440p. (C). 1973. 300.00 (*3-11-004246-0*) De Gruyter.

Saemtliche Werke, Vol. V. Biblische Dramen II. Christian Weise. LC 71-860995. (Ausgaben Deutscher Literatur des XV bis XVIII Jahrhunderts Ser.). (C). 1973. 330.75 (*3-11-003969-9*) De Gruyter.

Saemtliche Werke, Vol. 1: Trauerspiele 1; Theodoricus Veronensis, Marianne. Johann C. Hallmann. Ed. by Gerhard Spellerberg. (Ausgaben Deutscher Literatur des XV bis XVIII Jahrhunderts Ser.). (C). 1975. 284.65 (*3-11-004065-4*) De Gruyter.

Saemtliche Werke, Vol. 1: Von der Musica; Singschul. Wolfhart Spangenberg. Ed. by Andras Vizkelety. 173p. (C). 1971. 115.40 (*3-11-001846-2*) De Gruyter.

Saemtliche Werke, Vol. 21: Gedichte II. Christian Weise. Ed. by John D. Lindberg. (Ausgaben Deutscher Literatur des XV bis XVIII Jahrhunderts Ser.). (Illus.). (C). 1978. 423.10 (*3-11-006745-5*) De Gruyter.

Saemtliche Werke, 7 Baende Sechster Band: Briefwechsel und Dokumente Zu Leben und Werke. Daniel Czepko. Ed. by Hans-Gert Roloff & Marian Szyrocki. vi, 474p. (GER.). (C). 1995. lib. bdg. 326.15 (*3-11-013425-X*) De Gruyter.

Saemund Sigfusson & the Oddaverjar. Halldor Hermannsson. LC 33-5652. (Islandica Ser.: Vol. 22). 1932. pap. 25.00 (*0-527-00352-2*) Periodicals Srv.

Saenredam: The Art of Perspective. Rob Ruurs. LC 86-32669. (Illus.). 228p. 1987. 76.00 (*1-55619-015-8*) Benjamins North Am.

SAEP Practice Record Book Problem. 28p. 1992. 10.00 (*0-89606-301-1*); disk 25.00 (*0-89606-333-X*, 125CS) Am Assn Voc Materials.

Saeroun Sijak Eul Wihayeo see New Beginning: A Collection of Essays

Saeta Voladora. F. Sanchez. 58p. 0.90 (*0-318-14305-4*) Hispanic Inst.

***Saeulingsfuersorge Zwischen Sizialer Hygiene und Eugenik: Das Beispiel Berlins im Kaiserreich und in der Weimarer Republik.** Sigrid Stoeckel. (Veroeffentlichungen der Historischen Kommission zu Berlin Ser.: Vol. 91). xv, 445p. (GER.). (C). 1996. lib. bdg. 146.70 (*3-11-014539-1*) De Gruyter.

SAFAD: The Transition Period from the Termination of the British Mandate until the Implementation of the State of Israel Postal Service. A. Ben David. (Illus.). 140p. (C). 1995. 25.00 (*0-9647395-0-X*) WPIC.

Safari! LC 80-8799. (Books for World Explorers Series 3: No. 3). (Illus.). 104p. (J). (gr. 3-8). 1982. 8.95 (*0-87044-385-2*) Natl Geog.

Safari. B. Bull. (Illus.). 383p. 1988. 40.00 (*0-940143-65-8*) Safari Pr.

***Safari.** U. K. Macmillan. 1998. write for info. (*0-679-88985-X*) Knopf Bks Yng Read.

Safari. Michael Shapiro. 350p. (Orig.). (RUS.). 1992. pap. 3.00 (*1-881910-06-7*) Adventure NY.

Safari. Reginald O. Smythe. (Illus.). 80p. 1995. 24.95 (*0-9643771-0-1*) Traveling Bear.

Safari. Caren B. Stelson. (Carolrhoda Photo Bks.). 40p. (J). (ps-5). 1988. lib. bdg. 19.95 (*0-87614-324-9*, Carolrhoda) Lerner Group.

Safari. Roger Young & Rosemary Caggiano. 48p. (J). (gr. k-8). 1979. pap. 14.95 (*0-86704-006-8*) Clarus Music.

Safari. Caren B. Stelson. (Photo Bks.). (Illus.). 40p. (J). (ps-5). 1989. reprint ed. pap. 5.95 (*0-87614-512-8*, Lerner Publctns) Lerner Group.

Safari: A Chronicle of Adventure. Bartle Bull. (Illus.). 383p. 1992. pap. 29.95 (*0-14-016885-0*, Penguin Bks) Viking Penguin.

Safari: A Journey to the End. Dave Taylor. (Illus.). 120p. (Orig.). pap. 19.95 (*1-55046-016-1*, Pub. by Boston Mills Pr CN) Genl Dist Srvs.

Safari: A Saga of the African Blue. Martin Johnson. (Illus.). 1972. reprint ed. 40.00 (*1-55888-221-9*) Omnigraphics Inc.

Safari - The Last Adventure: How You Can Share in It. Peter H. Capstick. (Illus.). 352p. 1984. 22.95 (*0-312-69657-4*) St Martin.

Safari - the Last Adventure see Peter Capstick Collector's Library

Safari Adventure. (Pop-Up Bks.). (J). (ps-3). 1988. 9.95 (*0-8167-1444-4*) Troll Communs.

Safari Adventure. Don Bolognese. (How to Draw Your Own Story Ser.: No. 4). 1996. mass mkt. 3.50 (*0-8125-4314-9*) Tor Bks.

***Safari Adventure Company: Unlocking the 3 Treasures of Courage.** Rick Butts. 176p. (Orig.). 1997. pap. 14.98 (*0-9652991-4-7*) Coyote Creek Pr.

Safari Adventure in Legoland. Carol Matas. 96p. (J). (gr. 4-7). 1993. pap. 2.75 (*0-590-45876-0*) Scholastic Inc.

Safari Beneath the Sea: The Wonder World of the North Pacific Coast. Diane Swanson. (Sierra Club Books for Children Ser.). (Illus.). 64p. (J). (gr. 4-7). 1996. pap. 8.95 (*0-87156-860-8*) Sierra Club Childrens.

Safari Companion: A Guide to Watching African Mammals. Richard Estes. (Illus.). 470p. (Orig.). 1993. pap. 25.00 (*0-930031-49-0*) Chelsea Green Pub.

Safari Encounter. large type ed. Rosemary Carter. (Linford Romance Library). 283p. 1984. pap. 15.99 (*0-7089-6013-8*) Ulverscroft.

Safari! Endangered Species. Charlene Beeler. (Simulation Ser.). 44p. 1994. pap. 14.95 (*1-882664-11-6*) Prufrock Pr.

Safari Grammar. Mario Risso. 128p. 1995. pap. 5.95 (*0-8442-5466-5*, Natl Textbk) NTC Pub Grp.

Safari Jokes. Viki Woodworth. LC 92-38581. (Funny Side Up Ser.). (Illus.). 24p. (J). (gr. 1-4). 1995. lib. bdg. 19.93 (*1-56766-062-2*) Childs World.

Safari of African Cooking. Bill Odarty. LC 72-115155. 1971. pap. 12.00 (*0-910296-63-4*) Broadside Pr.

Safari Punctuation. Mario Risso. 128p. 1994. pap. 5.95 (*0-8442-5467-3*, Natl Textbk) NTC Pub Grp.

Safari Rifles. 2nd ed. C. T. Boddington. (Illus.). 423p. 1990. 37.50 (*0-940143-49-6*) Safari Pr.

Safari Ya Imani Ya Kanisa la Mennonite Tanzania 1934-1983. Mahlon M. Hess. (Illus.). 120p. (Orig.). 1984. pap. 5.00 (*0-9613368-0-3*) E Mennonite Bd.

Safarikleid. Lore Frobenius. 88p. (C). 1995. pap. text ed. 3.50 (*0-435-38321-3*, 38321) Heinemann.

Safarnama & Zafarnama. I. S. Nara. 327p. 1986. 25.00 (*0-8364-1793-3*, Pub. by Minerva II) S Asia.

Safavid Persia: The History & Politics of an Islamic Society. Ed. by Charles Melville. 256p. 1996. text ed. 59.50 (*1-86064-023-0*) St Martin.

Safavid Persia: The History & Politics of an Islamic Society. Ed. by Charles Melville. 256p. 1996. text ed. 19.95 (*1-86064-086-9*) St Martin.

SAFE: Security Audit & Field Evaluation for Computer Facilities & Information Systems. rev. ed. Leonard I. Krauss. LC 80-67963. 320p. reprint ed. pap. 91.20 (*0-317-27189-X*, 2023923) Bks Demand.

Safe Alternatives in Childbirth. 4th rev. ed. David Stewart et al. LC 76-19336. 268p. 1992. pap. 9.95 (*0-934426-47-3*) NAPSAC Reprods.

***Safe & Caring Nursery.** Jennifer R. Wilger. sp. (Orig.). 1998. pap. 15.99 (*0-7644-2025-9*) Group Pub.

***Safe & Easy Lawn Care.** (Taylor's Weekend Gardening Guide Ser.). 1997. write for info. (*0-614-27232-7*) HM.

Safe & Effective Use of Pesticides: Pesticide Application Compendium 1. Patrick J. Marer. LC 87-73550. 400p. 1988. 30.00 (*0-931876-83-4*, 3324) ANR Pubns CA.

Safe & Good Use of Blood in Surgery (Sanguis) Use of Blood Products & Artifical Colloids in 43 European Hospitals, No. EUR 15398. Girolamo Sirchia et al. (Illus.). 235p. 1994. 35.00 (*92-826-4118-X*, CD-NA-15-398ENC, Pub. by Europ Com UK) Bernan Associates.

Safe & Healthy: A Parent's Guide to Children's Illnesses & Accidents. William M. Sears. (Growing Family Ser.). 239p. (Orig.). 1989. pap. 8.75 (*0-912500-22-0*) La Leche.

***Safe & Secure.** John Williams. (Orig.). 1997. pap. 5.00 (*1-884838-15-4*) Walterick Pubs.

Safe & Secure - Office Building Commercial Safety. write for info. (*0-318-72635-1*, 730); 14.50 (*0-685-71700-3*); 27.50 (*0-685-71701-1*); 45.00 (*0-685-71702-X*) Inst Real Estate.

Safe & Simple Book of Electricity see Safe & Simple Electrical Experiments

Safe & Simple Electrical Experiments. Rudolf F. Graf. Orig. Title: Safe & Simple Book of Electricity. 1973. pap. 4.95 (*0-486-22950-5*) Dover.

Safe & Sound. Lucia Berlin. 104p. 1989. pap. 9.00 (*0-918395-10-0*) Poltroon Pr.

Safe & Sound. Kim M. Thompson & Karen M. Hilderbrand. (Illus.). 24p. (J). (gr. 1-5). 1995. 9.98 incl. audio (*1-882331-33-8*, TWIN 413) Twin Sisters.

***Safe & Sound.** rev. ed. Bosque. LC 96-34318. 1997. pap. 10.95 (*0-312-15204-3*) St Martin.

Safe & Sound: A Parent's Guide to Self-Protection for Kids. Gordon Franks. 1990. pap. 5.95 (*0-9625379-0-X*) Safe & Sound Prodns.

Safe & Sound: A Violence & AOD Prevention Program. Karen Vail-Smith & David M. White. 175p. (Orig.). (J). (gr. 4-8). 1995. student ed. 69.95 (*1-56688-275-3*) Bur For At-Risk.

***Safe & Sound: How Not to Get Lost in the Woods & How to Survive If You Do.** Gordon Snow. (Illus.). 80p. 1997. pap. 7.95 (*0-86492-222-1*, Pub. by Goose Ln Edits CN) Genl Dist Srvs.

Safe & Sound: How to Prevent & Treat the Most Common Childhood Emergencies. Elena Bosque & Sheila Watson. (Illus.). 128p. 1988. pap. 9.95 (*0-312-02276-X*) St Martin.

Safe & Sound: Protecting Your Child in an Unpredictable World. Vanessa L. Ochs. LC 94-45521. 216p. (Orig.). 1995. pap. 10.95 (*0-14-017880-5*, Penguin Bks) Viking Penguin.

Safe & Sound: Why You Can Stand Secure on the Future of the U. S. Economy. Bruce Howard. LC 95-42337. 1996. pap. 10.99 (*0-8423-7849-9*) Tyndale.

Safe & Sound Child: Keeping Your Child Safe Inside & Outside the Home. Larry Stone et al. 1996. pap. 12.95 (*0-673-36243-4*, GoodYrBooks) Addson-Wesley Educ.

***Safe & Sound Financial Systems: What Works for Latin America?** Ed. by Liliana Rojas-Suarez. 250p. (Orig.). 1997. pap. text ed. 18.50 (*1-886938-20-2*) IADB.

Safe & Sound Safety Program for Kids. Susan Erling & E. Gordon Franks. 1990. School curriculum. 99.95 (*0-9625379-2-6*) Safe & Sound Prodns.

Safe & Voluntary Surgical Contraception: Guidelines for Service Programs. AVSC International Staff. 105p. 1994. reprint ed. pap. text ed. 4.50 (*1-885063-06-7*) AVSC Int.

Safe As Houses. U. A. Fanthorpe. 72p. (Orig.). 1996. pap. 10.00 (*1-885266-26-X*, Pub. by Peterloo Poets UK) Story Line.

Safe As Houses. Alex Jeffers. 360p. 1995. 24.95 (*0-571-19860-0*) Faber & Faber.

Safe As Houses? Ill Health & Electro-Stress in the Home. David Cowan. (Illus.). 224p. (Orig.). 1995. pap. 13.95 (*1-85860-037-5*, Pub. by Gateway Books UK) ACCESS Pubs Network.

Safe at Any Speed: The Great Double Career of Joie Chitwood. Ed Watson & Jim Russell. (Illus.). 256p. 1992. 22.50 (*0-9627653-2-5*) Witness Prods.

Safe at Home! Peggy K. Anderson. LC 94-481. (J). 1995. pap. 3.95 (*0-689-71833-0*, Aladdin Paperbacks) S&S Childrens.

***Safe at Home: A Kate Henry Mystery.** Alison Gordon. 1996. mass mkt. 5.95 (*0-7710-3417-2*) McCland & Stewart.

Safe at Home, Safe Alone. Thomas J. Long. (Illus.). 64p. (Orig.). (J). (gr. 3-5). 1985. pap. 4.95 (*0-917917-01-4*) Miles River.

Safe at Home with Teddy Ruxpin. Michelle Baron. (Teddy Ruxpin Safe 'N' Sound Ser.). (Illus.). 34p. (J). (ps). 1988. audio write for info. (*0-934323-70-4*) Alchemy Comms.

***Safe at Home 2: More Winning Players Talk about Baseball & Their Faith, Vol. 2.** Dave Branon. 352p. (Orig.). 1997. pap. 11.99 (*0-8024-7904-9*) Moody.

Safe at Last: A Handbook for Recovery from Abuse. David J. Schopick. Ed. by Susanne Burr et al. LC 95-19355. 271p. (YA). (gr. 6-12). 1995. 15.95 (*0-914525-28-X*); pap. 9.95 (*0-914525-27-1*) Waterfront Bks.

Safe at Last in the Middle Years: The Invention of Midlife Progress Novel: Saul Bellow, Margaret Drabble, Anne Tyler, John Updike. Margaret M. Gullette. 300p. 1988. 30.00 (*0-520-06282-5*) U CA Pr.

Safe at School: Awareness & Action for Parents of Kids Grades K-12. Carol S. Saunders. Ed. by Pamela Espeland. LC 94-7165. 232p. (Orig.). 1994. pap. 14.95 (*0-915793-71-7*) Free Spirit Pub.

Safe Banks. Warren Weagant. 128p. 1988. pap. 19.95 (*0-933123-08-6*) Command Prods.

Safe Behavior Reinforcement. Daniel C. Petersen. Ed. by William G. Salo, Jr. LC 88-773. (Illus.). 175p. (Orig.). 1989. pap. 28.50 (*0-318-42046-5*) Aloray.

Safe Blood: Purifying the Nation's Blood Supply in the Age of AIDS. Joseph Feldshuh & Doron Weber. 1990. 22.95 (*0-02-910065-8*, Free Press) Free Pr.

Safe Blood & Blood Products: Distance Learning Materials, 5 Manuals, Set. 647p. 1993. pap. text ed. 108.00 (*0-614-08019-3*, 1930050) World Health.

Safe Bridge. large type ed. Frances P. Keyes. 1972. 25.99 (*0-85456-124-2*) Ulverscroft.

Safe Chain Saw Design. Thomas et al. (Illus.). 1983. 39.95 (*0-938830-02-3*) Inst Product.

Safe Child Book: A Commonsense Approach to Protecting Children & Teaching Children to Protect Themselves. Sherryll K. Kraizer. (Illus.). 160p. 1996. pap. 11.00 (*0-684-81423-4*, Fireside) S&S Trade.

Safe Choices Guide: AIDS & HIV Policies & Prevention Programs for High-Risk Youth. National Network of Runaway & Youth Services Staff. 252p. 1990. ring bd. 30.00 (*1-878848-01-1*) Natl Res Ctr.

Safe Cigarette? Ed. by Gio B. Gori & Fred G. Bock. LC 79-47999. (Banbury Reports: Vol. 3). (Illus.). 364p. 1980. 52.00 (*0-87969-202-2*) Cold Spring Harbor.

***Safe Computer Control Systems.** Taylor. (ITCP-UK Computer Science Ser.). 1997. text ed. 44.99 (*1-85032-332-1*) ITCP.

Safe Conduct. Elizabeth Benedict. LC 92-37077. 1993. 21.00 (*0-374-25341-2*) FS&G.

Safe Conduct. Boris Pasternak. LC 58-12799. 1958. pap. 9.95 (*0-8112-0135-X*, NDP77) New Directions.

Safe Conduct. Peter Vansittart. 184p. 9600. 30.00 (*0-7206-0953-4*, Pub. by P Owen Ltd UK) Dufour.

Safe Conduct. Peter Vansittart. 184p. 9600. pap. 18.95 (*0-7206-0977-1*, Pub. by P Owen Ltd UK) Dufour.

Safe Conduct: The Photographs of Paul Ickovic. Cornell Capa & Vaclav Havel. (Illus.). 96p. 1991. 29.95 (*0-933642-15-6*, U of Wash Pr) Intl Ctr Photo.

Safe Construction for the Future: Conference Proceedings. 120p. 1980. 30.00 (*0-7277-0105-3*, Pub. by T Telford UK) Am Soc Civil Eng.

Safe Current Limits for Electromedical Apparatus. 3rd ed. (AAMI - American National Standard Ser.). 14p. 1993. pap. 70.00 (*1-57020-007-6*, ES1-209) Assn Adv Med Instrn.

Safe Deposit & Other Stories About Grandparents, Old Lovers & Crazy Old Men. Afterword by Kerry M. Olitzky. 364p. 1992. pap. 12.95 (*1-55876-062-8*) Wiener Pubs Inc.

Safe Deposit & Other Stories about Grandparents, Old Lovers & Crazy Old Men. Grace Paley et al. LC 89-22412. (Masterworks of Modern Jewish Writings). 360p. 1989. 19.95 (*1-55876-013-X*) Wiener Pubs Inc.

Safe Design & Use of Chain Saws: An ILO Code of Practice. 72p. 1978. pap. 12.00 (*92-2-101927-6*, ILO90) Intl Labour Office.

Safe Dieting for Teens. Linda Ojeda. LC 92-26432. 128p. (Orig.). (YA). (gr. 7-12). 1992. pap. 9.95 (*0-89793-113-0*) Hunter Hse.

Safe Dieting for Teens. Linda Ojeda. (Illus.). 105p. (Orig.). (C). 1992. reprint ed. lib. bdg. 25.00 (*0-8095-6333-9*) Borgo Pr.

Safe Disposal of Hazardous Wastes: The Special Needs & Problems of Developing Countries, 3 vols. Ed. by Roger Batstone et al. (Technical Paper Ser.: No. 93). 854p. 1989. 25.95 (*0-8213-1144-1*, 11144) World Bank.

Safe Diving. Stracimir Gosovic. (Illus.). 496p. (C). 1993. 43.85 (*0-615-00268-4*, D627) Best Pub Co.

Safe Drinking Water: Current & Future Problems: Proceedings of a National Conference in Washington D. C. Ed. by Clifford S. Russell. LC 78-19840. (Resources for the Future Research Paper Ser.). 1978. pap. 30.00 (*0-8018-2181-9*) Johns Hopkins.

Safe Drinking Water: The Impact of Chemicals on a Limited Resource. Ed. by Rip G. Rice. LC 84-25105. (Illus.). 280p. 1984. 162.00 (*0-9614032-0-9*, CRC Reprint) Franklin.

Safe Drinking Water: The Impact of Chemicals on a Limited Resource. Ed. by Rip G. Rice. 275p. 1985. 34.95 (*0-317-01439-0*); 29.95 (*0-318-17815-X*) Intl Bottled Water.

Safe Drinking Water Act. Ed. by Edward J. Calabrese et al. (Illus.). 240p. 1989. 91.00 (*0-87371-138-6*, L138) Lewis Pubs.

Safe Drinking Water Act: A Case Study of an Unfunded Federal Mandate. Terry Dinan. (Illus.). 46p. (Orig.). 1995. pap. text ed. 20.00 (*0-7881-2612-1*) DIANE Pub.

Safe Driving Handbook: A Guide to Driving Defensively. 2nd ed. John C. Biardo. LC 95-90695. (Illus.). 128p. (Orig.). (YA). (gr. 10-12). 1996. pap. 9.95 (*0-933181-08-6*) Elmwood Park Pub.

Safe Eating. Earl Mindell. 1993. pap. 5.99 (*0-446-77690-4*) Warner Bks.

Safe Exercise Handbook. Toni T. Branner. 96p. 1995. per. 10.76 (*0-8403-8841-1*) Kendall-Hunt.

***Safe Exercise Handbook.** 3rd ed. Toni Branner. 100p. (C). 1996. per., pap. text ed. 20.94 (*0-7872-2695-5*) Kendall-Hunt.

***Safe Food.** Jacobson. 1993. pap. 4.99 (*0-425-13629-9*) Berkley Pub.

Safe Food. Michael F. Jacobson et al. 240p. (Orig.). 1993. mass mkt. 4.99 (*0-425-13621-3*) Berkley Pub.

Safe Food: Eating Wisely in a Risky World. Michael F. Jacobson et al. (Illus.). 235p. (Orig.). (J). 1991. pap. 9.95 (*1-879326-01-9*) Living Planet Pr.

Safe Food for You & Your Family. American Dietetic Association Staff. 1996. pap. text ed. 5.95 (*1-56561-094-6*) Chronimed.

***Safe Food Handling: A Training Guide for Managers of Food Service Establishments.** M. Jacob. 148p. 1989. 25.00 (*92-4-154245-4*) World Health.

Safe Food in a World of Risks: Eating Wisely. 1992. lib. bdg. 79.95 (*0-8490-5292-0*) Gordon Pr.

Safe for Democracy: A History of America, 1914-1945. Joseph M. Siracusa. LC 93-18839. 261p. 1993. 26.95 (*0-941690-49-0*); pap. 12.95 (*0-941690-50-4*) Regina Bks.

Safe for Democracy: The Anglo-American Response to Revolution, 1913-1923. Lloyd C. Gardner. 400p. (C). 1987. reprint ed. pap. 19.95 (*0-19-504155-0*) OUP.

Safe for Now. Margaret Mullen. 88p. (Orig.). 1993. pap. 11.95 (*0-9627007-1-1*) Monday Pr CA.

Safe from the Start. Cole. 1991. pap. 4.50 (*0-312-92455-0*) Tor Bks.

***Safe Handling Cytotoxic Drugs: An Independent Study Module.** rev. ed. Carol S. Blecher et al. Ed. by Jacqueline Welch & Joyce M. Silveria. (Illus.). 20p. 1997. pap. text ed. 10.00 (*1-890504-00-9*) Oncology Nursing.

***Safe Handling of Chemicals, Vol. 1 & 2.** Carson & Mumford. 1988. text ed. write for info. (*0-582-00304-0*, Pub. by Longman UK) Longman.

***Safe Handling of Chemicals in Industries, Vol. 13.** Carson. 1995. text ed. write for info. (*0-582-06307-8*, Pub. by Longman UK) Longman.

Safe Handling of Chemicals in Industry, 3 vols., Vol. 3. P. Carson & Clive J. Mumford. 496p. 1996. text ed. 185.00 (*0-470-23449-0*) Halsted Pr.

Safe Handling of Chemicals in Industry, 3 vols., Vol. 3. P. A. Carson & Clive J. Mumford. 1996. text ed. 375.00 (*0-470-23570-5*) Wiley.

Safe Handling of Flexible Intermediate Bulk Containers. ICHCA Staff. (C). 1988. 45.00 (*0-685-46514-4*, Pub. by ICHCA UK) St Mut.

Safe Handling of Flexible Intermediate Bulk Containers (FIBC's) An ICHCA Guide. ICHCA Staff. (C). 1985. 100.00 (*0-906297-50-8*, Pub. by ICHCA UK) St Mut.

Safe Handling of ISO Freight Containers by Hooks & General Guide to the Container Safety Convention. Ed. by ICHCA Staff. (C). 1988. 75.00 (*0-685-46490-3*, Pub. by ICHCA UK) St Mut.

Safe Handling of Plutonium. (Safety Ser.: No. 39). (Illus.). 135p. (Orig.). 1974. pap. 35.00 (*92-0-123473-2*, ISP358, Pub. by IAEA AU) Bernan Associates.

Safe Handling of Radioactive Materials. LC 63-60093. (Report Ser.: No. 30). 1964. pap. 20.00 (*0-913392-12-X*) NCRP Pubns.

Safe Harbor Regulations. Gerald D. Mills. 200p. (Orig.). pap. 39.95 (*0-07-600782-0*) Hlthcare Mgmt Grp.

Safe Harbour. large type ed. Brenda Parker. (Linford Romance Library). 288p. 1993. pap. 15.99 (*0-7089-7321-3*, Linford) Ulverscroft.

***Safe Haven.** Rowena Summers. 384p. 1996. 25.00 (*0-7278-4948-4*) Severn Hse.

Safe Haven: A Novel. Summer Allman. LC 93-49861. 1994. pap. 10.99 (*0-7852-8319-6*) Nelson.

Safe Haven: The Refugee Experience of Five Families. Ed. by Elizabeth McLuhan. (Illus.). 240p. 1995. pap. 28.75 (*0-919045-67-7*) U of Toronto Pr.

Safe Home for Manatees. Priscilla B. Jenkins. LC 96-3136. (Let's-Read-&-Find-Out Science Ser.: Stage 2). (Illus.). 32p. (J). (gr. k-4). 1997. 14.95 (*0-06-027149-3*); lib. bdg. 14.89 (*0-06-027150-7*) HarpC.

***Safe Home for Manatees.** Priscilla B. Jenkins. LC 96-3136. (Let's Read-&-Find-Out Science Ser.: Stage 2). (Illus.). 32p. (J). (gr. k-4). 1997. pap. 4.95 (*0-06-445164-X*, Trophy) HarpC Child Bks.

***Safe Home-Wiring Projects.** Rex Cauldwell. LC 97-5789. (Illus.). 160p. 1997. pap. 19.95 (*1-56158-164-X*, 070295) Taunton.

Safe Homes, Safe Neighborhoods. Stephanie Mann & M. C. Blakeman. 256p. 1993. pap. 14.95 (*0-87337-195-X*) Nolo Pr.

Safe Horse, Safe Rider: A Young Rider's Guide to Responsible Horsekeeping. Jessie Haas. Ed. by Amanda Haar. (Illus.). 160p. 1994. pap. 14.95 (*0-88266-700-9*, Storey Pub) Storey Comm Inc.

Safe House. Burton Shulman. 1996. pap. text ed. 12.00 (*1-887369-03-1*) Global Cty Pr.

Safe House: The Compelling Memoirs of the Only CIA Spy To Seek Asylum in Russia. Edward L. Howard. LC 95-757. 299p. 1995. 23.95 (*1-882605-15-2*) Natl Pr Bks.

Safe Houses. Rose Zwi. 160p. 1994. pap. 13.95 (*1-875559-21-3*, Pub. by SpiniFex Pr AT) LPC InBook.

Safe in America: A Novel. Marcie Hershman. LC 95-5737. 320p. 1995. 24.00 (*0-06-017144-8*, HarpT) HarpC.

Safe in America: A Novel. Marcie Hershman. 304p. 1996. pap. 12.50 (*0-06-092734-8*) HarpC.

Safe in His Care. Lily A. Bear. 1984. 8.15 (*0-318-03659-2*) Rod & Staff.

Safe in My Heart. Leigh Michaels. (Romance Ser.). 1993. pap. 2.89 (*0-373-03248-X*, 1-03248-1) Harlequin Bks.

***Safe in Paradise.** large type ed. Barbara Cartland. (Magna Large Print Ser.). 196p. 1997. 27.50 (*0-7505-1109-5*) Ulverscroft.

Safe in the City: A Streetwise Guide to Avoid Being Robbed, Raped, Ripped off, Or Run Over. Marc A. MacYoung & Chris Pfouts. 312p. 1994. pap. 21.95 (*0-87364-775-0*) Paladin Pr.

Safe in the Father's Arms: A 30-Day Devotional. Steve Fry. 96p. pap. 9.95 (*0-917143-34-5*) Sparrow TN.

Safe in the Sun. rev. ed. Mary E. Siegel. 1995. pap. 8.95 (*0-8027-7459-8*) Walker & Co.

Safe in the Sun: Your Skin Survival Guide for the 1990s. Mary E. Siegel. 258p. 1990. 21.95 (*0-8027-1100-6*); pap. 13.95 (*0-8027-7338-9*) Walker & Co.

Safe in the World. D. Martyn Lloyd-Jones. LC 87-70457. (John Seventeen Ser.). 160p. 1988. 14.99 (*0-89107-493-7*) Crossway Bks.

***Safe Inside the Sound.** Suzaine Rosenwasser. Date not set. write for info. (*0-688-05413-7*) Morrow.

Safe Investing: How to Make Money Without Losing Your Shirt. John Slatter. 1991. pap. 14.95 (*0-13-786195-8*, Busn) P-H.

Safe Journey Home. large type ed. Elisabeth Hargreaves. 400p. 1985. 25.99 (*0-7089-1295-8*) Ulverscroft.

Safe Kids: A Complete Child Safety Handbook & Resource Guide for Parents. Vivian K. Fancher. LC 90-21700. 209p. 1991. pap. text ed. 12.95 (*0-471-52973-7*) Wiley.

Safe Laboratories: Principle - Practices - Design - Remodeling. Ed. by Malcolm M. Renfrew & Peter C. Ashbrook. (Illus.). 184p. 1991. 71.95 (*0-87371-200-5*, L200) Lewis Pubs.

Safe Love & Other Political Acts. Lisa C. Taylor. LC 95-92152. (Illus.). 72p. 1995. pap. 10.00 (*0-9646195-0-4*) Plumeria Pr.

Safe Maintenance Guide for Robotic Workstations. 1995. lib. bdg. 255.75 (*0-8490-7521-1*) Gordon Pr.

Safe Maintenance Guide for Robotic Workstations. John R. Etherton. (Illus.). 53p. (Orig.). (C). 1994. pap. text ed. 20.00 (*0-7881-0398-9*) DIANE Pub.

Safe Medical Devices Act of 1990: A Legislative History of Public Law No. 101-629, 5 vols., Set. Ed. by Bernard D. Reams, Jr. LC 96-75096. (Federal Health Law Ser.: Pt. 10). 1996. 490.00 (*1-57588-093-8*, 309070) W S Hein.

Safe Medical Devices Act of 1990: Implications for Health Care Personnel - Information Package. 101p. (Orig.). 1992. pap. 95.00 (*1-57020-053-X*, MDR91-209) Assn Adv Med Instrn.

Safe Motorist's Guide to Speedtraps: State by State Listings to Keep Drivers Alert. John Tomerlin & Dru Whitledge. 367p. (Orig.). 1991. pap. 19.95 (*0-929387-26-0*) Bonus Books.

Safe Navigation Symposium Papers Washington, D. C. OCIMF Staff. 1978. 198.00 (*0-317-61463-0*, Pub. by Witherby & Co UK) St Mut.

Safe Not Sorry. Phyllis Schlafly. 1967. 1.00 (*0-934640-06-8*) Pere Marquette.

***Safe, Not Sorry: Keeping Yourself & Your Family Safe in a Violent Age.** Tanya Metaksa. LC 97-632. 256p. 1997. 23.00 (*0-06-039191-X*, ReganBooks) HarpC.

Safe Operation of Agricultural Equipment. Intro. by Thomas A. Silletto & Dale O. Hull. (Illus.). 1988. teacher ed., pap. text ed. 6.25 (*0-913163-21-X*, 10176) Hobar Pubns.

Safe Operation of Agricultural Equipment: Student Manual. Intro. by Thomas A. Silletto & Dale O. Hull. (Illus.). 1996. pap. text ed. 6.25 (*0-913163-27-9*, 10076) Hobar Pubns.

Safe Operations in Congested Airspace: Business & Commuter Flying in Europe: Proceedings of the Flight Safety Foundation European Corporate Aviation Safety Seminar (ECASS), March 1989, Zurich, Switzerland. Flight Safety Foundation Staff. LC 91-657078. (Flight Safety Digest Ser. Special Supplement: Vol. 8, No. 6, June 1989). 52p. reprint ed. pap. 25.00 (*0-7837-7006-5*, 2046820) Bks Demand.

Safe Passage. Ellyn Bache. 320p. 1995. cd-rom 7.50 (*1-886420-09-2*, Boson Bks) C & M Online.

Safe Passage. Ellyn Bache. LC 93-90159. 234p. 1993. reprint ed. pap. 8.95 (*0-9635967-7-2*) Banks Channel.

Safe Passage: Recovery for Adult Children of Alcoholics. Stephanie Brown. LC 91-4692. 288p. 1991. text ed. 47.50 (*0-471-54888-X*); pap. text ed. 12.95 (*0-471-53221-5*) Wiley.

Safe Passage: Words to Help the Grieving Hold Fast & Let Go. Molly Fumia. 288p. (Orig.). 1992. pap. 10.95 (*0-943233-39-9*) Conari Press.

Safe Passage: Words to Help the Grieving Hold Fast & Let Go. Molly Fumia. (Illus.). 288p. (Orig.). (C). 1993. reprint ed. lib. bdg. 31.00 (*0-8095-5871-8*) Borgo Pr.

Safe Passage into the Twenty-First Century: The United Nations' Quest for Peace, Equality, Justice & Development. Robert Muller & Douglas Roche. LC 95-20380. 146p. 1995. pap. text ed. 11.95 (*0-8264-0866-4*) Continuum.

Safe Passage on City Streets. Dorothy T. Samuel. LC 91-62085. 128p. 1991. pap. 6.00 (*0-9629905-0-7*) Liberty Literary.

Safe Passage to Healing: A Guide to Survivors of Ritual Abuse. Chrystine Oksana. LC 93-47635. 352p. (Orig.). 1994. pap. 15.00 (*0-06-096996-2*, PL) HarpC.

Safe People: How to Find Relationships That Are Good for You. Henry Cloud & John Townsend. 128p. 1995. wbk. ed. 8.99 (*0-310-49501-6*) Zondervan.

Safe People: How to Find Relationships That Are Good for You. Henry Cloud & John Townsend. 256p. 1995. 18.99 (*0-310-59560-6*) Zondervan.

Safe People: How to Find Relationships That Are Good for You & Avoid Those That Aren't. Henry Cloud & John Townsend. 208p. 1996. pap. 10.99 (*0-310-21084-4*) Zondervan.

Safe Place. Lorenzo Carcaterra. 1994. mass mkt. 6.99 (*0-345-38348-6*) Ballantine.

***Safe Place.** Lemieux. (Fair Lair Ser.: 2). (J). 1998. mass mkt. 3.99 (*0-689-81726-6*) S&S Childrens.

Safe Place. Tehila Peterseil. (Illus.). 144p. (YA). 1996. pap. 12.95 (*0-943706-72-6*) Pitspopany.

***Safe Place.** Tehila Peterseil. (Illus.). 144p. (YA). 1996. 16.95 (*0-943706-71-8*) Pitspopany.

Safe Place. Anne Rider. LC 73-22656. 192p. 1974. 6.95 (*0-672-51992-5*, Bobbs) Macmillan.

***Safe Place.** Maxine Trottier. LC 96-34555. (Illus.). 24p. (J). 1997. lib. bdg. 12.95 (*0-8075-7212-8*) A Whitman.

***Safe Place: A Journal for Women Diagnosed with Breast Cancer.** Jennifer Pike. 192p. (Orig.). 1997. pap. 12.95 (*1-55192-108-1*, Pub. by Raincoast Bks CN) Orca Bk Pubs.

Safe Place: Beyond Sexual Abuse. Jan Morrison. 216p. (Orig.). (YA). 1990. pap. 7.99 (*0-87788-747-0*) Shaw Pubs.

Safe Place: Laying the Groundwork of Psychotherapy. Leston L. Havens. LC 89-7571. 192p. 1989. 32.00 (*0-674-00085-4*) HUP.

Safe Place: Laying the GroundWork of Psychotherapy. Leston L. Havens. 192p. 1996. pap. 12.00 (*0-674-00086-2*) HUP.

Safe Place to Die. Janice Law. 1995. mass mkt. 3.99 (*0-373-26179-9*, 1-26179-1) Harlequin Bks.

Safe Place to Sleep. Jennifer L. Jordan. 171p. 1992. pap. 9.95 (*0-9634075-0-3*) Our Power Pr.

***Safe Places: Finding Security in the Passages of Your Life.** Stephen Arterburn et al. 256p. 1997. 16.99 (*0-7852-7867-2*) Nelson.

Safe Places? Security Planning & Litigation. Richard S. Kuhlman. 686p. 1989. 65.00 (*0-87473-507-6*) MICHIE.

Safe Practice in Obstetrics & Gynaecology. Ed. by Roger V. Clements. 492p. 1994. 95.00 (*0-443-04841-X*) Churchill.

Safe Practices Guide for Air Separation Plants. 3rd ed. 44p. 1989. 66.00 (*0-318-17555-X*, CGA P-8) Compress Gas.

Safe Practices in Chemical Laboratories. Royal Society of Chemistry Staff. 1989. 49.00 (*0-85186-309-4*) CRC Pr.

Safe Product Design in Law, Management & Engineering. Herman R. Heideklang. 272p. 1990. 95.00 (*0-8247-8462-6*) Dekker.

Safe Return. Catherine Dexter. 96p. (J). (gr. 4-7). 1996. 15.99 (*0-7636-0005-9*) Candlewick Pr.

Safe Road Transport in the Petroleum Industry: The Way Ahead: Papers Presented at a Conference-Organised by the Conveyance Panel of the Institute of Petroleum's Marketing Sub-Committee on 6 November 1990. Institute of Petroleum, London Staff. (Illus.). 120p. reprint ed. pap. 34.20 (*0-7837-6846-X*, 2046675) Bks Demand.

S

Safe Schools: A Handbook for Practitioners. Ed. by Robert Mahaffey. (Illus.). 200p. (Orig.). 1995. pap. 125.00 (*0-88210-304-0*) Natl Assn Principals.

Safe Schools: A Handbook for Violence Prevention. Ronald D. Stephens. 158p. (Orig.). 1995. pap. 25.00 (*1-879639-32-7*) Natl Educ Serv.

Safe Schools: A Security & Loss Prevention Plan. James B. Hylton. 234p. 1996. 34.95 (*0-7506-9759-8*, Focal) Buttrwrth-Heinemann.

Safe, Self-Confident Child. American Institute for Preventive Medicine Staff. LC 93-40577. (For Your Information Ser.). 1993. 8.95 (*1-56420-033-7*); audio 16.00 (*1-56420-034-5*) New Readers.

***Safe, Self-Confident Child: A Quick & Easy Guide.** Minnesota Early Learning Design Staff. (For Your Information Ser.). (Orig.). 1997. pap. 8.95 (*0-614-28111-3*, Signal Hill) New Readers.

Safe Sex: A Doctor Explains the Realities of AIDS & Other STDs. Joe S. McIlhaney, Jr. 176p. (YA). (gr. 9). 1992. pap. 8.99 (*0-8010-6294-2*) Baker Bks.

Safe Sex: A Guide to Condoms. 2nd ed. James Brackett. 1991. 5.95 (*0-929240-25-1*) EMIS.

Safe Sex see IVP Booklets

Safe Sex? see Save Sex

Safe Sex in the Age of AIDS. Ed. by Ted McIlvenna. 96p. 1986. pap. 3.95 (*0-8065-0996-1*, Citadel Pr) Carol Pub Group.

Safe Sex Never Tasted So Good. Susan L. Mintz. LC 90-188642. (Illus.). 144p. 1990. pap. write for info. (*0-9636037-0-1*) Boner Pubns.

Safe Ship - Safe Cargo, Vol. II. Ed. by Cargo Systems Staff. 1987. 195.00 (*0-907499-56-2*, Pub. by Cargo Systs UK) St Mut.

Safe Shopper's Bible: A Consumer Guide to Nontoxic Household Products, Cosmetics, & Food. David Steinman & Samuel S. Epstein. (Illus.). 464p. 1995. pap. 14.95 (*0-02-082085-2*) Macmillan.

Safe, Smart & Self-Reliant: Personal Safety for Women & Children. Foundation for Crime Prevention & Education Staff. Ed. by Gerri M. Dyer. LC 95-71363. (Illus.). 252p. 1996. 16.95 (*0-9648903-0-5*) Safety Press.

Safe Storage of Laboratory Chemicals. 2nd ed. Ed. by David A. Pipitone. LC 90-12949. 297p. 1991. text ed. 115.00 (*0-471-51581-7*) Wiley.

Safe Storage of Pyroxylin Plastics. National Fire Protection Association Staff. (Forty Ser.). 1993. 15.50 (*0-317-63073-3*, 40E-93) Natl Fire Prot.

Safe, Strong & Streetwise: The Teenager's Guide to Preventing Sexual Assault. Helen Benedict. (Joy Street Bks.). (Illus.). 192p. (YA). (gr. 7 up). 1987. pap. 6.95 (*0-87113-100-5*) Little.

SAFE, Student Assistance & Family Education Program: A Dynamic Program for Elementary Schools. Pamela Lemerand. LC 92-40065. 208p. 1993. pap. 39.95 (*1-56246-053-6*, P236) Johnsn Inst.

Safe Surfing: A Family Tour of the Net. Julie McKeehan. LC 96-8193. (Illus.). 326p. 1996. pap. text ed. 24.95 (*0-12-484834-6*, AP Prof) Acad Pr.

Safe Therapeutic Exercise for the Frail Elderly: An Introduction. Olga Hurley. (Illus.). 1988. pap. 14.95 (*0-937829-02-1*) Ctr Study Aging.

***Safe This Night.** 32p. (J). 1997. write for info. (*0-7459-3616-4*, Lion) Chariot Victor.

Safe to Let Out? The Current & Future Use of Secure Accommodation for Children & Young People. 72p. 1996. pap. 14.50 (*1-874579-63-6*, Pub. by Natl Childrens Bur UK) Paul & Co Pubs.

Safe Tourist - U. S. A. Hundreds of Proven Ways to Outsmart Trouble & Still Have a Wonderful Trip. Natalie Windsor. LC 94-42473. 224p. 1995. pap. 8.95 (*0-944042-27-9*) CorkScrew Pr.

Safe Tractor Operation & Daily Care. rev. ed. (Illus.). 120p. 1981. pap. 11.00 (*0-89606-056-X*, 103) Am Assn Voc Materials.

Safe Travel Book. rev. ed. Peter V. Savage. 222p. pap. 12.95 (*0-02-927726-4*, Free Press) Free Pr.

Safe Travel in Bear Country. Gary Brown. LC 95-40200. 152p. 1996. pap. 10.95 (*1-55821-349-X*) Lyons & Burford.

Safe Trip Abroad. 1994. lib. bdg. 250.00 (*0-8490-6475-9*) Gordon Pr.

Safe Use of Pesticides. (Technical Report Ser.: No. 720). 60p. 1985. pap. text ed. 6.00 (*92-4-120720-5*, 1100720) World Health.

An Asterisk (*) at the beginning of an entry indicates that the title is appearing in BIP for the first time.

Safe Use of Pesticides: Fourteenth Report of the WHO Expert Committee on Vector Biology & Control. (Technical Report Ser.: No. 813). iv, 27p. (ENG, FRE & SPA.). 1991. pap. text ed. 6.00 (*92-4-120813-9*, 1100813) World Health.

Safe Use of Pesticides: Proceedings of the WHO Expert Committee on Insecticides, 20th, Geneva, 1972. WHO Staff. (Technical Report Ser.: No. 513). 1973. pap. text ed. 6.00 (*92-4-120513-X*, 1100513) World Health.

***Safe Use of Pesticides: Third Report of the WHO Expert Committee on Vector Biology & Control.** (Technical Report Ser.: No. 634). 44p. 1979. pap. text ed. 5.00 (*92-4-120634-9*, 1100634) World Health.

***Safe Use of Pesticides in Public Health: Sixteenth Report of the WHO Expert Committee on Insecticides.** (Technical Report Ser.: No. 356). 0065p. 1967. pap. text ed. 5.00 (*92-4-120356-0*, 1100356) World Health.

Safe Use of Radioactive Tracers in Industrial Processes. (Safety Ser.: No. 40). 54p. (Orig.). 1974. pap. 16.00 (*92-0-123074-5*, ISP369, Pub. by IAEA AU) Bernan Associates.

Safe Use of Solvents. A. J. Collings & S. G. Luxon. 1982. text ed. 132.00 (*0-12-181250-2*) Acad Pr.

Safe Use of Vitamin A. J. Christopher Bauernfeind. Ed. by G. Arroyave et al. (Illus.). 44p. (Orig.). 1980. pap. text ed. 3.50 (*0-935368-24-8*) ILSI.

Safe Uses of Cortisol. 2nd ed. William M. Jefferies. (Illus.). 228p. 1996. 52.95 (*0-398-06620-5*); pap. 37.95 (*0-398-06621-3*) C C Thomas.

Safe Water from Every Tap: Improving Water Service to Small Communities. National Research Council Staff. 230p. (Orig.). (C). 1996. pap. text ed. 39.95 (*0-309-05527-X*) Natl Acad Pr.

Safe Within Your Love. rev. ed. Hannah W. Smith. Ed. by David Hazard. (Rekindling the Inner Fire Ser.: Vol. 4). 176p. 1992. pap. 8.99 (*1-55661-301-6*) Bethany Hse.

Safe Within Yourself: A Woman's Guide to Rape Prevention & Self-Defense. Doris Kaufman et al. LC 79-566334. (Illus.). 1980. pap. 15.00 (*0-916818-05-5*) Victimology.

***Safe Work Practices for Wastewater Treatment Plants.** Frank R. Spellman. 368p. 1996. pap. 49.95 (*1-56676-406-8*, 764068) Technomic.

***Safe Young Drivers: A Guide for Parents & Teens.** Phil Berardelli. LC 96-44731. (Illus.). 160p. 1996. spiral bd., pap. 12.00 (*1-889324-03-5*) EPM Pubns.

Safecomp 1993: The International Conference on Computer Safety, Reliability, & Security, 12th, Poznan, Poland, 27-29 October 1993. Ed. by Janusz Gorski. LC 93-35675. 1994. 107.95 (*0-387-19838-5*) Spr-Verlag.

SAFECOMP '95: The 14th International Conference on Computer Safety, Reliability & Security. Ed. by Gerhard Rabe. LC 95-37874. 528p. 1995. pap. 115.00 (*3-540-19962-4*) Spr-Verlag.

***Safecomp '96: The 15th International Conference on Computer Safety, Reliability, & Security, Vienna, Austria, October 23-25, 1996.** Ed. by E. Schoitsch. LC 96-44491. (Illus.). 425p. 1996. text ed. 109.00 (*3-540-76070-9*) Spr-Verlag.

Safecracking the Mortgage Secrets: The Complete Guide to Home Loans. Janet T. Freidman. Ed. by Marie-Louise Crozat. (Illus.). 192p. (Orig.). 1987. pap. 24.95 (*0-318-22506-9*) M A Enter.

Safed Spirituality: Rules of Mystical Piety, the Beginning of Wisdom. Safed. Tr. by Lawrence Fine. (Classics of Western Spirituality Ser.). 1984. pap. 15.95 (*0-8091-2612-5*) Paulist Pr.

Safed, the Mystical City. David Rosoff. 1991. 17.95 (*0-87306-566-2*) Feldheim.

Safeguard of Sailors, or Great Rutter. Tr. by Robert Norman. LC 76-57412. (English Experience Ser.: No. 827). 1977. reprint ed. lib. bdg. 30.00 (*90-221-0827-9*) Walter J Johnson.

***Safeguard of the Sea.** Nicholas Rodger. Date not set. write for info. (*0-393-04579-X*) Norton.

Safeguard Your Hard-Earned Savings. Ken Stern. 192p. (Orig.). 1995. pap. 11.99 (*1-56414-173-X*) Career Pr Inc.

Safeguarding Building Construction & Demolition Operations. National Fire Protection Association Staff. 1989. 15.50 (*0-317-63358-9*, 241-89) Natl Fire Prot.

Safeguarding Canada, Seventeen Sixty-Three to Eighteen Seventy-One. J. Mackay Hitsman. LC 68-95288. (Illus.). 262p. reprint ed. pap. 74.70 (*0-8357-8314-6*, 2034052) Bks Demand.

Safeguarding Civil Liberty Today. Carl L. Becker. 1949. 14.50 (*0-8446-1064-X*) Peter Smith.

Safeguarding Concepts Illustrated. 5th ed. National Safety Council Staff. LC 86-61185. (Illus.). 94p. reprint ed. pap. 26.80 (*0-7837-5569-4*, 2045346) Bks Demand.

Safeguarding Concepts Illustrated. 6th rev. ed. LC 92-85028. (Illus.). 130p. (Orig.). (C). 1992. pap. 37.50 (*0-87912-169-6*, 13004-0000) Natl Safety Coun.

Safeguarding Electronic Information: Law & Order on the Internet & Other Computer Security Quandries. Ed. by Jana Varlejs. LC 95-44767. 96p. 1996. pap. 19.95 (*0-7864-0189-3*) McFarland & Co.

Safeguarding Food Quality. Ed. by H. Sommer et al. LC 93-9392. 1993. 94.95 (*0-387-56368-7*) Spr-Verlag.

Safeguarding Liberty: The Constitution & Citizens Militias. James Pratt. 1995. pap. 14.00 (*1-880692-18-X*) Legacy Comms.

Safeguarding Our Children. Bill Allard. LC 95-90961. 109p. (Orig.). 1996. pap. 7.95 (*0-9649784-0-7*) Utopia Bks.

Safeguarding School Funds. Henry H. Linn. LC 76-176997. (Columbia University. Teachers College. Contributions to Education Ser.: No. 387). reprint ed. 37.50 (*0-404-55387-7*) AMS Pr.

Safeguarding Standards. Roy Parker. (C). 1990. 45.00 (*0-7855-0066-9*, Pub. by Natl Inst Soc Work); pap. 30.00 (*0-902789-68-6*, Pub. by Natl Inst Soc Work) St Mut.

Safeguarding the Atom: A Critical Appraisal. David Fischer & Paul Szasz. Ed. by Jozef Goldblat. 250p. 1985. 65.00 (*0-85066-306-7*) Taylor & Francis.

Safeguarding the Food Supply Through Irradiation Processing Techniques. 277p. (Orig.). (C). 1993. pap. text ed. 25.00 (*0-944919-05-7*) Agri Research Inst.

Safeguarding the Future. 40p. 1989. 6.00 (*0-89714-064-8*, 89.III.H.2) UN.

Safeguarding the Public: Historical Aspects of Medicinal Drug Control. Conference on the History of Medicinal Drug Control (1968: National Library of Medicine). Ed. by John B. Blake. LC 76-84651. 213p. reprint ed. pap. 60.80 (*0-317-19888-2*, 2023084) Bks Demand.

Safeguarding the Public Health. Stuart Galishoff. LC 75-66. (Illus.). 191p. 1975. text ed. 55.00 (*0-8371-7956-4*, GPH/, Greenwood Pr) Greenwood.

Safeguarding the Republic: Essays & Documents in American Foreign Relations, 1890-1991. Howard Jones. 1992. text ed. write for info. (*0-07-033016-6*) McGraw.

Safeguarding the School Board's Purchase of Architects' Working Drawings. Arthur M. Proctor. LC 73-177168. (Columbia University. Teachers College. Contributions to Education Ser.: No. 474). reprint ed. 37.50 (*0-404-55474-1*) AMS Pr.

Safeguarding Ukraine's Security: Dilemmas & Options. Ed. by Youri Matseiko & Steven E. Miller. (CSIA Studies in International Security: No. 9). (Illus.). 350p. 1997. 39.95 (*0-262-13310-5*) MIT Pr.

Safeguarding Ukraine's Security: Dilemmas & Options. Ed. by Youri Matseiko & Steven E. Miller. (CSIA Studies in International Security: Vol. No. 9). (Illus.). 350p. 1997. pap. 17.95 (*0-262-63164-4*) MIT Pr.

Safeguarding Your Teenager from the Dragons of Life: A Parent's Guide to the Adolescent Years. Bettie B. Youngs. 310p. (Orig.). 1993. pap. 11.95 (*1-55874-264-6*, 2646) Health Comm.

Safeguards for the Saints. rev. ed. Clay Sterrett. 126p. 1992. pap. 5.00 (*0-9621713-3-6*) CFC Literature.

Safeguards Systems Analysis: With Applications to Nuclear Material Safeguards & Other Inspection Problems. Rudolf Avenhaus. 380p. 1986. 95.00 (*0-306-42169-0*, Plenum Pr) Plenum.

Safehouse. Paula Inwood. LC 90-70901. 417p. 1991. pap. 10.95 (*1-55523-357-0*) Winston-Derek.

Safekeeping. Peg Sutherland. 1994. mass mkt. 3.50 (*0-373-70620-0*, 1-70620-9) Harlequin Bks.

Safelight. Linda C. Gray. 336p. (Orig.). 1992. pap. 4.99 (*0-451-17317-1*, Sig) NAL-Dutton.

Safely by Sea. Malcolm J. Kennedy & Michael J. O'Connor. 346p. (C). 1990. lib. bdg. 51.00 (*0-8191-7814-4*) U Pr of Amer.

Safely Sexual. Robert A. Hatcher et al. (Illus.). 250p. 1997. 22.95 (*0-8290-2454-9*); pap. 12.95 (*0-8290-2453-0*) Irvington.

Safer by Design. Howard Abbott. (Illus.). 240p. (C). 1987. 28.95 (*0-85072-204-7*, Pub. by Design Council Bks UK) Ashgate Pub Co.

***Safer by Design: A Guide to the Management & Law of Designing for Product Safety.** 2nd ed. Howard Abbott & Mark Tyler. LC 96-34694. (Design Council Ser.). 200p. 1997. text ed. 63.95 (*0-566-07707-8*, Pub. by Gower UK) Ashgate Pub Co.

Safer C: Development of High-Integrity & Safety-Critical Systems. Les Hatton. LC 94-23202. (Software Engineering Metaphysics Ser.). 1995. pap. text ed. 40.00 (*0-07-707640-0*) McGraw.

Safer Childbirth? A Critical History of Maternity Care. Marjorie Tew. 250p. 1990. pap. 32.50 (*0-412-33740-1*, A4423) Chapman & Hall.

Safer Childbirth? A Critical History of Maternity Care. 2nd ed. Marjorie Tew. 432p. 1994. pap. text ed. 47.75 (*1-56593-302-8*, 0626) Singular Publishing.

Safer Childbirth? A Critical History of Maternity Care. 2nd ed. Marjorie Tew. LC 94-68238. 414p. 1995. pap. 47.75 (*0-412-56100-X*) Chapman & Hall.

Safer Cities: Guidelines for Planning, Design, & Management. Carolyn Whitzman & Gerda R. Wekerle. 240p. 1994. text ed. 52.95 (*0-442-01269-1*) Van Nos Reinhold.

Safer Death: Multidisciplinary Aspects of Terminal Care. Ed. by A. Gilmore & S. Gilmore. LC 88-12414. (Illus.). 228p. 1988. 75.00 (*0-306-42912-8*, Plenum Pr) Plenum.

Safer Future: Reducing the Impacts of Natural Disasters. National Research Council Staff. 76p. 1991. pap. text ed. 12.95 (*0-309-04546-0*) Natl Acad Pr.

Safer Insecticides: Development & Use. Hodgson & Ronald J. Kuhr. (Drug & Chemical Toxicology Ser.: Vol. 7). 608p. 1990. 199.00 (*0-8247-7884-7*) Dekker.

Safer Lifting for Patient Care. 3rd ed. M. Hollis. 240p. 1990. pap. 29.95 (*0-632-02892-0*) Blackwell Sci.

Safer Planet Sex: The Handbook. Tuppy Owens. (Illus.). 270p. (Orig.). 1994. pap. 14.95 (*1-872819-11-7*, Pub. by Tuppy Owens UK) AK Pr Dist.

Safer Prescribing: A Guide to Some Problems in the Use of Drugs. 5th ed. Linda Beeley. 128p. 1991. pap. 16.95 (*0-632-03292-8*) Blackwell Sci.

Safer Roads: A Guide to Road Safety Engineering. Ken W. Ogden. 544p. 1996. 99.95 (*0-291-39829-4*, Pub. by Avebury Technical UK) Ashgate Pub Co.

Safer Sex: Guidelines to Live By. David Wiemers & Paul Turner. (Illus.). 32p. (Orig.). 1995. pap. 4.95 (*0-9648684-0-7*) InfoPlus.

Safer Sex: How Safe Is Safe? rev. ed. Christina Dye. 1995. pap. 0.50 (*0-89230-221-6*) Do It Now.

Safer Sexy: The Guide to Gay Sex Safely. Peter Tatchell. (Sexual Politics Ser.). (Illus.). 128p. 1994. pap. 19.95 (*1-86047-000-9*) LPC InBook.

***Safer Systems: Proceedings of the Fifth Safety-Critical Systems Symposium, 4-6 February 1997, Brighton, U. K.** Felix Redmill & Tom Anderson. LC 96-52064. 1997. pap. write for info. (*3-540-76134-9*) Spr-Verlag.

Safer Than a Known Way. Pamela R. Moore. LC 88-26514. 224p. 1990. pap. 9.99 (*0-8007-9175-4*) Chosen Bks.

Safer Than a Known Way. Pamela R. Moore. LC 88-26514. 224p. (gr. 10). 1996. mass mkt. 5.99 (*0-8007-8631-9*, Spire) Revell.

Safer Than a Known Way. 2nd rev. ed. John S. McConnell. (Illus.). 266p. 1988. 50.00 (*0-9588324-3-9*, Pub. by Delaware Grp AT) Am Overseas Bk Co.

Safest Creed. Octavius B. Frothingham. (Notable American Authors Ser.). 1992. reprint ed. lib. bdg. 75.00 (*0-7812-2904-9*) Rprt Serv.

Safety. (Illus.). 48p. (J). (gr. 6-12). 1986. pap. 1.85 (*0-8395-3347-0*, 33347) BSA.

Safety. 2nd ed. Alton L. Thygerson. 1991. pap. 30.00 (*0-86720-272-6*) Jones & Bartlett.

Safety: A Salute to Black Inventors. rev. ed. Ann C. Howell. Ed. by Evelyn L. Ivery. (Black Inventors Activity Bks.). (Illus.). 24p. (J). (gr. 3-7). 1992. reprint ed. pap. text ed. 1.50 (*1-877804-02-9*) Chandler White.

Safety: Principles & Issues. Dean F. Miller. 320p. (C). 1994. text ed. write for info. (*0-697-10943-7*) Brown & Benchmark.

***Safety: Principles & Issues.** 2nd ed. Miller. 1998. text ed. 30.00 (*0-697-29440-4*) McGraw.

Safety - Risk Analysis: Explosions. Thor E. Foyn. (C). 1989. 105.00 (*0-89771-726-0*, Pub. by Lorne & MacLean Marine) St Mut.

Safety Always Matters. Dottie Ahbe & Terry Pluta. (Fire Safety Education Ser.). (Illus.). 32p. (J). (gr. 1-3). 1988. student ed. 2.00 (*0-9620584-4-0*) Safety Always Matters.

Safety Always Matters. Dottie Ahbe & Terry Pluta. (Fire Safety Education Ser.). (Illus.). 32p. (J). (gr. 4-6). 1988. student ed. 2.00 (*0-9620584-5-9*) Safety Always Matters.

Safety Always Matters. Dottie Ahbe & Terry Pluta. (Fire Safety Education Ser.). (Illus.). 32p. (J). (ps). 1991. student ed. 2.00 (*0-9620584-3-2*) Safety Always Matters.

Safety Always Matters. Dottie Ahbe & Terry Pluta. (Fire Safety Education Ser.). (Illus.). 16p. (J). (ps). 1992. student ed. 0.59 (*0-9620584-0-8*) Safety Always Matters.

Safety Always Matters. Dottie Ahbe & Terry Pluta. (Fire Safety Education Ser.). (Illus.). 16p. (J). (gr. 1-3). 1992. student ed. 0.59 (*0-9620584-1-6*) Safety Always Matters.

Safety Always Matters. Dottie Ahbe & Terry Pluta. (Fire Safety Education Ser.). (Illus.). 16p. (J). (gr. 4-6). 1992. student ed. 0.59 (*0-9620584-2-4*) Safety Always Matters.

Safety & Clinical Efficacy of Implanted Neuroaugmentive Devices. Ed. by Philip L. Gildenberg. (Applied Neurophysiology Ser.: Vol. 40, Nos. 2-4). (Illus.). 1978. pap. 46.50 (*3-8055-2925-2*) S Karger.

Safety & Efficacy of Radiopharmaceuticals. Ed. by Knud Kristensen & Elisabeth Norbygaard. (Developments in Nuclear Medicine Ser.). 1983. lib. bdg. 171.00 (*0-89838-609-8*) Kluwer Ac.

Safety & Efficacy of Radiopharmaceuticals 1987. Ed. by Knud Kristensen & Elisabeth Norbygaard. (Developments in Nuclear Medicine Ser.). (C). 1987. lib. bdg. 194.00 (*0-89838-986-0*) Kluwer Ac.

Safety & Engineering Aspects of Spent Fuel Storage. I.A. E.A. Staff. 451p. 1995. pap. text ed. 160.00 (*92-0-101695-6*, STI/PUB/949, Pub. by IAEA AU) Bernan Associates.

***Safety & Environmental Issues in Rock Engineering, 1.** A. A. Balkema. 928p. 1995. pap. text ed. 75.00 (*90-5410-340-X*, Pub. by A A Balkema NE) Ashgate Pub Co.

Safety & Environmental Management. Dellagiustina. LC 96-19451. 400p. (C). 1996. text ed. 59.95 (*0-442-02117-8*) Van Nos Reinhold.

Safety & Environmental Training: Using Compliance to Improve Your Company. Dawn A. Baldwin. LC 92-15212. 1992. text ed. 57.95 (*0-442-01066-4*) Van Nos Reinhold.

Safety & Equipment Risks: Do You Prevent Injuries? Meridith B. Cox. (Orig.). (C). 1991. pap. text ed. 55.00 (*0-912665-24-6*) Cox Pubns.

Safety & Fire Protection. (Principles of Steam Generation Ser.: Module 1). 80p. 1982. spiral bd. 29.50 (*0-87683-251-6*) GP Courseware.

***Safety & Health.** Goetsch. 1997. pap. text ed. 29.33 (*0-13-674243-2*) P-H.

Safety & Health for Engineering. Brauer. (Industrial Health & Safety Ser.). 1992. teacher ed., pap. 20.95 (*0-442-01477-5*) Van Nos Reinhold.

Safety & Health for Engineering. Brauer. 1994. pap. 83.95 (*0-442-01856-8*) Van Nos Reinhold.

Safety & Health for Engineers. 2nd ed. Roger L. Brauer. 130p. 1994. pap. text ed. 79.95 (*0-442-02040-6*) Van Nos Reinhold.

Safety & Health for Production Agriculture. Dennis J. Murphy. LC 92-74464. 256p. 1992. 39.00 (*0-929355-32-6*, M0792) Am Soc Ag Eng.

Safety & Health Guide for Indiana Business. Ice M. Donadio & Ryan. 1996. 46.00 (*1-883698-04-9*) IN Chamber Comm.

***Safety & Health in Agriculture, Forestry & Fisheries.** Ricky L. Langley et al. LC 96-46442. 624p. 1997. text ed. 125.00 (*0-86587-552-9*) Gov Insts.

Safety & Health in Building & Civil Engineering Work: An ILO Code of Practice. xii, 386p. 1985. 36.00 (*92-2-100974-2*) Intl Labour Office.

Safety & Health in Coal Mines: An ILO Code of Practice. xiv, 176p. 1986. pap. 18.00 (*92-2-105339-3*) Intl Labour Office.

Safety & Health in Construction: An ILO Code of Practice. xiii, 162p. (Orig.). 1992. pap. 18.00 (*92-2-107104-9*) Intl Labour Office.

Safety & Health in Dock Work: An ILO Code of Practice. 2nd rev. ed. xvi, 221p. 1992. reprint ed. 24.75 (*92-2-101593-9*) Intl Labour Office.

Safety & Health in Opencast Mines: An ILO Code of Practice. xiii, 121p. (Orig.). 1991. pap. 18.00 (*92-2-107103-0*) Intl Labour Office.

Safety & Health in the Construction of Fixed Offshore Installations in the Petroleum Industry: An ILO Code of Practice. xi, 135p. (Orig.). 1982. pap. 18.00 (*92-2-102900-X*) Intl Labour Office.

Safety & Health in the Oil & Gas Extractive Industries. Commission of the European Communities Staff. 442p. 1983. pap. text ed. 129.00 (*0-86010-452-4*) G & T Inc.

Safety & Health in the Use of Agrochemicals: A Guide. v, 79p. (Orig.). 1991. pap. 22.50 (*92-2-107281-9*) Intl Labour Office.

Safety & Health in the Use of Chemicals at Work: A Training Manual. Abu B. Che Man & David Gold. v, 78p. (Orig.). 1993. pap. 15.75 (*92-2-106470-0*) Intl Labour Office.

Safety & Health in Wastewater Systems. (Manual of Practice Ser.: 1). 106p. 1983. pap. 35.00 (*0-943244-41-2*, MOOO1) Water Environ.

Safety & Health in Wastewater Systems. Task Force on Safety & Health in Wastewater Systems Staff. (Manual of Practice Ser.: Vol. 1). 1994. 45.00 (*0-614-01315-1*) Water Environ.

Safety & Health Inspector. Jack Rudman. (Career Examination Ser.: C-3143). 1994. pap. 29.95 (*0-8373-3143-9*) Nat Learn.

Safety & Health Management in the '90s: Creating a Winning Program. Milton J. Terrell. LC 95-6248. 1995. text ed. 57.95 (*0-442-02056-2*) Van Nos Reinhold.

Safety & Health of Migrant Workers: International Symposium. (Occupational Safety & Health Ser.: No. 41). 337p. 1983. 27.00 (*92-2-001906-X*) Intl Labour Office.

***Safety & Health on the Internet.** Ralph B. Stuart, 3rd. LC 96-47963. 220p. (Orig.). 1997. pap. text ed. 39.00 (*0-86587-523-5*) Gov Insts.

Safety & Health Practices of Multinational Enterprises. 2nd ed. viii, 90p. 1986. pap. 15.75 (*92-2-103742-8*) Intl Labour Office.

***Safety & Health Program.** Mark M. Moran. (OSHA Written Compliance Programs Ser.: No. 24). (Illus.). 37p. 1992. ring bd. 169.00 (*1-890966-18-5*) Moran Assocs.

Safety & Health Requirements Manual, 2 vols. 1994. lib. bdg. 650.95 (*0-8490-8509-8*) Gordon Pr.

***Safety & Health Training.** Richard K. Miller et al. (Market Research Survey Ser.: No. 240). 50p. 1996. 200.00 (*1-55865-272-8*) Future Tech Surveys.

***Safety & Infection Control.** SPC Staff. (Health Care Professional Review Ser.: Vol. 6). 1997. 24.95 (*0-87434-916-8*) Springhouse Pub.

Safety & Nutritional Adequacy of Irradiated Food. xv, 161p. (ENG, FRE & SPA.). 1994. pap. text ed. 42.00 (*92-4-156162-9*, 1150410) World Health.

Safety & Quality in Food. (Developments in Animal & Veterinary Science Ser.: Vol. 17). 1984. 114.50 (*0-444-42409-1*) Elsevier.

Safety & Reliability Assessment: An Integral Approach: Proceedings of the European Conference, Munich, Germany, 10-12 May, 1993. Ed. by Peter Kafka & Josefa Wolf. LC 93-1592. 1122p. 1993. 459.25 (*0-444-81561-9*) Elsevier.

Safety & Reliability in Emerging Control Technologies: A Postprint Volume from the IFAC Workshop, Florida, U.S.A., 1-3 November 1995. Hilburn et al. LC 96-44001. 298p. 1996. pap. 74.25 (*0-08-042610-7*, Pergamon Pr) Elsevier.

Safety & Reliability of Metal Structures: Specialty Conference, Pittsburgh, PA, Nov. 2-3, 1972. Speciality Conference on Safety & Reliability of Metal Structures Staff. LC 78-322838. (Illus.). 457p. reprint ed. pap. 130.30 (*0-317-08324-4*, 2019538) Bks Demand.

***Safety & Reliability of Software Based Systems: Twelfth Annual CSR Workshop (Bruges 12-15 September 1995)** City University Staff & Roger C. Shaw. LC 96-29238. (Illus.). 461p. 1996. pap. 89.50 (*3-540-76034-2*) Spr-Verlag.

Safety & Risk Management in Girl Scouting. Girl Scouts of the U. S. A. Staff. 144p. 1993. pap. 7.50 (*0-88441-477-9*) Girl Scouts USA.

Safety & Risk Management Tools & Techniques in the CPI. Ed. by by G. Sam Samdani. LC 96-11101. (Illus.). 304p. 1996. text ed. 55.00 (*0-07-057768-4*) McGraw.

***Safety & Seamanship.** John Chamier. Date not set. 22.95 (*0-8464-4473-9*) Beekman Pubs.

Safety & Seamanship. John Chamier. (Illus.). 1979. 3.75 (*0-229-11501-2*) S&S Trade.

Safety & Security Administration in Health Care Facilities: Forms, Checklists & Guidelines. Aspen Reference Group Staff. Ed. by Sara N. Di Lima & Dwayne E. Eutsey. LC 94-48768. ring bd. 189.00 (*0-8342-0657-9*) Aspen Pub.

Safety & Security Administration in School Facilities: Forms Checklist & Guidelines. Aspen Reference Group Staff. LC 96-20256. 1996. 129.00 (*0-8342-0821-0*) Aspen Pub.

Safety & Soundness Compliance Handbook: 1995 Edition. 3rd ed. Price Waterhouse Staff. 180p. (C). 1995. per. 65.00 (*1-55738-763-X*) Irwin Prof Pubng.

Safety & Soundness Compliance Handbook, 1994. Price Waterhouse Staff. 1994. per. 60.00 (*1-55738-705-2*) Irwin Prof Pubng.

Safety & Survival on the Fireground. Vincent Dunn. 377p. 1992. 39.95 (*0-912212-23-3*) Fire Eng.

An Asterisk (*) at the beginning of an entry indicates that the title is appearing in BIP for the first time.

Safety & Technology: Harmony or Discord?: Proceedings of the Flight Safety Foundation 45th Annual International Air Safety Seminar & the International Federation of Airworthiness 22nd International Conference, November 2-5, 1992, Long Beach, California. fac. ed. International Air Safety Seminar Staff. (Illus.). 407p. 1992. pap. 116.00 (*0-7837-7681-0*, 2047434) Bks Demand.

***Safety & the Bottom Line.** Frank E. Bird, Jr. & Ray J. Davies. (Illus.). 345p. 1996. 55.00 (*0-9656516-1-4*) FEBCO.

Safety & the Executive. James V. Findlay. LC 79-54954. (Illus.). 128p. 18.00 (*0-88061-008-5*) Intl Loss Cntrl.

Safety Assessment: A Quantitative Approach. B. S. Dhillon & A. Raouf. 208p. 1993. 69.95 (*0-87371-675-2*, L675) Lewis Pubs.

Safety Assessment for Pharmaceuticals. Shayne C. Gad. 1995. text ed. 88.95 (*0-442-00123-1*) Van Nos Reinhold.

Safety Assessment of Emergency Power Systems for Nuclear Power Plants. IAEA Staff. (Safety Ser.: No. 50-P-5). 85p. 1992. pap. 35.00 (*92-0-105092-5*, STI/PUB/887, Pub. by IAEA AU) Bernan Associates.

Safety Assessment of Genetically Engineered Fruits & Vegetables. 288p. 1992. 95.95 (*0-8493-4803-X*, SB) CRC Pr.

***Safety Assessment of Mobile Communications.** Ed. by Balzano et al. (Telecommunications Technology & Applications Ser.). (Illus.). 288p. 1997. text ed. 55.00 (*0-412-75000-7*, Chap & Hall NY) Chapman & Hall.

Safety Assurance for Environmental Introductions of Genetically-Engineered Organisms. Ed. by J. Fiksel & Vincent T. Covello. (NATO ASI Series F: Computer & Systems Science: Vol. 18). viii, 282p. 1988. 140.95 (*0-387-18561-5*) Spr-Verlag.

Safety at Work. 4th ed. John R. Ridley. LC 93-46862. 800p. 1994. 230.00 (*0-7506-0746-7*) Buttrwrth-Heinemann.

Safety at Work: The Limits of Self-Regulation. Sandra Dawson et al. (Cambridge Studies in Management: No. 12). 400p. 1988. 69.95 (*0-521-35497-8*) Cambridge U Pr.

Safety Audit: Designing Effective Strategies. Roger Saunders. (Financial Times Management Ser.). 304p. 1993. 77.50 (*0-273-03448-0*, Pub. by Pitman Pub Ltd UK) Trans-Atl Phila.

Safety Auditing: A Management Tool. D. Kase. 1990. text ed. 57.95 (*0-442-23746-4*) Van Nos Reinhold.

Safety Belts, Airbags, & Child Restraints. (Special Reports: No. 224). 69p. 1989. 12.00 (*0-309-04755-2*) Transport Res Bd.

Safety Bicycle. Ian Jones. 1989. pap. 25.00 (*0-85263-804-3*, Pub. by Shire UK) St Mut.

Safety Book for Active Kids: Teaching Your Child How to Avoid Everyday Dangers. Linda Schwartz. 200p. (J). (gr. k-3). 1995. 12.95 (*0-88160-270-1*, LW154) Learning Wks.

Safety by Objectives. Dan Peterson. LC 78-12057. 1978. 28.50 (*0-913690-07-4*) Aloray.

Safety Center: What to Do in an Emergency. Florence Weiner. (Illus.). 40p. (Orig.). 1997. pap. 19.95 (*1-888241-00-4*) Safety Ctr.

Safety Challenges in the 90s: Third Annual European Corporate & Regional Aircraft Operators Safety Seminar (ECARAOSS) Originally Scheduled for March 12-14 in Brussels, Belgium, Was Cancelled Because of Disruptions Caused by the Gulf War. Flight Safety Foundation Staff. LC 91-657078. (Flight Safety Digest Ser. Special Supplement: Vol. 10, No. 6, June 1991). 96p. reprint ed. pap. 27.40 (*0-7837-7028-6*, 2046843) Bks Demand.

Safety Code for Elevators & Escalators: ANS u-c17.1, 1987, No. AX9687. 1987. 85.00 (*0-685-37579-X*) ASME.

Safety Code for Elevators & Escalators: Handbook on A17.1. Ed. by E. A. Donoghue. 372p. 1987. 95.00 (*0-685-06265-1*, A00112) ASME.

Safety Considerations for Biotechnology: Scale-up of Crop Plants. 38p. (Orig.). 1994. pap. 12.00 (*92-64-14044-1*) OECD.

Safety Considerations for Biotechnology Scale-up of Micro-Organisms As Biofertilizers. 72p. (Orig.). 1995. pap. 19.00 (*92-64-14344-0*) OECD.

Safety Considerations of Energy Saving Materials & Devices. Steve Mazzoni. 1978. 3.25 (*0-686-12080-9*, TR 78-6) Society Fire Protect.

Safety Consultant. Jack Rudman. (Career Examination Ser.: C-2640). 1994. pap. 34.95 (*0-8373-2640-0*) Nat Learn.

Safety Coordinator. Jack Rudman. (Career Examination Ser.: C-1921). 1994. pap. 34.95 (*0-8373-1921-8*) Nat Learn.

***Safety Counts.** Joel Kupperstein. Ed. by Rozanne L. Williams. (Social Studies Learn to Read Ser.). (Illus.). 16p. (Orig.). (J). (ps-2). 1996. pap. 2.49 (*1-57471-143-1*, 3938) Creat Teach Pr.

***Safety Counts!** Joel Kupperstein. Ed. by Rozanne L. Williams. (Social Studies Big Bks.). (Illus.). 16p. (Orig.). (J). (ps-2). 1997. pap. 11.98 (*1-57471-189-X*, 3981) Creat Teach Pr.

Safety Critical Computer Systems. Neil Storey. (C). 1996. text ed. 29.95 (*0-201-42787-7*) Addison-Wesley.

Safety-Critical Systems: Current Issues, Techniques, & Standards. Ed. by Felix Redmill & Tom Anderson. LC 92-47352. 352p. (gr. 13). 1993. pap. text ed. 66.95 (*0-412-54820-8*) Chapman & Hall.

Safety-Critical Systems: The Convergence of High Tech & Human Factors: Proceedings of the Fourth Safety-Critical Systems Symposium, Leeds, 6-8 February 1996. Ed. by Felix Redmill & Tom Anderson. (Illus.). ix, 285p. 1996. pap. 75.00 (*3-540-76009-1*) Spr-Verlag.

Safety Design Criteria for Industrial Plants, 2 Vols. Ed. by Maurizio Cumo & Antonio Naviglio. 1989. 177.00 (*0-685-67693-5*, T55) CRC Pr.

Safety Design Criteria for Industrial Plants, 2 Vols., Vol. I. Ed. by Maurizio Cumo & Antonio Naviglio. 288p. 1989. 216.00 (*0-8493-6383-7*, T55) CRC Pr.

Safety Design Criteria for Industrial Plants, 2 Vols., Vol. II. Ed. by Maurizio Cumo & Antonio Naviglio. 304p. 1989. 215.95 (*0-8493-6384-5*, T55) CRC Pr.

Safety Directors Book of Letters. 40p. 1992. ring bd. 59.00 (*0-88711-221-8*) Am Trucking Assns.

Safety Diving Operations. 1986. pap. text ed. 129.00 (*0-86010-509-1*) Kluwer Ac.

Safety Engineer. Jack Rudman. (Career Examination Ser.: C-797). 1994. pap. 34.95 (*0-8373-0797-X*) Nat Learn.

Safety Engineering. James CoVan. LC 93-27077. (New Dimensions in Engineering Ser.). 320p. 1995. text ed. 69.95 (*0-471-55612-2*) Wiley.

Safety Engineering. Gilbert Marshall. LC 94-10722. 1994. 29.95 (*0-939874-99-7*) ASSE.

Safety Engineering & Risk Analysis. Ed. by F. A. Ellia & D. W. Pyatt. LC 93-73840. 265p. 1994. pap. 65.00 (*0-7918-1262-6*) ASME.

***Safety Engineering & Risk Analysis: Proceedings, ASME International Mechanical Engineering Congress & Exposition, Atlanta, GA, 1996.** F. J. Mintz. LC 96-78680. (SERA Ser.: Vol. 6). 147p. 1996. pap. 72.00 (*0-7918-1538-2*, T55) ASME.

Safety Engineering & Risk Analysis: 1994 International Mechanical Engineering Congress & Exposition, Chicago, Illinois - November 6-11, 1994. (SERA Ser.: Vol. 2). 236p. 1994. 807.00 (*0-7918-1457-2*, G00952) ASME.

Safety Engineering & Risk Analysis - 1995 Vol. 4: Safety Engineering & Risk Analysis - 1995. Ed. by D. W. Pyatt. (1995 ASME International Mechanical Engineering Congress & Exposition Ser.: SERA-Vol. 4). 148p. 1995. 60.00 (*0-7918-1727-X*, H01009) ASME.

Safety, Environmental Impact & Economic Prospects of Nuclear Fusion. Ed. by B. Brunelli & Heinz Knoepfel. (Ettore Majorana International Science Series, Life Sciences: Vol. 48). (Illus.). 360p. 1990. 105.00 (*0-306-43524-1*, Plenum Pr) Plenum.

Safety Evaluation: Toxicology, Methods, Concepts & Risk Assessment. Myron A. Mehlman. LC 87-609437. (Toxicology & Industrial Health Ser.: Vol. 10). (Illus.). 278p. 1987. 65.00 (*0-911131-13-2*) Princeton Sci Pubs.

Safety Evaluation & Regulation of Chemicals, No. 1. Ed. by F. Homburger. (Illus.). xiv, 294p. 1983. 158.50 (*3-8055-3578-3*) S Karger.

Safety Evaluation & Regulation of Chemicals, No. 2. Ed. by F. Homburger. (Illus.). xvi, 326p. 1985. 174.50 (*3-8055-3942-8*) S Karger.

Safety Evaluation & Regulation of Chemicals, No. 3. Ed. by F. Homburger. (Illus.). xiv, 242p. 1985. 135.25 (*3-8055-4017-5*) S Karger.

Safety Evaluation Based on Identification: Approaches Related to Time-Variant & Nonlinear Structures. Hans G. Natke et al. x, 324p. 1993. pap. 70.00 (*3-528-06535-4*, Pub. by Vieweg & Sohn GW) Informatica.

Safety Evaluation of Chemicals in Food Pt. 1: Toxicological Data Profiles for Pesticides: Carbamate & Organophosphorus Insecticides Used in Agriculture & Public Health. (Progress in Standardization: No. 3). 1975. pap. text ed. 10.00 (*92-4-068522-7*, 1260003) World Health.

Safety Evaluation of Drugs & Chemicals. Ed. by W. Eugene Lloyd. LC 84-12912. (Illus.). 487p. (C). 1986. text ed. 115.00 (*0-89116-352-2*) Hemisp Pub.

Safety Evaluation of Existing Dams: A Manual for the Safety Evaluation of Embankment & Concrete Dams. 1996. lib. bdg. 300.00 (*0-8490-6879-7*) Gordon Pr.

Safety Evaluation of Foods Derived by Modern Biotechnology: Concepts & Principles. OECD Staff. 72p. (Orig.). 1993. pap. 19.00 (*92-64-13859-5*) OECD.

***Safety Evaluation of Medical Devices.** A. Gad. LC 96-53470. 400p. 1997. 165.00 (*0-8247-9827-9*) Dekker.

Safety Features of Operating Light Reactors of Western Design. Mirela Gavrilas et al. 312p. 1994. 199.95 (*0-8493-7641-6*) CRC Pr.

***Safety First: Technology, Labor, & Business in the Building of American Work Safety, 1870-1939.** Mark Aldrich. LC 96-28998. (Studies in Industry & Society). (Illus.). 440p. 1997. text ed. 49.95 (*0-8018-5405-9*) Johns Hopkins.

Safety First - School. Cynthia F. Klingel. LC 86-72593. (Safety First Ser.). (J). (ps up). 1986. lib. bdg. 12.95 (*0-88682-084-7*) Creative Ed.

Safety First - Water. Cynthia F. Klingel. LC 86-72673. (Safety First Ser.). (J). (ps up). 1986. lib. bdg. 12.95 (*0-88682-083-9*) Creative Ed.

Safety First Checklist: Inspection Program for Children's Play Areas. 2nd ed. Sally McIntyre & Susan M. Goltsman. (Illus.). 136p. 1996. pap. text ed. 39.95 (*0-944661-19-X*) MIG Comns.

Safety for Carpenters & Woodworkers. Gaspar Lewis. LC 80-66859. (Carpentry-Cabinetmaking Ser.). (C). 1981. teacher ed. 13.50 (*0-8273-1870-7*); pap. 17.50 (*0-8273-1869-3*) Delmar.

Safety for Masons. Richard T. Kreh, Sr. LC 78-53663. 1979. teacher ed. 13.50 (*0-8273-1669-0*); pap. 17.50 (*0-8273-1668-2*) Delmar.

***Safety for Older Consumers: Home Safety Checklists.** (Illus.). 37p. (Orig.). 1996. pap. text ed. 15.00 (*0-7881-3083-8*) DIANE Pub.

Safety for Welders. Larry Jeffus. LC 78-73579. (Metalworking Ser.). (gr. 8). 1980. pap. 20.95 (*0-8273-1684-4*) Delmar.

Safety Guide for Health Care Institutions. 5th ed. Linda F. Chaff. LC 94-29435. 183p. 1994. pap. 52.00 (*1-55648-126-8*, 181149) AHPI.

Safety Guide for Terminals Handling Ships Carrying Liquefied Gases in Bulk. OCIMF Staff. (C). 1982. 275.00 (*0-900886-72-2*, Pub. by Witherby & Co UK) St Mut.

Safety Guide for Terminals Handling Ships Carrying Liquefied Gases in Bulk. OCIMF Staff. 1993. 72.00 (*1-85609-057-4*, Pub. by Witherby & Co UK) St Mut.

Safety Hazards & Ethics in Clinical Engineering. Ed. by Allan F. Pacela. (Journal of Clinical Engineering Reprint: No. 2). 56p. (Orig.). 1991. pap. 28.00 (*0-930844-30-0*) Quest Pub.

***Safety, Health, & Environmental Protection.** Charles A. Wentz. LC 97-16349. 1997. write for info. (*0-07-069310-2*) McGraw.

Safety, Health & Loss Prevention in Chemical Processes: Problems for Undergraduate Engineering Curriculum. Compiled by Center for Chemical Process Safety Staff. 479p. 1990. teacher ed., pap. 60.00 (*0-8169-0421-9*, G-16) Am Inst Chem Eng.

Safety, Health & Loss Prevention in Chemical Processes: Problems for Undergraduate Engineering Curriculum, Student Problems. Compiled by Center for Chemical Process Safety Staff. 180p. 1990. pap. 18.00 (*0-8169-0473-1*, G-17) Am Inst Chem Eng.

***Safety, Health & Welfare on Construction Sites: A Training Manual.** ix, 107p. 1995. pap. 22.50 (*92-2-109182-1*) Intl Labour Office.

Safety, Health & Working Conditions in the Transfer of Technology to Developing Countries: ILO Code of Practice. xi, 81p. (Orig.). 1988. pap. 13.50 (*92-2-106122-1*) Intl Labour Office.

***Safety in American Football, Vol. STP 1305.** Ed. by Earl F. Hoerner. LC 96-35836. (Illus.). 200p. 1997. text ed. 72.00 (*0-8031-2400-7*, 04-013050-47) ASTM.

Safety in Chemical Production. Whiston. 1992. 77.00 (*0-632-03255-3*) CRC Pr.

Safety in Chemical Tankers. ICS Staff. (C). 1977. 80.00 (*0-685-36225-6*, Pub. by Witherby & Co UK) St Mut.

***Safety in Clinical & Biomedical Laboratories.** Ed. by Collins. (Illus.). 176p. (Orig.). (C). (gr. 13 up). 1988. pap. text ed. 34.50 (*0-412-28370-0*) Chapman & Hall.

Safety in Electromedical Technology. Norbert Leitgeb. (Illus.). 184p. 1996. 119.00 (*1-57491-014-0*) Interpharm.

Safety in Gymnastics. Gerald A. Carr. (Illus.). 248p. pap. 9.95 (*0-88839-054-8*) Hancock House.

Safety in Ice Hockey. Ed. by C. R. Castaldi et al. LC 89-35946. (Special Technical Publication Ser.: Vol. 2, No. STP 1212). (Illus.). 230p. 1993. text ed. 94.00 (*0-8031-1873-2*, 04-012120-47) ASTM.

Safety in Industrial Microbiology. C. H. Collins & A. J. Beale. (Illus.). 257p. 1992. 175.00 (*0-7506-1105-7*) Buttrwrth-Heinemann.

Safety in Liquefied Gas Tankers. ICS Staff. (C). 1980. 90.00 (*0-685-36226-4*, Pub. by Witherby & Co UK) St Mut.

Safety in Mines Research: Proceedings, 21st International Conference of Safety in Mines Research Institutes, 21-25 Oct. 1985. A. R. Green. 798p. (C). 1985. text ed. 270.00 (*90-6191-610-0*, Pub. by A A Balkema NE) Ashgate Pub Co.

Safety in Mines Research: Proceedings, 22nd International Conference on Safety in Mines Research Institutes 1987. Ed. by Dai Guoquan. 1220p. (C). 1988. text ed. 208.00 (*7-5020-0041-0*, Pub. by A A Balkema NE) Ashgate Pub Co.

Safety in Numbers: Safer Sex & Gay Men. Edward King. (Lesbian & Gay Studies). 288p. 1993. 55.00 (*0-304-32699-2*) Cassell.

Safety in Numbers: Safer Sex & Gay Men. Edward King. 302p. (C). (gr. 13). 1994. pap. 16.95 (*0-415-90931-7*, Pub. by Tavistock UK) Routledge Chapman & Hall.

Safety in Offshore Drilling: The Roll of Shallow Gas Surveys. Ed. by D. A. Ardus & C. D. Green. (C). 1990. lib. bdg. 132.00 (*0-7923-0889-1*) Kluwer Ac.

Safety in Oil Tankers. ICS Staff. (C). 1978. 75.00 (*0-685-36227-2*, Pub. by Witherby & Co UK) St Mut.

Safety in Our Environment: Proceedings of the 31st Annual Meeting, Corporate Aviation Safety Seminar, April 14-16, 1986, Cincinnati, OH. Corporate Aviation Safety Seminar Staff. 212p. pap. 60.50 (*0-317-55564-2*, 2052214) Bks Demand.

Safety in Outdoor Recreational Activities. Ed. by Joseph Borozne et al. (Sports Safety Monographs: No. 6). 76p. reprint ed. pap. 25.00 (*0-685-15743-1*, 2026612) Bks Demand.

Safety in Process Plant Design. G. L. Wells. LC 80-509467. (Illus.). 293p. reprint ed. pap. 83.60 (*0-8357-2970-2*, 2039232) Bks Demand.

Safety in School Science Labs. Clair G. Wood. 137p. 1994. pap. 19.95 (*0-9647512-0-8*) Kaufman & Assocs.

Safety in the Artroom. Charles Qualley. LC 85-73421. 120p. 1986. 16.00 (*0-87192-174-X*) Davis Mass.

Safety in the Auto Body Shop. Robert Jenkins. LC 79-730992. (Orig.). 1979. student ed. 5.00 (*0-8064-0127-3*, 431); audio, vhs 89.00 (*0-8064-0128-1*) Bergwall.

Safety in the Built Environment. J. Sime. 350p. 1988. text ed. 72.50 (*0-419-14480-3*, E & FN Spon) Routledge Chapman & Hall.

Safety in the Chemical Laboratory, 2 vols, Vol. 2. Norman V. Steere. 1971. 17.00 (*0-910362-04-1*) Chem Educ.

Safety in the Chemical Laboratory, 2 vols, Vol. 3. Norman V. Steere. 1974. 17.00 (*0-910362-05-X*) Chem Educ.

Safety in the Chemical Laboratory, Vol. 4. Ed. by Malcolm M. Renfrew. 1981. pap. 20.00 (*0-910362-06-8*) Chem Educ.

Safety in the Chemistry & Biochemistry Laboratory. Andrew T. Prokopetz. Ed. by Andre Picot et al. Tr. by Robert H. Dodd. 1994. 49.95 (*1-56081-040-8*, VCH) Wiley.

Safety in the Elementary Science Classroom. rev. ed. Robert A. Dean et al. 22p. 1993. pap. 7.95 (*0-87355-117-6*) Natl Sci Tchrs.

Safety in the Handling of Cryogenic Fluids. F. J. Edeskuty & W. F. Stewart. (International Cryogenics Monographs). (Illus.). 228p. (C). 1996. 79.50 (*0-306-45161-1*, Plenum Pr) Plenum.

Safety in the Process Industries. Ralph W. King. 800p. 1990. pap. 84.95 (*0-7506-1970-8*) Buttrwrth-Heinemann.

Safety in the Salon. E. Almond. (C). 1986. 65.00 (*0-85950-202-3*, Pub. by S Thornes Pubs UK) St Mut.

Safety in the Skies. Percy Knauth. (Illus.). 166p. 1982. pap. 9.95 (*0-8306-2341-8*, 2341) McGraw-Hill Prof.

Safety in the Terminal Environment: Proceedings, 23rd Annual Meeting, April 9-12, 1978, Arlington Va. Corporate Aviation Safety Seminar Staff. 134p. reprint ed. pap. 38.20 (*0-317-10145-5*, 2010339) Bks Demand.

Safety in the Underground Construction & Operation of Exploratory Studies Facility at Yucca. 1995. pap. text ed. 34.00 (*0-309-05243-2*) Natl Acad Sci.

Safety in the Use of Asbestos: An ILO Code of Practice. xiii, 116p. 1990. pap. 18.00 (*92-2-103872-6*) Intl Labour Office.

Safety in the Use of Asbestos: Proceedings of the International Labour Conference, 72nd Session, 1986, Report IV. 68p. (Orig.). 1985. pap. 13.50 (*92-2-105174-9*) Intl Labour Office.

Safety in the Use of Chemicals at Work: An ILO Code of Practice. xi, 95p. (Orig.). 1993. pap. 15.75 (*92-2-108006-4*) Intl Labour Office.

Safety in the Use of Industrial Robots. (Occupational Safety & Health Ser.: No. 60). vii, 69p. (Orig.). 1989. pap. 11.25 (*92-2-106434-4*) Intl Labour Office.

Safety in the Use of Mineral & Synthetic Fibres: Working Document & Report of the Meeting of Experts on Safety in the Use of Mineral & Synthetic Fibres, Geneva, 17-25 April 1989. (Occupational Safety & Health Ser.: No. 64). v, 94p. (Orig.). 1990. pap. 13.50 (*92-2-106443-3*) Intl Labour Office.

Safety in Tritium Handling Technology: Based on the Lectures Given During the Eurocourse on 'Safety in Tritium Handling Technology' Held at the Joint Research Centre Ispra, Italy, April 28-30, 1993. Ed. by F. Mannone. LC 93-30126. (Eurocourses: Nuclear Science & Technology Ser.). 248p. (C). 1993. lib. bdg. 111.50 (*0-7923-2511-7*) Kluwer Ac.

Safety in Welding, Cutting, & Allied Processes (Z49.1-94) 50p. 1994. pap. 51.00 (*0-87171-450-7*) Am Welding.

Safety Inspection Guidelines & Terminal Safety Check List for Gas Carriers. OCIMF Staff. (C). 1979. 60.00 (*0-900886-43-9*, Pub. by Witherby & Co UK) St Mut.

Safety Instructions for Welding & Cutting. Nigel C. Balchin. (Safety Instruction Booklet Ser.). (Illus.). 16p. 1995. 60.00 (*1-85573-055-3*, Pub. by Woodhead Pubng UK) Am Educ Systs.

Safety Is No Accident: Children's Activities in Injury Prevention. William M. Kane & Kathleen E. Tritschler. LC 92-19798. (Illus.). 1992. 14.95 (*1-56071-085-3*) ETR Assocs.

Safety Issues: Pedestrians, Law Enforcement, Seat Belts, Elderly Drivers, & Economics. (Research Record Ser.: No. 1210). 65p. 1989. 12.00 (*0-309-04806-0*) Transport Res Bd.

Safety Kids Personal Safety, Vol. 1. Janeen Brady. (Illus.). 14p. (Orig.). (J). (gr. k-6). 1983. Set of 20. student ed. 12.00 (*0-944803-20-2*) Brite Music.

Safety Kids Personal Safety, Vol. 1. Janeen Brady. Tr. by Oscar Underwood. (Orig.). (SPA.). (J). (gr. k-6). 1984. 2.50 (*0-944803-16-4*); 10.95 incl. audio (*0-944803-17-2*); Trans. by Oscar Underwood, in Spanish, 1984, 6pgs. pap. text ed. 1.50 (*0-944803-19-9*); 6.95 (*0-944803-15-6*); audio 1.50 (*0-944803-18-0*) Brite Music.

Safety Kids Play it Smart: Stay Safe from Drugs, Vol. 2. Janeen Brady. (Illus.). 14p. (J). (gr. k-6). 1985. Set of 20. student ed. 12.00 (*0-944803-25-3*) Brite Music.

Safety Kids Play It Smart, Vol. 2: Stay Safe from Drugs. Janeen Brady. (Illus.). (Orig.). (J). (gr. k-6). 1985. 2.50 (*0-944803-22-9*); 10.95 incl. audio (*0-944803-23-7*); pap. text ed. 6.95 (*0-944803-21-0*); pap. text ed. 1.50 (*0-944803-24-5*); vhs 19.95 (*0-944803-72-5*) Brite Music.

Safety Kids, Vol. 3: Protect Their Minds. Janeen Brady. 24p. (Orig.). (J). (gr. k-6). pap. text ed. 1.50 (*0-944803-82-2*) Brite Music.

Safety Kids, Vol. 3: Protect Their Minds. Janeen J. Brady. (Illus.). 32p. (Orig.). (J). (gr. k-6). 1992. pap. 2.50 (*0-944803-78-4*); pap. 10.95 incl. audio (*0-944803-77-6*) Brite Music.

Safety Law Compliance Manual for California Businesses. John R. Spooner. Ed. by Melody Joachims. LC 92-53601. (Successful Business Library). 148p. (Orig.). 1992. pap. 24.95 (*1-55571-186-3*) Oasis Pr OR.

Safety Legislation: The Trade Union Response. P. B. Beaumont. (C). 1988. text ed. 30.00 (*0-685-22126-1*, Pub. by Univ Nottingham UK) St Mut.

Safety Licensable Computing Architecture. W. A. Halang et al. 272p. 1993. text ed. 109.00 (*981-02-1628-9*); pap. text ed. 61.00 (*981-02-1629-7*) World Scientific Pub.

Safety Made Easy: A Checklist Approach to OSHA Compliance. Weldon "Tex" Davis et al. LC 95-12508. 171p. 1995. pap. 49.00 (*0-86587-463-8*) Gov Insts.

Safety Management. K. Denton. 416p. 1982. text ed. write for info. (*0-07-016410-X*) McGraw.

Safety Management: A Human Approach. 2nd ed. Daniel C. Petersen. LC 88-10544. (Illus.). 380p. 1988. 32.50 (*0-913690-12-0*) Aloray.

Safety Management: Strategy & Practice. Roger Pybus. (Illus.). 192p. 1996. 66.95 (*0-7506-2519-8*) Buttrwrth-Heinemann.

***Safety Management & ISO 9000/QS-9000: A Guide to Alignment & Integration.** Robert J. Kozak & George Krafcisin. LC 96-41895. 184p. 1996. pap. 24.95 (*0-527-76317-9*) Qual Resc.

An Asterisk (*) at the beginning of an entry indicates that the title is appearing in BIP for the first time.

Safety Management at Girl Scout Sites & Facilities. Girl Scouts of the U. S. A. Staff. 112p. 1994. pap. 5.00 (*0-88441-481-7*) Girl Scouts USA.

Safety Management for Health Care Facilities. Linda D. Lee. (Management & Compliance Ser.: Vol. 5). (Illus.). 275p. 1989. ring bd. 110.00 (*0-87258-512-3*, 055204) Am Hospital.

Safety Management Practices for Hazardous Materials. Nicholas P. Cheremisinoff & Madelyn Graffia. LC 95-37548. 368p. 1995. 135.00 (*0-8247-9687-X*) Dekker.

Safety Manager's Guide, 1993-94. Bureau of Business Practice Staff. 1993. pap. 59.95 (*0-13-724584-X*) P-H.

Safety Manual. 64p. 4.06 (*0-318-14113-2*) Flat Glass Mktg.

Safety Manual for Municipalities. David Dodge. 82p. 1986. 25.00 (*0-939874-72-5*) ASSE.

Safety Manual on Magnetic Resonance Imaging Contrast Agents. Emanuel Kanal & Frank G. Shellock. LC 95-33162. 1995. pap. write for info. (*0-397-51619-3*) Lppncott-Raven.

Safety Margins in Criticality Safety International Meeting, San Francisco, CA, Nov. 26-30, 1989. 384p. 1989. 39.00 (*0-89448-145-2*, 700137) Am Nuclear Soc.

Safety Measures for Use in Outbreaks of Communicable Disease. Donald J. Dunsmore. 99p. 1986. pap. text ed. 17.00 (*92-4-154206-3*, 1150250) World Health.

Safety Meeting Repros. rev. ed. Chris Hocker. 1995. ring bd. 295.00 (*1-55645-029-X*, 1100007) Busn Legal Reports.

Safety Meetings Library. 1995. 495.00 incl. cd-rom (*0-614-08810-0*, 154002) Busn Legal Reports.

Safety Minute: How to Be Safe in the Streets, at Home, & Abroad So You Can Save Your Life! Robert L. Siciliano. Ed. by Chris Roerdan. (Illus.). 128p. (Orig.). Date not set. pap. 14.95 (*0-9648126-2-2*) Safety Zone.

Safety Needs in the Terminal Environment: Proceedings of the 30th Annual International Air Safety Seminar, Ottawa, 1977. International Air Safety Seminar Staff. 232p. reprint ed. pap. 66.20 (*0-317-10944-8*, 2006140) Bks Demand.

Safety Net. Heinrich Boll. Tr. by Leila Vennewitz from GER. LC 95-20769. (European Classics Ser.). 314p. 1995. pap. 15.95 (*0-8101-1210-8*) Northwestern U Pr.

Safety Net: Welfare & Social Security, 1929-1979. Blanche D. Coll. LC 94-32737. 400p. (C). 1995. text ed. 47.00 (*0-8135-2159-9*) Rutgers U Pr.

Safety Net as Ladder: Transfer Payments & Economic Development. Robert E. Friedman. LC 88-25687. 168p. 1988. 16.95 (*0-934842-42-6*) CSPA.

***Safety Net Programs & Poverty Reduction: Lessons from Cross-Country Experience.** K. Subbarao et al. (Directions in Development Ser.). 200p. 1997. 20.00 (*0-8213-3890-0*, 13890) World Bank.

***Safety Nets: Secrets of Effective Information Technology Controls.** Barbara J. Bashein et al. LC 96-61916. 150p. (Orig.). 1997. pap. 38.00 (*1-885065-08-6*, 097-03) Finan Exec.

Safety Nets, Politics, & the Poor: Transitions to Market Economies. Carol Graham. 378p. (C). 1994. 36.95 (*0-8157-3228-7*) Brookings.

Safety, Nutrition & Health. Robertson. (Early Childhood Education Ser.). 1998. pap. 42.50 (*0-8273-7329-5*) Delmar.

Safety, Nutrition & Health. Robertson. (Early Childhood Education Ser.). 1998. teacher ed. 12.95 (*0-8273-7330-9*) Delmar.

Safety of Appearing on the Day of Judgment in the Rightousness of Christ. rev. ed. Solomon Stoddard. Ed. by Don Kistler. 349p. 1995. 24.95 (*1-877611-92-1*) Soli Deo Gloria.

Safety of Chemical Batch Reactors & Storage Tanks. Ed. by A. Benuzzi & J. M. Zaldivar. (C). 1991. lib. bdg. 173.00 (*0-7923-1233-3*) Kluwer Ac.

Safety of Chemical in Food: Chemical Contaminants. Ed. by David H. Watson. 1993. write for info. (*0-318-70169-3*, Pub. by Tavistock-E Horwood UK) Routledge Chapman & Hall.

Safety of Chemicals in Foods: Chemical Contaminants. Ed. by David H. Watson. 193p. 1993. text ed. 99.95 (*0-13-787862-1*) Technomic.

Safety of Computer Control Systems, 1989: Safecomp: Proceedings of the IFAC-IFIP Workshop, Vienna Austria 5-7 December, 1989. Ed. by R. Genser et al. (IFAC Ser.). (Illus.). 164p. 1989. 78.00 (*0-08-037535-9*, Pergamon Pr) Elsevier.

Safety of Computer Control Systems, 1990: Safety, Security & Reliability Related Computers for the 1990's. Ed. by B. K. Daniels. (IFAC Symposia Ser.). (Illus.). 196p. 1990. 94.00 (*0-08-040953-9*, Pergamon Pr) Elsevier.

Safety of Computer Control Systems, 1991: Proceedings of the IFAC-IFIP-EWICS-SRE Symposium, Trondheim, Norway, 30 October - 1 November 1991. Ed. by J. F. Lindeberg. (IFAC Symposia Ser.). 200p. 1991. 73.00 (*0-08-041697-7*, Pergamon Pr) Elsevier.

Safety of Computer Control Systems 1992 (SAFECOMP '92) Computer Systems in Safety-Critical Applications: Proceedings of the IFAC Symposium, Zurich, Switzerland, 28-30 October 1992. Ed. by Heinz H. Frey. LC 92-40444. 332p. 1992. pap. 105.75 (*0-08-041893-7*, Pergamon Pr) Elsevier.

Safety of Dams: Flood & Earthquake Criteria. National Research Council Staff. 320p. 1985. pap. text ed. 29.95 (*0-309-03532-5*) Natl Acad Pr.

Safety of Dams: Proceedings of an International Conference, Coimbra, 23-28th April 1984, 2 vols. Ed. by J. Laginha Serafim. 599p. (C). 1984. text ed. 180.00 (*90-6191-521-X*, Pub. by A A Balkema NE) Ashgate Pub Co.

Safety of Elderly Drivers: Yesterday's Young in Today's Traffic. J. Peter Rothe. 250p. 1989. pap. 24.95 (*0-88738-728-4*) Transaction Pubs.

Safety of His Arms. Vivian Leiber. (Romance Ser.). 1995. pap. 2.99 (*0-373-19070-0*, 1-19070-1) Silhouette.

Safety of Hoists & Lifts. Shaw & Sons Ltd. Staff. (Shaway Guides Ser.). (C). 1988. 40.00 (*0-317-92364-1*, Pub. by Scientific UK) St Mut.

Safety of Irradiated Foods. Diehl. (Food Science & Technology Ser.: Vol. 68). 472p. 1995. 175.00 (*0-8247-9344-7*) Dekker.

Safety of Microbial Insecticides. Ed. by Marshall Laird et al. 288p. 1990. 218.00 (*0-8493-4793-9*, SB933) CRC Pr.

Safety of Next Generation Power Reactor International Topical Meeting, Seattle. WA, May 1-5, 1988. 946p. 1988. 95.00 (*0-89448-146-0*, 700138) Am Nuclear Soc.

Safety of Nuclear Power: Strategy for the Future. International Atomic Energy Agency Staff. 272p. 1992. pap. 95.00 (*92-0-100292-0*, STI/PUB/880, Pub. by IAEA AU) Bernan Associates.

Safety of Nuclear Power Insag Five. International Atomic Energy Agency Staff. (Safety Ser.: No. 75). 84p. 1992. pap. 40.00 (*92-0-100192-4*, STI/PUB/910, Pub. by IAEA AU) Bernan Associates.

Safety of Objects. A. M. Homes. LC 91-50019. (Vintage Contemporaries Ser.). 176p. 1991. pap. 11.00 (*0-679-73629-8*, Vin) Random.

Safety of Reactive Chemicals. T. Yoshida. (Industrial Safety Ser.: No. 1). 420p. 1987. 226.00 (*0-444-42748-1*) Elsevier.

Safety of Reactive Chemicals & Pyrotechnics. Tadao Yoshida et al. (Industrial Safety Ser.: Vol. 5). 346p. 1995. 261.75 (*0-444-88656-7*) Elsevier.

Safety of the Blood Supply: Report of a Roundtable Discussion. Robert E. Stein. 24p. 1992. pap. 20.00 (*0-933067-12-7*) Roscoe Pound Found.

***Safety of the Nuclear Fuel Cycle.** Ed. by K. Ebert & R. L. Ammon. 1989. pap. text ed. 170.00 (*3-527-27806-0*) Wiley.

Safety of Thermal Reactors Topical Meeting, Portland, OR, July 21-25, 1991. 832p. 1991. 85.00 (*0-89448-159-2*, 700155) Am Nuclear Soc.

Safety of Thermal Water Reactors. Ed. by E. Skuoinski et al. (Illus.). 624p. 1985. lib. bdg. 192.50 (*0-86010-678-0*) G & T Inc.

Safety of Tourist Submersibles. National Research Council Staff. 162p. 1991. pap. text ed. 19.00 (*0-309-04232-1*) Natl Acad Pr.

Safety of Water Disinfection: Balancing Chemical & Microbial Risks. Ed. by Gunther Craun. LC 93-61033. (Illus.). 690p. 1993. pap. 52.50 (*0-944398-11-1*) ILSI.

Safety Officer. Jack Rudman. (Career Examination Ser.: C-3061). 1994. pap. 27.95 (*0-8373-3061-0*) Nat Learn.

Safety Officer Trainee. Jack Rudman. (Career Examination Ser.: C-3062). 1994. pap. 23.95 (*0-8373-3062-9*) Nat Learn.

Safety on Tap: A Citizen's Drinking Water Handbook. League of Women Voters Education Fund Staff. 68p. 1987. pap. 7.95 (*0-89959-402-6*, 840) LWVUS.

Safety on the Rig. 2nd ed. Ed. by Vivian Carmona-Agosto. Tr. by Fernando Albornoz. (Rotary Drilling Ser.: Unit I, Lesson 10). (Illus.). 77p. (SPA.). 1981. pap. text ed. 14.00 (*0-88698-038-0*, 2.11032) PETEX.

Safety on the Rig. 3rd ed. Ed. by Jodie Leecraft. (Rotary Drilling Ser.: Unit I, Lesson 10). (Illus.). 76p. 1981. pap. text ed. 14.00 (*0-88698-014-3*, 2.11030) PETEX.

Safety on the Rig: Canadian Metric Version. 3rd ed. Ed. by Jodie Leecraft & Martha Greenlaw. (Rotary Drilling Ser.: Unit I, Lesson 10). (Illus.). 76p. 1980. pap. text ed. 14.00 (*0-88698-026-7*, 2.11031) PETEX.

Safety on Wheels. Boyer. LC 73-87802. (Safety Ser.). (Illus.). 32p. (J). (gr. k-5). 1974. ring bd. 12.35 (*0-87783-133-5*); audio 7.94 (*0-87783-199-8*) Oddo.

Safety on Wheels. deluxe ed. Boyer. LC 73-87802. (Safety Ser.). (Illus.). 32p. (J). (gr. k-5). 1974. pap. 3.94 (*0-87783-134-3*) Oddo.

Safety Patrol. Michael Martone. LC 87-26848. (Poetry & Fiction Ser.). 144p. 1988. 16.95 (*0-8018-3602-6*) Johns Hopkins.

Safety Performance Management. George L. Germain. (Illus.). 38p. Incl. transparency masters. ring bd. 57.50 (*0-88061-019-0*) Intl Loss Cntrl.

Safety Plays in Bridge. Terence Reese & Roger Trezel. (Master Bridge Ser.). (Illus.). 64p. 1976. pap. 9.95 (*0-575-02748-7*, Pub. by V Gollancz UK) Trafalgar.

Safety Policies & Procedures for Health Care Facilities. John S. Klare. (Orig.). 1992. pap. 100.00 (*0-87258-593-X*, 055452) Am Hospital.

Safety Practice for Water Utilities, No. M3. 160p. 1990. pap. 55.00 (*0-89867-534-0*, 30003) Am Water Wks Assn.

Safety Practices in the Chemistry Laboratory. J. N. Spencer. Ed. by H. Anthony Neidig. (Modular Laboratory Program in Chemistry Ser.). 8p. (C). 1994. pap. text ed. 1.35 (*0-87540-380-8*, TECH 380-8) Chem Educ Res.

***Safety Preparations for Cruising.** Jeremy R. Hood. (Illus.). 272p. 1997. 24.95 (*1-57409-022-4*) Sheridan.

Safety Problems Related to Chloramphenicol & Thiamphenicol. Ed. by Y. Najean et al. LC 80-5838. (Monographs of the Mairo Negri Institute for Pharmacological Research, Milan). (Illus.). 128p. 1981. reprint ed. pap. 36.50 (*0-7837-9562-9*, 2060311) Bks Demand.

Safety Problems Related to Sodium Handling in Liquid Metal Fast Breeder Reactors & Large Test Facilities, Vol. 3. Ed. by H. M. Kottowski. (Ispra Courses on Nuclear Engineering & Technology Ser.). 292p. 1981. text ed. 161.00 (*3-7186-0087-0*) Gordon & Breach.

Safety Profession: Year Two Thousand. Raymond P. Boylston, Jr. et al. 150p. (Orig.). 1991. pap. 6.95 (*0-939874-87-3*) ASSE.

Safety Provisions of Ocean Data Acquisition Systems, Aids & Devices. IMO Staff. (C). 1972. 22.00 (*0-7855-0030-8*, Pub. by Intl Maritime Org UK) St Mut.

***Safety Razors - A Price Guide.** (Orig.). 1995. pap. 19.95 (*0-89538-035-8*) L-W Inc.

Safety Recommendations: Operating Land Oil Well Drilling Rigs. French Oil & Gas Ind. Assoc. Publications Staff. (French Oil & Gas Industry Association Publications). (Illus.). 120p. (C). 1975. pap. 190.00 (*2-7108-0269-4*, Pub. by Edits Technip FR) St Mut.

Safety Recommendations for Lead-Acid Industrial Storage Batteries for Railway & Marine Starting Application. 1984. 5.50 (*0-318-18014-6*, IB 11-1984) Natl Elec Mfrs.

Safety Recommendations for Lead-Acid Industrial Storage Batteries Used for Motive Power Service. 1984. 5.50 (*0-318-18013-8*, IB 10-1984) Natl Elec Mfrs.

Safety Recommendations for Marine Operations. French Oil & Gas Ind. Assoc. Publications Staff. (French Oil & Gas Industry Association Publications). (Illus.). 200p. (C). 1971. pap. 195.00 (*2-7108-0166-3*, Pub. by Edits Technip FR) St Mut.

Safety Recommendations on the Use of Ports by Nuclear Merchants Ships. IMO Staff. (C). 1980. 40.00 (*0-7855-0008-1*, Pub. by Intl Maritime Org UK) St Mut.

Safety Related Systems for the Process Industries. EEMUA Staff. 1989. 125.00 (*0-85931-089-2*, Pub. by EEMUA UK) St Mut.

Safety, Reliability & Applications of Emerging Intelligent Control. Ng & Hung. 240p. 1995. pap. 74.75 (*0-08-042374-4*, Pergamon Pr) Elsevier.

Safety Relief Valves: Prepared at the Third National Congress on Pressure Vessels & Piping, San Francisco, CA, June 24-29, 1979. National Congress on Pressure Vessels & Piping Staff. Ed. by R. W. Haupt & R. A. Meyer. LC 79-50127. (PVP Ser.: No. 33). (Illus.). 200p. reprint ed. pap. 57.00 (*0-8357-3523-0*, 2056813) Bks Demand.

Safety Research: Accident Studies, Enforcement, EMS Management, & Simulation 1990. (Transportation Research Record Ser.: No. 1270). 113p. 1990. 18.00 (*0-309-05052-9*) Transport Res Bd.

Safety Research: Enforcement, Speed, Older Drivers, & Pedestrians. LC 92-46874. (Transportation Research Record Ser.: No. 1376). 1993. write for info. (*0-309-05418-4*) Transport Res Bd.

Safety Research: Heavy Vehicles, Information Systems, & Crash Studies & Methods. National Research Council, Transportation Research Board Staff. LC 92-45740. (Transportation Research Record Ser.: No. 1377). 1993. write for info. (*0-309-05417-6*) Transport Res Bd.

Safety Research for a Changing Highway Environment. (Special Reports: No. 229). 166p. 1990. 21.00 (*0-309-05056-1*) Transport Res Bd.

Safety Resource Catalog. 16p. 1985. pap. 14.00 (*0-318-19728-6*, SRC-1) P-PCI.

Safety Resource Manual for the Telecommunications Industry. MultiMedia Telecommunications Association Staff. 125p. 1990. pap. 53.00 (*0-685-52630-5*, 225) MultiMedia Telecomm.

Safety-Risk Analysis: Explosions. Thor E. Fayn. 1989. 125.00 (*90-6314-592-6*, Pub. by Lorne & MacLean Marine) St Mut.

Safety Scale Laboratory Experiments for General, Organic & Biochemistry. Spencer L. Seager & Michael R. Slabaugh. Ed. by Westby. 450p. (C). 1994. pap. text ed. 21.75 (*0-314-03619-9*) West Pub.

***Safety Scale Laboratory Experiments for General Organic & Biochemistry for Today.** 3rd ed. Spencer L. Seager. 1997. pap. text ed. 42.95 (*0-314-20612-4*) West Pub.

Safety Security Officer. Jack Rudman. (Career Examination Ser.: C-1459). 1994. pap. 23.95 (*0-8373-1459-3*) Nat Learn.

Safety Self-Inspection Program for Foodservice Operations. 32p. 1983. pap. 8.00 (*0-317-57924-X*, MG833) Natl Restaurant Assn.

***Safety Signs, Tags, & Labels.** Richard K. Miller et al. (Market Research Survey Ser.: No. 257). 50p. 1996. 200.00 (*1-55865-281-7*) Future Tech Surveys.

Safety Smart--Intermediate: Teaching Responsibility for Personal & Home Safety. Lori Miescke. Ed. by Judy Mitchell & Don Clerico. (Illus.). 144p. (Orig.). (J). (gr. 4-6). 1995. teacher ed., pap. 13.95 (*1-57310-016-1*) Teachng & Lrning Co.

Safety Smart--Primary: Teaching Responsibility for Personal & Home Safety. Susan Julio. Ed. by Judy Mitchell & Linda Karges-Bone. (Illus.). 144p. (Orig.). (J). (gr. k-3). 1995. teacher ed., pap. 13.95 (*1-57310-015-3*) Teachng & Lrning Co.

Safety Source, 1995: National Public Safety Yellow Pages. Tr. by Laura J. Gross. 200p. 1995. 15.00 (*1-880245-09-4*) NPCS Info.

Safety Source 1996. Tr. by Laura J. Gross. 225p. 1996. 17.00 (*1-880245-12-4*) NPCS Info.

Safety Standard for Electrical & Electronic Test, Measuring, Controlling & Related Equipment: General Requirements. 1994. pap. 120.00 (*1-55617-517-5*, S82.01) ISA.

Safety Standard for Electrical & Electronic Test, Measuring, Controlling, & Related Equipment - Electrical & Electronic Process Measurement & Control Equipment. 1988. pap. 25.00 (*1-55617-102-1*, S82.03) ISA.

Safety Standard for Electrical & Electronic Test, Measuring, Controlling & Related Equipment - Electrical & Electronic Test & Measuring Equipment. 1988. pap. 25.00 (*1-55617-101-3*, S82.02) ISA.

Safety, Status & Future of Non-Commercial Reactors & Irradiation Facilities Topical Meeting, Boise, ID, Sept. 31-Oct. 4, 1990, 2 vols., Set. 780p. 1990. 80.00 (*0-89448-155-X*, 700159) Am Nuclear Soc.

Safety Supervisor. Jack Rudman. (Career Examination Ser.: C-2641). 1994. pap. 34.95 (*0-8373-2641-9*) Nat Learn.

***Safety Swing B.** 1991. pap. write for info. (*0-425-13247-1*) Berkley Pub.

Safety Symbols. Nora Olgyay. 1994. pap. 49.95 (*0-442-01844-4*) Van Nos Reinhold.

Safety, Systems & People. Sue Cox & Tom Cox. (Illus.). 339p. 1996. 56.95 (*0-7506-2089-7*) Buttrwrth-Heinemann.

Safety Talks, 2 vols., Set. rev. ed. 1994. ring bd. 199.95 (*1-55645-022-2*, 110005) Busn Legal Reports.

Safety Technology: SAE International Congress & Exposition 1994, 14 papers. (Special Publications). 96p. 1994. pap. 44.00 (*1-56091-493-9*, SP-1041) Soc Auto Engineers.

***Safety Testing Technology.** 1997. 61.00 (*1-56091-976-0*) Soc Auto Engineers.

***Safety Training Materials.** Richard K. Miller et al. (Market Research Survey Ser.: No. 241). 50p. 1996. 200.00 (*1-55865-271-X*) Future Tech Surveys.

Safety Training Methods: Practical Solutions for the Next Millenniu, Second Edition. 2nd ed. Jack B. Re Ville & Joe Stephenson. LC 94-18137. 296p. 1995. text ed. 69.95 (*0-471-55230-5*) Wiley.

Safety Valve Stability & Capacity Test Results: Pressure Relief Valve Performance Study Final Report. Design Institute for Emergency Relief Systems Users Group Staff. 77p. 1987. spiral bd. 140.00 (*0-8169-0369-7*, B-5) Am Inst Chem Eng.

Safety-Wise. rev. ed. Girl Scouts of the U. S. A. Staff. 160p. 1993. pap. 2.00 (*0-88441-476-0*, 26-201) Girl Scouts USA.

Safety with Cryogenic Fluids. Michael G. Zabetakis. LC 66-12628. (International Cryogenics Monograph Ser.). 171p. reprint ed. pap. 48.80 (*0-317-27805-3*, 2055952) Bks Demand.

Safety with Lasers & Other Optical Sources: A Comprehensive Handbook. David H. Sliney & Myron A. Wilbarsht. LC 80-16591. 1060p. 1980. 125.00 (*0-306-40434-6*, Plenum Pr) Plenum.

Safety, Work & Life: An International View. H. Greenwood Thomas. (Illus.). 240p. (Orig.). 1991. pap. 14.95 (*0-939874-88-1*) ASSE.

Safety Zone. Linda D. Meyer. (Illus.). 32p. (J). 1985. pap. 3.50 (*0-446-38238-8*) Warner Bks.

Safety/Driver Education. (National Teacher Examination Ser.: NT-59). pap. 23.95 (*0-8373-8479-6*) Nat Learn.

Safeware: System Safety & Computers. Nancy G. Leveson. LC 94-19779. (Computer Science & Electrical Engineering Ser.). 680p. (C). 1995. text ed. 45.94 (*0-201-11972-2*) Addison-Wesley.

Safflower. Joseph Smith. (Illus.). 624p. 1996. 150.00 (*0-935315-61-6*) AOCS Pr.

Safflower Products: Utilization & Markets. A. Johnson & A. Marter. 1993. pap. 30.00 (*0-85954-329-3*, Pub. by Nat Res Inst UK) St Mut.

Saffo & Excerpts from Furio Cammila. Giovanni Pacini. (Italian Opera 1810-1840 Ser.). 330p. 1986. text ed. 30.00 (*0-8240-6585-9*) Garland.

Safford: The Ohio Valley Saffords. enl. rev. ed. R. H. Smith & S. M. Culbertson. 240p. 1993. reprint ed. pap. 37.50 (*0-8328-3399-1*); reprint ed. lib. bdg. 47.50 (*0-8328-3398-3*) Higginson Bk Co.

Saffron: An Elizabethan Tale. Thomas Westlake. Ed. by Stacey J. Weinberger. (Torches Ser.: Pt. One). (Illus.). 88p. (Orig.). 1989. pap. 7.95 (*0-9624996-0-9*) Poppinjay Pr.

Saffron & Currants: A Cornish Heritage Cookbook. Susan I. Pellowe. (Illus.). 52p. (Orig.). 1989. pap. 5.00 (*0-9623507-0-2*) Renard Prodns.

Saffron Scourge: A History of Yellow Fever in Louisiana, 1796-1905. Jo A. Carrigan. LC 93-73292. (Illus.). 480p. (C). 1993. 27.50 (*0-940984-86-5*) U of SW LA Ctr LA Studies.

Saffron's Trials. Frederick E. Smith. 256p. 1996. 22.00 (*0-7278-4877-1*) Severn Hse.

***Saffron's Trials.** large type ed. Frederick E. Smith. (Ulverscroft Large Print Ser.). 496p. 1997. 27.50 (*0-7089-3797-7*) Ulverscroft.

Safire's Usage Dictionary. W. Safire. 1996. write for info. (*0-679-44961-2*) Random.

SAFRA Papers, No. 1. David R. Jones. Incl. Advanced Guard. 1985. (*0-318-59307-6*); Mobility in Russian & Soviet Military Thought & Practice. 1985. (*0-318-59308-4*); 138p. 1985. 10.50 (*0-87569-085-8*) Academic Intl.

SAFRA Papers - Social Sciences in Soviet Armed Forces, No. 2. Ed. by David Jones. 1988. 11.00 (*0-87569-101-3*) Academic Intl.

***Safwa: Ein Ostrafrikanischer Volksstamm in Seinem Leben & Denken, Vol. 1.** Elise Kootz-Kretschmer. (B. E. Ser.: No. 138). (GER.). 1929. 23.00 (*0-8115-3061-2*) Periodicals Srv.

Sag Harbor: An American Beauty. 52.00 (*0-8488-0899-1*) Amereon Ltd.

***Sag Harbor in Earlier Days: A Series of Historical Sketches of the Harbor & Hampton Port.** Harry D. Sleight. (Illus.). 293p. 1997. reprint ed. lib. bdg. 36.00 (*0-8328-6217-7*) Higginson Bk Co.

Sag Mal. Gillian Taylor & Oliver Gray. 1989. pap. text ed. 10.00 (*0-582-22384-9*, 70932) Longman.

Sag Mir, o Hund - Wo der Hund Begraben Liegt. Helmut Hausle. (Spudasmata Ser.: Bd. XLIV). x, 74p. (GER.). 1989. write for info. (*3-487-09197-6*) G Olms Pubs.

***Saga.** Carlos R. Albet. LC 97-60043. 188p. (Orig.). (SPA.). 1997. pap. 14.95 (*1-882573-08-0*, Zinnia Bks) Serena Bay.

Saga. Lucia Fox. (Illus.). 66p. (SPA.). 1992. pap. text ed. 10.00 (*0-685-50240-6*) La Nueva Cronica.

Saga. Kelly Hamilton. (Illus.). 80p. 1983. pap. 5.95 (*0-88145-012-X*) Broadway Play.

S

An Asterisk (*) at the beginning of an entry indicates that the title is appearing in BIP for the first time.

Saga: Best New Writings on Mythology. Ed. & Pref. by Jonathan Young. (SAGA Annual Anthology Ser.). (Illus.). 232p. (Orig.). 1995. pap. 14.95 (*1-883991-13-7*) Whte Cloud Pr.

Saga: One Man's Battle with MS. Ron Snyder. Ed. by Merle Spector. 160p. (Orig.). 1995. spiral bd., pap. write for info. (*1-57502-030-0*) Morris Pubng.

Saga America. Barry Fell. LC 79-51440. (Illus.). 1983. 15. 00 (*0-8129-0847-3*, Times Bks) Random.

Saga Begins. Stan Campbell. (BibleLog Ser.: No.1). 156p. (YA). (gr. 8 up). 1988. pap. 6.50 (*0-89693-657-0*, Sonflower Bks) SP Pubns.

Saga Book, 1895-1977, 19 vols., Set. Viking Society for Northern Research Staff. (Illus.). 1980. reprint ed. 1,510. 50 (*0-404-60030-1*) AMS Pr.

Saga de Mexico. Ed. by Seymour Menton & Maria Herrera-Sobek. LC 91-33663. 348p. 1991. pap. 22.00 (*0-927534-11-8*) Biling Rev-Pr.

Saga in Steel & Concrete: Norwegian Engineers in America. Kenneth O. Bjork. 504p. 1947. 15.00 (*0-87732-028-4*) Norwegian-Am Hist Assn.

Saga Never Ends: Leader's Guide. Stan Campbell. (BibleLog Ser.: Bk. 8). 1989. pap. 5.99 (*0-89693-389-X*) SP Pubns.

Saga of a Crossroads - Florham Park. Eleanor Weis. Ed. by Carl Weis. (Illus.). 280p. 1988. 25.00 (*0-9621192-0-2*) Hist Soc Florham Pk.

Saga of a Frontier Seaport. Coleman McCampbell. 1993. reprint ed. lib. bdg. 75.00 (*0-7812-5945-2*) Rprt Serv.

Saga of a Great Soul. Swami Vividishananda. 1957. pap. 4.95 (*0-87481-584-3*, Pub. by Ramakrishna Math II) Vedanta Pr.

Saga of a Paper Mill. Laurence Pratt. LC 35-4692. 77p. reprint ed. pap. 25.00 (*0-317-41725-8*, 2052050) Bks Demand.

Saga of a Quiet Birdman: The Autobiography of Paul B. Jackson, Colonel USAF (Ret.) Ed. & Compiled by David G. Mayor. (Illus.). 320p. (Orig.). 1994. pap. 19.95 (*1-877633-20-8*) Luthers.

Saga of a Security Guard. James. 1994. 16.95 (*0-533-11135-8*) Vantage.

Saga of a Surgeon: The Life of Daniel Brainard, M.D. Janet Kinney. LC 87-62176. (Medical Humanities Ser.). (Illus.). 246p. (C). 1987. 17.95 (*0-931369-20-7*) Southern IL Univ Sch.

Saga of a Wayward Sailor. Tristan Jones. (Illus.). 276p. 1995. pap. 14.95 (*0-924486-79-1*) Sheridan.

Saga of American Society: A Record of Social Asperations, 1607-1937. Dixon Wecter. (BCL1 - U. S. History Ser.). 504p. 1991. reprint ed. lib. bdg. 109.00 (*0-7812-6004-3*) Rprt Serv.

Saga of an Entrepreneur: The Story of Mendis Spécial. W. M. Mendis. 1995. 16.95 (*0-533-10941-8*) Vantage.

Saga of an Irish Immigrant Family: The Descendants of John Mullanphy. Alice L. Cochran. LC 76-6328. (Irish Americans Ser.). 1976. 25.95 (*0-405-09325-X*) Ayer.

Saga of Anthropology in China: From Malinowski to Moscow to Mao. Gregory E. Guldin. LC 92-34292. (Studies on Modern China). 312p. (gr. 13). 1994. text ed. 69.95 (*1-56324-185-4*, East Gate Bk); pap. text ed. 26.95 (*1-56324-186-2*, East Gate Bk) M E Sharpe.

***Saga of Bjorn: Champion of the Men of Hitardale.** Alison Finlay. (Icelandic Saga Studies). 160p. 1996. 24.95 (*1-874312-26-5*, Pub. by Drake Intl Serv UK) Intl Spec Bk.

***Saga of Black Navy Veterans of World War II: An American Triumph.** James S. Peters, 2nd. LC 96-47070. 160p. 1996. pap. 12.95 (*1-57309-122-7*); text ed. 24.95 (*1-57309-123-5*) Intl Scholars.

Saga of California: Power & Glory. Robert Easton. 400p. 1996. reprint ed. mass mkt. 4.99 (*0-8439-4074-3*, Leisure Bks) Dorchester Pub Co.

Saga of Chief Joseph. Helen Addison Howard. LC 78-16138. (Illus.). 421p. 1978. reprint ed. pap. 12.00 (*0-8032-7202-2*, Bison Books) U of Nebr Pr.

Saga of Chrysodontis Pappas. John Kapsalis. LC 93-93510. 88p. (Orig.). 1994. pap. 8.00 (*1-56002-367-8*, Univ Edtns) Aegina Pr.

Saga of Cimba. Richard Maury. (Illus.). 1973. 7.25 (*0-8286-0063-5*) J De Graff.

Saga of Coe Ridge: A Study in Oral History. William L. Montell. LC 74-77846. (Illus.). 256p. 1970. 31.00 (*0-87049-096-6*); pap. 16.00 (*0-87049-315-9*) U of Tenn Pr.

Saga of Dazai Osamu: A Critical Study with Translations. Phyllis I. Lyons. LC 83-42542. (Illus.). 432p. 1985. 49. 50 (*0-8047-1197-6*) Stanford U Pr.

Saga of Denny McCune. Bird Arthur & Budd Arthur. 1993. 17.50 (*0-7451-4563-9*, Gunsmoke) Chivers N Amer.

Saga of Erik the Viking. Terry Jones. (Illus.). 192p. (J). (gr. 3-7). 1993. pap. 3.99 (*0-14-032261-2*, Puffin) Puffin Bks.

Saga of Erik the Viking. Terry Jones. (Storybooks Ser.). (Illus.). 144p. (J). (ps up). 1986. pap. 9.95 (*0-14-031713-9*, Puffin) Puffin Bks.

Saga of Felix Senac: Being the Legend & Biography of a Confederate Agent in Europe. Regina C. Rapier. (Illus.). 216p. 1972. 30.00 (*0-9600584-1-9*) R C Rapier.

Saga of Filster Stein. Gary Lovisi. (Illus.). 52p. (Orig.). 1988. 4.00 (*0-936071-07-9*) Gryphon Pubns.

Saga of Finnbogi the Strong. Tr. by W. Bryant Bachman, Jr. & Gudmundur Erlingsson. LC 89-22527. (Illus.). 130p. (Orig.). (C). 1990. pap. text ed. 15.00 (*0-8191-7595-1*); lib. bdg. 44.00 (*0-8191-7594-3*) U Pr of Amer.

Saga of Gisli the Outlaw. Tr. by George Johnston. LC 67-207. (Illus.). 146p. 1963. pap. 14.95 (*0-8020-6219-9*) U of Toronto Pr.

Saga of Gunnlaugur Snake's Tongue: With an Essay on the Structure & Translation of the Saga. E. Paul Durrenberger & Dorothy Durrenberger. LC 91-50425. 128p. 1992. 26.50 (*0-8386-3465-6*) Fairleigh Dickinson.

Saga of Hacon & a Fragment of the Saga of Magnus (Translation) see Icelandic Sagas, & Other Historical Documents on the British Isles

Saga of Han Lum Choy. David Y. Chan. 96p. 1995. pap. 9.00 (*0-8059-3816-8*) Dorrance.

***Saga of Havardur of Isafjord.** Tr. by Paul Durrenberger & Dorothy Durrenberger. (Icelandic Saga Studies). 104p. 1996. 22.95 (*1-874312-19-2*, Pub. by Drake Intl Serv UK) Intl Spec Bk.

Saga of Hog Island & Other Essays in Inconvenient History. James J. Martin. LC 76-62654. 1977. pap. 6.95 (*0-87926-021-1*) R Myles.

Saga of Hrafn Sveinbjarnarson. Hrafn Sveinbjarnarson. Tr. by Anne Tjomsland. (Islandica Ser.: Vol. 35). 1951. 25. 00 (*0-527-00365-4*) Periodicals Srv.

Saga of Hugh Glass: Pirate, Pawnee, & Mountain Man. John M. Myers. LC 75-38613. vii, 237p. 1976. reprint ed. pap. 10.95 (*0-8032-5834-8*, Bison Books) U of Nebr Pr.

Saga of Iron Mining in Michigan's Upper Peninsula. Burton H. Boyum. LC 77-150296. 1977. pap. 7.95 (*0-938746-03-0*) Marquette Cnty.

Saga of Jack Durant. unabridged ed. Mabel R. Leo. 208p. (Orig.). 1996. per., pap. 10.00 (*0-9650787-0-1*) M R Leo.

Saga of Jazz: A History. Collier. LC 97-3004. (J). 1997. 14. 95 (*0-8050-4121-4*) H Holt & Co.

Saga of Jesse James. Carl W. Breihan. LC 91-12985. (Illus.). 1991. pap. 14.95 (*0-87004-327-7*) Caxton.

Saga of Katy & the Gamblin' Lady. Ronald Burke. 32p. 1974. pap. 3.00 (*0-87129-687-X*, S10) Dramatic Pub.

Saga of Kettle Falls. Orville Dutro. (Illus.). 44p. (Orig.). 1988. pap. 4.95 (*0-940151-06-5*) Statesman-Exam.

Saga of Kosovo: Focus on Serbian-Albanian Relationships. Alex N. Dragnich & Slavko Todorovich. (East European Monographs). 1985. 22.50 (*0-317-18452-0*) Brooklyn Coll Pr.

Saga of Phil & the Red Piece of Meat. David E. Lindamood. LC 95-68516. (Illus.). 73p. 1995. pap. 9.95 (*1-57197-003-7*) Pentland Pr.

Saga of Prayer: The Poetry of Dylan Thomas. Robert K. Burdette. LC 68-23203. (Studies in English Literature: No. 67). 160p. 1973. text ed. 35.40 (*90-279-2072-9*) Mouton.

Saga of Saga: The Life & Death of an American Dream. William F. Scandling. LC 93-86913. (Illus.). 400p. 1994. 24.95 (*0-9639150-0-2*) Vista Linda Pr.

Saga of Sagebrush Sal. I. E. Clark. (Illus.). 20p. 1972. pap. 3.50 (*0-88680-167-2*); Director's Production Script. pap. 10.00 (*0-88680-168-0*) I E Clark.

Saga of Saint Mary of the Mills. Elizabeth L. Compton. 70p. 1993. 15.00 (*0-9636115-2-6*) St Mary Mills.

Saga of Saints. Sigrid Undset. Tr. by E. C. Ramsden. LC 68-22952. (Essay Index Reprint Ser.). 1977. reprint ed. 23.95 (*0-8369-0959-3*) Ayer.

Saga of Sammy-Cat. Ethel Mannin. (J). (gr. 1-3). 1969. reprint ed. 2.59 (*0-08-013397-5*, Pergamon Pr) Elsevier.

Saga of Shakespeare Pintlewood & the Great Silver Fountain Pen. James H. Lehman. LC 90-82303. (Illus.). 32p. (J). (gr. k-3). 1990. lib. bdg. 13.95 (*1-878925-00-8*) Brotherstone Pubs.

Saga of Sitting Bull's Bones: The Unusual Story Behind Sculptor Korczak Ziolkowski's Memorial to Chief Sitting Bull. Robb DeWall. LC 84-48122. (Illus.). 320p. 1984. 9.95 (*0-318-18779-5*) Crazy Horse.

Saga of South Kamrup. Indira Goswami. (C). 1993. 15.00 (*81-7201-152-0*, Pub. by Sahitya Akademi II) S Asia.

Saga of Swamp Thing. Alan Moore. 184p. (Orig.). 1987. pap. 10.95 (*0-446-38690-1*) Warner Bks.

Saga of Sydney A. Moore: A History of a Maryland Farming Family, 1820 to the Present. Robert E. Greene. LC 85-81232. (Illus.). 138p. 1985. pap. 9.95 (*0-9603320-6-5*) R E Greene.

Saga of the Air Mail. Carroll V. Glines, Jr. Ed. by James B. Gilbert. LC 79-2192. (Flight: Its First Seventy-Five Years Ser.). (Illus.). 1980. reprint ed. lib. bdg. 21.95 (*0-405-12213-6*) Ayer.

Saga of the All American. Buck Dawson. 400p. 1991. 27.95 (*1-880236-03-6*) Hoffman FL.

Saga of the Coeur D'Alene Indian Nation. Joseph Seltice. 1990. 24.95 (*0-87770-413-9*) Ye Galleon.

Saga of the Cotton Exchange. Madhav Pavaskar. 1985. 18. 00 (*0-8364-1405-5*, Pub. by Popular Prakashan II) S Asia.

Saga of the Electric Fork. Richard Blazey. 1990. pap. text ed. 5.00 (*1-879719-02-9*) Idea Connect.

Saga of the Grey Seal. Ronald M. Lockley. 8.50 (*0-8159-6801-9*) Devin.

Saga of the Jomsvikings. Ed. by Lee M. Hollander. LC 76-157341. (Select Bibliographies Reprint Ser.). (Illus.). 1977. reprint ed. 15.95 (*0-8369-5801-2*) Ayer.

Saga of the Jomsvikings. Tr. by Lee M. Hollander. (Illus.). 116p. 1989. reprint ed. pap. 6.95 (*0-292-77623-3*) U of Tex Pr.

Saga of the Mountain Legion (156th N. Y. Vols.) & the "Modest Hero Who Saved Our Flag" Seward R. Osborne. (Illus.). 40p. 1994. pap. text ed. 6.00 (*0-944413-31-5*) Longstreet Hse.

***Saga of the Nerve Growth Factor.** Rita Levi-Montalcini. 1997. 84.00 (*981-02-2604-7*) World Scientific Pub.

Saga of the Ridge. J. H. Pratt. 224p. 1983. pap. 9.50 (*1-55787-023-3*, NY76001) Hrt of the Lakes.

Saga of the Saints: An Illustrated History of the First 25 Seasons. Wayne A. Mack. LC 92-13809. 1992. pap. 29. 95 (*0-930892-18-6*) A Hardy & Assocs.

Saga of the Sea. Frederick B. Austin. LC 76-116930. (Short Story Index Reprint Ser.). 1977. reprint ed. 21.95 (*0-8369-3432-6*) Ayer.

Saga of the Soo Vol. I: West from Shoreham. John A. Gjevre. LC 90-90283. (Illus.). 216p. 1990. 39.00 (*0-9646134-1-7*); pap. 20.00 (*0-9646134-2-5*) Agassiz Pubns.

Saga of the South. Edward P. Lawton. LC 65-19041. (Illus.). 1974. 15.00 (*0-87208-005-6*) Shoeless Pub.

Saga of the Spotted Cow. Patricia Hail. (Illus.). 32p. (J). (gr. k-3). 1992. 9.95 (*1-879894-00-9*) Saratoga Pub.

Saga of the Sun Setters: The Illustrated History of the 38th Bombardment Group During WWII. Lawrence J. Hickey. LC 89-84158. (Eagles over the Pacific Ser.: Vol. 5). (Illus.). 480p. 1997. 75.00 (*0-913511-04-8*) Intl Res & Pub.

Saga of the Swamp Thing. Alan Moore. Ed. by Barry Marx. (Illus.). 88p. 1987. pap. 12.95 (*0-930289-22-6*, Vertigo) DC Comics.

Saga of the Sword. Frederick B. Austin. LC 75-106243. (Short Story Index Reprint Ser.). 1977. 21.95 (*0-8369-3279-X*) Ayer.

Saga of the Sword That Sings & Other Realities. Stephanie Stearns. (Illus.). 111p. (Orig.). 1988. pap. text ed. 7.98 (*0-317-90980-0*) Dubless Pubns.

Saga of the Tin Goose: The Story of the Ford Trimotor Airplane. David A. Weiss. LC 70-147340. (Illus.). (Orig.). 1995. pap. 19.00 (*0-9634299-2-2*) Cumberland Ent.

Saga of the Volsungs. Tr. by George K. Anderson. LC 80-65685. 272p. 1982. 38.50 (*0-87413-172-3*) U Delaware Pr.

Saga of the Volsungs: The Norse Epic of Sigurd the Dragon Slayer. Ed. & Tr. by Jesse L. Byock. 1990. 40.00 (*0-520-06683-9*); pap. 14.00 (*0-520-06904-8*) U CA Pr.

Saga of the Volsungs, the Saga of Ragnar Lodbrook, Together with the Lay of Kraka. Tr. by Margaret Schlauch. LC 75-41284. reprint ed. 27.50 (*0-404-14704-6*) AMS Pr.

Saga of Tom Horn: The Story of a Cattlemen's War. Dean F. Krakel. LC 87-33019. (Illus.). xi, 274p. 1988. pap. 12. 95 (*0-8032-7767-9*, Bison Books) U of Nebr Pr.

***Saga of Tristram & Isond.** Paul Schach. LC 73-76351. (Illus.). 227p. 1973. reprint ed. pap. 64.70 (*0-608-02683-2*, 2063336) Bks Demand.

Saga of Viga Glum. Tr. by George Johnston from ICE. 1990. write for info. (*0-921254-12-1*, Pub. by Penumbra Pr CN) U of Toronto Pr.

Saga of Walther of Aquitaine. Ed. by Marion D. Learned. LC 76-98848. 225p. 1970. reprint ed. text ed. 55.00 (*0-8371-3903-1*, LEWA, Greenwood Pr) Greenwood.

Saga of Walther of Aquitaine. Marion D. Learned. (BCL1-PR English Literature Ser.). 208p. 1992. reprint ed. lib. bdg. 79.00 (*0-7812-7165-7*) Rprt Serv.

Saga of '54: And More. Charles A. Hair. LC 87-50301. (Illus.). xiv, 210p. 1991. 37.95 (*0-918837-07-3*); 49.50 (*0-918837-08-1*) Robinson Typos.

***Saga School: Moribana Style.** Saga I. Ac. 1996. pap. 10.95 (*4-07-973234-1*) Shufu no Tomo-Sha.

***Saga School: Seika Style.** Saga I. Ac. 1996. pap. 10.95 (*4-07-973228-7*) Shufu no Tomo-Sha.

***Saga School: Shogonka Style.** Saga I. Ac. 1996. pap. 10.95 (*4-07-973211-2*) Shufu no Tomo-Sha.

***Saga School Heika.** Saka I. Ac. 1996. pap. 10.95 (*4-07-973240-6*) Shufu no Tomo-Sha.

***Saga School Ikebana in Living.** Saga I. Ac. 1996. pap. 10. 95 (*4-07-973257-0*) Shufu no Tomo-Sha.

***Saga School Principle Style.** Saga I. Ac. 1996. pap. 10.95 (*4-07-973205-8*) Shufu no Tomo-Sha.

Sagacity. Janet Hamilton. 135p. (Orig.). 1981. pap. 7.95 (*0-88784-087-6*, Pub. by Hse. of Anansi Pr CN) Genl Dist Srvs.

Sagada Reader. William H. Scott. 249p. (Orig.). (C). 1989. pap. 17.50 (*971-10-0330-9*, Pub. by New Day Pub PH) Cellar.

Sagadahoc Colony: Comprising the Relation of a Voyage into New England. Henry Thayer. LC 76-173865. (Illus.). 1972. reprint ed. 26.95 (*0-405-09026-9*) Ayer.

Sagalassos: Report on the Fourth Excavation Campaign of 1993, Vol. III. Ed. by M. Waelkens & J. Poblome. (Acta Archaeologica Lovaniensia Ser.: No. 7). (Illus.). 377p. (Orig.). 1995. pap. 147.50 (*90-6186-664-2*, Pub. by Leuven Univ BE) Coronet Bks.

Sagalassos II: Report on the Third Excavation Campaign of 1992. Ed. by M. Waelkens & J. Poblome. (Acta Archaeologica Lovaniensia Ser.: No. 6). 278p. (Orig.). 1993. pap. 117.50 (*90-6186-574-3*, Pub. by Leuven Univ BE) Coronet Bks.

Sagallassos I: First General Report on the Survey (1986-1989) & Excavations (1990-1991) Ed. by M. Waelkens. (Acta Archaeologica Lovaniensia Ser.: No. 5). 238p. (Orig.). 1993. pap. 117.50 (*90-6186-529-8*, Pub. by Leuven Univ BE) Coronet Bks.

***Sagamore: Omega Wolf.** W. David Speas. Ed. by J. L. Oberleitner. (Illus.). 43p. (YA). (gr. 7 up). 1997. 18.95 (*1-885092-00-8*) Forging Pathways.

Sagas & Popular Antiquarianism in Icelandic Archaeology. Adolph Fridriksson. Ed. by Ross Samson. (Worldwide Archaeology Ser.). 222p. 1994. 59.95 (*1-85628-709-2*, Pub. by Avebury Pub UK) Ashgate Pub Co.

***Sagas & Sagebrush.** Demitra A. Syrtis. 12p. 1995. pap. text ed. 7.00 (*1-886352-10-0*) Crow Feather.

Sagas Islandais. deluxe ed. Ed. by Regis Boyer. 2064p. (FRE.). 1987. 155.00 (*0-7859-3877-X*, 2070111172) Fr & Eur.

Sagas of Icelanders. Halldor Hermannsson. (Islandica Ser.: Vol. 24). 1935. 25.00 (*0-527-00354-9*) Periodicals Srv.

Sagas of King Half & King Hrolf. Tr. by W. Bryant Bachman, Jr. & Gudmundur Erlingsson from ICE. (Illus.). 144p. (Orig.). (C). 1991. pap. text ed. 24.50 (*0-8191-8123-4*); lib. bdg. 47.50 (*0-8191-8122-6*) U Pr of Amer.

Sagas of the Central Coast: History from the Pages of Central Coast Magazine. Ed. by Bob Nelson. (Illus.). 128p. (Orig.). 1995. pap. 14.95 (*0-9646930-0-3*) R J Nelson.

Sagattarius Whirl. J. May. pap. write for info. (*0-345-39518-2*) Ballantine.

Sage. Norah Hess. 448p. (Orig.). 1994. mass mkt., pap. text ed. 4.99 (*0-8439-3591-X*) Dorchester Pub Co.

Sage. Christopher Stasheff. (Star Stone Saga Ser.: Bk. 2). 384p. 1996. 22.00 (*0-345-39239-6*, Del Rey) Ballantine.

Sage: A Scholarly Journal on Black Women. fac. ed. (Illus.). 2000p. 1996. 150.00 (*0-926019-92-9*) Carlson Pub.

SAGE: Implementation Manual. Diane Modest & Sandra Cymerman. 1986. teacher ed., ring bd. 45.00 (*0-944584-05-5*, 28SAGE) Sopris.

SAGE: Mini-Study Units. Diane Modest & Sandra Cymerman. (Illus.). 652p. 1992. teacher ed., ring bd. 50. 00 (*0-944584-45-4*, 28MINI) Sopris.

Sage Brush Dentist. William Frackelton. (American Autobiography Ser.). 258p. 1995. reprint ed. lib. bdg. 79. 00 (*0-7812-8521-6*) Rprt Serv.

Sage Cottage Herb Garden Cookbook: Celebrations, Recipes, & Herb Gardening Tips for Every Month of the Year. 2nd ed. Dorry B. Norris. LC 95-15669. (Illus.). 320p. 1995. pap. 14.95 (*1-56440-727-6*) Globe Pequot.

Sage Counsels: Speeches on Indian Economy. B. D. Garware. 1990. 22.50 (*0-317-99585-5*, Pub. by Popular Prakashan II) S Asia.

Sage from Concord. Compiled by Virginia Hanson & Clarence Pedersen. LC 84-40510. 160p. (Orig.). 1985. pap. 5.95 (*0-8356-0593-0*, Quest) Theos Pub Hse.

Sage in Harlem: H. L. Mencken & the Black Writers of the 1920s. Charles Scruggs. LC 83-6246. 223p. reprint ed. pap. 63.60 (*0-7837-7056-1*, 2046868) Bks Demand.

Sage in Israel & the Ancient Near East. Ed. by John G. Gammie & Leo G. Perdue. LC 90-30764. xiv, 545p. 1990. text ed. 47.50 (*0-931464-46-3*) Eisenbrauns.

Sage Lake Road. Ron Rau. 126p. 1983. 15.00 (*0-932558-17-8*) Willow Creek Pr.

Sage Ninomiya's Evening Talks. Sontoku Ninomiya. Tr. by Isoh Yamagata. LC 70-98786. 139p. 1970. reprint ed. text ed. 38.50 (*0-8371-3134-0*, NIEV, Greenwood Pr) Greenwood.

Sage of Ananda: Shri Brahmananda Sarasvati, Vol. I. George Bailin & Daryl Bailin. 96p. (Orig.). 1993. pap. 9.95 (*0-942856-03-1*) Seaport Poets & Writers.

Sage of Bethany. Perry Gresham. 190p. 1988. 12.99 (*0-89900-289-7*) College Pr Pub.

Sage of San Diego Said Choose Quality & Reason. Malcom Dalgliesh. (Illus.). 100p. (Orig.). 1996. pap. 6.95 (*0-9646438-0-4*) New Enlightenment.

Sage, Priest, & Prophet: Religious & Intellectual Leadership in Ancient Israel. Joseph Blenkinsopp. Ed. by Douglas A. Knight. LC 95-1792. (Library of Ancient Israel). 208p. 1995. 19.00 (*0-664-21954-3*) Westminster John Knox.

Sage, Saint, & Sophist: Holy Men & Their Associates in the Early Roman Empire. Graham Anderson. LC 93-27965. 304p. (C). (gr. 13). 1994. text ed. 62.95 (*0-415-02372-6*, Routledge NY) Routledge.

***Sage Sayings.** Morris A. Inch. 1997. mass mkt. 4.99 (*1-55197-323-5*, Pub. by Comnwlth Pub CN) Partners Pubs Grp.

Sage Street: A Collection of Stories. David L. Roberts. LC 91-66153. 108p. (Orig.). (YA). (gr. 9 up). 1991. pap. 6.95 (*0-914767-20-8*) Skyline West Pr.

SAGE Trilogy. Lillian Stough. (Illus.). 130p. (Orig.). 1994. pap. 18.00 (*0-9615725-3-1*) Sage Pr.

SAGE Trilogy Introduction & Pt. One: A Desert Flower - the Beauty & Wonder of Special Days. Lillian Stough. (Illus.). 40p. (Orig.). 1994. pap. 7.00 (*0-9615725-4-X*) Sage Pr.

SAGE Trilogy, Pt. Three - Spice: Opinions, Criticism, Praise, Suspicions & Sound-offs. Lillian Stough. (Illus.). 50p. (Orig.). 1994. pap. 7.00 (*0-9615725-6-6*) Sage Pr.

SAGE Trilogy, Pt. Two - Wisdom: To Think, to Discover, to Plan for the Future. Lillian Stough. (Illus.). 40p. (Orig.). 1994. pap. 7.00 (*0-9615725-5-8*) Sage Pr.

Sage und Schreibe. Barbara Wotjak & Manfred Richter. 150p. 1993. 17.50 (*3-324-00304-0*) Langenscheidt.

***Sage und Schreibe: Inszenierungen Religioser Lesekultur.** Hermann Timm. (Innen und Auben Ser.: Vol. 2). 141p. 1995. pap. 21.50 (*90-390-0211-8*, Pub. by KOK Pharos NE) Eisenbrauns.

***Sage Woman Calendar for 1998: The Goddess of the Zodiac.** Ed. by Joanna P. Colbert. (Illus.). Date not set. pap. 8.95 (*0-9630360-7-6*) Sage Woman.

Sage Woman Cauldron: A Collection from Our First Five Years. Ed. by Lunaea Weatherstone. (Illus.). 152p. (Orig.). 1993. pap. 14.95 (*0-9630360-1-7*) Sage Woman.

Sagebrush. large type ed. Wade Hamilton. (Linford Western Library). 240p. 1988. pap. 15.99 (*0-7089-6608-X*, Linford) Ulverscroft.

Sagebrush & Cappuccino: Confessions of an LA Naturalist. David Wicinas. LC 95-4280. 160p. (Orig.). 1995. pap. 13.00 (*0-87156-435-1*) Sierra.

Sagebrush & Sunshine. Margot Dalton. (Superromance Ser.: No. 425). 1990. pap. 2.95 (*0-373-70425-9*) Harlequin Bks.

Sagebrush & Sunshine. Margot Dalton. (Western Lovers Ser.). 1995. mass mkt. 3.99 (*0-373-88518-0*, 1-88518-5) Harlequin Bks.

Sagebrush Bohemian: Mark Twain in California. Nigey Lennon. (Illus.). 203p. 1994. pap. 10.95 (*1-56924-946-6*) Marlowe & Co.

Sagebrush Bride. Tanya A. Crosby. 368p. (Orig.). 1993. mass mkt. 4.50 (*0-380-77060-1*) Avon.

Sagebrush, Buttes & Buffalo. Nancy E. Hanson. (North Dakota Centennial Ser.: Vol. IV). (Illus.). 128p. (Orig.). 1987. pap. 17.95 (*0-911007-08-3*) Prairie Hse.

Sagebrush Country: A Wildflower Sanctuary. Ronald J. Taylor. Ed. by Kathleen Ort. (Illus.). 221p. (Orig.). 1992. pap. 14.00 (*0-87842-280-3*) Mountain Pr.

S

Sagebrush Country: Land & the American West. Philip L. Fradkin. LC 90-25212. (Illus.). 296p. 1991. reprint ed. pap. 19.95 (0-8165-1236-1) U of Ariz Pr.

Sagebrush Girl. Margaret F. Garrison. 96p. 1981. 8.75 (0-930142-05-5) Merlin Pr.

Sagebrush Ocean: A Natural History of the Great Basin. Stephen A. Trimble. LC 87-19186. (Max C. Fleischmann Series in Great Basin Natural History). (Illus.). 264p. 1993. pap. 24.95 (0-87417-222-5) U of Nev Pr.

Sagebrush Reflections: The History of Amedee & Honey Lake. Tim I. Purdy. (Illus.). 66p. (Orig.). 1993. pap. 9.45 (0-938373-11-0) Lahontan Images.

Sagebrush Seed. Don I. Smith. (Illus.). 112p. 1987. pap. 7.99 (0-932773-02-8) High Country Bks.

Sagebrush Skeletons. Jon Sharpe. (Trailsman Ser.: No. 179). 176p. 1996. mass mkt. 4.99 (0-451-18693-1) NAL-Dutton.

Sagebrush Soldier: Private William Earl Smith's View of the Sioux War of 1876. Sherry L. Smith. LC 89-5408. (Illus.). 176p. 1989. 19.95 (0-8061-2209-9) U of Okla Pr.

Sagebrush State: Nevada's History, Government, & Politics. Michael W. Bowers. LC 96-15678. (Wilbur S. Shepperson Series in History & Humanities: No. 38). 1996. pap. text ed. 13.95 (0-87417-249-7) U of Nev Pr.

Sagebrush to Shakespeare. Carrol B. Howe. (Illus.). 216p. 1984. pap. 10.00 (0-8323-0489-1) Binford Mort.

Sagebrush to Shakespeare. Carrol B. Howe. (Illus.). 214p. 1984. 16.00 (0-939860-06-6) Tremaine Graph & Pub.

Sagebrush Trilogy: Idah Meacham Strobridge & Her Works. Idah M. Strobridge. LC 90-39026. (Vintage West Ser.). (Illus.). 452p. 1990. reprint ed. pap. 14.95 (0-87417-164-4) U of Nev Pr.

Sagebrush Wildflowers. J. E. Underhill. 64p. pap. 6.95 (0-88839-171-4) Hancock House.

Sages: Their Concepts & Beliefs. Ephraim E. Urbach. LC 87-8415. 1120p. 1987. pap. text ed. 27.50 (0-674-78523-1) HUP.

Sages: Their Concepts & Beliefs, 2 vols., Set. 2nd enl. ed. E. E. Urbach. Tr. by I. Abrahams. 1089p. 1979. text ed. 45.00 (965-223-319-6, Pub. by Magnes Press IS) Eisenbrauns.

Sages & Saints. Leo Jung. (Jewish Library: Vol. X). 1987. pap. 25.00 (0-88125-103-8) Ktav.

Sages & Schoolmen: Philosophers from Pythagoras to Eckhardt. Arland Ussher. LC 66-29650. 71p. 6700. 15.95 (0-8023-1139-3) Dufour.

Sages & Seers. Manly P. Hall. pap. 14.95 (0-89314-393-6) Philos Res.

Sages & Specialists. Matt Forbeck. 1996. 20.00 (0-7869-0410-0) TSR Inc.

Sages of China. Manly P. Hall. (Adepts Ser.). (Illus.). 114p. 1985. reprint ed. pap. 9.95 (0-89314-531-9) Philos Res.

***Sages of Roney Street: And Other Joys, Large & Small.** Jerry G. Gambill. Ed. by John A. Gentry. LC 95-90896. 304p. (Orig.). 1997. pap. 10.95 (1-56002-631-6, Univ Edtns) Aegina Pr.

Sages' Shooters: The Original Gelatin Shooter Recipe Book. Laurie S. Morris. LC 95-83133. 80p. (Orig.). 1995. pap. 11.95 (1-56167-237-8) Am Literary Pr.

Sages Speak: Rabbinic Wisdom & Jewish Values. William B. Silverman. LC 89-15142. 264p. 1996. reprint ed. pap. text ed. 24.95 (1-56821-410-3) Aronson.

Sages Speak about Immortality. Ed. by Margaret Leuverink. (Mananam Ser.). (Illus.). 106p. 1995. 7.00 (1-880687-08-9) Chinmaya Pubns.

Sages Speak about Life & Death. Ed. by Margaret Leuverink. LC 94-21223. (Mananam Ser.). (Illus.). 107p. pap. 7.00 (1-880687-07-0) Chinmaya Pubns.

Sages, Stories, Authors & Editors in Rabbinic Babylonia. Richard Kalmin. LC 94-33649. (Brown Judaic Studies: Vol. 300). 363p. 1994. 59.95 (0-7885-0045-7, 140300) Scholars Pr GA.

Sagesse. Paul M. Verlaine. (Illus.). 110.00 (0-685-37129-8) Fr & Eur.

Sagesse: Avec: Parallelement, Les Memoirs d'un Veuf. Paul M. Verlaine & Jean Gaudon. 247p. (FRE.). 1977. pap. 10.95 (0-7859-1434-X, 2080702912) Fr & Eur.

Sagesse, Amour, Bonheur. Paul M. Verlaine. (FRE.). 1975. pap. 10.95 (0-8288-3828-3, F102140) Fr & Eur.

Sagesse, Amour, Bonheur. Paul M. Verlaine. (Poesie Ser.). 256p. (FRE.). 1975. pap. 9.95 (2-07-032152-5) Schoenhof.

Sagesse de Rebbe Nachman. Nathan. Ed. & Tr. by A. Dimermanas from HEB. 334p. (FRE.). 1989. text ed. 15.00 (0-930213-31-9); pap. text ed. 13.00 (0-930213-32-7) Breslov Res Inst.

Sagesse Du Pere Brown. Gilbert K. Chesterton. 247p. (FRE.). 1985. pap. 10.95 (0-7859-2014-5, 2070376567) Fr & Eur.

Sagesses Barbares. Arnaldo D. Momigliano. (FRE.). 1991. pap. 11.95 (0-7859-3980-6) Fr & Eur.

Saggio di una Bibliografia Euclidea, 4 pts. in 1. Pietro Riccardi. 260p. 1974. reprint ed. write for info. (3-487-05407-8) G Olms Pubs.

Saggio Sopra la Pittura (Livorno, 1763) fac. ed. Francesco Algarotti. (Documents of Art & Architectural History Ser.: Ser II; Vol. 6). (Illus.). (ITA.). 1981. lib. bdg. 30.00 (0-89371-206-X) Broude Intl Edns.

Saggy Baggy Elephant. Illus. by Gustaf Tenggren. (Little Nugget Bks.). 28p. (J). 1994. write for info. (0-307-12545-9) Western Pub.

Saginaw: A History of the Land. Stuart A. Gross. 19.95 (0-89781-016-3) Am Historical Pr.

Saginaw: A Pictorial History. Jeremy W. Kilar. (Michigan Pictorial History Ser.). (Illus.). 1994. write for info. (0-943963-40-0) G Bradley.

Saginaw Chippewa & the Isabella "Reservation" A Research Report. James A. Clifton. 223p. reprint ed. pap. 63.60 (0-7837-6224-0, AU00444) Bks Demand.

Saginaw Paul Bunyan. James Stevens. LC 87-24395. (Great Lakes Bks.). 264p. 1987. reprint ed. 29.95 (0-8143-1929-7); reprint ed. pap. 14.95 (0-8143-1930-0) Wayne St U Pr.

Sagitario: Astro-Numerogia. Michael J. Kurban. Tr. by Loretta H. Kurban from ENG. LC 86-91275. (Illus.). (Orig.). (SPA.). 1992. pap. 8.00 (0-938863-53-3) Libra Press Chi.

Sagitarius Rising. Douglas M. Baker. (Esoteric Astrology: The Rising Signs Ser.). 1981. pap. 7.50 (0-906006-37-6, Pub. by Baker Pubns UK) New Leaf Dist.

Sagitarius Sun Sign. Douglas M. Baker. (Astrological Sun Sign Ser.). 1972. pap. 5.50 (0-906006-25-2, Pub. by Baker Pubns UK) New Leaf Dist.

Sagittar 97. Sydney Omarr. 1996. pap. 4.99 (0-451-18835-7, Sig) NAL-Dutton.

Sagittarius. (Super Horoscopes, 1995 Ser.). 256p. (Orig.). 1994. pap. text ed. 4.99 (0-7865-0034-4) Diamond.

Sagittarius. (Total Horoscopes, 1995 Ser.). 272p. (Orig.). 1994. pap. text ed. 4.50 (0-515-11419-7) Jove Pubns.

Sagittarius. (Love Signs Library). 64p. 1996. 8.95 (0-7894-1097-4) DK Pub Inc.

***Sagittarius.** (Parker's Love Signs Ser.). 1996. 8.95 (0-614-20708-8) DK Pub Inc.

***Sagittarius.** (Astrology Journals). (Illus.). 80p. 1997. pap. 6.50 (1-55670-576-X) Stewart Tabori & Chang.

***Sagittarius.** (Fisher-Price Little People Coloring & Activity Ser.). (Illus.). 24p. 1997. pap. write for info. (1-56144-968-7, Honey Bear Bks) Modern Pub NYC.

***Sagittarius.** Ariel Books Staff. (Tiny Tomes Ser.). 128p. 1997. 3.95 (0-8362-2670-4, Arie Bks) Andrews & McMeel.

Sagittarius. Lucille Callard. (Astro-Pups: Your Sign, Your Dogs Ser.). (Illus.). 60p. 1991. pap. 9.95 (1-881038-08-4) Penzance Pr.

***Sagittarius.** Jove Publications Incorporated, Staff. (Total Horoscopes Ser.). 272p. 1997. mass mkt. 5.99 (0-515-12116-9) Jove Pubns.

Sagittarius. Derek Parker & Julia Parker. LC 92-52792. (Sun & Moon Signs Library). (Illus.). 64p. 1992. 8.95 (1-56458-092-X) DK Pub Inc.

Sagittarius. Paula Taylor. (Sun Sign Ser.). 40p. (J). (gr. 4). 1989. lib. bdg. 13.95 (0-88682-251-3) Creative Ed.

***Sagittarius: A Little Book of Zodiac Wisdom, a Pop-Up Book.** Running Press Staff. (Zodiac Wisdom Ser.). 1997. 4.95 (0-7624-0031-5) Running Pr.

Sagittarius: Astro-Numerology. 2nd ed. Michael J. Kurban. (Illus.). 50p. 1991. pap. 8.00 (0-938863-17-7) Libra Press Chi.

Sagittarius: Little Birth Sign. Ariel Books Staff. 1994. 4.95 (0-8362-3077-9, Arie Bks) Andrews & McMeel.

***Sagittarius: Old Moore's Horoscopes & Astral Diaries.** W. Foulsham & Co. Staff. 1997. pap. text ed. 5.95 (0-572-02359-6, Pub. by W Foulsham UK) Trans-Atl Phila.

***Sagittarius: Your Sun-&-Moon Guide to Love & Life.** Ariel Books Staff. 374p. (Orig.). 1997. pap. 5.95 (0-8362-3564-9, Arie Bks) Andrews & McMeel.

Sagittarius 1994 Purse Book. 1994. mass mkt. 1.25 (0-440-60240-8) Dell.

Sagittarius 1995 Love Signs. 1995. mass mkt. 1.29 (0-440-22128-5) Dell.

Sagittarius 1995 Purse Book. 1994. mass mkt. 0.99 (0-440-60241-6) Dell.

Sagittarius 1996 Purse Book. 1995. mass mkt. 1.19 (0-440-60254-8) Dell.

SAGO: The Equatorial Swamp As a Natural Resource. Ed. by W. R. Stanton & M. Flach. 258p. 1981. lib. bdg. 112.00 (90-247-2470-8) Kluwer Ac.

Sago Saga. Gert Montague. LC 88-84093. (Illus.). 107p. (Orig.). reprint ed. 12.95 (0-9623565-0-6); reprint ed. pap. 9.95 (0-9623565-1-4) G Montague.

Sagouin. Francois Mauriac. (FRE.). 1963. pap. 10.95 (0-8288-9867-7, F113150) Fr & Eur.

Sagouin. Francois Mauriac. 9.95 (0-686-55477-9) Fr & Eur.

Sagrado Coran: Koran & Commentary in Spanish Translation. (ARA & SPA.). 1988. 54.50 (1-85372-118-2) Colton Bk.

Sag's auf Deutsch: A First Book for German Conversation. C. R. Goedsche. (Illus.). (GER.). (gr. 10 up). 1979. reprint ed. pap. text ed. 6.95 (0-8290-0026-7) Irvington.

***Saguache County Museum Presents Images of the Past, Vol. 1.** 79p. Date not set. pap. write for info. (0-9651079-1-4) Saguache Cnty.

Saguaro: A View of Saguaro National Monument & the Tucson Basin. Gary P. Nabhan. Ed. by T. J. Priehs & Carolyn Dodson. LC 86-61422. (Illus.). 76p. (Orig.). 1986. pap. 4.95 (0-911408-69-X) SW Pks Mnmts.

***Saguaro Cactus.** Paul Berquist. LC 96-37097. (Habitats Ser.). 1997. lib. bdg. 17.30 (0-516-20713-X) Childrens.

***Saguaro Cactus.** Paul Fleisher. LC 96-37810. (Webs of Life Ser.). (Illus.). 48p. (J). (gr. 1-3). 1997. lib. bdg. 14.95 (0-7614-0433-3, Benchmark NY) Marshall Cavendish.

Saguaro Cactus. Conrad J. Storad. LC 93-38913. (Early Bird Nature Bks.). 48p. (J). (gr. 2-3). 1994. lib. bdg. 18.95 (0-8225-3002-3, Lerner Publctns) Lerner Group.

Saguaro National Monument. Doris Evans. Ed. by T. J. Priehs & Sandra Scott. LC 93-86298. (Illus.). 16p. (Orig.). 1993. pap. 3.95 (1-877856-36-3) SW Pks Mnmts.

Saguaro National Park, AZ. (Illus.). 1995. 8.99 (1-56695-010-4) Trails Illustrated.

***Saguaro Riptide.** Norman Partridge. 256p. 1997. mass mkt. 5.99 (0-425-15699-0, Prime Crime) Berkley Pub.

Sahajayana: A Study of Tantric Buddhism. Ramprasad Mishra. (C). 1991. 45.00 (81-85094-45-4, Pub. by Punthi Pus II) S Asia.

Sahajayoga & Other Meditations. C. S. Pillai. 1987. 8.95 (0-318-37038-7) Asia Bk Corp.

Sahajiya Cult of Bengal & Pancha Sakha Cult of Orissa. Paritosh Das. (C). 1988. 17.50 (0-8364-2378-X, Pub. by Firma KLM II) S Asia.

Sahar: Dawn. 12th ed. Shah Maghsoud Sadegh Angha. 197p. (Orig.). (ENG, GER, JPN & PER.). 1984. 30.00 (0-910735-47-6); pap. 12.00 (0-910735-48-4) MTO Printing & Pubn Ctr.

Sahara. Clive Cussler. 1995. pap. 7.99 (0-671-52110-1) S&S Trade.

Sahara. Peter Murray. LC 93-25782. (Vision Bks.). 32p. (J). (gr. 2-6). 1993. lib. bdg. 22.79 (1-56766-023-1) Childs World.

Sahara. Peter Murray. LC 93-25782. (Libro Vision Ser.). 32p. (SPA.). (J). (gr. 2-6). 1993. lib. bdg. 22.79 (1-56766-040-1) Childs World.

Sahara. Jan Reynolds. (Illus.). 32p. (J). (gr. 2 up). 1991. 17.00 (0-15-269959-7); pap. 9.00 (0-15-269958-9) HarBrace.

Sahara: Vanishing Cultures. Reynolds. 1991. pap. 9.50 (0-15-200167-0) HarBrace.

Sahara Crosswind. T. Davis Bunn. LC 94-38348. (Rendezvous with Destiny Ser.: Bk. 3). 192p. 1994. pap. 8.99 (1-55661-381-4) Bethany Hse.

Sahara, Desert of Destiny. Georg Gerster. Tr. by Stewart Thomson. LC 70-133521. (Select Bibliographies Reprint Ser.). 1977. 28.95 (0-8369-5553-6) Ayer.

Sahara Sara - Sara Nohair: Saranohair. Gillian K. Johnson. (Picture Bks.). (Illus.). 32p. (FRE.). (J). 1996. 12.95 (1-55037-258-0, Pub. by Les Editions CN) Firefly Bks Ltd.

***Sahara Unveiled.** William Langewiesche. 1997. pap. 13.00 (0-679-75006-1, Vin) Random.

Sahara Unveiled: A Journey Across the Desert. William Langewiesche. LC 95-48864. 320p. 1996. 24.00 (0-679-42982-4) Pantheon.

Sahel: A Guide to the Microfiche Collection of Documents & Dissertations. University Microfilms International Staff. LC 80-28653. 1981. pap. 45.00 (0-8357-0534-X) Univ Microfilms.

Sahel Population: Integrated Rural Development Projects Research Components in Development Projects. Ed. by Annette Reenberg & Birgitte Markussen. (AAU Reports: No. 32). 182p. (C). 1994. pap. 12.95 (87-87600-41-2, Pub. by Aarhus Univ Pr DK) David Brown.

Sahel Visions: Planned Settlement & River Blindness Control in Burkina Faso. Della E. McMillan. LC 94-21940. (Studies in Human Ecology). 223p. 1995. pap. text ed. 15.95 (0-8165-1489-5); lib. bdg. 36.00 (0-8165-1487-9) U of Ariz Pr.

Sahibs & the Natives. Gomathi Narayanan. 174p. 1986. 18.50 (81-7001-016-0, Pub. by Chanakya II) S Asia.

***Sahibs, Nabobs & Boxwallahs: A Dictionary of the Words of Anglo-India.** Ivor Lewis. 278p. 1997. reprint ed. pap. 16.95 (0-19-564223-6) OUP.

Sahibs, Nabobs, & Boxwallahs: The Words of Anglo-India. Ivor Lewis. 350p. 1992. 39.95 (0-19-562582-X) OUP.

Sahih Al-Bukhari: Concise Version. Muhammad M. Khan. 1100p. 1995. 19.95 (1-56744-519-5) Kazi Pubns.

Sahih Al-Bukhari: The Early Years. Muhammad Asad. 306p. (Orig.). 1981. 24.95 (0-317-52458-5) New Era Publns MI.

Sahih Al-Bukhari: The Early Years of Islam. Bukhari. Tr. by Muhammad Asad from ARA. 306p. 1938. reprint ed. 33.00 (0-939660-05-9, Pub. by Dar Al-Andalus SP) Threshold VT.

Sahih-Al-Bukhari: U. S. A. Edition, Set, Vols. 1-9. M. M. Khan. Set. 240.00 (0-934905-23-1) Kazi Pubns.

Sahih al-Bukhari, Vols. I-IX: Foreign Edition, Set. Imam Bukhari. Tr. by M. Muhsin Khan. 1800p. (C). 1993. pap. 120.00 (1-56744-496-2) Kazi Pubns.

Sahih Muslim, 4 vols. Abdul H. Siddiqui. 59.00 (0-933511-44-2) Kazi Pubns.

Sahih Muslim. Abdul H. Siddiqui. 1613p. 1982. 80.00 (0-318-37192-8) Asia Bk Corp.

Sahitya, a Theory. Krishna Rayan. 88p. 1991. text ed. 15.95 (81-207-1175-0, Pub. by Sterling Pubs II) Apt Bks.

Sahitya Akademi Awards: Books & Writers 1955-1978. (C). 1990. 20.00 (81-7201-014-1, Pub. by Sahitya Akademi II) S Asia.

Sahitya-Darpana or Mirror of Composition of Visvanatha: A Treatise on Poetical Criticism. Tr. by J. R. Ballantyne & Pramada D. Mitra. (C). 1994. reprint ed. text ed. 32.00 (81-208-1145-3, Pub. by Motilal Banarsidass II) S Asia.

Sahtain, Middle East Cookbook. Arab Women Union Staff. (Illus.). 312p. 1995. vinyl bd. 19.95 (0-86685-036-8, AWUO36-8, Pub. by Librairie du Liban FR) Intl Bk Ctr.

Sai. Tadashi Yamashita. LC 87-50511. (Orig.). 1989. pap. write for info. (0-86568-090-6) Unique Pubns.

Sai Baba: Source of Light, Love & Bliss. Kailash Kumar & Jorgen Hovgard. (C). 1995. reprint ed. pap. 9.00 (81-207-1714-7, Pub. by Sterling Plns Pvt II) S Asia.

Sai Baba: The Embodiment of Love. 5th ed. Peggy Mason. 272p. 1982. pap. 13.95 (0-946551-52-9, Pub. by Gateway Books UK) ACCESS Pubs Network.

Sai Baba: The Holy Man & the Psychiatrist. Samuel H. Sandweiss. LC 75-28784. 240p. 1975. pap. 9.00 (0-9600958-1-0) Birth Day.

Sai Baba: The Ultimate Experience. Phyllis Krystal. 256p. 1994. pap. 12.95 (0-87728-794-5) Weiser.

Sai Baba & You: Practical Spirituality. 3rd ed. Mark H. Gardner & Barbara R. Gardner. (Illus.). 165p. (Orig.). 1995. pap. 8.00 (0-614-05176-2) Wisdom Works Pr.

Sai Baba Avatar: A New Journey into Power & Glory. Howard Murphet. LC 77-83643. 1977. pap. 6.30 (0-9600958-3-7) Birth Day.

Sai Baba Gita - The Way to Self-Realization & Liberation in This Age. Al Drucker. (Wisdom Teachings Ser.). 384p. 1993. pap. 12.50 (0-9638449-0-3) ATMA Pr.

Sai Baba, Man of Miracles. Howard Murphet. LC 90-24107. 216p. (Orig.). 1977. pap. 9.95 (0-87728-335-4) Weiser.

Sai Baba Manager Divine. Ajit Haksar. (Illus.). 136p. (Orig.). 1995. pap. 9.00 (0-9629835-5-1) Leela Pr.

Sai Baba's Mahavakya on Leadership. M. L. Chibber. (Illus.). 232p. (Orig.). 1995. pap. 12.00 (0-9629835-4-3) Leela Pr.

***Sai Inner Views & Insights: 30 Years with the Avatar.** Howard Murphet. LC 96-78608. 184p. (Orig.). 1996. pap. 12.00 (1-887906-00-2) Leela Pr.

Sai Karate Weapon of Self-Defense. Fumio Demura. LC 74-83597. (Weapons Ser.). (Illus.). 1974. pap. text ed. 10.95 (0-89750-010-5, 115, Wehman) Ohara Pubns.

***Sai Prophecy: A Novel.** Barbara Gardner. 1997. 19.95 (0-614-20712-6) Illum Arts.

***Sai Ram.** Charles Penn & Faith Penn. Date not set. pap. 4.50 (0-614-19084-3, BW-165) Sathya Sai Bk Ctr.

***Sai Spiritual Education - Teacher's Manual.** Date not set. pap. 11.00 (0-614-19118-1, BC-008) Sathya Sai Bk Ctr.

***Sai System of Education & World Crisis.** Ed. & Compiled by S. P. Ruhela. 223p. 1996. pap. 47.50 (81-85880-90-5, Pub. by Print Hse II) St Mut.

***Saicho: The Establishment of the Japanese Tendai School.** Paul Groner. (Berkeley Buddhist Studies). viii, 337p. 1984. 25.00 (0-87725-317-X) U of Cal IAS.

Said & the Unsaid: Mind Meaning & Culture. Stephen A. Tyler. 1978. text ed. 66.00 (0-12-705550-9) Acad Pr.

Said ibn Sultan (1791-1856), Ruler of Oman & Zanzibar. Ruete R. Said. (Illus.). xviii, 200p. reprint ed. write for info. (0-318-71560-0) G Olms Pubs.

Said Lands, Islands, & Premises. Mary M. Sloan. LC 95-21999. 1995. text ed. write for info. (0-925904-13-9) Chax Pr.

Saigo Takamori: The Man Behind the Myth. Charles L. Yates. LC 93-45592. 250p. 1995. 76.50 (0-7103-0484-6) Routledge Chapman & Hall.

Saigon Assignment. A. Frank Krause. 400p. (Orig.). (C). 1994. pap. 6.99 (0-9640228-1-8) ALCA VA.

Saigon Commandos: Dinky-Dau Death, No. 3. Jonathan Cain. 1984. mass mkt. 2.50 (0-317-02894-4, Zebra Kensgtn) Kensgtn Pub Corp.

Saigon Commandos: You Die, Du Ma, No. 8. Jonathan Cain. 320p. 1987. mass mkt. 2.50 (0-317-56089-1, Zebra Kensgtn) Kensgtn Pub Corp.

Saigon Dreaming. Tela Zasloff. 1990. 16.95 (0-312-04216-7) St Martin.

Saigon for a Song: The True Story of a Vietnam Gig to Remember. Reuben Noel & Nancy Noel. LC 87-16244. (Illus.). 264p. (Orig.). 1987. pap. 6.95 (0-943247-02-0) UCS Press.

Saigon Guidebook. Peter Leonard. (Illus.). 96p. (Orig.). 1995. pap. 9.95 (0-9645457-9-9) VietnAm Trading.

Saigon Merchant. large type ed. James A. Pattinson. 274p. 1994. pap. 17.99 (1-85389-468-0, Dales) Ulverscroft.

Saigon Singer. Mason. 1976. 24.95 (0-89190-352-6) Amereon Ltd.

Saigon to Jerusalem: Conversations with U. S. Veterans of the Vietnam War Who Emigrated to Israel. Eric Lee. LC 92-53501. (Illus.). 208p. 1992. pap. 29.95 (0-89950-727-1) McFarland & Co.

Saigyo: More Love Poems (101-200) Tr. by Howard S. Levy. (East Asian Poetry in Translation Ser.: No. 15). 1981. pap. 8.00 (0-686-37537-8) Oriental Bk Store.

Saigyo (1112-1190) As a Love Poet: One Hundred More Selections (201-300), Japanese Love Poems (1001-1100) Tr. by Howard S. Levy. (East Asian Poetry in Translation Ser.: No. 20). 1981. pap. 8.00 (0-686-37540-8) Oriental Bk Store.

Saigyo (1118-1190) As a Love Poet (Japanese Love Poems, 401-500) Tr. by Howard S. Levy. (East Asian Poetry in Translation Ser.: No. 12). 1980. pap. 8.00 (0-686-37534-3) Oriental Bk Store.

Saigyo (1118-1190) the Poet of Reflective Being & Natural Scene. Tr. by Howard S. Levy. (East Asian Poetry in Translation Ser.: No. 13). 1980. pap. 8.00 (0-686-37535-1) Oriental Bk Store.

***Saikei Basics.** Herb Gustafson. 1997. write for info. (0-8069-9737-0) Sterling.

***Saiki Koi & Other Stories.** Ogai Mori. Ed. by David Dilworth & J. Thomas Rimer. LC 77-4455. (Historical Literature of Mori Ogai Ser.: No. 2). 210p. 1977. reprint ed. pap. 59.90 (0-608-04394-X, 2065175) Bks Demand.

Sail! (J). (ps). 1995. 5.95 (1-885751-02-8) Wee Venture.

Sail. Eric Dlugokinski. LC 87-71724. (Illus.). 62p. (Orig.). 1988. pap. 5.00 (0-916383-43-1) Aegina Pr.

S.A.I.L. Self-Awareness in Language Arts. Rosemarie S. Hughes & Pamela C. Kloeppel. Ed. by Don L. Sorenson. (Illus.). 240p. 1994. teacher ed. 19.95 (0-932796-63-X) Ed Media Corp.

Sail & Power. 4th ed. Richard Henderson & William E. Brooks, III. LC 90-23229. (Illus.). 384p. 1991. 39.95 (1-55750-359-1) Naval Inst Pr.

Sail & Rail: Narrative History of Transportation in Western Michigan. 2nd ed. Lawrence M. Wakefield. 216p. 1996. reprint ed. pap. 24.95 (1-882376-31-5) Thunder Bay Pr.

Sail & Steam: A Century of Maritime Enterprise, 1840-1935. John Falconer. LC 93-78972. (Illus.). 192p. 1993. 50.00 (0-87923-995-6) Godine.

Sail Away. Donald Crews. LC 94-6004. (Illus.). 32p. (J). (ps up). 1995. 16.00 (0-688-11053-3); lib. bdg. 15.93 (0-688-11054-1) Greenwillow.

Sail Away. Ed. by Eleanor G. Locke. (Illus.). 164p. (Orig.). (J). 1987. pap. 17.00 (0-913932-24-8) Boosey & Hawkes.

Sail Away! large type ed. Alice Sharpe. LC 93-27182. 1993. pap. 13.95 (0-7862-0044-8) Thorndike Pr.

Sail Away Business Simulation Narrative, Century 21 1st Year Accounting. 4th ed. Kenton E. Ross. (BA - Accounting - First Year Ser.). 1987. 11.95 (0-538-02423-2) S-W Pub.

An Asterisk (*) at the beginning of an entry indicates that the title is appearing in BIP for the first time.

***Sail Better: 101 Tips & Techniques.** Roger Marshall. 1996. pap. text ed. 14.95 (0-07-041077-1) McGraw.

Sail Better: 101 Tips & Techniques. Roger Marshall. LC 95-36249. 208p. 1996. pap. 14.95 (0-312-14133-5) St Martin.

***Sail-Boat & Lake.** Robert Finch. 94p. 1988. pap. 8.95 (0-88984-124-1, Pub. by Porcupines Quill CN) Genl Dist Srvs.

Sail Ho. James Bisset & P. R. Stephensen. LC 58-5447. (Illus.). 1958. 42.95 (0-87599-015-0) S G Phillips.

Sail into the Sunset. Bill Cooper & Laurel Cooper. (Illus.). 160p. 1994. pap. 27.50 (0-7136-3951-2) Sheridan.

Sail Like a Champion: Advanced Racing & Cruising Techniques. Dennis Conner & Michael Levitt. (Illus.). 416p. 1992. 40.00 (0-312-07078-0) St Martin.

Sail Magazine Book of Sailing. Peter Johnson. (Illus.). 1989. 40.00 (0-685-30680-1) Knopf.

Sail On! And More Adventures & Absurdities. Pat Springle. 164p. (J). 1996. pap. 7.95 (1-888237-04-X) Baxter Pr.

Sail Performance: Design & Techniques to Maximize Sail Power. Czeslaw A. Marchaj. (Illus.). 416p. 1996. text ed. 54.95 (0-07-040250-7) McGraw.

Sail, Race & Win. 2nd rev. ed. Eric Twiname. (Illus.). 192p. 1993. pap. 17.50 (0-924486-53-8) Sheridan.

Sail Racer. Jack Knights. 236p. 1973. 27.95 (0-8464-1435-X) Beekman Pubs.

***Sail Tall Ships: A Directory of Sail Training & Adventure at Sea.** 9th ed. Midpoint Publishing Staff. 1997. pap. text ed. 12.95 (0-9636483-2-2) Am Sail Trng.

***Sail Through with Arabic Letters.** 2nd ed. Iqra' Foundation Staff. (Illus.). (J). 1991. reprint ed. pap. 4.00 (1-56316-000-5) Iqra Intl Ed Fdtn.

***Sail to Caribe.** Michael Hagen. (YA). (gr. 5 up). 1997. pap. 6.99 (0-88092-410-1) Royal Fireworks.

***Sail to Crinkle Island.** Arnosky. (J). Date not set. mass mkt. 5.99 (0-689-81605-7) S&S Childrens.

Sail to Freedom: A Handbook for Extended Cruising. Bill Raper & June Raper. 96p. (C). 1939. text ed. 59.00 (0-906754-91-7, Pub. by Fernhurst Bks UK) St Mut.

Sailaway Home. Bruce Degen. LC 95-15737. 32p. (J). 1996. 14.95 (0-590-46443-4) Scholastic Inc.

Sailboard Book. Jake Grubb. (Illus.). 208p. 1985. pap. 15.95 (0-393-30224-5) Norton.

***Sailboat Diesel Maintenance.** Peter Compton. LC 97-10745. (International Marine Sailboat Library). (Illus.). 160p. 1997. text ed. 21.95 (0-07-012354-3) McGraw.

***Sailboat Electrical Systems: Improvement, Wiring, & Repair.** William Laudeman. (International Sailboat Library). (Illus.). 160p. 1997. text ed. 21.95 (0-07-036649-7) McGraw.

Sailboat Hull & Deck Repair. Don Casey. (International Marine Sailboat Library). 1996. pap. text ed. 19.95 (0-07-013369-7) McGraw.

Sailboat Lost. Leonard E. Fisher. LC 90-21504. (Illus.). 32p. (J). (ps up). 1991. text ed. 15.95 (0-02-735351-6, Mac Bks Young Read) S&S Childrens.

Sailboat Refinishing: Painting, Varnishing, & Cosmetics. Don Casey. (International Marine Sailboat Library). 1995. text ed. 19.95 (0-07-013225-9) Intl Marine.

Sailboats, Flag Poles, Cranes: Using Pulleys as Simple Machines. Christopher Lampton. (Gateway Simple Machines Ser.). (Illus.). 32p. (J). (gr. 2-4). 1991. lib. bdg. 14.40 (1-56294-026-0) Millbrook Pr.

Sailing. (Take up Sports! Ser.). (Illus.). 64p. pap. 4.95 (1-56757-052-6) Appleton Comms.

Sailing. Donna Bailey. LC 90-36489. (Sports World Ser.). (Illus.). 32p. (J). (gr. 1-4). 1990. pap. 3.95 (0-8114-4709-X); lib. bdg. 21.40 (0-8114-2853-2) Raintree Steck-V.

Sailing. Norman S. Barrett. Ed. by Franklin Watts Ltd. (Picture Library). (Illus.). 32p. (J). (gr. 3-5). 1988. lib. bdg. 20.00 (0-531-10351-X) Watts.

Sailing. Henry Beard & Roy McKie. LC 80-54621. (Illus.). 96p. 1981. pap. 5.95 (0-89480-144-9, 448) Workman Pub.

Sailing. Roland Denk. (EP Sports Ser.). (Illus.). 1973. 6.95 (0-685-01038-4) Charles River Bks.

Sailing. Jeremy Evans. LC 91-12321. (Adventurers Ser.). (Illus.). 48p. (J). (gr. 5-6). 1992. lib. bdg. 13.95 (0-89686-682-3, Crstwood Hse) Silver Burdett Pr.

Sailing. Herbert I. Kavet. 64p. 1993. 8.95 (0-88032-350-7) Ivory Tower Pub.

Sailing. Phil Twining. LC 95-16682. (Know the Sport Ser.). (Illus.). 48p. 1996. pap. 5.95 (0-8117-2827-7) Stackpole.

Sailing: A Beginner's Manual. John Driscoll. (C). 1990. text ed. 59.00 (0-906754-28-3, Pub. by Fernhurst Bks UK) St Mut.

Sailing: A Parent's Handbook for Junior Sailing. Susan D. Artof. (Boating Made Simple Ser.). (Illus.). 120p. (Orig.). 1993. pap. 10.95 (0-9626888-3-5) Ctr Pr CA.

Sailing Against the Wind: African Americans & Women in U. S. Education. Ed. by Kofi Lomotey. LC 96-8703. (SUNY Series, Frontiers in Education). 186p. 1997. pap. text ed. 16.95 (0-7914-3192-4) State U NY Pr.

Sailing Against the Wind: African Americans & Women in U. S. Education. Ed. by Kofi Lomotey. LC 96-8703. (SUNY Series, Frontiers in Education). 186p. 1997. text ed. 49.50 (0-7914-3191-6) State U NY Pr.

Sailing Alone Around the World. Joshua Slocum. 294p. 1987. 80.00 (0-85937-283-9, Pub. by K Mason Pubns Ltd UK) St Mut.

***Sailing Alone around the World.** Joshua Slocum. 1996. text ed. 14.95 (0-07-058220-3) McGraw.

Sailing Alone Around the World. large type ed. Joshua Slocum. 448p. 1986. 27.99 (0-7089-8323-5, Charnwood) Ulverscroft.

Sailing Alone Around the World. Joshua Slocum. (Illus.). 294p. 1956. reprint ed. pap. 4.95 (0-486-20326-3) Dover.

Sailing Alone Around the World. Joshua Slocum. (Illus.). 294p. 1993. reprint ed. 14.95 (0-911378-20-0) Sheridan.

***Sailing Alone Around the World.** Joshua Slocum. (Adventure Library: Vol. 5). (Illus.). 256p. 1995. reprint ed. lib. bdg. 25.00 (1-885283-04-0) Advent Library.

Sailing Alone Around the World: Centennial Edition. Joshua Slocum. Ed. by Donald W. Davidson. LC 95-67094. (Coastline Collection: Vol. I). (Illus.). 240p. 1995. 14.95 (1-883684-06-4) Peninsula MA.

Sailing & Soldiering in Defence of India. Sureshwar D. Sinha. 1990. 29.00 (81-7001-057-8, Pub. by Chanakya II) S Asia.

Sailing at the U. S. Naval Academy: An Illustrated History. Robert W. McNitt. LC 96-13061. (Illus.). 224p. 1996. 41.95 (1-55750-573-X) Naval Inst Pr.

***Sailing Away from the Night.** John Digby. 56p. 1978. pap. 13.95 (0-85646-040-0, Pub. by Anvil Press UK) Dufour.

Sailing Back in Time: A Nostalgic Voyage on Canada's West Coast. Maria Coffey. (Illus.). 168p. 1996. 39.95 (1-55110-487-3) Gr Arts Ctr Pub.

Sailing Barges. Frank Carr. 464p. 1990. 83.00 (0-86138-060-6, Pub. by T Dalton UK) St Mut.

Sailing Barges. Martin Hazell. 1989. pap. 25.00 (0-85263-584-2, Pub. by Shire UK) St Mut.

***Sailing Basics.** Roger Clark. (Illus.). 84p. (C). 1994. pap. text ed. 12.95 (0-9639190-1-6) Time Traveler.

***Sailing Beyond the Sea.** Jim P. D'Urfe. LC 96-70985. 228p. (Orig.). 1996. pap. 8.95 (1-882972-86-4) Queenship Pub.

Sailing Big on a Small Sailboat. Jerry D. Cardwell. (Illus.). 200p. 1992. pap. 16.50 (0-924486-34-1) Sheridan.

***Sailing Big on a Small Sailboat.** 2nd ed. Jerry Cardwell. (Illus.). 192p. 1997. pap. 17.50 (1-57409-007-0) Sheridan.

Sailing Bright Eternity. Gregory Benford. 488p. 1996. mass mkt. 5.99 (0-553-57332-2) Bantam.

Sailing Circle: 19th Century Seafaring Women from New York. Joan Druett & Mary A. Wallace. (Illus.). 48p. 1995. 11.95 (0-9636361-1-1) Whaling Mus.

Sailing Craft of East Anglia. Roger Finch & Hervey Benham. (C). 1988. 120.00 (0-86138-049-5, Pub. by T Dalton UK) St Mut.

Sailing Cruiser Manual. John Mellor. (Illus.). 196p. 1989. 26.50 (0-911378-87-1) Sheridan.

Sailing Dictionary. 2nd ed. Joachim Schult. Tr. by Barbara Webb from GER. (Illus.). 352p. 1992. 29.95 (0-924486-37-6) Sheridan.

Sailing Doctor: The Essential Shipboard Companion. Martin Luray. 1992. 27.00 (0-679-40911-4, Villard Bks) Random.

Sailing Drills: How to Sail Better, Faster, Smarter, Safer. Rick White & Mary Wells. LC 94-73954. (Illus.). 160p. (Orig.). 1995. spiral bd. 29.95 (1-880871-01-7) Ram Pr.

Sailing for Beginners. Moulton M. Farnham. (Illus.). 256p. 1986. pap. 18.00 (0-02-079870-9) Macmillan.

Sailing for Beginners. Jeff E. Toghill. LC 76-30640. (Illus.). 1977. 5.95 (0-668-04223-0, Arco) Macmillan Gen Ref.

***Sailing for Dummies.** J. J. Isler. 1997. pap. 19.99 (0-7645-5039-X) IDG Bks.

Sailing for Kids. Gary Kibble & Steve Kibble. (C). 1990. pap. text ed. 59.00 (0-906754-77-1, Pub. by Fernhurst Bks UK) St Mut.

Sailing for the Sun: The Chinese in Hawaii, 1789-1989. Ed. by Arlene Lum. (Illus.). 200p. 1989. 39.95 (0-8248-1313-8) UH Pr.

Sailing Fundamentals. Gary L. Jobson. 208p. 1987. pap. 16.00 (0-671-60598-4) S&S Trade.

Sailing Haiti Single Handed. J. Arthur Rogers. (Illus.). 92p. 1995. pap. 8.00 (0-9633412-8-6, 184) Sailaway.

Sailing Illustrated: The Sailor's Bible since '56. 9th rev. ed. Patrick M. Royce. LC 82-6925. (Illus.). 368p. 1992. pap. 12.95 (0-930030-51-6) ProStar Pubns.

Sailing Illustrated Homestudy Guide. Patrick M. Royce. (Illus.). 164p. 1989. pap. 11.95 (0-930030-39-7) ProStar Pubns.

***Sailing in a Spoonful of Water.** Coomer. LC 96-53645. 1997. 22.00 (0-312-15646-4) St Martin.

***Sailing into Divine Presence.** Katie G. Brannon. (Orig.). 1997. write for info. (1-57553-451-7) Watermrk Pr.

Sailing Maryland's Internet: A Concise Guide to Sailor & the Maryland Library Gateways. Walter L. Smith. 230p. (Orig.). 1996. spiral bd. 17.95 (1-886019-03-7, Swift Feet Dancing) Waltech.

Sailing Mystique: The Challenges & Rewards of a Life under Sail. Bill Robinson. (Illus.). 250p. 1994. pap. 14.95 (0-924486-63-5) Sheridan.

***Sailing on a Budget.** Anne M. Johnson. 160p. 1997. pap. 14.99 (1-55870-410-8, Betrwy Bks) F & W Pubns Inc.

Sailing on a Dream. 100p. (Orig.). 1997. pap. 10.95 (1-57532-017-7) Press-Tige Pub.

***Sailing on Friday: The Perilous Voyage of America's Merchant Marine.** John A. Butler. LC 97-20850. (Illus.). 320p. 1997. 27.95 (1-57488-124-8) Brasseys Inc.

Sailing on Ice: & Other Stories from Old Squire's Farm. C. A. Stephens. Ed. by Charles G. Waugh & Larry Glatz. LC 96-30306. 384p. 1996. 18.95 (1-55853-424-5) Rutledge Hill Pr.

***Sailing on the Seas of Fate: Ships, Seafaring, Sailors.** Mark Morrison et al. (Elric Roleplaying Game Ser.). (Illus.). 80p. (Orig.). 1996. pap. 12.95 (1-56882-022-4, 2906) Chaosium.

Sailing on the Silver Screen: Hollywood & the U. S. Navy. Lawrence H. Suid. LC 95-46736. (Illus.). 352p. 1996. 45.00 (1-55750-787-2) Naval Inst Pr.

***Sailing on Winds of Change: Two Decades in the Life of the United Board for Christian Higher Education in Asia, 1969-1990.** Paul T. Lauby. Ed. by Anne L. Ellis. 213p. (Orig.). (C). 1996. pap. write for info. (0-9646943-1-X) United Board CHE.

Sailing Past. Renee M. Waite. (Illus.). 96p. (Orig.). 1992. pap. 7.95 (0-85036-428-0) Sheridan.

Sailing Savannah 1996. John Ramsey. LC 93-45965. (Illus.). 128p. 1996. pap. 15.95 (0-913720-96-8) Beil.

Sailing Ship: Six Thousand Years of History. Romola Anderson & R. C. Anderson. LC 79-177507. 1972. 24.95 (0-405-08205-3) Ayer.

Sailing Ship Eagle. Barbara Keeler & Don Keeler. LC 94-16736. (Those Daring Machines Ser.). (J). 1994. pap. 5.95 (0-382-24751-5, Crstwood Hse) Silver Burdett Pr.

Sailing Ship Rigs & Rigging: With Authentic Plans of Famous Vessels. Harold A. Underhill. (C). 1987. 80.00 (0-85174-176-2, Pub. by Brwn Son Ferg) St Mut.

Sailing Ship to Supertanker. W. H. Mitchell & L. A. Sawyer. 264p. 1990. 54.00 (0-86138-055-X, Pub. by T Dalton UK) St Mut.

***Sailing Ships: A Lift-the-Flap Discovery.** Sadie Fields. LC 97-12373. (Illus.). (J). 1998. write for info. (0-531-30065-X) Orchard Bks Watts.

***Sailing Ships: Pop-Up Book.** Intervisual Books Staff. (Illus.). 1997. 22.95 (1-888443-04-9, Piggytoes Pr) Intervisual Bks.

Sailing Ships: The Story of Their Development from the Earliest Times to the Present Day. E. Keble Chatterton. 1977. lib. bdg. 75.00 (0-8490-2554-0) Gordon Pr.

***Sailing Ships & Pine Cones (A Sojourner's Soul)** Claire Knowles. Ed. by Deborah Beeksma. (Illus.). (Orig.). 1996. pap. 9.99 (0-9648972-3-7, 0187-41) OnQ.

Sailing Ships & Their Story. E. Keble Chatterton. LC 68-54240. (Illus.). 1968. reprint ed. 25.00 (0-87266-004-4) Argosy.

Sailing Ships Stained Glass Coloring Book. John Green. (Illus.). (J). (gr. k-3). 1993. pap. 1.00 (0-486-27011-4) Dover.

Sailing Shorthanded. Geoff Hales. 96p. (C). 1993. text ed. 59.00 (0-906754-93-3, Pub. by Fernhurst Bks UK) St Mut.

***Sailing Small Cruisers.** J. C. Winters. 1996. pap. text ed. 19.95 (0-07-071172-0) McGraw.

***Sailing Small Cruisers: A Guide to Equipment, Safety & Seamanship.** J. C. Winters. (Illus.). 176p. 1996. pap. 22.50 (0-7136-3913-X) Sheridan.

Sailing Smart: Winning Techniques, Tactics & Strategies. Buddy Melges & Charles Mason. LC 82-15557. (Illus.). 208p. 1983. 16.95 (0-8050-0200-6) H Holt & Co.

Sailing Smart: Winning Techniques, Tactics & Strategies. Buddy Melges & Charles Mason. LC 82-15557. (Illus.). 208p. 1987. pap. 10.95 (0-8050-0351-7, Owl) H Holt & Co.

Sailing South. Nancy O'Malley. LC 94-68046. 1994. 17.95 (1-877978-68-X, FLF Pr) Woldt.

***Sailing South.** Judith Prior. LC 96-29689. 55p. (Orig.). 1996. pap. 10.00 (0-88734-018-0) Players Pr.

Sailing the Carolina Sounds: Historical Places & My Favorite People. James T. Cheatham. (Illus.). 80p. 1992. pap. 9.95 (0-9636714-3-X) Gan Prodns.

Sailing the Golden Sea: The Adventures of Two Sunset Sailors. Paul Keller. 231p. 1992. 19.95 (0-9631759-0-4) Portside Pub.

Sailing the Golden Sea: The Adventures of Two Sunset Sailors. Paul Keller. 236p. 1992. pap. 14.50 (0-9631759-1-2) Portside Pub.

Sailing the Inland Seas: Further Adventures of the Sunset Sailors. Paul H. Keller. 250p. 1993. 19.95 (0-9631759-2-0) Portside Pub.

Sailing the Inland Seas: Further Adventures of Two Sunset Sailors. Paul Keller. LC 93-85763. 1994. pap. 14.95 (0-9631759-3-9) Portside Pub.

Sailing the Mirror. Roy Partridge. (C). 1990. text ed. 59.00 (0-906754-01-1, Pub. by Fernhurst Bks UK) St Mut.

***Sailing the Seven "C's"** (J). teacher ed., pap. 49.95 (0-614-18237-9) Let Us Tch Kids.

***Sailing the 7 "C's" for Vacation Bible School.** (J). teacher ed., pap. 39.95 (0-614-18242-5) Let Us Tch Kids.

Sailing Through China. limited ed. Paul Theroux. (Illus.). 64p. 1984. 35.00 (0-395-35492-7) HM.

Sailing Through Dinner: The Shoreline Cookbook Featuring Mystic's Favorite Restaurants. Annice Estes. 128p. 9.95 (0-9638120-0-9) Three Sqs Pr.

Sailing Through the Storm: A Child's Journey Through Divorce. Edie Julik. (Illus.). 26p. (Orig.). (J). (ps-3). 1994. pap. 8.95 (0-9642223-0-2) Kidsail.

Sailing Through the Storm to the Ocean of Peace. Ed. by Monique Bondeux. (Illus.). 40p. (J). (gr. k-6). 1996. 14.95 (1-887494-08-1) Kidsail.

Sailing Through the Storms of Life - Practical Steps to Overcoming Your Crisis. Ron Clark. LC 94-77928. 96p. (Orig.). 1994. pap. 6.00 (0-9641920-0-4) Liv Water Pub.

Sailing Through the Streets of Home. Don C. France. LC 90-70442. 157p. (Orig.). 1991. pap. 8.00 (1-56002-074-1) Aegina Pr.

Sailing Tips. William M. Burr, Jr. 1989. pap. 10.95 (0-312-02977-2) St Martin.

Sailing Tips: One Thousand New Ways to Solve Old Problems. William M. Burr, Jr. 1989. pap. 9.95 (0-318-42736-2) St Martin.

Sailing to Australia: Shipboard Diaries by Nineteenth-Century British Emigrants. Andrew Hassam. LC 94-12596. 1995. text ed. 65.00 (0-7190-3929-0, Pub. by Manchester Univ Pr UK); text ed. 22.95 (0-7190-4546-0, Pub. by Manchester Univ Pr UK) St Martin.

Sailing to Australia: Shipboard Diaries of Nineteenth-Century British Immigrants. Andrew Hassam. 254p. 1995. pap. 24.95 (0-522-84672-6, Pub. by Melbourne Univ Pr AT) Paul & Co Pubs.

Sailing to Cythera. Nancy Willard. LC 74-5602. (Anatole Trilogy Ser.: Bk. 1). (Illus.). 72p. (J). (gr. 3-7). 1985. pap. 6.00 (0-15-269961-9, Voyager Bks) HarBrace.

Sailing to Paradise: The Discovery of the Americas in 5000 B.C. Jim Bailey. 1995. 32.50 (0-684-81297-5) S&S Trade.

Sailing to Pint Pot. Bess C. Haskell. (Wind, Waves & Away! Ser.). (Illus.). 72p. (Orig.). (J). (gr. 4 up). 1993. pap. 10.95 (0-9626857-4-7) Coastwise Pr.

***Sailing to Utopia.** Michael Moorcock. (Eternal Champion Ser.: Vol. 9). 1997. 21.99 (0-614-27880-5) White Wolf.

***Sailing to Utopia, Vol. 8.** Michael Moorcock. (The Eternal Champion: Vol. 8). (Illus.). 1997. 21.99 (1-56504-183-6, 12509, Borealis) White Wolf.

Sailing up the Stream. Tr. by Ta San Shih. 224p. (CHI.). (J). 1995. pap. text ed. write for info. (1-886925-00-3, Buddhist Bliss) Buddhist Ch.

Sailing Vessels in Authentic Early Nineteenth-Century Illustrations. Edward W. Cooke. (Illus.). 80p. 1989. pap. 6.95 (0-486-26141-7) Dover.

Sailing with Pride. Greg Pease. LC 90-80916. (Illus.). 128p. 1990. 49.95 (0-9626299-0-1) C A Baumgartner Pub.

Sailing with the Wind. Thomas Locker. LC 85-23381. (Illus.). 32p. (J). (ps up). 1986. lib. bdg. 14.89 (0-8037-0312-0) Dial Bks Young.

Sailing with the Wind. Thomas Locker. (J). (gr. 3 up). 1992. pap. 5.99 (0-14-054698-7, Puff Pied Piper) Puffin Bks.

Sailing Yacht Design: An Appreciation of a Fine Art. Robert G. Henry & Richareds T. Miller. LC 65-18207. (Illus.). 153p. reprint ed. pap. 43.70 (0-317-08203-5, 2022554) Bks Demand.

Sailing Yesterday. Andrew F. Willis. 72p. (Orig.). 1991. pap. 10.00 (0-9626857-1-2) Coastwise Pr.

***Sailing's a Breeze!, 3 pts.** Gary B. Soloman. Incl. . 2nd ed. (Illus.). 112p. 1996. pap. 14.95 (1-883085-01-2, 90020); 39.95 (1-883085-03-9, 90040) Aquatics Unltd.

Sailmaker's Apprentice: A Guide for the Self-Reliant Sailor. Emiliano Marino & Christine Chamberlain. 512p. 1994. text ed. 39.95 (0-07-157980-X) Intl Marine.

Sailmaker's Listing of IOR & IMS Yachts. 350p. pap. 75.00 (1-882502-29-9) US Sail Assn.

***Sailor.** John M. Denney. Ed. by Rose M. Denney. (Illus.). 24p. (Orig.). (YA). (gr. 9-12). 1996. pap. 4.95 (0-9654698-3-2) Denney Literary.

Sailor - The Bitter Years. Dragutin Domac. 1987. 13.95 (0-940168-10-3) Boxwood.

***Sailor Aviators: The Tale of the Men of Navy Patrol Bombing Squadron 21 in World War II.** enl. rev. ed. Donald H. Sweet. LC 97-66749. (Illus.). 264p. 1996. pap. 20.00 (0-923687-42-4) Celo Valley Bks.

Sailor Bear. Martin Waddell. LC 91-71822. (Illus.). 32p. (J). (ps up). 1992. 14.95 (1-56402-040-1) Candlewick Pr.

Sailor Bear. Martin Waddell. LC 91-71822. (Bear Hugs Ser.). (Illus.). 32p. (J). (ps up). 1993. 4.95 (1-56402-256-0) Candlewick Pr.

Sailor Bear. Martin Waddell. LC 91-71822. (J). (ps up). 1996. pap. 4.99 (1-56402-606-X) Candlewick Pr.

***Sailor Bear.** Martin Waddell. (Little Book Cards Ser.). (Illus.). (J). 1997. pap. 3.29 (0-7636-0218-3) Candlewick Pr.

Sailor Cats. Emily Whittle. LC 92-23418. (Illus.). (J). 1993. 14.00 (0-671-79933-9, Green Tiger S&S) S&S Childrens.

Sailor-Diplomat: A Biography of Commodore James Biddle, 1783-1848. David F. Long. LC 82-22236. (Illus.). 328p. 1983. text ed. 45.00 (0-930350-39-1) NE U Pr.

Sailor Dog. (Little Golden Story Book 'n' Tape Ser.). (Illus.). 24p. (J). (ps-3). 5.95 incl. audio (0-307-14452-6, 14452) Western Pub.

Sailor Dog. Margaret Wise Brown. (Little Golden Bks.). (Illus.). 24p. (J). (ps). 1992. write for info. (0-307-00143-1, 312-08, Golden Pr) Western Pub.

Sailor from Gibraltar. Marguerite Duras. 1986. pap. text ed. 11.95 (0-7145-0511-0) Riverrun NY.

Sailor in English Fiction & Drama: 1550-1800. Harold F. Watson. LC 31-32461. reprint ed. 22.50 (0-404-06873-1) AMS Pr.

Sailor Jerry Collins: American Tattoo Master. Donald E. Hardy. 1994. pap. 30.00 (0-945367-11-2) Hardy Marks Pubns.

***Sailor Jerry Tattoo Flash, Vol. 1.** Intro. by Don E. Hardy. (Illus.). 64p. 1996. pap. 50.00 (0-945367-18-X, 620272) Dist Art Pubs.

Sailor Moon: Friends & Foes. Naoko Takeuchi. Ed. by Chikako Noma. (Illus.). 16p. (J). 1995. pap. 4.95 (1-56836-118-1) Kodansha.

Sailor of Fortune. Ian Jackson. (C). 1989. text ed. 59.00 (1-85821-022-4, Pub. by Pentland Pr UK) St Mut.

Sailor of the Air: The 1917-1919 Letters & Diary of USN CMM/A Irving Edward Sheely. Lawrence D. Sheely. LC 93-146. 240p. 1993. 29.95 (0-8173-0709-5) U of Ala Pr.

Sailor on Horseback: The Biography of Jack London. Irving Stone. 1992. reprint ed. lib. bdg. 75.00 (0-7812-5096-X) Rprt Serv.

Sailor Pig Furry Face. Western Promotional Books Staff. (J). 1993. 6.99 (0-307-16453-5) Western Pub.

Sailor Remembers: His Voyage from Darkness into Light. Daniel G. Baldyga. 320p. (Orig.). 1989. pap. 9.95 (0-924142-00-6) Mystic Hse.

Sailor Song. Ken Kesey. 544p. 1993. pap. 12.95 (0-14-013997-4, Penguin Bks) Viking Penguin.

Sailor to Statesman. Miriam Hood. LC 89-395. (Illus.). 1990. pap. 15.95 (0-87949-299-6) Ashley Bks.

Sailor View of Live Yeshu. M. N. Lucey. 759p. (C). 1989. text ed. 75.00 (1-872795-55-2, Pub. by Pentland Pr UK) St Mut.

Sailor Who Fell from Grace with the Sea. Yukio Mishima. 1994. pap. 11.00 (0-679-75015-0, Vin) Random.

Sailor 1930-1945: The Image of an American Demigod. Thomas W. Sokolowski. LC 82-84472. (Illus.). 116p. (Orig.). 1982. pap. 12.50 (0-940744-41-4) Chrysler Museum.

***Sailors Alphabet.** Michael McCurdy. LC 97-20647. 1998. write for info. (0-395-84167-4) HM.

Sailors & Scholars: The Centennial History of the U. S. Naval War College. John B. Hattendorf et al. LC 84-8257. (Illus.). 354p. (C). 1984. text ed. 13.00 (0-9637973-9-5) Naval War Coll.

Sailors & Sexual Identity: Crossing the Line Between "Straight" & "Gay" in the U. S. Navy. Steven Zeeland. LC 94-28996. (Illus.). 296p. 1994. 39.95 (1-56024-850-5); pap. 14.95 (1-56023-850-X) Haworth Pr.

Sailor's Assistant: Reference Data For Maintenance, Repair, & Cruising. John Vigor. (Illus.). 144p. 1996. text ed. 21.95 (0-07-067476-0) McGraw.

Sailor's Book. Charlotte Agell. (Illus.). 32p. (J). (gr. 3-6). 1991. pap. 4.95 (0-920668-91-7); lib. bdg. 14.95 (0-920668-90-9) Firefly Bks Ltd.

Sailors' Folk-Art under Glass: A Story of Ships-in-Bottles. Louis R. Norton. (Illus.). 32p. (Orig.). 1995. pap. write for info. (0-9626162-8-1) Old Salt Box.

Sailor's Garland. Ed. by John Masefield. LC 70-80376. (Granger Index Reprint Ser.). 1977. 48.36 (0-8369-6108-0) Ayer.

Sailors Guide to the Windward Islands. 6th ed. Chris Doyle. (Illus.). 320p. 1992. pap. 17.95 (976-8063-07-6) F Papy Cruising Guide.

Sailors Guide to the Windward Islands. 7th rev. ed. Chris Doyle. (Illus.). 336p. 1994. pap. 19.95 (0-944428-28-2) Cruising Guide.

***Sailor's Guide to the Windward Islands, 1997-1998.** Chris Doyle. 1996. pap. text ed. 19.95 (0-944428-35-5) Cruising Guide.

Sailor's Handbook: A Clear & Comprehensive Guide to Sailing for Pleasure & Sport. Halsey C. Herreshoff. 1994. pap. 19.95 (0-316-35948-3) Little.

Sailor's Holiday: The Wild Life of Sailor & Lula. Barry Gifford. 1991. 17.95 (0-685-39015-2) Random.

Sailor's Holiday: The Wild Life of Sailor & Lula. Barry Gifford. 1992. pap. 12.00 (0-679-73490-2, Vin) Random.

Sailor's Home, & Other Stories. Clotilde I. Graves. LC 77-122711. (Short Story Index Reprint Ser.). 1977. 20.95 (0-8369-3544-6) Ayer.

Sailors in the Sky: Memoir of a Navy Aircrewman in the Korean War. Jack Sauter. LC 95-19567. (Illus.). 317p. 1995. pap. 25.95 (0-7864-0113-3) McFarland & Co.

Sailor's Lending Log: For Book Owners & Borrowers. David D. Hume. (Illus.). 1996. pap. 6.95 (1-880158-10-8) J N Townsend.

Sailor's Log: Recollections of Forty Years of Naval Life. Robley D. Evans. LC 93-31160. (Classics of Naval Literature Ser.). (Illus.). 352p. 1993. 32.95 (0-87021-587-6) Naval Inst Pr.

Sailors Odyssey, Vol. 1: At Peace & War, 1935-1945. Alvin P. Chester. Ed. by Barbara Feinberg et al. LC 91-172665. (Illus.). 289p. 1991. 19.95 (0-9631239-0-4) Odysseus Bks.

Sailors on Horseback. large type ed. Vivian Stuart. 1994. 25.99 (0-7089-3195-2) Ulverscroft.

Sailor's Pillow Tales. Guy Willard. (Illus.). 265p. 1991. pap. 14.95 (0-943383-03-X) FirstHand Ltd.

Sailors' Secrets: Advice from the Masters. Ed. by Mike Badham & Robby Robinson. LC 96-47681. (Illus.). 288p. 1997. text ed. 29.95 (0-07-039088-6) Intl Marine.

Sailor's Sketchbook. Bruce Bingham. LC 83-531. (Illus.). 144p. 1987. pap. text ed. 15.95 (0-915160-55-2) Seven Seas.

Sailor's Sketchbook. Bruce Bingham. 1987. pap. text ed. 15.95 (0-07-155096-8) Intl Marine.

Sailor's Songbag: An American Rebel in an English Prison, 1777-1779. Ed. by George G. Carey. LC 75-32483. (Illus.). 176p. 1976. reprint ed. pap. 50.20 (0-608-01707-8, 2062362) Bks Demand.

***Sailors Sourcebook.** Anthony C. Meisel. Date not set. write for info. (0-688-10456-8) Hearst Bks.

Sailor's Start-Up: A Beginner's Guide to Sailing. Doug Werner. LC 93-94343. (Start-up Sports Ser.: No. 3). (Illus.). 144p. (Orig.). 1994. pap. 9.95 (1-884654-03-7) Tracks Pubng.

Sailor's Story Book I. Sam Glanzman. 64p. 1987. 5.95 (0-87135-298-2) Marvel Entmnt.

Sailor's Story Book II. Sam Glanzman. 64p. 1989. 6.95 (0-87135-556-6) Marvel Entmnt.

Sailors' Union of the Pacific. Paul S. Taylor. LC 70-156427. (American Labor Ser., No. 2). 1978. reprint ed. 15.95 (0-405-02946-2) Ayer.

Sailors, Waterways & Tugboats I Have Known. Fred G. Godfrey. LC 92-42484. (Illus.). 146p. 1993. 28.50 (0-912526-61-0) Lib Res.

Sailor's Weather Guide. Jeff Markell. (Illus.). 285p. 1995. pap. 19.95 (0-924486-91-0) Sheridan.

***Sailor's Weather Guide.** Jeff Markell. 1996. pap. text ed. 19.95 (0-07-040574-3) McGraw.

***Sailor's Wind.** Stuart Walker. Date not set. write for info. (0-393-04555-2) Norton.

Sailor's Word Book: An Alphabetical Digest of Nautical Terms & an Authoritative Encyclopedia of Naval Science & Nomenclature. W. H. Smyth. 1977. pap. 75.00 (0-8490-2555-9) Gordon Pr.

Sails. Rochelle L. Holt. 1991. 3.50 (0-934536-46-5) Rose Shell Pr.

Sails. 2nd ed. John Heyes. 96p. (C). 1993. text ed. 59.00 (0-906754-73-9, Pub. by Fernhurst Bks UK) St Mut.

Sails. 5th ed. Jeremy Howard-Williams. LC 68-19075. (Illus.). 1983. 10.95 (0-8286-0107-0) J De Graff.

***Sails: The Way They Work & How to Make Them.** Derek Harvey. LC 96-52941. (Illus.). 188p. 1997. pap. 19.95 (1-57409-030-5) Sheridan.

Sails & Rigging. Gordon Trower & Nola Trower. 1996. 24.95 (1-85223-853-4, Pub. by Crowood UK) Motorbooks Intl.

Sails & Steam in the Mountains: A Maritime & Military History of Lake George & Lake Champlain. Russell Bellico. LC 92-25010. (Illus.). 400p. 1992. 45.00 (0-935796-33-9); pap. 25.00 (0-935796-32-0) Purple Mnt Pr.

Sails for Rent. Boyce. (DF - Computer Applications Ser.). 1990. pap. 20.95 (0-538-60300-3) S-W Pub.

Sails Full & By. Dom Degnon. (Illus.). 240p. 1995. 27.50 (0-924486-75-9) Sheridan.

Sail's Last Century: The Merchant Sailing Ship, 1830-1930. Ed. by Robert Gardiner & Basil Greenhill. (Conway's History of the Ship Ser.). (Illus.). 176p. 1993. 47.95 (1-55750-757-0) Naval Inst Pr.

Sails, Steamships & Sea Captains: Early Settlement, Trade & Transportation County, Washington. Kim Davis et al. (Illus.). 150p. (Orig.). 1993. pap. 15.95 (0-929186-02-8) Island Cnty Hist Soc.

Sail's, Things That Work: More Than One Hundred Sea-Tested Improvements for Your Boat. Sail Magazine Staff. 1993. pap. 12.95 (0-87742-374-1) Intl Marine.

SAIL's Things That Work: More Than 100 Sea-Tested Improvements for Your Boat. Ed. by Sail Magazine Staff. 1993. pap. text ed. 12.95 (0-07-054209-0) McGraw.

Saino Kaihatsu Wa Zero-Sai Kara see Ability Development from Age Zero

***Saint.** Mark Bailey. 1997. mass mkt. write for info. (0-515-12173-8) Jove Pubns.

***Saint.** Barer. 1997. mass mkt. 5.99 (0-671-00951-6, Pocket Books) PB.

Saint. Christine Bell. LC 85-12256. 256p. 1985. 14.95 (0-910923-21-3) Pineapple Pr.

Saint. Conrad F. Meyer. Tr. by E. F. Hauch from GER. 1976. reprint ed. 35.00 (0-86527-298-0) Fertig.

Saint: A Complete History in Print, Radio, Film & Television of Leslie Charteris' Robin Hood of Modern Crime, Simon Templar, 1928-1992. Burl Barer. LC 92-53509. (Illus.). 431p. 1993. lib. bdg. 55.00 (0-89950-723-9) McFarland & Co.

Saint: A Fictional Biography of Thomas Becket. Conrad F. Meyer. Tr. by W. F. Twaddell from GER. LC 77-7038. 137p. reprint ed. pap. 39.10 (0-685-20775-7, 2030027) Bks Demand.

Saint: A Novel. Christine Bell. 244p. 1996. pap. 11.00 (0-393-31350-6, Norton Paperbks) Norton.

Saint: Alias the Saint. Leslie Charteris. 192p. 1994. 3.95 (0-7867-0099-8) Carroll & Graf.

Saint: The Saint & Mr. Teal. Leslie Charteris. 176p. 1995. mass mkt. 4.50 (0-7867-0228-1) Carroll & Graf.

Saint - Adventurers of the Virginia Frontier. Klaus Wust. LC 76-48566. (Illus.). 1977. 12.00 (0-917968-29-8) Shenandoah Hist.

Saint Abroad. Leslie Charteris. 1993. reprint ed. lib. bdg. 21.95 (1-56849-130-1) Buccaneer Bks.

St. Agnes' Stand. Tom Eidson. 224p. 1994. pap. text ed. 4.99 (0-425-14396-1) Berkley Pub.

St. Agnes' Stand. large type ed. Tom Eidson. LC 93-38173. 282p. 1994. lib. bdg. 21.95 (0-7862-0246-7) Thorndike Pr.

St. Alban's College, Valladolid: Four Centuries of English Catholic Presence in Spain. Michael C. Williams. LC 86-17787. 278p. 1987. text ed. 39.95 (0-312-69736-8) St Martin.

St. Alexander Nevsky. pap. 0.50 (0-89981-082-9) Eastern Orthodox.

Saint-Alexis Santons: History, Humor, Poetry. Michele M. Saint-Alexis Scott. 330p. (ENG & FRE.). 1994. pap. 9.50 (0-9641097-0-0) M J S Pubns.

St. Alphonsus Liguori: Bishop, Confessor, Founder of the Redemptorist & Doctor of the Church. D. F. Miller & L. X. Aubin. LC 87-51071. Orig. Title: Saint Alphonsus Mary de' Liguori - Founder, Bishop, & Doctor (1696-1780). 388p. 1992. reprint ed. pap. 16.50 (0-89555-329-5) TAN Bks Pubs.

Saint Alphonsus Mary de' Liguori - Founder, Bishop, & Doctor (1696-1780) see St. Alphonsus Liguori: Bishop, Confessor, Founder of the Redemptorist & Doctor of the Church

St. Ambrose: His Life & Times. Angela Paredi. LC 63-19325. 495p. reprint ed. pap. 141.10 (0-317-26143-6, 2024372) Bks Demand.

Saint & a Half. Denis Meadows. 220p. 1963. 10.00 (0-8159-6803-5) Devin.

Saint & Hero: Andreas & Medieval Doctrine. Robert Boenig. LC 89-46401. 136p. 1991. 32.50 (0-8387-5187-3) Bucknell U Pr.

Saint & His Saviour. (Spurgeon Collection). 1995. 9.99 (1-871676-01-0, Pub. by Christian Focus UK) Spring Arbor Dist.

Saint & Mary Kate. Frank O'Connor. 301p. 1990. reprint ed. pap. 11.95 (0-85640-445-4, Pub. by Blackstaff Pr IE) Dufour.

Saint & Singer: Edward Taylor's Typology & the Poetics of Meditation. Karen E. Rowe. (Cambridge Studies in American Literature & Culture: No. 18). 320p. 1986. text ed. 69.95 (0-521-30865-8) Cambridge U Pr.

Saint & the Skeptics: Joan of Arc in the Work of Mark Twain, Anatole France, & Bernard Shaw. William Searle. LC 75-26709. 183p. reprint ed. pap. 52.20 (0-7837-3629-0, 2043495) Bks Demand.

St. Andrews & Golf. John M. Olman & Morton W. Olman. LC 93-78338. (Illus.). 208p. (Orig.). 1995. 55.00 (0-942117-20-4) Market St Pr.

St. Andrew's Church: Roker, Sunderland 1905 Edward Prior. Trevor Garnham. (Architecture in Detail Ser.). (Illus.). 60p. 1996. pap. text ed. 29.95 (0-7148-3344-4, Pub. by Phaidon Press UK) Chronicle Bks.

St. Andrews Golf Club: The Birthplace of American Golf. Desmond Tolhurst. (Illus.). 194p. 1989. 49.00 (0-685-27220-6) Karjan Pub Inc.

St. Andrews Golf Club: The Birthplace of American Golf. limited ed. Desmond Tolhurst. (Illus.). 194p. 1989. 175.00 (0-685-27221-4) Karjan Pub Inc.

St. Andrews Golf Links: The First 600 Years. Tom Jarrett. (Illus.). 192p. 1996. 29.95 (1-85158-665-2, Pub. by Mnstream UK) Trafalgar.

St. Andrews of Jo Grimond. Jo Grimond. (Illus.). 160p. 1992. 22.50 (0-7509-0207-8, Pub. by Sutton Pubng UK) Bks Intl VA.

St. Andrews Seven. Scotish Missions Promotion Staff. (Orig.). 1985. pap. 9.99 (0-85151-428-6) Banner of Truth.

St. Anne Soho: Parish of St. Anne Soho, 2 vols. Francis H. Sheppard. (Survey of London Ser.: Vol. 33-34). (C). 1966. text ed. 150.00 (0-485-48223-1, Pub. by Athlone Pr UK) Humanities.

St. Anselm: A Portrait in a Landscape. Richard W. Southern. 500p. (C). 1991. text ed. 69.95 (0-521-36262-8) Cambridge U Pr.

St. Anselm: A Portrait in a Landscape. Richard W. Southern. 525p. (C). 1992. pap. text ed. 24.95 (0-521-43818-7) Cambridge U Pr.

St. Anselm & His Biographer: A Study of Monastic Life & Thought, 1059c-1130. Richard W. Southern. (Birkbeck Lectures: 1959). 405p. reprint ed. pap. 115.50 (0-317-09510-2, 2022473) Bks Demand.

St. Anselm's Proslogion. Tr. by M. J. Charlesworth. LC 78-63300. 1979. reprint ed. pap. text ed. 13.00 (0-268-01697-6) U of Notre Dame Pr.

St. Anthony: Doctor of the Church. Sophronius Clasen. Tr. by Ignatius Brady from GER. LC 61-11200. Orig. Title: Antonius. 106p. 1973. reprint ed. pap. 4.95 (0-8199-0458-9, Frncscn Herld) Franciscan Pr.

Saint Anthony: Herald of the Good News: Excerpts from the "Sermones" of Saint Anthony. Claude M. Jarmak. LC 95-79039. 228p. (Orig.). 1995. pap. text ed. write for info. (0-9648076-0-2) Conventual Franciscan.

Saint Anthony: Words of Fire, Life of Light. Madeline P. Nugent. LC 95-23131. 412p. 1995. pap. 10.95 (0-8198-6984-8) Pauline Bks.

St. Anthony & Other Stories. Guy De Maupassant. Tr. by Lafcadio Hearn from FRE. LC 79-150479. (Short Story Index Reprint Ser.). 1977. reprint ed. 18.95 (0-8369-3820-8) Ayer.

***St. Anthony & the Christ Child.** Helen W. Homan. 1997. pap. text ed. 9.95 (0-89870-598-3) Ignatius Pr.

***Saint Anthony of Padua.** (Saint Joseph Picture Bks.). (Illus.). 1989. pap. 1.25 (0-89942-386-8, 386-00) Catholic Bk Pub.

St. Anthony of Padua. Mary F. Windeatt. (Catholic Story Coloring Bks.). (Illus.). 32p. (J). (gr. 1-5). 1992. reprint ed. wbk. ed. 3.00 (0-89555-369-4) TAN Bks Pubs.

Saint Anthony of Padua: Our Franciscan Friend. large type ed. (Illus.). 1993. pap. 4.75 (0-89942-110-5, 110/04) Catholic Bk Pub.

St. Anthony of Padua: The Story of His Life & Popular Devotions. 68p. 1993. pap. 3.95 (0-86716-202-3) St Anthony Mess Pr.

St. Anthony RBRVS & Hospital Seminar Manual. Ed. by Gay M. Boughton-Barnes. 200p. 1992. 149.00 (1-56329-080-4, HRCM) St Anthony Pub.

St. Anthony the Great, Founder of Monasticism. large type ed. St. Athanasius the Great. 1994. pap. 10.00 (0-89981-300-3) Eastern Orthodox.

St. Anthony's Ambulatory Surgery Coding Seminar Manual. Ed. by Gay M. Boughton-Barnes. Orig. Title: '. 200p. 1992. 180.00 (1-56329-041-3, OUCL) St Anthony Pub.

***St. Anthony's APG Guidebook Version 2.0 1997.** Lolita M. Jones. 400p. Date not set. 79.00 (1-56329-393-5) St Anthony Pub.

***St. Anthony's APG Implementation Guide: A Task Force Action Plan.** Kathy L. Brouch. Ed. by Lolita M. Jones. 400p. Date not set. 349.00 (1-56329-381-1) St Anthony Pub.

***St. Anthony's APG Sourcebook: A Comprehensive Guide to the Outpatient Prospective Payment System.** Lolita M. Jones et al. 300p. Date not set. 269.00 (1-56329-382-X) St Anthony Pub.

St. Anthony's B-W ICD-9-CM for Nursing Home & Hospice, 3 vols. E. Lorenz. 350p. (Orig.). (C). 1993. pap. 107.00 (1-56329-165-7) St Anthony Pub.

St. Anthony's Basic ICD-9-CM Coding: Self-Directed Training for the Physician Office Professional. Ed. by Gay Boughton-Barnes. 150p. 1991. 279.00 incl. audio (1-56329-071-5) St Anthony Pub.

St. Anthony's Clinical Coder. Ed. by Marleeta K. Jones et al. 200p. 1992. 89.00 (1-56329-051-0) St Anthony Pub.

***St. Anthony's Clinical Coder.** Ed. by Karen Schmidt et al. 218p. Date not set. pap. 75.00 (1-56329-412-5) St Anthony Pub.

St. Anthony's Clinical Coder: Orthopaedics. Ed. by Marleeta K. Jones et al. 250p. 1992. 70.00 (1-56329-025-1, ROR) St Anthony Pub.

St. Anthony's Clinical Reference to Diagnostic Coding: ADX. E. Lorenz. (Illus.). 300p. (C). 1993. ring bd. 95.00 (1-56329-115-0) St Anthony Pub.

St. Anthony's Clinical Reference to OB-GYN, '93-94: ATOB. E. Lorenz. (Illus.). 300p. (C). 1993. ring bd. 159.00 (1-56329-125-8) St Anthony Pub.

St. Anthony's Color-Coded ICD-9-CM Codebook, '94, 3 vols. E. Lorenz. 247p. (C). 1993. pap. 69.95 (1-56329-164-9) St Anthony Pub.

***St. Anthony's Complete Guide to Medicare Coverage Issues: A Reference to Covered & Non-Covered Services.** Ed. by Carol F. Endahl. 800p. Date not set. 149.00 (1-56329-403-6) St Anthony Pub.

***St. Anthony's Complete RBDVS.** rev. ed. Relative Value Studies, Inc. Staff. Ed. by Mark Paynter. 400p. Date not set. 99.95 (1-56329-397-8) St Anthony Pub.

***St. Anthony's DRG Analyzer for Health Information Management.** Ed. by Marleeta Jones & Susan White. 320p. (C). 1996. 229.00 (1-56329-386-2) St Anthony Pub.

St. Anthony's DRG Clinic-Seminar Manual. Ed. by Gay M. Boughton-Barnes. 200p. 1992. 149.00 (1-56329-040-5, D101) St Anthony Pub.

St. Anthony's DRG Optimizer. E. Lorenz. 175p. (Orig.). (C). 1993. 99.00 (1-56329-197-5) St Anthony Pub.

St. Anthony's DRG Optimizer: 1992 Edition. Ed. by Charlotte Bowers et al. 500p. 1991. 95.00 (1-56329-049-9) St Anthony Pub.

St. Anthony's DRG Working Guidebook. E. Lorenz. 135p. (Orig.). (C). 1993. 69.00 (1-56329-171-1) St Anthony Pub.

St. Anthony's DRG Working Guidebook: 1992 Edition. Ed. by Charlotte Bowers et al. 560p. 1991. 59.00 (1-56329-050-2) St Anthony Pub.

St. Anthony's DRG Working Guidebook: 1993 Edition. Ed. by Charlotte Bowers. 560p. 1992. 65.00 (1-56329-103-7, DRG) St Anthony Pub.

St. Anthony's Guide to ASC Payment Groups. Lolita Dickerson. 1991. 135.00 (1-56329-022-7) St Anthony Pub.

St. Anthony's Guide to ASC Payment Groups. E. Lorenz. 200p. (C). ring bd. write for info. (1-56329-132-0) St Anthony Pub.

***St. Anthony's Guide to Code Linkage for Laboratory Services.** 300p. (C). Date not set. 159.00 (1-56329-391-9) St Anthony Pub.

St. Anthony's Guide to Home Health Managed Care & Capitation: Home Health, Home Infusion, Home Medical Equipment, Prosthetics & Orthotics. Ed. by Jay Lechtman & John F. Persinos. 200p. Date not set. 249.00 (1-56329-311-0) St Anthony Pub.

St. Anthony's Guide to Radiology Managed Care & Capitation: Radiology, Diagnostic Imaging, Radiation Therapy. Michael J. Monea. Ed. by Jay Lechtman & John F. Persinos. 200p. (C). Date not set. 349.00 (1-56329-312-9) St Anthony Pub.

St. Anthony's HCFA 1500 Editor. Ed. by Carol B. Falconer. 200p. 1992. 129.00 (1-56329-068-5) St Anthony Pub.

St. Anthony's HCFA 1500 Editor. E. Lorenz. 150p. (C). 1993. ring bd. 129.00 (1-56329-134-7) St Anthony Pub.

St. Anthony's HCPCS Level II Code Book, 1992. Ed. by Kathy Brouch. 1992. 75.00 (1-56329-074-X) St Anthony Pub.

St. Anthony's HCPCS Level II Code Book. E. Lorenz. 175p. (C). 1994. pap. 29.95 (1-56329-169-X); spiral bd. 75.00 (1-56329-170-3) St Anthony Pub.

***St. Anthony's HCPCS Level II Codebook: HBK.** Ed. by Laurie Castillo & Carol Endahl. (C). 1997. 75.00 (1-56329-389-7) St Anthony Pub.

***St. Anthony's HCPCS Level II Codebook - Short Version: HBIN.** Ed. by Laurie Castillo & Carol Endahl. (C). 1997. write for info. (1-56329-390-0) St Anthony Pub.

St. Anthony's HCPCS Questions & Answers. Ed. by Lolita M. Dickerson. 150p. 1992. 99.00 (1-56329-070-7) St Anthony Pub.

St. Anthony's HCPCS Reference Manual for Medicare Outpatient Services. Ed. by Michael Grambo. 1987. 329.00 (1-56329-004-9) St Anthony Pub.

***St. Anthony's Home Health Agency Policy & Procedures Manual.** Marilyn Seiler. Ed. by Lolita R. Jones. 250p. Date not set. 349.00 (1-56329-379-X) St Anthony Pub.

***St. Anthony's Home Health Job Descriptions.** Marilyn Seiler. 200p. (C). 1997. 249.00 (1-56329-387-0) St Anthony Pub.

St. Anthony's ICD-9-CM Code Book, 3 vols. E. Lorenz. 387p. (C). ring bd. 139.00 (1-56329-130-4) St Anthony Pub.

St. Anthony's ICD-9-CM Code Book, 3 vols. annot. ed. E. Lorenz. (Illus.). 400p. (C). 1993. ring bd. 195.00 (1-56329-101-0, IAD) St Anthony Pub.

***St. Anthony's Integrated Health Care 100 Directory: The Most Comprehensive Financial & Contact Data for Integrated Delivery Systems.** 2nd ed. Ed. by Susan Namovicz-Peat. (Illus.). 700p. (Orig.). 1997. pap. text ed. 495.00 (1-56329-399-4) St Anthony Pub.

***St. Anthony's Medicare Billing & Compliance Guide.** Carol F. Endahl & Karen E. Schmidt. 350p. Date not set. 259.00 (1-56329-383-8) St Anthony Pub.

***St. Anthony's Medicare Correct Coding & Payment Manual for Procedures & Services.** Ed. by Anita Hart & Sheila R. Parvis. 450p. (C). 1997. 279.00 (1-56329-407-9) St Anthony Pub.

***St. Anthony's Medicare Coverage Manual.** Carol F. Endahl & Julia Palmer. 700p. Date not set. 149.00 (1-56329-384-6) St Anthony Pub.

***St. Anthony's Medicare Outpatient Reference Manual.** Sheila R. Parvis & Christi Sarasin. 1100p. Date not set. 329.00 (1-56329-380-3) St Anthony Pub.

***St. Anthony's Medicare Outpatient Reference Manual.** rev. ed. Christi Sarasin. Ed. by Sheila R. Parvis. Date not set. 329.00 (1-56329-410-9) St Anthony Pub.

***St. Anthony's Medicare Reimbursement Guide for Radiology Services: The Coding, Billing & Coverage Reference.** rev. ed. Sheila R. Parvis. Ed. by MaryAnne Kirk. 800p. Date not set. 249.00 (1-56329-411-7) St Anthony Pub.

***St. Anthony's Medicare Unbundling Guidebook.** rev. ed. Ed. by Anita Hart. 1997. 179.00 (1-56329-413-3) St Anthony Pub.

***St. Anthony's Toolkit for Managing Home Care Services: A Five-Step Plan Integrating Clinical & Financial Resources for Managed Care & Quality Assessment.** 2nd ed. Marilyn Seiler & Clarice J. Powers. (Illus.). 370p. Date not set. lab manual ed., wbk. ed. 299.00 (1-56329-398-6) St Anthony Pub.

***St. Anthony's UB-92 Editor.** Carol F. Endahl & Greg Britt. Ed. by Julia R. Palmer. (Illus.). 600p. Date not set. 199.00 (1-56329-385-4) St Anthony Pub.

***St. Anthony's Version 2.0 APG Guidebook 1997.** Lolita M. Jones. 410p. 1997. pap. 79.00 (1-56329-388-9) St Anthony Pub.

St. Anthony's 1996-97 Hospital Directory. Ed. by Susan Namovicz-Peat. 700p. (C). Date not set. 199.00 (*1-56329-320-X*) St Anthony Pub.

St. Augustine: The Greatness of the Soul. Augustine, Saint. Ed. by J. Quasten & J. Plumpe. Tr. by Joseph M. Colleran. LC 78-62455. (Ancient Christian Writers Ser.: No. 9). 255p. 1950. 16.95 (*0-8091-0060-6*) Paulist Pr.

St. Augustine - 1962, Vol. 25. Eugen Rosenstock-Huessy. (Eugen Rosenstock-Huessy Lectures). 149p. pap. 60.00 incl. audio (*0-614-05396-X*); pap. 30.00 (*0-912148-44-6*); audio 45.00 (*0-614-05395-1*) Argo Bks.

Saint Augustine & His Influence in the Middle Ages, No. 3. Edward B. King. Ed. by Jacqueline T. Schaefer. LC 92-50575. 130p. (Orig.). 1988. pap. 15.00 (*0-918769-24-8*) Univ South Pr.

St. Augustine on the Psalms, Vol. 1. Augustine, Saint. Ed. by J. Quasten & W. J. Burghardt. Tr. by Scholastica Hebgin & Felicitas Corrigan. LC 60-10722. (Ancient Christian Writers Ser.: No. 29). 360p. 1960. 22.95 (*0-8091-0104-1*) Paulist Pr.

St. Augustine on the Psalms, Vol. 2. Augustine, Saint. Ed. by J. Quasten & W. J. Burghardt. Tr. by D. Scholastica Hebgin & D. Felicitas Corrigan. LC 60-10722. (Ancient Christian Writers Ser.: No. 30). 425p. 1961. 26.95 (*0-8091-0105-X*) Paulist Pr.

St. Augustine, Sermons for Christmas & Epiphany. Saint Augustine. Ed. by J. Quasten & J. Plumpe. Tr. by Thomas C. Lawler. LC 78-62464. (Ancient Christian Writers Ser.: No. 15). 250p. 1952. 16.95 (*0-8091-0137-8*) Paulist Pr.

Saint Augustine the Bishop: A Book of Essays. Ed. by Fannie LeMoine & Christopher Kleinhenz. LC 94-7258. (Medieval Casebooks Ser.: Vol. 9). (Illus.). 232p. 1994. text ed. 39.00 (*0-8153-1639-9*, H1830) Garland.

St. Augustine, the First Catechetical Instruction. Augustine, Saint. Ed. by J. Quasten & J. Plumpe. Tr. by Joseph P. Christopher. LC 78-62449. (Ancient Christian Writers Ser.: No. 2). 170p. 1946. 14.95 (*0-8091-0047-9*) Paulist Pr.

***St. Augustine's Abbey.** Richard Gem. 1997. 35.00 (*0-7134-8144-7*, Pub. by Batsford UK) Trafalgar.

Saint Augustine's Confessions: The Odyssey of Soul. Robert J. O'Connell. LC 69-12731. 200p. 1989. pap. 19.95 (*0-8232-1265-3*) Fordham.

***St. Augustine's Confessions in Kwikscan.** St. Augustine & Kwikscan, Inc. Staff. LC 90-35315. 1990. write for info. (*0-941485-29-3*); write for info. (*0-941485-30-7*) KWIKSCAN.

Saint Augustine's Meter & George Herbert's Will. fac. ed. William H. Pahlka. LC 87-4252. 263p. 1987. pap. 75.00 (*0-7837-7629-2*, 2047381) Bks Demand.

Saint Babe. Linda Anderson. Date not set. pap. 5.99 (*0-451-19077-7*) NAL-Dutton.

Saint Barthelemy & the Swedish West India Company: A Selection of Printed Documents, 1784-1814. Ed. by John B. Hattendorf. LC 94-28791. (Maritime History Series, Scholar's Facsimiles & Reprints: 488). 1995. 55.00 (*0-8201-1488-X*) Schol Facsimiles.

***St. Bartholomew's Eve: A Tale of the Huguenot Wars.** G. A. Henty. (Illus.). 376p. 1997. write for info. (*1-887159-08-8*) Preston-Speed.

Saint Basil the Blessed, Fool for Christ's Sake, Wonderworker of Moscow. 1996. pap. 1.00 (*0-89981-163-9*) Eastern Orthodox.

***Saint Behind Enemy Lines.** Olga K. Campora. LC 97-12495. 1997. write for info. (*1-57345-227-0*) Deseret Bk.

Saint Ben. John Fischer. 288p. (Orig.). 1993. pap. 8.99 (*1-55661-259-1*) Bethany Hse.

Saint Benedict: The Story of the Father of the Western Monks. Mary F. Windeatt. LC 93-61378. Orig. Title: Hero of the Hills. (Illus.). 158p. (J). (gr. 5-8). 1994. pap. 8.00 (*0-89555-427-5*) TAN Bks Pubs.

St. Benedict's Prayer Book. Ampleforth Abbey Press Staff. 1994. 12.95 (*0-85244-258-0*, Pub. by Gracewing UK) Morehouse Pub.

***Saint Bernard.** Charlotte Wilcox. LC 97-16363. (Learning about Dogs Ser.). 1998. write for info. (*1-56065-544-5*) Capstone Pr.

Saint Bernard Champions, 1952-1989. Camino E. E. & Bk. Co. Staff. (Illus.). 200p. 1994. pap. 36.95 (*1-55893-001-9*) Camino E E & Bk.

Saint Bernard of Clairvaux: A Theory of Art Formulated from His Writings & Illustrated in Twelfth-Century Works of Art. M. Kilian Hufgard. LC 89-12798. (Medieval Studies). (Illus.). 196p. 1990. lib. bdg. 79.95 (*0-88946-266-6*) E Mellen.

***Saint Bernards.** Martin Weil. (Illus.). 1997. pap. 9.95 (*0-7938-2324-2*, KW-109S) TFH Pubns.

Saint Bonaventure: Etudes sur les Sources de sa Pensee. Jacques G. Bougerol. (Collected Studies: No. CS306). 310p. (FRE.). (C). 1989. reprint ed. text ed. 98.95 (*0-86078-254-9*, Pub. by Variorum UK) Ashgate Pub Co.

Saint Bonaventure's Day Affair & 7 More Weird Stories. Tony Rozycki. 104p. (Orig.). 1990. pap. text ed. 10.00 (*0-685-29065-4*) Black Riv MN.

Saint Bonaventure's Disputed Questions on the Knowledge of Christ, Vol. IV. Bonaventure Staff. (Works of Saint Bonaventure). 202p. 1992. pap. 12.00 (*1-57659-046-1*) Franciscan Inst.

Saint Bonaventure's Disputed Questions on the Mystery of the Trinity, Vol. III. Bonaventure Staff. (Works of Saint Bonaventure). 280p. 1979. pap. 11.00 (*1-57659-045-3*) Franciscan Inst.

Saint Brendan. Ed. by Iain MacDonald. (Celtic Studies Ser.). 62p. 1992. pap. 6.95 (*0-86315-141-8*) Dufour.

Saint Bride. Ed. by Iain MacDonald. (Celtic Studies Ser.). 62p. 1992. pap. 6.95 (*0-86315-142-6*) Dufour.

Saint Bride & Her Book: Birgitta of Sweden's Revelations. Ed. by Julia B. Holloway. (Focus Library of Medieval Women). 180p. (Orig.). (C). 1992. pap. 9.95 (*0-941051-18-8*, P27) Focus Pub-R Pullins.

***Saint Bride & Her Book: Birgitta of Sweden's Revelations.** Julia B. Holloway. (Library of Medieval Women). (Illus.). 184p. 1997. 23.00 (*0-85991-441-0*, DS Brewer) Boydell & Brewer.

Saint Bruno the Carthusian. Andre Ravier. LC 94-75668. 197p. (Orig.). 1995. pap. 11.95 (*0-89870-562-2*) Ignatius Pr.

***St. Burl's Obituary.** Daniel Akst. LC 96-43962. 1997. pap. 12.00 (*0-15-600514-X*, Harvest Bks) HarBrace.

St. Burl's Obituary. Daniel Akst. LC 95-52568. 370p. 1996. 22.95 (*1-878448-68-4*) MacMurray & Beck.

Saint Catherine of Siena: The Story of the Girl Who Saw Saints in the Sky. Mary F. Windeatt. LC 93-60320. (Illus.). 64p. (J). 1993. reprint ed. pap. 5.00 (*0-89555-421-6*) TAN Bks Pubs.

St. Charles Avenue Streetcar Line: A Self-Guided Tour. Text by Lynn Adams & John Magill. (Illus.). 16p. 1994. pap. 4.95 (*0-917860-38-1*) Historic New Orleans.

***St. Charles Streetcar: The History of the New Orleans & Carrollton Railroad.** 3rd rev. ed. James Guilbeau. LC 92-81388. (Illus.). 108p. 1992. pap. write for info. (*1-879714-02-7*) SW PF LA Land.

Saint Christopher. Margaret Hodges. (Illus.). (J). write for info. (*0-8028-5077-4*) Eerdmans.

***Saint Christopher's Monkey.** Andrew Zec. 36p. 1996. pap. 7.00 (*0-930502-22-1*) Pine Pr.

Saint Columba. Ed. by Iain MacDonald. (Celtic Studies Ser.). 62p. 1992. pap. 6.95 (*0-86315-143-4*) Dufour.

Saint Coran. Muhammad Hamidullah. 25.00 (*0-685-66747-2*, 13) Tahrike Tarsile Quran.

Saint Coran: Traduction et Commentaire de Muhammad Hamidullah Avec la Collaboration de M. Leturmy. rev. ed. Muhammad Hamidullah. 1312p. (ARA & FRE.). 1989. text ed. 15.00 (*0-915957-04-3*) amana pubns.

St. Cuthbert, His Cult & His Community to A.D. 1200. Ed. by Gerald Bonner et al. (Illus.). 540p. 1995. 89.00 (*0-85115-510-3*) Boydell & Brewer.

St. Cuthbert, His Cult & His Community to A.D. 1200. Ed. by Gerald Bonner et al. (Illus.). 544p. 1997. pap. 35.00 (*0-85115-610-X*) Boydell & Brewer.

***St. Cuthbert's Way.** Roger Smith. (Official Trail Guide Ser.). 144p. 1997. pap. 29.95 (*0-11-495762-2*, Pub. by Statnry Ofc UK) Seven Hills Bk.

St. Cyril of Alexandria Vol. 1: Letters 1-50. Cyril. Tr. by John I. McEnerney. LC 85-5692. (Fathers of the Church Ser.: Vol. 76-77). 253p. 1987. reprint ed. pap. 72.20 (*0-7837-9149-6*, 2049949) Bks Demand.

St. Cyril of Alexandria: The Christological Controversy: Its History, Theology, & Texts. John A. McGuckin. LC 94-11851. (Supplements to Vigiliae Christianae Ser.: Vol. 23). 1994. 173.00 (*90-04-09990-5*) E J Brill.

Saint Dominic: Preacher of the Hail Mary & Founder of the Dominican Order. Mary F. Windeatt. LC 93-61379. (Illus.). 156p. (J). (gr. 5-8). 1994. reprint ed. pap. 8.00 (*0-89555-430-5*) TAN Bks Pubs.

Saint-Dominique see Essais et Ecrits de Combat

***Saint Edmund Campion: Priest & Martyr.** Evelyn Waugh. LC 96-32720. 252p. 1996. reprint ed. pap. 15.95 (*0-918477-44-1*) Sophia Inst Pr.

Saint Endellion. Ed. by Edwin Stark. (C). 1989. 58.00 (*0-907566-62-6*, Pub. by Dyllansow Truran UK) St Mut.

Saint Ephrem's Commentary on Tatian's "Diatessaron" An English Translation of Chester Beatty Syriac MS 709 with Introduction & Notes. Ed. by Carmel McCarthy. (Journal of Semetic Studies Supplement: Suppl. No. 2). (Illus.). 388p. 1994. 59.00 (*0-19-922163-4*) OUP.

Saint-Evremond: Artiste de l'Euphorie. Leonard Rosmarin. LC 86-63080. 112p. (FRE.). 1987. 18.95 (*0-917786-52-1*) Summa Pubns.

Saint-Exupery: A Biography. Stacy Schiff. LC 94-4011. (Illus.). 525p. 1994. 30.00 (*0-679-40310-8*) Knopf.

***Saint-Exupery: A Biography.** Stacy Schiff. LC 96-49352. (Illus.). 559p. 1997. reprint ed. pap. 18.95 (*0-306-80740-8*) Da Capo.

Saint-Exupery: L'ecriture et la Pensee. Major. 28.90 (*0-685-37091-7*) Fr & Eur.

St. Famous. Jonathan Dee. 240p. 1996. 22.95 (*0-385-47459-8*) Doubleday.

Saint for Your Name: Saints for Boys. Albert J. Nevins. LC 79-92504. (Illus.). 120p. (YA). (gr. 7 up). 1980. pap. 6.95 (*0-87973-320-9*, 320) Our Sunday Visitor.

Saint for Your Name: Saints for Girls. Albert J. Nevins. LC 79-92502. (Illus.). 104p. (YA). (gr. 7 up). 1980. pap. 6.95 (*0-87973-321-7*, 321) Our Sunday Visitor.

Saint Foucault: Towards a Gay Hagiography. David M. Halperin. (Illus.). 224p. 1995. 25.00 (*0-19-509371-2*) OUP.

***Saint Foucault: Towards a Gay Hagiography.** David M. Halperin. (Illus.). 256p. 1997. reprint ed. pap. 13.95 (*0-19-511127-3*) OUP.

Saint Frances of Hollywood. Sally Clark. 128p. 1996. pap. text ed. 11.95 (*0-88922-366-1*) Genl Dist Srvs.

Saint Francis. Brian Wildsmith. 40p. (J). Date not set. write for info. (*0-19-279980-0*) OUP.

Saint Francis. Brian Wildsmith. (Illus.). 36p. (J). (gr. 4-7). 1996. 20.00 (*0-8028-5123-1*) Eerdmans.

Saint Francis & the Poet. Ed. by Elizabeth B. Patterson. 163p. 11.95 (*0-8159-6802-7*) Devin.

St. Francis for Today. Edmund O. Gorman. 1994. pap. 7.95 (*0-85244-130-4*, Pub. by Gracewing UK) Morehouse Pub.

***Saint Francis of Assisi.** (Saint Joseph Picture Bks.). (Illus.). 1975. pap. 1.25 (*0-89942-286-1*, 286-00) Catholic Bk Pub.

***Saint Francis of Assisi.** Jo F. Frazier. (Saints Alive Ser.: Vol. 2). (Illus.). 24p. (Orig.). (J). (gr. 3-6). 1997. pap. 4.00 (*0-9650704-1-7*) Saints Alive.

Saint Francis of the Seven Seas. Albert F. Nevins. LC 95-755666. (Vision Book Ser.). (Illus.). 130p. (Orig.). (J). (gr. 4-10). 1995. pap. 9.95 (*0-89870-519-3*) Ignatius Pr.

Saint Francis Solano: Wonder-Worker of the New World & Apostle of Argentina & Peru. Mary F. Windeatt. LC 93-61380. Orig. Title: Song in the South. (Illus.). 211p. (J). (gr. 5-8). 1994. pap. 11.00 (*0-89555-431-3*) TAN Bks Pubs.

Saint Frideswide's Monastary at Oxford. Christopher Blair. (Illus.). 300p. (C). 1991. text ed. 70.00 (*0-86299-773-9*, Pub. by Sutton Pubng UK) Bks Intl VA.

***Saint Gabriel Possenti, Passionist: A Young Man in Love.** Gabriele Cingolani. Tr. by S. B. Zak from ITA. LC 97-3129. (Illus.). 124p. (Orig.). 1997. pap. 12.95 (*0-8189-0790-8*) Alba.

Saint Gall Tractate: A Medieval Guide to Rhetorical Syntax. Ed. by Anna A. Grotans & David W. Porter. LC 95-12308. (GERM Ser.). ix, 150p. (C). 1995. 58.95 (*1-879751-19-4*) Camden Hse.

Saint Genet, Comedien et Martyr see Oeuvres Completes

***Saint George Chronicles: Containing an Historical Sketch from 1605 to 1932.** Compiled by Joseph T. Simmons & Mabelle A. Rose. (Illus.). 78p. 1997. reprint ed. pap. 15.50 (*0-8328-5908-7*) Higginson Bk Co.

Saint Germain: Prophecy to the Nations, Bk. I. Elizabeth C. Prophet. 594p. 1990. 24.95 (*0-922729-00-X*) Summit Univ.

Saint Germain: Prophecy to the Nations, Bk. II. Elizabeth C. Prophet. 680p. 1990. 24.95 (*0-922729-01-8*) Summit Univ.

St. Germain-des-Pres. Paul Webster & Nicholas Powell. LC 85-216795. 277p. reprint ed. pap. 79.00 (*0-318-34737-7*, 2031994) Bks Demand.

Saint Germain on Alchemy. Saint Germain. Ed. by Mark L. Prophet & Elizabeth C. Prophet. LC 81-52784. (Illus.). 544p. (Orig.). 1985. pap. text ed. 6.99 (*0-916766-68-3*) Summit Univ.

Saint-Glinglin. Raymond Queneau. (Imaginaire Ser.). 272p. (FRE.). 1948. 12.95 (*2-07-029151-0*) Schoenhof.

Saint Glinglin. Raymond Queneau. Tr. by James Sallis from FRE. LC 92-29479. 192p. 1993. 19.95 (*1-56478-027-9*) Dalkey Arch.

St. Gregory of Nyssa & the Tradition of the Fathers. Michael Azkoul. LC 94-45748. (Texts & Studies in Religion: Vol. 63). 238p. 1995. text ed. 89.95 (*0-7734-8993-2*) E Mellen.

St. Gregory Palamas: Treatise on the Spiritual Life. Daniel M. Rogich. 105p. (Orig.). 1994. pap. 9.95 (*1-880971-05-4*) Light&Life Pub Co MN.

St. Hilarion Calendar, Year of Our Lord 1995. rev. ed. Ed. & Frwd. by Aidan Keller. 120p. 1994. pap. 7.75 (*0-923864-06-7*) St Hilarion Pr.

Saint Hilary's School Cookbook. St. Hilary School Families. (Illus.). 282p. (Orig.). 1991. pap. 10.00 (*0-9631651-0-0*) St Hilary Schl.

Saint Honey & Oh David, Are You There? Paul Ritchie. 124p. 1968. 12.95 (*0-910278-45-8*) Boulevard.

St. Hyacinth of Poland: The Story of the Apostle of the North. Mary F. Windeatt. LC 93-83094. (Illus.). 189p. (J). 1993. reprint ed. pap. 11.00 (*0-89555-422-4*) TAN Bks Pubs.

Saint Hysteria: Neurosis, Mysticism, & Gender in European Culture. Christina Mazzoni. LC 96-13417. 248p. 1996. 42.50 (*0-8014-3229-4*) Cornell U Pr.

Saint in Europe. Leslie Charteris. 1975. reprint ed. lib. bdg. 20.95 (*0-89190-387-9*, Rivercity Pr) Amereon Ltd.

Saint in Miami. large type ed. Leslie Charteris. 454p. 1973. 25.99 (*0-85456-223-0*) Ulverscroft.

Saint in New York. Leslie Charteris. LC 88-82346. 229p. 1988. reprint ed. pap. 4.95 (*0-930330-97-8*, Lib Crime Classics) Intl Polygonics.

Saint in the Slums (Kagawa of Japan) Cyril Davey. 1979. pap. 3.95 (*0-87508-620-9*) Chr Lit.

Saint Intervenes. Leslie Charteris. 1976. 23.95 (*0-89190-384-4*) Amereon Ltd.

Saint Is Born in Chima: A Novel. Manuel Zapata Olivella. Tr. by Thomas E. Kooreman. (Texas Pan American Ser.). 124p. 1991. pap. 10.95 (*0-292-77644-6*); text ed. 21.95 (*0-292-77633-0*) U of Tex Pr.

St. Isaac & the Indians. 2nd rev. ed. Milton Lomask. LC 90-85767. (Vision Book Ser.). (Illus.). 170p. (J). (gr. 4-9). 1991. reprint ed. pap. 9.95 (*0-89870-355-7*) Ignatius Pr.

Saint Jack. Paul Theroux. 1997. pap. 11.95 (*0-14-004157-5*, Viking) Viking Penguin.

Saint Jack. Paul Theroux. 1994. reprint ed. lib. bdg. 32.95 (*1-56849-346-0*) Buccaneer Bks.

***St. James Film Directors Encyclopedia.** Andrew Sarris. 1997. 29.95 (*1-57859-028-0*) Visible Ink Pr.

St. James Guide to Crime & Mystery Writers. 4th ed. Jay P. Pederson & Taryn Benbow-Pfalzgraf. LC 96-18661. (St. James Guide to Writers Ser.). 264p. 1996. 140.00 (*1-55862-178-4*) St James Pr.

St. James Guide to Fantasy Writers. Ed. by David Pringle. (St. James Guide to Fantasy Writers Ser.). 711p. 1995. 140.00 (*1-55862-205-5*) St James Pr.

***St. James Guide to Horror, Ghost & Gothic Writers.** 600p. 1998. 95.00 (*1-55862-206-3*, 00007321) St James Pr.

***St. James Modern Masterpieces: The Best of Art, Architecture, Photography & Design Since 1945.** Udo Kultermann. 1997. 29.95 (*1-57859-023-X*) Visible Ink Pr.

***St. James Press Gay & Lesbian Almanac.** 1998. 100.00 (*1-55862-358-2*, 00157204) St James Pr.

***St. James Santee, Plantation Parish: History & Records, 1685-1925.** Anne B. Bridges & Roy Williams. LC 96-43877. 1996. write for info. (*0-87152-504-6*) Reprint.

Saint Jerome in the Renaissance. Eugene F. Rice, Jr. LC 84-21324. (Symposia in Comparative History Ser.: No. 13). (Illus.). 304p. 1988. reprint ed. pap. text ed. 15.95 (*0-8018-3747-2*) Johns Hopkins.

***Saint Joan.** Shaw. 1991. pap. text ed. write for info. (*0-582-07786-9*, Pub. by Longman UK) Longman.

***Saint Joan.** George Bernard Shaw. Date not set. lib. bdg. 20.95 (*0-8488-1653-6*) Amereon Ltd.

Saint Joan. George Bernard Shaw. 160p. 1989. pap. 7.95 (*0-14-045023-8*) Viking Penguin.

Saint Joan: The Girl in Armour. Dorothy Smith. (Illus.). (J). 1990. pap. 2.95 (*0-8091-6594-5*) Paulist Pr.

***Saint Joan of Arc.** Leon Cristiani. 160p. pap. 3.95 (*0-8198-0465-7*) Pauline Bks.

***Saint Joan of the Stockyards.** Bertolt Brecht. Ed. by Ralph Nanheim & John Willett. 160p. 1998. pap. 8.95 (*1-55970-420-9*) Arcade Pub Inc.

Saint John: The Making of a Colonial Urban Community. T. W. Acheson. 326p. 1992. pap. 24.95 (*0-8020-7380-8*) U of Toronto Pr.

St. John Beach Guide: The Complete Guide to the Beaches on the Island of St. John in the United States Virgin Islands. Gerald Singer. LC 94-66624. (Illus.). 112p. 1994. pap. 9.95 (*0-9641220-0-6*) Sombrero Pubng.

Saint John Bosco & the Children's Saint Dominic Savio. 2nd ed. Catherine Beebe. LC 92-71930. (Vision Book Ser.). 157p. (J). (gr. 4-9). 1992. pap. 9.95 (*0-89870-416-2*) Ignatius Pr.

Saint John Masias: Marvelous Dominican Gatekeeper of Lima, Peru. Mary F. Windeatt. LC 93-61382. Orig. Title: Warrior in White. (Illus.). 156p. (J). (gr. 5-8). 1994. pap. 8.00 (*0-89555-428-3*) TAN Bks Pubs.

Saint John Neumann, Wonder-Worker of Philadelphia: Recent Miracles 1961-1991. Timothy E. Byerley. Ed. by Charles Fehrenbach. 211p. 1992. pap. write for info. (*0-9634825-0-5*) Nat Shrine.

Saint John of the Cross: A Spirituality of Substance. Ed. by Peter O. Slattery. 147p. (Orig.). 1994. pap. 8.95 (*0-8189-0684-7*) Alba.

Saint John of the Cross: On the State of Beginners. Compiled by Bede Frost. (Basket of Tolerance Ser.). (Illus.). 3248p. (Orig.). 1992. pap. 4.95 (*0-918801-45-1*) Dawn Horse Pr.

St. John of the Cross: Understanding His Ascent & Dark Night in Easy Stages. Peter Bourne. LC 93-60166. (Illus.). 207p. (C). 1995. 19.95 (*0-930887-15-8*) Wenzel Pr.

***St. John off the Beaten Track: A Unique & Unusual Guide to St. John U. S. V. I.** Gerald Singer. LC 96-92640. (Illus.). 304p. 1997. pap. 19.95 (*0-9641220-1-4*) Sombrero Pubng.

St. John's Bestiary. William Babula. 264p. 1994. 19.95 (*1-885173-01-6*) Write Way.

Saint John's in Pictures. Michael Crouser. 80p. 1994. 39.00 (*0-9644200-0-7*) Veronica Press.

***St. John's Wort.** Roy Upton. 1997. pap. 4.95 (*0-87983-813-2*) Keats.

Saint Johnsbury, VT. C. Johnson. (Images of America Ser.). 128p. 1996. pap. 16.99 (*0-7524-0260-9*, Arcdia) Chalford.

***St. Joseph Annotated Catechism.** Anthony Schraner. 1987. pap. 4.25 (*0-89942-545-3*, 545/04) Catholic Bk Pub.

***St. Joseph Catholic Manual.** Thomas J. Donaghy. 1994. pap. 2.95 (*0-89942-268-3*, 268/04) Catholic Bk Pub.

St. Joseph Children's Missal for Boys. (Illus.). 1977. 3.95 (*0-89942-806-1*, 806/67B) Catholic Bk Pub.

St. Joseph Children's Missal for Boys. deluxe ed. (Illus.). 1977. 13.95 (*0-89942-802-9*, 806/82B) Catholic Bk Pub.

St. Joseph Children's Missal for Girls. (Illus.). 1977. 3.95 (*0-89942-805-3*, 806/67W) Catholic Bk Pub.

St. Joseph Children's Missal for Girls. deluxe ed. (Illus.). 1977. 13.95 (*0-89942-801-0*, 806/82W) Catholic Bk Pub.

St. Joseph Church History. large type ed. Lawrence G. Lovasik. (Illus.). (Orig.). 1989. pap. 5.95 (*0-89942-262-4*, 262/04) Catholic Bk Pub.

***St. Joseph Confirmation Book.** large type ed. Lawrence G. Lovasik. (Illus.). (J). 1978. 6.75 (*0-89942-249-7*, 249/04) Catholic Bk Pub.

***St. Joseph First Mass Book for Boys.** (Illus.). 1985. 9.95 (*0-89942-800-2*, 808/72B) Catholic Bk Pub.

***St. Joseph First Mass Book for Girls.** (Illus.). 1985. 9.95 (*0-89942-814-2*, 808/72W) Catholic Bk Pub.

***Saint Joseph "Guardian of the Redeemer" Apostolio Exhortation of John Paul II Text & Reflections.** Tarcisio Stramare. 120p. 1997. pap. 8.00 (*1-883839-06-8*) Guard Redeemer.

Saint Joseph in Spanish American Colonial Images of the Holy Family: Guardian of an Earthly Paradise. Christopher C. Wilson. LC 95-8103. 24p. 1992. write for info. (*0-916101-13-4*) St Joseph.

***St. Joseph in the Lives of Two Blesseds of the Church.** Larry Toschi. LC 94-76450. 152p. (Orig.). 1997. pap. 8.00 (*1-883839-05-X*) Guard Redeemer.

St. Joseph New American Catechism. large type ed. Lawrence G. Lovasik. (New American Catechism Ser.: No. 3). (Illus.). (YA). (gr. 9-12). 1978. student ed. 3.95 (*0-89942-253-5*, 253/05) Catholic Bk Pub.

***St. Joseph New American Catechism.** large type ed. Lawrence G. Lovasik. (New American Catechism Ser.: No. 1). (Illus.). (J). (gr. 3-5). 1989. student ed. 2.25 (*0-89942-251-9*, 251/05) Catholic Bk Pub.

***St. Joseph New American Catechism.** large type ed. Lawrence G. Lovasik. (New American Catechism Ser.: No. 2). (Illus.). (J). (gr. 6-8). 1989. student ed., pap. 3.25 (*0-89942-252-7*, 252/05) Catholic Bk Pub.

***St. Joseph New American Catechism: First Communion.** large type ed. Lawrence G. Lovasik. (New American Catechism Ser.: Vol. 0). (Illus.). (J). (gr. 1-2). 1989. student ed., pap. 2.25 (*0-89942-250-0*, 250/05) Catholic Bk Pub.

***St. Joseph People's Prayer Book.** 1975. im. lthr. 17.95 (*0-89942-901-7*, 900/22) Catholic Bk Pub.

St. Joseph People's Prayer Book. Francis Evans. vinyl bd. 15.75 (*0-89942-900-9*, 900/08) Catholic Bk Pub.

S

***St. Joseph Picture Books Boxed Gift Set: Twenty-Six Titles.** (Saint Joseph Picture Bks.). (Illus.). 1978. pap. 32.00 (*0-89942-300-0*, 300-00) Catholic Bk Pub.

***St. Joseph Pocket Catechism.** A. Lodders. 1975. 1.25 (*0-89942-047-8*, 46-00) Catholic Bk Pub.

Saint Joseph Weekday Missal Vol. 1: Advent ot Pentecost, Vol. I. 1306p. 1975. vinyl bd. 13.50 (*0-89942-920-3*, 920/09) Catholic Bk Pub.

***Saint Joseph Weekday Missal Vol. 2: Pentecost to Advent, Vol. II.** 1306p. 1975. vinyl bd. 13.50 (*0-89942-921-1*, 921/09) Catholic Bk Pub.

St. Joseph's Blues. John Detro. 63p. Date not set. pap. 10.00 (*0-932662-86-2*) St Andrews NC.

Saint Judas. James Wright. LC 59-12481. (Wesleyan Poetry Program Ser.: Vol. 4). 64p. 1959. pap. 11.95 (*0-8195-1110-2*, Wesleyan Univ Pr) U Pr of New Eng.

Saint Jude, Thank You. John W. Spencer. 224p. 1986. 12.95 (*0-941219-01-1*) Phillips Pub MA.

Saint-Just. Norman Hampson. 224p. 1991. 41.95 (*0-631-16233-X*) Blackwell Pubs.

Saint Justin Martyr: The First Apology, the Second Apology, Dialogue with Trypho, Exhortation to the Greeks, Discourse to the Greeks, the Monarchy, or the Rule of God. Justin Martyr. Ed. by Thomas B. Falls. LC 65-18317. (Fathers of the Church Ser.: Vol. 6). 486p. 1977. reprint ed. pap. 138.60 (*0-7837-9146-1*, 2049946) Bks Demand.

St. Lawrence River & Seaway. Terri Willis. LC 94-3023. (Wonders of the World Ser.). (Illus.). 64p. (J). (gr. 5-8). 1994. lib. bdg. 25.68 (*0-8114-6370-2*) Raintree Steck-V.

***St. Lawrence Seaway.** Ann Armbruster. (True Bks.). 48p. (J). 1997. pap. 6.95 (*0-516-26114-2*) Childrens.

***Saint Leibowitz & the Wild Horse Woman: A Novel.** Walter M. Miller, Jr. LC 97-3181. 432p. 1997. 23.95 (*0-553-10704-6*) Bantam.

St. Lo: Normandy. (Military History Ser.). 1995. lib. bdg. 251.95 (*0-8490-7417-7*) Gordon Pr.

Saint Louis: Crusader King of France. abr. ed. Jean Richard. Ed. by Simon Lloyd. Tr. by Jean Birrell. (Illus.). 408p. (C). 1992. text ed. 69.95 (*0-521-38156-8*) Cambridge U Pr.

St. Louis: Historic Churches & Synagogues. Mary M. Stiritz et al. (Illus.). (Orig.). 1995. pap. 22.00 (*0-937322-10-5*) St Louis Pub Lib.

St. Louis Blues. Bruce Brothers. LC 93-48456. (NHL Today Ser.). 32p. (J). 1995. lib. bdg. 15.95 (*0-88682-686-1*) Creative Ed.

St. Louis Blues. limited ed. Rex Miller. 160p. 1995. boxed 40.00 (*0-940776-30-8*) Maclay Assoc.

St. Louis Cardinals: Over 100 Years of Baseball Memories & Memorabilia. David M. Spindel. (Major League Memories Ser.). (Illus.). 132p. 1995. 29.95 (*1-55859-861-8*) Abbeville Pr.

Saint Louis Days...Saint Louis Nights. Junior League of St. Louis Staff. (Illus.). 288p. 1996. 19.95 (*0-9638298-1-5*) Jr Leag St Louis.

St. Louis de Montfort: The Story of Our Lady's Slave. Mary F. Windeatt. LC 90-71826. (Stories of the Saints for Young People Ages 10 to 100 Ser.). Orig. Title: Our Lady's Slave: The Story of St. Louis Mary Grignion de Montfort. (Illus.). 211p. (J). (gr. 5-9). 1994. reprint ed. pap. 12.00 (*0-89555-414-3*) TAN Bks Pubs.

St. Louis: Home on the River. Elaine Viets & Quinta Scott. (Urban Tapestry Ser.). (Illus.). 416p. 1995. 39.50 (*1-881096-18-1*) Towery Pub.

Saint Louis JobBank. 5th ed. Adams Publishing Staff. 384p. 1995. pap. 15.95 (*1-55850-462-1*) Adams Media.

St. Louis Lost: Uncovering the City's Architectural Treasures. Mary Bartley. (Illus.). 200p. 1994. 44.95 (*0-9631448-4-7*) VA Pub Corp.

St. Louis Souvenir Book. (Orig.). pap. text ed. write for info. (*1-56944-009-3*) Terrell Missouri.

St. Louis Union Station. Phoenix Publishing Staff. (Illus.). 96p. 1996. 34.95 (*1-886154-14-7*) Phoenix IL.

Saint Lucia Development Atlas. 42.00 (*0-8270-2619-6*) OAS.

Saint Luke. Ed. by Dennis E. Nineham & Howard C. Kee. LC 89-78459. (New Testament Commentaries Ser.). 960p. 1990. 39.95 (*0-334-00951-0*) TPI PA.

Saint Margaret Mary: And the Promises of the Sacred Heart of Jesus. Mary F. Windeatt. LC 90-71825. Orig. Title: Mission for Margaret. (J). (gr. 5-8). 1994. pap. 11.00 (*0-89555-415-1*) TAN Bks Pubs.

St. Martin Concise. Andrea L. Lunsford. 1997. pap. text ed. 19.50 (*0-312-09569-4*) St Martin.

Saint-Martin, Vol. VIII. Jacques Matter. Ed. by Robert Amadou. 329p. reprint ed. write for info. (*0-318-71419-1*) G Olms Pubs.

Saint Martin: The French Mystic. Arthur E. Waite. 78p. 1992. reprint ed. pap. 9.95 (*0-922802-93-9*) Kessinger Pub.

***St. Martin De Porres.** (Saint Joseph Picture Bks.). (Illus.). 1983. pap. 1.25 (*0-89942-383-3*, 383-00) Catholic Bk Pub.

St. Martin de Porres: The Little Stories & the Semiotics of Culture. Alexandro Garcia-Rivera. LC 95-17445. (Faith & Cultures Ser.). 160p. (Orig.). 1995. pap. 16.95 (*1-57075-033-5*) Orbis Bks.

St. Martin de Porres: The Story of the Little Doctor of Lima, Peru. Mary F. Windeatt. LC 93-83095. (Illus.). 122p. (J). 1992. reprint ed. pap. 7.00 (*0-89555-423-2*) TAN Bks Pubs.

St. Martin's Guide to Teaching Writing. 2nd ed. Robert J. Connors & Cheryl Glenn. 256p. (C). 1992. pap. text ed. write for info. (*0-318-68813-1*) St Martin.

***St. Martin's Guide to Writing.** 4th ed. Axelrod. Date not set. pap. text ed. 33.30 (*0-312-11230-0*) St Martin.

St. Martin's Handbook. 3rd ed. Andrea A. Lunsford & Robert Connors. 944p. (C). 1995. pap. text ed. 21.50 (*0-312-10212-7*) St Martin.

St. Martin's Handbook. 3rd ed. Andrea A. Lunsford. 1995. teacher ed., pap. text ed. 22.50 (*0-312-10213-5*) St Martin.

St. Martins Reader. Glenn. Date not set. pap. text ed. write for info. (*0-312-14917-4*) St Martin.

St. Martin's Source for Writing Tutors. Murphy. 1995. pap. text ed. 7.00 (*0-312-11729-9*) St Martin.

St. Martin's Workbook. 3rd ed. Lex Runciman. 592p. 1995. pap. text ed. 14.00 (*0-312-10216-X*) St Martin.

Saint Maybe. 1995. 5.99 (*0-517-10770-8*) Random Hse Value.

Saint Maybe. Anne Tyler. 337p. 1991. 22.00 (*0-679-40361-2*) Knopf.

***Saint Maybe.** Anne Tyler. 1996. pap. 12.00 (*0-449-91160-8*) Fawcett.

Saint Maybe: A Novel. large type ed. Anne Tyler. 512p. 1991. 25.00 (*0-679-40771-5*) Random Hse Lrg Prnt.

Saint-Memin & the Neoclassical Profile Portrait in America. Ellen G. Miles. LC 94-15239. (Illus.). 512p. 1994. text ed. 95.00 (*1-56098-411-2*) Smithsonian.

***Saint Menas of Egypt.** Ed. & Tr. by E. A. Budge from COP. 1997. pap. 7.50 (*0-89979-097-6*) British Am Bks.

***Saint Michael the Archangel Roman Catholic Parish, Lansford, PA 1891-1991 - A Century of Faith & Heritage - "Viera a Dedicstvo" Storocna Pamatnica.** Ed. by Thomas A. Derzack et al. (Illus.). 295p. 1995. 35.00 (*0-9643755-0-8*, TX 4-195-727) St Michael the Archangel.

Saint Monica & Her Son Augustine. 1994. pap. 5.95 (*0-8198-0462-2*) Pauline Bks.

Saint Mudd. Steve Thayer. Date not set. pap. 5.50 (*0-451-19178-1*, Sig) NAL-Dutton.

Saint Mudd: A Novel of Gangsters & Saints. Steve Thayer. LC 88-70735. 320p. 1988. 17.95 (*0-9620389-0-3*) Birchwood Page Publishing.

Saint Mudd: A Novel of Gangsters & Saints. Steve Thayer. LC 88-70735. 320p. 1990. pap. 5.95 (*0-9620389-1-1*) Birchwood Page Publishing.

Saint Mudd: A Novel of Gangsters & Saints. Steve Thayer. 416p. 1994. pap. 6.50 (*0-451-17682-0*, Sig) NAL-Dutton.

Saint Nektarios: A Saint for Our Times. Sotos Chondropoulos. Tr. by Peter Los & Alici Los from GRE. LC 89-15612. 289p. (Orig.). (YA). (gr. 10-12). 1989. pap. 14.95 (*0-917651-63-4*) Holy Cross Orthodox.

Saint Nicholas. Regine Schindler & Brother Kenneth. (Illus.). (C). 1990. text ed. 39.00 (*0-85439-335-8*, Pub. by St Paul Pubns UK) St Mut.

***St. Nicholas: His Legend & His Role in the Christmas Celebration & Other Popular Customs.** 3rd unabridged ed. George M. McKnight. (Illus.). 210p. 1996. reprint ed. pap. 15.95 (*0-87928-114-6*) Corner Hse.

***St. Nicholas & the Weir.** Conor McPherson. (Nick Hern Bks.). 1997. pap. text ed. 16.95 (*1-85459-347-1*, Pub. by N Hern Bks UK) Theatre Comm.

***Saint Nicholas Speaks.** Stephen M. Crotts. 1996. pap. 2.95 (*1-55673-399-2*) CSS OH.

Saint Oedipus: Psychocritical Approaches to Flaubert's Art. William J. Berg et al. LC 81-17441. 312p. 1982. 45.00 (*0-8014-1383-4*) Cornell U Pr.

Saint of Beersheba. Alex Weingrod. LC 89-4047. (SUNY Series in Anthropology & Judaic Studies). (Illus.). 148p. 1990. pap. text ed. 21.95 (*0-7914-0139-1*) State U NY Pr.

Saint of Beersheba. Alex Weingrod. LC 89-4047. (SUNY Series in Anthropology & Judaic Studies). (Illus.). 148p. 1990. text ed. 64.50 (*0-7914-0138-3*) State U NY Pr.

Saint of Bourbon Street: Men of the Black Watch. B. J. James. (Silhouette Desire Ser.: No. 951). 1995. mass mkt., pap. 3.25 (*0-373-05951-5*) Harlequin Bks.

***Saint of Circumstance.** Weller. 1997. 24.00 (*0-671-01437-4*, PB Hardcover) PB.

Saint of Jilan. S. A. Salik. Tr. by Muhammad Rahimuddin. 110p. (Orig.). 1985. pap. 3.00 (*1-56744-374-5*) Kazi Pubns.

***Saint of Jilan (Ghauth Al-Azam)** S. A. Salik. 110p. 1996. pap. 3.50 (*0-614-21715-6*, 1100) Kazi Pubns.

Saint of London: The Life & Miracles of St. Erkenwald: Text & Translation. Ed. & Tr. by E. Gordon Whatley. (Medieval & Renaissance Texts & Studies: Vol. 58). (Illus.). 272p. 1989. 25.00 (*0-86698-042-3*, MR58) MRTS.

Saint of Philadelphia: The Life of Bishop John Neumann. Philip Douglas. 1991. reprint ed. 13.95 (*0-911218-07-6*); reprint ed. pap. 7.95 (*0-911218-08-4*) Ravengate Pr.

***Saint of the Day: Lives & Lessons for Saints & Feasts of the New Missal.** Leonard Foley. 368p. 1997. pap. 13.95 (*0-86716-318-6*) St Anthony Mess Pr.

Saint Office. Maurice Rheims. (FRE.). 1985. pap. 17.95 (*0-7859-4230-0*) Fr & Eur.

***St. Olaf Choir - A Narrative.** Joseph M. Shaw. (Orig.). 1997. 29.95 (*0-9640020-1-9*) St Olaf Coll.

***St. Olaf Choir - A Narrative.** Joseph M. Shaw. (Orig.). 1997. pap. 22.95 (*0-9640020-2-7*) St Olaf Coll.

Saint on Guard. Leslie Charteris. 1975. reprint ed. lib. bdg. 22.95 (*0-89190-386-0*, Rivercity Pr) Amereon Ltd.

Saint or Sinner. Cheryl St. John. 1995. mass mkt. 4.50 (*0-373-28888-3*, 1-28888-5) Harlequin Bks.

Saint or Slaver. Glen L. Rickard. Ed. by Arelene D. Rickard. (Orig.). 1991. pap. 10.95 (*0-9627012-0-3*) G L Rickard Pub.

***St. Oscar & Other Plays.** Terry Eagleton. LC 96-26957. 236p. 1997. 49.95 (*0-631-20452-0*); pap. 22.95 (*0-631-20453-9*) Blackwell Pubs.

St. Oswald of Worcester: Life & Influence. Nicholas Brooks & Catherine Cubitt. LC 95-23869. (Studies in the Early History of Britain: No. 2). (Illus.). 352p. 1996. 70.00 (*0-7185-0003-2*, Pub. by Leicester Univ Pr) Bks Intl VA.

Saint Overboard. Leslie Charteris. 1993. reprint ed. lib. bdg. 20.95 (*1-56849-131-X*) Buccaneer Bks.

***Saint Overboard.** Leslie Charteris. Date not set. reprint ed. lib. bdg. 24.95 (*0-614-25287-3*, Am Repr) Amereon Ltd.

Saint-Pascal: Changing Leadership & Social Organization in a Quebec Town. Gerald L. Gold. (Illus.). 215p. (C). 1985. reprint ed. pap. text ed. 10.95 (*0-88133-164-3*) Waveland Pr.

***Saint Patrick.** Lawrence G. Lovasik. (Saint Joseph Picture Bks.). (Illus.). Date not set. pap. 1.25 (*0-89942-385-X*, 385-00) Catholic Bk Pub.

Saint Patrick. Ed. by Iain MacDonald. (Celtic Studies Ser.). 62p. 1992. pap. 6.95 (*0-86315-144-2*) Dufour.

Saint Patrick & the Leprechauns: A Riddle Story. (Step into a Story Bk.). 20p. (Orig.). 1996. pap. 3.50 (*1-889238-11-2*) Papa Joes.

Saint Patrick & the Peddler. Margaret Hodges. LC 92-44522. (Illus.). 40p. (J). (gr. k-3). 1993. 16.95 (*0-531-05489-6*) Orchard Bks Watts.

***Saint Patrick & the Peddler.** Margaret Hodges. LC 92-44522. (Illus.). 40p. (J). (gr. k-3). 1997. pap. 6.95 (*0-531-07089-1*) Orchard Bks Watts.

Saint Patrick & the Snakes. Patricia Egan. (Illus.). 28p. (J). (gr. 1-8). 1990. 9.95 (*1-85390-059-1*, Pub. by Veritas Pubns IE) Irish Bks Media.

St. Patrick's. Nancy M. Davis et al. (Davis Teaching Units Ser.: Vol. 1, No. 7). (Illus.). 29p. (Orig.). (J). (ps-4). 1986. pap. 4.95 (*0-937103-08-X*) DaNa Pubns.

St. Patrick's Daughter. Margaret Mulvihill. 252p. 1995. pap. 10.95 (*0-340-59774-7*, Pub. by H & S UK) Trafalgar.

Saint Patrick's Day. Gail Gibbons. (Illus.). (J). (ps-3). 1995. pap. 6.95 (*0-8234-1173-7*) Holiday.

St. Patrick's Day. Joyce K. Kessel. LC 82-1254. (Carolrhoda On My Own Bks.). (Illus.). 48p. (J). (gr. k-3). 1982. pap. 5.95 (*0-87614-482-2*, Carolrhoda); lib. bdg. 17.50 (*0-87614-193-9*, Carolrhoda) Lerner Group.

St. Patrick's Day. Janet Riehecky. LC 93-47640. (Circle the Year with Holidays Ser.). (Illus.). 32p. (J). (ps-2). 1994. pap. 3.95 (*0-516-40696-5*); lib. bdg. 17.50 (*0-516-00696-7*) Childrens.

St. Patrick's Day Shamrock Mystery. Marion M. Markham. LC 94-36716. 48p. (J). (gr. 2-5). 1995. 15.00 (*0-395-72137-7*) HM.

Saint Patrick's Purgatory: A Poem by Marie de France. Tr. by Michael Curley. (Medieval & Renaissance Texts & Studies: Vol. 94). 176p. 1993. 20.00 (*0-86698-108-X*, MR94) MRTS.

***Saint Patrick's World: The Christian Culture of Ireland's Apostolic Age.** Tr. by Liam De Paor. 352p. 1997. pap. 20.00 (*0-268-01757-3*) U of Notre Dame Pr.

Saint Paul. Carlo Cremona. Tr. by Paul Duggan from ITA. 225p. 1995. pap. 14.95 (*0-8198-6974-0*) Pauline Bks.

Saint Paul at the Movies: The Apostle's Dialogue with American Culture. Robert Jewett. LC 93-1315. 192p. (Orig.). 1993. pap. 15.00 (*0-664-25482-9*) Westminster John Knox.

St. Paul from the Trenches. G. Cornish. 1994. 10.95 (*0-933062-31-1*) R H Sommer.

***St. Paul Metro Business Directory 1997-1998.** rev. ed. American Business Directories Staff. 1408p. 1997. boxed 295.00 (*1-56105-984-6*) Am Busn Direct.

***St. Paul the Apostle.** Lawrence G. Lovasik. (Saint Joseph Picture Bks.). (Illus.). 1977. pap. 1.25 (*0-89942-289-6*, 289-00) Catholic Bk Pub.

Saint Paul the Apostle: The Story of the Apostle to the Gentiles. Mary F. Windeatt. LC 93-61076. Orig. Title: The Man on Fire. 231p. (J). (gr. 5-8). 1994. pap. 13.00 (*0-89555-426-7*) TAN Bks Pubs.

St. Paul vs. St. Peter: A Tale of Two Missions. Michael Goulder. LC 94-8767. 176p. (Orig.). 1995. pap. 16.00 (*0-664-25561-2*) Westminster John Knox.

St. Paul's Cathedral: London, 1675-1710: Christopher Wren. Vaughan Hart. (Architecture in Detail Ser.). (Illus.). 60p. (Orig.). (C). 1995. pap. 29.95 (*0-7148-2998-6*, Pub. by Phaidon Press UK) Chronicle Bks.

St. Paul's Theology of Rhetorical Style: An Examination of I Corinthians 2.1-5 - In the Light of First Century Graeco-Roman Rhetorical Culture. Michael A. Bullmore. (Christian Universities Press Ser.). (Orig.). 1995. pap. 49.95 (*1-57309-018-2*); text ed. 69.95 (*1-57309-019-0*) Intl Scholars.

Saint Peter: A Biography. Michael Grant. 224p. 1995. 23.00 (*0-684-19354-X*) S&S Trade.

Saint Peter Canisius. James Brodrick. (Request Reprint Ser.). (Illus.). 1962. 19.95 (*0-8294-0008-7*) Loyola Pr.

Saint Peter Canisius, S. J., 1521-1597. James Brodrick. LC 83-45589. reprint ed. 65.00 (*0-404-19882-1*) AMS Pr.

Saint Peter Related an Incident: Selected Poems. James W. Johnson. LC 92-30139. (Twentieth-Century Classics Ser.). 112p. 1993. pap. 8.95 (*0-14-018684-0*, Penguin Classics) Viking Penguin.

Saint Peter the Apostle. Lawrence G. Lovasik. (Saint Joseph Picture Bks.). (Illus.). pap. text ed. 1.25 (*0-89942-290-X*, 290-00) Catholic Bk Pub.

Saint Peter's Fair. Ellis Peters. 1995. pap. 17.95 (*0-7871-0374-8*, Dove Bks) Dove Audio.

Saint Peter's Wolf. Michael Cadnum. 432p. 1993. mass mkt. 4.99 (*0-8217-4183-7*, Zebra Kensgtn) Kensgtn Pub Corp.

St. Petersburg. Ed. by John Miller & Kirsten Miller. LC 94-34287. (Chronicles Abroad Ser.). 256p. 1995. 13.95 (*0-8118-0879-3*) Chronicle Bks.

***Saint Petersburg.** Parkstone Press Limited Staff. (Great Cities Ser.). 1996. 30.00 (*1-85995-178-3*) Parkstone Pr.

St. Petersburg. Steve Raymer. LC 94-8374. 1994. 39.95 (*1-878685-48-1*) Turner Pub GA.

Saint Petersburg. Solomon Volkov. 1995. 23.99 (*0-02-933431-4*, Free Press) Free Pr.

***St. Petersburg.** Solomon Volkov. 1997. pap. 17.00 (*0-684-83296-8*, Free Press) Free Pr.

St. Petersburg: City Guide. Nicholas Selby. (Illus.). 348p. 1996. pap. 11.95 (*0-86442-326-8*) Lonely Planet.

***St. Petersburg: Once Upon a Time: Memories of Places & People - 1890s to 1990s.** Del Marth & Martha J. Marth. (Illus.). 196p. (Orig.). 1996. pap. 19.95 (*1-885034-08-3*) Suwannee River.

St. Petersburg: Russia's Imperial City. 2nd ed. Marsha Nordbye. 168p. 1995. pap. 15.95 (*0-8442-9956-1*, Passport Bks) NTC Pub Grp.

St. Petersburg: A Cultural History. Solomon Volkov. Tr. by Antonina W. Bouis. (Illus.). 598p. 1995. 30.00 (*0-02-874052-1*) Free Pr.

St. Petersburg Mathematical Society: Proceedings. Ed. by O. A. Ladyzhenskaya. (Translations Ser.: Vol. 159). 225p. 1994. 115.00 (*0-8218-7510-8*, TRANS2/159) Am Math.

St. Petersburg Nights. William C. Douglass. 250p. 1995. 22.50 (*1-885236-06-9*) Second Opinion.

St. Petersburg "Swan" Manuscript. fac. ed. Ed. by Tim Crawford & Francois-Pierre Goy. (Monuments of the Luetnist Art Ser.: Vol. II). 280p. (Orig.). 1994. pap. 98.00 (*0-936186-82-8*, LUTE-2) Edit Orphee.

St. Philip Neri: A Portrait. Louis Bouyer. 94p. 1995. pap. 7.95 (*0-85244-299-8*, Pub. by Gracewing UK) Morehouse Pub.

St. Philip of the Joyous Heart. Francis X. Connolly. LC 92-74761. (Vision Book Ser.). (Illus.). 189p. (J). (gr. 4-9). 1993. pap. 9.95 (*0-89870-431-6*) Ignatius Pr.

***Saint Photios, Patriarch of Constantinople: The St. Photios Shrine Lectures.** LC 92-846. 1992. write for info. (*0-917651-92-8*) Holy Cross Orthodox.

Saint Pius X: The Farm Boy Who Became Pope. Walter Diethelm. LC 93-78530. (Illus.). 163p. (J). (gr. 4-9). 1996. pap. 9.95 (*0-89870-469-3*) Ignatius Pr.

Saint Play in Medieval Europe. Ed. by Clifford Davidson. (Early Drama, Art & Music Monograph: No. 8). 1987. pap. 15.95 (*0-918720-78-8*); boxed 25.95 (*0-918720-77-X*) Medieval Inst.

Saint-Porchaire Ceramics. Ed. by Daphne Barbour & Shelley Sturman. (Studies in the History of Art: No. 52). (Illus.). 162p. 1996. pap. 25.00 (*0-89468-213-X*) Natl Gallery Art.

Saint Raphael Kalinowski: An Introduction to His Life & Spirituality. Szczepan T. Praskiewicz. Tr. by Thomas Coonan & Michael Griffin from ITA. LC 94-29713. Date not set. pap. write for info. (*0-935216-53-7*) ICS Pubns.

Saint Ronan's Well. Walter Scott. Ed. by Mark Weinstein. (Edinburgh Edition of the Waverly Novels Ser.). 508p. 1995. 47.50 (*0-231-10398-0*) Col U Pr.

St. Rose of Lima: The Story of the First Canonized Saint of the Americas. Mary F. Windeatt. LC 93-83096. (Illus.). 132p. (J). 1993. reprint ed. pap. 8.00 (*0-89555-424-0*) TAN Bks Pubs.

Saint-Saens. Arthur Hervey. LC 70-94271. (Select Bibliographies Reprint Ser.). 1977. 21.95 (*0-8369-5045-3*) Ayer.

Saint-Saens. Arthur Hervey. LC 70-109746. 159p. 1970. reprint ed. text ed. 49.75 (*0-8371-4236-9*, HECS, Greenwood Pr) Greenwood.

Saint-Saens. Arthur Hervey. 159p. 1990. reprint ed. lib. bdg. 59.00 (*0-7812-9082-1*) Rprt Serv.

Saint-Saens & the Organ. Rollin Smith. LC 91-11626. (Illus.). 275p. 1993. lib. bdg. 48.00 (*0-945193-14-9*) Pendragon NY.

Saint-Saens, Camille, & Dvorak, Antonin: Great Romantic Cello Concertos in Full Score. Robert A. Schumann. (Music Ser.). 224p. (Orig.). 1983. pap. 8.95 (*0-486-24584-5*) Dover.

Saint Sees It Through. Leslie Charteris. 1976. 23.95 (*0-89190-389-5*) Amereon Ltd.

Saint Shah Waris Ali & Sai Baba. B. K. Narayan. (C). 1995. 14.00 (*0-7069-8755-1*, Pub. by Vikas II) S Asia.

Saint Sharbel. Mary C. Vincent. (Illus.). 80p. (Orig.). 1992. pap. 5.95 (*0-932506-94-1*) St Bedes Pubns.

Saint-Simonian Religion in Germany. E. M. Butler. 1968. reprint ed. 49.50 (*0-86527-177-1*) Fertig.

Saint-Simonism et Pensee Contemporaine see Saint-Simonisme et Pari pour l'Industrie, XIXe et XXe Siecles

Saint-Simonism in the Radicalism of Thomas Carlyle. David B. Cofer. (English Literature Ser.: No. 33). 1970. reprint ed. pap. 39.95 (*0-8383-0017-0*) M S G Haskell Hse.

Saint-Simonisme et Pari pour l'Industrie, XIXe et XXe Siecles, 4 tomes. Ed. by Pierre M. Schuhl & F. Perroux. Incl. Tome I. Theorie et Politique. 8.95 (*0-685-73331-9*); Tome II. Saint-Simonism et Pensee Contemporaine. 8.95 (*0-685-73332-7*); Tome III. Influence a l'Etranger. 8.95 (*0-685-73333-5*); Tome IV. Economie Politique. 8.95 (*0-685-73334-3*); (Cahiers de l'ISEA Ser.). write for info. (*0-318-52254-3*) Fr & Eur.

Saint, Site & Sacred Strategy: Ignatius, Rome, & Jesuit Urbanism. Ed. & Des. by Thomas M. Lucas. (Illus.). 232p. 1992. per., pap. 45.00 (*0-614-16766-3*, SSASS, Jesuit Way) Loyola Pr.

Saint Speaks for Another Saint see St. Joseph Cafasso: Priest of the Gallows

St. Stephen & the Hellenists in the Primitive Church. Marcel Simon. 1958. 59.50 (*0-614-00052-1*) Elliots Bks.

Saint Steps In. Leslie Charteris. 1976. reprint ed. lib. bdg. 21.95 (*0-89190-385-2*, Rivercity Pr) Amereon Ltd.

St. Teresa of Avila: Author of a Heroic Life. Carole Slade. LC 94-28476. (Illus.). 1995. 35.00 (*0-520-08802-6*) U CA Pr.

St. Teresa's Castle of the Soul: A Study of the Interior Castle. Peter Bourne. LC 94-31700. 144p. (C). 1995. 19.95 (*0-930887-19-0*) Wenzel Pr.

St. Thaddeus of Aiken: A Church & Its City. H. Addison McClearen & S. Owen Sheetz. LC 94-7187. (Illus.). 308p. 1994. 37.50 (*0-87152-481-3*) Reprint.

An Asterisk (*) at the beginning of an entry indicates that the title is appearing in BIP for the first time.

St. Therese & the Roses. Helen W. Homan. (Vision Book Ser.). (Illus.). 149p. (Orig.). (J). (gr. 4-9). 1996. pap. 9.95 (0-89870-520-7) Ignatius Pr.

St. Therese of Lisieux: A Life of Sister Therese of the Child Jesus & of the Holy Face. Christine Frost. (Illus.). 121p. (J). (gr. 6-10). 1994. reprint ed. pap. text ed. 5.95 (0-940147-29-7) Source Bks CA.

Saint Therese of the Child Jesus. Jo F. Frazier. (Saints Alive Ser.: Vol. 1). (Illus.). 24p. (Orig.). (J). (gr. 3-6). 1996. pap. text ed. write for info. (0-9650704-0-9) Saints Alive.

Saint Thomas Aquinas. Ralph McInerny. LC 81-16293. 197p. (C). 1982. reprint ed. pap. text ed. 11.50 (0-268-01707-7) U of Notre Dame Pr.

St. Thomas Aquinas: The Story of the Dumb Ox. Mary F. Windeatt. LC 92-82033. (Illus.). 81p. (J). 1993. reprint ed. pap. 6.00 (0-89555-420-8) TAN Bks Pubs.

Saint Thomas Aquinas Vol. 1: The Person & His Work. Jean-Pierre Torrell. Tr. by Robert Royal. 407p. 1996. 39.95 (0-8132-0852-1); pap. 25.95 (0-8132-0853-X) Cath U Pr.

Saint Thomas Aquinas on the Existence of God: The Collected Papers of Joseph Owens. Joseph Owens. Ed. by John R. Catan. LC 79-13885. 291p. 1980. text ed. 64.50 (0-87395-401-7); pap. text ed. 21.95 (0-87395-446-7) State U NY Pr.

St. Thomas Revisited. Stefan W. Swiezawski. Tr. by Theresa Sandok from POL. LC 94-16094. (Catholic Thought from Lublin Ser.: No. 8). 216p. (C). 1995. text ed. 46.95 (0-8204-1844-7) P Lang Pubng.

Saint-Tropez. Goscinny Sempe. (FRE.). 1975. pap. 10.95 (0-8288-3790-2, F70580) Fr & Eur.

Saint Valentine. Robert Sabuda. LC 91-25012. (Illus.). 32p. (J). (gr. 1-4). 1992. lib. bdg. 16.00 (0-689-31762-X, Atheneum Bks Young) S&S Childrens.

Saint-Venant's Problem. D. Iesan. (Lecture Notes in Mathematics Ser.: Vol. 1279). viii, 162p. 1987. 34.95 (0-387-18361-2) Spr-Verlag.

***Saint Veneration among the Jews of Morocco.** Issachar Ben-Ami. LC 97-15878. (Raphael Patai Series of Jewish Folklore & Anthropology). (Illus.). 384p. 1997. text ed. 49.95 (0-8143-2198-4) Wayne St U Pr.

Saint Vincent: A Benedictine Place. Ed. by Campion P. Gavaler. (Illus.). 120p. 1995. 29.95 (1-886565-03-1) St Vincent Spirit.

St. Vincent & the Grenadines. Lesley Sutty. (Illus.). 128p. (Orig.). 1995. pap. 11.95 (0-333-56818-4) Hunter NJ.

St. Vincent de Paul in Seattle - Seventy Five Years. Mary Seling. LC 94-61979. (Illus.). 136p. (Orig.). 1995. pap. 12.95 (1-879243-10-5, Unique Pr) Writers Helpers.

St. Vincent de Paul of Baltimore: The Story of a People & Their Home. Thomas W. Spalding & Katherine M. Kuranda. LC 94-47237. 1995. 24.95 (0-938420-49-6) MD Hist.

Saint Vitus' Dance. Jill Rubalcaba. LC 96-1260. (J). (gr. 4-9). 1996. 13.95 (0-395-72768-5, Clarion Bks) HM.

Saint Vitus Dances Eternity: A Sarajevo Ghost Story. Stewart Von Allmen. (Illus.). 1996. 21.99 (1-56504-947-0, 13404, Borealis) White Wolf.

Saint vs. Scotland Yard. Leslie Charteris. 21.95 (0-89190-390-9) Amereon Ltd.

Saint vs. Scotland Yard. Leslie Charteris. 1993. reprint ed. lib. bdg. 17.95 (1-56849-132-8) Buccaneer Bks.

Saint with a Gun: The Unlawful American Private Eye. William Ruehlman. 172p. (C). 1984. pap. text ed. 11.60 (0-8147-7393-1) NYU Pr.

Sainte Agnes et Poemes Inedits. Paul Claudel. (Illus.). 60.00 (0-686-54433-1) Fr & Eur.

Sainte-Beuve. Harold G. Nicolson. LC 77-20072. (Illus.). 274p. 1978. reprint ed. text ed. 59.75 (0-313-20013-0, NISB, Greenwood Pr) Greenwood.

Sainte-Beuve a l'Academie de Lausanne: Chronique du Cours sur Port-Royal (1837-1838) Bray. 9.95 (0-685-34976-4) Fr & Eur.

Sainte-Carmen of the Main. John Van Burek & Michel Tremblay. (NFS Canada Ser.). pap. 10.95 (0-88922-181-2) Genl Dist Srvs.

Sainte Genevieve. Charles Peguy. pap. 4.50 (0-685-37038-0) Fr & Eur.

Sainte Marguerite de Cortone. Francois Mauriac. pap. 9.95 (0-685-34304-9) Fr & Eur.

***Sainte-Marie among the Hurons.** James W. Nichol. 13.95 (0-88922-147-2, Pub. by Talonbooks CN) Genl Dist Srvs.

***Sainte Marie among the Iroquois: A Living History Museum of the French & the Iroquois at Onondaga in the 17th Century.** (Illus.). 118p. (Orig.). 1995. pap. text ed. 9.95 (0-9653973-0-0) E Metz.

Sainted Dead. Henry Harbaugh. (Notable American Authors Ser.). 1992. reprint ed. lib. bdg. 75.00 (0-7812-3005-5) Rprt Serv.

Sainted Women of the Dark Ages. Ed. by Jo A. McNamara et al. LC 91-24544. 357p. 1992. text ed. 49.95 (0-8223-1200-X); pap. text ed. 19.95 (0-8223-1216-6) Duke.

Sainthood: Its Manifestations in World Religions. Ed. by Richard Kieckhefer & George D. Bond. 275p. 1988. pap. 15.95 (0-520-07189-1) U CA Pr.

***Sainthood in the Later Middle Ages.** Andre Vauchez. Tr. by Jean Birrell. (Illus.). 680p. 1997. text ed. 95.00 (0-521-44559-0) Cambridge U Pr.

Saintly Buccaneer. Gilbert Morris. LC 88-33337. (House of Winslow Ser.: Vol. 5). 304p. (Orig.). 1989. pap. 9.99 (1-55661-048-3) Bethany Hse.

Saintly Companions. Ed. by Vincent J. O'Malley. LC 95-3115. 353p. (Orig.). 1995. pap. 9.95 (0-8189-0693-6) Alba.

***Saintly Death.** Jan A. Sainsbury. 270p. (Orig.). 1997. pap. 10.95 (1-881542-34-3) Book World Inc.

Saintly Scoundrel: The Life & Times of Dr. John Cook Bennett. Andrew F. Smith. LC 96-10147. 1997. 26.95 (0-252-02282-3) U of Ill Pr.

***Saints.** (St. Joseph's Coloring Bks.). (Illus.). 32p. (Orig.). (J). (ps-3). 1985. pap. 0.99 (0-89942-681-6, 681/00) Catholic Bk Pub.

Saints. Orson Scott Card. 720p. 1993. mass mkt. 5.99 (0-8125-3521-9) Tor Bks.

Saints. Alison Jones. (Compact Reference Ser.). (Illus.). 256p. (Orig.). 1992. pap. 9.95 (0-550-17014-6, Chambers LKC) LKC.

Saints: A Book of Days. Metropolitan Museum of Art Staff. (Illus.). 120p. 1995. 14.95 (0-8212-2173-6) Bulfinch Pr.

Saints: A Visual Almanac of the Virtuous, Pure, Praiseworthy, & Good. Tom Morgan. LC 94-7244. 176p. 1994. 16.95 (0-8118-0549-2) Chronicle Bks.

Saints: Poems. Reginald Gibbons. (National Poetry Ser.: 1985). 96p. 1986. 14.95 (0-89255-106-2); pap. 8.95 (0-89255-107-0) Persea Bks.

Saints: Studies in Hagiography. Ed. by Sandro Sticca. LC 95-4768. (Medieval & Renaissance Texts & Studies: Vol. 141). 370p. 1996. 28.00 (0-86698-179-9, MR141) MRTS.

Saints: Visible, Orderly & Catholic: The Congregational Idea of the Church. Alan P. Sell. LC 86-9457. (Princeton Theological Monographs: No. 7). (Orig.). 1986. pap. 12.00 (0-915138-89-1) Pickwick.

Saints: Who They Are & How They Help You. Elizabeth Hallam. 192p. 1994. 22.00 (0-671-88253-8) S&S Trade.

Saints Adrian & Natalie. Nina S. Seco & Anastasia D. Pilutik. (Cloud of Witnesses Ser.). (Illus.). (Orig.). (J). (ps-1). pap. write for info. (0-913026-29-8) St Nectarios.

Saints Alive. James R. Adair. LC 76-117319. (Biography Index Reprint Ser.). 1977. 20.95 (0-8369-8011-5) Ayer.

Saints Alive. Hilda Charlton. Ed. by Golden Quest Staff. (Golden Quest Ser.: Vol. 3). (Illus.). 304p. (Orig.). 1989. pap. 12.95 (0-927383-00-4) Golden Quest.

Saints Alive! Sheilah W. Ling. 240p. (C). 1990. 17.50 (0-85439-367-6, Pub. by St Paul Pubns UK) St Mut.

Saints Alive! A Book of Patron Saints. Enid B. Fisher. 128p. 1996. pap. 8.00 (0-00-627894-9) Harper SF.

Saints Alive: Stories & Activities for Young Children. Gayle Schreiber. LC 95-61491. 72p. (Orig.). (J). 1996. pap. 9.95 (0-89622-675-1) Twenty-Third.

Saints Alive! The Book. Ed. by Hal M. Helms. LC 85-71758. 414p. (Orig.). 1985. pap. 12.95 (0-941478-44-0) Paraclete MA.

Saints among Us. George H. Gallup, Jr. & Timothy Jones. LC 92-12681. 128p. (Orig.). 1992. pap. 8.95 (0-8192-1589-9) Morehouse Pub.

Saints & Angels All Around. Gregory J. Wismar. LC 95-9655. (Winners of the Race Ser.). 160p. 1995. pap. 8.99 (0-570-04816-8, 12-3258) Concordia.

Saints' & Angels' Song. John Fischer. LC 94-25132. 272p. 1995. pap. 8.99 (1-55661-474-8) Bethany Hse.

***Saints & Apostles.** Raymond Storey. LC 93-228338. 1997. pap. text ed. 10.95 (0-88754-514-9, Pub. by Playwrights CN Pr CN) Theatre Comm.

Saints & Feasts. Torkom Koushagian. Ed. by Elise Antreassian. Tr. by Haigazoun Melkonian from ARM. LC 88-18447. (Illus.). (Orig.). 1988. pap. text ed. 8.00 (0-934728-18-6) D O A C.

Saints & Festivals of the Christian Church. H. Pomeroy Brewster. LC 89-43339. (Illus.). 558p. 1990. reprint ed. lib. bdg. 45.00 (1-55888-878-0) Omnigraphics Inc.

Saints & Heroes since the Middle Ages. George Hodges. LC 75-107713. (Essay Index Reprint Ser.). 1977. 23.95 (0-8369-1515-1) Ayer.

Saints & Heroes to the End of the Middle Ages. George Hodges. LC 67-26749. (Essay Index Reprint Ser.). 1977. 23.95 (0-8369-0544-X) Ayer.

Saints & Heroes to the End of the Middle Ages. George Hodges. LC 67-26749. (Essay Index Reprint Ser.). (Illus.). 268p. 1982. reprint ed. lib. bdg. 19.00 (0-8290-0526-9) Irvington.

Saints & Houeholders: A Study of Hindu Ritual & Myth among the Kangra Rajputs. Gabriel Campbell. 1976. 60.00 (0-7855-0321-8, Pub. by Ratna Pustak Bhandar) St Mut.

Saints & Householdes: A Study of Hindu Ritual & Myth among the Kangra Rajputs. Gabriel Campbell. 1976. 75.00 (0-7855-0235-1, Pub. by Ratna Pustak Bhandar) St Mut.

Saints & Householdes: A Study of Hindu Ritual & Myth among the Kangra Rajputs. Ed. by Gabriel Campbell. 175p. (C). 1976. 65.00 (0-89771-121-1, Pub. by Ratna Pustak Bhandar) St Mut.

Saints & Innocents. Barbara Rex. 1972. 6.95 (0-393-08664-X) Norton.

Saints & Martyrs of Ireland. H. Patrick Montague. (Illus.). 138p. 1981. pap. 7.95 (0-86140-107-7, Pub. by Colin Smythe Ltd UK) Dufour.

Saints & Martyrs of Ireland. H. Patrick Montague. (Illus.). 138p. 8100. 18.95 (0-86140-106-9, Pub. by Colin Smythe Ltd UK) Dufour.

Saints & Non-Saints: Some Saintly & Not-So-Saintly Figures from Church History. Christa G. Habegger. 205p. (Orig.). 1987. pap. 11.95 (0-89084-388-0, 031807) Bob Jones Univ Pr.

Saints & Other Powerful Men in the Church. Bob Lord & Penny Lord. (Illus.). 528p. 1990. pap. 14.95 (0-926143-09-3) Journeys Faith.

Saints & Other Powerful Women in the Church. Bob Lord & Penny Lord. (Illus.). 400p. (Orig.). 1989. pap. 12.95 (0-926143-08-5) Journeys Faith.

Saints & Our Children. Mary R. Newland. 215p. 1995. pap. 12.50 (0-89555-517-4) TAN Bks Pubs.

Saints & Politicians: Essays in the Organisation of a Senegalese Peasant Society. Donal B. Cruise O'Brien. LC 74-82221. (African Studies Ser.: No. 15). 221p. reprint ed. pap. 63.00 (0-685-20564-9, 2030612) Bks Demand.

Saints & Postmodernism: Revisioning Moral Philosophy. Edith Wyschogrod. (Religion & Postmodernism Ser.). 326p. 1990. pap. text ed. 18.95 (0-226-92043-7) U Ch Pr.

Saints & Psychopaths. William L. Hamilton. 168p. 1995. pap. 9.95 (0-9644904-0-4) DANA.

Saints & Rebels. Eloise Lownsbery. LC 72-156682. (Essay Index Reprint Ser.). 1977. reprint ed. 24.95 (0-8369-2322-7) Ayer.

Saints & Revolutionaries: The Ascetic Hero in Russian Fiction. Marcia A. Morris. LC 92-279. 256p. (C). 1993. text ed. 64.50 (0-7914-1299-7); pap. text ed. 21.95 (0-7914-1300-4) State U NY Pr.

Saints & Runners: Stories & a Novella. Libby Scheier. 1993. per. 14.50 (1-55128-004-3) LPC InBook.

Saints & Sages of India. G. R. Sholapurkar. (C). 1992. 40.00 (81-217-0049-3, Pub. by Bharatiya Vidya Bhavan II) S Asia.

Saints & Scamps: Ethics in Academia. rev. ed. Steven M. Cahn. 136p. (C). 1993. pap. text ed. 9.95 (0-8226-3028-1) Littlefield.

Saints & Schemers: Opus Dei & Its Paradoxes. Joan Estruch. Tr. by Elizabeth L. Glick. LC 94-37014. 293p. 1995. 30.00 (0-19-508251-6) OUP.

Saints & Scholars. Terry Eagleton. LC 87-14991. 160p. 1987. 14.95 (0-86091-180-2, AO800, Pub. by Verso UK) Routledge Chapman & Hall.

Saints & Scholars: Twenty-Five Medieval Portraits. David Knowles. LC 87-29456. (Illus.). 232p. 1962. reprint ed. text ed. 59.75 (0-313-26219-5, KNSS, Greenwood Pr) Greenwood.

Saints & Scribes: Medieval Hagiography in Its Manuscript Context. Pamela Gehrke. LC 92-27741. (Publications in Modern Philology: Vol. 126). 1993. pap. 24.00 (0-520-09771-8) U CA Pr.

Saints & Shrews: Women & Aging in American Popular Film. Karen M. Stoddard. LC 82-15821. (Contributions in Women's Studies: No. 39). x, 174p. 1983. text ed. 49.95 (0-313-23391-8, STS/, Greenwood Pr) Greenwood.

Saints & Sinners. Lawrence Wright. 1995. pap. 12.00 (0-679-76163-2) Random.

***Saints & Sinners: A History of the Popes.** Eamon Duffy. 1997. 30.00 (0-300-07332-1) Yale U Pr.

Saints & Sinners in the Bible. Frank S. Mead. 256p. 1995. 7.98 (0-8317-6513-5) Smithmark.

Saints & Sisterhood. Eva C. Topping. 1990. pap. 10.95 (0-937032-75-1) Light&Life Pub Co MN.

Saints & Society: The Two Worlds of Western Christendom, 1000 to 1700. Donald Weinstein & Rudolph M. Bell. LC 82-7972. (Illus.). xii, 326p. (C). 1986. pap. text ed. 18.95 (0-226-89056-2) U Ch Pr.

Saints & Strangers. Angela Carter. 128p. 1987. pap. 10.95 (0-14-008973-X, Penguin Bks) Viking Penguin.

Saints & Strangers. George F. Willison. 520p. 1983. reprint ed. pap. 12.50 (0-940160-19-6) Parnassus Imprints.

Saints & the Union: Utah Territory During the Civil War. E. B. Long. LC 80-16775. (Illus.). 326p. 1981. text ed. 27.50 (0-252-00821-9) U of Ill Pr.

Saints & Their Authors: Studies in Medieval Spanish Hagiography in Honor of John K. Walsh. Ed. by Jane E. Connolly et al. xxviii, 216p. (SPA.). 1990. 30.00 (0-940639-61-0) Hispanic Seminary.

Saints & Their Miracles in Late Antique Gaul. Raymond Van Dam. LC 92-40285. (Illus.). 372p. 1993. text ed. 55.00 (0-691-03233-5); pap. text ed. 18.95 (0-691-02112-0) Princeton U Pr.

Saints & Vagabonds: A Charleston Christmas Storybook. Bruce Smith. (Illus.). 120p. (Orig.). (J). (ps up). Date not set. pap. 12.95 (0-9642620-2-9) Marsh Wind Pr.

***Saints & Villians.** Denise Giardina. LC 97-14749. Date not set. 25.00 (0-393-04571-4) Norton.

Saints & Virtues. Ed. by John S. Hawley. LC 86-24993. (Comparative Studies in Religion & Society: Vol. 2). 352p. 1987. pap. 14.00 (0-520-06163-2) U CA Pr.

Saints As Citizens: A Guide to Public Responsibilities for Christians. Timothy R. Sherratt. LC 94-23996. 128p. (Orig.). (gr. 10). 1995. pap. 7.99 (0-8010-8389-3) Baker Bks.

Saints As Models: Preaching & Prayer. rev. ed. David Q. Liptak. 159p. 1990. pap. 8.95 (0-940169-07-X) Liturgical Pubns.

Saints at War. Frank Hammond. 80p. (Orig.). 1986. pap. 5.00 (0-89228-104-9) Impact Christian.

Saints Beyond the White Cliffs: Stories of English Saints. Margaret Gibbs. LC 75-148211. (Biography Index Reprint Ser.). (Illus.). 1977. 23.95 (0-8369-8058-1) Ayer.

Saints Daily Exercise. John Preston. LC 76-57409. (English Experience Ser.: No. 824). 1977. reprint ed. lib. bdg. 60.00 (90-221-0824-4) Walter J Johnson.

Saints de France. Charles Peguy. pap. 1.95 (0-685-37039-9) Fr & Eur.

Saints de Notre Calendrier. Jules Romains. 256p. (FRE.). 1952. pap. 10.95 (0-7859-1404-8, 2080506234) Fr & Eur.

Saints, Demons, & Asses: Southern Preacher Anecdotes. Gary Holloway. LC 88-46036. 136p. 1989. 29.95 (0-253-32841-1); pap. 10.95 (0-253-20528-X, MB-528) Ind U Pr.

Saints' Encouragement to Diligence in Christ's Service. James Janeway. 119p. 1994. reprint ed. 15.95 (1-877611-87-5) Soli Deo Gloria.

Saints Euthymius, Ignatius & Acacius: Holy New Venerable-Martyrs of Athos. Tr. by Isaac E. Lambertsen from RUS. 32p. (Orig.). 1984. pap. 2.50 (0-912927-10-0, X010) St John Kronstadt.

Saints' Everlasting Rest. Richard Baxter. Ed. & Pref. by Timothy K. Beougher. (Collection of Classics Ser.). 71p. (Orig.). 1994. pap. text ed. 1.95 (1-879089-18-1) B Graham Ctr.

Saints for Contemporary Women. Mary H. Valentine. 1988. pap. 12.95 (0-88347-235-X) Res Christian Liv.

Saints for Now. Ed. by Clare Booth Luce. LC 93-78817. 300p. 1993. 12.95 (0-89870-476-6) Ignatius Pr.

Saints for Sinners. Alban Goodier. LC 70-99637. (Essay Index Reprint Ser.). 1977. 20.95 (0-8369-1504-6) Ayer.

Saints for Sinners. Alban Goodier. LC 93-77224. 172p. 1993. reprint ed. pap. 10.95 (0-89870-463-4) Ignatius Pr.

Saints for This Age. A. J. Muste. LC 62-21962. (Orig.). 1962. pap. 3.00 (0-87574-124-X) Pendle Hill.

Saints for Young Christians. David R. Previtali. LC 96-8390. (Illus.). 174p. (Orig.). 1996. pap. 9.95 (0-8189-0666-9) Alba.

Saints for Young Readers for Every Day, No. 1. 2nd ed. Ed. by Susan H. Wallace. LC 94-11927. (J). (gr. 4 up). 1994. Vol. 1. 8.95 (0-8198-6966-X); Vol. 1. pap. 5.95 (0-8198-6967-8) Pauline Bks.

Saints for Young Readers for Every Day, No. 2. 2nd ed. Ed. by Susan H. Wallace. LC 94-11927. (J). (gr. 4 up). 1994. Vol. 2. 8.95 (0-8198-6968-6); Vol. 2. pap. 5.95 (0-8198-6969-4) Pauline Bks.

Saints for Young Readers for Every Day, Set. 2nd ed. Ed. by Susan H. Wallace. LC 94-11927. (J). (gr. 4 up). 1995. 17.90 (0-8198-6970-8); pap. 11.90 (0-8198-6971-6) Pauline Bks.

Saints Galore. large type rev. ed. David L. Veal. 160p. (Orig.). 1990. pap. 5.95 (0-88028-106-5) Forward Movement.

Saints Galore: Character Sketches for the New Calendar of Saints. 3rd ed. David L. Veal. 184p. 1996. pap. 4.95 (0-88028-171-5, 405) Forward Movement.

Saints G'Lore: Our Shining Examples. Graci Dumelle. (Illus.). 32p. (Orig.). (J). (gr. k-6). 1992. pap. 5.95 (0-937739-12-X) Roman IL.

Saints, Goddesses & Kings: Muslims & Christians in South Indian Society, 1700-1900. Susan Bayly. (Cambridge South Asian Studies: No. 43). (Illus.). 520p. (C). 1990. text ed. 89.95 (0-521-37201-1) Cambridge U Pr.

Saints' Happiness: Sermons on the Beatitudes. Jeremiah Burroughs. 264p. 1988. reprint ed. 26.95 (1-877611-00-X) Soli Deo Gloria.

***Saints' Haven.** Dawn A. Poore. 256p. 1997. mass mkt. 4.99 (0-8217-5710-5, Zebra Kensgtn) Kensgtn Pub Corp.

Saints in Action. Dumas Malone. LC 70-142664. (Essay Index Reprint Ser.). 1977. 18.95 (0-8369-2062-7) Ayer.

Saints in Art. M. Tabor. 1972. 59.95 (0-8490-0986-3) Gordon Pr.

***Saints in Exile: A Day-By-Day Pioneer Experience.** David R. Crockett. LC 96-95323. (Pioneer Trek Ser.: Vol. 1). (Illus.). x, 448p. 1996. pap. 25.00 (0-9656108-0-2) LDS-Gems Pr.

Saints in Exile: The Holiness-Pentecostal Experience in African American Religion & Culture. Cheryl J. Sanders. (Illus.). 200p. 1996. 24.95 (0-19-509843-9) OUP.

Saints in Their Ox-Hide Boat. Brendan Galvin. LC 91-35822. 64p. 1992. pap. 7.95 (0-8071-1695-5); text ed. 14.95 (0-8071-1694-7) La State U Pr.

Saints Joke Book. John Deaux. (Illus.). 48p. (Orig.). (J). (gr. 6 up). 1981. pap. 2.95 (0-937552-08-9) Quail Ridge.

Saints, Knights & Llannau. T. Thornley Jones. 79p. (C). 1975. text ed. 35.00 (0-85088-325-3, Pub. by Gomer Pr UK) St Mut.

Saints Knowledge of Christ's Love. John Bunyan. pap. 1.59 (0-87377-985-1) GAM Pubns.

Saints' Legends. G. H. Gerould. 1973. 59.95 (0-8490-0987-1) Gordon Pr.

Saints Names for Boys & Girls. Veritas Publications Staff. 1989. pap. 25.00 (0-86217-249-7, Pub. by Veritas IE) St Mut.

***Saints Names for Your Baby.** Fiona MacMath. 1997. pap. 7.00 (0-551-03025-9, Pub. by Marshall Pickering) Harper SF.

Saints of Anglo-Saxon England. Vladimir A. Moss. (Orig.). pap. write for info. (0-913026-33-6) St Nectarios.

Saints of Anglo-Saxon England, Vol. I. Vladimir A. Moss. LC 92-82557. (Illus.). 112p. (Orig.). 1992. pap. 8.50 (0-913026-32-8) St Nectarios.

Saints of Anglo-Saxon England, Vol. II. Vladimir A. Moss. (Illus.). 128p. (Orig.). 1993. pap. 8.50 (0-913026-34-4) St Nectarios.

Saints of Anglo-Saxon England, Vol. III. Vladimir A. Moss. (Illus.). (Orig.). 1996. pap. 8.50 (0-913026-35-2) St Nectarios.

Saints of Another God. John M. Ball. LC 88-62794. 254p. (Orig.). 1989. pap. 10.99 (0-8100-0304-X, 15N0462) Northwest Pub.

Saints of Chaos. Peter Oliver. LC 67-23255. (Essay Index Reprint Ser.). 1977. 19.95 (0-8369-0752-3) Ayer.

Saints of Cornwall. Catherine R. John. (C). 1989. 78.00 (0-907566-14-6, Pub. by Dyllansow Truran UK) St Mut.

Saints of God Murders. Charles Meyer. 256p. (Orig.). 1995. mass mkt. 5.99 (0-425-14869-6, Prime Crime) Berkley Pub.

Saints of India. Satguru S. Keshavadas. 100p. (Orig.). 1975. pap. 8.00 (0-942508-05-X) Vishwa.

Saints of India. Anna A. Subramanian. (Illus.). 1978. pap. 2.95 (0-87481-479-0, Pub. by Ramakrishna Math II) Vedanta Pr.

Saints of Ireland. Mary R. D'Arcy. 241p. 1985. reprint ed. pap. 9.95 (0-9614900-0-4) Irish Am Cult.

Saints of Qumran: Stories & Essays on Jewish Themes. Rudolf Kayser. Ed. by Harry Zohn. LC 76-20273. 188p. 1977. 24.50 (0-8386-2024-8) Fairleigh Dickinson.

Saints of Sage & Saddle: Folklore among the Mormons. Austin E. Fife & Alta Fife. LC 81-137868. 385p. reprint ed. pap. 109.80 (0-8357-6845-7, 2035540) Bks Demand.

S

Saints of Scotland. Alexander P. Forbes. 1996. pap. 37.50 (0-89979-086-0) British Am Bks.

Saints of Scotland. Ed. by Edwin S. Towill. 258p. (C). 1989. pap. 35.00 (0-685-60674-0, Pub. by St Andrew UK) St Mut.

Saints of Scotland. Edwin S. Towill. 176p. 1993. pap. 24.00 (0-7152-0678-8) St Mut.

Saints of the California Missions. Norman Neuerburg. (Illus.). 48p. (Orig.). 1989. pap. 9.95 (0-88388-139-X) Bellerophon Bks.

Saints of the Eastern Orthodox Church. large type ed. Sabine Baring-Gould. 1994. pap. 5.00 (0-89981-301-1) Eastern Orthodox.

Saints of the Liturgical Year: Brief Biographies. Compiled by Joseph N. Tylenda. LC 89-27518. 200p. (Orig.). 1989. pap. 5.95 (0-87840-498-8) Georgetown U Pr.

Saints of the Roman Calender: Including Feasts Proper to the English-Speaking World. Tr. by Enzo Lodi & Jordan Auman. LC 92-20261. 444p. 1992. pap. 9.95 (0-8189-0652-9) Alba.

***Saints of the Seasons for Children.** Ethel Pochocki. (Illus.). 280p. (J). (gr. k-6). 1997. pap. 15.95 (0-86716-319-4, B3194) St Anthony Mess Pr.

Saints on the Seas: A Maritime History of Morman Migration, 1830-1890. Conway B. Sonne. LC 83-3604. (University of Utah Publications in the American West: No. 17). 230p. reprint ed. pap. 65.60 (0-317-58119-8, 2029672) Bks Demand.

Saints (One) December-May. Judi H. Winkowski. (C). 1990. text ed. 29.00 (0-85439-293-9, Pub. by St Paul Pubns UK) St Mut.

Saints Preserve Us! Everything You Need to Know About Every Saint You'll Ever Need. Sean Kelly & Rosemary Rogers. 1993. pap. 10.00 (0-679-75038-X) Random.

Saints Rest. Thomas Gifford. LC 96-20014. 480p. 1996. 22.95 (0-553-10134-X) Bantam.

***Saints Rest.** Thomas Gifford. 432p. 1997. mass mkt. 6.99 (0-553-57226-1) Bantam.

***Saint's Rest.** Thomas Gifford. 1996. 22.95 (0-614-20647-2, Viking) Viking Penguin.

Saints, Sages, Heroes, & Worthies of the World's Religions - A Dictionary: A Comprehensive Reference Guide to More Than 36,000 Ascetics, Blesseds, Confessors, Exemplars, Founders, Heroes, Martyrs, Masters, Mendicants, Preceptors, Prophets, Reformers, Sages, Saints, Spiritual Leaders, Teachers, Wonder-Workers, & Worthies of the World's Major Living Religions. Ed. by Frank R. Abate & Jacquelyn Goodwin. 1250p. 1998. lib. bdg. 65.00 (1-55888-304-5) Omnigraphics Inc.

Saints, Scholars & Schizophrenics: Mental Illness in Rural Ireland. Nancy Scheper-Hughes. 259p. 1979. pap. 15.95 (0-520-04786-9) U CA Pr.

Saints Show Us Christ: Daily Readings on the Spiritual Life. Rawley Myers. LC 95-75665. 364p. (Orig.). 1996. pap. 14.95 (0-89870-542-8) Ignatius Pr.

Saints, Signs & Symbols. 2nd ed. W. Ellwood Post. LC 62-19257. (Illus.). 96p. 1974. pap. 7.95 (0-8192-1171-0) Morehouse Pub.

Saints, Sinners & Beechers. Lyman B. Stowe. LC 71-117847. (Essay Index Reprint Ser.). 1977. 34.95 (0-8369-1720-0) Ayer.

Saints, Sinners & Comedians. Roger Sharrock. LC 81-40457. 304p. (C). 1984. text ed. 13.00 (0-268-01713-1) U of Notre Dame Pr.

Saints, Sinners & Comedians: The Novels of Graham Greene. Roger Sharrock. 304p. 1994. pap. 21.00 (0-86012-141-0, Pub. by Srch Pr UK) St Mut.

Saints, Sinners & Snake River Secrets: From Memories Recorded in Jessie's Journals. Lillian C. Densley. (Illus.). 136p. (Orig.). 1988. pap. 14.95 (0-9623748-0-6) Snake Riv Secrets.

Saints, Slaves, & Blacks: The Changing Place of Black People Within Mormonism. Newell G. Bringhurst. LC 81-1093. (Contributions to the Study of Religion Ser.: No. 4). (Illus.). 256p. 1981. text ed. 59.95 (0-313-22752-7, BSB/, Greenwood Pr) Greenwood.

Saints Syriaques. Jean-Maurice Fiey. (Studies in Late Antiquity & Early Islam: No. 6). (Illus.). 200p. 1996. 24.95 (0-87850-111-8) Darwin Pr.

Saints That Moved the World: Anthony, Augustine, Francis, Ignatius, Theresa. Rene Fulop-Miller. LC 72-13293. (Essay Index Reprint Ser.). 1977. reprint ed. 40.95 (0-8369-8159-6) Ayer.

Saints' Treasury. Jeremiah Burroughs. Ed. by Don Kistler. 175p. 1991. reprint ed. 15.95 (1-877611-30-1) Soli Deo Gloria.

Saints Who Saw Mary. Raphael Brown. LC 93-61596. Orig. Title: Mary Communes with the Saints. (Illus.). 145p. 1994. pap. 10.00 (0-89555-506-9) TAN Bks Pubs.

***Saints with Sinner's Problems.** T. D. Jakes. (Orig.). 1997. pap. write for info. (1-890521-02-7) Jakes Ent.

Saipan: The Beginning of the End. Carl W. Hoffman. (Elite Unit Ser.). (Illus.). 286p. 1988. reprint ed. 35.00 (0-89839-109-1) Battery Pr.

Saipan: The War Diary of John Ciardi. John Ciardi. LC 87-25564. 155p. 1988. pap. 12.00 (1-55728-018-5) U of Ark Pr.

Saisir le Plan - Scanning the Plan: Old Testament Survey. Kenneth F. McKinley. (Illus.). 210p. (FRE.). 1991. reprint ed. pap. 10.00 (0-9630161-0-5) Bible Study Min.

Saison au Congo. Aime Cesaire. 1975. pap. 10.95 (0-8288-9086-2) Fr & Eur.

Saison en Enfer see Illuminations

Saisons Pascal Collasse see Chefs-d'Oeuvres Classiques de l'Opera Francais

***Sait Faik, a Dot on the Map: Selected Stories & Poems.** rev. ed. Ed. by Talat Halman. LC 95-75323. (Turkish Studies: Vol. 4). 328p. (C). Date not set. pap. text ed. 16.95 (1-878318-08-X) IN Univ Turkish.

Saite & Persian Demotic Cattle Documents: A Study in Legal Forms & Principles in Ancient Egypt. Eugene Cruz-Uribe. (ASP Monographs). 126p. (C). 1985. 24.95 (0-89130-854-7, 31-00-26) Scholars Pr GA.

Saiva Art & Architecture in South India. C. Krishna Murthy. 1985. 48.00 (0-8364-1417-9, Pub. by Sundeep II) S Asia.

Saiva Dharma Sastras: The Book of Discipline of Saiva Siddhanta Church. 7th ed. Satguru S. Subramuniyaswami. 478p. 1996. pap. 24.95 (0-945497-69-5) Himalayan Acad.

Saivagamas: A Study in the Socio-Economic Ideas & Institutions of Kashmir. Vishva N. Drabu. (C). 1990. 52.00 (81-85182-38-8, Pub. by Indus Pub II) S Asia.

Saivism: A Perspective of Grace. S. Arulsamy. 252p. 1988. text ed. 27.50 (81-207-0757-5, Pub. by Sterling Pubs II) Apt Bks.

Saivism & the Phallic World, 2 vols. B. Bhattacharya. (C). 1993. text ed. 110.00 (81-215-0618-2, Pub. by Munshiram Manoharial II) S Asia.

Saivite Hindu Religion: The Master Course Level One. Satguru S. Subramuniyaswami. LC 95-78249. (Illus.). 166p. (ENG, HIN & TAM.). (J). (gr. 1). 1995. 12.95 (0-945497-54-7) Himalayan Acad.

Sajo & Her Beaver People. Grey Owl. 225p. (C). 1988. 50.00 (1-85219-035-3, Pub. by Bishopsgate Pr Ltd UK) St Mut.

Sajo & the Beaver People. Grey Owl. 188p. (YA). (gr. 7-12). 1991. reprint ed. pap. 4.95 (0-7736-7341-5, Pub. by Stoddart Pubng CN) Genl Dist Srvs.

Sakakura Associates. A. Komiyama. (Process Architecture Ser.: No. 110). (Illus.). 155p. 1993. pap. 44.95 (4-89331-110-7, Pub. by Process Archit JA) Bks Nippan.

Sakamoto Ryoma & the Meiji Restoration. Marius B. Jansen. LC 94-39075. 423p. 1995. pap. 17.50 (0-231-10173-2) Col U Pr.

Sake: A Drinker's Guide. Hiroshi Kondo. (Illus.). 128p. 1992. pap. 19.95 (4-7700-1654-9) Kodansha.

Sake Handbook. John Gaunter. (Illus.). 200p. (Orig.). 1996. pap. 10.95 (4-900737-44-5) C E Tuttle.

***Sake Jock.** 80p. 1995. pap. 8.95 (1-56097-188-6) Fantagraph Bks.

Sake (U. S. A.) A Complete Guide to American Sake, Sake Breweries & Homebrewed Sake. Fred Eckhardt. Ed. by Jeff Frane. (Illus.). 208p. (Orig.). 1993. pap. 14.95 (0-9606302-8-7) F Eckhardt.

Sakeema. Jack Cranford. 176p. (Orig.). 1994. pap. 4.95 (1-56167-183-5) Am Literary Pr.

Sakereg Studentehandboek. 2nd ed. N. J. Olivier et al. 355p. 1993. pap. write for info. (0-7021-2938-0, Pub. by Juta SA) Gaunt.

Sakereg Vonnisbundel. H. J. Delport & N. J. Olivier. 752p. 1985. pap. write for info. (0-7021-1559-2, Pub. by Juta SA) Gaunt.

***Sakha (Yakut) Republic: Economy, Industry, Government, Business.** 2nd rev. ed. Russian Information & Business Center, Inc. Staff. (Russian Regional Business Directories Ser.). (Illus.). 200p. 1997. pap. 99.00 (1-57751-367-3) Russ Info & Busn Ctr.

***Sakhalin Oblast: Economy, Industry, Government, Business.** 2nd rev. ed. Russian Information & Business Center, Inc. Staff. (Russian Regional Business Directories Ser.). (Illus.). 200p. 1997. pap. 99.00 (1-57751-411-4) Russ Info & Busn Ctr.

Sakharov Memorial Lectures on Physics: Proceedings of the First International Sakharov Conference on Physics, Vol. 204, Nos. 1 & 2. Ed. by L. V. Keldysh & V. Y. Fainberg. 1075p. (C). 1992. Set. lib. bdg. 295.00 (1-56072-073-5) Nova Sci Pubs.

Sakharov Remembered. Ed. by S. D. Drell et al. 320p. 1991. 29.95 (0-88318-853-8) Am Inst Physics.

Sakharov-Solzhenitsyn Fraud: What's Behind the Hue & Cry for Intellectual Freedom. Gus Hall. 32p. 1973. pap. 0.40 (0-87898-102-0) New Outlook.

***Saki: Great British & Irish Short Stories I.** Illus. by James McConnell. LC 94-75352. (Classic Short Stories Ser.). 80p. 1994. pap. 5.95 (0-7854-0640-9, 40042) Am Guidance.

Sakkara. Noel Barber. 1985. pap. 3.95 (0-380-70091-3) Avon.

Sakkara. Noel Barber. 1985. 18.95 (0-02-506820-2) Macmillan.

Saklatvala, a Political Biography. Judith Squires. (C). 1990. text ed. 39.95 (0-85315-711-1, Pub. by Lawrence & Wishart UK) NYU Pr.

Saksalais-Suomalais-Saksalainen Matkailusanakirja. P. Kostera. 474p. (FIN & GER.). 1982. 79.95 (0-8288-1073-7, F 120120) Fr & Eur.

Sakshi Gopal: A Witness for the Wedding. Illus. by Tom Foley. 16p. (J). (gr. 1-4). 1981. pap. 2.50 (0-89647-036-9) Bala Bks.

***Saktas: An Introductory & Comparative Study.** Ernest A. Payne. LC 97-24965. 1997. pap. write for info. (0-486-29866-3) Dover.

Sakti & Sakta. John Woodroffe. 28.50 (0-89744-116-8) Auromere.

Sakti Iconography. D. R. Rajeshwari. (C). 1988. 65.00 (81-7076-015-1, Pub. by Intellectual II) S Asia.

Sakti Iconography in Tantric Mahavidyas. Sarbeswar Satpathy. (C). 1991. 28.00 (81-85094-44-6, Pub. by Punthi Pus II) S Asia.

Sakti Sadhana: Steps to Samadhi. Tr. by Pandit R. Tigunait from SAN. 196p. (Orig.). 1996. pap. 10.95 (0-89389-140-1) Himalayan Inst.

Sakura: Cherry Blossom Paintings by Yoshiko Ishikawa. Keinosuke Murata et al. LC 92-62884. (Illus.). 104p. 1993. pap. text ed. 21.95 (0-940979-22-5) Natl Museum Women.

Sakya of Buddhist Origins. Rhys Davids. 1972. lib. bdg. 200.00 (0-87968-512-3) Krishna Pr.

Sakya or Buddhist Origins. Caroline A. Davids. 444p. 1931. reprint ed. text ed. 32.50 (0-685-13679-5) Coronet Bks.

Sakyadhita: Daughters of the Buddha. Intro. by Karma L. Tsomo. LC 88-31948. 95p. (Orig.). 1989. pap. 14.95 (0-937938-72-6) Snow Lion Pubns.

Sal A Cantar Jimmy Jo! - Come Sing, Jimmy Joe. Katherine Paterson. 1995. pap. text ed. 8.95 (84-204-4567-3) Santillana.

***Sal Salvador's Single String Studies.** Ed. by Aaron Stang. 180p. 1985. pap. text ed. 16.95 (0-7692-1298-0) Warner Bros.

Sal T. Dog: One Stormy Night at Pickle Light. Fred Clough. (Illus.). 48p. (J). (gr. 1-3). 1990. 12.95 (0-89272-281-9) Down East.

Sal y Entra (Out the Door) Catherine Matthias. LC 81-17060. (Rookie Readers Ser.). (Illus.). 32p. (SPA.). (J). (ps-2). 1989. pap. 3.50 (0-516-53560-9) Childrens.

Sal y Pimienta: A Culinary Education. Francisca M. Schneider. (Illus.). 120p. (Orig.). 1996. pap. 15.00 (0-9614304-3-5) Ariel Bks.

***Sala & the Nkesi.** Sandra Johnston-Smoake. (Illus.). 40p. (Orig.). (J). (gr. 1-3). 1997. pap. 8.99 (1-55237-061-5, Pub. by Comnwlth Pub CN) Partners Pubs Grp.

Sala Family Archives: A Handlist of Medieval & Early Modern Catalonian Charters. Joseph J. Gwara. LC 84-10134. 155p. (Orig.). reprint ed. pap. 44.20 (0-7837-6325-5, 2046040) Bks Demand.

Salaam New York: A Novel. Prem N. Chopra. 160p. (Orig.). (C). 1992. pap. 6.95 (81-207-1397-4, Pub. by Sterling Pubs II) Apt Bks.

Salad. Amy Nathan. LC 84-28519. (Illus.). 120p. (Orig.). 1985. pap. 17.95 (0-87701-348-9) Chronicle Bks.

Salad a Day: Scrumptious Salads for Every Day of the Week. Ruth Moorman & Lalla Williams. (Cookbook Ser.: No. 3). (Illus.). 80p. 1980. pap. 5.95 (0-937552-02-X) Quail Ridge.

Salad Bar Beef. Joel F. Salatin. (Illus.). 368p. (Orig.). 1996. pap. 35.00 (0-9638109-1-X) Polyface.

Salad Bar Recipe Pages: Restaurant, Catering & Food Business Edition. Data Notes Staff. (Illus.). 60p. 1992. ring bd. 29.95 (0-911569-26-X) Prosperity & Profits.

***Salad Book.** Clare Connery. (Illus.). 120p. 10.95 (0-8317-2512-5) Smithmark.

***Salad Chef.** Judith Bosley. (Illus.). 60p. (Orig.). 1993. pap. 8.95 (0-930809-16-5) Kitch Cupbd Cookbks.

Salad Cookbook. 1995. 6.99 (0-88705-849-3) Joshua Morris.

Salad Days: Super Salads & Delicious Dressings. Patricia B. Mitchell. 1993. pap. 4.00 (0-925117-71-4) Mitchells.

Salad Days in Baghdad. Clementina Owles. 130p. 1986. 45.00 (0-7212-0712-X, Pub. by Regency Press UK) St Mut.

***Salad Dressings.** Teresa H. Burns. (Speciality Cookbooks Ser.). 128p. (Orig.). 1997. pap. 6.95 (0-89594-895-8) Crossing Pr.

Salad Dressings! Jane C. Dieckmann. 1987. pap. 8.95 (0-89594-223-2) Crossing Pr.

Salad Garden. Joy Larkcom. 168p. 1990. pap. 19.95 (0-14-025144-8, Viking) Viking Penguin.

Salad Garden: Salads from Seed to Table; A Complete, Illustrated, Year-Round Guide. Joy Larkcom. LC 83-40382. (Home Gardening Book Shelf Ser.). (Illus.). 168p. 1984. pap. 12.95 (0-670-61573-0) Viking Penguin.

Salad Gardens: Gourmet Greens & Beyond. Ed. by Karan D. Cutler & Brooklyn Botanic Garden Staff. (21st-Century Gardening Ser.). (Illus.). 120p. 1995. per., pap. 9.95 (0-945352-89-1) Bklyn Botanic.

Salad Gardens: Simple Secrets for Glorious Gardens-Indoors & Out. Mimi Luebbermann. (Garden Style Ser.). (Illus.). 108p. 1996. pap. 12.95 (0-8118-1062-3) Chronicle Bks.

***Salad Sorcery: Julia Anita's Gourmet Magic.** Julia A. Strimple. (Illus.). 42p. (Orig.). 1996. pap. 12.95 (1-890359-00-9) Gourmet Magic.

***Salad Suppers: Fresh Inspirations for Satisfying One-Dish Meals.** Andrea Chesman. Ed. by Rux Martin. LC 96-37469. (Illus.). 160p. (Orig.). 1997. pap. 12.95 (1-57630-028-5) Chapters Pub.

Saladin. Stanley Lane-Poole. 528p. 1985. 300.00 (1-85077-068-9, Pub. by Darf Pubs Ltd UK) St Mut.

Saladin: And the Fall of the Kingdom of Jerusalem, Vol. 1. Stanley Lane-Poole. 1991. pap. text ed. 15.00 (0-916157-93-8) African Islam Miss Pubns.

Saladin: And the Fall of the Kingdom of Jerusalem, Vol. 2. Stanley Lane-Poole. 1991. pap. text ed. 15.00 (0-916157-94-6) African Islam Miss Pubns.

Saladin: And the Fall of the Kingdom of Jerusalem, Vol. 3. Stanley Lane-Poole. 1991. pap. text ed. 15.00 (0-916157-95-4) African Islam Miss Pubns.

***Saladin: The Politics of the Holy War.** Malcolm C. Lyons & D. E. Jackson. 468p. 1997. pap. text ed. 12.95 (0-521-58562-7) Cambridge U Pr.

Saladin: The Politics of the Holy War. Malcom C. Lyons & D. E. Jackson. LC 79-13078. (Cambridge University Oriental Publicstions: No. 30). (Illus.). 400p. 1985. pap. 26.95 (0-521-31739-8) Cambridge U Pr.

Saladin & the Fall of Jerusalem. Geoffrey B. Regan. 192p. 1988. lib. bdg. 55.00 (0-7099-4208-7, Pub. by Croom Helm UK) Routledge Chapman & Hall.

Saladin & the Fall of the Kingdom of Jerusalem. Stanley Lane-Poole. LC 73-14453. (Heroes of the Nations Ser.). reprint ed. 37.50 (0-404-58270-2) AMS Pr.

Saladin & the Saracens Armies of the Middle East 1100-1300. David Nicolle. (Men-at-Arms Ser.: No. 171). (Illus.). 48p. pap. 11.95 (0-85045-682-7, 9103, Pub. by Osprey UK) Stackpole.

Saladmaker. rev. ed. David McFadden. 1977. reprint ed. pap. 2.00 (0-916696-03-0) Cross Country.

Saladmaster Guide to Healthy & Nutritious Cooking. Brenda J. Shriver. LC 95-34643. 1995. ring bd. 19.95 (1-56530-186-2) Summit TX.

***Salado Platform Mound on Tonto Creek, Roosevelt Platform Mound Study: Report on the Cline Terrace Mound, Cline Terrace Complex.** David Jacobs & Owen Lindauer. LC 96-36976. (Anthropological Field Studies). 1996. write for info. (1-886067-07-4) ASU Office Cultural Res.

***Salads.** (Country Friends Ser.). (Illus.). 31p. pap. 6.95 (1-888052-13-9) Gooseberry Patch.

Salads. Jane Hann. LC 93-49609. (Cooking with Style Ser.). (Illus.). 96p. 1994. 6.99 (1-57145-001-7) Thunder Bay CA.

***Salads.** Sue Mullin. 1996. 12.98 (0-7858-0554-0) Bk Sales Inc.

Salads. Emanuela S. Prinetti. Ed. by Laurie Wertz. LC 92-18191. (Williams-Sonoma Kitchen Library). (Illus.). 108p. 1993. 17.95 (0-7835-0237-0); pap. write for info. (0-7835-0238-9) Time-Life.

Salads. Louise Stoltzfus. LC 94-14903. (Best of Favorite Recipes from Quilters Ser.). (Illus.). 64p. 1994. 7.95 (1-56148-113-0) Good Bks PA.

***Salads.** Time-Life Books Editors. LC 96-34317. (Fanfare Ser.). (Illus.). 60p. 1997. write for info. (0-7835-4871-0) Time-Life.

***Salads.** Time-Life Books Editors. (Fanfare Collection). 1997. 12.95 (0-614-27965-8) Time-Life.

Salads. braille large type ed. pap. 7.00 incl. audio (0-317-01860-4) Cath Guild Blind.

Salads: Cook Books from Amish Kitchens. Phyllis P. Good & Rachel T. Pellman. (From Amish Kitchens Ser.). 32p. 1996. mass mkt. 2.95 (1-56148-195-5) Good Bks PA.

Salads: Salads from A-Z. Virginia Clark & Margaret Clark. (Illus.). 160p. (Orig.). Date not set. pap. 13.00 (1-879415-25-9, Bearly Cooking) Mtn n Air Bks.

Salads - Les Salades. Illus. by Nadine Wickenden. LC 94-14123. (Marie-Pierre Moine's French Kitchen Ser.). (ENG & FRE.). 1994. 14.00 (0-671-89659-8) S&S Trade.

Salads & Dressing: Varied & Delicious. Ed. by G & R Publishing Staff. (Uni-Bks.). 160p. (Orig.). 1994. pap. text ed. 3.00 (1-56383-020-5, 2400) G & R Pub.

Salads & Small Meals. Corinne T. Netzer. (Corinne T. Netzer Good Eating Gourmet Ser.). 1997. mass mkt. 5.99 (0-440-22349-0) Dell.

Salads for All Occasions. Polly Dutery & Joanne Van Roden. 36p. (Orig.). 1992. pap. 3.25 (0-940844-48-6) Wellspring.

Salads for All Seasons. Barbara Gibbons. 1982. 13.95 (0-02-543130-7) Macmillan.

Salads from A to Z, Vol. 3. Frances Levine. 60p. 1996. spiral bd. 14.95 (0-685-24737-6) Indiv Educ Syst.

Salads from A to Z, Vol. 3. Frances Levine. 60p. 1996. spiral bd. 14.95 (0-938911-10-4) Indiv Educ Syst.

Sala'ilua, a Samoan Mystery. Bradd Shore. LC 81-24188. (Illus.). 358p. reprint ed. pap. 102.10 (0-8357-4586-4, 2037517) Bks Demand.

SALALM & the Area Studies Community. Ed. by David Block. xi, 235p. (Orig.). 1994. pap. 45.00 (0-917617-39-8) SALALM.

Salamanca. Tom Burns. (Everything under the Sun Ser.). (Illus.). 176p. 1995. pap. 6.95 (0-8442-9212-5, Passport Bks) NTC Pub Grp.

Salamandastron: A Tale from Redwall. Brian Jacques. 368p. (Orig.). 1994. pap. text ed. 5.99 (0-441-00031-2) Ace Bks.

***Salamandastron: A Tale from Redwall.** Brian Jacques. (Illus.). 400p. (J). 1993. 17.95 (0-399-21992-7, Philomel Bks) Putnam Pub Group.

Salamander. Ed. by Keith Bullen & John Cromer. LC 79-103084. (Granger Index Reprint Ser.). 1977. 19.95 (0-8369-6099-8) Ayer.

Salamander. large type ed. Morris West. 1977. 25.99 (0-85456-559-0) Ulverscroft.

Salamander: Selected Poems of Robert Marteau. Robert Marteau. LC 78-70307. (Lockert Library of Poetry in Translation). 127p. reprint ed. pap. 36.20 (0-8357-7013-3, 2052288) Bks Demand.

Salamander: The Story of the Mormon Forgery Murders. 2nd ed. Linda Sillitoe & Allen Roberts. LC 89-70093. (Illus.). xiii, 571p. 1988. mass mkt. 5.95 (0-941214-87-7) Signature Bks.

Salamander & Other Gothic Tales. Vladimir F. Odoevsky. Ed. & Tr. by Neil Cornwell from RUS. 250p. (Orig.). 1992. pap. 15.95 (0-8101-1062-8) Northwestern U Pr.

Salamander & Other Stories. Masuji Ibuse. Ed. by Shaw. Tr. by John Bester. LC 80-84421. (Japan's Modern Writers Ser.). 134p. (C). 1981. pap. 8.00 (0-87011-458-1) Kodansha.

***Salamander Distro: Hitler's Luftwaffe.** Salamander Press Staff. 1997. 17.99 (0-517-18771-X) Crown Pub Group.

Salamander Room. Anne Mazer. LC 90-33301. (Illus.). 32p. (J). (ps-3). 1991. 17.00 (0-394-82945-X); lib. bdg. 17.99 (0-394-92945-4) Knopf Bks Yng Read.

Salamander Room. Anne Mazer. (Dragonfly Bks.). (Illus.). 32p. (J). (ps-3). 1994. pap. 6.99 (0-679-86187-4) Knopf Bks Yng Read.

Salamanders. Emery Bernhard. LC 94-15306. (Illus.). 32p. (J). (ps-3). 1995. lib. bdg. 15.95 (0-8234-1148-6) Holiday.

Salamanders. James E. Gerholdt. LC 94-18430. (Amazing Amphibians Ser.). (J). 1994. lib. bdg. 14.98 (1-56239-313-8) Abdo & Dghtrs.

Salamanders. Edward J. Maruska. (Nature Bks.). 32p. (J). (gr. 2-6). 1996. lib. bdg. 22.79 (1-56766-273-0) Childs World.

Salamanders. Lynn M. Stone. LC 95-16558. (Creepy Crawlers Ser.). (J). 1995. write for info. (1-55916-164-7) Rourke Bk Co.

Salamanders. Cherie Winner. (J). (gr. 2-5). 1993. pap. 6.95 (0-87614-614-0, Carolrhoda); lib. bdg. 14.96 (0-87614-757-0, Carolrhoda) Lerner Group.

An Asterisk (*) at the beginning of an entry indicates that the title is appearing in BIP for the first time.

Salamanders & Newts. Byron Bjorn. (Illus.). 91p. pap. 8.95 (*0-86622-389-4*, CO-043S) TFH Pubns.

Salamanders & Newts As a Hobby. John Coborn. (Illus.). 96p. 1993. 8.95 (*0-86622-730-X*, TT020) TFH Pubns.

Salamanders & Newts As a New Pet. John Coborn. (Illus.). 64p. 1994. pap. 6.95 (*0-86622-538-2*, TU023) TFH Pubns.

***Salamander's Life.** John Himmelman. LC 97-9128. (Nature Upclose Ser.). (J). 1998. write for info. (*0-516-20820-9*) Childrens.

Salamanders of Ohio. Ed. by Ralph Pfingsten & Floyd L. Downs. LC 85-60845. (Bulletin New Ser.: Vol. 7, No. 2). (Illus.). 300p. (Orig.). 1989. pap. text ed. 30.00 (*0-86727-099-3*) Ohio Bio Survey.

Salamfestschrift: A Collection of Talks from the Conference on Highlights of Particle & Condensed Matter Physics. Ed. by A. Ali et al. (Series in 20th Century Physics: Vol. 4). (Illus.). 628p. 1994. pap. 67.00 (*981-02-1422-7*) World Scientific Pub.

Salammbo. Gustave Flaubert. Ed. by Maynial. (Coll. Prestige). (FRE.). 49.95 (*0-685-34902-0*); pap. 29.95 (*0-685-34901-2*) Fr & Eur.

Salammbo. Gustave Flaubert. (Coll. GF). (FRE.). 1961. pap. 10.95 (*0-8288-9981-9*, F62313) Fr & Eur.

Salammbo. Gustave Flaubert. (Folio Ser.: No. 608). (FRE.). pap. 12.95 (*2-07-036608-1*) Schoenhof.

Salammbo. Alban J. Krailsheimer. (Classics Ser.). 288p. 1977. pap. 9.95 (*0-14-044328-2*, Penguin Classics) Viking Penguin.

Salammbo. unabridged ed. Gustave Flaubert. (FRE.). pap. 7.95 (*2-87714-151-9*, Pub. by Bookking Intl FR) Distribks Inc.

Salamonie Farm. Noah Hershberger. LC 96-2695. (Illus.). 235p. 1996. pap. 12.95 (*1-879863-53-7*) Goosefoot Acres.

Salar the Salmon. Henry Williamson. LC 89-46181. (Illus.). 208p. (Orig.). (YA). (gr. 5 up). 1990. pap. 14.95 (*0-87923-845-3*) Godine.

Salar, Vol. 1: An Angling Guide to Landlocked Salmon. Al Raychard. LC 94-20776. 1994. pap. 14.95 (*0-945980-45-0*) Nrth Country Pr.

Salaried Professional: How to Make the Most of Your Career. Joseph A. Raelin. LC 83-24796. 304p. 1984. text ed. 65.00 (*0-275-91246-9*, C1246, Praeger Pubs) Greenwood.

Salaries & Bonuses in the Service Department - 1994. Ed. by Steven Langer. 74p. 1994. pap. 295.00 (*0-317-55974-5*) Abbott Langer Assocs.

Salaries & Fringe Benefits in Virginia's Cities, Counties & Selected Towns. Ed. by Mary Jo Fields. (Salary Surveys Ser.). 87p. 1985. pap. 15.00 (*0-932993-00-1*) VA Muni League.

Salaries & Fringe Benefits in Virginia's Small Towns. Ed. by Mary Jo Fields. (Salary Surveys Ser.). 1986. pap. 15. 00 (*0-932993-01-X*) VA Muni League.

Salaries & Wages in California Public Schools 1993-94. Education Research Service Staff. 151p. (Orig.). 1994. per. 36.00 (*0-943397-30-8*, 101) Assn Calif Sch Admin.

Salaries & Wages in California Public Schools 1994-95. Education Research Service Staff. 159p. (Orig.). 1995. pap. write for info. (*0-943397-31-6*, 101) Assn Calif Sch Admin.

Salaries & Wages in Michigan Municipalities over 1,000 Population. Michigan Municipal League Staff. (Information Bulletin Ser.: No. 109). 1995. 50.00 (*0-318-19474-0*) MI Municipal.

Salaries in Virginia's Cities & Selected Towns & Counties: 1990 Report. Ed. by Mary J. Fields. (Salary Surveys Ser.). 49p. (Orig.). 1991. pap. 15.00 (*0-932993-04-4*) VA Muni League.

Salaries in Virginia's Small Towns, 1987. Ed. by Mary Jo Fields. (Salary Surveys Ser.). 24p. 1988. pap. 10.00 (*0-932993-03-6*) VA Muni League.

Salaries Nineteen Eighty-Nine. 128p. 1989. pap. 150.00 (*0-8412-1680-0*) Am Chemical.

Salaries of Engineers in Education, 1994. AAES, Engineering Workforce Commission Staff. 175p. (Orig.). 1994. pap. 112.00 (*0-87615-160-8*, 0742-6143) AAES.

Salaries of Engineers in Education 1996. Engineering Workforce Commission Staff. 175p. (Orig.). 1996. pap. 115.00 (*0-87615-150-0*) AAES.

Salaries of Scientists, Engineers & Technicians: A Summary of Salary Surveys. 196p. 1987. pap. 45.00 (*0-317-01570-2*) Comm Prof Sci & Tech.

Salaries Paid Professional Personnel in Public Schools, 1987-88. 127p. 1988. 36.00 (*0-318-37602-4*) Ed Research.

Salary Administration. 4th ed. Gordon McBeath. 192p. 1989. text ed. 49.95 (*0-566-02811-5*, Pub. by Gower UK) Ashgate Pub Co.

Salary Administration Plan. Todd Tatlock & Bruce Harville. (Executive Performance Ser.). 54p. (Orig.). 1993. pap. 79.00 (*1-889394-03-3*) Credit Union Execs.

Salary & Fringe Benefit Study. 60p. 125.00 (*0-318-15775-6*) Natl Kitchen Cabinet.

Salary & Fringe Benefit Survey. Personnel & Professional Concerns Cmte Staff. 1996. 20.00 incl. cd-rom (*0-614-04670-X*) Wisc Lib Assn.

Salary Management for the Nonspecialist. Stanley B. Henrici. LC 80-65877. 253p. reprint ed. pap. 72.20 (*0-317-27190-3*, 2023924) Bks Demand.

Salary of the Khalifah. Abidullah Ghazi. Ed. by Bushra Y. Ghazi & Suhaib H. Ghazi. (Illus.). 16p. (Orig.). (YA). 1993. pap. text ed. 6.00 (*1-56316-370-5*) Iqra Intl Ed Fdtn.

Salary Success: Know What You're Worth & Get It! Ronald L. Krannich. 168p. (Orig.). 1990. 22.95 (*0-942710-34-7*); pap. 11.95 (*0-942710-35-5*) Impact VA.

Salary Survey, 1992. Medical Library Association Staff. 39p. 1992. pap. 52.00 (*0-912176-33-4*) Med Lib Assn.

Salary Systems in Public Higher Education: A Microeconomic Analysis. Marion S. Beaumont. LC 85-5671. 240p. 1985. text ed. 49.95 (*0-275-90059-2*, C0059, Praeger Pubs) Greenwood.

Salaryman in Japan. Ed. by Japan Travel Bureau Staff. (JTB's Illustrated Japan in Your Pocket Ser.: No. 8). (Illus.). 192p. 1986. pap. 17.95 (*4-533-00665-5*, Pub. by Japan Trvl Bur JA) Bks Nippan.

***Salaryman's Wife.** Sujata Massey. mass mkt. 4.99 (*0-06-104443-1*, Harp PBks) HarpC.

Salas & Hille's Calculus: One Variable, Early Transcendentals. 7th ed. Einar Hille & S. L. Salas. LC 95-7224. 831p. 1995. pap. text ed. 67.95 (*0-471-12307-2*) Wiley.

***Salas & Hille's Calculus: One Variable, Early Transcendentals.** 7th ed. Einar Hille & S. L. Salas. 1995. text ed. 129.95 (*0-471-12337-4*) Wiley.

Salas & Hille's Calculus: Several Variables. 7th ed. Einar Hille & S. L. Salas. LC 94-30557. 1258p. 1995. pap. text ed. 62.95 (*0-471-12366-8*) Wiley.

Salas & Hille's Calculus One & Several Variables: One & Several Variables. 7th ed. Garret J. Etgen. 1392p. 1995. text ed. 84.95 (*0-471-58719-2*) Wiley.

Salas & Hilles' Calculus One Variable: One Variable. 7th ed. Garrett Etgen. 880p. 1995. text ed. 70.95 (*0-471-58725-7*) Wiley.

Salat Iz Bulavok. Arkadii Averchenko. LC 82-60958. 230p. (C). 1982. pap. 9.95 (*0-89830-064-9*) Russica Pubs.

Salat ul-Tahajjud. Muhammad Imran. 165p. (Orig.). 1985. pap. 9.50 (*1-56744-377-X*) Kazi Pubns.

Salata Kalman: Dokumentumdrama. Istvan Csicsery-Ronay. LC 84-60250. 91p. (HUN.). 1984. 8.00 (*0-911050-55-8*); pap. 6.00 (*0-911050-54-X*) Occidental.

Salavador in Pictures. Nathan A. Haverstock. (Visual Geography Ser.). (Illus.). 64p. (YA). (gr. 5 up). 1987. lib. bdg. 19.95 (*0-8225-1806-6*, Lerner Publctns) Lerner Group.

Salavin. Georges Duhamel. 144p. (FRE.). 1972. 7.95 (*0-7859-0092-6*, M3393) Fr & Eur.

Salazar. F. C. Egerton. 1974. 59.95 (*0-8490-0988-X*) Gordon Pr.

Salazar's Dictatorship & European Fascism: Problems & Perspectives of Interpretation. Antonio Costa Pinto. (Social Science Monographs). 220p. 1996. 31.00 (*0-88033-968-3*, 382) East Eur Monographs.

Salcombe & River Dart. Imray, Laurie, Norie & Wilson Ltd. Staff. (Illus.). (C). 1990. text ed. 75.00 (*0-685-40211-8*, Pub. by Imray Laurie Norie & Wilson UK) St Mut.

Saldivar Codex No. 4: Santiago de Murcia Manuscript of Baroque Guitar Music. fac. ed. Santiago De Murcia et al. (Saldivar Codex Ser.: Vol. 1). (Illus.). 124p. (Orig.). (C). 1987. pap. text ed. 40.00 (*0-9618527-1-2*) M Lorimer Pubng.

***Saldo a Favor: Conversational Business Spanish.** Vicki Galloway et al. LC 96-44705. 320p. 1997. pap. text ed. write for info. (*0-471-00739-0*) Wiley.

Sale: 25 High Performance Selling Skills. Don Hutson. 369p. 1993. 21.95 (*0-937539-18-X*) Executive Bks.

Sale & Lease in the Louisiana Jurisprudence: A Coursebook. 2nd ed. Saul Litvinoff. LC 86-62791. 730p. 1986. lib. bdg. 38.00 (*0-940448-14-9*) LSU Law Pubns.

Sale & Management of Flats. 2nd ed. Hugh G. Barraclough. 516p. 1994. boxed 121.00 (*0-406-02281-X*, UK) MICHIE.

Sale & Purchase of Real Property in Malaysia. Visu Sinnadurai. 559p. 1984. 110.00 (*0-406-18118-7*) MICHIE.

Sale & Purchase of Restaurants. 2nd ed. John M. Stefanelli. LC 89-28901. (Professional Restauranteur Guides Ser.). 256p. 1990. text ed. 43.95 (*0-471-51209-5*) Wiley.

Sale & Supply of Goods. 2nd ed. Michael Furmston. 202p. 1995. pap. 30.00 (*1-85941-281-5*, Pub. by Cavendish UK) Gaunt.

Sale Catalogues of the Libraries of Samuel Johnson. limited ed. Hester L. Thrale & James Boswell. 320p. 1993. 215.00 (*0-938768-44-1*) Oak Knoll.

Sale el Oso (Big Book) Alma F. Ada. (Rimas y Risas Green Ser.). (Illus.). 16p. (Orig.). (SPA.). (J). (gr. k-3). 1988. pap. text ed. 29.95 (*0-917837-03-7*) Hampton-Brown.

Sale el Oso (Small Book) Alma F. Ada. (Rimas y Risas Green Ser.). (Illus.). 16p. (Orig.). (SPA.). (J). (gr. k-3). 1992. pap. text ed. 6.00 (*1-56334-079-8*) Hampton-Brown.

Sale Is Only the Beginning: Sell More Easily. Ted Spratt. 77p. 1993. pap. 30.00 (*1-85609-056-6*, Pub. by Witherby & Co UK) St Mut.

Sale of a Small Business. William H. Dunn. (Orig.). 1984. suppl. ed. 65.00 (*0-933808-02-X*) Busn Sale Inst.

Sale of Corporate Control. 2nd rev. ed. Colin K. Harley. (Corporate Practice Ser.: No. 19). 1991. ring bd. 92.00 (*1-55871-194-5*) BNA.

Sale of Foreign Bonds or Securities in the United States, 4 vols., Set. 1991. lib. bdg. 750.95 (*0-8490-4496-0*) Gordon Pr.

Sale of Gibraltar in Fourteen Seventy-Four. Diego Lamelas. (C). 1988. pap. text ed. 30.00 (*0-948466-20-0*, Pub. by Gibraltar Bks UK) St Mut.

***Sale of Goods.** 2nd ed. Michael Bridge. 700p. 1997. 155.00 (*0-19-825871-2*) OUP.

Sale of Goods Act, 1930. Praful R. Desai. (C). 1990. 95.00 (*0-89771-233-1*) St Mut.

***Sale of Goods & Consumer Credit in Practice.** (Inns of Court School of Law Ser.). 160p. 1997. pap. 48.00 (*1-85431-611-7*, Pub. by Blackstone Pr UK) Gaunt.

Sale of Goods & Credit. Ed. by P. A. Read. 365p. (C). 1991. 110.00 (*1-85352-907-9*, Pub. by HLT Pubns UK) St Mut.

Sale of Goods & Hire Purchase. 4th ed. Avtar Singh. (C). 1985. 60.00 (*0-685-37441-6*) St Mut.

Sale of Goods Carried by Sea. Charles DeBattista. 450p. 1990. 190.00 (*0-406-11360-2*, U.K.) MICHIE.

***Sale of Land in Queensland.** 4th ed. Bill Duncan & Stephen Jones. 370p. 1996. 110.00 (*0-455-21372-0*, Pub. by Law Bk Co AT); pap. 75.00 (*0-455-21373-9*, Pub. by Law Bk Co AT) Gaunt.

***Sale. Root & Branch of the Sale Tree in America: An Account of Ten Generations.** Dorothy S. Goodman. 144p. 1996. reprint ed. pap. 24.00 (*0-8328-5248-1*); reprint ed. lib. bdg. 34.00 (*0-8328-5247-3*) Higginson Bk Co.

Saleable Livestock Receipts. Everett A. Blackman. 88p. (C). lib. bdg. 10.95 (*0-9622469-6-4*) Norcor Enterprises.

Salekov Kill. Guy Richards. 256p. (Orig.). 1981. mass mkt. 2.50 (*0-449-14405-4*, GM) Fawcett.

***Salem.** Lorraine Zenka. 1998. pap. 24.95 (*0-525-94302-1*) NAL-Dutton.

Salem: Maritime Salem in the Age of Sail. LC 85-21545. (National Park Service Handbook Ser.: No. 126). (Illus.). 159p. 1987. pap. 5.00 (*0-16-003537-6*, 024-005-01014-9) USGPO.

***Salem: Maritime Salem in the Age of Sail.** 1997. lib. bdg. 250.95 (*0-8490-8170-X*) Gordon Pr.

Salem Church Embattled. Ralph Happel. (Illus.). 62p. 1980. pap. 4.75 (*0-915992-15-9*) Eastern Acorn.

Salem County Wills Recorded in the Office of the Surrogate at Salem, 1804-1830. Contrib. by H. Stanley Craig. 214p. 1995. reprint ed. pap. 21.00 (*0-8328-4706-2*) Higginson Bk Co.

Salem Days, Life in a Colonial Seaport. James E. Knight. LC 81-23076. (Illus.). 32p. (J). (gr. 5-9). 1982. pap. text ed. 3.50 (*0-89375-733-0*) Troll Communs.

Salem Electric Against the Odds! John R. Ross. (Illus.). 121p. (Orig.). 1991. pap. text ed. 12.95 (*0-945490-02-X*) Carolina Pacific.

Salem Evangelical Lutheran Church, Killinger, Upper Paxton Township, Dauphin County, PA, 1770-1859. Schuylkill Roots. 57p. 1996. pap. 6.00 (*1-55856-215-X*) Closson Pr.

Salem Fire. Arthur B. Jones. (Illus.). 137p. 1989. reprint ed. lib. bdg. 24.95 (*0-8328-1396-6*) Higginson Bk Co.

Salem in the Eighteenth Century. James D. Phillips. LC 37-36381. (Illus.). 533p. 1969. reprint ed. 30.00 (*0-88389-017-8*, Essx Institute) Peabody Essex Mus.

Salem Interiors: Two Centuries of New England Taste & Decoration. Samuel Chamberlain. (Illus.). 180p. 1995. 42.50 (*0-942655-34-6*) Archit CT.

Salem Is My Dwelling Place: A Life of Nathaniel Hawthorne. Edwin H. Miller. LC 91-14543. (Illus.). 648p. 1991. 37.95 (*0-87745-332-2*) U of Iowa Pr.

Salem Is My Dwelling Place: A Life of Nathaniel Hawthorne. Edwin H. Miller. LC 91-14543. (Illus.). 648p. 1991. reprint ed. pap. 18.95 (*0-87745-381-0*) U of Iowa Pr.

Salem Kirban Reference Bible. deluxe ed. (Illus.). 1979. 69. 95 (*0-912582-31-6*) Kirban.

Salem Kittredge, & Other Stories. Bliss Perry. LC 71-133165. (Short Story Index Reprint Ser.). 1977. 19.95 (*0-8369-3689-2*) Ayer.

Salem Light Guard. Lester L. Kempfer. LC 73-76068. (Illus.). 128p. 1973. 5.95 (*0-686-04916-0*); pap. 3.95 (*0-686-04917-9*) L Kempfer.

Salem, MA. Ken Turino. (Images of America Ser.). 128p. 1996. pap. 16.99 (*0-7524-0404-0*, Arcdia) Chalford.

***Salem, MA, Vol. II.** Ken Turino. (Images of America Ser.). 1997. pap. 16.99 (*0-7524-0581-0*, Arcdia) Chalford.

Salem, Massachusetts. Deborah Kent. LC 95-13276. (Places in American History Ser.). (Illus.). 63p. (YA). (gr. 4 up). 1995. pap. 7.95 (*0-382-39174-8*, Dillon Silver Burdett); lib. bdg. 14.95 (*0-87518-648-3*, Dillon Silver Burdett) Silver Burdett Pr.

Salem, Massachusetts, 1626-1683: A Covenant Community. Richard P. Gildrie. LC 74-20841. 199p. reprint ed. pap. 56.80 (*0-317-58137-6*, 2029686) Bks Demand.

Salem, NH. K. Khalife. (Images of America Ser.). 1996. pap. 16.99 (*0-7524-0438-5*, Arcdia); pap. 16.99 (*0-7524-0420-2*, Arcdia) Chalford.

Salem-Peoria, Eighteen Eighty-Three to Nineteen Eighty-Two. David R. Pichaske. (Illus.). 256p. (Orig.). 1982. pap. 6.95 (*0-933180-40-3*) Ellis Pr.

Salem Possessed: The Social Origins of Witchcraft. Paul Boyer & Stephen Nissenbaum. LC 73-84399. 320p. 1976. pap. 12.95 (*0-674-78526-6*) HUP.

Salem Remembered - a Picture Scrapbook. Dale E. Shaffer. (Illus.). 234p. (Orig.). 1991. pap. 15.00 (*0-915060-27-2*) D E Shaffer.

Salem Stories: A Backward Glance. Dale E. Shaffer. (Illus.). 294p. (Orig.). 1993. pap. 18.00 (*0-915060-29-9*) D E Shaffer.

Salem Story: Reading the Witch Trials of 1692. Bernard Rosenthal. (Studies in American Literature & Culture: No. 73). 297p. (C). 1993. 52.95 (*0-521-44061-0*) Cambridge U Pr.

Salem Story: Reading the Witch Trials of 1692. Bernard Rosenthal. (Studies in American Literature & Culture: No. 73). 288p. (C). 1995. pap. text ed. 17.95 (*0-521-55820-4*) Cambridge U Pr.

Salem Street. large type ed. Anna Jacobs. (Magna Large Print Ser.). 545p. 1996. 25.99 (*0-7505-0912-0*, Pub. by Magna Print Bks UK) Ulverscroft.

Salem to Moscow: An Actor's Odyssey. Brian Cox. (Illus.). 181p. (C). 1991. 34.95 (*0-413-62820-5*, A0545, Pub. by Methuen UK); pap. 17.95 (*0-413-66450-3*, A0644, Pub. by Methuen UK) Heinemann.

Salem, Transcendentalism, & Hawthorne. Alfred F. Rosa. LC 77-89784. 108p. 1978. 28.50 (*0-8386-2159-7*) Fairleigh Dickinson.

Salem Vessels & Their Voyages Vol. 2: A History of the "George", "Glide", "Taria Topan" & "St. Paul" in Trade with Calcutta, East Coast of Africa, Madagascar & the Phillippine Islands. George G. Putnam. LC 30-1353. 1925. Vol. 2. 19.95 (*0-88389-106-9*) Peabody Essex Mus.

Salem Vessels & Their Voyages Vol. 4: A History of the European, African, Australian & South Pacific Islands Trade As Carried on by Salem Merchants, Particularly the Firm of N. L. Rogers & Brothers. George G. Putnam. LC 30-1353. 1925. 19.95 (*0-88389-108-5*) Peabody Essex Mus.

Salem-Village Witchcraft: A Documentary Record of Local Conflict in Colonial New England. rev. ed. Ed. by Paul Boyer & Stephen Nissenbaum. 416p. 1993. text ed. 45. 00 (*1-55553-164-4*); pap. text ed. 16.95 (*1-55553-165-2*) NE U Pr.

Salem Witch Crisis. Larry Gragg. LC 91-47099. 248p. 1992. text ed. 49.95 (*0-275-94189-2*, C4189, Praeger Pubs) Greenwood.

Salem Witch Hunt: A One Act Play. Hilary Weisman. (Illus.). 15p. (Orig.). (J). (gr. 5-9). 1992. wbk. ed., pap. 10.00 (*1-878668-16-1*) Disc Enter Ltd.

Salem Witch Trials. Earle Rice, Jr. (Famous Trials Ser.). (Illus.). 1996. lib. bdg. 17.96 (*1-56006-272-X*) Lucent Bks.

Salem Witch Trials. Lori L Wilson. LC 96-21371. (How History is Invented Ser.). (J). 1996. lib. bdg. write for info. (*0-8225-4889-5*, Carolrhoda) Lerner Group.

Salem Witchcraft, 2 vols. Charles W. Upham. (Illus.). 1991. reprint ed. lib. bdg. 79.50 (*0-8328-6577-X*) Higginson Bk Co.

Salem Witchcraft, Vol. 1. Charles W. Upham. (Illus.). 468p. 1991. reprint ed. write for info. (*0-8328-2229-9*) Higginson Bk Co.

Salem Witchcraft, Vol. 2. Charles W. Upham. (Illus.). 552p. 1991. reprint ed. Vol 2, 552p. write for info. (*0-318-68827-1*) Higginson Bk Co.

Salem Witchcraft & Hawthorne's "House of the Seven Gables" Enders A. Robinson. (Illus.). 388p. (Orig.). 1992. pap. 29.50 (*1-55613-515-7*) Heritage Bk.

Salem Witchcraft Papers: Verbatim Transcripts, 3 vols., Set. Ed. by Paul Boyer & Stephen Nissenbaum. (Civil Liberties in American History Ser.). 1977. lib. bdg. 145. 00 (*0-306-70655-5*) Da Capo.

Salem Witchcraft Trials. Katherine W. Richardson. LC 83-81118. (Illus.). 28p. (Orig.). 1988. pap. 5.95 (*0-88389-089-5*, Essx Institute) Peabody Essex Mus.

Salem Witchcraft Trials. Karen Zeinert. LC 88-38941. (Illus.). 128p. 1989. lib. bdg. 22.00 (*0-531-10673-X*) Watts.

***Salem Witchcraft Trials: A Legal History.** Peter C. Hoffer. LC 97-19986. 160p. 1997. 25.00 (*0-7006-0858-3*) U Pr of KS.

***Salem Witchcraft Trials: A Legal History.** Peter C. Hoffer. LC 97-19986. 160p. 1997. pap. 10.95 (*0-7006-0859-1*) U Pr of KS.

***Salem World of Nathaniel Hawthorne.** Margaret B. Moore. 1997. 37.50 (*0-8262-1149-6*) U of Mo Pr.

***Saleman's Little Book of Wisdom.** Scott Power. LC 96-29839. (Little Books of Wisdom). 160p. (Orig.). 1997. pap. 5.95 (*1-57034-061-7*) ICS Bks.

***Salem's Guide to Life with Sabrina the Teenage Witch: A Spellbinding Trivia Book with Stickers.** Kitty Richards. (J). 1997. pap. text ed. 6.99 (*0-689-81745-2*) S&S Childrens.

Salem's Lot. Stephen King. LC 73-22804. 464p. 1990. 25.00 (*0-385-00751-5*) Doubleday.

Salem's Lot. large type ed. Stephen King. LC 93-30431. 1994. lib. bdg. 23.95 (*0-8161-5686-7*, GK Hall) Thorndike Pr.

Salem's Lot. Stephen King. (Illus.). 448p. (YA). (gr. 10). 1976. reprint ed. pap. 6.99 (*0-451-16808-9*, Sig) NAL-Dutton.

Saleratus & Sagebrush: The Oregon Trail Through Wyoming. 2nd ed. Robert L. Munkres. (Illus.). 156p. 1974. reprint ed. pap. 3.50 (*0-943398-02-9*) Wyoming St Mus.

Salerno - American Operations from the Beaches to the Volturno, 9 Sept.-6 Oct. 1943. (Illus.). 106p. 1990. reprint ed. per. 4.00 (*0-16-001998-2*, 008-029-00196-9) USGPO.

Salerno Ivories: Ars Sacra from Medieval Amalfi. Robert P. Bergman. LC 79-22616. (Illus.). 268p. 1981. 50.00 (*0-674-78528-2*) HUP.

Salerton Trilogy. Robertson Davies. 1990. pap. write for info. (*0-318-66792-4*, Penguin Bks) Viking Penguin.

Sales. James Brescoll. (Opportunities in...Ser.). 128p. 1993. pap. 7.95 (*0-8442-8688-5*, VGM Career Bks) NTC Pub Grp.

Sales. Robert L. Jordan & William D. Warren. (University Casebook Ser.). 1992. text ed. 36.00 (*0-88277-987-7*) Foundation Pr.

Sales: Suitable for Use with Benfield. Richard G. Bell. (Cambridge Ser.). 221p. 1986. pap. text ed. 14.00 (*0-685-54306-4*, Chicago Law Bk) Cambridge Law.

Sales: Suitable for Use with Whaley. Richard G. Bell. (Cambridge Ser.). 241p. 1990. pap. text ed. 14.50 (*0-685-54298-X*, Chicago Law Bk) Cambridge Law.

Sales: Teacher's Manual for Cases & Materials On. 3rd ed. Marion W. Benfield, Jr. & William D. Hawkland. (University Casebook Ser.). 103p. (C). 1992. pap. text ed. write for info. (*1-56662-028-7*) Foundation Pr.

Sales: Teaching Materials. 5th ed. Richard E. Speidel et al. (American Casebook Ser.). 1188p. 1993. text ed. 36.00 (*0-314-03510-9*) West Pub.

Sales: UCC Article 2. 2nd ed. Kimm Walton. (Law in a Flash Ser.). 295p. 1994. 16.95 (*1-56542-566-9*) E Pub Corp.

S

Sales Agency - A Comparative Analysis: A Survey of BOC Sales Agency Programs for Network Sales. Mary I. Bradshaw. 94p. 1992. pap. 253.00 (*0-940919-33-8*, 235) MultiMedia Telecomm.

Sales Alive! The "How to" Book of the Industry. Arthur Heal. (Illus.). xii, 140p. (Orig.). 1991. pap. 14.95 (*0-939923-14-9*) M & W Pub Co.

Sales & Bulk Transfers under the Uniform Commercial Code, 2 vols., Vol. 3 & 3a. Richard W. Duesenberg & Lawrence P. King. 1966. Updates. ring bd. write for info. (*0-8205-1612-0*) Bender.

Sales & Consumer Law in Australia & New Zealand. 4th ed. Kenneth C. Sutton. 1995. 125.00 (*0-455-21297-X*, Pub. by Law Bk Co AT) Gaunt.

Sales & Consumer Law in Australia & New Zealand. 4th ed. Kenneth C. Sutton. 660p. 1995. pap. 95.00 (*0-455-21298-8*, Pub. by Law Bk Co AT) Gaunt.

Sales & Credit Transactions Handbook. Tang T. Trai Le & Edward J. Murphy. 784p. 1985. text ed. 95.00 (*0-07-044069-7*) Shepards.

Sales & Distribution Guide to Thailand. P. Renard et al. (Southeast Asian Business Guides Ser.: No. 2). 144p. 1988. text ed. 59.00 (*0-08-035838-1*, Pub. by Pergamon Repr UK) Franklin.

Sales & Distribution Practices of Independent Presses, 1989-1990. Laing Research Services Staff. 56p. 1990. 45.00 (*0-938106-12-0*) Laing Res Servs.

Sales & Leases. Brook. 1994. 25.95 (*0-316-10985-1*) Little.

Sales & Leases: Problems & Materials on National & International Transactions. John E. Murray, Jr. & Harry M. Fletcher. LC 93-11497. (American Casebook Ser.). 399p. 1994. pap. text ed. 30.00 (*0-314-02457-3*) West Pub.

Sales & Leases: Problems & Materials on National & International Transactions. John E. Murray & Harry M. Flechtner. (American Casebook Ser.). 255p. 1994. pap. text ed. write for info. (*0-314-03487-0*) West Pub.

Sales & Leases in California Commercial Law Practice, Set, Vols. 1 & 2. Ed. by David L. Wold et al. LC 93-70675. 1072p. 1993. 195.00 (*0-88124-609-3*, BU-32070) Cont Ed Bar-CA.

Sales & Leases of Goods. Richard E. Speidel & Alfred W. Meyer. (Black Letter Ser.). 317p. (C). 1993. pap. text ed. 24.50 (*0-314-01068-8*) West Pub.

Sales & Leases of Goods in a Nutshell. 3rd ed. John M. Stockton & Frederick H. Miller. LC 92-5654. (Nutshell Ser.). 441p. 1992. pap. text ed. 16.00 (*0-314-00660-5*) West Pub.

Sales & Marketing. Generation X Staff. (First Books for Business Ser.). (Illus.). 128p. 1996. pap. text ed. 12.00 (*0-07-001568-6*) McGraw.

Sales & Marketing see Radio Book

Sales & Marketing Catalog No. 90002: Two Hundred Seventy-Nine Marketing Improvement Ideas. Laddie F. Hutar. (OnePage Way Ser.). 16p. 1995. pap. text ed. 10.00 (*0-918896-93-2*) Hutar.

***Sales & Marketing Checklist.** Jan Mitchell. LC 97-16957. 1997. write for info. (*0-86718-435-3*) Home Builder.

Sales & Marketing for the Travel Professional. Dennis L. Foster. 1990. 33.50 (*0-02-680867-6*) Macmillan.

Sales & Marketing for Travel & Tourism. Philip G. Davidoff & Doris S. Davidoff. (Illus.). 296p. 1983. pap. text ed. 19.75 (*0-935920-09-9*, Ntl Pubs Blck) P-H.

Sales & Marketing for Travel & Tourism. 2nd ed. Philip G. Davidoff & Doris S. Davidoff. LC 93-17461. 304p. 1994. pap. text ed. 46.00 (*0-13-786518-X*) P-H.

Sales & Marketing Tips. Ed. by Donald R. Taylor. (Orig.). 1993. pap. 3.95 (*0-9637314-0-8*) Quick Study.

Sales & Sales Financing Law: Cases & Materials. 5th ed. John O. Honnold. LC 84-13778. (University Casebook Ser.). 856p. 1991. reprint ed. text ed. 29.00 (*0-88277-189-2*) Foundation Pr.

***Sales & Sales Management.** Chris Horsman. (Marketing in Action Ser.). 1997. pap. 19.95 (*0-7494-1992-X*) Kogan Page Ltd.

Sales & Sales Management. Ralph W. Jackson & Robert D. Hisrich. LC 95-36814. 1995. text ed. 70.00 (*0-13-606161-3*) P-H.

Sales & Secured Financing, Manual for Teachers to Accompany Cases, Problems & Materials On. 6th ed. John O. Honnold et al. (University Casebook Ser.). 304p. 1993. pap. text ed. write for info. (*1-56662-125-9*) Foundation Pr.

Sales & Secured Transactions: Adaptable to Courses Utilizing Speidel, Summers & White's Casebook on Sales & Secured Transactions, Including the Companion Book on Payment Law. Casenotes Publishing Co., Inc. Staff et al. (Orig.). 1994. pap. text ed. write for info. (*0-318-72701-3*, 1310) Casenotes Pub.

Sales & Secured Transactions: Teaching Materials. 5th ed. Richard E. Speidel & Robert S. Summers. Ed. by James J. White. (American Casebook Ser.). 1191p. 1993. text ed. 50.50 (*0-314-02344-5*) West Pub.

Sales & Secured Transactions Teaching Materials: Teacher's Edition. 5th ed. Richard E. Speidel et al. (American Casebook Ser.). 170p. 1993. pap. text ed. write for info. (*0-314-03250-9*) West Pub.

Sales & Use Taxation of Computer Software: A State-by-State Guide (1995-1996 Edition) 4th ed. Ed. by Kutish Publications Staff. LC 95-76467. 400p. 1995. 450.00 (*1-880815-07-9*) Sftware Taxation.

***Sales & Use Taxation of Computer Software: A State-by-State Guide, 1996-97 Edition.** L. J. Kutten. LC 96-69567. 450p. Date not set. 450.00 (*1-880815-11-7*) Sftware Taxation.

Sales Artillery: How to Arm the Sales Force for Successful Selling. Gene Plotnik. 240p. 1989. pap. 16.95 (*0-13-786575-9*, Busn) P-H.

Sales Associate Book, Version 3: How to Use the PC in Sales. rev. ed. Joseph M. Cerra. (Illus.). 250p. 1994. spiral bd. 29.95 incl. disk (*0-927701-04-9*) Evergreen Ventures.

Sales Automation Software Compendium. Richard N. Bohn. 330p. (Orig.). 1995. pap. text ed. 97.00 (*1-885413-00-9*) Denali Grp.

Sales Automation Suppliers Directory 1996 Edition. Paul H. Selden. 476p. 1991. 129.00 (*0-9629991-5-6*) Sales Automtn Assn.

Sales Bible: The Ultimate Sales Resource. Jeffery H. Gitomer. LC 93-46305. 1994. 30.00 (*0-688-13364-9*) Morrow.

Sales Casenote Law Outlines. Robert E. Scott & Don B. King. Ed. by Peter Tenen et al. (Law Outlines Ser.). (Orig.). (C). 1992. pap. text ed. write for info. (*0-87457-187-1*, 5700) Casenotes Pub.

Sales, Cases & Materials On. 3rd ed. Marion W. Benfield, Jr. & William D. Hawkland. (University Casebook Ser.). 605p. 1992. text ed. 36.00 (*0-88277-975-3*) Foundation Pr.

***Sales Chameleon: Turning Green Prospects into Gold Customers.** 2nd rev. ed. 211p. 1996. 19.95 (*0-9653631-0-4*) J Hoops.

Sales Closing Book. Gerhard Gschwandtner. LC 88-90648. (Illus.). 145p. 1988. text ed. 99.00 (*0-939613-02-6*) Personal Selling.

Sales Closing Power. J. Douglas Edwards. LC 87-81171. 240p. 1987. reprint ed. pap. 19.95 (*0-942645-02-2*); reprint ed. audio 99.95 (*0-942645-03-0*) Hampton Hse Pub.

Sales Coaching: Making the Great Leap From Sales Manager to Sales Coach. Linda Richardson. 180p. 1996. text ed. 19.95 (*0-07-052382-7*) McGraw.

Sales Compensation & Performance, 1995: A Comprehensive Benchmark Study of Industry. William P. Kennan. 1994. 50.00 (*1-55738-833-4*) Irwin Prof Pubng.

Sales Compensation Handbook. John K. Moynahan. 400p. 1991. 69.95 (*0-8144-0110-4*) AMACOM.

***Sales Compensation in the Printing Industries.** 1996. 155.00 (*0-318-02608-2*) Print Indus Am.

Sales Connection: Selling. 6th ed. Manning. 1995. student ed., pap. text ed. 35.60 (*0-13-185422-4*) P-H.

Sales Cybernetics: New Scientific Techniques in Motivational Selling. Brian Adams. 1985. pap. 10.00 (*0-87980-412-2*) Wilshire.

Sales Department Gross Margin Based Compensation System: A Blue Print to Profit Base, an Equipment Dealership Sales Team. James P. Beal. Ed. by Lenore A. Beal. 25p. 1996. wbk. ed. 200.00 (*0-9634476-3-7*) Taking Care Of Busn.

***Sales Dragon: The Ancient Secrets of Sales Greatness.** John Scevola. LC 97-8557. (Illus.). 256p. (Orig.). 1997. pap. 14.95 (*0-8119-0860-7*) LIFETIME.

Sales Driven: Turning Your Company into a Marketing Machine. Jack L. Matthews. 250p. 1992. text ed. 24.95 (*1-55738-417-7*) Irwin Prof Pubng.

Sales-Driven Company: Transforming Your Company--from the Mail Room to the Board Room--into a Marketing Machine. Jack L. Matthews. 275p. 1995. per. 19.95 (*1-55738-894-6*) Irwin Prof Pubng.

Sales Effectiveness Training: The Breakthrough Method to Become Partners with Your Customers. Thomas Gordon & Carl D. Zaiss. 256p. 1995. pap. 11.95 (*0-452-27241-6*, Plume) NAL-Dutton.

Sales Engineering. Hugh N. Roser. (Instructional Resource Package Ser.). 140p. 1983. reprint ed. student ed., pap. 39.90 (*0-608-01352-8*, 2062092) Bks Demand.

Sales Esteem: The Inner Source of Sales Power. Marc Ferguson. Ed. by William Karneges. (Illus.). 349p. 1995. pap. 18.95 (*0-614-06063-X*) Pax Pub.

Sales Esteem: The Inner Source of Sales Power. Marc Ferguson. 1995. pap. 18.95 (*0-9614914-8-5*) Pax Pub.

Sales-Fax Travel Directory: Your Passport to Advertising Decision Makers. 200p. 1995. 950.00 (*0-9649670-0-6*, Sales-Fax) Ad-Fax Media.

Sales-Fax Travel Directory: Your Passport to Advertising Decision Makers. rev. ed. Ed. by Larry Ross & Gloria Wood. 200p. 1996. 950.00 (*0-9649670-1-4*) Ad-Fax Media.

Sales Finance Companies & Their Credit Practices. Wilbur C. Plummer & Ralph A. Young. (Financial Research Program II: Studies in Consumer Installment Financing: No. 2). 324p. 1940. reprint ed. 84.30 (*0-87014-461-8*); reprint ed. mic. film 42.20 (*0-685-61208-2*) Natl Bur Econ Res.

Sales Force: A Sales Management Simulation. Wesley E. Patton. 110p. (C). 1994. pap. 25.95 (*0-256-15009-5*) Irwin.

Sales Force Automation: Using the Latest Technology to Make Your Sales Force More Competitive. George W. Colombo. 1993. text ed. 27.95 (*0-07-011840-X*) McGraw.

Sales Force Dynamics: Motives, Management, Money, Marketplace. James E. Weitzul. LC 92-34940. 208p. 1993. text ed. 55.00 (*0-89930-807-4*, Q807, Quorum Bks) Greenwood.

Sales Force Management. 5th ed. G. A. Churchill & Neil M. Ford. 800p. (C). 1996. per. 67.95 (*0-256-13787-0*) Irwin.

Sales Force Management. Kenneth Davis & Frederick E. Webster. LC 68-20549. 776p. reprint ed. pap. 180.00 (*0-317-28587-4*, 2055189) Bks Demand.

Sales Forecasting Models: A Diagnostic Approach. Lester C. Sartorius et al. LC 76-9812. (Research Monograph: No. 69). 229p. (C). 1976. pap. 34.95 (*0-88406-105-1*) GA St U Busn Pr.

Sales Forecasting Systems. Eugene A. Imhoff, Jr. 104p. pap. 20.00 (*0-86641-127-5*, 85169) Inst Mgmt Account.

***Sales Games & Activities for Trainers.** Gary B. Connor & John A. Woods. LC 97-9590. 248p. 1997. pap. text ed. 24.95 (*0-07-071847-4*) McGraw.

Sales is a 5 Letter Word. Janet S. Slusser. 1987. pap. 7.95 (*0-614-05761-2*) Abbott Langer Assocs.

Sales Law & the Contracting Process. 2nd ed. Alan Schwartz & Robert E. Scott. (University Casebook Ser.). 544p. 1990. text ed. 31.95 (*0-88277-859-5*) Foundation Pr.

Sales Lead-Getting Model Letter Book. Luther A. Brock. LC 85-43236. 261p. 1986. 27.95 (*0-13-787599-1*, Busn) P-H.

Sales, Leases & Bulk Transfers. Alces & Hansford. 1989. teacher ed. write for info. (*0-8205-0387-8*) Bender.

Sales Letters Ready to Go. Eleanor Dugan. Ed. by William Bethel. 160p. (Orig.). 1995. pap. 12.95 (*0-8442-3566-0*, NTC Busn Bks) NTC Pub Grp.

Sales Letters That Sell. 1987. lib. bdg. 79.25 (*0-8490-3891-X*) Gordon Pr.

***Sales Letters That Sell.** Laura Brill. LC 97-2279. 208p. (Orig.). 1997. pap. 17.95 (*0-8144-7945-6*) AMACOM.

Sales Letters That Sizzle: All the Hooks, Lines & Sinkers You'll Ever Need to Close Sales. Herschell G. Lewis. LC 94-16176. 224p. 1994. 29.95 (*0-8442-3547-4*, NTC Busn Bks) NTC Pub Grp.

Sales Machine Direct Marketing Course, Pt. 1. rev. ed. John M. Cummuta. (Illus.). 123p. 1993. write for info. (*1-883113-01-6*) Marketline.

Sales Machine Direct Marketing Course, Pt. 2. rev. ed. John M. Cummuta. (Illus.). 62p. 1993. write for info. (*1-883113-02-4*) Marketline.

Sales Machine Direct Marketing Course, 2 pts., Set. rev. ed. John M. Cummuta. (Illus.). 1993. pap. 98.00 (*1-883113-00-8*) Marketline.

Sales Magic: Revolutionary New Techniques that will Double Your Sales Volume in 21 Days. Kerry L. Johnson. 1995. pap. 12.00 (*0-688-14233-8*, Quill) Morrow.

Sales Management. R. Abrah et al. 127p. 1990. pap. 34.95 (*0-409-11091-4*) Buttrwrth-Heinemann.

Sales Management. William C. Moncrief & Shannon Shipp. (C). 1997. text ed. 68.95 (*0-673-46903-4*) Addson-Wesley Educ.

***Sales Management.** 3rd ed. Ingram. (C). 1997. teacher ed., pap. text ed. 73.00 (*0-03-010477-7*) HB Coll Pubs.

Sales Management. 3rd rev. ed. Charles M. Futrell. (Illus.). 609p. (C). 1991. text ed. 59.00 (*0-03-042467-4*) Dryden Pr.

Sales Management. 4th ed. Charles Futrell. LC 93-37381. 690p. (C). 1993. text ed. 71.50 (*0-03-098667-2*) Dryden Pr.

***Sales Management.** 5th ed. Futrell. (C). 1996. teacher ed., pap. text ed. 70.00 (*0-03-024349-1*) HB Coll Pubs.

Sales Management: A Practitioner's Guide to Sales Force Development. Roger F. Smith. (Illus.). 288p. (C). 1987. text ed. 45.13 (*0-13-786534-1*) P-H.

Sales Management: A Review of the Current Literature. Danny N. Bellenger et al. LC 81-6559. (Research Monograph: No. 89). 90p. 1981. pap. 19.95 (*0-88406-147-7*) GA St U Busn Pr.

Sales Management: Analysis & Decision Making. 2nd ed. Thomas N. Ingram & Raymond W. Laforge. 768p. (C). 1992. text ed. 57.00 (*0-03-054168-9*) Dryden Pr.

Sales Management: Analysis & Decision Making. 3rd ed. Thomas N. Ingram et al. 642p. (C). 1997. pap. text ed. 58.25 (*0-03-098584-6*) Dryden Pr.

Sales Management: Concepts & Cases. 5th ed. Douglas J. Dalrymple & William L. Cron. 784p. 1994. text ed. write for info. (*0-471-05548-4*) Wiley.

***Sales Management: Concepts & Cases.** 5th ed. Douglas J. Dalrymple & William L. Cron. 1995. pap. text ed. 25.00 (*0-471-11477-4*); pap. text ed. 25.00 (*0-471-11495-2*) Wiley.

***Sales Management: Concepts & Cases.** 5th ed. Douglas J. Dalrymple & William L. Cron. 1995. text ed. write for info. (*0-471-08873-0*) Wiley.

Sales Management: Concepts, Practices & Cases. 2nd ed. Eugene M. Johnson et al. LC 93-6423. 1994. text ed. write for info. (*0-07-032652-5*) McGraw.

Sales Management: Decisions, Strategies, & Cases. 5th ed. Richard Still et al. (Illus.). 656p. (C). 1988. text ed. write for info. (*0-13-786542-2*) P-H.

Sales Management: People & Profit. James M. Comer. 750p. 1991. text ed. write for info. incl. disk (*0-318-68010-6*, H25976); boxed write for info. (*0-318-68009-2*, H25968); disk 54.00 (*0-685-47330-9*, H25984) P-H.

Sales Management: The Complete Marketeer's Guide. Chris Noonan. (C). 1986. text ed. 49.95 (*0-04-658254-1*) Routledge Chapman & Hall.

Sales Management see Retail Banking Series

***Sales Management-A Career-Path Approach.** Hughes & McKee. (Miscellaneous/Catalogs Ser.). (C). Date not set. text ed. 62.95 (*0-538-87866-5*) S-W Pub.

Sales Management Role Plays. Shipp & William C. Moncrief. (C). 1994. text ed. 31.95 (*0-673-46904-2*) Addson-Wesley Educ.

Sales Management Sourcebook. Ed. by Ira G. Asherman & Sandra V. Asherman. 437p. 1992. 44.95 (*0-87425-163-X*) HRD Press.

Sales Manager's Complete Manual of Forms Agreements, Policies, Procedures & Job Descriptions. Bob Carlsen & Ken Boxley. 624p. 1990. 69.95 (*0-13-786591-0*) P-H.

Sales Manager's Desk Book. Gene Garofalo. 384p. 1988. 59.95 (*0-13-786583-X*) P-H.

Sales Manager's Desk Book. 2nd ed. Gene Garofalo. LC 96-16098. 384p. 1996. 69.95 (*0-13-244625-1*) P-H.

Sales Managers Handbook. 14th ed. John P. Steinbrink. 1272p. 1989. 49.95 (*0-85013-162-6*) Dartnell Corp.

Sales Managers High-Performance Guide: The Only Reference You Need to Build a Powerful Sales Force. Ed. by Roger Fritz. LC 93-78228. 1993. ring bd. 149.00 (*0-9636633-0-5*) Greene Trng.

Sales Manager's Model Letter Desk Book. Hal Fahner. 1977. 32.95 (*0-13-787663-7*, Parker Publishing Co) P-H.

Sales Manager's Model Letter Desk Book. 2nd ed. Hal Fahner & Morris E. Miller. 240p. 1988. 39.95 (*0-13-787789-7*, Busn) P-H.

Sales Manager's Planner: Planning & Controlling the Selling Function. George Holmes. 144p. 1991. 39.95 (*0-7506-0087-X*) Buttrwrth-Heinemann.

***Sales Manager's Portable Answer Book.** Gene Garofalo. LC 96-39203. 320p. 1996. 59.95 (*0-13-493496-2*) P-H.

Sales Manager's Sales Training Workbook. Gene Garfalo. 1992. 59.95 (*0-13-786013-7*, Busn) P-H.

Sales Manual. Reid. Date not set. teacher ed., pap. text ed. write for info. (*0-314-88426-2*) West Pub.

***Sales, Marketing & Continuous Improvement: Six Best Practices to Achieve Revenue Growth & Increase Customer Loyalty.** Daniel M. Stowell. LC 96-45846. 1997. write for info. (*0-7879-0857-6*) Jossey-Bass.

***Sales, Marketing & Customer Service.** 83p. 1996. pap. text ed. 25.00 (*1-888198-12-5*) Construct Contracting.

Sales Mastery: A Novel. Barry Trailer. 342p. 1991. 16.95 (*0-9627660-5-4*) No Rush.

Sales Negotiation Skills That Sell. Robert E. Kellar. 192p. (Orig.). 1996. pap. 17.95 (*0-8144-7930-8*) AMACOM.

Sales Negotiation Strategies. Mack Hanan & James Cribbin. LC 76-44021. 172p. reprint ed. pap. 49.10 (*0-317-10211-7*, 2022622) Bks Demand.

Sales of Goods & Services. 2nd ed. National Consumer Law Center, Inc. Staff. LC 89-63232. (Consumer Credit & Sales Legal Practice Ser.). 790p. (Orig.). 1989. pap. 70.00 (*0-943116-67-8*) Nat Consumer Law.

Sales on the Line: Meeting the Business Demands of the '90s Through Phone Partnering. Sharon D. Morgen. 248p. (Orig.). 1993. pap. 14.95 (*1-55552-047-2*) Metamorphous Pr.

Sales, Persuasion Presentations: A Psychological Analysis. Ed. by Thomas J. Rundquist. 6p. (Orig.). 1994. pap. 6.95 (*0-9618567-9-3*) Nova Media.

Sales Power: The Silva Mind Method for Sales Professionals. Jose Silva & Ed Bernd, Jr. 288p. (Orig.). 1994. mass mkt. 5.99 (*0-425-13474-1*) Berkley Pub.

Sales Presentation Manual: Role Playing for Sales Effectiveness. David A. Reid. Ed. by Burvikovs. 231p. (C). 1992. pap. text ed. 27.25 (*0-314-92681-X*) West Pub.

***Sales Process Engineering: A Personal Workshop.** Paul H. Seldon. LC 96-3207. 310p. 1996. 36.00 (*0-87389-418-9*, H0944) ASQC Qual Pr.

Sales Productivity Measurement. George A. Smith, Jr. (Briefing Ser.). 119p. 1994. pap. 15.00 (*0-87389-333-6*, MB103) ASQC Qual Pr.

Sales Professional's Survival Guide: Or Things Your Sale Managers Never Told You. Gene Garofalo & Gary Drummond. 204p. 1987. 19.95 (*0-13-788076-6*) P-H.

Sales Promotion. Blattberg. 1995. pap. text ed. 29.80 (*0-13-442302-X*) P-H.

***Sales Promotion.** Julian Cummins. (Marketing & Sales Ser.). 1989. pap. 16.95 (*1-85091-843-0*) Kogan Page Ltd.

Sales Promotion. Didactic Systems Staff. (Simulation Game Ser.). 1969. pap. 26.25 (*0-89401-084-0*) Didactic Syst.

Sales Promotion, Advertising & PR. Richard Bagehot. (Waterlow Publications). 256p. 1991. pap. 40.01 (*0-08-040856-7*, Waterlow) Macmillan.

Sales Promotion & Merchandising. Euromonitor Staff. 84p. (C). 1988. 975.00 (*0-86338-312-2*, Pub. by Euromonitor Pubns UK) Gale.

Sales Promotion & Merchandising Skillbook. Educational Foundation of the National Restaurant Association Staff. (Management Skills Program Ser.). 50p. (Orig.). 1992. pap. text ed. 10.95 (*0-915452-49-9*) Educ Found.

Sales Promotion Essentials. 2nd ed. William A. Robinson & Don E. Schultz. (Illus.). 208p. 1994. 39.95 (*0-8442-3366-8*, NTC Busn Bks) NTC Pub Grp.

Sales Promotion Essentials. 2nd ed. Don E. Schultz. 208p. 1994. pap. 17.95 (*0-8442-3367-6*) NTC Pub Grp.

Sales Promotion Handbook. 8th ed. Tamara Brezen & William Robinson. 909p. 1994. 69.95 (*0-85013-212-6*) Dartnell Corp.

Sales Promotion in Postmodern Marketing. Alan Toop & Christian Petersen. LC 94-2296. 192p. 1994. 67.95 (*0-566-07450-8*, Pub. by Gower UK) Ashgate Pub Co.

Sales Promotion Law - A Practical Guide. Philip J. Circus. 1989. U.K. pap. 64.00 (*0-406-11800-0*) MICHIE.

Sales Promotion Management. John A. Quelch. 360p. 1989. text ed. 78.00 (*0-13-788118-5*) P-H.

Sales Quality Audit. George A. Smith, Jr. 94p. 1995. pap. 20.00 (*0-87389-337-9*, H0911) ASQC Qual Pr.

Sales Question Book. 2nd ed. Gerhard Gschwandtner & Donald J. Moine. LC 86-82538. 115p. 1986. 99.00 (*0-939613-00-X*) Personal Selling.

Sales Questions That Close the Sale: How to Uncover Your Customers Real Needs. Charles D. Brennan. 160p. 1994. pap. 17.95 (*0-8144-7815-8*) AMACOM.

Sales Reengineering: A Complete Guide for the Sales & Marketing Professional. Mark Blessington. 1995. text ed. 24.95 (*0-07-005950-0*) McGraw.

Sales Rep Navigator: How to Find the Perfect Sales Rep or Distributor for Your Business. William G. Radin. Ed. by Betsy Smith. 60p. 1996. wbk. ed., text ed. 59.95 (*0-9626147-6-9*) Innovative Consulting.

Sales Rep Strategies for Dealing with Principals Successfully: Negotiations, Contracts, Working Relationships & Terminations. Steven M. Sack & Jonathen S. Sack. 146p. (Orig.). 1991. pap. text ed. 79.95 (*0-915910-31-4*) Downtown Res.

Sales Reports, Records & Systems. Phillip R. Lund. (Illus.). 128p. 22.95 (*0-8464-0812-0*) Beekman Pubs.

An Asterisk (*) at the beginning of an entry indicates that the title is appearing in BIP for the first time.

Sales Representative's Business & Tax Handbook: How to Run Your Company & How to Sell It. Melvin H. Daskal. LC 94-2844. 444p. 1994. text ed. 85.00 (*0-7863-0312-3*) Irwin Prof Pubng.

Sales Scripts That Sell: ...On the Phone...on the Road. Teri Gamble & Michael W. Gamble. LC 92-19082. 160p. 1992. pap. 16.95 (*0-8144-7767-4*) AMACOM.

Sales Secrets from Your Customers. Barry J. Farber. 128p. (Orig.). 1995. pap. text ed. 8.99 (*1-56414-169-1*) Career Pr Inc.

Sales, Secured Trans. & Payment: Adaptable to Courses Utilizing Spiedel, Summers & White's Casebook on Sales & Secured Transactions. Casenotes Publishing Co., Inc. Staff. Ed. by Norman S. Goldenberg et al. (Legal Briefs Ser.). 1993. pap. write for info. (*0-87457-021-2*, 1310) Casenotes Pub.

Sales Shock! The End of Selling Products - The Rise of CoManaging Customers. 5th ed. Mack Hanan. 176p. 1996. 21.95 (*0-8144-0248-8*) AMACOM.

Sales Source. Kris Woods. 71p. 1991. 15.00 (*1-56461-042-X*, 29130) Rough Notes.

Sales Store Worker. Jack Rudman. (Career Examination Ser.: C-1460). 1994. pap. 23.95 (*0-8373-1460-7*) Nat Learn.

Sales Strategist: 6 Breakthrough Sales Strategies to Win New Business. Warren Kurzrock. LC 96-33883. (Illus.). 1996. write for info. (*0-7863-0738-2*) Irwin Prof Pubng.

Sales Strategy. Didactic Systems Staff. (Simulation Game Ser.). 1968. pap. write for info. (*0-89401-085-9*) Didactic Syst.

Sales Strategy: Cases & Readings. Ed. by Robert F. Gwinner & Edward M. Smith. LC 75-77534. (Illus.). (C). 1969. pap. text ed. 9.95 (*0-89197-388-5*) Irvington.

Sales Superstars: How They Made It & What They Can Teach You! David C. Forward. LC 95-3859. 1995. pap. 14.95 (*0-7615-0023-5*) Prima Pub.

Sales Survival Guide. Judy McKee. Ed. by Sandra Caton. (Sales Ser.). 135p. (Orig.). 1989. pap. 12.95 (*0-685-44400-7*) Motivations Pub.

Sales Talk in Japan & the United States: An Ethnographic Analysis of Contrastive Speech Events. fac. ed. Aoi Tsuda. LC 84-1568. 173p. 1984. reprint ed. pap. 49.40 (*0-7837-7787-6*, 2047542) Bks Demand.

Sales Tax: A Practical Guide to Simplification. Arthur Andersen. 258p. 1993. pap. 71.00 (*0-409-30764-5*, Austral) MICHIE.

Sales Tax Auditing: An Operational Approach. Jerrold Wollison. Ed. by Lee A. Campbell. 21p. 1991. pap. 15.00 (*0-89413-248-2*, A839) Inst Inter Aud.

Sales Tax Cases, Nineteen Thirty-Eight to Nineteen Eighty-Five, Set. Eastern Book Co. Staff. (C). 1987. 6,000.00 (*0-685-25177-2*) St Mut.

Sales Tax Guide: Canada. 34th ed. 1554p. 1990. 38.95 (*0-685-59635-4*, 4220) Commerce.

***Sales Tax in the 21st Century.** Ed. by Matthew N. Murray & William F. Fox. LC 96-37729. 1997. text ed. write for info. (*0-275-95827-2*, Praeger Pubs) Greenwood.

Sales Tax Strategies of Wisconsin Businesses. Percy Werner. Ed. by M. Fischer-Williams. LC 80-65336. 94p. (Orig.). 1980. pap. 12.75 (*0-936400-01-3*) Gearhart-Edwards.

Sales Taxation. B. J. Terra. (Series on International Taxation: Vol. 8). 172p. 1989. 91.00 (*90-6544-381-9*) Kluwer Law Tax Pubs.

Sales Taxation. 2nd ed. John F. Due & John L. Mikesell. 375p. (C). 1994. lib. bdg. 55.00 (*0-87766-627-X*) Urban Inst.

Sales Taxation: Critical Issues in Policy & Administration. Ed. by William F. Fox. LC 92-894. 200p. 1992. text ed. 47.95 (*0-275-94053-5*, C4053, Praeger Pubs) Greenwood.

Sales Taxation: State & Local Structure & Administration. John F. Due & John L. Mikesell. LC 82-13968. 352p. 1983. text ed. 54.00 (*0-8018-2842-2*) Johns Hopkins.

Sales Taxation in Madhya Pradesh. M. Govinda Rao et al. 1990. text ed. 22.50 (*0-7069-5327-4*, Pub. by Vikas II) S Asia.

Sales Taxation in Nepal. Raj B. Khadka. 144p. (C). 1986. 210.00 (*0-89771-057-6*, Pub. by Ratna Pustak Bhandar) St Mut.

Sales Taxes, 10 vols. 1987. write for info. (*0-318-57360-1*); ring bd. 783.00 (*0-685-07435-8*); ring bd. 699.00 (*0-685-07436-6*) P-H.

Sales Technique & Management. 2nd ed. Geoffrey Lancaster & David Jobber. 273p. (Orig.). 1990. pap. 33.50 (*0-273-03190-2*, Pub. by Pitman Pub Ltd UK) Trans-Atl Phila.

Sales Training: ASTD Trainer's Sourcebook. H. Miller. 1995. pap. text ed. 39.95 (*0-07-053436-5*) McGraw.

Sales Training: The Complete Guide. Eric J. Soares et al. 350p. 1994. 65.00 (*0-8144-5144-6*) AMACOM.

***Sales Training Basics.** Elwood N. Chapman. (Better Management Skills Ser.). 1988. pap. 12.95 (*1-85091-794-9*) Kogan Page Ltd.

Sales Training Basics: A Primer for Those New to Selling. 3rd rev. ed. Elwood N. Chapman. Ed. by Michael G. Crisp. LC 91-77081. (Fifty-Minute Ser.). (Illus.). 68p. (Orig.). 1992. pap. 10.95 (*1-56052-119-8*) Crisp Pubns.

Sales Training in America: A New National Benchmarking Report on the Practices of 235 Leading Corporations. Executive KnowledgeWorks Staff. (Illus.). 300p. 1988. ring bd. 150.00 (*0-943353-04-1*) Exec Knowledge.

Sales Transactions: Domestic & International Law, Cases & Materials. John O. Honnold & Curtis R. Reitz. 416p. 1992. text ed. write for info. (*0-318-69352-6*) Foundation Pr.

Sales Transactions: Domestic & International Law, Manual for Teacher's to Accompany Cases, Problems & Materials On. John O. Honnold & Curtis R. Reitz. (University Casebook Ser.). 78p. (C). 1992. pap. text ed. write for info. (*1-56662-040-6*) Foundation Pr.

***SalesCompass: Your Guide to Sales Success.** Russell H. Granger. (Illus.). 126p. (Orig.). 1997. pap. 19.95 (*0-9656305-0-1*) ProEd Pub.

Saleskids. Duane Magnani. 1986. 14.95 (*1-883858-19-4*) Witness CA.

Saleslady. Frances R. Donovan. LC 74-3942. (Women in America Ser.). 278p. 1974. reprint ed. 25.95 (*0-405-06088-2*) Ayer.

Salesman Calling. H. Gordon Bethards. 78p. (Orig.). 1984. pap. 4.95 (*0-930264-54-1*) Century Comm.

Salesman in Marketing Strategy. Leverett S. Lyon. Ed. by Henry Assael. LC 78-240. (Century of Marketing Ser.). 1979. reprint ed. lib. bdg. 36.95 (*0-405-11183-5*) Ayer.

***Salesman of Death.** large type ed. Charles Leader. (Linford Mystery Library). 384p. 1997. pap. 16.99 (*0-7089-5062-0*, Linford) Ulverscroft.

Salesman of the Century: Inventing, Marketing, & Selling on TV - How I Did It & How You Can, Too! Ron Popeil. LC 95-3043. (Illus.). 336p. 1995. 23.95 (*0-385-31378-0*) Delacorte.

Salesman of the Century: Inventing, Marketing & Selling on TV: How I Did It & How You Can Too! Ron Popeil & Jefferson Graham. 320p. 1996. pap. 12.95 (*0-440-50766-9*, Dell Trade Pbks) Dell.

Salesman Performance Appraisal: A National Study. Ferdinand F. Fournies. 1975. 25.00 (*0-917472-01-2*) F Fournies.

Salesman's Guide to More Effective Selling: The Handbook on Basic Selling Skills. rev. ed. Homer B. Smith. LC 88-92440. (Illus.). 88p. 1994. pap. 7.95 (*0-9621285-0-3*) Mktg Educ Assocs.

Salesmanship. Boy Scouts of America. LC 19-600. (Illus.). 40p. (J). (gr. 6-12). 1987. pap. 2.40 (*0-8395-3351-9*, 33351) BSA.

Salesmanship: A Contemporary Approach. Paul Preston & Ralph Nelson. (C). 1981. teacher ed. write for info. (*0-318-55522-0*, Reston) P-H.

Salesmanship: Syllabus. 2nd ed. Marvin W. Hempel. (gr. 11 up). 1980. pap. 11.95 (*0-89420-109-3*, 216782); audio 244.55 (*0-89420-182-4*, 130800) Natl Book.

Salespeak: Everybody Sells Something. Terri L. Sjodin. LC 95-40546. 1995. 19.95 (*1-56530-192-7*) Summit TX.

Salespower Manual. 150p. 1984. 95.00 (*0-318-17657-2*) Prof Ins Agents.

***Salford Lancaster.** Joseph Bamford. 1997. pap. text ed. 17.95 (*0-85052-519-5*, Pub. by L Cooper Bks UK) Trans-Atl Phila.

***Salford Pals: 15th, 16th, 19th & 20th Battalions Lancashire Fusilliers.** Michael Stedman. 1997. pap. text ed. 24.95 (*0-85052-356-7*, Pub. by L Cooper Bks UK) Trans-Atl Phila.

***Salgair: A Steelhead Odyssey.** Barry Thornton. (Illus.). 96p. (Orig.). 1997. pap. 9.95 (*0-88839-412-8*) Hancock House.

***Salgamos Pues - Let Go Us Them.** Frazier. (Serie Discipulado Ser.). 28p. (SPA.). 1995. write for info. (*1-56063-614-9*) Editorial Unilit.

***Salgan...Llenen Todas las Vasijas!** Marilyn Lashbrook. (SPA.). 1997. pap. 3.50 (*0-8254-1420-2*, Edit Portavoz) Kregel.

Sali de Paseo. Sue Williams. (Illus.). (SPA.). (J). (ps-2). 1996. pap. 15.95 incl. audio (*0-87499-365-2*) Live Oak Media.

Sali de Paseo, 4 bks., Set. Sue Williams. (Illus.). (J). (ps-2). 1996. pap. 31.95 incl. audio (*0-87499-366-0*) Live Oak Media.

Sali de Paseo: I Went Walking. Sue Williams. Tr. by Alma F. Ada. (Illus.). 32p. (SPA.). (J). (ps-2). 1995. pap. 5.00 (*0-15-200288-X*, Voyager Bks) HarBrace.

Salibhadra-Dhanna-Carita (The Tale of the Quest for Ultimate Release by Slibhadra & Dhanna) A Work in Old Gujarati. Ed. & Tr. by Ernest Bender. (American Oriental Ser.: Vol. 73). vi, 573p. 1992. 52.00 (*0-940490-73-0*) Am Orient Soc.

Salida - St. Elmo - Shavano Peak, CO. rev. ed. Ed. by Trails Illustrated Staff. 1995. 8.99 (*0-925873-50-0*) Trails Illustrated.

Salient Features & Trends in Foreign Direct Investment. pap. 8.50 (*92-1-104058-2*, E.83.II.A.8) UN.

Salient Points: Cameos of the Great War - Ypres Sector 1914-1918. Tony Spagnoly & Ted Smith. (Illus.). 192p. 1994. 27.50 (*0-85052-319-2*, Pub. by L Cooper Bks UK) Trans-Atl Phila.

Salinan Indians of California & Their Neighbors. Betty W. Brusa. LC 74-13249. (American Indian Map Book: Vol. 2). (Illus.). 96p. (C). 1975. pap. 7.95 (*0-87961-022-0*) Naturegraph.

Salinas: Archaeology, History, Prehistory. 2nd ed. Ed. by David G. Noble. LC 92-55035. (Illus.). 40p. (C). 1993. reprint ed. pap. 7.95 (*0-941270-78-5*) Ancient City Pr.

Salinas de los Nueve Cerros Guatemala: Preliminary Archaeological Investigations. Brian Dillon. (Studies in Mesoamerican Art, Archaeology & Ethnohistory: No. 2). 94p. 1977. pap. 3.00 (*0-87919-070-1*) Ballena Pr.

Salinas Pueble Missions: Abo Quarai, & Gran Quivira. Daniel O. Murphy. Ed. by Randolph Jorgen & Ronald Foreman. LC 91-60459. (Illus.). 64p. (YA). 1993. pap. 9.95 (*0-911408-98-3*) SW Pks Mnmts.

Saline Agriculture: Salt-Tolerant Plants for Developing Countries. National Research Council, International Affairs Office Staff. 152p. 1990. pap. text ed. 15.00 (*0-309-04189-9*) Natl Acad Pr.

Saline & Sodic Soils: Principles, Dynamics, Modeling. E. Bresler et al. (Advanced Series in Agricultural Sciences: Vol. 10). (Illus.). 280p. 1982. 109.95 (*0-387-11120-4*) Spr-Verlag.

Saline County, Arkansas Census, Eighteen-Fifty. Carolyn E. Billingsley. 260p. 1987. pap. 23.00 (*0-9618123-3-8*) C E Billingsley.

Saline County, Arkansas Census, 1860. Bobbie J. McLane. 92p. (Orig.). 1986. pap. 15.00 (*0-929604-41-5*) Arkansas Ancestors.

Saline County, Arkansas Marriage Records, 1836-1877. Bobbie J. McLane & Margaret Hubbard. 105p. (Orig.). 1978. pap. 15.00 (*0-929604-32-6*) Arkansas Ancestors.

Saline County, Arkansas, Probate Book D: March 25, 1862 to September 8, 1865. Sybil Crawford. 165p. 1988. ring bd. 14.00 (*0-945183-07-0*) Saline Cnty Hist Heritage Soc.

Saline County, Arkansas, Will & Probate Records, 1842-1905. Sybil Crawford. 291p. 1987. ring bd. 27.00 (*0-945183-08-9*) Saline Cnty Hist Heritage Soc.

Saline County Arkansas Will Book A-1: September 15, 1842 to December 27, 1861. Sybil Crawford. 54p. 1987. pap. 10.00 (*0-945183-04-6*) Saline Cnty Hist Heritage Soc.

Saline Lake Ecosystems of the World. Ulrich T. Hammer. (Monographiae Biologicae). 1986. lib. bdg. 340.00 (*90-6193-535-0*) Kluwer Ac.

Saline Lakes. Ed. by F. A. Comin & T. G. Northcote. (Developments in Hydrobiology Ser.). (C). 1990. lib. bdg. 236.00 (*0-7923-0767-4*) Kluwer Ac.

Saline Lakes. Ed. by John M. Melack. (Developments in Hydrobiology Ser.). (C). 1988. lib. bdg. 247.50 (*90-6193-648-9*) Kluwer Ac.

Saline Lakes V: Proceedings of the Vth International Symposium on Inland Saline Lakes, Held in Bolivia, 22-29 March 1993. Ed. by Stuart H. Hurlbert. LC 93-24192. (Developments in Hydrobiology Ser.). 336p. (C). 1993. lib. bdg. 222.00 (*0-7923-2416-1*) Kluwer Ac.

Saline Solution. Marco Vassi. 180p. 1993. pap. 16.95 (*0-933256-84-1*) Second Chance.

***Saline Solution.** Marco Vassi. 1997. mass mkt. 6.95 (*1-56333-568-9*) Masquerade.

Saline Solution. Marco Vassi. 1994. reprint ed. pap. 12.95 (*1-56333-180-2*, R Kasak Bks) Masquerade.

Saline Solutions: Policy Dynamics in the Murray-Darling Basin, Vol. 2. Aynsley Kellow. 80p. 1992. pap. 53.00 (*0-7300-1530-0*, PTSSSO, Pub. by Deakin Univ AT) St Mut.

Saline Water Conservation. G. Gillam. (C). 1991. text ed. 350.00 (*0-89771-625-6*, Pub. by Intl Bk Distr II) St Mut.

Saline Water Conservation II. Stefan Strobel. (C). 1991. text ed. 350.00 (*0-89771-662-0*, Pub. by Intl Bk Distr II) St Mut.

Saline Water Processing: Desalination & Treatment of Seawater, Brackish Water, & Industrial Waste Water. Ed. by Hans-Gunter Heitmann. LC 89-32599. 336p. 1989. 155.00 (*3-527-27826-5*, VCH) Wiley.

Saline, 1986. Ed. by Carolyn E. Billingsley. (Illus.). 132p. 1986. ring bd. 13.75 (*0-945183-00-3*) Saline Cnty Hist Heritage Soc.

Saline, 1987. Carolyn E. Billingsley. (Illus.). 201p. 1988. ring bd. 13.75 (*0-945183-09-7*) Saline Cnty Hist Heritage Soc.

Salinisation of Land & Water Resources. H. A. Nix et al. 544p. 1995. 115.00 (*0-85198-906-3*) CAB Intl.

Salinisation of Land & Water Resources: Human Causes, Extent, Management & Case Studies. F. Ghassemi et al. (Illus.). 384p. 1995. 69.95 (*0-86840-198-6*, Pub. by New South Wales Univ Pr AT) Intl Spec Bk.

Salinity & Irrigation Agriculture in Antiquity: Diyala Basin Archaeological Projects, Report on Essential Results, 1957-58. Thorkild Jacobsen. (Bibliotheca Mesopotamica Ser.: Vol. 14). (Illus.). xii, 129p. 1982. pap. 24.25 (*0-89003-092-8*) Undena Pubns.

Salinity Gradient Solar Ponds. John R. Hull et al. 288p. 1988. 163.00 (*0-8493-6914-2*, TJ812, CRC Reprint) Franklin.

Salinity in Irrigation & Water Resources. Bruno Yaron. (Civil Engineering Ser.: Vol. 4). 448p. 1981. 180.00 (*0-8247-6741-1*) Dekker.

Salinity Tolerance in Plants: Strategies for Crop Improvement. Richard C. Staples & Gary H. Toenniessen. LC 83-14759. (Environmental Science & Technology Ser.: 1-121). 443p. 1984. text ed. 99.95 (*0-471-89674-8*) Wiley.

Salinity Tolerance of the Tilapias. Wade Watanabe. 22p. 1985. pap. 7.00 (*971-10-2214-1*, Pub. by ICLARM PH) Intl Spec Bk.

Salior Man. Leo Simpson. 304p. 1996. pap. text ed. 18.95 (*0-88984-171-3*, Pub. by Porcupines Quill CN) Genl Dist Srvs.

Salisbury: History & Guide. John Chandler. (History & Guide Ser.). 128p. 1992. pap. 16.00 (*0-7509-0188-8*, Pub. by Sutton Pubng UK) Bks Intl VA.

Salisbury & the Mediterranean, 1886-1896. C. J. Lowe. 20.00 (*0-89979-072-0*) British Am Bks.

Salisbury Beach, 1954. Paul Estaver. LC 83-50965. (Series Eight). 50p. 1983. pap. 7.00 (*0-931846-24-2*) Wash Writers Pub.

Salisbury, Connecticut, Records, 2 vols., Set. 1983. pap. 28.00 (*0-914385-00-3*) Catoctin Pr.

Salisbury, MD. Historical Briefs, Inc. Staff. Ed. by Thomas Antonucci & Michael Antonucci. 176p. 1992. pap. 14.95 (*1-56864-003-4*) Hist Briefs.

Salisbury Plain Poems of William Wordsworth. William Wordsworth. Ed. by Stephen Gill. LC 74-4865. (Cornell Wordsworth Ser.). (Illus.). 352p. 1975. 85.00 (*0-8014-0892-X*) Cornell U Pr.

Salisbury Psalter. Ed. by Celia Sisam & Kenneth Sisam. (EETS Original Ser.: Vol. 242). 1963. reprint ed. 40.00 (*0-19-722242-0*, Pub. by EETS UK) Boydell & Brewer.

Salish: Okanogan-Colville Indian Language. Andy Joseph. 66p. (Orig.). 1994. pap. 14.95 incl. audio (*0-9640276-0-7*) Colville Tribal.

Salish Folk Tales. Katheryn Law. (Indian Culture Ser.). (J). (gr. 2-8). 1972. pap. 1.50 (*0-89992-028-4*) Coun India Ed.

Salish Indian Sweaters. Priscilla A. Gibson-Roberts. LC 89-8171. 1989. 17.50 (*0-932394-13-2*) Dos Tejedoras.

Salistamba Sutra: Tibetan Original Sanskrit Vreconstruction, English Translation Critical Notes Including Pali Parallels, Chinese Version & Ancient Tibetan Fragments. N. Ross Peat. (C). 1993. 14.50 (*81-208-1135-6*, Pub. by Motilal Banarsidass II) S Asia.

Saliva: Composition & Secretion. Ira L. Shannon & R. P. Suddick. Ed. by M. Myers Howard. (Monographs in Oral Science: Vol. 2). (Illus.). 135p. 1974. 39.25 (*3-8055-1455-7*) S Karger.

Saliva As a Diagnostic Fluid. Ed. by Daniel Malamud & Lawrence Tabak. LC 93-9077. (Annals Ser.: Vol. 694). 348p. 1993. write for info. (*0-89766-787-5*); pap. 95.00 (*0-89766-788-3*) NY Acad Sci.

Saliva Tree. Brian Aldiss. 1993. reprint ed. lib. bdg. 18.95 (*0-89968-326-6*, Lghtyr Pr) Buccaneer Bks.

Saliva Tree & Other Strange Growths. Brian W. Aldiss. LC 79-28703. 232p. 1981. reprint ed. 25.00 (*0-89366-147-3*) Ultramarine Pub.

Salivary Gland Tumours see International Histological Classification of Tumours

Salivary Glands: Radiology, Surgery, Pathology, 2. Dale Rice. Ed. by Hanafee & Ward. LC 94-30197. (Clinical Correlations in the Head & Neck Ser.: Vol. 2). (Illus.). 59p. 1994. 59.00 (*0-86577-364-5*) Thieme Med Pubs.

Salivary System. Ed. by Leo M. Sreebny. LC 87-5139. 256p. 1987. 140.00 (*0-8493-6689-5*, QP188, CRC Reprint) Franklin.

Salk Institute: La Jolla 1959-65 Louis I. Kahn. James Steele. (Architecture in Detail Ser.). (Illus.). 60p. (C). 1993. pap. 29.95 (*0-7148-2914-5*, Pub. by Phaidon Press UK) Chronicle Bks.

Salka. large type ed. Marcelle Bernstein. 576p. 1987. 27.99 (*0-7089-8385-5*, Charnwood) Ulverscroft.

Sallea Antiques. Sally B. Kaltman. (Illus.). 62p. (Orig.). 1991. pap. text ed. write for info. (*0-940429-09-8*) M B Glass Assocs.

Sallie: Civil War Dog: Eleventh Pennsylvania Regiment Mascot. large type ed. Helene Smith. LC 93-23315. (Illus.). 120p. (Orig.). 1996. pap. 19.95 (*0-945437-19-6*) MacDonald-Sward.

Sallie Dahmes Whitetail-Mule Deer Taxidermy System. Sallie Dahmes. Ed. by Bob Williamson & Ken Edwards. (Illus.). 160p. (C). 1987. pap. text ed. 24.95 (*0-925245-03-8*) WASCO Manufact.

Sallie Fox: The Story of a Pioneer Girl. Dorothy K. Leland. LC 95-61289. (Illus.). 128p. (Orig.). (J). (gr. 4-6). 1995. pap. 8.95 (*0-9617357-6-7*) Tomato Enter.

Sallie Robbin or a Lighted Candle in Her Heart. M. M Slappey. (Interspace Bks.). 212p. 1985. 9.95 (*0-317-39365-0*); audio write for info. (*0-318-60153-2*) Interspace Bks.

Sallie Southall Cotten: A Woman's Life in North Carolina. William Stephenson. 1987. pap. 11.95 (*0-943287-01-4*) Pamlico Pr.

Sallie Southall Cotton: A Woman's Life in North Carolina. William Stephenson. LC 87-60960. (Illus.). 224p. 1987. 17.95 (*0-317-59628-4*); pap. 11.95 (*0-685-18520-6*) P-H.

***Sallies of the Mind.** Francis Fergusson et al. LC 97-10247. 1997. 32.95 (*1-56000-312-X*) Transaction Pubs.

Sallust: Bellum Catilinae. Ed. by Patrick McGushin. (Bristol Latin Texts Ser.). 205p. (LAT.). 1980. pap. 18.95 (*0-906515-19-X*, Pub. by Brstl Class Pr UK) Focus Pub-R Pullins.

Sallust: Bellum Iugurthinum. Ed. by L. Watkiss. (Bristol Latin Texts Ser.). 396p. 1984. pap. 27.95 (*0-86292-143-0*, Pub. by Brstl Class Pr UK) Focus Pub-R Pullins.

Sallust: Catiline. Ed. by A. T. Davies. (Bristol Latin Texts Ser.). 128p. (LAT.). 1987. reprint ed. pap. 15.95 (*0-86292-258-5*, Pub. by Brstl Class Pr UK) Focus Pub-R Pullins.

Sallust: Rome & Jugurtha. Ed. by J. R. Hawthorne. (Bristol Latin Texts Ser.). 211p. (LAT.). 1992. pap. 17.95 (*0-906515-33-5*, Pub. by Brstl Class Pr UK) Focus Pub-R Pullins.

Sallust - Concordantia in Corpus Sallustianum, 2 vols., Set. Ed. by Jurgen Rapsch & Dietmar Najock. (Alpha-Omega, Reihe A Ser.: Bd. IX). xii, 1472p. (GER.). 1990. write for info. (*3-487-09384-7*) G Olms Pubs.

Sallust - Index Verborum Sallustianus. Ed. by Alva W. Bennett. xii, 280p. 1969. 65.00 (*0-318-70658-X*) G Olms Pubs.

Sallust on the Gods & the World & Other Works. Thomas Taylor. 15.95 (*0-89314-401-0*) Philos Res.

Sallust: The Conspiracy of Catiline: A Companion to the Penguin Translation. Patrick McGushin. (Classics Companions Ser.). 128p. 1987. pap. 14.95 (*0-86292-267-4*, Pub. by Brstl Class Pr UK) Focus Pub-R Pullins.

Sallustius: Concerning the Gods & the Universe. A. D. Nock. 1996. pap. 15.00 (*0-89005-550-5*) Ares.

Sallust's Bellum Catilinae. J. T. Ramsey. LC 81-21281. (American Philological Association Textbook Ser.). 262p. (C). 1984. pap. 15.00 (*0-89130-560-2*, 40 03 09) Scholars Pr GA.

Sally. Isaac Asimov. (Creative Short Stories Ser.). 40p. (J). (gr. 5). 1989. lib. bdg. 13.95 (*0-88682-230-0*) Creative Ed.

Sally: Unconventional Success. Sally Jesse Raphael & Pam Proctor. (Illus.). 264p. 1991. mass mkt. 4.99 (*0-312-92522-0*) St Martin.

Sally & Marsha: A Play in Two Acts. Sybille Pearson. 1985. pap. 5.25 (*0-8222-0980-2*) Dramatists Play.

Sally & Sam, Mike & Spike: Blend Book, 2 bks., Nos. 5 & 6. Debbie Strayer. (Bridge Story Bks.). (Illus.). 16p. (J). (gr. 1). 1992. pap. 8.00 (*1-880892-13-8*) Com Sense FL.

S

Sally & the Limpet. Simon James. LC 90-40088. (Illus.). 32p. (J). (ps-3). 1991. lib. bdg. 13.95 (*0-689-50528-0*, McElderry) S&S Childrens.

Sally-Ann in the Snow. Petronella Breinburg. 1989. pap. 8.95 (*0-370-01809-5*) Random.

Sally Ann Thunder Ann Whirlwind Crockett: A Tall Tale. Steven Kellogg. LC 94-43782. (Illus.). 48p. (J). (ps up). 1995. 15.00 (*0-688-14042-4*, Morrow Junior); lib. bdg. 14.93 (*0-688-14043-2*, Morrow Junior) Morrow.

Sally Arnold. Cheryl Ryan. LC 94-6455. (Illus.). 32p. (J). (ps-4). 1996. pap. 14.99 (*0-525-65176-4*, Cobblehill Bks) Dutton Child Bks.

Sally Blane, World's Greatest Girl Detective. Helen Sneed et al. 1991. spiral bd. 8.95 (*0-8222-0981-0*) Dramatists Play.

Sally Bradford: The Story of a Rebel Girl. Dorothy Hoobler & Thomas Hoobler. LC 96-16047. (Her Story Ser.). (Illus.). 128p. (J). (gr. 4-5). 1997. pap. 4.95 (*0-382-39259-0*); lib. bdg. 14.95 (*0-382-39258-2*) Silver Burdett Pr.

Sally Dows & Other Stories. Bret Harte. LC 79-113673. (Short Story Index Reprint Ser.). 1977. 20.95 (*0-8369-3402-4*) Ayer.

Sally Edwards' Heart Zone Training: Exercise Smart, Stay Fit, & Live Longer. Sally Edwards & Randy Saks. LC 96-19659. (Illus.). 224p. (Orig.). 1996. pap. 10.95 (*1-55850-552-0*) Adams Media.

Sally from Cork. Patricia Lynch. 230p. 1990. pap. 8.95 (*1-85371-070-9*, Pub. by Poolbeg Pr IE) Dufour.

***Sally Go Round the Moon: Revels Songs & Singing Games for Young Children.** Nancy Langstaff & John Langstaff. LC 86-90535. (Illus.). 127p. (J). (ps-4). 1986. pap. 14.95 (*0-9640836-3-9*, RI 10098) Revels Recs.

Sally Haley: A Lifetime of Painting. Terri M. Hopkins. (Illus.). 1993. pap. 10.00 (*0-914435-20-5*) Marylhurst Art.

Sally Hemings. Barbara Chase-Riboud. 416p. 1980. mass mkt. 4.95 (*0-380-48686-5*) Avon.

Sally Hemings. Barbara Chase-Riboud. 416p. 1994. reprint ed. pap. 12.00 (*0-345-38971-9*) Ballantine.

Sally Hemings. Barbara Chase-Riboud. 300p. 1992. reprint ed. lib. bdg. 29.95 (*0-89966-915-8*) Buccaneer Bks.

Sally Jane Got Married: (That Special Woman!) Celeste Hamilton. (Special Edition Ser.). 1994. mass mkt. 3.50 (*0-373-09865-0*, 5-09865-2) Silhouette.

Sally Learns about Cats. Matthew V. Smith. (Illus.). 18p. (J). (gr. k-3). 1994. pap. 10.95 (*1-56606-025-7*) Bradley Mann.

***Sally Mander, Incl. doll.** Gordon Henderson. (Illus.). 32p. (J). 1995. pap. 30.00 (*1-890414-04-2*) Bow Tie.

Sally of Sefton Grove. Dee Williams. 356p. 1996. pap. 11.95 (*0-7472-4880-X*, Pub. by Headline UK) Trafalgar.

***Sally Ride: A Space Biography.** Barbara Kramer. LC 97-21344. (Countdown to Space Ser.). 1997. write for info. (*0-89490-975-4*) Enslow Pubs.

***Sally Ride: First American Woman in Space.** Carole A. Camp. LC 97-9339. (People to Know Ser.). (Illus.). 128p. (YA). (gr. 6 up). 1997. lib. bdg. 18.95 (*0-89490-829-4*) Enslow Pubs.

Sally Ride: Shooting for the Stars. Jane Hurwitz & Sue Hurwitz. LC 89-90821. (Great Lives Biography Ser.). (Illus.). 115p. (J). (gr. 5-9). 1989. pap. 4.99 (*0-449-90394-X*, Columbine) Fawcett.

Sally Socolich's Bargain Hunting in the Bay Area: Completely Revised & Expanded. 11th expanded rev. ed. Sally Socolich. 448p. 1995. pap. 11.95 (*0-8118-1143-3*) Chronicle Bks.

Sally Thomas: Servant Girl. Phyllis Hemphill. LC 90-70040. 177p. 1990. pap. 6.95 (*1-55523-323-6*) Winston-Derek.

***Sally Warner.** (Author Bios Ser.). (J). 1997. pap. write for info. (*0-676-76198-4*) Knopf Bks Yng Read.

Sally Wister's Journal. Sally Wister. LC 94-43038. 64p. 1995. reprint ed. pap. 8.95 (*1-55709-114-5*) Applewood.

Sally Wister's Journal: A True Narrative. Sally Wister. 1993. reprint ed. lib. bdg. 89.00 (*0-7812-5859-6*) Rprt Serv.

Sally Wister's Journal: A True Narrative-Being a Quaker Maiden's Account of Her Experiences with Officers of the Continental Army, 1777- 1778. Sally Wister. (American Biography Ser.). 224p. 1991. reprint ed. lib. bdg. 69.00 (*0-7812-8424-4*) Rprt Serv.

Sally Wister's Journal: A True Narrative Being a Quaker Maiden's Account of Her Experiences with Officers of the Continental Army, 1777-1778. Sally Wister. Ed. by Albert C. Myers. LC 73-78039. (Eyewitness Accounts of the American Revolution Ser., No. 1). 1978. reprint ed. 18.95 (*0-405-01169-5*) Ayer.

Sally Writes a Letter to Santa Claus. Kaitlin M. Smith. (Illus.). 15p. (J). (gr. 1-4). 1992. pap. 10.95 (*1-56606-005-2*) Bradley Mann.

Sally's Beau. large type ed. Laurie Paige. LC 93-21001. 1993. pap. 13.95 (*0-7862-0059-6*) Thorndike Pr.

Sally's Christmas Miracle. Charles M. Schulz. LC 95-26453. (Illus.). 24p. (J). (ps-1). 1996. 11.95 (*0-694-00899-0*, Festival) HarpC Child Bks.

***Sally's Christmas Miracle.** Charles M. Schulz. (Illus.). 32p. (J). (ps-1). 1996. lib. bdg. 11.89 (*0-06-027448-4*) HarpC Child Bks.

Sally's Doorbell. William H. Payne. 192p. 1996. 16.00 (*0-8059-3894-X*) Dorrance.

***Sally's First Day at School.** Richard Scarry. (J). 1997. 4.99 (*0-689-81553-0*) S&S Childrens.

Sally's Holiday Cleaning. Price. (AB - Accounting Principles Ser.). 1991. 24.95 (*0-538-81487-X*) S-W Pub.

Sally's Shorts. Sally Nemeth. 1995. pap. 5.25 (*0-8222-1454-7*) Dramatists Play.

Sally's Submarine. Joan Anderson. LC 94-16644. (Illus.). 32p. (J). (gr. k up). 1995. 15.00 (*0-688-12690-1*, Morrow Junior); lib. bdg. 14.93 (*0-688-12691-X*, Morrow Junior) Morrow.

Salmagundi. Launcelott Langstaff. 1972. reprint ed. lib. bdg. 39.50 (*0-8422-8162-2*) Irvington.

Salmagundi: Second Series, 2 Vols. in 1. James K. Paulding. LC 70-144669. reprint ed. 49.50 (*0-404-04944-3*) AMS Pr.

Salmagundi: Second Series, 2 vols., Set. James K. Paulding. (BCL1-PS American Literature Ser.). 1992. reprint ed. lib. bdg. 150.00 (*0-7812-6825-7*) Rprt Serv.

Salmagundi (Contributor) William H. Irving. (Notable American Authors Ser.). 1992. reprint ed. lib. bdg. 75.00 (*0-7812-3342-9*) Rprt Serv.

Salmagundi Reader. Ed. by Robert Boyers & Peggy Boyers. LC 82-49294. 637p. reprint ed. pap. 180.00 (*0-685-23876-8*, 2056694) Bks Demand.

Salman Al-Farsi. write for info. (*0-940368-83-8*, 67) Tahrike Tarsile Quran.

Salman el-Farsi. Sayed A. Razwy. 1985. pap. 3.95 (*0-933543-02-6*) Aza Khana.

Salman El-Farsi. rev. ed. Sayed A. Razwy. LC 83-50152. 1990. pap. text ed. 5.95 (*0-940368-29-3*, 67) Tahrike Tarsile Quran.

***Salman El-Farsi: Friend of Prophet Muhammad.** Sayed A. Razwy. 124p. 1996. pap. 8.50 (*0-614-21716-4*, 1103) Kazi Pubns.

***Salman Rushdie.** Catherine Cundy. LC 96-9826. (Contemporary World Writers Ser.). 1997. text ed. 49.95 (*0-7190-4408-1*, Pub. by Manchester Univ Pr UK); text ed. 19.95 (*0-7190-4409-X*, Pub. by Manchester Univ Pr UK) St Martin.

Salman Rushdie. James Harrison. (Twayne's English Authors Ser.: No. 488). 160p. (C). 1991. 23.95 (*0-8057-7011-9*, Twayne) Scribnrs Ref.

Salman Rushdie Controversy in Inter-Religious Perspective. Ed. by Daniel Cohn-Sherbok. LC 90-6186. (Symposium Ser.: Vol. 27). 164p. 1990. lib. bdg. 79.95 (*0-88946-719-6*) E Mellen.

***Salmisto de Hamlin.** Ed. by Anna Hutchinson. Tr. by David Crowell. (Illus.). 20p. (Orig.). (ESP.). (J). (gr. 1-2). 1992. pap. 2.95 (*0-922852-17-0*, E018) Another Lang Pr.

***Salmo 119.** Jeff Adams. (SPA.). 1996. pap. 12.99 (*0-8254-1004-5*, Edit Portavoz) Kregel.

Salmon. (Magnet Gourmet Ser.). 10p. 1996. pap. 5.95 (*0-8069-4204-5*) Sterling.

Salmon. Sabrina Crewe. LC 96-4834. (Life Cycles Bks.). (J). 1996. lib. bdg. 21.40 (*0-8172-4371-2*) Raintree Steck-V.

***Salmon.** Elaine Elliot & Virginia Lee. (Maritime Flavours Ser.: No. 2). 64p. (Orig.). 1997. pap. 9.95 (*0-88780-352-0*, Pub. by Formac Pub CN) Seven Hills Bk.

Salmon. Paula Z. Hogan. LC 78-21178. (Life Cycles Bks.). (Illus.). 32p. (J). (gr. 1-4). 1979. pap. 4.95 (*0-8114-8178-6*) Raintree Steck-V.

Salmon: Life Cycles: A Circular Pop-up Book. David Hawcock. LC 94-73277. (Life Cycles Ser.). (Illus.). 12p. (J). (ps-3). 1995. 6.95 (*0-7868-0100-X*) Hyprn Child.

Salmon: Tireless Travelers. Andreu Llamas et al. LC 96-8199. (Secrets of the Animal World Ser.). (Illus.). (J). 1996. lib. bdg. 18.60 (*0-8368-1586-6*) Gareth Stevens Inc.

Salmon - The Complete Reference for the Commercial Use. Ian Dore. Ed. by Amy Spinthourakis. 320p. (gr. 13). 1990. text ed. 93.95 (*0-442-00197-5*) Chapman & Hall.

Salmon - Untitled, Bk. 1. Michael Salmon. (J). 1998. pap. 3.25 (*0-689-81211-6*) S&S Childrens.

Salmon - Untitled, Bk. 4. Michael Salmon. (J). 1998. pap. 3.25 (*0-689-81214-0*) S&S Childrens.

Salmon Aquaculture. Ed. by Knut Heen et al. 278p. 1993. text ed. 69.95 (*0-470-22139-9*) Halsted Pr.

Salmon Coast to Coast. Virgil Beck. LC 91-66690. (Complete Angler's Library). 250p. 1991. write for info. (*0-914697-43-9*) N Amer Outdoor Grp.

Salmon Cook: 99 Ways with Salmon. Hannah Sykes. (Illus.). 128p. 1995. 22.95 (*1-85223-842-9*, Pub. by Crowood Pr UK) Trafalgar.

Salmon Cookbook. Tessa Hayward. (Illus.). 192p. 1993. 29.95 (*0-09-177027-0*, Pub. by Ebury Pr UK) Trafalgar.

Salmon Cookbook. Teresa Kaye. LC 94-26714. 96p. 1994. 9.98 (*0-8317-7979-9*) Smithmark.

Salmon Fishers of the Columbia. Courtland L. Smith. (Illus.). 128p. 1979. 21.95 (*0-87071-313-2*) Oreg St U Pr.

Salmon Fishing: A Practical Guide. Hugh Falkus. (Illus.). 448p. 1989. 65.00 (*0-85493-144-9*, Pub. by V Gollancz UK) Trafalgar.

Salmon Fishing on River & Stream. Alexander B. Keachie. (Illus.). 228p. 1996. 45.00 (*1-85223-906-9*, Pub. by Crowood Pr UK) Trafalgar.

Salmon Flies: Their Character, Style, & Dressings. Poul Jorgensen. LC 78-17941. (Illus.). 192p. 1978. 39.95 (*0-8117-1426-8*) Stackpole.

Salmon Flyfishing: The Dynamics Approach. Francis T. Grant. (Illus.). 168p. 1993. 9.95 (*1-85310-394-2*, Pub. by Swan Hill UK) Voyageur Pr.

Salmon Handbook. Stephen D. Sedgwick. (Illus.). (C). 1982. 29.50 (*0-233-97331-1*, Pub. by A Deutsch UK) Scholium Intl.

Salmon in the Sea & New Enhancement Strategies. D. L. Mills. 1993. 49.95 (*0-85238-199-9*) Blackwell Sci.

Salmon Moon. Mark Karlins. LC 92-15702. (Illus.). (J). 1993. pap. 14.00 (*0-671-73624-8*, S&S Bks Young Read) S&S Childrens.

Salmon of Doubt. Douglas Adams. 1995. write for info. (*0-517-70117-0*) Random.

Salmon of Doubt. Douglas Adams. 1995. 23.00 (*0-517-57743-7*) Random.

Salmon of the Pacific. Adam Lewis. LC 94-16591. (Illus.). 96p. (Orig.). 1994. pap. 14.95 (*1-57061-016-9*) Sasquatch Bks.

Salmon on a Dry Fly. Derek Knowles. (Illus.). 124p. 1989. 39.95 (*0-85493-153-8*, Pub. by V Gollancz UK) Trafalgar.

Salmon on a Fly: The Essential Wisdom & Lore from a Lifetime of Salmon Fishing. Lee Wulff. Ed. by John Merwin. LC 95-32789. (Illus.). 224p. 1995. pap. 12.95 (*0-89272-372-6*, Silver Quill Pr) Down East.

Salmon on a Fly: The Essential Wisdom & Lore from a Lifetime of Salmon Fishing. Lee Wulff. Ed. by John Merwin. (Illus.). 208p. 1992. pap. 21.00 (*0-671-76065-3*) S&S Trade.

Salmon P. Chase. Albert B. Hart. 1993. reprint ed. lib. bdg. 89.00 (*0-7812-5369-1*) Rprt Serv.

Salmon P. Chase: A Life in Politics. Frederick J. Blue. LC 86-27664. 408p. 1987. 28.00 (*0-87338-340-0*) Kent St U Pr.

Salmon P. Chase: A Study in Paradox. John Niven. (Illus.). 544p. 1995. 39.95 (*0-19-504653-6*) OUP.

Salmon P. Chase Papers Vol. 1: Journals, 1829-1872. Ed. by John Niven et al. LC 93-16217. (Illus.). 880p. 1993. text ed. 55.00 (*0-87338-472-5*) Kent St U Pr.

Salmon P. Chase Papers Vol. 2: Correspondence, 1823-1857. Ed. by John Niven et al. LC 94-16217. (Illus.). 520p. 1995. text ed. 45.00 (*0-87338-508-X*) Kent St U Pr.

Salmon P. Chase Papers Vol. 3: Correspondence, 1858-March 1863. Ed. by John Niven et al. LC 93-16217. (Illus.). 492p. 1996. 45.00 (*0-87338-532-2*) Kent St U Pr.

***Salmon P. Chase Papers Vol. 4: Correspondence, April 1863-1864.** Ed. by John Niven et al. (Illus.). 503p. 1997. 45.00 (*0-87338-567-5*) Kent St U Pr.

Salmon Portland Chase. Albert Hart. LC 68-24981. (American Biography Ser.: No. 32). 1969. reprint ed. lib. bdg. 69.95 (*0-8383-0952-6*) M S G Haskell Hse.

Salmon Portland Chase. Ed. by Albert B. Hart. LC 79-128954. (American Statesmen Ser.: No. 28). reprint ed. 49.50 (*0-404-50878-2*) AMS Pr.

Salmon Portland Chase. Albert B. Hart. Ed. by John T. Morse, Jr. LC 74-108489. 1970. reprint ed. 20.00 (*0-403-00216-8*) Scholarly.

Salmon Production, Management, & Allocation: Biological, Economic, & Policy Issues. Ed. by William J. McNeil. LC 87-22135. (Illus.). 208p. 1988. 35.95 (*0-87071-354-X*) Oreg St U Pr.

Salmon Recipes from Alaska. Cecilia Nibeck. (Illus.). 190p. 1987. pap. text ed. 11.95 (*0-9622117-1-0*) AK Anchorage.

Salmon River, Digby County, Nova Scotia: Vital Records 1849-1907. Ed. by Leonard H. Smith, Jr. LC 77-79479. 24.00 (*0-932022-10-3*, 1484) Picton Pr.

Salmon River, NY. Rick Kustich. (River Journal Ser.: Vol. 3, No. 2). (Illus.). 48p. 1995. pap. 15.95 (*1-57188-004-6*) F Amato Pubns.

Salmon Run. Jack Charlton & Tony Francis. (Illus.). 95p. 1993. pap. 19.95 (*0-09-177264-8*, Pub. by S Paul UK) Trafalgar.

Salmon Run. Slightly Off Center Writers Group Staff. (Orig.). 1995. pap. 8.95 (*1-56721-109-7*) Twenty-Fifth Cent Pr.

***Salmon Rushdie Bibliography: A Bibliography of Salman Rushdie's Work & Rushdie Criticism.** Joel Kuortti. 241p. 1997. 44.95 (*3-631-31094-3*) P Lang Pubng.

***Salmon Shark Manual: The Development of a Commercial Salmon Shark (Lamnaditropis) Fishery in the North Pacific.** 2nd rev. ed. Ronald Smith & Brian C. Pust. (Report Ser.: No. 86-01). (Illus.). 391p. 1989. pap. 7.00 (*1-56612-043-8*) AK Sea Grant CP.

***Salmon Spawning Habitat Rehabilitation in the Merced, Tuolumne, & Stanislaus Rivers, California: An Evaluation of Project Planning & Performance.** G. Mathias Kondolf et al. 147p. 1996. pap. write for info. (*1-887192-04-2*) U Cal CWWR.

Salmon Story. Brenda Z. Guiberson. (Illus.). 64p. (J). (gr. 2-4). 1995. pap. 5.95 (*0-8050-4254-7*, Redfeather BYR) H Holt & Co.

Salmon to a Fly: Fly Fishing for a Pacific Salmon in the Open Ocean. Jim Crawford. (Illus.). 176p. 1995. pap. 19.95 (*1-57188-034-8*) F Amato Pubns.

Salmon/Dust. Douglas Adams. 1997. pap. 24.95 (*0-7871-0401-9*, Dove Bks) Dove Audio.

Salmonella. Rufus K. Guthrie. 248p. 1991. 97.00 (*0-8493-5419-6*, QR201) CRC Pr.

***Salmonellosis Control: The Role of Animal & Product Hygiene: Report of a WHO Expert Committee.** WHO Staff. (Technical Report Ser.: No. 774). 83p. 1988. 11.00 (*92-4-120774-4*) World Health.

Salmonia. Humphry Davy. (Illus.). 273p. 1970. boxed 10.75 (*0-88395-004-9*) Freshet Pr.

***Salmonid Culture.** William Pennell. (Developments in Aquaculture & Fisheries Science Ser.). Date not set. write for info. (*0-444-88804-7*) Elsevier.

Salmonid Ecosystems of the North Pacific. Ed. by William J. McNeil & Daniel C. Himsworth. LC 80-17800. (Illus.). 348p. 1980. pap. 26.95 (*0-87071-335-3*) Oreg St U Pr.

Salmonid Reproduction: Review Papers from an International Symposium. Ed. by Robert N. Iwamoto & Stacia Sower. LC 85-13764. (Illus.). viii, 167p. (Orig.). 1985. pap. text ed. 10.00 (*0-934539-00-6*, WSG-WO85-2) Wash Sea Grant.

Salo Wittmayer Baron: Architect of Jewish History. Robert Liberles. (Modern Jewish Masters Ser.). (C). 1995. 45.00 (*0-8147-5088-5*) NYU Pr.

Saloman Henning's Chronicle of Courland & Livonia. BSC Staff. 268p. 1992. per. 30.00 (*0-8403-7763-0*) Kendall-Hunt.

Salome. Mark Dunster. 16p. (Orig.). 1995. pap. 4.00 (*0-89642-251-8*) Linden Pubs.

Salome. Wilde. 1996. 1.99 (*0-679-77098-4*, Modern Lib) Random.

Salome. Oscar Wilde. LC 64-21052. (Illus.). 64p. 1989. pap. 4.95 (*0-8283-1467-5*, Intl Pocket Lib) Branden Pub Co.

***Salome.** Oscar Wilde. LC 96-33620. 55p. (Orig.). 1996. pap. 7.00 (*0-88734-367-8*) Players Pr.

Salome: A Tragedy in One Act. Aubrey Beardsley & Oscar Wilde. Tr. by Alfred Douglas. pap. 5.95 (*0-486-21830-9*) Dover.

Salome: Filmscript by Richard Lee. Ricardo Lee. Tr. by Rofel Brion. LC 92-72850. (Illus.). (Orig.). (C). 1992. lib. bdg. 27.95 (*1-881261-06-9*) U Wisc Ctr SE Asian.

Salome: Filmscript by Richard Lee. Ricardo Lee. Tr. by Rofel Brion. LC 92-72850. (Illus.). (Orig.). (C). 1992. pap. text ed. 8.95 (*1-881261-07-7*) U Wisc Ctr SE Asian.

Salome: Her Life & Work. Ed. by Angela Livingstone. (Illus.). 256p. 1987. pap. 9.95 (*0-918825-61-X*) Moyer Bell.

Salome see Selected Plays

Salome & Elektra. Richard Strauss. Ed. by Nicholas John. (English National Opera Guide Series: Bilingual Libretto, Articles: No. 37). (Illus.). 128p. (Orig.). 1989. pap. 9.95 (*0-7145-4131-1*) Riverrun NY.

Salome & Other Stories. Oscar Wilde. 17.95 (*0-8488-1223-9*) Amereon Ltd.

Salome & the Dance of Writing: Portraits of Mimesis in Literature. Francoise Meltzer. LC 86-24983. (Illus.). xii, 240p. (C). 1987. 29.95 (*0-226-51971-6*) U Ch Pr.

Salome & the Dance of Writing: Portraits of Mimesis in Literature. Francoise Meltzer. LC 86-24893. xii, 238p. 1989. reprint ed. pap. text ed. 16.95 (*0-226-51972-4*) U Ch Pr.

Salome & under the Hill. unabridged ed. Oscar Wilde & Audrey Beardsley. (Illus.). 128p. 1996. reprint ed. pap. 12.95 (*1-871592-12-7*) Creation Bks.

Salome by Salome. Salome. (Illus.). 332p. 1993. 65.00 (*3-89322-451-3*, Pub. by Edition Cantz GW) Dist Art Pubs.

Salome Libretto: After Oscar Wilde's Tragedy. J. Strauss. (ENG & GER.). 1986. pap. 4.95 (*0-7935-5384-9*, 50340370) H Leonard.

Salome of the Tenements. Anzia Yezierska. LC 95-6020. (Radical Novel Reconsidered Ser.). 160p. 1995. 15.95 (*0-252-06435-6*) U of Ill Pr.

Salomo Gabirol und seine Dichtungen. Abraham Geiger. Ed. by Steven Katz. LC 79-7130. (Jewish Philosophy, Mysticism & History of Ideas Ser.). 1980. reprint ed. lib. bdg. 17.95 (*0-405-12254-3*) Ayer.

***Salomon Formstecher - Ein Deutscher Reformrabbiner.** Bettina Kratz-Ritter. (Wissenschaftliche Abhandlungen des Salomon Ludwig Steinheim-Instituts Fur Deutsch-Judische Geschichte Ser.: Vol. 1). 223p. (GER.). 1991. write for info. (*3-487-09488-6*) G Olms Pubs.

***Salomon Ludwig Steinheim - Johanna Steinheim: Briefe.** Jutta Dick & Julius H. Schoeps. 446p. (GER.). 1996. write for info. (*3-487-10158-0*) G Olms Pubs.

***Salomon Maimon. Hiob der Aufklarung.** Konrad Pfaff. (Philosophische Texte und Studien: Vol. 41). viii, 320p. (GER.). 1995. write for info. (*3-487-10068-1*) G Olms Pubs.

Salomone on Mediation: A Practice & Procedure Handbook. William G. Salomone. 233p. 1993. pap. 45.50 (*0-9635912-0-7*) W G Salomone.

Salon Album of Vera Sudeikin-Stravinsky. Vera Stravinsky. Ed. & Tr. by John E. Bowlt from RUS. LC 95-10264. 256p. 1995. text ed. 75.00 (*0-691-04424-4*) Princeton U Pr.

Salon & English Letters. Chauncey B. Tinker. LC 67-21716. 300p. 1967. reprint ed. 45.00 (*0-87752-113-1*) Gordian.

Salon & English Letters: Chapters on the Interrelations of Literature & Society in the Age of Johnson. Chauncey B. Tinker. (BCL1-PR English Literature Ser.). 390p. 1992. reprint ed. lib. bdg. 79.00 (*0-7812-7045-6*) Rprt Serv.

Salon & Picturesque Photography in Cuba, 1860-1920. Gary R. Libby. Ed. by Sandra L. Miller. (Illus.). 50p. (C). 1988. pap. 5.00 (*0-933053-02-9*) Museum Art Sciences.

Salon Biz: Tips for Success. Geri Mataya. LC 92-9492. 136p. 1992. pap. 19.95 (*1-56253-048-8*) Milady Pub.

Salon de Espejos. Nomi Joval. (Concept Books Ser.). (Illus.). 16p. (SPA.). (J). (gr. k-4). 1992. lib. bdg. 13.95 (*1-879567-07-5*, Valeria Bks) Wonder Well.

Salon Dialogue. Hoffman. LC 97-11256. (Cosmetology Ser.). 1997. pap. 18.95 (*1-56253-322-3*) Van Nos Reinhold.

Salon du Wurtemberg. Pascal Quignard. (Folio Ser.: No. 1928). 432p. (FRE.). 1986. pap. 10.96 (*2-07-037928-0*) Schoenhof.

Salon Electromagnetic. Kenneth A. Connor. (C). 1996. text ed. write for info. (*0-201-52744-8*) Addison-Wesley.

Salon Life: A Comprehensive Guide to Professionalism & Communication for Today's Hairdresser. Mark R. Gehrman. (Illus.). 100p. (Orig.). (YA). (gr. 8 up). 1995. pap. text ed. 24.95 (*0-9645124-9-1*) Rasmus Publ.

Salon Management: For Hairdressers & Beauty Therapists. T. W. Masters. 250p. 1987. text ed. 46.95 (*0-291-39709-3*, Pub. by Gower UK) Ashgate Pub Co.

Salon Management for Cosmetology Students. 4th ed. Edward J. Tezak. (Illus.). 160p. 1991. pap. 23.95 (*1-56253-065-8*) Milady Pub.

Salon Management for Cosmetology Students. 4th ed. Edward J. Tezak. (Illus.). 32p. 1992. teacher ed., text ed. 13.50 (*1-56253-068-2*) Milady Pub.

Salon of 1765 & Notes on Painting see Diderot on Art

Salon of 1767 see Diderot on Art

Salon Ovations' Guide to Aromatherapy. 2nd rev. ed. Shelley Hess. Ed. by Marlene Pratt. LC 95-11525. 207p. (C). 1996. pap. text ed. 23.95 (*1-56253-313-4*) Milady Pub.

An Asterisk (*) at the beginning of an entry indicates that the title is appearing in BIP for the first time.

Salon Psychology: How to Succeed with People & Be a Positive Person. Lewis E. Losoncy. LC 87-63500. (Illus.). 242p. (Orig.). 1988. pap. text ed. 12.95 (*0-9619951-0-6*) Matrix Univ Pr.

Salon Receptionist Handbook. Salonovations Staff. (Career Development Ser.). 1996. pap. 16.95 incl. audio (*1-56253-308-8*) Milady Pub.

***Salon Women.** Gloria F. Orenstein. Date not set. write for info. (*0-688-03764-X*) Morrow.

Salona Travis in the Virgin Islands. Romeo Malone. LC 90-61069. 256p. 1990. 14.95 (*0-944957-05-6*) Rivercross Pub.

Salonavations' the Message of Makeup: Psychology, Personality & Application. Emily Harrell. (Cosmetology Ser.). (Illus.). 160p. 1996. 34.95 (*1-56253-253-7*) Milady Pub.

***Salonica, a Family Cookbook.** Nicholas Stavroulakis. 1996. 26.00 (*0-614-25432-9*, Pub. by Talos Pr GR) Bosphorus Bks.

Salonica Terminus: Travels into the Balkan Nightmare. Fred A. Reed. 288p. 1996. pap. 15.95 (*0-88922-368-8*) Genl Dist Srvs.

Salonika. Louise Page. (Methuen New Theatrescripts Ser.). 35p. (C). 1988. pap. 6.95 (*0-413-52180-X*, A0252, Pub. by Methuen UK) Heinemann.

Salonika: Jews & Dervishes. Nicholas P. Stavroulakis. (Illus.). xii, 83p. (Orig.). 1993. pap. text ed. 16.00 (*960-7459-02-4*, Pub. by Talos Pr GR) Bosphorus Bks.

***Salonika Bay Murder: Cold War Politics & the Polk Affair.** Edmund Keeley. LC 88-34039. (Illus.). 430p. 1990. reprint ed. pap. 122.60 (*0-608-02567-4*, 2063212) Bks Demand.

Salonika Bay Murder: Gold War Politics & the Polk Affair. Edmund Keekey. (Illus.). 400p. (Orig.). 1989. pap. text ed. 17.95 (*0-691-00858-2*) Princeton U Pr.

Salonikios: The Best Violin in the Balkans. Lisbet Torp. (Illus.). 229p. 1994. pap. 50.00 (*87-7289-224-2*, Pub. by Mus Tusculanum DK) Paul & Co Pubs.

***Salonique, 1830-1912: Une Ville Ottomane a l'Age des Reformes.** Meropi Anastassiadou. (Ottoman Empire & Its Heritage Ser.: Vol. 11). (Illus.). xii, 466p. (FRE.). 1997. 160.00 (*90-04-10798-3*) E J Brill.

Salonovations Beautiful Black Styles. Louise Cotter. 160p. 1995. text ed. 39.95 (*1-56253-222-7*) Delmar.

Salonovations' Children's Styles. Beverly Getschel & Cotter. (Cosmetology Ser.). 144p. 1996. text ed. 26.95 (*1-56253-310-X*) Milady Pub.

Salonovations' Cosmetology Dictionary. 2nd rev. ed. Milady Publishing Company Staff. LC 94-23230. 512p. 1995. 14.95 (*1-56253-214-6*) Milady Pub.

Salonovations Encyclopedia. Milady Publishing Company Staff. (Cosmetology Ser.). Date not set. text ed. 49.95 (*1-56253-364-9*) Milady Pub.

Salonovations' Nail Question & Answer Book. Vicki Peters. (Cosmetology Ser.). 224p. 1996. 15.95 (*1-56253-266-9*) Milady Pub.

Salonovations' Public Relations for the Salon. Jayne Morehouse. (Cosmetology Ser.). (Illus.). 192p. 1996. 24.95 (*1-56253-271-5*) Milady Pub.

SalonOvations' Shiatsu Massage: The Oriental Approach to Beauty Enhancement. 2nd rev. ed. Erica T. Miller. (Cosmetology Ser.). 160p. 1996. pap. 29.95 (*1-56253-264-2*) Milady Pub.

Salonovation's Tax & Financial Primer. Mark E. Battersby. LC 94-39613. (Illus.). 192p. 1996. text ed. 21.95 (*1-56253-215-4*) Milady Pub.

Salonovations' the Motivated Salon: Achieve Super Salon Income. Mark Foley. LC 96-15099. (Cosmetology Ser.). 256p. 1997. 19.95 (*1-56253-320-7*) Milady Pub.

Salonovations' the Multicultural Client: Cuts, Styles & Chemical Services. Victoria Wurdinger & Milady Publishing Company Staff. LC 95-9955. 352p. 1996. pap. 31.95 (*1-56253-178-6*) Milady Pub.

Salons. 2nd ed. Denis Diderot & R. Desne. 9.95 (*0-686-56029-9*) Fr & Eur.

Salons: Colonial & Republican. Anne H. Wharton. LC 75-172550. (Illus.). 1972. reprint ed. 24.95 (*0-405-09063-3*) Ayer.

***Salons der Romantik: Beitraege Eines Wiepersdorfer Kolloquiums Zu Theorie und Geschichte des Salons.** Ed. by Hartwig Schultz. (Illus.). viii, 378p. (GER.). (C). 1997. text ed. 104.30 (*3-11-014610-X*) De Gruyter.

Saloon Keeper's Daughter Saved. Bertha Mackey. 15p. 1982. pap. 0.15 (*0-686-36264-0*); pap. 0.25 (*0-686-37285-9*) Faith Pub Hse.

Saloon on Rocky Mountain Frontier. Elliott West. LC 78-24090. xvii, 199p. 1996. pap. 12.00 (*0-8032-9784-X*, Bison Books) U of Nebr Pr.

Saloon Problem & Social Reform. John M. Barker. LC 76-112521. (Rise of Urban America Ser.). 1970. reprint ed. 25.95 (*0-405-02434-7*) Ayer.

Saloon Tokens of the United States. Joseph Schmidt & Rich Hartzog. 400p. 1997. write for info. (*0-912317-06-X*) World Exo.

Saloons of the American West: An Illustrated Chronicle. Robert L. Brown & Ed Collman. (Illus.). 144p. 1978. 19.00 (*0-913582-24-7*) Sundance.

Saloons of the Old West. Richard Erdoer. 1997. 9.99 (*0-517-18173-8*) Random Hse Value.

Salsa. (Ballroom Dance Ser.). 1986. lib. bdg. 64.95 (*0-8490-3282-2*) Gordon Pr.

Salsa. (Ballroom Dance Ser.). 1985. lib. bdg. 250.00 (*0-87700-791-8*) Revisionist Pr.

Salsa. Earl Atkinson. (Ballroom Dance Ser.). 1986. lib. bdg. 250.00 (*0-8490-3639-9*) Gordon Pr.

Salsa. P. J. Birosik. LC 92-35699. 134p. 1993. pap. 10.00 (*0-02-041641-5*) Macmillan.

Salsa. Paul Bottomer. 1996. 12.95 (*1-85967-221-3*, Lorenz Bks) Anness Pub.

Salsa. Ed. by Raoul Gordon. 1976. lib. bdg. 59.95 (*0-8490-0989-8*) Gordon Pr.

Salsa. Reed Hearon. LC 92-25585. 84p. 1993. 12.95 (*0-8118-0328-7*) Chronicle Bks.

Salsa! Hernando C. Ospina. (Illus.). 180p. 1995. pap. 19.00 (*0-85345-956-8*, PB9568) Monthly Rev.

Salsa! The Rhythm of Latin Music. Charley Gerard & Marty Sheller. Ed. by Larry W. Smith. LC 88-17164. (Performance in World Music Ser.: No. 3). (Illus.). 160p. 1989. 14.95 (*0-941677-09-5*); spiral bd. 28.95 (*0-941677-35-4*) White Cliffs Media.

Salsa! The Rhythm of Latin Music. Charley Gerard & Marty Sheller. Ed. by Larry W. Smith. LC 88-17164. (Performance in World Music Ser.: No. 3). (Illus.). 154p. 1992. 39.95 (*0-941677-11-7*) White Cliffs Media.

***Salsa! The Rhythm of Latin Music.** Ed. by Larry W. Smith. (Performance in World Music Ser.: No. 3). 144p. 1989. pap. 12.95 incl. audio (*0-941677-19-2*) White Cliffs Media.

Salsa & Chips. Daniel Reveles. 1997. pap. 11.95 (*0-345-40509-9*) Ballantine.

Salsa & Related Genres: A Bibliographical Guide. Compiled by Rafael Figueroa. LC 92-23778. (Music Reference Collection: No. 38). 128p. 1992. text ed. 47.95 (*0-313-27883-0*, FSG, Greenwood Pr) Greenwood.

***SALSA Book.** Courtney Buchanan et al. Ed. by Kieran O'Mahony. (Illus.). 475p. (Orig.). 1996. pap. 19.95 (*1-889548-00-6*) Wall Data WA.

Salsa Book. Jacqueline H. McMahan. LC 85-63671. 160p. 1986. 12.95 (*0-9612150-2-X*); per. 9.95 (*0-9612150-3-8*) Olive Pr.

Salsa Book. rev. ed. Jacqueline H. McMahan. (Illus.). 170p. 1989. pap. 14.95 (*0-9612150-8-9*) Olive Pr.

Salsa Cooking. Marjie Lambert. 1994. 17.98 (*0-7858-0023-9*) Bk Sales Inc.

Salsa Guidebook for Piano & Ensemble. Rebeca Mauleon. (Illus.). 259p. (C). 1993. pap. 20.00 (*0-9614701-9-4*) Sher Music.

Salsa Lover's Cook Book. Lee Fischer & Bruce Fischer. Ed. by Susan K. Bollin. (Illus.). 128p. 1993. pap. 5.95 (*0-914846-80-9*) Golden West Pub.

Salsa Session. Birger Sulsbruck et al. pap. 34.95 (*0-685-69138-1*, WH29999); audio 13.95 (*0-685-69139-X*, TV29999) Shawnee Pr.

Salsas! Andrea Chesman. LC 85-17114. (Specialty Cookbook Ser.). (Illus.). 144p. (Orig.). 1985. pap. 8.95 (*0-89594-178-3*) Crossing Pr.

***Salsas! 88 Exciting Salsa Recipes & the Drinks to Go with Them.** Virginia Hoffman et al. (Illus.). 80p. (Orig.). 1997. pap. 6.95 (*0-9629927-2-0*) Hoffman CA.

Salsas & Ketchup. Silvana Franca. 1995. 14.98 (*0-7858-0350-5*) Bk Sales Inc.

Salsas, Sambals, Chutneys, & Chowchows. Chris Schlesinger & John Willoughby. 1995. pap. 15.00 (*0-688-14270-2*) Hearst Bks.

Salsbury Story: A Medical Missionary's Lifetime of Public Service. Clarence G. Salsbury. LC 72-101100. (Illus.). 285p. reprint ed. pap. 81.30 (*0-317-58773-0*, 2029657) Bks Demand.

Salse Di Pomodoro: Over 60 Recipes for Italy's Great Tomato Sauces. Julia Della Croce. (Illus.). 132p. 1996. pap. 14.95 (*0-8118-0930-7*) Chronicle Bks.

Salsiology: Afro-Cuban Music & the Evolution of Salsa in New York City. Vernon W. Boggs. LC 91-43983. (Contributions to the Study of Music & Dance Ser.: No. 26). 416p. 1992. text ed. 55.00 (*0-313-28468-7*, BSP/, Greenwood Pr) Greenwood.

Salsiology: Afro-Cuban Music & the Evolution of Salsa in New York City. Vernon W. Boggs. LC 91-20149. 420p. 1992. pap. 24.00 (*0-935016-63-5*) Zinn Pub Grp.

Salt. (Metals & Minerals Ser.). 1993. lib. bdg. 250.95 (*0-8490-8953-0*) Gordon Pr.

Salt. Renee Ashley. LC 91-12357. (Brittingham Prize in Poetry Ser.). 70p. (Orig.). (C). 1992. 17.95 (*0-299-13140-8*); pap. 10.95 (*0-299-13144-0*) U of Wis Pr.

Salt. Norma M. Bracy. (Illus.). 32p. (J). (ps-12). 1986. pap. text ed. 2.50 (*0-915783-03-7*) Book Binder.

***Salt.** Earl Lovelace. LC 96-50266. 260p. 1997. 23.00 (*0-89255-226-3*) Persea Bks.

Salt. Brenda Walpole. Ed. by Rebecca Stefoff. (Threads Ser.). (Illus.). 28p. (J). (gr. 2-4). 1995. lib. bdg. 15.93 (*1-56074-060-4*) Garrett Ed Corp.

Salt: A Book of Poems by MaryAnn Maggiore. MaryAnn Maggiore. (Orig.). 1989. pap. 6.95 (*0-9623396-0-1*) Express PA.

Salt: A Russian Folktale. Tr. by Alice Plume from RUS. LC 91-74007. (Illus.). 40p. (J). (gr. k-3). 1992. 14.95 (*1-56282-178-4*) Hyprn Child.

Salt: A Russian Folktale. Tr. by Alice Plume from RUS. LC 91-74007. (Illus.). 40p. (J). (gr. k-3). 1994. pap. 5.95 (*1-56282-681-6*) Hyprn Child.

Salt: Or, the Education of Griffith Adams. A Novel. Charles G. Norris. LC 80-25152. (Lost American Fiction Ser.). 394p. 1981. reprint ed. 19.95 (*0-8093-1011-2*) S Ill U Pr.

Salt-Affected Soils. Istvan Szabolcs. 272p. 1988. 162.00 (*0-8493-4818-8*, S595, CRC Reprint) Franklin.

Salt Affected Soils of India - A Source Book. G. P. Bhargava. (C). 1989. 30.00 (*81-204-0432-7*) S Asia.

SALT Agreements. Calvo. 1987. lib. bdg. 108.00 (*90-247-3547-5*, Pub. by M Nijhoff NE) Kluwer Ac.

Salt & Civilization. S. A. Adshead. 1992. text ed. 45.00 (*0-312-06785-2*) St Martin.

Salt & Honey. Cranfield & Humphries. 1995. per. 7.95 (*0-85449-101-5*, Pub. by Gay Mens Pr UK) LPC InBook.

Salt & Hypertension. Ed. by R. Rettig et al. 385p. 1989. 118.00 (*0-387-50063-4*) Spr-Verlag.

Salt & Light. Matthew De Brincat. 56p. (J). (gr. 6-p). 1983. pap. 3.00 (*0-911423-00-1*) Bible-Speak.

Salt & Light: Talks & Writings on the Sermon on the Mount. rev. ed. Eberhard Arnold. Ed. & Tr. by Hutterian Brethren Staff from GER. LC 77-1204. 338p. 1986. pap. 8.00 (*0-87486-174-8*) Plough.

Salt & Medium Effects on Reaction Rates in Concentrated Solutions of Acids & Bases see Progress in Reaction Kinetics

Salt & Pepper Shakers. Larry Carey & Sylvia Tompkins. LC 94-65428. (Illus.). 112p. (Orig.). 1994. pap. 19.95 (*0-88740-607-6*) Schiffer.

Salt & Pepper Shakers. Helene Guarnaccia. (Illus.). 176p. 1985. pap. 9.95 (*0-89145-295-8*) Collector Bks.

***Salt & Pepper Shakers, Bk. 2.** Guarnaccia. (Illus.). 192p. 1993. pap. 14.95 (*0-614-22639-2*, 1888) Collector Bks.

Salt & Pepper Shakers: Identifications & Price Guide. Gideon Bosker & Lena Lencek. (Illus.). 382p. (Orig.). 1994. pap. 15.00 (*0-380-76958-1*, Confident Collect) Avon.

Salt & Pepper Shakers II. Helene Guarnaccia. 1993. pap. 14.95 (*0-89145-371-7*) Collector Bks.

Salt & Pepper Shakers III. Helene Guarnaccia. 1995. pap. 14.95 (*0-89145-448-9*) Collector Bks.

Salt & Pepper Shakers IV: Identification & Values. Helene Guarnaccia. 240p. 1995. pap. 18.95 (*0-89145-547-7*, 3443) Collector Bks.

Salt & Sediment Dynamics. I. Lerche & K. Petersen. LC 95-2515. 336p. 1995. 178.95 (*0-8493-7684-X*) CRC Pr.

Salt & Sediment Dynamics. Ian Lerche & Kenneth Petersen. 320p. 1995. 169.95 (*0-614-07249-2*, 7684) CRC Pr.

Salt & the Alchemical Soul. Ernest Jones et al. Ed. & Intro. by Stanton Marlan. 184p. 1995. 17.50 (*0-88214-222-4*) Spring Pubns.

Salt & Water. Horacio J. Adrogue & Donald E. Wesson. LC 94-18242. (Basics of Medicine Ser.). (Illus.). 320p. 1994. pap. 19.95 (*0-86542-426-8*) Blackwell Sci.

***Salt Creek Killing.** large type ed. David Horsley. (Linford Western Library). 272p. 1996. pap. 15.99 (*0-7089-7911-4*) Ulverscroft.

***Salt Dancers.** Ursula Hegi. 1997. pap. 12.00 (*0-684-84482-6*) S&S Trade.

Salt Dancers: A Novel. Ursula Hegi. 240p. 1995. 22.00 (*0-684-80209-0*) S&S Trade.

Salt Deformation in the Paradox Region. Hellmut H. Doelling et al. (Bulletin of the Utah Geological Survey Ser.: No. 122). (Illus.). 93p. (Orig.). 1988. pap. 9.50 (*1-55791-089-8*, B-122) Utah Geological Survey.

Salt Desert Trails: A History of the Hastings Cutoff & Other Early Trails Which Crossed the Great Salt Desert Seeking a Shorter Road to California. Charles Kelly & Peter H. Delafosse. LC 96-26519. 1996. 13.95 (*0-914740-37-7*) Western Epics.

Salt Diapirs of the Great Kavir, Central Iran. M. P. Jackson et al. (Memoir Ser.: No. 177). (Illus.). 140p. 1991. 25.00 (*0-8137-1177-0*) Geol Soc.

***Salt Domes, Gulf Region, United States & Mexico.** 2nd ed. Michel T. Halbouty. LC 79-16044. (Illus.). 609p. 1979. reprint ed. pap. 173.60 (*0-608-04206-4*, 2064941) Bks Demand.

***Salt Dough: 20 Practical Projects for the Home.** (Inspirations Ser.). (Illus.). 96p. 1997. 12.95 (*1-85967-537-9*, Lorenz Bks) Anness Pub.

Salt Dough Fun. Lorenz Books Staff. 64p. (J). 1996. 7.95 (*1-85967-220-5*, Lorenz Bks) Anness Pub.

Salt Dough Models. Catherine Baillaud. (Crafty Hands Collection). 48p. 1995. pap. 9.99 (*1-85410-328-8*, Pub. by Aurum Pr UK) London Brdge.

Salt Dough Models. Sue Organ. (Illus.). 48p. (YA). 1993. pap. 12.95 (*0-85532-756-1*, 756-1, Pub. by Search Pr UK) A Schwartz & Co.

Salt Eaters. Toni Cade Bambara. 304p. 1992. pap. 11.00 (*0-679-74076-7*, Vin) Random.

Salt Ecstasies. James L. White. LC 81-82140. 53p. 1982. pap. 5.00 (*0-915308-32-0*) Graywolf.

Salt Effects in Organic & Organometallic Chemistry. Andre Loupy & Bianca Tchoubar. 322p. 1992. 125.00 (*3-527-28025-1*, VCH) Wiley.

***Salt Fluoridation.** (PAHO Scientific Publication Ser.: No. 501). 202p. 1986. text ed. 20.00 (*92-75-11501-X*) World Health.

Salt-Free Baking at Home. Prudence H. Ahrens. 1985. pap. 10.95 (*0-911506-19-5*) Thueson.

Salt Glands in Birds & Reptiles. M. Peaker & J. L. Linzell. LC 75-314900. (Monographs of the Physiological Society: No. 32). 318p. reprint ed. pap. 90.70 (*0-317-28146-1*, 2022465) Bks Demand.

Salt-Glaze Ceramics. Janet Mansfield. 144p. 1992. 39.95 (*0-8019-8344-4*) Chilton.

Salt Glaze Ceramics: An International Perspective. Janet Mansfield. 144p. 1991. text ed. write for info. (*976-8097-11-6*) Gordon & Breach.

Salt Hands. Jane C. Aragon. (Illus.). 24p. (J). (ps-2). 1994. pap. 5.99 (*0-14-050321-8*, Puff Unicorn) Puffin Bks.

SALT I: Breakthrough or Deadlock? Paul R. Bennet. (Pew Case Studies in International Affairs). 59p. (C). 1988. pap. text ed. 3.50 (*1-56927-303-0*) Geo U Inst Dplmcy.

SALT I: Getting from "Nyet" to "Yes" Nancy D. Kates. (Pew Case Studies in International Affairs). 50p. (C). 1995. pap. text ed. 3.50 (*1-56927-339-1*) Geo U Inst Dplmcy.

SALT I: The Limitations of Arms Negotiations. Jonathan Haslam & Theresa Osborne. (Pew Case Studies in International Affairs). 50p. (C). 1988. pap. text ed. 3.50 (*1-56927-304-9*) Geo U Inst Dplmcy.

Salt II & American Security. Jeffrey Record et al. 65p. 1980. 11.95 (*0-89549-024-2*) Inst Foreign Policy Anal.

SALT II & the Soviet First-Strike Threat. Paul R. Bennett. (Pew Case Studies in International Affairs). 50p. (C). 1993. pap. text ed. 3.50 (*1-56927-330-8*) Geo U Inst Dplmcy.

***Salt in His Blood: The Life of Michael De Ruyter.** William R. Rang. LC 96-39179. (J). 1996. write for info. (*0-921100-59-0*) Inhtce Pubns.

Salt in My Kitchen. Jeanette Lockerbie. (Quiet Time Books for Women). 1967. pap. 4.99 (*0-8024-7500-0*) Moody.

Salt in the Bible. Charles A. Tulga. 1989. reprint ed. pap. 3.99 (*0-88019-245-3*) Schmul Pub Co.

Salt Industry of Bengal Seventeen Fifty-Seven to Eighteen Hundred. Balai Barui. 1985. 17.50 (*0-8364-1478-0*, Pub. by KP Bagchi IA) S Asia.

Salt Is Leaving. J. B. Priestley. 224p. 1986. reprint ed. pap. 3.95 (*0-88184-227-3*) Carroll & Graf.

***Salt Lake & Surrounding Area.** Peak Media, Inc. Staff. (Trail Books Ser.). 1997. 24.95 (*1-889364-01-0*) Peak Media.

Salt Lake City. Becky Ayres. LC 90-2968. (Downtown America Ser.). (Illus.). 60p. (J). (gr. 3 up). 1990. lib. bdg. 13.95 (*0-87518-436-7*, Dillon Silver Burdett) Silver Burdett Pr.

Salt Lake City Candidate to Host the Nineteenth Olympic Winter Games, 2002. Mary Gaddie et al. Tr. by Charlotte Carlus. LC 93-87369. 1994. pap. write for info. (*0-9627533-3-5*) Salt Lake Olympics.

Salt Lake City Candidate to Host the 18th Olympic Winter Games, 1998, 2 vols., I. Mary Gaddie et al. LC 90-62615. (Illus.). 1990. write for info. (*0-9627533-0-0*) Salt Lake Olympics.

Salt Lake City Candidate to Host the 18th Olympic Winter Games, 1998, 2 vols., II. Mary Gaddie et al. LC 90-62615. (Illus.). 1990. write for info. (*0-9627533-1-9*) Salt Lake Olympics.

Salt Lake City Candidate to Host the 18th Olympic Winter Games, 1998, 2 vols., Set. Mary Gaddie et al. LC 90-62615. (Illus.). 1990. write for info. (*0-9627533-2-7*) Salt Lake Olympics.

***Salt Lake City in a Different Light.** Photos by Don Busath. LC 96-70254. 150p. 1996. text ed. 49.95 (*1-57636-025-3*) SunRise Pbl.

***Salt Lake City Jobbank.** Adams Media Staff. 1997. pap. text ed. 16.95 (*1-55850-738-8*) Adams Media.

Salt Lake City Meeting: Regular Meetings of the Division of Particles & Fields APS. Ed. by J. Ball & C. DeTar. 680p. 1987. pap. 70.00 (*9971-5-0244-5*); text ed. 148.00 (*9971-5-0243-7*) World Scientific Pub.

Salt Lake City Skyline. Thomas Babe. 1980. pap. 5.25 (*0-8222-0982-9*) Dramatists Play.

***Salt Lake City Uncovered.** Sierra Adare & Candy V. Moulton. LC 96-40200. 320p. 1997. pap. 16.95 (*1-55622-534-2*, Seaside Pr) Wordware Pub.

Salt Lake City Underfoot: Self-Guide Tours of Historic Neighborhoods (Centennial Edition) 2nd ed. Mark Angus. LC 96-6997. (Illus.). 220p. 1993. pap. 12.95 (*1-56085-105-8*) Signature Bks.

Salt Lake City, UT. (Streetfinder Ser.). (Illus.). 1994. pap. 12.95 (*0-528-91315-8*) Rand McNally.

Salt Lake Temple: A Monument to a People. Charles M. Hamilton & C. Nina Cutrubus. LC 83-81785. (Illus.). 208p. 1983. 50.00 (*0-913535-06-0*) Univ Servs Inc.

Salt Lake Temple: A Monument to a People. Ed. by Charles M. Hamilton & C. Nina Cutrubus. (Illus.). 208p. 1983. write for info. (*0-913535-01-X*); pap. write for info. (*0-913535-02-8*) Univ Servs Inc.

Salt Lake Temple: A Monument to a People. limited ed. Ed. by Charles M. Hamilton & C. Nina Cutrubus. (Illus.). 208p. 1983. 250.00 (*0-913535-00-1*) Univ Servs Inc.

Salt Lake Valley: Crossroads of the West. Cheryl A. Smith. 1989. 34.95 (*0-89781-306-5*) Am Historical Pr.

Salt Lakes. W. D. Williams. (Developments in Hydrobiology Ser.: No. 5). 458p. 1981. lib. bdg. 234.00 (*90-6193-756-6*) Kluwer Ac.

***Salt Lantern: Traces of an American Family.** William T. Morgan. LC 97-17333. (American Land & Life Ser.). (Illus.). 232p. 1997. text ed. 29.95 (*0-87745-613-5*) U of Iowa Pr.

***Salt Lantern: Traces of an American Family.** William T. Morgan. LC 97-17333. (American Land & Life Ser.). (Illus.). 232p. 1997. pap. 15.95 (*0-87745-614-3*) U of Iowa Pr.

Salt, Leaven & Light: The Community Called Church. T. Howland Sanks. 240p. 1992. 21.95 (*0-8245-1175-1*) Crossroad NY.

***Salt, Leaven & Light: The Community Called Church.** T. Howland Sanks. 264p. 1997. pap. 19.95 (*0-8245-1666-4*, Crossrd Herd) Crossroad NY.

Salt Line: A Novel. Elizabeth Spencer. LC 84-19043. (Voices of the South Ser.). 320p. (C). 1995. pap. 12.95 (*0-8071-2029-4*) La State U Pr.

Salt Maker of Maldon. Gillian Soudah. 1993. pap. 15.00 (*0-86025-414-3*, Pub. by Ian Henry Pubns UK) Empire Pub Srvs.

***Salt Marsh Reflections.** Aline Fourier. (Illus.). 16p. (Orig.). 1996. pap. 19.95 (*0-9653559-0-X*) Creat Response.

Salt Marshes & Salt Deserts of the World. 2nd ed. Valentie J. Chapman. 1974. 125.00 (*3-7682-0927-X*) Lubrecht & Cramer.

Salt of Common Life: Individuality & Choice in the Medieval Town, Countryside, & Church. Ed. by Edwin B. DeWindt. (Studies in Medieval Culture: Vol. 36). 1996. pap. 20.00 (*1-879288-47-8*); boxed 50.00 (*1-879288-46-X*) Medieval Inst.

***Salt of the Earth.** Batzinger. 1997. pap. text ed. 12.95 (*0-89870-640-8*) Ignatius Pr.

Salt of the Earth. Bernadette Pruitt. LC 87-83381. 71p. 1988. 12.00 (*0-934188-27-0*) Evans Pubns.

Salt of the Earth. Sally Spencer. 416p. 1994. 24.95 (*1-85797-173-6*) Trafalgar.

Salt of the Earth. Clarence M. Wagner. Ed. by Tru-Faith Publishers Staff. 80p. (Orig.). 1981. pap. 3.50 (*0-937498-01-7*) Tru-Faith.

S

An Asterisk (*) at the beginning of an entry indicates that the title is appearing in BIP for the first time.

Salt of the Earth. Michael Wilson. LC 78-4212. (Illus.). 208p. 1978. pap. 10.95 (*0-912670-45-2*) Feminist Pr.

Salt of the Earth: A History of Immaculate Conception Parish, Carnegie, Pa., 1893-1992. James W. Garvey. (Illus.). 80p. (Orig.). 1994. pap. 30.00 (*0-939332-21-3*) J Pohl Assocs.

Salt of the Earth: One Family's Journey Through the Violent American Landscape. Jack Olsen. (Illus.). 376p. 1996. 24.95 (*0-312-14406-7*) St Martin.

***Salt of the Earth: One Family's Journey Through the Violent American Landscape.** Jack Olsen. 1997. mass mkt. 6.99 (*0-312-95998-2*) St Martin.

Salt of the Earth: The History of the Catholic Church in Utah, 1776- 1987. 2nd rev. ed. Bernice Maher Mooney. (Illus.). 546p. 1992. 15.00 (*0-9619627-1-2*) Catholic Diocese SLC.

Salt of the Earth: The Political Origins of Protest & Communist Revolution in China. Ralph V. Thaxton. LC 96-20359. (Illus.). 1997. 65.00 (*0-520-20318-6*) U CA Pr.

Salt of the Earth: The Story of a Film. Herbert Biberman. Ed. by Carlos E. Cortes. LC 76-1248. (Chicano Heritage Ser.). (Illus.). 1977. reprint ed. 17.95 (*0-405-09486-8*) Ayer.

Salt on the Windowpane: Doggered, Counterpoint & Main Theme from the New England Seacoast. rev. ed. Garvin McCurdy. (Illus.). 90p. 1994. 11.00 (*0-9641979-0-1*) Info Age Handyman.

Salt One: The Limitations of Arms Negotiations. Jonathan Haslam & Theresa Osborne. 56p. (Orig.). (C). 1987. pap. text ed. 11.75 (*0-941700-09-7*) JH FPI SAIS.

Salt Production Techniques in Ancient China: The Aobo Tu. Yoshida Tora. Tr. by Hans U. Vogel from JPN. LC 92-31206. 1992. write for info. (*90-04-09657-4*) Little.

Salt Rakers. large type ed. Barbara Whitnell. 608p. 1987. 27.99 (*0-7089-8437-1*, Charnwood) Ulverscroft.

Salt-River Pima-Maricopa Indians. John L. Myers & Robert Gryder. (Illus.). 176p. (Orig.). (C). 1988. write for info. (*0-929690-01-X*); pap. write for info. (*0-929690-00-1*) Herit Pubs AZ.

Salt Satyagraha in Coastal Andhra. C. M. Naidu. 238p. 1986. 13.50 (*0-8364-2033-0*, Pub. by Mittal II) S Asia.

Salt Stone: Selected Poems. John Woods. LC 83-20747. 224p. 1985. 16.00 (*0-937872-18-0*); pap. 8.00 (*0-937872-19-9*) Dragon Gate.

Salt Tectonics. Ed. by G. I. Alsop et al. (Geological Society Special Publication Ser.: No. 100). 320p. 1995. 110.00 (*1-897799-44-6*, 343, Pub. by Geol Soc Pub Hse UK) AAPG.

Salt Tectonics: A Global Perspective: Based on the Hedberg International Research Conference, Bath, U. K., September 1993. Ed. by M. P. Jackson et al. (Memoir Ser.: No. 65). (Illus.). xiii, 454p. 1996. 119.00 (*0-89181-344-6*, 565) AAPG.

Salt Tectonics on the Continental Slope, Northeast Green Canyon Area, Northern Gulf of Mexico: Evolution of Stocks & Massifs from Reactivation of Salt Sheets. S. J. Seni. (Report of Investigations Ser.: No. RI 212). (Illus.). 102p. 1994. pap. 6.50 (*0-614-01861-7*) Bur Econ Geology.

Salt Tide: Cycles & Currents of Life along the Coast. Curtis J. Badger. LC 92-28804. (Illus.). 160p. 1993. 16.95 (*0-8117-1632-5*) Stackpole.

Salt Tolerance of Crops & Plant Metabolism in Saline Substrate: An Annotated Bibliography, 1940-1980. G. L. Maliwal. 1981. 75.00 (*0-685-21852-X*, Pub. by Intl Bk Distr II) St Mut.

Salt Tolerance of Crops & Plants Metabolism in Saline Substrate: An Annotated Bibliography. G. L. Maliwal. (C). 1989. text ed. 135.00 (*0-89771-581-0*, Pub. by Intl Bk Distr II) St Mut.

***Salt Water.** Andrew Motion. 1997. pap. 11.95 (*0-571-19019-7*) Faber & Faber.

Salt Water Fishing. Mark Sosin & George Poveromo. (Illus.). 88p. (Orig.). 1988. pap. 12.95 (*0-945443-00-5*) M Sosin Comns.

Salt Water Fishing for Fun & Food. M. John Powell. (Illus.). 1982. pap. 8.95 (*0-941238-03-2*) Penobscot Bay.

Salt-Water Fly Tying. Frank Wentink. (Illus.). 192p. 1991. 22.95 (*1-55821-133-0*) McGraw.

Salt Water Intrusion. Atkinson. 1986. 223.00 (*0-87371-054-1*, GB1197, CRC Reprint) Franklin.

Salt-Water Moon. David French. 1988. pap. 5.25 (*0-8222-1388-5*) Dramatists Play.

Salt-Water Salmon Angling. Bob Mottram. (Illus.). 140p. 1990. pap. 9.95 (*0-936608-89-7*) F Amato Pubns.

Salt-Water Trinnies: Afro-Trinidadian Immigrant Networks & Non-Assimilation in Los Angeles. Christine G. Ho. LC 91-2297. (Immigrant Communities & Ethnic Minorities in the U. S. & Canada Ser.: No. 73). 1991. 42.50 (*0-404-19483-4*) AMS Pr.

***Salt Weathering Hazard.** Andrew Goudie & Heather A. Viles. LC 97-20299. 1997. write for info. (*0-471-95842-5*) Wiley.

Salt Works: Ohio Review Books. Michale Chitwood. LC 92-27430. 72p. 1992. 16.95 (*0-942148-15-0*) Ohio Review.

***Salt 9, Vol. 9.** Ed. by John Kinsella. (Illus.). 240p. 1996. pap. 16.95 (*1-86368-169-8*, Pub. by Fremantle Arts AT) Intl Spec Bk.

Salta, Ranita, Salta. Robert Kalan. (Illus.). (SPA.). (J). (ps-3). 1996. 22.95 incl. audio (*0-87499-368-7*); pap. 15.95 incl. audio (*0-87499-367-9*) Live Oak Media.

Salta, Ranita, Salta, 4 bks., Set. Robert Kalan. (Illus.). (SPA.). (J). (ps-3). 1996. pap. 31.95 incl. audio (*0-87499-369-5*) Live Oak Media.

Salta, Ranita, Salta: Jump, Frog, Jump. Robert Kalan. Ed. by Amy Cohn. Tr. by Aida E. Marcuse. LC 81-1401. (Illus.). 32p. (SPA.). (J). (ps up). 1994. pap. 4.95 (*0-688-13804-7*, Mulberry) Morrow.

Salta, Ranita, Salta! - Jump, Frog, Jump! Robert Kalan. LC 81-1401. (J). (ps-3). 1994. 15.00 (*0-688-13805-5*, Mulberry) Morrow.

Salta y Brinca. Ellen S. Walsh. (J). 1996. pap. 6.00 (*0-15-201356-3*) HarBrace.

Saltair. Nancy D. McCormick & John S. McCormick. LC 85-665. (Bonneville Bks.). (Illus.). 117p. (Orig.). reprint ed. pap. 33.40 (*0-8357-4375-6*, 2037205) Bks Demand.

Saltair na Rann. Oengus the Culdee. Tr. by B. MacCarthy from IRI. 1987. reprint ed. pap. 9.95 (*0-89979-036-4*) British Am Bks.

Saltair Na Rann. Ed. by William H. Stokes. (Anecdota Oxoniensia Ser.: No. 3). 1988. reprint ed. 49.50 (*0-404-63953-4*) AMS Pr.

Saltamontes Va Da Viage. Arnold Lobel. Date not set. pap. text ed. 9.95 (*84-204-3053-6*) Santillana.

Saltarin: Hopper. Marcus Pfister. (Illus.). 32p. (J). (ps-3). Date not set. 15.95 (*1-55858-563-X*, Ediciones NY); pap. 6.95 (*1-55858-548-6*, Ediciones NY) North-South Bks NYC.

Saltasaurio. Janet Riehecky. (Libros Sobre Dinosaurios! Ser.). (Illus.). 32p. (SPA.). (J). (gr. k-4). 1990. lib. bdg. 21.36 (*1-56766-138-6*) Childs World.

Saltasaurus. Janet Riehecky. (Dinosaur Bks.). (Illus.). 32p. (J). (gr. k-4). 1990. lib. bdg. 21.36 (*0-89565-635-3*) Childs World.

Saltatoria (Bush-Crickets, Crickets & Grasshoppers) of Northern Europe. Knud T. Holst. (Fauna Entomologica Scandinavica Ser.: No. 16). (Illus.). 127p. 1986. 34.00 (*90-04-07860-6*) Lubrecht & Cramer.

Saltbox & Cape-Cod Houses. Stanley Schuler. LC 88-63932. 160p. 1989. text ed. 29.95 (*0-88740-156-2*) Schiffer.

Salted Tories: The Story of the Whaling Fleets of San Francisco. Lloyd C. Hare. LC 68-46999. (Marine Historical Association, Publication Ser.: No. 37). 136p. reprint ed. pap. 38.80 (*0-8357-2792-0*, 2039918) Bks Demand.

Salted with Fire. George MacDonald. (George MacDonald Original Works: Series VII). 325p. 1996. 18.00 (*1-881084-44-2*) Johannesen.

Salted with Fire. deluxe ed. George MacDonald. 1989. 26.50 (*0-940652-98-6*) Sunrise Bks.

Salted with Fire: Spirituality for the Faithjustice Journey. Fred Kammer. LC 94-33444. 1995. pap. 11.95 (*0-8091-3540-X*) Paulist Pr.

Salted with Fire: Unitarian Universalist Strategies for Sharing Faith & Growing Congregations. Ed. by Scott Alexander. 272p. 1994. pap. 18.00 (*1-55896-289-1*, Skinner Hse Bks) Unitarian Univ.

Salterton Trilogy. Robertson Davies. 784p. 1991. pap. 17.95 (*0-14-015910-X*, Penguin Bks) Viking Penguin.

Saltire Scottish Song Book. Hardie Press Staff. 105p. 1991. pap. 45.00 (*0-946868-07-7*, Pub. by Hardie Pr UK) St Mut.

Saltire Two-Part Scottish Song Book: 15 Traditional Scottish Songs for Two Voices with Piano Accompaniment, Suitable for Adults & Children Male & Female Voices, Duet or Group Singing. Hardie Press Staff. 1991. pap. 60.00 (*0-946868-05-0*, Pub. by Hardie Pr UK); pap. 45.00 (*0-946868-06-9*, Pub. by Hardie Pr UK) St Mut.

Saltmarsh Ecology. Paul Adam. (Cambridge Studies in Ecology). (Illus.). 400p. (C). 1990. text ed. 110.00 (*0-521-24508-7*) Cambridge U Pr.

Saltmarsh Ecology. Paul Adam. (Studies in Ecology). (Illus.). 432p. (C). 1993. pap. text ed. 39.95 (*0-521-44823-9*) Cambridge U Pr.

Saltonstall Papers Vol. 1: 1607-1815, Vol. 1. Ed. by Robert E. Moody. (Collections of the Massachusetts Historical Society Ser.: Vols. 80-81). (Illus.). 1972. Vol. 2 1974, 655 pps. 50.00 (*0-934909-24-5*) Mass Hist Soc.

Saltonstall Papers Vol. 2: 1607-1815, Vol. 2. Ed. by Robert E. Moody. (Collections of the Massachusetts Historical Society Ser.: Vols. 80-81). (Illus.). 574p. 1978. Vol. 1 1972, 574 pps. 50.00 (*0-934909-25-3*) Mass Hist Soc.

Saltonstalls of New England: 350 Years in Public Life. Ed. by Robert E. Moody. LC 78-106214. (Picture Bks.). 1978. pap. 4.00 (*0-934909-14-8*) Mass Hist Soc.

Salts & Brines '85: Proceeding of the Symposium Solution Mining of Salts & Brines, New York, New York, February 25-26, 1985. Society of Mining Engineers of AIME Staff. Ed. by W. Joseph Schlitt & William C. Larson. LC 84-52557. 218p. reprint ed. pap. 62.20 (*0-8357-2568-5*, 2040258) Bks Demand.

Salts & Solids. Robert C. Mebane & Thomas R. Rybolt. (Everyday Material Science Experiments Ser.). (Illus.). 64p. (J). (gr. 5-8). 1995. lib. bdg. 15.98 (*0-8050-2841-2*) TFC Bks NY.

Saltville Massacre. Thomas B. Mays. LC 95-23723. (Civil War Campaigns & Commanders Ser.). (Illus.). 91p. (Orig.). 1995. pap. 11.95 (*1-886661-05-7*, 61057) Ryan Place Pub.

***Saltwater.** Andrew Motion. (Orig.). 1997. pap. 12.95 (*0-614-25018-8*) Faber & Faber.

Saltwater Adventure in the Florida Keys: An Introduction to Fishing for Kids. Jacky Robinson. LC 94-60394. (Illus.). 104p. (J). (gr. 3-7). 1994. lib. bdg. 19.95 (*0-9641228-0-4*) White Heron.

Saltwater Aquarium Fishes. Herbert R. Axelrod & Warren Burgess. (Illus.). 1992. 23.95 (*0-86622-499-8*, H-914) TFH Pubns.

Saltwater Farm. Lutera B. Dawson. (Illus.). 109p. (Orig.). 1993. pap. 7.95 (*0-9637523-0-8*) Impatiens Pr.

Saltwater Fish Cookbook. A. D. Livingston. LC 96-47102. (Illus.). 288p. 1997. pap. 19.95 (*0-8117-2924-9*) Stackpole.

Saltwater Fisherman's Bible. Erwin A. Bauer. 176p. 1991. pap. 12.95 (*0-385-26444-5*) Doubleday.

***Saltwater Fishes of Texas: A Guide to Knowing & Catching Bay & Gulf Fishes.** Ed. by Georg Zappler. (Illus.). 42p. 1993. pap. 9.95 (*0-9636765-3-9*) TX Prks & Wldlife.

Saltwater Fishing. Robert Anderson. (Illus.). 120p. (Orig.). 1989. pap. 5.95 (*0-8200-0128-7*) Great Outdoors.

Saltwater Fishing. Barney Rowe. (Illus.). 36p. (Orig.) 1983. pap. 3.80 (*0-940844-55-9*) Wellspring.

Saltwater Fishing. Jack Zinzow. LC 91-65378. (Illus.). 64p. (Orig.). 1992. pap. 3.95 (*0-89317-041-0*) Windward Pub.

Saltwater Fishing Guide. Pete Barrett. Ed. by Linda Barrett. (Fisherman Library). (Illus.). 256p. (C). 1994. pap. text ed. 18.95 (*0-923155-14-7*) Fisherman Lib.

Saltwater Fishing in California: Secrets of the Pacific Experts. 4th ed. Ron Kovach. 1996. pap. 14.95 (*0-934061-29-7*) Marketscope Bks.

Saltwater Fishing in Washington. 2nd ed. Frank Haw & Raymond M. Buckley. Ed. by Stanton L. Jones. (Illus.). 200p. (Orig.). reprint ed. pap. 8.95 (*0-939936-00-3*) Jones Pub.

Saltwater Flats: A Silent Film. Elihu Blotnick. LC 74-18166. (Illus.). 64p. 1975. pap. 16.95 (*0-915090-00-7*) Calif Street.

Saltwater Flies: Over 700 of the Best. Deke Meyer. (Illus.). 120p. 1995. pap. 34.95 (*1-57188-020-8*) F Amato Pubns.

Saltwater Fly Fishing. John A. Kumiski. Ed. by Linda Barrett. (Illus.). 200p. (Orig.). 1994. pap. text ed. write for info. (*0-923155-23-6*) Fisherman Lib.

Saltwater Fly Fishing. Jack Samson. LC 90-23235. (Illus.). 240p. 1991. 27.95 (*0-8117-1653-8*) Stackpole.

Saltwater Fly Fishing for Pacific Salmon. Barry M. Thornton. 1995. pap. 17.95 (*0-88839-268-0*) Hancock House.

Saltwater Fly Fishing for Pacific Salmon. limited ed. Barry M. Thornton. 1995. 75.00 (*0-88839-372-5*) Hancock House.

Saltwater Fly-Fishing Magic. Neal Rogers & Linda Rogers. (Illus.). 144p. 1993. 45.00 (*1-55821-253-1*) Lyons & Burford.

Saltwater Fly Patterns. rev. ed. Lefty Kreh. (Illus.). 224p. 1995. 35.00 (*1-55821-336-8*); pap. 19.95 (*1-55821-337-6*) Lyons & Burford.

Saltwater Fly Tying. Frank Wentink. (Illus.). 192p. 1994. pap. 22.95 (*1-55821-355-4*) Lyons & Burford.

Saltwater Foodways: New Englanders & Their Food, at Sea & Ashore, in the Nineteenth Century. Sandra L. Oliver. (Illus.). xiii, 442p. 1995. 39.95 (*0-913372-72-2*) Mystic Seaport.

Saltwater Game Fish of North America. Herbert A. Schaffner. LC 94-27974. 144p. 1995. pap. 14.95 (*1-56799-158-0*, Friedman-Fairfax) M Friedman Pub Grp Inc.

Saltwater Game Fishing: Offshore & Onshore. Peter Goadby. 1992. text ed. 44.95 (*0-07-011544-3*) McGraw.

Saltwater Gamefishing: Offshore & Onshore. Peter Goadby. (Illus.). 352p. 1992. text ed. 44.95 (*0-87742-323-7*) Intl Marine.

Saltwater Seasonings: Good Food from Coastal Maine. Sarah L. Chase & Jonathan Chase. (Illus.). 192p. 1992. 29.95 (*0-316-13812-6*) Little.

Saltwater Stories (EV) Independent Reader 5-Pack, Unit 9. (Networks Ser.). 1991. 15.00 (*0-88106-774-1*, N316) Charlesbridge Pub.

Saltwater Village. Ed. by Margaret Leather. 140p. 1990. pap. 21.00 (*0-86138-022-3*, Pub. by T Dalton UK) St Mut.

***Saltwater Women at Work.** Vickie Jensen. (Illus.). 192p. (Orig.). 1997. pap. 14.95 (*1-55054-436-5*) Orca Bk Pubs.

Saltworks of Historic Cape Cod. William Quinn. LC 92-83913. (Illus.). 256p. 1993. 29.95 (*0-940160-56-0*) Parnassus Imprints.

Salty & Felicia. Lass Small. 1994. mass mkt. 2.99 (*0-373-05860-8*, 5-05860-7) Harlequin Bks.

***Salty Diamonds.** David C. Cable. 208p. (Orig.). 1997. mass mkt. 4.99 (*1-55237-355-X*, Pub. by Comnwlth Pub CN) Partners Pubs Grp.

Salty Dog. Gloria Rand. LC 88-13453. (Illus.). 32p. (J). (ps-2). 1991. pap. 4.95 (*0-8050-1847-6*, Bks Young Read) H Holt & Co.

***Salty Dog.** Brad Strickland. (Adventures of Wishbone Ser.: Vol. 2). (Illus.). 144p. (Orig.). (J). (gr. 3-6). 1997. mass mkt. 3.99 (*1-57064-194-3*, Big Red) Lyrick Pub.

Salty Dog Talk: The Nautical Origins of Everyday Expressions. Bill Beavis & Richard G. McCloskey. 1994. pap. 6.95 (*0-924486-82-1*) Sheridan.

***Salty Dog/Be a Wolf!** Brad Strickland. (Adventures of Wishbone Ser.). (Illus.). (J). 1997. pap. text ed. 7.88 (*1-57064-230-3*, Barney Publ) Lyrick Pub.

Salty Sails North. Gloria Rand. LC 89-39063. (Illus.). 32p. (J). (ps-3). 1992. pap. 4.95 (*0-8050-2188-4*, Owlet BYR) H Holt & Co.

Salty Scarecrow Solution. Nancy Levene. LC 89-31274. 128p. (J). (gr. 3-6). 1989. pap. 4.99 (*1-55513-523-4*, Chariot Bks) Chariot Victor.

Salty Seagull: A Tale of an Old Salt. Suzanne Tate. LC 92-60375. (Suzanne Tate's Nature Ser.: No. 12). (Illus.). 28p. (Orig.). (J). (gr. k-4). 1992. pap. 3.95 (*1-878405-06-3*) Nags Head Art.

Salty Shore: The Story of the River Blackwater. John Leather. 216p. 1990. 36.00 (*0-900963-52-2*, Pub. by T Dalton UK) St Mut.

Salty Stories of Cape Cod, No. 23. Noel W. Beyle. (Illus.). 48p. (Orig.). 1984. pap. 0.95 (*0-912609-06-0*) First Encounter.

Salty Water. Pat Ingoldsby. 1990. pap. 11.95 (*0-86278-178-7*) Dufour.

Salty Wisdom: Proverbs of the Sea. Wolfgang Mieder. LC 90-52966. (Illus.). 64p. (Orig.). 1990. pap. 6.95 (*0-933050-82-8*) New Eng Pr VT.

Saltykov & the Russian Squire. Nikander Strelsky. reprint ed. 21.00 (*0-404-06298-9*) AMS Pr.

***Salud! A Latina's Guide to Total Health, Body, Mind & Spirit.** Jane L. Delgado. 352p. 1997. 40.00 (*0-06-055367-7*); pap. 20.00 (*0-06-095187-7*, PL) HarpC.

***Salud! Guia Integral Para la Salud Fisca, Mental y Espiritual de la Mujer Latina.** Jane L. Delgado. 1997. pap. text ed. 20.00 (*0-06-095261-X*, PL) HarpC.

Salud, Amor y Pesetas! Basic Communication in Spanish. Frederick Suarez-Richard. 192p. (C). 1980. pap. text ed. 18.00 (*0-15-578050-6*) HB Coll Pubs.

Salud de Hombres. Loretta Hilsher-Kurban. (SPA.). 1991. 8.00 (*0-938863-43-6*) Libra Press Chi.

Salud de la Mujer. Loretta Hilsher-Kurban. (SPA.). 1991. 8.00 (*0-938863-44-4*) Libra Press Chi.

Salud Herbal de Hoy. Louise Tenney. (Today's Herbal Health Ser.). 308p. (SPA.). 1994. pap. 14.95 (*0-913923-93-1*) Woodland UT.

Salud Herbal de Hoy: La Guia de Referencia Esencial para Engender el Uso de las Plantas. Louise Tenney. 1994. pap. 14.95 (*0-913923-87-7*) Woodland UT.

Saluda County, South Carolina, Epitaphs: Still Villages. June A. Seay. LC 86-90675. (Registry of Tombstone Epitaphs Ser.: Vol. I). (Illus.). 227p. (Orig.). 1987. pap. 32.50 (*0-9617786-0-1*); write for info. (*0-9617786-1-X*) June A Seay.

***Saludo en el Siglo: Sobreviviran los Medicas?** Francisco Contreras. Ed. by Pamela M. Lowe. Tr. by Luisa Ruiz. (Illus.). 340p. (Orig.). (SPA.). 1997. mass mkt. 19.95 (*1-57946-001-1*) Interpacific Pr.

Saludos: Poemas de Nuevo Mexico, a Bilingual Poetry Anthology. Ed. by Jeanie C. Williams & Victor Di Suvero. LC 94-69459. (Anthology Ser.). 287p. (SPA.). 1995. pap. 15.00 (*0-938631-33-0*) Pennywhistle Pr.

Saluki Champions, 1952-1989. Camino E. E. & Bk. Co. Staff. (Illus.). 180p. 1991. pap. 36.95 (*0-940808-97-8*) Camino E E & Bk.

Saluki in History, Art & Sport. deluxe ed. David Waters & Hope Waters. (Illus.). 124p. 1995. 60.00 (*0-614-04546-0*) Donald R Hoflin.

Salukis. Virginia M. Burch. (Illus.). 1990. 9.95 (*0-86622-771-7*, KW-189) TFH Pubns.

Saluqi: Coursing Hound of the East. Ed. by Gail Goodman. 872p. (C). 1995. 150.00 (*0-9639224-0-8*) Midbar.

Saluqi: Coursing Hound of The East. deluxe limited ed. Ed. by Gail Goodman. 872p. 1995. lthr. 350.00 (*0-614-12731-9*) Midbar.

Saluso's Game. Bill Badke. 260p. 1996. pap. 9.99 (*0-88070-866-2*, Multnomah Bks) Multnomah Pubs.

Salut. (FRE.). 1989. 3.95 (*0-86508-375-4*) BCM Pubn.

Salut et Fraternite: Avec: Alain et R. Rolland. Romain Rolland. 184p. (FRE.). 1969. pap. 8.95 (*0-7859-5465-1*) Fr & Eur.

Salut! Stage 1 Textbook. ITE Staff. 160p. (C). 1985. pap. 11.95 (*0-521-26954-7*) Cambridge U Pr.

Salut (1944-1946) see Memoires de Guerre

Salutation. large type ed. Frances Turk. 466p. 1981. 25.99 (*0-7089-0693-1*) Ulverscroft.

Salutation to Five: Mrs. Fitzherbert, Edmund Warre, Sir William Butler, Leo Tolstoy, Sir Mark Sykes. Shane Leslie. LC 75-126231. (Biography Index Reprint Ser.). 1977. 19.95 (*0-8369-8027-1*) Ayer.

***Salutation to the Sun.** Date not set. 7.95 (*0-8464-4483-6*) Beekman Pubs.

***Salutation to the Sun: A Daily Exercise for a Vital Life.** Rita Beintema. Tr. by Jill Penton. (Illus.). 80p. 1997. pap. 7.95 (*0-85207-304-6*, Pub. by C W Daniel UK) Natl Bk Netwk.

Salute America. Arno Breker. (Illus.). 6p. 1985. 120.00 (*0-914301-02-0*) West-Art.

***Salute the Brave: A Pictorial Record of Queensland War Memorials.** Shirley Mcivor & Trevor Mcivor. (Illus.). 340p. (Orig.). 1994. pap. 54.95 (*0-949414-54-9*, Pub. by U Sthrn Queenslnd AT) Aubrey Bks.

Salute to a Sufferer: Insights on the Ever-Present Problem of Suffering. Leslie D. Weatherhead. (C). 1990. pap. 30.00 (*0-85305-268-9*, Pub. by J Arthur Ltd UK) St Mut.

Salute to African Kings & Queens. Ed. by Richard L. Green. LC 95-48502. (Empak "Black History" Publication: Vol. 6). (J). 1996. write for info. (*0-614-97955-2*) Empak Pub.

Salute to Bazarada & Other Stories. Sax Rohmer. 311p. 1972. 12.50 (*0-685-26828-4*) Bookfinger.

Salute to Black Civil Rights Leaders. Ed. by Richard L. Green et al. (Empak "Black History" Publication). (Illus.). (Orig.). pap. text ed. 1.00 (*0-9616156-3-X*) Empak Pub.

Salute to Black Civil Rights Leaders. Ed. by Richard L. Green. (Empak "Black History" Publication: Vol. 4). (Orig.). (J). 1996. write for info. (*0-922162-04-2*) Empak Pub.

Salute to Black Pioneers. (Empak "Black History" Publication: Vol. 3). (J). 1996. write for info. (*0-922162-03-4*) Empak Pub.

Salute to Black Scientists & Inventors. Empak "Black History" Publication: Vol. 2). (J). 1996. write for info. (*0-922162-02-6*) Empak Pub.

Salute to Blacks in the Federal Government. Ed. by Richard L. Green. (Empak "Black History" Publication: Vol. 9). (J). 1996. write for info. (*0-922162-09-3*) Empak Pub.

Salute to Cape Verdean Musicians & Their Music. Ed. by Ronald Barboza. (Illus.). 48p. (YA). (gr. 9-12). 1989. pap. 10.00 (*0-9627637-0-5*) D&C Cape Verdeans.

Salute to Ferrari. Louis Klemantaski & Jesse Alexander. (Illus.). 64p. (YA). 1994. 100.00 (*0-9641689-0-1*) Klemantaski.

Salute to Historic African Kings & Queens, Vol. 6. (Empak "Black History" Publication). (YA). 1996. write for info. (*0-922162-06-9*) Empak Pub.

Salute to Historic Black Abolitionists. Ed. by Richard L. Green. (Empak "Black History" Publication: Vol. 5). (J). 1996. write for info. (*0-922162-05-0*) Empak Pub.

An Asterisk (*) at the beginning of an entry indicates that the title is appearing in BIP for the first time.

Salute to Historic Black Educators. (Empak "Black History" Publication: Vol. 10). (J). 1996. write for info. (*0-922162-14-X*) Empak Pub.

Salute to Historic Black Firsts. (Empak "Black History" Publication: Vol. 7). (J). 1996. write for info. (*0-922162-07-7*) Empak Pub.

Salute to Historic Black Women. (Empak "Black History" Publication: Vol. 1). (J). 1996. write for info. (*0-922162-01-8*) Empak Pub.

Salute to Historic Blacks in the Arts. Ed. by Richard L. Green et al. LC 95-48500. (Empak "Black History" Publication: Vol. 9). (Illus.). (J). 1996. write for info. (*0-922162-08-5*) Empak Pub.

Salute to Imaginative Economic Development Programs. Jody Tompros. Ed. by Jenny Murphy. 123p. (Orig.). 1989. pap. 27.50 (*0-317-04844-9*) Natl Coun Econ Dev.

Salute to Roy Campbell. Alister Kershaw et al. (Illus.). 128p. 1984. 100.00 (*0-930126-14-9*) Typographeum.

Salute to Spring. Meridel Le Sueur. LC 75-38588. 192p. (Orig.). 1989. pap. 3.95 (*0-7178-0463-1*) Intl Pubs Co.

Salute to the Great American Chefs. LC 88-71045. 1988. write for info. (*0-87502-233-2*) Benjamin Co.

Salute to the Olympics Sports in Art. (Illus.). 24p. (Orig.). 1968. pap. 3.00 (*0-943526-39-6*) Parrish Art.

Salute to Truro. Kenneth Pelmear. (C). 1989. 22.00 (*0-907566-31-6*, Pub. by Dyllansow Truran UK) St Mut.

Salute to Valor: Heroes of the United Nations. Linton Wells. LC 73-167435. (Essay Index Reprint Ser.). 1977. reprint ed. 23.95 (*0-8369-2729-X*) Ayer.

Salute, Walt Whitman. Photos by Duane Michals. (Illus.). 112p. 1996. 50.00 (*0-944092-34-9*) Twin Palms Pub.

Salute, Walt Whitman. limited ed. Photos by Duane Michals. (Illus.). 96p. 1996. 150.00 (*0-944092-35-7*) Twin Palms Pub.

Salute Your Shorts: Life at Summer Camp. Thomas Hill & Steve Slavkin. LC 84-40677. (Illus.). 160p. 1986. pap. 5.95 (*0-89480-034-5*, 1034) Workman Pub.

***Salutogenese in der Onkologie Symposium, Freiburg, February 1996.** Ed. by Hans H. Bartsch & Juergen Bengel. (Illus.). viii, 126p. 1996. pap. 41.75 (*3-8055-6396-5*) S Karger.

Salvacion: Obra de Dios. Ruben A. Zorzoli. (Biblioteca de Doctrina Cristiana). 156p. (Orig.). (SPA.). 1988. pap. 7.99 (*0-311-09118-0*) Casa Bautista.

Salvacion: Su Seguridad, Creteza y Gozo. 2nd ed. Jorge Cutting. Ed. by Roger P. Daniel. Tr. by Sara Bautista from ENG. (Serie Diamante). (Illus.). 48p. (SPA.). 1982. pap. 0.85 (*0-942504-05-4*) Overcomer Pr.

***Salvacion Tan Grande: La Doctrina de la Salvacion.** Regular Baptist Press Staff. Ed. by Richard Meyer. (Adult Sunday School Ser.). 88p. (SPA.). 1992. 3.95 (*1-879892-28-6*) Editorial Bautista.

Salvacion y las Dudas de Algunas Personas. 2nd ed. Alejandro Marshall & Gordon H. Bennett. Tr. by Sara Bautista from SPA. (Serie Diamante). (Illus.). 36p. (ENG.). 1982. pap. 0.85 (*0-942504-01-1*) Overcomer Pr.

Salvador. Faren M. Bachelis. LC 89-25419. (Enchantment of the World Ser.). (Illus.). 128p. (J). (gr. 5-9). 1990. lib. bdg. 30.00 (*0-516-02718-2*) Childrens.

Salvador. Joan Didion. 1994. pap. 10.00 (*0-679-75183-1*, Vin) Random.

Salvador. Arnoldo Ramos. (C). 1990. pap. 19.95 (*0-393-30645-3*) Norton.

Salvador. Larry Towell. LC 97-272. (Illus.). 128p. 1997. 37.50 (*0-393-03944-7*) Norton.

Salvador. Larry Towell. LC 97-272. (Illus.). 128p. 1997. pap. 25.00 (*0-393-31428-6*) Norton.

***Salvador: Peace on Trial.** Kevin Murray. (Country Profiles Ser.). (Illus.). 64p. (C). 1997. pap. 9.95 (*0-85598-361-2*, Pub. by Oxfam UK) Humanities.

***Salvador: Statistical Appendix.** Ana M. Jul. (IMF Staff Country Report Ser.: Vol. 96/39). 56p. pap. 25.00 (*0-608-04863-1*, 2065522) Bks Demand.

Salvador see Statements of the Laws of the OAS Member States in Matters Affecting Business

Salvador Allende & the Peaceful Road to Socialism. Gregory A. Raymond. (Pew Case Studies in International Affairs). 50p. (C). 1992. pap. text ed. 3.50 (*1-56927-451-7*) Geo U Inst Dplmcy.

Salvador-Chordal Enrichment. Sal Salvador. 7.95 (*0-87166-527-1*, 94046); audio 9.98 (*0-87166-528-X*, 94046C) Mel Bay.

***Salvador-Chordal Enrichment.** Sal Salvador. (Sal Salvador Jazz Guitar Ser.). 16.95 incl. audio (*0-7866-0964-8*, 94046P) Mel Bay.

Salvador Dali. (Prestel Postcard Bks.). (Illus.). 18p. 1994. pap. 8.95 (*3-7913-1405-X*) te Neues.

Salvador Dali. Ades. Date not set. pap. 24.95 (*0-500-27845-8*) Thames Hudson.

Salvador Dali. Ed. by Andreas Huneke. 100p. 1995. text ed. 15.00 (*3-364-00339-4*) Gordon & Breach.

Salvador Dali. Mike Venezia. LC 92-35053. (Getting to Know the World's Greatest Artists Ser.). (Illus.). 32p. (J). (ps-4). 1993. pap. 6.95 (*0-516-42296-0*); lib. bdg. 19.50 (*0-516-02296-2*) Childrens.

Salvador Dali. Contrib. by Simon Wilson. (Illus.). 128p. 1980. pap. 19.95 (*0-295-96762-5*) U of Wash Pr.

Salvador Dali. James T. Soby. LC 68-8368. (Museum of Modern Art Publications in Reprint). (Illus.). 1969. reprint ed. 23.95 (*0-405-01522-4*) Ayer.

Salvador Dali: Catalogue Raisonne of Prints II Lithographs & Wood Engravings, 2 vols., Set. Ed. by Ralf Michler et al. (Illus.). 192p. 1995. text ed. 130.00 (*3-7913-1602-8*, Pub. by Prestel GW) te Neues.

Salvador Dali: Master of Surrealism & Modern Art. G. A. Cevasco. Ed. by D. Steve Rahmas. LC 79-185661. (Outstanding Personalities Ser.: No. 5). 32p. 1972. lib. bdg. 7.25 (*0-87157-505-1*) SamHar Pr.

Salvador Dali: Masterpieces from the Collection of the Salvador Dali Museum. Kenneth Wach. LC 96-3544. (Illus.). 128p. 1996. 35.00 (*0-8109-3235-0*) Abrams.

Salvador Dali: Spanish Painter. George Crisp. (Hispanics of Achievement Ser.). (Illus.). (YA). (gr. 5 up). 1994. lib. bdg. 19.95 (*0-7910-1778-8*) Chelsea Hse.

***Salvador Dali: Spanish Painter.** George Crisp. (Hispanics of Achievement Ser.). (Illus.). 128p. (YA). (gr. 5 up). 1995. pap. 8.95 (*0-7910-3015-6*) Chelsea Hse.

Salvador Dali: The Catalogue Raisonne of Etchings & Mixed-Media Print. Ed. by Lutz W. Lopsinger et al. (Illus.). 262p. 1995. 130.00 (*3-7913-1279-0*, Pub. by Prestel GW) te Neues.

Salvador Dali, or the Art of Spitting on Your Mother's Portrait. Carlos Rojas. Tr. by Alma Amell from SPA. 208p. (C). 1993. 29.95 (*0-271-00842-3*) Pa St U Pr.

***Salvador Dali, 1904-1989.** Gilles Neret. LC 97-6596. 1997. write for info. (*1-57145-096-3*) Thunder Bay CA.

Salvador Dali's Art & Writing 1927-1942: The Metamorphoses of Narcissus. Haim Finkelstein. (RES Monographs on Anthropology & Aesthetics). (Illus.). 350p. (C). 1996. text ed. 75.00 (*0-521-49747-7*) Cambridge U Pr.

Salvador De Buques. Rosa R. Rey. 98p. (Orig.). (SPA.). (C). 1993. pap. 7.00 (*0-9626221-3-3*) Vista Pubns FL.

Salvador-Four Part Harmony. Sal Salvador. 7.95 (*0-87166-648-0*, 94099); audio 9.98 (*0-87166-649-9*, 94099C) Mel Bay.

***Salvador-Four Part Harmony.** Sal Salvador. 16.95 incl. audio (*0-87166-650-2*, 94099P) Mel Bay.

Salvador in Transition. Enrique A. Baloyra. LC 82-4815. 254p. 1982. reprint ed. pap. 72.40 (*0-608-00197-X*, 2060980) Bks Demand.

Salvador Land Reform: Nineteen Eighty to Nineteen Eighty-One. Laurence R. Simon. Ed. by James C. Stephens, Jr. & Joseph N. Short. (Impact Audit Ser.: No. 2). 55p. (Orig.). 1981. pap. 5.00 (*0-910281-01-7*) Oxfam Am.

Salvador of the Twentieth Century. Percy F. Martin. 1977. lib. bdg. 59.95 (*0-8490-2562-1*) Gordon Pr.

Salvadorans in Suburbia: Symbiosis & Conflict. Sarah J. Mahler. Ed. by Nancy Foner. (New Immigrants Ser.). 176p. (C). 1996. pap. text ed. 11.25 (*0-205-16737-3*) Allyn.

Salvadorans in the United States: The Case for Extended Voluntary Departure. (Public Policy Report Ser.: No. 1). 1984. 2.00 (*0-86566-034-4*) ACLU DC.

Salvador's Children: A Song for Survival. Lea Marenn. (Helen Hooven Santmyer Prize in Women's Studies). 240p. 1993. 26.50 (*0-8142-0593-3*) Ohio St U Pr.

Salvador's Decade of Terror: Human Rights since the Assassination of Archbishop Romero. Human Rights Watch Staff & Americas Watch Staff. (Latin American Studies - Political Science). 227p. (C). 1993. pap. 17.00 (*0-300-05781-4*) Yale U Pr.

Salvage & Overhaul. 7th ed. IFSTA Committee. Ed. by Gene P. Carlson & David England. LC 85-70110. (Illus.). 225p. 1985. pap. text ed. 18.00 (*0-87939-058-1*) IFSTA.

Salvage Archaeology in Nimbus & Redbank Reservior Areas, Central California. fac. ed. Adam E. Treganza. (Reports of the University of California Archaeological Survey: No. 26). (Illus.). 49p. 1954. reprint ed. pap. 4.70 (*1-55567-346-5*) Coyote Press.

Salvage Archaeology in Painted Rocks Reservoir, Western Arizona. William W. Wasley & Alfred E. Johnson. LC 64-63815. (Anthropological Papers: No. 9). 123p. 1965. pap. 12.95 (*0-8165-0273-0*) U of Ariz Pr.

Salvage Archaeology in the Cow Springs Area, 1960. J. Richard Ambler & Alan P. Olson. (Technical Ser.). 57p. 1977. pap. 7.95 (*0-685-14718-5*, TS-15) Mus Northern Ariz.

Salvage Archaeology in the Trinity Reservoir Area - Northern California - Field Season 1958. fac. ed. Adam E. Treganza. (Reports of the University of California Archaeological Survey: No. 46). 60p. 1959. reprint ed. pap. 5.55 (*1-55567-363-5*) Coyote Press.

Salvage Archaeology in the Trinity Reservoir Area, Northern California - The Lagomarsino Petroglyph Group (Site 26-St-1) Near Virginia City, Nevada, Set, Pts. I & II. fac. ed. R. F. Heizer et al. (Reports of the University of California Archaeological Survey: No. 43). 108p. 1958. reprint ed. pap. 9.65 (*1-55567-360-0*) Coyote Press.

Salvage Archaeology of the Bear Creek Site (SJo-112) A Terminal Central California Early Horizon Site. fac. ed. William H. Olsen & Norman Wilson. (Sacramento Anthropological Society, Sacramento State College Ser.: No. 1). (Illus.). 61p. 1964. reprint ed. pap. text ed. 5.55 (*1-55567-557-3*) Coyote Press.

Salvage Excavations at the Fowler Site: Some Aspects of the Social Organization of the Northern Chumash; & Skeletal Analysis of 4-SLO-406. fac. ed. J. Tainter & G. L. Warren. (San Luis Obispo County Archaeological Society Occasional Papers: Nos. 3 & 4). (Illus.). 62p. (C). 1971. reprint ed. pap. text ed. 5.55 (*1-55567-498-4*) Coyote Press.

***Salvage from the Cynthia.** Jules Verne. lib. bdg. 22.95 (*0-8488-2068-1*) Amereon Ltd.

Salvage from the Sea. G. Forsberg. (C). 1987. 66.00 (*0-7100-8698-9*, Pub. by Brwn Son Ferg) St Mut.

***Salvage Job.** large type ed. Bill Knox. (Linford Mystery Library). 352p. 1997. pap. 16.99 (*0-7089-5022-1*) Ulverscroft.

***Salvage Man: Edward Ellsberg & the U. S. Navy.** John D. Alden. (Illus.). 384p. 1997. 37.50 (*1-55750-027-4*) Naval Inst Pr.

Salvage of the Rio Oso Site, Yuba County, California, No. 6. Francis A. Riddell & W. H. Olsen. (Publications of the Department of Parks & Recreation: No. 6). (Illus.). 29p. (C). 1962. reprint ed. pap. text ed. 2.75 (*1-55567-458-5*) Coyote Press.

Salvage of Water Damaged Books, Documents, Micrographic & Magnetic Media. Eric G. Lundquist. 144p. (Orig.). 1986. pap. 12.95 (*0-9616850-0-X*) Doc Reprocessors.

Salvage Operations: New & Selected Poems. Paul J. Mariani. 1991. pap. 9.95 (*0-393-30759-X*) Norton.

***Salvaged Memories: The Raising of the Minnehaha.** Jerry Provost. LC 96-94657. (Illus.). 110p. (Orig.). 1996. pap. 10.95 (*0-9653839-0-3*) In Depth Pub.

Salvaging a Land of Plenty: Garbage & the American Dream. Jennifer S. Whitaker. LC 93-36912. 1994. 25.00 (*0-688-10130-5*) Morrow.

Salvaging Damaged dBase Files. Paul W. Heiser. 350p. (C). 1989. pap. text ed. 340.00 (*0-273-03220-8*, Pub. by Pitman Pubng UK) St Mut.

Salvaging Damaged dBASE Files. 2nd ed. Paul W. Heiser. Ed. by Lance A. Leventhal. LC 89-4307. (Lance A. Leventhal Data Based Advisor Ser.). 320p. 1989. pap. 24.95 (*0-915391-33-3*, Microtrend) Slawson Comm.

Salvaging Democracy: Some Reflections. V. Krishna Iyer. 215p. 1990. text ed. 25.00 (*81-220-0175-0*, Pub. by Konark Pubs Pvt Ltd II) Advent Bks Div.

***Salvaging Spenser.** Willy Maley. LC 97-12088. 1997. text ed. 49.95 (*0-312-17234-6*) St Martin.

Salvaging the Future: Waste-Based Production. Caroline Rennie & Alair MacLean. LC 89-11209. (Illus.). 160p. 1989. pap. text ed. 20.00 (*0-917582-37-3*) Inst Local Self Re.

Salvajes En Puente San Gil. Jose M. Recuerda. 290p. (SPA.). 1978. 9.50 (*0-8288-7046-2*) Fr & Eur.

***Salvaltion: Is Jesus the Only Way to God?** John Ankerberg & John Weldon. (The Defenders Ser.). 48p. (Orig.). 1997. pap. 2.99 (*1-56507-539-0*) Harvest Hse.

***Salvaodr Dali: Exploring the Irrational.** Edmund Swinglehurst. 1996. 15.98 (*0-7651-9724-3*) Smithmark.

***Salvat Cuatro Enciclopedico Diccionario, 4 vols.** (Illus.). 1400p. (SPA.). (YA). (gr. 5 up). 1995. lib. bdg. 119.00 (*970-611-356-8*) Grolier Educ.

Salvat Encyclopedia of Cooking, 12 vols., Set. Salvat Staff. (SPA.). 1977. 395.00 (*0-8288-8238-X*, 847137515X) Fr & Eur.

Salvat Encyclopedia of Cooking, 12 vols., Set. 4th ed. Salvat Staff. 2800p. (SPA.). 1977. 395.00 (*0-8288-7577-4*, 847137515X) Fr & Eur.

Salvat Encyclopedia of Creative Photography, 18 vols., Set. Salvat Staff. (SPA.). 1989. 595.00 (*0-8288-8239-8*, 8434535866) Fr & Eur.

Salvat Encyclopedia of Creative Photography, 18 vols., Set. 2nd ed. Salvat Staff. 1872p. (SPA.). 1989. 595.00 (*0-8288-7578-2*, 8434535866) Fr & Eur.

Salvat Encyclopedia of Health, 10 vols., Set. Salvat Staff. (SPA.). 1983. 1,295.00 (*0-8288-8240-1*, 8471374803) Fr & Eur.

Salvat Encyclopedia of Science & Technology, 14 vols., Set. Salvat Staff. (SPA.). 1990. 1,995.00 (*0-8288-8237-1*, 8434544903) Fr & Eur.

Salvat Encyclopedia of Science & Technology, 14 vols., Set. 2nd ed. Salvat Staff. 3472p. (SPA.). 1990. 1,995.00 (*0-8288-7576-6*, 8434544903) Fr & Eur.

Salvat Medicina, Enciclopedia de Conocimientos Basicos, 10 vols., Set. 3000p. (SPA.). 1974. 1,200.00 (*0-8288-6210-9*, S-50559) Fr & Eur.

Salvat Student's Encyclopedia. Salvat Staff. (SPA.). 1988. 1,250.00 (*0-8288-7879-X*, 8477430470) Fr & Eur.

Salvat Student's Encyclopedia, 12 vols., Set. Salvat Staff. (SPA.). 1988. 1,250.00 (*0-8288-8241-X*, 8477430470) Fr & Eur.

Salvat Uno, Diccionario Enciclopedico Basico. Salvat Staff. 1571p. (SPA.). 1981. 95.00 (*0-8288-2026-0*, S7726) Fr & Eur.

Salvation. Debbie Bentley. (Basic Christian Doctrine Ser.: No. 1). 6p. (Orig.). (YA). 1995. pap. 1.00 (*1-885090-00-5*) Cosecha Latina.

Salvation. Perry A. Gaspard. 1983. pap. 2.00 (*0-931867-00-2*) Abundant Life Pubns.

***Salvation.** Charles R. Swindoll. (Growing Deep in the Christian Life Ser.). 1997. pap. text ed. 6.99 (*0-8054-0158-X*) Broadman.

Salvation. rev. ed. Richard E. Todd. (Wordbook Ser.). (Illus.). 26p. (J). (gr. 2-6). 1993. student ed. 2.45 (*0-9605324-6-3*) Crosswalk Res.

***Salvation, Vol. 3.** Christopher Golden. (X-Men: Mutant Empire Bk.: No. 3). 288p. 1997. mass mkt. 5.99 (*1-57297-247-5*) Blvd Books.

Salvation: A Comparative Analysis of Differing Theological Traditions. Kathleen McConnell. LC 94-17139. (Catholic Scholars Press Ser.). 350p. 1997. text ed. 69.95 (*1-883255-67-8*, Cath Scholar Pr); pap. text ed. 49.95 (*1-883255-66-X*) Intl Scholars.

Salvation: God's Marvelous Work of Grace. Lewis S. Chafer. LC 91-24545. 128p. 1991. reprint ed. pap. 8.99 (*0-8254-2343-0*) Kregel.

Salvation: Growing Strong on the Bread of Life. Dusty Kemp. (Foundations for a Balaced Christian Life Ser.). 25p. (Orig.). 1987. pap. 1.00 (*0-944970-00-1*) Kemp Ministries.

Salvation: The Bible & Roman Catholicism. William A. Webster. 176p. 1990. pap. 8.50 (*0-85151-571-1*) Banner of Truth.

Salvation: The Way Made Plain. James H. Brookes. pap. 4.99 (*0-87377-015-3*) GAM Pubns.

Salvation see Summa Contra Gentiles

Salvation, a Biblical Model for Counseling. James Stone. 250p. 1990. pap. text ed. 9.95 (*0-934942-83-8*, 6067) White Wing Pub.

Salvation & Behavior. W. Graham Scroggie. LC 80-8075. (W. Graham Scroggie Library). 104p. 1981. reprint ed. pap. 5.99 (*0-8254-3735-0*) Kregel.

Salvation & Grace. Irish Inter-Church Meeting, Dept. of Theological Questions Staff. 1993. pap. 24.95 (*1-85390-286-1*, Pub. by Veritas IE) St Mut.

Salvation & Liberation: In Search of a Balance Between Faith & Politics. Clodovis Boff & Leonardo Boff. Tr. by Robert R. Barr from POR. LC 84-7220. 128p. (Orig.). 1984. pap. 13.50 (*0-88344-451-8*) Orbis Bks.

Salvation & Nurture of the Child of God: The Story of Emma. G. Temp Sparkman. LC 82-21349. 272p. 1983. reprint ed. pap. 77.60 (*0-608-00294-1*, 2059322) Bks Demand.

Salvation & Suicide: An Interpretation of Jim Jones, the Peoples Temple, & Jonestown. David Chidester. LC 87-45015. (Religion in North America Ser.). (Illus.). 208p. 1988. 31.50 (*0-253-35056-5*) Ind U Pr.

Salvation & Suicide: An Interpretation of Jim Jones, the Peoples Temple, & Jonestown. David Chidester. LC 87-45015. (Religion in North America Ser.). (Illus.). 208p. 1991. reprint ed. pap. 6.95 (*0-253-20690-1*, MB-690) Ind U Pr.

Salvation & the Church: An Agreed Statement by the Second Anglican-Roman Catholic International Commission. ARCIC II Staff. (Lambeth Study Papers). 30p. 1987. pap. 1.40 (*0-88028-063-8*, 884) Forward Movement.

Salvation & the Perfect Society: The Eternal Quest. Alfred Braunthal. LC 79-4705. 448p. 1979. lib. bdg. 40.00 (*0-87023-273-8*) U of Mass Pr.

Salvation & the Savage: An Analysis of Protestant Missions & American Indian Response, 1787-1862. Robert F. Berkhofer, Jr. LC 77-22857. 186p. 1977. reprint ed. text ed. 55.00 (*0-8371-9745-7*, BESSA, Greenwood Pr) Greenwood.

Salvation Army Farm Colonies. Clark C. Spence. LC 85-8763. 151p. 1985. 28.50 (*0-8165-0897-6*) U of Ariz Pr.

Salvation Army in America: Selected Reports, 1899-1903. Frederick Booth-Tucker. LC 79-38439. (Religion in America, Ser. 2). 212p. 1976. reprint ed. 21.95 (*0-405-04060-1*) Ayer.

Salvation Audit. Colin Grant. LC 92-62490. 1994. write for info. (*0-940866-34-X*) U Scranton Pr.

Salvation by Grace Through Faith in Contrast to the Restorationist Doctrine. Bob L. Ross. 1979. pap. 2.00 (*1-56186-508-7*) Pilgrim Pubns.

Salvation for Sale: An Insider's View of Pat Robertson. Gerard T. Straub. 396p. 1988. pap. 24.95 (*0-87975-436-2*) Prometheus Bks.

Salvation from Despair: A Reappraisal of Spinoza's Philosophy. E. E. Harris. (International Archives of the History of Ideas Ser.: No. 59). 289p. 1973. lib. bdg. 100.50 (*90-247-5158-6*) Kluwer Ac.

Salvation from Sin. John H. Noyes. 1972. 59.95 (*0-8490-0990-1*) Gordon Pr.

Salvation from Sin, the End of Christian Faith see Male Continence

Salvation in Full Color: Twenty Sermons by Great Awakening Preachers. Ed. by Richard O. Roberts. LC 93-80172. xxii, 362p. (Orig.). 1994. pap. text ed. 17.95 (*0-926474-12-X*) Intl Awakening Pr.

***Salvation in Full Color: Twenty Sermons by Great Awakening Preachers.** Ed. by Richard O. Roberts. LC 93-80172. xxii, 362p. (Orig.). 1994. pap. text ed. 17.95 (*0-940033-46-1*) R O Roberts.

Salvation In Life In The Book Of Romans. Witness Lee. 57p. 2.25 (*0-87083-526-2*, 07025001) Living Stream Ministry.

Salvation in the Book of Acts. Frederick E. Kinzie. LC 88-20758. (Illus.). 192p. (Orig.). 1988. pap. 7.99 (*0-932581-40-4*) Word Aflame.

Salvation in the Killing Fields. Aileen Ludington. 1991. pap. 4.97 (*0-8163-0890-X*) Pacific Pr Pub Assn.

Salvation in the Slums: Evangelical Social Welfare Work, 1865-1920. Norris Magnuson. LC 76-54890. (American Theological Library Association Monograph: No. 10). 315p. 1977. 32.50 (*0-8108-1001-8*) Scarecrow.

Salvation Is Forever. Robert Gromacki. LC 89-10144. 188p. 1989. reprint ed. pap. text ed. 8.95 (*0-87227-130-7*, RBP5160) Reg Baptist.

Salvation Is Free (Romans 5:6-21) large type ed. Odethia L. Washington. 35p. 1993. pap. 14.25 (*0-9637574-0-7*) Odethia WA.

Salvation Is of the Jews. Blair Adams & Joel Stein. 223p. (Orig.). 1988. pap. 9.95 (*0-916387-14-3*) Truth Forum.

Salvation, Learning about God's Plan. (BMC Teaching Bks.). (Illus.). 19p. (Orig.). (J). (gr. 1-8). 1974. pap. text ed. 4.50 (*0-86508-151-4*) BCM Pubn.

Salvation of Jesus: What It Means to Me. Keith Hershey. (Christian Life Ser.). 28p. (Orig.). 1992. pap. 1.95 (*0-940487-03-9*) Jubilee CA.

Salvation of the Human & Angelic Soul. (Walk with Jesus Ser.). 213p. 1990. pap. 35.00 (*1-57277-502-5*) Script Rsch.

Salvation of the Soul. Watchman Nee. Tr. by Stephen Kaung. 115p. 1978. pap. 4.50 (*0-935008-31-4*) Christian Fellow Pubs.

Salvation of the Soul & Islamic Devotion. Muhammad A. Quasem. 1981. 19.95 (*0-318-00411-9*) Quasem.

Salvation of the Soul & Islamic Devotion. Muhammad A. Quasem. 200p. 1982. pap. 14.95 (*0-7103-0033-6*) Routledge Chapman & Hall.

Salvation on Sand Mountain. Photos by Jim Neel & Melissa Springer. (Illus.). 1996. write for info. (*0-944564-05-4*) Alex Mus.

Salvation on Sand Mountain: Snake Handling & Redemption in Southern Appalachia. Dennis Covington. 200p. 1995. 20.00 (*0-201-62292-0*) Addison-Wesley.

Salvation on Sand Mountain: Snake Handling & Redemption in Southern Appalachia. Dennis Covington. (Illus.). 256p. 1996. pap. 11.95 (*0-14-025458-7*) Viking Penguin.

Salvation Outside the Church? Tracing the History of the Catholic Response. Francis A. Sullivan. LC 92-7910. 240p. 1992. pap. 12.95 (*0-8091-3304-0*) Paulist Pr.

S

Salvation Peddler. Jerry Marcus. LC 87-71614. 235p. 1988. 15.95 (*0-941394-01-8*) Brittany Pubns.

Salvation, Present, Perfect, Now or Never. D. S. Warner. 63p. pap. 0.40 (*0-686-29138-7*); pap. 1.00 (*0-686-29139-5*) Faith Pub Hse.

Salvation Prison - a Novel. Chhote Bharany. 99p. 1992. text ed. 15.95 (*81-207-1139-4*, Pub. by Sterling Pubs II) Apt Bks.

Salvation, Scripture, & Sexuality. 2nd rev. ed. Mark S. Shirilau. 59p. 1995. pap. 5.00 (*1-881568-09-1*) Healing Spirit.

Salvation Song Index. 6p. (J). (gr. k-6). 1957. pap. 0.50 (*1-55976-204-7*) CEF Press.

Salvation Songs, Vol. I. Ruth P. Overholtzer. 100p. (J). (gr. k-6). 1975. pap. text ed. 2.99 (*3-901171-00-2*) CEF Press.

Salvation Songs, Vol. II. Ruth P. Overholtzer. 105p. (J). (gr. k-4). 1979. pap. text ed. 2.99 (*1-55976-201-2*) CEF Press.

Salvation Songs, Vol. III. Ruth P. Overholtzer. 100p. (J). (gr. k-6). 1975. pap. text ed. 2.99 (*1-55976-202-0*) CEF Press.

Salvation Songs, Vol. IV. Ruth P. Overholtzer. (Illus.). 96p. (J). (gr. k-6). 1979. pap. text ed. 2.99 (*1-55976-203-9*) CEF Press.

S

Salvation, Then What. Marjorie Soderholm. 1968. pap. 2.95 (*0-911802-14-2*) Free Church Pubns.

Salvation Through Inflation: The Economics of Social Credit. Gary North. LC 93-18285. 1993. student ed. 25.00 (*0-930464-66-4*); pap. 12.95 (*0-930464-64-8*) Inst Christian.

***Salvationist Samurai: Gunpei Yamamuro & the Rise of the Salvation Army in Japan.** R. David Rightmire. LC 96-49240. (Pietist & Wesleyan Studies: No. 8). (Illus.). 216p. 1997. 49.00 (*0-8108-3270-4*) Scarecrow.

Salvations: Truth & Difference in Religion. S. Mark Heim. LC 95-20401. (Faith Meets Faith Ser.). 225p. (Orig.). 1995. pap. 20.00 (*1-57075-040-8*) Orbis Bks.

Salvation's Sisters. Jonis Agee. LC 97-12896. 1997. pap. 23.95 (*0-670-85809-9*) Viking Penguin.

Salvator, 4 vols. Alexandre Dumas. 1976. pap. 9.95 (*0-685-73335-1*) Fr & Eur.

Salvator Mundi of Leonardo da Vinci. Joanne Snow-Smith. LC 82-21190. (Illus.). 96p. (Orig.). 1982. pap. 29.95 (*0-935558-11-X*) Henry Art.

Salvator Rosa: This Life & Times. Jonathan Scott. LC 95-7225. 1995. write for info. (*0-300-06416-0*) Yale U Pr.

Salvatore: Bull of Salvation. Eduard Pesek-Marous. Ed. by Tau Editors. LC 76-49340. (Illus.). 111p. 1976. pap. 4.95 (*0-916453-00-6*) TAU Pr.

Salvatore Di Giacomo & Neapolitan Dialectal Literature. Ferdinando D. Maurino. 1951. 15.95 (*0-913298-30-1*) S F Vanni.

Salvatore Pinto: Morocco Paintings. (Illus.). 12p. (Orig.). 1991. pap. 10.00 (*1-879173-01-8*) Locks Gallery.

Salvatore's Daughter. Maryfrances Wagner. 64p. (Orig.). 1995. pap. 10.00 (*1-886157-00-6*) BkMk.

Salve America! LC 86-80886. (Coleccion Espejo de Paciencia). 61p. (Orig.). 1986. pap. 5.95 (*0-89729-400-9*) Ediciones.

Salve Reginas of G. B. Pergolesi: Pergo Edition. Allan Atlas. (Complete Works of G. B. Pergolesi: No. 4, Vol. XV). 1994. 110.00 (*0-945193-58-0*) Pendragon NY.

Salve Venetia. Francis M. Crawford. (Works of Francis Marion Crawford Ser.). 1990. reprint ed. lib. bdg. 79.00 (*0-685-44768-5*) Rprt Serv.

Salvemos la Familia de Hoy. Floresmiro Perea. 201p. (SPA.). 1991. pap. 4.50 (*1-56063-302-6*, 498423) Editorial Unilit.

Salven A Mi Babucha. Gilles Gauthier. (Primeros Lectores Ser.). (Illus.). 60p. (SPA.). (J). (gr. 5 up). 1994. pap. 5.95 (*958-07-0077-X*) Firefly Bks Ltd.

***Salven Mi Selva.** Monica Zak. (Illus.). 29p. (SPA.). (J). (gr. 3 up). pap. 12.95 (*968-6048-23-5*) Volcano Pr.

***Salvete! Bk. 1: A First Course in Latin.** 81p. 1995. pap. text ed. 8.50 (*0-521-40683-8*) Cambridge U Pr.

***Salvete! Bk. 2: A First Course in Latin.** 92p. 1996. pap. text ed. 8.50 (*0-521-40684-6*) Cambridge U Pr.

***Salvinorin: The Psychedelic Essence of Salvia Divinorum.** D. M. Turner. 1996. pap. 9.95 (*0-9642636-2-9*) Panther Press.

Salvo! Classic Naval Gun Actions. Bernard Edwards. (Illus.). 240p. 1995. 31.95 (*1-55750-796-1*) Naval Inst Pr.

Salz und Licht. Ed. & Tr. by Hutterian Society of Brothers Staff. Tr. by Heini Arnold. 186p. (GER.). 1982. reprint ed. pap. 9.00 (*3-87067-166-1*) Plough.

Salzburg Connection. large type ed. Helen MacInnes. LC 92-23906. (All-Time Favorites Ser.). 698p. 1993. reprint ed. lib. bdg. 20.95 (*1-56054-455-4*) Thorndike Pr.

Salzburg Lutheran Expulsion & Its Impact. Carl Mauelshagen. (Illus.). 167p. 1994. pap. text ed. 17.50 (*0-7884-0002-9*) Heritage Bk.

Salzburg One Hundred One Zeichnungen. Marie Z. Greene-Mercier. 112p. 1969. pap. 6.00 (*0-910790-16-7*) Intl Bk Co IL.

Salzburg Seminar: The First Forty Years. Thomas H. Eliot & Lois J. Eliot. (Illus.). 168p. 1987. 15.95 (*0-938864-10-6*) Ipswich Pr.

Salzburg Transaction: Expulsion & Redemption in Eighteenth-Century Germany. Mack Walker. LC 92-52774. (Illus.). 248p. 1993. 37.50 (*0-8014-2777-0*) Cornell U Pr.

Salzburg under Siege: U. S. Occupation, 1945-1955. Donald R. Whitnah & Florentine E. Whitnah. LC 91-21194. (Contributions in Military Studies: No. 120). 184p. 1991. text ed. 49.95 (*0-313-28116-5*, WUG, Greenwood Pr) Greenwood.

Salzburgers & Their Descendants: Being the History of a Colony of German, Lutheran, Protestants Who Migrated to Georgia in 1734. P. A. Strobel. 320p. 1980. reprint ed. 15.00 (*0-89308-248-1*) Southern Hist Pr.

Sam. Lester S. Golub. LC 93-91584. 220p. (Orig.). 1993. pap. 12.00 (*0-9636212-0-3*) Lit Scriveners.

Sam. Ann H. Scott. (Illus.). 40p. (J). (ps-3). 1996. pap. 5.95 (*0-698-11387-X*, Paperstar) Putnam Pub Group.

Sam. large type ed. Philip Temple. 448p. 1986. 25.99 (*0-7089-1561-2*) Ulverscroft.

Sam. Jack Weyland. LC 81-682. 168p. (YA). (gr. 9-12). 1992. reprint ed. pap. 4.95 (*0-87579-122-0*) Deseret Bk.

Sam, a Goat. Bayard Dominick. (Illus.). (J). (gr. 3-5). 1968. 9.95 (*0-8392-3062-1*) Astor-Honor.

Sam Adams: Pioneer in Propaganda. John C. Miller. (Illus.). 437p. 1936. 52.50 (*0-8047-0024-9*); pap. 17.95 (*0-8047-0025-7*) Stanford U Pr.

Sam Alley: Excavations at 4-LAK-305 Near Upper Lake, California. fac. ed. Thomas Jackson et al. (California State University, San Francisco - Treganza Anthropology Museum Ser.: No. 11). (Illus.). 75p. 1973. reprint ed. pap. text ed. 6.85 (*1-55567-579-4*) Coyote Press.

***Sam & Dasher.** Charnan Simon. LC 96-40361. (Rookie Reader Ser.). (Illus.). (J). 1997. write for info. (*0-516-20702-4*) Childrens.

***Sam & Derek, Derek & Sam.** Michael Levin. 256p. 1997. mass mkt. 4.50 (*0-425-16041-6*) Berkley Pub.

Sam & His Brother Len. John Manderino. LC 94-9992. 248p. 1994. 19.95 (*0-89733-407-8*) Academy Chi Pubs.

Sam & Max Color Collection. Steve Purcell. 64p. 1992. 4.95 (*0-87135-938-3*) Marvel Entmnt.

***Sam & Pepper's Tree House.** (Ready Readers Stage I Ser.). (Illus.). 32p. (J). (gr. k-2). 1995. pap. write for info. (*1-56144-743-9*, Honey Bear Bks) Modern Pub NYC.

Sam & the Firefly. Philip D. Eastman. LC 58-11966. (Illus.). 72p. (J). (gr. 1-2). 1958. lib. bdg. 11.99 (*0-394-90006-5*) Beginner.

Sam & the Firefly. Philip D. Eastman. LC 58-11966. (Illus.). 72p. (J). (gr. 1-2). 1958. 7.99 (*0-394-80006-0*) Beginner.

Sam & the Golden People. Marjorie Vandervelde. (Indian Culture Ser.). (J). (gr. 4-9). 1972. pap. 4.95 (*0-89992-027-6*) Coun India Ed.

Sam & the Lucky Money. Karen Chinn et al. LC 94-11766. (Illus.). 32p. (J). (ps-4). 1995. 14.95 (*1-880000-13-X*) Lee & Low Bks.

***Sam & the Lucky Money.** Karen Chinn. (Illus.). 32p. (J). (gr. k up). 1997. pap. 6.95 (*1-880000-53-9*) Lee & Low Bks.

Sam & the Speaker's Chair. Maurine W. Liles. LC 93-42374. (J). 1994. 14.95 (*0-89015-946-7*) Sunbelt Media.

***Sam & the Tigers.** Julius Lester. 1996. pap. 15.99 (*0-8037-2216-8*) Dial Bks Young.

Sam & the Tigers: A Retelling of Little Black Sambo. Julius Lester. LC 95-43080. (Illus.). 40p. (J). (ps-3). 1996. pap. 15.99 (*0-8037-2028-9*); pap. 15.89 (*0-8037-2029-7*) Dial Bks Young.

Sam & Violet's Get Well Book. Nicole Robel. 1985. pap. 2.50 (*0-380-89821-7*, Camelot) Avon.

Sam, Bangs & Moonshine. Evaline Ness. LC 66-10113. (Illus.). 48p. (J). (ps-2). 1966. 14.95 (*0-8050-0314-2*, Bks Young Read) H Holt & Co.

Sam, Bangs & Moonshine. Evaline Ness. LC 66-10113. (Illus.). 48p. (J). (ps-2). 1971. pap. 5.95 (*0-8050-0315-0*, Bks Young Read) H Holt & Co.

Sam, Bangs & Moonshine. Evaline Ness. (J). (gr. 4 up). 1971. pap. 3.95 (*0-03-080111-7*) H Holt & Co.

Sam, Bangs & Moonshine Literature Mini-Unit. Janet Lovelady. (Illus.). 32p. (J). (gr. 3-5). 1990. student ed. 4.95 (*1-56096-012-4*) Mari.

***Sam Bangs & Moonshine (Old), Vol. 1.** Evaline Ness. Date not set. write for info. (*0-03-012716-5*) H Holt & Co.

Sam, Bangs y Hechizo de Luna. Evaline Ness. Tr. by Liwayway Alonso from ENG. (Illus.). 48p. (SPA.). (J). 1994. 14.95 (*1-880507-12-9*) Lectorum Pubns.

Sam Bass: A Novel. Bryan Woolley. LC 83-70812. 214p. 1983. 16.95 (*0-931722-25-X*) Corona Pub.

Sam Bass: A Novel. Bryan Woolley. LC 83-70812. 214p. 1991. pap. 9.95 (*0-931722-38-1*) Corona Pub.

***Sam Becketts Artistic Theory.** Acheson. LC 96-27677. 1997. text ed. 49.95 (*0-312-16547-1*) St Martin.

Sam Bell Maxey & the Confederate Indians. John C. Waugh. LC 95-12958. (Civil War Campaigns & Commanders Ser.). (Illus.). 100p. (Orig.). 1995. pap. 11.95 (*1-886661-03-0*, 61030) Ryan Place Pub.

Sam Brannan, Builder of San Francisco. 2nd ed. Louis J. Stellman. (Illus.). 254p. 1996. pap. 13.95 (*1-885852-05-3*) J D Stevenson.

Sam Chamberlain's Mexican War: The San Jacinto Museum of History Paintings. limited ed. (Illus.). 388p. 1994. boxed 150.00 (*0-87611-133-9*) Tex St Hist Assn.

Sam Chamberlain's Mexican War: The San Jacinto Museum of History Paintings. limited ed. William H. Goetzmann. LC 93-21480. (Illus.). 388p. 1993. 49.95 (*0-87611-131-2*) Tex St Hist Assn.

Sam Chance. Benjamin Capps. LC 87-9757. (Southwest Life & Letters Ser.). 282p. 1987. reprint ed. 22.50 (*0-87074-250-7*); reprint ed. pap. 10.95 (*0-87074-251-5*) SMU Press.

Sam Clemens of Hannibal. Dixon Wecter. LC 76-6595. reprint ed. 36.00 (*0-404-15328-3*) AMS Pr.

Sam Colt's Own Record, 1847. 24.50 (*1-879356-14-7*) Wolfe Pub Co.

Sam Cooke's Night Beat. Ed. by Carol Cuellar. 80p. (Orig.). 1995. pap. 18.95 (*0-89724-748-5*, PF9528) Warner Brothers.

***Sam Cooke's Sar Records Story.** Ed. by Carol Cuellar. 292p. (Orig.). (C). 1994. pap. text ed. 32.95 (*0-910957-80-0*, P1081SMX) Warner Brothers.

Sam Curd's Diary: The Diary of a True Woman. Ed. by Susan S. Arpad. LC 83-22082. viii, 172p. 1984. 19.95 (*0-8214-0730-9*) Ohio U Pr.

Sam Curtin. Doug Bowman. 320p. (Orig.). 1994. pap. 4.99 (*0-8125-3453-0*) Forge NYC.

Sam Dees: Master of Soul. Ed. & Illus. by Dave Edwards. (Masters of Soul Ser.: Vol. 1). 60p. 1996. pap. 15.95 (*1-888885-01-7*, JPMC-1502) JPMC.

***Sam-Different: Fairy Tales Version.** Spencer Kagan. (Illus.). 80p. 1997. pap. text ed. 12.00 (*1-879097-44-3*) Kagan Cooperative.

Sam-Dog & Tommy. J. Thomas, pseud. 1994. pap. 7.95 (*0-9637794-2-7*) Machia.

***Sam Dreben: The Fighting Jew.** Art Leibson. (Great West & Indian Ser.: No. 67). (Illus.). 208p. 1996. 26.95 (*0-87026-098-7*) Westernlore.

***Sam Francis: A Survey of Paintings 1965-1983.** Pierre Schneider. (Illus.). 64p. 1996. pap. write for info. (*1-880154-10-2*) Gagosian Gallery.

Sam Francis: The Edge Paintings. (Illus.). 36p. 1992. 45.00 (*1-56466-022-2*) J Corcoran Gallery.

Sam Francis: Works On Paper. 1979. 3.00 (*0-910663-20-3*) ICA Inc.

***Sam Francis Vol. 1: Edge Paintings.** Sam Francis. Ed. by James Corcorin. (Illus.). 1981. 40.00 (*0-614-24675-X*) J Corcoran Gallery.

Sam Francis in the Idemitsu. Sam Francis. 1990. 55.00 (*0-932499-41-4*) Lapis Pr.

Sam Francis, Lesson of Darkness. Jean-Francois Lyotard. Tr. by Geoffrey Bennington from FRE. (Illus.). 100p. 1993. 60.00 (*0-932499-70-8*) Lapis Pr.

Sam Fuller - Film Is a Battleground: A Critical Study, with Interviews, a Filmography & a Bibliography. Lee Server. LC 94-10983. (Illus.). 188p. 1994. lib. bdg. 32.50 (*0-7864-0008-0*) McFarland & Co.

***Sam Gets Ready for School.** Esther L. Roberts. (Illus.). 24p. (Orig.). (J). (ps-6). 1996. pap. 10.00 (*0-9655120-1-0*) Starlight Farm.

Sam Goes Trucking. Henry Horenstein. (Illus.). (J). (ps-3). 1989. 14.95 (*0-395-44313-X*) HM.

Sam Goes Trucking. Henry Horenstein. (J). (ps-3). 1990. pap. 6.95 (*0-395-54950-7*) HM.

Sam H. Moore's Lost Mineral Spring. Michael P. Jones et al. (Illus.). 1984. pap. text ed. write for info. (*0-89904-073-X*) Crumb Elbow Pub.

Sam Hamburg: Agricultural Pioneer in California & Israel. Alice Hamburg et al. LC 89-50555. (Illus.). 88p. (Orig.). 1989. pap. 10.00 (*0-943376-42-4*) Magnes Mus.

***Sam Hawkins' 520 Christmas Cross-Stitch Designs.** Sam Hawkins. LC 97-6985. (Illus.). 1997. write for info. (*0-8069-1390-8*) Sterling.

Sam Henry's "Songs of the People" Ed. by Gale Huntington & Lani Herrmann. LC 90-36866. 680p. 1990. pap. 35.00 (*0-8203-1259-2*) U of Ga Pr.

Sam Higginbottom of Allahabad. Gary R. Hess. LC 67-17631. 198p. reprint ed. 56.50 (*0-8357-9816-X*, 2015747) Bks Demand.

Sam Hill: Prince of Castle Nowhere. 2nd ed. John E. Tuhy. (Illus.). 305p. 1992. reprint ed. pap. 12.95 (*0-917304-77-2*) Maryhill Art.

Sam Hook. Richard S. Wheeler. 192p. 1986. 14.95 (*0-8027-4064-2*) Walker & Co.

Sam Houston. Herman Toepperwein. pap. 1.75 (*0-910722-09-9*) Highland Pr.

Sam Houston. rev. ed. Dan Zadra. (We the People Ser.). (J). (gr. 2-4). 1988. lib. bdg. 14.95 (*0-88682-187-8*) Creative Ed.

Sam Houston: A Biography of the Father of Texas. John H. Williams. (Illus.). 432p. 1993. 25.00 (*0-671-74641-3*) S&S Trade.

***Sam Houston: A Leader for Texas.** Judy Alter. LC 97-25199. (Community Builders Ser.). (J). 1998. write for info. (*0-516-20834-9*) Childrens.

Sam Houston: American Hero. Ann F. Crawford. LC 93-77618. (Illus.). 64p. (J). (gr. 3 up). 1993. reprint ed. 12.95 (*0-937460-88-5*) Hendrick-Long.

Sam Houston: Texas Hero. William R. Sanford & Carl R. Green. LC 95-32160. (Legendary Heroes of the Wild West Ser.). 48p. (J). (gr. 4-10). 1996. lib. bdg. 14.95 (*0-89490-651-8*) Enslow Pubs.

Sam Houston: The Great Designer. Llerena Friend. LC 54-13252. (Illus.). 408p. 1955. reprint ed. pap. 4.00 (*0-292-78422-8*) U of Tex Pr.

Sam Houston: The Life and Times of the Liberator of Texas, an Authentic American Hero. John H. Williams. 448p. 1994. 14.00 (*0-671-88071-3*, Touchstone Bks) S&S Trade.

Sam Houston & the American Southwest. Randolph B. Campbell. LC 92-26949. (Library of American Biography). (C). 1993. text ed. 16.95 (*0-06-500688-7*) Addson-Wesley Educ.

Sam Houston & the American Southwest. Randolph B. Campbell. LC 92-26949. (Library of American Biography). 176p. reprint ed. pap. 15.95 (*1-886746-29-X*, 93474) Talman.

Sam Houston with the Cherokees, 1829-1833. Jack Gregory & Rennard Strickland. LC 95-44919. (Illus.). 240p. (Orig.). 1996. pap. 14.95 (*0-8061-2809-7*) U of Okla Pr.

Sam Houston's Wife: A Biography of Margaret Lea Houston. William Seale. LC 77-123341. (Illus.). 328p. 1992. pap. 14.95 (*0-8061-2436-9*) U of Okla Pr.

Sam Huff: Tough Stuff. 1988. write for info. (*0-318-62734-5*) St Martin.

Sam in Flight: Further Adventures of Bad Sam. Raz Autry. LC 92-496. (Illus.). 64p. (Orig.). (J). (gr. 1-6). 1992. pap. 5.95 (*1-56474-029-3*) Fithian Pr.

Sam Johnson & the Blue Ribbon Quilt. Lisa C. Ernst. LC 82-9980. (Illus.). 32p. (J). (gr. k-3). 1983. lib. bdg. 13.93 (*0-688-01517-4*) Lothrop.

Sam Johnson & the Blue Ribbon Quilt. Lisa C. Ernst. LC 82-9980. (Illus.). 32p. (J). (gr. k up). 1992. pap. 4.95 (*0-688-11505-5*, Mulberry) Morrow.

Sam Lawson's Oldstown Fireside Stories. Harriet Beecher Stowe. LC 67-29279. (Americans in Fiction Ser.). (Illus.). 287p. reprint ed. pap. text ed. 12.95 (*0-89197-928-X*); reprint ed. lib. bdg. 27.50 (*0-8398-1874-2*) Irvington.

Sam Lloyd's Book of Tangram Puzzles. Sam Loyd. LC 68-19895. 1968. reprint ed. pap. 4.50 (*0-486-22011-7*) Dover.

Sam Lovel's Boy, with Forest & Stream Fables. Rowland E. Robinson. Ed. by Llewellyn R. Perkins. LC 70-160949. (Short Story Index Reprint Ser.). 1977. reprint ed. 20.95 (*0-8369-3928-X*) Ayer.

Sam Lovel's Camps: & Other Stories, Including 'In the Green Wood' Rowland E. Robinson. Ed. by Llewellyn R. Perkins. LC 77-37558. (Short Story Index Reprint Ser.). 1977. reprint ed. 21.95 (*0-8369-4117-9*) Ayer.

Sam Maloof: Woodworker. Sam Maloof. (Illus.). 228p. 1989. pap. 50.00 (*0-87011-910-9*) Kodansha.

Sam Martin Went to Prison. William Janzen & Frances Greaser. (Illus.). 64p. (Orig.). 1990. pap. 4.95 (*0-921788-09-6*) Kindred Prods.

***Sam Mihara's Fly Fishing Alaska: A Guide to Enjoying Alaska's Waters & Saving Money.** Sam Mihara & Vicki Hogue. (Illus.). 1997. pap. 19.95 (*0-9656258-0-X*, 100) Eskay Pub.

SAM Model of Senescence: Proceedings of the First International Conference on Senescence, the SAM Model, Kyoto, 17-18 March, 1994. Ed. by Toshio Takeda. LC 94-20411. (International Congress Ser.: No. 1062). 474p. 1994. 227.25 (*0-444-81695-X*, Excerpta Medica) Elsevier.

Sam Norkin: Drawings - Stories. Sam Norkin. LC 94-29122. 350p. 1994. pap. 29.95 (*0-435-08642-1*, 08642) Heinemann.

Sam Okamoto's Incredible Vegetables. Osamu Okamoto. LC 94-8520. 1993. 21.95 (*1-56554-025-5*) Pelican.

Sam, Old Kate & I. Monte Reichenberg. (Illus.). 32p. (Orig.). (J). (ps-4). 1994. pap. 3.95 (*0-9640260-2-3*) MM & I Ink.

Sam Panda & Thunder Dragon. Chris Conover. (J). (ps-3). 1992. 16.00 (*0-374-36393-5*) FS&G.

Sam Patch, the Big Time Jumper. Carol B. York. LC 79-66318. (Illus.). 48p. (J). (gr. 3-6). 1980. lib. bdg. 11.89 (*0-89375-306-8*) Troll Communs.

Sam Pezzo, P. I, Bk. 1. Vittorio Giardino. Ed. by Bernd Metz. Tr. by Tom Leighton from FRE. (Illus.). 48p. 1988. pap. 8.95 (*0-87416-057-X*) Catalan Communs.

Sam Pollard of Yunnan. E. H. Hayes. 1978. pap. 4.99 (*0-88019-106-6*) Schmul Pub Co.

Sam Rayburn: A Bio-Bibliography. Anthony Champagne. LC 88-21341. (Bio-Bibliographies in Law & Political Science Ser.: No. 4). 161p. 1988. text ed. 42.95 (*0-313-25864-3*, CSR/, Greenwood Pr) Greenwood.

Sam Shepard. Carol Rosen. (Modern Dramatists Ser.). (Illus.). 160p. 1991. text ed. 24.95 (*0-312-06051-3*) St Martin.

***Sam Shepard.** Don Shewey. (Illus.). 282p. 1997. pap. 14.95 (*0-306-80770-X*) Da Capo.

Sam Shepard. Bruce Weber. (Illus.). 32p. 1990. 35.00 (*0-9621658-1-6*) Lil Bear Films.

Sam Shepard: A Casebook. Kimball King. LC 88-24313. (Casebooks on Modern Dramatists Ser.: Vol. 2). 300p. 1989. text ed. 42.00 (*0-8240-4448-7*, H861) Garland.

***Sam Shepard: Between the Margin & the Center 1.** Ed. by Johan Callens. 1997. pap. text ed. 21.00 (*90-5702-151-X*, Harwood Acad Pubs) Gordon & Breach.

***Sam Shepard: Between the Margin & the Center 2.** Ed. by Johan Callens. 1997. pap. text ed. 21.00 (*90-5702-152-8*, Harwood Acad Pubs) Gordon & Breach.

Sam Shepard: Seven Plays. Sam Shepard. 368p. (Orig.). 1984. pap. 12.95 (*0-553-34611-3*, Bantam Classics) Bantam.

Sam Shepard: Theme, Image & the Director, Vol. 19. Laura J. Graham. LC 93-12390. (American University Studies: Series XXIV). 344p. (C). 1995. text ed. 58.95 (*0-8204-2121-9*) P Lang Pubng.

***Sam Shepard & the American Theatre.** Leslie A. Wade. LC 96-57537. 1997. pap. text ed. write for info. (*0-275-94584-7*, Praeger Pubs) Greenwood.

***Sam Shepard & the American Theatre.** Leslie A. Wade. LC 96-47537. (Contributions in Drama & Theatre Studies: Vol. 76). 1997. text ed. write for info. (*0-313-28944-1*, Greenwood Pr) Greenwood.

Sam Shepard on the German Stage: Critics, Politics, Myths. Carol Benet. LC 91-18762. (American University Studies: Comparative Literature: Ser. III, Vol. 41). 262p. (C). 1993. text ed. 41.95 (*0-8204-1624-X*) P Lang Pubng.

Sam Shepard's Dog. Dina VonZweck. 32p. (Orig.). 1984. pap. 4.00 (*0-931567-00-9*) White Deer Bks.

Sam Shepard's Metaphorical Stages. Lynda Hart. LC 86-4616. (Contributions in Drama & Theatre Studies: No. 22). 166p. 1987. text ed. 45.00 (*0-313-25373-0*, HSS/, Greenwood Pr) Greenwood.

***Sam Smith's Great American Political Repair Manual.** Sam Smith. LC 97-18636. 256p. (Orig.). 1997. 27.50 (*0-393-04122-0*); pap. 14.95 (*0-393-31627-0*) Norton.

Sam Sunday & the Mystery at the Ocean Beach Hotel. Robyn Supraner. LC 95-46305. (Illus.). 32p. (J). (ps-2). 1996. pap. 14.99 (*0-670-84797-6*, Viking) Viking Penguin.

Sam Szafran: Recent Works. James Lord. (Illus.). 1987. 10.00 (*0-936827-05-X*) C Bernard Gallery Ltd.

Sam, the Adirondack Railroad Cat. Nancy A. Douglas. LC 94-7690. (Illus.). 32p. (J). 1994. pap. 6.50 (*0-925168-28-9*) North Country.

An Asterisk (*) at the beginning of an entry indicates that the title is appearing in BIP for the first time.

Sam the Allergen. Charlotte L. Casterline. (Illus.). 26p. (Orig.). (J). (ps-6). 1985. pap. 4.95 (*0-9617218-1-2*) Info All Bk.

***Sam the Bear.** Marilee Burton. Date not set. write for info. (*0-688-12864-5*, Tambourine Bks) Morrow.

***Sam the Bear.** Marilee Burton. (J). Date not set. lib. bdg. write for info. (*0-688-12865-3*, Tambourine Bks) Morrow.

Sam the Big Blue Bear, Vol. 1. C. L. Bourne. (Illus.). 24p. (J). (gr. k-4). Date not set. pap. write for info. (*0-9651281-4-8*) Blue Bear.

Sam the Detective & the Alef Bet Mystery. Amye Rosenberg & Patrice G. Mason. Ed. by Seymour Rossel. (Illus.). 64p. (Orig.). (J). (gr. 1-3). 1980. pap. text ed. 5.50 (*0-87441-328-1*) Behrman.

Sam the Detective's Reading Readiness Book. Amye Rosenberg. (Illus.). 63p. (J). (ps). 1995. pap. text ed. 5.50 (*0-87441-362-1*) Behrman.

***Sam the Garbage Hound.** Charan Simon. (Rookie Readers Ser.). (Illus.). 32p. (J). 1997. pap. 4.95 (*0-516-26078-2*) Childrens.

Sam the Garbage Hound. Charnan Simon. LC 96-2085. (Rookie Reader Ser.). (Illus.). (J). 1996. lib. bdg. 15.00 (*0-516-02057-9*) Childrens.

***Sam the Horse.** Esther L. Roberts. (Illus.). 24p. (Orig.). (J). (ps). 1996. pap. 10.00 (*0-9655120-0-2*) Starlight Farm.

Sam the Minuteman. Nathaniel Benchley. LC 68-10211. (Harper I Can Read History Bk.). (Illus.). 64p. (J). (gr. k-3). 1969. lib. bdg. 14.89 (*0-06-020480-X*) HarpC Child Bks.

Sam the Minuteman. Nathaniel Benchley. LC 68-10211. (Trophy I Can Read Bk.). (Illus.). 64p. (J). (gr. k-3). 1987. pap. 3.50 (*0-06-444107-5*, Trophy) HarpC Child Bks.

Sam the Scarecrow. Sharon Gordon. (Illus.). 32p. (J). (gr. k-2). 1997. pap. 2.50 (*0-89375-287-8*) Troll Communs.

Sam the Sea Cow. Francine Jacobs. 32p. (J). (gr. 1-3). 1992. pap. 7.95 (*0-8027-7373-7*); lib. bdg. 14.85 (*0-8027-8147-0*) Walker & Co.

***Sam the Zamboni Man.** James Stevenson. LC 97-6946. 32p. (J). (ps up). Date not set. lib. bdg. write for info. (*0-688-14485-3*) Greenwillow.

***Sam the Zamboni Man.** James Stevenson. LC 97-6946. 32p. (J). (ps up). 1998. 15.00 (*0-688-14484-5*) Greenwillow.

Sam to the Rescue. (Read with Me Key Words to Reading Ser.: No. 9010-4). (Illus.). 1990. 3.50 (*0-7214-1317-X*, Ladybrd); teacher ed. 3.95 (*0-317-04028-6*, Ladybrd) Penguin.

Sam to the Rescue, Series 9011-4, No. 4. (Read with Me Key Words to Reading Ser.: No. 9010-4). (Illus.). 1990. student ed. 2.95 (*0-7214-3223-9*, Ladybrd) Penguin.

Sam Tuttle's Picture Book of Old Connecticut. Sam Tuttle, pseud. LC 78-73606. (Illus.). (Orig.). 1979. pap. 9.95 (*0-914166-20-4*) Americana Rev.

Sam Vole & His Brothers. Martin Waddell. LC 91-58755. (Illus.). 32p. (J). (ps up). 1992. 14.95 (*1-56402-082-7*) Candlewick Pr.

Sam Vole & His Brothers. Martin Waddell. LC 91-58755. (J). (ps up). 1996. pap. 4.99 (*1-56402-522-5*) Candlewick Pr.

Sam Walton. Keith Greenberg. LC 92-45123. (Made in America Ser.). (J). 1993. 15.93 (*0-86592-047-8*); 11.95 (*0-685-66419-8*) Rourke Enter.

Sam Walton: The Giant of Wal-Mart. Anne Canadeo. Ed. by Richard G. Young. LC 91-32776. (Wizards of Business Ser.). (Illus.). 64p. (J). (gr. 4-8). 1992. lib. bdg. 17.26 (*1-56074-025-6*) Garrett Ed Corp.

Sam Walton Story: The Retailing of Middle America. Austin Teutsch. Ed. by Sandra Bybee. (Illus.). 224p. 1991. pap. 9.95 (*0-9630346-0-X*) GldnTouch.

Sam Who Never Forgets. Eve Rice. LC 76-30370. 32p. (J). (ps-3). 1977. lib. bdg. 13.93 (*0-688-84088-4*) Greenwillow.

Sam Who Never Forgets. Eve Rice. LC 76-30370. (Illus.). 32p. (J). (ps up). 1987. pap. 3.95 (*0-688-07335-2*, Mulberry) Morrow.

Sam Who Was Swallowed by a Shark. Phyllis Root. LC 93-2884. (Illus.). 32p. (J). (ps up). 1994. 12.95 (*1-56402-198-X*) Candlewick Pr.

Sam Who Was Swallowed by a Shark. Phyllis Root. LC 93-2884. (Illus.). 32p. (J). (ps-2). 1996. reprint ed. pap. 5.99 (*1-56402-955-7*) Candlewick Pr.

Sam Williams. W. S. Harrison. LC 70-39088. (Black Heritage Library Collection). 1977. reprint ed. 27.95 (*0-8369-9026-9*) Ayer.

Sam Woods. Stanley E. Rushworth. Ed. by Peter Greenwood. LC 92-81553. 176p. (Orig.). (C). 1992. pap. 14.95 (*0-9632574-9-8*) Talk Leaves.

Sam Woods American Healing. Stan Rushworth. LC 92-81553. 1993. 11.95 (*0-88268-122-2*) Station Hill Pr.

Sama Veda. Bibek Debroy. (Great Epics of India Ser.: Veda 3). (C). 1992. pap. 3.00 (*0-8364-2779-3*, Pub. by BR Pub II) S Asia.

Samadhi: Self Development in Zen, Swordsmanship, & Psychotherapy. Mike Sayama. LC 85-9894. (SUNY Series in Transpersonal & Humanistic Psychology). 160p. 1985. pap. 14.95 (*0-88706-147-8*); text ed. 42.50 (*0-88706-146-X*) State U NY Pr.

Samadhi & Beyond. Sri S. Chakravarti. LC 74-79444. 1974. pap. 3.50 (*0-87707-135-7*) Ranney Pubns.

***Samah Conspiracy.** Ken Vegotsky. (Love Living & Live Loving Ser.). (Orig.). 1998. mass mkt. 6.99 (*1-886508-05-4*) Adi Gaia Esalen.

Samantha. Andrea Kane. Ed. by Carolyn Tolley. 384p. (Orig.). 1994. mass mkt. 5.50 (*0-671-86507-2*) PB.

Samantha. Ellen S. Walsh. LC 95-12809. 32p. (J). 1996. 14.00 (*0-15-252264-6*) HarBrace.

Samantha, 6 bks., Set. Susan S Adler et al. (American Girls Collection). (Illus.). 432p. (J). (gr. 2-5). 1991. pap. 34.95 (*0-937295-77-9*); boxed 74.95 (*1-56247-050-7*) Pleasant Co.

Samantha: A Soap Opers & Vocabulary Book for Adult Students of English As a Second Language. Meryl Becker. LC 92-63209. 146p. 1993. teacher ed. 9.95 (*0-472-08190-X*); pap. text ed. 14.95 (*0-472-08178-0*) U of Mich Pr.

Samantha Crane Crossing the Line. Linda A. Cooney. 224p. (YA). 1996. mass mkt. 4.50 (*0-06-106410-6*, Harp PBks) HarpC.

Samantha Crane on Her Own. Linda A. Cooney. 272p. (Orig.). (J). 1996. mass mkt. 4.50 (*0-06-106412-2*, Harp PBks) HarpC.

Samantha Crane on the Edge. Linda A. Cooney. 224p. (YA). 1996. mass mkt. 4.50 (*0-06-106411-4*, Harp PBks) HarpC.

Samantha Crane on the Run. Linda A. Cooney. 240p. (YA). 1996. mass mkt. 4.50 (*0-06-106409-2*, Harp PBks) HarpC.

Samantha Gill, Belly Dancer. Karen M. Coombs. 128p. (J). 1989. pap. 2.75 (*0-380-75737-0*, Camelot) Avon.

Samantha Learns a Lesson: A School Story. Susan S. Adler. Ed. by Jeanne Thieme. (American Girls Collection). (Illus.). 72p. (J). (gr. 2-5). 1986. pap. 5.95 (*0-937295-13-2*); lib. bdg. 12.95 (*0-937295-83-3*) Pleasant Co.

Samantha on the Race Problem. Marietta Holley. LC 71-91082. (American Humorists Ser.). (Illus.). 387p. reprint ed. lib. bdg. 39.50 (*0-8398-0786-4*) Irvington.

Samantha Press 'n Dress. (J). 1992. 34.99 (*1-888074-14-0*) Pckts Lrning.

Samantha Rastles the Woman Question. Marietta Holley. Ed. by Jane Curry. LC 82-13482. (Illus.). 256p. 1983. pap. text ed. 11.95 (*0-252-01306-9*); audio 9.95 (*0-252-01062-0*) U of Ill Pr.

Samantha Rastles the Woman Question. fac. ed. Marietta Holley. Ed. by Jane Curry. LC 82-13482. 255p. 1983. reprint ed. pap. 72.70 (*0-7837-8069-9*, 2047822) Bks Demand.

Samantha Saves the Day: A Summer Story. Valerie Tripp. Ed. by Jeanne Thieme. (American Girls Collection). (Illus.). 72p. (J). (gr. 2-5). 1988. pap. 5.95 (*0-937295-41-8*); lib. bdg. 12.95 (*0-937295-92-2*) Pleasant Co.

Samantha Smith: A Journey for Peace. Anne Galicich. LC 87-13614. (Taking Part Ser.). (Illus.). 64p. (J). (gr. 3 up). 1988. lib. bdg. 13.95 (*0-87518-367-0*, Dillon Silver Burdett) Silver Burdett Pr.

Samantha Smith: Little Ambassador. Patricia S. Martin. (Reaching Your Goal Bks.). (Illus.). 24p. (J). (gr. 1-4). 1987. 10.95 (*0-685-58131-4*); lib. bdg. 14.60 (*0-86592-173-3*) Rourke Corp.

Samantha the Snob: A Step 2 Book. Kathryn Cristaldi. LC 93-19649. (Step into Reading Bks.). (Illus.). 48p. (Orig.). (J). (gr. 1-3). 1994. pap. 3.99 (*0-679-84640-9*); lib. bdg. 11.99 (*0-679-94640-3*) Random Bks Yng Read.

Samantha Tylers. Cherie Bennett. Date not set. pap. 3.50 (*0-14-036504-4*) Viking Penguin.

Samantha, 1904: Teacher's Guide to Six Books about America's New Century. Roberta Johnson. (Illus.). 64p. (Orig.). 1995. teacher ed., pap. 7.95 (*1-56247-238-0*) Pleasant Co.

Samantha's Cookbook. Polly Athan et al. Ed. by Jodi Evert. LC 94-12059. (J). 1994. pap. 5.95 (*1-56247-114-7*) Pleasant Co.

Samantha's Craft Book. Geri K. Strigenz. LC 94-12058. (Illus.). (J). 1994. pap. 5.95 (*1-56247-115-5*) Pleasant Co.

Samantha's Craft Book & Kit. (American Girls Collection). (Illus.). 44p. (J). (gr. 2-5). 1996. 19.95 (*1-56247-145-7*) Pleasant Co.

***Samantha's Journey.** Joanna Campbell. (Thoroughbred Super Ser.: No. 4). (J). 1997. pap. 3.99 (*0-06-106494-7*) HarpC Child Bks.

Samantha's Paper Doll. (American Girls Collection). (Illus.). (J). (gr. 2-5). 1993. pap. 5.95 (*1-56247-056-6*) Pleasant Co.

Samantha's Pastimes Boxed Set, 4 bks., Set. Ed. by Pleasant Company Staff. (American Girls Collection). (Illus.). 168p. (Orig.). (J). (gr. 2-5). 1995. boxed, pap. text ed. 22.95 (*1-56247-262-3*) Pleasant Co.

Samantha's Pride. Joanna Campbell. (Thoroughbred Ser.: No. 7). 192p. 1993. mass mkt. 3.99 (*0-06-106163-8*, Harp PBks) HarpC.

Samantha's Surprise: A Christmas Story. Maxine R. Schur. Ed. by Jeanne Thieme. (American Girls Collection). (Illus.). 72p. (J). (gr. 2-5). 1986. pap. 5.95 (*0-937295-22-1*); lib. bdg. 12.95 (*0-937295-86-8*) Pleasant Co.

Samantha's Theater Kit. Pleasant Company Staff. (American Girls Collection). 48p. (Orig.). (J). (gr. 2-5). 1994. pap. 5.95 (*1-56247-116-3*) Pleasant Co.

***Samara Oblast: Economy, Industry, Government, Business.** 2nd rev. ed. Russian Information & Business Center, Inc. Staff. (Russian Regional Business Directories Ser.). (Illus.). 200p. 1997. pap. 99.00 (*1-57751-412-2*) Russ Info & Busn Ctr.

***Samarian Solution.** Glenn D. Ridenour. 305p. (Orig.). 1997. mass mkt. 4.99 (*1-55237-177-8*, Pub. by Comnwlth Pub CN) Partners Pubs Grp.

Samaritan. Ted Gibbons. (Personal Enrichment Ser.). 15p. 1991. write for info. (*0-929985-23-0*) Jackman Pubng.

Samaritan. Nancy N. Rue. (Christian Heritage Ser.: Vol. 5). (Orig.). (J). 1996. pap. 5.99 (*1-56179-442-2*) Focus Family.

Samaritan Chronicle No. 2 (or, Sepher Ha-Yamim) from Joshua to Nebuchadnezzar. John Macdonald. (Beiheft 107 zur Zeitschrift fuer die Alttestamentliche Wissenschaft Ser.). (C). 1969. 92.35 (*3-11-002582-5*) De Gruyter.

Samaritan Liturgy, 2 vols., Set. Ed. by Arthur E. Cowley. LC 77-87608. reprint ed. 87.50 (*0-404-16430-7*) AMS Pr.

Samaritan Oral Law & Ancient Traditions. Moses Gaster. LC 77-87609. reprint ed. 39.50 (*0-404-16433-1*) AMS Pr.

Samaritan Problem: Studies in the Relationship of Samaritanism, Judaism, & Early Christianity. John Bowman. Tr. by Alfred M. Johnson, Jr. from GER. LC 75-20042. (Pittsburgh Theological Monographs: No. 4). 1975. pap. 8.75 (*0-915138-04-2*) Pickwick.

Samaritan Treasure. Marianne Luban. LC 90-2690. 221p. (Orig.). 1990. pap. 9.95 (*0-918273-79-X*) Coffee Hse.

Samaritans. Reinhard Pummer. (Iconography of Religions Ser.: Vol. XXIII-5). (Illus.). xiv, 46p. 1987. pap. 51.50 (*90-04-07891-6*) E J Brill.

Samaritans: History, Doctrine & Literature. M. Gaster. 1976. lib. bdg. 134.95 (*0-8490-2563-X*) Gordon Pr.

Samaritans: Their History, Doctrines & Literature. M. Gaster. (British Academy, London, Schweich Lectures on Biblical Archaeology Series, 1930). 1974. reprint ed. pap. 30.00 (*0-8115-1265-7*) Periodicals Srv.

Samaritans: Their Religion, Literature, Society & Culture. Ed. by Alan D. Crown. 900p. 1988. 242.00 (*3-16-145237-2*, Pub. by J C B Mohr GW) Coronet Bks.

Samaritans: Their Testimony to the Religion of Israel. J. Thomson. 1976. lib. bdg. 59.95 (*0-8490-2564-8*) Gordon Pr.

Samaritans Documents Relating to Their History, Religion & Life. Ed. & Tr. by John Bowman. LC 77-4949. (Pittsburgh Original Texts & Translations Ser.: No. 2). 1977. pap. 15.00 (*0-915138-27-1*) Pickwick.

Samaritan's Hospital. large type ed. Alex Stuart. 352p. 1988. 25.99 (*0-7089-1858-1*) Ulverscroft.

Samaritan's Imperative: Compassionate Ministry to People Living with AIDS. Michael J. Christensen. LC 90-47212. 208p. 1991. pap. 9.95 (*0-687-36790-5*) Abingdon.

Samaritans of Molokai. Charles J. Dutton. (Select Bibliographies Reprint Ser.). 1977. reprint ed. 25.95 (*0-8369-5733-4*) Ayer.

Samarkand. Amin Maalouf. Tr. by Russell Harris from FRE. LC 95-42496. (Emerging Voices Ser.). 320p. 1996. 35.00 (*1-56656-200-7*); pap. 14.95 (*1-56656-194-9*) Interlink Pub.

Samarkand & Bukhara. John Lawton. (Travel to Landmarks Ser.). 1992. 24.95 (*1-85043-178-7*, Pub. by I B Tauris UK) St Martin.

Samarkand Dimension. David Wise. 272p. 1988. pap. 3.95 (*0-380-70518-4*) Avon.

Samas Religious Texts Classified in the British Museum Catalogue As Hymns, Prayers, & Incantations. Ed. by Clifton D. Gray. LC 78-72728. (Ancient Mesopotamian Texts & Studies). reprint ed. 29.50 (*0-404-18176-7*) AMS Pr.

***Samatimerisch Phonetik Grammatik Lexikographie: Geschichte der Mundart der Deutschen Gemeinde Sanktmartin am Nordlichen Rand des Rumanischen Banats.** Joseph Mileck. (Berkeley Models of Grammars Ser.: Vol. 3). 392p. (C). 1997. text ed. 58.95 (*0-8204-3655-0*) P Lang Pubng.

Samaveda: Sanskrit Text with English Translation. Tr. by Devichand from SAN. 304p. (C). 1981. 35.00 (*0-8364-2352-6*, Pub. by Munshiram Manoharial II) S Asia.

Samavedic Chant. Wayne Howard. LC 76-49854. (Illus.). 1977. 75.00 (*0-300-01956-4*) Yale U Pr.

Samayasara (the Soul Essence) Kundakunda Acharya. Tr. & Comment by Rai B. Jaini. LC 73-3843. (Sacred Books of the Jainas: No. 8). reprint ed. 37.50 (*0-404-57708-3*) AMS Pr.

Samba. Earl Atkinson. (Ballroom Dance Ser.). 1986. lib. bdg. 250.00 (*0-8490-3632-1*) Gordon Pr.

Samba. Earl Atkinson. (Ballroom Dance Ser.). 1983. lib. bdg. 250.00 (*0-87700-473-0*) Revisionist Pr.

Samba. Alma Guillermoprieto. LC 90-55687. 256p. 1991. pap. 12.00 (*0-679-73256-X*, Vin) Random.

Samba: A Bibliography: History, People, Lyrics, Recordings. Florencio O. De Rio. (Illus.). 110p. (Orig.). 1992. pap. 14.00 (*0-929928-11-3*) Fog Pubns.

Samba: The Body Articulate. Barbara Browning. LC 94-38586. (Arts & Politics of the Everyday Ser.). (Illus.). 192p. 1995. 29.95 (*0-253-32867-5*); pap. 14.95 (*0-253-20956-0*) Ind U Pr.

***Samba & Lambada.** Paul Bottomer. (Dance Crazy Ser.). (Illus.). 64p. 1997. 12.95 (*1-85967-395-3*, Lorenz Bks) Anness Pub.

***Samba for Sherlock.** Jo Soares. 1997. 23.00 (*0-375-40065-6*) Pantheon.

Samba in the Night: Spiritism in Brazil. David J. Hess. LC 93-30887. 214p. 1994. 29.50 (*0-231-08432-3*) Col U Pr.

Samba Larue Sextet. M. Mossman. 1995. pap. text ed. 20.00 (*0-7935-4837-3*, 00000508) H Leonard.

Samba Made Easy. (Ballroom Dance Ser.). 1985. lib. bdg. 74.95 (*0-87700-672-5*) Revisionist Pr.

Samba Shiva: A Farce. Chandrasekhar Kambar. (C). 1992. pap. text ed. 5.00 (*81-7046-090-5*, Pub. by Seagull Bks II) S Asia.

Sambalena Show-Off. Phillis Gershator. LC 94-14413. (J). (gr. k-3). 1995. 15.00 (*0-689-80314-1*, Mac Bks Young Read) S&S Childrens.

Sambaqui: A Novel of Prehistory. Stella C. Ribeiro. Tr. by Claudia Van der Heuvel. 144p. (POR.). 1987. pap. 3.95 (*0-380-89624-9*) Avon.

Sambia: Ritual & Gender in New Guinea. Gilbert Herdt. 227p. (C). 1987. pap. text ed. 13.50 (*0-03-068907-4*) HB Coll Pubs.

Sambuco Black Elderberry Extract: A Breakthrough in the Treatment of Influenza Viruses. Madeleine Mumcuoglu. 16p. 1995. 2.50 (*0-9646056-0-0*) R S S Pub Inc.

Samburu. Jon Holtzman. LC 94-19665. (Heritage Library of African Peoples: Set 1). (Illus.). 64p. (YA). (gr. 7-12). 1994. lib. bdg. 15.95 (*0-8239-1759-2*) Rosen Group.

Same: II Timothy 2: 2. Terry C. Wilson. 250p. (Orig.). (YA). (gr. 12). 1989. pap. 30.00 (*0-9623886-0-2*) T C Wilson.

Same & Different. Illus. by Pam Adams. (Motivation Ser.). 16p. (Orig.). (J). (ps-2). 1975. pap. 3.99 (*0-85953-043-4*, Pub. by Childs Play UK) Childs Play.

Same & Not the Same. Roald Hoffman. (Pegram Lectures). pap. write for info. (*0-231-10139-2*) Col U Pr.

Same & Not the Same. Roald Hoffman. (Pegram Lectures). (Illus.). 256p. 1995. 34.95 (*0-231-10138-4*) Col U Pr.

Same Bed, Different Dreams. Hugh Gross. 1991. 17.95 (*0-922811-10-5*); pap. 9.95 (*0-922811-11-3*) Mid-List.

Same Bed, Different Dreams: America & Japan - Societies in Transition. Alan D. Romberg. LC 90-1523. 152p. 1990. reprint ed. pap. 43.40 (*0-608-02005-2*, 2062661) Bks Demand.

Same Blue Chevy. Gale R. Walder. 74p. (Orig.). 1996. pap. 10.95 (*1-882688-10-4*) Tia Chucha Pr.

Same but Different. Tessa Dahl. (Illus.). 32p. (J). (ps-3). 1993. pap. 3.99 (*0-14-054823-8*) Puffin Bks.

Same but Different. Meish Goldish. (Real Readers Ser.: Level Green). (Illus.). 32p. (J). (gr. 1-4). 1989. lib. bdg. 21.40 (*0-8172-3528-0*) Raintree Steck-V.

Same Client: The Demographics of Education & Service Delivery Systems. Harold L. Hodgkinson. 28p. 1989. 12.00 (*0-937846-67-8*) Inst Educ Lead.

S

Same-Day Diagnosis of Human Virus Infections. Donald M. McLean & Kathleen K. Wong. 144p. 1984. 84.00 (*0-8493-6590-2*, QR387, CRC Reprint) Franklin.

***Same Difference: Feminism & Sexual Difference.** Bacchi. pap. 19.95 (*0-04-370189-2*) Paul & Co Pubs.

Same Difference: Feminism & Sexual Difference. Carol Bacchi. 1991. pap. text ed. 19.95 (*0-04-442152-4*, Pub. by Allen Unwin AT) Paul & Co Pubs.

Same-Different: Holidays Version. rev. ed. Spencer Kagan. (Illus.). 104p. 1992. pap. text ed. 12.00 (*1-879097-11-7*) Kagan Cooperative.

Same Fate As the Poor. rev. ed. Judith Noone. LC 95-20271. 175p. 1995. pap. 12.95 (*1-57075-031-9*) Orbis Bks.

Same Game, Different Name: The World Hockey Association. Jack Lautier & Frank Polnaszek. (Illus.). 288p. 1996. pap. 19.95 (*0-9650315-1-9*) Glacier Publng.

Same Jesus. Clarence M. Wagner. Ed. by Tru-Faith Publishers Staff. 72p. (Orig.). 1981. pap. 3.50 (*0-937498-00-9*) Tru-Faith.

Same Jesus: A Contemporary Christology. Ed. by Daniel A. Helminiak. 368p. 1986. 15.95 (*0-8294-0521-6*) Loyola Pr.

Same Old Song. Marilyn Kaye. LC 92-53936. (Little Mermaid Novels Ser.). (Illus.). 80p. (J). (gr. 1-4). 1992. pap. 3.50 (*1-56282-249-7*) Disney Pr.

Same or Different. Barbara Gregorich. Ed. by Joan Hoffman. (Get Ready! Bks.). (Illus.). 32p. (J). (ps). 1983. student ed. 1.99 (*0-938256-52-1*) Sch Zone Pub Co.

Same Place But Different. Perry Nodelman. (J). 1995. 15.00 (*0-671-89839-6*, S&S Bks Young Read) S&S Childrens.

Same Place, Same Things. Tim Gautreaux. LC 96-19622. 224p. 1996. 20.95 (*0-312-14727-9*) St Martin.

***Same Place Same Things.** Tim Gautreaux. Date not set. 11.00 (*0-312-16994-9*) St Martin.

***Same River Twice.** John Burns. Ed. by Lauren McHenry. 80p. (Orig.). 1997. pap. 15.00 (*1-882611-11-X*) Yardbird Bks.

Same River Twice: A Memoir. Chris Offutt. 192p. 1994. pap. 9.95 (*0-14-023253-2*, Penguin Bks) Viking Penguin.

Same River Twice: Honoring the Difficult. Alice Walker. LC 96-42455. 1997. pap. 14.00 (*0-671-00377-1*) PB.

Same River Twice: Honoring the Difficult. Alice Walker. (Illus.). 304p. 1996. 24.00 (*0-684-81419-6*) S&S Trade.

Same River Twice: Honoring the Difficult. large type ed. Alice Walker. LC 96-884. 1996. 24.95 (*1-56895-298-8*) Wheeler Pub.

Same Sea As Every Summer. Esther Tusquets. Tr. by Margaret E. Jones from SPA. LC 89-38371. (European Women Writers Ser.). viii, 194p. 1990. pap. 9.95 (*0-8032-9416-6*, Bison Books) U of Nebr Pr.

***Same Sex: The Ethics, Science & Culture of Homosexuality.** Ed. by John Corvino. (Studies in Social, Political, & Legal Philosophy: No. 70). 320p. Date not set. pap. 17.95 (*0-8476-8483-0*) Rowman.

***Same Sex: The Ethics, Science & Culture of Homosexuality.** Ed. by John Corvino. LC 97-22315. (Studies in Social, Political, & Legal Philosophy: No. 70). 320p. 1997. 58.00 (*0-8476-8482-2*) Rowman.

***Same Sex, Different Cultures.** Gilbert Herdt. LC 97-1839. 1997. text ed. 26.00 (*0-8133-3163-3*) Westview.

Same-Sex Dynamics Among Nineteenth-Century Americans: A Mormon Example. D. Michael Quinn. LC 95-32473. (Illus.). 416p. 1996. 29.95 (*0-252-02205-X*) U of Ill Pr.

Same-Sex Love: And the Path to Wholeness. Ed. by Robert H. Hopcke et al. LC 92-50443. 294p. (Orig.). 1993. pap. 18.00 (*0-87773-651-0*) Shambhala Pubns.

***Same-Sex Marriage: The Moral & Legal Debate.** Robert M. Baired. LC 96-53057. 1997. pap. 16.95 (*1-57392-129-7*) Prometheus Bks.

Same-Sex Unions in Premodern Europe. John Boswell. 1995. pap. 13.00 (*0-679-75164-5*, Vin) Random.

Same Song-Separate Voices: The Collective Memoirs of the Lennon Sisters. Dianne Lennon et al. LC 84-60761. (Illus.). 368p. 1985. 17.95 (*0-915677-10-5*) Roundtable Pub.

Same Sun Was in the Sky. Denise Webb. LC 94-40959. (Illus.). 32p. (J). (gr. k up). 1995. lib. bdg. 14.95 (*0-87358-602-6*) Northland AZ.

Same Sweet Yellow. Jean Dubois. 48p. (Orig.). 1994. pap. 12.50 (0-9622932-2-9) San Miguel Pr.

Same Task: Different Mask Fundraising Cookbook. Cookbook Consortium Staff. 1985. ring bd. 19.95 (0-318-04323-8) Prosperity & Profits.

Same Thing Happening Over & Over see Novella Box

Same Time, Next Year. Debbie Macomber. (Special Edition Ser.). 1995. pap. 3.75 (0-373-09937-1, 1-09937-3) Silhouette.

***Same Time, Next Year.** Debbie Macomber. (Silhouette Ser.). 1996. 19.95 (0-373-59754-1) Thorndike Pr.

Same Time...Same Station: An A-Z Guide to Radio from Jack Benny to Howard Stern. Ronald W. Lackmann. LC 95-5662. (Illus.). 304p. 1995. 45.00 (0-8160-2862-1) Facts on File.

Same Water: Poems. Joan Murray. LC 89-33954. (Wesleyan New Poets Ser.). 64p. 1990. pap. 11.95 (0-8195-1183-8, Wesleyan Univ Pr); text ed. 25.00 (0-8195-2181-7, Wesleyan Univ Pr) U Pr of New Eng.

Samed: Journal of a West Bank Palestinian. Raja Shehadeh. LC 83-25647. 144p. 1984. pap. 9.95 (0-915361-02-7) Hemed Bks.

Same/Different: Barney Pretends. Margie Larsen & Mary A. Dudko. (Barney's Beginnings Ser.). (Illus.). 16p. (J). (ps-3). 1996. wbk. ed., pap. 2.95 (1-57064-093-9) Lyrick Pub.

***Same/Different: Barney Pretnds.** Margie Larsen & Mary A. Dudko. (Barney's Beginnings Ser.). 32p. (J). (ps-3). 1997. wbk. ed., pap. 2.95 (1-57064-176-5) Lyrick Pub.

SamFow: The San Joaquin Chinese Lagacy. Sylvia S. Minnick. LC 87-63495. (Illus.). 320p. (C). 1988. 25.00 (0-944194-09-5); pap. 14.95 (0-944194-10-9) Heritage West.

Samhain & other Poems in Irish Metres of the Eighth: To the Sixteenth Centuries. Robin Skelton et al. 52p. 9500. pap. 12.95 (1-897648-13-8, Pub. by Salmon Poetry IE) Dufour.

Sami & the Time of the Troubles. Florence P. Heide & Judith Heide Gilliland. (Illus.). 32p. (J). (gr. k-4). 1992. 15.95 (0-395-55964-2, Clarion Bks) HM.

Samian Ware. Guy De la Bedoyere. 1989. pap. 25.00 (0-85263-930-9, Pub. by Shire UK) St Mut.

Samir Husni's Guide to New Consumer Magazines. Ed. by Samir Husni. 208p. 1995. 49.95 (0-688-14451-9) Hearst Bks.

***Samir Husni's Guide to New Consumer Magazines.** Ed. by Samir A. Husni. (Illus.). 306p. (Orig.). 1997. pap. 295.00 (0-917460-84-7) Oxbridge Comm.

Sami's Traditional Turkish Dictionary. Sami. 1992. 75.00 (0-85585-597-5) Intl Bk Ctr.

Sami's Turkish Traditional Dictionary. Sh. Sami. 1578p. (TUR.). 1992. 75.00 (0-86685-597-1, LDL5971, Pub. by Librairie du Liban FR) Intl Bk Ctr.

Samisdat Guide to Publishing Your Own Book. 1991. lib. bdg. 79.95 (0-8490-4693-9) Gordon Pr.

Samisdat Method: A Do-It-Yourself Guide to Offset Printing. 4th ed. Merritt Clifton. (Illus.). 56p. 1990. pap. 10.00 (0-318-50051-5) Samisdat.

Samit & the Dragon. (Wellinworld Tapes & Books for Children: 2-9). 36p. (J). (ps-4). 1985. 8.95 (0-88684-177-1); audio write for info. (0-318-59509-5) Listen USA.

Samizdat: Voices of the Soviet Opposition. Ed. by George Saunders. Tr. by Marilyn Vogt from RUS. LC 75-186692. 464p. 1974. pap. 22.95 (0-913460-28-1); lib. bdg. 55.00 (0-913460-27-3) Pathfinder NY.

Samizdat & an Independent Society in Central & Eastern Europe. H. Gordon Skilling. 288p. 1989. text ed. 45.00 (0-8142-0487-2) Ohio St U Pr.

Samizdat Press in China's Provinces, 1979-1981: An Annotated Guide. Compiled by Claude Widor. (Bibliographical Ser.: No. 70). 157p. 1987. pap. text ed. 11.95 (0-8179-2702-6) Hoover Inst Pr.

Samizdat Register. Ed. by Roy A. Medvedev. (C). 1977. text ed. 10.95 (0-393-05652-X) Norton.

Samkhya: A Dualist Tradition in Indian Philosophy. Ed. by Gerald J. Larson et al. LC 85-43199. (Encyclopedia of Indian Philosophies: Vol. 4). 800p. 1986. text ed. 84.00 (0-691-07301-5) Princeton U Pr.

Samkhya Philosophy. Kapila. Tr. by Nandalal Sinha. LC 73-3799. (Sacred Books of the Hindus: No. 11). reprint ed. 74.50 (0-404-57811-X) AMS Pr.

Samkhya System, a History of the Samkhya Philosophy. Arthur B. Keith. LC 78-72452. reprint ed. 24.00 (0-404-17319-5) AMS Pr.

Samkyha-Yoga: Proceedings of the IASWR Conference, 1981. Ed. by Christopher Chapple. 181p. 1983. pap. text ed. 10.00 (0-915078-04-X) Inst Adv Stud Wld.

Samman's the Nails in Disease. 5th ed. Peter D. Samman & David A. Fenton. LC 94-34926. (Illus.). 224p. 1995. text ed. 65.00 (0-7506-0189-2) Buttrwrth-Heinemann.

Sammelbuch griechischer Urkunden aus Aegypten, 3 vols. Friedrich Preisigke. 1530p. 1974. reprint ed. 500.00 (3-11-004756-X) De Gruyter.

Sammi. Ernest A. Joselovitz. 1975. pap. 3.25 (0-8222-0983-7) Dramatists Play.

Sammlung Alt- und Mitteldeutscher Worter Aus Lateinischen Urkunden. Joseph Kehrein. viii, 71p. 1966. reprint ed. write for info. (0-318-71261-X) G Olms Pubs.

Sammlung Architektonischer Entwurfe (Collection of Architectural Designs) Karl F. Schinkel. (Illus.). 272p. 1989. reprint ed. 60.00 (0-910413-56-8) Princeton Arch.

Sammlung Franz Trau: Munzen der Romischen Kaiser. (Illus.). 130p. (ENG & GER.). 1976. 15.00 (0-915018-12-8) Attic Bks.

***Sammlung Kleiner Juristischer Abhandlungen Band 38: Nebst Desselben Leben und Vollstandigem Verzeichni Seiner Schriften.** Daniel Nettelbladt. 556p. (GER.). 1996. 198.00 (3-487-10283-8) G Olms Pubs.

***Sammy: Dallas Detective.** Robin Hardy. LC 96-61281. 224p. (Orig.). (J). 1997. pap. 9.99 (1-56384-134-7) Vital Issues.

Sammy at the Farm see Set 5

Sammy Cahn's Rhyming Dictionary. Sammy Cahn. 1991. pap. 16.95 (0-943351-51-0, XW1509) Astor Bks.

Sammy Carducci's Guide to Women. Ronald Kidd. 1995. 5.25 (0-87129-522-9, S33) Dramatic Pub.

Sammy Davis Jr. My Father. Tracey Davis & Delores A. Barclay. (Illus.). 288p. 1996. 19.95 (1-881649-84-9) Genl Pub Grp.

Sammy Davis Jr., Songbook (Piano - Vocal) Leslie Bricusse. Ed. by Milton Okun. (Illus.). 176p. (Orig.). (YA). 1992. pap. 19.95 (0-89524-717-8) Cherry Lane.

***Sammy Gets a Ride.** large type ed. Karen Evans & Kathleen Urmston. (Illus.). 12p. (Orig.). (J). (gr. k-2). 1997. pap. 4.95 (1-879835-03-7) Kaeden Corp.

***Sammy Keyes & the Hotel Thief.** Wendelin Van Draanen. 1998. lib. bdg. 16.99 (0-679-98839-4) Knopf Bks Yng Read.

***Sammy Keyes & the Hotel Thief.** Wendelin Van Draanen. 1998. 15.00 (0-679-88839-X) Random Bks Yng Read.

Sammy Marks: "The Uncrowned King of the Transvaal" Richard Mendelsohn. LC 90-28333. (Illus.). 320p. 1991. pap. 19.95 (0-8214-0999-9); text ed. 39.95 (0-8214-0998-0) Ohio U Pr.

Sammy Miller on Trials. Sammy Miller. (Illus.). 1971. 5.95 (0-393-60015-7) Norton.

Sammy Saves the Day. Leslie McGuire. (Play Along Ser.). 16p. (J). (ps-2). 1995. write for info. (1-57234-060-6) YES Ent.

Sammy Seahorse Teaches Chess: A Light-Hearted Introduction. F. Donald Bloss & Andrew Kensler. (Illus.). 192p. (Orig.). 1995. pap. 11.95 (0-936015-61-6) Pocahontas Pr.

Sammy Seal. (Derrydale Bath Bks.). (Illus.). (J). (ps). 1.79 (0-517-46416-0) Random Hse Value.

Sammy Shrimp: A Tale of a Little Shrimp. Suzanne Tate. LC 90-61002. (Suzanne Tate's Nature Ser.: No. 8). (Illus.). 28p. (Orig.). (J). (gr. k-4). 1990. pap. 3.95 (1-878405-00-4) Nags Head Art.

Sammy Skunk. Ron Reese. (I Can Read Ser.). (Illus.). (J). (gr. k-3). 1984. 7.95 (0-89868-009-3, Read Res) ARO Pub.

Sammy Skunk. Ron Reese. Ed. by Alton Jordan. (I Can Read Ser.). (Illus.). (J). (gr. k-3). 1984. pap. 3.95 (0-89868-042-5, Read Res) ARO Pub.

Sammy Skunk. Dave Sargent & Pat L. Sargent. (Animal Pride Ser.: No. 9). (Illus.). 38p. (J). (gr. 2-8). 1996. pap. 2.95 (1-56763-011-1) Ozark Pub.

Sammy Skunk. Dave Sargent & Pat L. Sargent. LC 96-1491. (Animal Pride Ser.: No. 9). (Illus.). 38p. (J). 1996. 12.95 (1-56763-089-8) Ozark Pub.

Sammy Skunk Plays the Clown. Larue W. Selman. (Buppet Bks.). (Illus.). (J). (gr. 1-4). 1980. pap. 3.95 (0-89868-108-1, Read Res) ARO Pub.

Sammy Skunk Plays the Clown. Larue W. Selman. Ed. by Alton Jordan. (Buppet Bks.). (Illus.). (J). (gr. 1-4). 1980. 9.95 (0-89868-097-2, Read Res) ARO Pub.

Sammy Spider's First Hanukkah. Sylvia A. Rouss. LC 92-39639. (Illus.). (J). 1993. pap. 5.95 (0-929371-46-1) Kar-Ben.

Sammy Spider's First Passover. Sylvia Rouss. (Illus.). 32p. (J). (ps-2). 1995. pap. 5.95 (0-929371-82-8) Kar-Ben.

Sammy Spider's First Rosh Hashanah. Sylvia Rouss. (Illus.). 32p. (J). (ps-2). 1996. 14.95 (0-929371-98-4); pap. 5.95 (0-929371-99-2) Kar-Ben.

***Sammy Spider's First Shabbat.** Sylvia Rouss. LC 97-2616. (Illus.). 32p. (J). (ps-2). 1997. pap. 5.95 (1-58013-006-2) Kar-Ben.

***Sammy Spider's First Shabbat.** Sylvia Rouss. LC 97-2616. (Illus.). 32p. (J). (ps-2). 1997. 14.95 (1-58013-007-0) Kar-Ben.

***Sammy, the Dog Detective.** Colleen S. Bare. LC 97-3881. (Illus.). (J). 1997. write for info. (0-525-65253-1) Dutton Child Bks.

Sammy the Elephant & Mr. Camel: A Story to Help Children Overcome Bedwetting While Discovering Self-Appreciation. Joyce C. Mills & Richard J. Crowley. LC 88-13581. (Illus.). 48p. (J). (gr. 1 up). 1988. pap. 16.95 (0-945354-09-6); pap. 8.95 (0-945354-08-8) Magination Pr.

Sammy the Sea Otter. Illus. by Bob Storms. (World of Animals Ser.). 24p. (J). (gr. k-4). 1993. 4.95 (0-89346-528-3) Heian Intl.

Sammy the Seal. Syd Hoff. LC 59-5316. (Harper I Can Read Bk.). (Illus.). 64p. (J). (gr. k-3). 1959. lib. bdg. 14.89 (0-06-022526-2) HarpC Child Bks.

Sammy the Seal. Syd Hoff. LC 59-5316. (Trophy I Can Read Bk.). (Illus.). 64p. (J). (gr. k-3). 1980. pap. 3.50 (0-06-444028-1, Trophy) HarpC Child Bks.

***Sammy, the Seal.** Syd Hoff. (Illus.). (J). (ps-3). 1959. 17.02 (0-06-022525-4, 451871) HarpC.

Sammy the Squirrel. (Frog Pond Ser.). (Illus.). (J). (ps-1). 2.98 (0-517-46987-1) Random Hse Value.

Sammy the Steamroller. Eugene Coco. (Storytime Bks.). (Illus.). 24p. (J). (ps-2). 1993. pap. text ed. 1.29 (1-56293-347-7) McClanahan Bk.

Sammy Younge, Jr. The First Black College Student to Die in the Black Liberation Movement. James Forman. LC 85-32095. 285p. 1986. reprint ed. pap. 11.95 (0-940880-13-X) Open Hand.

Sammy Younge, Jr. The First Black College Student to Die in the Black Liberation Movement. James Forman. LC 85-32095. 285p. (YA). (gr. 10-12). 1986. reprint ed. 22.95 (0-940880-12-1) Open Hand.

Sammy's Gadget Galaxy. Michael P. Waite. LC 91-38874. 32p. (J). (ps-3). 1992. pap. 9.99 (0-7814-0036-8, Chariot Bks) Chariot Victor.

Sammy's Mommy Has Cancer. Sherry Kohlenberg. LC 93-22773. (Illus.). 32p. (J). (ps-3). 1993. 16.95 (0-945354-56-8); pap. 8.95 (0-945354-55-X) Magination Pr.

Sammy's Mommy Has Cancer: A Story For Children Who Have a Loved One with Cancer. Sherry Kohlenberg. LC 93-38213. (J). (gr. 2 up). 1994. lib. bdg. 18.60 (0-8368-1071-6) Gareth Stevens Inc.

Sammy's Special Day. Cyndy Szekeres. LC 85-81986. (Golden Naptime Tales Series - A Jim Henson Muppet Press Bk.). (Illus.). 18p. (J). (ps). 1992. bds. write for info. (0-307-12288-3, 12296, Golden Pr) Western Pub.

***Sammy's Story.** David Kooharian. (Illus.). 32p. (J). (gr. k up). 1997. 15.95 (0-7894-2466-5) DK Pub Inc.

Samna: Luxury Word Processing. Rubin Rabinovitz. (Illus.). 288p. 1986. 24.95 (0-8306-0634-3); pap. 16.95 (0-8306-2734-0, NO. 2734) McGraw-Hill Prof.

Samnyasa Upanisads: Hindu Scriptures on Asceticism & Renunciation. Patrick Olivelle. 320p. (C). 1992. pap. text ed. 20.95 (0-19-507045-3) OUP.

Samoa: A Photographic Essay. Frederick Sutter. (Illus.). 104p. 1982. 19.95 (0-87022-778-5) UH Pr.

Samoa, a Hundred Years Ago & Long Before. George Turner. LC 75-35213. 1976. reprint ed. 62.50 (0-404-14236-2) AMS Pr.

Samoa Islands Vol. 2: An Outline of a Monograph with Particular Consideration of German Samoa: (Material Culture), Vol. 2. Augustin Kramer. Tr. by Theodore Verhaaren from GER. LC 94-5739. (Illus.). 624p. 1995. text ed. 85.00 (0-8248-1634-X) UH Pr.

Samoa Reader: Anthropologists Take Stock. Ed. by Hiram Caton. 366p. (Orig.). (C). 1990. pap. text ed. 31.00 (0-8191-7721-0) U Pr of Amer.

Samoa under the Sailing Gods. Newton A. Rowe. LC 75-35209. reprint ed. 57.50 (0-404-14232-X) AMS Pr.

Samoa Western & American Samoa: Travel Survival Kit. 2nd ed. Deanna Swaney. (Illus.). 208p. 1994. pap. 12.95 (0-86442-225-3) Lonely Planet.

Samoan Dance of Life: An Anthropological Narrative. John D. Copp & Faafouina I. Pula. LC 83-26370. xvi, 176p. 1984. reprint ed. text ed. 49.75 (0-313-24244-5, COSD, Greenwood Pr) Greenwood.

Samoan Dictionary: Samoan-English, English-Samoan. G. B. Milner. 465p. 1994. text ed. 32.00 (0-908597-12-6) UH Pr.

Samoan Herbal Medicine: O La'au. W. Arthur Whistler. (Illus.). 128p. 1996. pap. text ed. 13.00 (0-9645426-2-5) A Whistler.

Samoan Material Culture. Peter H. Buck. (BMB Ser.). 1974. reprint ed. 105.00 (0-527-02181-4) Periodicals Srv.

Samoan Medical Belief & Practice. C. MacPherson & L. MacPherson. 280p. 1990. 32.95 (1-86940-045-3, Pub. by Auckland Univ NZ) Paul & Co Pubs.

Samoan Perception of Work: Moving up & Moving Around. Robert W. Franco. (Immigrant Communities & Ethnic Minorities in the U. S. & Canada Ser.: No. 72). 1991. 59.50 (0-404-19482-6) AMS Pr.

Samoan Planters: Tradition & Economic Development in Polynesia. Tim O'Meara. 200p. (C). 1990. pap. text ed. 13.50 (0-03-022847-6) HB Coll Pubs.

Samoan Proverbial Expressions: Alaga'upu Fa'a - Samoa. Tr. & Compiled by Erich Schultz. 140p. 1989. pap. text ed. 13.00 (0-908597-01-0) UH Pr.

Samoan Variations: Essays on the Nature of Traditional Oral Arts. Jacob W. Love. LC 91-6778. (Illus.). 310p. 1991. text ed. 25.00 (0-8240-2985-2) Garland.

Samoan Village: Then & Now. George D. Spindler. (Case Studies in Cultural Anthropology). 155p. (C). 1992. pap. text ed. 13.50 (0-03-031692-8) HB Coll Pubs.

***Samoan Word Book.** Fata Simanu-Klutz. (Rainbow International Word Bks.). (Illus.). 112p. (Orig.). 1997. pap. 11.95 (0-614-30685-X) Bess Pr.

***Samoan Word Book.** Fata Simanu-Klutz. (Rainbow International Word Book Ser.). (Illus.). 112p. (Orig.). 1997. pap. 19.95 incl. audio (1-57306-060-7) Bess Pr.

Samoans: A Global Family. Frederic K. Sutter. 1989. 29.95 (0-8248-1238-7) UH Pr.

***Samoas.** H. G. Hughes. (World Bibliographical Ser.). 275p. 1997. 80.25 (1-85109-253-6) ABC-CLIO.

Samogitian Crusade. William Urban. LC 89-84523. (Illus.). 304p. 1989. 28.50 (0-929700-03-1) Lith Res & Studies.

Samora Machel: A Biography. Iain Christie. LC 89-25035. (Panaf Great Lives Ser.). (Illus.). 200p. (C). 1989. pap. 15.00 (0-901787-52-3, Pub. by Zed Bks Ltd UK); text ed. 49.95 (0-901787-51-5, Pub. by Zed Bks Ltd UK) Humanities.

***Samos & Neaegean Islands.** (Groc's Candid Guides Ser.). 1996. pap. 18.95 (0-948762-01-2) Cimino Pub Grp.

Samos & Samian Coins. Percy Gardner. 1990. reprint ed. lib. bdg. 20.00 (0-915262-61-4) S J Durst.

Samothrace: The Temenos, Vol. 5. Phyllis W. Lehmann & Denys Spittle. 530p. 1981. text ed. 225.00 (0-691-09917-0) Princeton U Pr.

Samothrace - the Rotunda of Arisinoe, Vol. 7: Excavations Conducted by the Institute of Fine Arts, New York University. Ed. by Karl Lehmann & Phyllis W. Lehmann. (Bollingen Ser.: Vol. LX, Pt. 7). (Illus.). 416p. 1992. text ed. 250.00 (0-691-09919-7) Princeton U Pr.

Samothrace, a Guide to the Excavation & the Museum. 5th ed. Karl Lehmann. LC 55-8563. pap. 12.00 (0-685-73230-4) J J Augustin.

***Samothrace: Excavations Conducted by the Institute of Fine Arts of New York University Vol. 5, Pt. 1: The Temenos.** Phyllis W. Lehmann & Denys Spittle. Ed. by Karl Lehmann. LC 58-8985. (Bollingen Ser.: Vol. 60). reprint ed. pap. 133.40 (0-608-04570-5, 2065342) Bks Demand.

***Samothrace: Excavations Conducted by the Institute of Fine Arts of New York University Vol. 5, Pt. 2: The Temenos.** Phyllis W. Lehmann & Denys Spittle. Ed. by Karl Lehmann. LC 58-8985. (Bollingen Ser.: Vol. 60). reprint ed. pap. 25.00 (0-608-04571-3, 2065342) Bks Demand.

***Samothrace: Excavations Conducted by the Institute of Fine Arts of New York University Vol. 7, Pt. 1: The Rotunda of Arsinoe.** James R. McCredie et al. Ed. by Karl Lehmann. LC 58-8985. (Bollingen Ser.: Vol. 60). reprint ed. pap. 132.90 (0-608-04572-1, 2065342) Bks Demand.

***Samothrace: Excavations Conducted by the Institute of Fine Arts of New York University Vol. 7, Pt. 2: The Rotunda of Arsinoe.** James R. McCredie et al. Ed. by Karl Lehmann. LC 58-8985. (Bollingen Ser.: Vol. 60). reprint ed. pap. 30.80 (0-608-04573-X, 2065342) Bks Demand.

Samothrace, Vol. 10: The Propylon of Ptolemy II. Ed. by Phyllis W. Lehman & Alfred Frazer. (Bollingen Ser.: Vol. 60, No. 10). (Illus.). 224p. (C). 1990. text ed. 140.00 (0-691-09922-7) Princeton U Pr.

Samothracian Reflections: Aspects of the Revival of the Antique. Phyllis W. Lehmann & Karl Lehman. LC 71-163867. (Bollingen Ser.: No. 92). 216p. 1973. text ed. 85.00 (0-691-09909-X) Princeton U Pr.

Samovars: The Art of the Russian Metalworkers. Mehmet N. Israfil. LC 90-81722. (Illus.). 82p. (Orig.). 1990. pap. 25.00 (0-9629138-0-4) Fil Caravan.

Samovnushenie I Ego Vliianie Na Organizm Cheloveka see Self-Suggestion & Its Influence on the Human Organism

Samoyed Book. deluxe ed. (Illus.). 300p. 1995. 55.00 (0-614-04549-5) Donald R Hoflin.

Samoyed Champions, 1952-1987. Camino E. E. & Bk. Co. Staff. (Illus.). 309p. 1988. pap. 36.95 (0-940808-85-4) Camino E E & Bk.

Samoyeds. Joyce Reynaud. (Illus.). 192p. 1994. 9.95 (0-7938-1053-1, KW-072) TFH Pubns.

Samoyeds. deluxe ed. Lavallin Puxley. 80p. 1995. 20.00 (0-614-04550-9) Donald R Hoflin.

Sampan Sailor: A Navy Man's Adventures in WWII China. Clayton Mishler. (World War II Commemorative Ser.). 240p. 1994. 23.95 (0-02-881073-2) Brasseys Inc.

Sample Analysis of a Piping System: Class One Nuclear. 1972. pap. text ed. 4.50 (0-685-30778-6, E00063) ASME.

Sample Appraisal Guide: Appraisal Manual. 2nd ed. Robert K. Bell, Jr. 162p. 1993. pap. 50.00 (0-9635502-0-9) Bells Fl.

Sample By-laws for Community Schools of the Arts. 1986. 6.00 (0-318-21713-9) NGCSA.

Sample Cataloguing Forms: Illustrations of Solutions to Problems of Description (with Particular Reference to Chapters 1-13 of the Anglo-American Cataloguing Rules, Second Edition) 3rd ed. Robert B. Slocum. LC 80-21507. (Illus.). 121p. 1980. 32.50 (0-8108-1364-5) Scarecrow.

Sample CD-ROM Licensing Agreements for Museums. rev. ed. Ed. by Geoffrey Samuels. 35p. 1996. pap. text ed. 21.00 (0-931201-27-6) Am Assn Mus.

Sample Contracts Manual. 1988. 20.90 (0-318-42984-5, S286) Am Congrs Survey.

Sample Contracts Manual. ACSM Staff. 38p. 1988. pap. 20.00 (0-614-06087-7, S286) Am Congrs Survey.

Sample Design in Business Research. W. Edwards Deming. (Classics Library). 517p. 1990. pap. text ed. 49.95 (0-471-52370-4) Wiley.

Sample Employee Performance Measures. Jack Zigon. (Performance Management Ser.). 350p. 1995. wbk. ed. 200.00 (0-9649667-2-7) Zigon Perf Grp.

Sample Exam for Electrical Licensing: Based on 1996 NEC. Michael G. Owen. 42p. 1996. wbk. ed., pap. 19.95 (1-888512-02-4) Elect Trnging.

Sample Examination Manual. R. G. Swanson. (Methods of Exploration Ser.: No. 1). (Illus.). 118p. 1981. 5.00 (0-89181-650-X, 603) AAPG.

Sample Exams for Master Electricians: Based on 1996 NEC. Michael G. Owen. 52p. 1996. wbk. ed., pap. 19.95 (1-888512-01-6) Elect Trnging.

Sample Faculty Manuals & Personnel Policy Documents. 1986. 7.00 (0-318-21714-7) NGCSA.

Sample Incorporating Indenture: Model Debenture Indenture Provisions, 1965. LC 65-27691. (American Bar Foundation Publications). 113p. 1965. 30.00 (1-57588-359-7, 304750) W S Hein.

***Sample Incorporating Indenture: Model Debenture Indenture Provisions, 1967.** LC 65-27691. (American Bar Foundation Publications). 113p. 1965. pap. 20.00 (1-57588-360-0, 304760) W S Hein.

Sample Indicators for Evaluating Quality in Ambulatory Health Care. William F. Card et al. Ed. by Maureen Duffy & Karen L. Hill. 52p. 1987. pap. 12.50 (0-86688-139-5) Joint Comm Hlthcare.

Sample Introduction in Atomic Spectroscopy. Joseph Sneddon. (Analytical Spectroscopy Library: No. 4). 360p. 1990. 190.00 (0-444-88229-4) Elsevier.

Sample Jury Instruction in Criminal Antitrust Cases. LC 84-7125. 196p. 1984. pap. 35.00 (0-89707-144-1, 503-0055) Amer Bar Assn.

Sample Letters & Memos for Builders, Developers, & Remodelers: Business Writing for Everyday Use. John A. Kilpatrick. LC 91-43255. 115p. 1991. pap. 20.00 (0-86718-374-8) Home Builder.

Sample Letters of Recommendation for Students Applying to Colleges & Universities. Donald R. Wilson. 38p. 1992. lib. bdg. 13.95 (0-939136-07-4) School Admin.

Sample Lexicon of Pan-Arabic. Ernest T. Abdel-Massih. LC 75-18985. (ARA.). 1975. pap. text ed. 10.00 (0-932098-10-X) UM Ctr MENAS.

Sample Line Piping & Tubing Standard for Use in Nuclear Power Plants. 1994. pap. 40.00 (*1-55617-523-X*, S67. 10) ISA.
Sample Nursing Home Contract. 24p. 1991. 7.35 (*0-931207-27-4*) Natl Hospice.
Sample Pleadings for Use in Juvenile Deliquecy Proceedings. American Bar Association, Criminal Justice Staff. 55p. 1986. pap. 7.50 (*0-318-36209-0*, 509-0027) Amer Bar Assn.
Sample Preparation for Biomedical & Environmental Analysis. Ed. by D. Stevenson & I. D. Wilson. (Chromatographic Society Symposium Ser.). (Illus.). 234p. 1994. 75.00 (*0-306-44663-4*, Plenum Pr) Plenum.
Sample Preparation Products Application Bibliography. 52p. (Orig.). (C). 1993. pap. text ed. 20.00 (*0-7881-0162-5*) DIANE Pub.
Sample Pretreatment & Separation. Richard Anderson. LC 87-10655. (Analytical Chemistry by Open Learning Ser.). 632p. 1987. pap. text ed. 125.00 (*0-471-91361-8*) Wiley.
Sample Real Estate Forms: For Buyers, Sellers, Brokers, Lawyers. 4th ed. James R. Deal. 130p. 1994. pap. 34.95 (*1-884949-03-7*) Great Ideas.
***Sample Safety Plans User's Guide.** Ed. by Summers Press Inc. Staff. (Illus.). 24p. 1997. pap. 119.50 (*1-56759-019-5*) Summers Pr.
Sample Sales Letter Portfolio: How You Can Write Winning Sales Letters. Galen Stilson. 24p. 1986. pap. 6.95 (*0-915665-14-X*) Premier Publishers.
Sample Size Choice: Charts for Experiments with Linear Models. 2nd ed. Robert Oheh & M. Fox. (Statistics: Textbooks & Monographs: Vol. 122). 216p. 1991. 85.00 (*0-8247-8600-9*) Dekker.
Sample Size Choice: Charts for Experiments with Linear Models. Robert E. Odeh & Martin Fox. LC 75-10347. (Statistics, Textbooks & Monographs: No. 14). 204p. reprint ed. pap. 58.20 (*0-8357-3524-9*, 2052302) Bks Demand.
Sample Size Determination in Health Studies: A Practical Manual. Stephen K. Lwanga & S. Lemeshow. viii, 80p. (ENG, FRE & SPA.). 1991. pap. text ed. 16.00 (*92-4-154405-8*, 1150336) World Health.
Sample Size Methodology. M. M. Desu & D. Raghavarao. (Statistical Modeling & Decision Science Ser.). 135p. 1990. text ed. 48.00 (*0-12-212165-1*) Acad Pr.
Sample Student Workbook Math. 3rd ed. Jacobs. student ed. write for info. (*0-7167-2556-8*) W H Freeman.
Sample Survey: Principles & Methods. 2nd rev. ed. V. Barnett. 173p. 1994. pap. 29.95 (*0-340-54553-4*, Pub. by E Arnold UK) Routledge Chapman & Hall.
Sample Survey Methods & Theory, 2 vols., Vol. 2. Morris H. Hansen et al. (Classics Library: Vol. 1). 1016p. 1993. pap. text ed. 84.95 (*0-471-00628-9*) Wiley.
Sample Survey Methods & Theory, Vol. 2. Morris H. Hansen et al. LC 53-8112. (Wiley Publications in Statistics). (Illus.). 332p. reprint ed. pap. 98.70 (*0-685-23831-8*, 2056612) Bks Demand.
Sample Survey Methods & Theory Vol. 1: Methods & Applications, Vol. 1. Morris H. Hansen et al. (Classics Library). 664p. 1993. pap. text ed. 47.95 (*0-471-30967-2*) Wiley.
Sample Survey Methods & Theory Vol. 2: Theory, Vol. 2. Morris H. Hansen et al. (Classics Library). 352p. 1993. pap. text ed. 39.95 (*0-471-30966-4*) Wiley.
Sample Survey Methods & Theory, Vol. 1: Methods & Applications. Morris H. Hansen et al. LC 53-8112. 660p. reprint ed. pap. 180.00 (*0-685-16177-3*, 2056296) Bks Demand.
Sample Survey Principles & Methods. Vic Barnett. 173p. 1994. pap. text ed. 33.95 (*0-470-23389-3*) Wiley.
***Sample Surveys.** Thompson. (C). (gr. 13 up). 1997. text ed. 46.00 (*0-412-31780-X*) Chapman & Hall.
Sampled-Data Control Systems. J. Ackermann. LC 85-10012. (Communications & Control Engineering Ser.). (Illus.). 620p. 1985. 178.95 (*0-387-15610-0*) Spr-Verlag.
Sampler. 180p. 1994. pap. text ed. 9.95 (*0-9642300-0-3*) Muvag Trading.
Sampler: A Machine Sewn Quilt. Eleanor Burns. (Illus.). 125p. (Orig.). 1984. pap. 12.95 (*0-922705-08-9*) Quilt Day.
Sampler: Patterns for Composition. 2nd ed. Rance G. Baker & Billie R. Phillips. LC 85-80169. 203p. (C). 1986. pap. text ed. 29.56 (*0-669-07684-8*) HM College Div.
***Sampler American Promise.** Roark. Date not set. pap. text ed. write for info. (*0-312-15722-3*) St Martin.
Sampler & Antique Needlework: A Year in Stitches, 1994. Ed. by Barbara Cockerham & Diane Kennedy-Jackson. (Illus.). 144p. 1994. 24.95 (*0-932437-02-8*) Symbol Exc Pubs.
Sampler & Antique Needlework: A Year in Stitches, 1995. Ed. by Barbara Cockerham & Diane Kennedy-Jackson. (Illus.). 144p. 1995. write for info. (*0-932437-04-4*) Symbol Exc Pubs.
Sampler Collection, Vol. I. 1996. pap. 9.95 (*0-696-20534-3*) Meredith Bks.
Sampler Collection, Vol. II. 1996. pap. text ed. 9.95 (*0-696-20535-1*) Meredith Bks.
Sampler from Marcy's. Compiled by Marcella Widdoes. 256p. 15.95 (*0-89015-875-4*) Sunbelt Media.
***Sampler Motif Book.** Brenda Keyes. LC 96-42933. 1997. write for info. (*0-89577-918-8*) RD Assn.
Sampler of American Folk Art from Pennsylvania Collections. Paul A. Chew. LC 89-50234. (Illus.). 100p. (Orig.). 1989. pap. 8.00 (*0-931241-22-7*) Westmoreland.
***Sampler of Devotional Poems.** Ed. by Kenneth Christopher. LC 96-51591. (Spiritual Samplers Ser.). 96p. (Orig.). 1997. pap. 1.95 (*0-8091-3721-6*) Paulist Pr.
Sampler of English-Language Arts Assessment, High School. California Department of Education Staff. (Illus.). 152p. 1992. pap. 6.50 (*0-8011-1062-9*) Calif Education.
Sampler of English-Language Arts Assessment, Middle Grades. California Department of Education Staff. (Illus.). 132p. 1992. pap. 6.50 (*0-8011-1061-0*) Calif Education.
Sampler of Forms for Special Libraries. 2nd ed. Sla Staff. (Illus.). 1991. spiral bd. 35.00 (*0-87111-345-7*) SLA.
Sampler of Jewish-American Folklore. Josepha Sherman. 272p. 1992. 21.95 (*0-87483-194-6*); pap. 11.95 (*0-87483-193-8*) August Hse.
Sampler of Mathematics Assessment. California Department of Education Staff. (Illus.). 56p. 1991. pap. 6.00 (*0-8011-0972-8*) Calif Education.
Sampler of Plays by Women. Rhoda-Gale Pollack. LC 89-13033. (American University Studies: English Language & Literature: Ser. IV, Vol. 52). 410p. (C). 1990. text ed. 64.50 (*0-8204-1172-8*) P Lang Pubng.
Sampler of the Month. Ed. by Burda Staff. (Burda Bks.). 5.95 (*0-686-64664-9*, B805) Toggitt.
Sampler of Wayside Herbs: Rediscovering Old Uses for Familiar Wild Plants. Barbara Pond. LC 73-89773. (Illus.). 1974. 24.95 (*0-85699-096-5*) Chatham Pr.
Sampler of Writings of Mordecai Noah. Mordecai Noah. Ed. by Michael Schuldiner. (Masterworks of Literature Ser.). 1994. pap. 15.95 (*0-685-71559-0*) NCUP.
Sampler Quilt Blocks for Native American Designs. Joyce Mori. LC 95-38422. 1995. 14.95 (*0-89145-847-6*, Am Quilters Soc) Collector Bks.
***Samplers.** Carol Humphrey. (Fitzwilliam Museum Handbooks Ser.). (Illus.). 152p. (C). 1997. text ed. 59.95 (*0-521-57300-9*) Cambridge U Pr.
***Samplers.** Carol Humphrey. (Fitzwilliam Museum Handbooks Ser.). (Illus.). 152p. (C). 1997. pap. text ed. 19.95 (*0-521-57592-3*) Cambridge U Pr.
Samplers. Susan Mayor & Diane Fowle. Ed. by Stephen Calloway. LC 95-22585. (Illus.). 64p. 1996. 9.95 (*1-55921-154-7*) Moyer Bell.
Samplers. Christine Stevens. (Illus.). (C). 1992. pap. 30.00 (*0-86383-825-1*, Pub. by Gomer Pr UK) St Mut.
Samplers & Samplermakers: An American Schoolgirl Art 1700-1850. Mary J. Edmonds. LC 91-11425. (Illus.). 160p. 1991. 40.00 (*0-8478-1396-7*) Rizzoli Intl.
Samples & Pictorial. Betty Ring. (Illus.). 1993. 125.00 (*0-394-55009-9*) Knopf.
***Samples & Populations: Data & Statistics.** Glenda Lappan et al. Ed. by Catherine Anderson et al. (Connected Mathematics Ser.). (Illus.). 72p. (YA). (gr. 8 up). 1997. student ed., pap. text ed. 5.95 (*1-57232-190-3*, 21485) Seymour Pubns.
***Samples & Populations: Data & Statistics.** Glenda Lappan et al. Ed. by Catherine Anderson et al. (Investigations in Number, Data, & Space Ser.). (Illus.). 151p. (YA). (gr. 8 up). 1997. teacher ed., pap. text ed. 16.50 (*1-57232-191-1*, 21486) Seymour Pubns.
Samples & Standards. Brian W. Woodget & Derek Cooper. LC 86-19009. (Analytical Chemistry by Open Learning Ser.). 299p. 1987. pap. text ed. 59.95 (*0-471-91290-5*) Wiley.
Samples from the Love of King David & Fair Bethsabe: With Reference Portions of the Bible. George Peele. LC 79-56834. 71p. (Orig.). 1980. pap. 4.95 (*0-9601000-2-4*) Longshanks Bk.
Sampling. Juanita Casey. (Chapbooks Ser.). 1981. pap. 2.95 (*0-912262-72-9*) Proscenium.
Sampling. Ed. by P. R. Krishaiah & C. R. Rao. (Hanbook of Statistics Ser.: Vol. 6). 594p. 1988. 190.00 (*0-444-70289-X*, North Holland) Elsevier.
Sampling. Steven K. Thompson. LC 92-7099. (Analysis of Linear Models: Regression & Analysis of Variance Ser.). 368p. 1992. text ed. 74.95 (*0-471-54045-5*) Wiley.
Sampling: Microbiological Monitoring of Environments. Ed. by R. G. Board & D. W. Lovelock. (Society for Applied Bacteriology Technical Ser.: No. 7). 1973. text ed. 125.00 (*0-12-108250-4*) Acad Pr.
Sampling, Analysis & Monitoring Methods: A Guide to EPA Requirements. C. C. Lee. 350p. 1995. pap. text ed. 79.00 (*0-86587-477-8*) Gov Insts.
Sampling & Analysis, 4. Ostler & Holley. LC 96-48897. 1997. text ed. 49.00 (*0-02-389534-9*, Macmillan Coll) P-H.
Sampling & Analysis of Airborne Pollutants. Eric D. Winegar. 384p. 1993. 79.95 (*0-87371-606-X*, L606) Lewis Pubs.
Sampling & Analysis of Compressed Air to Be Used for Breathing Purposes. G. L. Lee et al. (C). 1985. 45.00 (*0-905927-17-6*, Pub. by H&H Sci Cnslts UK) St Mut.
Sampling & Analysis of Copper Cathodes - STP 831. Ed. by W. M. Tuddenham & R. J. Hibbeln. LC 83-72052. 179p. 1984. text ed. 29.00 (*0-8031-0217-8*, 04-831000-03) ASTM.
Sampling & Analysis of Rain - STP 823. Ed. by S. Campbell. 96p. 1984. pap. 18.00 (*0-8031-0266-6*, 04-823000-17) ASTM.
Sampling & Analysis of Toxic Organics in the Atmosphere -STP 721. Ed. by S. Verner. 192p. 1980. 28.00 (*0-8031-0604-1*, 04-721000-19) ASTM.
Sampling & Assay of the Precious Metals. E. Smith. 39.95 (*0-931913-23-3*) Met-Chem Rsch.
Sampling & Calibration for Atmospheric Measurements. Ed. by John K. Taylor. LC 87-12439. (Special Technical Publication Ser.: No. 957). (Illus.). viii, 225p. 1987. text ed. 39.00 (*0-8031-0955-5*, 04-957000-17) ASTM.
Sampling & Identifying Allergenic Pollens & Molds: An Illustrated Identification Manual for Air Samplers. E. Grant Smith. LC 86-70134. (Illus.). 196p. (Orig.). (C). 1990. pap. text ed. 125.00 (*0-930961-02-1*) Blewstone Pr.
Sampling & Monitoring of Environmental Contaminants. R. Barth & Andrew Topper. 1993. pap. text ed. write for info. (*0-07-005153-4*) McGraw.
***Sampling & Sample Preparation: Practical Guide for Analytical Chemists.** M. Stoeppler. LC 97-7253. 1997. write for info. (*0-387-61975-5*) Spr-Verlag.
***Sampling & Sample Preparation: Practical Guide for Analytical Chemists.** Ed. by M. Stoeppler. LC 97-7253. (Illus.). 200p. 1997. 109.00 (*3-540-61975-5*) Spr-Verlag.
Sampling & Statistics Handbook for Research. Chester H. McCall. LC 82-15290. (Illus.). 352p. 1982. reprint ed. pap. 100.40 (*0-608-00119-8*, 2060884) Bks Demand.
Sampling & Testing of Residual Soils: A Review of International Practices. Ed. by E. W. Brand & H. B. Phillipson. 194p. (C). 1985. text ed. 70.00 (*90-6191-640-2*, Pub. by A A Balkema NE) Ashgate Pub Co.
Sampling Asphalt Products for Specifications Compliance. 2nd ed. (MS Ser.). 44p. (C). 1981. pap. text ed. 6.00 (*0-317-03833-8*, MS-18) Asphalt Inst.
Sampling Basics. Bobby Maestas & Paul Goldfield. Ed. by Peter L. Alexander. 125p. (C). 1989. pap. text ed. 14.95 (*0-939067-82-X*) Alexander Pub.
Sampling Biological Populations. Ed. by R. M. Cormack et al. (Statistical Ecology Ser.: Vol. 5). 1979. 45.00 (*0-89974-002-2*) Intl Co-Op.
Sampling Book. Joe Scacciaferro & Steve DeFuria. (Ferro Technologies Ser.). (Illus.). 144p. (Orig.). 1988. pap. 17. 95 (*0-88188-966-0*, HL 00605666) H Leonard.
Sampling Design & Statistical Methods for Environmental Biologists. Roger H. Green. LC 78-24422. 257p. 1979. text ed. 69.95 (*0-471-03901-2*) Wiley.
***Sampling Environmental Media, Vol. 128.** Ed. by James H. Morgan. LC 92-27603. (STP Ser.: No. 1282). (Illus.). 385p. 1996. text ed. 79.00 (*0-8031-2043-5*, 04-012820-56) ASTM.
Sampling for Social Research Surveys, 1947-1980. Irene Hess. LC 84-26193. 304p. (Orig.). 1985. pap. text ed. 20.00 (*0-87944-299-9*) Inst Soc Res.
Sampling in Archaeology. Ed. by James W. Mueller. LC 74-26372. 300p. (C). 1975. pap. 18.95 (*0-8165-0482-2*) U of Ariz Pr.
Sampling in Digital Signal Processing & Control. Arie Feuer & Graham C. Goodwin. LC 96-24284. (Systems & Control Ser.). 541p. 1996. 74.50 (*0-8176-3934-9*) Birkhauser.
Sampling Inner Experience in Disturbed Affect. R. T. Hurlburt. (Emotions, Personality & Psychotherapy Ser.). (Illus.). 255p. (C). 1993. 47.50 (*0-306-44377-5*, Plenum Pr) Plenum.
Sampling Inspection Tables: Single & Double Sampling. 2nd ed. Harold F. Dodge & Harry G. Romig. (Probability & Mathematical Statistics Ser.). (Illus.). 224p. 1959. text ed. 74.95 (*0-471-21747-6*) Wiley.
Sampling Methods for Applied Research: Text & Cases. Peter Tryfos. LC 95-35575. 480p. 1996. text ed. 45.00 (*0-471-04727-9*) Wiley.
***Sampling Methods for Censuses & Surveys.** 4th ed. write for info. (*0-85264-253-9*) Lubrecht & Cramer.
Sampling Methods for Multiresource Forest Inventory. Hans T. Schreuder et al. LC 92-6752. 464p. 1993. text ed. 95.00 (*0-471-55245-3*) Wiley.
Sampling Methods for the Auditor: An Advanced Treatment. Herbert Arkin. LC 81-2735. (Illus.). 288p. 1982. text ed. 45.00 (*0-07-002194-5*) McGraw.
***Sampling Methods in Morbidity Surveys & Public Health Investigations.** (Technical Report Ser.: No. 336). 29p. 1966. pap. text ed. 5.00 (*92-4-120336-6*) World Health.
Sampling Methods in Soybean Entomology. Ed. by M. Kogan & D. C. Herzog. (Experimental Entomology Ser.). (Illus.). 550p. 1980. 71.40 (*3-540-90446-8*) Spr-Verlag.
Sampling Normal & Schizophrenic Inner Experience. R. T. Hurlburt. (Emotions, Personality, & Psychotherapy Ser.). (Illus.). 306p. 1990. 45.00 (*0-306-43284-6*, Plenum Pr) Plenum.
Sampling of Coal. 224p. 1995. pap. 84.50 (*0-929531-30-2*) Intertec.
Sampling of Populations: Methods & Applications. Paul S. Levy & Stanley Lemeshow. LC 90-13047. (Series in Probability & Mathematics). 420p. 1991. text ed. 69.95 (*0-471-50822-5*) Wiley.
Sampling of Powders & Bulk Materials. K. Sommer. (Illus.). 300p. 1985. 118.95 (*0-387-15891-X*) Spr-Verlag.
Sampling of Soil & Rock: A Symposium Presented at the Seventy-Third Annual Meeting, Toronto, Ont., Canada, June 21-26, 1970. LC 75-137453. (American Society for Testing & Materials Special Technical Publication Ser.: No. 483). 199p. reprint ed. pap. 56.80 (*0-317-07983-2*, 2015508) Bks Demand.
Sampling Opinions: An Analysis of Survey Procedure. Fredirick F. Stephen & Philip J. McCarthy. LC 73-6395. (Illus.). 451p. 1974. reprint ed. text ed. 75.00 (*0-8371-6901-1*, STSO, Greenwood Pr) Greenwood.
***Sampling Plans for Aflatoxin Analysis on Peanuts & Corn.** 79p. 1993. 10.00 (*92-5-103395-1*, F33951, Pub. by FAO IT) Bernan Associates.
Sampling Source Book: An Indexed Bibliography of the Literature of Sampling. C. R. Thomas & Helen Schofield. 1996p. 1995. 120.00 (*0-7506-1947-3*) Buttrwrth-Heinemann.
Sampling, Standards & Homogeneity-STP 540. 136p. 1988. 24.00 (*0-8031-0561-4*, 04-540000-34) ASTM.
Sampling Strategies for Airborne Contaminants in the Workplace. I. G. Guest et al. (Technical Guide Ser.: No. 11). 83p. (C). 1993. 165.00 (*0-948237-14-7*, Pub. by H&H Sci Cnslts UK) St Mut.
Sampling Strategy Guide for Evaluating Contaminants in the Welding Environment (F1.3-91) (Illus.). 11p. 1991. pap. 21.00 (*0-87171-352-7*) Am Welding.
Sampling Systems for Process Analysers. K. G. Carr-Brion et al. LC 94-2204. (Illus.). 400p. 1996. 130.00 (*0-7506-1247-9*) Buttrwrth-Heinemann.
Sampling Techniques. 3rd ed. William G. Cochran. (Probability & Mathematical Statistics Ser.). 428p. 1977. text ed. 57.50 (*0-471-16240-X*) Wiley.
Sampling Techniques for Forest Resource Inventory. Barry D. Shiver & Bruce E. Borders. LC 95-32955. 500p. 1995. text ed. 43.00 (*0-471-10940-1*) Wiley.
Sampling the Book: Renaissance Prologues & the French Conteurs. Debra N. Losse. LC 92-55052. 1994. 29.50 (*0-8387-5244-6*) Bucknell U Pr.
Sampling the Green World: Innovative Concepts of Collection, Preservation, & Storage of Plant Diversity. Seymour H. Sohmer. LC 96-3600. (Illus.). 386p. 1996. 49.50 (*0-231-10136-8*) Col U Pr.
Sampling the Psalms. Henry M. Morris. LC 78-55613. 269p. 1991. reprint ed. pap. 9.95 (*0-89051-049-0*) Master Bks.
Sampling the Psalms see Amostra de Salmos
Sampling Theory for Forest Inventory. P. G. De Vries. (Illus.). 420p. 1986. 64.95 (*0-387-17066-9*) Spr-Verlag.
Sampling Theory in Fourier & Signal Analysis: Foundations. John R. Higgins. (Illus.). 240p. (C). 1996. 70.00 (*0-19-859699-5*) OUP.
Sampling Theory of Surveys with Applications. 3rd ed. Pandurang V. Sukhatme et al. (Illus.). 542p. 1984. text ed. 31.95 (*0-8138-1617-3*) Iowa St U Pr.
***Sampras: A Legend in the Works.** H. A. Branham. 250p. 1996. 24.95 (*1-56625-062-5*) Bonus Books.
***Sampson & Tindall's Texas Family Code.** annot. ed. John J. Sampson et al. LC 96-77460. 950p. 1996. pap. text ed. write for info. (*0-7620-0093-7*) Lawyers Cooperative.
Sampson Horse. Wendy Kanno. (Funny Farm Ser.). (Illus.). (J). (gr. k-2). 1984. 9.95 (*0-89868-163-4*); pap. 3.95 (*0-89868-164-2*) ARO Pub.
Sampson Reed: Primary Source Material for Emerson Studies. Sampson Reed. (Swedenborg Studies: No. 1). 53, xiip. 1992. pap. text ed. 6.95 (*0-87785-180-8*) Swedenborg.
Sampson Rock of Wall Street. Edwin Lefevre. LC 85-70939. 394p. 1985. reprint ed. pap. 21.00 (*0-87034-076-X*) Fraser Pub Co.
***Sams America.** Date not set. pap. 9.95 (*0-8431-3852-1*) Putnam Pub Group.
Sam's Ball. Barbro Lindgren. LC 83-722. (Illus.). 32p. (J). (ps). 1983. pap. 6.95 (*0-688-02359-2*, Morrow Junior) Morrow.
Sam's Bath. Barbro Lindgren. LC 83-724. (Illus.). 32p. (J). (ps). 1983. pap. 6.95 (*0-688-02362-2*, Morrow Junior) Morrow.
***Sams Bible Songs.** Date not set. 9.95 (*0-8431-3853-X*) Putnam Pub Group.
Sam's Boo-Boo. Harriet Ziefert. (J). 1996. 16.95 (*0-7894-0587-3*) DK Pub Inc.
***Sam's Car.** Barbro Lindgren. Orig. Title: Max Bil. (Illus.). (J). Date not set. lib. bdg. write for info. (*0-688-01266-3*, Morrow Junior) Morrow.
Sam's Car. Barbro Lindgren. LC 82-3437. Orig. Title: Max Bil. (Illus.). 32p. (J). (gr. k-3). 1982. pap. 6.95 (*0-688-01263-9*, Morrow Junior) Morrow.
Sam's Chance. Horatio Alger, Jr. (Works of Horatio Alger Jr.). 1989. reprint ed. lib. bdg. 79.00 (*0-685-27559-0*) Rprt Serv.
Sam's Christmas Joy. (Happy Day Coloring Bks.). (Illus.). 16p. (J). 1988. pap. 1.49 (*0-87403-466-3*, 02026) Standard Pub.
***Sam's Cookie.** Barbro Lindgren. (J). Date not set. lib. bdg. write for info. (*0-688-01268-X*) Morrow.
Sam's Cookie. Barbro Lindgren. LC 82-3419. (Illus.). 32p. (J). (gr. k-3). 1982. pap. 6.95 (*0-688-01267-1*, Morrow Junior) Morrow.
Sam's Easy Reader Stories. Ruth Dyer. LC 93-60261. (Illus.). 44p. (J). (ps-3). 1994. pap. 5.95 (*1-55523-614-6*) Winston-Derek.
Sams Goes Trucking. Henry Horenstein. (Illus.). 32p. (J). (gr. k-3). 1990. pap. 4.95 (*0-685-45556-4*) HM.
Sams In a Dry Season. Ivan Gold. 19.95 (*0-685-38086-6*) HM.
Sams in a Dry Season. Ivan Gold. Ed. by Jane Rosenman. 256p. 1992. reprint ed. pap. 10.00 (*0-671-75537-4*, WSP) PB.
Sam's Lady. Muriel S. Wright. 196p. (Orig.). 1994. pap. 7.95 (*0-922510-09-1*) Lucky Bks.
Sam's Mission Call. Gary Brown. (Illus.). 24p. (J). 12.95 (*0-910523-13-4*) Grandin Bk Co.
Sam's Passover. Hannigan. (J). pap. 5.95 (*0-7136-4084-7*, 93342, Pub. by A&C Black UK) Talman.
Sam's Picture Puzzle Books. Tony Tallarico. (Picture Puzzle Bks.). (Illus.). 24p. (J). 1991. 3.98 (*1-56156-009-X*) Kidsbks.
Sam's Pizza. David Pelham. (Illus.). 11p. (J). (ps up). 1996. pap. 11.99 (*0-525-45594-9*) NAL-Dutton.
Sam's Potty. Barbro Lindgren. LC 86-864. (Illus.). 32p. (J). (ps). 1986. pap. 6.95 (*0-688-06603-8*, Morrow Junior) Morrow.
Sam's Sandwich. David Pelham. (Illus.). 22p. (J). (ps-4). 1991. pap. 9.95 (*0-525-44751-2*) Dutton Child Bks.
Sams Sandwich. David Pelham. 1990. write for info. (*0-224-03011-6*) Random.
***Sam's Shining Star.** Diane M. Bernardy. (Orig.). 1997. pap. write for info. (*1-57553-556-4*) Watermrk Pr.
***Sams Sing Along.** Date not set. pap. 9.95 (*0-8431-3851-3*) Putnam Pub Group.
Sam's Snack. David Pelham. (Illus.). 16p. (J). (ps-4). 1994. pap. 10.99 (*0-525-45266-4*) Dutton Child Bks.
Sam's Sneaker Search. Obrien. LC 96-2964. (J). 1997. 10. 95 (*0-689-80169-6*, S&S Bks Young Read) S&S Childrens.
Sam's Surprise. David Pelham. (Illus.). 22p. (J). (ps-4). 1992. pap. 11.99 (*0-525-44947-7*) Dutton Child Bks.

***Sam's Teddy Bear.** Barbro Lindgren. (Illus.). (J). Date not set. lib. bdg. write for info. (*0-688-01271-X*, Morrow Junior) Morrow.

Sam's Teddy Bear. Barbro Lindgren. LC 82-3418. (Illus.). 32p. (J). (gr. k-3). 1982. pap. 6.95 (*0-688-01270-1*, Morrow Junior) Morrow.

***Sam's Throne.** Clay Frisbie. (Classic Rock Climbs: Vol. 22). (Illus.). (Orig.). 1997. pap. 10.95 (*1-57540-047-2*) Chockstone Pr.

Sam's Valley Serenade. Jon Plaisted. 80p. (Orig.). 1992. pap. 5.95 (*0-9634702-0-5*) Goodwin Coffin Pubs.

Sam's Wagon. Barbro Lindgren. LC 86-865. (Illus.). 32p. (J). (ps). 1986. pap. 6.95 (*0-688-05802-7*, Morrow Junior) Morrow.

Sam's Wild West Show. Nancy Antle. LC 94-3358. (J). (ps-3). 1995. pap. 12.99 (*0-8037-1532-3*); pap. 12.89 (*0-8037-1533-1*) Dial Bks Young.

Sam's WIT: Water Interval Training for Fabulous People of Every Kind. large type ed. Sam Rettig & Drucie French. (Illus.). 118p. 1993. pap. 20.00 (*0-9637470-2-9*) DFC Seminars.

Sam's World. Ann Williams. (Intimate Moments Ser.). 1995. pap. 3.50 (*0-373-07615-0*, 1-07615-7) Silhouette.

Sam's Worries. Maryann MacDonald. LC 91-71379. (Illus.). 32p. (J). (ps-3). 1991. 13.95 (*1-56282-081-8*) Hyprn Child.

Sam's Worries. Maryann MacDonald. LC 91-71379. (Illus.). 32p. (J). (ps-3). 1994. pap. 4.95 (*1-56282-522-4*) Hyprn Child.

Samsad Bengali-English Dictionary. Biswas. 932p. (BEN & ENG.). 1992. 29.95 (*0-7859-7465-2*) Fr & Eur.

Samsad English-Bengali Dictionary. S. K. Biswas. 932p. (BEN & ENG.). 1992. 59.95 (*0-8288-1119-9*, M14243) Fr & Eur.

Samskara: A Rite for a Dead Man. U. R. Murthy. Tr. by A. K. Ramnujan. 168p. 1979. pap. 9.95 (*0-19-561079-2*) OUP.

Samskrta-Sangita-Jagadisvari: Jewels in Sanskrit & Musicology, Prof. Jagdish Sahai Kulshreshtha Felicitation Volume. Ed. by Sushma Kulshreshtha et al. lxxii, 560p. 1995. 79.00 (*81-85133-93-X*, Pub. by Estrn Bk Linkers II) Nataraj Bks.

***Samskrta-Sangita-Ratnasati: 100 Gems of Rare Musical Compositions.** Ed. by J. S. Kulshreshtha & Sushma Kulshreshtha. (Illus.). 288p. 1996. 39.00 (*81-86339-42-6*, Pub. by Estrn Bk Linkers II) Nataraj Bks.

Samskrta Sangita Vaijayanti: Studies in Sanskrit & Musicology: Smt. Kamlesh Kumari Kulshreshtha Commemoration Volume. S. Kulshreshtha. (C). 1992. 98.00 (*0-8364-2820-X*, Pub. by Eastern Bk Linkers II) S Asia.

Samskrta-Sangita-Vaijayanti: Studies in Sanskrit & Musicology: Smt. Kamlesh Kumari Kulshreshtha Commemoration Volume. Ed. by Sushma Kulshreshtha & Satya P. Narang. (Illus.). 532p. 1992. 99.00 (*0-685-62635-0*, Pub. by Estrn Bk Linkers II) Nataraj Bks.

Samskrta-Sangita-Vijayanti: Studies in Sanskrit & Musicology: Smt. Kamlesh Kumari Kulshreshtha Commemoration Volume. Sushma Kulshreshtha & Satyapal Narang. (Illus.). iix, 532p. (C). 1992. 99.00 (*81-85133-56-5*, Pub. by Estrn Bk Linkers II) Nataraj Bks.

Samson. Mark Dunster. 8p. 1994. pap. 4.00 (*0-89642-250-X*) Linden Pubs.

Samson. Everitt M. Fjordbak. 74p. 1975. pap. text ed. 2.45 (*1-882449-02-9*) Messenger Pub.

***Samson.** Phil Stanton. (Victor Bible Character Ser.). Date not set. 7.99 (*1-56476-715-9*, Victor Bks) Chariot Victor.

Samson. Ellen G. Traylor. 1995. pap. 5.99 (*1-56507-280-4*) Harvest Hse.

***Samson: A Personal Perception.** Wendy E. Hyland. 144p. (Orig.). 1997. pap. 12.00 (*1-56002-679-0*, Univ Edtns) Aegina Pr.

Samson: A Secret Betrayed, a Vow Ignored. James L. Crenshaw. LC 77-15748. 173p. 1981. text ed. 9.95 (*0-8042-0170-6*, MUP-H001) Mercer Univ Pr.

Samson: Judges 13-16. Arch Books Staff. (J). (ps-3). 1994. pap. 1.99 (*0-570-09042-3*, 59-1465) Concordia.

Samson: Last of the California Grizzlies. Robert M. McClung. LC 91-33350. (Animal Life Cycle Ser.). (Illus.). 96p. (J). (gr. 3-6). 1992. reprint ed. lib. bdg. 16.50 (*0-208-02327-5*, Linnet Bks) Shoe String.

***Samson: The Weak Strong Man.** John G. Butler. 179p. 1992. 12.50 (*1-889773-06-9*) LBC Publns.

Samson - A Type of the Church. David Crank. 64p. (Orig.). 1991. pap. 4.99 (*0-89274-864-8*, HH-864) Harrison Hse.

Samson Agonistes. John Milton. Ed. by F. T. Prince. 144p. 1970. pap. 11.95 (*0-19-831910-X*) OUP.

Samson Agonistes & Shorter Poems. John Milton. Ed. by A. E. Barker. (Crofts Classics Ser.). 128p. 1950. pap. text ed. write for info. (*0-88295-058-4*) Harlan Davidson.

Samson & Delilah: Vocal Score. Saint-Saens. 272p. (ENG & FRE.). 1986. pap. 28.95 (*0-7935-3021-0*, 50338420) H Leonard.

Samson & Delilah Libretto. Saint-Saens. 32p. (ENG & FRE.). 1986. pap. 4.95 (*0-7935-5375-X*, 50340350) H Leonard.

***Samson Complex.** Mark Johnson. LC 97-17004. 1997. pap. text ed. 11.99 (*0-87788-742-X*) Shaw Pubs.

Samson Occom & the Christian Indians of New England. W. DeLoss Love. LC 96-1792. (Iroquois & Their Neighbors Ser.). 379p. 1996. reprint ed. 49.95 (*0-8156-2728-9*, LOSO); reprint ed. pap. 16.95 (*0-8156-0436-X*, LOSOP) Syracuse U Pr.

Samson Riddle. Mankowitz. 8.95 (*0-87677-102-9*) Hartmore.

Samson Rides Alone. Lester Sumrall. 56p. (C). 1987. pap. text ed. 10.00 (*0-937580-04-X*) LeSEA Pub Co.

Samson Saga & Its Place in Comparative Religion. A. Smythe Palmer. 1977. lib. bdg. 59.95 (*0-8490-2565-6*) Gordon Pr.

Samson-Saga & Its Place in Comparative Religion. Abram S. Palmer. Ed. by Richard M. Dorson. LC 77-70613. (International Folklore Ser.). 1977. reprint ed. lib. bdg. 25.95 (*0-405-10112-0*) Ayer.

Samson's Riddle. John Ratti. 1985. pap. 6.00 (*0-914610-41-4*) Hanging Loose.

Samter's Immunologic Diseases, 2 vols. 5th rev. ed. Ed. by Michael M. Frank et al. LC 94-11310. Orig. Title: Immunological Diseases. (Illus.). 2211p. 1995. reprint ed. text ed. 295.00 (*0-316-29237-0*) Lppncott-Raven.

Samtliche Werke, 10 vols. Catharina Regina von Greiffenberg. Ed. by Martin Bircher & Friedhelm Kemp. (GER.). 1983. 715.00 (*0-527-35868-1*) Periodicals Srv.

***Samtliche Werke, 14 vols.** Paracelsus. (GER.). 1996. reprint ed. write for info. (*3-487-09916-0*) G Olms Pubs.

***Samtliche Werke, Vol. 26.** Charles Sealsfield. (GER.). 1995. reprint ed. write for info. (*3-487-08370-1*) G Olms Pubs.

Samtliche Werke, Vols. 1-24. Charles Sealsfield, pseud. Ed. by Karl J. Arndt. 1,528.80 (*3-487-08012-5*) G Olms Pubs.

Samtliche Werke: Anbind-oder Fangbriefe. Gelegenheitsdichtungen. Beschreibung des Gluckhafens, Vol. 4, Pt. 1. Wolfhart Spangenberg. Ed. by Andras Vizkelety & Bircher. iv, 393p. (GER.). 1981. 265.40 (*3-11-008030-3*) De Gruyter.

Samtliche Werke: Anmutiger Weisheit Lustgarten I, Vol. 5. Wolfhart Spangenberg. iv, 362p. (GER.). 1981. 246.15 (*3-11-008648-4*) De Gruyter.

Samtliche Werke: Antmutiger Weisheit Lustgarten II, Vol. 6. Wolfhart Spangenberg. 449p. (GER.). 1982. 308.85 (*3-11-008647-6*) De Gruyter.

Samtliche Werke: Dramenubersetzungen. Alcestis, Hecuba, Amphitruo, Aiax Lorarius, Vol. 7. Wolfhart Spangenberg. Ed. by A. Tarnai. iv, 633p. (GER.). 1979. 430.75 (*3-11-007937-2*) De Gruyter.

Samtliche Werke: Predigten - Meisterlieder - Kronung Matthiae, Vol. 4, Pt. 2. Wolfhart Spangenberg. Ed. by Andras Vizkelety. iv, 327p. (GER.). 1982. 223.10 (*3-11-008904-1*) De Gruyter.

Samtliche Werke: Textcritical Edition in Two Volumes, Set. Adolf Reinach. Ed. by Karl Schuhmann & Barry Smith. (Philosophia Resources Library). xviii, 848p. (GER.). 1989. 199.00 (*3-88405-015-X*) Philosophia Pr.

***Samtliche Werke Band XIII: Lustspiele IV.** Christian Weise. Ed. by Hans-Gert Roloff. (Ausgaben Deutscher Literatur des XV. bis XVIII. Jahrhunderts). iv, 325p. (GER.). (C). 1996. lib. bdg. 198.50 (*3-11-014625-8*) De Gruyter.

Samtliche Werke (Alte Reihe), 21. Orlando di Lasso. (Illus.). 1973. pap. 1,500.00 (*0-8450-1900-7*) Broude.

Samtliche Werke fur Klavier, 8 vols. Joseph Lanner. 1973. reprint ed. pap. 425.00 (*0-8450-1010-7*) Broude.

***Samuel.** Concordia Publishing Staff. (People's Bible Commentary Ser.). 334p. 1996. pap. 12.99 (*0-570-04831-1*) Concordia.

Samuel. Gene A. Getz. LC 96-20805. (Men of Character Ser.). 192p. 1997. pap. 10.99 (*0-8054-6171-X*, 4261-71) Broadman.

Samuel. David F. Payne. 292p. 1993. pap. 22.00 (*0-7152-0521-8*, Pub. by St Andrew UK) St Mut.

Samuel. Keith Quincy. 255p. (Orig.). 1991. pap. 5.95 (*0-9628648-0-3*) Smidgen Bks.

Samuel: Gadianton's Foe. Clair Poulson. LC 94-10385. 1994. pap. 9.95 (*1-55503-658-9*, 01111574) Covenant Comms.

Samuel: Hebrew Text, English Translation & Commentary Digest. 2nd rev. ed. Ed. by Ephraim Oratz. LC 93-14555. (Books of the Bible Ser.). 1996. 14.95 (*1-871055-90-3*) Soncino Pr.

Samuel: Moroni's Young Warrior. Clair Poulson. LC 92-70859. 1993. pap. 9.95 (*1-55503-553-1*, 29004799) Covenant Comms.

***Samuel: The Inspiring Story of How an Amish Boy's Tragedy Brought Two Worlds Together.** Robert J. Hastings. 1997. pap. text ed. 9.95 (*1-56352-437-6*) Longstreet Pr Inc.

Samuel: Thunder in Paradise. Clair Poulson. LC 96-33842. 1996. write for info. (*1-55503-921-9*) Covenant Comms.

Samuel - The People's Bible. John R. Mittelstaedt. LC 93-84456. (People's Bible Ser.). 336p. (Orig.). 1994. pap. 11.99 (*0-8100-0491-7*, 15N0499) Northwest Pub.

Samuel Adams. James K. Hosmer. Ed. by John T. Morse, Jr. LC 78-128927. (American Statesmen Ser.: No. 2). reprint ed. 49.50 (*0-404-50852-9*) AMS Pr.

Samuel Adams. James K. Hosmer. (Notable American Authors Ser.). 1992. reprint ed. lib. bdg. 75.00 (*0-7812-3173-6*) Rprt Serv.

Samuel Adams: Grandfather of His Country. Karin C. Farley. LC 94-12646. (American Troublemakers Ser.). (J). 1994. lib. bdg. 27.11 (*0-8114-2379-4*) Raintree Steck-V.

***Samuel Adams: Radical Puritan.** Lillian M. Fowler. LC 96-31033. (C). 1997. text ed. 15.50 (*0-673-99293-4*) Longman.

***Samuel Adams: The Father of American Independence.** Dennis B. Fradin. LC 97-20027. 1998. write for info. (*0-395-82510-5*, Clarion Bks) HM.

***Samuel Adams - Father of the American Revolution.** Annette Francis. pap. 3.95 (*1-889086-03-7*, SA-203) Pan Mass.

Samuel Adams, Promoter of the American Revolution: A Study in Psychology & Politics. Ralph V. Harlow. (BCL1 - U. S. History Ser.). 363p. 1991. reprint ed. lib. bdg. 89.00 (*0-7812-6123-6*) Rprt Serv.

Samuel & the Deuteronomist: A Literary Study of the Deuteronomic History, Pt. 2: 1 Samuel. Robert M. Polzin. LC 92-43856. (Indiana Studies in Biblical Literature: Pt. 2). 312p. (C). 1993. 35.00 (*0-253-34552-9*); pap. 15.95 (*0-253-20849-1*) Ind U Pr.

Samuel & the Strange Sound. Bruce Porter. (Illus.). 40p. (Orig.). (J). (gr. 3 up). 1987. pap. 3.95 (*0-939925-13-3*) R C Law & Co.

Samuel & the Wake-up Call: 1 Samuel 3. Ed. by Jane L. Fryar. (Arch Bks.). (Illus.). 24p. (Orig.). (J). (gr. k-4). 1994. pap. 1.99 (*0-570-09035-0*, 59-1458) Concordia.

Samuel Barber. Nathan Broder. LC 85-14803. (Illus.). 111p. 1985. reprint ed. text ed. 49.75 (*0-313-24984-9*, BRSB, Greenwood Pr) Greenwood.

Samuel Barber: A Bio-Bibliography. Don A. Hennessee. LC 84-29017. (Bio-Bibliographies in Music Ser.: No. 3). xii, 404p. 1985. text ed. 59.95 (*0-313-24026-4*, HSB/, Greenwood Pr) Greenwood.

Samuel Barber: The Composer & His Music. Barbara B. Heyman. (Illus.). 618p. 1994. reprint ed. pap. 19.95 (*0-19-509058-6*) OUP.

Samuel Beckett. Deirdre Bair. 784p. 1990. pap. 20.00 (*0-671-69173-2*) S&S Trade.

***Samuel Beckett.** Ed. by L. Graver & Raymond Federman. (Critical Heritage Ser.). 392p. (C). 1997. text ed. 15.00 (*0-415-15954-7*) Routledge.

Samuel Beckett. Aidan Higgins. (Illus.). 92p. (Orig.). 1996. pap. 18.50 (*0-8076-1410-6*) Braziller.

Samuel Beckett. Arthur K. Kennedy. (British & Irish Authors Ser.). 190p. (C). 1989. pap. text ed. 17.95 (*0-521-27488-5*) Cambridge U Pr.

Samuel Beckett. Charles R. Lyons. Ed. by Bruce King & Adele King. (Modern Dramatists Ser.). 209p. 1990. pap. 13.95 (*0-333-29466-1*) St Martin.

***Samuel Beckett.** Ed. by John O'Brien. (Review of Contemporary Fiction Ser.: Vol. 7, No. 2). 220p. 1987. pap. 15.00 (*1-56478-108-9*) Dalkey Arch.

Samuel Beckett: "Waiting for Godot" Lawrence Graver. (Landmarks of World Literature Ser.). (Illus.). 132p. (C). 1989. text ed. 29.95 (*0-521-35513-3*); pap. text ed. 11.95 (*0-521-35775-6*) Cambridge U Pr.

Samuel Beckett: A Checklist of Criticism. James T. Tanner & J. Don Vann. LC 70-626232. (Serif Series: Bibliographies & Checklists: No. 8). 91p. reprint ed. pap. 26.00 (*0-8357-5580-0*, 2035207) Bks Demand.

Samuel Beckett: A Collection of Critical Essays. Ed. by Martin Esslin. 1965. text ed. 12.95 (*0-13-072991-4*, Spectrum IN) Macmillan Gen Ref.

Samuel Beckett: A Critical Study. Hugh Kenner. 1968. reprint ed. pap. 9.95 (*0-520-00641-0*) U CA Pr.

Samuel Beckett: A Reference Guide. Cathleen Culotta-Andonian. 1988. 65.00 (*0-8161-8570-0*, Hall Reference) Macmillan.

Samuel Beckett: A Study of the Short Fiction. Bob Cochran. (Twayne's Studies in Short Fiction: No. 29). 180p. (C). 1992. 23.95 (*0-8057-8320-2*, Twayne) Scribnrs Ref.

***Samuel Beckett: Humanistic Perspectives.** Ed. by Morris Beja et al. LC 82-12468. (Illus.). 234p. 1983. reprint ed. pap. 66.70 (*0-608-04444-X*, 2064976) Bks Demand.

Samuel Beckett: New Works, 1976-1985. 1986. write for info. (*0-318-61569-X*) Peartree Bks.

Samuel Beckett: The Comic Gamut. Ruby Cohn. LC 62-13761. 340p. reprint ed. pap. 99.20 (*0-8357-7943-2*, 2057016) Bks Demand.

Samuel Beckett: The Complete Short Prose, 1929-1989. Samuel Beckett. Ed. & Intro. by S. E. Gontarski. LC 95-13074. 294p. 1996. 23.00 (*0-8021-1577-2*, Grove) Grove-Atltic.

Samuel Beckett: The Expressive Dilemma. Lawrence Miller. LC 91-45795. 192p. 1992. text ed. 45.00 (*0-312-07960-5*) St Martin.

Samuel Beckett see Modern Critical Views Series

***Samuel Beckett & Music.** Ed. by Mary Bryden. 260p. 1997. 65.00 (*0-19-818427-1*) OUP.

***Samuel Beckett & the End of Modernity.** Richard Begam. LC 96-27406. 1996. write for info. (*0-8047-2731-7*) Stanford U Pr.

Samuel Beckett & the Meaning of Being: A Study in Onthological Parable. Lance St. John Butler. LC 83-15942. 224p. 1984. text ed. 35.00 (*0-312-69855-0*) St Martin.

Samuel Beckett & the Pessimistic Tradition. Steven J. Rosen. LC 76-2506. 262p. 1976. reprint ed. pap. 74.70 (*0-7837-5662-3*, 2059088) Bks Demand.

Samuel Beckett, W. B. Yeats, & Jack Yeats: Images & Words. Gordon S. Armstrong. LC 87-48015. (Illus.). 272p. 1990. 42.50 (*0-8387-5141-5*) Bucknell U Pr.

Samuel Beckett's Company - Compagnie & a Piece of Monologue - Solo: A Bilingual Variorum Edition. Samuel Beckett. Ed. by Charles Krance. LC 91-37752. (Illus.). 232p. 1993. text ed. 40.00 (*0-8240-9610-X*, H1400) Garland.

Samuel Beckett's Endgame see Modern Critical Interpretations

***Samuel Beckett's Hidden Drives: Structural Uses of Depth Psychology.** J. D. O'Hara. LC 97-16090. (CrossCurrents). 432p. 1997. 49.95 (*0-8130-1527-8*) U Press Fla.

Samuel Beckett's Mal vu Mal dit/Ill Seen Ill Said: A Bilingual, Evolutionary, & Synoptic Variorum Edition. variorum ed. Ed. by Charles Krance. LC 96-20485. (Samuel Beckett's Late Prose Ser.). 232p. 1996. text ed. 40.00 (*0-8240-3449-X*, H1266) Garland.

Samuel Beckett's New Worlds: Style in Metafiction. Susan D. Brienza. LC 86-24919. (Illus.). 312p. 1987. 32.95 (*0-8061-2047-9*) U of Okla Pr.

Samuel Beckett's Novel "Watt" Gottfried Buttner. Tr. by Joseph Dolan. LC 84-7234. (Illus.). 144p. 1985. 35.95 (*0-8122-7932-8*) U of Pa Pr.

Samuel Beckett's Real Silence. Helene L. Baldwin. LC 80-21465. 184p. (C). 1981. 28.50 (*0-271-00301-4*) Pa St U Pr.

Samuel Beckett's Self-Referential Drama: The Three Is. Shimon Levy. LC 89-32607. 210p. 1990. text ed. 45.00 (*0-312-03245-5*) St Martin.

Samuel Beckett's Waiting for Godot see Modern Critical Interpretations

Samuel Beckett's Wake & Other Uncollected Prose. Edward Dahlberg. Ed. by Steven Moore. LC 89-7856. 345p. 1989. 19.95 (*0-916583-42-2*) Dalkey Arch.

Samuel Blade Benton, His Ancestors & Descendants, 1620-1901. Josiah H. Benton, Jr. (Illus.). 366p. 1988. reprint ed. pap. 55.00 (*0-8328-0243-3*); reprint ed. lib. bdg. 63.00 (*0-8328-0242-5*) Higginson Bk Co.

Samuel Bronfman: The Life & Times of Seagram's Mr. Sam. Michael R. Marrus. LC 91-31775. (Illus.). 551p. 1991. 40.00 (*0-87451-571-8*) U Pr of New Eng.

Samuel Butler. Paul Jordan-Smith. 1972. 59.95 (*0-8490-0991-X*) Gordon Pr.

Samuel Butler. Robert F. Rattray. LC 73-21671. (English Biography Ser.: No. 31). 1974. lib. bdg. 43.95 (*0-8383-1782-0*) M S G Haskell Hse.

Samuel Butler: A Biography. Peter Raby. LC 90-71600. (Illus.). 358p. 1991. 37.95 (*0-87745-331-4*) U of Iowa Pr.

Samuel Butler: A Critical Study. G. Cannan. LC 70-133284. (English Biography Ser.: No. 31). 1970. reprint ed. lib. bdg. 49.95 (*0-8383-1183-0*) M S G Haskell Hse.

Samuel Butler: An Annotated Bibliography of Writings about Him. Hans-Peter Breuer & Roger Parsell. LC 90-2749. 560p. 1990. text ed. 66.00 (*0-8240-2747-7*, H769) Garland.

Samuel Butler: Critic & Philosopher. P. J. De Lange. LC 68-716. (English Biography Ser.: No. 31). 1969. reprint ed. lib. bdg. 75.00 (*0-8383-0537-7*) M S G Haskell Hse.

Samuel Butler: Eighteen Thirty-Five to Nineteen Two. Cyril E. Joad. (Select Bibliographies Reprint Ser.). 1977. 23.95 (*0-8369-5133-6*) Ayer.

Samuel Butler & the Odyssey. Benjamin Farrington. LC 73-21626. (English Literature Ser.: No. 33). 1974. lib. bdg. 75.00 (*0-8383-1777-4*) M S G Haskell Hse.

Samuel Butler, Author of Erewhon (1835-1902) a Memoir, 2 vols., Set. Henry F. Jones. (BCL1-PR English Literature Ser.). 1992. reprint ed. lib. bdg. 150.00 (*0-7812-7471-0*) Rprt Serv.

Samuel Butler on the Resurrection. Ed. by Robert Johnstone. 64p. 8000. 12.95 (*0-901072-59-1*, Pub. by Colin Smythe Ltd UK) Dufour.

Samuel Butler Revalued. Thomas L. Jeffers. LC 80-24904. 152p. (C). 1981. 30.00 (*0-271-00281-6*) Pa St U Pr.

Samuel Carpenter & His Descendants. Edward Carpenter & Louis Carpenter. (Illus.). 320p. 1989. reprint ed. pap. 48.00 (*0-8328-0369-3*); reprint ed. lib. bdg/ 56.00 (*0-8328-0368-5*) Higginson Bk Co.

Samuel Clemens & Mark Twain. Agor. 1987. pap. text ed. 4.65 (*0-13-790890-3*) P-H.

Samuel Coleridge-Taylor: The Development of His Compositional Style. Jewel T. Thompson. LC 94-5136. 207p. 1994. 29.50 (*0-8108-2737-9*) Scarecrow.

Samuel Colt's Submarine Battery: The Secret & the Enigma. Philip K. Lundeberg. LC 74-7322. (Smithsonian Studies in History & Technology: No. 29). (Illus.). 96p. reprint ed. pap. 27.40 (*0-317-09446-7*, 2004227) Bks Demand.

Samuel Daniel, A Critical Study. George K. Brady. (BCL1-PR English Literature Ser.). 38p. 1992. reprint ed. lib. bdg. 59.00 (*0-7812-7196-7*) Rprt Serv.

Samuel Davis of Oxford, Mass. & Joseph Davis of Dudley, Mass., & Their Descendants. G. L. Davis. 618p. 1989. reprint ed. pap. 92.00 (*0-8328-0459-2*); reprint ed. lib. bdg. 100.00 (*0-8328-0458-4*) Higginson Bk Co.

Samuel E. Dyke Collection of Kentucky Pistols. Frank Klay. 30p. 1980. 3.50 (*0-88227-004-4*) Gun Room.

Samuel Eaton's Day: A Day in the Life of a Pilgrim Boy. Kate Waters. LC 92-32325. 40p. (J). (gr. 4 up). 1993. 14.95 (*0-590-46311-X*) Scholastic Inc.

Samuel Eaton's Day: A Day in the Life of a Pilgrim Boy. Kate Waters. (J). (gr. 2-4). 1996. pap. 5.99 (*0-590-48053-7*) Scholastic Inc.

Samuel el Espantapajaros. Sharon Gordon. (Illus.). 32p. (SPA.). (J). (gr. k-2). 1995. pap. 1.95 (*0-89375-958-9*) Troll Communs.

Samuel Eliot Morison's Historical World: In Quest of a New Parkman. Gregory M. Pfitzer. 384p. 1991. text ed. 47.50 (*1-55553-101-6*) NE U Pr.

Samuel F. B. Morse. Paul Staiti. (Cambridge Monographs on American Artists). (Illus.). 320p. (C). 1990. text ed. 90.00 (*0-521-32218-9*) Cambridge U Pr.

Samuel F. B. Morse: Artist with a Message. John H. Tiner. (Sower Ser.). (Illus.). (J). (gr. 3-6). 1987. pap. 7.99 (*0-88062-137-0*) Mott Media.

Samuel F. B. Morse: His Letters & Journals, 2 vols, Set. Samuel F. Morse. Ed. by Edward L. Morse. LC 76-75279. (Library of American Art). (Illus.). 1080p. 1973. reprint ed. lib. bdg. 110.00 (*0-306-71304-7*) Da Capo.

***Samuel F. B. Morse: Samuel Explores How.** William Kloss. 19.98 (*0-7651-0146-7*) Smithmark.

Samuel F. B. Morse see Discovery Biographies

Samuel Ferguson: The Literary Achievement. Peter Denman. 220p. (C). 1990. text ed. 59.50 (*0-389-20927-9*) B&N Imports.

Samuel First & Second. Joyce G. Baldwin. Ed. by Donald J. Wiseman. LC 88-32895. (Tyndale Old Testament Commentary Ser.). 299p. (Orig.). (C). 1989. pap. 11.99 (*0-87784-258-2*, 258) InterVarsity.

Samuel Foote: A Biography. Percy H. Fitzgerald. LC 72-84512. 1972. 20.95 (*0-405-08519-2*, Pub. by Blom Pubns UK) Ayer.

Samuel Francis Smith: My Country 'tis of Thee. Marguerite Fitch. (Sower Ser.). (Illus.). (J). (gr. 3-6). 1987. pap. 7.99 (*0-88062-049-8*) Mott Media.

S

An Asterisk (*) at the beginning of an entry indicates that the title is appearing in BIP for the first time.

Samuel French Morse Collected Poems. Samuel F. Morse. Ed. by Guy Rotella. 355p. 1995. 35.00 (*0-943373-34-4*); pap. 19.95 (*0-943373-35-2*) Natl Poet Foun.

Samuel Gompers: Founder of the American Labor Movement. Gerald Kurland. Ed. by D. Steve Rahmas. LC 72-190242. (Outstanding Personalities Ser.: No. 24). 32p. (Orig.). (J). (gr. 7-12). 1972. lib. bdg. 7.25 (*0-87157-524-8*) SamHar Pr.

Samuel Gompers, American Statesman. Florence C. Thorne. LC 70-90710. 175p. 1969. reprint ed. text ed. 49.75 (*0-8371-2293-7*, THSG, Greenwood Pr) Greenwood.

Samuel Gompers & Organized Labor in America. Harold C. Livesay. 195p. (C). 1993. reprint ed. pap. text ed. 10.50 (*0-88133-751-X*) Waveland Pr.

Samuel Gompers & the Origins of the American Federation of Labor, 1848-1896. Stuart B. Kaufman. LC 76-176430. (Contributions in Economics & Economic History Ser.: No. 8). 274p. 1973. text ed. 55.00 (*0-8371-6277-7*, KAP/, Greenwood Pr) Greenwood.

***Samuel Gompers Papers: The American Federation of Labor & the Rise of Progressivism, 1902, 6.** Date not set. text ed. 85.00 (*0-252-02303-X*) U of Ill Pr.

Samuel Gompers Papers Vol. 5: An Expanding Movement at the Turn of the Century, 1898-1902. Ed. by Stuart B. Kaufman et al. (Illus.). 640p. (C). 1995. text ed. 60.00 (*0-252-02008-1*) U of Ill Pr.

Samuel Gompers Papers, Vol. 1: The Making of a Union Leader, 1850-86. Ed. by Stuart B. Kaufman et al. LC 84-2469. (Illus.). 568p. 1986. text ed. 60.00 (*0-252-01137-6*) U of Ill Pr.

Samuel Gompers Papers, Vol. 2: The Early Years of the American Federation of Labor, 1887-90. Ed. by Stuart B. Kaufman et al. LC 84-2469. (Illus.). 536p. 1987. text ed. 60.00 (*0-252-01350-6*) U of Ill Pr.

Samuel Gompers Papers, Vol. 3: Unrest & Depression, 1891-94. Ed. by Stuart B. Kaufman & Peter J. Albert. LC 84-2469. (Illus.). 744p. 1989. text ed. 60.00 (*0-252-01546-0*) U of Ill Pr.

Samuel Gompers Papers, Vol. 4: A National Labor Movement Takes Shape, 1895-98. Samuel Gompers. Ed. by Stuart B. Kaufman et al. (Illus.). 632p. 1992. text ed. 60.00 (*0-252-01768-4*) U of Ill Pr.

***Samuel H. Kress Collection At Philbrook.** Richard P. Townsend. (Illus.). 38p. (Orig.). 1991. pap. 11.95 (*0-86659-016-1*) Philbrook Mus Art.

***Samuel H. Kress Collection at the Seattle Art Museum.** Seattle Art Museum Staff & Chiyo Ishikawa. LC 97-25152. 1997. write for info. (*0-932216-47-1*) Seattle Art.

Samuel Hartlib & Universal Reformation: Studies in Intellectual Communication. Ed. by Mark Greengrass et al. (Illus.). 400p. (C). 1995. text ed. 64.95 (*0-521-45252-X*) Cambridge U Pr.

Samuel Hopkins & the New Divinity Movement: Calvinism, the Congregational Ministry, & Reform in New England Between the Great Awakenings. Joseph A. Conforti. LC 80-28268. 249p. reprint ed. pap. 71.00 (*0-317-08398-8*, 2020840) Bks Demand.

Samuel Huntington, President of Congress "Longer Than Expected" A Narrative Essay on the Letters of Samuel Huntington, 1779-1781. George K. Dreher. LC 95-45949. (Illus.). 200p. (C). 1995. pap. 12.95 (*0-9601000-6-7*); lib. bdg. 18.95 (*0-9601000-5-9*) Longshanks Bk.

Samuel I: Volume Eight, a New Translation with Introduction & Commentary. P. Kyle McCarter, Jr. LC 79-7201. (Anchor Bible Ser.). 512p. 1980. 35.00 (*0-385-06760-7*) Doubleday.

Samuel I & II: Critical & Exegetical Commentary. Henry P. Smith. Ed. by Samuel R. Driver et al. LC 99-1607. (International Critical Commentary Ser.). 462p. 1898. 36.95 (*0-567-05005-X*, Pub. by T & T Clark UK) Bks Intl VA.

Samuel II. Ed. by P. Kyle McCarter, Jr. LC 81-43919. (Anchor Bible Ser.: Vol. 9). (Illus.). 576p. 1984. 35.00 (*0-385-06808-5*, Anchor NY) Doubleday.

Samuel Johnson. Samuel Johnson. Ed. by Donald Greene. (Oxford Authors Ser.). (Illus.). 872p. 1984. pap. 21.00 (*0-19-281340-4*) OUP.

Samuel Johnson. Hugh Kingsmill. LC 75-42205. (English Literature Ser.: No. 33). 1974. lib. bdg. 49.95 (*0-8383-2018-X*) M S G Haskell Hse.

Samuel Johnson. Leslie Stephen. Ed. by John Morley. LC 68-58398. (English Men of Letters Ser.). reprint ed. lib. bdg. 27.50 (*0-404-51729-3*) AMS Pr.

Samuel Johnson: A Layman's Religion. Maurice J. Quinlan. LC 64-10260. 256p. 1964. reprint ed. pap. 73.00 (*0-608-01975-5*, 2062630) Bks Demand.

Samuel Johnson: A Survey & Bibliography of Critical Studies. James L. Clifford & Donald J. Greene. LC 74-109940. 349p. reprint ed. pap. 99.50 (*0-7837-2970-7*, 2057484) Bks Demand.

Samuel Johnson: His Words & His Ways. Edward T. Mason. LC 72-2104. (Studies in Samuel Johnson: No. 97). 1972. reprint ed. lib. bdg. 49.95 (*0-8383-1491-0*) M S G Haskell Hse.

Samuel Johnson: Literature, Religion & English Cultural Politics from the Restoration to Romanticism. J. C. Clark. (Illus.). 272p. (C). 1994. pap. text ed. 17.95 (*0-521-47885-5*) Cambridge U Pr.

Samuel Johnson: Literature, Religion & English Cultural Politics from the Restoration to Romanticism. J. C. Clark. (Illus.). 272p. (C). 1995. text ed. 49.95 (*0-521-47304-7*) Cambridge U Pr.

Samuel Johnson: Selected Poetry & Prose. Ed. by Frank Brady & William K. Wimsatt. 1978. pap. 18.95 (*0-520-03552-6*) U CA Pr.

Samuel Johnson: The Complete English Poems. Samuel Johnson. Ed. by J. D. Fleeman. LC 82-22782. (English Poets Ser.). 260p. reprint ed. pap. 74.10 (*0-7837-3319-4*, 2057723) Bks Demand.

Samuel Johnson see 18th Century Literature Critical Heritage

Samuel Johnson after Deconstruction: Rhetoric & "The Rambler" Steven J. Lynn. LC 91-4951. 208p. (C). 1992. 24.95 (*0-8093-1770-2*) S Ill U Pr.

Samuel Johnson & Biographical Thinking. Catherine N. Parke. 200p. 1991. text ed. 34.95 (*0-8262-0789-8*) U of Mo Pr.

Samuel Johnson & Neoclassical Dramatic Theory: The Intellectual Context of the Preface to Shakespeare. Robert D. Stock. LC 72-77194. 250p. reprint ed. pap. 71.30 (*0-7837-0119-5*, 2040396) Bks Demand.

Samuel Johnson & Ric. Richard Holmes. Date not set. pap. 24.00 (*0-670-83392-4*) Viking Penguin.

***Samuel Johnson & the Essay.** Robert D. Spector. LC 96-27390. (Contributions to the Study of World Literature Ser.). 256p. 1997. text ed. 59.95 (*0-313-29775-4*) Greenwood.

Samuel Johnson & the Impact of Print. Alvin Kernan. (Illus.). 374p. (C). 1987. pap. text ed. 17.95 (*0-691-01475-2*) Princeton U Pr.

***Samuel Johnson & the Life of Reading.** Robert DeMaria, Jr. LC 96-38636. (Illus.). 256p. 1997. text ed. 39.95 (*0-8018-5479-2*) Johns Hopkins.

Samuel Johnson & the New Science. Richard B. Schwartz. 198p. 1971. 30.00 (*0-299-06010-1*) U of Wis Pr.

Samuel Johnson & the Problem of Evil. Richard B. Schwartz. LC 74-27314. 128p. 1975. 27.50 (*0-299-06790-4*) U of Wis Pr.

Samuel Johnson Encyclopedia. Pat Rogers. LC 95-33072. 512p. 1996. text ed. 85.00 (*0-313-29411-9*, Greenwood Pr) Greenwood.

Samuel Johnson in the Medical World: The Doctor & the Patient. John Wiltshire. (Illus.). 308p. (C). 1991. text ed. 69.95 (*0-521-38326-9*) Cambridge U Pr.

Samuel Johnson on Shakespeare. Karl Young. LC 75-37625. (Studies in Shakespeare: No. 24). 1976. lib. bdg. 75.00 (*0-8383-2109-7*) M S G Haskell Hse.

Samuel Johnson on Shakespeare: The Discipline of Criticism. Edward Tomarken. LC 90-23164. 216p. 1991. 40.00 (*0-8203-1358-0*) U of Ga Pr.

Samuel Johnson, President of King's College: His Career & Writings, 4 Vols, Set. Herbert W. Schneider. LC 72-153333. reprint ed. 150.00 (*0-404-03600-7*) AMS Pr.

Samuel Johnson, President of King's College, His Career & Writing, 4 vols. Samuel Johnson. (American Biography Ser.). 1991. reprint ed. lib. bdg. write for info. (*0-7812-8222-5*) Rprt Serv.

Samuel Johnson, the Moralist. Robert B. Voitle. LC 61-8842. 204p. reprint ed. pap. 58.20 (*0-7837-4198-7*, 2059048) Bks Demand.

Samuel Johnson, Vol. 4, A Dictionary of the English Language see Encyclopaedic Dictionary in the 18th Century: Architecture, Arts & Crafts

Samuel Johnson's Attitudes to the Arts. Morris R. Brownell. (Illus.). 240p. 1989. 65.00 (*0-19-812956-4*) OUP.

Samuel Johnson's Critical Opinions: A Reexamination. Arthur Sherbo. LC 94-43846. 216p. 1995. 36.50 (*0-87413-547-8*) U Delaware Pr.

Samuel Johnson's Early Biographers. Robert E. Kelley & O. M. Brack, Jr. LC 74-151649. 175p. reprint ed. pap. 49.90 (*0-317-42128-X*, 2025941) Bks Demand.

Samuel Johnson's Literary Criticism. Samuel Johnson. Ed. by R. D. Stock. LC 73-91398. (Regents Critics Ser.). 304p. 1974. reprint ed. pap. 86.70 (*0-7837-8891-6*, 2049602) Bks Demand.

Samuel Johnson's Translation of Sallust: A Facsimile & Transcription of the Hyde Manuscript. Samuel Johnson et al. 42p. 1993. pap. 25.00 (*1-883631-02-5*) Biblgraph Soc.

Samuel Jones Tilden: A Study in Political Sagacity. Alexander C. Flick & Gustav Lobrano. LC 73-7103. (Illus.). 597p. 1973. reprint ed. text ed. 65.00 (*0-8371-6912-7*, FLST, Greenwood Pr) Greenwood.

Samuel Joseph May & the Dilemmas of the Liberal Persuasion, 1797-1871. Donald Yacavone. 300p. 1991. 44.95 (*0-87722-760-8*) Temple U Pr.

Samuel Kelso (Kelsey) Seventeen Twenty to Seventeen Ninety-Six: Scotch-Irish Immigrant & Revolutionary Patriot of Chester County South Carolina. Mavis P. Kelsey, Sr. LC 84-80307. 1984. 75.00 (*0-9613308-0-5*) Kelsey-Seybold Found.

Samuel Kirk & Son: American Silver Craftsmen since Eighteen Fifteen. Norton, R. W., Art Gallery Staff. (Illus.). 32p. 1971. pap. 1.00 (*0-913060-17-8*) Norton Art.

Samuel L. Southard: Jeffersonian Whig. Michael J. Birkner. LC 82-48517. 1984. 37.50 (*0-8386-3160-6*) Fairleigh Dickinson.

Samuel Logan Brengle: Portrait of a Prophet. Clarence W. Hall. 1978. reprint ed. 4.95 (*0-86544-006-9*) Salv Army Suppl South.

Samuel Lorenzo Knapp & Early American Biography. Ben H. McClary. 30p. 1985. reprint ed. pap. 4.50 (*0-912296-80-1*) Am Antiquarian.

Samuel Lyle Criminologist. Arthur Crabb. LC 74-121531. (Short Story Index Reprint Ser.). (Illus.). 1977. 23.95 (*0-8369-3487-3*) Ayer.

Samuel Mareschal: Melodiae Suaves. J. M. Bonhote. (Wissenschaftliche Abhandlungen-Musicological Studies: Vol. 25). 36p. (FRE.). 1976. pap. 8.00 (*0-912024-77-1*) Inst Mediaeval Mus.

Samuel Marsden: The Great Survivor. A. T. Yarwood. 358p. 1977. pap. 19.95 (*0-522-84404-9*, Pub. by Melbourne Univ Pr AT) Paul & Co Pubs.

***Samuel Marsden: The Great Survivor.** A. T. Yarwood. 384p. 1997. pap. 24.95 (*0-522-84732-3*, Pub. by Melbourne Univ Pr AT) Paul & Co Pubs.

Samuel Maxwell Harrington, a Pioneer Judge. Julian D. Winslow. 1993. 16.95 (*0-533-10663-X*) Vantage.

Samuel May Williams: Early Texas Entrepreneur. Margaret S. Henson. LC 75-40894. 222p. 1976. 19.95 (*0-89096-009-7*) Tex A&M Univ Pr.

Samuel May Williams Home: The Home & Life of a Founder of Galveston, Texas. Margaret S. Henson. LC 92-28140. (Fred Rider Cotten Popular History Ser.: No. 7). 1992. pap. 5.95 (*0-87611-125-8*) Tex St Hist Assn.

Samuel Medary & the "Crisis" Testing the Limits of Press Freedom. Reed W. Smith. 216p. (C). 1995. 45.00 (*0-8142-0672-7*) Ohio St U Pr.

***Samuel Mendelsson: A Man Who Must Not Be Forgotten.** (Illus.). 112p. (Orig.). Date not set. pap. write for info. (*0-614-30252-8*) H A Fraenkel.

Samuel Mendelsson: A Man Who Must Not Be Forgotten. H. Alexander Fraenkel. (Illus.). 112p. (Orig.). Date not set. pap. write for info. (*0-9646867-0-8*) H A Fraenkel.

Samuel Morey & His Atmospheric Engine. Horst O. Hardenberg. 114p. 1991. pap. 12.00 (*1-56091-240-5*, SP-922) Soc Auto Engineers.

Samuel Morris. Kjersti H. Baez. (Young Reader's Christian Library). (Illus.). 224p. (J). 1995. pap. text ed. 1.39 (*1-55748-603-4*) Barbour & Co.

Samuel Morris. Lindley Baldwin. LC 86-72978. 96p. 1987. mass mkt. 4.99 (*0-87123-950-7*) Bethany Hse.

Samuel Morris: The Apostle of Simple Faith. W. Terry Whalin. (Heroes of the Faith Ser.). 208p. (YA). (gr. 9 up). 1996. pap. 3.97 (*1-55748-878-9*) Barbour & Co.

Samuel Morse. Mona Kerby. LC 90-13109. (First Bks.). (Illus.). 64p. (J). (gr. 3-5). 1991. lib. bdg. 21.00 (*0-531-20023-X*) Watts.

Samuel Oldknow & the Arkwrights: The Industrial Revolution at Stockport & Marple. George Unwin. LC 68-5554. (Illus.). xxii, 259p. 1968. reprint ed. 39.50 (*0-678-06767-8*) Kelley.

Samuel One & Two. Ed. by A. Cohen. 361p. 1989. 14.95 (*0-900689-26-9*) Soncino Pr.

Samuel Palmer: His Life & Art. Raymond Lister. (Illus.). 296p. 1987. text ed. 80.00 (*0-521-32850-0*) Cambridge U Pr.

Samuel Pepys. G. Bradford. LC 75-42291. (English Biography Ser.: No. 31). 1974. lib. bdg. 52.95 (*0-8383-2061-9*) M S G Haskell Hse.

Samuel Pepys. E. Hallam Moorhouse. LC 74-30375. (English Biography Ser.: No. 31). 1974. lib. bdg. 75.00 (*0-8383-1908-4*) M S G Haskell Hse.

Samuel Pepys. Arthur Ponsonby. LC 71-160987. (Select Bibliographies Reprint Ser.). 1977. reprint ed. 24.95 (*0-8369-5855-1*) Ayer.

Samuel Pepys & the London Booksellers. Charles A. Rivington. (C). 1989. pap. 39.00 (*1-85072-113-0*, Pub. by W Sessions UK) St Mut.

Samuel Pepys & the Royal Navy. Joseph R. Tanner. LC 79-163207. (English Literature Ser.: No. 33). 1971. reprint ed. lib. bdg. 44.95 (*0-8383-1314-0*) M S G Haskell Hse.

Samuel Pepys & the World He Lived In. P. Wheatley. LC 75-34323. (English Literature Ser.: No. 33). 1977. lib. bdg. 75.00 (*0-8383-1895-9*) M S G Haskell Hse.

Samuel Pepy's Biography. Christopher Hibbert. 1996. write for info. (*0-201-63232-2*) Addison-Wesley.

Samuel Pepys in the Diary. Percival Hunt. LC 78-2747. 178p. 1978. reprint ed. text ed. 49.75 (*0-313-20363-6*, HUSD, Greenwood Pr) Greenwood.

Samuel Pepys' Penny Merriments. Roger Thompson. LC 76-50544. 1977. text ed. 55.00 (*0-231-04280-9*); pap. text ed. 19.50 (*0-231-04281-7*) Col U Pr.

Samuel Peter Heintzelman & the Sonora Exploring & Mining Company. Diane M. North. LC 79-15307. 248p. 1980. 33.95 (*0-8165-0679-5*) U of Ariz Pr.

Samuel Proctor: My Moral Odyssey. Samuel D. Proctor. 176p. 1989. pap. 13.50 (*0-8170-1151-X*) Judson.

Samuel R. Delany. Jane B. Weedman. Ed. by Roger C. Schlobin. LC 82-5545. (Starmont Reader's Guide Ser.: Vol. 10). ii, 79p. 1982. lib. bdg. 25.00 (*0-916732-28-2*) Borgo Pr.

Samuel Reshevsky: A Compendium of 1768 Games with Diagrams, Crosstables, Some Annotations, & Indexes. Stephen W. Gordon. 424p. 1997. lib. bdg. 65.00 (*0-7864-0275-X*) McFarland & Co.

Samuel Richardson. Austin Dobson. 1902. 7.00 (*0-403-00018-1*) Scholarly.

Samuel Richardson. Austin Dobson. (BCL1-PR English Literature Ser.). 214p. 1992. reprint ed. lib. bdg. 79.00 (*0-7812-7397-8*) Rprt Serv.

Samuel Richardson: Master Printer. William M. Sale, Jr. LC 77-22446. (Cornell Studies in English: No.37). (Illus.). 389p. 1978. reprint ed. text ed. 65.00 (*0-8371-9732-5*, SASR, Greenwood Pr) Greenwood.

Samuel Richardson: Passion & Prudence. Ed. by Valerie G. Myer. LC 86-10809. 224p. 1986. 50.00 (*0-389-20650-4*, N8208) B&N Imports.

Samuel Richardson: Tercentenary Essays. Ed. by Margaret A. Doody & Peter Sabor. (Illus.). 324p. (C). 1989. text ed. 69.95 (*0-521-35383-1*) Cambridge U Pr.

Samuel Richardson: The Triumph of Craft. Elizabeth B. Brophy. LC 74-3248. 152p. 1974. 21.00 (*0-87049-153-9*) U of Tenn Pr.

***Samuel Richardson, a Man of Letters.** Carol H. Flynn. LC 81-47916. 361p. 1982. reprint ed. pap. 102.90 (*0-608-03351-0*, 2064063) Bks Demand.

***Samuel Richardson's Clarissa.** Harold Bloom. LC 87-37499. (Modern Critical Interpretations Ser.). 1988. 24. 50 (*1-55546-328-2*) Chelsea Hse.

Samuel Richardson's Fictions of Gender. Tassie Gwilliam. 214p. (C). 1994. pap. 14.95 (*0-8047-2522-5*) Stanford U Pr.

Samuel Richardson's Fictions of Gender. Tassie Gwilliam. LC 92-25186. 208p. (C). 1995. 39.50 (*0-8047-2116-5*) Stanford U Pr.

***Samuel Richardson's Published Commentary on Clarissa 1747-1765.** Samuel Richardson & Tom Keymer. 1997. write for info. (*1-85196-463-0*, Pub. by Pickering & Chatto UK); write for info. (*1-85196-464-9*, Pub. by Pickering & Chatto UK) Ashgate Pub Co.

***Samuel Richardson's Published Commentary on Clarissa 1747-1765.** Samuel Richardson et al. LC 97-17853. 1997. pap. write for info. (*1-85196-462-2*, Pub. by Pickering & Chatto UK) Ashgate Pub Co.

***Samuel Richardson's Published Commentary on Clarissa 1747-1765.** Samuel Richardson et al. LC 97-17853. 1997. write for info. (*1-85196-461-4*, Pub. by Pickering & Chatto UK) Ashgate Pub Co.

Samuel Ringgold Ward: Christian Abolitionist. Ronald K. Burke. LC 94-42751. (Studies in African American History & Culture). (Illus.). 176p. 1995. text ed. 45.00 (*0-8153-1930-4*) Garland.

Samuel Rutherford & His Friends. Faith Cook. 157p. 1993. reprint ed. pap. 8.99 (*0-85151-635-1*) Banner of Truth.

Samuel S. White Catalogue of Dental Instruments & Equipment. Samuel S. White. (Illus.). 408p. 1995. reprint ed. 150.00 (*0-930405-63-3*) Norman SF.

Samuel, Saul, & Jesus. Roger D. Aus. LC 94-9894. (South Florida Studies in the History of Judaism: No. 105). 222p. 1994. 69.95 (*1-55540-969-5*, 24 01 05) Scholars Pr GA.

***Samuel, Saul & the Son of Jesse.** Charles Ozanne. 32p. (Orig.). 1997. pap. 3.00 (*1-880573-37-7*) Grace WI.

Samuel Sewall Sails for Home. Robert M. Chute. (Illus.). 36p. (Orig.). 1986. pap. 5.95 (*0-913341-10-X*) Coyote Love.

Samuel Sewall Sails for Home: Poetry by Robert Chute. Robert Chute. 22p. 1986. pap. 5.95 (*0-614-14603-8*) Maine Writers.

Samuel Slater & the Origins of the American Textile Industry, 1790-1860. Barbara M. Tucker. LC 84-45145. (Illus.). 256p. 1984. 39.95 (*0-8014-1594-2*) Cornell U Pr.

Samuel Slater's Mill & the Industrial Revolution. Christopher Simonds. (Turning Points in American History Ser.). (Illus.). 64p. (J). (gr. 5 up). 1990. lib. bdg. 14.95 (*0-382-09951-6*) Silver Burdett Pr.

Samuel Slater's Mill & the Industrial Revolution. Christopher Simonds. (Turning Points in American History Ser.). (Illus.). 64p. (YA). (gr. 5 up). 1990. pap. 7.95 (*0-382-09947-8*) Silver Burdett Pr.

***Samuel Sloan, Architect of Philadelphia, 1815-1884.** Harold N. Cooledge. LC 85-22496. 274p. 1986. reprint ed. pap. 78.10 (*0-608-03636-6*, 2064462) Bks Demand.

***Samuel Smiles: And the Construction of Victorian Values.** Adrian Jarvis. (Illus.). 224p. 1997. boxed 28.95 (*0-7509-1128-X*, Pub. by Sutton Pubng UK) Bks Intl VA.

Samuel Smiles & Nineteenth Century Self-Help in Education. M. D. Stephens & G. W. Roderick. (C). 1983. 25.00 (*0-902031-86-4*, Pub. by Univ Nottingham UK); text ed. 60.00 (*0-685-22147-4*, Pub. by Univ Nottingham UK) St Mut.

Samuel Smiles & the Victorian Work Ethic. Timothy Travers. (Modern European History Ser.). 410p. 1987. text ed. 15.00 (*0-8240-7835-7*) Garland.

Samuel Sulser, Pioneer of Gadsden, Alabama & Allied Families. Mildred S. Wright. LC 86-51287. (Illus.). 108p. 1986. pap. 25.00 (*0-917016-29-7*); text ed. 32.50 (*0-917016-28-9*) M S Wright.

Samuel Taylor Coleridge. Samuel Taylor Coleridge. (Poets Ser.). 146p. 1993. 5.95 (*0-7117-0441-4*, Pub. by Jarrold Pub UK) Seven Hills Bk.

Samuel Taylor Coleridge. Hugh I. Fausset. 1988. reprint ed. lib. bdg. 49.00 (*0-7812-0557-3*) Rprt Serv.

Samuel Taylor Coleridge. Hugh I. Fausset. (BCL1-PR English Literature Ser.). 350p. 1992. reprint ed. lib. bdg. 89.00 (*0-7812-7500-8*) Rprt Serv.

Samuel Taylor Coleridge. Hugh I. Fausset. (Illus.). 1971. reprint ed. 39.00 (*0-403-00792-5*) Scholarly.

Samuel Taylor Coleridge: A Biographical Study. Edmund K. Chambers. LC 78-19152. 373p. 1978. reprint ed. text ed. 65.00 (*0-313-20539-6*, CHST, Greenwood Pr) Greenwood.

Samuel Taylor Coleridge: A Selection. Samuel Taylor Coleridge. Ed. by H. J. Jackson. (Oxford Authors Ser.). 750p. (C). 1986. pap. 19.95 (*0-19-281383-8*) OUP.

Samuel Taylor Coleridge: A Selective Bibliography of Criticism, 1935-1977. Ed. by Jefferson D. Caskey & Melinda M. Stapp. LC 78-57765. 174p. 1978. text ed. 42.95 (*0-313-20564-7*, CCO/, Greenwood Pr) Greenwood.

Samuel Taylor Coleridge: Annotated Bibliography Criticism & Scholarship, Vol. 3. Walter B. Crawford. 1996. 90.00 (*0-8161-8727-4*, Hall Reference) Macmillan.

Samuel Taylor Coleridge see Romantics: Critical Heritage

Samuel Taylor Coleridge see Modern Critical Views Series

Samuel Taylor Coleridge & the English Romantic School. Alois Brandl. LC 68-757. (Studies in Coleridge: No. 7). 1969. reprint ed. lib. bdg. 75.00 (*0-8383-0512-1*) M S G Haskell Hse.

Samuel Taylor Coleridge Revisited. Raymond E. Matlak. 1996. 23.95 (*0-8057-7064-X*, Twayne) Scribnrs Ref.

***Samuel Taylor Coleridge (1772-1834) Selected Poetry.** Ed. by William Empson & David Pirie. pap. write for info. (*0-85635-815-0*, Pub. by Carcanet Pr UK) Paul & Co Pubs.

Samuel, the Prophet. Gordon Lindsay. (Old Testament Ser.: Vol. 18). 1965. 1.95 (*0-89985-138-X*) Christ for the Nations.

Samuel to Solomon see Message of the Old Testament

Samuel Todd's Book of Great Inventions. E. L. Konigsburg. LC 90-23688. (Illus.). 32p. (J). (ps-2). 1991. lib. bdg. 13. 95 (*0-689-31680-1*, Atheneum Bks Young) S&S Childrens.

S

Samuel Ullman & "Youth" The Life, the Legacy. Margaret E. Armbrester. LC 92-37414. (Judaic Studies). 168p. (C). 1993. 24.95 (*0-8173-0685-4*) U of Ala Pr.

Samuel W. Houston & His Contemporaries: A Documentary History of Education. Naomi W. Lede. 348p. (Orig.). 1991. pap. 16.00 (*0-9630007-1-3*) Lede Consult.

Samuel Walker Griffith. Roger B. Joyce. LC 84-2263. (Illus.). 456p. 1985. 44.95 (*0-7022-1688-7*, Pub. by Univ Queensland Pr AT) Intl Spec Bk.

Samuel Walters - Marine Artist: Fifty Years of Sea, Sail & Steam. A. S. Davidson. 1992. 195.00 (*0-947764-46-1*, Pub. by Jones-Sands UK) St Mut.

*__Samuel Ward Sermons.__ Samuel Ward. 178p. 1996. reprint ed. 14.99 (*0-85151-697-1*) Banner of Truth.

Samuel Wesley, Musician: The Story of His Life. James T. Lightwood. LC 72-83745. 1972. reprint ed. 20.95 (*0-405-08748-9*) Ayer.

Samuel Whiskers. Beatrix Potter. (Little Hide-&-Seek Bks.). (Illus.). 12p. (J). (ps-1). 1994. pap. 3.50 (*0-7232-4108-2*) Warne.

Samuel Whitbread 1764-1815: A Social & Political Study. Dean Rapp. (Modern European History Ser.). 512p. 1987. text ed. 15.00 (*0-8240-7829-2*) Garland.

Samuel Willard: Selected Sermons see Library of American Puritan Writings. The Seventeenth Century: The Seventeenth Century

Samuel Willard: Selected Works see Millennium in America: From the Puritan Migration to the Civil War

Samuel Yellin in Context. Richard J. Wattenmaker. LC 85-70690. (Illus.). 35p. (Orig.). 1985. pap. 4.00 (*0-939896-06-0*) Flint Inst Arts.

Samuel Yellin, Metalworker. Jack Andrews. LC 92-90938. (Illus.). 1992. 40.00 (*1-879535-05-X*) Skipjack Pr.

Samuell Gorton: A Forgotten Founder of Our Liberties. Lewis G. Janes. (Notable American Authors Ser.). 1992. reprint ed. lib. bdg. 75.00 (*0-7812-3487-5*) Rprt Serv.

Samuel's Choice. Richard Berleth. Ed. by Judith Mathews. LC 89-77186. (Illus.). 40p. (J). (gr. 3-6). 1990. lib. bdg. 14.95 (*0-8075-7218-7*) A Whitman.

*__Samuel's Easton's Day.__ Bruce McMillan. (J). (gr. 1-4). Date not set. pap. 5.99 (*0-614-19198-X*, Apple Paperbacks) Scholastic Inc.

Samuelson & Neo-Classical Economics. Ed. by George R. Feiwel. (Recent Economic Thought Ser.). 384p. 1982. lib. bdg. 70.50 (*0-89838-069-3*) Kluwer Ac.

Samurai. Anthony Briant. (Elite Ser.: No. 23). (Illus.). 64p. pap. 12.95 (*0-85045-897-8*, 9423, Pub. by Osprey UK) Stackpole.

Samurai. Shusaku Endo. Tr. by Van C. Gessel from JPN. LC 82-57851. 272p. 1982. 12.95i (*0-06-859852-1*, HarpT) HarpC.

*__Samurai.__ Shusaku Endo. Tr. by Van C. Gessel from JPN. LC 96-52780. (Classic Ser.). 196p. (Orig.). 1997. 10.95 (*0-8112-1346-3*, 839) New Directions.

*__Samurai.__ Shusaku Endo. 1997. pap. 10.95 (*0-614-27283-1*) New Dir Pub.

Samurai. Saburo Sakai. 1996. mass mkt. 5.99 (*0-671-56310-6*) PB.

Samurai: A Military History. Stephen Turnbull. (Japan Library). (Illus.). 288p. (C). 1996. pap. text ed. 29.00 (*1-873410-38-7*, Pub. by Curzon Press UK) UH Pr.

Samurai: A Novel. Julia Kristeva. Tr. by Barbara Bray from FRE. 352p. (C). 1992. 29.95 (*0-231-07542-1*) Col U Pr.

Samurai: The Warrior Tradition. Stephen Turnbull. (Illus.). 336p. 1996. 29.95 (*1-85409-359-2*, Pub. by Arms & Armour UK) Sterling.

Samurai & Silk: A Japanese & American Heritage. Haru M. Reischauer. (Illus.). 400p. 1986. 35.00 (*0-674-78800-1*) Belknap Pr.

Samurai & Silk: A Japanese & American Heritage. Haru M. Reischauer. 400p. 1988. reprint ed. pap. text ed. 17.95 (*0-674-78801-X*) Belknap Pr.

Samurai Armies 1550-1615. (Men-at-Arms Ser.: No. 86). (Illus.). 48p. pap. 11.95 (*0-85045-302-X*, 9024, Pub. by Osprey UK) Stackpole.

Samurai Bulldog. Chibinosuke Dogizaemon. (Illus.). 96p. (Orig.). 1994. pap. 9.95 (*0-8348-0305-4*) Weatherhill.

Samurai Castle. Fiona MacDonald et al. LC 95-2181. (Inside Story Ser.). (Illus.). 48p. (YA). (gr. 5 up). 1995. lib. bdg. 18.95 (*0-87226-381-9*) P Bedrick Bks.

Samurai Cat. JoAnn Roe. (Illus.). 64p. 1992. pap. 6.95 (*0-931551-07-2*); lib. bdg. 11.95 (*0-931551-08-0*) Montevista Pr.

Samurai Cat Goes to the Movies. Mark E. Rogers. 288p. 1994. pap. 10.95 (*0-312-85744-6*) Tor Bks.

Samurai Cat in the Real World. Mark E. Rogers. (Illus.). 128p. (Orig.). 1989. pap. 12.95 (*0-312-93198-0*) St Martin.

Samurai Crusader: The Kumomaru Chronicles. Hiroi Oji. 1996. pap. text ed. 15.95 (*1-56931-130-7*) Viz Commns Inc.

Samurai Film. Alain Silver. LC 82-22288. (Illus.). 242p. 1986. pap. 12.95 (*0-87951-246-6*) Overlook Pr.

Samurai Films of Akira Kurosawa. David Desser. LC 83-15563. (Studies in Cinema: No. 23). 172p. reprint ed. pap. 49.10 (*0-8357-1495-0*, 2070633) Bks Demand.

Samurai from Outer Space: Understanding Japanese Animation. Antonia Levi. (Illus.). 224p. (Orig.). 1996. pap. 18.95 (*0-8126-9332-9*) Open Court.

Samurai in Valhalla - Past the Future. Paul H. Johnson. 367p. (Orig.). (YA). (gr. 9 up). 1993. pap. 5.95 (*0-9636833-1-4*) Piros Pr.

Samurai Magick. IGOOS Staff. Ed. by Thorguard Templar. 107p. (Orig.). 1993. 29.95 (*1-883147-66-2*) Intern Guild ASRS.

Samurai of Gold Hill. rev. ed. Yoshiko Uchida. LC 84-20424. (Illus.). 128p. (J). (gr. 4-12). 1985. reprint ed. pap. 8.95 (*0-916870-86-3*) Creat Arts Bk.

Samurai Press: A Bibliography. J. Howard Woolmer. (Illus.). 98p. 1986. 25.00 (*0-913506-16-8*) Woolmer-Brotherson.

Samurai Selling: The Ancient Art of Modern Service. Chuck Laughlin et al. LC 92-44201. 1993. 16.95 (*0-312-08885-X*) St Martin.

Samurai Selling: The Ancient Art of Modern Service. Chuck Laughlin. 1994. pap. 8.95 (*0-312-11885-6*) St Martin.

*__Samurai Shodown.__ Kyoichi Nanatsuki. 1997. pap. text ed. 15.95 (*1-56931-213-3*, Viz Comics) Viz Commns Inc.

Samurai Sword. John M. Yumoto. 21.95 (*0-685-63777-8*) Wehman.

Samurai Sword: A Handbook. John M. Yumoto. LC 58-7497. (Illus.). 191p. 1958. 21.95 (*0-8048-0509-1*) C E Tuttle.

Samurai Swordsmanship, Vol. I. Dale S. Kirby. (Illus.). 110p. (Orig.). 1985. pap. 9.95 (*0-89826-014-0*) Natl Paperback.

*__Samurai Swordsmanship, Vol. II.__ Dale S. Kirby. (Illus.). (Orig.). 1988. pap. 9.95 (*0-89826-024-8*) Natl Paperback.

Samurai, the Mountie & the Cowboy: Should America Adopt the Gun Controls of Other Democracies? David Kopel. 470p. (C). 1992. 29.95 (*0-87975-756-6*) Prometheus Bks.

Samurai Warfare. Stephen Turnbull. (Illus.). 160p. (J). 1996. 29.95 (*1-85409-280-4*, Pub. by Arms & Armour UK) Sterling.

*__Samurai Warfare.__ Stephen Turnbull. 1997. pap. text ed. 19.95 (*1-85409-432-7*, Pub. by Arms & Armour UK) Sterling.

Samurai 1550-1600. Tony Bryant. (Warrior Ser.). (Illus.). 64p. 1994. pap. 12.95 (*1-85532-345-1*, 9606, Pub. by Osprey UK) Stackpole.

Samurai's Daughter. Robert D. San Souci. LC 91-15585. (Illus.). 32p. (J). (ps-3). 1992. pap. 15.99 (*0-8037-1135-2*) Dial Bks Young.

*__Samurai's Daughter.__ Robert D. San Souci. (J). 1997. pap. 5.99 (*0-14-056284-2*, Puffin) Puffin Bks.

Samurai's Garden. Gail Tsukiyama. 1995. 18.95 (*0-312-11813-9*) St Martin.

*__Samurais in Salt Lake.__ Dean W. Collinwood et al. Tr. by Kazue Matsui-Haag from JPN. (Illus.). 72p. (Orig.). 1996. pap. 5.00 (*0-9651163-9-5*) Harkness Pubng.

Samurai's Tale. Erik C. Haugaard. (YA). 1990. pap. 6.95 (*0-395-54970-1*) HM.

Samvidha Vidhi: (Law of Contract) Avtar Singh. (HIN.). (C). 1989. 90.00 (*0-685-37468-8*) St Mut.

Samworth Books: A Descriptive Bibliography: Thomas G. Samworth & the Small Arms Technical Publishing Co. Brian R. Smith. LC 90-61552. (Illus.). 320p. 1990. 39.95 (*0-9626820-8-X*) Marksmans Bookshelf.

Samy y Sus Fantasticos. Daniel Hochstatter. (SPA.). (J). 8.99 (*0-88113-178-4*); 8.99 (*0-88113-179-2*) Edit Betania.

San. Megan Biesele & Kxao Loloo. LC 96-38235. (Heritage Library of African Peoples: Set 4). (Illus.). 64p. (YA). (gr. 7-12). 1997. lib. bdg. 15.95 (*0-8239-1997-8*, D1997-8) Rosen Group.

San Agustin 200 Anos, 1790-1990: Seminario - la Arqueologia del Macizo y el Suroccidente Colombianos. (Illus.). 132p. (SPA.). 1991. pap. 8.50 (*1-877812-32-3*) UPLAAP.

San Andreas Fault System: Displacement, Palinspastic Reconstruction, & Geologic Evolution. Ed. by R. E. Powell et al. (Memoir Ser.: No. 178). (Illus.). 1993. 57.50 (*0-8137-1178-9*) Geol Soc.

San Andreas Transform Belt. Ed. by Sylvester. (IGC Field Trip Guidebooks Ser.). 128p. 1989. 28.00 (*0-87590-623-0*, T309) Am Geophysical.

San Angelenos: Mexican Americans in San Angelo, Texas. Arnoldo De Leon. (Illus.). 176p. (Orig.). (C). 1985. pap. 12.95 (*0-938036-05-X*) Mulberry Ave Bks.

San Angelo Showdown. William W. Johnstone. (Blood Bond Ser.: No. 7). 288p. 1994. mass mkt. 3.99 (*0-8217-4466-6*, Zebra Kensgtn) Kensgtn Pub Corp.

*__San Antonio.__ Erik Ketcherside. (City Smart Guidebooks Ser.). (Illus.). 224p. 1998. pap. 12.95 (*1-56261-382-0*) John Muir.

San Antonio. Sally Lee. LC 91-34303. (Downtown America Ser.). (Illus.). 60p. (J). (gr. 4 up). 1992. lib. bdg. 13.95 (*0-87518-510-X*, Dillon Silver Burdett) Silver Burdett Pr.

San Antonio. Al Rendon. (Texas Sights & Scenes Ser.). 64p. 1995. 7.95 (*0-88415-261-8*) Gulf Pub.

San Antonio. Photos by Al Rendon. LC 94-43910. (Texas Monthly Sights & Scenes Ser.). (Illus.). 64p. 1995. 7.95 (*0-87719-261-8*, 9261) Gulf Pub.

San Antonio. 4th ed. N. Foster & B. Fairbanks. (Texas Monthly Guidebooks Ser.). 288p. 1994. pap. 12.95 (*0-87719-221-9*) Gulf Pub.

*__San Antonio.__ 5th ed. Nancy Foster & Benjamin Fairbank. (Texas Monthly Guidebooks Ser.). 1998. pap. 16.95 (*0-87719-319-3*, 9319) Gulf Pub.

*__San Antonio: A Cultural Tapestry.__ Jan J. Russell & Cathy Smith. (Urban Tapestry Ser.). (Illus.). 1998. 44.95 (*1-881096-55-6*) Towery Pub.

San Antonio: A Historical Portrait. John L. Davis. (Illus.). 1978. 25.00 (*0-88426-055-0*) Encino Pr.

San Antonio: Guide to the City & Its Environs. Texas Writer's Project Staff. 1993. reprint ed. lib. bdg. 75.00 (*0-7812-5979-7*) Rprt Serv.

San Antonio: Portrait of the Fiesta City. Susan Nawrocki & Gerald Lair. LC 91-40861. (Illus.). 96p. 1992. pap. 16.95 (*0-89658-204-3*) Voyageur Pr.

*__San Antonio: The Enchanted City.__ Frank W. Jennings. (Illus.). 384p. 1997. 22.95 (*1-890346-02-0*) San Antonio Express-News.

*__San Antonio: The Enchanted City.__ Frank W. Jennings. (Illus.). 384p. 1997. pap. 16.95 (*1-890346-03-9*) San Antonio Express-News.

*__San Antonio & Austin.__ 2nd ed. Arthur Frommer. (Frommer Travel Guides Ser.). 1997. 14.95 (*0-02-861584-0*) Macmillan.

San Antonio-Border. 2nd ed. Ray Miller. (Eyes of Texas Travel Guides Ser.). (Illus.). 252p. 1988. pap. 10.95 (*0-88415-234-0*) Gulf Pub.

San Antonio Cuisine: A Sampling of Restaurants & Their Recipes. Karen Haram. (Illus.). 144p. (Orig.). 1994. pap. 14.95 (*1-878686-11-9*) Two Lane Pr.

San Antonio de Bexar: A Community on New Spain's Northern Frontier. Jesus F. De La Tejas. (Illus.). 239p. 1996. pap. 18.95 (*0-8263-1751-0*) U of NM Pr.

*__San Antonio Dine-a-Mate Book.__ 152p. 1996. pap. text ed. 25.00 (*1-57393-028-8*) Dine-A-Mate.

San Antonio Missions & Their System of Land Tenure. Felix D. Almaraz, Jr. (Illus.). 118p. 1989. 17.95 (*0-292-74653-9*) U of Tex Pr.

San Antonio Missions National Historical Park. Luis Torres. Ed. by T. J. Priehs & Ronald J. Foreman. LC 92-62159. (Illus.). 64p. (Orig.). 1992. pap. 9.95 (*1-877856-17-7*) SW Pks Mnmts.

San Antonio on Foot. Diane Capito & Mark Willis. (Illus.). 192p. (Orig.). 1993. student ed., pap. 10.95 (*0-89672-309-7*) Tex Tech Univ Pr.

*__San Antonio on Foot.__ 2nd ed. Diane Capito & Mark Willis. LC 97-22289. (Illus.). 240p. (Orig.). 1997. pap. 13.95 (*0-89672-382-8*) Tex Tech Univ Pr.

San Antonio Private School Guide. Cheryl D. Jividen. LC 94-61447. (Illus.). viii, 168p. (Orig.). 1994. pap. 12.95 (*0-934955-27-1*) Watercress Pr.

San Antonio River. Mary A. Guerra. (Illus.). 64p. (Orig.). 1991. pap. text ed. 5.95 (*0-943260-03-5*) Alamo Pr TX.

San Antonio River. Fritz A. Toepperwein & Emilie Toepperwein. 1977. pap. 1.95 (*0-910722-11-0*) Highland Pr.

San Antonio Rose: The Life & Music of Bob Wills. Charles Townsend. LC 75-45431. (Music in American Life Ser.). (Illus.). 498p. 1986. 17.95 (*0-252-01362-X*) U of Ill Pr.

San Antonio Self-Guiding Auto Tour. Rodger Bourne & Joan Burrell. 1990. pap. 5.00 (*0-915266-21-0*) Awani Pr.

San Antonio Sonata: For Saxophone & Piano. 11.95 (*0-7935-4028-3*, 50482227) H Leonard.

*__San Antonio Spurs.__ Paul Joseph. LC 97-2101. (Inside the NBA Ser.). (J). 1997. write for info. (*1-56239-773-7*) Abdo & Dghtrs.

San Antonio Spurs. Richard Rambeck. (NBA Today Ser.). (YA). (gr. 5 up). 1993. lib. bdg. 14.95 (*0-88682-519-9*) Creative Ed.

*__San Antonio Spurs.__ Richard Rambeck. LC 96-52962. (NBA Today Ser.). (J). 1997. write for info. (*0-88682-890-2*) Creative Ed.

*__San Antonio Spurs Basketball Team.__ Glenn Rogers. LC 96-46527. (Great Sports Teams Ser.). (J). (gr. 4-10). 1997. lib. bdg. 16.95 (*0-89490-797-2*) Enslow Pubs.

San Antonio Uncovered. Mark L. Rybczyk. LC 91-20146. (Illus.). 304p. (Orig.). 1991. pap. 16.95 (*1-55622-145-2*, Seaside Pr) Wordware Pub.

*__San Bernadino National Forest - CA.__ (Illus.). 1997. 8.99 (*1-56695-049-X*) Trails Illustrated.

San Bernardino: The Rise & Fall of a California Community. Edward L. Lyman. LC 95-9698. (Illus.). xiii, 470p. 1996. 24.95 (*1-56085-067-1*) Signature Bks.

*__San Bernardino Contla: Marriage & Family Structure in a Tlaxcalan Municipio.__ Hugo G. Nutini. LC 68-21632. 436p. 1968. reprint ed. pap. 124.30 (*0-608-03994-2*, 2064730) Bks Demand.

*__San Bernardino County Street Guide & Directory: 1998 Edition.__ Thomas Bros. Maps Staff. 272p. 1997. pap. 16.95 (*0-88130-899-4*) Thomas Bros Maps.

San Bernardino Mountain Trails. 4th ed. John W. Robinson. LC 85-41027. (Illus.). 272p. (Orig.). 1986. pap. 12.95 (*0-89997-063-X*) Wilderness Pr.

*__San Bernardino/Riverside Counties Street Guide & Directory: Zip Code Edition, 1998.__ Thomas Bros. Maps Staff. 516p. 1997. pap. 35.95 (*0-88130-901-X*) Thomas Bros Maps.

*__San Bernardino/Riverside Counties Street Guide & Directory: 1998 Edition.__ Thomas Bros. Maps Staff. 512p. 1997. pap. 27.95 (*0-88130-900-1*) Thomas Bros Maps.

San Bernardino/Riverside Counties Street Guide & Directory Census Tract Edition: 1997 Edition. (Illus.). 514p. 1996. pap. 59.95 (*0-88130-850-1*) Thomas Bros Maps.

*__San Bernardinos.__ John W. Robinson. 256p. 32.95 (*0-9615421-2-8*) Big Santa Hist.

San Bornes. Holt Staff. 1990. text ed. 107.25 (*0-03-021604-4*) HR&W Schl Div.

San Bruno Mountain Habitat Conservation Scam. 2nd ed. Craig C. Dremann. 82p. 1987. pap. 15.00 (*0-933421-20-6*) Redwood Seed.

San Camilo, 1936: The Eve, Feast, & Octave of St. Camillus of the Year 1936 in Madrid. Camilo Jose Cela. Tr. by John H. Polt. LC 91-13388. 327p. 1991. pap. 16.95 (*0-8223-1196-8*); lib. bdg. 49.95 (*0-8223-1179-8*) Duke.

San Carlo Borromeo: Catholic Reform & Ecclesiastical Politics in the Second Half of the Sixteenth Century. Ed. by John M. Headley & John B. Tomaro. LC 86-83052. (Illus.). 320p. 1988. 45.00 (*0-918016-92-4*) Folger Bks.

San Carlos Apache Texts. Pliny E. Goddard. LC 76-44073. (AMNH. Anthropological Papers: Vol. 24, Pt. 3). reprint ed. 29.50 (*0-404-15777-7*) AMS Pr.

San-Chu: Its Technique & Imagery. Wayne Schlepp. LC 76-106037. 160p. 1970. reprint ed. pap. 45.60 (*0-608-01897-X*, 2062549) Bks Demand.

San Cipriano: Life in a Puerto Rican Community, Vol. 1. Anthony L. LaRuffa. LC 73-136765. (Library of Anthropology). (Illus.). xiv, 148p. 1971. text ed. 87.00 (*0-677-03470-9*) Gordon & Breach.

San Cristobal: Voices & Visions of the Galisteo Basin. Christina S. Mednick. 272p. 1996. 50.00 (*0-89013-292-5*) Museum NM Pr.

San Cristobal: Voices & Visions of the Galisto Basin. Christina S. Mednick. LC 96-22539. 1996. pap. 35.00 (*0-89013-294-1*) Museum NM Pr.

San Damiano Cross: An Explanation. Michael Scanlan. (Illus.). 16p. (Orig.). 1983. pap. 1.95 (*0-940535-01-7*, UP102) Franciscan U Pr.

*__San Diegan: San Diego Guide.__ 28th ed. (Illus.). 352p. 1996. mass mkt. 1.95 (*1-890226-00-9*) San Diegan.

San Diego. Karen O'Connor. (Downtown America Ser.). (Illus.). 60p. (J). (gr. 3 up). 1990. lib. bdg. 13.95 (*0-87518-439-1*, Dillon Silver Burdett) Silver Burdett Pr.

San Diego. Chuck Place. LC 96-23766. (California Sights & Scenes Ser.). 64p. (Orig.). 1997. pap. 14.95 (*0-88415-835-7*, 5835) Gulf Pub.

San Diego. Bill Ross et al. (Illus.). 94p. 1988. 19.95 (*1-55652-043-3*) Chicago Review.

San Diego: A California City. Federal Writers' Project, California. LC 73-3660. (American Guide Ser.). reprint ed. 39.50 (*0-404-57904-3*) AMS Pr.

San Diego: An Introduction to the Region. 3rd ed. Philip R. Pryde-Sunbelt. (Illus.). 320p. 1992. per. 18.95 (*0-8403-7094-6*) Kendall-Hunt.

*__San Diego: Sidewalk Offline Restaurant Guide.__ Ed. by Sidewalk.com Editors Staff. (Sidewalk Ser.). 256p. (Orig.). 1997. pap. write for info. (*1-57061-103-3*) Sasquatch Bks.

*__San Diego: World-Class City.__ Tom Blair & Ron Donoho. (Urban Tapestry Ser.). (Illus.). 1998. 44.95 (*1-881096-52-1*) Towery Pub.

San Diego Access. Richard S. Wurman. (Access Guides Ser.). (Illus.). 176p. (Orig.). 1991. pap. 16.95 (*0-06-772524-4*, Harper Ref) HarpC.

San Diego Appointment Calendar, 1991. Josiah Sand. (Illus.). 14p. (Orig.). 1990. pap. 5.95 (*1-878505-00-9*) Road Runner Card.

San Diego Artists. Robert Perine & I. Andrea. LC 88-70826. (Illus.). 224p. 1988. 35.00 (*0-936725-02-8*) Artra Pub.

San Diego, California: The Travel Guide for Kids. Mary E. Stack. (Colormore Travels Ser.). (Illus.). 32p. (J). (gr. k-4). 1991. pap. 4.95 (*0-945600-06-2*) Colormore Inc.

San Diego Chargers. Bob Italia. (Inside the NFL Ser.). (J). 1996. lib. bdg. 15.98 (*1-56239-540-8*) Abdo & Dghtrs.

San Diego Chargers. Richard Rambeck. (NFL Today Ser.). (J). (gr. 4 up). 1991. lib. bdg. 14.95 (*0-88682-382-X*) Creative Ed.

San Diego Chargers. 2nd rev. ed. Larry Sutin. (NFL Today Ser.). (Illus.). 32p. (J). (gr. 4-8). 1996. lib. bdg. 14.95 (*0-88682-811-2*) Creative Ed.

San Diego Children's Directory. Riviera Publications Staff. Ed. by Elizabeth A. Nelson. 96p. 1990. pap. text ed. 3.95 (*1-877609-03-X*) Riviera Pubns.

San Diego Children's Directory 1992. Elizabeth A. Nelson. 1991. pap. 3.95 (*1-877609-04-8*) Riviera Pubns.

San Diego Children's Directory 1993. Elizabeth A. Nelson & Nelson Enginering & Research, Inc. Staff. 1992. pap. 4.95 (*1-877609-06-4*) Riviera Pubns.

*__San Diego Coast.__ Sean O'Brien. (Twelve Short Hikes Ser.: No. 15). (Illus.). 32p. (Orig.). 1997. pap. 4.95 (*1-57540-080-4*) Chockstone Pr.

San Diego Cooks! Delicious Recipes from San Diego's 40 Best Restaurants. David Nelson. 208p. (Orig.). 1991. reprint ed. lib. bdg. 31.00 (*0-8095-5859-9*) Borgo Pr.

San Diego County. Sandy S. Brown. Ed. by Kristine Miller. 375p. 1995. pap. 11.95 (*1-56413-184-X*) Auto Club.

*__San Diego County Business Directory, 1997.__ 8th ed. 352p. 1997. pap. 75.00 (*1-57541-038-9*) Database Pub Co.

San Diego County Including Imperial County Street Guide & Directory: 1996 Large Print Edition. large type ed. Thomas Bros. Maps Staff. 234p. 1995. pap. 34.95 (*0-88130-811-0*) Thomas Bros Maps.

San Diego County Including Imperial County Street Guide & Directory, Census Tract Edition: 1996 Edition. Thomas Bros. Maps Staff. (Illus.). 236p. 1995. pap. 49.95 (*0-88130-786-6*) Thomas Bros Maps.

*__San Diego County Including Portions of Imperial County Street Guide & Directory: Zip Code Edition, 1998.__ Thomas Bros. Maps Staff. 234p. 1997. pap. 23.95 (*0-88130-903-6*) Thomas Bros Maps.

*__San Diego County Including Portions of Imperial County Street Guide & Directory: 1998 Edition.__ Thomas Bros. Maps Staff. 232p. 1997. pap. 16.95 (*0-88130-902-8*) Thomas Bros Maps.

San Diego County Indians As Farmers & Wage Earners. Ted Couro. reprint ed. pap. 2.00 (*0-686-69102-4*) Acoma Bks.

San Diego County Practical Guide to Divorce. John D. Magnin. 237p. (Orig.). 1994. 34.95 (*1-885558-00-7*) CA Pract Law.

San Diego County Practical Guide to Divorce. John D. Magnin. Ed. by Donna L. Rose. 237p. (Orig.). 1994. pap. text ed. 29.95 (*1-885558-14-7*) CA Pract Law.

San Diego County Writers & Publishers Resource Guide: The Writer's Red Book. 2nd ed. Margaret L. McWhorter. 336p. (C). 1995. pap. 24.95 (*0-941903-14-1*) Ransom Hill.

San Diego County 1977: McCormack's Guides. 1997. pap. 9.95 (*0-931299-69-1*) McCormacks Guides.

San Diego County 1995: McCormack's Guides. 1995. pap. 9.95 (*0-931299-53-5*) McCormacks Guides.

San Diego County 1996: McCormack's Guides. 1995. pap. 9.95 (*0-931299-60-8*) McCormacks Guides.

San Diego County's Special Species: Nature Essays Written by & for Children. San Diego County School Children Staff. Ed. by Barbara Moran. 44p. (J). (gr. 1-12). 1993. pap. 4.95 (*0-9634474-1-6*) Ms B Bks.

San Diego Creative Directory. 5th ed. Ed. by Alex Farnsley & Susan Farnsley. 44p. 1988. spiral bd. 32.50 (*0-940093-00-6*) Farnsley Grp.

San Diego Creative Directory. 6th ed. Ed. by Alex Farnsley & Susan Farnsley. 525p. 1989. spiral bd. 36.95 (*0-940093-01-4*) Farnsley Grp.

San Diego Creative Directory. 7th ed. Alex Farnsley & Susan Farnsley. 462p. 1990. spiral bd. 42.50 (*0-940093-02-2*) Farnsley Grp.

San Diego Creative Directory No. 10: The Source Book for Advertising & Marketing. 1992. spiral bd. 44.50 (*1-880846-03-9*) Blue Bk CA.

San Diego Cuisine. Ed. by Gwenn Jensen. (Orig.). 1993. pap. 12.95 (*1-878686-09-7*) Two Lane Pr.

San Diego Dine-a-Mate. 288p. 1994. pap. 30.00 (*1-57393-008-3*) Dine-A-Mate.

***San Diego Dine-a-Mate Book.** 232p. 1996. pap. text ed. 35.00 (*1-57393-066-0*) Dine-A-Mate.

San Diego Exhibition: Forty-Two Emerging Artists. Jeff Kelly et al. LC 84-52886. (Illus.). 36p. (Orig.). 1985. pap. text ed. 9.00 (*0-934418-22-5*) Mus Contemp Art.

San Diego Film & Video Resource Guide 1995. Ed. by Cathy Anderson. 306p. 15.00 (*0-9646317-0-9*) San Diego Film Comm.

San Diego Firefighters Centennial Cookbook. Ed. by Kathryn C. Benson. (Illus.). 184p. (Orig.). (C). 1989. pap. 8.00 (*0-9622550-0-9*) SDFDCCC.

San Diego-La Jolla Underwater Park Ecological Reserve, Vol. 1: A Field Guide. Judith L. Garfield. 64p. 1994. pap. text ed. 14.95 (*0-9640724-6-7*) Picaro Pubng.

San Diego (Lawson) rev. ed. Greg Lawson. LC 82-71547. (Sunbelt Pictoral Bks.). (Illus.). 72p. 1989. pap. 11.95 (*0-916251-38-1*) Sunbelt Pubns.

San Diego Lightfoot Sue & Other Stories. Tom Reamy. LC 79-54396. (Illus.). 1979. 16.95 (*0-935128-00-X*) Ursus Imprints.

San Diego Little Restaurant Guide. Camaro Editors. (Illus.). 1985. pap. 4.95 (*0-913290-87-4*) Camaro Pub.

San Diego Mission. Bellerophon Books Staff. (J). (gr. 4-7). 1996. pap. 3.95 (*0-88388-206-X*) Bellerophon Bks.

***San Diego Mountains.** Sean O'Brien. (12 Short Hikes Ser.: No. 16). (Illus.). 32p. (Orig.). 1997. pap. 4.95 (*1-57540-081-2*) Chockstone Pr.

San Diego on Foot. 9th rev. ed. Carol Mendel. (Illus.). 96p. 1994. pap. 6.95 (*0-935179-20-8*) Carol Mendel.

San Diego on My Mind. Falcon Press Staff. LC 89-80767. 120p. 1989. 29.95 (*1-56044-392-8*) Falcon Pr MT.

San Diego Originals: Profiles of the Movers & Shakers of California's First Community. Theodore W. Fuller. LC 87-1017. (Illus.). 280p. 1987. 19.95 (*0-943379-00-8*); pap. 12.95 (*0-943379-01-6*) CA Profiles.

San Diego Padres. Michael E. Goodman. (Baseball: The Great American Game Ser.). 48p. (J). (gr. 4-10). 1992. lib. bdg. 14.95 (*0-88682-463-X*) Creative Ed.

San Diego Padres. Chris W. Sehnert. (America's Game Ser.). (J). 1997. lib. bdg. 15.95 (*1-56239-674-9*) Abdo & Dghtrs.

***San Diego Padres.** rev. ed. Michael E. Goodman. LC 97-6340. (Baseball Ser.). (Illus.). 32p. (YA). (gr. 4 up). 1998. lib. bdg. 15.95 (*0-88682-923-2*) Creative Ed.

***San Diego Penny-Wise Parent Guide.** Julie S. Lin. 116p. 1996. spiral bd. 8.95 (*0-9656708-0-5*) J Lin Creative.

San Diego (Peterson) Lee Peterson. LC 91-73732. (Sunbelt Pictoral Bks.). (Illus.). 80p. (ENG, ITA, JPN & SPA.). 1991. 19.95 (*0-916251-45-4*) Sunbelt Pubns.

San Diego Relocation Guide. rev. ed. 1989. pap. 2.95 (*0-929617-01-0*) Garnet Pubns Group Inc.

San Diego Relocation Guide. 4th rev. ed. 1990. reprint ed. pap. 2.95 (*0-929617-02-9*) Garnet Pubns Group Inc.

***San Diego Retirement & Relocation Guide.** Arthur S. Grupe & Alene Christiano. (Illus.). 350p. (Orig.). 1996. pap. 19.95 (*1-56559-100-3*) HGI Mrktng.

San Diego Slattern. Dirk Fletcher. (Spur Giant Special Edition Ser.). 320p. 1996. mass mkt. 5.99 (*0-8439-4060-3*, Leisure Bks) Dorchester Pub Co.

San Diego Sports Guide. Ed. by Alex Farnsley. (Illus.). 384p. (Orig.). 1992. pap. 16.95 (*0-940093-04-9*) Farnsley Grp.

San Diego-Tijuana in Transition: A Regional Analysis. Ed. by Norris C. Clement & Eduardo Zepeda M. 130p. (Orig.). (C). 1993. pap. text ed. 15.00 (*0-925613-10-X*) SDSU Inst Reg Studies.

San Diego Trivia. Evelyn Kooperman. LC 88-61524. 406p. (Orig.). 1989. pap. 12.95 (*0-929629-01-9*) Silver Gate Pubns.

San Diego Trivia, No. II. Evelyn Kooperman. LC 93-93638. 762p. (Orig.). 1993. pap. 14.95 (*0-929629-02-7*) Silver Gate Pubns.

San Diego Trolley. Gena Holle. LC 90-46724. (Illus.). 104p. pap. 25.95 (*0-916374-92-0*, SPECIAL 114) Pentrex Pub.

San Diego Weddings. 2nd rev. ed. Gerri Samuels. (Coopwood & Fields Consumer Planning Guide Ser.). 250p. 1996. pap. 14.95 (*1-878991-15-9*) I Do Pub.

San Diego Where California Began. 5th rev. ed. James R. Mills. (Illus.). 84p. 1985. pap. 4.95 (*0-918740-04-5*) San Diego Hist.

San Diego Women's Haggadah. 2nd ed. Ed. by Jane S. Zones. LC 85-51376. (Illus.). 83p. 1986. pap. 7.95 (*0-9608054-5-1*) Womans Inst-Cont Jewish Ed.

***San Diego '98.** Fodors Travel Staff. 1997. pap. 14.00 (*0-679-03528-1*) Fodors Travel.

***San Diego/Orange Counties Street Guide & Directory: 1998 Edition.** Thomas Bros. Maps Staff. 376p. 1997. pap. 27.95 (*0-88130-904-4*) Thomas Bros Maps.

San Diego/Orange Counties Street Guide & Directory Including Imperial County: 1997 Edition. (Illus.). 376p. 1996. pap. 27.95 (*0-88130-841-2*) Thomas Bros Maps.

San Diego's Best Freebies & Bargains. 3rd ed. Sally Gary. 1995. pap. 12.95 (*0-933717-06-7*) Pacifica Bks.

San Diego's Best Freebies & Bargains. 3rd rev. ed. Sally R. Gary. 304p. 1995. pap. 12.95 (*0-933712-06-5*) Pacifica Bks.

***San Diego's Deals & Steals: A $ Money-Saving Resource Guide.** Sally R. Gary. 300p. (Orig.). 1997. pap. 14.95 (*0-933717-10-5*) Pacifica Bks.

San Diego's Historic Gaslamp Quarter: Then & Now. Susan H. Carrico & Kathleen Flanigan. (Illus.). 90p. (Orig.). 1990. pap. 7.95 (*0-685-36271-X*) S Carrico.

San Diego's Spirits: Ghosts & Hauntings in America's Southwest Corner. Richard L. Carrico. (Illus.). 95p. (Orig.). 1991. pap. text ed. 9.95 (*0-9625788-1-9*) S Carrico.

San Domingo: The Medicine Hat Stallion. Marguerite Henry. LC 91-46020. (Illus.). 240p. (J). (gr. 3-7). 1992. reprint ed. pap. 4.50 (*0-689-71631-1*, Aladdin Paperbacks) S&S Childrens.

San Fernando Valley: Past & Present. Lawrence C. Jorgensen et al. LC 81-83166. (Illus.). 264p. 1982. 22.50 (*0-941014-00-2*) Pac Rim Res.

San Franciscana Photographs of Playland. 1989. 12.50 (*0-934715-02-5*) San Franciscana.

San Franciscana Photographs of Sutro Baths. 1987. 10.00 (*0-934715-01-7*) San Franciscana.

San Franciscana Photographs of the Cliff House. LC 85-90624. 1985. 10.00 (*0-934715-00-9*) San Franciscana.

San Franciscana Photographs of Three World Fairs. 1994. 13.50 (*0-934715-04-1*) San Franciscana.

San Francisco. (Essential Guides Ser.). (Orig.). 1994. pap. 7.95 (*0-8442-8931-0*, Passport Bks) NTC Pub Grp.

San Francisco. (Fodor's Citypack Ser.). 1996. pap. 10.00 (*0-614-97926-9*) Fodors Travel.

San Francisco. Berlitz Staff. (Pocket Guides Ser.). 1994. pap. 7.95 (*2-8315-0739-1*) Berlitz.

San Francisco. Robert W. Cherny & William Issel. Ed. by Norris Hundley, Jr. & John A. Schutz. (Golden State Ser.). (Illus.). 136p. 1981. pap. 9.00 (*0-929651-20-0*) MTL.

San Francisco. Gerald L. French & Kelli French. LC 96-7275. (California Sights & Scenes Ser.). (Illus.). 64p. 1996. pap. 7.95 (*0-88415-836-5*, 5836) Gulf Pub.

San Francisco. Patricia Haddock. LC 88-20200. (Downtown America Bks.). (Illus.). 60p. (J). (gr. 3 up). 1988. lib. bdg. 13.95 (*0-87518-383-2*, Dillon Silver Burdett) Silver Burdett Pr.

San Francisco. Patricia Haddock. LC 88-20200. (Downtown America Bks.). (Illus.). 60p. (J). (gr. 3 up). 1988. pap. 7.95 (*0-382-24801-5*, Dillon Silver Burdett) Silver Burdett Pr.

***San Francisco.** Insight Guides Staff. (Insight Pocket Guides Ser.). 1996. pap. 12.95 (*0-395-81940-7*) HM.

***San Francisco.** Insight Guides Staff. (Insight Compact Guides Ser.). 1997. pap. 7.95 (*0-395-82935-6*) HM.

***San Francisco.** Deborah Kent. LC 96-54706. (Cities of the World Ser.). (J). 1997. write for info. (*0-516-20466-1*) Childrens.

***San Francisco.** St. Martin's Press Staff. (Marcellino's Restaurant Report Ser.). 1997. pap. 9.99 (*0-312-16922-1*) St Martin.

San Francisco. Santi Visalli. 1995. pap. 25.00 (*0-7893-0004-4*) Universe.

San Francisco. Photos by David Wakely. (Illus.). 112p. 1996. 35.00 (*1-55868-296-1*) Gr Arts Ctr Pub.

San Francisco. rev. ed. Herb Caen et al. (Illus.). 226p. 1993. 49.50 (*0-8109-3834-0*) Abrams.

San Francisco. Federal Writers' Project Staff. (American Guidebook Ser.). 538p. 1940. reprint ed. 59.00 (*0-403-02205-3*) Somerset Pub.

San Francisco: "The City" in Verse. Ruth Slonim. LC 92-8315. (Washington State University Press Art Ser.). 80p. 1992. reprint ed. pap. 9.95 (*0-87422-086-6*) Wash St U Pr.

San Francisco: A City Guide. Federal Writers' Project Staff & Writers Program-WPA Staff. (American Guide Ser.). 1989. reprint ed. lib. bdg. 69.00 (*0-7812-1059-3*, 1059) Rprt Serv.

San Francisco: A Photographic Journey. Carrie Williams. (Illus.). 1991. 15.99 (*0-517-05303-9*) Random Hse Value.

San Francisco: A Picture Memory. 1990. 8.99 (*0-517-01751-2*) Random Hse Value.

San Francisco: City Guide. Tony Wheeler. (Illus.). 288p. 1996. pap. 11.95 (*0-86442-333-0*) Lonely Planet.

San Francisco: International Port of Call: An Illustrated Maritime History of the Golden Gate. Robert J. Schwendinger. LC 84-25733. 176p. 1984. 22.95 (*0-89781-122-4*) Am Historical Pr.

***San Francisco: Sidewalk Offline Restaurant Guide.** Ed. by Sidewalk.com Editors. (Sidewalk Ser.). 336p. (Orig.). 1997. pap. 12.95 (*1-57061-102-5*) Sasquatch Bks.

San Francisco: The City's Sights & Secrets. Text by Leah Garchik. LC 94-42301. 120p. 1995. 29.95 (*0-8118-0942-0*); pap. 14.95 (*0-8118-0917-X*) Chronicle Bks.

San Francisco: The Ultimate Guide. Randolph Delehanty. LC 94-17964. 496p. 1995. pap. 15.95 (*0-8118-0443-7*) Chronicle Bks.

***San Francisco: Twenty Corner Markets & One in the Middle of the Block.** Photos by Paula Chamlee. (Illus.). 32p. Date not set. 50.00 (*1-888899-00-X*) Lodima.

San Francisco - Cooking with Betty Evans. Betty Evans. LC 90-70839. (Illus.). 96p. (Orig.). 1990. pap. 6.95 (*0-931104-29-7*) Sunflower Ink.

San Francisco - San Mateo 1995: McCormack's Guides. 1995. pap. 8.95 (*0-931299-50-0*) McCormacks Guides.

San Francisco - San Mateo 1996: McCormack's Guides. 1995. pap. 8.95 (*0-931299-57-8*) McCormacks Guides.

San Francisco--I Love It! Pace International Research, Inc. Staff. (AAA Video Ser.). (Illus.). 144p. 1984. text ed. 8.95 (*0-89209-047-2*); pap. text ed. 4.25 (*0-89209-076-6*); audio 3.25 (*0-89209-077-4*); vhs 60.00 (*0-89209-044-8*) Pace Intl Res.

San Francisco a Certain Style. Diane D. Saeks. Ed. by Nion McEvoy. (Illus.). 204p. (Orig.). 1989. 35.00 (*0-87701-570-8*) Chronicle Bks.

San Francisco a Certain Style. Diane D. Saeks. Ed. by Nion McEvoy. (Illus.). 204p. (Orig.). 1992. pap. 22.95 (*0-8118-0199-3*) Chronicle Bks.

San Francisco, a History of the Pacific Coast Metropolis, 2 vols. John P. Young. (Illus.). 969p. 1993. reprint ed. lib. bdg. 99.00 (*0-8328-3508-0*) Higginson Bk Co.

San Francisco a la Carte. 512p. 1991. pap. 19.95 (*0-385-41772-1*) Doubleday.

San Francisco, a Pageant. Charles C. Dobie. 1992. reprint ed. lib. bdg. 75.00 (*0-7812-5026-9*) Rprt Serv.

San Francisco Access. rev. ed. Richard S. Wurman. (Access Travel Guides Ser.). (Illus.). 192p. 1987. pap. 12.95 (*0-318-39987-3*, Access NY) HarpC.

San Francisco Adventures. Charles C. Dobie. LC 70-101800. (Short Story Index Reprint Ser.). 1977. 19.95 (*0-8369-3188-2*) Ayer.

San Francisco Almanac. Ed. by Walter Biller. (Illus.). 224p. (Orig.). 1992. pap. 6.95 (*0-9628427-1-0*) SF Almanac.

San Francisco Almanac. Gladys Hansen. LC 94-19753. 464p. 1995. pap. 16.95 (*0-8118-0841-6*) Chronicle Bks.

San Francisco Almanac. Samuel F. Hunter. Ed. by Walter Biller. (Illus.). 380p. (Orig.). 1991. pap. 12.95 (*0-9628427-0-2*) SF Almanac.

San Francisco & Beyond: 101 Affordable Excursions: Fun, Historic, Cultural & Outdoors Things to Do All for Seven Dollars or Less Per Person. 2nd ed. Pamela P. Hegarty. 272p. 1994. pap. 10.95 (*0-9630791-2-3*) Trvl For Less.

San Francisco & Northern California. LC 94-3379. (Eyewitness Travel Guides Ser.). (Illus.). 312p. 1994. pap. 22.95 (*1-56458-645-6*) DK Pub Inc.

San Francisco & the Bay Area. Barry Parr. Ed. by Deke Castleman. (Discover America Ser.). (Illus.). 396p. 1992. 22.95 (*1-878867-02-4*, Compass Amrcn); pap. 12.95 (*1-878867-00-8*, Compass Amrcn) Fodors Travel.

San Francisco & the Golden Empire. Basil Woon. 1992. reprint ed. lib. bdg. 75.00 (*0-7812-5104-4*) Rprt Serv.

San Francisco Architecture: The Illustrated Guide to Over 600 of the Best Buildings, Parks & Public Artworks in Bay Area. Sally B. Woodbridge. 240p. 1992. pap. 16.95 (*0-87701-897-9*) Chronicle Bks.

San Francisco at Its Best. Robert S. Kane. 300p. 1995. pap. 12.95 (*0-8442-9603-1*, Passport Bks) NTC Pub Grp.

San Francisco Bar Book. Ed. by William Ristow. LC 81-66873. (Illus.). 128p. 1981. pap. 3.95 (*0-913192-03-1*) SF Bay Guardian.

San Francisco Bay: Use & Protection. Ed. by W. J. Kockelman & Alan E. Leviton. LC 82-71291. 310p. (Orig.). 1982. 17.95 (*0-934394-04-0*) AAASPD.

San Francisco Bay Area: Its Problems & Future, 3 vols., 1. Ed. by Stanley Scott. LC 66-7975. (Franklin K. Lane Project Ser.). 351p. reprint ed. pap. 94.80 (*0-7837-2130-7*, 2042412) Bks Demand.

San Francisco Bay Area: Its Problems & Future, 3 vols., 2. Ed. by Stanley Scott. LC 66-7975. (Franklin K. Lane Project Ser.). 385p. reprint ed. pap. 109.80 (*0-7837-2352-0*) Bks Demand.

San Francisco Bay Area: Its Problems & Future, 3 vols., 3. Ed. by Stanley Scott. LC 66-7975. (Franklin K. Lane Project Ser.). 564p. reprint ed. pap. 160.80 (*0-7837-2353-9*) Bks Demand.

San Francisco Bay Area: The Best 200 Restaurants. 2nd ed. Ed. by Tom Demaree. (Menu Ser.). (Illus.). 448p. (Orig.). 1993. pap. 12.95 (*0-9628274-6-0*) D Thomas Pub.

***San Francisco Bay Area: The Nation's Laboratory for New ideas.** Coreen Murray. Ed. by Nancy M. Leichner. (Illus.). 180p. Date not set. text ed. 49.95 (*0-9634100-4-0*) Wyndham Pubns.

San Francisco Bay Area - On Shaky Ground. 32p. 1987. 7.00 (*0-317-05674-3*, P87001EQK) Assn Bay Area.

San Francisco Bay Area Coast. Nancy Salcedo. (Twelve Short Hikes Ser.). (Illus.). 32p. (Orig.). 1997. pap. 4.95 (*1-57540-021-9*) Chockstone Pr.

San Francisco Bay Area East Bay. Nancy Salcedo. (Twelve Short Hikes Ser.). (Illus.). 32p. (Orig.). 1997. pap. 4.95 (*1-57540-018-9*) Chockstone Pr.

San Francisco Bay Area Economy: Shifting Structure & Growth. 17p. 1989. 10.00 (*0-317-05664-6*, P89002PRO) Assn Bay Area.

San Francisco Bay Area North Bay. Nancy Salcedo. (Twelve Short Hikes Ser.). (Illus.). 32p. (Orig.). 1997. pap. 4.95 (*1-57540-020-0*) Chockstone Pr.

San Francisco Bay Area South Bay. Nancy Salcedo. (Twelve Short Hikes Ser.). (Illus.). (Orig.). 1997. pap. 4.95 (*1-57540-019-7*) Chockstone Pr.

San Francisco Bay Earthquake 1989: Portraits of Tragedy & Courage. Los Angeles Times Staff. Ed. by Craig Turner. (Illus.). 96p. (Orig.). 1989. pap. 10.95 (*0-9619095-1-X*) LA Times.

San Francisco Bay Shoreline Guide. California State Coastal Conservancy Staff. LC 94-17818. 1995. pap. 14.95 (*0-520-08878-6*) U CA Pr.

San Francisco Bay Tripper: Twenty Exciting Day Trips in the San Francisco Bay Area. Jocelyn Becker. (Illus.). 208p. (Orig.). 1994. pap. 10.00 (*0-9637073-0-2*) Brighter Bks.

San Francisco, CA. (Streetfinder Ser.). (Illus.). 1995. pap. 12.95 (*0-528-91355-7*) Rand McNally.

San Francisco Calamity by Earthquake & Fire. Charles Morris. (Illus.). 224p. 1986. pap. 9.95 (*0-8065-0984-8*, Citadel Pr) Carol Pub Group.

San Francisco Chinatown: A Walking Tour. Shirley Fong-Torres. LC 91-72060. (Illus.). 244p. (Orig.). 1991. pap. 10.95 (*0-8351-2436-3*) China Bks.

San Francisco Chronicle Cookbook. Ed. by Michael Bauer & Fran Irwin. (Illus.). 448p. 1997. pap. 18.95 (*0-8118-1445-9*) Chronicle Bks.

San Francisco Clearing House Certificates: Last of California's Private Money. Robert J. Chandler. 32p. (Orig.). 1986. pap. text ed. 3.95 (*0-932151-01-9*) Gypsyfoot Ent.

San Francisco Confidential: Tales of Scandal & Excess from the Town That's Seen Everything. Ray Mungo. LC 94-12615. 1994. 19.95 (*1-55972-246-0*) Carol Pub Group.

***San Francisco County Commerce & Industry Directory, 1997.** 27th ed. 272p. 1997. pap. 75.00 (*1-57541-037-0*) Database Pub Co.

San Francisco County Street Guide & Directory: 1997 Edition. (Illus.). 112p. 1996. pap. 16.95 (*0-88130-789-0*) Thomas Bros Maps.

***San Francisco County Street Guide & Directory: 1998 Edition.** Thomas Bros. Maps Staff. 96p. 1997. pap. 16.95 (*0-88130-905-2*) Thomas Bros Maps.

San Francisco Earthquake. Sue Hamilton. Ed. by John Hamilton. LC 88-71723. (Day of Disaster Ser.). (Illus.). 32p. (J). (gr. 4). 1989. lib. bdg. 12.98 (*0-939179-43-1*) Abdo & Dghtrs.

San Francisco, Eighteen Sixty-Five to Nineteen Thirty-Two: Politics, Power, & Urban Development. William Issel & Robert W. Cherny. (Illus.). 352p. 1986. pap. 22.50 (*0-520-06033-4*) U CA Pr.

San Francisco Encore. 464p. 1991. pap. 17.95 (*0-385-41773-X*) Doubleday.

San Francisco Engagement Calendar, 1991. (Illus.). 12p. (Orig.). 1991. pap. 3.50 (*1-878395-07-6*) Smith-Western.

San Francisco Fair: Treasure Island, 1939-1940. Pat Carpenter & Paul Totah. (Illus.). 168p. 1989. 20.00 (*0-942087-02-X*) Scottwall Assocs.

***San Francisco for Less: The Total Guidebook.** Christina Prostano. 1998. pap. text ed. 19.95 (*0-9525437-9-6*, Pub. by Metropolis Promotions UK) IPG Chicago.

San Francisco Forty Niners. Steve Potts. (NFL Today Ser.). (J). (gr. 4 up). 1991. lib. bdg. 14.95 (*0-88682-383-8*) Creative Ed.

San Francisco Forty Niners: Team of the Decade: The Inside Story of How They Came from Nowhere to Win Four Super Bowls, Updated to Include the 1989-90 Championship Season. rev. ed. Michael W. Tuckman & Jeff Schultz. 280p. 1990. reprint ed. pap. 13.95 (*1-55958-053-4*) Prima Pub.

San Francisco Free & Easy. rev. ed. Ed. by William Ristow. LC 80-66932. (Illus.). 352p. 1980. pap. 5.95 (*0-913192-02-3*) SF Bay Guardian.

San Francisco Gay Guide. 4th ed. Brett Thomas & William Wolf. LC 94-92385. (Illus.). 208p. (Orig.). 1996. pap. 10.95 (*0-9633794-1-0*) DELCOM.

San Francisco Giants. Michael E. Goodman. (Baseball: The Great American Game Ser.). 48p. (J). (gr. 4-10). 1992. lib. bdg. 14.94 (*0-88682-453-2*) Creative Ed.

***San Francisco Giants.** Chris W. Sehnert. LC 96-17921. (America's Game Ser.). 1997. lib. bdg. 15.95 (*1-56239-683-8*) Abdo & Dghtrs.

***San Francisco Giants.** rev. ed. Michael E. Goodman. LC 97-6341. (Baseball Ser.). (Illus.). 32p. (YA). (gr. 4 up). 1998. lib. bdg. 15.95 (*0-88682-924-0*) Creative Ed.

***San Francisco Giants: A 40-Year Anniversary.** Glenn Dickey. LC 96-6180. (Illus.). 208p. (Orig.). 1997. pap. 19.95 (*0-942627-48-2*) Woodford Pubng.

San Francisco Giants Almanac: Thirty Years of Baseball by the Bay. Nick Peters. (Illus.). 200p. (Orig.). 1988. 30.00 (*1-55643-041-8*); pap. 8.95 (*1-55643-040-X*) North Atlantic.

San Francisco Gold. Ann Zavala. 288p. 1995. 21.95 (*0-312-85441-2*) Forge NYC.

***San Francisco Gold.** Ann Zavala. 1996. mass mkt. 5.99 (*0-8125-2360-1*) Forge NYC.

San Francisco Graphic Design. Gerry Rosentswieg. 256p. 1993. 45.00 (*0-942604-29-6*) Madison Square.

San Francisco Green Guide. Ed. by Michelin Travel Publications, Staff. 1996. per. 18.00 (*2-06-159501-4*, 1595) Michelin.

San Francisco Guide. Stephanie Gold. (Illus.). 464p. (Orig.). 1996. pap. 14.95 (*1-883323-37-1*) Open Rd Pub.

San Francisco in Fiction: Essays in a Regional Literature. Ed. by David Fine & Paul Skenazy. LC 95-4389. 256p. 1995. pap. 16.95 (*0-8263-1621-2*) U of NM Pr.

San Francisco in the 1850's: 32 Photographic Views by G. R. Fardon. G. R. Fardon. (Illus.). 1977. reprint ed. pap. 7.95 (*0-486-23459-2*) Dover.

San Francisco Interiors. Diane D. Saeks. (Illus.). 204p. 1995. 35.00 (*0-8118-0869-6*) Chronicle Bks.

San Francisco Irish, 1884-1880. R. A. Burchell. LC 79-65764. 1980. 45.00 (*0-520-04003-1*) U CA Pr.

San Francisco Jobbank, 1996. Adams Publishing Staff. 1995. pap. text ed. 15.95 (*1-55850-569-5*) Adams Media.

San Francisco Jobbank, 1997. Adams Publishing Staff. 1996. pap. text ed. 15.95 (*1-55850-673-X*) Adams Media.

San Francisco Little Restaurant Guide. Camaro Editors. (Illus.). 1985. pap. 4.95 (*0-913290-86-6*) Camaro Pub.

San Francisco Memoirs 1835-1851: Eyewitness Accounts of the Birth of a City. Compiled & Intro. by Malcolm E. Barker. (Illus.). 320p. (Orig.). 1994. pap. 16.95 (*0-930235-04-5*) Londonborn Pubns.

San Francisco Murals: Community Creates Its Muse, 1914-1994. Timothy W. Drescher. LC 94-66695. (Illus.). 124p. (Orig.). 1994. pap. 19.95 (*1-880654-06-7*) Pogo Pr.

San Francisco Night & Day. Fodor's Travel Staff. 1998. pap. 18.00 (*0-679-03235-5*) Fodors Travel.

***San Francisco Nightlife Guide: Internet Edition.** 10th rev. ed. 95p. 1997. pap. 10.95 (*1-879642-06-9*) SF Insight.

San Francisco 97: On the Loose, on the Cheap, off the Beaten Path. Fodor's Travel Staff. (Berkeley Travel Guides Ser.). 1996. pap. 13.95 (*0-679-03185-5*) Fodors Travel.

***San Francisco Nude.** Hisaka Kojima. (Illus.). 135p. (Orig.). 1996. pap. 49.95 (*4-416-89509-7*, Pub. by Seibundo Shinkosh JA) Bks Nippan.

S

An Asterisk (*) at the beginning of an entry indicates that the title is appearing in BIP for the first time.

***San Francisco on a Shoestring.** 10th rev. ed. Louis E. Madison. 224p. 1997. pap. 8.95 (0-912125-08-X) L E Madison.

San Francisco on a Shoestring: The Intelligent Traveler's & Native's Guide to Budget Living. Louis E. Madison. 1995. pap. text ed. 8.95 (0-912125-07-1) L E Madison.

***San Francisco Opera: Celebrating the First Seventy-Five Years.** Joan Chatfield-Taylor. LC 97-5085. 1997. 50.00 (0-8118-1368-1) Chronicle Bks.

San Francisco Oracle Facsimile Edition. deluxe ed. Intro. by Allen Cohen. (Illus.). 420p. 1990. reprint ed. 700.00 (0-916147-12-6) Regent Pr.

San Francisco Oracle Facsimile Edition. Intro. by Allen Cohen. (Illus.). 420p. 1990. reprint ed. lib. bdg. 175.00 (0-916147-11-8) Regent Pr.

San Francisco Panoramic Cards: Postcard Bk. T Schrack. 1995. pap. 11.95 (0-8118-0890-4) Chronicle Bks.

San Francisco Passenger Departure Lists: 15 July to 31 December 1851. Peter E. Carr. (San Francisco Passenger Departure Lists Ser.: Vol. III). (Orig.). 1993. pap. 15.95 (0-9631209-7-2) TCI Gene Res.

San Francisco Passenger Departure Lists, Vol. I: September 30, 1850 to December 31, 1850. Peter E. Carr. LC 91-90704. 139p. 1991. pap. 15.95 (0-9631209-2-1) TCI Gene Res.

San Francisco Passenger Departure Lists, Vol. II: January 3 to June 14, 1851. Peter E. Carr. LC 92-90288. 160p. (Orig.). 1992. pap. 15.95 (0-9631209-4-8) TCI Gene Res.

San Francisco Passenger Departure Lists, Vol. IV: 15 January to 30 June 1852. Peter E. Carr. 175p. (Orig.). 1993. pap. 15.95 (0-9631209-8-0) TCI Gene Res.

San Francisco Peaks. 32p. 1985. 4.95 (0-89734-068-X, PL56-3) Mus Northern Ariz.

San Francisco Peninsula Bike Trails: Road & Mountain Bicycle Rides Through San Francisco & San Mateo Counties. Conrad J. Boisvert. (Bay Area Bike Trails Ser.). (Illus.). 128p. (Orig.). 1991. pap. 11.95 (0-9621694-3-9) Penngrove Pubns.

***San Francisco Peninsula Birdwatching.** Sequoia Audubon Society Staff. Ed. by Cliff Richer. (Illus.). 1996. pap. 14.95 (0-9614301-1-7) Sequoia Aud Soc.

San Francisco Plenary Meeting of the Trilateral Commission. Ed. by Andrew V. Frankel & Charles B. Heck. (Trialogue Ser.: No. 39). (Illus.). 64p. (Orig.). 1987. pap. 6.00 (0-930503-10-4) Trilateral Comm.

San Francisco Poetry Renaissance, 1955-1960. Warren French. (Twayne's United States Authors Ser.: No. 575). 168p. (C). 1991. 24.95 (0-8057-7621-4) Macmillan.

San Francisco Renaissance: Poetics & Community at Mid-Century. Michael Davidson. (Cambridge Studies in American Literature & Culture: No. 35). 248p. (C). 1991. pap. text ed. 18.95 (0-521-42304-X) Cambridge U Pr.

San Francisco Renaissance: Poetics & Community at Mid-Century. Michael Davison. (Cambridge Studies in American Literature & Culture: No. 35). 264p. (C). 1989. text ed. 59.95 (0-521-25880-4) Cambridge U Pr.

San Francisco Restaurant ACCESS. 2nd ed. HarperReference Staff. 240p. 1996. pap. 13.00 (0-06-277192-2, Harper Ref) HarpC.

San Francisco-San Mateo 1997: McCormack's Guides. 1996. pap. 9.95 (0-931299-66-7) McCormacks Guides.

San Francisco Scandal: The California of George Gordon. Albert Shumate. LC 76-17948. (Illus.). 271p. 1994. 27.50 (0-87062-118-1) A H Clark.

San Francisco School of Abstract Expressionism. Susan Landauer. LC 94-47988. (Illus.). 290p. 1996. pap. 34.95 (0-520-08611-2) U CA Pr.

San Francisco School of Abstract Expressionism. Susan Landauer. LC 94-47988. (Illus.). 290p. (C). 1996. 60.00 (0-520-08610-4) U CA Pr.

San Francisco Ship Passenger Lists, 4 vols. Incl. Vol. 2. April 6, 1850 to November 4, 1851. LC 65-13821. 1966. 24.95 (0-911792-01-5); Vol. 4. June 17, 1852 to 1853. LC 65-13821. 1970. 24.95 (0-911792-03-1); LC 65-13821. (Ship, Rail & Wagon Train Ser.). 1965. write for info. (0-318-55716-9) SF Hist Records.

San Francisco Shipping Conspiracies of World War One. David H. Grover. (Illus.). 170p. (Orig.). 1996. pap. 11.95 (0-9623935-3-3) West Maritime Pr.

***San Francisco Sourcebook.** Macmillan Services Group Staff. 1992. 39.95 (0-688-11770-8) Morrow.

San Francisco Stage: A History. Edmond M. Gagey. LC 77-104244. 264p. 1970. reprint ed. text ed. 59.75 (0-8371-3927-9, GAFS, Greenwood Pr) Greenwood.

San Francisco Stage, Pt. 1: From Gold Rush to Golden Spike, 1849-1869. Misha Berson. (Journals: No. 2). 100p. 1989. pap. 15.00 (1-881106-01-2) SF Perf Arts Lib.

San Francisco Stage, Pt. 2: From Golden Spike to Great Earthquake, 1869-1906. Misha Berson. Ed. by David Gere. (SF Palm Ser.: No. 4). (Illus.). 146p. (Orig.). (C). 1992. pap. 15.00 (1-881106-03-9) SF Perf Arts Lib.

San Francisco Stages: A Concise History, 1849-1986. Dean Goodman. LC 86-62236. (Illus.). 222p. 1986. pap. 10.95 (0-939477-01-7) Micro Pro Litera Pr.

San Francisco Stories: Great Writers on the City. Ed. by John Miller. LC 89-25337. 304p. (Orig.). 1990. pap. 11.95 (0-87701-669-0) Chronicle Bks.

San Francisco Street Secrets. David Eames. Ed. by April G. Ping. LC 94-76114. (Illus.). 192p. (Orig.). 1995. pap. 10.95 (0-935182-75-6) Gem Guides Bk.

San Francisco Survival Guide: A Complete Resource Guide. Molly Dick. 125p. 1993. pap. 11.95 (0-9635622-0-7) CrossRds Calif.

San Francisco, the Musical History Tour: A Guide to Over 200 of the Bay Area's Most Memorable Music Sites. Joel Selvin. LC 95-35977. 176p. 1996. pap. 12.95 (0-8118-1007-0) Chronicle Bks.

San Francisco, the Way It Was Then & Now. Phyllis Zauner. (Western Mini-Histories Ser.). (Illus.). 64p. (Orig.). 1980. pap. 7.95 (0-936914-04-1) Zanel Pubns.

San Francisco Thrillers: True Crimes & Dark Mysteries from the City by the Bay. Ed. by John Miller & Tim Smith. LC 95-12957. (Illus.). 272p. 1995. pap. 14.95 (0-8118-1043-7) Chronicle Bks.

San Francisco Tragedy: The Brevet Major George Taylor Story. Richard B. Taylor. (Illus.). 200p. (Orig.). 1993. pap. write for info. (0-9616633-5-9) Beehive NV.

San Francisco Uncovered. Larenda L. Roberts. LC 95-36591. 296p. 1996. pap. 16.95 (1-55622-395-1, Seaside Pr) Wordware Pub.

San Francisco Waterfront Cookbook. Joseph Orlando. (Illus.). 144p. 1991. reprint ed. pap. 9.95 (0-89087-652-5) Celestial Arts.

San Francisco, You're History! A Chronicle of the People Who Helped Create California's Wildest City. J. Kingston Pierce. (Illus.). 304p. (Orig.). 1995. pap. 14.95 (1-57061-007-X) Sasquatch Bks.

San Francisco, 1995: The Grandmaster Invitational Chess Tournament. James Eade. LC 95-78533. (Competitive Chess Ser.). (Illus.). 140p. (Orig.). Date not set. pap. 14.95 (1-886040-19-2) Hypermodern Pr.

San Francisco 49ers. Bob Italia. LC 95-16472. (J). 1996. lib. bdg. 15.98 (1-56239-466-5) Abdo & Dghtrs.

San Francisco 49ers. 2nd rev. ed. Jack Harris. (NFL Today Ser.). (Illus.). 32p. (J). (gr. 4-8). 1996. lib. bdg. 14.95 (0-88682-786-8) Creative Ed.

San Francisco 49ers: A Fiftieth Anniversary Celebration. Glenn Dickey. (Illus.). 256p. 1995. 34.95 (1-57036-199-1) Turner Pub GA.

San Francisco 49ers: A Fiftieth Anniversary Collection. Glenn Dickey. 1995. pap. 24.95 (1-57036-258-0) Turner Pub GA.

***San Francisco '98.** Fodors Travel Staff. 1997. pap. 14.50 (0-679-03529-X) Fodors Travel.

San Francisco/Alameda/Contra Costa Counties Street Guide & Directory: 1997 Edition. (Illus.). 384p. 1996. pap. 35.95 (0-88130-790-4) Thomas Bros Maps.

***San Francisco/Alameda/Contra Costa Counties Street Guide & Directory: 1998 Edition.** Thomas Bros. Maps Staff. 368p. 1997. pap. 35.95 (0-88130-942-7) Thomas Bros Maps.

San Francisco's Burning. Helen Adam. 1985. 25.00 (0-914610-43-0); pap. 15.00 (0-914610-33-3) Hanging Loose.

San Francisco's Cable Cars: Riding the Rope Through Past & Present. Joyce Jansen. Ed. by Kate Hanley. LC 95-60137. (Illus.). 152p. (Orig.). 1995. pap. 19.95 (0-942627-12-1) Woodford Pubng.

San Francisco's Cooking Secrets: Starring the Best Restaurants & Inns of San Francisco. 6th rev. ed. Kathleen D. Fish. Ed. by Fred Hernandez. (Illus.). 288p. 1997. pap. text ed. 14.95 (1-883214-00-9) Bon Vivant Pr.

San Francisco's Greek Colony: An Evolution of an Ethnic Community. George P. Daskarolis. 208p. (Orig.). 1995. pap. 10.95 (1-880971-13-5) Light&Life Pub Co MN.

San Francisco's International Expositions, a Bibliography, Including Listings for the Mechanics' Institute Exhibitions. Marvin R. Nathan. LC 95-78357. (Illus.). 128p. 1995. text ed. 25.95 (0-9647514-0-2); pap. text ed. 11.95 (0-9647514-1-0) Lawthorne Pr.

San Francisco/San Mateo Counties Street Guide & Directory: 1997 Edition. (Illus.). 200p. 1996. pap. 27.95 (0-88130-792-0) Thomas Bros Maps.

***San Francisco/San Mateo Counties Street Guide & Directory: 1998 Edition.** Thomas Bros. Maps Staff. 176p. 1997. pap. 27.95 (0-88130-906-0) Thomas Bros Maps.

***San Fransico Bay Area Jobbank.** Date not set. pap. 16.95 (1-55850-790-6) Adams Media.

San Gabriel del Yungue As Seen by an Archaeologist. Florence H. Ellis. LC 89-4212. (Illus.). (Orig.). 1989. pap. 10.95 (0-86534-129-X) Sunstone Pr.

San Gabriel Mountains. Roy Murphy & Julia Murphy. (Illus.). 88p. 1985. 25.00 (0-9615421-0-1) Big Santa Hist.

San Gabriel Valley: Chronicle of an Abundant Land. William King. 1990. 27.95 (0-89781-344-8) Am Historical Pr.

***San Gabriels.** John W. Robinson. 311p. 34.95 (0-9615421-5-2) Big Santa Hist.

San, Hunter-Gatherers of the Kalahari: A Study in Ecological Anthropology. Jiro Tanaka. 199p. 1980. 29.50 (0-86008-276-8, Pub. by U of Tokyo JA) Col U Pr.

San Isabel National Forest Recreation Guide. Outdoor Books & Maps, Inc. Staff. 160p. 1995. pap. 12.95 (0-930657-14-4) Outdr Bks & Maps.

San Jacinto Battleground State Historical Park: A Teacher's Curriculum Guide. Connie Carden & Patti Ballard. Ed. by Larry Spasic et al. (Illus.). 147p. ring bd. 10.75 (0-940803-01-1) SJ Mus Hist Assn.

***San Jacintos.** John W. Robinson & Risher. 251p. 32.95 (0-9615421-6-0) Big Santa Hist.

San Joaquin, the Sierra, & Beyond. Bill Sanford. LC 94-60922. (Illus.). (Orig.). 1994. pap. 12.95 (0-934136-53-X) Western Tanager.

San Jose: A Personal View. Wes Peyton. Ed. by Kathleen Muller. (Illus.). 100p. 1989. 12.95 (0-914139-08-8) Hist Mus San Jose.

San Jose: City with a Past. Ed. by Kathleen Muller. (Illus.). 112p. 1988. 22.95 (0-914139-07-X) Hist Mus San Jose.

San Jose - And Other Famous Places. Harry Farrell. (Illus.). 1983. 12.95 (0-914139-00-2) Hist Mus San Jose.

***San Jose & Silicon Valley: Primed for the 21st Century.** Chris DiSalvo & Judith H. Semas. LC 97-16064. 1997. write for info. (1-885352-56-5) Community Comm.

San Jose Bride Book. Deborah Wood. 240p. 1987. pap. 16.95 (0-937533-04-1) TEC Pubns.

San Jose de Gracia: Mexican Village in Transition. Luis E. Gonzalez. Tr. by John Upton from SPA. LC 73-11495. (Texas Pan American Ser.). (Illus.). 406p. 1974. pap. 18.95 (0-292-77571-7) U of Tex Pr.

***San Jose Historia Biblica Condensada.** A. Lodders. (SPA.). 1989. 4.75 (0-89942-771-5, 771/04S) Catholic Bk Pub.

San Jose Reflections. Edith Brackway. 1977. 13.00 (0-912314-18-4); pap. 4.90 (0-912314-17-6) Academy Santa Clara.

San Jose Sharks. Joan St. Peter. LC 93-48450. (NHL Today Ser.). (J). 1995. lib. bdg. 15.95 (0-88682-744-2) Creative Ed.

San Jose with Kids: A Family Guide to the Greater San Jose - Santa Clara Region. Dierdre W. Honnold et al. LC 95-60696. (Illus.). 212p. (Orig.). 1995. pap. 11.95 (0-9640370-2-5) Wrdwrights Intl.

San Juan. Kathryn Wilde. 32p. 1991. 5.95 (0-89734-107-4, PL62-4) Mus Northern Ariz.

San Juan: Evangelio Segun San Juan. (Noeva Version Internacional Ser.). 48p. 1990. pap. (1-880349-51-5) Pocket Testament.

San Juan & Gulf Islands Best Places: A Destination Guide. (Best Places Destination Guides Ser.). (Illus.). 192p. (Orig.). 1995. pap. 11.95 (1-57061-031-2) Sasquatch Bks.

San Juan Bautista: Gateway to Spanish Texas. Robert S. Weddle. (Illus.). 501p. 1968. 35.00 (0-292-73306-2) U of Tex Pr.

San Juan Bautista: Gateway to Spanish Texas. Robert S. Weddle. (Illus.). 501p. 1991. reprint ed. pap. 15.95 (0-292-77651-9) U of Tex Pr.

San Juan Bautista: The Town, Park & Mission. Charles Clough. LC 95-61174. (Illus.). 144p. (Orig.). 1995. pap. 18.95 (1-884995-07-1) Word Dancer.

San Juan Canyons. LC 86-70538. (Waterproof River Runners Guides Ser.). 64p. 1986. 12.95 (0-9616591-0-6) Canon Pubs.

San Juan County in the Eighteen Nineties. pap. 2.50 (0-9608000-0-X) San Juan County.

San Juan Current Guide: Including the Gulf Islands & Strait of Juan de Fuca. 3rd ed. Island Canoe, Inc. Staff. (Illus.). 5p. 1995. pap. 15.95 (0-918439-19-1) Island Canoe.

San Juan de la Cruz: Mysticism & Sartrean Existentialism. Robert R. Ellis. LC 91-31791. (Medieval & Early Modern Mysticism Ser.: Vol. 1). 197p. (C). 1992. text ed. 40.95 (0-8204-1732-7) P Lang Pubng.

San Juan de la Cruz & el Islam: Estudio Sobre las Filiaciones Semiticas de su Literatura. Luce B. Lopez. 1986. 13.00 (968-12-0294-5) U of PR Pr.

***San Juan de la Cruz & Fray Cuis de Leon.** Ed. by Mary M. Gaylord & Francisco M. Villanueva. 309p. (SPA.). 1996. 22.00 (0-936388-76-5) Juan de la Cuesta.

San Juan Hill. Will Henry. 320p. 1996. reprint ed. mass mkt. 4.99 (0-8439-4045-X, Leisure Bks) Dorchester Pub Co.

San Juan Historical Sites. C. Gregory Crampton. (Glen Canyon Ser.: No. 22). reprint ed. 24.50 (0-404-60709-8) AMS Pr.

San Juan Island Classics Cookbook. Janice Veal & Dawn Ashbach. (Illus.). 223p. (Orig.). 1987. pap. 16.95 (0-9615580-2-4) Island Pubs WA.

San Juan Islands, Afoot & Afloat. 3rd ed. Marge Mueller & Ted Mueller. LC 94-44878. 1995. pap. 14.95 (0-89886-434-8) Mountaineers.

San Juan Islands Wildlife: A Handbook for Exploring Nature Year Around. Evelyn Adams. (Illus.). 256p. 1995. pap. 14.95 (0-89886-420-8) Mountaineers.

San Juan Mountains: A Climbing & Hiking Guide. Robert F. Rosebrough. LC 86-4530. (Illus.). 274p. 1986. pap. 14.95 (0-917895-07-X) Johnson Bks.

***San Juan National Forest.** Outdoor Books & Maps Inc. Staff. 72p. 1997. 9.95 (0-930657-13-6) Outdr Bks & Maps.

San Juan National Historic Site. rev. ed. Mark Johnson. 32p. (SPA.). 1994. pap. 2.95 (0-915992-70-1) Eastern Acorn.

San Juan River Chronicle. Steven J. Meyers. (Illus.). 160p. 1994. 19.95 (1-55821-277-9) Lyons & Burford.

***San Juan River Chronicle: Personal Remembrances of One of America's Best-Inown Trout Streams.** 2nd ed. Steven J. Meyers. 160p. 1997. reprint ed. pap. 14.95 (1-55821-600-6) Lyons & Burford.

San Juan Skyway. Scott S. Warren. LC 90-60506. (Illus.). 64p. (Orig.). 1990. pap. 8.95 (1-56044-039-2) Falcon Pr MT.

San Juan the Powder Keg Island: The Settlers Own Stories. Joanne Bailey-Cummings & Alan Cummings. (Illus.). 208p. (Orig.). 1987. pap. 7.95 (0-944257-00-3) San Juan Ent.

San Lorenzo. Ed. by William E. Wallace. LC 95-4441. (Michelangelo: Selected Scholarship in English Ser.: Vol. 3). (Illus.). 496p. 1995. text ed. 99.00 (0-8153-1826-X) Garland.

San Lorenzo: Guide to the Laurentian Complex. Bruno Santi. (Illus.). 128p. 1992. 19.95 (0-8161-0610-X) G K Hall.

San Luis Obispo County: Looking Backward into the Middle Kingdom. rev. ed. Daniel E. Krieger. (Illus.). 134p. (C). 1990. reprint ed. pap. 17.95 (0-945092-11-3) EZ Nature.

San Luis Obispo County Coast & Castle. Vicki Leon. (Illus.). 72p. (Orig.). 1986. pap. 9.95 (0-918303-11-7) Blake Pub.

San Luis Obispo County Trail Guide. 2nd ed. Illus. by Margaret Foster. 160p. 1989. pap. 8.95 (0-914598-89-9) Padre Prods.

San Luis Obispo Discoveries. Paul Tritenbach. (Illus.). (Orig.). 1989. pap. 10.95 (0-945092-10-5) EZ Nature.

San Luis Valley: Rock Climbing & Bouldering Guide. Bob D'Antonio. (Illus.). 88p. (Orig.). 1994. pap. 12.00 (0-934641-79-X) Chockstone Pr.

San Manuel Bueno, Martir. Miguel De Unamuno. Ed. by Victor Garcia de la Concha. (Nueva Austral Ser.: Vol. 110). (SPA.). 1991. pap. text ed. 13.95 (84-239-1910-2) Elliots Bks.

San Manuel Bueno Martir. 23th ed. Miguel De Unamuno. 176p. 1991. pap. write for info. (0-7859-5145-8) Fr & Eur.

San Manuel Bueno, Martir: Como Se Hace una Novela. Miguel De Unamuno. (SPA.). 6.25 (0-8288-2578-5) Fr & Eur.

San Manuel Bueno, Martir & la Novela de Don Sandalio. Miguel De Unamuno. Ed. by C. A. Longhurst. LC 84-19415. (Spanish Texts Ser.). 160p. 1988. text ed. 14.95 (0-7190-1092-6, Pub. by Manchester Univ Pr UK) St Martin.

San Manuel Bueno, Martir, y Tres Historias Mas. Miguel De Unamuno. (SPA.). 9.95 (0-8288-2579-3) Fr & Eur.

***San Marco Florence: A Souvenir Guide to the Museum & Its Art.** Giovanna Damiani. (Illus.). 96p. 1997. 30.00 (0-85667-474-5) Scala Books.

***San Marco Florence: A Souvenir Guide to the Museum & Its Art.** Giovanna Damiani. (Illus.). 96p. 1997. 30.00 (0-614-18272-7, Pub. by P Wilson Pubs) Sothebys Pubns.

***San Marco, Florence: The Museum & Its Art.** Giovanna Damiani. 1997. 30.00 (1-85759-138-0) Antique Collect.

San Marcos: A Brief History. William Carroll. LC 75-26259. (Illus.). 1977. 20.00 (0-910390-24-X, Coda Pubns) Auto Bk.

***San Marino.** 100p. 1996. pap. text ed. 65.00 (1-85109-242-0, DG430) ABC-CLIO.

San Martin Papers. Cristian Garcia-Godoy. Tr. by Barbara Huntley & Pilar Liria from SPA. (Illus.). lxxxiii, 545p. 1988. pap. 50.00 (0-8270-2732-X) OAS.

San Mateo: A Centennial History. Mitchell P. Postel. (Illus.). 312p. 1994. 29.95 (0-942087-08-9) Scottwall Assocs.

***San Mateo County Commerce & Industry Directory, 1997.** 27th ed. 272p. 1997. pap. 75.00 (1-57541-041-9) Database Pub Co.

San Mateo County Street Guide & Directory: 1997 Edition. LC q. (Illus.). 88p. 1996. pap. 16.95 (0-88130-793-9) Thomas Bros Maps.

***San Mateo County Street Guide & Directory: 1998 Edition.** Thomas Bros. Maps Staff. 80p. 1997. pap. 16.95 (0-88130-907-9) Thomas Bros Maps.

San Mateo (Version Popular) 172p. (SPA.). write for info. (0-614-00642-2, 5001) LBW.

San Miguel: A Mexican Collective Ejido. Raymond Wilkie. LC 79-119504. (Illus.). xvii, 190p. 1971. 35.00 (0-8047-0739-1) Stanford U Pr.

San Miguel Acatan, 1938-1959: Konob' Samiel yet Peyxa. Morris Siegel & Francis X. Grollig. Tr. by Fernando Penalosa. 176p. (Orig.). (SPA.). 1995. pap. 10.95 (1-886502-05-6) Yax Te Found.

San Miguel Island: Santa Barbara's Fourth Island West. Lois J. Roberts. LC 91-73715. 224p. 1992. pap. 9.95 (0-9630370-0-5) Cal Rim.

San Min Chu I: The Three Principles of the People. Sun Yat-sen. Ed. by L. T. Chen. Tr. by Frank W. Price from CHI. LC 75-1033. (China in the 20th Century Ser.). xvii, 514p. 1975. reprint ed. lib. bdg. 59.50 (0-306-70698-9) Da Capo.

San Nicolas de Zurite: Religion & Daily Life of A Peruvian Andean Village in a Changing World. Fred Spier. 160p. 1996. pap. 20.00 (90-5383-419-2, Pub. by VU Univ Pr NE) Paul & Co Pubs.

San Pedro: A Pictorial History Updated Through 1990. 3rd enl. ed. Henry P. Silka. Ed. & Intro. by Irene M. Almeida. LC 84-5122. (Illus.). 160p. 1993. reprint ed. 34.95 (0-9611556-3-9) San Pedro Hist.

San Pedro, Colombia: Small Town in a Developing Society. Miles Richardson. (Illus.). 99p. (C). 1986. reprint ed. pap. text ed. 8.95 (0-88133-252-6) Waveland Pr.

San Quentin: The Evolution of a State Prison: An Historical Narrative of the Ten Years from 1851-1861. James H. Wilkins & Bonnie L. Petry. (West Coast Studies: No. 6). pap. write for info. (0-89370-436-9); lib. bdg. write for info. (0-89370-336-2) Borgo Pr.

San Quentin Massacre: A True Story of Race & Violence in the Radical New Left. Paul Liberatore. 1994. 22.95 (1-879360-32-2) Noble Pr.

San Quentin Point. Lewis Baltz. (Illus.). 252p. 1986. 85.00 (0-89381-247-1) Aperture.

San Quentin Prison - Inside the Walls. Nancy A. Nichols. Ed. by James T. Delahunty. (Illus.). 68p. (Orig.). 1991. pap. 9.95 (0-9630115-2-9) San Quentin Mus.

***San Quentin State Prison: Working in Hell.** William B. Whitney. (Orig.). Date not set. pap. write for info. (0-9625714-0-7) Spruce Gulch Pr.

San Rafael: Camba Town. Allyn M. Stearman. LC 73-15730. (Latin American Monographs: Series 2, No. 12). (Illus.). 143p. reprint ed. pap. 40.80 (0-8357-6723-X, 2035361) Bks Demand.

San Rafael, Camba Town: Life in a Lowland Bolivan Peasant Community. 2nd rev. ed. Allyn M. Stearman. (Illus.). 168p. (C). 1995. pap. text ed. 10.50 (0-88133-838-9) Waveland Pr.

San Rafael Reef & Swell, UT. Ed. by Trails Illustrated Staff. 1996. 8.99 (0-925873-88-8) Trails Illustrated.

San Ramon Chapel Pioneers & Their California Heritage. Erlinda Ontiueros. LC 90-7934. 572p. (Orig.). 1990. 50.00 (0-933380-06-2) Olive Pr Pubns.

San Remo Manual on International Law Applicable to Armed Conflicts at Sea. Ed. by Louise Doswald-Beck. 250p. (C). 1995. pap. text ed. 20.95 (0-521-55864-6) Cambridge U Pr.

An Asterisk (*) at the beginning of an entry indicates that the title is appearing in BIP for the first time.

S

An Asterisk (*) at the beginning of an entry indicates that the title is appearing in BIP for the first time.

Sand & Fog: Adventures in Southern Africa. Jim Brandenburg. LC 93-30425. (Illus.). 48p. (J). (gr. 3 up). 1994. 16.95 (0-8027-8232-9); lib. bdg. 17.85 (0-8027-8233-7) Walker & Co.

Sand & Fog: Adventures in Southern Africa. Jim Brandenburg. (Illus.). 48p. (YA). (gr. 3 up). 1996. pap. 6.95 (0-8027-7476-8) Walker & Co.

Sand & Other Poems. Mahmud Darweesh. Tr. by Rana Kagbbani. 112p. 1986. 19.95 (0-7103-0062-X, 0062X) Routledge Chapman & Hall.

Sand & Pebbles: The Tales of Muju Ichien, a Voice for Pluralism in Kamakura Buddhism. Robert E. Morrell. LC 84-16348. (SUNY Series in Buddhist Studies). 383p. 1985. text ed. 64.50 (0-88706-059-5); pap. text ed. 21.95 (0-88706-060-9) State U NY Pr.

Sand & Sandstone. 2nd ed. Raymond Siever. (Springer Study Edition Ser.). (Illus.). 500p. 1987. 84.95 (0-387-96350-2) Spr-Verlag.

Sand & Satin. Sax Rohmer. 1978. 8.50 (0-685-90566-7) Bookfinger.

***Sand & Shell, Carousels & Silver Bells: A Child's Seasons of Prayer.** Isabel Anders. 1997. 5.99 (0-570-04881-8) Concordia.

***Sand & the Stars.** Gillon. Date not set. 18.50 (0-85303-176-2, Pub. by Vallentine Mitchell UK) Intl Spec Bk.

S

Sand Art: Your Amazing Sand Craft Kit. Sarah Gross. (Books & Stuff). (Illus.). 24p. (Orig.). (J). (gr. 1 up). 1996. pap. 8.95 (0-448-41495-3, G&D) Putnam Pub Group.

Sand Art Craft Kit. Suzanne Lord. 1996. 9.95 (0-590-20252-9) Scholastic Inc.

***Sand Between Aphrodite's Toes.** John Burns. 36p. 1996. pap. 6.00 (0-930502-24-8) Pine Pr.

Sand Blind. Julian Rathbone. (Masks Ser.). 1994. pap. 12.99 (1-85242-281-5) Serpents Tail.

Sand Cake. Frank Asch. LC 93-15452. (Parents Magazine Read Aloud Original Ser.). (J). 1993. lib. bdg. 17.27 (0-8368-0973-4) Gareth Stevens Inc.

Sand Cake. Frank Asch. LC 78-11183. (Illus.). 48p. (J). (ps-3). 1979. 5.95 (0-8193-0985-0); lib. bdg. 5.95 (0-8193-0986-9) Parents.

Sand Canyon Archaeological Project: A Progress Report. Ed. by William D. Lipe. LC 91-76231. (Occasional Paper: No. 2). (Illus.). 160p. (Orig.). 1992. pap. 21.95 (0-9624640-1-5) Crow Canyon Archaeol.

Sand Carving Glass: A Beginner's Guide. L. S. Watson. (Illus.). 192p. (Orig.). 1986. 19.95 (0-8306-0668-8, 1668); pap. 15.95 (0-8306-1668-3) McGraw-Hill Prof.

Sand Castle & Three Other Plays. Lanford Wilson. 1970. pap. 5.25 (0-8222-0984-5) Dramatists Play.

***Sand Castle Surprise.** Lee Davis. LC 97-8524. (P.B. Bear Picture Bks.). (Illus.). (J). 1997. write for info. (0-7894-1412-0) DK Pub Inc.

Sand Castles. Jan McDaniel. 192p. 1994. 17.95 (0-8034-9042-9) Bouregy.

***Sand Castles.** M. Gary Neuman. 1997. pap. write for info. (0-679-77801-2, Villard Bks) Random.

Sand Castles & Fortresses: Christian Relationships. Lois Qualben. (Illus.). 140p. (Orig.). 1992. pap. text ed. 5.95 (1-880292-02-5) LangMarc.

Sand Closures. (Illus.). 285p. (C). 1993. text ed. 155.00 (90-5410-143-1, Pub. by A A Balkema NE) Ashgate Pub Co.

***Sand Control Handbook.** 2nd ed. George O. Suman, Jr. et al. LC 83-12628. (Illus.). 100p. pap. 28.50 (0-608-04875-5, 2065555) Bks Demand.

Sand County Almanac: And Sketches Here & There. Aldo Leopold. (Illus.). 269p. 1968. pap. 9.95 (0-19-500777-8) OUP.

Sand County Almanac: And Sketches Here & There. Aldo Leopold. (Illus.). 256p. 1989. pap. 9.95 (0-19-505928-X) OUP.

Sand County Almanac: With Essays on Conservation from Round River. Aldo Leopold. (Ecological Main Event Ser.). 295p. 1986. mass mkt. 6.99 (0-345-34505-3) Ballantine.

Sand County Almanac & Sketches Here & There: Commemorative Edition. Aldo Leopold. (Illus.). 272p. 1987. 25.00 (0-19-505305-2) OUP.

***Sand Crabs.** Lois M. Harrod. 1996. pap. 5.00 (1-889806-15-3) Devils Millhopper.

Sand Creatures. Ray K. Metzker. (Illus.). 56p. 1979. pap. 10.00 (0-89381-051-7) Aperture.

Sand Creek & the Rhetoric of Extermination: A Case Study in Indian-White Relations. David Svaldi. LC 88-38120. 392p. (C). 1989. lib. bdg. 48.00 (0-8191-7314-2) U Pr of Amer.

Sand Creek Fight. Fred H. Werner. 1993. pap. 10.95 (0-933147-12-0) Werner Pubn.

Sand Creek Massacre. Stan Hoig. LC 61-15141. (Illus.). 1977. pap. 13.95 (0-8061-1147-X) U of Okla Pr.

Sand Creek Massacre: A Documentary History, 1865-1867. Intro. by John M. Carroll. 1985. 41.95 (0-914074-03-2, J M C & Co) Amereon Ltd.

Sand Dollar. Bethany Campbell. (Romance Ser.: No. 211). 1992. pap. 2.89 (0-373-03211-0) Harlequin Bks.

Sand Dollar & the Slide Rule: Drawing Blueprints from Nature. Delta Willis. 256p. 1995. 23.00 (0-201-63275-6) Addison-Wesley.

Sand Dollar & the Slide Rule: Drawing Blueprints from Nature. Delta Willis. Ed. by Heather Mimnaugh. 256p. (C). 1996. pap. 12.00 (0-201-48831-0) Addison-Wesley.

***Sand Dreams.** William Allen. 1996. mass mkt. 4.99 (1-55197-002-3, Pub. by Comnwlth Pub CN) Partners Pubs Grp.

Sand Dune & Beach Vegetation Inventory of NZ: North Island, Vol. I. T. R. Partridge. 1992. 50.00 (0-477-02610-9, Pub. by Manaaki Whenua NZ) Balogh.

Sand Dune Pony. Franklin Folsom. (Illus.). 250p. (J). (gr. 3-6). 1991. reprint ed. pap. 8.95 (0-911797-99-8) R Rinehart.

***Sand Dune Stabilization, Shelterbelts & Afforestation in Dry Zones.** 247p. 1985. 30.00 (92-5-102261-5, Pub. by FAO IT) Bernan Associates.

***Sand Dunes of the Great Lakes.** Edna Elfont & C. J. Elfont. (Illus.). 144p. 1997. 35.00 (1-886947-16-3) Sleepng Bear.

Sand Fortress: A Novel. rev. ed. John Coriolan. 224p. 1984. reprint ed. pap. 8.95 (0-917342-46-1) Gay Sunshine.

Sand Horse. Ann Turnbull. LC 89-9. (Illus.). 32p. (J). (gr. k-3). 1989. lib. bdg. 13.95 (0-689-31581-3, Atheneum Bks Young) S&S Childrens.

Sand in My Eyes. Seigniora R. Laune. LC 86-40089. (Illus.). 264p. 1986. pap. 9.95 (0-8061-2016-9) U of Okla Pr.

Sand in My Shoe: Homestead Day's in Twenty-Nine Palms. 3rd ed. Helen G. Bagley. Ed. by Harold Weight & Lucile Weight. LC 77-949990. (Illus.). 269p. 1978. reprint ed. pap. 17.50 (0-912714-08-5) Adobe Road.

Sand in My Shoes. Jeannine B. Browning. 1990. 14.95 (0-9627729-0-9) J B Browning.

Sand in my Shoes. large type ed. Wendy Kesselman. LC 94-12038. (Illus.). 32p. (J). (ps-2). 1995. lib. bdg. 14.89 (0-7868-2045-4) Hyprn Child.

Sand in my Shoes. large type ed. Wendy Kesselman. LC 94-12038. (Illus.). 32p. (J). (ps-2). 1995. 14.95 (0-7868-0057-7) Hyprn Child.

Sand in My Shoes. rev. ed. Katharine B. Ripley. 332p. 1995. pap. 13.95 (1-878086-40-5) Down Home NC.

Sand in Our Shoes: A Guide Book to Pharaonic Egypt. Polly S. Price. (Illus.). 307p. 1979. pap. text ed. 8.50 (0-9604012-0-2) P S Price.

Sand in the Gears: How We Won World War II in Spite of Ourselves. 2nd rev. ed. John B. Graham. Ed. by Joan A. Scurlock. 136p. (Orig.). 1996. pap. 17.00 (1-882188-25-X) Magnolia Mktg.

Sand in the Wind. Kathleen O'Neal Gear. 320p. 1990. mass mkt. 4.99 (0-8125-0088-1) Tor Bks.

Sand in Your Shoes, the Indispensable Guide to the Palm Beaches. 2nd rev. ed. Pat Kayser. LC 95-92537. (Illus.). 329p. 1995. per. 14.95 (0-9635494-1-3) P Kayser Bks.

Sand Mandala of Vajrabhairava. Daniel Cozort. (Illus.). 40p. 1995. pap. 8.95 (1-55939-056-5) Snow Lion Pubns.

Sand Mountain. Anastasios Aslanis. 320p. (Orig.). 1996. mass mkt. 4.99 (1-55197-275-1, Pub. by Comnwlth Pub CN) Partners Pubs Grp.

Sand Mountain. Romulus Linney. 1985. pap. 5.25 (0-8222-0985-3) Dramatists Play.

Sand of Silence see **Peter Capstick Collector's Library**

***Sand on the Move: The Story of Dunes.** Roy A. Gallant. LC 96-52382. (First Bk.). (J). 1997. write for info. (0-531-20334-4) Watts.

Sand Patch: Clash of Titans (B&O-PRR) Charles S. Roberts. LC 93-90583. (Cumberland to Connellsville & Branches 1837-1993 Ser.). (Illus.). 224p. 1993. 50.00 (0-934118-20-5) Barnard Roberts.

Sand Pebbles. Richard McKenna. 1962. write for info. (0-318-66791-6) HarpC.

Sand Pebbles. Richard McKenna. 300p. 1991. reprint ed. lib. bdg. 37.95 (0-89966-857-7) Buccaneer Bks.

Sand Pebbles. Richard McKenna. LC 83-27007. (Classics of Naval Literature Ser.). 597p. 1984. reprint ed. 32.95 (0-87021-592-2) Naval Inst Pr.

Sand Resources of Texas Gulf Coast. L. E. Garner. (Report of Investigations Ser.: RI 60). (Illus.). 85p. 1967. pap. 1.50 (0-318-03161-2) Bur Econ Geology.

Sand Sculptures Activity Book, Unit 11. (Networks Ser.). (J). (gr. 3). 1991. 3.90 (0-88106-787-3, N334) Charlesbridge Pub.

Sand Sculptures Activity Book (EV), Unit 11. (Networks Ser.). (J). (gr. 3). 1991. 3.90 (0-88106-786-5) Charlesbridge Pub.

Sand Sculptures Anthology, Unit 11. (Networks Ser.). (J). (gr. 3). 1991. 7.45 (0-88106-784-9, N331) Charlesbridge Pub.

Sand Sharks. John F. Prevost. LC 95-3314. (Sharks Ser.). (J). (gr. k-3). 1995. lib. bdg. 13.98 (1-56239-470-3) Abdo & Dghtrs.

Sand-Small Book. G. Parscoe & Craig Foster-Lynam. 8p. (J). 1987. 3.95 (0-88679-554-0) Educ Insights.

Sand, Surf & Seduction: Summer #4. Katherine Applegate. (J). (gr. 7 up). 1996. pap. 3.99 (0-671-51037-1) S&S Trade.

Sand Swallows Our Land. Leif O. Manger. (Bergen Studies in Social Anthropology: No. 24). 137p. (Orig.). 1985. pap. text ed. 11.95 (0-936508-60-4, Pub. by Bergen Univ Dept Social Anthro NO) Barber Pr.

Sand-Tall Book. G. Parscoe & Craig Foster-Lynam. 8p. (J). 1987. 19.95 (0-88679-553-2) Educ Insights.

Sand Through My Fingers. large type ed. Lee Naughton. 1990. 25.99 (0-7089-2129-9) Ulverscroft.

Sand to Sea: Marine Life of Hawaii. Stephanie Feeney & Ann Fielding. LC 88-38669. (Illus.). (J). (gr. 2-5). 1989. 12.95 (0-8248-1180-1, Kolowalu Bk) UH Pr.

Sand Transport in Rivers, Estuaries & the Sea: Proceedings of the Euromech 262 Colloquium, Wallingford, UK, 26-29 June 1990. Ed. by R. Soulsby & R. Bettess. (Illus.). 294p. (C). 1991. text ed. 95.00 (90-6191-186-9, Pub. by A A Balkema NE) Ashgate Pub Co.

Sand Transportation & Desertification in Arid Lands. Ed. by Farouk El-Baz et al. 488p. (C). 1990. text ed. 151.00 (9971-5-0858-3) World Scientific Pub.

Sand, Wind, & War: Memoirs of a Desert Explorer. Ralph A. Bagnold. LC 90-46430. (Illus.). 209p. 1991. 36.00 (0-8165-1211-6) U of Ariz Pr.

Sand Witch. Steve Senn. 96p. (J). (gr. 3-7). 1987. pap. 2.75 (0-380-75298-0, Camelot) Avon.

Sandak Individual Slides. Sandak. 1990. 3.50 (0-8161-1576-1, Hall Reference) Macmillan.

Sandal. Tony Bradman. 1999. pap. 3.95 (0-14-054173-X) NAL-Dutton.

Sandal & the Cave: The Indians of Oregon. Luther S. Cressman. LC 81-915. (Illus.). 96p. 1981. reprint ed. pap. 8.95 (0-87071-078-8) Oreg St U Pr.

Sandaled Foot. David Craig. (Cleveland Poets Ser.: No. 27). 59p. (Orig.). 1980. pap. 3.50 (0-914946-25-0) Cleveland St Univ Poetry Ctr.

Sandalwood Box. Geraldine B. Siks. (J). (gr. 1-7). 1954. 5.00 (0-87602-199-2) Anchorage.

Sandalwood Door Poems. M. K. Kaw. 80p. 1991. text ed. 10.00 (81-220-0215-3, Pub. by Konark Pubs Pvt Ltd II) Advent Bks Div.

Sandalwood Princess. Loretta Chase. 224p. 1991. 18.95 (0-8027-1128-6) Walker & Co.

Sandalwood Princess. Loretta Chase. 240p. 1991. mass mkt. 3.99 (0-380-71455-8) Avon.

Sandalwood Tree. Margaret Chatterjee. 4.80 (0-89253-457-5); 4.00 (0-89253-458-3) Ind-US Inc.

***Sandbag, Stage Left (Or, One Dead Dolly)** John Anthony. 80p. 1996. 5.00 (0-87440-031-7) Bakers Plays.

Sandblaster. Jack Rudman. (Career Examination Ser.: C-1461). 1994. pap. 23.95 (0-8373-1461-5) Nat Learn.

Sandbox. Wassmer et al. 119p. (Orig.). 1991. student ed. 10.95 (0-931749-06-9) PJC Lrng Mtrls.

Sandbox: A Study in the Optimal Lifestyle. Conrad Manning. 175p. (Orig.). pap. 14.95 (0-9618479-0-5) Sandbox Inc.

Sandbox & the Death of Bessie Smith. Edward Albee. 1988. pap. 8.95 (0-452-26083-3, Plume) NAL-Dutton.

Sandbox & The Death of Bessie Smith. Edward Albee. 1989. pap. 6.95 (0-317-02810-3) NAL-Dutton.

Sandbox Betty. Catherine Petrie. LC 81-15547. (Rookie Reader Ser.). (Illus.). 32p. (J). (ps-2). 1982. pap. 3.50 (0-516-43578-7); lib. bdg. 15.00 (0-516-03578-9) Childrens.

Sandbox King. Susanne M. Swanson. (Illus.). 28p. (Orig.). (J). (ps-5). 1995. pap. 6.99 (1-885101-08-2) Writers Pr Srv.

Sandbox King, Large Class Set. Susanne M. Swanson. (Illus.). (Orig.). (J). 1995. pap. 244.65 (1-885101-35-X) Writers Pr Srv.

Sandbox King, Resource Room Set. Susanne M. Swanson. (Illus.). (Orig.). (J). 1995. pap. 69.90 (1-885101-33-3) Writers Pr Srv.

Sandbox King, 25 bks., Small Class Set. Susanne M. Swanson. (Illus.). (Orig.). (J). 1995. pap. 174.75 (1-885101-34-1) Writers Pr Srv.

Sandbox King: Library Set. Susanne M. Swanson. Ed. by John Bruyninckx. (Enrichment Collection: No. 1). (Illus.). (Orig.). (J). (gr. k-5). pap. 34.95 (1-885101-60-0) Writers Pr Srv.

Sandbox Scientist: Real Science Activities for Little Kids. Michael E. Ross. LC 95-13508. (Illus.). 144p. (J). (ps-3). 1995. pap. 12.95 (1-55652-248-7) Chicago Review.

Sandbox Society: Early Education in Black & White America - An Ethnographic Comparison. Sally Lubeck. LC 85-10422. 160p. 1985. 25.00 (1-85000-051-4, Falmer Pr) Taylor & Francis.

Sandburg Shelf: A Bibliography & Annotated Price Guide to the Works of Carl Sandburg. Kenan Heise. 72p. 1993. pap. 15.00 (0-924772-23-9) CH Bookworks.

Sandburrs. Alfred H. Lewis. LC 72-90585. (Short Story Index Reprint Ser.). (Illus.). 1977. 21.95 (0-8369-3068-1) Ayer.

Sandburrs. Alfred H. Lewis. LC 72-104512. (Illus.). 318p. reprint ed. lib. bdg. 18.00 (0-8398-1158-6) Irvington.

Sandburrs. Alfred H. Lewis. 318p. (C). 1986. reprint ed. pap. text ed. 7.95 (0-8290-2029-2) Irvington.

Sandcastle. Iris Murdoch. 1978. pap. 11.95 (0-14-001474-8, Penguin Bks) Viking Penguin.

***Sandcastle Bluff.** Cis Hawk. LC 96-90689. (Orig.). 1997. pap. 10.95 (0-533-12143-4) Vantage.

Sandcastle Seahorses. Nikia C. Leopold. LC 87-35978. 45p. (Orig.). (J). 1988. pap. 5.95 (0-913123-17-X) Galileo.

Sandcastles. Wayne Turiansky. 36p. 1975. pap. 2.00 (0-913028-35-5) North Atlantic.

Sandcastles: The Arabs in Search of the Modern World. Milton Viorst. 1994. 25.00 (0-679-40599-2) Knopf.

Sandcastles: The Arabs in Search of the Modern World. Milton Viorst. 452p. 1995. pap. 16.95 (0-8156-0362-2) Syracuse U Pr.

Sandcastles & Cucumber Ships Last Forever. LC 78-74555. 48p. (Orig.). (J). (gr. 3-8). 1978. pap. 2.95 (0-916872-06-8) Delafield Pr.

***Sandeha Nivarini (Mysteries of Spiritual Truths)** Sai S. Sathya. Date not set. pap. 2.00 (0-614-19043-6, BA-312) Sathya Sai Bk Ctr.

Sander's Fishing Guide One: Western New York Edition. rev. ed. John M. Sander. (Illus.). 304p. 1992. pap. 18.95 (0-9618057-1-4) Sanders Fish.

Sander's Fishing Guide Two: Finger Lakes Region Edition. John M. Sander. (Illus.). 328p. (Orig.). 1988. pap. 17.95 (0-9618057-0-6) Sanders Fish.

Sanders Price Guide to Autographs. 4th ed. George Sanders. 608p. 1996. pap. text ed. 24.95 (1-57090-032-9) Alexander Bks.

Sanders Price Guide to Autographs 1994. George Sanders et al. (Illus.). 512p. (Orig.). 1994. 29.95 (1-57090-001-9); pap. 21.95 (1-57090-003-5) Alexander Bks.

Sanders Price Guide to Sports Autographs. George Sanders et al. LC 95-76109. (Illus.). 512p. Date not set. pap. text ed. 21.95 (1-57090-010-8) Alexander Bks.

Sanders Quick Reference to Autograph Prices. George Sanders. Date not set. pap. text ed. 6.99 (1-57090-039-6) Alexander Bks.

Sanders Sports Autograph Price Guide,1994. 3rd ed. Mark Baker. 1993. pap. 19.95 (0-89487-198-6) Scott Pub Co.

Sanders Turbo Tax 94 Forms. Date not set. spiral bd. 32.75 (0-314-05911-3) West Pub.

Sanderson Flood of 1965: Crisis in a Rural Texas Community. Russell A. Scogin. Ed. by Earl H. Elam. (Illus.). 112p. (Orig.). (C). 1995. pap. text ed. 10.00 (0-9647629-0-0) Sul Ross St Univ.

Sandgrains on a Tray: Poems. Alan Brownjohn. LC 69-19125. 6900. 15.95 (0-8023-1212-8) Dufour.

Sandgropers: A Western Australian Anthology. Ed. by Dorothy Hewett. 19.95 (0-85564-070-7, Pub. by Univ of West Aust Pr AT) Intl Spec Bk.

Sandhi: The Theoretical, Phonetic, & Historical Bases of Word-Junction in Sanskrit. W. Sidney Allen. (Janua Linguarum, Series Minor: No. 17). 1972. reprint ed. pap. text ed. 24.65 (90-279-2360-4) Mouton.

Sandhi Phenomena in the Languages of Europe. Ed. by Henning Andersen. (Trends in Linguistics, Studies & Monographs: No. 33). (Illus.). xii, 616p. 1986. lib. bdg. 215.40 (0-89925-070-X) Mouton.

Sandhill Century, Eighteen Eighty-Three to Nineteen Eighty-Three, 2 vols. set, Bk. I. Ed. by Marianne Beel. LC 85-70605. (Illus.). 400p. 1986. Book I: The Land 400pp. write for info. (0-9614508-0-0) Cherry County Cent.

Sandhill Century, Eighteen Eighty-Three to Nineteen Eighty-Three, 2 vols. set, Bk. II. Ed. by Marianne Beel. LC 85-70605. (Illus.). 562p. 1986. Book II: The People 562pp. write for info. (0-9614508-1-9) Cherry County Cent.

Sandhill Century, Eighteen Eighty-Three to Nineteen Eighty-Three, 2 vols. set, Set. Ed. by Marianne Beel. LC 85-70605. (Illus.). 1986. 61.00 (0-9614508-2-7) Cherry County Cent.

***Sandhill Cranes.** Lynn M. Stone. LC 96-49981. (Early Bird Nature Bks.). 1997. write for info. (0-8225-3027-9, Lerner Publctns) Lerner Group.

Sandhill Sundays & Other Recollections. Mari Sandoz. LC 78-82707. x, 167p. 1970. reprint ed. pap. 9.95 (0-8032-9148-5, Bison Books) U of Nebr Pr.

Sandhills Beckon. Maxine B. Isackson. 1977. 13.00 (0-931068-08-8) Purcells.

Sandhills Classic: The Stories of Mid Pines & Pine Needles. Lee Pace. (Illus.). 144p. 1996. write for info. (0-9651076-0-4) Pine Needles.

Sandi Patti Anthology. (EZ Play Today Ser.). (Illus.). 176p. 1991. pap. 14.95 (0-7935-0535-6, 00102121) H Leonard.

Sandi Patti Anthology, No. 218. 1991. spiral bd. 14.95 (0-7935-0519-4, 00244124) H Leonard.

***Sandia: An Airline & Its Aircraft.** R. E. Davies. (Illus.). 64p. 1995. 30.00 (0-9626483-7-X) Paladwr Pr.

Sandia Mountain Sequence. Carl Mayfield. 20p. 1982. pap. 2.00 (0-913719-57-9) High-Coo Pr.

***Sandia National Laboratories: The Postwar Decade.** Necah S. Furman. LC 89-16726. (Illus.). 884p. 1990. reprint ed. pap. 180.00 (0-608-04139-4, 2064872) Bks Demand.

Sanding & Planing. Nick Engler. LC 93-29729. (Workshop Companion Ser.). 1993. 19.95 (0-87596-582-2) Rodale Pr Inc.

Sandinista Communism & Rural Nicaragua. Janusz Bugajski. LC 89-71093. (Washington Papers: No. 143). 144p. 1990. text ed. 45.00 (0-275-93535-3, C3535); pap. text ed. 14.95 (0-275-93536-1) Greenwood.

Sandinista Economics in Practice: An Insider's Critical Reflections. Alejandro M. Cuenca. 178p. (Orig.). 1992. 30.00 (0-89608-432-9); pap. 12.00 (0-89608-431-0) South End Pr.

Sandinista Legacy: Lessons from a Political Economy in Transition. Ilja A. Luciak. LC 95-6520. (Illus.). 248p. 1995. 49.95 (0-8130-1369-0) U Press Fla.

Sandinista Nicaragua, Pt. 1: Revolution, Religion, & Social Policy: An Annotated Bibliography with Analytical Introductions. Snarr, Neil & Associates Staff. LC 88-32093. 188p. 1989. pap. 40.00 (0-87650-255-9) Pierian.

Sandinista Nicaragua, Pt. 2: Economy, Politics, & Foreign Policy: an Annotated Bibliography with Analytical Introductions. Neil Snarr & Associates Staff. (Resources on Contemporary Issues Ser.: No. 5). 194p. 1990. pap. 40.00 (0-87650-256-7) Pierian.

Sandinista Revolution: National Liberation & Social Transformation in Central America. Carlos M. Vilas. Tr. by Judy Butler. LC 86-28560. 319p. reprint ed. pap. 91.00 (0-7837-6994-6, 2046806) Bks Demand.

Sandinistas Speak: Speeches & Writings of Nicaragua's Leaders. Tomas Borge et al. Tr. by Taber & Will Reissner from SPA. LC 82-82051. 160p. 1986. reprint ed. pap. 13.95 (0-87348-619-6) Pathfinder NY.

Sandino. Gregorio Selser. Tr. by Cedric Belfrage. LC 80-8086. 250p. reprint ed. pap. 71.30 (0-7837-6995-4, 2046807) Bks Demand.

Sandino Affair. Neill Macaulay. LC 85-20430. (Illus.). 320p. 1985. reprint ed. pap. text ed. 18.95 (0-8223-0696-4) Duke.

Sandino in the Streets. Joel C. Sheesley & Wayne G. Bragg. LC 90-25231. (Caribbean & Latin American Studies). (Illus.). 148p. 1991. 10.95 (0-253-35207-X) Ind U Pr.

***Sandino, the Testimony of a Nicaraguan Patriot, 1921-1934.** Ed. by Sergio Ramirez & Robert E. Conrad. Tr. & Intro. by Robert E. Conrad. LC 89-48567. (Illus.). 465p. 1990. reprint ed. pap. 132.60 (0-608-02578-X, 2063224) Bks Demand.

Sandino Without Frontiers: Selected Writings of Augusto Cesar Sandino on Internationalism, Pan-Americanism, & Social Questions. Augusto C. Sandino et al. Ed. & Tr. by Karl Bermann. LC 88-18974. 144p. (Orig.). (C). 1988. pap. 7.95 (0-944824-01-3) Compita Pub.

Sandino's Communism: Spiritual Politics for the Twenty-First Century. Donald C. Hodges. LC 91-44264. (Illus.). 264p. 1992. text ed. 37.50 (0-292-77657-8) U of Tex Pr.

An Asterisk (*) at the beginning of an entry indicates that the title is appearing in BIP for the first time.

Sandino's Daughters: Testimonies of Nicaraguan Women in Struggle. Margaret Randall. LC 95-8563. 224p. (C). 1995. pap. text ed. 18.95 (0-8135-2214-5) Rutgers U Pr.
Sandino's Daughters Revisited: Feminism in Nicaragua. Margaret Randall. LC 93-10819. (Illus.). 311p. (C). 1994. pap. 16.95 (0-8135-2025-8); text ed. 47.00 (0-8135-2024-X) Rutgers U Pr.
Sanditon & Other Stories. Jane Austen. 528p. 1996. 20.00 (0-679-44719-9, Everymans Lib) Knopf.
Sandlapper Cookbook. Ed. by Joseph T. Bruce, Jr. LC 73-88594. (Illus.). 241p. 1982. pap. 9.95 (0-87844-020-8) Sandlapper Pub Co.
***Sandler Heart Failure.** 1989. lib. bdg. write for info. (0-85200-678-0) Kluwer Ac.
Sandler Inquiry. Noel Hynd. 1990. mass mkt. 4.50 (0-8217-3070-3, Zebra Kensgtn) Kensgtn Pub Corp.
***Sandlot Game.** Ed. by Dick Wimmer. LC 96-53557. (Illus.). 256p. 1997. 20.00 (1-57028-120-3) Masters Pr IN.
Sandlot Seasons: Sport in Black Pittsburgh. Rob Ruck. LC 92-46304. 280p. 1993. pap. text ed. 13.50 (0-252-06342-2) U of Ill Pr.
Sandlot Summit. Richard A. Fishman. LC 85-63032. (Illus.). 197p. (Orig.). (J). (gr. 4-9). 1985. pap. 3.95 (0-9615884-0-3) Sunlakes Pub.
S&M Theory: Theory & Practices. Oliverios. Date not set. write for info. (0-312-09378-0) St Martin.
Sandman. Illus. by Judy Deykin. 16p. (J). (ps). 1994. 8.99 (1-881445-31-3) Sandvik Pub.
***Sandman.** Keith Floyd. (Illus.). 64p. 1997. 9.95 (0-89815-910-5) Ten Speed Pr.
***Sandman.** J. Robert Janes. LC 97-20991. 1998. write for info. (1-56947-106-1) Soho Press.
Sandman. Rien Poortvliet. 36p. 1996. boxed 13.95 (1-56937-130-X) Kabouter Prods.
Sandman. Rob Shepperson. (Illus.). 32p. (J). (ps-3). 1989. 13.95 (0-374-36405-2) FS&G.
***Sandman.** Rob Shepperson. (Illus.). 32p. (J). (ps-3). 1991. pap. 4.95 (0-374-46450-2) FS&G.
Sandman: A Game of You. Neil Gaiman. Ed. & Intro. by Bob Kahan. (Illus.). 192p. 1993. pap. 19.95 (1-56389-089-5, Vertigo) DC Comics.
***Sandman: Book of Dreams.** Ed. by Neil Gailman & Edward E. Kramer. 304p. 1997. pap. 12.00 (0-06-105354-6, HarperPrism) HarpC.
Sandman: Brief Lives. Neil Gaiman. Ed. by Bob Kahan. (Illus.). 256p. (Orig.). 1994. pap. 19.95 (1-56389-138-7, Vertigo) DC Comics.
Sandman: Dream Country. Neil Gaiman. Ed. by Bob Kahan. (Illus.). 160p. 1995. 29.95 (1-56389-226-X, Vertigo) DC Comics.
Sandman: Fables & Reflections. Neil Gaiman. Ed. by Bob Kahan. (Illus.). 264p. 1993. 29.95 (1-56389-106-9, Vertigo) DC Comics.
Sandman: Fables & Reflections. Neil Gaiman. Ed. by Bob Kahan. (Illus.). 264p. 1993. pap. 19.95 (1-56389-105-0, Vertigo) DC Comics.
Sandman: Preludes & Nocturnes. Neil Gaiman. Ed. by Michael Hill. (Illus.). 240p. 1991. pap. 14.95 (1-56389-011-9, Vertigo) DC Comics.
Sandman: Preludes & Nocturnes. Neil Gaiman. Ed. by Bob Kahan. (Illus.). 240p. 1995. 29.95 (1-56389-227-8) DC Comics.
Sandman: Season of Mists. Neil Gaiman. Ed. by Michael Hill. (Illus.). 224p. 1992. pap. 19.95 (1-56389-041-0, Vertigo) DC Comics.
Sandman: The Doll's House. Neil Gaiman. Ed. by K. C. Carlson. (Illus.). 256p. 1990. pap. 14.95 (0-930289-59-5, Vertigo) DC Comics.
Sandman: The Doll's House. Neil Gaiman. Ed. by Bob Kahan. (Illus.). 256p. 1995. 29.95 (1-56389-225-1, Vertigo) DC Comics.
Sandman: The Dream Country. Neil Gaiman. Ed. by Michael Hill. (Illus.). 160p. 1991. pap. 14.95 (1-56389-016-X, Vertigo) DC Comics.
Sandman: The Kindly Ones. Neil Gaiman. Ed. by Bob Kahan. (Illus.). 352p. 1996. 34.95 (1-56389-204-9, Vertigo) DC Comics.
Sandman: The Kindly Ones. Neil Gaiman. Ed. by Bob Kahan. (Illus.). 352p. 1996. pap. 19.95 (1-56389-205-7, Vertigo) DC Comics.
***Sandman: The Wake.** Neil Gaiman. Ed. by Bob Kahan & Karen Berger. (Illus.). 192p. 1996. 29.95 (1-56389-287-1) DC Comics.
***Sandman: The Wake.** Neil Gaiman. Ed. by Bob Kahan. (Illus.). 192p. 1997. pap. 19.95 (1-56389-279-0) DC Comics.
Sandman: World's End. Neil Gaiman. Ed. by Bob Kahan. (Illus.). 168p. (Orig.). 1995. pap. 19.95 (1-56389-171-9, Vertigo) DC Comics.
Sandman Blues. Stephane Bourguignon. 240p. (Orig.). Date not set. pap. 14.95 (0-7737-5783-X, Pub. by Stoddart Pubng CN) Genl Dist Srvs.
Sandman Midnight Theatre. Neil Gaiman & Matt Wagner. Ed. by K. Berger. (Illus.). 64p. 1995. pap. 6.95 (1-56389-208-1, Vertigo) DC Comics.
Sandman Mystery Theatre: The Tarantula. M. Wagner & Steven Seagle. Ed. by Bob Kahan. (Illus.). 112p. 1995. pap. 14.95 (1-56389-195-6, Vertigo) DC Comics.
Sandor Ferenczi: Reconsidering Active Intervention. Martin Stanton. LC 90-14523. 240p. 1991. 30.00 (0-87668-569-6) Aronson.
Sandor Ferenczi: The Psychotherapist of Tenderness & Passion. Arnold W. Rachman. LC 94-32540. 488p. 1997. 60.00 (1-56821-100-7) Aronson.
Sandostatin in the Treatment of Acromegaly: Consensus Round Table, Amsterdam 1987. (Illus.). 185p. 1988. 50.95 (0-387-19269-7) Spr-Verlag.
Sandostatin in the Treatment of GEP Endrocine Tumors. Ed. by T. M. O'Dorisio. 170p. 1989. 50.95 (0-387-50715-9) Spr-Verlag.
Sandow the Magnificent: Eugen Sandow & the Beginnings of Bodybuilding. David L. Chapman. LC 93-15736. (Illus.). 264p. 1994. 26.95 (0-252-02033-2) U of Ill Pr.
Sandoz Corp. A Report on the Company's Environmental Policies & Practices. (Illus.). 21p. (C). 1994. reprint ed. pap. text ed. 250.00 (0-7881-0925-1, Coun on Econ) DIANE Pub.
Sandpaint Native. Front Street Staff. Date not set. pap. 16.95 (0-525-45368-7) NAL-Dutton.
Sandpainting. Gray Jacobik. LC 80-50065. (Series Five). 50p. 1980. pap. 7.00 (0-931846-15-3) Wash Writers Pub.
Sandpapers. Frank M. Clark. (Illus.). 160p. (Orig.). 1994. pap. 14.95 (0-86534-211-3) Sunstone Pr.
Sandplay. K. Amatruda. 19.95 (1-879041-18-9) Sigo Pr.
Sandplay: A Psychotherapeutic Approach to the Psyche. rev. ed. Dora M. Kalff. Tr. by Hilde Kirsch & Wendayne Ackerman. LC 80-27195. (Illus.). 166p. 1981. pap. 16.95 (0-938434-00-4) Sigo Pr.
Sandplay: Past, Present, & Future. R. Rogers Mitchell & Harriet S. Friedman. LC 93-8079. 192p. (C). 1994. pap. 18.95 (0-415-10137-9); text ed. 69.95 (0-415-10136-0) Routledge.
Sandplay: Silent Workshop of the Psyche. Kay Bradway & Barbara McCoard. LC 96-16802. 256p. 1997. pap. write for info. (0-415-15075-2) Routledge.
Sandplay: Silent Workshop of the Psyche. Kay Bradway & Barbara McCoard. LC 96-16802. 256p. (C). 1997. text ed. write for info. (0-415-15074-4) Routledge.
Sandplay Bridges & Transcendent Function. Katherine Bradway. 1985. 5.00 (0-317-47621-1) C G Jung Frisco.
Sandplay Studies: Origins, Theory, & Practice. rev. ed. K. Bradway et al. Ed. by Gareth Hill. (Illus.). 240p. (C). 1991. reprint ed. pap. 19.95 (0-938434-40-3) Sigo Pr.
Sandplay Studies: Origins, Theory, & Practice. 2nd rev. ed. K. Bradway et al. Ed. by Gareth Hill. (Illus.). 240p. (C). 1991. reprint ed. 35.00 (0-938434-41-1) Sigo Pr.
***Sandra & the Scoundrel, Vol. 32.** Jacqueline Diamond. (Love & Laughter Ser.). 1997. mass mkt. 3.50 (0-373-44032-4) Harlequin Bks.
Sandra Brown: Three Complete Novels. Sandra Brown. 784p. 1992. Omnibus incl. Best Kept Secrets, Mirror Image, & Slow Heat in Heaven. 13.99 (0-517-07774-4) Random Hse Value.
Sandra Day O'Connor. Paul Deegan. Ed. by Bob Italia. LC 92-13716. (Supreme Court Justices Ser.). (J). 1992. lib. bdg. 14.98 (1-56239-089-9) Abdo & Dghtrs.
Sandra Day O'Connor. Beverly Gherman. (J). (gr. 4-7). 1991. pap. 10.95 (0-670-82756-8) Viking Child Bks.
Sandra Day O'Connor. Christopher Henry. LC 94-11287. (Illus.). 64p. (J). 1994. lib. bdg. 21.00 (0-531-20175-9) Watts.
Sandra Day O'Connor. Gini Holland. LC 96-19996. (First Biographies Ser.). (J). 1997. lib. bdg. 21.40 (0-8172-4455-7) Raintree Steck-V.
Sandra Day O'Connor: Equal Justice: A Biography of Sandra Day O'Connor. Harold Woods & Geraldine Woods. LC 84-23042. (People in Focus Ser.). (Illus.). 128p. (YA). (gr. 6 up). 1987. lib. bdg., pap. 13.95 (0-87518-292-5, Dillon Silver Burdett) Silver Burdett Pr.
Sandra Day O'Connor: Independent Thinker. D. J. Herda. LC 94-49566. (Justices of the Supreme Court Ser.). (Illus.). 104p. (YA). (gr. 6 up). 1995. lib. bdg. 18.95 (0-89490-558-9) Enslow Pubs.
Sandra Day O'Connor: Justice for All. Beverly Gherman. LC 92-42464. (Women of Our Time Ser.). (Illus.). 64p. (J). (gr. 2-6). 1993. pap. 4.99 (0-14-034100-5, Puffin) Puffin Bks.
Sandra Day O'Connor: Supreme Court Justice see American Women of Achievement
Sandra Leveson. Helen Ivory. 90p. 1993. text ed. 70.00 (976-8097-43-4) Gordon & Breach.
Sandra Mendelsohn Rubin: Paintings & Drawings, March 4-April 4, 1987. LC 87-70243. (Illus.). 36p. (Orig.). 1987. pap. 10.00 (0-936827-04-1) C Bernard Gallery Ltd.
Sandra Nichols Found Dead: A Jerry Kennedy Novel. George V. Higgins. LC 95-31689. 256p. 1996. 23.00 (0-8050-3747-0) H Holt & Co.
***Sandra Nichols Found Dead: A Jerry Kennedy Novel.** George V. Higgins. 1997. pap. 12.00 (0-8050-5222-4, Owl) H Holt & Co.
Sandragraph: Between Printing & Painting. Harry Reese. (Illus.). 20p. (C). 1987. 3,000.00 (0-923980-04-0) Arundel Pr.
Sands: Descendants of James Sands of Block Island, with Notes on the Walker, Hutchinson, Ray, Guthrie, Palgrave, Cornell (& Other) Families. Malcolm S. Wilson. (Illus.). 109p. 1995. reprint ed. pap. 19.00 (0-8328-4944-8); reprint ed. lib. bdg. 29.00 (0-8328-4943-X) Higginson Bk Co.
Sands & Shores. Samantha Kingsley. 144p. (Orig.). 1996. mass mkt. 4.99 (1-55197-126-7, Pub. by Comnwlth Pub CN) Partners Pubs Grp.
S&S Crossword, No. 180. Ed. by Eugene T. Maleska. 1994. pap. 7.50 (0-671-89268-1, Fireside) S&S Trade.
S&S Crossword, No. 187. John M. Samson. 1995. pap. 8.00 (0-684-81392-0, Fireside) S&S Trade.
S&S Crossword, No. 188. John M. Samson. 1995. pap. 8.00 (0-684-81394-7, Fireside) S&S Trade.
S&S Crossword No. 178. Eugene T. Maleska. 1994. pap. 7.50 (0-671-87197-8, Fireside) S&S Trade.
S&S Crossword Treasury. Eugene T. Maleska. 1995. pap. 9.00 (0-684-81187-1, Fireside) S&S Trade.
S&S Crossword Treasury. Eugene T. Maleska. 1995. pap. 8.00 (0-684-81393-9, Fireside) S&S Trade.
S&S Crosswords from the Times, No. 38. Margaret P. Farrar. 1980. 3.95 (0-686-62843-8, 25503, Fireside) S&S Trade.
S&S Crostics, No. 114. Thomas H. Middleton. 1995. pap. 8.00 (0-684-81380-7, Fireside) S&S Trade.
S&S Crostics Number 111. Thomas Middleton. 1994. pap. 7.00 (0-671-87193-5, Fireside) S&S Trade.
S&S Fun Crostics, No. 13. Charles A. Duerr. 1995. pap. 8.00 (0-684-81391-2, Fireside) S&S Trade.
S&S Fun with Crostics, No. 9. Charles Duerr. 1994. pap. 8.00 (0-671-88714-9, Fireside) S&S Trade.
S&S Fun with Crostics, No. 12. Charles A. Duerr. 1995. pap. 8.00 (0-684-80125-6, Fireside) S&S Trade.
S&S Hooked on Cryptics Treasury, No. 1. Henry Hook. 1995. pap. 9.00 (0-684-80892-7, Fireside) S&S Trade.
S&S Hooked on Puzzles, Vol 8. Henry Hook. 1995. pap. 9.00 (0-684-80264-3, Fireside) S&S Trade.
S&S Large Type Crossword No. 19, Vol 19. John M. Samson & Eugene T. Maleska. 1995. pap. 8.00 (0-684-80262-7, Fireside) S&S Trade.
Sands of Desire. large type ed. Julia Davis. (Linford Romance Library). 256p. 1993. pap. 15.99 (0-7089-7450-3, Trailtree Bookshop) Ulverscroft.
Sands of Destiny. Becky L. Weyrich. 1996. pap. 5.50 (0-8217-5311-8) NAL-Dutton.
Sands of Experience: One Man's Odyssey in Search of Self. Tony Vidal. 206p. (Orig.). 1992. pap. 10.95 (0-9632217-0-1) Rogue Wave Pr.
Sands of Kalahari. rev. ed. William Mulvihill. LC 60-8479. 246p. 1996. reprint ed. pap. 12.00 (0-9645875-3-X) Brickiln Pr.
Sands of Lamanna. large type ed. Jean Innes. (Dales Romance Ser.). 245p. 1992. pap. 17.99 (1-85389-310-2) Ulverscroft.
Sands of Mars. Arthur C. Clarke. (J). (gr. 7). pap. 2.50 (0-451-12312-3, AE2312, Sig) NAL-Dutton.
Sands of Silence: On Safari in Namibia. Peter H. Capstick. (Illus.). 288p. 1991. 35.00 (0-312-06459-4) St Martin.
Sands of Silence: Tales of Wisdom from the Desert 2: Christian Spirituality in Stories. Derek Webster. 118p. 1993. 25.00 (0-85439-460-5, Pub. by St Paul Pubns UK) St Mut.
Sands of the Hourglass, Vol. 1. Martha Webster. (Illus.). 59p. (Orig.). 1990. pap. 5.75 (0-9624950-1-8) M Webster.
Sands of the Well. Denise Levertov. LC 96-4324. 144p. 1996. 20.95 (0-8112-1316-1) New Directions.
***Sands of the Well.** Denise Levertov. LC 96-4324. 144p. 1998. pap. 9.95 (0-8112-1361-7) New Directions.
Sands of Time. Justin Richards. (Dr. Who Missing Adventures Ser.). 272p. (Orig.). 1996. mass mkt. 5.95 (0-426-20472-7) London Brdge.
Sands of Time. Sidney Sheldon. 448p. 1989. mass mkt. 6.99 (0-446-35683-2) Warner Bks.
Sands of Time. Sidney Sheldon. LC 88-25916. 320p. 1988. 22.95 (0-688-06571-6) Morrow.
Sands of Time. Sidney Sheldon. (Sheldon Continuity Ser.). 416p. 1994. 12.95 (1-56865-087-6, GuildAmerica) Dblday Direct.
Sands of Time. Sidney Sheldon. 1991. 5.99 (0-446-77479-0) Warner Bks.
Sands of Time. Terri Valentine. 448p. 1993. mass mkt. 4.50 (0-8217-4398-8, Zebra Kensgtn) Kensgtn Pub Corp.
Sands of Time, Vol. 1. Carolyn E. Cardwell. (Illus.). 225p. (Orig.). 1986. pap. 10.95 (0-916395-21-9, ST-1) Hieroglyphics.
Sands of Time, Vol. 1. Gaya Hughes. (Illus.). 194p. (Orig.). 1992. pap. 14.00 (0-9633636-0-3) G Hughes.
Sands of Time, Vol. 2. Carolyn E. Cardwell. (Illus.). 225p. (Orig.). 1986. pap. 10.95 (0-916395-23-5, ST-2) Hieroglyphics.
***Sands of Valour.** Geoffrey Wagner. (Echoes of War Military History Ser.). 1996. pap. 10.95 (0-907675-51-4, Pub. by Ashland Buchan & Enright UK) Cimino Pub Grp.
Sands of Windee. 2nd large type ed. Arthur Upfield. 282p. 1993. 21.95 (1-85695-345-9, Pub. by ISIS UK) Transaction Pubs.
Sands of Yesteryear: Arabia Petraea. Elias J. Marsh. (Transactions of the Connecticut Academy of Arts & Sciences Ser.: Vol. 52, Pt. 1). 104p. 1994. pap. 16.00 (1-878508-08-3) CT Acad Arts & Sciences.
***Sands Run Out.** (Great War Ser.). Date not set. pap. text ed. write for info. (0-582-39417-1, Pub. by Longman UK) Longman.
S&S Young Reader's Book of Science. Robin Kerrod. (YA). 1991. pap. 12.95 (0-671-73128-9, S&S Bks Young Read) S&S Childrens.
Sandscrapers: A Forgotten Navy. Griffin T. Garnett. Ed. by Robert H. Pruett. LC 95-30636. (Illus.). 432p. 1995. pap. 14.95 (1-883911-03-6) Brandylane.
***Sandscrapers: A Forgotten Navy.** 2nd ed. Griffin T. Garnett. LC 96-30510. 1996. write for info. (1-883911-10-9) Brandylane.
Sandscripts: Word Pictures of Life, Vol. I. W. L. Lambert. Ed. & Illus. by Mary H. Lambert. LC 88-91181. 102p. (C). 1991. reprint ed. pap. 7.95 (0-929357-00-0) Sandscript Creations.
Sandscripts: Word Pictures of Life, Vol. II. 104p. 1991. pap. 7.95 (0-929357-01-9) Sandscript Creations.
SandSpit: A Redwood Northcoast Notebook. Francesca Fryer. 292p. 1995. pap. 21.50 (0-9649748-1-9) Clr Creek Pub.
Sandspit Crossing. Noel Virtue. 182p. 9300. pap. 18.95 (0-7206-0907-0) Dufour.
Sandspit Crossing. Noel Virtue. 182p. 9400. 29.00 (0-7206-0906-2, Pub. by P Owen Ltd UK) Dufour.
Sandstone Depositional Environments. Darwin R. Spearing. (AAPG Memoir Ser.: No. 31). (Illus.). viii, 410p. 1982. 74.00 (0-89181-307-1, 627) AAPG.
Sandstone Depositional Models for Exploration. Klein. 209p. 1988. text ed. 64.00 (0-13-791179-3) P-H.
Sandstone Depositional Models for Exploration for Fossil Fuels. 3rd ed. George Klein. LC 84-29735. (Illus.). 218p. 1985. text ed. 48.00 (0-934634-82-3) Intl Human Res.
Sandstone Landforms. R. Young & A. Young. Ed. by Dietrich Barsch. (Physical Environment Ser.: Vol. 11). (Illus.). 160p. 1992. 123.95 (0-387-53946-8) Spr-Verlag.
Sandstone Papers: On the Crisis of Contemporary Life. Martin Glass. LC 86-50781. 192p. (Orig.). 1986. pap. 9.00 (0-939660-18-0) Threshold VT.
Sandstone Petroleum Reservoirs. Ed. by J. H. Barwis et al. (Casebooks in Earth Sciences Ser.). (Illus.). xv, 583p. 1990. 159.95 (0-387-97217-X) Spr-Verlag.
***Sandstone Sunsets: In Search of Everett Ruess.** Mark A. Taylor. LC 97-741. 1997. write for info. (0-87905-803-X) Gibbs Smith Pub.
Sandstorm. Laurence Gough. Date not set. pap. 4.95 (0-14-015723-9, Viking) Viking Penguin.
Sandstorm: Middle East Conflicts & America. Ed. by Daniel Pipes. LC 92-29688. 422p. (Orig.). (C). 1993. pap. text ed. 24.50 (0-8191-8894-8); lib. bdg. 71.50 (0-8191-8893-X) U Pr of Amer.
Sandstorms: Days & Nights in Arabia. Peter Theroux. 288p. 1991. pap. 12.00 (0-393-30797-2) Norton.
***Sandusky Bay: Poems.** Theodore Waterfield. 103p. (Orig.). 1996. pap. 9.95 (0-9657288-5-4) Coventry Pr.
Sandusky Tool Company Catalog, 1925. (Illus.). 72p. 1992. reprint ed. pap. 8.50 (1-879335-26-3) Astragal Pr.
Sandwich: The Town That Glass Built. Harriet B. Barbour. LC 72-153125. (Illus.). viii, 318p. 1972. reprint ed. lib. bdg. 39.50 (0-678-03564-4) Kelley.
***Sandwich Cemeteries.** Harriett V. Lighton. 161p. 1997. reprint ed. pap. 19.50 (0-8328-6023-9) Higginson Bk Co.
Sandwich Cuisine - Oregon Style. Jan Roberts-Dominguez. Ed. by Craig J. Battrick. LC 90-82414. (Illus.). 188p. 1991. pap. 15.95 (0-9626441-0-2) Drift Creek Pr.
Sandwich Generation: Caught Between Growing Children & Aging Parents. H. M. Zal. (Illus.). 235p. 1992. 25.95 (0-306-44124-1, Plenum Insight) Plenum.
Sandwich Maker Cookbook. Nancy Al-Khalidi & Leila Ahmed. viii, 217p. 1991. pap. 12.95 (0-9632393-0-9) NALA Pubs.
Sandwich Maker Cookbook. Donna R. German. (Illus.). 176p. (Orig.). 1992. pap. 7.95 (1-55867-039-4, Nitty Gritty Ckbks) Bristol Pub Ent CA.
Sandwich Man's Daughter. Robbie Gordon. 199p. 1978. pap. 4.95 (0-89924-012-7) Lynx Hse.
***Sandwiches.** unabridged ed. Robert F. Schissel. Ed. & Illus. by Krueger Graphics Staff. 100p. (Orig.). 1997. pap. 12.95 (0-9653916-2-0) Recipe Res Inst.
Sandwiches by Artemus Ward. Charles F. Browne. (Works of Charles Farrar Browne). 1989. reprint ed. lib. bdg. 79.00 (0-7812-2095-5) Rprt Serv.
***Sandwiches 101: Fish, Egg Salad, Meat, Nuts, Cheese.** 1996. 19.50 (0-87557-134-4) Saphrograph.
Sandwichman. Walter Brierley. (Radical Fiction Ser.). 304p. 1990. reprint ed. lib. bdg. 25.00 (0-929587-41-3) I R Dee.
Sandwoman. Madeleine Ouellete-Michalska. 1990. pap. 9.00 (0-920717-24-1) Guernica Editions.
Sandwriter. Hughes. pap. 2.95 (0-671-75031-3) S&S Trade.
Sandy. Helen B. King. (Illus.). 18p. (J). (ps-3). 1985. pap. 4.95 (0-9615366-4-0) King ME.
Sandy. Alice H. Rice. 24.95 (0-8488-1137-2) Amereon Ltd.
Sandy & the Rock Star. Walt Morey. LC 78-12375. (J). (gr. 4-7). 1979. pap. 13.95 (0-525-38785-4) Dutton Child Bks.
Sandy Autobiography. (J). pap. 1.95 (0-590-31303-7) Scholastic Inc.
***Sandy Bottom.** Garrison Keillor. 1998. pap. 4.95 (0-7868-1250-8) Hyprn Child.
Sandy Bottom Orchestra. Garrison Keillor. LC 96-41404. 272p. (J). (gr. 3-7). 1996. 14.95 (0-7868-0173-5); 14.89 (0-7868-2145-0) Hyprn Child.
Sandy Dallas. Wayne H. Miller. Ed. by Denise M. Smith. (Sandy Dallas Series of Books for Children, Parents, & Teachers). (Illus.). 100p. (Orig.). (YA). (gr. 6-12). 1995. pap. text ed. 4.95 (0-9634735-4-9) Hiram Charles.
Sandy Dallas Visits the Zoo. Wayne H. Miller. Ed. by Denise M. Smith. (Sandy Dallas Series of Books for Children, Parents, & Teachers). (Illus.). 100p. (Orig.). (YA). (gr. 6-12). 1995. pap. text ed. 4.95 (0-9634735-5-7) Hiram Charles.
***Sandy Dennis: A Personal Memoir.** Sandy Dennis. LC 96-30607. (Illus.). 112p. 1997. 14.95 (1-57601-001-5) Papier-Mache Press.
Sandy Hook--In 1879. George Houghton. Ed. by William R. Jones. (Illus.). 16p. 1978. reprint ed. pap. 2.95 (0-89646-047-9) Vistabooks.
Sandy Koufax. John Grabowski. (Baseball Legends Ser.). (Illus.). 64p. (J). (gr. 3 up). 1992. lib. bdg. 15.95 (0-7910-1180-1) Chelsea Hse.
Sandy Koufax. William R. Sanford & Carl R. Green. LC 92-31249. (Sports Immortals Ser.). (Illus.). 48p. (J). (gr. 5). 1993. lib. bdg. 11.95 (0-89686-780-3, Crstwood Hse) Silver Burdett Pr.
Sandy of Laguna. Joseph Bell. (Illus.). 72p. (Orig.). (J). (gr. k-8). 1992. pap. 10.95 (1-880812-01-0) S Ink WA.
Sandy Patch: A Biography of Lt. Gen. Alexander M. Patch. William K. Wyant. LC 91-8748. 264p. 1991. text ed. 59.95 (0-275-93454-3, C3454, Praeger Pubs) Greenwood.
Sandy Shore. John Hay. LC 68-18991. (Illus.). 1968. 9.95 (0-85699-006-X) Chatham Pr.
Sandy Walker: Woodblock Prints. Katy Kline. (Illus.). 47p. (Orig.). 1994. pap. 8.00 (0-938437-47-X) MIT List Visual Arts.
Sandy's Suitcase. Elsy Edwards. LC 92-34269. (Voyages Ser.). (Illus.). (J). 1993. 14.00 (0-383-03650-X) SRA McGraw.
Sandyvale Cemetery, Johnstown, PA: A Recreation of Burials, 1850-1906. Phyllis Oyler. 363p. 1989. pap. text ed. 30.00 (0-933227-72-8) Closson Pr.

Sane Alternative: A Choice of Futures. 3rd ed. James Robertson. 152p. (Orig.). 1983. pap. 4.95 (*0-936106-00-X*) River Basin.

Sane Sex Life. H. W. Long. 14.95 (*0-685-22094-X*) Wehman.

Sane Society. Erich Fromm. LC 55-8006. 384p. 1990. pap. 12.95 (*0-8050-1402-0*, Owl) H Holt & Co.

Sane Society Ideal in Modern Utopianism: A Study in Ideology. Kerry S. Walters. LC 87-28126. (Problems in Contemporary Philosophy Ser.: Vol. 7). 350p. 1989. lib. bdg. 99.95 (*0-88946-331-X*) E Mellen.

Sanfield, Inc. A Computerized Audit Case. 2nd ed. Noyan Arson & Naomi L. Satterfield. 170p. (C). 1994. pap. 30.85 incl. disk (*0-256-12909-6*) Irwin.

Sanford: Thomas Sanford, Emigrant to New England. Carlton E. Sanford. 768p. 1991. reprint ed. pap. 98.00 (*0-8328-2075-X*); reprint ed. lib. bdg. 108.00 (*0-8328-2074-1*) Higginson Bk Co.

Sanford Ballard Dole: Hawaii's Only President, 1844-1926. Helena G. Allen. LC 87-72591. (Illus.). 304p. 1988. 24.95 (*0-87062-184-X*) A H Clark.

***Sanford Guide to Antimicrobial Therapy & HIV-AIDS Therapy 1997.** large type rev. ed. Jay P. Sanford et al. 1997. pap. 25.00 (*0-933775-32-6*) Antimicrob Ther.

***Sanford Guide to Antimicrobial Therapy 1997.** rev. ed. Jay P. Sanford et al. 1997. pap. 7.00 (*0-933775-30-X*) Antimicrob Ther.

***Sanford Guide to HIV-AIDS Therapy 1997.** Merle A. Sande et al. 1997. pap. 7.00 (*0-933775-31-8*) Antimicrob Ther.

Sanford Hirsch: Painted Sculptures. Richard J. Wattenmaker. (Illus.). 16p. (Orig.). 1985. pap. 2.00 (*0-915511-04-5*) Ball St U Mus Art.

Sanford Meisner Approach: An Actor's Workbook. Larry Silverberg. 132p. 1994. pap. 12.95 (*1-880399-77-6*) Smith & Kraus.

***Sanford Meisner Approach Vol. II: Emotions.** Larry Silverberg. 160p. 1979. pap. 14.95 (*1-57525-074-8*) Smith & Kraus.

***Sanford Meisner Approach Vol. II: Emotions.** Larry Silverberg. 160p. 1996. 25.00 (*1-57525-082-9*) Smith & Kraus.

Sanford Meisner on Acting. Sanford Meisner & Dennis Longwell. LC 86-46187. 1987. pap. 12.00 (*0-394-75059-4*, Vin) Random.

***Sanfords' Guide to Brush-McCoy Pottery, Bk. 1.** 2nd ed. Martha A. Sanford & Steve E. Sanford. (Illus.). 144p. 1992. reprint ed. mass mkt. 40.00 (*0-9633531-1-X*) M S Sanford.

***Sanfords' Guide to Brush-McCoy Pottery, Bk. 2.** Martha A. Sanford & Steve E. Sanford. (Illus.). 80p. 1996. mass mkt. 29.95 (*0-9633531-2-8*) M S Sanford.

Sang d'Afrique. Guy Des Cars & Dominique Halbout. (FRE & TUR.). 1992. 125.00 (*0-7859-1189-8*, 2700501667) Fr & Eur.

Sang d'Afrique: L'Africain, Vol. 1. Guy Des Cars. (FRE.). 1971. 6.95 (*0-8288-9570-8*, M5741) Fr & Eur.

Sang d'Afrique: L'Amoureuse, Vol. 2. Guy Des Cars. (FRE.). 1971. 6.95 (*0-8288-9571-6*, M5742) Fr & Eur.

Sang d'Aquarelle. Francoise Sagan. (Folio Ser.: No. 2054). (FRE.). pap. 8.95 (*2-07-038142-0*) Schoenhof.

Sang d'Aquarelle. Francoise Sagan. (FRE.). 1989. pap. 10.95 (*0-8288-3728-7*, F85560) Fr & Eur.

Sang Des Autres. Simone De Beauvoir. 320p. (FRE.). 1973. pap. 11.95 (*0-7859-1740-3*, 2070363635) Fr & Eur.

Sang Des Autres. Simone De Beauvoir. (Folio Ser.: No. 363). 320p. (FRE.). 1973. pap. 9.95 (*2-07-036363-5*) Schoenhof.

Sang des Autres. Simone De Beauvoir. (FRE.). 1973. pap. 11.95 (*0-8288-3655-8*, M3058) Fr & Eur.

Sang Dore des Borgia. Francoise Sagan & Jacques Quoirez. 216p. (FRE.). 1978. pap. 19.95 (*0-7859-1416-1*, 2080640542) Fr & Eur.

Sang Maudit. Dashiell Hammett. 254p. (FRE.). 1987. pap. 10.95 (*0-7859-2545-7*, 2070378683) Fr & Eur.

Sang Noir. Louis Guilloux. 640p. (FRE.). 1980. pap. 13.95 (*0-7859-2641-0*, 207037226X) Fr & Eur.

Sangallensia in Washington: The Arts & Letters in Medieval & Baroque St. Gall Viewed from the Late Twentieth Century. Ed. by James C. King. LC 92-35644. 334p. (C). 1993. text ed. 52.95 (*0-8204-2081-6*) P Lang Pubng.

Sangam City: Delhi. Intro. by Khushwant Singh. (Illus.). 152p. (Orig.). 1983. pap. text ed. 5.00 (*0-86131-373-9*, Pub. by Orient Longman Ltd II) Apt Bks.

Sangamon. Edgar L. Masters. LC 88-17510. (Prairie State Bks.). (Illus.). 296p. 1988. 10.95 (*0-252-06038-5*) U of Ill Pr.

Sangaree. Frank Slaughter. 24.95 (*0-89190-283-X*) Amereon Ltd.

***Sangaya.** Silas S. Ncozana. 56p. 1996. pap. 24.95 (*99908-16-00-X*) Intl Scholars.

Sangha & State in Burma: A Study of Monastic Sectarianism & Leadership. E. Michael Mendelson. Ed. by John P. Ferguson. LC 75-13398. (Illus.). 416p. 1975. 55.00 (*0-8014-0875-X*) Cornell U Pr.

***Sangha, State, & Society: Thai Buddhism in History.** Yoneo Ishii. LC 86-673063. (Monographs of the Center for Southeast Asian Studies, Kyoto University: No. 16). (Illus.). 211p. 1986. reprint ed. pap. 60.20 (*0-608-04372-9*, 2065153) Bks Demand.

Sangi Bar Guri: A Gravestone. Jalal Al-E Ahmad. 102p. (Orig.). (PER.). 1991. pap. 8.95 (*0-936347-14-7*) Iran Bks.

Sangita Ratnakara of Sarngadeva, Vol. II. R. K. Shringy & Prem L. Sharma. (C). 1989. 60.00 (*0-685-30853-7*, Pub. by Munshiram Manoharial II) S Asia.

Sangitasiromani: A Medieval Handbook of Indian Music. Ed. & Tr. by Emmie Te Nijenhuis from SAN. LC 91-30664. (Brill's Indological Library: Vol. 5). ix, 620p. 1992. 178.50 (*90-04-09498-9*) E J Brill.

Sanglax A Persian Guide to the Turkish Language. Mahdi Xan. (Gibb Memorial New Ser.: Vol. 20). 1992. 29.85 (*0-906094-31-3*, Pub. by Aris & Phillips UK) David Brown.

Sangoma: My Odyssey into the Spirit World of Africa. James A. Hall. LC 95-157. 1995. pap. 12.00 (*0-684-81506-0*, Fireside) S&S Trade.

Sangre. Benny Hinn. Date not set. pap. text ed. 7.99 (*0-88113-217-9*) Edit Betania.

Sangre Bajo Las Banderas (de Rusia Vino el Martillo - y la Hoz de Mi Garganta) Joaquin E. Piedra. LC 85-81209. (Coleccion Espejo de Paciencia). 101p. (Orig.). (SPA.). 1986. pap. 9.95 (*0-89729-382-7*) Ediciones.

***Sangre Caliente.** Charlotte Lamb. (Bianca Ser.: No. 33399). (SPA.). 1997. mass mkt. 3.50 (*0-373-33399-4*, 1-33399-6) Harlequin Bks.

Sangre de Cristo: A Novel of Science & Faith. Martin Hewlett. LC 93-87725. 256p. (Orig.). 1994. pap. 13.95 (*0-9639790-0-0*) Spirit Rider Pr.

***Sangre de Cristo Wilderness: A Territory of the Heart.** Mary J. Porter. (Illus.). 48p. (Orig.). 1997. pap. 15.95 (*0-9656126-6-X*, MMP-6) Music Mtn Pr.

Sangre de Monstruo - Monster Blood. R. L. Stine. (Escalofrios - Goosebumps Ser.: No. 3). (SPA.). (J). 1996. pap. 3.99 (*0-590-50209-3*) Scholastic Inc.

***Sangre de Santa Agueda: Angiolillo, Betances y Canovas.** Frank Fernandez. (SPA.). pap. 18.00 (*0-89729-756-3*) Ediciones.

Sangre Del Monte. Roberto A. Lucero. 192p. (Orig.). 1994. pap. 12.95 (*0-9642480-3-4*) Mrningstar Bks.

Sangreal Ceremonies & Rituals. William G. Gray. LC 85-51169. (Sangreal Sodality Ser.: Vol. 4). 384p. 1986. pap. 12.95 (*0-87728-583-7*) Weiser.

Sangreal Sacrament. William G. Gray. LC 82-62847. (Sangreal Sodality Ser.: Vol. 2). 194p. 1983. pap. 8.95 (*0-87728-562-4*) Weiser.

Sangreal Tarot. William G. Gray. (Illus.). 194p. (Orig.). 1988. pap. 14.95 (*0-87728-665-5*) Weiser.

Sangrey Family History: (The Descendents of Mary & John Sangrey 1788-1838) Abram W. Sangrey. LC 89-62151. (Illus.). 1989. 18.00 (*0-685-27240-0*) A W Sangrey.

***Sanguine Dreams.** (Illus.). 104p. 1997. 15.00 (*0-9657681-0-4*) minimalist voyeur.

Sanhedrin, 2 vols. (ENG & HEB.). 30.00 (*0-910218-74-9*) Bennet Pub.

Sanibel Arcanum. Tom Cochrun. 250p. pap. 15.95 (*1-878208-41-1*) Guild Pr IN.

Sanibel Flats. Randy W. White. 1991. pap. 5.99 (*0-312-92602-2*) St Martin.

Sanibel Island. Lynn M. Stone. LC 90-44458. (Voyageur Wilderness Ser.). (Illus.). 96p. (Orig.). 1991. pap. 16.95 (*0-89658-139-X*) Voyageur Pr.

Sanibel Island Eyes: And Other Island Afflictions & Addictions. Chelle K. Walton. (Illus.). 104p. (Orig.). 1988. pap. write for info. (*0-318-64010-4*) Island Eyes.

***Sanidad de Adentro Hacia Afuera - Healing From the Inside Out.** Marshall. 211p. (SPA.). write for info. (*1-56063-513-4*) Editorial Unilit.

***Sanidad Del Alma Herida.** Arline Westmeier. 122p. (SPA.). 1989. pap. write for info. (*0-614-27137-1*) Editorial Unilit.

Sanidad del Alma Herida, Tomo 2. Arline Westmeier. 122p. (SPA.). 1989. pap. 6.50 (*1-56063-406-5*, 498537) Editorial Unilit.

Sanidad del Alma Herida, Vol. 1. Arline Westmeier. (SPA.). 1991. 4.50 (*1-56063-105-8*, 490264) Editorial Unilit.

***Sanidad Divina.** Yiye Avila. 170p. (SPA.). 1995. write for info. (*1-56063-634-3*) Editorial Unilit.

Sanidad Divina: Una Perspectiva Biblica Equilibrada - Divine Healing: A Balanced View. Robert G. Witty. Tr. by Nelda B. De Gaydou from ENG. 192p. (Orig.). (SPA.). 1991. pap. 8.50 (*0-311-09137-7*) Casa Bautista.

***Sanidad Emocional - Emotional Healing.** Mario Fumero. 130p. (SPA.). 1996. write for info. (*0-7899-0174-9*) Editorial Unilit.

***Sanidad Interior - Inner Healing.** Jorge A. Ovando. (SPA.). write for info. (*0-7899-0207-9*) Editorial Unilit.

***Sanidad Para Personas Angustiadas.** D. Harrison. (SPA.). 1.50 (*0-8297-1953-9*) Life Pubs Intl.

***Sanierung von Altlasten 1995.** H. L. Jessberger. 1995. 70.00 (*90-5410-546-1*, Pub. by A A Balkema NE) Ashgate Pub Co.

Sanitarian. Jack Rudman. (Career Examination Ser.: C-1462). 1994. pap. 27.95 (*0-8373-1462-3*) Nat Learn.

Sanitarian Trainee. Jack Rudman. (Career Examination Ser.: C-1463). 1994. pap. 23.95 (*0-8373-1463-1*) Nat Learn.

Sanitarians: A History of American Public Health. John Duffy. 344p. (C). 1992. pap. text ed. 15.95 (*0-252-06276-0*) U of Ill Pr.

Sanitarians: A History of American Public Health. fac. ed. John Duffy. LC 89-5107. 341p. 1990. pap. 97.20 (*0-7837-7622-5*, 2047374) Bks Demand.

Sanitary Centennial & Selected Short Stories. Fernando Sorrentino. Tr. by Thomas C. Meehan from SPA. (Texas Pan American Ser.). 216p. 1988. 19.95 (*0-292-77608-X*) U of Tex Pr.

Sanitary Chemist. Jack Rudman. (Career Examination Ser.: C-3266). 1994. pap. 29.95 (*0-8373-3266-4*) Nat Learn.

Sanitary Commission of the U. S. Army, a Succinct Narrative of Its Works & Purposes. U. S. Sanitary Commission Staff. LC 78-180567. (Medicine & Society in America Ser.). 326p. 1972. reprint ed. 23.95 (*0-405-03978-6*) Ayer.

Sanitary Condition of Boston: The Report of a Medical Commission. Boston Medical Commission. Ed. by Barbara G. Rosenkrantz. LC 76-25655. (Public Health in America Ser.). 1977. reprint ed. lib. bdg. 19.95 (*0-405-09808-1*) Ayer.

Sanitary Condition of the Laboring Population of New York, with Suggestions for Its Improvement. John H. Griscom. LC 75-125742. (American Environmental Studies). 1976. reprint ed. 15.95 (*0-405-02667-6*) Ayer.

Sanitary Construction Inspector. Jack Rudman. (Career Examination Ser.: C-3195). 1994. pap. 34.95 (*0-8373-3195-1*) Nat Learn.

Sanitary Engineer. Jack Rudman. (Career Examination Ser.: C-798). 1994. pap. 29.95 (*0-8373-0798-8*) Nat Learn.

Sanitary Engineer II. Jack Rudman. (Career Examination Ser.: C-2945). 1994. pap. 34.95 (*0-8373-2945-0*) Nat Learn.

Sanitary Engineer III. Jack Rudman. (Career Examination Ser.: C-2946). 1994. pap. 34.95 (*0-8373-2946-9*) Nat Learn.

Sanitary Engineer IV. Jack Rudman. (Career Examination Ser.: C-2947). 1994. pap. 39.95 (*0-8373-2947-7*) Nat Learn.

Sanitary Evolution of London. Henry Jephson. LC 70-173152. 1978. reprint ed. 36.95 (*0-405-08671-7*, Pub. by Blom Pubns UK) Ayer.

Sanitary Fairs: A Philatelic & Historical Study of Civil War Benevolences. Alvin R. Kantor & Marjorie S. Kantor. LC 92-61024. (Illus.). 300p. 1992. 75.00 (*0-9632603-0-8*) S F Pub IL.

Sanitary Improvement District As a Mechanism for Urban Development. Center for Applied Urban Research Staff. 126p. 1975. pap. 9.00 (*1-55719-027-5*) U NE CPAR.

Sanitary Laboratory Technician. Jack Rudman. (Career Examination Ser.: C-1037). 1994. pap. 29.95 (*0-8373-1037-7*) Nat Learn.

Sanitary Landfill Leachate: Generation, Control & Treatment. Sayed R. Qasim & W. Walter Chiang. LC 94-60645. 335p. 1994. pap. 59.95 (*1-56676-129-8*) Technomic.

Sanitary Lessons of the War & Other Papers. George M. Sternberg. Ed. by Barbara G. Rosenkrantz. LC 76-40647. (Public Health in America Ser.). 1977. reprint ed. lib. bdg. 19.95 (*0-405-09832-4*) Ayer.

Sanitary Ramblings: Sketches & Illustrations of Bethal Green. Hector Gavin. (Illus.). 132p. 1971. reprint ed. 27.50 (*0-7146-2417-9*, Pub. by F Cass Pubs UK) Intl Spec Bk.

Sanitation & Parking Violation Inspector. Jack Rudman. (Career Examination Ser.: C-1873). 1994. pap. 27.95 (*0-8373-1873-4*) Nat Learn.

Sanitation Aspects of Food Service Facility Plan Preparation & Review: Reference Guide. 100p. 2.00 (*0-317-35247-4*) Natl Sanit Foun.

Sanitation Dispatcher. Jack Rudman. (Career Examination Ser.: C-2881). 1994. pap. 23.95 (*0-8373-2881-0*) Nat Learn.

Sanitation Enforcement Agent. Jack Rudman. (Career Examination Ser.: C-3177). 1994. pap. 23.95 (*0-8373-3177-3*) Nat Learn.

Sanitation Harvesting, Processing & Distribution of Shellfish, 2 pts., Pt. 1. rev. ed. USFDA Staff. 1993. 49.00 (*0-8493-8724-8*, RA602) CRC Pr.

Sanitation Harvesting, Processing & Distribution of Shellfish, 2 pts., Pt. 2. rev. ed. USFDA Staff. 1993. 44.00 (*0-8493-8725-6*, RA602) CRC Pr.

Sanitation in Developing Countries. Ed. by Arnold Pacey. LC 78-4215. 252p. reprint ed. pap. 71.90 (*0-8357-6942-9*, 2039001) Bks Demand.

Sanitation in Food Processing. 2nd ed. John A. Troller. LC 93-9721. (Food Science & Technology Ser.). (Illus.). 478p. 1993. text ed. 69.00 (*0-12-700655-9*) Acad Pr.

Sanitation Inspector. Jack Rudman. (Career Examination Ser.: C-2152). 1994. reprint ed. pap. 27.95 (*0-8373-2152-2*) Nat Learn.

Sanitation Inspector Trainee. Jack Rudman. (Career Examination Ser.: C-2029). 1994. pap. 23.95 (*0-8373-2029-1*) Nat Learn.

Sanitation Man (Worker) Jack Rudman. (Career Examination Ser.: C-700). 1994. pap. 19.95 (*0-8373-0700-7*) Nat Learn.

Sanitation, Safety, & Maintenance Management. Bruce H. Axler. 1974. 13.25 (*0-672-96106-7*, Bobbs); teacher ed. 5.00 (*0-672-96108-3*, Bobbs); student ed. 6.45 (*0-672-96107-5*, Bobbs) Macmillan.

Sanitation Self-Inspection Program for Foodservice Operators. rev. ed. 32p. 1983. 8.00 (*0-317-57920-7*, MG869) Natl Restaurant Assn.

Sanitation Strategy for a Lakefront Metropolis: The Case of Chicago. Louis P. Cain. LC 76-14711. 173p. 1978. 22.50 (*0-87580-064-5*) N Ill U Pr.

Sanitation Supervisor. Jack Rudman. (Career Examination Ser.: C-2151). 1994. reprint ed. pap. 29.95 (*0-8373-2151-4*) Nat Learn.

Sanitation Worker. Susan C. Poskanzer. LC 88-10044. (What's It Like to Be a...Ser.). (Illus.). 32p. (J). (gr. k-3). 1997. pap. 3.95 (*0-8167-1437-1*) Troll Communs.

Sanitation Worker - Street Cleaner - Snow Remover. 7th ed. Hy Hammer. (Illus.). 160p. 1992. pap. 12.00 (*0-13-788316-1*, Arco) Macmillan Gen Ref.

Sanitation Worker Exam National Edition. Ed. by Jim Gish. LC 96-18176. (Civil Service Library). 208p. 1997. pap. 12.95 (*1-57685-047-1*) LrningExprss.

***Sanitation Worker Exam New York City.** Learning Express Staff. LC 96-48976. (Complete Preparation Guide Ser.). 192p. 1997. pap. 25.00 (*1-57685-092-7*) LrningExprss.

Sanitation Workers: A to Z. Jean Johnson. (Walker's Community Helpers Ser.). (Illus.). (J). (gr. k-3). 1988. 11.95 (*0-8027-6772-9*); lib. bdg. 12.85 (*0-8027-6773-7*) Walker & Co.

***Sanitatsdienst Im Romischen Reich.** Juliane C. Wilmanns. (Medizin der Antike Ser.: Vol. 2). 13p. (GER.). 1995. write for info. (*0-614-22122-6*) G Olms Pubs.

Sanity & Survival in the Nuclear Age: Psychological Aspects of War & Peace. Jerome D. Frank. 346p. (C). 1988. reprint ed. pap. 27.00 (*0-8191-6744-4*) U Pr of Amer.

Sanity in Bedlam: A Study of Robert Burton's "Anatomy of Melancholy" Lawrence A. Babb. LC 77-13309. 116p. 1977. text ed. 35.00 (*0-8371-9856-9*, BBSB, Greenwood Pr) Greenwood.

Sanity, Madness & the Family. R. D. Laing & A. Esterson. 1970. mass mkt. 6.95 (*0-14-021157-8*, Penguin Bks) Viking Penguin.

Sanity Manual: Therapeutic Uses of Writing. Allan Hunter. (Illus.). 175p. (Orig.). 1996. pap. 19.95 (*1-56072-318-1*) Nova Sci Pubs.

Sanity of Earth & Grass: Complete Poems. Robert Winner. Ed. by Thomas Lux & Sylvia Winner. LC 93-37897. 160p. (Orig.). 1994. 19.95 (*0-88448-139-5*); pap. 12.95 (*0-88448-140-9*) Tilbury Hse.

Sanity of William Blake. Greville Macdonald. (Studies in Blake: No. 3). 1970. reprint ed. pap. 24.95 (*0-8383-0097-9*) M S G Haskell Hse.

Sanity Plea: Schizophrenia in the Novels of Kurt Vonnegut. rev. ed. Lawrence R. Broer. LC 94-1075. 264p. 1994. pap. text ed. 19.95 (*0-8173-0752-4*) U of Ala Pr.

Sanity Plea: Schizophrenia in the Novels of Kurt Vonnegut. Lawrence Broer. Ed. by Robert Scholes. LC 88-39248. (Studies in Speculative Fiction: No. 18). 228p. reprint ed. 64.50 (*0-8357-1885-9*, 2070698) Bks Demand.

Sanity Savers for Parents: Tips for Tackling Homework. Daniel Olympia et al. (Homework Partners Ser.). (Illus.). 112p. (Orig.). 1996. pap. 16.50 (*1-57035-002-7*, 44SAN) Sopris.

Sanjay Story. Vinod Mehta. 192p. 1978. 9.95 (*0-318-37220-7*) Asia Bk Corp.

Sankar Company Limited: A Novel. Moni S. Mukherjee. Tr. by Achala Moulik from BEN. 162p. 1977. pap. text ed. 5.95 (*0-86125-336-1*, Pub. by Orient Longman Ltd II) Apt Bks.

Sankara: The Man & His Philosophy. T. S. Rukmani. (C). 1991. text ed. 3.50 (*81-85425-33-7*, Pub. by Manohar II) S Asia.

Sankara Digvijaya: The Traditional Life of Sri Sankaracharya. Madhava-Vidyaranya. Tr. by Tapasyananda. 1979. pap. 5.95 (*0-87481-484-7*, Pub. by Ramakrishna Math II) Vedanta Pr.

Sankara on the Yoga-Sutras: The Vivarana Sub-Commentary to Vyasa-Bhasya, 2 vols., 1. Tr. by Trevor P. Leggett. 220p. 1983. 30.00 (*0-7100-0826-0*, RKP) Routledge.

Sankara on the Yoga-Sutras: The Vivarana Sub-Commentary to Vyasa-Bhasya, 2 vols., 2. Tr. by Trevor P. Leggett. 220p. 1983. 30.00 (*0-7100-9539-2*, RKP) Routledge.

Sankara on the Yoga-Sutras: The Vivarana Sub-Commentary to Vyasa-Bhasya on the Yoga-Sultras of Pantanjali. Trevor P. Leggett. 600p. 1981. text ed. 30.00 (*0-7103-0277-0*) Routledge Chapman & Hall.

Sankaracharya. T. M. Mahadevan. 119p. 1968. 3.95 (*0-318-37165-0*) Asia Bk Corp.

Sankhya Philosophy: A Critical Evaluation of Its Origins & Development. S. G. Weerasinghe. (Sri Garib Dass Oriental Ser.: No. 167). 1993. 28.00 (*81-7030-361-3*) S Asia.

Sankofa: African Thought & Education. Elleni Tedla. LC 94-19876. (Studies in African & African-American Culture: Vol. 11). 1995. pap. 32.95 (*0-8204-2525-7*) P Lang Pubng.

***Sankofa: Celebrations for the African American Church.** Grenae D. Dudley & Carlyle F. Stewart, III. 120p. (Orig.). 1997. pap. 12.95 (*0-8298-1179-6*) Pilgrim OH.

Sankofa: Stories, Proverbs & Poems of An African Childhood. David Abdulai. Ed. by Hattie Portis et al. (Illus.). 128p. (Orig.). 1995. pap. 14.95 (*0-9647012-0-0*) Konkori Intl.

Sankofa: Thought & Education. Elleni Tedla. (Studies in African & African-American Culture: Vol. 11). 256p. (C). 1995. pap. text ed. 25.95 (*0-8204-2526-5*) P Lang Pubng.

Sankov Confession. P. S. Donoghue. 352p. 1992. mass mkt. 4.50 (*0-8217-3800-3*, Zebra Kensgtn) Kensgtn Pub Corp.

Sanku Kisuhsok: Treize Lunes - Thirteen Moons: A Passamaquoddy Translation. Robert M. Chute. Ed. by Robert M. Leavitt. Tr. by David A. Francis from ENG. 64p. (Orig.). (ENG & FRE.). 1990. pap. 3.00 (*0-9624912-1-7*) Ciderpress.

Sannazaro & Arcadia. C. Kidwell. 84.95 (*0-7156-2477-6*, Pub. by Duckworth UK) Focus Pub-R Pullins.

Sanni Mannitae: A Tall Tale for Our Times. Ian I. Smart. 195p. 1994. pap. 11.95 (*0-9641929-0-X*) Orig Wrld Pr.

Sanpete Scenes: A Guide to Utah's Heart. Gary B. Peterson & Lowell C. Bennion. LC 87-72694. (Illus.). 144p. (Orig.). 1987. pap. 16.95 (*0-9617133-0-5*) Basin-Plateau Pr.

Sanpoil & Nespelem: Salishan Peoples of Northeastern Washington. Verne F. Ray. LC 76-43809. (Univ. of Washington Publications in Anthropology: Vol. 5). reprint ed. 45.00 (*0-404-15663-0*) AMS Pr.

Sans Apres Abortement: Guide Practique pour Ameliorer Qualite des Soins. Ed. by Judith Winkler et al. (Illus.). (Orig.). (FRE.). 1996. pap. 15.00 (*0-929817-32-X*) JHPIEGO.

Sans Bornes. Jarvis. 1990. text ed. 57.25 (*0-03-021402-5*) HR&W Schl Div.

Sans-Culottes: The Popular Movement & Revolutionary Government, 1793-1794. Albert Soboul. 318p. 1981. pap. 18.95 (*0-691-00782-9*) Princeton U Pr.

Sans Detour: French for English Speakers. 2nd ed. Priscilla Gac-Artigas & Gustavo Gac-Artigas. LC 96-90413. (Innovative, Non-Traditional Grammars Ser.). (Illus.). 145p. (Orig.). (ENG & FRE.). 1997. pap. 11.95 (*0-9653060-1-1*) To the Pt Bks.

An Asterisk (*) at the beginning of an entry indicates that the title is appearing in BIP for the first time.

Sans Doute. Anne Nerenz & Ariew. 1992. pap. 15.95 (*0-8384-2379-5*) Heinle & Heinle.

Sans Famille. unabridged ed. F. Malot. (FRE.). pap. 7.95 (*2-87714-288-4*, Pub. by Bookking Intl FR) Distribks Inc.

Sans Famille, Tome 1. Hector Malot. (Folio - Junior Ser.: No. 612). (Illus.). 351p. (FRE.). (J). (gr. 5-10). 1990. pap. 10.95 (*2-07-033612-3*) Schoenhof.

Sans Famille, Tome 2. Hector Malot. (Folio - Junior Ser.: No. 617). (Illus.). 417p. (FRE.). (J). (gr. 5-10). 1991. pap. 10.95 (*2-07-033617-4*) Schoenhof.

Sans III Conference Proceedings: Washington, D. C. 1994. (Illus.). 146p. (Orig.). 1994. pap. text ed. write for info. (*1-880446-59-6*) USENIX Assn.

SANS IV Conference Proceedings: Washington, D. C. 140p. (Orig.). 1995. pap. text ed. write for info. (*1-880446-68-5*) USENIX Assn.

Sans le Misericorde Du Christ. Hector Bianciotti. 352p. (FRE.). 1987. pap. 11.95 (*0-7859-2066-8*, 2070378470) Fr & Eur.

Sans Moi, Que Deviendrait la Poesie? Florentin Smarandache. Ed. by Michele De Laplante. (Illus.). 66p. (Orig.). (FRE.). (C). 1992. pap. text ed. 6.95 (*1-879585-32-4*) Erhus Univ Pr.

Sans Rime Ni Raison. Marisa Carroll. (OR Ser.). (FRE.). 1994. pap. 4.50 (*0-373-38162-X*, 1-38162-3) Harlequin Bks.

Sans Serif Display Alphabets: 100 Complete Fonts. Ed. by Dan X. Solo. LC 78-74144. (Illus.). 1979. pap. 5.95 (*0-486-23785-0*) Dover.

***Sans Souci.** Dionne Brand. 150p. pap. 10.95 (*0-88961-196-3*, Pub. by Wmns Pr CN) LPC InBook.

Sans Souci & Other Stories. Dionne Brand. LC 89-23614. 150p. (Orig.). 1989. pap. 8.95 (*0-932379-70-2*); lib. bdg. 18.95 (*0-932379-71-0*) Firebrand Bks.

Sans Souci Spa Dining. Susanne Kircher. LC 93-78351. 1993. pap. 15.00 (*0-9611354-8-4*) T Knox Pub.

Sansad Evam Sansadiya Prakriya: (Parliament & Parliamentary Procedure in Hindi) B. L. Babel. (HIN.). (C). 1990. 50.00 (*0-685-39597-9*) St Mut.

Sansato. large type ed. LC 96-24044. (Classics of Fantastic Literature Ser.). 1996. write for info. (*0-913960-38-1*) Borgo Pr.

Sansato. large type ed. LC 96-24044. (Classics of Fantastic Literature Ser.). 1996. pap. write for info. (*0-913960-39-X*) Borgo Pr.

Sanseido's New Concise English-Japanese Dictionary. T. Sasaki. 1362p. (ENG & JPN.). 1985. 49.95 (*0-8288-0466-4*, M10006) Fr & Eur.

Sanseido's New Concise Japanese-English Dictionary. F. Nakajima. 1362p. (ENG & JPN.). 1985. 49.95 (*0-8288-0465-6*, M9989) Fr & Eur.

Sanskar Vidhi: The Procedure of Sacraments. Swami D. Saraswati. Tr. by Acharya V. Shastri. viii, 359p. (Orig.). 1985. pap. 8.95 (*0-685-72925-7*, Pub. by Sarvadeshik Arya II) Nataraj Bks.

Sanskrit & Indian Studies: Essays in Honour of Daniel H. H. Ingalls. Ed. by Masatoshi Nagatomi et al. (Studies in Classical India: No. 2). 278p. 1980. lib. bdg. 104.50 (*90-277-0991-2*, D Reidel) Kluwer Ac.

Sanskrit Buddhism in Burma. Nihar-Ranjan Ray. LC 78-70112. reprint ed. 41.50 (*0-404-17267-5*) AMS Pr.

Sanskrit by Cassette, 9 cass., Set, Vol. I. 497p. (YA). 1991. pap. 215.00 incl. audio (*1-57970-015-2*, AFSK10) Audio-Forum.

Sanskrit by Cassette, 4 cassettes, Set, Vol. II. 75p. (YA). 1991. pap. 110.00 incl. audio (*1-57970-016-0*, AFSK20) Audio-Forum.

Sanskrit-Chinese Dictionary. Ernest J. Eitel. 228p. 1981. 45.00 (*0-8288-1777-4*, M14248) Fr & Eur.

***Sanskrit Criticism.** V. K. Chari. LC 89-27965. 317p. 1990. reprint ed. pap. 90.40 (*0-608-04376-1*, 2065157) Bks Demand.

Sanskrit Drama: Its Origins & Decline. Indu Sekhar. (Illus.). 1977. 22.00 (*0-685-13819-4*) Coronet Bks.

Sanskrit Drama, in Its Origin, Development, Theory & Practice. A. Berriedale Keith. (C). 1992. text ed. 18.50 (*81-208-0977-7*, Pub. by Motilal Banarsidass II) S Asia.

Sanskrit Drama, Problems & Prospects. G. K. Bhat. 1986. 37.50 (*0-8364-1531-0*, Pub. by Ajanta II) S Asia.

Sanskrit-English Dictionary. Theodore Benfey. 1145p. (ENG, GRE, LAT & SAN.). 1982. 55.00 (*0-8288-1154-7*, M14104) Fr & Eur.

Sanskrit-English Dictionary. Monier Monier-Williams. 1372p. (ENG & SAN.). 95.00 (*0-7859-9821-7*) Fr & Eur.

Sanskrit-English Dictionary. rev. ed. Monier Monier-Williams et al. 1367p. (ENG & SAN.). 1920. 139.00 (*0-19-864308-X*) OUP.

Sanskrit-English Dictionary. 4th ed. Monier Monier-Williams. 1333p. 1986. 125.00 (*0-8288-4403-8*, M14103) Fr & Eur.

Sanskrit-English Dictionary. 4th ed. Monier M. Williams. 1367p. 1988. reprint ed. 54.00 (*81-208-0069-9*, Pub. by Motilal Banarsidass II) S Asia.

Sanskrit-English Dictionary: With References to the Best Edition of Sanskirt Author & Etymologies & Comparisons of Cognate Words Chiefly in Greek, Latin, Gothic & Anglo-Saxon. Theodore Benfey. (C). 1991. 28.00 (*81-206-0370-2*, Pub. by Asian Educ Servs II) S Asia.

Sanskrit-English Dictionary (A Comprehensive Sanskrit English Lexicon) Horace H. Wilson. (ENG & SAN.). 95.00 (*0-8288-8052-2*, M14120) Fr & Eur.

Sanskrit-English, Student's Dictionary. 2nd ed. Vaman S. Apte. 664p. (ENG & SAN.). 1988. Sanskrit-English, 2nd ed., 664p., 1988. 24.00 (*81-208-0044-3*) IBD Ltd.

Sanskrit-German Dictionary: Woerterbuch Sanskrit-Deutsch. 3rd ed. Klaus Mylius. 583p. (GER & SAN.). 1987. 150.00 (*0-8288-1157-1*, F60923) Fr & Eur.

Sanskrit Grammar. 2nd ed. William D. Whitney. 566p. 1989. 46.50 (*0-674-78810-9*) HUP.

Sanskrit Grammar. 5th ed. W. D. Whitney. 551p. 1989. reprint ed. 28.00 (*81-208-0620-4*) IBD Ltd.

Sanskrit Grammar: Including Both, the Classical Language & the Older Dialects of Veda & Brahmana. William D. Whitney. (C). 1993. reprint ed. text ed. 18.50 (*0-685-64759-5*, Pub. by Motilal Banarsidass II) S Asia.

Sanskrit Grammar for Students. Arthur A. Macdonell. (C). 12.50 (*81-208-0504-6*, Pub. by Motilal Banarsidass II); pap. 8.50 (*81-208-0505-4*, Pub. by Motilal Banarsidass II) S Asia.

Sanskrit Grammar for Students. 3rd ed. Arthur A. Macdonell. 284p. 1986. pap. 32.00 (*0-19-815466-6*) OUP.

Sanskrit Indeclinables of the Hindu Grammarians & Lexicographers. I. Dyen. (Language Dissertations Ser.: No. 31). 1939. pap. 25.00 (*0-527-00777-3*) Periodicals Srv.

Sanskrit Keys to the Wisdom-Religion. Judith M. Tyberg. 180p. 1976. pap. 10.95 (*0-913004-29-4*) Point Loma Pub.

Sanskrit Language: A Grammar & Reader, 2 vols., Set, Vols. 1 & 2. Walter Maurer. 838p. (C). 1995. text ed. 75.00 (*0-7007-0352-7*, Pub. by Curzon Press UK) UH Pr.

Sanskrit Love Lyrics. Tr. by P. Lal from SAN. 31p. 1973. 6.75 (*0-88253-265-0*); 4.80 (*0-89253-525-3*) Ind-US Inc.

Sanskrit Manual. Roderick S. Bucknell. (C). 1994. text ed. 17.00 (*81-208-1188-7*, Pub. by Motilal Banarsidass II) S Asia.

Sanskrit Play Production in Ancient India. Tarla Mahta. (C). 1995. 34.00 (*81-208-1057-0*, Pub. by Motilal Banarsidass II) S Asia.

Sanskrit Poems of Mayura. Mayura. Tr. by George P. Quackenbos. LC 77-181072. (Columbia University. Indo-Iranian Ser.: No. 9). reprint ed. 39.50 (*0-404-50479-5*) AMS Pr.

Sanskrit Poetry from Vidyakara's Treasury. Vidyakara. LC 67-29627. 356p. (ENG & SAN.). reprint ed. pap. 101.50 (*0-7837-4197-9*, 2059047) Bks Demand.

Sanskrit Primer. Ed Perry. 230p. (Orig.). 1986. reprint ed. 22.00 (*0-685-35381-8*, Pub. by Motilal Banarsidass II) S Asia.

Sanskrit Pronunciation. Bruce C. Hall. 1992. 10.00 incl. audio (*1-55700-021-2*) Theos U Pr.

Sanskrit Reader: Text & Vocabulary & Notes. Charles R. Lanman. LC 11-24320. 425p. 1984. 44.00 (*0-674-78900-8*) HUP.

Sanskrit Reader with Vocabulary & Notes. Charles R. Lanmann. (C). 1983. reprint ed. 16.00 (*0-8364-2860-9*) S Asia.

Sanskrit Speech: Habits & Panini. Vasant V. Bhandare. 387p. 1986. 16.00 (*0-8364-1674-0*, Pub. by Ajanta II) S Asia.

Sanskrit Studies of M. B. Emeneau: Selected Papers. Intro. by M. B. Emeneau. LC 87-72589. (Occasional Papers: No. 13). (Illus.). 224p. (Orig.). (C). 1988. pap. 5.40 (*0-944613-02-0*) UC Berkeley Ctrs SE Asia.

Sanskrit Syntax. J. S. Speijer. (C). 1989. 24.00 (*81-208-0482-1*, Pub. by Motilal Banarsidass II); pap. 15.00 (*81-208-0483-X*, Pub. by Motilal Banarsidass II) S Asia.

Sanskrit-Telugu Dictionary. 580p. (SAN & TEL.). 1943. 49.95 (*0-7859-9815-2*) Fr & Eur.

Sanskrit Tradition & Tantrism. Ed. by Teun Goudriaan & Johannes Bronkhorst. (Panels of the VIIth World Sanskrit Conference - Kern Institute, Leiden: August 23-29, 1987 Ser.: Vol. I). 121p. 1990. 53.50 (*90-04-09245-5*) E J Brill.

Sanson el Hombre Fuerte. Penny Frank & Tony Morris. (Serie Historias de la Biblia - Children's Bible Story Books Ser.). 24p. (SPA.). (J). 1984. 1.79 (*0-8423-6273-8*, 490314) Editorial Unilit.

Sansones's Police Photography. 3rd ed. Larry S. Miller. LC 91-76957. (Illus.). (C). 1992. pap. text ed. 29.95 (*0-87084-767-8*) Anderson Pub Co.

Sansoni Woerterbuch der Italienischen und Deutschen Sprache. 2nd ed. Vladimiro Macchi. 3178p. (GER & ITA.). 1989. 795.00 (*0-7859-8578-6*, 8838314535) Fr & Eur.

Sant' Ilario. Francis M. Crawford. (Works of Francis Marion Crawford Ser.). 1990. reprint ed. lib. bdg. 79.00 (*0-7812-2536-1*) Rprt Serv.

Sant Sai Baba. R. Mohan Rai. 1992. pap. 7.95 (*81-207-1509-8*, Pub. by Sterling Pubs II) Apt Bks.

Santa. Reader's Digest Editors. (J). 1995. 4.99 (*0-89577-813-0*) RD Assn.

***Santa - The Unauthorized Biography.** large type ed. Robert J. Youngs. Ed. by Michelle Nosco. (Illus.). 600p. (Orig.). (J). 1995. per. 19.95 (*0-9646561-0-8*) Feathertouch.

Santa Ana: The People, the Pueblo, & the History of Tamaya. Laura Bayer et al. LC 93-48899. (Illus.). 408p. 1994. 18.95 (*0-8263-1515-1*) U of NM Pr.

Santa Ana Mountains Trail Guide. 4th rev. ed. Kenneth S. Croker. LC 76-14649. (Illus.). 112p. 1991. pap. 7.95 (*0-9622184-1-3*) Whale & Eagle.

Santa Ana River Hydroelectric System. Mark T. Swanson & David De Vries. (Statistical Research Technical Ser.: No. 47). (Illus.). 162p. (Orig.). 1994. per. 18.00 (*1-879442-09-4*) Stats Res.

Santa & Friends. Waldon M. Geyer. 32p. (J). 1991. 14.95 (*1-880695-01-4*); 23.95 incl. audio (*1-880695-03-0*); pap. 8.95 (*1-880695-02-2*); pap. 15.95 incl. audio (*1-880695-04-9*); audio 7.95 (*1-880695-00-6*) Santa & Friends.

Santa & His Friends: Carving with Tom Wolfe. Tom Wolfe & Douglas Congdon-Martin. LC 90-61513. (Illus.). 64p. (Orig.). 1990. pap. 9.95 (*0-88740-277-1*) Schiffer.

Santa & Sams. Bobi Dolora. 96p. 1992. pap. text ed. 9.50 (*1-56770-258-9*) S Scheewe Pubns.

Santa & Son. Leandra Logan. 1996. pap. 3.50 (*0-373-44010-3*, 1-44010-6) Harlequin Bks.

Santa & the Captain: A Mystic Christmas Tale. Tom Tift. LC 89-81337. (Illus.). 24p. (Orig.). (J). (gr. 2-4). 1989. pap. 6.95 (*0-9624607-0-2*) Hickory Ridge Pr.

Santa & the Skipjack. Janie Meneely. (Illus.). 32p. (J). (gr. k-6). 1991. write for info. (*0-9618461-1-9*) BaySailor Bks.

Santa Anna: Patriot or Scoundrel. Ruby C. Tolliver. LC 93-33092. (Illus.). 112p. (J). (gr. 4 up). 1993. 13.95 (*0-937460-82-6*) Hendrick-Long.

Santa Anna: Prisoner of War in Texas. Ken Durham. Ed. by Skipper Steely. (Illus.). 125p. 1986. 13.95 (*0-915263-09-2*); pap. 9.95 (*0-915263-10-6*) Wright Pr.

Santa Anna: The Story of an Enigma Who Once Was Mexico. Wilfrid H. Callcott. LC 36-37514. 405p. reprint ed. pap. 115.50 (*0-317-28705-2*, 2055509) Bks Demand.

Santa Apolonia (Patrona Dental) Cesar A. Mena. LC 86-80092. (Illus.). 79p. (Orig.). (SPA.). 1985. pap. 10.00 (*0-89729-388-6*) Ediciones.

***Santa, Are You for Real?** Harold Myra. LC 97-25497. (Illus.). 32p. (J). (ps-2). 1997. 7.99 (*0-8499-1492-2*) Tommy Nelson.

Santa Barbara: A Guide to El Pueblo Viejo. Rebecca Conard & Christopher H. Nelson. LC 89-705. 160p. (Orig.). (C). 1988. reprint ed. 29.00 (*0-8095-4021-5*, 19263110) Borgo Pr.

Santa Barbara: A Guide to the Channel City & Its Environs. Federal Writers' Project Staff & Writers Program-WPA Staff. (American Guide Ser.). 1989. reprint ed. lib. bdg. 69.00 (*0-7812-1060-7*, 1060) Rprt Serv.

Santa Barbara: A Guide to the Channel City & Its Environs. Federal Writers' Project Staff. LC 73-4574. (American Guidebook Ser.). 1980. reprint ed. lib. bdg. 59.00 (*0-403-02216-9*) Somerset Pub.

Santa Barbara: A Photo-Essay by Tom Tuttle. Tom Tuttle. Ed. by Richard Lane. LC 89-90418. (Illus.). 112p. 1989. 24.95 (*0-930556-05-4*) Tom Tuttle.

***Santa Barbara - Secrets & Side Trips.** 2nd rev. ed. Laurie MacMillan. (Illus.). 139p. 1997. pap. 8.95 (*1-885375-03-4*, Shore Line Pr) Pacific Bks.

***Santa Barbara & California's Central Coast Region: Images & Encounters.** Ed. by Jeanette G. Betts et al. (Pathways in Geography Ser.: Vol. 15). (Illus.). 80p. 1996. pap. 8.00 (*1-884136-10-9*) NCFGE.

Santa Barbara & San Luis Obispo Counties Street Guide & Directory: 1997 Edition. (Illus.). 136p. 1996. pap. 16.95 (*0-88130-842-0*) Thomas Bros Maps.

***Santa Barbara & San Luis Obispo Counties Street Guide & Directory: 1998 Edition.** Thomas Bros. Maps Staff. 136p. 1997. pap. 16.95 (*0-88130-908-7*) Thomas Bros Maps.

Santa Barbara & San Luis Obispo/Ventura Counties Street Guide & Directory: Census Tract Edition. Thomas Bros. Maps Staff. (Illus.). 242p. 1991. 59.95 (*0-88130-551-0*) Thomas Bros Maps.

***Santa Barbara & San Luis Obispo/Ventura Counties Street Guide & Directory: Zip Code Edition, 1998.** Thomas Bros. Maps Staff. 242p. 1997. pap. 33.95 (*0-88130-910-9*) Thomas Bros Maps.

Santa Barbara & San Luis Obispo/Ventura Counties Street Guide & Directory: 1997 Edition. (Illus.). 240p. 1996. pap. 27.95 (*0-88130-843-9*) Thomas Bros Maps.

***Santa Barbara & San Luis Obispo/Ventura Counties Street Guide & Directory: 1998 Edition.** Thomas Bros. Maps Staff. 240p. 1997. pap. 27.95 (*0-88130-909-5*) Thomas Bros Maps.

Santa Barbara & San Luis Obispo/Ventura Counties Street Guide & Directory ZIP Code Edition: 1997 Edition. (Illus.). 242p. 1996. pap. 33.95 (*0-88130-844-7*) Thomas Bros Maps.

***Santa Barbara & Surrounding Area.** Peak Media, Inc. Staff. (Trail Books Ser.). 1997. 24.95 (*1-889364-03-7*) Peak Media.

Santa Barbara Architecture. 3rd ed. Herb Andree et al. Ed. by Bob Easton & Wayne McCall. LC 95-42956. (Illus.). 316p. 1995. 89.95 (*0-88496-400-0*) Capra Pr.

Santa Barbara Bargain Book. Cheri Rae. 94p. (Orig.). 1993. pap. 7.95 (*0-945092-33-4*) EZ Nature.

Santa Barbara by the Sea. Ed. by Rochelle Bookspan. (Illus.). 236p. pap. 10.00 (*0-87461-036-2*) McNally & Loftin.

Santa Barbara Collects. Santa Barbara Museum of Art Staff. LC 84-27608. (Illus.). 84p. (Orig.). 1984. pap. 12.00 (*0-89951-057-4*) Santa Barb Mus Art.

Santa Barbara Cooks! Original Recipes from Santa Barbara's Best Restaurants. Hilary D. Klein. 208p. 1991. reprint ed. lib. bdg. 31.00 (*0-8095-5860-2*) Borgo Pr.

Santa Barbara Day Hikes. Raymond Ford, Jr. LC 92-20956. 292p. 1992. pap. 12.50 (*0-87461-103-2*) McNally & Loftin.

Santa Barbara History Makers. Walker A. Tomkins. LC 83-17591. 423p. 1983. pap. 15.00 (*0-87461-059-1*) McNally & Loftin.

Santa Barbara Mountain Bikes. Raymond Ford, Jr. LC 92-11631. 1992. 9.95 (*0-87461-105-9*) McNally & Loftin.

Santa Barbara Neighborhoods. Walker A. Tompkins. Ed. by Barbara H. Tompkins. (Illus.). 179p. (Orig.). 1989. pap. text ed. 8.98 (*0-685-44891-6*) Santa Barbara Bd Realtors.

Santa Barbara Presidio Area Eighteen Forty to Present. Karen Schultz et al. Ed. by Catherine E. Rudolph. (Illus.). 174p. (Orig.). 1993. pap. 14.95 (*1-879208-01-6*) SB Trust Hist.

Santa Barbara Restaurant Guide. 2nd ed. 110p. 1994. pap. 8.95 (*0-945092-32-6*) EZ Nature.

Santa Barbara Restaurant Guide. 112p. (C). 1990. reprint ed. lib. bdg. 27.00 (*0-8095-4078-9*) Borgo Pr.

Santa Barbara Restaurant Guide, Vol. 1. Unknown Critic Staff. Ed. by Liz McClung. LC 89-82044. (Illus.). 160p. 1990. reprint ed. pap. 8.95 (*0-9624574-0-X*) Best Cellar Bks.

Santa Barbara Road Rides. Raymond Ford, Jr. LC 95-4238. 1995. 8.50 (*0-87461-109-1*) McNally & Loftin.

Santa Barbara Secrets & Sidetrips. Laurie MacMillan. (Illus.). 128p. (Orig.). 1991. pap. 8.95 (*0-945092-17-2*) EZ Nature.

Santa Barbara Snapshop. Tom Tuttle. (Illus.). 48p. (Orig.). (ENG, FRE, GER, JPN & SPA.). 1994. pap. write for info. (*0-318-72747-1*) Pacific Bks.

Santa Barbara with Kids! Places to Go, Things to Do. Susan A. Cann. LC 91-76064. (Illus.). 168p. (Orig.). 1992. pap. 10.95 (*0-9630810-0-4*) Chaparral.

***Santa Barbara's Flying a Studio.** Stephen Lawton. LC 96-39089. (Illus.). 160p. (Orig.). 1997. pap. 12.95 (*1-56474-210-5*) Fithian Pr.

Santa Bear. Marcia Leonard. 1996. pap. 2.95 (*0-8167-1495-9*) Troll Communs.

Santa Biblia: The Bible Through Hispanic Eyes. Justo L. Gonzalez. 144p. (Orig.). 1996. pap. 14.95 (*0-687-01452-2*) Abingdon.

Santa Biblia - Large Print Reference Bible: Edicion Especial Con Letra Grande, Reina-Valera 1909 Version. deluxe large type ed. 1986. 45.00 (*0-311-48731-9*) Casa Bautista.

Santa Calls. William Joyce. LC 92-52691. (Laura Geringer Bk.). (Illus.). 40p. (J). (ps-3). 1993. 15.95 (*0-06-021133-4*, Festival) HarpC Child Bks.

Santa Calls. William Joyce. LC 92-52691. (Laura Geringer Bk.). (Illus.). 40p. (J). (ps up). 1993. lib. bdg. 17.89 (*0-06-021134-2*) HarpC Child Bks.

Santa Calls Board Book. William Joyce. (Laura Geringer Bk.). (Illus.). 10p. (J). (ps-3). 1993. 6.95 (*0-694-00841-9*, Festival) HarpC Child Bks.

Santa Calls Gift Box. William Joyce. (Laura Geringer Bk.). (Illus.). 40p. (J). (ps-3). 1996. 15.95 (*0-694-00902-4*, Festival) HarpC Child Bks.

Santa Carving. Ron Ransom. (Illus.). 48p. 1987. pap. 8.95 (*0-88740-107-4*) Schiffer.

Santa Carving with Myron Bowman. 64p. pap. 12.95 (*1-56523-076-0*) Fox Chapel Pub.

Santa Catalina Cookbook, Vol. I. 2nd rev. ed. Ed. by Terri C. Branzinsky & Kathi Bowden. Tr. by Carlotta O'Donnell & Santa Catalina Students & Faculty Staff. (Illus.). 293p. 1983. 15.50 (*0-9612300-0-2*) Santa Catalina.

Santa Catalina Cookbook, Vol. II. Ed. by Terri C. Brazinsky & Kathi Bowden. (Illus.). 400p. 1983. 17.50 (*0-9612300-1-0*) Santa Catalina.

Santa Catalina Island: The Story Behind the Scenery. Terrence D. Martin. LC 83-83007. (Illus.). 48p. (Orig.). 1984. pap. 7.95 (*0-916122-97-2*) KC Pubns.

Santa Clara County, California Declarations of Intention, Bk. A, B, & C. Christine Rose. iv, 76p. 1990. Book A (1850-1857), Book B (1862-1867), Book C (1848-1870). per. 9.75 (*0-929626-03-6*) Rose Family Assn.

***Santa Clara County Commerce & Industry Directory, 1997.** 27th ed. 384p. 1997. pap. 75.00 (*1-57541-042-7*) Database Pub Co.

***Santa Clara County Street Guide & Directory: Zip Code Edition, 1998.** Thomas Bros. Maps Staff. 146p. 1997. pap. 23.95 (*0-88130-912-5*) Thomas Bros Maps.

Santa Clara County Street Guide & Directory: 1997 Edition. (Illus.). 136p. 1996. pap. 16.95 (*0-88130-797-1*) Thomas Bros Maps.

***Santa Clara County Street Guide & Directory: 1998 Edition.** Thomas Bros. Maps Staff. 144p. 1997. pap. 16.95 (*0-88130-911-7*) Thomas Bros Maps.

Santa Clara County Street Guide & Directory ZIP Code Edition: 1997 Edition. (Illus.). 138p. 1996. pap. 23.95 (*0-88130-851-X*) Thomas Bros Maps.

Santa Clara County 1977: McCormack's Guides. 1996. pap. 9.95 (*0-931299-68-3*) McCormacks Guides.

Santa Clara County 1995: McCormack's Guides. 1995. pap. 8.95 (*0-931299-51-9*) McCormacks Guides.

Santa Clara County 1996: McCormack's Guides. 1995. pap. 8.95 (*0-931299-59-4*) McCormacks Guides.

Santa Clara Pottery Today. Betty LeFree. LC 73-92996. (School of American Research Monograph: No. 29). (Illus.). 125p. 1975. pap. 11.95 (*0-8263-0322-6*) U of NM Pr.

***Santa Clara Sagas.** Austen D. Warburton. Ed. by Mary J. Ignoffo. LC 96-31645. (Local History Studies). 1996. 29.95 (*0-935089-20-9*) CA History Ctr.

***Santa Clara Sagas.** Austen D. Warburton. Ed. by Mary J. Ignoffo. LC 96-31645. (Local History Studies: Vol. 36). 1996. pap. 19.95 (*0-935089-19-5*) CA History Ctr.

Santa Clara/San Mateo Counties Street Guide & Directory: 1997 Edition. (Illus.). 224p. 1996. pap. 27.95 (*0-88130-798-X*) Thomas Bros Maps.

***Santa Clara/San Mateo Counties Street Guide & Directory: 1998 Edition.** Thomas Bros. Maps Staff. 224p. 1997. pap. 27.95 (*0-88130-913-3*) Thomas Bros Maps.

***Santa Clara/Santa Cruz Counties Street Guide & Directory: 1998 Edition.** Thomas Bros. Maps Staff. 1997. pap. 27.95 (*0-88130-914-1*) Thomas Bros Maps.

***Santa Claus.** Gail Gibbons. (J). Date not set. write for info. (*0-688-15528-6*, Morrow Junior); lib. bdg. write for info. (*0-688-15529-4*, Morrow Junior) Morrow.

Santa Claus. Charles Hardy. 1992. 12.98 (*1-55521-782-6*) Bk Sales Inc.

Santa Claus. Jerry Smath. (J). 1995. pap. 4.95 (*0-8167-3680-4*) Troll Communs.

Santa Claus. Illus. by Jennie Tulip. 12p. (J). (ps). 1996. bds. 4.98 (*1-85854-551-X*) Brimax Bks.

S

Santa Claus: The Tooth Fairy & Other Stories - A Child's Introduction to Religion. Ronald Gestwicki. Ed. by Sylvia Ashton. LC 77-80276. 1977. 22.95 (*0-87949-108-6*) Ashley Bks.

Santa Claus & His Works. George P. Webster & Thomas Nast. (Illus.). 12p. (J). (gr. 1-8). 1972. reprint ed. pap. 3.25 (*0-914510-03-7*) Evergreen.

Santa Claus & the Woodcutter. Kathrin Siegenthaler. Tr. by Elizabeth Crawford. LC 87-32203. (Illus.). 32p. (J). (gr. k-3). 1995. pap. 6.96 (*1-55858-505-2*) North-South Bks NYC.

Santa Claus Bank Robbery. A. C. Greene. 1988. pap. 4.95 (*0-318-37697-0*) St Martin.

Santa Claus Bank Robbery. A. C. Greene. LC 86-5976. 270p. 1986. reprint ed. pap. 9.95 (*0-87719-055-0*) Gulf Pub.

Santa Claus Book. Alden Perkes. (Illus.). 132p. 1996. reprint ed. pap. 14.95 (*0-8184-0381-0*, L Stuart) Carol Pub Group.

Santa Claus Cartoon Book. Donald Froelich. LC 92-82829. (Illus.). 176p. 1994. pap. 10.00 (*1-56002-279-5*, Univ Edtns) Aegina Pr.

Santa Claus Celebrates Jesus' Birthday. Elizabeth B. Fulgaro. LC 93-91731. (Illus.). 32p. (Orig.). (J). (gr. 3-7). 1994. pap. 5.95 (*0-9638891-0-9*) Holy Spir.

Santa Claus Doesn't Mop Floors. Debbie Dadey & Marcia Jones. 80p. (J). 1991. pap. 2.99 (*0-590-44477-8*) Scholastic Inc.

S

***Santa Claus Express.** Linda Kelm et al. 85p. (Orig.). 1997. pap. 10.00 (*1-57502-465-9*, P01397) Morris Pubng.

Santa Claus Forever! Carolyn Haywood. LC 83-1017. (Illus.). 32p. (J). (gr. k-3). 1999. pap. 11.95 (*0-688-10998-5*, Morrow Junior) Morrow.

Santa Claus Has a Busy Night. (Christmas Titles Ser.: No. S808-6). (Illus.). (J). 3.95 (*0-7214-5077-6*, Ladybrd) Penguin.

Santa Claus in My Kitchen. Candy Coleman. (Illus.). 48p. (Orig.). 1979. pap. text ed. 3.00 (*0-943768-01-2*) C Coleman.

Santa Claus Is Coming. M. J. Rodgers. (Intrigue Ser.). 1993. mass mkt. 2.99 (*0-373-22254-8*, 1-22254-6) Harlequin Bks.

Santa Claus Is Coming to Town. (Favorite Christmas Tales Ser.). (Illus.). 24p. (J). 1993. 4.98 (*1-56173-715-1*) Pubns Intl Ltd.

Santa Claus Is Coming to Town. (Christmas Classic Holiday Ser.). 24p. (J). (ps-3). Date not set. text ed. 3.50 (*1-56987-237-6*) Landoll.

Santa Claus Is Coming to Town. (Little Landoll Christmas Ser.). 32p. (J). (ps-6). Date not set. text ed. 1.29 (*1-56987-280-5*) Landoll.

Santa Claus Is Coming to Town. Illus. by Isobel Bushell. (Musical Board Bk.). 12p. (J). (ps). 1993. 5.95 (*0-694-00563-0*, Festival) HarpC Child Bks.

Santa Claus Is Coming to Town. Carolyn Quattrocki. (Favorite Christmas Tales Ser.). (Illus.). 24p. (J). (ps-4). 1992. lib. bdg. 10.95 (*1-56674-026-6*, HTS Bks) Forest Hse.

Santa Claus Is Missing! Sylvia Ashby. (Illus.). 22p. (Orig.). (J). (ps up). 1989. Piano Score. 7.50 (*0-88680-311-X*); pap. 3.25 (*0-88680-310-1*) I E Clark.

Santa Claus, Last of the Wild Men: The Origins & Evolution of Saint Nicholas, Spanning 50,000 Years. Phyllis Siefker. LC 96-38896. (Illus.). 227p. 1996. lib. bdg. 28.50 (*0-7864-0246-6*) McFarland & Co.

***Santa Claus of the 20th Century: Donald Franels Fournier.** Paul A. Fournier. Ed. by John Cole. (Illus.). 192p. 1997. 14.95 (*0-9656876-0-0*) Consolidated Pr.

Santa Claus-Paper Dolls in Full Color. Tom Tierney. (J). 1983. pap. 3.95 (*0-486-24546-2*) Dover.

Santa Claus' Snack. Robert L. Merriam. (Illus.). 14p. (J). (ps-6). 1970. pap. 2.00 (*0-686-32491-9*) R L Merriam.

Santa Claus Snowed Under. Victor G. Ambrus & Glenys Ambrus. 32p. (J). Date not set. write for info. (*0-19-279941-X*) OUP.

Santa Claus Stories: Broadcast on 1927 from Palais Royal Department Store, Washington DC. 1988. write for info. (*0-318-60429-9*) Interspace Bks.

Santa Clause. Adapted by Daphne Skinner. LC 94-78141. (Junior Novel Ser.). (Illus.). 96p. (J). (gr. 3-7). 1994. pap. 3.95 (*0-7868-1011-4*) Hyprn Ppbks.

Santa Clues. Ed. by Martin H. Greenberg & Carol-Lynn R. Waugh. 256p. 1993. pap. 5.99 (*0-451-17708-8*, Topaz) NAL-Dutton.

***Santa Cookie.** Jacqueline Joyce. LC 97-93808. (Illus.). 36p. (Orig.). (J). (ps-4). Date not set. pap. 7.95 (*0-9652211-6-4*, 11133) Bear Path.

***Santa Cookie.** Jacqueline Joyce. Tr. by DelMar Communications Int'l. Staff. LC 97-93807. (Illus.). 36p. (Orig.). (SPA.). (J). (ps-4). Date not set. pap. 7.95 (*0-9652211-7-2*, 11134) Bear Path.

Santa Cow Island. Cooper Edens. LC 93-30899. (Illus.). (J). 1994. 14.00 (*0-671-88319-4*, Green Tiger S&S) S&S Childrens.

Santa Cow Studios. Cooper Edens. (Illus.). (J). (ps-3). 1995. 14.00 (*0-689-80030-4*, S&S Bks Young Read) S&S Childrens.

***Santa Cowboy.** McMahon. 1997. mass mkt. 3.50 (*0-373-76116-3*) Harlequin Bks.

Santa Cows. Cooper Edens. LC 91-57. (Illus.). 40p. (J). (gr. 2 up). 1991. lib. bdg. 14.00 (*0-671-74863-7*, Green Tiger S&S) S&S Childrens.

Santa Cruz: The Early Years. Leon Rowland. Ed. by Michael S. Gant. LC 80-81418. (Illus.). 273p. 1980. pap. 7.95 (*0-934136-04-1*) Western Tanager.

***Santa Cruz County, California: Illustrations Descriptive of Its Scenery, Fine Residences, Public Buildings, Manufactories, Hotels, Farm Scenes, Business Houses, Schools, Churches, Mines Mills, Etc...With Historical Sketch of the County.** Leonard A. Greenberg et al. LC 96-50164. (Illus.). 1997. write for info. (*0-940283-08-5*) Santa Cruz Hist.

Santa Cruz County Place Names: A Geographical Dictionary. Donald T. Clark. LC 86-24840. (Illus.). 624p. 1986. 33.95 (*0-940283-00-X*); pap. 23.95 (*0-940283-01-8*) Santa Cruz Hist.

Santa Cruz Guru Murders. Marc Darrow. (Mystery in the Monterey Bay Area Ser.). 174p. (Orig.). 1995. pap. 9.95 (*0-9617681-8-5*) Otter B Bks.

Santa Cruz Haggadah: A Passover Haggadah, Coloring Book & Journal for the Evolving Consciousness. Karen Roekard. 1992. Participants Version. student ed. 5.95 (*0-9628913-8-X*) Hineni Concisus.

Santa Cruz Haggadah Kids Passover Fun Book. Karen Roekard. (Illus.). 56p. (Orig.). (J). (ps-10). 1994. pap. 4.95 (*0-9628913-0-4*) Hineni Concisus.

Santa Cruz Haggadah Leader's Edition: A Passover Haggadah, Coloring Book & Journal for the Evolving Consciousness. Karen Roekard. 1992. Leaders Version. 13.95 (*0-9628913-4-7*) Hineni Concisus.

Santa Cruz Is in the Heart. Geoffrey Dunn. 185p. 1990. 12.95 (*0-932319-02-5*) Capitola Bk.

***Santa Cruz Island: A History of Conflict & Diversity.** John Gherini. LC 97-904. (Illus.). 275p. 1997. 39.50 (*0-87062-264-1*) A H Clark.

Santa Cruz Island Anthology. 2nd ed. Ed. & Intro. by Marla Daily. 161p. pap. 10.95 (*1-886342-00-8*) Pacfic Bks.

Santa Cruz Mountain Poems. 2nd ed. Morton Marcus. (Illus.). 72p. reprint ed. pap. 12.95 (*0-932319-03-3*) Capitola Bk.

Santa Cruz Mountains Trail Book. 5th rev. ed. Tom Taber. (Illus.). 144p. 1988. pap. 7.95 (*0-9609170-3-9*) Oak Valley.

Santa Cruz Mountains Trail Book. 6th ed. Tom Taber. (Illus.). 160p. 1990. pap. 9.95 (*0-9609170-4-7*) Oak Valley.

Santa Cruz Mountains Trail Book: San Francisco to Santa Cruz. Tom Taber. 184p. 1994. pap. 11.95 (*0-9609170-5-5*) Oak Valley.

***Santa Crystal Valley.** Des. by Steve Kerhli. (Illus.). 24p. (Orig.). 1996. pap. 8.00 (*0-9654795-0-1*) FIGI.

Santa Dolls: Historical to Contemporary. Ann Bahar. 176p. 1992. 29.95 (*0-87588-397-4*) Hobby Hse.

Santa Dolls & Figurines Price Guide Antique to Contemporary. Polly Judd & Pam Judd. (Illus.). 160p. 1994. 14.95 (*0-87588-420-2*, 4702) Hobby Hse.

Santa Eucarista y Otros Servicios. 44p. (SPA.). 1983. pap. 1.50 (*0-935461-05-1*) St Alban Pr CA.

Santa Evita. Tomas E. Martinez. 1996. pap. 14.00 (*0-679-77629-X*, Vin) Random.

Santa Evita. Tomas E. Martinez. 1997. pap. 14.00 (*0-679-76814-9*) Random.

Santa Evita. Tomas E. Martinez. 1996. 23.00 (*0-679-44704-0*) Knopf.

***Santa Evita.** Tomas E. Martinez. Tr. by Helen Lane. 371p. Date not set. 23.00 (*0-614-21930-2*) Knopf.

Santa Fe. (Frommer's Irreverent Guides Ser.). 1996. pap. 12.95 (*0-614-12830-7*) Macmillan.

Santa Fe. Lawrence Cheek. LC 95-2933. (Compass American Guides Ser.). (Illus.). 1996. pap. 18.95 (*1-878867-75-X*) Fodors Travel.

Santa Fe. Laurence E. Parent. LC 96-5215. (New Mexico Sights & Scenes Ser.). (Illus.). 1996. 7.95 (*0-88415-839-X*, 5839) Gulf Pub.

Santa Fe: An Intimate View. Bill Jamison. LC 82-81390. (Illus.). (Orig.). 1982. pap. 7.95 (*0-9608504-0-6*) Milagro Pr Inc.

***Santa Fe: Dancing Ground of the Sun.** Lorraine Bonebrake. (Illus.). 64p. 1997. 14.95 (*1-56579-239-4*) Westcliffe Pubs.

Santa Fe: History of an Ancient City. Francis Levine et al. Ed. by David G. Noble. LC 89-4214. (Illus.). 155p. 1989. 29.95 (*0-933452-26-8*); pap. 16.95 (*0-933452-27-6*) Schol Am Res.

Santa Fe: History of an Ancient City. Ed. by David G. Noble. (Illus.). 168p. 1989. 29.95 (*0-295-96879-6*); pap. 16.95 (*0-295-96865-6*) U of Wash Pr.

Santa Fe: The Autobiography of a Southwestern Town. Oliver La Farge & Arthur N. Morgan. LC 59-7958. 436p. 1985. pap. 19.95 (*0-8061-1696-X*) U of Okla Pr.

Santa Fe: The Railroad Gateway to the American West. Donald Duke. LC 95-21413. 1995. 59.95 (*0-87095-110-6*) Gldn West Bks.

Santa Fe & Beyond. Shirley Phipps. LC 93-84179. 1993. 9.95 (*0-916809-61-7*) Scott Pubns MI.

Santa Fe & Taos: The Writers Era, 1916-1941. Marta Weigle & Kyle Fiore. LC 93-43122. (Illus.). 240p. (Orig.). 1994. pap. 12.95 (*0-941270-79-3*) Ancient City Pr.

Santa Fe & Taos: Under a Coyote Moon. Landt Dennis. LC 95-30891. (Illus.). 144p. 1996. pap. 19.95 (*0-8118-0896-3*) Chronicle Bks.

Santa Fe & Taos Book: A Complete Guide. 3rd ed. Brandt Morgan & Keith Easthouse. (Great Destinations Ser.). 352p. 1996. 17.95 (*0-936399-81-3*) Berkshire Hse.

Santa Fe & Taos Colonies: Age of the Muses, 1900-1942. Arrell M. Gibson. LC 82-40452. (Illus.). 328p. 1988. pap. 16.95 (*0-8061-2116-5*) U of Okla Pr.

Santa Fe & Taos, Eighteen Ninety-Eight to Nineteen Forty-Two: An American Cultural Center. Kay A. Reeve. (Southwestern Studies: No. 67). (Illus.). 72p. 1982. pap. 10.00 (*0-87404-126-0*) Tex Western.

Santa Fe Area Mountain Bike Trails. Craig Martin. (Illus.). 110p. (Orig.). 1994. pap. 10.95 (*0-9639040-1-9*) All Seasons.

Santa Fe Art Colony, 1900-1942. Sharyn R. Udall. Ed. by Nancy Pierson. LC 87-80960. (Illus.). 99p. 1987. pap. 18.00 (*0-935037-15-2*) G Peters Gallery.

Santa Fe Arts Directory see Santa Fe Directory of the Arts

Santa Fe Christmas. Christine Mather. LC 93-2736. 1993. 16.00 (*0-517-59246-0*, C P Pubs) Crown Pub Group.

Santa Fe Coast Lines Depots: Los Angeles Division. Lee Gustafson & Phil Serpico. LC 89-64471. (Illus.). 200p. (C). 1991. 49.95 (*0-88418-003-4*) Omni Hawthorne.

Santa Fe Design. Consumer Guide Editors. 1990. 29.99 (*0-517-02035-1*) Random Hse Value.

Santa Fe Directory of the Arts. 2nd rev. ed. Ed. by Santa Fe Arts Commission Staff. Orig. Title: Santa Fe Arts Directory. 288p. (Orig.). 1996. 9.95 (*0-9651314-0-8*) Santa Fe Arts.

Santa Fe Fantasy. Elmo Baca. LC 92-53959. (Illus.). 120p. 1993. 34.95 (*0-940666-14-6*) Clear Light.

Santa Fe Food Tour: A Guide to Good Eats. Michael Goldberg. 59p. (Orig.). 1993. pap. 5.95 (*0-9637919-0-7*) Blaze Pr.

Santa Fe Guide. 7th ed. Waite Thompson & Richard M. Gottlieb. LC 86-5769. (Illus.). 64p. 1994. pap. 6.95 (*0-86534-087-0*) Sunstone Pr.

Santa Fe Hot & Spicy Recipes: Hot New Recipes from Santa Fe Chefs. Joan Stromquist. Ed. by Carl Stromquist. (Recipe Ser.). (Illus.). 352p. (Orig.). 1993. pap. 16.95 (*0-9622807-5-5*) Tierra Pubns.

Santa Fe in the Mountains: Three Passes of the West: Raton, Cajon, & Tehachapi. George Drury. (Golden Years of Railroading Ser.). (Illus.). 128p. (Orig.). 1995. per. 18.95 (*0-89024-229-1*, 01060) Kalmbach.

Santa Fe Indian Market: Showcase of Native American Art. 2nd ed. Sheila Tryk. Ed. by Bruce Bernstein. (Illus.). 224p. 1993. 34.95 (*0-9622807-4-7*) Tierra Pubns.

***Santa Fe Lite & Spicy II: More Light & Healthy Recipes from Santa Fe's Renowned Chefs.** Joan Stromquist. (Illus.). 320p. 1997. 17.95 (*0-9622807-9-8*) Tierra Pubns.

Santa Fe Lite & Spicy Recipe: Lighter, Healthier Recipes from Santa Fe's Renowned Chefs. Joan Stromquist & Carl Stromquist. (Recipe Ser.). (Illus.). 336p. (Orig.). 1992. 16.95 (*0-9622807-2-0*) Tierra Pubns.

Santa Fe Meeting: Proceedings of 1984 Division of Particicles & Fields, American Physical Society. Ed. by T. Goldman & M. M. Neito. 600p. 1985. 108.00 (*9971-978-46-6*); pap. 60.00 (*9971-978-82-2*) World Scientific Pub.

Santa Fe Motive Pictorial-1987. Joseph W. Shine. 128p. (Orig.). 1988. 25.95 (*0-9616874-2-8*) Four Ways.

Santa Fe Motive Power Pictorial-1988. Joseph W. Shine. 128p. (Orig.). 1989. 25.95 (*0-9616874-3-6*) Four Ways.

Santa Fe, New Mexico: Sightseeing in Eighty-Eight Pictures. Lisa D. Hoff. (Cities in Color Pictorial Guidebooks Ser.). (Illus.). 80p. (Orig.). 1992. pap. 9.95 (*0-9617959-6-4*) Cities in Color.

Santa Fe on Foot: Running, Walking & Bicycling Adventures in the City Different. rev. ed. Elaine Pinkerton. Ed. by Richard L. Polese. LC 86-60510. (Adventure Roads Travel Ser.: No. 1). (Illus.). 144p. 1994. pap. 9.95 (*0-943734-25-8*) Ocean Tree Bks.

Santa Fe Recipe: A Cookbook of Recipes from Favorite Local Restaurants. Ed. by Joan Stromquist & Carl Stromquist. (Illus.). 320p. (Orig.). 1989. pap. 14.95 (*0-9622807-0-4*) Tierra Pubns.

Santa Fe Rembrandt. Cecil Dawkins. (Southwest Mysteries Ser.). 1993. mass mkt. 4.99 (*0-8041-1101-4*) Ivy Books.

Santa Fe Route to the Pacific. Phil Serpico. LC 87-46360. (Illus.). 150p. (YA). (gr. 6 up). 1988. 25.00 (*0-88418-000-X*) Omni Hawthorne.

Santa Fe Rules. Stuart Woods. 368p. 1993. mass mkt. 5.99 (*0-06-109089-1*, Harp PBks) HarpC.

Santa Fe Rules. large type ed. Stuart Woods. LC 92-23905. 501p. 1992. reprint ed. lib. bdg. 20.95 (*1-56054-513-5*) Thorndike Pr.

Santa Fe School of Cooking Cookbook: Spirited Southwestern Recipes. Susan Curtis. LC 95-11519. (Illus.). 176p. 1995. 24.95 (*0-87905-619-3*) Gibbs Smith Pub.

***Santa Fe Shadows Whisper: A History of the Alarid & Moya Families.** Waldo Alarid. Ed. by Charlene Garcia-Simms. (Illus.). 176p. (Orig.). 1997. pap. 14.95 (*0-9628974-5-0*) El Escrito.

Santa Fe Showdown. Frederic Bean. 256p. 1993. mass mkt. 3.50 (*0-8217-4065-2*, Zebra Kensgtn) Kensgtn Pub Corp.

Santa Fe Showdown. Wesley Ellis. (Lone Star Ser.: No. 120). 192p. (Orig.). 1992. mass mkt. 3.99 (*0-515-10902-9*) Jove Pubns.

Santa Fe Steam: The Last Decade: 1949-1959. Lloyd E. Stagner. (Illus.). 72p. 1995. reprint ed. pap. 18.95 (*0-942035-34-8*) South Platte.

Santa Fe Streamliners. Karl Zimmermann. 1987. pap. 17.95 (*0-915276-41-0*) Quadrant Pr.

Santa Fe Style. Christine Mather & Sharon Woods. LC 86-42715. (Illus.). 256p. 1993. 42.50 (*0-8478-0734-7*) Rizzoli Intl.

Santa Fe Sunshine. Preston Jones. 1977. pap. 5.25 (*0-8222-0986-1*) Dramatists Play.

Santa Fe Symposium on Jewelry Manufacturing Technology, 1987. Ed. by Dave Schneller. 45.00 (*0-931913-08-X*) Met-Chem Rsch.

Santa Fe Symposium on Jewelry Manufacturing Technology, 1988. Ed. by Dave Schneller. 45.00 (*0-931913-13-6*) Met-Chem Rsch.

Santa Fe Symposium on Jewelry Manufacturing Technology, 1989. Ed. by Dave Schneller. 45.00 (*0-931913-16-0*) Met-Chem Rsch.

Santa Fe Symposium on Jewelry Manufacturing Technology, 1990. Ed. by Dave Schneller. 45.00 (*0-931913-17-9*) Met-Chem Rsch.

Santa Fe Symposium on Jewelry Manufacturing Technology, 1991. Ed. by Dave Schneller. 49.95 (*0-931913-18-7*) Met-Chem Rsch.

Santa Fe Symposium on Jewelry Manufacturing Technology, 1995. Ed. by Dave Schneller. 49.95 (*0-931913-20-9*) Met-Chem Rsch.

***Santa Fe Symposium on Jewelry Manufacturing Technology 1996.** Ed. by Dave Schneller. 1996. 49.95 (*0-931913-24-1*) Met-Chem Rsch.

Santa Fe, Taos Albuquerque 97: The Best of New Mexico Including the Pueblos & Carlsbad Caverns. Fodor's Staff. (Illus.). 1997. pap. 13.50 (*0-679-03280-0*) Fodors Travel.

Santa Fe Tarot. Holly Huber & Tracey LeCocq. (Illus.). 224p. 1996. pap. 12.00 (*0-88079-756-8*, BK144) US Games Syst.

Santa Fe Tarot, Set, incl. deck. Holly Huber & Tracey LeCocq. (Illus.). 224p. 1996. pap. 28.00 (*0-88079-757-6*, SFE99) US Games Syst.

Santa Fe TASI-87: Proceedings of the 1987 Theoretical Advanced Study Institute in Elementary Partical Physics, 2 vols. R. Slansky. 1056p. 1988. text ed. 124.00 (*9971-5-0438-3*); pap. text ed. 61.00 (*9971-5-0439-1*) World Scientific Pub.

Santa Fe Then & Now. Sheila Morand. LC 84-2503. (Illus.). 96p. (Orig.). 1984. pap. 14.95 (*0-86534-046-3*) Sunstone Pr.

***Santa Fe Trail.** Ralph Compton. 1997. mass mkt. 5.99 (*0-312-96296-7*) St Martin.

Santa Fe Trail. James A. Crutchfield. 208p. 1995. pap. 12.95 (*1-55622-462-1*, Rep of TX Pr) Wordware Pub.

Santa Fe Trail. Linda Hatch. (Pathways of America Ser.). 96p. teacher ed. 10.99 (*0-86653-811-9*, GA1503) Good Apple.

Santa Fe Trail. David S. Lavender. LC 94-16638. (Illus.). 64p. (J). (gr. 3-7). 1995. lib. bdg. 15.95 (*0-8234-1153-2*) Holiday.

Santa Fe Trail. R. L. Duffus. (Illus.). 1971. reprint ed. 39.00 (*0-403-00918-9*) Scholarly.

Santa Fe Trail: New Perspectives. Colorado Historical Society Staff. LC 92-30677. 1992. pap. 11.95 (*0-87081-278-5*) Univ Pr Colo.

Santa Fe Trail: Voyage of Discovery. Dan Murphy. Tr. by Brigitte Morales. (Illus.). 48p. (Orig.). (GER.). 1994. pap. 8.95 (*0-88714-788-7*) KC Pubns.

Santa Fe Trail: Voyage of Discovery. Dan Murphy. Tr. by Carlos Marapodi. (Illus.). 48p. (Orig.). (SPA.). 1994. pap. 8.95 (*0-88714-787-9*) KC Pubns.

Santa Fe Trail: Voyage of Discovery. Dan Murphy. LC 94-75107. (Illus.). 64p. (Orig.). 1994. pap. 7.95 (*0-88714-086-6*) KC Pubns.

Santa Fe Trail: Yesterday & Today. William Hill. LC 92-13064. 1992. pap. 12.95 (*0-87004-354-4*) Caxton.

Santa Fe Trail Activity Book: Pioneer Settlers in the Southwest. Walter D. Yoder. 48p. (Orig.). (J). (gr. 3-9). 1994. pap. 7.95 (*0-86534-217-2*) Sunstone Pr.

***Santa Fe Trail by Air: A Pilot's Guide to the Santa Fe Trail.** William W. White. (Illus.). 128p. (Orig.). 1996. pap. 14.95 (*0-9655085-0-1*) Western Airtrails.

Santa Fe Trail by Bicycle: A Historic Adventure. Elaine Pinkerton. (Illus.). 176p. 1993. pap. 12.95 (*1-878610-24-4*) Red Crane Bks.

Santa Fe Trail National Historic Trail. Mark Gardner. Ed. by Ronald J. Foreman & T. J. Priehs. LC 92-62156. (Illus.). 16p. (Orig.). 1993. pap. 3.95 (*1-877856-20-7*) SW Pks Mnmts.

Santa Fe Trail Revisited. Gregory M. Franzwa. LC 89-39605. (Illus.). 275p. 1989. pap. 12.95 (*0-935284-74-5*) Patrice Pr.

Santa Fe Trail Revisited. Gregory M. Franzwa. LC 89-39605. (Illus.). 275p. 1989. audio 29.95 (*0-935284-91-5*) Patrice Pr.

Santa Fe Trail to California Eighteen Forty-Nine to Eighteen Fifty Two. Ed. by Douglas S. Watson. (Illus.). 1985. 300.00 (*0-8488-0225-X*, J M C & Co) Amereon Ltd.

Santa Fe Trail to California, 1849-1852. H. M. Powell. Ed. by Douglas S. Watson. LC 79-174284. (Illus.). reprint ed. lib. bdg. 125.00 (*0-404-05099-9*) AMS Pr.

Santa Fe Trail Trivia. 2nd ed. Leo E. Oliva & Bonita M. Oliva. iv, 56p. (Orig.). 1987. pap. 1.95 (*0-685-66153-9*) Western Bks.

Santa Fe Trail Trivia. 3rd ed. Leo E. Oliva & Bonita M. Oliva. viii, 68p. (Orig.). 1989. pap. 2.95 (*0-938463-04-7*) Western Bks.

Santa Fe Trails Postcards. 64p. 1995. pap. text ed. 9.95 (*0-89013-274-7*) Museum NM Pr.

Santa Fe, 1940-1971, in Color Vol. 2: Kansas City to Albuequerque. Lloyd E. Stagner. LC 92-64308. (Illus.). 128p. 1993. 49.95 (*1-878887-18-1*) Morning NJ.

Santa Fe, 1940-1971, in Color Vol. 3: Albuquerque to Los Angeles. Lloyd E. Stagner. LC 92-64308. (Illus.). 128p. 1993. 49.95 (*1-878887-22-X*) Morning NJ.

Santa Fe, 1940-1971, in Color Vol. 4: Texas-El Capitan, Set. Lloyd E. Stagner. (Illus.). 128p. 1994. 49.95 (*1-878887-35-1*) Morning NJ.

Santa Fe, 1940-1971, in Color, Vol. 1: Chicago to Kansas City. Lloyd E. Stagner. LC 92-64308. (Illus.). 128p. 1992. 49.95 (*1-878887-13-0*) Morning NJ.

Santa Flip Book. Jill Weber. (J). 1991. pap. 2.50 (*1-878689-03-7*) Frajil Farms.

***Santa in a Stetson.** Thompson. 1997. mass mkt. 3.50 (*0-373-25761-9*) Harlequin Bks.

***Santa in My Father's Shoes & Other Christmas Stories.** Illus. by Bob Newman. 1996. 19.95 (*1-885134-07-X*) Newsday.

Santa Is Coming. (Christmas Ser.). (J). (ps). 1983. 2.95 (*0-86112-229-1*, Brimax Bks) Borden.

***Santa Loves Snowmen.** 2nd ed. Jean Zawicki. 1997. pap. text ed. write for info. (*1-57377-013-2*) Easl Pubns.

Santa Lucia. large type ed. Ann Jennings. (Linford Romance Library). 224p. 1993. pap. 15.99 (*0-7089-7401-5*, Linford) Ulverscroft.

***Santa Misa: Mi Misal en Laminas.** Lawrence G. Lovasik. (San Jose de Libros en Laminas Ser.). (Illus.). (SPA.). 1988. pap. 1.25 (0-89942-467-8, 467/S) Catholic Bk Pub.

***Santa Monica Bay: Paradise by the Sea.** Fred Basten. LC 97-3461. (Illus.). 304p. 1997. 29.95 (1-57544-024-5) Genl Pub Grp.

***Santa Monica Mountains National Recreation Area - CA.** (Illus.). 1997. 8.99 (1-56695-050-3) Trails Illustrated.

Santa Monica Pier - a History from 1875-1990. Jeffrey W. Stanton. (Illus.). 172p. (Orig.). 1990. pap. 19.95 (0-9619849-1-0) Donahue Pub.

Santa Monica Poems. Steve Richmond. (Illus.). 48p. 1987. pap. 8.00 (0-941543-00-5) Sun Dog Pr.

***Santa, NASA & the Man in the Moon.** Richard Kaplan et al. (Illus.). (Orig.). (J). (ps-5). 1995. pap. 14.95 (0-9649608-0-X) Batyah Prodns.

***Santa, NASA y el Hombre en la Luna.** Richard Kaplan et al. (Illus.). (Orig.). (SPA.). (J). (ps-5). pap. 14.95 (0-9649608-1-8) Batyah Prodns.

***Santa Paws.** Victoria Alexander et al. 400p. (Orig.). 1997. mass mkt. 5.99 (0-505-52235-7, Love Spell) Dorchester Pub Co.

Santa Plus Martha. Bev Stone. (Illus.). 62p. (J). (gr. k-6). 1992. pap. 12.95 (0-9619791-1-9) Stone Studios.

Santa Remembered. 1989. 24.95 (0-942237-05-6) Leisure AR.

Santa Rita. Martin W. Schwettmann. 1958. 9.50 (0-87611-018-9) Tex St Hist Assn.

***Santa Rita Experimental Range: History & Annotated Bibliography (1903-1988)** Alvin L. Medina. (Illus.). 67p. (Orig.). 1997. pap. text ed. 30.00 (0-7881-3753-0) DIANE Pub.

Santa Rita Village Mortuary Complex (CA-ALA-413) Vol. 18: Evidence & Implications of a Meganos Intrusion. Randy S. Wiberg. (Archives of California Prehistory Ser.: Vol. 18). (Illus.). 106p. (Orig.). (C). 1988. pap. text ed. 9.65 (1-55567-052-0) Coyote Press.

Santa Romana Republica see Holy Roman Republic: A Historic Profile of the Middle Ages

Santa Roo: Peek-A-Pooh. Mouse Works Staff. 10p. (J). 1996. 6.98 (1-57082-331-6) Mouse Works.

Santa Rosa, a Nineteenth Century Town. Gaye LeBaron et al. LC 86-109023. (Illus.). 224p. 1992. reprint ed. pap. 24.95 (0-9615010-1-4) Historia Ltd.

Santa Rosa, a Twentieth Century Town, Vol. II. Gaye LeBaron & Joann Mitchell. LC 93-79227. (Illus.). 352p. 1993. 59.95 (0-9615010-2-2) Historia Ltd.

Santa Rosa Cemeteries: Gravestone Inscriptions for All Cemeteries in Santa Rosa County, Florida. Richard E. Jernigan. (Illus.). 844p. 1987. lib. bdg. 42.50 (0-9619014-1-1) West FL Geol Soc.

***Santa Rosa Cemeteries: Index & Introduction.** West Florida Genealogical Society Staff & Richard E. Jernigan. (Illus.). 128p. pap. text ed. write for info. (0-9646616-1-6) Beyreuth Enter.

***Santa Rosa Cemeteries Vol. 1: Allen-Howell Cemeteries.** West Florida Genealogical Society Staff & Richard E. Jernigan. (Illus.). 248p. pap. text ed. write for info. (0-9646616-2-4) Beyreuth Enter.

***Santa Rosa Cemeteries Vol. 2: Jay-Williams Cemeteries.** West Florida Genealogical Society Staff & Richard E. Jernigan. (Illus.). 293p. pap. text ed. write for info. (0-9646616-3-2) Beyreuth Enter.

Santa Sleuth: (Kids & Kisses Christmas) Heather Allison. (Romance Ser.). 1994. mass mkt. 2.99 (0-373-03341-9, 1-03341-4) Harlequin Bks.

Santa Stories. rev. ed. Lungago. 1989. write for info. (0-930061-26-8) Interspace Bks.

***Santa Suit.** Whittenburg. 1997. mass mkt. 3.75 (0-373-16708-3) Harlequin Bks.

***Santa Surprises.** (Illus.). 160p. 1997. 19.96 (1-57367-095-2) Needlecrft Shop.

***Santa Takes a Vacation - The Happy Adventures of Mr. & Mrs. Claus.** Ruthie M. Jones. (Illus.). 80p. (Orig.). (J). (ps-6). 1996. pap. 15.95 (0-9655010-2-7) Celebrity Pubs.

Santa Through the Window. Faith H. Byrnie. LC 95-3138. (Illus.). 36p. (J). (ps up). 1995. lib. bdg. 15.40 (1-56294-454-1) Millbrook Pr.

Santa Through the Window. Taro Gomi. LC 95-3138. (Illus.). 36p. (J). 1995. 12.95 (1-56294-934-9) Millbrook Pr.

Santa Will Love My Tree (Play Format) Humberto Almaraz. 12p. (Orig.). (J). (ps-3). 1982. pap. 5.00 incl. lp (0-9616528-1-0) Alpha Beto Music.

Santa Will Love My Tree (Story Format) Humberto Almaraz. 12p. (Orig.). (J). (ps-2). 1982. pap. 5.00 incl. lp (0-9616528-0-2) Alpha Beto Music.

Santabear's High Flying Adventure. Lenore Kletter. (Illus.). 32p. (J). (gr. 1-3). 1987. 12.99 (0-9619204-0-8) Santabear Bks.

Santaberry & the Snard. Joel Schick & Alice Schick. (J). (gr. 4). 1976. 15.00 (0-912846-23-2) Bookstore Pr.

Santal. Ronald Firbank. (Sun & Moon Classics Ser.: No. 58). 56p. (Orig.). 1995. pap. 7.95 (1-55713-174-0) Sun & Moon CA.

Santal: A Tribe in Search of a Great Tradition. Martin Orans. LC 65-12595. 168p. reprint ed. 47.90 (0-685-16243-5, 2027605) Bks Demand.

Santal Dictionary, 7 pts. in 5 vols., Set. P. O. Bodding. 1993. reprint ed. 240.00 (81-212-0423-2, Pub. by Gian Publng Hse II) S Asia.

Santal Folk Tales. A. Campbell. LC 78-67700. (Folktale Ser.). reprint ed. 29.50 (0-404-16066-2) AMS Pr.

Santal Theology of Liberation. V. Manuel Raj. 1990. 22.00 (81-85024-81-2, Pub. by Uppal Pub Hse II) S Asia.

Santali: A Look into Santal Morphology. Arun Ghosh. (C). 1994. 18.50 (81-212-0451-8, Pub. by Gian Publng Hse II) S Asia.

Santals: A Classified & Annotated Bibliography. J. Troisi. LC 76-901556. 1976. 14.50 (0-88386-816-4) S Asia.

Santals, Religion & Rituals. A. B. Chaudhri. (C). 1987. 26.50 (81-7024-085-9, Pub. by Ashish II) S Asia.

***Santamaria: Memoirs of a Political Outsider.** B. A. Santamaria. (Illus.). 400p. 1997. pap. 35.00 (0-19-554052-2) OUP.

Santan Dharma Ka Mahatva: (Uttarpara Speech) Sri Aurobindo. 14p. 1.00 (0-317-17480-0) Auromere.

Santana: Last War Chief of the Mescalero Apaches. Almer N. Blazer. Ed. by A. R. Pruit. LC 95-33158. (Illus.). 320p. 1997. 24.95 (0-940666-69-3); pap. 14.95 (0-940666-70-7) Clear Light.

Santana Vol. 1: Dance of the Rainbow Serpent, Heart. Ed. by Aaron Stang. 116p. (Orig.). (YA). 1996. pap. text ed. 22.95 (1-57623-302-2, PG9538) Warner Brothers.

Santana Vol. 2: Dance of the Rainbow Serpent, Soul. Ed. by Aaron Stang. 80p. (Orig.). (YA). 1996. pap. text ed. 22.95 (1-57623-303-0, PG9539) Warner Brothers.

Santana Vol. 3: Dance of the Rainbow Serpent Spirit. Ed. by Aaron Stang. 152p. (Orig.). (YA). 1996. pap. text ed. 22.95 (1-57623-304-9, PG9540) Warner Brothers.

***Santana Anthology.** Santana. pap. 19.95 (0-7935-6409-3) H Leonard.

Santana Formation Fossils. John G. Maisey. 1991. 200.00 (0-86622-549-8, H-1108) TFH Pubns.

Santander Regime in Gran Colombia. David Bushnell. LC 78-100248. 381p. 1970. reprint ed. text ed. 35.00 (0-8371-2981-8, BUSR, Greenwood Pr) Greenwood.

***Santanismo.** B. Larson. (SPA.). 10.95 (0-8297-1022-1) Life Pubs Intl.

Santas. Rick Butz & Ellen Butz. LC 95-3763. (Woodcarving Step by Step with Rick Butz Ser.). (Illus.). 128p. 1995. pap. 14.95 (0-8117-2566-9) Stackpole.

Santa's ABC. Florence Johnson. (Illus.). 16p. (J). (ps-3). 1993. pap. 3.95 (0-307-10360-9, Golden Books) Western Pub.

***Santas & Snowmen: Carving for Christmas.** Tina Toney. 1997. pap. text ed. 12.95 (1-56523-083-3) Fox Chapel Pub.

***Santas Anda Suelto.** N. Cruz. (SPA.). pap. 5.95 (0-8297-0595-3) Life Pubs Intl.

***Santa's Ark.** Cliff Wright. LC 97-11228. (Illus.). (J). 1997. write for info. (0-7613-0299-9) Millbrook Pr.

***Santa's Ark.** Cliff Wright. (Illus.). 36p. (J). (ps-2). 1997. lib. bdg. 15.90 (0-7613-0314-6) Millbrook Pr.

***Santa's Around the World.** Ed. by Fred L. Israel & Arthur M. Schlesinger, Jr. (Looking into the Past). (Illus.). 64p. (YA). (gr. 5 up). 1997. lib. bdg. 16.95 (0-7910-4678-8) Chelsea Hse.

Santa's Beard Is Soft & Warm. Bob Ottum & JoAnne Wood. (Golden Touch & Feel Bks.). (Illus.). 24p. (J). (ps-3). 1974. 6.50 (0-307-12148-8, Golden Books) Western Pub.

***Santa's Birthday.** Laurie A. Horn. (Illus.). 15p. (Orig.). (J). (gr. 1-2). 1997. pap. 8.99 (1-55237-390-8, Pub. by Comnwlth Pub CN) Partners Pubs Grp.

Santa's Book of Christmas Fun. rev. ed. Illus. by Stacy Venturi-Pickett. 24p. (J). (ps-3). 1995. pap. 2.49 (1-57102-079-9, Ideals Child) Hambleton-Hill.

Santa's Book of Names. David McPhail. LC 92-37279. (J). 1993. 14.95 (0-316-56335-8, Joy St Bks) Little.

***Santa's Book of Names.** David McPhail. 1997. pap. text ed. 5.95 (0-316-11534-7) Little.

Santa's Busy Christmas. Julie Chambers. (Illus.). 14p. (J). (ps-k). 1996. 7.95 (0-694-00905-9, Festival) HarpC Child Bks.

Santa's Busy Night. Illus. by Terry Burton. 20p. (J). (ps). 1996. bds. 3.49 (1-85854-545-5) Brimax Bks.

Santa's Cajun Christmas Adventure. Timothy J. Edler. (Tim Edler's Tales from the Atchafalaya Ser.). (Illus.). 48p. (J). (gr. k-8). 1981. pap. 6.00 (0-931108-07-1) Little Cajun Bks.

Santa's Christmas Journey. Roger Brooke. (Legends & Folktales Ser.). (J). (ps-3). 1993. pap. 4.95 (0-8114-8356-8) Raintree Steck-V.

Santa's Christmas Journey: A Scrolling Picture Book. Penny Ives. (Illus.). (J). (ps-3). 1995. 14.95 (0-7868-0023-2) Hyprn Child.

Santa's Christmas Ride: A Storybook with Real Presents. Louise B. Egan. (Illus.). 52p. (J). 1993. 16.95 (0-8362-4505-9) Andrews & McMeel.

Santa's Christmas Storybook. Sheila Black. LC 95-3010. 102p. (J). (gr. k up). 1995. 19.95 (1-57036-159-2) Turner Pub GA.

Santa's Christmas Surprise. Robert Bernardini. LC 94-12716. (Illus.). 32p. (J). 1994. 14.95 (1-56554-089-1) Pelican.

Santa's Christmas Surprise. Jamie McIntire. LC 93-24843. (Glow-in-the-Dark Bk.). (Illus.). (J). (gr. k-3). 1996. pap. 2.95 (0-8167-3257-4) Troll Communs.

Santa's Christmas Surprise. Lucinda McQueen. (Sparkling Christmas Tree Bks.). (Illus.). 10p. (J). (ps). 1994. bds. 4.95 (0-590-48041-3, Cartwheel) Scholastic Inc.

Santa's Cookie Surprise. Janet Craig. LC 88-19997. (First-Start Easy Readers Ser.). (Illus.). 32p. (J). (gr. k-2). 1989. lib. bdg. 9.79 (0-8167-1538-6) Troll Communs.

Santa's Cookie Surprise. Janet Craig. LC 88-19997. (First-Start Easy Readers Ser.). (Illus.). 32p. (J). (gr. k-2). 1997. pap. 2.50 (0-8167-1539-4) Troll Communs.

Santa's Crash-Bang Christmas. Steven Kroll. LC 77-3025. (Illus.). 32p. (J). (ps-3). 1977. lib. bdg. 15.95 (0-8234-0302-5) Holiday.

Santa's Dog & Other Stories. Clifton A. Cross. LC 94-93871. 128p. (Orig.). 1994. pap. 5.95 (1-885951-25-6) Pprbck Writer.

Santa's Favorite Cookies. Tracey Curtis. (Illus.). 24p. (J). 1995. pap. 7.99 (0-89577-796-7) RD Assn.

Santa's Favorite Questions from Kids. Larry L. Meyer. LC 95-94434. 60p. (Orig.). (J). pap. write for info. (0-9646762-0-6) Captain Blys.

Santa's Favorite Story. Hisako Aoki. (Illus.). 24p. (J). 1991. pap. 4.95 (0-590-44454-9, Blue Ribbon Bks) Scholastic Inc.

Santa's Favorite Story. 2nd ed. Hisako Aoki. LC 82-60895. (Pixies Ser.). (Illus.). 28p. (J). (gr. k up). 1991. reprint ed. pap. 4.95 (0-88708-153-3, Picture Book Studio) S&S Childrens.

Santa's Gone Away. Harold Ellison. LC 88-51034. 44p. (J). (gr. k-3). 1988. 6.95 (1-55523-180-2) Winston-Derek.

***Santas Great Book.** Oxmoor House Staff. 144p. 1996. pap. text ed. 19.95 (1-57486-039-9) Oxmoor Hse.

Santa's Hat. Jane Walker. (Little Christmas Window Book Ser.). (Illus.). 14p. (J). (gr. k-3). 1996. bds. 3.99 (1-57584-048-0) Rdrs Dgst Yng Fam.

Santa's Helper. Sherry C. Miller. LC 83-72493. (Molly Character - Color Me Ser.: No. 1). (Illus.). 32p. (Orig.). (J). (gr. k-5). 1983. pap. 1.95 (0-913379-00-X) Double M Pub.

Santa's Helper. Charnan Simon. 10p. (J). 1989. pap. 2.95 (0-8167-1885-7) Troll Communs.

***Santa's Holiday Treats: A Wilton Book of Recipes & Ideas.** (Illus.). 96p. (Orig.). 1995. pap. 7.99 (0-912696-91-5) Wilton.

***Santa's Lap.** Marilyn Whittaker. (J). (ps-4). 1997. 8.95 (0-533-12223-6) Vantage.

Santa's Lil' Gimp: A Book Not for Children. Gregory P. Dorr. LC 95-80767. (Illus.). 32p. (Orig.). 1995. pap. 9.95 (1-878044-47-8) Mayhaven Pub.

Santa's Little Elf. Illus. by Bettina Paterson. 12p. (J). (ps). 1995. bds. 2.50 (0-448-40932-1, G&D) Putnam Pub Group.

***Santa's Little Helper.** Matthuews. 1997. pap. 5.99 (0-7860-0459-2) Kensgtn Pub Corp.

Santa's Little Helpers. Janet Dailey et al. (Orig.). 1995. mass mkt. 4.99 (0-373-48311-2, 5-48311-0) Harlequin Bks.

Santa's Little Instruction Book: His Checklist to See Who's Been Naughty or Nice. Scott Matthews & Barbara Alpert. 96p. 1994. 4.99 (0-7860-0129-1, Pinncle Kensgtn) Kensgtn Pub Corp.

***Santa's Littlest Helper.** (J). (ps up). 1996. pap. 4.99 (0-614-18979-9) RD Assn.

Santa's Littlest Helper. Stewart Cowley. (Fluffy Tale Ser.). (Illus.). 10p. (J). (ps up). 1996. bds. 4.99 (0-88705-964-3) Rdrs Dgst Yng Fam.

Santa's Narrow Escape Christmas Sound Story. Sight & Sound Staff. (J). (ps). 1991. 30.50 (0-88704-205-8) Sight & Sound.

***Santa's New Boots.** Ralph W. Kiesling. (Illus.). (Orig.). (J). (ps-4). 1997. pap. 6.95 (0-533-12228-7) Vantage.

Santa's New Reindeer. Judie Schrecker. LC 96-18586. (Illus.). 40p. (J). (gr. 1-10). 1996. boxed 17.95 (1-880664-18-6) E M Pr.

Santa's New Sled. Sharon Peters. LC 81-5028. (Illus.). 32p. (J). (gr. k-2). 1997. pap. 3.95 (0-89375-524-9) Troll Communs.

Santa's New Sleigh. 10p. (J). (gr. k-2). 1991. pap. 3.95 (0-8167-2187-4) Troll Communs.

Santa's New Suit Funbook. Beverly A. Scott. (J). (ps-6). 1973. pap. 3.00 (0-686-11715-8) B A Scott.

Santa's New Suit Storybook. (J). (ps-6). 1972. 3.00 (0-686-00005-6) B A Scott.

Santa's Pockets. Illus. by Carolyn Bracken. (J). (ps). 1983. pap. 3.95 (0-671-47660-2, Litl Simon S&S) S&S Childrens.

***Santa's Price Guide to Contemporary Christmas Collectibles.** Beth Dees. (Illus.). 240p. (Orig.). 1997. pap. 24.95 (0-87341-528-0, XMCL) Krause Pubns.

Santa's Problem. Myra J. Jordan & Roy E. Grant. (Illus.). 30p. (Orig.). (J). (ps-1). 1980. pap. 5.00 (0-914562-08-8) Merriam-Eddy.

Santa's Red Toy Bag: (How it All Began) Francis Kapraun. (Illus.). 24p. (J). 1994. write for info. (0-9643313-0-6) Inspired.

***Santa's Reindeer.** A. V. McIntosh. (Illus.). 42p. (Orig.). (J). (ps-3). 1996. pap. 10.00 (1-57502-360-1, PO1165) Morris Pubng.

Santa's Scientific Christmas. Ann Veith et al. 1993. 35.00 incl. vdisk (1-883822-01-7) Terrific Sci.

***Santa's Scorekeeper's of the Naughty & the Nice.** James H. Mitchell. (Illus.). 22p. (Orig.). (J). (gr. 1-4). 1997. pap. 8.99 (1-55197-700-1, Pub. by Comnwlth Pub CN) Partners Pubs Grp.

Santa's Secret Helper. Andrew Clements. LC 93-20119. (Pixies Ser.: No. 27). (Illus.). (J). (gr. 1-8). 1993. 4.95 (0-88708-325-0, Picture Book Studio) S&S Childrens.

Santa's Secret Helper. Bill Graham. 18p. (J). (ps). 1987. 10.95 (1-879680-06-8) About You.

Santa's Secret Second String. Jim George. (J). 1996. write for info. (1-56844-045-6) Enchante Pub.

***Santa's Short Suit Shrunk & Other Christmas Tongue Twisters.** Nola Buck. LC 96-29077. (I Can Read Bk.). (Illus.). 32p. (J). (ps-2). 1997. 14.95 (0-06-026649-X); lib. bdg. 14.89 (0-06-026663-5) HarpC Child Bks.

***Santa's Sleigh.** Gill Davies. (Christmas Window Bks.). (Illus.). 14p. (J). (ps up). 1997. bds. 4.98 (1-85854-667-2) Brimax Bks.

Santa's Squeaky Boots. Funworks Staff. 18p. (J). 1996. 6.98 (1-57082-338-3) Mouse Works.

***Santa's Surprise: With Antique Changing Pictures.** Piggytoes Press Staff. (Ernest Nister's Mini Christmas Books Ser.). 1997. 4.95 (1-888443-34-0, Piggytoes Pr) Intervisual Bks.

Santa's Surprises. (J). (ps up). 1994. 9.95 (0-89577-633-2) RD Assn.

***Santa's Time Off.** Bill Maynard. LC 97-2081. (Illus.). 32p. (J). (gr. k-12). 1997. 15.95 (0-399-23138-2) Putnam Pub Group.

Santa's Tiny Workshop. Illus. by David Wenzel. (Little Little Golden Book Boxed Set Ser.). 24p. (J). (ps-3). 1994. boxed 11.95 (0-307-13695-7, Golden Books) Western Pub.

Santa's Toy Shop. (Christmas Classic Holiday Ser.). 24p. (J). (ps-3). Date not set. text ed. 3.50 (1-56987-239-2) Landoll.

Santa's Toy Shop. (Little Landoll Christmas Ser.: No. II). 32p. (J). (ps-6). Date not set. text ed. 1.29 (1-56987-278-3) Landoll.

Santa's Twin. Dean R. Koontz. (Illus.). 72p. 1996. 20.00 (0-06-105355-4, HarperPrism) HarpC.

Santa's Wheat Kernels. Ralph F. Parkison. Ed. by Marion O. Withrow. (Illus.). 60p. (Orig.). (J). (gr. 2-8). 1988. pap. write for info. (0-318-64005-8) Little Wood Bks.

***Santa's Wild Goose Chase.** Gilbert O. Twyman, III. (Illus.). 1997. 14.95 (1-886110-32-8) Addax Pubng.

Santa's Winter Vacation. Viveca L. Sundvall. Tr. by Kjersti Board. (Illus.). 26p. 1995. 13.00 (91-29-62953-5) FS&G.

Santa's Workshop. (Hidden Pictures Ser.). (Illus.). 24p. (J). 1992. 4.98 (0-8317-4681-5) Smithmark.

Santa's Workshop. Ann Braybrooks. LC 94-74819. (Illus.). 32p. (J). (gr. k-3). 1995. 12.95 (0-7868-3026-3) Disney Pr.

Santa's Workshop. Peter Lippman. (Mini House Bks.). (Illus.). 20p. (J). (ps-1). 1993. bds. 9.95 (1-56305-499-X, 3499) Workman Pub.

Santa's Workshop: A Magical Three-Dimensional Tour. Paul Stickland. (Illus.). 8p. (J). (ps up). 1995. pap. 18.99 (0-525-45343-1) Dutton Child Bks.

Santa's Workshop: A Punch-Out Village & Characters. Anne-Frisbie Malone. (Illus.). (J). (gr. 4-7). 1993. pap. 2.95 (0-486-27622-8) Dover.

Santasaurus. Mary Sheldon. 64p. (J). 1996. pap. 15.95 (0-7871-0470-1, Dove Bks) Dove Audio.

Santayana. Neal O'Sullivan. 112p. 1993. 19.95 (1-870626-33-8, Pub. by Claridge Pr UK); pap. 12.95 (1-870626-38-9, Pub. by Claridge Pr UK) Paul & Co Pubs.

Santayana: An Examination of His Philosophy. Timothy L. Sprigge. (Arguments of the Philosophers Ser.). 1974. 29.50 (0-7100-7721-1, RKP) Routledge.

Santayana: An Examination of His Philosophy. Timothy L. Sprigge. (Arguments of the Philosophers Ser.). 262p. (C). 1995. pap. 24.95 (0-415-11751-8, B4674) Routledge.

Santayana: Saint of the Imagination. Mossie M. Kirkwood. LC 61-65164. (Illus.). 252p. reprint ed. pap. 71.90 (0-8357-6382-X, 2035737) Bks Demand.

Santayana & the Sense of Beauty. W. E. Arnett. 1984. 14.50 (0-8446-0458-5) Peter Smith.

Santayana, Art, & Aesthetics. Jerome Ashmore. LC 66-16889. 153p. reprint ed. pap. 43.70 (0-317-08999-4, 2001348) Bks Demand.

Santayana, Pragmatism, & the Spiritual Life. Henry S. Levinson. LC 91-50785. (Illus.). xvi, 348p. (C). 1992. 49.95 (0-8078-2031-8) U of NC Pr.

Sante de la Mere et de l'Enfant: Nouveaux Concepts en Pediatrie Sociale. 2nd ed. M. Manciaux et al. (Illus.). 504p. 1984. lib. bdg. 35.00 (0-318-04482-X) S M P F Inc.

***Sante Fe Railroad.** Michael Blaszak. (Color History Ser.). (Illus.). 128p. 1997. pap. 19.95 (0-7603-0380-0) Motorbooks Intl.

***Sante Fe Rules.** Stuart Woods. 368p. 1995. mass mkt. 3.99 (0-06-109481-1, Harp PBks) HarpC.

***Sante Fe, Taos, Albuquerque.** 3rd ed. Access Guides Staff. (Access Travel Guides Ser.). 160p. 1997. pap. 18.50 (0-06-277194-9, Access NY) HarpC.

Sante Graziani: A Celebration. Text by Karen Papineau. (Illus.). 20p. 1977. 2.00 (0-916746-48-8) Springfield Lib & Mus.

Sante ou Maladie. rev. ed. S. I. McMillen. Orig. Title: None of These Diseases. 288p. (FRE.). 1987. pap. 2.95 (0-8297-0963-0) Life Pubs Intl.

Santee Sioux. Nancy Bonnvillain. (Indians of North America Ser.). (J). 1996. pap. 9.95 (0-7910-3482-8) Chelsea Hse.

Santee Sioux - Great Plains see Indians of North America

***Santee Sioux Indians.** Terrance Dolan. LC 96-25065. (Junior Library of American Indians). (J). 1996. pap. 7.95 (0-7910-4453-X) Chelsea Hse.

Santee Sioux Indians see Junior Library of American Indians

Santeria. Migene G. Wippler. 183p. 1984. pap. 8.95 (0-942272-04-8) Original Pubns.

Santeria: A Practical Guide to Afro-Caribbean Magic. Luis M. Nunez. LC 92-24219. 163p. (Orig.). 1995. pap. 16.00 (0-88214-349-2) Spring Pubns.

Santeria: African Spirits in America. Joseph M. Murphy. LC 92-8590. 224p. 1993. pap. 16.00 (0-8070-1021-9) Beacon Pr.

Santeria: An African Religion in America. Joseph M. Murphy. 208p. 1989. pap. 10.95 (0-942272-22-6) Original Pubns.

Santeria: Magia Africana en Latinoamerica. M. G. Wippler. (SPA.). 1987. pap. 8.95 (0-942272-39-0) Original Pubns.

Santeria: The Religion. 2nd ed. Migene Gonzalez-Wippler. LC 94-15747. (World Religion & Magic Ser.). (Illus.). 400p. 1994. pap. 12.95 (1-56718-329-8) Llewellyn Pubns.

Santeria: The Religion: A Legacy of Faith, Rites, & Magic. Migene Gonzalez-Wippler. 1989. 20.00 (0-517-57154-4, Harmony) Crown Pub Group.

Santeria Aesthetics in Contemporary Latin American Art. Ed. by Arturo Lindsay. (Illus.). 360p. 1996. text ed. 65.00 (1-56098-644-1); pap. text ed. 34.95 (1-56098-615-8) Smithsonian.

Santeria Experience. M. G. Wippler. 239p. 1988. pap. 6.95 (0-942272-15-3) Original Pubns.

***Santeria from Africa to the New World: The Dead Cell Memories.** George Brandon. (Blacks in the Diaspora Ser.). 1997. pap. text ed. 10.95 (*0-253-21114-X*) Ind U Pr.

Santeria from Africa to the New World: The Dead Sell Memories. George Brandon. LC 92-24251. (Blacks in the Diaspora Ser.). (Illus.). 228p. 1993. 31.50 (*0-253-31257-4*) Ind U Pr.

Santeria Garments & Altars: Speaking Without a Voice. Ysamur Flores-Pena & Roberta J. Evanchuk. (Folk Art & Artists Ser.). (Illus.). 64p. 1994. 32.50 (*0-87805-705-6*); pap. 16.95 (*0-87805-703-X*) U Pr of Miss.

Santeria in the Eastern United States. Jim Bailey. 88p. 1991. pap. text ed. 6.00 (*0-9630657-0-X*) Godolphin Hse.

Santeros Puertorriquenos. Teodoro Vidal. 1979. 6.95 (*0-9600714-2-3*) Edns Alba.

Santerra's Sin. Donna Kauffman. (Loveswept Ser.: No. 811). 240p. 1996. mass mkt. 3.50 (*0-553-44538-3*, Loveswept) Bantam.

Santha Rama Rau. S. K. Desai. (Indian Writers Ser.: Vo. 13). 1977. 8.50 (*0-89253-451-6*) Ind-US Inc.

Santhali: The Base of World Languages. Parimal C. Mitra. (C). 1988. 15.00 (*0-8364-2379-8*, Pub. by Firma KLM II) S Asia.

Santhali - English Dictionary. Campbell. 1988. 95.00 (*0-8288-8425-0*) Fr & Eur.

***Santiago.** Vernon Doerksen. (Comentario Biblico Portavoz Ser.). (SPA.). 1996. pap. 6.99 (*0-8254-1166-1*, Edit Portavoz) Kregel.

Santiago. Manuel Pereiras. 26p. 1993. pap. text ed. 2.95 (*1-885901-03-8*) Presbyters Peartree.

Santiago: C-Alumno. Gary Teja. (SPA.). 1994. 1.75 (*1-55955-140-2*) CRC Wrld Lit.

Santiago: C-Muestro. Gary Teja. (SPA.). 1994. 2.00 (*1-55955-141-0*) CRC Wrld Lit.

Santiago: Una Fe en Accion. Evis L. Carballosa. 352p. (Orig.). (SPA.). 1986. pap. 11.99 (*0-8254-1112-2*, Edit Portavoz) Kregel.

Santiago & the Drinking Party. Clay Morgan. (Contemporary American Fiction Ser.). 288p. 1993. reprint ed. pap. 10.00 (*0-14-016732-3*, Penguin Bks) Viking Penguin.

Santiago-bL-Alumno. Gary Teja. (SPA.). 1994. 1.75 (*1-55955-138-0*) CRC Wrld Lit.

Santiago-bL-Maestro. Gary Teja. (SPA.). 1994. 2.00 (*1-55955-139-9*) CRC Wrld Lit.

***Santiago Calatraua: Complete Works.** Ed. by Sergio Dolano. (Illus.). 326p. 1997. pap. 55.00 (*3-927258-37-7*) Gingko Press.

Santiago Calatrava. Ed. by Dennis Sharp. (Architectural Monographs). (Illus.). 120p. (Orig.). 1996. pap. 38.00 (*1-85490-454-X*) Academy Ed UK.

Santiago Calatrava. 2nd ed. Dennis Sharp. 1994. pap. 24.95 (*0-419-19570-X*, E & FN Spon) Routledge Chapman & Hall.

***Santiago Calatrava: Dynamic Equilibrium, Recent Projects.** Birkhauser Staff. 80p. 1996. pap. text ed. 39.95 (*3-7643-5525-5*) Birkhauser.

***Santiago Calatrava: Engineering Architecture.** 2nd ed. Werner Blaser. 1996. 68.00 (*3-7643-2460-0*) Birkhauser.

Santiago Calatrava: Engineering Architecture. 21th rev. ed. Werner Blaser. 176p. 1991. 62.00 (*0-8176-2460-0*) Birkhauser.

Santiago Calatrava: Secret Sketchbook. Santiago Calatrava. Ed. by Mirko Zardini. (Illus.). 96p. 1996. 40.00 (*1-885254-33-4*) Monacelli Pr.

Santiago Calatrava: Structure & Expression. Matilda McQuaid. (Illus.). 40p. 1993. pap. 9.95 (*0-685-65844-9*) Abrams.

Santiago Campaign of 1898: A Soldier's View of the Spanish-American War. A. B. Feuer. LC 93-6769. 216p. 1993. text ed. 49.95 (*0-275-94479-4*, C4479, Praeger Pubs) Greenwood.

Santiago Campaign, 1898. Joseph Wheeler. LC 75-130566. (Select Bibliographies Reprint Ser.). 1977. 24.95 (*0-8369-5539-0*) Ayer.

Santiago Db-Alumno. Gary Teja. (SPA.). 1994. 1.75 (*1-55955-136-4*) CRC Wrld Lit.

Santiago Db-Maestro. Gary Teja. (SPA.). 1994. 2.00 (*1-55955-137-2*) CRC Wrld Lit.

Santiago de Compostela: In the Age of the Great Pilgrimages. Marilyn Stokstad. LC 77-18612. (Illus.). 187p. reprint ed. pap. 53.30 (*0-8357-9740-6*, 2016270) Bks Demand.

***Santiago de Guatemala, 1541-1773: City, Caste, & the Colonial Experience.** Christopher H. Lutz. LC 93-46131. (Illus.). 368p. 1997. pap. 16.95 (*0-8061-2911-5*) U of Okla Pr.

Santiago de Murcia's "Codice Saldivar No. 4" A Treasury of Secular Guitar Music from Baroque Mexico, 2 vols. Craig H. Russell. (Music In American Life Ser.). 1995. text ed. 85.00 (*0-252-02093-6*) U of Ill Pr.

Santiago de Murcia's "Codice Saldivar No. 4" Vol. 2: Facsimile & Transcription: A Treasury of Secular Guitar Music from Baroque Mexico. Craig H. Russell. (Music in American Life Ser.). 328p. 1995. text ed. 39.95 (*0-252-02092-8*) U of Ill Pr.

Santiago De Murcia's "Codice Saldivar Number 4" Vol. 1: A Treasury of Secular Guitar Music from Baroque. Craig H. Russell. 320p. 1995. text ed. 59.95 (*0-252-02083-9*) U of Ill Pr.

Santiago Iglesias: Apostol de los Trabajadores. Clarence Senior. Tr. by Jesus Benitez. LC 72-91601. (Illus.). 110p. (Orig.). 1972. 2.95 (*0-913480-01-0*); pap. 1.95 (*0-913480-03-7*) Inter Am U Pr.

Santiago Iglesias: Creador del Movimiento Obrero de Puerto Rico. Gonzalo F. Cordova & Sara I. Concepcion. LC 78-14404. (Illus.). 231p. (SPA.). 1980. pap. 6.00 (*0-8477-0857-8*) U of PR Pr.

Santiago Iglesias: Labor Crusader. Clarence Senior. Ed. by John Zebrowski. Tr. by Jesus Benitez from ENG. LC 72-91601. (Illus.). 98p. (Orig.). 1972. 2.95 (*0-913480-00-2*); pap. 1.95 (*0-913480-02-9*) Inter Am U Pr.

Santiago Poems. James Scully. LC 81-5475. 32p. 1975. pap. 4.95 (*0-915306-21-2*) Curbstone.

Santiago por Judas (Version Popular) James Through Jude in Spanish. 88p. (SPA.). write for info. (*0-614-00650-3*, 5096) LBW.

Santiago Ramon & Cajal: Vida & Consejos de un Genio de la Ciencia. Francisco Gonzalez-Lima & Erika M. Gonzalez-Lima. (UPREX, Biografias Ser.: No. 77). 85p. 1986. pap. 3.00 (*0-8477-0077-1*) U of PR Pr.

Santiago Vidaurri & the Southern Confederacy. Ron Tyler. (Illus.). 196p. 1973. 14.95 (*0-87611-029-4*) Tex St Hist Assn.

Santidad de Dios. R. Charles Sproul. 190p. (SPA.). 1985. pap. 5.99 (*1-56063-177-5*, 490222) Editorial Unilit.

***Santidad de la Vida.** E. Dawn Swaby-Ellis. (SPA.). 1.50 (*0-8297-1960-1*) Life Pubs Intl.

Santidad para Todo Creyente. Keith Drury. Tr. by Roberto Crosby et al. 146p. 1995. pap. 9.95 (*0-89827-152-5*, BK799) Wesleyan Pub Hse.

Santideva's Bodhicharyavatara, 2 vols., Set. Prajnakarmiti. (C). 1990. 72.00 (*81-85179-13-1*, Pub. by Aditya Prakashan II) S Asia.

Santificados por Completo-Wholly Sanctified. A. B. Simpson. (Illus.). 136p. 1981. mass mkt. 2.99 (*0-87509-307-8*) Chr Pubns.

***Santillana Pictodiccionario.** Santillana Staff. (SPA.). 1996. 24.95 (*84-294-4545-5*) Santillana.

Santilli's Generalization of Galilei's & Einstein's Relativities. A. K. Arigazin et al. (Illus.). 388p. (Orig.). 1992. pap. text ed. 70.00 (*0-911767-56-8*) Hadronic Pr Inc.

Santilli's Isotopies of Contemporary Algebras, Geometries, & Relativities. J. Valdimir Kadeisvili. LC 92-5307. (Monographs in Mathematics). (Illus.). 310p. (Orig.). 1992. paph. text ed. 60.00 (*0-911767-52-5*) Hadronic Pr Inc.

Santimals: Carving with Tom Wolfe. Tom Wolfe. LC 92-60696. (Illus.). 64p. 1992. pap. 12.95 (*0-88740-440-5*) Schiffer.

Santini-Aichel's Design for the Baroque Convent at the Cistercian Monastery at Plasy in Western Bohemia. Michael Young. (Illus.). 144p. 1995. text ed. 32.00 (*0-88033-221-2*) Col U Pr.

Santo Domingo. S. Hazard. 1976. lib. bdg. 69.95 (*0-8490-2567-2*) Gordon Pr.

Santo Domingo: A Country with a Future. Otto Schoenrich. 1976. lib. bdg. 69.95 (*0-8490-0992-8*) Gordon Pr.

Santo Domingo & Beyond: Documents & Commentaries. Ed. by Alfred T. Hennelly. Tr. by Phillip Berryman from SPA. LC 93-36862. 300p. (Orig.). 1993. pap. 21.00 (*0-88344-920-X*) Orbis Bks.

***Santo Questo/The Holy Cheese: Cuentos/Stories.** Jim Sagel. 240p. 1996. pap. 13.95 (*0-8263-1707-3*) U of NM Pr.

***Santo Rosario.** Lawrence G. Lovasik. (San Jose de Libros en Laminas Ser.). (Illus.). (SPA.). 1989. pap. 1.25 (*0-89942-466-X*, 466/S) Catholic Bk Pub.

Santo Triduo Pascual. 80p. 1992. pap. 1.50 (*0-8146-6108-4*, Pueblo Bks) Liturgical Pr.

Santo y Humano: Como Enfrentar las Demandas del Ministerio Pastoral - Being Holy, Being Human Dealing with the Expections of Ministry. Jay Kesler. Tr. by Nelda B. De Gaydou from ENG. 160p. (Orig.). (SPA.). 1992. pap. 7.50 (*0-311-42089-3*) Casa Bautista.

Santorini. Alistair MacLean. 1988. mass mkt. 5.99 (*0-449-20974-1*, Crest) Fawcett.

Santorini: Stopping the Leak. James Merrill. (Metacom Limited Edition Ser.: No. 8). 24p. 1982. 37.50 (*0-911381-07-4*) Metacom Pr.

Santos & Saints: The Religious Folk Art of Hispanic New Mexico. Thomas J. Steele. LC 94-74274. (Illus.). 226p. (Orig.). 1994. pap. 15.95 (*0-941270-84-X*) Ancient City Pr.

Santos-Dumont: A Study in Obsession. Peter Wykeham. Ed. by James B. Gilbert. LC 79-7304. (Flight: Its First Seventy-Five Years Ser.). (Illus.). 1980. reprint ed. lib. bdg. 28.95 (*0-405-12210-1*) Ayer.

Santos Inocentes. Miguel Delibes. 176p. (SPA.). 1993. pap. 14.95 (*0-7859-0509-X*, 8408000187) Fr & Eur.

Santos of Spanish New Mexico Coloring Book. Al Chapman. (J). 1982. pap. 4.95 (*0-86534-238-5*) Sunstone Pr.

Santosha Avatara Gita: The Revelation of the Great Means of the Divine Heart-Way of No-Seeing & Non-Separateness. Adi Da. LC 90-44933. 332p. 1995. pap. 24.95 (*1-57097-009-2*) Dawn Horse Pr.

Sants: Studies in a Devotional Tradition of India. Ed. by Karine Schomer & W. H. McLeod. (C). 1987. 50.00 (*0-9612208-0-5*, Pub. by Motilal Banarsidass II) S Asia.

Santuario. William Faulkner. Tr. by Lino Novas Calvo. (Nueva Austral Ser.: Vol. 14). (SPA.). 1991. pap. text ed. 24.95 (*84-239-1814-9*) Elliots Bks.

Santuario de Chimayo. Stephen F. De Borhegyi & E. Boyd. (Illus.). 32p. 1987. pap. 3.95 (*0-941270-09-2*) Ancient City Pr.

Santuary: Carbon Typescript. Thomas Mchaney & Michael Millgate. (William Faulkner Manuscripts). 384p. 1987. text ed. 55.00 (*0-8240-6811-4*) Garland.

Santuc: Selected Poems & Memories. Thomas W. Christopher. LC 93-94128. (Illus.). 80p. (Orig.). 1994. pap. 8.00 (*1-56002-387-2*) Aegina Pr.

Sanuma Memories: Yanomani Ethnography in Times of Crisis. Alcida R. Ramos. LC 94-39614. (New Directions in Anthropological Writing Ser.). (Illus.). 320p. 1995. pap. text ed. 19.95 (*0-299-14654-5*); lib. bdg. 50.00 (*0-299-14650-2*) U of Wis Pr.

Sanvida Vidhi: (Law of Contract in Hindi) 4th ed. Avtar Singh. (HIN.). (C). 1989. 65.00 (*0-685-39764-5*) St Mut.

San'ya Blues: Laboring Life in Contemporary Tokyo. Edward Fowler. (Illus.). 296p. 1996. 29.95 (*0-8014-3247-2*) Cornell U Pr.

Sanyo Basic User's Handbook. Weber Systems, Inc. Staff. LC 85-5346. (User's Handbooks to Personal Computers Ser.). 250p. (Orig.). 1985. pap. 26.95 (*0-938862-02-2*) Weber Systems.

Sanyo MBC 550-555 User's Handbook. Weber Systems, Inc. Staff. LC 84-20954. (User's Handbooks to Personal Computers Ser.). 330p. (Orig.). 1985. pap. 26.95 (*0-938862-24-3*) Weber Systems.

Sanz, Promotor de la Conciencia Separatista en Puerto Rico. Labor Gomez de Acevedo. (UPREX, Humanidades Ser.: No. 35). 349p. (C). 1974. pap. 1.50 (*0-8477-0035-6*) U of PR Pr.

Sanza Mezzo. Frank Samperi. 1977. 5.00 (*0-685-89003-1*); bds., boxed 10.00 (*0-685-89002-3*) Elizabeth Pr.

Sao Paulo in the Brazilian Federation, 1889-1937. Joseph L. Love. LC 78-66177. (Illus.). xvii, 398p. 1980. 52.50 (*0-8047-0991-2*) Stanford U Pr.

Sao Paulo Law School & the Anti-Vargas Resistance (1938-1945) John W. Dulles. LC 85-15069. (Illus.). 286p. 1986. pap. 81.60 (*0-7837-8956-4*, 2049669) Bks Demand.

Sao Paulo Samba. (Ballroom Dance Ser.). 1986. lib. bdg. 79.95 (*0-8490-3407-8*) Gordon Pr.

Sao Paulo Samba. (Ballroom Dance Ser.). 1985. lib. bdg. 63.00 (*0-87700-788-8*) Revisionist Pr.

Sao Tome & Principe. Caroline S. Shaw. (World Bibliographical Ser.). 183p. 1995. lib. bdg. 54.00 (*1-85109-181-5*) ABC-CLIO.

Sap: Jar of Flies with Notes & Tablature. 56p. 1994. otabind 19.95 (*0-7935-3426-7*, 00694925) H Leonard.

***SAP Documentation & Training Development Guide: A Straight Forward Approach to Planning & Developing Documentation & Training for Your SAP Project.** Kathryn E. Park. Ed. by Robert S. Park. (Illus.). ix, 182p. (Orig.). 1997. pap. 44.95 (*0-9656621-2-8*) Bobkat Press.

***Sap of the Moon-Planet.** unabridged ed. Elias Siqueiros. (Orig.). 1996. mass mkt. 5.95 (*0-9653615-1-9*) Severed Head.

***SAP R-3 Unleashed: Design & Implementation, Vol. 1.** Torsten Schlabach. 1997. pap. text ed. 79.99 incl. cd-rom (*0-672-31120-8*) Sams.

***SAP R-3'S ABAP-4 Command Reference.** Dennis Barnett. 1997. 29.99 (*0-7897-1416-7*) Que.

***SAP R/3 Handbook.** Jose Hernandez. LC 97-18865. (Illus.). 608p. 1997. pap. text ed. 59.95 (*0-07-033121-9*) McGraw.

***Sap Security Clearly Explained.** Tammy Peoples. (Clearly Explained Ser.). (Illus.). 400p. pap. text ed. 59.95 (*0-12-550555-8*, AP Prof) Acad Pr.

Sapatq'ayn: Twentieth Century Nez Perce Artists. Intro. by P. Y. Minthorn. (Orig.). 1991. pap. text ed. 12.95 (*0-914019-27-9*) NW Interpretive.

Sapatq'ayn: Twentieth Century Nez Perce Artists. Ed. by Tim Nitz. LC 91-62472. 60p. 1991. 20.00 (*0-917652-95-9*) Confluence Pr.

Sapelo: A History. Buddy Sullivan. (Illus.). 88p. 1988. write for info. (*0-318-63374-4*) MC CC.

Sapelo's People: A Long Walk into Freedom. William S. McFeely. 208p. 1995. pap. 11.00 (*0-393-31377-8*, Norton Paperbks) Norton.

Sapho. Alphonse Daudet. 247p. (FRE.). 1992. pap. 28.95 (*0-7859-4667-5*) Fr & Eur.

Sapien Homo. Joe E. Pierce. LC 78-71820. 1978. pap. 7.95 (*0-913244-01-5*) Hapi Pr.

***Sapirstein Edition of Rashi: Bereishis.** Yisrael Herczeg. Ed. by Avie Gold. 24.99 (*0-89906-026-9*, RA1H) Mesorah Pubns.

Sapo. Robert Beatty. LC 96-83915. 285p. 1996. 18.95 (*0-9639705-4-2*) Ecopress.

***Sapo Duerme Fuera de Casa: The Toad Sleeps Over.** John Bianchi. 1997. pap. text ed. 5.95 (*0-921285-56-6*, Pub. by Bungalo Bks CN) Firefly Bks Ltd.

Sapo y Sepo un Ano Entero. Arnold Lobel. Date not set. pap. text ed. 11.50 (*84-204-3052-8*) Santillana.

Sapogonia. Ana Castillo. LC 89-933. 320p. 1990. 27.00 (*0-916950-95-6*); pap. 17.00 (*0-916950-96-4*) Biling Rev-Pr.

Sapogonia. Ana Castillo. 368p. 1994. pap. 11.95 (*0-385-47080-0*, Anchor NY) Doubleday.

Saponins. K. Hostettmann & A. Marston. (Chemistry & Pharmacology of Natural Products Ser.). (Illus.). 360p. (C). 1995. text ed. 130.00 (*0-521-32970-1*) Cambridge U Pr.

Saponins in Food & Health. Oakenfull. 1995. write for info. (*0-8493-6867-7*) CRC Pr.

***Saponins Used in Food & Agriculture: Proceedings of the 210th National Meeting of the American Chemical Society Symposium on Saponins: Chemistry & Biological Activity Held in Chicago, Illinois, August 20-24, 1995.** Ed. by George R. Waller & Kazuo Yamasaki. LC 96-32063. (Advances in Experimental Medicine & Biology Ser.: Vol. 405). 430p. 1996. 120.00 (*0-306-45394-0*) Plenum.

***Saponins Used in Traditional & Modern Medicine: Proceedings of the 20th National Meeting of the American Chemical Society Symposium on Saponins: Chemistry & Biological Activity Held in Chicago, Illinois, August 20-24, 1995.** Ed. by George R. Waller & Kazuo Yamasaki. LC 96-2902. (Advances in Experimental Medicine & Biology Ser.: Vol. 404). 570p. 1996. 145.00 (*0-306-45393-2*, Plenum Pr) Plenum.

Sapotaceae: Palynology. Terence D. Pennington. (Flora Neotropica Monographs: No. 52). (Illus.). 770p. 1990. pap. 136.00 (*0-89327-344-9*) NY Botanical.

Sappers in the Wire. Keith W. Nolan. 1996. mass mkt. 5.99 (*0-671-00254-6*) PB.

Sappers in the Wire: The Life & Death of Firebase Mary Ann. Keith W. Nolan. LC 95-12215. (Texas A&M University Military History Ser.: No. 45). (Illus.). 240p. (C). 1995. 24.95 (*0-89096-654-0*) Tex A&M Univ Pr.

Sapphic Songs: Eighteen to Eighty, the Love Poetry of Elsa Gidlow. Elsa Gidlow. LC 82-5144. (Illus.). 96p. (Orig.). 1982. pap. 8.00 (*0-912932-14-7*) Booklegger Pubng.

Sapphics Against Anger & Other Poems. Timothy Steele. LC 86-462. 80p. 1986. 12.45 (*0-394-55504-X*) Random.

Sapphics & Uncertainties: Poems 1970-1986. Timothy Steele. LC 95-6846. 96p. 1995. 22.00 (*1-55728-376-1*); pap. 14.00 (*1-55728-375-3*) U of Ark Pr.

Sapphira & the Slave Girl. Willa Cather. LC 74-20797. 1975. pap. 10.00 (*0-394-71434-2*, Vin) Random.

Sapphira & the Slave Girl. large type ed. Willa Cather. 295p. 1992. reprint ed. lib. bdg. 20.95 (*1-56054-482-1*) Thorndike Pr.

Sapphire. Helen Ashfield. 174p. 1985. pap. 3.95 (*0-685-43286-6*) St Martin.

Sapphire: A Wizard's Quest. Barry Blair. (Illus.). 107p. 1991. pap. 9.95 (*1-56398-003-7*) Malibu Comics Ent.

Sapphire: War of the Elves. Barry Blair. (Illus.). 96p. 1990. pap. 9.95 (*0-944735-64-9*) Malibu Comics Ent.

***Sapphire Princess Meets a Monster, No. 2.** Jahnna N. Malcolm. (The Jewel Kingdom Ser.: No. 1). (Illus.). (J). (gr. 1-4). 1997. mass mkt. 3.99 (*0-590-21284-2*) Scholastic Inc.

Sapphire Ring. large type ed. Marjorie Warby. 368p. 1986. 25.99 (*0-7089-1495-0*) Ulverscroft.

Sapphire Rose. David Eddings. (Elenium Ser.: Bk. 3). 512p. 1993. mass mkt. 6.99 (*0-345-37472-X*, Del Rey) Ballantine.

Sapphire Success. Gro Warling. 96p. 1993. pap. 6.95 (*1-879244-84-5*) Windom Bks.

Sapphires: Here & Otherwhere & Silver Nutmegs, 2 Vols. Vernon Knowles. Ed. by R. Reginald & Douglas Melville. LC 77-84243. (Lost Race & Adult Fantasy Ser.). (Illus.). 1978. reprint ed. lib. bdg. 44.95 (*0-405-10989-X*) Ayer.

Sapphistry: The Book of Lesbian Sexuality. 3rd rev. ed. Pat Califia. (Illus.). 208p. (Orig.). 1988. pap. 10.95 (*0-941483-24-X*) Naiad Pr.

Sappho. Tr. by Mary Barnard. LC 93-33398. (Pocket Classics Ser.). 1994. pap. 6.00 (*0-87773-991-9*, Sham Pocket Class) Shambhala Pubns.

Sappho. Franz Grillparzer. Tr. by Arthur Burkhard from GER. 100p. (Orig.). (C). 1953. pap. 5.00 (*0-686-74815-8*) Register Pr.

Sappho. Alphonse Daudet. Tr. by Eithne Wilkins from FRE. LC 88-60593. 183p. 8800. reprint ed. pap. 14.95 (*0-948166-12-6*, Pub. by Soho Bk Co UK) Dufour.

Sappho: A Garland. Jim Powell. 72p. 1994. pap. 9.00 (*0-374-52421-1*, Noonday) FS&G.

Sappho: A Garland; the Poems & Fragments of Sappho. Sappho. 1993. 15.00 (*0-374-25393-5*) FS&G.

Sappho: A New Translation. Sappho. Tr. by Mary Barnard. 1958. pap. 10.00 (*0-520-01117-1*) U CA Pr.

Sappho: Poems & Fragments. Sappho. 1992. pap. 16.95 (*1-85224-201-9*) Dufour.

Sappho: Poems & Fragments. Sappho. Tr. by Josephine Balmer. (Meadowland Ser.). 128p. 1988. reprint ed. pap. 6.95 (*0-8216-2000-2*) Carol Pub Group.

Sappho: The Poems. rev. ed. Sappho. Tr. & Pref. by Sasha Newborn. LC 86-72786. (Humanist Classics Ser.). (Illus.). 48p. 1993. pap. text ed. 5.00 (*0-942208-11-0*) Bandanna Bks.

Sappho: Tragedy in Five Acts. Franz Grillparzer. Tr. by Arthur Burkhard from GER. 99p. (C). 1953. pap. text ed. 8.50 (*0-917324-16-1*) German Bk Ctr.

Sappho see Notable Biographies

Sappho & Phaon: In a Series of Legitimate Sonnets (1796) fac. ed. Mary Robinson. LC 95-14726. (Scholars' Facsimiles & Reprints Ser.: Vol. 494). 1995. 50.00 (*0-8201-1494-4*) Schol Facsimiles.

Sappho & the Virgin Mary: Same-Sex Love & the English Literary Imagination. Ruth Vanita. LC 96-17768. (Between Men - Between Women Ser.). (Illus.). 304p. 1996. 49.50 (*0-231-10550-9*); pap. 17.50 (*0-231-10551-7*) Col U Pr.

***Sappho is Burning.** Page Duboia. 1997. pap. text ed. 14.95 (*0-226-16756-9*) U Ch Pr.

Sappho Is Burning. Page DuBois. LC 95-8407. 218p. 1995. 24.95 (*0-226-16755-0*) U Ch Pr.

***Sappho Through English Poetry.** Peter Jay & Caroline Lewis. (Poetica Ser.). 144p. 1996. pap. 15.95 (*0-85646-273-X*, Pub. by Anvil Press UK) Dufour.

Sappho to Valery: Poems in Translation. Tr. by John F. Nims. LC 89-38953. 435p. 1990. pap. 24.00 (*1-55728-141-6*) U of Ark Pr.

Sappho und Simonides. Ulrich Von Wilamowitz-Moellendorff. 330p. 1985. write for info. (*3-296-16160-0*) G Olms Pubs.

Sappho Was a Right-On Woman. Ed. by Abbott & Love. LC 77-160348. 1978. 8.95 (*0-8128-2406-7*, Scrbrough Hse) Madison Bks UPA.

Sappho's Gymnasium. Olga Broumas & T. Begley. LC 94-31304. 1994. pap. 12.00 (*1-55659-071-7*) Copper Canyon.

Sappho's Immortal Daughters. Margaret Williamson. LC 95-20124. (Illus.). 209p. (C). 1995. 24.95 (*0-674-78912-1*) HUP.

Sappho's Lyre: Archaic Lyric & Women Poets of Ancient Greece. Tr. by Diane Rayor. LC 90-48642. (Illus.). 234p. 1991. 38.00 (*0-520-07335-5*); pap. 13.95 (*0-520-07336-3*) U CA Pr.

Sappho's Sweetbitter Songs: Configurations of Female & Male in Ancient Greek Lyric. Lyn H. Wilson. LC 95-37772. 240p. (C). 1996. pap. 17.95 (*0-415-12671-1*); text ed. 69.95 (*0-415-12670-3*) Routledge.

Saprolegniaceae with Notes on Other Water Molds. W. C. Coker. (Illus.). 1969. reprint ed. pap. 50.00 (3-7682-0620-3) Lubrecht & Cramer.

Saprophytes Pro Parte. Paul J. Maas et al. (Flora Neotropica Monographs: No. 40-42). (Illus.). (Orig.). 1986. pap. 49.50 (0-89327-271-X) NY Botanical.

***Saps R-3 System Administrators Handbook.** William Lee. 1997. pap. text ed. 79.99 (0-7821-2051-2) Sybex.

SAPT: Diagnostic Radiology of the Dog & Cat. Lamb. 144p. (gr. 13). 1994. pap. text ed. 31.95 (0-8151-5323-6, Yr Bk Med Pubs) Mosby Yr Bk.

Sapt Clinical Medicine. Bouloux. (C). (gr. 13). 1993. 34.00 (0-8151-0436-7) Mosby Yr Bk.

SAPT in Veterinary Medicine: Exotics. Cooper. (gr. 13). 1994. 31.95 (0-8151-1861-9) Mosby Yr Bk.

SAQ's in Psychiatry: An Aid for MRCPsych Part II Candidates, Pt. II. Dinesh K. L. Bhugra. 112p. 1990. pap. text ed. 32.50 (0-407-01887-5) Buttrwrth-Heinemann.

SAR: Side Effects & Drug Design. David A. Lien. (Medicinal Research Ser.: Vol. 11). 384p. 1987. 199.00 (0-8247-7686-0) Dekker.

SAR Guide for a Better Sex Life. National Sex Forum Staff. 128p. 1975. 5.95 (0-317-34149-9) Specific Pr.

Sara. Eva Gibson. LC 84-71717. (Springsong Bks.). 160p. (Orig.). (YA). (gr. 7 up). 1996. mass mkt. 4.99 (1-55661-735-6, Hampshire MN) Bethany Hse.

***Sara & Gerald.** Donnelly. 1984. 7.95 (0-8050-1762-3) St Martin.

***Sara & Grandmother Rose.** Violet M. Ramos. (Illus.). v, 27p. (Orig.). (J). (ps-6). 1997. mass mkt. 3.95 (0-9658334-0-2) VR Pubns.

***Sara & Sam Series Set.** Ruth N. Moore. (YA). (gr. 7 up). 1994. pap. 48.95 (0-8361-9002-5) Herald Pr.

***Sara & the Foreverness of Friends of a Feather.** Esther W. Hicks & Jerry S. Hicks. (Illus.). 185p. (Orig.). 1995. reprint ed. pap. 15.00 (0-9621219-4-0) Crown Intle.

Sara Bear's Surprise. Carolyn R. Rathbun. (Land of Pleasant Dreams Ser.). (Illus.). (Orig.). (J). (ps). 1993. 12.95 (0-9634808-0-4); pap. 4.50 (0-9634808-1-2) Endless Love.

Sara Bishop. Houghton Mifflin Compamy Staff. (Literature Experience 1993 Ser.). (J). (gr. 8). 1992. pap. 9.84 (0-395-61875-4) HM.

Sara Coleridge, a Victorian Daughter: Her Life & Essays. Bradford K. Mudge. LC 88-37427. 312p. (C). 1989. text ed. 37.50 (0-300-04443-7) Yale U Pr.

Sara Crewe. Frances Hodgson Burnett. 96p. (J). (gr. 3-7). 1986. pap. 3.50 (0-590-42323-1) Scholastic Inc.

***Sara Crewe: Or What Happened at Miss Minchin's.** Frances H. Burnett. 59p. (J). (gr. 1 up). 1996. pap. 5.25 (0-87129-734-5, SB5) Dramatic Pub.

Sara Diamond: Memories Revisited, History Retold. Jean Gagnon & Karen Knights. (Illus.). 93p. (C). 1993. pap. 15.00 (0-88884-622-3, Pub. by CN Mus Contemporary Photo CN) U Ch Pr.

Sara Jeannette Duncan: Novelist of Empire. Thomas E. Tausky. 304p. 1980. 38.00 (0-88835-006-6) P D Meany.

Sara Jeannette Duncan & Her Works. Thomas E. Tausky. (Canadian Author Studies). 80p. (C). 1988. pap. text ed. 9.95 (0-920763-75-8, Pub. by ECW Press CN) Genl Dist Srvs.

Sara Kate Saves the World. Susan B. Pfeffer. (Illus.). (J). (gr. 2-4). 1995. 14.95 (0-8050-3148-0) H Holt & Co.

Sara Kate, Super Kid. Susan B. Pfeffer. (J). 1994. 14.95 (0-8050-3147-2) H Holt & Co.

Sara Lee Corp. A Report on the Company's Environmental Policies & Practices. (Illus.). 26p. (C). 1994. reprint ed. pap. text ed. 250.00 (0-7881-0948-0, Coun on Econ) DIANE Pub.

***Sara Midda's South of France: A Sketch Book.** Sara Midda. LC 90-50369. 96p. 1990. 13.95 (1-56305-367-5, 3367F) Workman Pub.

Sara Shriner's Selections. Compiled by Sara V. Shriner. LC 75-39400. (Granger Index Reprint Ser.). 1977. reprint ed. 20.95 (0-8369-6352-0) Ayer.

***Sara Squirrel & the Lost Acorns.** Julie Sykes. LC 96-32966. (Illus.). (J). 1996. 12.95 (1-888444-05-3) Little Tiger.

Sara Summer. Mary D. Hahn. 144p. (J). (gr. 4-5). 1995. reprint ed. pap. 4.50 (0-380-72354-9, Camelot) Avon.

Sara Teasdale: Woman & Poet. William Drake. LC 88-20726. (Illus.). 320p. 1989. reprint ed. pap. 16.95 (0-87049-595-X); reprint ed. lib. bdg. 34.00 (0-87049-606-9) U of Tenn Pr.

Sara Thornton. Jennifer Nadel. (Illus.). 256p. 1994. pap. 15.95 (0-575-05581-2, Pub. by V Gollancz UK) Trafalgar.

Sara Title III: Reporting Made Easy. 275p. 1992. 57.95 (0-87814-375-0, S4514) PennWell Bks.

SARA Title III Software: A Review of What's Available & What It Can Do for You. James W. Morentz. (Environmental Management Guides Ser.). 12p. 1994. pap. text ed. 17.50 (0-86587-438-7) Gov Insts.

Sara Title Three Compliance Handbook. 2nd ed. Ed. by W. Lawrence Wallace, Sr. (Environmental Compliance Handbook Ser.: Vol. 6). 1992. pap. 49.95 (0-7816-0186-X) Exec Ent Pubns.

Sara Videbeck-the Chapel. C. J. Almquist. Tr. by Adolph B. Benson from SWE. LC 77-185449. (Library of Scandinavian Literature). 1972. lib. bdg. 6.75 (0-8057-3354-X) Irvington.

Saraband: The Memoirs of E. L. Mascall. Eric L. Mascall. (Illus.). 392p. 1997. 24.95 (0-85244-222-X, Pub. by Gracewing UK) Morehouse Pub.

Saraband for Two Sisters. large type ed. Philippa Carr. 1981. 12.00 (0-7089-0609-5) Ulverscroft.

Sarabande. Madelyn Sanders. (Intrigue Ser.: 187). 1992. pap. 2.89 (0-373-22187-8, 1-22187-8) Harlequin Bks.

***Sarabands: Poems from Hollywood.** 26p. 1997. pap. 5.00 (0-89642-382-4) Linden Pubs.

Saracen Faris 1100-1250 A. D. David Nicolle. (Warrior Ser.). (Illus.). 64p. 1994. pap. 12.95 (1-85532-453-9, 9609, Pub. by Osprey UK) Stackpole.

Saracens. Edward Gibbon & S. Ockley. 450p. 1985. 250.00 (1-85077-048-4, Pub. by Darf Pubs Ltd UK) St Mut.

Saracen's Country: Some Southeast Arkansas History. James W. Leslie. (Illus.). 216p. 1974. 19.95 (0-914546-03-1) J W Bell.

***Saracen's Head.** Ed Skarda. 288p. (Orig.). 1997. mass mkt. 4.99 (1-55197-822-9, Pub. by Comnwlth Pub CN) Partners Pubs Grp.

Saracinesca. Francis M. Crawford. (Works of Francis Marion Crawford Ser.). 1990. reprint ed. lib. bdg. 79.00 (0-7812-2531-0) Rprt Serv.

Sarada Devi: A Biography in Pictures. Advaita Ashrama Staff. 108p. 1989. 7.95 (0-87481-234-8, Pub. by Advaita Ashrama II) Vedanta Pr.

Sarada Devi, Sri: The Great Wonder. 526p. 1985. pap. 13.50 (0-87481-569-X, Pub. by Ramakrishna Mission II) Vedanta Pr.

Saragarhi Battalion - Ashes to Glory: History of the Fourth Battalion, The Sikh Regiment XXXVI. Kanwaljit Singh. 300p. (C). 1987. 32.50 (81-7062-022-8, Pub. by Lancer II) S Asia.

Saragosa, Texas, Tornado, May 22, 1987: An Evaluation of the Warning System. National Research Council, Committee on Natural Disasters Staff. (Natural Disaster Studies: Vol. 2). 76p. 1991. pap. text ed. 19.00 (0-309-04435-9) Natl Acad Pr.

Sarah. 1987. pap. 20.95 incl. vhs (0-440-85194-7) Dell.

Sarah. Date not set. pap. 1.95 (0-590-05179-2) Scholastic Inc.

Sarah. Mary C. Borntrager. LC 95-7716. (Ellie's People Ser.: Vol. 8). 144p. 1995. pap. 7.99 (0-8361-9019-X) Herald Pr.

Sarah. Maura Seger. 400p. (Orig.). 1987. mass mkt. 3.95 (0-373-97041-2) Harlequin Bks.

Sarah. large type ed. Mary C. Borntrager. (Ellie's People Ser.: Bk. 8). 144p. (J). 1995. pap. 8.99 (0-8361-9020-3) Herald Pr.

Sarah. large type ed. Margaret Dickinson. 1996. 25.99 (0-7505-0787-X, Pub. by Magna Print Bks UK) Ulverscroft.

Sarah. large type ed. Joyce Marlow. 576p. 1989. 17.95 (0-7089-2029-2) Ulverscroft.

Sarah: A Novel of Sarah Bernhardt. Joel Gross. 352p. 1988. mass mkt. 4.50 (0-380-70277-0) Avon.

Sarah: A Sexual Biography. Paul R. Abramson. LC 83-17983. 142p. 1984. pap. text ed. 19.95 (0-87395-863-2) State U NY Pr.

Sarah: A Story of Love & Adoption. Kathie Nichols. (Illus.). 32p. (Orig.). (J). (gr. 2-4). 1992. pap. 6.95 (0-943861-21-7) Lone Tree.

Sarah: A Story of Love & Adoption. Kathie Nichols. LC 92-28414. (Illus.). (Orig.). 1992. 12.95 (0-943861-22-5) Lone Tree.

Sarah: God's Covenant Woman. Janice A. Duseau. 16p. (Orig.). 1989. pap. write for info. (0-318-65839-9) Word Power Pub.

Sarah: Sexual Abuse. Illana Katz. (J). (gr. k-7). 1994. pap. 9.95 (1-882388-08-9); lib. bdg. 16.95 (1-882388-07-0) Real Life Strybks.

Sarah: The Letters & Diaries of a Courtier's Wife, 1906-1936. Sarah H. Bradford. Ed. by Alfred Shaugnessy. LC 89-81665. (Illus.). 144p. 9000. 30.00 (0-7206-0757-4, Pub. by P Owen Ltd UK) Dufour.

Sarah, Also Known As Hannah. Lillian H. Ross. LC 93-29601. (Illus.). (J). 1994. lib. bdg. 11.95 (0-8075-7237-3) A Whitman.

Sarah & Me & Lady from the Sea. Patricia Beatty. LC 89-33624. 224p. (J). (gr. 5 up). 1989. 11.95 (0-688-08045-6, Morrow Junior) Morrow.

Sarah & Me & Lady from the Sea. Patricia Beatty. Ed. by Amy Cohn. LC 89-33624. 224p. (YA). (gr. 5 up). 1994. reprint ed. pap. 4.95 (0-688-13626-5, Morrow Junior) Morrow.

Sarah & Puffle: A Story for Children about Diabetes. Linnea Mulder. LC 92-25638. (Illus.). 32p. (J). 1992. pap. 11.95 (0-945354-42-8) Magination Pr.

Sarah & the Sandhorse. Andrew Baynes. (Illus.). 32p. (J). (ps-1). 1995. 19.95 (0-86264-476-3, Pub. by Andersen Pr UK) Trafalgar.

Sarah Anne Hartford. Kathleen Duey. LC 95-39249. (American Diaries Ser.: 1). (Illus.). 144p. (J). (gr. 3-7). 1996. pap. 3.99 (0-689-80384-2, Aladdin Paperbacks) S&S Childrens.

Sarah Bear & Sweet Sidney. Nancy Patz. LC 88-21300. (Illus.). 32p. (J). (ps-2). 1989. lib. bdg. 13.95 (0-02-770270-7, Four Winds Pr) S&S Childrens.

Sarah Bernhardt. Maurice Baring. LC 78-91893. 1972. 20.95 (0-405-08237-1, Pub. by Blom Pubns UK) Ayer.

Sarah Bernhardt. Maurice Baring. LC 70-98809. 162p. 1970. reprint ed. text ed. 49.75 (0-8371-3018-2, BASB, Greenwood Pr) Greenwood.

Sarah Bernhardt: A French Actress on the British Stage. Elaine Aston. LC 88-36911. (Women's Ser.). 192p. 1989. 12.95 (0-85496-019-8) Berg Pubs.

Sarah Bernhardt: The Art Within the Legend. Gerda Taranow. LC 70-90962. (Illus.). 321p. reprint ed. pap. 91.50 (0-685-23406-1, 2032630) Bks Demand.

Sarah Bernhardt, My Grandmother. Lysiane S. Bernhardt. Tr. by Vyvyan Holland. LC 79-8054. reprint ed. 26.50 (0-404-18365-4) AMS Pr.

Sarah Bernhardt's Leg. David Kirby. (CSU Poetry Ser.: No. XI). 56p. (Orig.). 1983. pap. 5.00 (0-914946-36-6) Cleveland St Univ Poetry Ctr.

Sarah Bishop. Scott O'Dell. (J). (gr. 7 up). 1980. 16.00 (0-395-29185-2) HM.

Sarah Bishop. Scott O'Dell. 240p. (J). (gr. 7-9). 1991. pap. 4.50 (0-590-44651-7, Point) Scholastic Inc.

***Sarah Brown's Fresh Vegetarian Cookery.** Sarah Brown. (Illus.). 256p. 1996. 28.95 (0-563-37055-6) BBC Pubns.

Sarah Camberwell Tring. large type ed. Janet Edmonds. 534p. 1994. pap. 17.99 (1-85389-471-0) Ulverscroft.

***Sarah Canary.** Karen J. Fowler. 1998. pap. write for info. (0-345-41644-9) Ballantine.

Sarah Canary. Karen J. Fowler. 384p. 1993. mass mkt. 5.99 (0-8217-4088-1, Zebra Kensgtn) Kensgtn Pub Corp.

***Sarah Childress Polk.** Susan Sinnott. LC 97-21381. (Encyclopedia of First Ladies Ser.). 1997. 32.50 (0-516-20601-X) Childrens.

***Sarah Childress Polk: A Biography of the Remarkable First Lady.** John R. Bumgarner. LC 97-9684. 176p. 1997. pap. 26.50 (0-7864-0366-7) McFarland & Co.

Sarah Childress Polk: Wife of the 11th President of the United States. Anson Nelson & Fanny Nelson. LC 93-74429. (Signature Ser.). (Illus.). 284p. 1994. reprint ed. 30.00 (0-945707-07-X) Amer Political.

Sarah Cobb. large type ed. Catherine M. Rae. LC 90-29874. 267p. 1991. reprint ed. lib. bdg. 17.95 (1-56054-125-3) Thorndike Pr.

***Sarah Conley: A Novel.** Ellen Gilchrist. LC 97-8207. 1998. 23.95 (0-316-31477-3) Little.

Sarah Elizabeth: A Tale of Old Colorado. J. G. Masters. 208p. 1985. 13.95 (0-940672-29-4) Shearer Pub.

Sarah Faulkner's Planning a Home: A Projects Manual. Ray Faulkner. 98p. (C). 1980. pap. text ed. 20.00 (0-03-045476-X) HB Coll Pubs.

Sarah Ferguson: The Royal Redhead. David Banks. LC 87-15567. (Taking Part Ser.). (Illus.). 64p. (J). (gr. 3 up). 1988. lib. bdg. 13.95 (0-87518-369-7, Dillon Silver Burdett) Silver Burdett Pr.

Sarah Fielding. Bree. 1996. 28.95 (0-8057-7051-8, Twayne) Scribnrs Ref.

Sarah Freeman Clark 1808-1896: A Woman of the Nineteenth Century. Joan A. Kopp & Scott Bowden. (Illus.). 112p. (Orig.). 1993. pap. 9.95 (0-9637925-0-4) Cobb Lndmrks.

Sarah Jane Foster, Teacher of the Freedmen: A Diary & Letters. Ed. by Wayne E. Reilly. 240p. 1990. text ed. 35.00 (0-8139-1284-9); pap. text ed. 16.50 (0-8139-1305-5) U Pr of Va.

***Sarah Kirsch.** Ed. by Mererid Hopwood & David Basker. 120p. 1997. pap. 14.95 (0-7083-1336-1, Pub. by Univ Wales Pr UK) Paul & Co Pubs.

Sarah Laughed: Women's Voices in the Old Testament. Trevor Dennis. LC 93-34719. 208p. (Orig.). 1994. pap. 16.95 (0-687-01371-2) Abingdon.

***Sarah Lucas.** Contrib. by Jan Van Adrichem & Angus Fairhurst. (Illus.). 72p. 1996. pap. 19.95 (90-6918-154-1, 620692, Pub. by Museum Boymans-van NE) Dist Art Pubs.

Sarah M. Peale: America's First Woman Artist. Joan King. (Illus.). 1987. 18.95 (0-8283-1999-5) Branden Pub Co.

Sarah McLachlan Collection. 168p. 1994. otabind 19.95 (0-7935-3697-9, 00308256) H Leonard.

Sarah Mildred Long Bridge: The History of the Maine-New Hampshire Interstate Bridge. Woodward D. Openo. (Portsmouth Marine Society Ser.: No. 13). (Illus.). 130p. 1989. 30.00 (0-915819-12-0) Portsmouth Marine Soc.

***Sarah Miles.** Charlotte Bronte. 1996. 24.00 (0-679-45715-1) Random.

Sarah Morgan: The Civil War Diary of a Southern Woman. Sarah Morgan. Ed. by Charles East. LC 92-21798. (Illus.). 688p. 1992. pap. 16.00 (0-671-78503-6, Touchstone Bks) S&S Trade.

Sarah Morton's Day: A Day in the Life of a Pilgrim Girl. Kate Waters. LC 88-35581. (Illus.). 32p. (J). (gr. k-4). 1989. pap. 14.95 (0-590-42634-6) Scholastic Inc.

Sarah Morton's Day: A Day in the Life of a Pilgrim Girl. Kate Waters. (Illus.). 32p. (J). 1991. pap. 4.95 (0-590-44871-4, Blue Ribbon Bks) Scholastic Inc.

Sarah Morton's Day: A Day in the Life of a Pilgrim Girl. Kate Waters. 32p. (J). 1993. pap. 4.95 (0-590-47400-6) Scholastic Inc.

Sarah of the Border Wars. James D. Yoder. LC 93-72125. 185p. (Orig.). 1993. pap. 9.95 (0-87303-213-6) Faith & Life.

Sarah on Her Own. Karen M. Coombs. (American Dreams Ser.). 240p. (Orig.). (YA). (gr. 7 up). 1996. pap. 3.99 (0-380-78275-8, Flare) Avon.

Sarah, or the Exemplary Wife. Susanna Rowson. LC 78-64090. reprint ed. 37.50 (0-404-17165-6) AMS Pr.

Sarah Orne Jewett. Richard Cary. (Twayne's United States Authors Ser.). 1962. pap. 13.95 (0-8084-0272-2, T19) NCUP.

Sarah Orne Jewett. Francis O. Matthiessen. 1929. 14.50 (0-8446-1305-3) Peter Smith.

Sarah Orne Jewett. Francis O. Matthiessen. (BCL1-PS American Literature Ser.). 159p. 1992. reprint ed. lib. bdg. 69.00 (0-7812-6775-7) Rprt Serv.

Sarah Orne Jewett. Margaret F. Thorp. LC 66-64594. (University of Minnesota Pamphlets on American Writers Ser.: No. 61). 48p. (Orig.). reprint ed. pap. 25.00 (0-7837-2860-3, 2057595) Bks Demand.

Sarah Orne Jewett: A Writer's Life. Elizabeth Silverthorne. LC 92-24589. (Illus.). 1993. 22.95 (0-87951-484-1) Overlook Pr.

***Sarah Orne Jewett: Great American Short Stories I.** Illus. by James Balkovek. LC 94-75019. (Classic Short Stories Ser.). 80p. 1994. pap. 5.95 (0-7854-0576-3, 40008) Am Guidance.

Sarah Orne Jewett: Her World & Her Work. Paula Blanchard. (Radcliffe Biography Ser.). (Illus.). 320p. 1994. 27.50 (0-201-51810-4) Addison-Wesley.

Sarah Orne Jewett: Her World & Her Work. Paula Blanchard. 416p. (YA). 1995. pap. 15.00 (0-201-48934-1) Addison-Wesley.

Sarah Orne Jewett: Reconstructing Gender. Margaret Roman. LC 90-20598. 264p. 1992. text ed. 28.95 (0-8173-0533-5) U of Ala Pr.

Sarah Orne Jewett, an American Persephone. Sarah W. Sherman. LC 88-40353. (Illus.). 347p. 1989. pap. 19.95 (0-87451-484-3) U Pr of New Eng.

Sarah Pardee Winchester - A Driven Woman: Her Compelling Story: The Winchester Mystery House. Genevieve Woelfl. Ed. by Sean McGuire. (Illus.). 32p. (Orig.). 1994. pap. 5.95 (0-917928-02-4, TX2020941) Redwood.

Sarah Phillips. Andrea Lee. (Northeastern Library of Black Literature). 144p. 1993. reprint ed. pap. text ed. 13.95 (1-55553-158-X) NE U Pr.

Sarah, Plain & Tall. Patricia MacLachlan. LC 83-49481. (Charlotte Zolotow Bk.). 64p. (J). (gr. 3-5). 1985. 12.95 (0-06-024101-2); lib. bdg. 12.89 (0-06-024102-0) HarpC Child Bks.

Sarah, Plain & Tall. Patricia MacLachlan. LC 83-49481. (Trophy Bk.). 64p. (J). (gr. 3 up). 1987. pap. 3.95 (0-06-440205-3, Trophy) HarpC Child Bks.

Sarah, Plain & Tall. large type ed. Patricia MacLachlan. 64p. (J). (gr. 4-7). 1995. reprint ed. lib. bdg. 16.95 (1-885885-12-1, Cornerstone FL) Pages Inc FL.

Sarah, Plain & Tall: A Study Guide. Norma Marsh. (Novel-Ties Ser.). 1988. student ed., teacher ed., pap. text ed. 15.95 (0-88122-063-9) Lrn Links.

Sarah, Plain & Tall & Journey: A Literature Unit. Kathee Gosnell. (Literature Units Ser.). (Illus.). 48p. 1993. student ed. 7.95 (1-55734-425-6) Tchr Create Mat.

Sarah Royce & the American West. Sarah Royce. Ed. & Intro. by Jane Shuter. (History Eyewitness Ser.). 48p. (J). (gr. 5-8). 1996. lib. bdg. 24.26 (0-8114-8286-3) Raintree Steck-V.

Sarah Scrap & Her Nature Trail. Wendy Lewis. (Illus.). 32p. (J). 1993. 13.95 (0-237-51216-5, Pub. by Evans Bros Ltd UK) Trafalgar.

Sarah Scrap & Her Wonderful Heap! Wendy Lewis. (Illus.). 32p. (J). (gr. k-2). 1992. 13.95 (0-237-51152-5, Pub. by Evans Bros Ltd UK) Trafalgar.

Sarah, Sencilla y Alta - Sarah, Plain & Tall. Patricia Maclachlan. 1996. pap. text ed. 9.50 (84-279-3421-1) Lectorum Pubns.

Sarah, Sissy Weed, & the Ships of the Desert. Paula Paul. (Illus.). 112p. (J). (gr. 5-6). 1985. 9.95 (0-89015-504-6) Sunbelt Media.

Sarah, Sissy Weed, & the Ships of the Desert. Paula Paul. (Illus.). 112p. (J). (gr. 5-6). 1985. pap. 5.95 (0-89015-552-6) Sunbelt Media.

Sarah Snail. Lowesdale School Children Staff. LC 92-27084. (Voyages Ser.). (Illus.). (J). 1993. 3.75 (0-383-03592-9) SRA McGraw.

Sarah T. Portrait of a Teenage Alcoholic. Robert Wagnen. (Orig.). 1986. mass mkt. 4.95 (0-345-34242-9) Ballantine.

Sarah the Dragon Lady. Martha B. Stiles. 96p. (J). (gr. 3-7). 1988. pap. 2.75 (0-380-70471-4, Camelot) Avon.

Sarah the Priestess: The First Matriarch of Genesis. Savina J. Teubal. LC 84-96. xx, 201p. 1984. pap. 12.95 (0-8040-0844-2, Swallow) Ohio U Pr.

***Sarah the Siamese Cat.** (Illus.). 30p. (Orig.). (J). 1996. mass mkt. write for info. (0-9658371-8-1) M Goloversic.

***Sarah Vaughan.** Marianne Ruuth. pap. 5.99 (0-87067-786-1, Melrose Sq) Holloway.

Sarah Vaughan: A Discography. Denis Brown. LC 91-27632. (Discographies Ser.: No. 47). 184p. 1991. text ed. 47.95 (0-313-28005-3, BVG/, Greenwood Pr) Greenwood.

Sarah Vaughan: Singer. Marianne Ruuth. (Black American Ser.). (Illus.). 208p. (Orig.). (YA). 1994. mass mkt. 3.95 (0-87067-592-3, Melrose Sq) Holloway.

Sarah Vaughan Sassy Jazz Songs. Ed. by John L. Haag. (Illus.). 160p. (Orig.). 1995. pap. 16.95 (1-56922-083-2, 07-1084) Creat Cncpts.

Sarah Whitcher's Story. Elizabeth Yates. LC 94-27185. (Pennant Ser.). (Illus.). 95p. (J). 1994. pap. 6.49 (0-89084-754-1, 080564) Bob Jones Univ Pr.

Sarah, Who Loved Laughter. France Quere. Tr. by Gwen Marsh from FRE. (Tales of Heaven & Earth Ser.). (Illus.). 40p. (YA). (gr. 5 up). 1997. lib. bdg. 14.95 (0-88682-826-0) Creative Ed.

Sarah Wilkins, in Search of a Song, Vol. 7. Sarah Wilkins. Ed. by Barbara Fisher. 22p. (Orig.). (J). (gr. 5-8). 1984. pap. 2.00 (0-934830-35-5) Ten Penny.

Sarah Winnemucca. Mary F. Morrow. (American Indian Stories Ser.). (Illus.). 32p. (J). (gr. 3-6). 1990. lib. bdg. 21.40 (0-8172-3402-0) Raintree Steck-V.

Sarah Winnemucca. Mary F. Morrow. (Raintree-Rivilo American Indian Stories Ser.). (Illus.). 32p. (J). (gr. 3-6). 1990. pap. 4.95 (0-8114-4095-8) Raintree Steck-V.

Sarah Winnemucca: Northern Paiute Writer & Diplomat see North American Indians of Achievement

Sarah Winnemucca: Northern Paiute Writer & Diplomat see North Americans Indians of Achievement

Sarah Winnemucca of the Northern Paiutes. Gae W. Canfield. LC 82-40448. (Illus.). 336p. (Orig.). 1988. pap. 14.95 (0-8061-2090-8) U of Okla Pr.

Sarah with an "H" Hadley Irwin. (J). 1996. 16.00 (0-689-80949-2, S&S Bks Young Read) S&S Childrens.

Sarah's Angel. Judith Stafford. (Regency Romance Ser.). 1993. mass mkt. 2.99 (0-373-31211-3, 1-31211-5) Harlequin Bks.

Sarah's Awakening. Susan V. Billings. (Orig.). 1979. mass mkt. 2.50 (0-89083-536-5, Zebra Kensgtn) Kensgtn Pub Corp.

Sarah's Bear. Marta Koci. LC 86-30241. (Illus.). 28p. (J). (ps). 1991. pap. 14.95 (0-88708-038-3, Picture Book Studio) S&S Childrens.

Sarah's Boat: A Young Girl Learns the Art of Sailing. Douglas Alvord. LC 93-37971. (Illus.). 48p. (J). (gr. 3-8). 1994. 16.95 (0-88448-117-4) Tilbury Hse.

Sarah's Child. Linda Howard. (Special Edition Ser.). 1991. mass mkt. 3.29 (0-373-15162-4) Silhouette.

S

An Asterisk (*) at the beginning of an entry indicates that the title is appearing in BIP for the first time.

S

Sarah's Child. Linda Howard. 1994. mass mkt. 4.50 (*0-373-48301-5*, 5-48301-1) Silhouette.

***Sarah's Child.** Linda Howard. 1997. mass mkt. 3.99 (*0-373-48362-7*, 1-48362-7) Harlequin Bks.

Sarah's Choice. Eleanor Wilner. LC 88-22317. 112p. 1989. pap. 13.95 (*0-226-90028-2*) U Ch Pr.

Sarah's Dad & Sophia's Mom. Francine Pascal. (Sweet Valley Twins Ser.: No. 62). 144p. (J). 1992. pap. 3.25 (*0-553-15944-5*) Bantam.

Sarah's Daughters: A Celebration of Jewish Women. Arthur Leipzig. Ed. by Nathan Gould & Jane K. Vitiello. (Illus.). 94p. 1988. 25.00 (*0-685-26588-9*) Womens Am ORT.

Sarah's Daughter's Sing: A Sampler of Poems by Jewish Women. Ed. by Henny Wenkart. (Illus.). 259p. 1990. 19.95 (*0-88125-348-0*); pap. 14.95 (*0-88125-349-9*) Ktav.

Sarah's Dilemma. Judy Baer. (Live! From Brentwood High Ser.: No. 4). 144p. (J). 1995. mass mkt. 4.99 (*1-55661-389-X*) Bethany Hse.

Sarah's Flag for Texas. Jane A. Knapik. LC 93-16171. (Illus.). (J). (gr. 3-6). 1994. 12.95 (*0-89015-900-9*) Sunbelt Media.

Sarah's Ghost. Tim Knutson. 177p. 1995. 12.00 (*0-8059-3693-9*) Dorrance.

Sarah's Growing-up Summer. Carmen P. Bobo. LC 88-62111. 52p. (J). 1989. 6.95 (*1-55523-187-X*) Winston-Derek.

Sarah's Holy Mountain. D. W. Hoffman. 764p. (Orig.). 1996. pap. 24.00 (*0-9650656-5-0*) Abandoned Orchard.

***Sarah's House.** Eric Thomas. (J). 19.95 (*0-614-19297-8*) DK Pub Inc.

***Sarah's House.** Eric Thomas. (Illus.). 1996. 19.95 (*0-7894-1007-9*) DK Pub Inc.

Sarah's Incredible Idea: A Brownie Girl Scout Book. Jane O'Connor. LC 92-36803. (Here Come the Brownies Ser.: No. 2). (Illus.). 64p. (J). (gr. 1-4). 1993. pap. 4.95 (*0-448-40162-2*, G&D) Putnam Pub Group.

***Sarah's Journey, No. 5.** 208p. (J). 1997. write for info. (*0-7814-0023-6*, Chariot Bks) Chariot Victor.

Sarah's Journey: One Child's Experience with the Death of Her Father. Alan D. Wolfelt. (Illus.). 121p. (Orig.). 1992. pap. 9.95 (*1-879651-03-3*) Companion CO.

Sarah's Life. Eunice V. Pike. LC 93-85571. xi, 53p. 1993. pap. 4.95 (*0-88312-618-4*); fiche 8.00 (*0-88312-855-1*) Summer Instit Ling.

Sarah's Lion. Margaret Greaves. (J). 1995. pap. text ed. 5.95 (*0-8120-9272-4*) Barron.

***Sarah's Psalm.** Ladd. LC 97-6784. 1997. pap. 13.00 (*0-684-83279-8*, Scribners PB Fict) S&S Trade.

Sarah's Psalm. Florence Ladd. 320p. 1996. 22.00 (*0-684-80410-7*) S&S Trade.

Sarah's Quest. Carol L. Williams. LC 95-33438. (Latter-Day Daughters Ser.). (Orig.). (J). 1995. pap. 4.95 (*1-56236-504-5*) Aspen Bks.

***Sarah's Rocking Chair.** Cynthia R. Erkel. LC 96-45292. (Illus.). (J). 1998. pap. write for info. (*0-525-65234-5*) Dutton Child Bks.

Sarah's Room. Leah Klein. (B. Y. Times Kid Sisters Ser.: No. 4). 106p. (J). Date not set. pap. 7.95 (*1-56871-008-9*) Targum Pr.

Sarah's Room. Doris Orgel. LC 63-13675. (Illus.). (J). (gr. k-3). 1963. 11.95 (*0-06-024605-7*) HarpC Child Bks.

***Sarah's Seasons: An Amish Diary & Conversation.** Martha M. Davis. LC 97-10556. (Bur Oak Original Ser.). (Illus.). 192p. 1997. 22.95 (*0-87745-596-1*) U of Iowa Pr.

***Sarah's Seasons: An Amish Diary & Conversation.** Martha M. Davis & Sarah Fisher. LC 97-10556. (Bur Oak Original Ser.). 1997. pap. write for info. (*0-87745-597-X*) U of Iowa Pr.

Sarah's Secret Plan. Linda Johns. LC 94-39167. (Illus.). 32p. (J). (ps-3). 1995. lib. bdg. 12.50 (*0-8167-3693-6*) Troll Communs.

Sarah's Secret Plan. Linda Johns. LC 94-39167. (Illus.). 32p. (J). (ps-3). 1995. pap. 2.95 (*0-8167-3512-3*) Troll Communs.

Sarah's Shovel. Debbie Mackinnon. 1997. pap. 4.99 (*0-8037-2101-3*) Dial Bks Young.

***Sarah's Shovel.** Debbie MacKinnon. (Illus.). (J). (ps-k). 1997. bds. 4.99 (*0-614-28687-5*) Dial Bks Young.

Sarah's Sin. Tami Hoag. 256p. 1992. mass mkt. 5.50 (*0-553-56050-6*) Bantam.

Sarah's Song: A True Story of Love & Courage. Janice A. Burns. 272p. 1996. mass mkt. 6.50 (*0-446-60343-0*) Warner Bks.

Sarah's Story. Lillian Cantleberry. (Continued Applied Christianity Ser.). 216p. 1983. pap. 5.99 (*0-570-03898-7*, 12-2980) Concordia.

Sarah's Story. Bill Harley. LC 96-4274. (Illus.). 32p. (J). (gr. 1-3). 1996. 15.95 (*1-883672-20-1*) Tricycle Pr.

Sarah's Story. Bobbie C. Jobe. 1987. pap. 3.95 (*0-89137-442-6*) Quality Pubns.

Sarah's Surprise. Nan Holcomb. (Illus.). 32p. (J). (ps-2). 1990. pap. 7.95 (*0-944727-07-7*) Jason & Nordic Pubs.

Sarah's Surprise. Nan Holcomb. (Illus.). 32p. (J). (ps-3). 1992. reprint ed. lib. bdg. 13.95 (*0-944727-18-2*) Jason & Nordic Pubs.

Sarah's Unicorn. Bruce Coville & Katherine Coville. LC 79-2408. (Lippincott I-Like-to-Read Bks.). (Illus.). 48p. (J). (ps-2). 1979. lib. bdg. 13.89 (*0-397-31873-1*, Lipp Jr Bks) HarpC Child Bks.

Sarah's Unicorn. Bruce Coville & Katherine Coville. LC 85-42749. (Trophy Picture Bk.). (Illus.). 48p. (J). (gr. 1-4). 1985. pap. 4.95 (*0-06-443084-7*, Trophy) HarpC Child Bks.

***Sarah's Unicorn.** Bruce Coville. (Illus.). (J). (ps-2). 1979. 7.66 (*0-397-31872-3*, 246042) Lppncott-Raven.

Sarajevo: A War Journal. Zlatko Dizdarevic. Ed. by Ammiel Alcalay et al. Tr. by Anselm Hollo from FRE. LC 94-26222. 1994. pap. 12.95 (*0-8050-3535-4*) H Holt & Co.

Sarajevo: A War Journal. Zlatko Dizdarevic. Tr. by Anselm Hollo. LC 93-36174. (Illus.). 208p. 1993. 19.95 (*0-88064-149-5*) Fromm Intl Pub.

Sarajevo: An Anthology for Bosnian Relief. Ed. by John Babbitt et al. 360p. 1993. pap. 14.95 (*0-9638516-0-8*) Elgin Comm Coll.

Sarajevo: Survival Guide. FAMA Staff. 96p. 1994. pap. 10.00 (*1-56305-688-7*, 3688) Workman Pub.

Sarajevo Daily: A City & Its Newspaper under Siege. Tom Gjelten. (Illus.). 288p. 1996. pap. 13.00 (*0-06-092662-7*) HarpC.

Sarajevo Days, Sarajevo Nights. Elma Softic. Tr. by Nada Conic. 200p. 1996. 20.00 (*1-886913-10-2*) Hungry Mind.

Sarajevo, Exodus of a City. Dzevad Karahasan. Tr. & Afterword by Slavenka Drakulic. 144p. 1994. pap. 10.00 (*1-56836-057-6*) Kodansha.

Sarajevo Shots: Studies in the Immediate Origin of World War I. C. Patrick Joyce. (Revisionist Historiography Ser.). 1979. lib. bdg. 250.00 (*0-87700-263-0*) Revisionist Pr.

Sarajevo's Home Cooking. Irena Popovic. 1991. pap. 10.00 (*0-533-09303-1*) Vantage.

Sarakhsi: Concepts of Treaties & the Doctrine of Juristic Preference in Islamic Jurisprudence. Husain Kassim. 480p. 1995. 74.95 (*1-880921-88-X*); pap. 54.95 (*1-880921-87-1*) Austin & Winfield.

Saral Nepali Shabda Kosh. 1991. 20.00 (*0-7855-0285-8*, Pub. by Ratna Pustak Bhandar) St Mut.

Saranac Lake: Pioneer Health Resort. Mark Caldwell. Ed. by Barbara Parnass et al. (Illus.). 40p. (Orig.). 1993. pap. 11.95 (*0-9615159-1-0*) Hist Saranac.

Saranohair. Gillian K. Johnson. (Illus.). 56p. (J). 1992. 12.95 (*1-55037-211-4*, Pub. by Annick CN) Firefly Bks Ltd.

Sarapiqui Chronicle: A Naturalist in Costa Rica. Allen M. Young. LC 90-39532. (Illus.). 384p. (C). 1991. pap. 16.95 (*1-56098-047-8*) Smithsonian.

Sarapis & Isis: Collected Essays. Thomas A. Brady. Ed. by Fordyce Mitchel. 129p. 1978. 25.00 (*0-89005-253-0*) Ares.

Sara's City. Sue Alexander. LC 94-24045. (Illus.). 31p. (J). 1995. 15.95 (*0-395-64483-6*, Clarion Bks) HM.

Sara's Father. Jennifer Mikels. (Special Edition Ser.). 1995. pap. 3.75 (*0-373-09947-9*, 1-09947-2) Silhouette.

Sara's Homecoming. Heather Conkie. (Road to Avonlea Ser.: No. 12). 128p. (J). (gr. 4-7). 1993. 3.99 (*0-553-48038-3*) Bantam.

Sara's Life & Testimonies-Plus Letters to God. Sara Flack. 1994. 10.95 (*0-533-10928-0*) Vantage.

Sara's Secret. Suzanne Wanous. LC 94-32234. (Illus.). (J). 1995. lib. bdg. 14.21 (*0-87614-856-9*, Carolrhoda) Lerner Group.

Sara's Summer. Naomi R. Stucky. LC 90-71017. 144p. (Orig.). (YA). (gr. 6-12). 1990. pap. 6.99 (*0-8361-3534-2*) Herald Pr.

***Sara's Trek.** Florence E. Schloneger. 1981. pap. 6.00 (*0-614-23871-4*) Am Hist Soc Ger.

Sara's World. Maria Mahoney. 1994. 8.95 (*0-533-10821-7*) Vantage.

Sarasota: Journey to Centennial: A Pictorial & Entertaining Commentary on Growth & Development of Sarasota. rev. ed. Janet S. Matthews. LC 88-93028. (Illus.). 232p. 1997. 29.95 (*0-9621986-2-5*) Coastal Pr FL.

Sarasota: Journey to Centennial: A Pictorial & Entertaining Commentary on the Growth & Development of Sarasota, Florida. Janet S. Matthews. LC 88-93028. 1989. reprint ed. 29.95 (*0-9621986-1-7*) Coastal Pr FL.

Sarasota, a Sentimental Journey. Jeff LaHurd. 120p. 1991. pap. 8.95 (*1-888438-75-4*) Sarasota Alliance.

Sarasota Chef du Jour: Chef Recipes from Popular Area Restaurants. 4th ed. Jan McCann. (Illus.). 38p. (Orig.). 1995. pap. 19.00 (*0-9640198-3-3*) Strawbry Press.

Sarasota School of Architecture. John Howey. LC 95-13652. (Illus.). 200p. (C). 1995. 35.00 (*0-262-08240-3*) MIT Pr.

***Sarasota School of Architecture.** John Howey. (Illus.). 224p. 1997. reprint ed. pap. 22.50 (*0-262-58156-6*) MIT Pr.

Sarasota, Then & Now. Jeff LaHurd. 96p. 1994. pap. 12.00 (*1-888438-25-8*) Sarasota Alliance.

Sarasota Times Past: A Reflective Collection of the Florida Gulf Coast. Bernice B. Bergen. (Illus.). 192p. 1993. pap. 19.95 (*0-9631461-3-X*) Valiant Pr.

***Sarasota's Chef Du Jour.** 5th rev. ed. Jan McCann. (Illus.). 210p. 1997. pap. 14.50 (*0-9640198-6-8*) Strawbry Press.

Saratoga. Michael J. Friedman. (Star Trek: Deep Space Nine Ser.). 1996. mass mkt. 5.99 (*0-671-56897-3*, Star Trek) PB.

Saratoga. Richard Ketchum. LC 97-2773. 1997. 27.50 (*0-8050-4681-X*) H Holt & Co.

Saratoga: Equine Tradition. Tom Killips. (Illus.). 96p. 1996. write for info. (*1-881275-26-4*) Pamco Pub.

Saratoga Backtalk. Stephen Dobyns. 224p. 1995. pap. 5.95 (*0-14-024708-4*, Penguin Bks) Viking Penguin.

Saratoga Backtalk. large type ed. Stephen Dobyns. LC 94-45328. (Large Print Bks.). 1995. pap. 21.95 (*1-56895-089-6*) Wheeler Pub.

Saratoga Backtalk: A Charlie Bradshaw Mystery. Stephen Dobyns. 1994. 19.95 (*0-393-03659-6*) Norton.

Saratoga County, Our County & Its People: A Descriptive & Biographical Record of Saratoga, Co., N. Y. Saratogian Staff & George B. Anderson. (Illus.). 787p. 1995. reprint ed. lib. bdg. 79.50 (*0-8328-4477-2*) Higginson Bk Co.

Saratoga Fleshpot. Stephen Dobyns. 224p. 1996. pap. 5.95 (*0-14-025535-4*, Penguin Bks) Viking Penguin.

Saratoga Fleshpot: A Charlie Bradshaw Mystery. Stephen Dobyns. 220p. 1995. 21.00 (*0-393-03805-X*) Norton.

Saratoga Haunting. Stephen Dobyns. 224p. 1994. pap. 5.95 (*0-14-017162-2*, Penguin Bks) Viking Penguin.

Saratoga Head Hunter. Stephen Dobyns. (Crime Monthly Ser.). 1986. pap. 3.50 (*0-14-007772-3*, Penguin Bks) Viking Penguin.

Saratoga Hexameter. large type ed. Stephen Dobyns. (General Ser.). 391p. 1991. lib. bdg. 20.95 (*0-8161-5133-4*, GK Hall) Thorndike Pr.

Saratoga Queen of Spas. Grace Swanner. (Illus.). 304p. 1988. 19.95 (*0-932052-67-3*); pap. 14.95 (*0-932052-66-5*) North Country.

***Saratoga Strongbox.** Sephen Dobyns. 1998. pap. 21.95 (*0-670-87692-5*) Viking Penguin.

Saratoga Trifecta. Stephen Dobyns. LC 95-10380. 1995. pap. 14.95 (*0-14-025196-0*, Penguin Bks) Viking Penguin.

Saratoga Yearling. Kevin J. Reed. Ed. by Meri G. Herold. (Illus.). 110p. (Orig.). (J). (gr. 5-9). 1985. pap. 3.95 (*0-9614546-0-1*) Chowder Pr.

***Saratov Oblast: Economy, Industry, Government, Business.** 2nd rev. ed. Russian Information & Business Center, Inc. Staff. (Russian Regional Business Directories Ser.). (Illus.). 200p. 1997. pap. 99.00 (*1-57751-413-0*) Russ Info & Busn Ctr.

***Sarava! Brazilian Magick - Roots of Afro-Brazilian Magick.** Carol Dow. LC 96-52081. (Illus.). 264p. (Orig.). 1997. pap. 14.95 (*1-56718-235-6*) Llewellyn Pubns.

Sarawak: Its Inhabitants & Productions. Hugh Low. (Asian Folk Tales Ser.). (Illus.). 440p. 1995. pap. 17.00 (*967-67-1009-1*, Pub. by Delta Edits MY) Weatherhill.

Sarawak: Its Inhabitants & Productions. Hugh Low. (Illus.). 416p. 1968. reprint ed. 35.00 (*0-7146-2017-3*, Pub. by F Cass Pubs UK) Intl Spec Bk.

Sarayacu Quichua Pottery. Carolyn Orr & Patricia Kelley. (Museum of Anthropology Publications: No. 1). 37p. 1976. fiche 4.00 (*0-88312-240-5*) Summer Instit Ling.

Sarcasm Does Not Become You, Ma'am. Charles M. Schulz. (Peanuts Classics Ser.). (Illus.). 128p. 1996. pap. 7.95 (*0-8050-3937-6*, Owlet BYR) H Holt & Co.

Sarcocystosis of Animals. J. P. Dubey et al. LC 88-15684. 224p. 1989. 130.00 (*0-8493-6364-0*, QR201, CRC Reprint) Franklin.

Sarcoidosis: Proceedings of the International Symposium on Sarcoidosis, Held November 14-16, 1979. International Symposium on Sarcoidosis Staff. Ed. by Riichiro Mikami & Yutaka Hosoda. LC 81-188866. (Japan Medical Research Foundation Publication: No. 13). 428p. 1981. reprint ed. pap. 122.00 (*0-608-01244-0*, 2061932) Bks Demand.

Sarcoidosis & Other Granulomatous Diseases of the Lung. Fanburg. (Lung Biology in Health & Disease Ser.: Vol. 20). 544p. 1983. 185.00 (*0-8247-1866-6*) Dekker.

Sarcoidosis & Other Granulomatous Disorders. James. (Lung Biology in Health & Disease Ser.: Vol. 73). 896p. 1994. 210.00 (*0-8247-9126-6*) Dekker.

Sarcoidosis & Other Granulomatous Disorders. D. Geraint James & W. Jones Williams. (Problems in Internal Medicine Ser.: Vol. 24). (Illus.). 256p. 1985. text ed. 93.00 (*0-7216-1044-7*) Saunders.

Sarcoidosis Resource Guide & Directory. Sandra Conroy. (Illus.). 304p. (Orig.). 1992. pap. 19.95 (*0-9631222-5-8*) PC Pubns.

Sarcoidosis Resource Guide & Directory for Health Care Professionals. Sandra Conroy. (Illus.). 250p. 1991. pap. write for info. (*0-9631222-6-6*) PC Pubns.

Sarcolemmal Biochemistry, 2 vols., Set. Ed. by Abdul M. Kidwai. 1987. 207.00 (*0-8493-5908-2*, QP321, CRC Reprint) Franklin.

Sarcolemmal Biochemistry, Vol. I. Abdul M. Kidwai. LC 86-26358. 1987. reprint ed. 106.00 (*0-8493-5909-0*, CRC Reprint) Franklin.

Sarcolemmal Biochemistry, Vol. II. Abdul M. Kidwai. 168p. 1987. 101.00 (*0-8493-5910-4*) CRC Pr.

Sarcolemmal Biochemistry, Vol. 2. Abdul M. Kidwai. LC 86-26358. 384p. 1987. reprint ed. 95.00 (*0-317-05750-2*, CRC Reprint) Franklin.

Sarcomas: Directory of Authors of New Medical & Scientific Reviews with Subject Index. Science & Life Consultants Association Staff. 160p. 1995. 47.50 (*0-7883-0608-1*); pap. 44.50 (*0-7883-0609-X*) ABBE Pubs Assn.

Sarcophagidae (Diptera) of Fennoscandia & Denmark. Thomas Pape. (Fauna Entomologica Scandinavica Ser.: No. 19). (Illus.). 203p. 1987. text ed. 51.00 (*90-04-08184-4*) Lubrecht & Cramer.

Sarcophagus. Vladimir Gubaryev. Tr. by Michael Glenny. 107p. 1990. pap. 5.95 (*0-87129-669-1*, S78) Dramatic Pub.

Sarcophagus & Other Stories. Jose Y. Dalisay, Jr. 144p. 1992. pap. text ed. 18.00 (*971-10-5074-9*, Pub. by U of Philippines Pr PH) UH Pr.

Sarcophagus Safety '94: The State of the Chernobyl Nuclear Power Plant, Unit 4. 474p. (Orig.). 1995. pap. 99.00 (*92-64-14437-4*, Pub. by Org for Econ FR) OECD.

Sarcoplasmic Reticulum in Muscle Physiology, Vol. I. Ed. by Mark L. Entman & W. Barry Van Winkle. 184p. 1986. 110.00 (*0-8493-6180-X*, QP321, CRC Reprint) Franklin.

Sarcoplasmic Reticulum in Muscle Physiology, Vol. II. Ed. by Mark L. Entman & W. Barry Van Winkle. 184p. 1986. 110.00 (*0-8493-6181-8*, QP321, CRC Reprint) Franklin.

Sarcosomataceae (Pezizales Sarcosyphgineae) Joseph Paden. LC 83-8056. (Flora Neotropica Monographs: No. 37). (Illus.). 16p. (Orig.). 1983. pap. 5.50 (*0-89327-250-7*) NY Botanical.

Sardar Patel: His Political Ideology. S. R. Bakshi. 1990. 42.00 (*81-7041-263-3*, Pub. by Anmol II) S Asia.

Sardar Sarovar Project. Ed. by Mahesh T. Pathak. (C). 1991. 12.50 (*81-204-0545-5*, Pub. by Oxford IBH II) S Asia.

Sardar Vallabhbhai Patel: India's Iron Man. Bimal Krishna. (C). 1995. 42.00 (*81-7223-211-X*, Pub. by Indus Pub II) S Asia.

Sardine Carriers & Seiners of the Maine Coast. Paul E. Bennett. LC 92-90763. (Illus.). 70p. 1992. 23.95 (*0-9632725-0-0*) P E Bennett.

Sardine Deception. Leif Davidsen. Tr. by Tiina Nunnally & Steven T. Murray from DAN. LC 86-2094. 199p. (Orig.). 1986. pap. 6.95 (*0-940242-15-X*) Fjord Pr.

Sardines. Nuruddin Farah. 263p. 1992. pap. 12.00 (*1-55597-161-X*) Graywolf.

Sardinia. (Insight Guides Ser.). 1993. pap. 22.95 (*0-395-66440-3*) HM.

Sardinia. Andrew Gravette. (Illus.). 304p. 1992. pap. 15.95 (*0-900075-47-3*, Pub. by Windrush Pr UK) Interlink Pub.

Sardinia in the Mediterranean: A Footprint in the Sea: Studies in Sardinian Archaeology Presented to Miriam S. Balmuth. Ed. by Andres Tykot. (Monographs in Mediterranean Archaeology: No. 3). (Illus.). 530p. 1992. 75.00 (*1-85075-386-5*, Pub. by Sheffield Acad UK) CUP Services.

***Sardinia Map.** 1996. 8.95 (*2-06-700433-6*, 433) Michelin.

Sardinian Chronicles. Bernard Lortat-Jacob. Tr. by Teresa L. Fagan. LC 94-10766. (Chicago Studies in Ethnomusicology). 128p. 1994. pap. text ed. 19.95 (*0-226-49341-5*) U Ch Pr.

Sardinian Chronicles. Bernard Lortat-Jacob. Tr. by Teresa L. Fagan. LC 94-10766. (Chicago Studies in Ethnomusicology). 128p. 1995. lib. bdg. 47.50 (*0-226-49340-7*) U Ch Pr.

Sardinian Syntax. Michael Jones. LC 93-13297. (Romance Linguistics Ser.). 240p. (C). (gr. 13). 1993. text ed. 99.95 (*0-415-04922-9*, A7887) Routledge.

Sardis: Twenty-Seven Years of Discovery. David G. Mitten et al. Ed. by Eleanor Guralnick. (Illus.). 123p. 1988. pap. 12.00 (*0-9609042-1-2*) Archaeol Chi.

Sardi's Bar Guide. Vincent Sardi, Jr. & George Shea. 1988. mass mkt. 5.99 (*0-345-32924-4*) Ballantine.

Sardis from Prehistoric to Roman Times: Results of the Archaeological Exploration of Sardis, 1958-1975. George M. Hanfmann & William E. Mierse. (Illus.). 512p. 1983. 58.00 (*0-674-78925-3*) HUP.

Sardis in the Age of Croesus. John G. Pedley. LC 67-64447. (Centers of Civilization Ser.). 155p. reprint ed. pap. 44.20 (*0-317-28329-4*, 2016247) Bks Demand.

Sardonic Humor of Ambrose Bierce. Ambrose Bierce. Ed. by George Barkin. 232p. (Orig.). 1963. pap. 4.50 (*0-486-20768-4*) Dover.

Sardonic Smile: Nonverbal Behavior in Homeric Epic. Donald Lateiner. LC 95-1704. 1995. 49.50 (*0-472-10598-1*) U of Mich Pr.

Sardonic Tales (Contes Cruels) Jean M. Villiers De l'Isle-Adam. Tr. by Hamish Miles. LC 77-11497. reprint ed. 34.50 (*0-404-16356-4*) AMS Pr.

Sarek. A. C. Crispin. Ed. by Kevin Ryan. (Star Trek Ser.). 416p. 1995. mass mkt. 5.99 (*0-671-79562-7*) PB.

Sarepta: A Preliminary Report on the Iron Age. James B. Pritchard et al. (University Museum Monographs: No. 35). (Illus.). ix, 114p. 1975. pap. 30.00 (*0-934718-24-5*) U PA Mus Pubns.

Sargam: An Introduction to Indian Music. Vishnudas Shirali. 1978. 37.00 (*0-88386-830-X*) S Asia.

Sargasso. Marjorie Agosin. Tr. by Cola Franzen. 1993. pap. 12.00 (*1-877727-27-X*) White Pine.

***Sargasso Sea & Other Stories.** Donn Byrne. 344p. 1972. 21.95 (*0-8369-4144-6*) Ayer.

***Sarge Reynolds: In the Time of His Life.** Andrew H. McCutcheon & Michael P. Gleason. (Illus.). vi, 180p. (Orig.). 1996. pap. 9.95 (*0-9655584-0-1*) Gleason Pub.

Sargent: Supplement to the 1895 Sargent Genealogy. Edward R. Sargent. 16p. 1994. reprint ed. pap. 5.00 (*0-8328-4186-2*) Higginson Bk Co.

***Sargent Abroad: Figures & Landscapes.** Warren Adelson et al. LC 97-10517. (Illus.). 256p. 1997. 75.00 (*0-7892-0384-7*) Abbeville Pr.

Sargent Portrait Drawings: 42 Works. John S. Sargent. (Art Library). (Illus.). 48p. (Orig.). 1983. pap. 3.95 (*0-486-24524-1*) Dover.

Sargent Record: William Sargent of New England, with His Descendants & Their Intermarriages, & Other Sargent Branches. Edward Sargent. (Illus.). 331p. 1989. reprint ed. lib. bdg. 57.50 (*0-8328-1048-7*) Higginson Bk Co.

Sargent Record: William Sargent of New England, with His Descendants & Their Intermarriages, & Other Sargent Branches. Edward E. Sargent. (Illus.). 331p. 1989. reprint ed. pap. 49.50 (*0-8328-1049-5*) Higginson Bk Co.

Sargent Tool Catalog Collection. Intro. by Paul Weidenschilling. (Illus.). 192p. 1993. pap. 17.95 (*1-879335-42-5*) Astragal Pr.

Sargonic & Gutian Periods (2334-2113 BC) Douglas R. Frayne. (Royal Inscriptions of Mesopotamia, Early Periods Ser.: No. 2). 356p. 1993. 175.00 (*0-8020-0593-4*) U of Toronto Pr.

Sargonic Texts from Telloh in the Istanbul Archaeological Museums. Veysel Donbaz & Benjamin R. Foster. (Occasional Publications of the Babylonian Fund: No. 5). (Illus.). xi, 17p. 1982. 20.00 (*0-934718-44-X*) U PA Mus Pubns.

Sargonic Texts in the Ashmolean Museum, Oxford. Ignace J. Gelb. LC 79-111601. (Materials for the Assyrian Dictionary Ser.: No. 5). 150p. 1970. pap. text ed. 15.00 (*0-226-62309-2*) U Ch Pr.

Sargonic Texts in the Louvre. Ignace J. Gelb. LC 79-111600. (Materials for the Assyrian Dictionary Ser.: No. 4). 150p. 1970. pap. text ed. 13.50 (*0-226-62308-4*) U Ch Pr.

Sargozasht-e Haji Baba-Ye Isfahani Haji Baba-Ye Isfahani. James Morier. Tr. by Mirza H. Isfahani. (Bibliotheca Iranica Ser.: No. 9). Orig. Title: The Adventures of Haji Baba of Isphahan. (Illus.). 432p. (Orig.). (PER.). 1996. pap. text ed. 24.95 (*1-56859-042-3*) Mazda Pubs.

An Asterisk (*) at the beginning of an entry indicates that the title is appearing in BIP for the first time.

Sari. large type ed. Bette Allan. (Linford Romance Library). 256p. 1994. pap. 15.99 (*0-7089-7517-8*, Linford) Ulverscroft.

Sari: Styles - Patterns - History - Technique. Linda Lynton & Sanjay K. Singh. LC 95-1590. (Illus.). 208p. 1995. 49.50 (*0-8109-4461-8*) Abrams.

***Sari: Styles, Patterns, History, Techniques.** Linda Lynton. 1995. 58.00 (*0-500-01672-0*) Thames Hudson.

Sari-Sari Store: A Philippine Scrapbook. Rebecca C. Asedillo & B. David Williams. (Illus.). 80p. (Orig.). 1989. pap. 4.95 (*0-377-00195-3*) Friendship Pr.

Sari-Sarna: Santhal Religion. P. C. Hembram. 129p. (C). 1988. 19.00 (*81-7099-044-0*, Pub. by Mittal II) S Asia.

Sariah: Mother of Nations. Elsje Chun. (Noble Women Ser.). (Illus.). 52p. (Orig.). (J). (gr. 1-6). 1995. pap. 5.95 (*1-57665-014-6*) Muggli Graphics.

Saris of India: Madhya Pradesh. Rta Kapur Chishti & Amba Sanyal. (Illus.). 276p. 1991. 125.00 (*81-224-0187-2*) U of Wash Pr.

Saris of India: Madya Pradesh. Ed. by Chishti R. Kapur & Amba Sanyal. (C). 1989. 130.00 (*0-8364-2489-1*) S Asia.

Sarista. Peter Adkison & Michael McDonald. (Talislanta Ser.). 72p. 1993. pap. 10.95 (*1-880992-15-9*) Wizards Coast.

Sarkis. Gordon Orear & Elizabeth Orear. LC 94-43015. (Illus.). 170p. 1995. text ed. 27.95 (*0-8143-2517-3*, Great Lks Bks) Wayne St U Pr.

SARK's Journal & Play!Book: A Place to Dream While Awake. Sark. (Illus.). 176p. 1995. 19.95 (*0-89087-702-5*) Celestial Arts.

Sarmiento & His Argentina. Ed. by Joseph T. Criscenti. LC 92-38372. 216p. 1993. lib. bdg. 30.00 (*1-55587-351-0*) Lynne Rienner.

Sarmiento, Author of a Nation. Tulo H. Donghi et al. LC 93-16613. 400p. 1994. 50.00 (*0-520-07531-5*); pap. 20.00 (*0-520-07532-3*) U CA Pr.

Sarmiento de Frente y Perfil. William H. Katra. LC 92-23540. (Iberica Ser.: Vol. 7). 273p. (SPA.). (C). 1993. text ed. 49.95 (*0-8204-2044-1*) P Lang Pubng.

Sarmiento's Travels in the United States in 1847. Domingo F. Sarmiento. Tr. & Intro. by Michael A. Rockland. LC 70-113009. 339p. reprint ed. pap. 96.70 (*0-8357-3525-7*, 2034283) Bks Demand.

***Sarn - The Story of an Otter in Spring.** Tessa Potter. LC 96-35466. (Animals Through the Year Ser.). (Illus.). (J). 1997. lib. bdg. 21.40 (*0-8172-4620-7*) Raintree Steck-V.

***Sarn, the Story of an Otter in Spring.** Tessa Potter. (J). 1997. pap. text ed. 5.95 (*0-8172-6901-0*) Raintree Steck-V.

Sarna Deep Sky Atlas. Thomas Sarna. 1984. pap. 29.95 (*0-943396-06-9*) Willmann-Bell.

Sarngadhara Samhita: A Trestise on Ayurveda. Sarngadhara. Tr. by Srikanata K. Murthy from SAN. 335p. 1984. text ed. 42.00 (*0-89744-056-0*) Auromere.

***Sarny, a Life Remembered.** Gary Paulsen. LC 96-53842. (J). 1997. write for info. (*0-385-32195-3*) Delacorte.

Sarojini Naidu: An Introduction to Her Life, Work & Poetry. Vishwanath S. Naravane. 160p. 1980. 20.00 (*0-86131-253-8*, Pub. by Orient Longman Ltd II) Apt Bks.

Saros Cycle Dates & Related Babylonian Astronomical Texts. Asger Aaboe et al. LC 91-55342. (Transactions Ser.: Vol. 81, Pt. 6). (Illus.). 80p. (C). 1991. pap. 12.50 (*0-87169-816-1*, T816-AAA) Am Philos.

***Sarowbi.** William F. Band. 241p. (Orig.). 1998. mass mkt. 4.99 (*1-55237-469-6*, Pub. by Comnwlth Pub CN) Partners Pubs Grp.

Saroyan Special. William Saroyan. LC 70-134979. (Short Story Index Reprint Ser.). (Illus.). 1977. 32.95 (*0-8369-3709-0*) Ayer.

Saroyan's Armenians. Alice K. Barter. LC 91-67767. 184p. (Orig.). 1994. pap. 12.50 (*1-56002-168-3*, Univ Edtns) Aegina Pr.

Sarrasine. Paul Tana & Bruno Ramirez. (Drama Ser.: No. 15). 166p. Date not set. pap. 15.00 (*1-55071-041-9*) Guernica Editions.

Sarraute Romanciere: Espaces intimes. Sabine Raffy. (American University Studies: Romance Languages & Literature: Ser. II, Vol. 60). 269p. (C). 1988. text ed. 47.00 (*0-8204-0479-9*) P Lang Pubng.

Sarsfield; or Wanderings of Youth: An Irish Tale, 3 vols. in 2, Set. John Gamble. LC 79-8268. reprint ed. 84.50 (*0-404-61859-6*) AMS Pr.

Sarsi Texts. fac. ed. Pliny E. Goddard. (University of California Publications in American Archaeology & Ethnology: Vol. 11: 3). 89p. (C). 1915. reprint ed. pap. text ed. 8.10 (*1-55567-196-9*) Coyote Press.

Sarsiellidae of the Western Atlantic & Northern Gulf of Mexico & Revision of the Sarsiellinae: Ostracoda: Myodocopina. LC 85-600238. (Smithsonian Contributions to Zoology Ser.: No. 415). 221p. reprint ed. pap. 63.00 (*0-685-16432-2*, 2027313) Bks Demand.

***Sartain. Annals of the Sartain Tribe, 1557 to 1886.** John Sartain. (Illus.). 77p. 1996. reprint ed. pap. 16.00 (*0-8328-5350-X*); reprint ed. lib. bdg. 26.00 (*0-8328-5349-6*) Higginson Bk Co.

Sartain's Union Magazine of Literature & Art, Set, Vols. 1-11. reprint ed. Set. lib. bdg. 525.00 (*0-404-19550-4*) AMS Pr.

***Sartogo Grenon.** Sartogo. LC 97-5768. 1997. pap. 40.00 (*1-885254-51-2*) Viking Penguin.

Sarton Selected: An Anthology of the Novels, Journals, & Poetry of May Sarton. Bradford D. Daziel. 1991. 22.95 (*0-393-02968-9*) Norton.

Sartor Resartus. Thomas Carlyle. Ed. by Kerry McSweeney & Peter Sabor. (World's Classics Ser.). 320p. 1987. pap. 9.95 (*0-19-281757-4*) OUP.

***Sartor Resartus: The Life & Opinions of Herr Teufelsdr Ockh in Three Books.** Thomas Carlyle et al. LC 97-3100. (Norman & Charlotte Strouse Edition of the Writings of Thomas Carlyle). 1998. write for info. (*0-520-20928-1*) U CA Pr.

Sartor-Shults Family History. A. F. Sartor, Jr. LC 89-50421. (Illus.). 312p. 1989. 20.00 (*0-9622693-0-1*) A F Sartor.

Sartoris. William Faulkner. 474p. (FRE.). 1977. pap. 11.95 (*0-7859-2638-0*, 207036920X) Fr & Eur.

Sartoris. William Faulkner. 1983. pap. 3.50 (*0-452-00646-5*, Mer) NAL-Dutton.

Sartoris, Le Bruit et le Fureur: Sanctuaire, Tandis Que J'Agonise. William Faulkner. (FRE.). 1977. 110.00 (*0-8288-3444-X*, M5094) Fr & Eur.

Sartre. Peter Caws. (Arguments of the Philosophers Ser.). 224p. 1984. pap. 11.95 (*0-7102-0233-4*, RKP) Routledge.

Sartre. Ronald Hayman. (Illus.). 576p. 1987. write for info. (*0-671-45942-2*) S&S Trade.

Sartre. Ed. & Intro. by Christina Howells. LC 94-45555. (Modern Literatures in Perspective Ser.). (C). 1995. text ed. 52.95 (*0-582-21412-2*, Pub. by Longman UK) Longman.

Sartre. Ed. by Christina Howells. (Modern Literatures in Perspective Ser.). 272p. (C). 1996. pap. text ed. 22.95 (*0-582-21413-0*, Pub. by Longman UK) Longman.

***Sartre: A Biography.** Ronald Hayman. 15.95 (*0-7867-0875-1*) Carroll & Graf.

Sartre: A Biography. Ronald Hayman. (Illus.). 576p. 1992. pap. 15.95 (*0-88184-875-1*) Carroll & Graf.

Sartre: A Philosophic Study. Anthony R. Manser. LC 81-765. 280p. 1981. reprint ed. text ed. 38.50 (*0-313-22827-2*, MASPS, Greenwood Pr) Greenwood.

Sartre: An Investigation of Some Major Themes. Simon Glynn. 200p. 1987. text ed. 63.95 (*0-566-05181-8*, Pub. by Avebury Pub UK) Ashgate Pub Co.

Sartre: Bibliography 1980-1992. Ed. by Michel Rybalka & Michel Contat. (Bibliographies of Famous Philosophers Ser.). 247p. 1993. 40.00 (*0-912632-96-8*) Philos Document.

***Sartre: Le Mur.** J. P. Sartre. Ed. by W. Redfern. (Bristol Classical Press French Texts Ser.). 128p. (FRE.). (C). 1997. pap. text ed. 18.95 (*1-85399-457-X*, Pub. by Duckworth UK) Focus Pub-R Pullins.

Sartre: Life & Works. Kenneth A. Thompson & Margaret Thompson. LC 82-15585. (Facts on File Chronology Ser.). 243p. reprint ed. pap. 69.30 (*0-685-23990-X*, 2031563) Bks Demand.

Sartre: The Origins of a Style. Fredric Jameson. (Morningside Bk.). 250p. 1984. reprint ed. pap. text ed. 17.00 (*0-231-05891-8*) Col U Pr.

Sartre: The Radical Conversion. James F. Sheridan. LC 69-15915. 182p. reprint ed. pap. 51.90 (*0-317-09227-8*, 2006444) Bks Demand.

Sartre Alive. Ed. by Ronald Aronson & Adrian Van Den Hoven. LC 90-12500. 390p. (C). 1991. pap. text ed. 24.95 (*0-8143-2177-1*) Wayne St U Pr.

Sartre Alive. Ed. by Ronald Aronson & Adrian Van Den Hoven. LC 90-12500. 390p. (C). 1991. text ed. 49.95 (*0-8143-2176-3*) Wayne St U Pr.

Sartre & Evil: Guidelines for a Struggle. Haim Gordon & Rivca Gordon. LC 94-30930. (Contributions in Philosophy Ser.: Vol. 54). 264p. 1995. text ed. 62.95 (*0-313-27861-X*, Greenwood Pr) Greenwood.

***Sartre & Existentialism: Philosophy, Politics, Ethics, the Psyche, Literature & Aesthetics, 8 vols.** Ed. & Intro. by William L. McBride. 1997. 520.00 (*0-8153-2440-5*) Garland.

Sartre & His Predecessors: The Self & the Other. William R. Schroeder. 350p. 1984. 55.00 (*0-7102-0274-1*, RKP) Routledge.

Sartre & Marxist Existentialism: The Test Case of Collective Responsibility. Thomas R. Flynn. LC 83-4994. 280p. (C). 1986. reprint ed. pap. text ed. 13.50 (*0-226-25466-6*) U Ch Pr.

Sartre & Psychoanalysis: An Existentialist Challenge to Clinical Metatheory. Betty Cannon. LC 90-12993. xviii, 398p. 1991. 35.00 (*0-7006-0445-6*) U Pr of KS.

Sartre & Psychology. Ed. by Keith Hoeller. LC 92-34508. (Studies in Existential Psychology & Psychiatry). 100p. (Orig.). (C). 1993. pap. 12.50 (*0-391-03776-5*) Humanities.

Sartre & Psychology. Ed. by Keith Hoeller. 101p. (Orig.). 1983. pap. 10.00 (*0-914857-01-0*) Rev Exist Psych.

Sartre & Surrealism. William Plank. LC 81-431. (Studies in the Fine Arts - Art Theory). 110p. reprint ed. pap. 31.40 (*0-8357-1175-7*, 2070253) Bks Demand.

Sartre & the Artist. George H. Bauer. LC 76-88232. 246p. reprint ed. pap. 70.20 (*0-317-26640-3*, 2024082) Bks Demand.

Sartre & the Media. Michael Scriven. 160p. 1993. text ed. 49.95 (*0-312-10617-3*) St Martin.

Sartre & the Problem of Morality. Francis Jeanson. Tr. by Robert V. Stone from FRE. LC 80-7807. (Studies in Phenomenology & Existential Philosophy). 320p. 1980. 31.50 (*0-253-16603-9*) Ind U Pr.

Sartre As Biographer. Douglas Collins. LC 79-25863. 230p. 1980. reprint ed. pap. 65.60 (*0-7837-4458-7*, 2057988) Bks Demand.

Sartre for Beginners. Donald Palmer. (Illus.). 176p. 1995. pap. 11.00 (*0-86316-177-4*) Writers & Readers.

***Sartre, Foucault & Reason in History: Toward an Existentialist Theory, Vol. 1.** Thomas R. Flynn. 1996. pap. text ed. 18.95 (*0-226-25468-2*); lib. bdg. 55.00 (*0-226-25467-4*) U Ch Pr.

Sartre on Cuba. Jean-Paul Sartre. LC 73-21102. 160p. 1974. reprint ed. text ed. 49.75 (*0-8371-5952-0*, SASA, Greenwood Pr) Greenwood.

Sartre Revisted. Minahen. LC 96-48925. 1997. text ed. write for info. (*0-312-16079-8*) St Martin.

Sartre, 1905-1980. Annie Cohen-Solal. (Folio Essais Ser.). (FRE.). pap. 19.95 (*2-07-032508-3*) Schoenhof.

Sartre's Concept of a Person: An Analytic Approach. Phyllis S. Morris. LC 75-8451. 184p. 1976. 25.00 (*0-87023-185-5*) U of Mass Pr.

Sartre's Ethics of Authenticity. Linda A. Bell. LC 86-19284. 224p. 1982. reprint ed. pap. 63.90 (*0-608-01660-8*, 2062315) Bks Demand.

Sartre's Existential Biographies. Michael Scriven. LC 83-16115. 200p. 1984. text ed. 35.00 (*0-312-69968-9*) St Martin.

Sartre's French Contemporaries & Enduring Influences: Camus, Merleau-Ponty, Debeauvoir & Enduring Influences. Ed. by William L. McBride. LC 96-48996. (Sartre & Existentialism Ser.: Vol. 8). 400p. 1996. reprint ed. text ed. 70.00 (*0-8153-2498-7*) Garland.

Sartre's Life, Times & Vision du Monde. Ed. by William L. McBride. LC 96-44914. (Sartre & Existentialism Ser.: Vol. 3). 400p. 1996. reprint ed. text ed. 75.00 (*0-8153-2493-6*) Garland.

Sartre's Marxism. Mark Poster. LC 81-18146. 136p. 1982. 22.95 (*0-521-24559-1*) Cambridge U Pr.

Sartre's Ontology: A Study of Being & Nothingness in the Light of Hegel's Logic. Klaus Hartmann. (Studies in Phenomenology & Existential Philosophy). 166p. 1966. pap. 19.95 (*0-8101-0610-8*) Northwestern U Pr.

Sartre's Philosophy of Social Existence. George J. Stack. (Modern Revivals in Philosophy Ser.). 154p. 1992. 49.95 (*0-7512-0058-1*, Pub. by Gregg Pub UK) Ashgate Pub Co.

Sartre's Philosophy of Social Existence. George J. Stack. (Illus.). 176p. 1978. 10.60 (*0-87527-153-7*) Green.

Sartre's Political Theory. William L. McBride. LC 90-25291. (Studies in Continental Thought). 260p. 1991. 37.50 (*0-253-33621-X*) Ind U Pr.

Sartre's Political Theory. William L. McBride. LC 90-25291. (Studies in Continental Thought). 260p. 1991. pap. 6.95 (*0-253-20655-3*, MB-655) Ind U Pr.

***Sarum.** Edward Rutherford. 1997. pap. 14.95 (*0-449-00072-9*) Fawcett.

Sarum. Edward Rutherford. 1990. 5.99 (*0-517-03389-5*) Random Hse Value.

Sarum. Edward Rutherford. 6.99 (*0-09-952730-8*) Random.

Sarum. Edward Rutherford. 1993. reprint ed. lib. bdg. 45.95 (*1-56849-114-X*) Buccaneer Bks.

Sarum: The Novel of England. Edward Rutherfurd. 1988. mass mkt. 6.99 (*0-8041-0298-8*) Ivy Books.

Sarum Mass Book: A New English Version with Gregorian Chant of the Sarum Missal & Tonale. Ed. & Tr. by Aidan Keller from LAT. (Old Catholic Missal & Ritual Sarum Rite Ser.: Vol. 4). (Illus.). 148p. 1990. 39.95 (*0-923864-03-2*) St Hilarion Pr.

Sarva Tathagata-Tattva Sangraha. Lokesh Chandra. (C). 1987. 50.00 (*81-208-0273-X*, Pub. by Motilal Banarsidass II) S Asia.

Sarvagi of Gopaldas: A Seventeenth Century Anthology of Bhakti Literature. Winand M. Callewaert. (C). 1993. 80.00 (*0-685-69769-X*, Pub. by Manohar II) S Asia.

***Sarx.** Pascal Quignard. Tr. by Keith Waldrop from FRE. (Serie d'Ecriture Ser.: Suppl. 2). 40p. (Orig.). (C). 1997. pap. 5.00 (*1-886224-20-X*) Burning Deck.

***SAS: Operation Bulbasket.** Paul McCue. 1997. pap. text ed. 18.95 (*0-85052-534-9*, Pub. by L Cooper Bks UK) Trans-Atl Phila.

SAS: Operation Oman. Tony Jeapes. (Elite Unit Ser.: No. 4). (Illus.). 245p. 1982. 29.95 (*0-89839-054-0*) Battery Pr.

SAS: Secret War in Southeast Asia. Peter Dickens. 1992. mass mkt. 5.99 (*0-8041-0833-1*) Ivy Books.

SAS: The British Special Air Service. Leroy Thompson. (Power Ser.). (Illus.). 128p. 1994. pap. 16.95 (*0-87938-940-0*) Motorbooks Intl.

***SAS: The Illustrated History.** Barry Davies. (Illus.). 224p. (Orig.). 1997. pap. 19.95 (*0-7535-0197-X*, Pub. by Virgin Pub UK) London Brdge.

SAS: With the Maquis: In Action with the French Resistance, June-September 1944. Ian Wellsted. 192p. 1994. 34.95 (*1-85367-186-X*, 5421) Stackpole.

SAS-AF Guide for Personal Computers, Version 6 Edition. SAS Institute, Inc. Staff. 303p. (C). 1993. pap. 14.95 (*1-55544-063-0*) SAS Inst.

SAS Applications Guide, 1987 Edition. 252p. (C). 1987. pap. 15.95 (*1-55544-032-0*, BR5661) SAS Inst.

SAS Applications Programming: A Gentle Introduction. Frank C. Dilorio. 684p. (C). 1998. pap. 39.95 (*0-534-92390-9*, BR56193) SAS Inst.

SAS Basics: From Installation to Operation. Rick Aster. LC 93-1130. 279p. 1993. pap. 28.95 (*0-8306-4316-8*, Windcrest) TAB Bks.

SAS-C C Plus Plus Development System User's Guide. 256p. (C). 1993. pap. 29.95 (*1-55544-446-6*, 56122) SAS Inst.

***SAS Companion for the AOS/VS Environment, Version 6.** 288p. (C). 1990. pap. 25.95 (*1-55544-407-5*) SAS Inst.

SAS Companion for the CMS Environment, Version 6. 352p. (C). 1994. pap. 25.95 (*1-55544-399-0*, BR56103) SAS Inst.

SAS Companion for the Macintosh, Version 6. 120p. (C). 1995. pap. 24.95 (*1-55544-671-X*, BR55112) SAS Inst.

***SAS Companion for the Microsoft Windows Environment, Version 6.** 2nd ed. 304p. (C). 1997. pap. 29.95 (*1-55544-771-6*, BR55268) SAS Inst.

***SAS Companion for the Microsoft Windows NT Environment: Version 6.** 408p. (C). 1993. pap. 25.95 (*1-55544-562-4*) SAS Inst.

SAS Companion for the Microsoft Windows NT Environment, Version 6. 382p. (C). 1993. pap. 29.95 (*1-55544-527-6*, BR56112) SAS Inst.

***SAS Companion for the MVS Environment, Version 6.** 2nd ed. 520p. (C). 1996. pap. 29.95 (*1-55544-794-5*, BR55108) SAS Inst.

***SAS Companion for the OpenVMS Environment, Version 6.** 2nd ed. 544p. (C). 1997. pap. 36.95 (*1-55544-775-9*, BR55113) SAS Inst.

***SAS Companion for the OS/2 Environment: Version 6.** 294p. (C). 1993. pap. 25.95 (*1-55544-417-2*) SAS Inst.

***SAS Companion for the OS/2 Environment: Version 6.** 2nd ed. 344p. (C). 1995. pap. 29.95 (*1-55544-517-9*) SAS Inst.

***SAS Companion for the Unix Environment & Derivatives.** 304p. (C). 1995. pap. 25.95 (*1-55544-420-2*) SAS Inst.

***SAS Companion for the VSE Environment: Version 6.** 592p. (C). 1993. pap. 52.95 (*1-55544-525-X*) SAS Inst.

SAS Companion for UNIX Environments: Language, Version 6. 256p. (C). 1993. pap. 25.95 (*1-55544-565-9*, BR56114) SAS Inst.

SAS Companion for UNIX Environments: User Interfaces, Version 6. 156p. (C). 1993. pap. 25.95 (*1-55544-560-8*, BR56113) SAS Inst.

***SAS Consultant's Guide: Supporting the SAS System.** 2nd ed. 72p. (C). 1996. pap. 12.00 (*1-55544-777-5*) SAS Inst.

SAS Escape, Evasion & Survival Manual. Barry Davis. (Illus.). 276p. 1996. pap. 19.95 (*0-7603-0302-9*) Motorbooks Intl.

SAS Foundations: From Installation to Operation. Rick Aster. 1993. pap. text ed. 28.95 (*0-07-001543-0*) McGraw.

SAS-FSP User's Guide: Release 6.03 Edition. SAS Institute, Inc. Staff. 331p. (C). 1993. pap. 12.95 (*1-55544-092-4*) SAS Inst.

SAS-GRAPH Hardware Interfaces for Personal Computers: Version 6 Edition. SAS Institute, Inc. Staff. 353p. (C). 1992. pap. 16.95 (*1-55544-093-2*) SAS Inst.

SAS-GRAPH User's Guide: Release 6.03 Edition. SAS Institute, Inc. Staff. 549p. (C). 1994. pap. 38.95 (*1-55544-087-8*) SAS Inst.

SAS Guide. Kilman Shin. 312p. (C). 1994. 20.54 (*0-256-15920-3*) Irwin.

SAS Guide. 2nd ed. Kilman Shin. (Irwin Statistical Software Ser.). 424p. (C). 1995. 20.54 (*0-256-20650-3*) Irwin.

SAS Guide to Macro Processing, Version 6. 2nd ed. 319p. 1990. 21.95 (*1-55544-382-6*, BR56041) SAS Inst.

SAS Guide to Macro Processing, Version 6. 2nd ed. 319p. (C). 1991. pap. 21.95 (*1-55544-061-4*) SAS Inst.

***SAS Guide to Report Writing: Examples, Version 6.** 232p. (C). 1994. pap. 32.95 (*1-55544-637-X*) SAS Inst.

SAS Guide to Tabulate Processing. 2nd ed. 208p. (C). 1990. pap. 13.95 (*1-55544-416-4*, BR56095) SAS Inst.

SAS Guide to the REPORT Procedure: Reference, Release 6.11. 136p. (C). 1997. pap. 14.95 (*1-55544-265-X*, BR55323) SAS Inst.

***SAS Guide to the Report Procedure: Usage & Reference.** 336p. (C). 1995. pap. 19.95 (*1-55544-422-9*) SAS Inst.

***SAS Guide to the SQL Procedure: Usage.** 232p. (C). 1997. pap. 12.95 (*1-55544-367-2*) SAS Inst.

SAS Guide to the SQL Query Window: Usage & Reference, Version 6. 176p. (C). 1995. pap. 14.95 (*1-55544-266-8*, BR55342) SAS Inst.

SAS Guide to VSAM Processing, Version 6. 152p. (C). 1992. pap. 24.95 (*1-55544-504-7*, BR56042) SAS Inst.

SAS-IML User's Guide: Release 6.03 Edition. SAS Institute, Inc. Staff. 357p. (C). 1988. pap. 20.95 (*1-55544-094-0*) SAS Inst.

SAS Introductory Guide for Personal Computers, Version 6.03 Edition. SAS Institute, Inc. Staff. 111p. (C). 1994. pap. 14.95 (*1-55544-095-9*) SAS Inst.

SAS Language: Reference, Version 6. 1042p. (C). 1997. pap. 25.95 (*1-55544-381-8*, BR56076) SAS Inst.

***SAS Language & Procedures.** 688p. (C). 1997. pap. 34.95 (*1-55544-445-8*) SAS Inst.

SAS Language & Procedures: Introduction, Version 6. 124p. (C). 1996. pap. 11.95 (*1-55544-410-5*, BR56074) SAS Inst.

SAS Language & Procedures: Syntax, Version 6. 175p. (C). 1997. pap. 10.95 (*1-55544-400-8*, BR56077) SAS Inst.

SAS Language & Procedures: Usage, Version 6. 638p. (C). 1997. pap. 19.95 (*1-55544-371-0*, BR56075) SAS Inst.

SAS Language Guide for Personal Computers: Release 6.03. SAS Institute, Inc. Staff. 550p. (C). 1993. pap. 22.95 (*1-55544-099-1*) SAS Inst.

SAS Macro Facility Tips & Techniques, Version 6. 319p. (C). 1997. pap. 25.95 (*1-55544-605-1*, BR55097) SAS Inst.

***SAS Macro Language: Reference.** 304p. (C). 1997. pap. 25.95 (*1-55544-953-0*) SAS Inst.

***SAS Operations.** James D. Ladd. 1997. pap. text ed. 29.95 (*0-7090-6043-2*, Hale-Parkwest) Parkwest Pubns.

***Sas Pagoda.** Anthony J. Pearson. Date not set. write for info. (*0-688-05379-3*) Morrow.

SAS, Phantoms in the Jungle: A History of the Australian Special Air Service. David Horner. (Elite Unit Ser.: No. 25). (Illus.). 527p. 1989. 39.95 (*0-89839-139-3*) Battery Pr.

SAS Procedures Guide: Release 6.03 Edition. SAS Institute, Inc. Staff. 441p. (C). 1994. pap. 18.95 (*1-55544-089-4*) SAS Inst.

SAS Procedures Guide, Version 6. 3rd ed. 705p. (C). 1997. pap. 21.95 (*1-55544-378-8*, BR56080) SAS Inst.

SAS Programmer's Pocket Reference. Rick Aster. LC 92-32890. 1992. pap. 19.95 (*0-8306-4317-6*, Windcrest) TAB Bks.

SAS Programming by Example. Ron Cody & Ray Pass. 337p. (C). 1997. pap. 32.95 (*1-55544-681-7*, BR55126) SAS Inst.

SAS Programming for Researchers & Social Scientists. Paul E. Spector. (Illus.). 192p. (C). 1993. text ed. 46.00 (*0-8039-4984-7*); pap. text ed. 19.50 (*0-8039-4985-5*) Sage.

SAS Programming Tips: A Guide to Efficient SAS Processing. 155p. (C). 1996. pap. 15.95 (*1-55544-431-8*, BR56150) SAS Inst.

S

SAS Recipes. Susanne Aref. 39p. (C). 1995. spiral bd. 6.00 (0-87563-601-2) Stipes.

*SAS Research Application User's Guide. 182p. (C). 1996. pap. 34.95 (1-55544-800-3) SAS Inst.

*SAS Screen Control Language: Reference, Version 6. 2nd ed. 648p. (C). 1996. pap. 42.95 (1-55544-659-0, BR55147) SAS Inst.

SAS Screen Control Language: Syntax, Version 6. 732p. (C). 1996. pap. 11.95 (1-55544-488-1, BR56032) SAS Inst.

SAS Screen Control Language: Usage, Version 6. 690p. (C). 1997. pap. 36.95 (1-55544-444-X, BR56031) SAS Inst.

SAS Software: Abridged Reference, Version 6. 607p. (C). 1994. pap. 40.95 (1-55544-582-9, BR56043) SAS Inst.

SAS Software: Changes & Enhancements, Release 6.10. 11p. (C). 1997. pap. 14.00 (1-55544-638-8, BR55120) SAS Inst.

SAS Software Roadmaps: Your Guide to Discovering the SAS System. 317p. (C). 1994. pap. 25.95 (1-55544-606-X, BR56195) SAS Inst.

*SAS Software Solutions. Thomas Miron. 240p. (C). 1993. pap. 28.95 (1-55544-536-5) SAS Inst.

SAS-STAT User's Guide: Release 6.03 Edition. SAS Institute, Inc. Staff. 1028p. (C). 1995. pap. 34.95 (1-55544-088-6) SAS Inst.

*Sas System: Information Delivery for Banking & Financial Services. 328p. (C). 1993. pap. 36.00 (1-55544-537-3) SAS Inst.

SAS System: Information Delivery for the Public Sector. 592p. 1993. 40.00 (1-55544-516-0, BR56554) SAS Inst.

SAS System: Information Delivery for the Utilities Sector. 384p. 1993. 35.00 (1-55544-515-2, BR56553) SAS Inst.

SAS System for Elementary Statistical Analysis. SAS Institute, Inc. Staff. 440p. (C). 1988. pap. 26.95 (1-55544-076-2, BR5619) SAS Inst.

SAS System for Forecasting Time Series, 1986 Edition. SAS Institute, Inc. Staff. 240p. (C). 1986. pap. 19.95 (1-55544-027-4, BR5612) SAS Inst.

SAS System for Linear Models. 3rd ed. 352p. (C). 1996. pap. 22.95 (1-55544-430-X, BR56140) SAS Inst.

*SAS System for Mixed Models. Ramon C. Littell et al. 656p. (C). 1996. pap. 39.95 (1-55544-779-1, BR55235) SAS Inst.

SAS System for Regression. 2nd ed. 232p. (C). 1995. pap. 22.95 (1-55544-429-6, BR56141) SAS Inst.

SAS System for Statistical Graphics. Michael Friendly. 697p. (C). 1997. pap. 53.95 (1-55544-441-5, BR56143) SAS Inst.

SAS System Guide. Fowler. 1993. pap. text ed. write for info. (0-07-020189-7) McGraw.

SAS Technical Report: P-173 Transporting & Converting Version 5.16 Full-Screen Catalogs to a Release 6.03 System. SAS Institute, Inc. Staff. 63p. (C). 1992. pap. 5.00 (1-55544-084-3) SAS Inst.

SAS Technical Report C-114: A Guide for the SAS/C Compiler Consultant. 64p. (C). 1993. pap. 18.00 (1-55544-540-3, BR59019) SAS Inst.

SAS Technical Report C-115: The Generalized Operating System Interface for the SAS/C Compiler Run-Time System, Release 5.50. 30p. (C). 1993. pap. 17.00 (1-55544-535-7, BR59025) SAS Inst.

SAS Technical Report P-208, SAS/GRAPH Software: Changes & Enhancements to Map Data Sets, Release 6. 07. 98p. (C). 1991. pap. 7.00 (1-55544-437-7, BR59125) SAS Inst.

SAS Technical Report P-212, SAS/SHARE Software for the MVS Environment, Release 6.07. 44p. (C). 1991. pap. 8.00 (1-55544-457-1, BR59129) SAS Inst.

SAS Technical Report P-213, SAS/SHARE Software for the CMS Environment, Release 6.07. 44p. (C). 1991. pap. 8.00 (1-55544-458-X, BR59130) SAS Inst.

SAS Technical Report P-214, Using the SAS System, Release 6. 07, on the NeXT Computer. 36p. 1991. 6.00 (1-55544-460-1, BR59131) SAS Inst.

SAS Technical Report P-215, SAS/GRAPH Software: Changes & Enhancements, Release 6. 07. 84p. (C). 1991. pap. 5.00 (1-55544-461-X, BR59132) SAS Inst.

SAS Technical Report P-216, SAS/AF Software, SAS/FSP Software, & SAS Screen Control Language: Changes & Enhancements, Release 6. 07. 332p. 1991. 12.00 (1-55544-468-7, BR59133) SAS Inst.

SAS Technical Report P-217, SAS - STAT Software: The PHREG Procedure, Version 6. 64p. (C). 1993. pap. 5.00 (1-55544-459-8) SAS Inst.

SAS Technical Report P-218, Changes & Enhancements to the SAS System, Release 6. 07, for the MVS Environment. 140p. 1991. 8.00 (1-55544-467-9, BR59135) SAS Inst.

SAS Technical Report P-219, Changes & Enhancements to the SAS System, Release 6. 07, for the CMS Environment. 92p. 1991. 6.00 (1-55544-464-4, BR59136) SAS Inst.

SAS Technical Report P-220, Changes & Enhancements to the SAS System, Release 6. 07, for the VMS Environment. 196p. 1991. 9.00 (1-55544-462-8, BR59137) SAS Inst.

SAS Technical Report P-221, SAS/ACCESS Software: Changes & Enhancements, Release 6. 07. 140p. (C). 1991. pap. 9.00 (1-55544-465-2, BR59138) SAS Inst.

SAS Technical Report P-222, Changes & Enhancements to Base SAS Software, Release 6. 07. 384p. (C). 1991. pap. 14.00 (1-55544-466-0, BR59139) SAS Inst.

SAS Technical Report P-228, Using SAS/CPE Software, Release 6.07, in the VMS Environment. 352p. (C). 1991. pap. 27.00 (1-55544-483-0, BR59145) SAS Inst.

SAS Technical Report P-230, SAS/IML Software: Changes & Enhancements, Release 6. 07. 53p. 1991. 5.00 (1-55544-478-4, BR59147) SAS Inst.

SAS Technical Report P-231, SAS Software: Summary of Changes & Enhancements, Release 6. 07. 107p. (C). 1992. pap. 6.00 (1-55544-479-2, BR59148) SAS Inst.

SAS Technical Report P-235, Using International Character Support with the SAS System, Release 6.07, under UNIX Operating Systems & Derivatives. 36p. (C). 1991. pap. 6.00 (1-55544-493-8, BR59152) SAS Inst.

SAS Technical Report P-242, SAS Software: Changes & Enhancements, Release 6.08. 11p. (C). 1997. pap. 13.00 (1-55544-522-5, BR59159) SAS Inst.

SAS Technical Report P-251, Changes & Enhancements to the SAS System, Release 6.09, for the Open VMS Environment. 22p. 1993. 11.00 (1-55544-568-3, BR59168) SAS Inst.

SAS Technical Report P-252, SAS Software: Changes & Enhancements, Release 6.09. 63p. (C). 1993. pap. 9.00 (1-55544-567-5, BR59169) SAS Inst.

SAS Technical Report P-253, User-Written Methods & Objects in SAS-EIS Software, Release 6.08. 70p. (C). 1996. pap. 12.00 (1-55544-559-4, 59170) SAS Inst.

SAS Technical Report P-257, International Character Support for UNIX Environments, Release 6.09. 22p. (C). 1993. pap. 7.00 (1-55544-569-1, BR59174) SAS Inst.

SAS Technical Report P-258, Using the REPORT Procedure in a Nonwindowing Environment, Release 6. 07. 276p. (C). 1993. pap. 17.00 (1-55544-572-1, BR59175) SAS Inst.

SAS Technical Report P-260, SAS/SHARE for the MVS Environment, Release 6.08. 36p. (C). 1993. pap. 10.00 (1-55544-577-2, BR59177) SAS Inst.

SAS Technical Report P-261, SAS/SHARE for the CMS Environment, Release 6.08. 34p. (C). 1993. pap. 12.00 (1-55544-578-0, BR59178) SAS Inst.

SAS Technical Report P-263: Image Extensions to SAS/GRAPH Software, Version 6. 134p. (C). 1995. pap. 10. 00 (1-55544-629-9, BR55037) SAS Inst.

SAS Technical Report P-264, SAS/ASSIST Software: Query & Reporting from DB2, Release 6.08. 138p. 1994. 17.00 (1-55544-652-3, BR55196) SAS Inst.

SAS Technical Report P-265, SAS/SHARE Software for the OpenVMS Environment, Releases 6.08 & 6.09. 58p. (C). 1994. pap. 14.00 (1-55544-651-5, BR55197) SAS Inst.

SAS Technical Report R-109, Conjoint Analysis Examples. 86p. (C). 1993. pap. 10.00 (1-55544-581-0, BR59041) SAS Inst.

*SAS Unleashed. Wayne Vovil. 1997. 59.99 (0-672-31180-1) Mac Comp Pub.

*SAS Urban Survival Handbook. John Wiseman. 1997. 22. 00 (0-00-255803-3) Harper SF.

*SAS with the Marquis: In Action with the French Resistance, June-September 1944. Ian Wellsted. LC 97-14670. 1997. pap. write for info. (1-85367-285-8) Stackpole.

SAS Workbook. Ron Cody. 243p. (C). 1996. pap. 23.95 (1-55544-757-0, BR55473) SAS Inst.

*SAS Workbook & Solutions, 2 vols. Ron Cody. 392p. (C). 1996. pap. 40.72 (1-55544-762-7, BR55594) SAS Inst.

SAS Workbook Solutions. Ron Cody. 129p. (C). 1997. pap. 23.95 (1-55544-758-9, BR55475) SAS Inst.

SAS/ACCESS Interface to ADABAS: Usage & Reference, Version 6. 272p. (C). 1991. pap. 28.95 (1-55544-411-3, BR56065) SAS Inst.

SAS/ACCESS Interface to CA-DATACOM DB: Usage & Reference, Version 6. 240p. (C). 1991. pap. 22.95 (1-55544-412-1, BR56066) SAS Inst.

SAS/ACCESS Interface to CA-IDMS: Reference, Version 6. 82p. (C). 1995. pap. 29.95 (1-55544-661-2, BR55180) SAS Inst.

SAS/ACCESS Interface to IMS-DL - I: Usage & Reference, Version 6. 280p. 1991. 29.95 (1-55544-456-3, BR56069) SAS Inst.

SAS/ACCESS Interface to IMS-DL/I: Usage & Reference, Version 6. 2nd ed. 365p. (C). 1995. pap. 29.95 (1-55544-227-7, BR55270) SAS Inst.

*SAS/Access Interface to Prime Information: Usage & Reference, Version 6. .p. (C). 1990. pap. 23.95 (1-55544-413-X) SAS Inst.

*SAS/Access Interface to System 2000 Data Management Software. 272p. (C). 1990. pap. 28.95 (1-55544-368-0) SAS Inst.

SAS/ACCESS Software Changes & Enhancements: SQL Procedure Pass-Through Facility, Version 6. 56p. (C). 1995. pap. 9.00 (1-55544-660-4, BR55237) SAS Inst.

SAS/ACCESS Software for PC File Formats: Reference, Version 6. 260p. (C). 1997. pap. 38.95 (1-55544-212-9, BR55206) SAS Inst.

SAS/ACCESS Software for Relational Databases: Reference, Version 6. 196p. (C). 1996. pap. 29.95 (1-55544-631-0, BR55144) SAS Inst.

*SAS/Access Software for Relational Databases: Reference, Version 6. 23p. (C). 1996. pap. 9.75 (1-55544-642-6) SAS Inst.

*SAS/Access Software for Relational Databases: Reference, Version 6. 40p. (C). 1997. pap. 9.75 (1-55544-649-3) SAS Inst.

*SAS/Access Software for Relational Databases: Reference, Version 6. 2nd ed. 52p. (C). 1996. pap. 9.75 (1-55544-714-7) SAS Inst.

*SAS/Access Software for Relational Databases: Reference, Version 6. 2nd ed. 48p. (C). 1995. pap. 9.75 (1-55544-715-5) SAS Inst.

*SAS/Access Software for Relational Databases: Reference, Version 6. 2nd ed. .p. (C). 1997. pap. 9.75 (1-55544-937-9) SAS Inst.

*SAS/Access Software for Relational Databases: Reference, Version 6. 2nd ed. 28p. (C). 1997. pap. 9.75 (1-55544-944-1) SAS Inst.

*SAS/Access Software for Relational Databases (Oracle) Reference, Version 6. 51p. (C). 1996. pap. 9.75 (1-55544-226-9) SAS Inst.

*SAS/Access Software for Relational Databases (SyBase & SQL Server) Reference, Version 6. 34p. (C). 1997. pap. 9.75 (1-55544-225-0) SAS Inst.

*SAS/AF & SAS/FSP Software: Changes & Enhancements, Release 6.07. 96p. (C). 1997. pap. 8.00 (1-55544-853-4) SAS Inst.

SAS/AF Software: FRAME Application Development Concepts, Version 6. 216p. (C). 1996. pap. 19.95 (1-55544-243-9, BR55376) SAS Inst.

SAS/AF Software: FRAME Class Dictionary, Version 6. 1158p. (C). 1995. pap. 63.95 (1-55544-206-4, BR55146) SAS Inst.

*SAS/AF Software: Frame Entry Usage & Reference, Version 6. 632p. (C). 1996. pap. 40.95 (1-55544-477-6) SAS Inst.

*SAS/AF Software: Usage & Reference, Version 6. 288p. (C). 1997. pap. 21.95 (1-55544-369-9) SAS Inst.

Sasakawa, the Warrior for Peace: Global Philanthropist. Paula Daventry. (Illus.). 143p. 1981. pap. 9.00 (0-08-028126-5, Pergamon Pr) Elsevier.

*Sasaki Associates: Integrated Environments. Melanie Simo. 1997. pap. text ed. 35.00 (1-888931-08-6) Spacemkr Pr.

Sasanian Coins. R. Gobl. LC 90-91495. (Illus.). 1990. reprint ed. lib. bdg. 25.00 (0-942666-63-1) S J Durst.

Sasanian Remains from Qasr-i Abu Nasr: Seals, Sealings, & Coins. Ed. by Richard N. Frye. LC 72-80657. (Harvard Iranian Ser.: No. 1). (Illus.). 148p. 1973. 14.00 (0-674-78960-1) HUP.

Sasanian Stamp Seals in the Metropolitan Museum of Art. Christopher J. Brunner. (Illus.). 152p. 1979. 35.00 (0-87099-176-0) Metro Mus Art.

*SAS/Assist Software: Changes & Enhancements, Version 6. 336p. (C). 1996. pap. 16.00 (1-55544-216-1) SAS Inst.

*SAS/Assist Software: Your Interface to the SAS System: Version 6. 64p. (C). 1993. pap. 9.95 (1-55544-375-3) SAS Inst.

SAS/C CICS User's Guide: Release 6.00. 2nd ed. 120p. (C). 1996. pap. 28.95 (1-55544-669-8, BR55117) SAS Inst.

SAS/C Compiler & Library Quick Reference Guide. 112p. (C). 1996. pap. 15.95 (1-55544-670-1, BR55182) SAS Inst.

SAS/C Compiler & Library User's Guide: Release 6.00. 4th ed. 433p. (C). 1996. pap. 54.95 (1-55544-668-X, BR55156) SAS Inst.

*SAS/C Compiler Interlanguage Communication Feature User's Guide. 280p. (C). 1989. pap. 15.95 (1-55544-323-0) SAS Inst.

SAS/C Cross-Platform Compiler & C++ Development System: Usage & Reference, Release 6.00. 140p. (C). 1996. pap. 29.95 (1-55544-259-5, BR55388) SAS Inst.

*SAS/C Debugger User's Guide & Reference. 3rd ed. 446p. (C). 1996. pap. 36.95 (1-55544-439-3) SAS Inst.

*SAS/C Full-Screen Support Library User's Guide. 192p. (C). 1997. pap. 13.95 (1-55544-334-6) SAS Inst.

SAS/C Full-Screen Support Library User's Guide. 2nd ed. 515p. (C). 1992. pap. 35.95 (1-55544-472-5, BR56124) SAS Inst.

SAS/C Library Reference, Release 6.00. 3rd ed. 767p. (C). 1996. pap. 63.95 (1-55544-666-3, BR55049) SAS Inst.

SAS/C Library Reference, Release 6.00. 3rd ed. 623p. (C). 1996. pap. 63.95 (1-55544-667-1, BR55178) SAS Inst.

SAS/C Software Diagnostic Messages: Release 6.00. 420p. (C). 1996. pap. 63.95 (1-55544-672-8, BR55184) SAS Inst.

*SAS/C Softwares: Changes & Enhancements to tje SAS/C Debugger & C++ Development System, Release 6. 85p. (C). 1996. pap. 15.00 (1-55544-720-1) SAS Inst.

SAS/CALC Software: Usage & Reference, Version 6. 720p. (C). 1991. pap. 35.95 (1-55544-455-5, BR56035) SAS Inst.

*SAs/Connect Software: Usage & Reference, Version 6. 2nd ed. 384p. (C). 1996. pap. 34.95 (1-55544-625-6) SAS Inst.

*SAS/CPE Software: Reference, Version 6. 2nd ed. 298p. (C). 1996. pap. 39.95 (1-55544-796-1, BR55642) SAS Inst.

*SAS/CPE User's Guide: Version 5. 220p. (C). 1989. pap. 11.95 (1-55544-328-1) SAS Inst.

SASE, a Mail Installation. Miekal And. (Samsara Congeries Ser.: Bk. 8). 35p. 1990. pap. 5.00 (0-945112-11-4) Generator Pr.

*SAS/EIS Software: Reference, Version 6. 368p. (C). 1996. pap. 42.95 (1-55544-470-9) SAS Inst.

SAS/EIS Software: Reference, Version 6. 2nd ed. 280p. (C). 1996. pap. 45.95 (1-55544-205-6, BR55249) SAS Inst.

SAS/ENGLISH Software: Knowledge Base Administrator's Guide, Version 6. 354p. (C). 1993. pap. 10.00 (1-55544-571-3, BR56083) SAS Inst.

SAS/ENGLISH Software: User's Guide, Version 6. 151p. (C). 1993. pap. 10.00 (1-55544-570-5, BR56084) SAS Inst.

SAS/ETS Software: Applications Guide 1, Version 6. 404p. (C). 1992. pap. 25.95 (1-55544-480-6, BR56008) SAS Inst.

*SAS/ETS Software: Applications Guide 2, Version 6. 472p. (C). 1993. pap. 36.95 (1-55544-549-7, BR56009) SAS Inst.

*SAS/ETS Software: Changes & Enhancements for Version 6.12. 112p. (C). 1997. pap. 8.00 (1-55544-875-5) SAS Inst.

*SAS/ETS Software: Changes & Enhancements, Release 6. 120p. (C). 1996. pap. 10.00 (1-55544-273-0) SAS Inst.

*SAS/ETS Software: Syntax, Version 6. 112p. (C). 1994. pap. 12.95 (1-55544-628-0) SAS Inst.

SAS/ETS Software: Times Series Forecasting System, Version 6. 264p. (C). 1996. pap. 24.95 (1-55544-275-7, BR55476) SAS Inst.

*SAS/ETS User's Guide: Version 6. 2nd ed. 1022p. (C). 1993. pap. 44.95 (1-55544-554-3, BR56010) SAS Inst.

SAS/FSP Software: Usage & Reference, Version 6. 451p. (C). 1996. pap. 29.95 (1-55544-365-6, BR56001) SAS Inst.

SAS/GIS Software: Usage & Reference, Version 6. 280p. (C). 1996. pap. 44.95 (1-55544-561-6, BR56585) SAS Inst.

*SAS/Graph Software: Examples, Version 6. 320p. (C). 1993. pap. 42.95 (1-55544-500-4) SAS Inst.

SAS/GRAPH Software: Graphics Editor, Version 6. 208p. (C). 1991. pap. 34.95 (1-55544-419-9, BR56023) SAS Inst.

SAS/GRAPH Software: Introduction, Version 6. 122p. (C). 1996. pap. 9.95 (1-55544-395-8, BR56019) SAS Inst.

SAS/GRAPH Software: Reference, Version 6, 2 vols., Set, Vols. 1 & 2. 1341p. (C). 1996. Set. pap. 65.95 (1-55544-379-6, BR56020) SAS Inst.

SAS/GRAPH Software: Syntax, Version 6. 188p. (C). 1992. pap. 11.95 (1-55544-487-3, BR56024) SAS Inst.

SAS/GRAPH Software: Usage, Version 6. 936p. (C). 1991. pap. 48.95 (1-55544-421-0, BR56021) SAS Inst.

SAS/GRAPH Software: Using Graphics Devices in the CMS Environment, Version 6. 224p. (C). 1992. pap. 17.95 (1-55544-501-2, BR56026) SAS Inst.

SAS/GRAPH Software: Using Graphics Devices in the MVS Environment, Version 6. 188p. (C). 1992. pap. 17.95 (1-55544-492-X, BR56025) SAS Inst.

SAS/GRAPH Software: Using Graphics Devices in the UNIX Environment & Derivatives, Version 6. 216p. (C). 1993. pap. 45.95 (1-55544-519-5, BR56027) SAS Inst.

SAS/GRAPH Software: Using Graphics Devices in the VMS Environment, Version 6. 200p. (C). 1993. pap. 22.95 (1-55544-558-6, BR56028) SAS Inst.

Sash, Doors, & Mouldings. Fulton & Libby Co. Staff. (Illus.). 200p. 1995. pap. 35.00 (0-87556-779-7) Saifer.

*Sash My Father Wore. Robert Greacen. 192p. 1997. 35.00 (1-85158-923-6, Pub. by Mnstream UK) Trafalgar.

Sasha & the Wiggly Tooth. Rhea Tregebov. (NFS Canada Ser.). 1993. 12.95 (0-929005-51-1, Pub. by Second Story Pr CN) LPC InBook.

Sasha & the Wiggly Tooth. Rhea Tregebov. (Illus.). 24p. (J). 1993. pap. 5.95 (0-929005-50-3, Pub. by Second Story Pr CN) LPC InBook.

*Sasha & the Wind. Rhea Tregebov. 24p. (J). (ps-2). 1996. mass mkt. 5.95 (0-929005-83-X, Pub. by Second Story Pr CN) LPC InBook.

*Sasha & the Wind. Rhea Tregebov. (Illus.). 24p. (J). 1996. 12.95 (0-929005-84-8, Pub. by Second Story Pr CN) LPC InBook.

*Sasha & the Wind. Rhea Tregebov & Helene Desputeaux. (FRE.). (J). pap. 6.99 (0-590-16018-4) Scholastic Inc.

Sasha's Trick. David Rosenbaum. 400p. 1996. mass mkt. 5.99 (0-446-40441-1, Mysterious Paperbk) Warner Bks.

*Sashiko: Blue & White Quilt Art of Japan. Kazuko Mende & Reiko Morishige. 1997. 45.50 (0-614-28075-3) Japan Pubns USA.

Sashiko: Blue & White Quilt Art of Japan. rev. ed. Kazuko Mende & Reiko Morishige. (Illus.). 120p. 1996. 29.00 (0-87040-978-6) Kodansha.

Sashiko: Traditional Japanese Quilt Designs. Nihon Vogue Staff. LC 88-80146. (Illus.). 42p. (Orig.). 1989. pap. 11. 95 (0-87040-769-4) Japan Pubns USA.

Sashiko & Beyond: Techniques for Quilting in the Japanese Style. Saikoh Takano. 128p. 1993. 19.95 (0-8019-8514-5) Chilton.

*Sashimi. Doreen Koto. LC 96-90445. 1997. 29.95 (0-533-12054-3) Vantage.

Sashone - Victim & Survivor. E. Bernardine Bayez-Sydner. LC 92-60290. 188p. 1992. pap. 8.95 (1-55523-525-5) Winston-Derek.

*SAS/IML Software: Changes & Enhancements Through Release 6.11. 312p. (C). 1996. pap. 16.00 (1-55544-281-1) SAS Inst.

SAS/IML Software: Usage & Reference, Version 6. 504p. (C). 1997. pap. 24.95 (1-55544-377-X, BR56040) SAS Inst.

*SAS/Insight Software: Changes & Enhancements, Version 6. 216p. (C). 1996. pap. 18.00 (1-55544-636-1) SAS Inst.

*SAS/Insight User's Guide: Version s. 456p. (C). 1993. pap. 30.95 (1-55544-418-0) SAS Inst.

*SAS/Insight User's Guide: Version 6. 2nd ed. 496p. (C). 1995. pap. 34.95 (1-55544-526-8) SAS Inst.

SAS/INSIGHT User's Guide, Version 6. 3rd ed. 582p. (C). 1996. pap. 35.95 (1-55544-751-1, BR55582) SAS Inst.

*Saskaid. Hall. Date not set. pap. write for info. (0-312-18171-X) St Martin.

*Saskatchewan. Harry Beckett. LC 97-12866. (Journey Across Canada Ser.). (J). 1997. write for info. (1-55916-204-X) Rourke Bk Co.

Saskatchewan. Suzanne LeVert. (Let's Discover Canada Ser.). (Illus.). 64p. (J). (gr. 3 up). 1991. lib. bdg. 16.95 (0-7910-1024-4) Chelsea Hse.

Saskatchewan. David Margoshes. (Discover Canada Ser.). (Illus.). 144p. (J). (gr. 4 up). 1992. lib. bdg. 29.30 (0-516-06618-8) Childrens.

Saskatchewan. Gillian Richardson. LC 94-44842. (Hello Canada Ser.). (J). 1995. lib. bdg. 14.21 (0-8225-2760-X) Lerner Group.

*Saskatchewan Business Directory 1997-1998. rev. ed. American Business Directories Staff. 512p. 1997. boxed 295.00 (1-56105-973-0) Am Busn Direct.

Saskatchewan Reports Vols. 1-25: 1908-1931. 1970. 725.00 (1-57588-361-9, 302590) W S Hein.

Saskiad. Brian Hall. LC 96-25841. 380p. 1997. 23.95 (0-395-82754-X) HM.

An Asterisk (*) at the beginning of an entry indicates that the title is appearing in BIP for the first time.

SAS/LAB Software: User's Guide, Version 6. 320p. (C). 1993. pap. 34.95 (*1-55544-486-5*, BR56098) SAS Inst.
SAS/NVISION Software: Language Usage & Reference, Version 6. 456p. 1992. 47.95 (*1-55544-192-0*, BR56134) SAS Inst.
***SAS/OR Software: Project Management Examples, Version 6.** 232p. (C). 1993. pap. 24.95 (*1-55544-544-6*) SAS Inst.
***SAS/OR Software: The Projman Menu System, Version 6.** 216p. (C). 1993. pap. 11.95 (*1-55544-543-8*) SAS Inst.
SAS/OR User's Guide, Version 6. 479p. (C). 1989. pap. 53. 95 (*1-55544-324-9*, BR5850) SAS Inst.
SAS/PH-Clinical Software: Usage & Reference, Version 2. 468p. (C). 1997. pap. 59.95 (*1-55544-744-9*, BR55511) SAS Inst.
SAS/QC Software: ADX Menu System for Design of Experiments, Version 6. 250p. (C). 1994. pap. 32.95 (*1-55544-443-1*, BR56039) SAS Inst.
SAS/QC Software: SQC Menu System for Quality Improvement, Version 6. 2nd ed. 200p. (C). 1995. pap. 32.95 (*1-55544-234-X*, BR55242) SAS Inst.
SAS/QC Software Vols. 1 & 2: Usage & Reference, Version 6. 1697p. (C). 1996. pap. 63.95 (*1-55544-658-2*, BR55140) SAS Inst.
Sasquatch: Bigfoot. Thomas Steenburg. 82p. 1993. pap. 11. 95 (*0-88839-312-1*) Hancock House.
Sasquatch: The Apes Among Us. John Green. (Illus.). 492p. pap. 12.95 (*0-88839-123-4*) Hancock House.
Sasquatch Apparitions: A Critique on the Pacific Northwest Hominoir. Barbara Wasson. (Illus.). 174p. (Orig.). 1979. pap. 8.95 (*0-9614105-0-7*) B Butler.
Sasquatch-Bigfoot: The Search for North America's Incredible Creature. Don Hunter & Rene Dahinden. (Illus.). 224p. 1993. pap. 14.95 (*1-895565-28-6*) Firefly Bks Ltd.
Sasquatch, Wild Man of the Woods. Elaine Landau. LC 92-35144. (Mysteries of Science Ser.). (Illus.). 48p. (J). (gr. 3-6). 1993. lib. bdg. 15.40 (*1-56294-348-0*) Millbrook Pr.
***SAS(R) Today! A Year of Terrific Tips.** 396p. (C). 1996. pap. 16.95 (*1-55544-880-1*, BR55662) SAS Inst.
Sass: Dieselmaschinen, Vol. 1. 1948. 58.95 (*0-387-01344-X*) Spr-Verlag.
Sass Menagerie. Robert L. Steed. LC 88-81797. (Illus.). 164p. 1988. 14.95 (*0-929264-06-1*) Longstreet Pr Inc.
Sassafras. Stephen Cosgrove. (Serendipity Ser.). (Illus.). 32p. (J). (ps-4). 1995. pap. 3.95 (*0-8431-3830-0*) Price Stern Sloan.
Sassafras. Audrey Penn. (Illus.). 32p. (J). (ps-3). 1995. 16. 95 (*0-87868-578-2*, Child-Family Pr) Child Welfare.
Sassafras! The Ozark's Cookbook. 7th ed. Junior League of Springfield, MO Staff. LC 84-81440. (Illus.). iv, 401p. 1997. reprint ed. 17.95 (*0-9613307-1-6*) Jr League MO.
Sassafras, Cypress & Indigo. Ntozake Shange. 224p. 1983. pap. 9.95 (*0-312-69972-7*) St Martin.
Sassafrass, Cypress, & Indigo. Ntozake Shange. LC 95-44945. 240p. 1996. pap. 12.00 (*0-312-14091-6*) St Martin.
SAS/SHARE Software: Usage & Reference, Version 6. 132p. (C). 1991. pap. 15.95 (*1-55544-454-7*, BR56014) SAS Inst.
Sassinak. Anne McCaffrey & Elizabeth Moon. (Planet Pirate Ser.). 352p. 1990. mass mkt. 6.99 (*0-671-69863-X*) Baen Bks.
Sassoon Dynasty. Cecil Roth. Ed. by Mira Wilkins. LC 76-29982. (European Business Ser.). (Illus.). 1977. reprint ed. lib. bdg. 25.95 (*0-405-09747-6*) Ayer.
Sassoon's Sketches. Elias Sassoon. LC 86-72870. 168p. (Orig.). 1987. pap. 8.00 (*0-916383-20-2*) Aegina Pr.
***SAS/Stat Software: Changes & Enhancements for Release 6.12.** 168p. (C). 1996. pap. 10.00 (*1-55544-874-7*) SAS Inst.
SAS/STAT Software: Changes & Enhancements Through Release 6.11. 1104p. (C). 1995. pap. 40.00 (*1-55544-274-9*, BR55356) SAS Inst.
***SAS/Stat Software: Changes & Enhancements Through Release 6.12.** 1176p. (C). 1997. pap. 43.00 (*1-55544-873-9*) SAS Inst.
***SAS/Stat Software: Syntax, Version 6.** 160p. (C). 1993. pap. 12.95 (*1-55544-545-4*) SAS Inst.
SAS/STAT User's Guide, Version 6, Set. Vols. 1 & 2. 4th ed. 1686p. (C). 1997. Set. pap. 44.95 (*1-55544-376-1*, BR56065) SAS Inst.
Sassy: The Life of Sarah Vaughan. Leslie Gourse. (Illus.). 327p. 1994. reprint ed. pap. 13.95 (*0-306-80578-2*) Da Capo.
***Sassy Lady.** Becky Barker. (Black Satin Romance Ser.). 289p. 1997. 25.99 (*1-86110-024-8*) Ulverscroft.
Sassy Sayin's & Mountain Badmouth. Jesse Masters & Don Johnston. (Illus.). 80p. (Orig.). 1985. pap. 3.95 (*0-9615347-0-2*) Sassy Sayings.
Sassy, Secure, & over Sixty. large type ed. Gwendolyn L. Baines. LC 96-68369. (Illus.). 128p. (Orig.). 1996. pap. 10.95 (*0-9614505-3-3*) Nevada Pub.
SAS/TOOLKIT Software: Usage & Reference, Version 6. 788p. (C). 1991. pap. 63.95 (*1-55544-453-9*, BR56049) SAS Inst.
***SAS/Trader Software: Product Administrator's Guide, Version 6.** 112p. (C). 1995. pap. 44.95 (*1-55544-221-8*) SAS Inst.
***Sastre de Panama.** 1997. pap. text ed. 18.95 (*0-553-06063-5*) Bantam.
Sastun: One Woman's Apprenticeship with a Maya Healer & their Efforts to Save the Vanishing Tradition of Rainforest Medicine. Rosita Arvigo & Nadine Epstein. LC 93-37439. 224p. 1995. pap. 12.00 (*0-06-250259-X*) Harper SF.
***SAS/Warehouse Administrator User's Guide, Release 1.1.** 146p. (C). 1997. pap. 32.95 (*1-55544-963-8*) SAS Inst.
SAT: See You at the Top. Daniel Alderson & Jon Simon. 120p. 1995. pap. 9.95 (*0-89087-747-5*) Celestial Arts.
***SAT & College Level English, Grammar & Usage.** Jack Rudman. (General Aptitude & Abilities Ser.: Vol. CS-56). 1997. pap. 23.95 (*0-8373-6756-5*) Nat Learn.
***SAT & College Level Mathematical Ability.** Jack Rudman. (General Aptitude & Abilities Ser.: Vol. CS-58). 1997. pap. 23.95 (*0-8373-6758-1*) Nat Learn.
***SAT & College Level Reading Comprehension.** Jack Rudman. (General Aptitude & Abilities Ser.: Vol. CS-57). 1997. pap. 23.95 (*0-8373-6757-3*) Nat Learn.
***SAT & College Level Vocabulary.** Jack Rudman. (General Aptitude & Abilities Ser.: Vol. CS-55). 1997. pap. 23.95 (*0-8373-6755-7*) Nat Learn.
SAT & PSAT. 13th ed. Davidson & Associates Staff. 1996. pap. 12.00 incl. disk (*0-02-861080-6*, Arco) Macmillan Gen Ref.
SAT & PSAT Computer Diagnostics 1995 Edition: Mac Version. Princeton Review Editors. 1995. 15.25 (*1-884536-10-7*, Villard Bks) Random.
***SAT & PSAT Power, 1998 Edition.** (Cambridge Review Test Preparation Guides Ser.). 496p. 1997. 16.95 (*0-02-861688-X*) Macmillan.
Sat at a Glance. Ronald G. Vlk. 3.95 (*0-668-06464-1*) S&S Trade.
Sat Chit Anand: Truth-Consciousness-Bliss. Rajneesh Osho Staff. (Mantra Ser.). 416p. 1989. 21.95 (*3-89338-042-6*, Pub. by Rebel Hse GW) Osho America.
SAT Cram Course. 3rd ed. Suzee J. Vlk. LC 93-22325. 1993. pap. 8.00 (*0-671-86399-1*) P-H Gen Ref & Trav.
SAT Gender Gap: Identifying the Causes. Phyllis Rosser. 190p. 1989. pap. 15.00 (*1-877966-00-2*) Ctr Women Policy.
***SAT I.** (YA). (gr. 10-12). 1996. pap. text ed. 31.25 incl. cd-rom (*0-8220-5601-1*) Cliffs.
SAT I Computer Study Program, Macintosh. 3rd ed. Samuel C. Brownstein et al. 1994. 24.95 incl. disk (*0-8120-8158-7*) Barron.
SAT I Computer Study Program, Windows. 3rd ed. Samuel C. Brownstein et al. 1994. 24.95 incl. disk (*0-8120-8157-9*) Barron.
SAT I for Dummies. Suzee J. Vlk. 300p. 1994. student ed., pap. 14.99 (*1-56884-213-9*) IDG Bks.
SAT I for Dummies. 2nd ed. Suzee J. Vlk. 1996. pap. 14.99 (*1-56884-398-4*) IDG Bks.
***SAT I for Dummies.** 3rd ed. Suzee Vlk. 1997. pap. 14.99 (*0-7645-5044-6*) IDG Bks.
SAT I Math Tutor. Research & Education Association Staff. 325p. 1995. pap. text ed. 15.95 (*0-87891-962-7*) Res & Educ.
***SAT I Performance Improvement.** Timothy Hall. (Illus.). xii, 315p. (Orig.). 1997. pap. text ed. 29.95 (*0-9658060-0-6*) PQIC Pr.
SAT I Preparation Guide: Scholastic Assessment Test. Jerry Bobrow. (Cliffs Test Preparation Ser.). (Illus.). 444p. (Orig.). 1994. pap. text ed. 9.95 (*0-8220-2074-2*) Cliffs.
SAT I Quick Study & Review. (Illus.). 300p. 1994. pap. text ed. 8.95 (*0-87891-938-4*) Res & Educ.
SAT I Reasoning Test. (Illus.). 1008p. 1996. pap. text ed. 15.95 (*0-87891-934-1*) Res & Educ.
SAT I Teacher's Manual. (Illus.). 288p. 1994. pap. text ed. 12.95 (*0-87891-937-6*) Res & Educ.
SAT I Verbal Tutor. Research & Education Association Staff. 256p. 1995. pap. text ed. 15.95 (*0-87891-963-5*) Res & Educ.
SAT I Wordmaster, Level I. George Ehrenhaft. 1996. 7.95 (*0-8120-6536-0*) Barron.
SAT I Wordmaster, Level II. George Ehrenhaft. 1996. 7.95 (*0-8120-6537-9*) Barron.
SAT II: English Language Proficiency Test. Vernon et al. 432p. 1996. pap. 24.95 incl. audio (*0-87891-641-5*) Res & Educ.
SAT II American History & Social Studies. rev. ed. Research & Education Association Staff. (Illus.). 508p. 1994. pap. text ed. 14.95 (*0-87891-845-0*) Res & Educ.
SAT II Biology. rev. ed. Research & Education Association Staff. (Illus.). 432p. 1996. pap. text ed. 14.95 (*0-87891-644-X*) Res & Educ.
SAT II Chemistry. rev. ed. Research & Education Association Staff. (Illus.). 368p. 1996. pap. text ed. 15.95 (*0-87891-603-2*) Res & Educ.
SAT II French. Research & Education Association Staff. 1995. pap. 14.95 (*0-87891-969-4*) Res & Educ.
SAT II German. Research & Education Association Staff. 1995. pap. 13.95 (*0-87891-970-8*) Res & Educ.
SAT II Literature. rev. ed. Research & Education Association Staff. (Illus.). 288p. 1996. pap. text ed. 14.95 (*0-87891-846-9*) Res & Educ.
Sat II Math Level IC: Math Level IC. SAT Research & Education Staff. 272p. 1995. pap. text ed. 14.95 (*0-87891-750-0*) Res & Educ.
SAT II Math Level IIC. Max Fogiel. 1996. pap. 14.95 (*0-87891-957-0*) Res & Educ.
***Sat II Math 1998.** Kaplan Staff. 1997. pap. 18.00 (*0-684-84163-0*) S&S Trade.
SAT II Physics. rev. ed. Research & Education Association Staff. (Illus.). 288p. 1994. pap. text ed. 14.95 (*0-87891-870-1*) Res & Educ.
SAT II Spanish. Research & Education Association Staff. 1994. pap. 14.95 (*0-87891-968-6*) Res & Educ.
SAT II Writing. 3rd ed. Leo Lieberman & Jeffrey Spielberger. LC 93-17593. 1993. pap. 12.00 (*0-671-86400-9*) P-H.
SAT II Writing Preparation Guide: Scholastic Assessment Test. Allan Casson & Cliff Notes Inc. Staff. (Test Preparation Ser.). 352p. (Orig.). (YA). (gr. 11-12). 1996. student ed., pap. text ed. 14.95 (*0-8220-2325-3*) Cliffs.
SAT II Writing Test. Research & Education Association Staff & E. Conner. 362p. 1995. pap. 14.95 (*0-87891-935-X*) Res & Educ.
***Sat II Writing 1998.** Kaplan Staff. 1997. pap. 18.00 (*0-684-84164-9*) S&S Trade.
SAT In-a-Week. Kaplan. 1996. pap. 11.00 (*0-684-83384-0*) S&S Trade.
SAT in a Week. Kaplan Educational Center, Ltd. Staff. 224p. 1994. pap. 9.95 (*0-385-31276-8*) Doubleday.
SAT Math Flash: The Quick Way to Build Math Power for the New SAT - & Beyond. Michael R. Crystal. LC 93-23413. 144p. (Orig.). 1993. pap. 7.95 (*1-56079-321-X*) Petersons.
SAT Math Workbook. 4th ed. Brigitte Saunders et al. LC 93-12203. 1993. pap. 10.00 (*0-671-79968-1*) P-H Gen Ref & Trav.
SAT Math Workbook: Scholastic Aptitude Test. 3rd ed. Brigitte Saunders et al. (Illus.). 288p. 1992. pap. 10.00 (*0-13-564097-0*, Arco) Macmillan Gen Ref.
***SAT Math Workbook: Scholastic Assessment Test.** 5th ed. Brigitte Saunders et al. (Illus.). 288p. 1997. pap. 10. 95 (*0-02-861704-5*, Arco) Macmillan Gen Ref.
SAT Math Workout. Cornelia Cooke. (Princeton Review Ser.). 1995. pap. 15.00 (*0-679-75363-X*, Villard Bks) Random.
***SAT or ACT.** Kaplan Staff. LC 97-16953. 1997. pap. 12.00 (*0-684-84162-2*) S&S Trade.
SAT Power. Cambridge Review Staff. 384p. 1996. 16.95 (*0-02-861074-1*) Macmillan.
SAT Prep Course. Jeff Kolby. Ed. by Scott Thornburg. (Prep Course Ser.). (Illus.). 608p. (Orig.). 1995. pap. 19. 95 (*0-9637371-5-5*) Nova Pr.
***SAT Prep Course.** Jeff Kolby. 624p. (Orig.). 1997. pap. 19. 95 incl. disk (*1-889057-03-7*) Nova Pr.
SAT Preparation for Critical Reading: The Touchstones Method. Geoffrey Comber et al. 128p. (YA). (gr. 11-12). 1995. teacher ed., pap. 12.95 (*1-878461-32-X*) CZM Pr.
***SAT Savvy: Last Minute Tips & Strategies.** Marian Martin & Sandra Martin. 72p. 1996. 6.00 (*1-57509-012-0*) Octameron Assocs.
SAT Success. 4th ed. Joan D. Carris et al. LC 94-2714. 474p. 1994. pap. 12.95 (*1-56079-393-7*) Petersons.
SAT Success. 4th rev. ed. Joan D. Carris et al. LC 94-2714. 474p. 1994. pap. 18.95 incl. disk (*1-56079-469-0*) Petersons.
SAT Success. 5th rev. ed. Joan D. Carris et al. LC 96-24534. (Test Success Ser.). 512p. 1996. pap. 12.95 (*1-56079-584-0*); pap. 24.95 incl. disk (*1-56079-606-5*) Petersons.
SAT Supercourse. 2nd ed. Thomas H. Martinson. 1994. pap. 17.00 (*0-671-86402-5*, Arco) Macmillan Gen Ref.
SAT Supercourse. 3rd ed. Thomas H. Martinson. 752p. 1996. 17.95 (*0-02-861185-3*) Macmillan.
SAT II, Math Level IC-IIC. 2nd ed. Morris Bramson & Norman Levy. LC 95-11513. 200p. 1996. pap. 20.00 (*0-02-860307-9*, Arco) Macmillan Gen Ref.
SAT Verbal Workbook. Adam Martz. (Princeton Review Ser.). 1995. pap. 16.00 (*0-679-75362-1*, Villard Bks) Random.
SAT Verbal Workbook. 4th ed. Walter J. Miller et al. LC 93-3538. 1993. pap. 10.00 (*0-671-86405-X*, Arco) Macmillan Gen Ref.
SAT Verbal Workbook. 5th ed. Walter J. Miller et al. LC 93-44287. 1994. 10.00 (*0-671-88813-7*, Arco) Macmillan Gen Ref.
SAT Verbal Workbook: Scholastic Aptitude Test. 3rd ed. Walter J. Miller et al. 400p. 1992. pap. 10.00 (*0-685-51950-3*, Arco) Macmillan Gen Ref.
***SAT Verbal Workbook: Scholastic Assessment Test.** 6th ed. Gabriel Freedman et al. 224p. 1997. pap. 10.95 (*0-02-861712-6*, Arco) Macmillan Gen Ref.
SAT Video Course. Ed. by Bruce Rind & Paul Marasa. 1993. student ed. 109.95 (*1-57004-010-9*); vhs 99.95 (*1-57004-008-7*); vhs 99.95 (*1-57004-011-7*) L Erlbaum Assocs.
SAT Video Course. Ed. by Bruce Rind & Paul Marasa. 1993. student ed., wbk. ed., pap. 129.95 incl. audio (*1-57004-007-9*) L Erlbaum Assocs.
SAT Video Course, Set. Ed. by Bruce Rind & Paul Marasa. 1993. pap. text ed. 149.95 (*1-57004-009-5*); lib. bdg. 169.95 (*1-57004-006-0*) L Erlbaum Assocs.
SAT Vocabulary Builder. Ewald Neumann. (Vocabulary Builder Ser.). 64p. (C). 1992. pap. text ed. 24.95 incl. audio (*0-9625001-2-7*) Spargo Comns.
***SAT with Testware.** Research & Education Association Staff. 1000p. 1997. pap. text ed. 29.95 incl. disk (*0-87891-468-4*) Res & Educ.
SAT Word Flash: The Quick Way to Build Verbal Power for the New SAT - & Beyond. Joan D. Carris. LC 93-27328. 144p. (Orig.). 1993. pap. 7.95 (*1-56079-320-1*) Petersons.
***SAT 1998.** 1997. 12.95 (*0-02-861698-7*) Macmillan.
***SAT 1998.** 1997. 29.95 incl. cd-rom (*0-02-861932-3*) Macmillan.
***SAT 1998.** Kaplan Staff. 1997. pap. 29.95 incl. cd-rom (*0-684-84159-2*); pap. 18.00 (*0-684-84158-4*) S&S Trade.
SATA Autobiography Series, Vol. 12. 1991. 96.00 (*0-8103-4461-0*) Gale.
SATA Autobiography Series, Vol. 13. 1991. 96.00 (*0-8103-4462-9*) Gale.
SATA Autobiography Series, Vol. 14. Joyce Nakamura. 1992. 96.00 (*0-8103-4463-7*) Gale.
SATA Autobiography Series, Vol. 15. Joyce Nakamura. 1992. 96.00 (*0-8103-4464-5*) Gale.
SATA Autobiography Series, Vol. 16. 1993. 96.00 (*0-8103-4465-3*) Gale.
SATA Autobiography Series, Vol. 17. 1993. 96.00 (*0-8103-4466-1*) Gale.
SATA Autobiography Series, Vol. 18. Joyce Nakamura. 1994. 96.00 (*0-8103-4467-X*) Gale.
SATA Autobiography Series, Vol. 19. Joyce Nakamura. 1994. 96.00 (*0-8103-4468-8*) Gale.
SATA Autobiography Series, Vol. 22. Gerald J. Senick. 1996. 96.00 (*0-8103-9332-8*) Gale.
Sata Autobiography Series, Vol. 23. Gerald J. Senick. 1996. 96.00 (*0-8103-9333-6*, Gale Res Intl) Gale.
SATA Autobiogrpahy Series, Vol. 21. Ed. by Gerard J. Senick. 400p. 1995. 96.00 (*0-8103-4470-X*, 002724) Gale.
SAT/ACT Practice Tests: Algebra 1. 1992. pap. text ed. 8.25 (*0-03-073336-7*) HR&W Schl Div.
SAT/ACT Practice Tests: Algebra 2. 1992. pap. text ed. 8.25 (*0-03-073337-5*) HR&W Schl Div.
Satan: A Defeated Foe. Charles H. Spurgeon. 192p. 1993. mass mkt. 4.99 (*0-88368-267-2*) Whitaker Hse.
Satan: His Motives & Methods. Lewis S. Chafer. LC 90-20616. 144p. 1991. reprint ed. pap. 8.99 (*0-8254-2344-9*) Kregel.
Satan: Sanctuary or System? O. Talmadge Spence. (Charismatic Ser.: Vol. 4). (Illus.). 282p. (Orig.). (C). 1989. pap. 10.95 (*1-882542-00-2*) Fndtns NC.
Satan: The Early Christian Tradition. Jeffrey B. Russell. LC 81-66649. (Illus.). 258p. 1981. 39.95 (*0-8014-1267-6*) Cornell U Pr.
Satan: The Early Christian Tradition. Jeffrey B. Russell. LC 81-66649. (Illus.). 258p. 1987. pap. 14.95 (*0-8014-9413-3*) Cornell U Pr.
Satan see Major Literary Characters
Satan, a Portrait: A Study of the Character of Satan Through All the Ages. Edward Langton. 1976. lib. bdg. 59.95 (*0-8490-2568-0*) Gordon Pr.
Satan & His Host. Blaine M. Yorgason & Brenton Yorgason. (Gospel Power Ser.). 45p. 1990. pap. text ed. 3.50 (*0-929985-17-6*) Jackman Pubng.
Satan & Israel. pap. 0.95 (*0-937408-13-1*) GMI Pubns Inc.
Satan, Bite the Dust. Carman. (J). 1996. pap. text ed. write for info. (*1-880089-34-3*) Albury Pub.
Satan Bug. Alistair MacLean. 1994. reprint ed. lib. bdg. 27. 95 (*1-56849-305-3*) Buccaneer Bks.
Satan Cast Out. Frederick S. Leahy. 200p. 1990. reprint ed. pap. 7.99 (*0-85151-234-8*) Banner of Truth.
Satan, Demon Manifestations & Delusions, Vol. 3. rev. ed. Gordon Lindsay. (Powers of Darkness Ser.). 1967. pap. 2.95 (*0-89985-955-0*) Christ for the Nations.
Satan, Fallen Angels & Demons. Gordon Lindsay. (Literature Crusade Ser.: Vol. 2). 1965. pap. 0.95 (*0-89985-350-1*) Christ for the Nations.
Satan, Fallen Angels & Demons, Vol. 2. Gordon Lindsay. (Powers of Darkness Ser.). 1960. pap. 1.95 (*0-89985-954-2*) Christ for the Nations.
Satan, Fallen Angels & Demons (Los Angeles Caidos) Gordon Lindsay. (Literature Crusade Ser.). (SPA.). 1965. pap. 0.95 (*0-89985-363-3*) Christ for the Nations.
Satan Hunter. Thomas W. Wedge & Robert L. Powers. LC 87-20219. (Illus.). 222p. (Orig.). (C). 1988. pap. 12.95 (*0-935878-08-4*) Calibre Pr.
Satan in Goray. Isaac B. Singer. 256p. 1996. pap. text ed. 10.00 (*0-374-52479-3*, Noonday) FS&G.
Satan in Society. Nicholas F. Cooke. LC 73-20617. (Sex, Marriage & Society Ser.). 412p. 1974. reprint ed. 34.95 (*0-405-05796-2*) Ayer.
Satan Is Alive & Well on Planet Earth. Hal Lindsey & C. C. Carlson. 255p. 1972. pap. 10.99 (*0-310-27791-4*, 18189P) Zondervan.
Satan Is Defeated. Shirley Greenslade. 32p. 1985. pap. write for info. (*1-886799-00-8*) Agape Word.
***Satan Is in Sales.** Michael Canion. 114p. (Orig.). 1997. pap. 10.00 (*1-57502-464-0*, PO1386) Morris Pubng.
Satan Is No Myth. J. Oswald Sanders. LC 74-15358. 1983. pap. 9.99 (*0-8024-7525-6*) Moody.
Satan Loves Tired People. Barbara H. Seguin. 46p. 1987. pap. 2.75 (*0-88144-110-4*) Christian Pub.
Satan Loves Tired People. Barbara H. Seguin. 48p. 1993. mass mkt. 3.99 (*0-88368-257-5*) Whitaker Hse.
Satan-Proof Your Home. 7.95 (*1-56441-015-3*) M Hickey Min.
Satan Revisited: The Old New England Blues. Richard E. Petitti. (Illus.). 150p. 1985. pap. 20.00 (*0-938582-02-X*) Sensitive Man.
***Satan Ring.** Charles E. Sodman. (Orig.). 1996. pap. 11.95 (*0-533-12026-8*) Vantage.
Satan Says. Sharon Olds. LC 79-24300. (Poetry Ser.). 72p. 1980. 19.95 (*0-8229-3413-2*); pap. 10.95 (*0-8229-5314-5*) U of Pittsburgh Pr.
Satan Sleeps with the Holy: Word Paintings. Carolyn M. Kleefeld. LC 82-80785. 109p. 1982. 13.95 (*0-9602214-9-2*) Atoms Mirror.
Satan Sleeps with the Holy: Word Paintings. Carolyn M. Kleefeld. LC 82-80785. 109p. 1982. reprint ed. pap. 11. 95 (*0-9602214-8-4*) Atoms Mirror.
Satan Stalking. Dorothy M. England. 88p. (Orig.). 1993. pap. 4.95 (*0-88028-145-6*, 1227) Forward Movement.
Satan the Adversary & His Kingdom of Darkness. (Walk with Jesus Ser.). 418p. 1993. pap. 40.00 (*1-57277-528-9*) Script Rsch.
Satan Unmasked. Earl Paulk. 344p. (Orig.). 1984. pap. 9.95 (*0-917595-03-3*) Kingdom Pubs.
Satan Unmasked. James B. Richards. 150p. (Orig.). 1997. pap. 10.00 (*0-924748-12-5*) Impact Ministries.
Satan Who/Enlightened Church. Karl A. Barden. 224p. (Orig.). 1994. pap. 8.95 (*1-56043-135-0*) Destiny Image.
Satan Worshiper's Guide to the American Northeast. Victor Mingovits. 79p. (Orig.). 1991. pap. 4.95 (*0-9630465-9-4*) Watershed.
Satan, You're Not Stealing My Marriage. Bob Christensen. 36p. (Orig.). 1989. pap. 2.00 (*1-886045-00-3*) Covenant Marriages.
Satan (5 Sermons) Charles H. Spurgeon. 1978. pap. 4.00 (*1-56186-412-9*) Pilgrim Pubns.
Satanas Escondido. Lauren Stratford. 288p. (SPA.). 1988. pap. 6.99 (*1-56063-263-1*, 490219) Editorial Unilit.
Satanas No Es Mito. J. Oswald Sanders. 160p. (SPA.). 1996. pap. 6.99 (*0-8254-1648-5*, Edit Portavoz) Kregel.
Satanic Bible. Anton S. La Vey. 1976. mass mkt. 6.99 (*0-380-01539-0*) Avon.

S

S

Satanic Chaos In The Old Creation & The Divine Economy For The New Creation. Witness Lee. 122p. per. 4.75 (*0-87083-661-7*, 04016001) Living Stream Ministry.

Satanic Conspiracy, Pts. 1 & 2: A Man Without Youth & A Dead Man Alive. Roman Corp. Staff. LC 90-91755. 612p. 1990. write for info. (*0-9627447-0-0*) Roman Corp.

Satanic Extracts. Aleister Crowley. Ed. by Cosmo Trelawney. (Orig.). 1995. pap. 6.95 (*1-55818-267-5*) Holmes Pub.

Satanic Mass. H. T. Rhodes. 254p. 1975. reprint ed. pap. 3.95 (*0-8065-0484-6*, Citadel Pr) Carol Pub Group.

Satanic Mill. Otfried Preussler. (J). (gr. 5-9). 1990. 19.50 (*0-8446-6196-1*) Peter Smith.

Satanic Murder: Chilling True Stories of Sacrificial Slaughter. Nigel Cawthorne. 288p. (Orig.). 1996. pap. 5.95 (*0-86369-978-2*, Pub. by Virgin Pub UK) London Brdge.

Satanic Nurses. Dee N. Rush. (Illus.). 168p. (Orig.). 1990. pap. 12.95 (*0-9627950-0-3*) ISOS PC.

Satanic Orgy. Robert Blandraex. Ed. by Thorguard Templar. Tr. by Robert Blanchard from FRE. 104p. (Orig.). 1993. 25.00 (*1-883147-72-7*) Intern Guild ASRS.

Satanic Panic: The Creation of a Contemporary Legend. Jeffrey S. Victor. LC 93-995. 418p. 1993. 38.95 (*0-8126-9191-1*); pap. 18.95 (*0-8126-9192-X*) Open Court.

Satanic Rampage: A Graphic Account of the Liberian Civil War. J. Talley Youboty. Ed. by Cyrus Cooper. (Illus.). 580p. (Orig.). 1993. pap. write for info. (*0-9635479-0-9*) Modern Wrld.

Satanic Reverses. Mary J. Rachner. LC 89-61567. (Illus.). 153p. (Orig.). 1989. pap. 9.95 (*0-9623133-0-0*) Oxner Inst.

Satanic Ritual Abuse: A Handbook for Therapists. Dee Brown. (Illus.). 136p. (Orig.). 1994. pap. 16.95 (*0-9642200-8-3*) Blue Moon CO.

Satanic Rituals. Anton S. LaVey. 1976. mass mkt. 6.99 (*0-380-01392-4*) Avon.

Satanic Rituals. Anton S. LaVey. (Illus.). 300p. 1991. reprint ed. lib. bdg. 23.95 (*0-89966-827-5*) Buccaneer Bks.

Satanic Verses. Salman Rushdie. 1992. pap. 14.00 (*0-9632707-0-2*) Consortium DE.

Satanic Verses. Salman Rushdie. LC 88-40266. 496p. 1989. pap. 19.95 (*0-670-82537-9*) Viking Penguin.

***Satanic Verses.** Salman Rushdie. LC 97-795. 1997. pap. 14.00 (*0-8050-5309-3*) H Holt & Co.

Satanic Visits. James M. Tennison. 1994. 17.95 (*0-533-11075-0*) Vantage.

Satanic Voices: A Surfeit of Blasphemy Including the Rushdie Report. David M. Pidcock. 1992. pap. text ed. 14.95 (*1-871012-03-1*, Pub. by Mustaquim-Islamic UK) Intl Spec Bk.

Satanic Whispers & Echoes of Truth: A Study in Interdependence of Dignity of Man & Just Social Order Based upon Rational & Reasonable Analysis of Truth. Aqeel Ansari. LC 94-71466. 208p. (Orig.). 1994. pap. 19.95 (*0-9641592-3-6*) Awareness PA.

Satanic Witch. 2nd ed. Anton Szandon LaVey. (Illus.). 280p. reprint ed. pap. 9.95 (*0-922915-00-8*) Feral Hse.

Satanism. Bruce G. Frederickson. LC 95-8597. (How to Respond Ser.). 64p. 1995. 3.99 (*0-570-04678-5*, 12-6011) Concordia.

Satanism. Bob Passantino & Gretchen Passantino. (Guide to Cults & Religious Movements Ser.). 64p. 1995. pap. 5.99 (*0-310-70451-0*) Zondervan.

Satanism: A Guide to the Awesome Power of Satan. Wade Baskin. 1988. pap. 7.95 (*0-8065-1090-0*, Citadel Pr) Carol Pub Group.

***Satanism: An Annotated Bibliography.** David G. Bromley & Diane G. Cutchin. Ed. by John G. Melton. (Sects & Cults in America Ser.). Date not set. text ed. 40.00 (*0-8153-0037-9*) Garland.

Satanism: The Not So New Problem. Lyle J. Rapacki. (Illus.). 65p. (Orig.). 1988. pap. 10.00 (*0-9621597-0-0*) Crossroads Ministries.

Satanism: The Seduction of America's Youth. Bob Larson. LC 89-38105. 1989. pap. 10.99 (*0-8407-3034-9*) Nelson.

Satanism & the Witch's Hammer. B. D. Wallace & M. J. Philippus. 57p. (YA). (gr. 7-12). 1991. pap. 6.95 (*1-57515-011-5*) PPI Pubng.

Satanism & Witchcraft. Jules Michelet. 352p. 1983. reprint ed. pap. 12.95 (*0-8065-0059-X*, 89, Citadel Pr) Carol Pub Group.

Satanism & Witchcraft see Witchcraft, Sorcery & Superstition

Satanism in French Romanticism. M. Rudwin. 1972. 59.59 (*0-8490-0993-6*) Gordon Pr.

Satanism in Prisons Story, Vol. 1. Alan H. Peterson. 100p. 1992. pap. 34.95 (*1-877858-22-6*, TSIPT) Amer Focus Pub.

Satanism Scare. Ed. by James T. Richardson et al. (Social Institutions & Social Change Ser.). 326p. 1991. pap. text ed. 29.95 (*0-202-30379-9*); lib. bdg. 49.95 (*0-202-30378-0*) Aldine de Gruyter.

Satanism, Vol. 1: Sacrilege, Silly or Serious? Steve Aiken. (Illus.). 48p. (Orig.). 1989. pap. text ed. 10.00 (*1-877858-02-1*) Amer Focus Pub.

Satanismo: Esta Tu Familia a Salvo? Ted Schwarz & Duane Emp. 215p. (SPA.). 5.99 (*1-56063-021-3*, 498465) Editorial Unilit.

Satanist: Anniversary Edition. 75th ed. Hugh Fraser & J. I. Stahlmann. Ed. by John C. Moran. (Worthies Library: No. 4). 480p. 1987. 10.00 (*0-318-22842-4*) F M Crawford.

***Satanization of America: Secular Humanism's Assault on America.** Bob Rosio. LC 93-87610. 208p. 1994. pap. 9.99 (*0-933451-26-1*) Prescott Pr.

Satanizing of the Jews: Origin & Development of Mystical Anti-Semitism. Joel Carmichael. 210p. 1993. pap. 10.95 (*0-88064-152-5*) Fromm Intl Pub.

Satanizing of the Jews: Origin & History of Mystical Anti-Semitism. Joel Carmichael. 210p. 1992. 18.95 (*0-88064-132-0*) Fromm Intl Pub.

Satan's Banker. Flann Foster. 189p. (Orig.). 1996. mass mkt. 4.99 (*1-55197-206-9*, Pub. by Comnwlth Pub CN) Partners Pubs Grp.

***Satan's Best.** Red J. Arobateau. 1997. mass mkt. 6.50 (*1-56333-539-5*, Rosebud) Masquerade.

Satan's Caravan. Grace Conlon. 1995. pap. 12.95 (*0-533-11094-7*) Vantage.

Satan's Children. Robert S. Mayer. 272p. 1992. mass mkt. 4.99 (*0-380-71830-8*) Avon.

Satan's Contract. Susanne McCarthy. (Presents Ser.). 1995. pap. 2.99 (*0-373-11717-5*, 1-11717-5) Harlequin Bks.

Satan's Devices see Occult ABC

***Satan's Diabolical Plot to Destroy Women.** Johnny Goodman, Jr. 156p. (Orig.). 1997. pap. write for info. (*1-57502-508-6*, P01509) Morris Pubng.

Satan's Ditches & Dog-Faced Baboons: Thoughts about Living the Faith of Jesus. Robert S. Folkenberg. LC 95-16475. 1995. pap. 2.99 (*0-8163-1272-9*) Pacific Pr Pub Assn.

Satan's Drummers. Sananda. 211p. (Orig.). 1995. pap. 6.00 (*1-56935-054-X*) Phoenix Source.

Satan's Fat Attack!!! Carrier M. Meeks. Ed. by Martha Williams. (Illus.). 168p. (Orig.). 1986. pap. 9.95 (*0-941513-00-9*) C & M Pubs & Distributors.

Satan's Fire. Doherty. LC 96-25615. 256p. 1996. 21.95 (*0-312-14728-7*) St Martin.

***Satan's High Priest.** Spencer. LC 97-12266. 1997. 23.00 (*0-671-72800-8*, PB Hardcover) PB.

Satan's Invisible World Discovered. George Sinclair. LC 68-17017. 1969. reprint ed. 50.00 (*0-8201-1068-X*) Schol Facsimiles.

Satan's Invisible World Displayed: A Study of Greater New York. William T. Stead. LC 73-19180. (Politics & People Ser.). (Illus.). 222p. 1974. reprint ed. 20.95 (*0-405-05901-9*) Ayer.

Satan's Kingdom & the Second Coming. Noah W. Hutchings. 52p. (Orig.). 1994. pap. 2.50 (*1-879366-60-6*) Hearthstone OK.

Satan's Lambs. Lynn S. Hightower. 256p. 1993. 19.95 (*0-8027-1229-0*) Walker & Co.

Satan's Little Instruction Book. Carmine DeSena. LC 95-38485. (Main Street Book Ser.). 112p. 1996. pap. 6.95 (*0-385-48217-5*) Doubleday.

Satan's Mark Exposed. Salem Kirban. 165p. 1981. pap. 6.99 (*0-912582-36-7*) Kirban.

Satan's Master. Joseph Nazel. 224p. (Orig.). 1983. mass mkt. 2.50 (*0-87067-259-2*, BH259) Holloway.

Satan's Master Plan to Destroy the Church. Charles D. Young. 123p. (Orig.). 1991. pap. 5.95 (*0-9628836-0-3*) C D Young NM.

Satan's Music Exposed. Salem Kirban. 1980. pap. 5.95 (*0-912582-35-9*) Kirban.

Satan's Oil. Joe Bumpas. 1995. 16.95 (*0-533-11514-0*) Vantage.

Satan's Rebellion & Fall, 7 vols., Vol. 1. Gordon Lindsay. (Powers of Darkness Ser.). 1967. 1.95 (*0-89985-953-4*) Christ for the Nations.

Satan's Seat: Adventures in Faith Pictorial, Vol. 1. Mike Francen. (Adventures in Faith Ser.). (Illus.). 29p. (Orig.). 1993. pap. 3.00 (*1-888079-09-6*) Francen Wrld.

Satan's Secret Revealed: From the Files of a Christian Exorcist. Frank M. Brim. 176p. 1983. pap. 5.00 (*0-9612676-0-7*) World Wide Mini.

***Satan's Silence.** Alex Matthews. Ed. by Lee Ellison. LC 96-79331. (Cassidy McCabe Mystery Ser.: No. 2). 304p. 1997. 22.50 (*0-9643161-5-3*) Columb Pub.

Satan's Silence: Ritual Abuse & the Making of a Modern American Witch-Hunt. Debbie Nathan & Michael Snedecker. 288p. 1995. 25.00 (*0-465-07180-5*) Basic.

Satan's Silence: Ritual Abuse & the Making of Modern American Witch Hunt. Debbie Nathan & Mike Snedeker. 366p. 1996. pap. text ed. 14.00 (*0-465-07181-3*) HarpC.

Satan's Snare. Peter Anderson. 1988. pap. 3.99 (*0-85234-245-4*, Pub. by Evangelical Pr) Presby & Reformed.

Satan's Spawn. Richard J. Silverthorn. 256p. (Orig.). 1988. pap. 3.95 (*0-380-75316-2*) Avon.

Satan's Stones. Moniru Ravanipur. Ed. by Mohammad R. Ghanoonparvar. Tr. by Karim et al. from PER. 93p. 1996. pap. 9.95 (*0-292-77076-6*) U of Tex Pr.

Satan's Stones. Moniru Ravanipur. Ed. by Mohammad R. Ghanoonparvar. Tr. by Karim et al. from PER. 93p. 1996. text ed. 25.00 (*0-292-77075-8*) U of Tex Pr.

Satans Suckhole. Willard Gellis. 1988. pap. 8.00 (*0-917455-05-3*) Big Foot NY.

Satan's Suckhole Trilogy. 2nd rev. ed. Willard Gellis. (Been to Hell & Ain't Come Back Yet Ser.). 1990. pap. write for info. (*0-917455-12-6*) Big Foot NY.

Satan's Ten Most Believable Lies. 2nd ed. David Breese. 1987. pap. 9.99 (*0-8024-7675-9*) Moody.

Satan's Thrust. Don Pendleton. (Stony Man Ser.: Vol. 21). 1996. mass mkt. 4.99 (*0-373-61905-7*, 1-61905-5, Wrldwide Lib) Harlequin Bks.

Satans Toe. James Fenimore Cooper. (Works of James Fenimore Cooper Ser.). 1990. reprint ed. lib. bdg. 79.00 (*0-7812-2393-8*) Rprt Serv.

***Satan's Tragedy & Redemption: Iblis in Sufi Psychology.** P. J. Awn. 246p. 1996. 59.50 (*0-614-21558-7*, 1105) Kazi Pubns.

Satan's Underground. Lauren Stratford. LC 91-20327. 240p. (Orig.). reprint ed. pap. 10.95 (*0-88289-876-0*) Pelican.

Satan's Whispers: Breaking the Lies That Bind. Robert D. Hughes. 176p. (Orig.). 1992. pap. 8.99 (*0-8054-6052-7*, 4260-52) Broadman.

Satanskin. James Havoc. (Illus.). 128p. (Orig.). 1996. pap. 13.95 (*1-871592-10-0*) Creation Bks.

Satanstoe. James Fenimore Cooper. LC 62-9515. (Bison Book Ser.: BB138). 442p. reprint ed. pap. 126.00 (*0-317-29729-5*, 2022205) Bks Demand.

Satanstoe, or the Littlepage Manuscripts: A Tale of the Colony. James Fenimore Cooper. LC 88-12196. (Writings of James Fenimore Cooper). 500p. (Orig.). 1990. pap. text ed. 19.95 (*0-88706-904-5*) State U NY Pr.

Satanstoe, or the Littlepage Manuscripts: A Tale of the Colony. James Fenimore Cooper. LC 88-12196. (Writings of James Fenimore Cooper). 500p. (Orig.). 1990. text ed. 59.50 (*0-88706-903-7*) State U NY Pr.

Satanta, the Great Chief of the Kiowas & His People. Clarence R. Wharton. LC 76-43889. reprint ed. 32.50 (*0-404-15748-3*) AMS Pr.

Satapancasatka of Matrceta: Sanskirt Text, Tibetan Translation & Commentary, & Chinese Translation. Ed. by Bailey Shackleton. LC 61-28529. 249p. reprint ed. pap. 71.00 (*0-317-10105-6*, 2051469) Bks Demand.

Satapatha Brahmana, 5 vols. Ed. by Julius Eggeling. 1974. lib. bdg. 500.00 (*0-8490-0994-4*) Gordon Pr.

Satasai. Bihari. Tr. & Intro. by K. P. Bahadur. 416p. 1992. pap. 11.95 (*0-14-044576-5*, Penguin Classics) Viking Penguin.

Satchel. Marilyn Mohr. Ed. by Stanley H. Barkan. (Review Jewish Writers Chapbook Ser.: No. 8). 48p. 1992. 15.00 (*0-89304-312-5*); pap. 5.00 (*0-89304-313-3*) Cross-Cultrl NY.

Satchel: Mini. Marilyn Mohr. Ed. by Stanley H. Barkan. (Review Jewish Writers Chapbook Ser.: No. 8). 48p. 1992. 15.00 (*0-89304-314-1*); pap. 5.00 (*0-89304-315-X*) Cross-Cultrl NY.

Satchel Paige. Norman L. Macht. (Baseball Legends Ser.). (Illus.). 64p. (J). (gr. 3 up). 1991. lib. bdg. 15.95 (*0-7910-1185-2*) Chelsea Hse.

***Satchel Paige.** Lesa Ransome. LC 97-13790. (Illus.). (J). 1998. write for info. (*0-689-81151-9*) S&S Childrens.

Satchel Paige: Baseball Great. David Shirley. Ed. by Nathan I. Huggins. (Black Americans of Achievement Ser.). (Illus.). 112p. (YA). (gr. 5 up). 1993. pap. 8.95 (*0-7910-1983-7*); lib. bdg. 19.95 (*0-7910-1880-6*) Chelsea Hse.

Satchel Paige: The Best Arm in Baseball. Patricia McKissack & Fredrick McKissack. LC 92-3583. (Great African Americans Ser.). (Illus.). 32p. (J). (gr. 1-4). 1992. lib. bdg. 12.95 (*0-89490-317-9*) Enslow Pubs.

Satchmo. Gary Giddins. LC 92-8584. 240p. 1992. pap. 15.00 (*0-385-24429-0*, Anchor NY) Doubleday.

Satchmo: My Life in New Orleans. Louise Armstrong. 220p. 1986. 13.95 (*0-306-80276-7*) Da Capo.

Satchmo My Life in New Orleans: My Life in New Orleans. Louise Armstrong. 240p. reprint ed. lib. bdg. 39.00 (*0-685-14803-3*) Rprt Serv.

Satchmo's Blues. Alan Schroeder. LC 93-41082. (Illus.). 32p. (J). 1996. 15.95 (*0-385-32046-9*) Doubleday.

Satellite Altimetry in Geodesy & Oceanography. Ed. by Reiner Rummel & Fernando Sanso. LC 93-17952. (Lecture Notes in Earth Sciences Ser.: Vol. 50). 1993. 118.95 (*0-387-56818-2*) Spr-Verlag.

***Satellite & Cable.** Mosteshar. 1989. pap. text ed. write for info. (*0-85121-204-2*) Addison-Wesley.

Satellite & Cable TV: Scrambling & Descrambling. 2nd rev. ed. Frank Baylin & Brent Gale. 272p. (Orig.). 1988. pap. text ed. 20.00 (*0-917893-07-7*) Baylin Pubns.

***Satellite & TV Handbook: Satellite Broadcasts & Terrestrial Television Information Guide.** 4th ed. Bart Kuperus. 1997. pap. text ed. 24.95 (*0-8230-7658-X*) Watsn-Guptill.

Satellite Anthology. 1994. pap. 10.00 (*0-87259-464-5*) Am Radio.

***Satellite Astronomy: The Principles & Practice of Astronomy from Space.** 2nd ed. John K. Davies. LC 96-28785. (Wiley-Praxis Series in Astronomy & Astrophysics). 1996. text ed. 64.95 (*0-471-96258-9*) Wiley.

Satellite Atlas. David Flint et al. LC 96-18051. 1996. lib. bdg. 25.27 (*0-8368-1677-3*) Gareth Stevens Inc.

Satellite Broadcasting: The Politics & Implications of the New Media. Ed. by Ralph M. Negrine. 320p. 1988. lib. bdg. 65.00 (*0-415-00109-9*) Routledge.

Satellite Cells of the Sensory Ganglia. E. Pannese. (Advances in Anatomy, Embryology & Cell Biology Ser.: Vol. 65). (Illus.). 98p. 1981. 48.95 (*0-387-10219-1*) Spr-Verlag.

Satellite Cities: A Study of Industrial Suburbs. Graham R. Taylor. LC 70-112576. (Rise of Urban America Ser.). (Illus.). 1973. reprint ed. 24.95 (*0-405-02478-9*) Ayer.

***Satellite Communication.** Bates. 1994. pap. text ed. write for info. (*0-85121-943-8*) Addison-Wesley.

Satellite Communication Applications Handbook. Bruce R. Elbert. 490p. 1996. 79.00 (*0-89006-781-3*) Artech Hse.

Satellite Communication System: Systems, Techniques & Technology. 2nd ed. G. Maral & M. Bousquet. Tr. by S. David. (Communication & Distributed Systems Ser.). 688p. 1993. text ed. 94.95 (*0-471-93032-6*) Wiley.

Satellite Communication Systems: Design Principles. M. Richharia. 1995. text ed. 55.00 (*0-07-052374-6*) McGraw.

Satellite Communication Systems Design. Ed. by S. Tirro. (Illus.). 868p. 1993. 110.00 (*0-306-44147-0*, Plenum Pr) Plenum.

Satellite Communication Systems Engineering. 2nd ed. Wilbur L. Pritchard et al. LC 92-2361. 544p. 1993. text ed. 99.00 (*0-13-791468-7*) P-H Gen Ref & Trav.

***Satellite Communications.** Calcutt. (Electrical Engineering). 1995. pap. 40.95 (*0-340-61448-X*) Van Nos Reinhold.

Satellite Communications. Richard G. Meadows. (C). 1989. 130.00 (*0-09-175903-X*, Pub. by S Thornes Pubs UK) St Mut.

***Satellite Communications.** Mostesnar. Date not set. pap. text ed. write for info. (*0-85121-240-9*) Addison-Wesley.

Satellite Communications. Timothy Pratt & Charles W. Postian. 472p. 1986. Net. text ed. 59.50 (*0-471-87837-5*) Wiley.

Satellite Communications. 2nd ed. Dennis J. Roddy. LC 95-22077. 1995. text ed. 60.00 (*0-07-053370-9*) McGraw.

Satellite Communications: A Practical Guide. D. I. Dalgleish & E. C. Johnson. 1989. 99.00 (*0-86341-132-0*, TE020) Inst Elect Eng.

Satellite Communications: Mobile & Fixed Services. Ed. by Michael J. Miller et al. LC 93-10183. (International Series in Engineering & Computer Science, VLSI, Computer Architecture, & Digital Screen Processing). 432p. (C). 1993. lib. bdg. 120.50 (*0-7923-9333-3*) Kluwer Ac.

Satellite Communications: Self Study Course. Timothy Pratt. (Illus.). 1989. student ed., teacher ed. 299.00 (*0-87942-459-1*, HL0410-1) Inst Electrical.

Satellite Communications: the First Quarter Century of Service. David W. Rees. LC 88-33948. 329p. 1990. text ed. 98.95 (*0-471-62243-5*) Wiley.

Satellite Communications & DBS Systems. James Wood. (Illus.). 288p. 1993. 94.95 (*0-240-51338-X*, Focal) Buttrwrth-Heinemann.

Satellite Communications at Frequencies. L. Ippolito. 1990. text ed. write for info. (*0-442-23934-3*) Van Nos Reinhold.

Satellite Communications in North American Commercial Systems (U. S.) Market Intelligence Staff. 200p. 1992. 2,900.00 (*1-56753-916-5*, A2473) Frost & Sullivan.

Satellite Communications in the Next Decade: Proceedings of the 14th Goddard Memorial Symposium. Ed. by Leonard Jaffe. (Science & Technology Ser.: Vol. 44). (Illus.). 1977. 20.00 (*0-87703-088-X*) Univelt Inc.

Satellite Communications Pocket Book. James Wood. LC 93-39894. (Newnes Pocket Bks.). 203p. 1994. 26.95 (*0-7506-1749-7*) Buttrwrth-Heinemann.

Satellite Communications Systems & Technology: Europe - Japan - Russia. Burton I. Edelson et al. LC 94-34035. (Advanced Computing & Telecommunications Ser.). (Illus.). 511p. 1995. 72.00 (*0-8155-1370-4*) Noyes.

Satellite Communications Systems & Technology: Executive Summmary. Ed. by Burton I. Edelson & Joseph N. Pelton. (Executive Summaries Ser.). (Illus.). 8p. (Orig.). 1993. pap. write for info. (*1-883712-25-4*) Intl Tech Res.

Satellite Communications Systems & Technology Report: Analytical Chapters & Site Reports. (Illus.). 508p. (Orig.). 1994. pap. text ed. 195.00 (*0-7881-0359-8*) DIANE Pub.

Satellite Communications Systems & Technology Report: Emerging Systems Concepts, Applications, Services & Technologies in Europe, Japan & Russia. (Illus.). 508p. (Orig.). (C). 1994. pap. text ed. 195.00 (*0-7881-0341-5*) DIANE Pub.

Satellite Communications Systems & Technology, Vol. II: Site Reports. Ed. by Burton I. Edelson & Joseph N. Pelton. (WTEC Panel Reports). (Illus.). ii, 186p. (Orig.). 1993. pap. write for info. (*1-883712-27-0*) Intl Tech Res.

Satellite Control: A Comprehensive Approach. John T. Garner. LC 95-49409. (Wiley-Praxis Series in Space Science & Technology). 1996. text ed. 69.95 (*0-471-96254-6*) Wiley.

Satellite Data for Atmosphere, Continent & Ocean Research. Ed. by V. V. Salomonson et al. 142p. 1995. pap. 92.75 (*0-08-042672-7*, Pergamon Pr) Elsevier.

***Satellite Dishes & Other Antennas: Model Rules & Guidelines for Planned Communities.** Lara E. Howley & Barbara A. Beach. LC 97-4021. 1997. write for info. (*0-941301-38-9*) CAI.

Satellite Down. Thomas. LC 97-20950. (J). 1998. 16.00 (*0-689-80957-3*, S&S Bks Young Read) S&S Childrens.

Satellite Environment Handbook. 2nd ed. Ed. by Francis S. Johnson. LC 64-8894. 120p. reprint ed. pap. 30.00 (*0-685-15963-9*, 2026811) Bks Demand.

Satellite Experimenter's Handbook. Martin Davidoff. LC 83-71699. 1990. pap. 20.00 (*0-87259-318-5*) Am Radio.

Satellite Geodesy: Foundations, Methods, & Applications. rev. ed. Gunter Seeber. LC 93-15112. (Illus.). xiv, 532p. 1993. lib. bdg. 94.95 (*3-11-012753-9*) De Gruyter.

***Satellite Gravity & the Geosphere: Contributions to the Study of the Solid Earth & Its Fluid Envelopes.** 125p. 1997. pap. 30.00 (*0-309-05792-2*) Natl Acad Pr.

Satellite Hydrocarbon Exploration: Interpretation & Integration Techniques. Zeev Berger. LC 94-8948. 1994. 111.95 (*0-387-57348-8*) Spr-Verlag.

Satellite Hydrology: Proceedings of the Fifth Annual William T. Pecora Memorial Symposium on Remote Sensing, Sioux Falls SD, June 10-15, 1979. Pecora, William T. Memorial Symposium On. LC 81-65679. (Technical Publications: No. TPS81-1). (Illus.). 744p. reprint ed. pap. 180.00 (*0-8357-4079-X*, 2036769) Bks Demand.

Satellite Imagery Indicators of Turbulence. National Environmental Satellite, Data & Information Service Staff & Satellite Applications Lab Staff. (NWA Publication: No. 1-91). 17p. (C). 1991. pap. text ed. 84.00 incl. sl. (*1-883563-08-9*) Natl Weather.

Satellite Imagery Interpretation for Forecasters, 3 vols., Set. Compiled by Peter S. Parke. (Monograph Ser.: No. 2-86). (C). 1993. reprint ed. pap. text ed. 51.00 (*1-883563-04-6*) Natl Weather.

Satellite Imagery Interpretation for Forecasters, Vol. 1. Compiled by Peter S. Parke. (Monograph Ser.: No. 2-86). 240p. (C). 1993. reprint ed. pap. text ed. 20.00 (*1-883563-01-1*) Natl Weather.

Satellite Imagery Interpretation for Forecasters, Vol. 2. Compiled by Peter S. Parke. (Monograph Ser.: No. 2-86). 248p. (C). 1993. reprint ed. pap. text ed. 20.00 (*1-883563-02-X*) Natl Weather.

Satellite Imagery Interpretation for Forecasters, Vol. 3. Compiled by Peter S. Parke. (Monograph Ser.: No. 2-86). (C). 1993. reprint ed. pap. text ed. 20.00 (*1-883563-03-8*) Natl Weather.

Satellite Images: Photographs of Canada from Outer Space. Brian Banks. 160p. 1989. 29.95 (*0-920656-72-2*, Pub. by Camden Hse CN) Firefly Bks Ltd.

Satellite Images of Carbonate Depositional Settings. Ed. by P. M. Harris & W. S. Kowalik. (AAPG Methods in Exploration Ser.: No. 11). (Illus.). xxi, 147p. 1994. spiral bd. 74.00 (*0-89181-661-5*, 503) AAPG.

Satellite Information Systems. Edward S. Binkowski. (Professional Librarian Ser.). 237p. (C). 1988. 45.00 (*0-8161-1856-6*, Hall Reference); 30.00 (*0-8161-1880-9*, Hall Reference) Macmillan.

***Satellite Integrated Communications Networks.** E. Del Re et al. xii, 436p. 1988. 218.25 (*0-444-70372-1*, North Holland) Elsevier.

Satellite Intelligence: Boston-San Diego New Art Exchange. Ronald J. Onorato et al. LC 90-61071. (Illus.). 36p. (Orig.). 1990. pap. 10.00 (*0-934418-35-7*) Mus Contemp Art.

Satellite Invasion of India. S. C. Bhatt. (C). 1996. 30.00 (*81-212-0483-6*, Pub. by Gian Publng Hse II) S Asia.

***Satellite Market & Opportunities, 1996.** (China Telecom-2000 Ser.: Vol. 6). 1995. 2,995.00 (*0-614-18328-6*, IGIC-06) Info Gatekeepers.

Satellite Meteorology: An Introduction. Stanley Q. Kidder & Thomas H. Vonder Haar. (Illus.). 466p. 1995. boxed 65.00 (*0-12-406430-2*) Acad Pr.

Satellite Microwave Remote Sensors. Allan. 1990. boxed write for info. (*0-318-68284-2*) P-H.

Satellite Monitoring of the Earth. Karl-Heinz Szekielda. LC 88-21978. (Remote Sensing & Image Processing Ser.). 326p. 1989. text ed. 113.50 (*0-471-61330-4*) Wiley.

Satellite Monitoring of the Earth's Surface & Atmosphere 16-10. Arnault. (Advances in Space Research Ser.: 16). 194p. 1995. pap. 97.75 (*0-08-042635-2*, Pergamon Pr) Elsevier.

Satellite Night Fever. Jack Hopkins. 240p. (Orig.). 1994. mass mkt. 4.99 (*0-441-00065-7*) Ace Bks.

Satellite Night Special. Jack Hopkins. 1993. mass mkt. 4.99 (*0-441-75047-8*) Ace Bks.

Satellite Oceanography: An Introduction for Oceanographers & Remote-Sensing Scientists. I. S. Robinson. (Wiley-Praxis Ser.). 455p. 1995. text ed. 170.00 (*0-471-95424-1*) Wiley.

Satellite Orbits, No. ASR 14/5. J. B. Zielinski. (Advances in Space Research Ser.: No. 14). 144p. 1994. pap. 165.00 (*0-08-042479-1*, Pergamon Pr) Elsevier.

***Satellite Orbits in an Atmosphere: Theory & Application.** D. G. King-Hele. (Illus.). 304p. (C). 1987. text ed. 159.00 (*0-216-92252-6*, Pub. by Blackie Acad & Prof UK) Routledge Chapman & Hall.

Satellite Personal Communications & Their Consequences for European Telecommunications, Trade & Industry: Report to the European Commission, 2 vols., Set. (Illus.). 475p. (Orig.). (C). 1995. pap. text ed. 95.00 (*0-7881-1929-X*) DIANE Pub.

Satellite Perturbations & Orbital Determination. Ed. by Parag K. Lal. (Advances in Space Research Ser.: Vol. 1, No. 6). (Illus.). 95p. 1981. pap. 14.50 (*0-08-028380-2*, Pergamon Pr) Elsevier.

Satellite Projects Handbook. Lawrence Harris. (Illus.). 192p. 1996. pap. 28.95 (*0-7506-2406-X*) Buttrwrth-Heinemann.

Satellite Reconnaissance: The Role of Informal Bargaining. Gerald M. Steinberg. LC 82-19020. 208p. 1983. text ed. 55.00 (*0-275-91085-7*, C1085, Praeger Pubs) Greenwood.

Satellite Regulatory Compendium. Christine A. Meagher. LC 85-206066. 1985. 197.00 (*0-934960-26-7*) Phillips Business.

Satellite Remote Sensing: An Introduction. Ray Harris. LC 87-4927. 256p. (C). 1987. text ed. 67.50 (*0-7102-0305-5*, RKP); pap. text ed. 27.50 (*0-7102-1312-3*, RKP) Routledge.

Satellite Remote Sensing for Agricultural Projects. Ed. by J. P. Gastellu-Etchegorry. (Technical Paper Ser.: No. 128). 236p. 1990. 13.95 (*0-8213-1625-7*, 11625) World Bank.

Satellite Remote Sensing for Hydrology & Water Management: The Mediterranean Coasts & Islands, Vol. 1. Ed. by E. C. Barrett et al. xiv, 322p. 1990. text ed. 234.00 (*2-88124-732-6*) Gordon & Breach.

Satellite Remote Sensing for Operational Hydrology, Vol. 4. F. Becker. (Remote Sensing Reviews Ser.). 472p. 1990. text ed. 246.00 (*3-7186-5056-8*, Harwood Acad Pubs) Gordon & Breach.

Satellite Remote Sensing in Climatology. Carleton. 1991. 99.95 (*0-8493-7720-X*) CRC Pr.

Satellite Remote Sensing of Natural Resources. David Verbyla. (Mapping Sciences Ser.). 224p. 1995. 59.95 (*1-56670-107-4*, L1107) Lewis Pubs.

Satellite Remote Sensing of Polar Regions. Massom. 1991. 83.00 (*0-87371-607-8*) CRC Pr.

Satellite Sensing of a Cloudy Atmosphere: Observing the Third Planet. Ed. by A. Sellers Henderson. (Illus.). 336p. 1984. 90.00 (*0-85066-254-0*) Taylor & Francis.

Satellite Services Sourcebook. Samuel L. Hoard & Consultants Beach Associates. LC 82-72850. 1982. 75.00 (*0-910339-00-7*) Drake's Ptg & Pub.

Satellite Surveillance. Harold Hough. LC 91-76488. (Illus.). 208p. (Orig.). 1991. pap. text ed. 21.95 (*1-55950-077-8*) Loompanics.

Satellite Technology: An Introduction. Andrew F. Inglis. (Electronic Media Guide Ser.). 112p. 1991. pap. 19.95 (*0-240-80078-8*, Focal) Buttrwrth-Heinemann.

***Satellite Technology: An Introduction.** 2nd ed. Andrew Inglis & Arch Luther. (Illus.). 144p. 1997. pap. 24.95 (*0-240-80295-0*) Buttrwrth-Heinemann.

Satellite Technology & Its Applications. 2nd ed. P. R. K. Chetty. (Illus.). 448p. 1991. 49.95 (*0-8306-9688-1*, 3688, TAB/TPR) TAB Bks.

Satellite Television in Indonesia. Godwin C. Chu. Ed. by Alfian. vi, 211p. (Orig.). 1981. pap. 6.00 (*0-86638-002-7*) EW Ctr HI.

Satellite Television Reception: A Personal User's Guide. Joel Goldberg. (Illus.). 128p. (C). 1984. pap. 23.25 (*0-13-791251-X*) P-H.

Satellite Transmission. Business Communications Co., Inc. Staff. 268p. 1987. pap. 1,750.00 (*0-89336-518-1*, G-094) BCC.

Satellite TV for Dummies: The Common Sense Guide to Home Installation of a Satellite Receiving System. David Lagarde. (Illus.). 90p. (Orig.). 1994. pap. 19.95 (*1-885913-00-1*) Sterling Pubng.

Satellite TV Installation Guide. Picton Publishing (Chippenham) Ltd. Staff. (C). 1987. 60.00 (*0-685-39331-3*, Pub. by Picton UK) St Mut.

Satellite Warfare a Challenge for the International Community. 42p. 1988. pap. 19.00 (*92-9045-018-5*, GV. E.87.0.1) UN.

Satellites. Ed. by Joseph A. Burns & Mildred S. Matthews. LC 86-19145. (Space Science Ser.). (Illus.). 1021p. 1986. 72.00 (*0-8165-0983-2*) U of Ariz Pr.

***Satellites.** Steve Parker. LC 96-27730. (20th Century Inventions Ser.). (J). 1997. lib. bdg. 24.25 (*0-8172-4810-2*) Raintree Steck-V.

***Satellites.** Seymour Simon. (J). Date not set. write for info. (*0-688-14646-5*); lib. bdg. write for info. (*0-688-14647-3*, Morrow Junior) Morrow.

Satellites: An Educational Coloring Book. Spizzirri Publishing Co. Staff. Ed. by Linda Spizzirri. (Illus.). 32p. (J). (gr. 1-8). 1986. pap. 1.99 (*0-86545-074-9*) Spizzirri.

Satellites & Broadcasting 1990: U. S. Domestic & International Market Directions & Issues. National Association of Broadcasters Staff. 42p. (Orig.). 1989. 60.00 (*0-89324-075-3*) Natl Assn Broadcasters.

Satellites & Commissars: Strategy & Conflict in the Politics of Soviet-Bloc Trade. Randall W. Stone. LC 95-17510. (Studies in International History & Politics). 288p. 1996. text ed. 39.50 (*0-691-04414-7*) Princeton U Pr.

Satellites & Forecasting of Solar Radiation. E. A. Aronson et al. Ed. by Raymond E. Bahm. LC 80-70943. (International Solar Energy Society, American Section, Workshop Ser.). 1982. pap. text ed. 32.50 (*0-89553-026-0*) Am Solar Energy.

***Satellites & Probes.** Bobbie Kalman. (Eye on the Universe Ser.). (Illus.). 32p. (J). 1997. lib. bdg. 18.64 (*0-86505-681-1*) Crabtree Pub Co.

***Satellites & Probes.** Bobbie Kalman. (Eye on the Universe Ser.). (Illus.). 32p. (J). 1997. pap. 5.95 (*0-86505-691-9*) Crabtree Pub Co.

Satellites & Radio Broadcasting: Historical Review & Market Developments. 65p. 1991. 60.00 (*0-89324-118-0*) Natl Assn Broadcasters.

***Satellites of Jupiter.** Ed. by David Morrison. 972p. 1982. write for info. (*0-8165-1768-1*) U of Ariz Pr.

Satellites of Jupiter. Ed. by David Morrison. LC 81-13050. (Space Science Ser.). (Illus.). 982p. reprint ed. pap. 180.00 (*0-7837-1909-4*, 2042113) Bks Demand.

Satellites of the Outer Planets: Worlds in Their Own Right. David A. Rothery. (Illus.). 208p. 1992. pap. 45.00 (*0-19-854290-9*) OUP.

***Sathya Sai Baba, Pt. 1: Birth - 1962.** N. Kasturi. (Series on the Life of Sathya Sai Baba). Date not set. pap. 4.25 (*0-614-19028-2*, BA-201) Sathya Sai Bk Ctr.

***Sathya Sai Baba, Pt. 2: Years 1962-1968.** N. Kasturi. (Series on the Life of Sathya Sai Baba). Date not set. pap. 3.00 (*0-614-19029-0*, BA-202) Sathya Sai Bk Ctr.

***Sathya Sai Baba, Pt. 3: Years 1969-1972.** N. Kasturi. (Series on the Life of Sathya Sai Baba). Date not set. pap. 4.00 (*0-614-19030-4*, BA-203) Sathya Sai Bk Ctr.

***Sathya Sai Baba, Pt. 4: Years 1973-1979.** N. Kasturi. (Series on the Life of Sathya Sai Baba). Date not set. pap. 2.50 (*0-614-19031-2*, BA-204) Sathya Sai Bk Ctr.

***Sathya Sai Baba Compendium: A Guide to the First 70 Years.** Ed. by Brian Steel. 360p. (Orig.). 1997. pap. 19.95 (*0-87728-884-4*) Weiser.

Sathya Sai Education in Human Values: An Integrated Curriculum for the Development of Character - Kindergarten Through Eighth Grade. Compiled by Bea Flaig & Ronne Marantz. (Illus.). 328p. (Orig.). 1995. wbk. ed. 5.00 (*0-9629835-7-8*) Leela Pr.

***Sathya Sai Speaks, Index, Vol. 1-11 (1953-1982)** Ed. by David Gries & Elaine Gries. Date not set. pap. 2.00 (*0-614-19018-5*, BA-021) Sathya Sai Bk Ctr.

***Sathya Sai Speaks, Vol. 1.** enl. rev. ed. Ed. by David Gries & Elaine Gries. Date not set. pap. 4.20 (*0-614-19003-7*, BA-001) Sathya Sai Bk Ctr.

***Sathya Sai Speaks, Vol. 2.** Ed. by David Gries & Elaine Gries. Date not set. pap. 3.75 (*0-614-19004-5*, BA-002) Sathya Sai Bk Ctr.

***Sathya Sai Speaks, Vol. 3.** Ed. by David Gries & Elaine Gries. Date not set. pap. 2.75 (*0-614-19005-3*, BA-003) Sathya Sai Bk Ctr.

***Sathya Sai Speaks, Vol. 4.** Ed. by David Gries & Elaine Gries. Date not set. pap. 3.75 (*0-614-19006-1*, BA-004) Sathya Sai Bk Ctr.

***Sathya Sai Speaks, Vol. 5.** Ed. by David Gries & Elaine Gries. Date not set. pap. 3.75 (*0-614-19007-X*, BA-005) Sathya Sai Bk Ctr.

***Sathya Sai Speaks, Vol. 6.** Ed. by David Gries & Elaine Gries. Date not set. pap. 3.75 (*0-614-19008-8*, BA-006) Sathya Sai Bk Ctr.

***Sathya Sai Speaks, Vol. 7.** Ed. by David Gries & Elaine Gries. Date not set. pap. 4.00 (*0-614-19009-6*, BA-007) Sathya Sai Bk Ctr.

***Sathya Sai Speaks, Vol. 8.** Ed. by David Gries & Elaine Gries. Date not set. pap. 3.00 (*0-614-19010-X*, BA-008) Sathya Sai Bk Ctr.

***Sathya Sai Speaks, Vol. 9.** Ed. by David Gries & Elaine Gries. Date not set. pap. 3.00 (*0-614-19011-8*, BA-009) Sathya Sai Bk Ctr.

***Sathya Sai Speaks, Vol. 10.** Ed. by David Gries & Elaine Gries. Date not set. pap. 4.00 (*0-614-19012-6*, BA-010) Sathya Sai Bk Ctr.

***Sathya Sai Speaks, Vol. 11.** Ed. by David Gries & Elaine Gries. Date not set. pap. 3.50 (*0-614-19013-4*, BA-011) Sathya Sai Bk Ctr.

***Sathya Sai Speaks, Vol. 12.** Ed. by David Gries & Elaine Gries. Date not set. pap. write for info. (*0-614-19016-9*, BA-012) Sathya Sai Bk Ctr.

***Sathya Sai Speaks, Vol. 13.** Ed. by David Gries & Elaine Gries. Date not set. pap. write for info. (*0-614-19014-2*, BA-013) Sathya Sai Bk Ctr.

***Sathya Sai Speaks, Vol. 14.** Ed. by David Gries & Elaine Gries. Date not set. pap. write for info. (*0-614-19015-0*, BA-014) Sathya Sai Bk Ctr.

***Sathya Sai Speaks, Vol. 15.** enl. rev. ed. Ed. by David Gries & Elaine Gries. Date not set. pap. 5.40 (*0-614-19017-7*, BA-015) Sathya Sai Bk Ctr.

***Sathya Sai Vahini (Writings on Basic Spiritual Values)** Sai B. Sathya. Date not set. pap. 4.00 (*0-614-19044-4*, BA-313) Sathya Sai Bk Ctr.

***Sathya Sai's Golden Jubilee Book of Thoughts.** Sai B. Sathya. Date not set. pap. 3.50 (*0-614-19087-8*, BW-170) Sathya Sai Bk Ctr.

Sati. Mulk R. Anand. (C). 1989. 21.50 (*81-7018-535-1*, Pub. by Renaiss Publng Hse II) S Asia.

Sati. Christopher Pike. 1991. mass mkt. 4.99 (*0-8125-1035-6*) Tor Bks.

Sati: Historical & Phenomenological Essays. Arvind Sharma. (C). 1988. 14.00 (*81-208-0464-3*, Pub. by Motilal Banarsidass II); pap. 8.75 (*0-685-22787-1*, Pub. by Motilal Banarsidass II) S Asia.

Sati & Social Reforms in India. Meena Gaur. 1989. 29.00 (*81-85263-57-4*, Pub. by Rawat II) S Asia.

Sati, the Blessing & the Curse: The Burning of Wives in India. Ed. by John S. Hawley. LC 92-23468. 240p. 1994. pap. 16.95 (*0-19-507774-1*) OUP.

Satie: His World Through His Letters. Erik Satie. (Illus.). 220p. 1990. 35.00 (*0-7145-2811-0*) M Boyars Pubs.

Satie: Seen Through His Letters. Ed. by Ornella Volta. (Illus.). 242p. 1994. reprint ed. pap. 19.95 (*0-7145-2980-X*) M Boyars Pubs.

Satie Guitar 3 Gymnopedies & 3 Gnossiennes. Erik Satie. 24p. 1986. pap. 7.95 (*0-7935-5543-4*, 50332780) H Leonard.

Satie, Ravel, Poulenc. Manuel Rosenthal & Virgil Thomson. 86p. (Orig.). 1987. pap. 5.95 (*0-937815-09-8*) Hanuman Bks.

Satie Remembered. Robert Orledge. (Illus.). 272p. 1995. 29.95 (*1-57467-000-X*, Amadeus Pr); pap. 19.95 (*1-57467-001-8*, Amadeus Pr) Timber.

Satie the Composer. Robert Orledge. (Music in the Twentieth Century Ser.: No. 1). (Illus.). 275p. (C). 1990. text ed. 80.00 (*0-521-35037-9*) Cambridge U Pr.

***SATIF-2 - Shielding Aspects of Accelerators, Targets, & Irradiation Facilities: Proceedings of the 2nd Specialists Meeting.** NEA Staff. 324p. (Orig.). 1996. pap. 69.00 (*92-64-15287-3*, 66-96-11-1) OECD.

Satillites. Mary V. Fox. (Inventors & Inventions Ser.). 64p. (J). (gr. 3-5). 1996. lib. bdg. 17.95 (*0-7614-0049-4*, Benchmark NY) Marshall Cavendish.

***Satin & Lace.** Danielle Shaw. 1997. pap. text ed. 3.99 (*1-85487-930-8*) London Brdge.

Satin Arcane. Jack Hirschman. 20p. (Orig.). 1991. pap. 3.00 (*0-929730-36-4*) Zeitgeist Pr.

Satin Dolls: The Women of Jazz. Friedman-Fairfax & Sony Music Staff. (Life, Times & Music Book/CD Ser.). 1995. pap. 16.98 incl. audio compact disk (*1-56799-125-4*, Friedman-Fairfax) M Friedman Pub Grp Inc.

***Satin Dolls: The Women of Jazz.** Andrew G. Hager. LC 96-34513. 1997. write for info. (*1-56799-353-2*, Friedman-Fairfax) M Friedman Pub Grp Inc.

***Satin in the Snow.** Jeanette Gilge-Barnes. LC 97-60465. 192p. (Orig.). 1997. pap. 9.95 (*1-57921-016-3*) WinePress Pub.

Satin Palms. Elizabeth Inness-Brown. LC 81-71001. 120p. (Orig.). 1981. pap. 6.95 (*0-931362-04-0*) SDSU Press.

Satin Roses. Sharon Miller. pap. 11.99 (*0-87377-001-3*) GAM Pubns.

Satin Sheets. Leigh. 1992. pap. write for info. (*0-312-92793-2*) St Martin.

***Satin Slipper, or, the Worst Is Not the Surest.** Paul Claudel. LC 90-34113. 1991. write for info. (*0-86527-397-9*) Fertig.

***Satin Street.** Merrill C. Gilfillan. LC 96-21118. 1997. pap. 12.95 (*1-55921-182-2*, Asphodel Pr) Moyer Bell.

Satin Tunnels. Beth Brown. LC 87-46317. 127p. 1989. per. 8.50 (*0-916418-69-3*) Lotus.

***Satipatthana Sutta Discourse Summaries.** S. N. Goenka. Ed. by Patrick Given-Wilson. 130p. (Orig.). Date not set. pap. write for info. (*0-614-30219-6*) Vipassana Res.

Satir Approach to Communication: A Workshop Manual. Johanna Schwab & Michele Baldwin. 1989. pap. 13.95 (*0-8314-0071-4*) Sci & Behavior.

Satir Model. John Banmen. LC 89-60194. 1991. pap. 23.95 (*0-8314-0078-1*) Sci & Behavior.

Satir Step by Step. Virginia M. Satir. 1984. 16.95 (*0-8314-0068-4*) Sci & Behavior.

Satira Hecha Por Mateo Rosas De Oquendo a las Cosas Que Pasan En el Piru, Ano De 1598. Ed. by Pedro Lasarte. (Colonial Spanish American Ser.: No. 2). cxx, 182p. 1990. 20.00 (*0-940639-52-1*) Hispanic Seminary.

Satirarum Liber. Flaccus A. Persius. ccxvi, 418p. 1967. reprint ed. write for info. (*0-318-71193-1*) G Olms Pubs.

Satire: A Critical Re-Introduction. Dustin Griffin. LC 93-32688. 256p. (C). 1994. 27.00 (*0-8131-1844-1*) U Pr of Ky.

Satire: A Critical Reintroduction. Dustin Griffin. 256p. 1995. pap. text ed. 15.95 (*0-8131-0829-2*) U Pr of Ky.

Satire: From Aesop to Buchwald. Frederick T. Kiley. 496p. (C). 1971. pap. text ed. 38.00 (*0-02-363590-8*, Macmillan Coll) P-H.

Satire: Spirit & Art. George A. Test. 304p. (C). 1991. lib. bdg. 49.95 (*0-8130-1087-X*) U Press Fla.

Satire & Allegory in Wynnere & Wastoure. Thomas H. Bestul. LC 73-77750. 135p. 1974. reprint ed. pap. 38.50 (*0-608-02043-5*, 2062696) Bks Demand.

Satire & Humor in Education: Selected Readings. Ed. by Rolland Callaway. 284p. (Orig.). (C). 1990. pap. text ed. 26.00 (*0-8191-7871-3*); lib. bdg. 50.00 (*0-8191-7870-5*) U Pr of Amer.

Satire & Irony: A Jr. High-Intermediate Language Arts Unit. Frances Corvasse. 1984. pap. 4.00 (*0-89824-103-0*); teacher ed., pap. 5.00 (*0-89824-102-2*) Trillium Pr.

Satire & Politischer Roman: Untersuchungen Zum Romanwerk Benjamin Disrealis. Ulrich C. Janiesch. (Bochum Studies in English: No. 1). vi, 300p. (Orig.). 1975. pap. 32.00 (*90-6032-055-7*) Benjamins North Am.

Satire & Sentiment, 1660-1830. Claude Rawson. LC 92-30428. 290p. (C). 1994. text ed. 69.95 (*0-521-38395-1*) Cambridge U Pr.

***Satire & Society in Ancient Rome.** Ed. by Susan H. Braund. 160p. (C). 1989. pap. 14.95 (*0-85989-331-6*, Pub. by Univ Exeter Pr UK) Northwestern U Pr.

Satire & the Correspondence of Swift. Craig H. Ulman. LC 72-95457. (LeBaron Russell Briggs Prize Honors Essays in English Ser.). 56p. 1973. pap. 2.50 (*0-674-78976-8*) HUP.

Satire & the Hebrew Prophets. Thomas Jemielity. (Literary Currents in Biblical Interpretation Ser.). 288p. (Orig.). 1992. pap. 19.00 (*0-664-25229-X*) Westminster John Knox.

Satire & the Transformation of Genre. Leon Guilhamet. LC 86-30715. 212p. 1987. pap. text ed. 18.95 (*0-8122-1308-4*) U of Pa Pr.

Satire Anthology. Ed. by Carolyn Wells. LC 70-128161. (Granger Index Reprint Ser.). 1977. 21.95 (*0-8369-6190-0*) Ayer.

Satire Anthology. Ed. by Carolyn Wells. LC 70-128161. (Granger Index Reprint Ser.). 369p. reprint ed. lib. bdg. 18.00 (*0-8290-0511-0*) Irvington.

Satire Caricature & Perspectivism in the Works of Georg Buchner. Henry J. Schmidt. 1970. text ed. 16.15 (*0-686-22398-5*) Mouton.

Satire Demystificatrice de la Bruyere Vol. 8: Essais Sur Les Caracteres ou Les Moeurs de ce Siecle. Homayoun Mazaheri. (Sociocriticism Ser.). 152p. (FRE.). (C). 1995. text ed. 42.95 (*0-8204-2873-6*) P Lang Pubng.

Satire in Colonial Spanish America: Turning the New World Upside Down. Julie G. Johnson. LC 92-42849. (Texas Pan American Ser.). 224p. (C). 1993. text ed. 32.50 (*0-292-77654-3*) U of Tex Pr.

Satire in Narrative: Petronius, Swift, Gibbon, Melville, & Pynchon. Frank Palmeri. 195p. 1990. text ed. 30.00 (*0-292-77631-4*) U of Tex Pr.

Satire in Persian Literature. Hasan Javadi. LC 84-46118. (Illus.). 336p. 1988. 39.50 (*0-8386-3260-2*) Fairleigh Dickinson.

Satire in the Comedies of Congreve, Sheridan, Wilde & Coward. Rose Snider. LC 79-159119. 145p. (C). 1971. reprint ed. 45.00 (*0-87753-055-6*) Phaeton.

***Satire, Lies, & Politics.** Condren. LC 97-7121. 1997. text ed. 59.95 (*0-312-17515-9*) St Martin.

Satire of John Marston. Morse S. Allen. LC 65-26460. (Studies in Drama: No. 39). 1969. reprint ed. lib. bdg. 55.95 (*0-8383-0500-8*) M S G Haskell Hse.

Satire of Jonathan Swift. Herbert J. Davis. LC 79-17603. 109p. 1979. reprint ed. text ed. 35.00 (*0-313-22068-9*, DAJS, Greenwood Pr) Greenwood.

Satire on Stone: The Political Cartoons of Joseph Keppler. Richard S. West. LC 87-19212. 518p. 1988. text ed. 39.95 (*0-252-01497-9*) U of Ill Pr.

Satire or Evasion? Black Perspectives on Huckleberry Finn. Ed. by James S. Leonard et al. LC 91-14315. 288p. 1991. lib. bdg. 45.00 (*0-8223-1163-1*) Duke.

Satire or Evasion? Black Perspectives on Huckleberry Finn. Ed. by James S. Leonard et al. LC 91-14315. 288p. 1992. pap. text ed. 19.95 (*0-8223-1174-7*) Duke.

Satire, Parodie, Calembour: Esquisse d'une Theorie des Devalues. Lionel Duisit. (Stanford French & Italian Studies: No. 11). vi, 164p. (FRE.). 1978. pap. 46.50 (*0-915838-26-5*) Anma Libri.

Satiren und Pasquille Aus der Reformationszeit, 3 vols. in 1. Oskar Schade. xxvi, 976p. 1966. reprint ed. write for info. (*0-318-71279-2*) G Olms Pubs.

Satires. Jenkinson & Flaccus A. Persius. 1981. 49.95 (*0-85668-159-8*, Pub. by Aris & Phillips UK); pap. 19.95 (*0-85668-173-3*, Pub. by Aris & Phillips UK) David Brown.

Satires. Juvenal & Flaccus A. Persius. (Loeb Classical Library: No. 91). 498p. 1918. 18.95 (*0-674-99102-8*) HUP.

Satires. Juvenal. Tr. by Niall Rudd. 296p. 1991. 95.00 (*0-19-814756-2*, 1643) OUP.

Satires. Juvenal. Ed. by Niall Rudd & William Barr. (World's Classics Ser.). 250p. 1992. pap. 8.95 (*0-19-281762-0*) OUP.

Satires. Quintus Horatius Flaccus. cxxviii, 623p. 1966. reprint ed. write for info. (*0-318-71147-8*); reprint ed. write for info. (*0-318-71356-X*) G Olms Pubs.

S

An Asterisk (*) at the beginning of an entry indicates that the title is appearing in BIP for the first time.

Satires, 3 pts. Paul Whitehead. LC 92-22719. (Augustan Reprints Ser.: No. 223). 1984. reprint ed. 14.50 (*0-404-70223-6*) AMS Pr.

Satires, Bk. I. Juvenal. Ed. by Susan M. Braund. (Greek & Latin Classics Ser.). 360p. (C). 1996. pap. text ed. 23.95 (*0-521-35667-9*) Cambridge U Pr.

Satires, Bk. I. Juvenal. Ed. by Susanna M. Braund. (Greek & Latin Classics Ser.). 332p. (C). 1996. text ed. 64.95 (*0-521-35566-4*) Cambridge U Pr.

Satires, Vol. I. Horace. Ed. by Brown. 1993. 49.95 (*0-85668-529-1*, Pub. by Aris & Phillips UK); pap. 24.95 (*0-85668-530-5*, Pub. by Aris & Phillips UK) David Brown.

Satires, Vol. II. Horace. Ed. by Douglas C. Muecke. 1992. 49.95 (*0-85668-531-3*, Pub. by Aris & Phillips UK); pap. 24.95 (*0-85668-532-1*, Pub. by Aris & Phillips UK) David Brown.

Satires: With the Satires of Persius. Juvenal. Tr. by William Gifford. 256p. 1994. reprint ed. pap. text ed. 8.95 (*0-460-87171-4*, Everyman's Classic Lib) C E Tuttle.

Satires Against Man: The Poems of Rochester. Dustin H. Griffin. LC 72-95304. 331p. reprint ed. pap. 94.40 (*0-7837-4808-6*, 2044455) Bks Demand.

Satires & Miscellaneous Poetry & Prose. Samuel Butler. Ed. by Rene Lamar. LC 76-29457. (BCL Ser. II). reprint ed. 42.50 (*0-404-15301-1*) AMS Pr.

S

Satires, Epistles & Ars Poetica. Horace. (Loeb Classical Library: No. 194). 540p. 1926. 18.95 (*0-674-99214-8*) HUP.

Satires, Epitres, Art Poetique. Nicolas Boileau. (Poesie Ser.). (FRE.). pap. 15.95 (*2-07-032293-9*) Schoenhof.

Satires, Epitres, l'Art Poetique. Nicolas Boileau. (FRE.). 1985. pap. 19.95 (*0-7859-2794-8*) Fr & Eur.

Satires, Le Lutrin see Oeuvres

Satires of A. Persius Flaccus. Flaccus A. Persius. Ed. by H. Nettleship. xxxix, 149p. 1987. reprint ed. 29.12 (*3-487-01781-4*) G Olms Pubs.

Satires of Decimus Junius Juvenalis. Juvenal. Tr. by John Dryden. LC 70-161788. (Augustan Translators Ser.). reprint ed. 58.00 (*0-404-54124-0*) AMS Pr.

Satires of Horace. Niall Rudd. (Bristol Classical Paperbacks Ser.). 336p. 1994. pap. 25.95 (*0-86292-041-8*, Pub. by Brstl Class Pr UK) Focus Pub-R Pullins.

Satires of Horace: A Study. Niall Rudd. LC 66-11031. 330p. reprint ed. pap. 94.10 (*0-317-26383-8*, 2024525) Bks Demand.

Satires of Horace & Persius. Horace et al. Tr. by Niall Rudd. (Classics Ser.). 304p. 1974. pap. 11.95 (*0-14-044279-0*, Penguin Classics) Viking Penguin.

Satires of Juvenal. Juvenal. Tr. by Rolfe Humphries. LC 58-12213. 192p. 1958. pap. 8.95 (*0-253-20020-2*, MB-20) Ind U Pr.

Satires of Juvenal. Juvenal. Tr. by William Gifford. LC 72-964. (Temple Greek & Latin Classics: No. 1). reprint ed. 27.00 (*0-404-07901-6*) AMS Pr.

Satires of Juvenal Translated. Juvenal. Tr. by Thomas Sheridan. LC 72-179336. (Augustan Translators Ser.). reprint ed. 63.00 (*0-404-54125-9*) AMS Pr.

Satires of Lodovico Sergardi. Lodovico Sergardi. Tr. by Ronald E. Pepin from LAT. LC 93-11272. (Seventeenth-Century Texts & Studies: Vol. 4). 144p. (C). 1994. text ed. 37.95 (*0-8204-2297-5*) P Lang Pubng.

***Satires of Persius.** C. Dessen. (Bristol Classical Paperbacks Ser.). 128p. (Orig.). 1996. pap. text ed. 20.95 (*1-85399-487-1*, Pub. by Brstl Class Pr UK) Focus Pub-R Pullins.

Satires of Persius Flaccus. Flaccus A. Persius. Ed. by W. R. Connor & Basil L. Gildersleeve. LC 78-67138. (Latin Texts & Commentaries Ser.). (ENG & LAT.). 1979. reprint ed. lib. bdg. 19.95 (*0-405-11605-5*) Ayer.

Satires on Women. Intro. by Felicity A. Nussbaum. LC 92-24348. (Augustan Reprints Ser.: No. 180). 1976. reprint ed. 14.50 (*0-404-70180-9*, PR1195) AMS Pr.

Satiric Allegory: Mirror of Man. Ellen D. Leyburn. LC 78-5886. (Yale Studies in English: Vol. 130). 142p. 1978. reprint ed. text ed. 45.00 (*0-313-20457-8*, LESM, Greenwood Pr) Greenwood.

Satiric Impersonations: From Aristophanes to the Guerrilla Girls. Joel Schecter. LC 93-7619. (Illus.). 208p. (C). 1994. 29.95 (*0-8093-1867-9*); pap. 19.95 (*0-8093-1868-7*) S Ill U Pr.

Satiric Inheritance: Rabelais to Sterne. Michael Seidel. LC 79-84016. 299p. 1979. reprint ed. pap. 85.30 (*0-7837-8182-2*, 2047887) Bks Demand.

Satiric Poems: The Progress of Dulness & M'Fingal. John Trumbull. Ed. by Edwin T. Bowden. LC 61-15829. 230p. reprint ed. pap. 65.60 (*0-8357-7726-X*, 2036083) Bks Demand.

Satiric Vision of Blas de Otero. Geoffrey R. Barrow. LC 88-4877. 168p. 1989. text ed. 26.00 (*0-8262-0687-5*) U of Mo Pr.

Satiric Voice: Program, Form & Meaning in Persius & Juvenal. William T. Wehrle. (Altertumswissenschaftliche Texte und Studien: Vol. 23). x, 156p. (GER.). 1992. 21.32 (*3-487-09613-7*) G Olms Pubs.

Satirical Apocalypse: An Anatomy of Melville's the Confidence Man. Jonathan A. Cook. LC 95-40033. (Contributions to the Study of World Literature Ser.: Vol. 67). 296p. 1996. text ed. 65.00 (*0-313-29404-6*, Greenwood Pr) Greenwood.

Satirical Element in the American Novel. Ernest J. Hall. 1972. 250.00 (*0-87968-033-4*) Gordon Pr.

Satirical Element in the American Novel. Ernest J. Hall. LC 76-98994. (American Literature Ser.: No. 49). (C). 1970. reprint ed. pap. 39.95 (*0-8383-0036-7*) M S G Haskell Hse.

Satirical Element in the American Novel. Ernest J. Hall. (BCL1-PS American Literature Ser.). 89p. 1992. reprint ed. lib. bdg. 59.00 (*0-7812-6636-X*); reprint ed. lib. bdg. 59.00 (*0-7812-6640-8*) Rprt Serv.

Satirical Etchings of James Gillray. James Gillray. Ed. by Draper Hill. (Illus.). 144p. (Orig.). 1976. pap. 9.95 (*0-486-23340-5*) Dover.

Satirical Literature. Mary E. Snodgrass. LC 96-47329. (Literary Companions Ser.). 600p. 1996. lib. bdg. 65.00 (*0-87436-856-1*) ABC-CLIO.

Satirical Rogue on Poetry. Robert Francis. LC 68-13940. 136p. 1968. 20.00 (*0-87023-034-4*) U of Mass Pr.

Satiricon. Petrone. (FRE.). 1972. pap. 10.95 (*0-7859-3983-0*) Fr & Eur.

Satiricon. 2nd rev. ed. Petronius. Ed. by Evan T. Sage & Brady B. Gilleland. LC 72-87112. (LAT.). (C). 1969. pap. text ed. 14.95 (*0-89197-338-9*) Irvington.

Satirische Kurzprosa Heinrich Bolls. Erhard Friedrichsmeyer. LC 80-26886. (University of North Carolina Studies in Comparative Literature: No. 97). 237p. reprint ed. pap. 67.60 (*0-7837-2075-0*, 2042349) Bks Demand.

Satirizing the Satirist: Critical Dynamics in Swift, Diderot & Jean Paul. Stephanie Hammer. LC 90-44344. (Studies in Comparative Literature). 152p. 1990. reprint ed. 15.00 (*0-8240-5474-1*) Garland.

Satisaptakam Saga of the Seven Mothers. K. R. Iyengar. 656p. 1991. 59.95 (*0-910261-15-6*, Pub. by Samata Bks II) Lotus Light.

***SATisfaction.** Milton Polsky. LC 96-30988. 55p. (Orig.). 1996. pap. 6.00 (*0-88734-426-7*) Players Pr.

***Satisfaction: A Behavioral Perspective on the Consumer.** Richard L. Oliver. 1996. text ed. write for info. (*0-07-048025-7*) McGraw.

Satisfaction Guaranteed. Susan Strasser. 1989. 24.95 (*0-394-55292-X*) Pantheon.

Satisfaction Guaranteed: Contentment. Henry Oursler. (Inter Acta Ser.). (Illus.). 6p. (C). 1994. teacher ed., ring bd. 1.25 (*1-885702-71-X*, 741-051t, Inter Acta); student ed., ring bd. 3.25 (*1-885702-70-1*, 741-051s, Inter Acta) WSN Pr.

Satisfaction Guaranteed: The Making of the American Mass Market. Susan Strasser. (Illus.). 339p. 1996. pap. 15.95 (*1-56098-654-9*) Smithsonian.

Satisfaction Guaranteed: Two-Hundred & Thirty-Six Ideas to Make Your Customers Feel Like. Byrd Baggett. LC 94-2500. 1994. 12.95 (*1-55853-286-2*) Rutledge Hill Pr.

***Satisfaction in Close Relationships.** Robert J. Sternberg & Mahzad Hojjat. LC 97-13530. 1997. lib. bdg. 45.00 (*1-57230-217-8*) Guilford Pubns.

Satisfaction in Parenting. Larry Larrabee. Ed. by Michael J. Goc. 128p. (Orig.). 1995. pap. 12.00 (*0-938627-24-4*) New Past Pr.

***Satisfaction in the Land of Opportunity: Answers for U.S. Immigrants & Refugees. Raimonda Mikatavage. LC 97-93344. (Pioneer Living Ser.). (Illus.). 192p. (Orig.). 1997. pap. 19.95 (*0-9647213-6-8*) Melodija Bks.**
The author & her family came to the U.S. as refugees. She has lived through the immigrant experience. SATISFACTION IN THE LAND OF OPPORTUNITY, in direct & simple English, covers topics of education, money, finding work, building relationships with Americans, fitting in, dealing with emergencies, making better decisions, buying a car, insurance, a home, avoiding scams & much more. Many important phone numbers, organizations, & Internet web pages listed. Whether you have been in the U.S. ten days, or ten years, you will find valuable advice in this book. "Full of resources & proven strategies for a quick adjustment," says Judy Priven, author of HELLO! USA. "Extremely valuable insights & explanations of cultural differences... expressed with neither hostility nor condescension," says Amy Southwick for ENGLISH LANGUAGE AMERICA. The author's first book, YOUR JOURNEY TO SUCCESS, is a bestseller in Lithuania, her country of origin. She also writes an advice column for newcomers. Order SATISFACTION IN THE LAND OF OPPORTUNITY from Melodija Books, P.O. Box 689, Hampstead, MD 21074. (410) 374-3117, FAX: (410) 374-3569. Available through Quality Books & Baker & Taylor. ***Publisher Provided Annotation.***

Satisfaction of Interest & the Concept of Morality. Steven A. Smith. LC 73-8305. 165p. 1975. 28.50 (*0-8387-1383-1*) Bucknell U Pr.

Satisfactions in White-Collar Job. Nancy C. Morse. Ed. by Leon Stein. LC 77-70518. (Illus.). 1977. reprint ed. lib. bdg. 23.95 (*0-405-10187-2*) Ayer.

***Satisfiability Problem: Theory & Applications: Proceedings of a DIMACS Workshop, March 11-13, 1996.** Du Dingzhu et al. LC 97-25448. (Dimacs Series In Discrete Mathematics And Theoretical Computer Science,). 1997. write for info. (*0-8218-0479-0*) Am Math.

Satisfied by the Promise of the Spirit: Affirming the Fullness of God's Provision for Spiritual Living. Thomas Edgar. 288p. 1996. pap. 12.99 (*0-8254-2510-7*) Kregel.

Satisfied Mind: The Country Music Life of Porter Wagoner. Steve Eng. LC 94-2500. (Illus.). 320p. 1992. 19.95 (*1-55853-133-5*) Rutledge Hill Pr.

Satisfied with Nothin' Ernest Hill. LC 91-91194. 297p. 1992. pap. 9.95 (*0-9630827-0-1*) Pickaninny.

Satisfied with Nothin' Ernest Hill. 304p. 1996. 22.00 (*0-684-82259-8*, S&S) S&S Trade.

***Satisfied with Nothin'** Ernest Hill. 1997. pap. text ed. 11.00 (*0-684-83405-7*, Scribners PB Fict) S&S Trade.

Satisfied...A Promise of Peace in a Troubled World. Rexella Van Impe. 142p. 1984. pap. 5.00 (*0-934803-15-3*) J Van Impe.

Satisfying Africa's Food Needs: Food Production & Commercialization in African Agriculture. Ed. by Ronald Cohen. LC 88-3164. 244p. 1988. lib. bdg. 35.00 (*1-55587-083-X*) Lynne Rienner.

Satisfying Customers. (Quality & Participation Ser.). 64p. 30.00 (*0-614-04829-X*, KSA 5) Assn Qual & Part.

Satisfying Internal Customers First! A Practical Guide to Improving Internal & External Customer Satisfaction. Richard Y. Chang & P. Keith Kelly. (Quality Improvement Ser.). (Illus.). 120p. 1994. pap. 12.95 (*1-883553-04-0*) R Chang Assocs.

Satisfying Reason: Studies in the Theory of Knowledge. Nicholas Rescher. LC 94-33491. (Episteme Ser.: Vol. 21). 256p. (C). 1995. lib. bdg. 99.00 (*0-7923-3148-6*, Pub. by Klwr Acad Pubs NE) Kluwer Ac.

Satisfying Soups: Homemade Bisques, Chowders, Gumbos, Stews & More. Phyllis Hobson. Ed. by Connie Oxley & Pat Art. LC 91-55015. (Illus.). 224p. 1991. pap. 13.95 (*0-88266-690-8*, Garden Way Pub) Storey Comm Inc.

Satisfying the Black Man Sexually Made Simple. Rosie Milligan. 1992. pap. text ed. 14.95 (*1-881524-04-3*) Prof Busn Cnslt.

Satisfying the Black Woman Made Simple. Rosie Milligan. 93p. 1990. pap. text ed. 14.95 (*1-881524-00-0*) Prof Busn Cnslt.

Satisfying Work: Christian Living from Nine to Five. R. Paul Stevens & Gerry Schoberg. (Fisherman Bible Studyguide Ser.). 96p. (Orig.). 1989. pap. text ed. 4.99 (*0-87788-752-7*) Shaw Pubs.

***Satmar: Two Generations of an Urban Island.** 2nd ed. Israel Rubin. 352p. (C). 1996. text ed. 39.95 (*0-8204-0759-3*) P Lang Pubng.

Satnami Story: A Thrilling Drama of Religious Change. Donald A. McGavran. LC 89-39652. 192p. (Orig.). 1990. pap. 8.95 (*0-87808-225-5*, WCL225-5) William Carey Lib.

Sato & the Elephants. Juanita Havill. LC 91-26096. (Illus.). (J). (ps-3). 1993. 15.00 (*0-688-11155-6*); lib. bdg. 14.93 (*0-688-11156-4*) Lothrop.

Satori. Rod Pelkey. 247p. (Orig.). 1996. mass mkt. 4.99 (*1-55197-194-1*, Pub. by Comnwlth Pub CN) Partners Pubs Grp.

Satori in Paris & PIC. Jack Kerouac. LC 58-6703. 240p. 1988. pap. 11.00 (*0-8021-3061-5*, Grove) Grove-Atltic.

Satori West. Thomas Krampf. Ed. by Edith Schrot. (Illus.). 78p. (Orig.). 1987. pap. 6.00 (*0-9616797-0-0*) Ischua Bks.

Satsang, Vol I. M. P. Pandit. Ed. by Vasanti R. Golikhere. 298p. (Orig.). 1979. pap. 11.00 (*0-941524-10-8*) Lotus Light.

Satsanga Veda. Hartmut Ballin. 128p. 1996. write for info. (*0-9649408-0-9*) Trillenium Pubng.

Satsuki. Alexander Kennedy. (Illus.). 128p. (Orig.). 1995. pap. 16.95 (*0-9525145-0-8*) Stone Lantern.

Satsuma Rebellion: An Episode of Modern Japanese History. Augustus H. Mounsey. LC 79-65367. (Studies in Japanese History & Civilization). 294p. 1979. reprint ed. text ed. 69.50 (*0-313-26993-9*, U6993, Greenwood Pr) Greenwood.

Sattukku dans l'Esumesa durant la periode d'Isin et Larsa. Rene M. Sigrist. LC 79-65002. (Bibliotheca Mesopotamica Ser.: Vol. 11). 166p. (FRE.). 1984. pap. 41.25 (*0-89003-048-0*) Undena Pubns.

***Satura.** Bernhard Fabian. (Olms Studien: Bd. 39). ix, 522p. (GER.). 1975. write for info. (*3-487-07001-4*) G Olms Pubs.

Saturae. Petronius. Ed. by Franz Buecheler. l, 377p. 1963. write for info. (*3-296-14900-7*) G Olms Pubs.

Saturae. Decimus J. Juvenalis. Ed. by Alfred E. Housman. LC 69-13957. 146p. 1969. reprint ed. text ed. 35.00 (*0-8371-2749-1*, JUSA, Greenwood Pr) Greenwood.

Saturarum Menippearum Reliquiae. Terentius Varro. Ed. by Alexander Riese. 309p. 1971. reprint ed. write for info. (*0-318-71235-0*) G Olms Pubs.

***Saturated Blue: Writings from the Notebooks.** Sam Francis. (Illus.). 272p. 1996. 60.00 (*0-932499-99-6*, 620503) Lapis Pr.

Saturated Flow & Soil Structure: A Review of the Subject & Laboratory Experiments on the Basic Relationship. H. Diestel. (Physical Environment Ser.: Vol. 14). (Illus.). vi, 125p. 1994. 118.95 (*0-387-55791-1*) Spr-Verlag.

Saturated Heterocyclic Chemistry, Vol. 2. M. F. Ansell & G. Pattenden. LC 72-83454. 1974. 47.00 (*0-85186-532-1*) Am Chemical.

Saturated Heterocyclic Chemistry, Vol. 3. M. F. Ansell & G. Pattenden. LC 72-83454. 1975. 43.00 (*0-85186-562-3*) Am Chemical.

Saturated Heterocyclic Chemistry, Vol. 4. M. F. Ansell & G. Pattenden. LC 72-83454. 1977. 77.00 (*0-85186-592-5*) Am Chemical.

Saturated Heterocyclic Chemistry, Vol. 5. M. F. Ansell & G. Pattenden. LC 72-83454. 1978. 66.00 (*0-85186-622-0*) Am Chemical.

Saturated Self: Delimmas of Identity in Contemporary Life. Kenneth J. Gergen. LC 90-55597. 1992. pap. 17.00 (*0-465-07185-6*) Basic.

Saturation & Material Balances. LC 80-25594. (AIChEMI Modular Instruction F Series: Vol. 2). 79p. 1981. pap. 44.00 (*0-8169-0181-3*, J-12) Am Inst Chem Eng.

Saturday Academy Concept. Ed. by Nellouise D. Watkins & William B. DeLauder. (Illus.). 250p. 1987. write for info. (*0-940823-24-1*) Bennett Coll.

Saturday Adoption. Ron Cowen. 1969. pap. 5.25 (*0-8222-0987-X*) Dramatists Play.

Saturday Afternoon Madness. Bob Waldstein & Phil Silverman. 288p. (Orig.). 1995. pap. 12.95 (*0-9648571-0-3*) Four Horsemen.

Saturday Afternoons at the Old Met: The Metropolitan Opera Broadcasts, 1931-1950. Paul Jackson. LC 91-33533. (Illus.). 586p. 1992. 49.95 (*0-931340-48-9*, Amadeus Pr) Timber.

Saturday & Sunday. Edmund K. Broadus. LC 67-23186. (Essay Index Reprint Ser.). 1977. 19.95 (*0-8369-0255-6*) Ayer.

Saturday at the New You. Barbara E. Barber. LC 93-5165. (Illus.). 32p. (J). (ps-3). 1994. 14.95 (*1-880000-06-7*) Lee & Low Bks.

Saturday at The New You. Barbara E. Barber. (Illus.). 32p. (J). (ps-3). 1996. reprint ed. pap. 5.95 (*1-880000-43-1*) Lee & Low Bks.

Saturday Bloody Saturday. V. Rockliff. 1987. 39.00 (*0-7223-2097-3*, Pub. by A H S Ltd UK) St Mut.

Saturday Collection. Pat Stewart. LC 94-48870. 64p. 1996. pap. 12.95 (*0-7734-2715-5*, Mellen Poetry Pr) E Mellen.

Saturday Evening Post, Vol. 1. Norman Rockwell. (Illus.). 120p. 1995. pap. 49.95 (*4-8457-0955-4*, Pub. by Treville JA) Bks Nippan.

Saturday Evening Post, Vol. 2. Norman Rockwell. (Illus.). 120p. 1995. pap. 49.95 (*4-8457-0961-9*, Pub. by Treville JA) Bks Nippan.

Saturday Evening Post Cookbook. Cory SerVaas. 288p. 1996. pap. 14.99 (*0-7852-7509-6*) Nelson.

Saturday Evening Post Norman Rockwell Book. Illus. by Norman Rockwell. 1987. 14.99 (*0-517-62607-1*) Random Hse Value.

Saturday Evening Post Vegetable Primer. Ed. by Saturday Evening Post Editors. (Illus.). 144p. 1982. 5.95 (*0-89387-045-5*) Curtis Pub Co.

Saturday Extra Special! Betty Brooke. (C). 1990. pap. text ed. 24.00 (*0-85305-301-4*, Pub. by J Arthur Ltd UK) St Mut.

Saturday Is Ballet Day. Karen Backstein. (My Pretty Ballerina Ser.: No. 1). (Illus.). 32p. (J). 1991. pap. 2.99 (*0-590-45143-X*) Scholastic Inc.

Saturday Is Cookouts: From Kebabs & Ribs to Potato Salad & More. Time-Life Books Editors. LC 95-51348. (Everyday Cookbooks Ser.). (Illus.). 128p. 1996. 14.95 (*0-7835-4788-9*) Time-Life.

***Saturday Is Pattyday.** Leslea Newman. (Illus.). 24p. (J). pap. 5.95 (*0-88961-181-5*, Pub. by Wmns Pr CN) LPC InBook.

Saturday Is Pattyday. Leslea Newman. (Illus.). 24p. (J). (ps-5). 1993. pap. 6.95 (*0-934678-51-0*); lib. bdg. 14.95 (*0-934678-52-9*) New Victoria Pubs.

Saturday Market. Patricia Grossman. LC 94-75730. (J). (ps-3). 1994. 15.00 (*0-688-12176-4*); lib. bdg. 14.93 (*0-688-12177-2*) Lothrop.

***Saturday Morning Fever.** Burke. Date not set. pap. write for info. (*0-312-16996-5*) St Martin.

Saturday Morning Murder: A Psychoanalytic Case. Batya Gur. Tr. by Dalya Bilu from HEB. LC 91-58346. 304p. 1993. reprint ed. pap. 10.00 (*0-06-099508-4*, PL) HarpC.

Saturday Mourning Fly in My Eye. Ed. by Niles. (Illus.). 1990. pap. 9.95 (*1-56060-022-5*) Eclipse Bks.

Saturday Night. Caroline B. Cooney. (Point Romance Ser.). 240p. (J). (gr. 7-9). 1992. pap. 3.25 (*0-590-45784-5*, Point) Scholastic Inc.

Saturday Night. Jerome Kass. 1978. pap. 5.25 (*0-8222-0988-8*) Dramatists Play.

Saturday Night. Susan Orlean. 1990. 19.95 (*0-317-99650-9*) Knopf.

Saturday Night & Sunday Morning. Alan Sillitoe. 1959. 16.95 (*0-394-44377-2*) Knopf.

Saturday Night & Sunday Morning. Alan Sillitoe. LC 92-53549. 256p. 1992. reprint ed. pap. 11.95 (*0-452-26909-1*, Plume) NAL-Dutton.

Saturday Night & Sunday Morning: An Easter Sunrise Drama. Pamela Urfer. 1992. pap. 3.95 (*1-55673-569-3*, 9316) CSS OH.

Saturday Night at Moody's Diner: Even More Stories from Tim Sample. 2nd ed. Tim Sample. LC 96-2239. (Illus.). 144p. 1996. reprint ed. pap. 12.95 (*0-89272-385-8*) Down East.

***Saturday Night at the Dinosaur Stomp.** Carol D. Shields. LC 97-536. (Illus.). 32p. (J). 1997. 15.99 (*1-56402-693-0*) Candlewick Pr.

Saturday Night at the Pahala Theatre. Lois-Ann Yamanaka. LC 93-9139. (Bamboo Ridge Ser.: Nos. 58-59). 143p. 1993. pap. 8.00 (*0-910043-31-0*) Bamboo Ridge Pr.

Saturday Night in Havana. Ron Bernthal. 96p. 1992. pap. 9.95 (*0-9631682-1-5*) Mariposa Pr.

Saturday Night Live: The First Twenty Years. Ed. by Michael Cader. (Illus.). 264p. 1994. 25.00 (*0-395-70895-8*) HM.

Saturday Night Live: The First Twenty Years. Ed. by Michael Cader. (Illus.). 211p. 1995. pap. 16.95 (*0-395-75284-1*) HM.

***Saturday Night Lives! Selected Diaries.** John Fraser. 1996. pap. text ed. 19.99 (*0-7710-3134-3*) McCland & Stewart.

Saturday Night Women. Michael Judge. (Contemporary Drama Ser.). 1977. pap. 2.50 (*0-912262-42-7*) Proscenium.

Saturday Nite-Mambo-Cha. (Ballroom Dance Ser.). 1986. lib. bdg. 79.95 (*0-8490-3409-4*) Gordon Pr.

Saturday of Glory. large type ed. David Serafin. 1981. 25.99 (*0-7089-0577-3*) Ulverscroft.

An Asterisk (*) at the beginning of an entry indicates that the title is appearing in BIP for the first time.

Saturday Review, Eighteen Fifty-Five to Eighteen Sixty-Eight: Representative Educated Opinion in Victorian England. Merle M. Bevington. LC 41-25970. reprint ed. 20.00 (0-404-00795-3) AMS Pr.

Saturday Sancocho. Leyla Torres. LC 94-31329. (J). (gr. 3-7). 1995. 15.00 (0-374-36418-4) FS&G.

Saturday Sancocho. Leyla Torres. (Illus.). 32p. (SPA.). (J). (gr. k-1). 1995. 15.00 (0-374-31997-9) FS&G.

Saturday School: A Model Early Education Program. Ed. by Ferguson-Florissant Schools Staff & Marion M. Wilson. (Illus.). 12p. 1990. 2.50 (0-939418-61-4) Ferguson-Florissant.

Saturday Special. Tr. by Betty Brooke. (C). 1990. pap. 24.00 (0-85305-286-7, Pub. by J Arthur Ltd UK) St Mut.

Saturday, Sunday, Monday: A Play in Three Acts. Eduardo De Filippo. Tr. by Keith Waterhouse & Willis Hall from ITA. 87p. 1974. 12.95 (0-435-23200-2) Boulevard.

Saturday-Sunday Shuffle. Russell Holt. (Discovery Ser.). 29p. 1987. pap. 0.89 (0-8163-0758-X) Pacific Pr Pub Assn.

Saturday Surprise, the February 23, 1991 Coup in Thailand: The Role of the Military in Politics & Thailand's Painful Path to Democracy. Gerald W. Fry. (Pew Case Studies in International Affairs). 50p. (C). 1992. pap. text ed. 3.50 (1-56927-353-7) Geo U Inst Dplmcy.

Saturday the Rabbi Went Hungry. Harry Kemelman. 224p. 1987. mass mkt. 5.99 (0-449-21392-7) Fawcett.

Saturday, the 14th. William Gleason. 1987. pap. 5.00 (0-87129-350-1, S77) Dramatic Pub.

Saturday Town. Thomas Thornburg. LC 76-15749. (Living Poets' Library). 1976. pap. 3.50 (0-686-17004-0) Dragons Teeth.

Saturday Treat. large type ed. Catherine C. Clark. (Magna Large Print Ser.). 1994. 25.99 (0-7505-0649-0, Pub. by Magna Print Bks UK) Ulverscroft.

Saturdays. Elizabeth Enright. LC 41-30925. 196p. (J). (gr. 4-6). 1988. 12.95 (0-8050-0291-X, Bks Young Read) H Holt & Co.

***Saturdays.** Elizabeth Enright. LC 96-53949. (J). 1997. pap. 4.99 (0-14-038395-6) Viking Penguin.

Saturday's Child. Janet O. Dallett. 1995. pap. 15.00 (0-919123-52-X, Pub. by Inner City CN) BookWorld Dist.

Saturday's Child. Suzanne Seed. LC 72-12599. (Illus.). (J). (gr. 6-12). 1973. pap. 6.95 (0-87955-203-4); lib. bdg. 8.95 (0-87955-803-2) O'Hara.

Saturday's Child: Hong Kong in the Sixties. Lynn Pan & Trea Wiltshire. (Illus.). 88p. 1995. 40.00 (962-7283-10-X, Pub. by FormAsia HK) Weatherhill.

Saturdays Forever. Harold Smith. 138p. 1985. 9.95 (0-89826-016-7) Natl Paperback.

Saturday's Heroes. Joe Mitchell. 128p. (Orig.). 1994. pap. 8.95 (1-898928-05-3) AK Pr Dist.

Saturdays with Ana Alicia Felicia. Tom Vannetta. (Illus.). 32p. (J). (gr. k-3). 1995. 16.95 (1-885340-22-2) Coming Age Pr.

Saturday's Women. Ed. by Charlotte Mandel et al. LC 82-10278. (Eileen W. Barnes Award Ser.). 102p. (Orig.). 1982. pap. 6.50 (0-938158-02-3) Saturday Pr.

Saturdee. Norman Lindsay. LC 75-41175. (Illus.). reprint ed. 39.50 (0-404-14716-X) AMS Pr.

Saturn. Duncan Brewer. LC 90-40811. (Planet Guides Ser.). (Illus.). 64p. (J). (gr. 5-9). 1992. lib. bdg. 17.95 (1-85435-374-8) Marshall Cavendish.

Saturn. Ed. by Tom Gehrels & Mildred S. Matthews. LC 84-2517. 968p. 1984. 72.00 (0-8165-0829-1) U of Ariz Pr.

Saturn. Elaine Landau. LC 90-13081. (First Bks.). (Illus.). 64p. (J). (gr. 3-5). 1991. lib. bdg. 21.00 (0-531-20013-2) Watts.

Saturn. Peter Murray. LC 92-41542. (Vision Bks.). 32p. (J). (gr. 2-6). 1993. lib. bdg. 22.79 (1-56766-014-2) Childs World.

***Saturn.** Peter Murray. LC 96-46674. (Nature Bks.). 32p. (J). (gr. 1-6). 1997. lib. bdg. 22.79 (1-56766-388-5) Childs World.

Saturn. Seymour Simon. LC 85-2995. (Illus.). 32p. (J). (ps-3). 1985. lib. bdg. 15.93 (0-688-05799-3, Morrow Junior) Morrow.

Saturn. Seymour Simon. LC 85-2995. (Illus.). 32p. (J). (ps-3). 1988. pap. 5.95 (0-688-08404-4, Morrow Junior) Morrow.

Saturn. Gregory L. Vogt. LC 92-30188. (Gateway Solar System Ser.). (Illus.). 32p. (J). (gr. 2-4). 1993. pap. 6.95 (1-56294-801-6); lib. bdg. 14.90 (1-56294-332-4) Millbrook Pr.

Saturn. rev. ed. Dennis B. Fradin. LC 88-39117. (New True Bks.). (Illus.). 48p. (J). (gr. k-4). 1993. pap. 5.50 (0-516-41166-7); lib. bdg. 19.00 (0-516-01166-9) Childrens.

Saturn. Elaine Landau. (First Books). (Illus.). 64p. (J). (gr. 4-6). 1996. reprint ed. pap. 6.95 (0-531-15771-7) Watts.

Saturn: A New Look at an Old Devil. Liz Greene. LC 76-15546. 186p. 1976. pap. 7.95 (0-87728-306-0) Weiser.

Saturn see Ringed Planet: Saturn

Saturn French-German, German-French Dictionary: Dictionnaire Saturne Francais-Allemand-Francais. P. Grappin. 1800p. (FRE & GER.). 1981. 75.00 (0-8288-0340-4, M6724) Fr & Eur.

Saturn in Transit: Boundaries of Mind, Body & Soul. Erin Sullivan. Ed. by Howard Sasportas. (Arkana Contemporary Astrology Ser.). 296p. 1991. pap. 12.95 (0-14-019284-0, Arkana) Viking Penguin.

Saturn is Mostly Weather: Selected & Uncollected Poems. Gene Frumkin. LC 91-72301. 96p. 1992. pap. 9.95 (0-938317-16-4) Cinco Puntos.

Saturn Larousse French-English, English-French Dictionary: Dictionnaire Larousse Saturne Francais-Anglais-Francais. Marguerite-Marie Dubois. 1632p. (ENG & FRE.). 1981. 59.95 (0-8288-0060-X, M6174) Fr & Eur.

Saturn-Pluto Phenomenon. Joy Michaud & Karen Hilverson. LC 91-35566. 208p. 1993. pap. 11.95 (0-87728-722-8) Weiser.

Saturn Return. Ehresman & Albaugh. LC 83-71150. 104p. 1984. write for info. (0-86690-240-6, E2298-014) Am Fed Astrologers.

Saturn Rukh. Robert L. Forward. LC 96-42527. 1997. 22.95 (0-312-86321-7) Tor Bks.

Saturn Split. Alan Glazen. 304p. 1994. pap. 13.95 (1-886094-02-0) Chicago Spectrum.

Saturnalia. Paul Fleischman. LC 89-36380. (Charlotte Zolotow Bk.). 128p. (YA). (gr. 7 up). 1990. 14.95 (0-06-021912-2); lib. bdg. 14.89 (0-06-021913-0) HarpC Child Bks.

Saturnalia. Paul Fleischman. LC 89-36380. (Charlotte Zolotow Bk.: A Trophy Keypoint Bk.). 128p. (YA). (gr. 7 up). 1992. pap. 4.50 (0-06-447089-X, Trophy) HarpC Child Bks.

Saturnalia. Carole Marsh. (Carole Marsh Short Story Ser.). (Illus.). (Orig.). (J). (gr. 4-12). 1994. 29.95 (1-55609-187-7); pap. 19.95 (1-55609-238-5) Gallopade Pub Group.

Saturnino Q. Cariaga: His American Dream. Ed. by Regina Cariaga-Barden & Michael P. Onorato. 1988. 12.50 (0-930046-11-0) CSUF Oral Hist.

Saturno. Peter Murray. LC 92-41542. (Libro Vision Ser.). 32p. (SPA.). (J). (gr. 2-6). 1993. lib. bdg. 22.79 (1-56766-037-1) Childs World.

***Saturn's Child.** Nichelle Nichols. 1996. mass mkt. 5.99 (0-441-00384-2) Ace Bks.

Saturn's Child. Nichelle Nichols. 352p. 1995. 21.95 (0-399-14113-8, Ace-Putnam) Putnam Pub Group.

Saturn's Garden. Tehane Brown. 16p. (J). (gr. 2). 1993. write for info. (0-9637099-0-9) T Brown.

Satvotpatti Vinischaya & Nirvana Vibhaga: An Enquiry into the Origin of Beings & Discussions about Nirvana. Tr. by Henry M. Gunasekera. LC 78-72424. reprint ed. 17.50 (0-404-17285-7) AMS Pr.

Satwant Kaur: A Fictional Account of an Abducted Sikh Girl. Vir S. Singh & Ujagar S. Bawa. LC 87-50241. (Books on Sikhism Ser.). 224p. (YA). (gr. 8-12). 1987. pap. 10.00 (0-942245-00-8) Wash Sikh Ctr.

Satya-Jatakam: Treatise on Horoscopy Based on the Principles of Satya Samhita. Sage Satyacharya. 1991. 18.00 (0-685-58911-0, Pub. by Ranjan Pubs II) S Asia.

Satya Sai Avatar: Glimpses of Divinity. R. Mohan Rai. (C). 1995. reprint ed. 9.00 (81-207-1849-6, Pub. by Sterling Plns Pvt II) S Asia.

Satya Sai Avtar: Glimpses of Divinity. R. Mohan Rai. 132p. 1988. text ed. 25.00 (81-207-0707-9, Pub. by Sterling Pubs II) Apt Bks.

Satyagraha: The Gandhian Approach to Nonviolent Social Change. 2nd ed. Wallis T. Milne. 100p. 1989. pap. 8.95 (0-938875-18-3) Pittenbruach Pr.

Satyagraha in South Africa. M. K. Gandhi. Tr. by V. G. Desai from GUJ. 1979. reprint ed. pap. 7.00 (0-934676-03-8) Greenlf Bks.

***Satyagraha in South Africa: The Making of Mahatma Gandhi: The Story in His Own Words (Authorized U. S. Edition)** M. K. Gandhi. Tr. by V. G. Desai. (Illus.). 1997. 29.95 (0-9651800-1-8) Free Hand.

***Satyagraha in South Africa: The Making of Mahatma Gandhi: The Story in His Own Words (Authorized U. S. Edition)** M. K. Gandhi. Tr. by V. G. Desai. (Illus.). 1997. pap. 16.95 (0-9651800-2-6) Free Hand.

Satyajit Ray: A Film. Shyam Benegal. (C). 1988. 14.00 (81-7046-021-2, Pub. by Seagull Bks II) S Asia.

Satyajit Ray: A Study of His Films. Ben Nyce. LC 88-6620. 223p. 1988. text ed. 49.95 (0-275-92666-4, C2666, Praeger Pubs) Greenwood.

***Satyajit Ray: Beyond the Frame.** Surabhi Banerjee. 1996. 18.00 (81-7023-545-6, Pub. by Allied II) S Asia.

Satyajit Ray: The Inner Eye. Andrew Robinson. 430p. 1990. 45.00 (0-520-06905-6) U CA Pr.

Satyajit Ray: The Inner Eye. Andrew Robinson. 430p. 1992. pap. 18.95 (0-520-06946-3) U CA Pr.

Satyam Shivam Sundram: Truth-Godliness-Beauty. Rajneesh Osho Staff. Ed. by Krishna Prabhu & Ma V. Shabda. (Mantra Ser.). (Illus.). 368p. 1989. 21.95 (3-89338-031-0, Pub. by Rebel Hse GW) Osho America.

Satyartha Prakash in English with Comments: Spot Light on Truth. Vande M. Ramachandra. xii, 328p. 1988. text ed. 25.00 (0-614-00504-3, Pub. by Sarvadeshik Arya II) Nataraj Bks.

Satyendra Nath Bose. Santimay Chatterjee & Enakshi Chatterjee. (National Biography Ser.). 1979. pap. 3.00 (0-89744-196-6) Auromere.

Satyr. Robert DeMaria. LC 91-39571. 176p. 1992. 22.00 (0-933256-78-7) Second Chance.

Satyr. Susan Hartman. Ed. by Stanley H. Barkan. (Cross-Cultural Review Chapbook Ser.: No. 7: American Poetry 4). (Illus.). 16p. 1980. 15.00 (0-89304-847-X, CCC132); pap. 5.00 (0-89304-806-2) Cross-Cultrl NY.

Satyric & Heroic Mimes: Attitude As the Way of the Mime in Ritual & Beyond. Kathryn Wylie. LC 92-51103. (Illus.). 264p. 1994. lib. bdg. 37.50 (0-89950-897-9) McFarland & Co.

Satyrica. Petronius. Ed. by R. Bracht Branham & Daniel Kinney. Tr. by Daniel Kinney. LC 95-53110. 304p. (C). 1996. 28.00 (0-520-20599-5) U CA Pr.

***Satyrica.** Petronius. 1997. pap. text ed. 10.95 (0-520-21118-9) U CA Pr.

Satyricon. Petronius. 1983. pap. 11.95 (0-452-01005-5, Mer) NAL-Dutton.

Satyricon. Petronius. Tr. by William Arrowsmith. 1983. mass mkt. 4.50 (0-452-00964-2, Mer) NAL-Dutton.

Satyricon. Petronius. Bd. with Apocolocyntosis. (Loeb Classical Library: No. 15). 15.50 (0-674-99016-1) HUP.

Satyricon. Petronius. LC 95-19062. 272p. (ENG & LAT.). (C). 1996. 55.00 (0-19-815012-1, Clarendon Pr) OUP.

***Satyricon.** Petronius. Tr. & Intro. by P. G. Walsh. (The World's Classics Ser.). (Illus.). 272p. 1997. pap. 8.95 (0-19-283305-7) OUP.

Satyricon. rev. ed. Lucius A. Seneca. Bd. with Apocolocyntosis. 240p. 1986. Set pap. 10.95 (0-14-044489-0, Penguin Classics) Viking Penguin.

Satyricon, 2 vols., Set. Petronius. Ed. by Petro Burmanno. 1294p. 1974. reprint ed. write for info. (3-487-05416-7) G Olms Pubs.

Satze, Geschichten, Aufsatze. Mentor Lernhilfen. (GER.). 17.50 (3-580-64090-9) Langenscheidt.

***Satzgliedstellung in den Bairischen Dialekten Osterreichs.** Franz Patocka. (Reihe Schriften zur Deutschen Sprache in Osterreich Ser.: Bd. 20). (Illus.). 433p. (GER.). 1997. 69.95 (3-631-30450-1) P Lang Pubng.

Satzlexicon der Handelskorrespondenz. Dusan Zavada. 388p. (GER & ITA.). 1972. 55.00 (0-8288-6420-9, M-7618, Pub. by O Brandstetter Verlag GW) Fr & Eur.

Satzlexikon der Handelskorrespondenz. Dusan Zavada. (ENG & GER.). 1969. 55.00 (0-8288-6614-7, M-7615) Fr & Eur.

Satzlexikon der Handelskorrespondenz. Dusan Zavada. (FRE & GER.). 1971. 55.00 (0-8288-6477-2, M-7613, Pub. by O Brandstetter Verlag GW) Fr & Eur.

Satzlexikon der Handelskorrespondenz. Dusan Zavada. (GER & SPA.). 1973. 55.00 (0-685-57723-6, S-32990, Pub. by O Brandstetter Verlag GW) Fr & Eur.

Satzmelodie und Sprachwahrnehmung: Psycholinguistische Untersuchungen zur Grundfrequenz. Hede Helfrich. (Grundlagen der Kommunikation-Bibliotheksausgabe Ser.). xviii, 400p. (GER.). 1985. 153.85 (3-11-009918-7) De Gruyter.

SAT2 Subject Tests Supercourse. 2nd ed. Thomas H. Martinson. 1994. pap. 17.00 (0-671-86403-3, Arco) Macmillan Gen Ref.

***Sauaro Cactus.** Paul Berquist. (Habitats Ser.). 1997. pap. 6.95 (0-516-26065-0) Childrens.

Sauce: The Poetry Virgins. Ed. by Linda France et al. 64p. 9500. pap. 12.95 (1-85224-316-3) Dufour.

Sauce Bible: A Guide to the Saucier's Craft. David P. Larousse. LC 92-37388. 400p. 1993. text ed. 54.95 (0-471-57228-4) Wiley.

Sauce Book: Enhancing Great Foods with Contemporary Sauces. Deirdre Davis. (Illus.). 320p. 1992. 27.00 (0-201-57710-0) Addison-Wesley.

Sauce for the Goose. Robert Campbell. 208p. 1996. mass mkt. 5.99 (0-446-40463-2, Mysterious Paperbk) Warner Bks.

Sauce for the Goose. large type ed. Robert Campbell. (Cloak & Dagger Ser.). 290p. 1995. 23.95 (0-7862-0547-4) Thorndike Pr.

Sauce for the Pigeon. large type ed. Gerald Hammond. (Linford Mystery Library). 305p. 1989. pap. 15.99 (0-7089-6631-4, Linford) Ulverscroft.

***Saucer Attack.** Eric Nesheim. LC 97-22098. 1997. pap. text ed. 16.95 (1-57544-066-0) Genl Pub Grp.

Saucer City. Laura A. Shamas. 1994. 5.25 (0-87129-460-5, S20) Dramatic Pub.

Saucer Eyes: A Story of Becoming in Hard Rock Mining Country. Eulah C. Laucks. (Illus.). 96p. (Orig.). 1996. pap. 9.95 (1-56474-153-2) Fithian Pr.

Saucerful of Secrets: A Pink Floyd Odyssey. Nicholas Schaffner. 368p. 1992. pap. 14.95 (0-385-30684-9, Delta) Dell.

Saucerful of Secrets: The Pink Floyd Odyssey. Nicholas Schaffner. 1991. 20.00 (0-517-57608-2, Harmony) Crown Pub Group.

Saucers of the Illuminati. Jay Katz. 68p. 1993. spiral bd. 10.00 (1-881531-01-5) Ed Arcas.

Sauces. Sonia Allison. 1994. 9.95 (0-572-01705-7, Pub. by W Foulsham UK) Trans-Atl Phila.

***Sauces.** 2nd rev. ed. Peterson. (Culinary Arts Ser.). (C). 1998. text ed. 50.00 (0-442-02615-3) Van Nos Reinhold.

Sauces: Classical & Contemporary Sauce Making. James Peterson. LC 90-39442. (Illus.). 512p. 1991. text ed. 44.95 (0-442-23773-1) Van Nos Reinhold.

Sauces & Dressing Markets. Market Intelligence Staff. 295p. 1993. 1,200.00 (1-56753-551-8) Frost & Sullivan.

Sauces & Dressings: Eighty-Five Light & Easy Recipes from Nouvelle to New American. Diane Rozas. 96p. 1988. pap. 6.95 (0-517-57117-X, Harmony) Crown Pub Group.

Sauces & Gravies Market. Ed. by Peter Allen. 200p. 1988. 995.00 (0-941285-19-7) FIND-SVP.

Sauces for Pasta! Kristie Trabant. 128p. (Orig.). 1990. pap. 8.95 (0-89594-403-0) Crossing Pr.

Sauces, Seasonings & Marinades for Fish & Wild Game. Duane R. Lund. 1991. pap. 8.95 (0-934860-74-2) Adventure Pubns.

Saucier's Apprentice: A Modern Guide to Classic French Sauces for the Home. Raymond Sokolov. (Illus.). 1976. 25.00 (0-394-48920-9) Knopf.

Saucy Sailor & Other Dramatized Ballads. Ed. by Janet E. Tobitt. LC 70-80381. (Granger Index Reprint Ser.). 1977. 18.95 (0-8369-6066-1) Ayer.

***Saucy Sisters Insider's Guide to the Best Places to Eat in Nashville.** Barbara Nowak & Beverly Wichman. 110p. (Orig.). 1997. pap. 9.95 (0-9658399-0-7) Saucy Sisters.

Saucy Songs. 14.95 (0-7935-4608-7, 00310033) H Leonard.

Saudade. Katherine Vas. write for info. (0-345-37992-6, Ballantine Trade) Ballantine.

Saudade. Katherine Vaz. LC 96-7132. 304p. 1996. pap. 12.95 (0-312-14408-3) St Martin.

Saudades do Brasil: A Photographic Memoir. Claude Levi-Strauss. Tr. by Sylvia Modelski. (Illus.). 224p. (C). 1995. 50.00 (0-295-97472-9) U of Wash Pr.

Saudades do Brasil: A Photographic Memoir. Claude Levi-Strauss. Tr. by Sylvia Modelski. LC 95-21579. (Illus.). 224p. 1996. pap. 29.95 (0-295-97566-0) U of Wash Pr.

Saudi Arabia. Berlitz Editors. (Pocket Guides Ser.). 1992. 7.95 (2-8315-2244-7) Berlitz.

Saudi Arabia. Susannah Honeyman. LC 94-17104. (Country Fact Files Ser.). (J). (gr. 4 up). 1995. lib. bdg. 24.26 (0-8114-2786-2) Raintree Steck-V.

Saudi Arabia. George A. Lipsky et al. LC 59-8227. (Area & Country Surveys Ser.). 381p. 1959. 20.00 (0-87536-907-3) HRAFP.

Saudi Arabia. E. Eugene Oliver. (Pelham Guides Ser.). 70p. (C). 1996. 22.00 (0-929851-85-4) Am Assn Coll Registrars.

***Saudi Arabia.** U. S. Government Staff. (Country Studies). 1993. 20.00 (0-614-30814-3, USAUDI) Claitors.

Saudi Arabia. rev. ed. Leila M. Foster. LC 92-8890. (Enchantment of the World Ser.). (Illus.). 128p. (J). (gr. 5-9). 1994. lib. bdg. 30.00 (0-516-02611-9) Childrens.

Saudi Arabia. 2nd rev. ed. Frank A. Clements. (World Bibliographical Ser.: No. 5). 310p. 1988. lib. bdg. 55.00 (1-85109-067-3) ABC-CLIO.

Sa'udi Arabia. Harry S. Philby. LC 72-4289. (World Affairs Ser.: National & International Viewpoints). (Illus.). 422p. 1978. reprint ed. 26.95 (0-405-04581-6) Ayer.

Saudi Arabia: A Case Study in Development. Fouad Al-Farsy. 300p. (Orig.). 1986. 59.50 (0-7103-0128-6, 01286) Routledge Chapman & Hall.

Saudi Arabia: A Desert Kingdom. Kevin McCarthy. LC 96-14962. (Discovering Our Heritage Ser.). (Illus.). 128p. (YA). (gr. 5 up). 1996. lib. bdg. 14.95 (0-382-39608-1, Dillon Silver Burdett) Silver Burdett Pr.

Saudi Arabia: A Personal Experience. Heidi Tawfik. LC 91-65404. 216p. (Orig.). 1991. pap. 13.00 (0-9629455-0-1) Windmill CA.

Saudi Arabia: A Study of the Educational System of Saudi Arabia & a Guide to the Academic Placement of Students in Educational Institutions of the United States. E. Eugene Oliver. LC 87-1204. (World Education Ser.). 132p. reprint ed. pap. 37.70 (0-8357-8660-9, 2035108) Bks Demand.

Saudi Arabia: All You Need to Know. Esber I. Shaheen. LC 95-5829. 1995. 39.95 (0-940485-02-8) Intl Inst Tech.

Saudi Arabia: An Artist's View of the Past. Safeya Binzagr. (Illus.). 1979. boxed 60.00 (2-88001-076-4, Three Contnts) Lynne Rienner.

Saudi Arabia: Forces of Modernization. Bob Abdrabboh. 125p. (Orig.). 1985. pap. 9.95 (0-915597-19-5) Amana Bks.

***Saudi Arabia: Guarding the Desert Kingdom.** Anthony H. Cordesman. LC 96-46048. 1997. text ed. 65.00 (0-8133-3241-9) Westview.

***Saudi Arabia: Guarding the Desert Kingdom.** Anthony H. Cordesman. LC 96-46048. (C). 1997. pap. text ed. 27.00 (0-8133-3242-7) Westview.

Saudi Arabia: Past & Present. Shirley Kay. 12.95 (0-7043-2223-4, Pub. by Quartet UK) Charles River Bks.

Saudi Arabia: Rush to Development. Ragaei El Mallakh. LC 81-48189. 480p. 1982. text ed. 68.50 (0-8018-2783-3) Johns Hopkins.

Saudi Arabia: Society, Government & the Gulf Crises. Mordechai Abir. 256p. (C). (gr. 13). 1993. text ed. 49.95 (0-415-09325-2, B0160) Routledge.

Saudi Arabia: Technocrats in a Traditional Society. Henry H. Albers. (American University Studies Anthropology & Sociology: Ser. XI, Vol. 33). 247p. (C). 1989. text ed. 35.95 (0-8204-1095-0) P Lang Pubng.

Saudi Arabia: The Ceaseless Quest for Security. Nadav Safran. 1988. pap. 17.95 (0-8014-9484-2) Cornell U Pr.

Saudi Arabia: The Ceaseless Quest for Security. Nadav Safran. (Illus.). 592p. 1985. 35.00 (0-674-78985-7) HUP.

Saudi Arabia: The Coming Storm. Peter W. Wilson & Douglas F. Graham. LC 94-12612. (Illus.). 302p. (gr. 13). 1994. 66.95 (1-56324-394-6); pap. 25.95 (1-56324-395-4) M E Sharpe.

Saudi Arabia see Cultures of the World - Group 5

Saudi Arabia - Kuwait - Middle East Jobs: The New Jobs Manual. 5th rev. ed. Richard M. Zink. (Illus.). 64p. 1995. pap. 14.95 (0-939446-49-9) Zinks Career Guide.

Saudi Arabia & Its Royal Family. William F. Powell. 384p. 1982. 14.95 (0-8184-0326-8) Carol Pub Group.

Saudi Arabia & the Gulf War. Nasser I. Rashid & Esber I. Shaheen. LC 92-9853. (Illus.). 564p. 1992. 22.95 (0-940485-01-X) Intl Inst Tech.

Saudi Arabia by the First Photographers. William Facey & Gillian Grant. (Illus.). 128p. 1995. write for info. (0-905743-74-1, Pub. by Stacey Intl UK) Intl Bk Ctr.

Saudi Arabia Country Studies: Area Handbook. Library of Congress Federal Research Division. Ed. by Helen C. Metz. LC 93-28506. (Area Handbook Ser.: No. 550-51). 1993. 20.00 (0-8444-0791-7) Lib Congress.

Saudi Arabia in the 1980's: Foreign Policy, Security, & Oil. William B. Quandt. LC 82-18086. 190p. 1981. 26.95 (0-8157-7286-6) Brookings.

Saudi Arabia-Kuwait-Middle East Jobs: The New Employment Manual. 5th rev. ed. Richard M. Zink. (Illus.). 64p. 1995. pap. text ed. 14.95 (0-939469-49-9) Zinks Career Guide.

Saudi Arabia Sociological Research Project. Center for Applied Urban Research Staff. 52p. (Orig.). 1977. pap. 3.50 (1-55719-070-4) U NE CPAR.

Saudi Arabia, the West & the Security of the Arab Gulf. Mazher A. Hameed. 192p. 1987. 42.50 (0-7099-4663-5, Pub. by Croom Helm UK) Routledge Chapman & Hall.

Saudi Arabia Through the Eyes of an Artist. Malin Basil. (Illus.). 84p. (C). 1995. 75.00 (0-907151-17-5, Pub. by IMMEL Pubng UK) St Mut.

Saudi Arabia, with an Account of the Development of Its Natural Resources. 3rd ed. Karl S. Twitchell. LC 69-14126. 281p. 1969. reprint ed. text ed. 45.00 (0-8371-2364-X, TWSA, Greenwood Pr) Greenwood.

***Saudi Arabia-Yemen Dispute, 6 vols.** Ed. by R. N. Schofield. (Arabian Geopolitics Ser.). 4000p. 1993. reprint ed. lib. bdg. 1,595.00 (1-85207-480-9, Pub. by Archive Editions UK) N Ross.

S

An Asterisk (*) at the beginning of an entry indicates that the title is appearing in BIP for the first time.

Saudi Arabian Dialects. Theodore Prochazka, Jr. 400p. 1987. text ed. 82.50 (0-7103-0204-5) Routledge Chapman & Hall.

Saudi Arabian Economy. Ali D. Johany et al. LC 85-45869. 256p. 1986. text ed. 28.50 (0-8018-3351-5) Johns Hopkins.

Saudi Arabian Industrial Investment: An Analysis of Government-Business Relationships. Wahib A. Soufi & Richard T. Mayer. LC 90-40698. 160p. 1990. text ed. 55.00 (0-89930-595-4, SUZ, Quorum Bks) Greenwood.

Saudi Arabian Modernization: The Impact of Change on Stability. John A. Shaw & David E. Long. LC 81-23356. (Washington Papers: No. 89). (Illus.). 110p. 1982. pap. text ed. 9.95 (0-275-91553-0, B1553, Praeger Pubs) Greenwood.

Saudi Arabian Revenues & Expenditures: The Potential for Foreign Exchange Savings. Donald A. Wells. LC 74-19945. 44p. reprint ed. pap. 25.00 (0-317-26486-9, 2023819) Bks Demand.

Saudi Arabian Seashells: Selected Red Sea & Arabian Gulf Molluscs. Doreen Sharabati. (Illus.). 120p. 1983. 35.00 (0-7103-0051-4) Routledge Chapman & Hall.

Saudi Arabian Women Writers: Short Stories. Aman Attieh. LC 96-23221. 284p. 1997. 30.00 (0-89410-377-6, Three Contnts); pap. 16.00 (0-89410-378-4, Three Contnts) Lynne Rienner.

Saudi Arabia's Oil Policy. William B. Quandt. LC 82-73524. 46p. 1982. pap. 7.95 (0-8157-7287-4) Brookings.

Saudi Arabic. Foreign Service Institute Staff. 288p. pap. text ed. 185.00 incl. audio (0-88432-037-5, AFA234) Audio-Forum.

Saudi Arabic Basic Course: Urban Hajazi Dialect. Margaret K. Omar. 288p. (Orig.). 1994. pap. 14.95 (0-7818-0257-1) Hippocrene Bks.

Saudi Arabic Familiarization Course. Karin C. Ryding & Margaret K. Nydell. 80p. 1990. pap. text ed. 24.95 incl. audio (0-9628410-1-3) DLS VA.

Saudi Aramco & Its World: Arabia & the Middle East. rev. ed. Ed. by Ismail I. Nawwab et al. LC 95-70752. (Illus.). 291p. 1995. 27.50 (0-9601164-3-5) Saudi Arab Oil Co.

Saudi Business & Labor Law: Its Interpretation & Application. 2nd ed. Q. Javed Mian & Alison Lerrick. 450p. 1987. lib. bdg. 407.50 (0-86010-573-3) G & T Inc.

Saudi Financial System: In the Context of Western & Islamic Finance. Adnan M. Abdeen & Dale N. Shook. 287p. 1984. text ed. 108.95 (0-471-90346-9) Wiley.

***Saudi Green Book 1934.** 500p. (ARA & ENG.). 1994. reprint ed. lib. bdg. 195.00 (1-85207-323-3, Pub. by Archive Editions UK) N Ross.

Saudi Oil Policy & the Changing World Energy Balance. Thomas R. McHale. 20p. 1986. pap. 10.00 (0-918714-09-5) Intl Res Ctr Energy.

Saudi-Yemeni Relations: Domestic Structures & Foreign Influences. F. Gregory Gause, III. 288p. 1990. text ed. 49.50 (0-231-07044-6) Col U Pr.

Saudia Arabia Medical Review. IMMEL Publishing Ltd. Staff. 98p. (C). 1995. pap. 33.00 (0-907151-57-4, Pub. by IMMEL Pubng UK) St Mut.

Saudia Arabia's Economy: Oil & the Search for Economic Development. Hossein Askari. LC 89-49104. (Contemporary Studies in Economic & Financial Analysis: Vol. 67). 248p. 1990. 73.25 (1-55938-002-0) Jai Pr.

***Sauerbruch Hutton: Ten Projects.** Robert Harbison. (Illus.). 144p. 1999. pap. text ed. 49.50 (3-7643-5348-1) Birkhauser.

Saugus Book. Thomas F. Sheehan. 1984. 8.00 (0-8233-0388-8) Golden Quill.

***Saugus, MA.** N. Down. (Images of America Ser.). 1997. pap. 16.99 (0-7524-0469-5, Arcdia) Chalford.

Sauks & the Black Hawk War. Perry A. Armstrong. LC 76-43643. (Illus.). reprint ed. 57.50 (0-404-15478-6) AMS Pr.

Saul & Jonathan. Gordon Lindsay. (Old Testament Ser.: Vol. 20). 1965. 1.95 (0-89985-140-1) Christ for the Nations.

***Saul Baizerman's "The City & the People"** Douglas Dreishpoon & Valerie Fletcher. Ed. by Sheila Schwartz. (Illus.). 64p. (Orig.). 1997. pap. 15.00 (0-9627541-9-6) UNC Greensboro.

Saul Bass: A Life in Film & Design. Joe Morgenstern. LC 96-48693. (Illus.). 240p. 1997. 75.00 (1-881649-96-2) Genl Pub Grp.

Saul Bellow. Peter Hyland. LC 91-39681. (Modern Novelists Ser.). 160p. 1992. text ed. 29.95 (0-312-07598-7) St Martin.

Saul Bellow. T. Tanner. (Writers & Critics Ser.). 120p. 1978. 24.50 (0-912378-05-0) Chips Bksearch.

Saul Bellow. Earl H. Rovit. LC 67-26665. (University of Minnesota Pamphlets on American Writers Ser.: No. 65). 46p. reprint ed. pap. 25.00 (0-317-29457-1, 2055934) Bks Demand.

Saul Bellow: A Mosaic. Ed. by Gloria L. Cronin & Ada Aharoni. LC 92-12971. (Twentieth Century American Jewish Writers Ser.: Vol. 3). 209p. (C). 1993. text ed. 46.95 (0-8204-1572-3) P Lang Pubng.

Saul Bellow: An Annotated Bibliography. 2nd ed. Gloria L. Cronin. LC 87-7607. 496p. 1990. text ed. 25.00 (0-8240-9421-2) Garland.

Saul Bellow: In Defense of Man. 2nd ed. John J. Clayton. LC 78-19554. 346p. reprint ed. pap. 98.70 (0-8357-6692-6, 2056872) Bks Demand.

Saul Bellow: Vision & Revision. Daniel Fuchs. LC 83-9061. xi, 345p. 1984. reprint ed. pap. text ed. 20.95 (0-8223-0420-1) Duke.

Saul Bellow Against the Grain. Ellen Pifer. LC 89-22596. (Pennsylvania Studies in Contemporary American Fiction). 222p. (C). 1990. pap. text ed. 16.95 (0-8122-1369-6) U of Pa Pr.

***Saul Bellow & the Critics.** Malin. (C). 1966. text ed. write for info. (0-8147-0286-4); pap. text ed. write for info. (0-8147-0287-2) NYU Pr.

Saul Bellow & the Struggle at the Center. Saul Bellow. Ed. by Eugene Hollahan. LC 91-58150. (Georgia State Literary Studies: No. 12). 1992. 55.00 (0-404-63212-2) AMS Pr.

Saul Bellow Estate. Chirantan Kulshrestha. (Writers Workshop Greybird Ser.). 63p. 1976. 12.00 (0-86578-105-2); text ed. 6.00 (0-86578-104-4) Ind-US Inc.

Saul Bellow in the 1980s: A Collection of Critical Essays. Ed. by L. H. Goldman & Gloria L. Cronin. LC 89-42698. 320p. (C). 1989. text ed. 27.95 (0-87013-270-9) Mich St U Pr.

Saul Bellow's Herzog see Modern Critical Interpretations

Saul Bellow's Moral Vision: A Critical Study of the Jewish Experience. L. H. Goldman. 1983. text ed. 29.50 (0-8290-1056-4); pap. text ed. 16.95 (0-8290-1535-3) Irvington.

Saul, Israel's First King. Gordon Lindsay. (Old Testament Ser.: Vol. 19). 1965. 1.95 (0-89985-139-8) Christ for the Nations.

Saul Steinberg. Christina M. Strassfield. (Illus.). 16p. 1993. pap. 3.00 (0-933793-26-X) Guild Hall.

Saul to Paul: Enlightened to Serve. Phyllis Vos Wezeman & Colleen A. Wiessner. (Celebrate: A Creative Approach to Bible Studies). 32p. (Orig.). (J). (gr. 1-6). 1989. pap. 5.95 (0-940754-74-6) Ed Ministries.

Saul's Book. Paul T. Rogers. 1983. 15.95 (0-916366-16-2) Pushcart Pr.

Saul's Book. Paul T. Rogers. 1996. reprint ed. mass mkt. 6.95 (1-56333-462-3, Hard Candy) Masquerade.

Saul's Death: And Other Poems. Joe Haldeman. LC 96-30542. 80p. (Orig.). 1997. pap. 10.95 (0-9631203-4-4) Anamnesis Pr.

Saul's Fall: A Critical Fiction. Herbert Lindenberger. LC 78-22003. 1979. 38.50 (0-8018-2176-2) Johns Hopkins.

Sauna. Rob Roy. LC 96-2761. (Illus.). 120p. (Orig.). 1996. pap. 20.00 (0-930031-87-3) Chelsea Green Pub.

***Sauna.** Rob Roy. 1997. pap. 20.00 (0-614-27393-5) Chelsea Green Pub.

Sauna. David W. Salmela. (Illus.). 42p. (Orig.). (J). 1996. pap. text ed. 9.95 (0-9649064-0-6) OTSA PR.

Sauna. Sauna Society of America Staff. (Illus.). 6p. 1965. pap. 3.00 (0-318-19014-1) Sauna Soc.

Sauna. deluxe limited ed. David W. Salmela. (Illus.). 44p. (Orig.). (J). (ps-3). Date not set. 21.95 (0-9649064-1-4) OTSA PR.

Sauna - And Your Health. Compiled by Finnish Medical Society Staff. (Illus.). 80p. 1988. pap. 17.50 (0-614-14410-8) Sauna Soc.

Sauna & the Heart: Arrhythmias & Other Cardiovascular Responses During Finnish Sauna & Exercise Testing in Healthy Men & Post-Myocardial Infarction Patients. Olavi J. Luurila. 60p. 1980. pap. 12.50 (951-99256-6-X) Sauna Soc.

Sauna As Symbol: Society & Culture in Finland. L. M. Edelsward. LC 90-46511. (American University Studies: Anthropology & Science: Ser. XI, Vol. 53). 270p. (C). 1991. text ed. 41.95 (0-8204-1395-X) P Lang Pubng.

***Sauna Detoxification Therapy: A Guide for the Chemically Sensitive.** Marilyn G. McVicker. LC 97-51802. (Illus.). 175p. 1997. pap. 29.95 (0-7864-0359-4) McFarland & Co.

Sauna in Central New York. Melissa Ladenheim. (Illus.). xiv, 25p. (Orig.). 1986. pap. 2.95 (0-942690-35-4) DeWitt Hist.

Sauna Is. Bernhard Hillila. 70p. 1988. pap. 5.95 (0-941016-57-9) Penfield.

Sauna Studies. 301p. 1976. pap. 19.50 (951-95328-0-3) Sauna Soc.

***Sauncey & Mr. King's Gallery.** Clara A. Simmons. (Illus.). 30p. (J). (gr. 1-4). 1997. 9.95 (0-87033-498-0, Tidewtr Pubs) Cornell Maritime.

Saundarya Lahari of Sri Sankara. Shankara. pap. 4.95 (0-87481-585-1, Pub. by Ramakrishna Math II) Vedanta Pr.

Saundaryalahari. Sri Sankaracharya. Ed. & Tr. by V. K. Subramanian. x, 112p. 1986. 9.50 (0-685-35380-X, Pub. by Motilal Banarsidass II) S Asia.

***Saunders Cardiology CD-ROM: Containing Braunwald, 5/E, Skorton et al., 2/E & Smith.** Ed. by Richard Zorab. 1997. text ed. 415.00 (0-7216-7168-3) Saunders.

Saunders Drugs for Nursing Practice. Linda Harner. LC 95-17704. 1024p. 1996. pap. text ed. write for info. (0-7216-5402-9) Saunders.

Saunders First Responder. Bovia. pap. text ed. write for info. (0-7216-8660-5) Saunders.

Saunders Fundamentals for Nursing Assistants. Arlene Polaski & Judith P. Warner. (Illus.). 944p. 1994. pap. text ed. 27.95 (0-7216-3608-X) Saunders.

***Saunders Fundamentals for Nursing Assistants.** Arlene L. Polaski & Judith P. Warner. (Illus.). 1994. teacher ed., pap. write for info. (0-7216-3612-8) Saunders.

***Saunders Fundamentals for Nursing Assistants.** Arlene L. Polaski & Judith P. Warner. (Illus.). 1994. student ed., pap. write for info. (0-7216-3613-6) Saunders.

***Saunders Fundamentals for Nursing Assistants.** Arlene L. Polaski & Judith P. Warner. (Illus.). 944p. 1994. student ed., pap. write for info. (0-7216-4516-X) Saunders.

Saunders General. Sauncobio. (C). 1995. 209.50 (0-03-011218-4) HB Coll Pubs.

Saunders General Biology. 2nd ed. Eberhard. (C). 1996. lab manual ed., pap. text ed. 36.75 (0-03-010213-8) HB Coll Pubs.

Saunders General Biology Laboratory Manual: 1990 Version. 2nd ed. Carolyn Eberhard. (C). 1989. pap. text ed. 32.25 (0-03-025384-5) SCP.

Saunders General Biology Laboratory Manual: 1991 Version. Carolyn Eberhard. (C). 1991. pap. text ed. 43.25 (0-03-033367-9) SCP.

Saunders Infection Control Reference Service. Elias Abrutyn. Ed. by Lisa Biello. LC 96-38025. 1536p. 1997. text ed. write for info. (0-7216-6443-1) Saunders.

Saunders International Medical Word Book. 1100p. 1991. text ed. 71.00 (0-7216-3620-9) Saunders.

Saunders Internet Guide. Randy Reddick. (C). 1996. text ed. 14.75 (0-03-018858-X) HarBrace.

Saunders Lewis: A Presentation of His Work. Saunders Lewis. Ed. by Harri P. Jones. 228p. 1990. pap. 14.95 (0-87243-187-8) Templegate.

***Saunders Manual for Veterinary Technology.** Peter. Date not set. text ed. write for info. (0-7216-4193-8) Saunders.

Saunders Manual of Medical Assisting Practice. Ed. by Karen Lane. LC 92-49703. (Illus.). 888p. 1992. text ed. 46.95 (0-7216-3063-4) Saunders.

Saunders Manual of Medical Office Management. Alice A. Andress. Ed. by Margaret Biblis. LC 95-4642. (Illus.). 352p. 1996. text ed. 40.00 (0-7216-4820-7) Saunders.

Saunders Manual of Medical Practice. Robert E. Rakel. Ed. by Darlene Pedersen. LC 95-6354. (Illus.). 1088p. 1996. text ed. 97.50 (0-7216-5192-5) Saunders.

Saunders Manual of Medical Transcription. Ed. by Sheila Sloane-Dusseau & Marilyn T. Fordney. (Illus.). 784p. 1993. text ed. 46.00 (0-7216-3675-6) Saunders.

Saunders Manual of Nursing Care. Saunders. Ed. by Joan Luckmann et al. LC 95-50014. 1888p. 1997. text ed. 49.00 (0-7216-5017-1) Saunders.

***Saunders Manual of Pediatric Practice.** Laurence Finberg. LC 97-5188. 1998. pap. text ed. write for info. (0-7216-6537-3) Saunders.

Saunders Manual of Physical Therapy Practice. Rose S. Myers. LC 94-452. (Illus.). 1072p. 1995. text ed. 83.00 (0-7216-3671-3) Saunders.

Saunders Manual of Small Animal Practice. Stephen J. Birchard & Robert G. Sherding. (Illus.). 1424p. 1993. text ed. 127.00 (0-7216-3219-X) Saunders.

Saunders Medical Assisting Review. Newsome. Date not set. pap. text ed. write for info. (0-7216-4331-0) HarBrace.

***Saunders Nursing Drug Book 200.** Saunders Publishing Staff. Date not set. pap. text ed. write for info. (0-7216-7399-6); pap. text ed. write for info. (0-7216-7400-3) Saunders.

***Saunders Nursing Drug Handbook 1998.** 98th ed. Barbara B. Hodgson & Robert J. Kizior. Ed. by Maura Connor. LC 97-15903. (Illus.). 1344p. 1997. pap. text ed. write for info. (0-7216-7397-X) Saunders.

Saunders. "Old Tobe" Some Lines of Descent of Tobias Saunders of Westerly, Rhode Island. Earl P. Crandall. (Illus.). 334p. 1995. pap. 48.00 (0-8328-4675-9); lib. bdg. 58.00 (0-8328-4674-0) Higginson Bk Co.

Saunders Ophthalmology Word Book. Laurie Adams. 368p. 1991. pap. text ed. 33.00 (0-7216-3672-1) Saunders.

Saunders Paramedic Care. Thomas. Date not set. wbk. ed., pap. text ed. write for info. (0-7216-6320-6) HarBrace.

Saunders Paramedic Care. Thomas. text ed. write for info. (0-7216-6274-9) Saunders.

***Saunders Pharmaceutical Word Book.** Ellen Drake & Randy Drake. Ed. by Margaret Biblis. 704p. 1996. pap. text ed. 29.00 (0-7216-7249-3) Saunders.

Saunders "Physics" Saundersco. (C). 1995. pap. text ed. 28.00 (0-03-010968-X) HB Coll Pubs.

***Saunder's Pocket Essentials of Clinical Medicine.** Ann Ballinger & Steve Patchett. (Illus.). 547p. 1995. pap. write for info. (0-7020-1921-6, Pub. by W B Saunders UK) Saunders.

Saunders Pocket Reference for Nurses. 2nd ed. Kathleen Melonakos. LC 94-20443. (Illus.). 656p. 1994. pap. text ed. 23.00 (0-7216-4459-7) Saunders.

Saunders Review for NCLEX-RN. 2nd ed. Esther Matassarin-Jacobs. LC 93-22879. (Illus.). 800p. 1994. pap. text ed. 29.95 (0-7216-4993-9) Saunders.

Saunders Review for NCLEX RN. 2nd ed. Esther Matassarin-Jacobs. 1995. pap. text ed. 31.50 (0-7216-6323-0) Saunders.

***Saunders Review of Dental Hygiene.** Nelson. Date not set. pap. text ed. write for info. (0-7216-7576-X) Saunders.

Saunders Review of Family Practice. 2nd ed. Edward T. Bope et al. Ed. by Ray Kersey. (Illus.). 416p. 1996. pap. text ed. 49.50 (0-7216-5817-2) Saunders.

Saunder's Review of Practical Nursing for NCLEX-PN. 3rd ed. Esther Matassarin-Jacobs. Ed. by Maura Connor. (Illus.). 480p. 1996. pap. text ed. 27.95 (0-7216-5872-5) Saunders.

***Saunders Self Assessment & Review Guide for Nursing.** 2nd ed. 379p. 1994. pap. write for info. (0-920513-07-7, Pub. by Saunders CN) Saunders.

Saunders Student Nurse Planner. Susan C. DeWit. LC 95-11490. 1995. pap. text ed. 13.95 (0-7216-5831-8) Saunders.

Saunterer's Rewards. Edward V. Lucas. LC 75-128271. (Essay Index Reprint Ser.). 1977. 19.95 (0-8369-1887-8) Ayer.

***Sauntering: A Soul-Journey in the Woods with Thoreau As My Guide.** Tom Owen-Towle. (Illus.). 180p. 1996. pap. 12.95 (0-9630636-2-6) Bald Eagle Mtn.

Sauntering into the Holiness. Douglas Vest. LC 95-3738. (Illus.). 128p. (Orig.). 1995. pap. 7.95 (0-940147-34-3) Source Bks CA.

Sauria Terrestria, Amphisbaenia. R. Estes. (Encyclopedia of Paleoherpetology Ser.: Pt. 10A). (Illus.). 249p. 1983. lib. bdg. 182.00 (3-437-30391-0) Lubrecht & Cramer.

Saurischia. R. Steel. (Encyclopedia of Paleoherpetology Ser.: Pt. 14). (Illus.). 87p. 1970. pap. text ed. 52.50 (3-437-30030-X) Lubrecht & Cramer.

Sauron Defeated: The History of the Lord of the Rings, Pt. Four; The Notion Club Papers, & The Drowning of Anadune. J. R. R. Tolkien. Ed. & Frwd. by Christopher Tolkien. LC 92-14587. (Illus.). 496p. 1992. 29.95 (0-395-60649-7) HM.

Sauropod Dinosaur Barosaurus Marsh. Richard S. Lull. (Connecticut Academy of Arts & Sciences Ser., Trans.: Vol. 6). 1919. pap. 150.00 (0-685-22867-3) Elliots Bks.

***Sausage.** A. D. Livingston. LC 97-17151. 1998. write for info. (1-55821-526-3) Lyons & Burford.

Sausage & Processed Meat Formulations. Herbert W. Ockerman. 608p. (gr. 13). 1991. text ed. 91.95 (0-442-23436-8) Chapman & Hall.

Sausage-Making Cookbook. Jerry Predika. LC 82-19679. (Illus.). 192p. 1983. 16.95 (0-8117-1693-7) Stackpole.

Sausage Tree. Rosalie Medcraft & Valda Gee. 200p. 1995. pap. 16.95 (0-7022-2783-8, Pub. by Univ Queensland Pr AT) Intl Spec Bk.

Sausalito, Moments in Time. Jack Tracy. Ed. by Wayne Bonnett. (Illus.). 200p. 1983. 32.00 (0-915269-00-7) Windgate Pr.

Sausalito Waterfront Stories. Derek Van Loan. (Illus.). 144p. (Orig.). 1992. pap. 9.95 (0-9614068-2-8) Epoch Pr.

Saussure: Signs, System & Arbitrariness. David Holdcroft. (Modern European Philosophy Ser.). (Illus.). 160p. (C). 1991. text ed. 59.95 (0-521-32618-4); pap. text ed. 17.95 (0-521-33918-9) Cambridge U Pr.

Saussure, Derrida, & the Metaphysics of Subjectivity. Robert M. Strozier. (Approaches to Semiotics Ser.: No. 80). xii, 304p. (C). 1989. lib. bdg. 103.50 (0-89925-344-X) Mouton.

Saussure for Beginners. W. Terrence Gordon. (Illus.). 160p. 1995. pap. 11.00 (0-86316-195-2) Writers & Readers.

***Saussures First & Second Courses of Lectures on General Linguistics, 2 vols.** F. De Saussure et al. 158.00 (0-08-042783-9) Elsevier.

Saussure's Second Course of Lectures on General Linguistics (1908-09) see Saussures 1st, 2nd & 3rd Course of Lectures on General Linguistics

***Saussures 1st, 2nd & 3rd Course of Lectures on General Linguistics, 3 vols.** Incl. Premier Cours de Linguistique Generale (1907): (Saussure's First Course of Lecture on General Linguistics, 1907): D'Apres les Cahiers D'Albert Riedlinger: (From the Notebooks of Albert Riedlinger. rev. ed. Ed. by Eisuke Komatsu & George Wolf. Tr. by George Wolf. (FRE.). 292p. 1996. 86.50 (0-08-042578-X, Pergamon Pr); Saussure's Second Course of Lectures on General Linguistics (1908-09). Eisuke Komatsu & George Wolf. 1997. (0-08-042579-8, Pergamon Pr); Troisieme Cours de Linguistique Generale (1910-1911) - Saussure's Third Course of Lectures on General Linguistics (1910-1911)-Cours de Linguistique Generale: Saussure's Third Course of Lectures on General Linguistics (1910-1911) from the Notebooks of Emil Constantin. F. De Saussure. Ed. by Eisuke Komatsu. Tr. by Roy Harris from FRE. LC 93-8253. 373p. 1993. text ed. 102.50 (0-08-041922-4, Pergamon Pr); 202.00 (0-08-042784-7) Elsevier.

Sauternes: And Other Sweet Wines of Bordeaux. Stephen Brook. 192p. 1995. 24.95 (0-571-17316-0); pap. 15.95 (0-571-17317-9) Faber & Faber.

Sautes. David DiResta & Joanne Foran. (Illus.). 160p. (Orig.). 1996. pap. 8.95 (1-55867-139-0, Nitty Gritty Ckbks) Bristol Pub Ent CA.

Sauvage. Jean Anouilh. Bd. with Invitation au Chateau. (Folio Ser.: No. 874). (FRE.). Set pap. 10.50 (2-07-036874-2, 748) Schoenhof.

Sauvage. Incl. Invitation au Chateau. (0-318-63598-4); write for info. (0-318-63597-6, 748) Fr & Eur.

Sauvage see Pieces Noires

Sauvage Suivi de l'Invitation au Chateau. Jean Anouilh. 384p. (FRE.). 1976. pap. 10.95 (0-7859-3472-3, F81898) Fr & Eur.

***Sauvages Americains: Representations of Native Americans in French & English Colonial Literature.** Gordon M. Sayre. LC 96-36993. (Illus.). 336p. (C). 1997. 45.00 (0-8078-2346-5); pap. 19.95 (0-8078-4652-X) U of NC Pr.

Sauve Qui Peut. Goscinny Sempe. (FRE.). 1972. pap. 10.95 (0-8288-3791-0, M11034) Fr & Eur.

Sauve Qui Peut. Jean-Jacques Sempe. (Folio Ser.: No. 81). (FRE.). pap. 8.95 (2-07-036081-4) Schoenhof.

***Sauve Qui Peut l'Amour.** Marie-Francine Hebert. (Novels in the Roman Plus Ser.). 160p. (FRE.). (YA). (gr. 8 up). 1996. pap. 7.95 (2-89021-168-1, Pub. by Les Editions CN) Firefly Bks Ltd.

***Sauvez Ma Babouche!** Gilles Gauthier. (Novels in the Premier Roman Ser.). 64p. (FRE.). (J). (gr. 2-5). 1996. pap. 7.95 (2-89021-110-X, Pub. by Les Editions CN) Firefly Bks Ltd.

Sauvignon Blanc TasteTour, Vol. 1, No. 5, White Wines of Distinction see TasteTour Collection: Fine Wines of the World

Sav, Shemini, Tazria, Negaim, Mesoram & Zabim. Jacob Neusner. 1988. 43.95 (1-55540-206-2) Scholars Pr GA.

Savage. Parris A. Bonds. 368p. (Orig.). 1995. mass mkt., pap. text ed. 4.99 (0-8439-3784-X) Dorchester Pub Co.

Savage. Nicole Jordan. 400p. (Orig.). 1994. mass mkt. 4.50 (0-380-77280-9) Avon.

Savage Acts: Four Plays (Ligazon, La Rosa De Papel, La Cabeza Del Bautista, Sacrilegio. Ramon Del Valle-Inclan. Ed. by Martha T. Halsey. Tr. by Robert Lima from SPA. LC 92-75690. (Contemporary Spanish Plays Ser.: Vol. 3). xvi, 68p. 1993. pap. 6.00 (0-9631212-2-7) Estreno.

Savage Amusement. David Bishop. (Judge Dredd Ser.). 256p. (Orig.). 1996. mass mkt. 5.95 (0-352-32874-6, Pub. by Virgin Pub UK) London Brdge.

S

An Asterisk (*) at the beginning of an entry indicates that the title is appearing in BIP for the first time.

***Savage & Barbarian: Historical Attitudes in the Criticism of Homer & Ossian in Britian, 1760-1800.** M. M. Rubel. (Verhandelingen der Koninklijke Nederlandse Akademie van Wetenschappen, Afd. Letterkunde, Nieuwe Reeks Ser.: No. 96). 128p. 1978. pap. text ed. 34.50 (*0-7204-8442-1*) Elsevier.

Savage & Beautiful Country: The Secret Life of the Mind. Alan McGlashan. 208p. 1995. pap. 15.95 (*3-85630-517-3*, Pub. by Daimon Pubs SZ) Continuum.

Savage & His Totem. Percival Hadfield. LC 75-32825. reprint ed. 32.50 (*0-404-14129-3*) AMS Pr.

Savage & Stevens Arms: Collector's History. 3rd rev. ed. Jay Kimmel. (Illus.). 252p. 1993. pap. 25.00 (*0-942893-00-X*) CoryStevens Pub.

Savage & Stevens, Arms & History, 1849-1971: All "Stevens" Arms. Bill West. LC 72-143773. (West Arms Library - Classic Bks.). (Illus.). 1971. 60.00 (*0-911614-10-9*) B West.

Savage Anomaly: The Power of Spinoza's Metaphysics & Politics. Antonio Negri. Tr. & Frwd. by Michael Hardt. 284p. 1990. pap. text ed. 18.95 (*0-8166-1877-1*) U of Minn Pr.

Savage Arena. Joe Tasker. (Illus.). 288p. 1982. 18.95 (*0-312-69984-0*) St Martin.

Savage Aristocrat. Roberta Leigh. 1980. pap. 1.75 (*0-449-14246-9*, GM) Fawcett.

Savage Arms & History, 1849-1989: Reduced "Stevens" Descriptions. Bill West. LC 89-90228. (West Arms Library - Classic Bks.). (Illus.). 1989. 52.00 (*0-911614-20-6*) B West.

Savage Art: A Biography of Jim Thompson. Robert Polito. LC 94-48455. 528p. 1995. 30.00 (*0-394-58407-4*) Knopf.

***Savage Art: A Biography of Jim Thompson.** Robert Polito. 1996. pap. 16.00 (*0-679-73352-3*, Vin) Random.

Savage Attack: Rage Player's Guide to Rage. (Rage Ser.). 1995. 7.95 (*1-56504-396-0*, 3906) White Wolf.

Savage Autumn. C. Obanyon. 1990. pap. 4.50 (*0-8217-3188-2*) NAL-Dutton.

Savage Autumn. Constance O'Banyon. 1988. mass mkt. 3.95 (*0-8217-1938-6*, Zebra Kensgtn) Kensgtn Pub Corp.

Savage Betrayal. Lynne Graham. (Harlequin Presents Ser.: No. 1824). 1996. mass mkt. 3.50 (*0-373-11824-4*, 1-11824-9) Harlequin Bks.

Savage Betrayal. Lynne Graham. (Harlequin Romance Ser.). 1996. 19.95 (*0-263-14478-X*, Pub. by Mills & Boon UK) Thorndike Pr.

***Savage Bliss.** Cassie Edwards. 336p. 1996. reprint ed. mass mkt. 5.50 (*0-505-52150-4*) Dorchester Pub Co.

Savage Blood. Duff McCoy. (Cutter Ser.: No. 3). 1991. mass mkt. 3.50 (*1-55817-482-6*, Pinncle Kensgtn) Kensgtn Pub Corp.

Savage Carrot. Ingrid Tomey. LC 93-7273. 192p. (J). (gr. 5-7). 1993. lib. bdg. 14.95 (*0-684-19633-6*, C Scribner Sons Young) S&S Childrens.

Savage Comedy since King Ubu: A Tangent to "The Absurd" Kenneth S. White. (C). 1977. pap. text ed. 15.50 (*0-8191-0152-4*) U Pr of Amer.

Savage Conquest. Janelle Taylor. 1992. mass mkt. 4.99 (*0-8217-3503-9*, Zebra Kensgtn) Kensgtn Pub Corp.

Savage Courtship. Susan Napier. (Presents Ser.). 1995. mass mkt. 3.25 (*0-373-11744-2*, 1-11744-9) Harlequin Bks.

Savage Courtship. large type ed. Susan Napier. (Harlequin Romance Ser.). 283p. 1995. lib. bdg. 18.95 (*0-263-14102-0*, Pub. by Mills & Boon UK) Thorndike Pr.

Savage Cut. Jo Dereske. 320p. 1996. mass mkt. 5.50 (*0-440-22221-4*) Dell.

***Savage Dance.** Cassie Edwards. 320p. 1997. reprint ed. mass mkt. 5.50 (*0-505-52242-X*, Love Spell) Dorchester Pub Co.

Savage Day. large type ed. Jack Higgins. 1995. 22.95 (*0-7862-0358-7*) Thorndike Pr.

Savage Days, Savage Nights. Soka Gakkai Youth Division Staff. 234p. 1984. pap. 4.95 (*0-8184-0362-4*, Citadel Pr) Carol Pub Group.

Savage Desire. Constance O'Banyon. 1983. mass mkt. 3.50 (*0-8217-1120-2*, Zebra Kensgtn) Kensgtn Pub Corp.

Savage Destiny, No. 5. F. Rosanne Bittner. 1985. mass mkt. 4.50 (*0-8217-3171-8*, Zebra Kensgtn) Kensgtn Pub Corp.

Savage Destiny: (Too Hot to Handle) Amanda Browning. (Presents Ser.). 1995. pap. 3.25 (*0-373-11724-8*, 1-11724-1) Harlequin Bks.

Savage Destiny, No. 6. F. Rosanne Bittner. 1986. mass mkt. 4.50 (*0-8217-3172-6*, Zebra Kensgtn) Kensgtn Pub Corp.

Savage Dilemma. John Patrick. 1972. pap. 5.25 (*0-8222-0989-6*) Dramatists Play.

Savage Dragon: Force to Be Reckoned With. Erik Larson. (Illus.). (Orig.). (YA). 1996. pap. 14.95 (*1-887279-12-1*); text ed. 39.95 (*1-887279-13-X*) Image Comics.

***Savage Dream.** Cassie Edwards. 336p. 1997. reprint ed. mass mkt. 5.50 (*0-505-52161-X*) Dorchester Pub Co.

Savage Dreams. Rebecca Solnit. 1995. pap. 13.00 (*0-679-76660-X*) Random.

Savage Dreams: A Journey into the Hidden Wars of the American West. Rebecca Solnit. LC 94-4103. (Illus.). 256p. 1994. 22.00 (*0-87156-526-9*) Sierra.

Savage Earth. large type ed. Helga Moray. 400p. 1984. 25.99 (*0-7089-1116-1*) Ulverscroft.

Savage Ecstasy. Janelle Taylor. 1991. mass mkt. 4.95 (*0-8217-3496-2*, Zebra Kensgtn) Kensgtn Pub Corp.

Savage Ecstasy. Janelle Taylor. 1996. pap. 5.99 (*0-8217-5453-X*) Kensgtn Pub Corp.

Savage Eden. Cassie Edwards. 336p. 1996. reprint ed. mass mkt. 5.50 (*0-505-52097-4*, Love Spell) Dorchester Pub Co.

Savage Embers. Cassie Edwards. 448p. (Orig.). 1994. mass mkt., pap. text ed. 4.99 (*0-8439-3568-5*) Dorchester Pub Co.

Savage Encounter. large type ed. George Goodchild. (Linford Mystery Library). 1995. pap. 15.99 (*0-7089-7803-7*, Linford) Ulverscroft.

Savage Eye: Melville & the Visual Arts. Ed. by Christopher Sten. LC 91-9994. (Illus.). 352p. 1992. 35.00 (*0-87338-444-X*) Kent St U Pr.

Savage Freud & Other Essays on Possible & Retrievable Selves. Ashis Nandy. LC 94-46626. (Studies in Culture/Power/History). 284p. 1995. text ed. 49.50 (*0-691-04411-2*); pap. text ed. 16.95 (*0-691-04410-4*) Princeton U Pr.

Savage Frontier: The Apache Wars Saga, Vol. 3. Frank Burleson. 352p. 1995. pap. 4.99 (*0-451-18091-7*, Sig) NAL-Dutton.

Savage Garden: A Journal. Paul Reed. 176p. 1994. 20.00 (*0-9641006-0-6*) Hse of Lillian.

***Savage Garden: Cultivating Carnivorous Plants.** Peter D'Amato. (Illus.). 192p. (Orig.). 1997. pap. 16.95 (*0-89815-915-6*) Ten Speed Pr.

Savage God: A Study of Suicide. A. Alvarez. 1990. pap. 9.95 (*0-393-30657-7*) Norton.

Savage Gun. large type ed. Dan Stewart. (Dales Western Ser.). 191p. 1993. pap. 17.99 (*1-85389-373-0*, Medcom-Trainex) Ulverscroft.

Savage Guns. Jon Sharpe. (Trailsman Ser.: No. 150). 176p. (Orig.). 1994. pap. 3.50 (*0-451-17886-6*) NAL-Dutton.

Savage H. Jerry Ahern. (Survivalist Ser.: No. 6). 1983. mass mkt. 2.50 (*0-8217-1243-8*, Zebra Kensgtn) Kensgtn Pub Corp.

Savage Heart. Cassie Edwards. 1985. mass mkt. 3.95 (*0-8217-1582-8*, Zebra Kensgtn) Kensgtn Pub Corp.

***Savage Heart.** Cassie Edwards. 384p. 1997. mass mkt. 5.99 (*0-8217-5635-4*, Zebra Kensgtn) Kensgtn Pub Corp.

***Savage Heart.** Diana Palmer. 1997. mass mkt. 10.00 (*0-449-00006-0*, Columbine) Fawcett.

***Savage Heart.** Diane Palmer. 1997. mass mkt. 10.00 (*0-8041-1589-3*) Ivy Books.

Savage Hits Back. Julius E. Lips. 1966. 10.00 (*0-8216-0147-4*, Univ Bks) Carol Pub Group.

Savage Holiday. Richard A. Wright. (Banner Bk.). 220p. 1995. reprint ed. pap. 16.95 (*0-87805-750-1*); reprint ed. lib. bdg. 37.50 (*0-87805-749-8*) U Pr of Miss.

Savage Horde. J. Ahern. 1989. pap. 2.95 (*0-8217-2937-3*) NAL-Dutton.

Savage in Judaism: An Anthropology of Israelite Religion & Ancient Judaism. Howard Eilberg-Schwartz. LC 89-45919. (Illus.). 304p. 1990. 35.00 (*0-253-31946-3*); pap. 17.95 (*0-253-20591-3*, MB-591) Ind U Pr.

Savage in Limbo. John P. Shanley. 1986. pap. 5.25 (*0-8222-0990-X*) Dramatists Play.

Savage Inequalities: Children in America's Schools. Jonathan Kozol. 288p. 1991. 20.00 (*0-517-58221-X*, Crown) Crown Pub Group.

Savage Inequalities: Children in America's Schools. Jonathan Kozol. LC 92-52636. 272p. 1992. pap. 13.50 (*0-06-097499-0*, PL) HarpC.

***Savage Innocence.** Cassie Edwards. 448p. 1997. mass mkt. 5.99 (*0-8217-5578-1*, Zebra Kensgtn) Kensgtn Pub Corp.

Savage Is My Name: A History of 13 Generations of a Savage Family in America. R. Blair Savage. LC 95-81031. (Illus.). 308p. 1995. 29.50 (*0-9649239-5-5*) Buffalo Run.

Savage Justice. Ron Handberg. 480p. 1995. mass mkt. 5.99 (*0-06-100684-X*, Harp PBks) HarpC.

***Savage Justice.** Ron Handberg. 374p. 4.98 (*0-8317-4956-3*) Smithmark.

Savage Justice: A Novel. Ron Handberg. 288p. 1992. 18.95 (*1-55972-116-2*, Birch Ln Pr) Carol Pub Group.

***Savage Land.** Matt Braun. 1997. mass mkt. 5.99 (*0-312-96004-2*) St Martin.

Savage Land. Janet Dailey. 1992. mass mkt. 3.59 (*0-373-89893-2*, 1-89893-1) Harlequin Bks.

Savage Land. John Killdeer. (Mountain Majesty Ser.: Bk. 8). 256p. 1995. mass mkt. 5.99 (*0-553-57434-5*, Bantam Domain) Bantam.

Savage Legacy. large type ed. Jean Chapman. 512p. 1988. 25.99 (*0-7089-1893-X*) Ulverscroft.

***Savage Longings.** Cassie Edwards. 400p. (Orig.). 1997. mass mkt. 5.99 (*0-8439-4176-6*) Dorchester Pub Co.

Savage Lost: Florida Garage Bands - The '60s & Beyond. Jeffrey M. Lemlich. LC 91-15241. (Illus.). 424p. 1992. pap. 19.95 (*0-942963-12-1*) Distinctive Pub.

***Savage Love.** Dan Savage. 1998. pap. 21.95 (*0-525-94294-7*) NAL-Dutton.

Savage Marquess. Marion Chesney. (Regency Romance Ser.). 224p. 1988. pap. 3.99 (*0-451-15240-9*, Sig) NAL-Dutton.

Savage Mind. Claude Levi-Strauss. LC 66-28197. (Nature of Human Society Ser.). 1968. pap. 16.95 (*0-226-47484-4*, P325) U Ch Pr.

***Savage Money: The Anthropology & Politics of Commodity Exchange.** Chris Gregory. (Studies in Anthropology & History: Vol. 21). 300p. 1997. text ed. 72.00 (*90-5702-091-2*, Harwood Acad Pubs); pap. text ed. 28.00 (*90-5702-092-0*, Harwood Acad Pubs) Gordon & Breach.

Savage Mountains. Robert Adams. (Horseclans Ser.: No. 5). (Orig.). 1983. pap. 2.95 (*0-451-12934-2*, AE2934, Sig) NAL-Dutton.

Savage My Kinsman. rev. ed. Elisabeth Elliot. (Illus.). 160p. 1996. pap. 10.99 (*1-56955-003-4*, Vine Bks) Servant.

Savage My Kinsman: The True Story of Elisabeth Elliot's Life among the Auca Indians. Elisabeth Elliot. (Illus.). 180p. 1981. reprint ed. pap. 9.99 (*0-89283-099-9*, Vine Bks) Servant.

Savage Night. Jim Thompson. LC 91-50072. (Vintage Crime - Black Lizard Ser.). 160p. 1991. pap. 9.00 (*0-679-73310-8*, Vin) Random.

Savage Nights. Cyril Collard. Tr. by William Rodarmor. LC 93-31881. 240p. 1994. 18.95 (*0-87951-534-1*) Overlook Pr.

Savage Nights. Cyril Collard. LC 93-31881. 223p. 1995. pap. 11.95 (*0-87951-580-5*) Overlook Pr.

Savage Oaks. Julie Ellis. 1981. pap. 2.25 (*0-449-23996-9*, Crest) Fawcett.

Savage Obsession. Cassie Edwards. 1985. mass mkt. 3.95 (*0-8217-1638-7*, Zebra Kensgtn) Kensgtn Pub Corp.

Savage Obsession. Cassie Edwards. 432p. 1997. mass mkt. 5.99 (*0-8217-5554-4*, Zebra Kensgtn) Kensgtn Pub Corp.

Savage Obsession. Diana Hamilton. (Presents Ser.). 1993. mass mkt. 2.99 (*0-373-11588-1*, 1-11588-0) Harlequin Bks.

Savage Obsession. large type ed. Diana Hamilton. (Harlequin Ser.). 1993. 19.95 (*0-263-13404-0*) Thorndike Pr.

Savage on Selling: Secrets from an Insurance Great. John Savage. 172p. 1994. 19.95 (*0-7931-0913-2*, 24015601) Dearborn Finan.

***Savage Paradise.** Cassie Edwards. 480p. 1997. mass mkt. 5.99 (*0-8217-5637-0*, Zebra Kensgtn) Kensgtn Pub Corp.

***Savage Paradise.** large type ed. Sheila Belshaw. (Linford Romance Library). 304p. 1997. pap. 16.99 (*0-7089-7980-7*, Linford) Ulverscroft.

Savage Passions. Cassie Edwards. 448p. (Orig.). 1996. mass mkt., pap. text ed. 5.99 (*0-8439-3902-8*) Dorchester Pub Co.

Savage Peace: Americans at War in the 1990s. Daniel P. Bolger. LC 95-5842. 448p. 1995. 27.95 (*0-89141-452-5*) Presidio Pr.

Savage Persuasion. Cassie Edwards. 448p. (Orig.). 1993. mass mkt., pap. text ed. 4.99 (*0-8439-3543-X*) Dorchester Pub Co.

Savage Persuasion. Cassie Edwards. 1995. mass mkt. 5.99 (*0-8439-4010-7*) Dorchester Pub Co.

Savage Pilgrimage: A Narrative by D. H. Lawrence. Catherine Carswell. 1988. reprint ed. lib. bdg. 49.00 (*0-7812-0593-X*) Rprt Serv.

Savage Pilgrimage: A Narrative by D. H. Lawrence. Catherine M. Carswell. LC 75-144937. 307p. 1972. reprint ed. 39.00 (*0-403-01760-2*) Scholarly.

***Savage Pilgrims: On the Road to Santa Fe.** Henry Shukmkan. LC 96-47446. 240p. 1997. 20.00 (*1-56836-170-X*) Kodansha.

Savage Place. Robert B. Parker, Jr. 192p. 1992. mass mkt. 6.50 (*0-440-18095-3*) Dell.

Savage Place. large type ed. Frank G. Slaughter. 1971. 25.99 (*0-85456-651-1*) Ulverscroft.

Savage Plains. David W. Ross. 480p. (Orig.). 1996. mass mkt. 5.99 (*0-380-78324-X*) Avon.

Savage Pride. Cassie Edwards. 448p. (Orig.). 1995. mass mkt., pap. text ed. 5.99 (*0-8439-3732-7*) Dorchester Pub Co.

Savage Promise. Cassie Edwards. 1995. mass mkt. 5.99 (*0-8439-3978-8*) Dorchester Pub Co.

Savage Range. large type ed. Luke Short. LC 95-32669. 250p. 1995. pap. 20.95 (*0-7838-1460-7*, GK Hall) Thorndike Pr.

Savage Rendezvous. David Thompson. (Wilderness Ser.: No. 3). 1995. mass mkt. 3.99 (*0-8439-3924-9*) Dorchester Pub Co.

***Savage Rendezvous & Blood Fury.** David Thompson. (Wilderness Ser.). 352p. 1997. reprint ed. mass mkt. 4.99 (*0-8439-4208-8*) Dorchester Pub Co.

***Savage Revenge.** Theresa Scott. 448p. 1997. mass mkt. 5.99 (*0-8439-4255-X*, Leisure Bks) Dorchester Pub Co.

Savage Rock: The History of a Parish. Peter Kavanagh. 60p. 1978. 40.00 (*0-914612-09-3*) Kavanagh.

Savage Sam. Fred Gipson. (J). (gr. 1-5). 1976. mass mkt. 6.00 (*0-06-080377-0*, P377, PL) HarpC.

Savage Sands. Christina Nicholson. 1978. pap. 2.25 (*0-449-23762-1*, Crest) Fawcett.

***Savage Scruple: A Woman's Life.** Thelma Klein. LC 97-65990. (Illus.). 128p. 1997. pap. 13.50 (*0-88739-107-9*) Creat Arts Bk.

Savage Season. Joe R. Lansdale. 192p. 1995. mass mkt. 5.50 (*0-446-40431-4*, Mysterious Paperbk) Warner Bks.

***Savage Season: Hurricanes Bertha & Fran Summer of 1996.** Ed. by Wilmington Star-News Staff. (Illus.). 64p. (Orig.). 1996. pap. 16.95 (*0-9655164-0-7*) Wilmington Star.

Savage Secrets. Cassie Edwards. 448p. (Orig.). 1995. mass mkt., pap. text ed. 5.99 (*0-8439-3823-4*) Dorchester Pub Co.

Savage Shadows. Cassie Edwards. 400p. (Orig.). 1996. mass mkt. 5.99 (*0-8439-4051-4*, Leisure Bks) Dorchester Pub Co.

Savage Shadows: Eileen Ross's True Story of Blindness, Rape - & Courage. Eileen Ross et al. LC 91-66895. 1992. 21.95 (*0-88282-105-9*) New Horizon NJ.

Savage Shore. Cynthia S. Roberts. 448p. 1993. lib. bdg. 22.00 (*0-7278-4477-6*) Severn Hse.

Savage Shore. large type ed. Cynthia S. Roberts. (Charnwood Large Print Ser.). 1995. 27.99 (*0-7089-8841-5*, Charnwood) Ulverscroft.

Savage Spirit. Cassie Edwards. 448p. (Orig.). 1994. mass mkt., pap. text ed. 4.99 (*0-8439-3639-8*) Dorchester Pub Co.

Savage Splendor. Constance O'Banyon. 1983. mass mkt. 3.50 (*0-8217-1292-6*, Zebra Kensgtn) Kensgtn Pub Corp.

Savage Splendor. Cassie Edwards. 336p. 1996. reprint ed. mass mkt. 5.50 (*0-505-52112-1*, Love Spell) Dorchester Pub Co.

Savage Spring. Constance O'Banyon. 1988. mass mkt. 3.95 (*0-8217-1715-4*, Zebra Kensgtn) Kensgtn Pub Corp.

Savage Strategy for Independence. Richard A. Savage. LC 83-90321. (Illus.). 204p. 1983. lib. bdg. 16.95 (*0-912889-01-2*) Essex Pub Ltd.

Savage Summer. Constance O'Banyon. 448p. 1986. mass mkt. 3.95 (*0-8217-1922-X*, Zebra Kensgtn) Kensgtn Pub Corp.

***Savage Sun.** Axler. (Outlanders Ser.: No. 3). 1997. mass mkt. 5.50 (*0-373-63816-7*) Harlequin Bks.

Savage Surrender. Cassie Edwards. 352p. 1996. reprint ed. mass mkt., pap. text ed. 5.50 (*0-505-52093-1*, Love Spell) Dorchester Pub Co.

Savage Systems: Colonialism & Comparative Religion in Southern Africa. David Chidester. LC 96-12909. (Studies in Religion & Culture). 352p. 1996. 49.50 (*0-8139-1664-X*); pap. text ed. 19.50 (*0-8139-1667-4*) U Pr of Va.

***Savage Tears.** Cassie Edwards. 400p. (Orig.). 1997. mass mkt. 5.99 (*0-8439-4281-9*, Leisure Bks) Dorchester Pub Co.

Savage Thunder. Johanna Lindsey. 416p. (Orig.). 1989. mass mkt. 6.99 (*0-380-75300-6*) Avon.

Savage Thunder. large type ed. Johanna Lindsey. LC 90-38576. 490p. (Orig.). 1990. reprint ed. 19.95 (*1-56054-029-X*) Thorndike Pr.

***Savage Torment.** Cassie Edwards. 384p. 1997. mass mkt. 5.99 (*0-8217-5581-1*, Zebra Kensgtn) Kensgtn Pub Corp.

Savage Trail. James Persak. 1985. mass mkt. 2.25 (*0-8217-1594-1*, Zebra Kensgtn) Kensgtn Pub Corp.

Savage Trail: A Novel. Charles E. Friend. LC 92-33213. 128p. (Orig.). 1992. pap. 8.95 (*1-56474-043-9*) Fithian Pr.

Savage Vengeance. C. G. King. Date not set. pap. 4.99 (*0-7860-0208-5*) Kensgtn Pub Corp.

Savage Vengeance. Gary C. King. 1996. mass mkt. 5.99 (*0-7860-0251-4*, Pinncle Kensgtn) Kensgtn Pub Corp.

Savage View: Charles Savage, Mormon Pioneer Photographer. Bradley W. Richards. Ed. by Jean Chapman. LC 94-77983. (Illus.). 192p. 1995. 65.00 (*0-9621940-5-0*) C Mautz Pubng.

Savage View: Charles Savage, Pioneer Mormon Photographer. Bradley W. Richards. Ed. by Jean Chapman. LC 94-77983. (Illus.). 182p. 1995. pap. 29.95 (*0-9621940-6-9*) C Mautz Pubng.

***Savage Wars of Peace: England, Japan & the Malthusian Trap.** Alan Macfarlane. LC 96-28823. 1997. 59.95 (*0-631-18117-2*) Blackwell Pubs.

Savage Whispers. Cassie Edwards. 320p. 1996. reprint ed. mass mkt. 5.50 (*0-505-52142-3*, Love Spell) Dorchester Pub Co.

***Savage Wilderness.** Harold Coyle. LC 97-13257. 1997. 26.00 (*0-684-83433-2*) S&S Trade.

Savage Winter. Constance O'Banyon. 1988. mass mkt. 3.95 (*0-8217-2372-3*, Zebra Kensgtn) Kensgtn Pub Corp.

Savage Within: The Social History of British Anthropology, 1885-1945. Henrika Kuklick. (Illus.). 320p. (C). 1992. text ed. 59.95 (*0-521-41109-2*) Cambridge U Pr.

Savage Within: The Social History of British Anthropology, 1885-1945. Henrika Kuklick. (Illus.). 335p. (C). 1993. pap. text ed. 19.95 (*0-521-45739-4*) Cambridge U Pr.

Savagely Gross Jokes. Julius Alvin. 1995. mass mkt. 4.50 (*0-8217-5149-2*, Zebra Kensgtn) Kensgtn Pub Corp.

***Savages.** W. James Allred. 180p. (Orig.). 1997. mass mkt. 4.99 (*1-55197-930-6*, Pub. by Comnwlth Pub CN) Partners Pubs Grp.

Savages. Shirley Conran. Ed. by Julie Rubenstein. 1990. mass mkt. 5.99 (*0-671-72719-2*) PB.

Savages. James Douglas. (Irish Play Ser.). 1979. 6.95 (*0-912262-60-5*); pap. 2.95 (*0-912262-61-3*) Proscenium.

Savages. Christopher Hampton. 86p. 1974. pap. 8.95 (*0-571-10348-0*) Faber & Faber.

Savages. Joe Kane. 304p. 1996. pap. 13.00 (*0-679-74019-8*) Fodors Travel.

Savages. Joe Kane. LC 95-4258. (Illus.). 1995. 25.00 (*0-679-41191-7*) Knopf.

Savages & Civilization: Who Will Survive? Jack M. Weatherford. 320p. 1995. pap. 12.00 (*0-449-90957-3*) Fawcett.

Savages & Naturals: Black Portraits by White Writers in Modern American Literature. John Cooley. 208p. 1982. 32.50 (*0-87413-167-7*) U Delaware Pr.

Savages & Scientists see Smithsonian & the American Indian: Making a Moral Anthropology in Victorian America

Savages & Shakespeare Wallah: Two Films. James Ivory. (Illus.). 152p. (Orig.). 1986. pap. 7.95 (*0-936839-54-6*) Applause Theatre Bk Pubs.

Savage's Romance: The Poetry of Marianne Moore. John M. Slatin. LC 85-43250. 276p. 1986. 35.00 (*0-271-00425-8*) Pa St U Pr.

Savagism & Civilization: A Study of Indians & the American Mind. Roy H. Pearce. 1988. pap. 12.95 (*0-520-06227-2*) U CA Pr.

Savanna. Janice H. Giles. 1976. 24.95 (*0-8488-0502-X*) Amereon Ltd.

Savanna Ecology & Management, Australian Perspectives & Intercontinental Comparisons. Patricia A. Werner. (Journal of Biogeography Ser.: Vol. 17, Nos. 4-5). (Illus.). 232p. 1991. reprint ed. pap. 76.95 (*0-632-03199-9*) Blackwell Sci.

Savanna Plants, an Illustrated Guide. Shahina A. Ghazanfar. (Illus.). 225p. (Orig.). (C). 1990. pap. text ed. 20.50 (*0-333-45940-7*) Scholium Intl.

***Savannah.** Eugenia Price. 1997. mass mkt. 6.99 (*0-312-96232-0*) St Martin.

Savannah. Federal Writers' Project, Georgia. LC 73-3608. (American Guide Ser.). reprint ed. 12.50 (*0-404-57912-4*) AMS Pr.

Savannah: A History of Her People since 1733. Preston Russell & Barbara Hines. LC 91-45219. 1994. pap. 18.00 (*0-913720-81-X*) Beil.

Savannah: Her History As Seen by the Artist. Louise Y. Streed. 128p. 1996. 29.95 (*0-9648581-0-X*) Nostalgia GA.

Savannah: Proud As a Peacock. Savannah Junior Auxiliary Staff. Ed. by Carol Barker & Lynn Patrick. 320p. 1982. pap. 9.95 (*0-939114-45-3*) Savannah Jr Aux.

Savannah & the Lowcountry. Ray Ellis. 1995. 30.00 (*0-9641967-0-0*) Compass Publng.

An Asterisk (*) at the beginning of an entry indicates that the title is appearing in BIP for the first time.

Savannah Blue. large type ed. William Harrison. 528p. 1983. 25.99 (*0-7089-1015-7*) Ulverscroft.

Savannah Brown. Erma Winfield. Ed. by Renais Hill. LC 93-85868. 261p. 1994. pap. 12.95 (*1-55666-090-1*) Pubs Grp Toluca.

Savannah Collection: Favorite Recipes from Savannah Cooks. Martha G. Nesbit. (Illus.). 250p. 1986. bds. 10.95 (*0-9617126-0-0*) M Nesbit.

Savannah Entertains. Martha G. Nesbit. (Illus.). 1996. 29.95 (*0-941711-35-8*) Wyrick & Co.

Savannah Experience: An Artistic Expression of My Life in Savannah. Myrtle Jones. Ed. by Polly P. Stramm. (Illus.). 1995. 40.00 (*0-9650927-0-4*) M J King.

Savannah in Eighty-Eight Pictures: Sightseeing in 88 Pictures. Lisa D. Hoff. (Cities in Color Pictorial Guidebooks Ser.). 80p. (Orig.). 1994. pap. 10.95 (*0-9617959-8-0*) Cities in Color.

***Savannah in the Time of Peter Tondee: A Man, a Town & the Fight for Freedom in Colonial Georgia.** Carl Solana Weeks. 1997. 27.95 (*1-887714-13-8*) Summerhse Pr.

Savannah Monitors. J. Coborn. (Illus.). 1995. pap. text ed. 9.95 (*0-7938-0278-4*, RE113) TFH Pubns.

Savannah Purchase. Jane A. Hodge. 1979. pap. 1.95 (*0-449-24097-5*, Crest) Fawcett.

***Savannah Purchase.** large type ed. Jane Hodge. LC 96-44925. 1997. 21.95 (*0-7862-0937-2*) Thorndike Pr.

Savannah Revisited: History & Architecture. 4th ed. Mills Lane. (Illus.). 218p. 1994. 35.00 (*0-88322-021-0*) Beehive GA.

Savannah River Chiefdoms: Political Change in the Late Prehistoric Southeast. David G. Anderson. LC 93-48393. 488p. 1994. pap. text ed. 29.95 (*0-8173-0725-7*) U of Ala Pr.

Savannah River Plantations. Writers Program, Georgia Staff. LC 73-3610. (American Guide Ser.). reprint ed. 27.50 (*0-404-57913-2*) AMS Pr.

Savannah Safari: A Self-Guided Walking Adventure in Search of Architectural Animals. Polly Cooper & Emmeline Cooper. 16p. 1995. pap. text ed. 5.00 (*0-9647471-0-3*) Perry St Bks.

Savannah Sampler Cookbook. Margaret W. DeBolt & Emma Law. LC 78-1078. (Illus.). 298p. 1978. pap. 8.95 (*0-915442-49-3*) Donning Co.

Savannah Scarlett. Becky L. Weyrich. 352p. 1996. mass mkt. 5.50 (*0-8217-5528-5*, Zebra Kensgtn) Kensgtn Pub Corp.

Savannah Seasons: Food & Stories from Elizabeth on 37th. Elizabeth Terry & Alexis Terry. (Illus.). 352p. 1996. 30.00 (*0-385-48236-1*) Doubleday.

Savannah Spectres. Margaret W. DeBolt. Ed. by Robert Friedman. LC 82-23455. (Illus.). (Orig.). 1984. pap. 7.95 (*0-89865-201-4*) Donning Co.

Savannah Style. Junior League Staff. 1996. reprint ed. 18.95 (*0-9613411-0-6*) Jr Leag Savannah.

Savannah Trivia. Susan H. Albu & Elizabeth E. Arndt. 58p. 1993. pap. 7.95 (*0-9640597-0-3*) Albu & Arndt.

***Savannah's Passion: A Novel.** Thomas E. Campbell. 250p. (Orig.). (YA). (gr. 10 up). Date not set. pap. write for info. (*0-614-29751-6*) J M Emory.

Savannas: Biogeography & Geobotany. Monica Cole. 1986. text ed. 159.00 (*0-12-179520-9*) Acad Pr.

Savant. James Follett. 1996. mass mkt. 5.99 (*0-7493-2476-7*, Reed Trade) Buttrwrth-Heinemann.

Savantasse of Montparnasse. Allen Mandelbaum. (Illus.). 203p. 1987. 19.95 (*0-935296-70-0*); pap. 12.95 (*0-935296-71-9*) Sheep Meadow.

Savard - Lee International Symposium on Bath Smelting. Ed. by J. K. Brimacombe et al. (Illus.). 661p. 1992. 142.00 (*0-87339-191-8*, 1918) Minerals Metals.

Savatage - Gutter Ballet. (Play-It-Like-It-Is Guitar Ser.). pap. 17.95 (*0-89524-617-1*) Cherry Lane.

Savate. 3rd rev. ed. Bruce Tegner. (Illus.). 109p. 1983. pap. 7.00 (*0-87407-042-2*, T-2) Thor.

***Savayajnas.** J. Gonda. (Verhandelingen der Koninklijke Nederlandse Akademie van Wetenschappen, Afd. Letterkunde, Nieuwe Reeks Ser.: No. 71(2)). 462p. pap. 53.25 (*0-7204-8367-0*) Elsevier.

Save! Alan Silverstein's Guide to Mortgage Payment Tables. Alan Silverstein. 160p. 1993. pap. 9.95 (*0-7737-5562-4*) Genl Dist Srvs.

Save! Biographies of Greatness in Goalkeeping. Mark A. Newman. (Illus.). 200p. (Orig.). 1993. pap. text ed. 12.95 (*0-9636916-2-7*) Minds Eye Pr.

Save a Fortune: A Common Sense Guide to Building Wealth. Phillip Godwin. 209p. 1988. 12.95 (*0-945332-05-X*) Agora Inc MD.

Save a Fortune on Your Estate Taxes: Wealth Creation & Preservation. Barry Kaye. 1992. per. 17.00 (*1-55623-968-8*) Irwin Prof Pubng.

Save & Survive in a Difficult Economy: 429 Ways to Save Money. Sherri L. Eskesen. Ed. by James C. Aker. 130p. (Orig.). 1993. pap. 6.95 (*1-884745-42-3*) SLE Pubng.

Save Big Money on a New Car: A Common Sense Buyers Guide. Peter A. Ciullo. LC 90-91633. 64p. (Orig.). 1990. pap. 6.95 (*0-9626043-4-8*) Maradia Pr.

Save Brave Ted. Heather Maisner. (Illus.). 32p. (J). (ps-1). 1996. 14.99 (*1-56402-878-X*) Candlewick Pr.

Save Brave Ted. Heather Maisner. (Candlewick Gamebook Ser.). (Illus.). 32p. (J). (gr. k-2). 1997. reprint ed. pap. 5.99 (*0-7636-0136-5*) Candlewick Pr.

***Save $50,000 on Your New Home: Yes! You Can Be Your Own General Contractor.** William J. Molloy. LC 96-40985. 300p. 1997. pap. text ed. 18.95 (*0-471-15562-4*) Wiley.

***Save Halloween!** Stephanie S. Tolan. (J). Date not set. pap. 4.95 (*0-688-15497-2*, Beech Tree Bks) Morrow.

Save Halloween! Stephanie S. Tolan. LC 93-10635. 176p. (J). (gr. 4 up). 1993. 15.00 (*0-688-12168-3*, Morrow Junior) Morrow.

Save Jerusalem. Michael D. Evans. 323p. 1995. pap. 8.00 (*0-935199-00-4*) Bedfrd Books.

Save Lives! Report Recommendations & Community Action Guide of the Join Together Public Policy Panel on Underage Access to Alcohol. (Illus.). 56p. (Orig.). (C). 1994. pap. text ed. 20.00 (*0-7881-0778-X*) DIANE Pub.

Save Me a Place at Forest Lawn. Lorees Yerby. 1963. pap. 3.25 (*0-8222-0992-6*) Dramatists Play.

Save Me, Joe Louis. Madison Smartt Bell. LC 93-233. 1993. 23.95 (*0-15-179432-4*) HarBrace.

Save Me, Joe Louis. Madison Smartt Bell. (Contemporary American Fiction Ser.). 368p. 1994. pap. 10.95 (*0-14-023633-3*, Penguin Bks) Viking Penguin.

Save Money & Save the Earth: How Your Business Can Do Both. Kathi A. Haas. 160p. 1992. pap. 8.95 (*0-9624798-4-5*); lib. bdg. 14.95 (*0-9624798-3-7*) Mktg Methods Pr.

Save More So You Can Spend More: Hundreds of Tips to Save Thousands of Dollars. Anahid. 168p. (Orig.). 1996. pap. 14.95 (*0-918751-47-0*) Delta Pr.

Save My Rainforest. Monica Zak. Tr. by Nancy Schimmel. LC 91-40179. (Illus.). 32p. (J). 1992. pap. 14.95 (*0-912078-94-4*) Volcano Pr.

***Save Our Earth: A Musical Story.** Connie Anderson. Tr. by Lindsay Anderson. (Illus.). 28p. (Orig.). (SPA.). (J). (ps-5). 1997. write for info. incl. audio (*0-614-30093-2*) Iguana Prodns.

Save Our Land, Save Our Towns: A Plan for Pennsylvania. Thomas Hylton. LC 94-74070. (Illus.). 128p. (Orig.). 1995. pap. 24.95 (*1-879441-44-6*) RB Bks.

Save Our Schools: 66 Things You Can Do to Improve Your School Without Spending an Extra Penny. Mary S. Miller. LC 92-56416. 1993. pap. 8.00 (*0-06-250733-8*) Harper SF.

***Save Our Tree.** (Young Dragon Readers 2 Ser.). (J). 1995. pap. text ed. write for info. (*962-359-533-6*) Addison-Wesley.

Save Queen of Sheba. Louise Moeri. 112p. 1982. pap. 2.95 (*0-380-58529-4*, Flare) Avon.

Save Queen of Sheba. Louise Moeri. 112p. (J). 1990. pap. 3.50 (*0-380-71154-0*, Camelot) Avon.

Save Queen of Sheba. Louise Moeri. 128p. (J). (gr. 3-7). 1994. pap. 3.99 (*0-14-037148-6*) Puffin Bks.

Save Room for Dessert! Sensational Sweets: A Serious Cookbook. Selene Ganek. (Illus.). 178p. 1986. reprint ed. 11.95 (*0-9616186-0-4*) S Ganek.

Save Sam. A. Brown. (J). 4.99 (*1-85792-021-X*, Pub. by Christian Focus UK) Spring Arbor Dist.

Save Save Save Save. Nichola Manning. 1986. 14.95 (*0-930090-27-6*); pap. 7.95 (*0-930090-26-8*) Applezaba.

Save Save Save Save. deluxe limited ed. Nichola Manning. 1986. Signed & Lettered. 20.00 (*0-930090-25-X*) Applezaba.

Save Sex. 2nd ed. George B. Eager. Orig. Title: Safe Sex?. (Illus.). 29p. (YA). (gr. 6-12). 1993. pap. 3.00 (*1-879224-07-0*) Mailbox.

Save That Dog! Liz Palika. LC 96-30038. 1997. 14.95 (*0-87605-737-7*) Macmillan.

Save That House. A. J. Hupp. LC 83-72006. (Illus.). 88p. (Orig.). 1984. pap. 8.95 (*0-9611744-0-4*) D J Pub.

Save the Animals. Wendy Lewis. (Illus.). 32p. (J). (gr. k-2). 1992. 15.95 (*0-237-51153-3*, Pub. by Evans Bros Ltd UK) Trafalgar.

Save the Animals. Annalisa Suid. (Illus.). 48p. (J). (gr. 1-3). 1993. pap. 9.95 (*1-878279-46-7*) Monday Morning Bks.

Save the Animals, Save the Earth. L. Skiera. 80p. 1993. teacher ed., pap. 19.95 (*0-7935-2895-X*) H Leonard.

Save the Babies: American Public Health Reform & the Prevention of Infant Mortality, 1850-1929. Richard A. Meckel. LC 89-15389. (Henry E. Sigerist Series in the History of Medicine). (Illus.). 360p. 1990. text ed. 49.95 (*0-8018-3879-7*) Johns Hopkins.

Save the Beloved Country. Alan Paton. 336p. 1989. 22.50 (*0-684-19127-X*) S&S Trade.

Save the Children & Yourself! Guide to a Healthier Future Generation by Avoiding Toxins in Today's Foods & Waters. Nikolaus J. Smeh. (Health Ser.). 44p. 1996. pap. 12.95 (*0-9637755-2-9*) Alliance VA.

Save the Democracy: Winning the Ultimate Bowl. Dinesh Shah. (Save the Democracy Ser.: Vol. II). 200p. 1995. 18.00 (*0-9634764-7-5*) TwentyTwenty Bks.

Save the Dolphins. Michael Donoghue & Annie Wheeler. (Illus.). 160p. 1990. 24.95 (*0-924486-07-4*) Sheridan.

Save the Earth: An Action Handbook for Kids. Betty Miles. LC 90-46514. (Illus.). 128p. (Orig.). (J). (gr. 5 up). 1991. pap. 6.95 (*0-679-81731-X*) Knopf Bks Yng Read.

***Save the Earth Maze Book.** Roger Moreau. 1996. pap. text ed. 59.50 (*0-8069-9625-0*) Sterling.

Save the Earth Maze Book. Roger Moreau. (Illus.). 64p. (J). 1996. pap. 5.95 (*0-8069-9456-8*) Sterling.

Save the Everglades! Judith B. Stamper. LC 92-18085. (Stories of America Ser.). (Illus.). 56p. (J). (gr. 2-5). 1992. lib. bdg. 24.26 (*0-8114-7219-1*) Raintree Steck-V.

Save the Family Promise Book. deluxe ed. Marilyn Hickey. 137p. 1991. 14.95 (*1-56441-020-X*) M Hickey Min.

Save the Family, Save the Child. Vincent J. Fontana. 320p. 1992. pap. 5.99 (*0-451-17362-7*, Ment) NAL-Dutton.

Save the Goldfish. 1988. pap. 3.50 (*0-19-421914-3*) OUP.

Save the Haunted House. Robert F. Wedell. (Rolf the Green Ghost Ser.: Bk. 3). (Illus.). 124p. (Orig.). (J). 1991. pap. 6.95 (*0-9625221-2-0*) Milrob Pr.

Save the Inch! Aron Breslow. 2.00 (*0-918430-02-X*) Happy History.

Save the Last Dance for Me. Dyan Sheldon. (YA). (gr. 5 up). 1995. pap. 3.95 (*0-8167-3794-0*) Troll Communs.

Save the Last Dance for Me: The Musical Legacy of the Drifters 1953-1992. Tony Allan & Faye Treadwell. Ed. by Thomas Schultheiss. LC 92-81113. (Rock & Roll Remembrances Ser.: No. 11). (Illus.). 180p. 1993. lib. bdg. 45.00 (*1-56075-028-6*) Popular Culture.

Save the Macaw. Jill Bailey. LC 91-19871. (Save Our Species Ser.). (Illus.). 48p. (J). (gr. 3-7). 1992. pap. 4.95 (*0-8114-6549-7*); lib. bdg. 24.26 (*0-8114-2712-9*) Raintree Steck-V.

Save the Males. Kenneth Wetcher et al. 176p. (Orig.). 1991. pap. 8.95 (*0-929162-42-0*) PIA Pr.

Save the Males: Why Men Are Mistreated, Misdiagnosed, & Misunderstood. Kenneth Wetcher et al. 176p. 1991. 14.95 (*0-929162-48-X*) PIA Pr.

Save the Past for the Future II: Report for the Working Conference. Society for American Archaeology Staff. 64p. 1996. pap. 3.00 (*0-932839-13-4*) Soc Am Arch.

Save the Rain Forests. Allan Fowler. LC 96-16972. (Rookie Read-About Science Ser.). 32p. (J). 1996. lib. bdg. 17.30 (*0-516-20029-1*) Childrens.

***Save the Rain Forests.** Allan Fowler. (Rookie Read about Science Ser.). 32p. (J). 1997. pap. 4.95 (*0-516-26084-7*) Childrens.

Save the Rainforest. (SPA.). (J). 1992. pap. 1.95 (*0-590-45830-2*) Scholastic Inc.

***Save the Rivers, Rain Forests & Ravioli.** Jim Davis. LC 96-86674. (Illus.). 80p. 1997. 4.95 (*0-8362-2876-6*) Andrews & McMeel.

Save the Snow Leopard. Jill Bailey. LC 90-45917. (Save Our Species Ser.). (Illus.). 48p. (J). (gr. 3-7). 1991. pap. 4.95 (*0-8114-6557-8*); lib. bdg. 24.26 (*0-8114-2709-9*) Raintree Steck-V.

Save the Tiger. Jill Bailey. LC 89-48770. (Save Our Species Ser.). (Illus.). 48p. (J). (gr. 3-7). 1990. pap. 4.95 (*0-8114-6551-9*); lib. bdg. 24.26 (*0-8114-2703-X*) Raintree Steck-V.

Save the Turkey! Francine Pascal. (Sweet Valley Kids Super Special Ser.: Vol. 4). (Illus.). 112p. (Orig.). (J). (gr. k-3). 1995. lib. bdg. 3.99 (*0-553-48286-6*, Sweet Valley) BDD Bks Young Read.

Save the Unicorns. Shelagh Jones. (Illus.). 140p. (J). (gr. 4-7). 1989. 11.95 (*0-947962-48-4*, Pub. by Childrens Pr IE) Irish Bks Media.

Save the Unicorns! Francine Pascal. (Unicorn Club Ser.: No. 1). 176p. (J). (gr. 4-7). 1994. pap. 3.50 (*0-553-48202-5*) Bantam.

Save the Whales! Richard Roberts. (Illus.). (Orig.). 1991. pap. 10.95 (*0-942380-12-6*) Vernal Equinox.

Save Thirty Percent on Your Casualty Insurance: Yet Improve Coverage. Robert A. Wilson. Ed. by Irving L. Blackman. (Special Report Ser.: No. 130). 52p. 1985. pap. 23.00 (*0-916181-22-7*) Blackman Kallick Bartelstein.

Save Thousands of Dollars Buying Your New Car. Dick Krol. LC 86-91246. (Illus.). 288p. (Orig.). 1986. pap. 19.95 (*0-938879-00-6*) RMK Pub.

Save Thousands on Your Wedding. 153p. (Orig.). 1988. pap. 9.95 (*0-945739-00-1*) Hart Pub VA.

Save Thousands When You Buy or Sell Your Home. John D. Bowers. 132p. (Orig.). (C). 1974. pap. 8.95 (*0-685-02679-5*) J D Bowers.

***Save Time & Money Through Chemistry.** Kenneth P. Carpenter. LC 96-90852. (Illus.). x, 261p. (Orig.). 1997. pap. 24.95 (*0-9655667-1-4*) Useful Chemistry.

***Save Time, & Peace of Mind: Just Cook It Ahead.** Bettie L. Howard. Ed. by Willa Gray. (Illus.). 220p. 1997. spiral bd. 9.95 (*1-881636-12-7*) Windsor Hse Pub Grp.

Save Tomorrow for the Children. E. Paul Torrance et al. 234p. (Orig.). 1987. pap. 14.95 (*0-943456-22-3*) Bearly Ltd.

Save Your Baby! The Hygienic Care of Children. Herbert M. Shelton. 467p. 1993. reprint ed. spiral bd. 20.00 (*0-7873-0782-3*) Hlth Research.

Save Your Back. H. Duane Saunders & Michael S. Melnick. Ed. by Robin Saunders & Beth Solheim. (Illus.). (Orig.). 1981. pap. text ed. 5.00 (*0-9616461-4-4*) Saunders Grp.

Save Your Business a Bundle: 202 Ways to Cut Costs & Boost Profits Now-For Companies of Any Size. Daniel M. Kehrer. 272p. 1994. 22.00 (*0-671-78893-0*) S&S Trade.

Save Your Business Book: A Survival Manual for Small Business Owners. John D. Goldhammer. LC 92-32074. 235p. 22.95 (*0-02-912115-9*, Free Press) Free Pr.

Save Your Hands! Lauriann Greene. (Illus.). (Orig.). 1995. text ed. 17.95 (*1-883195-03-9*) Infinity WA.

Save Your Heart Wine Guide. Frank Jones. LC 96-9455. 288p. 1996. 22.95 (*0-312-14729-5*) St Martin.

Save Your Home: How to Protect Your Home & Property from Foreclosure. 2nd ed. Steven L. Porter. LC 90-30371. (Illus.). 160p. 1990. pap. 16.00 (*0-941599-14-0*) Piccadilly Bks.

Save Your Horse Handbook. Ed. by Bill Weikel. 1979. pap. 4.95 (*0-87505-386-6*) Borden.

Save Your Knees. James Fox & Rick Mcguire. 288p. (Orig.). 1988. pap. 11.95 (*0-440-50011-7*, Dell Trade Pbks) Dell.

Save Your License: A Driver's Survival Guide. Gene Mason. LC 78-2218. (Illus.). 150p. 1978. text ed. 14.95 (*0-87364-103-5*) Paladin Pr.

Save-Your-Life Defense Handbook. Matthew Braun. (Illus.). 1977. 12.95 (*0-8159-5711-4*) Devin.

Save Your Money, Save Your Face: What Every Cosmetics Buyer Needs to Know. Elaine Brumberg. LC 84-4134. 368p. reprint ed. pap. 104.90 (*0-8357-4247-4*, 2037036) Bks Demand.

Save Your Skin: With Vital Oils. Liz Earle. (Illus.). 192p. 1993. pap. 15.95 (*0-09-177172-2*, Pub. by Ebury Pr UK) Trafalgar.

Save Yourself from Breast Cancer: Life Choices That Can Help You Reduce the Odds. Robert M. Kradjian. (Illus.). 272p. (Orig.). 1994. pap. 12.00 (*0-425-14390-2*, Berkley Trade) Berkley Pub.

Save Yourself Save Your Nation Save the World. John White & C. B. White. 96p. 1994. per. 10.00 (*0-9620798-7-1*) ScanFan Pubns.

Saved. Edward Bond. 123p. 1983. pap. 5.95 (*0-87129-099-5*, S64) Dramatic Pub.

Saved. Edward Bond. (Methuen Modern Plays Ser.). 123p. (C). 1988. pap. 9.95 (*0-413-31360-3*, A0254, Pub. by Methuen UK) Heinemann.

***Saved! A Guide to Success with Your Shelter Dog.** Myrna L. Papurt. LC 97-7744. 1997. pap. 9.95 (*0-7641-0062-9*) Barron.

Saved: The Gospel Speeches of Bob Dylan. Ed. by Clinton Heylin. 116p. (Orig.). 1990. pap. 5.95 (*0-937815-38-1*) Hanuman Bks.

Saved by a Saint. Barbara Cartland. (Camfield Ser.: No. 136). 176p. (Orig.). 1994. mass mkt. 3.99 (*0-515-11508-8*) Jove Pubns.

Saved by a Saint. large type ed. Barbara Cartland. LC 95-52454. (Orig.). 1996. 19.95 (*0-7862-0646-2*) Thorndike Pr.

***Saved by Development: Preserving Environmental Areas, Farmland & Historic Landmarks with Transfer of Development Rights.** Rick Pruetz. LC 97-70105. (Illus.). 600p. (Orig.). 1997. pap. 37.00 (*0-9658314-0-X*) Arje Pr.

Saved by Fire. G. D. Lehmann. (Asha's Adventures Ser.). (Illus.). 125p. (J). (gr. 4-8). 1992. pap. 4.95 (*0-87508-441-9*) Chr Lit.

Saved by Grace. Anthony A. Hoekema. 1994. pap. 18.00 (*0-8028-0857-3*) Eerdmans.

Saved by Grace...for Service. Robert L. Sumner. 1979. 8.95 (*0-87398-797-7*) Sword of Lord.

Saved by Hope: Essays in Honor of Richard C. Oudersluys. Ed. by James I. Cook. LC 78-5416. 198p. reprint ed. 56.50 (*0-8357-9132-7*, 2016060) Bks Demand.

Saved by Mr. F. Scott Fitzgerald. Allen Woodman. 128p. (Orig.). (C). 1997. 19.95 (*0-942979-42-7*); pap. 9.95 (*0-942979-41-9*) Livingston U Pr.

***Saved by Soup.** Judith Barrett. Date not set. write for info. (*0-688-15300-3*) Morrow.

***Saved by the Bell.** 24p. (J). 1997. pap. write for info. (*0-7814-3025-9*, Chariot Bks) Chariot Victor.

Saved by the Bell. 56p. otabind 12.95 (*0-7935-4986-8*, 00313023) H Leonard.

Saved by the Bell. Barbara Davoll. (Illus.). 24p. (J). 1988. audio 11.99 (*0-89693-614-7*, 3-1614, Victor Bks) Chariot Victor.

Saved by the Bell. Barbara Davoll. (Christopher Churchmouse Classics Ser.). (Illus.). 24p. (J). 1988. 8.99 (*0-89693-403-9*, 6-1403, Victor Bks) Chariot Victor.

***Saved by the Judge.** DeLoris Crain. (Judge Ser.). 132p. (Orig.). 1995. pap. 8.99 (*0-9627099-4-8*) Zephyr Pub Corp.

Saved by the Lamp. (Giant Carousel Book). 12p. (J). (ps-1). 1995. pap. 6.98 (*1-57082-243-3*) Mouse Works.

Saved by the Light. Dannion Brinkley. 224p. 1995. mass mkt. 5.99 (*0-06-100889-3*, Harp PBks) HarpC.

Saved by the Light. large type ed. Dannion Brinkley & Paul Perry. 1994. 24.95 (*1-56895-119-1*) Wheeler Pub.

Saved from Drowning. Scott Heim. Ed. by Michael Hathaway. 45p. (Orig.). 1993. pap. 10.00 (*0-943795-24-9*) Chiron Rev.

Saved from Oblivion: Interdependency Theory in the First Half of the 20th Century: A Study on the Causality Between War & Complex Interdependence. Jaap De Wilde. 298p. 1991. text ed. 59.95 (*1-85521-141-6*, Pub. by Dartmth Pub UK) Ashgate Pub Co.

Saved from Obscurity. Tom Mardirosian. 1989. pap. 5.25 (*0-8222-0991-8*) Dramatists Play.

Saved from Satanism: The Life & Conversion of a Sorcerer. 1991. pap. 2.95 (*0-89981-124-8*) Eastern Orthodox.

Saved from the Sea: The Story of Life-Saving Services on the East Anglian Coast. Robert Malster. 296p. 1990. 42.00 (*0-900963-32-8*, Pub. by T Dalton UK) St Mut.

Saved from the Very Start: Growing up in New Jersey Projects. Kaye P. Brooks. 102p. (YA). 1995. pap. 3.95 (*1-886663-04-1*) Chatman Pub.

Saved in Eternity: The Assurance of Our Salvation. D. Martyn Lloyd-Jones. LC 87-70457. (John Seventeen Ser.). 192p. 1988. 14.99 (*0-89107-448-1*) Crossway Bks.

Saved on Monday. Vivian D. Gunderson. (J). (gr. k-8). 1964. pap. 3.25 (*0-915374-14-5*, 14-5) Rapids Christian.

***Saved Sex: Chastity - Because You're Worth It.** Molly Kelly. LC 97-7817. 200p. (YA). 1997. pap. 10.99 (*0-89283-996-1*, Charis) Servant.

***Saved Sex: Chastity--Because You're Worth It.** Molly Kelly. LC 97-7817. (YA). 1997. write for info. (*1-56077-516-5*) Ctr Learning.

***Saved, Single & Sanctified.** Cynthia T. Pugh. 50p. (Orig.). 1996. pap. 5.00 (*1-57502-356-3*, PO1159) Morris Pubng.

***Saved to Serve: The Treasure in Earthen Vessels.** John B. Martin. Ed. by J. Boyd Nicholson. 60p. 1994. 4.95 (*1-882701-09-7*) Uplook Min.

Saved? What Do You Mean Saved? A Journalist's Report on Salvation. Joe Ortiz. Ed. by Mark D. Feldstein. (Illus.). 95p. (Orig.). (C). 1983. pap. 4.95 (*0-912695-00-5*) GBM Bks.

Saved Without a Doubt. John MacArthur, Jr. (MacArthur Study Ser.). 192p. (Orig.). 1992. pap. 9.99 (*1-56476-017-0*, 6-3017, Victor Bks) Chariot Victor.

Saveiz-Vous? Francois Cavanna. 316p. (FRE.). 1990. pap. 16.95 (*0-7859-2138-9*, 2070382354) Fr & Eur.

Savidge Brothers, Sandhills Aviators. Duane Hutchinson. (Illus.). 332p. 1982. 19.95 (*0-934988-06-4*); pap. 9.95 (*0-934988-14-5*) Foun Bks.

Savile Correspondence. Henry Savile. LC 17-3795. (Camden Society, London. Publications, First Ser.: No. 71). reprint ed. 75.00 (*0-404-50171-0*) AMS Pr.

***Saving: Good or Bad? A Pilot Study on Public Attitudes Toward Saving, Investment, & Competitiveness.** John Immerwahr & Daniel Yankelovich. 15p. (Orig.). 1989. pap. 6.00 (*1-889483-25-7*) Public Agenda.

S

An Asterisk (*) at the beginning of an entry indicates that the title is appearing in BIP for the first time.

Saving a Continent: Towards a Sustainable Future. David Smith. (Illus.). 216p. 1995. pap. 29.95 (*0-86840-214-1*, Pub. by New South Wales Univ Pr AT) Intl Spec Bk.

Saving a Fallen World. Michael Bentley. 1992. pap. 13.99 (*0-85234-300-0*, Pub. by Evangelical Pr) Presby & Reformed.

Saving a Generation: A Twentieth Century Fund Paper. Blanche Bernstein. 63p. (Orig.). (C). 1986. pap. text ed. 7.50 (*0-87078-206-1*) TCFP-PPP.

***Saving Across the World: Puzzles & Policies.** Klaus Schmidt-Hebbel & Luis Serven. LC 96-37903. (Discussion Paper Ser.: No. 354). 176p. 1997. pap. 10.95 (*0-8213-3852-8*, 13852) World Bank.

Saving All the Parts: Reconciling Economics & the Endangered Species Act. Rocky Barker. LC 93-4640. 220p. 1993. pap. 15.95 (*1-55963-201-1*); text ed. 30.00 (*1-55963-202-X*) Island Pr.

Saving American Birds: T. Gilbert Pearson & the Founding of the Audubon Movement. Oliver H. Orr, Jr. (Illus.). 272p. 1992. lib. bdg. 39.95 (*0-8130-1129-9*) U Press Fla.

Saving America's Countryside: A Guide to Rural Conservation. Samuel N. Stokes et al. LC 88-19941. (Illus.). 320p. 1989. pap. 18.95 (*0-8018-3696-4*); text ed. 47.50 (*0-8018-3695-6*) Johns Hopkins.

***Saving America's Countryside: A Guide to Rural Conservation.** 2nd ed. National Trust for Historic Preservation Staff et al. LC 96-45398. 1997. write for info. (*0-8018-5547-0*) Johns Hopkins.

***Saving America's Countryside: A Guide to Rural Conservation.** 2nd ed. Samuel N. Stokes et al. LC 96-45398. 1997. pap. write for info. (*0-8018-5548-9*) Johns Hopkins.

Saving America's Wildlife. Thomas R. Dunlap. 238p. 1988. pap. text ed. 15.95 (*0-691-00613-X*) Princeton U Pr.

Saving & Credit for Development. 384p. 1992. 35.00 (*92-1-104379-4*, E.92.II.A.1) UN.

Saving & Investment in a Global Economy. Barry P. Bosworth. 188p. (C). 1993. 34.95 (*0-8157-1044-5*); pap. 14.95 (*0-8157-1043-7*) Brookings.

Saving & Spending. Jeffrey P. Mark. 1980. lib. bdg. 59.95 (*0-8490-3083-8*) Gordon Pr.

Saving & the Accumulation of Wealth: Essays on Italian Household & Government Saving Behavior. Ed. by Albert Ando et al. LC 93-34758. 432p. (C). 1994. text ed. 49.95 (*0-521-45208-2*) Cambridge U Pr.

Saving Beauty: Further Studies in Hopkins. Michael E. Allsopp & David A. Downes. LC 93-41179. (Origins of Modernism Ser.). 368p. 1994. text ed. 59.00 (*0-8153-0834-5*, H1587) Garland.

Saving Behavior & the Asset Price "Bubble" in Japan: Analytical Studies. Ed. by Ulrich Baumgartner et al. LC 95-10141. (Occasional Paper Ser.: No. 124). 86p. 1995. pap. 15.00 (*1-55775-462-4*) Intl Monetary.

Saving Belief: A Critique of Physicalism. Lynne R. Baker. 192p. 1988. pap. text ed. 14.95 (*0-691-02050-7*) Princeton U Pr.

***Saving Belief: A Critique of Physicalism.** Lynne R. Baker. LC 87-25926. reprint ed. pap. 54.20 (*0-608-04631-0*, 2065318) Bks Demand.

Saving Belief: A Discussion of Essentials. Austin Farrer. Ed. by Susan Howatch. (Library of Anglican Spirituality Ser.). 152p. 1994. reprint ed. pap. 9.95 (*0-8192-1625-9*) Morehouse Pub.

***Saving Biological Diversity: Economic Incentives.** OECD Staff. 126p. (Orig.). 1996. pap. 39.00 (*92-64-14807-8*, Pub. by Org for Econ FR) OECD.

Saving California's Coast: Army Engineers at Oceanside & Humboldt Bay. Susan P. O'Hara & Gregory Graves. (Western Lands & Waters Ser.: No. 16). (Illus.). 278p. 1991. 38.50 (*0-87062-201-3*) A H Clark.

Saving Casey. Karen M. Coombs. 192p. (Orig.). (J). 1992. pap. 3.50 (*0-380-76634-5*, Camelot) Avon.

Saving Challenge of Religion. Budhananda. 272p. (Orig.). 1982. pap. 4.95 (*0-87481-567-3*) Vedanta Pr.

Saving Children: A Guide to Injury Prevention. Ed. by Modena Wilson et al. (Illus.). 264p. 1991. 39.95 (*0-19-506115-2*) OUP.

Saving Children: Diary of a Buchenwald Survivor & Rescuer. Jack Werber & William B. Helmreich. 129p. 1995. text ed. 29.95 (*1-56000-250-6*) Transaction Pubs.

Saving Children at Risk: Poverty & Disabilities. Travis Thompson & Susan C. Hupp. (Focus Editions Ser.: Vol. 131). (Illus.). 230p. 1991. text ed. 54.00 (*0-8039-3967-1*); pap. text ed. 24.95 (*0-8039-3968-X*) Sage.

***Saving Children at Risk: Poverty & Disabilities.** Ed. by Travis Thompson & Susan C. Hupp. LC 91-10630. (Sage Focus Editions Ser.: No. 131). (Illus.). 203p. 1992. reprint ed. pap. 57.90 (*0-608-04322-2*, 2065102) Bks Demand.

Saving China: Canadian Missionaries in the Middle Kingdom, 1888-1959. Alvyn J. Austin. 413p. reprint ed. pap. 117.80 (*0-7837-0604-9*, 2040952) Bks Demand.

Saving Cities, Saving Money: Environmental Strategies That Work. John Hart. 116p. (Orig.). 1992. pap. 15.95 (*0-932857-08-6*) Ag Access.

Saving Endangered Animals. Virginia B. Silverstein et al. LC 92-1765. (Better Earth Ser.). (Illus.). 128p. (YA). (gr. 6 up). 1993. lib. bdg. 18.95 (*0-89490-402-7*) Enslow Pubs.

Saving Endangered Birds: Ensuring a Future in the Wild. Thane Maynard. (Cincinnati Zoo Bks.). (Illus.). 56p. (J). (gr. 5-7). 1993. 15.95 (*0-531-15260-X*); lib. bdg. 22.70 (*0-531-11094-X*) Watts.

Saving Endangered Mammals: A Field Guide to Some of the Earth's Rarest Animals. Thane Maynard. LC 92-14439. (Cincinnati Zoo Bks.). 1992. 15.95 (*0-531-15253-7*) Watts.

Saving Endangered Mammals: A Field Guide to Some of the Earth's Rarest Animals. Thane Maynard. (Illus.). 64p. (J). (gr. 3-8). 1992. lib. bdg. 22.70 (*0-531-11076-1*) Watts.

***Saving Endangered Species: The New NOAHS.** Elaine Pascoe. LC 96-43531. (New Explorers Ser.). (Illus.). 48p. (YA). (gr. 5 up). 1997. lib. bdg. 16.95 (*1-56711-230-7*) Blackbirch.

Saving Energy. Dineen. (What about...? Ser.). (J). 1995. lib. bdg. 21.40 (*0-8172-5534-6*) Raintree Steck-V.

Saving Energy in U. S. Transporation. (Illus.). 266p. (Orig.). (C). 1995. pap. text ed. 50.00 (*0-7881-2497-8*) DIANE Pub.

Saving Energy in United States Transportation. 1996. lib. bdg. 253.99 (*0-8490-6005-2*) Gordon Pr.

***Saving Energy in United States Transportation.** 1997. lib. bdg. 251.95 (*0-8490-7684-6*) Gordon Pr.

Saving Face. Nancy Lane. write for info. (*0-318-58989-3*) World Pr Ltd.

Saving Face: The Politics of Shame & Guilt. Stuart Schneiderman. LC 95-22998. 336p. 1996. 25.00 (*0-679-40969-6*) Knopf.

Saving Face Through Surrender & Grace: A First Step Guide for Codependents. Evelyn Leite. 24p. (Orig.). 1988. pap. 3.95 (*0-945485-03-4*) Comm Intervention.

***Saving Faces: Photographic Portraits & Musings.** Jane Rosemont. (Illus.). v, 75p. (Orig.). 1996. pap. 18.95 (*0-9654500-7-4*) Wom-in-the-Moon.

Saving Farmland. John Kolesar & Jaye Scholl. 1975. 4.25 (*0-943136-17-2*) Ctr Analysis Public Issues.

Saving for America's Economic Future: Parables & Policies. Laurence S. Seidman. LC 89-24219. 232p. (C). 1990. pap. text ed. 28.95 (*0-87332-579-6*) M E Sharpe.

Saving for America's Economic Future: Parables & Policies. Laurence S. Seidman. LC 89-24219. 232p. (C). (gr. 13). 1990. 57.95 (*0-87332-578-8*) M E Sharpe.

Saving for College: It's Just What You Need to Know. Marc Robinson & Time-Life Books Editors. LC 96-34250. (Your Money Matters Ser.). 40p. 1996. 4.95 (*0-7835-4793-5*) Time-Life.

Saving for Economic Recovery in Africa. Ed. by J. H. Frimpong-Ansah & Barbara Ingham. LC 92-13771. 210p. (C). 1992. text ed. 50.00 (*0-435-08075-X*, 08075) Heinemann.

Saving for Prosperity: The U. S. Saving Rate. B. Douglas Bernheim. 112p. 1990. 18.95 (*0-87078-312-2*); pap. 8.95 (*0-87078-313-0*) TCFP-PPP.

Saving for Retirement: A Complete Guide with Work Forms. Clifford R. Simms & John B. Moore. 1994. pap. 18.95 (*0-533-11082-3*) Vantage.

Saving Free Trade: A Pragmatic Approach. Robert Z. Lawrence & Robert E. Litan. LC 86-14705. 132p. 1986. 29.95 (*0-8157-5178-8*); pap. 11.95 (*0-8157-5177-X*) Brookings.

Saving Grace. Jennifer Fulton. 224p. 1993. pap. 9.95 (*1-56280-051-5*) Naiad Pr.

Saving Grace. Carole Mortimer. (Presents Ser.). 1993. pap. 2.89 (*0-373-11543-1*, 1-11543-5) Harlequin Bks.

Saving Grace. Lee Smith. LC 94-43904. 273p. (YA). 1995. 22.95 (*0-399-14050-6*, Putnam) Putnam Pub Group.

Saving Grace. Lee Smith. 288p. 1996. pap. 11.00 (*0-345-40333-9*) Ballantine.

Saving Grace. large type ed. Julie Garwood. LC 93-32414. 1993. lib. bdg. 22.95 (*0-8161-5890-8*, GK Hall) Thorndike Pr.

Saving Grace. Julie Garwood. Ed. by Linda Marrow. 416p. 1994. reprint ed. mass mkt. 6.99 (*0-671-87011-4*, Pocket Star Bks) PB.

Saving Graces. David Robinson. (Illus.). 128p. 1995. pap. 14.95 (*0-393-31333-6*, Norton Paperbks) Norton.

Saving Graces: Sojourns of a Backyard Biologist. Roger B. Swain. 1991. 17.95 (*0-316-82471-2*) Little.

***Saving Graces: The Inspirational Writings of Laura Ingalls Wilder.** Ed. by Stephen Hines. Date not set. 19.99 (*0-8054-0148-2*) Broadman.

***Saving Grandma.** Frank Schaeffer. 368p. 1997. pap. 12.00 (*0-425-15776-8*, Berkley Trade) Berkley Pub.

***Saving Historic Roads: Design & Policy Guidelines.** Paul D. Marriott. LC 97-14443. 224p. 1997. 44.95 (*0-471-19762-9*) Wiley.

Saving History. Fanny Howe. (Sun & Moon Classics Ser.: No. 27). 232p. 1990. pap. 12.95 (*1-55713-100-7*) Sun & Moon CA.

Saving in Postwar Japan. Tuvia Blumenthal. LC 78-119071. (East Asian Monographs: No. 35). 129p. 1970. pap. 11.00 (*0-674-78997-0*) HUP.

Saving Jessica. Lurlene McDaniel. (Seasonal Inspiration Ser.: No. 3). 160p. (J). 1996. mass mkt. 4.50 (*0-553-56721-7*) Bantam.

Saving Life of Christ. W. Ian Thomas. 143p. 1989. pap. 4.99 (*0-310-33262-1*, 10908S) Zondervan.

Saving Life of Christ & the Mystery of Godliness, 2 vols. Ian W. Thomas. 208p. 1988. pap. 10.99 (*0-310-33261-3*, 10910P) Zondervan.

Saving Lives. Brian McKibbin et al. (C). 1991. text ed. 59.95 (*0-255-36269-2*, Pub. by Inst Economic Affairs UK) St Mut.

Saving Money Any Way You Can: How to Become a Frugal Family. Mike Yorkey. 284p. 1994. pap. 10.99 (*0-89283-864-7*, Vine Bks) Servant.

Saving Money, Saving Lives: The Documented Benefits of Federal Health & Safety Protections. John Canham-Clyne et al. 40p. 1995. pap. text ed. 15.00 (*0-937188-88-3*) Pub Citizen Inc.

***Saving Money Sensibly.** unabridged ed. Paul E. Hadinger. 220p. (Orig.). 1997. pap. text ed. 22.95 (*0-9655026-1-9*) THINC Corp.

Saving Nature's Legacy: Protecting & Restoring Biodiversity. Allen Cooperrider & Reed F. Nosee. 1994. text ed. 48.00 (*1-55963-247-X*) Island Pr.

Saving Nature's Legacy: Protecting & Restoring Biodiversity. Allen Cooperrider & Reed F. Noss. 1994. pap. text ed. 27.50 (*1-55963-248-8*) Island Pr.

***Saving of a Nation at Risk: A Dissertation on the Destruction of a Nation from Within, the Raping of the Constitution & the Lynching of America by the Supreme Court of the United States.** Mat Arashiro. LC 96-90509. 300p. (Orig.). 1997. pap. 12.95 (*0-533-12082-9*) Vantage.

***Saving of Arma Armadillo.** John Harms, II. LC 96-86419. (Illus.). 32p. (J). (gr. 3-7). 1996. 18.95 (*0-9653871-1-9*) Frederick Pr.

Saving Oiled Seabirds. rev. ed. Anne S. Williams. Ed. by Meryl L. Kane. LC 87-70495. (Illus.). 50p. 1987. pap. 20.00 (*0-89364-057-3*, 841-44470) Am Petroleum.

***Saving "Old Glory"** Robert J. Goldstein. (C). 1996. pap. text ed. 21.00 (*0-8133-3300-8*) Westview.

Saving on a Shoestring. Barbara O'Neill. 224p. 1994. pap. 15.95 (*0-7931-1118-8*, 568009-01) Dearborn Finan.

Saving on a Shoestring. Barbara O'Neill. 1995. pap. text ed. 34.95 incl. cd-rom (*0-7931-1708-9*, 1800-4301) Dearborn Trade.

Saving on a Shoestring: How to Cut Expenses, Reduce Debt, Stash More Cash. Barbara O'Neil. 352p. 1996. reprint ed. mass mkt. 6.99 (*0-425-15344-4*) Berkley Pub.

Saving Our Ancient Forests. Seth Zuckerman. (Illus.). 118p. (Orig.). (YA). 1991. pap. 5.95 (*0-9626072-9-0*) Living Planet Pr.

Saving Our Animal Friends. National Geographic Society Staff. (Illus.). 32p. (J). 1996. pap. text ed. 4.95 (*0-7922-3602-5*) Natl Geog.

Saving Our Animal Friends see Books for Young Explorers

***Saving Our Architectural Heritage: The Conservation of Historic Stone Structures: Report of the Dahlem Workshop on Saving Our Architectural Heritage: The Conservation of Historic Stone Structures, Berlin, March 3-8, 1996.** Norbert S. Baer & Rolf Snethlage. LC 96-49091. (Dahlem Workshop Reports). 1997. write for info. (*0-471-96526-X*) Wiley.

Saving Our Children from Poverty: What the United States Can Learn from France. Barbara R. Bergmann. 184p. (C). 1996. text ed. 34.95 (*0-87154-114-9*) Russell Sage.

***Saving Our Cities: You Can Change Your City for God.** Happy Caldwell. 1997. pap. text ed. 6.99 (*0-89274-698-X*) Harrison Hse.

Saving Our Planet: A Study Guide. Alice Sheff. (Thematic Units Ser.). 1991. pap. text ed. 20.95 (*0-88122-562-2*) Lrn Links.

Saving Our Planet: Challenges & Hopes. Kostafa K. Tolba. LC 92-14657. (Illus.). 296p. (ENG, FRE & SPA.). (gr. 13). 1992. English version. pap. text ed. 29.95 (*0-412-47370-4*, A9452) Chapman & Hall.

Saving Our Planet: Challenges & Hopes. Kostafa K. Tolba. LC 92-14657. (Illus.). 296p. (ENG, FRE & SPA.). (gr. 13). 1992. Spanish version. pap. text ed. 41.95 (*0-412-47390-9*, A9460); French version. pap. text ed. 41.95 (*0-412-47380-1*, A9456) Chapman & Hall.

Saving Our Soil: Solutions for Sustaining Earth's Vital Resource. James Glanz. LC 95-10257. (Illus.). 192p. 1995. pap. 15.95 (*1-55566-136-X*) Johnson Bks.

Saving Our Sons: Raising Black Children in a Turbulent World. Marita Golden. 208p. 1996. pap. 10.95 (*0-385-47303-6*, Anchor NY) Doubleday.

Saving Our Wetlands & Their Wildlife. Karen Liptak. LC 91-4682. (First Bks.). (Illus.). 64p. (J). (gr. 5-8). 1991. lib. bdg. 21.00 (*0-531-20092-2*) Watts.

Saving Our Wetlands & Their Wildlife. Karen Liptak. (First Bks.). (Illus.). 64p. (J). (gr. 5-8). 1992. pap. 6.95 (*0-531-15648-6*) Watts.

Saving Owen's Toad. Juanita Havill. LC 94-8794. (Illus.). 128p. (J). (gr. 3-6). 1994. 14.95 (*0-7868-0029-1*); lib. bdg. 14.89 (*0-7868-2024-1*) Hyprn Child.

Saving Plants & Jobs: Union-Management Negotiations in the Context of Threatened Plant Closing. Paul F. Gerhart. LC 87-10527. 107p. 1987. pap. text ed. 10.00 (*0-88099-046-5*) W E Upjohn.

Saving Presence: Exploring the Ministry of Jesus in His Church. 2nd ed. David M. Knight. (Spiritual Growth Through Matthew's Gospel Ser.: Vol. 4). 247p. 1985. reprint ed. pap. 6.95 (*0-942971-07-8*) His Way.

Saving Public Housing from Demolition or Sale: A Description of Relevant Laws. 34p. 1988. 37.00 (*0-685-30170-2*, 43,830) NCLS Inc.

Saving Quetico-Superior: A Land Set Apart. rev. ed. R. Newell Searle. LC 77-21883. (Illus.). xv, 275p. 1979. reprint ed. 11.50 (*0-87351-116-6*); reprint ed. pap. 7.95 (*0-87351-140-9*) Minn Hist.

Saving Rain. Elsie Webber. (Illus.). 220p. 1989. 17.95 (*0-8283-1911-1*) Branden Pub Co.

Saving Remnant: Religion & the Settling of New England. Cedric B. Cowing. 320p. 1995. 19.95 (*0-252-06440-2*); text ed. 39.95 (*0-252-02138-X*) U of Ill Pr.

Saving Remnants: Feeling Jewish in America. Sara Bershtel & Allen Graubard. LC 93-1852. 1993. reprint ed. pap. 15.95 (*0-520-08512-4*) U CA Pr.

Saving San Antonio: The Precarious Preservation of a Heritage. Lewis F. Fisher. LC 96-9582. (Illus.). 544p. (C). 1996. 35.00 (*0-89672-372-0*) Tex Tech Univ Pr.

Saving Seeds: The Gardner's Guide to Growing & Storing Vegetable & Flower Seeds. Marc Rogers. Ed. by Ben Watson. LC 90-50353. 176p. 1990. pap. 12.95 (*0-88266-634-7*) Storey Comm Inc.

***Saving Serenity.** Jenna Jones. 256p. 1998. mass mkt. 4.99 (*0-8217-5851-9*, Zebra Kensgtn) Kensgtn Pub Corp.

***Saving Shiloh.** Naylor. (J). Date not set. mass mkt. 4.50 (*0-689-81461-5*) S&S Childrens.

***Saving Shiloh.** Phyllis R. Naylor. LC 96-37373. (J). 1997. 15.00 (*0-689-81460-7*, Atheneum S&S) S&S Trade.

Saving Signs, Wondrous Words. David Philippart. LC 96-41455. 140p. (Orig.). 1996. pap. 10.00 (*1-56854-103-1*, SAVING) Liturgy Tr Pubns.

Saving Special Places: A Centennial History of the Trustees of Reservations: Pioneer of the Land Trust Movement. Gordon Abbott, Jr. (Illus.). 352p. 1994. 35.00 (*0-938864-20-3*); pap. 20.00 (*0-938864-19-X*) Ipswich Pr.

Saving St. Germ. Carol M. Dukes. 304p. 1995. pap. 10.95 (*0-14-023913-8*, Penguin Bks) Viking Penguin.

***Saving Susannah.** Beverly Bird. 1997. mass mkt. 3.99 (*0-373-07814-5*, 1-07814-6) Silhouette.

Saving Sweetness. Diane Stanley. LC 95-10621. (Illus.). 32p. (J). (ps-3). 1996. 15.95 (*0-399-22645-1*, Putnam) Putnam Pub Group.

Saving the Animals. Stonehouse. 1981. 21.95 (*0-02-614750-5*) Macmillan.

Saving the Appearances: A Study in Idolatry. 2nd ed. Owen Barfield. LC 88-5563. 191p. 1988. pap. 13.95 (*0-8195-6205-X*, Wesleyan Univ Pr) U Pr of New Eng.

Saving the Atmosphere: International Law, Developing Countries & Air Pollution. Frank Biermann. LC 95-9226. (European University Studies; Ser. 2, Law: Vol. 1737). 174p. 1995. pap. 37.95 (*3-631-48537-9*) P Lang Pubng.

"Saving the Badlands" Adventure: Buffalo Biff & Farley's Raiders. Joe Loesch. Ed. by Cheryl J. Hutchinson. (Backyard Adventures Ser.: Vol. 2). (Illus.). 56p. (Orig.). (J). (gr. 1-5). 1995. pap. 14.95 incl. audio (*1-887729-02-X*) Toy Box Prods.

***Saving the Badlands Adventure Vol. 2: Buffalo Biff & Farley's Raiders.** Joe Loesch. Ed. by Cheryl J. Hutchinson. (Backyard Adventures Ser.). (Illus.). 54p. (Orig.). (J). (gr. 1-5). 1995. pap. 16.95 incl. audio compact disk (*1-887729-03-8*) Toy Box Prods.

Saving the Best of Texas: A Partnership Approach to Conservation. Richard C. Bartlett. LC 94-43734. (Illus.). 240p. (Orig.). 1995. 40.00 (*0-292-70834-3*) U of Tex Pr.

Saving the Best of Texas: A Partnership Approach to Conservation. Richard C. Bartlett. LC 94-43734. (Illus.). 240p. (Orig.). 1995. pap. 19.95 (*0-292-70835-1*) U of Tex Pr.

Saving the Constitution from the Courts. William Gangi. LC 94-43089. 352p. 1995. 45.00 (*0-8061-2732-5*) U of Okla Pr.

Saving the Earth: The History of a Middle Class Millenarian Movement. Steven M. Gelber & Martin L. Cook. 1990. 47.50 (*0-520-06762-2*) U CA Pr.

Saving the Environment. Kathlyn Gay. (Impact Bks.). (Illus.). 112p. (YA). (gr. 9-12). 1996. lib. bdg. 22.70 (*0-531-11263-2*) Watts.

Saving the Forests: A Rabbit's Story. Janet Riehecky. LC 89-28122. (Discovery World Ser.). (Illus.). 32p. (J). (ps-2). 1990. lib. bdg. 21.36 (*0-89565-561-6*) Childs World.

Saving the Forests: What Will It Take? Alan T. Durning. 70p. (Orig.). 1993. pap. 5.00 (*1-878071-18-1*) Worldwatch Inst.

Saving the Great Stone Face. Frances Hancock. LC 83-22961. (Illus.). 1984. 14.95 (*0-914659-02-2*) Phoenix Pub.

Saving the Great Swamp: The People, the Power Brokers & an Urban Wilderness. Cam Cavanaugh. LC 78-8132. (Illus.). 1978. 11.95 (*0-914366-11-4*) Columbia Pub.

Saving the Hidden Treasure: The Evolution of Groundwater Policy. Henry C. Kenski. (Contemporary Issues in Natural Resources & Environmental Policy Ser.). 174p. (C). 1991. reprint ed. text ed. 22.95 (*0-8138-1682-3*) Iowa St U Pr.

***Saving the Medicare System with Medical Savings Accounts.** 29p. 1995. pap. 10.00 (*1-56808-065-4*, 199) Natl Ctr Pol.

Saving the Mediterranean: The Politics of International Environmental Cooperation. Peter M. Haas. 288p. 1990. text ed. 49.50 (*0-231-07012-8*) Col U Pr.

Saving the Mediterranean: The Politics of International Environmental Cooperation. Peter M. Haas. 288p. 1992. pap. text ed. 17.50 (*0-231-07013-6*) Col U Pr.

Saving the Middle Class, the American Way. J. S. Norris. LC 96-90086. (Orig.). 1996. pap. 8.95 (*0-533-11886-7*) Vantage.

Saving the Neighborhood: You Can Fight Developers & Win. National Park Service Staff. (Illus.). 428p. (Orig.). 1995. pap. text ed. 16.95 (*0-471-14420-7*) Wiley.

Saving the Oceans. Ed. by Joseph MacInnis. 1992. 50.00 (*1-55013-416-7*) U of Toronto Pr.

Saving the Oceans. Ed. by Joseph MacInnis. (Illus.). 180p. 1996. 40.00 (*1-55209-076-0*) Firefly Bks Ltd.

Saving the Peregrine Falcon. Caroline Arnold. LC 84-15576. (Nature Watch Bks.). (Illus.). 48p. (J). (gr. 2-5). 1985. pap. 7.95 (*0-87614-523-3*, Carolrhoda) Lerner Group.

Saving the Planet: How to Shape an Environmentally Sustainable Global Economy. Lester R. Brown et al. (Illus.). 224p. 1991. pap. 8.95 (*0-393-30823-5*) Norton.

Saving the Planet with Pesticides & Plastic: The Environmental Triumph of High-Yield Farming. Dennis T. Avery. (Illus.). 432p. (Orig.). 1995. pap. text ed. 19.95 (*1-55813-051-9*) Hudson Instit IN.

Saving the Plenty: Pickling & Preserving. Richard Humphrey. LC 85-51151. (Antique Eating Ser.: Vol. 14). 126p. (Orig.). 1986. pap. 4.95 (*0-9610602-3-9*) Teaparty Bks.

Saving the Queen. William F. Buckley, Jr. 288p. 1981. pap. 3.95 (*0-380-55111-X*) Avon.

***Saving the Queen.** William F. Buckley, Jr. LC 96-51926. 320p. 1997. reprint ed. pap. 10.95 (*1-888952-27-X*) Cumberland Hse.

Saving the Rain Forest - Why? Shirley Jones. 36p. (YA). (gr. 7-12). 1995. pap. 6.95 (*1-57515-040-9*) PPI Pubng.

Saving the River: The St. Croix River Association. James T. Dunn. (Illus.). 56p. (Orig.). 1986. pap. 7.50 (*0-9617292-0-1*) St Croix River Assn.

S

An Asterisk (*) at the beginning of an entry indicates that the title is appearing in BIP for the first time.

Saving the Savings & Loan: The American Thrift Industry & the Texas Experience, 1950-1988. M. Manfred Fabritius. LC 88-32942. 173p. 1989. text ed. 49.95 (*0-275-93161-7*, C3161, Praeger Pubs) Greenwood.

Saving the Seed. Renee Vellve. 1991. 19.95 (*1-85383-150-6*, Pub. by Erthscan Pubns UK) Island Pr.

Saving the Text: Literature-Derrida-Philosophy. Geoffrey H. Hartman. LC 80-21748. 216p. (Orig.). 1995. pap. text ed. 14.95 (*0-8018-2453-2*) Johns Hopkins.

Saving the Tropical Forests. Judith Gradwohl & Russell Greenberg. LC 88-31267. (Illus.). 207p. (C). 1988. text ed. 24.95 (*0-933280-81-5*) Island Pr.

***Saving the Village.** Kathleen Ragan. Date not set. write for info. (*0-393-04598-6*) Norton.

Saving the Young Men of Vienna. David Kirby. LC 87-40148. (Brittingham Prize in Poetry, 1987 Ser.). (C). 1987. 17.95 (*0-299-11220-9*); pap. 10.95 (*0-299-11224-1*) U of Wis Pr.

Saving Thousands on Your Mortgage. Dome Financial Services Staff. Ed. by Nick Picchione. 256p. (Orig.). 1990. pap. 7.95 (*0-02-028345-8*) Macmillan.

Saving Water from the Ground Up: A Pilot Study of Irrigation Scheduling on Four California Fields. Gail Richardson. LC 85-60576. 69p. reprint ed. pap. 25.00 (*0-7837-0335-X*, 2040654) Bks Demand.

Saving Water in a Desert City. William E. Martin et al. LC 83-43263. 127p. reprint ed. pap. 36.20 (*0-7837-2180-3*, 2042518) Bks Demand.

Saving Water in the Home & Garden. Jonathan Erickson. 1993. pap. 12.95 (*0-8306-4413-X*) McGraw-Hill Prof.

Saving Wildlife: A Century of Conservation. Ed. by Donald Goddard. LC 94-22874. 1995. 49.50 (*0-8109-3674-7*) Abrams.

Saving Work: Feminist Practices of Theological Education. Rebecca S. Chopp. LC 94-36761. 160p. (Orig.). 1995. pap. 13.00 (*0-664-25539-6*) Westminster John Knox.

Saving Your Business: How to Survive Chapter 11 Bankruptcy & Successfully Reorganize Your Company. Suzanne Caplan. LC 92-11279. 1992. pap. 17.95 (*0-13-832684-3*) P-H.

Saving Your Library: A Guide to Getting, Using & Keeping the Power You Need. Sally G. Reed. LC 91-51207. 144p. 1992. pap. 26.50 (*0-89950-719-0*) McFarland & Co.

Saving Your Life With Sunlight. (Alternative Medicine Ser.). 1992. lib. bdg. 88.00 (*0-8490-5413-3*) Gordon Pr.

Saving Your Marriage Before It Starts: A Marriage Curriculum for Engaged, About-to-Be-Engaged, & the Very Newly Married. Les Parrott, III. 48p. 1995. teacher ed. 7.99 (*0-310-20448-8*); teacher ed. 159.99 incl. vdisk (*0-310-20451-8*) Zondervan.

Saving Your Marriage Before It Starts: Seven Questions to Ask Before (& After) You Marry. 2nd ed. Iii L. Parrott. 1995. audio 14.99 (*0-310-49248-3*) Zondervan.

Saving Your Marriage Before it Starts: Seven Questions to Ask Before & after You Marry. 2nd ed. Les Parrott, III. 208p. 1995. 15.99 (*0-310-49240-8*) Zondervan.

Saving Your Marriage Before It Starts, a Workbook for Women: Seven Questions to Ask Before (& After) You Marry. 2nd ed. Les Parrott, III. 48p. 1995. wbk. ed., pap. 4.99 (*0-310-48741-2*) Zondervan.

Saving Your Marriage Before It Starts, for Men: Seven Questions to Ask Before (& After) You Marry. 2nd ed. Les Parrott, III. 48p. 1995. wbk. ed., pap. 4.99 (*0-310-48731-5*) Zondervan.

Saving Your Skin: Early Detection, Treatment & Prevention of Melanoma & Other Skin Cancers. Barney Kenet & Patricia Lawler-Kenet. LC 94-908. (Illus.). 224p. (Orig.). 1994. pap. 14.95 (*1-56858-009-6*) FWEW.

Saving Your Skin: Secrets of Healthy Skin & Hair. Eric A. Mein. (Natural Remedies for Common Ailments & Conditions Ser.). 72p. (Orig.). 1991. pap. 4.95 (*0-87604-262-0*, 349) ARE Pr.

***Saving Your Time, Your Money, Your Energy, Your Steps, Your Life.** Barbara D. Isaacson. 100p. (Orig.). 1997. reprint ed. pap. 24.95 (*0-9630456-7-9*) S Moskowitz.

***Saving Your Time Your Money Your Energy Your Steps Your Life.** Barbara D. Isaacson. 100p. 1997. reprint ed. 29.95 (*0-9630456-6-0*) S Moskowitz.

Saving Yourself from the Disease-Care Crises. Walt Stoll. (Illus.). 210p. (Orig.). 1996. pap. 9.95 (*0-9653171-0-2*) Sunrise Hlth.

Savings. Linda Hogan. LC 88-11819. 74p. (Orig.). 1988. pap. 10.95 (*0-918273-41-2*) Coffee Hse.

Savings & Bequests. Toshiaki Tachibanaki. 460p. 1994. text ed. 65.00 (*0-472-10498-5*) U of Mich Pr.

Savings & Investment in Farm Household: Analysis Using Life Cycles Models. Euan Phimister. 100p. 1993. 54.95 (*1-85628-596-0*, Pub. by Avebury Pub UK) Ashgate Pub Co.

Savings & Investment Requirements for the Resumption of Growth in Latin America. Ed. by Edmar L. Bacha. 200p. (C). 1993. pap. text ed. 15.95 (*0-940602-61-X*) IADB.

Savings & Loam. Ralph McInerny. (Worldwide Library Mystery: No. 91). 1992. mass mkt. 3.99 (*0-373-26091-1*, 1-26091-8) Harlequin Bks.

Savings & Loan Associations: An AICPA Audit & Accounting Guide. 4th rev. ed. American Institute of Certified Public Accountants Staff. LC 87-161844. 246p. reprint ed. pap. 70.20 (*0-7837-1922-1*, 2042130) Bks Demand.

Savings & Loan Bailout: Valiant Rescue or Hysterical Reaction? Hans F. Sennholz. 57p. 1989. pap. 4.95 (*0-910884-23-4*) Libertarian Press.

Savings & Loan Crisis. Richard J. Cebula-Hung. 128p. (C). 1992. pap. text ed. 13.59 (*0-8403-7620-0*) Kendall-Hunt.

Savings & Loan Crisis: An Annotated Bibliography. Compiled by Pat L. Talley. LC 93-12910. (Bibliographies & Indexes in Economics & Economic History Ser.: No. 14). 192p. 1993. text ed. 59.95 (*0-313-28833-X*, GR8833, Greenwood Pr) Greenwood.

Savings & Loan Industry: Current Problems & Possible Solutions. Walter J. Woerheide. LC 83-13686. (Illus.). xviii, 216p. 1984. text ed. 55.00 (*0-89930-038-3*, WOL/, Quorum Bks) Greenwood.

Savings & Withdrawal Tables for Retirement Accounts. Financial Publishing Co. Staff. 130p. 1982. pap. 15.00 (*0-87600-148-7*) Finan Pub.

Savings Bank Life Insurance. Donald Johnson. (C). 1963. 10.95 (*0-256-00647-4*) Irwin.

Savings Bank of Baltimore, 1818-1866: A Historical & Analytical Study. Peter L. Payne & Lance E. Davis. LC 75-41778. (Companies & Men: Business Enterprises in America Ser.). (Illus.). 1976. reprint ed. 23.95 (*0-405-08093-X*) Ayer.

Savings Behavior: Theory, International Evidence & Policy Implications. Ed. by Erkki Koscela & Jouko Paunio. 224p. 1992. pap. 38.95 (*0-631-18266-7*) Blackwell Pubs.

Savings Institutions: Mergers, Acquisitions & Conversions. Julie L. Williams. 750p. 1988. 98.00 (*0-317-01810-8*) NY Law Pub.

Savings Mobilization. WCCU (World Council of Credit Unions, Inc.) Staff. 160p. 1989. per. 10.00 (*0-8403-5606-4*) Kendall-Hunt.

Savio: A Study Guide for Parents, Priests & Educators. Joseph Aubry. Tr. by Joe Boenzi from ITA. LC 79-50460. 69p. (Orig.). 1979. pap. 2.50 (*0-89944-038-X*) Salesiana Pubs.

***Savion!** Savion Glover. (J). Date not set. write for info. (*0-688-15629-0*, Morrow Junior); lib. bdg. write for info. (*0-688-15630-4*, Morrow Junior) Morrow.

Savior. Carlos Morton. LC 93-15619. 1993. pap. 6.00 (*0-88734-271-X*) Players Pr.

Savior Is Born. Brian Gleeson. LC 92-4577. (Greatest Stories Ever Told Ser.). (Illus.). 40p. (J). 1992. pap. 14.95 (*0-88708-283-1*, Rabbit) S&S Childrens.

Savior is Born. Brian Gleeson. (J). 1996. 19.95 (*0-689-81098-9*) S&S Childrens.

Savior Is Born: Three Beautiful Adaptations of Artwork by Francis Hook (Counted Cross-Stitch) Jean D. Crowther. 1984. 5.98 (*0-88290-257-1*) Horizon Utah.

***Savior Is Here-Listen & Cheer: Christmas.** Carolyn Bergt. 1997. pap. text ed. 22.00 (*0-570-05519-9*) Concordia.

Savior of Fire. Robert B. Boardman. 294p. (Orig.). 1991. pap. 5.95 (*1-878398-11-3*) Blue Note Pubns.

Savior or Servant? Putting Government in Its Place. David W. Hall. LC 95-82126. 399p. (Orig.). 1996. 23.95 (*0-9650367-1-5*); pap. 18.95 (*0-9650367-0-7*) Covenant Fnd.

Savior Partage: Semiotique et Theorie de la Connaissance Chez Marcel Proust. Jacques Fontanille. LC 87-30929. (Actes Semiotiques Ser.: 4). 227p. (Orig.). (FRE.). (C). 1987. pap. 53.00 (*90-272-2265-7*) Benjamins North Am.

Savior-Sinless, Yet Tempted. A. J. Pollock. 16p. pap. 0.50 (*0-88172-158-1*) Believers Bkshelf.

Saviors of Mankind. William R. Van Buskirk. LC 71-86790. (Essay Index Reprint Ser.). 1977. 35.95 (*0-8369-1432-5*) Ayer.

Saviors of the Earth? The Politics & Religion of the Enviromental Movement. Michael S. Coffman. (Orig.). 1994. pap. 11.99 (*1-881273-27-5*) Northfield Pub.

Saviors of the Islamic Spirit, Set, Nos. I & II. Abul H. Nadwi. 820p. (C). 1995. text ed. 39.95 (*0-934905-65-7*) Kazi Pubns.

Savior's Touch. Charles Stanley. 560p. 1996. 29.99 (*0-310-21037-2*) Zondervan.

Saviour. R. Kent Hughes. LC 95-23642. (Illus.). 48p. 1995. 14.99 (*0-89107-853-3*) Crossway Bks.

Saviour God: Comparative Studies in the Concept of Salvation Presented to Edwin Oliver James. Ed. by Samuel G. Brandon. LC 80-14924. xxii, 242p. 1980. reprint ed. text ed. 55.00 (*0-313-22416-1*, BRSG, Greenwood Pr) Greenwood.

Saviour of the World. Benjamin B. Warfield. 280p. 1991. text ed. 16.99 (*0-85151-593-2*) Banner of Truth.

Saviour of the World: The Humanity of Christ in the Light of the Everlasting Gospel. Jack Sequeira. 1996. pap. 11.99 (*0-8163-1342-3*) Pacific Pr Pub Assn.

Savitri: A Legend & a Symbol. Sri Aurobindo. LC 94-72970. 826p. 1995. pap. 24.95 (*0-941524-80-9*) Lotus Light.

Savitri: A Legend & a Symbol. Sri Aurobindo. 816p. 1988. 19.00 (*81-7058-017-X*); pap. 15.00 (*81-7058-340-3*) Aurobindo Assn.

Savitri: A Legend & a Symbol. Sri Aurobindo. (Life Companion Library). 1978. 19.00 (*0-89744-933-9*); pap. 15.00 (*0-89744-934-7*) Auromere.

Savitri: A Legend & a Symbol, 2 vols., Set. Sri Aurobindo. (Life Companion Library). 1978. lib. bdg. 30.00 (*0-89744-953-3*) Auromere.

Savitri: A Tale of Ancient India. Aaron Shepard. Ed. by Judith Mathews. LC 91-16591. (Illus.). 38p. (J). (gr. 1-6). 1992. lib. bdg. 16.95 (*0-8075-7251-9*) A Whitman.

Savitri & Satyavan. Savitri. (Illus.). (J). (gr. 1-9). 1979. pap. 2.75 (*0-89744-160-5*) Auromere.

Savitri Unveiled. Mehdi Imam. 1981. 10.00 (*0-8364-0768-7*, Pub. by Motilal Banarsidass II) S Asia.

Savoir Accorder le Verbe. Henri Briet. 94p. (FRE.). 1986. pap. 19.95 (*0-8288-3353-2*) Fr & Eur.

Savoir Commander dans les Restaurants du Monde Entier. Giuseppe Tome. 401p. (ENG, FRE, ITA & SPA.). 1992. pap. 49.95 (*0-7859-1011-5*, 2855655455) Fr & Eur.

Savoir Dire: Cours de Phonetique et de Prononciation. Diane M. Dansereau. LC 89-82765. 240p. (FRE.). (C). 1990. pap. text ed. 46.36 (*0-669-20996-1*); Text with 7 cassettes. pap. text ed. 61.96 (*0-669-21830-8*); Instr.'s manual. teacher ed. 45.16 (*0-669-20997-X*); Demotape. 2.66 (*0-669-20999-6*); Cassettes. audio 31.16 (*0-669-20998-8*) HM College Div.

Savoir-Faire: Great Traditions in French Elegance. Francois Baudot & Pierre Rival. (Illus.). 240p. 1995. 65.00 (*2-08-013552-X*, Pub. by Flammarion FR) Abbeville Pr.

Savoir-Faire En Assurance et En Reassurance. Witherby & Co. Ltd. Staff. 163p. (C). 1977. 80.00 (*0-900886-18-8*, Pub. by Witherby & Co UK) St Mut.

Savoir Magrir: Dictionnaire des Aliments et des Calories. Jeanlouis Yaich. 369p. (FRE.). 1989. pap. 39.95 (*0-7859-8108-X*, 2856165206) Fr & Eur.

Savoir Rire: The Humorists' Guide to France. Intro. by Robert Wechsler. LC 88-15972. (Humorists' Guides Ser.). (Illus.). 208p. (Orig.). 1988. pap. 10.95 (*0-945774-00-1*, PN6231.F743S28) Catbird Pr.

Savoir Vivre en Francais: Culture et Communication. Howard L. Nostrand et al. 196p. 1988. Net. student ed., pap. 17.00 (*0-471-82725-8*); Net. pap. text ed. 33.50 (*0-471-82724-X*) Wiley.

Savoir Vivre en Francais: Culture et Communication. Howard L. Nostrand et al. 1988. audio 81.50 (*0-471-84571-X*) Wiley.

***Savon.** Ginette Anfousse. (Jiji et Pichou Ser.). (Illus.). 24p. (FRE.). (J). (ps up). 1996. pap. 4.95 (*2-89021-023-5*, Pub. by Les Editions CN) Firefly Bks Ltd.

Savon. Francis Ponge. 140p. (FRE.). 1992. pap. 10.95 (*0-7859-1390-4*, 2070725537) Fr & Eur.

Savonarola, His Life & Times. William R. Clark. LC 83-45654. reprint ed. 34.50 (*0-404-19804-X*) AMS Pr.

Savonarola: or The Unarmed Prophet: An Historical Drama. Augusto Croce. 72p. (Orig.). 1995. pap. 7.50 (*0-9635358-2-X*) ARS Historica.

Savonius Rotor Construction. Josef A. Kozlowski. (Illus.). 54p. 1977. English, 54pp. pap. 9.50 (*0-86619-062-7*) Vols Tech Asst.

Savor of the Salt. Ione Martens. LC 94-70089. 144p. 1994. pap. 9.95 (*0-9637515-1-4*) Dageforde Pub.

Savor Superior. Judy Kreag. LC 93-79453. 224p. 1993. 14.95 (*0-913383-29-5*) McClanahan Pub.

Savor the Brandywine Valley. Wilmington, DE Junior League Staff. LC 93-70327. 1993. 16.95 (*0-87197-363-4*) Favorite Recipes.

Savor the Flavor of Oregon. (Illus.). 319p. 1990. spiral bd. 17.95 (*0-9607976-1-0*) Jr League Eugene.

***Savor the Flavor of the Edina Country Club.** Ed. by Heather King. 290p. 1996. 21.25 (*0-9654991-0-3*) Edina Country Club.

Savor the Inns of Kansas: Recipes from Kansas Bed & Breakfast Inns. Tracy Winters & Phyllis Winters. LC 93-61573. (Illus.). 96p. (Orig.). 1993. pap. 9.95 (*0-9625329-9-1*) Winters IN.

***Savoring Grace: A Year at Peace House.** Rose W. Tillemans. Ed. by Carl Koch. 104p. (Orig.). 1997. pap. 12.95 (*0-88489-428-2*) St Marys.

Savoring San Diego: An Evolving Regional Cuisine. University of California San Diego Medical Center Auxiliary Staff. LC 95-60027. (Illus.). 254p. 1995. 24.95 (*0-9636158-0-7*) UCSD Med Ctr.

Savoring Spices & Herbs: Recipe Secrets of Flavor, Aroma, & Color. Julie Sahni. 412p. 1996. 25.00 (*0-688-06976-2*) Morrow.

Savoring the Day: Recipes & Remedies to Enhance Your Natural Rhythms. Judith B. Hurley. 352p. 1997. 27.50 (*0-688-14292-3*) Morrow.

Savoring the Past: The French Kitchen & Table from 1300 to 1789. Barbara K. Wheaton. (Illus.). 368p. (Orig.). 1996. 40.00 (*0-684-81566-4*, Touchstone Bks); pap. 16.00 (*0-684-81857-4*, Touchstone Bks) S&S Trade.

Savoring the Seasons. Diana Shaw. 1992. 20.00 (*0-517-58269-4*) Random Hse Value.

Savoring the Seasons of the Northern Heartland. Beth Dooley & Lucia Watson. LC 94-9629. (Cooks American Ser.: Vol. 14). 1994. 25.00 (*0-679-41175-5*) Knopf.

Savoring the Southwest. Roswell Symphony Guild, Board of Directors Staff. LC 83-62041. (Illus.). 332p. 1994. 18.95 (*0-9612466-0-X*) Roswell Symphony Guild.

Savoring the Wild. Falcon Press Staff. LC 95-61747. 96p. 1989. pap. text ed. 7.95 (*1-56044-414-2*) Falcon Pr MT.

Savoring the Wine Country: Recipes from the Finest Restaurants of Northern California's Wine Regions. Ed. by Meesha Halm & Dayna Macy. LC 94-30073. 144p. 1995. pap. 20.00 (*0-00-638287-8*) Collins SF.

Savory Flavors. Tilak W. Nagodawithana. (Illus.). 480p. (C). 1995. write for info. (*0-9646172-3-4*) Esteekay Assocs.

***Savory Scottish Recipes.** Julie J. McDonald. 140p. 1996. 5.95 (*1-57216-026-8*) Penfield.

Savory Soups. Ellen Ratner. LC 88-70045. (Allergy Kitchen Ser.: Vol. 1). (Illus.). 128p. 1988. pap. 7.95 (*0-9616708-7-8*) Allergy Pubns.

Savory Soups & Salads: Great-Tasting Recipes in Minutes. Frank R. Blenn. (Healthy Selects Cookbook Ser.). (Illus.). 80p. 1996. pap. 8.95 (*0-945448-41-4*) Am Diabetes.

Savory Southwest: Prize-Winning Recipes from the Arizona Republic. Judy H. Walker. LC 89-63748. (Illus.). 144p. (Orig.). 1990. spiral bd. 12.95 (*0-87358-501-1*) Northland AZ.

Savory Stews. Jacques Burdick. LC 94-27242. 1995. 23.00 (*0-449-90545-4*) Fawcett.

Savory Suppers & Fashionable Feasts: Dining in Victorian America. Susan Williams. LC 95-4391. (Illus.). 368p. 1996. pap. 30.00 (*0-87049-912-2*) U of Tenn Pr.

Savory Way. Deborah Madison. 464p. 1990. 27.50 (*0-553-05780-4*) Bantam.

***Savory Way Recipeasel.** Deborah Madison. 1997. 14.95 (*0-8118-1619-2*) Chronicle Bks.

Savour of Life. Arnold Bennett. LC 74-17048. (Collected Works of Arnold Bennett: Vol. 72). 1977. reprint ed. 26.95 (*0-518-19153-2*) Ayer.

Savour of Salt: A Henry Salt Anthology. George Hendrick & Willene Hendrick. 208p. (C). 1989. 100.00 (*0-900001-30-5*, Pub. by Centaur Pr UK) St Mut.

Savouring the East: Feasts & Stories from Istanbul to Bali. David Burton. 240p. 1996. 24.95 (*0-571-17810-3*) Faber & Faber.

Savouron Petit Dictionnaire Gourmand. Modeste Savouron. 232p. (FRE.). 1988. pap. 39.95 (*0-7859-8220-5*, 2903515050) Fr & Eur.

Savoy Book. Harlan Ellison. (Illus.). 144p. (Orig.). 1980. pap. 2.50 (*0-86130-001-7*, Pub. by Savoy Bks UK) AK Pr Dist.

Savoy Label: A Discography. Michel Ruppli. LC 79-7727. (Discographies Ser.: No. 2). (Illus.). 442p. 1980. text ed. 105.00 (*0-313-21199-X*, RUS/, Greenwood Pr) Greenwood.

Savoy Operas. 740p. pap. 5.00 (*1-85326-313-3*) Publishers Group.

Savoyard Scrapbook: A Selection. W. S. Gilbert. 1976. 19.95 (*0-8488-1009-0*) Amereon Ltd.

Savoy/Savoie/Savois Families of Louisiana: A History of the Savoy Family from 1641 to the Twentieth Century. rev. ed. Harry J. Savoy. 180p. 1995. pap. 15.00 (*0-926764-92-6*) LAcadie Pubng.

***Savrola.** Winston Churchill. 1997. 24.95 (*0-85052-255-2*, Pub. by L Cooper Bks UK) Trans-Atl Phila.

Savrola. Winston S. Churchill. 241p. 1976. reprint ed. lib. bdg. 24.95 (*0-88411-074-5*, Queens House) Amereon Ltd.

Savta Simcha & the Cinnamon Tree. Yaffa Ganz. (J). (gr. 6-10). 1983. 13.95 (*0-87306-354-6*) Feldheim.

Savta Simcha & the Incredible Shabbes Bag: Jewish Mary Poppins. Yaffa Ganz. (Illus.). (gr. 1-5). 1980. 13.95 (*0-87306-187-X*) Feldheim.

Savta Simcha & the Seven Splendid Gifts. Yaffa Gauz. LC 87-3643. (Illus.). (J). (gr. 4-7). 1987. 13.95 (*0-87306-437-2*) Feldheim.

Savta Simcha, Uncle Nechemya, & the Very Strange Stone in the Garden. Yaffa Ganz. LC 92-26165. (Illus.). (J). 1992. 13.95 (*0-87306-618-9*) Feldheim.

Savushun: A Novel about Modern Iran. Simin Daneshvar. Tr. by M. R. Ghanoonparvar from PER. 392p. (C). 1991. pap. 12.95 (*0-934211-31-0*) Mage Pubs Inc.

Savvy Business Travel: Management Tips from the Pros. Darryl Jenkins. 336p. 1992. 25.00 (*1-55623-752-9*) Irwin Prof Pubng.

***Savvy Investors: Picking the Right Stockbroker for Maximum Profits.** Francis Miller. LC 96-18822. 1997. pap. text ed. 14.95 (*0-935016-20-1*, Dunhill Pub Co) Zinn Pub Grp.

***Savvy Medical Consumer.** Charles B. Inlander & People's Medical Society (U. S.) Staff. LC 97-8923. 1997. pap. write for info. (*1-882606-31-0*) Peoples Med Soc.

Savvy Secs: Street Wise & Book Smart. Lynda R. Abegg & Peggy J. Grillot. Ed. by Millicent Treloar. LC 84-91839. 140p. (Orig.). 1985. pap. 9.95 (*0-9614131-0-7*) Abegg Grillot Ent.

Savvy Survivor's Sprouting Guide. John R. Sauer. Ed. by Anderson & Shirley Jurjovec. (Illus.). 30p. (Orig.). 1996. mass mkt. 5.95 (*1-889399-01-9*) SAI Pubng.

Savvy the Burro: The Hamilton-Swagerty, Murray-Griswold Family History. Patricia Hamilton et al. (Illus.). 388p. 1994. spiral bd. 125.00 (*1-877809-53-5*) Park Pl Pubns.

***Savvy Woman's Success Bible: How to Find the Right Job, the Right Man, the Right Life.** Tina S. Flaherty & Kay I. Gilman. LC 96-38803. 336p. 1997. pap. 13.00 (*0-399-52299-9*, Perigee Bks) Berkley Pub.

Savy Consumer's Sourcebook: Where to Get Anything for Less. Ed Hart. 316p. 1992. pap. 15.95 (*0-9634443-0-1*) Savy Consumer.

Saw. Patricia Armentrout & David Armentrout. LC 94-46475. (Learning about Tools Ser.). (J). (gr. 2-6). 1995. write for info. (*1-55916-122-1*) Rourke Bk Co.

Saw a Star: A Christmas Story. Tedi T. Wixom. (Illus.). 32p. (Orig.). (J). (ps-8). 1995. pap. 6.95 (*1-885227-25-6*) TNT Bks.

Saw Palmetto Story. rev. ed. Michael Murray. 14p. reprint ed. pap. 2.95 (*0-9647080-2-7*) Healing Wisdom.

Saw the House in Half: A Novel. Oliver Jackman. LC 73-88971. 337p. 1974. 14.95 (*0-88258-010-8*) Howard U Pr.

***Sawah Cultivation in Ancient Java: Aspects of Development During the Indo-Javanese Period, 5th to 15th Century.** N. C. Van Setten van der Meer. (Oriental Monograph Ser.: Vol. 22). 188p. 1997. pap. text ed. 20.00 (*0-7081-0767-2*, Pub. by Aust Nat Univ AT) UH Pr.

Sawai Jai Singh & His Astronomy. Virendra N. Sharma. (C). 1995. 22.50 (*81-208-1256-5*, Pub. by Motilal Banarsidass II) S Asia.

Sawanih: Inspiration from the World of Pure Spirits. Ahmad Ghazzali. Tr. by Nasrollah Pourjavady. (Ancient Persian Treatise on Love Ser.). 132p. 1986. 37.50 (*0-7103-0091-3*) Routledge Chapman & Hall.

Sawdust & Sixguns. Max Brand. 246p. 1976. reprint ed. lib. bdg. 22.95 (*0-89190-208-2*, Rivercity Pr) Amereon Ltd.

Sawdust Ceaser: The Untold Story of Mussolini & Fascism. George H. Seldes. LC 70-180277. reprint ed. 44.50 (*0-404-56197-7*) AMS Pr.

Sawdust "Fair Dinkum" Ronald P. Cole. LC 92-91125. 88p. (J). 1993. pap. 8.00 (*1-56002-256-6*, Univ Edtns) Aegina Pr.

Sawdust in His Shoes. Eloise J. McGraw. 1994. reprint ed. lib. bdg. 27.95 (*1-56849-310-X*) Buccaneer Bks.

Sawdust Trail. Jon Sharpe. (Trailsman Ser.: No. 156). 176p. 1994. pap. 3.99 (*0-451-18160-3*, Sig) NAL-Dutton.

An Asterisk (*) at the beginning of an entry indicates that the title is appearing in BIP for the first time.

Sawdust Trail Preacher: The Story of Billy Sunday. Betty S. Everett & Billy Sunday. (Stories of Faith & Fame Ser.). 98p. (Orig.). (J). 1987. mass mkt. 3.95 (*0-87508-499-0*) Chr Lit.

Sawdust Trails in the Truckee Basin: A History of Logging Operations, 1856-1936. Dick Wilson. LC 91-34500. (Illus.). xiv, 90p. (Orig.). 1992. pap. 11.95 (*0-915641-04-6*) Nevada County Hist Society.

Sawdust War: Poems by Jim Barnes. Jim Barnes. 136p. (Orig.). 1992. 12.95 (*0-252-06239-6*) U of Ill Pr.

Sawfin Stickleback. Catherine Friend. LC 93-47151. (Illus.). 32p. (J). (ps-3). 1994. 13.95 (*1-56282-473-2*); lib. bdg. 13.89 (*1-56282-474-0*) Hyprn Child.

Sawfly Life History Adaptations to Woody Plants. Ed. by Michael Wagner & Kenneth F. Raffa. (Illus.). 581p. 1993. text ed. 67.00 (*0-12-730030-9*) Acad Pr.

Sawgrass Poems: A View of the Everglades. Frank Asch. LC 95-22762. (Illus.). 52p. (J). (gr. k-4). 1996. 18.00 (*0-15-200180-8*, Gulliver Bks) HarBrace.

Sawhorse Layout with the Framing Square. rev. ed. Intro. by W. Forrest Bear & Thomas A. Hoerner. (Illus.). 8p. 1971. pap. text ed. 2.20 (*0-913163-01-5*, 165) Hobar Pubns.

Sawing Technology: The Key to Improved Profits. 108p. (Orig.). 1985. pap. 18.00 (*0-935018-23-9*) Forest Prod.

Sawmill: The Story of Cutting the Last Great Virgin Forest East of the Rockies. Kenneth L. Smith. LC 86-1453. 264p. 1986. 32.00 (*0-938626-68-X*) U of Ark Pr.

Sawn Bench: Poems. David Appelbaum. LC 92-19966. 72p. 1993. pap. 12.95 (*0-7734-9517-7*, Mellen Poetry Pr) E Mellen.

Saws: Design, Selection, Operation, Maintenance. 2nd ed. Ed M. Williston. LC 89-45889. (Illus.). 450p. 1990. spiral bd. 48.00 (*0-87930-221-6*, 470) Miller Freeman.

Sawtooth National Recreation Area. 2nd ed. Luther Linkhart. LC 87-40156. (Illus.). 224p. 1988. pap. 14.95 (*0-89997-085-0*) Wilderness Pr.

***Sawtooth Tales.** Dick D'Easum. LC 76-24379. (Illus.). 294p. pap. 83.80 (*0-608-05050-4*, 2059711) Bks Demand.

Sawtooth Wolves. Richard Ballantine. LC 96-83437. (Illus.). 192p. 1996. 40.00 (*0-9649915-0-0*) Rufus Pubns Inc.

Sawyer: Genealogical Index of the Sawyer Families of New England Prior to 1900. Fred E. Sawyer. 394p. 1991. reprint ed. pap. 39.50 (*0-8328-2059-8*); reprint ed. lib. bdg. 49.50 (*0-8328-2058-X*) Higginson Bk Co.

Sawyer Brown: Cafe on the Corner. (Illus.). 48p. 1993. pap. 14.95 (*0-8256-1346-9*, AM91044) Music Sales.

Sawyer Brown: Outskirts of Town. 56p. 1994. otabind 12. 95 (*0-7935-3334-1*, 00308234) H Leonard.

Sawyer Brown: This Thing Called Wantin' & Havin' It All. Ed. by Milton Okun. 64p. (YA). 1995. pap. 15.95 (*0-89524-992-8*) Cherry Lane.

Sawyer Brown Greatest Hits P-V-G 1990-1995. Ed. by Milton Okun. 64p. (YA). 1995. pap. 15.95 (*0-89524-935-9*) Cherry Lane.

Sawyer. Descendants of Betfield Sawyer of Hill, N.H. Continuation of the Work of Roland Douglas Sawyer. Jay Norwalk. (Illus.). 110p. 1995. 35.00 (*0-8328-4731-3*) Higginson Bk Co.

Sawyer. Descendants of Betfield Sawyer of Hill, N.H. Continuation of the Work of Roland Douglas Sawyer. Jay Norwalk. (Illus.). 98p. 1995. pap. 18.00 (*0-8328-4732-1*) Higginson Bk Co.

Sawyer Family of Elliotsville, Piscataquis County, Maine: Descendants of James Sawyer of Gloucester, Massachusetts, & Their Kinfolk, the Drakes. 2nd ed. Fred E. Sawyer. 98p. 1994. reprint ed. pap. 19.00 (*0-8328-4234-6*); reprint ed. lib. bdg. 29.00 (*0-8328-4233-8*) Higginson Bk Co.

Sawyer's Australian Constitutional Cases. 4th ed. Leslie Zines. xxxv, 774p. 1982. pap. 73.00 (*0-455-20460-8*, Pub. by Law Bk Co AT) Gaunt.

Sawyer's Gas Turbine Engineering Handbooks, 3 Vols. 3rd ed. Ed. by John W. Sawyer & David Japikse. Vol. 2 : Selection & Application. 79.50 (*0-937506-15-X*); Vol. 3 : Accessories & Support. 79.50 (*0-937506-16-8*) Turbo Intl Pubn.

Sawyer's Gas Turbine Engineering Handbooks, 3 Vols., Set. 3rd ed. Ed. by John W. Sawyer & David Japikse. 248. 50 (*0-937506-13-3*) Turbo Intl Pubn.

Sawyer's Gas Turbine Engineering Handbooks, 3 Vols., Vol. 1. 3rd ed. Ed. by John W. Sawyer & David Japikse. 89. 50 (*0-937506-14-1*) Turbo Intl Pubn.

Sawyer's Internal Auditing: The Practice of Modern Internal Auditing. 4th ed. Lawrence B. Sawyer & M. Dittenhofer. Ed. by Marlene Greil. 1479p. 1996. pap. text ed. 100.00 (*0-89413-178-8*) Inst Inter Aud.

Sawyer's Internal Auditing: The Practice of Modern Internal Auditing,4th Edition. 4th enl. rev. ed. Lawrence B. Sawyer & M. Dittenhofer. 1479p. 1996. teacher ed. write for info. (*0-89413-336-5*) Inst Inter Aud.

Sawyers Survival Guide for Information Brokers. Deborah C. Sawyer. 85p. 1995. pap. text ed. 39.50 (*0-938519-12-3*) Burwell Ent.

Sawyer's Turbomachinery Maintenance Handbook, Vol. I: Gas Turbines-Turbocompressors. Ed. by John W. Sawyer & Kurt Hallberg. (Illus.). 375p. 1980. 60.00 (*0-937506-01-X*) Turbo Intl Pubn.

Sawyer's Turbomachinery Maintenance Handbook, Vol. II: Steam Turbines-Power Recovery Turbines. Ed. by John W. Sawyer & Kurt Hallberg. (Illus.). 350p. 1981. 60.00 (*0-937506-00-1*) Turbo Intl Pubn.

Sawyer's Turbomachinery Maintenance Handbook, Vol. III: Support Services & Equipment. Ed. by John W. Sawyer & Kurt Hallberg. (Illus.). 340p. 1981. 60.00 (*0-937506-02-8*) Turbo Intl Pubn.

Sawyer's Turbomachinery Maintenance Handbooks, 3 vols., Set. Ed. by John W. Sawyer & Kurt Hallberg. LC 80-53539. (Illus.). 1060p. 1981. 180.00 (*0-937506-03-6*) Turbo Intl Pubn.

Sax JamTrax. Ralph Agresta. (Illus.). 1993. pap. 9.95 (*0-8256-1353-1*, AM90042) Music Sales.

Sax Rohmer: Two Complete Fu Manchu Adventures. Sax Rohmer. Ed. by Tom Mason. (Illus.). 112p. 1990. pap. 12.95 (*0-944735-24-X*) Malibu Comics Ent.

Sax Scales, Chords & Solos. W. Herman. 48p. 1982. pap. 5.95 (*0-7935-3214-0*, 00384685) H Leonard.

Saxe Holm's Stories, 2 vols. Helen H. Jackson. 1972. Vol. 1 (First Ser.). lib. bdg. 16.00 (*0-8290-0660-5*); Vol. 2 (Second Ser.). lib. bdg. 16.00 (*0-8290-0670-2*) Irvington.

Saxe Holm's Stories. Helen H. Jackson. (Notable American Authors Ser.). 1992. reprint ed. lib. bdg. 75.00 (*0-7812-3348-8*) Rprt Serv.

Saxe Holm's Stories, Vol. 1. Helen H. Jackson. (First Ser.). (C). 1988. reprint ed. pap. text ed. 5.95 (*0-8290-2251-1*) Irvington.

Saxe Holm's Stories, Vol. 2. Helen H. Jackson. (Second Ser.). (C). 1988. reprint ed. pap. text ed. 5.95 (*0-8290-1946-4*) Irvington.

Saxe Holm's Stories, First Series. Helen M. Jackson. LC 74-110225. (Short Story Index Reprint Ser.). 1977. 21. 95 (*0-8369-3375-3*) Ayer.

Saxe Holm's Stories, Second Series. Helen M. Jackson. LC 74-110225. (Short Story Index Reprint Ser.). 1977. reprint ed. 20.95 (*0-8369-3817-8*) Ayer.

Saxicolen Arten der Flechtengattung Rinodina in Europa. H. Mayrhofer & J. Poelt. (Bibliotheca Lichenologica Ser.: No. 12). (Illus.). (GER.). 1979. lib. bdg. 30.00 (*3-7682-1237-8*) Lubrecht & Cramer.

Saxicolous Species of PorinaMuell. Aeg., Trichotheliae, in the Southern Hemisphere. Patrick McCarthy. (Bibliotheca Lichenologica Ser.: Vol. 52). (Illus.). 134p. 1993. pap. 48.00 (*3-443-58031-9*, Pub. by Cramer-Borntraeger GW) Lubrecht & Cramer.

Saxo Grammaticus Bks. I-IX: The History of the Danes. Ed. by Hilda E. Davidson. Tr. by Peter Fisher. 528p. 1996. 89.00 (*0-85991-509-3*) Boydell & Brewer.

Saxo Grammaticus & the Life of Hamlet: A Translation, History, & Commentary. William F. Hansen. LC 82-2671. (Illus.). xvi, 206p. 1983. text ed. 25.00 (*0-8032-2318-8*) U of Nebr Pr.

Saxon. Margaret Moore. (Historical Ser.). 1995. pap. 4.50 (*0-373-28868-9*, 1-28868-7) Harlequin Bks.

Saxon. Daniel Torres. Ed. by Bernd Metz. Tr. by David Rosenthal from SPA. (Astral Adventures of Rocco Vargas Ser.). (Illus.). 56p. (Orig.). 1991. pap. 9.95 (*0-87416-114-2*) Catalan Communs.

Saxon Bride. Tamara Leigh. 448p. 1996. mass mkt. 5.99 (*0-553-56534-6*, Fanfare) Bantam.

Saxon Genesis: An Edition of the West Saxon Genesis B & the Old Saxon Vatican Genesis. A. N. Doane. LC 90-50641. 416p. 1991. 45.00 (*0-299-12800-8*) U of Wis Pr.

Saxon Savior: The Germanic Transformation of the Gospel in the Ninth-Century Heliand. G. Ronald Murphy. 144p. (C). 1995. pap. text ed. 15.95 (*0-19-509720-3*) OUP.

Saxon Shore. Ed. by Maxfield. (Illus.). 192p. 1989. pap. text ed. 17.95 (*0-85989-330-8*, Pub. by Univ Exeter Pr UK) Northwestern U Pr.

Saxon Shore. David Rudkin. (Methuen Modern Plays Ser.). 52p. (C). 1988. pap. 8.95 (*0-413-14100-4*, A0255) Heinemann.

Saxon Thegn. Mark Harrison. (Warrior Ser.). (Illus.). 64p. 1993. pap. 12.95 (*1-85532-349-4*, 9604, Pub. by Osprey UK) Stackpole.

Saxon Tithing Men in America. Herbert B. Adams. (Principle Works of Herbert Baxter Adams). 1989. reprint ed. lib. bdg. 79.00 (*0-7812-1464-5*) Rprt Serv.

Saxon, Viking & Norman. Terence Wise. (Men-at-Arms Ser.: No. 85). (Illus.). 48p. pap. 11.95 (*0-85045-301-1*, 9023, Pub. by Osprey UK) Stackpole.

Saxons & the Normans. (History of Britain Ser.: No. F895-2). (Illus.). (YA). (gr. 5 up). 1990. pap. 3.95 (*1-85543-007-X*, Ladybrd) Penguin.

Saxons & Vikings: Openings in History. W. Wenham. (C). 1989. 40.00 (*0-09-138551-2*, Pub. by S Thornes Pubs UK) St Mut.

Saxons in England, 2 Vols. rev. ed. John Kemble. Ed. by Walter D. Birch. LC 72-151600. reprint ed. 115.00 (*0-404-03647-3*) AMS Pr.

Saxophone Bk. 1. (Breeze Easy Method Ser.). 32p. (Orig.). 1994. pap. 6.50 (*0-89724-195-9*, BE0015) Warner Brothers.

Saxophone Bk. 2. (Breeze Easy Method Ser.). 32p. 1994. pap. 6.50 (*0-89724-371-4*, BE0016) Warner Brothers.

Saxophone Fingering Chart. Brenda Murphy. (Illus.). 1984. pap. 3.95 (*0-8256-2384-7*, AM35742) Music Sales.

***Saxophone Method.** Bob Cooper. 1993. 9.95 (*0-7866-0530-8*, 93472) Mel Bay.

Saxophone Pocket Book Bk. 2. William Bay. pap. 0.95 (*0-87166-555-7*, 93748) Mel Bay.

Saxophone Primer. Louis Hittler. 1993. 4.95 (*0-87166-374-0*, 93424) Mel Bay.

Saxophone Recital Music: A Discography. Ed. by Stanley L. Schleuter. LC 93-2588. (Discographies Ser.: No. 53). 304p. 1993. text ed. 69.50 (*0-313-29001-6*, Greenwood Pr) Greenwood.

Saxophone Soloists & Their Music, 1844-1985: An Annotated Bibliography. Harry R. Gee. LC 85-45537. 318p. 1986. 23.95 (*0-253-35091-3*) Ind U Pr.

Saxophone Soloists & Their Music, 1844-1985: An Annotated Bibliography. Harry R. Gee. LC 85-45537. 315p. 1986. reprint ed. pap. 89.80 (*0-608-01061-8*, 2059369) Bks Demand.

Saxophone Technique. Danny Wilensky. (Illus.). 88p. 1989. pap. 14.95 (*0-8256-2551-3*, AM71374) Music Sales.

Sax's Dangerous Properties of Industrial Materials: 1993 Update. N. Irving Sax & Richard J. Lewis. 1994. text ed. 99.95 (*0-442-01675-1*) Van Nos Reinhold.

Say. Barbara L. McCombs & Linda Brannan. (Skills for Job Success Ser.). (Illus.). 32p. (Orig.). 1990. student ed., pap. 4.95 (*1-56119-003-9*) Educ Pr MD.

Say. Barbara L. McCombs & Linda Brannan. (Skills for Job Success Ser.). (Illus.). 32p. (Orig.). (YA). (gr. 7-12). 1990. teacher ed. 1.95 (*1-56119-004-7*); disk 39.95 (*1-56119-102-7*) Educ Pr MD.

SAY! deluxe limited ed. Lyn Mandelbaum. (Illus.). 1982. pap. 10.00 (*0-935694-02-1*) St Edns.

Say, Set. Barbara L. McCombs & Linda Brannan. (Skills for Job Success Ser.). (Illus.). 32p. (Orig.). (YA). (gr. 7-12). 1990. student ed., teacher ed. 44.95 (*1-56119-060-8*) Educ Pr MD.

Say a Fast Goodbye to Fat Forever! Mary E. McNeil. (Illus.). 272p. (Orig.). 1987. pap. 9.95 (*0-915451-08-5*) New Start Pubns.

Say a Little Mantra for Me. Yvonne Burgess. (Writers Ser.). 166p. 1995. reprint ed. pap. text ed. 12.95 (*0-86975-467-X*, Pub. by Ravan Pr ZA) Ohio U Pr.

Say Aah (Hah)! A Medical Educator Mouths Off. Herbert L. Fred. LC 91-27294. (Illus.). 1991. 25.00 (*0-86554-400-X*, H326) Mercer Univ Pr.

Say Again, Please: Guide to Radio Communications. Bob Gardner. (Illus.). (Orig.). 1995. pap. 14.95 (*1-56027-224-4*, ASA-SAP) Av Suppl & Acad.

***Say Amen! The African-American Family's Book of Prayers.** Chestina M. Archibald. LC 97-20403. 1997. pap. 23.95 (*0-525-94215-7*) NAL-Dutton.

Say Amen, Brother! Old-Time Negro Preaching: A Study in American Frustration. William H. Pipes. LC 91-19572. (African American Life Ser.). 230p. 1992. 29.95 (*0-8143-2383-9*); pap. 15.95 (*0-8143-2384-7*) Wayne St U Pr.

Say Amen Brother, Old-Time Negro Preaching: A Study in American Frustration. William H. Pipes. LC 73-111585. 210p. 1970. reprint ed. text ed. 35.00 (*0-8371-4611-9*, PSA&, Negro U Pr) Greenwood.

Say & Spell: The Bridge from Speaking to Spelling. Jeannette M. Dewey. LC 95-92563. 464p. (Orig.). 1995. pap. 10.95 (*0-9648519-0-3*) Seneca Pubng.

***Say Boo!** Lynda Graham-Barber. (Illus.). 24p. (J). 1997. reprint ed. pap. 2.99 (*0-7636-0343-0*) Candlewick Pr.

Say Bye-Bye. Anna Ross. LC 90-52915. (Sesame Street Toddler Bks.). (Illus.). 24p. (J). (ps). 1992. 3.95 (*0-394-85485-3*) Random Bks Yng Read.

Say Can You Deny Me: A Guide to Surviving Music by Women from the 16th Through the 18th Centuries. Barbara G. Jackson. LC 94-6332. 480p. (C). 1994. 45.00 (*1-55728-303-6*) U of Ark Pr.

Say Cheese! Vassily Aksyonov. Tr. by Aksyonov Bouis. 1989. 19.95 (*0-394-54363-7*) Random.

***Say Cheese.** Judith Bosley. (Illus.). 60p. 1990. pap. 8.95 (*0-930809-06-8*) Kitch Cupbd Cookbks.

Say "Cheese", No. 10. Patricia R. Giff. (Kids of the Polk Street School Ser.). (Illus.). 80p. (J). (gr. 6-9). 1985. mass mkt. 3.99 (*0-440-47639-9*, YB BDD) BDD Bks Young Read.

***Say Cheese & Die!** R. L. Stine. LC 97-19369. (Goosebumps Ser.). (J). 1997. write for info. (*0-8368-1976-4*) Gareth Stevens Inc.

Say Cheese & Die! R. L. Stine. (Goosebumps Ser.: No. 4). 160p. (J). (gr. 4-6). 1992. pap. 3.99 (*0-590-45368-8*, Apple Paperbacks) Scholastic Inc.

Say Cheese & Die, Again! R. L. Stine. (Goosebumps Ser.: No. 44). (J). (gr. 4-7). 1996. pap. text ed. 3.99 (*0-590-56881-7*) Scholastic Inc.

Say Cheese & Milk Please. Marjorie A. Fontana & Jean L. Larson. LC 78-67289. (Illus.). 62p. (Orig.). 1978. 7.95 (*0-9603596-0-5*); pap. 5.95 (*0-9603596-1-3*) Fontastic.

Say Cheesecake & Smile. 2nd rev. ed. Elvira Monroe. LC 80-54453. (Illus.). 176p. 1983. pap. 6.95 (*0-933174-17-9*) Wide World-Tetra.

***Say Good-Bye to Discouragement.** Nancy Gray. 1996. pap. text ed. 8.99 (*0-89274-993-8*) Harrison Hse.

Say Good Night. Barbara Gregorich. Ed. by Joan Hoffman. (Start to Read! Ser.). (Illus.). 16p. (Orig.). (J). (gr. k-2). 1984. pap. 2.25 (*0-88743-010-4*, 06010) Sch Zone Pub Co.

Say Good Night. Barbara Gregorich. Ed. by Joan Hoffman. (Start to Read! Ser.). (Illus.). 32p. (Orig.). (J). (gr. k-2). 1992. pap. 3.95 (*0-88743-408-8*, 06060) Sch Zone Pub Co.

Say Good Night. Anna Ross. LC 90-52914. (Sesame Street Toddler Bks.). (Illus.). 24p. (J). (ps). 1992. 5.99 (*0-394-85491-8*) Random Bks Yng Read.

Say Good Night! Harriet Ziefert & Catherine Siracusa. (Easy-to-Read Ser.: Level 1, Blue). (Illus.). (J). (ps-2). 1995. pap. 3.50 (*0-14-036839-6*) Puffin Bks.

Say Good Night, Scooter. (Little Golden Sound Story Bks.). (Illus.). 24p. (J). 1995. bds. 6.95 (*0-307-74826-X*, Golden Pr) Western Pub.

Say Goodbye to Back Pain: A Successful Alternative for the Treatment of Back Pain. Richard Stuckey. (Illus.). 122p. (Orig.). 1994. pap. 14.95 (*0-85572-248-7*) Seven Hills Bk.

Say Goodbye to Illness. Devi S. Nambudripad. 300p. 1993. pap. text ed. 21.00 (*0-9637570-0-8*) Delta Pubng CA.

Say Goodbye to Shy: Change Your Thinking, Change Your Life. Jean Ann Stevens. 128p. (Orig.). 1995. pap. 11.95 (*0-9642402-7-0*) Sndpiper Pr.

Say Goodbye to Yesterday. large type ed. Jacqui Bennett. (Linford Romance Library). 1989. pap. 15.99 (*0-7089-6774-4*) Ulverscroft.

Say Goodnight, Gracie. Julie R. Deaver. LC 87-45278. (Charlotte Zolotow Bks.). 224p. (YA). (gr. 7 up). 1988. 15.00 (*0-06-021418-X*); lib. bdg. 14.89 (*0-06-021419-8*) HarpC Child Bks.

Say Goodnight, Gracie. Julie R. Deaver. LC 87-45278. (Charlotte Zolotow Bks.). 224p. (YA). (gr. 7 up). 1989. pap. 3.95 (*0-06-447007-5*, Trophy) HarpC Child Bks.

Say Goodnight, Gracie. Ralph Pape. 1979. pap. 5.25 (*0-8222-0993-4*) Dramatists Play.

Say Hello to Cactus Flats: A Fox Trot Collection. Bill Amend. (Illus.). 128p. (Orig.). 1993. pap. 8.95 (*0-8362-1720-9*) Andrews & McMeel.

Say Hey: The Autobiography of Willie Mays. Willie May & Lou Sahadi. 1989. mass mkt. 4.50 (*0-671-67836-1*) PB.

Say Hola, Sarah. Patricia R. Giff. (Friends & Amigos Ser.: No. 2). (Illus.). 48p. (Orig.). (J). (gr. 1-4). 1995. pap. 3.50 (*0-440-41077-0*, YB BDD) BDD Bks Young Read.

Say Hola to Spanish. Susan Middleton Elya. LC 95-478. (Illus.). 32p. (ENG & SPA.). (J). (ps-5). 1996. 14.95 (*1-880000-29-6*) Lee & Low Bks.

***Say Hola to Spanish, Otra Vez (Again!)** Susan M. Elya. LC 97-6851. (Illus.). 32p. (J). (gr. k-5). 1997. 15.95 (*1-880000-59-8*) Lee & Low Bks.

Say I Am You: Poetry Interspersed with Stories of Rumi & Shams. Telalvddim Rumi. Tr. by Coleman Barks & John Moyne. 128p. (Orig.). 1994. pap. 12.00 (*1-884237-00-2*) Maypop.

Say, Is This the U. S. A. M. Bourke-White & E. Caldwell. LC 77-9598. (Photography Ser.). (Illus.). 1977. reprint ed. pap. 8.95 (*0-306-80071-3*); reprint ed. lib. bdg. 35.00 (*0-306-77434-8*) Da Capo.

Say It. Roland Flint. LC 78-5149. 1979. pap. 8.95 (*0-931848-21-0*) Dryad Pr.

Say It Again Sam. Sam Churchill. Ed. by Samuel J. Churchill & Dorothy L. Churchill. 196p. (Orig.). 1991. pap. 9.95 (*0-9630536-0-4*) S Dot S.

Say It Ain't So, Joe: The True Story of Shoeless Joe Jackson. rev. ed. Donald Gropman. 256p. 1992. pap. 10.95 (*0-8065-1336-5*, Citadel Pr) Carol Pub Group.

Say It & Live It. Patricia Jones. 288p. 1995. pap. 14.95 (*0-385-47630-2*) Doubleday.

Say It Clearly. English. 1988. pap. 22.95 (*0-8384-3353-7*); audio 22.95 (*0-8384-3354-5*) Heinle & Heinle.

Say It Graciously. Marion Boyd. iv, 35p. 1992. reprint ed. pap. 4.00 (*0-88053-321-8*, S-296) Macoy Pub.

Say It in Arabic. Farouk El-Baz. pap. 3.50 (*0-486-22026-5*) Dover.

Say It in Chinese. Nancy D. Lay. (Say It Ser.). (Orig.). 1980. pap. 3.50 (*0-486-23325-1*) Dover.

Say It in Croatian: Phrase Book & Dictionary. Ruzica Kapetanovic. (Illus.). 256p. (Orig.). (CRO.). 1994. pap. 6.95 (*0-910164-26-6*) Assoc Bk Pubs.

Say It in Czech. Milan Fryscak. LC 76-173447. (Orig.). 1973. pap. text ed. 3.95 (*0-486-21538-5*) Dover.

Say It in Danish. Gerda M. Andersen. 165p. (Orig.). 1958. pap. 3.50 (*0-486-20818-4*) Dover.

Say It in Dutch. Anna M. Hunningher. (Orig.). pap. 3.50 (*0-486-20817-6*) Dover.

Say It in Finnish. Aili Flint. (Language & Linguistics Ser.). 192p. (Orig.). 1984. pap. 3.95 (*0-486-24591-8*) Dover.

Say It in French. Leon J. Cohen. (Orig.). pap. 2.95 (*0-486-20803-6*) Dover.

Say It in German. Gustave B. Mathieu & Guy Stern. (Orig.). 1957. pap. 3.50 (*0-486-20804-4*) Dover.

Say It in Hawaiian: My Body. Wren & Maile. (Keiki's First Bks.). (Illus.). 10p. (ENG & HAW.). (J). (ps). 1992. bds. 4.95 (*1-880188-03-1*) Bess Pr.

Say It in Hindi. Veena T. Oldenburg. (Say It Ser.). 192p. (Orig.). 1981. pap. 4.95 (*0-486-23959-4*) Dover.

Say It in Hungarian. Juliette Victor-Rood. (Say It Ser.). (Illus.). 224p. (Orig.). 1983. pap. 3.95 (*0-486-24423-7*) Dover.

Say It in Indonesian: Malay. John U. Wolff. (Language & Linguistics Ser.). 192p. (Orig.). 1983. pap. 3.95 (*0-486-24424-5*) Dover.

Say It in Italian. Olga Ragusa. pap. 3.50 (*0-486-20806-0*) Dover.

Say It in Japanese. Miwa Kai. (Say It Ser.). 220p. (Orig.). 1984. pap. 3.50 (*0-486-20807-9*) Dover.

Say It in Japanese, No. 15. Japan Travel Bureau Staff. (Illustrated Japan in Your Pocket Ser.). (Illus.). 192p. 1993. pap. 17.95 (*4-533-01956-0*, Pub. by Japan Trvl Bur JA) Bks Nippan.

Say It in Modern Greek. George Pappageotes. 1956. pap. 2.95 (*0-486-20813-3*) Dover.

Say It in Modern Hebrew. Aleeza Cerf. (Orig.). pap. 3.50 (*0-486-20805-2*) Dover.

Say It in Norwegian. Samuel Abrahamsen. (Orig.). 1957. pap. 2.95 (*0-486-20814-1*) Dover.

Say It in Polish. Victor Raysman. (Orig.). 1954. pap. 2.95 (*0-486-20808-7*) Dover.

Say It in Portuguese. M. M. Mickle & Francisco Da Costa. (Orig.). 1954. pap. 3.95 (*0-486-20809-5*) Dover.

Say It in Portuguese (European Usage) Alexander R. Prista. LC 77-73311. 1979. pap. 3.95 (*0-486-23676-5*) Dover.

Say It in Russian. N. C. Stepanoff & Michael S. Flier. (Say It Ser.). 256p. (J). (gr. 6 up). pap. 3.95 (*0-486-20810-9*) Dover.

Say It in Serbo-Croatian. Prod. by Vasa D. Mihailovich. (Say It Ser.). 160p. 1987. pap. 3.95 (*0-486-25261-2*) Dover.

Say It in Sign: A Workbook of Sign Language Exercises. Carol B. Carpenter & Sue F. Rakow. (Illus.). 266p. (C). 1983. spiral bd., pap. 37.95 (*0-398-04779-0*) C C Thomas.

Say It in Six: How to Say Exactly What You Mean in Six Minutes or Less: a New Communications System for the Time-Hungry 90s. Ron Hoff. LC 95-42234. (Illus.). 176p. (Orig.). 1996. pap. 10.95 (*0-8362-1041-7*) Andrews & McMeel.

Say It in Spanish. Leon J. Cohen & A. C. Rogers. (Orig.). 1951. pap. 2.95 (*0-486-20811-7*) Dover.

Say It in Spanish: A Guide for Health Care Professionals. Esperanza V. Joyce & Maria E. Villanueva. 304p. 1995. pap. text ed. 15.00 (*0-7216-4955-6*) Saunders.

Say It in Spanish! Language & Activities for the Elementary Classroom. Marianne Mitchell. 125p. 1997. pap. text ed. 18.50 (*1-56308-434-1*) Teacher Ideas Pr.

Say It in Swahili. Sharifa M. Zawawi. (Say It Ser.). 205p. (Orig.). 1972. pap. 3.50 (*0-486-22792-8*) Dover.

Say It in Swedish. Kerstin Norris. LC 72-94755. 1979. pap. 3.50 (*0-486-20812-5*) Dover.

Say It in Turkish. Jeanne M. Blackburn & Refah Seniz. (Orig.). pap. 2.95 (*0-486-20821-4*) Dover.

Say It in Yiddish. Uriel Weinreich & Beatrice Weinreich. (Orig.). pap. 3.95 (*0-486-20815-X*) Dover.

Say It Loud! The Story of Rap Music. K. Maurice Jones. LC 93-1939. (Illus.). 128p. (YA). (gr. 7 up). 1994. lib. bdg. 20.90 (*1-56294-386-3*) Millbrook Pr.

Say It Loud: The Story of Rap Music. K. Maurice Jones. 128p. (YA). (gr. 7 up). 1994. pap. 12.95 (*1-56294-724-9*) Millbrook Pr.

Say It Naturally. Allie P. Wall. 288p. (C). 1987. pap. text ed. 16.00 (*0-03-002873-6*) HB Coll Pubs.

***Say It Right: (NLP Focused)** S. A. Brown. Ed. by W. R. VanHoozer. (Illus.). 82p. 1996. ring bd. 15.95 (*1-889530-01-8*) McClure-Brown.

Say It Right: A Guide to Effective Oral Business Presentations. Garth A. Hanson et al. LC 94-26273. 304p. (C). 1994. per. 29.95 (*0-256-14546-6*) Irwin.

Say It Right: A Practical, User-Friendly, Totally Unintimidating Guide to Speaking Good English. Diane Kaiser. LC 94-11472. (Illus.). 72p. (Orig.). (C). 1994. pap. 8.95 (*0-913515-95-7*, Starhill Pr) Black Belt Comm.

Say It Right: American English Pronunciation, 2 vols., Set. Dorothy M. Taguchi. 507p. 1994. 99.95 incl. audio (*1-880822-07-5*) Linguistic Edge.

Say It Right, Write It Right: The Secretary's Guide to Solving Business Communications Problems. Marta Been. 1994. text ed. 29.95 (*0-13-791492-X*) P-H.

Say It Straight. Virginia M. Satir. 1991. 18.95 (*0-8314-0074-9*) Sci & Behavior.

***Say It Straight - Learn by Doing.** 58p. wbk. ed., pap. 3.95 (*0-926632-04-3*) A Wagner & Assocs.

Say It Straight or You'll Show It Crooked. Abe Wagner. 116p. (Orig.). 1988. pap. 7.95 (*0-926632-00-0*) A Wagner & Assocs.

Say It Straight or You'll Show It Crooked. Abe Wagner. (Orig.). 1993. pap. 7.95 (*0-926632-05-1*) A Wagner & Assocs.

***Say It Strong: Motion in Poetry.** Lawrence Schulz. (Illus.). 42p. (Orig.). 1997. pap. 8.00 (*1-885021-05-4*) Orange Ocean.

Say It with Charts: The Executive's Guide to Successful Presentations. 2nd ed. Gene Zelazny. 160p. 1991. text ed. 45.00 (*1-55623-447-3*) Irwin Prof Pubng.

Say It with Charts: The Executive's Guide to Visual Communication. 3rd ed. Gene Zelazny. 198p. 1996. text ed. 45.00 (*0-7863-0894-X*) Irwin Prof Pubng.

Say It with Clip-Art, No. I. Margaret Yorgason & Annette Ward. (Personal Enrichment Ser.). (Illus.). 37p. (Orig.). 1991. pap. write for info. (*0-929985-78-8*) Jackman Pubng.

Say It with Clip-Art, No. II. Margaret Yorgason & Annette Ward. (Personal Enrichment Ser.). (Illus.). 37p. (Orig.). 1991. pap. write for info. (*0-929985-79-6*) Jackman Pubng.

Say It with Confidence: Overcome the Mental Blocks That Keep You from Making Great Presentations & Speeches. Margo T. Krasne. LC 96-9246. 240p. (Orig.). 1997. pap. 13.99 (*0-446-67288-2*) Warner Bks.

Say It with Hands. Louie J. Fant, Jr. (Illus.). 1964. 8.95 (*0-913072-02-8*) Natl Assn Deaf.

Say It with Music: A Story about Irving Berlin. Thomas Streissguth. LC 93-4376. (Carolrhoda Creative Minds Bks.). (Illus.). (J). (gr. 3-6). 1993. lib. bdg. 14.21 (*0-87614-810-0*, Carolrhoda) Lerner Group.

Say It with Music: Music Games & Trivia. Beckie Karras. 76p. (Orig.). 1990. pap. text ed. 10.95 (*1-879633-05-1*) Eldersong.

Say It with Myrder. large type ed. Edward S. Aarons. (Linford Mystery Library). 368p. 1994. pap. 15.99 (*0-7089-7477-5*, Linford) Ulverscroft.

Say it with Poison. Ann Granger. 224p. 1993. mass mkt. 5.50 (*0-380-71823-5*) Avon.

***Say It with Power & Confidence.** Collins. 1997. text ed. 29.95 (*0-13-614272-9*); pap. text ed. 16.95 (*0-13-614280-X*) P-H.

***Say It with Quilts.** Laura Nownes & Diana McClun. Ed. by Barbara K. Kuhn. LC 96-38606. (Illus.). 144p. 1997. 29.95 (*1-57120-023-1*, 10147) C & T Pub.

Say It with Sign. Silent Network Staff. 208p. 1982. per. 29.95 (*0-8403-2863-X*) Kendall-Hunt.

Say It with Style. rev. ed. Christine A. Robinson. (Plus Ser.). 320p. (C). 1991. pap. text ed. 42.16 (*1-56226-088-X*) CT Pub.

Say It with Zest. M. Shapiro. (Middos Ser.). 1993. 7.99 (*0-89906-513-9*) Mesorah Pubns.

Say Jesus & Come to Me. Ann A. Shockley. 288p. 1987. reprint ed. pap. 8.95 (*0-930044-98-3*) Naiad Pr.

Say No & Fly Away! Rita Friedman & Elaine Weimann. (Fables from the Letter People Ser.). (Illus.). 30p. (J). (ps-1). 1988. lib. bdg. 12.95 (*0-89796-013-0*) New Dimens Educ.

Say No & Know Why: Kids Learn About Drugs. Wendy Wax. 64p. (J). (gr. 2-5). 1992. 12.95 (*0-8027-8140-3*); lib. bdg. 13.85 (*0-8027-8141-1*) Walker & Co.

Say No, Little Fish. Carla Dijs. (J). (gr. 2 up). 1995. 7.95 (*0-671-50742-7*, Litl Simon S&S) S&S Childrens.

Say No to Cancer. Barbara Waters. LC 83-90862. (Illus.). 453p. (Orig.). (C). 1984. pap. 12.00 (*0-930107-01-2*) Waters Pub.

Say No to Circumcision! 40 Compelling Reasons. 2nd ed. Thomas J. Ritter & George C. Denniston. (Illus.). 108p. (Orig.). 1996. pap. 9.95 (*0-934061-30-0*) Marketscope Bks.

Say No to Drugs Color & Learn Book. Merle E. Woolley. (Illus.). 20p. (J). (gr. k-6). 1988. student ed. 1.50 (*0-9623773-0-9*) Mapakam Inc.

Say No to Drugs Color & Learn Book. Merle E. Woolley. Tr. by Ruben Guitterez. (Illus.). 20p. (SPA.). (J). (gr. k-6). 1990. 1.50 (*0-9623773-1-7*) Mapakam Inc.

Say No to Murder. Nancy Pickard. Ed. by Linda Marrow. 1988. mass mkt. 4.95 (*0-671-73431-8*) PB.

Say "No!" to Violence see Breaking Free from Partner Abuse: Voices of Battered Women Caught in the Cycle of Domestic Violence

Say, Pastor, I Was Wondering... Karl S. Peterson. 48p. (Orig.). 1984. student ed., pap. 3.50 (*0-8100-0182-9*, 22N0793); teacher ed., pap. 5.50 (*0-8100-0183-7*, 22N0794) Northwest Pub.

Say Please. Virginia Austin. LC 94-10576. (Illus.). (J). 1996. pap. 4.99 (*1-56402-833-X*) Candlewick Pr.

Say Please! Shari Lewis' Baby Lamb Chop. Teddy S. Margulies. (Illus.). 18p. (J). (ps). 1995. bds. 3.95 (*0-307-12874-1*, Golden Books) Western Pub.

***Say Please & Thank You.** Stan Berenstain & Jan Berenstain. (Berenstain Bears Family Time Storybks.). (J). (ps-1). 1996. 3.95 (*0-614-20241-8*, GT Publng) GT Pubng Corp.

Say Something. rev. ed. Mary Stolz. LC 92-8317. (Illus.). 32p. (J). (ps-3). 1993. lib. bdg. 14.89 (*0-06-021159-8*) HarpC Child Bks.

Say, Spell & Write. E. W. Ellis. (C). 1982. 40.00 (*0-85950-373-9*, Pub. by S Thornes Pubs UK) St Mut.

Say That Again, Please! Insights in Dealing with a Hearing Loss. Thomas H. Bradford. LC 91-92991. (Illus.). 382p. (Orig.). 1991. 23.95 (*0-9630738-4-2*); 89.95 (*0-9630738-9-3*); pap. 16.95 (*0-9630738-5-0*) Bradford Pubns.

Say That the River Turns: The Impact of Gwendolyn Brooks. Ed. by Haki R. Madhubuti. (Orig.). 1987. pap. 8.95 (*0-88378-118-2*) Third World.

***Say the Magic Word, Please.** Marc Brown. 1997. 4.99 (*0-679-86736-8*) Random Bks Yng Read.

Say the Magic Word, Please. Anna Ross. LC 89-34544. (Sesame Street Toddler Bks.). (Illus.). 24p. (J). (ps). 1990. 5.99 (*0-394-85857-3*) Random Bks Yng Read.

Say the Right Thing! C. Meloni et al. 1982. pap. text ed. 15.76 (*0-201-10205-6*) Addison-Wesley.

***Say the Silence.** Doreen G. Wiley. LC 96-92831. 120p. 1997. pap. 10.95 (*0-9614529-1-9*) Celilo Pubns.

Say the Sound. (Key Words Readers Ser.: C Series, No. 641-4c). (Illus.). (J). (ps-5). 3.50 (*0-7214-0028-0*, Ladybrd) Penguin.

***Say the Sound.** Ladybird Staff. (J). 1997. pap. 3.50 (*0-7214-5770-3*) Dutton Child Bks.

Say the Sound, Ser. S705, No. 4. (Key Words Readers Ser.: C Series, No. 641-4c). (Illus.). (J). (ps-5). student ed. 1.95 (*0-317-00419-7*, Ladybrd) Penguin.

Say the Word! A Guide to Improving Word Recognition Skills. Barbara Rosenberg Loss. 1993. teacher ed. 7.95 (*0-88336-154-X*); student ed., text ed. 14.00 (*0-88336-152-3*); 29.95 (*0-88336-153-1*) New Readers.

Say These Names (Remember Them) Betty S. Cummings. LC 84-11422. 300p. 1984. 14.95 (*0-910923-15-9*) Pineapple Pr.

Say to the Moment: Poems by Millicent Whitt. Millicent Whitt. LC 96-68140. 64p. (Orig.). 1996. pap. 7.95 (*1-889087-00-9*) P S A Pr.

Say to This Mountain. Bodie Thoene. (Shiloh Legacy Ser.: Vol. 3). 448p. (Orig.). 1993. pap. 12.99 (*1-55661-191-9*) Bethany Hse.

Say to This Mountain: Mark's Story of Discipleship. Ched Myers et al. Ed. by Karen Lattea. LC 96-33153. 256p. (Orig.). 1996. pap. 14.00 (*1-57075-100-5*) Orbis Bks.

Say Uncle. Eric S. Quinn. 1995. pap. 10.95 (*0-452-27166-5*, Plume) NAL-Dutton.

Say Uncle. P. J. Speir. 1994. pap. 15.00 (*0-9639956-0-X*) ISI Press.

Say What? The Three Hundred Five Best Things Ever Said about Service, Sales, & Supervision. Jim Sullivan. 72p. 1993. pap. 9.95 (*1-879239-03-5*) Pencom.

Say What You Feel! Weinstein. 1989. pap. 21.95 (*0-8384-3323-5*); audio 28.95 (*0-8384-3324-3*) Heinle & Heinle.

Say What You Mean/Get What You Want: A Businessperson's Guide to Direct Communication. Judith C. Tingley. 176p. 1996. pap. 15.95 (*0-8144-7904-9*) AMACOM.

***Say Yes.** Wakeman. 13.95 (*0-340-62151-6*, Pub. by H & S UK) Trafalgar.

Say Yes! How to Renew Your Spiritual Passion. Luis Palau. LC 95-23200. 176p. (Orig.). 1995. pap. 10.99 (*0-929239-96-2*) Discovery Hse Pubs.

Say Yes to It. Elisabeth Kubler-Ross. LC 96-48973. (Kubler-Ross In-Person Ser.). 1997. pap. text ed. 5.95 (*1-886449-27-9*) Barrytown Ltd.

Say Yes! to Life: A Musical Drama about the Dangers Drugs Pose to the Joys of Living. Tobin J. Mueller. (Illus.). (J). (gr. 4-9). 1990. Audio tape incl. pap. 14.95 (*1-56213-045-5*) Ctr Stage Prodns.

***Say Yes to Life: Daily Meditations for Recovery.** 2nd rev. ed. Leo Booth. 380p. Date not set. pap. 10.00 (*0-9623282-3-5*) SCP Ltd.

***Say Yes to Life: Get Out of Your Own Way.** Ivan G. Burnell. (Illus.). 168p. (Orig.). 1997. pap. 7.95 (*0-9625806-2-7*) Intl Pers Dev.

Say Yes to Success. R. Gregory Alonzo. ii, 114p. 1996. pap. 10.00 (*0-9651822-0-7*) Candu.

Say "Yes" to Success: The Wellness Way to Living. Candace I. Jennings. LC 83-51482. 160p. 1983. spiral bd. 15.95 (*0-934104-05-0*) Woodland.

Say Yes to Tomorrow. Dale E. Rogers & Lloyd W. Thatcher. LC 96-20403. 128p. (gr. 10). 1996. mass mkt. 5.99 (*0-8007-8638-6*, Spire) Revell.

Say You Love Me. Trisha Alexander. 1994. mass mkt. 3.50 (*0-373-09875-8*, 5-09875-1) Silhouette.

Say You Love Me. Patricia Hagan. 384p. 1995. mass mkt. 5.50 (*0-06-108222-8*, Harp PBks) HarpC.

Say You Love Me. Johanna Lindsey. LC 96-28812. 352p. 1996. 22.00 (*0-688-14287-7*) Morrow.

Say You Love Me. Dave Sargent. Ed. by Debbie Bowen. (Illus.). 31p. (J). (gr. k-6). lib. bdg. 12.95 (*1-56763-129-0*) Ozark Pub.

Say You Love Me. Dave Sargent. Ed. by Debbie Bowen. (Illus.). 31p. (J). (gr. k-6). pap. text ed. 2.95 (*1-56763-130-4*) Ozark Pub.

***Say You Love Me.** large type ed. Johanna Lindsey. LC 96-42002. 1998. pap. 24.95 (*0-7838-1927-7*) G K Hall.

***Say You Love Me.** large type ed. Johanna Lindsey. LC 96-42002. (Core Ser.). 477p. 1997. lib. bdg. 26.95 (*0-7838-1928-5*, GK Hall) Thorndike Pr.

Say, You Want a Revolution. Eric Johnson. LC 93-86238. (Orig.). 1994. pap. 9.95 (*0-685-71900-6*) Longwood.

Say You Want Me. Richard Cohen. LC 88-4492. 268p. 1988. 17.95 (*0-939149-12-5*) Soho Press.

***Sayagyi U Ba Khin Journal: An Anthology of Articles from the Vipassana Research Institute.** 320p. pap. 13.95 (*81-7414-016-6*) Vipassana Res.

Sayahane Urupani dar Iran see European Travelers to Iran: From the Earliest Times to the 17th Century

Sayajirao of Baroda. Fatesinghrao Gaekwad. (C). 1989. 44.00 (*0-86132-214-2*) S Asia.

Saybrook at the Mouth of the Connecticut River: The First One Hundred Years. Gilman C. Gates. (Illus.). 246p. 1995. reprint ed. lib. bdg. 32.50 (*0-8328-4989-8*) Higginson Bk Co.

SAYdee. Denise Grigas. (Illus.). (J). (ps-12). 1993. 20.00 (*0-937857-47-5*, 1546) Speech Bin.

Say...Do You Know a Good Place to Eat? Bob Bowman. 133p. 12.95 (*1-878096-16-8*) Best E TX Pubs.

Sayeh-ye Omr (The Shadow of Life) Rahi Moayeri. 244p. (PER.). 1988. pap. 10.00 (*0-936347-44-9*) Iran Bks.

Saying & Meaning in Puerto Rico: Some Problems in the Ethnography of Discourse. Marshall Morris. (Language & Communication Library: Vol. 1). 186p. 1981. text ed. 79.00 (*0-08-025822-0*, CRC Reprint) Franklin.

Saying Enough. Yvonne M. Hardenbrook. (Amelia Chapbooks Ser.). 16p. (Orig.). 1990. pap. 4.50 (*0-936545-15-1*) Amelia.

Saying Good-Bye. Marjorie Wilkov. (Illus.). (J). 1995. 7.95 (*0-533-11452-7*) Vantage.

Saying Good-Bye. unabridged ed. Linda Holeman. 176p. (YA). (gr. 7 up). 1995. 12.95 (*1-895555-47-7*, Pub. by Stoddart Kids CN) Genl Dist Srvs.

Saying Good-Bye to Grandma. Jane R. Thomas. LC 87-20826. 40p. (J). (ps-3). 1990. pap. 6.95 (*0-395-54779-2*, Clarion Bks) HM.

Saying Goodbye. Marie G. Lee. LC 93-26092. (J). 1994. 14.95 (*0-395-67066-7*) HM.

Saying Goodbye. rev. ed. Jim Boulden. (Illus.). 32p. (Orig.). (J). (gr. 1-7). 1991. reprint ed. pap. 3.95 (*1-878076-12-4*) Boulden Pub.

Saying Goodbye. 2nd ed. Jim Boulden. (Illus.). (Orig.). (SPA.). (J). (gr. 1-7). 1991. pap. 3.95 (*1-878076-02-7*) Boulden Pub.

Saying Goodbye: A Casebook of Termination in Child & Adolescent Analysis & Therapy. Ed. by Anita G. Schmukler. 400p. 1991. text ed. 49.95 (*0-88163-106-X*) Analytic Pr.

Saying Goodbye: A Time of Growth for Congregations & Pastors. Edward A. White. LC 89-82321. 124p. (Orig.). 1990. pap. 12.25 (*1-56699-037-8*, AL118) Alban Inst.

Saying Goodbye to a Baby, Vol. 1: A Book about Loss & Grief in Adoption, Vol. 1. 1989. pap. 12.95 (*0-87868-387-9*) Child Welfare.

Saying Goodbye to a Baby, Vol. 2: A Counselor's Guide to Birthparent Grief & Loss, Vol. 2. Patricia Roles. 34p. 1990. pap. 10.95 (*0-87868-393-3*) Child Welfare.

Saying Goodbye to Daddy. Judith Vigna. Ed. by Abby Levine. LC 90-12757. (Albert Whitman Concept Bks.). (Illus.). 32p. (J). (gr. k-2). 1991. lib. bdg. 14.95 (*0-8075-7253-5*) A Whitman.

Saying Goodbye to Daniel: When Death Is the Best Choice. Juliet C. Rothman. LC 95-32338. 180p. 1995. 18.95 (*0-8264-0857-5*) Continuum.

Saying Goodbye to Disappointments. David Stoop & Jan Stoop. LC 93-19118. 1993. 16.99 (*0-8407-6741-2*) Nelson.

***Saying Goodbye to Grandma.** Moshe Spero. 1997. 14.95 (*0-943706-46-7*) Pitspopany.

***Saying Goodbye to Grandpa.** Moshe Spero. 1997. 14.95 (*0-943706-38-6*) Pitspopany.

Saying Goodbye to Your Grief. Hardy Clemons. 96p. (Orig.). 1994. pap. 8.95 (*1-880837-99-4*) Smyth & Helwys.

Saying Grace: A Novel. Beth Gutcheon. 320p. 1996. pap. 13.00 (*0-06-092727-5*) HarpC.

Saying "I Do" - The Wedding Ceremony: The Complete Guide to a Perfect Wedding. Steven M. Neel. Ed. by Rhonda Wray. LC 95-31890. (Illus.). 238p. 1995. pap. 10.95 (*1-56608-012-6*, B122) Meriwether Pub.

Saying I'm Sorry. Laura Alden. LC 82-19945. (Moods & Emotions Ser.). (Illus.). 32p. (J). (ps-2). 1983. lib. bdg. 21.36 (*0-89565-247-1*) Childs World.

Saying It Ain't So: American Values As Revealed in Children's Baseball Stories 1880-1950. Debra A. Dagavarian. (American University Studies: Anthropology & Sociology: Ser. XI, Vol. 16). 223p. 1988. text ed. 32.50 (*0-8204-0583-3*) P Lang Pubng.

Saying My Name Out Loud. Arthur Dobrin. (Illus.). 1978. pap. 2.50 (*0-918870-05-4*) Pleasure Dome.

Saying My Name Out Loud. deluxe limited ed. Arthur Dobrin. (Illus.). 1978. 3.50 (*0-918870-06-2*) Pleasure Dome.

Saying "No" Its Meaning in Child Development, Psychoanalysis, Linguistics & Hegel. Wilfried Ver Eecke. LC 84-1617. 224p. 1984. text ed. 18.50 (*0-8207-0169-6*) Duquesne.

Saying No Is Not Enough: Raising Children Who Make Wise Decisions about Drugs & Alcohol. Robert Schwebel. LC 89-33775. 256p. 1991. 18.95 (*1-55704-041-9*); pap. 10.95 (*1-55704-078-8*) Newmarket.

***Saying No Is Not Enough: What to Say & How to Listen to Your Kids about Alcohol, Tobacco & Other Drugs - A Guide for Parents.** Robert Schwebel. 1997. pap. 14.95 (*1-55704-318-3*) Newmarket.

***Saying No is Not Enough: What to Say & How to Listen to Your Kids About Alcohol, Tobacco & Other Drugs- A Guide for Parents.** Robert Schwebel. 1997. 23.95 (*1-55704-324-8*) Newmarket.

Saying "No" to Negativity: How to Manage Negativity in Yourself, Your Boss & Your Co-Workers. Zoie Kaye. Ed. by Kelly Scanlon & Jane D. Guthrie. LC 95-73270. (Illus.). 68p. (Orig.). 1996. pap. 12.95 (*1-57294-017-4*, 12-0028) SkillPath Pubns.

Saying of Confucius. 1989. pap. 3.95 (*0-451-62672-9*) NAL-Dutton.

Saying Please. Jane B. Moncure. LC 82-19927. (Moods & Emotions Ser.). (Illus.). 32p. (J). (ps-2). 1983. lib. bdg. 21.36 (*0-89565-248-X*) Childs World.

Saying So Out Loud. Betsy Struthers. 70p. 1995. lib. bdg. 27.00 (*0-8095-4580-2*) Borgo Pr.

Saying Something: Jazz Improvisation & Interaction. Ingrid Monson. LC 96-23224. (Chicago Studies in Ethnomusicology). (Illus.). 253p. 1997. pap. text ed. 14.95 (*0-226-53478-2*); lib. bdg. 39.95 (*0-226-53477-4*) U Ch Pr.

***Saying Tehillim.** 6th ed. Yosef Y. Schneersohn. Tr. by Zalman I. Posner. 60p. (Orig.). 1975. reprint ed. pap. 3.00 (*0-8266-0426-9*) Kehot Pubn Soc.

Saying Thank You. Colleen L. Reece. LC 82-21992. (Moods & Emotions Ser.). (Illus.). 32p. (J). (ps-2). 1983. lib. bdg. 21.36 (*0-89565-249-8*) Childs World.

Saying Thank You Makes Me Happy. Wanda Hayes. (Illus.). 24p. (J). (ps). 1994. pap. 1.99 (*0-7847-0270-5*, 04220) Standard Pub.

***Saying the Right Thing: The Four Secrets of Powerful Communication.** Raymond DiZazzo. LC 97-1711. 120p. 1997. 12.95 (*1-57071-141-0*) Sourcebks.

Saying Yes. Diana Chang. Ed. by Stanley H. Barkan. Tr. by Parker P. Huang. (Review Women Writers Chapbook Ser.: No. 10). 48p. (CHI & ENG.). 1991. 15.00 (*0-89304-445-8*); 15.00 (*0-89304-447-4*); pap. 5.00 (*0-89304-446-6*); pap. 5.00 (*0-89304-448-2*) Cross-Cultrl NY.

Saying Yes & Saying No: On Rendering to God & Caesar. Robert M. Brown. LC 85-29575. 144p. (Orig.). 1986. pap. 10.00 (*0-664-24695-8*, Westminster) Westminster John Knox.

Saying Yes, Saying No: You & Drugs--A Positive Approach to Staying Drug Free. Community Intervention, Inc. Staff. 24p. (Orig.). (YA). (gr. 8-12). 1986. pap. 3.95 (*0-9613416-4-5*) Comm Intervention.

Saying Yes to Change. Barbara M. Johnson. LC 81-65649. 128p. 1981. 5.00 (*0-8066-1885-X*) B M Johnson.

Saying Yes to God: Esther. Linda R. McGinn. (Women in the Word Ser.). 96p. (Orig.). (YA). (gr. 10). 1995. pap. 3.99 (*0-8010-5044-8*) Baker Bks.

Saying Yes to God Leader's Guide: Esther. Linda R. McGinn. (Women in the Word Ser.). 112p. (Orig.). 1995. teacher ed., pap. 7.99 (*0-8010-5246-7*) Baker Bks.

Saying Yes to Japanese Investment: How You Can Benefit by Doing Business with the Japanese. Simon Partner. 1992. pap. 19.95 (*0-13-785049-2*, Busn) P-H.

Saying Yes to Know. William P. Haiber & Robert Haiber. (Illus.). 160p. 1996. pap. text ed. 24.95 (*0-944089-24-0*) Info Devels.

***Sayings.** David O. Finney. 155p. (Orig.). 1996. pap. write for info. (*0-9651997-1-1*) D O Finney.

Sayings: The Wisdom of Zen. Ed. by Manuela Dunn. LC 96-33725. (Box of Zen Ser.). 64p. 1996. 9.95 (*0-7868-6253-X*) Hyperion.

Sayings & Doings & an Eastward Look. rev. ed. Wendell Berry. LC 90-81977. 64p. 1990. reprint ed. pap. 10.00 (*0-917788-43-5*) Gnomon Pr.

Sayings & Portraits of John Wesley. unabridged ed. Ed. by John Telford. (Illus.). 150p. 1995. reprint ed. pap. 10.99 (*0-88019-336-0*) Schmul Pub Co.

Sayings & Riddles in New Mexico. Arthur L. Campa. LC 37-28299. 67p. 1982. reprint ed. lib. bdg. 27.00 (*0-89370-731-7*) Borgo Pr.

***Sayings for Teachers.** Ed. by David C. Jones. 68p. (Orig.). 1997. pap. 9.95 (*1-55059-144-4*, Pub. by Detselig CN) Temeron Bks.

Sayings of Anthony Trollope. Ed. by R. Mullen. (Sayings Ser.). 64p. pap. 9.95 (*0-7156-2420-2*, Pub. by Duckworth UK) Focus Pub-R Pullins.

Sayings of Benjamin Franklin. Ed. by E. Wright. (Sayings Ser.). 64p. pap. 9.95 (*0-7156-2620-5*, Pub. by Duckworth UK) Focus Pub-R Pullins.

Sayings of Buddha: The Iti-Vuttaka. Itivuttaka. LC 09-4569. (Columbia University. Indo-Iranian Ser.: No. 5). reprint ed. 34.50 (*0-404-50475-2*) AMS Pr.

Sayings of Charles Dickens. Ed. by Watts. (Sayings Ser.). 64p. pap. 9.95 (*0-7156-2666-3*, Pub. by Duckworth UK) Focus Pub-R Pullins.

Sayings of Charlotte Bronte. (Sayings Ser.). 64p. 1996. pap. 9.95 (*0-7156-2744-9*, Pub. by Duckworth UK) Focus Pub-R Pullins.

Sayings of Confucius. 70p. 1990. pap. 4.95 (*9971-947-22-6*) Heian Intl.

An Asterisk (*) at the beginning of an entry indicates that the title is appearing in BIP for the first time.

Sayings of D. H. Lawrence. Ed. by S. Martin. (Sayings Ser.). 64p. pap. 9.95 (*0-7156-2639-6*, Pub. by Duckworth UK) Focus Pub-R Pullins.

Sayings of Disraeli. Ed. by R. Blake. (Sayings Ser.). pap. 9.95 (*0-7156-2424-5*, Pub. by Duckworth UK) Focus Pub-R Pullins.

Sayings of Dr. Johnson. Ed. by B. O'Cascy. (Sayings Ser.). 64p. pap. 9.95 (*0-7156-2352-4*, Pub. by Duckworth UK) Focus Pub-R Pullins.

Sayings of E. Stanley Jones: A Treasury of Wisdom & Wit. Ed. by Whitney J. Dough. 144p. (Orig.). 1994. pap. 12.95 (*1-881576-29-9*) Providence Hse.

Sayings of Evelyn Waugh. (Sayings Ser.). 64p. 1996. pap. 9.95 (*0-7156-2742-2*, Pub. by Duckworth UK) Focus Pub-R Pullins.

Sayings of F. Scott Fitzgerald. Ed. by R. Pearce. (Sayings Ser.). 64p. pap. 9.95 (*0-7156-2648-5*, Pub. by Duckworth UK) Focus Pub-R Pullins.

Sayings of George Bernard Shaw. Ed. by J. Spence. (Sayings Ser.). 64p. pap. 9.95 (*0-7156-2491-1*, Pub. by Duckworth UK) Focus Pub-R Pullins.

Sayings of Goethe. (Sayings Ser.). 64p. 1996. pap. 9.95 (*0-7156-2745-7*, Pub. by Duckworth UK) Focus Pub-R Pullins.

Sayings of Henrik Ibsen. Ed. by R. Huntford. (Sayings Ser.). 64p. 1996. pap. 9.95 (*0-7156-2668-X*, Pub. by Duckworth UK) Focus Pub-R Pullins.

Sayings of James Joyce. Ed. by S. Sheehan. (Sayings Ser.). 64p. pap. 9.95 (*0-7156-2637-X*, Pub. by Duckworth UK) Focus Pub-R Pullins.

Sayings of Jane Austen. Ed. by M. McKernan. (Sayings Ser.). pap. 9.95 (*0-7156-2461-X*, Pub. by Duckworth UK) Focus Pub-R Pullins.

Sayings of Jesus. Ed. by Andrew Linzey. (Sayings Ser.). 64p. pap. 9.95 (*0-7156-2364-8*, Pub. by Duckworth UK) Focus Pub-R Pullins.

Sayings of Jesus. Edward Dumbauld. (Illus.). 196p. (C). 1988. reprint ed. pap. text ed. 20.00 (*0-8191-6753-3*) U Pr of Amer.

Sayings of Jesus in the Epistle of James. Dean B. Deppe. 1994. 29.95 (*0-317-05949-1*) Dove Bkslrs.

Sayings of Jesus in the Pseudo-Clementine Homilies. Leslie L. Kline. LC 75-1645. (Society of Biblical Literature. Dissertation Ser.: No. 14). 208p. reprint ed. 59.30 (*0-8357-9579-9*, 2017517) Bks Demand.

Sayings of Jesus in the Teaching of the Twelve Apostles. Clayton N. Jefford. LC 89-37998. (Supplements to Vigiliae Christianae Ser.: No. XI). xvi, 185p. 1989. text ed. 71.50 (*90-04-09127-0*) E J Brill.

Sayings of John Keats. Ed. by J. Peerless. (Sayings Ser.). 64p. pap. 9.95 (*0-7156-2638-8*, Pub. by Duckworth UK) Focus Pub-R Pullins.

Sayings of Jonathan Swift. Ed. by J. Spence. (Sayings Ser.). 64p. pap. 9.95 (*0-7156-2633-7*, Pub. by Duckworth UK) Focus Pub-R Pullins.

Sayings of K'ung the Master. Allen Upward. LC 78-64056. (Des Imagistes: Literature of the Imagist Movement Ser.). reprint ed. 27.50 (*0-404-17110-9*) AMS Pr.

Sayings of Leo Tolstoy. Ed. by R. Pearce. (Sayings Ser.). 64p. pap. 9.95 (*0-7156-2671-X*, Pub. by Duckworth UK) Focus Pub-R Pullins.

***Sayings of Lewis Carroll.** Ed. by R. Pearce. (Duckworth Sayings Ser.). 64p. (Orig.). 1996. pap. 9.95 (*0-7156-2743-0*, Pub. by Duckworth UK) Focus Pub-R Pullins.

Sayings of Lord Byron. Ed. by G. Martin. (Sayings Ser.). 64p. pap. 9.95 (*0-7156-2351-6*, Pub. by Duckworth UK) Focus Pub-R Pullins.

Sayings of Mark Twain. Ed. by J. Munson. (Sayings Ser.). 64p. pap. 9.95 (*0-7156-2421-0*, Pub. by Duckworth UK) Focus Pub-R Pullins.

***Sayings of Master Chao-Chou.** Green. 18.00 (*0-06-063474-X*) HarpC.

Sayings of Menahem Mendel of Kotsk. Simcha Raz. Tr. by Edward Levin. LC 94-28313. 224p. 1995. 25.00 (*1-56821-297-6*) Aronson.

Sayings of Moses. Ed. by D. Cohn-Sherbok. (Sayings Ser.). 64p. pap. 9.95 (*0-7156-2375-3*, Pub. by Duckworth UK) Focus Pub-R Pullins.

Sayings of Muhammad. Ghazi Ahmad. pap. 3.50 (*0-933511-47-7*) Kazi Pubns.

Sayings of Muhammad. Allama Al-mamun. 1990. pap. 6.95 (*0-8065-1169-9*, Citadel Pr) Carol Pub Group.

Sayings of Muhammad. Ed. by N. Robinson. (Sayings Ser.). 64p. pap. 9.95 (*0-7156-2365-6*, Pub. by Duckworth UK) Focus Pub-R Pullins.

Sayings of Muhammad. Allama Sir Abdullah Al-Mamun Al-Suhrawardy. LC 91-78174. (Wisdom of the East Ser.). 128p. 1992. reprint ed. 12.95 (*0-8048-1797-9*) C E Tuttle.

Sayings of Muhammad. Allama Sir Abdullah al-Mamun alsuhrawardy. LC 79-52559. (Islam Ser.). 1980. reprint ed. lib. bdg. 17.95 (*0-8369-9266-0*) Ayer.

Sayings of Muhammad, the Last Prophet. S. A. Hussain. pap. 3.50 (*0-933511-49-3*) Kazi Pubns.

Sayings of Nietzsche. Ed. by S. Martin. (Sayings Ser.). 64p. pap. 9.95 (*0-7156-2475-X*, Pub. by Duckworth UK) Focus Pub-R Pullins.

Sayings of Oscar Wilde. Ed. by H. Russell. (Sayings Ser.). 64p. pap. 9.95 (*0-7156-2305-2*, Pub. by Duckworth UK) Focus Pub-R Pullins.

Sayings of Paramahansa Yogananda. Self-Realization Fellowship Editorial Staff & Paramahansa Yogananda. LC 79-66287. (Illus.). 136p. 1980. pap. 6.50 (*0-87612-116-4*) Self Realization.

Sayings of Paramahansa Yogananda. Paramahansa Yogananda & Self-Realization Fellowship Editorial Staff. LC 79-66287. (Illus.). 136p. 1980. 10.50 (*0-87612-115-6*) Self Realization.

Sayings of R. L. Stevenson. Ed. by K. Steele. (Sayings Ser.). 63p. 1994. pap. 9.95 (*0-7156-2613-2*, Pub. by Duckworth UK) Focus Pub-R Pullins.

Sayings of Rudyard Kipling. Ed. by A. Rutherford. (Sayings Ser.). 64p. pap. 9.95 (*0-7156-2621-3*, Pub. by Duckworth UK) Focus Pub-R Pullins.

Sayings of Samuel Pepys. Ed. by R. L. Ollard. (Sayings Ser.). 64p. 1996. pap. 9.95 (*0-7156-2667-1*, Pub. by Duckworth UK) Focus Pub-R Pullins.

Sayings of Shakespeare. Ed. by A. Rowse. (Sayings Ser.). 64p. pap. 9.95 (*0-7156-2458-X*, Pub. by Duckworth UK) Focus Pub-R Pullins.

Sayings of Shigeo Shingo: Key Strategies for Plant Improvement. Shigeo Shingo. Tr. by Andrew P. Dillon from JPN. LC 87-60547. (Illus.). 207p. 1987. 45.00 (*0-915299-15-1*) Prod Press.

Sayings of Somerset Maugham. Ed. by C. Hewetson. (Sayings Ser.). 64p. pap. 9.95 (*0-7156-2440-7*, Pub. by Duckworth UK) Focus Pub-R Pullins.

Sayings of Sri Ramakrishna. Sri Ramakrishna. pap. 4.95 (*0-87481-431-6*, Pub. by Ramakrishna Math II) Vedanta Pr.

Sayings of Sydney Smith. Ed. by A. Bell. (Sayings Ser.). 64p. pap. 9.95 (*0-7156-2391-5*, Pub. by Duckworth UK) Focus Pub-R Pullins.

Sayings of the Ancestors: The Spiritual Life of the Sibundoy Indians. John H. McDowell. LC 89-5435. 216p. 1989. 24.00 (*0-8131-1671-6*) U Pr of Ky.

Sayings of the Ancient One. Patrick G. Bowen. 1972. lib. bdg. 250.00 (*0-87968-490-9*) Krishna Pr.

Sayings of the Bible. Ed. by M. Grant. (Sayings Ser.). 64p. 1994. pap. 9.95 (*0-7156-2448-2*, Pub. by Duckworth UK) Focus Pub-R Pullins.

Sayings of the Buddha. Ed. by Geoffrey Parrinder. (Sayings Ser.). pap. 9.95 (*0-7156-2374-5*, Pub. by Duckworth UK) Focus Pub-R Pullins.

Sayings of the Desert Fathers. (Cistercian Studies: No. 59). 1972. pap. 12.95 (*0-87907-959-2*) Cistercian Pubns.

Sayings of the Fathers. E. A. Budge. 1975. pap. 6.95 (*0-89981-089-6*) Eastern Orthodox.

Sayings of the Hour. Salvatore Cipparone. 4.95 (*0-686-20575-8*) Ivory Scroll.

Sayings of the Jewish Fathers. Charles W. Taylor. 1973. 59.95 (*0-8490-0995-2*) Gordon Pr.

Sayings of the Jewish Fathers, 2 Vols. in 1. rev. ed. Charles Taylor. (Library of Jewish Classics). 1969. 35.00 (*0-87068-114-1*) Ktav.

Sayings of the Prophet Muhammad: 40 Hadith. (Hadith Qudsi Ser.). (ARA & ENG.). 1982. 8.95 (*0-86685-285-9*) Intl Bk Ctr.

***Sayings of the Sufi Sages.** Ed. by Lynn Wilcox. LC 96-71230. 104p. (Orig.). 1997. pap. 5.95 (*0-910735-86-7*) MTO Printing & Pubn Ctr.

Sayings of Thomas Hardy. Ed. by R. Pearce. (Sayings Ser.). 64p. 1996. pap. 9.95 (*0-7156-2699-X*, Pub. by Duckworth UK) Focus Pub-R Pullins.

Sayings of W. B. Yeats. Lewis Spence. (Sayings Ser.). pap. 9.95 (*0-7156-2457-1*, Pub. by Duckworth UK) Focus Pub-R Pullins.

Sayings of Walter Scott. Ed. by E. Anderson. (Sayings Ser.). 64p. pap. 9.95 (*0-7156-2680-9*, Pub. by Duckworth UK) Focus Pub-R Pullins.

Sayings of Winston Churchill. Ed. by J. Sutcliffe. (Sayings Ser.). 1992. pap. 9.95 (*0-7156-2389-3*, Pub. by Duckworth UK) Focus Pub-R Pullins.

Sayings of Women. Ozouf. LC 97-2648. 1997. 29.95 (*0-226-64333-6*) U Ch Pr.

Sayles Complex: A Late Milling Stone Assemblage from Cajon Pass & the Ecological Implications of Its Scraper Planes, Vol. 6. Makoto Kowta. (University of California Publications in American Archaeology & Ethnology: Vol. 6). (Illus.). 105p. 1969. reprint ed. pap. text ed. 9.65 (*1-55567-478-X*) Coyote Press.

Sayles Country: A Social History, 1600-1986, & Some Descendants of John & Mary (Williams) Sayles of Providence, R.I. Judith A. Hurst. (Illus.). 319p. 1995. reprint ed. pap. 47.50 (*0-8328-4832-8*); reprint ed. lib. bdg. 57.50 (*0-8328-4831-X*) Higginson Bk Co.

Sayonara. James A. Michener. 1983. mass mkt. 5.95 (*0-449-20414-6*, Crest) Fawcett.

Sayonara, Michelangelo: The Sistine Chapel Restored & Repackaged. Waldemar Januszczak. 224p. 1991. pap. 10.00 (*0-201-56750-4*) Addison-Wesley.

Sayonara, Mrs. Kackleman. Maira Kalman. 32p. (J). 1991. pap. 5.99 (*0-14-054159-4*, Puffin) Puffin Bks.

Sayonara, Mrs. Kackleman. Maira Kalman. (Illus.). 40p. (J). (ps-5). 1989. pap. 16.99 (*0-670-82945-5*) Viking Child Bks.

Sayonara My Friend Love Annie. Charlotte Manassen-Mori. (Illus.). 247p. 1994. 22.50 (*0-85572-239-8*) Seven Hills Bk.

Sayonara, Sweet Amaryllis. large type ed. James Melville. 304p. 1986. 25.99 (*0-7089-1433-0*) Ulverscroft.

Sayre Family: Lineage of Thomas Sayre, a Founder of Southampton. Theodore M. Banta. (Illus.). 774p. 1989. reprint ed. lib. bdg. 124.00 (*0-8328-1050-9*) Higginson Bk Co.

Sayre Family: Lineage of Thomas Sayre, a Founder of Southampton. Theordore M. Banta. (Illus.). 774p. 1989. reprint ed. pap. 116.00 (*0-8328-1051-7*) Higginson Bk Co.

Says I, Says He. Ron Hutchinson. (Phoenix Theatre Ser.). 1980. pap. 6.95 (*0-912262-69-9*) Proscenium.

Say's Law: An Historical Analysis. Thomas Sowell. LC 78-38515. 256p. 1972. text ed. 45.00 (*0-691-04166-0*) Princeton U Pr.

Says Who? Scott Huber. (Inter Acta Ser.). (Illus.). 4p. (C). 1994. student ed., ring bd. 3.25 (*1-885702-30-2*, 741-009s, Inter Acta) WSN Pr.

Says Who? A Guide to the Quotations of the Century. Jonathan Green. 1989. 14.95 (*0-582-89336-4*) Longman.

Says Who? Relativism. Scott Huber. (Illus.). 6p. (C). 1994. teacher ed., ring bd. 1.25 (*1-885702-31-0*) WSN Pr.

Sayula Popoluca Verb Derivation. Lawrence Clark. (Language Data, Amerindian Ser.: No. 8). 80p. (Orig.). 1983. fiche 4.00 (*0-88312-508-0*) Summer Instit Ling.

Sayyid Qutb & Islamic Activism: A Translation & Critical Analysis of Social Justice in Islam. William E. Shepard. LC 96-2064. (Social, Economic, & Political Studies of the Middle East: Vol. 54). 1996. 112.00 (*90-04-10152-7*) E J Brill.

SB 198 Handbook. James T. Dufour. 300p. (Orig.). (C). 1995. pap. text ed. 45.00 (*1-878630-63-6*) CA Chamber Commerce.

***SBA: The Reawakening of the African Mind.** Asa G. Hilliard. Ed. by Patricia Hilliard-Nuny. LC 96-94987. xviii, 220p. 1997. write for info. (*0-9655402-0-0*) Makare Pub.

***SBA: The Reawakening of the African Mind.** Asa G. Hilliard. Ed. by Patricia Hilliard-Nuny. LC 96-94987. xviii, 220p. (Orig.). 1997. pap. write for info. (*0-9655402-1-9*) Makare Pub.

SBA Hotline Answer Book. Gustav Berle. LC 91-4622. 288p. 1991. pap. text ed. 14.95 (*0-471-54297-0*) Wiley.

SBA Loan Guide. Jack Fox. (Illus.). 250p. 1989. 45.00 (*0-685-25954-4*) Jack Fox Assocs.

SBA Loans: A Step-by-Step Guide. 2nd ed. Patrick D. O'Hara. 282p. 1994. pap. text ed. 19.95 (*0-471-30331-3*) Wiley.

SBA Microloan & Specialty Handbook. Patrick O'Hara. LC 95-53995. 220p. 1996. text ed. 49.95 (*0-471-13915-7*); pap. text ed. 19.95 (*0-471-13914-9*) Wiley.

SBA's Section Five Hundred Three Program. Mia Purcell. Ed. by Stephanie Sampson. 24p. (Orig.). 1983. pap. 11.00 (*0-317-04826-0*) Natl Coun Econ Dev.

SBC Helldiver in Action. Thomas Doll. (Aircraft in Action Ser.). (Illus.). 50p. 1995. pap. 7.95 (*0-89747-331-0*) Squad Sig Pubns.

SBC Warburg Euromoney Directory, 1996. 1996. pap. 395.00 (*1-85564-378-2*, Pub. by Euromoney UK) Am Educ Systs.

SBC's One Hundred & One Laws - & Perhaps More: Like Supplements 102 to 151 - & Perhaps More. 2nd ed. Austin M. Elliott. 164p. 1991. ring bd. 151.00 (*0-914285-01-7*) Sm Busn Clinic.

SBC's One Hundred & One Laws--& Perhaps More. Austin M. Elliott & R. W. Dorst. 109p. 1984. 101.00 (*0-914285-00-9*) Sm Busn Clinic.

SBC4 Harnessing 3D Studio, Version 5.0. G. Hilley. (ID - CAD/CAM Ser.). 608p. 1996. pap. 49.95 incl. cd-rom (*0-8273-7249-3*) Delmar.

SBD Dauntless in Action. Robert Stern. (Aircraft in Action Ser.). (Illus.). 50p. (Orig.). 1984. pap. 7.95 (*0-89747-153-9*) Squad Sig Pubns.

SBEG: Integrated Logistics Support Handbook. 2nd ed. James V. Jones. 1995. text ed. 57.50 (*0-07-033079-4*) McGraw.

Sb'eyb'al Jun Naq Maya' Q'anjob'al: La Otra Cara. Gaspar P. Gonzalez. 375p. (Orig.). (MYN & SPA.). 1996. pap. 19.95 (*1-886502-13-7*, Ediciones Yax Te) Yax Te Found.

SBL, 1987: Seminar Papers. Ed. by Kent H. Richards. 720p. 1987. 22.95 (*1-55540-200-3*, 06 09 26) Scholars Pr GA.

***SBL 1988: Seminar Papers.** Ed. by David J. Lull. 644p. 1988. pap. 20.95 (*1-55540-297-6*) Scholars Pr GA.

***SBL 1989: Seminar Papers.** Ed. by David J. Lull. 1989. pap. 20.95 (*1-55540-421-9*) Scholars Pr GA.

***SBL 1990: Seminar Papers.** Ed. by David J. Lull. 644p. 1990. pap. 19.95 (*1-55540-548-7*) Scholars Pr GA.

***SBL 1991: Seminar Papers.** Ed. by Eugene H. Lovering, Jr. 839p. 1991. pap. 25.00 (*1-55540-624-6*) Scholars Pr GA.

SBL 1995: Seminar Papers. Ed. by Eugene H. Lovering, Jr. (SBL Seminar Papers). 721p. (C). 1995. pap. 25.00 (*0-7885-0156-9*, 060934) Scholars Pr GA.

***SBL 1996: Seminar Papers.** LC 96-9567. (SBL Seminar Papers Ser.). 517p. pap. 25.00 (*0-7885-0292-1*, 063511) Scholars Pr GA.

SBMO International Microwave Conference - Brazil, 1993. IEEE, (Microwave Theory & Techniques Society) Staff. Ed. by IEEE, (Institute of Electrical & Electronics Engineers, Inc.) Staff. LC 93-78203. 650p. 1993. pap. write for info. (*0-7803-1288-0*, 93TH0555-3); fiche write for info. (*0-7803-1289-9*) Inst Electrical.

Sborniki Dukhovno-Muzikal'nikh Proizvjedenij Borisa Mikhajlovicha Ledkovskago, 3 Vols., Vol. 1. 47p. 1972. 5.00 (*0-317-30399-6*) Holy Trinity.

Sborniki Dukhovno-Muzikal'nikh Proizvjedenij Borisa Mikhajlovicha Ledkovskago, 3 Vols., Vol. 2. 88p. 1972. 8.00 (*0-317-30400-3*) Holy Trinity.

Sborniki Dukhovno-Muzikal'nikh Proizvjedenij Borisa Mikhajlovicha Ledkovskago, 3 Vols., Vol. 3. 185p. 1972. 15.00 (*0-317-30401-1*) Holy Trinity.

SBS: Container Gardening. Sue Phillips & Sutherland. (Illus.). 112p. 1995. 14.98 (*0-8317-7790-7*) Smithmark.

SBS: Roses. John Mattock et al. (Illus.). 112p. 1995. 14.98 (*0-8317-7791-5*) Smithmark.

***SBS Basic Carpentry.** Ben Allen. (Illus.). 112p. 1997. pap. 12.95 (*0-696-20665-X*) Meredith Bks.

***SBS Bed & Bath Projects.** (Do-It-Yourself Ser.). (Illus.). 96p. 12.95 (*0-696-20733-8*) Meredith Bks.

***SBS Masonry & Concrete.** Ben Allen. (Illus.). 112p. 1997. pap. 12.95 (*0-696-20666-8*) Meredith Bks.

***SBS Pillows & Cushions.** (Do-It-Yourself Ser.). (Illus.). 96p. 12.95 (*0-696-20732-X*) Meredith Bks.

***SBS Window Treatments.** (Do-It-Yourself Ser.). (Illus.). 96p. 12.95 (*0-696-20734-6*) Meredith Bks.

SBS World Guide. 5th ed. Ed. by Thorpe, D. W., Staff. 800p. 1996. pap. 30.00 (*1-875589-97-X*, 80500) D W Thorpe.

SBT-IEEE International Telecommunications Symposium, 1994. IEEE, Communications Society Staff. Ed. by IEEE Staff. LC 94-78173. 1994. pap. text ed. write for info. (*0-7803-2097-2*); lib. bdg. write for info. (*0-7803-2098-0*, 94CH3484-3); fiche write for info. (*0-7803-2099-9*) Inst Electrical.

SBus: TELOS: The Electronic Library of Science. Jim Lyle. LC 92-18701. (Illus.). ix, 351p. 1992. 54.95 (*0-387-97862-3*) Spr-Verlag.

SB2U Vindicator in Action. Thomas Doll. (Aircraft in Action Ser.). (Illus.). 50p. 1992. pap. 7.95 (*0-89747-274-8*, 1122) Squad Sig Pubns.

***Sc Assist Fly Tying.** D. Meyer. 1995. pap. 9.45 (*1-878175-65-3*) F Amato Pubns.

SC, Y, La-Lu Rare Earth Elements, 12-B, C. 8th ed. (Compounds with Carbon Ser.). 362p. 1994. 1,595.00 (*0-387-93689-0*) Spr-Verlag.

Sc, Y, La-Lu Rare Earth Elements Supplement Vol. C 12a: Compounds wuth Carbons. 8th ed. H. Hein et al. Ed. by J. Jouanne et al. (Gmelin Handbook of Inorganic & Organmetallic Chemicals). (Illus.). xx, 459p. 1995. 2,029.00 (*3-540-93718-8*) Spr-Verlag.

***SCA Guide to Graduate Environmental Programs.** Student Conservation Association Staff. LC 97-5603. 384p. 1997. 29.95 (*1-55963-339-5*, Shearwater Bks); pap. 16.95 (*1-55963-340-9*, Shearwater Bks) Island Pr.

Scaasi: A Cut Above. Arnold Scaasi & Bernadine Morris. LC 96-18119. (Illus.). 192p. 1996. 55.00 (*0-8478-1987-6*) Rizzoli Intl.

S

Scab. Jack London. (Illus.). 42p. 1992. pap. 1.95 (*0-932458-23-8*) Star Rover.

Scab Pie. Pat Pollari. (Barf-O-Rama Ser.: No. 7). 128p. (YA). 1996. mass mkt. 3.50 (*0-553-48413-3*) BDD Bks Young Read.

Scabies. K. Mellanby. 87p. 1972. 20.00 (*0-317-07173-4*) St Mut.

Scacciato. William Maddox. 128p. (Orig.). 1996. pap. 10.00 (*0-916620-97-2*) Portals Pr.

***SCADA: Supervisory Control & Data Acquisition.** Stuart A. Boyer. LC 93-123. 254p. 1993. 68.00 (*1-55617-210-9*) ISA.

***SCADA/Control Systems in Municipal Water & Wastewater Facilities.** Richard K. Miller et al. (Market Research Survey Ser.: No. 284). 50p. 1996. 200.00 (*1-55865-303-1*) Future Tech Surveys.

Scaenicae Romanorum Poesis Fragmenta, Bd. I: Tragicorum Fragmenta. Ed. by Otto Ribbeck. ccxiv, 876p. 1978. reprint ed. write for info. (*0-318-71215-6*) G Olms Pubs.

Scaenicae Romanorum Poesis Fragmenta, Bd. II: Comicorum Fragmenta. Ed. by Otto Ribbeck. ccxiv, 876p. 1978. reprint ed. write for info. (*0-318-71216-4*) G Olms Pubs.

Scaenicae Romanorum Poesis Fragmenta, 2 vols., Set. Ed. by Otto Ribbeck. ccxiv, 876p. 1978. reprint ed. write for info. (*0-318-71214-8*) G Olms Pubs.

Scaffolding: Selected Poems. Jane M. Cooper. 144p. (Orig.). 1993. reprint ed. pap. 12.95 (*0-88448-108-5*) Tilbury Hse.

Scaffolding Children's Learning: Vygotsky & Early Childhood Education. Laura E. Berk & Adam Winsler. LC 95-69457. (Illus.). 182p. (Orig.). 1995. pap. text ed. 8.00 (*0-935989-68-4*, 146) Natl Assn Child Ed.

Scaffolding Reading Experiences: Designs for Student Success. Michael Graves & Bonnie Graves. (Illus.). 252p. (Orig.). (J). (gr. 3-8). 1994. pap. text ed. 28.95 (*0-926842-35-8*) CG Pubs Inc.

***Scaffolding Student Learning: Instructional Approaches & Issues.** Ed. by Kathleen Hogan & Michael Pressley. LC 96-29940. (Advances in Learning & Teaching Ser.). 180p. (Orig.). 1997. pap. text ed. 21.95 (*1-57129-036-2*) Brookline Bks.

Scagel: The Man & his Knives. Harry K. McEvoy. (Illus.). 28p. 1985. pap. 3.95 (*0-940362-09-0*) Knife World.

SCAI '95. Aamodt & Komorowski. LC 95-75771. (Frontiers in Artificial Intelligence & Applications Ser.). (gr. 12). 1995. 98.00 (*90-5199-221-1*) IOS Press.

Scala Di Seta: Farsa Comica in One Act, 2 vols., Set. Gioachino Rossini. Ed. by Anders Wiklund. (Works of Gioachino Rossini Critical Edition Ser.). 600p. 1992. lib. bdg. 180.00 (*0-226-72845-5*) U Ch Pr.

Scalable Choice Models. Tony E. Smith. (Discussion Paper Ser.: No. 84). 1975. pap. 10.00 (*1-55869-110-3*) Regional Sci Res Inst.

Scalable High-Performance Computing Conference (SHPCC-94) LC 93-81316. 872p. 1994. pap. text ed. 160.00 (*0-8186-5680-8*, 5680) IEEE Comp Soc.

Scalable Object-Oriented Database Design. Peter Heinckiens. LC 96-43507. (Advances in Object Technology Ser.). (Orig.). 1996. 40.00 (*1-884842-36-4*, 2364) SIGS Bks & Multimedia.

***Scalable Performance Data Server User's Guide: Version 1.** 101p. (C). 1996. pap. 25.95 (*1-55544-844-5*) SAS Inst.

Scalable Shared Memory Multiprocessing. Dan Lenoski & Wolf-Dietrich Weber. 341p. 1995. 59.95 (*1-55860-315-8*) Morgan Kaufmann.

Scalable Shared Memory Multiprocessors. Ed. by Michel Dubois & Shreekant S. Thakkar. 352p. 1991. lib. bdg. 119.00 (*0-7923-9219-1*) Kluwer Ac.

Scalabrinian Mission among Polish Immigrants in Boston, 1893-1909. Silvano M. Tomasi. (Pastoral Ser.). 25p. 1985. 5.00 (*0-934733-01-5*) CMS.

Scalabrinians in North America (1887-1934) Mary E. Brown. LC 95-37420. 420p. 1996. pap. 19.95 (*0-934733-88-0*) CMS.

Scalacronica: A Chronicle of England & Scotland from A.D. 1066 to A. D. 1362. Thomas Gray. Ed. by Joseph Stevenson. LC 70-168186. (Maitland Club, Glasgow. Publications: No. 40). reprint ed. 57.50 (*0-404-53015-X*) AMS Pr.

An Asterisk (*) at the beginning of an entry indicates that the title is appearing in BIP for the first time.

***Scalar Interpretation in Deontic Speech Acts.** rev. ed. Eugene Rohrbaugh. (Outstanding Dissertations in Linguistics Ser.). (Illus.). 250p. 1997. 50.00 (*0-8153-2885-0*) Garland.

Scalar Wave Theory: Green's Functions & Applications. J. A. DeSanto. Ed. by L. M. Brekhovskikh et al. LC 92-15953. (Wave Phenomena Ser.: No. 12). (Illus.). xiii, 193p. 1992. 69.95 (*0-387-55263-4*) Spr-Verlag.

Scalawag in Alabama Politics, 1865-1881. Sarah W. Wiggins. 248p. 1991. pap. 16.95 (*0-8173-0557-2*) U of Ala Pr.

Scalawagons in Oz. John R. Neill. (Illus.). 309p. (J). (gr. 3 up). 1991. 24.95 (*0-929605-12-8*) Books Wonder.

Scalded to Death by the Steam: Authentic Stories of Railroad Disasters & the Ballads That Were Written about Them. Katie L. Lyle. LC 88-830. (Illus.). 224p. 1988. pap. text ed. 12.95 (*0-945575-01-7*) Algonquin Bks.

Scale Aircraft Drawings: World War One. Model Airplane News Staff. (Illus.). 154p. 1986. pap. 14.95 (*0-911295-02-X*) Air Age.

Scale Aircraft Drawings Vol. 2: World War II. Peter M. Bowers. 151p. 1991. 14.95 (*0-911295-14-3*) Air Age.

Scale & Administrative Performance: The Governance of Small States & Microstates. Randall Baker. Ed. by Dennis Conway. (Series on Environment & Development). 41p. (Orig.). 1992. pap. 2.00 (*1-881157-08-3*) In Ctr Global.

Scale & Conformal Symmetry in Hadron Physics. Ed. by R. Gatto. LC 73-4324. 240p. reprint ed. pap. 68.40 (*0-317-09058-5*, 2011957) Bks Demand.

Scale & Mode Techniques. (Four Bass Superchops Ser.). 1992. pap. 12.95 incl. audio (*0-7935-1031-7*, 00660306) H Leonard.

Scale & Mode Techniques. (Four Bass Superchops Ser.). 1992. pap. 14.95 incl. audio compact disk (*0-7935-1032-5*, 00660307) H Leonard.

Scale & Scope: The Dynamics of Industrial Capitalism. Alfred D. Chandler, Jr. (Illus.). 860p. 1990. text ed. 42.50 (*0-674-78994-6*) HUP.

Scale & Scope: The Dynamics of Industrial Capitalism. Alfred D. Chandler. 860p. (C). 1994. pap. text ed. 16.95 (*0-674-78995-4*) HUP.

Scale Book: Piano. D. Glover. 36p. 1986. pap. 4.95 (*0-7935-2571-3*) H Leonard.

Scale-Chord Synopticon. K. Powell et al. 634p. (Orig.). (C). 1987. pap. 29.95 (*0-926954-00-8*) Synopticon Pub.

***Scale, Cost & Effectiveness in University Distance Teaching.** Ed. by Chris Curran. (Illus.). 226p. 1997. text ed. 59.95 (*1-85972-468-X*, Pub. by Ashgate UK) Ashgate Pub Co.

Scale Development: Theories & Applications. Robert F. Devellis. (Applied Social Research Methods Ser.: Vol. 26). (Illus.). 160p. 1991. text ed. 39.95 (*0-8039-3775-X*); pap. text ed. 17.95 (*0-8039-3776-8*) Sage.

Scale Effects in Rock Masses: Proceedings of the First International Workshop, Loen, 7 - 8 June 1990. Ed. by A. Pinto da Cunha. (Illus.). 352p. (C). 1990. text ed. 105.00 (*90-6191-126-5*, Pub. by A A Balkema NE) Ashgate Pub Co.

Scale Effects in Rock Masses 93: Proceedings of the Second International Workshop on Scale Effects in Rock Masses, Lisbon, Portugal, June 1993. Ed. by A. Pinto Da Cunha. (Illus.). 350p. 1993. text ed. 105.00 (*90-5410-322-1*, Pub. by A A Balkema NE) Ashgate Pub Co.

Scale for Measuring the Antero-Posterior Posture of Ninth Grade Boys. C. L. Brownell. LC 74-176601. (Columbia University. Teachers College. Contributions to Education Ser.: No. 325). reprint ed. 37.50 (*0-404-55325-7*) AMS Pr.

Scale in Conscious Experience: Is the Brain Too Important to Be Left to the Specialists to Study? Ed. by Joseph King & Karl H. Pribram. (INNS Series of Texts, Monographs, & Proceedings). 452p. 1995. pap. 95.00 (*0-8058-2178-3*) L Erlbaum Assocs.

***Scale in Remote Sensing & GIS.** Dale A. Quattrochi & Michael F. Goodchild. LC 96-27156. 1996. write for info. (*1-56670-104-X*) Lewis Pubs.

Scale Insect Family Coccidae: An Indentification Manual to Genera. C. J. Hodgson. 656p. 1994. 150.00 (*0-85198-882-2*) CAB Intl.

Scale Insects of Central Europe. Michael Kosztarab & F. Kozar. (Entomologica Ser.). (C). 1988. lib. bdg. 203.00 (*90-6193-623-3*) Kluwer Ac.

Scale Insects of Northeastern North America: Identification, Biology, & Distribution. Michael Kosztarab. (UMNH Special Publications: No. 3). (Illus.). 660p. 1996. 59.95 (*1-884549-01-2*) VA Mus Natl Hist.

Scale Insects of the Tropical South Pacific Region, Pt. 2: The Mealybugs (Pseudococcidae) D. J. Williams & G. W. Watson. 264p. (Orig.). 1988. pap. 60.00 (*0-85198-625-0*, Pub. by CAB Intntl UK) OUP.

Scale Insects of the Tropical South Pacific Region, Pt. 3 Pt. 3: The Soft Scales (Coccidae) & Other Families. D. J. Williams & G. W. Watson. 272p. (Orig.). 1990. pap. 60.00 (*0-85198-659-5*, Pub. by CAB Intntl UK) OUP.

Scale Invariance, Interfaces, & Non-Equilibrium Dynamics. Ed. by Alan McKane et al. LC 95-17265. (NATO ASI Ser.: Ser. B, Vol. 344). 344p. 1995. 105.00 (*0-306-45005-4*, Plenum Pr) Plenum.

Scale Issues in Hydrological Modelling. Ed. by J. D. Kalma & M. Sivapalan. (Advances in Hydrological Processes Ser.). 489p. 1995. pap. text ed. 67.95 (*0-471-95847-6*) Wiley.

Scale Model Detailing: Projects You Can Do. Kalmbach Publishing Co. Staff. 1995. pap. 14.95 (*0-89024-209-7*, 12139) Kalmbach.

Scale Model of Human Surface Anatomy & Musculature. Leon Schlossberg. 1979. 42.50 (*0-8018-2165-7*) Johns Hopkins.

Scale Modeling Tips & Techniques. FineScale Modeler Staff. Ed. by Michael Emmerich. (Illus.). 48p. (Orig.). 1992. per. 6.95 (*0-89024-127-9*, 12102) Kalmbach.

Scale of Imprisonment. Franklin E. Zimring & Gordon J. Hawkins. LC 90-44613. (Studies in Crime & Justice). (Illus.). xiv, 264p. 1993. pap. text ed. 12.95 (*0-226-98354-4*) U Ch Pr.

Scale of Perfection & the English Mystical Tradition. Joseph E. Milosh. LC 66-22857. 226p. reprint ed. pap. 64.50 (*0-317-07863-1*, 2010975) Bks Demand.

Scale Operator. Jack Rudman. (Career Examination Ser.: C-3008). 1994. pap. 27.95 (*0-8373-3008-4*) Nat Learn.

***Scale Patterns.** Ed. by Aaron Stang. 76p. (Orig.). (C). 1991. pap. text ed. 9.95 (*0-7692-0958-0*, F3092GTX) Warner Brothers.

Scale Problems in Hydrology. Ed. by V. K. Gupta et al. 1986. lib. bdg. 106.00 (*90-277-2258-7*) Kluwer Ac.

Scale Removal. Wire Association International Staff. 15.00 (*0-318-03183-3*, 7514) Wire Assn Intl.

***Scale-Space Theory for Computer Vision: First International Conference, Scale-Space '97, Utrecht, the Netherlands, July 2-4, 1997 : Proceedings, Vol. 125.** LC 97-23262. (Lecture Notes in Computer Science). 1997. pap. write for info. (*3-540-63167-4*) Spr-Verlag.

Scale-Space Theory in Computer Vision. Tony Lindeberg. LC 93-23648. 440p. (C). 1993. lib. bdg. 130.00 (*0-7923-2636-9*) Kluwer Ac.

Scale-Space Theory in Computer Vision. Tony Lindeberg. 440p. (C). 1994. lib. bdg. 161.00 (*0-7923-9418-6*) Kluwer Ac.

Scale Studies & Etudes for Guitar. Allen Hanlon. 1993. 9.95 (*0-87166-783-5*, 94031) Mel Bay.

Scale Studies for the Violin. J. Hrimaly. 40p. 1986. pap. 3.95 (*0-7935-2568-3*) H Leonard.

Scale Studies for Viola: Based on Hrimaly Scale Studies for the Violin. L. Mogill. 40p. 1987. pap. 9.95 (*0-7935-5446-2*, 50262330) H Leonard.

Scale Studies for Violin. J. Hrimaly. (Carl Fischer Music Library: No. 114). 1994. pap. 5.95 (*0-8258-0020-X*, L114) Fischer Inc NY.

Scale Studies for Violin. Henry Schradieck. Ed. by Gustav Saenger. (Carl Fischer Music Library: No. 641). pap. 7.95 (*0-8258-0085-4*, L641) Fischer Inc NY.

Scale System. Carl Flesch. 112p. 1942. pap. 18.95 (*0-8258-0231-8*, 02921) Fischer Inc NY.

Scale System for Young: EZ Scales. Yoon-Il Auh. (Auh School of Violin Ser.). 45p. (J). (gr. 1-12). 1993. student ed. 10.00 (*1-882858-10-7*) Yoon-il Auh.

Scale-up & Design of Industrial Mixing Processes. Gary B. Tatterson. LC 93-31551. 1993. text ed. 56.00 (*0-07-062939-0*) McGraw.

Scale-up in Biotechnology. Business Communications Co., Inc. Staff. 240p. 1987. pap. 1,950.00 (*0-89336-504-1*, C-061) BCC.

Scale-Up Methodology for Chemical Processes. Jean-Paul Euzen et al. (Illus.). 248p. 1993. 125.00 (*0-88415-188-3*, 5188) Gulf Pub.

Scale-Up Methodology for Chemical Processes. Jean-Paul Euzen et al. 248p. (C). 1993. 420.00 (*2-7108-0646-0*, Pub. by Edits Technip FR) St Mut.

Scaleable Object-Oriented Database Design. Peter Heinckiens. LC 96-43507. 1996. pap. text ed. 40.00 (*0-13-490376-5*) P-H.

Scalehunter's Beautiful Daughter. Lucius Shepard. LC 87-5193. 160p. 1988. 16.95 (*0-9612970-8-5*) Mark Ziesing.

Scales & Arpeggios for Five String Banjo. 2nd ed. Peter W. Pardee. (Illus.). 180p. (Orig.). 1985. pap. 25.00 (*0-933611-00-5*) Harbinger Pubns.

Scales & Arpeggios in Letter Format: One Octave, Bk. 1. Teresa A. Krosnick. 32p. (Orig.). (J). 1992. pap. text ed. 10.00 (*1-882176-00-6*) Theory Aids Keybd.

Scales & Balances. J. T. Graham. (Orig.). 1989. pap. 25.00 (*0-7478-0227-0*, Pub. by Shire UK) St Mut.

Scales & Exercises. Jerry Hahn. (Jerry Hahn Contemporary Guitar Ser.: Vol. 1). 1993. 9.95 (*0-87166-298-1*, 94183); audio 9.98 (*0-87166-299-X*, 94183C) Mel Bay.

***Scales & Exercises.** Jerry Hahn. (Jerry Hahn Contemporary Guitar Ser.: Vol. 1). 1993. 18.95 incl. audio (*0-87166-325-2*, 94183P) Mel Bay.

Scales & Modes for Bass: A Fun & Easy Way to Use Scales & Modes. Steve Hall & Ron Manus. (Alfred Handy Guide Ser.). 32p. (Orig.). 1992. pap. 4.95 (*0-88284-546-2*, 4434) Alfred Pub.

Scales & Modes for Guitar: A Fun & Easy Way to Use Scales & Modes. Steve Hall & Ron Manus. (Alfred Handy Guide Ser.). 32p. (Orig.). 1992. pap. 4.95 (*0-88284-545-4*, 4433) Alfred Pub.

Scales & Weights: A Historical Outline. Bruno Kisch. LC 65-12545. (Yale Studies in the History of Science & Medicine: No. 1). 318p. reprint ed. pap. 90.70 (*0-8357-8315-4*, 2033782) Bks Demand.

Scales, Arpeggios, & Exercises for the Recorder. Margaret Donington & Robert Donington. 80p. (YA). (gr. 9 up). 1968. 19.95 (*0-19-322160-8*) OUP.

Scales for Rating Behavioral Characteristics of Superior Students. Joseph S. Renzulli et al. 1977. pap. 8.95 (*0-936386-00-2*) Creative Learning.

Scales, Intervals, Keys, Triads, Rhythm & Meter. rev. ed. John Clough & Joyce Conley. (C). 1983. pap. text ed. 25.95 (*0-393-95189-8*) Norton.

Scales Made Easy. 2nd ed. Virginia Taylor & Eva T. Kozak. 48p. 1984. pap. 7.95 (*0-938170-04-X*) Wimbledon Music.

Scales, Norms, & Equivalent Scores. William H. Angoff. 1988. 6.00 (*0-317-67895-7*) Educ Testing Serv.

***Scales of Injustice.** Gary Russell. (Dr. Who Missing Adventures Ser.). 280p. 1996. mass mkt. 5.95 (*0-426-20477-8*, Pub. by Virgin Pub UK) London Brdge.

Scales of Justice. Robert Caswell. 176p. (C). 1993. pap. 17.95 (*0-86819-097-7*) Aubrey Bks.

Scales of Justice. Ngaio Marsh. 1994. mass mkt. 4.99 (*0-425-14487-9*) Berkley Pub.

Scales of Justice: Exploring the Wilderness of Health Care & Society's Moral Conscience. Emerita T. Gueson. LC 92-50204. vii, 213p. (Orig.). (C). 1992. pap. text ed. 19.95 (*1-55605-204-9*) Wyndham Hall.

Scales Out of Balance. Lawrence Schug. 55p. 1990. pap. 6.95 (*0-87839-062-6*) North Star.

Scales over Chords: How to Improvise...& Never Play Bad Notes! Wilbur M. Savidge & Randy L. Vradenburg. 160p. 1994. pap. text ed. write for info. (*1-884848-05-2*) Praxis Music.

Scales Over Chords Audio Companion. Wilbur M. Savidge. 8p. 1994. pap. text ed. write for info. (*1-884848-06-0*) Praxis Music.

Scaleup in the Chemical Process Industries: Conversion from Laboratory Scale Tests to Successful Commercial Size Design. Attilio Bisio & Robert L. Kabel. LC 84-25767. 712p. 1985. text ed. 140.00 (*0-471-05747-9*) Wiley.

Scaling: Why Is Animal Size So Important? Knut Schmidt-Nielsen. LC 84-5841. (Illus.). 240p. 1984. pap. text ed. 19.95 (*0-521-31987-0*) Cambridge U Pr.

Scaling & Renormalization in Statistical Physics. John Cardy. (Cambridge Lecture Notes in Physics Ser.: No. 5). 256p. 1996. pap. 32.95 (*0-521-49959-3*) Cambridge U Pr.

Scaling & Self-Similarity in Physics. Jurg Frohlich. (Progress in Physics Ser.: Vol. 8). 434p. (C). 1983. 69.00 (*0-8176-3168-2*) Birkhauser.

Scaling Concepts in Polymer Physics. Pierre-Gilles De Gennes. LC 78-21314. 319p. 1979. 69.95 (*0-8014-1203-X*) Cornell U Pr.

Scaling Fisheries: A Science Driven by Economics & Politics 1855-1955. Tim D. Smith. LC 93-38292. (Cambridge Studies in Applied Ecology & Resource Management). (Illus.). 360p. (C). 1994. text ed. 80.00 (*0-521-39032-X*) Cambridge U Pr.

Scaling in Soil Physics. Ed. by Daniel Hillel & David Elrick. 122p. 1990. 24.00 (*0-89118-792-8*) Am Soc Agron.

Scaling in Two-Phase Flows: Presented at the Winter Annual Meeting of the American Society of Mechanical Engineers, Chicago, Illinois, November 16-21, 1980. American Society of Mechanical Engineers Staff. Ed. by P. Saha & N. M. Farukhi. LC 80-69193. (HTD Ser.: Vol. 14). (Illus.). 59p. reprint ed. pap. 25.00 (*0-8357-2817-X*, 2039056) Bks Demand.

Scaling of Water Flux Rate in Animals. Kenneth A. Nagy & Charles C. Peterson. LC 88-10791. (University of California Publications in Zoology: No. 120). 186p. 1988. pap. 53.10 (*0-7837-7496-6*, 2049218) Bks Demand.

Scaling Phenomena in Disordered Systems. Ed. by Roger Pynn & Arne Skjeltorp. (NATO ASI Series B, Physics: Vol. 133). 592p. 1986. 120.00 (*0-306-42112-7*, Plenum Pr) Plenum.

Scaling Phenomena in Fluid Mechanics: Inaugural Lecture. G. I. Barenblatt. (Illus.). 50p. (C). 1995. pap. text ed. 7.95 (*0-521-46920-1*) Cambridge U Pr.

Scaling Physiological Processes: Leaf to Globe. Ed. by James R. Ehleringer & Christopher B. Field. (Physiological Ecology Ser.). (Illus.). 388p. 1993. text ed. 72.50 (*0-12-233440-X*) Acad Pr.

Scaling, Self-Similarity & Intermediate Asymptotics. G. I. Barenblatt. (Cambridge Texts in Applied Mathematics Ser.: No. 14). 300p. (C). 1996. text ed. 95.00 (*0-521-43516-1*); pap. text ed. 34.95 (*0-521-43522-6*) Cambridge U Pr.

Scaling the Dragon. Janice Moulton & George Robinson. LC 94-71584. 210p. (Orig.). 1994. pap. 19.95 (*0-940121-29-8*, P209, Cross Roads Bks) Cross Cultural Pubns.

Scaling the High Cs: The Musical Life of Tenor John L. Brecknock. John L. Brecknock & John K. Melling. LC 96-17495. 144p. 1996. 44.00 (*0-8108-3137-6*) Scarecrow.

***Scaling the Ivory Tower: Merit & Its Limits in Academic Careers.** Lionel S. Lewis. LC 97-7926. (Foundations of Higher Education Ser.). 1997. 24.95 (*1-56000-958-6*) Transaction Pubs.

***Scaling the Ivory Tower: Merit & Its Limits in Academic Careers.** Lionel S. Lewis. LC 75-11358. 256p. 1975. reprint ed. pap. 73.00 (*0-608-04031-2*, 2064767) Bks Demand.

Scaling the Ivory Tower: Stories from Women in Business School Faculties. Ed. by Dianne H. Cyr & Blaize H. Reich. LC 95-45416. 224p. 1996. text ed. 55.00 (*0-275-95085-9*, Praeger Pubs) Greenwood.

Scaling the Ivory Tower: Stories from Women in Business School Faculties. Ed. by Dianne H. Cyr & Blaize H. Reich. LC 95-45416. 224p. 1996. pap. text ed. 19.95 (*0-275-95673-3*, Praeger Pubs) Greenwood.

Scaling the Ivy Wall in the 90's: Twelve Essential Steps to Winning Admission to America's Most Selective Colleges & Universities. Howard Greene & Robert Minton. LC 94-5159. 1994. pap. 12.95 (*0-316-32736-0*) Little.

Scaling the Secular City: A Defense of Christianity. J. P. Moreland. LC 87-70626. 280p. (Orig.). (C). 1987. pap. 14.99 (*0-8010-6222-5*) Baker Bks.

Scaling the Wall: Talking to Eastern Europe: The Best of Radio Free Europe. Radio Free Europe Staff. Ed. by George R. Urban. LC 64-18955. 303p. reprint ed. pap. 86.40 (*0-7837-3801-3*, 2043621) Bks Demand.

Scaling the Walls: Poems Nineteen Sixty-Seven to Nineteen Seventy-Four. Jonathan Greene. LC 74-18770. 1975. pap. 12.50 (*0-917788-05-2*) Gnomon Pr.

Scaling the Walls: Poems Nineteen Sixty-Seven to Nineteen Seventy-Four. limited ed. Jonathan Greene. LC 74-18770. 1975. 25.00 (*0-917788-06-0*) Gnomon Pr.

***Scaling Up.** Ed. by Martin Greenberger. (Technologies for the 21st Century Ser.: Vol. 7). 292p. (Orig.). 1996. pap. 29.95 (*1-886313-96-2*) Coun For Tech.

***Scaling-Up.** Ed. by P. R. Van Gardingen et al. LC 96-51105. (Society for Experimental Biology Seminar Ser.: No. 63). (Illus.). 294p. (C). 1997. text ed. 85.00 (*0-521-47109-5*) Cambridge U Pr.

Scaling Up: A Research Agenda for Software Engineering. National Research Council Staff. 100p. 1989. pap. text ed. 15.00 (*0-309-04131-7*) Natl Acad Pr.

Scaling Up: Science, Engineering, & the American Chemical Industry. John A. Heitmann & David J. Rhees. (BCHOC Publication: No. 2). (Illus.). 24p. (Orig.). 1984. pap. 6.00 (*0-941901-01-7*) Chem Heritage Fnd.

Scaling up in Hydrology Using Remote Sensing. J. B. Stewart. LC 96-27878. 1996. write for info. (*0-471-96829-3*) Wiley.

Scallion Stone. deluxe ed. Basil A. Smith. (Illus.). 1980. boxed 35.00 (*0-918372-06-2*) Whispers.

Scallop Estuary: The Natural History Features of the Niantic River. Nelson Marshall. (Illus.). 150p. 1994. pap. write for info. (*0-9628730-1-2*) Th Anchorage.

Scallops: Biology, Ecology & Aquaculture. Ed. by S. E. Shumway. (Developments in Aquaculture & Fisheries Science Ser.: No. 21). 1096p. 1991. 225.50 (*0-444-88954-X*) Elsevier.

Scalp Ceremonial of Zuni. Elsie C. Parsons. LC 25-1663. (American Anthropological Association Memoirs Ser.). 1924. pap. 25.00 (*0-527-00530-4*) Periodicals Srv.

***Scalpdance: Indian Warfare on the High Plains, 1865-79.** Thomas Goodrich. LC 97-15471. (Illus.). 320p. 1997. pap. 32.95 (*0-8117-1523-X*) Stackpole.

Scalpel. I Corn. 1985. pap. 3.50 (*0-8217-1682-4*) NAL-Dutton.

Scalpel. Ira Corn, Jr. 1984. mass mkt. 3.50 (*0-8217-1371-X*, Zebra Kensgtn) Kensgtn Pub Corp.

Scalpel. Horace McCoy. (FRE.). 1984. pap. 11.95 (*0-7859-4203-3*) Fr & Eur.

Scalpel. Horace McCoy. 1995. reprint ed. lib. bdg. 24.95 (*1-56849-583-8*) Buccaneer Bks.

Scalpel & the Sword: The Story of Doctor Norman Bethune. rev. ed. Ted Allan & Sydney Gordon. LC 73-8059. 336p. 1974. reprint ed. pap. 10.00 (*0-85345-302-0*) Monthly Rev.

Scalphunters. Patrick E. Andrews. 256p. 1993. mass mkt. 3.50 (*0-8217-4101-2*, Zebra Kensgtn) Kensgtn Pub Corp.

Scalping in America. Tr. by Georg Friederici from GER. reprint ed. 14.95 (*0-8488-0034-6*, J M C & Co) Amereon Ltd.

Scaly & Slimy. Rick Sammon & Susan Sammon. (3-D Children's Ser.). (Illus.). 28p. (J). (gr. k up). 1996. 9.95 (*1-57359-008-8*, Starhill Pr) Black Belt Comm.

Scaly Babies: Reptiles Growing Up. Ginny Johnston & Judy Cutchins. LC 87-18599. (Illus.). 48p. (J). (gr. 2-5). 1988. lib. bdg. 15.93 (*0-688-07306-9*, Morrow Junior) Morrow.

Scaly Facts. Ivan Chermayeff et al. LC 94-2958. (Illus.). 32p. (J). (ps-1). 1995. 11.00 (*0-15-200109-3*, Gulliver Bks) HarBrace.

***Scaly Reptiles: Sticker Activity Book.** Time Life Books Staff. (The Nature Company Discoveries Library). 1997. pap. text ed. 7.95 (*0-7835-4898-2*) Time-Life.

Scaly Things. Klay Lamprell. LC 96-12346. (Young Discoveries Ser.). (Illus.). 32p. (J). (ps-2). 1996. write for info. (*0-7835-4842-7*) Time-Life.

Scam. Parnell Hall. LC 96-31673. 320p. 1997. 22.00 (*0-89296-623-8*) Warner Bks.

***Scam.** Parnell Hall. 336p. 1998. pap. 6.50 (*0-446-40469-1*, Mysterious Paperbk) Warner Bks.

Scam. Peter Lloyd. 72p. 1996. pap. 15.95 (*1-85411-150-7*, Pub. by Seren Bks UK) Dufour.

Scam! Inside America's Con Artist Clans. Don Wright. 520p. 1996. pap. 19.95 (*0-937877-18-2*) Cottage Pubns Inc.

Scam: Shams, Stings, & Shady Business Practices & How You Can Avoid Them. Peter H. Engel. 160p. 1996. pap. 9.95 (*0-312-14409-1*) St Martin.

Scam: The Cover-Up & Compromise. S. Mustafa & A. M. Chenoy. 1995. write for info. (*81-224-0713-7*, Pub. by Wiley Estrn II) Franklin.

Scam, Who Won, Who Lost, Who Got Away. Debashish Basu. (C). 1993. 24.00 (*81-85944-10-5*, Pub. by UBS Pubs Dist II) S Asia.

SCAMC: Proceedings of the 17th Annual Symposium. American Medical Informatics Association Staff. 1992. pap. text ed. 18.95 (*0-07-001519-8*) McGraw-Hill Prof.

Scammell & Densham's Law of Agricultural Holdings. 7th ed. H. A. Densham. 1989. 190.00 (*0-406-36813-9*, U.K.) MICHIE.

***Scammell & Densham's Law of Agricultural Holdings.** 8th ed. H. A. Densham & Della Evans. 1200p. 1996. write for info. (*0-406-00904-X*) Buttrwrth-Heinemann.

Scamp. Linda T. Brandon. 24p. (J). (gr. k-3). 1994. pap. 1.99 (*0-87406-684-0*) Willowisp Pr.

Scamper. Bob Eberle. 51p. 1997. pap. 14.95 (*1-882664-24-8*) Prufrock Pr.

Scamper: A Gray Tree Squirrel. Edna Miller. (Illus.). 32p. (J). (gr. k-3). 1991. lib. bdg. 15.95 (*0-945912-12-9*) Pippin Pr.

Scamper On. Bob Eberle. 55p. (Orig.). 1997. pap. 14.95 (*1-882664-25-6*) Prufrock Pr.

Scamper Sam see Take Along Stories

Scamper Strategies: Fundamental Activities for Narrative Development. Carol E. Esterreicher. LC 94-29659. 1994. pap. 33.00 (*0-930599-31-4*) Thinking Pubs.

Scampering Marmoset. Ken Morrice. 60p. 1990. pap. text ed. 12.00 (*0-08-040927-X*, Pub. by Aberdeen U Pr) Macmillan.

***Scamper's Year.** Jeff Kindley. (Ready-to-Read Ser.). (Illus.). (J). 1997. pap. 4.50 (0-553-37582-2, Bank St); pap. 4.50 (0-553-53132-8, Bank St) BDD Bks Young Read.

***Scams from the Great Beyond: How to Make Easy Money off of ESP, Astrology, UFOs, Crop Circles, Cattle Mutilations, Alien Abductions, Atlantis, Channeling, & Other New-Age Nonsense.** Peter Huston. (Illus.). 208p. 1997. pap. 20.00 (0-87364-912-5) Paladin Pr.

Scams in India: From Ancient Times to 1992 Mega Bank Scam. M. Halayya. (C). 1992. 20.00 (81-7018-727-3, Pub. by BR Pub II) S Asia.

***Scams, Scandals & Skulduggery: A Selection of the World's Most Outrageous Frauds.** Andreas Schroeder. 1996. pap. text ed. 19.99 (0-7710-7952-4) McCland & Stewart.

Scams, Swindles, & Rip-Offs: How to Recognize & Avoid. rev. ed. Graham M. Mott. (Illus.). 208p. 1994. pap. 14.95 (0-9633155-1-X) Gldn Shadows.

Scan This Book. Ed. by John Mendenhall. LC 91-77465. (Illus.). 120p. 1991. pap. text ed. 15.95 (0-88108-099-3) Art Dir.

***Scan This Book, Vol. 2.** Ed. by John Mendenhall. (Illus.). 1991. pap. text ed. 15.95 (0-88108-193-0) Art Dir.

Scandal. Joanna Elm. 1996. mass mkt. 6.99 (0-8125-4471-4) Forge NYC.

Scandal. Shusaku Endo. 238p. 8800. 30.00 (0-7206-0682-9, Pub. by P Owen Ltd UK) Dufour.

Scandal. Shusaku Endo. Tr. by Van C. Gessel. (Vintage International Ser.). 1989. pap. 10.00 (0-679-72355-2, Vin) Random.

Scandal. Amanda Quick. 352p. 1991. pap. 6.50 (0-553-28932-2) Bantam.

Scandal. large type ed. Amanda Quick. 564p. 1991. reprint ed. lib. bdg. 21.95 (1-56054-176-8) Thorndike Pr.

Scandal: Essays in Islamic Heresy. Peter L. Wilson. 224p. Date not set. 12.00 (0-936756-15-2) Autonomedia.

Scandal! Inside Stories of Power, Intrigue & Corruption. A. Summers. 1992. 19.99 (0-517-07341-2) Random Hse Value.

Scandal & Aftereffect: The Study of France since 1930. Steven Ungar. LC 94-22019. 1995. text ed. 49.95 (0-8166-2526-3); pap. text ed. 19.95 (0-8166-2527-1) U of Minn Pr.

Scandal & Reform: Controlling Police Corruption. Lawrence W. Sherman. LC 77-79236. 315p. reprint ed. pap. 89.80 (0-7837-4689-X, 2044436) Bks Demand.

***Scandal & the Shame: Poverty & Underdevelopment.** Bertrand Schneider. (C). 1995. 22.50 (0-7069-9468-X, Pub. by Vikas II) S Asia.

Scandal & the Star. W. Robert McClelland. 128p. (Orig.). 1988. pap. 8.99 (0-8272-3430-9) Chalice Pr.

Scandal Annual, 1993. Paragon Project Staff. 1992. pap. 6.99 (0-312-92936-6) St Martin.

Scandal at High Chimneys. John D. Carr. 192p. 1988. pap. 3.50 (0-88184-394-6) Carroll & Graf.

Scandal in Bohemia. Arthur Conan Doyle. (Sherlock Holmes Ser.). 20p. 1996. pap. 2.50 (1-57514-261-9, 3069) Encore Perform Pub.

Scandal in Fair Haven. Carolyn G. Hart. 336p. 1995. mass mkt. 4.99 (0-553-56537-0) Bantam.

Scandal in Paradise. Marilyn Kaye. 224p. (Orig.). (YA). (gr. 5 up). 1996. pap. 3.95 (0-8167-3974-9) Troll Communs.

***Scandal in the Church: Dr. Edward Drax Free, 1764-1843.** R. B. Outhwaite. LC 97-22833. 1997. write for info. (1-85285-165-1) Hambledon Press.

Scandal in the Ink. Christopher Robinson. 1995. 60.00 (0-304-32703-4) LPC InBook.

Scandal of a Crucified World: Perspectives on the Cross & Suffering. Ed. by Jacob Tesfai. LC 94-17224. 168p. (Orig.). 1994. pap. 17.00 (0-88344-976-5) Orbis Bks.

Scandal of Father Brown. Gilbert K. Chesterton. 1982. pap. 3.50 (0-14-004739-5, Penguin Bks) Viking Penguin.

Scandal of Pleasure: Art in an Age of Fundamentalism. Wendy Steiner. (Illus.). 263p. 1995. 24.95 (0-226-77223-3) U Ch Pr.

Scandal of Pre-Forgiveness. Richard S. Taylor. 1993. pap. 5.99 (0-88019-300-X) Schmul Pub Co.

Scandal of the Cross & Its Triumph. rev. ed. Bob Lord & Penny Lord. 320p. 1992. reprint ed. pap. 12.95 (0-926143-15-8) Journeys Faith.

Scandal of the Evangelical Mind. Mark A. Noll. 283p. 1995. pap. 16.00 (0-8028-4180-5) Eerdmans.

Scandal of the Fabliaux. R. Howard Bloch. LC 85-16428. 166p. 1986. lib. bdg. 27.00 (0-226-05975-8) U Ch Pr.

Scandal of the Gospels: Jesus, Story, & Offense. David McCracken. 240p. 1994. 35.00 (0-19-508428-4) OUP.

Scandal of the Incarnation: Irenaeus Against the Heresies. St. Irenaeus. Ed. by Hans U. Von Balthasar. Tr. by John Saward from GER. LC 90-82992. 117p. (Orig.). 1990. pap. text ed. 10.95 (0-89870-315-8) Ignatius Pr.

Scandal of Ulysses: The Sensational Life of a Twentieth Century Masterpiece. Bruce Arnold. 228p. 1993. pap. 14.95 (0-312-09379-9) St Martin.

Scandal Point. John Patrick. 1969. pap. 13.00 (0-8222-0994-2) Dramatists Play.

Scandalabra. limited ed. Zelda Fitzgerald. 1980. 50.00 (0-89723-022-1) Bruccoli.

Scandale D'Amour. Anne-Marie Villefranche. 1995. mass mkt. 5.95 (0-7867-0293-1) Carroll & Graf.

Scandale de la Verite see Essais et Ecrits de Combat

Scandale de la Vertie. Georges Bernanos. (FRE.). 1984. pap. 19.95 (0-7859-2696-8) Fr & Eur.

***Scandalized!** Lori Foster. 1997. mass mkt. 3.50 (0-373-25757-0, 1-25757-5) Harlequin Bks.

Scandalous. Candace Camp. 1996. mass mkt. 5.99 (1-55166-166-7, Mira Bks) Harlequin Bks.

Scandalous. Donna Hill. 320p. 1995. mass mkt. 4.99 (0-8217-0148-7, Zebra Kensgtn); mass mkt. 4.99 (0-7860-0148-8, Pinncle Kensgtn) Kensgtn Pub Corp.

Scandalous. Sonia Simone. 384p. (Orig.). 1994. mass mkt. 4.50 (0-380-77496-8) Avon.

Scandalous No. 2: Eden's Story. Jude Watson. (Brides of Wildcat County Ser.). 179p. (J). (gr. 7-10). 1995. pap. 3.95 (0-689-80327-3, Aladdin Paperbacks) S&S Childrens.

Scandalous Affair. large type ed. Clarissa Ross. 304p. 1995. 25.99 (0-7089-3248-7) Ulverscroft.

Scandalous Charade. Mona Gedney. 288p. 1994. mass mkt. 3.99 (0-8217-4697-9, Zebra Kensgtn) Kensgtn Pub Corp.

Scandalous Courtship. Barbara Reeves. 190p. 1993. 19.95 (0-8027-1258-4) Walker & Co.

Scandalous Courtship. Barbara Reeves. 208p. 1994. mass mkt. 3.99 (0-380-72151-1) Avon.

Scandalous Ghost: Sartre's Existentialism As Related to Vitalism, Humanism, Mysticism, Marxism. Jacques L. Salvan. LC 67-15733. 217p. reprint ed. pap. 61.90 (0-7837-3777-7, 2043596) Bks Demand.

Scandalous Life of Cesar Moro in His Own Words: Peruvian Surrealist Poetry. Cesar Moro. Tr. by Philip Ward. (Modern Poets Ser.: Vol. 6). 1976. pap. 4.95 (0-902675-73-7) Oleander Pr.

Scandalous Love. Brenda Joyce. 416p. (Orig.). 1992. mass mkt. 5.99 (0-380-76536-5) Avon.

Scandalous Marquis. Julie Caille. 384p. 1993. mass mkt. 3.99 (0-8217-4203-5, Zebra Kensgtn) Kensgtn Pub Corp.

Scandalous Penton: A Biography of Brian Penton. Patrick Buckridge. LC 94-226034. 350p. 1994. pap. 29.95 (0-7022-2602-5, Pub. by Univ Queensland Pr AT) Intl Spec Bk.

Scandalous Proposal. Teresa DesJardien. 320p. 1994. mass mkt. 3.99 (0-8217-4504-2, Zebra Kensgtn) Kensgtn Pub Corp.

Scandalous Providence: The Jesus Story of the Compassion of God. E. Frank Tupper. LC 95-5765. 468p. 1995. 35.00 (0-86554-469-7, MUP/H372) Mercer Univ Pr.

***Scandalous Return of Jake Walker.** Myrna MacKenzie. 1997. mass mkt. 3.25 (0-373-19256-8, 1-19256-6) Silhouette.

Scandalous Risks. Susan Howatch. 1991. mass mkt. 5.99 (0-449-21982-8, Crest) Fawcett.

Scandalous Schoolmistress. Rita Boucher. 256p. (Orig.). 1992. mass mkt. 3.99 (0-380-76529-2) Avon.

Scandalous Season. Nancy Lawrence. 224p. 1996. mass mkt. 4.50 (0-8217-5466-1, Zebra Kensgtn) Kensgtn Pub Corp.

Scandalous Seduction. Miranda Lee. (Presents Ser.). 1993. mass mkt. 2.99 (0-373-11589-X, 1-11589-8) Harlequin Bks.

Scandalous Spirits. Erin Yorke. 464p. 1988. mass mkt. 4.50 (0-373-97054-4) Harlequin Bks.

Scandalous Suzanne. Glenda Sanders. 384p. (Orig.). 1996. mass mkt. 5.50 (0-380-77589-1) Avon.

Scandalous Woman: The Story of Caroline Norton. Alan Chedzoy. 320p. 1995. pap. 10.95 (0-7490-0166-6, Pub. by A & B UK) London Brdge.

Scandals. Georgina Devon. 1996. pap. 4.99 (0-373-83322-9, 1-83322-7) Harlequin Bks.

Scandals & Secrets (Hearts of Fire) Miranda Lee. 1995. mass mkt. 3.25 (0-373-11778-7) Harlequin Bks.

***Scandal's Captive.** Mandalyn Kaye. 352p. 1998. mass mkt. 5.50 (0-8217-5819-5, Zebra Kensgtn) Kensgtn Pub Corp.

Scandal's Darling. Nancy Bush. Ed. by Carolyn Tolley. 320p. (Orig.). 1993. mass mkt. 4.99 (0-671-75177-8) PB.

Scandal's Darling. Anne Caldwell. 400p. 1991. mass mkt. 4.50 (0-380-76110-6) Avon.

Scandal's Daughter. Carola Dunn. 320p. 1996. mass mkt. 4.50 (0-8217-5273-1, Zebra Kensgtn) Kensgtn Pub Corp.

Scandal's Daughter. Phylis A. Warady. 172p. 1990. 17.95 (0-8027-1133-2) Walker & Co.

***Scandals in the House of Birds: Shamans & Priests on Lake Atitlan.** Nathaniel Tarn. 1997. 24.00 (1-56886-044-7) Marsilio Pubs.

Scandal's Lady. Mary Kingsley. 304p. 1994. mass mkt. 3.99 (0-8217-4472-0, Zebra Kensgtn) Kensgtn Pub Corp.

Scandal's Reward. Jean R. Ewing. 256p. 1994. mass mkt. 3.99 (0-8217-4666-9, Zebra Kensgtn) Kensgtn Pub Corp.

Scandia Plan: A Cooperative Acquisition Scheme for Improving Access to Research Publications in Four Nordic Countries. Sigrun K. Hannesdottir. LC 92-1070. (Illus.). 340p. 1992. 42.50 (0-8108-2540-6) Scarecrow.

Scandinavia. (Driving Tours Ser.). 1995. pap. 18.00 (0-671-51753-8, P-H Travel) P-H Gen Ref & Trav.

Scandinavia. Driving Tours. (Driving Tours Ser.). 1995. 18.00 (0-02-860072-X) Macmillan.

Scandinavia. Brian Fullerton & Richard Knowles. (Western Europe: Economic & Social Studies Ser.). 192p. 1991. pap. 29.50 (1-85396-083-7, Pub. by P Chapman Pub UK) Taylor & Francis.

Scandinavia. Dan Garrett. LC 91-6422. (World in View Ser.). (Illus.). 96p. (J). (gr. 6-11). 1991. lib. bdg. 25.68 (0-8114-2444-8) Raintree Steck-V.

Scandinavia. rev. ed. Frank Hill. (TravelCard Pac Ser.). 1992. Incl. 4 language cards, 1 phrasecard. 4.00 (0-88699-014-9) Travel Sci.

Scandinavia. rev. ed. Franklyn D. Scott. LC 75-2818. (American Foreign Policy Library). 426p. 1975. 44.50 (0-674-79000-6) HUP.

Scandinavia. 16th ed. Frommer Staff. (Frommer's Travel Guides Ser.). 1995. 19.95 (0-02-860077-0, P-H Travel) P-H Gen Ref & Trav.

Scandinavia: A New Geography. Brian S. John. LC 82-24930. (Illus.). 383p. reprint ed. pap. 109.20 (0-8357-3526-5, 2034441) Bks Demand.

Scandinavia: Between East & West. Ed. by Henning K. Friis. LC 78-21137. 388p. 1979. reprint ed. text ed. 65.00 (0-313-20864-6, FRSB, Greenwood Pr) Greenwood.

***Scandinavia: Country-Living.** Hearst Books Staff. LC 97-21331. 1997. write for info. (0-688-15096-9) Hearst Bks.

Scandinavia: New Focus of Soviet Pressures. Boleslaw A. Boczek. (C). 1990. 50.00 (0-907967-99-X, Pub. by Inst Euro Def & Strat UK) St Mut.

Scandinavia: Off the Beaten Track. Margaret Rogers & Robin Rogers. LC 93-10709. (Off the Beaten Track Ser.). (Illus.). 317p. (Orig.). 1993. pap. 14.95 (1-56440-303-3, Pub. by Moorland Pubng UK) Globe Pequot.

Scandinavia & Finland see Encyclopedia of World Geography

***Scandinavia & Finland Map.** 1996. 10.95 (2-06-700985-0, 985) Michelin.

***Scandinavia & the Great Powers 1890-1940.** Patrick Salmon. 396p. (C). 1997. text ed. 69.95 (0-521-41161-0) Cambridge U Pr.

Scandinavia & the United States. Hanhimaki. 1997. 14.95 (0-8057-4600-5, Twayne) Scribnrs Ref.

Scandinavia & the United States. large type ed. Hanhimaki. 1997. 22.95 (0-8057-4601-3, GK Hall) Thorndike Pr.

***Scandinavia & the United States: An Insecure Friendship.** Jussi M. Hanhim Aki. LC 96-44455. (Twayne's International History Ser.). 1997. write for info. (0-8057-7935-3) Scribnrs Ref.

Scandinavia During the Second World War. Ed. by Henrik S. Nissen. Tr. by Thomas Munch-Petersen. LC 82-2779. (Nordic Ser.: No. 9). 417p. reprint ed. pap. 118.90 (0-7837-2932-4, 2057522) Bks Demand.

Scandinavia in a New Europe: A Challenge for Sociology. Ed. by Thomas P. Boje & Sven E. Hort. (Scandinavian University Press Publication). 427p. (C). 1993. 39.50 (82-00-21183-5, 14460) Scandnvan Univ Pr.

Scandinavia in the European World-Economy, Ca. 1570-1625: Some Local Evidence of Economic Integration. John P. Maarbjerg. (American University Studies, Series IX: Vol. 169). 320p. (C). 1995. text ed. 49.95 (0-8204-2532-X) P Lang Pubng.

Scandinavia Living Design. Elizabeth Gaynor. LC 87-9966. (Illus.). 256p. 1987. 50.00 (1-55670-009-1) Stewart Tabori & Chang.

Scandinavia Living Design. Elizabeth Gaynor. 1994. pap. 27.50 (1-55670-364-3) Stewart Tabori & Chang.

Scandinavia 97: The Complete Guide to Denmark, Finland, Iceland, Norway & Sweden. Fodor's Staff. (Illus.). 1996. pap. 21.00 (0-679-03281-9) Fodors Travel.

Scandinavia/Finland Green Guide. Michelin Travel Publications, Staff. (Illus.). 1996. per. 20.00 (2-06-156701-0, 1567) Michelin.

***Scandinavian.** Emms. 1997. pap. 19.95 (1-901259-02-1) Macmillan.

Scandinavian Adventure. Arland O. Fiske. (Illus.). 232p. (Orig.). 1990. pap. 9.95 (0-942323-11-4) N Amer Heritage Pr.

***Scandinavian American Family Album.** Dorothy Hoobler & Thomas Hoobler. (American Family Albums Ser.). (Illus.). 128p. (J). 1997. 19.95 (0-19-510579-6); lib. bdg. 22.95 (0-19-510578-8) OUP.

Scandinavian & Baltic Europe. 3rd ed. Glenda Bendure et al. (Illus.). 576p. 1997. pap. 17.95 (0-86442-434-5) Lonely Planet.

***Scandinavian & Slavonic Literature, Vol. 10.** Various. Date not set. write for info. (0-8369-4801-7) Ayer.

Scandinavian Archaeology. Haakon Shetelig. Tr. by E. V. Gordon. LC 75-41251. reprint ed. 57.50 (0-404-14600-7) AMS Pr.

Scandinavian Art. Carl Laurin et al. LC 69-13242. (Illus.). 1972. reprint ed. 52.95 (0-405-08735-7) Ayer.

Scandinavian Caledonides. Trygve Strand & O. Kulling. LC 77-78474. (Regional Geology Ser.). 323p. reprint ed. pap. 92.10 (0-317-29870-4, 2016158) Bks Demand.

Scandinavian Christmas Charted Designs. Jana Hauschild. 48p. (Orig.). 1985. pap. 3.50 (0-486-24914-X) Dover.

Scandinavian Christmas Recipes & Traditions. Ed. by Sue Roemig. (Illus.). 40p. 1985. pap. 5.00 (0-941016-28-5) Penfield.

Scandinavian Cinema. Peter Cowie. 1992. pap. 24.95 (0-573-69911-9) French.

Scandinavian Conference on Artificial Intelligence '88. Ed. by Thore Danielsen. (Frontiers in Artificial Intelligence & Applications Ser.). 382p. (gr. 12). 1988. pap. 68.00 (90-5199-003-0, Pub. by IOS Pr NE) IOS Press.

Scandinavian Conference on Artificial Intelligence '89: Proceedings of the Second SCAI, Tempere, Finland, June 12-15, 1989. Ed. by H. Jaakkola & S. Linnainmaa. (Frontiers in Artificial Intelligence & Applications Ser.). 960p. (gr. 12). 1989. pap. 150.00 (90-5199-017-0, Pub. by IOS Pr NE) IOS Press.

Scandinavian Conference on Artificial Intelligence '91: Proceedings of the SCAI '91, Roskilde, Denmark, 21-24 May, 1991. Ed. by Brian Mayoh. (Frontiers in Artificial Intelligence & Applications Ser.: Vol. 12). 350p. 1991. 66.00 (90-5199-056-1, Pub. by IOS Pr NE) IOS Press.

Scandinavian Conference on Artificial Intelligence '93: Proceedings of the Fourth Scandinavian Conference on Artificial Intelligence, Electrum, Stockholm, Sweden, 4-7 May 1993. Ed. by Erik Sandewall & Carl G. Jansson. LC 93-78258. 270p. (gr. 12). 1993. pap. 80.00 (90-5199-134-7, Pub. by IOS Pr NE) IOS Press.

Scandinavian Cookbook. Duane R. Lund. 1992. pap. 8.95 (0-934860-88-2) Adventure Pubns.

Scandinavian Cooking. Sonia Maxwell. 1995. (0-7858-0186-3) Bk Sales Inc.

Scandinavian Country. House Beautiful Magazine Editors & JoAnn Barwick. (Illus.). 240p. 1991. 45.00 (0-517-57661-9, C P Pubs) Crown Pub Group.

Scandinavian Country. Norma Skurka. Ed. by JoAnn Barwick & House Beautiful Magazine Editors. LC 95-2557. (Little Style Bks.). 1995. pap. 12.00 (0-517-88460-7, Clarkson Potter) Crown Bks Yng Read.

Scandinavian Cross Stitch Designs: Over 50 Delightful Designs. Jana H. Lindberg. (Illus.). 128p. 1996. 24.95 (0-304-34389-7, Pub. by Cassell UK) Sterling.

Scandinavian Cross Stitch on Linen & Cotton. Inga Bergfeldt. Tr. by Lars Malmberg & Seymour Bress from SWE. 64p. 1989. 19.95 (0-9623468-0-2); pap. 14.95 (0-9623468-1-0) Stellar Pub Hse.

Scandinavian Cultural Radicalism: Literary Commitment & the Collective Novel in the 1930's. Scott De Francesco. LC 90-5877. (American University Studies: General Literature: Ser. XIX, Vol. 7). 152p. (C). 1990. text ed. 39.50 (0-8204-1263-5) P Lang Pubng.

***Scandinavian Defence 4...Nb6 (B01)** Ed. by S. L. Edritrice. (Illus.). 60p. 1996. pap. 15.50 (88-86127-51-0) Thinkers Pr.

Scandinavian Defense Anderssen Counter Attack. W. John Lutes. 148p. (Orig.). 1992. pap. 14.95 (0-945470-21-5) Chess Ent.

Scandinavian Element in the United States. Kendric C. Babcock. LC 69-18757. (American Immigration Collection. Series 1). 1969. reprint ed. 12.95 (0-405-00505-9) Ayer.

Scandinavian Film. Forsyth Hardy. Ed. by Roger Manvell. LC 79-169330. (National Cinema Ser.). (Illus.). 108p. 1974. reprint ed. 12.95 (0-405-03895-X) Ayer.

Scandinavian Folk & Fairy Tales. Ed. by Claire Booss. (Illus.). 704p. (YA). (gr. 7-10). 1988. 12.99 (0-517-43620-5) Random Hse Value.

Scandinavian Folk Belief & Legend. Ed. by Reimund Kvideland & Henning K. Sehmsdorf. (Nordic Ser.: Vol. 15). (Illus.). 451p. (C). 1991. pap. 18.95 (0-8166-1967-0) U of Minn Pr.

Scandinavian Folk Belief & Legend. Reimund Kvideland & Henning K. Sehmsdorf. 429p. 1991. pap. write for info. (82-00-21299-8) Scandnvan Univ Pr.

Scandinavian Folk Designs. Lis Bartholm. (Design Library). (Illus.). 48p. (Orig.). 1988. pap. 4.95 (0-486-25578-6) Dover.

Scandinavian Folklore. W. A. Craigie. 1973. 59.95 (0-8490-0996-0) Gordon Pr.

Scandinavian Ghost Stories. Retold by Joanne Asala. 1995. pap. 12.95 (1-57216-015-2) Penfield.

Scandinavian Girl & Boy Paper Dolls. Kathy Allert. (Illus.). (J). (gr. 4-7). 1993. pap. 2.95 (0-486-27684-8) Dover.

Scandinavian Heritage. Arland O. Fiske. (Illus.). 248p. (Orig.). 1987. pap. 11.95 (0-942323-00-9) N Amer Heritage Pr.

***Scandinavian Heritage Cookbook.** 2nd rev. ed. Jackson Scandinavian American Society Staff. Ed. by Janice R. Matthews et al. (Illus.). 152p. 1997. 11.95 (1-888499-00-1) Riverview GA.

Scandinavian Holiday Recipes. Spencer. 159p. 1989. spiral bd. 5.95 (0-941016-60-9) Penfield.

Scandinavian Humour & Other Myths. John L. Anderson. 218p. 1987. pap. 9.95 (0-9616967-0-2) Nordbook.

Scandinavian Hymnody from the Reformation to the Present. Howard C. Smith. LC 87-1001. (American Theological Library Association Monograph). (Illus.). 343p. 1987. 45.00 (0-8108-1938-4) Scarecrow.

Scandinavian Immigrant Literature. Christer L. Mossberg. (Western Writers Ser.: No. 47). (Illus.). 52p. (Orig.). 1981. pap. 4.95 (0-88430-071-4) Boise St U W Writ Ser.

Scandinavian Immigrants & Education in North America. Ed. by Phililp J. Anderson et al. LC 95-68623. (Illus.). 224p. 1995. 19.95 (0-914819-01-1) Swedish-Am.

Scandinavian Immigrants in N. Y. 1630-1674. John O. Erjen. xxiv, 438p. 1992. reprint ed. lib. bdg. 45.50 (0-8328-6548-6) Higginson Bk Co.

Scandinavian Immigrants in New York, 1630-1674. John O. Evjen. (Illus.). 464p. 1996. reprint ed. pap. 36.50 (0-614-16590-3, 1730) Clearfield Co.

Scandinavian Immigrants in New York 1630-1674. John O. Evjen. (Illus.). 438p. 1994. reprint ed. lib. bdg. 49.00 (0-8328-3880-2) Higginson Bk Co.

Scandinavian Influences in the English-Romantic Movement. Frank Farley. 1972. lib. bdg. 59.95 (0-8490-0997-9) Gordon Pr.

Scandinavian Knitting Designs. Pauline Chatterton. LC 76-27879. (Encore Edition Ser.). (Illus.). 272p. 1982. 5.95 (0-684-16538-4) S&S Trade.

Scandinavian Language Contacts. P. Sture Ureland & Iain Clarkson. (Illus.). 350p. 1984. 74.95 (0-521-25685-2) Cambridge U Pr.

Scandinavian Languages: Fifty Years of Linguistic Research (1918-1968) Hinar G. Haugen. (Janua Linguarum, Series Practica). 1972. pap. text ed. 47.70 (90-279-2358-2) Mouton.

Scandinavian Legends & Folk-Tales. Illus. by Joan Kiddell-Monroe. (Oxford Myths & Legends Ser.). 192p. (YA). (gr. 4 up). 1992. pap. 12.95 (0-19-274150-0) OUP.

Scandinavian Loan-Words in Middle English. E. Bjorkman. LC 68-24897. (Studies in Language: No. 41). 1969. reprint ed. lib. bdg. 75.00 (0-8383-0913-5) M S G Haskell Hse.

Scandinavian Loan-Words in Middle English. Erik Bjorkman. LC 75-107161. 360p. 1972. reprint ed. 14.00 (0-403-00450-0) Scholarly.

Scandinavian Misadventure: The Campaign in Norway 1940. Maurice Harvey. 308p. (C). 1991. 105.00 (0-946771-44-8, Pub. by Spellmount UK) St Mut.

Scandinavian Model: Welfare States & Welfare Research. Robert Erikson et al. LC 85-10912. (Comparative Public Policy Analysis Ser.). 262p. (gr. 13). 1987. text ed. 72.95 (0-87332-348-3); pap. text ed. 25.95 (0-87332-500-1) M E Sharpe.

Scandinavian Music: A Short History. John Horton. LC 73-7673. (Illus.). 180p. 1975. reprint ed. text ed. 55.00 (0-8371-6944-5, HOSM, Greenwood Pr) Greenwood.

Scandinavian Music: Finland & Sweden. Antony Hodgson. LC 84-47547. 224p. 1985. 32.50 (0-8386-2346-8) Fairleigh Dickinson.

An Asterisk (*) at the beginning of an entry indicates that the title is appearing in BIP for the first time.

Scandinavian Painted Furniture: A Step-by-Step Workbook. Jocasta Innes. (Illus.). 160p. 1995. 29.95 (*0-304-34385-4*, Pub. by Cassell UK) Sterling.

Scandinavian Proverbs. Ed. by Julie J. McDonald. 30p. 1993. pap. 10.95 (*0-941016-27-7*) Penfield.

Scandinavian Reformation: From Evangelical Movement to Institutionalisation of Reform. Ed. by Ole P. Grell. LC 94-14116. (Illus.). 232p. (C). 1995. text ed. 59.95 (*0-521-44162-5*) Cambridge U Pr.

Scandinavian Revenue Stamps: Denmark. Peter Poulsen. Ed. by Paul A. Nelson. (Illus.). 96p. (Orig.). (C). 1989. pap. text ed. 14.00 (*0-929850-00-9*) SPLOSC.

Scandinavian, Russian & Eastern European Paintings: 1820-1920. (Illus.). 1985. pap. write for info. (*0-318-58131-0*) W Whitney.

Scandinavian Settlement. write for info. (*0-8386-3620-9*) Fairleigh Dickinson.

Scandinavian Settlement in Northern Britain: Place-Name Studies in Their Historical Context. Ed. by Barbara Crawford. LC 95-10299. 1995. 79.95 (*0-7185-1923-X*, Pub. by Leicester Univ Pr) St Martin.

Scandinavian Smorgasbord Recipes. 158p. 1991. spiral bd. 5.95 (*0-941016-85-4*) Penfield.

Scandinavian Smorgasbord, Soups, Savories & Sweets. M. Savonius. 1980. 10.00 (*0-87557-107-7*) Saphrograph.

Scandinavian Snickerfest: A Book of Jokes from the Northern Folks. J. Edward Thornberg. (Illus.). 60p. (Orig.). 1989. pap. 3.00 (*0-929082-09-5*) Natl Hall Humor.

Scandinavian Spirit. Arland O. Fiske. (Illus.). 246p. (Orig.). 1989. pap. 9.95 (*0-942323-08-4*) N Amer Heritage Pr.

Scandinavian States & the League of Nations. Samuel S. Jones. LC 39-8287. 316p. reprint ed. pap. 90.10 (*0-317-26669-1*, 2055992) Bks Demand.

Scandinavian Studies: Essays Presented to Dr. Henry Goddard Leach. Ed. by Carl F. Bayerschmidt & Erik J. Friis. LC 65-22388. (American-Scandinavian Foundation Scandinavian Studies). (Illus.). 472p. 1965. 25.00 (*0-295-73924-X*) U of Wash Pr.

Scandinavian-Style Feltmaking: A Three Dimensional Approach to Hats, Boots, Mittens & Other Useful Objects. Patricia Spark. LC 92-60848. (Illus.). 56p. 1992. pap. 10.95 (*0-916658-90-2*) Shuttle Craft.

Scandinavian Sweet Treats. Karen B. Douglas. (Illus.). 120p. 1992. spiral bd. 5.95 (*0-941016-88-9*) Penfield.

***Scandinavian Texts for Handel's Messiah: A Study of Translation Technique Applied to a Libretto.** Alan Bower. x, 194p. (Orig.). 1996. pap. 24.00 (*0-9643394-3-9*) Stonehill MI.

Scandinavian Treasury: Cookery & Culture of Scandinavia. 6.95 (*0-87741-010-0*) Makepeace Colony.

Scandinavian Women Writers: An Anthology from the 1880s to the 1980s. Ed. by Ingrid Claréus. LC 89-2147. (Contributions in Women's Studies: No. 95). 246p. 1989. text ed. 55.00 (*0-313-25884-8*, CSV/, Greenwood Pr) Greenwood.

Scandinavian World. Arland O. Fiske. LC 87-60604. (Illus.). 252p. (Orig.). 1988. pap. 9.95 (*0-942323-02-5*) N Amer Heritage Pr.

Scandinavian Writers. Ed. by Stanley H. Barkan & Siv Cedering. 1991. boxed 75.00 (*0-89304-951-4*); boxed 50.00 (*0-685-49067-X*) Cross-Cultrl NY.

Scandinavian York & Dublin. Alfred P. Smyth. 512p. 1987. 45.00 (*0-7165-2365-5*, Pub. by Irish Acad Pr IE) Intl Spec Bk.

Scandinavians & America. Ed. by H. Arnold Barton. 1974. pap. 1.50 (*0-318-03682-7*) Swedish-Am.

***Scandinavians & South Africa.** Alan H. Winquist. (South African Biographical & Historical Studies: No. 24). 286p. 1978. 60.00 (*0-86961-096-1*, Pub. by A A Balkema NE) Ashgate Pub Co.

Scandinavians in America Series, 36 bks., Set. Ed. by Franklyn D. Scott. (Illus.). 1979. lib. bdg. 920.00 (*0-405-11628-4*) Ayer.

Scandinavians in History. Stanley M. Toyne. LC 79-114898. (Select Bibliographies Reprint Ser.). 1977. 31.95 (*0-8369-5302-9*) Ayer.

Scandinavians in History. S. M. Toyne. 352p. 1982. reprint ed. lib. bdg. 21.50 (*0-8290-0833-0*) Irvington.

Scandium: Its Geochemistry & Mineralogy. Leonid F. Borisenko. LC 62-15551. 82p. reprint ed. pap. 25.00 (*0-317-10633-3*, 2003358) Bks Demand.

Scandium, Yttrium, Lanthanum & Lanthanide Halides in Nonaqueous Solvents. Ed. by T. Mioduski & M. Salomon. (Illus.). 418p. 1985. 142.00 (*0-08-030709-4*, Pub. by PPL UK) Elsevier.

ScanFan Southern California. 6th ed. Fred K. White. Ed. by C. B. White. 416p. 1995. per. 19.95 (*0-9620798-8-X*) ScanFan Pubns.

Scanlin's Law. Amarillas. 1995. mass mkt. 4.50 (*0-373-28883-2*) Harlequin Bks.

Scanlon Plan for Organization Development: Identity, Participation, & Equity. Carl F. Frost et al. 200p. 1996. reprint ed. pap. 19.95 (*0-87013-408-6*) Mich St U Pr.

Scannable Resumes. (Illus.). 36p. 1994. pap. 6.00 (*1-884783-17-1*) Eclecon.

Scanned Image Microscopy. Ed. by Eric Ash. LC 80-41580. 1981. text ed. 152.00 (*0-12-065180-7*) Acad Pr.

Scanned Probe Microscopy. Ed. by H. Kumar Wickramasinghe. (AIP Conference Proceedings Ser.: No. 241). (Illus.). 600p. 1992. lib. bdg. 95.00 (*0-88318-816-3*) Am Inst Physics.

Scanner Book: A Complete Guide to the Use & Applications of Desktop Scanners. Stephen Beale & James Cavuoto. 224p. 1989. pap. 22.95 (*0-941845-02-8*) Micro Pub Pr.

Scanner Darkly. Philip K. Dick. LC 91-50090. 256p. 1991. pap. 11.00 (*0-679-73665-4*, Vin) Random.

Scanner Listener's Handbook - How to Hear More on Your Scanned Radio. Edward Soomre. 130p. (Orig.). 1989. pap. 14.95 (*0-936653-19-1*) Tiare Pubns.

Scanner Master Chicagoland Guide. Richard Carlson & Ted Moran. 168p. 1995. pap. 13.95 (*0-939430-32-0*) Scanner Master.

Scanner Master D. C., Delaware, Maryland & Virginia Guide: The Public Safety/Radio Communications Reference. 4th ed. Lynne Burke & John McColman. 432p. 1996. pap. 29.95 (*0-939430-34-7*) Scanner Master.

Scanner Master Greater Philadelphia-South Jersey Pocket Guide. Ed. by Chuck Gysi. (Frequency Guide Ser.: No. 5A). 160p. 1991. 13.95 (*0-939430-14-2*) Scanner Master.

Scanner Master Maine Guide. Ed. by Edward Soomre & Richard Barnett. (Frequency Guide Ser.: No. 12). 280p. 1987. 9.95 (*0-939430-13-4*) Scanner Master.

Scanner Master Massachusetts Communications Guide: The Commonwealth's Reference Guide. Richard Barnett & Edward Soomre. 692p. 1995. pap. 29.95 (*0-939430-25-8*) Scanner Master.

Scanner Master Massachusetts Guide. 4th ed. Ed. by Richard Barnett. (Frequency Guide Ser.: No. 10). (Illus.). 520p. 1989. 29.95 (*0-685-34567-X*) Scanner Master.

Scanner Master Massachusetts Pocket Guide. 3rd ed. Ed. by Richard Barnett. (Frequency Guide Ser.: No. 1A). 142p. 1990. 12.95 (*0-685-34568-8*) Scanner Master.

Scanner Master Metro D. C.-Virginia Guide. 3rd ed. Ed. by John McColman. (Frequency Guide Ser.: No. 6). (Illus.). 350p. 1991. 29.95 (*0-685-51888-4*) Scanner Master.

Scanner Master Metropolitan New York Guide. 4th ed. Warren M. Silverman. (Frequency Guide Ser.: No. 11). (Illus.). 400p. 1990. 29.95 (*0-685-34569-6*) Scanner Master.

Scanner Master New Hampshire & Vermont Guide. Ed. by Edward Soomre & Richard Barnett. (Frequency Guide Ser.: No. 13). 330p. 1987. 9.95 (*0-939430-12-6*) Scanner Master.

Scanner Master New York Metro - Northern New Jersey Guide. Warren M. Silverman. 660p. 1995. pap. 38.95 (*0-939430-33-9*) Scanner Master.

Scanner Master Ohio Pocket Guide. Dave Marshall. 168p. 1995. pap. 13.95 (*0-939430-20-7*) Scanner Master.

Scanner Master Upstate New York Guide. David T. Stark. 320p. 1995. pap. 29.95 (*0-939430-28-2*) Scanner Master.

Scanner Modification & Antennas: Everything You Ever Wanted to Know But Were Afraid to Ask. Jerry Pickard. LC 95-81303. (Illus.). 164p. (Orig.). 1997. pap. 22.95 (*1-56866-120-7*) Index Pub Grp.

Scanner Modification Handbook, Vol. 2. Bill Cheek. (Illus.). 220p. (Orig.). 1991. pap. 18.95 (*0-939780-14-3*) CRB Res.

Scanner Modification Handbook: Upgrade Your Scanner. Bill Cheek. (Illus.). 160p. (Orig.). 1990. pap. 18.95 (*0-939780-11-9*) CRB Res.

Scanner Radio Guide 1994. Larry M. Barker. 128p. 1993. pap. 14.95 (*1-878707-10-8*) HighText.

Scanners & Secret Frequencies. Henry L. Eisenson. LC 93-78786. (Electronic Underground Ser.: Vol. 3). (Illus.). 320p. (Orig.). 1993. pap. 19.95 (*1-56866-038-3*) Index Pub Grp.

Scanning & Image Processing for the PC. Frank Baeseler & Bruce Bovill. 1993. pap. text ed. 27.95 (*0-07-707594-3*) McGraw.

Scanning & Image Processing for the PC. Frank Baeseler & Bruce Bovill. LC 93-31120. 1993. write for info. (*0-07-707819-5*) McGraw.

Scanning & OCR Devices (U. S.) Market Intelligence Staff. 385p. 1992. 2,900.00 (*1-56753-917-3*, A2524) Frost & Sullivan.

Scanning & OCR Market (Europe) Market Intelligence Staff. 270p. 1992. 3,700.00 (*1-56753-918-1*, E1595) Frost & Sullivan.

Scanning & Printing: Perfect Pictures with Desktop Publishing. rev. ed. Peter Kammermeier. (Illus.). 350p. 1995. pap. 39.95 (*0-240-51400-9*, Focal) Buttrwrth-Heinemann.

Scanning Electron Microscope Atlas of the Honey Bee. Eric H. Erickson, Jr. et al. LC 85-19727. (Illus.). 292p. (C). 1986. text ed. 59.95 (*0-8138-0546-5*) Iowa St U Pr.

Scanning Electron Microscope Studies of the Brain Ventricular Surfaces. Walter E. Stumpf. (Illus.). 1978. reprint ed. pap. text ed. 15.00 (*0-931288-03-7*) Scanning Microscopy.

Scanning Electron Microscope Survey of the Epidermis of East African Grasses, Vol. 4. Patricia G. Palmer & Susan Gerbeth-Jones. LC 80-19201. (Smithsonian Contributions to Botany Ser.: No. 62). 124p. reprint ed. pap. 35.40 (*0-317-55524-3*, 2029551) Bks Demand.

Scanning Electron Microscope Survey of the Epidermis of East African Grasses, Pt. 3. Patricia G. Palmer et al. LC 80-19201. (Smithsonian Contributions to Botany Ser.: No. 55). 142p. reprint ed. pap. 40.50 (*0-317-42001-1*, 2025684) Bks Demand.

Scanning Electron Microscopic Studies of Embryogenesis. Ed. by Gary C. Schoenwolf. (Illus.). 368p. 1986. reprint ed. pap. 36.00 (*0-931288-36-3*) Scanning Microscopy.

Scanning Electron Microscopy. Ludwig Reimer. (Optical Sciences Ser.: Vol. 45). (Illus.). 480p. 1985. 106.95 (*0-387-13530-8*) Spr-Verlag.

Scanning Electron Microscopy: Atlas of Corneal Pathology. Frank M. Polack. (Illus.). 168p. (gr. 13). 1983. 74.50 (*0-89352-203-1*, Yr Bk Med Pubs) Mosby Yr Bk.

Scanning Electron Microscopy & X-Ray Microanalysis: A Text for Biologists, Materials Scientists & Geologists. 2nd ed. Patrick Echlin et al. LC 92-9840. (Illus.). 800p. (C). 1992. 55.00 (*0-306-44175-6*, Plenum Pr) Plenum.

***Scanning Electron Microscopy As a Tool for the Analysis of Wool Speciality Fiber Blends.** F. J. Wortmann & G. Wortmann. 1991. pap. 42.00 (*0-614-20892-0*, Pub. by Textile Inst UK) St Mut.

Scanning Electron Microscopy Atlas of Normal & Malignant Leukocytes. Aaron Polliack et al. LC 92-49075. 95p. 1993. text ed. 88.00 (*3-7186-5362-1*) Gordon & Breach.

Scanning Electron Microscopy of Cells in Culture. Ed. by Paul B. Bell, Jr. (Illus.). vi, 314p. 1984. reprint ed. pap. 29.00 (*0-931288-31-2*) Scanning Microscopy.

Scanning Electron Microscopy of Vascular Casts: Methods & Applications. Ed. by P. M. Motta et al. (Electron Microscopy in Biology & Medicine Ser.). 416p. (C). 1992. lib. bdg. 289.50 (*0-7923-1297-X*) Kluwer Ac.

Scanning Electron Microscopy, X-Ray Microanalysis & Analytical Electricity: A Laboratory Workbook. C. E. Lyman et al. (Illus.). 420p. 1990. spiral bd. 34.50 (*0-306-43591-8*, Plenum Pr) Plenum.

Scanning Electron Microscopy 1978: International Review of Advances in Techniques & Applications of the Scanning Electron Microscope, 1978, 2 pts., Pt. I. Ed. by Om Johari & Robert P. Becker. LC 72-626068. (Illus.). 1978. text ed. 37.00 (*0-931288-01-0*) Scanning Microscopy.

Scanning Electron Microscopy 1978: International Review of Advances in Techniques & Applications of the Scanning Electron Microscope, 1978, 2 pts., Pt. II. Ed. by Om Johari & Robert P. Becker. LC 72-626068. (Illus.). 1978. text ed. 37.00 (*0-931288-02-9*) Scanning Microscopy.

Scanning Electron Microscopy 1978: International Review of Advances in Techniques & Applications of the Scanning Electron Microscope, 1978, 2 pts., Set. Ed. by Om Johari & Robert P. Becker. LC 72-626068. (Illus.). 1978. text ed. 65.00 (*0-931288-00-2*) Scanning Microscopy.

Scanning Electron Microscopy 1979: International Review of Advances in Techniques & Applications of the Scanning Electron Microscope, 1979, 3 pts. Ed. by Om Johari & Robert P. Becker. LC 72-626068. (Illus.). 1979. Pt. III. write for info. (*0-931288-06-1*) Scanning Microscopy.

Scanning Electron Microscopy 1979: International Review of Advances in Techniques & Applications of the Scanning Electron Microscope, 1979, 3 pts., Pt. II. Ed. by Om Johari & Robert P. Becker. LC 72-626068. (Illus.). 1979. text ed. 37.00 (*0-931288-05-3*) Scanning Microscopy.

Scanning Electron Microscopy 1979: International Review of Advances in Techniques & Applications of the Scanning Electron Microscope, 1979, 3 pts., Pts. I & II. Ed. by Om Johari & Robert P. Becker. LC 72-626068. (Illus.). 1979. text ed. 65.00 (*0-931288-08-8*) Scanning Microscopy.

Scanning Electron Microscopy, 1980, Pt. I. Om Johari. LC 72-626068. (Illus.). xvi, 608p. 1980. 52.00 (*0-931288-11-8*) Scanning Microscopy.

Scanning Electron Microscopy, 1980, Pt. II. R. P. Becker & Om Johari. LC 72-626068. (Illus.). xiv, 658p. 1980. 52.00 (*0-931288-12-6*) Scanning Microscopy.

Scanning Electron Microscopy, 1980, Pt. III. Ed. by Om Johari & R. P. Becker. LC 72-62608. (Illus.). xx, 670p. 1980. 52.00 (*0-931288-13-4*) Scanning Microscopy.

Scanning Electron Microscopy, 1980, Pt. IV. Ed. by Om Johari & R. P. Becker. (Scanning Electron Microscopy Ser.). (Illus.). iv, 220p. 1981. 52.00 (*0-931288-14-2*) Scanning Microscopy.

Scanning Electron Microscopy, 1980, 4 pts., Set. 1980. 109.00 (*0-931288-15-0*) Scanning Microscopy.

Scanning Electron Microscopy, 1981, Pt. I. 1981. 52.00 (*0-931288-17-7*) Scanning Microscopy.

Scanning Electron Microscopy, 1981, Pt. III. Ed. by Om Johari et al. (Illus.). xvi, 624p. 1981. 52.00 (*0-931288-19-3*); 109.00 (*0-931288-21-5*) Scanning Microscopy.

Scanning Electron Microscopy, 1981, Pt. IV. Ed. by Om Johari et al. LC 72-626068. viii, 312p. 1982. 52.00 (*0-931288-20-7*) Scanning Microscopy.

Scanning Electron Microscopy, 1982, Pt. I. Ed. by Om Johari et al. LC 72-626068. (Illus.). xvi, 464p. 1983. 52.00 (*0-931288-23-1*) Scanning Microscopy.

Scanning Electron Microscopy 1982, Pt. II. Ed. by Om Johari et al. LC 72-626068. (Illus.). xvi, 432p. 1983. 52.00 (*0-931288-24-X*) Scanning Microscopy.

Scanning Electron Microscopy, 1982, Pt. III. Ed. by Om Johari et al. LC 72-626068. (Scanning Electron Microscopy Ser.). (Illus.). xviii, 462p. 1983. 52.00 (*0-931288-25-8*); 109.00 (*0-685-07006-9*) Scanning Microscopy.

Scanning Electron Microscopy, 1982, Pt. IV. Ed. by Om Johari et al. LC 72-626068. (Scanning Electron Microscopy Ser.). (Illus.). xxii, 458p. 1983. 52.00 (*0-931288-26-6*) Scanning Microscopy.

Scanning Electron Microscopy, 1982, 4 pts., Set. Ed. by Om Johari et al. LC 72-626068. (Illus.). xvi, 464p. 1983. 109.00 (*0-931288-27-4*) Scanning Microscopy.

Scanning Electron Microscopy, 1982, 4 pts., Set. Ed. by Om Johari et al. LC 72-626068. (Scanning Electron Microscopy Ser.). (Illus.). xxii, 458p. 1983. 109.00 (*0-685-06980-X*) Scanning Microscopy.

Scanning Electron Microscopy 1982, 4 pts., Set. Ed. by Om Johari et al. LC 72-626068. (Illus.). xvi, 432p. 1983. 109.00 (*0-685-06690-8*) Scanning Microscopy.

Scanning Force Microscopy: With Applications to Electric, Magnetic, & Atomic Forces. 2nd ed. Dror Sarid. (Series on Optical & Imaging Sciences). (Illus.). 288p. 1994. reprint ed. 65.00 (*0-19-509204-X*) OUP.

Scanning Microscopy: Symposium Proceedings, Wetzlar, October 1990. Ed. by Commission of the European Communities Staff. LC 92-24849. (ESPRIT Basic Research Ser.). 220p. 1992. 64.95 (*0-387-55696-6*) Spr-Verlag.

Scanning Microscopy of Vertebrate Mineralized Tissues: A Compilation in Memory of Edward J. Reith. Lawrence Martin et al. (Illus.). viii, 384p. 1989. pap. text ed. 43.00 (*0-931288-41-X*) Scanning Microscopy.

Scanning Patterns of Human Infants: Implications for Visual Learning. Gordon Bronson. LC 81-20543. (Monographs on Infancy: Vol. 2). 136p. 1982. text ed. 73.25 (*0-89391-114-3*) Ablex Pub.

Scanning Probe Microscopy & Spectroscopy: Methods & Applications. R. Wiesendanger. LC 93-31700. (Illus.). 659p. (C). 1994. text ed. 120.00 (*0-521-41810-0*); pap. text ed. 42.95 (*0-521-42847-5*) Cambridge U Pr.

Scanning Probe Microscopy of Clay Minerals. Ed. by K. R. Nagy & A. E. Blum. (CMS Workshop Lectures: Vol. 7). (Illus.). 256p. (Orig.). (C). 1994. pap. text ed. 23.00 (*1-881208-08-7*) Clay Minerals.

***Scanning the Global Environment: A Framework & Methodology for Integrated Environmental Reporting & Assessment.** National Institute of Public Health & the Environment Staff. 58p. 1995. 99.00 (*92-807-1491-0*) UN.

Scanning the Plan Vol. 1: Old Testament Survey. Kenneth F. McKinley. (Illus.). 210p. 1995. reprint ed. pap. 10.00 (*0-9630161-1-3*) Bible Study Min.

Scanning the Professional Way. Sybil Ihrig & Emil Ihrig. (Illus.). 148p. 1995. pap. text ed. 21.95 (*0-07-882145-2*) McGraw.

Scanning Tunneling Microscopy. Ed. by Henning Neddermeyer. LC 92-38479. (Perspectives in Condensed Matter Physics Ser.: Vol. 6). 272p. (C). 1993. lib. bdg. 144.00 (*0-7923-2065-4*) Kluwer Ac.

Scanning Tunneling Microscopy. Ed. by Joseph Stroscio & William Kaiser. (Illus.). 459p. 1994. pap. text ed. 48.00 (*0-12-674050-X*) Acad Pr.

Scanning Tunneling Microscopy & Its Application, Vol. 32. Chunli Bai. Ed. by G. Ertl et al. LC 95-34587. (Springer Series in Surface Sciences: Vol. 32). 320p. 1995. 99.50 (*3-540-59346-2*) Spr-Verlag.

***Scanning Tunneling Microscopy & Spectroscopy: Theory, Techniques & Applications.** Ed. by D. A. Bonnell. 1993. text ed. 135.00 (*0-471-18735-6*) Wiley.

Scanning Tunneling Microscopy & Spectroscopy: Theory, Techniques, & Applications. Ed. by Dawn A. Bonnell. LC 92-46997. 400p. 1993. 125.00 (*0-89573-768-X*, VCH) Wiley.

Scanning Tunneling Microscopy I: General Principles & Applications to Clean & Adsorbate-Covered Surfaces. Ed. by H. J. Guntherodt et al. (Surface Sciences Ser.: Vol. 20). (Illus.). 264p. 1992. text ed. 59.00 (*0-387-54308-2*) Spr-Verlag.

Scanning Tunneling Microscopy I: General Principles & Applications to Clean & Adsorbate-Covered Surfaces. 2nd ed. Ed. by H. J. Guntherodt & R. Wiesendanger. (Springer Series in Surface Sciences: Vol. 20). xii, 280p. 1994. 53.95 (*3-540-58415-3*) Spr-Verlag.

Scanning Tunneling Microscopy II: Further Applications & Related Scanning Techniques. Ed. by R. Wiesendanger & H. J. Guntherodt. LC 95-32274. (Springer Series in Surface Sciences: Vol. 28). 1995. 54.00 (*3-540-58589-3*) Spr-Verlag.

Scanning Tunneling Microscopy III: Theory of Stm & Related Scanning Probe Methods. 2nd ed. R. Wiesendanger & H. J. Guntherodt. LC 96-21459. (Springer Series in Surface Sciences). 450p. 1996. pap. 69.95 (*3-540-60824-9*) Spr-Verlag.

Scanning Tunneling Microscopy Three: Theory of STM & Related Scanning Probe Methods. Ed. by R. Wiesendanger & H. J. Guntherodt. LC 92-46679. (Surface Sciences Ser.: No. 29). 1993. 79.00 (*0-387-56317-2*) Spr-Verlag.

Scanning Tunneling Microscopy Two: Further Applications & Related Scanning Techniques. Ed. by G. Ertl et al. (Surface Sciences Ser.: Vol. 28). (Illus.). 324p. 1992. 69.00 (*0-387-54555-7*) Spr-Verlag.

Scanty Plot of Ground: Studies in the Victorian Sonnet. William T. Going. (Studies in English Literature: No. 106). 1976. text ed. 33.85 (*90-279-3015-5*) Mouton.

Scapegoat. Johan Borgen. Tr. by Elizabeth Rokkan from NOR. 187p. 9400. pap. 23.00 (*1-870041-21-6*, Pub. by Norvik Pr UK) Dufour.

Scapegoat. Jocelyn Brooke. LC 96-60142. 128p. (Orig.). 1998. pap. 12.95 (*1-885983-09-3*) Turtle Point Pr.

Scapegoat. Daphne Du Maurier. 348p. 1988. pap. 4.50 (*0-88184-409-8*) Carroll & Graf.

Scapegoat. Daphne Du Maurier. 1976. 21.95 (*0-89190-154-X*, Queens House) Amereon Ltd.

Scapegoat. Daphne Du Maurier. 1976. 24.95 (*0-89233-037-6*) Queens Hse-Focus Serv.

Scapegoat. Bruce H. Joffe. LC 94-96162. 168p. 1994. pap. 7.95 (*0-9642145-0-4*) Mentor Press.

Scapegoat. Mary Lee Settle. (Beulah Quintet Ser.: Bk. IV). 278p. 1996. pap. 12.95 (*1-57003-117-7*) U of SC Pr.

***Scapegoat.** Mary Lee Settle. 1996. pap. 12.95 (*0-614-19480-6*, Harvest Bks) HarBrace.

Scapegoat. Daphne Du Maurier. 1977. reprint ed. lib. bdg. 25.95 (*0-88411-149-0*, Queens House) Amereon Ltd.

Scapegoat. Daphne Du Maurier. 1994. reprint ed. lib. bdg. 24.95 (*1-56849-550-1*) Buccaneer Bks.

Scapegoat. Rene Girard. Tr. by Yvonne Freccero from FRE. LC 86-2699. 232p. 1989. reprint ed. pap. text ed. 14.95 (*0-8018-3917-3*) Johns Hopkins.

Scapegoat: A Novel on the Life of Moses. Joan Lawrence. 188p. 8800. 26.00 (*0-7206-0708-6*, Pub. by P Owen Ltd UK) Dufour.

Scapegoat: A Romance, 2 vols. in 1. Hall Caine. LC 79-8244. reprint ed. 44.50 (*0-404-61802-2*) AMS Pr.

***Scapegoat: General Percival of Singapore.** Clifford Kinvig. (Illus.). 288p. 1996. 31.95 (*1-85753-171-X*, Pub. by Brasseys UK) Brasseys Inc.

An Asterisk (*) at the beginning of an entry indicates that the title is appearing in BIP for the first time.

Scapegoat: The Impact of Death-Fear on an American Family. Eric Bermann. LC 73-80573. 371p. 1973. reprint ed. pap. 105.80 (*0-7837-4712-8*, 2059064) Bks Demand.

Scapegoat see **Golden Bough**

Scapegoat Complex. Sylvia B. Perera. 1995. pap. 15.00 (*0-919123-22-8*, Pub. by Inner City CN) BookWorld Dist.

Scapegoat General: The Story of General Benjamin Huger C. S. A. Jeffrey L. Rhoades. LC 85-18530. (Illus.). xi, 164p. (C). 1986. lib. bdg. 29.50 (*0-208-02069-1*, Archon Bks) Shoe String.

Scapegoat Generation: America's War Against Adolescents. Mike Males. 300p. (Orig.). 1996. pap. 17.95 (*1-56751-080-9*) Common Courage.

Scapegoat Generation: America's War Against Adolescents. Mike Males. 300p. (Orig.). 1996. lib. bdg. 29.95 (*1-56751-081-7*) Common Courage.

Scapegoat in the New Wilderness. Frederic C. Jaher. LC 93-34822. 351p. 1994. 32.00 (*0-674-79006-5*) HUP.

Scapegoat in the New Wilderness: The Origins & Rise of Anti-Semitism in America. Frederic C. Jaher. 352p. 1996. pap. 16.95 (*0-674-79007-3*) HUP.

Scapegoat on Trial. Mendel Beilis. (C). 1993. 16.95 (*1-56062-166-4*); pap. 13.95 (*1-56062-167-2*) CIS Comm.

Scapegoats. Ed. by Dan Garrett. (Drama Workshop Plays Ser.). (Illus.). 96p. (Orig.). (YA). 1990. pap. 15.00 (*0-333-36055-9*, Pub. by Macmillan Ed UK) Players Pr.

Scapegoats: A Defense of Kimmel & Short at Pearl Harbor. Edward L. Beach. (Illus.). 240p. 1995. 26.95 (*1-55750-059-2*) Naval Inst Pr.

Scapegoats: The Exodus of the Remnants of Polish Jewry. Josef Banas. Tr. by Tadeusz Szafar. 221p. 1979. 37.95 (*0-8419-6303-7*) Holmes & Meier.

Scapegoats: Transferring Blame. Tom Douglas. LC 95-30567. 224p. (C). 1995. pap. 18.95 (*0-415-11019-X*) Routledge.

Scapegoats: Transferring Blame. Tom Douglas. LC 95-30567. 224p. (C). (gr. 13). 1995. text ed. 62.95 (*0-415-11018-1*) Routledge.

***Scapegoats & Social Actors.** Joly. Date not set. text ed. 65.00 (*0-312-17723-2*) St Martin.

Scapegrace. Sylvia Thorpe. 1978. pap. 1.50 (*0-449-23478-9*, Crest) Fawcett.

Scapel & the Cross. Wilbur L. Creech. (Illus.). 270p. (Orig.). 1993. pap. 19.95 (*1-880994-08-9*) Mt Olive Coll Pr.

Scapes. Phyllis Plous. (Illus.). 59p. 1985. 15.00 (*0-942006-10-0*) U of CA Art.

Scaphoid Fractures & Complications. Ed. by James H. Herndon. 88p. 1994. pap. 35.00 (*0-89203-084-4*) Amer Acad Ortho Surg.

***Scapin.** Bill Irwin & Mark O'Donnell. 1997. pap. 5.25 (*0-8222-1603-5*) Dramatists Play.

Scapin & Don Juan. Moliere. Tr. & Adapted by Albert Bermel. (Actor's Moliere Ser.: Vol. 3). 1987. pap. 6.95 (*0-936839-80-5*) Applause Theatre Bk Pubs.

Scapino! Frank Dunlop & Jim Dale. 94p. 1975. pap. 5.95 (*0-87129-639-X*, S12) Dramatic Pub.

Scapino! One Act Version. Frank Dunlop & Jim Dale. 1975. pap. 3.95 (*0-87129-183-5*, S11) Dramatic Pub.

Scapino! - Special Book. Frank Dunlop & Jim Dale. 1975. pap. 9.95 (*0-87129-374-9*, S13) Dramatic Pub.

Scapular of Carmel. 2nd rev. ed. Kilian F. Lynch. 48p. 1996. 1.95 (*0-911988-11-4*, 42972) AMI Pr.

Scar. Thomas L. McComb. (Illus.). 138p. 1993. pap. text ed. write for info. (*1-883517-00-1*) Alef Bet Comns.

Scar Lover. Harry Crews. 288p. 1993. pap. 10.00 (*0-671-79786-7*, Touchstone Bks) S&S Trade.

Scar Mirror. Derek Pell. (Illus.). 1979. pap. 2.50 (*0-916866-05-X*) Cats Pajamas.

Scar of Race. Paul M. Sniderman & Thomas Piazza. LC 93-17063. 224p. 1993. text ed. 18.95 (*0-674-79010-3*) Belknap Pr.

Scar of Race. Paul M. Sniderman & Thomas Piazza. (Illus.). 224p. 1995. pap. 12.00 (*0-674-79011-1*, SNISCX) Belknap Pr.

Scar of Revolution: Custine, Tocqueville, & the Romantic Imagination. Irena G. Gross. LC 91-9336. 217p. 1991. 34.95 (*0-520-07351-7*) U CA Pr.

Scar Tissue. Michael Ignatieff. LC 93-34990. 1994. 20.00 (*0-374-25428-1*) FS&G.

Scar Tissue. Leonard Randolph. (Hollow Spring Poetry Ser.). (Illus.). 64p. (C). 1984. pap. text ed. 5.00 (*0-318-00815-7*) Hollow Spring Pr.

Scarabs: The History, Manufacture, & Religious Symbolism of the Scarabaeus, in Ancient Egypt, Phoenicia, Sardinia, Etruria, Etc. Isaac Meyer. 205p. 1995. pap. 17.95 (*1-56459-491-2*) Kessinger Pub.

Scaramouche. large type ed. Rafael Sabatini. LC 93-40527. 1994. lib. bdg. 21.95 (*0-7862-0157-6*) Thorndike Pr.

Scaramouche. Rafael Sabatini. 1990. reprint ed. lib. bdg. 21.95 (*0-89968-547-1*) Buccaneer Bks.

Scaramouche. Raphael Sabatini. 1976. reprint ed. lib. bdg. 25.95 (*0-89190-744-0*, Rivercity Pr) Amereon Ltd.

Scaramouche the King Maker. Raphael Sabatini. 25.95 (*0-8488-0879-7*) Amereon Ltd.

Scaramutza in Germany: The Dramatic Works of Caspar Stieler. Judith P. Aikin. LC 88-25238. 239p. 1989. lib. bdg. 35.00 (*0-271-00656-0*) Pa St U Pr.

Scarboro, Maine, Marriages of the Second Congregational Church. Michael J. Denis. 21p. 1983. pap. 3.50 (*0-935207-12-0*) Danbury Hse Bks.

***Scarboro Register, 1905 (Town History & Directory)** Compiled by Mitchell & Campbell. 95p. 1997. reprint ed. pap. 18.00 (*0-8328-5910-9*) Higginson Bk Co.

Scarborough (Maine) Town Records-Births. 62p. 1986. reprint ed. pap. 7.50 (*0-935207-45-7*) Danbury Hse Bks.

Scarborough, ME. R. Laughton. (Images of America Ser.). 128p. 1996. pap. 16.99 (*0-7524-0262-5*, Arcdia) Chalford.

Scarce Medical Resources & Justice: Proceedings of 1987 Bishops' Workshop. Ed. by Donald G. McCarthy. LC 87-18302. 308p. (Orig.). 1987. pap. 17.95 (*0-935372-21-0*) Pope John Ctr.

Scarce Natural Resources: The Challenge to Public Policymaking. Ed. by Susan Welch & Robert Miewald. LC 83-2898. (Sage Yearbooks in Politics & Public Policy Ser.: No. 11). 288p. 1983. reprint ed. pap. 82.10 (*0-608-01469-9*, 2059513) Bks Demand.

Scarce Truth Enough Alive: Shakespeare's Contemporary Search for Truth & Trust. Max H. James. (Illus.). 232p. 1995. text ed. 20.00 (*0-8059-3701-3*) Dorrance.

Scarce Water & Institutional Change. Ed. by Kenneth D. Frederick. LC 85-20999. 207p. 1986. text ed. 22.50 (*0-915707-21-7*) Resources Future.

Scarcity & Choice in History. William H. Court. LC 74-113460. viii, 256p. 1970. lib. bdg. 39.50 (*0-678-08017-8*) Kelley.

Scarcity & Growth: The Economics of Natural Resource Availability. Harold J Barnett & Chandler Morse. LC 63-9742. 288p. 1963. 32.00 (*0-8018-0056-0*) Resources Future.

Scarcity & Growth Reconsidered. Ed. by V. Kerry Smith. LC 78-27236. xvi, 298p. 1979. 30.00 (*0-8018-2232-7*); pap. 14.95 (*0-8018-2233-5*) Resources Future.

Scarcity & Opportunity in an Indian Village. James M. Freeman. (Illus.). 177p. (C). 1985. reprint ed. pap. text ed. 10.50 (*0-88133-165-1*) Waveland Pr.

Scarcity & Survival in Central America: Ecological Origins of the Soccer War. William H. Durham. LC 78-55318. (Illus.). xx, 209p. 1979. 35.00 (*0-8047-1000-7*); pap. 13.95 (*0-8047-1154-2*) Stanford U Pr.

Scarcity by Design: The Legacy of New York City's Housing Policies. Peter D. Salins & Gerard C. Mildner. LC 92-15981. 168p. 1992. text ed. 32.00 (*0-674-79018-9*) HUP.

***Scarcity of Love.** Anna Kavan. write for info. (*0-614-20081-4*, Pub. by P Owen Ltd UK) Dufour.

***Scarcity of Water: Emerging Legal & Policy Responses.** Edward H. Brans. LC 97-9640. (International Environmental Law & Policy Ser.). 1997. write for info. (*90-411-0657-X*) Kluwer Law Tax Pubs.

***Scare Bare.** Betsy Haynes. (Bone Chillers Ser.: No. 20). (J). 1997. pap. 3.99 (*0-06-106452-1*) HarpC Child Bks.

Scare Tactics. John Farris. 320p. 1989. mass mkt. 4.95 (*0-8125-0300-7*) Tor Bks.

Scare Tactics. Elizabeth Manz. 1996. pap. 5.99 (*0-312-95792-0*) St Martin.

Scare the Moon. Harriet Ziefert. (Illus.). (J). (ps up). 1995. 12.95 (*1-56402-657-4*) Candlewick Pr.

Scarebird. Sid Fleischman. LC 87-4099. 32p. (J). (gr. k-3). 1988. 16.00 (*0-688-07317-4*); lib. bdg. 15.93 (*0-688-07318-2*) Greenwillow.

Scarebird. Sid Fleischman. LC 93-11726. (Illus.). 32p. (J). (ps up). 1994. reprint ed. pap. 4.95 (*0-688-13105-0*, Mulberry) Morrow.

Scarecrow. Richie T. Cusick. Ed. by Claire Zion. 288p. (Orig.). 1990. mass mkt. 4.99 (*0-671-69020-5*) PB.

Scarecrow! Valerie Littlewood. 32p. (J). (gr. 2-6). 1995. pap. 4.99 (*0-14-055614-1*, Puff Unicorn) Puffin Bks.

Scarecrow. Jaime Manrique. 1990. pap. 7.00 (*0-922792-63-1*) Gnosis Pr.

Scarecrow. Cynthia Rylant. LC 96-7652. (Illus.). 1998. write for info. (*0-15-201084-X*) HarBrace.

***Scarecrow: How the Scarecrow Came About.** Martha H. Nitschke. Ed. by Debbie Christie. (Illus.). 20p. (J). 1997. 2.99 (*0-9630077-3-4*) Entrepress.

Scarecrow of Oz. L. Frank Baum. (J). 20.95 (*0-8488-0707-3*) Amereon Ltd.

***Scarecrow of Oz.** L. Frank Baum. 1997. 22.00 (*0-688-14719-4*, Morrow Junior) Morrow.

Scarecrow of Oz. L. Frank Baum. (J). pap. 4.95 (*0-8167-2897-6*) Troll Communs.

Scarecrow Poetry: The Muse in Post-Middle Age. Ed. by Robert McGovern & Stephen H. Haven. LC 94-71673. 178p. (Orig.). 1994. pap. 19.00 (*0-912592-36-2*) Ashland Poetry.

***Scarecrow Santa.** Carole A. Huebner. (Illus.). 20p. (Orig.). (J). (ps-1). 1998. pap. 8.99 (*1-55237-456-4*, Pub. by Comnwlth Pub CN) Partners Pubs Grp.

Scarecrow, the Lion & the Tinman: A Novelette about Forbidden Friendships. Alicia Williams. ix, 127p. (Orig.). 1996. pap. 11.00 (*1-889316-00-8*) Ecrivez.

Scarecrow Walks at Midnight. R. L. Stine. (Goosebumps Ser.: No. 20). 160p. (J). (gr. 4-6). 1994. pap. 3.99 (*0-590-47742-0*) Scholastic Inc.

Scarecrows. George D. Gribble. (Illus.). 32p. 1985. 30.00 (*0-930126-16-5*) Typographeum.

Scarecrow's Secret. H. Amery. (Farmyard Tales Ser.). (Illus.). 16p. (J). (ps-3). 1992. pap. 3.95 (*0-7460-0584-9*) EDC.

***Scarecrow's Secret Sticker Book.** Alastair Smith. (Farmyard Tales Sticker Storybook Ser.). (Illus.). 18p. (Orig.). (J). (ps up). 1997. pap. 5.95 (*0-7460-2993-4*, Usborne) EDC.

Scarecrow's Spooky Night. Susan Hood. (Illus.). 24p. (Orig.). (J). (ps-3). 1996. pap. 3.95 (*0-8167-4114-X*, Whistlstop) Troll Communs.

Scared & the Doomed: The Jewish Establishment vs. the Six Million. M. J. Nurenberger. (Illus.). 350p. 24.95 (*0-88962-290-6*); pap. 14.95 (*0-88962-289-2*) Mosaic.

Scared Chaos. Kane. (Studies in Jungian Psychology). 1995. pap. 16.00 (*0-919123-65-1*, Pub. by Inner City CN) BookWorld Dist.

Scared Child: Helping Kids Overcome Traumatic Events. Barbara Brooks & Paula M. Siegel. LC 96-10330. 176p. 1996. pap. text ed. 14.95 (*0-471-08284-8*) Wiley.

Scared Generation. Ed. by Natasha Perova & Arch Tait. (Glas Ser.: No. 9). (Illus.). 224p. pap. 14.95 (*0-939010-49-6*) I R Dee.

Scared Growing Up in America. George H. Gallup. LC 96-3210. (Illus.). 92p. 1996. pap. 9.95 (*0-8192-1662-3*) Morehouse Pub.

***Scared in School.** Roberta S. Brown. LC 97-23602. 1997. write for info. (*0-87483-496-1*) August Hse.

Scared Money. Mark Cramer. LC 94-68302. 134p. 1994. 19.95 (*0-933944-15-2*) City Miner Bks.

Scared or Prepared: Preventing Conflict & Violence in Your Classroom. Lee Canter & Ron Garrison. 125p. (Orig.). 1994. pap. text ed. 10.95 (*0-939007-97-5*) Lee Canter & Assocs.

***Scared Out of My Skin.** Roger Ethier. Ed. by Arlene Smith. (Illus.). 72p. (YA). (gr. 4 up). 1997. 14.95 (*0-9644924-6-6*) Folklore VA.

Scared Silly. Eth Clifford. 128p. (J). 1989. pap. 2.75 (*0-590-42382-7*) Scholastic Inc.

Scared Silly. James Howe. 48p. (J). 1990. reprint ed. pap. 5.99 (*0-380-70446-3*, Camelot) Avon.

Scared Silly! A Collection of Stories, Rhymes, & Riddles to Laugh Your Fears Away. Illus. & Compiled by Marc T. Brown. LC 93-13501. (J). 1994. 18.95 (*0-316-11360-3*) Little.

Scared Silly: A Halloween Treat. James Howe. LC 88-7837. (Illus.). 48p. (J). (gr. k up). 1989. 16.00 (*0-688-07666-1*, Morrow Junior) Morrow.

Scared Speechless: Public Speaking Step by Step. Rebecca McDaniel. (C). 1994. text ed. 42.00 (*0-8039-5173-6*); pap. text ed. 17.50 (*0-8039-5174-4*) Sage.

Scared Stiff. Jahnna N. Malcolm. 128p. (J). 1995. pap. 3.50 (*0-590-44996-6*, Apple Paperbacks) Scholastic Inc.

Scared Stiff. Willo D. Roberts. LC 90-37732. 192p. (J). (gr. 3-7). 1991. lib. bdg. 15.00 (*0-689-31692-5*, Atheneum Bks Young) S&S Childrens.

Scared Stiff: Seven Tales of Seduction & Terror. Ramsey Campbell. 192p. 1988. pap. 8.95 (*0-446-38783-5*) Warner Bks.

Scared to Death. Jahnna N. Malcolm. 144p. (J). 1992. pap. 2.95 (*0-590-44995-8*, Apple Paperbacks) Scholastic Inc.

Scared to Death. Jahnna N. Malcolm. 144p. (J). (gr. 3-7). 1995. pap. 3.50 (*0-590-55217-1*) Scholastic Inc.

Scared to Life. Douglas Rumford. 180p. 1994. pap. 9.99 (*1-56476-413-3*, 6-3413, Victor Bks) Chariot Victor.

Scared Woman: True Expose, Vol. I. Beulah S. Kershaw. (Illus.). 44p. (Orig.). 1981. pap. 3.00 (*0-911870-03-2*) Beulah.

Scaredy Cat. Joan Rankin. (Illus.). (J). (ps-3). 1996. 16.00 (*0-689-80948-4*, S&S Bks Young Read) S&S Childrens.

Scaredy Cat. Rozanne L. Williams. (Emergent Reader Bks.). 16p. 1994. 2.49 (*0-916119-71-8*) Creat Teach Pr.

Scaredy Cat. Rozanne L. Williams. (Emergent Reader Big Bks.). (Illus.). 16p. (Orig.). (J). 1995. pap. 11.98 (*1-57471-083-4*) Creat Teach Pr.

Scaredy-Cat Elizabeth. Francine Pascal. (Sweet Valley Kids Ser.). (Illus.). 96p. (Orig.). (J). (gr. k-3). 1995. pap. 3.50 (*0-553-48213-0*, Sweet Valley) BDD Bks Young Read.

Scaredy-Cat Kitten. Roz Rosenbluth. (Storytime Bks.). (Illus.). 24p. (J). (ps-2). 1993. pap. text ed. 1.29 (*1-56293-352-3*) McClanahan Bk.

***Scaredy Cat Reading System Vol. I: Level I PreReading Kit.** Joyce M. Herzog. Ed. by Tom J. Herzog. 85p. (Orig.). (J). (gr. k-1). 1992. pap. text ed. 39.95 (*1-887225-00-5*) Simplified Lrn.

***Scaredy Cat Reading System Vol. II: Level II Beginner's Book.** Joyce M. Herzog. Ed. by Tom J. Herzog. (Illus.). 113p. (Orig.). (J). (gr. k-3). 1995. pap. text ed. 39.95 (*1-887225-01-3*) Simplified Lrn.

Scaredy Cat Reading System Vol. III: Level III Advanced Beginner's Book. Joyce M. Herzog. Ed. by Tom J. Herzog. (Illus.). 135p. (Orig.). (J). (gr. k-6). 1993. pap. text ed. 49.95 (*1-887225-02-1*) Simplified Lrn.

***Scaredy Cat Reading System Vol. IV: Level IV Rules... & Fun!** Joyce M. Herzog. Ed. by Tom J. Herzog. (Illus.). 155p. (Orig.). (J). (gr. k-6). 1995. pap. text ed. 49.95 (*1-887225-03-X*) Simplified Lrn.

Scaredy Cat Reading System Level 1: A Story-Based Phonics Instruction Program. Joyce Herzog. 85p. (Orig.). (J). 1997. pap. 29.95 (*1-882514-31-9*) Greenleaf TN.

Scaredy Cat Reading System Level 2: A Story-Based Phonics Instruction Program. Joyce Herzog. 102p. (Orig.). (J). 1997. pap. 34.95 (*1-882514-32-7*) Greenleaf TN.

Scaredy Cat Reading System Level 3: A Story-Based Phonics Instruction Program. Joyce Herzog. 140p. (Orig.). (J). 1997. pap. 49.95 (*1-882514-33-5*) Greenleaf TN.

Scaredy Cat Reading System Level 4: A Story-Based Phonics Instruction Program. Joyce Herzog. 156p. (Orig.). (J). 1997. pap. 49.95 (*1-882514-34-3*) Greenleaf TN.

Scaredy Cat Runs Away. Rozanne L. Williams. (Emergent Reader Bks.). (Illus.). 8p. (Orig.). (J). (gr. k-2). 1995. pap. 1.59 (*1-57471-003-6*) Creat Teach Pr.

Scaredy Cat Runs Away. Rozanne L. Williams. (Emergent Reader Big Bks.). (Illus.). 8p. (Orig.). (J). (gr. k-2). 1996. pap. 7.98 (*1-57471-107-5*) Creat Teach Pr.

***Scaredy Cats.** Audrey Wood. (ITA.). (J). 1989. pap. 3.99 (*0-85953-575-4*) Childs Play.

Scaredy Cats. Audrey Wood. LC 90-46913. (Illus.). 32p. (J). (ps-2). 1989. 7.99 (*0-85953-110-4*); pap. 3.99 (*0-85953-323-9*) Childs Play.

***Scaredy Cats.** Audrey Wood. (J). 1996. lib. bdg. 11.95 (*0-85953-895-8*) Childs Play.

***Scaredy Cats, 10.** Stanley. (J). 1998. mass mkt. 3.99 (*0-689-81617-0*) S&S Childrens.

***Scaredy Cats, 11.** Stanley. (J). 1998. mass mkt. 3.99 (*0-689-81618-9*) S&S Childrens.

***Scaredy Cats, 12.** Stanley. 1998. mass mkt. 3.99 (*0-689-81619-7*) S&S Childrens.

Scaredy Cats No. 4: Mrs. O'Dell's Third-Grade Class Is Shrinking, Bk. 4. George E. Stanley. 1996. pap. 3.99 (*0-689-80860-7*, S&S Bks Young Read) S&S Childrens.

Scaredy Cat's Guide to Teamwork & Empowerment. Filomena D. Warihay. 108p. 1995. pap. 12.95 (*0-9641834-1-2*) Take Charge Cnslts.

Scaredy Dog. Jane R. Thomas. LC 95-49312. (Illus.). 64p. (J). (gr. 1-3). 1996. pap. 3.95 (*0-7868-1148-X*) Hyprn Child.

Scaredy Ghost. Mary Packard. LC 93-24845. (Illus.). 24p. (J). (gr. k-2). 1994. pap. 1.50 (*0-8167-3246-9*) Troll Communs.

Scaredy-Ghost. Bettina Paterson. (Illus.). 12p. (J). (ps). 1993. bds. 2.50 (*0-448-40574-1*, G&D) Putnam Pub Group.

Scaredy Kitten. (Kitten Tales Ser.). (Illus.). 28p. (J). (ps-2). 1992. 3.95 (*0-7214-5309-0*, S915-2, Ladybrd) Penguin.

Scareforce. Charles D. Hough. 208p. (Orig.). 1995. mass mkt. 5.99 (*0-446-60128-4*) Warner Bks.

Scarf Juggling. Dave Finnigan. (Illus.). 20p. (Orig.). (J). (gr. 2-7). 1991. pap. 10.00 (*0-9615521-8-2*, 133730) Jugglebug.

Scarf Magic. (Illus.). 64p. 1993. spiral bd. 5.98 (*1-56173-291-5*, 3612200) Pubns Intl Ltd.

Scarf Tying Made Easy: It's the Easy Way to Look Good! Julie C. Reagan. (Illus.). 210p. (Orig.). (C). 1988. pap. 14.95 (*0-317-93908-4*) J Claire Inc.

Scarface Al & the Crime Crusaders: Chicago's Private War Against Capone. Dennis E. Hoffman. LC 93-16865. (Illus.). 209p. (C). 1993. 24.95 (*0-8093-1925-X*) S Ill U Pr.

Scariest Night. Betty R. Wright. LC 91-55030. 166p. (J). (gr. 3-7). 1991. 15.95 (*0-8234-0904-X*) Holiday.

Scariest Place on Earth: Eye to Eye with Hurricanes. David E. Fisher. 1994. 23.00 (*0-679-42775-9*) Random.

Scaring Myself Again: Far-Flung Adventures of a TV Journalist. Allen Abel. 249p. (Orig.). 1993. pap. 12.00 (*0-00-637908-7*, Pub. by HarpC CN) HarpC.

Scaring Us to Death: The Impact of Stephen King on Popular Culture. 2nd expanded rev. ed. Michael R. Collins. LC 95-5023. (Milford Series: Popular Writers of Today: Vol. 63). pap. write for info. (*0-930261-38-0*); lib. bdg. write for info. (*0-930261-37-2*) Borgo Pr.

Scarlatti: Solo Piano Literature-A Comprehensive Guide Annotated & Evaluated with Thematics. Ed. by Carolyn Maxwell. (Maxwell Music Evaluation Bks.). (Illus.). 412p. (Orig.). 1985. pap. 13.95 (*0-912531-02-9*) Maxwell Mus Eval.

Scarlatti Inheritance. Robert Ludlum. 368p. 1982. mass mkt. 7.50 (*0-553-27146-6*) Bantam.

Scarlet & Black. Stendhal. Tr. by Margaret R. Shaw. (Classics Ser.). 512p. (Orig.). 1953. pap. 8.95 (*0-14-044030-5*, Penguin Classics) Viking Penguin.

Scarlet & Black. M. Stendhal. 656p. (Orig.). 1991. 20.00 (*0-679-40565-8*, Everymans Lib) Knopf.

Scarlet & the Beast, 3 vols., Set. John Daniel. 1275p. 1995. 58.00 (*0-9635079-6-6*) J Kregal Inc.

Scarlet & the Beast, 3 vols., Set. 2nd ed. John Daniel. (Illus.). 1343p. (C). 1995. 57.00 (*0-9635079-9-0*) J Kregal Inc.

Scarlet & the Beast: A History of the War Between English & French, Vol. I. 2nd ed. John Daniel. (Illus.). 947p. (C). 1995. 43.00 (*0-9635079-8-2*) J Kregal Inc.

Scarlet & the Beast: English Freemasonry, Banks, & the Illegal Drug Trade, Vol. 3. John Daniel. 175p. 1995. 12.00 (*0-9635079-4-X*) J Kregal Inc.

Scarlet & the Beast: Freemasonry & the Illegal Drug Trade, Vol. 3. John Daniel. 175p. 1992. pap. 10.00 (*0-9635079-5-8*) J Kregal Inc.

Scarlet & the Beast: Freemasonry, Mother of Modern Cults, Vis-a-Vis Mystery Babylon, Mother of Harlots, Vol. 2. John Daniel. 200p. 1992. pap. 10.00 (*0-9635079-3-1*) J Kregal Inc.

Scarlet & the Beast: Mother of Modern Cults, Viv-a-Vis, Mystery Babylon, Mother of Harlots, Vol. 2. John Daniel. 200p. 1994. 12.00 (*0-9635079-2-3*) J Kregal Inc.

Scarlet & the Beast: The War Between English & French Freemasonry. 2nd ed. John Daniel. (Illus.). 1000p. 1995. write for info. (*0-614-07570-X*) J Kregal Inc.

Scarlet & the Beast: The War Between English & French Freemasonry, Vol. 1. John Daniel. 900p. 1992. 43.00 (*0-9635079-0-7*); pap. 30.00 (*0-9635079-1-5*) J Kregal Inc.

Scarlet Angel. Palmer. Date not set. 3.98 (*0-8317-4618-1*) Smithmark.

Scarlet Angel. Elizabeth Palmer. 1993. 19.95 (*0-312-09917-7*, Thomas Dunne Bks) St Martin.

***Scarlet Apples & Cream.** K. B. Fedorev Vanderkleed. 37p. (Orig.). 1996. pap. 5.95 (*1-889724-00-9*) Scarlet Apple Ent.

Scarlet Arena 30303. Silas Moore. Ed. by Genevieve Oddo. LC 74-190272. (Illus.). 196p. (J). (gr. 8-12). 1972. lib. bdg. 3.95 (*0-87783-063-0*) Oddo.

Scarlet Author. Pauline Angelakis. (Illus.). 20p. (Orig.). 1992. pap. 4.95 (*0-915992-56-6*) Eastern Acorn.

Scarlet Book of Freemasonry: Containing, a Thrilling & Authentic Account of the Imprisonment, Torture, & Martyrdom of Freemasons & Knights Templars, for the Past Six Hundred Years; Also an Authentic Account of the Education, Remarkable Career & Tragic Death of the Renowned Philospher Pythagoras, Recent Remarkable Discovery of Masonic Emblems on an Ancient Obelisk in Egypt. M. W. Redding. 517p. 1992. pap. 36.00 (*1-56459-283-9*) Kessinger Pub.

Scarlet Christmas: Abortion: The Grandparent Connection. Joy Parker. 32p. (Orig.). 1991. pap. 2.95 (*0-9628088-1-4*) Laser Pr Pubs.

S

Scarlet City: A Novel of Sixteenth-Century Italy. Hella S. Haasse. Tr. & Intro. by Anita Miller. 594p. 1990. 22.95 (*0-89733-349-7*) Academy Chi Pubs.

Scarlet City: A Novel of 16th Century Italy. 2nd ed. Hella S. Haasse. Tr. by Anita Miller from DUT. 368p. 1997. reprint ed. pap. 15.95 (*0-89733-372-1*) Academy Chi Pubs.

Scarlet Dawn. large type ed. Amber Dana. (Nightingale Ser.). 1996. 20.00 (*0-7838-1888-2*, GK Hall) Thorndike Pr.

***Scarlet Diaries: Poems from the Darkside.** Carson Gabel. LC 96-71879. (Illus.). 108p. (Orig.). 1997. pap. 7.95 (*0-9654194-0-1*) Oasis in Print.

Scarlet Domino. Sylvia Thorpe. 224p. 1978. pap. 1.50 (*0-449-23220-4*, Crest) Fawcett.

Scarlet Dream. C. L. Moore. (Illus.). 1981. 20.00 (*0-937986-42-9*) D M Grant.

Scarlet Empire. David M. Parry. LC 77-154456. (Utopian Literature Ser.). (Illus.). 1976. reprint ed. 33.95 (*0-405-03538-1*) Ayer.

Scarlet Feather. Joan Grant. 290p. 1990. pap. 10.95 (*0-89804-148-1*) Ariel GA.

Scarlet Feather. Joan M. Grant. 1980. 25.95 (*0-405-11789-2*) Ayer.

***Scarlet Fever.** Mitchell Smith. 1996. 23.95 (*0-614-20637-5*) NAL-Dutton.

Scarlet Fish & Other Stories. Joan M. Grant. 1980. 17.95 (*0-405-11790-6*) Ayer.

Scarlet Flower. 8.00 (*0-686-23329-8*) Rochester Folk Art.

***Scarlet Generation.** Christopher Nicole. (Russian Saga Ser.: No. 5). 320p. 1996. 24.00 (*0-7278-4968-9*) Severn Hse.

Scarlet Ibis: A Classic Story of Brotherhood. James Hurst. (Creative Short Stories Ser.). (Illus.). (J). (gr. 4 up). 1987. lib. bdg. 13.95 (*0-88682-000-6*) Creative Ed.

Scarlet Kisses. Patricia Camden. 384p. (Orig.). 1992. mass mkt. 4.50 (*0-380-76825-9*) Avon.

***Scarlet Lady.** Sandra Chastain. (Loveswept Ser.: No. 855). 1997. mass mkt. 3.50 (*0-553-44551-0*, Loveswept) Bantam.

Scarlet Lady. Georgina Devon. 352p. 1991. mass mkt. 3.95 (*0-8217-3400-8*, Zebra Kensgtn) Kensgtn Pub Corp.

***Scarlet Lady.** Marlene Suson. 384p. (Orig.). 1997. mass mkt. 5.99 (*0-380-78912-4*) Avon.

***Scarlet Lady.** Sara Wood. 1997. mass mkt. 3.50 (*0-373-11916-X*, 1-11916-3) Harlequin Bks.

***Scarlet Lady.** large type ed. Sara Wood. (Mills & Boon Large Print Ser.). 288p. 1996. 21.50 (*0-263-14801-7*, Pub. by M & B UK) Ulverscroft.

***Scarlet Leaves.** Sonya Birmingham. 368p. (Orig.). 1996. mass mkt. 5.50 (*0-8439-4081-6*, Leisure Bks) Dorchester Pub Co.

Scarlet Legacy. V. Helton. 352p. 1994. mass mkt. 4.50 (*0-06-108091-8*, Harp PBks) HarpC.

Scarlet Letter. Created by Harcourt Brace Staff. 1990. student ed., pap. 10.00 (*0-15-348523-X*) HR&W Schl Div.

Scarlet Letter. Created by Harcourt Brace Staff. 1990. student ed., teacher ed., pap. 22.75 (*0-15-348529-9*) HR&W Schl Div.

Scarlet Letter. Nathaniel Hawthorne. 200p. pap. 4.00 (*1-85326-029-0*, Pub. by Wrdsworth Edits UK) Publishers Group.

Scarlet Letter. Nathaniel Hawthorne. (Classics Ser.). (YA). (gr. 9 up). 1962. mass mkt. 3.95 (*0-8049-0007-8*, CL-7) Airmont.

***Scarlet Letter.** Nathaniel Hawthorne. (Illustrated Classics Collection 2). 64p. 1994. pap. 4.95 (*0-7854-0722-7*, 40412) Am Guidance.

Scarlet Letter. Nathaniel Hawthorne. 256p. 1981. mass mkt. 2.95 (*0-553-21009-2*, Bantam Classics) Bantam.

Scarlet Letter. Nathaniel Hawthorne. (Book Notes Ser.). (C). 1984. pap. 2.95 (*0-8120-3442-2*) Barron.

Scarlet Letter. Nathaniel Hawthorne. LC 91-70969. (Literary Classics Ser.). 208p. 1991. pap. 5.98 (*1-56138-036-9*) Courage Bks.

Scarlet Letter. Nathaniel Hawthorne. 1970. pap. 1.50 (*0-06-080620-6*, Harp PBks) HarpC.

***Scarlet Letter.** Nathaniel Hawthorne. 1997. pap. 7.75 (*0-03-051497-5*) HR&W Schl Div.

Scarlet Letter. Nathaniel Hawthorne. Ed. by Harry T. Levin. LC 60-2662. (YA). (gr. 9 up). 1960. pap. 10.36 (*0-395-05142-8*, RivEd) HM.

Scarlet Letter. Nathaniel Hawthorne. LC 95-4307. (Illus.). 288p. 1995. pap. 12.95 (*0-7868-8093-7*) Hyperion.

Scarlet Letter. Nathaniel Hawthorne. 1959. pap. 3.95 (*0-451-52522-1*) NAL-Dutton.

Scarlet Letter. Nathaniel Hawthorne. Ed. & Intro. by Throp Willard. (Four Classic American Novels). 1969. pap. write for info. (*0-318-54486-5*) NAL-Dutton.

***Scarlet Letter.** Nathaniel Hawthorne. 1999. pap. 3.99 (*0-14-038239-9*) Penguin.

Scarlet Letter. Nathaniel Hawthorne. 276p. 1996. pap. 6.95 (*1-57392-047-9*) Prometheus Bks.

Scarlet Letter. Nathaniel Hawthorne. 1995. pap. 9.95 (*0-312-13846-6*) St Martin.

Scarlet Letter. Nathaniel Hawthorne. 288p. 1989. pap. 2.50 (*0-8125-0483-6*) Tor Bks.

Scarlet Letter. Nathaniel Hawthorne. LC 92-52902. 1992. 17.00 (*0-679-41731-1*, Everymans Lib) Knopf.

Scarlet Letter. Nathaniel Hawthorne. 220p. 1984. lib. bdg. 25.95 (*0-89968-258-8*, Lghtyr Pr) Buccaneer Bks.

Scarlet Letter. Nathaniel Hawthorne. (Classics Illustrated Ser.). (Illus.). 52p. (YA). 1990. pap. 4.95 (*1-57209-006-5*) First Classics.

Scarlet Letter. Nathaniel Hawthorne. Ed. by Austin Warren. 254p. (C). 1947. pap. text ed. 22.50 (*0-03-009860-2*) HB Coll Pubs.

Scarlet Letter. Nathaniel Hawthorne. Ed. by William Charvat et al. (Centenary Edition of the Works of Nathaniel Hawthorne: Vol. 1). (Illus.). 292p. 1963. 50.00 (*0-8142-0059-1*) Ohio St U Pr.

Scarlet Letter. Nathaniel Hawthorne. Ed. & Intro. by Brian Harding. (World's Classics Ser.). 352p. 1990. pap. 4.95 (*0-19-281753-1*) OUP.

Scarlet Letter. Nathaniel Hawthorne. 1994. mass mkt. 4.99 (*0-671-51011-8*, WSP) PB.

Scarlet Letter. Nathaniel Hawthorne. (Portland House Illustrated Classics Ser.). (Illus.). 312p. (YA). 1991. 9.99 (*0-517-64302-2*) Random Hse Value.

Scarlet Letter. Nathaniel Hawthorne. Ed. by Ross C. Murfin. (Case Studies in Contemporary Criticism). 416p. 1991. text ed. 39.95 (*0-312-06024-6*) St Martin.

Scarlet Letter. Nathaniel Hawthorne. (American Library). 256p. 1983. pap. 5.95 (*0-14-039019-7*, Penguin Classics) Viking Penguin.

Scarlet Letter. Nathaniel Hawthorne. 1988. pap. 4.50 (*0-8220-1165-4*) Cliffs.

Scarlet Letter. Nathaniel Hawthorne. Ed. by John S. Martin. 260p. 1995. pap. 9.95 (*1-55111-046-6*) Broadview Pr.

Scarlet Letter. Nathaniel Hawthorne. 224p. 1995. write for info. (*1-56865-139-2*, GuildAmerica) Dbldy Direct.

Scarlet Letter. Nathaniel Hawthorne. 1997. pap. 2.95 (*0-89375-994-5*) NAL-Dutton.

Scarlet Letter. Nathaniel Hawthorne. LC 96-31365. 160p. 1996. pap. 6.95 (*1-55783-243-9*) Applause Theatre Bk Pubs.

***Scarlet Letter.** Nathaniel Hawthorne. write for info. (*0-614-22115-3*, Sig Classics) NAL-Dutton.

***Scarlet Letter, 2 vols.** Nathaniel Hawthorne. 20.00 (*0-614-30539-X*) NAVH.

Scarlet Letter. Holt. 1989. student ed., pap. 10.00 (*0-03-023454-9*) HR&W Schl Div.

Scarlet Letter. Meyer. (Bedford Introduction to Literature Ser.). Date not set. pap. text ed. 36.90 (*0-312-13892-X*) St Martin.

***Scarlet Letter.** Ed. by Eileen Morey. (Literary Companion Ser.). (YA). (gr. 9-12). 1997. pap. 12.96 (*1-56510-756-X*) Greenhaven.

***Scarlet Letter.** Ed. by Eileen Morey. (Literary Companion Ser.). (YA). (gr. 9-12). 1997. lib. bdg. 20.96 (*1-56510-757-8*) Greenhaven.

Scarlet Letter. 3rd ed. Nathaniel Hawthorne. Ed. by Seymour L. Gross et al. (Critical Editions Ser.). 480p. (C). 1988. pap. text ed. 8.95 (*0-393-95653-9*) Norton.

Scarlet Letter. Nathaniel Hawthorne. 523p. 1984. reprint ed. lib. bdg. 25.95 (*0-89966-494-6*) Buccaneer Bks.

Scarlet Letter. Nathaniel Hawthorne. 320p. 1994. reprint ed. pap. text ed. 6.95 (*0-460-87183-8*, Everyman's Classic Lib) C E Tuttle.

Scarlet Letter. Nathaniel Hawthorne. LC 94-5440. 192p. reprint ed. pap. 2.00 (*0-486-28048-9*) Dover.

Scarlet Letter. Nathaniel Hawthorne. (Notable American Authors Ser.). 1992. reprint ed. lib. bdg. 75.00 (*0-7812-3038-1*) Rprt Serv.

Scarlet Letter: A Case Study in Contemporary Criticism. Nathaniel Hawthorne. LC 89-63918. 416p. (Orig.). (C). 1990. pap. text ed. 6.50 (*0-312-03546-2*, Bedford Bks) St Martin.

Scarlet Letter: A Reading. Nina Baym. (Twayne's Masterwork Studies: No. 1). 20.95 (*0-685-40583-4*, 500, Twayne) Scribnrs Ref.

Scarlet Letter: A Reading. Nina Baym. 152p. 1986. 17.95 (*0-685-19706-9*, Twayne) Scribnrs Ref.

Scarlet Letter: A Study Guide. Henry Chupack. (Novel-Ties Ser.). 1983. student ed., teacher ed., pap. text ed. 15.95 (*0-88122-032-9*) Lrn Links.

Scarlet Letter: Student Activity Book. Marcia Sohl & Gerald Dackerman. (Now Age Illustrated Ser.). (Illus.). (J). (gr. 4-10). 1976. student ed. 1.25 (*0-88301-194-8*) Pendulum Pr.

Scarlet Letter & Other Tales of the Puritans. Nathaniel Hawthorne. Ed. by Harry T. Levin. LC 61-2662. (C). 1972. pap. 11.56 (*0-395-05153-3*, Hill Stead Mus) HM.

Scarlet Letter & Selected Writings. Nathaniel Hawthorne. Ed. by Stephen Nissenbaum. (Modern Library College Editions). 400p. (C). 1984. pap. text ed. write for info. (*0-07-555475-5*) McGraw.

Scarlet Letter & the Custom House. Nathaniel Hawthorne. 1976. 23.95 (*0-8488-0520-8*) Amereon Ltd.

***Scarlet Letter Readalong.** Nathaniel Hawthorne. (Illustrated Classics Collection 2). 64p. 1994. pap. 14.95 incl. audio (*0-7854-0688-3*, 40414) Am Guidance.

***Scarlet Master of the House.** Margaret Callaghan. 1997. pap. text ed. 3.99 (*1-85487-928-6*) London Brdge.

Scarlet Memorial: Tales of Cannibalism in Modern China. Zheng Yi. 256p. 1996. text ed. 32.00 (*0-8133-2615-X*) Westview.

Scarlet Memorial: Tales of Cannibalism in Modern China. Zheng I. Ed. & Tr. by T. P. Sym from CHI. LC 96-33948. 256p. (C). 1997. pap. text ed. 19.50 (*0-8133-2616-8*) Westview.

Scarlet Monster Lives Here. Marjorie W. Sharmat. LC 78-19484. (I Can Read Bk.). (Illus.). 64p. (J). (gr. k-3). 1986. pap. 3.50 (*0-06-444098-2*, Trophy) HarpC Child Bks.

***Scarlet Music: A Life of Hildegard Von Bingen.** Joan Ohanneson. LC 96-47125. 228p. 1997. pap. 17.95 (*0-8245-1646-X*) Crossroad NY.

Scarlet Pansy. 2nd ed. (Orig.). 1994. mass mkt. 4.95 (*1-56333-189-6*, Badboy) Masquerade.

Scarlet Pimpernel. Orczy. 1997. pap. 3.99 (*0-14-037454-X*, Puffin) Puffin Bks.

Scarlet Pimpernel. Baroness E. Orczy. 20.95 (*0-8488-0601-8*) Amereon Ltd.

***Scarlet Pimpernel.** Baroness E. Orczy. (Illustrated Classics Collection 4). 64p. 1994. pap. 4.95 (*0-7854-0755-3*, 40518) Am Guidance.

Scarlet Pimpernel. Emmuska Orczy. (Airmont Classics Ser.). (J). (gr. 7 up). 1964. mass mkt. 2.95 (*0-8049-0028-0*, CL-28) Airmont.

Scarlet Pimpernel. Emmuska Orczy. 272p. 1992. mass mkt. 4.95 (*0-553-21402-0*, Bantam Classics) Bantam.

Scarlet Pimpernel. Emmuska Orczy. 256p. (J). (gr. 7). 1974. pap. 4.95 (*0-451-52315-6*, Sig Classics) NAL-Dutton.

Scarlet Pimpernel. Emmuska Orczy. Ed. by Naunerle Farr. (Now Age Illustrated IV Ser.). (Illus.). (gr. 4-12). 1978. student ed. 1.25 (*0-88301-345-2*); pap. text ed. 2.95 (*0-88301-321-5*) Pendulum Pr.

Scarlet Pimpernel. Emmuska Orczy. 256p. 1984. reprint ed. lib. bdg. 21.95 (*0-89966-508-X*) Buccaneer Bks.

Scarlet Pimpernel: Vocal Selections. 64p. (Orig.). 1994. pap. 16.95 (*0-89724-211-4*, VF1801) Warner Brothers.

***Scarlet Pimpernel Readalong.** Baroness E. Orczy. (Illustrated Classics Collection 4). 64p. 1994. pap. 14.95 incl. audio (*0-7854-0771-5*, 40520) Am Guidance.

Scarlet Pimpernell. 1994. pap. 16.95 (*1-57007-035-0*, XW1650) Astor Bks.

Scarlet Place. Pamela Jane. LC 96-11065. (Illus.). (J). 1997. write for info. (*0-385-32241-0*) Delacorte.

Scarlet Place in the Church. V. Tyler. 32p. 1993. pap. 4.95 (*0-9630779-3-7*) PPC Bks.

Scarlet Plague. Jack London. LC 74-16506. (Science Fiction Ser.). (Illus.). 181p. 1978. reprint ed. 20.95 (*0-405-06304-0*) Ayer.

Scarlet Plume. Frederick Manfred. (Buckskin Man Tales Ser.: Bk. 3). 368p. 1995. 4.50 (*0-451-18423-8*, Sig) NAL-Dutton.

Scarlet Poppy & Other Stories. Harriet P. Spofford. (C). 1972. reprint ed. lib. bdg. 24.00 (*0-8422-8111-8*) Irvington.

Scarlet Poppy & Other Stories. Harriet P. Spofford. (C). 1986. reprint ed. pap. text ed. 7.95 (*0-8290-2017-9*) Irvington.

Scarlet Q: Anarchy, Religion & the Cult of Science. Michael V. Ziesing. (Illus.). 150p. (Orig.). 1990. pap. 7.50 (*0-929480-17-1*) Mark Ziesing.

Scarlet Ribbons. Judith E. French. 384p. 1989. pap. 3.95 (*0-380-75552-1*) Avon.

Scarlet Rider. Lucy Sussex. LC 96-18115. 352p. 1996. 23.95 (*0-312-85293-2*) Forge NYC.

Scarlet Riders, No. 6: The Flying Patrol. Ian Anderson. 240p. 1988. mass mkt. 2.50 (*0-8217-2437-1*, Zebra Kensgtn) Kensgtn Pub Corp.

Scarlet Ruse. John D. MacDonald. 320p. 1987. mass mkt. 4.95 (*0-449-13247-1*) Fawcett.

Scarlet Ruse. John D. MacDonald. 1996. mass mkt. 5.99 (*0-449-22477-5*) Fawcett.

Scarlet Scourge. Johnston McCully. reprint ed. lib. bdg. 22.95 (*0-89190-998-2*, Rivercity Pr) Amereon Ltd.

Scarlet Season. Laura Gordon. (Intrigue Ser.). 1993. mass mkt. 2.99 (*0-373-22255-6*, 1-22255-3) Harlequin Bks.

***Scarlet Sister Mary.** Julia Peterkin. 352p. 1997. reprint ed. pap. 15.95 (*0-8203-1956-2*) U of Ga Pr.

Scarlet Slipper Mystery. rev. ed. Carolyn Keene. LC 74-3869. (Nancy Drew Ser.: Vol. 32). (Illus.). 196p. (J). (gr. 4-7). 1955. 5.95 (*0-448-09532-7*, G&D) Putnam Pub Group.

Scarlet Song. Mariama Ba. (Longman African Writers Ser.). (C). 1986. pap. text ed. 11.95 (*0-582-26455-3*) Addison-Wesley.

***Scarlet Survey.** Kevin Sherlock. 272p. (Orig.). 1997. pap. 19.95 (*0-9654036-1-0*, VSC497) Brennyman Bks.

Scarlet Tanager. Diana M. Amadeo. LC 94-90511. 144p. (Orig.). 1995. pap. 7.00 (*1-56002-502-6*, Univ Edtns) Aegina Pr.

Scarlet Temptress. Sue Rich. 336p. (Orig.). 1991. mass mkt. 5.50 (*0-671-73625-6*) PB.

Scarlet Thread. Francine Rivers. LC 96-3721. (Illus.). 462p. 1996. pap. 12.99 (*0-8423-3568-4*) Tyndale.

Scarlet Thread. large type ed. Evelyn Anthony. LC 90-22836. 668p. 1991. reprint ed. lib. bdg. 20.95 (*1-56054-096-6*) Thorndike Pr.

Scarlet Thread. large type ed. Evelyn Anthony. LC 90-22836. 668p. 1991. lib. bdg. 15.95 (*1-56054-994-7*) Thorndike Pr.

Scarlet Thread: Collected Writings on Culture & the Arts. Elizabeth G. Sayad. (Illus.). 163p. 1991. 9.95 (*0-935284-94-X*) Patrice Pr.

Scarlet Thread Special Education. Rivers. 1996. 18.99 (*0-8423-3563-3*) Tyndale.

Scarlet Tree. Osbert Sitwell. 4.95 (*0-7043-3157-8*, Pub. by Quartet UK) Charles River Bks.

Scarlet Whispers. Diana Whitney. 1994. mass mkt. 3.50 (*0-373-07603-7*, 1-07603-3) Harlequin Bks.

Scarlet Woman. Barbara Faith. (Special Edition Ser.). 1995. mass mkt. 3.75 (*0-373-09975-4*, 1-09975-3) Silhouette.

Scarlet Woman. Louisa Rawlings. (Historical Ser.). 1993. mass mkt. 3.99 (*0-373-28794-1*, 1-28794-5) Harlequin Bks.

Scarlet Women. J. D. Christillian. 1997. pap. 5.99 (*0-451-19096-3*) NAL-Dutton.

Scarlet Women. J. D. Christillian. 294p. 1996. pap. 22.95 (*1-55611-475-3*) D I Fine.

Scarlet Women. large type ed. J. D. Christillian. Date not set. 25.95 (*1-56895-349-6*) Wheeler Pub.

Scarlett. large type unabridged ed. 1992. lib. bdg. 11.97 (*0-8161-5535-6*, GK Hall) Thorndike Pr.

Scarlett, Vol. 2. large type unabridged ed. 1992. lib. bdg. 11.97 (*0-8161-5536-4*, GK Hall) Thorndike Pr.

Scarlett: The Sequel to Margaret Mitchell's Gone with the Wind. Alexandra Ripley. 1992. pap. 6.99 (*0-446-78168-1*); mass mkt. 6.99 (*0-446-36325-1*) Warner Bks.

Scarlett: The Sequel to Margaret Mitchell's Gone with the Wind. deluxe limited ed. Alexandra Ripley. 1992. 100.00 (*0-446-51718-6*) Warner Bks.

Scarlett: The Sequel to Margaret Mitchell's Gone with the Wind. large type ed. Alexandra Ripley. (General Ser.). 1184p. 1992. pap. 21.95 (*0-8161-5528-3*, GK Hall) Thorndike Pr.

Scarlett Angelina Wolverton-Manning. Jacqueline K. Ogburn. LC 92-41930. (Illus.). (J). 1994. pap. 14.99 (*0-8037-1376-2*); pap. 14.89 (*0-8037-1377-0*) Dial Bks Young.

Scarlett Doesn't Live Here Anymore: The Essential Guidebook to Atlanta. Charlotte Soutter & Michael T. Roe. Ed. by John English. (Illus.). 82p. (Orig.). 1996. pap. 5.95 (*0-9650562-0-1*) Spiral Bks.

***Scarlett Letter.** Nathaniel Hawthorne. Ed. by Susan Cockcroft. (Cambridge Literature Ser.). 288p. 1997. pap. text ed. 7.95 (*0-521-56783-1*) Cambridge U Pr.

***Scarlett Letters 1990s.** White. LC 96-51669. 1997. text ed. 65.00 (*0-312-17307-5*) St Martin.

***Scarlett Saves Her Family.** J. C. Suares. 1997. 20.00 (*0-684-84288-2*, S&S) S&S Trade.

Scarlett's Women: Gone with the Wind & Its Female Fans. Helen Taylor. 258p. (Orig.). 1989. pap. 14.95 (*0-8135-1496-7*); text ed. 40.00 (*0-8135-1480-0*) Rutgers U Pr.

Scarne on Card Tricks. John Scarne. 352p. 1986. pap. 5.99 (*0-451-15864-4*, Sig) NAL-Dutton.

Scarne on Cards. John Scarne. 1986. pap. 5.99 (*0-451-16765-1*, ROC) NAL-Dutton.

Scarne on Dice. John Scarne. 528p. 1992. pap. 15.00 (*0-87980-431-9*) Wilshire.

***Scarne's Encyclopedia of Card Games.** John Scarne. (Illus.). 475p. 1995. pap. 16.00 (*0-06-273155-6*) HarpC.

Scarne's Guide to Modern Poker. John Scarne. 308p. 1984. pap. 11.00 (*0-671-53076-3*, Fireside) S&S Trade.

Scarne's New Complete Guide to Gambling. John Scarne. (Illus.). 896p. 1986. pap. 18.00 (*0-671-63063-6*, Fireside) S&S Trade.

Scarne's on Cards. John Scarne. 1989. pap. 4.95 (*0-451-14949-1*) NAL-Dutton.

***Scarpa.** Sergio Los. 1994. pap. 24.99 (*3-8228-9441-9*) Taschen Amer.

Scarperer. Brendan Behan. reprint ed. lib. bdg. 18.95 (*0-89190-573-1*, Rivercity Pr) Amereon Ltd.

Scarred. William Heffernan. 384p. (Orig.). 1993. pap. 5.99 (*0-451-17863-7*, Sig) NAL-Dutton.

Scarred. David Roever & Kathy Koch. (Illus.). 200p. 1995. pap. 15.00 (*0-9648148-0-3*) Roever Commun.

Scarred: General Fiction Ser. large type ed. Monica Dickens. 288p. 1992. 27.99 (*0-7089-8655-2*) Ulverscroft.

Scarred Man. large type ed. Philip Daniels. (Linford Mystery Library). 273p. 1989. pap. 15.99 (*0-7089-6637-3*, Linford) Ulverscroft.

***Scarred Soul: Understanding & Ending Self-Inflicted Violence.** Tracy Alderman. (Illus.). 216p. (Orig.). 1997. pap. 13.95 (*1-57224-079-2*) New Harbinger.

Scars. Peter Meinke. (Poetry Ser.). 88p. (Orig.). (C). 1996. text ed. 24.95 (*0-8229-3935-5*) U of Pittsburgh Pr.

Scars. Peter Meinke. (Poetry Ser.). 88p. (Orig.). 1996. pap. 10.95 (*0-8229-5592-X*) U of Pittsburgh Pr.

***Scars.** Caroline Spector. (Earthdawn Ser.: No. 6). 1999. pap. 4.99 (*0-451-45390-5*, ROC) NAL-Dutton.

Scars. Steven D. Spratt & Lee G. Spratt. 128p. (Orig.). 1993. pap. 9.95 (*0-89407-107-6*) Strawberry Hill.

Scars: American Poetry in the Face of Violence. Ed. by Cynthia D. Edelberg. LC 95-2952. 232p. (C). 1995. pap. 24.95 (*0-8173-0787-7*) U of Ala Pr.

Scars Vol. 1: Chronicles of the Ancients, Vol. 1. (Chronicles of the Ancients Ser.). (Illus.). 256p. (Orig.). 1996. pap. 5.99 (*1-55560-280-0*, 6502) FASA Corp.

Scars & Memories. Odie Hawkins. 224p. 1987. mass mkt. 2.50 (*0-87067-277-0*, BH277) Holloway.

Scars & Stripes. Thomas C. Jones. 42p. (Orig.). (YA). 1994. pap. 3.00 (*1-57514-104-3*, 3043) Encore Perform Pub.

Scars & Stripes: Healing the Wounds of War. Gail A. Olson & Michael J. Robbins. 210p. 1992. 17.95 (*0-8306-3946-2*, 3979, TAB-Human Servs Inst); pap. 8.95 (*0-8306-3088-0*, 3979, TAB-Human Servs Inst) TAB Bks.

Scars Make Your Body More Interesting & Other Stories. Sherril Jaffe. LC 89-27143. 184p. (C). 1989. reprint ed. 20.00 (*0-87685-779-9*); reprint ed. pap. 13.00 (*0-87685-778-0*) Black Sparrow.

Scars Make Your Body More Interesting & Other Stories, signed ed. deluxe ed. Sherril Jaffe. LC 89-27143. 184p. (C). 1989. reprint ed. 30.00 (*0-87685-780-2*) Black Sparrow.

Scars of a Soldier: Vernon Heppe's True Story. Gordon Galloway. 226p. 1994. pap. 10.00 (*0-9644077-0-1*) Deerfield Pubng.

Scars of Christ. Rodney L. Johnson, Sr. LC 95-90977. (Orig.). 1996. pap. 8.95 (*0-533-11803-4*) Vantage.

Scars of Conquest - Masks of Resistance: The Invention of Cultural Identities in African, African-American, & Caribbean Drama. Tejumola Olaniyan. 224p. 1995. 42.00 (*0-19-509405-0*); pap. 16.95 (*0-19-509406-9*) OUP.

Scars of Dyslexia: A Case Studies in Emotional Reactions. Janice H. Edwards. LC 93-48376. (Cassell Education Ser.). (Illus.). 160p. 1994. pap. 26.00 (*0-304-32944-4*) Cassell.

Scars of Dyslexia: A Case Studies in Emotional Reactions. Janice H. Edwards. LC 93-48376. (Cassell Education Ser.). (Illus.). 160p. 1995. 70.00 (*0-304-32946-0*) Cassell.

Scars of Evolution: What Our Bodies Tell Us about Human Origin. Elaine Morgan. (Illus.). 208p. 1994. reprint ed. pap. 13.95 (*0-19-509431-X*) OUP.

***Scars of Racism.** Christopher D. Handy. 112p. (Orig.). 1996. pap. 12.99 (*1-885921-00-4*) Harvest Time.

Scars of the Soul. Mary A. Woodward. LC 85-70207. 200p. 1985. pap. 8.95 (*0-89804-903-2*) Ariel GA.

S

An Asterisk (*) at the beginning of an entry indicates that the title is appearing in BIP for the first time.

Scars of Venus: A History of Venereology. J. D. Oriel. LC 93-34554. vii, 248p. 1994. 98.00 (*0-387-19844-X*) Spr-Verlag.

*__Scars of Venus: A History of Venereology.__ J. D. Oriel. (Illus.). 248p. 1994. 98.00 (*3-540-19844-X*) Spr-Verlag.

Scars of Vietnam: Personal Accounts by Veterans & Their Families. Harry Spiller. LC 94-33860. (Illus.). 240p. 1994. pap. 19.95 (*0-7864-0010-2*) McFarland & Co.

Scars of War. Paul Tribus. 112p. (Orig.). 1992. pap. 6.99 (*1-56043-493-7*) Destiny Image.

Scars on the Soul. Enid Vien. 80p. (Orig.). 1996. pap. text ed. 10.95 (*0-9648330-1-8*) Dynamism Pubns.

Scars, Pleasure & Sacrifice: Argentina - Colombia Video Creations. Rodger Larson et al. LC 94-66181. (Illus.). 64p. (Orig.). (ENG & SPA.). 1994. pap. write for info. (*1-883592-08-9*) Perm Mission.

Scars Within. large type ed. Hope Colbere. 1991. pap. 15. 99 (*0-7089-6971-2*) Ulverscroft.

Scarsdale: or Life on the Lancashire & Yorkshire Border, 3 vols. in 2, Set. Kay-Shuttleworth. LC 79-8146. reprint ed. 84.50 (*0-404-61956-8*) AMS Pr.

Scary Animals. Jean De Sart. LC 93-20963. (Illus.). 48p. (J). 1994. 14.95 (*0-88106-674-5*); lib. bdg. 15.88 (*0-88106-694-X*) Charlesbridge Pub.

Scary Book. Ed. by Joanna Cole & Stephanie Calmenson. LC 90-26330. (Illus.). 128p. (J). (gr. 2 up). 1991. 12.95 (*0-688-10654-4*, Morrow Junior) Morrow.

Scary Book. Ed. by Joanna Cole et al. LC 90-26330. (Illus.). 128p. (J). (gr. 2 up). 1994. reprint ed. pap. 4.95 (*0-688-04594-4*, Morrow Junior) Morrow.

*__Scary Creatures Sticker Storybook.__ Cathy Beylon. (Illus.). 16p. (Orig.). (J). 1997. pap. text ed. 1.00 (*0-486-29721-7*) Dover.

Scary Day. Doreen Rappaport. (J). (ps-1). 1988. 8.49 (*0-87386-056-X*); pap. 1.95 (*0-87386-052-7*); audio 16.99 (*0-685-25200-0*); audio 9.95 (*0-685-25201-9*) Jan Prods.

Scary Facts to Blow Your Mind. Judith F. Clark. LC 93-12249. (Facts to Blow Your Mind Ser.). (Illus.). 48p. (Orig.). (J). (gr. 1-6). 1993. pap. 4.95 (*0-8431-3580-8*) Price Stern Sloan.

*__Scary Fairies.__ Patricia Ludlow. LC 97-12757. (Illus.). 24p. (J). (gr. k-3). 1997. 16.90 (*0-7613-0258-1*) Millbrook Pr.

*__Scary Fairies.__ Dug Steer. LC 97-12757. (Illus.). (J). 1997. write for info. (*0-7613-0298-0*) Millbrook Pr.

Scary Harry the Tooth Fairy. Trevor Raven. LC 93-94127. (Illus.). 64p. (Orig.). (J). 1995. pap. 4.95 (*1-56002-386-4*, Univ Edtns) Aegina Pr.

Scary Howl of Fame. Sheryl Scarborough & Sharon McCoy. LC 94-49530. (Illus.). 96p. (J). (gr. 5-7). 1995. 14.95 (*0-8069-1312-6*) Sterling.

Scary Howl of Fame. Sheryl Scarborough. (Illus.). 80p. (J). 1996. pap. 4.95 (*0-8069-1313-4*) Sterling.

*__Scary Journey.__ Christine Leeson. LC 96-27750. (Illus.). (J). 1997. 12.95 (*1-888444-10-X*) Little Tiger.

Scary Masks: 6 Punch-Out Designs. Carolyn Bracken. (Illus.). (J). (gr. k-3). 1992. pap. 2.95 (*0-486-27240-0*) Dover.

Scary Mazes. Dave Phillips. LC 93-18312. 1993. 2.95 (*0-486-27608-2*) Dover.

Scary Monster House. (Play - a - Sound Ser.). (Illus.). 24p. (J). 1993. 12.98 (*0-7853-0139-9*) Pubns Intl Ltd.

Scary Monsters & Other Creatures. (Look & Find Ser.). (Illus.). 24p. (J). 1993. 7.98 (*1-56173-522-1*) Pubns Intl Ltd.

Scary Mysteries for Sleep-Overs. Allen B. Ury. LC 95-49290. (Illus.). (J). (gr. 1 up). 1996. 5.95 (*0-8431-8220-2*) Price Stern Sloan.

*__Scary Myths & Legends from around the World.__ Neal Yamamoto. LC 97-11748. (J). 1997. write for info. (*1-56565-778-0*) Lowell Hse.

Scary Night Visitors: A Story for Children with Bedtime Fears. Irene W. Marcus & Paul Marcus. LC 92-56874. (Books to Help Children Ser.). (J). 1993. lib. bdg. 18.60 (*0-8368-0935-1*) Gareth Stevens Inc.

Scary Night Visitors: A Story for Children with Bedtime Fears. Irene W. Marcus & Paul Marcus. LC 90-41919. (Illus.). 32p. (J). (ps-2). 1990. 11.95 (*0-945354-26-6*) Magination Pr.

Scary Origami. Jill Smolinski. LC 95-21112. (Illus.). 64p. (J). 1995. pap. 5.95 (*1-56565-353-X*) Lowell Hse.

Scary Poems for Rotten Kids. Sean O. Huigin. (Illus.). 32p. (J). (ps-8). 1988. pap. 4.95 (*0-88753-177-6*, Pub. by Black Moss Pr CN) Firefly Bks Ltd.

Scary Readers Theatre. Suzanne I. Barchers. (Illus.). xiii, 157p. 1994. pap. text ed. 22.00 (*1-56308-292-6*) Teacher Ideas Pr.

Scary, Scary Halloween. Eve Bunting. LC 86-2642. (Illus.). 32p. (J). (ps-3). 1986. 15.00 (*0-89919-414-1*, Clarion Bks) HM.

Scary, Scary Halloween. Eve Bunting. LC 86-2642. (Illus.). 32p. (J). (ps-3). 1988. pap. 5.95 (*0-89919-799-X*, Clarion Bks) HM.

Scary Science: The Truth Behind Vampires, Witches, UFOs Ghosts, & More. Sylvia Funston. (Illus.). 64p. (Orig.). (YA). (gr. 3 up). 1996. 19.95 (*1-895688-52-3*, Pub. by Owl Bks CN); pap. 9.95 (*1-895688-53-1*, Pub. by Owl Bks CN) Firefly Bks Ltd.

Scary Search a Word Puzzles. Elvira Gamiello. (Illus.). (Orig.). (J). (gr. 4-6). 1988. pap. 1.95 (*0-942025-39-3*) Kidsbks.

*__Scary Shark Stories.__ Scott Ingram. LC 97-4977. (J). 1997. pap. 5.95 (*1-56565-614-8*) Contemp Bks.

Scary Sights & Funny Frights Rubber Stamp Set: A Rubber Stamp Storybook. Doris Tomaselli. (Rubber Stamp Ser.). (Illus.). 24p. (J). (ps-3). 1996. boxed, pap. 9.99 (*1-57584-040-5*) Joshua Morris.

Scary Spiders. Steve Parker. LC 93-27876. (Creepy Creatures Ser.). (Illus.). (J). 1993. lib. bdg. 24.26 (*0-8114-2345-X*) Raintree Steck-V.

Scary, Spooky Hunt Activity Book. 48p. (Orig.). (YA). 1994. pap. 2.99 (*0-8125-9436-3*) Tor Bks.

*__Scary Stories.__ Gordon Armstrong. pap. 10.95 (*0-921368-63-1*, Pub. by Blizzard Pub CN) Genl Dist Srvs.

Scary Stories. Schwartz. (J). 1990. mass mkt. 3.50 (*0-06-107016-5*, Harp PBks) HarpC.

Scary Stories, No. 1. Neal Shusterman. (YA). 1995. 7.99 (*0-312-55197-5*) Forge NYC.

*__Scary Stories Vols. 1-3.__ Querida L. Pearce. (Illus.). 128p. (J). (gr. 2-8). Date not set. boxed, pap. 4.95 (*0-8431-3956-0*) Price Stern Sloan.

Scary Stories, Boxed set. Alvin Schwartz. (Trophy Bk.). (Illus.). (J). (gr. 4-7). 1992. pap. 11.85 (*0-06-440465-X*, Trophy) HarpC Child Bks.

Scary Stories for Sleep-Overs. Robert Welch. LC 91-18587. (Scary Stories Ser.). (Illus.). 128p. (Orig.). (J). (gr. 3-6). 1991. pap. 4.95 (*0-8431-2914-X*) Price Stern Sloan.

*__Scary Stories for Sleep-Overs Tomb of Eternity.__ Allen B. Ury. (J). Date not set. pap. 5.95 (*1-56565-604-0*) Contemp Bks.

Scary Stories for Stormy Nights. R. C. Welch. LC 94-39591. 128p. (J). (gr. 2 up). 1995. pap. 5.95 (*1-56565-262-2*) Lowell Hse.

*__Scary Stories for Stormy Nights, No. 5.__ Q. L. Pearce. LC 97-15693. (Illus.). (J). 1997. write for info. (*1-56565-718-7*) Lowell Hse.

Scary Stories for When You're Home Alone. Allen B. Ury. LC 96-33902. (Illus.). 96p. (J). (gr. 3-7). 1996. pap. 5.95 (*1-56565-382-3*) Lowell Hse Juvenile.

Scary Stories from 1313 Wicked Way. Craig Strickland. LC 96-2984. (Illus.). 128p. (J). (gr. 3-7). 1996. pap. 5.95 (*1-56565-484-6*) Lowell Hse Juvenile.

*__Scary Stories of Sleep-Overs, No. VIII.__ LC 97-17225. (J). 1997. write for info. (*1-56565-714-4*) Lowell Hse.

Scary Stories Three: More Tales to Chill Your Bones. Illus. by Stephen Gammell. LC 90-47474. (Trophy Bk.). 128p. (J). (gr. 4 up). 1991. pap. 3.95 (*0-06-440418-8*, Trophy) HarpC Child Bks.

Scary Stories Three: More Tales to Chill Your Bones. Alvin Schwartz. LC 90-47474. (Illus.). 128p. (J). (gr. 4 up). 1991. 14.95 (*0-06-021794-4*); lib. bdg. 14.89 (*0-06-021795-2*) HarpC Child Bks.

Scary Stories to Drive You Batty. Devra Newberger. LC 94-21667. (Illus.). 32p. (J). (gr. 2-6). 1994. pap. text ed. 2.95 (*0-8167-3534-4*) Troll Communs.

Scary Stories to Tell in the Dark. Alvin Schwartz. (Trophy Bk.). (Illus.). 128p. (J). (gr. 4 up). 1986. pap. 3.95 (*0-06-440170-7*, Trophy) HarpC Child Bks.

Scary Stories to Tell in the Dark: Collected from American folklore. Alvin Schwartz. LC 80-8728. (Illus.). 128p. (J). (gr. 5 up). 1981. 14.95 (*0-397-31926-6*, Lipp Jr Bks); lib. bdg. 14.89 (*0-397-31927-4*, Lipp Jr Bks) HarpC Child Bks.

Scary Story Reader. Richard Young & Judy D. Young. 174p. 1994. 19.00 (*0-87483-271-3*) August Hse.

Scary Story Reader. Richard Young & Judy D. Young. 174p. 1994. pap. 11.95 (*0-87483-382-5*) August Hse.

Scary Story Starters. Diane Cuneo. 64p. (J). 1995. pap. 4.95 (*1-56565-313-0*) Lowell Hse.

Scary Storytime. (Storytime Ser.: No. 887-6). (Illus.). (J). (ps-2). 1990. 3.50 (*0-7214-1340-4*, Ladybrd) Penguin.

Scary Tales. Ed. by Bobbie Wanamaker. (Reading Resources Ser.). (J). (gr. 2-5). 1995. pap. text ed. 299.00 (*0-941217-00-0*) Reading Resources Inc.

*__Scary Things.__ 1997. 3.99 (*0-679-88584-6*) Random Bks Yng Read.

*__Scary Things.__ (Halloween Coloring & Activity Bks.). (Illus.). 32p. (J). (gr. k-2). 1996. pap. write for info. (*1-56144-881-8*, Honey Bear Bks) Modern Pub NYC.

Scat! Wil Perkins. (Open Mouth Poetry Ser.). 100p. (Orig.). 1997. pap. 9.95 (*1-884773-04-4*) Heat Press.

Scat! Vocal Improvisational Techniques. Bob Stoloff. 120p. 1996. pap. 25.00 (*0-9628467-5-9*) Gerard Sarzin Pub.

Scathatch & Maeve's Daughter. Mary A. Walker. LC 90-141. 128p. (J). (gr. 6-9). 1990. lib. bdg. 13.95 (*0-689-31638-0*, Atheneum Bks Young) S&S Childrens.

Scatology in Modern Drama. Sidney Shrager. 128p. 1981. 24.50 (*0-8290-0261-8*) Irvington.

Scatology in Modern Drama. Sidney Shrager. 128p. 1986. reprint ed. pap. text ed. 9.95 (*0-8290-2015-2*) Irvington.

Scatter Diagrams: Leader Manual & Instructional Guide. rev. ed. Donald L. Dewar. (Illus.). 58p. 1993. pap. 14.00 (*0-937670-22-7*) QCI Intl.

*__Scatter Matrix.__ Abigail Child. pap. 9.95 (*0-937804-63-0*) Segue NYC.

Scatter Me: Poems - Nineteen Eighty to Nineteen Eighty-Nine. D. R. Osborne. Ed. by P. E. Duthie. 95p. (Orig.). 1990. pap. 8.00 (*0-9626451-0-9*) Laughing Coyote.

Scatter Plots: Plain & Simple. Joiner Assocs., Inc. Staff. Ed. by Sue Reynard. (Illus.). 140p. (Orig.). 1995. student ed. pap. 19.95 (*1-884731-08-2*) Joiner Assoc.

Scatterbrain Sam. Lucien-Guy. (Child's World Library). (Illus.). 32p. (J). (gr. 3-5). 1991. lib. bdg. 18.50 (*0-89565-754-6*) Childs World.

Scattered: Like Chaff in the Wind. Claudia Nichol et al. (Illus.). 340p. (Orig.). 1989. pap. 13.95 (*0-9623121-0-X*) CompuWords.

Scattered: Poems. Michel F. Sarda. LC 92-73300. 128p. 1992. pap. 9.95 (*0-927015-08-0*) Bridgewood Pr.

Scattered among the Nations: Documents Affecting Jewish History 49 to 1975. Ed. by Alexis P. Rubin. LC 94-17497. 360p. 1995. 30.00 (*1-56821-237-2*) Aronson.

Scattered Blossoms. Barbara Michaels. 1992. 20.00 (*0-685-53583-5*) S&S Trade.

Scattered Brains. Darrell Gray. LC 74-32028. (Illus.). 78p. 1975. pap. 5.00 (*0-915124-04-1*, Toothpaste) Coffee Hse.

Scattered Debris: Bikhare Moti. Subhadra K. Chauhan. (C). 1994. text ed. 14.00 (*81-7001-102-7*, Pub. by Chanakya II) S Asia.

Scattered Hegemonies: Postmodernity & Transnational Feminist Practices. Ed. by Inderpal Grewal & Caren Kaplan. LC 93-14232. 1994. text ed. 49.95 (*0-8166-2137-3*); pap. text ed. 19.95 (*0-8166-2138-1*) U of Minn Pr.

Scattered Light. Doraine Poretz. 32p. (Orig.). 1987. pap. 3.95 (*0-941017-09-5*) Bombshelter Pr.

Scattered People: An American Family Moves West. Gerald W. McFarland. LC 91-16751. (Illus.). 304p. (C). 1991. reprint ed. pap. 16.95 (*0-87023-765-9*) U of Mass Pr.

Scattered Poems. Jack Kerouac. (Pocket Poets Ser.: No. 28). 1971. pap. 6.95 (*0-87286-064-7*) City Lights.

Scattered Radiation in the Ozone Absorbtion Bands at Selected Levels of a Terrestrial, Rayleigh Atmospheres. Jitendra V. Dave & P. M. Furukawa. (Meteorological Monograph: Vol. 7, No. 29). (Illus.). 353p. 1966. 27.00 (*0-933876-21-1*); pap. 25.00 (*0-933876-22-X*) Am Meteorological.

Scattered Seed. Maisie Mosco. 608p. 1991. mass mkt. 4.95 (*0-06-100185-6*, Harp PBks) HarpC.

Scattered to All the Winds: 1685-1720, Migrations of the Dauphine French Hugeunots into Italy, Switzerland, & Germany. Willis L. Schalliol. LC 83-70252. Orig. Title: Zerstreut in alle Winde. (Illus.). 284p. (Orig.). 1997. reprint ed. pap. 21.10 (*0-9605732-1-6*) Belle Pubns.

Scattered Tracks on the Lawrence Trail: Twelve Essays on T. E. Lawrence. J. N. Lockman. LC 96-85429. (Illus.). xix, 208p. 1996. 24.00 (*0-9648897-1-4*) Falcon Books.

Scattered Voice: Christians at Odds in the Public Square. James W. Skillen. 252p. 1993. reprint ed. spiral bd. 18. 95 (*1-57383-015-1*) Regent College.

Scattergun-Apache Rifles. Kit Dalton. (Buckskin Double Edition Ser.). 384p. 1995. mass mkt., pap. text ed. 4.99 (*0-8439-3791-2*) Dorchester Pub Co.

Scattering - Structural Foams see Encyclopedia of Polymer Science & Engineering

Scattering & Attenuation of Seismic Waves, Pt. I. Ru-Shan Wu & Keiiti Aki. 454p. 1988. 34.50 (*0-8176-2254-3*) Birkhauser.

Scattering & Attenuation of Seismic Waves, Pt. II. Ed. by Ru-Shan Wu & Keiiti Aki. 198p. 1989. 27.50 (*0-8176-2341-8*) Birkhauser.

Scattering & Attenuation of Seismic Waves, Pt. III. Ed. by Ru-Shan Wu & Keiiti Aki. 446p. 1989. 34.50 (*0-8176-2342-6*) Birkhauser.

Scattering & Diffraction in Physical Optics. M. Nieto-Vesperinas. LC 91-8261. (Series In Pure & Applied Optics). 416p. 1991. text ed. 110.00 (*0-471-61529-3*) Wiley.

Scattering & Diffraction of Waves. LC 59-11511. (Harvard Monographs in Applied Science: No. 7). (Illus.). 236p. reprint ed. pap. 67.30 (*0-317-09160-3*, 2002784) Bks Demand.

Scattering & Localization of Classical Waves in Random Media. Ping Sheng. (Series on Directions in Condensed Matter Physics: Vol. 8). 648p. 1990. text ed. 76.00 (*9971-5-0539-8*); pap. text ed. 47.00 (*9971-5-0540-1*) World Scientific Pub.

*__Scattering & Surface Roughness.__ Ed. by Zu-Han Gu & Alexei A. Maradudin. 29p. 1997. pap. 69.00 (*0-8194-2563-X*) SPIE.

Scattering by a Groove in an Impedance Plane. Sunil Bindiganavale & John L. Volakis. (University of Michigan Reports: No. 030601-2-T). 21p. reprint ed. pap. 25.00 (*0-7837-6784-6*, 2046616) Bks Demand.

Scattering by a Planar Resistive Strip Array. rev. ed. John L. Volakis & Y. C. Lin. (University of Michigan Reports: No. 390968-1-T). 43p. reprint ed. pap. 25.00 (*0-7837-4623-7*, 2044346) Bks Demand.

Scattering by Obstacles. A. G. Ramm. 1986. lib. bdg. 205. 00 (*90-277-2103-3*) Kluwer Ac.

Scattering, Deformation & Fracture in Polymers. George D. Wignall. (MRS Symposium Proceedings Ser.: Vol. 79). 1987. text ed. 17.50 (*0-931837-44-8*) Materials Res.

Scattering from Black Holes. J. A. Futterman et al. (Cambridge Monographs on Mathematical Physics). (Illus.). 230p. 1988. 64.95 (*0-521-32986-8*) Cambridge U Pr.

Scattering in Quantum Field Theories: Axiomatic & Constructive Approaches. Daniel Iagolnitzer. (Physics Ser.). (Illus.). 256p. 1992. text ed. 59.50 (*0-691-08589-7*) Princeton U Pr.

Scattering Methods in Polymer Science. 2nd ed. G. Richards. 350p. 1996. text ed. 105.00 (*0-13-791567-5*) P-H.

Scattering of Dust: Some Favorite Readings. Charles D. Floro. 80p. (Orig.). 1991. pap. 10.00 (*1-879765-01-2*) Earth & Sky.

Scattering of Electromagnetic Waves from Rough Surfaces. Andre Spizzichino. LC 63-10108. (International Series of Monographs on Electronics & Instrumentation: Vol. 4). 1963. 224.00 (*0-08-010007-4*, Pub. by Pergamon Repr UK) Franklin.

Scattering of Electromagnetic Waves from Rough Surfaces. Petr Beckmann & Andre Spizzichino. LC 87-70042. (Artech House Radar Library). (Illus.). 511p. reprint ed. pap. 145.70 (*0-8357-4231-8*, 2037018) Bks Demand.

Scattering of Jades: Stories, Poems, & Prayers of the Aztecs. T. J. Knab & Thelma D. Sullivan. 1994. 23.00 (*0-671-86414-9*, Touchstone Bks); pap. 12.00 (*0-671-86413-0*, Touchstone Bks) S&S Trade.

Scattering of Salts. James Merrill. 1995. 20.00 (*0-679-44158-1*) Knopf.

Scattering of Salts: Poems. James Merrill. 1996. pap. 14.00 (*0-679-76590-5*) Knopf.

Scattering of Thermal Energy Atoms from Disordered Surfaces. B. Poelsema & G. Comsa. (Tracts in Modern Physics Ser.: Vol. 115). (Illus.). 170p. 1989. 80.95 (*0-387-50358-7*) Spr-Verlag.

Scattering of Transient Diffusive Electromagnetic Fields. E. C. Slob. 188p. (Orig.). 1994. pap. 52.50 (*90-6275-968-8*, Pub. by Delft U Pr NE) Coronet Bks.

Scattering Operator, Eisenstein Series, Inner Product Formula & "Maass-Selberg" Relations for Kleinian Groups. N. Mandouvalos. LC 89-180. (Memoirs Ser.: Vol. 78/400). 87p. 1989. pap. 16.00 (*0-8218-2463-5*, MEMO/78/400) Am Math.

Scattering Parameters of Microwave Networks with Coupled Transmission Lines. A. Djordjevic et al. (Artech House Microwave Software Library). 158p. 1990. 300.00 incl. disk (*0-89006-404-0*) Artech Hse.

Scattering Seeds. Corinne H. Webb. 1994. 12.95 (*0-533-10840-3*) Vantage.

*__Scattering Sunshine.__ 145p. (Orig.). (J). (gr. 1-5). 1996. pap. 6.95 (*0-87813-565-0*) Christian Light.

Scattering Theory. 1984. 101.50 (*0-8176-1519-9*) Spr-Verlag.

Scattering Theory. A. G. Sitenko. Ed. by M. K. Gaillard et al. Tr. by O. D. Kocherga from RUS. (Series in Nuclear & Particle Physics). (Illus.). 302p. 1991. 64.95 (*0-387-51953-X*) Spr-Verlag.

Scattering Theory. rev. ed. Ed. by Peter D. Lax & Ralph S. Phillips. (Pure & Applied Mathematics Ser.: Vol. 26). 309p. 1990. text ed. 81.00 (*0-12-440051-5*) Acad Pr.

Scattering Theory see Methods of Modern Mathematical Physics

Scattering Theory by the Enss Method, Vol. 1. P. Perry. (Mathematical Reports: Vol. 1, No. 1). xiv, 348p. 1983. text ed. 274.00 (*3-7186-0093-5*) Gordon & Breach.

Scattering Theory for Diffraction Gratings. C. H. Wilcox. (Applied Mathematical Sciences Ser.: Vol. 46). (Illus.). 170p. 1983. 52.95 (*0-387-90924-9*) Spr-Verlag.

Scattering Theory for Hyperbolic Operators. V. Petkov. (Studies in Mathematics & Its Applications: No. 21). 374p. 1989. 149.50 (*0-444-88056-9*, North Holland) Elsevier.

Scattering Theory for Many-Body Quantum Mechanical Systems. I. M. Sigal. (Lecture Notes in Mathematics Ser.: Vol. 1011). 132p. 1983. 29.95 (*0-387-12672-4*) Spr-Verlag.

Scattering Theory in Mathematical Physics: Proceedings of the NATO Advanced Study Institute, Denver, Colorado, June, 1973. NATO Advanced Study Institute Staff. Ed. by J. A. LaVita & J. P. Marchand. LC 73-91205. 1974. lib. bdg. 123.50 (*90-277-0414-7*) Kluwer Ac.

*__Scattering Theory of Classical & Quantum N-Particle Systems, Vol. XII.__ Jan Derezinski & Christian Gerard. LC 96-46757. (Texts & Monographs in Physics). (Illus.). 443p. 1997. 89.95 (*3-540-62066-4*) Spr-Verlag.

Scattering Theory of Waves & Particles. 2nd ed. R. G. Newton. (Texts & Monographs in Physics). 800p. 1982. 117.95 (*0-387-10950-1*) Spr-Verlag.

Scattering Time: Turkana Responses to Colonial Rule. John Lamphear. 336p. 1992. 75.00 (*0-19-820226-1*) OUP.

Scatterings (Based upon a True Story) A. D. Printup, II. LC 85-71343. 192p. 1986. pap. 6.95 (*0-685-10438-9*, TS-027) DeWitt & Sheppard.

*__Scavenger.__ Scott Peterson. (Dragon Flyz Ser.). (Illus.). 24p. (J). (ps). 1997. 2.50 (*0-694-01020-0*, Festival) HarpC Child Bks.

*__Scavenger.__ Dennison Smith. 1997. pap. text ed. 14.99 (*1-895837-15-4*) Login Pubs Consort.

Scavenger Hunt. Christopher Pike. (Orig.). (J). (gr. 9 up). 1990. pap. 3.99 (*0-671-73686-8*, Archway) PB.

Scavenger in Indian Society Marginality, Identity & Politicization of the Community: Marginality, Identity & Politicization of the Community. Rama Sharma. 268p. 1995. pap. 175.00 (*81-85880-70-0*, Pub. by Print Hse II) St Mut.

Scavenger Reef. Laurence Shames. LC 93-30625. 1994. 21. 00 (*0-671-86493-9*) S&S Trade.

Scavenger Reef. Laurence Shames. 336p. 1995. mass mkt. 4.99 (*0-440-21797-0*) Dell.

Scavengers. Yvonne Montgomery. 256p. 1990. pap. 3.50 (*0-380-71002-1*) Avon.

*__Scavengers at War.__ large type ed. Charles Leader. (Linford Mystery Library). 352p. 1997. pap. 16.99 (*0-7089-5068-X*) Ulverscroft.

Scavengers, Recyclers, & Solutions for Solid Waste Management in Indonesia. Daniel T. Sicular. LC 92-1504. (Center for Southeast Asia Studies: No. 32). 201p. (Orig.). (C). 1992. pap. text ed. 16.50 (*0-944613-13-6*) UC Berkeley Ctrs SE Asia.

Scavenger's Son. T. Sivasankara Pillai. (Asian Writers Ser.). 124p. 1994. pap. 9.95 (*0-435-95082-7*, 95082) Heinemann.

Scavenging the Country for a Heartbeat. Neil Shepard. (First Poetry Ser.). 80p. 1993. pap. 9.95 (*0-922811-16-4*) Mid-List.

Scavnicky: Portrait of an Anthracite Family Nelson Morris, Photographer. Judith H. O'Toole et al. (Illus.). 47p. (Orig.). (C). 1992. pap. 5.00 (*0-942945-02-6*) Sordoni Gal.

*__Scavullo: Photographs, 50 Years.__ Francesco Scavullo & Enid Nemy. LC 97-9537. 1997. write for info. (*0-8109-4180-5*) Abrams.

SCCS Reference Card. 2nd ed. Anatole Olczak. 8p. 1991. pap. 2.95 (*0-935739-04-1*) ASP.

SCD - The Sports Card Explosion. Ed. by Mark K. Larson. LC 93-77541. (Illus.). 304p. (Orig.). 1993. pap. 16.95 (*0-87341-254-0*, BS93) Krause Pubns.

SCD Baseball Autograph Handbook: A Comprehensive Guide to Authentication & Valuation of Hall of Fame Autographs. 2nd ed. Mark Baker. LC 89-83583. (Illus.). 352p. 1991. pap. 19.95 (*0-87341-169-2*, BA02) Krause Pubns.

S

SCD Minor League Baseball Card Price Guide. Mark K. Larson. LC 92-74798. (Illus.). 480p. (Orig.). 1993. pap. 14.95 (*0-87341-239-7*, SG01) Krause Pubns.
Sceince of Bharata Natyam. S. Vaidyanathan. (Illus.). 80p. 1984. 19.95 (*0-318-36313-5*) Asia Bk Corp.
Scelomo Solomon Rhapsodie Hebraique: Violoncelle & Piano. E. Bloch. 36p. 1986. pap. 18.95 (*0-7935-5213-3*, 50274500) H Leonard.
Scenario. Jean Anouilh. 192p. (FRE.). 1984. pap. 10.95 (*0-7859-2001-3*, 2070376109) Fr & Eur.
Scenario see Pieces Secretes
Scenario-Based Design: Envisioning Work & Technology in System Development. John M. Carroll. LC 94-23772. 408p. 1995. text ed. 44.95 (*0-471-07659-7*) Wiley.
***Scenario Development & Costing in Health Care: Methodological Accomplishments & Practical Guidelines.** STG Foundation for Future Health Scenarios Staff. 96p. (Orig.). 1997. pap. 25.00 (*90-6224-877-2*, Pub. by Uitgeverij Arkel NE) LPC InBook.
Scenario-Driven Planning: Learning to Manage Strategic Uncertainty. Nicholas C. Georgantzas & William Acar. LC 94-8540. 432p. 1995. text ed. 65.00 (*0-89930-825-2*, Quorum Bks) Greenwood.
Scenario Educational Software: Design & Development of Discovery Learning. Mark Keegan. LC 94-30857. 1995. 44.95 (*0-87778-282-2*) Educ Tech Pubns.
***Scenario of Mythos: From Unified Field Theory to Unitary Mythos.** James A. Green. (Literature Ser.: Vol. 4). (Illus.). 150p. (Orig.). 1997. 68.88 (*1-890121-28-2*) Grnwd Resch.
***Scenario of Mythos: From Unified Field Theory to Unitary Mythos.** large type ed. James A. Green. (Literature Ser.: Vol. 4). (Illus.). 150p. (Orig.). 1997. 55.88 (*1-890121-29-0*) Grnwd Resch.
Scenario of the Savior as Sovereign: The Book of Revelation As a Christian World View & Philosophy of History. Arthur Northup. 345p. 1991. pap. write for info. (*1-881909-18-2*) Advent Christ Gen Conf.
Scenario Studies for the Rural Environment: Selected & Edited Proceedings of the Symposium "Scenario Studies for the Rural Environment," Wageningen, the Netherlands, 12-15 September 1994. Ed. by Job F. Schoute et al. (Environment & Policy Ser.: Vol. 5). 776p. (C). 1995. lib. bdg. 285.00 (*0-7923-3748-4*) Kluwer Ac.
Scenario Techniques. Ute Von Reibnitz. 1989. pap. text ed. 12.95 (*0-07-065931-1*) McGraw.
Scenario 2000: A Personal Forecast of the Prospects for World Evangelization. Tom Houston. 47p. 1992. pap. 2.50 (*0-912552-78-6*) MARC.
Scenarios. Ed. by Richard Kostelanetz. LC 80-68155. (Illus.). 704p. (C). 1981. pap. 20.00 (*0-915066-49-1*) Assembling Pr.
Scenarios: The Art of Strategic Conversation. Kees Van Der Heijden. LC 96-3246. 1996. text ed. 29.95 (*0-471-96639-8*) Wiley.
Scenarios for a Mixed Landscape. John Allman. LC 86-2421. 80p. (Orig.). 1986. pap. 7.95 (*0-8112-0989-X*, NDP619) New Directions.
Scenarios for Teaching Writing: Contexts for Discussion & Reflective Practice. Chris M. Anson et al. (Illus.). 160p. (Orig.). 1993. pap. 16.95 (*0-8141-4255-9*) NCTE.
Scenarios in Self-Defense. Mary Brandl & Anita Bendickson. (Illus.). 57p. (Orig.). (C). 1990. pap. 7.00 (*1-878479-00-8*) BPS Commns.
Scenarios of Change: Advocacy & the Diffusion of Job Redesign in Organizations. Lyle Yorks & David A. Whitsett. LC 89-16079. 240p. 1989. text ed. 59.95 (*0-275-93209-5*, C3209, Praeger Pubs) Greenwood.
Scenarios of Modernist Disintegration: Tryggve Andersen's Prose Fiction. Timothy Schiff. LC 85-12493. (Contributions to the Study of World Literature Ser.: No. 11). xiii, 147p. 1985. text ed. 45.00 (*0-313-24818-4*, SFM/, Greenwood Pr) Greenwood.
Scenarios of Power: Myth & Ceremony in Russian Monarchy. Richard S. Wortman. LC 94-21537. (Studies of the Harriman Institute, Columbia University). 432p. 1994. 52.50 (*0-691-03484-2*) Princeton U Pr.
Scenarios of State Government in the Year 2010: Thinking about the Future. Thomas W. Bonnett & Robert L. Olson. LC 92-41392. 1992. 10.00 (*0-934842-72-8*) CSPA.
Scenarios of the Commedia Dell'Arte: A Theatrical Repertory of Fables. Ed. & Frwd. by Henry F. Salerno. LC 89-12943. 413p. 1989. reprint ed. pap. 22.50 (*0-87910-133-4*) Limelight Edns.
Scenarios of the Commedia Dell'Arte: Flaminio Scala's "Il Teatro Delle Favole Rappresentative" Flaminio Scala. Tr. by Henry F. Salerno from ITA. LC 67-10693. 413p. 1967. 24.95 (*0-910278-82-2*) Boulevard.
Scenarios of the Imaginary: Theorizing the French Englightenment. Josue V. Harari. LC 86-24247. 240p. (C). 1987. 37.50 (*0-8014-1842-9*) Cornell U Pr.
Scenas Infantis: Memories of Childhood: Five Pieces for the Piano. O. Pinto. 16p. 1986. pap. 7.95 (*0-7935-0585-2*, 50327100) H Leonard.
Scene. Clarence L. Cooper, Jr. LC 96-8036. (Old School Bks.). 1996. pap. 11.00 (*0-393-31463-4*, Norton Paperbks) Norton.
Scene. Edward G. Craig. LC 65-20498. (Illus.). 1972. reprint ed. 20.95 (*0-405-08381-5*, Pub. by Blom Pubns UK) Ayer.
Scene: And Other Stories. Jim Reagan. 176p. 1994. pap. 9.95 (*1-56474-103-6*) Fithian Pr.
Scene - Four. Ed. by Stanley Nelson. LC 77-70415. (Scene Award Ser.). (Illus.). 272p. 1977. pap. 8.00 (*0-912292-42-3*) Smith.
Scene - One. Ed. by Stanley Nelson. LC 72-89382. (Scene Award Ser.). 212p. 1972. pap. 8.00 (*0-912292-27-X*) Smith.
Scene - Three. Ed. by Stanley Nelson. LC 72-89382. (Scene Award Ser.). 196p. 1975. pap. 8.00 (*0-912292-38-5*) Smith.
Scene - Two. Ed. by Stanley Nelson. LC 70-94633. (Scene Award Ser.). 192p. 1974. pap. 8.00 (*0-912292-34-2*) Smith.
Scene & Structure. Jack H. Bickham. (Elements of Fiction Writing Ser.). 176p. 1993. 14.99 (*0-89879-551-6*, Wrtrs Digest Bks) F & W Pubns Inc.
Scene Change: A Theatre Diary Prague, Moscow, Leningrad Spring 1991. Joanna Rotte. LC 94-67. (Illus.). 176p. (Orig.). 1994. 25.00 (*0-87910-175-X*); pap. 12.95 (*0-87910-171-7*) Limelight Edns.
***Scene Design.** Ed. by Bellman. (C). 1994. text ed. write for info. (*0-06-501335-2*) Addison-Wesley.
Scene Design: A Guide to the Stage. Henning Nelms. LC 74-25249. (Illus.). 96p. 1975. reprint ed. pap. 5.95 (*0-486-23153-4*) Dover.
Scene Design & Stage Lighting. 6th ed. W. Oren Parker & R. Craig Wolf. (Illus.). 624p. (C). 1990. text ed. 41.25 (*0-03-028777-4*) HB Coll Pubs.
Scene Design & Stage Lighting. 7th ed. W. Oren Parker & R. Craig Wolf. 690p. (C). 1996. text ed. 46.75 (*0-15-501620-2*) HB Coll Pubs.
Scene Design for Stage & Screen. Ed. by Orville K. Larson. LC 76-10460. (Illus.). 334p. 1976. reprint ed. text ed. 35.00 (*0-8371-8320-0*, LASS, Greenwood Pr) Greenwood.
Scene Design in the American Theatre: Nineteen-Fifteen to Nineteen Sixty. Orville K. Larson. LC 88-27628. (Illus.). 405p. (C). 1989. 55.00 (*1-55728-064-9*); pap. 40.00 (*1-55728-065-7*) U of Ark Pr.
Scene Design in the Theatre. Dennis J. Sporre & Robert C. Burroughs. 368p. 1989. text ed. 72.00 (*0-13-791682-5*) P-H.
Scene from the Movie Giant. Tino Villanueva. LC 93-26423. 56p. (Orig.). 1993. pap. 9.95 (*1-880684-12-8*) Curbstone.
Scene of Linguistic Action & Its Perspectivization by SPEAK, TALK, SAY & TELL. Rene Dirven et al. (Pragmatics & Beyond Ser.: Vol. III, No. 6). vi, 186p. (Orig.). 1983. pap. 53.00 (*90-272-2528-1*) Benjamins North Am.
Scene of the Crime. Franklin W. Dixon. (Hardy Boys Casefiles Ser.: No. 24). (YA). (gr. 7 up). 1989. pap. 2.95 (*0-671-69377-8*, Archway) PB.
Scene of the Crime. Marvin Miller. (Skeleton Returns Ser.: No. 2). 1996. pap. text ed. 3.50 (*0-590-56872-8*) Scholastic Inc.
***Scene of the Crime.** Jane R. Ransom. 1997. pap. 11.00 (*0-614-29456-8*) Story Line.
***Scene of the Crime.** Ed. by Ralph Rugoff. (Illus.). 176p. 1997. pap. 25.00 (*0-262-68099-8*) MIT Pr.
Scene of the Crime. Doug Wilhelm. (Choose Your Own Adventure Ser.: No. 137). 128p. (J). (gr. 4-7). 1993. pap. 3.25 (*0-553-56004-2*) Bantam.
Scene of the Crime: A Writer's Guide to Crime-Scene Investigations. Anne Wingate. (Howdunit Writing Ser.). 240p. 1992. pap. 15.99 (*0-89879-518-4*, Wrtrs Digest Bks) F & W Pubns Inc.
***Scene of the Crime: Poems.** Jane R. Ransom. LC 97-17496. 1997. write for info. (*1-885266-56-1*) Story Line.
Scene Painting for the Theatre. Crabtree. 1997. pap. write for info. (*0-240-80187-3*, Focal) Buttrwrth-Heinemann.
Scene Safety Video (Generic) Video Brady. 1993. pap. 63.00 (*0-89303-842-3*) P-H.
Scene Technology. 3rd ed. Richard L. Arnold. LC 93-16748. 1993. text ed. 55.00 (*0-13-501073-X*) P-H.
Scene under the Suntree. Meng Wang. (CHI.). pap. 9.95 (*7-5004-1706-3*, Pub. by China Intl Bk CH) Distribks Inc.
Scenebook for Actors: Great Monologs & Dialogs from Contemporary & Classical Theatre. Norman A. Bert. Ed. by Arthur L. Zapel. LC 90-52983. 256p. (Orig.). 1990. pap. text ed. 14.95 (*0-916260-65-8*, B177) Meriwether Pub.
Scenery in Shakespeare's Plays & Other Studies. David W. Rannie. LC 70-153346. reprint ed. 45.00 (*0-404-05225-8*) AMS Pr.
Scenery Manual: Terrain & Landscape Modeling the Woodland Scenics Way. Woodland Scenics Staff. LC 93-61065. (Illus.). 158p. 1995. reprint ed. pap. 9.95 (*1-887436-00-6*) Woodland Scenics.
Scenery of Great Britain & Ireland in Aquatint & Lithography, 1770-1860: A Bibliographical Catalogue. J. R. Abbey. (Illus.). 488p. 1991. reprint ed. 175.00 (*1-55660-130-1*) A Wofsy Fine Arts.
Scenery of Scotland: The Structure Beneath. W. J. Baird. (Illus.). 64p. 1995. pap. 6.95 (*0-948636-24-6*, 6246, Pub. by Natl Mus Scotland UK) A Schwartz & Co.
Scenery, Set & Staging in the Italian Renaissance: Studies in the Practice of Theatre. Ed. by Christopher Cairns. LC 96-3909. (Illus.). 340p. 1996. text ed. 99.95 (*0-7734-8814-6*) E Mellen.
Scenery Tips & Techniques from Model Railroader Magazine. Model Railroader Magazine Staff. Ed. by Michael Emmerich. (Illus.). 116p. (Orig.). 1989. per. 14.95 (*0-89024-095-7*, 12084) Kalmbach.
Scenes. John Irwin. LC 77-528. (City & Society Ser.: Vol. 1). 236p. reprint ed. pap. 67.30 (*0-317-09003-8*, 2021914) Bks Demand.
***Scenes along the Line of the San Jose & Los Gatos Injerurban Railroad.** Illus. by Judith Henderson. 101p. 1994. pap. 18.95 (*0-914139-11-8*) Hist Mus San Jose.
Scenes along the Rails Vol. I: The Anthracite Region of Pennsylvania. John W. Hudson, 2nd & Suzanne C. Hudson. (Illus.). iv, 108p. 1996. 25.00 (*0-9651364-1-8*) Depot Sq.
Scenes & Actions: Unpublished Manuscripts. Christopher Caudwell et al. (Illus.). 224p. 1987. pap. 19.95 (*0-7102-0985-1*, 09851, RKP) Routledge.
Scenes & Adventures in the Army: or Romance of Military Life. Philip St. George Cooke. LC 72-9436. (Far Western Frontier Ser.). 436p. 1973. reprint ed. 29.95 (*0-405-04966-8*) Ayer.
Scenes & Characters of the Middle Ages. Edward L. Cutts. 1977. lib. bdg. 59.95 (*0-8490-2569-9*) Gordon Pr.
Scenes & Legends of the North of Scotland: Traditional History of Cromarty. 2nd rev. ed. Hugh G. Miller. Ed. by Richard M. Dorson. (International Folklore Ser.). 1977. reprint ed. lib. bdg. 41.95 (*0-405-10110-4*) Ayer.
Scenes & Monologs from the Best New Plays: An Anthology of New Dramatic Writing from Professionally Produced American Plays. Roger Ellis. Ed. by Theodore O. Zapel. LC 92-32989. 256p. (Orig.). 1992. pap. text ed. 14.95 (*0-916260-93-3*, B140) Meriwether Pub.
Scenes & Monologues for Teenaged Actors, Vol. 1. Ed. by C. Michael Perry. (Scene Bks.). 60p. (YA). (gr. 7-12). 1994. pap. 8.95 (*1-57514-001-2*, 5006) Encore Perform Pub.
Scenes & Monologues for Teenaged Actors, Vol. 2. Ed. by C. Michael Perry. (Scene Bks.). 67p. (YA). (gr. 7-12). 1994. pap. 8.95 (*1-57514-000-4*, 5009) Encore Perform Pub.
Scenes & Monologues from the New American Theater. Frank Pike & Thomas G. Dunn. 304p. 1988. pap. 5.99 (*0-451-62547-1*, Ment) NAL-Dutton.
Scenes & Sequences - Eric Fischl - E. L. Doctorow. limited ed. Illus. by Eric Fischl. 125p. 1989. 325.00 (*0-935875-07-7*) P Blum Edit.
Scenes & Silhouettes. David L. Murray. LC 68-16959. (Essay Index Reprint Ser.). 1977. reprint ed. 20.95 (*0-8369-0727-2*) Ayer.
Scenes & Themes. Gaynor Ramsey & Michael Rutman. 64p. (C). 1985. 40.00 (*0-7175-1306-8*, Pub. by S Thornes Pubs UK) St Mut.
Scenes & Themes. Stanley Thornes. (C). 1985. audio 85.00 (*0-7175-1324-6*, Pub. by S Thornes Pubs UK) St Mut.
Scenes Beyond the Grave. Marietta Davis. Ed. by Gordon Lindsay. 1961. per. 4.95 (*0-89985-091-X*) Christ for the Nations.
Scenes Choisies. Andre Malraux. 8.50 (*0-685-34268-9*) Fr & Eur.
Scenes de France. C. Neamat. (C). 1982. 35.00 (*0-7175-1005-0*, Pub. by S Thornes Pubs UK) St Mut.
Scenes de la Vie de Boheme. Henry Murger. (Folio Ser.: No. 1968). 476p. (FRE.). 1988. pap. 13.95 (*2-07-038055-6*) Schoenhof.
Scenes de la Vie Francaise. Gaston Mauger. 6.95 (*0-685-36697-9*) Fr & Eur.
Scenes de la Vie Parisienne. Guy De Maupassant. 192p. (FRE.). 1985. pap. 10.95 (*0-7859-4690-X*) Fr & Eur.
Scenes for a Raja: Study of an Indian Kalamkari Found in Indonesia. Nina W. Gwatkin. (Monographs: No. 27). (Illus.). 24p. (Orig.). 1986. pap. text ed. 5.00 (*0-930741-06-4*) UCLA Fowler Mus.
Scenes for Acting & Directing, Vol. 1. Samuel Elkind. LC 91-52952. (Illus.). 176p. (Orig.). 1991. pap. 17.00 (*0-88734-617-0*) Players Pr.
Scenes for Acting & Directing, Vol. 2. Samuel Elkind. LC 91-52952. (Illus.). 176p. (Orig.). 1993. pap. 17.00 (*0-88734-623-5*) Players Pr.
***Scenes for Drama Ministry.** Ed. by Celia Schall. (Orig.). 1996. pap. text ed. 16.50 (*0-8309-0726-2*) Herald Hse.
Scenes for Kids. Ruth M. Roddy. 64p. (Orig.). (J). (gr. 2-6). 1990. pap. 8.95 (*0-940669-14-5*, D-9) Dramaline Pubns.
Scenes for Mandarins: The Elite Theater of the Ming. Tr. & Comment by Cyril Birch. LC 95-3382. (Translations from the Asian Classics Ser.). (CHI & ENG.). 1995. 35.00 (*0-231-10262-3*) Col U Pr.
Scenes for Student Actors, 6 Vols, 1. Frances Cosgrove. 5.00 (*0-573-69025-1*) French.
Scenes for Student Actors, 6 Vols, 2. Frances Cosgrove. 5.00 (*0-573-69026-X*) French.
Scenes for Student Actors, 6 Vols, 3. Frances Cosgrove. 5.00 (*0-573-69027-8*) French.
Scenes for Student Actors, 6 Vols, 4. Frances Cosgrove. 5.00 (*0-573-69028-6*) French.
Scenes for Student Actors, 6 Vols, 5. Frances Cosgrove. 5.00 (*0-573-69029-4*) French.
Scenes for Student Actors, 6 Vols, 6. Frances Cosgrove. 5.00 (*0-573-69030-8*) French.
Scenes for Teenagers. Roger Karshner. 64p. (Orig.). 1986. pap. 7.95 (*0-9611792-9-5*, D-11) Dramaline Pubns.
Scenes for Teenagers. Roger Karshner. LC 95-49189. (Orig.). 1995. pap. 7.95 (*0-09-617929-5*, D-11) Dramaline Pubns.
Scenes for Young Actors. Lorraine Cohen. 384p. (J). (gr. 6 up). 1982. mass mkt. 5.99 (*0-380-00997-8*) Avon.
Scenes for Young Actors: From the World of Literature & Modern Day Plays. Ed. by C. Michael Perry. (Scene Bks.). 51p. (J). (gr. 3-10). 1993. pap. 8.95 (*1-57514-002-0*, 5007) Encore Perform Pub.
Scenes from a Disturbed Childhood. Adam Czerniawski. (Illus.). 192p. (Orig.). 1992. pap. 15.99 (*1-85242-241-6*) Serpents Tail.
Scenes from a Marriage. David Barker. 40p. (Orig.). 1979. pap. 4.00 (*0-935390-04-9*) Wormwood Bks & Mag.
Scenes from a Second Adolescence, & Other Poems. Gerald Locklin. 1979. pap. 4.95 (*0-930090-08-X*) Applezaba.
Scenes from a Sistah. Lolita Files. 288p. 1997. 22.00 (*0-446-52100-0*) Warner Bks.
***Scenes from a Sistah.** Lolita Files. 320p. 1998. pap. 6.50 (*0-446-60539-5*, Warner Vision) Warner Bks.
Scenes from African Urban Life: Collected Copperbelt Essays. A. L. Epstein. 233p. 1992. 42.50 (*0-7486-0321-2*, Pub. by Edinburgh U Pr UK) Col U Pr.
Scenes from an Unfinished War: Low-Intensity Conflict in Korea, 1966-1969. (Illus.). 177p. (Orig.). (C). 1994. pap. text ed. 35.00 (*0-7881-1208-2*) DIANE Pub.
Scenes from an Unfinished War: Low-Intensity Conflict in Korea, 1966-1969, Successful Low-Intensity Conflict. 1995. lib. bdg. 253.95 (*0-8490-6758-8*) Gordon Pr.
Scenes from Classic Plays 468 B.C. to 1970 A.D. Ed. by Jocelyn A. Beard. (Scene Study Ser.). 320p. 1993. pap. 11.95 (*1-880399-36-9*) Smith & Kraus.
Scenes from Day Care: How Teachers Teach & What Children Learn. Elizabeth Platt. (Early Childhood Education Ser.: No. 35). 128p. (C). 1992. pap. text ed. 16.95 (*0-8077-3131-5*) Tchrs Coll.
Scenes from Deep Time: Early Pictorial Representations of the Prehistoric World. Martin J. Rudwick. LC 91-47677. (Illus.). 294p. 1992. 49.50 (*0-226-73104-9*) U Ch Pr.
Scenes from Deep Time: Early Pictorial Representations of the Prehistoric World. Martin J. Rudwick. xiv, 294p. 1995. pap. 20.00 (*0-226-73105-7*) U Ch Pr.
Scenes from Peter Rabbit. Beatrix Potter. 5p. (J). 1996. pap. 4.99 (*0-7232-4183-X*) Warne.
Scenes from Provincial Life: Knightly Families in Sussex, 1280-1400. Nigel Saul. (Illus.). 204p. 1987. 55.00 (*0-19-820077-3*) OUP.
Scenes from Russian Life. Vladimir Soloukhin. Tr. by D. Martin from RUS. LC 88-51685. 174p. 8900. 30.00 (*0-7206-0712-4*, Pub. by P Owen Ltd UK) Dufour.
Scenes from Seasons Past. Claudia Nice. 96p. 1988. pap. text ed. 9.50 (*1-56770-183-5*) S Scheewe Pubns.
Scenes from Shakespeare: Fifteen Cuttings for the Classroom. Michael Wilson. Ed. by Theodore O. Zapel. LC 93-223. 144p. (Orig.). 1993. pap. text ed. 10.95 (*0-916260-90-9*, B120) Meriwether Pub.
Scenes from Surgical Life. David LeVay. 200p. 1976. 22.95 (*0-8464-0813-9*) Beekman Pubs.
Scenes from the Anti-Nazi War. Basil Davidson. LC 81-81696. 294p. reprint ed. pap. 83.80 (*0-7837-3920-6*, 2043768) Bks Demand.
Scenes from the Bathhouse: And Other Stories of Communist Russia. Mikhail Zoshchenko. 1959. pap. 16.95 (*0-472-06070-8*, 70, Ann Arbor Bks) U of Mich Pr.
Scenes from the History of Real Functions. F. A. Medvedev. (Science Networks - Historical Studies: Vol. 7). 268p. 1992. 156.00 (*0-8176-2572-0*) Birkhauser.
Scenes from the Holy Infancy: A Cappella. V. Thomson. 16p. 1994. pap. 1.25 (*0-7935-3541-7*, 50482206) H Leonard.
Scenes from the Homefront. Stories. Sara Vogan. LC 87-4996. (Illinois Short Fiction Ser.). 144p. 1987. 14.95 (*0-252-01430-8*) U of Ill Pr.
Scenes from the Life of a City: Corruption & Conscience in Old New York. Eric Homberger. LC 94-3334. 1994. 32.50 (*0-300-06041-6*) Yale U Pr.
Scenes from the Life of a City: Corruption & Conscience in Old New York. Eric Homberger. 1996. pap. 16.00 (*0-300-06882-4*) Yale U Pr.
Scenes from the Life of a Faun. Arno B. Schmidt. LC 82-12901. 160p. 1983. 13.95 (*0-7145-2762-9*) M Boyars Pubs.
Scenes from the Life of a Faun. Arno B. Schmidt. 160p. 1987. reprint ed. pap. 8.95 (*0-7145-2763-7*) M Boyars Pubs.
Scenes from the Life of an Actor. George H. Hill. LC 75-81204. 258p. 1972. lib. bdg. 24.95 (*0-405-08617-2*, Pub. by Blom Pubns UK) Ayer.
Scenes from the Life of Cleopatra. Mary Butts. (Sun & Moon Classics Ser.: No. 72). 288p. (Orig.). 1994. pap. 13.95 (*1-55713-140-6*) Sun & Moon CA.
Scenes from the Light Years. Anne C. Bromley. LC 94-70460. (Poetry Ser.). 72p. 1995. pap. 11.95 (*0-88748-197-3*) Carnegie-Mellon.
Scenes from the Music of Charles Ives: A Critical Analysis. Jill Beck. (Educational Performance Collection). 59p. (C). 1985. pap. text ed. write for info. (*0-932582-43-5*) Dance Notation.
Scenes from the Music of Charles Ives: Labanotation Score. Anna Sokolow & Ilene Fox. (Educational Performance Collection). 154p. 1985. pap. write for info. (*0-932582-44-3*) Dance Notation.
Scenes from the Nineteenth-Century Stage in Advertising Woodcuts. Ed. by Stanley Appelbaum. (Pictorial Archive Ser.). (Illus.). 152p. 1977. pap. 10.95 (*0-486-23434-7*) Dover.
Scenes from the Past of Nevada, Missouri. Betty Sterett. Ed. by Donna Logan. (Illus.). 288p. (Orig.). 1985. 15.00 (*0-9614944-0-9*); pap. 10.00 (*0-9614944-1-7*) DGL InfoWrite.
Scenes from the Tale of Peter Rabbit. Beatrix Potter. (Illus.). (J). 1989. pap. 6.95 (*0-7232-3547-3*) Warne.
Scenes from Tom Kitten. Beatrix Potter. (Little Carousels Ser.). (J). 1996. 4.99 (*0-614-15581-9*); pap. 4.99 (*0-7232-4213-5*) Warne.
Scenes in Black & White. James Penzi. (Chapbook Ser.). (Illus.). 32p. (Orig.). 1982. pap. 3.00 (*0-936556-06-4*) Contact Two.
Scenes in Memory see Sprigs of Lilacs
Scenes in Nineteenth Century English Fiction. R. N. Sarkar. 216p. 1989. text ed. 30.00 (*81-7045-036-5*, Pub. by Associated Pub Hse II) Advent Bks Div.
Scenes in the Life of Harriet Tubman. Sarah H. Bradford. LC 70-154071. (Black Heritage Library Collection). 1980. 22.95 (*0-8369-8782-9*) Ayer.
Scenes in The South, & Other Miscellaneous Pieces. James R. Creecy. 1977. 20.95 (*0-8369-9186-9*, 9055) Ayer.
Scenes of American Life. 2nd ed. Martha E. Kendall. 124p. (C). 1987. student ed. 12.95 (*0-945783-00-0*) Highland Pub Group.
Scenes of Approaching Death, America Leading the Procession: War, Aids, Drugs, Disease, Depression, Homelessness, Crime & the Coming Social Disintegration of the United States. 1991. lib. bdg. 75.00 (*0-8490-4064-7*) Gordon Pr.

An Asterisk (*) at the beginning of an entry indicates that the title is appearing in BIP for the first time.

Scenes of Beautiful Japan: Memories of a U. S. Airman's 1969 Tour of Duty. Destin Pass. LC 90-45924. (Illus.). 80p. (Orig.). 1990. pap. 9.95 (*0-912526-50-5*) Lib Res.

Scenes of Beaver Creek. Gary Winterburn. (Illus.). 130p. 1992. 29.00 (*0-685-60831-X*) Beavr Crk OH.

Scenes of Childhood, Op. 15. Robert A. Schumann. Ed. by Maxwell Eckstein. (Carl Fischer Music Library: No. 256). 1949. pap. 4.50 (*0-8258-0100-1*, L256) Fischer Inc NY.

Scenes of Clerical Life. George Eliot. (World's Classics Ser.). 336p. 1989. pap. 4.95 (*0-19-281786-8*) OUP.

Scenes of Clerical Life. George Eliot. Ed. by David Lodge. (English Library). 432p. 1973. pap. 7.95 (*0-14-043087-3*, Penguin Classics) Viking Penguin.

Scenes of Clerical Life. Intro. by Graham Handley. 304p. 1994. 4.95 (*0-460-87463-2*, Everyman's Classic Lib) C E Tuttle.

Scenes of Jewish Life in Alsace. Daniel Stauben. Tr. & Intro. by Rose Choron. LC 91-52906. (Illus.). 160p. 1991. reprint ed. 23.50 (*0-934710-26-0*) J Simon.

Scenes of Life at the Capital. Philip Whalen. LC 72-163756. 84p. (Orig.). 1971. pap. 2.50 (*0-912516-00-3*) Grey Fox.

Scenes of Madness: A Psychiatrist at the Theatre. Derek R. Davis. LC 95-18951. 224p. (C). 1995. pap. 18.95 (*0-415-13173-1*) Routledge.

Scenes of Madness: Psychiatrist At the Theatre. Derek R. Davis. 224p. (C). 1991. text ed. 62.95 (*0-415-05678-0*, Routledge NY) Routledge.

Scenes of Nature, Signs of Man: Essays in 19th & 20th Century American Literature. Tony Tanner. (Cambridge Studies in American Literature & Culture: No. 31). 288p. (C). 1989. pap. text ed. 24.95 (*0-521-31155-1*) Cambridge U Pr.

Scenes of Seduction: Prostitution, Hysteria, & Reading Difference in Nineteenth-Century France. Jann Matlock. LC 93-13966. 422p. 1994. 60.00 (*0-231-07206-6*); pap. 18.50 (*0-231-07207-4*) Col U Pr.

*__Scenes of Subjection.__ Saidiya V. Hartman. LC 97-5808. (Race & American Culture Ser.). 304p. 1997. 45.00 (*0-19-508983-9*); pap. 19.95 (*0-19-508984-7*) OUP.

Scenes of the World to Come: European Architecture & the American Challenge 1893-1960. Jean-Louis Cohen. (Illus.). 224p. 1995. 45.00 (*2-08-013576-7*, Pub. by Flammarion FR) Abbeville Pr.

Scenes of Wonder & Curiosity. Ted Orland. LC 88-45333. (Illus.). 128p. 1988. 35.00 (*0-87923-768-6*) Godine.

Scenes That Happen: Dramatized Snapshots about the Real Life of High Schoolers. Mary Krell-Oishi. Ed. by Theodore O. Zapel. LC 91-26778. 176p. (Orig.). (YA). (gr. 9-12). 1991. pap. 10.95 (*0-916260-79-8*, B156) Meriwether Pub.

Scenes They Haven't Seen. Roger Karshner. 53p. (Orig.). 1983. pap. 7.95 (*0-9611792-1-X*, D-6) Dramaline Pubns.

Scenes Unseen: Unreleased & Uncompleted Films from the World's Master Filmmakers, 1912-1990. Harry Waldman. LC 90-53611. (Illus.). 286p. 1991. lib. bdg. 45.00 (*0-89950-601-1*) McFarland & Co.

Scenic & Costume Design for the Ballets Russes. Robert C. Hansen. LC 85-14029. (Theater & Dramatic Studies: No. 30). (Illus.). 247p. reprint ed. pap. 70.40 (*0-8357-1681-3*, 2070551) Bks Demand.

Scenic Art. Hugh Hood. 254p. 1984. 18.95 (*0-7737-2023-5*) Genl Dist Srvs.

Scenic Byways. LC 92-30681. (Transportation Research Record Ser.: No. 1363). 1992. 14.00 (*0-309-05401-X*) Transport Res Bd.

Scenic Byways I. Beverly Magley. LC 90-80040. (Falcon Guide Ser.). (Illus.). 240p. (Orig.). 1990. pap. 14.95 (*0-937959-94-4*) Falcon Pr MT.

Scenic Byways II. Beverly Magley. Ed. by Malcolm Bates. LC 91-77726. (Falcon Guide Ser.). (Illus.). 207p. (Orig.). 1992. pap. 14.95 (*1-56044-112-7*) Falcon Pr MT.

Scenic Daguerreotype: Romanticism & Early Photography. John Wood. LC 94-49126. (Illus.). 238p. 1995. 55.00 (*0-87745-511-2*) U of Iowa Pr.

Scenic Design on Broadway: Designers & Their Credits, 1915-1990. Bobbi Owen. LC 91-25254. (Bibliographies & Indexes in the Performing Arts Ser.: No. 10). 320p. 1991. text ed. 65.00 (*0-313-26534-8*, OSN, Greenwood Pr) Greenwood.

*__Scenic Drafting for Theatre, Film & Television: Principles & Professional Examples.__ Patricia Woodbridge. (Illus.). 220p. 1997. pap. write for info. (*0-89676-145-2*, By Design Pr) QSMG Ltd.

Scenic Driving Alaska & the Yukon. Erik Molvar. LC 96-8579. (Illus.). 296p. (Orig.). 1996. pap. 15.95 (*1-56044-489-4*) Falcon Pr MT.

Scenic Driving Arizona. Stewart Green. LC 96-39245. (Falcon Guide Ser.). (Illus.). 176p. 1997. pap. 12.95 (*1-56044-449-5*) Falcon Pr MT.

*__Scenic Driving California.__ Stewart Green. LC 97-5566. 222p. 1996. pap. text ed. 14.95 (*1-56044-450-9*) Falcon Pr MT.

Scenic Driving Colorado. Stuart Green. 262p. 1996. reprint ed. pap. 14.95 (*1-56044-451-7*) Falcon Pr MT.

Scenic Driving Georgia. Donald W. Pfitzer & LeRoy Powell. LC 96-2544. 196p. 1996. pap. 14.95 (*1-56044-411-8*) Falcon Pr MT.

*__Scenic Driving Hawaii.__ Richard A. McMahon. LC 97-9800. (Illus.). 152p. (Orig.). 1997. pap. 14.95 (*1-56044-556-4*) Falcon Pr MT.

*__Scenic Driving Michigan.__ Kathy-Jo Wargin & Ed Wargin. LC 97-9802. (Illus.). 200p. (Orig.). 1997. pap. 14.95 (*1-56044-518-1*) Falcon Pr MT.

*__Scenic Driving Minnesota.__ Phil Davies. LC 97-10979. (Illus.). 208p. (Orig.). 1997. pap. 14.95 (*1-56044-557-2*) Falcon Pr MT.

*__Scenic Driving Montana.__ Sarah A. Snyder. 176p. 1996. pap. 14.95 (*1-56044-452-5*) Falcon Pr MT.

*__Scenic Driving New England.__ Stewart Green. LC 96-49931. (Illus.). 224p. (Orig.). 1997. pap. 14.95 (*1-56044-511-4*) Falcon Pr MT.

Scenic Driving New Mexico. Laurence E. Parent. LC 96-19634. Orig. Title: New Mexico Scenic Drives. (Illus.). 160p. 1997. reprint ed. pap. 14.95 (*1-56044-453-3*) Falcon Pr MT.

*__Scenic Driving Oregon.__ Tom Barr. LC 96-33019. 1996. pap. 14.95 (*1-56044-440-1*) Falcon Pr MT.

Scenic Driving Texas. Laurence E. Parent. 178p. 1996. pap. 14.95 (*1-56044-462-2*) Falcon Pr MT.

*__Scenic Driving the Beartooth Highway.__ H. L. James. (Illus.). 80p. (Orig.). 1997. pap. 14.95 (*1-56044-555-6*) Falcon Pr MT.

Scenic Driving the Ozarks, Including the Ouachita Mountains. Donald Kurz. LC 96-8581. (Illus.). 261p. (Orig.). 1996. pap. 14.95 (*1-56044-485-1*) Falcon Pr MT.

Scenic Driving Utah. Joe Benson. (Illus.). 248p. (Orig.). 1996. pap. 14.95 (*1-56044-486-X*) Falcon Pr MT.

*__Scenic Driving Washington.__ Steve Giordano. LC 97-14787. (Illus.). 176p. (Orig.). 1995. pap. 14.95 (*1-56044-577-7*) Falcon Pr MT.

*__Scenic Driving Wisconsin.__ Aaron Cieslicki. LC 97-9801. (Illus.). 184p. (Orig.). 1997. pap. 14.95 (*1-56044-558-0*) Falcon Pr MT.

*__Scenic Driving Wyoming.__ Laurence E. Parent. LC 97-10042. (Illus.). 200p. (Orig.). 1997. pap. 12.95 (*1-56044-536-X*) Falcon Pr MT.

Scenic Drowning. Robert Sommer & Barbara B. Sommer. (Illus.). 40p. (Orig.). 1984. pap. text ed. 1.00 (*0-9613339-0-1*) Grey Cats Pr.

Scenic Highway One: Monterey to Morro Bay. rev. ed. Vicki Leon. (Illus.). 64p. (Orig.). 1984. pap. 8.95 (*0-918303-02-8*) Blake Pub.

*__Scenic Highways.__ Reader's Digest Association Staff. LC 97-14290. (Explore America Ser.). 1997. write for info. (*0-89577-906-4*) RD Assn.

*__Scenic, Historic Lookout Mountain.__ 3rd ed. (Illus.). 162p. 1977. write for info. (*0-9608494-2-4*) John Wilson.

Scenic Parks & Landscape Value. Ellen H. Makoski. LC 90-39467. (Environment: Problems & Solutions Ser.: Vol. 15). 283p. 1990. text ed. 25.00 (*0-8240-0470-1*) Garland.

Scenic Relief Carving. Georg Keilhofer. LC 95-26285. (Illus.). 64p. (YA). (gr. 10-13). 1996. pap. 12.95 (*0-88740-788-9*) Schiffer.

Scenic Route. Bruce Francis. 100p. 1987. 20.00 (*0-935716-45-9*) Lord John.

Scenic San Diego. Leslie Bergstrom. (Illus.). 68p. 1990. pap. 4.95 (*0-9612668-4-8*) Talk Town.

Scenic Sedona. rev. ed. Arizona Highways Staff. 64p. 1995. pap. 9.95 (*0-916179-52-4*) Ariz Hwy.

Scenic South Carolina. 2nd rev. ed. Eugene B. Sloan. LC 79-183143. (Illus.). (C). 1971. text ed. 12.95 (*0-915114-00-3*) Lewis-Sloan.

Scenic Tours of Lancaster County. 98p. (Orig.). 1994. pap. 9.95 (*0-9642225-0-7*) Lancaster Bicycle.

Scenic Tucson: A Guide to Seeing the Best of the Tucson Area. Bob Kerry. 208p. 1994. pap. 19.95 (*0-9641137-0-8*) Backcntry Bks.

Scenic Tunnels. Louise O. Neaderland. (Illus.). 16p. (Orig.). 1983. pap. 12.00 (*0-942561-03-1*) Bone Hollow.

Scenic Washington Engagement Calendar, 1991. (Illus.). 12p. (Orig.). 1991. pap. 3.50 (*1-878395-09-2*) Smith-Western.

Sceno-Graphic Techniques. 3rd ed. W. Oren Parker. LC 86-17859. (Illus.). 158p. (C). 1987. pap. 19.95 (*0-8093-1350-2*) S Ill U Pr.

Scenographic Imagination. 3rd ed. Darwin R. Payne. LC 92-13216. (Illus.). 400p. (C). 1993. 39.95 (*0-8093-1850-4*); pap. 24.95 (*0-8093-1851-2*) S Ill U Pr.

Scenotest Manual: A Practical Technique for Understanding Unconscious Problems & Personality Structure. rev. ed. G. Von Staabs. Tr. by Joseph A. Smith from GER. LC 91-21226. (Illus.). 120p. 1991. text ed. 35.00 (*0-920887-71-6*) Hogrefe & Huber Pubs.

Scent: The Mysterious & Essential Powers of Smell. Annick Le Guerer. Ed. by Philip Turner. Tr. by Richard Miller. 272p. 1994. pap. 13.00 (*1-56836-024-X*) Kodansha.

Scent: Training to Track, Search, & Rescue. Milo D. Pearsall & Hugo Verbruggen. (Illus.). 240p. 1982. 16.95 (*0-931866-11-1*) Alpine Pubns.

Scent & Fragrances: The Fascination of Odors & Their Chemical Perspectives. Gunther Ohloff. Tr. by W. Pickenhagen from GER. LC 93-44959. (Illus.). 260p. 1994. 103.95 (*0-387-57108-6*) Spr-Verlag.

Scent & the Scenting Dog. 3rd ed. William G. Syrotuck. LC 72-94862. (Illus.). 102p. 1972. pap. 9.95 (*0-914124-03-X*) Arner Pubns.

Scent Bottles. Alexandra Walker. 1989. pap. 25.00 (*0-85263-909-0*, Pub. by Shire UK) St Mut.

Scent in Your Garden. Stephen Lacey. 1991. 40.00 (*0-316-51169-2*) Little.

*__Scent of Apple: An Anthology of Poetry on Family Relationships.__ John Bourne et al. Ed. by Teddy Milne. LC 96-72545. 53p. 1997. pap. 9.95 (*0-938875-37-X*) Pittenbruach Pr.

Scent of Apples: A Collection of Stories. Bienvenido N. Santos. LC 79-4857. 250p. 1979. pap. 14.95 (*0-295-95695-X*) U of Wash Pr.

Scent of Cloves. Norah Lofts. reprint ed. lib. bdg. 24.95 (*0-89190-228-7*, Rivercity Pr) Amereon Ltd.

Scent of Death. large type ed. Emma Page. (Mystery Ser.). 352p. 1987. 25.99 (*0-7089-1579-5*) Ulverscroft.

Scent of Death. Emma Page. 224p. 1989. reprint ed. mass mkt. 3.50 (*0-373-26012-1*) Harlequin Bks.

Scent of Eternity: The Life of Harris Elliott Kirk. Donald G. Miller. LC 89-35945. (Illus.). xvi, 730p. (C). 1990. 31.95 (*0-86554-332-1*, MUP/H246) Mercer Univ Pr.

Scent of Eucalyptus. Barbara Hanrahan. 188p. 1990. pap. 11.95 (*0-7012-0855-4*, Pub. by Hogarth Pr UK) Trafalgar.

Scent of Fear. large type ed. Patricia Matthews & Clayton Matthews. LC 92-23099. 351p. 1992. reprint ed. lib. bdg. 19.95 (*1-56054-336-1*) Thorndike Pr.

Scent of Flowers. James Saunders. 1970. pap. 5.25 (*0-8222-0995-0*) Dramatists Play.

Scent of Flowers: A Journey Through Grief, Healing, & Love. Gloria J. Roy. 160p. (Orig.). 1995. pap. 11.00 (*1-57502-065-3*) Morris Pubng.

Scent of Gold. large type ed. Hilary London. (General Ser.). 416p. 1993. 25.99 (*0-7089-2845-5*) Ulverscroft.

Scent of Heather. Jane Peart. (International Romance Ser.). 192p. (Orig.). 1993. pap. 7.99 (*0-8007-5462-X*) Revell.

Scent of Ink: The Roy & Marilyn Papp Collection of Chinese Painting. Ju-Hsi Chou. (Illus.). 176p. 1994. pap. text ed. write for info. (*0-910407-30-4*) Phoenix Art.

Scent of Jasmine: Reflections for Peace in Everyday Life. Carmel McCarthy. LC 95-30480. 216p. (Orig.). 1995. pap. 14.95 (*0-8146-2332-8*, Liturg Pr Bks) Liturgical Pr.

Scent of Mimosa. large type ed. Jade Shannon. 464p. 1985. 25.99 (*0-7089-1354-7*) Ulverscroft.

*__Scent of Murder.__ Barbara Block. 336p. 1997. 18.95 (*1-57566-195-0*, Knsington) Kensgtn Pub Corp.

*__Scent of Orchids.__ R. Kaiser. 260p. 1993. 190.75 (*0-444-89841-7*) Elsevier.

*__Scent of Saffron.__ Shafii Rouhi. 1997. pap. 19.95 (*1-85727-088-6*, Pub. by Scarlet Pr UK) LPC InBook.

Scent of Snow Flowers. Regina L. Klein. 528p. 1989. 19.95 (*0-87306-498-4*); pap. 16.95 (*0-87306-499-2*) Feldheim.

Scent of Spring. large type ed. Tracy Davis. 1990. pap. 15. 99 (*0-7089-6874-0*, Trailtree Bookshop) Ulverscroft.

Scent of the Beast. Jonathan Tweet. (Talislanta Ser.). 72p. 1992. pap. 10.00 (*1-880992-04-3*) Wizards Coast.

Scent of the Gods. Fiona Cheong. 256p. 1993. pap. 8.95 (*0-393-31012-4*) Norton.

Scent of the Sea. large type ed. Geoffrey Jenkins. 1974. 25. 99 (*0-85456-267-2*) Ulverscroft.

Scent of Water. Vera J. Nelson. (Western Americana Bks.). 104p. (Orig.). 1973. pap. 5.00 (*0-913626-19-8*) S S S Pub Co.

Scented Age: The Biology & Culture of Human Odour. D. Michael Stoddart. (Illus.). 320p. (C). 1990. pap. text ed. 30.95 (*0-521-39561-5*) Cambridge U Pr.

Scented Christmas. Dawn Cusick. (Illus.). 112p. 1990. pap. 9.95 (*0-8069-7470-2*) Sterling.

Scented Christmas: Fragrant Decorations, Gifts, & Cards for the Festive Season. Gail Duff. LC 91-6494. (Illus.). 128p. 1992. 17.95 (*0-87857-974-5*, 11-020-0) Rodale Pr Inc.

Scented Garden. David Squire. 1996. 19.99 (*0-517-15929-5*) Random.

Scented Garden. Eleanor S. Rohde. 1974. reprint ed. 46.00 (*1-55888-222-7*) Omnigraphics Inc.

Scented Garden: Choosing, Growing & Using the Plants that Bring Fragrance to Your Life, Your Home, Your Table. Rosemary Verey. LC 89-42535. (Illus.). 168p. 1989. 29.95 (*0-394-57990-9*) Random.

Scented Garden of Abdullah the Satirist of Shiraz: A Facsimile Edition. Aleister Crowley. LC 91-8493. 160p. 1991. 29.95 (*0-933429-05-3*) Teitan Pr.

Scented Gardens for the Blind. Janet Frame. LC 64-10786. 252p. 1980. pap. 10.95 (*0-8076-0985-4*) Braziller.

Scented Garlands & Bouquets. (Illus.). 80p. 1992. pap. 12. 95 (*0-7137-2227-4*, Pub. by Blandford Pr UK) Sterling.

Scented Geraniums: Knowing, Growing, & Enjoying More Than 100 Varieties. Jim Becker & Faye Brawner. (Illus.). 96p. 1996. pap. 14.95 (*1-883010-18-7*) Interweave.

Scented Herb Papers: How to Use Natural Scents & Colours in Hand-Made Recycled & Plant Papers. Polly Pinder. (Illus.). 64p. 1995. pap. 14.95 (*0-85532-789-8*, 7898X, Pub. by Search Pr UK) A Schwartz & Co.

Scented Room: Cherchez's Book of Dried Flowers, Fragrance, & Potpourri. Barbara M. Ohrbach. 1986. 18. 00 (*0-517-56081-X*, C P Pubs) Crown Pub Group.

Scented Room Gardening Notebook. Barbara M. Ohrbach. LC 89-7993. (Illus.). 519p. 1990. 15.95 (*0-517-57577-9*, C P Pubs) Crown Pub Group.

Scented Treasures: Aromatic Gifts from the Kitchen & Garden. Stephanie Donaldson. LC 96-10642. (Illus.). 128p. 1996. 24.95 (*0-88266-930-3*) Storey Comm Inc.

Scenterpieces of Fragrance: Creative Recipe Pages. rev. ed. Bibliotheca Press Staff. (Illus.). 60p. 1991. student ed., ring bd. 25.95 (*0-939476-88-6*) Prosperity & Profits.

Scentimental Journey: Reflections on Life. Ron Papcun. 128p. (Orig.). 1994. pap. 7.95 (*0-9641644-0-X*) Regenerat Concepts.

*__Scentouri Guide to Wild Fragrances for Potpourri, Etc.__ 29.95 (*1-890928-20-8*) F Carrol.

Scents Appeal: The Silent Persuasion of Aromatic Encounters. Gabrielle J. Dorland. (Illus.). 324p. 1993. text ed. 34.50 (*0-9603250-4-2*) Dorland Pub Co.

*__Scents for Success.__ Bill Bynum. Ed. by Craig Boddington. (Whitetail Secrets Ser.: No. 7). (Illus.). 194p. (YA). (gr. 10 up). 1995. 17.95 (*1-56416-157-9*) Derrydale Pr.

*__Scents of Eden: A Narrative of the Spice Trade.__ Charles Corn. 352p. 1998. 25.00 (*1-56836-202-1*) Kodansha.

Scents of Place: Season of the St. Croix Valley. Cynthia B. Gustavson. (Illus.). (Orig.). (YA). (gr. 9-12). 1987. pap. 8.95 (*0-317-91094-9*) Country Messenger Inc.

Scents of Wood & Silence: Short Stories by Latin American Women Writers. Ed. by Yvette E. Miller & Kathleen Ross. LC 91-30002. (Discoveries Ser.). 224p. 1991. pap. 16.95 (*0-935480-55-2*) Lat Am Lit Rev Pr.

*__Scentual Touch.__ Jackson. 1986. 22.95 (*0-8050-2148-5*) H Holt & Co.

Scentuous Cookery: Or How to Make It in the Kitchen. Jane Johnston & Phyllis Jedlicka. LC 76-174740. (Illus.). 1971. 15.00 (*0-87832-004-0*) Piper.

Scepsis Scientifica, or Confest Ignorance, the Way to Science & Scire - I Tuum Nihil Est, or The Authors Defence of the Vanity of Dogmatizing. Joseph Glanvill. Ed. by Bernhard Fabian. (Collected Works: Vol. III). 1985. reprint ed. 55.12 (*3-487-02689-9*) G Olms Pubs.

Scepter & the Spear: Studies on Forms of Repetition in the Homeric Poems. Steven Lowenstam. LC 93-19243. (Greek Studies: Interdisciplinary Approaches). 280p. (C). 1992. text ed. 62.50 (*0-8476-7772-9*); pap. text ed. 28.50 (*0-8476-7790-7*) Rowman.

Scepter & the Star: Jewish Messianism in Light of the Dead Sea Scrolls. John J. Collins. LC 94-16886. (Bible Reference Library Ser.). 228p. 1995. 30.00 (*0-385-47457-1*, Anchor NY) Doubleday.

Scepter of Egypt, Vol. 1: From the Earliest Times to the End of the Middle Kingdom. rev. ed. William C. Hayes. (Illus.). 421p. 1990. pap. 25.00 (*0-87099-190-6*, 0-8109-6479-1) Metro Mus Art.

Scepter of Egypt, Vol. 2: The Hyksos Period & the New Kingdom. rev. ed. William C. Hayes. (Illus.). 526p. 1990. pap. 25.00 (*0-87099-191-4*, 0-8109-6480-5) Metro Mus Art.

Scepters, Swords, & Fire from Heaven. (Bible Adventure Bks.). (J). (gr. 4-6). 1990. 2.19 (*0-89636-113-6*, JB 2B) Accent CO.

Sceptical Challenge. Ruth Weintraub. LC 96-1507. (International Library of Philosophy). 144p. (C). 1997. text ed. 55.00 (*0-415-13946-5*) Routledge.

Sceptical Chemist. Robert Boyle. 442p. 1992. reprint ed. pap. 36.00 (*0-922802-90-4*) Kessinger Pub.

Sceptical Essays. Bertrand Russell. (Unwin Paperbacks Ser.). 1960. pap. 19.95 (*0-04-104003-1*) Routledge Chapman & Hall.

Scepticism. Christopher Hookway. (Problems of Philosophy: Their Past & Present Ser.). 258p. (C). 1992. pap. 16.95 (*0-415-08764-3*, A9616) Routledge.

Scepticism. Michael Williams. (International Research Library of Philosophy). 504p. 1993. 136.95 (*1-85521-335-4*, Pub. by Dartmth Pub UK) Ashgate Pub Co.

Scepticism & Animal Faith: Introduction to a System of Philosophy. George Santayana. 1955. pap. text ed. 7.95 (*0-486-20236-4*) Dover.

Scepticism & Belief in Hume's Dialogues Concerning Natural Religion. Stanley Tweyman. 1986. lib. bdg. 97. 00 (*90-247-3090-2*) Kluwer Ac.

Scepticism & Hope in Twentieth-Century Fantasy Literature. Kath Filmer. LC 92-72464. 160p. (C). 1992. 26.95 (*0-87972-553-2*); pap. 13.95 (*0-87972-554-0*) Bowling Green Univ Popular Press.

Scepticism & Irreligion in the 17th & 18th Centuries. Ed. by Richard H. Popkin & Arjo Vanderjagt. LC 92-44598. (Brill's Studies in Intellectual History: Vol. 37). 1993. 113.00 (*90-04-09596-9*) E J Brill.

Scepticism & Poetry: An Essay on the Poetic Imagination. David G. James. LC 80-21749. 274p. 1980. reprint ed. text ed. 59.75 (*0-313-22840-X*, JASP, Greenwood Pr) Greenwood.

*__Scepticism & the Foundation of Epistemology: A Study in the Metalogical Fallacies.__ Luciano Floridi. (Brill's Studies in Intellectual History: No. 70). xx, 372p. 1996. 126.50 (*90-04-10533-6*) E J Brill.

*__Scepticism in the Enlightenment.__ Richard H. Popkin et al. LC 97-21896. (International Archives of the History of Ideas Ser.). 1997. write for info. (*0-7923-4643-2*) Kluwer Ac.

Scepticism in the History of Philosophy: A Pan-American Dialogue. Ed. by Richard H. Popkin. (Archives Internationales D'Histoire des Idees Ser.: Vol. 145). 296p. (C). 1996. lib. bdg. 157.00 (*0-7923-3769-7*) Kluwer Ac.

Scepticism, Man & God: Selections from the Major Writings Of Sextus Empiricus. Sextus Empiricus. Ed. by Philip P. Hallie. Tr. by Sanford G. Etheridge. LC 64-22377. 248p. reprint ed. pap. 70.70 (*0-317-08988-9*, 2001959) Bks Demand.

Scepticisms: Notes on Contemporary Poetry. Conrad P. Aiken. LC 67-30170. (Essay Index Reprint Ser.). 1977. 18.95 (*0-8369-0140-1*) Ayer.

Sceptics. R. J. Hankinson. LC 94-4592. (Arguments of the Philosophers Ser.). 432p. (C). (gr. 13). 1995. text ed. 85. 00 (*0-415-04772-2*, B4675) Routledge.

Sceptics, Millenarians & Jews. Ed. by David S. Katz & Jonathan I. Israel. LC 89-49704. (Studies in Intellectual History: Vol. 17). x, 293p. 1989. 103.50 (*90-04-09160-2*) E J Brill.

Sceptics of the Old Testament. Emile J. Dillon. LC 73-16064. (Studies in Comparative Literature: No. 35). 1974. reprint ed. lib. bdg. 75.00 (*0-8383-1723-5*) M S G Haskell Hse.

Sceptre & the Rose. large type ed. Doris Leslie. (Shadows of the Crown Ser.). 1974. 25.99 (*0-85456-618-X*) Ulverscroft.

Sceptre D'ottokar. Herge. (Illus.). (FRE.). (J). (gr. 7-9). ring bd. 19.95 (*0-8288-5060-7*) Fr & Eur.

Sceve Celebration: Delie, 1544-1994. Ed. by Jerry C. Nash. (Stanford French & Italian Studies: No. 77). 200p. 1993. pap. 46.50 (*0-915838-93-1*) Anma Libri.

Schachnovelle. Stefan Zweig. 110p. (GER.). 1995. pap. 9.00 (*3-596-21522-6*, Pub. by Fischer Taschbch Verlag GW) Intl Bk Import.

Schachspiel. Siegbert Tarrasch. (Praxis Schach Ser.: Bd. 5). (Illus.). 412p. (GER.). 1992. write for info. (*3-283-00253-3*) G Olms Pubs.

Schadenersatz im Internationalen Seefrachtrecht. Alexander Von Ziegler. 236p. (GER.). 1990. pap. 65.00 (*3-7890-1960-7*, Pub. by Nomos Verlags GW) Intl Bk Import.

S

S

Schaeffer: Memoirs & Reminiscences Together with the Sketches of the Early History of Sussex County, NJ, with Notes & Genealogical Record of the Schaeffer, Shaver or Shafer Family. William M. Johnson. (Illus.). 187p. 1994. reprint ed. pap. 29.50 (*0-8328-4052-1*); reprint ed. lib. bdg. 39.50 (*0-8328-4051-3*) Higginson Bk Co.

Schaffer & Avery's Diseases of the Newborn. 6th ed. H. William Taeusch et al. (Illus.). 1104p. 1991. text ed. 157.00 (*0-7216-2476-6*) Saunders.

Schaldach. Etchings. The Sporting Art of William J. Schaldach. limited ed. Ed. by Edward Gray & DeCourcy Taylor. LC 87-82427. (Illus.). 160p. 1987. 45.00 (*0-9609842-9-1*) GSJ Press.

Schalliol Is Our Family Name: Its History from 1323 to 1985. Willis L. Schalliol. Tr. by Paul Challiol & Helga C. Gay from ENG. (Illus.). 502p. (Orig.). (ENG, FRE & GER.). 1985. pap. 22.00 (*0-9605732-3-2*); lib. bdg. 30.00 (*0-9605732-4-0*) Belle Pubns.

Schalliol Is Our Family Name: 1323-1991. Willis L. Schalliol. Tr. by Paul Challiol & Helga C. Gay. (Illus.). 27p. (Orig.). (ENG, FRE & GER.). 1991. pap. 5.00 (*0-9605732-6-7*) Belle Pubns.

Schalm's Veterinary Hematology. 4th ed. Nemi C. Jain. LC 84-27811. (Illus.). 1221p. 1986. text ed. 149.00 (*0-8121-0942-2*) Williams & Wilkins.

Schambach-Kaston Collection of Musical Instruments. Richard T. Rephann. (Illus.). 88p. (Orig.). 1988. pap. 15.00 (*0-929530-05-5*) Yale U Coll Musical Instruments.

Schammachanat: Poetry & Stories. Nat Scammacca. 94p. (ENG & ITA.). 1985. 20.00 (*0-89304-597-7*); pap. 10.00 (*0-89304-572-1*) Cross-Cultrl NY.

Scharansky: Hero of Our Time. Martin Gilbert. 512p. 1986. 24.95 (*0-317-46605-4*) Viking Penguin.

Schatz Rackhams des Roten. Herge. (Illus.). 62p. (GER.). (J). pap. 19.95 (*0-8288-5062-3*) Fr & Eur.

Schatzbehalter. Michael Wolgemut & Stephan Fridolin. (Illus.). 708p. (GER.). 1981. reprint ed. boxed 75.00 (*0-915346-69-9*) A Wofsy Fine Arts.

***Schatzsuche Im Buchstaben Land.** Illus. by Hella Soyka. 18p. (GER.). (J). (gr. k-2). 1989. 4.95 (*3-614-29651-2*) Another Lang Pr.

Schau-Buehne Englischen und Frantzosischer Comoedianten, 1670 see Spieltexte der Wanderbuehne

Schaubuhne - die Weltbuhne 1905-1933, 3 vols. Joachim Bergmann. 1200p. 1991. lib. bdg. 375.00 (*3-598-10831-1*) K G Saur.

Schaufelein (Hans) The Graphic Work, 2 vols., Set. Karl H. Schreyl. (Illus.). 676p. (GER.). 1990. 275.00 (*1-55660-169-7*) A Wofsy Fine Arts.

Schauffler Chronicle: Roster & Biographical Sketches of the Schauffler Family in America, William Gottlieb Schauffler & Mary Reynolds Schauffler & Their Descendants. R. M. Schauffler. 121p. 1993. reprint ed. pap. 22.00 (*0-8328-3745-8*); reprint ed. lib. bdg. 32.00 (*0-8328-3744-X*) Higginson Bk Co.

Schaum Boolean Algebra & Switching Circuits. Elliot Mendelson. (Schaum's Outline Ser.). 1970. pap. text ed. 12.95 (*0-07-041460-2*) McGraw.

Schaum Three Thousand Solved Problems in Organic Chemistry. Herbert Meislich. (Schaum's Solved Problems Ser.). 1993. pap. text ed. 22.95 (*0-07-056424-8*) McGraw.

Schaum's College Physics. Dennison. (C). 1996. pap. text ed. 39.95 incl. disk (*0-07-844268-0*) McGraw.

Schaum's Education & Enseignement: Education & the School Lectures & Vocabulary. Conrad J. Schmitt. (FRE.). 1995. text ed. 11.95 (*0-07-056822-7*) McGraw.

Schaum's Electric Power Systems. Syed A. Masar. 1990. pap. text ed. 12.95 (*0-07-045917-7*) McGraw.

***Schaum's Electronic Tutor for College Algebra.** 2nd ed. Jean H. Bevis & Cheryl Stratton. (Schaum's Outline Ser.). 1997. pap. text ed. 38.95 (*0-07-913620-6*) McGraw.

***Schaum's Electronic Tutor of Electric Circuits.** 3rd ed. Joseph A. Edminister & Mahmood S. Nahvi. (Schaum's Outline Ser.). 1996. pap. text ed. 38.95 (*0-07-844696-1*) McGraw.

Schaum's Engineering Mechanics. 5th ed. McLean. 1997. pap. text ed. 39.95 incl. disk (*0-07-844097-1*) McGraw.

Schaum's General Biology. George Fried. 448p. 1990. pap. text ed. 14.95 (*0-07-022401-3*) McGraw.

Schaum's Mechanical Vibrations. Kelly. 1996. pap. text ed. 39.95 incl. disk (*0-07-844266-4*) McGraw.

Schaum's Microprocessor Fundamentals. 2nd ed. Roger L. Tokheim. 1990. pap. text ed. 12.95 (*0-07-064999-5*) McGraw.

Schaums Outline Electromagnetics. Joseph Edminister. 1995. pap. text ed. 38.95 incl. disk (*0-07-842713-4*) McGraw.

Schaums Outline Feedback & Control Systems. Distefano. 1994. pap. text ed. 38.95 incl. disk (*0-07-842709-6*) McGraw.

Schaums Outline Fluid Mechanics & Hydraulics. Giles. 1995. pap. text ed. 38.95 incl. disk (*0-07-842715-0*) McGraw.

Schaum's Outline for Physical Chemistry. 2nd ed. Clyde R. Metz. 512p. 1988. pap. text ed. 14.95 (*0-07-041715-6*) McGraw.

Schaum's Outline of Advanced Cost Accounting see Schaum's Outline of Cost Accounting II

Schaum's Outline of Analytical Chemistry. A. A. Gordus. 256p. 1985. pap. text ed. 13.95 (*0-07-023795-6*) McGraw.

Schaum's Outline of Assembly Language: Including 1695 Solved Problems. David E. Goldberg. 1988. text ed. 14.95 (*0-07-033011-5*) McGraw.

Schaum's Outline of Basic Circuit Analysis. 2nd ed. John O'Malley. (Schaum's Outline Ser.). 448p. 1992. pap. text ed. 14.95 (*0-07-047824-4*) McGraw.

Schaum's Outline of Basic Electrical Engineering. J. J. Cathey & Syed A. Nasar. 1983. pap. text ed. 14.95 (*0-07-010234-1*) McGraw.

***Schaum's Outline of Basic Electrical Engineering.** 2nd ed. Syed A. Nasar. Ed. by Jimmy J. Cathey. LC 96-47056. (Schaum's Outline Ser.). 1997. pap. text ed. 14.95 (*0-07-011355-6*) McGraw.

Schaum's Outline of Basic Electricity. W. Gussow. (Schaum's Outline Ser.). 448p. 1983. pap. text ed. 14.95 (*0-07-025240-8*) McGraw.

Schaum's Outline of Beginning Linear Algebra. Seymour Lipschutz. LC 96-9004. 1996. pap. text ed. 13.95 (*0-07-038037-6*) McGraw.

***Schaum's Outline of Beginning Statistics.** Larry J. Stephens. (Schaum's Outline Ser.). 1998. pap. 14.95 (*0-07-061259-5*) McGraw.

Schaum's Outline of Biochemistry. Philip W. Kuchel. 1988. pap. text ed. 14.95 (*0-07-035579-7*) McGraw.

***Schaum's Outline of Biochemistry.** 2nd ed. Philip W. Kuchel. LC 97-23525. (Schaum's Ser.). 1997. pap. text ed. 14.95 (*0-07-036149-5*) McGraw.

Schaum's Outline of Bookkeeping & Accounting. 2nd ed. Joel J. Lerner. 1988. pap. text ed. 12.95 (*0-07-037231-4*) McGraw.

Schaum's Outline of Calculus. 3rd ed. Frank Ayres, Jr. & Elliot Mendelson. 1990. pap. text ed. 14.95 (*0-07-002662-9*) McGraw.

Schaum's Outline of Chemistry Foundations. David E. Goldberg. (Schaum's Outline Ser.). 1991. pap. text ed. 13.95 (*0-07-023679-8*) McGraw.

***Schaum's Outline of College Algebra.** 2nd ed. Murray R. Siegel & Roert E. Moyer. (Schaum's Outline Ser.). 1997. pap. text ed. 14.95 (*0-07-060266-2*) McGraw.

Schaum's Outline of College Chemistry. 8th ed. Jerome L. Rosenberg & Lawrence M. Epstein. LC 96-46610. (Illus.). 384p. 1996. pap. text ed. 14.95 (*0-07-053709-7*) McGraw.

Schaum's Outline of College Physics. 8th ed. Frederick J. Bueche. (Schaum's Outline Ser.). 1989. pap. text ed. 13.95 (*0-07-008874-8*) McGraw.

Schaum's Outline of College Physics. 9th ed. Frederick J. Bueche & Eugene Hecht. (Illus.). 448p. 1997. pap. text ed. 14.95 (*0-07-008941-8*) McGraw.

Schaum's Outline of Combinatorics. V. K. Balakrishnan. (Schaum's Outline Ser.). 1995. pap. text ed. 13.95 (*0-07-003575-X*) McGraw.

Schaum's Outline of Computer Graphics. R. A. Plastock & G. Kalley. (Schaum's Outline Ser.). 352p. 1986. pap. text ed. 14.95 (*0-07-050326-5*) McGraw.

Schaum's Outline of Core Concepts of Calculus: A Friendly Approach. Eli Passow. 1996. pap. text ed. 11.95 (*0-07-048738-3*) McGraw.

Schaum's Outline of Cost Accounting I. 2nd ed. Ralph S. Polimeni & James A. Cashin. 272p. 1984. pap. text ed. 11.95 (*0-07-010273-2*) McGraw.

Schaum's Outline of Cost Accounting II. James A. Cashin et al. (Schaum's Outline Ser.). Orig. Title: Schaum's Outline of Advanced Cost Accounting. 240p. (C). 1982. pap. text ed. 10.95 (*0-07-010207-4*) McGraw.

Schaum's Outline of Differential Equations. 2nd ed. Richard Bronson. (Schaum's Outline Ser.). 1993. pap. text ed. 14.95 (*0-07-008019-4*) McGraw.

***Schaum's Outline of Discrete Mathematics.** 2nd ed. Seymour Lipschutz & Marc Lipson. LC 97-19341. (Schaum's Outline Ser.). 1997. pap. text ed. 14.95 (*0-07-038045-7*) McGraw.

Schaum's Outline of Electric Circuits. 2nd ed. Joseph Edminster. 1995. pap. text ed. 13.95 (*0-07-021233-3*) McGraw.

Schaum's Outline of Electric Circuits. 3rd ed. Joseph Edminister & Mahmood S. Nahvi. (Schaum's Outline Ser.). 1996. pap. text ed. 13.95 (*0-07-018999-4*) McGraw.

Schaum's Outline of Electric Machines & Electromechanics. Syed A. Nasar. (Schaum's Outline Ser.). (Illus.). 208p. (C). 1981. pap. text ed. 12.95 (*0-07-045886-3*) McGraw.

***Schaum's Outline of Electric Machines & Electromechanics.** 2nd ed. Syed A. Nasar. LC 97-23529. (Schaum's Outline Ser.). 1997. pap. text ed. 14.95 (*0-07-045994-0*) McGraw.

Schaum's Outline of Electromagnetics. 2nd ed. Joseph Edminister. 1993. pap. text ed. 12.95 (*0-07-018993-5*) McGraw.

***Schaum's Outline of Electromagnetics.** 2nd rev. ed. Joseph Edminister. (Schaum's Outline Ser.). 1993. pap. text ed. 13.95 (*0-07-021234-1*) McGraw.

Schaum's Outline of Electronic Communication. 2nd ed. Lloyd Temes & Mitchel Schultz. (Schaum's Outline Ser.). 1997. pap. text ed. 11.95 (*0-07-063496-3*) McGraw.

Schaum's Outline of Electronic Devices & Circuits. J. J. Cathey. 352p. 1989. pap. text ed. 12.95 (*0-07-010274-0*) McGraw.

Schaum's Outline of Engineering Mechanics. 4th ed. William G. McLean & E. W. Nelson. (Schaum's Outline Ser.). 448p. 1988. pap. text ed. 14.95 (*0-07-044822-1*) McGraw.

***Schaum's Outline of Engineering Mechanics.** 5th ed. E. W. Nelson et al. LC 97-24244. (Illus.). 480p. 1997. pap. text ed. 15.95 (*0-07-046193-7*) McGraw.

Schaum's Outline of English Grammar. 2nd ed. Eugene H. Ehrlich & Daniel J. Murphy. (Schaum's Outline Ser.). 160p. 1991. pap. text ed. 9.95 (*0-07-019484-X*) McGraw.

Schaum's Outline of Essential Computer Mathematics. Seymour Lipschutz. 256p. (C). 1982. pap. text ed. 14.95 (*0-07-037990-4*) McGraw.

Schaum's Outline of Feedback & Control Systems. 2nd ed. Joseph J. DiStefano & Allen J. Stubberud. (Schaum's Outline Ser.). 1990. pap. text ed. 15.95 (*0-07-017052-5*) McGraw.

Schaum's Outline of Financial Accounting. Joel G. Siegel & Jae K. Shim. (Schaum's Outline Ser.). 272p. (C). 1983. pap. text ed. 14.95 (*0-07-057304-2*) McGraw.

Schaum's Outline of Finite Element Analysis. George R. Buchanan. (Schaum's Outline Ser.). 1994. pap. text ed. 14.95 (*0-07-008714-8*) McGraw.

Schaum's Outline of Finite Mathematics: Including Hundreds of Solved Problems. 2nd ed. Seymour Lipschutz. (Schaum's Outline Ser.). 1994. pap. text ed. 14.95 (*0-07-038002-3*) McGraw.

Schaum's Outline of Fluid Dynamics. 2nd ed. William F. Hughes & John A. Brighton. (Schaum's Outline Ser.). 1991. pap. text ed. 14.95 (*0-07-031117-X*) McGraw.

Schaum's Outline of Fluid Mechanics & Hydraulics. 3rd ed. Ranald V Giles & Cheng Liu. (Schaum's Outline Ser.). 1993. pap. text ed. 13.95 (*0-07-020509-4*) McGraw.

Schaum's Outline of French Grammar. 3rd ed. Mary C. Crocker. (Schaum's Outline Ser.). 336p. 1990. pap. text ed. 13.95 (*0-07-013885-0*) McGraw.

Schaum's Outline of French Vocabulary. Mary E. Coffman. (Schaum's Outline Ser.). 256p. 1985. pap. text ed. 12.95 (*0-07-011561-3*) McGraw.

***Schaum's Outline of French Vocabulary.** 2nd ed. Mary E. Crocker. (Schaum's Ser.). 1997. pap. text ed. 14.95 (*0-07-013886-9*) McGraw.

Schaum's Outline of General, Organic, & Biological Chemistry. George Odian. 1994. pap. text ed. 14.95 (*0-07-047609-8*) McGraw.

Schaum's Outline of Genetics. 3rd ed. William D. Stansfield. (Schaum's Outline Ser.). 1991. pap. text ed. 14.95 (*0-07-060877-6*) McGraw.

Schaum's Outline of Geometry. 2nd ed. Barnett Rich. (Outline Ser.). 272p. 1989. pap. text ed. 12.95 (*0-07-052246-4*) McGraw.

Schaum's Outline of German Grammar. 3rd ed. Elke Gschossmann-Hendershot & Lois Feuerle. LC 96-35002. 288p. 1996. pap. text ed. 11.95 (*0-07-025134-7*) McGraw.

Schaum's Outline of German Vocabulary. Edda Weiss. 1986. text ed. 12.95 (*0-07-069128-2*) McGraw.

Schaum's Outline of Graph Theory. V. K. Balakrishnan. 256p. 1997. pap. text ed. 14.95 (*0-07-005489-4*) McGraw.

Schaum's Outline of Heat Transfer. 2nd ed. Donald R. Pitts & Leighton E. Sissom. 1997. pap. text ed. 13.95 (*0-07-050207-2*) McGraw.

Schaum's Outline of Human Anatomy & Physiology. 2nd ed. Kent Van De Graaff & R. Ward Rhees. LC 97-8163. (Illus.). 448p. 1997. pap. text ed. 14.95 (*0-07-066887-6*) McGraw.

Schaum's Outline of Human Anatomy & Physiology: Including 1450 Problems & Questions. Kent M. Van De Graaff & R. Ward Rhees. (Schaum's Outline Ser.). 368p. 1987. text ed. 13.95 (*0-07-066884-1*) McGraw.

Schaum's Outline of Intermediate Accounting. 2nd rev. ed. James A. Cashin et al. (Schaum's Outline Ser.). 288p. 1989. pap. text ed. 12.95 (*0-07-010204-X*) McGraw.

Schaum's Outline of Intermediate Accounting I. Baruch Englard. (Schaum's Outline Ser.). 1995. pap. text ed. 14.95 (*0-07-019579-X*) McGraw.

Schaum's Outline of Intermediate Accounting Two. Baruch Englard. 1992. pap. text ed. 13.95 (*0-07-019483-1*) McGraw.

***Schaum's Outline of Intermediate Algebra.** Ray Steege & Kerry Bailey. LC 97-6801. (Illus.). 416p. 1997. pap. text ed. 14.95 (*0-07-060839-3*) McGraw.

Schaum's Outline of Introduction to Digital Systems: Including 183 Solved Problems. James E. Palmer. 1992. pap. text ed. 13.95 (*0-07-048439-2*) McGraw.

Schaum's Outline of Introduction to Psychology. Arno F. Wittig. (Schaum's Outline Ser.). 1977. pap. text ed. 14.95 (*0-07-071194-1*) McGraw.

Schaum's Outline of Introductory Geology. R. Ojakangas. (Schaum's Outline Ser.). 1991. pap. text ed. 12.95 (*0-07-047704-3*) McGraw.

Schaum's Outline of Introductory Surveying. R. H. Wirshing & J. R. Wirshing. 368p. 1985. pap. text ed. 14.95 (*0-07-071124-0*) McGraw.

Schaum's Outline of Investments: Including Hundreds of Solved Problems. Jack C. Francis. 1992. pap. text ed. 14.95 (*0-07-021807-2*) McGraw.

Schaum's Outline of Italian Grammar. 2nd ed. Joseph Germano & Conrad J. Schmitt. (Schaum's Outline Ser.). 288p. (C). 1982. pap. text ed. 12.95 (*0-07-023031-5*) McGraw.

Schaum's Outline of Italian Grammar. 2nd ed. Joseph E. Germano & Conrad J. Schmitt. LC 93-40652. 1994. pap. text ed. 13.95 (*0-07-023033-1*) McGraw.

Schaum's Outline of Italian Vocabulary. F. C. Clark & Conrad J. Schmitt. (Schaum's Outline Ser.). 256p. 1987. pap. text ed. 12.95 (*0-07-023032-3*) McGraw.

Schaum's Outline of Linear Algebra. 2nd ed. Seymour Lipschutz. (Schaum's Outline Ser.). 1991. pap. text ed. 13.95 (*0-07-038007-4*) McGraw.

Schaum's Outline of Logic. John E. Nolt & Dennis A. Rohatyn. 384p. 1988. pap. text ed. 13.95 (*0-07-053628-7*) McGraw.

Schaum's Outline of Machine Design. Joseph F. Shelley. (Schaum's Outline Ser.). 1998. pap. text ed. 13.95 (*0-07-056837-5*) McGraw.

Schaum's Outline of Macroeconomic Theory. 2nd ed. Eugene A. Diulio. 1990. pap. text ed. 12.95 (*0-07-017051-7*) McGraw.

***Schaum's Outline of Macroeconomics.** 3rd ed. Eugene Diulio. (Schaum's Outline Ser.). 1997. pap. text ed. 14.95 (*0-07-017053-3*) McGraw.

Schaum's Outline of Managerial Finance. Jae K. Shim & Joel G. Siegel. 432p. (C). 1986. pap. text ed. 14.95 (*0-07-057306-9*) McGraw.

Schaum's Outline of Mathematical Economics. 2nd ed. Edward T. Dowling. 480p. 1992. pap. text ed. 14.95 (*0-07-017674-4*) McGraw.

Schaum's Outline of Mathematical Methods for Business & Economics. Edward T. Dowling. 1992. pap. text ed. 12.95 (*0-07-017697-3*) McGraw.

Schaum's Outline of Mathematics for Nurses. E. Nishiura. 208p. 1986. pap. text ed. 12.95 (*0-07-046100-7*) McGraw.

Schaum's Outline of Mathematics of Finance & Actuarial Science. 2nd rev. ed. Petr Zima & Robert L. Brown. 304p. 1996. pap. text ed. 12.95 (*0-07-008203-0*) McGraw.

Schaum's Outline of Matrix Operations. (Schaum's Outline Ser.). 288p. 1989. pap. text ed. 12.95 (*0-07-007978-1*) McGraw.

Schaum's Outline of Mechanical Vibrations: Including Hundreds of Solved Problems. S. Graham Kelly. 1996. pap. text ed. 14.95 (*0-07-034041-2*) McGraw.

Schaum's Outline of Microbiology. I. Edward Alcamo. LC 97-12020. (Illus.). 352p. 1997. pap. text ed. 14.95 (*0-07-000967-8*) McGraw.

Schaum's Outline of Microeconomic Theory. 3rd ed. Dominick Salvatore. (Schaum's Outline Ser.). 1992. pap. text ed. 14.95 (*0-07-054515-4*) McGraw.

Schaum's Outline of Modern Physics. Ronald Gautreau & William Savin. (Schaum's Outline Ser.). (Illus.). (C). 1978. pap. text ed. 12.95 (*0-07-023062-5*) McGraw.

Schaum's Outline of Molecular Biology. William D. Stansfield et al. (Schaum's Outline Ser.). 1996. pap. text ed. 13.95 (*0-07-060898-9*) McGraw.

Schaum's Outline of Numerical Analysis. 2nd ed. Francis Scheid. (Outline Ser.). 480p. 1988. pap. text ed. 13.95 (*0-07-055221-5*) McGraw.

Schaum's Outline of Operations Management. 2nd ed. Joseph G. Monks. (Schaum's Outline Ser.). 1996. pap. text ed. 14.95 (*0-07-042764-X*) McGraw.

Schaum's Outline of Operations Research. Richard Bronson. (Schaum Paperback Ser.). 1982. pap. text ed. 13.95 (*0-07-007977-3*) McGraw.

Schaum's Outline of Organic Chemistry. 2nd ed. Herbert Meislich et al. (Schaum's Outline Ser.). 1991. pap. text ed. 14.95 (*0-07-041458-0*) McGraw.

Schaum's Outline of Partial Differential Equations. Paul C. DuChateau & D. W. Zachmann. 224p. 1986. pap. text ed. 13.95 (*0-07-017897-6*) McGraw.

Schaum's Outline of Physical Science. 2nd ed. Arthur Beiser. 352p. 1988. pap. text ed. 14.95 (*0-07-004419-8*) McGraw.

Schaum's Outline of Physics for Engineering & Science. Dare A. Wells & H. S. Slusher. (Schaum's Outline Ser.). 336p. 1983. pap. text ed. 14.95 (*0-07-069254-8*) McGraw.

***Schaum's Outline of Physics for Pre-Med, Allied Health & Biology Students.** George Hademenos. (Schaum's Outline Ser.). 1998. pap. 14.95 (*0-07-025474-5*) McGraw.

Schaum's Outline of Preparatory Physics II: Electritity & Magnetism, Optics, Modern Physics. Alvin Halpern. (Schaum's Outline Ser.). 1997. pap. text ed. 14.95 (*0-07-025707-8*) McGraw.

Schaum's Outline of Preparatory Physics 1: Mechanics, Heat, & Sound. Alvin Halpern. 1995. pap. text ed. 13.95 (*0-07-025653-5*) McGraw.

***Schaum's Outline of Principles of Accounting I.** 5th ed. Joel J. Lerner. (Schaum's Outline Ser.). 1998. pap. text ed. 14.95 (*0-07-038149-6*) McGraw.

Schaum's Outline of Principles of Accounting II. 4th ed. Joel J. Lerner & James A. Cashin. LC 92-4387. (Schaum's Outline Ser.). 1993. pap. text ed. 12.95 (*0-07-037589-5*) McGraw.

Schaum's Outline of Principles of Economics. Dominick Salvator & Eugene A. Diulio. (Schaum's Outline Ser.). 1980. pap. text ed. 12.95 (*0-07-054487-5*) McGraw.

Schaum's Outline of Principles of Economics. 2nd ed. Dominick Savatore & Eugene Diulio. (Schaum's Outline Ser.). 1995. pap. text ed. 14.95 (*0-07-054629-0*) McGraw.

Schaum's Outline of Probability, Random Variables, & Random Processes. Hwei P. Hsu. LC 96-18245. 336p. 1996. pap. text ed. 14.95 (*0-07-030644-3*) McGraw.

Schaum's Outline of Programming With C. 2nd rev. ed. Byron Gottfried. LC 96-2724. 544p. 1996. pap. text ed. 13.95 (*0-07-024035-3*) McGraw.

Schaum's Outline of Programming with C Plus Plus: Including Hundreds of Solved Problems. John R. Hubbard. 1996. pap. text ed. 13.95 (*0-07-030837-3*) McGraw.

Schaum's Outline of Programming with FORTRAN. William E. Mayo & Martin Cwiakala. (Schaum's Outline Ser.). 1994. pap. text ed. 13.95 (*0-07-041155-7*) McGraw.

Schaum's Outline of Programming with FORTRAN IV. Seymour Lipschutz & Arthur C. Poe. (Schaum's Outline Ser.). 1978. pap. text ed. 12.95 (*0-07-037984-X*) McGraw.

Schaum's Outline of Punctuation, Capitalization, & Spelling. 2nd ed. Eugene H. Ehrlich. LC 91-4108. 208p. 1992. pap. text ed. 12.95 (*0-07-019487-4*) McGraw.

***Schaum's Outline of Quantum Mechanics.** Eliahu Zaarur & Reuven Phini. (Illus.). 320p. 1997. pap. text ed. 14.95 (*0-07-054018-7*) McGraw.

***Schaum's Outline of Review of Elementary Mathematics.** 2nd ed. Barnett Rich. LC 97-8029. (Illus.). 352p. 1997. pap. text ed. 14.95 (*0-07-052279-0*) McGraw.

Schaum's Outline of Signals & Systems. Hwel P. Hse. (Schaum's Outline Ser.). 1995. pap. text ed. 14.95 (*0-07-030641-9*) McGraw.

An Asterisk (*) at the beginning of an entry indicates that the title is appearing in BIP for the first time.

Schaum's Outline of Spanish Grammar. 3rd ed. Conrad J. Schmitt. (Schaum's Outline Ser.). 224p. (C). 1989. pap. text ed. 12.95 (*0-07-055437-4*) McGraw.

Schaum's Outline of Spanish Vocabulary. 2nd rev. ed. Conrad J. Schmitt. LC 96-35001. 352p. 1996. pap. text ed. 13.95 (*0-07-057227-5*) McGraw.

Schaum's Outline of Statics & Strength of Materials. John J. Jackson & Harold G. Wirtz. (Schaum's Outline Ser.). 416p. (C). 1983. pap. text ed. 14.95 (*0-07-032121-3*) McGraw.

Schaum's Outline of Statistics. 2nd ed. Murray R. Spiegel. (Outline Ser.). 400p. 1989. pap. text ed. 14.95 (*0-07-060234-4*) McGraw.

Schaum's Outline of Statistics & Econometrics. Dominick Salvatore. (Illus.). 176p. (C). 1982. pap. text ed. 12.95 (*0-07-054505-7*) McGraw.

Schaum's Outline of Strength of Materials. 3rd ed. William A. Nash. 1994. pap. text ed. 14.95 (*0-07-045903-7*) McGraw.

Schaum's Outline of Structural Steel Design. Abraham J. Rokach. (Schaum's Outline Ser.). 1991. pap. text ed. 13.95 (*0-07-053563-9*) McGraw.

Schaum's Outline of Structured COBOL Programming. 2nd ed. Lawrence R. Newcomer. (Schaum's Outline Ser.). 1994. pap. text ed. 13.95 (*0-07-038019-8*) McGraw.

Schaum's Outline of Tensor Calculus. David C. Kay. (Schaum's Outline Ser.). 240p. 1988. text ed. 13.95 (*0-07-033484-6*) McGraw.

Schaum's Outline of Theory & Problems of Applied Physics. 3rd ed. Arthur Beiser. LC 94-24928. (Schaum's Outline Ser.). 1995. pap. text ed. 13.95 (*0-07-005201-8*) McGraw.

Schaum's Outline of Theory & Problems of Basic Mathematics for Electricity & Electronics. 2nd ed. Arthur Beiser. LC 92-30096. 1993. text ed. 12.95 (*0-07-004439-2*) McGraw.

Schaum's Outline of Theory & Problems of Bookkeeping & Accounting. 3rd ed. Joel J. Lerner. LC 93-41304. 1994. pap. text ed. 13.95 (*0-07-037593-3*) McGraw.

Schaum's Outline of Theory & Problems of Business Mathematics. Joel J. Lerner & P. Zima. 320p. 1985. pap. text ed. 12.95 (*0-07-037212-8*) McGraw.

Schaum's Outline of Theory & Problems of Business Statistics. 3rd ed. Leonard J. Kazmier. LC 95-9265. (Schaum's Outline Ser.). 1996. pap. text ed. 14.95 (*0-07-034026-9*) McGraw.

Schaum's Outline of Theory & Problems of Cost Accounting. 3rd ed. Ralph S. Polimeni et al. LC 93-23908. (Schaum's Outline Ser.). 1994. pap. text ed. 13.95 (*0-07-011026-3*) McGraw.

Schaum's Outline of Theory & Problems of Digital Principles. 3rd ed. Roger L. Tokheim. LC 93-64. (Schaum's Outline Ser.). 1993. pap. text ed. 14.95 (*0-07-065050-0*) McGraw.

Schaum's Outline of Theory & Problems of Elementary Algebra. 2nd rev. ed. Barnett Rich. LC 92-18533. 1993. pap. text ed. 13.95 (*0-07-052262-6*) McGraw.

Schaum's Outline of Theory & Problems of Engineering Economics. William E. Souder et al. 192p. 1984. pap. text ed. 12.95 (*0-07-023834-0*) McGraw.

Schaum's Outline of Theory & Problems of Fluid Mechanics & Hydraulics. 3rd ed. Ronald V. Giles et al. LC 92-35841. (Schaum's Outline Ser.). 1993. reprint ed. pap. text ed. 13.95 (*0-07-023316-0*) McGraw.

Schaum's Outline of Theory & Problems of International Economics. 4th ed. Dominick Salvatore. LC 95-14740. (Schaum's Outline Ser.). (C). 1996. pap. text ed. 13.95 (*0-07-054950-8*) McGraw.

Schaum's Outline of Theory & Problems of Managerial Accounting. Jae K. Shim. 1983. pap. text ed. 14.95 (*0-07-057305-0*) McGraw.

Schaum's Outline of Theory & Problems of Operations Management. Joseph G. Monks. 38p. 1985. pap. text ed. 13.95 (*0-07-042726-7*) McGraw.

***Schaum's Outline of Theory & Problems of Operations Research.** 2nd ed. Richard Bronson & Govindsami Naadimuthu. LC 97-9538. 1997. pap. text ed. 14.95 (*0-07-008020-8*) McGraw.

Schaum's Outline of Theory & Problems of Principles of Accounting I. 4th ed. Joel J. Lerner & James A. Cashin. LC 92-2432. 1993. pap. text ed. 14.95 (*0-07-037278-0*) McGraw.

Schaum's Outline of Theory & Problems of Programming with PASCAL. 2nd ed. Byron S. Gottfried. LC 93-4710. (Schaum's Outline Ser.). 1994. pap. text ed. 14.95 (*0-07-023924-X*) McGraw.

Schaum's Outline of Theory & Problems of Programming with Structured COBOL. Lawrence R. Newcomer. (Illus.). 375p. (C). 1984. pap. text ed. 12.95 (*0-07-037998-X*) McGraw.

Schaum's Outline of Theory & Problems of Reinforced Concrete Design: Including Hundreds of Solved Problems. 3rd ed. Noel J. Everard & John L. Tanner, III. LC 92-23615. (Schaum's Outline Ser.). 1993. pap. text ed. 13.95 (*0-07-019772-5*) McGraw.

Schaum's Outline of Theory & Problems of Zoology see Zoology, the Animal Kingdom: A Complete Course in 1000 Questions & Answers

Schaum's Outline of Thermodynamics. 2nd rev. ed. Michael M. Abbott & Hendrick Van Ness. 400p. (C). 1990. pap. text ed. 14.95 (*0-07-000042-5*) McGraw.

Schaum's Outline of Thermodynamics for Engineers. Craig W. Somerton. 1993. pap. text ed. 13.95 (*0-07-050707-4*) McGraw.

Schaum's Outline of Trigonometry. 2nd rev. ed. Frank Ayres, Jr. & Robert E. Moyer. 288p. (C). 1990. pap. text ed. 11.95 (*0-07-002659-9*) McGraw.

Schaum's Outline of Unix. Harley Hahn. (Schaum's Outline Ser.). 1995. pap. text ed. 7.38 (*0-07-025515-6*) McGraw.

Schaums Outline Thermodynamics for Engineers. Beatrix Potter. 1995. pap. text ed. 38.95 (*0-07-842717-7*) McGraw.

Schaum's Outline to Beginning Calculus. 2nd ed. Elliot Mendelson. LC 96-39852. (Illus.). 400p. 1996. pap. text ed. 13.95 (*0-07-041733-4*) McGraw.

Schaum's Personal Finance. Jae K. Shim. (Schaum's Outline Ser.). 1991. pap. text ed. 12.95 (*0-07-057559-2*) McGraw.

Schaum's Principles of Economics. Diulio Salvatore. 1996. pap. text ed. 39.95 incl. disk (*0-07-843966-3*) McGraw.

Schaum's Probability. Schaum. 1968. pap. text ed. 12.95 (*0-07-037982-3*) McGraw.

Schaum's Programming in Structured BASIC. 4th ed. Byron S. Gottfried. 1993. pap. text ed. 13.95 (*0-07-023899-5*) McGraw.

***Schaum's Quick Guide to Business Formulas.** Joel G. Siegel. (Schaum's Quick Guides). 1997. pap. text ed. 14.95 (*0-07-058031-6*) McGraw.

Schaum's Statistics. 2nd ed. Di. 1996. pap. text ed. 39.95 incl. disk (*0-07-843990-6*) McGraw.

Schaum's Three Thousand Solved Problems in Chemistry. David E. Goldberg. 1992. pap. text ed. 20.95 (*0-07-023684-4*) McGraw.

Schaum's Three Thousand Solved Problems in Electrical Circuits. Syed Nassar. (Illus.). 1992. pap. text ed. 22.95 (*0-07-045936-3*) McGraw.

Schaum's Three Thousand Solved Problems in Linear Algebra. Seymour Lipschutz. 4960p. 1989. pap. text ed. 19.95 (*0-07-038023-6*) McGraw.

Schaum's Twenty-Five Hundred Solved Problems in Differential Equations. Richard Bronson. (Schaum's Solved Problems Ser.). 448p. 1989. pap. text ed. 19.95 (*0-07-007979-X*) McGraw.

Schaum's Two Thousand Solved Problems in Mechanical Engineering Thermodynamics. Peter E. Liley. 416p. 1989. pap. text ed. 19.95 (*0-07-037863-0*) McGraw.

Schaum's Two Thousand Solved Problems in Physical Chemistry. Clyde R. Metz. (Schaum's Solved Problem Ser.). 672p. (C). 1989. pap. text ed. 21.95 (*0-07-041716-4*) McGraw.

Schaum's Vector Analysis. Murray R. Spiegel. 1959. pap. text ed. 14.95 (*0-07-060228-X*) McGraw.

Schauspieltexte im Theatermuseum der Universitat zu Koln, 8 vols. Ed. by Roswitha Flatz. 3900p. (GER.). 1990. Set. lib. bdg. 2,000.00 (*3-598-32890-7*) K G Saur.

Schawacker's Greater Philadelphia Special Events Resource Directory: 1996 Edition. Virginia Schawacker. 300p. 1995. pap. 29.95 (*1-887025-02-2*) Buffington Bks.

Schawacker's L.A. Metro Special Events Resource Directory. Peter E. Schawacker. 500p. 1995. pap. 29.95 (*1-887025-01-4*) Buffington Bks.

Schawacker's Special Events Resource Directory: Greater Philadelphia Edition. Virginia Schawacker. 1995. pap. 29.95 (*1-887025-00-6*) Buffington Bks.

Schechem II, No. 2. Edward F. Campbell. (Archaeological Reports: No. 2). xii, 123p. 1992. reprint ed. 74.95 (*1-55540-639-4*, 85 00 02) Scholars Pr GA.

Schede di Lavoro, No. 1. Raffaella Maiguashea et al. 1985. teacher ed. 5.00 (*0-8020-6599-6*) U of Toronto Pr.

Schede di Lavoro, No. 2. Raffaella Maiguashea et al. 1985. teacher ed. 5.00 (*0-8020-6601-1*) U of Toronto Pr.

Schede di Lavoro, Pt. 1. Raffaella Maiguashea et al. 276p. 1985. Part 1. Wkbk. 276p. student ed. 23.95 (*0-8020-6598-8*) U of Toronto Pr.

Schede di Lavoro, Pt. 2. Raffaella Maiguashea et al. 200p. 1985. Part 2. Wkbk. 200p. student ed. 21.95 (*0-8020-6600-3*) U of Toronto Pr.

Schede di Lavoro 1. 2nd ed. Marina S. Frescura et al. (Italian Studies). 152p. (C). 1994. student ed. 24.95 (*0-8020-7213-5*); teacher ed. 20.00 (*0-8020-7226-7*) U of Toronto Pr.

Schedulae Orchidiacae, 10 pts. Oakes Ames. 594p. (C). 1922. 120.00 (*0-685-22353-1*, Pub. by Scientific UK) St Mut.

Schedule Castes & National Integration. Suresh Rajaram Kakade. 165p. 1990. text ed. 25.00 (*81-7027-136-3*, Pub. by Radiant Pubs II) S Asia.

Schedule Two, Vol. 1. Gaylord Dold. 256p. 1996. 21.95 (*0-312-14730-9*) St Martin.

Schedule 40 & 80 Rigid PVC Conduit UL 651. 6th ed. 1995. pap. text ed. 95.00 (*1-55989-867-4*) Underwrtrs Labs.

Scheduled Caste & Scheduled Tribes in India. H. C. Upandhyay. (C). 1991. 34.00 (*81-7041-452-0*, Pub. by Anmol II) S Asia.

Scheduled Caste Girls: Educational Backwardness & Prospects. Lalita Kabra. (C). 1991. 21.00 (*81-7099-329-6*, Pub. by Mittal II) S Asia.

Scheduled Caste Panchayat Pradhans in India. Vijay Kumar. (C). 1989. 21.50 (*81-202-0262-7*, Pub. by Ajanta II) S Asia.

Scheduled Caste Women: Studies in Exploitation. H. M. Trivedi. 256p. 1977. 18.95 (*0-318-37079-4*) Asia Bk Corp.

Scheduled Castes: History of Elevation, Tamil Nadu, 1900-1955. P. E. Mohan. 1993. 19.00 (*0-8364-2875-7*, Pub. by New Era) S Asia.

Scheduled Castes: Socio-Economic Changes. Nirupama Prakash. (C). 1988. 44.00 (*81-85076-58-8*, Pub. by Chugh Pubns II) S Asia.

Scheduled Castes & Scheduled Tribes in Industrial Training Institutes. Kusum K. Premi. 150p. 1988. text ed. 25.00 (*0-7069-4263-9*, Pub. by Vikas II) S Asia.

Scheduled Castes & Their Status in India. Ali K. Mumtaz. 276p. 1980. 23.50 (*0-940500-23-X*) Asia Bk Corp.

Scheduled Castes & Tribes: A Socio-Economic Survey. C. Parvathamma. 1985. 37.50 (*0-8364-1253-2*, Pub. by Ashish II) S Asia.

Scheduled Castes & Tribes: Socio-Economic Upliftment Programmes. Hemlata Rao. Ed. by M. Devendra Babu. (Illus.). vi, 150p. (C). 1994. 16.00 (*81-7024-566-4*, Pub. by Ashish Pub Hse II) Nataraj Bks.

Scheduled Castes at the Crossroads. C. Parvathamma. (C). 1989. 24.00 (*81-7024-257-6*, Pub. by Ashish II) S Asia.

Scheduled Castes in India. E. S. Yurlova. (C). 1990. 35.00 (*81-7050-115-6*, Pub. by Patriot II) S Asia.

Scheduled Salaries for Professional Personnel in Public Schools, 1987-88. 113p. 1988. 36.00 (*0-318-37601-6*) Ed Research.

Scheduled Tribes. Govind S. Ghurye. (C). 1995. 32.00 (*81-7154-661-7*, Pub. by Popular Prakashan II) S Asia.

Scheduled Tribes in Rajasthan Below Poverty-Line. Bhupinder Singh & S. L. Batra. (C). 1994. 16.00 (*0-7069-7321-6*, Pub. by Vikas II) S Asia.

Scheduled Tribes of Himachal Pradesh: Marriage & Divorce Customs. Suresh Kapur. (C). 1993. text ed. 20.00 (*81-7013-092-1*, Pub. by Navrang) S Asia.

Scheduled Tribes of India. Govind S. Ghurye. LC 79-66430. 399p. 1980. pap. 24.95 (*0-87855-692-3*); text ed. 49.95 (*0-87855-308-8*) Transaction Pubs.

Scheduler's Notebook: A Guide to School Scheduling Using the Mac School Administrative Package. Lawrence Bickford. 163p. 1990. pap. 44.00 (*0-9637294-0-3*) Sugar Hill Pr.

Schedules Castes of India. Sohan Singh. (C). 1987. 48.50 (*81-212-0084-9*, Pub. by Gian Publng Hse II) S Asia.

Schedules for Clinical Assessment in Neuropsychiatry, Version 2.0 (SCAN) Glossary. World Health Organization Staff. 237p. 1994. spiral bd. 43.95 (*0-88048-984-7*, 8984) Am Psychiatric.

Schedules for Clinical Assessment in Neuropsychiatry, Version 2.0 (SCAN) Manual. 332p. 1994. spiral bd. 49.95 (*0-88048-976-6*, 8976) Am Psychiatric.

Schedules for Clinical Assessment in Neuropsychiatry, Version 2.0 (SCAN) Recording Booklets. World Health Organization Staff. 103p. 1994. pap. text ed. 39.95 (*0-88048-985-5*, 8985) Am Psychiatric.

***Schedules of Reinforcement.** C. B. Ferster & B. F. Skinner. (Illus.). 776p. 1997. reprint ed. pap. 20.00 (*0-87411-828-X*) Copley Pub.

Schedules 000-599 see Dewey Decimal Classification & Relative Index

Schedules 600-999 see Dewey Decimal Classification & Relative Index

Scheduling. J. K. Lenstra et al. Date not set. text ed. 49.95 (*0-471-90549-6*) Wiley.

Scheduling: Theory, Algorithms & Systems. Michael Pinedo. LC 94-8256. (International Industrial & Sytems Engineering Ser.). 416p. 1994. text ed. 75.00 (*0-13-706757-7*) P-H.

Scheduling Algorithms, Vol. X. Peter Brucker. (Illus.). 326p. 1995. 98.00 (*3-540-60087-6*) Spr-Verlag.

Scheduling & Control. Mel Tainiter. 120p. 1985. 95.00 incl. disk (*0-934577-07-2*) Softext Pub.

Scheduling & Load Balancing in Parallel & Distributed Systems. Ed. by Behrooz A. Shirazi et al. LC 95-3159. 520p. 1995. pap. 50.00 (*0-8186-6587-4*, BP06587) IEEE Comp Soc.

***Scheduling Computer & Manufacturing Processes.** Jacek Blazewicz. LC 96-29227. 488p. 1996. 129.50 (*3-540-61496-6*) Spr-Verlag.

Scheduling Construction Projects. Edward M. Willis. LC 85-26589. 462p. 1986. text ed. 43.95 (*0-471-80869-5*) P-H.

Scheduling Control for Industry & Government. Melvin Tainiter. LC 74-185676. 56p. (Orig.). pap. 3.25 (*0-87974-000-0*) Timetable Pr.

Scheduling Divisible Loads in Parallel & Distributed Systems. Veeravalli Bharadwaj et al. LC 96-177. 292p. 1996. 50.00 (*0-8186-7521-7*) IEEE Comp Soc.

Scheduling in Computer & Manufacturing Systems. Jacek Blazewicz et al. LC 92-37487. 1992. 109.00 (*0-387-55958-2*) Spr-Verlag.

Scheduling in Computer & Manufacturing Systems. 2nd rev. ed. Jacek Blazewicz et al. LC 94-17909. 1994. 99.95 (*0-387-58049-2*) Spr-Verlag.

Scheduling Module 3" - Parsifal Workbench. Morton. (GC - Principles of Management Ser.). 1997. pap. 39.95 (*0-87709-533-7*) S-W Pub.

Scheduling Multifamily Maintenance. Frank Basile. LC 88-62050. 96p. 1988. pap. 20.00 (*0-86718-322-5*) Home Builder.

Scheduling Patients & Appointment Book Control: A Complete How-to Manual for the Doctor & Staff. Robert D. Westerman. (Classic Practice Ser.: Vol. 1). 290p. 1991. ring bd. 295.00 (*0-9629983-0-3*) R Westerman.

Scheduling Residential Construction for Builders & Remodelers. Thomas A. Love. LC 94-41539. (Illus.). 128p. (Orig.). 1995. pap. 29.00 (*0-86718-401-9*) Home Builder.

Scheduling the Secondary School. fac. ed. Richard A. Dempsey & Henry P. Traverso. LC 83-215584. (Illus.). 88p. (Orig.). 1983. reprint ed. pap. 25.10 (*0-7837-7836-8*, 2047596) Bks Demand.

***Scheduling the 24-Hr. Operation: The Manual of Shift Scheduling - Planning, Implementation & Evaluation.** Glenn N. McBride. (Illus.). 280p. 1996. ring bd. 99.50 (*0-9638482-1-6*) McBride Pubns.

Scheduling Theory: Multi-Stage Systems. Viacheslav S. Tanaev. (Mathematics & Its Applications Ser.). 416p. (C). 1994. lib. bdg. 225.50 (*0-7923-2854-X*) Kluwer Ac.

Scheduling Theory: Single-State Systems, 2 vols. Viacheslav S. Tanaev et al. LC 94-14887. (Mathematics & Its Applications Ser.: Vol. 284). 384p. (C). 1994. lib. bdg. 316.00 (*0-7923-2872-8*) Kluwer Ac.

Scheduling Theory: Single-State Systems. Viacheslav S. Tanaev et al. LC 94-14887. (Mathematics & Its Applications Ser.: Vol. 284). 384p. (C). 1994. lib. bdg. 208.00 (*0-7923-2853-1*) Kluwer Ac.

Scheduling Theory & Its Applications. Ed. by Philippe Chretienne et al. 350p. 1995. text ed. 72.95 (*0-471-94059-3*) Wiley.

***Scheduling Time for Music.** Milton Goldberg et al. 80p. (Orig.). 1995. pap. 17.00 (*1-56545-094-9*, 1640) Music Ed Natl.

***Scheewe Art Workshop - Watercolor & Acrylic, Vol. 30.** Susan S. Brown. (Illus.). 100p. (Orig.). 1997. pap. 11.95 (*1-56770-398-4*) S Scheewe Pubns.

Scheherazade. Marisha Chamberlain. 1985. pap. 5.25 (*0-8222-0996-9*) Dramatists Play.

Scheherazade. Jules Supervielle. 186p. (FRE.). 1949. pap. 10.95 (*0-7859-1329-7*, 2070261468) Fr & Eur.

Scheherazade in England: A Study of Nineteenth-Century English Criticism of the Arabian Nights. Muhsin J. Ali. LC 80-53382. (Illus.). 187p. (Orig.). 1981. pap. 10.00 (*0-89410-247-8*, Three Contnts) Lynne Rienner.

Scheherazade in England: A Study of Nineteenth-Century English Criticism of the Arabian Nights. Mushin J. Ali. Ed. by Philip Noss. LC 80-53382. (Illus.). 187p. (Orig.). 1981. pap. 20.00 (*0-89410-246-X*, Three Contnts) Lynne Rienner.

Scheherazade in Full Score. Nikolai Rimsky-Korsakov. 240p. 1984. pap. 9.95 (*0-486-24734-1*) Dover.

Scheherazade's Cat: And Other Fables from Around the World. Amy Zerner & Jessie S. Zerner. (Illus.). 64p. 1993. 16.95 (*0-8048-1807-X*) C E Tuttle.

Scheherezade in the Marketplace: Elizabeth Gaskell & the Victorian Novel. Hilary M. Schor. 240p. 1992. 45.00 (*0-19-507388-6*) OUP.

Scheimpflung Lens Documentation. New Developments & Applications. Ed. by A. Wegener. (Journal: Ophthalmic Research: Vol. 24, Suppl. 1, 1992). (Illus.). iv, 72p. 1992. pap. 23.50 (*3-8055-5702-7*) S Karger.

Scheisse! The Real German You Were Never Taught in School. Gertrude Besserwisser. LC 93-48608. (Illus.). 96p. (Orig.). 1994. pap. 8.95 (*0-452-27221-1*, Plume) NAL-Dutton.

Scheler's Critique of Kant's Ethics. Philip Blosser. (Continental Thought Ser.: No. 22). 270p. (C). 1995. text ed. 39.95 (*0-8214-1108-X*) Ohio U Pr.

Schelling & Modern European Philosophy: An Introduction. Andrew Bowie. LC 93-13079. 192p. (C). (gr. 13). 1993. text ed. 69.95 (*0-415-10346-0*) Routledge.

Schelling & Modern European Philosophy: An Introduction. Andrew Bowie. LC 93-13079. 192p. (C). 1994. pap. 16.95 (*0-415-10347-9*) Routledge.

***Schelling & Swedenborg: Mysticism & German Idealism.** Friedemann Horn. Tr. by George F. Dole. (Orig.). (C). 1997. pap. 13.95 (*0-87785-186-7*) Swedenborg.

***Schelling & Swedenborg: Mysticism & German Idealism.** Friedemann Horn. Tr. by George F. Dole. (Orig.). (C). 1997. 17.95 (*0-87785-187-5*) Swedenborg.

Schelling & the End of Idealism. Dale E. Snow. LC 95-4245. (Hegelian Studies). 271p. (C). 1996. pap. text ed. 16.95 (*0-7914-2746-3*) State U NY Pr.

Schelling & the End of Idealism. Dale E. Snow. LC 95-4245. (SUNY Series in Hegelian Studies). 271p. (C). 1996. text ed. 49.50 (*0-7914-2745-5*) State U NY Pr.

***Schelling und Nietzsche: Zur Auslegung der Fruehen Werke Friedrich Nietzsches.** John E. Wilson. (Monographien und Texte Zur Nietzsche-Forschung Ser.: Vol. 33). xi, 400p. (GER.). (C). 1996. lib. bdg. 176.30 (*3-11-015128-6*) De Gruyter.

Schelling's Idealism & Philosophy of Nature. Joseph L. Esposito. 294p. 1978. 38.50 (*0-8387-1904-X*) Bucknell U Pr.

***Schelling's Transcendental Idealism: 1882 Edition.** John Watson. 266p. 1996. reprint ed. write for info. (*1-85506-155-4*) Bks Intl VA.

Schelling's Treatise on the Deities of Samothrace: A Translation & an Interpretation. Robert F. Brown. LC 76-42239. (American Academy of Religion. Studies in Religion: No. 12). 75p. reprint ed. pap. 25.00 (*0-7837-5480-9*, 2045245) Bks Demand.

Schelling's Treatise on the Essence of Human Freedom. Martin Heidegger. Tr. by Joan Stambaugh. LC 83-19472. (Series in Continental Thought: Vol. 8). viii, 200p. 1985. pap. 17.95 (*0-8214-0691-4*) Ohio U Pr.

Schells' Guide to Eastern Mexico. rev. ed. Rolfe F. Schell. (Illus.). 302p. 1975. pap. 6.95 (*0-87208-024-2*) Shoeless Pub.

Schells' Guide to Yucatan & Neighboring States. Lois W. Schell & Rolfe F. Schell. LC 85-52459. (Illus.). 292p. 1986. pap. 8.95 (*0-87208-101-X*) Shoeless Pub.

Schelmuffsky. Christian Reuter. Tr. by Wayne Wonderley. LC 62-62959. (North Carolina. University. Studies in the Germanic Languages & Literatures: No. 33). reprint ed. 27.00 (*0-404-50933-9*) AMS Pr.

Schema in Clinical Psychoanalysis. Joseph Slap & Laura Slap-Shelton. 184p. 1991. 29.95 (*0-88163-089-6*) Analytic Pr.

Schema Theory Based Analysis of Voter Intent in 1980: Use of a Schema-Model in a Qualitative Choice Estimation. L. L. Loeffler. Ed. by M. E. Nelson. (Illus.). 617p. 1996. 995.00 (*1-56471-004-1*) Annenberg.

Schemamonk Mark of Sarov. 1996. pap. 0.50 (*0-89981-167-1*) Eastern Orthodox.

Schemas. Beauvois. (C). 1996. pap. text ed. 26.75 (*0-15-501282-7*) HB Coll Pubs.

Schemas. Beauvois. (C). 1996. teacher ed., pap. text ed. 28.00 (*0-15-501702-0*) HB Coll Pubs.

Schemas in Problem Solving. Sandra P. Marshall. (Illus.). 350p. (C). 1995. text ed. 49.95 (*0-521-43072-0*) Cambridge U Pr.

Schemata. Beverly Moser et al. 304p. (C). 1996. pap. text ed. 23.75 (*0-03-010104-2*) HB Coll Pubs.

S

S

*Schematic Capture with Microsim PSpice. 3rd ed. Herniter. LC 97-22470. (C). 1998. pap. 37.33 (0-13-629494-4) P-H.

Schematic Capture with PSpice. 2nd ed. Marc E. Herniter. LC 95-38051. 448p. (C). 1995. pap. text ed. 46.00 (0-13-233982-X) P-H.

Schematic Diagrams: The Basics of Interpretation & Use. J. Richard Johnson. (Illus.). 208p. 1994. pap. 16.95 (0-7906-1059-0) Prompt Publns.

Schematic Replica of the Cardiac Cycle. Bernard M. Bane. 45p. 1981. pap. 3.00 (0-930924-11-8) BMB Pub Co.

Schematic Wiring, a Step-by-Step Guide. Stanley Aglow. LC 91-39158. 248p. 1991. 22.95 (0-912524-66-9) Busn News.

Schematics Computation. Little & Vincent C. Manis. 1995. lab manual ed., pap. text ed. 16.80 (0-13-834714-X) P-H.

Schematics of Computation. Vincent C. Manis & James J. Little. LC 94-21432. 608p. 1995. text ed. 59.00 (0-13-834284-9) P-H.

Schematics Reading for Beginners in Electronics. 1991. lib. bdg. 63.95 (0-8490-4765-X) Gordon Pr.

SCHEME. Patrick H. Winston. (Programming Languages Library). (C). 1996. pap. text ed. write for info. (0-201-58041-1) Addison-Wesley.

Scheme & the Art of Programming. George Springer & Daniel P. Friedman. 400p. 1989. 57.50 (0-262-19288-8); pap. 28.50 (0-262-69136-1) MIT Pr.

SCHEME & the Art of Programming. George Springer & Daniel P. Friedman. 596p. (C). 1990. pap. text ed. write for info. (0-07-060522-X) McGraw.

Scheme of Economic Theory. George L. Shackle. LC 65-14346. 221p. reprint ed. pap. 63.00 (0-317-20820-9, 2024538) Bks Demand.

Scheme of Redemption: Fifteenth Annual Spiritual Sword Lectureship. Ed. by Jim Laws. 618p. 1990. 24.00 (0-9615751-7-4) Getwell Church.

Scheme Programming Language. 2nd ed. Kent Dybbig. 272p. (C). 1996. pap. text ed. 42.00 (0-13-454646-6) P-H.

Schemer's Guide. Iain Ferguson et al. LC 91-60023. 328p. (Orig.). 1991. pap. text ed. 39.95 (0-9628745-7-4) Schemers.

Schemer's Guide. 2nd ed. Iain Ferguson et al. LC 94-62149. 330p. (Orig.). (C). 1995. pap. text ed. 39.95 (0-9628745-2-3) Schemers.

Schemer's Guide to C++ Iain Ferguson. 92p. (Orig.). (C). 1996. pap. text ed. 17.95 (1-888579-11-0) Schemers.

Schemes: The Language of Modern Algebric Geometry. David Eisenbud & Joe Harris. LC 91-45534. 160p. (C). 1992. text ed. 49.95 (0-534-17606-2); pap. text ed. 19.95 (0-534-17604-6) Chapman & Hall.

Schemes & Scams: A Practical Guide for Outwitting Today's Con Artist. Douglas P. Shadel & John T. Ed. by Gina Misiroglu. (Illus.). 256p. (Orig.). 1994. pap. 12.95 (0-87877-186-7) Newcastle Pub.

Schemes & Truth. Sharon M. Alston. 32p. 1989. write for info. (0-8062-3587-X) Macmillan.

Schemes & Undertakings: A Study of English Politics in the Seventeenth Century. Clayton Roberts. LC 85-25572. 347p. 1985. 52.50 (0-8142-0377-9); pap. 30.00 (0-8142-0402-3) Ohio St U Pr.

Schemes for the Federation of the British Empire. Seymour C. Cheng. LC 68-59048. (Columbia University. Studies in the Social Sciences: No. 335). reprint ed. 32.50 (0-404-51335-2) AMS Pr.

Schemes in the Month of March. Emilio Diaz Valcarcel. Tr. by Nancy A. Sebastiani from SPA. LC 76-45296. Orig. Title: Figuraciones en el mes de marzo. 1979. pap. text ed. 17.00 (0-916950-05-0); lib. bdg. 27.00 (0-916950-06-9) Biling Rev-Pr.

Schemes of Satan. Mike Warnke. 312p. (Orig.). 1991. pap. 9.95 (0-932081-28-2) Victory Hse.

Schemes, Scams, & Frauds: How to Protect Yourself. Wilbur Cross. 192p. 1996. mass mkt. 5.99 (0-06-101027-8) HarpC.

Scheming for the Poor: The Politics of Redistribution in Latin America. William Ascher. LC 83-12866. (Illus.). 360p. 1984. 37.00 (0-674-79085-5) HUP.

Scheming for Youth: A Study of the YTS in the Enterprise Culture. David Lee et al. 208p. 1990. 90.00 (0-335-15193-0); pap. 34.00 (0-335-15192-2) Taylor & Francis.

Scheming Papists & Lutheran Fools: Five Reformation Satires. Tr. & Intro. by Erika Rummel. LC 92-34382. 112p. (Orig.). (C). 1993. 25.00 (0-8232-1482-6); pap. 15.00 (0-8232-1483-4) Fordham.

Scheming Women: Poetry, Privilege, & the Politics of Subjectivity. Cynthia Hogue. LC 94-47463. (SUNY Series in Feminist Criticism & Theory). 262p. (C). 1995. text ed. 59.50 (0-7914-2621-1); pap. text ed. 19.95 (0-7914-2622-X) State U NY Pr.

*Schenbeck - Shanebeck - Shanbeck Family Record, 1798-1959. Safara Shanebeck. (Illus.). 142p. 1996. reprint ed. pap. 25.00 (0-8328-5424-7); reprint ed. lib. bdg. 35.00 (0-8328-5423-9) Higginson Bk Co.

Schenectady: A Pictorial History. Larry Hart. (Illus.). 252p. (Orig.). 1984. pap. text ed. 16.95 (0-932035-07-8) Old Dorp Bks.

Schenectady: Facts & Stuff. Larry Hart. 20p. 1991. pap. text ed. 1.75 (0-932035-12-4) Old Dorp Bks.

*Schenectady, Ancient & Modern: A Complete & Connected History of Schenectady from the Granting of the First Patent in 1661 to 1914. Joel H. Monroe. (Illus.). 285p. 1997. reprint ed. lib. bdg. 35.00 (0-8328-6227-4) Higginson Bk Co.

*Schenectady County: Its History to the Close of the Nineteenth Century. With Biographical Sketches. Ed. by Austin A. Bates. (Illus.). 721p. 1997. reprint ed. lib. bdg. 75.00 (0-8328-6231-2) Higginson Bk Co.

Schenectady's Golden Era: 1880-1930. Larry Hart. (Illus.). 351p. 1996. pap. 19.95 (0-932035-02-7) Old Dorp Bks.

Schenker's Argument & the Claims of Music Theory. Leslie D. Blasius. (Cambridge Studies in Music Theory & Analysis: No. 9). 200p. (C). 1996. text ed. 44.95 (0-521-55085-8) Cambridge U Pr.

*Schenker's Interpretive Practice. Robert Snarrenberg. (Cambridge Studies in Music Theory & Analysis: No. 11). 250p. (C). 1997. 59.95 (0-521-49726-4) Cambridge U Pr.

*Scherenschnitte: Designs & Techniques for Traditional Papercutting. Susanne Schlapfer-Geiser. Ed. by Carol Taylor. (Illus.). 144p. 1996. 18.95 (1-887374-18-3) Lark Books.

Scherenscnitte: Traditional Paper Cutting Reminiscent of the Pennsylvania Germans. 1977. 3.00 (0-911410-44-9) Applied Arts.

Schering Symposium on Biodynamics & Mechanism of Action of Steroid Hormones, Berlin 1968 see Advances in the Biosciences

Schering Symposium on Immunopathology see Advances in the Biosciences

Schering Symposium on Intrinsic & Extrinsic Factors in Early Mammalian Development, Venice 1970 see Advances in the Biosciences

Schering Symposium on Mechanisms Involved in Conception, Berlin 1969 see Advances in the Biosciences

Schering Workshop in Pharmacokinetics, Berlin 1969 see Advances in the Biosciences

Schering Workshop on Central Action of Estrogenic Hormones see Advances in the Biosciences

Schering Workshop on Prognostic Factors in Human Acute Leukemia see Advances in the Biosciences

Schering Workshop on Steroid Hormone "Receptors," Berlin, 1970 see Advances in the Biosciences

Schering Workshop on Virus - Cell Interaction see Advances in the Biosciences

*Schermerhorn Family Dutch Connection. K. C. Koster. Ed. by Horace S. Schermerhorn. 43p. 1996. reprint ed. pap. 9.50 (0-8328-5224-4); reprint ed. lib. bdg. 19.50 (0-8328-5223-6) Higginson Bk Co.

*Schernoff Discoveries. LC 96-45390. (J). 1997. 15.95 (0-385-32194-5) Delacorte.

Scherz und Ernst: A German Intermediate Oral Reader. Ed. by Kenneth E. Keeton. LC 67-15832. (Orig.). (GER.). 1967. pap. text ed. 6.95 (0-89197-389-3) Irvington.

*Scherzi, I Believe. Lance Olsen. 130p. 1994. 9.95 (1-877655-11-2) Wordcraft Oregon.

Scherzo (Hommage A'Prokofieff) Piano Duet. Harold Zabrack. (Orig.). 1979. pap. 3.95 (0-934286-14-0) Kenyon.

Scherzo Tartantelle, Op. 16: For Violin & Piano. H. Wieniawski. Ed. by Theodore Spiering. (Carl Fischer Music Library: No. 806). 1917. pap. 6.95 (0-8258-0090-0, L806) Fischer Inc NY.

Scherzofrenia. Georgette W. Amowitz. 1990. spiral bd. 15.00 (1-878084-04-6) Danscores.

*Schiaparelli. Baudot. Date not set. 18.95 (0-7893-0116-4) St Martin.

*Schiaparelli Fashion Review Paper Dolls. Tom Tierney. (Illus.). pap. 4.95 (0-486-25658-8) Dover.

Schick Anatomy Charts. (WC Ser.). 8.95 (0-685-12055-4) Am Map.

Schick Anatomy Set. Schick. 1993. pap. 29.95 (0-8416-1444-X, 61444X) Am Map.

Schicksal und Dichtung: Goethe Aufsaetze Ed. by Wieland Schmidt. Edwin Redslob. 145p. (GER.). 1985. 63.10 (3-11-010472-5) De Gruyter.

Schiedsgericht. Menander. Ed. by Ulrich Von Wilamowitz-Moellendorff. viii, 219p. 1974. write for info. (3-296-14600-8) G Olms Pubs.

Schiele. Tim Marlow. 112p. 1994. 14.98 (0-8317-6115-6) Smithmark.

*Schiele. Christopher Short. (Color Library). (Illus.). 128p. 1997. pap. 14.95 (0-7148-3393-2, Pub. by Phaidon Press UK) Chronicle Bks.

*Schiele. R. Steiner. 1994. pap. text ed. 9.99 (3-8228-0553-X) Taschen Amer.

Schiele Drawings: Forty Four Works. Egon Schiele. LC 94-20436. (Art Library). (Illus.). 1994. write for info. (0-486-28150-7) Dover.

Schiff. (Meyers Klien Kinderbibliothek). 24p. (GER.). (J). 13.25 (3-411-08571-1) Langenscheidt.

Schildburger. Marchen. unabridged ed. Tieck. (World Classic Literature Ser.). (GER.). pap. 5.95 (3-89507-041-6, Pub. by Bookking Intl FR) Distribks Inc.

Schilddruesentumoren. Ed. by K. Krisch. (Beitraege zur Onkologie, Contributions to Oncology Ser.: Vol. 16). (Illus.). vi, 82p. 1983. pap. 33.00 (3-8055-3695-X) S Karger.

Schilder: Preserver of the Faith. 1996. 15.00 (0-533-11637-6) Vantage.

Schilder's Struggle for the Unity of the Church. Rudolf Van Reest. Tr. & Intro. by Theodore Plantinga. 464p. 1990. 26.60 (0-921100-23-X) Inhtce Pubns.

Schildkrotenspiel see Mensch und Zeit: An Anthology of German Radio Plays

Schildt's Advanced Windows 95 Programming in C & C++ Herbert Schildt. 512p. 1996. pap. text ed. 29.95 (0-07-882174-6) McGraw.

Schildt's Expert C++ Herbert Schildt. 540p. 1996. pap. text ed. 34.95 (0-07-882209-2) McGraw.

Schildt's Windows 95 Programming in C & C++ Programming in C & C++ Herbert Schildt. 512p. 1995. pap. text ed. 29.95 (0-07-882081-2) McGraw.

Schillebeeckx. Philip Kennedy. Ed. by Brian Davies. (Outstanding Christian Thinkers Ser.). 160p. (Orig.). 1993. pap. text ed. 12.95 (0-8146-5502-5, M Glazier) Liturgical Pr.

Schillebeeckx Case. Ed. by Ted Schoof. (Orig.). 1990. 15.25 (0-8446-6132-5) Peter Smith.

Schiller. William Witte. LC 74-31030. (Studies in German Literature: No. 13). 1974. lib. bdg. 49.95 (0-8383-1946-7) M S G Haskell Hse.

Schiller. Henry B. Garland. LC 76-39809. (Illus.). 280p. 1977. reprint ed. text ed. 59.75 (0-8371-9084-3, GASC, Greenwood Pr) Greenwood.

Schiller: Die Rauber. Ed. by F. Lamport. (German Texts Ser.). 192p. (GER.). 1996. pap. 16.95 (1-85399-318-2, Pub. by Brstl Class Pr UK) Focus Pub-R Pullins.

Schiller & His Poetry. William H. Hudson. LC 71-120989. (Poetry & Life Ser.). reprint ed. 16.00 (0-404-52519-9) AMS Pr.

Schiller, Hegel, & Marx: State, Society, & the Aesthetic Ideal of Ancient Greece. Phillip J. Kain. 1982. 55.00 (0-7735-1004-4, Pub. by McGill CN) U of Toronto Pr.

*Schiller in Italy: Schiller's Reception in Italy: 19th & 20th Centuries. Edmund Kostka. LC 96-7119. (California Studies in German & European Romanticism & in the Age of Goethe: Vol. 3). 176p. (C). 1997. text ed. 41.95 (0-8204-3332-2) P Lang Pubng.

Schiller, Poet of Freedom, Vol. II. William F. Wertz. (Illus.). (Orig.). (C). 1988. 15.00 (0-9621095-1-7) Schiller Inst.

Schiller, Poet of Freedom, Vol. III. William F. Wertz. LC 90-62731. (Illus.). (Orig.). 1990. pap. 15.00 (0-9621095-2-5) Schiller Inst.

Schiller, Sein Leben, und Seine Werke, Set, Vols. 1 & 2. rev. ed. Karl Berger. LC 70-178909. (BCL Ser. I). (Illus.). reprint ed. Set. 165.00 (0-404-00790-2) AMS Pr.

Schiller Seventeen Fifty-Nine to Nineteen Fifty-Nine: Commemorative American Studies. Johann C. Schiller. Ed. by John R. Frey. LC 59-10551. (Illinois Studies in Language & Literature: Vol. 46). 222p. reprint ed. pap. 63.30 (0-317-08234-5, 2004186) Bks Demand.

Schiller to Derrida: Idealism in Aesthetics. Juliet Sychrava. 264p. (C). 1989. text ed. 69.95 (0-521-36027-7) Cambridge U Pr.

Schiller's Aesthetic Essays: Two Centuries of Criticism. Lesley Sharpe. (LCGERM Ser.). xiii, 138p. (C). 1995. 55.95 (1-57113-058-6) Camden Hse.

*Schiller's Historical Dramas: The Critical Legacy. Kathy Saranpa. (LCGERM Ser.). Date not set. write for info. (1-57113-047-0) Camden Hse.

Schillers Junge Idealisten. Rolf N. Linn. LC 71-182546. (University of California Publications in Social Welfare: Vol. 106). 96p. reprint ed. pap. 27.40 (0-317-29557-8, 2021258) Bks Demand.

Schillers Personlichkeit, 3 vols. in 1. Max Hecker & Julius Petersen. 1976. reprint ed. write for info. (3-487-05969-X) G Olms Pubs.

*Schillinger System of Musical Compsition, 2 vols. Joseph Schillinger. Incl. 2. . LC 77-21709. 1978. reprint ed. lib. bdg. 115.00 (0-306-77522-0); 205.00 (0-306-77552-2) Da Capo.

Schimmelreiter. Erzahlungen. unabridged ed. Storm. (World Classic Literature Ser.). (GER.). pap. 7.95 (3-89507-013-0, Pub. by Bookking Intl FR) Distribks Inc.

Schimmelreiter, Storm: Critical Monographs in English. Mark G. Ward. 64p. 1993. pap. 32.00 (0-85261-256-7, Pub. by Univ of Glasgow UK) St Mut.

Schindler's Legacy: True Stories of the List Survivors. Elinor J. Brecher. (Illus.). 442p. 1994. pap. 14.95 (0-452-27353-6, Plume) NAL-Dutton.

Schindler's List. Thomas Keneally. 400p. 1993. pap. 12.00 (0-671-88031-4, Touchstone Bks) S&S Trade.

Schindler's List. Thomas Keneally. 1994. 25.00 (0-671-51688-4) S&S Trade.

Schinkel Guide. (Illus.). (Orig.). pap. 19.95 (1-878271-10-5) Princeton Arch.

Schinkel's Berlin: A Study in Environmental Planning. Hermann G. Pundt. LC 75-172325. (Illus.). 283p. reprint ed. pap. 80.70 (0-7837-4181-2, 2059030) Bks Demand.

Schippel the Plumber. C. P. Taylor. 1994. pap. 5.95 (0-87129-240-8, SA2) Dramatic Pub.

Schipperke Champions, 1952-1987. Camino E. E. & Bk. Co. Staff. 242p. 1989. pap. 36.95 (0-940808-86-2) Camino E E & Bk.

Schipperke Champions, 1988-1993. Camino E. E. & Bk. Co. Staff. (Illus.). 90p. 1994. pap. 32.95 (1-55893-035-3) Camino E E & Bk.

Schipperkes, AKC Rank No. 50. Darwin J. Martin. (KW Dog Ser.). (Illus.). 224p. 1996. pap. 9.95 (0-7938-2352-8, KW161S) TFH Pubns.

Schirmer Biographical Dictionary of Dance. Mcquade. 1998. 95.00 (0-02-864677-0) Mac Lib Ref.

Schirmer Biographical Dictionary of Dance. Mcquade. 1998. 95.00 (0-02-860306-0) Schirmer Bks.

Schirmer Biographical Dictionary of Dance. Mcquade. Date not set. 95.00 (0-02-864511-1) Schirmer Bks.

Schirmer Guide to Schools of Music & Conservatories Throughout the World. Nancy Uscher. 635p. 1988. 90.00 (0-02-873030-5) Schirmer Bks.

*Schirmer Inheritance. Eric Ambler. 3.95 (0-7867-0767-4) Carroll & Graf.

Schirmer Inheritance. Eric Ambler. 208p. 1991. pap. 3.95 (0-88184-767-4) Carroll & Graf.

Schirmer Pronouncing Pocket Manual of Musical Terms. 5th ed. Ed. by Theodore Baker. 350p. 1995. 5.95 (0-02-874567-1) Schirmer Bks.

*Schirmer Pronouncing Pocket Manual of Musical Terms. 5th rev. ed. 1997. pap. 5.95 (0-8256-9390-X, GS 10026) Music Sales.

Schirra's Space. Walter M. Schirra. LC 95-24817. (Bluejacket Bks.). (Illus.). 240p. 1995. pap. 14.95 (1-55750-792-9) Naval Inst Pr.

Schism & Continuity in an African Society: A Study of Ndembu Life. Victor Turner. 352p. 1996. pap. 22.95 (0-85496-282-4) Berg Pubs.

Schism & Continuity in an African Society: A Study of Ndembu Life. Victor Turner. 652p. 1996. reprint ed. 52.95 (1-85973-110-4) Berg Pubs.

Schism in Accounting. Robert Bloom et al. LC 93-5445. 168p. 1994. text ed. 55.00 (0-89930-699-3, Quorum Bks) Greenwood.

Schism in England: La Cisma de Inglaterra. Calderon De la Barca. (Hispanic Classics Ser.). 1990. 49.95 (0-85668-331-0, Pub. by Aris & Phillips UK); pap. 22.00 (0-85668-332-9, Pub. by Aris & Phillips UK) David Brown.

Schism in High Society: Granville Waldergrave Lord Radstock & His Followers. Nikolai Leskov. Tr. by James Muckle. 1995. 30.00 (0-9517853-5-4, Pub. by Bramcote Pr UK) Intl Spec Bk.

Schism in High Society: Granville Waldergrave Lord Radstock & His Followers. Nikolai Leskov. Tr. by James Muckle. 1995. pap. 19.95 (0-9517853-4-6, Pub. by Bramcote Pr UK) Intl Spec Bk.

Schism in the Early Church: Edward Cadbury Lectures, 1949-50. Stanley L. Greenslade. LC 82-45818. (Orthodoxies & Heresies in the Early Church Ser.). reprint ed. 28.50 (0-404-62384-0) AMS Pr.

Schism in the Methodist Episcopal Church, 1844. John H. Norwood. LC 76-10284. (Perspectives in American History Ser.: No. 33). 255p. 1976. reprint ed. lib. bdg. 37.50 (0-87991-357-6) Porcupine Pr.

Schism or Not? The Episcopal Consecrations of Archbishop Marcel Lefebore. Francois Pivert. 50p. 1995. pap. text ed. 3.95 (0-935952-54-3) Angelus Pr.

Schismatics, Sectarians, Dissidents, Deviants: The First One Hundred Years of Jewish-Christian. Jack T. Sanders. LC 93-24087. 428p. 1993. pap. 30.00 (1-56338-065-X) TPI PA.

*Schismatrix Plus: Includes Schismatrix & Selected Stories from Crystal Express. Bruce Sterling. 304p. 1996. pap. 13.00 (0-441-00370-2) Ace Bks.

Schistosoma Mansoni: The Parasite Surface in Relation to Host Immunity. Diane J. McLaren. LC 80-40955. (Tropical Medicine Research Studies: No. 1). (Illus.). 245p. reprint ed. pap. 69.90 (0-8357-3527-3, 2034247) Bks Demand.

Schistosomes: Development, Reproduction & Host Relations. Paul F. Basch. (Illus.). 264p. 1991. 69.00 (0-19-505807-0) OUP.

Schistosomes, Liver Flukes, & Helicobacter Pylori. (IARC Monographs on the Evaluation of Carcinogenic Risks to Humans: Vol. 61). 270p. 1994. pap. text ed. 70.00 (92-832-1261-4, 1720061) World Health.

Schistosomiasis Control: Proceedings of the WHO Expert Committee, Geneva, 1972. WHO Staff. (Technical Report Ser.: No. 515). 1973. pap. text ed. 6.00 (92-4-120515-6, 1100515) World Health.

Schistosomiasis in Egypt. Ed. by M. F. Abd-El-Wahab. 256p. 1982. 142.00 (0-8493-6220-2, RC182, CRC Reprint) Franklin.

Schistosomiasis in Twentieth Century Africa: Historical Studies on West Africa & Sudan. K. David Patterson & Gerald W. Hartwig. 1984. pap. 15.00 (0-918456-54-1) African Studies Assn.

Schiwetz Legacy: An Artist's Tribute to Texas, 1910-1971. E. M. Schiwetz. (Illus.). 144p. 1972. 32.50 (0-292-77502-4) U of Tex Pr.

Schizoid Phenomena, Object Relations & the Self. Harry Guntrip. LC 68-56426. 438p. 1969. 65.00 (0-8236-5985-2) Intl Univs Pr.

Schizophrenia. Ed. by Steven Hirsch & Daniel Weinberger. LC 94-26616. (Illus.). 656p. 1995. 135.00 (0-632-03276-6, Pub. by Blckwell Sci Pubns UK) Blackwell Sci.

Schizophrenia. Douglas W. Smith. LC 92-21140. (Venture Bks.). (Illus.). 112p. (YA). (gr. 7-12). 1993. lib. bdg. 22.00 (0-531-12514-9) Watts.

Schizophrenia. Ed. by Eckart R. Straube & Kurt Hahlweg. (Illus.). 256p. 1990. 70.00 (0-387-50573-3) Spr-Verlag.

Schizophrenia. John S. Strauss & William T. Carpenter. (Critical Issues in Psychiatry Ser.). 232p. 1981. 49.50 (0-306-40704-3, Plenum Med Bk) Plenum.

Schizophrenia. Patrick Young. (Encyclopedia of Health Ser.). (Illus.). 120p. (YA). (gr. 7 up). 1988. lib. bdg. 19.95 (0-7910-0052-4) Chelsea Hse.

Schizophrenia: A Guide for Sufferers, Family & Friends. Jacqueline M. Atkinson. 144p. (Orig.). 1985. pap. 8.99 (0-85500-216-6, Pub. by Turnstone Pr) HarpC.

Schizophrenia: A Neuropsychological Perspective. Christos Pantelis et al. LC 96-25494. 470p. 1996. text ed. 89.95 (0-471-96644-4) Wiley.

Schizophrenia: A Scientific Delusion. Mary Boyle. 256p. (C). 1993. pap. 24.95 (0-415-09700-2, B2359) Routledge.

Schizophrenia: An Integrated Approach to Research & Treatment. Max Birchwood et al. 432p. (C). 1989. text ed. 36.00 (0-8147-1125-1) NYU Pr.

Schizophrenia: An Integrated Approach to Research & Treatment. Max Birchwood et al. 432p. (C). 1992. pap. 18.50 (0-8147-1181-2) NYU Pr.

Schizophrenia: An International Follow-up Study. World Health Organization Staff. LC 78-17808. 456p. reprint ed. pap. 130.00 (0-685-20662-9, 2030448) Bks Demand.

Schizophrenia: An Overview & Practical Handbook. Kavanagh. 478p. 1992. 76.50 (1-56593-054-1, 0360) Singular Publishing.

*Schizophrenia: Breaking Down the Barriers. Stephen G. Holliday et al. LC 96-2847. 1996. text ed. write for info. (0-471-96703-3) Wiley.

An Asterisk (*) at the beginning of an entry indicates that the title is appearing in BIP for the first time.

Schizophrenia: Current Concepts & Research. D. Siva Sankar. LC 70-95390. 1969. 49.95 (0-9600290-0-1) PJD Pubns.

Schizophrenia: Emperical Research and Findings. Eckart R. Straube. (Personality, Psychopathology & Psychotherapy Ser.). (Illus.). 637p. 1992. text ed. 69.00 (0-12-673010-5) Acad Pr.

Schizophrenia: Exploring the Spectrum of Psychosis. Ed. by R. J. Ancill et al. LC 94-21813. 376p. 1995. text ed. 125.00 (0-471-95255-9) Wiley.

Schizophrenia: From Mind to Molecule. Ed. by Nancy C. Andreasen. LC 93-9585. (American Psychopathological Association Ser.). 278p. 1994. text ed. 34.00 (0-88048-950-2, 8950) Am Psychiatric.

***Schizophrenia: From the Mind of a Black Man.** unabridged ed. Antwan Worsham. 160p. (Orig.). 1996. pap. 10.00 (1-56411-155-5, 4BBG157) Untd Bros & Sis.

***Schizophrenia: Latest Advances in Understanding & Drug Development.** Ed. by Lori Dirks. (Biomedical Library). 296p. 1996. pap. 795.00 (1-57936-016-5) IBC USA.

Schizophrenia: Manifestation, Incidence & Course in Different Cultures. A. Jablensky et al. (Psychological Medicine Monograph Supplements Ser.: No. 20). (Illus.). 50p. (C). 1993. pap. 23.95 (0-521-42328-7) Cambridge U Pr.

Schizophrenia: Medical & Psychological Subject Index with Bibliography. Harold P. Drummond. LC 87-31833. 150p. 1987. 44.50 (0-88164-496-X); pap. 39.50 (0-88164-497-8) ABBE Pubs Assn.

Schizophrenia: Origins, Processes, Treatment, & Outcome. Ed. by Rue L. Cromwell & C. R. Snyder. LC 92-48996. 384p. 1993. 110.00 (0-19-506922-6) OUP.

Schizophrenia: Psychotic Continuum or Distinct Entities. Ed. by Ming T. Tsuang et al. LC 94-47536. 1995. write for info. (0-387-58820-5) Spr-Verlag.

Schizophrenia: Psychotic Continuum or Distinct Entities. Ed. by Ming T. Tsuang et al. LC 94-47536. 1995. 77.95 (3-540-58820-5) Spr-Verlag.

Schizophrenia: Recent Biosocial Developments. Costas N. Stefanis & Andreas D. Rabuilas. LC 86-27353. 286p. 1987. 43.95 (0-89885-345-1) Human Sci Pr.

Schizophrenia: Science & Practice. Ed. by John C. Shershow. LC 78-6317. (Illus.). 256p. 1978. 29.00 (0-674-79112-6) HUP.

Schizophrenia: Scientific Progress. Ed. by S. Charles Schulz & Carol A. Tamminga. (Illus.). 448p. 1989. 65.00 (0-19-505527-6) OUP.

Schizophrenia: Selected Papers. David Shakow. LC 76-45548. (Psychological Issues Monograph: No. 38). 354p. 1977. 50.00 (0-8236-6003-6); pap. 42.50 (0-8236-6002-8) Intl Univs Pr.

Schizophrenia: Symptoms, Causes, Treatments. Kayla F. Bernheim & Richard R. Lewine. (Illus.). (C). 1979. pap. text ed. 11.95 (0-393-09017-5) Norton.

Schizophrenia: The Experience & Its Treatment. Werner M. Mendel et al. LC 76-20083. (Jossey-Bass Behavioral Science Ser.). 192p. reprint ed. pap. 54.80 (0-8357-4995-9, 2037928) Bks Demand.

***Schizophrenia: The Facts.** Stanley Farraone & Ming T. Tsuang. (The Facts Ser.). 176p. 1997. pap. 17.95 (0-19-262760-0) OUP.

Schizophrenia: The First Ten Dean Award Lectures. Ed. by Stanley R. Dean. LC 73-6815. 1973. text ed. 29.50 (0-8422-7115-5) Irvington.

Schizophrenia: The Major Issues. Bebbington. 262p. 1988. 95.00 (0-433-00045-7) Buttrwrth-Heinemann.

***Schizophrenia: The Positive Perspective, in Search of Dignity for Schizophrenic People.** Peter K. Chadwick. LC 96-40143. 240p. (C). 1997. pap. write for info. (0-415-14288-1); text ed. write for info. (0-415-14287-3) Routledge.

Schizophrenia: The Sacred Symbol of Psychiatry. Thomas Szasz. LC 87-26769. (Illus.). 237p. (C). 1988. reprint ed. pap. 14.95 (0-8156-0224-3) Syracuse U Pr.

Schizophrenia: Treatment of Acute Psychotic Episodes. Ed. by Stephen T. Levy & Philip T. Ninan. LC 89-17556. 224p. 1990. text ed. 36.00 (0-88048-164-1, 8164) Am Psychiatric.

Schizophrenia: Treatment Process & Outcome. Thomas H. McGlashan & Christopher J. Keats. LC 88-24228. 207p. 1989. text ed. 32.00 (0-88048-281-8, 8281) Am Psychiatric.

***Schizophrenia & Bipolar Disease: Often Misdiagnosed, often Mistreated.** Herbert Wagemaker. Ed. by Ann Bucholz. (Illus.). 160p. (Orig.). 1996. pap. 12.00 (0-9654996-1-8) Ponte Vedra Pub.

Schizophrenia & Civilization. E. Fuller Torrey. LC 79-51931. 240p. 1979. 30.00 (0-87668-380-4) Aronson.

Schizophrenia & Manic-Depressive Disorder: The Biological Roots of Mental Illness as Revealed by the Landmark Study of Identical Twins. E. Fuller Torrey et al. (Illus.). 304p. 1995. pap. 16.50 (0-465-07285-2) Basic.

***Schizophrenia & Primitive Mental States: Structural Collapse & Creativity.** Peter L. Giovacchini. LC 96-26148. 288p. 1997. pap. 45.00 (0-7657-0027-1) Aronson.

Schizophrenia & Related Syndromes. P. J. McKenna. (Illus.). 352p. 1994. bds. 89.50 (0-19-261780-X) OUP.

Schizophrenia & the Family. rev. ed. Theodore Lidz & Stephen Fleck. LC 65-23613. 494p. 1985. 62.50 (0-8236-6001-X, 06001) Intl Univs Pr.

Schizophrenia & the Family: A Practitioner's Guide to Psychoeducation & Management. Carol M. Anderson et al. LC 85-17218. 365p. 1986. lib. bdg. 41.95 (0-89862-065-1) Guilford Pr.

Schizophrenia As a Brain Disease. Ed. by Fritz A. Henn & Henry A. Nasrallah. (Illus.). 320p. (C). 1982. text ed. 39.95 (0-19-503088-5) OUP.

Schizophrenia at Home. Jacqueline M. Atkinson. 200p. (C). 1986. text ed. 36.00 (0-8147-0586-3) NYU Pr.

***Schizophrenia from a Neurocognitive Perspective: Probing the Impenetrable Darkness.** Michael F. Green. 1997. 50.25 (0-205-18477-4) Allyn.

Schizophrenia Genesis: The Origins of Madness. Irving L. Gottesman. (C). 1995. pap. text ed. write for info. (0-7167-2147-3) W H Freeman.

Schizophrenia in Focus: Guidelines for Treatment & Rehabilitation. David Dawson et al. 190p. 1983. 32.95 (0-89885-096-7) Human Sci Pr.

Schizophrenia Simplified: A Field Guide to the Social, Medical, & Legal Complexities. Ed. by Mary V. Seeman & J. F. Thornton. LC 91-20806. (Illus.). 160p. 1995. reprint ed. spiral bd. 16.95 (0-920887-17-1) Hogrefe & Huber Pubs.

Schizophrenia, Theory, Diagnosis, & Treatment: Proceedings. International Symposium on Psychopharmacology Staff. Ed. by Herman C. Denber. LC 78-14831. 256p. reprint ed. pap. 73.00 (0-7837-0824-6, 2041138) Bks Demand.

***Schizophrenia 1993: A Special Report.** Ed. by David Shore & Samuel J. Keith. (Illus.). 273p. (C). 1996. reprint ed. pap. 45.00 (0-7881-3152-4) DIANE Pub.

Schizophrenias: A Biological Approach to the Schizophrenia Spectrum Disorders. Mary Coleman & Christopher Gillberg. (Series on Psychiatry). (Illus.). 320p. 1996. 46.95 (0-8261-9290-4) Springer Pub.

Schizophrenic Disorders: Long-Term Patient & Family Studies. Manfred Bleuler. Tr. by Siegfried M. Clemens. LC 75-43303. 553p. reprint ed. pap. 157.70 (0-7837-3283-X, 2057685) Bks Demand.

Schizophrenic Disorders: Sense & Nonsense. L. C. Whitaker. (Perspectives on Individual Differences Ser.). (Illus.). 270p. 1992. 39.50 (0-306-44156-X, Plenum Pr) Plenum.

Schizophrenic Disorders: Theory & Treatment from a Psychodynamic Point of View. Ping-Nie Pao. LC 77-92180. 456p. 1979. 70.00 (0-8236-5990-9) Intl Univs Pr.

Schizophrenic Psychology: Index of New Information with Authors, Subjects & Bibliography. Harold P. Drummond. 180p. 1993. 47.50 (1-55914-810-1); pap. 44.50 (1-55914-811-X) ABBE Pubs Assn.

Schizophrenics in the Community: An Experimental Study in the Prevention of Hospitalization. Benjamin Pasamanick et al. LC 66-25455. (Illus.). 1967. 29.50 (0-89197-390-7) Irvington.

Schizophrenics in the New Custodial Community: Five Years after the Experiment. Ann E. Davis et al. LC 74-11383. 242p. 1974. 35.00 (0-8142-0215-2) Ohio St U Pr.

Schizophyceen der Plankton-Expedition der Humboldt-Stiftung. N. Wille. (Illus.). 1968. reprint ed. 25.20 (3-7682-0808-7) Lubrecht & Cramer.

Schizotext & Other Poems: Esquizotexto y Otros Poemas. Gonzalo Rojas. Ed. by Howard Quackenbush & Russel Cluff. 135p. (ENG & SPA.). (C). 1988. text ed. 34.00 (0-8204-0561-2) P Lang Pubng.

Schizotypal Personality. Ed. by Adrian Raine et al. (Illus.). 300p. (C). 1995. text ed. 95.00 (0-521-45422-0) Cambridge U Pr.

***Schizotypy: Implications for Illness & Health.** Ed. by Gordon Claridge. (Illus.). 336p. 1997. 105.00 (0-19-852353-X) OUP.

Schlaf, Kindchen, Schlaf! Mesopotamische Baby-Beschworungen und-Rituale. Walter Farber. LC 88-8012. (Mesopotamian Civilizations Ser.: Vol. 2). xii, 196p. (GER.). (C). 1989. text ed. 39.50 (0-931464-44-7) Eisenbrauns.

Schlag Nach Uber Rotary. David H. Bailey & Louise Gottlieb. Ed. by Willmon L. White & Mark Perlberg. (Illus.). 506p. (GER.). 1982. 16.75 (0-915062-11-9) Rotary Intl.

Schlagwortkatalog der Universitatsbibliothek Kiel Bis, 1988. (GER.). 1992. write for info. incl. fiche (0-318-70557-5) G Olms Pubs.

***Schlangen: Grundlagen Erfolgreicher Haltung und Zucht.** Friedrich Golder. (Illus.). 200p. (Orig.). 1996. pap. 32.95 (3-930612-04-6, Pub. by Edition Chimaira GW) Bibliomania.

Schleiermacher als Kirchengeschichtler: Mit Edition der Nachschrift Karl Rudolf Hagenbachs von 1821-22. Joachim Boekels. (Schleiermacher-Archiv Ser.: Vol. 13). xii, 488p. (GER.). (C). 1994. lib. bdg. 183.10 (3-11-014203-1) De Gruyter.

Schleiermacher & die Wissenschaftliche Kultur des Christentums. Guenter Meckenstock. (Theologische Bibliothek Toepelmann Ser.: Vol. 51). xvi, 521p. (GER.). (C). 1991. lib. bdg. 152.35 (3-11-012857-8) De Gruyter.

Schleiermacher & Feminism: Sources, Evaluations, & Responses. Ed. by Iain G. Nicol. LC 92-26504. (Schleiermacher Studies & Translations: Vol. 12). 140p. 1992. text ed. 69.95 (0-7734-9587-8) E Mellen.

Schleiermacher in Context: Papers from the 1988 International Symposium on Schleiermacher at Herrnhut, the German Democratic Republic. Ed. by Ruth D. Richardson. LC 91-3611. (Schleiermacher Studies & Translations: Vol. 6). (Illus.). 472p. 1991. lib. bdg. 109.95 (0-7734-9793-5) E Mellen.

***Schleiermacher-Studien.** Hans-Joachim Birkner. Ed. by Hermann Fischer. (Schleiermacher-Archiv Ser.: Vol. 16). (Illus.). xvi, 421p. (GER.). (C). 1996. lib. bdg. 146.70 (3-11-014253-8, 125/96) De Gruyter.

Schleiermacher the Theologian: The Construction of the Doctrine of God. Robert R. Williams. LC 77-78650. 218p. reprint ed. pap. 62.20 (0-685-15499-8, 2026892) Bks Demand.

Schleiermacher und Claus Harms: Von den Reden "Uber die Religion" zur Nachfolge an der Dreifaltigkeitskirche. Hans-Friedrich Traulsen. (Schleiermacher Archiv Ser.: Vol. 7). ix, 320p. (C). 1989. lib. bdg. 86.95 (3-11-012056-9) De Gruyter.

Schleiermachers Bibliothek: Bearbeitung des Faksimilierten Rauchschen Auktionskatalogs & der Hauptbuecher des Verlages G. Reimer. Ed. by Guenter Meckenstock. (Schleiermacher-Archiv Ser.: Bd 10). vii, 349p. (GER.). (C). 1993. lib. bdg. 152.35 (3-11-013619-8) De Gruyter.

Schleiermachers Briefwechsel, Verzeichnis, Nebst Einer Liste Seiner Vorlesungen. Ed. by Andreas Arndt & Wolfgang Virmond. vii, 337p. (GER.). (C). 1992. lib. bdg. 98.50 (3-11-013189-7) De Gruyter.

***Schleiermachers Hermeneutische Dialektik.** Maciej Potepa. (Studies in Philosophical Theology: Vol. 15). 226p. 1993. pap. 37.50 (90-390-0221-5, Pub. by KOK Pharos NE) Eisenbrauns.

***Schleiermacher's Introductions to the Dialogue of Plato.** Friedrich D. Schleiermacher. Tr. by William Dobson. 454p. write for info. (1-85506-176-7) Bks Intl VA.

Schleiermachers Philosophie. Wolfgang H. Pleger. x, 207p. (GER.). (C). 1988. lib. bdg. 26.15 (3-11-011706-1) De Gruyter.

Schleiermacher's Philosophy & the Philosophical Tradition. Ed. by Sergio Sorrentino. LC 92-29515. (Schleiermacher Studies & Translations: Vol. 11). 160p. 1992. text ed. 69.95 (0-7734-9168-6) E Mellen.

Schleiermachers Predigt. 2nd ed. Wolfgang Trillhaas. (Theologische Bibliothek Toepelmann Ser.: Vol. 28). (C). 1975. 63.10 (3-11-005739-5) De Gruyter.

Schleiermachers Programm der Philosophischen Theologie. Martin Roessler. (Schleiermacher-Archiv Ser.: Bd. 14). 247p. (GER.). (C). 1994. lib. bdg. 121.55 (3-11-014171-X) De Gruyter.

Schleiermachers System als Philosophie und Theologie see Leben Schleiermachers

Schleiermachers Theorie der Froemmigkeit: Ihr Wissenschaftlicher Ort und Ihr Systematischer Gehalt In den Reden, In der Glausbenslehre und In der Dialektikk. Christian Albrecht. (Schleiermacher-Archiv Ser.: No. 15). xvii, 350p. (GER.). 1993. lib. bdg. 152.35 (3-11-014172-8) De Gruyter.

Schleitheim Confession. Tr. by John H. Yoder. 32p. 1977. pap. 2.99 (0-8361-1831-6) Herald Pr.

Schlemiel As Metaphor: Studies in Yiddish & American Jewish Fiction. enl. rev. ed. Sanford Pinsker. 216p. (C). 1991. 29.95 (0-8093-1581-5) S Ill U Pr.

Schlemiel Comes to America. Ezra Greenspan. LC 83-14399. 258p. 1983. 25.00 (0-8108-1646-6) Scarecrow.

Schlesisches Tonkunstler-Lexikon. Ed. by Kobmaly & Carlo. 322p. 1982. reprint ed. write for info. (3-487-07237-8) G Olms Pubs.

Schlichten Papers. Donald Wirtshafter. 116p. 1994. pap. 19.95 (0-9642097-2-1) Ohio Hempery.

***Schlichtung Bd. 2: Konfliktstoff: Gespraechsanalyse der Konfliktbearbeitung in Schlichtungsgespraechen.** Werner Nothdurft. (Schriften Des Instituts Fuer Deutsche Sprache: Vol. 5.2). vi, 195p. (GER.). (C). 1996. lib. bdg. 91.45 (3-11-013623-6) De Gruyter.

Schlichtung Vol. 1: Streit Schlichten - Gespraechsanalytische Untersuchungen Zu Institutionellen Formen Konsensueller Konfliktregelung. Ed. by Werner Nothdurft. (Schriften Des Instituts Fuer Deutsche Sprache: Vol. 5.1). viii, 431p. (GER.). 1996. lib. bdg. 158.50 (3-11-013508-6) De Gruyter.

Schlieffen Plan & the Strategy of the Central Powers in the East. Graydon A. Tunstal, Jr. write for info. (0-318-60325-X) Brooklyn Coll Pr.

Schlieffen Plan, Critique of a Myth. Gerhard A. Ritter & B. Liddell Hart. LC 78-9962. (Illus.). 195p. 1979. reprint ed. text ed. 35.00 (0-313-20757-7, RISCH, Greenwood Pr) Greenwood.

Schliemann Defense. Leonid Shamkovich & Eric Schiller. 125p. (Orig.). 1993. pap. 9.95 (0-945470-32-0) Chess Ent.

***Schliemann Defense Vol. 2: Classical Variation.** Legnid Shamkovich & Eric Schiller. 100p. (Orig.). 1996. pap. 9.95 (0-945470-60-6) Chess Ent.

***Schliemann of Troy.** Traill. 1997. pap. 16.95 (0-312-15647-2) St Martin.

Schliemann of Troy: Treasure & Deceit. David A. Traill. LC 95-40767. 320p. 1995. 24.95 (0-312-14042-8) St Martin.

Schliemann's Excavations. Carl Schuchhardt. Tr. by Eugenie Sellers. LC 74-77893. (Illus.). 419p. 1975. pap. 20.00 (0-89005-034-1) Ares.

Schliemann's Excavations: An Archaeological & Historical Study. Charles Schuchardt. LC 74-173145. (Illus.). 1972. reprint ed. 42.95 (0-405-08938-4) Ayer.

Schlo Pillnitz. 2nd ed. H. G. Hartman. 64p. 1994. pap. text ed. 11.00 (3-364-00222-3) Gordon & Breach.

Schloss. Franz Kafka. 416p. (GER.). 1994. pap. 13.50 (3-596-12444-1, Pub. by Fischer Taschbch Verlag GW) Intl Bk Import.

Schluessel zum Werk von Paul Tillich: Textgeschichte und Bibliographie sowie Register zu den Gesammelten Werken. Ed. by Renate Albrecht & Werner Schussler. (Gesammelte Werke Ser.: Band 14). 344p. (C). 1990. lib. bdg. 67.70 (3-11-012039-9) De Gruyter.

Schlumberger Cambridge Research Centre: Cambridge 1985 Michael Hopkins & Partners. David Jenkins. (Architecture in Detail Ser.). (Illus.). 60p. (C). 1993. pap. 29.95 (0-7148-2774-6, Pub. by Phaidon Press UK) Chronicle Bks.

Schlumpf Automobile Collection. Ed. by Halwart Schrader. LC 89-61985. (Illus.). 182p. 1989. pap. 19.95 (0-88740-192-9) Schiffer.

Schmalkald Articles. Martin Luther. 1994. pap. 10.00 (0-8006-2661-3, Fortress Pr) Augsburg Fortress.

Schmerzbehandlung in der Rheumatologie. Ed. by G. Kaganas et al. (Fortbildungskurse fuer Rheumatologie Ser.: Vol. 8). (Illus.). xii, 248p. 1989. 50.50 (3-8055-4901-6) S Karger.

Schmerzmessung und Schmerzdiagnostik: Methoden, Analysen, Ergebnisse am Beispiel Rheumatischer Erkrankungen. O. B. Scholz. (Illus.). xiv, 288p. 1994. 80.00 (3-8055-5792-2) S Karger.

Schmetterlinge Baden-Wuerttembergs, Vol. 1: Tagfalter One. G. Ebert et al. (Illus.). 552p. (GER.). 1991. lib. bdg. 55.00 (3-8001-3451-9, Pub. by Ulmer Verlog GW) Lubrecht & Cramer.

Schmick's Mahican Dictionary. Carl Masthay. LC 86-90530. (Memoirs Ser.: Vol. 197). 188p. (C). 1992. 30.00 (0-87169-197-3, M197-MAC) Am Philos.

Schmidt American Government 95-96. Date not set. teacher ed., pap. text ed. write for info. (0-314-05467-7); student ed., pap. text ed. 20.00 (0-314-05468-5) West Pub.

Schmidt-Focke's Discus Book. Eduard Schmidt-Focke. 1991. 35.95 (0-86622-077-1, TS-135) TFH Pubns.

Schmidt's Anatomy of a Successful Dental Practice. Duane A. Schmidt. LC 96-33681. 1996. 44.95 (0-87814-585-0) PennWell Bks.

***Schmidts von Plettenberg: A Chronicle of a German-American Family.** Frederick P. Schmidt. (Illus.). 544p. 1996. write for info. (0-614-20344-9) Aardvark.

Schmitty's Short Stories & Poems, Vol. II. Lloyd Schmidt. LC 86-90506. 128p. 1987. per. 10.00 (0-8187-0100-5) Harlo Press.

Schmo Must Go On. Mike Thaler. LC 93-4317. (Funny Firsts Ser.). (Illus.). 32p. (J). (gr. k-3). 1994. lib. bdg. 11.89 (0-8167-3519-0) Troll Communs.

Schmo Must Go On. Mike Thaler. LC 93-4317. (Funny Firsts Ser.). (Illus.). 32p. (J). (gr. k-3). 1994. pap. 2.95 (0-8167-3520-4) Troll Communs.

***Schmoe White & the Seven Dorfs.** Mike Thaler. (Happily Ever Laughter Ser.). 1997. pap. 2.99 (0-590-89824-8, Cartwheel) Scholastic Inc.

***Schmoozing: The Private Conversations of Amerian Jews.** Joshua Halberstam. LC 97-3530. 272p. 1997. pap. 13.00 (0-399-52157-7, Perigee Bks) Berkley Pub.

Schmuck der Achameniden. Ellen Rehm. (Altertumskunde des Vorderen Orients Ser.: Vol. 2). (Illus.). xii, 468p. (GER.). 1992. 91.00 (3-927120-11-1, Pub. by UGARIT GW) Eisenbrauns.

Schnabel House: Brentwood, California 1990 Frank Gehry. James Steele. (Architecture in Detail Ser.). (Illus.). 60p. (C). 1993. pap. 29.95 (0-7148-2749-5, Pub. by Phaidon Press UK) Chronicle Bks.

Schnauzers: Everything about Purchase, Care, Nutrition, & Breeding. Fredric L. Frye. 1988. pap. 6.95 (0-8120-3949-1) Barron.

Schneider on Schneider: The Conversion of the Jews & Other Anthropological Stories. David M. Schneider. Ed. & Told to Richard Handler. LC 95-10338. (Illus.). 224p. 1995. text ed. 44.95 (0-8223-1679-X); pap. text ed. 14.95 (0-8223-1691-9) Duke.

Schnell Was Feines, Natuerlich Frisch fuer Dich und Mich. Olli Leeb. (Illus.). 209p. (GER.). 1989. 20.50 (3-921799-81-3, Pub. by Olli Leeb GW) Lubrecht & Cramer.

Schnetterlinge Badeb-Wuerttembergs, Vol. 2: Tagfalter Two. G. Ebert et al. (Illus.). 535p. (GER.). 1991. lib. bdg. 55.00 (3-8001-3459-4, Pub. by Ulmer Verlog GW) Lubrecht & Cramer.

Schnitzel Von Krumm's Basketwork. Lynley Dodd. LC 94-14560. (Illus.). 32p. (J). (gr. 1 up). 1994. lib. bdg. 18.60 (0-8368-1149-6) Gareth Stevens Inc.

Schnitzler, Hofmannsthal, & the Austrian Theatre. W. E. Yates. (Illus.). 320p. (C). 1992. text ed. 40.00 (0-300-05742-3) Yale U Pr.

Schnorky the Wave Puncher. Jeff Raglus. LC 95-40887. 40p. (J). (gr. 1 up). 1996. 15.00 (0-517-70924-4, Crown) Crown Pub Group.

Schocken Book of Contemporary Jewish Fiction. Ed. by Ted Solotaroff & Nessa Rapoport. 416p. 1996. reprint ed. pap. 14.00 (0-8052-1065-2) Schocken.

***Schocken Book of Jewish Mystical Testimonies: A Unique & Inspiring Collection of Accounts by People Who Have Encountered God, from Biblical Times to the Present.** Louis Jacobs. 1998. pap. 15.00 (0-8052-1091-1) Schocken.

***Schocken Book of Jewish Mystical Testimonies: Personal Testimonies from Across the Ages.** Louis Jacobs. 1997. 25.00 (0-8052-4143-4) Schocken.

Schocken Passover Haggadah. Ed. by Nahum N. Glatzer. (Illus.). 176p. 1996. reprint ed. pap. 11.00 (0-8052-1067-9) Schocken.

Schoenberg. (Dent Master Musicians Ser.). (Illus.). (C). pap. write for info. (0-614-07881-4) OUP.

Schoenberg: "Pierrot Lunaire" Jonathan Dunsby. (Cambridge Music Handbooks Ser.). (Illus.). 100p. (C). 1992. 29.95 (0-521-38279-3); pap. text ed. 11.95 (0-521-38715-9) Cambridge U Pr.

Schoenberg: Articles by Arnold Schoenberg, Erwin Stein & Others, 1929-1937. Ed. by Merle Armitage. LC 79-106709. 319p. 1977. reprint ed. text ed. 59.75 (0-8371-3439-0, ARSC); reprint ed. fiche 11.80 (0-8371-9600-0); reprint ed. fiche 20.65 (0-8371-9599-3) Greenwood.

Schoenberg: Nineteen Twenty-Nine to Nineteen Thirty-Seven. Ed. by Merle Armitage. LC 77-157360. (Select Bibliographies Reprint Ser.). 1980. reprint ed. 23.95 (0-8369-5783-0) Ayer.

Schoenberg & His School: The Contemporary Stage of the Language of Music. Rene Leibowitz. Tr. by Dika Newlin from FRE. LC 75-115338. (Music Ser.). 1970. reprint ed. lib. bdg. 37.50 (0-306-71930-4) Da Capo.

Schoenberg & the God-Idea: The Opera "Moses und Aron" Pamela C. White. Ed. by George Buelow. LC 85-1033. (Studies in Musicology: No. 83). 340p. reprint ed. 100.70 (0-8357-1647-3, 2070447) Bks Demand.

Schoenberg & the New Music. Carl Dahlhaus. Tr. by Derrick Puffett & Alfred Clayton. (Illus.). 300p. 1989. pap. text ed. 23.95 (0-521-33783-6) Cambridge U Pr.

An Asterisk (*) at the beginning of an entry indicates that the title is appearing in BIP for the first time.

Schoenberg Discography. 2nd expanded rev. ed. R. Wayne Shoaf. LC 94-29347. (Reference Books in Music: Vol. 18). x, 264p. (Orig.). 1994. 45.00 (*0-914913-24-7*) Fallen Leaf.

Schoenberg Remembered: Diaries & Recollections 1938-1976. Dika Newlin. LC 79-19128. (Illus.). 1980. 36.00 (*0-918728-14-2*) Pendragon NY.

Schoenberg's Error. William Thomson. LC 90-28313. (Studies in the Criticism & Theory of Music). (Illus.). 288p. (C). 1991. text ed. 41.95 (*0-8122-3088-4*) U of Pa Pr.

Schoenberg's Serial Odyssey: The Evolution of His Twelve-Tone Method, 1914-1928. Ethan Haimo. (Illus.). 208p. 1993. reprint ed. pap. 23.00 (*0-19-816352-5*) OUP.

Schoenberg's Twelve-Tone Harmony: The Suite Op. 29 & the Compositional Sketches. Martha M. Hyde. LC 81-16369. (Studies in Musicology: No. 49). 171p. reprint ed. pap. 48.80 (*0-685-20814-1*, 2070030) Bks Demand.

Schoene Ist Angekommen: Ein Grammatikkrimi. L. M. Brand et al. 80p. (GER.). (C). 1995. pap. text ed. 17.00 (*3-12-675318-3*, Pub. by Klett Edition GW) Intl Bk Import.

Schoenhut Dolls: A Collector's Encyclopedia. Carol Corson. 272p. 1993. pap. 39.95 (*0-87588-400-8*) Hobby Hse.

Schoepfung aus dem Nichts: Die Entstehung der Lehre von der Creatio Ex Nihilo. Gerhard May. (Arbeiten zur Kirchengeschichte Ser.: Vol. 48). (C). 1978. 86.95 (*3-11-007204-1*) De Gruyter.

Schofer: Johan Georg Schofer Family History, Containing Records of Antecedents in Europe, Account of Migration to America in 1832, Biographical Sketches of Members of the Family in This Country. Henry M. Schofer. (Illus.). 180p. 1993. reprint ed. pap. 29.50 (*0-8328-2981-1*); reprint ed. lib. bdg. 39.50 (*0-8328-2980-3*) Higginson Bk Co.

Schoffler-Weis German & English Dictionary. 1062p. (ENG & GER.). 1994. 19.95 (*0-8442-2878-8*, Natl Textbk) NTC Pub Grp.

Schofield's Election Law. Ed. by A. J. Little. (C). 1982. ring bd. 650.00 (*0-7219-0344-4*, Pub. by Scientific UK) St Mut.

Schola Illustris: The Roxbury Latin School, 1645-1995. F. Washington Jarvis. (Illus.). 640p. 1996. 40.00 (*1-56792-066-7*) Godine.

Scholae Academicae: Some Account of Studies at English Universities in the 18th Century. Christopher Wordsworth. LC 79-93271. xii, 435p. 1969. reprint ed. 49.50 (*0-678-05085-6*) Kelley.

Scholae Academicae: Some Account of the Studies at the English Universities in the Eighteenth Century. Christopher Wordsworth. 435p. 1968. reprint ed. 35.00 (*0-7146-1450-5*, Pub. by F Cass Pubs UK) Intl Spec Bk.

Scholae in Liberales Artes. Petrus Ramus. Ed. by Walter J. Ong. xvi, 1166p. 1970. reprint ed. write for info. (*0-318-71275-X*) G Olms Pubs.

Scholae in Liberales Artes. Petrus Ramus. xvi, 1166p. (GER.). 1970. reprint ed. write for info. (*0-318-70504-4*); reprint ed. write for info. (*0-318-71467-1*) G Olms Pubs.

Scholar Adventurer: A Tribute to John D. Gordan (1907-1968) on the Eightieth Anniversary of His Birth with Six of His Essays. John D. Gordan. LC 87-18136. (Illus.). xxvi, 133p. (Orig.). 1987. pap. 10.00 (*0-87104-294-0*) NY Pub Lib.

Scholar Adventurers. Richard D. Altick. LC 87-11064. 340p. 1987. reprint ed. pap. 22.50 (*0-8142-0435-X*) Ohio St U Pr.

***Scholar & the Serving Maid.** Fang Ai. 209p. 1994. pap. 6.95 (*0-8351-3141-6*) China Bks.

Scholar & the Serving Maid: A Qing Dynasty Mystery. Fang Ai. Tr. by Yu Fanquin & Esther Samson. 210p. 1994. pap. 10.95 (*7-5071-0224-6*) Cheng & Tsui.

Scholar & the State: And Other Orations & Addresses. Henry C. Potter. LC 72-4509. (Essay Index Reprint Ser.). 1977. reprint ed. 23.95 (*0-8369-2969-1*) Ayer.

Scholar at Work: An Exhibit. Sally Leach. 53p. 1975. 12.00 (*0-87959-119-6*); pap. 6.00 (*0-87959-120-X*) U of Tex H Ransom Ctr.

Scholar Gardens of China: A Study & Analysis of the Spatial Design of the Chinese Private Garden. R. Stewart Johnston. (Illus.). 360p. (C). 1991. 159.95 (*0-521-39477-5*) Cambridge U Pr.

Scholar of Decay. Tanya Huff. (Ravenloft Ser.). 320p. (Orig.). 1995. pap. 5.99 (*0-7869-0206-X*) TSR Inc.

Scholar Painters of Japan: The Nanga School. James Cahill. LC 74-27413. (Asia Society Ser.). (Illus.). 1976. reprint ed. lib. bdg. 36.95 (*0-405-06562-0*) Ayer.

Scholar, Patriot, Mentor. Ed. by Richard B. Spence & Linda L. Nelson. 320p. 1992. text ed. 56.50 (*0-88033-217-4*) Col U Pr.

Scholar Warrior: An Introduction to the Tao in Everyday Life. Dang Ming-Dao. LC 89-46453. (Illus.). 320p. (Orig.). 1990. pap. 22.00 (*0-06-250232-8*) Harper SF.

***Scholarly Book Reviewing in the Social Sciences & Humanities: The Flow of Ideas Within & among Disciplines.** Ylva Lindholm-Romantschuk. (Contributions in Librarianship & Information Science: 91). 1998. text ed. write for info. (*0-313-29514-X*, Greenwood Pr) Greenwood.

***Scholarly Communication: The Report of the National Enquiry.** LC 79-51420. 192p. 1979. reprint ed. pap. 54.80 (*0-608-04078-9*, 2064810) Bks Demand.

Scholarly Communication & Bibliometrics. Ed. by Christine L. Borgman. (Illus.). 336p. (C). 1990. 49.95 (*0-8039-3879-9*) Sage.

Scholarly Communication & Serials Prices. Ed. by Karen Brookfield. (British Library Research Ser.). 160p. 1991. lib. bdg. 45.00 (*0-86291-478-7*) Bowker-Saur.

Scholarly Disciplines see **Asia in the Making of Europe**

Scholarly Editing: A Guide to Research. Ed. by D. C. Greetham. LC 94-30207. vii, 740p. (Orig.). 1995. pap. 23.00 (*0-87352-561-2*, T127P); lib. bdg. 45.00 (*0-87352-560-4*, T127) Modern Lang.

Scholarly Editing in the Computer Age: Theory & Practice. 3rd ed. Peter L. Shillingsburg. LC 96-18342. 1995. 42.50 (*0-472-09600-1*) U of Mich Pr.

Scholarly Editing in the Computer Age: Theory & Practice. 3rd ed. Peter L. Shillingsburg. LC 96-18342. 1995. pap. 17.95 (*0-472-06600-5*) U of Mich Pr.

Scholarly Information & Standardization: Proceedings of the 12th Open Forum on the Study of the International Exchange of Japanese Information... Ed. by William E. Moen. (National Information Standards Ser.). 123p. 1994. 40.00 (*1-880124-06-8*) NISO.

Scholarly Journals at the Crossroads: A Subversive Proposal for Electronic Publishing. Ed. by Ann Okerson & James O'Donnell. 250p. 1995. pap. 20.00 (*0-918006-26-0*) ARL.

Scholarly Means to Evangelical Ends: The New Haven Scholars & the Transformation of Higher Learning in America, 1830-1890. Louise L. Stevenson. LC 85-27502. (New Studies in American Intellectual & Cultural History). 240p. 1986. text ed. 38.50 (*0-8018-2695-0*) Johns Hopkins.

Scholarly Priviledges in the Middle Ages. Pearl Kibre. LC 60-16435. (Medieval Academy Bks.: No. 72). 1962. 35.00 (*0-910956-46-4*) Medieval Acad.

Scholarly Publishing: The Electronic Frontier. Gregory B. Newby. Ed. by Robin P. Peek. (Illus.). 450p. (C). 1996. 35.00 (*0-262-16157-5*) MIT Pr.

***Scholarly Religious Libraries in North America: A Statistical Examination.** John F. Harvey & Jo Ann Mourides. LC 97-8405. 1997. write for info. (*0-8108-3341-7*) Scarecrow.

Scholarly Writing for Law Students-Seminar Papers, Law Review Notes & Law Review Competition Papers. Elizabeth Fajans & Mary R. Falk. 177p. (C). 1994. pap. 13.50 (*0-314-05661-0*) West Pub.

Scholarmanship: Or How to Succeed in College Without Really Trying. John Fox. 1986. 12.95 (*0-940416-04-2*) Bacchus Pr.

Scholars. Wu Ching-tzu. Tr. by Yang Hsien-yi & Glagys Yang from CHI. LC 92-24471. (Illus.). 448p. (C). 1993. pap. 22.00 (*0-231-08153-7*, Mrngside); text ed. 45.00 (*0-231-08152-9*, Mrngside) Col U Pr.

Scholars & Dollars: Politics, Economics, & the Universities of Ontario 1945-1980. Paul Axelrod. (State & Economic Life Ser.). 388p. 1982. pap. 17.95 (*0-8020-6492-2*) U of Toronto Pr.

Scholars & Gentlemen. John Priest. 336p. (C). 1990. 78.00 (*0-86439-013-0*, Pub. by Boolarong Pubns AT) St Mut.

Scholars & Gentlemen: Shakespearean Textual Criticism & Representations of Scholarly Labour, 1725-1765. Simon Jarvis. 240p. 1995. text ed. 49.95 (*0-19-818295-3*) OUP.

Scholars & Gypsies: An Autobiography. Walter Starkie. LC 63-22845. 336p. reprint ed. pap. 95.80 (*0-685-44497-X*, 2031516) Bks Demand.

Scholars & Personal Computers: Microcomputing in the Human & Social Sciences. George M. Kren. LC 86-27615. 209p. 1988. 35.95 (*0-89885-358-3*) Human Sci Pr.

Scholars & Scholarship: The Interaction Between Judaism & Other Cultures. Ed. by Leo Landman. 1991. 25.00 (*0-88125-344-8*) Ktav.

Scholars & Their Publishers. Ed. by Weldon A. Kefauver. LC 77-91126. 59p. (Orig.). 1977. pap. text ed. 10.00 (*0-87352-005-X*, S3100) Modern Lang.

Scholars' Bedlam: Menippean Satire in the Renaissance. W. Scott Blanchard. LC 94-19757. 208p. 1995. 35.00 (*0-8387-5281-0*) Bucknell U Pr.

Scholar's Conscience: Selected Writings of J. Saunders Redding. Ed. by Faith Berry. (Illus.). 248p. 1992. text ed. 37.00 (*0-8131-1770-4*); pap. text ed. 15.00 (*0-8131-0806-3*) U Pr of Ky.

Scholars, Dollars, & Bureaucrats. Chester E. Finn, Jr. LC 78-13363. (Studies in Higher Education Policy). 238p. 1978. 9.95 (*0-8157-2828-X*) Brookings.

Scholar's Guide to Academic Journals in Religion. James Dawsey. LC 88-18104. (American Theological Library Association Monograph). 316p. 1989. 32.50 (*0-8108-2135-4*) Scarecrow.

Scholar's Guide to Geographical Writing on the American & Canadian Past. Ed. by Michael P. Conzen et al. (Geography Research Papers: No. 235). 760p. 1993. pap. text ed. 33.00 (*0-226-11569-0*) U Ch Pr.

Scholar's Guide to Intelligence Literature: Bibliography of the Russell J. Bowen Collection. Ed. by Marjorie W. Cline et al. LC 83-80922. 256p. 1983. text ed. 69.50 (*0-313-27048-1*, U7048, Greenwood Pr) Greenwood.

Scholar's Guide to the Humanities & Social Sciences in the Soviet Successor States: The Academies of Sciences of Russia, Armenia, Azerbaidzhan, Belarus, Estonia, Georgia, Kazakhstan, Kyrgyzstan, Latvia, Lithuania, Moldova, Tadzhikistan, Turkmenistan, Ukraine & Uzbekistan. 2nd ed. Compiled by Institute of Scientific Information in the Social Sciences Staff et al. LC 92-6306. 256p. (gr. 13). 1993. text ed. 215.00 (*0-87332-831-0*) M E Sharpe.

Scholars' Guide to Washington, D. C. for African Studies. Purnima M. Bhatt. LC 79-607774. (Scholar's Guide to Washington D.C. Ser.: No. 4). 348p. (Orig.). 1980. text ed. 29.95 (*0-87474-238-2*, Johns Hopkins); pap. text ed. 12.95 (*0-87474-239-0*, Johns Hopkins) W Wilson Ctr Pr.

Scholars' Guide to Washington, D. C. for Cartography & Remote Sensing Imagery. Ralph E. Ehrenberg. LC 86-600371. (Scholar's Guide to Washington D.C. Ser.). 420p. 1987. 29.95 (*0-87474-406-7*, Johns Hopkins); pap. 15.00 (*0-87474-407-5*, Johns Hopkins) W Wilson Ctr Pr.

Scholars' Guide to Washington, D. C., for Central & East European Studies: Albania, Austria, Bulgaria, Czechoslovakia, Germany (FRG & GDR), Greece (Ancient & Modern), Hungary, Poland, Romania, Switzerland, & Yugoslavia. Kenneth J. Dillon. Ed. by Zdenek V. David. LC 80-607019. 330p. 1991. 27.50 (*0-87474-368-0*, Johns Hopkins); pap. text ed. 11.95 (*0-87474-367-2*, Johns Hopkins) W Wilson Ctr Pr.

Scholars' Guide to Washington, D. C., for East Asian Studies: China, Japan, Korea, & Mongolia. Hong N. Kim. Ed. by Zdenek V. David. LC 79-17344. 414p. 1991. 22.50 (*0-87474-582-9*, Johns Hopkins); pap. text ed. 12.95 (*0-87474-581-0*, Johns Hopkins) W Wilson Ctr Pr.

Scholars' Guide to Washington, D. C., for Latin American & Caribbean Studies. rev. ed. Michael Grow. Ed. by Craig VanGrasstek. LC 92-12589. (Scholars' Guide to Washington, D. C. Ser.: No. 2). 380p. 1992. pap. 19.95 (*0-943875-37-4*) Johns Hopkins.

Scholars' Guide to Washington, D. C., for Latin American & Caribbean Studies. 2nd rev. ed. Michael Grow. Ed. by Craig VanGrasstek. LC 92-12589. (Scholars' Guide to Washington, D. C. Ser.: No. 2). 380p. 1992. 60.00 (*0-943875-36-6*) Johns Hopkins.

Scholars' Guide to Washington, D. C., for Middle Eastern Studies: Egypt, Sudan, Jordan, Lebanon, Syria, Iraq, the Arabian Peninsula, Israel, Turkey, & Iran. Steven R. Dorr. Ed. by Zdenek V. David. LC 81-607073. 564p. 1991. 29.95 (*0-87474-372-9*, Johns Hopkins); pap. text ed. 15.00 (*0-87474-371-0*, Johns Hopkins) W Wilson Ctr Pr.

Scholars' Guide to Washington, D. C., for Northwest European Studies: Belgium, Denmark, Finland, Great Britain, Greenland, Iceland, Ireland, Luxembourg, the Netherlands, Norway, & Sweden. Louis A. Pitschmann. Ed. by Zdenek V. David. LC 84-600036. 452p. 1991. 29.95 (*0-87474-754-6*, Johns Hopkins); pap. text ed. 15.00 (*0-87474-753-8*, Johns Hopkins) W Wilson Ctr Pr.

Scholar's Guide to Washington, D. C., for Peace & International Security Studies. Robert W. Janes & Katherine R. Tromble. LC 95-14677. (Scholars' Guide to Washington, D. C. Ser.). 436p. 1995. pap. text ed. 24.95 (*0-8018-5219-6*) Johns Hopkins.

Scholar's Guide to Washington, D. C., for Peace & International Security Studies. Robert W. Janes et al. LC 95-14677. (Scholars' Guide to Washington, D. C. Ser.: No. 15). 436p. 1995. text ed. 65.00 (*0-8018-5218-8*) Johns Hopkins.

Scholars' Guide to Washington, D. C. for South Asian Studies: Afghanistan, Bangladesh, Bhutan, India, Maldives, Nepal, Pakistan, & Sri Lanka. Enayetur Rahim. LC 81-607847. (Scholar's Guide to Washington D.C. Ser.: No. 8). 438p. 1991. pap. 12.95 (*0-87474-777-5*, Johns Hopkins); text ed. 29.95 (*0-87474-778-3*, Johns Hopkins) W Wilson Ctr Pr.

Scholars' Guide to Washington, D. C., for Southeast Asian Studies: Brunei, Burma, Cambodia, Indonesia, Laos, Malaysia, Philippines, Singapore, Thailand, & Vietnam. Patrick M. Mayerchak. Ed. by Zdenek V. David. LC 82-19454. 412p. 1991. 29.95 (*0-87474-626-4*, Johns Hopkins); pap. text ed. 12.95 (*0-87474-625-6*, Johns Hopkins) W Wilson Ctr Pr.

Scholars' Guide to Washington, D. C. for Southwest European Studies. Joan F. Higbee. (Scholar's Guide to Washington D.C. Ser.: Vol. 13). 500p. (C). 1989. pap. text ed. 27.50 (*0-943875-11-0*, Johns Hopkins); lib. bdg. 49.50 (*0-943875-12-9*, Johns Hopkins) W Wilson Ctr Pr.

Scholar's Guide to Washington, D.C. for Audio Resources: Sound Recordings in the Arts, Humanities, & Social, Physical, & Life Sciences. James R. Heintze. LC 84-600234. (Scholar's Guide to Washington D.C. Ser.). 410p. 1985. 29.95 (*0-87474-516-0*, Johns Hopkins); pap. 15.00 (*0-87474-517-9*, Johns Hopkins) W Wilson Ctr Pr.

Scholars' Guide to Washington, D.C., for Media Collections. Bonnie G. Rowan & Cynthia Wood. (Woodrow Wilson Center Press Ser.). 208p. (C). 1994. text ed. 45.00 (*0-943875-54-4*); pap. text ed. 19.95 (*0-943875-55-2*) Johns Hopkins.

Scholars' Guide to Washington, D.C., for Russian, Central Eurasian, & Baltic Studies. 3rd ed. Steven A. Grant. (Woodrow Wilson Center Press Ser.). 336p. (C). 1994. text ed. 60.00 (*0-943875-51-X*); pap. text ed. 22.75 (*0-943875-52-8*) Johns Hopkins.

Scholar's Haggadah: Ashkenazic, Sephardic, & Oriental Version. Heinrich Guggenheimer. LC 94-26392. 432p. 1995. 40.00 (*1-56821-287-9*) Aronson.

Scholars Manque & Freeway Students: Repercussions of the Baby Boom at American State Colleges. Frank A. Darknell. LC 96-85164. (Illus.). 350p. (Orig.). 1997. pap. 19.95 (*0-9647412-7-X*) Capitola Hall Pr.

***Scholars of Byzantium.** rev. ed. N. G. Wilson. 296p. (C). 1996. pap. 25.00 (*0-915651-08-4*, IND01) Medieval Acad.

Scholars of the Law: English Jurisprudence from Blackstone to Hart. Richard A. Cosgrove. LC 95-41782. 296p. (C). 1996. 45.00 (*0-8147-1533-8*) NYU Pr.

Scholars on Parade. David A. Lockmiller. 290p. 1993. pap. 15.95 (*1-57087-002-0*) Prof Pr NC.

Scholars, Savants & Their Tests: Studies in Philosophy & Religious Thought: Essays in Honor of Arthur Hyman. Ed. by Ruth Link-Salinger & Robert Herrera. 271p. (C). 1989. text ed. 48.95 (*0-8204-0834-4*) P Lang Pubng.

Scholar's Testament: Two Letters from George Edward Woodberry to J. E. Spingarn. George E. Woodberry. (American Biography Ser.). 110p. 1991. reprint ed. lib. bdg. 59.00 (*0-7812-8425-2*) Rprt Serv.

Scholars Who Teach: The Art of College Teaching. Ed. by Steven M. Cahn. LC 78-944. 258p. 1978. pap. 26.95 (*0-88229-598-5*) Nelson-Hall.

Scholars, Writers, & Professionals. Jonathan W. Bolton & Claire M. Wilson. LC 93-31683. (American Indian Lives Ser.). (Illus.). 160p. (J). (gr. 4-11). 1994. 17.95 (*0-8160-2896-6*) Facts on File.

Scholar's Zulu Dictionary (English-Zulu - Zulu-English) 4th ed. G. R. Dent. 519p. 1993. pap. 39.95 (*0-7859-8719-3*) Fr & Eur.

Scholarship. (Illus.). 80p. (J). (gr. 6-12). 1988. pap. 2.40 (*0-8395-3384-5*, 33384) BSA.

Scholarship: Extracts from the Writings of Baha'u'llah & Abdu'l-Baha & from the Letters of Shoghi Effendi & the Universal House of Justice. 64p. 1995. pap. 3.95 (*0-909991-92-8*) Bahai.

***Scholarship Advisor: The Scholarship Expert Shares His Secrets to Winning Big Money for College.** Christopher Vuturo. (Princeton Review Ser.). 1997. pap. 23.00 (*0-679-77881-0*) Random.

Scholarship & Education in Bengal. Katherine S. Diehl. (Printers & Printing in the East Indies to 1850 Ser.: Vol. VII). write for info. (*0-89241-396-4*) Caratzas.

Scholarship & Its Survival: Questions on the Idea of Graduate Education. Jaroslav J. Pelikan. LC 83-15211. 93p. 1983. pap. text ed. 6.50 (*0-931050-24-3*) Carnegie Fnd Advan Teach.

Scholarship & Nation Building: The Universities of Strasbourg & Alsatian Society, 1871-1939. John E. Craig. LC 83-24341. 528p. (C). 1984. 36.00 (*0-226-11670-0*) U Ch Pr.

Scholarship & Partisanship: Essays on Max Weber. Reinhard Bendix & Guenther Roth. 1980. reprint ed. 50.00 (*0-520-04171-2*) U CA Pr.

Scholarship & Service: The Policies & Ideals of a National University in a Modern Democracy. Nicholas M. Butler. LC 78-134066. (Essay Index Reprint Ser.). 1977. reprint ed. 23.95 (*0-8369-2220-4*) Ayer.

Scholarship & Technology in the Humanities. Ed. by Mary Katzen. (British Library Research Ser.). 196p. 1991. 50.00 (*0-86291-625-9*) Bowker-Saur.

***Scholarship Assessed: Evaluation of the Professoriate.** Charles Glassick. LC 97-4849. 1997. pap. 15.95 (*0-7879-1091-0*) Jossey-Bass.

Scholarship Book. 5th ed. Daniel J. Cassidy. 400p. 1996. text ed. 32.95 (*0-13-476078-6*); pap. text ed. 24.95 (*0-13-476060-3*) P-H.

Scholarship Book: The Complete Guide to Private Scholarships, Grants, & Loans for Undergraduates. 4th ed. Daniel J. Cassidy, & Michael J. Alves. 1993. text ed. 32.95 (*0-13-799537-7*); pap. text ed. 21.95 (*0-13-799545-8*) P-H.

Scholarship Book: The Complete Guide to Private-Sector Scholarships, Grants, & Loans for Undergraduates. 2nd ed. Daniel J. Cassidy & Michael J. Alves. 1987. 29.95 (*0-13-792425-9*); 19.95 (*0-13-792417-8*) P-H.

Scholarship Consulting Packet. Catherine A. Gullo. 61p. 1993. spiral bd. 19.95 (*1-883374-03-0*) Scholar Cnslt.

Scholarship in Museums: Roles & Responsibilities. Wayne Craven, Jr. et al. 73p. (C). 1989. pap. 12.00 (*0-925050-02-4*) U Del Mus Studies Prog.

Scholarship of William Foxwell Albright. Gus W. Van Beek. (Harvard Semitic Studies). 73p. 1989. 17.95 (*1-55540-314-X*, 04 04 33) Scholars Pr GA.

Scholarship Reconsidered: Priorities of the Professoriate. Ernest L. Boyer. LC 90-22684. 147p. (Orig.). 1990. pap. 8.00 (*0-931050-43-X*) Carnegie Fnd Advan Teach.

Scholarship, Research Libraries & Global Publishing. 159p. 1996. 30.00 (*0-614-16511-3*) ARL.

Scholarship, Research Libraries, & Global Publishing: The Result of a Study Funded by the Andrew W. Mellon Foundation. Jutta Reed-Scott et al. 159p. 1996. 30.00 (*0-918006-78-3*) Assn Res Lib.

Scholarship, Sacraments & Service: Historical Studies in Protestant Tradition (Essays in Honor of Bard Thompson) Ed. by Daniel B. Clendenin & W. David Buschart. LC 89-78415. (Texts & Studies in Religion: Vol. 49). 320p. 1990. lib. bdg. 99.95 (*0-88946-838-9*) E Mellen.

***Scholarships.** Kaplan Staff. 1997. pap. 25.00 (*0-684-84579-2*) Kaplan Educ.

Scholarships & Grants for Study or Research in U. S. A. A Scholarship Handbook for Foreign Nationals. 3rd ed. Ed. by Walter Wickremasinghe. LC 95-83556. 206p. (Orig.). 1996. pap. 31.95 (*0-940937-04-2*) Amer Coll Serv.

Scholarships & Loans for Nursing Education 1990-1991 (Annual) 104p. 1991. pap. 10.95 (*0-88737-505-7*) Natl League Nurse.

Scholarships & Loans for Nursing Education, 1992-1993. rev. ed. Ed. by National League for Nursing Staff. 112p. 1992. pap. text ed. 12.95 (*0-88737-560-X*) Natl League Nurse.

Scholarships & Loans for Nursing Education 1993-1994. NLN Staff. 1993. 14.00 (*0-88737-580-4*, 41-1964) Natl League Nurse.

Scholarships & Loans for Nursing Education 1994-1995. rev. ed. Rev. by National League for Nursing Staff. 118p. 1994. 15.95 (*0-88737-614-2*) Natl League Nurse.

Scholarships & Loans for Nursing Education 1996-1997. Regina Fawcett. 1996. pap. 16.95 (*0-88737-678-9*) Natl League Nurse.

Scholarships & Loans 95-96. 1995. pap. 13.95 (*0-88737-643-6*) Natl League Nurse.

Scholarships, Fellowships & Grants for Programs Aboard - A Handbook of Awards for U. S. Nationals for Study or Research Abroad. Ed. by Walter Wickremasinghe. LC 89-84074. 300p. (Orig.). 1989. pap. 29.75 (*0-940937-02-6*) Amer Coll Serv.

Scholarships Fellowships & Loans: 1997. 97th ed. Jaszczak. 1996. 155.00 (*0-7876-0092-X*) Gale.

Scholarships, Fellowships & Loans 1996, Vol. 11. 96th ed. Jaszczak. 1995. 145.00 (*0-8103-9217-0*) Gale.

S

An Asterisk (*) at the beginning of an entry indicates that the title is appearing in BIP for the first time.

***Scholarships Fellowships & Loans, 1998.** 1997. 155.00 (*0-7876-1675-3*, 00157032) Gale.

Scholarships Fellowships & Loans 92-93, Vol. 9. 92th ed. Kirby. 1991. 110.00 (*0-8103-8347-0*) Gale.

Scholarships Fellowships & Loans 94-95. 94th ed. Kirby. 1993. 140.00 (*0-8103-8532-5*) Gale.

Scholarships, Grants, Fellowships & Endowments: Free Money; Get Your Slice of the Pie (A Comprehensive Resource Guide) Loretta Johnson. (Illus.). 200p. 1996. per. 29.95 (*0-9651524-0-5*) LoKee Pub.

***Scholarships 1998.** Kaplan Staff. 1997. 25.00 (*0-684-83675-0*) S&S Trade.

Scholarum Mathematicarum Libri Unus et Triginta. Petrus Ramus. 314p. reprint ed. write for info. (*0-318-71468-X*) G Olms Pubs.

Scholary Publishers Guide: Financial & Legal Aspects. Ed. by Primary Comm. Research Centre Staff. 1979. 40.00 (*0-906083-08-7*) St Mut.

Scholastic Aptitude Test (SAT) Practice Examination Number 1. David M. Tarlow. (Practice Examination Ser.). 40p. 1992. pap. 16.95 (*0-931572-61-4*) Datar Pub.

Scholastic Aptitude Test (SAT) Practice Examination Number 3. David M. Tarlow. (Practice Examination Ser.). 40p. 1992. pap. 16.95 (*0-931572-62-2*) Datar Pub.

Scholastic Aptitude Test (SAT) Practice Examination Number 5. David M. Tarlow. (Practice Examination Ser.). 40p. 1992. pap. 16.95 (*0-931572-63-0*) Datar Pub.

Scholastic Aptitude Test (SAT) Student Guide. David M. Tarlow. (Student Guide Ser.). 120p. 1992. pap. 12.95 (*0-931572-60-6*) Datar Pub.

Scholastic Aptitude Test/SAT I (SAT) Jack Rudman. (Admission Test Ser.: ATS-21). 1994. pap. 23.95 (*0-8373-5021-2*) Nat Learn.

Scholastic Behavior of a Selected Group of Undergraduate Home Economics Students. Ruth Connor. LC 70-176667. (Columbia University. Teachers College. Contributions to Education Ser.: No. 497). reprint ed. 37.50 (*0-404-55497-0*) AMS Pr.

Scholastic Children's Dictionary. Scholastic Inc. Staff. LC 95-26237. (Illus.). 656p. (J). (gr. 3 up). 1996. text ed. 16.95 (*0-590-25271-2*, Scholastic Ref) Scholastic Inc.

***Scholastic Children's Thesaurus.** John K. Bollard. LC 97-25049. (Illus.). (J). 1998. write for info. (*0-590-96785-1*) Scholastic Inc.

Scholastic Communications & Aptitude Test. (General Aptitude & Abilities Ser.: CS-52). pap. 29.95 (*0-8373-6752-2*) Nat Learn.

***Scholastic Culture of the Middle Ages, 1000-1300.** John W. Baldwin. (Illus.). 125p. (C). 1997. reprint ed. pap. text ed. 11.95 (*0-88133-942-3*) Waveland Pr.

Scholastic Debater. Royce E. Flood & Nicholas Cripe. 99p. (C). 1990. pap. text ed. 12.95 (*0-9616489-2-9*) Educ Vid Grp.

Scholastic Dictionary of Idioms: More Than 600 Phrases, Sayings, & Expressions. Marvin Terban. (J). 1996. write for info. (*0-590-27552-6*) Scholastic Inc.

Scholastic Dictionary of Idioms: More Than 600 Phrases, Sayings, & Expressions. Marvin Terban. LC 95-16593. (Illus.). 245p. (J). (gr. 4 up). 1996. 15.95 (*0-590-27549-6*, Scholastic Ref) Scholastic Inc.

Scholastic Discovery Boxes: Animal Tracks. Scholastic Staff. (First Discovery Bks.). 32p. (J). (gr. 1-5). 1996. 11.95 (*0-590-89652-0*, Scholastic Ref) Scholastic Inc.

Scholastic Discovery Boxes: Compass. Scholastic Staff. (First Discovery Bks.). 32p. (J). (gr. 1-5). 1996. 11.95 (*0-590-89663-6*, Scholastic Ref) Scholastic Inc.

Scholastic Discovery Boxes: Movies. Scholastic Staff. (First Discovery Bks.). 32p. (J). (gr. 1-5). 1996. 11.95 (*0-590-89655-5*, Scholastic Ref) Scholastic Inc.

Scholastic Discovery Boxes: Optical Illusions. Scholastic Staff. (First Discovery Bks.). 32p. (J). (gr. 1-5). 1996. 11.95 (*0-590-89667-9*, Scholastic Ref) Scholastic Inc.

Scholastic Discovery Boxes: Planets. Scholastic Staff. (First Discovery Bks.). 32p. (J). (gr. 1-5). 1996. 11.95 (*0-590-89651-2*, Scholastic Ref) Scholastic Inc.

Scholastic Discovery Boxes: Stars. Scholastic Staff. (First Discovery Bks.). 32p. (J). (gr. 1-5). 1996. 11.95 (*0-590-89653-9*, Scholastic Ref) Scholastic Inc.

Scholastic Discovery Boxes: Temples. Scholastic Staff. (First Discovery Bks.). 32p. (J). (gr. 1-5). 1996. 11.95 (*0-590-89662-8*, Scholastic Ref) Scholastic Inc.

Scholastic Discovery Boxes: Trees. Scholastic Staff. (First Discovery Bks.). 32p. (J). (gr. 1-5). 1996. 11.95 (*0-590-89654-7*, Scholastic Ref) Scholastic Inc.

***Scholastic Encyclopedia of Sports in America.** LC 96-39775. (J). 1997. 17.95 (*0-590-69264-X*) Scholastic Inc.

Scholastic Encyclopedia of the American Indian. James Ciment. LC 95-26171. 1996. write for info. (*0-590-22791-2*) Scholastic Inc.

Scholastic Encyclopedia of the North American Indian. James Ciment. LC 95-26171. 224p. (J). (gr. 4 up). 1996. 17.95 (*0-590-22790-4*, Scholastic Ref) Scholastic Inc.

Scholastic Encyclopedia of the Presidents & Their Times. David Rubel. LC 93-11810. (Illus.). 224p. (J). (gr. 4 up). 1994. 17.95 (*0-590-49366-3*, Scholastic Ref) Scholastic Inc.

***Scholastic Encyclopedia of the United States.** Judy Bock & Rachel Kranz. LC 96-39774. (J). 1997. 17.95 (*0-590-94747-8*) Scholastic Inc.

Scholastic Encyclopedia of U. S. Women. Sheila Keenan. LC 95-26236. (Illus.). (J). 1996. write for info. (*0-590-22793-9*) Scholastic Inc.

Scholastic Encyclopedia of U. S. Women. Sheila Keenan. LC 95-26236. (Illus.). 208p. (YA). (gr. 5 up). 1996. 17.95 (*0-590-22792-0*, Scholastic Ref) Scholastic Inc.

Scholastic Environmental Atlas of the United States. Mark T. Mattson. LC 92-46757. 80p. 1993. 14.95 (*0-590-49354-X*, Scholastic Ref) Scholastic Inc.

***Scholastic First Dictionary.** Judith S. Levey & Scholastic Inc., Staff. LC 97-25050. (J). 1998. write for info. (*0-590-96786-X*) Scholastic Inc.

***Scholastic First Encyclopedia, 4 vols.** (Illus.). (J). 60.00 (*0-590-24498-1*) Scholastic Inc.

Scholastic Guide to Balanced Reading: Making It Work for You!, Grades K-2. Scholastic Staff. 1996. pap. text ed. 12.95 (*0-590-96051-2*) Scholastic Inc.

Scholastic Guide to Balanced Reading: Making It Work for You!, Grades 3-6. Scholastic Staff. 1996. pap. text ed. 12.95 (*0-590-96053-9*) Scholastic Inc.

Scholastic Guide to Checking Your Grammar. Marvin Terban. LC 92-47493. 144p. (J). 1993. 10.95 (*0-590-49454-6*) Scholastic Inc.

***Scholastic Humanism & the Unification of Europe Vol. I: Foundations.** Richard W. Southern. LC 93-47307. pap. 26.95 (*0-631-20527-6*) Blackwell Pubs.

Scholastic Humanism & the Unification of Europe Vol. I: Foundations. Richard W. Southern. LC 93-47307. (Scholastic Humanism & the Integration of Western Europe Ser.: No. 1). (Illus.). 288p. 48.95 (*0-631-19111-9*) Blackwell Pubs.

Scholastic Integrated Language Arts & Source Book. Valerie SchifferDanoff. 1995. pap. 34.95 (*0-590-49800-2*) Scholastic Inc.

Scholastic Journalism. 9th ed. Earl English et al. LC 96-7341. 376p. 1996. text ed. 32.95 (*0-8138-1356-5*); pap. text ed. 22.95 (*0-8138-1357-3*) Iowa St U Pr.

Scholastic Journalism. 9th ed. Earl English et al. LC 96-7341. (Illus.). 1996. teacher ed., pap. text ed. 5.95 (*0-8138-1358-1*) Iowa St U Pr.

Scholastic Magic: Ritual & Revelation in Early Jewish Mysticism. Michael D. Swartz. LC 96-33720. 260p. 1996. text ed. 35.00 (*0-691-01098-6*) Princeton U Pr.

Scholastic Miscellany: Anselm to Ockham. Ed. by Eugene R. Fairweather et al. LC 56-5104. (Library of Christian Classics). 454p. (C). 1982. reprint ed. pap. 25.00 (*0-664-24418-1*, Westminster) Westminster John Knox.

Scholastic Newspaper Fundamentals. Ed. by Helen F. Smith. (Illus.). 48p. (Orig.). 1986. pap. text ed. 8.50 (*0-916084-16-7*) Columbia Scholastic.

Scholastic NF F95. (J). 1995. pap. write for info. (*0-590-47943-1*) Scholastic Inc.

Scholastic Ordering & Dependence in Applied Probability. R. Szekli. LC 94-46763. (Lecture Notes in Statistics Ser.: Vol. 97). 1995. 43.95 (*0-387-94450-8*) Spr-Verlag.

Scholastic Philosophy. Jack Rudman. (Undergraduate Program Field Tests Ser.: UPFT-22). 1994. pap. 23.95 (*0-8373-6022-6*) Nat Learn.

Scholastic Rabbinism: A Literary Study of the Fathers According to Rabbi Nathan. Anthony J. Saldarini. LC 81-13564. (Brown Judaic Studies). 161p. 1982. pap. text ed. 13.95 (*0-89130-523-8*, 14-00-14) Scholars Pr GA.

Scholastic Ready-to-Use Reading Assessment Kit. Adele Fiderer. 1996. pap. text ed. 16.95 (*0-590-74401-1*) Scholastic Inc.

Scholastic Rhyming Dictionary. Sue K. Young. (Illus.). 224p. (J). (gr. 3 up). 1994. 14.95 (*0-590-49460-0*, Scholastic Ref) Scholastic Inc.

***Scholastic Rhyming Dictionary.** Sue K. Young. 1997. pap. text ed. 6.95 (*0-590-96393-7*) Scholastic Inc.

Scholastic Roots of the Spanish American Revolution. O. Carlos Stoetzer. LC 77-75797. 312p. reprint ed. pap. 89.00 (*0-7837-5620-8*, 2045529) Bks Demand.

Scholastic Student. (J). Date not set. pap. 2.95 (*0-590-26633-0*) Scholastic Inc.

Scholastic Timelines: The United States in the 20th Century. David Rubel. LC 94-45702. (J). 1995. pap. write for info. (*0-590-27135-0*, Scholastic Ref) Scholastic Inc.

Scholastic World Atlas: No. 9552, No. 695520. American Map Corp. Staff. (J). (gr. 7-9). 1993. pap. 3.95 (*0-8416-9552-0*) Am Map.

Scholastic Yearbook Fundamentals. Ed. by Charles E. Savedge. (Illus.). 68p. (Orig.). 1985. pap. text ed. 8.50 (*0-916084-13-2*) Columbia Scholastic.

Scholastica Commentaria in Primam Partem Summae Theologicae S. Thomae Aquinatis, De Deo Uno. F. Dominico Banes. Ed. by Luis Urbano. (Medieval Studies Reprint Ser.). (LAT & SPA.). reprint ed. lib. bdg. 45.00 (*0-697-00028-1*) Irvington.

Scholasticism & Politics. Jacques Maritain. LC 72-353. (Essay Index Reprint Ser.). 1977. reprint ed. 18.95 (*0-8369-2805-9*) Ayer.

Scholasticism in the Modern World. Ed. by George F. McLean. (Proceedings of the American Catholic Philosophical Association Ser.: Vol. 40). 1966. pap. 20.00 (*0-918090-00-8*) Am Cath Philo.

***Scholastic's Children's Guide to Dinosaurs.** Philip Whitfield. (Illus.). (J). 21.95 (*0-590-24329-2*) Scholastic Inc.

Schole: A Journal of Leisure Studies & Recreation Education. 3rd ed. Karla Henderson. 1991. pap. write for info. (*0-910251-41-X*) Venture Pub PA.

Scholemaster. Roger Ascham. Ed. by John E. Mayor. LC 75-161717. reprint ed. 31.50 (*0-404-00409-1*) AMS Pr.

Scholemaster: Or, Plaine & Perfite Way of Teachyng Children the Latin Tong. Roger Ascham. LC 68-54609. (English Experience Ser.: No. 15). 134p. 1968. reprint ed. 60.00 (*90-221-0015-4*) Walter J Johnson.

***Scholemaster: 1570 Edition.** Roger Ascham. Ed. & Intro. by Jeffrey Stern. (Classics in Education Ser.). 80p. 1996. reprint ed. write for info. (*1-85506-266-6*) Bks Intl VA.

Scholia: Studia ad Criticam. Ed. by W. J. Aerts et al. vi, 168p. 1985. pap. 35.00 (*90-6980-001-2*, Pub. by Egbert Forsten NE) Benjamins North Am.

Scholia Ad Libros E - I Continens see Scholia Graeca in Homeri Iliadem: Scholia Vetera

Scholia Ad Libros K-(Z) Continens see Scholia Graeca in Homeri Iliadem: Scholia Vetera

Scholia Ad Libros Y-Continens see Scholia Graeca in Homeri Iliadem: Scholia Vetera

Scholia Bernensia Ad Vergilii Bucolica Atque Georgica. Hermann Hagen. 344p. 1967. reprint ed. write for info. (*0-318-71140-0*) G Olms Pubs.

Scholia Graeca Ex Codicibus Aucta Et Emendata. Aeschylus. xviii, 548p. 1962. reprint ed. 120.00 (*0-318-70848-5*) G Olms Pubs.

Scholia Graeca in Aristophanem. Aristophanes. Ed. by Friedrich Dubner. xxxi, 726p. 1969. reprint ed. 160.00 (*0-318-70855-8*) G Olms Pubs.

Scholia Graeca in Homeri Iliadem: Scholia Vetera, 6 vols. Incl. Vol 1. Praefationem et Scholia ad libros A-D continens. Ed. by Hartmut Erbse. 545p. 1969. 415.00 (*3-11-002558-2*); Vol 2. Scholia Ad Libros E - I Continens. Hartmut Erbse. 550p. 1971. 378.00 (*3-11-003882-X*); Vol. 3. Scholia Ad Libros K-(Z) Continens. Ed. by Hartmut Erbse. 1974. 459.00 (*3-11-004641-5*); Vol. 4. Scholia Ad Libros Y-Continens. Ed. by Hartmut Erbse. 1977. 422.00 (*3-11-005770-0*); Vol. 5. Volumen Quintum, Scholia ad Libros y Continens. Ed. by Hartmut Erbse. 1977. 511.00 (*3-11-006911-3*); write for info. (*0-318-51646-2*) De Gruyter.

Scholia in Apollonium Rhodium Vetera. Apollonius Rhodius. Ed. by Karl Wendel. xxviii, 402p. (GER.). 1974. write for info. (*3-296-15400-0*) G Olms Pubs.

***Scholia in Aristophanem III 4b: Scholia in Thesmophoriazusas; Ranas; Ecclesiazusas et Plutum.** Ed. by M. Chantry. xxx, 318p. (GRE & LAT.). 1996. lib. bdg. 157.00 (*90-6980-084-5*, Pub. by Egbert Forsten NE) Benjamins North Am.

Scholia in Aristophanem. Pars I Prolegomena de Comoedia. Scholia in "Acharnenses," "Equites," "Nubes," Fasc. 1b: Scholia in Aristophanis "Acharnenses" Ed. by N. G. Wilson. ix, 153p. 1992. 65.00 (*90-6088-050-1*, Pub. by Egbert Forsten NE) Benjamins North Am.

Scholia in Aristophanem, Pars II: Scholia in 'Vespas', 'Aves', et Lysistratam. Ed. by D. Holwerda. (Fasc II: Scholia Vetera et Recentiora in Aristophanis 'Pacem' Ser.). (Illus.). xxxii, 194p. 1982. 96.00 (*90-6088-076-5*, Pub. by Boumas Boekhuis NE) Benjamins North Am.

Scholia in Aristophanem, Pars, II: Scholia in 'Vespas', 'Aves', et 'Lysistratem' Ed. by D. Holwerda & W. J. Koster. (Fasc I: Scholia Vetera et Recentiora in Aristophanis 'Vespas' Ser.). (Illus.). li, 248p. 1978. 109.50 (*90-6088-058-7*, Pub. by Boumas Boekhuis NE) Benjamins North Am.

Scholia in Aristophanem Pars II, Fasc. III: Scholia in Vespas, Pacem, Aves et Lysistratam Scholia Vetera et Recentiora in Aristophanis "Aves" Ed. by D. Holwerda. xxxviii, 249p. (GRE & LAT.). 1992. 138.00 (*90-6088-033-1*, Pub. by Egbert Forsten NE) Benjamins North Am.

Scholia in Artistophanem. Pars I Prolegomena de Comoedia. Scholia in "Acharnenses," "Equites," "Nubes," Fasc. Two: Scholia Vetera in Aristophanis "Equites" Ed. by D. M. Jones. xxv, 279p. 1992. 75.00 (*0-685-62460-9*, Pub. by Egbert Forsten NE) Benjamins North Am.

Scholia in Homeri Odysseae A 1-309. Ed. by Arthur Ludwich. iv, 120p. 1966. reprint ed. write for info. (*0-318-71024-2*) G Olms Pubs.

Scholia in Lucani Bellum Civile. Hermann Usener. x, 338p. (GER.). 1967. reprint ed. write for info. (*0-318-70416-1*) G Olms Pubs.

Scholia in Thesmophoriazusas: Ranasi Ecclesiazusas et Plutum. Ed. by M. Chantry. (Scholia in Aristophanem III 4a in Plutum Ser.). xxx, 202p. (GEC & LAT.). 1994. lib. bdg. 127.00 (*90-6980-055-1*, Pub. by Egbert Forsten NE) Benjamins North Am.

Scholia in Thucydidem: Ad Optimos Codices Collata, Edidit Carolus Hude. Thucydides. LC 72-7895. (Greek History Ser.). (GRE.). 1977. reprint ed. 35.95 (*0-405-04801-7*) Ayer.

***Scholia in Vespas, Pacem, Aves & Lysistratam.** Ed. by D. Holwerda. (Scholia in Aristophanem Ser.: Pars II, Fasc IV). xvi, 58p. (GRE & LAT.). 1996. lib. bdg. 57.00 (*90-6980-083-7*, Pub. by Egbert Forsten NE) Benjamins North Am.

Scholia on the Aves. John W. White. cxii, 378p. 1974. reprint ed. lib. bdg. 110.00 (*3-487-05318-7*) G Olms Pubs.

Scholia Platonica. Ed. by William C. Greene. (Philological Monographs: Bd. VIII). xlii, 569p. 1988. reprint ed. write for info. (*3-487-07930-5*) G Olms Pubs.

Scholl Presents Ozzy Osbourne Guitar. 16.95 (*0-7935-4311-8*, 00660022) H Leonard.

Schollers Purgatory, Discovered in the Stationers Common-Wealth. George Wither. LC 77-7441. (English Experience Ser.: No. 900). 1977. reprint ed. lib. bdg. 20.00 (*90-221-0900-3*) Walter J Johnson.

Scholls Ferry Tales. Margaret P. Hesse. LC 94-44064. (Illus.). 112p. (Orig.). 1994. pap. 10.95 (*0-936738-06-5*) Webb Research.

Scholtes - Fonck Family History. Jean S. Zielinski. LC 88-50096. (Illus.). 575p. 1990. 45.00 (*0-9620035-0-6*) J S Zielinski.

Schomburg Center Guide to Black Literature. Denise Valade-Kasinec. Ed. by Roger Valade, 3rd. LC 95-36733. 550p. 1995. 75.00 (*0-7876-0289-2*, 109232) Gale.

Schomburg Essential Black Literature Guide. Galens. LC 95-32724. (African American Literature Encyclopedia Ser.). (Illus.). 450p. 1995. 17.95 (*0-7876-0734-7*) Visible Ink Pr.

Schomburg Library of Nineteenth-Century Black Women Writers, 30 vols., Set. Ed. by Henry L. Gates, Jr. 1988. 650.00 (*0-19-505267-6*) OUP.

Schomer Lichtner Drawings. Schomer Lichtner. (Illus.). 72p. (Orig.). 1964. pap. 5.00 (*0-941074-00-5*) Lichtner.

***Schonsten Hollywoodfilme.** Ed. by Eberhard Mertens. (Filmprogramme Ser.: Vol. 7). (Illus.). 130p. (GER.). 1982. write for info. (*3-487-08240-3*) G Olms Pubs.

Schonsten Sagen des Klassischen Altertums. unabridged ed. Schwab. (World Classic Literature Ser.). (GER.). pap. 7.95 (*3-89507-012-2*, Pub. by Bookking Intl FR) Distribks Inc.

***Schonsten Teddys und Tiere von Steiff.** 2nd ed. Rolf Pistorius & Christel Pistorius. (Illus.). 160p. (GER.). (C). 1993. 67.00 (*3-8170-1008-7*, Pub. by Knstvrlag Weingrtn GW) Intl Bk Import.

School. Greg Lee. LC 92-44073. (J). (gr. 3 up). 1993. 12.67 (*0-86593-269-7*); 9.50 (*0-685-66359-0*) Rourke Corp.

School. Emily A. McCully. LC 87-156. (Trophy Picture Bk.). (Illus.). 32p. (J). (ps-1). 1990. pap. 4.95 (*0-06-443233-5*, Trophy) HarpC Child Bks.

***School.** Emily A. McCully. (Illus.). (J). (ps-1). 14.89 (*0-06-024132-2*, 622645) HarpC Child Bks.

School. Emily A. McCully. LC 87-156. (Illus.). 32p. (J). (ps-2). 1987. lib. bdg. 14.89 (*0-06-024133-0*) HarpC Child Bks.

School. T. M. Wright. 288p. 1994. mass mkt. 4.99 (*0-8125-1335-5*) Tor Bks.

School, Vol. 3. Ed. by Eleanor C. Goldstein. (Social Issues Resources Ser.). 1989. suppl. ed. 95.00 (*0-89777-079-X*) Sirs Inc.

School: All about Language Ser. Harris Winitz. (Illus.). 50p. (Orig.). (YA). (gr. 7 up). 1987. pap. text ed. 31.00 incl. audio (*0-939990-49-0*) Intl Linguistics.

School Vol. 5: Including 1994 Supplement. Ed. by Eleanor C. Goldstein. (Social Issues Resources Ser.). 1995. 57.00 (*0-89777-189-3*) Sirs Inc.

School - College Connection: Relationships & Standards. National Association of Secondary School Principals Staff. 89p. reprint ed. pap. 25.40 (*0-8357-4664-X*, 2037604) Bks Demand.

School Achievement of Minority Children: New Perspectives. Ed. by Ulric Neisser. 208p. (C). 1986. text ed. 39.95 (*0-89859-685-8*) L Erlbaum Assocs.

School Acres: An Adventure in Rural Education. Rossa B. Cooley. LC 71-106853. (Illus.). 166p. 1970. reprint ed. text ed. 45.00 (*0-8371-3475-7*, CSC&, Greenwood Pr) Greenwood.

School Activities & the Law. John L. Strope. LC 84-174586. (Illus.). 78p. (Orig.). reprint ed. pap. 25.00 (*0-7837-0592-1*, 2040938) Bks Demand.

School Administration: Leadership & Interaction. Stanley W. Williams. 380p. 1984. text ed. 24.50 (*0-8290-0533-1*) Irvington.

School Administration: Persistent Dilemmas in Preparation & Practice. Ed. by Stephen L. Jacobson et al. LC 96-15328. 312p. 1996. text ed. 65.00 (*0-275-95247-9*, Praeger Pubs) Greenwood.

School Administration As a Craft: Foundations of Practice. Arthur Blumberg. 312p. 1988. text ed. 62.50 (*0-205-11674-4*, H1674-4) Allyn.

School Administrative Aide. Jack Rudman. (Career Examination Ser.: C-1069). 1994. pap. 27.95 (*0-8373-1069-5*) Nat Learn.

School Administrative & Supervisory Organizations in Cities of 20,000 to 50,000 Population. William N. McGinnis. LC 71-177024. (Columbia University. Teachers College. Contributions to Education Ser.: No. 392). reprint ed. 37.50 (*0-404-55392-3*) AMS Pr.

***School Administrators.** Ed. by William J. Evans, Jr. (Case Citation Ser.: Vol. 18). 66p. (Orig.). 1996. pap. text ed. 40.00 (*1-56534-089-2*) Ed Law Assn.

School Administrator's Budget Handbook: A Step-by-Step Guide for Preparing & Managing Your School Budget. George E. Ridler & Robert J. Shockley. 288p. 1989. text ed. 49.95 (*0-13-793332-0*) P-H.

School Administrator's Complete Letter Book. Gerald Tomlinson. LC 83-24409. 294p. 1984. text ed. 32.95 (*0-13-792367-8*, Busn) P-H.

School Administrator's Encyclopedia. P. Susan Mamchak & Steven R. Mamchak. LC 81-22492. 414p. 1982. text ed. 27.95 (*0-13-792390-2*, Parker Publishing Co) P-H.

School Administrator's Factomatic. Robert J. Shockley et al. LC 92-16140. 1992. write for info. (*0-13-793399-1*) P-H.

School Administrator's Faculty Supervision Handbook. Ronald T. Hyman. LC 85-28249. 223p. 1986. 24.95 (*0-13-792409-7*, Busn) P-H.

School Administrator's Guide to Computers in Education. Cheever et al. 1985. pap. text ed. write for info. (*0-318-59749-7*) Addison-Wesley.

School Administrator's Guide to Early Childhood Programs. Lawrence J. Schweinhart. LC 88-11073. 91p. 1988. pap. text ed. 12.95 (*0-931114-77-2*) High-Scope.

***School Administrator's Handbook of Internet Sites.** Ed. by Leslie A. Ramsey. 186p. 1996. spiral bd. 54.00 (*1-56925-045-6*, NET) Capitol Publns.

***School Administrator's Handbook of Internet Sites.** 2nd ed. Ed. by James DeAngelis & Annette Licitka. 235p. 1997. pap. 69.00 (*1-56925-084-7*, NET2) Capitol VA.

School Administrators' Mailbox, 4 vols., Vols. 1-4. Donald R. Wilson. 1993. Set, Vol. 1, 38p., Vol. 2, 31p., Vol. 3, 30p., Vol. 4, 31p. lib. bdg. 40.00 (*0-939136-18-X*) School Admin.

School Administrators' Mailbox Vol. 1: Sample Letters to Students. Donald R. Wilson. 38p. 1993. lib. bdg. 11.00 (*0-939136-03-1*) School Admin.

School Administrators' Mailbox Vol. 2: Sample Letters to Faculty & Staff. Donald R. Wilson. 31p. 1993. lib. bdg. 11.00 (*0-939136-04-X*) School Admin.

School Administrators' Mailbox, Vol. 3: Sample Letters of Recommendation & Academic Oriented Letters to Faculty & Staff. Donald R. Wilson. 30p. 1993. lib. bdg. 11.00 (*0-939136-05-8*) School Admin.

School Administrators' Mailbox, Vol. 4: Sample Letters to Parents & Community. Donald R. Wilson. 31p. 1993. lib. bdg. 11.00 (*0-939136-06-6*) School Admin.

S

School Administrator's Public Speaking Portfolio: With Model Speeches & Anecdotes. P. Susan Mamchak & Steven R. Mamchak. 360p. 1983. 34.95 (*0-13-792556-5*, Parker Publishing Co) P-H.

School Administrator's Staff Development Activities Manual. Ronald T. Hyman. LC 85-28250. 153p. 1986. pap. 16.95 (*0-13-792607-3*, Busn) P-H.

School Adventures: Aventuras Escolares. Armando B. Rico. 27p. (Orig.). (J). 1989. pap. text ed. 4.95 (*1-879219-04-2*) Veracruz Pubs.

School-Age Child Care: An Action Manual for the 90's & Beyond. 2nd ed. Michelle Seligson & Michael Allenson. LC 92-18359. 328p. 1993. text ed. 55.00 (*0-86569-024-3*, T024, Auburn Hse); pap. text ed. 19.95 (*0-86569-025-1*, R025, Auburn Hse) Greenwood.

School-Age Child Care: Getting Started. (Illus.). 330p. (Orig.). (C). 1994. pap. text ed. 50.00 (*0-7881-0316-4*) DIANE Pub.

School-Age Children with Special Needs: What Do They Do When School Is Out? Dale B. Fink. LC 88-82290. (Illus.). 160p. 1988. pap. 12.95 (*0-930958-05-5*) Excptnl Parent.

School-Age Children with Special Needs: What Do They Do When School Is Out? Dale B. Fink. LC 88-82290. 152p. 1988. pap. text ed. 15.95 (*0-313-28384-2*) Greenwood.

School Age Demographics: Recent Trends & New Educational Challenges. (Illus.). 91p. (Orig.). (C). 1994. pap. text ed. 30.00 (*0-7881-0214-1*) DIANE Pub.

School-Age Environment Rating Scale (SACERS) Thelma Harms et al. 48p. (C). 1995. pap. text ed. 8.95 (*0-8077-3507-8*) Tchrs Coll.

School-Age Environment Rating Scale (SACERS), Scoring Sheets. Thelma Harms et al. 48p. (C). 1995. pap. 8.95 (*0-8077-3508-6*) Tchrs Coll.

School-Age Ideas & Activities for after School Programs. Karen Haas-Foletta & Michele Cogley. LC 90-63115. (Illus.). 168p. (Orig.). (C). 1990. pap. text ed. 16.95 (*0-917505-03-4*) School Age.

School-Age Parents: The Challenge of Three-Generation Living. Jeanne W. Lindsay. LC 90-6039. (Illus.). 224p. (Orig.). 1990. 17.95 (*0-930934-37-7*); pap. 10.95 (*0-930934-36-9*); teacher ed., pap. 2.50 (*0-930934-56-3*) Morning Glory.

School & Classroom Organization. Ed. by Robert E. Slavin. 288p. 1988. 59.95 (*0-89859-998-9*) L Erlbaum Assocs.

School & College: Partnerships in Education. Gene I. Maeroff. LC 83-70359. 83p. 1983. pap. text ed. 4.50 (*0-931050-22-7*) Carnegie Fnd Advan Teach.

School & College Speaker. Ed. by Wilmot B. Mitchell. LC 78-74820. (Granger Poetry Library). 1979. reprint ed. 35.00 (*0-89609-139-2*) Roth Pub Inc.

School & Commonwealth. Henry C. Morrison. LC 73-142673. (Essay Index Reprint Ser.). 1977. 20.95 (*0-8369-2063-5*) Ayer.

School & Community History of Dickenson County, Virginia. Ed. by Dennis Reedy. (Illus.). 520p. 1994. 21.95 (*1-57072-010-X*) Overmountain Pr.

School & Community Relations. 6th ed. Donald R. Gallagher & Bagin. 352p. 1996. 62.00 (*0-205-26414-X*) Allyn.

School & Community Resources for the Behaviorally Handicapped. Ed. by Thomas J. Kelly et al. 333p. 1974. text ed. 29.50 (*0-8422-5163-4*); pap. text ed. 9.75 (*0-8422-0392-3*) Irvington.

School & Divorce. Lucia Vail. 40p. (Orig.). 1992. pap. text ed. 6.00 (*0-935493-80-8*) Programs Educ.

School & Family Partnerships: Parent/Teacher Relationship I. Buzzell. (Teaching Methods Ser.). 64p. 1996. teacher ed., pap. 8.50 (*0-8273-7164-0*) Delmar.

School & Family Partnerships: Preparing Educators & Improving Schools. Joyce L. Epstein. 275p. (C). 1998. text ed. 55.00 (*0-8133-8754-X*); pap. text ed. 19.95 (*0-8133-8755-8*) Westview.

School & Home Guide to Apple Macintosh Computer. Everett E. Murdock & Susan Sudbury. LC 85-530. (Illus.). 204p. 1985. pap. 15.95 (*0-13-793605-2*) P-H.

School & Home Guide to IBM Compatible Personal Computers. Everett E. Murdock & Susan Sudbury. LC 84-24786. 292p. 1985. pap. 18.95 (*0-13-793662-1*) P-H.

School & Home Guide to the IBM PCjr. Everett E. Murdock & Susan Sudbury. (Illus.). 224p. 1985. text ed. 29.00 (*0-13-793654-0*); pap. text ed. 15.95 (*0-13-793647-8*) P-H.

School & Play in the Parrish of Vaynor: From 1650 to the Present. T. J. Harris & Jack Evans. 112p. (C). 1989. 75.00 (*0-905928-07-5*, Pub. by D Brown & Sons Ltd UK) St Mut.

School & Society. John Dewey. LC 79-26919. (Arcturus Books Paperbacks). 124p. 1980. pap. 9.95 (*0-8093-0967-X*) S Ill U Pr.

School & Society. 2nd ed. Jonas F. Soltis. (Thinking about Education Ser.). 168p. (C). 1992. pap. text ed. 12.95 (*0-8077-3174-9*) Tchrs Coll.

School & Society: Educational Practice As Social Expression. Steven E. Tozer. LC 92-26492. 1992. teacher ed. write for info. (*0-07-557195-1*) McGraw.

School & Society: Educational Practice As Social Expression. Steven E. Tozer. LC 92-26492. 1993. pap. text ed. write for info. (*0-07-557043-2*) McGraw.

School & Society: Historical & Contemporary Perspectives. 2nd ed. Steven E. Tozer et al. LC 94-40706. 1995. pap. text ed. write for info. (*0-07-065282-1*) McGraw.

School & Society: Learning Content Through Culture. Ed. by Henry T. Trueba & Concha Delgado-Gaitan. LC 87-32880. 239p. 1988. text ed. 55.00 (*0-275-92860-8*, C2860, Praeger Pubs) Greenwood.

School & Society in Chicago. George S. Counts. LC 71-165715. (American Education Ser, No. 2). 1975. reprint ed. 30.95 (*0-405-03704-X*) Ayer.

School & Society in Tsarist & Soviet Russia: Selected Papers from the Fourth World Congress for Soviet & East European Studies, Harrogate, 1990. Ed. by Ben Eklof. LC 92-19909. 1993. text ed. 39.95 (*0-312-08555-9*) St Martin.

School & Society in Victorian Britain: Joseph Payne & the New World of Education. Richard Aldrich. LC 94-17106. (Studies in the History of Education: Vol. 935, Vol. 1). (Illus.). 317p. 1994. text ed. 49.00 (*0-8153-1558-9*, SS935) Garland.

School & Society Through Science Fiction. Ed. by Joseph D. Olander et al. LC 81-40587. (Illus.). 404p. 1982. reprint ed. pap. text ed. 31.00 (*0-8191-1997-0*) U Pr of Amer.

School & the Immigrant. Herbert A. Miller. LC 71-129507. (American Immigration Collection. Series 2). 1980. reprint ed. 13.95 (*0-405-00561-X*) Ayer.

School & the Military Family. Robin Wuebker-Battershell. (Family Forum Library Ser.). 16p. 1993. 1.95 (*1-56688-071-8*) Bur For At-Risk.

School & the Social Order. Frank Musgrave. LC 79-40738. 210p. reprint ed. pap. 59.90 (*0-685-20598-3*, 2030532) Bks Demand.

School & the University: An International Perspective. Ed. by Burton R. Clark. LC 85-1158. 400p. 1985. 50.00 (*0-520-05423-7*); pap. 15.00 (*0-520-06177-2*) U CA Pr.

School Answers Back: Responding to Student Drug Abuse. Richard Hawley. LC 83-73198. 148p. 1984. pap. 5.00 (*0-942348-14-1*) Am Council Drug Ed.

School Archival Records Search (SARS) User's Guide & Technical Manual. Herbert H. Severson et al. 1991. pap. text ed. 35.00 (*0-944584-38-1*, 33KIT) Sopris.

School Around Us: 25 Years. Claudia Berman. (Illus.). 195p. (Orig.). 1994. pap. text ed. 18.95 (*0-9643758-0-X*) Schl Around Us.

School Art in American Culture, 1820-1970. Foster L. Wygant. LC 93-77475. (Illus.). 240p. (Orig.). (C). 1993. pap. 21.95 (*0-9610376-1-X*) Interwood Pr.

School Art Programs: A Guide for School Board Members & Superintendents. 28p. 1992. pap. text ed. 10.00 (*0-937652-64-4*) Natl Art Ed.

School As a Home for the Mind: A Collection of Articles by Arthur L. Costa. Arthur L. Costa. LC 91-61609. 192p. 1991. pap. text ed. 19.95 (*0-932935-33-8*) IRI-SkyLght.

School As a Journey: The Eight-Year Odyssey of a Waldorf Teacher & His Class. Torin M. Finser. LC 94-35018. 256p. (Orig.). 1995. pap. 14.95 (*0-88010-389-2*) Anthroposophic.

***School As a Tool for Survival for Homeless Children.** rev. ed. K. L. Lively & Paul F. Kleine. LC 96-36705. (Children of Poverty Ser.). (Illus.). 112p. 1996. text ed. 34.00 (*0-8153-2619-X*) Garland.

***School As Sign: An Introduction to Semiotic Inquiry in Education.** David G. Smith. Ed. by Joe Kincheloe & Shirley R. Steinberg. (Critical Education Practice Ser.). 200p. Date not set. text ed. 30.00 (*0-8153-1165-6*); pap. text ed. 18.95 (*0-8153-2316-6*) Garland.

School Assessment Survey (SAS) Information for School Improvement. Bruce L. Wilson. 61p. 1985. pap. 16.95 (*1-56602-004-2*) Research Better.

School at Home, Teach Your Own Child. Ingeborg U. Kendall. LC 80-85435. 190p. 1982. 6.95 (*0-914704-03-6*) ICER Pr.

School at Mopass: A Problem of Identity. George D. Spindler. (Case Studies in Education & Culture). 112p. 1983. reprint ed. pap. text ed. 6.95 (*0-8290-0319-3*) Irvington.

School Attendance Aide. Jack Rudman. (Career Examination Ser.: C-3264). 1994. pap. 23.95 (*0-8373-3264-8*) Natl Learn.

School Attendance As a Factor in School Progress. Carl W. Ziegler. LC 70-177608. (Columbia University. Teachers College. Contributions to Education Ser.: No. 297). reprint ed. 37.50 (*0-404-55297-8*) AMS Pr.

School Attendance, Truancy & Dropping Out. Marilyn Dreilinger. (Family Forum Library Ser.). 16p. 1992. 1.95 (*1-56688-043-2*) Bur For At-Risk.

School-Based Affective & Social Interventions. Ed. by Susan G. Foreman. LC 87-25151. (Special Services in the Schools Ser.: Vol. 3, Nos. 3 & 4). 169p. 1988. text ed. 39.95 (*0-86656-702-X*) Haworth Pr.

***School-Based Budgets: Getting, Spending & Accounting.** Jerry J. Herman & Janice L. Herman. LC 96-61791. 125p. 1997. pap. text ed. 39.95 (*1-56676-508-0*) Technomic.

School-Based Change. LC 93-40578. (Teacher to Teacher Ser.). 1994. pap. 12.95 (*0-8106-2905-4*) NEA.

***School-Based Clinics: The Abortion Connection.** Richard D. Glasow. LC LB3432.5.G58. 149p. 1990. reprint ed. 2.25 (*0-9619452-0-6*) National Right to Life Educational.

School Based Clinics That Work. Jane K. Martin. (Illus.). 74p. (Orig.). (C). 1995. pap. text ed. 20.00 (*0-7881-1885-4*) DIANE Pub.

School-Based Collaboration with Families: Constructing Family-School-Agency Partnerships That Work. J. Brien O'Callaghan. LC 93-6573. (Social & Behavioral Sciences Ser.). 224p. 1993. text ed. 27.95 (*1-55542-527-5*) Jossey-Bass.

School-Based Decision-Making & Management. Ed. by Judith D. Chapman. 372p. 1990. 80.00 (*1-85000-780-2*, Falmer Pr); pap. 38.00 (*1-85000-781-0*, Falmer Pr) Taylor & Francis.

School-Based Enterprise: Productive Learning in American High Schools. David Stern et al. LC 93-29489. (Education-Higher Education Ser.). 245p. text ed. 30.95 (*1-55542-597-6*) Jossey-Bass.

School-Based Evaluation: A Dialogue for School Improvement. David Nevo. LC 94-46676. 214p. 1995. text ed. 69.25 (*0-08-041942-9*, Pergamon Pr) Elsevier.

School-Based HIV Prevention: A Multidisciplinary Approach. 1991. 24.95 (*0-614-06294-2*) Am Sch Health.

School-Based Leadership: Challenges & Opportunities. 3rd ed. Richard A. Gorton & Gail L. Schneider. 656p. (C). 1991. per. write for info. (*0-697-10404-4*) Brown & Benchmark.

School Based Management: A Detailed Guide for Successful Implementation. Richard G. Neal. 211p. (Orig.). 1991. pap. 21.95 (*1-879639-15-7*) Natl Educ Serv.

School-Based Management: Current Thinking & Practice. Jerry J. Herman & Janice L. Herman. (Illus.). 294p. 1992. pap. 40.95 (*0-398-06387-7*) C C Thomas.

School-Based Management: Current Thinking & Practice. Jerry J. Herman & Janice L. Herman. (Illus.). 294p. (C). 1992. text ed. 57.95 (*0-398-05817-2*) C C Thomas.

School-Based Management: Organizing for High Performance. Susan A. Mohrman & Priscilla Wohlstetter. LC 94-17756. (Education Ser.). 330p. text ed. 34.95 (*0-7879-0035-4*) Jossey-Bass.

School Based Management & School Effectiveness. Clive Dimmock. LC 93-2933. (Educational Management Ser.). 272p. (C). 1993. pap. 18.95 (*0-415-08314-1*, B0769) Routledge.

School Based Management & School Effectiveness. Clive Dimmock. LC 93-2933. (Educational Management Ser.). 272p. (C). (gr. 13). 1993. text ed. 69.95 (*0-415-08313-3*, B0765) Routledge.

School-Based Management As School Reform: Taking Stock. Joseph Murphy & Lynn G. Beck. LC 95-7733. (Illus.). 232p. 1995. 51.95 (*0-8039-6175-8*); pap. 23.95 (*0-8039-6176-6*) Corwin Pr.

School-Based Prevention for Children at Risk: The Primary Mental Health Project. Emory L. Cowen. LC 96-23913. 1996. 39.95 (*1-55798-353-4*); pap. 29.95 (*1-55798-374-7*) Am Psychol.

School-Based Prevention Programs for Children & Adolescents. Joseph A. Durlak. (Development Clinical Psychology & Psychiatry Ser.: Vol. 34). 136p. (C). 1995. 39.95 (*0-8039-5631-2*); pap. 17.95 (*0-8039-5632-0*) Sage.

School Behind Bars. 2nd ed. Leone Hineline & Jane Jablonski. LC 91-61080. (Illus.). 232p. (Orig.). 1991. 17.95 (*0-9628384-0-3*) O M Pub.

School Behind Bars. 2nd ed. Leone Hineline & Jane Jablonski. LC 91-61080. (Illus.). 232p. (Orig.). 1991. reprint ed. pap. 9.95 (*0-9628384-1-1*) O M Pub.

School Bell Memories: Horse & Buggy to Space Age. Ferol M. Slotte. (Illus.). 55p. reprint ed. pap. text ed. 8.00 (*0-9617960-0-6*) Del Monte Pr.

School Bits. 2nd rev. ed. Donna Martin. (Love 'n Hug Notes Ser.). (Illus.). 10p. (J). 1993. write for info. (*1-879127-45-8*) Lighten Up Enter.

***School Board Development: Needs & Opportunities.** 25p. (Orig.). 1996. pap. write for info. (*0-925299-58-8*) Natl Ctr Nonprofit.

School Board Member Handbook. (Illus.). 131p. 1995. pap. 22.50 (*1-56452-049-8*) NY Boards Assoc.

School Board Member Liability under Section 1983. David B. Rubin. Ed. by Naomi E. Gittens. 44p. 1992. pap. text ed. 15.00 (*0-88364-134-8*) Natl Sch Boards.

School Board Primer: A Guide for School Board Members. John Wiles & Joseph Bondi, Jr. 300p. 1984. pap. text ed. 39.95 (*0-205-08331-5*, H83314) Allyn.

School Board Studies. Maurice E. Stapley & Francis S. Chase. 1957. pap. 4.00 (*0-931080-00-2*) U Chicago Midwest Admin.

School Board Study Programs: Board Member's Manual, Series II. Daniel Brent & Carolyn Jurkowitz. 55p. 1988. reprint ed. pap. 6.60 (*1-55833-004-6*) Natl Cath Educ.

School Boards: Changing Local Control. Ed. by Patricia F. First & Herbert J. Walberg. LC 91-66583. 195p. 1992. 30.70 (*0-8211-0508-6*) McCutchan.

School Boards: Strengthening Grass Roots Leadership. 58p. 1986. 8.00 (*0-937846-89-9*) Inst Educ Lead.

School Boards & School Policy: An Evaluation of Decentralization in New York City. Marilyn Gittell et al. LC 72-92475. (Special Studies in U. S. Economic, Social & Political Issues). (Illus.). 1973. text ed. 29.00 (*0-89197-929-8*) Irvington.

School Book: A Comprehensive Guide to Elementary Schools in the Twin Cities. 560p. (Orig.). 1989. pap. text ed. 12.95 (*1-878222-00-7*) Cits League.

School Book: Everything Parents Should Know about Their Child's Education. Mary S. Miller. 1991. pap. 14.95 (*0-312-05508-0*) St Martin.

School Budget: A Handbook for School Board Members. 81p. 1990. 22.50 (*1-56452-028-5*) NY Boards Assoc.

School Bullying: Insights & Perspectives. Peter K. Smith & Sonia Sharp. LC 94-4418. 288p. (C). 1994. pap. 19.95 (*0-415-10373-8*, B4353) Routledge.

School Bullying: Insights & Perspectives. Peter K. Smith & Sonia Sharp. LC 94-4418. 224p. (C). (gr. 13). 1994. text ed. 59.95 (*0-415-10372-X*, B4349) Routledge.

***School Bus.** (Fisher-Price Little People Coloring & Activity Ser.). (Illus.). 48p. (J). (gr. k-2). 1997. pap. write for info. (*1-56144-959-8*, Honey Bear Bks) Modern Pub NYC.

School Bus. Donald Crews. LC 83-18681. (Illus.). 32p. (J). (gr. k-3). 1984. 16.00 (*0-688-02807-1*); lib. bdg. 15.93 (*0-688-02808-X*) Greenwillow.

School Bus. Donald Crews. LC 92-43766. (Illus.). 32p. (J). (ps up). 1993. pap. 4.95 (*0-688-12267-1*, Mulberry) Morrow.

***School Bus Adventure.** Judith Jango-Cohen. (Illus.). 12p. (J). (ps up). 1997. bds. 7.99 (*1-57584-178-9*) Rdrs Dgst Yng Fam.

School Bus Comes at Eight O'Clock. David McKee. LC 93-79583. (Illus.). 32p. (J). (ps-3). 1994. 14.95 (*1-56282-662-X*); lib. bdg. 14.89 (*1-56282-663-8*) Hyprn Child.

***School Bus Drivers.** Dee Ready. LC 97-2957. (Community Helpers Ser.). (J). 1998. write for info. (*1-56065-560-7*) Capstone Pr.

School Bus Law: A Case Study in Education, Religion & Politics. Theodore Powell. LC 60-13155. 1960. 28.95 (*0-89197-392-3*); pap. text ed. 6.95 (*0-8290-2016-0*) Irvington.

***School Buses.** Dee Ready. LC 97-12197. (J). 1998. write for info. (*1-56065-612-3*) Capstone Pr.

School Business Administration. Guilbert C. Hentschke. LC 84-61507. 604p. 1986. 43.30 (*0-8211-0768-2*) McCutchan.

***School Business Administration.** 6th ed. Hack & Candoli. LC 97-11426. 1997. text ed. 51.00 (*0-205-27354-8*) P-H.

***School Business Administration.** Kenneth F. Jordan. LC 84-24877. 416p. 1985. reprint ed. pap. 118.60 (*0-608-02692-1*, 2063345) Bks Demand.

School Business Administration: A Planning Approach. 3rd ed. I. Carl Candoli et al. 421p. 1984. text ed. 42.95 (*0-205-08152-5*, H81524) Allyn.

School Business Administration: A Planning Approach. 5th ed. Walter G. Hack et al. LC 94-28856. 1994. text ed. 58.00 (*0-205-16366-1*) Allyn.

School Business Executive. Jack Rudman. (Career Examination Ser.: C-2887). 1994. pap. 34.95 (*0-8373-2887-X*) Nat Learn.

School Business Management. Thelbert L. Drake & William H. Roe. LC 93-18857. 1993. text ed. 67.00 (*0-205-14699-6*) Allyn.

School Business Management in the 21st Century, No. 9004. Ed. by Kenneth Stevenson & John Lane. 166p. (Orig.). (C). 1990. pap. 20.00 (*0-910170-55-X*) Assn Sch Busn.

School Business Office Job Description Handbook. 2nd ed. 614p. 1995. pap. 75.00 (*0-910170-67-3*) Assn Sch Busn.

School Busing - Constitutional & Political Developments Vol. 2: The Public Debate over School Busing & Attempts to Restrict Its Use, 2 vols. Davison M. Douglas. LC 94-27194. (Controversies in Constitutional Law Ser.). 992p. 1994. 130.00 (*0-8153-1853-7*) Garland.

School Carnival. Danae Dobson. LC 95-42264. (Sunny Street Kids' Club Ser.: Vol. 4). (Illus.). 32p. (J). (ps-3). 1995. pap. 4.99 (*0-8499-5115-1*) Word Pub.

School-Centred Management Training. Mike Wallace. 1991. pap. 37.50 (*1-85396-099-3*, Pub. by P Chapman Pub UK) Taylor & Francis.

School Change: The Personal Development of a Point of View. Seymour B. Sarason. LC 94-44041. (Series on School Reform). 240p. (C). 1995. text ed. 48.00 (*0-8077-3449-7*); pap. text ed. 23.95 (*0-8077-3448-9*) Tchrs Coll.

***School Change Checklist.** Nicole Zocchetti & Miche Zocchetti. (Checklist Ser.). (Orig.). 1997. pap. write for info. (*0-614-30861-5*) NEA.

School Children at Risk. Virginia Richardson-Koehler et al. 286p. 1989. 75.00 (*1-85000-514-1*, Falmer Pr); pap. 31.00 (*1-85000-515-X*, Falmer Pr) Taylor & Francis.

School Choice. Frwd. by Ernest L. Boyer. LC 92-40895. 129p. 1992. 8.00 (*0-931050-45-6*) Carnegie Fnd Advan Teach.

School Choice: Issues & Answers. Ruth Randall & Keith Geiger. 228p. (Orig.). 1991. pap. 21.95 (*1-879639-02-5*) Natl Educ Serv.

***School Choice: Making Your Decision & Making It Work.** Ed. by Dennis Rainey & Barbara Rainey. 73p. 19.95 (*1-57229-056-0*) FamilyLife.

School Choice: The Struggle for the Soul of American Education. Peter W. Cookson, Jr. LC 93-35450. 184p. 1994. 25.00 (*0-300-05791-1*) Yale U Pr.

School Choice: The Struggle for the Soul of American Education. Peter W. Cookson. 1995. pap. 10.00 (*0-300-06499-3*) Yale U Pr.

School Choice: Why We Need It, How We Get It. David Harmer. LC 94-30046. 200p. 1994. 22.95 (*1-882577-14-0*); pap. 12.95 (*1-882577-15-9*) Cato Inst.

***School Choice in an Established Market.** Stephen Gorard. (Illus.). 290p. 1997. text ed. 59.95 (*1-84014-106-9*, Pub. by Ashgate UK) Ashgate Pub Co.

School Choice in Massachusetts. Abigail M. Thernstrom. (Pioneer Paper Ser.: No. 5). 141p. (Orig.). 1991. pap. 10.00 (*0-929930-05-3*) Pioneer Inst.

School Class Size: Research & Policy. Gene V. Glass et al. LC 81-23308. 160p. 1982. reprint ed. pap. 45.60 (*0-608-01470-2*, 2059514) Bks Demand.

School Clerk. Jack Rudman. (Career Examination Ser.: C-1984). 1994. pap. 23.95 (*0-8373-1984-6*) Nat Learn.

School Climate & Restructuring for Low-Achieving Students. Barbara Smey-Richman. 130p. 1991. pap. text ed. 21.95 (*1-56602-040-9*) Research Better.

School-College Collaboration: A Way of Redesigning the Educational Pipeline. Ed. by Nancy Carriuolo. (Freshman Year Experience Monograph: No. 16). 172p. (Orig.). 1996. pap. 30.00 (*1-889271-13-6*) Nat Res Ctr.

School-College Collaborative Programs in English. Ed. by Ronald J. Fortune. LC 86-711. (Options for Teaching Ser.: No. 8). xxii, 128p. 1986. pap. 19.75 (*0-87352-361-X*, J208P); lib. bdg. 37.50 (*0-87352-360-1*, J208C) Modern Lang.

School-College Partnerships: A Look at the Major National Models. Franklin P. Wilbur et al. LC 88-131040. 64p. (Orig.). 1988. reprint ed. pap. 25.00 (*0-608-02082-6*, 2062735) Bks Demand.

School Colors. Tulsky. 1998. 22.00 (*0-684-81307-6*) S&S Trade.

School Communication Workshop Kit. 1986. 119.00 (*0-87545-049-0*, 418-13950) Natl Sch PR.

School Community Centers: Guidelines for Interagency Planners. Joseph Ringers, Jr. & Larry E. Decker. 96p. (Orig.). 1995. pap. 14.95 (*0-930388-11-9*) Comm Collaborators.

An Asterisk (*) at the beginning of an entry indicates that the title is appearing in BIP for the first time.

School-Community Connections: Exploring Issues for Research & Practice. Ed. by Margaret C. Wang et al. (Education-Social & Behavioral Sciences Ser.). 470p. text ed. 45.00 (*0-7879-0099-0*) Jossey-Bass.

School-Community Relations in Transition. rev. ed. Richard W. Saxe. LC 83-62771. 361p. 1984. 29.25 (*0-8211-1859-5*) McCutchan.

School-Community Relations, under Reform. Robert L. Crowson. LC 91-66582. 317p. 1992. 32.00 (*0-8211-0231-1*) McCutchan.

School Consultancy in the U K: Its Role & Contribution to Educational Change. Ed. by Carol Aubrey. 225p. 1990. 70.00 (*1-85000-434-X*, Falmer Pr); pap. 30.00 (*1-85000-435-8*, Falmer Pr) Taylor & Francis.

School Consultation. Conoley. (Practitioner Guidebook Ser.). (C). 1982. 64.95 (*0-205-14431-4*, H4431, Longwood Div) Allyn.

School Consultation. 2nd ed. Conoley. (C). 1992. pap. text ed. 31.50 (*0-205-14561-2*, H4561) Allyn.

***School Consultation: Conceptual & Empirical Bases of Practice.** William P. Erchul & Brian K. Martens. LC 96-45186. (Issues in Clinical Child Psychology Ser.). 246p. 1997. 39.50 (*0-306-45456-4*) Plenum.

School Controversy Eighteen Ninety-One to Eighteen Ninety-Three. Daniel F. Reilly. LC 76-89221. (American Education: Its Men, Institutions, & Ideas. Series 1). 1975. reprint ed. 26.95 (*0-405-01460-0*) Ayer.

School Counseling Assistant. Jack Rudman. (Career Examination Ser.: C-3469). 1994. pap. 27.95 (*0-8373-3469-1*) Nat Learn.

School Counseling for the Twenty-First Century. 2nd ed. Stanley B. Baker. LC 95-11573. 1995. text ed. 67.00 (*0-02-305371-2*, Macmillan Coll) P-H.

School Counseling Renewal: Strategies for the Twenty-First Century. Rosemary Thompson. LC 91-70333. xvi, 424p. (Orig.). 1992. pap. text ed. 32.95 (*1-55959-026-2*) Accel Devel.

School Counselors & Censorship: Facing the Challenge. Greg Brigman & Peggy Moore. LC 94-14215. 184p. 1995. pap. text ed. 24.95 (*1-55620-140-0*, 72571) Am Coun Assn.

***School Counselor's Book of Lists.** Dorothy J. Blum. 1997. pap. text ed. 29.95 (*0-87628-129-3*) Ctr Appl Res.

School Counselor's Letter Book. Kenneth Hitchner et al. 240p. 1991. 29.95 (*0-87628-786-0*) Ctr Appl Res.

School, Court, Public Administration. Jacob Neusner. LC 87-4632. (Brown Judaic Studies). 306p. 1987. 36.95 (*1-55540-115-5*, 14-00-83) Scholars Pr GA.

***School Crime & Juvenile Justice.** Richard Lawrence. (Illus.). 256p. (C). 1997. pap. text ed. 18.95 (*0-19-510165-0*) OUP.

***School Crime & Juvenile Justice.** Richard Lawrence. (Illus.). 256p. (C). 1997. text ed. 45.00 (*0-19-510164-2*) OUP.

School Crime & Violence: Problems & Solutions. Joseph I. Grealy. LC 79-55399. 1980. 29.95 (*0-918214-05-X*) F E Peters.

***School Crisis Management.** Judie Smith. 160p. 1997. pap. 23.95 (*1-55691-127-0*, 270) Learning Pubns.

School Crisis Management: A Team Training Guide. Kendall Johnson. 192p. 1992. lib. bdg. 49.00 (*0-8095-6337-1*) Borgo Pr.

School Crisis Management: A Team Training Guide. Kendall Johnson. LC 92-32783. (Illus.). 192p. 1993. pap. 19.95 (*0-89793-099-1*); spiral bd. 24.95 (*0-89793-142-4*) Hunter Hse.

School Crisis Survival Guide: Management Techniques & Materials for Counselors & Administrators. Suni Petersen & Ronald Straub. 256p. 1991. spiral bd. 34.95 (*0-87628-806-9*) Ctr Appl Res.

School Crossing Guard. Jack Rudman. (Career Examination Ser.: C-702). 1994. pap. 23.95 (*0-8373-0702-3*) Nat Learn.

School Cultures: Universes of Meaning in Private Schools. Mary E. Henry. LC 92-42686. (Interpretive Perspectives on Education & Policy Ser.). 272p. 1993. pap. 39.50 (*1-56750-023-4*); text ed. 73.25 (*1-56750-022-6*) Ablex Pub.

School, Curriculum, & the Individual. John I. Goodlad. LC 66-17796. (Blaisdell Book in Education Ser.). 267p. reprint ed. pap. 76.10 (*0-317-09498-X*, 2055148) Bks Demand.

School Custodial Supervisor. Jack Rudman. (Career Examination Ser.: C-1581). 1994. pap. 29.95 (*0-8373-1581-6*) Nat Learn.

School Custodian. Jack Rudman. (Career Examination Ser.: C-799). 1994. pap. 23.95 (*0-8373-0799-6*) Nat Learn.

School Custodian-Engineer. Jack Rudman. (Career Examination Ser.: C-701). 1994. pap. 27.95 (*0-8373-0701-5*) Nat Learn.

School Day. Monica Stoppleman. (Turn of the Century Ser.). (Illus.). 32p. (J). (gr. 3-6). 1992. 12.95 (*0-7136-3185-6*, Pub. by A&C Black UK) Talman.

School Day Poetry & a Family Tree. Jerrold J. Rotwein. (Orig.). 1996. pap. write for info. (*1-57553-223-9*) Watermrk Pr.

School Days. (J). (ps-3). 1994. pap. 9.95 (*0-8167-1564-5*) Troll Communs.

School Days. Patrick Chamoiseau. Tr. by Linda Coverdale. LC 96-24210. ix, 146p. 1997. pap. 13.00 (*0-8032-6376-7*, Bison Books); text ed. 35.00 (*0-8032-1477-4*) U of Nebr Pr.

School Days. Steven Heller & Steven Guarnaccia. LC 92-12833. (Illus.). 96p. 1992. 9.98 (*1-55859-397-7*) Abbeville Pr.

School Days. B. G. Hennessy. LC 92-12008. (J). (gr. 4 up). 1992. pap. 4.99 (*0-14-054179-9*, Puffin) Puffin Bks.

School Days. B. G. Hennessy. (J). (ps-3). 1990. pap. 13.95 (*0-670-83025-9*) Viking Child Bks.

School Days. B.G. Hennessy. 1995. pap. 3.99 (*0-14-055808-X*) NAL-Dutton.

School Days. Shirley J. Miller. (Illus.). 80p. (Orig.). (J). (gr. 2-6). 1993. pap. 6.95 (*1-878580-90-6*) Asylum Arts.

***School Days.** Laura Ingalls Wilder. LC 96-31240. (Little House Bks.). (Illus.). 80p. (J). (gr. 2-5). 1997. pap. 3.95 (*0-06-442049-3*, Trophy); lib. bdg. 13.89 (*0-06-027146-9*) HarpC Child Bks.

School Days: An Essay on the Hoover Institution Conference "Choice & Vouchers - The Future of American Education?" Peter Robinson. LC 93-35680. (Essays in Public Policy Ser.: No. 45). 1993. 5.00 (*0-8179-5502-X*) Hoover Inst Pr.

School Days: Spanish Edition. B. G. Hennessy. 1995. pap. 3.99 (*0-14-055814-4*) NAL-Dutton.

School Days, Fun Days: Creative Ways to Teach Humor Skills in the Classroom. Deborah J. Hill. LC 93-7241. (Illus.). 178p. 1993. pap. 27.95 (*0-398-06395-8*) C C Thomas.

School Days, Fun Days: Creative Ways to Teach Humor Skills in the Classroom. Deborah J. Hill. LC 93-7241. (Illus.). 178p. (C). 1993. text ed. 41.95 (*0-398-05862-8*) C C Thomas.

School Days in Paris. 2nd ed. 1995. mass mkt. 5.95 (*1-56333-325-2*) Masquerade.

School Days in the Wallowas: A History of the Ninety-One Schools & Communities That Have Been in Wallowa County Oregon. Irene Barklow. Ed. by Kathy Sterbentz. (Illus.). 567p. (Orig.). 1992. 49.95 (*0-9618185-4-9*); pap. write for info. (*0-9618185-3-0*) Enchant Pub Oregon.

***School Days Memories.** C. R. Gibson Company, Staff. 1997. 37.00 (*0-7667-1245-1*) Gibson.

School Days, Rule Days: The Legalization & Regulation of Education. Ed. by David L. Kirp & Donald Jessen. LC 85-1537. (Stanford Series on Education & Public Policy: Vol. 1). 390p. 1986. pap. 30.00 (*1-85000-018-2*, Falmer Pr) Taylor & Francis.

School Days with the Millers. Mildred A. Martin. (Miller Family Ser.). (J). (gr. 3-8). 1995. pap. text ed. 6.00 (*1-884377-01-7*) Green Psturs Pr.

School Daze: Jokes Your Teacher Will Hate! Louis Phillips. (Illus.). 64p. (J). (gr. 2-6). 1996. pap. 3.99 (*0-14-036415-3*, Puffin) Puffin Bks.

School Daze & the Education Maze: A Teacher Talks to Parents. Chuck Cascio. 173p. (Orig.). 1992. pap. 25.00 (*1-878907-39-5*) TechBooks.

School-Dazed Parents. Charles S. Mueller. LC 94-13042. 224p. 1994. pap. 10.99 (*0-570-04667-X*, 12-3239) Concordia.

School Decentralization: Lessons from the Study of Bureaucracy. Bruce A. Bimber. LC 93-11802. 1993. pap. 15.00 (*0-8330-1354-8*, MR-157-GGS/LE) Rand Corp.

School Desegregation: Cross-Cultural Perspectives. Yehuda Amir & Shlomo Sharan. 288p. 1984. text ed. 59.95 (*0-89859-335-2*) L Erlbaum Assocs.

School Desegregation: Shadow & Substance. Ed. by Florence H. Levinsohn & Benjamin D. Wright. LC 76-17291. 224p. reprint ed. pap. 63.90 (*0-685-15771-7*, 2026781) Bks Demand.

School Desegregation, Enough Is Enough. William R. Moss. 216p. 1992. 19.95 (*0-9634115-0-0*) Danmo Pub Co.

School Desegregation in Texas: The Implementation of United States vs. State of Texas. Contrib. by Richard L. Schott. LC 82-82981. (Policy Research Project Report: No. 51). 75p. 1982. pap. 6.50 (*0-89940-653-X*) LBJ Sch Pub Aff.

***School Desegregation in the Twenty-First Century: The Focus Must Change.** Brian L. Fife. LC 96-51742. (Symposium Ser.: Vol. 41). 146p. 1997. text ed. 69.95 (*0-7734-8725-5*) E Mellen.

School Desegregation Plans That Work. Charles V. Willie. LC 83-12685. (Contributions to the Study of Education Ser.: No. 10). (Illus.). xi, 239p. 1984. text ed. 39.95 (*0-313-24051-5*, WDP/, Greenwood Pr) Greenwood.

School Desegregation Research: New Directions in Situational Analysis. Ed. by Jeffrey Prager et al. (Critical Issues in Social Justice Ser.). 284p. 1986. 49.50 (*0-306-42151-8*, Plenum Pr) Plenum.

School Design. Henry Sanoff. LC 93-7904. 215p. 1994. text ed. 59.95 (*0-442-01096-6*) Van Nos Reinhold.

School Development Planning. G. B. Giles. 1990. pap. 30.00 (*0-7463-0626-1*, Pub. by Northcote UK) St Mut.

School Dictionary. 2nd ed. Created by Harcourt Brace Staff. 1985. wbk. ed., pap. 7.00 (*0-15-321136-9*) HB Schl Dept.

School Dictionary. 2nd ed. Harcourt Brace Staff. 1985. 41.50 (*0-15-321135-0*) HB Schl Dept.

School Disaster Planning. Stoffel et al. (Illus.). 178p. 1991. ring bd. 25.00 (*0-913724-44-0*) Emerg Response Inst.

***School Discipline: Best Practices for Administrators.** Louis Rosen. LC 96-51307. (Illus.). 136p. 1997. 54.95 (*0-8039-6572-9*) Corwin Pr.

***School Discipline: Best Practices for Administrators.** Louis Rosen. LC 96-51307. (Illus.). 136p. 1997. pap. 24.95 (*0-8039-6573-7*) Corwin Pr.

School Discipline-A Planning & Resource Guide. James K. Nighswander. 500p. 1987. teacher ed. 2.50 (*0-932957-92-7*); teacher ed. 200.00 (*0-932957-93-5*) Natl School.

School Discipline & School Violence: The Teacher Variance Approach. Irwin A. Hyman et al. LC 96-10506. 384p. 1996. 38.00 (*0-205-15812-9*) Allyn.

School Discipline & Student Rights: An Advocate's Manual. Paul Weckstein. LC 83-111264. ix, 544p. 1982. 25.00 (*0-912585-00-5*) Ctr Law & Ed.

School Discipline Desk Book: With Model Programs & Tested Procedures. Eugene R. Howard. (Illus.). 1977. 18.50 (*0-13-793000-3*, Parker Publishing Co) P-H.

School Discipline Guidebook: Theory into Practice. Frank A. Johns et al. 224p. 1988. pap. text ed. 57.50 (*0-205-11828-3*, H18286) Allyn.

School Discipline Policies & Procedures: A Practical Guide. rev. ed. Kelly Frels et al. Ed. by Naomi Gittins. 40p. 1990. reprint ed. pap. 25.00 (*0-88364-154-2*) Natl Sch Boards.

School Discourse Problems. 2nd ed. Ed. by Danielle N. Ripich & Nancy A. Craighead. LC 93-36789. (School-Age Children Ser.). 352p. (Orig.). 1994. 49.95 (*1-56593-096-7*, 0400) Singular Publishing.

School District Instructional Computer-Use Evaluation Manual. Chris Morton & Don Beverly. LC 88-24682. (Illus.). 61p. 1989. pap. 24.95 (*0-87778-214-8*) Educ Tech Pubns.

School District Library Media Director's Handbook. Betty Martin & Frances Hatfield. LC 81-14292. (Illus.). x, 236p. (C). 1982. pap. 27.50 (*0-208-01890-5*, Lib Prof Pubns) Shoe String.

School District Organization Handbook. California Department of Education Staff. 222p. 1993. pap. 17.50 (*0-8011-1088-2*) Calif Education.

School Dropouts: Everybody's Problem. Sheppard Rambon. Ed. by Anne Lewis & Michael D. Usdan. 58p. (Orig.). 1986. pap. 7.50 (*0-937846-91-0*) Inst Educ Lead.

School Dropouts: Patterns & Policies. enl. ed. Ed. by Gary Natriello. 192p. 1986. reprint ed. pap. 17.95 (*0-8077-2835-7*) Tchrs Coll.

School Dropouts: Patterns & Policies. Ed. by Gary Natriello. LC 86-22978. 191p. 1987. reprint ed. pap. 54.50 (*0-608-01657-8*, 2062309) Bks Demand.

School Dropouts: The Tragedy of America's Undereducated Youth. Carlos A. Bonilla & Jana L. Brazda. LC 91-70837. (Illus.). 224p. (Orig.). 1993. per. 29.95 (*1-879774-00-3*) ICA Pub Co.

School Earthquake Preparedness Guidebook. (Illus.). 154p. (Orig.). (C). 1994. pap. text ed. 35.00 (*0-7881-0771-2*) DIANE Pub.

School Education in India: Contemporary Issues & Trends. H. S. Singha. 196p. 1991. text ed. 27.95 (*81-207-1308-7*, Pub. by Sterling Pubs II) Apt Bks.

School Effectiveness: Research, Policy & Practice. Ed. by David Reynolds & Peter Cuttance. (School Development Ser.). 208p. 1992. text ed. 65.00 (*0-304-32295-4*); pap. text ed. 24.95 (*0-304-32276-8*) Cassell.

School Effectiveness & School-Based Management: A Mechanism for Development. Yin-Cheong Cheng. LC 96-18260. 256p. 1996. 69.95 (*0-7507-0457-8*, Falmer Pr); pap. 24.95 (*0-7507-0458-6*, Falmer Pr) Taylor & Francis.

School Effectiveness & School Improvement. Ed. by H. M. Creemers et al. xii, 384p. 1989. 54.75 (*90-265-1008-X*) Swets.

School Emergencies Manual. Mesd School Health Services Staff. 1992. 25.00 (*1-880118-05-X*) MESD Pr.

School Empowerment. Ed. by Mike Richardson et al. LC 95-60051. 369p. 1995. text ed. 39.95 (*1-56676-269-3*) Technomic.

School Energy Management. Shirley Hansen Associates Staff. 1977. 10.00 (*0-87652-046-8*, 021-00520) Am Assn Sch Admin.

School Enrollment: Social & Economic Characteristics of Students. (Illus.). 85p. (Orig.). (C). 1993. pap. text ed. 20.00 (*1-56806-464-0*) DIANE Pub.

School Enrollment, Social & Economic Characteristics of Students. 1994. lib. bdg. 250.00 (*0-8490-8578-0*) Gordon Pr.

School Events. Tanya Kaufman & Judith Wishny. Ed. by Benjamin Piltch. (Skyview Ser.). (Illus.). 64p. (J). (gr. 2-5). 1983. 4.00 (*0-934618-04-6*) Learning Well.

School Exercises for Flatwork & Jumping. Eleanor Ross. (Illus.). 95p. 1992. pap. 20.95 (*1-872082-31-9*) Half Halt Pr.

School Experience. Ed. by Peter Woods & Martyn Hammersley. LC 76-44644. 1977. text ed. 29.95 (*0-312-70140-3*) St Martin.

***School Facilities: Accessibility for the Disabled Still an Issue.** (Illus.). 37p. (Orig.). (C). 1996. pap. 20.00 (*0-7881-3114-1*) DIANE Pub.

School Facilities: America's Schools Not Designed or Equipped for the 21st Century. (Illus.). 67p. (Orig.). (C). 1995. pap. text ed. 20.00 (*0-7881-1808-0*) DIANE Pub.

***School Facilities: America's Schools Report Differing Conditions.** (Illus.). 105p. (Orig.). (C). 1996. pap. 35.00 (*0-7881-3482-5*) DIANE Pub.

School Facilities: Condition of America's Schools. (Illus.). 65p. (Orig.). (C). 1995. pap. text ed. 25.00 (*0-7881-1787-4*) DIANE Pub.

***School Facilities: Profiles of School Condition by State.** (Illus.). 191p. (Orig.). (C). 1996. pap. 35.00 (*0-7881-3481-7*) DIANE Pub.

***School Facilities: States' Financial & Technical Support Varies.** (Illus.). 31p. (Orig.). (C). 1996. pap. 20.00 (*0-7881-3109-5*) DIANE Pub.

School Facilities Maintenance & Operations Manual. Irene Lober. 125p. (Orig.). 1988. pap. text ed. 16.00 (*0-910170-51-7*) Assn Sch Busn.

School Failure. Ed. by David W. Kaplan. (Journal: Pediatrician: Vol. 13, No. 2-3, 1986). (Illus.). 88p. 1987. pap. 47.25 (*3-8055-4550-9*) S Karger.

***School, Family, & Community Partnerships: Your Handbook for Action.** Joyce L. Epstein et al. 216p. 1997. 69.95 (*0-8039-6570-2*) Sage.

***School, Family, & Community Partnerships: Your Handbook for Action.** Joyce L. Epstein et al. 216p. 1997. pap. 29.95 (*0-8039-6571-0*) Sage.

***School, Family & Media: Their Impact on Political Socialization of Children.** 1995. 28.00 (*0-614-25275-X*, Pub. by Rawat II) S Asia.

School, Family & Neighborhood: The Theory & Practice of School-Community Relations. Eugene Litwak & Henry J. Meyer. LC 73-17274. 316p. reprint ed. pap. 90.10 (*0-8357-4275-X*, 2037073) Bks Demand.

School Figures. Cathy Song. (Poetry Ser.). 128p. (Orig.). (C). 1994. 19.95 (*0-8229-3773-5*); pap. 10.95 (*0-8229-5517-2*) U of Pittsburgh Pr.

School Finance. 2nd ed. Austin D. Swanson. LC 96-17355. (C). 1997. text ed. 69.50 (*0-8013-1516-6*) Addison-Wesley.

***School Finance.** 3rd ed. Guthrie & Pierce. 1997. text ed. 71.00 (*0-205-27339-4*) P-H.

School Finance: A California Perspective. 4th ed. June Schmeider & Arthur Townley. 224p. (C). 1996. per., pap. text ed. 35.64 (*0-7872-2478-2*) Kendall-Hunt.

School Finance: A California Perspective. 4th ed. June Schmieder. 224p. (C). 1996. per., pap. text ed. 35.64 (*0-8403-9754-2*) Kendall-Hunt.

School Finance: A Policy Perspective. Allan R. Odden & Lawrence O. Picus. 1992. text ed. write for info. (*0-07-047486-9*) McGraw.

School Finance: Its Economics & Politics. Austin D. Swanson & Richard A. King. 384p. (C). 1991. text ed. 65.95 (*0-8013-0296-X*, 75946) Longman.

***School Finance: Options for Improving Measures of Effort & Equity in Title I.** (Illus.). 46p. (Orig.). (C). 1996. pap. 25.00 (*0-7881-3640-2*) DIANE Pub.

***School Finance: State Efforts to Reduce Funding Gaps Between Poor & Wealthy Districts.** (Illus.). 320p. 1997. pap. text ed. 65.00 (*1-57979-229-4*) BPI Info Servs.

School Finance: The Economics & Politics of Public Education. Walter I. Garms et al. (Illus.). 1978. text ed. write for info. (*0-13-793315-0*) P-H.

***School Finance: Three States Experiences with Equity in School Funding.** (Illus.). 56p. (Orig.). (C). 1996. pap. 20.00 (*0-7881-3117-6*) DIANE Pub.

School Finance: Trends in U. S. Education Spending. (Illus.). 55p. (Orig.). (C). 1996. pap. text ed. 20.00 (*0-7881-2755-1*) DIANE Pub.

School Finance Manager. Jack Rudman. (Career Examination Ser.: C-2886). 1994. pap. 34.95 (*0-8373-2886-1*) Nat Learn.

School Finance Policies & Practices: The Nineteen-Eighties: Decade of Conflict. James W. Guthrie. LC 80-19707. (American Education Finance Association Ser.). 312p. 1982. 24.50 (*0-88410-195-9*) Harper Busn.

School Finances & Education Policy. 2nd ed. Guthrie & Garms. 1988. text ed. 77.00 (*0-13-793324-X*) P-H.

School Financing in Nepal. Kedar N. Shrestha. 22p. 1981. pap. 3.00 (*0-318-23182-4*) Am-Nepal Ed.

School-Focused Staff Development: Guidelines for Policy Makers. Eric Hewton. 155p. 1988. 60.00 (*1-85000-273-8*, Falmer Pr); pap. 31.00 (*1-85000-274-6*, Falmer Pr) Taylor & Francis.

School Food Service Supervisor. (National Teacher Examination Ser.: NT-60). pap. 23.95 (*0-8373-8480-X*) Nat Learn.

School Foodservice Handbook. Dorothy V. Pannell. 96p. (Orig.). 1987. pap. text ed. 13.00 (*0-910170-48-7*) Assn Sch Busn.

School for Ambassadors & Other Essays. Jean A. Jusserand. LC 68-57325. (Essay Index Reprint Ser.). 1977. 23.95 (*0-8369-0581-4*) Ayer.

School for Colored Girls in Washington, D. C. see Myrtilla Miner: A Memoir

***School for Crusoes.** Jules Verne. lib. bdg. 22.95 (*0-8488-2071-1*) Amereon Ltd.

***School for Diplomats: The Paris Peace Conference of 1919.** Clifford R. Lovin. LC 97-9796. 182p. 1997. 32.50 (*0-7618-0755-1*) U Pr of Amer.

School for Fools. Sasha Sokolov. Tr. by Carl R. Proffer. LC 87-33009. 228p. 1988. pap. 9.95 (*0-941423-07-7*) FWEW.

School for Hope. Michael McLaverty. 256p. 1993. reprint ed. pap. 11.95 (*1-85371-172-1*, Pub. by Poolbeg Pr IE) Dufour.

School for Husbands. Moliere. (Illus.). 43p. 1966. pap. 3.25 (*0-88680-169-9*) I E Clark.

School for Husbands. Moliere. Tr. by Richard Wilbur. 1991. pap. 5.25 (*0-8222-0998-5*) Dramatists Play.

School for Husbands: Director's Script. Moliere. (Illus.). 43p. 1966. pap. 10.00 (*0-88680-170-2*) I E Clark.

School for Husbands & Sganarelle, or the Imaginary Cuckold. Moiiere. Tr. by Richard Wilbur. 1994. pap. 12.95 (*0-15-679500-0*) HarBrace.

School for Husbands by Moliere. Richard Wilbur. 1992. 18.95 (*0-15-179577-0*) HarBrace.

School for Murder. Robert Barnard. 208p. reprint ed. pap. 6.00 (*0-88150-320-7*) Countryman.

School for One. Judith Weil. (J). (gr. 4 up). 1992. 11.95 (*0-87306-620-0*); pap. 9.95 (*0-87306-621-9*) Feldheim.

School for Pagan Lovers. Edmund Keeley. LC 92-28943. (Fiction Ser.). 302p. (C). 1993. 19.95 (*0-8135-1935-7*) Rutgers U Pr.

School for Pompey Walker. Michael J. Rosen. LC 94-6240. (Illus.). 48p. (J). (gr. 2-7). 1995. 16.00 (*0-15-200114-X*, HB Juv Bks) HarBrace.

School for Quality Learning: Managing the School & Classroom the Deming Way. Donna K. Crawford et al. LC 93-84097. 296p. (Orig.). (C). 1993. pap. text ed. 21.95 (*0-87822-341-X*, 4674) Res Press.

School for Scandal. Richard B. Sheridan. 1977. pap. 6.95 (*0-8120-0155-9*) Barron.

School for Scandal. Richard B. Sheridan. Ed. by John Loftis. (Crofts Classics Ser.). 128p. 1966. pap. text ed. write for info. (*0-88295-092-4*) Harlan Davidson.

School for Scandal. Richard B. Sheridan. Ed. by Richard Adams. 1988. pap. 5.72 (*0-582-33149-8*, 72055) Longman.

School for Scandal. Richard B. Sheridan. 21.95 (*0-8488-1163-1*) Amereon Ltd.

School for Scandal. Richard B. Sheridan. 1991. pap. 1.00 (*0-486-26687-7*) Dover.

S

School for Scandal. Richard B. Sheridan. Ed. by C. J. Price. 146p. 1971. pap. 10.95 (*0-19-911008-5*) OUP.

*__School for Scandal.__ Richard B. Sheridan. 21.95 (*1-56723-090-3*) Yestermorrow.

School for Scandal. Richard B. Sheridan. Ed. & Intro. by William-Alan Landes. LC 95-35798. (Illus.). 82p. 1995. pap. 7.00 (*0-88734-284-1*) Players Pr.

School for Scandal. 3rd ed. Richard B. Sheridan. Ed. by Frederick W. Bateson. (New Mermaid Ser.). (C). 1995. pap. text ed. 7.95 (*0-393-90077-0*) Norton.

School for Scandal & Other Plays: And Other Plays. Richard B. Sheridan. Ed. & Intro. by Eric S. Rump. 288p. 1989. pap. 9.95 (*0-14-043240-X*, Penguin Classics) Viking Penguin.

School for Slaughter. George G. Gilman. (Edge Ser.: No. 48). 192p. 1993. mass mkt. 3.50 (*1-55817-682-9*, Pinncle Kensgtn) Kensgtn Pub Corp.

School for Terror: Going to School Can Be Murder. Peter Beere. 160p. (YA). (gr. 7-9). 1994. pap. 3.50 (*0-590-48319-6*) Scholastic Inc.

School for the Blind. Dennis McFarland. 1994. 21.95 (*0-395-64497-6*) HM.

School for the Blind. Dennis McFarland. 272p. 1995. mass mkt. 6.99 (*0-8041-1350-5*) Ivy Books.

School for Wives. Moliere. Tr. by Richard Wilbur. 1991. pap. 5.25 (*0-8222-0999-3*) Dramatists Play.

*__School for Wives: After Moliere.__ Derek Mahon. 76p. 1986. pap. 12.95 (*1-85235-004-0*) Dufour.

School for Wives: An Adaptation in Rhymed Verse. Moliere. Tr. by Eric M. Steel. LC 75-154426. 1977. pap. 4.95 (*0-8120-0436-1*) Barron.

School for Wives & the Learned Ladies. Tr. by Richard Wilbur. 1991. pap. 10.95 (*0-15-679502-7*, Harvest Bks) HarBrace.

School for Wives-Robert-Genevieve or the Unfinished Confidence. Andre Gide. Tr. by Dorothy Bussy from FRE. LC 79-23993. 1980. reprint ed. lib. bdg. 18.00 (*0-8376-0454-0*) Bentley.

School for Young Children: Developmentally Appropriate Practices. Charles H. Wolfgang & Mary E. Wolfgang. 336p. (C). 1991. pap. text ed. 36.00 (*0-205-13122-0*) Allyn.

School Foundation Workbook. K. B. Rasmussen. 1993. 72.00 (*1-56925-015-4*, TSFW) Capitol Publns.

*__School Fun.__ (Berenstain Bears Family Time Coloring & Activity Bks.). (J). (ps-2). 1996. pap. 1.95 (*0-614-20247-7*, GT Pubing) GT Pubng Corp.

School Fun. Al Hartley. (Barbour Activity Bks.). (Illus.). (J). (gr. 1). 1988. reprint ed. pap. text ed. 1.29 (*1-55748-003-6*) Barbour & Co.

School Fun Activity Book. Anthony John. (Illus.). 64p. (Orig.). (J). 1991. pap. 1.95 (*1-56156-036-7*) Kidsbks.

School Funds & Their Apportionment, a Consideration of the Subject with Reference to a More General Equalization of Both the Burdens & the Advantages of Education. Ellwood P. Cubberley. LC 72-176681. (Columbia University. Teachers College. Contributions to Education Ser.: No. 2). reprint ed. 37.50 (*0-404-55002-9*) AMS Pr.

School Funds in the Province of Quebec. George J. Trueman. LC 75-177695. (Columbia University. Teachers College. Contributions to Education Ser.: No. 106). reprint ed. 37.50 (*0-404-55106-8*) AMS Pr.

*__School Governors.__ Brooksbank. Date not set. pap. text ed. write for info. (*0-900313-76-5*) Addison-Wesley.

School Governors: What Governors Need to Know, 3 pts., Pt. 1. Jeff Jones. 64p. 1993. pap. 16.00 (*1-85346-263-2*, Pub. by D Fulton UK) Taylor & Francis.

School Governors: What Governors Need to Know, 3 pts., Pt. 2. Jeff Jones. 64p. 1993. pap. 17.00 (*1-85346-264-0*, Pub. by D Fulton UK) Taylor & Francis.

School Governors: What Governors Need to Know, 3 pts., Pt. 3. Jeff Jones. 64p. 1993. pap. 17.00 (*1-85346-265-9*, Pub. by D Fulton UK) Taylor & Francis.

School Greenhouse Guide. Eve Pranis & Joreen Hendry. (Growing Ideas Ser.). (Illus.). 24p. (Orig.). 1995. pap. 7.95 (*0-915873-37-0*) Natl Gardening Assn.

School Guard. Jack Rudman. (Career Examination Ser.: C-1923). 1994. pap. 23.95 (*0-8373-1923-4*) Nat Learn.

School Hammond World Almanac. (J). pap. 2.50 (*0-590-05437-6*) Scholastic Inc.

School Handbooks: Some Legal Considerations. Mary A. Shaughnessy. 100p. 1989. pap. 8.00 (*1-55833-022-4*) Natl Cath Educ.

*__School Health.__ 5th ed. Schalle. (C). 1981. write for info. (*0-03-057702-0*) HB Coll Pubs.

School Health: Findings from Evaluated Programs. 1994. lib. bdg. 250.00 (*0-8490-8408-3*) Gordon Pr.

School Health: Helping Children Learn. (Illus.). 73p. 1991. pap. text ed. 15.00 (*0-88364-138-0*) Natl Sch Boards.

School Health: Policy & Practice. 5th ed. American Academy of Pediatrics Staff. 428p. 1993. pap. 44.95 (*0-910761-42-6*) Am Acad Pediat.

School Health Education to Prevent AIDS & Sexually Transmitted Diseases. WHO Staff. (WHO AIDS Ser.: Vol. 10). v, 79p. (CHI, FRE, RUS & SPA.). 1992. pap. text ed. 18.00 (*92-4-121010-9*, 1870010) World Health.

School Health Handbook: A Ready Reference for School Nurses & Educators. Jerry Newton. LC 84-8382. 300p. 1984. 27.95 (*0-13-793639-7*, Busn) P-H.

School Health in America. 5th ed. 1986. 18.00 (*0-917160-20-7*) Am Sch Health.

*__School Health Instruction Lessons.__ 3rd ed. Marion Pollock. 184p. (C). 1994. per. write for info. (*0-8151-6683-4*) Wm C Brown Pubs.

School Health Program. 3rd ed. Jessie H. Haag. LC 70-175461. (Health Education, Physical Education, & Recreation Ser.). 297p. reprint ed. pap. 84.70 (*0-685-15869-1*, 2056187) Bks Demand.

School History of Mississippi. Franklin L. Riley. LC 76-68. (Illus.). 448p. 1976. reprint ed. 17.50 (*0-87152-219-5*) Reprint.

School History of the Negro Race in America, 2 Vols. in 1. Edward A. Johnson. LC 73-100532. reprint ed. 26.50 (*0-404-00176-9*) AMS Pr.

School-Home Notes: Promoting Children's Classroom Success. Mary L. Kelley. LC 89-49686. (Guilford School Practitioner Ser.). 198p. 1990. pap. text ed. 20.95 (*0-89862-235-2*) Guilford Pr.

School-Home Notes: Promoting Children's Classroom Success. Mary L. Kelley. LC 89-49686. (Guilford School Practitioner Ser.). 198p. 1990. lib. bdg. 49.95 (*0-89862-356-1*) Guilford Pr.

*__School House Humor & Insight.__ Chuck Sodergren. Ed. by June G. Krehbiel. LC 96-70118. 112p. (Orig.). 1996. pap. 9.95 (*0-9645085-9-1*) Prtnrshp Bk Servs.

*__School House of Quality.__ Richard Hammond. 130p. 1996. pap. text ed. write for info. (*0-07-057270-4*) McGraw.

School Improvement. Ed. by Creemers. 168p. (C). 1996. pap. 17.95 (*0-415-13024-7*); text ed. 59.95 (*0-415-13023-9*) Routledge.

School Improvement: Theory & Practice, a Book of Readings. Ed. by Robert V. Carlson & Edward R. Ducharme. (Illus.). 1228p. (Orig.). (C). 1987. lib. bdg. 99.00 (*0-8191-5815-1*) U Pr of Amer.

School Improvement in an Era of Change. Mel Ainscow et al. LC 94-12563. 1994. pap. 21.95 (*0-8077-3390-3*) Tchrs Coll.

School Improvement in an Era of Change. Ed. by David Hopkins et al. (School Development Ser.). (Illus.). 192p. 1994. 70.00 (*0-304-32608-9*); pap. text ed. 22.50 (*0-304-32610-0*) Cassell.

School Improvement in Practice: Schools Make a Difference. Ed. by Kate Myers. LC 95-23592. 1996. write for info. (*0-7507-0439-X*, Falmer Pr); pap. write for info. (*0-7507-0440-3*, Falmer Pr) Taylor & Francis.

School in Belmont. large type ed. Sheila Bishop. 1995. 25.99 (*0-7089-3305-X*) Ulverscroft.

School in Every County: The Partnership of Jewish Philanthropist Julius Rosenwald & American Black Communities. Jeffrey Sosland. Ed. by Lawrence Goldmuntz & Steven Kurzman. (Illus.). 50p. (Orig.). 1995. pap. 1.00 (*0-9646528-0-3*) Econs & Sci.

School in Rose Valley: A Parent Venture in Education. Grace Rotzel. LC 70-144200. (Illus.). 159p. (C). reprint ed. 45.40 (*0-8357-9284-6*, 2015739) Bks Demand.

School in the Multicultural Society. Ed. by Alan James & Rob Jeffcoate. 324p. (C). 1982. 52.00 (*0-06-318195-9*, Pub. by P Chapman Pub UK); pap. 30.00 (*0-06-318196-7*, Pub. by P Chapman Pub UK) St Mut.

School in the Service of Evangelization: The Catholic Educational Impact in Eastern Nigeria 1886-1950. Nicholas I. Omenka. LC 88-37555. (Studies on Religion in Africa - Supplements to the Journal of Religion in Africa: Vol. 6). xv, 317p. 1989. 91.50 (*90-04-08632-3*) E J Brill.

School in the Social Setting. Alan Gorr. 392p. 1974. text ed. 37.50 (*0-8422-5162-6*); pap. text ed. 14.95 (*0-8422-0177-7*) Irvington.

School Industry Links. Bronte Price. (C). 1990. 59.00 (*0-86431-100-1*, Pub. by Aust Council Educ Res AT) St Mut.

School Inequality & the Welfare State. John D. Owen. LC 74-6834. 222p. reprint ed. pap. 63.30 (*0-685-23647-1*, 2027901) Bks Demand.

School Interventions for Children of Alcoholics. Bonnie K. Nastasi & Denise Dezolt. LC 94-853. (Guilford School Practitioner Ser.). 275p. 1994. lib. bdg. 27.95 (*0-89862-367-7*) Guilford Pubns.

School Is Hell. Matt Groening. LC 86-62859. (Illus.). 48p. 1987. pap. 7.95 (*0-394-75091-8*) Pantheon.

*__School Is Not a Four-Letter Word: How to Help Your Child Make the Grade.__ Louanne Johnson. LC 96-46150. 304p. 1997. 19.95 (*0-7868-6274-2*) Hyperion.

School Is Out: Late Elementary Piano Solos. B. Gallagher. 32p. 1993. pap. 5.95 (*0-7935-2347-8*, 00290421) H Leonard.

School Isn't Fair! Patricia Baehr. LC 88-21461. (Illus.). 32p. (J). (ps-k). 1989. lib. bdg. 13.95 (*0-02-708130-3*, Four Winds Pr) S&S Childrens.

School Isn't Fair. Patricia Baehr. LC 91-38485. (Illus.). 32p. (J). (ps). 1992. reprint ed. pap. 4.95 (*0-689-71544-7*, Aladdin Paperbacks) S&S Childrens.

School Jokes. Viki Woodworth. (Funny Side up Ser.). (Illus.). 32p. (J). (gr. 1-4). 1991. lib. bdg. 19.93 (*0-89565-726-0*) Childs World.

School Kit: Individual Sets in Four Kits. Marion W. Stuart. text ed. write for info. (*0-943343-60-7*) Lrn Wrap-Ups.

School Laboratory Assistant. Jack Rudman. (Career Examination Ser.: C-3333). 1994. pap. 27.95 (*0-8373-3333-4*) Nat Learn.

School Language Policy for Puerto Rico. Pedro A. Cebollero. LC 74-14224. (Puerto Rican Experience Ser.). (Illus.). 148p. 1974. reprint ed. 12.95 (*0-405-06214-1*) Ayer.

School Law. 3rd ed. Michael Lamorte. 480p. (C). 1990. Casebound. boxed write for info. (*0-13-793704-0*) P-H.

*__School Law.__ 25th ed. 586p. 1994. 45.00 (*0-614-26702-1*, 4227) NYS Bar.

*__School Law.__ 26th ed. 1996. 45.00 (*1-56452-051-X*) NY Boards Assoc.

School Law: Cases & Concepts. Michael W. La Morte. (Illus.). 448p. (C). 1982. write for info. (*0-13-793695-8*) P-H.

School Law: Cases & Concepts. 5th ed. Michael W. La Morte. LC 95-7736. 1995. text ed. 74.00 (*0-205-16568-0*) Allyn.

School Law: Leading Your District into the 21st Century. 800p. 1990. student ed. 200.00 (*0-88364-151-8*) Natl Sch Boards.

School Law: The Legal Challenges of Change. NSBA Council of School Attorney Staff. 150p. 1996. pap. 30.00 (*0-88364-202-6*, 06-158) Natl Sch Boards.

School Law: Theoretical & Case Perspectives. Julius Menacker. 480p. (C). 1987. text ed. write for info. (*0-13-793753-9*) P-H.

School Law for Counselors, Psychologists, & Social Workers. 3rd ed. Louis Fischer & Gail P. Sorenson. LC 95-7932. 400p. (C). 1996. pap. text ed. 26.36 (*0-8013-1522-0*) Longman.

School Law for the Florida Educator. Kenneth T. Murray & Barbara A. Murray. 246p. (C). 1995. pap. text ed. 46.50 (*0-9644512-0-4*) IntraCoast Pub.

School Law for the Practitioner. Robert C. O'Reilly & Edward T. Green. LC 82-11982. (Contributions to the Study of Education Ser.: No. 6). (Illus.). xiv, 314p. 1983. text ed. 36.95 (*0-313-23639-9*, ORS/, Greenwood Pr) Greenwood.

School Law for the 1990s: A Handbook. Robert C. O'Reilly & Edward T. Green. LC 91-27237. 312p. 1992. text ed. 49.95 (*0-313-27817-2*, OSL/, Greenwood Pr) Greenwood.

*__School Law in New York State: A Manual for Parents.__ 2nd rev. ed. Seth Rockmuller. LC 96-78424. 156p. (Orig.). 1996. pap. 14.95 (*0-9636096-7-X*) Longview NY.

School Law in Review. 150p. 1992. pap. text ed. 35.00 (*0-88364-133-X*) Natl Sch Boards.

School Law in Review, 1989. 140p. (Orig.). 1989. pap. 35.00 (*0-88364-152-6*) Natl Sch Boards.

School Law in Review, 1990. 1990. 35.00 (*0-88364-155-0*) Natl Sch Boards.

School Law in Review, 1991. 164p. 1991. 35.00 (*0-88364-131-3*) Natl Sch Boards.

School Law in Review, 1993. National School Boards Association Staff. 130p. (Orig.). 1993. pap. 35.00 (*0-88364-148-8*) Natl Sch Boards.

School Law in Review, 1994: 1994. NSBA Council of School Attorneys Staff. 156p. (Orig.). 1994. pap. 35.00 (*0-88364-182-8*) Natl Sch Boards.

School Law in Review 1995. NSBA Council of School Attorneys Staff. (Orig.). 1995. pap. 35.00 (*0-88364-193-3*) Natl Sch Boards.

School Law in Review 1996. NSBA Council of School Attorneys Staff. 160p. (Orig.). 1996. pap. 35.00 (*0-88364-201-8*) Natl Sch Boards.

*__School Law in Review 1997.__ NSBA Council of School Attorneys Staff. 146p. 1997. pap. text ed. 35.00 (*0-88364-208-5*, 06-191) Natl Sch Boards.

School Leader in Action: Discovering the Golden Mean. David Cattanach. LC 95-61925. 538p. 1995. text ed. 49.95 (*1-56676-343-6*) Technomic.

School Leadership: A Blueprint for Change. Ed. by Scott D. Thomson. LC 91-32152. 64p. 1991. pap. text ed. 11.95 (*0-8039-6013-1*, 60131) Corwin Pr.

School Leadership: A Contemporary Reader. Ed. by Joel L. Burdin. LC 88-19104. 448p. 1989. 59.95 (*0-8039-3362-2*, 33622); pap. 27.95 (*0-8039-3363-0*, 33630) Corwin Pr.

*__School Leadership: Handbook for Excellence.__ 3rd ed. Stuart C. Smith et al. LC 96-34636. 1997. 29.95 (*0-86552-134-4*); pap. 19.95 (*0-86552-135-2*) U of Oreg ERIC.

School Leadership - Beyond Education Management: An Essay in Policy Scholarship. Gerald Grace. LC 95-2112. 184p. 1995. 75.00 (*0-7507-0414-4*, Falmer Pr); pap. 24.95 (*0-7507-0415-2*, Falmer Pr) Taylor & Francis.

School Leadership & Administration: Important Concepts, Case Studies, & Simulations. 4th ed. Richard A. Gorton & Petra E. Snowden. 336p. (C). 1992. per. write for info. (*0-697-10317-X*) Brown & Benchmark.

*__School Leadership & Administration: Important Concepts, Case Studies & Simulations.__ 5th ed. Petra E. Snowden & Richard A. Gorton Richard. 352p. (C). 1997. per. write for info. (*0-697-24143-2*) Wm C Brown Pubs.

School Leadership & Instructional Improvement. Daniel L. Duke. 280p. (C). 1986. pap. text ed. write for info. (*0-07-554970-0*) McGraw.

School Leadership for the 21st Century: A Competency & Knowledge Approach. Brent Davies & Linda Ellison. LC 96-2156. 1997. write for info. (*0-415-13366-1*) Routledge.

School Leavers & Their Prospects: Youth & the Labor Market in the 1980's. Kenneth Roberts. 169p. 1984. pap. 25.00 (*0-335-10418-5*, Open Univ Pr) Taylor & Francis.

*__School Leaver's Handbook.__ Joanna Grigg. (Careers & Testing Ser.). 1996. pap. 19.95 (*0-7494-1668-8*) Kogan Page Ltd.

School Leaver's Handbook. Ann Jones. 128p. (Orig.). 1989. pap. 14.95 (*0-8464-1414-7*) Beekman Pubs.

School-Leaving Youth & Employment: Some Factors Associated with the Duration of Early Employment of Youth Whose Formal Education Ended at High School Graduation or Earlier. Cloyd D. Long. LC 74-177006. (Columbia University. Teachers College. Contributions to Education Ser.: No. 845). reprint ed. 37.50 (*0-404-55845-3*) AMS Pr.

School Lessons, Work Lessons: Recruiting & Sustaining Employer Involvement in School-to-Work Programs. Irene Lynn & Loan L. Wills. 100p. 1994. 12.00 (*0-937846-48-1*) Inst Educ Lead.

School Letters in English & Spanish. Barbara Thuro. 285p. 1993. pap. 24.95 (*0-932825-04-4*) Ammie Enter.

School Librarian's Book of Lists. Jane E. Streiff. LC 92-12720. 240p. 1992. text ed. 29.95 (*0-87628-811-5*) Ctr Appl Res.

School Librarian's Sourcebook. Claire Rudin. 504p. 1990. 38.00 (*0-8352-2711-1*) Bowker.

School Librarianship. Ed. by John Cook. (Illus.). 272p. 1981. 34.00 (*0-08-024814-4*, Pergamon Pr); pap. 22.00 (*0-08-024813-6*, Pergamon Pr) Elsevier.

*__School Librarianship.__ 2nd ed. James E. Herring. LC 88-26009. (Illus.). 93p. 1988. reprint ed. pap. 26.60 (*0-608-02483-X*, 2063126) Bks Demand.

*__School Librarianship: International Perspectives & Issues.__ Ed. by Ken Haycock & Blanche Woolls. 300p. 1997. 35.00 (*1-890861-19-7*) IASL.

School Libraries: International Developments. 2nd ed. Ed. by Jean E. Lowrie & Mieko Nagakura. LC 91-10920. (Illus.). 403p. 1991. 45.00 (*0-8108-2390-X*) Scarecrow.

School Libraries & the Electronic Community: The Internet Connection. Laurel A. Clyde. LC 97-14506. 368p. 1997. pap. 29.95 (*0-8108-3193-7*) Scarecrow.

*__School Libraries for All? Conference Proceedings of the 10th Annual Conference of the International Association of School Librarianship, Aberystwyth, Wales, U. K., July 30-August 4, 1981.__ 167p. 25.00 (*0-9617248-0-3*) IASL.

*__School Libraries in a Diverse World: Selected Papers from the 20th Annual Conference of the International Association of School Librarianship, Everett, Washington, U. S. A., July 22-27, 1991.__ 221p. 25.00 (*1-890861-13-8*) IASL.

*__School Library - Centre of Communication: Conference Proceedings of the 12th Annual Conference of the International Association of School Librarianship, Bad Segeberg, Germany, August 10-15, 1983.__ Ed. by Anke Matthies. 225p. 25.00 (*1-890861-02-2*) IASL.

*__School Library - Children's Culture in the International Year of the Child: Conference Proceedings of the 8th Annual Conference of the International Association of School Librarianship, Middlefart, Denmark, July 30-August 4, 1979.__ 145p. 25.00 (*0-9617248-8-9*) IASL.

*__School Library - Gateway to Knowledge: Conference Proceedings of 16th Annual Conference of the International Association of School Librarianship, Reykjavik, Iceland, July 26-31, 1987.__ Ed. by Sigrun Hannesdottir. 280p. 25.00 (*1-890861-08-1*) IASL.

*__School Library - Window on the World: Conference Proceedings of 15th Annual Conference of the International Association of School Librarianship, Halifax, Nova Scotia, Canada, July 27-August 1, 1986.__ 392p. 1986. 25.00 (*1-890861-07-3*) IASL.

*__School Library: Centre for Life Long Learning: Conference Proceedings of the 18th Annual Conference of the International Association of School Librarianship, Kuala Lumpur, Malaysia, July 22-26, 1989.__ Ed. by Wong Kim Siong et al. 571p. 25.00 (*1-890861-11-1*) IASL.

School Library Journal's Best: A Reader for Children's, Young Adult, & School Librarians. Ed. by Marilyn L. Miller et al. LC 96-23856. 475p. 1997. pap. 39.95 (*1-55570-203-1*) Neal-Schuman.

School Library Management. 3rd ed. Ed. by Catherine Andronik. LC 93-47159. (Professional Growth Ser.). (Illus.). 300p. 1994. ring bd. 36.95 (*0-938865-29-3*) Linworth Pub.

School Library Media Annual, 1993, Vol. 11. Carol C. Kuhlthau et al. 350p. 1993. lib. bdg. 42.50 (*1-56308-099-0*) Libs Unl.

School Library Media Annual, 1994, 12. Ed. by Elspeth Goodin et al. xx, 380p. 1994. lib. bdg. 45.00 (*1-56308-317-5*) Libs Unl.

School Library Media Annual, 1995 Vol. 13: The Future of School Libraries. Ed. by Betty J. Morris et al. 400p. 1995. lib. bdg. 45.00 (*1-56308-388-4*) Libs Unl.

School Library Media Centers in the 21st Century: Changes & Challenges. Kathleen Craver. LC 94-5146. 216p. 1994. text ed. 35.00 (*0-313-29100-4*) Greenwood.

School Library Media Manager. Blanche Woolls. (Library Science Text Ser.). xvi, 336p. 1994. pap. text ed. 31.50 (*1-56308-318-3*); lib. bdg. 38.50 (*1-56308-304-3*) Libs Unl.

School Library Media Services to the Handicapped. Ed. by Myra Macon. LC 81-4262. (Illus.). xii, 208p. 1982. text ed. 49.95 (*0-313-22684-9*, MAL/, Greenwood Pr) Greenwood.

*__School Library Media Specialist As Manager: A Book of Case Studies.__ Amy G. Job & MaryKay Schnare. LC 97-20841. (School Librarianship Ser.). 1997. write for info. (*0-8108-3363-8*) Scarecrow.

School Library Reference Services in the 90's: Where We Are, Where We're Heading. Ed. by Carol Truett. LC 94-13311. (Reference Librarian Ser.: No. 44). (Illus.). 199p. 1994. 49.95 (*1-56024-673-1*) Haworth Pr.

School Life & Organizational Psychology. American Psychological Association Staff. (Human Behavior Curriculum Project Ser.). 64p. (Orig.). 1981. teacher ed. 9.95 (*0-8077-2618-4*); pap. text ed. 3.95 (*0-8077-2617-6*) Tchrs Coll.

*__School-Linked Comprehensive Services for Children & Families.__ 1997. lib. bdg. 250.95 (*0-8490-8238-2*) Gordon Pr.

School-Linked Human Services: A Comprehensive Strategy for Aiding Students at Risk of School Failure. 66p. (Orig.). (C). 1994. pap. text ed. 25.00 (*0-7881-0685-6*) DIANE Pub.

School Lunch Coordinator. Jack Rudman. (Career Examination Ser.: C-317). 1994. pap. 34.95 (*0-8373-0317-6*) Nat Learn.

School Lunch Director. Jack Rudman. (Career Examination Ser.: C-2088). 1994. pap. 34.95 (*0-8373-2088-7*) Nat Learn.

School Lunch Manager. Jack Rudman. (Career Examination Ser.: C-703). 1994. pap. 34.95 (*0-8373-0703-1*) Nat Learn.

*__School Lunch Program: Cafeteria Managers' Views on Food Wasted by Students.__ (Illus.). 44p. (Orig.). (C). 1996. pap. 25.00 (*0-7881-3434-5*) DIANE Pub.

An Asterisk (*) at the beginning of an entry indicates that the title is appearing in BIP for the first time.

***School Lunch Program: Role & Impacts of Private Food Service Companies.** (Illus.). 62p. (Orig.). (C). 1996. pap. 25.00 (*0-7881-3669-0*) DIANE Pub.

School-Maister to the Art of Stenographie. John Willis. LC 74-80225. (English Experience Ser.: No. 702). 176p. 1974. reprint ed. 20.00 (*90-221-0702-7*) Walter J Johnson.

School Management & Pupil Behaviour. Ed. by Neville Jones. (Education & Alienation Ser.). 280p. 1989. 70.00 (*1-85000-591-5*, Falmer Pr); pap. 35.00 (*1-85000-592-3*, Falmer Pr) Taylor & Francis.

School Management by Wandering Around. Larry Frase & Robert Hetzel. LC 89-51778. 212p. 1990. 39.95 (*0-87762-640-5*) Technomic.

School Management in Nepal. Kedar N. Shrestha. 25p. 1981. pap. 3.00 (*0-318-23181-6*) Am-Nepal Ed.

School Managers: Power & Conflict in American Public Education. Donald J. McCarty et al. LC 70-105975. (Illus.). 281p. 1971. text ed. 65.00 (*0-8371-3299-1*, MSM/, Greenwood Pr) Greenwood.

School-Marm Tree. O'Hagan. (NFS Canada Ser.). 1993. pap. 14.95 (*0-88922-129-4*) Genl Dist Srvs.

School Materials Safety Manual: A Collection of Material Safety Data Sheets (Plus Updating Service) John H. Bartsch. LC 87-14889. 439p. 1987. 195.00 (*0-931690-22-6*) Genium Pub.

School Mathematics: The Challenge to Change. Nerida F. Ellerton & M. A. Clements. 328p. (C). 1995. pap. 75.00 (*0-7300-0705-7*, ECS807, Pub. by Deakin Univ AT) St Mut.

School Matters. (Cross Training Ser.: Vol. 4). 56p. (J). (gr. 7-9). 1995. pap. 29.95 (*1-57405-030-3*) CharismaLife Pub.

School Matters. Peter Mortimore et al. 1988. 48.00 (*0-520-06502-6*); pap. 17.00 (*0-520-06503-4*) U CA Pr.

School Matters: The Junior Years. Peter Mortimore et al. 314p. 1988. pap. 22.00 (*0-7291-0194-0*, Pub. by Paul Chapman UK) Taylor & Francis.

School Meals Service. B. Berger. 1990. pap. 30.00 (*0-7463-0518-4*, Pub. by Northcote UK) St Mut.

School Mentor Handbook: Essential Skills & Strategies for Working with Student Teachers. Hazel Hagger et al. 128p. 1995. pap. 26.00 (*0-7494-1601-7*) Taylor & Francis.

School Misery. Jim Grant. 40p. 1992. pap. 6.00 (*0-935493-28-X*) Modern Learn Pr.

School Misery. Jim Grant. 40p. 1992. pap. text ed. 6.00 (*0-935493-88-3*) Programs Educ.

School Mouse. Dick King-Smith. LC 94-48443. (Illus.). 128p. (J). (gr. 2-5). 1995. 13.95 (*0-7868-0036-4*); lib. bdg. 13.89 (*0-7868-2029-2*) Hyprn Child.

School Mouse. Dick King-Smith. LC 94-48443. (Illus.). 128p. (J). (gr. 2-5). 1997. pap. 4.50 (*0-7868-1156-0*) Hyprn Child.

***School Mural.** Sarah Vazquez. LC 97-25426. (Illus.). (J). 1998. write for info. (*0-8172-7286-0*) Raintree Steck-V.

School Museum Collection Text & Prints. (Illus.). 120p. 1992. pap. text ed. 542.00 (*0-935493-75-1*) Modern Learn Pr.

School Music Program: A New Vision. Music Educators National Conference Staff. 48p. (C). 1994. pap. 14.50 (*1-56545-039-6*, 1618) Music Ed Natl.

School Myth-Takes (Myths & Mistakes About School) Margarita V. Hamada. 219p. 1987. pap. 13.75 (*971-10-0320-1*, Pub. by New Day Pub PH) Cellar.

School News Shows: Video Production with a Focus. Virginia Wallace & Ramona Gorham. LC 96-10480. (Professional Growth Ser.). 107p. 1996. pap. text ed. 24.95 (*0-938865-49-8*) Linworth Pub.

School Newspaper. Serena K. Bond. (Language Arts Ser.). 24p. (gr. 8-12). 1982. student ed. 5.00 (*0-8209-0328-0*, J-1) ESP.

***School Newspaper Adviser's Survival Guide.** Patricia Osborn. LC 97-23288. 1997. pap. text ed. 29.95 (*0-87628-891-3*) Ctr Appl Res.

School Newspaper Management. Campbell. 2.00 (*0-318-19222-5*) Quill & Scroll.

School Nurse from the Black Lagoon. Mike Thaler. (J). 1995. pap. 2.99 (*0-590-50312-X*) Scholastic Inc.

School Nurse Practitioner. Jack Rudman. (Certified Nurse Examination Ser.: CN-3). 1994. pap. 23.95 (*0-8373-6103-6*) Nat Learn.

School Nurse's Source Book of Individualized Healthcare Plans. Marykay B. Haas. LC 92-48666. 1993. pap. 39.95 (*0-9624814-1-6*) Sunrise River Pr.

School Nurse's Survival Guide: Ready-to-Use Tips, Techniques, & Materials for the School Health Professional. Richard M. Adams. LC 95-18454. 354p. 1995. spiral bd. 34.95 (*0-13-186727-X*) P-H.

School Nursing. Slack. 1978. pap. text ed. 22.95 (*0-7020-0672-6*) HarBrace.

***School Nursing & Health Services: A Resource & Planning Guide.** Cindy S. Ericksen. 200p. 1997. pap. 27.00 (*1-57337-048-7*) WI Dept Pub Instruct.

School Nutrition & Food Service Techniques: for Children with Exceptional Needs. California Department of Education Staff. 56p. 1982. pap. 4.50 (*0-8011-0261-8*) Calif Education.

School Nutrition Facility Planning Guide. California Department of Education Staff. (Illus.). 106p. 1992. spiral bd. 10.00 (*0-8011-1042-4*) Calif Education.

School of Abuse. Stephen Gosson. Ed. by John P. Collier. LC 77-126658. reprint ed. write for info. (*0-404-02886-1*) AMS Pr.

School of Abuse: A Pleasant Invective Against Poets, Pipers, Players, Jesters, Etc. see Stage Attacked. Northbrooke & Gosson: A Treatise Against Dicing, Dancing, Plays & Interludes

***School of Assassins: The Case for Closing the School of the Americas & for Fundamentally Changing U. S. Foreign Policy.** Jack Nelson-Pallmeyer. LC 97-3390. 128p. (Orig.). 1997. pap. 12.00 (*1-57075-134-X*) Orbis Bks.

School of Bowing Technic Book 1 Part 1: For the Violin. Otakar Sevcik. 32p. 1986. pap. 4.95 (*0-7935-5441-1*) H Leonard.

School of Calvary. J. H. Jowett. 1988. pap. 2.99 (*0-88019-238-0*) Schmul Pub Co.

School of Charity: Meditations on the Christian Creed. Evelyn Underhill. LC 90-19825. 124p. 1990. reprint ed. pap. 8.95 (*0-8192-1548-1*) Morehouse Pub.

School of Charity: The Letters of Thomas Merton on Religious Renewal & Spiritual Direction. Selected by Patrick Hart. 1990. 27.95 (*0-374-25449-4*) FS&G.

School of Charity: The Letters of Thomas Merton on Religious Renewal & Spiritual Direction. Selected by Patrick Hart. LC 92-33541. 1993. pap. 15.95 (*0-15-679515-9*) HarBrace.

School of Chartres. Pierre Morizot. 1987. pap. 6.95 (*0-916786-97-8*, Saint George Pubns) R Steiner Col Pubns.

School of Chemical Engineering at Cornell: A History of the First Fifty Years. Julian C. Smith. 101p. 1988. 15.00 (*0-918531-02-0*) Cornell Coll Eng.

School of Christian Rejections see Twelve Steps ot Holiness & Salvation

School of Classical Dance. Vera S. Kostrovitskaya & Alexei Pisarev. Tr. by John Barker. (Illus.). 488p. 1995. pap. text ed. 35.00 (*1-85273-044-7*, Pub. by Dance Bks UK) Princeton Bk Co.

School of Darkness. Bella V. Dodd. 1963. pap. 6.95 (*0-8159-6804-3*) Devin.

School of Education As a Workplace. Ed. by Ayers Bagley. 1986. 3.00 (*0-933669-36-4*) Soc Profs Ed.

School of English Murder. large type ed. Ruth D. Edwards. (Mystery Ser.). 432p. 1992. 25.99 (*0-7089-2765-3*) Ulverscroft.

***School of Faith.** Thomas F. Torrance. 485p. 1996. pap. 35.00 (*1-57910-020-1*) Wipf & Stock.

School of Fine Arts 1995: American Academy in Rome. Fellows of American Academy in Rome, School of Fine Arts Staff. (Illus.). 96p. 1995. pap. text ed. write for info. (*1-879549-03-4*) Am Acad Rome.

***School of Fish.** Eileen Myles. LC 97-11773. 200p. (Orig.). 1997. pap. 14.00 (*1-57423-031-X*) Black Sparrow.

***School of Fish.** Eileen Myles. LC 97-11773. 200p. 1997. 25.00 (*1-57423-032-8*) Black Sparrow.

***School of Fish.** deluxe limited ed. Eileen Myles. LC 97-11773. 200p. 1997. 35.00 (*1-57423-033-6*) Black Sparrow.

School of Franz Brentano. Ed. by Liliana Albertazzi et al. LC 95-39650. (Nijhoff International Philosophy Ser.: No. 52). 1995. lib. bdg. 199.00 (*0-7923-3766-2*) Kluwer Ac.

School of Guitar: The Guitar in Pedagogy, Practice, Performance, 2 vols., Set. Richard Pick. LC 92-14177. 1992. pap. 25.00 (*0-936186-73-9*) Edit Orphee.

***School of Hard Knocks: A Dead Letter Mystery.** Donna H. Murray. 1997. mass mkt. 5.99 (*0-312-96104-9*) St Martin.

School of Hawthorne. Richard H. Brodhead. 272p. 1990. reprint ed. pap. 19.96 (*0-19-506070-9*) OUP.

School of Her Own. Arleta Richardson. LC 85-29050. (Grandma's Attic Ser.). 173p. (J). (gr. 3-7). 1995. pap. 3.99 (*1-55513-670-2*, Chariot Bks) Chariot Victor.

School of Horsemanship. Francois R. De La Gueriniere. Tr. by Tracy Boucher. 482p. (C). 1993. 175.00 (*0-85131-575-5*, Pub. by J A Allen & Co UK) St Mut.

School of Jesus. James A. Mohler. LC 72-11835. 280p. 1973. 5.95 (*0-8189-0262-0*) Alba.

School of Law. Robert J. Shoop. 1996. pap. text ed. 25.95 (*0-205-19558-X*) P-H.

School of Learning - August. Dottie Henneberry. 48p. 1979. pap. 0.50 (*1-882825-13-6*) Hse of Prayer.

School of Learning - November. Dottie Henneberry. 44p. 1979. pap. 0.50 (*1-882825-16-0*) Hse of Prayer.

School of Learning - October. Dottie Henneberry. 48p. 1979. pap. 0.50 (*1-882825-15-2*) Hse of Prayer.

School of Learning - September. Dottie Henneberry. 44p. 1979. pap. 0.50 (*1-882825-14-4*) Hse of Prayer.

School of Living for Adult Education: A Pioneer of the New Age, Selections from the Interpreter, Balanced Living & a Way Out, 3 vols., Set. 1991. lib. bdg. 695.75 (*0-8490-5178-9*) Gordon Pr.

School of Love: Short Stories. Phyllis Barber. LC 89-38861. 120p. 1990. 14.95 (*0-87480-337-3*) U of Utah Pr.

School of Mechanism Opus 74: For the Violin. L. Dancla. 20p. 1986. pap. 3.95 (*0-7935-5459-4*) H Leonard.

School of Medieval England. Arthur F. Leach. 1976. lib. bdg. 59.95 (*0-8490-2570-2*) Gordon Pr.

School of Moses: Studies in Philo & Hellenistic Religion. Ed. by John P. Kenney. LC 95-37978. (Brown Judaic Studies: No. 304). 200p. (C). 1995. 34.95 (*0-7885-0162-3*, 140304) Scholars Pr GA.

School of Natural Healing. John R. Christopher. LC 90-205323. 724p. 1996. 39.95 (*1-879436-01-9*, 99101) Christopher Pubns.

School of Obedience see Escuela de la Obediencia

School of Obedience; Believer's Secret of Obedience see Blessings of Obedience

School of Paris: Paintings from the Florene May Schoenborn & Samuel A. Marx Collection. James T. Soby. LC 65-25727. (Illus.). 56p. 1965. pap. 7.95 (*0-87070-575-X*) Mus of Modern Art.

School of Plato: Its Origin, Development, & Revival under the Roman Empire (1896) F. W. Bussell. 361p. 1996. pap. 29.95 (*1-56459-633-8*) Kessinger Pub.

School of Practical Composition, 3 vols., Set. Carl Czerny. LC 79-21105. (Music Reprint Ser.). 1979. reprint ed. lib. bdg. 110.00 (*0-306-79595-7*) Da Capo.

School of Prague: Painting at the Court of Rudolf II. Thomas D. Kaufmann. (Illus.). xxx, 336p. 1988. 54.00 (*0-226-42727-7*) U Ch Pr.

School of Prayer: An Introduction to the Divine Office for All Christians. John Brook. 480p. (Orig.). 1992. pap. text ed. 14.95 (*0-8146-2028-0*) Liturgical Pr.

School of Salernum: Regimen Sanitatis Salernitanum, the English Version with a History of the School of Salernum by Francis R. Packard & a Note on the Prehistory of the Regimen Sanitatis by Fielding H. Garrison. John Harington et al. LC 79-95627. (Illus.). 214p. 1970. reprint ed. 35.00 (*0-678-03751-5*) Kelley.

School of Shakespeare, 2 vols, Set. Ed. by Richard Simpson. LC 78-176026. reprint ed. 115.00 (*0-404-06058-7*) AMS Pr.

School of Sight Singing: Vocal Practical Method for Young Beginners. G. Concone. 64p. 1986. pap. 7.95 (*0-7935-5102-1*) H Leonard.

School of St. Matthew & Its Use of the Old Testament. Krister Stendahl. 249p. 1991. 25.00 (*0-9623642-4-X*); pap. 18.00 (*0-9623642-3-1*) Sigler Pr.

School of Technic for Violin: Op. 1 Part 1. Otakar Sevcik. (Carl Fischer Music Library: No. 282). (ENG, FRE & GER.). (YA). (gr. 6-12). 1993. pap. 9.50 (*0-8258-0034-X*, L 282) Fischer Inc NY.

School of Technic for Violin, Op. 1, Part 2. Otakar Sevcik. (Carl Fischer Music Library: No. 283). 49p. (ENG, FRE & GER.). (J). 1991. pap. 9.95 (*0-8258-0035-8*, L 283) Fischer Inc NY.

School of the Church: Worship & Christian Formation. Philip H. Pfatteicher. LC 94-47514. 160p. 1994. pap. 14.00 (*1-56338-110-9*) TPI PA.

School of the French Revolution: A Documentary History of the College of Louis-le-Grand & Its Director, Jean-Francois Champagne, 1762-1814. Tr. by Robert R. Palmer. LC 74-25625. 311p. 1975. reprint ed. pap. 88.70 (*0-7837-9412-6*, 2060157) Bks Demand.

School of the Future. Ed. by Wayne H. Holtzman. 190p. (Orig.). 1992. pap. 19.95 (*0-943463-11-4*) Hogg Found.

School of the Soul: Its Path & Pitfalls. Z'ev Ben Shimon Halevi. LC 85-50635. 194p. (Orig.). 1993. pap. 14.00 (*0-87728-801-1*) Weiser.

School of the South - La Escuela del Sur: El Taller Torres-Garcia & Its Legacy. Florencia B. Nelson. LC 91-73445. (Illus.). 22p. 1991. pap. 5.00 (*0-614-02733-0*) A M Huntington Art.

School of the Spirit. Roberts Liardon. 1994. pap. 8.99 (*0-88419-360-8*) Creation House.

School of the Sun. Ana M. Matute. 256p. 1989. text ed. 52.50 (*0-231-06916-2*); pap. text ed. 15.50 (*0-231-06917-0*) Col U Pr.

School of Thought & Action. Ali Shariati. Tr. by Cyrus Bakhtiar from PER. 56p. (Orig.). (C). 1988. pap. 5.50 (*1-871031-10-9*) Abjad Bk.

***School of Thought & Action.** Ali Shariati. Tr. by Cyrus Bakhtiar. 55p. (Orig.). 1996. pap. 5.50 (*0-614-21448-3*, 1108) Kazi Pubns.

School of UDHRA. Nathaniel Mackey. 144p. (Orig.). 1993. pap. 9.95 (*0-87286-278-X*) City Lights.

School of Velocity for Piano, Op. 299, Complete Edition. Carl Czerny. 101p. (J). 1903. pap. 7.50 (*0-8258-0108-7*, L 338) Fischer Inc NY.

School of Venice. Ed. by Luciano Semerani. (Academy Architecture Ser.). (Illus.). 88p. 1986. pap. 19.95 (*0-312-70188-8*) St Martin.

School of Violin-Technic, Bk. 2: Exercises in Double Stops. Henry Schradieck. (Carl Fischer Music Library: No. 178). pap. 7.50 (*0-8258-0031-5*, L178) Fischer Inc NY.

School of Violin Technics Opus 1 First Position, Bk. 1. Otakar Sevcik. 44p. 1986. pap. 5.95 (*0-7935-5435-7*) H Leonard.

School of Visual Arts Gold: Fifty Years of Creative Graphic Design. School of Visual Arts, Staff. LC 96-20306. 192p. 1997. 55.00 (*0-86636-337-8*) St Martin.

School of Visual Arts Gold: Fifty Years of Creative Graphic Design. School of Visual Arts Staff. LC 96-20306. 1996. pap. write for info. (*0-86636-312-2*) PBC Intl Inc.

School of Visual Arts Guide to Careers see Careers in the Visual Arts: A Guide to Jobs, Money, Opportunities, & an Artistic Life

School Office Spanish. Barbara Thuro. LC 95-94882. 170p. (Orig.). pap. 19.95 (*0-932825-07-9*) Ammie Enter.

School Officials & the Courts: Update 1987. Joseph C. Beckham. (ERS Monograph Ser.). 66p. 1987. 18.00 (*0-318-37598-2*) Ed Research.

School on Qualitative Aspects & Applications of Nonlinear Evolution Equations. T. T. Li & P. De Mottoni. 250p. 1991. text ed. 93.00 (*981-02-0504-X*) World Scientific Pub.

***School on 103rd Street.** Roland S. Jefferson. LC 97-5669. 208p. (YA). 1997. pap. 11.00 (*0-393-31662-9*) Norton.

School Organization: A Sociological Analysis. William Tyler. (Social Analysis Ser.). 272p. 1988. lib. bdg. 55.00 (*0-7099-4333-4*, Pub. by Croom Helm UK) Routledge Chapman & Hall.

School Partnerships Handbook: How to Set up & Administer Programs with Business, Government & Your Community. Susan D. Otterbourg. 336p. 1986. 29.95 (*0-13-793852-7*) P-H.

School Phobia & Its Treatment. Nigel Blagg. 240p. 1987. pap. 22.95 (*0-7099-5050-0*, Pub. by Croom Helm UK); lib. bdg. 49.95 (*0-7099-3938-8*, Pub. by Croom Helm UK) Routledge Chapman & Hall.

School Phobia & Other Anxieties in Youth. Ron Kerner. (Family Forum Library Ser.). 16p. 1992. 1.95 (*1-56688-002-5*) Bur For At-Risk.

School Picnic. Jan Steffy. LC 87-14867. (Illus.). 32p. (J). (ps-3). 1987. 12.95 (*0-934672-52-0*) Good Bks PA.

School Planner: A Time Management Program. Deanda. (CA - Career Development Ser.). 1992. pap. 9.95 (*0-538-61396-3*) S-W Pub.

School Planning: A Guide for Parents of Children with Seizure Disorders. Epilepsy Foundation of America Staff. 125p. 1994. pap. 12.95 (*0-916570-14-2*) Epilepsy Foundation of America.

School Plant Facilities Supervisor. (Career Examination Ser.: C-3744). 1994. pap. 34.95 (*0-8373-3744-5*) Nat Learn.

School Play: A Source Book. James H. Block & Nancy R. King. LC 86-33491. (Source Books on Education: Vol. 10). 360p. 1987. text ed. 53.00 (*0-8240-8632-5*) Garland.

***School Poems.** Ed. by Bruce Lanskey. (J). 1997. write for info. (*0-614-29265-4*) Meadowbrook.

School Policy. Duke & Canady. 1991. text ed. write for info. (*0-07-018028-8*) McGraw.

School Portfolio: A Comprehensive Framework for School Improvement. Victoria L. Bernhardt. LC 94-34145. 1994. 36.95 (*1-883001-11-0*) Eye On Educ.

School Power: Implications of an Intervention Project. James P. Comer. 336p. 1995. pap. 17.95 (*0-02-874053-X*) Free Pr.

School Power: Strategies for Succeeding in School. Jeanne S. Schumm & Marguerite C. Radencich. Ed. by Pamela Espeland. LC 92-10907. (Illus.). 132p. (Orig.). (YA). (gr. 5 up). 1992. pap. 13.95 (*0-915793-42-3*) Free Spirit Pub.

S

School PR: The Complete Book. National School Public Relations Association Staff. 1986. 29.95 (*0-87545-051-2*, 411-13346) Natl Sch PR.

***School Prayer: A History of the Debate.** Tricia Andryszewski. LC 96-51951. (Issues in Focus Ser.). (Illus.). (J). 1997. lib. bdg. 18.95 (*0-89490-904-5*) Enslow Pubs.

School Prayer: The Court, the Congress & the First Amendment. Robert Alley. 273p. 1993. 28.95 (*0-87975-843-0*) Prometheus Bks.

School Principal. Jalal A. Ahmad. Tr. by John K. Newton. (Studies in Middle Eastern Literatures: No. 4). 1983. pap. 12.00 (*0-88297-032-1*) Bibliotheca.

School Principal As an Entrepreneur. M. Ann Grooms. 91p. 1994. pap. text ed. 11.95 (*0-9647893-0-2*) Educ Servs.

School Principals & Change. Michael D. Richardson et al. LC 92-28436. (Source Books on Education: Vol. 33). 288p. 1993. text ed. 46.00 (*0-8153-0383-1*, SS783) Garland.

School Programs in Speech-Language: Organization & Management. Elizabeth A. Neidecker. (Illus.). 1980. text ed. write for info. (*0-13-794321-0*) P-H.

School Programs in Speech-Language: Organization & Management. 3rd ed. Elizabeth A. Neidecker & Jean L. Blosser. 400p. 1992. text ed. 65.00 (*0-13-792268-X*) P-H.

School Promotion, Publicity & Public Relations...Nothing but Benefits. Tracey H. MacPhee & Robert L. DeBruyn. LC 87-60751. 320p. (Orig.). 1987. text ed. 29.95 (*0-914607-24-3*) Master Tchr.

School Psychologist. Jack Rudman. (Teachers License Examination Ser.: GT-4). 1994. pap. 39.95 (*0-8373-8124-X*) Nat Learn.

School Psychologist: An Introduction. Ed. by George W. Hynd. 352p. 1983. text ed. 44.95 (*0-8156-2289-9*); pap. text ed. 16.95 (*0-8156-2290-2*) Syracuse U Pr.

School Psychologist & the Exceptional Child. Ed. by Geraldine T. Scholl. 256p. 1985. pap. text ed. 10.00 (*0-86586-153-6*, P300) Coun Exc Child.

School Psychologist in Nontraditional Settings: Integrating Clients, Services, & Settings. Ed. by R. C. D'Amato & R. S. Dean. 240p. 1989. 49.95 (*0-89859-996-2*) L Erlbaum Assocs.

School Psychologist-in-Training. Jack Rudman. (Teachers License Examination Ser.: GT-5). 1994. pap. 34.95 (*0-8373-8125-8*) Nat Learn.

School Psychologists at Mid-Century: A Report. Thayer Conference on the Functions, Qualifications, & Training of School Psychologists Staff. Ed. by Norma E. Cutts. LC 55-9034. 240p. reprint ed. pap. 68.40 (*0-7837-0494-1*, 2040818) Bks Demand.

School Psychology. Jack Rudman. (National Teacher Examination Ser.: NT-40). 1994. pap. 23.95 (*0-8373-8450-8*) Nat Learn.

School Psychology: A Developmental & Social Systems Approach. Robert H. Woody et al. 432p. (C). 1992. text ed. 81.00 (*0-205-13502-1*) Allyn.

School Psychology: A Social Psychological Perspective. Ed. by Frederic Medway & Thomas Cafferty. 496p. 1991. text ed. 89.95 (*0-8058-0536-2*) L Erlbaum Assocs.

School Psychology: Essentials of Theory & Practice. Cecil R. Reynolds et al. LC 83-21918. 496p. (C). 1984. Net. text ed. 47.50 (*0-471-08327-5*) Wiley.

School Psychology: Past, Present, & Future. Thomas K. Fagan & Paula S. Wise. LC 93-19105. 368p. (C). 1994. text ed. 65.95 (*0-8013-1020-2*, 79325) Longman.

School Psychology at a Turning Point: Ensuring a Bright Future for the Profession. Beeman N. Phillips. LC 89-27510. (Social & Behavioral Sciences Ser.). 324p. text ed. 35.95 (*1-55542-195-4*) Jossey-Bass.

School Public Relations: Communicating to the Community. Jack Kinder. LC 82-60802. (Fastback Ser.: No. 182). 50p. 1982. pap. 3.00 (*0-87367-182-1*) Phi Delta Kappa.

School Purchasing Agent. Jack Rudman. (Career Examination Ser.: C-863). 1994. pap. 29.95 (*0-8373-0863-1*) Nat Learn.

School Quality, Achievement Bias, & Dropout Behavior in Egypt, 107. Eric A. Hanushek & Victor Lavy. LC 94-32798. (LSMS Working Paper Ser.: No. 107). 50p. 1995. 6.95 (*0-8213-2998-7*, 12998) World Bank.

School Readiness: Assessment & Educational Issues. Gilbert R. Gredler. LC 91-72062. 264p. (Orig.). (C). 1992. pap. text ed. 29.95 (*0-88422-112-1*) Clinical Psych.

School Readiness: Assessment & Educational Issues. Gilbert R. Gredler. 296p. 1996. pap. text ed. 32.50 (*0-471-16200-0*) Wiley.

School Readiness & Transition Programs: Real Facts from Real Schools. James K. Uphoff. 106p. (Orig.). 1991. pap. 9.95 (*0-935493-47-6*) Modern Learn Pr.

School Recess & Playground Behavior: Educational & Developmental Roles. Anthony D. Pellegrini. LC 93-50547. (SUNY Series, Children's Play in Society). 187p. 1995. text ed. 59.50 (*0-7914-2183-X*); pap. text ed. 19.95 (*0-7914-2184-8*) State U NY Pr.

School Record of McLean County & Other Papers. John H. Burnham et al. (Transactions of the Mclean County Historical Society Ser.: Vol. II). (Illus.). 695p. 1903. 25.00 (*0-943788-02-1*) McLean County.

School Records: Kindergarten - 12th Grade. Tom Cox & Sherri Cox. (Illus.). 27p. (J). (gr. k-12). 1990. spiral bd. 9.95 (*0-9626932-0-0*) TCA Pub.

***School Recycling Programs: A Handbook for Educators.** (Illus.). 24p. 1996. reprint ed. pap. 15.00 (*0-7881-3162-1*) DIANE Pub.

School Reform: Lessons from England. Kathryn Stearns. 150p. 1996. pap. 12.00 (*0-931050-57-X*) Carnegie Fnd Advan Teach.

School Reform Handbook How to Improve Your Schools. Jeanne Allen & Angela Dale. LC 95-68282. 166p. (Orig.). 1995. 9.95 (*0-9646028-0-6*) Ctr Educ Reform.

School Reform in the Deep South: A Critical Appraisal. Ed. by David J. Vold & Joseph L. DeVitis. LC 90-44661. 208p. 1991. text ed. 29.95 (*0-8173-0553-X*) U of Ala Pr.

School Reform in the Information Age. Howard D. Mehlinger. LC 95-92373. (Illus.). 165p. (Orig.). 1995. pap. 14.95 (*0-9645857-0-7*) IN Univ Excell.

School Refusal: Assessment & Treatmenet. Neville J. King et al. (Practitioner Guidebook Ser.). 1995. text ed. 34.50 (*0-205-16071-9*, Longwood Div) Allyn.

School Renovation Handbook: Investing in Education. Glen I. Earthman. LC 94-60644. 188p. 1994. pap. 34.95 (*1-56676-153-0*) Technomic.

School Research Assistant. Jack Rudman. (Teachers License Examination Ser.: GT-6). 1994. pap. 34.95 (*0-8373-8126-6*) Nat Learn.

School Research Associate. Jack Rudman. (Teachers License Examination Ser.: GT-7). 1994. pap. 34.95 (*0-8373-8127-4*) Nat Learn.

School Research Technician. Jack Rudman. (Teachers License Examination Ser.: GT-8). 1994. pap. 34.95 (*0-8373-8128-2*) Nat Learn.

School Restructuring: A Practitioner's Guide. John H. Hansen & Elaine Liftin. LC 91-65221. (Illus.). 258p. (Orig.). (C). 1991. pap. text ed. 35.95 (*0-9628917-0-3*) Watersun MA.

School Restructuring & Cost Implications. (State Legislative Reports: Vol. 14, No. 14). 1989. 5.00 (*1-55516-255-X*, 7302-1414) Natl Conf State Legis.

School Restructuring, Chicago Style. G. Alfred Hess, Jr. LC 90-27612. 248p. 1991. 53.95 (*0-8039-6001-8*, 60018); pap. 24.95 (*0-8039-6002-6*, 60026) Corwin Pr.

School Rights: A Parent's Legal Handbook & Action Guide. Thomas Condon & Patricia Wolff. 1994. pap. 14.95 (*0-02-075890-1*) Macmillan.

School Safety. Cynthia F. Klingel. LC 86-72593. (Safety First Ser.). (J). (ps up). 1986. lib. bdg. 12.95 (*0-87191-737-8*) Creative Ed.

School Safety. Nancy Loewen. LC 95-25898. (Safety Sense Ser.). (Illus.). 24p. (J). (gr. k-3). 1996. lib. bdg. 18.50 (*1-56766-255-2*) Childs World.

***School Safety: Promising Initiatives for Addressing School Violence.** 46p. (Orig.). 1996. pap. 20.00 (*0-7881-2989-9*) DIANE Pub.

School Safety Handbook: Taking Action for Student & Staff Protection. Kenneth E. Lane et al. 357p. 1996. pap. 49.95 (*1-56676-397-5*, 763975) Technomic.

School Safety Handbook, 1986. 160p. 1986. 13.00 (*0-910170-44-4*) Assn Sch Busn.

School Savvy. Diane Harrington & Laurette Young. 1993. 10.00 (*0-374-52380-0*) FS&G.

School Science Safety: Secondary. Flinn Scientific Staff. (Illus.). (Orig.). 1989. pap. text ed. 19.95 (*1-877991-19-8*, AP4272) Flinn Scientific.

School Science Safety, Elementary. Flinn Scientific Staff. (Elementary Ser.). (Illus.). (Orig.). 1989. pap. text ed. 17.95 (*1-877991-20-1*, AP4273) Flinn Scientific.

School Search Guide to Private Schools in the Northeast. Marjorie B. Lipkin. 351p. 1988. pap. text ed. 12.95 (*0-9620326-0-3*) Schoolsearch Pr.

School Secretary. Jack Rudman. (Teachers License Examination Ser.: T-52). 1994. pap. 27.95 (*0-8373-8052-9*) Nat Learn.

School Secretary's Encyclopedic Dictionary. Cherie Fehrman. 300p. 24.95 (*0-13-794446-2*, Busn) P-H.

School Secretary's Survival Guide: With Reproducible Letters, Forms & Checklists. Muriel K. Trachman. LC 93-4452. 1993. write for info. (*0-13-792276-0*) P-H.

School Security Screening. Charles Garrett. LC 91-65614. (Illus.). 122p. 1991. pap. 5.95 (*0-915920-76-X*) Ram Pub.

School Security Supervisor. Jack Rudman. (Career Examination Ser.: C-3182). 1994. pap. 29.95 (*0-8373-3182-X*) Nat Learn.

School Segregation Decision: A Report to the Governor of North Carolina on the Decision of the Supreme Court of the United States on the 17th of May 1954. Albert Coates & James C. Paul. (Law & Government Ser.). x, 132p. 1981. reprint ed. lib. bdg. 22.50 (*0-8377-2607-7*) Rothman.

School Segregation in Malmo, Sweden. Harald Swedner. LC 70-158358. 1971. 2.35 (*0-912008-08-3*) Equity & Excel.

School Site Budgeting: Decentralized School Management. John Greenhalgh. (Illus.). 206p. (C). 1984. lib. bdg. 46.00 (*0-8191-3774-X*) U Pr of Amer.

School Site Management & School Restructuring. Grover H. Baldwin. 92p. (Orig.). (C). 1993. pap. 25.95 (*1-56534-055-8*) Ed Law Assn.

School-Site Management Applied. William J. Bailey. LC 90-71264. 195p. 1990. 39.95 (*0-87762-743-6*) Technomic.

School Smart: Behaviors & Skills for Student Success, 93-94. Steven D. Spainhower. Ed. by Dana Wilson & Steven J. Brown. (Illus.). 205p. (Orig.). (YA). (gr. 7-12). 1993. pap. text ed. 18.95 (*0-9637573-0-X*) Education Res.

School Smart see Parent Power: A Guide to Your Child's Success

School Smart Parent: A Guide for Knowing What Your Child Should Know - From Infancy Through the End of Elementary School. Gene I. Maeroff. 1989. 19.95 (*0-8129-1631-X*, Times Bks) Random.

***School-Smart Parenting: Raising Children for Success & Happiness in School.** Michael L. Brock. LC 96-90616. 300p. (Orig.). 1997. pap. 14.95 (*0-533-12110-8*) Vantage.

***School Smarts: A Frustrated Parent's Guide to Navigating California.** Judy Goddess. 224p. Date not set. pap. write for info. (*1-887836-10-1*, Schl Wise Pr) Pubng Twenty-Twenty.

School Smarts: Two Thousand Things Students Need to Know, Ages 10 Plus. Jay Amberg. (Illus.). 400p. (Orig.). 1994. 13.95 (*0-673-36175-6*, GoodYrBooks); pap. 9.95 (*0-673-36136-5*, GoodYrBooks) Addson-Wesley Educ.

School Social Work: A Practitioner's Guidebook - A Community-Integrated Approach to Practice. Evelyn H. Ginsburg. (Illus.). 244p. 1989. pap. 38.95 (*0-398-06149-1*) C C Thomas.

School Social Work: A Practitioner's Guidebook - A Community-Integrated Approach to Practice. Evelyn H. Ginsburg. (Illus.). 244p. (C). 1989. text ed. 58.95 (*0-398-05560-2*) C C Thomas.

School Social Work: Practice & Research Perspectives. 3rd ed. Ed. by Robert Constable et al. LC 95-32132. 448p. (C). 1995. pap. text ed. 36.95 (*0-925065-11-0*) Lyceum IL.

School Social Worker. (National Teacher Examination Ser.: NT-65). pap. 23.95 (*0-8373-8485-0*) Nat Learn.

School Social Worker. Jack Rudman. (Teachers License Examination Ser.: GT-9). 1994. pap. 34.95 (*0-8373-8129-0*) Nat Learn.

School Social Workers in the Multicultural Environment: New Roles, Responsibilities, & Educational Enrichment. Ed. by Paul R. Keys. LC 94-34120. (Journal of Multicultural Social Work). (Illus.). 150p. 1994. lib. bdg. 29.95 (*1-56024-696-0*) Haworth Pr.

School Social Problems: An Interdisciplinary Analysis. Harry R. White. 202p. (C). 1995. pap. text ed. 12.95 (*0-9645543-0-5*) Bell Publ.

School Songs of America's Colleges & Universities: A Directory. Robert F. O'Brien. LC 91-11337. 208p. 1991. text ed. 42.95 (*0-313-27890-3*, OSS/, Greenwood Pr) Greenwood.

School Spirit. 176p. (J). 1995. pap. 3.50 (*0-590-22332-1*) Scholastic Inc.

School Spirit. Johanna Hurwitz. LC 93-37685. (Illus.). 144p. (J). (gr. 2 up). 1994. 14.00 (*0-688-12825-4*, Morrow Junior) Morrow.

School Spirit & Self-Esteem Bulletin Boards. Marianne V. Standley. (Easy-To-Make-&-Use Ser.). (Illus.). 64p. (J). (gr. k-6). 1986. pap. text ed. 7.95 (*0-86530-135-2*, IP-112-4) Incentive Pubns.

School Spirit Sabotage: Starring Brian & Pea Brain. Elizabeth Levy. LC 93-23029. (Trophy Chapter Bk.). (Illus.). 96p. (J). (gr. 2-5). 1995. pap. 3.95 (*0-06-442013-2*, Trophy) HarpC Child Bks.

***School Spirits.** Michael O. Tunnell. 160p. (J). (gr. 3-7). 1997. lib. bdg. 15.95 (*0-8234-1310-1*) Holiday.

School, State, & Society: The Growth of Elementary Schooling in Nineteenth-Century France - A Quantitative Analysis. Raymond Grew & Patrick J. Harrigan. (Illus.). 350p. 1991. text ed. 47.50 (*0-472-10095-5*) U of Mich Pr.

School Stinks. Frank O'Keefe. 132p. (YA). (gr. 7-12). 1991. pap. 4.95 (*0-7736-7294-X*, Pub. by Stoddart Pubng CN) Genl Dist Srvs.

School Store: Experience in Entrepreneurship. Myers. (General Business & Business Education Ser.). 1995. pap. 13.00 (*0-8273-6254-4*) Delmar.

School Stress & Anxiety. Beeman N. Phillips. LC 77-21658. 165p. 1978. 32.95 (*0-87705-324-3*) Human Sci Pr.

School Strikes in Prussian Poland, 1901 to 1907: The Struggle Over Bilingual Education. John J. Kulczycki. (East European Monographs: No. 82). 279p. 1981. text ed. 59.00 (*0-914710-76-1*) East Eur Monographs.

School Subjects & Curriculum Change. 3rd rev. ed. Ivor F. Goodson. (Studies in Curriculum History Ser.). 324p. 1993. pap. 29.00 (*0-7507-0098-X*, Falmer Pr) Taylor & Francis.

School Success: The Inside Story. Peter Kline & Laurence D. Martel. LC 92-8120. (Illus.). 128p. (Orig.). 1993. reprint ed. pap. 14.95 (*0-915556-25-1*) Great Ocean.

School Superintendency. M. Scott Norton et al. LC 95-34819. 1996. text ed. 44.95 (*0-205-15933-8*) Allyn.

School Superintendency: Leading Education into the 21st Century. M. William Konnert & John J. Augenstein. LC 95-60956. 310p. 1995. text ed. 39.95 (*1-56676-286-3*) Technomic.

***School Superintendent: The Profession & the Person.** William L. Sharp & James K. Walter. LC 96-61025. 239p. 1996. pap. text ed. 39.95 (*1-56676-435-1*) Technomic.

School Superintendent's Complete Handbook: Practical Techniques & Materials for the Inservice Administrator. Patricia C. Conran. 560p. 1989. text ed. 49.95 (*0-13-794462-4*) P-H.

School Supplies: A Book of Poems. Illus. by Renee Flower. (J). 1996. 17.00 (*0-671-51172-6*, S&S Bks Young Read) S&S Childrens.

School Supplies: A Book of Poems. Lee B. Hopkins & Renee Flowers. (J). (ps-3). 1996. 17.00 (*0-689-80497-0*) S&S Childrens.

School Survival Guide for Kids with LD (Learning Differences) Ways to Make Learning Easier & More Fun. Rhoda Cummings & Gary Fisher. LC 91-14489. (Illus.). 176p. (J). (gr. 2 up). 1991. pap. 10.95 (*0-915793-32-6*) Free Spirit Pub.

***School Survival Skills: Student Syllabus.** Kathleen L. McDonough. 1985. audio 36.25 (*0-89420-245-6*, 340000) Natl Book.

School Survival Skills: Student Syllabus. Kathleen L. McDonough. (Illus.). 64p. (YA). (gr. 8 up). 1985. pap. 8.95 (*0-89420-246-4*, 340025) Natl Book.

School System Administration: A Strategic Plan for Site-Based Management. I. Carl Candoli. LC 90-71213. 245p. 1990. 39.95 (*0-87762-728-2*) Technomic.

***School Tales: Stories by Young Women.** Ed. by Jill Dawson. (Livewire Ser.). (YA). (gr. 6-9). pap. 7.95 (*0-7043-4922-1*, Pub. by Womens Press UK) Trafalgar.

School Talk: Gender & Adolescent Culture. Donna Eder et al. LC 94-25220. 225p. (C). 1995. text ed. 40.00 (*0-8135-2178-5*); pap. text ed. 15.00 (*0-8135-2179-3*) Rutgers U Pr.

School Teacher in England & the United States. R. K. Kelsall & H. M. Kelsall. 1969. 95.00 (*0-08-006519-8*, Pub. by Pergamon Repr UK) Franklin.

School Teacher in Old Alaska: The Story of Hannah Breece. Ed. by Jane Jacobs. (Illus.). 366p. 1995. 24.00 (*0-679-44134-4*) Random.

School Teacher in Old Alaska: The Story of Hannah Breece. Ed. by Jane Jacobs. 1997. pap. 13.00 (*0-679-77633-8*) Random.

***School Teachers Forum Highlights.** Karen Tuttle et al. (Highlights from the American String Teacher Forums Ser.). 25.00 (*0-614-25496-5*, 1941S) Am String Tchrs.

***School Teacher's Pay & Conditions Documents, 1996.** HMSO Staff. 52p. 1996. pap. 16.00 (*0-11-270952-4*, HM09524, Pub. by Stationery Ofc UK) Bernan Associates.

School Teaching in Canada. Alexander Lockhart. 224p. 1991. 40.00 (*0-8020-2748-2*); pap. 19.95 (*0-8020-6788-3*) U of Toronto Pr.

***School Technology Planner (STP) Software.** Allison Rossett. 1997. pap. text ed. 74.95 (*0-205-27027-1*) P-H.

School Terminology Handbook (English-Spanish) Barbara Thuro. LC 93-90771. 167p. (Orig.). 1993. pap. 16.95 (*0-932825-05-2*) Ammie Enter.

School Testing: What Parents & Educators Need to Know. Estelle S. Gellman. LC 94-28003. 192p. 1995. text ed. 45.00 (*0-275-94800-5*, Praeger Pubs) Greenwood.

School That Refused to Die: Continuity & Change at Thomas Jefferson High School. Daniel L. Duke. LC 94-10030. (SUNY Series, Educational Leadership). 291p. (C). 1994. pap. text ed. 18.95 (*0-7914-2332-8*) State U NY Pr.

School That Refused to Die: Continuity & Change at Thomas Jefferson High School. Daniel L. Duke. LC 94-10030. (SUNY Series, Educational Leadership). 291p. (C). 1995. text ed. 57.50 (*0-7914-2331-X*) State U NY Pr.

School That Was: A School Marm's Tale. Rose H. Tennis. LC 90-70254. (Illus.). 88p. (Orig.). (YA). 1990. pap. text ed. 6.95 (*0-923568-08-5*) Wilderness Adventure Bks.

School Ties. Deborah Chiel. Ed. by Sally Peters. 224p. (Orig.). 1992. mass mkt. 4.50 (*0-671-77715-7*) PB.

School Time Fun. Barbara Gregorich. Ed. by Joan Hoffman. (Get Ready! Bks.). (Illus.). 32p. (J). (ps). 1983. student ed. 1.99 (*0-938256-67-X*) Sch Zone Pub Co.

School-to-Work. Arnold H. Packer & Marion W. Pines. (Illus.). 280p. (C). 1996. 41.95 (*1-883001-18-8*) Eye On Educ.

School-to-Work: A Guide for State Policymakers. Jobs for the Future Staff. (Investing in People Ser.). 40p. 15.00 (*1-55516-348-3*, 3125) Natl Conf State Legis.

School to Work: What Does Research Say about It? (Illus.). 184p. (Orig.). (C). 1995. pap. text ed. 35.00 (*0-7881-1320-8*) DIANE Pub.

***School to Work: What Does Research Say about It.** 1997. lib. bdg. 250.99 (*0-8490-7668-4*) Gordon Pr.

School-To-Work: What Does Research Say about School-To-Work Programs. 1995. lib. bdg. 250.75 (*0-8490-6856-8*) Gordon Pr.

***School-to-Work Opportunities Act of 1994: A Guide to the Law & How to Use It.** Lauren Jacobs. 50p. 1995. pap. text ed. 10.00 (*0-912585-14-5*) Ctr Law & Ed.

***School to Work Opportunities Through the Lens of Youth Development.** Shepherd Zeldin & Ivan Charner. (Education Reform & School-to-Work Transition Ser.). 20p. 1995. teacher ed., pap. text ed. 12.00 (*0-614-24523-0*) Natl Inst Work.

School to Work Planner. 3rd ed. Stull. (CA = Career Development Ser.). 1997. student ed., pap. 15.95 (*0-538-64970-4*) S-W Pub.

School-to-Work Programs Vols. 1 & 2: A State-by-State Guide. (Career Dollar Ser.: Vol. 2). 1994. ring bd. 50.00 (*1-884669-04-2*) Conway Greene.

***School-to-Work Revolution: How Employers & Educators Are Joining Forces to Prepare Tomorrow's Skilled Workforce.** Olson. 1997. write for info. (*0-201-14940-0*) Addison-Wesley.

School-to-Work Toolkit: Building a Local Program. Andrew Churchill et al. 1994. 191.00 (*1-887410-52-X*) Jobs for Future.

School-to-Work Toolkit: Building a State-Wide System. John Niles. 1994. 150.00 (*1-887410-50-3*) Jobs for Future.

School-to-Work Transition: Reaching for Scale in Big Cities: A Background Paper Prepared for Linking School & Work in Urban Areas: A Three-City Conference. Basil J. Whiting. 50p. 1993. pap. 10.00 (*1-887410-58-9*) Jobs for Future.

***School to Work Transition & Its Role in the Systemic Reform of Education: The Experience of Jefferson County, Ky. & Ky. Education Reform Act.** Regina Kyle. (Education Reform & School-to-Work Transition Ser.). 21p. 1995. teacher ed., pap. text ed. 12.00 (*0-614-24522-2*) Natl Inst Work.

School-to-Work Transition for At-Risk Youth. Sheila H. Feichtner. 1989. 8.75 (*0-317-03012-4*, IN339) Ctr Educ Trng Employ.

School to Work Transition in Japan: An Ethnographic Study. Kaori Okano. LC 92-20817. (Language & Education Library: No. 3). 1992. 99.00 (*1-85359-163-7*, Pub. by Multilingual Matters UK) Taylor & Francis.

***School to Work Transitions.** 23p. (YA). (gr. 10 up). 1994. wbk. ed., pap. 7.00 (*0-8064-1508-8*, C15) Bergwall.

School Tradition of the Old Testament. Eric W. Heaton. 192p. 1994. 58.00 (*0-19-826362-7*) OUP.

School Transportation Coordinator. Jack Rudman. (Career Examination Ser.: C-1513). 1994. pap. 29.95 (*0-8373-1513-1*) Nat Learn.

School Transportation Supervisor. Jack Rudman. (Career Examination Ser.: C-113). 1994. pap. 29.95 (*0-8373-0113-0*) Nat Learn.

School Trip. (J). 1993. pap. 2.99 (*0-440-40823-7*) Dell.

School Trip. Ewa Lipniacka. LC 92-33325. (Jamie & Luke Ser.). (Illus.). (J). 1993. 6.95 (*1-56656-121-3*, Crocodile Bks) Interlink Pub.

School Trivia: Funny (& Not So Funny) Stuff about Schools, Teachers & Students. Carole Marsh. (Quantum Leap Ser.). (Illus.). 1994. 29.95 (*0-7933-0007-X*); pap. 19.95 (*0-7933-0008-8*) Gallopade Pub Group.

School-University Partnerships in Action: Concepts, Cases & Concerns. Ed. by Kenneth A. Sirotnik & John I. Goodlad. 256p. 1988. pap. text ed. 19.95 (*0-8077-2892-6*) Tchrs Coll.

School Violence. Arnold P. Goldstein et al. (Illus.). 272p. (C). 1984. text ed. 47.00 (*0-13-794545-0*) P-H.

School Violence. Deborah L. Kopka. LC 97-8977. (Contemporary World Issues Ser.). 1997. lib. bdg. 39.50 (*0-87436-861-8*) ABC-CLIO.

***School Violence Intervention Handbook.** Ed. by Arnold P. Goldstein & Jane C. Conoley. LC 96-36922. 1997. lib. bdg. 55.00 (*1-57230-175-9*) Guilford Pr.

***School Visual Arts.** PBC International Staff. Date not set. 55.00 (*0-688-15416-6*) Morrow.

School, Vol. 4: Incl. 1989-1993 Supplements. Ed. by Eleanor C. Goldstein. (Social Issues Resources Ser.). 1994. 95.00 (*0-89777-153-2*) Sirs Inc.

School Volunteer Management. Whaley. 1996. 119.00 (*0-8342-0516-5*) Aspen Pub.

School Volunteer's Handbook. rev. ed. Mary L. Veele. 32p. 1987. pap. 4.95 (*1-55691-003-7*, 037) Learning Pubns.

School Wars: When World Views Collide. Barbara B. Gaddy et al. (Education Ser.). 272p. 1996. 25.00 (*0-7879-0236-5*) Jossey-Bass.

School with Forest & Meadow. Ikue Tezuka. Ed. by Dayle M. Bethel. Tr. by Katsusuke Hori from JPN. (Illus.). 150p. (Orig.). (C). 1995. pap. 17.95 (*1-880192-15-2*) Caddo Gap Pr.

***School Within Us: The Creation of an Innovative Public School.** James Nehring. (SUNY Series, Restructuring & School Change). 160p. (C). 1997. text ed. 34.50 (*0-7914-3589-X*) State U NY Pr.

***School Within Us: The Creation of an Innovative Public School.** James Nehring. (SUNY Series, Restructuring & School Change). 160p. (C). 1997. pap. text ed. 10.95 (*0-7914-3590-3*) State U NY Pr.

School Work: Gender & the Cultural Construction of Teaching. Sari K. Biklen. (Series on School Reform). 216p. (C). 1994. text ed. 44.00 (*0-8077-3408-X*); pap. text ed. 19.95 (*0-8077-3407-1*) Tchrs Coll.

School, Work, & Equity: Educational Reform in Rwanda. Susan Hoben. (African Research Studies: No. 16). xvi, 134p. (Orig.). (C). 1989. pap. text ed. 13.00 (*0-915118-15-7*) Boston U African.

School Writing: Discovering the Ground Rules. Yanina Sheeran & Douglas Barnes. (English, Language & Education Ser.). 160p. 1991. pap. 29.00 (*0-335-09453-8*, Open Univ Pr) Taylor & Francis.

School Yard-Backyard, Cycles of Science. Jerry DeBruin. 160p. (J). (gr. 3-9). 1989. 12.99 (*0-86653-489-X*, GA1084) Good Apple.

School Year 1968-1969 see Readings on Equal Education, Vol. 10: Critical Issues for a New Administration and Congress

School Year 1969-1970 see Readings on Equal Education, Vol. 10: Critical Issues for a New Administration and Congress

School Year 1970-1971 see Readings on Equal Education, Vol. 10: Critical Issues for a New Administration and Congress

School Year 1971-72 see Readings on Equal Education, Vol. 10: Critical Issues for a New Administration and Congress

School Year 1972-1975 see Readings on Equal Education, Vol. 10: Critical Issues for a New Administration and Congress

School Year 1977-1979 see Readings on Equal Education, Vol. 10: Critical Issues for a New Administration and Congress

School Years. Carriage House Staff. 1993. Red Stamped Binding. 14.95 (*0-89786-140-X*); Printed in Full Color. 14.95 (*0-89786-141-8*) CHP Ltd Redding.

School Years. 2nd ed. Ed. by John Coleman. LC 91-28498. (Illus.). 192p. (C). 1992. pap. 17.95 (*0-415-06170-9*, A7784) Routledge.

School Years. 2nd ed. Ed. by John Coleman. LC 91-28498. (Illus.). 208p. (C). (gr. 13). 1992. text ed. 85.00 (*0-415-06169-5*, A7780) Routledge.

School Zone. John Duckworth. 96p. (YA). (gr. 7-9). 1986. teacher ed. 2.80 (*0-89693-198-6*, Victor Bks); student ed., pap. 0.60 (*0-89693-558-2*, 6-2558, Victor Bks) Chariot Victor.

School Zone: Learning Environments for Children. Anne P. Taylor & George Vlastos. LC 83-50868. (Illus.). 144p. (C). 1983. reprint ed. pap. 9.95 (*0-913947-00-8*) Schl Zone Inc.

Schoolbook Protest Movement: Forty Questions & Answers. Edward B. Jenkinson. LC 85-62729. 150p. (Orig.). 1986. pap. 11.00 (*0-87367-432-4*) Phi Delta Kappa.

Schoolbooks & Krags: The United States Army in the Philippines, 1898-1902. John M. Gates. LC 77-140917. (Contributions in Military History Ser.: No. 3). 320p. 1973. text ed. 59.95 (*0-8371-5818-4*, GSK/, Greenwood Pr) Greenwood.

Schoolcraft's Expedition to Lake Itasca: The Discovery of the Source of the Mississippi. 2nd ed. Henry R. Schoolcraft. Ed. by Philip P. Mason. LC 58-6358. (Schoolcraft Ser.). (Illus.). 390p. (C). 1993. reprint ed. 35.00 (*0-87013-334-9*) Mich St U Pr.

Schoolcraft's Expedition to Lake Itasca: The Discovery of the Source of the Mississippi. Henry R. Schoolcraft. Ed. by Philip P. Mason. LC 58-6358. (Schoolcraft Ser.). (Illus.). 390p. (C). 1993. reprint ed. pap. 19.95 (*0-87013-335-7*) Mich St U Pr.

Schoolcraft's Indian Legends from Algic Researches, The Myth of Hiawatha, Oneota, The Red Race in America, & Historical & Statistical Information Respecting...the Indian Tribes of the United States. Henry R. Schoolcraft. LC 55-11688. (Michigan State University Schoolcraft Ser.). 322p. (C). 1991. reprint ed. 35.00 (*0-87013-300-4*); reprint ed. pap. 19.95 (*0-87013-301-2*) Mich St U Pr.

Schoolcraft's Narrative Journal of Travels. 2nd ed. Henry R. Schoolcraft. Ed. by Mentor L. Williams & Philip P. Mason. (Schoolcraft Ser.). 520p. (C). 1992. reprint ed. 35.00 (*0-87013-313-6*) Mich St U Pr.

Schoolcraft's Narrative Journal of Travels. Henry R. Schoolcraft. Ed. by Mentor L. Williams & Philip P. Mason. (Schoolcraft Ser.). 520p. (C). 1992. reprint ed. pap. 19.95 (*0-87013-314-4*) Mich St U Pr.

Schoolcraft's Ojibwa Lodge Stories: Life on the Lake Superior Frontier. Henry R. Schoolcraft. Ed. by Philip P. Mason. (Schoolcraft Ser.: Vol. 4). 193p. (Orig.). 1995. pap. 19.95 (*0-87013-457-4*, 0-87013-457-4) Mich St U Pr.

Schoolday Dialogues. Ed. by Alexander Clark. LC 72-103085. (Granger Index Reprint Ser.). 1977. 19.95 (*0-8369-6100-5*) Ayer.

Schooldays in Imperial Japan: A Study in the Culture of a Student Elite. Donald T. Roden. LC 79-64477. (Illus.). 314p. reprint ed. pap. 89.50 (*0-7837-4842-6*, 2044489) Bks Demand.

Schoole of Abuse: 1579 & A Short Apologie of the Schoole of Abuse, 1868. Stephen Gosson. 80p. 1984. pap. 15.00 (*0-87556-104-7*) Saifer.

Schoole of Abuse, Conteining a Pleasaunt Invective Against Poets, Pipers, Plaiers, Iesters & Such Like Catepillers of the Commonwelth. Stephen Gosson. LC 72-5998. (English Experience Ser.: No. 523). 104p. 1973. reprint ed. 35.00 (*90-221-0523-7*) Walter J Johnson.

Schoole of Musicke, Wherein Is Taught the Perfect Method of True Fingering of the Lute, Pandora, Orpharion & Viol da Gamba. Thomas Robinson. LC 73-6122. (English Experience Ser.: No. 589). 1973. reprint ed. 25.00 (*90-221-0589-X*) Walter J Johnson.

Schooled to Order: A Social History of Public Schooling in the United States. David Nasaw. 302p. 1981. pap. 11.95 (*0-19-502892-9*) OUP.

Schoolgirl Fictions. Valerie Walkerdine. 320p. (C). 1990. pap. 19.00 (*0-86091-517-4*, A4981, Pub. by Vrso UK) Norton.

SchoolGirls: Young Women, Self-Esteem, & the Confidence Gap. Peggy Orenstein. 368p. 1995. reprint ed. pap. 12.95 (*0-385-42576-7*, Anchor NY) Doubleday.

Schoolground Science see Beyond the Classroom: Exploration of Schoolground & Backyard

Schoolhome: Rethinking Schools for Changing Families. Jane R. Martin. 237p. (Orig.). (C). 1992. text ed. 24.95 (*0-674-79265-3*) HUP.

Schoolhome: Rethinking Schools for Changing Families. Jane R. Martin. 248p. (Orig.). (C). 1995. pap. text ed. 14.95 (*0-674-79266-1*) HUP.

Schoolhouse. (Chubby Shape Bks.). (Illus.). 8p. (J). (ps). 1984. pap. 3.50 (*0-671-49717-0*, Litl Simon S&S) S&S Childrens.

Schoolhouse. Ed. by Karen C. Soltys. (Classic American Quilt Collection Ser.). 1995. 19.95 (*0-87596-685-3*) Rodale Pr Inc.

Schoolhouse Applique: Reverse Techniques & More. Charlotte Patera. (Illus.). 80p. 1995. pap. 19.95 (*0-914881-99-X*, 10121) C & T Pub.

***Schoolhouse Decisions of the United States Supreme Court.** Ed. by Maureen Harrison & Steve Gilbert. 240p. (Orig.). (C). 1997. pap. 16.95 (*0-9628014-9-6*) Excellent Bks.

Schoolhouse Door: Segregation's Last Stand at the University of Alabama. E. Culpepper Clark. 352p. 1993. 30.00 (*0-19-507417-3*) OUP.

Schoolhouse Door: Segregation's Last Stand at the University of Alabama. E. Culpepper Clark. 352p. 1995. pap. 16.95 (*0-19-509658-4*) OUP.

Schoolhouse in the Red: A Guidebook for Cutting Our Losses. Shirley Hansen. 40p. 1992. pap. 6.95 (*0-87652-174-X*, 21-00142) Am Assn Sch Admin.

Schoolhouse Mystery. Gertrude C. Warner. LC 65-23889. (Boxcar Children Mysteries Ser.: No. 10). (Illus.). 128p. (J). (gr. 2-7). 1965. reprint ed. pap. 3.95 (*0-8075-7263-2*); reprint ed. lib. bdg. 13.95 (*0-8075-7262-4*) A Whitman.

Schoolhouse Planning. rev. ed. Ed. by C. William Day & Karl V. Hertz. 96p. (Orig.). 1987. pap. text ed. 13.00 (*0-910170-50-9*) Assn Sch Busn.

Schoolhouse Politicians: Locality & State During the Chinese Republic. Helen R. Chauncey. LC 92-28367. 378p. 1992. text ed. 40.00 (*0-8248-1415-0*) UH Pr.

Schoolhouse Politics: Lessons from the Sputnik Era. Peter B. Dow. 299p. (C). 1991. 38.00 (*0-674-79240-8*) HUP.

Schoolhouse Rock! The Official Guide. Tom Yohe & George Newall. (Illus.). 112p. (Orig.). 1996. pap. 9.95 (*0-7868-8170-4*) Hyperion.

Schoolhousing: Planning & Designing Educational Facilities. Flora I. Ortiz. LC 92-47103. 195p. (C). 1993. text ed. 64.50 (*0-7914-1727-1*); pap. text ed. 21.95 (*0-7914-1728-X*) State U NY Pr.

Schooling. Sylvia Farnham-Diggory. (Developing Child Ser.). (Illus.). 256p. 1990. 23.50 (*0-674-79271-8*); pap. text ed. 8.95 (*0-674-79272-6*) HUP.

Schooling & Cognitive Achievements of Children in Morocco: Can The Government Improve Outcomes. Shahidur R. Khandker et al. LC 94-33983. (World Bank Discussion Papers). 1994. 7.95 (*0-8213-3046-2*, 13046) World Bank.

Schooling & Disability. Ed. by Douglas P. Biklen et al. (National Society for the Study of Education Publication Ser.: No. 88, Pt. 2). 302p. 1989. 27.00 (*0-226-60150-1*, Natl Soc Stud Educ) U Ch Pr.

Schooling & Innovation: The Rhetoric & the Reality. Angela E. Fraley. LC 81-169045. 250p. (C). 1981. text ed. 12.00 (*0-9605520-0-6*) Tyler-Gibson.

Schooling & Scholars in Nineteenth-Century Ontario. Susan E. Houston & Alison Prentice. (Ontario Historical Studies). (Illus.). 432p. 1988. 40.00 (*0-8020-5801-9*); pap. 24.95 (*0-8020-6717-4*) U of Toronto Pr.

***Schooling & Social Change, 1964-1990.** Roy Lowe. LC 96-51714. 240p. (C). 1997. pap. write for info. (*0-415-16689-6*); text ed. write for info. (*0-415-02397-1*) Routledge.

Schooling & Society. 2nd ed. Rodman B. Webb & Robert R. Sherman. 901p. (C). 1988. text ed. 86.00 (*0-02-424900-9*, Macmillan Coll) P-H.

Schooling & Society. 3rd ed. Rodman B. Webb & Robert R. Sherman. 656p. (C). 1997. text ed. write for info. (*0-02-424922-X*, Macmillan Coll) P-H.

***Schooling & Society: Studies in the History of Education.** Ed. by Lawrence Stone. LC 76-15005. 288p. 1976. reprint ed. pap. 82.10 (*0-608-03655-2*, 2064481) Bks Demand.

Schooling & Society in Australia: Sociological Perspectives. Lawrence J. Saha & John P. Keeves. (Illus.). 288p. 1991. pap. text ed. 33.00 (*0-08-034409-7*, Pergamon Pr) Elsevier.

Schooling & Society in Nineteenth-Century Germany: The Politics of Education in Prussia & Bavaria, 1750-1900. Karl A. Schleunes. 278p. 1989. 19.95 (*0-85496-267-0*) Berg Pubs.

Schooling & the Silenced "Others" Race & Class in Schools. Lois Weis et al. LC 92-19805. (Special Studies in Teaching & Teacher Education: No. 7). 73p. (Orig.). 1992. pap. 10.00 (*0-937033-50-2*) SUNY GSE Pubns.

Schooling & the Struggle for Public Life: Critical Pedagogy in the Modern Age. Henry A. Giroux. LC 88-4746. (American Culture Ser.). xiii, 257p. (Orig.). 1988. pap. text ed. 15.95 (*0-8166-1706-6*) U of Minn Pr.

Schooling & Work in the Democratic State. Martin Carnoy & Henry M. Levin. LC 83-40697. 320p. 1985. 45.00 (*0-8047-1242-5*); pap. 17.95 (*0-8047-1289-1*) Stanford U Pr.

Schooling As a Ritual Performance: Towards a Political Economy of Symbols & Gestures. 2nd rev. ed. Peter McLaren. LC 92-45839. 280p. (C). 1993. pap. 18.95 (*0-415-08265-X*, B2392) Routledge.

Schooling Christians: "Holy Experiments" in American Education. fac. ed. Ed. by Stanley Hauerwas & John H. Westerhoff. LC 92-17171. 293p. 1992. reprint ed. pap. 83.60 (*0-7837-7957-7*, 2047713) Bks Demand.

***Schooling Desire: Literacy, Cultural Politics & Pedagogy.** Ursula A. Kelly. LC 96-50349. 178p. (C). 1997. pap. write for info. (*0-415-91549-X*); text ed. write for info. (*0-415-91548-1*) Routledge.

Schooling Disadvantaged Children: Racing Against Catastrophe. Gary Natriello. 272p. (C). 1990. pap. text ed. 19.95 (*0-8077-3014-9*) Tchrs Coll.

Schooling, Experience, & Earnings. Jacob Mincer. (Studies in Human Behavior & Social Institutions: No. 2). 167p. 1974. 45.50 (*0-87014-265-8*) Natl Bur Econ Res.

Schooling for Change: Reinventing Education for Early Adolescents. Andy Hargreaves et al. LC 96-12558. 208p. 1996. 69.95 (*0-7507-0489-6*, Falmer Pr); pap. 22.95 (*0-7507-0490-X*, Falmer Pr) Taylor & Francis.

Schooling for "Good Rebels" Socialism, American Education, & the Search for Radical Curriculum. Kenneth Teitelbaum. 272p. (C). 1995. pap. text ed. 22.95 (*0-8077-3486-1*) Tchrs Coll.

Schooling for "Good Rebels" Socialist Education for Children in the United States, 1900-1920. Kenneth Teitelbaum. 304p. (C). 1993. 54.95 (*0-87722-980-5*) Temple U Pr.

Schooling for Jobs: Changes in the Career Preparation of British Secondary School Children. Andy Furlong. 118p. 1993. 55.95 (*1-85628-345-3*, Pub. by Avebury Pub UK) Ashgate Pub Co.

***Schooling for Ruling: A Training Manual for the Development of Effective Leadership & the Growth of Strong Local Churches.** John Tetsola. 98p. (Orig.). 1997. pap. 11.99 (*1-889389-07-2*) End-Time Wave.

Schooling for Servitude: Some Aspects. E. Jefferson Murphy. 38p. 1972. 4.50 (*0-317-65386-5*) I N Thut World Educ Ctr.

Schooling for Social Order: Democracy, Equality & Social Mobility in Education. Ed. by Lawrence Angus. 94p. (C). 1986. 51.00 (*0-7300-0397-3*, Pub. by Deakin Univ AT) St Mut.

Schooling for the New Slavery: Black Industrial Education, 1868-1915. Donald Spivey. LC 77-87974. (Contributions in Afro-American & African Studies: No. 38). 162p. 1978. text ed. 38.50 (*0-313-20051-3*, SSN/, Greenwood Pr) Greenwood.

Schooling for the People: Comparative Local Studies of Schooling History in France & Germany, 1750-1850. Mary J. Maynes. LC 84-10929. 272p. 1985. 49.75 (*0-8419-0966-0*) Holmes & Meier.

Schooling for Work in Capitalist Britain. Chris Shilling. 220p. 1989. 70.00 (*1-85000-518-4*, Falmer Pr); pap. 35.00 (*1-85000-519-2*, Falmer Pr) Taylor & Francis.

Schooling German Girls & Women: Secondary & Higher Education in the Nineteenth Century. James C. Albisetti. 320p. 1989. text ed. 62.50 (*0-691-05535-1*) Princeton U Pr.

Schooling Homeless Children: A Qualitative Study of One Urban School. Sharon Quint. LC 94-28783. 176p. (C). 1994. pap. 14.95 (*0-8077-3391-1*); text ed. 30.00 (*0-8077-3392-X*) Tchrs Coll.

Schooling in a Plural Canada. John R. Mallea. 120p. 1989. 69.00 (*1-85359-030-4*, Pub. by Multilingual Matters UK); pap. 24.95 (*1-85359-029-0*, Pub. by Multilingual Matters UK) Taylor & Francis.

Schooling in a "Total Institution" Critical Perspectives on Prison Education. Howard S. Davidson. LC 94-36221. (Critical Studies in Education & Culture). 248p. 1995. pap. text ed. 21.95 (*0-89789-426-X*, Bergin & Garvey) Greenwood.

Schooling in a "Total Institution" Critical Perspectives on Prison Education. Ed. by Howard S. Davidson. LC 94-36221. (Critical Studies in Education & Culture). 248p. 1995. text ed. 59.95 (*0-89789-347-6*, Bergin & Garvey) Greenwood.

Schooling in America. Frank McKenna. 256p. (C). 1993. per. 28.29 (*0-8403-8699-0*) Kendall-Hunt.

Schooling in Capitalist America: Educational Reform & the Contradictions of Economic Life. Samuel Bowles & Herbert Gintis. LC 75-7267. 352p. 1977. pap. text ed. 16.00 (*0-465-09718-9*) Basic.

Schooling in English: Critical Episodes in the Struggle to Shape Literary & Cultural Studies. John Dixon. 192p. 1991. 95.00 (*0-335-09322-1*, Open Univ Pr); pap. 36.00 (*0-335-09321-3*, Open Univ Pr) Taylor & Francis.

Schooling in Mexico: Educational Austerity in a Developing Country. Christopher Martin. 235p. 1994. 55.95 (*1-85628-665-7*, Pub. by Avebury Pub UK) Ashgate Pub Co.

Schooling in Modern European Society: A Report to the Academia Europaea. Ed. by Torsten Husen et al. 414p. 1992. text ed. 65.00 (*0-08-041393-5*, Pergamon Pr) Elsevier.

Schooling in Renaissance Italy: Literacy & Learning, 1300-1600. Paul F. Grendler. LC 88-73568. (Studies in Historical & Political Science). 592p. 1991. pap. text ed. 24.95 (*0-8018-4229-8*) Johns Hopkins.

Schooling in Social Context: Qualitative Studies. Ed. by George W. Noblit & William T. Pink. LC 86-10890. 352p. (C). 1987. text ed. 73.25 (*0-89391-326-X*) Ablex Pub.

***Schooling in Sub-Saharan Africa: Contemporary Issues & Future Concerns.** Cynthia S. Sunal. Ed. by Edward R. Beauchamp. (Reference Books on International Education). 350p. Date not set. text ed. 52.50 (*0-8153-1645-3*) Garland.

Schooling in the Asian Region: Primary & Secondary Education in Indonesia, Malaysia, the Philippines, Singapore & Thailand. Ed. by T. Neville Postlethwaite & R. Murray Thomas. LC 79-41357. (Illus.). 348p. 1980. 151.00 (*0-08-024289-8*, Pub. by Pergamon Repr UK) Franklin.

Schooling in the Light of Popular Culture. Ed. by Paul Farber et al. LC 93-28209. (SUNY Series, Education & Culture: Critical Factors in the Formation of Character & Community in American Life). 276p. (C). 1994. pap. text ed. 19.95 (*0-7914-1872-3*) State U NY Pr.

Schooling in Western Europe: A Social History. Mary J. Maynes. LC 84-8847. 177p. 1985. text ed. 64.50 (*0-87395-978-7*); pap. text ed. 21.95 (*0-87395-977-9*) State U NY Pr.

Schooling Jobs, & Cultural Identity: Minority Education in Quebec. Linda Kahn. LC 91-41998. (Studies in Education & Culture: Vol. 2). 272p. 1992. text ed. 45.00 (*0-8240-7138-7*, SS639) Garland.

Schooling of the Horse. rev. ed. John R. Young. LC 81-11539. (Illus.). 376p. 1982. 34.95 (*0-8061-1787-7*) U of Okla Pr.

Schooling of the Immigrant see Americanization Studies: The Acculturation of Immigrant Groups into American Society

Schooling Reform in Hard Times. Ed. by Bob Lingard et al. LC 92-38081. 324p. 1993. 90.00 (*0-7507-0119-6*, Falmer Pr); pap. 33.00 (*0-7507-0120-X*, Falmer Pr) Taylor & Francis.

***Schooling Sexualities.** Debbie Epstein & Richard Johnson. LC 97-23198. 1997. write for info. (*0-335-19537-7*, Open Univ Pr); pap. write for info. (*0-335-19536-9*, Open Univ Pr) Taylor & Francis.

***Schooling That Works: A Superintendent's Proven Model.** Richard Scardamaglia. 112p. 1997. pap. 9.00 (*0-938453-06-8*, SAN660-9805) Small Helm Pr.

Schooling the Daughters of Marianne: Textbooks & the Socialization of Girls in Modern French Primary Schools. Linda L. Clark. LC 83-5035. 224p. 1984. text ed. 74.50 (*0-87395-787-3*); pap. text ed. 24.95 (*0-87395-786-5*) State U NY Pr.

Schooling the New South: Pedagogy, Self, & Society in North Carolina, 1880-1920. James L. Leloudis. LC 95-26137. (Fred W. Morrison Series in Southern Studies). (Illus.). 352p. (C). 1996. text ed. 39.95 (*0-8078-2265-5*) U of NC Pr.

Schooling the Poor: A Social Inquiry into the American Educational Experience. Stanley W. Rothstein. 1994. write for info. (*0-318-72276-3*, Bergin & Garvey) Greenwood.

Schooling the Poor: A Social Inquiry into the American Educational Experience. Stanley W. Rothstein. LC 93-40161. (Critical Studies in Education & Culture). 189p. 1994. text ed. 49.95 (*0-89789-372-7*, Bergin & Garvey) Greenwood.

Schooling the Poorer Child: Elementary Education in Sheffield 1560-1902. Malcolm V. Mercer. (Illus.). 328p. 1996. pap. 19.95 (*1-85075-534-5*, Pub. by Sheffield Acad UK) CUP Services.

Schooling the Preachers: The Development of Protestant Theological Education in the United States, 1740-1875. James W. Fraser. LC 88-20714. 174p. (Orig.). (C). 1988. pap. text ed. 20.00 (*0-8191-7161-1*); lib. bdg. 40.50 (*0-8191-7160-3*) U Pr of Amer.

Schooling, the School Effectiveness Movement & Educational Reform. Lawrence Angus. 100p. (C). 1986. 48.00 (*0-7300-0375-2*, Pub. by Deakin Univ AT) St Mut.

Schooling the Spirit. Geoffrey Clark. LC 92-72709. 208p. (Orig.). 1993. pap. 11.95 (*1-878580-36-1*) Asylum Arts.

Schooling the Violent Imagination. John F. Schostak. 208p. 1986. 35.00 (*0-7102-0365-9*, 03659, RKP) Routledge.

Schooling to Working: Exploring the Connections. Richard Lyons et al. LC 90-40764. (American University Studies: Vol. 30). 200p. (C). 1991. text ed. 34.95 (*0-8204-1344-5*) P Lang Pubng.

Schooling, Welfare, & Parental Responsibility. Michael G. Wyness. (New Prospects Ser.: Vol. 2). 224p. 1996. 72.95 (*0-7507-0437-3*, Falmer Pr); pap. 24.95 (*0-7507-0438-1*, Falmer Pr) Taylor & Francis.

Schooling Without Labels: Parents, Educators & Inclusive Education. Douglas Biklen. (Health, Society, & Policy Ser.). (C). 1992. 59.95 (*0-87722-875-2*); pap. 19.95 (*0-87722-876-0*) Temple U Pr.

Schooling Young Children: A Feminist Pedagogy for Liberatory Learning. Jeanne Brady. LC 94-28901. 108p. (C). 1995. text ed. 39.50 (*0-7914-2501-0*); pap. text ed. 12.95 (*0-7914-2502-9*) State U NY Pr.

Schooling Young Horses. Werner Storl. (Illus.). 120p. 1990. 22.50 (*0-914327-36-4*) Breakthrgh NY.

Schooling Your Young Horse. George Wheatley. 1977. pap. 7.00 (*0-87980-201-4*) Wilshire.

Schoolland. Max Martinez. LC 87-35127. 250p. (Orig.). 1988. pap. 9.50 (*0-934770-87-5*) Arte Publico.

Schoolma'am. Frances R. Donovan. LC 74-3943. (Women in America Ser.). 368p. 1974. reprint ed. 29.95 (*0-405-06087-4*) Ayer.

Schoolmaker: Sawney Webb & the Bell Buckle Story. Laurence McMillin. LC 72-144336. 218p. reprint ed. pap. 62.20 (*0-7837-2065-3*, 2042340) Bks Demand.

Schoolmarm All My Life: Personal Narratives from Frontier Utah. Ed. & Intro. by Joyce Kinkead. LC 96-18067. (Illus.). 300p. (Orig.). 1997. pap. 17.95 (*1-56085-083-3*) Signature Bks.

Schoolmarms: Women in America's Schools. Edwina Walsh. 235p. (Orig.). (C). 1995. pap. 19.95 (*1-880192-14-4*) Caddo Gap Pr.

Schoolmaster. Boyce Mouton. LC 85-62798. 138p. 1985. pap. 5.99 (*0-89900-209-9*) College Pr Pub.

Schoolmaster. Earl Lovelace. (Caribbean Writers Ser.). 171p. (C). 1983. reprint ed. pap. 7.95 (*0-435-98550-7*, 98550) Heinemann.

Schoolmaster. Rose Moss. (Writers Ser.). 239p. 1995. reprint ed. pap. text ed. 12.95 (*0-86975-470-X*, Pub. by Ravan Pr ZA) Ohio U Pr.

Schoolmaster & Other Stories. Anton P. Chekhov. Tr. by Constance Garnett from RUS. (Tales of Anton Chekhov Ser.: Vol. 11). 302p. 1986. reprint ed. pap. 9.50 (*0-88001-058-4*) Ecco Pr.

Schoolmaster Ni Huan-Chi. 2nd ed. Yeh Sheng-Tao. Tr. by A. C. Barnes from CHI. 337p. (C). 1978. 7.95 (*0-917056-98-1*, Pub. by Foreign Lang Pr CH) Cheng & Tsui.

Schoolmaster to an Empire: Richard Henry Brunton in Meiji Japan, 1868-1876. Ed. by Richard H. Brunton & Edward R. Beauchamp. LC 90-19931. (Contributions in Asian Studies: No. 1). 200p. 1991. text ed. 59.95 (*0-313-27795-8*, BHW/, Greenwood Pr) Greenwood.

Schoolmasters. Leonard E. Fisher. LC 96-16609. (Colonial Craftsmen Ser.). (Illus.). (J). 1997. lib. bdg. write for info. (*0-7614-0480-5*, Benchmark) B K Pickard.

S

***Schoolmasters.** 2nd ed. Leonard E. Fisher. LC 96-16609. (Colonial Craftsmen Ser.). (Illus.). (YA). (gr. 4 up). 1996. reprint ed. lib. bdg. 14.95 (*0-614-24095-6*, Benchmark NY) Marshall Cavendish.

Schoolmaster's Son. Jesus Otero. (American Autobiography Ser.). 130p. 1995. reprint ed. lib. bdg. 69.00 (*0-7812-8605-0*) Rprt Serv.

Schoolmaster's Stories for Boys & Girls. Edward Eggleston. (Collected Works of Edward Eggleston). (YA). 1988. reprint ed. lib. bdg. 59.00 (*0-7812-1176-X*) Rprt Serv.

Schoolmaster's Stories for Boys & Girls see Collected Works of Edward Eggleston

Schoolmistress & Other Stories. Anton P. Chekhov. Tr. by Constance Garnett from RUS. (Tales of Chekhov Ser.: Vol. 9). 305p. 1986. reprint ed. pap. 9.95 (*0-88001-056-8*) Ecco Pr.

Schoolmistress in History, Poetry & Romance. Thomas W. Field. 1972. 59.95 (*0-8490-0998-7*) Gordon Pr.

Schoolproof: How to Help Your Family Beat the System & Learn to Love Learning the Easy, Natural Way. Mary Pride. LC 87-72953. 1988. pap. 10.99 (*0-89107-480-5*) Crossway Bks.

Schoolroom Poets: A Bibliography of Bryant, Holmes, Longfellow, Lowell & Whittier with Selective Annotation. Jeanetta Boswell. LC 83-19276. 311p. 1983. 29.50 (*0-8108-1659-8*) Scarecrow.

Schools. Diane Yancey. LC 94-40039. (Overview Ser.). 80p. (J). (gr. 6-10). 1995. lib. bdg. 17.96 (*1-56006-167-7*) Lucent Bks.

Schools: An Education in Charity Law. Debra Morris. (Illus.). 288p. 1996. 62.95 (*1-85521-444-X*, Pub. by Dartmth Pub UK) Ashgate Pub Co.

Schools--Progress, Activities, & Trends: Index of New Information with Authors, Subjects, & References. Chester M. Lukeman. 1995. 47.50 (*0-7883-0464-X*); pap. 44.50 (*0-7883-0465-8*) ABBE Pubs Assn.

Schools Abroad of Interest to Americans. 8th ed. Ed. by Porter Sargent Staff. LC 67-18844. (Handbook Ser.). (Illus.). 592p. 1991. 35.00 (*0-87558-127-7*) Porter Sargent.

***Schools Abroad of Interest to Americans.** 9th ed. Porter Sargent Staff. LC 67-18844. (Handbook Ser.). (Illus.). 600p. 1997. 45.00 (*0-87558-138-2*) Porter Sargent.

Schools & Business - a New Partnership. 110p. (Orig.). 1992. pap. 20.00 (*92-64-13632-0*) OECD.

Schools & Colleges Directory. 1996. 9.50 (*0-614-12924-9*) Assn Exper Ed.

Schools & Disruptive Pupils. D. Galloway & Stephen J. Ball. LC 81-15601. 1982. pap. 10.95 (*0-582-49707-8*) Longman.

Schools & Drugs: A Guide to Drug & Alcohol Abuse Prevention Curricula & Programs. 144p. (Orig.). (C). 1993. pap. text ed. 30.00 (*0-7881-0163-3*) DIANE Pub.

Schools & Drugs: A Handbook for Parents & Educators. 2nd rev. ed. Joyce M. Tobias. LC 89-48781. 48p. (Orig.). (C). 1989. 4.00 (*0-9616700-4-5*) Panda Press VA.

Schools & Employment Law. Patricia Leighton. Ed. by John Sayer. (Education Management Ser.). 192p. 1992. pap. text ed. 29.95 (*0-304-32445-0*) Cassell.

Schools & External Relations. John Sayer & Vivian Williams. 192p. 1989. pap. text ed. 24.95 (*0-304-31720-9*) Cassell.

Schools & Families: Issues & Actions. Dorothy Rich. 128p. 1987. pap. 11.95 (*0-8106-0276-8*) NEA.

***Schools & Family Therapy: Using Systems Theory & Family Therapy in the Resolution of School Problems.** William M. Walsh & G. Robert Williams. LC 97-12058. 1997. write for info. (*0-398-06777-5*); pap. write for info. (*0-398-06778-3*) C C Thomas.

Schools & Health: Our Nation's Investment. Ed. by Diane Allensworth et al. 350p. 1997. 39.95 (*0-309-05435-4*) Natl Acad Pr.

Schools & Parents. John Partington & Ted Wragg. (Education Matters Ser.). 96p. 1989. text ed. 45.00 (*0-304-31714-4*); pap. text ed. 17.95 (*0-304-31712-8*) Cassell.

Schools & Politics No. 50: The Kaum Muda Movement in West Sumatra 1927-1933. Taufik Abdullah. 257p. 1971. pap. 6.00 (*0-87763-010-0*) Cornell Mod Indo.

Schools & Quality: An International Report. OECD Staff. 140p. (Orig.). 1989. pap. 20.00 (*92-64-13254-6*) OECD.

Schools & Scholars in Fourteenth-Century England. William J. Courtenay. (Illus.). 416p. 1988. text ed. 69.50 (*0-691-05500-9*) Princeton U Pr.

***Schools & Scholars in Fourteenth-Century England.** William J. Courtenay. LC 87-14808. reprint ed. 130.00 (*0-608-04592-6*, 2065362) Bks Demand.

Schools & Social Justice. R. W. Connell. LC 93-1616. 144p. (C). 1993. 44.95 (*1-56639-137-7*); pap. 16.95 (*1-56639-138-5*) Temple U Pr.

Schools & Society: A Unified Reader. Jeanne H. Ballantine. LC 88-33384. 593p. (Orig.). (C). 1989. pap. text ed. 37.95 (*0-87484-907-1*, 907) Mayfield Pub.

Schools & Society: New Perspectives in American Education. Rothstein. 1995. pap. text ed. 40.00 (*0-02-403993-4*, Macmillan Coll) P-H.

***Schools & Society: Teleclass Study Guide.** GSU (Schmidt) Staff. 342p. (C). 1996. per., pap. text ed. 24.95 (*0-7872-2446-4*) Kendall-Hunt.

***Schools & Staffing in the United States: A Statistical Profile.** 1997. lib. bdg. 258.99 (*0-8490-6256-X*) Gordon Pr.

Schools & Students at Risk: Context & Framework for Positive Change. Robert J. Rossi. LC 93-44316. 336p. (C). 1994. pap. 23.95 (*0-8077-3325-3*); text ed. 48.00 (*0-8077-3326-1*) Tchrs Coll.

***Schools & Students in Industrial Society: Japan & the West, 1870-1940.** Peter N. Stearns. (Bedford Series in Comparative History). 160p. 1997. 35.00 (*0-312-16381-9*) St Martin.

***Schools & the Changing World: Struggling Towards the Future.** Benjamin Levin & Anthony Riffel. (Education Policy Perspectives Ser.). 224p. 1997. 72.95 (*0-7507-0662-7*, Falmer Pr); pap. 24.95 (*0-7507-0617-1*, Falmer Pr) Taylor & Francis.

Schools & the Culturally Diverse Exceptional Student: Promising Practices & Future Directions. Ed. by Bruce A. Ramirez & Alba A. Ortiz. 176p. 1988. pap. text ed. 21.70 (*0-86586-182-X*, P326) Coun Exc Child.

Schools & the Law. 5th ed. E. Edmund Reutter. LC 81-80361. 126p. reprint ed. pap. 36.00 (*0-685-23754-0*, 2032797) Bks Demand.

Schools & Work. David Coffey. 224p. 1992. text ed. 60.00 (*0-304-32599-6*); pap. text ed. 19.95 (*0-304-32583-X*) Cassell.

Schools & Workplaces: An Overview of Successful & Unsuccessful Practices. (Illus.). 100p. (Orig.). 1996. pap. text ed. 25.00 (*0-7881-2886-8*) DIANE Pub.

Schools As Collaborative Cultures: Creating the Future Now. Ann Lieberman. (School Development & the Management of Change Ser.). 256p. 1990. 75.00 (*1-85000-672-5*); pap. 31.00 (*1-85000-673-3*) Taylor & Francis.

Schools As Learning Communities: Transforming Education. David Clark. (Cassell Education Ser.). (Illus.). 176p. 1996. 90.00 (*0-304-33075-2*); pap. 21.00 (*0-304-33073-6*) Cassell.

Schools As Sorters: Lewis M. Terman, Applied Psychology, & the Intelligence Testing Movement, 1890-1930. Paul D. Chapman. (American Social Experience Ser.: No. 11). (Illus.). 284p. (C). 1988. text ed. 20.00 (*0-8147-1420-X*) NYU Pr.

Schools As Sorters: Lewis M. Terman, Applied Psychology, & the Intelligence Testing Movement, 1890-1930. Paul D. Chapman. (American Social Experience Ser.: No. 11). (Illus.). 284p. (C). 1990. pap. text ed. 14.80 (*0-8147-1436-6*) NYU Pr.

Schools at the Centre? A Study of Decentralisation. Alison Bullock & Hywel Thomas. LC 96-26284. 248p. (C). 1997. pap. write for info. (*0-415-12911-7*, Routledge NY) Routledge.

School's Choice: Guidelines for Dropout Prevention at the Middle & Junior High School. 1988. 13.25 (*0-318-40017-0*, SP700DP02) Ctr Educ Trng Employ.

Schools, Communities, & the Arts: A Research Compendium. Nancy Welch. (Illus.). 164p. 1995. write for info. (*0-9647870-0-8*) AZ State U MIPP.

Schools, Conflict, & Change. Ed. by Mike M. Milstein. LC 79-20327. 320p. reprint ed. pap. 91.20 (*0-318-34884-5*, 2031205) Bks Demand.

Schools Count: World Bank Project Designs & the Quality of Primary Education in Sub-Saharan Africa. Ward Heneveld & Helen Craig. LC 95-36253. (Technical Paper Ser.: No. 303). 152p. 1996. 9.95 (*0-8213-3460-3*, 13460) World Bank.

Schools Flunk...Kids Don't. Joe Petterle. (Orig.). 1992. pap. 15.95 (*1-881805-22-0*) Copernicus Systs.

Schools Flunk...Kids Don't. Joe Petterle. (Orig.). 1993. pap. 15.95 (*1-882180-16-X*) Griffin CA.

Schools for a New Century: A Conservative Approach to Radical School Reform. Dwight W. Allen. LC 91-39815. 200p. 1992. text ed. 45.00 (*0-275-93649-X*, C3649, Praeger Pubs) Greenwood.

Schools for All: Educating Children in a Diverse Society. Lyn Lachmann-Miller & Lorraines Taylor. LC 94-26265. (Illus.). 416p. 1995. text ed. 38.95 (*0-8273-5957-8*) Delmar.

Schools for All: The Blacks & Public Education in the South, 1865-1877. William P. Vaughn. LC 73-86408. 192p. reprint ed. pap. 54.80 (*0-8357-9793-7*, 2013517) Bks Demand.

***Schools for All: 1812 Edition.** James Mill. Ed. & Intro. by Jeffrey Stern. (Classics in Education Ser.). 88p. 1996. reprint ed. write for info. (*1-85506-294-1*) Bks Intl VA.

Schools for All Learners: Beyond the Bell Curve. Renfro C. Manning. LC 94-34139. 1994. 29.95 (*1-883001-06-4*) Eye On Educ.

Schools for an Information Age: Reconstructing Foundations for Learning & Teaching. Byrd L. Jones & Robert W. Maloy. LC 95-34417. 416p. 1996. text ed. 59.95 (*0-275-95395-5*, Praeger Pubs) Greenwood.

Schools for an Information Age: Reconstructing Foundations for Learning & Teaching. Byrd L. Jones & Robert W. Maloy. LC 95-34417. 416p. 1996. pap. text ed. 29.95 (*0-275-95396-3*, Praeger Pubs) Greenwood.

Schools for Cities. 156p. (Orig.). 1995. pap. 25.00 (*92-64-14324-6*, Pub. by Org for Econ FR) OECD.

***Schools for Growth: Radical Alternatives to Current Educational Models.** Lois Holzman. LC 97-13494. 208p. 1997. write for info. (*0-8058-2356-5*) L Erlbaum Assocs.

***Schools for Growth: Radical Alternatives to Current Educational Models.** Lois Holzman. LC 97-13494. 208p. 1997. pap. write for info. (*0-8058-2357-3*) L Erlbaum Assocs.

Schools for Sale. Thomas Toch. 1996. write for info. (*0-201-62718-3*) Addison-Wesley.

Schools for Talent Development: A Practical Plan for Total School Improvement. Joseph S. Renzulli. 1994. pap. 39.95 (*0-936386-65-7*) Creative Learning.

Schools for the Shires: The Reform of Middle-Class Education in Mid-Victorian England. David Allsobrook. 308p. 1988. text ed. 24.95 (*0-7190-2271-1*, Pub. by Manchester Univ Pr UK) St Martin.

Schools for the Twenty-First Century. California Department of Education Staff. (Illus.). 48p. 1990. pap. 5.25 (*0-8011-0911-6*) Calif Education.

Schools for the Twenty-First Century: Leadership Imperatives for Educational Reform. Phillip C. Schlechty. LC 89-29662. (Education-Higher Education Ser.). 190p. text ed. 29.95 (*1-55542-208-X*) Jossey-Bass.

Schools for the Twenty-First Century: Leadership Imperatives for Educational Reform. Phillip C. Schlechty. LC 89-29662. (Education-Higher Education Ser.). 164p. 1991. reprint ed. pap. 18.00 (*1-55542-366-3*) Jossey-Bass.

Schools for Thought: A Science of Learning in the Classroom. John T. Bruer. 336p. 1994. pap. 17.50 (*0-262-52196-2*, Bradford Bks) MIT Pr.

***Schools for Today & Tomorrow: An International Compendium of Exemplary Educational Facilities.** OECD Staff. (Illus.). 150p. (Orig.). 1996. pap. 30.00 (*92-64-15291-1*, 95-96-05-1) OECD.

Schools for Young Disadvantaged Children. Ruth Hamlin et al. LC 67-21504. (Early Childhood Education Ser.). 186p. reprint ed. pap. 53.10 (*0-317-41960-9*, 2026019) Bks Demand.

Schools in Cities: Consensus & Conflict in American Educational History. Ed. by Ronald K. Goodenow & Diane Ravitch. LC 83-8374. 326p. 1983. 45.00 (*0-8419-0850-8*) Holmes & Meier.

Schools in Conflict: The Politics of Education. 3rd ed. Frederick M. Wirt & Michael Kirst. LC 92-64196. 400p. 1992. 34.00 (*0-8211-2266-5*) McCutchan.

Schools in Crisis: Training for Success or Failure? 2nd ed. Carl Sommer. LC 83-71106. 335p. (Orig.). (C). 1984. pap. 8.95 (*0-9610810-0-7*) Advance Pub.

Schools in Partnership: Current Initiatives in School-Based Teacher-Training. Ed. by Vivienne Griffiths & Patricia Owen. 192p. 1995. pap. 26.95 (*1-85396-275-9*, Pub. by Paul Chapman UK) Taylor & Francis.

Schools in the Great Depression. Dominic W. Moreo. LC 95-44760. (Studies in the History of Education: No. 2). 224p. 1996. text ed. 45.00 (*0-8153-2039-6*, SS1037) Garland.

Schools in the Middle: Developing a Middle-Level Orientation. Jack A. McKay. Ed. by Jerry J. Herman & Janice L. Herman. LC 95-1463. (Road Maps to Success Ser.). (Illus.). 80p. 1995. pap. 11.95 (*0-8039-6232-0*) Corwin Pr.

Schools in the West: Essays in Canadian Educational History. Ed. by Nancy M. Sheehan et al. 323p. (Orig.). (C). 1986. pap. text ed. 18.95 (*0-920490-57-3*) Temeron Bks.

Schools in Tudor England. Craig R. Thompson. LC 59-1347. (Folger Guides to the Age of Shakespeare Ser.). 1959. 4.95 (*0-918016-28-2*) Folger Bks.

Schools into Fields & Factories: Anarchists, the Guomindang, & the National Labor University in Shanghai, 1927-1932. Ming K. Chan & Arif Dirlik. LC 91-7379. 351p. 1991. text ed. 52.95 (*0-8223-1154-2*) Duke.

Schools Make a Difference: Lessons Learned from a 10-Year Study of School Effects. Samuel Stringfield. LC 92-44888. 272p. (C). 1993. text ed. 35.00 (*0-8077-3237-0*) Tchrs Coll.

Schools, Mathematics, & the World of Reality. Ed. by Robert B. Davis & Carolyn A. Maher. LC 92-11678. 336p. 1993. text ed. 61.95 (*0-205-13445-9*, Longwood Div) Allyn.

Schools, Mathematics & Work. Ed. by Mary Harris. 224p. 1991. 70.00 (*1-85000-893-0*, Falmer Pr); pap. 33.00 (*1-85000-894-9*, Falmer Pr) Taylor & Francis.

***Schools of Architecture.** John Hejduk. 1997. pap. text ed. 22.95 (*90-5662-032-0*, Pub. by NAi Uitgevers NE) Dist Art Pubs.

Schools of Cincinnati & Its Vicinity. John P. Foote. LC 75-112545. (Rise of Urban America Ser.). (Illus.). 1970. reprint ed. 18.95 (*0-405-02454-1*) Ayer.

Schools of Griswold, Connecticut in Historical Perspective. Lucille A. Lupinacci. (Connecticut Educational History Ser.). 16p. 1987. 2.00 (*0-318-32532-2*) I N Thut World Educ Ctr.

Schools of Hope: Developing Mind & Character in Today's Youth. Douglas H. Heath. LC 93-36594. (Education Ser.). 466p. 32.95 (*1-55542-616-6*) Jossey-Bass.

Schools of Linguistics. Geoffrey Sampson. LC 80-81140. 283p. 1980. 42.50 (*0-8047-1084-8*); pap. 14.95 (*0-8047-1125-9*) Stanford U Pr.

Schools of Medieval England. A. F. Leach. LC 68-56478. (Illus.). 1972. reprint ed. 23.95 (*0-405-08740-3*) Ayer.

Schools of Quality: An Introduction to Total Quality Management in Education. 2nd ed. John J. Bonstingl. LC 96-12294. 150p. 1996. pap. 20.95 (*0-87120-263-8*, 196019) Assn Supervision.

Schools of Reconciliation: Issues in Joint Roman Catholic-Anglican Education. Priscilla Chadwick. LC 94-6804. 1995. pap. 22.95 (*0-304-33142-2*, Pub. by Cassell Publng UK) Morehouse Pub.

***Schools of the Americas: U. S. Military Training for Latin American Countries.** (Illus.). 24p. (Orig.). (C). 1996. pap. 25.00 (*0-7881-3638-0*) DIANE Pub.

***Schools of Their Own: The Education of Hispanos in New Mexico, 1850 -1940.** Lynne M. Getz. LC 96-51266. 1997. 34.95 (*0-8263-1812-6*) U of NM Pr.

Schools of Thought. Olga Amsterdamska. (C). 1987. lib. bdg. 129.50 (*90-277-2391-5*) Kluwer Ac.

Schools of Thought: How the Politics of Literacy Shape Thinking in the Classroom. Rexford G. Brown. LC 90-19892. (Education-Higher Education Ser.). 320p. text ed. 27.95 (*1-55542-314-0*) Jossey-Bass.

Schools of Thought: How the Politics of Literacy Shape Thinking in the Classroom. Rexford G. Brown. LC 90-19892. (Education-Higher Education Ser.). 320p. reprint ed. pap. 18.00 (*1-55542-558-5*) Jossey-Bass.

Schools of Thought in International Relations: Interpreters, Issues, & Morality. Kenneth W. Thompson. LC 96-26852. (Political Traditions in Foreign Policy Ser.). 200p. 1996. text ed. 40.00 (*0-8071-2097-9*); pap. text ed. 14.95 (*0-8071-2131-2*) La State U Pr.

Schools of Winchester, Virginia. 64p. 1964. pap. write for info. (*0-318-64326-X*) Winchester-Frederick Cty Hist Soc.

Schools on Trial: The Trials of Democratic Comprehensives. Colin Fletcher et al. 128p. 1985. pap. 25.00 (*0-335-15022-5*, Open Univ Pr) Taylor & Francis.

School's Out. Johanna Hurwitz. LC 90-13446. (Illus.). 128p. (J). (gr. 2 up). 1991. 12.95 (*0-688-09938-6*, Morrow Junior) Morrow.

School's Out! Johanna Hurwitz. (Illus.). 96p. (J). 1992. pap. 3.50 (*0-590-45053-0*, Little Apple) Scholastic Inc.

School's Out! Anne Logan. (Illus.). 80p. 22.95 (*0-919783-72-4*, Pub. by Boston Mills Pr CN) Genl Dist Srvs.

***School's Out!** Laura E. Williams. (Let's Have a Party Ser.: No. 1). (J). (gr. 1-4). Date not set. mass mkt. 3.99 (*0-380-78925-6*, Camelot) Avon.

School's Out! rev. ed. Joan M. Bergstrom. (Illus.). 330p. (J). 1990. pap. 16.95 (*0-89815-349-2*) Ten Speed Pr.

***School's Out: Poems Not for School.** Benjamin Zephaniah. 64p. (Orig.). (YA). 1997. pap. 6.95 (*1-873176-49-X*) AK Pr Dist.

School's Out: The End of Education & the New Technology. Lewis J. Perelman. 368p. 1993. reprint ed. pap. 12.50 (*0-380-71748-4*) Avon.

School's Out: The Impact of Gay & Lesbian Issues on America's Schools. Dan Woog. LC 95-5763. (Illus.). 383p. (Orig.). 1995. pap. 11.95 (*1-55583-249-0*) Alyson Pubns.

School's Out - It's Summer! Joan Bergstrom. (Illus.). 96p. (Orig.). 1992. pap. 7.95 (*0-89815-463-4*) Ten Speed Pr.

***School's Out Hell High.** David V. Mason. (Illus.). 108p. (Orig.). (YA). (gr. 9-12). 1996. pap. 5.00 (*0-88092-400-4*) Royal Fireworks.

Schools That Work. Judith Gelber. LC 89-51316. 256p. (Orig.). 1990. pap. 12.95 (*0-9624020-0-1*) Uriel Pub PA.

Schools That Work: America's Most Innovative Public Education Programs. George H. Wood. LC 91-29607. 320p. 1993. pap. 12.95 (*0-452-26959-8*, Plume) NAL-Dutton.

Schools That Work: Where All Children Read & Write. Richard L. Allington & Patricia M. Cunningham. LC 95-15798. (Illus.). 288p. (C). 1996. text ed. 27.95 (*0-673-99881-9*) Addson-Wesley Educ.

Schools under Scrutiny. OECD CERI Staff. 156p. (Orig.). 1995. pap. 40.00 (*92-64-14567-2*, Pub. by Org for Econ FR) OECD.

Schools under Siege. Knox et al. 240p. (C). 1992. pap. text ed. 47.19 (*0-8403-8232-4*) Kendall-Hunt.

***Schools under Siege: Guns, Gangs, & Hidden Dangers.** Carl W. Bosch. LC 96-36363. (Issues in Focus Ser.). (Illus.). 112p. (YA). (gr. 6 up). 1997. lib. bdg. 18.95 (*0-89490-908-8*) Enslow Pubs.

Schools, Violence, & Society. Ed. by Allan M. Hoffman. LC 95-40089. 368p. 1996. text ed. 65.00 (*0-275-94978-8*, Praeger Pubs); pap. text ed. 24.95 (*0-275-95506-0*, Praeger Pubs) Greenwood.

Schools We Have, the Schools We Want: An American Teacher on the Front Line. James Nehring. LC 92-14016. (Education-Higher Education Ser.). 200p. text ed. 28.95 (*1-55542-457-0*) Jossey-Bass.

Schools We Need & Why We Don't Have Them: And Why We Don't Have Them. E. D. Hirsch, Jr. 317p. 1996. 24.95 (*0-385-48457-7*) Doubleday.

Schools Where Children Learn. Joseph Featherstone. LC 75-148664. 1971. pap. 2.95 (*0-87140-251-3*) Liveright.

Schools with a Purpose. John W. Friesen. 142p. (Orig.). (C). 1983. pap. text ed. 10.95 (*0-920490-34-4*) Temeron Bks.

Schools Without Drugs: What Works. 95p. (Orig.). (C). 1993. pap. text ed. 20.00 (*0-7881-0084-X*) DIANE Pub.

Schools Without Failure. William Glasser. 320p. 1975. pap. 11.00 (*0-06-090421-6*, CN421, PL) HarpC.

Schools Without Fear: Group Activities for Building Community. Judy B. Lehr & Craig Martin. LC 94-72561. (Illus.). 192p. (Orig.). (C). 1994. pap. text ed. 19.95 (*0-932796-68-0*) Ed Media Corp.

Schoolsearch Guide to Colleges with Programs or Services for Students with Learning Disabilities. Midge Lipkin. 928p. (Orig.). 1993. pap. text ed. 34.95 (*0-9620326-5-4*) Schoolsearch Pr.

Schoolsearch Guide to Private Schools with Programs or Services for Students with Learning Disabilities. Midge Lipkin. 650p. (Orig.). 1992. pap. 34.95 (*0-9620326-4-6*) Schoolsearch Pr.

***Schoolsmart & Motherwise: Working-Class Women's Identity & Schooling.** Wendy Luttrell. LC 96-39655. 176p. (C). 1997. pap. write for info. (*0-415-91012-9*) Routledge.

***Schoolsmart & Motherwise: Workingclass Women's Identity & Schooling.** Wendy Luttrell. (Perspectives on Gender Ser.). 176p. (C). 1997. text ed. 59.95 (*0-415-91011-0*, Routledge NY) Routledge.

Schoolteacher: A Sociological Study. Dan C. Lortie. LC 74-11428. 296p. 1977. reprint ed. pap. text ed. 12.95 (*0-226-49354-7*, P748) U Ch Pr.

Schoolteachers & Schooling: Ethoses in Conflict. Ed. by Eugene F. Provenzo, Jr. & Gary N. McCloskey. LC 96-22351. (Social & Policy Issues in Education Ser.). 194p. 1996. pap. 39.50 (*1-56750-248-2*); text ed. 73.25 (*1-56750-247-4*) Ablex Pub.

***Schoolwide Enrichment Model: A How-To Guide for Educational Excellence.** 2nd rev. ed. 424p. 1997. pap. text ed. 42.95 (*0-936386-70-3*) Creative Learning.

An Asterisk (*) at the beginning of an entry indicates that the title is appearing in BIP for the first time.

Schoolwise: Teaching Academic Patterns of Mind. Joan E. Barickman. LC 92-22088. 136p. 1992. pap. text ed. 19.50 (*0-86709-309-9*, 0309) Boynton Cook Pubs.

***Schoolwomen of the Prairies & Plains: Personal Narratives from Iowa, Kansas, & Nebraska.** Mary H. Cordier. 365p. 1997. pap. text ed. 17.95 (*0-8263-1774-X*) U of NM Pr.

Schoolwork: Approaches to the Labor of Teaching, Vol. 1. Ed. by Jenny Ozga. 224p. 1987. 90.00 (*0-335-15554-5*, Open Univ Pr) Taylor & Francis.

***Schoolwork for Work: Integrated Classroom Activities.** 180p. (J). (gr. 3-5). 1997. spiral bd. 89.95 (*1-878172-73-5*, 397NGCSSFW) Wintergrn-Orchard Hse.

SchoolWorks: Reinventing Public Schools to Create the Workforce for the Future. William E. Nothdurft. 104p. 1990. pap. 9.95 (*0-8157-6201-1*) Brookings.

Schoolyard Mystery. Elizabeth Levy. (Hello Reader!, Invisible Inc. Ser.: Level 4, Bk. 1). (Illus.). 48p. (J). (gr. 2-3). 1994. pap. 3.99 (*0-590-47483-9*, Cartwheel) Scholastic Inc.

Schoolyard of Broken Dreams. Marvin Tate. 72p. 1994. pap. 7.95 (*1-882688-03-1*) Tia Chucha Pr.

Schoolyard Science, Grades 2-4: Schoolyard Science, Grades 2-4. Peggy K. Perdue. 1990. pap. 8.95 (*0-673-38967-7*, GoodYrBooks) Addson-Wesley Educ.

Schoom. Jonathan Wilson. LC 95-1322. 224p. (Orig.). 1995. pap. 10.95 (*0-14-023827-1*, Penguin Bks) Viking Penguin.

***Schooner: Its Design & Development from 1600 to the Present.** David R. MacGregor. (Illus.). 192p. 1997. 42.95 (*1-55750-847-X*) Naval Inst Pr.

***Schooner Bertha L. Downs.** Basil Greenhill & Sam Manning. 1996. text ed. 37.95 (*0-07-024514-2*) McGraw.

Schooner Bertha L. Downs. Basil Greenhill & Sam Manning. (Anatomy of the Ship Ser.). (Illus.). 128p. 1995. 39.95 (*1-55750-790-2*) Naval Inst Pr.

Schooner Integrity. Frank Mulville. (Illus.). 184p. 1992. pap. 14.95 (*0-85036-425-6*, Pub. by Seafarer Bks UK) Sheridan.

Schooner Master: A Portrait of David Stevens. Peter Carnahan. LC 89-32336. 207p. 1989. reprint ed. pap. 59.00 (*0-608-00549-5*, 2061428) Bks Demand.

***Schooner Pilgrim's Progress: A Voyage Around the World, 1932-1934.** Donald C. Starr. (Illus.). 371p. 1996. 19.95 (*0-913372-79-X*) Mystic Seaport.

***Schooner Sail to Starboard: Confederate Blockade-Running on the Louisiana-Texas Coast Lines.** large type ed. W. T. Block. (Illus.). 258p. (Orig.). (C). 1997. pap. 15.00 (*1-887745-08-4*) Dogwood TX.

Schooners & Schooner Barges. Paul C. Morris. LC 84-81110. (Illus.). 160p. 1984. 25.00 (*0-936972-06-8*) Lower Cape.

Schooners in Peril: True & Exciting Stories about Tall Ships on the Great Lakes. 2nd ed. James L. Donahue. (Illus.). 237p. (Orig.). 1995. reprint ed. pap. 14.95 (*1-882376-23-4*) Thunder Bay Pr.

Schopenhauer. David W. Hamlyn. (Arguments of the Philosophers Ser.). 192p. 1985. pap. 15.95 (*0-7102-0543-0*, RKP) Routledge.

Schopenhauer. Christopher Janaway. LC 93-40149. (Past Masters Ser.). 128p. 1994. pap. 8.95 (*0-19-287685-6*) OUP.

Schopenhauer. Vivian J. McGill. LC 77-159487. (Studies in Philosophy: No. 40). 1971. lib. bdg. 75.00 (*0-8383-1258-6*) M S G Haskell Hse.

Schopenhauer: New Essays in Honor of His 200th Birthday. Ed. by Eric Von der Luft. LC 88-26733. (Studies in German Thought & History: Vol. 10). 459p. 1989. lib. bdg. 119.95 (*0-88946-311-5*) E Mellen.

Schopenhauer: The Human Character. John E. Atwell. 240p. 1990. 39.95 (*0-87722-748-9*) Temple U Pr.

Schopenhauer & Nietzsche. Georg Simmel. Tr. by Helmut Loiskandl et al. 248p. 1991. pap. text ed. 15.95 (*0-252-06228-0*) U of Ill Pr.

Schopenhauer & the Ground of Existence. Bernard Bykhovsky. Tr. by Philip Moran from RUS. (Philosophical Currents Ser.: Vol. 30). vi, 194p. 1984. pap. 24.00 (*90-6032-208-8*, Pub. by Gruner NE) Benjamins North Am.

Schopenhauer & the Wild Years of Philosophy. Rudiger Safranski. 408p. (C). 1991. pap. text ed. 14.95 (*0-674-79276-9*) HUP.

Schopenhauer on the Character of the World: The Metaphysics of Will. John E. Atwell. LC 94-18811. 1995. 35.00 (*0-520-08770-4*) U CA Pr.

Schopenhauer, Philosophy & the Arts. Ed. by Dale Jacquette. (Studies in Philosophy & the Arts). 323p. (C). 1996. text ed. 54.95 (*0-521-47388-8*) Cambridge U Pr.

Schopenhauerian Critique of Nietzsche's Thought: Toward a Restoration of Metaphysics. Harry J. Ausmus. LC 95-19349. (Studies in the History of Philosophy: Vol. 38). 440p. 1996. text ed. 109.95 (*0-7734-8891-X*) E Mellen.

***Schopenhauer's Early Four-Fold Root: Translation & Commentary.** F. C. White. (Avebury Series in Philosophy). 108p. 1997. text ed. 55.95 (*1-85972-656-9*, Pub. by Avebury Pub UK) Ashgate Pub Co.

***Schopenhauer's System in Its Philosophical Significance: 1896 Edition.** William Caldwell. 560p. 1996. reprint ed. write for info. (*1-85506-185-6*) Bks Intl VA.

***Schopfung Als Evolution: Die Bedeutung des Komplementaritatsprinzips und der Synchronizitatsphanomene Fur ein Neuverstandnis der Evolution.** Ingeborg Hus. (Europaische Hochschulschriften Ser.: Reihe 20, Bd. 508). (Illus.). 168p. (GER.). 1996. 35.95 (*3-631-30566-4*) P Lang Pubng.

Schott at Sunrise. Carol Schott. (Orig.). 1987. pap. 5.00 (*0-944754-00-7*) Pudding Hse Pubns.

Schott Guide to Glass. 2nd ed. H. Pfaender. 224p. (gr. 13). 1995. text ed. 46.95 (*0-412-62060-X*) Chapman & Hall.

Schpountz. Marcel Pagnol. pap. 9.95 (*0-685-37008-9*) Fr & Eur.

Schprountz. Marcel Pagnol. (Illus.). 288p. (FRE.). 1976. 10.95 (*0-7859-0119-1*, M3842) Fr & Eur.

Schrader Automobil - Worterbuch. Heiko Schrader. 200p. (ENG & GER.). 1991. lib. bdg. 75.00 (*0-8288-3593-4*, F41074) Fr & Eur.

Schrader on Schrader. Paul Schrader. Ed. by Kevin Jackson. (Illus.). 192p. 1992. pap. 10.95 (*0-571-16370-X*) Faber & Faber.

Schreber: Father & Son. Han Israels. LC 88-35654. 400p. 1989. 57.50 (*0-8236-6011-7*, BN#06011) Intl Univs Pr.

Schreber Case: Psychoanalytic Profile of a Paranoid Personality. William G. Niederland. (Illus.). 196p. 1984. reprint ed. pap. text ed. 29.95 (*0-88163-025-X*) Analytic Pr.

***Schreib- und Leseubungen fur Sprachgestorte: Ein Ubungsbuch fur Patienten und Angehorige.** Berthold Simons. (GER.). 1996. 34.95 (*3-631-30116-2*) P Lang Pubng.

***Schreiben im Heutigen Deutschland: Die Literarische Szene nach der Wende.** Ed. by Ursula Beitter. (Loyola College in Maryland Berlin Seminar). 224p. (GER.). (C). 1997. text ed. 46.95 (*0-8204-3319-5*) P Lang Pubng.

Schreiben macht Spass: Heft 2. Gerhard Neuner. 40p. (GER.). (J). 1992. pap. text ed. 29.00 (*3-12-675431-7*, Pub. by Klett Edition GW) Intl Bk Import.

Schreiben macht Spass: Heft 3. Gerhard Neuner. 40p. (GER.). (J). 1993. pap. text ed. 29.00 (*3-12-675432-5*, Pub. by Klett Edition GW) Intl Bk Import.

Schreiben macht Spass. Kopiervorlagen: Heft 1. Gerhard Neuner. 44p. (GER.). (J). 1991. pap. text ed. 29.00 (*3-12-675430-9*, Pub. by Klett Edition GW) Intl Bk Import.

***Schreibkompetenz: Schreiben Als Intelligentes Handeln.** Karin Steffen. (Germanistische Texte und Studien: Vol. 52). viii, 224p. (GER.). 1995. write for info. (*3-487-10031-2*) G Olms Pubs.

Schreibung und Aussprache Im Aelteren Fruehneuhochdeutschen: Zum Verhaeltnis von Graphem - Phonem - Phon Am Bairisch-Oesterreichischen Beispiel von Andreas Kurzmann Um 1400. Peter Wiesinger. (Studia Linguistica Germanica). x, 265p. (GER.). (C). 1996. lib. bdg. 131.85 (*3-11-013727-5*) De Gruyter.

Schreiner Festschrift, George E. Journal: Mineral & Electrolyte Metabolism, Vol. 13, No. 6, 1987. Ed. by J. M. Letteri. (Illus.). vi, 118p. 1987. pap. 64.00 (*3-8055-4651-3*) S Karger.

Schrier's Publishing Cookbook Series: A Collection of Favorite Recipes, 2 vols., Set. rev. ed. Martha S. Schrier. 1992. write for info. (*0-9628403-2-7*) M S Schrier.

***Schrifsteller aus der DDR: Ausburgerungen und Ubersiedlungen von 1961 bis 1989 Autorenlexikon.** Andrea Jager. (GER.). 1995. 85.95 (*3-631-48646-4*) P Lang Pubng.

***Schrifsteller aus der DDR: Ausburgerungen und Ubersiedlungen von 1961 bis 1989 Studie.** Andrea Jager. (GER.). 1995. 37.95 (*3-631-48643-X*) P Lang Pubng.

Schrift ist Unveraenderlich: Essays zu Kafka. Malcolm Pasley. 224p. (GER.). 1995. pap. 18.00 (*3-596-12251-1*, Pub. by Fischer Taschbch Verlag GW) Intl Bk Import.

***Schrift und Schriftlichkeit - Writing & Its Use: Ein Interdisziplinaeres Handbuch Internationaler Forschung - An Interdisciplinary Handbook of International Research, 2 vols., Set.** Ed. by Hartmut Guenther & Otto Ludwig. (Handbooks of Linguistics & Communication Science: Vol. 10.2). xiv, 851p. (ENG & GER.). (C). 1996. lib. bdg. 570.40 (*3-11-014744-0*, 102/96) De Gruyter.

Schrift und Schriftlichkeit - Writing & Its Use: Ein Interdisziplinaeres Handbuch Internationaler Forschung - An Interdisciplinary Handbook of International Research. Ed. by Hartmut Gunther & Otto Ludwig. (Handbooks of Linguistics & Communication Science: Bd. 10.1). 950p. (GER.). (C). 1994. lib. bdg. 653.85 (*3-11-011129-2*) De Gruyter.

Schriftbilder. Catherine C. Baumann et al. Ed. by Helga M. Thorson et al. (Illus.). 147p. (Orig.). (GER.). (C). 1988. pap. text ed. 10.00 (*0-317-93404-X*) IP Inc MN.

Schriften: Collected Writings of Arno Breker. Volker G. Probst. (Illus.). 192p. 1983. text ed. 20.00 (*0-914301-28-4*, Pub. by Marco GW) West-Art.

Schriften: Institutio Elementaris; Capita Philosophica, Dialectica: Als Anhang: Die Philosophischen Stuecke Aus Cod. Oxon. Johannes Von Damaskos. Ed. by Bonifatius Kotter. (Patristische Texte und Studien: No. 7). (C). 1969. 110.00 (*3-11-002661-9*) De Gruyter.

Schriften der Romischen Feldmesser. Ed. by Karl Lachmann et al. xx, 952p. 1967. reprint ed. 225.00 (*0-318-71222-9*) G Olms Pubs.

Schriften des Johannes von Damaskos, Vol. 3: Contra imaginum columniatores orationes tres. Ed. by P. Bonifatius Kotter. (Patristische Texte und Studien: Vol. 17). xvi, 224p. (GER & LAT.). (C). 1975. 126.95 (*3-11-005971-1*) De Gruyter.

Schriften von 1517 bis 1520 see Luthers Werke in Auswahl

Schriften von 1520 bis 1524 see Luthers Werke in Auswahl

Schriften von 1524 bis 1528 see Luthers Werke in Auswahl

Schriften von 1529 bis 1545 see Luthers Werke in Auswahl

Schriften zur griechischen und Roemischen Verfassungsgeschichte und Verfassungstheorie. Kurt Von Fritz. 1976. 176.95 (*3-11-006567-3*) De Gruyter.

Schriften 1828 Bis 1854, 28 Vols. Ludwig Tieck. (C). reprint ed. 1,157.70 (*3-11-005009-9*) De Gruyter.

Schriftgelehrte Prophetie in Jes 56-66: Eine Untersuchung zu den Literarischen Bezuegen in den Letzten Elf Kapiteln des Jesajabuches. Wolfgang Lau. (Beihefte zur Zeitschrift fuer die Alttestamentliche Wissenschaft Ser.: Vol. 225). ix, 357p. (GER.). (C). 1994. lib. bdg. 132.35 (*3-11-014239-2*) De Gruyter.

Schrifttafeln zur Erlernung der Lateinischen Palaeographie. Wilhelm Arndt & Michael Tangl. 64p. 1976. reprint ed. 145.00 (*3-487-05940-1*) G Olms Pubs.

***Schrifttanz.** Alfred Schlee. 273p. (GER.). 1991. reprint ed. write for info. (*3-487-09537-8*) G Olms Pubs.

Schrifttanz: German Modern Dance Writings of the 1920s & 1930s. Ed. by Valerie Preston-Dunlop. (Illus.). 136p. 1990. pap. text ed. 24.95 (*1-85273-016-1*, Dance Horizons) Princeton Bk Co.

***Schrifttum Uber das Deutschtum in Russland.** Karl Stumpp. 1980. pap. 8.50 (*0-614-23873-0*) Am Hist Soc Ger.

Schriftwort in der Rabbinischen Literatur. rev. ed. Victor Aptowitzer. (Library of Biblical Studies). 1970. 50.00 (*0-87068-005-6*) Ktav.

Schritte auf dem Mond. Herge. (Illus.). 62p. (GER.). (J). pap. 19.95 (*0-8288-5063-1*) Fr & Eur.

Schritte-Steps-Pas-Pasos. Seibert & Stollenwerk. 96p. 1986. 19.95 (*3-468-49884-5*) Langenscheidt.

Schrodinger: Centenary Celebration of a Polymath. Ed. by C. W. Kilmister. 300p. 1989. pap. text ed. 38.95 (*0-521-37929-6*) Cambridge U Pr.

Schrodinger: Life & Thought. Walter Moore. (Illus.). 528p. (C). 1989. text ed. 64.95 (*0-521-35434-X*) Cambridge U Pr.

Schrodinger: Life & Thought. Walter Moore. (Illus.). 513p. (C). 1992. pap. text ed. 24.95 (*0-521-43767-9*) Cambridge U Pr.

Schrodinger Centenary: Surveys in Physics. Ed. by S. Lal & V. Singh. 312p. 1988. text ed. 84.00 (*9971-5-0694-7*) World Scientific Pub.

Schrodinger Diffusion Processes. Ed. by J. Gani et al. 200p. 1996. 79.50 (*3-7643-5386-4*) Spr-Verlag.

Schrodinger Diffusion Processes: Probability & Its Applications. Robert Aebi. 186p. 1996. 79.50 (*0-8176-5386-4*) Birkhauser.

Schrodinger Equation. F. A. Berezin & M. A. Shubin. (C). 1991. lib. bdg. 319.00 (*0-7923-1218-X*) Kluwer Ac.

Schrodinger Equations & Diffusion Theory. Masao Nagasawa. LC 93-1170. xii, 319p. 1993. 115.00 (*0-8176-2875-4*) Birkhauser.

Schrodinger Operators. Ed. by H. Holden & A. A. Jensen. (Lecture Notes in Physics Ser.: Vol. 345). v, 458p. 1989. 63.95 (*0-387-51783-9*) Spr-Verlag.

Schrodinger Operators: The Quantum Mechanical Many-Body Problem: Proceedings of a Workshop Held at Aarhus, Denmark, 15 May-1 August 1991. Ed. by Erik Balslev et al. LC 92-14018. (Lecture Notes in Physics Ser.: Vol. 403). viii, 264p. 1992. 66.95 (*0-387-55490-4*) Spr-Verlag.

Schrodinger Operators: With Application to Wuantum Mechanics & Global Geometry. Ed. by H. L. Cycon et al. (Texts & Monographs in Physics). (Illus.). ix, 319p. 1987. 49.95 (*0-387-16758-7*) Spr-Verlag.

Schrodinger Operators, Aarhus 1985. Ed. by E. Balslev. (Lecture Notes in Mathematics Ser.: Vol. 1218). v, 222p. 1986. pap. 25.30 (*0-387-16826-5*) Spr-Verlag.

Schrodinger Operators, Como 1984. Ed. by S. Graffi. (Lecture Notes in Mathematics Ser.: Vol. 1159). 272p. 1985. 42.95 (*0-387-16035-3*) Spr-Verlag.

Schrodinger Operators, Standard & Non-Standard. Ed. by P. Exner & P. Seba. 424p. (C). 1989. text ed. 125.00 (*9971-5-0840-0*) World Scientific Pub.

Schrodinger's Cat Trilogy. Robert A. Wilson. 560p. (J). 1988. pap. 14.95 (*0-440-50070-2*, Dell Trade Pbks) Dell.

Schrodinger's Kittens & the Search for Reality: Solving the Quantum Mysteries. John Gribbin. (Illus.). 261p. 1995. 23.95 (*0-316-32838-3*) Little.

Schrodinger's Kittens & the Search for Reality: Solving the Quantum Mysteries. John Gribbin. 1996. pap. 12.95 (*0-316-32819-7*) Little.

Schrodinger's Mechanics. Ed. by D. B. Cook. (Lecture Notes in Physics Ser.: Vol. 28). 164p. (C). 1989. text ed. 40.00 (*9971-5-0760-9*) World Scientific Pub.

***Schrodinger's Philosophy of Quantum Mechanics.** Michel Bitbol. (Boston Studies in the Philosophy of Science: Vol. 188). 300p. (C). 1996. lib. bdg. 117.00 (*0-7923-4266-6*) Kluwer Ac.

Schroeder's Antiques Price Guide. 15th rev. ed. Bob Huxford. (Illus.). 608p. 1996. pap. 12.95 (*0-89145-734-8*, 4727) Collector Bks.

***Schroeder's Antiques Price Guide.** 16th ed. Schroeder. 608p. 1997. pap. 12.95 (*1-57432-025-4*, 4949) Collector Bks.

Schroeder's Collectible Toys: Antiques to Modern Price Guide. 3rd rev. ed. Bob Huxford. (Illus.). 512p. 1996. pap. 17.95 (*0-89145-735-6*) Collector Bks.

***Schroeder's Collectible Toys - Antique to Modern.** 4th rev. ed. Bob Huxford & Sharon Huxford. (Illus.). 512p. 1997. pap. 17.95 (*1-57432-026-2*, 4953) Collector Bks.

Schroeder's Favorite Classics, Vol. 1. Ed. by John Welch. (Peanuts Piano Course Ser.). (Illus.). 38p. (Orig.). (J). (gr. 1-6). 1989. pap. 5.50 (*1-56516-047-9*) H Leonard.

Schroeder's Favorite Classics, Vol. 2. Ed. by John Welch. (Peanuts Piano Course Ser.). (Illus.). 38p. (Orig.). (J). (gr. 1-6). 1989. pap. 5.50 (*1-56516-048-7*) H Leonard.

Schroeder's Favorite Classics, Vol. 1: Clavinova Software. Ed. by John Welch. (Peanuts Piano Course for Clavinova Ser.). (Illus.). 38p. (Orig.). (J). (gr. 1-6). 1992. pap. 34.95 (*1-56516-021-5*) H Leonard.

Schroeder's First Recital. Ed. by John Welch. (Peanuts Piano Course Ser.). (Illus.). 38p. (Orig.). (J). (gr. 1-6). 1989. pap. 5.50 (*1-56516-050-9*) H Leonard.

Schroeder's First Recital Encores. Ed. by John Welch. (Peanuts Piano Course Ser.). (Illus.). 38p. (Orig.). (J). (gr. 1-6). 1989. pap. 5.50 (*1-56516-051-7*) H Leonard.

Schroedinger Equation: Proceedings of the International Symposium, Vienna, June 10-12, 1976. International Symposium "Fifty Years Schroedinger Equation" Staff. Ed. by W. Thirring & P. Urban. (Acta Physica Austriaca Ser.: Suppl. 17). (Illus.). 1977. 52.95 (*0-387-81437-X*) Spr-Verlag.

Schubert. (Masterpieces of Piano Music Ser.). (Illus.). 192p. 1986. pap. 14.95 (*0-8256-1087-7*, AM65103) Music Sales.

Schubert. Peter Hartling. Tr. by Rosemary Smith from GER. 260p. 1995. 25.00 (*0-8419-1347-1*) Holmes & Meier.

Schubert. Ann Rachlin. (Famous Children Ser.). (Illus.). 24p. (J). (gr. k-3). 1994. pap. 5.95 (*0-8120-1995-4*) Barron.

***Schubert.** Reed. (Master Musician Ser.). 1997. 35.00 (*0-02-864814-5*) S&S Trade.

***Schubert.** Reed. (Master Musicians Ser.). 1997. 35.00 (*0-02-864867-6*) S&S Trade.

***Schubert.** Mark Rowlinson. 1998. 47.50 (*0-375-40073-7*, Everymans Lib) Knopf.

Schubert. Tutti Staff. (TuTTi Ser.: No. 8). 176p. pap. 16.95 incl. disk (*1-57301-022-7*) TuTTi USA.

Schubert. Peggy Woodford. (Illustrated Lives of the Great Composers Ser.). (Illus.). 160p. 1996. 14.95 (*0-7119-0255-0*, OP 42415) Omnibus NY.

Schubert. 2nd ed. LC 96-34211. (Dent Master Musicians Ser.). (Illus.). (C). 1996. pap. write for info. (*0-19-816494-7*) OUP.

Schubert: "Die Schone Mullerin" Susan Youens. (Cambridge Music Handbooks Ser.). (Illus.). 120p. (C). 1992. pap. text ed. 11.95 (*0-521-42279-5*) Cambridge U Pr.

Schubert: A Critical Biography. Maurice J. Brown. (Quality Paperbacks Ser.). (Illus.). 414p. 1988. reprint ed. pap. 14.95 (*0-306-80329-1*) Da Capo.

Schubert: A Documentary Biography. Otto E. Deutsch. Tr. by Eric Blom. LC 77-5499. (Music Reprint Ser.). (Illus.). 1977. reprint ed. lib. bdg. 125.00 (*0-306-77420-8*) Da Capo.

Schubert: Critical & Analytical Studies. Ed. by Walter Frisch. LC 85-8445. xiv, 256p. 1996. pap. text ed. 12.00 (*0-8032-6892-0*, Bison Books) U of Nebr Pr.

Schubert: Second Quartet in D Minor & Octet. Alexander Brent-Smith. 55p. 1990. reprint ed. lib. bdg. 59.00 (*0-7812-9166-6*) Rprt Serv.

Schubert: The Complete Song Texts. Tr. by Richard Wigmore. 380p. 1988. 40.00 (*0-02-872911-0*) Schirmer Bks.

***Schubert: The Music & the Man.** Brian Newbould. LC 96-49876. (Illus.). 1997. 39.95 (*0-520-21065-4*) U CA Pr.

Schubert: 100 Sings - High. pap. 27.95 (*0-7935-4642-7*, 00740027) H Leonard.

Schubert: 100 Songs - Low. pap. 27.95 (*0-7935-4643-5*, 00740028) H Leonard.

Schubert - Solo Piano Literature: A Comprehensive Guide: Annotated & Evaluated with Thematics. Ed. by Carolyn Maxwell. (Maxwell Music Evaluation Bks.). (Illus.). (Orig.). 1986. pap. 12.95 (*0-912531-03-7*) Maxwell Mus Eval.

***Schubert & His World: A Biographical Dictionary.** Peter Clive. (Illus.). 344p. 1997. 45.00 (*0-19-816582-X*) OUP.

***Schubert Chamber Music.** Jack A. Westrup. 64p. 1996. 5.95 (*0-563-20516-4*, BB 11149, Pub. by BBC UK) Parkwest Pubns.

Schubert Club Museum. Ed. by Bruce Carlson. (Illus.). 64p. (Orig.). 1990. pap. 10.00 (*0-912373-05-9*) Schubert.

***Schubert, Muller, & Die Schone Mullerin.** Susan Youens. (Illus.). 225p. (C). 1997. text ed. 59.95 (*0-521-56364-X*) Cambridge U Pr.

Schubert Reader: Music Book Index. Otto E. Deutsch. 1039p. 1993. reprint ed. lib. bdg. 119.00 (*0-7812-9618-8*) Rprt Serv.

***Schubert Song Companion.** Reed. Date not set. pap. 23.95 (*1-901341-00-3*) St Martin.

Schubert Studies: Problems of Style & Chronology. Ed. by Eva Badura-Skoda & Peter Branscombe. LC 81-38528. (Illus.). 350p. 1982. 75.00 (*0-521-22606-6*) Cambridge U Pr.

Schubert Symphony in B Minor (Unfinished) Franz Schubert. Ed. by Martin Chusid. (Critical Scores Ser.). (C). 1971. pap. text ed. 7.95 (*0-393-09731-5*) Norton.

Schubert, the Man. Oscar Bie. LC 77-107794. (Select Bibliographies Reprint Ser.). 1977. 26.95 (*0-8369-5177-8*) Ayer.

Schubert, the Man. Oskar Bie. 215p. 1990. reprint ed. lib. bdg. 69.00 (*0-7812-9086-4*) Rprt Serv.

Schubert Thematic Catalogue. unabridged ed. Otto E. Deutsch. LC 95-14500. Orig. Title: Schubert, Thematic Catalogue of All His Works in Chronological Order. 592p. 1995. reprint ed. pap. text ed. 16.95 (*0-486-28685-1*) Dover.

Schubert, Thematic Catalogue of All His Works in Chronological Order see Schubert Thematic Catalogue

Schubert Very Best for Piano. Ed. by John L. Haag. (Illus.). 144p. (Orig.). 1996. pap. 14.95 (*1-56922-105-7*, 07-2042) Creat Cncpts.

***Schubert's Complete Song Texts, Vol. 1.** Beaumont Glass. (C). 1996. text ed. 60.00 (*1-878617-19-2*) Leyerle Pubns.

***Schubert's Complete Song Texts, Vol. 2.** Beaumont Glass. (C). 1997. text ed. 60.00 (*1-878617-20-6*) Leyerle Pubns.

Schubert's Dramatic Lieder. Marjorie W. Hirsch. LC 92-31440. 192p. (C). 1993. text ed. 59.95 (*0-521-41820-8*) Cambridge U Pr.

Schubert's Music for Piano Four-Hands. Dallas A. Weekley & Nancy Arganbright. (Illus.). 148p. 1990. pap. 23.50 (*0-912483-55-5*) Pro-Am Music.

Schubert's Poets & the Making of Lieder. Susan Youens. (Illus.). 350p. (C). 1996. text ed. 64.95 (0-521-55257-5) Cambridge U Pr.

Schubert's Songs to Texts by Goethe. Franz Schubert. Tr. by Stanley Appelbaum from GER. LC 78-58220. 1979. reprint ed. pap. 11.95 (0-486-23752-4) Dover.

***Schubert's Vienna.** Raymond Erickson. LC 97-10707. 1997. write for info. (0-300-07080-2) Yale U Pr.

Schuelerduden Die Literatur. Duden. 480p. (GER.). 1980. 39.95 (0-8288-1566-6, M15163) Fr & Eur.

Schuelerduden-Die Psychologie: Scholar's Psychology Duden. Karl-Heinz Ahlheim. 408p. (GER.). 1981. 35.00 (0-8288-2205-0, M15377) Fr & Eur.

Schuelerduden-Geeschichte: Scholar's Duden Dictionary of History. Duden. 603p. (GER.). 1983. 39.95 (0-8288-1491-0, M15148) Fr & Eur.

Schuelerduden-Politik und Gesellschaft. Duden. 468p. (GER.). 1985. 35.00 (0-8288-2253-0, M15260) Fr & Eur.

Schuetzen Rifles - History & Loadings. Gerald O. Kelver. 1995. pap. 12.50 (1-877704-20-2) Pioneer Pr.

Schuldrecht. Wolfgang Fikentscher. xxvi, 858p. 1985. 90.80 (3-11-010527-6); pap. 60.00 (3-11-007158-4) De Gruyter.

Schule & Absolutismus in Preussen: Akten zum Preussischen Elementarschulwesen Bis 1806. Ed. by Wolfgang Neugebauer. (Veroeffentlichungen der Historischen Kommission zu Berlin, Band 67, Beitraege zu Inflation und Wiederaufbau in Deutschland und Europa 1914-1924: Vol. 33). vii, 814p. (C). 1992. lib. bdg. 195.40 (3-11-012304-5) De Gruyter.

Schuler-Bobenmyer Clan Book, 1758-1917. 2nd ed. A. B. Schuyler. (Illus.). 166p. 1992. reprint ed. pap. 24.00 (0-8328-2595-6); reprint ed. lib. bdg. 34.00 (0-8328-2594-8) Higginson Bk Co.

Schulkinder unter Stress: Theoretische Ueberlegungen zum Stressmodell. Hans R. Mueller. Ed. by G. Ritzel. (Sozialmedizinische und Paedagogische Jugendkunde Ser.: Band 12). 140p. 1976. 19.25 (3-8055-2299-1) S Karger.

Schulschwierigkeiten bei Kindern. A. Hundsalz & B. Fachinger. (Psychologische Praxis Ser.: Vol. 53). (Illus.). 1980. pap. 29.00 (3-8055-0148-X) S Karger.

***Schulthess, Friedrich - Enno Littmann: Grammatik des Christlich - Palastinischen Aramaisch.** Ed. by Enno Littmann. xvi, 159p. (GER.). 1983. reprint ed. 48.00 (3-487-01136-0) G Olms Pubs.

Schultz Cousins in Florida: Including John's Diary & Isaac's Search. Anno. by Andrew S. Schultz, Jr. (Illus.). 109p. (Orig.). 1989. pap. 10.00 (0-935980-07-5) Schwenkfelder Lib.

Schultz Site at Green Point: A Stratified Occupation Area in the Saginaw Valley of Michigan. Ed. by James E. Fitting. (Memoirs Ser.: No. 4). (Illus.). 1972. pap. 2.00 (0-932206-66-2) U Mich Mus Anthro.

Schulwerk, Vol. 3. Carl Orff. Tr. by Margaret Murray from GER. (Carl Orff Documentation Ser.). 1978. pap. 25.00 (0-930448-06-5, STAP065) Eur-Am Music.

Schumacher: The Life of the New Formula 1 Champion. Timothy Collings. (Illus.). 200p. 1996. pap. 15.95 (0-7603-0257-X) Motorbooks Intl.

Schuman Plan & the British Abdication of Leadership in Europe. Edmund Dell. 320p. 1995. 59.00 (0-19-828967-7) OUP.

Schumann. (Masterpieces of Piano Music Ser.). (Illus.). 192p. 1986. pap. 14.95 (0-8256-1086-9, AM65111) Music Sales.

Schumann. (Dent Master Musicians Ser.). (Illus.). (C). pap. write for info. (0-19-816471-8) OUP.

Schumann. Tim Dowley. (Illustrated Lives of the Great Composers Ser.). (Illus.). 144p. 1996. 14.95 (0-7119-0261-5, OP 42472) Omnibus NY.

Schumann. Ann Rachlin. LC 92-26965. (Famous Children Ser.). (Illus.). 24p. (J). (gr. k-3). 1993. pap. 5.95 (0-8120-1544-4) Barron.

Schumann: "Fantasie, Op. 17" Nicholas Marston. (Cambridge Music Handbooks Ser.). (Illus.). 136p. (C). 1992. text ed. 34.95 (0-521-39284-5); pap. text ed. 11.95 (0-521-39892-4) Cambridge U Pr.

Schumann: A Symposium. Ed. by Gerald E. Abraham. LC 77-8051. 319p. 1977. reprint ed. text ed. 67.50 (0-8371-9050-9, SCSY, Greenwood Pr) Greenwood.

Schumann: The Inner Voices of a Musical Genius. Peter F. Ostwald. (Illus.). 390p. 1987. reprint ed. pap. text ed. 16.95 (1-55553-014-1) NE U Pr.

Schumann - Solo Piano Literature: A Comprehensive Guide: Annotated & Evaluated with Thematics. Ed. by Carolyn Maxwell & William DeVan. (Maxwell Music Evaluation Bks.). (Illus.). 339p. (Orig.). 1984. pap. 11.95 (0-912531-01-0) Maxwell Mus Eval.

Schumann, a Life of Suffering. Victor Basch. Tr. by Catherine A. Phillips. LC 76-107791. (Select Bibliographies Reprint Ser.). 1977. 24.95 (0-8369-5175-1) Ayer.

Schumann, a Life of Suffering. Victor Basch. (Music Book Index Ser.). 243p. 1992. reprint ed. lib. bdg. 79.00 (0-7812-9468-1) Rprt Serv.

Schumann & His World. Ed. by Larry Todd. LC 94-9686. 408p. 1994. pap. text ed. 22.50 (0-691-03698-5) Princeton U Pr.

Schumann-Heink: The Last of the Titans. Mary Lawton. Ed. by Andrew Farkas. LC 76-29945. (Opera Biographies Ser.). (Illus.). 1977. reprint ed. lib. bdg. 41.95 (0-405-09687-9) Ayer.

***Schumann on Music.** Robert A. Schumann. pap. 6.95 (0-486-25748-7) Dover.

***Schumann Orchestral Music.** Hans Gal. (BBC Music Guides Ser.). 64p. 1996. 2.95 (0-563-12423-7, BB 11129, BBC-Parkwest) Parkwest Pubns.

***Schumann Piano Music.** Joan Chissell. (BBC Music Guides Ser.). 72p. 1996. 5.95 (0-563-20495-8, BB 11130, Pub. by BBC UK) Parkwest Pubns.

***Schumann Songs.** Astra Desmond. (BBC Music Guides Ser.). 64p. 1996. 7.95 (0-563-20556-3, BB 11131, Pub. by BBC UK) Parkwest Pubns.

Schumanns & Johannes Brahms. Eugenie Schumann. LC 75-124256. (Select Bibliographies Reprint Ser.). 1977. 18.95 (0-8369-5444-0) Ayer.

Schumann's Piano Album: Selected Pieces & Rules for Young Musicans. Laura Francesca. 32p. (YA). 1996. pap. text ed. 5.95 (0-85692-178-5, Pub. by East-West NE) Omega Pubns NY.

Schumann's Pianoforte Works. John A. Fuller-Maitland. 1988. reprint ed. lib. bdg. 49.00 (0-7812-0759-2) Rprt Serv.

Schumann's Pianoforte Works. John A. Fuller-Maitland. 59p. 1990. reprint ed. lib. bdg. 59.00 (0-7812-9168-2) Rprt Serv.

Schumann's Pianoforte Works. John A. Fuller-Maitland. LC 76-181159. 59p. 1927. reprint ed. 49.00 (0-403-01561-8) Scholarly.

***Schumpeter & the Idea of Social Science.** Yuichi Shionoya. (Historical Perspectives on Modern Economics Ser.). 384p. 1997. text ed. 54.95 (0-521-43034-8) Cambridge U Pr.

Schumpeter & the Political Economy of Change. David L. McKee. LC 90-44404. 164p. 1991. text ed. 45.00 (0-275-93679-1, C3679, Praeger Pubs) Greenwood.

Schumpeter in the History of Ideas. Ed. by Yuichi Shionoya & Mark Perlman. 150p. 1994. text ed. 39.50 (0-472-10548-5) U of Mich Pr.

Schumpeter, Social Scientist. Ed. by Seymour E. Harris. LC 71-80387. (Essay Index Reprint Ser.). 1977. 26.95 (0-8369-1138-5) Ayer.

Schumpeterian Puzzles: Technological Competition & Economic Evolution. Maria Brouwer. 228p. 1991. text ed. 54.50 (0-472-10254-0) U of Mich Pr.

Schumpeter's Capitalism, Socialism & Democracy Revisited. Ed. by Arnold Heertje. LC 81-84245. 208p. 1981. text ed. 49.95 (0-275-90641-8, C0641, Praeger Pubs) Greenwood.

Schur Algebras & Representation Theory. Stuart Martin. (Studies in Advanced Mathematics: No. 40). 200p. (C). 1994. text ed. 47.95 (0-521-41591-8) Cambridge U Pr.

***Schur Functions, Operator Colligations, & Reproducing Kernel Pontryagin Spaces.** Daniel Alpay. LC 97-17908. (Operator Theory, Advances, & Applications Ser.). 1997. write for info. (0-8176-5763-0); write for info. (3-7643-5763-0) Birkhauser.

Schur Lectures (1992) Ed. by Ilya Piatetski-Shapiro & Stephen Gelbart. (Israel Mathematical Conference Proceedings Ser.: Vol. 8). 236p. 1995. pap. 52.00 (0-614-08385-0, IMCP/8) Am Math.

Schur Methods in Operator Theory & Signal Processing. Ed. by I. Gohberg. (Operator Theory Ser.: Vol. 18). 328p. 1986. 118.00 (0-8176-1776-0, Pub. by Birkhauser Vlg SZ) Birkhauser.

Schur Parameters, Factorization, & Dilation Problems. LC 96-15524. (Operator Theory, Advances, & Applications Ser.). 1996. write for info. (0-8176-5285-X) Birkhauser.

Schur Parameters, Factorization, & Dilation Problems. Tiberiu Constantinescu. LC 96-15524. (Operator Theory, Advances & Application Ser.: Vol. 82). 264p. 1996. 122.50 (3-7643-5285-X) Birkhauser.

Schureman: The Schuremans of New Jersey. Richard Wynkoop. 142p. 1992. reprint ed. pap. 24.00 (0-8328-2719-3); reprint ed. lib. bdg. 34.00 (0-8328-2718-5) Higginson Bk Co.

Schuss Von der Kanzel. unabridged ed. Meyer. (World Classic Literature Ser.). (GER.). pap. 7.95 (3-89507-032-7, Pub. by Bookking Intl FR) Distribks Inc.

Schuster Fleck's October Guide to Frangokastello. R. C. Kenedy. LC 81-69727. (Illus.). 101p. (Orig.). 1982. pap. 7.00 (0-940066-02-5) Dalmas & Ricour.

***Schutz des Geistigen Eigentums in den Schriften von Winfried Schulz: Festgabe Fur Theodor Schmitz Zur Vollendung des 80.** Winfried Schulz. Ed. by Elmar Guthoff & Karl-Heinz Selge. (Adnotationes in ius Canonicum Ser.: Bd. 2). (Illus.). 200p. (GER.). 1997. 44.95 (3-631-31137-0) P Lang Pubng.

Schutzenpanzerwagen: War Horse of the Panzer-Grenadiers. Horst Scheibert. Tr. by Edward Force from GER. (Illus.). 48p. 1992. pap. 8.95 (0-88740-402-2) Schiffer.

Schutzhund: Theory & Training Methods. Susan Barwig & Stewart Hilliard. (Illus.). 256p. 1991. pap. 24.95 (0-87605-731-8) Howell Bk.

Schutz's Theory of Relevance: A Phenomenological Critique. R. R. Cox. (Phaenomenologica Ser.: Vol. 77). 246p. 1978. lib. bdg. 135.00 (90-247-2041-9, Pub. by M Nijhoff NE) Kluwer Ac.

Schuykill County, PA. L. Ward. (Images of America Ser.). 1996. pap. 16.99 (0-7524-0231-5, Arcdia) Chalford.

Schuyler Colfax, the Changing Fortunes of a Political Idol. Willard H. Smith. 475p. 1952. 6.50 (1-885323-12-3) IN Hist Bureau.

***Schuylkill County Death Records, Vol. 2.** Stephen J. Dellock. LC 96-85586. 195p. (Orig.). 1996. pap. 19.95 (1-55856-236-2) Closson Pr.

Schuylkill County Death Records, 1893-1895. Stephen J. Dellock. 201p. 1995. pap. 19.95 (1-55856-183-8) Closson Pr.

Schuylkill County, PA Archives, Vol. I. Schuylkill Roots Staff. 560p. 1995. 39.95 (1-55856-182-X) Closson Pr.

Schuylkill County, PA Archives, Vol. 2. Compiled by Jean A. Dellock & Phillip A. Rice. 577p. (Orig.). 1996. pap. 39.95 (1-55856-219-2) Closson Pr.

Schuylkill County, PA Archives, Vol. 3. Compiled by Jean A. Dellock & Phillip A. Rice. 573p. (Orig.). 1996. pap. 39.95 (1-55856-220-6) Closson Pr.

Schuylkill Navigation: A Photographic History. Harry L. Rinker. LC 90-85567. (Illus.). 96p. 1991. pap. 16.00 (0-9613675-2-0) Canal Captains.

Schwa. Bill Barker. (Illus.). 38p. 1993. pap. 6.00 (0-9635914-1-X) Schwa Pr.

***Schwa: A Sightings Journal.** Schwa Coporation Staff. 1997. pap. text ed. 9.95 (0-8118-1713-X) Chronicle Bks.

***SCHWA: World Operations Manual.** SCHWA Corporation. LC 97-15990. 1997. pap. write for info. (0-8118-1585-4) Chronicle Bks.

Schwager's Car Nicobar Foraminifera in the Reports of the Novara Expedition. rev. ed. M. S. Srininvasan. (Illus.). 91p. 1980. 12.00 (0-88065-195-4, Messers Today & Tomorrow) Scholarly Pubns.

Schwan Artist. 17th ed. 1991. pap. 9.95 (1-57598-002-9) Schwann Pubns.

Schwann Artist. 18th ed. 1995. pap. 12.95 (1-57598-007-X) Schwann Pubns.

Schwann Artist. 19th ed. 1996. pap. 12.95 (1-57598-020-7) Schwann Pubns.

Schwann CD Review Digest - Classical, Vol. 8, No. 4. 1995. pap. 24.95 (1-57598-000-2) Schwann Pubns.

Schwann CD Review Digest - Classical, Vol. 9, No. 1. 1995. pap. 12.95 (1-57598-008-8) Schwann Pubns.

Schwann CD Review Digest - Classical, Vol. 9, No. 2. 1995. pap. 12.95 (1-57598-013-4) Schwann Pubns.

Schwann CD Review Digest - Classical, Vol. 9, No. 3. 1996. pap. 12.95 (1-57598-016-9) Schwann Pubns.

Schwann CD Review Digest - Classical, Vol. 9, No. 4. 1996. pap. 24.95 (1-57598-021-5) Schwann Pubns.

Schwann CD Review Digest - Classical, Vol. 10, No. 1. 1996. pap. 12.95 (1-57598-026-6) Schwann Pubns.

Schwann CD Review Digest - Classical, Vol. 10, No. 2. 1996. pap. 12.95 (1-57598-029-0) Schwann Pubns.

Schwann CD Review Digest - Rock, Pop, Jazz, Etc. 1996. pap. 12.95 (1-57598-030-4) Schwann Pubns.

Schwann CD Review Digest - Rock, Pop, Jazz, Etc., Vol. 8, No. 4. 1995. pap. 24.95 (1-57598-001-0) Schwann Pubns.

Schwann CD Review Digest - Rock, Pop, Jazz, Etc., Vol. 9, No. 1. 1995. pap. 12.95 (1-57598-009-6) Schwann Pubns.

Schwann CD Review Digest - Rock, Pop, Jazz, Etc., Vol. 9, No. 2. 1995. pap. 12.95 (1-57598-014-2) Schwann Pubns.

Schwann CD Review Digest - Rock, Pop, Jazz, Etc., Vol. 9, No. 3. 1996. pap. 12.95 (1-57598-017-7) Schwann Pubns.

Schwann CD Review Digest - Rock, Pop, Jazz, Etc, Vol. 9, No. 4. 1996. pap. 24.95 (1-57598-022-3) Schwann Pubns.

Schwann CD Review Digest - Rock, Pop, Jazz, Etc., Vol. 10, No. 1. 1996. pap. 12.95 (1-57598-027-4) Schwann Pubns.

Schwann CDRD Best-Rated CD's - Classical: 1995 Edition. 1995. pap. 17.95 (1-57598-010-X) Schwann Pubns.

Schwann CDRD Best-Rated CD's - Classical: 1996 Edition. 1996. pap. 17.95 (1-57598-023-1) Schwann Pubns.

Schwann CDRD Best-Rated CD's - Rock, Pop, Jazz, Etc. 1995 Edition. 1995. pap. 17.95 (1-57598-011-8) Schwann Pubns.

Schwann CDRD Best-Rated Cd's - Rock, Pop, Jazz, Etc. 1996 Edition. 1996. pap. 17.95 (1-57598-024-X) Schwann Pubns.

Schwann Opus: 1995 Edition. 848p. 1995. pap. 12.95 (1-57598-004-5) Schwann Pubns.

Schwann Opus: 1995-96 Edition, Vol. 7, No. 1. 1995. pap. 12.95 (1-57598-015-0) Schwann Pubns.

Schwann Opus: 1996 Edition, Vol. 7, No. 2. 1996. pap. 12.95 (1-57598-019-3) Schwann Pubns.

Schwann Opus Vol. 6, No. 4: 1995 Edition. 1995. pap. 12.95 (1-57598-006-1) Schwann Pubns.

Schwann Opus Vol. 7, No. 3: 1996 Edition. 1996. pap. 12.95 (1-57598-028-2) Schwann Pubns.

***Schwann Opus 4, Vol. 7.** Schwann Publications Staff. 1996. pap. 12.95 (1-57598-037-1) Schwann Pubns.

Schwann Spectrum: 1995 Edition. 570p. 1995. pap. 9.95 (1-57598-003-7) Schwann Pubns.

Schwann Spectrum: 1996 Edition, Vol. 7, No. 2. 1996. pap. 9.95 (1-57598-018-5) Schwann Pubns.

Schwann Spectrum Vol. 6, No. 4: 1995 Edition. 1995. pap. 9.95 (1-57598-005-3) Schwann Pubns.

Schwann Spectrum Vol. 7, No. 1: 1995-96 Edition. 1995. pap. 9.95 (1-57598-012-6) Schwann Pubns.

Schwann Spectrum Vol. 7, No. 3: 1996 Edition. 1996. pap. 9.95 (1-57598-025-8) Schwann Pubns.

***Schwann Spectrum, 1996-1997, Vol. 8.** Schwann Publications Staff. 1996. pap. text ed. 9.95 (1-57598-038-X) Schwann Pubns.

***Schwann Spectrum 4: Life Beyond the Dead, Vol. 7.** Schwann Publications Staff. 1996. pap. text ed. 9.95 (1-57598-036-3) Schwann Pubns.

***Schwanritter - Das Turner von Nantes.** Edward Schroeder & Ludwig Wolff. (Konrad von Wurzburg Ser.: Teil 2). xii, 83p. (GER.). 1974. write for info. (0-614-27204-1, Pub. by Weidmann GW) Lubrecht & Cramer.

Schwartz Family of El Paso: The Story of a Pioneer Jewish Family in the Southwest. Floyd S. Fierman. (Southwestern Studies: No. 61). 1980. pap. 5.00 (0-87404-120-1) Tex Western.

Schwarz Function & Its Applications. P. J. Davis. (Carus Mathematical Monograph: No. 17). 241p. 1974. 10.00 (0-88385-017-6, CAM-17) Math Assn.

Schwarz Function & Its Generalization to Higher Dimensions. Harold S. Shapiro. LC 91-41118. (University of Arkansas Lecture Notes in the Mathematical Sciences Ser.: No. 1655). 128p. 1992. text ed. 99.95 (0-471-57127-X) Wiley.

Schwarz Lemma. Sean Dineen. (Oxford Mathematical Monographs). (Illus.). 264p. 1989. 55.00 (0-19-853571-6) OUP.

Schwarz Rot Gold: German Handbook. Paul Webster. 224p. 1986. pap. text ed. 17.95 (0-521-27883-X) Cambridge U Pr.

Schwarz Rot Gold: German Handbook. Paul Webster. 128p. 1987. pap. text ed. 13.95 (0-521-27882-1) Cambridge U Pr.

Schwarz Rot Gold: German Handbook, Set. Paul Webster. 1987. pap. 69.95 (0-521-26248-8) Cambridge U Pr.

Schwarz Rot Gold: The Course Book. Paul Webster. 272p. (C). 1990. pap. text ed. 37.95 (0-521-27884-8) Cambridge U Pr.

Schwarze Insel. Herge. (Illus.). 62p. (GER.). (J). pap. 19.95 (0-8288-5064-X) Fr & Eur.

Schwarze Intelligenz: Ein Literarisch-Politischer Streifzug durch Sudafrika. Peter Sulzer. (B. E. Ser.: No. 61). (GER.). 1955. 30.00 (0-8115-3012-4) Periodicals Srv.

Schwarzkopf in His Own Words. Richard Pyle. 1991. pap. 4.50 (0-451-17205-1, Sig) NAL-Dutton.

***Schwarzwald Church Register, Exeter Township, Berks Co., PA, Pts. 1 & 2.** Compiled by Schuylkill Roots Staff. LC 96-85602. 445p. (Orig.). 1997. pap. 39.95 (1-55856-240-0) Closson Pr.

Schwatka: The Life of Frederick Schwatka 1849-1892. R. E. Johnson et al. LC 84-81684. (Illus.). (Orig.). 1984. pap. text ed. 3.50 (0-9614070-9-3) Horn Moon Ent.

***Schwatka's Last Search: New-York Ledger Expedition Through Unknown Alaska & British America: Including the Journal of Charles Willard Hayes, 1891.** Frederick Schwatka et al. LC 96-38514. 1996. pap. 20.00 (0-912006-87-0) U of Alaska Pr.

Schwatka's Search: Sledging in the Arctic in Quest of the Franklin Records. William H. Gilder. LC 74-5839. reprint ed. 47.50 (0-404-11644-2) AMS Pr.

Schwedisch Ohne Muhe (One) Swedish for German Speakers (1) Assimil Staff. (GER & SWE.). 28.95 (0-8288-4456-9, F55570); audio 125.00 (0-685-53052-3) Fr & Eur.

Schwedisch Ohne Muhe (Two) Intermediate Swedish for German Speakers (2) Assimil Staff. (GER & SWE.). 28.95 (0-8288-4457-7, F55580); audio 125.00 (0-685-53053-1) Fr & Eur.

Schwedische Sprachgeschichte, 3 vols. Elias Wessen. Incl. Vol. 1. Lautlehre und Flexionslehre. x, 314p. 1970. 111.00 (3-11-006361-1); Vol. 2. Wortbildungslehre. x, 186p. 1970. 74.10 (3-11-006362-X); Vol. 3. Grundriss einer historischen Syntax. x, 378p. 1970. 137.00 (3-11-006363-8); (Grundriss der Germanischen Philologie Ser.: Vol. 18, Nos. 1-3). (GER.). (C). 1970. write for info. (0-318-51647-0) De Gruyter.

Schweigenden Gotter. Klaus Schneider. 115p. (GER.). 1966. write for info. (0-318-70614-8) G Olms Pubs.

Schweinekrankheiten. Ed. by H. D. Dannenberg. (Illus.). 400p. 1987. 40.00 (3-8055-4547-9) S Karger.

Schweitzer: Shadow of a Star. Gene Schulze. LC 92-73296. 252p. 1992. 21.95 (0-9634202-0-8) Houston Hse.

Schweitzer Returns. Robert R. Leichtman. (From Heaven to Earth Ser.). (Illus.). 104p. (Orig.). 1980. pap. 3.50 (0-89804-063-9) Ariel GA.

Schweizer Woerterbuch der Deutschen Sprache. Ingrid Bigler. 400p. (GER.). 1987. 39.95 (0-7859-8674-X, 325202201x) Fr & Eur.

Schweizerische Gesellschaft fuer Dermatologie und Venerologie, Genf, September 30-October 1, 1977: 59 Jahresversammlung - Journal: Dermatologica, Vol. 157, No. 5. Ed. by R. Schuppli. (Illus.). 1978. pap. 21.00 (3-8055-2964-3) S Karger.

Schweizerische Gesellschaft fuer Dermatologie und Venerologie 61. Jahresversammlung, Lausanne, Okber 1979. Ed. by R. Schuppli. (Journal: Dermatologica: Vol. 161, No. 6). (Illus.). xx, 68p. 1981. 9.00 (3-8055-2367-X) S Karger.

Schweizerische Gesellschaft fuer Gynaekologie, Bericht ueber die Jahresversammlung Davos 1976. (Journal: Gynaekologische Rundschau: Vol. 16, Suppl. 1). (Illus.). 1977. 22.50 (3-8055-2669-5) S Karger.

Schweizerische Gesellschaft fuer Gynaekologie, Bericht ueber die Jahresversammlung, Montreux, Juni 1979. Ed. by E. Dreher. (Journal: Gynaekologische Rundschau: Vol. 19, Suppl. 2). 1980. pap. 26.50 (3-8055-0456-X) S Karger.

Schweizerische Gesellschaft fuer Gynaekologie Bericht ueber die Jahresversammlung, St. Gallen. J 1980. Ed. by E. Dreher. (Journal: Gynaekologische Rundschau: Vol. 20, No. 1). (Illus.). iv, 144p. 1981. pap. 26.50 (3-8055-2126-X) S Karger.

Schweizerische Gesellschaft fuer Gynaekologie und Geburtshilfe: Societe Suisse de Gynecologie et Obstetrique , Bericht ueber die Jahresversammlung, St. Moritz, April 1984. Ed. by E. Dreher. (Journal: Gynaekologische Rundschau: Vol. 24, Suppl. 1). iv, 160p. 1985. pap. 38.50 (3-8055-3964-9) S Karger.

Schweizerische Gesellschaft fuer Gynaekologie und Geburtshilfe: Societe Suisse de Gynecologie et Obstetrique, Bericht ueber die Jahresversammlung Lugano, Juni 1, 1985. Ed. by E. Dreher. (Journal: Gynaekologische Rundschau: Vol. 25, Suppl. 2, 1985). (Illus.). ii, 92p. 1986. pap. 22.50 (3-8055-4242-9) S Karger.

Schweizerische Gesellschaft fuer Gynaekologie und Geburtshilfe, Bericht ueber die Jahresversammlung, Lausanne, Juni 1983. Ed. by E. Dreher. (Journal: Gynaekologische Rundschau: Vol. 23, Suppl. 4). (Illus.). iv, 116p. 1984. pap. 26.50 (3-8055-3815-4) S Karger.

An Asterisk (*) at the beginning of an entry indicates that the title is appearing in BIP for the first time.

Schweizerische Gesellschaft fuer Gynaekologie und Geburtshilfe unter Mitkirkung der Schweizerischen Gesellschaft fuer Medizinische Genetik. Bericht ueber die Jahresversammlung, Zuerich, 1982. Ed. by E. Dreher. (Journal: Gynaekologische Rundschau: Vol. 22, Suppl. 3). (Illus.). xiv, 104p. 1983. pap. 31.25 (*3-8055-3656-9*) S Karger.

Schweizerische Gesellschaft fuer Senologie, Kongress in Zuerich, November Nineteen Seventy-Nine. Ed. by W. E. Schreiner. (Journal: Gynaekologische Rundschau: Vol. 21, Suppl. 1). (Illus.). vi, 198p. 1981. pap. 48.00 (*3-8055-2837-X*) S Karger.

Schweizerisches Erythropoietin Symposium: Beatenberg-CH, Maerz 1988. Ed. by U. Binswanger & G. Kretschmer. (Journal: Nephron: Vol. 51, Suppl. 1, 1989). (Illus.). vi, 46p. 1988. pap. 15.25 (*3-8055-4941-5*) S Karger.

***Schwellenzeit: Beitraege zur Geschichte des Christentums in Spaetantike und Fruehmittelalter.** Knut Schaeferdiek. Ed. by Winrich A. Loehr & Hanns C. Brennecke. (Arbeiten zur Kirchengeschichte Ser.: Vol. 64). xiv, 546p. (GER.). (C). 1996. lib. bdg. 191.15 (*3-11-014968-0*, 119/96) De Gruyter.

Schwenk: Genealogy of the Schwenk Family. rev. ed. E. S. Schwenk & J. K. Schwenk. Ed. by R. B. Strassburger. (Illus.). 282p. 1991. reprint ed. pap. 44.00 (*0-8328-1874-7*); reprint ed. lib. bdg. 54.00 (*0-8328-1873-9*) Higginson Bk Co.

Schwenkfeld & Early Schwenkfeldianism: Papers Presented at the Colloquium on Schwenkfeld & the Schwenkfelders. Peter C. Erb. 428p. (Orig.). 1986. pap. 10.00 (*0-935980-05-9*) Schwenkfelder Lib.

Schwenkfelder, 2 vols. Ed. by S. K. Brecht. 1752p. 1991. reprint ed. pap. 215.00 (*0-8328-2079-2*); reprint ed. lib. bdg. 225.00 (*0-8328-2078-4*) Higginson Bk Co.

Schwenkfelder Hymnology. A. A. Seipt. LC 77-134414. reprint ed. 34.50 (*0-404-09908-4*) AMS Pr.

Schwenkfelders in America. Ed. by Peter C. Erb. (Illus.). 274p. (Orig.). 1987. pap. text ed. 15.00 (*0-935980-06-7*) Schwenkfelder Lib.

Schwenkfelders in Pennsylvania. Howard W. Kriebel. LC 73-134413. reprint ed. 32.50 (*0-404-07219-4*) AMS Pr.

Schwenkfelders in Pennsylvania. Howard W. Kriebel. 1993. reprint ed. lib. bdg. 89.00 (*0-7812-5478-7*) Rprt Serv.

Schwenkfelders in Pennsylvania: A Historical Sketch. Howard W. Kriebel. (Illus.). 246p. 1995. reprint ed. lib. bdg. 35.00 (*0-8328-4719-4*) Higginson Bk Co.

Schwenkfelders in Silesia. Horst Weigelt. Tr. by Peter C. Erb from GER. 1985. pap. 10.00 (*0-935980-04-0*) Schwenkfelder Lib.

Schwermetallaufnahme von Monium hornum Hedw. im Hinblick auf Seine Eignung als Biomonitor. Marion Clement. (Dissertationes Botanicae Ser.: Vol. 164). (Illus.). 184p. (GER.). 1990. pap. text ed. 65.00 (*3-443-64076-1*, Pub. by Cramer-Borntraeger GW) Lubrecht & Cramer.

Schwertertrager der Wehrmacht: Recipients of the Knight's Cross with Oakleaves & Swords. David A. Miller. (World War II Historical Society Monograph Ser.). 52p. 1995. pap. 7.00 (*1-57638-025-4*) Merriam Pr.

Schwierige. Hugo V. Hofmannsthal. Ed. by W. E. Yates. 1966. text ed. 7.50 (*0-521-05283-1*) Cambridge U Pr.

Schwierige. Hugo Von Hofmannsthal. 120p. (GER.). 1996. pap. 11.75 (*3-596-27111-8*, Pub. by Fischer Taschbch Verlag GW) Intl Bk Import.

Schwindel. P. Liard et al. (Illus.). x, 102p. 1994. pap. 30.50 (*3-8055-5814-7*) S Karger.

Schwingen: The Official Austrian Ski Method. Franz Hoppichler. 1983. pap. 12.95 (*0-935240-07-1*) Poudre Pr.

Schwinn Bicycles: The First 100 Years. Jay Pridmore & Jim Hurd. LC 96-21887. (Illus.). 160p. 1996. 29.95 (*0-7603-0127-1*) Motorbooks Intl.

***Schwinn Sting-Ray.** Liz Fried. (Enthusiast Color Ser.). (Illus.). 1997. pap. 12.95 (*0-7603-0330-4*); pap. text ed. 12.95 (*0-933201-88-5*, Bicycle Bks) Motorbooks Intl.

***Sci-Fi Aesthetics.** Ed. by Rachel Armstrong. (Art & Design Ser.: Vol. 56). (Illus.). 96p. 1997. pap. 29.95 (*1-85490-528-7*) Academy Ed UK.

***Sci-Fi Channel Trivia Book.** John G. Betancourt. 400p. (Orig.). 1996. pap. 15.00 (*1-57297-110-X*) Blvd Books.

***Sci-Fi on Tape: A Comprehensive Guide to Science Fiction & Fantasy Films on Video.** James O'Neill. LC 96-52599. 1997. write for info. (*0-8230-7659-8*, Billboard Bks) Watsn-Guptill.

***Sci-Fi Private Eye.** Ed. by Martin H. Greenberg. (Orig.). 1997. mass mkt. 5.99 (*0-614-27776-0*, ROC) NAL-Dutton.

Sci-Math: Applications in Proportional Problem Solving. M. Goldstein. 1983. text ed. 12.95 (*0-201-20073-2*) Addison-Wesley.

Sci-Math: Applications in Proportional Problem Solving, Module 1. Madeline P. Goodstein. 1983. text ed. 10.95 (*0-201-20072-4*) Addison-Wesley.

Sci Tech: Reading & Writing the English of Science & Technology. Karl Drobnic et al. 132p. (Orig.). (gr. 10-12). 1981. pap. text ed. 4.95 (*0-89285-156-2*) ELS Educ Servs.

Sci-Tech Archives & Manuscript Collections. Intro. by Ellis Mount. LC 89-19779. (Science & Technology Libraries: Vol. 9, No. 4). (Illus.). 144p. 1989. text ed. 32.95 (*0-86656-950-2*) Haworth Pr.

Sci-Tech Libraries in Museums & Aquariums. Ed. by Ellis Mount. LC 85-16436. (Science & Technology Libraries: Vol. 6, Nos. 1-2). 204p. 1985. text ed. 32.95 (*0-86656-484-5*) Haworth Pr.

Sci-Tech Libraries of the Future. Intro. by Cynthia A. Steinke. LC 93-3151. (Science & Technology Libraries: Vol. 12(No. 4) & 13(No. 1)). (Illus.). 238p. 1993. lib. bdg. 39.95 (*1-56024-447-X*) Haworth Pr.

Sci-Tech Libraries Serving Societies & Institutions. Ellis Mount. (Science & Technology Libraries: Vol. 7, No. 2). 149p. 1987. 29.95 (*0-86656-618-X*) Haworth Pr.

Sci-Tech Libraries Servng Zoological Gardens. Ed. by Ellis Mount. LC 88-17548. (Science & Technology Libraries: Vol. 8, No. 4). (Illus.). 111p. 1989. text ed. 29.95 (*0-86656-837-9*) Haworth Pr.

Sci-Tech Library Networks Within Organizations. Ed. by Ellis Mount. LC 88-540. (Science & Technology Libraries: Vol. 8, No. 2). (Illus.). 162p. 1988. text ed. 29.95 (*0-86656-747-X*) Haworth Pr.

Sci-Tech Selling. Michael Wayne. (Illus.). 192p. 1987. 30.95 (*0-13-794587-6*) P-H.

***Sciapodinae, Medeterinae (Insecta: Diptera) with a Generic Review of the Dolichopodidae.** D. J. Bickel. (Fauna of New Zealand Ser.: Vol. 23). (Illus.). 73p. 1991. pap. 27.45 (*0-477-02627-3*, Pub. by Manaaki Whenua NZ) Balogh.

Sciatic Syndrome. H. F. Farfan. LC 95-30024. 300p. 1996. 65.00 (*1-55642-243-1*, 12431) SLACK Inc.

Sciatica. William Hunter. 48p. 1985. 4.00 (*0-8187-0060-2*) Harlo Press.

***Sciatica Relief Handbook.** Chet Cunningham. LC 97-60209. (Illus.). 272p. 1997. pap. 14.95 (*1-887053-09-3*) United Res CA.

Science. (Encyclopaedia Britannica Fascinating Facts Ser.). (Illus.). 32p. (J). 1993. 8.98 (*1-56173-319-9*) Pubns Intl Ltd.

Science. (J). write for info. (*0-7894-0020-0*) DK Pub Inc.

Science. (Regents Competency Test Ser.). 1997. pap. 23.95 (*0-8373-6402-7*, RCT-2) Nat Learn.

***Science.** (Bip Quiz Ser.). (J). 1997. pap. 16.95 (*0-8069-0946-3*) Sterling.

***Science.** Addison-Wesley, Inc. Staff. 1997. 319.00 (*0-201-31600-5*) Addison-Wesley.

Science. F. F. Blackwell & C. Hohmann. LC 90-22885. (K-Three Curriculum Ser.). 216p. 1991. Field Test Ed. pap. 22.95 (*0-929816-25-0*) High-Scope.

Science. Jane Kelsey. 96p. (J). 1996. 13.95 (*0-8442-4377-9*, VGM Career Bks) NTC Pub Grp.

Science. Ed. by Diana Maine. LC 92-54482. (Picturepedia Ser.). (Illus.). (J). 1993. write for info. (*1-56458-248-5*) DK Pub Inc.

Science. David Rubel. LC 94-46529. (Illus.). (J). 1995. write for info. (*0-590-49368-X*) Scholastic Inc.

Science. David Rubel. LC 94-46529. (Kid's Encyclopedia Ser.). (Illus.). 192p. (J). (gr. 2 up). 1995. 18.95 (*0-590-49367-1*, Scholastic Ref) Scholastic Inc.

Science. J. Sheen. 250p. 1987. 50.00 (*1-85313-002-8*, Pub. by Checkmate Pubns UK) St Mut.

Science. Brenda Walpole. (Funstations Ser.). (Illus.). 48p. (J). (gr. 4 up). 1995. pap. 21.95 (*0-8431-3730-4*) Price Stern Sloan.

Science. Janice Weiss. LC 92-43466. (Contemporary's Foundations Ser.). 1993. pap. 11.26 (*0-8092-3832-2*) Contemp Bks.

Science. Steve Woolgar. 160p. (C). 1988. pap. 9.95 (*0-7458-0042-4*, Pub. by Tavistock UK); text ed. 19.95 (*0-7458-0041-6*, Pub. by Tavistock UK) Routledge Chapman & Hall.

Science, 4 vols. unabridged ed. (Learning Works). (Illus.). 32p. (J). 16.95 (*1-57145-117-X*) Thunder Bay CA.

Science. 89th ed. Abruscato. 1989. teacher ed., pap. text ed. 61.25 (*0-03-011398-9*) HR&W Schl Div.

Science, Grade 7. 86th ed. Abruscato. 1986. text ed. 96.25 (*0-03-003924-X*) HR&W Schl Div.

Science, Level 1. Cooper. 1985. 26.50 (*0-15-365491-0*) HB Schl Dept.

Science, Level 2. Cooper. 1985. 29.50 (*0-15-365492-9*) HB Schl Dept.

Science, Level R. enl. ed. Cooper. 1985. 323.25 (*0-15-365488-0*) HB Schl Dept.

Science: A Curriculum Profile for Australian Schools. Curriculum Corporation Staff. 121p. 1994. pap. text ed. 27.50 (*1-86366-208-1*, 00775) Heinemann.

Science: A First Course. M. Meadows. (C). 1989. 120.00 (*0-09-182361-7*, Pub. by S Thornes Pubs UK) St Mut.

Science: A History of Discovery in the Twentieth Century. Trevor I. Williams. 256p. 1990. 40.00 (*0-19-520843-9*) OUP.

Science: Good, Bad & Bogus. Martin Gardner. LC 80-84405. (Science & the Paranormal Ser.). 412p. 1990. reprint ed. pap. 18.95 (*0-87975-573-3*) Prometheus Bks.

Science: Growth & Change. Henry W. Menard. LC 77-156138. (Illus.). 227p. reprint ed. pap. 64.70 (*0-7837-4171-5*, 2059020) Bks Demand.

***Science: Insects & Spiders.** Kim Merlino. (Illus.). 32p. (J). (gr. 2-3). 1997. pap. 2.25 (*0-88743-292-1*, 02160) Sch Zone Pub Co.

Science: It's Changing Your World. Paul D. Martin. Ed. by Donald J. Crump. LC 85-2936. (Books for World Explorers Series 6: No. 3). (Illus.). 104p. (J). (gr. 3-8). 1985. lib. bdg. 12.50 (*0-87044-521-9*) Natl Geog.

Science: Its History & Development among the World's Cultures. Colin A. Ronan. LC 82-12176. 543p. reprint ed. pap. 154.80 (*0-7837-2675-9*, 2043046) Bks Demand.

Science: Just Add Salt. Sandras Markle. 64p. (J). (gr. 4-7). 1994. pap. 2.99 (*0-590-46537-6*) Scholastic Inc.

Science: Level 3. Cooper. 1985. 29.95 (*0-15-365493-7*) HB Schl Dept.

Science: Level 5. Cooper. 1985. 34.50 (*0-15-365494-5*) HB Schl Dept.

***Science: Seeds & Plants.** Diane O'Hanesian. (Illus.). 32p. (J). (gr. 2-3). 1997. wbk. ed., pap. 2.25 (*0-88743-293-X*, 02161) Sch Zone Pub Co.

Science: Sense & Nonsense. John L. Synge. LC 72-8534. (Essay Index Reprint Ser.). 1977. reprint ed. 19.95 (*0-8369-7332-1*) Ayer.

Science: Some Sociological Perspectives. Nicholas Mullins. LC 72-12826. (Studies in Sociology). 42p. (C). 1973. pap. text ed. write for info. (*0-672-61205-4*, Bobbs) Macmillan.

Science: Studies in the Life Sciences in Ancient Greece. G. E. Lloyd. LC 82-19808. 300p. 1983. text ed. 80.00 (*0-521-25314-4*); pap. text ed. 27.95 (*0-521-27307-2*) Cambridge U Pr.

Science: The Renaissance of a History: (Proceedings of the International Conference, Paris, June 1986) Ed. by Pietro Redondi. (History & Technology Ser.: Vol. 4, Nos. 1-4). iv, 582p. 1987. pap. text ed. 161.00 (*3-7186-0441-8*) Gordon & Breach.

***Science: Weather.** Julie Hall. (Science Workbooks Ser.). (Illus.). 32p. (J). (gr. 2-3). 1997. wbk. ed., pap. 2.25 (*0-88743-294-8*, 02162) Sch Zone Pub Co.

Science see Ideas for Teaching Gifted Students

Science - Science: Sound Bites & Insights. Howard A. Royle. 160p. (Orig.). 1996. pap. 6.50 (*0-9649118-0-9*) Canyn Pubng.

***Science - Technology - Society Investigating & Evaluating STS: Issues & Solutions.** Harold Hungerford et al. (Illus.). 185p. 1997. spiral bd. 12.60 (*0-87563-717-5*) Stipes.

***Science - Technology - Society Investigating & Evaluating STS: Issues & Solutions.** Harold Hungerford et al. (Illus.). 265p. 1997. teacher ed., spiral bd. 24.20 (*0-87563-718-3*) Stipes.

Science - Technology - Society Projects for Young Scientists. David E. Newton. LC 91-17825. (Projects for Young Scientists Ser.). (Illus.). 128p. (YA). (gr. 9-12). 1991. lib. bdg. 22.00 (*0-531-11047-8*) Watts.

Science - The False Messiah & Holier Than Thou. C. E. Ayres. LC 71-130660. 1973. reprint ed. 49.50 (*0-678-00774-8*) Kelley.

Science a la Mode: Physical Factions & Fictions. Tony Rothman. (Illus.). 224p. 1989. pap. text ed. 13.95 (*0-691-02521-5*) Princeton U Pr.

Science According to Moses: Building Your Worldview on the Knowledge Presented in Genesis. G. Thomas Sharp. (Illus.). 442p. pap. text ed. 14.95 (*0-9634981-0-X*) Creat Truth.

***Science Achievement in the Primary School Years: IEA's Third International Mathematics & Science Study.** Michael O. Martin et al. 200p. (Orig.). 1997. pap. write for info. (*1-889938-05-X*) Boston Coll.

Science Achievement of Year 12 Students in Australia. Malcoln E. Rosier. (C). 1992. 75.00 (*0-86431-089-7*, Pub. by Aust Council Educ Res AT) St Mut.

***Science Achievet in the Middle School Years: IEA's Third International Mathematics & Science Study.** Albert E. Beaton et al. LC 96-71250. (Illus.). 240p. (Orig.). 1996. pap. 30.00 (*1-889838-03-9*) Boston Coll.

Science, Action, & Fundamental Theology: Toward a Theology of Communicative Action. Helmut Peukert. Tr. by James Bohman. (Studies in Contemporary German Social Thought). 360p. 1986. pap. 14.95 (*0-262-66060-1*) MIT Pr.

Science, Action, & Reality. Raimo Tuomela. 288p. 1985. lib. bdg. 112.00 (*90-277-2098-3*, D Reidel) Kluwer Ac.

Science Activities, Vol. II. M. Unwin. (Illus.). 24p. (J). (gr. 1-4). 1993. text ed. 12.95 (*0-7460-0978-X*) EDC.

Science Activities, Vol. III. Rebecca Heddle & Paul Shipton. (Illus.). 72p. (J). (gr. k-5). 1993. pap. text ed. 12.95 (*0-7460-1428-7*, Usborne) EDC.

***Science Activities for Children.** 10th ed. George C. Lorbeer & Leslie W. Nelson. 416p. (J). 1997. spiral bd. write for info. (*0-07-114996-1*) McGraw.

Science Activities for Children, Vol. I. 9th ed. George C. Lorbeer & Leslie W. Nelson. 448p. (C). 1991. spiral bd. write for info. (*0-697-10416-8*) Brown & Benchmark.

Science Activities for Children, Vol. I. 10th ed. George C. Lorbeer & Leslie W. Nelson. 416p. (C). 1995. spiral bd. 30.05 (*0-697-24150-5*) Brown & Benchmark.

Science Activities for Children, Vol. II. George C. Lorbeer. 416p. (C). 1992. spiral bd. write for info. (*0-697-14691-X*) Brown & Benchmark.

Science Activities for Christian Children. 3rd ed. Clifton Keller & Jeanette Appel. (Illus.). 128p. 1989. pap. text ed. 6.50 (*0-930192-22-2*) Gazelle Pubns.

Science Activities Pre-K-3: Leaves Are Falling in Rainbows. Michael E. Knight & Terry L. Graham. LC 83-81429. 192p. (Orig.). (J). (ps-3). 1984. pap. 16.95 (*0-89334-045-6*) Humanics Ltd.

Science Activities Pre-K-3: Leaves Are Falling in Rainbows. Michael E. Knight & Terry L. Graham. LC 83-81429. (Illus.). 192p. 1984. lib. bdg. 26.95 (*0-89334-204-1*, 204-1) Humanics Ltd.

Science Activities with Simple Things. Howard R. Munson. (J). (gr. 4-8). 1972. pap. 8.99 (*0-8224-6320-2*) Fearon Teach Aids.

Science Adventure II. pap. 22.00 (*1-56997-092-0*) Knowldge Adv.

Science Adventures. Fred Justus. (Science Ser.). 24p. (gr. 4). 1977. student ed. 5.00 (*0-8209-0142-3*, S-4) ESP.

Science Advice to the President. 2nd ed. William T. Golden. 329p. (C). 1994. reprint ed. pap. 24.95 (*0-87168-509-4*, 93-08S) Transaction Pubs.

Science after 'Forty. Ed. by Arnold Thackray. (Oiris Ser.: Vol. 7). 320p. 1992. pap. text ed. 25.00 (*0-226-79375-3*); lib. bdg. 39.00 (*0-226-79374-5*) U Ch Pr.

Science after the Cold War: International Seminar on Nuclear War & Planetary Emergencies - 19th Session. K. Goebel. (The Science & Culture Series). 364p. 1995. text ed. 94.00 (*981-02-2277-7*) World Scientific Pub.

***Science, Agriculture, & Food Security.** Joseph H. Hulse. 242p. (Orig.). (C). 1995. pap. 45.00 (*0-660-16210-5*, Pub. by NRC Res Pr CN) Aubrey Bks.

Science, Air & Space Activities: Folder Games for the Classroom Adapted for Preschool. rev. ed. Jane Hodges-Caballero. LC 85-81658. 152p. (J). (ps-3). 1993. pap. 16.95 (*0-89334-158-4*) Humanics Ltd.

Science, Air & Space Activities: Folder Games for the Classroom Adapted for Preschool. rev. ed. Jane Hodges-Caballero. LC 85-81658. 160p. 1994. lib. bdg. 26.95 (*0-89334-232-7*) Humanics Ltd.

Science Almanac for Kids. Querida L. Pearce. (Illus.). 128p. (J). (gr. 3-7). 1993. pap. 7.95 (*1-56293-356-6*) McClanahan Bk.

Science Alternative Animal Experiments. Fred Lembeck. 1990. boxed write for info. (*0-318-68271-0*) P-H.

Science, American Style. Nathan Reingold. LC 90-9068. 414p. (C). 1991. text ed. 42.00 (*0-8135-1660-9*); pap. text ed. 18.00 (*0-8135-1661-7*) Rutgers U Pr.

***Science & Absolute Value: Twenty Addresses.** Sun M. Moon. LC 97-22323. 1997. write for info. (*0-89226-201-X*) ICF Pr.

Science & Academic Life in Transition. Emanuel Piore. 96p. (C). 1990. 29.95 (*0-88738-337-8*) Transaction Pubs.

Science & Agricultural Development. Ed. by Lawrence Busch. LC 81-65005. 198p. 1981. text ed. 48.00 (*0-86598-022-5*) Rowman.

Science & Agriculture. Arden A. Andersen. LC 92-71951. 370p. 1992. pap. 20.00 (*0-911311-35-1*) Acres USA.

Science & Anti-Science. Gerald Holton. (Illus.). 215p. 1994. pap. text ed. 14.95 (*0-674-79299-8*, HOLSCX) HUP.

Science & Anti-Science. Gerald J. Holton. LC 93-272. 215p. 1993. Alk. paper. 32.00 (*0-674-79298-X*) HUP.

Science & Applications of Conducting Polymers: Papers from the 6th European Industrial Workshop. Ed. by W. R. Salaneck et al. (Illus.). 196p. 1991. 100.00 (*0-7503-0049-3*) IOP Pub.

Science & Art of Dental Ceramics, Vol. II. John McLean. (Illus.). 496p. 1980. text ed. 160.00 (*0-931386-11-X*) Quint Pub Co.

Science & Art of Elocution. Frank H. Fenno. LC 78-139760. (Granger Index Reprint Ser.). 1977. 25.95 (*0-8369-6214-1*) Ayer.

Science & Art of Healing. Ralph Twentyman. (Illus.). 320p. 1992. pap. 27.95 (*0-86315-149-3*, Pub. by Floris Books UK) Anthroposophic.

***Science & Art of Living a Longer & Healthier Life.** Carl E. Bartecchi & Robert W. Schrier. (Illus.). 201p. (Orig.). 1997. pap. 14.95 (*0-929240-80-4*) EMIS.

Science & Art of Regeneration. 1992. lib. bdg. 249.95 (*0-8490-8830-5*) Gordon Pr.

Science & Art of Regeneration. Ida Mingle. 65p. 1984. reprint ed. spiral bd. 12.50 (*0-7873-0618-5*) Hlth Research.

***Science & Art of Renaissance Music.** James Haar & Paul E. Corneilson. LC 97-13032. 1997. write for info. (*0-691-02874-5*) Princeton U Pr.

Science & Art of the Pendulum: A Complete Course in Radiesthesia. Gabriele Blackburn. LC 83-83220. (Illus.). 96p. (Orig.). (C). 1984. pap. 10.00 (*0-9613054-1-X*) Idylwild Bks.

Science & Astrology: The Relationship Between the Measure Formulae & the Zodiac. Arthur M. Young. (Broadside Editions Ser.). (Illus.). 47p. (Orig.). 1988. pap. 5.95 (*0-931191-06-8*) Rob Briggs.

Science & Babies: Private Decisions, Public Dilemmas. Suzanne Wymelenberg & Institute of Medicine Staff. 184p. 1990. pap. 14.95 (*0-309-04136-8*) Natl Acad Pr.

Science & Behavior: An Introduction to Methods of Psychological Research. 4th rev. ed. Robert M. Liebert & Lynn L. Liebert. LC 94-40698. 336p. 1995. text ed. 59.00 (*0-13-142721-0*) P-H.

Science & Belief. Jean P. Lonchamp. 160p. (C). 1993. text ed. 50.00 (*0-85439-434-6*, Pub. by St Paul Pubns UK) St Mut.

Science & Biblical Faith: A Science Documentation. Thomas G. Barnes. (Illus.). 196p. (Orig.). 1993. pap. 13.00 (*0-9637550-0-5*) T G Barnes.

***Science & Biology.** Ed. by Baker. (C). Date not set. student ed., pap. text ed. 19.95 (*0-673-39681-9*) Addison-Wesley.

Science & Blindness: Retrospective & Prospective. International Symposium on Science & Blindness Staff. Ed. by Milton D. Graham. LC 72-82240. 224p. reprint ed. pap. 63.90 (*0-7837-0138-1*, 2040427) Bks Demand.

Science & British Liberalism: Locke, Bentham, Mill & Popper. Struan Jacobs. (Avebury Series in Philosophy). 260p. 1991. 63.95 (*1-85628-073-X*, Pub. by Avebury Pub UK) Ashgate Pub Co.

Science & Ceremony: The Institutional Economics of C. E. Ayres. Ed. by William Breit & William P. Culbertson, Jr. LC 76-8238. (Dan Murphy Sports Ser.). 228p. reprint ed. pap. 65.00 (*0-8357-7727-8*, 2036084) Bks Demand.

Science & Christian. Robert Whitelaw. pap. 1.49 (*0-87377-114-1*) GAM Pubns.

Science & Christianity. 2nd ed. John D. Callahan. (Illus.). 120p. 1986. pap. 5.95 (*0-9615767-0-7*) Callahan CA.

S

An Asterisk (*) at the beginning of an entry indicates that the title is appearing in BIP for the first time.

Science & Civilisation in China, 6 vols. Joseph Needham. Incl. Vol. 1. Introductory Orientations. (Illus.). xxxiv, 318p. 1956. text ed. 110.00 (*0-521-05799-X*); Vol. 2. History of Scientific Thought. (Illus.). xxiv, 698p. 1991. text ed. 150.00 (*0-521-05800-7*); Vol. 3. Mathematics & the Sciences of the Heavens & the Earth. (Illus.). xlviii, 878p. 1959. text ed. 200.00 (*0-521-05801-5*); Vol. 4. Physics & Physical Technology Pt. 1: Physics. (Illus.). xxxiv, 434p. 1962. text ed. 125.00 (*0-521-05802-3*); Vol. 4. Physics & Physical Technology Pt. 2: Mechanical Engineering. (Illus.). lvi, 760p. 1991. text ed. 170.00 (*0-521-05803-1*); Vol. 4. Physics & Physical Technology Pt. 3: Civil Engineering & Nautics. (Illus.). lviii, 932p. 1971. text ed. 200.00 (*0-521-07060-0*); Vol. 5. Chemistry & Chemical Technology Pt. 1: Paper & Printing. (Illus.). 350p. 1985. text ed. 135.00 (*0-521-08690-6*); Vol. 5. Chemistry & Chemical Technology Pt. 2: Spagyrical Discovery & Invention: Magisteries of Gold & Immortality. (Illus.). xlviii, 600p. 1974. text ed. 140.00 (*0-521-08571-3*); Vol. 5. Chemistry & Chemical Technology Pt. 3: Spagyrical Discovery & Invention: Historical Survey from Cinnabar Elixirs to Synthetic Insulin. (Illus.). xxxv, 481p. 1976. text ed. 135.00 (*0-521-21028-3*); Vol. 4. Chemistry & Chemical Technology Pt. 4: Spagyrical Discovery & Invention: Apparatus & Theory. (Illus.). xlviii, 756p. 1980. text ed. 170.00 (*0-521-08573-X*); Vol. 5. Chemistry & Chemical Technology Pt. 5: Spagyrical Discovery & Invention: Physiological Alchemy. (Illus.). 550p. 1983. text ed. 145. 00 (*0-521-08574-8*); Vol. 5. Military Technology Pt. 7: The Gunpowder Epic. (Illus.). 600p. 1987. text ed. 150. 00 (*0-521-30358-3*); Vol. 6. Biology & Biological Technology Pt. 1: Botany. (Illus.). 756p. 1986. text ed. 150.00 (*0-521-08731-7*); Vol. 6. Biology & Biological Technology Pt. 2: Agriculture. (Illus.). 724p. 1984. text ed. 150.00 (*0-521-25076-5*); write for info. (*0-318-51294-7*) Cambridge U Pr.

Science & Civilisation in China: Textile Technology: Spinning & Reeling, Vol. 5, Pt. 7. Dieter Kuhn. (Illus.). 900p. 1988. text ed. 135.00 (*0-521-32021-6*) Cambridge U Pr.

***Science & Civilisation in China Vol. 5, Pt. 13: Chemistry & Chemical Technology: Mining.** Peter Golas. (Illus.). 850p. (C). 1997. write for info. (*0-521-58000-5*) Cambridge U Pr.

***Science & Civilisation in China Vol. 7, Pt. 1: The Social Background: Language & Logic in Traditional China.** Christoph Harbsmeier. 600p. (C). 1997. write for info. (*0-521-57143-X*) Cambridge U Pr.

Science & Civilization. Ed. by Francis S. Marvin. LC 70-105030. (Essay Index Reprint Ser.). 1977. 23.95 (*0-8369-1581-X*) Ayer.

Science & Civilization in China: Military Technology, Pt. 6, Missiles & Sieges; Vol. 5 Chemistry & Chemical Technology. Joseph Needham & Robin D. Yates. (Science & Civilization in China Ser.). (Illus.). 552p. (C). 1995. text ed. 140.00 (*0-521-32727-X*) Cambridge U Pr.

Science & Civilization in China Vol. 6, Pt. 3: Biology & Biological Technology: Agro-Industries & Forestry. Christian Daniels & Nicholas K. Menzies. (Illus.). 750p. (C). 1996. text ed. 155.00 (*0-521-41999-9*) Cambridge U Pr.

Science & Civilization in India, Vol. 1: Harappan Period, c. 3000 BC-1500 BC. A. K. Bag. 175p. 1986. 32.50 (*0-8364-1549-3*, Pub. by Navrang) S Asia.

***Science & Civilization in Islam.** Seyyed H. Nasr. 388p. 1996. 22.50 (*0-614-21606-0*, 1109) Kazi Pubns.

Science & Civilization in Islam. 2nd ed. Seyyed H. Nasr. 138p. 1987. 29.95 (*0-946621-11-X*, Pub. by Islamic Texts UK) Intl Spec Bk.

Science & Civilization in Islam. Seyyed H. Nasr. LC 68-25616. 384p. reprint ed. pap. 109.50 (*0-7837-4122-7*, 2057945) Bks Demand.

Science & Clinical Judgment in Orthodontics. Ed. by Katherine A. Ribbens & Peter S. Vig. (Craniofacial Growth Ser.: Vol. 19). (Illus.). 251p. 1986. 49.00 (*0-929921-15-1*) UM CHGD.

Science & Comparative Philosophy. David E. Shaner et al. LC 88-34854. 291p. (Orig.). 1989. pap. text ed. 114.00 (*90-04-08953-5*) E J Brill.

Science & Computer Activities for Children 3 to 9 Years Old. 2nd rev. ed. Bonnie E. Nelson. (Illus.). 146p. (J). (gr. k-3). 1988. 28.00 (*0-931642-21-3*) Lintel.

Science & Convention: Essays on the Origin & Significance of the Conventionalist Philosophy of Science. Jerzy Giedymin. (Foundations & Philosophy of Science & Technology Ser.). 260p. 1982. 99.00 (*0-08-025790-9*, Pub. by Pergamon Repr UK) Franklin.

Science & Cooperative Learning: Science Units for: Weather, Insects, Plants, Dinosaurs, Space. Betty Ehret. (Illus.). 112p. (Orig.). 1994. pap. 21.95 (*1-878347-43-8*) NL Assocs.

Science & Corporate Strategy: Du Pont R&D, 1902-1980. David A. Hounshell & John K. Smith, Jr. (Studies in Economic History & Policy: The United States in the Twentieth Century). (Illus.). 832p. 1988. text ed. 52.95 (*0-521-32767-9*) Cambridge U Pr.

Science & Creation: From Eternal Cycles to an Oscillating Universe. Stanley L. Jaki. 386p. (C). 1990. reprint ed. pap. text ed. 35.50 (*0-8191-7839-X*) U Pr of Amer.

Science & Creation: Geological, Theological, & Educational Perspectives. Ed. by Robert W. Hanson. LC 83-50822. (AAAS Issues in Science & Technology Ser.). 238p. reprint ed. pap. 67.90 (*0-7837-6750-1*, 2046378) Bks Demand.

Science & Creation in the Middle Ages: Henry of Langenstein (D. 1397) on Genesis. Nicholas H. Steneck. LC 75-19881. 1977. pap. 16.50 (*0-268-01691-7*) U of Notre Dame Pr.

Science & Creationism. Ed. by Ashley Montagu. LC 82-14173. 434p. 1984. 35.00 (*0-19-503252-7*) OUP.

Science & Creationism. Ed. by Ashley Montagu. LC 82-14173. 434p. 1984. pap. 20.95 (*0-19-503253-5*) OUP.

Science & Creationism: A View from the National Academy of Sciences. National Research Council Staff. 28p. (C). 1984. pap. 5.00 (*0-309-03440-X*) Natl Acad Pr.

***Science & Criticism: The Humanistic Tradition in Contemporary Thought.** Herbert J. Muller. 303p. Date not set. 20.95 (*0-8369-2327-8*) Ayer.

Science & Cultivation of Edible Fungi: Proceedings of the Thirteenth International Congress, Dublin, 1-6 September 1991, 2 vols. Ed. by Michael J. Maher. (Illus.). 880p. 1991. text ed. 140.00 (*90-5410-021-4*, Pub. by A A Balkema NE) Ashgate Pub Co.

Science & Cultivation of Edible Fungi: Proceedings of the 14th International Congress on the Science & Cultivation of Edible Fungi, Oxford, 17-22 September 1995, 2 vols., Set. Ed. by T. J. Elliott. (Illus.). 960p. (C). 1995. text ed. 165.00 (*90-5410-570-4*, Pub. by A A Balkema NE) Ashgate Pub Co.

Science & Cultural Context: Soviet Scientists in Comparative Perspective. Nina Toren. (Worcester Polytechnic Institute Studies in Science, Technology, & Culture: Vol. 1). 201p. (C). 1988. text ed. 37.50 (*0-8204-0668-6*) P Lang Pubng.

Science & Cultural Crisis: An Intellectual Biography of Percy Williams Bridgman (1882-1961) Maila L. Walter. LC 90-30511. 384p. 1990. 47.50 (*0-8047-1796-6*) Stanford U Pr.

Science & Culture: Popular & Philosophical Essays. Hermann Von Helmholtz. Ed. & Intro. by David Cahan. LC 95-12217. 436p. 1995. pap. text ed. 17.95 (*0-226-32659-4*); lib. bdg. 52.00 (*0-226-32658-6*) U Ch Pr.

***Science & Culture under William & Mary.** Ed. by J. D. North & P. W. Klein. (Mededelingen der Koninklijke Nederlandse Akademie van Wetenschappen, Afd. Letterkunde Ser.: No. 55(2)). 48p. 1992. pap. text ed. 17.50 (*0-444-85748-6*) Elsevier.

Science & Design of Engineering Materials. rev. ed. James P. Schaffer et al. 864p. (C). 1995. text ed. 80.95 (*0-256-19580-3*) Irwin.

***Science & Design of Engineering Materials.** 2nd ed. James P. Schaffer. LC 96-49670. 832p. (C). 1998. text ed. 62. 40 (*0-256-24766-8*) Irwin.

Science & Disssent in Post-Mao China: The Politics of Knowledge. H. Lyman Miller. LC 95-24846. (Illus.). 366p. 1996. 38.00 (*0-295-97505-9*); pap. 18.95 (*0-295-97532-6*) U of Wash Pr.

Science & Earth History: The Evolution-Creation Controversy. Arthur N. Strahler. (Illus.). 522p. 1988. 51.95 (*0-87975-414-1*) Prometheus Bks.

Science & Ecosystem Management in the National Parks. Ed. by William L. Halvorson & Gary E. Davis. LC 95-32530. (Illus.). 384p. 1996. 40.00 (*0-8165-1566-2*) U of Ariz Pr.

Science & Empire: East Coast Fever in Rhodesia & the Transvaal. Paul F. Cranefield. (Cambridge History of Medicine Ser.). (Illus.). 300p. (C). 1991. text ed. 79.95 (*0-521-39253-5*) Cambridge U Pr.

Science & Empires: Historical Studies about Scientific Development & European Expansion. Ed. by Patrick Petitjean. (Boston Studies in the Philosophy of Science). 428p. (C). 1991. lib. bdg. 145.00 (*0-7923-1518-9*, Pub. by Klwr Acad Pubs NE) Kluwer Ac.

Science & Engineering Conference Proceedings: A Guide to Sources for Identification & Verification. Ed. by Barbara DeFelice. 84p. (C). 1995. pap. 16.50 (*0-8389-7790-1*) Assn Coll & Res Libs.

Science & Engineering Degrees: 1966-90. (Illus.). 65p. (Orig.). (C). 1993. pap. text ed. 20.00 (*1-56806-292-3*) DIANE Pub.

Science & Engineering Degrees: 1966-93. Susan T. Hill. (Illus.). 99p. (Orig.). (C). 1995. pap. text ed. 25.00 (*0-7881-2416-1*) DIANE Pub.

Science & Engineering Degrees, by Race-Ethnicity of Recipients: 1977-91. Susan T. Hill. (Illus.). 126p. (Orig.). (C). 1995. pap. text ed. 30.00 (*0-7881-2253-3*) DIANE Pub.

Science & Engineering Dictionary: Russian-English. Eugene A. Carpovich & Vera V. Carpovich. (ENG & RUS.). 1988. 90.00 (*0-911484-05-1*) Tech Dict.

Science & Engineering Indicators, 2 vols., Set. 1995. lib. bdg. 625.95 (*0-8490-7440-1*) Gordon Pr.

***Science & Engineering Indicators (1993)** (Illus.). 514p. (Orig.). (C). 1996. reprint ed. pap. text ed. 35.00 (*0-7881-2977-5*) DIANE Pub.

***Science & Engineering Indicators, 1996.** 352p. (Orig.). (C). 1996. pap. 50.00 (*0-7881-3360-8*) DIANE Pub.

Science & Engineering of Compositng: Deisgn, Environmental, Microbiological & Utilization Aspects. Ed. by Harry A. Hoitink & Harold M. Keener. LC 92-53882. 728p. 1992. 125.00 (*0-936645-15-6*) Renaissance Pubns.

Science & Engineering of Materials. 2nd ed. Donald R. Askeland. 800p. (C). 1989. text ed. 68.95 (*0-534-91657-0*) PWS Pubs.

Science & Engineering of Materials. 3rd ed. Donald R. Askeland. LC 93-21416. 1994. text ed. 81.95 (*0-534-93423-4*) PWS Pubs.

***Science & Engineering of Materials Solutions Manual.** (Illus.). 416p. (Orig.). 1996. pap. text ed. 55.00 (*0-412-72610-6*, Chap & Hall NY) Chapman & Hall.

Science & Engineering of One & Zero-Dimensional Semiconductors. Clivia M. Sotomayor-Torres. (NATO ASI, Series B: Physics: Vol. 214). (Illus.). 214p. 1990. 95.00 (*0-306-43417-2*, Plenum Pr) Plenum.

Science & Engineering of Semiconductor Fabrication. Stephen A. Campbell. (Oxford Series in Electrical & Computer Engineering). (Illus.). 560p. (C). 1996. text ed. 71.00 (*0-19-510508-7*) OUP.

Science & Engineering of Thermal Spray Coatings. Lech Pawlowski. LC 94-19287. 414p. 1995. text ed. 99.95 (*0-471-95253-2*) Wiley.

Science & Engineering on Supercomputers. Ed. by Eric J. Pitcher. LC 90-84073. 628p. 1990. 212.00 (*0-945824-99-8*) Computational Mech MA.

Science & Engineering on Supercomputers: Fifth International Symposium October 22-24, 1990, London, England. E. J. Pitcher. ix, 628p. 1990. 223.95 (*0-387-53226-9*) Spr-Verlag.

Science & Engineering Programs: On Target for Women? National Research Council Staff. Ed. by Marsha L. Matyas & Linda S. Dix. LC 92-61248. (Illus.). 240p. (Orig.). (C). 1992. pap. text ed. 29.00 (*0-309-04778-1*) Natl Acad Pr.

Science & Engineering Sourcebook. Cass R. Lewart. LC 82-80269. (Illus.). 96p. (Orig.). 1982. pap. 9.95 (*0-942412-02-8*); audio 8.95 (*0-686-98227-4*) Micro Text Pubns.

Science & English Poetry: A Historical Sketch, 1590-1950. Douglas Bush. LC 80-18161. (Patten Lectures Ser., 1949, Indiana Univ.). viii, 166p. 1980. reprint ed. text ed. 49.75 (*0-313-22654-7*, BUSC, Greenwood Pr) Greenwood.

Science & Epilepsy: Neuroscience Gains in Epilepsy Research. James L. O'Leary & Sidney Goldring. LC 75-21860. 303p. 1976. text ed. 62.00 (*0-89004-072-9*) Lppncott-Raven.

Science & Ethical Values. Hiram B. Glass. LC 81-13170. ix, 101p. 1981. reprint ed. text ed. 49.75 (*0-313-23141-9*, GLSE, Greenwood Pr) Greenwood.

Science & Everyday Life. John B. Haldane. LC 74-26267. (History, Philosophy & Sociology of Science Ser.). 1975. reprint ed. 28.95 (*0-405-06595-7*) Ayer.

Science & Faith. Ed. by Vladimir Vukanovic. 120p. (Orig.). 1995. pap. text ed. 9.95 (*1-880971-06-2*) Light&Life Pub Co MN.

Science & Faith: The Anthropology of Revelation. Eric Gans. 144p. (C). 1990. lib. bdg. 47.50 (*0-8476-7659-5*) Rowman.

Science & Fine Art of Fasting. 5th ed. Herbert M. Shelton. LC 77-99219. 384p. 1934. reprint ed. pap. 14.95 (*0-914532-21-9*) Amer Natural Hygiene.

***Science & Fine Art of Food & Nutrition.** 6th rev. ed. Herbert M. Shelton. LC 96-85470. 1984. pap. 14.95 (*0-914532-39-1*) Amer Natural Hygiene.

Science & Fine Art of Natural Hygiene. 3rd ed. Herbert M. Shelton. LC 94-79571. 424p. 1934. reprint ed. pap. 14. 95 (*0-914532-36-7*) Amer Natural Hygiene.

Science & First Principles. F. S. Northrop. LC 79-89840. 1979. reprint ed. 32.00 (*0-918024-08-0*) Ox Bow.

Science & Football. Ed. by T. Reilly et al. 500p. 1988. text ed. 57.50 (*0-419-14360-2*, E & FN Spon) Routledge Chapman & Hall.

Science & Football, No. 2. 2nd ed. Ed. by T. Reilly et al. 768p. (gr. 13). 1992. text ed. 145.95 (*0-419-17850-3*, A9478, E & FN Spon) Chapman & Hall.

Science & Founding Fathers: Science in the Political Thought of Thomas Jefferson, Benjamin Franklin, John Adams, & James Madison. Bernard Cohen. 368p. 1997. pap. 15.95 (*0-393-31510-X*) Norton.

Science & Freedom. Ed. by Lyman Bryson. LC 71-156620. (Essay Index Reprint Ser.). 1977. reprint ed. 20.95 (*0-8369-2385-5*) Ayer.

Science & Gender: A Critique of Biology & Its Theories on Women. Ruth Bleier. (Athene Ser.). (Illus.). 250p. 1984. text ed. 45.00 (*0-08-030972-0*, Pergamon Pr); pap. text ed. 18.95 (*0-08-030971-2*, Pergamon Pr) Elsevier.

Science & Gender: A Critique of Biology & Its Theories on Women. Ruth Bleier. LC 97-7367. (Athene Ser.). 240p. (C). 1984. pap. text ed. 18.95 (*0-8077-6200-8*) Tchrs Coll.

***Science & God.** Saiyid S. Ahmed. 11p. 1996. pap. 2.00 (*0-614-21607-9*, 1110) Kazi Pubns.

Science & God. Shamim A. Saiyid. 11p. (Orig.). 1985. pap. 3.00 (*1-56744-379-6*) Kazi Pubns.

Science & Golf: The Proceedings of the First World Scientific Congress of Golf. Ed. by Alastair J. Cochran. 352p. 1990. 72.50 (*0-419-15130-3*, A5019, E & FN Spon) Routledge Chapman & Hall.

Science & Golf 2: Proceedings of the World Scientific Congress of Golf. A. J. Cochran. 1994. 59.95 (*0-419-18790-1*, E & FN Spon) Routledge Chapman & Hall.

Science & Government: Godkin Lectures. C. P. Snow. 17.95 (*0-8488-0937-8*) Amereon Ltd.

Science & Health. Mary M. Eddy. (Notable American Authors Ser.). 1992. reprint ed. lib. bdg. 75.00 (*0-7812-2746-1*) Rprt Serv.

Science & Health Experiments & Demonstrations in Smoking Education. 1989. 11.85 (*0-917160-19-3*) Am Sch Health.

Science & Health with Key to the Scriptures. Mary Baker Eddy. 700p. 1989. reprint ed. pap. 15.95 (*0-930227-11-5*) Bookmark CA.

Science & Health with Key to the Scriptures: Authorized Edition. Mary B. Eddy. 700p. 1994. reprint ed. pap. 18. 00 (*0-87952-038-8*) Eddy Wrtngs M B Eddy.

Science & Health with Key to the Scriptures: 1910 Edition. Mary B. Eddy. (Illus.). 700p. 1987. reprint ed. 9.95 (*1-878641-00-X*) Aequus Inst Pubns.

Science & Health with Key to the Scriptures-French. Mary Baker Eddy. (FRE.). pap. 24.00 (*0-87952-116-3*) Eddy Wrtngs M B Eddy.

Science & Health with Key to the Scriptures-German. Mary Baker Eddy. (GER.). pap. 24.00 (*0-87952-150-3*) Eddy Wrtngs M B Eddy.

Science & Health with Key to the Scriptures-Portuguese. Mary Baker Eddy. (POR.). pap. 24.00 (*0-87952-209-7*) Eddy Wrtngs M B Eddy.

Science & Health with Key to the Scriptures-Spanish. Mary Baker Eddy. (SPA.). pap. 24.00 (*0-87952-225-9*) Eddy Wrtngs M B Eddy.

Science & Hermeneutics. Vern S. Poythress. (Foundations of Contemporary Interpretation Ser.: Vol. 6). 1988. 18. 99 (*0-310-40971-3*) Zondervan.

Science & History. Ed. by Dwight W. Hoover & John T. Koumoulides. (Conspectus of History Ser.). (Orig.). 1982. pap. 4.95 (*0-937994-02-2*) Ball State Univ.

***Science & Homosexualities.** Vernon A. Rosario. LC 96-9673. 288p. 1996. pap. 18.95 (*0-415-91502-3*) Routledge.

***Science & Homosexualities.** Vernon A. Rosario. LC 96-9673. 288p. (C). 1997. text ed. 69.95 (*0-415-91501-5*) Routledge.

Science & Human Behavior. B. F. Skinner. 1965. reprint ed. pap. 12.95 (*0-02-929040-6*, Free Press) Free Pr.

Science & Human Life. John B. Haldane. LC 72-142638. (Essay Index Reprint Ser.). 1977. 21.95 (*0-8369-2161-5*) Ayer.

***Science & Human Transformation: Subtle Energies, Intentionality, & Consciousness.** William A. Tiller. LC 97-66498. (Illus.). 320p. (Orig.). 1997. per., pap. 24.95 (*0-9642637-4-2*) Pavior Pubng.

Science & Human Values. J. Bronowski. 1992. 21.50 (*0-8446-6518-5*) Peter Smith.

Science & Human Values. Jacob Bronowski. LC 89-45631. 128p. 1990. reprint ed. pap. 10.00 (*0-06-097281-5*, PL) HarpC.

***Science & Humanities, 10 bks.** (American Women of Achievement Ser.). (YA). (gr. 5 up). 199.50 (*0-7910-3502-6*) Chelsea Hse.

Science & Hypothesis. Henri Poincare. 1905. pap. 6.95 (*0-486-60221-4*) Dover.

Science & Hypothesis: Historical Essays on Scientific Methodology. Larry Laudan. (University of Western Ontario Series in Philosophy of Science WONS: No. 19). 269p. 1981. lib. bdg. 93.00 (*90-277-1315-4*) Kluwer Ac.

Science & Ideology in the Policy Sciences. Paul Diesing. 464p. 1982. lib. bdg. 49.95 (*0-202-30301-2*) Aldine de Gruyter.

Science & Immortality. Manly P. Hall. pap. 4.95 (*0-89314-351-0*) Philos Res.

Science & Immortality. William Osler. Ed. by Robert J. Kastenbaum. LC 76-19586. (Death & Dying Ser.). 1977. reprint ed. lib. bdg. 17.95 (*0-405-09581-3*) Ayer.

Science & Innovation: The U. S. Pharmaceutical Industry During the 1980s. Alfonso Gambardella. (Illus.). 199p. (C). 1995. text ed. 44.95 (*0-521-45118-3*) Cambridge U Pr.

Science & Innovation As Strategic Tools for Industrial & Economic Growth: Proceedings of the NATO Advanced Research Workshop, Moscow, Russia, October 24-26, 1994. Ed. by Carlo Corsi. LC 95-26544. (NATO ASI: Partnership Sub-Series 4: Science & Technology Policy: Vol. 4). 192p. (C). 1996. lib. bdg. 99.00 (*0-7923-3903-7*) Kluwer Ac.

Science & Inquiry in Social Work Practice. Ben A. Orcutt. 256p. 1990. text ed. 42.50 (*0-231-07040-3*) Col U Pr.

Science & Instruments in Seventeenth Century Italy. Silvio A. Bedini. LC 94-8292. (Collected Studies: No. CS 449). 1994. 109.95 (*0-86078-442-8*, Pub. by Variorum UK) Ashgate Pub Co.

Science & International Security: New Perspectives for a Changing World Order. Ed. by Eric H. Arnett. 298p. 1991. 15.00 (*0-87168-431-4*, 91-40S) AAAS.

***Science & Invention.** Diane K. Moser. LC 97-9873. (American Historical Places Ser.). 1997. 18.95 (*0-8160-3402-8*) Facts on File.

Science & Its Critics. J. Passmore. 1986. pap. 18.95 (*0-7156-1326-X*, Pub. by Duckworth UK) Focus Pub-R Pullins.

Science & Its Fabrication. Alan Chalmers. 160p. (C). 1990. pap. text ed. 14.95 (*0-8166-1888-7*) U of Minn Pr.

***Science & Its Fabrication.** Alan F. Chalmers. 160p. 1990. 37.50 (*0-335-09318-3*, Open Univ Pr); pap. 11.99 (*0-335-09317-5*, Open Univ Pr) Taylor & Francis.

Science & Its Public: The Changing Relationship. Ed. by Gerald J. Holton & W. Blanpied. LC 75-41391. (Boston Studies in the Philosophy of Science: No. 33). 315p. 1975. pap. text ed. 52.00 (*90-277-0658-1*, D Reidel); lib. bdg. 100.50 (*90-277-0657-3*, D Reidel) Kluwer Ac.

***Science & Its Ways of Knowing.** John Hatton & Paul B. Plouffe. 256p. (C). 1996. text ed. 30.67 (*0-13-205576-7*) P-H.

Science & Judgement in Risk Assessment: Student Edition. National Academy of Sciences Staff. 352p. 1996. pap. text ed. 29.95 (*1-56032-589-5*) Taylor & Francis.

Science & Judgment in RIsk Assessment. National Research Council Staff. 672p. (Orig.). (C). 1994. text ed. 69.95 (*0-309-04894-X*) Natl Acad Pr.

Science & Justice: The Massachusetts Witchcraft Trials. Sanford J. Fox. LC 68-18771. (Illus.). 144p. reprint ed. 41.10 (*0-8357-9285-4*, 2016570) Bks Demand.

***Science & Key of Life: Planetary Influences, 7 vols.** Alvidas. Incl. Vol. 7. . (Illus.). 160p. 1997. reprint ed. pap. 15.00 (*0-87728-918-2*); Vol. 6. . (Illus.). 264p. 1997. reprint ed. pap. 15.00 (*0-87728-917-4*); Vol. 5. . (Illus.). 288p. 1997. reprint ed. pap. 15.00 (*0-87728-916-6*); Vol. 4. . (Illus.). 328p. 1997. reprint ed. pap. 15.00 (*0-87728-915-8*); Vol. 3. . (Illus.). 264p. 1997. reprint ed. pap. 15.00 (*0-87728-914-X*); Vol. 2. . (Illus.). 272p. 1997. reprint ed. pap. 15.00 (*0-87728-913-1*); Vol. 1. . (Illus.). 280p. 1997. reprint ed. pap. 15.00 (*0-87728-912-3*); LC 97-367. 1997. 99.00 (*0-87728-911-5*) Weiser.

An Asterisk (*) at the beginning of an entry indicates that the title is appearing in BIP for the first time.

Science & Knowledge: Proceedings of a Conference Sponsored by Sociedad Filosofica Ibero-Americana. Ed. by Enrique Villanueva. (Philosophical Issues Ser.: No. 3, 1993). viii, 320p. (Orig.). 1993. pap. text ed. 25.00 (*0-924922-14-1*); lib. bdg. 42.00 (*0-924922-64-8*) Ridgeview.

Science & Language Links: Classroom Implications. Ed. by Johanna Scott. LC 92-44250. (Illus.). 91p. 1993. pap. text ed. 16.00 (*0-435-08338-4*, 08338) Heinemann.

Science & Liberal Education. Hiram B. Glass. LC 60-8285. (Davis Washington Mitchell Lectures). 127p. reprint ed. pap. 36.20 (*0-317-09391-6*, 2003383) Bks Demand.

Science & Liberal Education in the Space Age. Glenn T. Seaborg. LC 60-214. (Augustana College Library Occasional Papers, Wallin Lecture: No. 5). 15p. 1960. pap. 1.00 (*0-910182-26-4*) Augustana Coll.

***Science & Liberation.** Ed. by Rita Arditti et al. 398p. 41.99 (*0-919618-97-9*, Pub. by Black Rose Bks CN); pap. 12.99 (*0-919618-96-0*, Pub. by Black Rose Bks CN) Consort Bk Sales.

Science & Life. Cummings. Date not set. write for info. (*0-314-09586-1*) West Pub.

Science & Life. Robert A. Millikan. LC 76-93360. (Essay Index Reprint Ser.). 1977. 17.95 (*0-8369-1307-8*) Ayer.

Science & Literature. Ed. by Harry R. Garvin. LC 81-72026. (Bucknell Review Ser.: Vol. 27, No. 2). 192p. 1983. 22.00 (*0-8387-5051-6*) Bucknell U Pr.

Science & Math. Joy Evans. (How to Make Books with Children Ser.: Vol. 3). (Illus.). 160p. (J). (gr. 1-6). 1995. teacher ed., pap. text ed. 16.95 (*0-614-06231-4*, EMC 298) Evan-Moor Corp.

Science & Math, Techknowledge Reference Series. Barrowman. (TP - Technology Education Ser.). (J). (gr. k-12). 1997. pap. 21.95 (*0-538-64484-2*) S-W Pub.

Science & Mathematics. (National Teacher Examination Ser.: NC-5). pap. 23.95 (*0-8373-8405-2*) Nat Learn.

Science & Mathematics Education in the United States: Eight Innovations. OECD Staff. 180p. (Orig.). 1993. pap. text ed. 28.00 (*92-64-13918-4*, 96-93-01-1) OECD.

Science & Mathematics in Early Childhood Education. Donna M. Wolfinger. (C). 1993. text ed. 36.50 (*0-06-501262-3*) Addson-Wesley Educ.

Science & Medicine. Walter Oleksy. (Information Revolution Ser.). (Illus.). 128p. (J). (gr. 5-12). 1995. 17.95 (*0-8160-3076-6*) Facts on File.

Science & Medicine in Imperial Russia. Anatoly Bezkorovainy. (Illus.). 271p. 1980. spiral bd., pap. 12.00 (*0-9607600-0-8*) Bezkorovainy.

***Science & Medicine in Islam.** Franz Rosenthal. 250p. 1996. 79.95 (*0-614-21608-7*, 1111) Kazi Pubns.

Science & Medicine in Islam: A Collection of Essays. Franz Rosenthal. (Collected Studies: No. 330). 250p. 1991. text ed. 79.95 (*0-86078-282-4*, Pub. by Variorum UK) Ashgate Pub Co.

Science & Medicine in Shakespeare's Time: A Guide to the Microfiche Collection. (Shakespeariana Ser.). 43p. (Orig.). 1991. pap. 20.00 (*0-8357-2175-2*) Univ Microfilms.

Science & Medicine in Sport. 2nd ed. Ed. by John Bloomfield. 648p. 1995. pap. 69.95 (*0-86793-321-6*) Blackwell Sci.

Science & Medicine in the Old South. fac. ed. Ed. by Ronald L. Numbers & Todd L. Savitt. LC 88-32648. (Illus.). 382p. 1989. reprint ed. pap. 108.90 (*0-7837-7768-X*, 2047524) Bks Demand.

Science & Medicine in Twentieth-Century China: Research & Education. Ed. by John Z. Bowers et al. (Science, Medicine, & Technology in East Asia Ser.: No. 3). 283p. 1989. text ed. 50.00 (*0-89264-077-4*); pap. text ed. 25.00 (*0-89264-078-2*) Ctr Chinese Studies.

Science & Medieval Thought. Thomas C. Allbutt. LC 75-23673. reprint ed. 29.50 (*0-404-13226-X*) AMS Pr.

Science & Metaphysics: Variations on Kantian Themes. Wilfrid Sellars. x, 278p. 1991. reprint ed. pap. text ed. 22.00 (*0-924922-11-7*); reprint ed. lib. bdg. 39.00 (*0-924922-61-3*) Ridgeview.

Science & Method. Henri Poincare. (Key Texts Ser.). 288p. 1996. pap. 24.95 (*1-85506-431-6*) Bks Intl VA.

Science & Modern Life. Edward J. Russell. LC 70-117833. (Essay Index Reprint Ser.). 1977. reprint ed. 17.95 (*0-8369-2440-1*) Ayer.

Science & Moral Choice: An Examination of the Foundations of Moral Philosophy. Ronald D. Icenogle. 280p. 1995. 29.00 (*0-87527-518-4*) Green.

Science & Morals, & Other Essays. Bertram C. Windle. LC 70-156731. (Essay Index Reprint Ser.). 1977. reprint ed. 19.95 (*0-8369-2301-4*) Ayer.

Science & Music. James Jeans. (Illus.). 1968. reprint ed. pap. 6.95 (*0-486-61964-8*) Dover.

Science & Mysticism: A Comparative Study of Western Natural Science, Theravada Buddhism, & Advaita Vedanta. Richard H. Jones. LC 84-46098. 272p. 1986. 40.00 (*0-8387-5093-1*) Bucknell U Pr.

Science & Nature: How They Work. Frank Schaffer Publications, Inc. Staff. (Middle School Bks.). (Illus.). 1996. wbk. ed. 12.95 (*0-7647-0021-9*, FS-10197) Schaffer Pubns.

Science & Nature: The Annual of Marxist Philosophy for Natural Scientists, Nos. 7-8. Ed. by Lester Talkington. 160p. (Orig.). 1986. pap. 6.50 (*0-939275-00-7*) Dialectics Workshop.

***Science & Nature in Motion - Birds of North America.** Stan Freeman. LC 96-75349. (Illus.). 112p. (Orig.). 1996. pap. 11.95 (*0-9636814-2-7*) Hampshire House.

Science & Nature, Nos. 1 to 6: Adventures in Marxist Philosophy for Natural Scientists. Intro. by Lester Talkington & Stephen J. Gould. 544p. 1989. pap. 19.95 (*0-939275-02-3*) Dialectics Workshop.

Science & Nature, Nos. 9-10: A Letter to Gorbachev & Other Adventures in Marxist Philosophy for Natural Scientists. Ed. by Lester Talkington. 188p. 1989. pap. 7.50 (*0-939275-01-5*) Dialectics Workshop.

Science & Necessity. John Bigelow & Robert Pargetter. (Cambridge Studies in Philosophy). 375p. (C). 1991. text ed. 80.00 (*0-521-39027-3*) Cambridge U Pr.

Science & Objectivity: Episodes in the History of Astronomy. Norriss S. Hetherington. LC 87-3140. (Illus.). 180p. 1988. reprint ed. pap. 51.30 (*0-608-00039-6*, 2060805) Bks Demand.

Science & Other Poems. Alison H. Deming. LC 93-39187. 96p. 1994. pap. 9.95 (*0-8071-1915-6*); text ed. 17.95 (*0-8071-1914-8*) La State U Pr.

***Science & Our Global Heritage: Multidisciplinary Perspectives on Sustainable Development.** James H. Barton et al. (Illus.). 400p. (C). Date not set. pap. text ed. 49.95 (*1-884687-04-0*) N Horzns Pub.

Science & Our Troubled Conscience. J. Robert Nelson. LC 80-8045. 187p. (Orig.). 187p. reprint ed. pap. 53.30 (*0-317-55550-2*, 2029619) Bks Demand.

Science & Philosophy: Past & Present. Derek Gjertsen. 304p. 1990. pap. 8.95 (*0-14-022674-5*, Penguin Bks) Viking Penguin.

Science & Philosophy, & Other Essays. Bernard Bosanquet. LC 67-23180. (Essay Index Reprint Ser.). 1977. 20.95 (*0-8369-0224-6*) Ayer.

Science & Philosophy in Aristotle's Biological Works. Anthony Preus. (Studien und Materialien Zur Geschichte der Philosophie Ser.: No. 1). ix, 404p. 1975. 83.20 (*3-487-05832-4*) G Olms Pubs.

Science & Philosophy in the Light of the New Church. (Words for the New Church Ser.: Vols. IV-VI). 289p. 1976. reprint ed. 14.95 (*0-915221-24-1*) Swedenborg Sci Assn.

Science & Philosophy in the Twentieth Century: Basic Works of Logical Empiricism, 6 vols., Set. Ed. & Intro. by Sahotra Sarkar. 1996. 420.00 (*0-8153-2261-5*) Garland.

Science & Philosophy of the Organism, 2 vols., Set. Hans A. Driesch. LC 77-27217. (Gifford Lectures: 1907-08). reprint ed. 89.50 (*0-404-60500-1*) AMS Pr.

Science & Poetry. I. A. Richards. LC 74-6484. (Studies in Poetry: No. 38). 1974. lib. bdg. 75.00 (*0-8383-1916-5*) M S G Haskell Hse.

Science & Policy Reader. Lance R. Clark & R. Neil Sampson. write for info. (*0-614-16429-X*) Am Forests.

Science & Politics. Quintin M. Hailsham. LC 73-16740. 110p. 1974. reprint ed. 49.75 (*0-8371-7227-6*, HASC, Greenwood Pr) Greenwood.

Science & Politics: The Dual Vision of Feminist Policy Research, the Example of Family & Medical Leave. rev. ed. Roberta M. Spalter-Roth & Heidi Hartmann. 24p. 1991. pap. 5.00 (*0-685-29936-8*) Inst Womens Policy Rsch.

Science & Politics in Canada. G. Bruce Doern. LC 79-180255. 252p. reprint ed. pap. 71.90 (*0-317-26055-3*, 2023842) Bks Demand.

Science & Politics of Food. Ed. by Robert A. Brungs & Marianne Postiglione. (Illus.). 244p. (Orig.). (C). 1995. pap. 15.95 (*1-885583-01-X*) ITEST Faith.

Science & Politics of I. Q. Leon J. Kamin. LC 74-13883. 183p. (C). 1974. text ed. 39.95 (*0-89859-129-5*) L Erlbaum Assocs.

Science & Politics of Racial Research. William H. Tucker. 384p. 1996. 17.95 (*0-252-06560-3*) U of Ill Pr.

Science & Politics of Racial Research: Race, Science, & Politics. William H. Tucker. LC 93-47673. 384p. (C). 1996. 36.95 (*0-252-02099-5*) U of Ill Pr.

Science & Polity in France at the End of the Old Regime. Charles C. Gillispie. LC 80-7521. 615p. reprint ed. pap. 175.30 (*0-7837-3408-5*, 2043368) Bks Demand.

Science & Practice in Clinical Neurology. Ed. by Simon C. Gandevia et al. (Illus.). 350p. (C). 1994. text ed. 69.95 (*0-521-43119-0*) Cambridge U Pr.

***Science & Practice of Cognitive Behaviour Therapy.** Ed. by David M. Clark & Christopher G. Fairburn. (Illus.). 448p. 1996. pap. 47.50 (*0-19-262725-2*) OUP.

Science & Practice of Gerontology: A Multidisciplinary Guide. Ed. by Nancy J. Osgood & Ann H. Sontz. LC 88-25100. 204p. 1989. text ed. 55.00 (*0-313-26161-X*, OSP/, Greenwood Pr) Greenwood.

Science & Practice of Intramedullary Nailing. 2nd ed. Ed. by Bruce D. Browner. LC 95-14195. 374p. 1995. 135.00 (*0-683-01123-5*) Williams & Wilkins.

Science & Practice of Intramedullary Nailing. Bruce D. Browner & Charles C. Edwards. LC 86-15292. 383p. reprint ed. pap. 109.20 (*0-7837-2693-7*, 2043071) Bks Demand.

Science & Practice of Iridology, Vol. I. Bernard Jensen. 1952. pap. 24.50 (*0-9608360-5-5*) B Jensen.

Science & Practice of Liquid-Liquid Extraction, Vol. 1. John D. Thornton. (Oxford Engineering Science Ser.: No. 27). (Illus.). 528p. 1992. 135.00 (*0-19-856236-5*) OUP.

Science & Practice of Liquid-Liquid Extraction, Vol. 2. Ed. by John D. Thornton. (Engineering Science Ser.: No. 27). (Illus.). 450p. 1992. 135.00 (*0-19-856237-3*) OUP.

***Science & Practice of Occlusion.** Ed. by Charles McNeill. (Illus.). 500p. Date not set. write for info. (*0-86715-304-0*) Quint Pub Co.

Science & Practice of Pediatric Cardiology, 3 vols. Arthur Garson, Jr. et al. LC 90-5544. (Illus.). 2557p. 1990. text ed. 395.00 (*0-8121-1167-2*) Williams & Wilkins.

Science & Practice of Pediatric Cardiology. 2nd ed. Arthur Garson. 1997. write for info. (*0-683-03417-0*) Williams & Wilkins.

Science & Practice of Strength Training. Vladimir M. Zatsiorsky. LC 94-40135. (Illus.). 264p. 1995. text ed. 30.00 (*0-87322-474-4*, BZAT0474) Human Kinetics.

Science & Practice of Welding, Vol. 1: Welding Science & Technology. 10th ed. A. C. Davies. (Illus.). 360p. (C). 1993. text ed. 80.00 (*0-521-43403-3*); pap. text ed. 28.95 (*0-521-43565-X*) Cambridge U Pr.

Science & Practice of Welding, Vol. 2: The Practice of Welding. 10th ed. A. C. Davies. (Illus.). 500p. (C). 1993. text ed. 95.00 (*0-521-43404-1*); pap. text ed. 34.95 (*0-521-43566-8*) Cambridge U Pr.

Science & Practice of Yoga. Swami Paramananda. 1918. pap. 0.75 (*0-911564-31-4*) Vedanta Ctr.

Science & Praxis of Complexity. 384p. 1985. 25.00 (*92-808-0560-6*, E.85.III.A.7) UN.

Science & Psychical Phenomena. G. N. Tyrrell. LC 75-7406. (Perspectives in Psychical Research Ser.). 1975. reprint ed. 34.95 (*0-405-06993-6*) Ayer.

Science & Psychotherapy, Vol. 1. Ed. by Raphael Stern & Louise Horowitz. (Philosophy & Science Ser.). 1979. text ed. 50.00 (*0-930586-02-6*) Haven Pubns.

Science & Psychotherapy, Vol. 2. Raphael Stern. (Philosophy & Science Ser.). 1984. 65.00 (*0-930586-39-5*) Haven Pubns.

Science & Psychotherapy, Vol. 2. Raphael Stern & Esther Robison. (Philosophy & Science Ser.). 1984. pap. 35.00 (*0-317-00882-X*) Haven Pubns.

Science & Public Policy: A Report to the President, 5 Vols. President's Scientific Research Board Staff & John R. Steelman. Ed. by I. Bernard Cohen. LC 79-7998. (Three Centuries of Science in America Ser.). (Illus.). 1980. reprint ed. lib. bdg. 94.95 (*0-405-12586-0*) Ayer.

Science & Public Policy: Uses & Control of Knowledge. Laurel R. Singleton. (Public Issues Ser.). (Illus.). 68p. (YA). (gr. 9-12). 1993. teacher ed., pap. 2.00 (*0-89994-375-6*); pap. 3.50 (*0-89994-376-4*) Soc Sci Ed.

Science & Public Policy II. Intro. by Frances Sterret & Bianca Rosenberg. (Annals Ser.: Vol. 387). 130p. 1982. pap. 28.00 (*0-89766-165-6*) NY Acad Sci.

Science & Public Policy III. 1983. 24.00 (*0-89766-198-2*); pap. 24.00 (*0-89766-199-0*, VOL. 403) NY Acad Sci.

Science & Quiet Art: The Role of Medical Research in Health Care. David Weatherall. 384p. 1996. pap. 15.95 (*0-393-31564-9*) Norton.

***Science & Racket Sports.** Hughes et al. (Illus.). 304p. 1994. text ed. 88.95 (*0-419-18500-3*, E & FN Spon) Routledge Chapman & Hall.

Science & Rationalism in the Government of Louis XIV: 1661-1683. James E. King. LC 78-64207. (Johns Hopkins University. Studies in the Social Sciences. Thirtieth Ser. 1912: 2). reprint ed. 37.50 (*0-404-61312-8*) AMS Pr.

Science & Reason. Henry E. Kyburg, Jr. 304p. 1990. 48.00 (*0-19-506253-1*) OUP.

Science & Reform: Selected Works of Charles Babbage. Charles Babbage. Ed. by Anthony Hyman. (Illus.). 400p. (C). 1989. text ed. 74.95 (*0-521-34311-9*) Cambridge U Pr.

Science & Relativism: Some Key Controversies in the Philosophy of Science. Larry Laudan. LC 90-32112. (Science & Its Conceptual Foundations Ser.). 194p. 1990. pap. text ed. 13.95 (*0-226-46949-2*) U Ch Pr.

Science & Religion. Julian S. Huxley et al. LC 75-84336. (Essay Index Reprint Ser.). 1977. 17.95 (*0-8369-1106-7*) Ayer.

Science & Religion. Swami Ranganathananda. 1979. pap. 3.50 (*0-87481-190-2*, Pub. by Advaita Ashrama II) Vedanta Pr.

Science & Religion: Baden Powell & the Anglican Debate, 1800-1860. Pietro Corsi. 350p. 1988. text ed. 69.95 (*0-521-24245-2*) Cambridge U Pr.

Science & Religion: From Conflict to Conversation. John F. Haught. LC 95-32124. 240p. (Orig.). 1996. pap. 14.95 (*0-8091-3606-6*) Paulist Pr.

Science & Religion: From Conflict to Conversation. John F. Haught. 240p. 1996. 24.95 (*0-8091-0478-4*) Paulist Pr.

Science & Religion: One World - Changing Perspectives on Reality. Ed. by Jan Fennema & Iain Paul. 242p. (C). 1990. lib. bdg. 129.00 (*0-7923-0731-3*, Pub. by Klwr Acad Pubs NE) Kluwer Ac.

Science & Religion: Opposing Viewpoints. Janelle Rohr. LC 87-38066. (Opposing Viewpoints Ser.). (Illus.). 240p. (YA). (gr. 10 up). 1988. pap. text ed. 12.96 (*0-89908-406-0*) Greenhaven.

Science & Religion: Some Historical Perspectives. John H. Brooke. (Cambridge History of Science Ser.). (Illus.). 330p. (C). 1991. text ed. 54.95 (*0-521-23961-3*); pap. text ed. 18.95 (*0-521-28374-4*) Cambridge U Pr.

Science & Religion in the Thought of Nicolas Malebranche. Michael E. Hobart. LC 81-7419. 205p. reprint ed. pap. 58.50 (*0-7837-0306-6*, 2040628) Bks Demand.

Science & Religion Series, 4 Vols. Incl. Threshold of Eternity. John Zachary. (Illus.). 213p. 1994. pap. 9.99 (*0-9640404-1-7*); Scientific Evidence for the Second Coming of Christ. John Zachary. Ed. by Donald Webster. (Illus.). 77p. (Orig.). 1994. pap. 4.99 (*0-9640404-3-3*); Mysterious Numbers of the Sealed Revelation. John Zachary. Ed. by Donald Webster. (Illus.). 87p. (Orig.). 1994. pap. 4.99 (*0-9640404-4-1*); Prophecies of Nostradamus & a Scientific Approach to Scripture. John Zachary. 3.99 (*0-9640404-6-8*); 17.97 (*0-9640404-0-9*) Harvard House.

Science & Religious Thought: A Darwinism Case Study. Walter J. Wilkins. Ed. by Margaret R. Miles. LC 86-24946. (Studies in Religion: No. 3). 224p. reprint ed. 63.60 (*0-8357-1778-X*, 2070477) Bks Demand.

Science & Romance of Selected Herbs Used in Medicine & Religious Ceremony. Anthony K. Andoh. LC 86-617535. (Illus.). 324p. 1986. 27.95 (*0-916299-01-5*) North Scale Co.

Science & Romance of Selected Herbs Used in Medicine & Religious Ceremony. Anthony K. Andoh. (Illus.). 324p. 1991. pap. 19.95 (*0-916299-24-4*) North Scale Co.

Science & Russian Culture in an Age of Revolutions: V. I. Vernadsky & His Scientific School, 1863-1945. Kendall E. Bailes. LC 89-45358. (Indiana-Michigan Series in Russian & East European Studies). (Illus.). 252p. 1990. 12.95 (*0-253-31123-3*) Ind U Pr.

Science & Scepticism. John Watkins. LC 84-42555. (Illus.). 408p. 1984. pap. text ed. 19.95 (*0-691-10171-X*) Princeton U Pr.

Science & Scholarship in Hungary. 2nd ed. Ed. by Tibor Erdey-Gruz & Kalman Kulcsar. 1975. 24.95 (*0-8464-0816-3*) Beekman Pubs.

Science & Science Policy in the Arab World. A. B. Zahlan. LC 79-3380. 1980. text ed. 29.95 (*0-312-70232-9*) St Martin.

Science & Scientists in an Agricultural Research Organization: A Sociological Study. Norman W. Storer. Ed. by Harriet Zuckerman & Robert K. Merton. LC 79-9029. (Dissertations on Sociology Ser.). 1980. lib. bdg. 23.95 (*0-405-12996-3*) Ayer.

Science & Secrets of Wheat Trading, Vol. 6. Burton H. Pugh. 234p. 1980. pap. text ed. 60.00 (*0-939093-10-3*) Lambert Gann Pub.

Science & Secrets of Winning in Futures. Henry Clasing. 400p. 1992. 50.00 (*0-930233-52-2*, W72) Windsor.

Science & Security: Nuclear & Conventional Forces in Europe: Colloquium Proceedings, September 28-29, 1987, Arlington, Virginia. Ed. by W. Thomas Wander & Kenneth N. Luongo. (AAAS Publication Ser.: No. 88-3). 314p. reprint ed. pap. 89.50 (*0-7837-0056-3*, 2040303) Bks Demand.

Science & Security: The Future of Arms Control. American Association for the Advancement of Science Staff. Ed. by W. James Wander et al. (AAA Publication: No. 86-16). 229p. reprint ed. pap. 65.30 (*0-8357-6435-4*, 2035806) Bks Demand.

Science & Security: The Future of Arms Control: Colloquium Proceedings. Ed. by W. Thomas Wander & Kenneth N. Luongo. (AAAS Miscellaneous Publications: No. 86-17). 334p. reprint ed. pap. 95.20 (*0-7837-0071-7*, 2040318) Bks Demand.

Science & Sense in the Book of Books. John Stout. (Illus.). 235p. 1992. 15.95 (*0-9626122-0-0*) Stout Pub.

Science & Sensibility. G. R. Dunstan & F. D. Maruice. 1982. 30.00 (*0-317-43865-4*) St Mut.

Science & Serendipity. Wendy B. Murphy. LC 93-74286. write for info. (*0-87502-249-9*) Benjamin Co.

Science & Service: A History of the Land-Grant University & Agriculture in California. Ann F. Scheuring. LC 94-60131. (Illus.). 288p. 1995. write for info. (*1-879906-17-1*, 3360) ANR Pubns CA.

Science & Service in Mental Retardation: Proceedings of the Seventh Congress of the International Association for the Scientific Study of Mental Deficiency. Ed. by Joseph M. Berg. 512p. 1986. text ed. 47.50 (*0-416-40650-5*, 1042) Routledge Chapman & Hall.

***Science & Skiing.** Muller et al. (Illus.). 626p. 1997. text ed. 94.95 (*0-419-20850-X*, E & FN Spon) Routledge Chapman & Hall.

***Science & Soccer.** T. Reilly. (Illus.). 408p. 1995. pap. text ed. 36.50 (*0-419-18880-0*, E & FN Spon) Routledge Chapman & Hall.

Science & Social Change. Compiled by Jesse E. Thornton. LC 72-357. (Essay Index Reprint Ser.). 1977. reprint ed. 31.95 (*0-8369-2830-X*) Ayer.

Science & Social Science Research in British India, 1780-1880: The Role of Anglo-Indian Associations & Government. Edward W. Ellsworth. LC 90-38421. (Contributions in Comparative Colonial Studies: No. 28). 240p. 1991. text ed. 59.95 (*0-313-26674-3*, EIN, Greenwood Pr) Greenwood.

Science & Social Status: The Members of the Academie des Sciences 1666-1750. David Sturdy. (Illus.). 477p. (C). 1995. 117.00 (*0-85115-395-X*) Boydell & Brewer.

Science & Social Structure: A Festschrift for Robert K. Merton. LC 80-13464. (Transaction Ser.: Vol. 39). 173p. 1980. 17.00 (*0-89766-043-9*) NY Acad Sci.

Science & Socialist Construction in China. Liang-Ying Hsu & Fan Dainian. Ed. by Pierre M. Perrolle. Tr. by John C. Hsu. LC 81-23250. (China Book Project). 253p. 1982. reprint ed. pap. 72.20 (*0-7837-9975-6*, 2060702) Bks Demand.

Science & Society. Ed. & Intro. by Martin Moskovits. (John C. Polanyi Nobel Laureates Lectures). 168p. 1995. 19.95 (*0-88784-170-8*, Pub. by Hse of Anansi Pr CN) Genl Dist Srvs.

Science & Society. 2nd ed. Joan Y. Gregg & Joan Russell. 384p. (C). 1996. pap. text ed. 26.46 (*0-7872-1226-1*) Kendall-Hunt.

Science & Society. Ed. by Norman Kaplan. LC 74-26271. (History, Philosophy & Sociology of Science Ser.). 1975. reprint ed. 51.95 (*0-405-06599-X*) Ayer.

Science & Society: Historical Essays on the Relations of Science, Technology & Medicine. A. Rupert Hall. (Collected Studies: No. CS 434). (Illus.). 350p. 1994. 89.95 (*0-86078-400-2*, Pub. by Variorum UK) Ashgate Pub Co.

Science & Society: Knowing, Teaching, Learning. Cheryl Charles. Ed. by Bob Samples. LC 78-70847. (National Council for the Social Studies Bulletin: No. 57). 96p. reprint ed. pap. 27.40 (*0-317-39643-9*, 2023190) Bks Demand.

***Science & Society: Redefining the Relationship.** 88p. 1996. pap. 7.50 (*0-614-30593-4*) Ed Comm States.

Science & Society: Selected Essays in the Sociology of Science. Joseph Agassi. 550p. 1981. lib. bdg. 175.00 (*90-277-1244-1*, D Reidel) Kluwer Ac.

Science & Society: Some Perspectives. Ed. by Yash Pal et al. (C). 32.00 (*81-212-0458-5*, Pub. by Gian Publng Hse II) S Asia.

S

***Science & Society: The John C. Polanyi Nobel Laureates Lectures.** Martin Moskivits. 168p. 1997. 13.95 (0-88784-589-4, Pub. by Hse of Anansi Pr CN) Genl Dist Srvs.

Science & Society: Writer's Library. HarperCollins Staff. (C). 1993. text ed. 9.50 (0-06-501126-0) Addson-Wesley Educ.

Science & Society General Index: Volumes 26-50 (1962 to 1986-87) Ed. by David Laibman. LC 88-83178. 230p. 1989. lib. bdg. 50.00 (0-89862-380-4) Guilford Pr.

Science & Society in Early America: Essays in Honor of Whitfield J. Bell, Jr. Ed. by Randolph S. Klein. LC 85-71740. (Memoirs Ser.: Vol. 166). 300p. 1986. 30.00 (0-87169-166-3, M166-KLR) Am Philos.

Science & Society in Restoration England. Michael Hunter. (Modern Revivals in History Ser.). 260p. 1992. 59.95 (0-7512-0075-1, Pub. by Gregg Revivals UK) Ashgate Pub Co.

Science & Society Sixteen Hundred to Nineteen Hundred. Ed. by Peter Mathias. LC 76-172833. 174p. reprint ed. pap. 49.60 (0-318-34821-7, 2031688) Bks Demand.

Science & Sociological Practice. Steven Yearley. 160p. 1984. 63.00 (0-335-10584-X, Open Univ Pr); pap. 25.00 (0-335-10581-5, Open Univ Pr) Taylor & Francis.

Science & Spirit. Ed. by Ravi Ravindra. LC 90-6962. (ICUS Ser.). 433p. (C). 1990. text ed. 29.95 (0-89226-085-8, ICUS); pap. text ed. 14.95 (0-89226-082-3, ICUS) Paragon Hse.

Science & Spirit: The Meaning of Psychical Research for Religion, Set. Ed. by Frank C. Tribbe. (Spiritual Frontiers Fellowship Thirtieth Anniversary Booklet Ser.: Vol. I, No. 3). 1986. 12.00 (0-317-68876-6) Spirit Front Fellow.

Science & Stewardship in the Antarctic. National Research Council Staff. 127p. (Orig.). (C). 1993. pap. text ed. 25.00 (0-309-04947-4) Natl Acad Pr.

***Science & Stonehenge.** Ed. by Barry Cunliffe & Colin Renfrew. (Proceedings of the British Academy: Vol. 92). (Illus.). 384p. 1997. 70.00 (0-19-726174-4) OUP.

Science & Stories: Integrating Science & Literature, Grades 4-6. Hilarie N. Staton & Tara McCarthy. (Illus.). 160p. (Orig.). 1994. pap. 12.95 (0-673-36084-9, GoodYrBooks) Addson-Wesley Educ.

Science & Stories: Integrating Science & Literature, K-3. Hilarie N. Staton & Tara McCarthy. (Illus.). 152p. (Orig.). 1994. pap. 12.95 (0-673-36083-0, GoodYrBooks) Addson-Wesley Educ.

Science & Subjectivity. 2nd ed. Israel Scheffler. LC 81-85414. 178p. (C). 1982. reprint ed. pap. text ed. 8.95 (0-915145-30-8); reprint ed. lib. bdg. 27.95 (0-915145-31-6) Hackett Pub.

Science & Supernature: A Critical Appraisal of Parapsychology. James Alcock. 186p. 1989. 30.95 (0-87975-548-2) Prometheus Bks.

Science & Technical Library. Creeh. 1994. pap. text ed. 39.95 incl. cd-rom (1-57176-058-X) Walnut Creek.

Science & Technical Writing: A Manual of Style. Philip Rubens. LC 91-36422. 544p. 1994. pap. 19.95 (0-8050-3091-3) H Holt & Co.

Science & Technlogy in China, Vol. II. Chinese Academy of Sciences Staff. (International Academic Publishers Ser.). (Illus.). 550p. 1989. 200.00 (0-08-036386-5, Pergamon Pr) Elsevier.

Science & Technology. (Illus.). 160p. (J). 1993. 35.00 (0-19-910143-4) OUP.

***Science & Technology.** Central Office of Info. (Aspects of Britain Ser.). (Illus.). 115p. 1995. pap. 9.95 (0-11-701947-X, Pub. by Stationery Ofc UK) Seven Hills Bk.

Science & Technology. Frank H. Osborne. 80p. (C). 1994. pap. text ed., spiral bd. 17.85 (0-8403-9569-8) Kendall-Hunt.

Science & Technology. Lisa Watts. (Illustrated Encyclopedia Ser.). (Illus.). 96p. (J). (gr. 4 up). 1996. 16.95 (0-7460-1796-0, Usborne) EDC.

Science & Technology. Brian Williams. LC 92-46589. (Visual Factfinders Ser.). (Illus.). 96p. 1993. pap. 9.95 (1-85697-849-4, Kingfisher LKC) LKC.

Science & Technology: Between Civilian & Military Research & Development. (UNIDIR Research Papers: No. 7). 23p. 1992. 10.00 (0-685-52976-2) UN.

Science & Technology: Pocket Data Book (1993) (Illus.). 58p. (Orig.). (C). 1993. pap. text ed. 25.00 (1-56806-611-2) DIANE Pub.

Science & Technology: Pocket Data Book (1994) Ed. by Deborah A. Collins. (Illus.). 57p. (Orig.). (C). 1995. pap. text ed. 25.00 (0-7881-1745-9) DIANE Pub.

Science & Technology: Vital National Resources. Ed. by Ralph Sanders. LC 74-17562. 146p. 1975. 12.50 (0-912338-11-3); fiche 9.50 (0-912338-12-1) Lomond.

Science & Technology Advice: To the President, Congress, & Judiciary. 2nd ed. Ed. & Intro. by William T. Golden. LC 92-36148. 529p. (C). 1994. reprint ed. pap. 27.95 (0-87168-510-8, 93-09S) Transaction Pubs.

Science & Technology Advice to the President, Congress & Judiciary. Ed. by William T. Golden. LC 95-10334. 1995. pap. 29.95 (1-56000-829-6) Transaction Pubs.

Science & Technology & the Changing World Order (Fiscal Year 1991) Susan L. Sauer. 297p. 1990. 12.00 (0-87168-386-5, 90-32S) AAAS.

Science & Technology & the Implications for Peace & Security. (Disarmament Topical Papers: No. 2). 159p. 1990. 13.50 (92-1-142159-4, 90.IX.8) UN.

Science & Technology Centers. Victor J. Danilov. (Illus.). 416p. (C). 1982. 52.50 (0-262-04068-9) MIT Pr.

Science & Technology Desk Reference: Answers to Frequently Asked & Difficult to Answer Reference Questions in Science & Technology. Carnegie Library of Pittsburgh, Department of Science & Technology Staff. 375p. 1992. 45.00 (0-8103-8884-7, 101535) Gale.

Science & Technology Desk Refrence: 1,700 Answers to Frequently-Asked or Difficult to Answer Questions. 2nd ed. Carnegie Library of Pittsburgh Staff. LC 96-26601. 1996. 50.00 (0-8103-9176-7) Gale.

Science & Technology Education & Future Human Needs, Vol. 1. Ed. by J. L. Lewis & P. J. Kelly. LC 87-7020. (STEF Ser.: No. 1). (Illus.). 130p. 1987. 93.00 (0-08-033909-3, Pub. by Pergamon Repr UK) Franklin.

Science & Technology Firsts. Len Bruno. LC 96-43595. 1996. 65.00 (0-7876-0256-6) Gale.

Science & Technology for Rural Development. Upendra Kunwar. (C). 1991. 22.50 (81-7100-299-4, Pub. by Deep II) S Asia.

***Science & Technology in a Developing World.** Terry Shinn et al. LC 96-52464. (Sociology of the Sciences Yearbook Ser.). 1997. lib. bdg. write for info. (0-7923-4419-7) Kluwer Ac.

Science & Technology in a Multicultural World: The Cultural Politics of Facts & Artifacts. David J. Hess. LC 94-34733. 1995. 49.50 (0-231-10196-1); pap. 18.00 (0-231-10197-X) Col U Pr.

Science & Technology in Africa. 1994. write for info. (0-8103-9701-3, Pub. by Longman Grp UK) Gale.

Science & Technology in Africa. 281p. 1989. text ed. 115.00 (0-582-00086-6) Longman.

Science & Technology in African History with Case Studies from Nigeria, Sierra Leone, Zimbabwe, & Zambia. Ed. by Gloria Thomas-Emeagwali. LC 92-19201. (Illus.). 216p. (ENG & FRE.). 1992. lib. bdg. 89.95 (0-7734-9557-6) E Mellen.

Science & Technology in Australasia, Antartica, & Pacific Islands. Ed. by D. Alsmeyer & A. G. Atkins. 540p. 1989. 95.00 (0-582-90060-3, Pub. by Longman Grp UK) Gale.

Science & Technology in British Politics. N. Vig. LC 68-21389. 1968. 92.00 (0-08-012737-1, Pub. by Pergamon Repr UK) Franklin.

Science & Technology in Canada. 1993. 175.00 (0-582-10106-9, 101871, Pub. by Longman Grp UK) Gale.

Science & Technology in Catalysis 1994. Ed. by Yushiko Izumi et al. (Studies in Surface Science & Catalysis: Vol. 92). 496p. 1995. 324.25 (0-444-82189-9) Elsevier.

Science & Technology in Central & Eastern Europe: The Reform of Higher Education. Anthony Tillet & Barry Lesser. Ed. by Philip Altbach. LC 95-48374. (Studies in Higher Education: Vol. 8). (Illus.). 232p. 1996. text ed. 45.00 (0-8153-1768-9, SS991) Garland.

Science & Technology in China. Tong B. Tang. (Guides to World Science & Technology Ser.). 269p. 1900. pap. text ed. 88.00 (0-582-90056-5, 076398-99584) Longman.

Science & Technology in China. 2nd ed. Denis F. Simon. 500p. 1996. 95.00 (1-56159-134-3, Stockton Pr) Groves Dictionaries.

Science & Technology in China: A Source Guide. 1991. lib. bdg. 72.00 (0-8490-4900-8) Gordon Pr.

Science & Technology in China Vol. 3: Selections from the Bulletin of the Chinese Academy of Sciences. Ed. by Chinese Academy of Sciences Bulletin Editorial Department Staff. 592p. 1990. lib. bdg. 130.00 (3-527-28106-1, VCH) Wiley.

Science & Technology in China, Vol. 4: Selections from the Bulletin of the Chinese Academy of Sciences. Ed. by Department of the Bulletin of the Chinese Academy of Sciences Staff. 583p. 1990. lib. bdg. 120.00 (3-527-28107-X, VCH) Wiley.

Science & Technology in China, Vol. 5: Selections from the Bulletin of the Chinese Academy of Sciences. (Bulletin of the Chinese Academy of Sciences). 540p. 1992. lib. bdg. 105.00 (3-527-28406-0, VCH) Wiley.

Science & Technology in Chinese Civilization: Proceedings of the Workshop held at the University of California, San Diego, California, September 1985. Ed. by C. Y. Chen. 372p. 1987. text ed. 89.00 (9971-5-0192-9) World Scientific Pub.

Science & Technology in Eastern Europe. Ed. by Gyorgy Darvas. 283p. 1988. 114.00 (0-582-90054-9, Longman) Gale.

Science & Technology in Fact & Fiction: A Guide to Children's Books. DayAnn M. Kennedy et al. 319p. 1990. 38.00 (0-8352-2708-1) Bowker.

Science & Technology in Fact & Fiction: A Guide to Young Adult Books. DayAnn M. Kennedy et al. 363p. 1990. 38.00 (0-8352-2710-3) Bowker.

Science & Technology in France - Belgium. 2nd ed. 1991. 100.00 (0-685-48430-0, 076464, Pub. by Longman Grp UK) Gale.

Science & Technology in France & Belgium. E. Walter Kellermann. (Guides to World Science & Technology Ser.). 131p. 1988. 100.00 (0-582-00084-X, 076401-99584) Longman.

Science & Technology in Germany. (Guides to World Science & Technology Ser.). 550p. 1990. 115.00 (0-685-49085-8, 076418-M99406) Longman.

Science & Technology in Germany. Wilhelm Krull & Frieder Meyer-Krahmer. 500p. 1996. 95.00 (1-56159-196-3, Stockton Pr) Groves Dictionaries.

Science & Technology in History: An Approach to Industrial Development. Ian Inkster. LC 90-24557. 400p. (C). 1991. text ed. 50.00 (0-8135-1680-3) Rutgers U Pr.

Science & Technology in India. 1991. 138.00 (0-582-06469-4) Longman.

Science & Technology in India. Ed. by Vadilal Dagli. 345p. 1982. text ed. 22.00 (0-685-13747-3) Coronet Bks.

Science & Technology in India. Ed. by B. R. Nanda. 1978. 9.00 (0-8364-0170-0) S Asia.

Science & Technology in India. 2nd ed. 1996. write for info. (0-8103-9714-5, 076471, Pub. by Longman Grp UK) Gale.

Science & Technology in Japan. Alun M. Anderson. (Guides to World Science & Technology Ser.). 421p. 1984. 88.00 (0-582-90015-8, 076403-99584) Longman.

Science & Technology in Japan. 2nd ed. Alun M. Anderson. 350p. 1991. text ed. 149.00 (0-582-03684-4) Longman.

Science & Technology in Japan. 3rd ed. 1995. write for info. (0-8103-9710-2, 076465, Pub. by Longman Grp UK) Gale.

Science & Technology in Japan. 3rd ed. Jon Sigurdson. 500p. 1995. 95.00 (1-56159-135-1, Stockton Pr) Groves Dictionaries.

Science & Technology in Judicial Decision Making: Creating Opportunities & Meeting Challenges. Carnegie Commission on Science, Technology, & Government Staff & Helene L. Kaplan. 92p. (Orig.). 1993. pap. write for info. (1-881054-08-X) Carnegie Comm Sci.

Science & Technology in Latin America. 1983. 88.00 (0-582-90057-3, Pub. by Longman Grp UK) Gale.

Science & Technology in Latin America. 3rd ed. 1995. write for info. (0-8103-9704-8, 0763920, Pub. by Longman Grp UK) Gale.

Science & Technology in Latin America. 93th ed. 1994. fiche 399.00 (0-8103-9909-1, 076391, Pub. by Longman Grp UK) Gale.

Science & Technology in Medieval Society. Intro. by Pamela O. Long. (Annals Ser.: Vol. 441). 224p. 1984. pap. 50.00 (0-89766-277-6); lib. bdg. 50.00 (0-89766-276-8) NY Acad Sci.

Science & Technology in New York City for the 21st Century: Report by the Mayor's Commission for Science & Technology. George Bugliarello. 20p. (Orig.). 1989. pap. text ed. write for info. (0-918902-26-6) Polytechnic Pr.

Science & Technology in Post-Mao China. Ed. by Denis F. Simon & Merle R. Goldman. LC 88-28456. (Contemporary China Ser.: No. 5). 460p. 1989. pap. 18.00 (0-674-79475-3) Coun East Asian Stud.

Science & Technology in Providence, 1760-1914: An Essay in the History of Brown University in the Metropolitan Community. Donald Fleming. LC 52-9555. (Brown University Papers: No. 26). 52p. reprint ed. 25.00 (0-685-15639-7, 2027504) Bks Demand.

Science & Technology in Relation to Rural Women. Ed. by Anjali Bahuguna. (C). 1995. 28.00 (81-241-0359-3, Pub. by Har-Anand Pubns II) S Asia.

Science & Technology in Saudi Arabia. Tarek A. Fadaak et al. LC 95-30696. (Illus.). 187p. 1995. pap. 15.00 (0-915957-30-2) amana pubns.

Science & Technology in Scandinavia. 1989. 115.00 (0-582-01892-7, Pub. by Longman Grp UK) Gale.

Science & Technology in Scandinavia. 2nd ed. 1994. write for info. (0-8103-9700-5, 076467, Pub. by Longman Grp UK) Gale.

Science & Technology in South Asia. Ed. by Peter Gaeffke & David A. Utz. LC 85-29476. (Proceedings of the South Asia Seminar Ser.: No. 2). (Illus.). x, 171p. (Orig.). 1985. pap. text ed. 10.00 (0-936115-01-7) U Penn South Asia.

Science & Technology in Southeast Asia. 93th ed. 1994. 263.00 incl. fiche (0-8103-9911-3, 076393, Pub. by Longman Grp UK) Gale.

Science & Technology in the Academic Enterprise: Status, Trends, & Issues. National Academy of Engineering Staff et al. 120p. 1989. pap. text ed. 15.00 (0-309-04175-9) Natl Acad Pr.

Science & Technology in the Developing World: Liberation or Dependence? Ed. by Thomas F. Gieryn & Hollis R. Johnson. (Lecture Ser.). 250p. (Orig.). 1992. pap. 5.00 (1-881157-19-9) In Ctr Global.

Science & Technology in the Early Years: An Equal Opportunities Approach. Ed. by Naima Browne. (Gender & Education Ser.). 160p. 1990. 27.00 (0-335-09229-2, Open Univ Pr) Taylor & Francis.

Science & Technology in the Federal Republic of Germany. Frieder Meyer-Krahmer. (Guides to World Science & Technology Ser.). 480p. 1990. 115.00 (0-582-05439-7, 076418-99584) Longman.

Science & Technology in the Federal Republic of Germany 2. 1995. write for info. (0-8103-9705-6, Pub. by Longman Grp UK) Gale.

Science & Technology in the Industrial Revolution. Ed. by A. E. Musson & E. Robinson. (Classics in the History & Philosophy of Science Ser.: Vol. 3). xii, 534p. 1969. pap. text ed. 62.00 (2-88124-382-7) Gordon & Breach.

Science & Technology in the Mid East. 93th ed. 1994. 672.00 incl. fiche (0-8103-9910-5, 076396, Pub. by Longman Grp UK) Gale.

Science & Technology in the Middle East: A Guide to Issues, Organizations & Institutions. Ed. by Ziauddin Sardar. (Longman Guide to World Science & Technology Ser.: Vol. 1). 324p. 1993. 88.00 (0-582-90052-2, Pub. by Longman Grp UK) Gale.

Science & Technology in the U. K. 2nd ed. 1996. write for info. (0-8103-9713-7, 076470, Pub. by Longman Grp UK) Gale.

Science & Technology in the U. S. A. 93th ed. 1994. 764.00 incl. fiche (0-8103-9912-1, 076416, Pub. by Longman Grp UK) Gale.

Science & Technology in the U. S. S. R. Michael J. Berry. (Guides to World Science & Technology Ser.). 405p. 1988. text ed. 95.00 (0-582-90053-0, 076405-99584) Longman.

Science & Technology in the U. S. S. R. 2nd ed. 1995. write for info. (0-8103-9711-0, 076466, Pub. by Longman Grp UK) Gale.

Science & Technology in the United Kingdom. 1990. pap. text ed. 162.00 (0-582-90051-4) Longman.

Science & Technology in the United States of America. Albert H. Teich & Jill H. Pace. (Guides to World Science & Technology Ser.). 408p. 1986. 95.00 (0-582-90061-1, 076406-99584) Longman.

Science & Technology in U. S. International Affairs. Carnegie Commission on Science, Technology, & Government Staff. (Illus.). 125p. (Orig.). 1992. pap. write for info. (1-881054-00-4) Carnegie Comm Sci.

Science & Technology Issues in Coastal Ecotourism. 1994. lib. bdg. 250.00 (0-8490-6476-7) Gordon Pr.

Science & Technology Leadership in America Government: Ensuring the Best Presidential Appointments. National Academy of Sciences Staff et al. 104p. (C). 1992. pap. text ed. 12.95 (0-309-04727-7) Natl Acad Pr.

Science & Technology Museums. Stella Butler. (Leicester Museum Studies Ser.). 256p. (C). 1992. text ed. 54.00 (0-7185-1357-6) St Martin.

Science & Technology of Adhesive Bonding: Proceedings of the Thirty-Fifth Sagamore Army Materials Research Conference Held June 25-30, 1988, at Bedford, New Hampshire. Ed. by L. H. Sharpe & S. E. Wentworth. viii, 370p. 1990. text ed. 152.00 (2-88124-388-6) Gordon & Breach.

Science & Technology of Agriculture: A Biological Approach. H. R. Herren. (Agriculture Ser.). 560p. 1996. text ed. 37.95 (0-8273-5811-3) Delmar.

***Science & Technology of Atomically Engineered Materials: Proceedings of the International Symposium.** 664p. 1996. 94.00 (981-02-2609-8) World Scientific Pub.

Science & Technology of Building Seals, Sealants, Glazing, & Waterproofing, Vol. 2. Ed. by Jerome M. Klosowski. (Special Technical Publication Ser.: No. STP 1200). (Illus.). 330p. 1992. text ed. 53.00 (0-8031-1857-0, 04-012000-10) ASTM.

***Science & Technology of Building Seals, Sealants, Glazing, & Waterproofing, Vol. 4.** Ed. by D. H. Nicastro. 149p. 1995. pap. 48.00 (0-8031-2008-7) ASTM.

***Science & Technology of Building Seals, Sealants, Glazing & Waterproofing, Vol. 5.** Ed. by Michael A. Lacasse. (Special Technical Publication Ser.: No. 1271). (Illus.). 320p. Date not set. text ed. 63.00 (0-8031-2049-4, 04-012710-10) ASTM.

***Science & Technology of Building Seals, Sealants, Glazing & Waterproofing, Vol. 6.** James C. Myers. (STP 1286 Ser.). (Illus.). 163p. 1996. pap. text ed. 47.00 (0-8031-2044-3, 04-012860-10) ASTM.

Science & Technology of Building Seals, Sealants, Glazing & Waterproofing Vol. 3. Ed. by James C. Myers. (Special Technical Publication: No. 1254). (Illus.). 106p. 1994. text ed. 59.00 (0-8031-1993-3, 04-012540-10) ASTM.

Science & Technology of Ceramic Fuel Cells. Nguyen Q. Minh & Takehiko Takahashi. LC 95-21137. 378p. 1995. 181.50 (0-444-89568-X) Elsevier.

***Science & Technology of Civil Engineering Materials.** J. F. Young et al. 432p. (C). 1997. pap. text ed. 81.00 (0-13-659749-1) P-H.

Science & Technology of Coal & Coal Utilization. Ed. by Bernard R. Cooper & William A. Ellingson. 682p. 1984. 135.00 (0-306-41436-8, Plenum Pr) Plenum.

Science & Technology of Electroceramic Thin Films. LC 94-48303. 1995. lib. bdg. 211.00 (0-7923-3332-2) Kluwer Ac.

Science & Technology of Fast Ion Conductors. Ed. by H. L. Tuller & M. Balkanski. (NATO ASI, Series B: Physics: Vol. 199). (Illus.). 372p. 1990. 110.00 (0-306-43218-8, Plenum Pr) Plenum.

Science & Technology of Fructan. Michio Suzuki. Ed. by N. J. Chatterton. 384p. 1993. 218.00 (0-8493-5111-1, QP702) CRC Pr.

Science & Technology of Glazing Systems. Ed. by Charles J. Parise. LC 89-28496. (Special Technical Publication Ser.: No. 1054). (Illus.). 150p. 1990. text ed. 29.00 (0-8031-1286-6, 04-010540-10) ASTM.

Science & Technology of Mesoscopic Structures. Ed. by S. Namba et al. LC 92-30098. 1993. write for info. (4-431-70090-0); write for info. (3-540-70090-0); 218.95 (0-387-70090-0) Spr-Verlag.

Science & Technology of Microfabrication. Ed. by S. Namba et al. (MRS Symposium Proceedings Ser.: Vol. 76). 1987. text ed. 17.50 (0-931837-42-1) Materials Res.

Science & Technology of Nanostructured Magnetic Materials. Ed. by G. C. Hadjipanayis & G. Prinz. (NATO ASI, Series B: Physics: Vol. 259). (Illus.). 690p. 1991. 159.50 (0-306-43924-7, Plenum Pr) Plenum.

***Science & Technology of Photography.** K. Keller. (Illus.). xiii, 260p. 1993. 140.00 (3-527-28611-X, VCH) Wiley.

Science & Technology of Polymer Processing: Proceedings of the International Conference on Polymer Processing. Ed. by Nam P. Suh & Nak-Ho Sung. (Illus.). 1979. 85.00 (0-262-19179-2) MIT Pr.

Science & Technology of Rapid Solidification & Processing: Proceedings of the NATO Advanced Research Workshop, West Point Military Academy, New York, NY, U. S. A., June 21-24, 1994. Ed. by Monde A. Otooni. (NATO Advanced Science Institutes: Series E). 392p. (C). 1994. lib. bdg. 194.00 (0-7923-3203-2) Kluwer Ac.

Science & Technology of Rapidly Quenched Alloys. Ed. by M. Tenhover et al. (MRS Symposium Proceedings Ser.: Vol. 80). 1987. text ed. 17.50 (0-931837-45-6) Materials Res.

Science & Technology of Rubber. 2nd ed. Ed. by James E. Mark et al. (Illus.). 751p. 1994. text ed. 90.00 (0-12-472525-2) Acad Pr.

***Science & Technology of Semiconductor Surface Preparation: Materials Research Society Symposium Proceedings, Vol. 477.** Ed. by G. S. Higashi et al. 1997. text ed. 68.00 (1-55899-381-9) Materials Res.

Science & Technology of the Undercooled Melt: Rapid Solidification Materials & Technologies. Ed. by P. R. Sahm et al. 1986. lib. bdg. 139.00 (*90-247-3386-3*) Kluwer Ac.

Science & Technology of Thin Film Superconductors. Ed. by R. D. McConnell & Stuart A. Wolf. (Illus.). 572p. 1989. 125.00 (*0-306-43215-3*, Plenum Pr) Plenum.

Science & Technology of Thin Film Superconductors 2. Ed. by R. D. McConnell & Rommel Noufi. (Illus.). 650p. 1990. 135.00 (*0-306-43803-8*, Plenum Pr) Plenum.

Science & Technology of Thin Films. Ed. by F. C. Matacotta & G. Ottaviani. LC 95-24958. 300p. 1995. text ed. 86.00 (*981-02-2193-2*) World Scientific Pub.

Science & Technology of Traditional & Modern Roofing Systems: "The New Bible of Roofing", 2 Vols. Heshmat O. Laaly. LC 91-90263. (Illus.). 3152p. (C). 1992. 350.00 (*0-9629669-0-8*) Laaly Sci.

Science & Technology of Tributyl Phosphate, 2 vols., Set. James D. Navratil. Ed. by Wallace W. Schultz. LC 83-7774. 1987. 177.00 (*0-8493-6397-7*, QD305, CRC Reprint) Franklin.

Science & Technology of Tributyl Phosphate, 5 vols., Set. Wallace W. Schultz & James D. Navratil. 1991. reprint ed. 742.00 (*0-8493-6395-0*, CRC Reprint) Franklin.

Science & Technology of Tributyl Phosphate, 2 vols., Vol. I. Ed. by Wallace W. Schulz. 352p. 1987. write for info. (*0-318-62348-X*) CRC Pr.

Science & Technology of Tributyl Phosphate, 2 vols., Vol. II. Ed. by Wallace W. Schulz. 295p. 1987. write for info. (*0-318-62349-8*) CRC Pr.

Science & Technology of Tributyl Phosphate: Application of Tributyl Phosphate in Nuclear Fuel Reprocessing, Vol. 3. rev. ed. Ed. by Wallace W. Schultz et al. LC 83-7774. (Science & Technology of Tributyl Phosphate Ser.). 256p. 1990. 154.00 (*0-8493-6389-6*, QD305) Franklin.

Science & Technology of Tributyl Phosphate: Extraction of Water & Acids, Vol. 4. rev. ed. Wallace W. Schultz et al. LC 83-7774. (Illus.). 352p. 1991. 218.00 (*0-8493-6393-4*, QD305) Franklin.

Science & Technology of Tributyl Phosphate: Selected Technical & Industrial Uses, Vol. II. Ed. by Wallace W. Schultz & James D. Navratil. 295p. 1987. 190.00 (*0-317-61081-3*, CRC Reprint) Franklin.

Science & Technology of Tributyl Phosphate Vol. 1: Synthesis, Properties, Reactions, & Analysis. James D. Navratil & Wallace W. Schulz. LC 83-774. 1984. 194.00 (*0-8493-6396-9*, QD305, CRC Reprint) Franklin.

Science & Technology of Tributyl Phosphate Vol. 2, Pt. A: Selected Technical & Industrial Uses. James D. Navratil & Wallace W. Schultz. LC 83-7774. 1987. 84.00 (*0-8493-6398-5*, QD305, CRC Reprint) Franklin.

Science & Technology of Tributyl Phosphate Vol. 2, Pt. B: Selected Technical & Industrial Uses. James D. Navratil & Wallace W. Schultz. LC 83-7774. 1987. 94.00 (*0-8493-6399-3*, QD305, CRC Reprint) Franklin.

Science & Technology of Wood. George T. Tsoumis. (Illus.). 400p. 1991. text ed. 67.95 (*0-442-23985-8*) Chapman & Hall.

***Science & Technology of Wood.** George T. Tsoumis. (Illus.). 494p. (C). (gr. 13 up). 1991. text ed. 67.95 (*0-412-07851-1*) Chapman & Hall.

Science & Technology of Zirconia II. International Conference on the Science & Technology of Zirconia Staff. Ed. by Nils Claussen et al. LC 84-14498. (Advances in Ceramics Ser.: No. 12). (Illus.). 856p. reprint ed. pap. 180.00 (*0-7837-4340-8*, 2044050) Bks Demand.

Science & Technology on the Internet: An Instructional Guide. Gail P. Clement. 228p. 1995. pap. 45.00 (*1-882208-12-9*) Library Solns.

Science & Technology on the Internet PLUS: Instructor's Supplement, Incl. inst. guide. variorum ed. Gail P. Clement. (Internet Workshop Ser.: No. 4). vi, 40p. 1995. disk 60.00 (*1-882208-13-7*) Library Solns.

Science & Technology Planning & Policy. F. Bilich. 304p. 1989. 136.25 (*0-444-87491-7*) Elsevier.

Science & Technology Policies in Finland & Hungary: A Comparative Study. R. O. Donner & L. Pal. 372p. 1985. 225.00 (*0-569-08860-7*, Pub. by Collets) St Mut.

***Science & Technology Policy.** Ed. by Feller. (C). 1998. text ed. write for info. (*0-321-01127-9*) Addson-Wesley Educ.

Science & Technology Policy. Ed. by Joseph Haberer. (C). 1976. pap. 15.00 (*0-918592-17-8*) Pol Studies.

Science & Technology Policy: Perspectives & Developments. Joseph Haberer. 240p. 1985. reprint ed. lib. bdg. 44.50 (*0-8191-5147-5*, Pol Studies) U Pr of Amer.

Science & Technology Policy: Review & Outlook 1994. OECD Staff. 250p. (Orig.). 1994. pap. 46.00 (*92-64-14237-1*) OECD.

Science & Technology Policy: U. S. Dept. of Agriculture. 56p. (Orig.). (C). 1993. pap. text ed. 30.00 (*1-56806-661-9*) DIANE Pub.

Science & Technology Policy for Economic Development in Africa. Ed. by Aqueil Ahmad. LC 92-40437. (International Studies in Sociology & Social Anthropology: Vol. 61). 1992. pap. 46.50 (*90-04-09659-0*) E J Brill.

Science & Technology Policy in Interdependent Economies. David C. Mowery. LC 93-41058. 320p. (C). 1994. lib. bdg. 128.00 (*0-7923-9422-4*) Kluwer Ac.

Science & Technology Policy in the U. S. A. 2nd ed. Chris Hill. 1996. 95.00 (*1-56159-133-5*, Stockton Pr) Groves Dictionaries.

Science & Technology Programs in the States, 1992. Paul B. Phelps & Paul R. Brockman. 96p. 1992. pap. 30.00 (*0-9632443-0-2*) Adv Develop.

Science & Technology Today. Mackenzie. 1994. teacher ed., pap. text ed. 0.42 (*0-312-09690-9*) St Martin.

Science & Technology Today. Nancy MacKenzie. 560p. 1994. pap. text ed. 21.00 (*0-312-09692-5*) St Martin.

Science & Technology Under Free Trade. Ed. by John De La Mothe & Louis Ducharme. 250p. 1990. text ed. 39.00 (*0-86187-728-4*) St Martin.

Science & Technology Year Book 1992. Collier. 1992. 45.00 (*0-02-527175-X*) Mac Lib Ref.

Science & the Art see Notes on Nursing

Science & the Arts: A Study in Relationships from 1600-1900. Jacob Opper. LC 70-178042. 226p. 1973. 32.50 (*0-8386-1054-4*) Fairleigh Dickinson.

Science & the Arts in the Renaissance. Ed. by John Shirley & F. David Hoeniger. LC 82-49312. (Illus.). 224p. 1985. 38.50 (*0-918016-69-X*) Folger Bks.

Science & the Bible. expanded rev. ed. Henry M. Morris. 1986. pap. 9.99 (*0-8024-0656-4*) Moody.

Science & the Bible. rev. ed. Richard M. Greene, Jr. (Examines the Bible - Is Today's Science "Right" or "Wrong" Ser.). (Illus.). 370p. 1997. spiral bd. 49.95 (*0-934487-54-5*) R M Greene.

Science & the Bible: 30 Scientific Demonstrations Illustrating Scriptural Truths. Donald B. DeYoung. LC 93-21085. (Illus.). 112p. (Orig.). (J). (gr. 10). 1994. pap. 8.99 (*0-8010-3023-4*) Baker Bks.

***Science & the Bible: 30 Scientific Demonstrations Illustrating Scriptural Truths.** Donald B. Deyoung. 96p. 1997. pap. 8.99 (*0-8010-5773-6*) Baker Bks.

Science & the Business of Living. James G. Vail. (C). 1953. pap. 3.00 (*0-87574-070-7*) Pendle Hill.

Science & the Canadian Arctic: A Century of Exploration, 1918-1920. Trevor H. Levere. (Illus.). 400p. (C). 1993. text ed. 69.95 (*0-521-41933-6*) Cambridge U Pr.

Science & the Catholic Church. National Conference of Catholic Bishops. 6p. (Orig.). 1995. mass mkt., pap. 1.00 (*1-55586-085-0*) US Catholic.

Science & the Cure of Diseases: Letters to Members of Congress. Efraim Racker. LC 79-84012. 121p. reprint ed. pap. 34.50 (*0-8357-7014-1*, 2033403) Bks Demand.

***Science & the Detective: Selected Reading in Forensic Science.** Brian H. Kaye. (Illus.). xviii, 388p. 1995. 90.00 (*3-527-29251-9*, VCH) Wiley.

Science & the Detective: Selected Reading in Forensic Science. Brian H. Kaye. 388p. 1995. pap. 39.95 (*3-527-29252-7*, VCH) Wiley.

Science & the Endangered Species Act. Committee on Scientific Issues in the Endangered-Act, Board on Environmental Studies & Toxecology, Commission of Life Sciences Staff. LC 95-33322. 1995. text ed. 39.95 (*0-309-05291-2*) Natl Acad Pr.

Science & the Enlightenment. Thomas L. Hankins. (Cambridge History of Science Ser.). (Illus.). 200p. 1985. pap. text ed. 17.95 (*0-521-28619-0*) Cambridge U Pr.

Science & the Evolution of Public Policy. Ed. by James A. Shannon. LC 73-76398. (Illus.). 278p. 1973. 15.00 (*0-87470-017-5*) Rockefeller.

Science & the Founding Fathers: Science in the Political Thought of Thomas Jefferson, Benjamin Franklin, John Adams, & James Madison. I. Bernard Cohen. 256p. 1992. 25.00 (*0-393-03501-8*) Norton.

Science & the Goals of Man: A Study in Semantic Orientation. Anatol Rapoport. LC 70-138126. 262p. 1971. reprint ed. text ed. 35.00 (*0-8371-4142-7*, RASG, Greenwood Pr) Greenwood.

Science & the Human Comedy: Natural Philosophy in French Literature from Rabelais to Maupertuis. Harcourt Brown. LC 74-84353. (University of Toronto Romance Ser.: No. 30). 244p. reprint ed. pap. 69.60 (*0-685-16257-5*, 2026427) Bks Demand.

Science & the Human Condition in India & Pakistan. Ed. by Ward Morehouse. LC 68-56606. (Illus.). 252p. 1968. 7.50 (*0-87470-010-8*) Rockefeller.

Science & the Human Imagination: Albert Einstein. Henry B. Hass & A K. Bose. Incl. New Jersey's Contributions to the Chemical Industry & Chemical Education. LC 77-92565. 1978. (*0-318-51878-3*); LC 77-92565. (Leverton Lectures: No. 5). 1978. 14.50 (*0-8386-2223-2*) Fairleigh Dickinson.

Science & the Humanities. Moody E. Prior. LC 62-13293. 136p. reprint ed. 38.80 (*0-8357-9470-9*, 2015306) Bks Demand.

Science & the Making of the Modern World. John Marks. 507p. 1984. pap. text ed. 35.00 (*0-435-54781-X*, 54781) Heinemann.

Science & the Management of Protected Areas. Ed. by J. H. Willison et al. LC 91-45580. (Developments in Landscape Management & Urban Planning Ser.: No. 7). 548p. 1992. 246.50 (*0-444-89163-3*, QH75) Elsevier.

Science & the Modern Mind: A Symposium. American Academy of Arts & Sciences Staff. Ed. by Gerald J. Holton. LC 70-167304. (Essay Index Reprint Ser.). 1977. reprint ed. 15.95 (*0-8369-2446-0*) Ayer.

***Science & the Modern World.** Whitehead. 1997. pap. 16.95 (*0-684-83639-4*) S&S Trade.

Science & the Modern World. Alfred N. Whitehead. LC 67-2244. 1967. pap. 16.95 (*0-02-935190-1*, Free Press) Free Pr.

Science & the Nation, Essays by Cambridge Graduates. Ed. by Albert C. Seward. LC 67-26780. (Essay Index Reprint Ser.). 1977. 20.95 (*0-8369-0864-3*) Ayer.

Science & the National Parks. National Research Council Staff et al. LC 92-26303. (Illus.). 136p. (C). 1992. pap. text ed. 19.95 (*0-309-04781-1*) Natl Acad Pr.

Science & the Navy: The History of the Office of Naval Research. Harvey M. Sapolsky. (Illus.). 158p. 1990. text ed. 32.50 (*0-691-07847-5*) Princeton U Pr.

Science & the New Civilization. Robert A. Millikan. LC 76-142671. (Essay Index Reprint Ser.). 1977. reprint ed. 20.95 (*0-8369-2418-5*) Ayer.

Science & the New Zealand Environment. Ed. by M. J. Taylor et al. (C). 1992. pap. text ed. 30.00 (*0-86469-152-1*) Intl Spec Bk.

Science & the Paranormal. Leonard Lewin. 16p. 1979. pap. 4.00 (*0-904674-07-X*, Pub. by Octagon Pr UK) ISHK.

Science & the Past. Ed. by Sheridan Bowman. (Illus.). 192p. 1991. 40.00 (*0-8020-5997-X*) U of Toronto Pr.

Science & the Practice of Medicine in the Nineteenth Century. W. F. Bynum. (Cambridge History of Science Ser.). (Illus.). 288p. (C). 1994. text ed. 59.95 (*0-521-25109-5*); pap. text ed. 17.95 (*0-521-27205-X*) Cambridge U Pr.

***Science & the Public, 3 vols.** Incl. Vol. III. Global Warming Caused by the Greenhouse Effect. John Doble et al. 188p. 1990. pap. 25.00 (*1-889483-36-2*); Vol. II. The Disposal of Solid Waste. John Doble et al. 109p. (Orig.). 1990. pap. 25.00 (*1-889483-35-4*); Vol. I. Searching for Common Ground on Issues Related to Science & Technology. John Doble & Jean Johnson. 76p. (Orig.). 1990. pap. 15.00 (*1-889483-34-6*); 65.00 (*1-889483-42-7*) Public Agenda.

Science & the Quest for Meaning. Donald M. MacKay. LC 81-17504. 87p. reprint ed. pap. 25.00 (*0-317-30150-0*, 2025333) Bks Demand.

Science & the Quest for Reality. Alfred I. Tauber. (Main Trends of the Modern World Ser.). 419p. (C). 1997. 55.00 (*0-8147-8218-3*); pap. 17.50 (*0-8147-8220-5*) NYU Pr.

Science & the Quiet Art: The Role of Medical Research in Health Care. David J. Weatherall. LC 94-16483. (Commonwealth Fund Ser.). Orig. Title: No Spell to Cast on Nature. (Illus.). 378p. 1995. 25.00 (*0-393-03744-4*) Norton.

***Science & the Raj 1857-1905.** Deepak Kumar. (Illus.). 300p. 1997. pap. 11.95 (*0-19-564194-9*) OUP.

***Science & the Retreat from Reason.** John Gillot & Manjit Kumar. 288p. 1997. 38.00 (*0-85345-986-X*) Monthly Rev.

***Science & the Retreat from Reason.** John Gillot & Manjit Kumar. 288p. 1997. pap. 18.00 (*0-85345-987-8*) Monthly Rev.

Science & the Revenge of Nature: Marcuse & Habermas. C. Fred Alford. LC 85-627. x, 226p. 1985. 39.95 (*0-8130-0817-4*) U Press Fla.

Science & the Sciences in Plato. Ed. by John P. Anton. LC 78-13418. 1980. 35.00 (*0-88206-301-4*) Caravan Bks.

Science & the Secrets of Nature: Books of Secrets in Medieval & Early Modern Culture. William Eamon. LC 93-31794. 512p. 1994. text ed. 65.00 (*0-691-03402-8*) Princeton U Pr.

Science & the Secrets of Nature: Books of Secrets in Medieval & Early Modern Culture. William Eamon. 510p. 1994. pap. text ed. 19.95 (*0-691-02602-5*) Princeton U Pr.

Science & the Shabby Curate of Poetry: Essays about the Two Cultures. Martin B. Green. LC 77-27419. 159p. 1978. reprint ed. text ed. 49.75 (*0-313-20191-9*, GRSS, Greenwood Pr) Greenwood.

Science & the Shape of Orthodoxy: Intellectual Change in Late-Seventeenth-Century Britain. Michael Hunter. (Illus.). 357p. (C). 1995. 99.00 (*0-85115-594-4*, Boydell Pr) Boydell & Brewer.

Science & the Social Order. Bernard Barber. LC 78-1569. 228p. 1978. reprint ed. text ed. 59.75 (*0-313-20356-3*, BASSO, Greenwood Pr) Greenwood.

Science & the Soviet Social Order. Ed. by Loren R. Graham. (Illus.). 443p. 1990. text ed. 42.50 (*0-674-79420-6*) HUP.

Science & the Superconscious State. Anthony Kassir. (Einstein's Chalkboard Ser.). 60p. 1992. pap. 2.00 (*1-56543-009-3*) Mt SA Coll Philos.

Science & the Theory of Rationality. John Wright. 153p. 1991. 63.95 (*1-85628-220-1*, Pub. by Avebury Pub UK) Ashgate Pub Co.

Science & the Third World. Abdus Salam. 1991. pap. 7.00 (*0-7486-0144-9*, Pub. by Edinburgh U Pr UK) Col U Pr.

***Science & Theology.** Rae. pap. 29.95 (*0-567-29265-7*, Pub. by T & T Clark UK) Bks Intl VA.

Science & Theology: Questions at the Interface. Ed. by Murray Rae et al. LC 94-12331. 272p. (Orig.). 1994. pap. 30.00 (*0-8028-0816-6*) Eerdmans.

Science & Unreason. Daisie Radner & Michael Radner. 110p. (C). 1982. pap. 18.95 (*0-534-01153-5*) Wadsworth Pub.

Science & Values. Joseph Grunfeld. 210p. (Orig.). 1973. pap. 29.00 (*90-6032-016-6*, Pub. by Gruner NE) Benjamins North Am.

Science & Values: An Essay on the Aims of Science & Their Role in Scientific Debate. Larry Laudan. LC 84-249. (Pittsburgh Series in Philosophy & History of Science: No. 3). 160p. 1984. pap. 16.00 (*0-520-05743-0*) U CA Pr.

Science & Your Body. Rebecca Heddle. (Science Activities Ser.). (Illus.). 24p. (J). (gr. 1-4). 1993. pap. 4.95 (*0-7460-1425-2*); lib. bdg. 12.95 (*0-88110-632-1*) EDC.

Science, Animals & Evolution: Reflections on Some Unrealized Potentials of Biology & Medicine. Catherine Roberts. LC 79-52322. (Contributions in Philosophy Ser.: No. 14). 221p. 1980. text ed. 49.95 (*0-313-21479-4*, RSA/, Greenwood Pr) Greenwood.

Science Antique et Medievale, des Origines a 1450 see Histoire Generale des Sciences

Science Anxiety. Jeffry V. Mallow. Ed. by Robert Hackworth & Joseph W. Howland. (Illus.). 200p. (Orig.). 1986. 12.95 (*0-943202-18-3*) H & H Pub.

Science Anytime. 1995. student ed., pap. text ed. 9.00 (*0-15-306166-9*) HB Schl Dept.

Science Anytime. 1995. student ed., pap. text ed. 9.25 (*0-15-306168-5*) HB Schl Dept.

Science Anytime. 1995. student ed., pap. text ed. 9.25 (*0-15-306170-7*) HB Schl Dept.

Science Anytime. 1995. student ed., pap. text ed. 9.25 (*0-15-306172-3*) HB Schl Dept.

Science Anytime. 95th ed. HB Staff. (J). (gr. 1-1). 1996. wbk. ed., pap. text ed. 5.75 (*0-15-306777-2*) HarBrace.

Science Anytime. 95th ed. HB Staff. (J). (gr. 6). 1996. wbk. ed., pap. text ed. 11.00 (*0-15-306800-0*) HarBrace.

Science Anytime: Grade 3. 1995. teacher ed., pap. text ed. 44.00 (*0-15-306472-2*) HB Schl Dept.

Science Anytime: Grade 3 Unit B. 1995. teacher ed., pap. text ed. 44.00 (*0-15-306473-0*) HB Schl Dept.

Science Anytime: Unit A. 1995. student ed., pap. text ed. 9.25 (*0-15-306167-7*) HB Schl Dept.

Science Anytime: Unit A Grade 4. 1995. teacher ed., pap. text ed. 44.00 (*0-15-306477-3*) HB Schl Dept.

Science Anytime: Unit A Grade 5. 1995. teacher ed., pap. text ed. 44.00 (*0-15-306482-X*) HB Schl Dept.

Science Anytime: Unit A Grade 6. 1995. teacher ed., pap. text ed. 44.00 (*0-15-306488-9*) HB Schl Dept.

Science Anytime: Unit B Grade 4. 1995. teacher ed., pap. text ed. 44.00 (*0-15-306478-1*) HB Schl Dept.

Science Anytime: Unit B Grade 6. 1995. teacher ed., pap. text ed. 44.00 (*0-15-306489-7*) HB Schl Dept.

Science Anytime: Unit C. 1995. student ed., pap. text ed. 9.00 (*0-15-306163-4*) HB Schl Dept.

Science Anytime: Unit C. 1995. student ed., pap. text ed. 9.25 (*0-15-306169-3*) HB Schl Dept.

Science Anytime: Unit C Grade 3. 1995. teacher ed., pap. text ed. 44.00 (*0-15-306474-9*) HB Schl Dept.

Science Anytime: Unit C Grade 4. 1995. teacher ed., pap. text ed. 44.00 (*0-15-306479-X*) HB Schl Dept.

Science Anytime: Unit C Grade 5. 1995. teacher ed., pap. text ed. 44.00 (*0-15-306484-6*) HB Schl Dept.

Science Anytime: Unit C Grade 6. 1995. teacher ed., pap. text ed. 44.00 (*0-15-306490-0*) HB Schl Dept.

Science Anytime: Unit D. 1995. student ed., pap. text ed. 9.00 (*0-15-306164-2*) HB Schl Dept.

Science Anytime: Unit D Grade 3. 1995. teacher ed., pap. text ed. 44.00 (*0-15-306475-7*) HB Schl Dept.

Science Anytime: Unit D Grade 4. 1995. teacher ed., pap. text ed. 44.00 (*0-15-306480-3*) HB Schl Dept.

Science Anytime: Unit D Grade 5. 1995. teacher ed., pap. text ed. 44.00 (*0-15-306485-4*) HB Schl Dept.

Science Anytime: Unit D Grade 6. 1995. teacher ed., pap. text ed. 44.00 (*0-15-306491-9*) HB Schl Dept.

Science Anytime: Unit E. 1995. student ed., pap. text ed. 9.00 (*0-15-306165-0*) HB Schl Dept.

Science Anytime: Unit E. 1995. student ed., pap. text ed. 9.25 (*0-15-306171-5*) HB Schl Dept.

Science Anytime: Unit E Grade 3. 1995. teacher ed., pap. text ed. 44.00 (*0-15-306476-5*) HB Schl Dept.

Science Anytime: Unit E Grade 4. 1995. teacher ed., pap. text ed. 44.00 (*0-15-306481-1*) HB Schl Dept.

Science Anytime: Unit E Grade 5. 1995. teacher ed., pap. text ed. 44.00 (*0-15-306486-2*) HB Schl Dept.

Science Anytime: Unit E Grade 6. 1995. teacher ed., pap. text ed. 44.00 (*0-15-306492-7*) HB Schl Dept.

Science Anytime: Unit F Grade 5. 1995. teacher ed., pap. text ed. 44.00 (*0-15-306487-0*) HB Schl Dept.

Science Anytime: Unit F Grade 6. 1995. teacher ed., pap. text ed. 44.00 (*0-15-306493-5*) HB Schl Dept.

Science Anytime Videodisc Series Library, Set. Pegasus Learning Company Staff. (J). (gr. k-6). 1996. write for info. incl. vdisk (*1-881259-37-4*) Pegasus Lrn.

Science Anytime 1995. 95th ed. HB Staff. (J). (gr. 3-3). 1996. wbk. ed., pap. text ed. 5.75 (*0-15-306785-3*) HarBrace.

Science Anytime 1995. 95th ed. HB Staff. (J). (gr. 4-4). 1996. wbk. ed., pap. text ed. 5.75 (*0-15-306786-1*) HarBrace.

Science Anytime 1995. 95th ed. HB Staff. (J). (gr. 5-5). 1996. wbk. ed., pap. text ed. 5.75 (*0-15-306787-X*) HarBrace.

Science Anytime 1995. 95th ed. HB Staff. (J). (gr. 6-6). 1996. wbk. ed., pap. text ed. 5.75 (*0-15-306788-8*) HarBrace.

Science Anytime 95. 95th ed. HB Staff. (J). (gr. 2-2). 1996. wbk. ed., pap. text ed. 5.75 (*0-15-306784-5*) HarBrace.

Science Anytime 95. 95th ed. HB Staff. (J). (gr. 1-1). 1996. wbk. ed., pap. text ed. 11.00 (*0-15-306789-6*) HarBrace.

Science Anytime 95. 95th ed. HB Staff. (J). (gr. 2-2). 1996. wbk. ed., pap. text ed. 11.00 (*0-15-306796-9*) HarBrace.

Science Anytime 95. 95th ed. HB Staff. (J). (gr. 3-3). 1996. wbk. ed., pap. text ed. 11.00 (*0-15-306797-7*) HarBrace.

Science Anytime 95. 95th ed. HB Staff. (J). (gr. 4). 1996. teacher ed., pap. text ed. 11.00 (*0-15-306798-5*) HarBrace.

Science Anytime 95. 95th ed. HB Staff. (J). (gr. 5-5). 1996. teacher ed., pap. text ed. 11.00 (*0-15-306799-3*) HarBrace.

Science Arabe & Son Role Dans l'Evolution Scientifique Mondiale. Aldo Mieli. (Medieval Studies Reprint Ser.). (FRE.). reprint ed. lib. bdg. 44.00 (*0-697-00044-3*) Irvington.

Science Around the House. Robert Gardner. (Robert Gardner's Science Activity Bks.). (Illus.). 136p. (J). (gr. 4-8). 1989. pap. 4.95 (*0-671-68129-X*, Julian Messner) Silver Burdett Pr.

Science around the House. Robert Gardner. (Robert Gardner's Science Activity Bks.). (Illus.). 136p. (J). (gr. 4-8). 1989. pap. 4.95 (*0-671-68139-7*, Julian Messner) Silver Burdett Pr.

Science Around the World: Travel Through Time & Space with Fun Experiments & Projects. Shar Levine & Leslie Johnstone. LC 95-44029. (Illus.). 96p. (J). (gr. 3-6). 1996. pap. text ed. 10.95 (*0-471-11916-4*) Wiley.

***Science Around You Bk. 3.** Atherton. 1992. pap. text ed. write for info. (*0-582-87554-4*, Pub. by Longman UK) Longman.

Science, Art & Nature in Medieval & Modern Thought. A. C. Crombie. LC 95-49964. 1996. boxed 65.00 (*1-85285-067-1*) Hambledon Press.

S

Science As a Career Choice: Theoretical & Empirical Studies. Ed. by Bernice T. Eiduson & Linda Beckman. LC 72-83833. 752p. 1973. 70.00 (*0-87154-230-7*) Russell Sage.

Science As a Cultural Process. Maurice N. Richter, Jr. 160p. 1972. pap. text ed. 13.95 (*0-87073-073-8*) Schenkman Bks Inc.

Science As a Human Endeavor. George F. Kneller. LC 77-19167. 345p. reprint ed. pap. 98.40 (*0-317-26145-2*, 2024374) Bks Demand.

***Science, As a Matter Fact.** Jerome Agel. Date not set. lib. bdg. write for info. (*0-688-13184-0*, Tambourine Bks) Morrow.

Science as a Process: An Evolutionary Account of the Social & Conceptual Development of Science. David L. Hull. LC 88-2743. (Science & Its Conceptual Foundations Ser.). (Illus.). 600p. 1990. pap. text ed. 27.95 (*0-226-36051-2*) U Ch Pr.

Science As a Questioning Process. N. Sanitt. LC 96-15832. (Illus.). 184p. 1996. 40.00 (*0-7503-0369-7*) IOP Pub.

Science As a Way of Knowing: The Foundations of Modern Biology. John A. Moore. 1993. text ed. 34.50 (*0-674-79481-8*) HUP.

Science As a Way of Knowing: The Foundations of Modern Biology. John A. Moore. (Illus.). 544p. (C). 1993. text ed. 29.95 (*0-674-79480-X*) HUP.

Science As Intellectual Property: Who Controls Research? Dorothy Nelkin. LC 83-3805. (AAAS Series on Issues in Science & Technology). 142p. reprint ed. pap. 40.50 (*0-7837-6741-2*, 2046369) Bks Demand.

Science As Intellectual Property: Who Controls Scientific Research. Dorothy Nelkin. (AAAS Issues in Science & Technology Ser.). 130p. 1983. pap. text ed. 15.95 (*0-02-949090-1*, Free Press) Free Pr.

Science As Intellectual Property: Who Controls Scientific Research. Dorothy Nelkin. 130p. 1983. text ed. write for info. (*0-318-57876-X*) Macmillan.

Science As Power: Discourse & Ideology in Modern Society. Stanley Aronowitz. LC 88-4782. xii, 384p. (Orig.). 1988. pap. text ed. 16.95 (*0-8166-1659-0*) U of Minn Pr.

Science as Practice & Culture. Andrew Pickering. (Illus.). 482p. 1992. pap. text ed. 24.95 (*0-226-66801-0*); lib. bdg. 75.00 (*0-226-66800-2*) U Ch Pr.

Science as Public Culture: Chemistry & Enlightenment in Britain, 1760-1820. Jan Golinski. (Illus.). 330p. (C). 1992. text ed. 59.95 (*0-521-39414-7*) Cambridge U Pr.

Science As Salvation: A Modern Myth & Its Meaning. Mary Midgley. LC 91-30984. 256p. (C). (gr. 13). 1992. text ed. 29.95 (*0-415-06271-3*, A7063) Routledge.

Science As Salvation: A Modern Myth & Its Meaning. Mary Midgley. 256p. (C). 1994. pap. 15.95 (*0-415-10773-3*) Routledge.

Science As Social Knowledge: Value & Objectivity in Scientific Inquiry. Helen E. Longino. 252p. (Orig.). 1990. pap. text ed. 16.95 (*0-691-02051-5*) Princeton U Pr.

Science As Writing. David Locke. 256p. (C). 1992. text ed. 32.50 (*0-300-05452-1*) Yale U Pr.

Science Assessment in the Service of Reform. Ed. by Gerald Kulm & Shirley M. Malcom. 400p. 1991. 24.95 (*0-87168-426-8*, 91-33S) AAAS.

Science Assessment in the Service of Reform. Ed. by Gerald Kulm & Shirley M. Malcom. 408p. 1994. pap. 32.50 (*0-8058-1875-8*) L Erlbaum Assocs.

Science Astray. Time-Life Books Editors. LC 92-19180. (Library of Curious & Unusual Facts). 1992. write for info. (*0-8094-7691-6*); lib. bdg. write for info. (*0-8094-7692-4*) Time-Life.

Science at Harvard University: Historical Perspectives. Ed. by Clark A. Elliott & Margaret W. Rossiter. LC 89-64067. (Illus.). 384p. 1992. 55.00 (*0-934223-12-2*) Lehigh Univ Pr.

***Science at Oxford: Transforming an Arts University.** Jack Morrell. (Illus.). 320p. 1997. 95.00 (*0-19-820657-7*) OUP.

***Science at the Bar: Law, Science & Technology in America.** Shelia Jasanoff. 1997. pap. text ed. 17.95 (*0-674-79303-X*) HUP.

Science at the Bar: Science & Technology in American Law. Sheila S. Jasanoff. LC 95-9192. (Twentieth Century Fund Bks.). 240p. (C). 1995. text ed. 29.95 (*0-674-79302-1*) HUP.

Science at the Bedside: Clinical Research in American Medicine, 1905-1945. A. McGehee Harvey. LC 80-28786. 496p. 1981. text ed. 48.00 (*0-8018-2562-8*) Johns Hopkins.

Science at the Crossroads. Nikolai Dukharin. 228p. 1971. 35.00 (*0-7146-2868-9*, Pub. by F Cass Pubs UK) Intl Spec Bk.

Science at the Frontier. Addison Greenwood & National Academy of Sciences Staff. (Illus.). 288p. (C). 1992. 24.95 (*0-309-04592-4*) Natl Acad Pr.

Science at the White House: A Political Liability. Edward J. Burger, Jr. LC 80-81425. 208p. 1981. text ed. 32.50 (*0-8018-2433-8*) Johns Hopkins.

Science at War. George W. Gray. LC 72-4531. (Essay Index Reprint Ser.). 1977. reprint ed. 23.95 (*0-8369-2944-6*) Ayer.

Science at Work. Ed. by Richard Gillespie. (C). 1982. pap. 38.00 (*0-86828-148-4*, Pub. by Deakin Univ AT) St Mut.

***Science at Work: Balance in life.** 3rd ed. Rowlands. 1995. pap. text ed. write for info. (*0-582-24708-X*) Addison-Wesley.

***Science at Work: Communication.** 3rd ed. Snape & Rowlands. 1995. pap. text ed. write for info. (*0-582-24707-1*) Addison-Wesley.

***Science at Work: Patterns in Life.** 3rd ed. Snape & Rowlands. 1995. pap. text ed. write for info. (*0-582-24706-3*, Pub. by Longman UK) Longman.

Science Awakening I: Egyptian, Babylonian, & Greek Mathematics. B. L. Van der Waerden. (Illus.). 310p. (C). 1988. reprint ed. pap. text ed. 14.95 (*0-945726-05-8*); reprint ed. lib. bdg. 40.00 (*0-945726-04-X*) Scholars Bookshelf.

Science-Based Dating in Archaeology. Martin J. Aitken. (Archaeology Ser.). (Illus.). 288p. (C). 1989. text ed. 49.95 (*0-582-05498-2*) Longman.

***Science-Based Economic Development: Case Studies Around the World.** Susan U. Raymond. LC 96-45942. (Annals of the New York Academy of Sciences). 1996. 125.00 (*1-57331-052-2*); pap. write for info. (*1-57331-053-0*) NY Acad Sci.

Science-Based Risk Assessment: A Piece of the Superfund Puzzle. Steven J. Milloy. (Orig.). 1995. pap. 25.00 (*0-9647463-0-1*) Nat Environ Policy.

Science, Belief & Behavior. Ed. by D. H. Mellor. LC 79-41614. (Illus.). 240p. 1980. text ed. 47.95 (*0-521-22960-X*) Cambridge U Pr.

Science Between the Superpowers: A Twentieth Century Fund Paper. Yakov M. Rabkin. 119p. 1988. 18.95 (*0-87078-223-1*); pap. 8.95 (*0-87078-222-3*) TCFP-PPP.

Science Between Utopia & Dystopia, 1984. Ed. by Everett I. Mendelsohn & Helga Nowotny. (Sociology of the Sciences Yearbook Ser.: No. 8). 310p. 1984. pap. text ed. 61.00 (*90-277-1721-4*); lib. bdg. 122.50 (*90-277-1719-2*) Kluwer Ac.

Science Book. Sara Stein. LC 79-64786. (Illus.). 288p. (J). (gr. 4-7). 1980. pap. 9.95 (*0-89480-120-1*, 291) Workman Pub.

***Science Book for Girls & Other Intelligent Beings: And Other Intelligent Beings.** unabridged ed. Valerie Wyatt. (Illus.). 80p. (Orig.). (J). (gr. 3-7). 1997. pap. 8.95 (*1-55074-113-6*, Pub. by Kids Can Pr CN) Genl Dist Srvs.

Science Book of Air. Neil Ardley. 29p. (J). (gr. 2-5). 1991. 10.00 (*0-15-200578-1*) HarBrace.

Science Book of Color. 1993. pap. text ed. 11.00 (*0-15-365401-5*) HB Schl Dept.

Science Book of Color. Neil Ardley. 29p. (J). (gr. 2-5). 1991. 10.00 (*0-15-200576-5*) HarBrace.

Science Book of Electricity. 1993. pap. text ed. 11.00 (*0-15-365406-6*) HB Schl Dept.

Science Book of Electricity. Neil Ardley. 29p. (J). (ps-3). 1991. 10.00 (*0-15-200583-8*, HB Juv Bks) HarBrace.

Science Book of Energy. 1993. pap. text ed. 11.00 (*0-15-365408-2*) HB Schl Dept.

Science Book of Energy. Neil Ardley. (J). (gr. 2-5). 1992. 10.00 (*0-15-200611-7*, HB Juv Bks) HarBrace.

Science Book of Gravity. 1993. pap. text ed. 11.00 (*0-15-365415-5*) HB Schl Dept.

Science Book of Gravity. Neil Ardley. (J). 1992. 10.00 (*0-15-200621-4*, Gulliver Bks) HarBrace.

Science Book of Hot & Cold. 1993. pap. text ed. 11.00 (*0-15-365411-2*) HB Schl Dept.

Science Book of Hot & Cold. Neil Ardley. (Illus.). 28p. (J). (gr. 2-5). 1992. 10.00 (*0-15-200612-5*, HB Juv Bks) HarBrace.

Science Book of Light. 1993. pap. text ed. 11.00 (*0-15-365402-3*) HB Schl Dept.

Science Book of Light. Neil Ardley. (Illus.). 29p. (J). (gr. 2-5). 1991. 10.00 (*0-15-200577-3*) HarBrace.

Science Book of Machines. 1993. pap. text ed. 11.00 (*0-15-365410-4*) HB Schl Dept.

Science Book of Machines. Neil Ardley. (Illus.). 28p. (J). (gr. 2-5). 1992. 10.00 (*0-15-200613-3*, HB Juv Bks) HarBrace.

Science Book of Magnets. 1993. pap. text ed. 11.00 (*0-15-365405-8*) HB Schl Dept.

Science Book of Magnets. Neil Ardley. 29p. (J). (ps-3). 1991. 9.95 (*0-15-200581-1*, HB Juv Bks) HarBrace.

Science Book of Motion. 1993. pap. text ed. 11.00 (*0-15-365412-0*) HB Schl Dept.

Science Book of Motion. Neil Ardley. 28p. (J). (ps-3). 1992. 10.00 (*0-15-200622-2*, Gulliver Bks) HarBrace.

Science Book of Numbers. 1993. pap. text ed. 11.00 (*0-15-365413-9*) HB Schl Dept.

Science Book of Numbers. J. Challoner. 28p. (J). (ps-3). 1992. 10.00 (*0-15-200623-0*, Gulliver Bks) HarBrace.

Science Book of Senses. 1993. pap. text ed. 11.00 (*0-15-365409-0*) HB Schl Dept.

Science Book of Sound. 1993. pap. text ed. 11.00 (*0-15-365404-X*) HB Schl Dept.

Science Book of Sound. Neil Ardley. 29p. (J). (ps-3). 1991. 10.00 (*0-15-200579-X*, HB Juv Bks) HarBrace.

Science Book of the Senses. Neil Ardley. 28p. (J). (gr. 2-5). 1992. 10.00 (*0-15-200614-1*, HB Juv Bks) HarBrace.

Science Book of Things That Grow. Neil Ardley. 29p. (J). (ps-3). 1991. 10.00 (*0-15-200586-2*, HB Juv Bks) HarBrace.

Science Book of Water. 1993. pap. text ed. 11.00 (*0-15-365400-7*) HB Schl Dept.

Science Book of Water. Neil Ardley. 29p. (J). (gr. 2-5). 1991. 10.00 (*0-15-200575-7*) HarBrace.

Science Book of Weather. 1993. pap. text ed. 11.00 (*0-15-365414-7*) HB Schl Dept.

Science Book of Weather. Neil Ardley. 28p. (J). (ps-3). 1992. 10.00 (*0-15-200624-9*, Gulliver Bks) HarBrace.

Science Book of Wonder Drugs. Donald G. Cooley. LC 72-99627. (Essay Index Reprint Ser.). (Illus.). 1977. 23.95 (*0-8369-1562-3*) Ayer.

Science Books & Films' Best Books for Children 1988-1991. Ed. by Maria Sosa & Shirley M. Malcom. 312p. 1994. 19.95 (*0-8058-1879-0*) L Erlbaum Assocs.

Science Books & Films' Best Books for Children, 1988-91. Ed. by Maria Sosa & Shirley M. Malcom. LC 92-27208. 350p. 1992. 40.00 (*0-87168-505-1*, 92-30H) AAAS.

Science Boosters. Deborah McMillian. (Illus.). 64p. (J). (gr. 2-6). 1988. teacher ed., pap. 6.95 (*0-912107-82-0*, MM 998) Monday Morning Bks.

Science Brainstretchers: Creative Problem-Solving Activities in Science, Grades 4-6. Anthony D. Fredericks. 1990. pap. 9.95 (*0-673-46345-1*, GoodYrBooks) Addson-Wesley Educ.

Science Bulletin Board Ideas with a Bible Background. John H. Tiner. 1983. pap. 7.25 (*0-89137-614-3*) Quality Pubns.

Science Bulletin Boards. Imogene Forte. (Easy-To-Make-&-Use Ser.). 64p. (J). (gr. k-6). 1986. pap. text ed. 7.95 (*0-86530-131-X*, IP 112-1) Incentive Pubns.

Science Business: Report of the Twentieth Century Fund Task Force on the Commercialization of Scientific Research. 84p. (Orig.). 1984. pap. text ed. 7.50 (*0-87078-156-1*) TCFP-PPP.

***Science Calculations.** Sang et al. 1995. pap. text ed. write for info. (*0-582-23730-0*, Pub. by Longman UK) Longman.

Science Centennial Review. Ed. by Philip H. Abelson & Ruth Kulstad. LC 80-69480. (AAAS Publication Ser.: No. 80-10). 192p. reprint ed. pap. 54.80 (*0-7837-0069-5*, 2040316) Bks Demand.

***Science Challenge Bk. 1.** Davenport & Sellwood. Date not set. pap. text ed. write for info. (*0-582-07008-2*, Pub. by Longman UK) Longman.

Science Challenging AIDS. Ed. by G. Giraldo et al. (Illus.). xx, 300p. 1992. 191.50 (*3-8055-5485-0*) S Karger.

Science Chef: One Hundred Fun Food Experiments & Recipes for Kids. J. D'Amico & Karen E. Drummond. 180p. (J). 1994. pap. text ed. 12.95 (*0-471-31045-X*) Wiley.

Science Chef Travels Around the World: Fun Food Experiments & Recipes for Kids. Joan D'Amico & Karen E. Drummond. LC 95-32952. (Illus.). 165p. (J). (gr. 3-9). 1996. pap. text ed. 12.95 (*0-471-11779-X*) Wiley.

Science, Churchill & Me: The Autobiography of Hermann Bondi. Hermann Bondi. (Illus.). 154p. 1990. 51.25 (*0-08-037235-X*, Pergamon Pr) Elsevier.

***Science City in a Global Context.** Kunio Goto & David V. Gibson. Ed. by Heidi Lopez-Cepero & Graham Stewart. (Orig.). 1997. pap. 20.00 (*1-887406-07-7*) ICTwo Inst.

***Science Class You Wish You Had... The Seven Greatest Scientific Discoveries in History & the People Who Mad Them.** David E. Brody & Arnold R. Brody. LC 96-45097. 400p. 1997. pap. 14.00 (*0-399-52313-8*, Perigee Bks) Berkley Pub.

Science Close-Up: Gemstones. Gina Ingoglia. (Deluxe Science Close-Up Kits Ser.). (Illus.). 24p. (J). (ps-3). 1995. pap. 8.95 (*0-307-12859-8*, Golden Books) Western Pub.

Science Close-Up: Magnets. Robert Bell. (Science Close-up Ser.). (Illus.). 24p. (J). (ps-3). 1995. pap. 6.50 (*0-307-12862-8*, Golden Books) Western Pub.

Science Close-Up: Minerals. Robert Bell. (Deluxe Science Close-Up Kits Ser.). (Illus.). 24p. (J). (ps-3). 1995. pap. 8.95 (*0-307-12860-1*, Golden Books) Western Pub.

Science Close-Up: Rocks. Lin Bass. (Deluxe Science Close-Up Kits Ser.). (Illus.). 24p. (J). (ps-3). 1995. pap. 8.95 (*0-307-12858-X*, Golden Books) Western Pub.

Science Close-Up: Seashells. Gina Ingoglia. (Deluxe Science Close-Up Kits Ser.). (Illus.). 24p. (J). (ps-3). 1995. pap. 8.95 (*0-307-12861-X*, Golden Books) Western Pub.

Science Communication & Development. J. V. Vilanilam. LC 92-25088. 232p. (C). 1993. text ed. 32.00 (*0-8039-9447-8*) Sage.

Science, Community & the Transformation of American Philosophy, 1860-1930. Daniel J. Wilson. LC 89-35929. 239p. 1990. 35.95 (*0-226-90143-2*) U Ch Pr.

Science Computer Programs for Kids... & Other People: Apple Version. Tom Speitel & Dan Speitel. (Illus.). 1984. 14.50 (*0-8359-6901-0*, Reston) P-H.

Science, Computers, & People: From the Tree of Mathematics, Stanislaw Ulam. Ed. by Mark Reynolds & Gian-Carlo Rota. (Illus.). 1986. 48.00 (*0-8176-3276-X*) Birkhauser.

Science Confronts the Paranormal. Ed. by Kendrick Frazier. 367p. 1985. pap. 23.95 (*0-87975-314-5*) Prometheus Bks.

Science Contemporaine see Histoire Generale des Sciences

Science Content Picture Dictionary. Weiss. (Global ESL/ELT Ser.). 1997. pap. 25.95 (*0-8384-6696-6*); wbk. ed., pap. 12.95 (*0-8384-6697-4*) Heinle & Heinle.

Science Continuum of Concepts: For Grades K-6. Karen D. Olsen. 55p. (Orig.). 1995. teacher ed., pap. 9.95 (*0-9630547-3-2*) Bks Educators.

Science Cookbook. Julia B. Waxter. LC 79-57431. (J). (gr. 4-8). 1981. pap. 9.99 (*0-8224-6292-3*) Fearon Teach Aids.

Science Crafts for Kids: 50 Fantastic Things to Invent & Create. Gwen Diehn & Terry Krautwurst. LC 93-39112. 144p. (J). 1994. 21.95 (*0-8069-0283-3*) Sterling.

***Science Crafts for Kids: 50 Fantastic Things to Invent & Create.** Gwen Diehn & Terry Krautwurst. (Illus.). 144p. (J). 1997. pap. 14.95 (*0-8069-0284-1*) Sterling.

Science Crafts for Kids Book & Kit. (Illus.). (J). 1994. 29.95 (*0-8069-0900-5*) Sterling.

Science Critic: A Critical Analysis of the Popular Presentation of Science. Maurice Goldsmith. (Illus.). 256p. 1986. 37.50 (*0-7102-0467-1*, 04671, RKP) Routledge.

***Science, Culture & Politics in Britain, 1750-1870.** Jack Morrell. LC 96-52706. (Collected Studies: Vol. CS567). 350p. 1997. 98.95 (*0-86078-633-1*, Q127.G4M67, Pub. by Variorum UK) Ashgate Pub Co.

Science, Culture & Popular Belief in Renaissance Europe. Ed. by Stephen Pumfrey et al. 352p. 1994. text ed. 24.95 (*0-7190-4322-0*, Pub. by Manchester Univ Pr UK) St Martin.

Science Curriculum: The Report of the 1986 National Forum for School Science. National Forum for School Science Staff. (This Year in School Science Ser.: No. 1986). 285p. reprint ed. pap. 81.30 (*0-8357-2823-4*, 2039059) Bks Demand.

Science, Curriculum, & Liberal Education: Selected Essays. Joseph J. Schwab. Ed. by Ian Westbury & Neil J. Wilkof. LC 78-5848. 400p. 1978. 28.95 (*0-226-74186-9*) U Ch Pr.

Science, Curriculum, & Liberal Education: Selected Essays. Joseph J. Schwab. Ed. by Ian Westbury & Neil J. Wilkof. LC 78-5848. 394p. 1982. pap. text ed. 12.00 (*0-226-74187-7*) U Ch Pr.

Science Curriculum Resource Handbook: A Practical Guide for K-12 Science Curriculum. LC 92-28471. (Teacher Resource Handbook Ser.). (Illus.). 384p. 1992. pap. 29.95 (*0-8039-6373-4*) Corwin Pr.

Science, Decision & Value. Ed. by J. J. Leach et al. LC 72-77877. (Western Ontario Ser.: Vol. 1). 220p. 1973. lib. bdg. 80.00 (*90-277-0239-X*, D Reidel) Kluwer Ac.

Science, Decision & Value. Ed. by J. J. Leach et al. LC 72-77877. (Western Ontario Ser.: Vol. 1). 220p. 1973. pap. text ed. 46.00 (*90-277-0327-2*, D Reidel) Kluwer Ac.

Science Deified & Science Defied: The Historical Significance of Science in Western Culture: Vol 1, From the Bronze Age to the Beginnings of the Modern Era ca. 3500 B. C. to ca. A. D. 1640. Richard Olson. LC 82-40093. (Illus.). 375p. 1982. pap. 16.00 (*0-520-04716-8*) U CA Pr.

Science Deified & Science Defied Vol. 2: The Historical Significance of Science in Western Culture: From the Early Modern Age Through the Early Romantic Era ca. 1640-ca.1820. Richard Olson. (Illus.). 445p. 1995. pap. 17.00 (*0-520-20167-1*) U CA Pr.

Science, Democracy, & Islam: And Other Essays. Humayun Kabir. LC 80-2195. reprint ed. 27.50 (*0-404-18967-9*) AMS Pr.

Science Demonstrations for the Elementary Classroom. Dorothea Allen. 288p. 1988. pap. text ed. 24.95 (*0-13-794652-X*, Parker Publishing Co) P-H.

Science des Comptes Mise a la Portee de Tous: The Science of Accounting Put Within Reach of Us All. Eugene Leautey & Adolfe Guilbaut. Ed. by Richard P. Brief. LC 80-1508. (Dimensions of Accounting Theory & Practice Ser.). (FRE.). 1980. reprint ed. lib. bdg. 50.95 (*0-405-13533-5*) Ayer.

Science Detectives. SETI Institute Staff. LC 95-38936. (Life in the Universe Ser.). 225p. 1996. pap. text ed. 54.00 incl. vdisk (*1-56308-323-X*) Teacher Ideas Pr.

Science, Development, & Violence: The Revolt Against Modernity. Claude Alvares. (Oxford India Paperbacks Ser.). 198p. 1995. pap. 7.95 (*0-19-563281-8*) OUP.

Science Dictionary. Longman. 136p. 1983. 39.95 (*0-8288-2096-1*, F34210) Fr & Eur.

Science Dictionary. Seymour Simon. LC 94-9962. (Illus.). 266p. (J). (gr. 4 up). 1994. 29.95 (*0-06-025629-X*) HarpC Child Bks.

Science Dictionary of Animals. James Richardson. LC 91-18826. (Science Dictionary Ser.). (Illus.). 48p. (YA). (gr. 3-7). 1992. pap. 3.95 (*0-8167-2440-7*); lib. bdg. 11.95 (*0-8167-2521-7*) Troll Communs.

Science Dictionary of Dinosaurs. James Richardson. LC 91-4110. (Science Dictionary Ser.). (Illus.). 48p. (YA). (gr. 3-7). 1992. lib. bdg. 11.95 (*0-8167-2522-5*) Troll Communs.

Science Dictionary of Dinosaurs. James Richardson. LC 91-4110. (Science Dictionary Ser.). (Illus.). 48p. (YA). (gr. 3-7). 1997. pap. 3.95 (*0-8167-2441-5*) Troll Communs.

Science Dictionary of Space. James Richardson. LC 91-16551. (Science Dictionary Ser.). (Illus.). 48p. (YA). (gr. 3-7). 1992. lib. bdg. 11.95 (*0-8167-2524-1*) Troll Communs.

Science Dictionary of Space. James Richardson. LC 91-16551. (Science Dictionary Ser.). (Illus.). 48p. (YA). (gr. 3-7). 1997. pap. 3.95 (*0-8167-2443-1*) Troll Communs.

Science Dictionary of the Human Body. James Richardson. LC 91-19162. (Science Dictionary Ser.). (Illus.). 48p. (YA). (gr. 3-7). 1992. pap. 3.95 (*0-8167-2442-3*); lib. bdg. 11.95 (*0-8167-2523-3*) Troll Communs.

***Science Discoveries.** Steve Parker. Incl. Aristotle & Scientific Thought. (Illus.). 32p. (J). (gr. 3 up). 1995. lib. bdg. 15.95 (*0-7910-3005-9*); Alexander Graham Bell & the Telephone. LC 94-8263. (Illus.). 32p. (J). (gr. 3 up). 1995. lib. bdg. 15.95 (*0-7910-3004-0*); Marie Curie & Radium. LC 94-20657. (Illus.). 32p. (J). (gr. 3 up). 1995. lib. bdg. 15.95 (*0-7910-3011-3*); Charles Darwin & Evolution. LC 94-20656. (Illus.). 32p. (J). (gr. 3 up). 1995. lib. bdg. 15.95 (*0-7910-3007-5*); Thomas Edison & Electricity. LC 94-20658. (Illus.). 32p. (J). (gr. 3 up). 1995. lib. bdg. 15.95 (*0-7910-3012-1*); Albert Einstein & the Laws of Relativity. LC 94-43924. (Illus.). 32p. (J). (gr. 3 up). 1995. lib. bdg. 15.95 (*0-7910-3003-2*); Benjamin Franklin & Electricity. LC 94-25255. (Illus.). 32p. (J). (gr. 3 up). 1995. lib. bdg. 15.95 (*0-7910-3006-7*); Galileo & the Universe. LC 94-20659. (Illus.). 32p. (J). (gr. 3 up). 1995. lib. bdg. 15.95 (*0-7910-3008-3*); Guglielmo Marconi & Radio. LC 94-8253. (Illus.). (J). (gr. 3 up). 1995. lib. bdg. 15.95 (*0-7910-3009-1*); Isaac Newton & Gravity. LC 94-8260. (Illus.). 32p. (J). (gr. 3 up). 1995. lib. bdg. 15.95 (*0-7910-3010-5*); Louis Pasteur & Germs. LC 94-8262. (Illus.). 32p. (J). (gr. 3 up). 1995. lib. bdg. 15.95 (*0-7910-3002-4*); Wright Brothers & Aviation. LC 94-25254. (Illus.). 32p. (J). (gr. 3 up). 1995. lib. bdg. 15.95 (*0-7910-3013-X*); 179.40 (*0-7910-3001-6*) Chelsea Hse.

Science Discovers the Physiological Value of Continence. Raymond W. Bernard. 46p. 1994. reprint ed. spiral bd. 6.50 (*0-7873-1025-5*) Hlth Research.

Science Discovery Book: Grades 4 - 6. Anthony D. Fredericks et al. (Illus.). 60p. (Orig.). 1986. pap. 9.95 (*0-673-18344-0*, GoodYrBooks) Addson-Wesley Educ.

An Asterisk (*) at the beginning of an entry indicates that the title is appearing in BIP for the first time.

Science Du Droit En Grece: Platon, Aristote, Theophraste. Rodolphe de la Chavanne Dareste. LC 75-13259. (History of Ideas in Ancient Greece Ser.). (FRE.). 1976. reprint ed. 23.95 (*0-405-07301-1*) Ayer.

Science Education: A Minds-on Approach for the Elementary Years. Eleanor Duckworth et al. 216p. (C). 1990. text ed. 49.95 (*0-8058-0543-5*) L Erlbaum Assocs.

Science Education: Exploring the Tension. Ian M. Robottom. 70p. (C). 1988. 41.00 (*0-7300-0562-3*, Pub. by Deakin Univ AT) St Mut.

Science Education & Information Transfer. J. Lewis. Ed. by C. A. Taylor. LC 86-25229. (Science & Technology Education & Future Human Needs Ser.: Vol. 9). (Illus.). 244p. 1987. 112.00 (*0-08-033954-9*, Pub. by Pergamon Repr UK) Franklin.

Science Education for a Pluralist Society. Michael J. Reiss. LC 92-47138. (Developing Science & Technology Education Ser.). 1993. 75.00 (*0-335-15761-0*, Open Univ Pr); pap. 23.00 (*0-335-15760-2*, Open Univ Pr) Taylor & Francis.

Science Education in the States: A Survey. (State Legislative Reports: Vol. 15, No. 16). 8p. 1990. 5.00 (*1-55516-272-X*, 7302-1516) Natl Conf State Legis.

Science Education in the United States: Issues, Crises, Priorities. Ed. by Shyamal K. Majumdar et al. LC 91-60096. (Illus.). 550p. 1991. text ed. 45.00 (*0-945809-04-2*) Penn Science.

***Science Education in the 21st Century.** D. L. Thompson et al. LC 97-12191. 264p. 1997. text ed. 56.95 (*1-85742-382-8*, Pub. by Arena UK) Ashgate Pub Co.

Science Education Partnerships: Manual for Scientists & K - 12 Teachers. Ed. by Art Sussman. LC 93-84434. 256p. 1993. pap. 14.95 (*0-9635683-1-0*); lib. bdg. 24.95 (*0-9635683-0-2*) UCSF Sci Ed.

Science Encounters the Indian, Eighteen Twenty to Eighteen Eighty: The Early Years of American Ethnology. Robert E. Bieder. LC 86-40068. (Illus.). 320p. 1986. 29.95 (*0-8061-1995-0*) U of Okla Pr.

Science Encounters the Indian, 1820-1880: The Early Years of American Ethnology. Robert E. Bieder. LC 86-40068. (Illus.). 304p. 1989. pap. 14.95 (*0-8061-2176-9*) U of Okla Pr.

Science Encyclopedia. A. Craig & C. Rosney. (Encyclopedias Ser.). (Illus.). 128p. (J). 1989. pap. 14.95 (*0-7460-0419-2*); lib. bdg. 22.95 (*0-88110-390-X*) EDC.

Science Enrichment Activities for the Elementary School. Joseph Crescimbeni. LC 80-28026. 272p. 1981. 24.95 (*0-13-794693-7*, Parker Publishing Co) P-H.

Science et Christ. Pierre Teilhard De Chardin. (FRE.). 1965. pap. 24.95 (*0-7859-1244-4*, 2020028654) Fr & Eur.

Science, Ethics, & Food: Papers & Proceedings of a Colloquium Organized by the Smithsonian Institution. Ed. by Brian W. LeMay. LC 88-18399. (Illus.). 144p. (Orig.). 1988. pap. text ed. 14.95 (*0-87474-605-1*) Smithsonian.

Science, Ethics, & Technology. 2nd ed. Donald Hatcher. 324p. (C). 1995. pap. text ed. 24.95 (*0-89641-233-4*) American Pr.

Science Everywhere: Opportunities for Very Young Children. Barbara Taylor. LC 91-78063. (Illus.). 288p. (C). 1993. pap. text ed. 24.00 (*0-03-054194-8*) HB Coll Pubs.

Science Expalined: The World of Science in Everyday Life. Ed. by Colin A. Ronan. (Illus.). 240p. 1996. pap. 22.50 (*0-8050-4236-9*, Owl) H Holt & Co.

***Science Experiences.** Koch. (C). Date not set. pap. write for info. (*0-395-70800-1*) HM.

Science Experiences: Cooperative Learning & the Teaching of Science. Jack Hassard. 1990. text ed. 27.00 (*0-201-23134-4*) Addison-Wesley.

Science Experiences for the Early Childhood Years: An Integrated Approach. 6th ed. Jean D. Harlan & Mary S. Rivkin. 1995. pap. text ed. 33.00 (*0-02-350180-4*, Macmillan Coll) P-H.

Science Experiences for Young Children. Viola S. Carmichael. Ed. by Robert D. Reed. LC 81-85434. (Orig.). 1982. spiral bd. 9.95 (*0-88247-633-5*) R & E Pubs.

Science Experiences for Young Children: Air. Rosemary Althouse & Cecil Main. LC 74-23257. (Illus.). 38p. 1975. reprint ed. pap. 25.00 (*0-608-00845-1*, 2061636) Bks Demand.

Science Experiences for Young Children: As We Grow. Rosemary Althouse & Cecil Main. LC 74-23257. (Illus.). 40p. 1975. reprint ed. pap. 25.00 (*0-608-00850-8*, 2061641) Bks Demand.

Science Experiences for Young Children: Colors. Rosemary Althouse & Cecil Main. LC 74-23257. (Illus.). 49p. 1975. reprint ed. pap. 25.00 (*0-608-00851-6*, 2061642) Bks Demand.

Science Experiences for Young Children: Food. Rosemary Althouse & Cecil Main. LC 74-23257. (Illus.). 37p. 1975. reprint ed. pap. 25.00 (*0-608-00849-4*, 2061640) Bks Demand.

Science Experiences for Young Children: Magnets. Rosemary Althouse & Cecil Main. LC 74-23257. (Illus.). 57p. 1975. reprint ed. pap. 25.00 (*0-608-00846-X*, 2061637) Bks Demand.

Science Experiences for Young Children: Pets. Rosemary Althouse & Cecil Main. LC 74-23257. (Illus.). 45p. 1975. pap. 25.00 (*0-608-00852-4*, 2061643) Bks Demand.

Science Experiences for Young Children: Seeds. Rosemary Althouse & Cecil Main. LC 74-23257. (Illus.). 38p. 1975. reprint ed. pap. 25.00 (*0-608-00853-2*, 2061644) Bks Demand.

Science Experiences for Young Children: Senses. Rosemary Althouse & Cecil Main. LC 74-23257. (Illus.). 41p. 1975. reprint ed. pap. 25.00 (*0-608-00844-3*, 2061635) Bks Demand.

Science Experiences for Young Children: Water. Rosemary Althouse & Cecil Main. LC 74-23257. (Illus.). 39p. 1975. reprint ed. pap. 25.00 (*0-608-00847-8*, 2061638) Bks Demand.

Science Experiences for Young Children: Wheels. Rosemary Althouse & Cecil Main. LC 74-23257. (Illus.). 29p. 1975. reprint ed. pap. 25.00 (*0-608-00848-6*, 2061639) Bks Demand.

Science Experiences with Everyday Things. Howard R. Munson. (J). (gr. 4-8). 1988. pap. 10.99 (*0-8224-6846-8*) Fearon Teach Aids.

Science Experiments. J. Bingham. (Illus.). 64p. (J). (gr. 5 up). 1992. pap. 8.95 (*0-7460-0806-6*, Usborne); lib. bdg. 16.95 (*0-88110-515-5*, Usborne) EDC.

Science Experiments. Vera Webster. LC 82-4429. (New True Bks.). 48p. (J). (gr. k-4). 1982. pap. 5.50 (*0-516-41646-4*); lib. bdg. 19.00 (*0-516-01646-6*) Childrens.

Science Experiments & Amusements for Children. Charles Vivian. LC 67-28142. Orig. Title: Science Games for Children, Il. (J). (ps-6). 1967. reprint ed. pap. 2.95 (*0-486-21856-2*) Dover.

Science Experiments & Projects for Students. Julia Cothron et al. 198p. (C). 1996. per., pap. 18.84 (*0-7872-1590-2*) Kendall-Hunt.

Science Experiments & Projects Index. Ed. by Lisa Holonitch. 330p. (J). (gr. k-12). 1994. text ed. 40.00 (*0-917846-31-1*, 95577) Highsmith Pr.

Science Experiments for the Primary Grades. Robert W. Reid. 1962. pap. 3.99 (*0-8224-6300-8*) Fearon Teach Aids.

Science Experiments for Young People Series, 3 bks., Set. Thomas R. Rybolt & Robert C. Mebane. (Illus.). (J). (gr. 4-9). 1993. lib. bdg. 53.85 (*0-89490-448-5*) Enslow Pubs.

Science Experiments Index for Young People. Mary A. Pilger. xiv, 240p. 1988. lib. bdg. 35.00 (*0-87287-671-3*) Libs Unl.

Science Experiments Index for Young People. 2nd ed. Mary A. Pilger. 400p. 1996. lib. bdg. 60.00 (*1-56308-341-8*) Libs Unl.

Science Experiments Index for Young People: Update 91. Mary A. Pilger. xiv, 133p. 1992. lib. bdg. 21.00 (*0-87287-858-9*) Libs Unl.

Science Experiments on File: Experiments, Demonstrations & Projects for School & Home. Facts on File Staff. (On File Ser.). (Illus.). 288p. 1988. ring bd. 155.00 (*0-8160-1888-X*) Facts on File.

Science Experiments You Can Eat. rev. ed. Vicki Cobb. LC 93-13679. (Illus.). 224p. (J). (gr. 5-9). 1994. 15.00 (*0-06-023534-9*); lib. bdg. 14.89 (*0-06-023551-9*) HarpC Child Bks.

Science Experiments 100's Middle School. Cothon et al. 160p. (C). 1996. per., pap. 18.84 (*0-7872-1574-0*) Kendall-Hunt.

Science Explained: The World of Science in Everyday Life. Ed. by Colin A. Ronan. LC 93-15439. (Reference Bks.). (Illus.). 240p. 1993. 45.00 (*0-8050-2551-0*, Bks Young Read) H Holt & Co.

Science Explained: The World of Science in Everyday Life. Ed. by Colin A. Ronan. 1995. pap. 19.95 (*0-614-15514-2*, Owl) H Holt & Co.

Science Explorer: The Best Family Activities & Experiments from the World's Farovite Hands-On. Pat Murphy et al. LC 96-16847. (Exploration-at-Home Bk.: No. 1). (Illus.). 144p. (YA). (gr. 8 up). 1996. pap. 12.95 (*0-8050-4536-8*) H Holt & Co.

Science Express. Ontario Science Center Staff. 1991. 14.38 (*0-201-57773-9*); pap. 8.95 (*0-201-57725-9*) Addison-Wesley.

Science Facilities Design for California Public Schools. California Department of Education Staff. (Illus.). 72p. 1992. pap. 8.25 (*0-8011-1038-6*) Calif Education.

Science Facts. Fred Justus. (Science Ser.). 24p. (gr. 6). 1978. student ed. 5.00 (*0-8209-0144-X*, S-6) ESP.

Science Facts. Steve Setford. LC 95-42182. (Pockets Ser.). 160p. (J). 1996. pap. 6.95 (*0-7894-0604-7*) DK Pub Inc.

Science Facts Puzzles. Fred Justus. (Puzzles Ser.). 24p. (gr. 6). 1980. student ed. 5.00 (*0-8209-0298-5*, PU-12) ESP.

***Science Facts Wow!** Jerome Agel. (J). Date not set. pap. 6.95 (*0-688-13183-2*) Morrow.

***Science Fair.** Ann M. Martin. (Kids in Ms. Coleman's Class Ser.: No. 7). (J). 1997. mass mkt. 3.50 (*0-590-69203-8*) Scholastic Inc.

Science Fair: Developing a Successful & Fun Project. Maxine H. Iritz. 1987. 16.95 (*0-07-156181-1*); pap. text ed. 11.95 (*0-07-156194-3*) McGraw.

Science Fair: Developing a Successful & Fun Project. Maxine H. Iritz. LC 87-10030. (Illus.). 96p. 1987. 16.95 (*0-8306-0936-9*, 2936); pap. 9.95 (*0-8306-2936-X*) McGraw-Hill Prof.

Science Fair for Non-Scientists. Carl Tant. (Illus.). 144p. (Orig.). (YA). (gr. 7-12). 1996. pap. 16.95 (*1-880319-16-0*) Biotech.

***Science Fair Project in Energy.** Bob Bonnet. (J). 1997. 16. 95 (*0-8069-9793-1*) Sterling.

Science Fair Project Index: Nineteen Seventy-Three to Nineteen Eighty. Ed. by Akron-Summit County Public Library, Science & Technology Division Staff. LC 83-3353. 729p. 1983. 59.50 (*0-8108-1605-9*) Scarecrow.

Science Fair Project Index: 1985-1989, for Grades K-8. Akron-Summit County Public Library Staff. Ed. by Cynthia Bishop et al. LC 92-22221. 563p. 1992. 55.00 (*0-8108-2555-4*) Scarecrow.

Science Fair Project Index, Nineteen Eighty-One to Nineteen Eighty-Four. Ed. by Akron-Summit County Public Library Staff et al. LC 86-6571. 692p. 1986. 47.50 (*0-8108-1892-2*) Scarecrow.

Science Fair Projects: A Source Guide. 1991. lib. bdg. 69. 00 (*0-8490-4859-1*) Gordon Pr.

***Science Fair Projects: Flight, Space & Astronomy.** Robert L. Bonnet & Dan Keen. LC 96-39281. (Illus.). (J). 1997. 16.95 (*0-8069-9450-9*) Sterling.

Science Fair Projects for the Environment. Dan Keen & Bob Bonnet. LC 94-46331. (Illus.). 96p. (Orig.). (J). (gr. 2 up). 1996. pap. 8.95 (*0-8069-0543-3*) Sterling.

Science Fair Projects for the Environment. Frances W. Zweifel. LC 94-46331. (Illus.). 96p. (Orig.). (J). (gr. 3-5). 1995. 16.95 (*0-8069-0542-5*) Sterling.

Science Fair Projects with Electricity & Electronics. Bob Bonnet & Dan Keen. LC 95-51492. (Illus.). 96p. (J). 1996. 16.95 (*0-8069-1300-2*) Sterling.

***Science Fair Projects with Electricity & Electronics.** Bob Bonnet & Dan Keen. (Illus.). 96p. (J). 1997. pap. 8.95 (*0-8069-1301-0*) Sterling.

Science Fair Spelled W-I-N. 2nd ed. Carl Tant. LC 95-75899. (Illus.). 240p. (Orig.). (YA). (gr. 7-12). 1995. pap. 19.95 (*1-880319-12-8*) Biotech.

Science Fair Success. Ruth Bombaugh. LC 89-7798. (Illus.). 96p. (YA). (gr. 6 up). 1990. lib. bdg. 17.95 (*0-89490-197-4*) Enslow Pubs.

Science Fair Workshop. Marcia J. Daab. (J). (gr. 4-8). 1990. pap. 7.99 (*0-8224-6374-1*) Fearon Teach Aids.

Science Fairs & Projects, 7-12. (Illus.). 72p. 1988. 9.50 (*0-87355-072-2*) Natl Sci Tchrs.

Science Fairs with Style. Jerry DeBruin. 336p. (J). (gr. 5-12). 1991. 20.99 (*0-86653-606-X*, GA1325) Good Apple.

Science, Faith, & Politics: Francis Bacon & the Utopian Roots of the Modern Age. Jerry Weinberger. LC 85-47707. 336p. (C). 1985. 45.00 (*0-8014-1817-8*) Cornell U Pr.

Science, Faith & Society. Polanyi. 1964. pap. text ed. 7.95 (*0-226-67298-0*) U Ch Pr.

Science, Faith & Society. Michael Polanyi. 96p. 1964. pap. text ed. 8.95 (*0-226-67290-5*, P155) U Ch Pr.

Science Fantasy Voices & Visions of Cosmic Religion. William W. Mountcastle. LC 96-10674. 172p. 1996. pap. text ed. 26.00 (*0-7618-0297-5*); lib. bdg. 46.00 (*0-7618-0296-7*) U Pr of Amer.

Science Fare: Chemistry at the Table see Science in Our World

Science Fiction. Compiled by Lin Haire-Sargeant. 240p. (Orig.). (C). 1996. pap. text ed. write for info. (*1-57790-015-4*) Book Tech.

Science Fiction. Andrew Joron. 65p. 1991. pap. 8.95 (*1-880766-02-7*) Pantograph Pr.

Science Fiction. Ed. by Jim Villani & Rose Sayre. (Pig Iron Ser.: No. 10). (Illus.). 96p. (Orig.). 1982. pap. 5.95 (*0-917530-18-7*) Pig Iron Pr.

Science Fiction, 61 vols, Set. (Illus.). 1975. 1,428.50 (*0-405-06270-2*) Ayer.

Science Fiction: A Critical Guide. Ed. by Patrick Parrinder. LC 78-40686. 252p. reprint ed. pap. 71.90 (*0-8357-3528-1*, 2034476) Bks Demand.

Science Fiction: A Teacher's Guide & Resource Book. Ed. by Marshall B. Tymn. LC 87-10143. (Starmont Reference Guide Ser.: No. 5). x, 140p. (Orig.). 1988. pap. 19.00 (*1-55742-020-3*); lib. bdg. 29.00 (*1-55742-021-1*) Borgo Pr.

Science Fiction: An Historical Anthology. Ed. by Eric S. Rabkin. 540p. 1983. pap. 14.95 (*0-19-503272-1*) OUP.

Science Fiction: Imagining Worlds. rev. ed. Patricia Payson. 79p. (J). (gr. k-8). 1980. spiral bd. 19.95 (*1-56976-002-0*) Zephyr Pr AZ.

Science Fiction: Ten Explorations. Colin N. Manlove. LC 85-14738. 224p. 1986. 22.50 (*0-87338-326-5*) Kent St U Pr.

Science-Fiction: The Early Years. Everett F. Bleiler. LC 90-4839. 1024p. 1991. 75.00 (*0-87338-416-4*) Kent St U Pr.

Science Fiction: The Future. 2nd ed. Dick Allen. 432p. (Orig.). (C). 1983. pap. text ed. 20.00 (*0-15-578651-2*) HB Coll Pubs.

Science Fiction: The Illustrated Encyclopedia. John Clute. LC 95-8083. (Illus.). 312p. (J). 1995. 39.95 (*0-7894-0185-1*, 6-70499) DK Pub Inc.

Science Fiction: The Mythos of a New Romance. Janice Antczak. Ed. by Jane Anne Hannigan. LC 84-14726. (Diversity & Direction in Children's Literature Ser.). 233p. 1985. 27.95 (*0-918212-43-X*) Neal-Schuman.

Science Fiction: The One Hundred Best Novels. David Pringle. 1987. pap. 7.95 (*0-88184-346-6*) Carroll & Graf.

Science Fiction: The SFRA Anthology. Ed. by Patricia S. Warrick et al. 522p. (C). 1987. pap. text ed. 33.95 (*0-06-046941-2*) Addison-Wesley Educ.

***Science Fiction: The 100 Best Novels.** David Pringle. 224p. 1997. pap. 10.95 (*0-7867-0481-0*) Carroll & Graf.

Science Fiction: The 100 Best Novels; An English-Language Selection, 1949-1984. David Pringle. 220p. 1986. 15.95 (*0-88184-259-1*) Carroll & Graf.

Science Fiction: Visions of Tomorrow. Isaac Asimov. LC 95-7233. (New Library of the Universe). (J). (gr. 3 up). 1995. lib. bdg. 18.60 (*0-8368-1224-7*) Gareth Stevens Inc.

Science Fiction after 1900. London. LC 96-44851. 1997. 22.95 (*0-8057-0962-2*, Twayne) Scribnrs Ref.

***Science Fiction & Fant Awards.** Hartwell. Date not set. pap. 14.95 (*0-312-85892-2*) St Martin.

Science Fiction & Fantasy. Library of Congress, National Library Service for the Blind & Physically Handicapped Staff. LC 94-35460. 1994. write for info. (*0-8444-0842-5*) Lib Congress.

Science Fiction & Fantasy see Young Adult Reading Activities Library

Science Fiction & Fantasy Authors: A Bibliography of First Printings of Their Fiction & Selected Fiction. L. W. Currey. 579p. 1979. pap. 78.50 (*0-89366-285-2*) Ultramarine Pub.

Science Fiction & Fantasy Book Review, Nos. 1-13 1979-1980. Ed. by Neil Barron & R. Reginald. LC 78-2211. 1983. reprint ed. lib. bdg. 35.00 (*0-89370-624-8*) Borgo Pr.

Science Fiction & Fantasy Book Review Annual, 1990. Robert A. Collins & Robert Latham. 728p. 1991. text ed. 85.00 (*0-313-28150-5*, SF90, Greenwood Pr) Greenwood.

Science Fiction & Fantasy Book Review Annual 1991. Robert A. Collins & Robert Latham. 896p. 1993. text ed. 115.00 (*0-313-28326-5*, Greenwood Pr) Greenwood.

Science Fiction & Fantasy Book Review Annual, 1988. Ed. by Robert A. Collins & Robert Latham. 496p. 1988. text ed. 75.00 (*0-313-28069-X*, SF88, Greenwood Pr) Greenwood.

Science Fiction & Fantasy Book Review Annual, 1989. Ed. by Robert A. Collins & Robert Latham. 625p. 1990. text ed. 75.00 (*0-313-28070-3*, SF89, Greenwood Pr) Greenwood.

Science Fiction & Fantasy Book Review Index, Vol. 10, 1979. Ed. by H. W. Hall. LC 72-625320. 1980. pap. 7.50 (*0-935064-05-2*) SFBRI.

Science Fiction & Fantasy Book Review Index, Vol. 11. Hal W. Hall. 64p. 1981. lib. bdg. 25.00 (*0-89370-076-2*) Borgo Pr.

Science Fiction & Fantasy Book Review Index, Vol. 11, 1980. H. W. Hall. LC 72-625320. 54p. 1981. pap. text ed. 7.50 (*0-935064-06-0*) SFBRI.

Science Fiction & Fantasy Book Review Index, Vol. 12. Hal W. Hall. 64p. 1982. lib. bdg. 25.00 (*0-89370-077-0*) Borgo Pr.

Science Fiction & Fantasy Book Review Index, Vol. 13. Hal W. Hall. 64p. 1983. lib. bdg. 27.00 (*0-89370-078-9*) Borgo Pr.

Science Fiction & Fantasy Book Review Index, Vol. 14. Hal W. Hall. 80p. 1984. reprint ed. lib. bdg. 27.00 (*0-89370-773-2*) Borgo Pr.

Science Fiction & Fantasy Book Review Index, Vol. 15. Hal W. Hall. 80p. 1985. lib. bdg. 27.00 (*0-89370-570-5*) Borgo Pr.

Science Fiction & Fantasy Book Review Index, Vol. 16. Hal W. Hall. 1988. lib. bdg. 27.00 (*0-89370-531-4*) Borgo Pr.

Science Fiction & Fantasy Book Review Index, vol. 17. Hal W. Hall. 1988. lib. bdg. 27.00 (*0-8095-6800-4*) Borgo Pr.

Science Fiction & Fantasy Book Review Index, Vol. 18. Hal W. Hall. v, 70p. 1987. lib. bdg. 27.00 (*0-8095-6801-2*) Borgo Pr.

Science Fiction & Fantasy Book Review Index, Vol. 19. Hal W. Hall. 85p. 1988. lib. bdg. 27.00 (*0-8095-6802-0*) Borgo Pr.

Science Fiction & Fantasy Book Review Index, Vol. 20. Hal W. Hall. vi, 90p. 1989. lib. bdg. 27.00 (*0-8095-6804-7*) Borgo Pr.

Science Fiction & Fantasy Book Review Index, Vol. 21. Hal W. Hall. 105p. 1990. lib. bdg. 29.00 (*0-8095-6805-5*) Borgo Pr.

Science Fiction & Fantasy Book Review Index 1980-1984. 84th ed. H. W. Hall. 794p. 1985. 195.00 (*0-8103-1646-3*) Gale.

Science Fiction & Fantasy BRI 1985- 85th ed. Donald Hall. 1900. 195.00 (*0-8103-5488-8*) Gale.

Science Fiction & Fantasy Film Handbook. Alan Frank. LC 82-8802. (Illus.). 194p. 1982. 41.50 (*0-389-20319-X*, N7157) B&N Imports.

Science Fiction & Fantasy Literature: A Checklist from 1700 to 1974...with Contemporary Science Fiction Authors II, 2 vols. Ed. by Robert Reginald. LC 76-46130. 1167p. 1994. 260.00 (*0-8103-1051-1*) Gale.

Science Fiction & Fantasy Literature: Nineteen Seventy-Five to Nineteen Ninety-One Supplement, 2 vols. 86th ed. Ed. by Robert Reginald. 1500p. 1992. 199.00 (*0-8103-1825-3*) Gale.

Science Fiction & Fantasy Literature Supplement 87. 87th ed. R. Reginald. 1901. 140.00 (*0-8103-5511-6*) Gale.

Science Fiction & Fantasy Paperbacks: A Complete List (1943-1973) C. P. Stephens. 150p. 1991. pap. 22.95 (*0-89366-162-7*) Ultramarine Pub.

Science Fiction & Fantasy Reference Index, 1878-1985: An International Author & Subject Index to History & Criticism, 2 vols., Set. 78th ed. Ed. by Hal W. Hall. 1511p. 1987. 185.00 (*0-8103-2129-7*) Gale.

Science Fiction & Fantasy Reference Index 1985-1991: An International Author & Subject Index to History & Criticism. Hal W. Hall. LC 92-43531. xxi, 677p. 1993. lib. bdg. 90.00 (*1-56308-113-X*) Libs Unl.

***Science Fiction & Fantasy Reference Index, 1992-1995: An International Subject & Author Index to History & Criticism.** Hal Hall. 400p. 1997. lib. bdg. 75.00 (*1-56308-527-5*) Libs Unl.

Science Fiction & Fantasy Research Index, Vol. 1. Hal W. Hall. (Orig.). 1981. lib. bdg. 25.00 (*0-89370-062-2*) Borgo Pr.

Science Fiction & Fantasy Research Index, Vol. 1. Hal W. Hall. 30p. (Orig.). 1981. pap. 5.00 (*0-935064-11-7*) SFBRI.

Science Fiction & Fantasy Research Index, Vol. 2. Hal W. Hall. (Orig.). 1982. lib. bdg. 27.00 (*0-89370-063-0*) Borgo Pr.

Science Fiction & Fantasy Research Index, Vol. 2. Ed. by Hal W. Hall. 72p. (Orig.). 1982. pap. 10.00 (*0-935064-12-5*) SFBRI.

Science Fiction & Fantasy Research Index, Vol. 3. Ed. by Hal W. Hall. 74p. (Orig.). 1983. pap. 10.00 (*0-935064-13-3*) SFBRI.

Science Fiction & Fantasy Research Index, Vol. 3. Hal W. Hall. (Orig.). 1983. reprint ed. lib. bdg. 27.00 (*0-89370-064-9*) Borgo Pr.

Science Fiction & Fantasy Research Index, Vol. 4. Hal W. Hall. (Orig.). 1985. lib. bdg. 27.00 (*0-89370-774-0*) Borgo Pr.

S

Science Fiction & Fantasy Research Index, Vol. 4. Ed. by Hal W. Hall. 83p. (Orig.). 1985. pap. 10.00 (*0-935064-15-X*) SFBRI.

Science Fiction & Fantasy Research Index, Vol. 5. Hal W. Hall. (Orig.). 1985. lib. bdg. 27.00 (*0-89370-775-9*) Borgo Pr.

Science Fiction & Fantasy Research Index, Vol. 6. Hal W. Hall. (Orig.). 1987. lib. bdg. 27.00 (*0-89370-530-6*) Borgo Pr.

Science Fiction & Fantasy Research Index, Vol. 7. Hal W. Hall. (Orig.). 1988. lib. bdg. 35.00 (*0-8095-6103-4*) Borgo Pr.

Science Fiction & Fantasy Research Index, Vol. 8. Hal W. Hall. (Orig.). 1988. lib. bdg. 27.00 (*0-8095-6111-5*) Borgo Pr.

Science Fiction & Fantasy Research Index, Vol. 9. Hal W. Hall. v, 97p. (Orig.). (C). 1992. lib. bdg. 27.00 (*0-8095-6112-3*) Borgo Pr.

Science Fiction & Fantasy Research Index, Vol. 10. Hal W. Hall. iv, 153p. (Orig.). 1994. lib. bdg. 33.00 (*0-8095-6803-9*) Borgo Pr.

Science Fiction & Fantasy Writer's Sourcebook: Where to Sell Your Manuscripts. 2nd ed. Ed. by David H. Borcherding. 480p. 1996. 19.99 (*0-89879-762-4*, Wrtrs Digest Bks) F & W Pubns Inc.

Science Fiction & Heroic Author Index. Compiled by Stuart W. Wells. 15.95 (*0-931998-00-X*); pap. 9.95 (*0-931998-01-8*) Purple Unicorn.

Science-Fiction & Horror Movie Posters in Full Color. Ed. by Alan Adler. 48p. 1977. pap. 9.95 (*0-486-23452-5*) Dover.

Science Fiction & Postmodern Fiction: A Genre Study. Barbara Puschmann-Nalenz. LC 91-21112. (American University Studies: General Literature: Ser. XIX, Vol. 29). 268p. (C). 1992. text ed. 46.95 (*0-8204-1670-3*) P Lang Pubng.

Science Fiction & Space Futures: Past & Present. Ed. by Eugene M. Emme. (AAS History Ser.: Vol. 5). (Illus.). 278p. 1982. pap. text ed. 25.00 (*0-87703-173-8*); lib. bdg. 35.00 (*0-87703-172-X*) Univelt Inc.

Science Fiction & the Theatre. Ralph Willingham. LC 93-4276. 232p. 1993. text ed. 59.95 (*0-313-28951-4*, Greenwood Pr) Greenwood.

Science Fiction Audiences: Doctor Who, Star Trek, & Their Fans. John Tulloch & Henry Jenkins. LC 94-29962. (Pupular Fictions Ser.). (Illus.). 288p. (C). (gr. 13). 1995. pap. 16.95 (*0-415-06141-5*, C0360); text ed. 62.95 (*0-415-06140-7*, C0359) Routledge.

Science Fiction Before 1900: Imagination Discovers Technology. Alkon. 1995. pap. 14.95 (*0-8057-9237-6*, Hall Reference) Macmillan.

Science Fiction Book Review Index, 1923-1973. 73th ed. Ed. by Hal W. Hall. LC 74-29085. 456p. 1975. 195.00 (*0-8103-1054-6*) Gale.

Science Fiction Book Review Index, 1974 to 1979. 79th ed. Ed. by Hal W. Hall. 416p. 1981. 195.00 (*0-8103-1107-0*) Gale.

***Science Fiction Century.** David G. Hartwell. LC 96-54591. 1997. 40.00 (*0-312-86338-1*) St Martin.

Science Fiction Classics. Edgar Rice Burroughs. 1992. 7.98 (*0-89009-582-5*) Bk Sales Inc.

Science Fiction Collections: Fantasy, Supernatural & Weird Tales. Ed. by Hal W. Hall. LC 82-21355. (Special Collections: Vol. 2, Nos. 1-2). 181p. 1983. 44.95 (*0-917724-49-6*) Haworth Pr.

Science Fiction Criticism: An Annotated Checklist. Thomas D. Clareson. LC 71-181084. (Serif Series: Bibliographies & Checklists: No. 23). 239p. reprint ed. pap. 68.20 (*0-7837-0568-9*, 2040912) Bks Demand.

Science Fiction Design Book. Bradford R. Hamann. (International Design Library). (Illus.). 48p. 1982. pap. 5.95 (*0-916144-49-6*) Stemmer Hse.

Science Fiction Detective Tales: A Brief Overview of Futuristic Detective Fiction in Paperback. Gary Lovisi. (Illus.). 107p. (Orig.). 1986. pap. 7.95 (*0-936071-01-X*) Gryphon Pubns.

Science Fiction Fandom. Ed. by Joe Sanders. LC 94-16126. (Contributions to the Study of Science Fiction & Fantasy Ser.: No. 62). 312p. 1994. text ed. 59.95 (*0-313-23380-2*, Greenwood Pr) Greenwood.

Science Fiction, Fantasy & Horror: 1984. Charles N. Brown & William G. Contento. (Science Fiction, Fantasy & Horror Ser.: No. 4). 300p. 1990. 50.00 (*0-9616629-5-6*) Locus Pr.

Science Fiction, Fantasy, & Horror: 1986. Charles N. Brown & William G. Contento. (Science Fiction, Fantasy & Horror Ser.: No. 2). 347p. 1987. 45.00 (*0-9616629-3-X*) Locus Pr.

Science Fiction, Fantasy, & Horror: 1987. Charles N. Brown & William G. Contento. (Science Fiction, Fantasy & Horror Ser.: No. 3). 420p. 1987. 45.00 (*0-9616629-4-8*) Locus Pr.

Science Fiction, Fantasy, & Horror: 1988. Charles N. Brown & William G. Contento. 1989. 50.00 (*0-9616629-6-4*) Locus Pr.

Science Fiction, Fantasy & Horror: 1990. Charles N. Brown & William G. Contento. 587p. 1991. 50.00 (*0-9616629-8-0*) Locus Pr.

Science Fiction, Fantasy & Horror Film Series & Remakes: An Illustrated Filmography, with Plot Synopses & Critical Commentary. Kim R. Holston & Tom Winchester. LC 96-51433. (Illus.). 608p. 1997. lib. bdg. 75.00 (*0-7864-0155-9*) McFarland & Co.

Science Fiction, Fantasy & Horror Reference: An Annotated Bibliography of Works about Literature & Film. Keith L. Justice. LC 89-2841. 240p. 1989. lib. bdg. 45.00 (*0-89950-406-X*) McFarland & Co.

Science Fiction, Fantasy, & Horror Writers, 2 vols. Marie J. MacNee. 480p. (J). 1994. 43.00 (*0-8103-9865-6*, UXL) Gale.

Science Fiction, Fantasy & Horror, 1986. Charles N. Brown & William G. Contento. 347p. 1987. 45.00 (*0-88736-071-8*) Locus Pr.

Science Fiction, Fantasy & Horror, 1989. Charles N. Brown & William G. Contento. 515p. 1990. 50.00 (*0-9616629-7-2*) Locus Pr.

Science Fiction, Fantasy, & Horror, 1991: A Comprehensive Bibliography of Books & Short Fiction Published in the English Language. Charles N. Brown & William G. Contento. 1992. 60.00 (*0-9616629-9-9*) Locus Pr.

Science Fiction, Fantasy, & Weird Fiction Magazines. Ed. by Marshall B. Tymn & Mike Ashley. LC 85-17360. (Historical Guides to the World's Periodicals & Newspapers Ser.). (Illus.). xxx, 970p. 1985. text ed. 105.00 (*0-313-21221-X*, TFM/) Greenwood.

Science Fiction Filmmaking in the 1980s: Interviews with Actors, Directors, Producers & Writers. Lee Goldberg et al. LC 94-30909. (Illus.). 279p. 1995. lib. bdg. 37.50 (*0-89950-918-5*) McFarland & Co.

Science Fiction for Young Readers. Ed. by C. W. Sullivan, III. LC 92-26667. (Contributions to the Study of Science Fiction & Fantasy Ser.: No. 56). 232p. 1993. text ed. 55.00 (*0-313-27289-1*, SYD/, Greenwood Pr) Greenwood.

Science Fiction from China: Eight Stories. Ed. by Patrick D. Murphy & Dingbo Wu. LC 89-1986. 217p. 1989. text ed. 18.95 (*0-275-93343-1*, C3343, Praeger Pubs) Greenwood.

Science Fiction from China: Eight Stories. Ed. by Dingbo Wu & Patrick D. Murphy. (Contributions to the Study of Science Fiction & Fantasy Ser.: No. 39). 1989. write for info. (*0-313-26544-5*, WUS, Greenwood Pr) Greenwood.

Science Fiction Hall of Fame, Vol. 1. Ed. by Robert Silverberg. 672p. 1976. mass mkt. 6.99 (*0-380-00795-9*) Avon.

Science Fiction Hall of Fame, Vol. IV. Ed. by Terry Carr. 432p. 1986. mass mkt. 4.95 (*0-380-89710-5*) Avon.

Science Fiction Horizons, 2 Vols. Ed. by Brian W. Aldiss & Harry Harrison. LC 74-15942. (Science Fiction Ser.). (Illus.). 64p. 1977. reprint ed. 17.95 (*0-405-06320-2*) Ayer.

Science Fiction, Horror & Fantasy Film & Television Credits, Suppl. 2: Through 1993. Harris M. Lentz, III. LC 93-33878. 864p. 1994. lib. bdg. 85.00 (*0-89950-927-4*) McFarland & Co.

Science Fiction in America, Eighteen Seventies-Nineteen Thirties: An Annotated Bibliography of Primary Sources. Compiled by Thomas D. Clareson. LC 84-8934. (Bibliographies & Indexes in American Literature Ser.: No. 1). xiii, 305p. 1984. text ed. 69.50 (*0-313-23169-9*, CSF/) Greenwood.

Science Fiction in Print 1985. Charles N. Brown & William G. Contento. 237p. 1986. 35.00 (*0-9616629-2-1*) Locus Pr.

Science Fiction in the Real World. Norman Spinrad. LC 89-19705. (Alternatives Ser.). 248p. 1990. 29.95 (*0-8093-1538-6*); pap. 16.95 (*0-8093-1671-4*) S Ill U Pr.

Science Fiction in the Twentieth Century. Edward James. 160p. 1994. pap. 12.95 (*0-19-289244-4*) OUP.

Science Fiction Legal Series, Bk. 1. limited ed. J. Pero Wexler. 183p. 1995. 88.00 (*1-887695-00-1*) L G Scolish.

Science Fiction Magazines: A Bibliographical Checklist of Titles & Issues Through 1982. Hal W. Hall. LC 84-11192. 89p. 1984. lib. bdg. 29.00 (*0-89370-772-4*) Borgo Pr.

Science Fiction Market Realities. Ed. by Eric S. Rabkin et al. LC 94-23971. 1996. 40.00 (*0-8203-1726-8*) U of Ga Pr.

Science Fiction Movies. Andrea Staskowski. (Silver Screen Ser.). (Illus.). 80p. (YA). (gr. 5 up). 1991. lib. bdg. 9.50 (*0-8225-1638-1*, Lerner Publctns) Lerner Group.

Science Fiction, Myth, & Jungian Psychology. Kenneth L. Golden. LC 95-3015. 1995. write for info. (*0-7734-9023-X*) E Mellen.

Science Fiction Novel: Imagination & Social Criticism. 3rd ed. Basil Davenport et al. LC 58-7492. 1969. reprint ed. 15.00 (*0-911682-02-3*); reprint ed. pap. 8.00 (*0-911682-13-9*) Advent.

Science Fiction of Edgar Allan Poe. Edgar Allan Poe. Ed. by Harold Beaver. (English Library). 430p. 1976. pap. 10.95 (*0-14-043106-3*, Penguin Classics) Viking Penguin.

Science Fiction of Konstantin Tsiolkovsky. Konstantin Tsiolkovsky. Ed. by Adam Starchild. 455p. reprint ed. pap. 129.70 (*0-8357-2800-5*, AU00410) Bks Demand.

Science Fiction of Kris Neville. Kris Neville. Ed. by Barry N. Malzberg & Martin H. Greenberg. LC 83-10514. (Alternatives Ser.). 254p. (C). 1984. 19.95 (*0-8093-1112-7*) S Ill U Pr.

Science Fiction of Mark Clifton. Ed. by Barry N. Malzberg & Martin H. Greenberg. LC 80-20977. (Alternatives Ser.). 318p. 1980. 19.95 (*0-8093-0985-8*) S Ill U Pr.

Science Fiction of Mark Twain. Mark Twain. LC 84-6282. xxxiii, 385p. (C). 1984. lib. bdg. 40.00 (*0-208-02036-5*, Archon Bks) Shoe String.

Science Fiction on Radio: A Revised Look at 1950-1975. James F. Widner & Meade Frierson, III. LC 96-83951. 200p. (Orig.). 1996. pap. 15.00 (*0-9639544-4-X*) A F A B.

Science Fiction Private Eye. Martin Greenberg. 1997. pap. 5.99 (*0-451-45592-4*, ROC) NAL-Dutton.

Science Fiction Reference Book: A Comprehensive Handbook & Guide. Ed. by Marshall B. Tymm. LC 80-28888. (Illus.). viii, 536p. 1981. pap. 43.00 (*0-916732-24-X*); lib. bdg. 53.00 (*0-916732-49-5*) Borgo Pr.

Science Fiction Roots & Branches: Contemporary Critical Approaches. Rhys Garnett & R. J. Ellis. LC 89-36454. 210p. 1990. text ed. 39.95 (*0-312-03598-5*) St Martin.

Science Fiction Stars & Horror Heroes: Interviews with Actors, Directors, Producers & Writers of the 1940s Through 1960s. Tom Weaver. LC 90-53528. (Illus.). 462p. 1991. lib. bdg. 38.50 (*0-89950-594-5*) McFarland & Co.

***Science Fiction Stories.** Ursula K. Le Guin. write for info. (*0-06-105202-7*, HarperPrism) HarpC.

Science Fiction Stories. Illus. by Karin Littlewood. LC 92-26453. (Story Library). 256p. (J). (gr. 4-9). 1993. 6.95 (*1-85697-889-3*, Kingfisher LKC) LKC.

Science Fiction Stories. Jack London. 1976. 23.95 (*0-8488-1081-3*) Amereon Ltd.

***Science Fiction Stories.** Robinson Publishing Staff. (J). 1997. pap. 9.99 (*0-679-88527-7*) Random.

Science Fiction Stories of Jack London. Compiled by James Bankes. LC 92-39510. 1993. 9.95 (*0-8065-1407-8*, Citadel Pr) Carol Pub Group.

Science Fiction Stories of Jack London. Jack London. 1994. reprint ed. lib. bdg. 27.95 (*1-56849-303-7*) Buccaneer Bks.

Science Fiction Stories of Rudyard Kipling. Ed. by John Brunner. LC 93-45379. 1994. 9.95 (*0-8065-1508-2*, Citadel Pr) Carol Pub Group.

Science Fiction Story Index, 1950-1968. Frederick Siemon. LC 70-162470. 286p. reprint ed. pap. 81.60 (*0-317-27835-5*, 2024219) Bks Demand.

Science Fiction Story Index, 1950-1979. 2nd ed. Marilyn Fletcher. LC 80-28685. 623p. reprint ed. pap. 177.60 (*0-7837-5950-9*, 2045750) Bks Demand.

Science Fiction-Syndicat see Grande Encyclopedie

Science Fiction Television Series: Episode Guides, Histories, & Casts & Credits for 62 Prime Time Shows, 1959-1989. Mark Phillips & Frank Garcia. LC 95-47667. (Illus.). 703p. 1996. lib. bdg. 75.00 (*0-7864-0041-2*) McFarland & Co.

Science Fiction TV: From the Twilight Zone to Deep Space Nine. James Van Hise. 272p. 1995. mass mkt. 4.99 (*0-06-105436-4*, HarperPrism) HarpC.

Science Fiction Voices: No. 1. Darrell Schweitzer. LC 82-640033. (Milford Ser.: Popular Writers of Today: Vol. 23). 63p. 1979. pap. 13.00 (*0-89370-233-1*); lib. bdg. 23.00 (*0-89370-133-5*) Borgo Pr.

Science Fiction Voices: No. 2. Jeffrey M. Elliot. LC 82-640033. (Milford Ser.: Popular Writers of Today: Vol. 25). 62p. 1979. pap. 13.00 (*0-89370-237-4*); lib. bdg. 23.00 (*0-89370-137-8*) Borgo Pr.

Science Fiction Voices: No. 3. Jeffrey M. Elliot. LC 82-640033. (Milford Ser.: Popular Writers of Today: Vol. 29). 64p. 1980. pap. 13.00 (*0-89370-243-9*); lib. bdg. 23.00 (*0-89370-143-2*) Borgo Pr.

Science Fiction Voices No. 4: Interviews with Science-Fiction Authors. Jeffrey M. Elliot. LC 82-640033. (Milford Series: Vol. 33). 63p. (Orig.). 1982. pap. 13.00 (*0-89370-248-X*); lib. bdg. 23.00 (*0-89370-148-3*) Borgo Pr.

Science Fiction Voices, No. 5: Interviews with Science-Fiction Writers. Darrell Schweitzer. LC 82-640033. (Milford Series: Popular Writers of Today: Popular Writers of Today: Vol. 35). 64p. 1981. pap. 13.00 (*0-89370-251-X*); lib. bdg. 23.00 (*0-89370-151-3*) Borgo Pr.

Science Fiction Writers of the Golden Age see Writers of English: Lives & Works

Science Fiction Writer's Workshop-1: An Introduction to Fiction Mechanics. Barry B. Longyear. 168p. 1980. pap. 9.50 (*0-913896-18-7*) Owlswick Pr.

Science Fiction Yearbook. Ed. by Jerry Pournelle et al. 344p. 1985. 15.95 (*0-317-27055-9*, Baen Bks) PB.

Science Fictionisms. Ed. by William Rotsler. LC 95-13162. 144p. 1995. pap. 6.95 (*0-87905-693-2*) Gibbs Smith Pub.

Science Fictions: Orshi Drozdik & Jon Tower. Katy Kline & Helaine Posner. LC 92-54122. (Illus.). 48p. (Orig.). 1992. pap. 12.00 (*0-938437-41-0*) MIT List Visual Arts.

Science for a Polite Society: Gender, Culture, & the Demonstration of Enlightenment. Geoffrey V. Sutton. (C). 1997. pap. text ed. 19.00 (*0-8133-1576-X*) Westview.

Science for Agriculture: A Long-Term Perspective. Wallace E. Huffman & Robert E. Evanson. LC 93-16097. (Illus.). 280p. (C). 1993. text ed. 47.95 (*0-8138-1359-X*) Iowa St U Pr.

Science for All: Access to the National Curriculum for Children with Special Needs. 2nd ed. Sue Fagg & Sue Skelton. 96p. 1993. pap. 22.00 (*1-85346-256-X*, Pub. by D Fulton UK) Taylor & Francis.

Science for All: Studies in the History of Victorian Science & Education. William H. Brock. (Collected Studies: No. CS518). 320p. 89.95 (*0-86078-542-4*, Pub. by Variorum UK) Ashgate Pub Co.

Science for All Americans. F. James Rutherford & Andrew Ahlgren. 272p. 1991. pap. 12.95 (*0-19-506771-1*) OUP.

Science for All Children. Anthony D. Fredericks & G. R. Cheeseborough. (C). 1992. 56.50 (*0-673-46485-7*) Addson-Wesley Educ.

***Science for All Children.** Martin & Sexton. 1997. text ed. 32.00 (*0-205-27573-7*) P-H.

Science for All Children: A Guide to Improving Elementary Science Education in Your School District. rev. ed. Smithsonian Institution, National Academy of Sciences, National Science Resources Center Staff. 240p. 1997. pap. 19.95 (*0-309-05297-1*) Natl Acad Pr.

Science for All Cultures. Shelley J. Carey. (Illus.). 72p. 1993. pap. text ed. 16.50 (*0-87355-122-2*) Natl Sci Tchrs.

Science for Children: A Book for Teachers. 2nd ed. Willard J. Jacobson & Abby B. Bergman. (Illus.). 448p. (C). 1987. text ed. write for info. (*0-13-795014-4*) P-H.

Science for Children: A Book for Teachers. 3rd ed. Willard J. Jacobson & Abby B. Bergman. 416p. 1990. text ed. 65.00 (*0-13-794843-3*) P-H.

Science for Children see Physics Experiments for Children

Science for Conservators Series: Adhesives & Coatings, Vol. 3. Conservation Unit Staff & Museums & Galleries Commission Staff. (Heritage: Care-Preservation-Management Program Ser.). 140p. (C). 1992. pap. 19.95 (*0-415-07163-1*, A9587) Routledge.

Science for Conservators Series: An Introduction to Materials, Vol. 1. Conservation Unit Staff & Museums & Galleries Commission Staff. (Heritage: Care-Preservation-Management Program Ser.). 116p. (C). 1992. pap. 19.95 (*0-415-07167-4*, A9604) Routledge.

Science for Conservators Series: An Introduction to Materials, Vol. 1. Conservation Unit Staff & Museums & Galleries Commission Staff. (Heritage: Care-Preservation-Management Program Ser.). 116p. (C). (gr. 13). 1992. text ed. 49.95 (*0-415-07166-6*, A9600) Routledge.

Science for Conservators Series: Cleaning, Vol. 2. Conservation Unit Staff & Museums & Galleries Commission Staff. (Heritage: Care-Preservation-Management Program Ser.). 132p. (C). 1992. pap. 19.95 (*0-415-07165-8*, A7855) Routledge.

Science for Curriculum Leaders. Ed. by Elizabeth Clayden & Alan Peacock. LC 93-44875. (Primary Inset Ser.). (Illus.). 128p. (C). (gr. 13). 1994. text ed. 49.95 (*0-415-10390-8*, B3588) Routledge.

Science for Deaf Children. Allan Leitman. LC 68-58037. 1968. pap. text ed. 7.95 (*0-88200-109-4*, D2668) Alexander Graham.

Science for Democracy. Conference On the Scientific Spirit & Democratic Faith - 3rd. LC 70-121459. (Essay Index Reprint Ser.). 1977. 20.95 (*0-8369-1793-6*) Ayer.

Science for Elementary School. 8th ed. Victor. LC 96-22861. 1996. text ed. 65.00 (*0-13-457037-5*) P-H.

Science for Engineering. J. O. Bird. 380p. 1995. pap. 28.95 (*0-7506-2150-8*) Buttrwrth-Heinemann.

Science for Floodplain Management into the 21st Century. 1996. lib. bdg. 255.75 (*0-8490-5982-8*) Gordon Pr.

Science for Fun Experiments. Gary Gibson. LC 96-13908. (Illus.). 224p. (J). (gr. 2-4). 1996. 16.95 (*0-7613-0517-3*, Copper Beech Bks) Millbrook Pr.

Science for Girls. Ed. by Alison Kelly. 192p. 1987. pap. 24.95 (*0-335-10294-8*, Open Univ Pr) Taylor & Francis.

Science for Hobbyists Bk. 3. Exploratorium Staff. 1997. pap. 12.00 (*0-8050-4541-4*) H Holt & Co.

Science for Hobbyists Bk. 4. Exploratorium Staff. 1997. pap. 12.00 (*0-8050-4542-2*) H Holt & Co.

Science for Kids: Thirty Nine Easy Animal Biology Experiments. Robert W. Wood. 1991. pap. text ed. 9.95 (*0-07-071726-5*) McGraw.

Science for Kids: Thirty-Nine Easy Astronomy Experiments. Robert W. Wood. 1990. pap. text ed. 10.95 (*0-07-156195-1*) McGraw.

Science for Kids: Thirty-Nine Easy Chemistry Experiments. Robert W. Wood. 1991. pap. text ed. 10.95 (*0-07-156180-3*) McGraw.

Science for Kids: Thirty-nine Easy Engineering Experiments. Robert W. Wood. (J). (gr. 3-8). 1991. 16.95 (*0-8306-1946-1*); pap. 9.95 (*0-8306-1943-7*) McGraw-Hill Prof.

Science for Kids: Thirty Nine Easy Engineering Experiments. Robert W. Wood. 1991. pap. text ed. 10.95 (*0-07-071740-0*) McGraw.

Science for Kids: Thirty-Nine Easy Geography Activities. Robert W. Wood. 1991. pap. text ed. 10.95 (*0-07-157869-2*) McGraw.

Science for Kids: Thirty Nine Easy Geology Experiments. Robert W. Wood. 1991. text ed. 16.95 (*0-07-071724-9*) McGraw.

Science for Kids: Thirty Nine Easy Plant Biology Experiments. Robert W. Wood. 1991. pap. text ed. 10.95 (*0-07-071728-1*) McGraw.

Science for Kids: 39 Easy Meteorology Experiments. Robert W. Wood. 1991. pap. text ed. 10.95 (*0-07-071723-0*) McGraw.

Science for Life & Living: Integrating Science, Technology & Health. BSCS Staff. 368p. (J). (gr. 5). 1991. boxed 29.90 (*0-8403-5998-5*) Kendall-Hunt.

Science for Life & Living: Integrating Science, Technology & Health. BSCS Staff. 560p. 1991. teacher ed., ring bd. 59.90 (*0-8403-5999-3*) Kendall-Hunt.

Science for Life & Living: Integrating Science, Technology & Health Grade 2. BSCS Staff. 240p. 1991. 24.90 (*0-8403-5992-6*); ring bd. 59.90 (*0-8403-5991-8*) Kendall-Hunt.

Science for Life & Living: Integrating Science, Technology & Health Grade 2. BSCS Staff. 208p. 1995. per. 11.90 (*0-8403-5990-X*) Kendall-Hunt.

Science for Life & Living: Integrating Science, Technology, & Health, Grade 2. BSCS Staff. 320p. 1991. boxed 28.90 (*0-8403-5996-9*) Kendall-Hunt.

Science for Life & Living: Integrating Science, Technology, & Health, Grade 2. BSCS Staff. 368p. 1991. boxed 27.90 (*0-8403-5994-2*) Kendall-Hunt.

Science for Life & Living: Integrating Science, Technology, & Health, Grade 2. BSCS Staff. 464p. (J). (gr. 2). 1991. teacher ed., ring bd. 59.90 (*0-8403-5993-4*) Kendall-Hunt.

Science for Life & Living: Integrating Science, Technology, & Health, Grade 2. BSCS Staff. 480p. 1991. teacher ed., ring bd. 59.90 (*0-8403-5995-0*); teacher ed., ring bd. 59.90 (*0-8403-5997-7*) Kendall-Hunt.

Science for Life & Living Grade 6. BSCS Staff. 352p. 1991. 29.90 (*0-8403-6000-2*) Kendall-Hunt.

Science for Life & Living Teachers Edition: Grade 6. BSCS Staff. 416p. 1991. ring bd. 59.90 (*0-8403-6001-0*) Kendall-Hunt.

Science for Me. Linda Diebert. 112p. (J). (ps-2). 1991. 12.99 (*0-86653-597-7*, GA1318) Good Apple.

***Science for Motor Vehicle Engineers.** Twigg. (Mechanical Engineering Ser.). 1996. pap. 27.50 (*0-340-64527-X*) Van Nos Reinhold.

An Asterisk (*) at the beginning of an entry indicates that the title is appearing in BIP for the first time.

Science for Sane Societies. Paulos Mar Gregorios. LC 86-25282. (Patterns of World Spirituality Ser.). 247p. 1987. pap. 8.95 (0-913757-70-5, New Era Bks) Paragon Hse.

Science for the Beauty Therapist. J. F. Rounce. 314p. (C). 1983. pap. 42.00 (0-85950-331-3, Pub. by S Thornes Pubs UK) St Mut.

Science for the Earth: Can Science Make the World a Better Place? Ed. by Tom Wakeford & Martin Walters. LC 94-43583. 370p. 1995. pap. text ed. 14.95 (0-471-95284-2) Wiley.

Science for the Food Industry of the 21st Century: Biotechnology, Supercritical Fluids, Membranes & Other Advanced Technologies for Low Calorie, Healthy Food Alternatives. Ed. by Manssur Yalpani. 420p. (C). 1993. 187.00 (1-882360-45-1) ATL Pr Sci.

Science for the Fun of It. Ed. by Marvin Druger. (Illus.). 142p. 1988. 11.00 (0-87355-074-9) Natl Sci Tchrs.

*Science for the Twenty-First Century: The Vannevar Bush Report. Ed. by Claude E. Barfield. 125p. 1997. pap. 14.95 (0-8447-4015-2) Am Enterprise.

*Science for the Twenty-First Century: The Vannevar Bush Report Revisited. Ed. by Claude E. Barfield. 100p. 1997. 29.95 (0-8447-4014-4) Am Enterprise.

Science for You - One Hundred & Twelve Illustrated Experiments. Brown. 1988. 12.95 (0-8306-0325-5, 3025); pap. 7.95 (0-8306-9325-4) McGraw-Hill Prof.

Science Framework for California Public Schools, K-12. California Department of Education Staff. (Illus.). 220p. 1990. pap. 9.50 (0-8011-0870-5) Calif Education.

Science Friction: Grins & Groans among the Titles of Scientific Studies. Lubertus Berrens. LC 95-4088. (Illus.). 92p. 1995. pap. 19.50 (0-88937-146-6) Hogrefe & Huber Pubs.

Science from an Easy Chair, First Series. Edwin R. Lankester. LC 79-152185. (Essay Index Reprint Ser.). 1977. 26.95 (0-8369-2194-1) Ayer.

Science from an Easy Chair, Second Series. Edwin R. Lankester. LC 79-152185. (Essay Index Reprint Ser.). 1977. 23.95 (0-8369-2210-7) Ayer.

Science from Your Airplane Window. rev. ed. Elizabeth A. Wood. LC 75-14762. 256p. 1975. pap. 5.95 (0-486-23205-0) Dover.

Science Front, 1939. Frank S. Taylor. LC 77-156722. (Essay Index Reprint Ser.). 1977. reprint ed. 23.95 (0-8369-2430-4) Ayer.

Science Frontiers: Some Anomalies & Curiosities of Nature. William R. Corliss. LC 93-92800. 356p. (Orig.). (C). 1994. pap. text ed. 18.95 (0-915554-28-3) Sourcebook.

Science Fun. Imogene Forte. LC 84-62935. (Tabletop Learning Ser.). (Illus.). 80p. (J). (gr. k-6). 1985. pap. text ed. 4.95 (0-86530-100-X, IP 91-4) Incentive Pubns.

Science Fun. M. Johnson et al. (Pocket Scientist Ser.). (Illus.). 192p. (J). (gr. 4 up). 1993. pap. 9.95 (0-7460-0361-7) EDC.

Science Fun in Chicagoland: A Guide for Parents & Teachers with Over Eight-Hundred Resource Descriptions. Thomas W. Sills. (Illus.). 193p. (Orig.). 1995. pap. 14.95 (0-9644096-0-7) Dearborn Res.

Science Fun Series, 5 vols., Set. Rose Wyler. (Illus.). 288p. (J). (gr. 2-4). 1988. pap. 24.70 (0-382-24533-4, Julian Messner) Silver Burdett Pr.

Science Fun with Drums, Bells, & Whistles. Rose Wyler. LC 87-7838. (Science Fun Ser.). (Illus.). 48p. (J). (gr. 2-4). 1987. pap. 4.95 (0-671-64760-1, Julian Messner) Silver Burdett Pr.

Science Fun With Mud & Dirt. Rose Wyler. (Science Fun Ser.). (Illus.). 48p. (J). (gr. 3). 1987. pap. 4.95 (0-317-56794-2) S&S Trade.

Science Fun with Mud & Dirt. Rose Wyler. LC 86-8388. (Science Fun Ser.). (Illus.). 48p. (J). (gr. 2-4). 1986. pap. 4.95 (0-671-62904-2, Julian Messner) Silver Burdett Pr.

Science Fun with Peanuts & Popcorn. Rose Wyler. (Science Fun Ser.). (Illus.). 48p. (J): (gr. 2-4). 1986. pap. 4.95 (0-671-62452-0, Julian Messner) Silver Burdett Pr.

Science Fun with Toy Boats & Planes. Rose Wyler. LC 85-8842. (Science Fun Ser.). (Illus.). 48p. (J). (gr. 2-4). 1986. pap. 4.95 (0-671-62453-9, Julian Messner) Silver Burdett Pr.

Science Fun with Toy Boats & Planes. Rose Wyler. (Science Fun Ser.). (Illus.). 48p. (J). (gr. 3). 1987. pap. 4.95 (0-317-56816-7) S&S Trade.

Science Fun with Toy Cars & Trucks. Rose Wyler. LC 87-20326. (Science Fun Ser.). (Illus.). 48p. (J). (gr. 2-4). 1988. pap. 4.95 (0-671-65854-9, Julian Messner) Silver Burdett Pr.

Science Fundamentals: A Background for Household Equipment. Louise J. Peet. LC 70-171171. (Illus.). 140p. 1972. reprint ed. pap. 39.90 (0-608-00157-0, 2060938) Bks Demand.

Science Funding: Politics & Porkbarrel. Joseph P. Martino. 336p. (C). 1992. 44.95 (1-56000-033-3) Transaction Pubs.

Science Game: An Introduction to Research in the Social Science. 6th ed. Sandra W. Pyke & Neil McKagnew. LC 93-40931. 384p. 1993. pap. text ed. 26.80 (0-13-098583-X) P-H.

Science Games. Arnold R. Davis & Donald C. Miller. (J). (gr. 1-6). 1974. pap. 4.99 (0-8224-6303-2) Fearon Teach Aids.

Science Games & Puzzles. Laurence B. White, Jr. LC 84-40786. (J). 1979. pap. 4.95 (0-201-08606-9, Lipp Jr Bks) HarpC Child Bks.

Science Games for Children, II see Science Experiments & Amusements for Children

Science Gap: Dispelling the Myths & Understanding the Reality of Science. Milton A. Rothman. 254p. 1991. 29.95 (0-87975-710-8) Prometheus Bks.

Science Goals. Fred Justus. (Science Ser.). 24p. (gr. 5). 1980. student ed. 5.00 (0-8209-0143-1, S-5) ESP.

Science, God, & Nature in Victorian Canada. Carl Berger. (Joanne Goodman Lectures: No. 1982). (Illus.). 112p. reprint ed. pap. 32.00 (0-8357-3631-8, 2036359) Bks Demand.

Science Grade 2 1989. Abruscato. 1989. student ed. 36.00 (0-03-011419-5) HB Schl Dept.

Science Grade 2 89. Abruscato. 1989. student ed. 26.50 (0-03-011389-X) HB Schl Dept.

Science Grade 3 1989. Abruscato. 1989. 30.75 (0-03-011392-X) HB Schl Dept.

Science Grade 4 89. Abruscato. 1989. student ed. 35.25 (0-03-011393-8) HB Schl Dept.

Science Grade 6 1989. Abruscato. 1989. 36.00 (0-03-011394-6) HB Schl Dept.

Science Graphs & Word Games. Lorraine Conway. (Superific Science Ser.: Bk. V). 48p. (J). (gr. 5 up). 1981. 8.99 (0-86653-029-0, GA 257) Good Apple.

Science Has No National Borders: Harry C. Kelly & the Reconstruction of Science & Technology in Postwar Japan. Hideo Yoshikawa & Joanne Kauffman. LC 93-29741. (Illus.). 160p. 1994. 26.00 (0-262-24037-8) MIT Pr.

Science, Hegemony & Violence: A Requiem for Modernity. Ed. by Ashis Nandy. (Oxford India Paperbacks Ser.). (Illus.). 314p. 1990. reprint ed. pap. 12.95 (0-19-562580-3) OUP.

Science, History & Faith. Alan Richardson. LC 86-22863. 216p. 1986. reprint ed. text ed. 55.00 (0-313-25325-0, RISHF, Greenwood Pr) Greenwood.

Science Horizons Year Book 1993. Ed. by Collier Staff. 1993. 45.00 (0-02-942579-4) Mac Lib Ref.

Science, Ideology & the Media: The Cyril Burt Scandal. Ronald Fletcher. 196p. (C). 1990. 44.95 (0-88738-376-9) Transaction Pubs.

*Science Imagined: An Exhibition of the Book As Art. Ed. by Susannah Hays. (Illus.). 32p. (Orig.). Date not set. pap. 15.00 (0-942744-05-5) Berkeley Art.

Science in a Bag. Forbes. (Illus.). 80p. (J). (ps-4). 1995. wbk. ed., pap. text ed. 9.95 (1-55734-197-4) Tchr Create Mat.

Science in a Bag: Discovery Experiences Using Resealable Bags. Esther Egley. 64p. (J). (gr. k-2). 10.99 (0-86653-884-4, FE0884) Fearon Teach Aids.

Science in a Bottle. Sandra Markle. 64p. (J). 1995. pap. 2.99 (0-590-47595-9) Scholastic Inc.

Science in a Nanosecond: Illustrated Answers to 100 Basic Science Questions. James A. Haught. (Young Readers Ser.). (Illus.). 110p. (Orig.). (J). (gr. 4 up). 1991. pap. 14.95 (0-87975-637-3) Prometheus Bks.

Science in a Nutshell for Kids: Over 100 Experiments You Can Do in Ten Minutes or Less. Jean Potter. 144p. (J). 1995. pap. text ed. 10.95 (0-471-04456-3) Wiley.

Science in Action: How to Follow Scientists & Engineers Through Society. Bruno Latour. 288p. 1988. reprint ed. pap. 16.50 (0-674-79291-2) HUP.

Science in Action: The Marshall Cavendish Guide to Projects & Experiments, 6 vols., Set. LC 87-36819. (Illus.). 288p. (J). (gr. 4-9). 1989. 89.70 (0-86307-020-5) Marshall Cavendish.

Science in America: A Documentary History, 1900-1939. Ed. by Nathan Reingold & Ida H. Reingold. LC 81-2584. 504p. 1981. 45.00 (0-226-70946-9) U Ch Pr.

*Science in Ancient China. George Beshore. LC 97-3519. (First Book Ser.). (J). 1998. write for info. (0-531-11334-5) Watts.

Science in Ancient China: Researches & Reflections. Nathan Sivin. LC 95-30588. (Collected Studies: Vol. 506). 328p. 1995. 89.95 (0-86078-492-4, Pub. by Variorum UK) Ashgate Pub Co.

*Science in Ancient Egypt. Geraldine Woods. LC 97-649. (First Book Ser.). (J). 1998. write for info. (0-531-20341-7) Watts.

*Science in Ancient Rome. Jacqueline L. Harris. LC 97-1901. (Science of the Past Ser.). (J). 1998. write for info. (0-531-20354-9) Watts.

Science in Art. George Coulter & Shirley Coulter. LC 94-49347. (Science Projects Ser.). (Illus.). 32p. (J). (gr. 3-4). 1995. lib. bdg. 15.93 (0-86625-519-2) Rourke Pubns.

Science in Cinema: Teaching Science Fact Through Science Fiction Films. Leroy W. Dubeck et al. 204p. (C). 1988. pap. text ed. 17.95 (0-8077-2915-9) Tchrs Coll.

Science in Contemporary China. Ed. by Leo A. Orleans. LC 79-65178. 640p. 1980. 75.00 (0-8047-1078-3) Stanford U Pr.

Science in Context. B. Barnes & D. Edge. 384p. 1982. pap. 34.00 (0-335-10054-6, Open Univ Pr) Taylor & Francis.

*Science in Early Islamic Culture. George Beshore. LC 97-5012. (First Book Ser.). (J). 1998. write for info. (0-531-20355-7) Watts.

Science in Elementary Education. 7th ed. Peter C. Gega. LC 92-43308. (Illus.). 713p. (C). 1993. text ed. 70.00 (0-02-341302-6, Macmillan Coll) P-H.

*Science in Elementary Education. 8th ed. Peter C. Gega & Joseph M. Peters. LC 97-3542. 1997. 62.00 (0-13-613852-7) P-H.

Science in Europe. Ed. by E. Amaldi & G. Ghirardi. 280p. (C). 1989. text ed. 108.00 (9971-5-0842-7) World Scientific Pub.

*Science in Evidence. D. H. Kaye. 430p. (C). 1997. pap. 29.95 (0-87084-480-6) Anderson Pub Co.

Science in Food. George Coulter & Shirley Coulter. LC 94-49348. (Science Projects Ser.). 32p. (J). (gr. 3-4). 1995. lib. bdg. 15.93 (0-86625-518-4) Rourke Pubns.

Science in Geography Series, 4 vols. Peter Davis. Incl. Vol 3. Data Description & Presentation. (Illus.). 1974. pap. text ed. 10.95 (0-19-913067-1); (C). 1974. write for info. (0-318-54891-7) OUP.

Science in History. George Coulter & Shirley Coulter. LC 95-7209. (Science Projects Ser.). 32p. (J). (gr. 3-4). 1995. lib. bdg. 15.93 (0-86625-521-4) Rourke Pubns.

Science In Its Youth. Andrei V. Anikin. Tr. by K. M. Cook from RUS. LC 78-31568. 389p. (C). 1979. pap. 3.50 (0-7178-0503-4) Intl Pubs Co.

*Science in Medieval Islam: An Illustrated Introduction. Howard R. Turner. LC 97-7733. (Illus.). 248p. 1997. 40.00 (0-292-78147-4); pap. 19.95 (0-292-78149-0) U of Tex Pr.

Science in Music. George Coulter & Shirley Coulter. LC 95-6591. (Science Projects Ser.). (J). (gr. 2-6). 1995. write for info. (0-86625-522-2) Rourke Pubns.

Science in Nature. George Coulter & Shirley Coulter. LC 95-2399. (Rourke Science Projects Ser.). (J). 1995. write for info. (0-86625-520-6) Rourke Pubns.

Science in Nineteenth-Century America: A Documentary History. Ed. by Nathan Reingold. LC 85-1021. xii, 352p. 1985. pap. text ed. 15.00 (0-226-70947-7) U Ch Pr.

Science in Nursing. 3rd rev. ed. Cree. 1995. pap. text ed. 51.50 (0-7295-1422-6) Saunders.

Science in Orbit: The Shuttle & Spacelab Experience. 1994. lib. bdg. 250.95 (0-8490-6408-2) Gordon Pr.

*Science in Our World, 31 vols. (Illus.). 1488p. (J). (gr. 4-8). 1996. lib. bdg. 349.00 (0-7172-7279-6) Grolier Educ.

*Science in Our World, 5 vols. Ed. by Mickey Sarquis. Incl. Strong Medicine: Chemistry at the Pharmacy. (Illus.). 92p. (Orig.). 1995. pap. 13.95 (1-883822-10-6); Chain Gang: The Chemistry of Polymers. (Illus.). 159p. (Orig.). 1995. pap. 13.95 (1-883822-13-0); Dirt Alert: The Chemistry of Cleaning. (Illus.). 66p. (Orig.). 1995. pap. 13.95 (1-883822-11-4); Fat Chance: The Chemistry of Lipids. (Illus.). 96p. (Orig.). 1995. pap. 13.95 (1-883822-09-2); Science Fare: Chemistry at the Table. (Illus.). 76p. (Orig.). 1995. pap. 13.95 (1-883822-12-2); 59.75 (0-614-29796-6) Terrific Sci.

Science in Our World, 16 vols., Set I. (Illus.). 48 ea.p. (J). (gr. 4-8). 1994. lib. bdg. 199.00 (0-7172-7368-7) Grolier Educ.

Science in Our World, 15 vols., Set II. (Illus.). 48 ea.p. (J). (gr. 4-8). 1994. lib. bdg. 199.00 (0-7172-7257-5) Grolier Educ.

Science in Participatory Development: The Achievements & Dilemmas of a Development Movement: The Case of Kerala. R. Sooryamoorthy. 192p. (C). 1994. pap. 19.95 (1-85649-272-9, Pub. by Zed Bks Ltd UK); text ed. 55.00 (1-85649-271-0, Pub. by Zed Bks Ltd UK) Humanities.

Science in Progress. LC 78-37534. (Eleventh Ser.). 1977. reprint ed. 31.95 (0-8369-7241-4) Ayer.

Science in Progress, Eighth Series. George Gamow et al. Ed. by George A. Baitsell. LC 78-37534. (Essay Index Reprint Ser.). 1977. reprint ed. 36.95 (0-8369-2533-5) Ayer.

Science in Progress, Fifth Series. Frank B. Jewett et al. Ed. by George A. Baitsell. LC 78-37534. (Essay Index Reprint Ser.). 1977. reprint ed. 39.95 (0-8369-2530-0) Ayer.

Science in Progress, First Series. Ernest O. Lawrence. Ed. by George A. Baitsell. LC 78-37534. (Essay Index Reprint Ser.). 1977. reprint ed. 39.95 (0-8369-2526-2) Ayer.

Science in Progress, Fourteenth Series. Ed. by Wallace R. Brode. LC 78-37534. (Essay Index Reprint Ser.). 1977. reprint ed. 23.95 (0-8369-7274-0) Ayer.

Science in Progress, Fourth Series. Walter R. Miles et al. Ed. by George A. Baitsell. LC 78-37534. (Essay Index Reprint Ser.). 1977. reprint ed. 46.95 (0-8369-2529-7) Ayer.

Science in Progress, Ninth Series. Laurence H. Snyder et al. Ed. by George A. Baitsell. LC 78-37534. (Essay Index Reprint Ser.). 1977. reprint ed. 36.95 (0-8369-2534-3) Ayer.

Science in Progress, Second Series. L. J. Stadler et al. Ed. by George A. Baitsell. LC 78-37534. (Essay Index Reprint Ser.). 1977. reprint ed. 39.95 (0-8369-2527-0) Ayer.

Science in Progress, Seventh Series. Bradley M. Patten et al. Ed. by George A. Baitsell. LC 78-37534. (Essay Index Reprint Ser.). 1977. reprint ed. 44.95 (0-8369-2532-7) Ayer.

Science in Progress, Sixth Series. H. D. Smyth et al. Ed. by George A. Baitsell. LC 78-37534. (Essay Index Reprint Ser.). 1977. reprint ed. 37.95 (0-8369-2531-9) Ayer.

Science in Progress, Third Series. Harlow Shapley et al. Ed. by George A. Baitsell. LC 78-37534. (Essay Index Reprint Ser.). 1977. reprint ed. 36.95 (0-8369-2528-9) Ayer.

Science in Progress, Thirteenth Series. Alan T. Waterman et al. Ed. by Wallace R. Brode. LC 78-37534. (Essay Index Reprint Ser.). 1977. reprint ed. 24.95 (0-8369-7240-6) Ayer.

Science in Progress, Twelfth Series. Ed. by Wallace R. Brode. LC 78-37534. (Essay Index Reprint Ser.). 1977. reprint ed. 25.95 (0-8369-7275-9) Ayer.

Science in Reflection. Ed. by Edna Ullmann-Margalit. 239p. (C). 1988. pap. text ed. 55.00 (90-277-2713-9, Pub. by Klwr Acad Pubs NE); lib. bdg. 130.00 (90-277-2712-0, Pub. by Klwr Acad Pubs NE) Kluwer Ac.

Science in Rhyme Without Reason. Ralph Barton. 1972. 59.95 (0-8490-1000-4) Gordon Pr.

Science in Russia & the Soviet Union: A Short History. Loren R. Graham. (Cambridge History of Science Ser.). (Illus.). 375p. (C). 1993. 34.95 (0-521-24566-4) Cambridge U Pr.

Science in Russia & the Soviet Union: A Short History. Loren R. Graham. (Illus.). 351p. (C). 1994. pap. text ed. 18.95 (0-521-28789-8) Cambridge U Pr.

Science in Russian Culture: A History to 1860. Alexander S. Vucinich. xv, 463p. 1963. 62.50 (0-8047-0157-1) Stanford U Pr.

Science in Russian Culture, 1861-1917. Alexander S. Vucinich. LC 75-107650. xvi, 576p. 1970. 69.50 (0-8047-0738-3) Stanford U Pr.

Science in Schools. Ed. by Joan Brown et al. LC 86-16336. 416p. 1987. 95.00 (0-335-15982-6, Open Univ Pr); pap. 36.00 (0-335-15981-8, Open Univ Pr) Taylor & Francis.

*Science in Seconds with Toys: Over 100 Experiments You Can Do in Ten Minutes or Less. Jean Potter. LC 97-20000. 128p. (J). 1998. pap. 12.95 (0-471-17900-0) Wiley.

Science in Soviet Russia. National Council of American Soviet Friendship Staff. LC 74-25151. (History, Philosophy & Sociology of Science Ser.). 1975. reprint ed. 18.95 (0-405-06635-X) Ayer.

Science in Sports. George Coulter & Shirley Coulter. LC 94-43479. (Science Projects Ser.). (J). (gr. 2-6). 1995. write for info. (0-86625-517-6) Rourke Pubns.

S

Science in Sweden: Seventeen Thirty-Nine to Nineteen Eighty-Nine. Ed. by Tore Frangsmyr. 1989. 45.00 (0-88135-092-3) Watson Pub Intl.

Science in the Arab Countries & Its Role in Solving Environmental Problems in the Region Vols. I & II: Proceedings of the Fourth General Conference of the Third World Academy of Sciences, 2 vols. Fourth General Conference of the Third World Academy of Sciences Staff. Ed. by Mohamed H. Hassan et al. 1000p. 1996. 255.00 (0-7103-0510-9, KP5109) Col U Pr.

Science in the British Colonies of America. Raymond P. Stearns. LC 78-122915. (Illus.). 780p. 1970. text ed. 49.95 (0-252-00120-6) U of Ill Pr.

Science in the Changing World. Ed. by Mary Adams. LC 68-29188. (Essay Index Reprint Ser.). 1977. reprint ed. 20.95 (0-8369-0136-3) Ayer.

Science in the Creation Week: Content & "Hands-On" Science Skills Curriculum Grades 2-5. David Unfred. (Illus.). 136p. (J). (gr. 2-5). 19.95 (1-56857-006-6) Noble Pub Assocs.

Science in the Early Roman Empire: Pliny the Elder, His Sources & His Influence. Ed. by Roger French & Frank Greenaway. LC 86-7919. (Illus.). 298p. 1986. 64.50 (0-389-20634-2, N8192) B&N Imports.

Science in the Federal Government: A History of Policies & Activities. A. Hunter Dupree. LC 86-45456. 488p. 1986. reprint ed. pap. text ed. 18.95 (0-8018-3381-7) Johns Hopkins.

Science in the Federal Government: A History of Policies & Activities to 1940. A. Hunter Dupree. Ed. by I. Bernard Cohen. LC 79-7959. (Three Centuries of Science in America Ser.). (Illus.). 1980. reprint ed. lib. bdg. 42.95 (0-405-12540-2) Ayer.

Science in the Field Vol. 11: Osiris, Vol.11. Ed. by Henrika Kuklick & Robert E. Kohler. 254p. 1996. pap. text ed. 25.00 (0-226-46003-7) U Ch Pr.

Science in the Field Vol. 11: Osiris, Vol.11. Ed. by Henrika Kuklick & Robert E. Kohler. 254p. 1996. lib. bdg. 39.00 (0-226-46002-9) U Ch Pr.

Science in the Kitchen. K. Woodward. (Science Activities Ser.). (Illus.). 24p. (J). (gr. 1-4). 1992. pap. 4.95 (0-7460-0974-7); lib. bdg. 12.95 (0-88110-284-9) EDC.

Science in the Kitchen & the Art of Eating Well. Pellegrino Artusi. 450p. (C). 1997. 32.50 (1-56886-040-4); pap. 19.95 (1-56886-039-0) Marsilio Pubs.

Science in the Light of Torah: A B'Or Ha'Torah Reader. Ed. by Herman Branover & Ilana C. Attia. LC 93-29371. 352p. 1994. 35.00 (1-56821-034-5) Aronson.

Science in the Making. Joel H. Hildebrand. LC 84-25250. (Bempton Lectures in America Ser.: No. 9). viii, 116p. 1985. reprint ed. text ed. 57.50 (0-313-24737-4, HISC, Greenwood Pr) Greenwood.

Science in the Making: Scientific Development As Chronicled by Historic Papers in the Philosophical Magazine, with Commentaries & Illustrations, Vol. 1: 1798-1850. Ed. by E. A. Davis. 300p. 1995. 99.00 (0-7484-0219-5, Pub. by Tay Francis Ltd UK) Taylor & Francis.

*Science in the Making: Scientific Development As Chronicled by Historic Papers in the Philosophical Magazine with Commentaries & Illustrations, Vol. 2: 1851-1900. Ed. & Frwd. by Nevill F. Mott. 448p. 1997. 99.00 (0-7484-0642-5, Pub. by Tay Francis Ltd UK) Taylor & Francis.

Science in the Marketplace: Consumer Science. 5th rev. ed. Florence G. Korchin. Ed. by Robert Woolfe. (Illus.). 380p. (YA). (gr. 7-12). 1995. text ed. 35.00 (0-9611318-5-3) Tiger Pubn.

Science in the Medieval World: "Book of the Categories of Nations" Sa'id Al-Andalusi. Tr. by Sema'an I. Salem & Alok Kumar. (History of Science Ser.: No. 5). (Illus.). 144p. (C). 1991. text ed. 35.00 (0-292-71139-5) U of Tex Pr.

Science in the Medieval World: Book of the Categories of Nations. Sa'id Al-Andalusi. Tr. by Sema'an I. Salem & Alok Kumar from ARA. (History of Science Ser.). 118p. (Orig.). (C). 1996. pap. 11.95 (0-292-70469-0) U of Tex Pr.

*Science in the Medieval World: Book of the Categories of Nations. Said Al-Andalusi. Ed. by Alok Kumar. Tr. by Sema'an I. Salem. 144p. 1996. 29.00 (0-614-21609-5, 1112) Kazi Pubns.

Science in the Middle Ages. Ed. by David C. Lindberg. LC 78-5367. (Chicago History of Science & Medicine Ser.). (Illus.). 568p. 1980. pap. text ed. 22.50 (0-226-48233-2, P870) U Ch Pr.

Science in the Multicultural Classroom: A Guide to Teaching & Learning. Roberta H. Barba. LC 94-14852. 1994. text ed. 61.00 (0-205-15105-1) Allyn.

***Science in the Multicultural Classroom: A Guide to Teaching & Learning.** 2nd ed. Roberta H. Barba. LC 97-10531. 1997. 50.67 (*0-205-26737-8*) Allyn.

Science in the National Curriculum. Mike Watts. 192p. 1991. text ed. 50.00 (*0-304-32348-9*); pap. text ed. 16.95 (*0-304-32349-7*) Cassell.

Science in the New Age: The Paranormal, Its Defenders, & Debunkers, & American Culture. David J. Hess. LC 93-18890. (Science & Literature Ser.). (Illus.). 256p. (C). 1993. pap. 17.95 (*0-299-13824-0*); lib. bdg. 42.50 (*0-299-13820-8*) U of Wis Pr.

Science in the Pleasure Ground: A History of the Arnold Arboretum. Ida Hay. (Illus.). 416p. 1994. text ed. 39.95 (*1-55553-201-2*) NE U Pr.

Science in the Service of Physical Education & Sport: The Story of the International Council for Sic< Sport Science & Physical Education, 1956-1996. Steve Bailey. LC 96-22600. 1996. text ed. write for info. (*0-471-96924-9*) Wiley.

Science in the Streets: Report of the Twentieth Century Fund Task Force on the Communication of Scientific Risk. 97p. (Orig.). 1985. pap. text ed. 7.50 (*0-87078-154-5*) TCFP-PPP.

Science in the Subarctic: Trappers, Traders, & the Smithsonian Institution. Debra Lindsay. LC 92-29811. (Illus.). 192p. (C). 1993. text ed. 34.00 (*1-56098-233-0*) Smithsonian.

***Science in the Twentieth Century.** Ed. by John Krige & Dominique Pestre. 1200p. 1997. 120.00 (*90-5702-172-2*, Harwood Acad Pubs) Gordon & Breach.

Science in the Twentieth Century. Walter Sullivan. LC 77-18144. 1976. 27.95 (*0-405-06672-4*, 1754) Ayer.

Science in the Twentieth Century. large type ed. Glick. 1997. 27.95 (*0-8057-9520-0*, GK Hall) Thorndike Pr.

Science in the University. University of California Faculties Staff. LC 68-20331. (Essay Index Reprint Ser.). 1977. 23.95 (*0-8369-0856-2*) Ayer.

Science in the Worlds. Dale McCreedy & Kate Tabachnick. (National Science Partnership for Girl Scouts & Science Museums Ser.). (Illus.). 80p. (Orig.). 1995. pap. 8.00 (*0-9625622-2-X*) Franklin PA.

***Science in the 20th Century.** (Twentieth Century Ser.). (Illus.). (YA). (gr. 6 up). 29.95 (*0-614-21969-8*) Random.

Science in Traditional China. Joseph Needham. (Illus.). 144p. (C). 1982. pap. text ed. 11.95 (*0-674-79439-7*) HUP.

Science in Utopia: A Mighty Design. Nell Eurich. LC 67-14339. 344p. reprint ed. pap. 98.10 (*0-317-09457-2*, 2017014) Bks Demand.

Science in Victorian Manchester: Enterprise & Expertise. Robert H. Kargon. LC 77-4556. 1978. text ed. 46.00 (*0-8018-1969-5*) Johns Hopkins.

Science in Western & Eastern Civilization in Carolingian Times. Ed. by Paul L. Butzer & Dietrich Lohrmann. LC 93-20519. xii, 609p. 1993. 81.50 (*0-8176-2863-0*) Birkhauser.

Science in Working Lives. Secord. 300p. (C). 1990. lib. bdg. 34.95 (*0-226-74412-4*) U Ch Pr.

Science in Your Backyard. William R. Wellnitz. 1992. pap. text ed. 10.95 (*0-07-157871-4*) McGraw.

Science in Your Backyard. William R. Wellnitz. 128p. 1992. 16.95 (*0-8306-2495-3*); pap. 9.95 (*0-8306-2494-5*) McGraw-Hill Prof.

Science in Your Salon. Bronwyn Cozens. LC 91-3555. (Illus.). 220p. (C). 1991. pap. 15.95 (*1-56253-035-6*) Milady Pub.

***Science Incarnate.** Lawrence. 1997. 18.95 (*0-226-47014-8*) U Ch Pr.

***Science Incarnate.** Lawrence. 1998. lib. bdg. 55.00 (*0-226-47012-1*) U Ch Pr.

Science, Industry & the Social Order in Post-Revolutionary France. Robert Fox. LC 95-2625. (Collected Studies: No. CS489). 1995. 92.95 (*0-86078-481-9*, Pub. by Variorum UK) Ashgate Pub Co.

Science Instruction in the Middle & Secondary Schools. 3rd ed. Alfred T. Collette. (Illus.). 514p. (C). 1993. text ed. 69.00 (*0-02-323551-9*, Macmillan Coll) P-H.

***Science Instruction in the Middle & Secondary Schools.** 4th ed. Chiappetta & Alfred T. Collette. LC 97-14717. (C). 1997. pap. text ed. 56.00 (*0-13-651118-X*) P-H.

***Science International: A History of the International Council of Scientific Unions.** Frank Greenaway. (Illus.). 291p. (C). 1997. text ed. 49.95 (*0-521-58015-3*) Cambridge U Pr.

Science, Internationalism & War: An Original Anthology. Yahuda Elkana et al. Ed. by Robert K. Merton et al. LC 74-25185. (History, Philosophy & Sociology of Science Ser.). 1975. reprint ed. 18.95 (*0-405-06633-3*) Ayer.

***Science Is... A Source Book of Fascinating Facts, Projects & Activities.** Susan V. Bosak. (Illus.). 515p. (J). pap. 29.95 (*0-590-74070-9*) Scholastic Inc.

Science Is an Action Word! Grades 1-3. Peggy K. Perdue. 1990. pap. 8.95 (*0-673-38968-5*, GoodYrBooks) Addson-Wesley Educ.

Science is Fun. Oppenheim. 32p. 1996. teacher ed. 12.50 (*0-8273-7337-6*) Delmar.

Science Is Fun: For Families & Classroom Groups. Carol Oppenheim. (Early Childhood Education Ser.). 416p. (J). 1996. pap. 18.95 (*0-8273-7336-8*) Delmar.

***Science Is Not a Quiet Life.** 450p. 1997. 19.85 (*981-02-3057-5*) World Scientific Pub.

Science, Jews, & Secular Culture: Studies in Mid-Twentieth-Century American Intellectual History. David A. Holinger. 216p. 1996. text ed. 24.95 (*0-691-01143-5*) Princeton U Pr.

Science, Knowledge, & Mind: A Study in the Philosophy of C. S. Peirce. C. F. Delaney. LC 92-53743. (C). 1993. text ed. 33.50 (*0-268-01748-4*) U of Notre Dame Pr.

Science, Law, & Hudson River Power Plants: A Case Study in Environmental Impact Assessment. Ed. by Lawrence W. Barnthouse et al. LC 88-72144. (AFS Monograph Ser.: No. 4). 347p. 1988. pap. 36.00 (*0-913235-51-2*) Am Fisheries Soc.

Science, Law, & Society. Christopher Arup. (Orig.). (C). pap. 19.95 (*1-86324-014-4*, Pub. by LaTrobe Univ AT) Intl Spec Bk.

Science Learning: Processes & Applications. Ed. by Carol M. Santa & Donna E. Alvermann. LC 91-2473. 173p. 1991. reprint ed. pap. 49.40 (*0-608-01419-2*, 2062182) Bks Demand.

Science Learning Centers for the Primary Grades. Carol A. Poppe & Nancy A. Van Matre. 1985. pap. 27.95 (*0-87628-749-6*) Ctr Appl Res.

Science Learning in Victorian Schools, 1990. Raymond Adams. (C). 1992. 75.00 (*0-86431-108-7*, Pub. by Aust Council Educ Res AT) St Mut.

Science Lecture Room: A Planning Study to Examine the Principles of Location & Design of Lecture Rooms in the Development of University Science Areas. Jeremy R. Taylor. LC 67-24941. 127p. reprint ed. pap. 36.20 (*0-317-27100-8*, 2024548) Bks Demand.

Science Librarianship at America's Liberal Arts Colleges: Working Librarians Tell Their Stories. Ed. by Tony Stankus. LC 92-18021. (Science & Technology Libraries: Vol. 12, No. 3). 137p. 1992. text ed. 39.95 (*1-56024-357-0*) Haworth Pr.

***Science Lives for Geniuses: Journal & Calendar Set.** Katherine E. Anderson. (Illus.). (Orig.). 1996. spiral bd., pap. 21.95 (*1-57876-897-7*) Triple U Prods.

***Science Lives for Health Care Workers: Journal & Calendar Set.** Katherine E. Anderson. (Illus.). (Orig.). 1996. spiral bd., pap. 21.95 (*1-57876-899-3*) Triple U Prods.

***Science Lives for Intellectuals: Journal & Calendar Set.** Katherine E. Anderson. (Illus.). (Orig.). 1996. spiral bd., pap. 21.95 (*1-57876-896-9*) Triple U Prods.

***Science Lives for Researchers: Journal & Calendar Set.** Katherine E. Anderson. (Illus.). (Orig.). 1996. spiral bd., pap. 21.95 (*1-57876-898-5*) Triple U Prods.

***Science Lives for Students: Journal & Calendar Set.** Katherine E. Anderson. (Illus.). (Orig.). 1996. spiral bd., pap. 21.95 (*1-57876-894-2*) Triple U Prods.

***Science Lives for Teachers: Journal & Calendar Set.** Katherine E. Anderson. (Illus.). (Orig.). 1996. spiral bd., pap. 21.95 (*1-57876-895-0*) Triple U Prods.

***Science Lives Journal for Health Care Workers.** Katherine E. Anderson. (Illus.). 150p. (Orig.). 1994. spiral bd., pap. 15.95 (*1-57876-805-5*) Triple U Prods.

***Science Lives Journal for Intellectuals.** Katherine E. Anderson. (Illus.). 150p. (Orig.). 1994. spiral bd., pap. 15.95 (*1-57876-802-0*) Triple U Prods.

***Science Lives Journal for Researchers.** Katherine E. Anderson. (Illus.). 150p. (Orig.). 1994. spiral bd., pap. 15.95 (*1-57876-804-7*) Triple U Prods.

***Science Lives Journal for Students.** Katherine E. Anderson. (Illus.). 150p. (Orig.). 1994. spiral bd., pap. 15.95 (*1-57876-800-4*) Triple U Prods.

***Science Lives Journal for Teachers.** Katherine E. Anderson. (Illus.). 150p. (Orig.). 1994. spiral bd., pap. 15.95 (*1-57876-801-2*) Triple U Prods.

Science Made Stupid! Tom Weller. 1985. pap. 10.95 (*0-395-36646-1*) HM.

Science Magic. (J). 1987. write for info. (*0-318-61082-5*) P-H.

***Science Magic: Martin Gardner's Tricks & Puzzles.** Martin Gardner. LC 96-39314. (J). 1997. 14.95 (*0-8069-9543-2*) Sterling.

Science Magic for Kids: Simple & Safe Experiments. William R. Wellnitz. (Illus.). 128p. (J). 1990. 17.95 (*0-8306-8423-9*, 3423); pap. 9.95 (*0-8306-3423-1*) McGraw-Hill Prof.

Science Magic with Forces. Chris Oxlade. LC 94-32052. (Science Magic Ser.). (J). 1994. 10.95 (*0-8120-6502-6*); pap. 4.95 (*0-8120-9191-4*) Barron.

Science Magic with Light. Chris Oxlade. LC 94-5549. (Science Magic Ser.). (Illus.). 30p. (J). (gr. 2-5). 1994. 9.95 (*0-8120-6445-3*); pap. 4.95 (*0-8120-1984-9*) Barron.

Science Magic with Machines. Chris Oxlade. LC 94-40702. (Science Magic Ser.). (Illus.). 32p. (J). 1995. 10.95 (*0-8120-6517-4*); pap. 4.95 (*0-8120-9368-2*) Barron.

Science Magic with Magnets. Chris Oxlade. LC 94-32055. (Science Magic Ser.). (J). 1994. pap. 4.95 (*0-8120-9190-6*) Barron.

Science Magic with Magnets. Chris Oxlade. LC 94-32055. (Science Magic Ser.). (J). 1994. 10.95 (*0-8120-6501-8*) Barron.

Science Magic with Shapes & Materials. Chris Oxlade. LC 94-40701. (Science Magic Ser.). (Illus.). 32p. (J). 1995. pap. 4.95 (*0-8120-9369-0*); lib. bdg. 10.95 (*0-8120-6518-2*) Barron.

Science Magic with Sound. Chris Oxlade. LC 94-5550. (Science Magic Ser.). (Illus.). 30p. (J). (gr. 2-5). 1994. pap. 4.95 (*0-8120-1985-7*); lib. bdg. 9.95 (*0-8120-6446-1*) Barron.

Science Magic with Water. Chris Oxlade. LC 94-5548. (Science Magic Ser.). (Illus.). 30p. (J). (gr. 2-5). 1994. pap. 4.95 (*0-8120-1986-5*); lib. bdg. 9.95 (*0-8120-6448-8*) Barron.

Science Manual: The Process & Communication. Ed. & Illus. by William A. Muller. 78p. 1991. pap. text ed. 10.95 (*0-9625187-3-5*) Wavecrest Comns.

Science Mate, Set, Vols. 1-6. 1992. Set. 110.00 (*1-56638-199-1*) Math Sci Nucleus.

Science Mate, Vols. 1-6. 1992. 500.00 (*1-56638-198-3*) Math Sci Nucleus.

Science, Materialism, & the Study of Culture. Ed. by Martin F. Murphy & Maxine L. Margolis. (Illus.). 256p. (Orig.). (C). 1995. 49.95 (*0-8130-1413-1*) U Press Fla.

Science, Materialism, & the Study of Culture. Ed. by Martin F. Murphy & Maxine L. Margolis. (Illus.). 256p. (Orig.). (C). 1996. pap. text ed. 22.95 (*0-8130-1414-X*) U Press Fla.

Science Matrix: Past, Present & Future. Frederick Seitz. 160p. 1993. 48.95 (*0-387-97677-9*) Spr-Verlag.

Science Matters: Achieving Scientific Literacy. Robert M. Hazen & James S. Trefil. 320p. 1991. reprint ed. pap. 12.95 (*0-385-26108-X*, Anchor NY) Doubleday.

Science, Meaning, & Evolution: The Cosmology of Jacob Boehme. Basarab Nicolescu. Tr. by Rob Baker from FRE. (Illus.). 231p. 1991. reprint ed. 17.95 (*0-930407-20-2*) Parabola Bks.

***Science Medicale Occidentale Entre Deux Renaissances, Vols. XII-XV.** Danielle Jacquart. LC 96-40471. (Variorum Collected Studies: Vol. 567). 336p. (FRE.). 1997. 99.95 (*0-86078-621-8*, Pub. by Ashgate UK) Ashgate Pub Co.

Science, Medicine & Cultural Imperialism. Ed. by Teresa Meade & Mark Walker. LC 90-45331. 190p. 1991. text ed. 45.00 (*0-312-04779-7*) St Martin.

Science, Medicine, & History, 2 Vols., Set. Ed. by E. Ashworth Underwood. LC 74-26300. (History, Philosophy & Sociology of Science Ser.). (Illus.). 1975. reprint ed. 108.95 (*0-405-06624-4*) Ayer.

Science, Medicine, & History, 2 Vols., Vol. 1. Ed. by E. Ashworth Underwood. LC 74-26300. (History, Philosophy & Sociology of Science Ser.). (Illus.). 1975. reprint ed. 54.95 (*0-405-06640-6*) Ayer.

Science, Medicine, & History, 2 Vols., Vol. 2. Ed. by E. Ashworth Underwood. LC 74-26300. (History, Philosophy & Sociology of Science Ser.). (Illus.). 1975. reprint ed. 54.95 (*0-405-06641-4*) Ayer.

Science, Medicine & Technology: English Grammar & Technical Writing. Peter A. Master. (Illus.). 320p. (C). 1986. pap. text ed. 16.00 (*0-13-795469-7*) P-H.

Science, Medicine, & the State in Germany: The Case of Baden, 1815-1871. Arleen M. Tuchman. LC 92-23470. 216p. 1993. 42.50 (*0-19-508047-5*) OUP.

Science Medievale d'Espagne et D'alentour. Guy Beaujouan. (Collected Studies: No. CS374). 336p. 1992. 98.95 (*0-86078-304-9*, Pub. by Variorum UK) Ashgate Pub Co.

Science, Metaphysics, & the Chance of Salvation: An Interpretation of the Thought of William James. Henry S. Levinson. LC 78-7383. (American Academy of Religion. Dissertation Ser.: No. 24). 266p. reprint ed. pap. 75.90 (*0-7837-5467-1*, 2045232) Bks Demand.

Science Methods for Elementary & Middle School Teachers. William J. Bluhm et al. 1995. spiral bd. 24.40 (*0-87563-579-2*) Stipes.

Science, Mind, & Art: Essays on Science & the Humanistic Understanding in Art, Epistemology, Religion & Ethics in Honor of Robert S. Cohen. Ed. by Kostas Gavroglu et al. LC 94-48184. (Boston Studies in the Philosophy of Science: Vol. 165). 456p. 1995. lib. bdg. 170.00 (*0-7923-2990-2*, Pub. by Klwr Acad Pubs NE) Kluwer Ac.

Science, Mind & Art: Essays on Science & the Humanistic Understanding in Art, Epistemology, Religion & Ethics in Honor of Robert S. Cohen. Ed. by Kostas Gavroglu. (Boston Studies in the Philosophy of Science). 456p. (C). 1996. lib. bdg. 249.00 (*0-7923-3990-8*) Kluwer Ac.

Science, Mind, & Psychology: Essays in Honor of Grover Maxwell. Ed. by Mary L. Maxwell & C. Wade Savage. LC 89-36360. 476p. (Orig.). (C). 1989. lib. bdg. 65.00 (*0-8191-7557-9*) U Pr of Amer.

Science Mind Stretchers. Imogene Forte & Sandra Schurr. (Illus.). 128p. (J). (gr. 4-7). 1987. pap. text ed. 10.95 (*0-86530-165-4*, 165-4) Incentive Pubns.

Science Miscellany. David McNaughton. 1991. 14.95 (*0-533-09464-X*) Vantage.

Science Moderne, de 1450 a 1800 see Histoire Generale des Sciences

Science, Morality & Feminist Theory. Ed. by M. Hanen & K. Nielsen. 434p. 1993. pap. 12.00 (*0-919491-13-8*) Paul & Co Pubs.

Science Mysteries. Jerome Luine. LC 94-5355. 80p. (J). 1994. pap. 5.95 (*1-56565-173-1*) Lowell Hse Juvenile.

Science, Myth, & the Fictional Creation of Alien Worlds. Albert Wendland. LC 84-16474. (Studies in Speculative Fiction: No. 12). 208p. reprint ed. pap. 59.30 (*0-8357-1608-2*, 2070526) Bks Demand.

Science, Myth, Reality: The Black Family in One-Half Century of Research. Eleanor Engram. LC 81-1262. (Contributions in Afro-American & African Studies: No. 64). (Illus.). xviii, 216p. 1982. text ed. 55.00 (*0-313-22835-3*, ESM/, Greenwood Pr) Greenwood.

Science, Non-Science & Pseudo-Science. Ed. by Max Charlesworthy. (C). 1982. 35.00 (*0-949823-05-8*, Pub. by Deakin Univ AT) St Mut.

Science, Nonscience, & Nonsense: Approaching Environmental Literacy. Michael Zimmerman. LC 95-5006. 232p. 1995. 25.95 (*0-8018-5090-8*) Johns Hopkins.

***Science, Nonscience & Nonsense: Approaching Environmental Literacy.** Michael Zimmerman. 1997. pap. text ed. 14.95 (*0-8018-5774-0*) Johns Hopkins.

Science Nova: Level 1. Coper. 1989. student ed. 26.25 (*0-15-364321-8*) H Holt & Co.

Science Nova: Level 2. Cooper. 1989. student ed. 29.95 (*0-15-364322-6*) H Holt & Co.

Science Now: Body in Action. J. Jenkins. (C). 1990. text ed. 30.00 (*0-7487-0204-0*, Pub. by Stanley Thornes UK) Trans-Atl Phila.

Science Now: Chemicals on the Farm. B. McDuell. (C). 1990. 40.00 (*0-7487-0212-1*, Pub. by Stanley Thornes UK) Trans-Atl Phila.

Science Now: Electricity. E. Fogden. (C). 1989. text ed. 40.00 (*0-7487-0208-3*, Pub. by S Thornes Pubs UK) St Mut.

Science Now: Energy. E. Fogden. (C). 1985. text ed. 40.00 (*0-7487-0209-1*, Pub. by S Thornes Pubs UK) St Mut.

Science Now: Health Physics. A. McCormick. (C). 1989. 50.00 (*0-7487-0205-9*, Pub. by Stanley Thornes UK) Trans-Atl Phila.

Science Now: Inheritance. J. Jenkins. (C). 1990. 40.00 (*0-7487-0203-2*, Pub. by Stanley Thornes UK) Trans-Atl Phila.

Science Now: Leisure Physics. E. Fogden. (C). 1989. text ed. 35.00 (*0-7487-0207-5*, Pub. by S Thornes Pubs UK) St Mut.

Science Now: Metals & Corrosion. B. McDuell. (C). 1985. 30.00 (*0-7487-0211-3*, Pub. by S Thornes Pubs UK) St Mut.

Science Now: Plastics a Plenty. B. McDuell. (C). 1990. 30.00 (*0-7487-0210-5*, Pub. by Stanley Thornes UK) Trans-Atl Phila.

Science Now: Space Physics. E. Fogden. (C). 1989. text ed. 30.00 (*0-7487-0206-7*, Pub. by S Thornes Pubs UK) St Mut.

Science Now: The Biosphere. T. Steven & D. Wright. (C). 1989. 30.00 (*0-7487-0202-4*, Pub. by S Thornes Pubs UK) St Mut.

Science of a Legislator: The Natural Jurisprudence of David Hume & Adam Smith. Knud Haakonssen. (Illus.). 256p. (C). 1989. pap. text ed. 19.95 (*0-521-37625-4*) Cambridge U Pr.

Science of a Witches Brew. William Wilks. 208p. 1979. pap. 11.95 (*0-919017-01-0*) Hancock House.

Science of Agriculture: A Biological Approach. Herren. (Agriculture Ser.). 304p. 1996. lab manual ed., pap. 17.00 (*0-8273-6839-9*) Delmar.

Science of Agriculture: A Biological Approach. Herren. (Agriculture Ser.). 1996. lab manual ed. 12.75 (*0-8273-6840-2*) Delmar.

Science of Agriculture: A Biological Approach. H. R. Herren. (Agriculture Ser.). 48p. 1996. 12.75 (*0-8273-7580-8*) Delmar.

Science of Agriculture: Biological Applications. Cooper. (Agriculture Ser.). 1996. 100.00 (*0-8273-7490-9*) Delmar.

Science of Agriculture: Biological Applications. Herren. (Agriculture Ser.). 1997. teacher ed. 89.95 (*0-8273-7495-X*) Delmar.

Science of AIDS. Scientific American Staff. LC 88-3221. (Illus.). 135p. (C). 1995. text ed. 13.95 (*0-7167-2036-1*) W H Freeman.

Science of Alchemy. A. S. Raleigh. 172p. 1992. reprint ed. pap. 16.95 (*1-56459-007-0*) Kessinger Pub.

Science of Alchymy. William W. Westcott. 1983. reprint ed. pap. 3.95 (*0-916411-02-8*) Holmes Pub.

Science of Allelopathy. Ed. by A. R. Putnam & C. S. Tang. 317p. 1986. text ed. 87.95 (*0-471-83027-5*) Wiley.

Science of Animal Agriculture. Ray V. Herren. LC 92-21483. 335p. 1993. text ed. 35.95 (*0-8273-4546-1*) Delmar.

Science of Animal Agriculture. Ray V. Herren. LC 92-21483. 335p. 1994. disk 105.95 (*0-8273-6158-0*) Delmar.

Science of Animal Agriculture: Lab Manual Answer Key. Frank Flanders & Ray V. Herren. 32p. 1994. 12.75 (*0-8273-6683-3*) Delmar.

Science of Animal Husbandry. 4th ed. James Blakely & David H. Bade. (C). 1985. teacher ed. write for info. (*0-8359-6898-7*, Reston) P-H.

Science of Animal Husbandry. 5th ed. Blakely & David H. Bade. 1989. text ed. 62.00 (*0-13-794702-X*) P-H.

Science of Animal Husbandry. 5th ed. James Blakely & David H. Bade. 736p. 1989. boxed 43.00 (*0-685-44714-6*) P-H.

Science of Animal Husbandry. 6th ed. James Blakely & David H. Bade. LC 93-7574. 656p. (C). 1993. text ed. 86.00 (*0-13-793365-7*) P-H.

Science of Animal Life. A. W. Lindsey. 656p. 1984. pap. 175.00 (*0-7855-0389-7*, Pub. by Intl Bks & Periodicals II) St Mut.

Science of Animals That Serve Humanity. 3rd ed. John R. Campbell & John F. Lasley. LC 84-7950. 880p. 1985. text ed. write for info. (*0-07-009700-3*) McGraw.

Science of Art: Optical Themes in Western Art from Brunelleschi to Seurat. Martin Kemp. (Illus.). 383p. (C). 1992. reprint ed. pap. text ed. 27.50 (*0-300-05241-3*) Yale U Pr.

Science of Ascension: A Study of Our Being. Lillian De Waters. 181p. 1975. reprint ed. spiral bd. 7.00 (*0-7873-0278-3*) Hlth Research.

Science of Ascension: A Study of Our Being (1929) Lillian De Waters. 190p. 1996. pap. 17.95 (*1-56459-919-1*) Kessinger Pub.

Science of Ball Lightning (Fire Ball) Ed. by Y. H. Ohtsuki. 352p. (C). 1989. text ed. 98.00 (*9971-5-0723-4*) World Scientific Pub.

Science of Becoming Excellent. rev. ed. Judith L. Powell & Wallace D. Wattles. LC 92-41455. 160p. 1993. pap. 8.95 (*0-914295-96-9*) Top Mtn Pub.

Science of Being. Eugene Fersen. 328p. 1986. reprint ed. spiral bd. 24.50 (*0-7873-1237-1*) Hlth Research.

Science of Being & Art of Living: Transcendental Meditation. Mahesh Yogi. 352p. 1994. pap. 13.95 (*0-452-01142-6*, Meridian) NAL-Dutton.

Science of Being Well. Wallace D. Wattles. 155p. 1968. reprint ed. spiral bd. 7.00 (*0-7873-0938-9*) Hlth Research.

Science of Being Well: Principles of Health, Uses of the Will, When to Eat, What to Eat, How to Eat, Breathing & Sleeping. Wallace D. Wattles. 1991. lib. bdg. 75.00 (*0-87700-948-1*) Revisionist Pr.

Science of Being Well: When to Eat, How to Eat, What to Eat. Wallace D. Wattles. 1991. lib. bdg. 79.95 (*0-8490-4131-7*) Gordon Pr.

S

S

An Asterisk (*) at the beginning of an entry indicates that the title is appearing in BIP for the first time.

Science of Linguistics in the Art of Translation: Some Tools from Linguistics for the Analysis & Practice of Translation. Joseph L. Malone. LC 87-13888. (SUNY Series in Linguistics). 241p. 1988. text ed. 89.50 (*0-88706-653-4*); pap. text ed. 29.95 (*0-88706-654-2*) State U NY Pr.

Science of Logic: or, An Analysis of the Laws of Thought. Intro. by Asa Mahan. 1986. reprint ed. pap. 14.95 (*0-935005-84-6*) Lincoln-Rembrandt.

Science of Love. John Baines. Ed. by Judith Hipskind. Tr. by Josephine Bregazzi from SPA. LC 92-97419. (Illus.). 401p. (Orig.). 1993. pap. 12.95 (*1-882692-00-4*) J Baines Inst.

Science of Love: Understanding Love & Its Effects on Mind & Body. Anthony Walsh. LC 96-8954. 276p. 1996. reprint ed. pap. 19.95 (*1-57392-091-6*) Prometheus Bks.

Science of Love with Key to Immortality, 2 vols., Set. Ida Mingle. 1976. reprint ed. spiral bd. 49.00 (*0-7873-0616-9*) Hlth Research.

Science of Love with Key to Immortality (1926) Ida Mingle. 590p. 1996. pap. 33.00 (*1-56459-716-4*) Kessinger Pub.

Science of Magnetic, Mental & Spiritual Healing, with Instructions How to Heal by Laying on of Hands. E. W. Sprague. 155p. 1974. reprint ed. spiral bd. 10.00 (*0-7873-0811-0*) Hlth Research.

Science of Man. Mary M. Eddy. (Notable American Authors Ser.). 1992. reprint ed. lib. bdg. 75.00 (*0-7812-2747-X*) Rprt Serv.

Science of Man in the Scottish Enlightenment: Hume, Reid & Their Contemporaries. Ed. by Peter Jones. 216p. 1991. pap. text ed. 29.00 (*0-7486-0146-5*, Pub. by Edinburgh U Pr UK) Col U Pr.

Science of Managing Organized Technology, 4 vols. M. Cetron & J. D. Goldhar. 1698, lvip. 1970. text ed. 582.00 (*0-677-02320-0*) Gordon & Breach.

Science of Materials. Witold Brostow. LC 84-15484. 460p. (C). 1985. reprint ed. lib. bdg. 55.50 (*0-89874-780-5*) Krieger.

Science of Materials Used in Advanced Technology. Ed. by Earl R. Parker & Umberto Colombo. LC 73-1065. 572p. reprint ed. pap. 163.10 (*0-317-08187-X*, 2015173) Bks Demand.

Science of Matter: A Historical Survey. Ed. by Maurice Crosland. LC 92-21727. (Classics in the History & Philosophy of Science Ser.: Vol. 9). 217p. 1992. pap. text ed. 41.00 (*2-88124-570-6*) Gordon & Breach.

***Science of Measurement.** Herbert A. Klein. pap. 16.95 (*0-486-25839-4*) Dover.

Science of Meat & Meat Products. 3rd ed. Ed. by James F. Price & Bernard S. Schweigert. 639p. 1987. 98.00 (*0-917678-21-4*) Food & Nut Pr.

Science of Mechanics. 6th ed. Ernst Mach. Tr. by T. J. McCormack from GER. (Illus.). 666p. 1960. pap. 22.00 (*0-87548-202-3*) Open Court.

Science of Mechanics in the Middle Ages. Marshall Clagett. (Illus.). 742p. 1959. text ed. 50.00 (*0-299-01900-4*) U of Wis Pr.

Science of Meditation. 3rd ed. Torkom Saraydarian. LC 77-158995. 1982. 16.00 (*0-911794-29-8*) Aqua Educ.

Science of Meditation. 4th ed. Torkom Saraydarian. LC 77-158995. 1993. pap. 15.00 (*0-911794-30-1*) Aqua Educ.

Science of Meditation. Rohit Mehta. (C). 1991. reprint ed. 12.50 (*81-208-0297-7*, Pub. by Motilal Banarsidass II) S Asia.

Science of Meditation. Rohit Mehta. (C). 1995. reprint ed. pap. 9.00 (*81-208-0298-5*, Pub. by Motilal Banarsidass II) S Asia.

Science of Mental Illness. Ethan E. Gorenstein. (Illus.). 158p. 1992. text ed. 32.00 (*0-12-291745-6*) Acad Pr.

***Science of Mind.** Ernest Holmes. (New Thought Library). 672p. 1997. 25.95 (*0-87477-865-4*, Tarcher Putnam) Putnam Pub Group.

Science of Mind. Kenneth A. Klivington. 256p. 1989. 45.00 (*0-262-11141-1*) MIT Pr.

Science of Mind: The Quest of Psychological Reality. Peter Du Preez. 228p. 1991. text ed. 61.00 (*0-12-224960-7*) Acad Pr.

Science of Mind Skills. Jane Claypool. 154p. 1994. pap. 14.95 (*0-9643948-0-4*) Cornucopia CA.

Science of Money. Alexander Del Mar. 1973. 59.95 (*0-8490-1002-0*) Gordon Pr.

Science of "Muddling Through" Charles E. Lindblom. (Reprint Series in Social Sciences). (C). 1993. reprint ed. pap. text ed. 1.00 (*0-8290-3504-4*, PS-169) Irvington.

***Science of Music.** Robin Maconie. (Illus.). 238p. 1997. 29.95 (*0-19-816648-6*) OUP.

Science of Musical Sound. John R. Pierce. LC 91-46742. 1995. pap. text ed. write for info. (*0-7167-6005-3*) W H Freeman.

Science of Musical Sounds. Ed. by Johan Sundberg. (Cognition & Perception Ser.). (Illus.). 237p. 1991. text ed. 53.00 (*0-12-676948-6*) Acad Pr.

Science of Musical Sounds. 2nd ed. Dayton C. Miller. LC 76-181211. 286p. 1926. reprint ed. 59.00 (*0-403-01622-3*) Scholarly.

Science of Musical Sounds. Dayton C. Miller. 286p. 1990. reprint ed. lib. bdg. 69.00 (*0-7812-9127-5*) Rprt Serv.

***Science of Mystic Lights.** John Walbridge. 296p. 1996. pap. 14.95 (*0-614-21240-5*, 1345); pap. 14.95 (*0-614-21338-X*, 1345) Kazi Pubns.

Science of Mystic Lights: Qutb al-Din Shirazi & the Illuminationist Tradition of Islamic Philosophy. John Walbridge. (Middle Eastern Monographs: No. 27). 312p. (Orig.). (C). 1992. pap. text ed. 14.95 (*0-932885-06-3*) Harvard CMES.

Science of Natural Theology. Asa Mahan. LC 75-3273. reprint ed. 37.50 (*0-404-59261-9*) AMS Pr.

Science of Nature. Oluf Tyberg. 85p. 1993. pap. 10.00 (*0-913004-87-1*) Point Loma Pub.

Science of New Materials. Ed. by Andrew Briggs. (Wolfson College Lectures). (Illus.). 224p. 1992. 38.95 (*0-631-18246-2*) Blackwell Pubs.

Science of Numbers & Their Meaning in Scripture. 77p. 1989. pap. 15.00 (*1-57277-426-6*) Script Rsch.

Science of Numerology: Discerning What Numbers Mean to You. Walter B. Gibson. 196p. 1995. pap. 12.95 (*0-87877-230-8*) Newcastle Pub.

Science of Numerology Through the Law of Vibration. John C. Laurie. 75p. 1959. reprint ed. spiral bd. 9.00 (*0-7873-0537-5*) Hlth Research.

Science of Nutrition of Farm Livestock. D. Cuthbertson & H. Sinclair. LC 69-14229. (International Encyclopedia of Food & Nutrition Ser.: Vol. 17, Pt. 1). 1969. 263.00 (*0-08-012709-6*, Pub. by Pergamon Repr UK) Franklin.

Science of Olfaction. Ed. by M. J. Serby & K. L. Chobor. (Illus.). 632p. 1992. 200.00 (*0-387-97688-4*) Spr-Verlag.

Science of Optical Finishing. LC 89-64038. (Technical Digest Series, 1990: Vol. 9). 300p. 1990. lib. bdg. 75.00 (*1-55752-136-0*) Optical Soc.

Science of Opticianry see Opticianry: The Practice & the Art

Science of Organic Dietetics Series, 4 vols., Vols. 1 - 4. Raymond W. Bernard. 49p. 1994. reprint ed. spiral bd. 22.00 (*0-7873-1050-6*) Hlth Research.

***Science of Overabundance: Deer Ecology & Population Management.** Ed. by William J. McShea et al. LC 97-3327. (Illus.). 432p. 1997. text ed. 37.50 (*1-56098-681-6*) Smithsonian.

Science of Palmistry. Eugene Lawrence. 138p. 1973. reprint ed. spiral bd. 10.00 (*0-7873-0538-3*) Hlth Research.

Science of Palmistry & Its Relations to Astrology & Phrenology. Irene Smith. 150p. 1973. reprint ed. spiral bd. 10.00 (*0-7873-0803-X*) Hlth Research.

Science of Personal Success: How to Turn Your Life into a World of Endless Success. 2nd rev. ed. Leroy W. Smith, Jr. Ed. by Carolyn McKay. (Illus.). 101p. (Orig.). 1985. pap. 6.95 (*0-915455-01-3*) Prestige Ent.

Science of Personality. Lawrence A. Pervin. LC 95-5144. 1995. text ed. write for info. (*0-471-57850-9*) Wiley.

Science of Photobiology. 2nd ed. Ed. by Kendric C. Smith. LC 88-31624. (Illus.). 434p. 1989. 85.00 (*0-306-43049-5*, Plenum Pr); pap. 42.50 (*0-306-43059-2*, Plenum Pr) Plenum.

Science of Photomedicine. Ed. by James D. Regan et al. LC 82-9072. (Photobiology Ser.). 680p. 1982. 125.00 (*0-306-40924-0*, Plenum Pr) Plenum.

Science of Pleasure: Cosmos & Psyche in the Bourgeois World View. Harvie Ferguson. 384p. (C). 1992. pap. 18.95 (*0-415-04458-8*, A5432) Routledge.

Science of Pocket Billiards. Jack H. Koehler. LC 88-62401. (Illus.). 262p. (Orig.). (C). 1989. 26.95 (*0-9622890-0-0*) Sportology Pubns.

Science of Pocket Billiards. 2nd ed. Jack H. Koehler. LC 88-62401. (Illus.). (Orig.). 1995. pap. 22.95 (*0-9622890-2-7*) Sportology Pubns.

Science of Political Economy. Henry George. LC 81-5939. 545p. 1992. reprint ed. 15.00 (*0-911312-51-X*) Schalkenbach.

Science of Political Economy. Henry George. (Notable American Authors Ser.). 1992. reprint ed. lib. bdg. 75.00 (*0-7812-2920-0*) Rprt Serv.

Science of Polymer Molecules. Richard H. Boyd & Paul J. Phillips. (Solid State Science Ser.). (Illus.). 420p. (C). 1994. text ed. 90.00 (*0-521-32076-3*) Cambridge U Pr.

Science of Polymer Molecules. Richard H. Boyd & Paul J. Phillips. (Cambridge Solid State Science Ser.). 428p. 1996. pap. text ed. 32.95 (*0-521-56508-1*) Cambridge U Pr.

Science of Powder Coatings Vol. 2: Applications. John Copland & David A. Bate. Ed. by Ashley J. Scott. (Illus.). 333p. 1994. text ed. 100.00 (*0-947798-27-7*) Scholium Intl.

Science of Powder Coatings, Vol. 1: Chemistry, Formulation, Manufacture & Application. David A. Bate. (Illus.). 350p. 1990. text ed. 100.00 (*0-947798-00-5*, Pub. by SITA Tech UK) Scholium Intl.

***Science of Prevention: Methodological Advances from Alcohol & Substance Abuse Research.** Kendall J. Bryant et al. LC 97-14910. (Illus.). 504p. 1997. text ed. 49.95 (*1-55798-439-5*) Am Psychol.

Science of Problem-Solving: A Practical Guide for Science Teachers. Mike Watts. 160p. 1991. pap. text ed. 21.00 (*0-435-08314-7*, 08314) Heinemann.

Science of Programming. David Gries. (Texts & Monographs in Computer Science). 366p. 1987. 40.00 (*0-387-90641-X*) Spr-Verlag.

Science of Programming. David Gries. (Texts & Monographs in Computer Science). xiii, 366p. 1995. reprint ed. 34.95 (*0-387-96480-0*) Spr-Verlag.

***Science of Prophecy, Vol. 1.** 3rd ed. E. Bernard Jordan. Ed. by Deborah Jones. 80p. (Orig.). 1988. reprint ed. pap. 10.00 (*0-939241-07-2*) Faith Print.

Science of Psychic Healing. Yogi Ramacharaka. 190p. 1972. reprint ed. spiral bd. 8.00 (*0-7873-0689-4*) Hlth Research.

Science of Psychic Phenomena. Swami Abhedananda. 101p. 1987. 5.95 (*0-87581-642-8*, Pub. by Rama Ved Math II) Vedanta Pr.

Science of Psychometry. Ida Ellis. 1993. reprint ed. pap. 15.95 (*1-872736-49-1*, Pub. by Mandrake Pr UK) Holmes Pub.

Science of Psychotherapy. Harvey J. Fischer. 288p. 1990. 40.00 (*1-56032-122-9*) Taylor & Francis.

Science of Radio. Paul J. Nahin. 1995. pap. 19.00 (*1-56396-347-7*) Spr-Verlag.

Science of Reading & Spelling: Teacher's Manual for Use with Sure Steps to Reading & Spelling. M. Herbert Weiss. 1976. The Science of Reading & Spelling. pap. text ed. 2.00 (*0-916720-01-2*) Weiss Pub.

***Science of Reciting the Quran.** Muhammad I. Surty. 256p. 1996. 29.95 (*0-614-21071-2*, 1113); pap. 23.95 (*0-614-21070-4*, 1113) Kazi Pubns.

Science of Regeneration: Physiological Methods of Male & Female Regeneration, Pts. I & II. Raymond W. Bernard. 44p. 1955. spiral bd. 11.00 (*0-7873-1216-9*) Hlth Research.

Science of Regeneration: Physiological, Nutritional & Blood Methods of Regeneration. Universal Research Staff. Ed. by Manuel Grace. (Illus.). 150p. (Orig.). 1995. lib. bdg. 10.95 (*0-942951-04-2*) Universal Res MA.

Science of Regeneration of Sex Enlightenment (1911) Advance Thought Pub. Staff. 162p. 1996. pap. 16.95 (*1-56459-932-9*) Kessinger Pub.

Science of Religion. Paramahansa Yogananda. LC 81-52892. (Illus.). 102p. 1982. 10.50 (*0-87612-004-4*); English ed. pap. 6.50 (*0-87612-005-2*) Self Realization.

Science of Religion: Paramhansa Yogananda. LC 84-71200. 1993. pap. 10.95 (*0-937134-16-3*) Amrita Found.

Science of Religion, Studies in Methodology. Ed. by Lauri Honko. (Religion & Reason Ser.). 1979. text ed. 100.80 (*90-279-7854-9*) Mouton.

Science of Revolution: An Introduction. Lenny Wolff. LC 80-51229. 252p. (Orig.). 1983. 15.95 (*0-89851-035-X*); pap. 7.95 (*0-89851-036-8*) RCP Pubns.

Science of Revolution: Fundamentals of Marxism-Leninism, Mao Tse Tung Thought & the Line of the Revolutionary Communist Party, U. S. A. Victor Wild. (Orig.). 1980. pap. 1.50 (*0-89851-038-4*) RCP Pubns.

Science of Revolutionary Warfare. Johann Most. (Explosives, Incendiaries & Demolitions Ser.: No. 2). 1990. lib. bdg. 79.95 (*0-8490-3993-2*) Gordon Pr.

Science of Revolutionary Warfare: A Guide for Would-Be Anarchists. J. Most. (Anarchists & Anarchism Ser.). 1990. lib. bdg. 250.00 (*0-87700-887-6*) Revisionist Pr.

Science of Seating. Ed. by Kageyu Noro. 250p. 1994. 99.00 (*0-85066-802-6*, Pub. by Tay Francis Ltd UK) Taylor & Francis.

Science of Seership. 5th ed. Geoffrey Hodson. 224p. 1985. reprint ed. spiral bd. 21.00 (*0-7873-0412-3*) Hlth Research.

Science of Self Realization. Bhaktivedanta Swami. (Illus.). 412p. 1977. 9.95 (*0-89213-101-2*) Bhaktivedanta.

Science of Selling Alarm Systems. Norman C. Eisenstat. 208p. 1984. 34.95 (*0-7506-9174-3*) Buttrwrth-Heinemann.

Science of Sintering: New Directions for Materials Processing & Microstructural Control. Ed. by D. P. Uskokovic et al. (Illus.). 640p. 1990. 145.00 (*0-306-43528-4*, Plenum Pr) Plenum.

***Science of Snow Goose Hunting.** Dennis Hunt & Bob Guist. (Illus.). 120p. (Orig.). 1994. pap. 19.95 (*0-9653908-0-2*) D Hunt Huntg.

Science of Soap Films & Soap Bubbles. Cyril Isenberg. (Illus.). 220p. 1992. reprint ed. pap. 9.95 (*0-486-26960-4*) Dover.

Science of Social Redemption: McGill, The Chicago School, & the Origins of Social Research in Canada. Marlene Shore. 1987. 40.00 (*0-8020-5733-0*); pap. 18.95 (*0-8020-6645-3*) U of Toronto Pr.

Science of Society. Stephen Andrews. Ed. by Charles Shively. 184p. 1970. 15.00 (*0-87730-004-6*) M&S Pr.

Science of Society. Stephen P. Andrews. 1972. 250.00 (*0-8490-1003-9*) Gordon Pr.

Science of Society: Toward an Understanding of the Life & Work of Karl August Wittfogel. G. L. Ulman. 1978. 192.35 (*90-279-7766-6*) Mouton.

Science of Soul: A Practical Exposition of Ancient Method of Visualisation of Soul. Atma-Vijnana. Yogeshwaranand S. Maharaj. xx, 280p. 1987. 18.00 (*0-614-06349-3*, Pub. by Yoga Niketan II) Nataraj Bks.

Science of Sound. 2nd ed. Thomas D. Rossing. (C). 1990. text ed. 54.50 (*0-201-15727-6*) Addison-Wesley.

Science of Sound: Musical, Electronic, Environmental. Thomas D. Rossing. LC 80-12028. (Chemistry Ser.). (Illus.). 512p. 1982. text ed. write for info. (*0-201-06505-3*) Addison-Wesley.

Science of Sound Physics of Hi-Fi. Orest Symko. 384p. (C). 1994. per., pap. text ed. 52.95 (*0-8403-8823-3*) Kendall-Hunt.

Science of Space-Time. Derek J. Raine & Michael Heller. (Astronomy & Astrophysics Ser.: Vol. 9). (Illus.). 256p. 1981. text ed. 38.00 (*0-912918-12-8*, 0012) Pachart Pub Hse.

Science of Spiritual Alchemy. R. Swinburne Clymer. 235p. 1959. 9.95 (*0-932785-44-1*) Philos Pub.

Science of Success. Julia Seton. 217p. 1972. reprint ed. spiral bd. 8.50 (*0-7873-0772-6*) Hlth Research.

Science of Success (1914) Julia Seton. 217p. 1996. pap. 17.95 (*1-56459-795-4*) Kessinger Pub.

Science of Successful Living. Raymond C. Barker. LC 57-11392. 145p. 1984. reprint ed. pap. 7.95 (*0-87516-536-2*) DeVorss.

Science of Superconductivity & New Materials. Ed. by S. Nakajima. 348p. (C). 1989. text ed. 86.00 (*9971-5-0885-0*) World Scientific Pub.

Science of Survival. L. Ron Hubbard. 580p. 1989. 50.00 (*0-88404-418-1*) Bridge Pubns Inc.

Science of Tennis. David J. Anderson & Robert M. Anderson. (Illus.). 146p. (Orig.). (C). 1985. pap. 12.75 (*0-9617528-0-7*) Racquet Pr.

Science of the Mind. 2nd ed. Owen Flanagan. (Illus.). 128p. (Orig.). 1991. pap. 19.00 (*0-262-56056-9*, Bradford Bks) MIT Pr.

Science of the Mind: 2001 & Beyond. Ed. by Robert L. Solso & Dominic W. Massaro. (Illus.). 336p. 1995. 35.00 (*0-19-508064-5*) OUP.

Science of the Oneness of Being in the Christian Science Textbook. Max Kappeler. LC 82-81131. 276p. 1983. 24.00 (*0-942958-03-9*) Kappeler Inst Pub.

Science of the Sacraments. Charles W. Leadbeater. 1988. 29.95 (*81-7059-181-3*) Theos Pub Hse.

Science of the Singing Voice. Johan Sundberg. LC 87-5499. 1987. pap. 22.00 (*0-87580-542-6*) N Ill U Pr.

Science of the Singing Voice. Johan Sundberg. 228p. 1987. pap. 34.95 (*1-56593-583-7*, 0809) Singular Publishing.

Science of the Soul. R. Swinburne Clymer. 1993. 17.50 (*0-686-00828-6*) Philos Pub.

Science of the Soul: Consciousness: The Bridge Between Energy & Substance, 2 vols. 2nd ed. Luis F. Zapata & Christopher J. Hibbard. 420p. (Orig.). 1992. pap. 18.00 (*0-9623614-4-5*) Disciples Pr.

Science of the Spoken Word. Ed. by Mark L. Prophet & Elizabeth C. Prophet. LC 74-82293. (Illus.). 218p. 1965. reprint ed. pap. 12.95 (*0-916766-07-1*) Summit Univ.

Science of the Summer Games. Vincent P. Mallette. (Illus.). 300p. (Orig.). 1996. pap. 19.95 (*1-886801-14-2*) Chrles River Media.

Science of the Times: No. 4. 1981. write for info. (*0-318-50887-7*) Ayer.

Science of the Times, Vol. 3: A New York Times Survey. Ed. by Arleen Keylin. 1980. 19.95 (*0-405-13094-5*) Ayer.

***Science of the Times, 1: A New York Times Survey.** Ed. by Leslie Parr. Date not set. write for info. (*0-405-19030-1*) Ayer.

Science of the Water Planet. Lansing Community College, Science Department Staff. (C). 1993. student ed. 12.00 (*1-881592-16-2*) Hayden-McNeil.

Science of Theology. Gillian R. Evans et al. Ed. by Paul Avis. LC 86-19645. (History of Christian Theology Ser.: Vol. 1). 375p. reprint ed. pap. 106.90 (*0-7837-0509-3*, 2040833) Bks Demand.

Science of Thought. Friedrich M. Mueller. LC 73-18813. reprint ed. 69.50 (*0-404-11453-9*) AMS Pr.

***Science of Time: The Time & the Judgement.** Elijah Muhammad. Ed. by Nasie Hakim. 96p. (Orig.). 1997. pap. 7.95 (*1-884855-27-X*) Secretarius.

Science of Today & the Problems of Genesis. Patrick O'Connell. LC 90-71913. 382p. 1993. pap. 18.50 (*0-89555-438-0*) TAN Bks Pubs.

Science of Trapping. E. Kreps. (Illus.). 229p. pap. 4.00 (*0-936622-19-9*) A R Harding Pub.

Science of Tridosha. B. Bhattacharyya. 57p. 1978. reprint ed. spiral bd. 6.50 (*0-7873-0109-4*) Hlth Research.

Science of Tridosha: An Analysis of the Three Cosmic Elements in Medicines, Foods, & Diseases & Homeopathy. Bhaskar Bhattacharyya. 1991. lib. bdg. 79.95 (*0-87700-961-9*) Revisionist Pr.

Science of Vine & Wine in France, 1750-1990. Harry W. Paul. (Illus.). 432p. (C). 1996. text ed. 64.95 (*0-521-49745-0*) Cambridge U Pr.

Science of Virtual Reality. 2nd ed. Roy Kalawsky. (C). 1997. text ed. write for info. (*0-201-42773-7*) Addison-Wesley.

Science of Virtual Reality & Virtual Environments. Roy Kalawsky. (C). 1993. text ed. 47.50 (*0-201-63171-7*) Addison-Wesley.

Science of Vision. Ed. by K. N. Leibovic. (Illus.). 472p. 1990. 72.00 (*0-387-97270-6*) Spr-Verlag.

Science of Vital Force: A New Research of Self & God-Realisation by the Medium of Prana. Yogeshwaranand S. Maharaj. Tr. by Muktanand Saraswati. v, 143p. 1980. 12.00 (*0-614-06352-3*, Pub. by Yoga Niketan II) Nataraj Bks.

Science of Vocal Pedagogy: Theory & Application. D. Ralph Appelman. LC 67-10107. (Illus.). 448p. 1967. pap. 23.95 (*0-253-20378-3*) Ind U Pr.

Science of Vocal Pedagogy: Theory & Application, Tape 1. D. Ralph Appelman. LC 67-10107. 1967. 8.95 (*0-253-35112-X*) Ind U Pr.

Science of Vocal Pedagogy: Theory & Application, Tape 2. D. Ralph Appelman. LC 67-10107. 1967. 8.95 (*0-253-35113-8*) Ind U Pr.

Science of Vocal Pedagogy: Theory & Application, Tape 3. D. Ralph Appelman. LC 67-10107. 1967. 8.95 (*0-253-35114-6*) Ind U Pr.

Science of Vocal Percussion in the Gan-Tone Method of Singing. Robert Gansert. LC 93-78487. (Illus.). 220p. 24.95 (*0-939458-01-2*) Gan-Tone Pub.

Science of War. G. F. Henderson. 1977. lib. bdg. 59.95 (*0-8490-2572-9*) Gordon Pr.

Science of War: Back to First Principles. Ed. by W. E. Rous & Brian H. Reid. LC 92-15504. (Operational Level of War Ser.). 208p. (C). (gr. 13). 1993. text ed. 69.95 (*0-415-07995-0*, B0307) Routledge.

Science of Water: The Foundation of Modern Hydraulics. Enzo Levi. Tr. by Daniel E. Edina from SPA. LC 94-44189. 1995. 100.00 (*0-7844-0005-9*) Am Soc Civil Eng.

Science of Well-Being. Judith L. Powell & Wallace D. Wattles. LC 93-17454. 160p. (Orig.). 1993. pap. 8.95 (*1-56087-059-1*) Top Mtn Pub.

Science of Whitewares. Ed. by Victoria E. Henkes et al. (Illus.). 446p. 1996. 90.00 (*1-57498-011-4*, G025) Am Ceramic.

Science of Woman: Gynaecology & Gender in England, 1800-1929. Ornella Moscucci. (History of Medicine Ser.). (Illus.). 296p. (C). 1993. pap. text ed. 19.95 (*0-521-44795-X*) Cambridge U Pr.

Science of Words. George A. Miller. (Illus.). 267p. (C). 1996. pap. text ed. 19.95 (*0-7167-6016-9*) W H Freeman.

Science of Words: A Scientific American Library Book. George A. Miller. 250p. 1995. text ed. 32.95 (*0-7167-5027-9*) W H Freeman.

Science of Writing. Ed. by C. Michael Levy & Sarah Ransdell. 456p. 1996. text ed. 69.95 (*0-8058-2108-2*); pap. text ed. 34.50 (*0-8058-2109-0*) L Erlbaum Assocs.

Science of Yoga. I. K. Taimni. LC 67-4112. 1986. pap. 11.95 (*0-8356-0023-8*, Quest) Theos Pub Hse.

An Asterisk (*) at the beginning of an entry indicates that the title is appearing in BIP for the first time.

Science of Yoga. I. K. Taimni. 1986. 15.95 (81-7059-001-9) Theos Pub Hse.
Science on a Shoestring. Herb Strongin. 1976. pap. text ed. 16.00 (0-201-07329-3) Addison-Wesley.
Science on a Shoestring, 1992. Herb Strongin. 1991. pap. 20.00 (0-201-25760-2) Addison-Wesley.
Science on Amazon. Anthony Smith. 1999. pap. 19.95 (0-670-81311-7) Viking Penguin.
Science on Form. Ed. by S. Ishizaka et al. 1987. lib. bdg. 285.50 (90-277-2390-7) Kluwer Ac.
Science on Ice: Research in the Antarctic. Michael Woods. LC 94-12055. (Illus.). 96p. (YA). (gr. 6 up). 1995. lib. bdg. 20.90 (1-56294-498-3) Millbrook Pr.
Science on Stage Anthology. Ed. by Tessa Bridal & Susan McCormick. (Illus.). 116p. 1991. pap. 14.00 (0-944040-26-8) AST Ctrs.
Science on the Connection Machine: Proceedings of the 1st European Users Meeting. T. Lippert et al. 236p. 1992. text ed. 81.00 (981-02-1206-2) World Scientific Pub.
Science on the Ice: An Antarctic Journal. Rebecca L. Johnson. LC 94-41487. (YA). (gr. 5 up). 1995. lib. bdg. 19.13 (0-8225-2852-5) Lerner Group.
Science on the Run: Information Management & Industrial Geophysics at Schlumberger, 1920-1940. Geoffrey C. Bowker. LC 93-29647. (Inside Technology Ser.). 200p. 1994. 27.50 (0-262-02367-9) MIT Pr.
***Science on the Texas Frontier: Observations of Dr. Gideon Lincecum.** Gideon Lincecum et al. LC 97-10939. (Illus.). 224p. 1997. 35.00 (0-89096-768-7); pap. 17.95 (0-89096-790-3) Texas A&M Univ.
Science on the Web: A Connoisseur's Guide to over 500 of the Best, the Most Useful, & Most Fun Web Sites. Edward J. Renehan. LC 96-18688. 392p. 1996. pap. 19. 95 (0-387-94795-7) Spr-Verlag.
***Science on Trial.** Marcia Angell. Date not set. pap. 13.95 (0-393-31672-6) Norton.
Science on Trial. Douglas Futuyma. 1982. 16.50 (0-394-52371-7) Pantheon.
Science on Trial: The Case for Evolution. Douglas J. Futuyma. LC 95-5980. 1995. pap. 16.95 (0-87893-184-8) Sinauer Assocs.
Science on Trial: The Clash of Medical Evidence & the Law in the Breast Implant Case. Marcia Angell. 288p. 1996. 27.50 (0-393-03973-0) Norton.
Science, Optics & Music in Medieval & Early Modern Thought. A. C. Crombie. 450p. 1990. boxed 65.00 (0-907628-79-6) Hambledon Press.
Science, Paradox, & the Moebius Principle: The Evolution of a "Transcultural" Approach to Wholeness. Steven M. Rosen. LC 93-3091. (SUNY Series in Science, Technology, & Society). 317p. (C). 1994. pap. text ed. 21.95 (0-7914-1770-0) State U NY Pr.
Science, Paradox, & the Moebius Principle: The Evolution of a "Transcultural" Approach to Wholeness. Steven M. Rosen. LC 93-3091. (SUNY Series in Science, Technology, & Society). 317p. (C). 1994. text ed. 64.50 (0-7914-1769-7) State U NY Pr.
Science Parks & Innovation Centres: Their Economic & Social Impact: Proceedings of the International Conference Held in Berlin, 13-15 Feb. 1985. Ed. by J. M. Gibb. 478p. 1985. 148.25 (0-444-42544-6) Elsevier.
Science Parks & the Growth of High Technology Firms. C. S. Monck et al. 224p. (C). 1988. text ed. 72.50 (0-415-00092-0) Routledge.
Science: People, Concepts, Processes see Gateways to Science
Science, Perception & Reality. Wilfrid Sellars. 384p. 1991. pap. text ed. 22.00 (0-924922-00-1); lib. bdg. 39.00 (0-924922-50-8) Ridgeview.
Science, Philosophy, & Culture: Historical Perspective. Ed. by Debiprasad Chattopadhyaya & Ravinder Kumar. (C). 1995. 15.00 (81-215-0686-7, Pub. by Munshiram Manoharial II) S Asia.
***Science Philosophy & Culture: Multi-Disciplinary Explorations, Pt. 1.** Ed. by Debiprasad Chattopadhyaya & Ravinder Kumar. (C). 1996. 82.00 (81-215-0718-9, Pub. by Munshiram Manoharial II) S Asia.
Science, Philosophy, & Human Behavior in the Soviet Union. Loren R. Graham. LC 86-26357. 672p. 1987. text ed. 66.00 (0-231-06442-X) Col U Pr.
Science, Philosophy, & Human Behavior in the Soviet Union. Loren R. Graham. LC 86-26357. 672p. 1989. pap. text ed. 32.50 (0-231-06443-8) Col U Pr.
Science, Philosophy & Religion. John Bascom. LC 75-3041. reprint ed. 42.50 (0-404-59039-X) AMS Pr.
Science Plus: Technology & Society. 97th ed. McFadden. 1997. teacher ed., text ed. 109.50 (0-03-095091-0) HR&W Schl Div.
Science Plus: Technology & Society 1997. 97th ed. McFadden. 1997. student ed., text ed. 59.75 (0-03-095093-7) HR&W Schl Div.
Science Plus Sentiment: Cesar Daly's Formula for Modern Architecture. Richard J. Becherer. LC 84-2453. (Studies in the Fine Arts - Architecture: No. 7). (Illus.). 451p. reprint ed. pap. 128.60 (0-8357-1566-3, 2070493) Bks Demand.
Science Plus 1997: Technology & Society. 97th ed. McFadden. 1997. teacher ed., text ed. 109.50 (0-03-095094-5) HR&W Schl Div.
Science Policies in International Perspective: The Experience of India & the Netherlands. Ed. by P. J. Lavakare & J. G. Waardenburg. 280p. 1992. text ed. 49. 00 (0-86187-826-4) St Martin.
Science Policy: A Behavioral Approach. Cornelius A. Hazeu. 190p. 1990. text ed. 63.95 (1-85628-057-8, Pub. by Avebury Pub UK) Ashgate Pub Co.
Science Policy: A Source Guide. 1991. lib. bdg. 71.00 (0-8490-4874-5) Gordon Pr.
Science Policy - Foreign & International: A Source Guide. 1991. lib. bdg. 69.95 (0-8490-4861-3) Gordon Pr.
Science Policy - New Mechanisms for Scientific Collaboration Between East & West: Proceedings of the NATO Advanced Research Workshop, Novosibirsk, Russia, November 22-25, 1993. Tr. by Valentin A. Koptyug. 292p. (C). 1994. lib. bdg. 158.50 (0-7923-3227-X) Kluwer Ac.
Science Policy & Business: The Changing Relations of Europe & the United States. Ed. by David W. Ewing. LC 72-86387. 160p. 1973. 37.50 (0-674-79460-5) HUP.
Science Policy & Development. E. Tal & Y. Ezrachi. 362p. 1971. 68.00 (0-677-60185-9) Gordon & Breach.
Science Policy & National Development. Vikram A. Sarabhai. Ed. by Kamla Chowdhry. LC 74-903458. 1974. 9.00 (0-333-90057-X) S Asia.
Science Policy & Politics. Alexander J. Morin. 208p. 1992. pap. text ed. 29.80 (0-13-795246-5) P-H.
Science Policy & Research Management in the Balkan Countries: Proceedings of the NATO Advanced Research Workshop, Athens, Greece, November 23-25, 1994. Ed. by George Parissakis. (NATO ASI - Partnership Sub-Series 4). 248p. (C). 1995. lib. bdg. 157. 00 (0-7923-3599-6) Kluwer Ac.
Science Policy, Biotechnology, & American State Government: Recommendations for State Action. James W. O'Brien. (Studies in Technology & Social Change: No. 12). 76p. (Orig.). (C). 1989. pap. 8.00 (0-945271-17-4) ISU-CIKARD.
Science Policy, Ethics, & Economic Methodology. Kristin S. Shrader-Frechette. 336p. 1984. pap. text ed. 46.00 (90-277-1845-8, D Reidel); lib. bdg. 117.50 (90-277-1806-7, D Reidel) Kluwer Ac.
Science Policy for Britain. Tam Dalyell. LC 83-190946. 141p. reprint ed. pap. 40.20 (0-685-16352-0, 2027714) Bks Demand.
Science Policy Research: Implications & Applications. Ed. by Darcy F. De Almeida. 1991. text ed. 39.00 (0-86187-130-8) St Martin.
***Science, Politics & Gnosticism.** Eric Voegelin. LC 97-13501. 1997. pap. text ed. 9.95 (0-89526-419-6) Regnery Pub.
Science, Politics, & International Conferences: A Functional Analysis of the Moscow Political Science Congress. Richard L. Merritt & Elizabeth C. Hanson. LC 88-18322. (GSIS Monograph in World Affairs). 1989. lib. bdg. 20.00 (1-55587-134-8) Lynne Rienner.
Science, Politics, & International Ocean Management: The Uses of Scientific Knowledge in International Negotiations. Edward L. Miles. LC 87-81999. (Policy Papers in International Affairs: No. 33). (Illus.). viii, 70p. 1987. pap. text ed. 6.50 (0-87725-533-4) U of Cal IAS.
Science, Politics, & Morality: Scientific Uncertainty & Decision Making. Ed. by Rene Von Schomberg. LC 92-31872. (Theory & Decision Library, Series A, Philosophy & Methodology of the Social Sciences: Vol. 17). 246p. (C). 1993. lib. bdg. 102.00 (0-7923-1997-4, Pub. by Klwr Acad Pubs NE) Kluwer Ac.
Science, Politics & Social Practice: Essays on Marxism & Science, Philosophy of Culture & the Social Sciences: In Honor of Robert S. Cohen. Ed. by Kostas Gavroglu et al. LC 94-3703. (Boston Studies in the Philophy of Science: Vol. 164). 404p. 1995. lib. bdg. 150.00 (0-7923-2989-9, Pub. by Klwr Acad Pubs NE) Kluwer Ac.
Science, Politics & Society in Eighteenth-Century Italy: The Giornale de Letterati d'Italia & Its World. Brendan M. Dooley. LC 91-3337. (Modern European History Outstanding Studies & Dissertations). 216p. 1991. text ed. 15.00 (0-8153-0471-4) Garland.
Science, Politics & the Cold War. Greta Jones. 208p. 1988. lib. bdg. 52.50 (0-415-00356-3) Routledge.
Science, Politics, & the Pharmaceutical Industry. John Abraham. LC 95-9025. 1995. text ed. 55.00 (0-312-12873-8) St Martin.
***Science Power, 2 vols.** (World Book Power Ser.). (Illus.). 480p. (YA). (gr. 5-12). 1996. write for info. (0-7166-2994-1, 186) World Bk.
Science Pre GED Series. Steck-Vaughn Co., Staff. 1994. pap. text ed. 9.96 (0-8114-4487-2) Raintree Steck-V.
Science Probe 2. Susan S. Thee & Gary Sokolis. LC 96-26771. (UK - Science Ser.). (J). 1997. text ed. 61.95 (0-538-66901-2) S-W Pub.
Science Probe 10. Bullard et al. (UK - Science Ser.). 1992. text ed. 57.95 (0-471-79534-8) S-W Pub.
Science Probe 9. Beckett et al. (UK - Science Ser.). 1995. text ed. 62.95 (0-17-604716-6) S-W Pub.
***Science Problem Solving.** Hook & Ingram. 1990. pap. text ed. write for info. (0-582-86944-7, Pub. by Longman UK) Longman.
Science Profession in the Third World: Studies from India & Kenya. Thomas O. Eisemon. Ed. by Philip G. Altbach. LC 82-7662. (Special Studies in Comparative Education). 186p. 1982. text ed. 45.00 (0-275-90785-6, C0785, Praeger Pubs) Greenwood.
Science Project. Nicholas Pine. (Terror Academy Ser.: No. 8). 192p. (Orig.). 1994. mass mkt. 3.50 (0-425-14152-7) Berkley Pub.
***Science Project Ideas about Air.** Robert Gardner. LC 97-7389. (Science Projects Ideas Ser.). (Illus.). 96p. (J). (gr. 4-9). 1997. lib. bdg. 17.95 (0-89490-838-3) Enslow Pubs.
***Science Project Ideas about Animals.** Robert Gardner. LC 97-13136. (Science Projects Ideas Ser.). (Illus.). 96p. (J). (gr. 4-9). 1997. lib. bdg. 17.95 (0-89490-842-1) Enslow Pubs.
***Science Project Ideas about Rain.** Robert Gardner. LC 96-42411. (Science Projects Ideas Ser.). (Illus.). 96p. (J). (gr. 4-9). 1997. lib. bdg. 17.95 (0-89490-843-X) Enslow Pubs.
***Science Project Ideas about the Moon.** Robert Gardner. LC 97-6486. (Science Projects Ideas Ser.). (Illus.). 96p. (J). (gr. 4-9). 1997. lib. bdg. 17.95 (0-89490-844-8) Enslow Pubs.
***Science Project Ideas about the Sun.** Robert Gardner. LC 96-42693. (Science Projects Ideas Ser.). (Illus.). 96p. (J). (gr. 4-9). 1997. lib. bdg. 17.95 (0-89490-845-6) Enslow Pubs.
***Science Project Ideas about Trees.** Robert Gardner. LC 97-6515. (Science Projects Ideas Ser.). (Illus.). 96p. (J). (gr. 4-9). 1997. lib. bdg. 17.95 (0-89490-846-4) Enslow Pubs.
Science Projects about Chemistry. Robert Gardner. LC 94-959. (Science Projects Ser.). (Illus.). 128p. (YA). (gr. 6 up). 1994. lib. bdg. 18.95 (0-89490-531-7) Enslow Pubs.
Science Projects about Electricity & Magnets. Robert Gardner. LC 93-45252. (Science Projects Ser.). (Illus.). 128p. (YA). (gr. 6 up). 1994. lib. bdg. 18.95 (0-89490-530-9) Enslow Pubs.
Science Projects about Light. Robert Gardner. LC 93-23719. (Science Projects Ser.). (Illus.). 128p. (YA). (gr. 6 up). 1994. lib. bdg. 18.95 (0-89490-529-5) Enslow Pubs.
Science Projects about Temperature & Heat. Robert Gardner & Eric Kemer. LC 93-48800. (Science Projects Ser.). (Illus.). 128p. (YA). (gr. 6 up). 1994. lib. bdg. 18. 95 (0-89490-534-1) Enslow Pubs.
Science Projects about the Human Body. Robert Gardner. LC 92-43802. (Science Projects Ser.). (Illus.). 104p. (YA). (gr. 6 up). 1993. lib. bdg. 18.95 (0-89490-443-4) Enslow Pubs.
Science Projects about Weather. Robert Gardner & David Webster. LC 93-48720. (Science Projects Ser.). (Illus.). 128p. (YA). (gr. 6 up). 1994. lib. bdg. 18.95 (0-89490-533-3) Enslow Pubs.
Science Projects for the Intermediate Grades. Maxine S. Schneider. LC 70-132146. 1971. pap. 8.99 (0-8224-6310-5) Fearon Teach Aids.
Science Projects for Young People. George Barr. 153p. (J). (gr. 5 up). 1986. reprint ed. pap. 4.95 (0-486-25235-3) Dover.
***Science Projects Ideas, 6 vols.** Robert Gardner. (Science Projects Ser.). (Illus.). (J). (gr. 4-9). 1997. lib. bdg. 107. 70 (0-89490-998-3) Enslow Pubs.
Science Projects Series, 6 bks. (Illus.). (YA). (gr. 6 up). 1993. lib. bdg. 113.70 (0-89490-581-3) Enslow Pubs.
***Science Projects with Computers.** Elayne Schulman et al. write for info. (0-668-06251-7) S&S Trade.
Science Projects with Computers. Elayne E. Schulman et al. write for info. (0-668-06245-2) S&S Trade.
Science, Pseudo-Science, & Utopianism in Early Modern Thought. Ed. by Stephen A. McKnight. (Illus.). 240p. (C). 1992. text ed. 37.95 (0-8262-0835-5) U of Mo Pr.
Science, Psychology & Communication: Essays Honoring William Stephenson. Ed. by Steven R. Brown & Donald J. Brenner. LC 73-165607. (Foresight Books in Psychology Ser.). 493p. reprint ed. pap. 140.60 (0-317-42024-0, 2025996) Bks Demand.
Science Puzzlers! 150 Ready-to-Use Activities to Make Learning Fun. Robert G. Hoehn. 255p. 1995. spiral bd. 27.95 (0-87628-859-X) Ctr Appl Res.
Science Puzzlers see Entertaining Science Experiments with Everyday Objects
Science Puzzles. Jo E. Moore. (Illus.). 48p. (J). (gr. 3-6). 1991. teacher ed., pap. text ed. 4.95 (1-55799-205-3, EMC 823) Evan-Moor Corp.
Science Question in Feminism. Sandra Harding. LC 85-48197. 296p. 1986. pap. 14.95 (0-8014-9363-3) Cornell U Pr.
***Science Question in Feminism.** Sandra Harding. 272p. 1986. 42.50 (0-335-15360-7, Open Univ Pr); pap. 13.99 (0-335-15359-3, Open Univ Pr) Taylor & Francis.
Science Quizbook. P. Dowswell & M. Claridge. (Quizbooks Ser.). (Illus.). 32p. (J). (gr. 3 up). 1994. pap. 6.95 (0-7460-1357-4, Usborne); lib. bdg. 14.95 (0-88110-652-6, Usborne) EDC.
Science, Radiation Protection, & The NCRP. Warren K. Sinclair. LC 93-27826. (Taylor Lectures: No. 17). 56p. 1993. pap. 25.00 (0-929600-31-2) NCRP Pubns.
Science, Rationality, & Neoclassical Economics. Lance D. Keita. LC 90-50455. 192p. 1992. 35.00 (0-87413-410-2) U Delaware Pr.
Science, Reality, & Language. Michele Marsonet. LC 94-22357. (SUNY Series in Philosophy). 170p. (C). 1995. text ed. 44.50 (0-7914-2475-8); pap. text ed. 14.95 (0-7914-2476-6) State U NY Pr.
***Science, Reason, & Anthropology: A Guide to Critical Thinking.** James Lett. 160p. 1997. 55.00 (0-8476-8592-6) Rowman.
***Science, Reason, & Anthropology: A Guide to Critical Thinking.** James Lett. 160p. 1997. pap. 16.95 (0-8476-8593-4) Rowman.
Science, Reason & Religion. Derek Stanesby. 224p. 1988. pap. 12.95 (0-415-02657-1) Routledge.
Science, Reason, & Rhetoric. Ed. by Henry Krips et al. (Pittsburgh-Konstanz Series in the Philosophy & History of Science). 318p. (C). 1995. 49.95 (0-8229-3912-6) U of Pittsburgh Pr.
Science Rediscovered: A Daily Chronicle of Highlights in the History of Science. Leanne Stiffler. (Illus.). 112p. (J). (gr. 6-8). 1998. pap. text ed. write for info. (0-89089-940-1) Carolina Acad Pr.
Science, Religion & Belief: The Clerical Virtuosi of the Royal Society of London, 1663-1687. Rogers B. Miles. LC 91-16763. (American University Studies: Theology & Religion: Ser. VII, Vol. 106). 207p. 1993. 41.95 (0-8204-1564-2) P Lang Pubng.
Science, Religion, & Mormon Cosmology. Erich R. Paul. (Illus.). 312p. (C). 1992. text ed. 29.95 (0-252-01895-8) U of Ill Pr.
Science, Religion & the Future. Charles Raven. Ed. by Susan Howatch. LC 94-31712. (Yes: Library of Anglican Spirituality Ser.). 144p. 1995. pap. 9.95 (0-8192-1633-X) Morehouse Pub.
Science, Religion & the Search for God: Bridging the Gap. Richard V. Sidy. 148p. (Orig.). 1996. pap. text ed. 8.95 (0-9633744-2-7) SNS Pr.
Science Reorganized. James F. McClellan. 1985. text ed. 72.00 (0-231-05996-5) Col U Pr.
Science Report on Solar Energy in America. William D. Metz & Allen L. Hammond. LC 78-69957. (AAAS Publication Ser.: No. 78-10). 256p. reprint ed. pap. 73.00 (0-7837-0070-9, 2040317) Bks Demand.
Science Research Experiments for Young People. George Barr. 1989. pap. 3.50 (0-486-26111-5) Dover.
***Science Research Programs: Showing Intractable Decision Conflict.** Ronald Cutburth. (Illus.). 65p. 1997. spiral bd. 9.00 (1-878291-35-1) Love From Sea.
***Science Resource Guide.** Kathy Burdick et al. Ed. by Rozanne L. Williams. (Learn to Read Resource Guide Ser.). (Illus.). 80p. (Orig.). 1996. pap. text ed. 25.98 (1-57471-144-X, 3497) Creat Teach Pr.
Science Responds to Environmental Threats: Synthesis Report. OECD Staff. 142p. (Orig.). 1992. pap. 18.00 (92-64-03687-3) OECD.
Science, Revolution & Discontinuity. John Krige. (Modern Revivals in Philosophy Ser.). 232p. 1994. 55.95 (0-7512-0294-0, Pub. by Gregg Revivals UK) Ashgate Pub Co.
Science-Royal Society of Chemistry Medicinal Chemistry Symposium, 2nd, No. 50. Emmett. 1989. 62.00 (0-85186-935-1) CRC Pr.
Science Safety Handbook for California High Schools. California Department of Education Staff. (Illus.). 184p. 1987. pap. 7.25 (0-8011-0669-9) Calif Education.
Science Sampler. Sandra Markle. (Computers & Science Ser.). 112p. (J). (gr. 4-8). 1980. 10.95 (0-88160-031-8, LW 216) Learning Wks.
Science, Satire & Wit: The Essays of Georg Christoph Lichtenberg. Ralph W. Buechler. LC 90-36002. (Studies in Modern German Literature: Vol. 41). 311p. (C). 1991. text ed. 52.95 (0-8204-1367-4) P Lang Pubng.
***Science, Science Everywhere: A Supplement to Childcraft - The How & Why Library.** LC 97-3509. (Illus.). 224p. (J). (gr. 1-6). 1997. write for info. (0-7166-0697-6) World Bk.
Science Secrets. Robyn Supraner. LC 80-23794. (Illus.). 48p. (J). (gr. 1-5). 1981. lib. bdg. 12.50 (0-89375-426-9) Troll Communs.
Science Sensations: An Activity Book from the Children's Museum, Boston. Diane Willow & Emily Curran. 1989. 16.95 (0-201-51747-7) Addison-Wesley.
Science Sensations: An Activity Book from the Children's Museum, Boston. Diane Willow & Emily Curran. (J). 1989. pap. 11.00 (0-201-07189-4) Addison-Wesley.
Science Sequencing Activities. Joy Evans & Jo E. Moore. (Illus.). 48p. (J). (ps-1). 1987. teacher ed., pap. text ed. 4.95 (1-55799-118-9, EMC 815) Evan-Moor Corp.
Science Serving Faith: Henry Nelson Wieman. Ed. by Creighton Peden & Charles L. Willig. LC 87-9441. (American Academy of Religion, Studies in Religion). 200p. 1987. 22.95 (1-55540-131-7, 01-00-46); pap. 16.95 (1-55540-132-5) Scholars Pr GA.
Science Seven-Eleven: Developing Primary Teaching Skills. Clive Carre & Carrie Ovens. LC 93-49489. (Curriculum in Primary Practice Ser.). (Illus.). 112p. (Orig.). (C). 1994. pap. text ed. 17.95 (0-415-10509-9, B4356, Routledge NY) Routledge.
Science since Fifteen-Hundred: A Short History of Mathematics, Physics, Chemistry, Biology. H. T. Pledge. 1990. 14.50 (0-8446-0850-5) Peter Smith.
Science Sketches. enl. ed. David S. Jordan. (Essay Index Reprint Ser.). 1977. reprint ed. 20.95 (0-518-10181-9) Ayer.
Science Skills Assessment Tests. P. J. Holme. (C). 1985. text ed. 190.00 (0-7175-1354-8, Pub. by S Thornes Pubs UK) St Mut.
Science Sleuth. Dale McCreedy et al. (National Science Partnership for Girl Scouts & Science Museums Ser.). (Illus.). 72p. (Orig.). 1995. pap. 8.00 (0-9625622-3-8) Franklin PA.
***Science Sleuth - Einstein.** Seymour Simon. (J). Date not set. 14.00 (0-688-14435-7, Morrow Junior); lib. bdg. write for info. (0-688-14436-5, Morrow Junior) Morrow.
***Science Smart Junior.** (Princeton Review Ser.). 1997. pap. 10.00 (0-679-77538-2) Random.
Science Snapshots: Brief Looks at Common Science Phenomena. Fred Beyer. (Illus.). 200p. (J). (gr. 6-8). 1998. pap. text ed. write for info. (0-89089-680-1) Carolina Acad Pr.
Science, Society & Philosophy: A New Radical Humanist Approach. Oroon K. Ghosh. 1986. 28.00 (0-8364-1563-9, Pub. by Ajanta II) S Asia.
Science, Society, & Values: Toward a Sociology of Objectivity. Sal P. Restivo. LC 92-85310. 1994. 39.50 (0-934223-21-1) Lehigh Univ Pr.
***Science Sources 1992-1995.** Ed. by Tracy Gath & Maria Sosa. (J). pap. 24.00 (0-87168-586-8) AAAS.
Science Spook. Hanya Bloom. (Vic the Vampire Ser.: No. 2). 80p. (J). (gr. 4-7). 1990. mass mkt. 2.95 (0-06-106020-8, PL) HarpC.
***Science Stamps.** R. W. Truman. (Illus.). 119p. (Orig.). Date not set. pap. 7.00 (0-614-25043-9) Am Topical Assn.
Science Starter. (Child's First Library of Learning). (Illus.). 88p. (J). (gr. 1-4). 1990. 14.95 (0-8094-4881-5) Time-Life.
Science Starter. (Child's First Library of Learning). (Illus.). 88p. (J). (ps-3). 1990. lib. bdg. 21.27 (0-8094-4882-3) Time-Life.
Science Starters! Over One Thousand Ready-to-Use Attention-Grabbers That Make Science Fun. Robert Hoehn. 288p. 1993. spiral bd. 27.95 (0-87628-860-3) Ctr Appl Res.

S

An Asterisk (*) at the beginning of an entry indicates that the title is appearing in BIP for the first time.

Science Stew: First Discoveries. Laurie Steding. (Great Beginnings Ser.: Level 2). (J). 1997. pap. 1.95 (*0-8167-3446-1*) Troll Communs.

***Science Studies: An Advanced Introduction.** David J. Hess. LC 97-4782. 1998. 50.00 (*0-8147-3563-0*); pap. 16.95 (*0-8147-3564-9*) NYU Pr.

Science Study Skills Workshop Kit. HM Study Skills Group Staff. (J). (gr. 7-9). 1983. pap. 21.50 (*0-88210-152-8*) Natl Assn Principals.

Science Success for Students with Disabilities. American Institute for Research. (YA). 1993. pap. text ed. 18.50 (*0-201-81939-2*) Addison-Wesley.

Science Surprises. Sandra Markle. (J). 1996. pap. 2.99 (*0-590-48401-X*) Scholastic Inc.

Science Surprises! Ready-to-Use Experiments & Activities for Young Learners. Jean R. Feldman. 256p. 1995. pap. 27.95 (*0-87628-871-9*) Ctr Appl Res.

Science, Systems, & Psychoanalysis. Robert J. Langs. 262p. 1992. pap. text ed. 34.95 (*1-85575-036-8*, Pub. by Karnac Bks UK) Brunner-Mazel.

Science Teacher's Almanac: Practical Ideas & Activities for Every Month of the School Year. Julie Moutran. 1992. pap. text ed. 27.95 (*0-87628-809-3*) Ctr Appl Res.

Science Teachers "Autorad" Pair & Edvotek Twleve Page Explanatory Guide. 19.95 (*0-614-13042-5*) Genelex.

***Science Teacher's Book of Lists.** Fran Barhydt. 1997. pap. text ed. 29.50 (*0-13-673518-5*) P-H.

Science Teacher's Book of Lists. Frances B. Barhydt & Paul Morgan. LC 92-26920. 1993. 29.95 (*0-13-793381-9*) P-H.

Science Teacher's Choice: Research Activities that Work. Nancy Williamson. 200p. 1989. teacher ed., pap. 19.95 (*0-921149-41-7*) Broadview Pr.

Science Teacher's Guide. (Spanish Storybooks Ser.). 65p. (Orig.). (ENG & SPA.). 1992. 12.00 (*1-56334-147-6*) Hampton-Brown.

Science Teacher's Instant Labs Kit. Michael Fleming. 288p. 1991. pap. 24.95 (*0-87628-861-1*) Ctr Appl Res.

Science Teaching: The Report of the 1985 National Forum for School Science. National Forum for School Science Staff. Ed. by Audrey B. Champagne & Leslie E. Hornig. (AAAS Publication Ser.: No. 86-6). 250p. reprint ed. pap. 71.30 (*0-7837-0060-1*, 2040307) Bks Demand.

Science Teaching & the Development of Thinking. Anton E. Lawson. LC 94-6339. 593p. 1995. text ed. 53.95 (*0-534-23994-3*) Wadsworth Pub.

Science Teaching in Schools. R. C. Das. 1986. text ed. 27.50 (*81-207-0037-6*, Pub. by Sterling Pubs II) Apt Bks.

***Science Teaching in the Secondary School.** Dawson. 1994. pap. text ed. write for info. (*0-582-80129-X*, Pub. by Longman UK) Longman.

***Science Teaching Methods for Elementary School.** Bentley. Date not set. text ed. 47.95 (*0-534-12912-9*) Brooks-Cole.

Science Teaching Reconsidered: A Handbook. National Research Council Staff. LC 97-4492. 104p. (Orig.). (C). 1997. pap. text ed. 10.00 (*0-309-05498-2*) Natl Acad Pr.

Science Teasers. Dilip M. Salwi. (Illus.). xiii, 121p. 1989. text ed. 17.95 (*81-220-0140-8*, Pub. by Konark Pubs Pvt Ltd II) Advent Bks Div.

Science Tech & Industrial Development in India. S. C. Pakrashi & G. P. Phondke. 1995. write for info. (*81-7236-101-7*, Pub. by Wiley Estrn II) Franklin.

Science-Technology-Abstraction: Art at the End of the Decade. University Art Galleries Staff. Ed. by Wright State University Staff. (Illus.). 40p. (Orig.). 1989. pap. text ed. 12.00 (*0-932706-15-0*) WSU Art Gallrs.

Science, Technology, & American Diplomacy. 412p. (Orig.). (C). 1993. pap. text ed. 50.00 (*1-56806-369-5*) DIANE Pub.

***Science, Technology, & American Diplomacy (1995)** 16th ed. 421p. (Orig.). (C). 1996. pap. 50.00 (*0-7881-3564-3*) DIANE Pub.

Science, Technology, & American Foreign Policy. Eugene B. Skolnikoff. 1969. reprint ed. pap. 6.95 (*0-262-69019-5*) MIT Pr.

Science, Technology, & Applications of Colloidal Suspensions. Ed. by James H. Adair et al. LC 95-34341. (Ceramic Transactions Ser.: Vol. 54). 278p. 1995. 83.00 (*0-944904-96-3*) Am Ceramic.

Science, Technology & China's Drive for Modernization. Richard P. Suttmeier. LC 79-88587. (Publication Ser.: No. 223). 121p. 1980. pap. 3.58 (*0-8179-7232-3*) Hoover Inst Pr.

Science, Technology & Commercialization of Powder Synthesis & Shape Forming Processes: Proceedings: 97th Annual Meeting of the American Ceramic Society, Cincinnati, Ohio, April 30-May 3, 1995. Ed. by J. J. Kingsley et al. (Ceramic Transactions Ser.: Vol. 62). 1996. 90.00 (*1-57498-005-X*) Am Ceramic.

Science, Technology, & Culture. Ed. by Henry J. Steffens & H. N. Mueller, III. LC 74-580. (Studies in Modern Society: Political & Social Issues: No. 5). 32.50 (*0-404-11275-7*) AMS Pr.

Science, Technology & Development: North-South Co-operation. Ed. by Mozammel Huq et al. 1992. text ed. 30.00 (*0-7146-3455-7*, Pub. by F Cass Pubs UK) Intl Spec Bk.

Science, Technology & Development: Political Economy of Technical Advance in Underdeveloped Countries. Ed. by Charles Cooper. 204p. 1973. 30.00 (*0-7146-2999-5*, Pub. by F Cass Pubs UK) Intl Spec Bk.

Science, Technology & Development in Afghanistan. D. Gopa & M. A. Qureshi. (C). 1987. 25.00 (*81-7013-042-5*, Pub. by Navrang) S Asia.

Science, Technology & Economic Development in China. V. P. Karbandha. 226p. 1987. 31.00 (*81-7013-043-3*, Pub. by Navrang) S Asia.

Science, Technology, & Ecopolitics in the U. S. S. R. Miron Rezun. LC 95-22010. 240p. 1996. text ed. 59.95 (*0-275-95383-1*, Praeger Pubs) Greenwood.

Science, Technology & Global Problems: The United Nations Advisory Committee on the Application of Science & Technology to Development. United Nations, Office for Science & Technology Staff. 62p. 1979. 40.00 (*0-08-025131-5*, Pub. by Pergamon Repr UK) Franklin.

Science, Technology, & Government for a Changing World. (Illus.). 94p. (Orig.). (C). 1993. pap. text ed. 30.00 (*1-56806-708-9*) DIANE Pub.

Science, Technology, & Government for a Changing World: The Concluding Reports of the Carnegie Commission on Science, Technology, & Government. John Brademas et al. (Illus.). 96p. (Orig.). 1993. pap. write for info. (*1-881054-11-X*) Carnegie Comm Sci.

***Science, Technology, & Industry Outlook 1996.** OECD Staff. 312p. (Orig.). 1996. pap. 72.00 (*92-64-14910-4*, 92-96-07-1) OECD.

Science, Technology & Innovation: A Research Bibliography. Ed. by Felicity Henwood & Graham P. Thomas. LC 83-40179. 264p. 1984. text ed. 39.95 (*0-312-70281-7*) St Martin.

Science, Technology & Innovation Policies: Denmark. 187p. (Orig.). 1995. pap. 30.00 (*92-64-14374-2*, Pub. by Org for Econ FR) OECD.

Science, Technology & Innovation Policies: Iceland. OECD Staff. 200p. (Orig.). 1993. pap. 34.00 (*92-64-23947-2*) OECD.

Science, Technology & Innovation Policy, Federation of Russia, Vol. 1: Evaluation Report. 87p. (Orig.). 1994. pap. 16.00 (*92-64-14081-6*) OECD.

Science, Technology & National Socialism. Monkia Renneberg & Mark Walker. LC 92-41633. (Illus.). 416p. (C). 1993. text ed. 69.95 (*0-521-40374-X*) Cambridge U Pr.

Science, Technology, & Public Policy. Encel. 1979. text ed. 44.00 (*0-08-024268-5*, Pergamon Pr) Elsevier.

Science, Technology, & Religious Ideas. Ed. by Mark H. Shale. 254p. (Orig.). (C). 1994. pap. text ed. 28.00 (*0-8191-9347-X*); lib. bdg. 62.50 (*0-8191-9346-1*) U Pr of Amer.

Science, Technology, & Reparations: Exploitation & Plunder in Postwar Germany. John Gimbel. LC 89-37835. 304p. 1990. 37.50 (*0-8047-1761-3*) Stanford U Pr.

Science, Technology, & Social Progress. Ed. by Steven L. Goldman. LC 88-45718. (Research in Technology Studies: Vol. 2). (Illus.). 304p. 1989. 42.50 (*0-934223-05-X*) Lehigh Univ Pr.

Science, Technology & Society. David Andrews. 192p. (C). 1994. 150.00 (*0-7478-1293-4*, Pub. by Stanley Thornes UK) Trans-Atl Phila.

Science, Technology & Society. Robert E. McGinn. 304p. (C). 1990. pap. text ed. 32.00 (*0-13-794736-4*) P-H.

Science, Technology & Society. Shipman. 1993. pap. text ed. write for info. (*0-07-056912-6*) McGraw.

***Science, Technology, & Society.** 2nd ed. John Dewey & Julius A. Sigler. LC 97-22237. (Lynchburg College Symposium Readings Ser.). 1997. pap. write for info. (*0-7618-0835-3*) U Pr of Amer.

Science, Technology, & Society: A Historical Perspective. Martin Fichman. LC 93-24429. 316p. (C). 1996. pap. text ed. 33.54 (*0-8403-8621-4*) Kendall-Hunt.

Science, Technology & Society: A Japanese Perspective. Kunio Goto. 237p. 1993. pap. 16.95 (*1-887406-02-6*) ICTwo Inst.

Science, Technology, & Society: Emerging Relationships. Ed. by Rosemary Chalk. LC 88-26204. 262p. 1988. pap. 19.95 (*0-87168-332-6*, 88-12S) AAAS.

Science, Technology & Society: New Directions. Andrew Webster. LC 91-16801. 212p. (C). 1991. pap. 16.00 (*0-8135-1723-0*); text ed. 36.00 (*0-8135-1722-2*) Rutgers U Pr.

Science, Technology, & Society Education & Citizen Participation. Leonard J. Waks. (Working Papers on Citizenship). 1988. 2.50 (*0-318-33328-7*, PC1) IPPP.

Science, Technology & Society in Postwar Japan. Shigeru Nakayama. (Japanese Studies). 296p. 1992. 89.95 (*0-7103-0428-5*, A6701) Routledge Chapman & Hall.

Science, Technology & Society in Seventeenth Century England. Robert K. Merton. LC 79-82308. 1970. 40.00 (*0-86527-178-X*) Fertig.

Science, Technology, & Society in the Third World: An Annotated Bibliography. Wesley Shrum et al. LC 94-6256. 403p. 1995. 47.50 (*0-8108-2871-5*) Scarecrow.

Science, Technology & Society in the Time of Alfred Nobel: Proceedings of a Nobel Symposium 52 Held at Bjorkborn, Karlskoga, Sweden, August 17-22, 1981. Ed. by C. G. Bernhard et al. LC 82-11254. (Illus.). 440p. 1982. 197.00 (*0-08-027939-2*, Pub. by Pergamon Repr UK) Franklin.

Science, Technology, & the Art of Medicine: European-American Dialogues. Ed. by Corinna Delkeskamp-Hayes & Mary A. Cutter. Tr. by Ruth W. Moskop & S. G. Engelhardt. LC 92-18579. (Philosophy & Medicine Ser.: Vol. 44). 346p. (C). 1993. lib. bdg. 133.00 (*0-7923-1869-2*, Pub. by Klwr Acad Pubs NE) Kluwer Ac.

Science, Technology & the British Industrial 'Decline', 1870-1970. David Edgerton. (New Studies in Economic & Social History: No. 29). 80p. (C). 1996. text ed. 34.95 (*0-521-57127-8*); pap. text ed. 10.95 (*0-521-57778-0*) Cambridge U Pr.

Science, Technology, & the Environment: Multidisciplinary Perspectives. Ed. by James R. Fleming & Henry A. Gemery. LC 94-34905. (Series on Technology & the Environment). (Illus.). 340p. (C). 1994. text ed. 39.95 (*0-9622628-9-7*); pap. text ed. 21.95 (*1-884836-00-3*) U Akron Pr.

Science, Technology & the Nuclear Arms Race. Dietrich Schroeer. LC 84-7379. 414p. 1984. Net. pap. text ed. 36.00 (*0-471-88141-4*) Wiley.

Science, Technology & the Quality of Life. Alexander King. 8p. 1972. pap. 4.00 (*0-9500029-8-4*, Pub. by Octagon Pr UK) ISHK.

Science-Technology Education in Church-Related Colleges & Universities. Frwd. by Robert A. Brungs. (Illus.). 271p. (Orig.). 1990. pap. 15.95 (*0-9625431-0-1*) ITEST Faith.

Science-Technology-Society: Training Manual. Ed. by Laurel R. Singleton. 168p. (Orig.). 1988. pap. 4.50 (*0-89994-314-4*) Soc Sci Ed.

Science Tests & Reviews. Ed. by Oscar K. Buros. LC 75-8114. xxiii, 296p. 1975. 35.00 (*0-910674-21-3*) U of Nebr Pr.

Science That Colonizes: A Critique of Fertility Studies in Africa. Agnes Riedmann. LC 92-26098. 256p. 1993. 44.95 (*1-56639-042-7*) Temple U Pr.

Science the Endless Frontier: A Report to the President. Vannevar Bush. Ed. by I. Bernard Cohen. LC 79-7953. (Three Centuries of Science in America Ser.). 1980. reprint ed. lib. bdg. 18.95 (*0-405-12534-8*) Ayer.

***Science, Theology & Consciousness: The Search for Unity.** John B. Arden. LC 97-18723. 1997. text ed. write for info. (*0-275-96032-3*, Praeger Pubs) Greenwood.

Science, Theology, & the Transcendental Horizon: Einstein, Kant, & Tillich. Roy D. Morrison. LC 94-12336. (AAR Reflection & Theory in the Study of Religion Ser.: Vol. 67). 486p. 1994. 59.95 (*1-55540-678-5*, 010067); pap. 39.95 (*1-55540-679-3*, 010067) Scholars Pr GA.

Science Through Children's Literature: An Integrated Approach. Carol M. Butzow & John W. Butzow. 200p. 1989. pap. text ed. 24.50 (*0-87287-667-5*) Teacher Ideas Pr.

***Science Times Book of Birds.** Ed. by Nicholas Wade. (Illus.). 288p. 1997. 25.00 (*1-55821-605-7*) Lyons & Burford.

***Science Times Book of Fish.** Ed. by Nicholas Wade. LC 97-19471. (Illus.). 288p. 1997. 25.00 (*1-55821-604-9*) Lyons & Burford.

Science Times with Nursery Rhymes. Stephanie K. Burton & Phyllis Campbell. (Illus.). (Orig.). (J). (ps-2). 1996. teacher ed., pap. 16.95 (*1-889163-01-5*) Panda Bear Pub.

Science To-Day & To-Morrow, Compiled from a Series of Lectures Delivered at Morley College. Morley College for Working Men & Women, London Staff. LC 67-30231. (Essay Index Reprint Ser.). 1977. 19.95 (*0-8369-0857-0*) Ayer.

Science to the Home - Beauty & Health. L. M. Gawthorpe. (C). 1970. 65.00 (*0-7175-0515-4*, Pub. by S Thornes Pubs UK) St Mut.

Science to the Rescue. Sandra Markle. LC 92-41096. (Illus.). 48p. (J). (gr. 3-7). 1994. lib. bdg. 15.95 (*0-689-31783-2*, Atheneum Bks Young) S&S Childrens.

***Science Today: Problem or Crisis?** Ralph Levinson & Jeffrey N. Thomas. LC 96-43790. 248p. (C). 1997. pap. write for info. (*0-415-13531-1*) Routledge.

Science Toolbox: Making & Using the Tools of Science. Jean Stangl. LC 93-29389. (J). (ps-3). 1993. 17.95 (*0-8306-4605-1*); pap. 9.95 (*0-8306-4352-4*) McGraw-Hill Prof.

Science, Tools, & Magic. Francis Maddison et al. (Nasser D. Khalili Collection of Islamic Art: Vol. XII). (Illus.). 320p. 1997. 260.00 (*0-19-727610-5*) OUP.

Science Toys & Tricks. Laurence B. White, Jr. LC 84-40787. (J). 1980. pap. 4.95 (*0-201-08659-X*, Lipp Jr Bks) HarpC Child Bks.

Science Tracer Bullets: A Reference Guide to Scientific, Technological, Health, & Environmental Information Sources, 4 vols., Set. Ed. by Helene Henderson. liv, 402p. 1990. lib. bdg. 180.00 (*1-55888-925-6*) Omnigraphics Inc.

Science Tracer Bullets, Vol. 1: Earth & Natural Sciences, Vol. 1. Ed. by Helene Henderson. liv, 396p. 1990. lib. bdg. 53.00 (*1-55888-260-X*) Omnigraphics Inc.

Science Tracer Bullets, Vol. 2: High Technology. Ed. by Helene Henderson. liv, 460p. 1990. lib. bdg. 53.00 (*1-55888-261-8*) Omnigraphics Inc.

Science Tracer Bullets, Vol. 3: Medical & Biological Sciences. Ed. by Helene Henderson. liv, 430p. 1990. lib. bdg. 53.00 (*1-55888-262-6*) Omnigraphics Inc.

Science Tracer Bullets, Vol. 4: Socio-Political Aspects of Science & Technology. Ed. by Helene Henderson. liv, 402p. 1990. lib. bdg. 53.00 (*1-55888-263-4*) Omnigraphics Inc.

Science Tricks & Magic for Young People. George Barr. (Illus.). 126p. (J). (gr. 3-11). 1987. reprint ed. pap. 3.95 (*0-486-25453-4*) Dover.

Science Trivia: From Anteaters to Zeppelins. Charles J. Cazeau. 296p. 1986. 19.95 (*0-306-42353-7*, Plenum Pr) Plenum.

Science Trivial Pursuit: Intermediate Grades 4-6. Kino Learning Center Staff et al. (Illus.). 64p. (J). (gr. 4-6). teacher ed. 12.99 (*0-86653-649-3*, GA1386) Good Apple.

Science Trivial Pursuit: Junior High Grades 7-9. Kino Learning Center Staff & Judith Bisignano. (Illus.). 64p. (J). (gr. 7-9). teacher ed. 12.99 (*0-86653-651-5*, GA1387) Good Apple.

Science Trivial Pursuit: Primary Grades 1-3. Kino Learning Center Staff & Elizabeth Prohaska. (Illus.). 64p. (J). (gr. 1-3). teacher ed. 12.99 (*0-86653-647-7*, GA1385) Good Apple.

Science under Control: The French Academy of Sciences, 1795-1914. Maurice P. Crosland. (Illus.). 472p. (C). 1992. text ed. 130.00 (*0-521-41373-7*) Cambridge U Pr.

Science under Scarcity: Principles & Practice for Agricultural Research Evaluation & Priority Setting. Julian M. Alston et al. (Food Systems & Agrarian Change Ser.). (Illus.). 585p. 1994. 39.95 (*0-8014-2937-4*) Cornell U Pr.

Science under Siege: How the Environmental Misinformation Campaign Is Affecting Our Laws,... Michael Fumento. LC 96-17757. 1996. pap. 16.00 (*0-688-14766-6*, Quill) Morrow.

Science under Siege: The Myth of Objectivity in Scientific Research. Beth Savan. 192p. 1988. 14.95 (*0-88794-336-5*) Genl Dist Srvs.

Science Underground. Ed. by Michael M. Nieto et al. LC 83-70377. (AIP Conference Proceedings Ser.: No. 96). 446p. 1983. lib. bdg. 38.75 (*0-88318-195-9*) Am Inst Physics.

***Science Validates Spiritual Healing.** Daniel Benur. (Healing Research Ser.). (Illus.). 350p. 1997. write for info. (*1-886785-11-2*) Vision Pub.

***Science, Values, & the American West.** Ed. by Stephen Tchudi. 272p. (Orig.). 1997. pap. 14.95 (*1-890591-00-9*) NV Humanities.

Science vs. Crime. Eugene B. Block. LC 79-21941. (Illus.). 1980. 12.95 (*0-89666-007-9*) Cragmont Pubns.

Science vs. Crime. Eugene B. Block. LC 79-21941. (Illus.). 208p. 1980. pap. 6.95 (*0-89666-010-9*) Cragmont Pubns.

Science vs. Pseudoscience? Nathan Aaseng. LC 93-30014. (Illus.). 112p. (YA). (gr. 9-12). 1994. lib. bdg. 22.70 (*0-531-11182-2*) Watts.

Science vs. Religion. Tad S. Clements. 264p. 1990. 31.95 (*0-87975-593-8*) Prometheus Bks.

Science Wars. Ed. by Andrew Ross. LC 96-22506. 352p. 1996. text ed. 49.95 (*0-8223-1881-4*); pap. text ed. 16.95 (*0-8223-1871-7*) Duke.

***Science with a Human Face: In Honor of Roger Randall Revelle.** Roger Revelle et al. LC 97-20687. 1997. pap. write for info. (*0-674-79483-4*) HUP.

Science with a Smile. R. Weber. (Illus.). 460p. 1992. 44.00 (*0-7503-0211-9*) IOP Pub.

Science with a Vengeance: How the Military Created the U. S. Space Sciences after World War II. David H. DeVorkin. LC 93-30683. (Illus.). 432p. 1995. 39.95 (*0-387-94137-1*) Spr-Verlag.

Science with a Vengeance: The Military Origins of the Space Sciences in the American V-2 Era. D. H. DeVorkin. (Illus.). 376p. 1992. 69.00 (*0-387-97770-8*) Spr-Verlag.

Science with Air. (Science Activities Ser.). (Illus.). 24p. (J). 1992. pap. 4.95 (*0-7460-0972-0*); lib. bdg. 12.95 (*0-88110-581-3*) EDC.

Science with Batteries. P. Shipton. (Science Activities Ser.). (Illus.). 24p. (J). (gr. 1-4). 1993. pap. 4.95 (*0-7460-1423-6*); lib. bdg. 12.95 (*0-88110-633-X*) EDC.

***Science with Large Millimetre Arrays: Proceedings of the ESO-IRAM-NFRA-ONSALA Workshop, Held at Garching, Germany, 11-13 December 1995.** P. A. Shaver. LC 96-35785. (ESO Astrophysics Symposia Ser.). 408p. 1996. 38.00 (*3-540-61582-2*) Spr-Verlag.

Science with Light & Mirrors. H. Edom. (Science Activities Ser.). (Illus.). 24p. (J). (gr. 1-4). 1992. pap. 4.95 (*0-7460-0696-9*, Usborne); lib. bdg. 12.95 (*0-88110-545-7*, Usborne) EDC.

Science with Magnets. H. Edom. (Starting Point Science Ser.). (Illus.). 24p. (J). (gr. 1-4). 1991. pap. 4.95 (*0-7460-1259-4*, Usborne); lib. bdg. 12.95 (*0-88110-629-1*, Usborne) EDC.

Science with Plants. M. Unwin. (Science Activities Ser.). (Illus.). 24p. (J). (gr. 1-4). 1993. pap. 4.95 (*0-7460-0976-3*); lib. bdg. 12.95 (*0-88110-620-8*) EDC.

Science with Pocket Calculators. David R. Green & John Lewis. LC 78-57665. (Wykeham Science Ser.: No. 48). 220p. (C). 1977. 36.00 (*0-8448-1361-3*, Crane Russak) Taylor & Francis.

Science with Practice: Charles E. Bessey & the Maturing of American Botany. Richard A. Overfield. LC 91-16180. (History of Technology & Science Ser.). (Illus.). 276p. 1993. text ed. 39.95 (*0-8138-1822-2*) Iowa St U Pr.

Science with Reason: A Developmental Approach. Ed. by Sue Atkinson & Marilyn Fleer. LC 95-24700. 179p. 1995. pap. text ed. 19.50 (*0-435-08381-3*, 08381) Heinemann.

Science with the VLT: Proceedings of the ESO Workshop Held at Garching, Germany, 28 June-1 July 1994. Ed. by Jeremy R. Walsh et al. LC 95-10529. (ESO Astrophysics Symposia Ser.). 504p. 1995. 39.95 (*3-540-59169-9*) Spr-Verlag.

Science with Water. H. Edom. (Starting Point Science Ser.). (Illus.). 24p. (J). (gr. 1-4). 1991. pap. 4.95 (*0-7460-1261-6*, Usborne); lib. bdg. 12.95 (*0-88110-630-5*, Usborne) EDC.

Science with Weather. Rebecca Heddle & Paul Shipton. (Science Activities Ser.). (Illus.). 24p. (J). (gr. k-5). 1993. pap. 4.95 (*0-7460-1421-X*, Usborne); lib. bdg. 12.95 (*0-88110-654-2*, Usborne) EDC.

Science Within Art. Lynette I. Rhodes. LC 79-93193. (Illus.). 72p. reprint ed. pap. 25.00 (*0-317-10007-6*, 2022660) Bks Demand.

Science Without Answers. B. K. Hixson. 59p. 1989. pap. text ed. 14.99 (*1-57156-007-6*) Wild Goose UT.

***Science Without Common Sense.** Steven J. Milloy. 68p. 1996. pap. 8.00 (*1-882577-34-5*) Cato Inst.

Science Without Limits: Toward a Theory of Interaction Between Nature & Knowledge. James S. Perlman. 358p. 1995. 29.95 (*0-87975-962-3*) Prometheus Bks.

Science Without Myth: On Constructions, Reality, & Social Knowledge. Sergio Sismondo. LC 95-14015. (Science, Technology, & Society Ser.). 199p. 1995. pap. text ed. 14.95 (*0-7914-2734-X*) State U NY Pr.

Science Without Myth: On Constructions, Reality, & Social Knowledge. Sergio Sismondo. LC 95-14015. (SUNY Series in Science, Technology, & Society). 199p. 1995. text ed. 44.50 (*0-7914-2733-1*) State U NY Pr.

Science Wizardry for Kids. Phyllis S. Williams. (J). (gr. 4-7). 1992. 13.95 (*0-8120-4766-4*) Barron.

Science Wizardry for Kids Activity Kit, Incl. microscope in pkg. Margaret E. Kenda & Phyllis S. Williams. (Illus.). 320p. (J). (gr. 3 up). 1995. pap. 21.95 (*0-8120-8364-4*) Barron.
Science Wonders. Dale McCreedy & Jean N. Kuhn. (National Science Partnership for Girl Scouts & Science Museums Ser.). (Illus.). 40p. (Orig.). 1995. pap. 8.00 (*0-9625622-4-6*) Franklin PA.
Science Workout Teacher's Guide, No. 1. R. Purnell. (C). 1989. 60.00 (*0-7487-0198-2*, Pub. by S Thornes Pubs UK); 220.00 (*0-7487-0486-8*, Pub. by S Thornes Pubs UK); 300.00 (*0-7487-0197-4*, Pub. by S Thornes Pubs UK) St Mut.
Science Workout Teacher's Guide, No. 2. R. Purnell. (C). 1990. 75.00 (*0-7487-0200-8*, Pub. by Stanley Thornes UK); 220.00 (*0-7487-0487-6*, Pub. by Stanley Thornes UK); 300.00 (*0-7487-0199-0*, Pub. by Stanley Thornes UK) Trans-Atl Phila.
Science Works. Elizabeth Rieth & Carol Johmann. 120p. (J). (gr. 3-6). 1997. 12.95 (*0-88160-242-6*, LW337) Learning Wks.
***Science Workshop.** 2nd ed. I. Finch. Date not set. pap. text ed. write for info. (*0-582-18350-2*, Pub. by Longman UK) Longman.
Science Workshop: A Whole Language Approach. Wendy Saul et al. LC 92-21468. 168p. (C). 1993. pap. text ed. 19.50 (*0-435-08336-8*, 08336) Heinemann.
Science World. Fred Justus. (Science Ser.). 24p. (gr. 4-7). 1978. student ed. 5.00 (*0-8209-0156-3*, S-18) ESP.
Science Writing Through Critical Thinking. Marilyn F. Moriarty. 1996. 20.00 (*0-86720-510-5*) Jones & Bartlett.
Science Year - 1993: The World Book Annual Science Supplement. Ed. by World Book Editors. LC 65-21776. (Illus.). 400p. (YA). (gr. 6 up). 1992. lib. bdg. write for info. (*0-7166-0593-7*) World Bk.
Science Year, 1992: The World Book Annual Science Supplement. Ed. by World Book Editors. LC 65-21776. (Illus.). 400p. (YA). (gr. 7-12). 1991. lib. bdg. write for info. (*0-7166-0592-9*) World Bk.
Science Year, 1994: The World Book Annual Science Supplement. Ed. by World Book Editors. LC 65-21776. (Illus.). 368p. (YA). (gr. 6 up). 1993. lib. bdg. write for info. (*0-7166-0594-5*) World Bk.
Science Year 1995: The World Book Annual Supplement. Ed. by World Bank Staff. LC 65-21776. 368p. 1994. 28. 40 (*0-7166-0595-3*) World Bk.
***Science Year 1997.** LC 65-21776. (Illus.). 352p. (YA). 1996. text ed. write for info. (*0-7166-0597-X*) World Bk.
Science Yellow Pages for Students & Teachers. LC 87-82070. (Yellow Pages Ser.). 64p. (J). (gr. k-8). 1988. pap. text ed. 8.95 (*0-318-32626-4*, IP 89-2) Incentive Pubns.
Science 1 Anthology. 1993. 10.00 (*0-88336-121-3*); teacher ed. 7.50 (*0-88336-122-1*); 31.99 (*0-88336-123-X*) New Readers.
Science 1985. Cooper. 1985. wbk. ed., pap. 9.00 (*0-15-365522-4*); wbk. ed., pap. 9.00 (*0-15-365523-2*); teacher ed., wbk. ed., pap. 12.75 (*0-15-365527-5*); teacher ed., wbk. ed., pap. 12.75 (*0-15-365528-3*); teacher ed., wbk. ed., pap. 13.25 (*0-15-365529-1*); teacher ed., wbk. ed., pap. 13.25 (*0-15-365530-5*); teacher ed., wbk. ed., pap. 13.50 (*0-15-365531-3*); teacher ed., wbk. ed., pap. 13.50 (*0-15-365532-1*) HB Schl Dept.
Science 1985. Cooper. 1985. pap. 12.25 (*0-15-365489-9*) HB Schl Dept.
Science 1985: Tests. Cooper. 1985. pap. 5.75 (*0-15-365538-0*); pap. 5.75 (*0-15-365539-9*); pap. 5.75 (*0-15-365540-2*); pap. 5.75 (*0-15-365541-0*) HB Schl Dept.
Science 1986. Abruscato. 1986. wbk. ed., pap. 8.25 (*0-03-003448-5*); teacher ed., wbk. ed., pap. 13.50 (*0-03-003449-3*); teacher ed., wbk. ed., pap. 13.50 (*0-03-003453-1*); wbk. ed., pap. 9.50 (*0-03-003454-X*); teacher ed., wbk. ed., pap. 14.25 (*0-03-003457-4*); wbk. ed., pap. 9.50 (*0-03-003458-2*); teacher ed., wbk. ed., pap. 14.25 (*0-03-003459-0*); teacher ed., text ed. 58.50 (*0-03-003163-X*); teacher ed., text ed. 61.25 (*0-03-003164-8*); teacher ed., text ed. 67.25 (*0-03-003167-2*); teacher ed., text ed. 70.50 (*0-03-003168-0*); teacher ed., text ed. 73.25 (*0-03-003169-9*); teacher ed., text ed. 81.00 (*0-03-003172-9*) HB Schl Dept.
Science 1986: Grade 8. 86th ed. Abruscato. 1986. text ed. 96.25 (*0-03-003927-4*) HR&W Schl Div.
Science 1989. Abruscato. 1989. teacher ed. 61.75 (*0-03-011399-7*); teacher ed. 61.75 (*0-03-011402-0*); teacher ed. 73.00 (*0-03-011403-9*); teacher ed. 73.00 (*0-03-011404-7*); teacher ed. 80.00 (*0-03-011407-1*); teacher ed. 80.00 (*0-03-011408-X*); teacher ed. 252.00 (*0-03-011974-X*); teacher ed. 263.25 (*0-03-011979-0*); teacher ed. 319.25 (*0-03-011984-7*); teacher ed. 325.00 (*0-03-011989-8*); teacher ed. 325.00 (*0-03-011994-4*); teacher ed. 325.00 (*0-03-011999-5*); wbk. ed., pap. 9.25 (*0-03-011414-4*); wbk. ed., pap. 9.50 (*0-03-011417-9*); wbk. ed., pap. 9.50 (*0-03-011418-7*); teacher ed., wbk. ed., pap. 14.25 (*0-03-011423-3*); teacher ed., wbk. ed., pap. 14.25 (*0-03-011424-1*); teacher ed., wbk. ed., pap. 15.50 (*0-03-011427-6*); teacher ed., wbk. ed., pap. 15.50 (*0-03-011428-4*) HB Schl Dept.
Science 2 Anthology. 1993. 10.00 (*0-88336-124-8*); teacher ed. 7.50 (*0-88336-125-6*); 31.99 (*0-88336-126-4*) New Readers.
Science 85: Level R. Cooper. 1985. teacher ed. 57.00 (*0-15-365501-1*) HB Schl Dept.
Science 85: Level 1. Cooper. 1985. 69.00 (*0-15-365502-X*) HB Schl Dept.
Science 85: Level 5. Cooper. 1985. teacher ed. 96.75 (*0-15-365506-2*) HB Schl Dept.
Science 85: Level 6. Cooper. 1985. student ed. 35.00 (*0-15-365495-3*) HB Schl Dept.
Science 89: Level 5. Cooper. 1989. student ed. 34.25 (*0-15-364325-0*) HB Schl Dept.
Science 89: Nova Level R. Cooper. 1989. teacher ed. 57.00 (*0-15-364327-7*) HB Schl Dept.
Science 89: Nova Level 1. Harcourt Brace Staff. 1989. teacher ed. 69.00 (*0-15-364328-5*) HB Schl Dept.
Science 89: Nova Level 2. Harcourt Brace Staff. 1989. teacher ed. 70.75 (*0-15-364329-3*) HB Schl Dept.
Science 89: Nova Level 3. Cooper. 1989. 29.95 (*0-15-364323-4*) H Holt & Co.
Science 89: Nova Level 3. Harcourt Brace Staff. 1989. teacher ed. 77.50 (*0-15-364330-7*) HB Schl Dept.
Science 89: Nova Level 4. Cooper. 1989. student ed. 33.00 (*0-15-364324-2*) H Holt & Co.
Science 89: Nova Level 4. Harcourt Brace Staff. 1989. teacher ed. 92.75 (*0-15-364331-5*) HB Schl Dept.
Science 89: Nova Level 5. Harcourt Brace Staff. 1989. teacher ed. 96.75 (*0-15-364332-3*) HB Schl Dept.
Science 89: Nova Level 6. Cooper. 1989. 35.25 (*0-15-364326-9*) HB Schl Dept.
ScienceArts: Discovering Science Through Art Experiences. Jean Potter & Maryann F. Kohl. LC 93-90056. (Bright Ideas for Learning Ser.). (Illus.). 144p. (Orig.). (J). (ps-5). 1993. pap. 15.95 (*0-935607-04-8*) Bright Ring.
Sciences: An Integrated Approach. James S. Trefil & Robert M. Hazen. 576p. 1993. pap. text ed. 23.50 (*0-471-30300-3*) Wiley.
Sciences: An Integrated Approach. James S. Trefil et al. 208p. 1995. lab manual ed., pap. write for info. (*0-471-07647-3*) Wiley.
***Sciences: An Integrated Approach.** 2nd ed. James Trefil & Robert M. Hazen. LC 97-24248. 720p. 1997. pap. text ed. write for info. (*0-471-16117-9*) Wiley.
Sciences: An Integrated Approach - A Preliminary Edition. Robert M. Hazen & James S. Trefil. 752p. 1994. pap. text ed. 50.95 (*0-471-58931-4*) Wiley.
Sciences see Career Employment Opportunities Directory
Sciences see Comprehensive Dissertation Index, 1988: Supplement
Sciences see Comprehensive Dissertation Index, 1989: Supplement
Sciences & Philosophy. John S. Haldane. LC 77-27199. (Gifford Lectures: 1927-28). reprint ed. 34.50 (*0-404-60479-X*) AMS Pr.
Sciences & the Self in Medieval Poetry: Alan of Lille's "Anticlaudianus" & John Gower's "Confessio Amantis" James Simpson. (Studies in Medieval Literature: No. 25). 304p. (C). 1995. text ed. 64.95 (*0-521-47181-8*) Cambridge U Pr.
Sciences & the Vedas. Ed. by Ishwarbhai Patel. 1986. 12.50 (*0-8364-1663-5*, Pub. by Somaiya II) S Asia.
Sciences Basic to Orthopaedics. Hughes. 1997. text ed. write for info. (*0-7020-1973-9*) Saunders.
Sciences Basic to Psychiatry. Basant Puri & Peter Tyrer. (Illus.). 334p. (Orig.). 1992. pap. text ed. 45.00 (*0-443-04478-3*) Churchill.
Sciences de la Terre a l'Heure des Satellites see Earth's Science in the Age of the Satellite
Sciences in Communist China: A Symposium Presented at the New York Meeting of the American Association for Advanced Science. Sidney H. Gould. LC 74-7534. 872p. 1975. reprint ed. text ed. 175.00 (*0-8371-7583-6*, GOSC, Greenwood Pr) Greenwood.
Sciences in the Fourteenth & Fifteenth Centuries. Shank. 1997. 26.95 (*0-8057-9516-2*, Hall Reference) Macmillan.
Sciences of Cognition: Theory & Research in Psychology & Artificial Intelligence. Morton Wagman. LC 94-28001. 184p. 1995. text ed. 55.00 (*0-275-94948-6*, Praeger Pubs) Greenwood.
Sciences of Fish Health Management: Master Volume. John Gratzek. (Aquariology Ser.). 34.95 (*1-56465-105-3*, 16855) Tetra Pr.
Sciences of Man in the Making. Edwin A. Kirkpatrick. LC 75-156672. (Essay Index Reprints - International Library of Psychology, Philosophy, & Scientific Method). 1977. reprint ed. 24.95 (*0-8369-2282-4*) Ayer.
Sciences of the Artificial. 3rd ed. Herbert A. Simon. (Illus.). 215p. 1996. 30.00 (*0-262-19374-4*); pap. 14.50 (*0-262-69191-4*) MIT Pr.
Sciences of the Earth: An Encyclopedia of Events, People & Phenomena. Gregory A. Good. Ed. by Marc Rothenberg. LC 97-25163. (Encyclopedias on the History of Science Ser.). 654p. 1997. text ed. 150.00 (*0-8153-0062-X*) Garland.
Sciences of the Times: A New York Times Survey. Intro. by Walter Sullivan. LC 77-11053. 1978. lib. bdg. 27.95 (*0-405-10747-1*) Ayer.
Sciences Process Skills. Karen Ostlund. 144p. (J). 1995. pap. text ed. write for info. (*0-201-29092-8*) Addison-Wesley.
***Sciences, Social.** Ken Poyner. 28p. 1995. pap. 5.00 (*1-889806-10-2*) Devils Millhopper.
Sciences Sociales Dans L'encyclopedie: The Social Sciences in the Encyclopedie. Rene Hubert. LC 74-24867. (European Sociology Ser.). 368p. 1975. reprint ed. 31.95 (*0-405-06548-5*) Ayer.
Sciences Sociales, 1. Ed. by Roger Caratini. 160p. (FRE.). 1971. 49.95 (*0-8288-6478-0*, M-6510) Fr & Eur.
Sciences Sociales, 2: Linguistique. Ed. by Roger Caratini. 160p. (FRE.). 1971. 49.95 (*0-8288-6479-9*, M-6511) Fr & Eur.
Sciences Today. Ed. by Mortimer J. Adler. LC 75-4350. (Great Ideas Anthologies Ser.). (Illus.). 564p. 1977. 23. 95 (*0-405-07173-6*) Ayer.
Science's Trickiest Questions: 402 Questions that will Stump, Amuse, & Surprise. Paul Kuttner. LC 94-5954. 240p. 1994. pap. 10.95 (*0-8050-2873-0*) H Holt & Co.
Science/Technology/Society: Activities & Resources for Secondary Science & Social Studies. Laurel R. Singleton. (Illus.). (Orig.). 1994. pap. 23.95 (*0-89994-379-9*) Soc Sci Ed.
Science/Technology/Society as Reform in Science Education. Ed. by Robert E. Yager. LC 95-10191. (SUNY Series in Science Education). 339p. 1996. text ed. 59.50 (*0-7914-2769-2*); pap. text ed. 19.95 (*0-7914-2770-6*) State U NY Pr.
Scienceworks: Sixty-Five Experiments That Introduce the Fun & Wonder of Science. Ontario Science Center Staff. (Illus.). (J). (gr. 2-7). 1986. pap. 11.95 (*0-201-16780-8*) Addison-Wesley.
Sciencing: An Involvement Approach to Elementary Science Methods. 3rd ed. Sandra E. Cain & Jack M. Evans. 432p. (C). 1990. pap. text ed. 47.00 (*0-675-20869-6*, Merrill Coll) P-H.
Sciennes & the Grange. Malcolm Cant. 250p. (C). 1989. pap. 24.00 (*0-85976-253-X*, Pub. by J Donald UK) St Mut.
Scientia & Ars im Hoch- & Spaetmittelalter, Pts. 1-2, Pt. 1, xxx, 513p, Pt. 2, xii, 1065p. Ed. by Ingrid Craemer-Ruegenberg & Andreas Speer. (Miscellanea Mediaevalia Ser.: Band 22). (GER.). (C). 1993. Pt. 1: xxx, 513p.; Pt. 2: xii, 1065p. lib. bdg. 446.15 (*3-11-014058-6*) De Gruyter.
Scientia Rerum Natura Occultarum Methodologische Studien Zur Physik Pierre Gassendis. Wolfgang Detel. (Quellen und Studien zur Philosophie Ser.: Vol. 14). (C). 1978. 100.00 (*3-11-007320-X*) De Gruyter.
Scientiae Draconis Project Book. Ed. by Einar Lutemaker, pseud. (Illus.). (Orig.). 1989. pap. 2.00 (*1-877934-02-X*) Rose & Nefr Pr.
Scientific - Technological Challenge & East European Socialism. Anton A. Bebler. (CISA Working Papers: No. 65). 25p. (Orig.). 1989. pap. 15.00 (*0-86682-082-5*) Ctr Intl Relations.
Scientific Achievement of the Middle Ages. Richard C. Dales. LC 73-77801. (Middle Ages Ser.). (Illus.). 184p. 1973. pap. text ed. 16.95 (*0-8122-1057-3*) U of Pa Pr.
Scientific Advances & Clinical Experience with the Edwards TEKNA Bileaflet Valve. Silent Partners, Inc. Staff. (Illus.). 144p. (Orig.). 1994. pap. write for info. (*1-878353-33-0*) Silent Partners.
Scientific Advances in Alternative Demilitarization Technologies. Ed. by Francis W. Holm. (NATO ASI Ser.: Vol. 6). 1996. lib. bdg. 99.00 (*0-7923-4035-3*) Kluwer Ac.
Scientific Adventure. Herbert Dingle. LC 71-121462. (Essay Index Reprint Ser.). 1977. 26.95 (*0-8369-1749-9*) Ayer.
Scientific Alternative to Neo-Darwinian Evolutionary Theory. A. E. Wilder-Smith. 206p. 1987. pap. 6.99 (*0-614-11250-8*) Word for Today.
Scientific Alternatives to Animal Experiments. Ed. by Fred Lembeck. Tr. by Jacqui Welch from GER. (Ellis Horwood Series in Biochemistry & Biotechnology). 300p. 1990. 69.95 (*0-412-02771-2*, A4476, Chap & Hall NY) Chapman & Hall.
Scientific American Activity Book. Ginns. 128p. (J). 1994. text ed. write for info. (*0-7167-6558-6*) W H Freeman.
Scientific American Cumulative Index, 1978-1988. Ed. by Scientific American Staff. 228p. (Orig.). 1989. pap. 24.95 (*0-89454-010-6*) Scientific Am Inc.
Scientific American Introduction to Molecular Medicine. Ed. by Edward Rubenstein et al. (Basic Science for Clinicians Ser.). (Illus.). 300p. (C). 1994. text ed. 49.00 (*0-89454-015-7*) Sci Am Medicine.
Scientific American Medicine, 3 Vols. Ed. by D. Dale & D. Federman. LC 77-92625. (Illus.). 1996. ring bd. 328.00 (*0-89454-000-9*) Sci Am Medicine.
Scientific American Medicine: Pocket Edition. Ed. by Edward Rubenstein & Daniel D. Federman. (Illus.). 900p. (C). 1993. pap. text ed. 34.95 (*0-89454-013-0*) Sci Am Medicine.
Scientific American Molecular Cardiovascular Medicine. Ed. by Edgar Haber. LC 95-15502. 1995. 49.00 (*0-89454-021-1*) Sci Am Medicine.
Scientific American Sourcebooks Series, 3 Vol., Set. (Illus.). 96p. (J). (gr. 5-8). 1995. lib. bdg. 56.94 (*0-8050-4280-6*) TFC Bks NY.
Scientific American Surgery, 2 vols., Set. Ed. by Douglas Wilmore et al. (Illus.). 1996. ring bd. 250.00 (*0-89454-019-X*) Sci Am Medicine.
***Scientific Americans.** John Moghton. LC 90-175652. 1997. pap. text ed. 10.95 (*0-88754-488-6*, Pub. by Playwrights CN Pr CN) Theatre Comm.
Scientific Analysis of Genesis. Edward F. Blick. (Illus.). 150p. (Orig.). 1991. pap. 8.95 (*1-879366-12-6*) Hearthstone OK.
Scientific Analysis on the Pocket Calculator. 2nd ed. Jon M. Smith. LC 77-6662. (Illus.). 457p. 1977. reprint ed. pap. 130.30 (*0-7837-3474-3*, 2057806) Bks Demand.
***Scientific & Clinical Applications of Magnetic Carriers.** Urs Hafeli. LC 97-23537. 1997. write for info. (*0-306-45687-7*) Plenum.
Scientific & Clinical Literature for the Decade of the Brain. Ed. by Tony Stankus. LC 93-4490. (Science & Technology Libraries: Vol. 13, Nos. 3-4). 254p. 1994. lib. bdg. 49.95 (*1-56024-481-X*) Haworth Pr.
Scientific & Common Names for the Amphibians & Reptiles of Mexico. Liner. 1994. pap. write for info. (*0-916984-32-X*) SSAR.
Scientific & Common Names of 7,000 Vascular Plants in the United States. Amy Y. Rossman et al. LC 94-79381. (U. S. National Fungus Collections). 304p. (Orig.). 1995. pap. 29.00 (*0-89054-171-X*) Am Phytopathol Soc.
Scientific & Cultural Development: From the Seventh Century BC to the Seventh Century AD. 7th ed. Erik J. Zurcher. (History of Humanity Ser.: Vol. 3). 736p. (C). 1996. text ed. 150.00 (*0-415-09307-4*) Routledge.
Scientific & Engineering Aspects of Nondestructive Evaluation. Ed. by M. N. Srinivasan. (PVP Ser.: Vol. 257). 128p. 1993. 40.00 (*0-7918-0984-6*, H00816) ASME.
Scientific & Engineering Programming in C Plus Plus. John J. Barton & Lee R. Nackman. (Illus.). 576p. (C). 1994. pap. text ed. 54.95 (*0-201-53393-6*) Addison-Wesley.
Scientific & Engineering Research Facilities at Universities & Colleges Vol. 1: Analysis. Ann T. Lanier. (Illus.). 200p. (Orig.). (C). 1995. pap. text ed. 30.00 (*0-7881-2288-6*) DIANE Pub.
Scientific & Engineering Sourcebook: Professional Programs for the Timex Sinclair 1000. Cass R. Lewart. LC 82-62818. (Illus.). 120p. (Orig.). 1983. pap. text ed. 15.95 (*0-07-037444-9*, BYTE Bks) McGraw.
Scientific & Humanistic Contributions of Frank Pierce Jones on the F. Matthias Alexander Technique. Brown & Thompson. 64p. 1988. pap. 5.95 (*0-913111-10-4*) Centerline.
Scientific & Humanistic Dimensions of Language: Festschrift for Robert Lado. Kurt R. Jankowsky. LC 85-13397. lii, 614p. 1985. 118.00 (*90-272-2013-1*) Benjamins North Am.
Scientific & Philosophical Treatises (1716-1740) 2nd ed. Emanuel Swedenborg. Ed. by Alfred H. Stroh. (Illus.). 171p. 1992. 12.95 (*0-915221-68-3*) Swedenborg Sci Assn.
Scientific & Philosophical Writings. Ed. by Jonathan Edwards & Wallace E. Anderson. LC 78-26663. (Works of Jonathan Edwards: Vol. 6). (Illus.). 1980. 75.00 (*0-300-02282-4*) Yale U Pr.
Scientific & Primordial Knowing. Terry J. Tekippe. LC 96-21569. 544p. 1996. pap. text ed. 44.00 (*0-7618-0390-4*); lib. bdg. 64.00 (*0-7618-0389-0*) U Pr of Amer.
Scientific & Regulatory Basis for the Geological Disposal of Radioactive Waste. David N. Savage. LC 95-20220. 1996. pap. text ed. 80.00 (*0-471-96090-X*) Wiley.
Scientific & Religious Belief. Ed. by Paul A. Weingartner. (Philosophical Studies in Philosophy). 192p. (C). 1993. lib. bdg. 111.50 (*0-7923-2595-8*, Pub. by Klwr Acad Pubs NE) Kluwer Ac.
Scientific & Statistical Database Management, 7th International Working Conference On. LC 94-77463. 304p. 1994. pap. 40.00 (*0-8186-6610-2*, PR06610) IEEE Comp Soc.
Scientific & Statistical Database Management, 8th International Conference on (SSDBM '96) LC 96-76648. 300p. 1996. pap. 60.00 (*0-8186-7264-1*, PRO7264) IEEE Comp Soc.
***Scientific & Statistical Database Management, 9th International Conference.** 300p. 1997. pap. 70.00 (*0-8186-7952-2*) IEEE Comp Soc.
Scientific & Technical Careers, 6 vols., Set. 98.00 (*0-685-23040-6*, CG110S) Ready Ref Pr.
Scientific & Technical Communication: Theory, Practice & Policy. Ed. by James H. Collier. LC 96-2537. 420p. 1996. 58.00 (*0-7619-0320-8*); pap. 26.95 (*0-7619-0321-6*) Sage.
Scientific & Technical Education in Early Industrial Britain. M. D. Stephens & G. W. Roderick. (C). 1981. 40.00 (*0-902031-61-9*, Pub. by Univ Nottingham UK); pap. 35.00 (*0-685-66072-9*, Pub. by Univ Nottingham UK) St Mut.
Scientific & Technical Information Resources. Bhadriraju Subramanyam. (Books in Library & Information Science: Vol. 33). 432p. 1981. 85.00 (*0-8247-8297-6*) Dekker.
Scientific & Technical Issues Facing Post-1987 Ozone Control Strategies: Transactions of an APCA Specialty Conference. Ed. by George T. Wolff et al. TR-12. (Illus.). 352p. (Orig.). (C). 1988. pap. text ed. write for info. (*0-318-64318-9*) Air & Waste.
Scientific & Technical Journals. Jill Lambert. LC 85-116142. (Illus.). 191p. reprint ed. pap. 54.50 (*0-7837-5324-1*, 2045063) Bks Demand.
Scientific & Technical Libraries, Vol. 2. Nancy J. Pruett. (Library & Information Science Ser.). 1986. text ed. 83. 00 (*0-12-566042-1*) Acad Pr.
Scientific & Technical Libraries: Administration & Management: A Source Guide. 1991. lib. bdg. 75.00 (*0-8490-4879-6*) Gordon Pr.
***Scientific & Technical Libraries in the 70s.** 1981. 65.00 (*0-8103-1491-6*, 00010108, Gale Res Intl) Gale.
Scientific & Technical Library Budget & Expenditure Report. Primary Research Staff. 120p. 1993. ring bd. 65.00 (*0-9626749-5-8*) Primary Research.
***Scientific & Technical Library Budget & Expenditure Report, 1995.** Primary Research Staff. Date not set. pap. 80.00 (*1-57440-001-0*) Primary Research.
Scientific & Technical Literature: An Introduction for Communication. Richard D. Walker & C. D. Hurt. LC 90-687. (Illus.). (C). 1990. text ed. 15.00 (*0-8389-0539-0*) ALA.
Scientific & Technical Organizations & Agencies Directory, 2 vols. 2nd ed. Ed. by Margaret L. Young. 1670p. 1987. 195.00 (*0-8103-2103-3*) Gale.
Scientific & Technical Organizations & Agencies Directory. 3rd ed. 1993. 195.00 (*0-8103-5464-0*) Gale.
Scientific & Technical Organizations & Agencies Directory. 4th ed. 1999. 195.00 (*0-8103-5465-9*) Gale.
Scientific & Technical Periodicals of the Seventeenth & Eighteenth Centuries: A Guide. David A. Kronick. LC 91-32012. 352p. 1991. 42.50 (*0-8108-2492-2*) Scarecrow.
Scientific & Technical Reports: Elements, Organization, & Design, Z39.18-1995. National Information Standards Organization Staff. LC 95-22240. (National Information Standards Ser.). 44p. 1995. 49.00 (*1-880124-24-6*) NISO.
Scientific & Technical Reports-Organization, Preparation, & Production. (National Information Standards Ser.). 1987. 26.00 (*0-88738-984-8*, Z30.18) Transaction Pubs.

S

An Asterisk (*) at the beginning of an entry indicates that the title is appearing in BIP for the first time.

Scientific & Technical Research Centres in Australia. Commonwealth Scientific & Industrial Research Organization Staff. Ed. by I. Crump. 332p. 1975. 63.00 (*0-677-65210-0*) Gordon & Breach.

Scientific & Technical Translation. Ed. by Sue E. Wright & Leland D. Wright. (American Translators Association Scholarly Monograph Ser.: Vol. VI). viii, 298p. 1993. 45.00 (*1-55619-625-3*) Benjamins North Am.

Scientific & Technical Vocabulary: Vocabulario Cientifico y Tecnico. Real Academia De Ciencias Staff. 503p. (SPA.). 1983. 175.00 (*0-8288-2145-3*, S60131) Fr & Eur.

Scientific & Technical Writing. Peter M. Sandman et al. LC 84-19740. 512p. (C). 1985. pap. text ed. 26.75 (*0-03-041056-8*) HB Coll Pubs.

***Scientific & Technological Achievements Related to the Development of European Cities: Proceedings of the NATO Advanced Research Workshop Held in Kishinev, Republic of Moldova, May 22-24, 1996.** Ed. by Sergei Radautsan. LC 96-49531. (NATO ASI Series Partnership Sub-Series 4). 352p. (C). 1996. lib. bdg. 185.00 (*0-7923-4340-9*) Kluwer Ac.

Scientific & Technological Information for Development: Proceedings of the Ad-hoc Panel of Experts on Information Systems for Science & Technology for Development, Held in Rome, Italy, 21-25 January 1985. 179p. 1985. pap. 17.50 (*92-1-104236-4*, E.85.II.A.7) UN.

Scientific & Technological Revolution: A Study of the Soviet Union, Capitalist, & Third World Countries. M. Millionschikov et al. 279p. 1975. 25.00 (*0-8464-0818-X*) Beekman Pubs.

Scientific Answer to Human Relations: A Blueprint for Harmony in Industry. Walter Russell & Lao Russell. (Illus.). 68p. 1978. text ed. 7.00 (*1-879605-15-5*) U Sci & Philos.

Scientific Application of Baseline Observations of Atmospheric Composition. Ed. by Dieter Ehhalt et al. (C). 1987. lib. bdg. 180.50 (*90-277-2533-0*) Kluwer Ac.

Scientific Applications for the Next Computer System: Technical Examples & Methodology. Richard E. Crandall & Marianne M. Colgrove. 300p. 1989. pap. 22.95 (*0-201-51732-9*) Addison-Wesley.

Scientific Applications of Lunar Laser Ranging. Ed. by J. Derral Mulholland. (Astrophysics & Space Science Library: No. 62). 1977. lib. bdg. 117.50 (*90-277-0790-1*) Kluwer Ac.

Scientific Applications of the Connection Machine. Ed. by H. Simon. 364p. (C). 1989. text ed. 113.00 (*9971-5-0969-5*) World Scientific Pub.

Scientific Applications of the Connection Machine. 2nd ed. H. Simon. 400p. 1991. text ed. 99.00 (*981-02-0928-2*) World Scientific Pub.

Scientific Approach. Carlo Lastrucci. 257p. 1967. pap. 16.95 (*0-87073-042-8*) Schenkman Bks Inc.

Scientific Approach to Biblical Mysteries. Robert Faid. LC 92-85131. 208p. (Orig.). 1993. pap. 9.95 (*0-89221-231-4*) New Leaf.

Scientific Approach to Christianity. Robert W. Faid. LC 90-63010. 196p. 1990. pap. 9.95 (*0-89221-186-5*) New Leaf.

Scientific Approach to More Biblical Mysteries. Robert Faid. LC 94-69838. 208p. (Orig.). 1995. pap. 9.95 (*0-89221-283-7*) New Leaf.

Scientific Approach to the Metaphysics of Astrology. Enrique Linares. Ed. by Arlene Robertson. 170p. (Orig.). 1982. per. 7.95 (*0-930706-10-2*) Seek-It Pubns.

Scientific Approaches to Consciousness. Ed. by Jonathan D. Cohen & Jonathan W. Schooler. (Carnegie Mellon Symposia on Cognition Ser.). 300p. 1996. text ed. 99.95 (*0-8058-1471-X*); pap. text ed. 39.95 (*0-8058-1472-8*) L Erlbaum Assocs.

Scientific Approaches to Health & Health Care. Ed. by B. Z. Nizetic et al. 186p. 1986. pap. text ed. 15.00 (*92-890-1032-0*, 1340030) World Health.

Scientific Aspects of European Expansion. Ed. by William K. Storey. (Expanding World Ser.: Vol. 6). 368p. 1996. 109.95 (*0-86078-524-6*, Pub. by Variorum UK) Ashgate Pub Co.

Scientific Aspects of Graphology: A Handbook. Ed. by Baruch Nevo. (Illus.). 362p. (C). 1987. 56.95 (*0-398-05245-X*) C C Thomas.

Scientific Aspects of Graphology: A Handbook. Ed. by Baruch Nevo. (Illus.). 362p. 1987. pap. 39.95 (*0-398-06304-4*) C C Thomas.

Scientific Aspects of Luther Burbank's Work. David S. Jordan. 1992. reprint ed. lib. bdg. 75.00 (*0-7812-5058-7*) Rprt Serv.

Scientific Aspects of the Race Problem. H. S. Jennings et al. LC 73-127591. (Essay Index Reprint Ser.). 1977. 23.95 (*0-8369-1774-X*) Ayer.

Scientific Aspects of the Race Problem. H. S. Jennings et al. (Essay Index Reprint Ser.). 312p. 1982. reprint ed. lib. bdg. 20.00 (*0-8290-0824-1*) Irvington.

Scientific Aspects of the Welfare of Food Animals. (Reports Ser.: No. 91). 54p. 1981. 3.50 (*0-318-13837-9*) CAST.

***Scientific Assessment of Stratospheric Ozone: 1989, Vol. 1.** Daniel L. Albritton & Robert T. Watson. (Illus.). 486p. 1996. reprint ed. pap. 50.00 (*0-7881-3205-9*) DIANE Pub.

Scientific Attitude. 2nd ed. Frederick Grinnell. LC 91-43226. (Conduct of Science Ser.). 179p. 1992. reprint ed. pap. text ed. 18.95 (*0-89862-018-X*) Guilford Pr.

Scientific Attitudes in Mary Shelley's "Frankenstein" Samuel H. Vasbinder. Ed. by Robert Scholes. LC 84-8438. (Studies in Speculative Fiction: No. 8). 120p. reprint ed. 34.00 (*0-8357-1580-9*, 2070462) Bks Demand.

***Scientific Authority & Twentieth-Century America.** Ed. by Ronald C. Walters. LC 96-46908. (Illus.). 320p. 1997. text ed. 35.00 (*0-8018-5389-3*) Johns Hopkins.

Scientific Autobiography. Aldo Rossi. Tr. by Lawrence Venuti from ITA. (Illus.). 128p. 1984. pap. 13.95 (*0-262-68041-6*) MIT Pr.

Scientific Autobiography & Other Papers. Max K. Planck. Tr. by Frank Gaynor. LC 68-23319. 192p. 1968. reprint ed. text ed. 35.00 (*0-8371-0194-8*, PLAP, Greenwood Pr) Greenwood.

Scientific Automobile Accident Reconstruction, 6 vols., Set. Martin E. Barzelay & George W. Lacy. 1964. ring bd. write for info. (*0-8205-1343-1*) Bender.

Scientific Background of International Sanitary Conferences 1851-1938. N. Howard-Jones. (History of International Public Health Ser.: No. 1). (Illus.). 1975. pap. text ed. 12.00 (*92-4-156055-X*, 1290001) World Health.

Scientific Background to Modern Philosophy: Selected Readings. Ed. by Michael R. Matthews. LC 88-32012. 174p. (C). 1989. 24.95 (*0-87220-075-2*); pap. 5.95 (*0-87220-074-4*) Hackett Pub.

Scientific Ballooning. W. Riedler & K. M. Torkar. (Advances in Space Research Ser.). 122p. 1995. pap. 97.75 (*0-08-042653-0*, Pergamon Pr) Elsevier.

***Scientific Ballooning.** W. Riedler & K. M. Torkar. (Advances in Space Research (RJ) Ser.: Vol. 13). 226p. 1992. 165.00 (*0-08-042048-6*, Pergamon Pr) Elsevier.

Scientific Ballooning: Proceedings of a Symposium of the 21st Plenary Meeting of the Committee on Space Research, Innsbruck, Austria, May 29-June 10 1978. Ed. by W. Riedler. LC 78-41182. (Illus.). 226p. 1979. 76.00 (*0-08-023420-8*, Pergamon Pr) Elsevier.

Scientific Ballooning: Proceedings of Symposium 7 of the COSPAR Twenty-Fifth Plenary Meeting Held in Graz, Austria, 25 June -7 July 1984, No. IV. Ed. by W. Riedler & K. M. Torkar. (Illus.). 140p. 1985. pap. 54.00 (*0-08-032753-2*, Pub. by PPL UK) Elsevier.

Scientific Ballooning-II. Ed. by W. Riedler & M. Friedrich. (Advances in Space Research Ser.: Vol. 1, No. 11). (Illus.). 274p. 1981. pap. 42.00 (*0-08-028390-X*, Pergamon Pr) Elsevier.

***Scientific Bases for Preservation of the Mariana Crow.** National Research Council Staff. 104p. (Orig.). 1997. pap. text ed. 29.00 (*0-309-05581-4*) Natl Acad Pr.

Scientific Bases for the Preservation of the Hawaiian Crow. Commission on Life Sciences, National Research Council Staff. 148p. (Orig.). (C). 1992. pap. text ed. 21.00 (*0-309-04775-7*) Natl Acad Pr.

***Scientific Bases of Cancer Chemoprevention: Proceedings of the International Forum on the Scientific Bases of Cancer Chemoprevention, 31 March-2 April 1996.** Cesare Maltoni et al. LC 96-36161. (International Congress Ser.). 310p. 1996. 184.50 (*0-444-82453-7*) Elsevier.

Scientific Basis & Clinical Applications. Williams. Date not set. write for info. (*0-7236-2087-3*, Pub. by John Wright UK) Buttrwrth-Heinemann.

Scientific Basis for Nuclear Waste Management VIII, Vol. 44. Ed. by C. M. Jantzen et al. LC 85-5023. (MRS Symposium Proceedings Ser.). 1985. text ed. 17.50 (*0-931837-09-X*) Materials Res.

Scientific Basis for Nuclear Waste Management X. Ed. by J. K. Bates & W. B. Seefeldt. (MRS Symposium Proceedings Ser.: Vol. 84). 1987. text ed. 17.50 (*0-931837-49-9*) Materials Res.

Scientific Basis for Nuclear Waste Management XI. Ed. by M. J. Apted & R. E. Westerman. (Symposium Proceedings Ser.: Vol. 112). 1988. text ed. 30.00 (*0-931837-80-4*) Materials Res.

Scientific Basis for Nuclear Waste Management XII, Vol. 127. Ed. by W. Lutze. (Materials Research Society Symposium Proceedings Ser.). 1989. text ed. 30.00 (*0-931837-97-9*) Materials Res.

Scientific Basis for Nuclear Waste Management XIII Vol. 176: Materials Research Society Symposium Proceedings. Ed. by V. M. Oversby & P. W. Brown. 804p. 1990. text ed. 17.50 (*1-55899-064-X*) Materials Res.

Scientific Basis for Nuclear Waste Management XIX: Materials Research Society Symposium Proceedings, Vol. 412. Ed. by W. M. Murphy & D. A. Knecht. 937p. 1996. 65.00 (*1-55899-315-0*) Materials Res.

Scientific Basis for Nuclear Waste Management XV. Ed. by C. G. Sombret. (Materials Research Society Symposium Proceedings Ser.: Vol. 257). 766p. 1992. text ed. 30.00 (*1-55899-151-4*) Materials Res.

Scientific Basis for Nuclear Waste Management XVI. Ed. by C. G. Interrante & R. T. Pabalan. (Materials Research Society Symposium Proceedings Ser.: Vol. 294). 951p. 1993. text ed. 63.00 (*1-55899-189-1*) Materials Res.

Scientific Basis for Nuclear Waste Management XVII, Vol. 333: Materials Research Society Symposium Proceedings. Ed. by A. Barkatt & R. Van Konynenburg. 969p. 1994. text ed. 78.00 (*1-55899-232-4*) Materials Res.

Scientific Basis for Nuclear Waste Management XVIII: Materials Research Society Symposium Proceedings. Ed. by Takashi Murakami & C. Ewing. (Proceedings from the Eighteenth Symposium on Nuclear Waste Management Ser.: Vol. 353). 1455p. 1995. 85.00 (*1-55899-253-7*) Materials Res.

***Scientific Basis for Nuclear Waste Management XX.** Ed. by W. J. Gray & I. R. Triay. (Materials Research Society Symposium Proceedings Ser.: No. 465). 1997. 75.00 (*1-55899-369-X*) Materials Res.

***Scientific Basis for Selected Environmental Medicine Techniques.** Sherry A. Rogers. LC 94-69079. 130p. 1994. reprint ed. pap. 17.95 (*0-9618821-6-6*) Prestige NY.

Scientific Basis for the Treatment of Parkinson's Disease. Ed. by Charles W. Olanow & Abraham Lieberman. (Illus.). 250p. 1992. 68.00 (*1-85070-355-8*) Prthnon Pub.

Scientific Basis for Vitamin Intake in Human Nutrition. P. J. Walter. (Bibliotheca Nutritio et Dieta Ser.: No. 52). (Illus.). vi, 178p. 1995. 198.25 (*3-8055-6166-0*) S Karger.

Scientific Basis of Air Conditioning. Ken-Ichi Kimura. (Illus.). vii, 273p. 1977. 79.25 (*0-85334-732-8*, Pub. by Elsevier Applied Sci UK) Elsevier.

***Scientific Basis of Eating: Taste, Smell, Mastication, Salvation & Swallowing & Their Dysfunctions.** Ed. by Robert W. Linden. (Frontiers in Oral Biology Ser.: Vol. 9, 1997). (Illus.). viii, 180p. 1997. 156.50 (*3-8055-6498-8*) S Karger.

Scientific Basis of Flotation. K. J. Ives. 1983. lib. bdg. 175.00 (*90-247-2907-6*) Kluwer Ac.

Scientific Basis of Health & Safety Regulation. Ed. by Robert W. Crandall & Lester B. Lave. LC 81-10227. (Studies in the Regulation of Economic Activity). 309p. 1981. 34.95 (*0-8157-1600-1*); pap. 14.95 (*0-8157-1599-4*) Brookings.

***Scientific Basis of Health Services.** Ed. by Michael Peckham & Richard Smith. 186p. 1996. pap. text ed. 42.00 (*0-7279-1029-9*, Pub. by BMJ Pubng Grp UK) Amer Coll Phys.

Scientific Basis of Joint Replacement. Ed. by Sydney A. Swanson et al. LC 76-51524. (Illus.). 190p. reprint ed. pap. 54.20 (*0-317-07938-7*, 2020342) Bks Demand.

Scientific Basis of National Progress, Including That of Morality. G. Gore. 218p. 1970. reprint ed. 26.00 (*0-7146-2407-1*, BHA-02407, Pub. by F Cass Pubs UK) Intl Spec Bk.

Scientific Basis of Noise-Induced Hearing Loss. Ed. by Alf Axelsson et al. LC 95-45011. 472p. 1995. 85.00 (*0-86577-596-6*) Thieme Med Pubs.

Scientific Basis of Phototherapy. Grossweiner. 227p. 1994. 139.00 (*0-8493-4980-X*) CRC Pr.

Scientific Basis of Psychiatry. 2nd ed. Barbara F. Weller. 1992. pap. text ed. 66.00 (*0-7020-1448-6*) HarBrace.

Scientific Basis of the Art of Teaching. Nathaniel L. Gage. LC 78-6250. 1978. pap. text ed. 13.95 (*0-8077-2537-4*) Tchrs Coll.

Scientific Basis of Transfusion Medicine. Ed. by Kenneth C. Anderson & Paul Ness. LC 92-49439. 1994. text ed. 135.00 (*0-7216-3302-1*) Saunders.

Scientific Basis of Vegetarianism. William Harris. 218p. (Orig.). 1995. pap. 15.95 (*0-9646538-0-X*) Hawaii Hlth Pubs.

Scientific Basis of Vegetarianism. R. T. Trall. 23p. 1961. reprint ed. spiral bd. 5.50 (*0-7873-1120-0*) Hlth Research.

Scientific Basis of Vegetarianism: Determining Our Natural Dietary Needs. Arthur M. Baker. 30p. (Orig.). 1994. pap. 7.95 (*1-883989-46-9*) Self Hlth Care.

Scientific Blacksmith. Mortimer E. Cooley. LC 72-5041. (Technology & Society Ser.). (Illus.). 290p. 1972. reprint ed. 20.95 (*0-405-04693-6*) Ayer.

Scientific Bodies in Motion: The Domestic & International Consequences of the Current & Emergent Brain Drain from the Former U. S. S. R. Vladimir D. Shkolnikov. LC 94-11386. 1994. pap. text ed. 13.00 (*0-8330-1538-9*, MR-433-EAC/FFNA) Rand Corp.

Scientific C Plus Plus: Building Numerical Libraries the Object Oriented Way. Guido Buzzi-Ferraris. (C). 1993. text ed. 39.75 (*0-201-63192-X*) Addison-Wesley.

Scientific Christian Mental Practice. Emma C. Hopkins. 279p. 1974. reprint ed. pap. 10.95 (*0-87516-199-5*) DeVorss.

Scientific Colonialism: A Cross-Cultural Comparison - Papers at a Conference at Melbourne, May 25-30, 1981. Ed. by Nathan Reingold & Marc Rothenberg. LC 85-43238. 264p. (Orig.). (C). 1986. pap. text ed. 19.95 (*0-87474-785-6*) Smithsonian.

Scientific Communication & National Security. National Academy of Sciences Staff. 188p. (C). 1982. pap. text ed. 19.95 (*0-309-03332-2*) Natl Acad Pr.

Scientific Communities in the Developing World. Ed. by Jacques Gaillard et al. LC 96-17807. 430p. 1996. 45.00 (*0-8039-9330-7*) Sage.

Scientific Community. Warren O. Hagstrom. LC 74-18379. (Arcturus Books Paperbacks). 319p. 1975. pap. 9.95 (*0-8093-0720-0*) S Ill U Pr.

Scientific Companion: Exploring the Physical World with Facts, Figures & Formulas. 2nd ed. Cesare Emilinai. LC 95-35530. (Illus.). 320p. 1995. pap. text ed. 19.95 (*0-471-13324-8*) Wiley.

Scientific Computation: Proceedings of International Conference. Zhong-Ci Shi. (Applied Mathematics Ser.). 288p. 1992. text ed. 92.00 (*981-02-1091-4*) World Scientific Pub.

Scientific Computations in Engineering & Applied Science: DOE, PDE, & DAE's. William E. Schiesser. LC 93-17599. 464p. 1993. 81.95 (*0-8493-7373-5*, TA347) CRC Pr.

Scientific Computations on Mathematical Problems & Conjectures. Richard Varga. LC 90-34761. (CBMS-NSF Regional Conference Series in Applied Mathematics: No. 60). vi, 122p. 1990. pap. 25.00 (*0-89871-257-2*) Soc Indus-Appl Math.

Scientific Computer Graphics in C. Shoichiro Nakamura & Peter Carswell. 1993. text ed. write for info. (*0-13-795790-4*) P-H.

Scientific Computing: An Introduction with Parallel Computing. Gene H. Golub & James M. Ortega. (Illus.). 442p. 1993. text ed. 56.00 (*0-12-289253-4*) Acad Pr.

***Scientific Computing: An Introductory Survey.** Michael T. Heath. LC 96-43722. 1996. text ed. write for info. (*0-07-027684-6*) McGraw.

Scientific Computing & Automation (Europe) 1990: Proceedings of the Conference, 12-15 June, 1990, Maastricht, The Netherlands. Ed. by E. J. Karjalainen. (Data Handling in Science & Technology Ser.: No. 6). 514p. 1991. 267.50 (*0-444-88949-3*) Elsevier.

Scientific Computing & Differential Equations: An Introduction to Numerical Methods. Gene H. Golub & James M. Ortega. (Illus.). 352p. 1991. text ed. 61.00 (*0-12-289255-0*) Acad Pr.

***Scientific Computing & Validated Numerics: Proceedings of the International Symposium on Scientific Computing, Computer Arithmetic & Validated Numbers SCAN-95 Held in Wuppertal, Germany, September 26-29, 1995.** Ed. by Gotz Alefeld et al. (Mathematical Research Ser.: Vol. 90). (Illus.). 300p. 1996. 95.00 (*3-05-501737-4*, VCH) Wiley.

Scientific Computing in Chemical Engineering. Ed. by F. Keil et al. LC 96-15898. 259p. 1996. 99.00 (*3-540-60940-7*) Spr-Verlag.

Scientific Computing on Supercomputers II. Ed. by J. T. Devreese. (Illus.). 260p. 1990. 89.50 (*0-306-43712-0*, Plenum Pr) Plenum.

Scientific Computing on Supercomputers III. Ed. by J. T. Devreese & P. E. Van Camp. (Illus.). 224p. 1992. 89.50 (*0-306-44118-7*, Plenum Pr) Plenum.

Scientific Computing on Vector Computers. W. Schonauer. (Special Topics in Supercomputing Ser.: No. 2). 488p. 1987. 157.00 (*0-444-70288-1*, North Holland) Elsevier.

Scientific Computing with Supercomputers. Ed. by J. T. Devreese & P. E. Van Camp. (Illus.). 292p. 1989. 89.50 (*0-306-43217-X*, Plenum Pr) Plenum.

Scientific Conference Russian-English Phrase Book. L. Stupin & A. Lapitskii. (C). 1990. text ed. 70.00 (*0-569-09366-X*, Pub. by Collets) St Mut.

Scientific Conscience: Reflections on the Modern Biologist & Humanism. Catherine Roberts. 1974. 22.95 (*0-8464-0819-8*) Beekman Pubs.

Scientific Consideration in Monitoring & Evaluating Toxicological Research. E. J. Gralla. 1981. text ed. 29.50 (*0-07-024047-7*) McGraw.

Scientific Controversies: Case Studies in the Resolution & Closure of Disputes in Sciences & Technology. Ed. by H. Tristram Engelhardt, Jr. & Arthur L. Caplan. 704p. 1987. text ed. 85.00 (*0-521-25565-1*) Cambridge U Pr.

Scientific Controversies: Case Studies in the Resolution & Closure of Disputes in Sciences & Technology. Ed. by H. Tristram Engelhardt, Jr. & Arthur L. Caplan. 704p. 1987. pap. text ed. 38.95 (*0-521-27560-1*) Cambridge U Pr.

Scientific Cooperation for Development: Search for New Directions. Ed. by P. J. Lavakare et al. 216p. 1980. text ed. 20.00 (*0-7069-0955-0*, Pub. by Vikas II) S Asia.

Scientific Correspondence During the Chemical Revolution: Louis-Bernard Guyton de Morveau & Richard Kirwan, 1782-1802. Ed. by Emmanuel Grison et al. LC 94-66475. (Berkeley Papers in History of Science: No. 17). 257p. (Orig.). 1994. pap. text ed. 10.00 (*0-918102-21-9*) U Cal Hist Sci Tech.

Scientific Creationism. Morris. 281p. 1986. 10.95 (*0-89051-003-2*) Master Bks.

Scientific Creationism - Chinese Edition. Henry M. Morris. Tr. by Paul Han. 223p. (CHI.). 1997. pap. 7.00 (*1-56582-039-8*) Christ Renew Min.

***Scientific Credibility & Technical Standards.** Ed. by Jed Z. Buchwald. (Archimedes New Studies in the History & Philosophy of Science & Technology: No. 1). 192p. (C). 1996. lib. bdg. 110.00 (*0-7923-4241-0*) Kluwer Ac.

Scientific Credibility of Folk Psychology. Garth Fletcher. 105p. 1995. pap. 14.50 (*0-8058-1571-6*); text ed. 27.50 (*0-8058-1570-8*) L Erlbaum Assocs.

Scientific Credibility of Freud's Theories & Therapy. Seymour Fisher & Roger P. Greenberg. LC 85-9722. 502p. 1985. pap. text ed. 22.00 (*0-231-06215-X*) Col U Pr.

***Scientific Culture & the Making of the Industrial West.** Margaret C. Jacob. (Illus.). 304p. (C). 1997. text ed. 47.00 (*0-19-508219-2*); pap. text ed. 19.95 (*0-19-508220-6*) OUP.

Scientific Data Analysis. R. L. Branham, Jr. (Illus.). 250p. 1990. 65.95 (*0-387-97201-3*) Spr-Verlag.

Scientific Dating Methods. Ed. by H. Y. Goksu et al. 368p. (C). 1991. lib. bdg. 153.50 (*0-7923-1461-1*) Kluwer Ac.

Scientific Demonstration of the Future Life. Thomas Hudson. 1979. mass mkt. 2.50 (*0-89083-464-4*, Zebra Kensgtn) Kensgtn Pub Corp.

Scientific Design of Exhaust & Intake Systems. 3rd rev. ed. Philip H. Smith & John C. Morrison. LC 72-86569. (Illus.). 274p. 1972. 22.95 (*0-8376-0309-9*) Bentley.

Scientific Development & Higher Education: The Case of Newly Industrializing Nations. Philip G. Altbach et al. LC 88-38101. 396p. 1989. text ed. 69.50 (*0-275-93264-8*, C3264, Praeger Pubs) Greenwood.

Scientific Dialogue: From Basic Research to Clinical Intervention. Ed. by H. G. Zapotoczky & T. Wenzel. (Annual Series of European Research in Behavior Therapy: Vol. 5). xii, 316p. 1990. 49.75 (*90-265-1106-X*) Swets.

***Scientific Discoveries & Soviet Law: A Sociohistorical Analysis.** James M. Swanson. LC 84-12020. (University of Florida Monographs: Vol. 70). 160p. reprint ed. pap. 45.60 (*0-608-04512-8*, 2065257) Bks Demand.

Scientific Discovery: Case Studies. Ed. by Thomas Nickles. (Boston Studies in the Philosophy of Science: No. 60). 404p. 1980. pap. text ed. 52.00 (*90-277-1093-7*, D Reidel); lib. bdg. 93.00 (*90-277-1092-9*, D Reidel) Kluwer Ac.

Scientific Discovery: Computational Explorations of the Creative Processes. Patrick Langley et al. (Illus.). 344p. 1987. pap. 17.50 (*0-262-62052-9*) MIT Pr.

Scientific Discovery: Logic & Tinkering. Aharon Kantorovich. LC 92-1766. (SUNY Series in Philosophy & Biology). 281p. (C). 1993. text ed. 59.50 (*0-7914-1477-9*); pap. text ed. 19.95 (*0-7914-1478-7*) State U NY Pr.

An Asterisk (*) at the beginning of an entry indicates that the title is appearing in BIP for the first time.

Scientific Discovery: The Erice Lectures 1977. Ed. by M. D. Grmek et al. (Boston Studies in the Philosophy of Science Ser.: No. 34). 342p. 1980. pap. text ed. 55.00 (*90-277-1123-2*) Kluwer Ac.

Scientific Discovery, Logic & Rationality. Ed. by Thomas Nickles. (Boston Studies in the Philosophy of Science: No. 56). 397p. 1980. lib. bdg. 93.00 (*90-277-1069-4*, D Reidel) Kluwer Ac.

*__Scientific Diving: A General Code of Practice.__ 2nd ed. Ed. by N. C. Fleming & M. D. Max. (Illus.). 278p. 1996. pap. 39.95 (*0-941332-51-9*, D399) Best Pub Co.

*__Scientific Document Examination Manual.__ Katherine M. Koppenhauer. (Illus.). 56p. (Orig.). 1997. wbk. ed., pap. text ed. 25.00 (*0-9632206-7-5*) Foren Pubs Joppa.

Scientific Elite: Nobel Laureates in the United States. Harriet Zuckerman. 335p. (C). 1995. pap. text ed. 24.95 (*1-56000-855-5*) Transaction Pubs.

Scientific Encounters of the...Series, 4 bks., Set. Lynn Embry. teacher ed. 34.99 (*1-56417-151-5*, GA1132) Good Apple.

Scientific Encyclopedia of the Universe: Encyclopedie Scientifique de l'Univers: La Physique. Gauthiers-vil. 480p. (FRE.). 1981. 75.00 (*0-8288-2231-X*, M14354) Fr & Eur.

Scientific Endeavor. Ed. by H. Jordan & E. Kone. LC 65-18302. (Illus.). 340p. 1965. 6.00 (*0-87470-004-3*) Rockefeller.

Scientific Engineering of Materials with Theorist Notebook. 3rd ed. Askeland. (General Engineering Ser.). 1994. suppl. ed. 28.95 (*0-534-94250-4*) PWS Pubs.

Scientific Engineering of Materials with Theorist Notebook. 3rd ed. Askeland. (General Engineering Ser.). 1994. text ed. 103.95 (*0-534-94230-X*) PWS Pubs.

Scientific English: A Guide for Scientists & Other Professionals. 2nd ed. Robert A. Day. LC 95-370. (Illus.). 160p. 1995. pap. 15.95 (*0-89774-989-8*) Oryx Pr.

Scientific Enterprise. Ed. by Edna Ullmann-Margalit. LC 92-31007. (Bar-Hillel Colloquium Ser.: Vol. 4). 312p. (C). 1992. lib. bdg. 121.50 (*0-7923-1992-3*, Pub. by Klwr Acad Pubs NE) Kluwer Ac.

Scientific Enterprise in America: Readings from Isis. Ronald L. Numbers & Charles E. Rosenberg. LC 95-47657. 320p. (C). 1996. pap. text ed. 17.95 (*0-226-60838-7*) U Ch Pr.

Scientific Enterprise in America: Readings from Isis. Ed. by Ronald L. Numbers & Charles E. Rosenberg. LC 95-47657. (C). 1996. lib. bdg. 35.00 (*0-226-60837-9*) U Ch Pr.

Scientific Enterprise in Antiquity & the Middle Ages: Readings from Isis. Ed. by Michael H. Shank. 240p. 1996. pap. text ed. 17.95 (*0-226-74951-7*); lib. bdg. 35.00 (*0-226-74950-9*) U Ch Pr.

Scientific Enterprise in Early Modern Europe: Readings from Isis. Ed. by Peter Dear. LC 96-42535. 340p. 1997. lib. bdg. 37.50 (*0-226-13946-8*) U Ch Pr.

Scientific Enterprise in Early Modern Europe: Readings from Isis. Ed. by Peter Dear. LC 96-42535. 340p. 1996. pap. text ed. 17.95 (*0-226-13947-6*) U Ch Pr.

Scientific Essentials of Reproduction. Hillier. 1996. text ed. 119.00 (*0-7020-1826-0*) Saunders.

Scientific Establishments & Hierarchies. N. Elias et al. 1982. pap. text ed. 61.00 (*90-277-1323-5*) Kluwer Ac.

Scientific Estate. Don K. Price. LC 65-22047. 343p. 1965. 37.00 (*0-674-79485-0*) Belknap Pr.

Scientific Evidence, 2 vols., Set. 2nd ed. Paul C. Gianelli & Edward J. Imwinkelried. 1341p. 1993. 160.00 (*1-55834-055-6*) MICHIE.

*__Scientific Evidence & Expert Testimony Handbook: A Guide for Lawyers, Criminal Investigators & Forensic Specialists.__ Ronald F. Becker. LC 96-53287. 246p. 1997. text ed. 55.95 (*0-398-06761-9*); pap. text ed. 42.95 (*0-398-06762-7*) C C Thomas.

Scientific Evidence for Dietary Targets in Europe. Ed. by J. C. Somogyi & A. Trichopoulou. (Bibliotheca Nutritio et Dieta Ser.: No. 37). (Illus.). vi, 162p. 1985. 120.00 (*3-8055-4161-9*) S Karger.

Scientific Evidence for the Second Coming of Christ see Science & Religion Series

Scientific Evidence in Civil & Criminal Cases. 4th ed. Andre A. Moenssens et al. 1230p. 1994. text ed. 48.95 (*1-56662-233-6*) Foundation Pr.

Scientific Evidence in Criminal Cases. 3rd ed. Andre A. Moenssens et al. (University Textbook Ser.). 805p. 1986. 38.95 (*0-88277-281-3*) Foundation Pr.

Scientific Evidence with 1991 Cumulative Supplement. Paul C. Giannelli & Edward J. Imwinkelried. (Contemporary Litigation Ser.). 1252p. 1991. suppl. ed. 95.00 (*0-87215-936-1*) MICHIE.

*__Scientific Examination of Documents.__ 2nd ed. David Ellen. 182p. 1996. 79.95 (*0-7484-0580-1*, Pub. by Tay Francis Ltd UK) Taylor & Francis.

Scientific Examination of Questioned Documents. rev. ed. O. Hilton. (Forensic & Police Science Ser.: Vol. 2). 424p. 1981. 82.00 (*0-444-00628-1*, HV8074) CRC Pr.

Scientific Excellence: Origins & Assessment. Ed. by Douglas N. Jackson & J. Philippe Rushton. LC 86-1839. 381p. 1987. reprint ed. pap. 108.60 (*0-608-01471-0*, 2059515) Bks Demand.

Scientific Expedition of Leon De Cessac to California, 1877-1879 & a Bibliography of the Chumash & Their Predecessors. fac. ed. H. Reichlen et al. (Reports of the University of California Archaeological Survey: No. 61). (Illus.). 74p. 1964. reprint ed. pap. 6.85 (*1-55567-376-7*) Coyote Press.

Scientific Experiments for Manned Orbital Flight: Proceedings of the Goddard Memorial Symposium, 3rd, Washington, D.C., 1965. Ed. by P. C. Badgley. (Science & Technology Ser.: Vol. 4). 1965. 30.00 (*0-87703-032-4*) Univelt Inc.

*__Scientific Explanation: 1953 Edition.__ R. B. Braithwaite. 388p. 1996. reprint ed. write for info. (*1-85506-327-1*) Bks Intl VA.

*__Scientific Explanation & the Casual Structure of the World.__ Wesley C. Salmon. LC 84-42562. 320p. 1984. reprint ed. pap. 91.20 (*0-608-03757-5*, 2064580) Bks Demand.

Scientific Explanation of Sex. 1991. write for info. (*1-879605-16-3*) U Sci & Philos.

Scientific Explorers. Rebecca Stefoff. (Extraordinary Explorers Ser.). (Illus.). 144p. (J). 1993. lib. bdg. 26.00 (*0-19-507689-3*) OUP.

Scientific Failure. Ed. by Tamara Horowitz & Allen I. Janis. 240p. (C). 1993. lib. bdg. 42.50 (*0-8476-7806-7*) Rowman.

*__Scientific Farm Animal Production.__ 6th ed. Taylor & Field. 1997. text ed. 83.00 (*0-13-456591-6*) P-H.

Scientific Farm Animal Production: An Introduction to Animal Production. 5th ed. Robert E. Taylor. (Illus.). 650p. 1995. text ed. 90.00 (*0-02-419291-0*, Macmillan Coll) P-H.

Scientific Fasting. Linda B. Hazzard. 360p. 1963. reprint ed. spiral bd. 25.00 (*0-7873-0390-9*) Hlth Research.

Scientific Fasting: The Ancient & Modern Key to Health. Linda B. Hazzard. 360p. 1996. pap. 24.95 (*1-56459-826-8*) Kessinger Pub.

Scientific Forecasting & Human Needs: Trends, Methods & Message. Ed. by UNESCO Staff. LC 83-25046. (Illus.). 228p. 1984. 101.00 (*0-08-027970-8*, Pub. by Pergamon Repr UK); pap. 5.50 (*0-08-030867-8*, Pub. by Pergamon Repr UK) Franklin.

Scientific Forth: A Modern Language for Scientific Computing. Julian V. Noble. (Illus.). 330p. (Orig.). (C). 1992. pap. text ed. 39.95 (*0-9632775-0-2*) Mechum Banks.

Scientific Foundation of Sports Medicine. Teitz. 408p. (gr. 13). 1989. 64.95 (*1-55664-081-1*) Mosby Yr Bk.

Scientific Foundations of Biochemistry in Clinical Practice. 2nd ed. Ed. by David L. Williams & Vincent Marks. (Scientific Foundations of Clinical Biochemistry Ser.). (Illus.). 896p. 1995. 195.00 (*0-7506-0167-1*) Buttrwrth-Heinemann.

Scientific Foundations of Jainism. K. V. Mardia. 1990. 23.00 (*81-208-0658-1*, Pub. by Motilal Banarsidass II) S Asia.

Scientific Foundations of Neurology. A. Norman Guthkelch & Karl E. Misulis. LC 96-14099. (Illus.). 512p. 1996. text ed. 85.00 (*0-86542-408-X*) Blackwell Sci.

Scientific Foundations of Surgery. 4th ed. James Kyle & Larry C. Carey. 696p. 1989. write for info. (*0-433-18902-9*) Buttrwrth-Heinemann.

Scientific Foundations of the Ovulation Method. Thomas W. Hilgers. LC 95-69119. (Illus.). 81p. 1995. pap. 16.00 (*0-9626485-3-1*) Pope Paul Sixth.

Scientific Foundations of Trauma. Graham Cooper et al. (Illus.). 600p. 1993. write for info. (*0-7506-1585-0*) Buttrwrth-Heinemann.

Scientific Foundations of Urology. 3rd ed. G. D. Chisholm & William R. Fair. 820p. 1989. write for info. (*0-433-05497-2*) Mosby Yr Bk.

Scientific Fraud. 1991. lib. bdg. 79.95 (*0-8490-4711-0*) Gordon Pr.

Scientific French: A Concise Description of the Structural Elements of Scientific & Technical French. William N. Locke. LC 78-11669. 124p. 1978. reprint ed. pap. 9.50 (*0-88275-771-7*) Krieger.

Scientific Fundamentals of Robotics 3: Kinematics & Trajectories Synthesis of Manipulation Robots. M. Vukobratovic & N. Kircanski. (Communications & Control Engineering Ser.). (Illus.). x, 267p. 1985. 103.95 (*0-387-13071-3*) Spr-Verlag.

Scientific Fundamentals of Robotics 4: Real-Time Dynamics of Manipulation Robots. M. Vukobratovic & N. Kircanski. (Communications & Control Engineering Ser.). (Illus.). xii, 239p. 1985. 91.95 (*0-387-13072-1*) Spr-Verlag.

Scientific Fundamentals of Robotics 5. M. Vukobratovic et al. (Communications & Control Engineering Ser.). (Illus.). x, 383p. 1985. 139.95 (*0-387-13073-X*) Spr-Verlag.

Scientific Fundamentals of Robotics 6. M. Vukobratovic & V. Potkonjak. (Communications & Control Engineering Ser.). (Illus.). xiii, 305p. 1985. 94.00 (*0-387-13074-8*) Spr-Verlag.

Scientific Fur Servicing: Storage, Cleaning, Repairing & Restyling. Gaetan J. Lapick & Jack Geller. (Illus.). 145p. reprint ed. pap. 41.40 (*0-317-10808-5*, 2011751) Bks Demand.

Scientific Genius: A Psychology of Science. Dean K. Simonton. (Illus.). 200p. 1988. text ed. 42.95 (*0-521-35287-8*) Cambridge U Pr.

Scientific Genius & Creativity. Owen Gingerich. LC 86-31920. (Readings from Scientific American Ser.). (Illus.). 110p. (C). 1995. text ed. write for info. (*0-7167-1857-X*) W H Freeman.

Scientific Genius & Creativity. Owen Gingerich. LC 86-31920. (Readings from Scientific American Ser.). (Illus.). 110p. (C). 1995. text ed. write for info. (*0-7167-1858-8*) W H Freeman.

Scientific German by the Method of Discovery. Kurt F. Leidecker. 1947. 15.00 (*0-913298-67-0*) S F Vanni.

Scientific Goofs. Billy Aronson. LC 94-4492. (Illus.). (J). (gr. 3-7). 1994. text ed. 14.95 (*0-7167-6537-3*, Sci Am Yng Rdrs); pap. text ed. 7.95 (*0-7167-6553-5*, Sci Am Yng Rdrs) W H Freeman.

Scientific Graphics with Lotus 1-2-3. Oleg D. Jefimenko. (Illus.). 194p. 1987. pap. 16.00 (*0-917406-05-2*) Electret Sci.

Scientific Growth: Essays on the Social Organization & Ethos of Science. Joseph Ben-David. (California Studies in the History of Science: No. 8). 576p. 1991. 65.00 (*0-520-06925-0*) U CA Pr.

Scientific Guide to Peaceful Living. Betty Y. Ho. LC 77-142457. (System of Government in the Living Body Ser.). (Illus.). 170p. (Orig.). 1973. pap. 20.00 (*0-9600148-2-9*) Juvenescent.

Scientific Habit of Thought. Frederick Barry. reprint ed. 31.50 (*0-404-00666-3*) AMS Pr.

Scientific Healing Affirmations. Paramahansa Yogananda. LC 81-53040. (Illus.). 100p. 1981. pap. 1.95 (*0-87612-144-X*) Self Realization.

Scientific Healing Affirmations: Paramhansa Yogananda. LC 84-71199. 1993. pap. 9.95 (*0-937134-15-5*) Amrita Found.

Scientific Highlights in Memory of Leon Van Hove, Napoli, Italy, October 25-26, 1991. Ed. by F. Nicodemi. LC 93-17108. (Twentieth Century Physics Ser.: Vol. 2). 180p. 1993. text ed. 67.00 (*981-02-1399-9*) World Scientific Pub.

Scientific Horseshoeing. 2nd ed. William Rusell. LC 87-82868. 490p. 1995. 45.00 (*0-944707-01-7*) Loose Change.

Scientific Horticulture, 2 vols. S. P. Singh. (C). 1991. text ed. 135.00 (*0-318-69684-3*, Pub. by Scientific Pubs II) St Mut.

Scientific Horticulture, 1. S. P. Singh. (C). 1991. text ed. 125.00 (*81-7233-019-7*, Pub. by Scientific Pubs II) St Mut.

Scientific Horticulture, 2. S. P. Singh. (C). 1991. text ed. 125.00 (*0-685-63523-6*, Pub. by Scientific Pubs II) St Mut.

Scientific Hydrotherapy. William L. McKie. 134p. 1993. reprint ed. spiral bd. 12.50 (*0-7873-0599-5*) Hlth Research.

Scientific Ideas of G. K. Gilbert: An Assessment on the Occasion of the Centennial of the United States Geological Survey (1879-1979) Ed. by Ellis L. Yochelson. LC 80-67676. (Geological Society of America, Special Paper Ser.: No. 183). (Illus.). 156p. reprint ed. pap. 44.50 (*0-7837-1849-7*, 2042049) Bks Demand.

Scientific Identification of Disputed Documents, Fingerprints & Ballistics. R. A. Gregory. 155p. 1984. 105.00 (*0-317-54703-8*) St Mut.

Scientific Illustration. John L. Ridgway. (Illus.). xiv, 173p. 1938. 35.00 (*0-8047-0996-3*) Stanford U Pr.

Scientific Illustration. 2nd ed. Phyllis Wood. LC 93-3317. 1994. pap. 29.95 (*0-442-01316-7*) Van Nos Reinhold.

Scientific Image. B. C. VanFrassen. (Clarendon Library of Logic & Philosophy). 248p. 1980. pap. text ed. 26.00 (*0-19-824427-4*) OUP.

Scientific Image: From Cave to Computer. Harry Robin. LC 93-48053. 1995. pap. text ed. write for info. (*0-7167-2504-5*) W H Freeman.

Scientific Imagination. Gerald J. Holton. LC 76-47196. (Illus.). 1978. pap. 25.95 (*0-521-29237-9*) Cambridge U Pr.

Scientific Information & Society. Gyorgy Rozsa. 1973. bds. 29.25 (*90-279-7181-1*) Mouton.

Scientific Information in Wartime: An Allied-German Rivalry, 1939-1945. Pamela S. Richards. LC 93-25050. (Contributions in Military Studies: No. 151). 192p. 1994. text ed. 49.95 (*0-313-29062-8*) Greenwood.

Scientific Information Systems & the Principle of Selectivity. William Goffman & Kenneth Warren. LC 80-49. 202p. 1980. text ed. 55.00 (*0-275-90489-X*, C0489, Praeger Pubs) Greenwood.

Scientific Inquiry & the Social Sciences. Ed. by Marilynn B. Brewer & Barry E. Collins. LC 81-6023. (Jossey-Bass Social & Behavioral Science Ser.). 543p. reprint ed. pap. 154.80 (*0-8357-4971-1*, 2037904) Bks Demand.

Scientific Inquiry in Philosophical Perspective. Ed. by Nicholas Rescher. (CPS Publications in Philosophy of Science). (Illus.). 308p. (Orig.). 1987. pap. text ed. 26.00 (*0-8191-5799-6*, Ctr Philos Sci) U Pr of Amer.

Scientific Instrument Manufacturer. Ed. by ICC Information Group Staff. 1987. 695.00 (*1-85319-044-6*, Pub. by ICC Info Group Ltd UK) St Mut.

Scientific Instruments & Experimental Philosophy 1550-1850. G. L. Turner. (Collected Studies: No. CS331). 352p. 1991. text ed. 103.95 (*0-86078-280-8*, Pub. by Variorum UK) Ashgate Pub Co.

Scientific Intellectual: The Psychological & Sociological Origins of Modern Science. Lewis S. Feuer. 497p. (C). 1991. text ed. 24.95 (*1-56000-571-8*) Transaction Pubs.

Scientific Intelligentsia in the U. S. S. R. Structure & Dynamics of Personnel. D. M. Gvishiani et al. Tr. by Jane Sayers from RUS. 1976. 19.95 (*0-8464-0820-1*) Beekman Pubs.

Scientific Interfaces & Technological Applications. National Research Council, Physics Survey Committee Staff. LC 85-32039. (Physics Through the 1990's Ser.). 284p. reprint ed. pap. 81.00 (*0-7837-3570-7*, 2043428) Bks Demand.

Scientific Investigator. Richard O. Arther. (Illus.). 248p. 1976. 31.95 (*0-398-00055-7*) C C Thomas.

Scientific Investment Analysis. Austin Murphy. 588p. 1994. 74.95 incl. disk (*0-914061-51-8*) Orchises Pr.

Scientific Issues in Quantitative Cancer Risk Assessment. Suresh H. Moolgavkar. 320p. 1990. 64.00 (*0-8176-3501-7*) Birkhauser.

Scientific Journals: Improving Library Collections Through Analysis of Publishing Trends. Tony Stankus. LC 90-40988. (Serials Librarian Supplement Ser.: No. 6). 206p. 1990. text ed. 39.95 (*0-86656-905-7*) Haworth Pr.

Scientific Journals: Issues in Library Selection & Management. Tony Stankus. LC 87-7047. (Serials Librarian Supplement Ser.: No. 3). 218p. 1987. text ed. 39.95 (*0-86656-616-3*) Haworth Pr.

Scientific Karatedo. Masayuki K. Hisataka. (Illus.). 296p. (Orig.). 1995. pap. 24.95 (*0-8048-2019-8*) C E Tuttle.

Scientific Kid: Projects, Experiments, Adventures. Mary S. Carson. LC 88-45551. 80p. (Orig.). (J). 1989. pap. 15.00 (*0-06-096316-6*, PL 6316, PL) HarpC.

Scientific Knowledge. James H. Fetzer. 339p. 1981. pap. text ed. 46.00 (*90-277-1336-7*, D Reidel); lib. bdg. 135.00 (*90-277-1335-9*, D Reidel) Kluwer Ac.

Scientific Knowledge. 2nd ed. Janet A. Kourany. (Philosophy Ser.). 1997. pap. 27.75 (*0-534-52530-X*) Course Tech.

Scientific Knowledge: A Sociological Analysis. Barry Barnes et al. 1996. lib. bdg. 38.00 (*0-226-03730-4*) U Ch Pr.

Scientific Knowledge: A Sociological Analysis. Ed. by Barry Barnes et al. 288p. 1996. pap. text ed. 15.95 (*0-226-03731-2*) U Ch Pr.

Scientific Knowledge: Basic Issues in the Philosophy of Science. Ed. by Janet A. Kourany. 399p. (C). 1987. pap. 40.95 (*0-534-06444-2*) Wadsworth Pub.

Scientific Knowledge: Discovery of Nature or Mental Construction? Harry Settanni. LC 92-10052. 1992. pap. 8.95 (*0-8191-8673-2*) U Pr of Amer.

Scientific Knowledge a Sociological Analysis. Barnes & Bloor. (C). Date not set. text ed. write for info. (*0-485-11404-6*) Humanities.

Scientific Knowledge & Its Social Problems. Jerome R. Ravetz. 480p. (C). 1995. pap. text ed. 29.95 (*1-56000-851-2*) Transaction Pubs.

Scientific Knowledge & Philosophic Thought. Harold Himsworth. LC 85-24118. 128p. 1986. text ed. 28.50 (*0-8018-3316-7*) Johns Hopkins.

Scientific Knowledge & Sociological Theory. Barry Barnes. (Monographs in Social Theory). 204p. 1975. pap. 13.95 (*0-7100-7962-1*, RKP) Routledge.

Scientific Knowledge As a Cultural & Historical Process: The Cultural Prospects of Science. Vladimir A. Zviglyanich. Ed. by Andrew Blasko & Hilary H. Brandt. LC 93-19191. 284p. 1993. text ed. 89.95 (*0-7734-9865-6*) E Mellen.

Scientific Knowledge in Controversy: The Social Dynamics of the Fluoridation Debate. Brian Martin. LC 90-34740. (SUNY Series in Science, Technology, & Society). 266p. 1991. text ed. 64.50 (*0-7914-0538-9*); pap. text ed. 21.95 (*0-7914-0539-7*) State U NY Pr.

Scientific Knowledge Socialized. Ed. by Imre Hronszky et al. 432p. (C). 1989. lib. bdg. 203.00 (*90-277-2284-6*, D Reidel) Kluwer Ac.

Scientific Lectures. John Lubbock. LC 72-4522. (Essay Index Reprint Ser.). 1977. reprint ed. 20.95 (*0-8369-2960-8*) Ayer.

Scientific Letters & Papers of James Clerk Maxwell, Vol. 2: 1862-1873, Vol. 2. James C. Maxwell. Ed. by P. M. Harman. (Illus.). 1056p. (C). 1995. text ed. 295.00 (*0-521-25626-7*) Cambridge U Pr.

Scientific Letters & Papers, Vol. 1: 1846-1862. James C. Maxwell. Ed. by P. M. Harman. (Illus.). 750p. (C). 1990. text ed. 235.00 (*0-521-25625-9*) Cambridge U Pr.

Scientific Literacy & Environmental Policy: The Missing Prerequisite for Sound Decision Making. Dorothy J. Howell. LC 91-36028. 200p. 1992. text ed. 49.95 (*0-89930-616-0*, HPB/, Quorum Bks) Greenwood.

Scientific Literacy & the Myth of the Scientific Method. Henry H. Bauer. 192p. 1992. 24.95 (*0-252-01856-7*) U of Ill Pr.

Scientific Literacy & the Myth of the Scientific Method. Henry H. Bauer. 192p. 1994. 13.95 (*0-252-06436-4*) U of Ill Pr.

Scientific Literacy of Australian Students. Malcoln E. Rosier. (C). 1992. 75.00 (*0-86431-069-2*, Pub. by Aust Council Educ Res AT) St Mut.

Scientific London. Bernard H. Becker. 340p. 1968. reprint ed. 30.00 (*0-7146-2328-8*, Pub. by F Cass Pubs UK) Intl Spec Bk.

Scientific Malpractice. Ivan Zabilka. 160p. 1992. pap. 8.95 (*0-917851-17-X*) Bristol Hse.

Scientific Man & the Bible: A Personal Testimony. unabridged ed. Howard A. Kelly. LC 95-78100. 158p. 1996. reprint ed. 12.95 (*1-886787-01-8*) Messengers Hope.

Scientific Management. 2nd rev. ed. Horace B. Drury. LC 68-56654. (Columbia University. Studies in the Social Sciences: No. 157). 1922. 37.50 (*0-404-51157-0*) AMS Pr.

Scientific Management: Frederick Winslow Taylor's Gift to the World? Ed. by J. C. Spender & Hugo J. Kijne. LC 96-28080. 191p. (C). 1996. lib. bdg. 105.00 (*0-7923-9758-4*) Kluwer Ac.

Scientific Management & Labor. Robert F. Hoxie. LC 66-21677. (Reprints of Economic Classics Ser.). x, 302p. 1966. reprint ed. pap. text ed. 39.50 (*0-678-00169-3*) Kelley.

Scientific Management, Comprising Shop Management, the Principles of Scientific Management, & Testimony Before the Special House Committee, 3 vols. in 1. Frederick W. Taylor. LC 77-138133. (Illus.). 207p. 1972. reprint ed. text ed. 115.00 (*0-8371-5706-4*, TASM) Greenwood.

*__Scientific Management in Action: Taylorism at Watertown Arsenal, 1908-1915.__ Hugh G. Aitken. LC 84-26462. 288p. 1985. reprint ed. pap. 82.10 (*0-608-02940-8*, 2064006) Bks Demand.

Scientific Management in Education. J. M. Rice. LC 70-89225. (American Education). 1975. reprint ed. 23.95 (*0-405-01462-7*) Ayer.

Scientific Management of Library Operations. 2nd ed. Richard M. Dougherty et al. LC 81-18200. 286p. 1982. 27.50 (*0-8108-1485-4*) Scarecrow.

Scientific Management of Temperate Communities for Conservation. Ian F. Spellerberg et al. 1991. pap. 65.00 (*0-632-03186-7*) Blackwell Sci.

Scientific Management, Socialist Discipline, & Soviet Power. Mark R. Beissinger. LC 87-30887. (Russian Research Center Studies: No. 84). 376p. 1988. 39.95 (0-674-79490-7) HUP.

Scientific Manual of Clinical Virology. Taylor & Ronalds. 350p. Date not set. write for info. (0-7506-1469-2) Buttrwrth-Heinemann.

Scientific Marketing Management. Percival White. Ed. by Henry Assael. LC 78-272. (Century of Marketing Ser.). 1979. reprint ed. lib. bdg. 29.95 (0-405-11163-0) Ayer.

Scientific Materialism. Mario Bunge. 233p. 1981. lib. bdg. 112.00 (90-277-1304-9, D Reidel) Kluwer Ac.

Scientific Measurement of International Conflict: Handbook of Datasets on Crises & Wars, 1495-1988 A. D. Claudio Cioffi-Revilla. LC 89-39491. 88p. 1990. pap. text ed. 15.95 (1-55587-194-1) Lynne Rienner.

*Scientific Measurements. Roberts. Date not set. 1.20 (0-7167-9171-4) W H Freeman.

*Scientific Meeting on Rehabilitation in Leprosy. (Technical Report Ser.: No. 221). 37p. 1961. pap. text ed. 3.00 (92-4-120221-1) World Health.

Scientific Memoirs. John W. Draper. LC 72-9194. (Literature of Photography Ser.). 1973. reprint ed. 35.95 (0-405-04904-8) Ayer.

Scientific Memoirs. John W. Draper. (Notable American Authors Ser.). 1992. reprint ed. lib. bdg. 75.00 (0-7812-2705-4) Rprt Serv.

Scientific Metaphysics see Collected Papers of Charles Sanders Peirce

Scientific Method: A Historical & Philosophical Introduction. Barry Gower. LC 96-7865. 288p. (C). 1996. pap. 18.95 (0-415-12282-1); text ed. 65.00 (0-415-12281-3) Routledge.

Scientific Method: The Hypothetico-Experimental Laboratory Procedure of the Physical Sciences. James K. Feibleman. 254p. 1972. pap. text ed. 64.50 (90-247-1200-9, Pub. by M Nijhoff NE) Kluwer Ac.

Scientific Method & Social Research. 3rd ed. B. N. Ghosh. 254p. (C). 1984. text ed. 30.00 (0-86590-723-4, Pub. by Sterling Pubs II) Apt Bks.

Scientific Methods: Conceptual & Historical Problems. Ed. by Peter Achinstein & Laura J. Snyder. LC 93-47265. (Open Forum Ser.). 168p. (Orig.). (C). 1994. pap. 19.50 (0-89464-822-5) Krieger.

Scientific Methods for the Study of Polymer Colloids & Their Applications: Proceedings of the NATO Advanced Study Institute on Polymer Colloids Held in Strasbourg, France, July 3-15, 1988. Ed. by Francoise Candau & Ronald H. Ottewill. (C). 1990. lib. bdg. 247.00 (0-7923-0599-X) Kluwer Ac.

Scientific Methods of Urban Analysis. Anthony J. Catanese. LC 71-160384. 352p. reprint ed. pap. 100.40 (0-7837-5733-6, 2045394) Bks Demand.

Scientific Model of Social & Cultural Evolution. Robert B. Graber. 206p. (Orig.). (C). 1994. lib. bdg. 36.50 (0-943549-19-1) TJU Pr.

Scientific Monitoring Strategies for Ocean Waste Disposal. Ed. by Hood et al. LC 84-29701. (Oceanic Processes in Marine Pollution Ser.: Vol. 4). 302p. (C). 1989. lib. bdg. 62.50 (0-89874-813-5) Krieger.

Scientific Nature of Geomorphology: Proceedings of the 27th Binghamton Symposium in Geomorphology, Held 27-29 September 1996. Ed. by Bruce L. Rhoads & Colin E. Thorn. LC 96-14602. 1996. text ed. 145.00 (0-471-96811-0) Wiley.

Scientific Nihilism: On the Loss & Recovery of Physical Explanation. Daniel Athearn. LC 93-12869. (SUNY Series in Philosophy). 387p. 1994. text ed. 64.50 (0-7914-1807-3); pap. text ed. 21.95 (0-7914-1808-1) State U NY Pr.

Scientific Objectives, Philosophy & Management of the MOCAT Project. John A. Dutton. LC 77-136104. 141p. 1969. 19.00 (0-403-04497-9) Scholarly.

Scientific 100: A Ranking of the Most Influential Scientists Past & Present. John Simmons. (Illus.). 400p. Date not set. 25.95 (0-8065-1749-2, Citadel Pr) Carol Pub Group.

Scientific Palm Reading. Gopi Sharma. (Orig.). (C). 1993. 15.00 (81-202-0371-2, Pub. by Ajanta II) S Asia.

Scientific Papers, 4 vols. Bruce G. Batchelor & George K. Batchelor. Incl. Vol. 1. Mechanics of Solids. 95.00 (0-521-06608-5); write for info. (0-318-51295-5) Cambridge U Pr.

Scientific Papers: Ed. by C. S. Sargent. Asa Gray. (Notable American Authors Ser.). 1992. reprint ed. lib. bdg. 75.00 (0-7812-2951-0) Rprt Serv.

*Scientific Papers & Presentations. Martha Davis. LC 96-28241. (Illus.). 296p. 1996. pap. 19.95 (0-12-206370-8, AP Prof) Acad Pr.

Scientific Papers of Arthur Holly Compton. Arthur H. Compton. Ed. by Robert S. Shankland. 816p. 1974. lib. bdg. 60.00 (0-226-11430-9) U Ch Pr.

Scientific Papers of C. V. Raman, Vol. 1: Scattering of Light. Chandrasekhara V. Raman. Ed. by S. Ramaseshan. (Illus.). 608p. 1989. 55.00 (81-85324-01-8) OUP.

Scientific Papers of C. V. Raman, Vol. 2: Acoustics. Chandrasekhara V. Raman. Ed. by S. Ramaseshan. (Illus.). 668p. 1989. 55.00 (81-85324-02-6) OUP.

Scientific Papers of C. V. Raman, Vol. 3: Optics. Chandrasekhara V. Raman. Ed. by S. Ramaseshan. (Illus.). 576p. 1989. 55.00 (81-85324-03-4) OUP.

Scientific Papers of C. V. Raman, Vol. 4: Optics of Minerals & Diamond. Chandrasekhara V. Raman. Ed. by S. Ramaseshan. (Illus.). 766p. 1989. 55.00 (81-85324-04-2) OUP.

Scientific Papers of C. V. Raman, Vol. 5: Physics of Crystals. Chandrasekhara V. Raman. Ed. by S. Ramaseshan. (Illus.). 874p. 1989. 55.00 (81-85324-05-0) OUP.

Scientific Papers of C. V. Raman, Vol. 6: Floral Colors & Visual Perception. Chandrasekhara V. Raman. Ed. by S. Ramaseshan. (Illus.). 636p. 1989. 55.00 (81-85324-06-9) OUP.

Scientific Papers of J. Willard Gibbs: Dynamics, Vector Analysis, Multiple Algebra, Electromagnetic Theory of Light, Vol. 2. Josiah W. Gibbs. LC 93-19391. viii, 284p. 1994. pap. 34.00 (1-881987-06-X) Ox Bow.

Scientific Papers of J. Willard Gibbs: Thermodynamics, Vol. 1. Josiah W. Gibbs. LC 93-19391. xxviii, 434p. 1993. reprint ed. pap. 32.00 (0-918024-77-3) Ox Bow.

Scientific Papers of Tjalling C. Koopmans, Vol. 2. Tjalling C. Koopmans. 320p. 1985. 42.00 (0-262-11106-3) MIT Pr.

Scientific Papers of William F. Giauque, 1950-1968 Vol. II: Low Temperature, Chemical, & Magneto Thermodynamics. W. F. Giauque. xxxvi, 419p. 1995. 35.00 (0-9647359-0-3) Giauque Sci Papers Found.

Scientific Papers of William F. Giauque, 1968-1978 Vol. III: Low Temperature, Chemical, & Magneto Thermodynamics. W. F. Giauque. xxx, 515p. 1995. 35.00 (0-9647359-1-1) Giauque Sci Papers Found.

Scientific Pascal. 2nd ed. Harley Flanders. LC 95-35243. 1995. write for info. (3-7643-3760-5) Birkhauser.

Scientific Pascal. 2nd rev. ed. Harley Flanders. LC 95-35243. 600p. 1995. 42.50 incl. 3.5 hd (0-8176-3760-5) Birkhauser.

Scientific Philosophy: Origins & Developments. Ed. by Friedrich Stadler. (Vienna Circle Institute Yearbook Ser.). 324p. (C). 1993. lib. bdg. 122.00 (0-7923-2526-5, Pub. by Klwr Acad Pubs NE) Kluwer Ac.

Scientific Philosophy Today. Ed. by Joseph Agassi & Robert S. Cohen. 523p. 1981. lib. bdg. 171.00 (90-277-1262-X, D Reidel) Kluwer Ac.

Scientific Photomacrography: Recording Specimens at Magnifications Between x1 & x50. B. Bracegirdle. (Royal Microscopial Society Handbook Ser.: No. 31). (Illus.). 160p. (Orig.). 1995. pap. 42.50 (1-872748-49-X, Pub. by Bios Scientific UK) Coronet Bks.

Scientific Practice: Theories & Stories of Doing Physics. Ed. by Jed Z. Buchwald. LC 94-49715. 412p. 1995. pap. text ed. 24.95 (0-226-07890-6); lib. bdg. 65.00 (0-226-07889-2) U Ch Pr.

*Scientific Practice & Ordinary Action: Ethnomethodology & Social Studies of Science. 355p. 1997. pap. text ed. 21.95 (0-521-59742-0) Cambridge U Pr.

Scientific Practice & Ordinary Action: Ethnomethodology & Social Studies of Science. Michael Lynch. (Illus.). 350p. (C). 1994. text ed. 59.95 (0-521-43152-2) Cambridge U Pr.

Scientific Principles & Practices of Health-Related Fitness. Allen W. Jackson. (Illus.). 304p. (Orig.). 1994. pap. text ed. 22.95 (0-87322-864-2, BJAC0864) Human Kinetics.

*Scientific Principles of Anesthesia. Debra Schwinn. LC 97-11333. (Atlas of Anesthesia Ser.). 1997. write for info. (0-443-07901-3) Churchill.

Scientific Problem Solving: An Introduction to Technology. John Aitken & George Mills. (J). (gr. 4-6). 1989. pap. 12.99 (0-8224-6324-5) Fearon Teach Aids.

Scientific Problems of Coal Utilization: Proceedings. Ed. by Bernard R. Cooper. LC 78-9553. (DOE Symposium Ser.). 409p. 1978. pap. 18.50 (0-87079-400-0, CONF-770509); fiche 9.00 (0-87079-378-0, CONF-770509) DOE.

Scientific Proceedings American Animal Hospital Association Annual Meeting. 662p. 1986. 42.00 (0-9616498-5-2) Am Animal Hosp Assoc.

Scientific Proceedings of the Annual Meeting of the American Animal Hospital Association. American Animal Hospital Association Staff. 467p. 1984. 9.50 (0-9616498-7-9) Am Animal Hosp Assoc.

Scientific Proceedings of the Annual Meeting of the American Animal Hospital Association, 1981. American Animal Hospital Association Staff. 408p. 1981. 9.50 (0-685-43407-9) Am Animal Hosp Assoc.

Scientific Process. S. D. Ross. 163p. 1971. pap. text ed. 47.00 (90-247-5026-1, Pub. by M Nijhoff NE) Kluwer Ac.

Scientific Process & the Computer. Donald N. Streeter. LC 73-21744. 480p. reprint ed. pap. 136.80 (0-317-08515-8, 2007078) Bks Demand.

Scientific Processes: Origin of Knowledge. Robert C. Anderson. 92p. 1992. student ed. 13.35 (0-9634298-4-1) Cricket Sci.

Scientific Processes: Origin of Knowledge. Robert C. Anderson. (Illus.). 102p. (C). 1994. 18.95 (0-9634298-9-2) Cricket Sci.

Scientific Processing Using FORTRAN 77. T. Turner. (C). 1989. 100.00 (0-09-161601-8, Pub. by S Thornes Pubs UK) St Mut.

Scientific Program & Abstracts: International CODATA Conference, 10th, July 14-17, 1986, Ottawa, Canada. Ed. by CODATA Staff. (CODATA Bulletin Ser.). 102p. 1986. pap. 15.00 (0-08-032529-7, Pergamon Pr) Elsevier.

Scientific Programmer's Toolkit: Turbo Pascal Edition. M. H. Beilby et al. (Illus.). 438p. 1990. 198.00 incl. disk (0-7503-0038-8) IOP Pub.

Scientific Programmer's Toolkit: Turbo Pascal Edition. M. H. Beilby et al. (Illus.). 438p. 1991. 240.00 incl. disk (0-7503-0127-9) IOP Pub.

Scientific Progress. 2nd ed. Craig Dilworth. 1986. lib. bdg. 101.50 (90-277-2215-3) Kluwer Ac.

Scientific Progress: A Study Concerning the Nature of the Relation Between Successive Scientific Theories. 3rd ed. Ed. by Craig Dilworth. LC 93-6199. (Synthese Library). 242p. (C). 1994. pap. text ed. 43.50 (0-7923-2488-9, Pub. by Klwr Acad Pubs NE); lib. bdg. 102.00 (0-7923-2487-0, Pub. by Klwr Acad Pubs NE) Kluwer Ac.

Scientific Progress Goes "Boink" Bill Watterson. (Illus.). 128p. (Orig.). 1991. pap. 9.95 (0-8362-1878-7) Andrews & McMeel.

Scientific Publication System in Social Science. Duncan Lindsey. LC 78-62570. (Jossey-Bass Social & Behavioral Science Ser.). 189p. reprint ed. pap. 53.90 (0-8357-4994-0, 2037927) Bks Demand.

Scientific Publications of Charles Wilkins Short: Original Anthology. Ed. by Keir B. Sterling. LC 77-81125. (Biologists & Their World Ser.). 1978. lib. bdg. 35.95 (0-405-10721-8) Ayer.

Scientific Racism in Modern South Africa. Saul Dubow. (Illus.). 384p. (C). 1995. text ed. 64.95 (0-521-47343-8); pap. text ed. 22.95 (0-521-47907-X) Cambridge U Pr.

Scientific Rationality: Studies in the Foundations of Science & Ethics. Ed. by Risto Hilpinen. (Philosophical Studies in Philosophy: No. 21). 263p. 1980. lib. bdg. 112.00 (90-277-1112-7, D Reidel) Kluwer Ac.

Scientific Realism: A Critical Reappraisal. Nicholas Rescher. (University of Western Ontario Series in Phylosophy of Science: No. 40). 182p. 1900. pap. text ed. 51.50 (90-277-2528-4) Kluwer Ac.

Scientific Realism: A Critical Reappraisal. Nicholas Rescher. (University of Western Ontario Series in Phylosophy of Science: No. 40). 182p. 1987. lib. bdg. 110.00 (90-277-2442-3) Kluwer Ac.

Scientific Realism & Human Emancipation. Roy Bhaskar. 308p. (C). 1986. text ed. 19.00 (0-86091-143-8, Pub. by Vrso UK) Norton.

Scientific Realism & the Plasticity of Mind. P. M. Churchland. LC 78-73240. (Cambridge Studies in Philosophy). (Illus.). 178p. 1979. text ed. 59.95 (0-521-22632-5) Cambridge U Pr.

Scientific Realism & the Plasticity of Mind. P. M. Churchland. LC 78-73240. (Cambridge Studies in Philosophy). (Illus.). 168p. 1986. pap. text ed. 20.95 (0-521-33827-1) Cambridge U Pr.

Scientific, Reasoning & Epistemic Attitudes. Laszlo Harsing. 148p. (C). 1982. pap. 30.00 (963-05-3003-1, Pub. by Akad Kiado HU) St Mut.

Scientific Reasoning for Social Workers. Leonard E. Gibbs. 314p. (C). 1990. text ed. 55.00 (0-675-21079-8, Merrill Coll) P-H.

Scientific Reinterpretation of Form. Norma E. Emerton. LC 84-45139. (Cornell History of Science Ser.). 320p. 1984. 47.50 (0-8014-1583-7) Cornell U Pr.

Scientific Renaissance, 1450-1630. Marie B. Hall. (Illus.). 876p. 1994. reprint ed. pap. 9.95 (0-486-28115-9) Dover.

Scientific Research: Continued Vigilance Critical to Protecting Human Subjects. 46p. (Orig.). (C). 1996. pap. text ed. 20.00 (0-7881-2869-8) DIANE Pub.

*Scientific Research - Military & Civilian, Vol. 1. Louis Gerken. (Illus.). 300p. (C). 1997. 40.00 incl. trans. (0-9617163-6-3, Helvetica) Amer Scientific.

Scientific Research in the Federal Republic of Germany: Essays on the Constitutional, Administrative & Financial Problems. Ed. by Andrea Orsi-Battaglini & Ulrich Karpen. 279p. 1990. 53.00 (3-7890-1913-5, Pub. by Nomos Verlags GW) Intl Bk Import.

Scientific Research on Maharishi's Transcendental Meditation & TM-Sidhi Program, Vol. 5. 830p. 1990. 60.00 (0-923569-07-3, B-05) Maharishi U Mgmt Pr.

Scientific Results of Cruise VII of the "Carnegie" During 1928-1929, under Command of Captain J. P. Ault: The Work of the Carnegie & Suggestions for Future Scientific Cruises. 1946. pap. 7.00 (0-87279-582-9) Carnegie Inst.

Scientific Results of the Viking Project. Ed. by E. Flinn. (Illus.). 725p. 1977. 15.00 (0-87590-207-3) Am Geophysical.

Scientific Reviews of Arid Zone Research. Ed. by Hony et al. (C). 1988. 400.00 (0-317-92352-8, Pub. by Scientific UK) St Mut.

Scientific Reviews on Arid Zone Research, 5 vols., 4. H. S. Maan. (C). 1991. 350.00 (0-685-60029-7, Pub. by Scientific Pubs II) St Mut.

Scientific Reviews on Arid Zone Research, 5 vols., Set, Vols. 1-6. H. S. Maan. (C). 1991. Set. write for info. (81-85046-06-9, Pub. by Scientific Pubs II) St Mut.

Scientific Reviews on Arid Zone Research, 5 vols., Vols. 1-3 & 5-6. H. S. Maan. (C). 1991. Vols. 1-3 & Vols. 5-6. 250.00 (0-685-74447-7, Pub. by Scientific Pubs II) St Mut.

Scientific Revolution. James A. Corrick. (ABC-CLIO World Companions Ser.). (Illus.). 256p. 1997. lib. bdg. 55.00 (0-87436-875-8) ABC-CLIO.

Scientific Revolution. Harry Henderson & Lisa Yount. LC 95-51342. (World History Ser.). 112p. (J). 1996. lib. bdg. 17.96 (1-56006-283-5) Lucent Bks.

Scientific Revolution. W. E. Middleton. 88p. 1965. pap. 11.95 (0-87073-851-8) Schenkman Bks Inc.

Scientific Revolution. Steven Shapin. LC 96-13196. (Illus.). 200p. 1996. 19.95 (0-226-75020-5) U Ch Pr.

Scientific Revolution. Steven Shapin. LC 96-13196. 1996. pap. write for info. (0-226-75021-3) U Ch Pr.

Scientific Revolution: A Historiographical Inquiry. H. Floris Cohen. LC 93-41784. 680p. 1994. pap. text ed. 26.95 (0-226-11280-2) U Ch Pr.

Scientific Revolution: A Historiographical Inquiry. H. Floris Cohen. LC 93-41784. 680p. 1994. lib. bdg. 75.00 (0-226-11279-9) U Ch Pr.

*Scientific Revolution: An Annotated Bibliography. S. A. Jayawardene. LC 95-43553. (Illus.). 383p. (C). 1996. lib. bdg. 60.00 (0-933951-71-X) Locust Hill Pr.

Scientific Revolution: Aspirations & Achievements, 1500-1700. James R. Jacob. LC 97-17851. (Control of Nature Ser.). (Illus.). (C). 1997. 39.95 (0-391-03977-6) Humanities.

Scientific Revolution: Aspirations & Achievements, 1500-1700. James R. Jacob. LC 97-17851. (Control of Nature Ser.). (Illus.). (C). 1997. pap. 12.50 (0-391-03978-4) Humanities.

*Scientific Revolution & the Origins of Modern Science. John Henry. LC 96-2760. (Studies in European History). 1997. text ed. 10.95 (0-312-16540-4) St Martin.

Scientific Revolution in National Context. Ed. by Roy Porter & Mikulas Teich. 400p. (C). 1992. text ed. 69.95 (0-521-39510-0); pap. text ed. 24.95 (0-521-39699-9) Cambridge U Pr.

Scientific Revolution in Victorian Medicine. Youngson. (Australian National University Press Ser.). 1996. text ed. write for info. (0-08-032982-9, Pergamon Pr) Elsevier.

Scientific Revolutions. Ian Hacking. (Oxford Readings in Philosophy Ser.). 186p. (C). 1981. pap. text ed. 16.95 (0-19-875051-X) OUP.

Scientific Revolutions: What Science Actually Is, Myth & Reality. 1991. lib. bdg. 76.95 (0-8490-4637-8) Gordon Pr.

*Scientific Romance. Wright. Date not set. write for info. (0-312-18172-8) St Martin.

Scientific Romances: First & Second Series, 2 vols, in 1. Howard C. Hinton. LC 75-36841. (Occult Ser.). 1976. reprint ed. 34.95 (0-405-07954-0) Ayer.

Scientific Russian. George E. Condoyannis. LC 77-16615. 238p. 1978. reprint ed. pap. 17.50 (0-88275-643-5) Krieger.

Scientific Russian: Readings in Russian Science & Technology. ACTR Staff & Simes-Timofejeva. 176p. 1993. per. 30.00 (0-8403-8586-2) Kendall-Hunt.

Scientific Satellite Programmed During the International Magnetospheric Study: Proceedings, Vol. 57. Astrophysics & Space Science Staff. Ed. by K. Knott & Bruce Battrick. LC 75-44353. 1975. lib. bdg. 152.00 (90-277-0688-3) Kluwer Ac.

Scientific Satellites - Mission & Design. Ed. by I. E. Jeter. (Advances in the Astronautical Sciences Ser.: Vol. 12). 1962. 25.00 (0-87703-013-8) Univelt Inc.

Scientific Socialism & Self-Reliance. Jan M. Haakonsen. (Bergen Studies in Social Anthropology: No. 34). (Illus.). 172p. 1985. pap. text ed. 13.95 (0-936508-66-3, Pub. by Bergen Univ Dept Social Anthro NO) Barber Pr.

Scientific Societies: Conversations on Change. Task Force of Scientists Staff. (Special Publications: Vol. 20). (Illus.). 23p. (Orig.). 1996. pap. 10.00 (1-887383-06-9) CAST.

Scientific Software Systems. Ed. by J. C. Mason. 200p. (gr. 13). 1990. text ed. 74.95 (0-412-34570-6, 836) Chapman & Hall.

Scientific Space Selection. Audit Bureau of Circulations Staff. LC 75-22798. (America in Two Centuries Ser.). 1976. reprint ed. 18.95 (0-405-07669-X) Ayer.

Scientific Spirit & Democratic Faith: Conference on the Scientific Spirit & Democratic Faith, 1st, New York, 1943. LC 72-121457. (Essay Index Reprint Ser.). 1977. 17.95 (0-8369-1872-X) Ayer.

Scientific Standards of Psychological Practice: Issues & Recommendations. Ed. by Steven C. Hayes et al. (Illus.). 288p. (C). 1995. text ed. 34.95 (1-878978-23-3) Context Pr.

Scientific Strategies to Save Your Life. Bross. (Statistics: Textbooks & Monographs: Vol. 35). 272p. 1981. 99.75 (0-8247-1273-0) Dekker.

Scientific Studies Vol. 12. Johann W. Von Goethe. Ed. & Tr. by Douglas Miller. LC 95-36597. (Princeton Paperbacks Ser.). 370p. (C). 1994. pap. text ed. 19.95 (0-691-04347-7) Princeton U Pr.

Scientific Studies in Special Creation. 2nd ed. Intro. by Walter E. Lammerts. LC 70-150955. (Illus.). 343p. 1990. reprint ed. pap. 9.95 (0-940384-08-6) Creation Research.

*Scientific Study of Human Nature: Tribute to Hans J. Eysenck at Eighty. Helmuth Nyborg. LC 97-15771. 1997. write for info. (0-08-042787-1) Elsevier.

Scientific Study of Human Society. Franklin H. Giddings. LC 73-14155. (Perspectives in Social Inquiry Ser.). 264p. 1974. reprint ed. 16.95 (0-405-05501-3) Ayer.

Scientific Study of Marihuana. Ed. by Ernest L. Abel. LC 76-4508. 320p. 1976. 40.95 (0-88229-144-0) Nelson-Hall.

Scientific Study of Peace & War. John Vasquez. 479p. Date not set. pap. 17.95 (0-669-20105-7, Lexington) Jossey-Bass.

Scientific Study of Personality. Hans J. Eysenck. LC 81-20077. xiii, 320p. 1982. reprint ed. text ed. 45.50 (0-313-23241-5, EYSS, Greenwood Pr) Greenwood.

Scientific Study of Social Behaviour. Michael Argyle. LC 73-13021. (Illus.). 239p. 1974. reprint ed. text ed. 59.75 (0-8371-7108-3, ARSS, Greenwood Pr) Greenwood.

Scientific Study of the College Student. Harry D. Kitson. Bd. with Whole vs. Part Methods in Motor Learning. L. A. Pechstein. ; Vol. 2, No. 2. Yale Psychology Studies. Ed. by R. P. Angier. ; Vertical-Horizontal Illusion. S. M. Ritter. (Psychological Monographs General & Applied: Vol. 23). 1974. reprint ed. 55.00 (0-8115-1422-6) Periodicals Srv.

Scientific Style & Format: The CBE Manual for Authors, Editors, & Publishers. 6th rev. ed. CBE Style Manual Committee. LC 83-7172. (Council of Biology Editors Manual Ser.). (Illus.). 825p. (C). 1995. text ed. 39.95 (0-521-47154-0) Coun Biology Eds.

Scientific Success. Harvey A. Cook & Duane E. Pederson. Ed. by Samila S. Nickell & Holly W. Bushnell. (Scientific Selling Ser.). 179p. (Orig.). 1989. pap. write for info. (0-9626547-0-1) Sell Perfect.

Scientific Support for Scriptural Stories. R. Clayton Brough & Rodney D. Griffin. 1992. 18.98 (0-88290-450-7) Horizon Utah.

Scientific Survey of Puerto Rico & the Virgin Islands: An Eighty-Year Reassessment of the Islands' Natural History. Julio C. Fugueroa Colon. LC 95-52608. (Annals of the New York Academy of Sciences Ser.: Vol. 776). 1996. text ed. write for info. (0-89766-949-5) NY Acad Sci.

An Asterisk (*) at the beginning of an entry indicates that the title is appearing in BIP for the first time.

Scientific Survey of Puerto Rico & the Virgin Islands: An Eighty-Year Reassessment of the Islands' Natural History. Ed. by Julio C. Figueroa Colon. LC 95-52608. (Annals of the New York Academy of Sciences Ser.: Vol. 776). 273p. 1996. pap. 80.00 (*0-89766-950-9*) NY Acad Sci.

Scientific-Technical Backgrounds for Biotechnology Regulations: Based on the Lectures Given During the Eurocourse on 'Scientific-Technical Backgrounds for Biotechnology Regulations' Held at the Joint Research Centre Ispra, Italy, June 4-7, 1991. Ed. by F. Campagnari et al. LC 94-1388. (Eurocourses: Technological Innovation Ser.: Vol. 2). 196p. (C). 1994. lib. bdg. 106.00 (*0-7923-1587-1*) Kluwer Ac.

Scientific Temper: An Empirical Study. Binay K. Pattnaik. (C). 1992. 22.00 (*81-7033-176-5*, Pub. by Rawat II) S Asia.

Scientific Terms, Aeronautics: Japanese-English, English-Japanese. Ministry of Education Staff. 235p. (ENG & JPN.). 1973. 39.95 (*0-8288-6328-8*, M-9347) Fr & Eur.

Scientific Terms, Chemistry: Japanese-English, English-Japanese. Japan, Ministry of Education Staff. 630p. (ENG & JPN.). 1974. 95.00 (*0-7859-0791-2*, M-9335) Fr & Eur.

Scientific Terms Electrical Engineering. Japan, Ministry of Education Staff. 675p. (ENG & JPN.). 1979. 125.00 (*0-8288-4835-1*, M9330) Fr & Eur.

Scientific Terms Mathematics: Japanese-English, English-Japanese. deluxe ed. Japan, Ministry of Education Staff. 146p. (ENG & JPN.). 1954. 95.00 (*0-8288-6874-3*, M-9346) Fr & Eur.

Scientific Terms Meteorology: Japanese-English, English-Japanese. deluxe ed. Japan, Ministry of Education Staff. 140p. (ENG & JPN.). 1975. 49.95 (*0-8288-5944-2*, M9338) Fr & Eur.

Scientific Terms Naval Architecture & Marine Engineering: Japanese-English, English-Japanese. deluxe ed. Japan, Ministry of Education Staff. 526p. (ENG & JPN.). 1955. 59.95 (*0-8288-6868-9*, M-9337) Fr & Eur.

Scientific Terms Nuclear Engineering: Japanese-English, English-Japanese. deluxe ed. Japan, Ministry of Education Staff. 282p. (ENG & JPN.). 1977. 49.95 (*0-8288-5516-1*, M9336) Fr & Eur.

Scientific Terms Physics: Japanese-English, English-Japanese. Japan, Ministry of Education Staff. 221p. (ENG & JPN.). 1954. 95.00 (*0-8288-6875-1*, M-9343) Fr & Eur.

Scientific Terms Spectroscopy: Japanese-English, English-Japanese. Japan, Ministry of Education Staff. 165p. (ENG & JPN.). 1974. 75.00 (*0-8288-6211-7*, M-9341) Fr & Eur.

Scientific Theism. Arvid Reuterdahl. 1926. 25.00 (*0-8159-6805-1*) Devin.

Scientific Theism. Francis E. Abbot. LC 75-3012. (Philosophy in America Ser.). reprint ed. 39.50 (*0-404-59004-7*) AMS Pr.

Scientific Theist: A Life of Francis Ellingwood Abbot. Sydney E. Ahlstrom & Robert B. Mullin. LC 86-33128. 208p. 1987. 29.95 (*0-86554-236-8*, H208) Mercer Univ Pr.

***Scientific Theory & Religious Belief: An Essay on the Rationality of Views of Life.** Eberhard Herrmann. (Studies in Philosophical Theology: Vol. 16). 128p. 1995. pap. 37.50 (*90-390-0222-3*, Pub. by KOK Pharos NE) Eisenbrauns.

Scientific Theory of Culture. Bronislaw Malinowski. LC 44-8385. x, 228p. (C). 1990. reprint ed. pap. 14.95 (*0-8078-4283-4*) U of NC Pr.

***Scientific Theory of Culture, & Other Essays by Bronislaw Malinowski with a Preface by Huntington Cairns.** Bronislaw Malinowski. LC 44-8385. 238p. pap. 67.90 (*0-608-05213-2*, 2065750) Bks Demand.

***Scientific Thinking.** Robert M. Martin. 180p. 1997. pap. 16.95 (*1-55111-130-6*) Broadview Pr.

***Scientific Thought: 1923 Edition.** C. D. Broad. 560p. 1996. reprint ed. write for info. (*1-85506-230-5*) Bks Intl VA.

Scientific Thought & Social Reality: Essays by Michael Polanyi. Michael Polanyi. Ed. by Fred Schwartz. LC 74-5420. (Psychological Issues Monograph: No. 32, Vol. 8, No. 4). 168p. (C). 1974. 27.50 (*0-8236-6005-2*) Intl Univs Pr.

Scientific Thought in Poetry. Ralph B. Crum. LC 31-29142. reprint ed. 20.00 (*0-404-01868-8*) AMS Pr.

Scientific Training for Girls: An Education Above All Suspicion? Ed. by UNESCO, French National Commission Staff. 150p. 1995. pap. 39.95 (*1-85302-346-9*, Pub. by J Kingsley Pubs UK) Taylor & Francis.

Scientific Traveler: A Guide to the People, Places, & Institutions of Europe. Charles Tanford & Jacqueline Reynolds. (Science Editions Ser.). 352p. 1992. pap. text ed. 16.95 (*0-471-55566-5*) Wiley.

Scientific Traveler Guide. Charles Tanford. (Science Editions Ser.). 1992. write for info. (*0-471-57698-0*) Wiley.

Scientific Truth & Statistical Method. M. Boldrini. 1972. 35.00 (*0-85264-197-4*) Lubrecht & Cramer.

Scientific Uncertainty & Environmental Problem Solving. Ed. by John Lemons. LC 95-36595. (Environmental Sciences Library). 512p. 1996. 80.00 (*0-86542-476-4*) Blackwell Sci.

***Scientific Uncertainty & Its Influence on the Public Communication Process: Proceedings of the NATO Advanced Research Workshop, Paris, France, September 8-10, 1994.** Vincent T. Covello & Tim L. Tinker. Ed. by Virginia H. Sublet. LC 96-28467. (NATO ASI Series D: Behavioural & Social Sciences). 248p. (C). 1996. lib. bdg. 127.00 (*0-7923-4180-5*) Kluwer Ac.

Scientific Unit Conversion: Practical Guide to Metrication, Vol. XVI. Francois Cardarelli. (Illus.). 456p. 1997. pap. 39.95 (*3-540-76022-9*) Spr-Verlag.

Scientific Uses of Earth Satellites. James A. Van Allen. LC 56-11813. 326p. reprint ed. pap. 93.00 (*0-317-07811-9*, 2055659) Bks Demand.

Scientific Validation of Herbal Medicine. Daniel B. Mowrey. 336p. (Orig.). 1990. pap. 14.95 (*0-87983-534-6*) Keats.

Scientific Vegetarianism. Edmond B. Szekely. (Illus.). 56p. 1977. pap. 3.50 (*0-89564-041-4*) IBS Intl.

***Scientific Visualization.** Crane & Naqui. 1997. text ed. 68.00 (*0-13-861683-3*) P-H.

Scientific Visualization. William Schroeder. 816p. 1996. pap. 59.95 (*0-13-199837-4*) P-H.

Scientific Visualization: Advanced Software Techniques. Ed. by Patrizia Palamidese. LC 93-19127. (Ellis Horwood Workshop Ser.). 1993. 59.50 (*0-13-710337-9*, Pub. by Tavistock-E Horwood UK) Routledge Chapman & Hall.

Scientific Visualization: Advances & Challenges. Gregory M. Nielson et al. (Illus.). 532p. 1994. boxed 49.95 (*0-12-227742-2*) Acad Pr.

***Scientific Visualization: Overviews, Methodologies, & Techniques.** Gregory M. Nielson et al. LC 97-5922. 400p. 1997. 69.00 (*0-8186-7777-5*, BP07777) IEEE Comp Soc.

Scientific Visualization: Techniques & Applications. Ed. by K. W. Brodlie et al. (Illus.). xxv, 284p. 1992. 91.95 (*0-387-54565-4*) Spr-Verlag.

Scientific Visualization & Graphics Simulation. Ed. by Daniel Thalmann. LC 90-12445. 264p. 1990. text ed. 62.95 (*0-471-92742-2*) Wiley.

Scientific Visualization in Mathematics & Science Teaching. Ed. by David A. Thomas. (Illus.). 350p. (Orig.). 1994. pap. 35.00 (*1-880094-09-6*) Assn Advan Comput Educ.

Scientific Visualization of Physical Phenomena. Ed. by N. M. Patrikalakis. (Illus.). c, 706p. 1991. 216.95 (*0-387-70081-1*) Spr-Verlag.

***Scientific Visualization '95: Proceedings of the International Symposium.** 160p. 1995. 30.00 (*981-02-2461-3*) World Scientific Pub.

Scientific Voice. Montgomery. LC 95-43660. (Conduct of Science Ser.). 460p. 1995. lib. bdg. 40.00 (*1-57230-016-7*, 0016) Guilford Pr.

Scientific Voice. Scott L. Montgomery. LC 95-43660. (Conduct of Science Ser.). 460p. 1995. pap. text ed. 19.95 (*1-57230-019-1*, 0019) Guilford Pr.

***Scientific Vortex Information: How to Easily Understand, Find & Tap Vortex Energy in Sedona & Wherever You Travel.** Pete A. Sanders, Jr. (Illus.). 64p. (Orig.). 1992. pap. 9.95 (*0-9641911-3-X*) Free Soul.

Scientific Watergate - Dyslexia: How & Why Countless Millions Are Deprived of Breakthrough Medical Treatment. Harold N. Levinson. LC 93-87064. (Illus.). 455p. 1994. 24.95 (*0-9639303-0-3*) Stonebrdge Pubng.

Scientific Ways in the Study of Ego Development. Ed. by J. Loevinger. (Heinz Werner Lectures: No. 12). 1978. pap. 6.00 (*0-914206-14-1*) Clark U Pr.

Scientific Words: Their Structure & Meaning. W. E. Flood. LC 74-6707. 220p. 1974. reprint ed. text ed. 55.00 (*0-8371-7541-0*, FLOW, Greenwood Pr) Greenwood.

Scientific Work of John Winthrop: An Original Anthology. Michael Shute. Ed. by I. Bernard Cohen. LC 79-8005. (Three Centuries of Science in America Ser.). (Illus.). 1980. lib. bdg. 25.95 (*0-405-12593-3*) Ayer.

Scientific Works. David R. Iriarte. LC 82-82544. (Illus.). 544p. (Orig.). 1983. pap. 39.00 (*0-89729-316-9*) Ediciones.

Scientific World Perspective & Other Essays: 1931-1963. Kazimierz Ajdukiewicz. Ed. by Jerzy Giedymin. (Synthese Library: No. 108). 1977. lib. bdg. 171.00 (*90-277-0527-5*) Kluwer Ac.

Scientific World View in Dystopia. Alexandra Aldridge. LC 84-2724. (Studies in Speculative Fiction: No. 3). 107p. reprint ed. pap. 30.50 (*0-8357-1572-8*, 2070531) Bks Demand.

Scientific Worldview. Glenn Borchardt. (Illus.). xiii, 343p. (Orig.). (C). 1984. 49.95 (*0-917929-01-2*); pap. 29.95 (*0-917929-00-4*) Progressive Sci Inst.

Scientific Writings of David Rittenhouse: An Original Anthology. Ed. by Brooke Hindle & I. Bernard Cohen. LC 79-7987. (Three Centuries of Science in America Ser.). (Illus.). 1980. lib. bdg. 49.95 (*0-405-12568-2*) Ayer.

Scientific Yoga for the Man of Today. Sri S. Chakravarti. 1971. pap. 3.50 (*0-685-58385-6*) Ranney Pubns.

Scientifica Hermetica: An Introduciton to the Science of Alchemy. A. S. Raleigh. 109p. 1974. reprint ed. spiral bd. 10.00 (*0-7873-1049-2*) Hlth Research.

Scientifica Hermetica: An Introduction to the Science of Alchemy. A. S. Raleigh. 115p. 1995. reprint ed. pap. 15.95 (*1-56459-492-0*) Kessinger Pub.

Scientifically Soured Milk: Its Influence in Arresting Intestinal Putrefaction. Elie Metchnikoff. 1991. lib. bdg. 69.00 (*0-8490-4298-4*) Gordon Pr.

Scientifically Soured Milk: Its Influence in Arresting Intestinal Putrefaction. Elie Metchnikoff. 11p. 1969. reprint ed. spiral bd. 5.00 (*0-7873-0610-X*) Hlth Research.

Scientism: Philosophy & the Infatuation with Science. Tom Sorell. 208p. (C). 1994. pap. 16.95 (*0-415-10771-7*) Routledge.

Scientism & Humanism: Two Cultures in Post-Mao China, 1978-1989. Shiping Hua. LC 94-21098. 206p. (C). 1995. text ed. 54.50 (*0-7914-2421-9*); pap. text ed. 17.95 (*0-7914-2422-7*) State U NY Pr.

Scientism & Values. Ed. by Helmut Schoeck & James W. Wiggins. LC 78-172228. (Right Wing Individualist Tradition in America Ser.). 1972. reprint ed. 23.95 (*0-405-00436-2*) Ayer.

Scientism in Chinese Thought 1900-1950. D. W. Kwok. 244p. 1992. reprint ed. pap. 19.95 (*1-879176-11-4*) Imprint Pubns.

Scientist: A Metaphysical Autobiography. rev. ed. John C. Lilly. LC 78-3545. (Illus.). 320p. (Orig.). 1996. pap. 14.95 (*0-914171-72-0*) Ronin Pub.

Scientist & Activist, Phyllis Stearner. Mary E. Verheyden-Hilliard. LC 87-82597. (American Women in Science Biographies Ser.). (Illus.). 32p. (Orig.). (J). (gr. 1-4). 1988. pap. 5.00 (*0-932469-15-9*) Equity Inst.

Scientist & Administrator, Antoinette Rodez Schiesler. Mary E. Verheyden-Hilliard. LC 84-25978. (American Women in Science Biographies Ser.). (Illus.). 32p. (Orig.). (J). (gr. 1-4). 1985. pap. 5.00 (*0-932469-08-6*) Equity Inst.

Scientist & Astronaut, Sally Ride. Mary E. Verheyden-Hilliard. LC 84-25940. (American Women in Science Biographies Ser.). (Illus.). 32p. (Orig.). (J). (gr. 1-4). 1985. pap. 5.00 (*0-932469-07-8*) Equity Inst.

Scientist & Catholic: Pierre Duhem. Stanley L. Jaki. 280p. 1991. pap. 9.95 (*0-931888-44-1*) Christendom Pr.

Scientist & Engineer in Court. Michael D. Bradley. LC 83-10582. (Water Resources Monograph Ser.: Vol. 8). (Illus.). 111p. (Orig.). 1983. pap. 14.00 (*0-87590-309-6*) Am Geophysical.

Scientist & Governor, Dixy Lee Ray. Mary E. Verheyden-Hilliard. LC 84-25986. (American Women in Science Biographies Ser.). (Illus.). 32p. (Orig.). (J). (gr. 1-4). 1985. pap. 5.00 (*0-932469-06-X*) Equity Inst.

Scientist & Physician, Judith Pachciarz. Mary E. Verheyden-Hilliard. LC 87-82599. (American Women in Science Biographies Ser.). (Illus.). 32p. (Orig.). (J). (gr. 1-4). 1988. pap. 5.00 (*0-932469-13-2*) Equity Inst.

Scientist & Planner, Ru Chih Cheo Huang. Mary E. Verheyden-Hilliard. LC 84-25982. (American Women in Science Biographies Ser.). (Illus.). 32p. (Orig.). (J). (gr. 1-4). 1985. pap. 5.00 (*0-932469-03-5*) Equity Inst.

Scientist & Puzzle Solver, Constance Tom Noguchi. Mary E. Verheyden-Hilliard. LC 84-25924. (American Women in Science Biographies Ser.). (Illus.). 32p. (Orig.). (J). (gr. 1-4). 1985. pap. 5.00 (*0-932469-05-1*) Equity Inst.

Scientist & Strategist, June Rooks. Mary E. Verheyden-Hilliard. LC 87-82596. (American Women in Science Biographies Ser.). (Illus.). 32p. (Orig.). (J). (gr. 1-4). 1988. pap. 5.00 (*0-932469-14-0*) Equity Inst.

Scientist & Teacher, Anne Barrett Swanson. Mary E. Verheyden-Hilliard. LC 87-82598. (American Women in Science Biographies Ser.). (Illus.). 32p. (Orig.). (J). (gr. 1-4). 1988. pap. 5.00 (*0-932469-16-7*) Equity Inst.

***Scientist As Consultant: Building New Career Opportunities.** C. J. Sindermann & T. K. Sawyer. (C). 1997. write for info. (*0-306-45637-0*, Plenum Pr) Plenum.

Scientist at the White House. George B. Kistiakowsky & Charles S. Maier. 515p. 1976. 42.50 (*0-674-79496-6*) HUP.

***Scientist Explores Spirit.** George Dole & Robert Kirven. LC 97-614. 112p. 1997. pap. 9.95 (*0-87785-241-3*) Swedenborg.

Scientist from Puerto Rico, Maria Cordero Hardy. Mary E. Verheyden-Hilliard. LC 84-25979. (American Women in Science Biographies Ser.). (Illus.). 32p. (Orig.). (J). (gr. 1-4). 1985. pap. 5.00 (*0-932469-02-7*) Equity Inst.

Scientist from the Santa Clara Pueblo, Agnes Naranjo Stroud-Lee. Mary E. Verheyden-Hilliard. LC 84-25959. (American Women in Science Biographies Ser.). (Illus.). 32p. (Orig.). (J). (gr. 1-4). 1985. pap. 5.00 (*0-932469-09-4*) Equity Inst.

Scientist in Action: A Scientific Study of His Methods. William H. George. LC 74-26264. (History, Philosophy & Sociology of Science Ser.). 1975. reprint ed. 30.95 (*0-405-06592-2*) Ayer.

Scientist in the City. James S. Trefil. LC 93-24961. 288p. 1994. 23.95 (*0-385-24797-4*) Doubleday.

Scientist in the City. James S. Trefil. 288p. 1995. pap. 12.95 (*0-385-26109-8*, Anchor NY) Doubleday.

Scientist Looks at Christianity: A Probability Analysis of the Claims & Teachings Attributed to Christ. 2nd ed. George B. Whatmore. LC 94-70708. 244p. 1995. pap. 25.00 (*0-9631576-7-1*) Bridgenorth.

Scientist Looks at Research Management. John W. Koning, Jr. LC 74-30016. (American Management Associations Ser.). 24p. reprint ed. pap. 25.00 (*0-317-10666-X*, 2051519) Bks Demand.

***Scientist Looks at the Bible Spiritual Healing: Fact or Fiction.** George Walton. Ed. by William C. Burkle & John Kozloff. 112p. (Orig.). 1997. pap. 10.95 (*0-9658739-0-0*, 111) Turquite Pr.

Scientist of the Empire: Sir Roderick Murchison, Scientific Exploration & Victorian Imperialism. Robert A. Stafford. (Illus.). 305p. (C). 1990. text ed. 59.95 (*0-521-33537-X*) Cambridge U Pr.

Scientist on the Trail. Adolf F. Bandelier. Ed. by George P. Hammond. LC 67-24721. (Quivira Society Publications, Vol. 10). 1967. reprint ed. 19.95 (*0-405-00084-7*) Ayer.

Scientist on the Trail. Adolph F. Bandelier. (American Autobiography Ser.). 142p. 1995. reprint ed. lib. bdg. 69.00 (*0-7812-8448-1*) Rprt Serv.

Scientist Practitioner. Barlow. (C). 1992. pap. text ed. 55.00 (*0-205-14269-9*, H4269) Allyn.

Scientist Sam. Donna L. Pape. LC 68-56826. (Sound Ser.). (Illus.). 48p. (J). (gr. 2-5). 1968. lib. bdg. 10.95 (*0-87783-034-7*) Oddo.

Scientist Speaks Out, a Personal Perspective on Science, Society & Change. Glenn T. Seaborg. 350p. 1996. text ed. 44.00 (*981-02-2204-1*) World Scientific Pub.

Scientist with Determination, Elma Gonzalez. Mary E. Verheyden-Hilliard. LC 84-25981. (American Women in Science Biographies Ser.). (Illus.). 32p. (Orig.). (J). (gr. 1-4). 1985. pap. 5.00 (*0-932469-01-9*) Equity Inst.

Scientist Within You Vol. 1: Experiments & Biographies of Distinguished Women in Science. 2nd rev. ed. Rebecca L. Warren & Mary H. Thompson. LC 93-74855. (Illus.). 192p. (Orig.). (J). (gr. 3-8). 1996. pap. 21.95 (*1-884414-16-8*) ACI Pubng.

Scientist Within You Vol. 2: Women Scientists from Seven Continents - Biographies & Activities. Rebecca L. Warren & Mary H. Thompson. LC 95-78055. (Illus.). 224p. (Orig.). (J). (gr. 5-10). 1995. pap. 24.95 (*1-884414-12-5*) ACI Pubng.

Scientists. S. Reid & P. Fara. (Famous Lives Ser.). (Illus.). 48p. (J). (gr. 4 up). 1993. pap. 7.95 (*0-7460-1009-5*); lib. bdg. 15.95 (*0-88110-587-2*) EDC.

Scientists: The Lives & Works of 150 Physical & Social Scientists. Peggy Saari & Stephen Allison. LC 96-25579. 1100p. 1996. 99.95 (*0-7876-0959-5*, UXL) Gale.

Scientists: Tips for Giving Presentations to Teachers. Norman D. Anderson. (Illus.). 15p. 1993. write for info. (*0-935577-58-0*) Acid Rain Found.

Scientist's & Engineer's Guide to Workstations & Supercomputers: Coping with UNIX, RISC, Vectors, & Programming. Rubin H. Landau et al. LC 92-19556. 416p. 1992. pap. text ed. 63.95 (*0-471-53271-1*) Wiley.

Scientists & Human Rights in Guatemala: Report of a Delegation. Institute of Medicine Staff & National Academy of Sciences Staff. 80p. (Orig.). (C). 1992. pap. text ed. 21.00 (*0-309-04793-5*) Natl Acad Pr.

S

Scientists & Journalists: Reporting Science As News. Ed. by Sharon M. Friedman et al. LC 88-7874. 334p. 1986. pap. 19.95 (*0-87168-340-7*, 86-20S) AAAS.

Scientists & Technologists. Irene M. Franck & David M. Brownstone. LC 87-19959. (Work Throughout History Ser.). 224p. reprint ed. pap. 63.90 (*0-7837-2674-0*, 2043045) Bks Demand.

Scientists & the Development of Nuclear Weapons: From Fission to the Limited Test Ban Treaty, 1939-1963. Lawrence Badash. LC 94-17471. (Control of Nature Ser.). 144p. (C). 1995. pap. 12.50 (*0-391-03874-5*) Humanities.

***Scientists & the Sea, 1650-1900: A Study of Marine Science.** Margaret Deacon. 480p. 1997. 84.95 (*1-85928-352-7*, Pub. by Ashgate UK) Ashgate Pub Co.

Scientists & the State: Domestic Structures & the International Context. Etel Solingen. LC 93-44407. 200p. (C). 1994. text ed. 52.50 (*0-472-10486-1*) U of Mich Pr.

Scientists Are Human. David L. Watson. LC 74-26305. (History, Philosophy & Sociology of Science Ser.). 1975. reprint ed. 26.95 (*0-405-06629-5*) Ayer.

Scientists Around the World. Jerry DeBruin. (Illus.). 160p. (J). (gr. 4-12). 1987. pap. 12.99 (*0-86653-416-4*, GA1005) Good Apple.

Scientists Confront Creationism. Ed. by Laurie R. Godfrey. 352p. 1984. reprint ed. pap. 12.95 (*0-393-30154-0*) Norton.

Scientists Confront Scientists Who Confront Velikovsky. 2nd ed. Velikovsky et al. Ed. by Lewis M. Greenberg et al. (Illus.). (Orig.). 1978. pap. 10.00 (*0-917994-06-X*) Kronos Pr.

Scientists Confront Velikovsky. Ed. by Donald Goldsmith. 1979. reprint ed. pap. 3.95 (*0-393-00928-9*) Norton.

Scientists, Educators & National Standards: Action at the Local Level: Sigma Xi Forum Proceedings, April 14-15, 1994. (Illus.). 275p. (Orig.). 1994. pap. 5.00 (*0-914446-08-8*) Sigma Xi.

Scientists, Engineers & Technicians in Manufacturing Industries. Richard E. Morrison. (Illus.). 129p. (Orig.). (C). 1995. pap. text ed. 30.00 (*0-7881-2414-5*) DIANE Pub.

Scientists, Engineers, & Technicians in Nonmanufacturing Industries. 86p. (Orig.). (C). 1993. pap. text ed. 20.00 (*1-56806-474-8*) DIANE Pub.

Scientist's Handbook for Writing Papers & Dissertations. Antoinette M. Wilkinson. 1990. text ed. 77.00 (*0-13-969411-0*) P-H.

Scientists in Conference: The Congress Organizer's Handbook, The Congress Visitor's Companion. Volker Neuhoff. Tr. by Robert Schoenfeld from GER. LC 88-20974. 223p. 1987. 55.00 (*3-527-26579-1*, VCH) Wiley.

Scientists in Conflict: The Beginnings of the Oil Industry in California. Gerald T. White. LC 68-31651. (Huntington Library Publications). 286p. reprint ed. pap. 81.60 (*0-7837-6682-3*, 2046298) Bks Demand.

Scientists in Industry: Conflict & Accommodation. William Kornhauser. LC 82-1001. (Publication of the Institute of Industrial Relations Ser.). xii, 230p. 1982. reprint ed. text ed. 59.75 (*0-313-23491-4*, KOSC, Greenwood Pr) Greenwood.

Scientists in Organizations Revised Edition: Productive Climates for Research & Development. Donald C. Pelz & Frank M. Andrews. LC 76-620038. 400p. 1976. 22.00 (*0-87944-208-5*) Inst Soc Res.

Scientists in Power. Spencer R. Weart. LC 78-21670. (Illus.). 356p. 1981. 37.00 (*0-674-79515-6*) HUP.

Scientists in the Third World. Jacques Gaillard. LC 90-47574. (Agrarian Questions Ser.). 208p. 1991. text ed. 32.00 (*0-8131-1731-3*) U Pr of Ky.

Scientists Look at Our World. W. V. Houston et al. LC 71-142694. (Essay Index Reprint Ser.). 1977. reprint ed. 18.95 (*0-8369-2859-8*) Ayer.

Scientists Must Write: A Guide to Better Writing for Scientists, Engineers & Students. Robert Barrass. 176p. (gr. 13). 1978. pap. text ed. 16.50 (*0-412-15430-7*, NO. 6385) Chapman & Hall.

Scientists of Faith: 48 Biographies of Historic Scientists & Their Christian Faith. Dan Graves. 192p. 1996. pap. 9.99 (*0-8254-2724-X*) Kregel.

Scientists of the Mind: Intellectual Founders of Modern Psychology. Clarence J. Karier. LC 85-996. (Illus.). 368p. 1986. text ed. 29.95 (*0-252-01182-1*) U of Ill Pr.

Scientists, Peace & Disarmament. Ed. by Guillermo A. Lemarchand. 396p. (C). 1988. text ed. 89.00 (*9971-5-0761-7*) World Scientific Pub.

***Scientists since 1660: A Bibliography of Biographies.** Leslie Howsam. LC 96-41789. 300p. 1997. text ed. 93. 95 (*1-85928-035-8*, Pub. by Scolar Pr UK) Ashgate Pub Co.

***Scientists, Society, & State: The Social Relations of Science Movement in Great Britain, 1931-1947.** William McGucken. LC 83-8320. 395p. 1984. reprint ed. pap. 112.60 (*0-608-04448-2*, 2064980) Bks Demand.

Scientists Starred Nineteen Hundred & Three to Nineteen Forty-Three in American Men of Science. Stephen S. Visher. LC 74-26301. (History, Philosophy & Sociology of Science Ser.). 1975. reprint ed. 46.95 (*0-405-06625-2*) Ayer.

Scientists, the Arms Race & Disarmament. Ed. by Joseph Rotblat. 320p. 1982. 39.00 (*0-85066-234-6*) Taylor & Francis.

Scientist's Thesaurus: A Treasury of the Stockwords of Science. 4th ed. George F. Steffanides. 156p. 1978. pap. 3.00 (*0-9600114-0-4*) Steffanides.

***Scientist's Tools for Business: Metaphors & Modes of Thought.** Robert L. Sproull. 384p. 1997. write for info. (*1-878822-84-5*) Univ Rochester Pr.

Scientists under Hitler: Politics & the Physics Community in the Third Reich. Alan D. Beyerchen. LC 77-2167. (Illus.). 309p. reprint ed. pap. 88.10 (*0-7837-4526-5*, 2080189) Bks Demand.

Scientist's Voice in American Culture: Simon Newcomb & the Rhetoric of Scientific Method. Albert E. Moyer. (C). 1992. 40.00 (*0-520-07689-3*) U CA Pr.

Scientists Who Believe: 21 Tell Their Own Stories. Ed. by Eric C. Barrett & David Fisher. 1984. mass mkt., pap. 5.99 (*0-8024-7634-1*) Moody.

Scientists Who Changed the World. Illus. by Robert R. Ingpen. (Turning Points in History Ser.). 96p. (YA). (gr. 5 up). 1994. lib. bdg. 19.95 (*0-7910-2763-5*) Chelsea Hse.

Scientists Who Study Ancient Temples & Tombs. Mel Higginson. LC 94-6996. (Scientists Ser.). (J). 1994. write for info. (*0-86593-376-6*) Rourke Corp.

Scientists Who Study Fossils. Mel Higginson. LC 94-6995. (Scientists Ser.). (J). 1994. write for info. (*0-86593-375-8*) Rourke Corp.

Scientists Who Study Ocean Life. Mel Higginson. LC 94-6999. (Scientists Ser.). (J). 1994. write for info. (*0-86593-371-5*) Rourke Corp.

Scientists Who Study Plants. Mel Higginson. LC 94-6998. (Scientists Ser.). (J). 1994. write for info. (*0-86593-373-1*) Rourke Corp.

Scientists Who Study the Earth. Mel Higginson. LC 94-7000. (Scientists Ser.). (J). (gr. 4 up). 1994. write for info. (*0-86593-372-3*) Rourke Corp.

Scientists Who Study Wild Animals. Mel Higginson. LC 94-6997. (Scientists Ser.). (J). 1994. write for info. (*0-86593-374-X*) Rourke Corp.

Scientology: A History of Man. L. Ron Hubbard. 1989. 35. 00 (*0-88404-024-0*) Bridge Pubns Inc.

***Scientology: A New Slant on Life.** L. Ron Hubbard. Date not set. pap. 12.95 (*1-57318-037-8*) Bridge Pubns Inc.

***Scientology: The Fundamentals of Thought.** L. Ron Hubbard. 30.00 (*0-88404-956-6*); mass mkt. 5.99 (*0-88404-104-2*) Bridge Pubns Inc.

Scientology: The Fundamentals of Thought. L. Ron Hubbard. 212p. 1995. mass mkt. 5.99 (*0-88404-503-X*) Bridge Pubns Inc.

Scientology Handbook. L. Ron Hubbard. 988p. 1994. 100. 00 (*0-88404-899-3*) Bridge Pubns Inc.

***Scientology 0-8.** L. Ron Hubbard. 32.50 (*0-88404-952-3*) Bridge Pubns Inc.

Scientology 0-8. L. Ron Hubbard. 274p. 1989. 22.00 (*0-88404-376-2*) Bridge Pubns Inc.

Scientology 8-80. L. Ron Hubbard. 1989. 35.00 (*0-88404-428-9*) Bridge Pubns Inc.

Scientology 8-80: The Discovery & Increase of Life Energy. L. Ron Hubbard. 182p. 1995. 35.00 (*0-88404-954-X*) Bridge Pubns Inc.

Scientology 8-8008. L. Ron Hubbard. 276p. 1989. 35.00 (*0-88404-429-7*) Bridge Pubns Inc.

Scientology 8-8008: How to Increase Your Spiritual Ability from Zero to Infinity. L. Ron Hubbard. 276p. 1995. 35. 00 (*0-88404-953-1*) Bridge Pubns Inc.

Scientometric Indicators: A Thirty-Two Country Comparative Evaluation of Publishing Performance & Citation Impact. T. Braun et al. 250p. 1985. text ed. 47. 00 (*9971-966-69-7*) World Scientific Pub.

***Scienza e Terminologia Medica Nella Letteratura Latina di eta Neroniana: Seneca, Lucano, Persio, Petronio.** Paola Migliorini. (Studien Zur Klassischen Philologie Ser.: Bd. 104). 229p. 1997. 44.95 (*3-631-31229-6*) P Lang Pubng.

SCIL: Systematic Curriculum for Independent Living, 4 vols, Set. Marta Hannah et al. 1977. ring bd. 165.00 (*0-87879-187-6*) Acad Therapy.

Scimidar: Feast & Famine, Vol. 2. R. A. Jones. Ed. by Chris Ulm. (Illus.). 102p. 1990. pap. 9.95 (*0-944735-54-1*) Malibu Comics Ent.

Scimidar: The Twilight Men. R. A. Jones. (Illus.). 99p. 1991. pap. 9.95 (*0-944735-85-1*) Malibu Comics Ent.

Scimidar, Vol. 1: Pleasure & Pain. R. A. Jones. (Illus.). 118p. 1989. pap. 9.95 (*0-944735-29-0*) Malibu Comics Ent.

Scimitar. Picton Publishing (Chippenham) Ltd. Staff. (FAA Ser.). (C). 1987. 50.00 (*0-948251-39-5*, Pub. by Picton UK) St Mut.

Scimitar. Scott Stone. 384p. (Orig.). 1989. mass mkt. 3.95 (*0-373-97102-8*) Harlequin Bks.

Scimitar Cat: Homotherium Serum Cope. Viola R. Schatzinger. (Reports of Investigations: No. 47). (Illus.). 80p. 1992. pap. 6.00 (*0-89792-136-4*) Ill St Museum.

Scintigraphic Evaluation of Coronary Thrombolysis. L. Mortelmans. No. 25. 148p. (Orig.). 1990. pap. 39.50 (*90-6186-370-8*, Pub. by Leuven Univ BE) Coronet Bks.

Scintigraphy of Inflammation with Nanometer-Sized Colloidal Tracers. Marc De Schrijver. (Developments in Nuclear Medicine Ser.). (C). 1989. lib. bdg. 112.00 (*0-7923-0272-9*) Kluwer Ac.

Scintillae Juris Meditations in the Tea Room: Meditations in the Tea Room. Justice Darling. LC 88-80854. 225p. 1988. reprint ed. 43.00 (*0-912004-64-9*) Gaunt.

Scintilla's Journal, 12 vols., Vol. 1. Laura J. Lustig et al. 100p. 1996. pap. 40.00 (*1-889008-00-1*) Projects.

Scintillating Fiber Detectors: Proceedings of the SCIFI '93 Workshop, 2 vols. D. Bross et al. 684p. 1995. text ed. 129.00 (*981-02-1818-4*) World Scientific Pub.

Scintillation Detectors. (Advanced Health Physics Training Ser.). (Illus.). 170p. 1983. ring bd. 60.00 (*0-87683-193-5*) GP Courseware.

Scintillations Three. Ed. by Joann M. Everett & Jo S. Dufton. (Scintillations Ser.). 51p. (Orig.). 1985. pap. 5.75 (*0-930069-03-X*) Jasmine Pr.

Scintillations Two. Ed. by Ron Zettlemoyer. (Scintillations Ser.). (Illus.). 60p. (Orig.). 1984. pap. 5.00 (*0-930069-01-3*) Jasmine Pr.

Scintillator & Phosphor Materials Vol. 348: Materials Research Society Symposium Proceedings. Ed. by M. J. Weber et al. 565p. 1994. text ed. 63.00 (*1-55899-248-0*) Materials Res.

Sciomyzidae (Diptera) of Fennoscandia & Denmark. R. Rozkosny. (Fauna Entomologica Scandinavica Ser.: No. 14). (Illus.). 224p. 1984. text ed. 47.00 (*90-04-07592-5*) Lubrecht & Cramer.

Scions of Shannara. Terry Brooks. LC 89-37935. 544p. 1990. 23.00 (*0-345-35695-0*, Del Rey) Ballantine.

Scions of Shannara. Terry Brooks. 432p. 1991. mass mkt. 6.99 (*0-345-37074-0*, Del Rey) Ballantine.

***Scions of Shannara.** Terry Brooks. (Shannara Ser.). 1997. pap. 6.99 (*0-345-91130-X*, Del Rey) Ballantine.

Scipio Africanus: Greater Than Napoleon. Basil H. Liddell-Hart. 288p. 1992. 37.50 (*1-85367-132-0*) Stackpole.

Scipio Africanus: Greater Than Napoleon. B. Liddell Hart. (Illus.). 304p. 1994. reprint ed. pap. 14.95 (*0-306-80583-9*) Da Capo.

Scipio Africanus: The Conqueror of Hannibal, Selections from Livy, Bks. XXIV-XXX. T. A. Buckney. (Illus.). 112p. (ENG & LAT.). 1987. reprint ed. pap. 11.00 (*0-86516-208-5*) Bolchazy-Carducci.

Scipio Africanus & Rome's Invasion of Africa, Bk. XXIX: A Historical Commentary on Titus Livius. Philip J. Smith. (McGill University Monographs in Classical Archaeology & History: No. 13). xii, 105p. 1992. pap. 37.00 (*90-5063-090-1*, Pub. by Gieben NE) Benjamins North Am.

Scipio Storytelling: Talk in a Southern Indiana Community. Margaret R. MacDonald. LC 96-15649. 248p. 1996. pap. text ed. 34.00 (*0-7618-0350-5*); lib. bdg. 54.00 (*0-7618-0349-1*) U Pr of Amer.

SCIS Subject Headings List. 3rd ed. Compiled by Schools Cataloguing Information Service Staff. 900p. 1994. 58.00 (*1-875589-08-2*) D W Thorpe.

Scissor Skill Patterns. Linda Milliken. (Illus.). 72p. (J). (ps-2). 1993. Grades ps-2. pap. 7.95 (*1-56472-009-8*) Edupress.

Scissor Skills. Carson & Dellosa. (Home Workbooks Ser.). (Illus.). 64p. (Orig.). (J). (ps-1). 1995. wbk. ed., pap. 2.49 (*0-88724-310-X*, CD6807) Carson-Dellos.

Scissor Sorcery: Cutting Activities for Early Childhood. Sharon Carpenter. LC 83-83236. (Illus.). 241p. (J). (ps-2). 1985. lib. bdg. 26.95 (*0-89334-170-3*, 170-3) Humanics Ltd.

Scissor Sorcery: Cutting Activities for Early Childhood Programs. Sharon Carpenter. LC 83-83236. 241p. (Orig.). (J). (ps-2). 1985. pap. 16.95 (*0-89334-076-6*) Humanics Ltd.

Scissor-Tales for Any Day: Storytelling Cutups, Activities, & Extensions. Jan G. Philpot. Ed. by Leslie Britt. (Illus.). 80p. (Orig.). 1994. pap. text ed. 9.95 (*0-86530-285-5*) Incentive Pubns.

Scissor-Tales for Special Days: Storytelling Cutups, Activities, & Extensions. Jan G. Philpot. Ed. by Jan Keeling. (Illus.). 80p. (Orig.). 1994. pap. text ed. 9.95 (*0-86530-284-7*) Incentive Pubns.

Scissors. (Five-Minute Art Ideas Ser.). (Illus.). 24p. (Orig.). (J). (ps up). 1995. pap. 6.95 (*1-57102-037-3*, Ideals Child) Hambleton-Hill.

Scissors & Comb Haircutting: A Cut-by-Cut Guide for Home Haircutters. Bob Ohnstad. LC 84-90072. (Illus.). 186p. (Orig.). 1985. pap. 15.95 (*0-916819-01-9*) You Can Pub.

Scissors, Glue, & Concepts, Too! Interactive Activities for Practicing Basic Concepts. Susan Boegler & Debbie Abruzzini. 1992. spiral bd. 31.95 (*1-55999-237-9*) LinguiSystems.

Scissors of Meter: Grammetrics & Reading. Donald Wesling. LC 96-9950. (C). 1996. 42.50 (*0-472-10715-1*) U of Mich Pr.

Scissors, Paper, Rock. Larry Smith. (Cleveland Poets Ser.: No. 31). 32p. (Orig.). 1982. pap. 3.50 (*0-914946-30-7*) Cleveland St Univ Poetry Ctr.

Scissors, Paper, Rock. Fenton Johnson. Ed. by Jane Rosenman. 240p. 1994. reprint ed. pap. 10.00 (*0-671-79542-2*, WSP) PB.

***Scissors Paper Rock: Stories by Troy Riser.** Troy Riser. 74p. (Orig.). 1993. per. 5.95 (*1-880649-31-4*) Writ Ctr Pr.

Scitech Ch1: Environmental Issues Around the World. Vannaerssen. (College ESL Ser.). 1995. pap. 2.95 (*0-8384-6491-2*) Heinle & Heinle.

Scitech Ch10: Bicycles - Transportation to the Future? Vannaerssen. (College ESL Ser.). 1995. pap. 1.95 (*0-8384-6501-3*) Heinle & Heinle.

Scitech Ch11: Manufacturing, Recycling & the Community. Vannaerssen. (College ESL Ser.). 1995. pap. 1.95 (*0-8384-6502-1*) Heinle & Heinle.

Scitech Ch12: Solar Energy & Water. Vannaerssen. (College ESL Ser.). 1995. pap. 1.95 (*0-8384-6503-X*) Heinle & Heinle.

Scitech Ch13: Introduction - Safety in the Workplace. Vannaerssen. (College ESL Ser.). 1995. pap. 1.95 (*0-8384-6504-8*) Heinle & Heinle.

Scitech Ch14: Safety in Action. Vannaerssen. (College ESL Ser.). 1995. pap. 1.95 (*0-8384-6505-6*) Heinle & Heinle.

Scitech Ch15: Becoming Safety Smart. Vannaerssen. (College ESL Ser.). 1995. pap. 1.95 (*0-8384-6506-4*) Heinle & Heinle.

Scitech Ch16: Career Choices - Science & Technology. Brennan. (College ESL Ser.). 1995. pap. 2.95 (*0-8384-6507-2*) Heinle & Heinle.

Scitech Ch17: Scientific Education & Training. Brennan. (College ESL Ser.). 1995. pap. 1.95 (*0-8384-6508-0*) Heinle & Heinle.

Scitech Ch18: Preparing Science on the Job. Brennan. (College ESL Ser.). 1995. pap. 1.95 (*0-8384-6509-9*) Heinle & Heinle.

Scitech Ch19: Trends in Science & Technology. Brennan. (College ESL Ser.). 1995. pap. 1.95 (*0-8384-6510-2*) Heinle & Heinle.

Scitech Ch2: Science DPTS & Environment. Vannaerssen. (College ESL Ser.). 1995. pap. 2.95 (*0-8384-6492-0*) Heinle & Heinle.

Scitech Ch20: Opportunity for Advancement. Brennan. (College ESL Ser.). 1995. pap. 1.95 (*0-8384-6511-0*) Heinle & Heinle.

Scitech Ch21: Skills on the Job. Brennan. (College ESL Ser.). 1995. pap. 1.95 (*0-8384-6512-9*) Heinle & Heinle.

Scitech Ch22: Scientist & Technology. Brennan. (College ESL Ser.). 1995. pap. 1.95 (*0-8384-6513-7*) Heinle & Heinle.

Scitech Ch23: The Scientist & the Community. Brennan. (College ESL Ser.). 1995. pap. 1.95 (*0-8384-6514-5*) Heinle & Heinle.

Scitech Ch24: Moral Dilemmas for the Scientist. Brennan. (College ESL Ser.). 1995. pap. 1.95 (*0-8384-6515-3*) Heinle & Heinle.

Scitech Ch25: Professional Behavior for the Scientist. Brennan. (College ESL Ser.). 1995. pap. 1.95 (*0-8384-6516-1*) Heinle & Heinle.

Scitech Ch3: Unheard Voices - Environmental Issues. Vannaerssen. (College ESL Ser.). 1995. pap. 2.95 (*0-8384-6493-9*) Heinle & Heinle.

Scitech Ch4: Hidden Dangers - Clean up the Environment. Vannaerssen. (College ESL Ser.). 1995. pap. 2.95 (*0-8384-6494-7*) Heinle & Heinle.

Scitech Ch5: Professional Ethics & the Computer. Vannaerssen. (College ESL Ser.). 1995. pap. 2.95 (*0-8384-6496-3*) Heinle & Heinle.

Scitech Ch6: Language & Culture of Electronic Communication. Vannaerssen. (College ESL Ser.). 1995. pap. 1.95 (*0-8384-6497-1*) Heinle & Heinle.

Scitech Ch7: Computer Spies & Terrorists. Vannaerssen. (College ESL Ser.). 1995. pap. 1.95 (*0-8384-6498-X*) Heinle & Heinle.

Scitech Ch8: Academic Writing in the Computer Age. Vannaerssen. (College ESL Ser.). 1995. pap. 1.95 (*0-8384-6499-8*) Heinle & Heinle.

Scitech Ch9: What is Appropriate Technology? Vannaerssen. (College ESL Ser.). 1995. pap. 1.95 (*0-8384-6500-5*) Heinle & Heinle.

SciTech Front Matter. Brennan. (College ESL Ser.). 1995. pap. 1.75 (*0-8384-4119-X*) Heinle & Heinle.

Scitech 1: Communicating in English about Science & Technology. Margaret Van Naerssen. (College ESL Ser.). 208p. 1994. pap. 7.95 (*0-8384-4267-6*) Heinle & Heinle.

Scitech 2: Communicating in English about Science & Technology. Moya Brennen. 208p. 1994. pap. 27.95 (*0-8384-4081-9*) Heinle & Heinle.

***Sckraight from the Ghetto: You Know You're Ghetto If--** Bertice Berry & Joan Coker. LC 96-37232. 1996. pap. 7.95 (*0-312-15448-8*) St Martin.

Sclera. C. Stephen Foster & Maria Sainz De La Maiza. LC 93-10235. 1993. 163.00 (*0-387-94058-8*) Spr-Verlag.

Scleroderma: Caring for Your Hands & Face. Jeanne L. Melvin. (Illus.). 32p. 1994. pap. text ed. write for info. (*1-56900-006-9*) Am Occup Therapy.

Scleroderris Canker in Conifers. Paul D. Manion. (Forestry Sciences Ser.). 1984. lib. bdg. 122.50 (*90-247-2912-2*) Kluwer Ac.

Sclerosis: Index of New Information & Research Bible of Current Reviews. Leonard F. Selinsky. 150p. 1994. 47. 50 (*0-7883-0038-5*); pap. 44.50 (*0-7883-0039-3*) ABBE Pubs Assn.

***Sclerosis: Index of New Information & Research Bible of Current Reviews.** Leonard F. Selinsky. 143p. 1997. 44. 95 (*0-7883-1612-5*) ABBE Pubs Assn.

***Sclerosis: Index of New Information & Research Bible of Current Reviews.** Leonard F. Selinsky. 143p. 1997. pap. 39.95 (*0-7883-1613-3*) ABBE Pubs Assn.

***Sclerosis: Index of New Medical Information.** Leonard F. Selinsky. 155p. 1997. 44.50 (*0-7883-1624-9*) ABBE Pubs Assn.

***Sclerosis: Index of New Medical Information.** Leonard F. Selinsky. 155p. 1997. pap. 39.50 (*0-7883-1625-7*) ABBE Pubs Assn.

Sclerotherapy: Treatment of Varicose & Telangiectatic Leg Virus. 2nd ed. Mitchel P. Goldman. LC 94-44914. 544p. (C). (gr. 13). 1995. text ed. 179.00 (*0-8151-4011-8*) Mosby Yr Bk.

Sclerotherapy of Spider Veins. Victoria. (Illus.). 142p. 1995. 125.00 (*0-7506-9459-9*, Focal) Buttrwrth-Heinemann.

Sclerotherapy of Varicose & Telangiectatic Leg Veins. Robert A. Weiss. (Illus.). 350p. 1997. text ed. 115.00 (*0-07-069201-7*) McGraw.

Sclerotinaceae Two: Lambertella. K. P. Dumont. (Memoirs Ser.: Vol. 22 (1)). (Illus.). 178p. 1971. pap. 10.50 (*0-89327-074-1*) NY Botanical.

SCO: The Windows 95 Server. Charlie Russel. LC 96-24172. 1996. pap. 34.95 (*0-13-459421-5*) P-H.

Sco Application Developer's Handbook. David Bacon. 1994. pap. text ed. 27.00 (*0-13-122789-0*) P-H.

***SCO CMW Plus Administrator Tutorial, Vol. II.** Stephen A. Sutton. Ed. by Stephanie C. Bury. (Illus.). 370p. (Orig.). 1995. pap. 68.00 (*1-889827-06-1*) Trusted Systs.

***SCO CMW Plus Application Programming Guide, Vol. III.** Stephen A. Sutton. Ed. by Stephanie C. Bury. 310p. (Orig.). 1995. pap. 82.00 (*1-889827-07-X*) Trusted Systs.

***SCO CMW Plus User Tutorial, Vol. I.** Stephen A. Sutton. Ed. by Stephanie C. Bury. (Illus.). 275p. (Orig.). 1995. pap. 62.00 (*1-889827-05-3*) Trusted Systs.

SCO Companion: The Essential Guide for Users & System Administrators. James Mohr. LC 96-18098. 792p. 1996. pap. 39.95 (*0-13-451683-4*) P-H.

Sco Email Configuration Guide. John DuBois. 1994. pap. text ed. 24.00 (*0-685-70621-4*) P-H.

SCO Open DeskTop-SCO Open Server User's Guide. Santa Cruz Operations Staff. 320p. 1994. pap. text ed. 32.20 (*0-13-106816-4*) P-H.

Sco Performance Tuning Handbook. Gina Miscovich & David Simons. 640p. 1994. Incl. Disk. pap. text ed. 56. 00 (*0-13-102690-9*) P-H.

Sco Security Handbook. Peter Rosencrantz. 1994. pap. text ed. 26.25 (*0-13-123423-4*) P-H.

SCO System Administration. Timothy Parker. 1996. 29.95 (*0-13-443664-4*) P-H.

SCO UNIX in a Nutshell. O'Reilly & Assocs. & Ellie Cutler. 590p. 1994. pap. 19.95 (*1-56592-037-6*) OReilly & Assocs.

SCO UNIX System Administration. Timothy Parker. 1996. 29.95 (*0-614-14495-7*); 29.95 (*0-614-14496-5*) P-H.

SCO Users Companion. James Mohr. 1996. 34.95 (*0-614-14494-9*) P-H.

Scogin, Elam, & Bray: A Critical Monograph. Contrib. by Mark Linder et al. LC 92-15638. (Illus.). 224p. 1992. 40. 00 (*0-8478-1534-X*); pap. 40.00 (*0-8478-1535-8*) Rizzoli Intl.

Scoja Story: Jobbers Working Together. Richard H. DeMontmollin. LC 86-62676. (Illus.). 203p. 1986. 30.00 (*0-9617613-0-X*) SC Oil Job Assn.

Scold's Bridle. Minette Walters. 1995. mass mkt. 5.99 (*0-312-95612-6*) St Martin.

Scold's Bridle. large type ed. Minette Walters. LC 94-33719. 1995. 22.95 (*0-7838-1131-4*, GK Hall) Thorndike Pr.

Scolies Genevoises de l'Iliade, 2 vols. in 1. Jules Nicole. lxxxiii, 574p. 1966. reprint ed. write for info. (*0-318-70987-2*); reprint ed. write for info. (*0-318-71382-9*) G Olms Pubs.

Scoliosis: Diagnosis & Management. Rene Cailliet. LC 75-6709. (Illus.). 121p. 1975. text ed. 22.95 (*0-8036-1640-6*) Davis Co.

Scoliosis: Identifiable Causes Detection & Correction, Vol. III. 2nd expanded ed. Fredrick H. Barge. 347p. 1996. text ed. 75.00 (*1-885048-02-5*) Barge Chiropract.

Scoliosis: Subject, Reference & Research Guidebook. Corey S. York. LC 87-47648. 160p. 1987. 44.50 (*0-88164-596-6*); pap. 39.50 (*0-88164-597-4*) ABBE Pubs Assn.

Scoliosis Handbook: A Consultation with a Specialist. Michael Neuwirth & Kevin Osborn. LC 95-32801. 1996. 25.00 (*0-8050-3793-4*) H Holt & Co.

Scoliosis Prevention. Manijeh H. Mehta. LC 84-26400. (Proceedings of the Seventh Phillip Zorab Symposium). 316p. 1985. text ed. 65.00 (*0-275-91327-9*, C1327, Praeger Pubs) Greenwood.

SCOLMA Directory of Libraries & Special Collections on Africa in the United Kingdom & Europe. 5th enl. rev. ed. Ed. by Tom French. LC 92-45187. 367p. 1993. 85.00 (*0-905450-89-2*, Pub. by H Zell Pubs UK) Bowker-Saur.

Scolosaurus. D. White. (Dinosaur Library). (Illus.). 24p. (J). (gr. 3 up). 1989. 10.95 (*0-685-58286-8*); lib. bdg. 14.60 (*0-86592-519-4*) Rourke Corp.

Scones, Muffins, & Tea Cakes: Breakfast Breads & Teatime Spreads. Ed. & Intro. by Heidi Cusick. LC 95-24699. (Illus.). 96p. 1996. 12.95 (*0-00-225201-5*) Collins SF.

Scooby-Doo 1, 2, 3. (Shaped Hanna Barbera Board Bks.). (Illus.). 12p. (J). (ps-6). Date not set. bds. write for info. (*1-56987-435-2*) Landoll.

Scoop. Evelyn Waugh. 1977. pap. 12.95 (*0-316-92610-8*) Little.

Scoop! Fishbowl Fun, Simple Addition. Monica Weiss. LC 91-18657. (Frimble Family First Learning Adventures Ser.). (Illus.). 24p. (J). (gr. k-2). 1992. lib. bdg. 10.95 (*0-8167-2484-9*) Troll Communs.

Scoop! Fishbowl Fun, Simple Addition. Monica Weiss. LC 91-18657. (Frimble Family First Learning Adventures Ser.). (Illus.). 24p. (J). (gr. k-2). 1997. pap. 3.50 (*0-8167-2485-7*) Troll Communs.

Scoop Doogan Mysteries, 5 novels in ea. set, Set 1. Don Keown. (Illus.). (J). 1984. pap. 17.00 (*0-87879-466-2*) High Noon Bks.

Scoop Doogan Mysteries, 5 novels in ea. set, Set 2. Don Keown. (Illus.). 48p. 1985. Set 1, 48p. pap. 17.00 (*0-87879-433-6*) High Noon Bks.

***Scoop of Plays.** Groves. Date not set. pap. text ed. write for info. (*0-582-20689-8*, Pub. by Longman UK) Longman.

Scoop on Frogs & Princes. Greta B. Lipson & Eric Lipson. 128p. teacher ed. 12.99 (*0-86653-740-6*, GA1455) Good Apple.

An Asterisk (*) at the beginning of an entry indicates that the title is appearing in BIP for the first time.

Scoops from the Bay. Ed. by Cookbook Committee Staff & Cape Cod Academy Staff. (Illus.). 376p. 1989. 15.95 (*0-9623316-1-9*) Cape Cod Acad.

Scoops vs. Business-Aide, Inc., a Case File. Henry L. Hecht. 1991. pap. 19.50 (*0-685-69489-5*) PLI.

Scoopy the Lop-Eared Rabbit. John Maruhnich. LC 93-93765. (Illus.). 64p. 1994. pap. 7.00 (*1-56002-298-1*, Univ Edtns) Aegina Pr.

Scoor-oot: A Dictionary of Scots Words & Phrases in Current Use. James A. Stevenson. LC 89-34103. (Illus.). 220p. (C). 1989. pap. 19.95 (*0-485-12068-2*, Pub. by Athlone Pr UK); text ed. 45.00 (*0-485-11373-2*, Pub. by Athlone Pr UK) Humanities.

Scooter. Vera B. Williams. LC 90-38489. (Illus.). 160p. (J). (gr. 4-7). 1993. 15.00 (*0-688-09376-0*); lib. bdg. 14.93 (*0-688-09377-9*) Greenwillow.

***Scooter & the Stranger.** Dennis B. Harris. Ed. by Kay Harris. (Illus.). 44p. (J). (gr. 1-5). 1997. 12.95 (*0-614-29707-9*) Lfestyle Min.

***Scooter & the Stranger.** Dennis B. Harris. Ed. by Kay Harris. (Illus.). 44p. (J). (gr. 1-5). 1997. 12.95 (*1-890022-01-2*) Lfestyle Min.

***Scooter Boys.** Gareth Brown. 128p. pap. 15.95 (*0-7119-6159-X*) Omnibus NY.

Scooter Thomas Makes It to the Top of the World. Peter Parnell. 1982. pap. 3.25 (*0-8222-1000-2*) Dramatists Play.

Scooters! Michael Dregni & Eric Dregni. LC 95-24758. (Crestline Ser.). (Illus.). 360p. 1995. pap. 19.95 (*0-7603-0072-0*, Crestline Pub) Motorbooks Intl.

***Scooter's Days...& Other Days: A History of Sports in Lawrence County PA from 1922-1971.** Bob Vosburg. 276p. (Orig.). 1997. pap. text ed. 39.95 (*1-884687-06-7*) N Horzns Pub.

Scooter's Tail of Terror: A Fable of Addiction & Hope. Larry Shles. Ed. by Marie Ciconte. (Scooter Ser.: No. 1). (Illus.). 80p. (Orig.). (J). (gr. 2 up). 1992. pap. 9.95 (*0-915190-89-3*, JP9089-3) Jalmar Pr.

Scope & History of Commutative & Noncommutative Harmonic Analysis. Ed. by G. W. Mackey. LC 92-12857. (History of Mathematics Ser.: Vol. 5). 370p. 1992. 52.00 (*0-8218-9903-1*, HMATH/5C) Am Math.

Scope & Method of Political Economy. 4th ed. John Maynard Keynes. LC 86-105057. (Reprints of Economic Classics Ser.). xvi, 382p. 1986. reprint ed. 45.00 (*0-678-00010-7*) Kelley.

Scope & Method of Sociology. Paul H. Furfey. LC 65-17182. 556p. reprint ed. lib. bdg. 65.00 (*0-8154-0075-6*) Cooper Sq.

***Scope & Specificity.** Feng-hsi Liu. LC 97-16442. (Linguistik Aktuell - Linguistics Today Ser.: Vol. 16). viii, 183p. 1997. lib. bdg. 84.00 (*1-55619-900-7*) Benjamins North Am.

Scope & Variety of U. S. Diplomatic History, Vol. II: Readings Since 1900. Edward W. Chester. 384p. (C). 1989. pap. text ed. write for info. (*0-318-65459-8*) P-H.

Scope for Macroeconomic Policy to Alleviate Unemployment in Western Europe. 34p. 1992. pap. 25.00 (*92-1-100386-5*, E.GV.92.0.27) UN.

Scope IV of the Nursery Industry. 19p. (C). 1982. pap. text ed. 15.00 (*0-935336-02-8*) Horticult Research.

Scope of Ambulatory Monitoring in Ischemic Heart Disease: Proceedings. Conference on Ambulatory Monitoring, 3rd, 1977. Ed. by Nancy K. Jacobsen et al. 1978. 18.50 (*0-917054-15-6*) Med Communications.

Scope of American Linguistics: The First Golden Anniversary Symposium of the Linguistic Society of America. Ed. by Robert Austerlitz. v, 209p. (Orig.). (C). 1975. pap. text ed. 46.15 (*3-11-013343-1*) Mouton.

Scope of Astrological Prediction: An Introduction to the Dynamic Horoscopy. Marc E. Jones. (Illus.). 461p. 1969. 19.50 (*0-87878-012-2*) Sabian Pub.

Scope of Epidemiological Psychiatry: Essays in Honor of Michael Shepherd. Ed. by Paul Williams et al. 200p. 1989. 53.00 (*0-415-01814-5*) Routledge.

Scope of Faculty Collective Bargaining: An Analysis of Faculty Union Agreements at Four-Year Institutions of Higher Education. Ed. by Ronald L. Johnstone. LC 80-27440. (Contributions to the Study of Education Ser.: No. 2). (Illus.). 240p. 1981. text ed. 49.95 (*0-313-22918-X*, JBA/) Greenwood.

Scope of Geography. 3rd ed. Rhoads Murphey. 228p. 1982. pap. 13.95 (*0-416-33410-5*, NO. 6354) Routledge Chapman & Hall.

Scope of Government. Ed. by Ole Borre & Elinor Scarbrough. (Beliefs in Government Ser.: Vol. 3). (Illus.). 464p. 1996. 65.00 (*0-19-827954-X*) OUP.

Scope of Grammar: A Study of Modern English. Stanley J. Cook & Richard W. Suter. Ed. by William A. Talkington. (Illus.). 1980. text ed. write for info. (*0-07-012460-4*) McGraw.

Scope of History: Studies in the Historiography of Alfonso el Sabio. Charles F. Fraker. LC 96-10298. (C). 1996. 42.50 (*0-472-10669-4*) U of Mich Pr.

Scope of Morality. Peter A. French. LC 79-19026. 236p. 1979. reprint ed. pap. 67.30 (*0-7837-2962-6*, 2057492) Bks Demand.

Scope of Music. Percy C. Buck. LC 70-93321. (Essay Index Reprint Ser.). 1977. 17.95 (*0-8369-1276-4*) Ayer.

Scope of Practice for Nursing Informatics. American Nurses Association Staff. 15p. 1994. pap. 9.50 (*0-614-02736-5*, NP-90) Am Nurses Pub.

Scope of Reincarnation. William Q. Judge. 98p. 1987. pap. 3.00 (*0-938998-30-7*) Theosophy.

Scope of State Power in China. Ed. by Stuart R. Schram. LC 85-8299. 1985p. 1986. text ed. 39.95 (*0-312-70338-4*) St Martin.

Scope of the Fantastic-Culture, Biography, Themes, Children's Literature: Selected Essays from the First International Conference on the Fantastic in Literature & Film. Ed. by Robert A. Collins & Howard D. Pearce. LC 84-530. (Contributions to the Study of Science Fiction & Fantasy Ser.: No. 11). (Illus.). xiii, 284p. 1985. text ed. 59.95 (*0-313-23448-5*, COF/02) Greenwood.

Scope of the Fantastic-Theory, Technique, Major Authors: Selected Essays from the First International Conference on the Fantastic in Literature & Film. Ed. by Robert A. Collins & Howard D. Pearce. LC 84-538. (Contributions to the Study of Science Fiction & Fantasy Ser.: No. 10). (Illus.). xii, 295p. 1985. text ed. 59.95 (*0-313-23447-7*, COF/01) Greenwood.

Scope of the Shopping Center Industry in the United States, 1993-1994: Basic Facts & Economic Impacts. rev. ed. 106p. 1993. pap. 129.95 (*0-927547-32-5*) Intl Coun Shop.

Scope of Words: In Honor of Albert S. Cook. Ed. by Peter Baker et al. LC 90-27661. 440p. (C). 1991. text ed. 54.00 (*0-8204-1417-4*) P Lang Pubng.

Scope Play Books, No. 3. pap. 3.47 (*0-590-04596-2*) Scholastic Inc.

SCOPE Testability Products Applications Guide. Texas Instruments Engineering Staff. 194p. 1990. 9.95 (*0-685-62523-0*, SSYA006) Tex Instr Inc.

Scope V of the Nursey Industry. 32p. 1985. pap. text ed. 25.00 (*0-935336-06-0*) Horticult Research.

Scopes of Dimensions. Janet McClure. 159p. (Orig.). 1989. pap. 11.95 (*0-929385-09-8*) Light Tech Comns Servs.

***Scopes Trial.** Edward J. Larson. 336p. 1998. pap. write for info. (*0-465-07510-X*) Basic.

Scopes Trial. Don Nardo. (Famous Trials Ser.). (Illus.). (YA). 1996. lib. bdg. 17.96 (*1-56006-268-1*) Lucent Bks.

Scopes Trial: Defending the Right to Teach. Arthur Blake. LC 93-37018. (Spotlight on American History Ser.). (Illus.). 64p. (J). (gr. 4-6). 1994. lib. bdg. 16.40 (*1-56294-407-X*) Millbrook Pr.

Scoping: A Teen's Star Guide to School, Friends &, of Course, Guys. Barbara Stepko. 144p. (Orig.). (YA). 1995. mass mkt. 3.99 (*0-380-77828-9*, Flare) Avon.

Scoptocratic. Nancy Shaw. 93p. (C). 1992. pap. 12.00 (*1-55022-175-2*, Pub. by ECW Press CN) Genl Dist Srvs.

Scorched Earth. Louis Hooban. 180p. 1989. pap. 13.00 (*1-884710-03-4*) Indian Heritage.

Scorched Earth. Warren Murphy & Sapir. (Destroyer Ser.: No. 105). 1996. pap. 5.50 (*0-373-63220-7*, 1-63220-7, Wrldwide Lib) Harlequin Bks.

Scorched Earth: The Military's Assault on the Environment. William Thomas. (Illus.). 224p. 1995. pap. 18.95 (*0-86571-294-8*) New Soc Pubs.

Scorched Earth: The Military's Assault on the Environment. William Thomas. (Illus.). 224p. 1995. lib. bdg. 44.95 (*0-86571-293-X*) New Soc Pubs.

Scorched Earth: The Russian-German War 1943-1944. Paul Carell. LC 93-87471. (Illus.). 556p. 1994. 39.95 (*0-88740-598-3*) Schiffer.

Scorcher. John Lutz. 256p. 1988. pap. 3.95 (*0-380-70526-5*) Avon.

***Scorches Hands: An Anthology of Verse & Rage.** Ed. by Richard D. Houff. (Illus.). 120p. (Orig.). 1996. pap. 12.50 (*1-886895-05-8*) Poetry Harbor.

Scord of Brouster: An Early Agricultural Settlement on Shetland. Alasdair Whittle et al. (Illus.). 160p. 1987. pap. 19.98 (*0-947816-09-7*, Pub. by Oxford Univ Comm Arch UK) David Brown.

***Score.** large type ed. Jane Morell. (Linford Romance Large Print Ser.). 352p. 1996. pap. 15.99 (*0-7089-7971-8*) Ulverscroft.

Score! My Twenty-Five Years with the Broad Street Bullies. Gene Hart & Buzz Ringe. (Illus.). 342p. 1990. 18.95 (*0-929387-17-1*) Bonus Books.

Score! Soccer Tactics & Techniques for a Better Offense. Wiel Coerver. LC 94-45495. (Illus.). 192p. (DUT & ENG.). 1995. pap. 16.95 (*0-8069-0976-5*) Sterling.

SCORE: Solving Community Obstacles & Restoring Employment. Lynn Wechsler Kramer. LC 83-26555. (Occupational Therapy in Mental Health Ser.: Vol. 4, No. 1). 135p. 1984. text ed. 32.95 (*0-86656-295-8*) Haworth Pr.

Score - All Basketball Scorebook. S. D. Uslan. (Illus.). 64p. 1984. spiral bd. 3.95 (*0-88041-004-3*) Avalon Comm.

Score - All Soccer Scorebook. S. D. Uslan. (Illus.). 64p. 1984. spiral bd. 3.95 (*0-88041-005-1*) Avalon Comm.

Score - All Softball - Baseball Scorebook. S. D. Uslan. (Illus.). 64p. 1983. spiral bd. 3.95 (*0-88041-003-5*) Avalon Comm.

Score & Parts see Six Fantasias for Four Viols

***Score & Podium, 2 vols.** Frederik Prausnitz. Incl. A Complete Guide to Conducting. rev. ed. 544p. 1998. 49.50 (*0-8108-3420-0*); The Workbook. (Illus.). 96p. 1998. 23.50 (*0-8108-3421-9*); 65.00 (*0-8108-3425-1*) Scarecrow.

Score of Composers see Famous Composers

Score Reading, 4 vols. Roger Fiske. Incl. Vol. 1. Orchestration. 72p. 1968. 11.95 (*0-19-321301-X*); Vol. 2. Musical Form. 104p. 1968. 11.95 (*0-19-321302-8*); (YA). (gr. 9-p). write for info. (*0-318-54892-5*) OUP.

Score Reading, Bk. 5: Twentieth-Century Music. Malcolm Barry & Roger Parker. (Illus.). 88p. 1987. pap. text ed. 11.95 (*0-19-321030-4*) OUP.

SCORE That Counts: The Story of the Service Corps of Retired Executives. Elwyn A. Nellis. (Illus.). 188p. 1989. 7.50 (*0-9623466-0-8*) SCOREA.

Scoreboard Alert, April-May 1989. 1989. 1.95 (*0-89921-054-6*) Biblical News Serv.

Scoreboard Alert, August-October 1989. 1989. 1.95 (*0-89921-056-2*) Biblical News Serv.

Scoreboard Alert, June-July 1989. 1989. 1.95 (*0-89921-055-4*) Biblical News Serv.

Scoreboard Series: Fast Break, The Lunch Bowl, Side Kick, Strike Zone, In the Running, 5 bks., Set. Steven A. Boga & Bob Wright. Ed. by Betty L. Kratoville. (Illus.). 48p. (J). (gr. 2 up). 1994. pap. text ed. 17.00 (*0-87879-989-3*) Acad Therapy.

***Scoreboards: The Golf Professional's Complete Guide for Developing & Presenting Scoreboards.** Randy Houseman. (Illus.). 136p. (Orig.). 1997. pap. write for info. (*0-9656240-0-5*) Green Grass.

Scorebuilder for Principles of Accounting, Vol. I. Bruce Baldwin. 181p. (C). 1989. pap. text ed. 19.95 (*0-256-07831-9*, 01-3037-01) Irwin.

Scorebuilder for Principles of Accounting, Vol. II. Bruce Baldwin. 179p. (C). 1989. pap. text ed. 19.95 (*0-256-07832-7*, 01-3038-01) Irwin.

***Scorecard.** Gutfeld. LC 97-11894. 1997. pap. 9.95 (*0-8050-5450-2*) H Holt & Co.

Scorecard, Set. J. Richard Aronson. (C). 1979. pap. text ed. 17.75 (*0-7216-1409-4*) Dryden Pr.

Scorecard on the Israeli Economy: A Review of 1989. Alvin Rabushka. xvi, 73p. (Orig.). 1990. pap. write for info. (*0-923791-01-9*) IASPS.

***ScoreKeepers: Catalog Your Music from A to Z.** Will Limkemann et al. (Software-in-a-Book Ser.: No. 4). (Illus.). 192p. (Orig.). 1997. pap. 49.95 (*1-887155-03-1*) Doubleware Pubns.

Scores. Robert W. Miller. (Illus.). 47p. (Orig.). 1995. pap. 7.95 (*0-9649807-0-3*) R W Miller.

Scores & Recordings at the Indiana University Latin American Music Center. Ed. by Richardo Lorenz et al. LC 94-945. 1995. 75.00 (*0-253-33273-7*) Ind U Pr.

Scoring for Films. Earle Hagen. 1989. text ed. 49.95 incl. cd-rom (*0-88284-388-5*, 3399); pap. text ed. 39.95 incl. cd-rom (*0-88284-387-7*, 3398) Alfred Pub.

Scoring for Films. Earle Hagen. 1990. pap. 39.95 incl. cd-rom (*0-88284-447-4*, 3400) Alfred Pub.

Scoring for Voice: A Guide to Writing Vocal Arrangements. Jimmy Joyce. 82p. (Orig.). 1990. reprint ed. pap. text ed. 17.95 incl. cd-rom (*0-88284-471-7*, 3401) Alfred Pub.

Scoring Guide GED Assessment. Ed Swartz. 1988. pap. 7.60 (*0-8092-4656-2*) Contemp Bks.

Scoring Guidelines for the Home Care Accreditation Program. 120p. 1988. pap. 35.00 (*0-86688-168-9*) Joint Comm Hlthcare.

Scoring High on Bar Exam Essays: 80 Full-Length Sample Bar Exam Questions. 2nd rev. ed. Mary C. Gallagher. 306p. (Orig.). 1996. pap. 24.99 (*1-57613-001-0*) Sulzburger & Graham Pub.

Scoring High on College Entrance Examinations. Nicholas S. Vazzana & Carol J. Theil. (gr. 11-12). 1976. teacher ed. 39.95 (*0-89507-000-6*); student ed. 5.50 (*0-685-85067-6*) Multi Dimen.

Scoring in Heaven: Gravestones & Cemetery Art of the American Sunbelt States. Lucinda Bunnen & Virginia W. Smith. (Illus.). 176p. 1991. 40.00 (*0-89381-474-1*) Aperture.

***Scoring Load Capacity of Gears Lubricated with EP-Oils.** Hans Winter & K. Michaelis. (Technical Papers). 10p. 1983. pap. text ed. 30.00 (*1-55589-071-7*) AGMA.

Scorn for the World: Bernard of Cluny's De Contemptu Mundi: The Latin Text with English Translation. Bernard of Cluny. Ed. & Tr. by Ronald E. Pepin. (Medieval Texts & Studies: No. 8). 189p. 1991. 39.95 (*0-937191-35-3*) Colleagues Pr Inc.

Scornflakes. Attila the Stockbroker. (Illus.). 63p. 9400. pap. 13.95 (*1-85224-231-0*, Pub. by Bloodaxe Bks UK) Dufour.

Scornfyl Lady. Francis Beaumont & John Fletcher. LC 73-38152. (English Experience Ser.: No. 432). 70p. 1972. reprint ed. 15.00 (*90-221-0432-X*) Walter J Johnson.

Scorpian Shards. Neal Shusterman. 191p. (J). (gr. 6-9). 1995. 18.95 (*0-312-85506-0*) Tor Bks.

Scorpianne. Emily Devenport. 256p. (Orig.). 1994. pap. 4.99 (*0-451-45318-2*, ROC) NAL-Dutton.

Scorpio. (Super Horoscopes, 1995 Ser.). 256p. 1994. pap. 4.99 (*0-7865-0033-6*) Diamond.

Scorpio. (Total Horoscopes, 1995 Ser.). 272p. 1994. pap. text ed. 4.50 (*0-515-11418-9*) Jove Pubns.

Scorpio. (Love Signs Library). 64p. 1996. 8.95 (*0-7894-1096-6*) DK Pub Inc.

***Scorpio.** (Parker's Love Signs Ser.). 1996. 8.95 (*0-614-20709-6*) DK Pub Inc.

***Scorpio.** (Astrology Journals). (Illus.). 80p. 1997. pap. 6.50 (*1-55670-575-1*) Stewart Tabori & Chang.

***Scorpio.** (Fisher-Price Little People Coloring & Activity Ser.). (Illus.). 24p. 1997. pap. write for info. (*1-56144-967-9*, Honey Bear Bks) Modern Pub NYC.

***Scorpio.** Ariel Books Staff. (Tiny Tomes Ser.). 128p. 1997. 3.95 (*0-8362-2671-2*, Arie Bks) Andrews & McMeel.

***Scorpio.** Berkley Publishing Staff. (Berkley Super Horoscopes Ser.). 256p. 1997. pap. 6.99 (*0-425-15893-4*) Berkley Pub.

Scorpio. Lucille Callard. (Astro-Pups: Your Sign, Your Dogs Ser.). (Illus.). 60p. 1991. pap. 9.95 (*1-881038-07-6*) Penzance Pr.

Scorpio. Paula Harris. (Sun Sign Ser.). 40p. (J). (gr. 4). 1989. lib. bdg. 13.95 (*0-88682-260-2*) Creative Ed.

Scorpio. Derek Parker & Julia Parker. LC 92-52791. (Sun & Moon Signs Library). (Illus.). 64p. 1992. 8.95 (*1-56458-091-1*) DK Pub Inc.

***Scorpio: A Little Book of Zodiac Wisdom, a Pop-Up Book.** Running Press Staff. (Zodiac Wisdom Ser.). 1997. 4.95 (*0-7624-0029-3*) Running Pr.

Scorpio: Astro-Numerology. 2nd ed. Michael J. Kurban. (Illus.). 50p. 1991. pap. 8.00 (*0-938863-16-9*) Libra Press Chi.

Scorpio: Death Grip. Jahnna N. Malcolm. (Zodiac Ser.: No. 4). 192p. 1995. mass mkt. 3.99 (*0-06-106270-7*) HarpC.

Scorpio: Little Birth Sign. Ariel Books Staff. 1994. 4.95 (*0-8362-3078-7*) Andrews & McMeel.

***Scorpio: Old Moore's Horoscopes & Astral Diaries.** W. Foulsham & Co. Staff. 1997. pap. text ed. 5.95 (*0-572-02358-8*, Pub. by W Foulsham UK) Trans-Atl Phila.

Scorpio: Scorpio. (Total Horoscopes Ser.). 272p. 1997. mass mkt. 5.99 (*0-515-12115-0*) Jove Pubns.

***Scorpio: Your Sun-&-Moon Guide to Love & Life.** Ariel Books Staff. 374p. (Orig.). 1997. pap. 5.95 (*0-8362-3565-7*, Arie Bks) Andrews & McMeel.

Scorpio Ghosts & the Black Hole Gang see Ghostmobile

Scorpio III. Robert Ludlum. 544p. 1994. pap. 8.99 (*0-553-56838-8*) Bantam.

Scorpio Illusion. 6.98 (*0-8317-4693-9*) Smithmark.

Scorpio Illusion. Robert Ludlum. 672p. 1994. mass mkt. 7.50 (*0-553-56603-2*) Bantam.

***Scorpio Illusion.** large type ed. Robert Ludlum. pap. 18.95 (*0-7451-3550-1*, Pub. by Chivers Lrg Print UK) Chivers N Amer.

Scorpio Rising. Douglas M. Baker. (Esoteric Astrology: The Rising Signs Ser.). 1980. pap. 7.50 (*0-906006-54-6*, Pub. by Baker Pubns UK) New Leaf Dist.

Scorpio Six: Dragon Claw. Alex McDonough. 176p. (Orig.). 1993. mass mkt. 4.99 (*0-441-75514-3*) Ace Bks.

Scorpio Society, No. 2. Carol Ellis. 176p. (J). 1995. pap. 3.99 (*0-679-87305-8*) McKay.

Scorpio Sun Sign. Douglas M. Baker. (Astrological Sun Sign Ser.). 1972. pap. 5.50 (*0-906006-24-4*, Pub. by Baker Pubns UK) New Leaf Dist.

S

Scorpio 1994 Purse Book. 1994. mass mkt. 1.25 (*0-440-60237-8*) Dell.

Scorpio 1995 Love Signs. 1995. mass mkt. 1.29 (*0-440-22127-7*) Dell.

Scorpio 1995 Purse Book. 1994. mass mkt. 0.99 (*0-440-60239-4*) Dell.

Scorpio 1996 Purse Book. 1995. mass mkt. 1.19 (*0-440-60253-X*) Dell.

Scorpio 97. Sydney Omarr. 1996. pap. 4.99 (*0-451-18837-3*, Sig) NAL-Dutton.

Scorpion. Albert Memmi. (Folio Ser.: No. 1715). 270p. (FRE.). 1986. pap. 10.95 (*2-07-037715-6*) Schoenhof.

Scorpion. 2nd ed. Albert Memmi. LC 79-114950. 242p. 1975. reprint ed. 9.95 (*0-87955-908-X*); reprint ed. pap. 7.95 (*0-87955-906-3*) O'Hara.

Scorpion. Anna E. Weirauch. Tr. by Whittaker Chambers from GER. LC 75-12357. (Homosexuality Ser.). (ENG.). 1975. reprint ed. 18.95 (*0-405-07375-5*) Ayer.

Scorpion Affair. Dick Beyer. LC 93-71006. 304p. 1993. pap. 5.95 (*0-9635404-8-3*) TwoForYou Bks.

Scorpion CITV 1972-1994. Christopher F. Foss. (New Vanguard Ser.). (Illus.). 48p. 1995. pap. 12.95 (*1-85532-390-7*, Pub. by Osprey UK) Stackpole.

***Scorpion Files: Lies Satan Tells to Young Catholics.** Michelle Willis & Jackie Cole. LC 96-68758. 188p. (J). 1997. pap. 12.00 (*0-9607028-5-7*, 5-7) Ocean East.

Scorpion God: Three Short Novels. William Golding. 1984. pap. 6.00 (*0-15-679658-9*, Harvest Bks) HarBrace.

Scorpion in the Sea. P. T. Deutermann. 1994. mass mkt. 6.99 (*0-312-95179-5*) St Martin.

Scorpion in the Sea. P. T. Deutermann. Date not set. pap. write for info. (*0-451-18303-7*) NAL-Dutton.

Scorpion in the Sea: The Goldsborough Incident. P. T. Deutermann. LC 92-30827. 496p. 1992. 19.95 (*0-913969-49-4*, G Mason Univ Pr) Univ Pub Assocs.

Scorpion Man: Exploring the World of Scorpions. Laurence Pringle. LC 93-34936. (Illus.). (YA). (gr. 5 up). 1994. 15.95 (*0-684-19560-7*) S&S Trade.

Scorpion Sapphire: A Novel of Suspense. J. Bruce Monson. LC 89-38510. 256p. 1990. 17.95 (*0-931832-40-3*) Fithian Pr.

***Scorpion Shards, Vol. 1.** Neal Shusterman. 1996. mass mkt. 4.99 (*0-8125-2465-9*) Tor Bks.

Scorpion Strike. John J. Nance. 1994. mass mkt. 5.99 (*0-449-22221-7*, Crest) Fawcett.

Scorpion Trap. large type ed. Alfred Handley. (Linford Mystery Library). 288p. 1989. pap. 15.99 (*0-7089-6726-4*, Linford) Ulverscroft.

Scorpions. Jason Cooper. (Animals Without Bones Ser.). (J). 1996. write for info. (*0-86625-573-7*) Rourke Pubns.

Scorpions. Michael Golden. Ed. by J. Friedland & R. Kessler. (Novel-Ties Ser.). 1993. pap. text ed. 15.95 (*0-88122-912-1*) Lrn Links.

Scorpions. Tamara Green. (New Creepy Crawly Collection). (Illus.). (J). 1996. lib. bdg. 18.60 (*0-8368-1580-7*) Gareth Stevens Inc.

Scorpions. Robert Kelly. 1996. pap. text ed. 10.95 (*1-886449-20-1*) Barrytown Ltd.

Scorpions. Peter Murray. (Nature Bks.). 32p. (J). (gr. 2-6). 1996. lib. bdg. 22.79 (*1-56766-217-X*) Childs World.

Scorpions. Walter D. Myers. LC 85-45815. 160p. (YA). (gr. 7 up). 1988. 14.95 (*0-06-024364-3*); lib. bdg. 14.89 (*0-06-024365-1*) HarpC Child Bks.

Scorpions. Walter D. Myers. LC 85-45815. (Trophy Bk.). 224p. (YA). (gr. 7 up). 1996. pap. 4.50 (*0-06-440623-7*, Trophy) HarpC Child Bks.

Scorpions. Conrad J. Storad. LC 94-4634. (Early Bird Nature Bks.). (Illus.). 48p. (J). (gr. 3-5). 1994. lib. bdg. 18.95 (*0-8225-3004-X*, Lerner Publctns) Lerner Group.

Scorpions. Robert Kelly. LC 84-8785. 192p. (Orig.). 1985. reprint ed. pap. 7.95 (*0-88268-018-8*) Station Hill Pr.

Scorpions: Face the Heat with Notes & Tablature. 80p. 1994. per. 19.95 (*0-7935-3221-3*, 00694916) H Leonard.

***Scorpions - World Wide Live.** Ed. by Carol Cuellar. 96p. (Orig.). (C). 1985. pap. text ed. 12.95 (*0-7692-0496-1*, VF1258) Warner Brothers.

Scorpions & Venomous Insects of the Southwest. Erik D. Stoops. LC 95-1918. 1995. pap. 9.95 (*0-914846-87-6*) Golden West Pub.

Scorpions (Arachnida) from Costa Rica: Special Publications of the Museum. Oscar F. Francke & Scott A. Stockwell. (Illus.). 64p. 1987. 20.00 (*0-89672-147-7*); pap. 12.00 (*0-89672-146-9*) Tex Tech Univ Pr.

An Asterisk (*) at the beginning of an entry indicates that the title is appearing in BIP for the first time.

Scorpion's Dance. Warren Murphy. 1990. mass mkt. 4.95 (*1-55817-333-1*, Pinncle Kensgtn) Kensgtn Pub Corp.

***Scorpion's Dark Dance.** Alfredo De Palchi. Tr. by Sonia Raiziss from ITA. Date not set. write for info. (*0-614-24576-1*) Xenos Riverside.

Scorpion's Dark Dance: A Xenos Dual-Language Book. Alfredo De Palchi. Ed. by Karl Kvitko. Tr. by Sonia Raiziss. LC 93-16133. (Illus.). xiii, 130p. (Orig.). (ENG & ITA.). 1993. pap. 13.00 (*1-879378-05-1*); lib. bdg. 25.00 (*1-879378-06-X*) Xenos Riverside.

***Scorpions in a Bottle: Ethnic Conflict in Northern Ireland.** John Darby. 300p. 1997. 54.95 (*1-873194-11-0*, Pub. by Minority Rts Pubns UK); pap. 19.95 (*1-873194-16-1*, Pub. by Minority Rts Pubns UK) Paul & Co Pubs.

***Scorpion's Tongue.** Gail Collins. Date not set. write for info. (*0-688-14914-6*) Morrow.

Scorpius Connection. Craig L. Etka. 304p. (Orig.). 1994. pap. 16.95 (*1-56167-175-4*) Am Literary Pr.

Scorpius Equation. Larry Townsend. (Orig.). 1993. mass mkt. 4.95 (*1-56333-119-5*, Badboy) Masquerade.

Scorsese Connection. Stern. 1995. 47.00 (*0-85170-512-X*, Pub. by British Film Inst UK); 35.00 (*0-614-11863-8*); pap. 14.95 (*0-85170-513-8*, Pub. by British Film Inst UK) Ind U Pr.

Scorsese Connection. Lesley Stern. LC 95-38574. (Perspectives Ser.). 1995. 35.00 (*0-253-32952-3*); pap. 14.95 (*0-253-21011-9*) Ind U Pr.

Scorsese on Scorsese. Martin Scorsese. Ed. by David Thompson & Ian Christie. (Illus.). 200p. 1990. pap. 13.95 (*0-571-15243-0*) Faber & Faber.

Scorsese on Scorsese: The Update. 2nd ed. Ed. by David Thompson & Ian Christie. (Illus.). 240p. 1996. reprint ed. pap. 14.95 (*0-571-17827-8*) Faber & Faber.

Scorsese Picture: The Art & Life of Martin Scorsese. David Ehrenstein. (Illus.). 256p. 1992. 30.00 (*1-55972-152-9*, Birch Ln Pr) Carol Pub Group.

Scot & His Oats: A Survey of the Part Played by Oats & Oatmeal in Scottish History, Legend, Romance, & the Scottish Character. G. W. Lockhart. 72p. 1989. pap. 35.00 (*0-946487-05-7*, Pub. by Luath Pr UK) St Mut.

Scot Free. large type ed. Alastair Scott. (Illus.). 512p. 1987. 25.99 (*0-7089-1647-3*) Ulverscroft.

Scot Free: New Scottish Plays. Ed. by Alasdair Cameron. 275p. 1994. pap. 19.95 (*1-85459-017-0*, Pub. by N Hern Bks UK) Theatre Comm.

Scot Gallery Eccentric: Wry Tales of a Little-Known Realm. Tom Roy. LC 92-30161. (Orig.). 1993. 14.95 (*1-879094-22-3*) Momentum Bks.

Scot Goes South: A Journey from Mexico to Ayers Rock. large type ed. Alastair Scott. (Illus.). 1991. 27.99 (*0-7089-8621-8*) Ulverscroft.

Scot in History. Wallace Notestein. LC 76-104225. xvii, 371p. 1970. reprint ed. text ed. 59.75 (*0-8371-3342-4*, NOSH, Greenwood Pr) Greenwood.

Scot Returns: A Journey from Bali to Skye. large type ed. Alastair Scott. (Illus.). 448p. 1992. 27.99 (*0-7089-8628-5*) Ulverscroft.

Scotch Ale. Gregory J. Noonan. (Classic Beer Style Ser.). (Illus.). 197p. 1993. pap. 11.95 (*0-937381-35-7*) Brewers Pubns.

Scotch & Holy Water. John D. Tumpane. LC 81-84788. 348p. (Orig.). 1981. pap. 10.00 (*0-9607382-0-7*) St Giles.

Scotch in Miniature. rev. ed. Picton Publishing Staff & Alan Keegan. (Illus.). (C). 1987. 30.00 (*0-317-90426-4*, Pub. by Picton UK) St Mut.

Scotch-Irish. William Durning & Mary Durning. Ed. by Margaret Harris. LC 91-72478. (Illus.). 192p. 1991. pap. 15.95 (*0-9601868-2-4*) Irish Family Names.

Scotch-Irish: A Social History. James G. Leyburn. LC 62-16063. xx, 397p. (C). 1989. reprint ed. pap. 15.95 (*0-8078-4259-1*) U of NC Pr.

Scotch-Irish: Or the Scot in North Britain, North Ireland, & North America, 2 Vols., Set. Charles A. Hanna. (Illus.). 1225p. 1995. 75.00 (*0-8063-0168-6*) Genealog Pub.

Scotch-Irish & Their First Settlements on the Tyger River. George D. Howe. 31p. 1992. reprint ed. pap. 10.00 (*0-89308-475-1*, SC 53) Southern Hist Pr.

Scotch-Irish Family Research Made Simple. rev. ed. R. G. Campbell. (Illus.). 65p. 1992. pap. 10.00 (*1-878311-14-X*, Heritge Hse) Ye Olde Genealogie Shoppe.

Scotch-Irish in America. Henry J. Ford. 1972. 59.95 (*0-8490-1004-7*) Gordon Pr.

Scotch-Irish in America. Henry J. Ford. LC 69-18775. (American Immigration Collection. Series 1). 1969. reprint ed. 23.95 (*0-405-00523-7*) Ayer.

Scotch-Irish in America. Henry J. Ford. 607p. 1995. reprint ed. pap. 39.95 (*0-685-62600-8*, 9085) Clearfield Co.

Scotch-Irish in America. Henry J. Ford. (BCL1 - U. S. History Ser.). 607p. 1991. reprint ed. lib. bdg. 109.00 (*0-7812-6080-9*) Rprt Serv.

Scotch Irish Pioneers in Ulster & America. Charles K. Bolton. (Illus.). 412p. 1989. reprint ed. pap. 21.50 (*1-55613-235-2*) Heritage Bk.

Scotch-Irish Sources of Research. Afton E. Reintjes. 50p. 1986. pap. 16.50 (*0-940764-46-6*) Genealog Inst.

Scotch Phantasy Opus 46: Violin & Piano. M. Bruch. 36p. 1986. pap. 7.95 (*0-7935-5132-3*) H Leonard.

Scotch Plains, NJ. R. Bousquet. (Images of America Ser.). 1995. pap. 16.99 (*0-7524-0235-8*, Arcdia) Chalford.

Scotch Verdict. Lillian Faderman. 1994. pap. 16.00 (*0-231-08443-9*) Col U Pr.

***Scotch 4...QH4: The Steinitz Variation.** Sid Pickard. 103p. 1995. pap. 4.95 (*1-886846-02-2*) Pickard & Son.

Scotching the Myths: An Alternative Route Map to Scottish History. Jim Hewitson. (Illus.). 322p. 1996. 22.95 (*1-85158-701-2*, Pub. by Mnstream UK) Trafalgar.

Scotec Level Two Electrical Engineering Mathematics. Ed. by B. Buchan. (C). 1980. 50.00 (*0-85950-477-8*, Pub. by S Thornes Pubs UK) St Mut.

Scotec Level Two Mechanical Engineering Mathematics. Ed. by Stanley Thornes. (C). 1980. 50.00 (*0-85950-467-0*, Pub. by S Thornes Pubs UK) St Mut.

Scotichronicon, Vol. 6, Bks. 11-12. Walter Bower. Ed. by D. E. Watt. 570p. 1991. text ed. 68.00 (*0-08-041222-X*, Pergamon Pr) Elsevier.

Scotichronicon: Books XV & XVI, Vol. 8. Walter Bower. Ed. by D. R. Watt. 440p. 1987. text ed. 70.00 (*0-08-034527-1*, Pub. by Aberdeen U Pr) Macmillan.

Scoticisms, Arranged in Alphabetical Order, Designed to Correct Improprieties of Speech & Writing. James Beattie. LC 78-67647. (Scottish Enlightenment Ser.). reprint ed. 37.50 (*0-404-17177-X*) AMS Pr.

Scotish Poems, 3 vols., Set. Ed. by John Pinkerton. LC 70-144531. reprint ed. 165.00 (*0-404-08680-2*) AMS Pr.

Scotland. (Insight Guides, Windows on the World Ser.). (Illus.). 350p. 1993. pap. 22.95 (*0-395-66191-9*) HM.

***Scotland.** LC 96-44934. (Origins Ser.). (J). 1997. lib. bdg. write for info. (*0-531-14441-0*) Watts.

Scotland. Photos by Colin Baxter. (Illus.). 96p. pap. 16.95 (*0-948661-23-2*, Pub. by Colin Baxter Ltd UK) Voyageur Pr.

Scotland. Edizioni White Star Staff. (World Traveler Ser.). 1996. 14.98 (*0-8317-4303-4*) Smithmark.

Scotland. Eric G. Grant. (World Bibliographical Ser.: No. 34). 408p. 1982. lib. bdg. 55.00 (*0-903450-64-X*) ABC-CLIO.

***Scotland.** Hill. Date not set. pap. text ed. write for info. (*0-582-53346-5*, Pub. by Longman UK) Longman.

Scotland. HMSO Staff. (Aspects of Britain Ser.). 102p. 1993. pap. 9.95 (*0-11-701728-0*, HM17280, Pub. by Stationery Ofc UK) Bernan Associates.

***Scotland.** David Lyons. (Land of the Poets Ser.). (Illus.). 64p. 1996. 9.99 (*1-57215-141-2*, JG1140) World Pubns.

Scotland. Richard V. Smith & Alistair Cruickshank. (Around the World Program Ser.). (Illus.). 64p. (Orig.). 1997. pap. 13.95 (*0-939923-62-9*) M & W Pub Co.

Scotland. Richard V. Smith & Alistair Cruickshank. (Around the World Program Ser.). (Illus.). 64p. (Orig.). 1997. 18.95 (*0-939923-63-7*) M & W Pub Co.

Scotland. Donald Sommerville. (Illus.). 80p. 1995. 9.98 (*0-8317-7167-4*) Smithmark.

Scotland. Dorothy B. Sutherland. LC 84-23227. (Enchantment of the World Ser.). (Illus.). 128p. (J). (gr. 5-9). 1985. lib. bdg. 30.00 (*0-516-02787-5*) Childrens.

Scotland. Doreen Taylor. LC 90-10028. (World in View Ser.). (Illus.). 96p. (YA). (gr. 6-11). 1990. lib. bdg. 25.26 (*0-8114-2431-6*) Raintree Steck-V.

Scotland. Tr. by Maureen Walker. LC 95-12370. (Tintin's Travel Diaries). (Illus.). 80p. (J). 1995. pap. 6.95 (*0-8120-9238-4*) Barron.

Scotland. Tr. by Maureen Walker. LC 95-12370. (Tintin's Travel Diaries). (Illus.). 80p. (J). 1995. 11.95 (*0-8120-6503-4*) Barron.

Scotland. 2nd ed. Martin Belford & Belford. (Rough Guide Ser.). (Illus.). 512p. 1996. pap. 16.95 (*1-85828-166-0*, Penguin Bks) Viking Penguin.

***Scotland.** 2nd ed. Jarrold Printing Staff. 1997. 24.95 (*0-02-861874-2*) Macmillan.

Scotland. 11th ed. John Tomes. (Blue Guides Ser.). (Illus.). 512p. 1996. pap. 24.95 (*0-393-31417-0*, Norton Paperbks) Norton.

Scotland: A Concise History. rev. ed. Fitzroy Maclean. LC 92-62136. (Illus.). 240p. 1993. pap. 15.95 (*0-500-27706-0*) Thames Hudson.

Scotland: A Literary Guide. Alan N. Bold. 384p. 1989. 75.00 (*0-415-00731-3*) Routledge.

Scotland: An Intimate Portrait. Geddes MacGregor. 288p. 1990. pap. 12.95 (*0-395-56236-8*) HM.

Scotland: Archaeology & Early History. Graham Ritchie & Anna Ritchie. (Illus.). 208p. 1992. pap. 25.00 (*0-7486-0291-7*, Pub. by Edinburgh U Pr UK) Col U Pr.

***Scotland: Environment & Archaeology, 8000 B. C.-A. D. 1000.** Kevin J. Edwards & Ian Ralston. LC 96-36113. 1997. text ed. 80.00 (*0-471-94873-X*) Wiley.

Scotland: From the Earliest Times to the Present Century. John J. Mackintosh. LC 75-39198. (Select Bibliographies Reprint Ser.). 1977. reprint ed. 29.95 (*0-8369-6800-X*) Ayer.

Scotland: Land of Mountains. Colin Baxter & Desin Thompson. (Illus.). 128p. 29.95 (*0-948661-61-5*, Pub. by Colin Baxter Ltd UK) Voyageur Pr.

***Scotland: Myths & Legends.** B. Beare. 1996. 7.98 (*0-7858-0537-0*) Bk Sales Inc.

Scotland: Off the Beaten Track. Patrick Thorne. LC 94-29280. (Off the Beaten Track Ser.). (Illus.). 300p. 1994. pap. 14.95 (*1-56440-478-1*, Pub. by Moorland Pubng UK) Globe Pequot.

Scotland: The Land & the Whisky. Roddy Martine. (Illus.). 224p. 1995. 55.00 (*0-7195-5351-2*, Pub. by John Murray UK) Trafalgar.

***Scotland - The Movie.** David Bruce. 320p. (Orig.). 1996. pap. 22.00 (*0-7486-6209-X*, Pub. by Polygon UK) Subterranean Co.

***Scotland Address Book.** Photos by Colin Baxter. (Illus.). 72p. 1997. 8.95 (*1-900455-14-5*, Pub. by Colin Baxter Ltd UK) Voyageur Pr.

***Scotland after Enlightenment.** Craig Beveridge & Ronald Turnbull. 184p. 1997. 20.00 (*0-7486-6223-5*, Pub. by Polygon UK) Subterranean Co.

***Scotland & Its First American Colony, 1683-1765.** Ned C. Landsman. LC 84-42891. 375p. 1985. reprint ed. pap. 106.90 (*0-608-02509-7*, 2063153) Bks Demand.

Scotland & Its Neighbours in the Middle Ages. Geoffrey W. Barrow. LC 92-21984. 228p. 1992. boxed 55.00 (*1-85285-052-3*) Hambledon Press.

Scotland & Nationalism: Scottish Society & Politics, 1707-1977. Christopher T. Harvie. 318p. (C). 1986. pap. 35.00 (*0-317-89988-0*) St Mut.

Scotland & Nationalism: Scottish Society & Politics, 1707-1977. Christopher T. Harvie. LC 77-368131. 318p. reprint ed. pap. 90.70 (*0-317-20063-1*, 2023328) Bks Demand.

Scotland & Nationalism: Scottish Society & Politics, 1707-1994. Christopher T. Harvie. LC 93-2532. 236p. (C). 1994. pap. 18.95 (*0-415-09041-5*) Routledge.

Scotland & Scandinavia, 800-1800. Grant G. Simpson. (Mackie Monographs). 250p. (C). 1996. 75.00 (*0-85976-220-3*, Pub. by J Donald UK) St Mut.

Scotland & Scotsmen in the Eighteenth Century, 2 vols., Set. John Ramsay. Ed. by Alexander Allerdyce. (Contemporary Memoirs Ser.: Ser. 5 & 6). 578p. 1996. 200.00 (*1-85506-400-6*) Bks Intl VA.

Scotland & Scotsmen in the Eighteenth Century: From the Memoirs of John Ramsay Esq. of Ochtertyre, 2 vols. John Ramsay. Ed. by Alexander Allardyce. LC 78-67537. reprint ed. 97.50 (*0-404-17520-1*) AMS Pr.

Scotland & the Age of the Disruption. Ed. by Stewart J. Brown & Michael Fry. (Illus.). 256p. 1993. pap. 35.00 (*0-7486-0433-2*, Pub. by Edinburgh U Pr UK) Col U Pr.

Scotland & the French Revolution. Henry W. Meikle. LC 68-56255. xix, 317p. 1969. reprint ed. 45.00 (*0-678-00588-5*) Kelley.

Scotland & the Lowland Tongue: Studies in the Language & Literature of Lowland Scotland in Honour of David Donald Murison. Ed. by J. Derrick McClure. 248p. 1983. text ed. 38.00 (*0-08-028482-5*, Pergamon Pr) Elsevier.

Scotland & the Sea. Ed. by T. C. Smout. (C). 1991. text ed. 59.00 (*0-389-20969-4*) B&N Imports.

Scotland & the Sea. Ed. by T. C. Smout. 240p. (C). 1989. text ed. 75.00 (*0-85976-338-2*, Pub. by J Donald UK) St Mut.

Scotland & the Union. Ed. by Patrick S. Hodge. (Hume Papers on Public Policy). 152p. 1996. pap. 16.50 (*0-7486-0510-X*, Pub. by Edinburgh U Pr UK) Col U Pr.

Scotland & the United Kingdom: The Economy & the Union in the Twentieth Century. Clive Lee. LC 95-5482. (Insights from Economic History Ser.). 1995. text ed. 59.95 (*0-7190-4100-7*, Pub. by Manchester Univ Pr UK); text ed. 19.95 (*0-7190-4101-5*, Pub. by Manchester Univ Pr UK) St Martin.

Scotland & Wales on Twenty-Five Dollars a Day. Darwin Porter. 300p. 1986. pap. 10.95 (*0-685-11259-4*) S&S Trade.

Scotland & War. Norman MacDougall. 232p. 1991. text ed. 66.00 (*0-685-58963-3*) B&N Imports.

Scotland & War. Norman MacDougall. 200p. (C). 1996. 75.00 (*0-85976-248-3*, Pub. by J Donald UK) St Mut.

***Scotland at a Glimpse 1997.** Peter Little. (Illus.). 76p. (Orig.). 1996. pap. 12.95 (*0-9525277-6-6*, Pub. by P Little Pub IE) Irish Bks Media.

***Scotland Bed & Breakfast 1997.** Stilwell Publishing Staff. 1997. pap. text ed. 11.95 (*0-9521909-9-0*, Pub. by Stilwell Pubng UK) Seven Hills Bk.

***Scotland Bed & Breakfast 1998.** annuals Tim Stilwell. (Stilwell's Bed & Breakfasts 1998 Ser.). (Illus.). 150p. 1998. pap. 11.95 (*1-900861-04-6*, Pub. by Stilwell Pubng UK) Seven Hills Bk.

***Scotland Before History.** Stuart Piggott. 1990. 14.00 (*0-7486-6067-4*, Pub. by Polygon UK) Subterranean Co.

Scotland Before Seventeen Hundred: From Contemporary Documents. Ed. by Peter H. Brown. LC 77-87675. reprint ed. 65.00 (*0-404-16467-6*) AMS Pr.

Scotland Before the Industrial Revolution: An Economic & Social History, c.1500-c.1750. Ian D. Whyte. LC 94-35109. (Economic & Social History of Britain Ser.). 416p. (C). 1996. pap. text ed. 31.95 (*0-582-05091-X*, 77007) Longman.

Scotland County, Missouri, U. S. A., Community at Large: A Focus on Lawn Ridge, Historical, Biographical, Pictorial. Ellen K. Davison. LC 93-72626. (Illus.). 224p. 1993. lib. bdg. 39.50 (*0-9638069-0-4*) E K Davison.

Scotland Delineated, Seventeen Ninety-Nine. R. Heron. 398p. (C). 1986. 52.00 (*0-901824-40-2*, Pub. by Mercat Pr Bks UK) St Mut.

Scotland, Fascicule 4. Lawrence J. Keppie & Beverly J. Arnold. (Corpus Signorum Imperii Romani, Great Britain: Vol. I). (Illus.). 110p. 1984. 19.98 (*0-19-726026-8*) David Brown.

***Scotland for Backpackers 1997.** Ed. by Erica Brock. (Illus.). 280p. (Orig.). 1997. pap. 14.95 (*0-9524913-9-7*, Pub. by Reel Pubng UK) Seven Hills Bk.

Scotland for Kids. Anne Shade. 320p. 1996. 19.95 (*1-85158-679-2*, Pub. by Mnstream UK) Trafalgar.

Scotland from the Eleventh Century to 1603. Bruce Webster. LC 76-360512. (Sources of History: Studies in the Uses of Historical Evidence). 240p. reprint ed. pap. 68.40 (*0-317-27079-6*, 2024563) Bks Demand.

Scotland Green Guide. 2nd ed. Michelin Staff. 1994. pap. 19.95 (*0-7859-9132-8*) Fr & Eur.

Scotland Green Guide. 3rd ed. Ed. by Michelin Travel Publications, Staff. (Orig.). 1996. per. 20.00 (*2-06-157503-X*, 1575) Michelin.

Scotland Green Guide English Edition. Michelin Staff. pap. 17.95 (*0-7859-7192-0*, 2060157528) Fr & Eur.

Scotland in Film. Forsyth Hardy. (Illus.). 200p. 1990. 40.00 (*0-7486-0160-0*, Pub. by Edinburgh U Pr UK) Col U Pr.

Scotland in Film. Forsyth Hardy. (Illus.). 200p. 1991. pap. 15.00 (*0-7486-0183-X*, Pub. by Edinburgh U Pr UK) Col U Pr.

Scotland in Modern Times. William H. Marwick. (Illus.). 209p. 1964. 35.00 (*0-7146-1342-8*, Pub. by F Cass Pubs UK) Intl Spec Bk.

Scotland in Music. Roger Fiske. LC 82-14583. (Illus.). 300p. 1983. text ed. 69.95 (*0-521-24772-1*) Cambridge U Pr.

Scotland in Pictures. Ed. by Lerner Publications, Department of Geography Staff. (Visual Geography Ser.). (Illus.). 64p. (YA). (gr. 5 up). 1991. lib. bdg. 19.95 (*0-8225-1875-9*, Lerner Publctns) Lerner Group.

Scotland in the Nineteenth Century: An Analytical Bibliography of Material Relating to Scotland in Parliamentary Papers 1800-1900. Philip J. Haythornthwaite. 360p. 1993. 84.95 (*0-85967-870-9*, Pub. by Scolar Pr UK) Ashgate Pub Co.

***Scotland in the Second World War.** Helen McLullich & Sheena Bedborough. (Scottie Bks.). (Illus.). 40p. (J). 1998. pap. 8.95 (*0-11-495814-9*, Pub. by Statnry Ofc UK) Seven Hills Bk.

Scotland in the Twentieth Century. Ed. by T. M. Devine & Richard J. Finlay. 352p. Date not set. 68.00 (*0-7486-0751-X*, Pub. by Edinburgh U Pr UK) Col U Pr.

Scotland in the Twentieth Century. Ed. by T. M. Devine & Richard J. Finlay. 352p. 1996. pap. 25.00 (*0-7486-0839-7*, Pub. by Edinburgh U Pr UK) Col U Pr.

***Scotland Map.** 1996. 8.95 (*2-06-700401-8*, 401) Michelin.

***Scotland Nelles Guide.** (Nelles Guides Ser.). (Illus.). 256p. 1997. pap. 14.95 (*3-88618-049-2*, Pub. by Nelles Verlag GW) Seven Hills Bk.

***Scotland of One Hundred Years Ago.** Raymond Lamont-Brown. (Illus.). 128p. 1997. 33.95 (*0-7509-1421-1*, Pub. by Sutton Pubng UK) Bks Intl VA.

Scotland of Queen Mary & the Religious Wars, 1513-1638. Agnes M. Mackenzie. LC 75-41506. (Illus.). 404p. 1976. reprint ed. text ed. 65.00 (*0-8371-8704-4*, MASQ, Greenwood Pr) Greenwood.

***Scotland on a Shoestring: Scotland's Best for Less.** Anna Fenge. 240p. 1997. pap. 13.95 (*1-85158-937-6*, Pub. by Mnstream UK) Trafalgar.

Scotland Pocket Guide. rev. ed. Berlitz Editors. (Pocket Guides Ser.). 160p. 1995. pap. 7.95 (*2-8315-0999-8*) Berlitz.

Scotland Road. Jeffrey Hatcher. 1996. pap. 5.25 (*0-8222-1493-8*) Dramatists Play.

***Scotland Saw His Glory: A History of Revivals in Scotland.** W. J. Couper et al. Ed. by Richard O. Roberts. LC 95-78264. (Illus.). 351p. 1995. lib. bdg. 21.95 (*0-940033-51-8*) R O Roberts.

Scotland Saw His Glory: A History of Revivals in Scotland. Ed. by Richard O. Roberts. LC 95-78264. Date not set. lib. bdg. 21.95 (*0-926474-16-2*) Intl Awakening Pr.

Scotland since 1707. 3rd ed. R. H. Campbell. 288p. (C). 1996. pap. 45.00 (*0-85976-122-3*, Pub. by J Donald UK) St Mut.

Scotland the Best! The Essential Guide: New Edition. Peter Irvine. (Illus.). 288p. 1996. 19.95 (*1-85158-801-9*, Pub. by Mnstream UK) Trafalgar.

Scotland the Brand: The Heritage Industry. David McCrone et al. 160p. 1995. pap. 19.50 (*0-7486-0615-7*, Pub. by Edinburgh U Pr UK) Col U Pr.

***Scotland the Green: The Alternative to Vegetarian & Vegan Hideaways in Scotland.** Jackie Redding. (Illus.). 96p. (Orig.). 1997. pap. 9.95 (*1-899171-41-X*, Pub. by Findhorn Pr UK) Words Distrib.

Scotland the What? Buff Hardie et al. 272p. (C). 1989. 49.00 (*0-903065-59-2*, Pub. by G Wright Pub Ltd) St Mut.

Scotland Yard Files: One Hundred Fifty Years of the CID 1842-1992. Paul Begg & Keith Skinner. (Illus.). 320p. 1993. pap. 11.95 (*0-7472-3963-0*, Pub. by Headline UK) Trafalgar.

Scotland Yes. Alan Bold. 64p. 1978. 11.95 (*0-8464-1292-6*) Beekman Pubs.

Scotland, 1841: Clackmannan County. 1990. 40.00 (*0-89593-603-8*) Accelerated Index.

***Scotland '98.** Fodors Travel Staff. 1997. pap. 18.50 (*0-679-03532-X*) Fodors Travel.

Scotlands Issue 2: Gender & Identity. Ed. by Christopher MacLachlan. 120p. 1996. pap. 22.50 (*0-7486-0702-1*, Pub. by Edinburgh U Pr UK) Col U Pr.

Scotlands Issue One: Canons. Ed. by Christopher MacLachlan. 120p. 1996. pap. 22.50 (*0-7486-0486-3*, Pub. by Edinburgh U Pr UK) Col U Pr.

Scotland's Age of Improvement: A Survey of Eighteenth-Century Literary Clubs & Societies. Davis D. McElroy. LC 73-9172. 183p. reprint ed. pap. 52.20 (*0-8357-4567-8*, 2037477) Bks Demand.

Scotland's Distilleries. Picton Publishing Staff. (Illus.). (C). 1987. 45.00 (*0-317-90427-2*, Pub. by Picton UK) St Mut.

Scotland's First Settlers. Caroline Wickham-Jones. (Historic Scotland Ser.). (Illus.). 152p. 1994. pap. 34.95 (*0-7134-7371-1*, Pub. by Batsford UK) Trafalgar.

Scotland's Future: An Essay on the Economics of Nationalism. Gavin McCrone. LC 71-92501. 111p. 1969. 24.95 (*0-678-06252-8*) Kelley.

Scotland's Gift - Golf. rev. ed. Charles MacDonald. (Classics of Golf Ser.). (Illus.). 340p. 28.00 (*0-940889-07-2*) Classics Golf.

Scotland's Glory. (Scotland in Words & Pictures Ser.). (Illus.). 64p. (Orig.). (SPA.). 1995. pap. 7.95 (*0-7117-0649-2*) Seven Hills Bk.

Scotland's Glory. Jarrold Publishing Staff. (Illus.). 64p. 1993. pap. 7.95 (*0-7117-0554-2*, Pub. by Jarrold Pub UK) Seven Hills Bk.

Scotland's Golf Courses: An Extraordinary Variety of Experience. Robert Price. (Illus.). 254p. 1989. 25.00 (*0-08-036591-4*, Pub. by Aberdeen U Pr) Macmillan.

***Scotland's Golf Courses: The Complete Guide.** Vic Robbie. (Illus.). 224p. 1997. 24.95 (*1-85158-945-7*, Pub. by Mnstream UK) Trafalgar.

***Scotland's Heraldic Heritage: The Lion Rejoicing.** Charles Burnett & Mark Dennis. (Discovering Historic Scotland Ser.). (Illus.). 96p. 1997. pap. 14.95 (*0-11-495784-3*, Pub. by Statnry Ofc UK) Seven Hills Bk.

An Asterisk (*) at the beginning of an entry indicates that the title is appearing in BIP for the first time.

***Scotland's Kings & Queens: Their Lives & Times.** Richard Oram. (Discovering Historic Scotland Ser.). (Illus.). 96p. 1997. pap. 14.95 (*0-11-495783-5*, Pub. by Statnry Ofc UK) Seven Hills Bk.

Scotland's Malt Whiskies. Picton Publishing Staff. (C). 1987. 25.00 (*0-317-90429-9*, Pub. by Picton UK) St Mut.

Scotland's North Sea Gateway: Aberdeen Harbour AD 1136-1986, Section 123. Ed. by John Turner. 224p. 1986. 25.00 (*0-08-032463-0*, R130, R145, K150, Pergamon Pr); pap. 15.75 (*0-08-032464-9*, Pergamon Pr) Elsevier.

Scotland's Place Names. David Dorward. 64p. (C). 1986. pap. 35.00 (*0-901824-73-9*, Pub. by Mercat Pr Bks UK) St Mut.

Scotland's Relations with England: A Survey to 1707. William Ferguson. (C). 1994. pap. 50.00 (*0-85411-058-5*, Pub. by Saltire Soc) St Mut.

Scotland's Roman Remains: An Introduction & Handbook. Lawrence J. Keppie. 200p. (C). 1996. pap. 26.00 (*0-85976-157-6*, Pub. by J Donald UK) St Mut.

Scotland's Shifting Population: 1770-1850. Donald F. Macdonald. LC 78-15153. (Illus.). vii, 172p. 1978. reprint ed. lib. bdg. 35.00 (*0-87991-860-8*) Porcupine Pr.

***Scotland's Society & Economy in Transition, c. 1500-c. 1760.** Ian Whyte. LC 96-2943. (Social History in Perspective Ser.). 1997. text ed. 45.00 (*0-312-16514-5*) St Martin.

Scotland's Threatened Lines. Picton Publishing Staff. (C). 1987. 28.00 (*0-317-90402-7*, Pub. by Picton UK) St Mut.

Scotland's Top Five Hundred Companies, 1993. Jordon Dataquest Staff. 1991. pap. text ed. 600.00 (*0-686-25496-1*) St Mut.

***Scotland's Traditional Houses: Country, Town & Coastal Homes.** Elizabeth Beaton. (Discovering Historic Scotland Ser.). (Illus.). 96p. 1997. pap. 14.95 (*0-11-495785-1*, Pub. by Statnry Ofc UK) Seven Hills Bk.

Scotland's Voice in International Affairs. Ed. by Clive Archer & John Main. 160p. 1980. 44.95 (*0-7735-0512-1*, Pub. by McGill CN) U of Toronto Pr.

Scotland's War. Seona Robertson & Leslie Wilson. (Illus.). 192p. 1996. 35.00 (*1-85158-700-4*, Pub. by Mnstream UK) Trafalgar.

Scotland's Weather: An Illustrated Anthology. Andrew Martin. (Illus.). 112p. (Orig.). 1995. pap. 14.95 (*0-948636-71-8*, 671-8, Pub. by Natl Mus Scotland UK) A Schwartz & Co.

Scots Abolitionists, 1833-1861. fac. ed. Charles D. Rice. LC 81-3789. 235p. 1981. reprint ed. pap. 67.00 (*0-7837-7818-X*, 2047574) Bks Demand.

Scots & Britons: Scottish Political Thought & the Union of 1603. Ed. by Roger A. Mason. LC 93-32399. 328p. (C). 1994. text ed. 59.95 (*0-521-42034-2*) Cambridge U Pr.

Scots & Its Literature. Derrick J. McClure. LC 95-43671. (Varieties of English Around the World General Ser.: Vol. G14). vi, 218p. 1996. 52.00 (*1-55619-445-5*) Benjamins North Am.

Scots & Scotch-Irish in America. James E. Johnson. LC 66-10151. (In America Bks.). (Illus.). 88p. (YA). (gr. 5 up). 1991. lib. bdg. 18.95 (*0-8225-0242-9*, Lerner Publctns) Lerner Group.

Scots & Scotch-Irish in America. James E. Johnson. (YA). (gr. 5 up). 1992. pap. 5.95 (*0-8225-1038-3*, Lerner Publctns) Lerner Group.

***Scots Baronial.** John Dixon. 1991. 14.00 (*0-7486-6124-7*, Pub. by Polygon UK) Subterranean Co.

Scots Confession of Fifteen Sixty. Tr. by James Bulloch. (C). 1989. pap. 25.00 (*0-86153-063-2*, Pub. by St Andrew UK) St Mut.

Scots Gaelic: A Brief Introduction. G. McLennan. 28p. (ENG & GAE.). 1987. 12.95 (*0-8288-3345-1*, F132982) Fr & Eur.

Scots Gospel. Jamie Stuart. 112p. (Orig.). 1993. 50.00 incl. audio (*0-7152-0674-5*, Pub. by St Andrew UK); pap. 22.00 (*0-7152-0673-7*); audio 22.00 (*0-7152-0675-3*) St Mut.

Scots in Burma: Golden Times in a Golden Land. Alister McCrae. (Illus.). 120p. (C). 1995. pap. 25.00 (*1-870838-50-5*, Pub. by Kiscadale UK) Weatherhill.

***Scots of Chicago: Quiet Immigrants & Their New Society.** ISAS Staff. 240p. Date not set. pap. text ed. write for info. (*0-7872-2837-0*) Kendall-Hunt.

Scots on Scotch: The Scotch Whisky Society Book of Whisky. Philip Hills. (Illus.). 192p. 1992. 34.95 (*1-85158-416-1*, Pub. by Mnstream UK) Trafalgar.

Scots on the Chesapeake, 1607-1830. David Dobson. 169p. 1992. 20.00 (*0-8063-1328-5*, 1476) Genealog Pub.

Scots Proverbs & Rhymes. Forbes Macgregor. 80p. (C). 1989. 30.00 (*0-903065-39-8*, Pub. by G Wright Pub Ltd) St Mut.

Scots Thesaurus. Ed. by Iseabail Macleod et al. (Illus.). 556p. 1991. 37.00 (*0-08-036582-5*, Pub. by Aberdeen U Pr); pap. 19.90 (*0-08-036583-3*, Pub. by Aberdeen U Pr) Macmillan.

Scots Thesaurus. deluxe ed. Ed. by Iseabail Macleod et al. (Illus.). 556p. 1991. lib. bdg. 76.50 (*0-08-040926-1*, Pub. by Aberdeen U Pr) Macmillan.

Scots Worthies. John Howie. 627p. 1995. reprint ed. 33.95 (*0-85151-686-6*) Banner of Truth.

Scotsman from Lumber River: Angus Wilton McLean, Farmer, Industrialist, Public Servant. Evelyn Underwood. LC 96-67043. (Illus.). 208p. 1996. 16.95 (*1-57197-019-3*) Pentland Pr.

***Scotsman Wore Spurs.** Patricia Potter. 448p. 1997. mass mkt. 5.99 (*0-553-57506-6*, Fanfare) Bantam.

Scotswoman. Inglis Fletcher. (Carolina Ser.). 414p. reprint ed. lib. bdg. 32.95 (*0-89244-008-2*, Queens House) Amereon Ltd.

Scotswood Road. Jimmy Forsyth. 8600. pap. 17.95 (*1-85224-014-8*, Pub. by Bloodaxe Bks UK) Dufour.

Scott: An Aid to Clinical Surgery. 5th ed. R. C. Williamson & B. P. Waxman. (Illus.). 448p. 1993. pap. text ed. 29.95 (*0-443-04566-6*) Churchill.

Scott: Hugh Scott, an Immigrant of 1670. J. Scott. (Illus.). 314p. 1991. reprint ed. pap. 46.50 (*0-8328-2164-0*); reprint ed. lib. bdg. 57.50 (*0-8328-2163-2*) Higginson Bk Co.

Scott: The Critical Heritage. Ed. by John O. Hayden. 1978. 69.50 (*0-7100-6724-0*, RKP) Routledge.

Scott & His Circle. Donald Carswell. LC 72-175692. (Select Bibliographies Reprint Ser.). 1977. reprint ed. 21.95 (*0-8369-6607-4*) Ayer.

Scott & His Poetry. Arthur E. Morgan. LC 79-120980. (Poetry & Life Ser.). reprint ed. 16.00 (*0-404-52526-1*) AMS Pr.

Scott & Scotland: The Predicament of the Scottish Writer. Edwin Muir. 114p. 8200. 13.95 (*0-904919-60-9*) Dufour.

***Scott Baldwin on Jury Arguments.** Scott Baldwin & Francis H. Hare. LC 97-13281. (Trial Practice Library). 304p. 1997. 145.00 (*0-471-16462-3*) Wiley.

Scott Brown's Otolaryngology, 6 Vols. 6th ed. Incl. Vol. 1. Scott Brown's Otolaryngology. , 6 vols. 6th ed. Wright & Gleeson. 1996. 195.00 (*0-7506-0595-2*); Vol. 2. Scott Brown's Otolaryngology. , 6 vols. 6th ed. Stephens. 1996. 195.00 (*0-7506-0596-0*); Vol. 3. Scott Brown's Otolaryngology. , 6 vols. 6th ed. Booth. 1996. 195.00 (*0-7506-0597-9*); Vol. 5. Scott Brown's Otolaryngology. , 6 Vols. 6th ed. Mackay. 1996. 195.00 (*0-7506-0598-7*); Vol. 4. Scott Brown's Otolaryngology. , 6 Vols. 6th ed. Hibbert. 1996. 195.00 (*0-7506-0599-5*); Vol. 6. Scott Brown's Otolaryngology. , 6 Vols. 6th ed. Michael J. Cinnamond & David A. Adams. 592p. 1996. 195.00 (*0-7506-0600-2*); 995.00 (*0-7506-1935-X*) Buttrwrth-Heinemann.

Scott Brown's Otolaryngology, 6 vols., Set. 5th ed. Ed. by Alan G. Kerr. 1988. 700.00 (*0-407-00510-2*) Buttrwrth-Heinemann.

Scott Brown's Otolaryngology: Adult Audiology, Vol. 2. 5th ed. Ed. by Dafydd Stephens. (Illus.). 677p. 1988. 150.00 (*0-407-00512-9*) Buttrwrth-Heinemann.

Scott Brown's Otolaryngology: Basic Sciences, Vol. 1. 5th ed. Ed. by David A. Wright. (Illus.). 637p. 1988. 150.00 (*0-407-00511-0*) Buttrwrth-Heinemann.

Scott Brown's Otolaryngology: Laryngology, Vol. 5. 5th ed. Ed. by P. M. Stell. (Illus.). 459p. 1988. 120.00 (*0-407-00515-3*) Buttrwrth-Heinemann.

Scott Brown's Otolaryngology: Otology, Vol. 3. 5th ed. Ed. by John B. Boothe. (Illus.). 637p. 1988. 150.00 (*0-407-00513-7*) Buttrwrth-Heinemann.

Scott Brown's Otolaryngology: Pediatric Otolaryngology, Vol. 6. 5th ed. Ed. by N. G. Evans. (Illus.). 571p. 1988. 145.00 (*0-407-00516-1*) Buttrwrth-Heinemann.

Scott Brown's Otolaryngology: Rhinology, Vol. 4. 5th ed. Ed. by T. R Bull & Ian S. Mackay. (Illus.). 385p. 1988. 100.00 (*0-407-00514-5*) Buttrwrth-Heinemann.

Scott Brown's Otolaryngology see Scott Brown's Otolaryngology

Scott Buchanan: Recollections & Essays. Ed. by Charles A. Nelson. 160p. 1996. 14.95 (*0-9603690-5-8*) SJC Annapolis.

Scott Burton. Brenda Richardson. LC 86-22235. (Illus.). 92p. 1986. pap. 12.95 (*0-912298-61-8*) Baltimore Mus.

Scott, Chaucer, & Medieval Romance: A Study in Sir Walter Scott's Indebtedness to the Literature of the Middle Ages. Jerome Mitchell. LC 87-8294. 280p. 1987. 31.00 (*0-8131-1609-0*) U Pr of Ky.

Scott County, Arkansas. Michael Cate. (Illus.). 354p. 1991. 60.00 (*0-88107-183-8*) Curtis Media.

Scott County, Arkansas Census, 1860. Bobbie J. McLane & Bill Hanks. 147p. (Orig.). 1989. pap. 16.00 (*0-929604-62-8*) Arkansas Ancestors.

Scott County, Arkansas Census, 1870. Bobbie J. McLane & Bill Hanks. 221p. (Orig.). 1989. pap. 22.00 (*0-929604-63-6*) Arkansas Ancestors.

Scott County, Illinois Marriage Licenses - 1 January 1900 - 30 December 1915. pap. 8.00 (*0-685-65757-4*) E McMahan Secrest.

Scott County, Illinois Marriage Licenses - 28 March 1839 - 30 December 1899. pap. 16.00 (*0-9602120-1-9*) E McMahan Secrest.

Scott County, Kentucky: A History. Ed. by Lindsey Apple et al. LC 93-87203. 496p. 1993. text ed. 28.50 (*0-9639910-0-0*) Scott County Hist.

Scott County Virginia Marriages, 1815-1853. Mary D. Fugate. (Virginia Historic Marriage Register Ser.). x, 109p. 1990. pap. 12.00 (*0-935931-49-X*) Borgo Pr.

Scott County Virginia Marriages, 1815-1853. Mary D. Fugate. (Virginia Historic Marriage Register Ser.). x, 109p. (C). 1990. reprint ed. lib. bdg. 33.00 (*0-8095-8242-2*) Borgo Pr.

Scott Dramatized. H. Philip Bolton. (Novels on Stage Ser.). 608p. 1992. text ed. 170.00 (*0-7201-2060-8*, Mansell Pub) Cassell.

Scott E. Haselton & His Abbey Garden Press. D. W. Davies. (Illus.). 26p. 1985. 25.00 (*0-87093-182-2*) Dawsons.

***Scott Enquiry Report - Report of Inquiry into Export of Defence Equipment & Dual, 6 vols.** 1996. boxed, pap. 90.00 (*0-10-262796-7*, HM27967, Pub. by Stationery Ofc UK) Bernan Associates.

Scott Family Finding Aids Vol. 1: Marriages, 1700-1900. Craig R. Scott. 204p. 1992. pap. 15.00 (*0-8095-8689-4*); lib. bdg. 39.00 (*0-8095-8167-1*) Borgo Pr.

***Scott, Foresman English in Tune Level 4.** 1983. pap. text ed. 11.38 (*0-673-19104-4*) Addison-Wesley.

Scott, Foresman Handbook. 4th ed. John J. Ruszkiewicz & Maxine C. Hairston. Date not set. teacher ed. write for info. (*0-673-97448-0*) Addson-Wesley Educ.

Scott, Foresman Handbook: Reading Critically. Maxine C. Hairston et al. (C). 1993. 5.50 (*0-673-46849-6*) Addson-Wesley Educ.

Scott, Foresman Handbook: Teaching in Multicultural Classroom. 3rd ed. Maxine C. Hairston & Steer. (C). 1993. 5.00 (*0-673-46852-6*) Addson-Wesley Educ.

Scott, Foresman Handbook: Teaching Writing. 4th ed. Maxine C. Hairston & John J. Ruszkiewicz. (C). 1993. pap. text ed. 7.95 (*0-673-46865-8*) Addson-Wesley Educ.

***Scott Foresman Handbook: Writing & Designing Documents.** 4th ed. Hairston. (C). 1996. pap. text ed. 9.95 (*0-673-97453-7*) Addison-Wesley.

***Scott Foresman Handbook for Writers.** 3rd ed. Maxine Hairston & John J. Ruszkiewicz. LC 92-33586. 1992. write for info. (*0-673-46708-2*) Addison-Wesley.

Scott, Foresman Handbook for Writers. 4th ed. Maxine Hairston & John J. Ruszkiewicz. 880p. (C). 1996. pap. text ed. 30.50 (*0-673-99728-6*) Addson-Wesley Educ.

Scott, Foresman Handbook For Writers. 4th ed. Maxine C. Hairston & John J. Ruszkiewicz. (Illus.). 814p. 1995. bds. 31.00 (*0-8230-5008-4*) Watsn-Guptill.

***Scott Foresman Handbook Model Research Papers.** 4th ed. Hairston. (C). 1996. pap. text ed. 9.95 (*0-673-97470-7*) Addison-Wesley.

Scott-Franks: Pioneer Families of Coryell County, Texas. B. D. Scott & Janet W. Scott. LC 92-70295. (Illus.). 333p. 1992. text ed. 45.00 (*0-942309-04-9*) N Two S Pub.

Scott Genealogy. M. L. Holman. (Illus.). 410p. 1993. reprint ed. pap. 63.50 (*0-8328-3056-9*); reprint ed. lib. bdg. 73.50 (*0-8328-3055-0*) Higginson Bk Co.

Scott Gustafson's Animal Orchestra: A Counting Book. Illus. by Scott Gustafson. (J). 1995. bds. 14.95 (*0-86713-030-X*) Greenwich Wrkshop.

***Scott Hamilton: Fireworks on Ice.** Linda Shaughnessy. LC 96-46016. (Figure Skaters Ser.). 1997. pap. 6.95 (*0-382-39444-5*, Crstwood Hse); lib. bdg. 13.95 (*0-382-39443-7*, Crstwood Hse) Silver Burdett Pr.

Scott Henderson Guitar Book. 136p. 1993. otabind 19.95 (*0-7935-1125-9*, 00699330) H Leonard.

Scott Joplin. Katherine Preston. (Black American Ser.). (Illus.). 192p. (Orig.). (YA). 1990. mass mkt. 3.95 (*0-87067-557-5*, Melrose Sq) Holloway.

Scott Joplin: A Life in Ragtime. Steven Otfinoski. LC 95-8526. (Impact Biographies Ser.). (Illus.). 112p. (YA). (gr. 7-12). 1995. lib. bdg. 22.70 (*0-531-11244-6*) Watts.

Scott Joplin: Composer. Kitty Preston. Ed. by Nathan I. Huggins. (Black Americans of Achievement Ser.). (Illus.). 112p. (Orig.). (YA). (gr. 5 up). 1988. pap. 8.95 (*0-7910-0205-5*); lib. bdg. 19.95 (*1-55546-598-6*) Chelsea Hse.

Scott Joplin: The Man Who Made Ragtime. James Haskins. LC 76-50768. (Illus.). 264p. (Orig.). 1980. pap. 6.95 (*0-8128-6066-7*, Scrbrough Hse) Madison Bks UPA.

Scott Joplin for Fingerstyle Guitar. Jerry Silverman. 56p. 1995. pap. 11.95 (*0-89524-968-5*) Cherry Lane.

***Scott Joplin for Guitar.** Ed. by Aaron Stang. 40p. 1985. pap. text ed. 14.95 (*0-7692-1293-X*) Warner Bros.

Scott Joplin Greatest Hits. (Easy Play Ser.: Vol. 118). 1991. pap. 5.95 (*0-7935-0575-5*, 00001545) H Leonard.

Scott Joplin Greatest Hits. 48p. 1991. pap. 6.95 (*0-7935-0577-1*, 00102179) H Leonard.

Scott Joplin Melody Dicer. Carousel Staff. (Orig.). 1983. pap. text ed. 8.95 (*0-935474-16-1*) Carousel Pubns Ltd.

Scott Joplin Piano Music. (Carl Fischer's "All Time Favorites" Music Ser.). 132p. (Orig.). 1992. pap. 11.95 (*0-8258-0378-0*, ATF109) Fischer Inc NY.

Scott Nearing: An Intellectual Biography. John A. Saltmarsh. (C). 1991. 40.00 (*0-87722-844-2*) Temple U Pr.

Scott Nearing: Apostle of American Radicalism. Stephen J. Whitfield. LC 74-10641. 1974. text ed. 49.50 (*0-231-03816-X*) Col U Pr.

Scott Nearing Reader: The Good Life in Bad Times. Scott Nearing. Ed. by Steve Sherman. LC 88-29528. (Illus.). 333p. 1989. 32.50 (*0-8108-2144-3*) Scarecrow.

***Scott Nearing Reader: The Good Life in Bad Times.** Scott Sherman. 1989. 30.00 (*0-614-30479-2*) Scarecrow.

Scott 95 Stamp Catalog, Vol. 3: Countries of the World D-I. 1994. pap. 33.00 (*0-89487-202-8*) Scott Pub Co.

***Scott of the Antarctic.** Michael De-la-Noy. (Get a Life... Pocket Biographies Ser.). (Illus.). 128p. Date not set. pap. 10.95 (*0-7509-1512-9*, Pub. by Sutton Pubng UK) Bks Intl VA.

Scott of the Antarctic. Elspeth Huxley. LC 89-24956. (Illus.). xiv, 322p. 1990. reprint ed. pap. 17.95 (*0-8032-7248-0*, Bison Books) U of Nebr Pr.

Scott of the Shan Hills: Orders & Impressions. James G. Scott. Ed. by G. E. Mitton. LC 77-87056. reprint ed. 38.50 (*0-404-16858-2*) AMS Pr.

Scott on Trusts, 9 vols., Set. 4th ed. Austin W. Scott, Jr. & William F. Fratcher. 425.00 (*0-318-36122-1*) Little.

Scott Paper Co. A Report on the Company's Environmental Policies & Practices. (Illus.). 61p. (C). 1994. reprint ed. pap. text ed. 250.00 (*0-7881-0967-7*, Coun on Econ) DIANE Pub.

Scott Postage Stamp--1868: Reprint. John W. Scott. 1971. reprint ed. pap. 3.50 (*0-912574-27-5*) Collectors.

Scott Shaw's! Oddball Comics. Scott Shaw. Ed. by Dave Schreiner. 36p. 1993. ring bd. 10.95 (*0-87816-182-1*) Kitchen Sink.

Scott Sonniksen Paintings 1972-1982. George Lechner & Terri M. Hopkins. (Illus.). 1983. pap. 2.00 (*0-914435-02-7*) Marylhurst Art.

Scott Stamp Catalog, 1994, Vol. 2: Countries of the World A-C. 1993. pap. 32.00 (*0-89487-191-9*) Scott Pub Co.

Scott Stamp Catalog, 1994, Vol. 3. 1993. pap. 32.00 (*0-89487-192-7*) Scott Pub Co.

Scott Stamp Catalog, 1994, Vol. 4: Countries of the World J-Q. 1993. pap. 32.00 (*0-89487-193-5*) Scott Pub Co.

Scott Stamp Catalog, 1994, Vol. 5: Countries of the World R-Z. 1993. pap. 32.00 (*0-89487-194-3*) Scott Pub Co.

Scott Standard Postage Stamp Catalog, 4 vols. Incl. Vol. 1. U. S., U. N. & British Commonwealth. 32.00 (*0-685-70738-5*); Vol. 2. Europe, Africa, Asia, Latin America: A to F. 32.00 (*0-685-70739-3*); Vol. 3. . 32.00 (*0-685-70740-7*); Vol. 4. Europe, Africa, Asia, Latin America: P to Z. 32.00 (*0-685-70741-5*); write for info. (*0-318-56394-0*) Wehman.

Scott the Rhymer. Nancy M. Goslee. LC 88-5513. 264p. 1988. 29.00 (*0-8131-1650-3*) U Pr of Ky.

Scott Tinley's Winning Guide to Sports Endurance: How to Maximize Speed, Strength & Stamina. Scott Tinley & Ken McAlpine. LC 93-28410. 1994. pap. 14.95 (*0-87596-106-1*) Rodale Pr Inc.

Scott Tinley's Winning Triathlon. Scott Tinley & Mike Plant. (Illus.). 192p. (Orig.). 1986. pap. 19.95 (*0-8092-5117-5*) Contemp Bks.

Scott Trust, No. 1A. William F. Fratcher. 1986. 145.00 (*0-316-29226-5*) Little.

Scott Trust, No. 2. Fratcher. 1987. 145.00 (*0-316-29310-5*) Little.

Scott Trust, No. 2A. Fratcher. 1987. 145.00 (*0-316-29314-8*) Little.

Scott Trust, No. 3. Fratcher. 1987. 145.00 (*0-316-29300-8*) Little.

Scott Trust, No. 3A. Fratcher. 1987. 145.00 (*0-316-29301-6*) Little.

Scott Trust, No. 4. Fratcher. 1988. 145.00 (*0-316-29227-3*) Little.

Scott Trust, No. 4A. Fratcher. 1988. 145.00 (*0-316-29231-1*) Little.

Scott Trust, No. 5. Fratcher. 1989. 145.00 (*0-316-29239-7*) Little.

Scott Trust, No. 5A. Fratcher. 1989. 145.00 (*0-316-29240-0*) Little.

Scott Trust, No. 6. Fratcher. 1990. 145.00 (*0-316-29241-9*) Little.

Scott Trust, No. 6A. Fratcher. 1990. 145.00 (*0-316-29242-7*) Little.

Scott Turow. Derek Lundy. 1995. pap. 9.95 (*1-55022-234-1*) LPC InBook.

Scott U. S. First Day Cover Catalog: 1996 Edition. Michael Malone. 1995. pap. text ed. 6.95 (*0-89487-217-6*) Scott Pub Co.

Scott U. S. Specialized Catalog, 1994: Includes Extensive Coverage on U. S. Issues. 1993. pap. 32.00 (*0-89487-195-1*) Scott Pub Co.

***Scott Walker: A Deep Shade of Blue.** Mike Watkinson & Pete Anderson. (Illus.). 288p. (Orig.). 1996. pap. 14.95 (*0-86369-877-8*, Pub. by Virgin Pub UK) London Brdge.

Scott 1996 Stamp Catalogue Vol. 4: Countries of the World J-Q. Scott Publishing Company Staff. 1995. pap. text ed. 34.00 (*0-89487-212-5*) Scott Pub Co.

Scott 1996 Stamp Catalogue Vol. 5: Countries of the World R-Z. Scott Publishing Company Staff. 1995. pap. text ed. 34.00 (*0-89487-213-3*) Scott Pub Co.

Scott 1996 Stamp Catalogue Vol. 3: Countries of the World D-I. Scott Publishing Company Staff. 1995. pap. text ed. 34.00 (*0-89487-211-7*) Scott Pub Co.

Scott 1996 U. S. Specialized Catalogue. Scott Publishing Company Staff. 1995. pap. text ed. 34.00 (*0-89487-215-X*) Scott Pub Co.

Scott 95 Stamp Catalog, Vol. 1: British Commonwealth, United States, United Nations. 1994. pap. 33.00 (*0-89487-200-1*) Scott Pub Co.

Scott 95 Stamp Catalog, Vol. 2: Countries of the World A-C. 1994. pap. 33.00 (*0-89487-201-X*) Scott Pub Co.

Scott 95 Stamp Catalog, Vol. 4: Countries of the World J-Q. 1994. pap. 33.00 (*0-89487-203-6*) Scott Pub Co.

Scott 95 Stamp Catalog, Vol. 5: Countries of the World R-Z. 1994. pap. 33.00 (*0-89487-204-4*) Scott Pub Co.

Scott 95 U. S. First Day Cover Catalogue & Checklist. Michael A. Mellone. 1994. pap. 6.95 (*0-89487-199-4*) Scott Pub Co.

Scott 95 U. S. Specialized Catalogue. Scott Staff. 1994. pap. 33.00 (*0-89487-206-0*) Scott Pub Co.

Scott 95 U. S. Stamp Pocket Catalogue. Scott Staff. 1994. pap. 6.95 (*0-89487-207-9*) Scott Pub Co.

Scott 96 Stamp Catalogue Vol. 1A: United States, United Nations, Canada & British America. Scott. 1995. pap. 34.00 (*0-89487-208-7*) Scott Pub Co.

Scott 96 Stamp Catalogue Vol. 2: Countries of the World A-C. Scott. 1995. pap. 34.00 (*0-89487-210-9*) Scott Pub Co.

Scott 96 U. S. Pocket Stamp Catalogue & Checklist. 1995. pap. text ed. 9.95 (*0-89487-216-8*) Scott Pub Co.

Scottie. Towana J. Brown. LC 88-93029. (One Ser.). (Illus.). 150p. (Orig.). (J). (gr. 5-6). 1989. pap. 3.50 (*0-9622060-1-6*) T J Brown.

***Scottie Pippen.** Bill Gutman. LC 97-1090. (Sports World Ser.). (Illus.). 48p. (J). (gr. 3-6). 1997. 14.90 (*0-7613-0223-9*) Millbrook Pr.

Scottie Pippen. Fred McMane. LC 95-18518. (Basketball Legends Ser.). (Illus.). 64p. (J). (gr. 3 up). 1996. lib. bdg. 15.95 (*0-7910-2498-9*) Chelsea Hse.

Scottie Pippen: Prince of the Court. Howard Reiser. LC 92-42023. (Sports Stars Ser.). (Illus.). 48p. (J). (gr. 2-8). 1993. pap. 4.50 (*0-516-44366-6*); lib. bdg. 17.50 (*0-516-04366-8*) Childrens.

***Scottie Pippen: Reluctant Superstar.** Bob Schnakenberg. LC 96-52834. (J). 1997. pap. write for info. (*0-8225-9767-5*); lib. bdg. write for info. (*0-8225-3653-6*) Lerner Group.

***Scottie Pippen Memoirs.** Scottie Pippen. 288p. 1997. 23.00 (*0-06-018792-1*) HarpC.

***Scottie Pippin Memoirs.** Scottie Pippin. mass mkt. 5.99 (*0-06-109624-5*, Harp PBks) HarpC.

S

An Asterisk (*) at the beginning of an entry indicates that the title is appearing in BIP for the first time.

Scottie the Daughter Of... The Life of Frances Scott Fitzgerald Lanahan Smith. Eleanor Lanahan. (Illus.). 672p. 1996. pap. 18.00 (0-06-092738-0) HarpC.

Scottish Abbeys & Priories. Richard Fawcett. (Historic Scotland Ser.). (Illus.). 152p. 1995. pap. 29.95 (0-7134-7372-X, Pub. by Batsford UK) Trafalgar.

Scottish Abbeys & Social Life. G. G. Coulton. 1977. lib. bdg. 59.95 (0-8490-2573-7) Gordon Pr.

Scottish Agricultural Implements. Bob Powell. 1989. pap. 25.00 (0-85263-925-2, Pub. by Shire UK) St Mut.

Scottish-American Court Records, 1733-1783. David Dobson. 105p. 1991. 18.00 (0-8063-1312-9, 1477) Genealog Pub.

Scottish-American Heirs, 1683-1883. David Dobson. 165p. 1992. 21.50 (0-8063-1278-5, 1479) Genealog Pub.

Scottish-American Wills, 1650-1900. David Dobson. 137p. 1991. 20.00 (0-685-48615-X, 1478) Genealog Pub.

Scottish & English Spiers-Norris Metal Planes. 2nd rev. ed. Kenneth D. Roberts. (Illus.). 100p. 1991. pap. text ed. 15.00 (0-913602-69-8) K Roberts.

Scottish & Irish Terriers. William Haynes. 1991. lib. bdg. 79.95 (0-8490-5226-2) Gordon Pr.

Scottish & Jacobite Glass. Arnold Fleming. (Illus.). 1977. reprint ed. 35.00 (0-7158-1207-6) Charles River Bks.

Scottish & Other Miscellanies. Thomas Carlyle. (BCL1-PR English Literature Ser.). 339p. 1992. reprint ed. lib. bdg. 89.00 (0-7812-7485-0) Rprt Serv.

Scottish & Welsh Wars 1250-1400. Christopher Rothero. (Men-at-Arms Ser.: No. 151). (Illus.). 48p. pap. 11.95 (0-85045-542-1, 9083, Pub. by Osprey UK) Stackpole.

Scottish Archaeology: New Perceptions. Ed. by W. S. Hanson & E. A. Slater. (Aberdeen University Press Bks.). (Illus.). 192p. 1991. pap. 29.90 (0-08-041212-2, Pub. by Aberdeen U Pr) Macmillan.

Scottish Art in the 20th Century. Duncan Macmillan. (Illus.). 192p. 1996. 40.00 (1-85158-630-X, Pub. by Mnstream UK) Trafalgar.

Scottish Art 1460-1990. Duncan Macmillan. (Illus.). 432p. 1992. 95.00 (1-85158-251-7, Pub. by Mnstream UK) Trafalgar.

***Scottish Art 1460-1990.** Duncan Macmillan. (Illus.). 432p. 1996. pap. 40.00 (1-85158-862-0, Pub. by Mnstream UK) Trafalgar.

Scottish Assembly. Robert Crawford. (Illus.). 64p. 1992. pap. 15.95 (0-7011-3595-6, Pub. by Chatto & Windus UK) Trafalgar.

Scottish Autumn of Frederick Chopin. P. Zaluski & Iwo Zaluski. 180p. (C). 1996. pap. 25.50 (0-85976-389-7, Pub. by J Donald UK) St Mut.

***Scottish Bakehouse Cookbook.** Isabel M. White. 12.50 (0-932384-07-2) Tashmoo.

Scottish Ballads. Ed. & Intro. by Emily B. Lyle. (Canongate Classics Ser.). 224p. 1994. pap. 13.95 (0-86241-477-6) Interlink Pub.

Scottish Ballads. Robert Chambers. LC 77-144549. reprint ed. 44.50 (0-404-08628-4) AMS Pr.

Scottish Ballads & Ballad Writing. Lauchlan M. Watt. LC 71-144542. reprint ed. 21.50 (0-404-08616-0) AMS Pr.

Scottish Ballads & Songs, Historical & Traditionary, 2 Vols, Set. James Maidment. LC 78-144497. reprint ed. 67.50 (0-404-08670-5) AMS Pr.

Scottish Books: A Brief Bibliography. 51p. 1985. 22.00 (0-317-39144-5, Pub. by Saltire Soc) St Mut.

***Scottish Borders.** (Illus.). 112p. 1997. pap. 16.95 (0-11-495218-3, Pub. by Statnry Ofc UK) Seven Hills Bk.

Scottish Bride. Peggy Hanchar. 1996. mass mkt. 5.99 (0-449-14866-1) Fawcett.

Scottish Building Regulations: Explained & Illustrated. W. N. Hamilton et al. LC 93-34575. 1993. 64.95 (0-632-03234-0) Blackwell Sci.

***Scottish Building Regulations: Explained & Illustrated.** 2nd ed. W. N. Hamilton. LC 96-3200. 1996. pap. 49.95 (0-632-04115-3) Blackwell Sci.

Scottish Burgh & County Heraldry. R. M. Urquhart. LC 72-12491. (Illus.). 272p. 1973. 38.00 (0-8103-2005-3) Gale.

***Scottish Business Law.** 3rd ed. Moira McMillan. 480p. 1997. pap. 59.50 (0-273-62035-5, Pub. by Pitman Pub Ltd UK) Trans-Atl Phila.

Scottish Business Law: Text, Cases & Materials. C. F. Willet & A. O'Donnell. (C). 1991. 125.00 (0-685-50350-X) St Mut.

Scottish Business Law: Text, Cases & Materials. Chris Willett & Aidan O'Donnell. 442p. 1991. pap. 43.00 (1-85431-091-7, Pub. by Blackstone Pr UK) Gaunt.

Scottish Business Law: Text, Cases & Materials. 2nd ed. Chris Willett & Aidan O'Donnell. 544p. 1996. pap. 50.00 (1-85431-440-8, Pub. by Blackstone Pr UK) Gaunt.

Scottish Capital on the American Credit Frontier. W. G. Kerr. LC 75-16575. (Illus.). xviii, 246p. 1976. 16.95 (0-87611-035-9) Tex St Hist Assn.

Scottish Cat: An Anthology. Hamish Whyte. (Illus.). 192p. 1987. 26.00 (0-08-035077-1, Pub. by Aberdeen U Pr); pap. 14.00 (0-08-035078-X, Pub. by Aberdeen U Pr) Macmillan.

Scottish Catholic Secular Clergy, 1879-1989. Christine Johnson. 526p. (C). 1996. 90.00 (0-85976-345-5, Pub. by J Donald UK) St Mut.

***Scottish Ceilidh Dancing.** David Ewart & May Ewart. (Illus.). 176p. 1997. pap. 11.95 (1-85158-845-0, Pub. by Mnstream UK) Trafalgar.

Scottish Chiefs. Jane Porter. LC 91-8521. (Scribner's Illustrated Classics Ser.). (Illus.). 528p. (YA). 1991. lib. bdg. 28.00 (0-684-19340-X, C Scribner Sons Young) S&S Childrens.

Scottish Chiefs. Jane Porter. (Illus.). 1994. reprint ed. lib. bdg. 49.95 (1-56849-533-1) Buccaneer Bks.

Scottish Clan & Family Names: Their Arms, Origins & Tartans. Roddy Martine. (Illus.). 224p. 1993. pap. 22.95 (1-85158-418-8, Pub. by Mnstream UK) Trafalgar.

Scottish Clans & Tartans. Ian Grimble. (Illus.). 272p. 1986. pap. 14.00 (0-517-54827-5, Harmony) Crown Pub Group.

***Scottish Clans & Tartans.** Ed. by Fred L. Israel & Arthur M. Schlesinger. (Looking into the Past). (Illus.). 64p. (YA). (gr. 5 up). 1997. lib. bdg. 16.95 (0-7910-4676-1) Chelsea Hse.

Scottish Clans & Their Tartans. W. Johnson. 1992. 10.98 (1-55521-797-4) Bk Sales Inc.

Scottish Clans Notecards. 1985. pap. 8.95 (0-88289-325-4) Pelican.

Scottish Coalmining Ancestors. Lindsay S. Reeks. LC 86-81614. (Illus.). 292p. 1986. 25.00 (0-9616950-0-5) L S Reeks.

Scottish Coinage. I. H. Stewart. 1977. 20.00 (0-685-51519-2) S J Durst.

***Scottish Colourists: Cadell, Fergusson, Hunter & Peploe.** Roger Billcliffe. (Illus.). 176p. 1997. pap. 40.00 (0-7195-5437-3, Pub. by John Murray UK) Trafalgar.

Scottish Common Sense in Germany, 1768-1800: A Contribution to the History of Critical Philosophy. Manfred Kuehn. (McGill-Queen's Studies in the History of Religion). 300p. (C). 1987. text ed. 55.00 (0-7735-1009-5, Pub. by McGill CN) U of Toronto Pr.

Scottish Company Law. Nicholas Bourne & Brian Pillans. 338p. 1996. pap. 36.00 (1-85941-204-1, Pub. by Cavendish UK) Gaunt.

Scottish Contribution to Modern Economic Thought. Ed. by Douglas Mair. 1990. text ed. 39.00 (0-08-037723-8, Pub. by Aberdeen U Pr) Macmillan.

Scottish Country: Living in Scotland's Private Houses. Charles Maclean & Christopher S. Sykes. (Illus.). 240p. 1992. 45.00 (0-517-58273-2, C P Pubs) Crown Pub Group.

Scottish Country Houses, 1600-1914. Ed. by Ian Gow & Alistair Rowan. (Illus.). 350p. 1994. 60.00 (0-7486-0499-5, Pub. by Edinburgh U Pr UK) Col U Pr.

Scottish Covenanters. J. G. Vos. LC 93-74256. 240p. 1995. pap. 11.00 (1-884527-06-X) Crown & Covenant.

Scottish Crafts. Ian Finlay. (Illus.). 1977. reprint ed. 29.00 (0-7158-1171-1) Charles River Bks.

Scottish Crofters: A Historical Ethnography of a Celtic Village. Susan Parman. Ed. by Dawn Youngblood. LC 89-15392. (George & Louise Spindler Series in Anthropology). 160p. (C). 1990. pap. text ed. 13.50 (0-03-030754-6) HB Coll Pubs.

Scottish Curiosities. Robert Henderson. 220p. (C). 1992. pap. text ed. 30.00 (0-85976-383-8, Pub. by J Donald UK) St Mut.

Scottish Declaration of Independence. enl. rev. ed. E. Raymond Capt. (Illus.). 64p. 1996. pap. 4.00 (0-934666-11-3) Artisan Sales.

Scottish Deerhound Champions, 1952-1991. Camino E. E. & Bk. Co. Staff. (Illus.). 175p. 1998. pap. 36.95 (1-55893-003-5) Camino E E & Bk.

Scottish Doocot. Tim Buxbaum. 1989. pap. 25.00 (0-85263-848-5, Pub. by Shire UK) St Mut.

***Scottish Economic Bulletin No. 54: March 1997, No. 54, March 1997.** Stationery Office. 80p. 1997. pap. 25.00 (0-11-495845-9, HM58459, Pub. by Stationery Ofc UK) Bernan Associates.

***Scottish Economic Bulletin, Septembere 1996, No. 53.** 80p. 1996. pap. 25.00 (0-11-495822-X, HM95822X, Pub. by Stationery Ofc UK) Bernan Associates.

Scottish Economic Literature to 1800. William R. Scott. LC 77-125362. (Reprints of Economic Classics Ser.). 72p. 1971. reprint ed. lib. bdg. 25.00 (0-678-00717-9) Kelley.

Scottish Ecstasy. 1996. pap. 5.96 (1-57566-074-1) Kensgtn Pub Corp.

Scottish Emigration to Colonial America, 1607-1785. David Dobson. LC 92-14211. (Illus.). 216p. 1994. 35.00 (0-8203-1492-7) U of Ga Pr.

Scottish Endings: Writings on Death. Ed. by Andrew Martin. (Illus.). 128p. (Orig.). 1996. pap. 15.95 (0-948636-86-6, 6866, Pub. by Natl Mus Scotland UK) A Schwartz & Co.

Scottish Enlightenment, 6 vols. (History of British Philosophy Ser.). 2212p. (C). (gr. 13 up). 1994. text ed. 580.00 (0-415-08106-8, Routledge NY) Routledge.

Scottish Enlightenment. David Daiches. 48p. 1986. 22.00 (0-85411-032-1, Pub. by Saltire Soc) St Mut.

Scottish Enlightenment: An AMS Press Reprint Series. Ed. by Coleman O. Parsons. reprint ed. write for info. (0-404-17120-6) AMS Pr.

***Scottish Enlightenment I, 8 vols.** Intro. by Godfrey Vesey & John V. Price. 1911p. 1989. boxed 435.00 (0-415-07768-0) Routledge.

***Scottish Enlightenment Rhetoric & Its Influence on America.** Ed. by Lynee L. Gaillet. LC 97-21434. 400p. 1997. pap. write for info. (1-880393-27-1) L Erlbaum Assocs.

***Scottish Epitaphs & Images.** Betty Willsher. (Illus.). 112p. 1997. pap. 13.95 (0-86241-591-8, Pub. by Canongate Bks UK) Interlink Pub.

Scottish Fairy & Folk Tales. Ed. by George B. Douglas & Richard M. Dorson. LC 77-70591. (International Folklore Ser.). (Illus.). 1977. reprint ed. lib. bdg. 25.95 (0-405-10092-2) Ayer.

***Scottish Fairy Tales.** Donald A. MacKenzie. LC 97-19553. (Dover Children's Thrift Classics Ser.). (J). 1997. pap. write for info. (0-486-29900-7) Dover.

Scottish Family History. David Moody. 219p. 1989. pap. 18.95 (0-614-03821-9, 3860) Genealog Pub.

Scottish Family History: A Guide to Works of Reference on the History & Genealogy of Scottish Families. Margaret Stuart. LC 77-90813. 386p. 1994. reprint ed. 25.00 (0-8063-0795-1, 5650) Genealog Pub.

Scottish Family Research. rev. ed. J. Konrad. (Illus.). 56p. 1989. pap. 10.00 (1-878311-11-5, Heritge Hse) Ye Olde Genealogie Shoppe.

Scottish Fare. Norma Latimer & Gordon Latimer. (Traditional Cooking of Scotland Ser.). (Illus.). 105p. (Orig.). 1983. pap. 6.95 (0-941869-02-4) Latimers.

Scottish Farm Animals. Picton Publishing Staff. (C). 1987. 22.00 (0-317-90417-5, Pub. by Picton UK) St Mut.

Scottish Finance Sector. Neil Hood et al. (Scottish Industrial Policy Ser.: No. 4). 300p. 1988. 80.00 (0-85224-550-5, Pub. by Edinburgh U Pr UK) Col U Pr.

***Scottish Fishing Boats.** Matthew Tanner. 1996. pap. 25.00 (0-7478-0317-X, Pub. by Shire UK) St Mut.

Scottish Fold Cats: Everything about Acquisition, Care, Nutrition, Behavior, Health Care, & Breeding. Phil Maggitti. LC 92-36729. (Complete Pet Owner's Manuals Ser.). 88p. 1993. pap. 6.95 (0-8120-4999-3) Barron.

Scottish Folk Tales. Ruth Ratcliff. 1977. 40.00 (0-685-87557-1) St Mut.

Scottish Folk-Tales & Legends. Barbara K. Wilson. (Oxford Myths & Legends Ser.). (Illus.). 224p. (YA). (ps-7). 1990. pap. 12.95 (0-19-274141-1) OUP.

Scottish Football Quotations. Kenny MacDonald. 244p. 1995. pap. 15.95 (1-85158-643-1, Pub. by Mnstream UK) Trafalgar.

Scottish Gael: Or, Celtic Manners As Preserved among the Highlanders, 2 vols., Set. James Logan. LC 77-87679. reprint ed. 59.50 (0-404-16560-5) AMS Pr.

Scottish Gaelic-English English-Scottish Gaelic Dictionary. R. W. Renton & J. A. MacDonald. 162p. (Orig.). 1994. pap. 8.95 (0-7818-0316-0) Hippocrene Bks.

***Scottish Gaelic in 3 Months.** (Hugo's 3 Months Language Courses Ser.). 192p. (Orig.). 1997. pap. 8.95 (0-85285-234-7) Hunter NJ.

***Scottish Gaelic in 3 Months.** (Hugo's 3 Months Language Courses Ser.). 192p. (Orig.). 1997. pap. 29.95 incl. audio (0-85285-235-5) Hunter NJ.

Scottish Garden: Book of the Scottish Garden. Brinsley Burbidge. (Illus.). 168p. (C). 1989. 31.00 (0-948473-12-6, Pub. by Royal Botanic Edinburgh UK) Balogh.

Scottish Ghost Stories. (Ghost Ser.). (Illus.). 180p. 1993. pap. 7.95 (0-7117-0532-1) Seven Hills Bk.

Scottish Gold & Silver Work. Ian Finlay. (Illus.). 336p. 1991. 52.50 (0-88289-852-3) Pelican.

Scottish Golf & Golfers. S. L. McKinlay. 203p. 1992. lib. bdg. 28.00 (0-940889-37-4) Classics Golf.

Scottish Government Yearbook, 1990. Ed. by Alice Brown & Richard Parry. 323p. 1990. 39.00 (0-7486-0174-0, Pub. by Edinburgh U Pr UK) Col U Pr.

Scottish Government Yearbook, 1991. Ed. by Alice Brown & David McCrone. 272p. 1991. text ed. 39.00 (0-7486-0264-X, Pub. by Edinburgh U Pr UK) Col U Pr.

Scottish Gypsies under the Stewarts. David MacRitchie. LC 75-3463. reprint ed. 27.50 (0-404-16892-2) AMS Pr.

Scottish High Church Tradition in America: An Essay in Scotch-Irish Ethnoreligious History. William L. Fisk. 168p. (C). 1994. pap. text ed. 27.50 (0-8191-9761-0); lib. bdg. 46.00 (0-8191-9760-2) U Pr of Amer.

Scottish Highland Estate: Preserving an Environment. Michael Wigan. (Illus.). 208p. 1992. 35.95 (1-85310-162-1, Pub. by Swan Hill UK) Voyageur Pr.

Scottish Highland Games in America. Emily A. Donaldson. LC 85-28479. (Orig.). 1986. 18.95 (0-88289-474-9) Pelican.

Scottish Highlanders: A People & Their Place. James Hunter. (Illus.). 192p. 1993. 34.95 (1-85158-443-9, Pub. by Mnstream UK) Trafalgar.

***Scottish Highlanders in Colonial Georgia: The Recruitment, Emigration, & Settlement at Darien, 1735-1748.** Anthony W. Parker. 192p. 1997. text ed. 35.00 (0-8203-1915-5) U of Ga Pr.

***Scottish Highlanders, Indian Peoples: Thirty Generations of a Montana Family.** James Hunter. LC 97-13453. (Illus.). 224p. 1997. 29.95 (0-917298-51-9); pap. 18.95 (0-917298-52-7) MT Hist Soc.

***Scottish Highlands.** Insight Guides Staff. (Insight Compact Guides Ser.). 1997. pap. 7.95 (0-395-82936-4) HM.

Scottish Highlands. Jarrold Publishing Staff. (Illus.). 64p. 1993. pap. 7.95 (0-7117-0575-5, Pub. by Jarrold Pub UK) Seven Hills Bk.

Scottish Highlands & Islands. John Baxter et al. (Passport's Regional Guides of Great Britain Ser.). (Illus.). 128p. 1996. pap. 12.95 (0-8442-4880-0, Passport Bks) NTC Pub Grp.

Scottish Home. Ed. by Annette Carruthers. (Illus.). 232p. 1996. 25.00 (0-948636-72-6, 6726, Pub. by Natl Mus Scotland UK) A Schwartz & Co.

***Scottish Houses & Gardens: From the Archives of Country Life.** Ian Gow. (Illus.). 192p. 1997. 60.00 (1-85410-488-8, Pub. by Aurum Pr UK) London Brdge.

Scottish Housing: Policy & Politics, 1885-1985. Ed. by Richard Rodger. 250p. 1990. text ed. 45.00 (0-7185-1278-2) St Martin.

Scottish Housing in the Twentieth Century. Ed. by Richard Rodger. 264p. 1993. pap. 20.00 (0-7185-1493-9) St Martin.

Scottish Infantry Units in the World Wars. Mike Chappell. (Elite Ser.). (Illus.). 64p. 1995. pap. 12.95 (1-85532-469-5, Pub. by Osprey UK) Stackpole.

Scottish Insurrection of Eighteen Twenty. Peter B. Ellis & Seamus Mac A'Ghobhainn. 384p. 1989. pap. text ed. 19.95 (0-7453-0285-8) Routledge Chapman & Hall.

Scottish Interior: Gregorian & Victorian Decor. Ian Gow. (Illus.). 216p. (C). 1993. 45.00 (0-7486-0220-8, Pub. by Edinburgh U Pr UK) Col U Pr.

Scottish Interiors Series, 4 vols. Moubray House Publishing Ltd. Staff. (Illus.). 384p. (C). 1989. Scottish Renaissance Interiors. 35.00 (0-948473-06-1); Scottish Georgian Interiors. 35.00 (0-948473-05-3); Scottish Victorian Interiors. 35.00 (0-948473-04-5); Scottish Edwardian Interiors. 35.00 (0-948473-07-X) St Mut.

Scottish Interiors Series, 4 vols., Set. Moubray House Publishing Ltd. Staff. (Illus.). 384p. (C). 1989. 140.00 (0-685-40597-4) St Mut.

Scottish Internationalists' Who's Who, 1872-1986. Douglas Lamming. 250p. 1987. 60.00 (0-907033-47-4) St Mut.

***Scottish Island Hopping: A Guide for the Independent Traveller.** MacLean. 208p. (Orig.). 1994. pap. 17.00 (0-7486-6164-6, Pub. by Polygon UK) Subterranean Co.

Scottish Journey: A Modern Classic. Edwin Muir. 250p. 1996. pap. 13.95 (1-85158-841-8, Pub. by Mnstream UK) Trafalgar.

***Scottish Kings & Queens.** Elizabeth Douglas. (Scottie Bks.). (Illus.). 40p. (J). 1998. pap. 8.95 (0-11-495753-3, Pub. by Statnry Ofc UK) Seven Hills Bk.

Scottish Land Court: Practice & Procedure. K. H. Graham. 200p. 1993. boxed 90.00 (0-406-02981-4, UK) MICHIE.

Scottish Legal System. Robin White & Ian Willock. 290p. 1992. pap. 44.00 (0-406-00571-0) MICHIE.

Scottish Legal Tradition. 4th ed. Lord Cooper. Ed. by Michael C. Meston. 36p. 1986. 22.00 (0-85411-023-2, Pub. by Saltire Soc) St Mut.

Scottish Legends, Folklore & Superstitiion. Christian H. McKee. LC 83-80904. (Illus.). 56p. (Orig.). 1983. pap. 4.75 (0-9611046-0-0) C H McKee.

Scottish Life & Poetry. Lauchlan M. Watt. LC 75-144543. reprint ed. 42.50 (0-404-08617-9) AMS Pr.

Scottish Literacy & the Scottish Identity: Illiteracy & Society in Scotland & Northern England, 1600-1800. Rab A. Houston. (Cambridge Studies in Population, Economy & Society in Past Time: No. 4). (Illus.). 336p. 1985. text ed. 65.00 (0-521-26598-3) Cambridge U Pr.

Scottish Literature: An Anthology, Vol I. Ed. by David D. McCordick. 1280p. (C). 1996. text ed. 55.95 (0-8204-2880-9) P Lang Pubng.

***Scottish Literature: An Anthology, Vol. 2.** Ed. by David D. McCordick. 1272p. (C). 1997. 55.95 (0-8204-3399-3) P Lang Pubng.

Scottish Literature in English & Scots: A Guide to Information Sources. Ed. by W. R. Aitken. LC 73-16971. (American Literature, English Literature, & World Literatures in English Information Guide Ser.: Vol. 37). 448p. 1982. 68.00 (0-8103-1249-2) Gale.

***Scottish Literature Since 1707.** Walker. (C). 1997. pap. text ed. 25.95 (0-582-02892-2) Addison-Wesley.

Scottish Local History. David Moody. 178p. 1994. 18.95 (0-8063-1269-6, 3861) Genealog Pub.

Scottish Lore & Folklore. Ronald M. Douglas. 1990. 6.99 (0-517-03759-9) Random Hse Value.

Scottish Love Poems: A Personal Anthology. Ed. by Antonia Fraser. 253p. 1995. pap. 14.95 (0-7818-0406-X) Hippocrene Bks.

***Scottish Love Stories.** Ed. by Susie Maguire. 288p. (Orig.). 1995. pap. 20.00 (0-7486-6202-2, Pub. by Polygon UK) Subterranean Co.

***Scottish Magic.** Kaye et al. 256p. 1997. 21.95 (1-57566-182-9, Knsington) Kensgtn Pub Corp.

Scottish Medical Societies, 1731-1939: Their History & Records. Jacqueline Jenkinson. 256p. 1993. text ed. 60.00 (0-7486-0390-5, Pub. by Edinburgh U Pr UK) Col U Pr.

Scottish Metrical Romance of Lancelot Du Lak with Miscellaneous Poems. Ed. by Joseph Stevenson. LC 70-165337. reprint ed. 37.50 (0-404-53029-X) AMS Pr.

Scottish Ministers Widows Fund, 1743-1993. Ed. by Alan Dunlop. 160p. (C). 1992. 85.00 (0-86153-153-1, Pub. by St Andrew UK) St Mut.

Scottish Monasteries: Monastic Life in the Sixteenth Century. Mark Dilworth. (Illus.). 198p. (Orig.). 1995. pap. 25.00 (0-7486-0527-4, Pub. by Edinburgh U Pr UK) Col U Pr.

Scottish Moralists on Human Nature & Society. Louis Schneider. LC 67-15316. (Heritage of Sociology Ser.). 358p. reprint ed. pap. 102.10 (0-317-26687-X, 2025113) Bks Demand.

Scottish Motor Industry. Michael Worthington-Williams. 1989. pap. 25.00 (0-7478-0038-3, Pub. by Shire UK) St Mut.

Scottish Museums & Galleries: A Guide. Scottish Museums Council Staff. (Illus.). 100p. 1990. pap. 9.95 (0-08-037974-5, Pergamon Pr) Elsevier.

Scottish Nation, Vol. C. Ed. by William Anderson. (Illus.). 241p. 1995. reprint ed. pap. 30.00 (0-7884-0309-5) Heritage Bk.

Scottish Nation, Vol. D-F. William Anderson. (Illus.). 280p. (Orig.). 1995. reprint ed. pap. 34.50 (0-7884-0310-9) Heritage Bk.

Scottish Nation, Vol. M. William Anderson. 286p. (Orig.). 1995. pap. 35.50 (0-7884-0362-1, A00M) Heritage Bk.

Scottish Nation, Vol. G-L. William Anderson. (Illus.). 439p. (Orig.). 1995. pap. 51.00 (0-7884-0361-3, A00G) Heritage Bk.

Scottish Nation Vol. A: Or the Surnames, Families, Literature, Honours, & Biographical History of the People of Scotland. William Anderson. (Illus.). 172p. 1995. pap. text ed. 24.00 (0-7884-0245-5) Heritage Bk.

Scottish Nation Vol. T-Z: Or the Surnames, Families, Literature, Honours, & Biographical History of the People of Scotland. (Illus.). 193p. 1996. reprint ed. pap. 28.00 (0-7884-0381-8, A00T) Heritage Bk.

Scottish Nation; or the Surnames, Families, Literature, Honours, & Biographical History of the People of Scotland, Vol. B. William Anderson. (Illus.). 345p. 1995. pap. text ed. 41.50 (0-7884-0246-3) Heritage Bk.

Scottish Nation or the Surnames, Families, or Literature, Honours & Biographical History of the People of Scotland, Vol. N-5. (Illus.). 320p. 1996. pap. 41.00 (0-7884-0380-X, A00N) Heritage Bk.

Scottish National Convenant in Its British Context 1638-51. Ed. by John Morrill. 240p. 1991. 55.00 (0-7486-0203-8, Pub. by Edinburgh U Pr UK) Col U Pr.

An Asterisk (*) at the beginning of an entry indicates that the title is appearing in BIP for the first time.

Scottish Nationalism. Henry J. Hanham. 250p. 1969. 29.00 (*0-674-79580-6*) HUP.

Scottish Nationalism & Cultural Identity in the Twentieth Century: An Annotated Bibliography of Secondary Sources. Compiled by Gordon Bryan. LC 84-4667. (Bibliographies & Indexes in Law & Political Science Ser.: No. 1). (Illus.). xii, 180p. 1984. text ed. 49.95 (*0-313-23998-3*, BNA/) Greenwood.

Scottish Nature Diary. Douglas Willis. 188p. (C). 1989. text ed. 43.00 (*0-85976-316-1*, Pub. by J Donald UK) St Mut.

Scottish Office & Other Scottish Government Departments. David Milne. LC 84-24792. (New Whitehall Ser.). v, 140p. 1986. reprint ed. text ed. 59.75 (*0-313-23655-0*, MISO, Greenwood Pr) Greenwood.

Scottish Philosophy, Bibliographical, Expository, Critical, from Hutcheson to Hamilton. James McCosh. ix, 481p. 1966. reprint ed. 89.70 (*0-685-66492-9*, 05101276); reprint ed. write for info. (*0-318-71927-4*) G Olms Pubs.

***Scottish Philosophy, Biographical, Expository, Critical: From Hutcheson to Hamilton (1875 Edition)** James McCosh. 494p. 1996. reprint ed. write for info. (*1-85506-079-5*) Bks Intl VA.

Scottish Philosophy, Biographical, Expository, Critical, from Hutcheson to Hamilton. James McCosh. LC 75-3266. (Philosophy in America Ser.). 496p. 1980. reprint ed. 69.50 (*0-404-59254-6*) AMS Pr.

Scottish Philosophy of Common Sense. S. A. Grave. LC 72-7859. 262p. 1973. reprint ed. text ed. 35.00 (*0-8371-6539-3*, GRSC, Greenwood Pr) Greenwood.

***Scottish Pistol: Its History, Design & Manufacture.** Martin Kelvin. LC 96-42417. (Illus.). 250p. 1996. 49.50 (*0-8386-3745-0*) Fairleigh Dickinson.

Scottish Planning Law. Angus McAllister & Raymond McMaster. 230p. 1994. pap. text ed. 51.00 (*0-406-02012-4*, UK) MICHIE.

***Scottish Plants for Scottish Gardens.** Jill, Duchess of Hamilton. (Discovering Historic Scotland Ser.). (Illus.). 124p. 1997. pap. 22.95 (*0-11-495803-3*, Pub. by Statnry Ofc UK) Seven Hills Bk.

Scottish Poems & Ballads. (Poets Ser.). 146p. 1993. 5.95 (*0-7117-0403-1*, Pub. by Jarrold Pub UK) Seven Hills Bk.

Scottish Poets in America. Compiled by John D. Ross. LC 72-80502. 1972. reprint ed. lib. bdg. 24.95 (*0-405-08899-X*, Pub. by Blom Pubns UK) Ayer.

Scottish Political System. 4th ed. James G. Kellas. (Illus.). 320p. (C). 1989. pap. text ed. 29.95 (*0-521-36864-2*) Cambridge U Pr.

Scottish Pottery. Graeme Cruickshank. 1989. pap. 25.00 (*0-85263-849-3*, Pub. by Shire UK) St Mut.

Scottish Pottery. J. Arnold Flemming. (Illus.). 1976. reprint ed. 24.00 (*0-85409-778-3*) Charles River Bks.

***Scottish Prison Service Annual Report, 1995-96.** HMSO Staff. 62p. 1996. pap. 35.00 (*0-10-258396-X*, HM8396X, Pub. by Stationery Ofc UK) Bernan Associates.

Scottish Proverbs. A. Henderson. 1972. 59.95 (*0-8490-1005-5*) Gordon Pr.

Scottish Proverbs. Julie McDonald. Ed. by John Zug & Joan Liffring-Zug. (Illus.). 30p. (Orig.). 1987. pap. 10.95 (*0-941016-42-0*) Penfield.

Scottish Regency of the Earl of Arran: A Study in the Failure of Anglo-Scottish Relations. David Franklin. LC 94-41356. (Studies in British History: Vol. 35). (Illus.). 228p. 1995. text ed. 89.95 (*0-7734-8971-1*) E Mellen.

***Scottish Regiments.** Diana Henderson. (Illus.). 183p. (Orig.). 1997. pap. 15.00 (*0-00-471025-8*) HarperColl Wrld.

Scottish Regiments: 1633-1996. 2nd rev. ed. Patrick Mileham. (Illus.). 328p. 1996. 45.00 (*1-885119-24-0*) Sarpedon.

***Scottish Rite Ceremony for Maundy Thursday & Easter Sunday.** 1996. pap. 9.95 (*1-56459-991-4*) Kessinger Pub.

Scottish Rite Masonry, 2 vols., Set. pap. 30.00 (*0-685-19498-1*) Powner.

Scottish Rite Masonry, 2 vols., Set. E. A. Cook. 32.00 (*0-685-22097-4*) Wehman.

Scottish Roots. Alwyn James. (C). 1989. 39.00 (*0-904265-46-3*, Pub. by Saltire Soc) St Mut.

***Scottish Roots.** Alwyn James. 1996. pap. 39.95 (*0-85411-066-6*, Pub. by Saltire Soc) St Mut.

Scottish Roots: A Step-by-Step Guide for Ancestor-Hunters. Alwyn James. 1991. pap. 13.95 (*0-88289-802-7*) Pelican.

***Scottish Rose.** Jill Jones. 1997. mass mkt. write for info. (*0-614-20525-5*, St Martins Paperbacks) St Martin.

***Scottish Rose.** Jill Jones. 1997. mass mkt. 5.99 (*0-312-96099-9*) St Martin.

Scottish Salt Industry, 1570-1850: An Economic & Social History. C. A. Whately. 200p. 1987. text ed. 30.00 (*0-08-034528-X*, Pub. by Aberdeen U Pr) Macmillan.

***Scottish Scene.** Mike Parker. (Illus.). 200p. (Orig.). 1997. pap. 11.95 (*0-85449-248-8*, Pub. by Gay Mens Pr UK) LPC InBook.

***Scottish Sea Stories.** Ed. by Glen Murray. 1996. pap. 20.00 (*0-7486-6208-1*, Pub. by Polygon UK) Subterranean Co.

Scottish Sketches. Amelia E. Barr. LC 70-157771. (Short Story Index Reprint Ser.). 1977. reprint ed. 21.95 (*0-8369-3883-6*) Ayer.

Scottish Soldier. large type ed. Barbara Allen. 384p. 1988. 25.99 (*0-7089-1814-X*) Ulverscroft.

Scottish Soldier Abroad. Ed. by Grant G. Simpson. 224p. (C). 1992. text ed. 56.50 (*0-685-55038-9*) B&N Imports.

Scottish Soldier Abroad, 1247-1967. Grant G. Simpson. 250p. (C). 1996. 75.00 (*0-85976-341-2*, Pub. by J Donald UK) St Mut.

Scottish Song. John S. Blackie. LC 70-144563. reprint ed. 52.50 (*0-404-08579-2*) AMS Pr.

Scottish Songs, 2 vols. in 1. 2nd ed. Joseph Ritson. LC 77-144573. reprint ed. 74.50 (*0-404-08688-8*) AMS Pr.

Scottish Songs, 2 vols. in 1. Ed. by Robert Chambers. LC 70-144547. reprint ed. 76.50 (*0-404-08624-1*) AMS Pr.

Scottish Songs, Ballads, & Poems. Hew Ainslie. LC 75-144578. reprint ed. 37.50 (*0-404-08550-4*) AMS Pr.

Scottish Songs for Harmonica. Ed. by Pat Conway. (Illus.). 48p. 1992. pap. 7.95 (*0-7119-2791-X*, AM86520) Music Sales.

Scottish Songs of Robert Burns. 1994. 7.95 (*0-946005-81-8*, OS00096) Omnibus NY.

Scottish Sport in the Making of the Nation. Grant Jarvie & Graham Walker. (Sport, Politics & Culture Ser.). 256p. 1994. 55.00 (*0-7185-1454-8*, Pub. by Leicester Univ Pr) St Martin.

***Scottish Stained Glass.** Michael Donnelly. (Discovering Historic Scotland Ser.). (Illus.). 96p. 1998. pap. 14.95 (*0-11-495793-2*, Pub. by Statnry Ofc UK) Seven Hills Bk.

Scottish Stories from MacGregor's Gathering. Ed. by Stephen Mulrine. 63p. 1992. pap. 6.95 (*0-563-20739-6*, BBC-Parkwest) Parkwest Pubns.

Scottish Surnames. David Dorward. 64p. (C). 1986. pap. 40.00 (*0-901824-77-1*, Pub. by Mercat Pr Bks UK) St Mut.

Scottish Swords from the Battlefield at Culloden. Archibald Campbell. Ed. by Andrew Mowbray. (Illus.). 63p. 1971. 15.00 (*0-917218-04-3*) A Mowbray.

Scottish Tartans in Full Color. James Grant. (Illus.). 80p. 1992. pap. 14.95 (*0-486-27046-7*) Dover.

Scottish Terrier. Dorothy S. Caspersz. 1991. lib. bdg. 75.00 (*0-8490-5213-0*) Gordon Pr.

Scottish Terrier: Its Breeding & Management. Dorothy Gabriel. 1992. lib. bdg. 75.00 (*0-8490-5212-2*) Gordon Pr.

Scottish Terrier Champions, 1952-1990. Camino E. E. & Bk. Co. Staff. (Illus.). 175p. 1992. pap. 36.95 (*1-55893-005-1*) Camino E E & Bk.

Scottish Terriers. T. H. Snethen. (Illus.). 192p. 1995. 9.95 (*0-7938-1477-4*, KW103) TFH Pubns.

Scottish Textile History. Ed. by J. Butt. (Illus.). 256p. 1987. text ed. 42.00 (*0-08-034511-5*, Pub. by Aberdeen U Pr) Macmillan.

Scottish Texts & Calendars: An Analytic Guide to Serial Publications. David Stevenson & Wendy B. Stevenson. (Royal Historical Society Guides & Handbooks Ser.: No. 14). 245p. 27.00 (*0-86193-111-4*) David Brown.

Scottish Theatre since the Seventies. Ed. by Randall Stevenson & Gavin Wallace. 256p. 1996. pap. 22.50 (*0-7486-0781-1*, Pub. by Edinburgh U Pr UK) Col U Pr.

***Scottish Theology: From John Knox to John McLeod Campbell.** Thomas F. Torrance. 352p. 1996. 49.95 (*0-567-08532-5*, Pub. by T & T Clark UK) Bks Intl VA.

Scottish Theology in Relation to Church History Since the Reformation. John Macleod. 350p. (C). 1995. reprint ed. pap. text ed. 10.95 (*1-884416-14-4*, Reformed Acad Pr) A Press.

Scottish Thirties. Charles McKean. 200p. (C). 1987. pap. 35.00 (*0-7073-0493-8*, Pub. by Rutland Pr UK) St Mut.

Scottish Toasts & Graces. Charles MacLean. (Illus.). 60p. 1994. 7.95 (*0-8118-0622-7*) Chronicle Bks.

Scottish Tradition in Literature. Kurt Wittig. 360p. (C). 1986. 39.00 (*0-901824-47-X*, Pub. by Mercat Pr Bks UK) St Mut.

Scottish Tradition in Printed Books. William Beattie. 50p. 1986. 20.00 (*0-85411-004-6*, Pub. by Saltire Soc) St Mut.

***Scottish Traditional Tales.** Ed. by A. J. Bruford & D. A. MacDonald. 1994. pap. 26.00 (*0-7486-6150-6*, Pub. by Polygon UK) Subterranean Co.

Scottish Trip. Colin Palfey. 1986. 30.00 (*0-86243-041-0*, Pub. by Y Lolfa UK) St Mut.

***Scottish Tunes for Piano.** Alfred A. Moffat. 88p. 14.95 (*0-946005-27-3*, OS 10690, Pub. by Ossian Publns IE) Music Sales.

Scottish Universities: Distinctiveness & Diversity. J. J. Carter & D. J. Withrington. 250p. (C). 1996. 75.00 (*0-85976-375-7*, Pub. by J Donald UK) St Mut.

Scottish Urban History. Ed. by G. Gordon & B. Dicks. (Illus.). 280p. 1983. text ed. 33.00 (*0-08-025762-3*, Pergamon Pr) Elsevier.

Scottish Vernacular Literature. T. Henderson. 1972. 59.95 (*0-8490-1006-3*) Gordon Pr.

Scottish Visitors: A Story about 'Abdu'l-Baha in Britain. Anthony A. Lee. (Stories About 'Abdu'l-Baha Ser.). (Illus.). 24p. (Orig.). (J). (gr. k-5). 1981. pap. 3.00 (*0-933770-04-9*) Kalimat.

***Scottish Wild Plants: Their History, Ecology & Conservation.** Phil Lusby & Jenny Wright. (Illus.). 116p. 1996. 40.00 (*1-872291-17-1*, Pub. by Royal Botanic Edinburgh UK) Balogh.

***Scottish Wild Plants: Their History, Ecology & Conservation.** Phil Lusby & Jenny Wright. (Discovering Historic Scotland Ser.). (Illus.). 124p. 1997. pap. 22.95 (*0-11-495802-5*, Pub. by Statnry Ofc UK) Seven Hills Bk.

Scottish Witchcraft: The History & Magick of the Picts. Raymond Buckland. LC 91-32832. (Illus.). 256p. (Orig.). 1991. pap. 9.95 (*0-87542-057-5*) Llewellyn Pubns.

Scottish Witches. (Ghost Ser.). (Illus.). 144p. 1993. pap. 7.95 (*0-7117-0451-1*) Seven Hills Bk.

***Scottish Wonder Tales from Myth & Legend.** Donald A. Mackenzie. LC 96-42204. (Illus.). 224p. 1997. reprint ed. pap. text ed. 6.95 (*0-486-29677-6*) Dover.

Scotts. Jean Dunlop. (Johnston & Bacon Clan Histories Ser.). (Illus.). 32p. 1993. reprint ed. pap. 8.95 (*0-685-69993-5*, 9604) Clearfield Co.

Scott's English Law for GCSE. 5th ed. Ed. by Marianne Giles. 1987. U.K. pap. 14.00 (*0-406-65307-0*) MICHIE.

Scott's Fingerprint Mechanics. Robert D. Olsen, Sr. (Illus.). 480p. 1978. 73.95 (*0-398-03730-2*); pap. 44.95 (*0-398-06308-7*) C C Thomas.

Scott's Last Edition: A Study in Publishing History. Jane Millgate. (Illus.). 160p. 1987. 25.00 (*0-85224-541-6*, Pub. by Edinburgh U Pr UK) Col U Pr.

Scott's Last Expedition: The Journals. Robert F. Scott. (Illus.). 464p. 1996. pap. 14.95 (*0-7867-0382-2*) Carroll & Graf.

Scott's Official History of Reggae, the Original Wailers, & the Trench-Town Experience: Cornerstone Reggae Legends. Ricardo A. Scott. (Reggae Cornerstone Ser.). (Illus.). 140p. (Orig.). 1993. 35.00 (*1-883427-00-2*); teacher ed. 30.00 (*1-883427-05-3*); student ed. 30.00 (*1-883427-06-1*); pap. 30.00 (*1-883427-03-7*); text ed. 30.00 (*1-883427-02-9*); pap. text ed. 30.00 (*1-883427-04-5*); lib. bdg. 30.00 (*1-883427-01-0*) Crnerstone GA.

Scott's Official History of the American Negro in the World War. Emmett J. Scott. LC 69-18556. (American Negro: His History & Literature. Series 2). 1969. reprint ed. 23.95 (*0-405-01892-4*) Ayer.

Scotts See & Do Solutions: Flower Gardens. Sara Godwin & Linda J. Smith. Ed. by Jim Blume & Lisa Kingsley. (Illus.). 128p. 1995. 14.95 (*0-9644782-0-X*) Scotts Co.

Scotts See & Do Solutions: Lawns & Groundcovers. Sara Godwin. Ed. by Jim Blume & Lisa Kingsley. (Illus.). 128p. 1995. 14.95 (*0-9644782-1-8*) Scotts Co.

Scottsboro: Tragedy of the American South. rev. ed. Dan T. Carter. LC 79-1090. (Illus.). 512p. 1979. pap. text ed. 16.95 (*0-8071-0498-1*) La State U Pr.

Scottsboro Case in Mississippi: The Supreme Court & Brown vs. Mississippi. Richard C. Cortner. LC 85-20174. 188p. reprint ed. pap. 53.60 (*0-7837-1073-9*, 2041597) Bks Demand.

Scottsdale. Alan Korwin & William Franklin. LC 93-39618. (Illus.). 112p. (Orig.). 1994. pap. 9.95 (*1-56037-019-X*) Am Wrld Geog.

Scottsdale: A Portrait in Color. Michel F. Sarda. LC 91-71662. 136p. 1991. pap. 29.95 (*0-927015-03-X*) Bridgewood Pr.

Scottsdale: A Portrait in Color. 2nd ed. Michel F. Sarda. 136p. 1992. 39.95 (*0-927015-04-8*) Bridgewood Pr.

Scottsdale: Jewel in the Desert. Patricia M. McElfresh. LC 84-19605. (Illus.). 136p. 1988. 22.95 (*0-89781-105-4*) Am Historical Pr.

***Scottsdale - A Portrait in Color.** 3rd ed. Michel F. Sarda. LC 92-73301. (Illus.). 144p. 1996. 39.95 (*0-927015-13-7*) Bridgewood Pr.

Scottsdale Pain Relief Program: The Revolutionary Seven Day Program To Reduce Pain. Neal H. Olshan. 208p. 1987. 16.95 (*0-317-55019-5*) Beaufort Bks NY.

Scottsdale Pain Relief Program: The Seven Day Program to Reduce Pain. Neal H. Olshan. 1989. 2.98 (*0-8253-0423-7*) Beaufort Bks NY.

Scotty II: Born to Be Mild. Michael Fry. LC 88-82338. (Illus.). (Orig.). 1988. pap. 7.95 (*0-929828-44-5*) Fine Toon Pr.

Scotty's Castle. Ed. by Hank Johnston. 1974. 3.95 (*0-685-28951-6*) Flying Spur Pr.

Scotty's Pictorial Motorcycle Toy Price Guide. (Illus.). 80p. (Orig.). 1996. pap. 17.95 (*0-9652650-0-5*) Antique Toys.

Scotus Americanus: A Study of 18th Century Sources. William R. Brock. 293p. 1982. 35.00 (*0-85224-420-7*, Pub. by Edinburgh U Pr UK) Col U Pr.

Scoundrel. Ann Carberry. 352p. (Orig.). 1995. mass mkt. 5.50 (*0-515-11705-6*) Jove Pubns.

***Scoundrel.** Bernard Cornwell. mass mkt. write for info. (*0-06-109188-X*, Harp PBks) HarpC.

Scoundrel. Debra Dier. 400p. (Orig.). 1996. mass mkt., pap. text ed. 5.50 (*0-8439-3894-3*) Dorchester Pub Co.

Scoundrel. Elizabeth Elliott. 352p. 1996. mass mkt. 5.50 (*0-553-56911-2*) Bantam.

Scoundrels All. Ferdinand Lundberg. LC 68-18764. 1968. 3.95 (*0-8184-0072-2*) Carol Pub Group.

Scoundrel's Bride. Emily Hendrickson. (Signet Regency Romance Ser.). 224p. (Orig.). 1994. pap. 3.99 (*0-451-17935-8*, Sig) NAL-Dutton.

Scoundrel's Captive. JoAnn DeLazzari. 416p. (Orig.). 1991. mass mkt. 4.50 (*0-380-76420-2*) Avon.

Scoundrel's Desire. JoAnn DeLazzari. 384p. (Orig.). 1993. mass mkt. 4.50 (*0-380-76421-0*) Avon.

Scoundrel's Luck: Solitaire. 80p. 13.00 (*0-87431-112-8*, 40102) West End Games.

***Scourage of Guns: The Diffusion of Small Arms & Light Weapons in Latin America.** Michael T. Klare & David Andersen. LC 96-85376. (Illus.). iv, 112p. (Orig.). 1996. pap. 15.00 (*0-9653386-0-6*) Fed Am Scientists.

Scourge & Minister: A Study of Hamlet As Tragedy of Revengefulness & Justice. George R. Elliott. LC 78-166021. reprint ed. 27.50 (*0-404-02307-X*) AMS Pr.

Scourge of Christendom: Annals of British Relations with Algiers Prior to the French Conquest. Robert L. Playfair. LC 72-3987. (Black Heritage Library Collection). 1977. reprint ed. 35.95 (*0-8369-9104-4*) Ayer.

Scourge of Monetarism. 2nd ed. Nicholas Kaldor. (Illus.). 128p. 1986. pap. 13.95 (*0-19-877248-3*) OUP.

Scourge of Secrecy: A Personal Testimony & Appeal. Richard Harger. LC 80-50239. 218p. 1980. pap. 6.80 (*0-936472-00-6*) Gordy Pr.

Scourge of the Indies: Buccaneers, Corsairs & Filibusters. Maurice Besson. 1977. lib. bdg. 250.00 (*0-8490-2574-5*) Gordon Pr.

Scourge of the Rio Bravo. large type ed. Jack Greer. (Linford Western Library). 256p. 1995. pap. 15.99 (*0-7089-7750-2*, Linford) Ulverscroft.

Scourge of Villanie. John Marston. LC 73-21779. (English Literature Ser.: No. 33). 1974. lib. bdg. 57.95 (*0-8383-1828-2*) M S G Haskell Hse.

Scourging of Iraq. Simons. 1996. text ed. 45.00 (*0-312-16182-4*) St Martin.

Scourging of W. H. D. Wretched Hutchinson. George Chambers. Ed. by Richard Lyons. 162p. (Orig.). 1995. pap. 14.00 (*0-9638099-1-1*) SPSHR.

Scouring. Arved J. Raudkivi & H. N. Breusers. (Hydraulic Structures Design Manual Ser.: No. 2). (Illus.). 152p. (C). 1991. text ed. 85.00 (*90-6191-983-5*, Pub. by A A Balkema NE) Ashgate Pub Co.

Scout. Harry Combs. 1996. mass mkt. 6.50 (*0-440-21729-6*) Dell.

Scout. Ion L. Idriess. 128p. 1977. pap. 12.00 (*0-87364-135-3*) Paladin Pr.

Scout. Julie Nye. Ed. by Suzette Jordan. (Light Line Ser.). 178p. (Orig.). (J). 1987. pap. 6.49 (*0-89084-413-5*, 032839) Bob Jones Univ Pr.

Scout: Mount Fire. Timothy Truman. (Illus.). 1990. 34.95 (*0-913035-14-9*); pap. 14.95 (*0-913035-15-7*) Eclipse Bks.

Scout: Savage Spread, No. 33. Buck Gentry. 1991. mass mkt. 3.50 (*0-8217-3477-6*, Zebra Kensgtn) Kensgtn Pub Corp.

Scout: Searching for the Best in Baseball. Red Murff & Mike Capps. 256p. 1996. 19.99 (*0-8499-1299-7*) Word Pub.

Scout: The Four Monsters. Timothy Truman. (Illus.). 1990. 34.95 (*0-913035-35-1*); pap. 14.95 (*0-913035-33-5*) Eclipse Bks.

***Scout: The Secret of the Swamp.** Piet Prins. LC 97-19929. (J). 1997. pap. write for info. (*0-921100-50-7*) Inhtce Pubns.

Scout & Cody. Lark Carrier. LC 86-883. (Illus.). 28p. (J). (ps up). 1991. pap. 14.95 (*0-88708-013-8*, Picture Book Studio) S&S Childrens.

Scout & Ranger. James Pike. LC 74-39282. (American Scene Ser.). (Illus.). 164p. 1972. reprint ed. lib. bdg. 25.00 (*0-306-70458-7*) Da Capo.

Scout & Ranger: Being the Personal Adventures of James Pike of the Texas Rangers in 1859-60. James Pike. (American Biography Ser.). 164p. 1991. reprint ed. lib. bdg. 59.00 (*0-7812-8314-0*) Rprt Serv.

Scout Dog Training & Employment. 1986. lib. bdg. 150.00 (*0-8490-3825-1*) Gordon Pr.

Scout Dog Training & Employment: How to Choose & Train Your Own Attack Dog. 1986. lib. bdg. 150.00 (*0-8490-3670-4*) Gordon Pr.

Scout, No. 15: Texas Tease. Buck Gentry. 240p. 1984. mass mkt. 2.50 (*0-685-08593-7*, Zebra Kensgtn) Kensgtn Pub Corp.

Scout, or the Black Riders of Congaree. William G. Simms. LC 68-20021. (Americans in Fiction Ser.). 480p. reprint ed. lib. bdg. 19.00 (*0-8398-1860-2*) Irvington.

Scout, or the Black Riders of Congaree. William G. Simms. (Americans in Fiction Ser.). 480p. (C). 1986. reprint ed. pap. text ed. 5.75 (*0-8290-1944-8*) Irvington.

Scout, Vol. 32: Stiff Justice. Buck Gentry. 256p. 1991. mass mkt. 3.50 (*0-8217-3321-4*, Zebra Kensgtn) Kensgtn Pub Corp.

Scout with Custer. D. Dickson. 1976. 30.95 (*0-8488-0224-1*, J M C & Co) Amereon Ltd.

Scouting & Tracking. Randolph B. Marcy. (Buckaroos Ser.). (Illus.). 32p. (Orig.). (J). (gr. 2 up). 1996. pap. 1.50 (*1-55709-367-9*) Applewood.

Scouting, Cavorting, & Other World War II Memories. Robert G. Raymond. (Illus.). (Orig.). pap. write for info. (*0-9645021-0-0*) R G Raymond.

***Scouting Coordinator.** 1996. pap. 0.90 (*0-8395-3118-4*, 33118) BSA.

Scouting Expeditions of McCulloch's Texas Rangers: Or, the Summer & Fall Campaign of the Army of the United States in Mexico 1846. Samuel C. Reid, Jr. LC 72-126252. (Select Bibliographies Reprint Ser.). 1977. 20.95 (*0-8369-5479-3*) Ayer.

Scouting for Boys: A Handbook for Instruction in Good Citizenship. Robert Baden-Powell. (Illus.). 273p. (Orig.). (YA). 1992. pap. 17.95 (*0-9632054-1-2*) Stevens Pub.

Scouting for the Physically Disabled. 34p. 1971. pap. 5.50 (*0-8395-3057-9*, 33057) BSA.

Scouting in the Santa Clara Valley: The Seventy Year Adventure, 1920-1990. Council History Task Force Staff & James P. Sturrock. Ed. by Mardi Bennett. (Illus.). 232p. 1990. 29.95 (*0-9628133-0-3*) Santa Clara Cnty BSA.

Scouting in the Schools: A Study of the Relationship Between the Schools & the Boy Scouts of America. Ray O. Wyland. LC 70-177616. (Columbia University. Teachers College. Contributions to Education Ser.: No. 631). reprint ed. 37.50 (*0-404-55631-0*) AMS Pr.

Scouting Notebook 1995. John Dewan. 1995. pap. 16.00 (*1-884064-12-4*) STATS.

Scouting Notebook 1996. Stats Publishing Staff. 1996. pap. 16.95 (*1-884064-22-1*) STATS.

Scouting Notebook 1997. 3rd ed. 680p. 1997. pap. 19.95 (*1-884064-35-3*) STATS.

Scouting on Two Continents. Fredrick Burnham. 1993. reprint ed. 35.00 (*1-879356-31-7*) Wolfe Pub Co.

***Scouting Report 1997: The "Original" Scouting Report of Major League Players & Teams.** David Srinivasan. 480p. (Orig.). 1997. pap. 18.95 (*0-06-273055-X*, Harper Ref) HarpC.

Scouting Round the World. Lord Baden-Powell. (Illus.). 200p. 1992. pap. 16.95 (*0-9632054-6-3*) Stevens Pub.

Scoutmaster Handbook. Boy Scouts of America Staff. (Illus.). 268p. (YA). 1992. pap. 7.15 (*0-8395-3002-1*, 33002) BSA.

Scoutmaster Remembers. Dan C. Stowe. 1991. pap. 4.95 (*1-55673-381-X*, 7789) CSS OH.

S

An Asterisk (*) at the beginning of an entry indicates that the title is appearing in BIP for the first time.

***Scoutmastership Fundamentals: A Training Course for Scoutmasters, Assistant Scoutmasters, Troop Committee Members, & Parents.** rev. ed. Boy Scouts of America Staff. (Illus.). 180p. 1996. pap. 14.95 (0-8395-4549-5, 34549) BSA.

***Scouts.** (Star Wars Galaxy Guides Ser.: No. 8). 15.00 (0-87431-188-8, 40061) West End Games.

Scouts. Gail Stewart. (Wild West in American History Ser.: Set 11). (Illus.). 32p. (J). (gr. 3-8). 1990. 13.50 (0-685-58651-0); lib. bdg. 18.00 (0-86625-404-8) Rourke Corp.

Scouts & Raiders: The Navy's First Special Warfare Commandos. John B. Dwyer. LC 92-30384. 224p. 1993. text ed. 52.95 (0-275-94409-3, C4409, Praeger Pubs) Greenwood.

***Scout's Bride.** Kate Kingsley. (Historical Ser.). 1997. 4.99 (0-373-28954-5, 1-28954-5) Harlequin Bks.

Scout's Honor. Malacai Black. 432p. 1988. mass mkt. 3.95 (0-8217-2508-4, Zebra Kensgtn) Kensgtn Pub Corp.

Scout's Honor: Mystery Jigsaw Puzzle Thriller. Al Carusone. (Spider Tales Ser.). (Orig.). (J). (gr. 3-7). 1996. pap. 13.50 (1-57561-011-6, 00907HON) Bepuzzled.

Scout's Honor: Sexual Abuse in America's Most Trusted Institution. Patrick Boyle. LC 93-23556. 1994. 22.95 (1-55958-365-7) Prima Pub.

Scout's Honor: Sexual Abuse in Americas Most Trusted Institution. Patrick Boyle. 1995. pap. 12.95 (0-7615-0024-3) Prima Pub.

Scouts of Stonewall. Joseph Altsheler. 1976. lib. bdg. 19.95 (0-89968-004-6, Lghtyr Pr) Buccaneer Bks.

Scouts of Stonewall. Joseph Altsheler. 1990. reprint ed. lib. bdg. 21.95 (0-89968-466-1) Buccaneer Bks.

Scouts of Stonewall: The Story of the Great Valley Campaign. Joseph A. Altsheler. (Joseph A. Altsheler Civil War Ser.). 1985. 25.95 (0-8488-0070-2) Amereon Ltd.

***Scouts of the Heart.** Susan R. Shreve. Date not set. write for info. (0-688-05047-6) Morrow.

Scouts of the Valley. Joseph A. Altsheler. 26.95 (0-8488-1241-7) Amereon Ltd.

Scouts of the Valley. Joseph Altsheler. 345p. 1981. reprint ed. lib. bdg. 25.95 (0-89968-227-8, Lghtyr Pr) Buccaneer Bks.

Scouts of the Valley. Joseph Altsheler. (Young Trailer Ser.). 319p. 1984. reprint ed. lib. bdg. 25.95 (0-89966-484-9) Buccaneer Bks.

***Scouts of the Wild West.** Jeff Savage. LC 94-33361. (Trailblazers of the Wild West Ser.). (Illus.). 48p. (J). (gr. 4-10). 1995. lib. bdg. 14.95 (0-89490-605-4) Enslow Pubs.

Scovell: Arthur Scovell & His Descendants in America, 1660-1900. J. M. Holley & H. W. Brainard. 285p. 1991. reprint ed. pap. 45.50 (0-8328-1729-5); reprint ed. lib. bdg. 55.50 (0-8328-1728-7) Higginson Bk Co.

***Scow Schooners of San Francisco Bay.** Roger Olmsted. Ed. by Nancy Olmsted. (Local History Studies: Vol. 33). 112p. 1988. pap. 14.95 (0-935089-12-8) CA History Ctr.

SCPA & EPTL. 340p. 1997. ring bd. 19.95 (0-930137-47-7) Looseleaf Law.

SCR & New Technology in Electric Rig Drilling: A Safety & Efficiency Handbook. Will L. McNair. 296p. 1991. 25.00 (0-87814-368-8) PennWell Bks.

SCR Manual. 6th ed. General Electric Company Staff. (Illus.). 656p. 1982. 18.50 (0-13-796763-2) P-H.

Scrabble Brand Word Guide. Edmund Jacobson & Jacob S. Orleans. 112p. 1990. pap. 7.50 (0-399-51645-X, Perigee Bks) Berkley Pub.

***Scrabble Creek.** Patricia Wittman. (Illus.). (J). 4.98 (0-7651-0094-0) Smithmark.

Scrabble Creek. Patricia Wittmann. LC 92-10810. (Illus.). 32p. (J). (gr. k-3). 1993. lib. bdg. 14.95 (0-02-793225-7, Mac Bks Young Read) S&S Childrens.

Scrabble Crossword Puzzle Book, No. 4. William Lutwiniak. 1988. pap. 4.95 (0-02-688817-3) Macmillan.

***Scrabble Game Puzzle Book.** Edley. 1997. pap. 14.00 (0-671-56900-7, PB Trade Paper) PB.

Scrabble Word-Building Book. Saleem Ahmed. Ed. by Paul McCarthy. 608p. (Orig.). 1991. pap. 6.99 (0-671-73456-3) PB.

Scraboolee Jubilee. Tony Marino. LC 92-12840. (Widgets Ser.). (YA). 1992. lib. bdg. 13.99 (1-56239-153-4) Abdo & Dghtrs.

Scraggly's New Home. Thomas E. Bradbury. Tr. by Ron Goyette & Nancy C. Funk. (Scraggly, The Stowaway Cat Ser.). (Illus.). 32p. (Orig.). (J). (gr. k-5). 1987. pap. text ed. write for info. (0-9618945-0-4) Tern Pubns.

Scram: Relocating under a New Identity. James S. Martin. LC 93-78605. 83p. (Orig.). 1993. pap. 12.95 (1-55950-094-8, 61138) Loompanics.

Scramble for Africa. M. E. Chamberlain. LC 74-177119. (Seminar Studies in History). (C). 1974. pap. text ed. 13.50 (0-582-35204-5) Longman.

Scramble for Africa: The Great Trek to the Boer War. Anthony Nutting. (Illus.). 454p. 1994. pap. 37.50 (0-09-473820-3, Pub. by Constable Pubs UK) Trans-Atl Phila.

Scramble for Africa: The White Man's Conquest of the Dark Continent from 1876 to 1912. Thomas Pakenham. LC 91-52681. (Illus.). 784p. 1991. 31.50 (0-394-51576-5) Random.

Scramble for Africa: The White Man's Conquest of the Dark Continent from 1876 to 1912. Thomas Pakenham. 800p. 1992. reprint ed. pap. 17.50 (0-380-71999-1) Avon.

Scramble for Southern Africa, 1877-1895: The Politics of Partition Reappraised. Deryck M. Schreuder. LC 78-58800. (Cambridge Commonwealth Ser.). 398p. reprint ed. pap. 113.50 (0-318-34666-4, 2031722) Bks Demand.

***Scrambled Brains: A Cooking Guide for the Reality Impaired.** Robin Konstabaris. 1997. pap. text ed. 14.95 (1-55152-042-7, Pub. by Arsenal Pulp CN) LPC InBook.

Scrambled Eggheads. Illus. by Bill Ross. 14p. (J). (ps-2). 1995. pap. 3.50 (1-57102-031-4, Ideals Child) Hambleton-Hill.

Scrambled Eggs. B. B. Calhoun. (Dinosaur Detective Ser.: Vol. 5). (Illus.). 112p. (J). (gr. 3-7). 1995. text ed. 12.95 (0-7167-6584-5, Sci Am Yng Rdrs); pap. text ed. 3.95 (0-7167-6585-3, Sci Am Yng Rdrs) W H Freeman.

Scrambled Eggs. 95th ed. HB Staff. (J). (gr. 6). 1995. text ed., lib. bdg., pap. text ed. 12.25 (0-15-305236-8) HB Coll Pubs.

Scrambled Eggs & Whiskey: Poems 1991-1995. Hayden Carruth. LC 96-4487. 150p. 1996. 25.00 (1-55659-109-8); pap. 14.00 (1-55659-110-1) Copper Canyon.

Scrambled Eggs Super! Dr. Seuss. (Illus.). (J). (gr. k-3). 1953. lib. bdg. 13.99 (0-394-90085-5) Random Bks Yng Read.

Scrambled Eggs Super! Dr. Seuss. LC 53-5013. (Dr. Seuss Bks.). (Illus.). 64p. (J). (gr. 1-4). 1966. 14.00 (0-394-80085-0) Random Bks Yng Read.

Scrambled Home Evenings: A Novel. Joni Hilton. LC 93-42592. 1994. 9.95 (1-55503-651-1) Covenant Comms.

Scrambles Amongst the Alps: In the Years 1860-69. 5th unabridged ed. Edward Whymper. LC 95-45713. (Illus.). 512p. 1996. reprint ed. pap. text ed. 13.95 (0-486-28972-9) Dover.

Scrambling & Barriers. Ed. by Gunther Grewendorf & Wolfgang Sternefeld. LC 89-18427. (Linguistik Aktuell Ser.: Vol. 5). vi, 442p. 1990. 103.00 (90-272-2725-X) Benjamins North Am.

Scrambling for Protection: The New Media & the First Amendment. Patrick M. Garry. (Policy & Institutional Studies). 208p. (C). 1994. text ed. 35.00 (0-8229-3798-0) U of Pittsburgh Pr.

Scrambling for Protection: The New Media & the First Amendment. Patrick M. Garry. (Policy & Institutional Studies). 208p. (C). 1996. pap. text ed. 15.95 (0-8229-5582-2) U of Pittsburgh Pr.

Scrambling Techniques for Digital Transmission. Byeong G. Lee. 1994. 59.00 (0-387-19863-6) Spr-Verlag.

Scrambling Techniques for Digital Transmission: Telecommunications Networks & Computer. Byeong G. Lee. 1994. 59.00 (3-540-19863-6) Spr-Verlag.

Scrambling to Master Basic English Sentence Structure. Elizabeth Branch & Jeanette Adkins. 141p. (C). 1995. pap. text ed. 28.38 (1-56226-272-6) CT Pub.

Scramcat. Linda Jennings. LC 93-2911. (Illus.). 1993. 13.95 (1-56656-137-X, Crocodile Bks) Interlink Pub.

Scranton: Genealogical Register of Descendants of John Scranton of Guilford, Connecticut, Who Dies in the Year 1671. E. Scranton. 104p. 1993. reprint ed. pap. 17.00 (0-8328-3401-7); reprint ed. lib. bdg. 27.00 (0-8328-3400-9) Higginson Bk Co.

Scrap Basket Crafts: Over Fifty Quick & Easy Projects to Make from Fabric Scraps. Nancy Reames. (Illus.). 288p. 1994. 23.95 (0-87596-620-9) Rodale Pr Inc.

Scrap Book, Vol. II. B. H. Roberts. 578p. 1991. 34.95 (0-9622545-9-2) L Pulsipher.

Scrap-Book Recitation Series: A Miscellaneous Collection of Prose & Poetry for Recitation & Reading Designed for Schools, Home & Literary Circles, 2 Vols., Vol. 1. Henry M. Soper. text ed. 113.95 (0-8369-9364-0, 19735) Ayer.

Scrap Crafts. LC 83-51233. (McCall's Needlework & Crafts Ser.). (Illus.). 112p. 1984. write for info. (0-02-496700-9, Macmillan Coll) P-H.

Scrap Crafts Year 'Round: More Than 70 Projects to Make with Less Than a Yard of Fabric. Chris Rankin. LC 96-6015. (Illus.). 128p. 1996. 24.95 (0-8069-8166-0) Lark Books.

Scrap Fun for Everyone see It's Fun to Make Things from Scrap Materials

Scrap Materials. Mike Roussel. (Craft Projects Ser.). (Illus.). 32p. (J). (gr. 2-6). 1990. 11.95 (0-685-36305-8); lib. bdg. 15.94 (0-86592-487-2) Rourke Corp.

***Scrap of Pride: How to Use Quilting As a Tool to Bring People Together.** Luanne Bole-Becker. (Illus.). ii, 30p. (Orig.). 1996. wbk. ed., pap. 24.95 incl. vhs (0-9654560-0-5) BB Sound.

Scrap of Time: And Other Stories. Ida Fink. Tr. by Francine Prose & Madeline Levine from POL. LC 95-15281. (Jewish Lives Ser.). 174p. 1995. pap. 12.95 (0-8101-1259-0) Northwestern U Pr.

Scrap-Paper Miracle. Don Madaris. Ed. by Cathy Butler. 85p. (Orig.). 1993. reprint ed. pap. text ed. 6.95 (1-56309-022-8, New Hope AL) Womans Mission Union.

Scrap Quilt Memories. Aliske Webb. 176p. 1998. 18.00 (0-06-017462-5) HarpC.

Scrap Quilt, Strips & Spider Webs. Marcia Lasher. (Illus.). 64p. 1991. 8.95 (0-922705-26-7) Quilt Day.

Scrap Quilts. Judy Martin. LC 85-72392. (Illus.). 96p. (Orig.). 1985. pap. 12.95 (0-9602970-9-X) Leman Pubns.

Scrap Quilts & How to Make Them. Judy Florence. LC 94-40102. (Illus.). 96p. 1995. pap. text ed. 7.95 (0-486-28477-8) Dover.

Scrap Quilts Using Fast Patch. Anita Hallock. LC 90-55876. (Illus.). 208p. 1991. pap. 19.95 (0-8019-8116-6) Chilton.

Scrap Saver's Bazaar Stitchery. Sandra L. Foose. 1990. 19.95 (0-8487-0753-2) Oxmoor Hse.

Scrap Saver's Country Stitchery. Sandra Foose. LC 93-83173. 160p. 1993. pap. 14.95 (0-8487-1178-5) Oxmoor Hse.

Scrap Saver's Gift Stitchery. Sandra L. Foose. LC 83-51240. (Illus.). 168p. 1984. write for info. (0-02-496680-0, Macmillan Coll) P-H.

Scrap Savers One Hundred One Great Little Gifts. Sandra Foose. 1994. pap. 14.95 (0-8487-1419-9) Oxmoor Hse.

Scrap Tire Technology & Markets. U. S. Environmental Protection Agency, Office of Wetlands, Oceans, & Watersheds Staff et al. LC 92-25264. (Pollution Technology Review Ser.: No. 211). (Illus.). 316p. 1993. 54.00 (0-8155-1317-8) Noyes.

Scrapbook. Sean Martin. (Orig.). 1994. mass mkt. 4.95 (1-56333-224-8, Badboy) Masquerade.

Scrapbook: Some Family Reminiscences of a Native Nashville Septuagenarian. Emma W. Bragg. LC 85-73699. (Illus.). 50p. (Orig.). 1985. pap. 25.00 (0-9611930-2-6) E W Bragg.

Scrapbook of a Haight Ashbury Pilgrim: Spirit, Sacraments, & Sex in 1967-68. Elizabeth Gips. (Illus.). 218p. (Orig.). 1995. pap. 15.00 (0-9639056-0-0) Changes CA.

Scrapbook of Snowdonia. Vernon Hall. 312p. 1982. 20.00 (0-7223-1622-4, Pub. by A H S Ltd UK) St Mut.

Scrapbook on America. Francis R. Line. (Orig.). 1990. pap. 8.95 (0-938109-07-3) Wide Horiz Pr.

***Scrapbook Sensations.** Cathy Sexton. (Illus.). 24p. (Orig.). 1997. pap. 9.99 (1-58050-003-X, 40-6123) Provo Craft.

Scrapbook Stories: Character Building Stories from Yesteryear. Ed. by Ernest Lloyd. (Pioneer Ser.). (Illus.). 96p. (YA). (gr. 5 up). 1990. reprint ed. pap. 5.95 (0-945460-08-2) Upward Way.

Scrapcrafts from A to Z. Better Homes & Gardens Editors Staff. (Better Homes & Gardens Ser.). 1996. 24.95 (0-696-20379-0) Meredith Bks.

***Scrape Hunting from A to Z.** J. Wayne Fears. Ed. by Craig Boddington. (Whitetail Secrets Ser.: No. 3). (Illus.). 173p. (YA). (gr. 10 up). 1994. 17.95 (1-56416-153-6) Derrydale Pr.

Scrapie & Mad Cow Disease: The Smallest & Most Lethal Living Thing. G. D. Hunter. 1993. 14.95 (0-533-10230-8) Vantage.

Scrapie Disease in Sheep: Historical, Clinical, Epidemiological, Pathological & Practical Aspects of the Natural Disease. Herbert B. Parry. 1984. text ed. 99.00 (0-12-545750-2) Acad Pr.

Scraping up Pennsylvania's Past. Patrick M. Reynolds. (Pennsylvania Profiles Ser.: Vol. 8). (Illus.). 56p. (Orig.). 1984. pap. 3.95 (0-932514-10-3) Red Rose Studio.

ScrapLook: A Past & Present View of Designing & Piecing Multi-Fabric Quilts. Jinny Beyer. LC 85-16153. (Illus.). 131p. (Orig.). 1985. pap. 19.95 (0-914440-86-1) EPM Pubns.

Scrapper John: Rendezvous at Skull Mountain. Paul Bagdon. 128p. (Orig.). (J). 1992. pap. 3.50 (0-380-76418-0, Camelot) Avon.

Scrapper John: Showdown at Burnt Rock. Paul Bagdon. 128p. (Orig.). (J). (gr. 6). 1992. pap. 3.50 (0-380-76417-2, Camelot) Avon.

Scrapper John: Valley of the Spotted Horse. Paul Bagdon. (J). (gr. 4-7). 1992. pap. 3.50 (0-380-76416-4, Camelot) Avon.

Scrapple. Craig Czury. Ed. by Roy Zarucchi. (Chapbook Ser.). (Illus.). 24p. (Orig.). 1995. pap. 6.00 (1-879205-61-0) Nightshade Pr.

Scrappy: A Rodeo Bull. Jim Darden. (Illus.). iv, 169p. (Orig.). 1985. pap. 5.95 (0-9614570-0-7) Rodeo Studio.

Scrappy the Squabbler: A Beastie Book about Getting along with Others. Ron Berry et al. (Good Behavior Builders Ser.). (Illus.). 161p. (J). (ps-1). 1993. 5.95 (1-883761-04-2) Fmly Life Prods.

Scraps. Lori Baker. 96p. (Orig.). 1996. pap. 10.00 (0-945926-33-2) Paradigm RI.

***Scraps.** Lori Baker. 96p. (Orig.). 1996. pap. 25.00 (0-945926-34-0) Paradigm RI.

***Scraps.** Michel Leiris. Tr. by Lydia Davis from FRE. LC 96-41035. (Rules of the Game Ser.). 256p. 1997. pap. 15.95 (0-8018-5489-X); text ed. 35.00 (0-8018-5488-1) Johns Hopkins.

Scraps. Trevor Moore. 160p. 1994. pap. 8.95 (0-9643369-0-1) Poindexter Pr.

Scraps, Blocks & Quilts. Judy Martin. (Illus.). 192p. (Orig.). 1990. pap. 19.95 (0-929589-01-7) Crosley-Griffith.

Scraps of Life: The Chilean Arpilleras: Chilean Women & the Pinochet Dictatorship. Marjorie Agosin. Tr. by Cola Franzen from SPA. LC 87-61508. (Illus.). 190p. (C). 1987. 29.95 (0-932415-28-8); pap. 9.95 (0-932415-29-6) Red Sea Pr.

***Scraps of Paper.** Thomas E. Moser, Jr. (Orig.). 1996. pap. write for info. (1-57553-435-5) Watermrk Pr.

Scraps! The Ragtime Girl of Oz. V. Glasgow Koste. 54p. 1984. reprint ed. pap. 3.45 (0-87129-033-2, S88) Dramatic Pub.

Scratch & Bruise Sale. 1991. 9.95 (0-8306-5336-8) TAB Bks.

***Scratch & the Sniffs.** Chris Lynch. LC 96-47437. (He-Man Women Haters Club Ser.: Vol. 3). 128p. (J). (gr. 3-7). 1997. pap. 4.50 (0-06-440657-1, Trophy); lib. bdg. 13.89 (0-06-027416-6) HarpC Child Bks.

Scratch-Building R-C Airplanes. Richard Uravitch. (Illus.). 70p. (Orig.). 1991. pap. 12.95 (0-911295-18-6) Air Age.

Scratch Built! A Celebration of the Static Scale Airplane Modeller's Craft. John Alcorn et al. LC 93-83060. (Illus.). 144p. (Orig.). 1993. pap. 24.95 (0-88740-417-0) Schiffer.

Scratch Cooking. Benita M. Lyons. 154p. (Orig.). 1990. pap. 12.95 (0-9616911-6-6) M F Sohn Pubns.

Scratch Modelers Log. Henry Bridenbecker. Ed. by Ernest J. Gentle. (Moonraker Bks.). 112p. 1985. 17.95 (0-8168-0014-6, 20014, TAB-Aero) TAB Bks.

Scratches. Michel Leiris. Tr. by Lydia Davis. LC 96-23196. (Rules of the Game Ser.). 272p. 1997. pap. 15.95 (0-8018-5486-5); text ed. 35.00 (0-8018-5485-7) Johns Hopkins.

Scratches on Our Minds: American Images of China & India. Harold R. Isaacs. LC 73-9211. (Illus.). 416p. 1973. reprint ed. text ed. 65.00 (0-8371-6983-6, ISSM, Greenwood Pr) Greenwood.

Scratches on Our Minds: American Views of China & India. Harold R. Isaacs. LC 80-214. 452p. (gr. 13). 1980. reprint ed. pap. text ed. 24.95 (0-87332-161-8) M E Sharpe.

Scratchin' on the Eight Ball. Tom Frye. 240p. (YA). (gr. 6 up). 1993. reprint ed. pap. 9.95 (1-881663-16-7) Poudre Canyon Pr.

Scratchin' with Fay. Fay Brewer. 438p. 1994. 18.00 (1-885507-01-1) Fundco Printers.

Scratching Life's Itch: An Exhilarating Roller Coaster Ride. Lynn B. Welch. 320p. 1993. 15.95 (0-9639200-0-6) L B Welch.

Scratching the Beat Surface: Essays on New Vision from Blake to Kerouac. Michael McClure. 192p. 1994. pap. 10.95 (0-14-023252-4, Penguin Bks) Viking Penguin.

***Scratching the Woodchuck: Nature on an Amish Farm.** David Kline. LC 97-8221. 232p. 1997. 22.95 (0-8203-1938-4) U of Ga Pr.

Scrawl! Writing in Ancient Times. Geography Department, Runestone Press. LC 94-11980. (Buried Worlds Ser.). (YA). (gr. 6 up). 1994. lib. bdg. 22.95 (0-8225-3209-3, Lerner Publctns) Lerner Group.

Scrawny, the Classroom Duck. Susan Clymer. (Illus.). 96p. (J). (gr. 2-5). 1991. pap. 3.50 (0-590-43729-1) Scholastic Inc.

Scraypers: Heroes Unlimited. Kevin Siembieda & John Zeleznik. Ed. by James Osten & Alex Marciniszyn. (Rifts Dimension Bk.). (Illus.). (Orig.). 1997. pap. 15.95 (0-916211-78-9) Palladium Bks.

Scream Around the Campfire. J. R. Black. (Shadow Zone Ser.). 132p. (Orig.). (J). (gr. 3-7). 1995. pap. 3.99 (0-679-87080-6) Random Bks Yng Read.

Scream at the Sea. large type ed. Christopher Murphy. 432p. 1985. 25.99 (0-7089-1241-9) Ulverscroft.

***Scream Factory.** Michael O'Rourke. (Halloween Ser.: No. 1). 160p. 1997. mass mkt. 4.50 (1-57297-298-X) Blvd Books.

Scream for Jeeves: A Parody. P. H. Cannon. (Illus.). 86p. 1994. 20.00 (0-940884-61-5); pap. 7.50 (0-940884-60-7) Necronomicon.

Scream Machines. Herma Silverstein. 112p. (J). 1991. reprint ed. pap. 2.95 (0-380-71461-2, Camelot) Avon.

Scream of a Dove. large type ed. Robert Charles. (Linford Mystery Library). 368p. 1996. pap. 15.99 (0-7089-7864-9, Linford) Ulverscroft.

Scream of Eagles. William W. Johnstone. 1996. pap. 19.95 (0-8217-5253-7) NAL-Dutton.

***Scream of Eagles.** William W. Johnstone. 320p. 1997. mass mkt. 5.99 (0-7860-0447-9, Pinncle Kensgtn) Kensgtn Pub Corp.

Scream of Eagles. Robert K. Wilcox. Ed. by Paul McCarthy. 312p. 1992. reprint ed. pap. 6.50 (0-671-74566-2) PB.

Scream of Eagles: The Creation of the Top Gun & the U. S. Air Victory in Vietnam. Robert K. Wilcox. 295p. 1990. text ed. 22.95 (0-471-52641-X) Wiley.

Scream of the Cat. Lynn Beach. Ed. by Patricia MacDonald. (Phantom Valley Ser.). 128p. (Orig.). (YA). 1992. pap. 2.99 (0-671-74090-3, Minstrel Bks) PB.

Scream of the Eagle. Bert Byfield. (Russalka Trilogy Ser.: Vol. 2). 300p. Date not set. pap. 9.00 (1-887121-02-1) Caravela Bks.

***Scream of the Evil Genie.** R. L. Stine. (Give Yourself Goosebumps Ser.: No. 13). (J). 1997. mass mkt. 3.99 (0-590-84773-2) Scholastic Inc.

***Scream on the Water.** Margaret Press Staff. 1997. mass mkt. 5.99 (0-312-96299-1) St Martin.

***Scream on the Water: A Murder in Massachusetts Bay.** Margaret Press. 1997. mass mkt. 5.99 (0-614-27791-4) St Martin.

Scream Team. Diane Hoh. (Nightmare Hall Ser.: No. 5). 176p. (YA). (gr. 7-9). 1993. pap. 3.50 (0-590-47137-6) Scholastic Inc.

Scream, Team! Tom B. Stone. (Graveyard School Ser.: No. 12). (J). 1996. pap. 3.99 (0-553-48488-5) Bantam.

Scream When You Burn: A Pound of Seared Flesh from the Lap of Coffee Culture. Ed. by Rob Cohen. 240p. (Orig.). 1996. pap. 14.00 (1-888277-00-9) Incommcdo San Diego.

Screamers. Franklin W. Dixon. Ed. by Anne Greenberg. (Hardy Boys Casefiles Ser.: No. 72). 160p. (Orig.). (J). (gr. 6 up). 1993. pap. 3.75 (0-671-73108-4, Archway) PB.

Screaming Eagle. Scott Deschaine. (Illus.). 296p. (YA). 1997. pap. 14.95 (1-878181-04-1) Discovery Comics.

Screaming Eagles. Peg Kehret. (Frightmares Ser.: No. 7). (J). 1996. 14.00 (0-671-53525-0, PB Hardcover) PB.

Screaming Eagles. Peg Kehret. (Frightmares Ser.: No. 7). (J). (gr. 3-6). 1996. pap. 3.99 (0-671-53526-9, PB Trade Paper) PB.

Screaming Hawk: The Training of a Mystic Warrior, a Narrative. Patton L. Boyle. LC 93-48778. 1994. pap. 9.95 (0-88268-159-1) Station Hill Pr.

Screaming Hawk Returns to Flying Eagle: The Many Paths of a Mystic Warrior. Patton Boyle. LC 95-19718. 1995. pap. text ed. 9.95 (0-88268-192-3) Station Hill Pr.

Screaming Knife. Robert E. Vardeman. 224p. 1990. pap. 3.50 (0-380-75856-3) Avon.

Screaming Mean Machine. Joy Cowley. (J). (gr. 4-7). 1994. pap. 4.95 (0-590-48013-8) Scholastic Inc.

Screaming Mimi. Fredric Brown. 166p. 1989. pap. 3.50 (0-88184-449-7) Carroll & Graf.

***Screaming Poems: In the Night.** Demetrios Dolios. 56p. (Orig.). 1996. pap. 5.00 (1-885778-16-3) Seaburn.

Screaming Room: A Mother's Journal of Her Son's Struggle with AIDS. Barbara Peabody. 288p. 1987. mass mkt. 4.99 (0-380-70345-9) Avon.

Screaming S. (Clue Ser.: No. 10). (YA). 1995. pap. 3.50 (*0-590-48936-4*) Scholastic Inc.

Screaming Skull & Other Stories. Ed. by David G. Hartwell. 224p. (Orig.). (YA). (gr. 5 up). 1995. 4.99 (*0-8125-5178-8*) Tor Bks.

Screaming Skulls: 101 of the World's Greatest Ghost Stories. Daniel Cohen. LC 96-6280. (Camelot Bks.). (J). 1996. pap. 3.99 (*0-380-78349-5*) Avon.

Screaming to Be Heard: Hormonal Connections Women Suspect...& Doctors Ignore. Elizabeth L. Vliet. LC 94-49419. 512p. 1995. 24.95 (*0-87131-784-2*) M Evans.

Screaming Trees - Sweet Oblivion. (Play-It-Like-It-Is Guitar Ser.). 1994. pap. 19.95 (*0-89524-788-7*) Cherry Lane.

*__Screamplays.__ Chizmar & Greenberg. 1997. pap. 12.00 (*0-345-39429-1*, Del Rey) Ballantine.

*__Screamplays.__ Richard Chizmar & Martin Greenberg. 1997. pap. write for info. (*0-614-27456-7*, Del Rey) Ballantine.

Screams. Joyce Mansour. Tr. & Intro. by Serge Gavronsky. 100p. (Orig.). 1995. pap. 10.00 (*0-942996-25-9*) Post Apollo Pr.

Screams from the Balcony: Selected Letters 1960-1970. Charles Bukowski. LC 93-36411. 372p. 1995. reprint ed. 25.00 (*0-87685-915-5*); reprint ed. pap. 15.00 (*0-87685-914-7*) Black Sparrow.

Screams in the Night. Paul Hutchens. (Sugar Creek Gang Ser.: Vol. 10). (J). (gr. 3-7). 1967. mass mkt., pap. 3.99 (*0-8024-4812-7*) Moody.

*__Screams in the Night.__ Paul Hutchens. (Sugar Creek Gang Ser.: No. 12). (J). 1997. mass mkt. 4.99 (*0-8024-7016-5*) Moody.

Screams of Protest. Spurgeon E. Crayton. (Illus.). 1982. 10.00 (*0-8315-0188-X*) Speller.

*__Screams of Reason.__ David Skal. Date not set. write for info. (*0-393-04582-X*) Norton.

Scree Garden. Beverly F. Stoughton. Ed. by Shirley Warren. (Illus.). 28p. (Orig.). 1989. pap. 4.95 (*1-877801-04-6*) Still Waters.

*__Screech Bat: Creepy Creatures.__ Jan Pienkowski. (Creepy Creatures Ser.). (J). 1997. 5.95 (*0-8362-5156-3*) Andrews & McMeel.

Screech Owl at Midnight Hollow. C. Drew Lamm. (Smithsonian's Backyard Ser.). (Illus.). 32p. (J). (ps-3). 1996. 15.95 (*1-56899-264-5*); 19.95 incl. audio (*1-56899-268-8*) Soundprints.

Screech Owl at Midnight Hollow, Incl. stuffed animal toy. C. Drew Lamm. (Smithsonian's Backyard Ser.). (Illus.). 32p. (J). (ps-3). 1996. 32.95 (*1-56899-266-1*) Soundprints.

Screech Owl at Midnight Hollow, Mini edition. C. Drew Lamm. (Illus.). 32p. (J). 1996. 4.95 (*1-56899-265-3*) Soundprints.

Screech Owl at Midnight Hollow, Mini Edition, incl. stuffed animal toy. C. Drew Lamm. (Smithsonian's Backyard Ser.). (Illus.). 32p. (J). (ps-3). 1996. 12.95 (*1-56899-267-X*) Soundprints.

*__Screech Owls.__ Roy MacGregor. (Screech Owls Ser.). 1996. pap. text ed. 14.99 (*0-7710-5636-2*) McCland & Stewart.

*__Screech Owls' Northern Adventure.__ Roy MacGregor. (Illus.). 112p. (J). (gr. 6-9). Date not set. 4.99 (*0-7710-5628-1*) McCland & Stewart.

Screed. Jack Saunders. LC 80-53288. 250p. 1981. 12.95 (*0-912824-23-9*); pap. 5.95 (*0-912824-24-7*) Vagabond Pr.

Screen Acting. Mae Marsh. 1976. lib. bdg. 59.95 (*0-8490-2575-3*) Gordon Pr.

Screen Acting: How to Succeed in Motion Pictures. Brian Adams. (Illus.). 378p. 1987. pap. 17.95 (*0-943728-20-7*) Lone Eagle Pub.

Screen Adaptation: A Scriptwriting Handbook. Kenneth Portnoy. 196p. 1991. pap. 26.95 (*0-240-80095-8*, Focal) Buttrwrth-Heinemann.

Screen & Society: The Impact of Television upon Aspects of Contemporary Civilization. Ed. by Frank J. Coppa. LC 79-13500. 248p. 1980. 34.95 (*0-88229-413-X*) Nelson-Hall.

*__Screen Dreams.__ Whatling. Date not set. text ed. 59.95 (*0-7190-5066-9*); text ed. 19.95 (*0-7190-5067-7*) St Martin.

Screen Education Reader: Cinema, Television, Culture. Richard L. Collins et al. Ed. by Edward Buscombe & Richard Collins. LC 92-25729. (Communications & Culture Ser.). 320p. (C). 1993. pap. 18.50 (*0-231-08111-1*); text ed. 42.00 (*0-231-08110-3*) Col U Pr.

Screen Film Mammography: Imaging Considerations & Medical Physics Responsibilities. Ed. by Gary Barnes & G. Donald Frey. (Illus.). 242p. (C). 1991. reprint ed. pap. text ed. 43.95 (*0-944838-12-X*) Med Physics Pub.

Screen Gems: A History of Columbia Pictures Television from Cohn to Coke, 1948-1983. Jeb H. Perry. LC 91-33388. 385p. 1991. 42.50 (*0-8108-2487-6*) Scarecrow.

Screen Greats: Hollywood Nostalgia. M. Samuels. 1980. pap. 2.00 (*0-931064-30-9*) Starlog Pr.

Screen Image of Youth: Movies about Children & Adolescents. Ruth M. Goldstein & Edith Zornow. LC 80-14053. (Illus.). xxi, 363p. 1980. 30.00 (*0-8108-1316-5*) Scarecrow.

Screen Kisses: Quotes of Love, Sex & Romance from the Movies. Ian Hardy & Gretchen Zufall. LC 96-1918. 160p. 1997. pap. 10.00 (*0-399-52270-0*, Perigee Bks) Berkley Pub.

Screen Memories: Hollywood Cinema on the Psychoanalytic Couch. Harvey R. Greenberg. (Illus.). 304p. (C). 1993. 34.50 (*0-231-07286-4*) Col U Pr.

Screen Memories: Hollywood Cinema on the Psychoanalytic Couch. Harvey R. Greenberg. 1994. pap. 14.95 (*0-231-07287-2*) Col U Pr.

Screen Memories: The Hungarian Cinema of Marta Meszaros. Catherine Portuges. LC 92-2359. (International Women Filmmakers Ser.). 208p. 1993. 35.00 (*0-253-34558-8*); pap. 15.95 (*0-253-20782-7*) Ind U Pr.

Screen Monographs One. LC 75-124020. (Literature of Cinema, Ser. 1). 1970. reprint ed. 12.95 (*0-405-01626-3*) Ayer.

Screen Monographs Two. LC 75-124020. (Literature of Cinema, Ser. 1). 1970. reprint ed. 15.95 (*0-405-01627-1*) Ayer.

Screen of Frogs: An Old Tale. Illus. & Retold by Sheila Hamanaka. LC 92-24172. 32p. (J). (ps-2). 1993. 15.95 (*0-531-05464-0*) Orchard Bks Watts.

Screen Personalities of 1933. V. Trotta & C. Lewis. 1976. lib. bdg. 75.95 (*0-8490-2576-1*) Gordon Pr.

Screen Printer's Tip Book. Jeff Russ. (Illus.). 52p. 1996. pap. 14.95 (*0-944094-18-X*) ST Pubns.

Screen Printing. Samuel Hoff. LC 96-36589. (Graphic Communications Ser.). 1996. text ed. 35.95 (*0-8273-7128-4*) Delmar.

Screen Printing for Quilters. Hallie H. O'Kelley. 1995. pap. 17.95 (*1-881320-44-8*, Black Belt) Black Belt Comm.

Screen Printing Production Management. Richard C. Webb. LC 89-6142. 128p. (Orig.). 1989. pap. 14.95 (*0-911380-78-7*) ST Pubns.

Screen Printing Techniques. Albert Kosloff. (Illus.). 1981. pap. 21.95 (*0-911380-52-3*) ST Pubns.

Screen Printing Technology. Dennis. (Graphic Communications Ser.). 1990. pap. 28.95 (*0-8273-3772-8*); teacher ed., pap. 12.00 (*0-8273-3773-6*) Delmar.

Screen Process Printing. Robert A. Banzhaf. 1983. text ed. 15.32 (*0-02-672270-4*) Glencoe.

Screen Shakespeare: Academic Essays on Shakespearean Films. Ed. by Michael Skovmand. (Dolphin Ser.: No. 24). (Illus.). 148p. (C). 1994. pap. text ed. 19.95 (*87-7288-375-8*, Pub. by Aarhus Univ Pr DK) David Brown.

Screen Sleuths: A Filmography. Joseph J. Cocchiarelli. LC 91-28737. (Filmographies Ser.: Vol. 3). 249p. 1992. text ed. 42.00 (*0-8240-5427-X*, 1322) Garland.

Screen Smarts: Raising Media-Literate Kids. Gloria DeGaetano & Kathleen Bander. 256p. 1996. pap. 12.95 (*0-395-71550-4*) HM.

*__Screen Tastes: From Soap Opera to Satellite Dishes.__ Charlotte Brunsdon. LC 96-35327. 192p. 1997. pap. write for info. (*0-415-12155-8*) Routledge.

*__Screen Tastes: From Soap Opera to Satellite Dishes.__ Charlotte Brunsdon. LC 96-35327. 192p. (C). 1997. text ed. write for info. (*0-415-12154-X*) Routledge.

*__Screen Test.__ David Klass. LC 96-48174. (J). 1997. write for info. (*0-590-48592-X*) Scholastic Inc.

Screen Test. Elle Wolfe. 1990. pap. 106.20 (*0-8125-2846-8*) Tor Bks.

Screen Test Handbook. Shauna Crowley. 282p. (C). 1990. pap. 19.95 (*0-86819-227-9*) Aubrey Bks.

*__Screen Works: Practical & Inspirational Ideas for Making & Using Screens in the Home.__ Marion Elliot. (Illus.). 60p. 1997. 27.50 (*1-85967-373-2*, Lorenz Bks) Anness Pub.

Screen World, 10 vols. 1949, 1951-1959, Set. Daniel Blum. LC 70-84068. (Illus.). 1969. 200.00 (*0-8196-0255-8*) Biblo.

Screen World: Volumes 11-20, 1960 to 1969, The Complete Pictorial & Statistical Record of the Movies, 10 vols., Set. Incl. Vol. 11. Daniel Blum. LC 75-612827. (Illus.). 240p. 1960. 25.00 (*0-8196-0301-5*); Vol. 12. Daniel Blum. LC 75-612827. (Illus.). 240p. 1961. 25.00 (*0-8196-0302-3*); Vol. 13. Daniel Blum. LC 75-612827. (Illus.). 240p. 1962. 25.00 (*0-8196-0303-1*); Vol. 14. Daniel Blum. LC 75-612827. 240p. 1963. 25.00 (*0-8196-0304-X*); Vol. 15. Daniel Blum. LC 75-612827. 240p. 1964. 25.00 (*0-8196-0305-8*); Vol. 16. Daniel Blum. LC 75-612827. 240p. 1965. 25.00 (*0-8196-0306-6*); Vol. 17. John Willis. LC 75-612827. 256p. 1966. 25.00 (*0-8196-0307-4*); Vol. 18. John Willis. LC 75-612827. 256p. 1967. 25.00 (*0-8196-0308-2*); Vol. 19. John Willis. LC 75-612827. 256p. 1968. 25.00 (*0-8196-0309-0*); Vol. 20. John Willis. LC 75-612827. 256p. 1969. 25.00 (*0-8196-0310-4*); LC 75-612827. (Illus.). 256p. 1983. reprint ed. 200.00 (*0-517-52583-6*) Biblo.

Screen World 1991, Vol. 42. John Willis. (Illus.). 272p. 1991. 40.00 (*0-517-58645-2*, C P Pubs) Crown Pub Group.

Screen World 1992 Vol. 43: Film Annual, a Comprehensive Pictorial & Statistical Record of the 1991 Movie Season. Ed. by John Willis. (Illus.). 1992. 45.00 (*1-55783-135-1*) Applause Theatre Bk Pubs.

Screen World, 1993: Film Annual, a Comprehensive Pictorial & Statistical Record of the 1992 Movie Season, Vol. 44. John Willis. (Illus.). 272p. 1993. 45.00 (*1-55783-175-0*) Applause Theatre Bk Pubs.

Screen World 1994 Vol. 45: Film Annual, a Comprehensive Pictorial & Statistical Record of the 1993 Movie Season. Ed. by John Willis. (Screen World Ser.). (Illus.). (Orig.). cd-rom 49.95 (*1-55783-209-9*) Applause Theatre Bk Pubs.

Screen World 1994 Vol. 45: Film Annual, a Comprehensive Pictorial & Statistical Record of the 1993 Movie Season. Ed. by John Willis. (Illus.). 336p. (Orig.). 1995. 49.95 (*1-55783-201-3*) Applause Theatre Bk Pubs.

Screen World 1994 Vol. 45: Film Annual, a Comprehensive Pictorial & Statistical Record of the 1993 Movie Season. Ed. by John Willis. (Illus.). 336p. (Orig.). 1994. pap. 27.95 (*1-55783-202-1*) Applause Theatre Bk Pubs.

Screen World 1995 Vol. 46: Film Annual, a Comprehensive Pictorial & Statistical Record of the 1994 Movie Season. Ed. by John Willis. (Screen World Ser.). (Illus.). 352p. (Orig.). 1996. 49.95 (*1-55783-233-1*); pap. 27.95 (*1-55783-234-X*) Applause Theatre Bk Pubs.

Screen World 1996 Vol. 47: Film Annual, a Complete Pictorial & Statistical Record of the 1995 Movie Season. Ed. by John Willis & Barry Monush. (Screen World Ser.). (Illus.). 272p. 1996. pap. 27.95 (*1-55783-253-6*) Applause Theatre Bk Pubs.

Screen World 1996 Vol. 47: Film Annual, a Complete Pictorial & Statistical Record of the 1995 Movie Season, Vol. 47. Ed. by John Willis & Barry Monush. (Screen World Ser.). (Illus.). 272p. 1996. 49.95 (*1-55783-252-8*) Applause Theatre Bk Pubs.

*__Screen-Writing.__ Victor West. 110p. (Orig.). 1996. pap. write for info. (*1-57502-334-2*, PO1116) Morris Pubng.

Screen Writings: Scripts & Texts from Independent Filmmakers. Ed. by Scott MacDonald. LC 92-30429. 1994. 50.00 (*0-520-08024-6*); pap. 20.00 (*0-520-08025-4*) U CA Pr.

Screening America: Using Hollywood Films to Teach History. Marlette Rebhorn. (American University Studies: History: Ser. IX, Vol. 42). 211p. 1988. 34.50 (*0-8204-0726-7*) P Lang Pubng.

Screening American Reflections: Critical Contexts of Five Classic Films. Richard A. Blake. 1991. pap. 14.95 (*0-8091-3193-5*) Paulist Pr.

*__Screening & Assessment: Guidelines for Identifying Young Disabled & Developmentally Vulnerable Children & Their Families.__ Samuel J. Meisels et al. 68p. (Orig.). 1989. reprint ed. pap. 8.00 (*0-943657-15-6*, 07) Zero To Three.

Screening & Assessment for Alcohol & Other Drug Abuse among Adults in the Criminal Justice System. 1995. lib. bdg. 250.95 (*0-8490-6824-X*) Gordon Pr.

Screening & Assessment of Alcohol & Other Drug-Abusing Adolescents: A Treatment Improvement Protocol. (Illus.). 201p. (Orig.). (C). 1994. pap. text ed. 35.00 (*0-7881-1167-1*) DIANE Pub.

Screening & Diagnostic Procedures. 1983. 1.50 (*0-939418-50-9*) Ferguson-Florissant.

Screening & Management of Potentially Treatable Genetic Metabolic Disorders. Ed. by P. F. Benson. 176p. 1984. lib. bdg. 137.00 (*0-85200-784-1*) Kluwer Ac.

Screening & Surveillance in General Practice. Ed. by Cyril Hart & John Bain. (Illus.). 392p. 1992. text ed. 119.00 (*0-443-04160-1*) Churchill.

Screening Children for Auditory Function. Ed. by Fred H. Bess & James W. Hall, III. LC 92-70246. (Illus.). 560p. (C). 1992. text ed. 55.00 (*0-9631439-0-5*) B Wilkerson Ctr Pr.

*__Screening, Diagnosis, Management & Counseling, Clinical Practice Guideline for Sickle Cell Disease in Newborns & Infants.__ 1997. lib. bdg. 250.95 (*0-8490-8139-4*) Gordon Pr.

Screening Equipment Handbook. 2nd ed. Tom M. Pankratz. LC 94-62045. 300p. 1995. text ed. 89.95 (*1-56676-256-1*) Technomic.

Screening Equipment Handbook: For Industrial & Municipal Water & Wastewater Treatment. Tom M. Pankratz. LC 88-50738. 272p. 1988. 24.95 (*0-87762-630-8*) Technomic.

Screening Europe. Ed. by Duncan Petrie. (Working Papers: Vol. 1). (Illus.). 176p. 1992. pap. 16.95 (*0-85170-321-6*, Pub. by British Film Inst UK) Ind U Pr.

Screening for Biological Response Modifiers: Methods & Rationale. James E. Talmadge et al. (Developments in Oncology Ser.). 1985. lib. bdg. 71.50 (*0-89838-712-4*) Kluwer Ac.

Screening for Brain Impairment: A Manual for Mental Health Practice. Richard A. Berg et al. 264p. 1994. 33.95 (*0-8261-5741-6*) Springer Pub.

Screening for Cancer of the Uterine Cervix. Ed. by M. Hakama et al. (IARC Scientific Publications: No. 76). 300p. 1987. 55.00 (*92-832-1176-6*) OUP.

Screening for Colorectal Carcinoma: Proceedings of International Meeting Organized by the United Kingdom Coordinating Committee on Cancer Research. Ed. by J. D. Hardcastle. (Illus.). 110p. 1990. pap. 15.00 (*0-926592-03-3*) Normed Verlag.

Screening for Complications in Diabetes. Michael Edmonds. (Illus.). 192p. (Orig.). 1997. pap. text ed. 49.95 (*0-86542-982-0*) Blackwell Sci.

Screening for Down's Syndrome. Ed. by J. G. Grudzinskas et al. (Illus.). 286p. (C). 1995. text ed. 95.00 (*0-521-45271-6*) Cambridge U Pr.

Screening for Inborn Errors of Metabolism: Proceedings of the WHO Scientific Group, Geneva, 1967. WHO Staff. (Technical Report Ser.: No. 401). 57p. 1968. pap. text ed. 5.00 (*92-4-120401-X*, 1100401) World Health.

Screening for Infectious Diseases among Substance Abusers. 1995. lib. bdg. 251.95 (*0-8490-6825-8*) Gordon Pr.

Screening for Infectious Diseases among Substance Abusers: A Treatment Improvement Protocol. (Illus.). 160p. (Orig.). (C). 1994. pap. text ed. 35.00 (*0-7881-1162-0*) DIANE Pub.

Screening for Risk of Coronary Heart Disease: Proceedings of a Workshop on Strategies for Screening for Risk of Coronary Heart Disease, Held at the King Khalid Conference Centre, Royal College of Surgeons, Edinburgh, on 14-15 November 1985. Workshop on Strategies for Screening for Risk of Coronary Heart Disease Staff. Ed. by Michael Oliver et al. LC 86-18887. 144p. reprint ed. pap. 41.10 (*0-7837-3238-4*, 2043257) Bks Demand.

Screening Handbook. John Fry et al. 160p. 1990. pap. text ed. 49.00 (*0-7923-8926-3*) Kluwer Ac.

Screening History. Gore Vidal. (William E. Massey Sr. Lectures in the History of American Civilization). (Illus.). 97p. 1992. text ed. 14.95 (*0-674-79586-5*) HUP.

Screening History. Gore Vidal. 97p. (C). 1994. pap. text ed. 9.95 (*0-674-79587-3*) HUP.

Screening in Chronic Disease. 2nd ed. Alan S. Morrison. (Monographs in Epidemiology & Biostatistics: No. 19). (Illus.). 256p. 1992. 49.50 (*0-19-506390-2*) OUP.

Screening in Primary Health Care: Setting Priorities with Limited Resources. P. A. Braveman & E. Tarimo. viii, 196p. (CHI, ENG, FRE & SPA.). 1994. pap. text ed. 30.00 (*92-4-154473-2*, 1150424) World Health.

Screening Mammography: Breast Cancer Diagnosis in Asymptomatic Women. James Potchen et al. LC 92-49262. 556p. (C). (gr. 13). 1992. text ed. 142.00 (*0-8016-6488-8*) Mosby Yr Bk.

Screening Models for Releases of Radionuclides to Atmosphere, Surface Water & Ground, 2 vols., Set. LC 95-50691. (Reports Ser.: No. 123). 521p. 1996. pap. 75.00 (*0-929600-47-9*) NCRP Pubns.

Screening Models for Releases of Radionuclides to Atmosphere, Surface Water & Ground, Vol. 1. LC 95-50691. (Reports Ser.: No. 123). 316p. 1996. pap. 75.00 (*0-929600-48-7*) NCRP Pubns.

Screening Models for Releases of Radionuclides to Atmosphere, Surface Water & Ground - Work Sheets, Vol. 2. LC 95-50691. (Reports Ser.: No. 123). 205p. 1996. wbk. ed., pap. 75.00 (*0-929600-49-5*) NCRP Pubns.

Screening of Australia: Anatomy of a Film Industry, 2 vols., Vol. 1. Susan Dermody & Elizabeth Jacka. 256p. (C). 1987. pap. 24.95 (*0-86819-152-3*) Aubrey Bks.

Screening of Australia: Anatomy of a National Cinema, 2 vols., Vol. 2. Susan Dermody & Elizabeth Jacka. 290p. (C). 1988. pap. 24.95 (*0-86819-187-6*) Aubrey Bks.

Screening out the Past: The Birth of Mass Culture & the Motion Picture Industry. Larry May. LC 83-4927. (Illus.). 320p. (C). 1983. reprint ed. pap. text ed. 14.95 (*0-226-51173-1*) U Ch Pr.

Screening Shakespeare from Richard II to Henry V. Ace G. Pilkington. LC 90-50310. 216p. 1991. 39.50 (*0-87413-412-9*) U Delaware Pr.

Screening Space: The American Science Fiction Film. Vivian Sobchack. 352p. 1986. pap. text ed. 18.95 (*0-8044-6886-9*) F Ungar Bks.

*__Screening Space: The American Science Fiction Film.__ 2nd ed. Vivian C. Sobchack. LC 97-16074. 1997. pap. write for info. (*0-8135-2492-X*) Rutgers U Pr.

Screening Techniques for Determining Compliance with Environmental Standards. LC 86-5283. (Commentary Ser.: No. 3). 1986. 50.00 (*0-913392-82-0*) NCRP Pubns.

Screening the Blues: Aspects of the Blues Tradition. Paul Oliver. (Quality Paperbacks Ser.). (Illus.). 302p. 1989. reprint ed. pap. 13.95 (*0-306-80344-5*) Da Capo.

Screening the Body: Tracing Medicine's Visual Culture. Lisa Cartwright. LC 94-30340. 1995. text ed. 49.95 (*0-8166-2289-2*); pap. text ed. 17.95 (*0-8166-2290-6*) U of Minn Pr.

Screening the Holocaust: Cinema's Images of the Unimaginable. Ilan Avisar. LC 87-45400. (Jewish Literature & Culture Ser.). (Illus.). 240p. 1988. reprint ed. pap. 68.40 (*0-7837-9644-7*, 2059277) Bks Demand.

*__Screening the Los Angeles 'Riots' Race, Seeing, & Resitance.__ Darnell M. Hunt. (Cambridge Cultural Social Studies). 328p. (C). 1996. text ed. 59.95 (*0-521-57087-5*); pap. text ed. 19.95 (*0-521-57814-0*) Cambridge U Pr.

Screening the Male: Exploring Masculinities in the Hollywood Cinema. Ed. by Steven Cohan & Ina M. Hark. LC 92-5815. 224p. (gr. 13). 1993. pap. 16.95 (*0-415-07759-1*, A7262, Routledge NY) Routledge.

Screening the Male: Exploring Masculinities in the Hollywood Cinema. Ed. by Steven Cohan & Ina M. Hark. LC 92-5815. 224p. (C). (gr. 13). 1993. text ed. 59.95 (*0-415-07758-3*, Routledge NY) Routledge.

Screening the Sacred: Myth, Ritual, & Religion in Popular American Film. Joel W. Martin. (C). 1995. pap. text ed. 19.95 (*0-8133-8830-9*) Westview.

Screening the Sexes: Homosexuality in the Movies. Andrew X. Sarris. (Illus.). 419p. 1993. reprint ed. pap. 15.95 (*0-306-80543-X*) Da Capo.

Screening the Text: Intertextuality in New Wave French Cinema. T. Jefferson Kline. (Illus.). 320p. 1992. text ed. 40.00 (*0-8018-4267-0*) Johns Hopkins.

Screening Tool Kit: Keeping Bad Apples Out of Your Organization. John Patterson. LC 94-68617. 1994. pap. 15.00 (*0-9637120-1-2*) Nonprof Risk Mgmt Ctr.

Screenmaking for Screen Printers. Ed. by Mark Goodridge. 52p. 1996. pap. 14.95 (*0-944094-19-8*, 4520) ST Pubns.

Screenplay: A Blend of Film Form & Content. Margaret Mehring. (Illus.). 296p. 1989. pap. 34.95 (*0-240-80007-9*, Focal) Buttrwrth-Heinemann.

Screenplay: The Foundations of Screenwriting. enl. ed. Ed. by Syd Field. 272p. 1984. pap. 12.95 (*0-440-57647-4*, Dell Trade Pbks) Dell.

*__Screenplay Companion: A Workbook for Screenwriters.__ 2nd rev. ed. W. L. Davis, Jr. (Illus.). 110p. (C). 1996. pap. 18.95 (*0-9639177-1-4*) Write-Side Prods.

Screenplays of the African American Experience. Ed. by Phyllis R. Klotman. LC 90-43511. 280p. 1991. 39.95 (*0-253-33145-5*); pap. 15.95 (*0-253-20633-2*, MB-633) Ind U Pr.

Screenplay's the Thing: Movie Criticism, 1986-1990. Bruce Bawer. LC 92-7219. 298p. (C). 1992. lib. bdg. 32.50 (*0-208-02332-1*, Archon Bks) Shoe String.

Screenprinting: Design & Technique. Nicholas Bristow. (Illus.). 160p. 1991. pap. 24.95 (*0-7134-6631-6*, Pub. by Batsford UK) Trafalgar.

Screenprinting: Water-Based Techniques. Roni Henning. (Illus.). 144p. 1994. 29.95 (*0-8230-5644-9*, Watson-Guptill Bks) Watsn-Guptill.

Screens. Jean Genet. Tr. by Bernard Frechtman from FRE. LC 62-13055. 210p. 1987. pap. 7.95 (*0-8021-5158-2*, Grove) Grove-Atltic.

S

Screens of Power: Ideology, Domination, & Resistance in Informational Society. Timothy W. Luke. LC 88-37528. 280p. 1989. text ed. 34.95 (*0-252-01629-7*); pap. text ed. 14.95 (*0-252-06154-3*) U of Ill Pr.

Screenwriter As Collaborator. Kent R. Brown. Ed. by Garth S. Jowett. LC 79-6669. (Dissertations on Film, 1980 Ser.). 1980. lib. bdg. 20.95 (*0-405-12903-3*) Ayer.

Screenwriter Looks at the Screenwriter. rev. ed. William Froug. LC 91-21894. 362p. 1991. pap. 16.95 (*1-879505-01-0*) Silman James Pr.

Screenwriter's Bible: A Complete Guide to Writing, Formatting, & Selling Your Script. David Trottier. 195p. (Orig.). 1995. pap. 18.95 (*1-879505-26-6*) Silman James Pr.

Screenwriter's Bible: A Complete Guide to Writing, Formatting & Selling Your Spec Script. David Trottier. LC 94-67006. 184p. (Orig.). 1994. pap. 17.95 (*1-885655-03-7*) Clearstream.

Screenwriter's Bible: A Complete Guide to Writing, Formatting, & Selling Your Spec Script. rev. ed. David Trottier. 200p. 1995. pap. 18.95 (*1-885655-04-5*) Clearstream.

Screenwriter's Handbook: What to Write, How to Write It, Where to Sell It. Constance Nash & Virginia Oakey. LC 77-76031. 160p. 1978. pap. 10.00 (*0-06-463454-X*, EH 454) HarpC.

Screenwriters on Screenwriting: The Best in the Business Discuss Their Craft. Joel Engel. 320p. 1995. pap. 12.95 (*0-7868-8057-0*) Hyperion.

Screenwriter's Software Guide. Cahlin. 1997. pap. write for info. (*0-240-80213-6*, Focal) Buttrwrth-Heinemann.

Screenwriter's Workbook. Syd Field. 224p. (Orig.). 1988. pap. 12.95 (*0-440-58225-3*, Dell Trade Pbks) Dell.

Screenwriting: The Art, Craft & Business of Film & Television Writing. Richard Walter. LC 88-1813. 224p. 1988. pap. 12.95 (*0-452-26347-6*, Plume) NAL-Dutton.

Screenwriting for Television & Film. Ronald D. Dyas. 368p. (C). 1993. per. write for info. (*0-697-13761-9*) Brown & Benchmark.

Screenwriting Tricks of the Trade. William Froug. LC 92-26613. 150p. (Orig.). 1992. pap. 10.95 (*1-879505-13-4*) Silman James Pr.

***Screw.** Patricia Armentrout. LC 97-15152. (Simple Machines Ser.). (J). 1997. write for info. (*1-57103-179-0*) Rourke Pr.

Screw. Michael McLaughlin et al. LC 89-61207. 300p. 1989. 22.95 (*0-88282-048-6*) New Horizon NJ.

Screw Conveyors. (CEMA Standards Ser.: No. 350). (Illus.). 150p. 1988. 25.00 (*0-318-13805-0*) Conveyor Equip Mfrs.

Screw Driver. Patricia Armentrout & David Armentrout. LC 94-46471. (Learning about Tools Ser.). (J). (gr. 2-6). 1995. write for info. (*1-55916-119-1*) Rourke Bk Co.

***Screw Helicoid Pitch Diameter Formulas for the Measurement of the Exact Over-Wire Dimension.** J. H. Gehrung. (Technical Papers). 1976. pap. text ed. 30.00 (*1-55589-309-0*) AGMA.

Screw the Bitch! Divorce Tactics for Men. Victor Santoro. LC 91-61587. 192p. (C). 1991. pap. text ed. 17.95 (*1-55950-069-7*, 19174) Loompanics.

***Screw the Golden Years: I'd Rather Live in the Past.** V. Keith Thorne. Ed. by Aliza Caillou & Kate Thorne. (Illus.). 64p. (Orig.). 1996. pap. 6.95 (*0-9628329-4-4*) Thorne Enterprises.

Screw the Roses, Send Me the Thorns: The Romance & Sexual Sorcery of Sadomasochism. Philip Miller & Molly Devon. LC 95-79674. (Illus.). 277p. (Orig.). 1995. pap. 24.95 (*0-9645960-0-8*) Mystic Rose.

Screw Thread Gaging Systems for Determining Conformance to Thread Standards. (CRTD Ser.: Vol. 37). 72p. 1996. 48.00 (*0-7918-1228-6*, I00391) ASME.

Screw Threads & Gaskets for Fire Hose Connections. National Fire Protection Association Staff. 1993. 20.25 (*0-317-63568-9*, 1963-85) Natl Fire Prot.

Screw Unto Others: Revenge Tactics for All Occasions. George Hayduke. 252p. 1987. text ed. 19.95 (*0-87364-405-0*) Paladin Pr.

Screwball Comedy: A Genre of Madcap Romance. Wes D. Gehring. LC 85-12703. (Contributions to the Study of Popular Culture Ser.: No. 13). (Illus.). 228p. 1986. text ed. 49.95 (*0-313-24650-5*, GSE/, Greenwood Pr) Greenwood.

Screwball Comedy Films: A History & Filmography, 1934-1942. Duane Byrge & Robert M. Miller. LC 90-52654. (Illus.). 156p. 1991. lib. bdg. 32.50 (*0-89950-539-2*) McFarland & Co.

Screwball Express. Turner Publishing Company Staff. LC 92-85015. 168p. 1992. 48.00 (*1-56311-095-4*) Turner Pub KY.

Screwcutting in the Lathe. Martin Cleeve. (Workshop Practice Ser.: No. 3). (Illus.). 176p. (Orig.). 1984. pap. 18.50 (*0-85242-838-3*, Pub. by Nexus Special Interests UK) Trans-Atl Phila.

Screwdriver Expert's Guide to Peaking Out & Repairing CB Radios. Lou Franklin. (Illus.). 105p. (Orig.). 1997. pap. 22.00 (*0-943132-39-8*) CBC Intl.

Screwing the System & Making It Work: Juvenile Justice in the No-Fault Society. Mark D. Jacobs. LC 90-30126. (Illus.). 304p. 1990. 39.00 (*0-226-38980-4*) U Ch Pr.

Screwing the System & Making It Work: Juvenile Justice in the No-Fault Society. Mark D. Jacobs. (Illus.). viii, 304p. 1993. pap. text ed. 14.95 (*0-226-38981-2*) U Ch Pr.

Screws. David Glover. LC 96-15800. (Simple Machines Ser.). (J). 1997. lib. bdg. write for info. (*1-57572-085-X*) Rigby Interact Libr.

***Screwtape.** James Forsyth & C. S. Lewis. 123p. 1961. pap. 5.00 (*0-87129-754-X*, S18) Dramatic Pub.

Screwtape: Letters on Alcohol. Ira W. Hutchison. LC 92-18606. 120p. (Orig.). 1992. pap. 8.95 (*1-55612-565-8*, LL1565) Sheed & Ward MO.

Screwtape Letters. C. S. Lewis. 20.95 (*0-89190-989-3*) Amereon Ltd.

***Screwtape Letters.** C. S. Lewis. 112p. 1995. mass mkt. 4.50 (*0-553-21443-8*, Bantam Classics) Bantam.

Screwtape Letters. C. S. Lewis. 156p. 1985. 8.97 (*0-916441-33-4*, Christian Lib) Barbour & Co.

***Screwtape Letters.** C. S. Lewis. 160p. 1990. pap. 3.97 (*1-55748-142-3*) Barbour & Co.

Screwtape Letters. C. S. Lewis. 160p. 1992. mass mkt. 1.99 (*1-55748-315-9*) Barbour & Co.

Screwtape Letters. C. S. Lewis. LC 76-17707. (Illus.). 144p. 1978. student ed., mass mkt. 4.99 (*0-8007-8336-0*, Spire) Revell.

Screwtape Letters. C. S. Lewis. 160p. 1988. pap. 2.95 (*0-451-62610-9*, Ment) NAL-Dutton.

***Screwtape Letters.** C. S. Lewis. 1996. mass mkt. 4.95 (*0-684-83117-1*, Touchstone Bks) S&S Trade.

***Screwtape Letters.** C. S. Lewis. 96p. 1994. pap. 9.99 (*0-8407-6261-5*) Nelson.

Screwtape Letters. C. S. Lewis. (Value Bks.). 128p. 1996. mass mkt. 0.99 (*1-55748-811-8*) Barbour & Co.

Screwtape Letters. C. S. Lewis. 1988. pap. 5.99 (*0-451-62821-7*, Ment) NAL-Dutton.

Scriabin. Alfred J. Swan. LC 75-76423. (Music Ser.). 1969. reprint ed. lib. bdg. 22.50 (*0-306-71322-5*) Da Capo.

Scriabin. Alfred J. Swan. LC 76-109859. 119p. 1970. reprint ed. text ed. 38.50 (*0-8371-4350-0*, SWSC, Greenwood Pr) Greenwood.

Scriabin. Alfred J. Swan. 119p. 1990. reprint ed. lib. bdg. 59.00 (*0-7812-9090-2*) Rprt Serv.

Scriabin: Artist & Mystic. Boris Schloezer. Tr. by Nicolas Slonimsky from RUS. 336p. 1987. 45.00 (*0-520-04384-7*) U CA Pr.

Scriabin, a Biography. 2nd rev. ed. Faubion Bowers. (Illus.). 656p. 1996. pap. text ed. 14.95 (*0-486-28897-8*) Dover.

Scribal Publication in Seventeenth-Century England. Harold Love. (Illus.). 392p. 1993. 69.00 (*0-19-811219-X*) OUP.

Scribble Art: Independent Creative Art Experiences for Children. 2nd ed. MaryAnn F. Kohl. LC 94-94502. (Bright Ideas for Learning Ser.). (Illus.). 160p. (Orig.). (J). (ps-7). 1994. pap. 14.95 (*0-935607-05-6*) Bright Ring.

Scribble Art: Kindergarten & Preschool. Gretchen D. Albert. (Illus.). 85p. (J). (ps-3). 1980. pap. text ed. 5.80 (*0-686-28105-5*) GDA Pubns.

Scribble Death. Franz Kamin. LC 85-17230. 160p. (Orig.). 1986. pap. 6.95 (*0-930794-94-X*) Station Hill Pr.

Scribble-Foolers. Bernard Hamber. LC 79-92052. 175p. (Orig.). 1980. pap. 6.95 (*0-9604896-8-1*) BH Ent.

Scribble Scrabble: Ready-in-a-Minute Math Games. Vicki F. Sharp et al. LC 94-48315. 1995. pap. text ed. 12.95 (*0-07-057110-4*) McGraw-Hill Prof.

Scribble, Scribble, Scribble... Don Hendrie, Jr. LC 76-27963. 63p. 1976. pap. 7.00 (*0-89924-007-0*) Lynx Hse.

Scribbles & Bits. Dianne K. Zulkoski. Ed. by Linda J. Dageforde. LC 95-83822. (Illus.). 76p. (Orig.). 1996. pap. 9.95 (*1-886225-10-9*) Dageforde Pub.

Scribbling & More. Shirley Campbell. 200p. 1996. pap. 10.95 (*0-941092-32-1*) Mtn St Pr.

Scribbling in the Dark. Barry Oakley. LC 85-14090. 160p. 1993. reprint ed. pap. text ed. 14.95 (*0-7022-2524-X*, Pub. by Univ Queensland Pr AT) Intl Spec Bk.

***Scribbling Women.** Showalt. pap. 7.95 (*0-460-87770-4*, Everyman's Classic Lib) C E Tuttle.

***Scribbling Women: Short Stories by 19th Century American Women.** Ed. & Intro. by Elaine Showalter. LC 96-38915. 500p. (C). 1997. pap. 17.95 (*0-8135-2393-1*); text ed. 50.00 (*0-8135-2392-3*) Rutgers U Pr.

Scribe, Griot, & Novelist: Narrative Interpreters of the Songhay Empire. Thomas A. Hale. 288p. 1990. lib. bdg. 49.95 (*0-8130-0981-2*) U Press Fla.

Scribe Who Lived in a Tree. Michael Muchnik. (Illus.). 48p. (J). 1984. reprint ed. 7.00 (*0-8266-0351-3*, Merkos LInyonei Chinuch) Kehot Pubn Soc.

Scribes & Illuminators. Christopher De Hamel. (Medieval Craftsmen Ser.). (Illus.). 72p. 1992. pap. 19.95 (*0-8020-7707-2*) U of Toronto Pr.

Scribes & Scholars: A Guide to the Transmission of Greek & Latin Literature. 3rd ed. Leighton D. Reynolds & N. G. Wilson. (Illus.). 352p. 1991. pap. 39.95 (*0-19-872146-3*) OUP.

Scribes & Scholars at Salisbury Cathedral c. 1075- c. 1125. Teresa Webber. (Oxford Historical Monographs). 340p. 1992. 65.00 (*0-19-820308-X*) OUP.

Scribes & Schools in Monarchic Judah: A Socio-Archaeological Approach. David Jamieson-Drake. (Journal for the Study of the Old Testament Supplement Ser.: Vol. 109). 240p. 48.50 (*1-85075-275-3*, Pub. by Sheffield Acad UK) CUP Services.

Scribes & Scripture: New Testament Essays in Honor of J. Harold Greenlee. Ed. by David A. Black. LC 92-2921. xvi, 128p. 1992. text ed. 32.50 (*0-931464-70-6*) Eisenbrauns.

Scribes & Translators: Septuagint & Old Latin in the Books. Natalio F. Marcos. LC 94-9717. (Supplements to Vetus Testamentum Ser.). 1994. 68.00 (*90-04-10043-1*) E J Brill.

***Scribe's Family: A Golden Age Saga Spanning Five Millenia.** Don Jacobson. (Illus.). 336p. (Orig.). 1997. pap. 12.00 (*0-9657196-0-X*) Hypatia Pr CA.

***Scribe's Family: A Golden Age Saga Spanning Five Millenium.** Don Jacobson. (Illus.). 336p. 1997. 22.00 (*0-9657196-1-8*) Hypatia Pr CA.

Scribes, Script & Books: The Book Arts from Antiquity to the Rennaissance. Leila Avrin. LC 89-18024. (Illus.). 350p. 1991. 80.00 (*0-8389-0522-6*) ALA.

Scribes, Scripts & Readers. M. B. Parkes. 304p. 1991. boxed 65.00 (*1-85285-050-7*) Hambledon Press.

Scribes, Warriors & Kings: The City of Copan & the Ancient Maya. William L. Fash. LC 91-65316. (Illus.). 192p. 1993. pap. 19.95 (*0-500-27708-7*) Thames Hudson.

***Scribing the Center: Organization & Redaction in Deuteronomy 14:1-17:13.** William Morrow. 284p. 1995. pap. 33.95 (*0-7885-0065-1*, 060049) Scholars Pr GA.

Scribing the Center: Organization & Redaction in Deuteronomy 14:1-17:13. William S. Morrow. (Society of Biblical Literature Ser.: No. 49). 284p. 1995. 49.95 (*0-7885-0064-3*, 06 00 49) Scholars Pr GA.

Scribleriad - Being an Epistle to the Dunces, on Renewing Their Attack upon Mr. Pope: And The Difference Between Verbal & Practical Virtue. Scriblerus & Lord Hervey. LC 92-22020. (Augustan Reprints Ser.: No. 125 (1967)). reprint ed. 14.50 (*0-404-70125-6*, PR3634) AMS Pr.

Scribner-Bantam English Dictionary. Ed. by Edwin B. Williams. 1120p. 1984. mass mkt. 5.50 (*0-553-26496-6*) Bantam.

***Scribner ESL Workbook for Writers.** Moore. (C). 1900. pap. text ed. 8.25 (*0-02-382763-7*) Scribnrs Ref.

Scribner Handbook for Writers. Nickerson. 1995. pap. text ed. 24.00 (*0-02-387482-1*, Macmillan Coll) P-H.

***Scribner Handbook for Writers.** 2nd ed. Diyanni & Hoy. 1997. text ed. 28.00 (*0-205-19838-4*) P-H.

Scribner Handbook for Writers: Instructor's Annotated Editorial. Robert Diyanni & Pat C. Hoy, II. (Illus.). 848p. (C). 1994. teacher ed. write for info. (*0-318-72457-X*) Macmillan.

Scribner Handbook for Writers: Instructor's Annotated Editorial. Robert Diyanni & Pat C. Hoy, II. (Illus.). 848p. (C). 1995. text ed. 29.00 (*0-02-329864-2*, Macmillan Coll) P-H.

Scribner Writers Series: DOS or Macintosh Network Version. 1995. 715.00 (*0-684-19778-2*) S&S Trade.

Scribner Writers Series: DOS or Macintosh Single-User Version. 1995. 595.00 (*0-684-19776-6*) S&S Trade.

Scribner's American Biography 1981-1985. Jackson. 1998. lib. bdg. 95.00 (*0-684-80492-1*) Scribnrs Ref.

Scribner's American Biography 1986-1990. large type ed. Jackson. 1998. lib. bdg. 95.00 (*0-684-80491-3*) Scribnrs Ref.

***Scribner's Best of the Fiction Workshops 1997.** Ed. by John Kulka & Danford. LC 96-47122. 1997. pap. 13.00 (*0-684-83314-X*, Scribners PB Fict) S&S Trade.

Scribonius Largus - Concordantia in Scribonium Largum. Scribonius Largus. Ed. by Sergio Sconocchia. (Alpha-Omega, Reihe A Ser.: Bd. XCII). xi, 390p. (GER.). 1988. write for info. (*3-487-09116-X*) G Olms Pubs.

Scrieri Defecte. Florentin Smarandache. Ed. by Xiquan Publishing House Staff. 200p. (Orig.). (RUM.). (C). 1992. pap. 18.99 (*1-879585-09-X*) Erhus Univ Pr.

Scrimmage of Appetite. Jon Davis. LC 95-24381. 102p. (Orig.). (C). 1995. 24.95 (*1-884836-11-9*); pap. 12.95 (*1-884836-12-7*) U Akron Pr.

Scrimshaw: A Traditional Folk Art, a Contemporary Craft. Leslie Linsley. (Illus.). 1979. pap. 14.95 (*0-8015-6609-6*, Dutton) NAL-Dutton.

Scrimshaw & Ivory-Working Techniques. Harvey Shell. Ed. by Roxanna Chamberlin. (Illus.). (Orig.). 1986. pap. 2.50 (*0-914347-03-9*) Ahio Pub Co.

Scrimshaw of Manuel Cunha: Late Work from Madeira Revealed. Joshua T. Basseches. Ed. by Stuart M. Frank. (Museum Monograph Ser.). (Illus.). 19p. 1988. pap. text ed. 5.00 (*0-937854-26-3*) Kendall Whaling.

Scrimshaw, the Whaler's Legacy. Martha Lawrence. LC 93-85225. (Illus.). 240p. 1993. 69.95 (*0-88740-455-3*) Schiffer.

Scrip. Trade Tokens Issued by United States Coal Mining Companies & Company Store. Compiled by Stuart E. Brown, Jr. (Illus.). 1978. ring bd. 22.50 (*0-686-50094-6*) VA Bk.

Scripophily: The Art of Finance. 2nd rev. ed. Keith Hollender. (Illus.). 160p. 1994. 29.95 (*0-9642630-0-9*) Mus Am Finan.

***Scripps.** Jack Casserly. 236p. 4.98 (*0-8317-5544-X*) Smithmark.

Scrips & Scraps: Scrapbook Abstracts Venango County & Surrounding Counties. Nancy B. Romig. 318p. 1995. pap. 24.95 (*1-55856-191-9*) Closson Pr.

Script Alphabet. Arthur Baker & Don Barron. LC 78-56103. (Illus.). 1978. pap. 8.95 (*0-910158-47-9*) Art Dir.

Script Analysis for Actors, Directors & Designers. James Thomas. 208p. 1992. pap. 32.95 (*0-240-80129-6*, Focal) Buttrwrth-Heinemann.

Script & Cursive Alphabets: One Hundred Fonts. Dan X. Solo. 104p. (Orig.). 1987. pap. 5.95 (*0-486-25306-6*) Dover.

Script Book: Telephone - Letter Scripts for Direct Sales - Network Marketing Professionals. Dennis Windsor. 50p. 1991. pap. 7.95 (*0-9626791-2-7*) Windward TX.

Script Ease: A Step-by-Step Guide from Manuscript to Calligraphy. Christine Parkhurst & Marian Fellows. (Illus.). 64p. (gr. 1-12). 1982. 6.95 (*0-9607366-5-4*) Kino Pubns.

Script Ease: Manuscript of Calligraphy. Marian Fellows & Christine Parkhurst. (Illus.). 61p. (J). (gr. 2-6). 1982. pap. text ed. 9.95 (*0-317-62675-2*) Kino Pubns.

Script Ease: Simple Step by Step Guide from Ms to Calligraphy. Kino Learning Center Staff. 1982. pap. 9.99 (*0-685-34598-X*) Trillium Pr.

Script Formatting with Microsoft Word on the Apple Macintosh: The Complete Idiot's Guide to Make TV & Film Scripting Automatic! Larry Hussar. (Illus.). 95p. (Orig.). (C). 1989. pap. 10.95 (*0-685-25983-8*) Canard Pr.

Script from a Flask Found on the Beach at St. Pete: Collected Poems 1971-1991. James A. Green. LC 94-96184. (Illus.). 114p. 1994. 24.40 (*1-890121-33-9*) Grnwd Resch.

Script Girls: Women Writers in Hollywood. Lizzie Francke. 192p. 1994. 45.00 (*0-85170-477-8*, Pub. by British Film Inst UK); pap. 18.95 (*0-85170-478-6*, Pub. by British Film Inst UK) Ind U Pr.

Script, Grammar, & the Hungarian Writing System. John Lotz. LC 74-167265. (Hungarian-English Contrastive Linguistics Project, Working Papers: No. 2). 61p. reprint ed. pap. 25.00 (*0-8357-3344-0*, 2039574) Bks Demand.

Script into Performance: A Structuralist Approach. Richard Hornby. 228p. (Orig.). (C). 1995. pap. 16.95 (*1-55783-237-4*) Applause Theatre Bk Pubs.

***Script Is Finished, Now What Do I Do? The Scriptwriter's Resource Book & Agent Guide.** K. Callan. 300p. 1997. pap. 17.95 (*1-878355-08-2*) Sweden Pr.

Script, Kid & Fantasyland: The Truth That Makes You Free. Barbara M. Muhl. 1995. 18.95 (*0-615-00767-8*) Christus Pub.

Script, Kid, & Fantasyland: The Truth That Makes You Free. Barbara M. Muhl. 350p. 1995. pap. 18.95 (*1-880863-26-X*) Christus Pub.
This book is a culmination of the immensely successful workshop classes of the same name, taught by the author since 1986. The acceptance & practice of the Principles & Steps of the SCRIPT, KID & FANTASYLAND work have drastically improved the quality of life & relationships for hundreds of people. This work is designed to "break the chains" which keep us in "bondage" to the painful (& unproductive) reactions & emotions we experience as human beings & which actually "block" love & spiritual unfoldment. By "clearing away the wreckage of the past once & for all," we free ourselves to experience an "unhindered spiritual growth" &, as a result, a harmonious & loving human experience. The truth that makes you feel "REAL," is the truth that makes you "FREE." To order, write, phone, or FAX: Christus Publishing, P.O. Box 802649, Santa Carita, CA 91380-2649. U.S.A. Order line: 805-296-7836, FAX: 805-296-2182. ***Publisher Provided Annotation.***

Script Lettering for Artists. rev. ed. Tommy Thompson. (Illus.). 1955. pap. 3.95 (*0-486-21311-0*) Dover.

Script Models: A Handbook for the Media Writer. Robert Lee & Robert Misiorowski. 1978. pap. 10.00 (*0-8038-6754-9*) Hastings.

Script-O-Quotes - Word Grams Derived from Holy Scriptures. Betty J. Hudson. 25p. 1993. pap. 2.00 (*1-882581-04-0*) Campbell Rd Pr.

Script of Cologne, from Hildebald to Hermann. L. W. Jones. (Mediaeval Academy of America Publications: Vol. 10). 1932. 155.00 (*0-527-01684-5*) Periodicals Srv.

Script of Decadence: Essays on the Fictions of Flaubert & the Poetics of Romanticism. Eugenio Donato. 224p. 1993. 45.00 (*0-19-505724-4*) OUP.

Script of Harappa & Mohenjodaro & Its Connection with Other Scripts. G. R. Hunter. 242p. 1993. 43.50 (*81-215-0600-X*, Pub. by M Manoharial II) Coronet Bks.

Script of Life in Modern Society: Entry into Adulthood in a Changing World. Marlis Buchmann. LC 88-23928. (Illus.). 264p. 1989. 33.00 (*0-226-07835-3*) U Ch Pr.

Script Planning: Positioning & Developing Scripts for TV & Film. Tony Zaza. 248p. 1992. pap. 29.95 (*0-240-80121-0*, Focal) Buttrwrth-Heinemann.

Script Supervising & Film Continuity. 2nd ed. Pat P. Miller. (Illus.). 288p. 1990. pap. 37.95 (*0-240-80018-4*, Focal) Buttrwrth-Heinemann.

Script Tease: The Treasury of Surprise Endings. Ed. by Robert L. Loeffelbein. (Illus.). 192p. (Orig.). 1979. pap. 4.95 (*0-9601258-2-5*) Golden Owl Pub.

***Script to Screen: From Z Cars to the Charmer.** Allan Prior. (Distributed for the British Film Institute Ser.). (Illus.). 256p. 1996. pap. 17.50 (*0-9527512-0-8*, Pub. by British Film Inst UK) Ind U Pr.

Scripta - Ichenologica: Lichenological Papers Dedicated to Antonin Vezda. Ed. by E. E. Farkas et al. (Bibliotheca Lichenologica Ser.: Vol. 58). (Illus.). 501p. (ENG & GER.). 1995. pap. 140.00 (*3-443-58037-8*, Pub. by Cramer-Borntraeger GW) Lubrecht & Cramer.

Scripta Diversa. George O. Sayles. 360p. (C). 1983. text ed. 60.00 (*0-907628-12-5*) Hambledon Press.

Scripta Latina. Ed. by Adriano la Regina. (Illus.). 682p. 1993. 125.00 (*88-7097-023-X*) J P Getty Trust.

Scripta Minora, Vol. VII. Xenophon. (Loeb Classical Library: No. 183). 564p. 1925. 18.95 (*0-674-99202-4*) HUP.

***Scripta Minora Vol. 2: Ad Linquam Graecam Pertinentia.** Ed. by A. Rijksbaron & F. M. Waanders. xxiv, 852p. (FRE, GER & SPA.). 1997. lib. bdg. 183.00 (*90-5063-366-8*, Pub. by Gieben NE) Benjamins North Am.

Scripta Minora, (a Festschrift for C.J. Ruijgh) Ad Linguam Graecam Pertinentia. Ed. by F. M. Waanders et al. xiii, 871p. (FRE, GRE & LAT.). 1991. 167.00 (*90-5063-065-0*, Pub. by Gieben NE) Benjamins North Am.

Scripta Numaria Romana. Colin M. Kraay. 1979. 40.00 (*0-686-63876-X*) S J Durst.

Scripta Signa Vocis: Studies about Scripts, Scriptures Scribes & Languages in the Near East, Presented to H. Hospers. Ed. by F. Leemhuis et al. (Illus.). 336p. (Orig.). 1986. pap. 46.00 (*90-6980-008-X*, Pub. by Egbert Forsten NE) Benjamins North Am.

Scripted Drama. A. England. 260p. 1981. 54.95 (0-521-23235-X) Cambridge U Pr.

***Scripted Self: Textual Identities in Contemporary Spanish Narrative.** Ruth Christie et al. (Re-Reading Hispanic Literature Ser.). 208p. (Orig.). 1995. pap. 19.95 (0-85668-664-6, Pub. by Aris & Phillips UK) David Brown.

Scripting: Social Communication for Adolescents. 2nd ed. Patty Mayo & Pattii Waldo. 292p. (YA). (gr. 5-12). 1994. pap. 35.00 (0-930599-08-X) Thinking Pubns.

Scripting for the New AV Technologies. 2nd ed. Dwight V. Swain & Joye R. Swain. 336p. 1991. pap. 42.95 (0-240-80071-0, Focal) Buttrwrth-Heinemann.

***Scripting Languages: Automating the Web.** O'Reilly Publishing Staff. 1997. 29.95 (1-56592-265-4) OReilly & Assocs.

***Scripting with SALSA for the Desktop Vol. 1: Scripting Guide.** Patrick King. Ed. by Kieran O'Mahony. (Illus.). 100p. (Orig.). 1996. pap. 19.95 (1-889548-02-2) Wall Data WA.

***Scripting with SALSA for the Desktop Vol. 2: Language Reference.** Ellen Zehr. Ed. by Patrick King & Kieran O'Mahony. 400p. (Orig.). 1996. pap. 24.95 (1-889548-01-4) Wall Data WA.

***Scriptores Ecclesia Stici de Musica Sacra Potissimum.** Martin Gerbert. 1166p. (GER.). 1990. reprint ed. write for info. (3-487-00359-7) G Olms Pubs.

Scriptores Historiae Augustae, 3 vols. Ed. by E. H. Warmington. Tr. by David Magie. No. 139-140, 263. (ENG & LAT.). write for info. (0-318-53183-6) HUP.

Scriptores Historiae Augustae, 3 vols., 1. Ed. by E. H. Warmington. Tr. by David Magie. (Loeb Classical Library: No. 139-140, 263). (ENG & LAT.). 15.50 (0-674-99154-0) HUP.

Scriptores Historiae Augustae, 3 vols., 2. Ed. by E. H. Warmington. Tr. by David Magie. (Loeb Classical Library: No. 139-140, 263). (ENG & LAT.). 15.50 (0-674-99155-9) HUP.

Scriptores Historiae Augustae, 3 vols., 3. Ed. by E. H. Warmington. Tr. by David Magie. (Loeb Classical Library: No. 139-140, 263). (ENG & LAT.). 15.50 (0-674-99290-3) HUP.

Scriptores Originum Constantino-Politanarum. Ed. by Theodorus Preger. LC 75-7335. (Roman History Ser.). (GRE.). 1975. reprint ed. 35.95 (0-405-07054-3) Ayer.

Scriptores Rerum Mythicarum, Latini Tres Romae Nuper Reperti, 2 vols. in 1. Ed. by Georg H. Bode. xlvi, 472p. 1967. reprint ed. 120.00 (0-318-71225-3) G Olms Pubs.

Scriptorum Arabum Loci de Abbadidis, 3 vols. in 1. Reinhard P. Dozy. xxxvi, 970p. (GER.). 1992. reprint ed. write for info. (3-487-09566-1) G Olms Pubs.

Scriptorum de Musica Medii Aevi Novam Seriem a Gerbertina Alteram Collegit Nuncque Primum Edidit, 4 vols., Set. Charles E. Coussemaker. 1988. reprint ed. 560.00 (3-487-05126-5) G Olms Pubs.

Scriptorum Historiae Augustae Lexicon. Carl Lessing. iii, 747p. 1964. reprint ed. write for info. (0-318-71160-5); reprint ed. write for info. (0-318-72038-8) G Olms Pubs.

Scripts: Writing for Radio & Television. Arthur A. Berger. (Illus.). 160p. (C). 1990. 45.00 (0-8039-3761-X); pap. 19.95 (0-8039-3762-8) Sage.

Scripts & Literacy: Reading & Learning to Read Alphabets, Syllabaries & Characters. Ed. by Insup Taylor. LC 94-20325. (Neuropsychology & Cognition Ser.). 384p. (C). 1995. lib. bdg. 145.00 (0-7923-2912-0) Kluwer Ac.

Scripts & Scenarios: The Performed Comic Text in Renaissance Italy. Richard Andrews. LC 92-23446. 288p. (C). 1993. text ed. 74.95 (0-521-35357-2) Cambridge U Pr.

***Scripts of the World.** 2nd ed. (Illus.). 91p. (YA). reprint ed. 19.95 (0-9656274-1-1) Another Lang Pr.

Scripts People Live: Transactional Analysis of Life Scripts. Claude Steiner. LC 90-47229. 288p. 1990. pap. 12.95 (0-8021-3210-3, Grove) Grove-Atltic.

Scripts, Plans, Goals, & Understanding: An Inquiry into Human Knowledge Structures. Roger C. Schank. 256p. (C). 1977. pap. 29.95 (0-89859-138-4) L Erlbaum Assocs.

***Scripts to Accompany Earth Science.** 8th ed. Gould et al. 88p. 1994. ring bd. 10.95 (0-88725-214-1) Hunter Textbks.

Scriptural & Seasonal Indexes of the United Methodist Hymnal. Robert D. Ingram. (Orig.). 1992. pap. 13.95 (0-687-37066-3) Abingdon.

Scriptural & Statistical Views in Favor of Slavery. Thorton Stringfellow. LC 72-6593. (Black Heritage Library Collection). 1977. reprint ed. 21.95 (0-8369-9177-X) Ayer.

***Scriptural & Topical Indices LBW.** T. Bartsch et al. 6.75 (0-89536-727-0) CSS OH.

Scriptural Choreography: Biblical Dance Forms in Shaping Contemporary Worship. Linda K. Seaton. 1979. pap. 3.00 (0-941500-15-2) Sharing Co.

Scriptural Eating Patterns see Diet Alternative

Scriptural Examination of the Institution of Slavery in the United States: With Its Objects & Purposes. Howell Cobb. LC 72-6455. (Black Heritage Library Collection). 1977. reprint ed. 18.95 (0-8369-9163-X) Ayer.

Scriptural Freedom from Sin. Henry E. Brockett. 1980. pap. 6.99 (0-88019-107-4) Schmul Pub Co.

Scriptural Guide to a Fulfilling Marriage. Gary K. Hardley. LC 86-7175. 173p. 1987. pap. 8.95 (0-932990-01-0) IDEALS PA.

Scriptural Holiness & Keswick Teaching Compared. A. M. Hills. pap. 6.99 (0-88019-108-2) Schmul Pub Co.

Scriptural Images of Stress in the Ministry. James R. Ryan. pap. 24.95 (1-56699-091-2, OD81) Alban Inst.

Scriptural Index to the Hymnal 1982. Marion J. Hatchett. (Hymnal Studies: 8). 308p. 1988. pap. 19.95 (0-89869-146-X) Church Pub Inc.

Scriptural Interpretation in the Fathers. Ed. by Thomas Finan & Vincent Twomey. 370p. 1995. 49.50 (1-85182-162-7, Pub. by Four Cts Pr IE) Intl Spec Bk.

Scriptural Light on Speaking in Tongues. Wesley Bouterse. 1980. pap. 2.95 (0-86544-010-7) Salv Army Suppl South.

Scriptural Meditations for the Rosary. Peter H. Huyck. (Greeting Book Line Ser.). (Illus.). 32p. 1982. pap. 1.95 (0-89622-157-1) Twenty-Third.

Scriptural Outline of the Baptism of the Holy Spirit. George Gillies & Harriet Gillies. 32p. 1972. mass mkt. 1.99 (0-88368-062-9) Whitaker Hse.

Scriptural Principles of Gathering. A. P. Gibbs. 1935. pap. 3.00 (0-937396-37-0) Walterick Pubs.

Scriptural Proofs for Creative Evolution & the Role of Gayness in the Divine Economy of Salvation. Thomas J. Kuna-Jacob. 10p. ring bd. 2.00 (1-878030-09-4) Assn World Peace.

Scriptural Refutation of the Pope's Primacy. Apostolos Makrakis. Tr. by Denver Cummings. 171p. (Orig.). 1952. reprint ed. pap. 4.95 (0-938366-40-8) Orthodox Chr.

Scriptural Rosary (English) Christianica Staff. LC 64-66463. (Illus.). 1961. 8.95 (0-911346-01-5) Christianica.

Scriptural Teachings of the Prophet Joseph Smith. Joseph Smith, Jr. LC 92-41964. xvii, 539p. 1993. 19.95 (0-87579-647-8) Deseret Bk.

Scriptural Way To Meet And To Serve For The Building Up Of The Body Of Christ. Witness Lee. 285p. per. 10.75 (0-87083-379-0, 12018001) Living Stream Ministry.

Scripture. John R. Stott. (Christian Basics Bible Studies). 64p. (Orig.). 1994. wbk. ed., pap. 4.99 (0-8308-2001-9, 2001) InterVarsity.

***Scripture Alive: Role-Plays for Youth.** Robert P. Stamschror. (Illus.). 120p. (Orig.). 1997. pap. 19.95 (0-88489-491-6) St Marys.

Scripture & Christology: A Statement of the Pontifical Biblical Commission with A Commentary. Joseph A. Fitzmyer. 128p. 1986. pap. 8.95 (0-8091-2789-X) Paulist Pr.

Scripture & Community in Comparative Religion: Collected Essays on the Jains. Kendall W. Folkert. Ed. by John E. Cort. (Studies in World Religions). 450p. 1993. pap. 89.95 (1-55540-858-3, 030006) Scholars Pr GA.

Scripture & Discernment: Decisionmaking in the Church. Luke T. Johnson. 168p. 1996. pap. text ed. 19.95 (0-687-01238-4) Abingdon.

***Scripture & Ethics: Twentieth-Century Portraits.** Jeffrey Siker. LC 96-8899. 304p. 1996. 45.00 (0-19-510104-9); pap. 16.95 (0-19-511099-4) OUP.

Scripture & Homosexuality: Biblical Authority & the Church Today. Marion L. Soards. LC 95-2524. 84p. (Orig.). 1995. pap. 10.00 (0-664-25595-7) Westminster John Knox.

Scripture & Memory: The Ecumenical Hermeneutic of the Three-Year Lectionaries. Frederick West. LC 96-51883. 232p. (Orig.). 1997. pap. 24.95 (0-8146-6157-2, M Glazier) Liturgical Pr.

Scripture & Other Artifacts: Essays on Archaeology & the Bible in Honor of Philip J. King. Ed. by Michael D. Coogan et al. LC 94-9998. 480p. 1994. 25.00 (0-664-22036-3) Westminster John Knox.

Scripture & Science: A Physician's Reflections on Judaic Doctrine. Harold Speert. LC 95-18835. 1995. 10.00 (1-57059-256-X) R G Landes.

Scripture & Strategy: The Use of the Bible in Postmodern Church & Mission. David J. Hesselgrave. LC 94-36869. (EMS Ser.: No. 1). (Illus.). 208p. (Orig.). 1994. pap. 11.95 (0-87808-375-8, WCL375-8) William Carey Lib.

Scripture & Tradition. Archimandrite Chrysostomos & Hieromonk Auxentios. 96p. 1984. pap. 5.00 (0-911165-04-5) Ctr Trad Orthodox.

Scripture & Translation. Martin Buber & Franz Rosenzweig. Tr. by Lawrence Rosenwald & Everett Fox. LC 93-32629. (Indiana Studies in Biblical Literature). 292p. 1994. 26.50 (0-253-31272-8) Ind U Pr.

Scripture & Truth. Ed. by D. A. Carson & John D. Woodbridge. LC 92-15722. 448p. (C). 1992. reprint ed. pap. 24.99 (0-8010-2570-2) Baker Bks.

Scripture at Weddings: Choosing & Proclaiming the Word of God. Graziano Marcheschi & Nancy S. Marcheschi. 128p. (Orig.). 1992. pap. 4.00 (0-929650-62-X, READ/W) Liturgy Tr Pubns.

Scripture-Based Ideas for Reaching Out to Others. Pat King. LC 92-82794. 128p. (Orig.). 1993. pap. text ed. 4.95 (0-89243-451-1) Liguori Pubns.

Scripture Bulletin Boards. Tom Orange. (Bulletin Board Ser.). 96p. (J). (gr. 2-7). 1987. 10.95 (0-86653-397-4, SS1826, Shining Star Pubns) Good Apple.

Scripture by Picture: Make Memorizing the Bible Fun & Easy. Diantha S. Cavin. (Illus.). 78p. (Orig.). (J). (ps-6). 1992. pap. 10.95 (0-9628012-3-2) Dexter KS.

Scripture, Cannon & Commentary: A Comparison of Confucian & Western Exegesis. John B. Henderson. 256p. 1991. text ed. 45.00 (0-691-06832-1) Princeton U Pr.

Scripture Catechism. Hiram Bingham. (Works of Hiram Bingham). 1989. reprint ed. lib. bdg. 79.00 (0-685-27263-X) Rprt Serv.

Scripture Club of Valley Rest: or Sketches of Everybody's Neighbours. John Habberton. LC 75-165172. (American Fiction Reprint Ser.). 1977. reprint ed. 23.95 (0-8369-7038-1) Ayer.

Scripture Concepts for Children Activity-Story Book: Building Godly Character, Vol. 2. Joyce L. Burkhart & Deborah B. Mercer. (Illus.). 43p. (J). (ps-2). 1994. pap. 8.00 (0-9633166-1-3) Penta Ent.

Scripture Concepts for Children Activity-Story Book, Vol. 1: Building Godly Self-Esteem. Joyce L. Burkhart & Deborah B. Mercer. (Illus.). 43p. (Orig.). (J). (ps-2). 1991. pap. 8.00 (0-9633166-0-5) Penta Ent.

***Scripture Cryptograms.** Wanda S. Brookshire. Ed. by Cecillee Ramirez & Jean Starr. (Illus.). iv, 47p. (Orig.). 1997. pap. write for info. (0-9656802-0-7) Brooks Pub OK.

Scripture from Scratch: A Basic Bible Study Program - Facilitator's Manual. Virginia Smith & Elizabeth McNamer. 52p. 1991. pap. text ed. 3.95 (0-86716-145-0) St Anthony Mess Pr.

Scripture from Scratch: A Basic Bible Study Program - Participant's Manual. Elizabeth McNamer & Virginia Smith. 130p. 1991. spiral bd. 11.95 (0-86716-146-9) St Anthony Mess Pr.

***Scripture from Scratch No. II: The World of the Bible.** Elizabeth McNamer & Virginia Smith. 96p. (Orig.). 1997. student ed., pap. 8.95 (0-86716-276-7, B2767) St Anthony Mess Pr.

Scripture in Context: Essays on the Comparative Method. Ed. by Carl D. Evans et al. LC 80-10211. (Pittsburgh Theological Monographs: No. 34). 1980. pap. 15.00 (0-915138-43-3) Pickwick.

Scripture in Context II: More Essays on the Comparative Method. Ed. by William W. Hallo et al. LC 82-13868. xv, 250p. (C). 1983. text ed. 29.50 (0-931464-14-5) Eisenbrauns.

Scripture in History & Theology: Essays in Honor of J. Coert Rylaarsdam. Ed. by Arthur L. Merrill & Thomas W. Overholt. LC 77-12106. (Pittsburgh Theological Monographs: No. 17). 1977. pap. 10.00 (0-915138-32-8) Pickwick.

Scripture in the Streets: Reflections on Holy Week, Contemporary Spirituality. Anthony T. Padovano. LC 92-20687. 88p. 1992. pap. 5.95 (0-8091-3335-0) Paulist Pr.

Scripture in the Thought of Soren Kierkegaard. Joseph Rosas, III. LC 93-15865. 1994. 24.99 (0-8054-1624-2, 4216-24) Broadman.

***Scripture Index for Christian Theology.** 32p. 1969. 1.00 (0-8341-1034-2) Nazarene.

Scripture Index to John Milton's "De doctrina christiana" Ed. by Michael Bauman. (Medieval & Renaissance Texts & Studies: Vol. 67). 192p. 1989. 18.00 (0-86698-076-8, MR67) MRTS.

Scripture Index to the Works of St. Augustine in English Translation. James W. Wiles. LC 94-46780. 244p. (C). 1995. pap. text ed. 34.50 (0-8191-9848-X); lib. bdg. 53.00 (0-8191-9847-1) U Pr of Amer.

***Scripture Kit: Scripture Study at Its Best.** 11th ed. Bruce Barton. (Illus.). 200p. 1996. 29.95 (0-9645314-0-2) B Barton.

Scripture Lessons for the Deaf & Dumb. Harvey P. Peet. 1972. 59.95 (0-8490-1007-1) Gordon Pr.

Scripture Notes: Series B (Common Consensus Lectionary) Norman A. Beck. 1984. 10.50 (0-89536-687-8, 4863) CSS OH.

Scripture Notes: Series C (Common Consensus Lectionary) Norman A. Beck. 1985. 10.50 (0-89536-755-6, 5861) CSS OH.

Scripture of Leaves. William Stafford. LC 89-38154. 64p. (Orig.). 1989. pap. 8.95 (0-87178-531-5, 8315) Brethren.

Scripture of the Blind. Yannis Ritsos. Tr. by Kimon Friar & Kostas Myrsiades from GRE. LC 78-14319. 277p. 1979. 47.50 (0-8142-0298-5) Ohio St U Pr.

Scripture of the Golden Eternity. Jack Kerouac. LC 94-2796. (Pocket Poets Ser.: Vol. 51). 62p. (Orig.). 1995. reprint ed. pap. 6.95 (0-87286-291-7) City Lights.

Scripture of Venus. Robert Bensen. (Illus.). 60p. (C). 1988. 35.00 (0-934714-03-7); pap. 4.00 (0-934714-04-5) Swamp Pr.

Scripture on the Ten Kings & the Making of Purgatory in Medieval Chinese Buddhism. Stephen F. Teiser. LC 94-2531. (Studies in East Asian Buddhism: No. 9). (Illus.). 376p. (C). 1994. text ed. 46.00 (0-8248-1587-4) UH Pr.

Scripture One: An Introduction to the Scriptures. Angeline Bukowiecki & Brigid Meierotto. (Evangelizer's Handbook, Evangelistic Series Sisters of the New Covenant). 112p. (Orig.). (C). 1984. pap. text ed. 11.00 (0-924333-08-1) Sisters New Covenant.

Scripture Pathways to Inner Healing. Victor M. Parachin. LC 94-75227. 144p. (Orig.). 1994. pap. 6.95 (0-89243-591-7) Liguori Pubns.

Scripture Plays: Ten Plays from the Holy Bible. Dan Neidermyer. Ed. by Arthur L. Zapel. LC 88-37687. (Illus.). 192p. (Orig.). 1989. pap. text ed. 9.95 (0-916260-57-7, B150) Meriwether Pub.

Scripture Principle. Clark Pinnock. 250p. 1992. reprint ed. pap. 14.99 (1-57383-000-3) Regent College.

Scripture Readings: Advent to Pentecost. Rev. by Carmelites of Indianapolis Staff. 420p. 1989. pap. 19.95 (1-886873-00-3) Carmelites IN.

Scripture Readings: Ordinary Time Weeks 10-34. Rev. by Carmelites of Indianapolis Staff. 356p. 1990. pap. 19.95 (1-886873-01-1) Carmelites IN.

Scripture Readings in Orthodox Worship. Georges A. Barrois. 197p. 1977. pap. 10.95 (0-913836-41-9) St Vladimirs.

Scripture Reflections Day by Day. Joseph Donders. LC 91-65954. 384p. (Orig.). 1992. pap. 9.95 (0-89622-494-5) Twenty-Third.

***Scripture Scenes for Advent.** Janet S. Carr. 44p. 1995. pap. 7.95 (1-877871-91-5, 6465) Ed Ministries.

Scripture Sculpture: A Do-It-Yourself Manual for Biblical Preaching. Ramesh Richard. LC 94-34615. 224p. (C). 1995. pap. 10.99 (0-8010-7774-5) Baker Bks.

Scripture Sharing on Bishops' Economic Pastoral. James E. Hug. (Illus.). 48p. 1985. pap. text ed. 2.95 (0-934134-19-7) Sheed & Ward MO.

Scripture Sketches. Beth Sharpton & Tim Miller. 1986. 6.99 (0-685-68724-4, MP-614) Lillenas.

Scripture Stories for Tiny Tots: Read-Aloud Stories from the Bible for Children 1 to 6. Louise A. Randall. LC 83-83429. 38p. (Orig.). (J). (gr. k-3). 1983. pap. 5.98 (0-88290-209-1) Horizon Utah.

***Scripture, Teens, & Values.** Kate Deehr. 80p. 1997. teacher ed., pap. text ed. 12.95 (0-937997-41-2) Hi-Time Pub.

Scripture, the Soul of Theology. Joseph A. Fitzmyer. LC 94-15539. 144p. 1994. pap. 10.95 (0-8091-3509-4) Paulist Pr.

Scripture, Tradition & Infallibility. Dewey M. Beegle. LC 79-84557. Orig. Title: The Inspiration of Scripture. 332p. reprint ed. pap. text ed. 8.95 (0-933462-04-2) Pryor Pettengill.

Scripture, Tradition & Reason: A Study in the Criteria of Christian Doctrine. Ed. by Benjamin Drewery & Richard J. Bauckham. 308p. (C). 1997. 49.95 (0-567-09482-0, Pub. by T & T Clark UK) Bks Intl VA.

***Scripture, Tradition & Reason: A Study in the Criteria of Christian Doctrine.** Ed. by Benjamin Drewery & Richard Bauckham. 308p. 1997. pap. 24.95 (0-567-08557-0, Pub. by T & T Clark UK) Bks Intl VA.

Scripture Twisting: Twenty Ways the Cults Misread the Bible. James W. Sire. LC 80-19309. 180p. (Orig.). 1980. pap. 11.99 (0-87784-611-1, 611) InterVarsity.

Scripture Two: The Formation & Exile of God's People. Angeline Bukowiecki & Brigid Meierotto. (Evangelizer's Handbook, Evangelistic Series Sisters of the New Covenant). 153p. (Orig.). (C). 1987. pap. text ed. 25.00 (0-924333-16-2) Sisters New Covenant.

Scripture Way of Salvation: Sermons by John Wesley. John Wesley. Ed. & Intro. by Robert E. Coleman. (Collection of Classics Ser.). 73p. 1994. pap. text ed. 1.95 (1-879089-17-3) B Graham Ctr.

***Scripture Way of Salvation: The Heart of John Wesley's Theology.** Kenneth J. Collins. LC 97-16419. 256p. 1997. pap. 18.95 (0-687-00962-6) Abingdon.

Scripture Within Scripture: The Interrelationship of Form & Function in the Explicit Old Testament Citations in the Gospel of John. Bruce G. Schuchard. LC 92-32117. (Society of Biblical Literature Dissertation Ser.). 192p. 1992. 39.95 (1-55540-711-0, 062133); pap. 24.95 (1-55540-712-9) Scholars Pr GA.

Scriptures: How Shall I Read Them? 1970. pap. 2.25 (0-8100-0025-3, 12-0338) Northwest Pub.

Scriptures & Knowledge. Shlomo Biderman. (Numen Bookseries: No. 69). 250p. 1995. 90.50 (90-04-10154-3) E J Brill.

Scriptures & the Scrolls: Studies in Honour of A. S. Van Der Woude on the Occasion of His 65th Birthday. F. Garcia Martinez et al. LC 92-33127. (Supplements to Vetus Testamentum Ser.: Vol. 49). 1992. 109.50 (90-04-09746-5) E J Brill.

Scriptures are Fulfilled: The Phoenix Has Come! Kristina Gale-Kumar. (Illus.). 276p. (Orig.). 1992. pap. 12.95 (0-9611204-7-9) Cardinal Enter.

Scriptures Come Alive. Grace Bradford. 48p. (Orig.). 1995. pap. 5.95 (0-687-00560-4) Abingdon.

Scriptures for a Generation: What We Were Reading in the 60's. Philip D. Beidler. LC 94-4172. (C). 1995. pap. 12.95 (0-8203-1787-X) U of Ga Pr.

Scriptures for the Modern World. Ed. by Cheesman & Griggs. (Monograph Ser.: Vol. 11). 1984. 7.95 (0-88494-538-3) Bookcraft Inc.

Scriptures Jesus Knew: A Guide to the Old Testament. Charles Hill. 1994. pap. 12.95 (0-85574-365-4, Pub. by E J Dwyer AT) Morehouse Pub.

Scriptures of an African People: The Sacred Utterances of the Anlo. Christian Gaba. LC 73-85557. 189p. 1973. text ed. 14.95 (0-88357-018-1) NOK Pubs.

***Scriptures of Faith: Cornerstone of Catholicism.** Albert J. Nevins. 112p. 1996. pap. 4.95 (0-87973-480-9) Our Sunday Visitor.

Scriptures of the Church: Selections from the Encyclopedia of Mormonism. Ed. by Daniel H. Ludlow. LC 94-24006. 768p. (Orig.). 1995. pap. 18.95 (0-87579-923-X) Deseret Bk.

Scriptures of the Oral Torah: An Anthology of the Sacred Books of Judaism. Jacob Neusner. 256p. 1996. 43.95 (0-06-066106-2) Bks Intl VA.

Scriptures of the Oral Torah: Sanctification & Salvation in the Sacred Books of Judaism. Tr. by Jacob Neusner. (Brown Judaic Studies). 410p. 1990. 74.95 (1-55540-499-5, 14 02 07) Scholars Pr GA.

Scriptures of the World: 1996. L. Lupas & E. Rhodes. (Illus.). 145p. 1997. pap. text ed. 3.25 (0-8267-0304-6, 106063) Untd Bible Soc.

Scriptures Prayers for Intercessors. Peggy Yuna. 120p. 1989. reprint ed. pap. 14.95 (0-9619618-0-5) Peg Yuna.

Scriptures to Success. L. Lionel Kendrick. ix, 99p. 1993. pap. 6.95 (0-87579-825-X) Deseret Bk.

Scriptures (5 Sermons) Charles H. Spurgeon. 1978. pap. 4.00 (1-56186-409-9) Pilgrim Pubns.

Scriptwork: A Director's Approach to New Play Development. David Kahn & Donna Breed. LC 94-5425. 160p. (C). 1995. 29.95 (0-8093-1985-3) S Ill U Pr.

Scriptwork: A Director's Approach to New Play Development. David Kahn & Donna Breed. LC 94-5425. (C). 1995. pap. 14.95 (0-8093-1759-1) S Ill U Pr.

Scriptwriter's Handbook: Corporate & Educational Media Writing. rev. ed. William J. Van Nostran. LC 96-5084. Orig. Title: The Nonbroadcast Television Writer's Handbook. 403p. 1996. pap. 34.95 (0-240-80252-7, Focal) Buttrwrth-Heinemann.

Scriptwriter's Handbook: New Techniques for Media Writers. William J. Van Nostran. 402p. (C). 1989. student ed., pap. 29.95 (0-86729-292-X, Focal) Buttrwrth-Heinemann.

Scriptwriter's Journal. Mary C. Johnson. 208p. 1994. pap. 15.95 (0-240-80198-9, Focal) Buttrwrth-Heinemann.

S

S

Scriptwriters Market: How & Where to Sell What You Write for Film & TV. 8th rev. ed. Leslie Gates & Buffum David. 345p. 1988. pap. 28.95 (*0-910665-04-4*) Script Writers.

Scriptwriter's Workbook: A Media Writer's Companion. William J. Van Nostran. (Illus.). 192p. 1996. pap. 24.95 (*0-240-80273-X*, Focal) Buttrwrth-Heinemann.

Scriptwriting for Effective Telemarketing. Judy McKee. Ed. by Telemarketing Magazine Editorial Staff. 100p. (Orig.). pap. write for info. (*0-936840-12-9*) Tech Marketing.

Scriptwriting for High-Impact Videos: Imaginative Approaches to Delivering Factual Information. John Morley. 272p. (C). 1992. pap. 36.95 (*0-534-15066-7*) Wadsworth Pub.

ScriptX Architecture Guide. Kaleida Labs, Inc. Staff. 1994. pap. write for info. (*0-201-40729-9*) Addison-Wesley.

ScriptX Core Classes Reference. Kaleida Labs, Inc. Staff. 1994. pap. write for info. (*0-201-40730-2*) Addison-Wesley.

ScriptX Design Guidelines. Kaleida Labs, Inc. Staff. 1994. pap. write for info. (*0-201-40733-7*) Addison-Wesley.

ScriptX Excellent Examples. Kaleida Labs, Inc. Staff. 1994. pap. write for info. (*0-201-40732-9*) Addison-Wesley.

ScriptX Language Guide. Kaleida Labs, Inc. Staff. 1994. pap. write for info. (*0-201-40731-0*) Addison-Wesley.

Scrisori Din Tinerete Catre Eduard Silberstein, 1871-1881. Sigmund Freud. Ed. by Florin V. Vladescu. Tr. by Ioan Milea. (Illus.). 196p. (Orig.). 1993. pap. text ed. 19.95 (*1-883881-01-3*) S Freud RT&PF.

Scritti Scelti e Lettere, Set, Vols. I-III. Philip Mazzei. (ITA.). 1984. write for info. (*0-614-10131-X*) Am Inst Ital Stud.

Scrittura Latina Nell'Eta Romana. Luigi Schiaparelli. (Auxilia Ad Res Italicas Medii Aevi Exquirendas in Usum Scholarum Instructa et Collecta Ser.: No. 1). (Illus.). xi, 208p. 1979. reprint ed. write for info. (*3-487-06738-2*) G Olms Pubs.

***Scrivener.** Thomas R. Haggard. 138p. (Orig.). 1996. pap. 20.00 (*0-943856-71-X*, 590) SC Bar CLE.

***Scroll.** Donald Nasser. 368p. Date not set. pap. write for info. (*0-9642463-2-5*) ICAM Pub Co.

***Scroll.** unabridged ed. Donald Nasser. 368p. Date not set. 24.95 (*0-9642463-3-3*) ICAM Pub Co.

***Scroll, a Little Magazine.** Ed. by Mary G. Hamilton. (Seasonal Magazine Ser.). 56p. 1996. 4.95 (*0-9644683-2-8*) Sunporch Prods.

Scroll of Adam & Eve. Comment by J. J. Hurtak. 126p. 1989. 7.00 (*0-685-47188-8*) Acad Future Sci.

Scroll of Exalted Kingship: Diwan Malkuta 'Laita. Tr. by Jorunn J. Buckley. (American Oriental Society Translation Ser.: Vol. 3). xix, 110p. 1993. 22.00 (*0-940490-83-8*) Am Orient Soc.

Scroll of Time. J. A. Savage. pap. 6.95 (*0-88172-120-4*) Believers Bkshelf.

Scroll Ornaments of the Early Victorian Period. F. Knight. LC 77-88652. (Pictorial Archive Ser.). (Illus.). 1978. pap. 3.95 (*0-486-23596-3*) Dover.

Scroll Ornaments of the Early Victorian Period. F. Knight. 1990. 11.75 (*0-8446-5689-5*) Peter Smith.

Scroll Saw Basics. Patrick Spielman. LC 90-7669. (Basics Ser.). (Illus.). 128p. 1991. pap. 10.95 (*0-8069-7224-6*) Sterling.

Scroll Saw Book. Frank Pozsgai. LC 95-1944. (Illus.). 64p. (Orig.). 1995. pap. 12.95 (*0-88740-774-9*) Schiffer.

Scroll-Saw Christmas with Frank Pozsgai: Step-by-Step to a 3-D Sleight & Reindeer, Plus 30 Tree Ornament Patterns. Photos & Text by Douglas Congdon-Martin. LC 95-19424. (Illus.). 64p. (Orig.). 1995. pap. 12.95 (*0-88740-786-2*) Schiffer.

Scroll Saw Country Patterns. Patrick Spielman. LC 89-78351. (Illus.). 196p. 1990. pap. 14.95 (*0-8069-7220-3*) Sterling.

Scroll Saw Fretwork Patterns. Patrick Spielman & James Reidle. LC 88-30813. (Illus.). 256p. (Orig.). 1989. pap. 14.95 (*0-8069-6998-9*) Sterling.

Scroll Saw Fretwork Techniques & Projects. Patrick Spielman & James Reidle. LC 89-35458. (Illus.). 196p. 1990. pap. 16.95 (*0-8069-6874-5*) Sterling.

Scroll Saw Handbook. Patricia Spielman. (Sterling Publishing Co. Ser.). 1986. pap. 14.95 (*0-8273-5396-0*) Delmar.

Scroll Saw Handbook. Patrick Spielman. LC 86-14352. (Illus.). 256p. (Orig.). 1986. pap. 16.95 (*0-8069-4770-5*) Sterling.

Scroll Saw Holiday Patterns. Patrick Spielman & Patricia Spielman. LC 91-21981. (Illus.). 160p. 1991. pap. 14.95 (*0-8069-8476-7*) Sterling.

Scroll Saw Pattern. Patricia Spielman. (Sterling Publishing Co. Ser.). 1986. pap. 12.95 (*0-8273-5395-2*) Delmar.

Scroll Saw Pattern Book. Patrick Spielman & Patricia Spielman. LC 86-14358. (Illus.). 256p. (Orig.). 1986. pap. 14.95 (*0-8069-4772-1*) Sterling.

Scroll Saw Patterns for the Country Home. Patrick Spielman et al. LC 93-2329. (Illus.). 200p. 1993. pap. 14.95 (*0-8069-0481-X*) Sterling.

Scroll Saw Pictures. Frank Pozsgai. LC 95-4998. (Illus.). 64p. (Orig.). 1995. pap. 12.95 (*0-88740-775-7*) Schiffer.

Scroll Saw Projects, Bk. 756. Donald R. Brann. LC 75-3911. 1975. pap. 7.95 (*0-87733-756-X*); lib. bdg. 5.95 (*0-87733-056-5*) Easi-Bild.

Scroll Saw Puzzle Patterns. Patrick Spielman. LC 88-19968. (Illus.). 264p. (Orig.). 1988. pap. 14.95 (*0-8069-6586-X*) Sterling.

Scroll Saw Scandinavian Patterns & Projects. Patrick Speilman & Gosta Dahlqvist. LC 94-47990. (Illus.). 168p. 1995. pap. 14.95 (*0-8069-0986-2*) Sterling.

Scroll Saw Shelf Patterns. Patrick Spielman & Loren Raty. LC 92-17027. (Illus.). 132p. 1992. pap. 14.95 (*0-8069-8586-0*) Sterling.

Scroll Saw Silhouette Patterns. Patrick Spielman & James Reidle. LC 92-41352. (Illus.). 128p. 1993. pap. 14.95 (*0-8069-0306-6*) Sterling.

Scroll Saw Woodcrafting Magic. rev. ed. Joanne Lockwood. 312p. 1994. pap. 16.95 (*1-56523-054-X*) Fox Chapel Pub.

Scrolls & Christian Origins: Studies in the Jewish Background of the New Testament. Matthew W. Black. LC 83-11519. (Brown Judaic Studies). 232p. (C). 1983. pap. 15.00 (*0-89130-639-0*, 14 00 48) Scholars Pr GA.

Scrolls & the New Testament. Krister Stendahl. (Christian Origins Library). 320p. 1991. pap. 16.95 (*0-8245-1136-0*) Crossroad NY.

Scrolls from the Dead Sea: An Exhibition of Scrolls & Archeological Artifacts from the Collections of the Israel Antiquities Authority. Ed. by Ayala Sussmann & Ruth Peled. LC 93-20476. 1993. write for info. (*0-8444-0786-0*) Lib Congress.

Scrooge. (Look & Find Ser.). (Illus.). 24p. (J). 1993. 7.98 (*0-7853-0329-4*) Pubns Intl Ltd.

Scrooge. Mark Dunster. 16p. (Orig.). 1983. pap. 4.00 (*0-89642-101-5*) Linden Pubs.

Scrooge. adapted ed. Charles Dickens. 1959. pap. 5.25 (*0-8222-1001-0*) Dramatists Play.

Scrooge - The Musical. Ed. by Milton Okun. pap. 14.95 (*0-89524-726-7*) Cherry Lane.

Scrooge & the Golden Eggs. Walt Disney Productions Staff. (Mickey's Young Readers Library Ser.: Vol. 5). (Illus.). (J). (gr. 1-6). 1990. reprint ed. 3.49 (*1-885222-38-6*) Advance Pubs.

Scrooge & the Magic Fish. Walt Disney Productions Staff. (Walt Disney's Fun-to-Read Library Ser.: Vol. 12). (Illus.). 44p. (J). (gr. 1-6). 1986. reprint ed. 3.49 (*1-885222-24-6*) Advance Pubs.

Scrooge Investing: The Bargain Hunter's Guide to Discounts, Free Services, Special Privileges & 99 other Money-Saving Tips. rev. ed. Mark Skousen. 169p. 1994. 19.95 (*0-7931-0944-2*, 5608-691A) Dearborn Finan.

Scrooge Investings: The Bargain Hunter's Guide to More Than 120 Things you Can Do to Cut the Cost of Investing. 2nd ed. Mark Skousen. LC 95-4479. 1996. pap. 10.95 (*0-316-80000-7*) Little.

Scrooge Revised Vocal Selections. Ed. by Milton Okun. 88p. (YA). 1995. pap. 19.95 (*0-89524-988-X*) Cherry Lane.

***Scrooge Wore Spurs.** Dailey. 1997. mass mkt. 6.99 (*1-55166-293-0*, Mira Bks) Harlequin Bks.

Scrooge's Cryptic Carol: Visions of Energy, Time & Quantum Nature. Robert Gilmore. LC 96-15529. (Illus.). 200p. 1996. 22.00 (*0-387-94800-7*) Spr-Verlag.

Scrooge's Silly Day. Walt Disney Productions Staff. (Mickey's Young Readers Library Ser.: Vol. 14). (Illus.). (J). (gr. 1-6). 1990. reprint ed. 3.49 (*1-885222-47-5*) Advance Pubs.

Scrophulariaceae of Eastern Temperate North America. Francis W. Pennell. (Monograph: No. 1). (Illus.). 650p. (Orig.). 1935. pap. 7.00 (*0-910006-08-3*) Acad Nat Sci Phila.

Scrophulariaceae of the Western Himalayas. Francis W. Pennell. (Monograph: No. 5). (Illus.). 163p. (Orig.). 1943. pap. 5.00 (*0-910006-14-8*) Acad Nat Sci Phila.

Scrophulariaceae, Pt. I: Calceolarieae. Ulf Molau. (Flora Neotropica Monographs: No. 47). 326p. 1988. pap. 59.00 (*0-89327-327-9*) NY Botanical.

***Scrub-a-Dub-Dub.** Joanne Barkan. (J). 1998. write for info. (*0-679-89021-1*) Random Bks Yng Read.

***Scrub-a-Dub-Dub Bath Book: And Soap Gift Set.** (Berenstain Bears Ser.). (Illus.). (J). Date not set. 5.95 (*1-57719-101-3*) GT Pubng Corp.

Scrub Dog of Alaska. Walt Morey. (Walt Morey Adventure Library). 160p. (YA). (gr. 4-9). 1989. reprint ed. pap. 7.95 (*0-936085-13-4*) Blue Heron OR.

Scrubber Strategy. Mary A. Baviello et al. Ed. by Richard C. Allen. LC 82-81547. 188p. reprint ed. pap. 53.60 (*0-7837-0336-8*, 2040655) Bks Demand.

***Scrubs on Skates.** Scott Young. 233p. (J). mass mkt. 5.99 (*0-7710-9088-9*) McCland & Stewart.

Scruffy. Peggy Parish. LC 87-45564. (Harper Early I Can Read Bk.). (Illus.). 64p. (J). (gr. k-3). 1988. lib. bdg. 14.89 (*0-06-024660-X*) HarpC Child Bks.

Scruffy. Peggy Parish. LC 87-45564. (Trophy I Can Read Bk.). (Illus.). 64p. (J). (gr. k-3). 1990. pap. 3.50 (*0-06-444137-7*, Trophy) HarpC Child Bks.

Scruffy: A Wolf Finds His Place in the Pack. Jim Brandenburg. Ed. by JoAnn B. Guernsey. LC 96-5446. (Illus.). 32p. (J). 1996. 15.95 (*0-8027-8445-3*); lib. bdg. 16.85 (*0-8027-8446-1*) Walker & Co.

Scrumptious. Houston Junior Forum Staff. (Illus.). 373p. 1980. 11.95 (*0-317-89768-3*) Cookbook Collection Inc.

Scrumptious Brunches. Anne Tallman. Ed. by Kristina Evelyn. (Illus.). 90p. (Orig.). 1990. pap. 9.95 (*0-9626746-0-5*) Willoughby NY.

Scrumptious Recipes for Sizzling Sex. Linda K. Clemons. 50p. 1993. ring bd., vinyl bd. 19.95 (*0-9640375-0-5*) L Clemons Promot.

Scrumptious Swedish Recipes. Tatjana Cosko. Ed. by Lizette Cosko. 104p. 1996. spiral bd., pap. 8.95 (*1-889028-00-2*, 1001) TALI Bks.

Scrumpy. Elizabeth Dale. (Illus.). 32p. (J). (ps-1). 1996. 12.95 (*0-86264-510-7*, Pub. by Anderson Pr UK) London Bridge.

Scruples. Gilbert Kilpack. 1956. pap. 3.00 (*0-87574-089-8*) Pendle Hill.

Scruples. Judith Krantz. 592p. 1989. mass mkt. 7.50 (*0-553-28465-7*) Bantam.

Scruples. Judith Krantz. 512p. (SPA.). 1992. pap. 5.95 (*1-56780-056-4*) La Costa Pr.

***Scruples.** large type ed. Judith Krantz. pap. 18.95 (*0-7451-3632-X*, Pub. by Chivers Lrg Print UK) Chivers N Amer.

***Scruples.** large type ed. Judith Krantz. 21.95 (*0-7451-7771-9*, Pub. by Chivers Lrg Print UK) Chivers N Amer.

Scruples Two. Judith Krantz. 1993. pap. 6.99 (*0-685-67800-8*) Bantam.

***Scruples Two.** Judith Krantz. 544p. 1993. mass mkt. 6.99 (*0-553-56111-1*) Crown Pub Group.

Scruples Two. large type ed. Judith Krantz. 1992. 25.00 (*0-679-41380-4*) Random Hse Lrg Prnt.

Scrupules de Maigret. Georges Simenon. pap. 3.95 (*0-685-11557-7*) Fr & Eur.

Scrupulous Meanness: A Study of Joyce's Early Work. Edward Brandabur. LC 71-131057. 197p. reprint ed. pap. 56.20 (*0-317-28998-5*, 2020241) Bks Demand.

Scrut. George Roberts. LC 82-81349. 64p. 1983. pap. 4.00 (*0-930100-10-7*) Holy Cow.

Scrutinies of Simon Iff. Aleister Crowley. Ed. by Martin P. Starr. LC 87-7122. (Illus.). 200p. 1987. 19.95 (*0-933429-02-9*) Teitan Pr.

Scrutinizing Science. Arthur Donovan et al. 400p. (C). 1988. lib. bdg. 162.50 (*90-277-2608-6*) Kluwer Ac.

Scrutinizing Science: Empirical Studies of Scientific Change. Ed. by Arthur Donovan et al. 407p. 1992. reprint ed. pap. text ed. 24.95 (*0-8018-4517-3*) Johns Hopkins.

Scrutiny at a Glance. (Illus.). 60p. (Orig.). 1980. pap. 6.95 (*0-9616013-3-7*) Midwest Media.

Scrutiny of Cinema. William Hunter. LC 70-169328. (Literature of Cinema, Ser. 2). (Illus.). 92p. 1972. reprint ed. 18.95 (*0-405-03896-8*) Ayer.

Scrying: The Art of Female Divination. Raymond A. Moody. 175p. 1995. pap. 9.95 (*0-89176-999-4*) R Bemis Pub.

***Scrying for Beginners: Tapping into the Supersensory Powers of Your Subconscious.** Donald Tyson. LC 96-50071. 1997. pap. 12.95 (*1-56718-746-3*) Llewellyn Pubns.

SCSA: The Complete Reference Guide. Edwin Margulies. 34.95 (*0-936648-77-5*) Flatiron Pubng.

***SCSA: The Complete Reference to Using Signal Computing System Architecture in Computer Telephony.** 2nd ed. Edwin Margulies. 450p. 1996. 34.95 (*0-936648-43-0*, P90063) Flatiron Pubng.

SCSC-95: Summer Computer Simulation Proceedings. Ed. by Birta Oren. (Illus.). 900p. (Orig.). 1995. 180.00 (*0-614-10091-7*, SCSC-95) Soc Computer Sim.

SCSI Bench Reference. 3rd ed. Jeffrey D. Stai. (SCSI Ser.). 212p. (Orig.). 1996. pap. 99.00 (*1-879936-30-5*) ENDL Pubns.

SCSI Bench Reference: A Technical Guide to SCSI-2 & SCSI-3. 2nd ed. Jeffrey Stai. LC 91-17070. (ENDL SCSI Ser.). 224p. 1995. student ed. 195.00 (*1-879936-07-0*) ENDL Pubns.

SCSI Bus & IDE Interface: Protocols, Applications & Programming. Friedhelm Schmidt. Tr. by Michael Schultz. LC 94-23813. 304p. (ENG & GER.). 1994. pap. 34.95 incl. disk (*0-201-42284-0*) Addison-Wesley.

SCSI Encyclopedia Vol. I: Phases & Protocols (A-M) Jeffrey Stai. LC 91-17070. (ENDL SCSI Ser.). 304p. 1994. text ed. 495.00 (*1-879936-11-9*) ENDL Pubns.

SCSI Encyclopedia Vol. I: Phases & Protocols (N-Z) Jeffrey Stai. LC 91-17070. (ENDL SCSI Ser.). 274p. 1994. text ed. 495.00 (*1-879936-12-7*) ENDL Pubns.

SCSI Encyclopedia, Vol. II: Disk Operations (A-L) Jeffrey Stai et al. LC 91-17070. (ENDL SCSI Ser.). 344p. 1994. text ed. 495.00 (*1-879936-13-5*) ENDL Pubns.

SCSI Encyclopedia, Vol. II: Disk Operations (M-Z) Jeffrey Stai et al. LC 91-17070. (ENDL SCSI Ser.). 356p. 1994. text ed. 495.00 (*1-879936-23-2*) ENDL Pubns.

SCSI Handbook. L. Brett Glass. (Illus.). (Orig.). 1991. pap. 29.95 (*0-13-792136-5*) Brady Pub.

SCSI Tutor: An In-Depth Exploration of SCSI. David Deming. LC 91-17070. (ENDL SCSI Ser.). 390p. 1995. student ed. 395.00 (*1-879936-08-9*) ENDL Pubns.

***SCTV: Behind the Scenes.** Dave Thomas. Date not set. write for info. (*0-7710-8566-4*) McCland & Stewart.

***SCTV: Behind the Scenes.** Dave Thomas. 1997. pap. text ed. 17.95 (*0-7710-8568-0*) St Martin.

***Scuba.** Access Press Staff. 1997. pap. 18.50 (*0-06-277210-4*, Access NY) HarpC.

Scuba Divers Sign Language Manual. Leann G. Smith & James P. Smith. (Illus.). 103p. 1994. 12.95 (*0-941332-38-1*, D474) Best Pub Co.

Scuba Diving. Norman S. Barrett. LC 88-50372. (Picture Library). (Illus.). 32p. (J). (gr. k-6). 1990. lib. bdg. 20.00 (*0-531-10631-4*) Watts.

Scuba Diving. Dennis K. Graver. LC 92-43353. (Illus.). 224p. 1993. pap. 19.95 (*0-87322-431-0*, PGRA0431) Human Kinetics.

Scuba Diving. Bob Italia. (Action Sports Ser.). (J). (gr. 1-8). 1994. lib. bdg. 14.98 (*1-56239-345-6*) Abdo & Dghtrs.

Scuba Diving. Dave Saunders. LC 95-18039. (Know the Sport Ser.). 48p. 1996. pap. 5.95 (*0-8117-2826-9*) Stackpole.

Scuba Diving Explained: Questions & Answers on Physiology & Medical Aspects of Scuba Diving. Lawrence Martin. LC 93-79817. (Illus.). 280p. (Orig.). 1995. pap. 20.00 (*1-879653-12-5*) Lakeside Pr.

Scuba Diving First Aid. National Safety Council Staff. LC 94-48302. (Emergency Care Ser.). 65p. 1995. pap. 12.50 (*0-86720-944-5*) Jones & Bartlett.

Scuba Diving for Fun & Profit. Eric Tackett. Ed. by Ruth Hunsinger. (Illus.). 130p. 1989. pap. 10.95 (*0-943155-04-5*) Laser Tech.

Scuba Diving for Safety. Duekek. 1978. pap. 6.95 (*0-02-499750-1*, Macmillan Coll) P-H.

Scuba Diving with Disabilities. Jill Robinson & A. Dale Fox. LC 86-18532. (Illus.). 144p. (Orig.). 1987. pap. text ed. 20.00 (*0-88011-280-8*, PROB0280) Human Kinetics.

Scuba Duba. Bruce J. Friedman. 1968. pap. 5.25 (*0-8222-1002-9*) Dramatists Play.

Scuba Equipment: The Diver's Field Guide to Maintenance & Care for Scuba Diving Equipment. Mike Wood. 29p. 1985. pap. text ed. 5.50 (*0-943717-26-4*) Concept Sys.

Scuba Life Saving. Albert Pierce. LC 86-10308. (Illus.). 192p. 1985. reprint ed. pap. text ed. 20.00 (*0-88011-279-4*, PPIE0279) Human Kinetics.

Scuba Lifesaving & Accident Management. 2nd ed. Tom Leaird. 80p. 1988. pap. text ed. 12.00 (*0-87322-132-X*, 4929, YMCA USA) Human Kinetics.

Scuba Northeast, Vol. 2: Shipwrecks, Dive Sites & Dive Activities-Rhode Island to New Jersey. Robert G. Bachand. 130p. (Orig.). 1986. pap. 9.95 (*0-9616399-0-3*) Sea Sports Pubns.

Scuba Rescue: Skills & Techniques. National Association Of Underwater Instructors Staff. 208p. (gr. 13). 1995. pap. text ed. 7.25 (*0-8151-6289-8*) Mosby Yr Bk.

***Scuba Skills Update.** Laurie C. Humpal. 32p. 1996. pap. text ed. write for info. (*1-880229-36-6*) Concept Sys.

Scuba Skills Update Field Guide. Laurie Clark & Ed Christini. 43p. 1988. pap. text ed. 5.95 (*0-943717-59-0*) Concept Sys.

Scuba Skills Update Instructor Outline. Laurie Clark & Ed Christini. 34p. 1988. pap. text ed. 8.95 (*0-943717-60-4*) Concept Sys.

***Scuba Skills Update Teaching Outline.** 32p. 1996. pap. text ed. write for info. (*1-880229-37-4*) Concept Sys.

Scuba Talk: A Guide to Underwater Communication. Keith A. Ellenbogen. LC 95-94363. (Florida, Bahamas & Caribbean Ser.). (Illus.). 72p. (Orig.). 1996. spiral bd. 14.95 (*0-9645407-4-6*) Blue Reef Pubns.

***Scuba Talk: Coloring Book.** Keith A. Ellenbogen. (Illus.). 48p. (Orig.). (J). (ps-6). 1997. pap. 1.00 (*0-9645407-1-1*) Blue Reef Pubns.

Scudder's White Mountain Viewing Guide. Brent E. Scudder. LC 95-94325. (Illus.). 268p. (Orig.). 1995. pap. 15.95 (*0-9645856-9-3*) High Top.

Scuds or Butter? The Political Economy of Arms Control in the Middle East. Yahya M. Sadowski. LC 92-28969. 112p. 1993. pap. 9.95 (*0-8157-7663-2*) Brookings.

***Scuffing Resistance of Vehicle Transmission Gears Collenberg.** Franz J. Joachim. (1996 Fall Technical Meeting Ser.: Vol. 10). 1996. pap. text ed. 30.00 (*1-55589-677-4*) AGMA.

Scuffy the Tugboat. Gertrude Crampton. (Little Golden Sound Story Bks.). (Illus.). 24p. 1993. 6.95 (*0-307-74813-8*, 64813, Golden Pr) Western Pub.

Scuffy the Tugboat. Golden Books Staff. (Little Golden Bks.). (Illus.). 24p. (J). (ps-2). 1995. 1.49 (*0-307-02046-0*, Golden Pr) Western Pub.

Sculler at Ease: What Makes Boats Go. Frank Cunningham. (Illus.). 168p. 1993. write for info. (*0-937321-02-8*) Avery Pr CO.

Sculler, Rowing from Tiber to Thames. John Taylor. LC 72-235. (English Experience Ser.: No. 283). 48p. 1970. reprint ed. 15.00 (*90-221-0283-1*) Walter J Johnson.

***Scully X-Posed: The Unauthorized Biography of X-Files Superstar Gillian Anderson.** John K. Walters. LC 97-19730. 244p. 1997. per. 16.00 (*0-7615-1111-3*) Prima Pub.

***Sculpted Object, 1400-1700.** Ed. by Stuart Currie & Peta Motture. LC 96-33443. (Illus.). 224p. 1997. text ed. 68.95 (*1-85928-270-9*, Pub. by Ashgate UK) Ashgate Pub Co.

Sculpted Saints of a Borderland Mission. Richard Ahlborn. LC 74-18171. (Illus.). 124p. 1974. pap. 7.50 (*0-915076-03-9*) SW Mission.

Sculpted Stones (Piedas Labradas) Victor Montejo. Tr. by Victor Perera from SPA. 128p. 1995. pap. 11.95 (*1-880684-14-4*) Curbstone.

Sculpted Word: Keats, Ekphrasis, & the Visual Arts. Grant F. Scott. LC 94-1267. (Illus.). 246p. 1994. 37.50 (*0-87451-679-X*) U Pr of New Eng.

Sculpting Clay. Leon I. Nigrosh. (Illus.). 192p. 1992. 27.50 (*0-87192-236-3*) Davis Mass.

Sculpting Dolls in Cernit. Marleen Engeler. LC 91-62227. 68p. 1991. pap. text ed. 17.95 (*0-916809-52-8*) Scott Pubns MI.

Sculpting Dolls in Paperclay. Robert McKinley. Ed. by Barbara Campbell. LC 94-66878. 76p. (Orig.). 1994. pap. text ed. 24.95 (*0-916809-78-1*) Scott Pubns MI.

Sculpting Dolls in Super Sculpey. Cheryl Riello. Ed. by Kim Shields. (Illus.). 80p. (Orig.). 1995. pap. text ed. 14.95 (*1-879825-20-1*) Jones Publish.

Sculpting in Time: Reflections on the Cinema. Andrey Tarkovsky. Tr. by Kitty Hunter-Blair from RUS. (Illus.). 256p. 1989. reprint ed. pap. 19.95 (*0-292-77624-1*) U of Tex Pr.

Sculpting Miniature Military Figures. Kim Jones. LC 94-23513. (Illus.). 96p. (Orig.). 1995. pap. 17.95 (*0-88740-626-2*) Schiffer.

Sculpting the Learning Organization: Lessons in the Art & Science of Systemic Change. Karen E. Watkins & Victoria J. Marsick. (Management Ser.). 324p. text ed. 29.95 (*1-55542-576-3*) Jossey-Bass.

Sculpting the Original Doll: The BluFrogg Method. Ralph Gonzales & Mary Gonzales. (Illus.). 192p. (Orig.). (C). 1994. pap. text ed. 25.00 (*1-886204-05-5*) Pollywogg Pubns.

Sculpting Traditional Bowls. Rip Mann & Tammi Mann. LC 94-66374. (Illus.). 48p. (Orig.). 1994. pap. 12.95 (*0-88740-698-X*) Schiffer.

Sculpting with Cement: Direct Modeling in a Permanent Medium. Lynn Olson. LC 81-708. (Illus.). 109p. (Orig.). (C). 1995. reprint ed. pap. 24.95 (*0-9605678-0-1*) Steelstone.

Sculpting With the Environment. Baile Oakes. 256p. 1995. text ed. 64.95 (*0-442-01642-5*) Van Nos Reinhold.

Sculpting Wood: Contemporary Tools & Techniques. Mark Lindquist. LC 86-70901. (Illus.). 304p. (Orig.). 1986. pap. 31.50 (*0-87192-228-2*) Davis Mass.

Sculpting/Making a Toddler Doll-Head to Toe. Susan Dunham. (Illus.). 128p. 1996. 19.95 (*0-87588-457-1*, 5038) Hobby Hse.

Sculptor in Wood: The Collected Woodcarvings of Fred Cogelow. Fred Cogelow. 1991. 24.95 (*0-9622663-4-5*) Heart Prairie Pr.

Sculptor Speaks: A Series of Conversations on Art. Jacob Epstein & Arnold L. Haskell. LC 73-172922. (Illus.). 1972. reprint ed. 20.95 (*0-405-08487-0*) Ayer.

Sculptors & Physicians in Fifth-Century Greece: A Preliminary Study. Guy P. Metraux. (Illus.). 176p. 1995. 39.95 (*0-7735-1231-4*, Pub. by McGill CN) U of Toronto Pr.

Sculptor's Clay: Charles Grafly (1862-1929) Dorothy Grafly et al. LC 95-61556. (Illus.). 153p. (Orig.). 1996. pap. 35.00 (*1-887883-00-2*) Ulrich KS. This catalog for the exhibition THE SCULPTOR'S CLAY: CHARLES GRAFLY (1862-1929) is the first published study of the sculptor's life & work. The catalogue & exhibition are based on the extensive collection of Grafly materials at Wichita State University. It is comprised of two sections. The first is a biographical sketch of the artist by his daughter, art critic Dorothy Grafly Drummond, that highlights his years as a student at the Academie Julian (1888-1891) & his teaching career at the Pennsylvania Academy of the Fine Arts. The second section is the exhibition catalog & deals with the sculptor's work in portrait busts, memorials, & major public commissions, such as the PIONEER MOTHER MONUMENT in San Francisco (1913-1915) & the MEMORIAL TO MAJOR GENERAL GEORGE GORDON MEADE in Washington, D.C. (1916-1927). The catalog has 153 pages & 91 photographs, many of which are archival & have never been published.
Publisher Provided Annotation.

Sculptor's Eye: Looking at Contemporary American Art. Jan Greenberg & Sandra Jordan. LC 92-16323. 128p. (J). 1993. 19.95 (*0-385-30902-3*) Delacorte.

Sculptor's Eye: The African Art Collection of Chaim Gross. Arnold Rubin. (Illus.). 1976. 9.00 (*0-686-25966-1*) Mus African Art.

Sculptors O'Connor. Doris F. Soderman. (Illus.). 160p. 1994. 27.95 (*0-9642863-0-0*); pap. 24.95 (*0-9642863-3-5*) Gundi Pubng.

Sculptors of the Cyclades: Individual & Tradition in the Third Millennium B.C. Pat Getz-Preziosi. (Illus.). 288p. 1987. text ed. 89.00 (*0-472-10067-X*) U of Mich Pr.

Sculptors of the West Portals of Chartres Cathedral. Whitney S. Stoddard. (Illus.). 272p. 1992. pap. 22.50 (*0-393-30043-9*) Norton.

Sculptor's Society of Canada: 65th Anniversary Catalogue. (Illus.). 100p. (FRE.). pap. 24.95 (*0-88962-562-X*) Mosaic.

Sculptor's Son: Lincoln Borglum & Mount Rushmore. Tom D. Griffith. (Illus.). 48p. (Orig.). (J). (gr. 4-7). 1995. pap. 4.95 (*0-9646798-1-7*) Mt Rushmore.

Sculptor's Testimony in Bronze & Stone: The Sacred Sculpture of Avard T. Fairbanks. 2nd ed. Eugene F. Fairbanks. (Illus.). 147p. 1994. 21.95 (*0-916095-58-4*) Pubs Pr UT.

Sculptress. large type ed. Minette Walters. 488p. 1994. 25.99 (*0-7505-0625-3*, Pub. by Magna Print Bks UK) Ulverscroft.

Sculptress Vol. 1. Minette Walters. 1994. mass mkt. 5.99 (*0-312-95361-5*) St Martin.

Sculptura Humana. Norberto Torriente. (Illus.). 28p. 1992. 17.95 (*0-9632987-0-4*) NTD Photo.

Sculptural Art of Khajuraho. Krishna Deva. (Illus.). 160p. 1991. 39.00 (*81-7107-002-7*, Pub. by Bamboo Pub UK) Antique Collect.

Sculptural Ceramics. Ian Gregory. 160p. 1992. 34.95 (*0-8019-8387-8*) Chilton.

***Sculptural Ceramics.** Ian Gregory. (Illus.). 160p. 1992. 49.95 (*1-889250-09-0*) Gentle Br.

Sculptural Decoration of the Henry VII Chapel, Westminster Abbey. Helen J. Dow. 118p. (C). 1989. text ed. 65.00 (*1-872795-59-5*, Pub. by Pentland Pr UK) St Mut.

Sculptural Idea. 3rd ed. James J. Kelly. (Illus.). 232p. (C). 1991. reprint ed. pap. text ed. 22.95 (*0-88133-605-X*) Waveland Pr.

Sculptural Monuments in an Outdoor Environment: A Conference Held at the Penn. Academy of the Fine Arts. 2nd ed. Ed. by Virginia N. Naude. (Illus.). 116p. (Orig.). 1986. reprint ed. pap. 14.95 (*0-943836-04-2*) Penn Acad Art.

Sculptural Programs of Chartres Cathedral: Christ, Mary, Ecclesia. Adolf E. Katzenellenbogen. LC 59-14894. 230p. reprint ed. pap. 65.60 (*0-317-10764-X*, 2007368) Bks Demand.

Sculpture. (Illus.). 24p. (J). (gr. 6-12). 1969. pap. 2.40 (*0-8395-3322-5*, 33322) BSA.

Sculpture. (Illus.). text ed. write for info. (*1-56290-066-8*) Crystal.

Sculpture. 20p. 1963. pap. 2.00 (*0-939594-42-0*) Menil Collect.

***Sculpture.** Ed. by Andrew Benjamin. (Illus.). 96p. (Orig.). 1997. pap. 29.95 (*1-85490-527-9*) Academy Ed UK.

Sculpture. Mary-Jane Opie. LC 94-2593. (Eyewitness Art Ser.). (Illus.). 64p. 1994. 16.95 (*1-56458-495-X*) DK Pub Inc.

Sculpture. Andrew Pekarik. LC 92-52988. (Behind the Scenes Ser.). (Illus.). 64p. (J). (gr. 3-7). 1992. 18.95 (*1-56282-294-2*); lib. bdg. 18.89 (*1-56282-295-0*) Hyprn Child.

Sculpture. Andrew Pekarik. LC 92-52988. (Behind the Scenes Ser.). (Illus.). 64p. (J). (gr. 3-7). 1995. pap. 8.95 (*0-7868-1032-7*) Hyprn Child.

Sculpture. Stephen Ratcliffe. 96p. 1996. pap. 10.95 (*1-55713-297-6*) Sun & Moon CA.

***Sculpture.** Philip S. Rawson. LC 96-28432. (Illus.). 162p. 1997. 34.95 (*0-8122-8258-2*) U of Pa Pr.

Sculpture. Carmela Thiele. (Crash Course Ser.). 192p. 1996. pap. 12.95 (*0-8120-9775-0*) Barron.

Sculpture: A Fifteen-Week Multimedia Program. Judith Peck. (Illus.). 144p. 1986. pap. 14.95 (*0-671-61426-6*) P-H.

Sculpture: An Illustrated Catalogue. LC 93-29268. 1993. write for info. (*0-89468-187-7*) Natl Gallery Art.

***Sculpture: An Illustrated Summary Catalogue of the Collections of the J. Paul Getty Museum.** J. Paul Getty Museum Staff & Peter Fusco. LC 97-16753. 1997. write for info. (*0-89236-488-2*, J P Getty Museum) J P Getty Trust.

Sculpture: Principles & Practice. Louis Slobodkin. (Illus.). 256p. 1973. reprint ed. pap. 9.95 (*0-486-22960-2*) Dover.

Sculpture: Technique, Form, Content. rev. ed. Arthur Williams. LC 93-74648. (Illus.). 368p. 1995. 47.20 (*0-87192-277-0*) Davis Mass.

Sculpture: Tools, Materials, & Techniques. Wilbert Verhelst. (Illus.). 304p. 1973. 35.00 (*0-13-796615-6*) P-H.

Sculpture & Casting of Equestrian Statues: Translated from the Original French of 1784. Ed. by Helen Tullberg. 1990. pap. 18.00 (*0-902633-29-5*, Pub. by Picton UK) St Mut.

Sculpture & Enlivened Space: Aesthetics & History. F. David Martin. LC 79-4006. (Illus.). 352p. 1981. 38.00 (*0-8131-1386-5*) U Pr of Ky.

***Sculpture & Its Reproductions.** Ed. by Erich Ranfft & Anthony Hughes. (Critical Views Ser.). (Illus.). 224p. 1997. pap. 24.95 (*1-86189-002-8*, Pub. by Reaktion Bks UK) Consort Bk Sales.

Sculpture & Sculptors of Yazilikaya. Robert L. Alexander. LC 84-40804. (Illus.). 168p. 1986. 39.50 (*0-87413-279-7*) U Delaware Pr.

Sculpture As Experience. Judith Peck. LC 88-43308. (Illus.). 208p. 1989. pap. 14.95 (*0-8019-7978-1*) Chilton.

Sculpture by Anna Hyatt Huntington. Beatrice G. Proske. (Illus.). 24p. 1957. pap. text ed. 0.50 (*0-87535-093-3*) Hispanic Soc.

Sculpture by Antoine-Louise Barye in the Collection in the Fogg Art Museum. John M. Rosenfield. (Fogg Art Museum Handbooks Ser.: Vol. 4). (Illus.). 103p. (Orig.). 1995. pap. 9.95 (*0-916724-53-0*, 453-0) Harvard Art Mus.

Sculpture by Bill Woodrow: Natural Produce, an Armed Response. Hugh Davies. LC 85-81552. (Illus.). 20p. 1985. 5.00 (*0-934418-24-1*) Mus Contemp Art.

Sculpture Conservation: Preservation or Interference. Ed. by Phillip Lindley. LC 96-4097. (Illus.). 300p. 1996. 59.95 (*1-85928-254-7*, Pub. by Scolar Pr UK) Ashgate Pub Co.

Sculpture from Arcadia & Laconia: Proceedings from the International Conference Held at the American School of Classical Studies at Athens (1992) Ed. by Olga Palagia & William Coulson. (Oxbow Monographs in Archaeology: No. 30). (Illus.). 293p. 1993. 95.00 (*0-946897-54-9*, Pub. by Oxbow Bks UK) David Brown.

***Sculpture from the Collections of Minnesota Museums.** Steven Klindt. (Illus.). 36p. (Orig.). 1988. pap. write for info. (*1-889523-04-6*) Tweed Mus.

Sculpture I: 1952-1967. Mary C. Sturgeon. LC 76-362971. (Isthmia Ser.: No. 4). (Illus.). xxiii, 200p. 1987. 60.00 (*0-87661-934-0*) Am Sch Athens.

***Sculpture II: Marble Sculpture, 1967-1980.** Steven Lattimore. (Isthmia Ser.: No. 6). xviii, 64p. 1996. 55.00 (*0-87661-936-7*) Am Sch Athens.

Sculpture in America. 2nd ed. Wayne Craven. LC 82-40439. (Illus.). 808p. 1984. 60.00 (*0-8453-4776-4*, Cornwall Bks) Assoc Univ Prs.

Sculpture in America. 2nd ed. Wayne Craven. LC 82-40439. (Illus.). 808p. 1984. 60.00 (*0-87413-225-8*) U Delaware Pr.

Sculpture in Britain: 1530-1830. Margaret Whinney. (Pelican History of Art Ser.: No. 23). (Illus.). 1964. 50.00 (*0-670-62436-5*) Viking Penguin.

Sculpture in Britain: 1530-1830. 2nd ed. Margaret Whinney. (Pelican History of Art Ser.). (Illus.). 522p. (C). 1988. reprint ed. text ed. 55.00 (*0-300-05317-7*); reprint ed. pap. text ed. 26.50 (*0-300-05318-5*) Yale U Pr.

Sculpture in Clay from Puerto Rico. (Illus.). 63p. 1980. 3.50 (*0-916746-49-6*) Springfield Lib & Mus.

Sculpture in Italy: 1400-1500. Charles Seymour, Jr. (Pelican History of Art Ser.). (Illus.). 295p. (C). 1976. reprint ed. text ed. 50.00 (*0-300-05303-7*) Yale U Pr.

Sculpture in Miniature: The Chess Sets at Maryhill Museum of Art. Colleen Schafroth. LC 89-63457. (Illus.). 100p. (Orig.). 1990. pap. 9.95 (*0-9617180-1-3*) Maryhill Art.

Sculpture in Paper. Nicholas Roukes. LC 92-72329. (Illus.). 160p. 1993. 26.95 (*0-87192-246-0*) Davis Mass.

Sculpture in Siam. Alfred Salmony. LC 79-143362. (Illus.). 1972. reprint ed. 50.00 (*0-87817-081-2*) Hacker.

Sculpture in Silver. Bill Harmsen. 1992. 19.95 (*0-9601322-8-7*) Harmsen.

Sculpture in Stone. Paul Cummings. (Illus.). 76p. (Orig.). (C). 1989. pap. 9.00 (*0-9624620-0-4*) Tree Gallery.

Sculpture in Stone & Bronze: Additions to the Collections of Greek, Etruscan, & Roman Art 1971-1988. Cornelius C. Vermeule, III & Mary B. Comstock. 132p. 1988. pap. text ed. 25.00 (*0-87846-264-3*) Mus Fine Arts Boston.

Sculpture in the Huntington Collection. Henry E. Huntington Library & Art Gallery Staff & Robert R. Wark. LC 58-10419. (Huntington Library Publications). 85p. reprint ed. pap. 25.00 (*0-685-16397-0*, 2027300) Bks Demand.

Sculpture in the Isabella Stewart Gardner Museum. Cornelius C. Vermeule, Jr. et al. LC 77-94517. (Illus.). 1978. 15.00 (*0-914660-03-9*); pap. 10.00 (*0-914660-04-7*) I S Gardner Mus.

Sculpture in the Netherlands, Germany, France, & Spain: 1400-1500. Theodor Muller. (Pelican History of Art Ser.). (Illus.). 262p. (C). 1976. reprint ed. text ed. 60.00 (*0-300-05309-6*) Yale U Pr.

Sculpture in the Parthian Empire: A Study in Chronology, 2 vols., Set. Hans E. Mathiesen. (Illus.). 232p. (C). 1993. 51.00 (*87-7288-311-1*, Pub. by Aarhus Univ Pr DK) David Brown.

Sculpture in the Sun: Hawaii's Art for Open Spaces. Georgia F. Radford & Warren H. Radford. LC 77-92972. 117p. 1978. pap. 4.95 (*0-8248-0526-7*) UH Pr.

***Sculpture in Verse.** Robert A. Mercer. (Illus.). 54p. (Orig.). 1996. pap. 12.95 (*0-9655433-0-7*) Merwood Pr.

Sculpture in Wood. Jack C. Rich. (Illus.). 176p. 1992. reprint ed. pap. 9.95 (*0-486-27109-9*) Dover.

Sculpture in Wood. John Rood. LC 50-9725. 191p. reprint ed. pap. 54.50 (*0-317-39699-4*, 2055902) Bks Demand.

Sculpture Inspired by Kalidasa. C. Sivaramamurti. (Illus.). 1986. 29.95 (*0-318-36258-9*) Asia Bk Corp.

Sculpture: Italian see Frick Collection: An Illustrated Catalogue

Sculpture Machine. Budd. (C). 1997. pap. 18.95 (*0-8147-1267-3*) NYU Pr.

Sculpture Machine: Physical Culture & Body Politics in the Age of Empire. Michael A. Budd. (Illus.). 218p. (C). 1997. 40.00 (*0-8147-1266-5*) NYU Pr.

Sculpture of Africa: Selections from a Private Collection. Intro. by Evan E. Maurer. (Illus.). 52p. 1984. 5.00 (*0-912303-41-7*) Michigan Mus.

Sculpture of Andrea & Nino Pisano. Anita F. Moskowitz. (Illus.). 504p. 1987. text ed. 225.00 (*0-521-30754-6*) Cambridge U Pr.

***Sculpture of Ankor & Ancient Cambodia: Millennium of Glory.** Ed. by Helen I. Jessup & Thierry Zephir. LC 96-61815. (Illus.). 400p. 1997. 80.00 (*0-500-23738-7*) Thames Hudson.

Sculpture of Auguste Rodin: The Collection of the Rodin Museum, Philadelphia. Evan H. Turner. LC 75-5211. (Illus.). 664p. 1990. reprint ed. pap. 25.00 (*0-685-04030-5*) Phila Mus Art.

Sculpture of Austin Wright. James Hamilton. (British Sculptors & Sculpture Ser.). (Illus.). 144p. (C). 1994. 70.00 (*0-85331-651-1*, Pub. by Lund Humphries UK) Antique Collect.

Sculpture of Bette Fast. Bette Fast. LC 94-44370. 56p. (C). 1995. pap. 32.95 (*1-56324-587-6*) M E Sharpe.

Sculpture of Clement Meadmore. Eric Gibson. LC 94-13836. (Illus.). 144p. 1994. 50.00 (*1-55595-098-1*) Hudson Hills.

Sculpture of David Wynne 1974-1992. Jonathan Stone. (British Sculptors & Sculpture Ser.). (Illus.). 176p. (C). 1993. reprint ed. 80.00 (*0-85331-638-4*, Pub. by Lund Humphries UK) Antique Collect.

***Sculpture of Early Medieval Rajasthan.** Cynthia P. Atherton. LC 97-5133. (Studies in South Asian Culture: No. 21). (Illus.). 138p. 1997. 81.25 (*90-04-10789-4*, NLG 143) E J Brill.

Sculpture of Epstein. Evelyn Silber. LC 85-41060. (Illus.). 240p. 1987. 90.00 (*0-8387-5103-2*) Bucknell U Pr.

Sculpture of Frank Dobson. Neville Jason. (British Sculptors & Sculpture Ser.). (Illus.). 168p. (C). 1994. 90.00 (*0-85331-641-4*, Pub. by Lund Humphries UK) Antique Collect.

Sculpture of Gaston Lachaise. LC 67-17017. (Illus.). 86p. 1967. 85.00 (*0-87130-016-8*) Eakins.

Sculpture of India, Three Thousand BC-AD Thirteen Hundred. Pramod Chandra. (Illus.). 224p. 1985. 75.00 (*0-674-79590-3*) HUP.

Sculpture of Indonesia. Jan Fontein et al. LC 89-13678. (Illus.). 312p. 1990. 13.99 (*0-89468-141-9*) Natl Gallery Art.

Sculpture of Jacob Epstein. LC 76-28788. (Smithsonian Institution Traveling Exhibition Service Ser.). (Illus.). 1976. pap. 2.00 (*0-913060-25-9*) Norton Art.

Sculpture of Jacopo Sansovino, 2 vols., Set. Bruce Boucher. (Illus.). 652p. (C). 1991. text ed. 150.00 (*0-300-04759-2*) Yale U Pr.

Sculpture of Jacques Lipchitz: A Catalogue Raisonne: The Paris Years. Alan G. Wilkinson. LC 96-60239. (Illus.). 248p. 1996. 60.00 (*0-500-09262-1*) Thames Hudson.

Sculpture of Kenneth Arimitage. Tamsyn Woollcombe. (Illus.). 160p. 1996. 90.00 (*0-85331-702-X*, Pub. by Lund Humphries UK) Antique Collect.

Sculpture of Life. Ernest Borek. LC 73-6831. (Illus.). 181p. 1973. text ed. 45.00 (*0-231-03425-3*) Col U Pr.

Sculpture of Life. Ernest Borek. LC 73-6831. (Illus.). 203p. reprint ed. pap. 57.90 (*0-8357-4589-9*, 2037520) Bks Demand.

Sculpture of Love & Anguish: The Holocaust Memorial. Kenneth Treister. 168p. 1993. 50.00 (*1-56171-251-5*, S P I Bks) Sure Seller.

Sculpture of Maurice Lowe: Selected Works, 1956-1990. Maurice Lowe. LC 91-60772. (Illus.). 110p. (Orig.). 1991. pap. text ed. 24.95 (*0-9629150-0-9*, U of Pa Pr) M Lowe.

***Sculpture of Palenque Vol. 2: The Early Buildings of the Palace & the Wall Paintings.** Merle G. Robertson. LC 82-341. reprint ed. pap. 86.10 (*0-608-04646-9*, 2065333) Bks Demand.

***Sculpture of Palenque Vol. 3: The Late Buildings of the Palace.** Merle G. Robertson. LC 82-341. reprint ed. pap. write for info. (*0-608-04647-7*, 2065333) Bks Demand.

Sculpture of Palenque, Vol. IV: The Cross Group, the North Group, the Olvidado, & Other Pieces. Merle G. Robertson. (Illus.). 228p. 1991. text ed. 175.00 (*0-691-03572-5*) Princeton U Pr.

Sculpture of Phillip King. Tim Hilton. (British Sculptors & Sculpture Ser.). (Illus.). 128p. (C). 1992. reprint ed. 70.00 (*0-85331-622-8*, Pub. by Lund Humphries UK) Antique Collect.

Sculpture of Pol Bury: Shapes in Space & Time. Deborrah Lewis. 1978. pap. 4.95 (*0-614-02731-4*) A M Huntington Art.

Sculpture of Robert Adams. Alastair Grieve. (British Sculptors & Sculpture Ser.). (Illus.). 280p. (C). 1992. reprint ed. 120.00 (*0-85331-624-4*, Pub. by Lund Humphries UK) Antique Collect.

Sculpture of Stephen Cox. Stephen Bann. (Illus.). 144p. 1995. 90.00 (*0-85331-675-9*, Pub. by Lund Humphries UK) Antique Collect.

Sculpture of Thailand. Ed. by Theodore Bowie et al. LC 74-27410. (Asia Society Ser.). (Illus.). 1976. reprint ed. 36.95 (*0-405-06559-0*) Ayer.

Sculpture of the Inuit. George Swinton. (Illus.). 288p. 1994. pap. 35.00 (*0-7710-8370-X*) McCland & Stewart.

Sculpture of the Kamakura Period. Hisashi Mori. Tr. by Katherine A. Eickmann. LC 73-88470. (Heibonsha Survey of Japanese Art Ser.: Vol. 11). (Illus.). 176p. 1974. 20.00 (*0-8348-1017-4*) Weatherhill.

***Sculpture of the Sanctuary of Athena Polias at Priene.** J. C. Carter. (Illus.). 448p. 1984. 39.98 (*0-85431-238-2*, Pub. by Soc Antiquaries UK) David Brown.

Sculpture of the Twentieth Century. Andrew C. Ritchie. LC 78-169311. (Museum of Modern Art Publications in Reprint). (Illus.). 288p. 1972. reprint ed. 42.95 (*0-405-01570-4*) Ayer.

Sculpture of Thomas Eakins. (Illus.). 1969. 3.50 (*0-686-20539-1*) Corcoran.

Sculpture of Ursula von Rydingsvard. Dore Ashton et al. LC 96-8209. (Illus.). 108p. 1996. 45.00 (*1-55595-122-8*) Hudson Hills.

***Sculpture Projects in Munster, 1997.** Klaus Bubmann. 1996. 65.00 (*3-7757-0667-4*, Pub. by Gerd Hatje GW) Dist Art Pubs.

***Sculpture Space: Celebrating 20 Years.** Mary E. Murray. (Illus.). 72p. 1995. pap. 15.95 (*0-915895-18-8*) Munson Williams.

Sculpture Space Recent Trends. Sarah Clark-Langager. (Illus.). 48p. 1984. pap. 5.00 (*0-915895-01-3*) Munson Williams.

Sculpture Symposium Nineteen Eighty-Seven: Alice Aycock, Michael McCafferty, George Trakas. Lawrence Hanson. (Illus.). 24p. 1989. pap. 10.00 (*1-878237-00-4*) WWU Western Gallery.

Sculpture, the Reliefs from the Theater. Mary C. Sturgeon. LC 77-383. (Corinth Ser.: Vol. 9, Pt. 2). (Illus.). xvii, 148p. 1977. 40.00 (*0-87661-092-0*) Am Sch Athens.

Sculpture to Bronze. Ed. by W. D. Harmsen. (Illus.). 1981. 18.95 (*0-9601322-3-6*) Harmsen.

Sculpture to Resemblance: Work by Eight American Sculptors. (Illus.). 80p. 1987. pap. 20.00 (*0-914782-64-9*) Buffalo Fine-Albrght-Knox.

Sculpture Today. (Art & Design Profiles Ser.). (Illus.). 80p. 1988. pap. 21.95 (*0-312-01903-5*) St Martin.

Sculpture Today. Ed. by Andreas Papadakis. (Art & Design Ser.: No. 6). (Illus.). 96p. (Orig.). 1987. pap. 21.95 (*0-85670-931-X*) Academy Ed UK.

Sculpture with a Torch. John Rood. LC 63-13883. (Illus.). 117p. reprint ed. pap. 33.40 (*0-318-39691-2*, 2033286) Bks Demand.

Sculptured Capital in Spain. M. Byne. 1976. lib. bdg. 59.95 (*0-8490-2577-X*) Gordon Pr.

Sculptured Hyacinths. Charles N. Aronson. (Illus.). (C). 1973. 20.00 (*0-915736-02-0*) C N Aronson.

Sculptured Portraits of Greek Statesmen. Elmer G. Suhr. LC 78-19294. 1979. 17.95 (*0-405-10630-0*) Ayer.

Sculptured Pottery From Koptos. Adams. (Petrie Collection). 1986. pap. 39.95 (*0-85668-389-2*, Pub. by Aris & Phillips UK) David Brown.

Sculptured Surfaces in Engineering & Medicine. James P. Ducan & Susan G. Mair. LC 82-1116. (Illus.). 400p. 1983. 120.00 (*0-521-23450-6*) Cambridge U Pr.

Sculptured Tombs of Hellas. Percy Gardner. Date not set. write for info. (*0-8434-0133-8*, Pub. by McGrath NH) Ayer.

Sculpturen des Vaticanischen Museums Band I Text. Band II Text. Fotomechanischer Nachdruck in Einem Band Mit Einem Neuen Vorwort Von Bernard Andreae. Ed. by Walther Amelung. (GER.). (C). 1995. lib. bdg. 453.85 (*3-11-014767-X*) De Gruyter.

Sculptures & Monuments. Nathan Rapoport. LC 80-52914. (Illus.). 96p. 1981. 30.00 (*0-88400-072-9*) Shengold.

Sculptures by Duane Hanson. Martin H. Bush. LC 84-82245. (Illus.). 128p. 1985. 25.00 (*0-317-01521-4*) Edwin Ulrich.

Sculptures Negres: Sculptures d'Afrique, d'Amerique, d'Oceanie, 2 vols. in 1. Andre Breton & Paul Eluard. 1973. 40.00 (*0-87817-056-1*) Hacker.

***Sculptures of Andrea del Verrocchio.** Andrew Butterfield. LC 97-13650. 1997. write for info. (*0-300-07194-9*) Yale U Pr.

Sculptures of Assam. Monoranjan Dutta. 1990. 96.00 (*81-7186-001-X*, Pub. by Agam II) S Asia.

Sculptures of Kashmir. Bansilal Malla. 1990. 73.00 (*0-8364-2521-9*, Pub. by Agam Kala Prakashan) S Asia.

S

Sculptures of the Ganga-Yamuna Valley. Mihir M. Mukhopakhyaya. 1986. 40.00 (0-8364-1627-9, Pub. by Abhinav II) S Asia.

Sculptures of Vajrayana Buddhism. K. Krishna Murthy. (C). 1989. 32.50 (81-85132-06-2, Pub. by Classics India Pubns II) S Asia.

Sculpturing. Domenico Mazzone. (Artist's Library). (Illus.). 64p. (Orig.). 1994. pap. 7.95 (1-56010-124-5, AL21) W Foster Pub.

Sculpturing of Zion: Guide to the Geology of Zion. Wayne L. Hamilton. Ed. by Victor L. Jackson & James Staebler. (Illus.). 132p. 1984. pap. 14.95 (0-915630-13-3) Zion.

Sculpturing Totem Poles: Pattern & Instruction Manual. Walt Way. (Illus.). 26p. pap. 12.95 (1-56523-061-2) Fox Chapel Pub.

Sculputure of the Nike Temple Parapet. Rhys Carpender. Date not set. write for info. (0-8434-0126-5, Pub. by McGrath NH) Ayer.

Scultura del Cinquecento see Storia dell'Arte Italiana: 1901-1940

Scultura del Quattrocento see Storia dell'Arte Italiana: 1901-1940

Scultura del Trecento e le Sue Origini see Storia dell'Arte Italiana: 1901-1940

Scultures du Moyen Age. Marcel Aubert. (Illus.). (ENG & FRE.). 1948. lib. bdg. 24.95 (0-8288-3991-3) Fr & Eur.

Scum. Isaac B. Singer. Tr. by Rosaline D. Schwartz. 224p. 1991. 19.95 (0-374-25511-3) FS&G.

Scum. Isaac B. Singer. 1996. pap. 11.95 (0-14-018842-8, Viking) Viking Penguin.

Scum. Isaac B. Singer. 224p. 1992. reprint ed. pap. 9.95 (0-452-26786-2, Plume) NAL-Dutton.

Scum Also Rises. Skip Williamson. (Illus.). 144p. (Orig.). 1988. pap. 14.95 (0-930193-67-9) Fantagraph Bks.

***Scum Manifesto.** Valerie Solanas. 62p. (Orig.). 1996. pap. 5.00 (1-873176-44-9) AK Pr Dist.

Scumbler. William Wharton. 288p. 1985. pap. 3.95 (0-88184-135-8) Carroll & Graf.

Scumbler: A Novel. William Wharton. 288p. 1996. pap. 12.95 (1-55704-258-6) Newmarket.

'Scuse Me While I Kiss the Sky: The Life of Jimi Hendrix. rev. ed. David Henderson. (Illus.). 400p. 1996. pap. 12.95 (0-553-37785-X, Bantam Trade Bks) Bantam.

Scuttle Flies: The Phoridae. R. H. Disney. 480p. (gr. 13). 1994. text ed. 125.95 (0-412-56520-X) Chapman & Hall.

Scuttle Your Ships Before Advancing: And Other Lessons from History on Leadership & Change for Today's Managers. Richard A. Luecke. (Illus.). 224p. 1995. pap. 10.95 (0-19-509642-8) OUP.

Scuttlebutt. Jana Williams. LC 90-3775. 200p. (Orig.). 1990. pap. 8.95 (0-932379-88-5); lib. bdg. 18.95 (0-932379-89-3) Firebrand Bks.

Scylla & Charybdis. Bernard Evslin. (Monsters of Mythology Ser.). (Illus.). 100p. 1989. lib. bdg. 19.95 (1-55546-257-X) Chelsea Hse.

Scymnini: Coleoptera: Coccinellidae, of the United States & Canada: Key to Genera & Revision of Scymnus, Nephus & Diomus. Robert D. Gordon. LC 79-317413. (Bulletin Ser.: Vol. 28). (Illus.). 362p. (Orig.). (C). 1976. pap. 8.50 (0-944032-36-2) Buffalo SNS.

Scythe Book. David Tresemer. LC 96-36958. 1997. pap. 15.00 (0-911469-14-1) A C Hood.

Scythe of Saturn: Shakespeare & Magical Thinking. Linda Woodbridge. LC 93-11755. 344p. 1994. text ed. 47.50 (0-252-02080-4); pap. text ed. 17.95 (0-252-06370-8) U of Ill Pr.

Scythian Art. T. Piotrovsky. (C). 1990. 250.00 (0-685-34383-9, Pub. by Collets) St Mut.

Scythian Period: An Approach to the History, Art, Epigraphy, & Palaeography of North India from the First Century BC to the Third Century AD. Johanna E. Van Lohuizen-De Leeuw. 900p. (C). 1995. 82.00 (81-215-0664-6, Pub. by Munshiram Manoharial II) S Asia.

Scythian Treasures. M. Vickers. (Illus.). 56p. 1995. pap. 6.95 (0-900090-61-8, 0618, Pub. by Ashmolean Mus UK) A Schwartz & Co.

Scythians & Greeks. Ellis H. Minns. LC 65-15248. (Illus.). 1913. 60.00 (0-8196-0277-9) Biblo.

Scythians & Greeks: A Survey of Ancient History & Archaeology on the North Coast of the Euxine from the Danube to the Caucasus. Ellis H. Minns. 1976. lib. bdg. 59.95 (0-8490-2578-8) Gordon Pr.

Scythians 700-300 BC. E. N. Cernenko & M. V. Gorelik. (Men-at-Arms Ser.: No. 137). (Illus.). 48p. pap. 11.95 (0-85045-478-6, 9069, Pub. by Osprey UK) Stackpole.

Scythrididae (Lepidoptera) of Northern Europe. B. A. Bengtsson. (Fauna Entomologica Scandinavica Ser.: No. 13). (Illus.). 138p. 1984. text ed. 35.00 (90-04-07312-4) Lubrecht & Cramer.

SD. John D. Whitney. 1973. pap. 6.00 (0-685-82999-5) Elizabeth Pr.

SD. John D. Whitney. 66p. 1988. pap. 5.95 (0-944024-03-3) Spoon Riv Poetry.

Sd & Done. J. D. Whitney. Ed. by Robert Bixby. 40p. (Orig.). 1995. pap. 6.00 (1-882983-19-X) March Street Pr.

SDA Organizational Structure: Past, Present, & Future. Barry D. Oliver. (Andrews University Seminary Doctoral Dissertation Ser.: Vol. 15). 488p. (Orig.). 1989. pap. 19.99 (0-943872-97-9) Andrews Univ Pr.

SDE & F1: Proceedings of the First International Conference on System Development Environments & Factories, Berlin, May 1989. Ed. by N. Madhavji et al. 240p. (C). 1990. pap. text ed. 300.00 (0-273-08829-7, Pub. by Pitman Pubng UK) St Mut.

SDI: A View from Europe. Robert C. Hughes. 255p. (Orig.). (C). 1995. pap. text ed. 40.00 (0-7881-2152-9) DIANE Pub.

SDI: The Case for the Defence. Alun Chalfont. (C). 1990. 60.00 (0-907967-55-8, Pub. by Inst Euro Def & Strat UK) St Mut.

SDI & European Security Interests. Louis Deschamps. (Atlantic Papers: No. 62). 80p. 1987. pap. 12.95 (0-7099-4549-3, Pub. by Croom Helm UK) Routledge Chapman & Hall.

SDI & Industrial Technology Policy: Threat or Opportunity. Walter Zegveld & Christian Einzing. 300p. 1987. text ed. 39.95 (0-312-00464-8) St Martin.

SDI & Stability: The Role of Assumptions & Perceptions. Klaus Gottstein. 396p. 1988. 72.00 (3-7890-1558-X, Pub. by Nomos Verlags GW) Intl Bk Import.

SDI, Computer Simulations, New Proposals to Stop the Arms Race: Fifth International Seminar on Nuclear War. W. S. Newman & S. Stipcich. (Science & Culture Ser.). 396p. 1992. text ed. 121.00 (981-02-1188-0) World Scientific Pub.

SDI Critical Technologies. Jeff W. Schomisch. Ed. by Doug Rekenthaler, Jr. (Illus.). 138p. 1992. pap. 245.00 (0-935453-47-4) Pasha Pubns.

SDI Debate As a Continuation of History. Robert A. Levine. (CISA Working Papers: No. 55). 57p. (Orig.). 1986. pap. 15.00 (0-86682-070-1) Ctr Intl Relations.

SDK-85 System Design Kit User's Guide. rev. ed. Intel Corporation Staff. (C). pap. 15.00 (0-917017-25-0, 980451) Intel Corp.

SDL '89: The Language at Work: Proc. of the 4th SDL Forum, Lisbon, Portugal, 9-13 Oct. 1989. Ed. by O. Faergemand & M. M. Marques. 430p. 1989. 144.50 (0-444-88337-1, North Holland) Elsevier.

***SDL '91.** O. Faergemand & R. Reed. xii, 524p. 1991. 157.00 (0-444-88976-0, North Holland) Elsevier.

SDL '93: Busing Objects, Proceedings of the Sixth SDL Forum, Darmstadt, Germany, 11-15 October 1993. Ed. by Ove Frgemand & Armadeo Sarma. LC 93-26348. 534p. 1993. 180.25 (0-444-81486-8, North Holland) Elsevier.

SDL '95 with MSC in CASE: Proceedings of the Seventh SDL Forum, Oslo, Norway, 26-29 September 1995. SDL Forum Staff. Ed. by Rolv Brok & Amardeo Sarma. LC 95-35583. 412p. 1995. 178.50 (0-444-82269-0) Elsevier.

SDP: The Birth, Life, & Death of the Social Democratic Party. Ivor Crewe & Anthony King. (Illus.). 704p. 1996. 49.95 (0-19-828050-5) OUP.

***SDP: The Birth, Life, & Death of the Social Democratic Party.** Ivor Crewe & Anthony King. (Illus.). 652p. 1997. reprint ed. pap. 30.00 (0-19-829313-5) OUP.

Sdq, Mispat, & the Social Critique of the Eighth-Century Prophets. Hemchand Gossai. LC 92-32162. (American University Studies: Theology & Religion: Ser. VII, Vol. 141). 1993. 59.95 (0-8204-2029-8) P Lang Pubng.

SDR System & the Issue of Resource Transfers. Warren L. Coats, Jr. et al. Ed. by Margaret B. Riccardi. LC 90-28340. (Essays in International Finance Ser.: No. 180). 30p. (Orig.). 1990. pap. text ed. 8.00 (0-88165-087-0) Princeton U Int Finan Econ.

***SDS Resource Book.** Robert C. Reardon & Janet G. Lenz. 320p. 1997. pap. text ed. 23.95 (0-911907-28-9) Psych Assess.

SDWA Advisor: Regulatory Update Service. annuals Frederick W. Pontius. (Illus.). ring bd. 225.00 (0-89867-736-X, 74000); cd-rom 595.00 (0-614-10248-0, SDWACD) Am Water Wks Assn.

Se Banba. Michael Scott. Date not set. pap. write for info. (0-451-18378-9) NAL-Dutton.

Se Cosecha Lo Que Se Siembra: Dramatizando Se Aprende Mejor Practique el Espanol Conversando una Novela Para Adultos. Ana L. Jaramillo. LC 92-70963. (Coleccion Textos). 308p. (Orig.). (SPA.). 1993. pap. 19.95 (0-89729-640-0) Ediciones.

Se Encontraron Con Jesus. Catherine Schell & Marilyn Kunz. (Serie Encuentros - Bible Studies). 56p. (SPA.). 1989. pap. 1.50 (0-945792-56-5, 490454) Editorial Unilit.

Se Esta Divorciando Sin Saberlo. Pilar O. Bon & Jorge Sola. Ed. by Editorial Concepts Staff. 152p. (SPA.). 1985. pap. 4.95 (0-939193-07-8) Edit Concepts.

Se Hizo Hombre. Paul Hoff. 324p. (SPA.). 1990. pap. 12.95 (0-8297-1027-2) Life Pubs Intl.

***Se Humillo a Si Mismo.** Kenneth C. Fleming. (SPA.). 1.50 (0-8297-1090-6) Life Pubs Intl.

***Se Kele's Secret.** Tolowa Mollel. (Illus.). (J). 1997. pap. 14.99 (0-525-67559-0) Dutton Child Bks.

Se Leer Colores. Nellie Edge. Tr. by Marissa Zamora-Pearson from ENG. (Illus.). (SPA.). (J). (ps-2). 1993. pap. text ed. 14.00 (0-922053-28-6) N Edge Res.

Se-lu's Song. Wade Blevins. LC 96-6324. (Cherokee Indian Legend Ser.: Vol. 7). (Illus.). 53p. (J). 1996. 12.95 (1-56763-133-9) Ozark Pub.

Se Me Olvido - I Just Forgot. Mercer Mayer. (Spanish Language Look-Look Bks.). (Illus.). 24p. (SPA.). (J). 1994. 2.25 (0-307-71975-8) Western Pub.

Se Mueren por un Trago. Anderson Spickard & Barbara Thompson. 168p. (SPA.). 1991. pap. 1.50 (0-8297-0393-4) Life Pubs Intl.

Se Necesita Esposa-The Wilde Bunch. Barbara Boswell. 1996. mass mkt. 3.50 (0-373-35136-4) Harlequin Bks.

Se Positiva: Meditaciones Para Convertirte En la Mejor Amiga De Ti Misma. Sue P. Thoele. 290p. 1995. lib. bdg. 27.00 (0-8095-5894-7) Borgo Pr.

Se Positiva: Meditaciones Para Convertirte En la Mejor Amiga De Ti Misma. 2nd ed. Sue P. Thoele. 290p. (SPA.). 1995. pap. 8.95 (0-943233-95-X) Conari Press.

Se Puede Confiar en Dios? large type ed. Jorge Muller. 37p. (SPA.). 1989. pap. 2.99 (1-56063-341-7, 494026) Editorial Unilit.

Se-Quo-Yah, the American Cadmus & Modern Moses. George E. Foster. LC 76-43709. (Illus.). reprint ed. 45.00 (0-404-15544-8) AMS Pr.

Se Rencontrer Paysage Avec Joseph Sema. Rene Char. 20p. 1974. 8.95 (0-686-54170-7) Fr & Eur.

Se Salpica Todo/Wet All Over. (Autobus Magico Ser.). (ENG & SPA.). (J). (gr. 4-7). 1996. pap. text ed. 2.99 (0-590-85951-X) Scholastic Inc.

Se Sano Ahora! rev. ed. Mary K. MacDougall. LC 93-61519. (SPA.). 1994. 12.95 (0-87159-195-2) Unity Bks.

***Se Spirit Level.** Seamus Heaney. 1997. pap. write for info. (0-14-086413-X) Viking Penguin.

***Se Utterly Yours, Booker Jones.** Betsy Duffey. 1997. write for info. (0-14-038099-X, Puffin) Puffin Bks.

Se Venden Gorras. Esphyr Slobodkina. Tr. by Teresa Mlawer. LC 94-78493. (Illus.). 48p. (SPA.). (J). (ps-2). 1995. 14.95 (0-06-025330-4); pap. 5.95 (0-06-443401-X, HpArco Iris) HarpC Child Bks.

Se Venden Gorras: A Study Guide. Marina Petralia. Ed. by J. Friedland & R. Kessler. (Novel-Ties Ser.). (SPA.). (J). (gr. k-2). 1996. pap. text ed. 14.95 (1-56982-721-4) Lrn Links.

Se Venden Gorras: La Historia de un Vendedor Ambulante, unos Monos y Sus Travesuras. Esphry Slobodkina. Tr. by Teresa Mlawer. LC 94-78493. (Illus.). 48p. (SPA.). (J). (ps-2). 1995. pap. text ed. 10.95 incl. audio (0-694-70025-8, HpArco Iris) HarpC Child Bks.

Sea. (Information Ser.). 32p. (J). 3.50 (0-7214-1750-7, Ladybrd) Penguin.

Sea. (Information Activity Ser.). 24p. (J). 3.50 (0-7214-3442-8, Ladybrd) Penguin.

Sea. (World of Knowledge Ser.). (Illus.). 48p. (J). (gr. 1-6). 1995. text ed. 8.95 (1-56144-609-2) Modern Pub NYC.

Sea. (J). (gr. 2-6). 1996. pap. 4.99 (0-7214-5655-3, Ladybrd) Penguin.

***Sea.** Paul Aston. LC 97-24266. (True Stories Ser.). 1997. pap. text ed. 7.95 (0-8069-9661-7) Sterling.

***Sea.** Edward Bond. 80p. 1974. pap. 5.95 (0-87129-759-0, S19) Dramatic Pub.

Sea. Brian Williams. LC 92-53090. (World Around Us Ser.). (Illus.). 48p. (J). (gr. 3-8). 1992. pap. 5.95 (1-85697-815-X, Kingfisher LKC) LKC.

Sea: Excerpts from Herman Melville. Illus. by Joyce Alexander. 1970. pap. 9.00 (0-912020-15-6) Turtles Quill.

Sea: Its History & Romance, 4 vols., Set. F. Bowen. 1977. lib. bdg. 800.00 (0-8490-2581-8) Gordon Pr.

***Sea: Ocean Engineering Science, Vol. 9.** Bernard Lemehaute & Daniel M. Hanes. 1990. text ed. 0.01 (0-471-52855-2); text ed. write for info. (0-471-52856-0) Wiley.

Sea: The Earth Beneath the Sea; History, Vol. 3. Ed. by M. N. Hill. LC 80-248. 980p. 1981. reprint ed. lib. bdg. 98.00 (0-89874-099-1) Krieger.

***Sea: The Global Coastal Ocean: Processes & Methods, Vol. 10.** Kenneth H. Brink & Allan R. Robinson. (Ideas & Observations on Progress in the Study of the Sea Ser.). 416p. 1997. 79.95 (0-471-11544-4) Wiley.

Sea: The Poetry of the Earth. Michelle Levric. (Illus.). 64p. 1996. 9.98 (1-56138-506-9) Courage Bks.

Sea: Vol. 1, Physical Oceanography. Ed. by M. N. Hill. LC 80-248. 880p. 1982. reprint ed. lib. bdg. 88.00 (0-89874-097-5) Krieger.

Sea: Vol. 2, Composition of Sea Water. Ed. by M. N. Hill. LC 80-248. 570p. 1982. reprint ed. lib. bdg. 62.00 (0-89874-098-3) Krieger.

***Sea Aflame.** Nathan Miller. Date not set. write for info. (0-688-10792-3) Morrow.

Sea Aflame: A Naval History of World War II. Miller. 1995. 30.00 (0-02-584995-6) Macmillan.

Sea Alguien! Como Lograr lo Mejor de Uno Mismo. Alan L. McGinnis. Tr. by Arnoldo Canclini from ENG. 176p. (Orig.). (SPA.). 1988. pap. 7.50 (0-311-46115-8) Casa Bautista.

***Sea Alphabet.** Frederic C. Duncan. LC 91-77421. (Illus.). 1991. pap. 6.95 (0-932212-72-7) Avery Color.

Sea among the Cupboards. Maureen Seaton. 1992. pap. 7.00 (0-89823-134-5) New Rivers Pr.

Sea & Cedar: How the Northwest Coast Indians Lived. Lois McConkey. (Illus.). 32p. (J). (gr. 3-7). 1991. pap. 7.95 (0-88894-371-7) Firefly Bks Ltd.

***Sea & Coast.** Patience Coster. LC 96-44285. (Step-by-Step Ser.). (J). 1997. lib. bdg. write for info. (0-516-20353-3) Childrens.

Sea & History. Ed. by E. E. Rice. (Illus.). 224p. 1996. 63.00 (0-7509-1096-8, Pub. by Sutton Pubng UK) Bks Intl VA.

Sea & I. Harutaka Nakawatari. (Illus.). 32p. (J). (ps-3). 1992. 15.00 (0-374-36428-1) FS&G.

Sea & I. Harutaka Nakawatari. Tr. by Susan Matsui. (Illus.). 32p. (J). (ps-3). 1994. pap. 4.95 (0-374-46454-5, Sunburst Bks) FS&G.

Sea & Its Living Wonders, with Three Hundred Woodcuts & Plates. G. Hartwig. 1972. lib. bdg. 95.00 (0-8490-3066-8) Gordon Pr.

***Sea & Its Marvels.** (World Book Looks At Ser.). (J). 10.95 (0-7166-1803-6) World Bk.

***Sea & Its Marvels.** (World Book Looks At Ser.). (J). pap. 6.95 (0-7166-1811-7) World Bk.

Sea & Land: Cultural & Biological Adaptations in the Southern Coastal Plain. Ed. by James L. Peacock & James C. Sabella. LC 87-13284. (Southern Anthropological Society Proceedings Ser.: No. 21). 176p. 1988. pap. 20.00 (0-8203-0978-8) U of Ga Pr.

Sea & Me Library, 5 bks., Vols. 1 - 5. John Sammis. (Shamu's Little Library). (Illus.). 50p. (J). (ps). 1994. pap. 8.95 (1-884506-12-7) Third Story.

Sea & Other Water. rev. ed. Marlene J. McCracken & Robert A. McCracken. (Themes Ser.). (Illus.). 80p. (J). (gr. k-4). 1985. pap. 12.00 (0-920541-80-1) Peguis Pubs Ltd.

Sea & Poison. Shusaku Endo. Tr. by Michael Gallagher from JPN. LC 91-41413. (Revived Modern Classics Ser.). 176p. 1992. reprint ed. pap. 10.95 (0-8112-1198-3, NDP737) New Directions.

***Sea & Sardinia.** D. H. Lawrence. Ed. by Mara Kalnins. (Edition of the Works of D. H. Lawrence Ser.). 284p. (C). 1997. text ed. 64.95 (0-521-24275-4) Cambridge U Pr.

Sea & Shore Birds of California: California Birds. Gregory L. Foote. (Illus.). 32p. 1995. pap. 1.25 (0-935810-56-0) Primer Pubs.

Sea & the Bells. Pablo Neruda. Tr. by William O'Daly from SPA. LC 88-70585. 136p. (Orig.). 1988. pap. 10.00 (1-55659-019-9) Copper Canyon.

Sea & the Ice: A Naturalist in Antarctica. Louis J. Halle. LC 88-43303. (Illus.). 304p. 1989. pap. 15.95 (0-8014-9575-X) Cornell U Pr.

Sea & the Jungle. H. M. Tomlinson. (Marlboro Travel Ser.). 258p. 1996. pap. 14.95 (0-8101-6011-0) Marlboro Pr.

Sea & the Sand. Christopher Nicole. 1986. 19.00 (0-7278-1350-1) Severn Hse.

Sea Anemones As a Hobby. U. Erich Reiese. (Illus.). 320p. 1993. 47.95 (0-86622-539-0, TT027) TFH Pubns.

Sea Angling. Ed. by Michael Prichard. (Know the Game Ser.). (Illus.). 1976. pap. 2.50 (0-7158-0521-5) Charles River Bks.

Sea Angling: Kent to Cornwall. Mel Russ. (Illus.). 208p. 1992. pap. 8.95 (0-09-174244-7, Pub. by S Paul UK) Trafalgar.

Sea Animals. LC 91-27724. (Eye Openers Ser.). (Illus.). 24p. (J). (ps up). 1992. 8.99 (0-689-71565-X, Aladdin Paperbacks) S&S Childrens.

Sea Animals. Rick Detorie. (Magic Answer Bks.). (J). 1990. pap. 1.95 (0-8125-7319-6) Tor Bks.

Sea Animals. Amy Ericksen. LC 94-10110. (J). 1995. 5.95 (0-8118-0459-3) Chronicle Bks.

Sea Animals. Snapshot Staff. 16p. (J). 1996. pap. 4.95 (0-7894-0647-0) DK Pub Inc.

Sea Animals: A Thematic Unit. Diane Williams. Ed. by Patricia Miriani. (Thematic Units Ser.). (Illus.). 80p. (Orig.). (J). (ps-1). 1993. student ed., pap. 9.95 (1-55734-254-7) Tchr Create Mat.

Sea Animals Coloring Book. Lisa Bonforte. (Illus.). (J). (gr. k-3). 1993. pap. 1.00 (0-486-27729-1) Dover.

Sea Around Us. Rachel L. Carson. (Illus.). 278p. 1991. reprint ed. pap. 11.95 (0-19-506997-8, 6464) OUP.

Sea Around Us: Special Edition. Rachel L. Carson. (Illus.). 288p. 1989. 24.95 (0-19-506186-1) OUP.

Sea Around Us Laboratory Manual. Mark Pagani et al. 152p. (C). 1996. pap. text ed., spiral bd. 24.15 (0-7872-2001-9) Kendall-Hunt.

Sea As a Variable Star - Solar & Stellar Irradiance Variations: Proceedings of the 143rd Colloquim of the International Astronomical Union Held in Clarion Harvest House, Boulder, California, June 20-25, 1993. Ed. by Judit M. Pap. 328p. (C). 1994. lib. bdg. 155.00 (0-7923-3040-4) Kluwer Ac.

***Sea Babies: And Their Friends.** Cathleen Arone. (Illus.). 32p. (J). (ps-3). 1997. 15.95 (0-915009-56-0) World Leis Corp.

Sea Bass: Biology, Exploitation & Conservation. M. G. Pawson. 368p. (gr. 13). 1994. text ed. 99.95 (0-412-40090-1) Chapman & Hall.

Sea Battle & the Master Argument: Aristotle & Diodorus Cronus on the Metaphysics of the Future. Richard Gaskin. (Quellen und Studien zur Philosophie: Vol. 40). xii, 406p. (C). 1995. lib. bdg. 176.95 (3-11-014430-1) De Gruyter.

***Sea Battles.** John C. Wideman. LC 96-34370. (The Civil War Chronicles). 1997. write for info. (1-56799-424-5, MetroBooks) M Friedman Pub Grp Inc.

Sea Battles in Close-up: The Age of Nelson. David Lyon. (Illus.). 224p. 1996. 29.95 (1-55750-746-5) Naval Inst Pr.

Sea Battles in Close-Up: World War II. rev. ed. Martin Stephen. Ed. by Eric Grove. (Illus.). 225p. 1988. 27.95 (0-87021-556-6) Naval Inst Pr.

Sea Battles in Close-up: World War II, Vol. 2. Eric Grove. (Illus.). 224p. 1993. 27.95 (1-55750-758-9) Naval Inst Pr.

Sea-Beach at Ebb-Tide. Augusta F. Arnold. LC 68-20554. (Illus.). 490p. 1968. reprint ed. pap. 9.95 (0-486-21949-6) Dover.

Sea-Bed Nineteen Sixty-Eight, 5 Vols & Index. Ed. by Moshe Y. Sachs. 1969. 55.00 (0-685-00515-1) Ayer.

Sea-Bed Nineteen Sixty-Eight, 5 Vols & Index. Ed. by Moshe Y. Sachs. 1970. Index. 114.95 (0-405-02581-5) Ayer.

Sea-Bed Nineteen Sixty-Eight, 5 Vols & Index, Set. Ed. by Moshe Y. Sachs. 1970. 418.95 (0-405-02580-7) Ayer.

Sea-Bed Nineteen Sixty-Nine, 7 vols. Ed. by Moshe Y. Sachs. LC 73-171925. 1971. 71.50 (0-685-00516-X) Ayer.

Sea-Bed Nineteen Sixty-Nine, 7 vols. Ed. by Moshe Y. Sachs. LC 73-171925. 1971. Index. 96.95 (0-405-02595-5) Ayer.

Sea-Bed Nineteen Sixty-Nine, 7 vols, Set. Ed. by Moshe Y. Sachs. LC 73-171925. 1971. 590.00 (0-405-02587-4) Ayer.

Sea Bella con la Ayuda de la Naturaleza. Editorial America, S. A. Staff. Ed. by Maria E. Del Real. (Illus.). 264p. (Orig.). (SPA.). 1990. pap. 3.95 (0-944499-56-2) Editorial Amer.

Sea Between Us. Denise Chalem. Tr. by Danielle Brunon et al. from FRE. (Publications: No. 19). 64p. (Orig.). 1986. pap. text ed. 8.95 (0-913745-26-X) Ubu Repertory.

Sea Birds. Beth W. Brust. (Zoobooks Ser.). (J). 1991. lib. bdg. 14.95 (0-88682-416-8) Creative Ed.

Sea Birds Are Still Alive. Toni Cade Bambara. LC 82-40018. 224p. 1982. pap. 10.00 (0-394-71176-9) Random.

An Asterisk (*) at the beginning of an entry indicates that the title is appearing in BIP for the first time.

Sea Breeze & Local Winds. John E. Simpson. LC 93-29979. (Illus.). 200p. (C). 1994. text ed. 48.95 (*0-521-45211-2*) Cambridge U Pr.

Sea-Breeze Hotel. Marcia Vaughan & Patricia Mullins. LC 91-22303. (Willa Perlman Bks.). (Illus.). 32p. (J). (ps-2). 1992. 14.95 (*0-06-020488-5*); lib. bdg. 14.89 (*0-06-020504-0*) HarpC Child Bks.

Sea-Breeze Hotel. Marcia Vaughan. LC 91-22303. (Illus.). 32p. (J). (ps-2). 1995. pap. 4.95 (*0-06-443406-0*, Trophy) HarpC Child Bks.

Sea Bright Skiff & Other Shore Boats. rev. ed. Peter J. Guthorn. LC 82-62951. (Illus.). 256p. 1983. pap. 13.95 (*0-916838-73-0*) Schiffer.

Sea-Brothers: The Tradition of American Sea Fiction from Moby-Dick to the Present. Bert Bender. LC 88-17321. (Illus.). 282p. (C). 1988. pap. 18.95 (*0-8122-1339-4*) U of Pa Pr.

Sea Castles Activity Book, Unit 9. (Networks Ser.). (J). (gr. 3). 1991. 3.90 (*0-88106-772-5*, N314) Charlesbridge Pub.

Sea Castles Anthology, Unit 9. (Networks Ser.). (J). (gr. 3). 1991. 7.45 (*0-88106-770-9*, N311) Charlesbridge Pub.

Sea Cave. large type ed. Alan Scholefield. 512p. 1984. 27. 99 (*0-7089-8184-4*) Ulverscroft.

Sea Caves of Anacapa Island. David Bunnell. LC 93-22206. 207p. 1993. pap. 15.00 (*0-87461-093-1*) McNally & Loftin.

Sea Caves of Santa Cruz Island. David E. Bunnell. LC 88-37249. (Illus.). 124p. 1991. 12.00 (*0-87461-076-1*) McNally & Loftin.

Sea Chain. John E. Duncan. LC 85-73918. (Illus.). 439p. 1986. pap. 12.95 (*0-914166-23-9*) Americana Rev.

***Sea Change.** Jeannie Baker. Date not set. write for info. (*0-688-15760-2*); lib. bdg. write for info. (*0-688-15761-0*) Greenwillow.

Sea-Change. Muna Lee de Munoz-Marin. 1977. lib. bdg. 59. 95 (*0-8490-2580-X*) Gordon Pr.

Sea Change. Angela Lewis. 1971. 5.95 (*0-393-08641-0*) Norton.

***Sea Change.** Peter Nichols. LC 96-51569. 1997. 23.95 (*0-670-87179-6*) Viking Penguin.

***Sea Change.** Peter Nichols. 1998. pap. write for info. (*0-14-026413-2*) Penguin.

Sea Change. Ed. by Ralph E. West, Jr. 1980. teacher ed. 9.28 (*0-8013-0100-9*, 75764); student ed. 14.60 (*0-88334-126-3*, 76100) Longman.

***Sea Change: Across the Atlantic in a Wooden Boat.** Peter Nichols. 1997. 23.95 (*0-614-28022-2*, Viking) Viking Penguin.

Sea Change: Pacific Asia As the New World Industrial Center. James Abegglen. 320p. 1994. 27.95 (*0-02-900155-2*, Free Press) Free Pr.

Sea Change: The Message of the Oceans. Sylvia A. Earle. 384p. 1996. pap. 12.95 (*0-449-91065-2*) Fawcett.

Sea-Change of the Old Testament in the New. J. Duncan Derrett. (Studies in the New Testament: Vol. 5). xii, 245p. 1989. text ed. 80.00 (*90-04-09110-6*) E J Brill.

Sea Changes: British Emigration & American Literature. Stephen Fender. (Cambridge Studies in American Literature & Culture: No. 55). (Illus.). 300p. (C). 1992. text ed. 59.95 (*0-521-41175-0*) Cambridge U Pr.

Sea Changes: Culture & Feminism. Cora Kaplan. Ed. by Michele Barrett et al. (Questions for Feminism Ser.). 240p. 1987. 44.95 (*0-86091-151-9*, Pub. by Verso UK) Routledge Chapman & Hall.

Sea Changes: Culture & Feminism. Cora Kaplan. Ed. by Michele Barrett et al. (Questions for Feminism Ser.). 240p. (C). 1987. pap. text ed. 19.00 (*0-86091-864-5*, Pub. by Vrso UK) Norton.

Sea City, Here We Come! Ann M. Martin. (Baby-Sitters Club Super Special Ser.: No. 10). 240p. (J). (gr. 4-6). 1993. pap. 4.50 (*0-590-45674-1*) Scholastic Inc.

Sea Cliffs, Beaches, & Coastal Valleys of San Diego County: Some Amazing Histories & Some Horrifying Implications. Gerald G. Kuhn & Francis P. Shepard. (Illus.). 204p. 1991. pap. 15.95 (*0-520-07433-5*) U CA Pr.

Sea Coast of Bohemia: Literary Life in Sydney's Roaring Twenties. Peter Kirkpatrick. (Orig.). 1992. pap. 16.95 (*0-7022-2432-4*, Pub. by Univ Queensland Pr AT) Intl Spec Bk.

Sea Commonwealth, & Other Papers. Imperial Studies. Ed. by Arthur P. Newton. LC 68-22114. (Essay Index Reprint Ser.). 1977. 12.95 (*0-8369-0742-6*) Ayer.

Sea Condor - Dusty Sun. Eugenia Macer-Story. 62p. 1994. pap. 12.95 (*1-879980-06-1*) Magick Mirror.

Sea Creatures. LC 92-54274. (What's Inside? Ser.). (Illus.). 24p. (J). (gr. k-3). 1993. 8.95 (*1-56458-221-3*) DK Pub Inc.

Sea Creatures. Judy Nayer. (At Your Fingertips Ser.). (Illus.). 10p. (J). (ps-3). 1992. bds. 6.95 (*1-56293-222-5*) McClanahan Bk.

Sea Creatures. Lorna Read. (Look & Learn Ser.). (Illus.). 12p. (J). (ps). 1996. bds. 4.98 (*1-85854-388-6*) Brimax Bks.

Sea Cries over My Shoulder. Jonathan Russell. LC 91-70968. 1991. 12.95 (*0-8158-0472-5*) Chris Mass.

***Sea Cucumbers of British Columbia: Including Puget Sound & Southern Alaska.** Philip Lambert. (Illus.). 192p. 1997. pap. 24.95 (*0-7748-0607-9*, Pub. by U BC Pr) U of Wash Pr.

Sea Devil. Richard P. Henrick. 1990. mass mkt. 4.50 (*0-8217-3089-4*, Zebra Kensgtn) Kensgtn Pub Corp.

***Sea Devils.** Skip Williams. 1997. 20.00 (*0-7869-0643-X*) TSR Inc.

Sea Devils: Italian Navy Commandos in World War II. J. Valerio Borghese. Ed. by Jack Sweetman. LC 95-32082. (Classics of Naval Literature Ser.). (Illus.). 264p. 1995. 32.95 (*1-55750-072-X*) Naval Inst Pr.

Sea Dogs, Clowns, & Gypsies. Fatty Goodlander. 64p. 1991. pap. 8.50 (*0-9631060-2-3*) Am Paradise.

Sea-Doo Water Vehicles, 1988-1994. Intertec Publishing Staff. 1993. pap. 34.95 (*0-89287-646-8*, W809) Clymer Pub.

***Sea-Doo Water Vehicles, 1988-1996.** (Illus.). (Orig.). Date not set. pap. 34.95 (*0-89287-691-3*, W809-3) Intertec Pub.

Sea Dragons & Rainbow Runners: Exploring Fish with Children. Suzanne Samson. LC 95-69269. (Illus.). 40p. (J). (gr. 1-5). 1995. pap. 10.95 (*1-57098-052-7*) R Rinehart.

Sea Dream. Kerry J. Baidin. LC 96-96000. (Illus.). iv, 125p. (Orig.). 1996. pap. 15.95 (*0-9651110-0-8*) K J Baidin.

Sea Drift: Full Score for Orchestra. A. Carpenter. 40p. 1989. pap. 15.00 (*0-7935-3610-3*, 50488512) H Leonard.

Sea-Dumped Chemical Weapons - Aspects, Problems & Solutions: Proceedings of the NATO Advanced Research Workshop on 'Sea-Dumped Chemical Munitions', Kaliningrad (Moscow Region), Russia, Jan. 12-15. North Atlantic Treaty Organization Staff. Ed. by Alexander V. Kaffka. LC 96-18909. (NATO Advanced Science Institutes). 184p. (C). 1996. lib. bdg. 99.00 (*0-7923-4090-6*) Kluwer Ac.

Sea Edge. large type ed. W. Phillip Keller. (Large Print Inspirational Ser.). 176p. 1986. pap. 9.95 (*0-8027-2533-3*) Walker & Co.

Sea Elf. Ed. by Joanne Ryder. LC 92-27608. (Just for a Day Book). (Illus.). 32p. (J). (gr. k up). 1993. 15.00 (*0-688-10060-0*, Morrow Junior) Morrow.

Sea Exploring Manual. Boy Scouts of America. 272p. (YA). (gr. 6-12). 1987. pap. 12.85 (*0-8395-3239-3*, 33239) BSA.

Sea Fairies. L. Frank Baum. (Illus.). 240p. (J). (gr. 3 up). 1987. 24.95 (*0-929605-03-9*); pap. 12.95 (*0-929605-00-4*) Books Wonder.

Sea Fare Cookbook. Ed. by G. Carmichael et al. 184p. 1992. pap. 17.50 (*0-913235-82-2*) Am Fisheries Soc.

Sea Fever. large type unabridged ed. (Harlequin Ser.). 1990. lib. bdg. 18.95 (*0-263-12378-2*, Pub. by Mills & Boon UK) Thorndike Pr.

Sea Fighters from Drake to Farragut. Jessie P. Frothingham. LC 67-26743. (Essay Index Reprint Ser.). 1977. 27.95 (*0-8369-0461-3*) Ayer.

Sea Fighters from Drake to Farragut. Jessie P. Frothingham. LC 67-26743. (Essay Index Reprint Ser.). reprint ed. lib. bdg. 18.00 (*0-8290-0838-1*) Irvington.

Sea Fire. 1994. pap. 17.95 (*0-7871-0245-8*, Dove Bks) Dove Audio.

Sea Fire. Karen Robards. 416p. 1991. mass mkt., pap. text ed. 4.95 (*0-8439-3121-3*) Dorchester Pub Co.

***Sea Fisheries in Scotland.** James R. Coull. 336p. 1996. 90. 00 (*0-85976-410-9*, Pub. by J Donald UK) St Mut.

Sea Flame. Katharine Kincaid. 1989. pap. 3.75 (*0-8217-2567-X*) NAL-Dutton.

Sea Flavor. Hayden S. Pearson. LC 68-58809. (Essay Index Reprint Ser.). 1977. 15.95 (*0-8369-0051-0*) Ayer.

Sea Flavor. Hayden S. Pearson. (American Autobiography Ser.). 178p. 1995. reprint ed. lib. bdg. 69.00 (*0-7812-8613-1*) Rprt Serv.

Sea Floor: An Introduction to Marine Biology. E. Seibold & W. H. Berger. (Illus.). 288p. 1982. pap. 43.00 (*0-387-11256-1*) Spr-Verlag.

Sea Floor: An Introduction to Marine Geology. 2nd ed. E. Seibold & W. H. Berger. (Illus.). 320p. 1993. 49.00 (*0-387-56884-0*) Spr-Verlag.

Sea Floor: An Introduction to Marine Geology. 3rd ed. E. Seibold & W. H. Berger. (Illus.). 372p. 1996. 54.95 (*3-540-60191-0*) Spr-Verlag.

Sea Floor Spreading & Continental Drift. J. Coulomb. Tr. by R. W. Tanner from FRE. LC 79-179891. (Geophysics & Astrophysics Monographs: No. 2). 184p. 1972. lib. bdg. 82.50 (*90-277-0232-2*) Kluwer Ac.

Sea Foam, Jacquard. 80p. 1990. 3.00 (*0-9620519-6-9*) Iris Bks.

Sea Fog. B. Wang. (Illus.). 336p. 1985. 139.00 (*0-387-13150-7*) Spr-Verlag.

Sea Forces of the World: Military Force. 1990. 9.99 (*0-517-69129-9*) Random Hse Value.

Sea Full of Sharks. 1997. pap. 4.99 (*0-590-43101-3*) Scholastic Inc.

***Sea Full of Sharks.** Betsy Maestro & Giulio Maestro. (Illus.). (FRE.). (J). pap. 7.99 (*0-590-74409-7*) Scholastic Inc.

Sea Fury, Firefly & Sea Venom in Australian Service. Stewart Wilson. (Illus.). 155p. 1994. pap. 22.95 (*1-875671-05-6*, Pub. by Australian Aviation AT) Motorbooks Intl.

***Sea Gift.** Ashby. 1997. 14.95 (*0-395-77603-1*) Ticknor & Fields.

Sea Girl: Playscript. Francis Elitzig. (Orig.). (J). 1993. pap. 5.00 (*0-87602-318-9*) Anchorage.

Sea Girl & the Dragon King: A Chinese Folktale. Hildebrandt. 1998. 16.00 (*0-689-80540-3*) S&S Childrens.

Sea Grammar. John Smith. LC 68-54664. (English Experience Ser.: No. 5). 76p. 1968. reprint ed. 30.00 (*90-221-0005-7*) Walter J Johnson.

***Sea Gull.** rev. ed. Jean-Claude Van Itallie. 1997. pap. 5.25 (*0-8222-1588-8*) Dramatists Play.

Sea Gypsies of Malaya: An Account of the Nomadic Mawken Pople of the Mergui Archipelago. Walter G. White. LC 77-87082. (Illus.). 318p. reprint ed. 52.50 (*0-404-16878-7*) AMS Pr.

Sea Gypsy. R. Anderson. 1980. pap. 1.50 (*0-373-58052-5*) Harlequin Bks.

Sea Gypsy. Fern Michaels. (Best of the Best Ser.). (C). 1993. mass mkt. 4.50 (*0-373-48275-2*, 5-48275-7) Silhouette.

***Sea Hag's Treasure.** Melody Carlson. LC 96-37886. (Illus.). 48p. (J). (ps-3). 1997. 12.99 (*1-57673-055-7*, Gold & Honey) Multnomah Pubs.

Sea Harrier: BAe Sea Harrier, FRS Mk1. (Aeroguide Ser.: No. 3). 1984. pap. 6.00 (*0-918805-02-3*) Pac Aero Pr.

Sea Harrier over the Falklands: A Maverick at War. Sharkey Ward. 299p. 1993. 29.95 (*1-55750-756-2*) Naval Inst Pr.

Sea-Harrower. Abigail Clements. (Orig.). 1980. pap. 2.25 (*0-449-14326-0*, GM) Fawcett.

Sea Has Many Voices: Oceans Policy for a Complex World. Ed. by Cynthia Lamson. 368p. 1994. 49.95 (*0-7735-1112-1*, Pub. by McGill CN) U of Toronto Pr.

Sea Hawk. Ed. by Rudy Behlmer. LC 81-70418. (Wisconsin-Warner Bros. Screenplay Ser.). (Illus.). 244p. 1982. 11.95 (*0-299-09010-8*); pap. 6.95 (*0-299-09014-0*) U of Wis Pr.

Sea Hawk. Manohar Malgonkar. (Orient Paperbacks Ser.). 293p. 1980. 9.95 (*0-86578-136-2*); pap. 4.95 (*0-86578-069-2*) Ind-US Inc.

Sea-Hawk. Rafael Sabatini. 1994. lib. bdg. 21.95 (*1-56849-483-1*) Buccaneer Bks.

Sea History's Guide to American & Canadian Maritime Museums. 2nd ed. Joseph M. Stanford. (Illus.). 113p. 1990. pap. 11.50 (*0-930248-03-1*) Sea Hist Pr.

Sea Horse. Bonnie Bryant. (Saddle Club Ser.: No. 14). 144p. (J). (gr. 4-7). 1991. mass mkt. 3.99 (*0-553-15847-3*) Bantam.

Sea Horse. Rebecca Stefoff. LC 96-6212. (Living Things Ser.). (Illus.). 32p. (J). (gr. 1 up). 1996. lib. bdg. 14.95 (*0-7614-0116-4*, Benchmark NY) Marshall Cavendish.

Sea Horse, Sea Horse. Abbie Dee & Annie Scott. (Emergent Reader Ser.). 10p. (J). (ps-1). 1991. pap. text ed. 4.25 (*1-56843-079-5*) BGR Pub.

Sea Horse, Sea Horse: Big Book. Abbie Dee & Annie Scott. (Emergent Reader Ser.). 10p. (J). (ps-1). 1991. pap. text ed. 21.00 (*1-56843-031-0*) BGR Pub.

***Sea Hunt.** Berres et al. (Deep Sea Adventure Ser.). 10.00 (*0-614-30522-5*) NAVH.

***Sea Hunters.** Cussler. 1997. mass mkt. 7.99 (*0-671-00180-9*) PB.

Sea Hunters. Clive Cussler & Craig Dirgo. LC 96-28656. 368p. 1996. 24.00 (*0-684-83027-2*) S&S Trade.

***Sea Hunters.** Clive Cussler. 1997. mass mkt. 7.99 (*0-614-27775-2*, Pocket Star Bks) PB.

***Sea Hunters: True Adventures with Famous Shipwrecks.** large type ed. Clive Cussler & Craig Dirgo. LC 96-49136. 1997. 26.95 (*1-56895-407-7*) Wheeler Pub.

***Sea Hunters of Indonesia: Fishers & Weavers of Lamalera.** R. H. Barnes. (Oxford Studies in Social & Cultural Anthropology). (Illus.). 448p. 1997. 98.00 (*0-19-828070-X*) OUP.

Sea, Ice & Rock. Chris Bonington & Robin Knox-Johnston. LC 93-14786. (Illus.). 144p. 1993. 24.95 (*0-924486-48-1*) Sheridan.

Sea Ice Biota. Ed. by Rita A. Horner. 224p. 1985. 130.00 (*0-8493-6578-3*, QH95, CRC Reprint) Franklin.

Sea Ice Ecosystem. I. A. Melnikov. 220p. 1997. text ed. 75. 00 (*2-919875-04-3*) Gordon & Breach.

Sea in Soviet Strategy. 2nd ed. Bryan Ranft & Geoffrey Till. LC 88-61128. (Illus.). 275p. 1988. 32.95 (*0-87021-992-8*) Naval Inst Pr.

Sea in the Desert: Explorer's Guide to the Gulf of California Seaside. Nonie McKibbin. Ed. by Jenean Thomson et al. (Illus.). 130p. (Orig.). 1989. 10.00 (*0-685-34742-7*) Golden Puffer.

Sea in the Pre-Columbian World: Conference at Dumbarton Oaks, October 26 & 27, 1974. Ed. by Elizabeth P. Benson. LC 76-58217. (Illus.). 188p. 1977. 18.00 (*0-88402-071-1*) Dumbarton Oaks.

Sea Is All about Us: A Guide to Marine Environments of Cape Ann & Other Northern New England Waters. Sarah F. Robbins & Clarice Yentsch. 1973. pap. 10.95 (*0-87577-046-0*, Peabody Museum) Peabody Essex Mus.

Sea Is My Blanket. Helen Webber. (Illus.). (J). (gr. k-6). 1968. 8.95 (*0-8392-3057-5*) Astor-Honor.

Sea Island Lady. Francis Griswold. 24.95 (*0-685-06833-1*) Beaufort SC.

Sea Island Mathematical Manual: Surveying & Mathematics in Ancient China. Frank J. Swetz. 80p. 1992. text ed. 25.00 (*0-271-00795-8*); pap. text ed. 9.95 (*0-271-00799-0*) Pa St U Pr.

Sea Island Roots: African Presence in the Carolinas & Georgia: Testimonies of African Cultural Continuity. Keith E. Baird & Mary A. Twining. LC 88-70201. 325p. 1990. 45.00 (*0-86543-068-3*); pap. 12.95 (*0-86543-069-1*) Africa World.

Sea Island Seasons Cookbook. Ed. by Pearson & Trask. (Illus.). 1995. reprint ed. 14.95 (*0-9647460-1-8*) Beaufort County.

Sea Island to City: A Study of St. Helena Islanders in Harlem & Other Urban Centers. Clyde V. Kiser. LC 32-34112. (Columbia University. Studies in the Social Sciences: No. 368). reprint ed. 20.00 (*0-404-51368-9*) AMS Pr.

Sea Island Yankee. Clyde Bresee. (Illus.). 300p. (C). 1995. reprint ed. pap. 12.95 (*1-57003-095-2*) U of SC Pr.

Sea Jewel. Penelope Neri. 496p. 1986. mass mkt. 3.95 (*0-8217-1888-6*, Zebra Kensgtn) Kensgtn Pub Corp.

***Sea Kayaker's Deep Trouble: True Stories & Their Lessons from Sea Kayaker Magazine.** George Gronseth & Matt Broze. Ed. by Chris Cunningham. LC 97-15179. (Illus.). 176p. 1997. pap. text ed. 14.95 (*0-07-008499-8*) McGraw.

Sea Kayaker's Guide to Mt. Desert Island. Jennifer Paigen. LC 97-6534. (Illus.). 160p. (Orig.). 1997. pap. 14.95 (*0-89272-380-7*) Down East.

Sea Kayakers Trip Planner & Log Book. Richard S. Hendey, III et al. (Illus.). 96p. (Orig.). 1996. 16.00 (*0-9651229-1-3*) Go There.

Sea Kayaking. Nigel Foster. 96p. (C). 1990. text ed. 59.00 (*0-906754-60-7*, Pub. by Fernhurst Bks UK) St Mut.

Sea Kayaking: A Manual for Long-Distance Touring. enl. rev. ed. John Dowd. LC 88-2744. (Illus.). 304p. 1988. pap. 18.95 (*0-295-96630-0*) U of Wash Pr.

***Sea Kayaking: A Manual for Long-Distance Touring.** expanded rev. ed. John Dowd. (Illus.). 304p. 1997. pap. 18.95 (*0-295-97622-5*) U of Wash Pr.

Sea Kayaking along the Mid-Atlantic Coast: Coastal Paddling Adventures from New York to Chesapeake Bay. Tamsin Venn. (Illus.). 240p. 1994. pap. 14.95 (*1-878239-31-7*) AMC Books.

Sea Kayaking along the New England Coast. Tamsin Venn. LC 90-41633. (Illus.). 240p. 1990. pap. 14.95 (*1-878239-04-X*) AMC Books.

Sea Kayaking Canada's West Coast. John Ince & Hedi Kottner. (Illus.). 240p. (Orig.). 1989. pap. 14.95 (*0-9691064-0-8*) Gordon Soules Bk.

Sea Kayaking Canada's West Coast. John Ince & Hedi Kottner. (Orig.). 1992. pap. 14.95 (*0-89886-342-2*) Mountaineers.

Sea Kayaking in Baja. Andromeda Romano-Lax. LC 93-27790. 144p. 1993. pap. 13.95 (*0-89997-157-1*) Wilderness Pr.

Sea Kayaking in Florida. David Gluckman. LC 94-39198. (Illus.). 186p. (Orig.). 1995. pap. 14.95 (*1-56164-071-9*) Pineapple Pr.

***Sea Kayaking the Carolinas.** James Bannon & Morrison Giffen. (Illus.). 220p. (Orig.). 1997. pap. 15.00 (*0-9648584-3-6*) Out There Pr.

Sea King: Sir Francis Drake and His Times. Albert Marrin. (J). (gr. 5-9). 1995. 20.00 (*0-689-31887-1*, Atheneum Bks Young) S&S Childrens.

Sea King: Westland Sea King HAR Mk3. (Aeroguide Ser.: No. 10). 1985. pap. 5.50 (*0-918805-09-0*) Pac Aero Pr.

Sea King's Daughter. Shepard. 1997. 17.00 (*0-689-80759-7*) S&S Childrens.

Sea Kings of the Purple Towns. Mark Morrison. (Elric Roleplaying Game Ser.). (Illus.). 1993. pap. 18.95 (*1-56882-000-3*, 2114) Chaosium.

Sea Language Comes Ashore. Joanna C. Colcord. Ed. by Richard M. Dorsen. (International Folklore Ser.). 1977. reprint ed. lib. bdg. 19.95 (*0-405-10089-2*) Ayer.

Sea-Launched Cruise Missiles & U. S. Security. Eric H. Arnett. LC 90-27515. 224p. 1991. text ed. 55.00 (*0-275-93716-X*, C3716, Praeger Pubs) Greenwood.

***Sea Law.** 1994. 22.00 (*1-55806-202-5*) Iron Crown Ent Inc.

Sea-Lawyers. H. G. Kildore. 250p. 1995. 85.00 (*1-882727-09-6*) Bells & Whistles.

***Sea Legs: Hitch-Hiking the Coast of Ireland Alone.** Rosita Boland. 272p. 9200. pap. 14.95 (*1-874597-00-6*) Dufour.

Sea Leopard. Craig Thomas. 528p. 1990. mass mkt. 5.50 (*0-06-100088-4*, Harp PBks) HarpC.

Sea Leopard. large type ed. Craig Thomas. 1984. 27.99 (*0-7089-8197-6*) Ulverscroft.

Sea Level. Suzanne Matson. LC 90-4952. 72p. (Orig.). 1990. pap. 9.95 (*0-914086-84-7*) Alicejamesbooks.

Sea-Level Change. National Research Council Staff. (Studies in Geophysics). 256p. 1990. text ed. 29.95 (*0-309-04039-6*) Natl Acad Pr.

Sea Level Changes: An Integrated Approach. Ed. by Cheryl K. Wilgus et al. (Special Publications: No. 42). 400p. 1988. text ed. 75.50 (*0-918985-74-9*) SEPM.

Sea Level Changes: Determination & Effects. Ed. by P. L. Woodworth et al. LC 92-38038. (Geophysical Monograph Ser.: Vol. 69). 1993. 30.00 (*0-87590-460-2*) Am Geophysical.

Sea Level Changes: The Last 20,000 Years. Pirazzoli. LC 96-25986. (Coastal Morphology & Research Ser.). 1996. pap. text ed. 35.00 (*0-471-96913-3*) Wiley.

Sea-Level Fluctuations & Coastal Evolution. Ed. by Dag Nummedal et al. (Special Publications: No. 41). 276p. 1987. 45.00 (*0-918985-71-4*) SEPM.

***Sea-Level Research: A Manual for the Collection & Evaluation of Data.** Ed. by Van De Plassche. (Illus.). 1986. text ed. 140.95 (*0-86094-187-6*, Chap & Hall NY) Chapman & Hall.

Sea-Level Rise & Coastal Subsidence: Causes, Consequences, & Strategies. Ed. by John D. Milliman & Bilil U. Haq. (Coastal Systems & Continental Margins Ser.: Vol. 2). 384p. (C). 1996. lib. bdg. 189.00 (*0-7923-3933-9*) Kluwer Ac.

Sea Levels, Land Levels, & Tide Gauges. K. O. Emery & D. G. Aubrey. (Illus.). 432p. 1994. 71.95 (*0-387-97449-0*) Spr-Verlag.

Sea Life. (Quizmasters Ser.). (Illus.). 96p. (J). (ps-4). 1994. write for info. (*1-56458-795-9*) DK Pub Inc.

Sea Life. (Science Safari Ser.). (Illus.). 20p. (J). (gr. k up). 1990. 4.95 (*0-88679-818-3*) Educ Insights.

Sea Life. (Giant Step Picture Library). (Illus.). 16p. (J). (gr. k up). 1990. 9.95 (*0-88679-662-8*) Educ Insights.

Sea Life. (Animal Fun Bks.). 48p. (J). (gr. 3 up). 1990. 1.95 (*0-88679-812-4*) Educ Insights.

Sea Life. 85p. 1981. write for info. (*0-9607580-3-8*) S Stafford.

***Sea Life.** Carol Wawrychuk & Cherie McSweeney. (Hands-On Projects Ser.). (Illus.). 40p. (Orig.). (J). (ps-k). 1997. pap. 7.95 (*1-57612-015-5*, MM2046) Monday Morning Bks.

Sea Life at the Ocean's Edge. Julia Corbett. Ed. by Shirley T. Moore & Hank Warren. (Illus.). 24p. (J). (gr. 4-6). 1984. pap. text ed. 2.95 (*0-914019-04-X*) NW Interpretive.

***Sea Life Follow the Dots.** B. A. Levy. (J). (ps-3). 1997. mass mkt. 1.00 (*0-486-29446-3*) Dover.

Sea Life in Nelson's Time. John Masefield. LC 75-75513. (Select Bibliographies Reprint Ser.). 1977. 24.95 (*0-8369-5011-9*) Ayer.

Sea Life in 5-D Stereograms. Ed. by Stephen Schutz & Susan P. Schutz. 1995. 12.95 (*0-88396-414-7*) Blue Mtn Pr CO.

S

***Sea Life Mazes.** Phillip. (J). (ps-3). 1997. mass mkt. 1.00 (*0-486-29422-6*) Dover.

Sea Life of Britain & Ireland. Elizabeth Wood. (Illus.). 240p. (C). 1995. pap. 45.00 (*0-907151-33-7*, Pub. by IMMEL Pubng UK) St Mut.

Sea Life Stained Glass Coloring Book. Llyn Hunter. (Illus.). (J). (gr. k-3). 1990. pap. 3.95 (*0-486-26492-0*) Dover.

Sea Lion. Caroline Arnold. LC 93-27007. (Illus.). 48p. (J). 1994. 15.00 (*0-688-12027-X*, Morrow Junior); lib. bdg. 14.93 (*0-688-12028-8*, Morrow Junior) Morrow.

Sea Lion. Ken Kesey. (Illus.). 48p. (J). 1995. pap. 4.99 (*0-14-054950-1*) Puffin Bks.

Sea Lion. Ken Kesey. (Illus.). 48p. (J). (ps up). 1991. pap. 14.95 (*0-670-83916-7*) Viking Child Bks.

Sea Lion: A Mischievous Mermaid. Joelle Pichon. LC 96-17855. (Animal Close-ups Ser.). (Illus.). 28p. (J). (ps-3). 1997. pap. 6.95 (*0-88106-438-6*) Charlesbridge Pub.

Sea Lion Called Salena. Dayle C. Gaetz. (Illus.). 128p. (Orig.). (J). 1994. pap. 7.95 (*0-88865-069-8*, Pub. by Pacific Educ Pr CN) Orca Bk Pubs.

***Sea Lion Roars.** C. Drew Lamm. (Smithsonian Oceanic Collection). (Illus.). 32p. (J). (gr. 1-4). 1997. 15.95 (*1-56899-400-1*); 4.95 (*1-56899-401-X*); 19.95 incl. audio (*1-56899-406-0*); audio 5.00 (*1-56899-402-8*) Soundprints.

***Sea Lion Roars, Incl. Large Toy.** C. Drew Lamm. (Smithsonian Oceanic Collection). (Illus.). 32p. (J). (gr. 1-4). 1997. 34.95 incl. audio (*1-56899-405-2*) Soundprints.

***Sea Lion Roars, Incls. Large Book & Large Toy.** C. Drew Lamm. (Smithsonian Oceanic Collection). (Illus.). (J). (gr. 1-4). 1997. 29.95 (*1-56899-403-6*) Soundprints.

***Sea Lion Roars, Incls. Small Book & Small Toy.** C. Drew Lamm. (Smithsonian Oceanic Collection). (Illus.). 32p. (J). (gr. 1-4). 1997. 9.95 (*1-56899-404-4*) Soundprints.

Sea Lions. Sarah Palmer. (Sea Mammal Discovery Library). (Illus.). 24p. (J). (gr. k-5). 1989. lib. bdg. 11.94 (*0-86592-362-0*); lib. bdg. 8.95 (*0-685-58622-7*) Rourke Corp.

Sea Lions. James Fenimore Cooper. Ed. by Warren S. Walker. LC 65-18416. (Illus.). 533p. reprint ed. 152.00 (*0-8357-9714-7*, 2016027) Bks Demand.

Sea Loads on Ships & Offshore Structures. O. Faltinsen. (Ocean Technology Ser.: No. 1). (Illus.). 300p. (C). 1993. pap. text ed. 44.95 (*0-521-45870-6*) Cambridge U Pr.

Sea-Lords of Gondor. John B. Morin. Ed. by Peter C. Fenlon, Jr. (Middle-Earth Campaign Module Ser.). 64p. (Orig.). (YA). (gr. 10-12). 1987. pap. 12.00 (*0-915795-88-4*, 3400) Iron Crown Ent Inc.

Sea-Lulled Rocky Mountain Isle. Cynthia Frank. Ed. by Stella Monday. (Illus.). 1977. pap. 2.00 (*0-918510-00-7*) Monday Bks.

Sea Maiden. Doris J. Bayles. 360p. 1995. mass mkt. 5.99 (*1-896329-08-X*, Pub. by Comnwlth Pub CN) Partners Pubs Grp.

Sea Maidens of Japan. Lili Bell. LC 96-16132. (Illus.). 32p. (J). 1997. 14.95 (*1-57102-095-0*, Ideals Child) Hambleton-Hill.

Sea Mammal Discovery Library, 6 bks., Reading Level 2. Sarah Palmer. (Illus.). 144p. (J). (gr. k-5). 1989. lib. bdg. 53.70 (*0-685-58759-2*) Rourke Corp.

Sea Mammal Discovery Library, 6 bks., Set, Reading Level 2. Sarah Palmer. (Illus.). 144p. (J). (gr. k-5). 1989. Set. lib. bdg. 71.60 (*0-86592-357-4*) Rourke Corp.

Sea Mammals. Anita Ganeri. LC 93-19706. (Pointers Ser.). (Illus.). 32p. (J). (gr. 4-6). 1993. lib. bdg. 22.83 (*0-8114-6159-9*) Raintree Steck-V.

Sea Mammals. Anita Ganeri. (Pointers Ser.). (J). 1995. pap. text ed. 4.95 (*0-8114-9361-X*) Raintree Steck-V.

Sea Mammals Activity Book. (Illus.). (J). (ps-6). pap. 2.95 (*0-565-00974-5*, Pub. by Natural Hist Mus UK) Parkwest Pubns.

Sea Mammals-Coloring Book. (J). 1985. pap. 4.95 (*0-88388-067-9*) Bellerophon Bks.

Sea Man. Jane Yolen. LC 95-52051. (Illus.). (J). 1997. 14.95 (*0-399-22939-6*, Philomel Bks) Putnam Pub Group.

Sea-Mans Practice. Richard Norwood. LC 74-28877. (English Experience Ser.: No. 755). 1975. reprint ed. 30.00 (*90-221-0755-8*) Walter J Johnson.

***Sea-Mark: The Metaphorical Voyage, Spenser to Milton.** Philip Edwards. 240p. 1997. 41.95 (*0-85323-512-0*, Pub. by Lverpool Univ Pr UK) Intl Spec Bk.

***Sea-Mark: The Metaphorical Voyage, Spenser to Milton.** Philip Edwards. 240p. 1997. pap. 19.95 (*0-85323-522-8*, Pub. by Lverpool Univ Pr UK) Intl Spec Bk.

***Sea Mistress.** large type ed. Iris Gower. (Magna Large Print Ser.). 539p. 1996. 25.99 (*0-7505-1028-5*, Pub. by Magna Print Bks UK) Ulverscroft.

Sea Modes. S. Glick. 1994. pap. 4.95 (*0-7935-4292-8*, 00372362) H Leonard.

Sea Monster: A Tale from the Pacific Northwest. Illus. by Christopher Aja. LC 96-5123. (J). 1998. write for info. (*0-15-200619-2*) HarBrace.

***Sea Monster Tattoo.** Ruth Thomas. 176p. (Orig.). 1997. pap. 16.00 (*0-7486-6226-X*, Pub. by Polygon UK) Subterranean Co.

Sea Monsters, Ancient Reptiles That Ruled the Sea. David Eldridge. LC 79-87964. (Illus.). 32p. (J). (gr. 3-6). 1980. pap. 2.95 (*0-89375-244-4*) Troll Communs.

Sea Moods. Margery M. Johnson. (Illus.). 128p. 1994. pap. 10.00 (*1-56474-107-9*) Fithian Pr.

Sea-Mountain: Cascade Head-Salmon River Anthology. The Oregon Coast. Fred Barrett. LC 93-71456. (Illus.). 108p. 1993. pap. 19.95 (*0-9636614-8-5*) Alder Pr OR.

Sea Nation. Karl Roebling. (Illus.). 245p. 1987. 14.95 (*0-942910-14-1*) Dynapress.

Sea Never Changes: My Singlehanded Trimaran Race Around the World. Olivier De Kersauson. Tr. by Alison Anderson from FRE. (Illus.). 212p. 1992. pap. 17.95 (*0-924486-22-8*) Sheridan.

Sea of Becoming: Approaches to the Fiction of Esther Tusquets. Ed. by Mary S. Vasquez. LC 90-38409. (Contributions in Women's Studies: No. 118). 248p. 1990. text ed. 49.95 (*0-313-26332-9*, VAA, Greenwood Pr) Greenwood.

***Sea of Blood.** TSR Inc. Staff. 1997. 12.95 (*0-7869-0772-X*) TSR Inc.

***Sea of Connection.** Beatrice Ganley. (Illus.). 195p. 1996. 30.00 (*0-9657009-0-9*) Heirloom Pub NY.

***Sea of Connection.** Beatrice Ganley. (Illus.). 195p. (Orig.). 1996. pap. 20.00 (*0-9657009-1-7*) Heirloom Pub NY.

Sea of Cortez: A Leisurely Journal of Travel & Research. John Steinbeck & Edward F. Ricketts. (Illus.). 640p. 1972. reprint ed. 40.00 (*0-911858-08-3*) Appel.

Sea of Cortez & Other Plays. John Steppling. LC 96-31616. (Sun & Moon Classics/American Theater in Literature Ser.: No. 96). 350p. 1996. pap. 14.95 (*1-55713-237-2*) Sun & Moon CA.

Sea of Death. Jorge Amado. Tr. by Gregory Rabassa. 288p. 1989. pap. 7.95 (*0-380-75478-9*) Avon.

Sea of Death. Richard P. Henrick. 1992. mass mkt. 4.99 (*0-8217-3742-2*, Zebra Kensgtn) Kensgtn Pub Corp.

Sea of Faith. Don Cupitt. (Illus.). 286p. 1988. text ed. 54.95 (*0-521-34420-4*) Cambridge U Pr.

***Sea of Fire.** Carol Caldwell. 352p. 1997. mass mkt. 4.99 (*0-7860-0363-4*, Pinncle Kensgtn) Kensgtn Pub Corp.

Sea of Galilee Boat: An Extraordinary 2000 Year Old Discovery. Shelley Wachsmann. (Illus.). 418p. 1995. 24.95 (*0-306-44950-1*) Da Capo.

Sea of Glass. Barry B. Longyear. 384p. 1988. pap. 3.50 (*0-380-70055-7*) Avon.

Sea of Gold & Other Tales from Japan. Marianne Yamaguchi. LC 87-72797. (Illus.). 144p. (J). (gr. 7-12). 1988. reprint ed. pap. 8.95 (*0-88739-056-0*) Creat Arts Bk.

Sea of Grass. Conrad Richter. 1937. 13.95 (*0-394-44397-7*) Knopf.

Sea of Grass. Conrad Richter. LC 92-5181. 149p. (C). 1992. reprint ed. pap. 9.95 (*0-8214-1026-1*) Ohio U Pr.

Sea of Grass: The Maritime Drug War, 1970-1990. Charles M. Fuss, Jr. LC 96-16534. (Illus.). 352p. 1996. 31.95 (*1-55750-276-5*) Naval Inst Pr.

Sea of Lentils. Antonio Benitez-Rojo. Tr. by James E. Maraniss from SPA. LC 90-31381. 204p. 1990. 30.00 (*0-87023-723-3*); pap. 15.95 (*0-87023-754-3*) U of Mass Pr.

Sea of Light. Jenifer Levin. LC 93-45971. 400p. 1994. pap. 10.95 (*0-452-27059-6*, Plume) NAL-Dutton.

Sea of My Infancy. Ernesto Diaz-Rodriguez. Ed. by Belkis C. Male. Tr. by Idrana Klee from SPA. Orig. Title: Mar de Mi Infancia. (Illus.). 96p. (Orig.). (C). 1991. pap. 10.00 (*0-913827-04-5*) Linden Ln Pr.

Sea of Mystery. G. Arthur Rahman. (Illus.). 1981. 5.95 (*0-940244-14-4*) Flying Buffalo.

***Sea of Precious Virtues.** Tr. by Julie S. Meisami. 330p. 1996. 39.95 (*0-614-21339-8*, 1451) Kazi Pubns.

Sea of Precious Virtues: A Medieval Islamic Mirror for Princes. Ed. & Tr. by Julie S. Meisami from PER. LC 88-27858. 468p. 1990. lib. bdg. 39.95 (*0-87480-313-6*) U of Utah Pr.

Sea of Regret: Two Turn-of-the Century Chinese Romantic Novels. Tr. by Patrick Hanan from CHI. LC 94-49173. 216p. 1995. text ed. 32.00 (*0-8248-1666-8*); pap. text ed. 15.95 (*0-8248-1709-5*) UH Pr.

***Sea of Sage.** Melvin B. Banner. LC 96-95235. (Illus.). 334p. 19.95 (*1-888106-80-8*) Custom Fmly.

Sea of Shadow: A Storytellers Guide to the Tempest. White Wolf Staff & Nicky Rea. (Wraith). 96p. 1995. per., pap. 12.00 (*1-56504-612-9*, 6006/4612) White Wolf.

Sea of Slaughter: A Chronicle of the Destruction of Animal Life in the North Atlantic. Farley Mowat. Ed. by Cristen Brooks. LC 96-21050. (Illus.). 448p. 1996. reprint ed. pap. 13.95 (*1-57630-019-6*) Chapters Pub.

Sea of Small Boats. Ed. by John Cordell. (Cultural Survival Reports: No. 26). 300p. 1988. 34.95 (*0-939521-37-7*); pap. 15.00 (*0-939521-31-8*) Cultural Survival.

Sea of Stones. Florence Cohen. 1993. 25.00 (*0-916366-88-X*) Pushcart Pr.

Sea of Suspicion. Carolyn Keene. Ed. by Ann Greenberg. (Nancy Drew Files Ser.: No. 85). 160p. (Orig.). (YA). (gr. 6 up). 1993. mass mkt. 3.99 (*0-671-79477-9*, Archway) PB.

Sea of Talk. Ed. by John Dwyer. LC 90-27279. 106p. (Orig.). 1991. pap. text ed. 16.50 (*0-435-08582-4*, 08582) Heinemann.

Sea of the Bear. M. A. Ransom & Eloise K. Engle. LC 79-6122. (Navies & Men Ser.). (Illus.). 1980. reprint ed. lib. bdg. 24.95 (*0-405-13076-7*) Ayer.

Sea of the Ravens. Harold Lamb. (Illus.). 1983. 15.00 (*0-937986-58-5*); 35.00 (*0-937986-59-3*) D M Grant.

***Sea of Thirst.** Brian Gilliland. Ed. by Ginny Ballor & Carrie Neumann. 40p. (Orig.). (C). 1996. pap. 3.00 (*1-882294-19-X*) Green Gate.

Sea of Tranquility. Don Gordon. LC 88-71458. 48p. (Orig.). 1989. pap. 5.95 (*0-915306-79-4*) Curbstone.

Sea of Tranquility. Paul Russell. 416p. 1995. pap. 12.95 (*0-452-27311-0*, Plume) NAL-Dutton.

Sea of Tranquillity. Mark Haddon. LC 95-41267. (J). 1997. pap. write for info. (*0-15-201301-6*) HarBrace.

Sea of Tranquillity. Mark Haddon. (Illus.). (J). (ps-7). 1996. 16.00 (*0-15-201285-0*) HarBrace.

Sea of Treasures. Ed. by Caroline Sullivan. 1995. 69.95 (*1-56167-274-2*) Nat Lib Poetry.

***Sea of Trees.** Yannick Murphy. 1997. 22.95 (*0-614-27952-6*) HM.

***Sea of Trees, Qigong Adventure.** Linhai. Date not set. lib. bdg. 23.95 (*0-8488-1820-2*) Amereon Ltd.

Sea of Troubles. Janet L. Smith. 224p. (Orig.). 1991. mass mkt. 4.99 (*0-8041-0759-9*) Ivy Books.

Sea of Troubles. Janet L. Smith. LC 89-63605. 197p. (Orig.). 1990. pap. 8.95 (*0-9602676-9-7*) Persevrnce Pr.

Sea of Troubles Sources of Dispute. 1989. 15.25 (*0-08-037592-8*) Macmillan.

Sea of Upturned Faces: Proceedings of the Third Pacific Rim Conference on Children's Literature. Ed. by Winifred Ragsdale. LC 88-26534. 306p. 1989. 35.00 (*0-8108-2108-7*) Scarecrow.

Sea of Words. Dean King. LC 97-10440. 1997. 27.50 (*0-8050-5115-5*) H Holt & Co.

Sea of Words. 2nd ed. Dean King. LC 97-10440. 1997. pap. 14.95 (*0-8050-5116-3*) H Holt & Co.

Sea of Words: A Lexicon & Companion for Patrick O'Brian's Seafaring Tales. Dean King. LC 95-3924. 1995. 27.50 (*0-8050-3812-4*); pap. 14.00 (*0-8050-3816-7*) H Holt & Co.

Sea of Zanj. large type ed. Roumelia Lane. 1977. 25.99 (*0-7089-0067-4*) Ulverscroft.

***Sea Officer.** Kenneth Waters. Ed. by Nancy Padua. LC 96-35984. 272p. 1996. 19.95 (*0-941540-23-5*, 1025) Blacksmith Corp.

Sea on Its Side. Ambar Past. Tr. & Intro. by Jack Hirschman. 30p. (Orig.). 1994. pap. 7.00 (*0-942996-19-4*) Post Apollo Pr.

Sea Otter. Virginia B. Silverstein et al. LC 94-17998. (Endangered in America Ser.). (Illus.). 64p. (Orig.). (J). (gr. 4-6). 1995. lib. bdg. 16.90 (*1-56294-418-5*) Millbrook Pr.

Sea Otter. Virginia B. Silverstein et al. (Endangered in America Ser.). (Illus.). 64p. (Orig.). (J). (gr. 4-6). 1996. pap. 6.95 (*0-7613-0165-8*) Millbrook Pr.

Sea Otter Pup. Victoria Miles. (Illus.). 24p. (Orig.). (J). (gr. 1-4). 1995. pap. 5.95 (*1-55143-002-9*) Orca Bk Pubs.

Sea Otter, River Otter: A Story & Activity Book. Sandra C. Robinson. LC 92-62078. (Wonder Ser.). (Illus.). 64p. (Orig.). (J). (gr. 1-6). 1993. pap. 7.95 (*1-879373-41-6*) R Rinehart.

Sea Otters. Beth W. Brust. (Zoobooks Ser.). (J). 1991. lib. bdg. 14.95 (*0-88682-415-X*) Creative Ed.

***Sea Otters.** Bobbie Kalman. (Crabapple Ser.). 32p. 1996. pap. 5.95 (*0-86505-734-6*) Crabtree Pub Co.

***Sea Otters.** Bobbie Kalman. LC 96-36375. (Crabapple Ser.). 32p. (J). 1996. lib. bdg. 18.08 (*0-86505-634-X*) Crabtree Pub Co.

Sea Otters. John A. Love. LC 92-53032. (Illus.). 148p. (Orig.). 1992. pap. 12.95 (*1-55591-123-4*) Fulcrum Pub.

Sea Otters. Peter Murray. LC 93-42. (Nature Bks.). 32p. (J). (gr. 2-6). 1993. lib. bdg. 22.79 (*1-56766-007-X*) Childs World.

Sea Otters. Sarah Palmer. (Sea Mammal Discovery Library). (Illus.). 24p. (J). (gr. k-5). 1989. lib. bdg. 11.94 (*0-86592-361-2*) Rourke Corp.

Sea Otters. Marianne Riedman. (Natural History Ser.). (Illus.). 80p. (Orig.). 1990. pap. 9.95 (*1-878244-03-5*) Monterey Bay Aquarium.

Sea Otters. Walter Stuart. (Zoobooks Ser.). (Illus.). (J). 1992. pap. 2.75 (*0-937934-70-4*) Wildlife Educ.

Sea Otters. Wildlife Education, Ltd. Staff. (Zoobooks Ser.). (Illus.). (J). 1992. 13.95 (*0-937934-87-9*) Wildlife Educ.

Sea Otters: A Natural History & Guide. rev. ed. Roy Nickerson. (Illus.). 96p. (Orig.). (C). 1989. pap. 14.95 (*0-87701-567-8*) Chronicle Bks.

Sea Otters Cruz & Slick. Mary Craft. (Illus.). 24p. (Orig.). (J). (ps-3). 1991. pap. 4.00 (*0-9624842-2-9*) M Craft.

***Sea Otters of California.** Joan Duden. LC 97-11368. (Animals of the World Ser.). (J). 1998. write for info. (*1-56065-578-X*) Capstone Pr.

Sea Pacific: Two Hundred Eighty Points on the Compass of Prayer. Ed. by John Fandel. 56p. (Orig.). 1991. pap. 1.95 (*0-88028-118-9*, 1107) Forward Movement.

***Sea Picnic.** Melissa Mathis. Date not set. write for info. (*0-688-13568-4*, Tambourine Bks); lib. bdg. write for info. (*0-688-13569-2*, Tambourine Bks) Morrow.

Sea Plants. Jason Cooper. LC 92-16076. (Discovery Library of the Sea). (J). 1992. 12.67 (*0-86593-232-8*); 9.50 (*0-685-66141-5*) Rourke Corp.

Sea Plays. Ed. by Colin C. Clements. LC 79-50022. (One-Act Plays in Reprint Ser.). (Illus.). 1980. reprint ed. 30.00 (*0-8486-2046-1*) Roth Pub Inc.

Sea Poems. Selected by Ron Hawkins. (Jarrold Poets Ser.). 146p. (Orig.). 1994. pap. 5.95 (*0-7117-0679-4*) Seven Hills Bk.

Sea Power: A Global Journey. Luc Cuyvers. LC 93-4470. 247p. 1993. 45.00 (*1-55750-145-9*); pap. 28.95 (*1-55750-146-7*) Naval Inst Pr.

Sea Power: A Naval History. 2nd rev. ed. Ed. by E. B. Potter. LC 81-81668. (Illus.). 419p. 1981. Avail. bulk rates. 27.95 (*0-87021-607-4*) Naval Inst Pr.

Sea Power & British North America, 1783-1820: A Study in British Colonial Policy. Gerald S. Graham. LC 69-10101. 302p. 1969. reprint ed. text ed. 35.00 (*0-8371-0453-X*, GRBP, Greenwood Pr) Greenwood.

Sea Power & Influence: Old Issues & New Challenges. Ed. by Jonathan Alford. LC 80-67840. (Adelphi Library: Vol. 2). 224p. 1981. text ed. 52.00 (*0-916672-72-7*) Rowman.

Sea Power & Strategy in the Indian Ocean. Alvin J. Cottrell et al. LC 80-28415. 148p. reprint ed. pap. 42.20 (*0-8357-8450-9*, 2034714) Bks Demand.

Sea Power & the Nuclear Fallacy: A Reevaluation of Global Strategy. Robert E. Walters. LC 75-15754. 214p. 1975. reprint ed. 25.00 (*0-8419-0214-3*) Holmes & Meier.

Sea Power & Western Security. 1989. 15.25 (*0-08-037591-X*) Macmillan.

Sea Power in Its Relations to the War of 1812, 2 Vols. Alfred T. Mahan. LC 68-26362. (World History Ser.: No. 48). 1969. reprint ed. lib. bdg. 150.00 (*0-8383-0181-9*) M S G Haskell Hse.

Sea Power in Relation to the War of 1812, 2 vols., Set. Alfred T. Mahan. 1993. reprint ed. lib. bdg. 150.00 (*0-7812-5190-7*) Rprt Serv.

Sea Power in the Falklands. Charles W. Koburger, Jr. LC 83-17823. (Illus.). 128p. 1983. text ed. 55.00 (*0-275-91028-8*, C1028, Praeger Pubs) Greenwood.

Sea Power in the Falklands. Maritime Books Staff. (C). 1986. text ed. 100.00 (*0-03-069534-1*, Pub. by Maritime Bks UK) St Mut.

Sea Power in the Modern World. Herbert W. Richmond. LC 72-4293. (World Affairs Ser.: National & International Viewpoints). 318p. 1972. reprint ed. 23.95 (*0-405-04585-9*) Ayer.

Sea-Power in the Pacific: A Study of the American-Japanese Naval Problem. Hector C. Bywater. LC 75-111749. (American Imperialism: Viewpoints of United States Foreign Policy, 1898-1941 Ser.). 1970. reprint ed. 24.95 (*0-405-02006-6*) Ayer.

***Sea Power in the Twenty-First Century: Projecting a Naval Revolution.** Charles W. Koburger. LC 97-3629. 1997. text ed. write for info. (*0-275-95300-9*, Praeger Pubs) Greenwood.

Sea Power Library, 6 bks., Reading Level 5. Max Walmer & Jon Rawlinson. (Illus.). 288p. (J). (gr. 3-8). 1989. 18.60 (*0-685-58760-6*); 13.95 (*0-685-58761-4*) Rourke Corp.

Sea Power Library, 6 bks., Set, Reading Level 5. Max Walmer & Jon Rawlinson. (Illus.). 288p. (J). (gr. 3-8). 1989. Set. lib. bdg. 111.60 (*0-86625-087-5*) Rourke Corp.

Sea Power of the State. Sergei G. Gorshkov. (Illus.). 290p. 1979. 114.25 (*0-08-021944-6*, Pergamon Pr) Elsevier.

Sea Prick. R. T. Greig. (Illus.). 9p. (Orig.). 1989. 50.00 (*1-877886-01-7*) dG Printers.

Sea Priestess. Dion Fortune. LC 83-159136. 186p. (Orig.). 1979. reprint ed. pap. 10.95 (*0-87728-424-5*) Weiser.

Sea Princess. Wanda Owen. 400p. 1995. mass mkt. 4.99 (*0-8217-5084-4*, Zebra Kensgtn) Kensgtn Pub Corp.

Sea-Rabbit: Or, the Artist of Life. Wendy Walker. (Sun & Moon Classics Ser.: No. 57). 272p. 1995. pap. 12.95 (*1-55713-001-9*) Sun & Moon CA.

Sea-Rabbit: Or, the Artist of Life. deluxe ed. Wendy Walker. (New American Fiction Ser.: No. 14). 272p. 1988. 30.00 (*1-55713-040-X*) Sun & Moon CA.

***Sea Ranch.** Kathryn M. Wayne & John V. Maciuika. 29p. 1994. pap. 10.00 (*0-86602-307-0*, Sage Prdcls Pr) Sage.

Sea Raven. Patricia McAllister. 352p. 1996. mass mkt. 4.99 (*0-8217-5236-7*, Zebra Kensgtn) Kensgtn Pub Corp.

***Sea Resembling Glass.** Arlo McDaniel. (Illus.). 198p. (Orig.). 1996. pap. write for info. (*1-57502-338-5*, PO1121) Morris Pubng.

***Sea-Road of the Saints: Celtic Holy Men in the Hebrides.** John Marsden. 1996. reprint ed. 16.95 (*0-86315-210-4*, Pub. by Floris Bks UK) Gryphon Hse.

Sea Road to the Indies: An Account of the Voyages & Exploits of the Portuguese Navigators, Together with the Life & Times of Dom Vasco De Gama, Capitao-Mor, Viceroy of India & Count of Vidigueira. Henry H. Hart. LC 70-135246. (Illus.). 296p. 1971. reprint ed. text ed. 59.75 (*0-8371-5165-1*, HARO) Greenwood.

Sea Room. Maria Flook. LC 89-14831. (Wesleyan Poetry Ser.). 70p. 1990. pap. 11.95 (*0-8195-1185-4*, Wesleyan Univ Pr); text ed. 25.00 (*0-8195-2183-3*, Wesleyan Univ Pr) U Pr of New Eng.

Sea Routes to the Gold Fields. Oscar Lewis. 256p. 1987. reprint ed. 4.50 (*0-89174-044-9*) Comstock Edns.

***Sea Rover: Adventuring in America in 1605, Fighting Pirates & Indians.** unabridged ed. Lobo Blanco. LC 96-90526. ii, 140p. (Orig.). 1996. pap. 12.50 (*1-890492-05-1*) Univ Pr of Copperas.

Sea Run Cutthroat Trout. Les Johnson. (Illus.). 77p. (Orig.). 1979. pap. 11.95 (*0-936608-02-1*) F Amato Pubns.

Sea Runners. Ivan Doig. 1992. 22.25 (*0-8446-6538-X*) Peter Smith.

Sea Runners. Ivan Doig. 288p. 1983. pap. 11.95 (*0-14-006780-9*, Penguin Bks) Viking Penguin.

***Sea, Salt & Air.** Mirian Bat-Ami. (Illus.). 32p. (J). 4.98 (*0-7651-0095-9*) Smithmark.

***Sea Sayings: With Keychain.** Walt Disney Staff. 1997. 2.98 (*1-57082-762-1*) Mouse Works.

Sea Scape. large type ed. Mary Lide. LC 92-26852. (Popular Ser.). 310p. 1993. reprint ed. lib. bdg. 17.95 (*1-56054-552-6*) Thorndike Pr.

Sea Scapes: In Kairos Time. Joan W. Hollenbeck. Ed. by Doris Banks. (Illus.). 112p. 1996. reprint ed. pap. 14.95 (*0-936822-01-5*) Peppertree.

***Sea Scribe & Other Poems.** Mary B. Beyenka. (Illus.). 63p. (C). 1996. spiral bd. 8.00 (*1-57193-201-1*, AP-815) Alliance Pubns.

Sea Searcher's Handbook: Activities from the Monterey Bay Aquarium. Ed. by Pam Armstrong. LC 96-27100. (Illus.). 224p. (Orig.). (J). (gr. k up). 1996. pap. 16.95 (*1-878244-15-9*) Monterey Bay Aquarium.

Sea Serpent Journal: Hugh McCulloch Gregory's Voyage Around the World in a Clipper Ship, 1854-55. Hugh M. Gregory. Ed. by Robert H. Burgess. LC 74-12382. (Illus.). 1975. text ed. 19.50 (*0-8139-0589-3*) U Pr of Va.

Sea Serpents. Charles Bright. (Illus.). 112p. (C). 1991. 17.95 (*0-87972-539-7*) Bowling Green Univ Popular Press.

Sea Serpent's Daughter: A Brazilian Legend. Margaret H. Lippert. LC 92-21438. (Legends of the World Ser.). (Illus.). 32p. (J). (gr. 2-5). 1993. pap. 4.95 (*0-8167-3054-7*); lib. bdg. 13.95 (*0-8167-3053-9*) Troll Communs.

Sea Shadows: In Depth Perspectives of Nature. Carlos Eyles. 1992. pap. 24.95 (*0-922769-19-2*) Watersport Pub.

An Asterisk (*) at the beginning of an entry indicates that the title is appearing in BIP for the first time.

Sea Shall Not Have Them. Evans E. Kerrigan. (Illus.). 120p. 1972. 14.00 (0-9624663-0-1) Medallic Pub.

***Sea Shapes.** MacDonald. (J). 1998. pap. write for info. (0-15-201700-3, HB Juv Bks) HarBrace.

Sea Shapes. Suse MacDonald. LC 93-27957. (Illus.). 32p. (J). (ps-2). 1994. 14.00 (0-15-200027-5, Gulliver Bks) HarBrace.

Sea Shells. Jason Cooper. LC 92-16075. (Discovery Library of the Sea). (J). 1992. 12.67 (0-86593-233-6); 9.50 (0-685-66140-7) Rourke Corp.

Sea Shells of Tropical West America: Marine Mollusks from Baja California to Peru. 2nd ed. A. Myra Keen & James H. McLean. (Illus.). xvi, 1076p. 1971. 79.50 (0-8047-0736-7) Stanford U Pr.

Sea Shore Ecology of Hong Kong. Brian Morton & John Morton. (Illus.). 366p. 1983. 62.50 (962-209-028-1, Pub. by Hong Kong Univ Pr HK) Coronet Bks.

Sea Shore Ecology of Hong Kong. Brian Morton & John Morton. 366p. (C). 1983. text ed. 75.00 (0-685-65778-7, Pub. by Hong Kong U Pr HK); pap. text ed. 60.00 (962-209-027-3, Pub. by Hong Kong U Pr HK) St Mut.

Sea Skater. Helen Dunmore. 72p. 8600. pap. 11.95 (1-85224-006-7, Pub. by Bloodaxe Bks UK) Dufour.

Sea-Slug Gastropods. Wesley M. Farmer. (Illus.). 157p. (Orig.). 1980. pap. 5.00 (0-937772-00-3) W M Farmer.

Sea Snake Toxinology. P. Gopalakrishnakone. (Illus.). 260p. (Orig.). 1994. pap. 49.50 (9971-69-193-0, Pub. by Sgapore Univ SI) Coronet Bks.

***Sea Snakes.** Sneed B. Collard, III. LC 91-77604. (Illus.). 32p. (J). (gr. 2 up). 1997. pap. text ed. 7.95 (1-56397-690-0) Boyds Mills Pr.

Sea Snakes Toxinology. P. Gopalakrishnakone. 1994. 55.00 (9971-69-191-4, Pub. by Singapore Univ Pr SI) Intl Spec Bk.

Sea Soldiers in the Cold War: Amphibious Warfare, 1945-1991. Joseph H. Alexander & Merrill L. Bartlett. LC 94-20845. (Illus.). 320p. 1994. 34.95 (1-55750-055-X) Naval Inst Pr.

***Sea Song.** (J). 1997. 8.98 (1-57082-526-2) Mouse Works.

Sea Songs & Shanties. Compiled by R. H. Whall. (C). 1987. 100.00 (0-85174-181-9, Pub. by Brwn Son Ferg) St Mut.

Sea Spun Ecstasy. Allison Knight. 1990. mass mkt. 4.25 (0-8217-3057-6, Zebra Kensgtn) Kensgtn Pub Corp.

Sea Squares. Joy N. Hulme. LC 91-71381. (Illus.). 32p. (J). (ps-3). 1993. pap. 4.95 (1-56282-520-8) Hyprn Child.

Sea Squirt. Jenny E. Tesar. LC 94-27858. (What on Earth Is...? Ser). 32p. (J). (gr. 2-5). 1994. lib. bdg. 14.95 (1-56711-091-6) Blackbirch.

Sea Squirts of the Atlantic Continental Shelf from Maine to Texas. Harold H. Plough. LC 76-47388. (Illus.). 128p. reprint ed. pap. 36.50 (0-317-41676-6, 2025851) Bks Demand.

Sea Star: Orphan of Chincoteague. Marguerite Henry. LC 49-11474. (Illus.). 176p. (J). (gr. 3-7). 1991. lib. bdg. 15.00 (0-02-743627-6, Mac Bks Young Read) S&S Childrens.

Sea Star: Orphan of Chincoteague. Marguerite Henry. LC 49-11474. (Illus.). 176p. (J). (gr. 3-7). 1991. pap. 3.95 (0-689-71530-7, Aladdin Paperbacks) S&S Childrens.

Sea Starr's Day at the Beach. Alexandra Reid. (Sky Dancer Ser.). (Illus.). 24p. (J). (ps up). 1996. pap. 2.50 (0-694-00945-8, Festival) HarpC Child Bks.

Sea Stars. Jason Cooper. LC 95-26011. (Animals Without Bones Ser.). (Illus.). (J). 1996. write for info. (0-86625-569-9) Rourke Pubns.

Sea Stars & Dragons. Phyllis J. Perry. (First Bks.). (Illus.). 64p. (J). (gr. 4-6). 1996. lib. bdg. 21.00 (0-531-20223-2) Watts.

Sea Stars, Sea Urchins, & Allies: Echinoderms of Florida & the Caribbean. Gordon Hendler et al. LC 94-31424. (Illus.). 392p. 1995. 39.95 (1-56098-450-3) Smithsonian.

Sea Stories. Joseph Conrad. 272p. (Orig.). 1985. pap. 8.95 (0-88184-177-3) Carroll & Graf.

Sea Stories. Captain Olivey. (C). 1989. text ed. 59.00 (1-85821-031-3, Pub. by Pentland Pr UK) St Mut.

Sea Stories: Of Dolphins & Dead Sailors. John P. Barrett & Fred Wolleson. LC 87-82430. (Illus.). 128p. 1988. 15.00 (0-9619629-0-9) Gaff Pr.

Sea Stories, Bk. Two: Seagods & Sundogs. John P. Barrett. LC 87-82430. (Illus.). 160p. 1991. 15.00 (0-9619629-1-7) Gaff Pr.

Sea Stories from Searsport to Singapore: Selected Works of Lincoln Colcord. Lincoln Colcord. Ed. by Donald Mortland. LC 87-5643. (Illus.). 217p. 1987. 17.95 (0-89621-104-5); pap. 8.95 (0-945980-29-9) Nrth Country Pr.

Sea Stories of a Wily Sailor, Vol. 1. (Illus.). 176p. 19.50 (0-9652537-0-8) Sea Stories.

***Sea Stories of the Inside Passage: In the Wake of the Nid.** Iain Lawrence. Ed. & Photos by Reanne Hemingway-Douglass. LC 97-283. (Illus.). 160p. (Orig.). 1997. pap. 16.95 (0-938665-47-2) Fine Edge Prods.

***Sea Strike.** James H. Cobb. LC 97-23466. 480p. 1998. 24.95 (0-399-14324-6) Putnam Pub Group.

Sea Sums. Joy Hulme. LC 95-5935. (Illus.). 32p. (J). (ps-3). 1996. 13.95 (0-7868-0170-0); lib. bdg. 13.89 (0-7868-2142-6) Hyprn Child.

Sea Surface & Global Change. Ed. by Peter S. Liss & Robert A. Duce. LC 96-9377. (Illus.). 496p. (C). 1997. text ed. 95.00 (0-521-56273-2) Cambridge U Pr.

Sea Surface Sound: Natural Mechanisms of Surface Generated Noise in the Ocean. Ed. by B. R. Kerman. (C). 1988. lib. bdg. 252.00 (90-277-2761-9) Kluwer Ac.

Sea Surface Sound '94. M. J. Buckingham & J. R. Potter. 600p. 1996. text ed. 118.00 (981-02-1891-5) World Scientific Pub.

Sea Surface Studies: A Global View. Ed. by R. J. Devoy. 650p. 1987. lib. bdg. 110.00 (0-7099-0871-7, Pub. by Croom Helm UK) Routledge Chapman & Hall.

Sea Surface Topography & the Geoid. Hans Sunkel. (International Association of Geodesy Symposia Ser.: Vol. 104). x, 187p. 1990. 71.95 (0-387-97268-4) Spr-Verlag.

Sea Surveying, 2 vols., 1. Alan E. Ingham. LC 74-3066. (Illus.). reprint ed. pap. 82.20 (0-317-58206-2, 2052215) Bks Demand.

Sea Surveying, 2 vols., 2. Alan E. Ingham. LC 74-3066. (Illus.). reprint ed. pap. 61.70 (0-317-58207-0) Bks Demand.

Sea Survival: The Boatman's Emergency Manual. Robb Huff & Michael Farley. (Illus.). 224p. 1989. pap. 14.95 (0-8306-9377-7, 3077P) McGraw-Hill Prof.

***Sea Swept.** Nora Roberts. 352p. 1998. mass mkt. 6.99 (0-515-12184-3) Jove Pubns.

Sea Sword. Adrienne Martine-Barnes. 196p. (Orig.). 1989. pap. 3.50 (0-380-75456-8) Avon.

Sea Tales: The Pilot; The Red Rover. James Fenimore Cooper. Ed. by Kay S. House & Thomas L. Philbrick. 900p. 1991. 35.00 (0-940450-70-4) Library of America.

Sea the Land & the Heart: Verse by Thomas Martin Kurti. Thomas M. Kurti et al. (Illus.). 59p. (Orig.). 1983. pap. 10.00 (0-935886-01-X) East & West Pubns.

Sea, the Land, the Life Through the Cameras of The Cape Codder. Cape Codder Staff. (Illus.). 120p. (Orig.). 1988. pap. 14.95 (0-9619737-0-6) Cape Codder Pr.

Sea, the Sea. Iris Murdoch. 1980. pap. 12.95 (0-14-005199-6, Penguin Bks) Viking Penguin.

Sea Tiger. Terry Jones. LC 94-7546. (Twentieth Century Fairy Tales Ser.). (Illus.). 32p. (J). (gr. k up). 1994. 9.95 (0-87226-378-9) P Bedrick Bks.

***Sea Tiger.** Terry Jones. (Illus.). 24p. (J). 3.98 (0-7651-0179-3) Smithmark.

Sea to Shining Sea. Michael Phillips & Judith Pella. (Journals of Corrie Belle Hollister: Vol. 5). 320p. (Orig.). 1992. pap. 9.99 (1-55661-227-3) Bethany Hse.

***Sea to Shining Sea.** Lisa Shapiro. LC 97-10803. 288p. (Orig.). 1997. pap. 11.95 (1-56280-177-5) Naiad Pr.

Sea to Shining Sea: People, Travel, Places. Berton Roueche. 288p. 1987. mass mkt. 4.50 (0-380-70265-7) Avon.

Sea to Shore. Jan Robinson. 288p. 1989. pap. 14.95 (0-9612686-3-8) Ship-Shore.

Sea Treasure. Johanna Hailey. 448p. 1994. mass mkt. 4.50 (1-55817-790-6, Pinncle Kensgtn) Kensgtn Pub Corp.

***Sea Treasures.** Amanda Wallwork. (Illus.). 12p. (J). (gr. k up). 1997. 9.95 (0-8431-7891-4) Price Stern Sloan.

Sea Trek. Martha Holmes. (Illus.). 240p. 1993. reprint ed. 29.95 (0-563-36091-7, BBC-Parkwest); reprint ed. pap. 19.95 (0-563-36736-9, BBC-Parkwest) Parkwest Pubns.

Sea Turn, & Other Matters. Thomas B. Aldrich. LC 76-81258. (Short Story Index Reprint Ser.). 1977. 20.95 (0-8369-3010-X) Ayer.

Sea Turn & Other Matters. Thomas B. Aldrich. (Works of Thomas Bailey Aldrich). 1989. reprint ed. lib. bdg. 79.00 (0-7812-1677-X) Rprt Serv.

Sea Turtle: So Excellent a Fishe. rev. ed. Archie Carr. 292p. 1986. pap. 16.95 (0-292-77595-4) U of Tex Pr.

Sea Turtle Journey: The Story of a Loggerhead Turtle. Lorraine A. Jay. (Smithsonian Oceanic Collection). (Illus.). 32p. (J). (ps-3). 1995. 15.95 (1-56899-189-4); 4.95 (1-56899-190-8); 29.95 (1-56899-191-6); 9.95 (1-56899-192-4); 19.95 incl. audio (1-56899-193-2) Soundprints.

Sea Turtles. Caroline Arnold. LC 93-6353. 32p. (J). 1994. pap. 3.95 (0-590-46945-2) Scholastic Inc.

Sea Turtles. Robert L. Buyer & Thomas E. Gilbert. LC 96-13622. (Carving Sea Life Ser.). (Illus.). 48p. 1996. pap. 7.95 (0-8117-2470-0) Stackpole.

Sea Turtles. Gail Gibbons. LC 94-48579. (Illus.). 32p. (J). (gr. k-3). 1995. lib. bdg. 15.95 (0-8234-1191-5) Holiday.

Sea Turtles. Emilie U. Lepthien. (True Bk.). 48p. (J). 1996. lib. bdg. 19.00 (0-516-20161-1) Childrens.

***Sea Turtles.** Emilie U. Lepthien. (True Bks.). 48p. (J). 1997. pap. 6.95 (0-516-26113-4) Childrens.

Sea Turtles. Don Patton. LC 95-7858. (Nature Bks.). (Illus.). 32p. (J). (gr. 2-6). 1995. lib. bdg. 22.79 (1-56766-188-2) Childs World.

Sea Turtles. Jeff Ripple. LC 95-22059. (WorldLife Library). (Illus.). 84p. 1996. pap. 16.95 (0-89658-315-5) Voyageur Pr.

***Sea Turtles.** Anne Rudlue & Jack Rudlue. 1998. pap. write for info. (0-609-80008-6) Crown Pub Group.

Sea Turtles. Frank Staub. LC 94-4630. (Early Bird Nature Bks.). (Illus.). 48p. (J). (gr. 2-3). 1994. lib. bdg. 18.95 (0-8225-3005-8, Lerner Publctns) Lerner Group.

Sea Turtles. Lynn M. Stone. LC 93-15691. (Nighttime Animals Ser.). (J). 1993. write for info. (0-86593-296-4) Rourke Corp.

Sea Turtles: The Watchers Guide. M. Timothy O'Keefe. LC 95-75545. (Illus.). 128p. (Orig.). 1993. pap. text ed. 8.95 (0-936513-47-0) Larsens Outdoor.

Sea Turtles & the Turtle Industry of the West Indies, Florida, & the Gulf of Mexico. Thomas P. Rebel. LC 73-159293. 224p. 1990. pap. 14.95 (0-87024-217-2) U of Miami Pr.

Sea un Cristiano Autentico - Honest to God? Becoming an Authentic Christian. Bill Hybels. Tr. by Rafael C. Bustamante from ENG. 192p. (Orig.). (SPA.). 1993. pap. 6.99 (0-311-46132-8) Casa Bautista.

Sea Urchin: Molecular Biology, 3 vols., Vol. 2. John B. Chamberlain et al. 188p. (C). 1973. text ed. 28.50 (0-8422-7121-X) Irvington.

Sea Urchin: Molecular Biology, Vol. 3. S. A. Terman et al. 1973. 28.50 (0-8422-7122-8) Irvington.

Sea Urchin Development Cell Use. L. Stearns. 58.95 (0-317-64273-1) Van Nos Reinhold.

Sea Urchin Harakiri. Bernard Bador. Tr. by Clayton Eshleman. (Illus.). 120p. 1986. 16.95 (0-915572-77-X); pap. 6.95 (0-915572-76-1) Panjandrum.

Sea Urchins. Jason Cooper. LC 95-26009. (Animals Without Bones Ser.). (Illus.). (J). 1996. write for info. (0-86625-570-2) Rourke Pubns.

Sea Vegetable Gelatin Cookbook. Judith Cooper Madlener. LC 80-29228. (Illus.). (Orig.). 1981. pap. 7.95 (0-912800-76-3) Woodbridge Pr.

Sea Vegetable Gourmet Cookbook & Wildcrafter's Guide. Eleanor Lewallen & John Lewallen. 128p. 1996. pap. 19.95 (0-9647643-7-7) Mendocino Sea.

Sea Vegetables: Harvesting Guide & Cookbook. Evelyn McConnaughey. LC 85-18828. (Illus.). 244p. 1985. pap. 9.95 (0-87961-151-0) Naturegraph.

Sea Venture. F. Van Wyck Mason. 1976. reprint ed. lib. bdg. 25.95 (0-89190-353-4, Rivercity Pr) Amereon Ltd.

Sea Verse in a Sailor's Locker. James Tazelaar. LC 72-13085. (Illus.). 64p. 1972. reprint ed. pap. 25.00 (0-7837-9087-2, 2049837) Bks Demand.

Sea View Hotel. James Stevenson. LC 78-2749. (Illus.). 48p. (J). 1994. reprint ed. 15.00 (0-688-13469-6); reprint ed. lib. bdg. 14.93 (0-688-13470-X) Greenwillow.

Sea Vixen. Brian Fiddler. 24p. (C). 1987. pap. 30.00 (0-948251-03-4, Pub. by Picton UK) St Mut.

Sea, Vol. 9: Ocean Engineering Science, 2 vols., Set. Bernard Lemehaute & Daniel M. Hanes. 1344p. 1990. text ed. 300.00 (0-471-63393-3) Wiley.

Sea Voyage Narratives. Foulke. LC 97-15226. 1997. 24.95 (0-8057-0968-1) Macmillan.

Sea Wall. Eilis Dillon et al. 119p. (J). (gr. 4-10). 1994. reprint ed. pap. 8.95 (1-85371-304-X, Pub. by Poolbeg Pr IE) Dufour.

Sea War: Great Naval Battles of World War Two. large type ed. Frank Pearce. (Illus.). 384p. 1991. 21.95 (1-85089-505-8, Pub. by ISIS UK) Transaction Pubs.

Sea War: Nineteen Thirty-Nine to Nineteen Forty-Five. Janusz Piekalkiewicz. Tr. by Tek Translation & International Print Ltd. from GER. Orig. Title: Seekrieg 1939-1945. (Illus.). 353p. 1987. 19.95 (0-918678-17-X) Natl Hist Soc.

Sea War in Korea. Malcolm W. Cagle & Frank A. Manson. LC 79-6104. (Navies & Men Ser.). (Illus.). 1980. reprint ed. lib. bdg. 41.95 (0-405-13033-3) Ayer.

Sea Was My Last Chance: Memoir of an American Captured on Bataan in 1942 Who Escaped in 1944 & Led the Liberation of Western Mindanao. Donald H. Wills & Reyburn W. Myers. LC 92-50423. 187p. 1992. lib. bdg. 25.95 (0-89950-760-3) McFarland & Co.

Sea Watch: A Book of Poetry. Jane Yolen. (Illus.). 30p. (J). (ps-4). 1996. 15.95 (0-399-22734-2, Philomel Bks) Putnam Pub Group.

Sea Waves, Wind & Stars. 1995. pap. write for info. (0-930061-56-X) Interspace Bks.

Sea Waves, Winds & Stars: True Story of the First Waves Approved by the Navy. 1986. write for info. (0-318-60430-2) Interspace Bks.

Sea Where I Swim. Gwen Pascoe. LC 93-6647. (J). 1994. write for info. (0-383-03712-3) SRA McGraw.

***Sea Whisp & the Wasnizzle.** Tim Zahniser. Ed. by Jennifer W. Kranz. (Illus.). 30p. (Orig.). (J). (gr. 3-6). 1996. pap. 10.95 (0-9652232-0-5) Insty-Prints.

Sea Wing Disaster. Frederick L. Johnson. LC 90-81430. (Illus.). 115p. 1990. 7.95 (0-9617197-1-0) Goodhue County Hist Soc.

Sea Witch. Sara Blayne. 1988. mass mkt. 3.75 (0-8217-2542-4, Zebra Kensgtn) Kensgtn Pub Corp.

Sea Within. Ed. by Onesimo T. Almeida. Tr. by George Monteiro from POR. LC 83-80877. (Illus.). 115p. (Orig.). 1983. pap. 3.50 (0-943722-09-8) Gavea-Brown.

Sea Without a Shore. Sean Russell. (Moontide & Magic Rise Ser.: Vol. 2). 608p. 1996. mass mkt. 5.99 (0-88677-665-1) DAW Bks.

Sea Wolf. Elaine Kirn. (Regents Illustrated Classics Ser.). (Illus.). 62p. (gr. 7-12). 1987. pap. text ed. 4.00 (0-13-796798-5, 20545) Prentice ESL.

Sea Wolf. Jack London. (Airmont Classics Ser.). (J). (gr. 6 up). 1965. mass mkt. 2.50 (0-8049-0064-7, CL-64) Airmont.

Sea Wolf. Jack London. 1985. 15.95 (0-02-574630-8) Macmillan.

Sea Wolf. Jack London. (Illus.). 370p. 1981. pap. 9.95 (0-932458-05-X) Star Rover.

Sea Wolf. Jack London. (Bantam Classics Ser.). 256p. (gr. 7 up). 1984. pap. 3.95 (0-553-21225-7) Bantam.

Sea Wolf. Jack London. Ed. by John C. Fago. (Now Age Illustrated IV Ser.). (Illus.). (gr. 4-12). 1978. student ed. 1.25 (0-88301-346-0); pap. text ed. 2.95 (0-88301-322-3) Pendulum Pr.

Sea Wolf. Jack London. 320p. 1993. pap. 2.50 (0-8125-2276-1) Tor Bks.

Sea-Wolf. Jack London. 430p. 1993. pap. 5.95 (0-19-282931-9) OUP.

***Sea Wolf.** Jack London. (Illustrated Classics Collection 4). 64p. 1994. pap. 4.95 (0-7854-0756-1, 40521) Am Guidance.

***Sea Wolf.** Jack London. 1998. pap. 3.99 (0-14-038279-8) Viking Penguin.

***Sea Wolf.** Jack London. 1997. pap. 7.00 (0-7871-1366-2, Dove Bks) Dove Audio.

***Sea-Wolf.** large type ed. Jack London. 504p. 1997. reprint ed. lib. bdg. 24.00 (0-939495-19-8) North Bks.

***Sea Wolf.** unabridged ed. Jack London. 146p. 1997. reprint ed. pap. 14.95 (1-57002-023-X) Univ Publng Hse.

Sea Wolf. Jack London. 351p. reprint ed. lib. bdg. 23.95 (0-89190-657-6, Rivercity Pr) Amereon Ltd.

Sea-Wolf & Other Selected Stories. Jack London. 1990. reprint ed. lib. bdg. 24.95 (0-89968-539-0) Buccaneer Bks.

Sea-Wolf & Other Stories. Jack London. 320p. 1989. pap. 8.95 (0-14-018357-4, Penguin Classics) Viking Penguin.

Sea Wolf & Selected Stories. Jack London. 352p. (J). (gr. 8). 1964. pap. 4.95 (0-451-52356-3, Sig Classics) NAL-Dutton.

***Sea Wolf Readalong.** Jack London. (Illustrated Classics Collection 4). 64p. 1994. pap. 14.95 incl. audio (0-7854-0772-3, 40523) Am Guidance.

Sea Wolves. Edwin P. Hoyt. 208p. 1987. pap. 3.50 (0-380-75249-2) Avon.

Seabeck: Tide's Out; Table's Set. Fredi Perry et al. (Illus.). 256p. 1993. 26.00 (0-9622337-2-2); pap. 16.00 (0-9622337-3-0) Perry Pub WA.

Seabed Arms Control. David W. Felder. 44p. 1996. pap. text ed. 8.95 (0-910959-59-5, B&G 11E) Wellington Pr.

Seabed Mechanics. Ed. by Bruce Denness. 296p. 1985. lib. bdg. 163.00 (0-86010-504-0) G & T Inc.

Seabed Minerals: Selection of Sites for Seabed Manganese Nodule Processing Plants, Vol. 5. United Nations Staff. (C). 1990. lib. bdg. 104.50 (0-86010-395-1, Pub. by Graham & Trotman UK) Kluwer Ac.

Seabed Minerals Series: Vol. 3, Analysis of Processing Technology for Manganese Nodules. Ed. by Graham & Trotman, Ltd. Staff. 104p. 1986. lib. bdg. 67.50 (0-86010-349-8) G & T Inc.

Seabed Reconnaissance & Offshore Soil Mechanics for the Installation of Petroleum Structures. Pierre Le Tirant. 512p. 1979. 685.00 (2-7108-0333-X, Pub. by Edits Technip FR) St Mut.

Seabird. Holling C. Holling. (Illus.). (J). (gr. 4-6). 1973. 17.95 (0-395-18230-1) HM.

Seabird. Holling C. Holling. (Illus.). (J). (gr. 4-6). 1978. pap. 8.95 (0-395-26681-5) HM.

Seabird on Ocean Routes. Gerald Turb. 1987. 14.95 (0-685-43771-X) Viking Penguin.

Seabirds. Alice K. Flanagan. LC 95-25804. (New True Bk.). (Illus.). 48p. (J). (gr. 2-3). 1996. lib. bdg. 19.00 (0-516-01088-3) Childrens.

Seabirds. Alice K. Flanagan. (New True Bks.). (J). 1996. pap. 5.50 (0-516-20076-3) Childrens.

Seabirds. John P. Mackenzie. (Birds of the World Ser.). (Illus.). 144p. 1987. 24.95 (0-942802-52-7) NorthWord.

***Seabirds.** John P. Mackenzie. (Birds of the World Ser.). (Illus.). 144p. (Orig.). 1997. pap. 19.95 (1-55013-797-2, Pub. by Key Porter Bks CN) Firefly Bks Ltd.

Seabirds. Mark J. Rauzon. LC 96-7185. (First Books-Animals). 64p. (J). (gr. 4-6). 1996. lib. bdg. 21.00 (0-531-20246-1) Watts.

***Seabirds.** Mark J. Rauzon. (First Bks.). 64p. (J). 1997. pap. 6.95 (0-531-15817-9) Watts.

Seabirds. Paul Sterry. (Pointers Ser.). (Illus.). (J). 1994. lib. bdg. 22.83 (0-8114-6188-2) Raintree Steck-V.

Seabirds. Paul Sterry. (Pointers Ser.). (J). 1995. pap. text ed. 4.95 (0-8114-9360-1) Raintree Steck-V.

Seabirds. Wildlife Education, Ltd. Staff. (Zoobooks Ser.). (Illus.). 24p. (J). 1992. 13.95 (0-937934-90-9); pap. 2.75 (0-937934-66-6) Wildlife Educ.

Seabirds: An Identification Guide. Peter Harrison. (Illus.). 432p. 1991. pap. 29.95 (0-395-60291-2) HM.

Seabirds: An Unofficial Illustrated Encyclopedia of Naval Aviation. Illus. & Text by Hank Caruso. 96p. 1996. pap. 17.95 (1-57427-046-X) Howell Pr VA.

Seabirds & Other Marine Vertebrates: Competition, Predation, & Other Interactions. Ed. by Joanna Burger. 312p. 1989. text ed. 65.50 (0-231-06362-8) Col U Pr.

Seabirds of Hawaii: Natural History & Conservation. Craig S. Harrison. LC 89-71222. (Illus.). 288p. 1990. 47.50 (0-8014-2449-6); pap. 17.95 (0-8014-9722-1) Cornell U Pr.

Seabirds of the Farallon Islands: Ecology, Dynamics, & Structure of an Upwelling-System Community. Ed. by David G. Ainley & Robert J. Boekelheide. (Illus.). 488p. 1990. 69.50 (0-8047-1530-0) Stanford U Pr.

***Seabirds of the World: A Photographic Guide.** Peter Harrison. LC 96-43336. (Illus.). 317p. 1997. pap. text ed. 24.95 (0-691-01551-1) Princeton U Pr.

***Seabirds of the World: The Complete Reference.** Jim Enticott & David Tipling. LC 97-10077. (Birds of the World Ser.). (Illus.). 240p. 1997. 49.95 (0-8117-0239-1) Stackpole.

Seabirds on Islands: Threats, Case Studies & Action Plans. Ed. by David N. Nettleship et al. (Birdlife Conservation Ser.). (Illus.). 350p. 1994. pap. text ed. 32.00 (1-56098-526-7) Smithsonian.

Seaboard Air Line: Steam Trains & Locomotives 1935 to 1937. Robert K. Durham. LC 96-96170. (Steam of the Thirties Ser.). (Illus.). 52p. 1996. pap. 14.95 (0-9644480-5-X) R K Durham.

Seaboard Air Line Motive Power. Paul K. Withers & Warren C. Calloway. 240p. 1988. 39.95 (0-9618503-1-0) Withers Pub.

Seaboard Air Line Railway Album. Albert M. Langley, Jr. et al. LC 88-50417. (Illus.). 184p. (Orig.). 1988. pap. 27.95 (0-9615257-2-X) Union Sta.

***Seaboard Coast Line Railroad.** Douglas B. Nuckles. (Illus.). 108p. 1996. 19.95 (1-883089-13-1) TLC VA.

Seaboard Parish. George MacDonald. (George MacDonald Original Works: Series V). 650p. 1995. reprint ed. 20.00 (1-881084-30-2) Johannesen.

Seaborne Deception: The History of U. S. Navy Beach Jumpers. John B. Dwyer. LC 91-27817. 192p. 1992. text ed. 49.95 (0-275-93800-X, C3800, Praeger Pubs) Greenwood.

Seabourne: A Guide to Inner Strength. Seabourne. 184p. 1993. pap. text ed. 19.95 (0-88725-192-7) Hunter Textbks.

Seabrook & the Nuclear Regulatory Commission: The Licensing of a Nuclear Power Plant. Donald W. Steven. LC 79-56160. 264p. reprint ed. pap. 75.30 (0-317-39645-5, 2023233) Bks Demand.

Seabrook Station: Citizen Politics & Nuclear Power. Henry F. Bedford. LC 89-77123. (Illus.). 248p. (C). 1990. 30.00 (0-87023-711-X) U of Mass Pr.

S

Seabrook Station: Citizen Politics & Nuclear Power. Henry F. Bedford. LC 89-77123. (Illus.). 248p. (C). 1992. reprint ed. pap. 17.95 (*0-87023-785-3*) U of Mass Pr.

Seabuckthorn: The Vitamin Berry. Bryce Finley & Richard Walker. (Healing Plants Ser.). (Illus.). 100p. (Orig.). 1996. pap. 7.95 (*1-896245-05-6*) BRYCEFINLEY.

Seachnadh: The Avoiding & Other Poems. Aonghas Macneacail. (C). 1989. 39.00 (*0-86334-058-X*, Pub. by Saltire Soc) St Mut.

Seacliff. John W. De Forest. (Collected Works of John W. De Forest). 1988. reprint ed. lib. bdg. 59.00 (*0-7812-1157-3*) Rprt Serv.

Seacliff see Collected Works of John W. De Forest

Seacoast Fortifications of the United States: An Introductory History. Emanuel R. Lewis. (Illus.). 145p. 1993. pap. 18.95 (*1-55750-502-0*) Naval Inst Pr.

Seacoast Life: An Ecological Guide to Natural Seashore Communities in North Carolina. Judith M. Spitsbergen. LC 83-80687. (Illus.). 114p. 1983. reprint ed. pap. 7.95 (*0-8078-4109-9*) U of NC Pr.

Seacoast of Bohemia. large type ed. Nicolas Freeling. 312p. 1995. pap. 20.95 (*0-7838-1567-0*, GK Hall) Thorndike Pr.

Seacoast of Bohemia: A Henri Castang Mystery. Nicolas Freeling. 208p. 1996. mass mkt. 5.99 (*0-446-40371-7*, Mysterious Paperbk) Warner Bks.

Seacoast Poets: An Anthology of Sixteen San Diego Poets. Ed. by Kathleen Iddings. 54p. 1986. pap. write for info. (*0-936367-00-8*) Seacoast Poets.

Seacraft of Prehistory. Paul Johnstone. Ed. by Sean McGrail. (Illus.). 278p. 1980. 36.00 (*0-674-79595-4*) HUP.

***Seafare: A Collection of Favorite Recipes of Those Who Serve in the United States Navy.** Kim Orr. (Illus.). 200p. 1997. spiral bd. 16.95 (*0-9657312-0-0*) SFN Inc.

Seafarer. Ed. by I. L. Gordon. (Old English Ser.). 1966. pap. text ed. 6.95 (*0-89197-570-5*) Irvington.

***Seafarer.** Ed. by I. L. Gordon. 80p. 1996. pap. 13.95 (*0-85989-507-6*, Pub. by Univ Exeter Pr UK) Northwestern U Pr.

Seafarer. Tr. by Kevin C. Holland. 96p. 1993. 150.00 (*0-907664-21-0*, Pub. by Old Stiles UK) St Mut.

Seafarer. Tr. by John Wain. (C). 1990. 60.00 (*0-906887-05-4*, Pub. by Greville Pr UK) St Mut.

***Seafarer, B.Q.E., & Other Poems.** Frank Kuenstler. 105p. (Orig.). 1996. pap. 13.95 (*1-886044-05-8*) Cairn Editions.

Seafarers. large type ed. Vivian Stuart. 572p. 1989. 27.99 (*0-7089-8519-X*, Charnwood) Ulverscroft.

Seafarers: Chronicles of the Suspense & Romance of the Sea. Claudio O. Niedworok. Ed. by Tori Knight. (Illus.). 80p. (Orig.). (YA). Date not set. pap. text ed. 11.95 (*1-882133-05-6*) Barefoot Pr.

Seafarers' Conditions in India & Pakistan see Labour Courts in Latin America

***Seafaring Beggar & Other Tales.** 2nd ed. Yahiya Emerick. (Illus.). 89p. (J). (gr. 5-7). 1995. reprint ed. mass mkt. 3.95 (*1-889720-06-2*) Amirah Pubng.

Seafaring in Colonial Massachusetts. Ed. by Philip C. Smith. LC 80-51256. (Illus.). xvii, 240p. 1980. text ed. 30.00 (*0-8139-0897-3*) U Pr of Va.

Seafaring in the Contemporary Pacific Islands: Studies in Continuity & Change. Ed. by Richard Feinberg. LC 95-11622. (Illus.). 260p. 1995. lib. bdg. 35.00 (*0-87580-201-X*) N Ill U Pr.

Seafaring in the Sixteenth Century: The Letter of Eugenio de Salazar, 1573. Tr. by John Frye from SPA. LC 91-27391. 74p. 1991. pap. 39.95 (*0-7734-9880-X*) E Mellen.

Seafaring Labour: The Merchant Marine of Atlantic Canada, 1820-1914. Eric W. Sager. (Illus.). 352p. (C). 1989. text ed. 55.00 (*0-7735-0670-5*, Pub. by McGill CN) U of Toronto Pr.

***Seafaring Labour: The Merchant Marine of Atlantic Canada, 1820-1914.** Eric W. Sager. 1996. pap. text ed. 22.95 (*0-7735-1523-2*, Pub. by McGill CN) U of Toronto Pr.

Seafire. large type ed. Bill Knox. 1974. 25.99 (*0-85456-271-0*) Ulverscroft.

***Seafire.** large type ed. Sarah Westleigh. (Mills & Boon Large Print Ser.). 350p. 1997. 22.50 (*0-263-14902-1*) Ulverscroft.

Seafire: A James Bond Novel. John Gardner. 304p. 1995. mass mkt. 5.99 (*0-425-14775-4*) Berkley Pub.

***Seafire: James Bond.** John Gardner. 286p. 5.98 (*0-7651-0182-3*) Smithmark.

Seafishing Yarns. Zane Grey. 276p. reprint ed. lib. bdg. 23.95 (*0-89190-766-1*, Rivercity Pr) Amereon Ltd.

Seafloor Hydrothermal Systems: Physical, Chemical, Biological, & Geological Interactions. Ed. by Susan Humphris et al. (Geophysical Monograph Ser.: Vol. 91). 1995. write for info. (*0-87590-048-8*) Am Geophysical.

Seafloor Scour: Design Guidelines for Ocean-Founded Structures. John B. Herbich et al. LC 83-26325. (Ocean Engineering, a Wiley Ser.: No. 4). (Illus.). 336p. reprint ed. pap. 95.80 (*0-7837-0843-2*, 2041156) Bks Demand.

Seafood. (Spotlight on Resources Ser.). (Illus.). (J). (gr. 5 up). 1984. 12.95 (*0-685-58240-X*); lib. bdg. 17.27 (*0-86592-265-9*) Rourke Corp.

Seafood. (Popular Brands Cookbooks Ser.). (Illus.). 24p. 1995. pap. write for info. (*1-56144-674-2*) Modern Pub NYC.

Seafood. Joyce L. Young. 1990. pap. 16.95 (*0-942084-20-9*) SeaSide Pub.

Seafood. 2nd ed. Lonnie Gandara. (Kitchen Arts Ser.). 128p. 1995. reprint ed. pap. 11.95 (*1-56426-064-X*) Cole Group.

Seafood: A Collection of Heart-Healthy Recipes. 2nd rev. ed. Janis Harsila & Evie Hansen. Ed. by Diane Baker. LC 90-61209. (Illus.). 276p. (Orig.). 1990. pap. 13.95 (*0-9616426-2-9*) Nat Seafood Educ.

Seafood: Effects of Technology on Nutrition. Pigott & Tucker. (Food Science & Technology Ser.: Vol. 39). 384p. 1990. 140.00 (*0-8247-7922-3*) Dekker.

Seafood: Resources, Nutritional Composition & Preservation. Z. Sikorski. 256p. 1990. 211.00 (*0-8493-5985-6*, SH337) CRC Pr.

***Seafood-Analysis & Research for Health & Disease: Index of New Information with Authors, Subjects & References.** Marvin H. Vensko. 164p. 1997. 47.50 (*0-7883-1362-2*); pap. 39.50 (*0-7883-1363-0*) ABBE Pubs Assn.

Seafood & Fish: Delicious Recipes. Ed. by G & R Publishing Staff. (Uni-Bks.). 160p. (Orig.). 1994. pap. text ed. 3.00 (*1-56383-023-X*, 3100) G & R Pub.

Seafood Baja-Style: Postcard Recipes to Send Or Save. Patti Higginbotham. 48p. 1994. pap. text ed. 7.95 (*0-9632222-2-8*) Somethins Fishy.

Seafood Celebration: Healthful, Festive, Easy-to-Prepare Recipes for the Casual Cook or the Connoisseur. Sheryl London & Mel London. LC 93-19727. (Illus.). 1993. 30.00 (*0-671-76813-1*) S&S Trade.

***Seafood Cookbook.** Edward Brown & A. Boeum. Date not set. write for info. (*0-688-12456-9*) Hearst Bks.

Seafood Cookbook. Pierre Franey. LC 86-5779. (Illus.). 296p. 1986. 27.50 (*0-8129-1604-2*, Times Bks) Random.

Seafood Expressions. Normand J. Leclair. (Illus.). 312p. (Orig.). 1991. pap. 12.95 (*0-9620331-2-X*) Normand Pub.

Seafood Fishing for Amateur & Professional. R. C. O'Farrell. 1978. 35.00 (*0-685-63452-3*) St Mut.

Seafood Industry. Ed. by Roy F. Martin & George J. Flick, Jr. 520p. (C). (gr. 13). 1990. text ed. 101.95 (*0-442-23915-7*) Chapman & Hall.

Seafood Irradiation. Kilgen. 1993. write for info. (*0-8493-8988-7*) CRC Pr.

Seafood List: FDA's Guide to Acceptable Market Names for Seafood Sold in Interstate Commerce (1993) Spring Randolph & Mary Snyder. 69p. (Orig.). (C). 1994. pap. text ed. 30.00 (*0-7881-1324-0*) DIANE Pub.

Seafood Lovers Cookbook. Gloria J. Bass. LC 93-73153. 194p. (Orig.). 1993. pap. 15.95 (*0-935132-22-8*) C H Fairfax.

***Seafood Meals in Minutes! 150 Simple Recipes to Make Low-Fat Seafood Dishes.** M. J. Smith. (Meals in Minutes! Ser.). 288p. (Orig.). 1997. pap. 13.95 (*1-56561-126-8*) Chronimed.

Seafood of the Florida Suncoast. Tom Bailey. (Illus.). 80p. (Orig.). 1986. pap. 2.50 (*0-685-63151-6*) Seacoast AL.

Seafood of the Northern Gulf. Tom Bailey. (Illus.). 80p. (Orig.). 1984. pap. 2.50 (*0-685-63150-8*) Seacoast AL.

Seafood Pasta & Noodles: The New Classics. Rosina T. Wilson. LC 93-49012. (Illus.). 144p. 1994. pap. 15.95 (*0-89815-603-3*) Ten Speed Pr.

Seafood Product Safety. Steven Otwell. 1994. write for info. (*0-8493-4296-1*) CRC Pr.

***Seafood Proteins.** Z. Sikorski. (Illus.). 192p. 1994. text ed. 83.95 (*0-412-98481-4*, Chap & Hall NY) Chapman & Hall.

***Seafood Recipes, 2 vols.** Marjorie Standish. (Best of Marjorie Standish Ser.). (Illus.). 64p. (Orig.). 1997. reprint ed. pap. 8.95 (*0-89272-423-4*) Down East.

Seafood Regulations Compliance Manual. Andrew R. Welt. LC 94-41208. 768p. (C). (gr. 13). 1994. pap. text ed. 154.00 (*0-412-98751-1*) Chapman & Hall.

Seafood Restaurant Operations. Ad Wittemann. 59p. (Orig.). (C). 1988. pap. 25.00 (*0-938481-49-5*) Camelot Consult.

Seafood Safety. Institute of Medicine, Committee on Evaluation of the Safety of Fishery Products Staff. 452p. 1991. text ed. 49.95 (*0-309-04387-5*) Natl Acad Pr.

***Seafood Safety, Processing, & Biotechnology.** Fereidoon Shahidi et al. LC 97-60621. 272p. 1997. pap. text ed. 129.95 (*1-56676-573-0*) Technomic.

Seafood Sampler. Jan Siegrist. (Illus.). 48p. (Orig.). 1989. pap. 3.95 (*0-933050-75-5*) New Eng Pr VT.

Seafood Sampler of Canned Seafoods. R. Marilyn Schmidt. 110p. (Orig.). 1994. pap. 10.95 (*0-937996-26-2*) Barnegat.

***Seafood Savvy: A Consumer's Guide to Seafood Nutrition, Safety, Handling & Preparation.** Ken Gall. (Information Bulletin Ser.). (Illus.). 34p. (Orig.). 1992. pap. 5.50 (*1-57753-028-4*, 1041B226) Corn Coop Ext.

Seafood Scams & Frauds & How to Protect Yourself. Ian Dore. 160p. 1992. 39.00 (*1-881693-00-7*) Urner Barry Pubns.

Seafood Science & Technology. Ed. by E. G. Bligh. (Illus.). 416p. 1992. 125.00 (*0-85238-173-5*) Blackwell Sci.

Seafood Secrets Cookbook. 1994. pap. 14.95 (*0-939510-08-1*) Mystic Sea Mus.

Seafood Smoking. R. Marilyn Schmidt. (Illus.). 58p. (Orig.). 1987. pap. 5.95 (*0-937996-09-2*) Barnegat.

Seafood Sourcebook: A Consumer's Guide to Information on Food from Our Oceans & Lakes. New England Marine Advisory Service Staff. 46p. 1978. 1.00 (*0-686-36979-3*, P762) Sea Grant Pubns.

***Seafood Toxins.** Ed. by Edward P. Ragelis. LC 84-18551. (ACS Symposium Ser.: No. 262). (Illus.). 472p. 1984. reprint ed. pap. 134.60 (*0-608-03254-9*, 2063773) Bks Demand.

Seafood-Twice a Week, Vol. I. Evie Hansen & Cindy W. Snyder. LC 95-70435. (Illus.). (Orig.). 1995. pap. 14.95 (*0-9616426-4-5*) Nat Seafood Educ.

Seafood Yellow Pages: A Business to Business Directory. 1989. 79.95 (*0-9625591-0-5*) Amer Seafood.

Seafoods: Chemistry, Processing Technology & Quality. F. Shahidi. 1994. 136.00 (*0-7514-0218-4*, Pub. by Blackie Acad & Prof UK) Routledge Chapman & Hall.

Seaforth. Dean Robinson. (Illus.). 84p. (Orig.). pap. 10.95 (*0-919783-53-8*, Pub. by Boston Mills Pr CN) Genl Dist Srvs.

Seaghost. William H. Lovejoy. 256p. (Orig.). 1991. mass mkt. 3.99 (*0-380-76577-2*) Avon.

Seagoing Hitchhiker's Handbook: Roaming the Earth on Other People's Yachts. Greg Becker. Ed. by Estela Marin. 224p. (Orig.). 1994. pap. 11.95 (*0-9639712-0-4*) High Adventure.

***Seagoing Ships & Seamanship in the Bronze Age Levant.** Shelley Wachsmann. LC 96-49815. (Illus.). 448p. (C). 1997. text ed. 80.00 (*0-89096-709-1*) Tex A&M Univ Pr.

Seagram Museum. 46p. (Orig.). pap. 9.95 (*1-55046-068-4*, Pub. by Boston Mills Pr CN) Genl Dist Srvs.

Seagram's Bartending Guide. Seagram Company, Ltd. Staff. LC 95-31023. (Illus.). 272p. 1995. pap. 9.95 (*0-670-86397-1*, Viking) Viking Penguin.

***Seagram's Perfect Party Guide.** Summit Editors. 150p. 12.99 (*1-56530-253-2*) Summit TX.

Seagrapes. Roy King. 259p. (YA). 1996. 15.95 (*1-880664-13-5*) E M Pr.

Seagrass Ecosystems: A Scientific Perspective. Ed. by C. Peter McRoy & Carla Helfferich. LC 76-9466. (Marine Science Ser.: No. 4). 328p. reprint ed. pap. 93.50 (*0-318-35008-4*, 2030868) Bks Demand.

Seagrasses. Ronald C. Phillips & Ernani G. Menez. LC 87-23245. (Smithsonian Contributions to the Marine Sciences Ser.: No. 34). (Illus.). 110p. reprint ed. pap. 31.40 (*0-8357-8316-2*, 2034077) Bks Demand.

Seagrave Fire Apparatus. Richard Baker. write for info. (*0-318-62388-9*) E Hass.

Seagull. Anton Chekhov. Tr. by Fred Eisemann & Oliver F. Murphy. Bd. with Tragedian in Spite of Himself. (Orig.). Set pap. 4.95 (*0-8283-1454-3*) Branden Pub Co.

***Seagull.** Anton Chekhov. (Nick Hern Books, Drama Classics). 1997. pap. text ed. 6.95 (*1-85459-193-2*, Pub. by N Hern Bks UK) Theatre Comm.

Seagull. Anton P. Chekhov. Tr. by Pam Gems. 96p. Date not set. pap. 12.95 (*1-85459-261-0*, Pub. by N Hern Bks UK) Theatre Comm.

Seagull. Anton P. Chekhov. (Plays for Performance Ser.). 89p. (Orig.). 1992. pap. 7.95 (*0-929587-88-X*, Elephant Paperbacks) I R Dee.

Seagull. Anton P. Chekhov. (Plays for Performance Ser.). 89p. 1992. text ed. 15.95 (*0-929587-89-8*) I R Dee.

Seagull. Anton P. Chekhov. Ed. & Intro. by William-Alan Landes. 50p. (Orig.). 1996. pap. 7.00 (*0-88734-299-X*) Players Pr.

Seagull. Anton P. Chekhov. Tr. by Michael H. Heim from RUS. 1992. pap. 5.00 (*0-87129-123-1*, S85) Dramatic Pub.

Seagull. Anton P. Chekhov. Tr. by Michael Frayn from RUS. (Methuen Theatre Classics Ser.). 67p. (Orig.). (C). 1988. pap. 9.95 (*0-413-42140-6*, A0258, Pub. by Methuen UK) Heinemann.

Seagull. Anton P. Chekhov. Tr. by David French from RUS. 112p. 1993. pap. 10.95 (*0-88922-324-6*) Genl Dist Srvs.

Seagull: A New Version. John Murrell. 57p. (Orig.). 1989. 7.95 (*0-317-91355-7*) Playsmith.

***Seagull: After Chekhov.** Thomas Kilroy. 88p. 1993. pap. 12.95 (*1-85235-120-9*) Dufour.

Seagull: Chaika. Anton P. Chekhov. Tr. by Nicholas Saunders & Frank Dwyer. LC 94-7990. (Great Translations for Actors Ser.). 112p. 1994. pap. 11.95 (*1-880399-53-9*) Smith & Kraus.

Seagull see Plays

Seagull & the Pigeon: For the Children in Your Life. Bob Christensen. (Illus.). 42p. (Orig.). (YA). (gr. 4-12). 1991. pap. 5.95 (*1-886045-02-X*) Covenant Marriages.

Seagull Beach. Gary Metras. 35p. 1995. 10.00 (*0-938566-69-5*) Adastra Pr.

Seagull Beach. deluxe limited ed. Gary Metras. 35p. 1995. 30.00 (*0-938566-68-7*) Adastra Pr.

Seagull Produced by Stanislavski. Constantin Stanislavski. Ed. by S. D. Balukhaty. 1984. pap. write for info. (*0-317-11832-3*, Thtre Arts Bks) Routledge.

Seagull, Uncle Vanya... unabridged ed. Anton P. Chekhov. (World Classic Literature Ser.). (RUS.). pap. 6.95 (*2-87714-265-5*, Pub. by Bookking Intl FR) Distribks Inc.

Seagull Who Liked Cricket. Leslie Rees. (Illus.). 40p. (J). 1996. 18.95 (*1-875560-60-2*, Pub. by Cygnet AT) Intl Spec Bk.

Seagulls Don't Fly into the Bush: Cultural Identity & Development in Melanesia. Alice Pomponio. 242p. (C). 1992. pap. 22.95 (*0-534-16260-6*) Wadsworth Pub.

***Seagulls in My Soup.** Tristan Jones. 1996. pap. text ed. 14.95 (*0-07-033122-7*) McGraw.

Seagulls in My Soup: Further Adventures of a Wayward Sailor. Tristan Jones. (Illus.). 299p. 1991. 22.95 (*0-924486-17-1*) Sheridan.

Seagulls in My Soup: Further Adventures of a Wayward Sailor. Tristan Jones. (Illus.). 312p. 1996. pap. 14.95 (*1-57409-005-4*) Sheridan.

Seahorse: A Novel. Graham Petrie. LC 95-8673. 169p. 1996. 21.00 (*1-56947-077-4*) Soho Press.

Seal. (Animal World Bks.). (J). (gr. 2-5). 1996. pap. 3.50 (*0-8167-1575-0*) Troll Communs.

Seal. (Illus.). 64p. 1991. pap. 17.95 (*0-7119-2833-9*, AM86915) Music Sales.

Seal. Judy Allen. LC 93-3642. (Illus.). 32p. (J). (ps up). 1994. 14.95 (*1-56402-145-9*) Candlewick Pr.

Seal. Mary Hoffman. LC 86-17806. (Animals in the Wild Ser.). (Illus.). 24p. (J). (gr. k-5). 1987. pap. 3.95 (*0-8114-6887-9*) Raintree Steck-V.

Seal. Joelle Soler. LC 92-72904. (Animal Close-ups Ser.). (Illus.). 28p. (J). (gr. 3-8). 1992. pap. 6.95 (*0-88106-428-9*) Charlesbridge Pub.

Seal. Judy Allen. LC 93-3642. (Illus.). 32p. (J). (gr. k-5). 1996. reprint ed. pap. 5.99 (*1-56402-956-5*) Candlewick Pr.

***Seal, No. 2.** 1996. 17.95 (*0-7119-4315-X*, AM 92189) Omnibus NY.

Seal, Reading Level 3-4. Dalmais. (World Animal Library). (Illus.). 28p. (J). (gr. 2-5). 1983. 12.50 (*0-685-58825-4*); lib. bdg. 16.67 (*0-86592-867-3*) Rourke Corp.

Seal: People of the Sea. Fiona Middleton. (Illus.). 192p. 1996. 35.00 (*1-85158-744-6*, Pub. by Mnstream UK) Trafalgar.

Seal Called Andre: The Two Worlds of a Maine Harbor Seal. Lew Dietz & Harry Goodridge. LC 74-30996. 182p. 1980. pap. 9.95 (*0-89272-076-X*) Down East.

***Seal Child.** Sylvia Peck. (J). Date not set. lib. bdg. write for info. (*0-688-08683-7*, Morrow Junior) Morrow.

Seal Child. Sylvia Peck. 208p. (J). (gr. 3-7). 1991. reprint ed. mass mkt. 3.99 (*0-553-15868-6*, Skylark BDD) BDD Bks Young Read.

SEAL Combat Boarding Manual. (Illus.). 144p. 1992. pap. 20.00 (*0-87364-686-X*) Paladin Pr.

Seal Cylinders of Western Asia. William H. Ward. LC 78-72772. (Ancient Mesopotamian Texts & Studies). reprint ed. 72.50 (*0-404-18228-3*) AMS Pr.

Seal Islands of Alaska. Henry W. Elliott. (Alaska History Ser.: No. 9). (Illus.). 1976. reprint ed. 18.00 (*0-919642-72-1*) Limestone Pr.

Seal Journey. Richard Sobol & Jonah Sobol. LC 92-25974. (Illus.). 32p. (J). (gr. 1-5). 1993. pap. 14.99 (*0-525-65126-8*, Cobblehill Bks) Dutton Child Bks.

Seal Killers. Susannah Brin. Ed. by Liz Parker. (Take Ten Bks.). (Illus.). 45p. (Orig.). (J). (gr. 6-12). 1992. pap. text ed. 3.95 (*1-56254-051-3*) Saddleback Pubns.

Seal-Less Centrifugal Pumps: Class 1. EEMUA Staff. 1994. 125.00 (*0-85931-114-7*, Pub. by EEMUA UK) St Mut.

Seal Mother. Mordicai Gerstein. LC 82-29295. (Illus.). 32p. (J). (ps-3). 1986. lib. bdg. 10.89 (*0-8037-0303-1*) Dial Bks Young.

Seal of Approval, Set. Kenneth G. Mills. 1979. pap. 10.95 incl. audio (*0-919842-03-8*, KGOM9) Sun-Scape Ent.

***Seal of Approval: The History of the Comics Code.** Amy K. Nyberg. (Studies in Popular Culture). 256p. 1998. text ed. 45.00 (*0-87805-974-1*) U Pr of Miss.

***Seal of Approval: The History of the Comics Code.** Amy K. Nyberg. (Studies in Popular Culture). 256p. 1998. pap. 18.00 (*0-87805-975-X*) U Pr of Miss.

Seal of Orestes: Self-Reference & Authority in Sophocles' Electra. Ann G. Batchelder. 180p. (C). 1994. pap. text ed. 22.95 (*0-8476-7991-8*); lib. bdg. 52.50 (*0-8476-7990-X*) Rowman.

Seal of Renewal. Catharose De Petri. (Orig.). 1986. pap. 11.00 (*90-70196-39-5*) Rosycross Pr.

Seal of the End Times. Nils W. Hammaren. 319p. 1992. pap. 34.50 (*0-9632353-0-3*) End Times Pr.

Seal of the Prophets & His Message. Mujtaba L. Sayyid. 1990. 12.00 (*0-685-66734-0*, 66) Tahrike Tarsile Quran.

***Seal of the Saints.** Michel Chodkiewicz. 192p. 1996. pap. 17.95 (*0-614-21340-1*, 192) Kazi Pubns.

Seal of the Saints: Prophethood & Sainthood in the Doctrine of Ibn'Arabi. Michel Chodkiewicz. Tr. by Liadain Sherrard from FRE. (Golden Palm Ser.). 138p. 1995. 44.95 (*0-946621-39-X*, Pub. by Islamic Texts UK); pap. 21.95 (*0-946621-40-3*, Pub. by Islamic Texts UK) Intl Spec Bk.

Seal of the State of South Carolina: A Short History. David C. Heisser. Ed. by Judith M. Brimelow. (Illus.). 36p. pap. 4.00 (*1-880067-11-0*, PH8) SC Dept of Arch & Hist.

Seal Oil Lamp. Retold by Dale DeArmond. (Illus.). 48p. (J). (gr. k-4). 1997. reprint ed. pap. 7.95 (*0-87156-858-6*) Sierra Club Childrens.

Seal-Oil System. Center for Occupational Research & Development Staff. (EUTEC Power Plant Operator Curriculum Ser.). (Illus.). 20p. (C). 1985. pap. text ed. write for info. (*1-55502-214-6*) CORD Commns.

Seal Prince. Sheila MacGill-Callahan. LC 93-16248. (J). 1995. pap. 15.99 (*0-8037-1486-6*) Dial Bks Young.

Seal Pup Grows Up: The Story of a Harbor Seal. Kathleen W. Zoehfeld. LC 93-27269. (Smithsonian Oceanic Collection). (Illus.). 32p. (J). (ps-2). 1994. 15.95 (*1-56899-026-X*) Soundprints.

Seal Pup Grows Up: The Story of a Harbor Seal. Kathleen W. Zoehfeld. LC 93-27269. (Smithsonian Oceanic Collection). (Illus.). 32p. (J). (ps-2). 1994. 19.95 incl. audio (*1-56899-039-1*); 4.95 (*1-56899-027-8*); audio write for info. (*1-56899-037-5*) Soundprints.

Seal Pup Grows Up: The Story of a Harbor Seal, Incl. toy. Kathleen W. Zoehfeld. LC 93-27269. (Smithsonian Oceanic Collection). (Illus.). 32p. (J). (ps-2). 1994. 29.95 (*1-56899-038-3*); 9.95 (*1-56899-040-5*) Soundprints.

Seal Rock. John Haislip. LC 85-72583. 52p. (Orig.). 1987. pap. 5.95 (*0-935306-40-4*) Barnwood Pr.

SEAL Sniper Training Program. (Illus.). 288p. 1992. pap. 30.00 (*0-87364-683-5*) Paladin Pr.

Seal Surfer. Michael Foreman. (J). 1997. 16.00 (*0-15-201399-7*) HarBrace.

SEAL Team Combat Missions: Search & Destroy. Mark Roberts. 1994. pap. 4.99 (*1-56171-328-7*) Sure Seller.

Seal Team One. Dick Couch. 288p. (Orig.). 1991. mass mkt. 5.99 (*0-380-76115-7*) Avon.

Seal Team Seven. Keith Douglass. 336p. (Orig.). 1994. pap. text ed. 5.99 (*0-425-14340-6*) Berkley Pub.

Seal Team Seven: Nucflash. Keith Douglass. 304p. (Orig.). 1995. pap. text ed. 5.99 (*0-425-14881-5*) Berkley Pub.

***Seal Team Seven No. 5.** Keith Douglass. 304p. 1997. mass mkt. 5.99 (*0-425-16139-0*) Berkley Pub.

Seal Team 7: Specter. Keith Douglass. 304p. (Orig.). 1995. pap. text ed. 5.99 (*0-425-14569-7*) Berkley Pub.

Seal upon My Heart. E. M. Budd. LC 95-79070. 485p. 1996. pap. 12.95 (*1-885487-18-5*) Brownell & Carroll.

***Seal Wife.** large type ed. Eleanor Rees. (Magna Large Print Ser.). 219p. 1997. 27.50 (*0-7505-1059-5*) Ulverscroft.

Sealand of Ancient Arabia. Raymond P. Dougherty. LC 78-63564. (Yale Oriental Series: Researches: No. 19). reprint ed. 40.00 (*0-404-60289-4*) AMS Pr.

 An Asterisk (*) at the beginning of an entry indicates that the title is appearing in BIP for the first time.

Sealant Technology in Glazing Systems: A Symposium. American Society for Testing & Materials Staff. LC 77-83433. (ASTM Special Technical Publication Ser.: 638). 116p. reprint ed. pap. 33.10 (*0-317-20575-7*, 2022516) Bks Demand.

Sealants in Construction. Klosowski. (Civil Engineering Ser.: Vol. 7). 328p. 1988. 140.00 (*0-8247-7677-1*) Dekker.

Sealed & Dispatched. large type ed. Freda Bream. (Linford Mystery Large Print Ser.). 288p. 1995. pap. 15.99 (*0-7089-7728-6*, Linford) Ulverscroft.

Sealed Angel & Other Stories. Nikolai S. Leskov. Ed. by K. A. Lantz. LC 83-14547. 267p. reprint ed. pap. 76.10 (*0-7837-7080-4*, 2046892) Bks Demand.

Sealed Battery Selection for Designers & Users. Michael R. Meurer. 1996. text ed. 55.00 (*0-07-041824-1*) McGraw.

Sealed Containers. Kevin Beary. 28p. 1991. pap. 4.00 (*1-881355-03-9*) Intemprte Stage.

Sealed in Parchment: Rereadings of Knighthood in the Illuminated Manuscripts of Chretien de Troyes. Sandra Hindman. LC 93-5300. (Illus.). 240p. 1994. pap. text ed. 16.95 (*0-226-34156-9*); lib. bdg. 45.00 (*0-226-34155-0*) U Ch Pr.

Sealed Knot. Elizabeth Law. 224p. 1989. 18.95 (*0-8027-1085-9*) Walker & Co.

Sealed Orders. Elizabeth S. Ward. 1972. reprint ed. lib. bdg. 29.00 (*0-8422-8123-1*) Irvington.

Sealed Orders. Elizabeth S. Ward. (C). 1986. reprint ed. pap. text ed. 7.95 (*0-8290-1876-X*) Irvington.

Sealed Orders: The Autobiography of a Christian Mystic. Agnes Sanford. LC 72-76592. 312p. 1972. pap. 8.95 (*0-88270-048-0*) Bridge-Logos.

Sealed with a Kiss. Gwynne Forster. 1995. mass mkt. 4.99 (*0-7860-0189-5*, Pinncle Kensgtn) Kensgtn Pub Corp.

Sealed with a Kiss. Beverly Lewis. (Holly's Heart Ser.: Vol. 3). 160p. (J). (gr. 6-9). 1993. pap. 6.99 (*0-310-38071-5*) Zondervan.

Sealed with a Kiss. Sean McGrady. Ed. by Jane Chelius. 256p. (Orig.). 1995. mass mkt. 5.50 (*0-671-86941-8*) PB.

Sealed with a Loving Kill. large type ed. Roger Ormerod. (Linford Mystery Library). 288p. 1994. pap. 15.99 (*0-7089-7480-5*, Linford) Ulverscroft.

Sealers. Peter Tutein. Tr. by Eugene Gay-Tifft. (Seafaring Men: Their Ships & Times Ser.). (Illus.). 1980. reprint ed. text ed. 22.50 (*0-930576-28-4*) E M Coleman Ent.

Seali: From Vietnam's Phoenix Program to Central America's Drug Wars - Twenty-Six Years of Combat with a Special Forces Warrior. Mike Walsh & Greg Walter. Ed. by Eric Tobias. 288p. (Orig.). 1995. mass mkt. 6.50 (*0-671-86853-5*) PB.

SeaLife: A Guide to the Marine Environment. Marc Dando & Michael Burchett. Ed. by Geoffrey Waller. (Illus.). 432p. 1996. 49.95 (*1-56098-633-6*) Smithsonian.

Sealing & Seals on Texts form Kultepe Karen Level 2. B. Teissier. xiv, 280p. 1994. pap. text ed. 52.50 (*90-6258-070-X*, Pub. by Netherlands Inst NE) Eisenbrauns.

Sealless Centrifugal Pumps Standard for Nomenclature, Definitions, Application, Operation, & Test Standard, No. 5.4-5.6. (Hydraulic Institute Ser.: No. 5.4-5.6). 39p. 1994. 39.00 (*1-880952-09-2*, S108) Hydraulic Inst.

Sealless Rotary Pump Standard for Nomenclature, Definitions, Application, Operation, & Test Standard, No. 4.1-4.6. (Hydraulic Institute Ser.: No. 4.1-4.6). 23p. 1994. 39.00 (*1-880952-08-4*, S113) Hydraulic Inst.

SeAlphabet Encyclopedia. Keith A. McConnell. (NaturEncyclopedia Library). (Illus.). 48p. (Orig.). (J). (gr. 4 up). 1982. pap. 6.95 (*0-88045-016-9*) Stemmer Hse.

Seals. Annette Barkhausen & Franz Geiser. LC 92-10684. (Animal Families Ser.). 1992. lib. bdg. 19.93 (*0-8368-0842-8*) Gareth Stevens Inc.

Seals. Cousteau Society Staff. LC 91-34459. (Illus.). 24p. (J). (ps-1). 1992. pap. 4.95 (*0-671-77061-6*, Litl Simon S&S) S&S Childrens.

Seals. Eric S. Grace. (Sierra Club Bks.). (Illus.). 64p. (J). (gr. 3-6). 1994. pap. text ed. 7.95 (*0-316-32291-1*) Little.

Seals. Highlights for Children Editors. (Highlights Animal Bks.). (Illus.). 32p. (Orig.). (J). (gr. 2-5). 1993. pap. 3.95 (*1-56397-286-7*) Boyds Mills Pr.

Seals. L. Martin. (Wildlife in Danger Ser.). (Illus.). 24p. (J). (gr. k-5). 1988. lib. bdg. 11.94 (*0-86592-999-8*) Rourke Corp.

Seals. David Miller. (Illus.). 48p. (Orig.). 1994. pap. 9.95 (*0-948661-24-0*, Pub. by Colin Baxter Ltd UK) Voyageur Pr.

Seals. Two Can Publishing Ltd. Staff. (Animal Bks.). (Illus.). 32p. (J). (gr. 2-7). 1991. pap. 2.95 (*0-87534-218-3*) Highlights.

Seals: An Action Plan for Their Conservation. Ed. by P. Reijnders. 80p. write for info. (*2-8317-0044-2*, Pub. by IUCN SZ) Island Pr.

SEALs: UDT - Seal Operations in Vietnam. T. L. Bosiljevac. (Library of Vietnam Literature). 755p. (Orig.). 1991. mass mkt. 5.95 (*0-8041-0722-X*) Ivy Books.

SEALs: UDT-SEAL Operations in Vietnam. T. L. Bosiljevac. (Illus.). 272p. 1990. text ed. 26.95 (*0-87364-531-6*) Paladin Pr.

SEALs No. 1: Ambush. Steve MacKenzie. 192p. 1987. pap. 2.50 (*0-380-75189-5*) Avon.

SEALs No. 4: Target. Steve MacKenzie. 192p. 1987. pap. 2.95 (*0-380-75193-3*) Avon.

SEALs No. 7: Recon. Steve MacKenzie. 160p. 1988. pap. 2.95 (*0-380-75529-7*) Avon.

SEALs No. 8: Infiltrate. Steve MacKenzie. 160p. (Orig.). 1988. pap. 2.95 (*0-380-75530-0*) Avon.

SEALs No. 9: Assault! Steve MacKenzie. 160p. 1988. pap. 2.95 (*0-380-75532-7*) Avon.

SEALs No. 10: Sniper. Steve MacKenzie. 1988. pap. 2.95 (*0-380-75533-5*) Avon.

SEALs No. 11: Attack. Steve MacKenzie. 160p. 1989. pap. 2.95 (*0-380-75582-3*) Avon.

SEALs No. 12: Stronghold. Steve MacKenzie. 160p. (Orig.). 1989. pap. 2.95 (*0-380-75583-1*) Avon.

SEALs No. 13: Crisis! Steve MacKenzie. 160p. (Orig.). 1989. pap. 2.95 (*0-380-75771-0*) Avon.

SEALs No. 14: Treasure. Steve MacKenzie. 176p. 1989. pap. 2.95 (*0-380-75772-9*) Avon.

Seals & Man: A Study of Interactions. W. Nigel Bonner. LC 81-69684. (Illus.). 184p. 1982. pap. 9.95 (*0-295-95890-1*) U of Wash Pr.

Seals & Plus: Self-Esteem & Life Skills. Kathy K. Korb-Khalsa et al. (Illus.). 176p. 1992. spiral bd. 49.95 (*0-9622022-3-1*) Wellness Reprodns.

***Seals & Sea Lions.** (Portrait of the Animal World Ser.). 1996. 10.98 (*0-7651-9966-1*) Smithmark.

***Seals & Sea Lions.** (WorldLife Library). (Illus.). 84p. (Orig.). (YA). (gr. 5 up). 1998. pap. 14.95 (*0-89658-371-6*) Voyageur Pr.

Seals & Sea Lions. David G. Gordon. (Natural History Ser.). (Illus.). 64p. (Orig.). 1994. pap. 9.95 (*1-878244-06-X*) Monterey Bay Aquarium.

Seals & Sea Lions. Charles Rotter. (Nature Bks.). 32p. (J). (gr. 2-6). 1991. lib. bdg. 22.79 (*0-89565-714-7*) Childs World.

Seals & Sea Lions. Wildlife Education, Ltd. Staff. (Illus.). 20p. (Orig.). (YA). (gr. 5 up). 1985. pap. 2.75 (*0-937934-33-X*) Wildlife Educ.

Seals & Sea Lions. John Woodward. LC 96-7223. (Endangered! Ser.). (J). (gr. 3-5). 1996. 14.95 (*0-7614-0292-6*, Benchmark NY) Marshall Cavendish.

Seals & Sea Lions: An Affectionate Portrait. Vicki Leon. LC 94-31827. (Close Up Ser.). (Illus.). 40p. (YA). (gr. 5 up). 1994. pap. 7.95 (*0-382-24890-2*); lib. bdg. 14.95 (*0-382-24889-9*) Silver Burdett Pr.

Seals & Sea Lions of the World. Nigel Bonner. LC 92-46594. (Illus.). 224p. 1994. (*0-8160-2955-5*) Facts on File.

***Seals & Sealing Handbook.** 4th ed. 500p. 1995. 201.95 (*1-85617-232-5*, Pub. by Elsvr Adv Tech UK) Elsevier.

Seals & Sealing in the Ancient Near East. Ed. by M. Gibson & R. D. Biggs. LC 76-44923. (Bibliotheca Mesopotamica Ser.: Vol. 6). 160p. 1978. pap. 29.00 (*0-89003-022-7*) Undena Pubns.

***Seals & Sealing in the Ancient Near East.** Ed. by Joan G. Westenholz. (Illus.). 145p. pap. 42.00 (*965-7027-01-2*, Pub. by Bible Lands Mus IS) Eisenbrauns.

Seals & Talismans. Ludvik Kalus. (Nasser D. Khalili Collection of Islamic Art: Vol. XIII). (Illus.). 304p. 1998. 260.00 (*0-19-727611-3*) OUP.

Seals at War: The Story of U. S. Navy Special Warfare from the Frogmen to the SEALs. Edwin P. Hoyt. 272p. 1993. mass mkt. 5.99 (*0-440-21497-1*) Dell.

Seals, Fur Seals, Sea Lions & Walruses: An Action Plan for Their Conservation. Ed. by Peter J. Reijinders. 88p. (C). 1993. pap. text ed. 20.00 (*2-8317-0141-4*, Pub. by IUCN SZ) Island Pr.

Seals II: Self-Esteem & Life Skills, Too! Kathy K. Korb-Khalsa et al. (Illus.). 176p. 1996. spiral bd. 49.95 (*0-9622022-8-2*) Wellness Reprodns.

SEALs in Action. Kevin Dockery. 392p. 1991. mass mkt. 5.99 (*0-380-75886-5*) Avon.

Seals in the Far East. Hawley. 1991. pap. 5.95 (*0-910704-21-X*) Hawley.

Seals in the Inner Harbor. Brendan Galvin. LC 85-71692. (Poetry Ser.). 1985. 20.95 (*0-88748-050-0*); pap. 9.95 (*0-88748-076-4*) Carnegie-Mellon.

***Seals in the Inner Harbor.** Brendan Galvin. LC 85-71692. 1985. pap. 11.95 (*0-88748-051-9*) Carnegie-Mellon.

Seals of Chinese Painters & Collectors of the Ming & Ch'ing Periods. Victoria Contag & Wang Chi-ch'ien. (Illus.). 794p. (C). 1982. pap. text ed. 75.00 (*962-209-034-6*, Pub. by Hong Kong U Pr HK) St Mut.

Seals of the Order of St. John of Jerusalem, 3 vols., Vols. 1 - 3. Edwin J. King. LC 78-63355. (Crusades & Military Orders Ser.: Second Series). (Illus.). reprint ed. 44.00 (*0-404-16248-7*) AMS Pr.

Seals of Wisdom. Muhyiddin Al-Arabi. (Sacred Texts Ser.). (Illus.). (Orig.). (C). 1983. pap. 8.75 (*0-88695-010-4*) Concord Grove.

Seals, Sea Lions, & Walruses. Victoria Sherrow. LC 91-4663. (First Bks.). (Illus.). 64p. (J). (gr. 3-4). 1991. lib. bdg. 11.90 (*0-685-52512-0*) Denison.

Seals, Sea Lions, & Walruses: A Review of the Pinnipedia. Victor B. Scheffer. (Illus.). x, 179p. 1958. 19.50 (*0-8047-0544-5*) Stanford U Pr.

Seals, Sea Lions, & Walruses: A Review of the Pinnipedia. Victor B. Scheffer. LC 58-7844. (Illus.). 221p. reprint ed. pap. 30.00 (*0-7837-5128-1*, 2044856) Bks Demand.

Seals, Sea Lions, Walruses. John B. Wexo. (Zoobooks Ser.). 24p. (J). (gr. 4). 1989. lib. bdg. 14.95 (*0-88682-271-8*) Creative Ed.

SEALs, the Warrior Breed No. 1: Silver Star. H. Jay Riker. 400p. (Orig.). 1993. mass mkt. 5.99 (*0-380-76967-0*) Avon.

SEALs, the Warrior Breed No. 2: Purple Heart. H. Jay Riker. 512p. (Orig.). 1994. mass mkt. 5.99 (*0-380-76969-7*) Avon.

SEALs, the Warrior Breed No. 3: Bronze Star. H. Jay Riker. 464p. (Orig.). 1995. mass mkt. 5.99 (*0-380-76970-0*) Avon.

***Seals, Traps, & the Petroleum System.** Ronald C. Surdam. LC 97-20684. (AAPG Memoirs). 1997. write for info. (*0-89181-347-0*) Am Soc Clinical.

SEALs, UDT, Frogmen: Men under Pressure. Darryl Young. (Orig.). 1994. mass mkt. 5.99 (*0-8041-1064-6*) Ivy Books.

***Seal,Sea Lions & Otters.** HarBrace Staff. 1995. pap. 11.00 (*0-15-305616-9*) HarBrace.

Sealskin & Shoddy: Working Women in the American Nineteenth Century Labor Press, 1870-1920. Intro. by Ann Schofield. LC 87-36065. (Contributions in Women's Studies: No. 96). 272p. 1988. text ed. 55.00 (*0-313-25453-2*, SSK/, Greenwood Pr) Greenwood.

Sealy: Cases & Materials in Company Law. 6th ed. L. S. Sealy. 704p. 1996. write for info. (*0-406-06327-3*) MICHIE.

Sealy & Hooley: Cases & Materials in Commercial Law. L. S. Sealy & Richard Hooley. 640p. 1993. pap. write for info. (*0-406-01619-4*, UK) MICHIE.

***Sealyham Terrier: AKC Rank # 137.** Seymour L. Weiss. (Rare Breed Ser.). (Illus.). 96p. 1997. 19.95 (*0-7938-0771-9*, RX-121) TFH Pubns.

Sealyham Terrier Champions, 1911-1987. Camino E. E. & Bk. Co. Staff. 144p. 1988. pap. 36.95 (*0-940808-90-0*) Camino E E & Bk.

***Seam Allowance: Industrial Home Sewing in Canada.** Laura C. Johnson & Robert E. Johnson. 128p. pap. 5.95 (*0-88961-072-X*, Pub. by Wmns Pr CN) LPC InBook.

Seamaid. Mark Dunster. 10p. 1992. pap. 4.00 (*0-89642-208-9*) Linden Pubs.

Seaman: History of the Seaman Family in PA, with Genealogical Tables. G. S. Seaman. (Illus.). 135p. 1991. reprint ed. pap. 22.00 (*0-8328-1744-9*); reprint ed. lib. bdg. 32.00 (*0-8328-1743-0*) Higginson Bk Co.

Seaman A. Knapp: Schoolmaster of American Agriculture. Joseph C. Bailey. LC 73-165702. (American Education, Ser, No. 2). 1972. reprint ed. 19.95 (*0-405-03691-4*) Ayer.

Seaman's Friend. Richard Dana. LC 79-4623. 1979. reprint ed. lib. bdg. 50.00 (*0-8201-1330-1*) Schol Facsimiles.

Seaman's Friend. Richard H. Dana, Jr. (Notable American Authors Ser.). 1992. reprt ed. lib. bdg. 75.00 (*0-7812-2614-7*) Rprt Serv.

Seaman's Rights in the United States When Involved in an Accident. Charles R. Lipcon. Tr. by Professional Translating Services, Inc. Staff. 50p. (Orig.). (FRE, GER, GRE, ITA, KOR, POR & SPA.). 1989. pap. 9.95 (*0-932557-01-5*) Adels Inc.

Seamans Secrets. John Davis. LC 92-21729. 1992. 75.00 (*0-8201-1475-8*) Schol Facsimiles.

Seamanship: A Handbook for Oceanographers. Carvel H. Blair. LC 76-56349. (Illus.). 238p. 1977. text ed. 9.00 (*0-87033-228-7*) Cornell Maritime.

Seamanship: Fundamentals for the Deck Officer. 2nd ed. David O. Dodge & S. E. Kyriss. LC 80-5684. (Fundamentals of Naval Science Ser.: No. 2). 272p. 1981. text ed. 19.95 (*0-87021-613-9*) Naval Inst Pr.

Seamanship, Eighteen Sixty-Two. J. G. Nares. 368p. 1984. 49.00 (*0-905418-37-9*, Pub. by Gresham Bks UK) St Mut.

Seamanship for New Skippers. George H. Ludins. (Illus.). 1980. pap. 5.95 (*0-916224-54-6*) Banyan Bks.

Seamanship for Yachtsmen. Francis B. Cooke. 1977. lib. bdg. 69.95 (*0-8490-2582-6*) Gordon Pr.

Seamanship Notes. 5th ed. Kemp & Young. (Illus.). 144p. (Orig.). 1992. pap. 34.95 (*0-7506-0281-3*) Buttrwrth-Heinemann.

Seamanship Techniques: Shipboard Practice & Ship Handling. D. J. House. (Illus.). 580p. 1994. pap. 68.95 (*0-7506-2203-2*) Buttrwrth-Heinemann.

Seamen Ashore: A Study of the United Seamen's Service & of Merchant Seamen in Port. Elmo P. Hohman. (Merchant Seamen's Ser.: Vol. 2). 1952. 20.00 (*0-686-17410-0*) R S Barnes.

Seamen's Articles of Agreement, Vol. 64. International Labour Office Staff. (International Labour Office Studies & Reports: No. 1). 1974. reprint ed. bds. 80.00 (*0-8115-3296-8*) Periodicals Srv.

Seamen's Missions: Their Origins & Early Growth. Roald Kverndal. LC 85-25508. (Illus.). 903p. (C). 1986. 39.95 (*0-87808-440-1*, WCL440-1) William Carey Lib.

Seamen's Wages Calculator in Rupees. Compiled by C. A. Yates. (Illus.). (C). 1987. 35.00 (*0-85174-184-3*, Pub. by Brwn Son Ferg) St Mut.

***Seamless Connections: Refocusing Your Organization to Create a Successful Continuum of Care.** Connie Evashwick. LC 96-29703. (Illus.). 120p. (Orig.). 1997. pap. 32.00 (*1-55648-183-7*, 067105) AHPI.

Seamless Enterprise: Making Cross-Functional Management Work. Dan Dimancescu. LC 93-61003. 249p. (Orig.). 1994. pap. 18.00 (*0-939246-51-1*) Wiley.

Seamless Enterprise: Making Cross-Functional Management Work. Dan Dimancescu. 250p. 1995. pap. text ed. 19.95 (*0-471-13193-8*) Wiley.

Seamless Government: A Practical Guide to Re-Engineering in the Public Sector. Russell M. Linden. (Public Administration Ser.). 314p. text ed. 25.95 (*0-7879-0015-X*) Jossey-Bass.

Seamless Networks: Interoperating Wireless & Wireline Networks. Arkady Grinberg. LC 96-34043. (Illus.). 256p. 1996. text ed. 50.00 (*0-07-024844-3*) McGraw.

Seamless Object-Oriented Software Architecture: Analysis & Design of Reliable System. Jean-Marc Nerson & Kum Walden. LC 94-30456. (Object-Oriented Ser.). 302p. 1994. pap. text ed. 49.00 (*0-13-031303-3*) P-H.

Seamless Serial Hour. Robert Miltner. 1993. pap. 6.95 (*0-685-70583-8*) Pudding Hse Pubns.

Seamless Web. rev. ed. Stanley Burnshaw. 1991. reprint ed. pap. 12.50 (*0-8076-0534-4*) Braziller.

Seamounts, Islands, & Atolls. Ed. by B. H. Keating et al. (Geophysical Monograph Ser.: Vol. 43). (Illus.). 400p. 1987. 31.00 (*0-87590-068-2*) Am Geophysical.

Seams: Art as a Philosophical Context. Stephen Melville. Ed. & Intro. by Jeremy Gilbert-Rolfe. 160p. 1996. pap. 18.95 (*90-5701-021-6*, 610381, Pub. by G & B SZ) Dist Art Pubs.

Seams: Art as a Philosophical Context. Stephen Melville. Ed. & Intro. by Jeremy Gilbert-Rolfe. (Critical Voices in Art, Theory, & Culture Ser.: Vol. 2). (Illus.). 160p. 1996. 35.00 (*90-5701-031-3*, 610382, Pub. by G & B SZ) Dist Art Pubs.

Seams: Poetry. Kerry S. Keys. 168p. 1984. pap. 12.95 (*0-930502-05-1*) Pine Pr.

Seams Fishy. Ruth Seeley-Scheel. (Illus.). 1990. pap. 6.95 (*0-9619815-4-7*) Laugh Goose.

Seams, Threads & Needles. 1976. 50.00 (*0-317-43774-7*) St Mut.

Seamstress. Jack Rudman. (Career Examination Ser.: C-1619). 1994. pap. 34.95 (*0-8373-1619-7*) Nat Learn.

***Seamstress: A Memoir of Survival.** Sara T. Bernstein. LC 97-9461. (Illus.). 320p. 1997. 24.95 (*0-399-14322-X*) Putnam Pub Group.

***Seamus Heaney.** Allen. 1997. text ed. 39.95 (*0-312-16502-1*); text ed. 17.95 (*0-312-16503-X*) St Martin.

Seamus Heaney. Robert Buttel. Ed. by James F. Carens. (Irish Writers Ser.). 1990. pap. 1.95 (*0-8387-1568-0*) Bucknell U Pr.

Seamus Heaney. Andrew Murphy. (Writers & Their Work Ser.). 95p. (Orig.). 1996. pap. text ed. 17.00 (*0-7463-0783-7*, Pub. by Nrthcote House UK) U Pr of Miss.

Seamus Heaney. Ronald Tamplin. 1990. pap. 22.00 (*0-335-15261-9*, Open Univ Pr) Taylor & Francis.

Seamus Heaney: A Faber Student Guide. Neil Corcoran. 160p. (Orig.). 1986. pap. 9.95 (*0-571-13955-8*) Faber & Faber.

Seamus Heaney: A Reference Guide. Durkan & Brandes. 1996. 45.00 (*0-8161-7389-3*, GK Hall) Thorndike Pr.

Seamus Heaney: Poet & Critic. Arthur E. McGuinness. LC 92-43156. (Irish Studies: Vol. 3). 199p. (C). 1994. text ed. 39.95 (*0-8204-2065-4*) P Lang Pubng.

Seamus Heaney: The Making of the Poet. Michael W. Parker. LC 92-61949. (Illus.). 306p. 1993. text ed. 27.95 (*0-87745-398-5*) U of Iowa Pr.

Seamus Heaney: The Shaping Spirit. Ed. by Catharine Malloy & Phyllis Carey. LC 95-33643. (Illus.). 200p. 1996. 24.50 (*0-87413-581-8*) U Delaware Pr.

Seamus Heaney, Poet of Contrary Progressions. Henry Hart. (Irish Studies). 272p. pap. text ed. 16.95 (*0-8156-2612-6*) Syracuse U Pr.

Seamus Heaney, Poet of Contrary Progressions. Henry Hart. (Irish Studies: No. 1). 272p. 39.95 (*0-8156-2536-7*) Syracuse U Pr.

Seamy Side of Denver: Tall Tales of the Mile High City. Phil Goodstein. (Illus.). 288p. (Orig.). 1996. reprint ed. pap. 18.95 (*0-9622169-1-7*) New Social.

***Sean & David's Drive Thru America.** Sean Condon. (Illus.). 300p. (Orig.). 1998. pap. 12.95 (*0-86442-506-6*) Lonely Planet.

Sean & David's Long Drive: Travel Literature. Sean Condon. 304p. 1996. pap. 10.95 (*0-86442-371-3*) Lonely Planet.

Sean Connery: A Biography. Michael Freedland. (Illus.). 336p. 1995. pap. 9.95 (*1-85797-871-4*, Weidenfeld) Trafalgar.

Sean Connery: From 007 to Hollywood Icon. Andrew Yule. 1993. mass mkt. 4.50 (*1-55817-742-6*, Pinncle Kensgtn) Kensgtn Pub Corp.

Sean Connery: The Untouchable Hero. Michael F. Callan. 1995. mass mkt. 6.95 (*0-86369-755-0*) London Brdge.

Sean Donovan. Lori Wick. (Californians Ser.: Bk. 3). 1993. pap. 8.99 (*1-56507-046-1*) Harvest Hse.

Sean O'Casey. Bernard Benstock. LC 72-124101. (Irish Writers Ser.). 123p. 1975. 8.50 (*0-8387-7748-1*); pap. 1.95 (*0-8387-7618-3*) Bucknell U Pr.

Sean O'Casey. James Simmons. Ed. by Bruce King & Adele King. (Modern Dramatists Ser.). 197p. 1990. pap. 11.95 (*0-333-30897-2*) St Martin.

Sean O'Casey: A Bibliography. Ronald Ayling & Michael J. Durkan. LC 77-83181. 436p. 1978. 50.00 (*0-295-95566-X*) U of Wash Pr.

Sean O'Casey: A Bibliography of Criticism. E. H. Mikhail. LC 76-37007. 164p. 1972. text ed. 30.00 (*0-295-95167-2*) U of Wash Pr.

Sean O'Casey: A Collection of Critical Essays. Ed. by T. Kilroy. 7.95 (*0-13-628941-X*) P-H.

Sean O'Casey: A Research & Production Sourcebook. Bernice W. Schrank. LC 96-5254. (Modern Dramatists Research & Production Sourcebooks Ser.: Vol. 11). 320p. 1996. text ed. 75.00 (*0-313-27844-X*, Greenwood Pr) Greenwood.

Sean O'Casey & His Critics: An Annotated Bibliography, 1916-1982. E. H. Mikhail. LC 84-14166. (Author Bibliographies Ser.: No. 67). 362p. 1985. 32.50 (*0-8108-1747-0*) Scarecrow.

Sean O'Casey, Centenary Essays. Ed. by David Krause & Robert G. Lowery. (Irish Literary Studies: Vol. # 7). 258p. 8000. 54.95 (*0-86140-008-9*, Pub. by Colin Smythe Ltd UK) Dufour.

Sean O'Casey-Columbia Essays on Modern Writers, No. 73. John P. Frayne. 1976. pap. text ed. 10.00 (*0-231-03655-8*) Col U Pr.

Sean O'Casey's Autobiographies: An Annotated Index. Robert G. Lowery. LC 83-826. xxxi, 487p. 1983. text ed. 65.00 (*0-313-23765-4*, LYS/, Greenwood Pr) Greenwood.

Sean O'Casey's Bridge of Vision: Four Essays on Structure & Perspective. Carol Kleiman. 160p. 1982. 25.00 (*0-8020-2431-9*) U of Toronto Pr.

Sean O'Casey's Drama: Verisimilitude & Vision. Ronald G. Rollins. LC 77-14462. (Illus.). 150p. 1979. pap. 42.80 (*0-7837-8401-5*, 2059212) Bks Demand.

Sean O'Casey's Tragi-Comic Vision. Donald D. Wilson. 1975. lib. bdg. 250.00 (*0-87700-237-1*) Revisionist Pr.

S

An Asterisk (*) at the beginning of an entry indicates that the title is appearing in BIP for the first time.

S

Sean O'Faolain: A Critical Introduction. Maurice Harmon. LC 67-12124. 242p. reprint ed. pap. 69.00 (0-317-29672-8, 2022076) Bks Demand.
Sean O'Faolain's Irish Vision. Richard Bonaccorso. LC 87-10014. 167p. 1987. text ed. 64.50 (0-88706-536-8); pap. text ed. 21.95 (0-88706-537-6) State U NY Pr.
Sean Rafferty: Collected Poems. Ed. by Nicholas Johnson. 160p. 1996. pap. 24.95 (1-85754-124-3, Pub. by Carcanet Pr UK) Paul & Co Pubs.
Sean Scully. John Caldwell et al. LC 85-4203. (Illus.). 36p. 1985. pap. 6.95 (0-88039-010-7) Mus Art Carnegie.
***Sean Scully.** Donilo Eccher. 1996. pap. 35.00 (88-8158-087-X, Pub. by Charta IT) Dist Art Pubs.
Sean Scully. Maurice Poirier. LC 90-80946. (Illus.). 208p. 1990. 75.00 (1-55595-040-X) Hudson Hills.
Sean Scully: The Catherine Paintings. Sean Scully. (Illus.). 112p. (Orig.). 1993. pap. 29.95 (0-929865-09-X) Mod Art Mus Ft Worth.
Sean Scully: Twenty Years, 1976-1995. Ned Rifkin. LC 94-61651. (Illus.). 144p. 1995. 45.00 (0-500-09249-4) Thames Hudson.
Seance. Joan L. Nixon. 176p. (YA). (gr. 7 up). 1981. mass mkt. 3.99 (0-440-97937-4, LLL BDD) BDD Bks Young Read.
Seance. Susan Northrop. 1995. mass mkt. 5.99 (0-440-22176-5) Dell.
Seance: A Guide for Living. Suzane Northrop & Kate McLoughlin. LC 94-17689. 208p. 1994. text ed. 18.00 (0-9641509-0-5) Allian Pubng.
Seance: And Other Stories. Isaac B. Singer. LC 68-32742. 258p. 1980. pap. 6.95 (0-374-50832-1) FS&G.
Seance: Healing Messages from Beyond. Suzanne Northrop & Kate McLoughlin. 1995. mass mkt. 5.99 (0-614-15542-8) Dell.
Seance for a Vampire. Fred Saberhagen. 288p. 1994. 21.95 (0-312-85562-1) Tor Bks.
***Seance on a Wet Afternoon.** Mark McShane. 3.95 (0-7867-0615-5) Carroll & Graf.
Seance on a Wet Afternoon. Mark McShane. 189p. 1990. pap. 3.95 (0-88184-615-5) Carroll & Graf.
Sean's Book. Sean Hughes. 125p. 1996. pap. 11.95 (1-85793-465-2, Pub. by Pavilion UK) Trafalgar.
Sean's Legacy: An AIDS Awakening. Robert Hopkins. LC 95-41501. 192p. 1996. text ed. 19.95 (0-89243-875-4, Triumph Books) Liguori Pubns.
***Sean's War.** Leone C. Anderson. (Illus.). 192p. (J). (gr. 3-9). 1998. 16.95 (0-9638819-4-9) ShadowPlay Pr.
***Sean's War.** Leone C. Anderson. (Illus.). 192p. (J). (gr. 3-9). 1998. pap. 10.95 (0-9638819-5-7) ShadowPlay Pr.
***Seaplane Operations: Basic & Advanced Techniques for Floatplanes, Amphibians & Flying Boats from Around the World.** Dale DeRemer & Cesare Baj. (Illus.). 450p. (Orig.). (C). 1996. pap. write for info. (0-9622159-4-5) D De Remer.
Seaplanes - Felixstowe: The Story of the Air Station, 1913-1963. Gordon Kinsey. 240p. 1990. 42.00 (0-86138-039-8, Pub. by T Dalton UK) St Mut.
Seaport: A Waterfront at Work. Jack Leigh. LC 96-21783. (Illus.). 144p. 1996. 45.00 (0-941711-34-X) Wyrick & Co.
Seaport: Architecture & Townscape of Liverpool. F. Quentin Hughes. 26.00 (0-685-20625-4) Transatl Arts.
***Seaport Economy: A Study of the Singapore Experience.** David H. Hin. (Illus.). 210p. (Orig.). 1996. pap. 41.50 (9971-69-199-X, Pub. by Sgapore Univ SI) Coronet Bks.
Seaport in Virginia: George Washington's Alexandria. Gay M. Moore. LC 73-188711. 288p. reprint ed. 82.10 (0-8357-9817-8, 2019203) Bks Demand.
Seaport Sydney. Peter Proudfoot. (Illus.). 267p. 1995. pap. 39.95 (0-86840-007-6, Pub. by New South Wales Univ Pr AT) Intl Spec Bk.
Seaports. L. G. Taylor. (C). 1987. 45.00 (0-685-45080-5, Pub. by Brwn Son Ferg) St Mut.
Seaports & Development: The Experience of Kenya & Tanzania, Vol. 3. B. S. Hoyle. LC 82-12128. (Transportation Studies: Vol. 3). xviii, 254p. 1983. text ed. 207.00 (0-677-06030-0) Gordon & Breach.
***Seaports of the Americas: The 1997 AAPA Directory.** annuals 4th ed. Orig. Title: Seaports of the Western Hemisphere. 144p. 1997. pap. 79.00 (1-888817-07-0) Compass NAmer.
Seaports of the Western Hemisphere see Seaports of the Americas: The 1997 AAPA Directory
Seapower: Theory & Practice. Geoffrey Till. LC 94-28122. (Illus.). 206p. (C). 1994. 37.50 (0-7146-4604-0, Pub. by F Cass Pubs UK) Intl Spec Bk.
Seapower: Theory & Practice. Ed. by Geoffrey Till. LC 94-28122. (Illus.). (C). 1994. pap. 18.50 (0-7146-4122-7, Pub. by F Cass Pubs UK) Intl Spec Bk.
Seapower in Global Politics: 1494-1993. George Modelski & William R. Thompson. LC 87-10472. (Illus.). 384p. 1987. 35.00 (0-295-96502-9) U of Wash Pr.
Seapower in the Nuclear Age: The United States Navy & NATO 1949-80. Joel L. Sokolsky. (Illus.). 240p. 1991. 34.95 (1-55750-754-6) Naval Inst Pr.
Seaquake - Maremoto. Pablo Neruda. Tr. by Dennis Maloney & Maria Giacchetti. 64p. 1993. pap. 9.00 (1-877727-32-6) White Pine.
Seaquest DSV: Fire Below. Michael Jan-Friedman. (Orig.). 1994. mass mkt. 4.99 (0-441-00039-8) Ace Bks.
Seaquest DSV: The Ancient. David Bishoff. 240p. (Orig.). 1994. mass mkt. 4.99 (0-441-00042-8) Ace Bks.
Seaquest DSV: The Novel. Berkley. 1993. mass mkt. 4.99 (0-441-00037-1) Ace Bks.
Search. William Badke. (Ben Sylvester Mystery Ser.: No. 1). 256p. 1995. pap. 9.99 (0-88070-719-4) Multnomah Pubs.
Search. Tom Brown, Jr. & William Owen. 1986. pap. 12.00 (0-425-10251-3, Berkley Trade) Berkley Pub.
Search. Ruth Domino. (C). 1983. pap. 3.00 (0-87574-052-9) Pendle Hill.
Search. Mark Dunster. 10p. (Orig.). 1992. pap. 4.00 (0-89642-212-7) Linden Pubs.
Search. Dorothy Fournier. LC 81-8201. (Illus.). 1981. 8.95 (0-917002-71-7) Joyce Media.
Search. Bobby Griffin. (Irish Culture & History Ser.). pap. 1.75 (0-686-12739-0) Grace Pub Co.
Search. Naguib Mahfouz. 144p. 1991. pap. 9.95 (0-385-26460-7) Doubleday.
Search. Melanie McAllester. 240p. 1996. pap. 10.95 (1-56280-150-3) Naiad Pr.
Search. Snow. 23.95 (0-8488-0633-6) Amereon Ltd.
***Search.** Latifa Zayyat. 128p. 1997. pap. 11.95 (0-7043-0204-7, Pub. by Quartet UK) Interlink Pub.
Search. Grace L. Hill. reprint ed. lib. bdg. 23.95 (0-89190-048-9, Rivercity Pr) Amereon Ltd.
Search, Vol 39. Grace L. Hill. (Grace Livingston Hill Ser.: Vol. 39). 1992. pap. 4.99 (0-8423-5831-5) Tyndale.
Search: A Handbook for Adoptees & Birthparents. 2nd ed. Jayne Askin. LC 92-4210. 336p. 1992. pap. 24.50 (0-89774-717-8) Oryx Pr.
Search: A Young Person's Quest for Understanding. J. Donald Walters. LC 88-154807. (Illus.). 214p. (Orig.). 1988. pap. 9.95 (0-916124-46-0, CCP7) Crystal Clarity.
Search! How to Find Hidden Valuables in Homes & Yards. enl. rev. ed. James R. Warnke. (Illus.). 160p. 1992. pap. 10.95 (0-9631693-0-0) Warnke Pub.
Search: Information Gathering for the Mass Media. 2nd ed. Lauren Kessler & Duncan McDonald. 241p. (C). 1992. pap. 26.95 (0-534-16278-9) Wadsworth Pub.
Search: Talks on the Ten Bulls of Zen. Osho. Ed. by Ma Yoga Anurag. (Zen Ser.). 320p. 1993. 19.95 (3-89338-116-3, Pub. by Rebel Hse GW) Osho America.
Search - Manchurian Candidate. John D. Marks. 1980. write for info. (0-394-59583-1) Random.
Search a New Dawn. Barbara Delinsky. 1983. pap. 2.25 (0-373-47449-0, Harlequin) Harlequin Bks.
Search-A-Picture Puzzles. Elvira Gamiello. (Illus.). (Orig.). (J). (gr. 4-6). 1987. pap. 1.95 (0-942025-07-5) Kidsbks.
Search after Truth. Thomas H. Chivers. (Works of Thomas Holley Chivers Ser.). 1990. reprint ed. lib. bdg. 79.00 (0-7812-2285-0) Rprt Serv.
***Search after Truth: With "Elucidations of the Search after Truth"** Ed. by Thomas M. Lennon & Paul J. Olscamp. (Cambridge Texts in the History of Philosophy Ser.). 800p. (C). 1997. 79.95 (0-521-58004-8); pap. 29.95 (0-521-58995-9) Cambridge U Pr.
Search after Truth & Elucidations of the Search after Truth. Nicolas Malebranche. Tr. by Thomas M. Lennon & Paul J. Olscamp from FRE. LC 79-23881. Orig. Title: De la Recherche de la Verite & Eclaircissements. 893p. 1980. 95.00 (0-8142-0246-2) Ohio St U Pr.
Search after Truth, 1848, The Lost Pleiad, 1845, & Atlanta, 1853. Thomas H. Chivers & Charles M. Lombard. LC 76-18173. 1976. reprint ed. lib. bdg. 50.00 (0-8201-1269-0) Schol Facsimiles.
Search & Clear: Critical Responses to Literature & Films of the Vietnam War. Ed. by William J. Searle. LC 88-79749. 224p. (C). 1988. pap. 17.95 (0-87972-429-3); text ed. 34.95 (0-87972-428-5) Bowling Green Univ Popular Press.
Search & Destroy. Howard Korder. 1992. pap. 5.25 (0-8222-1315-X) Dramatists Play.
Search & Destroy. Gar Wilson. (Super Phoenix Force Ser.: No. 2). 352p. (Orig.). 1989. mass mkt. 3.95 (0-373-62202-3) Harlequin Bks.
Search & Destroy: A Play. Howard Korder. LC 91-28951. 104p. 1992. pap. 9.95 (0-8021-3274-X, Grove) Grove-Atltic.
***Search & Destroy: African American Males in the Criminal Justice System.** 320p. 1997. pap. text ed. 16.95 (0-521-59858-3) Cambridge U Pr.
Search & Destroy: African American Males in the Criminal Justice System. Jerome G. Miller. (Illus.). 344p. (C). 1996. text ed. 24.95 (0-521-46021-2) Cambridge U Pr.
***Search & Destroy, 1-6, the Complete Reprint: The Authoratative Guide to Punk Culture.** Vale Vale. LC 96-61780. (Illus.). 148p. (C). 1996. reprint ed. pap. 19.95 (0-9650469-4-X) V Search.
***Search & Destroy, 7-11, the Complete Reprint: The Authoritative Guide to Punk Culture.** Vale Vale. LC 96-61780. (Illus.). 148p. (C). 1997. reprint ed. pap. 19.95 (1-889307-00-9) V Search.
Search & Detection. Alan R. Washburn. (Topics in Operations Research Ser.). viii, 359p. 1981. pap. 12.00 (1-877640-01-8) INFORMS.
Search & Find: Theosophical Reference Index. Elsie Benjamin. Ed. by W. Emmett Small & Helen Todd. (Study Ser.: No. 1). 1978. pap. 7.95 (0-913004-32-4) Point Loma Pub.
Search & Re-Search: What the Inquiring Teacher Needs to Know. Ed. by Rita S. Brause & John S. Mayher. 224p. 1991. 65.00 (1-85000-855-8, Falmer Pr); pap. 26.00 (1-85000-856-6, Falmer Pr) Taylor & Francis.
***Search & Rescue.** M. Pesaresi & S. Glenn. 1997. mass mkt. 5.99 (0-449-22578-X, Crest) Fawcett.
Search & Rescue: Aircrew Survival. 1994. lib. bdg. 250.95 (0-8490-6430-9) Gordon Pr.
Search-&-Rescue Dogs: Expert Trackers & Trailers. Elizabeth Ring. LC 93-42278. (Good Dogs! Ser.). (Illus.). 32p. (J). (gr. 2-4). 1994. lib. bdg. 14.90 (1-56294-294-8) Millbrook Pr.
Search & Rescue Dogs: Training Methods. American Rescue Dog Association Staff. 256p. 1991. pap. 24.95 (0-87605-733-4) Howell Bk.
Search & Rescue Fundamentals. Robert C. Stoffel et al. (Illus.). 396p. per. 30.00 (0-913724-37-8) Emerg Response Inst.
Search & Rescue Survival: Survival on Land, Sea, Sea Ice, & in Areas Contaminated by Radiation. 1986. lib. bdg. 79.95 (0-8490-3797-2) Gordon Pr.
Search & Research. Linda Schwartz. (Study Skills Ser.). 48p. (J). (gr. 4-6). 1984. 6.95 (0-88160-116-0, LW 248) Learning Wks.
Search & Retrieval Index to EOS-ESD Symposium Proceedings 1979 to 1988. LC 89-83419. 102p. (Orig.). 1989. 10.00 (1-878303-18-X, SRI-7988) EOS ESD.
Search & Seizure, Vol. 2. 2nd ed. John W. Hall, Jr. LC 91-77443. 1991. 220.00 (0-685-59850-0) Clark Boardman Callaghan.
Search & Seizure: A Dilemma of the Supreme Court. Erwin N. Griswold. LC 74-15275. 87p. reprint ed. pap. 25.00 (0-8357-2951-6, 2039207) Bks Demand.
Search & Seizure: A Treatise on the Fourth Amendment, 4 vols. 2nd ed. Wayne R. LaFave. 2400p. 1986. text ed. write for info. (0-314-30073-2) West Pub.
Search & Seizure, a Treatise on the Fourth Amendment, Vol. 1. 3rd ed. Wayne R. LaFave. 800p. 1995. text ed. write for info. (0-314-07613-1) West Pub.
Search & Seizure, a Treatise on the Fourth Amendment, Vol. 2. 3rd ed. Wayne R. LaFave. 800p. 1995. text ed. write for info. (0-314-07614-X) West Pub.
Search & Seizure, a Treatise on the Fourth Amendment, Vol. 3. 3rd ed. Wayne R. LaFave. 800p. 1995. text ed. write for info. (0-314-07615-8) West Pub.
Search & Seizure, a Treatise on the Fourth Amendment, Vol. 4. 3rd ed. Wayne R. LaFave. 800p. 1995. text ed. write for info. (0-314-07612-3) West Pub.
Search & Seizure & the Supreme Court: A Study in Constitutional Interpretation. Jacob W. Landynski. LC 65-13523. (Johns Hopkins University Studies in Historical & Political Science: Ser. 84: No. 1). 296p. reprint ed. pap. 84.40 (0-317-09094-1, 2005193) Bks Demand.
Search & Seizure at a Rock Concert. FBI Staff. 8p. 1994. pap. 10.00 (0-930179-32-3) Johns Enter.
Search & Seizure for N.Y.S. Law Enforcement Officers. John J. Sullivan. 64p. 1997. 6.95 (0-930137-82-5) Looseleaf Law.
Search & Seizure Handbook. 5th rev. ed. Devallis Rutledge. LC 95-72123. (Illus.). 195p. (C). 1995. pap. 19.95 (0-942728-68-8) Copperhouse.
Search & Seizure in the Public Schools. 2nd ed. Lawrence F. Rossow & Jacqueline A. Stefkovich. 70p. (Orig.). (C). 1995. pap. 19.95 (1-56534-067-1) Ed Law Assn.
Search & Succeed: A Guide to Using the Classifieds. Bruce McGlothlin. LC 93-47545. (Life Skills Library). (Illus.). 48p. (YA). 1994. lib. bdg. 14.95 (0-8239-1695-2) Rosen Group.
Search & Support Directory. Mary J. Rillera. 216p. (Orig.). 1991. pap. 19.95 (0-910143-01-3) Pure CA.
Search & the Human Observer. Ed. by J. N. Clare & M. A. Sinclair. (Illus.). 198p. 1979. pap. 31.00 (0-85066-193-5) Taylor & Francis.
Search Committee. large type ed. Ralph McInerny. 1991. 27.99 (0-7089-8613-7, Trail West Pubs) Ulverscroft.
***Search Committee: Life, Death, Education, & God at a Struggling Church College.** Boyd W. Johnson. 352p. (Orig.). Date not set. pap. 12.95 (0-9641528-1-9) Direct Imaging.
Search Committee Handbook. Theodore J. Marchese. 56p. 1988. 12.00 (0-685-45302-2) Coll & U Personnel.
Search Conference: A Comprehensive Guide to Theory & Practice. Merrelyn Emery & Ronald E. Purser. (Public Administration Ser.). 358p. 1995. 28.95 (0-614-95641-2) Jossey-Bass.
Search Conference: A Powerful Method for Planning Organizational Change & Community Action. Merrelyn Emery & Ronald E. Purser. LC 95-38959. (Jossey-Bass Public Administration Ser.). 358p. 1996. 28.95 (0-7879-0192-X) Jossey-Bass.
Search Consultant's Handbook. Patricia Sanders. 32p. (Orig.). 1983. pap. 3.50 (0-942916-02-6) ISC Pubns.
Search Dog Training. Sandy Bryson. (Illus.). 359p. (Orig.). 1984. pap. 12.95 (0-910286-94-9) Boxwood.
***Search Engine Technologies for the World Wide Web & Intranets.** Computer Technology Research Corp. Staff. (Illus.). (Orig.). Date not set. pap. 295.00 (1-56607-993-4) Comput Tech Res.
***Search Engines for the World Wide Web: Visual Quickstart Guide.** Alfred Glossbrenner & Emily Glossbrenner. 208p. (C). 1997. pap. text ed. 19.95 (0-201-69642-8) Peachpit Pr.
Search-Equilibrium Approach to the Micro Foundations of Macroeconomics. Peter A. Diamond. (Illus.). 40p. 1984. 15.00 (0-262-04076-X) MIT Pr.
Search Find & Kill: Coastal Command's U-Boat Successes in World War Two. 2nd rev. ed. Norman Franks. (Illus.). 192p. 1995. 34.95 (1-898697-35-3, Pub. by Grub St Pubns UK) Seven Hills Bk.
Search for a Black Nationality: Black Emigration & Colonization, 1787-1863. Floyd J. Miller. LC 75-4650. (Blacks in the New World Ser.). 311p. reprint ed. pap. 88.70 (0-317-10832-8, 2020247) Bks Demand.
Search for a Just Society. John Huddleston. (Illus.). 528p. 1989. 44.50 (0-85398-288-0) G Ronald Pub.
Search for a Method. Jean-Paul Sartre. Tr. by Hazel E. Barnes. 1968. pap. 7.96 (0-394-70464-9, Vin) Random.
Search for a Method in American Studies. Cecil F. Tate. LC 73-77714. (Illus.). 178p. 1973. reprint ed. pap. 50.80 (0-608-00841-9, 2061632) Bks Demand.
Search for a National Retirement Income Policy. Ed. by Jack L. VanDerhei. (Pension Research Council Publications). 216p. (C). 1991. text ed. 32.95 (0-256-05606-4) U of Pa Pr.
Search for a Naturalistic World View, Vol. 1: Scientific Method & Epistemology. Abner Shimony. 368p. (C). 1993. text ed. 74.95 (0-521-37352-2); pap. text ed. 21.95 (0-521-37744-7) Cambridge U Pr.
Search for a Naturalistic World View, Vol. 2: Natural Science & Metaphysics. Abner Shimony. 360p. (C). 1993. text ed. 69.95 (0-521-37353-0); pap. text ed. 21.95 (0-521-37745-5) Cambridge U Pr.
Search for a Negotiated Settlement of the Vietnam War. Allan E. Goodman. LC 86-81533. (Indochina Research Monograph: No. 2). (Illus.). xii, 136p. (Orig.). 1986. pap. 10.00 (0-912966-90-4) IEAS.
Search for a New Alphabet: Literary Studies in a Changing World in Honor of Douwe Fokkema. Ed. by Harald Hendrix et al. LC 96-14855. x, 326p. 1996. pap. 39.95 (1-55619-510-9) Benjamins North Am.
***Search for a New Beginning: Developing a New Civilization.** Mikhail S. Gorbachev. write for info. (0-06-251326-5) HarpC.
Search for a New Dawn. Barbara Delinsky. 240p. 1995. mass mkt. 5.50 (0-06-100874-5, Harp PBks) HarpC.
***Search for a New Dawn.** Barbara Delinsky. (Five Star Romances Ser.). 1996. lib. bdg. 23.95 (0-7862-0850-3, Five Star) Mac Lib Ref.
***Search for a New Dawn.** large type ed. Barbara Delinsky. LC 97-10501. 1997. write for info. (0-7862-1112-1) Thorndike Pr.
Search for a Patron in the Middle Ages & the Renaissance. Ed. by David G. Wilkins & Rebecca L. Wilkins. LC 95-4602. (Medieval & Renaissance Studies: Vol. 12). (Illus.). 276p. 1996. text ed. 89.95 (0-7734-8867-7) E Mellen.
Search for a Postmodern Theatre: Interviews with Contemporary Playwrights. John L. DiGaetani. LC 91-3936. (Contributions in Drama & Theatre Studies: No. 41). 336p. 1991. text ed. 59.95 (0-313-27364-2, DTS, Greenwood Pr) Greenwood.
Search for a Rational Ethic. George D. Snell. (Illus.). 320p. 1988. 96.00 (0-387-96767-2) Spr-Verlag.
Search for a Shadow. Grace Thompson. 320p. 1995. 20.00 (0-7278-4736-8) Severn Hse.
Search for a Soul: Taylor Caldwell's Past Lives. Jess Stearn. 288p. 1994. mass mkt. 5.99 (0-425-14366-X) Berkley Pub.
Search for a Supertheory: From Atoms to Superstrings. Barry Parker. (Illus.). 302p. 1987. 21.95 (0-306-42702-8, Plenum Pr) Plenum.
Search for a Theory of Plan-Making Method: An Annotated Bibliography, Nos. 781-782. Richard C. Williams. 1975. 9.00 (0-686-20350-X, Sage Prdcls Pr) Sage.
Search for a Woman-Centered Spirituality. Annette Van Dyke. (Cutting Edge: Lesbian Life & Literature Ser.). 256p. (C). 1992. 45.00 (0-8147-8769-X); pap. 15.00 (0-8147-8770-3) NYU Pr.
Search for Ability: Standardized Testing in Social Perspective. David A. Goslin. LC 63-12591. 204p. 1963. 29.95 (0-87154-357-5) Russell Sage.
Search for Acceptance: Consumerism, Sexuality & Self among American Woman. Jerry Jacobs. LC 88-40539. 181p. (C). 1989. pap. text ed. 19.95 (1-55605-042-9) Wyndham Hall.
Search for Adele Parker. Robert C. Hull. LC 74-82751. (Illus.). 1975. 6.95 (0-87212-046-5) Libra.
Search for Africa: History, Culture, Politics. Basil Davidson. 1995. pap. 14.00 (0-8129-2527-0, Times Bks) Random.
Search for Aladdin's Lamp. Jay Leibold. (Choose Your Own Adventure Ser.: No. 117). 128p. (YA). 1991. pap. 3.50 (0-553-29185-8) Bantam.
Search for Aladdin's Lamp. large type ed. Jay Leibold. (Choose Your Own Adventure Ser.: No. 117). (Illus.). 128p. (J). (gr. 4 up). 1995. lib. bdg. 15.93 (0-8368-1311-1) Gareth Stevens Inc.
***Search for Amelia Earhart.** Rebecca P. Janney. (Impossible Dreams Ser.: Vol. 3). 128p. (J). (gr. 4-7). 1997. pap. 5.99 (1-57673-026-3) Multnomah Pubs.
***Search for America.** Frederick P. Grove. 1996. pap. text ed. 8.95 (0-7710-9957-6) McCland & Stewart.
Search for an AIDS Vaccine: Ethical Issues in the Development & Testing of a Preventive HIV Vaccine. Christine Grady. LC 94-35650. (Medical Ethics Ser.). 192p. 1995. text ed. 26.50 (0-253-32619-2) Ind U Pr.
Search for an American Indian Identity: Modern Pan-Indian Movements. Hazel W. Hertzberg. LC 77-140889. (C). 1971. 42.50 (0-8156-0076-3) Syracuse U Pr.
Search for an American Indian Identity: Modern Pan-Indian Movements. Hazel W. Hertzberg. 380p. (C). 1981. pap. 16.95 (0-8156-2245-7) Syracuse U Pr.
Search for an American Public Theology: The Contribution of John Courtney Murray. Robert W. McElroy. 1989. pap. 10.95 (0-8091-3051-3) Paulist Pr.
Search for an Ideal: Six Canadian Intellectuals & Their Convictions in an Age of Transition, 1890-1930. Samuel E. Shortt. LC 76-26507. 226p. reprint ed. pap. 64.50 (0-685-15846-2, 2026373) Bks Demand.
Search for Ancestors: A Swedish-American Family Saga. H. Arnold Barton. LC 78-15537. (Illus.). 189p. 1979. 19.95 (0-8093-0893-2) S Ill U Pr.
Search for Ancestors: A Swedish-American Family Saga. H. Arnold Barton. 178p. 1979. pap. 11.95 (0-318-16621-6) Swedish-Am.
Search for Ancient Egypt. Jean Vercoutter. (Discoveries Ser.). (Illus.). 220p. 1992. pap. 12.95 (0-8109-2817-5) Abrams.
Search for Ancient Greece. Roland Etienne & Francoise Etienne. Tr. by Anthony Zielonka. (Discoveries Ser.). (Illus.). 176p. 1992. pap. 12.95 (0-8109-2804-3) Abrams.
Search for Ancient Rome. Claude Moatti. Tr. by Anthony Zielonka. (Discoveries Ser.). (Illus.). 208p. 1993. pap. 12.95 (0-8109-2839-6) Abrams.
Search for Anti-Inflammatory Drugs: Case Histories from Concept to Clinic. Ed. by Vincent J. Merluzzi & Julian Adams. LC 95-1583. (Illus.). 314p. 1995. 87.50 (0-8176-3685-4) Birkhauser.

An Asterisk (*) at the beginning of an entry indicates that the title is appearing in BIP for the first time.

Search for Antiviral Drugs: Case Histories from Concept to Clinic. Ed. by Julian Adams & Vincent J. Merluzzi. LC 93-16405. (Illus.). xiii, 240p. 1993. 57.50 (*0-8176-3606-4*) Birkhauser.

Search for Archerland. H. R. Coursen. (Illus.). 245p. (Orig.). (YA). (gr. 8 up). 1993. pap. 12.50 (*1-880664-02-X*) E M Pr.

Search for Authenticity: An Existential-Analytic Approach to Psychotheraphy. enl. ed. James F. Bugental. 477p. 1989. reprint ed. text ed. 49.50 (*0-8290-0108-5*) Irvington.

Search for Authenticity: An Existential-Analytic Approach to Psychotheraphy. enl. ed. James F. Bugental. 477p. 1997. reprint ed. pap. text ed. 19.95 (*0-8290-1298-2*) Irvington.

Search for Available Jobs Module, Connections: School & Work Transitions - Work Skills-Job Search Skills. National Center for Research in Vocational Education Staff. 1987. write for info. (*0-318-67188-3*, SP100CB03) Ctr Educ Trng Employ.

Search for Beauty: Arts & Music. Lisa Sita. Ed. by Bruce Glassman. LC 95-43329. (Our Human Family Ser.). (Illus.). 80p. (YA). (gr. 5 up). Date not set. lib. bdg. 21.95 (*1-56711-129-7*) Blackbirch.

Search for Belief in the Poetry of Robert Frost. Rajendra N. Mishra. (C). 1992. 18.00 (*81-7017-291-8*, Pub. by Abhinav II) S Asia.

Search for Big Chub. Tony Miles. (Illus.). 192p. 1996. 45.00 (*1-85223-959-X*, Pub. by Crowood Pr UK) Trafalgar.

Search for Bioactive Compounds from Microorganisms. Ed. by Satoshi Omura. (Contemporary Bioscience Ser.). (Illus.). 376p. 1992. 92.95 (*0-387-97755-4*) Spr-Verlag.

***Search for Bridey Murphy.** Morey Bernstein. Date not set. lib. bdg. 22.95 (*0-8488-1955-1*) Amereon Ltd.

Search for Brotherhood, Peace, & Justice: The Story of Icaria. Lillian M. Snyder. (Illus.). 130p. (Orig.). 1996. pap. write for info. (*0-9653040-0-0*) F Baxter Pr.

***Search for Camp Olden, Hamilton Township.** Joseph F. Seliga. (Illus.). 52p. (Orig.). 1995. pap. text ed. 7.00 (*0-944413-39-0*, NB 130) Longstreet Hse.

Search for Certainty. Emma Smiley. 1972. pap. 4.95 (*0-87516-159-6*) DeVorss.

***Search for Charlie Holden.** Alden R. Bracewell. 236p. (Orig.). 1997. mass mkt. 4.99 (*1-55197-972-1*, Pub. by Comnwlth Pub CN) Partners Pubs Grp.

Search for Cheops & His Treasure. W. O. Bazhaw. (Illus.). 158p. 1988. pap. 12.95 (*0-929566-01-7*) Post Point Pr.

Search for Chess Perfection. Hammond & Jamieson. 1997. pap. write for info. (*0-938650-78-5*) Thinkers Pr.

Search for Christian America. Mark A. Noll et al. 208p. 1989. reprint ed. pap. 17.95 (*0-939443-15-5*) Helmers Howard Pub.

Search for Christian Doppler. 2nd ed. A. Eden. (Illus.). 140p. 1992. 46.95 (*0-387-82367-0*) Spr-Verlag.

Search for Cindy Austin. Carolyn Keene. (Nancy Drew Mystery Stories Ser.: No. 88). (Orig.). (J). (gr. 3-7). 1989. pap. 3.50 (*0-671-66313-5*, Minstrel Bks) PB.

Search for Common Ground. Howard Thurman. LC 86-25807. 108p. 1986. reprint ed. pap. 9.50 (*0-913408-94-8*) Friends United.

***Search for Common Ground in Sex Education: A Call for Community Action.** Ed Crawford. (Illus.). 85p. (Orig.). 1996. pap. 11.00 (*0-9644389-2-5*) Smoky Water Pr.

Search for Community. Ed. by David Cernic & Linda Longmire. LC 88-20488. 152p. (Orig.). (C). 1988. pap. text ed. 19.50 (*0-8191-7126-3*) U Pr of Amer.

Search for Community: From Utopia to a Cooperative Society. George Melnyk. 200p. 1985. pap. 36.95 (*0-920057-53-5*, Pub. by Black Rose Bks CN); pap. 16.95 (*0-920057-52-7*, Pub. by Black Rose Bks CN) Consort Bk Sales.

Search for Community in a Withering Tradition. Kai Nielsen & Hendrik Hart. 254p. (C). 1991. pap. text ed. 27.50 (*0-8191-7990-6*); lib. bdg. 48.50 (*0-8191-7989-2*) U Pr of Amer.

Search for Compassion: Spirituality & Ministry. Andrew Purves. 156p. (Orig.). 1989. pap. 11.00 (*0-664-25065-3*) Westminster John Knox.

Search for Concreteness-Reflections on Hegel & Whitehead: A Treatise on Self-Evidence & Critical Method in Philosophy. Darrel E. Christensen. LC 85-63421. 516p. 1986. 50.00 (*0-941664-22-8*) Susquehanna U Pr.

Search for Connections: Studies of Regeneration in the Nervous System of the Leech. John G. Nicholls. LC 86-22061. (Magnes Memorial Lectures: Vol. 2). (Illus.). 86p. (Orig.). 1987. pap. text ed. 21.95 (*0-87893-577-0*) Sinauer Assocs.

Search for Consensus: The Story of the Democratic Party. Ralph M. Goldman. LC 79-1207. 417p. 1979. 34.95 (*0-87722-152-9*) Temple U Pr.

Search for Corporate Strategic Credibility: Concepts & Cases in Global Strategy Communications. Richard B. Higgins. LC 95-50747. 200p. 1996. text ed. 55.00 (*0-89930-988-7*, Quorum Bks) Greenwood.

Search for Data in the Physical & Chemical Sciences. Linda Ray Arny. LC 83-20376. 158p. reprint ed. pap. 45.10 (*0-7837-1181-6*, 2041710) Bks Demand.

Search for David: A Cosmic Journey of Love. George Schwimmer. 304p. (Orig.). 1996. pap. 12.99 (*1-57174-051-1*, Heartsfire) Hampton Roads Pub Co.

Search for Delicious. Natalie Babbitt. LC 69-20374. (Illus.). 176p. (J). (gr. 3 up). 1969. 16.00 (*0-374-36534-2*) FS&G.

Search for Delicious. Carole Osterink. Ed. by J. Friedland & R. Kessler. (Novel-Ties Ser.). 1994. student ed., pap. text ed. 15.95 (*1-56982-061-9*) Lrn Links.

Search for Delicious. large type ed. Natalie Babbitt. 1995. 45.50 (*0-614-09608-1*, L-34852-00) Am Printing Hse.

***Search for Digital Excellence: Paradigms for Building the Webbed Organization.** Amir Hartman et al. 1997. 24.95 (*0-07-027057-0*) Osborne-McGraw.

Search for E. T. Bell: Also Known As John Taine. Constance Reid. LC 93-78369. (MAA Spectrum Ser.). (Illus.). 384p. 1993. 37.50 (*0-88385-508-9*, BELL) Math Assn.

Search for Economics: An Annotated Bibliography. Ed. by Lynn Turgeon. LC 95-48937. 440p. 1996. text ed. 55.00 (*0-8108-3120-1*) Scarecrow.

Search for Eden: Rebecca Searches for True Meaning in Life. Barbara Michel. (Eden Ser.: Vol. 2). 244p. (Orig.). 1996. pap. 8.95 (*0-614-16020-0*) Son-Rise Pubns.

Search for Effectiveness & Efficiency in Government: Policy Analysis, Program Evaluation, Social Indicator, & Quality of Life Research. Mitchel J. Beville & Kenneth Meyer. 1983. 5.00 (*1-55614-112-2*) U of SD Gov Res Bur.

Search for Efficiency in the Adjustment Process: Spain in the 1980s. Augusto Lopez-Claros. (Occasional Paper Ser.: No. 57). 43p. 1988. pap. 7.50 (*1-55775-009-2*) Intl Monetary.

Search for El Dorado. Ed. by Dale Brown. (Lost Civilizations Ser.). (Illus.). 168p. 1994. 19.95 (*0-8094-9033-1*) Time-Life.

Search for Emily. J. Dennis Deitz. (Illus.). 188p. 1989. pap. 6.95 (*0-938985-04-3*) Mntn Memories Bks.

Search for Emma's Story: A Model For Humanities Detective Work. Marian L. Martinello. LC 86-30005. (Illus.). 224p. (Orig.). 1987. pap. 12.95 (*0-87565-070-8*) Tex Christian.

Search for Enemies: America's Alliances after the Cold War. Ted G. Carpenter. 228p. 1992. 15.95 (*0-932790-96-8*); pap. 12.95 (*0-932790-95-X*) Cato Inst.

Search for English-Canadian Literature: An Anthology of Critical Articles from the Nineteenth & Early Twentieth Centuries. Ed. by Carl Ballstadt. LC 75-15779. (Literature of Canada, Poetry & Prose in Reprint Ser.: No. 16). 263p. reprint ed. pap. 75.00 (*0-317-26829-5*, 2023490) Bks Demand.

***Search for Enlightened Leadership: Applying New Administrative Theory.** unabridged ed. Richard J. Spady & Cecil H. Beel, Jr. (Civilization of Tomorrow Ser.). 160p. (Orig.). 1996. pap. 19.95 (*1-881908-14-3*) PanPress.

Search for Enlightenment: The Working Class & Adult Education. Simon & Schuster Staff. (C). 1990. text ed. 49.95 (*0-85315-683-2*, Pub. by Lawrence & Wishart UK) NYU Pr.

Search for Environment: The Garden City, Before & After. 2nd ed. Walter L. Creese. (Illus.). 420p. 1992. reprint ed. pap. text ed. 29.95 (*0-8018-4363-4*) Johns Hopkins.

Search for Equality: The National Urban League, 1910-1961. Jesse T. Moore, Jr. LC 80-24302. (Illus.). 264p. 1981. 30.00 (*0-271-00302-2*) Pa St U Pr.

Search for Equity: The Funding of Additional Educational Needs under LMS. Tim Lee. 151p. 1996. text ed. 55.95 (*1-85972-413-2*, Pub. by Avebury Pub UK) Ashgate Pub Co.

Search for Excellence: The Christian College in an Age of Educational Competition. Robert T. Sandin. LC 82-12482. vi, 242p. 1982. text ed. 13.50 (*0-86554-037-3*, MUP-H039) Mercer Univ Pr.

Search for Existential Identity: Patient-Therapist Dialogues in Humanistic Psychotherapy. James F. Bugental. LC 75-44882. (Social & Behavioral Science Ser.). 349p. 50.00 (*0-87589-273-6*) Jossey-Bass.

***Search for Extra-Solar Terrestrial Planets: Techniques & Technology.** 1997. lib. bdg. 95.00 (*0-7923-4474-X*) Kluwer Ac.

Search for Extraterrestrial Life. Ed. by J. S. Hanrahan. (Advances in the Astronautical Sciences Ser.: Vol. 22). 1967. 30.00 incl. fiche (*0-87703-025-1*) Univelt Inc.

Search for Extraterrestrial Life: Recent Developments. Ed. by Michael Papagiannis. 1985. lib. bdg. 182.50 (*90-277-2113-0*) Kluwer Ac.

Search for Fierra. Stephen R. Lawhead. (Empyrion Saga Ser.: Vol. 1). 432p. 1996. pap. 13.00 (*0-310-20509-3*) Zondervan.

***Search for Forgotten Origins.** Atlantis Rising Editors. (Paradigm Busters Ser.). (Illus.). 210p. (Orig.). 1996. pap. 14.95 (*0-9653310-0-8*) Atlan Rising.

Search for Form in Art & Architecture. Eliel Saarinen. 377p. 1985. reprint ed. pap. 9.95 (*0-486-24907-7*) Dover.

Search for Freedom: Demolishing the Strongholds That Diminish Your Faith, Hope, & Confidence in God. Robert S. McGee. 220p. (Orig.). 1995. pap. 12.99 (*0-89283-862-0*, Vine Bks) Servant.

Search for Fundamentals: The Process of Modernization & the Quest for Meaning. Ed. by Lieteke Van Vocht Tijssen. 296p. (C). 1995. lib. bdg. 128.00 (*0-7923-3542-2*) Kluwer Ac.

Search for General Miles. Newton F. Tolman. 24.50 (*0-8488-0234-9*, J M C & Co) Amereon Ltd.

Search for God. M. Chute. 1979. pap. 11.95 (*0-933062-04-4*) R H Sommer.

Search for God. David M. White. 448p. 1983. 23.99 (*0-02-627110-9*); 75.00 (*0-686-48308-1*) Macmillan.

Search for God, Bk. I. Ed. by Association for Research & Enlightenment, Readings Research Dept. et al. 146p. 1950. 8.95 (*0-87604-000-8*, 279) ARE Pr.

Search for God, Bk. I. rev. ed. Edgar Cayce et al. 218p. 1992. pap. 8.95 (*0-87604-296-5*, 376) ARE Pr.

Search for God, Bk. II. Ed. by Association for Research & Enlightenment, Readings Research Dept. et al. 147p. 1950. Bk. 1, 134p. 8.95 (*0-87604-001-6*, 280) ARE Pr.

Search for God Bks. 1 & 2: Anniversary Edition. (Illus.). 257p. 1992. text ed. 24.95 (*0-87604-290-6*, 370) ARE Pr.

Search for God at Harvard. Ari L. Goldman. (Illus.). 304p. 1992. pap. 10.00 (*0-345-37706-0*) Ballantine.

Search for God in Time & Memory. John S. Dunne. LC 76-20165. 1977. reprint ed. pap. 15.00 (*0-268-01673-9*) U of Notre Dame Pr.

***Search for God's Law.** Bernard G. Weiss. 745p. 1996. 69.00 (*0-614-21209-X*, 1115) Kazi Pubns.

Search for God's Law: Islamic Jurisprudence in the Writings of Sayf al-Din al-Amidi. Bernard G. Weiss. LC 90-48326. (Illus.). 752p. 1992. 65.00 (*0-87480-356-X*) U of Utah Pr.

***Search for Gold.** Treasure Hunter's Staff. LC 96-37564. (Treasure Hunters Ser.). (J). 1998. write for info. (*0-8172-4837-4*) Raintree Steck-V.

Search for Grace: A Documented Case of Murder & Reincarnation. Bruce Goldberg. Ed. by Tomi Keitlen & Ed Whalen. LC 94-76641. (Illus.). 276p. 1994. pap. 13.95 (*0-9630485-8-9*) In Print.

***Search for Grace: The True Story of Murder & Reincarnation.** Bruce Goldberg. 1997. pap. text ed. 12.95 (*1-56718-318-2*) Llewellyn Pubns.

Search for Grissi. Mary F. Shura. 128p. (J). 1987. pap. 3.50 (*0-380-70305-X*, Camelot) Avon.

Search for Haigwood-Hagood-Haygood, Et Cetera, 1650-1984, Vol. 1. John E. Haigwood. LC 84-63018. (Illus.). 850p. 1985. 65.00 (*0-9614500-0-2*) J E Haigwood.

Search for Happily-Ever-After. Patricia Baehr. LC 94-37415. 144p. (J). (gr. 3-5). 1997. pap. 13.95 (*0-8167-3658-8*) BrdgeWater.

Search for Harmony: Essays on Science & Mormonism. Ed. by Gene A. Sessions & Craig J. Oberg. LC 92-16811. (Essays on Mormonism Ser.: No. 6). xxii, 297p. 1993. pap. 17.95 (*1-56085-020-5*) Signature Bks.

Search for Health: A Classic Anthology. Tom Valentine et al. (Illus.). 520p. 1995. pap. 35.00 (*0-9648325-0-X*) Valentine Commun.

Search for Historical Meaning: Hegel & the Postwar American Right. Paul Gottfried. LC 86-5279. 1986. 29.00 (*0-87580-114-5*) N Ill U Pr.

Search for Holmes, Robson, Hind, Steele & Graham Families of Cumberland & Northumberland, England. Anne H. Christian. (Illus.). 184p. 1985. 12.95 (*0-9613723-0-3*) Search CA.

Search for Home. Sashthi Brata. 152p. 1975. pap. 2.50 (*0-88253-771-7*) Ind-US Inc.

Search for Identity. Robert L. Friedly & D. Duane Cummins. 192p. (Orig.). 1987. pap. 12.99 (*0-8272-3427-9*) Chalice Pr.

Search for Identity. Ed. by Arnold T. Olson. LC 80-66030. (Heritage Ser.: Vol. 1). 160p. 1980. 8.95 (*0-911802-46-0*); pap. 6.95 (*7-100-07621-8*) Free Church Pubns.

Search for Identity: Canonical Sponsorship of Catholic Healthcare. 100p. 1993. pap. 7.50 (*0-87125-210-4*, 800) Cath Health.

Search for Identity: Five American Indian Stories. Royce Q. Holland et al. Ed. by Jon Reyhner & Rachel Schaffer. (J). (gr. 4-9). 1991. pap. 6.95 (*0-89992-432-8*) Coun India Ed.

Search for Immortality. Time-Life Books Editors. Ed. by Jim Hicks. (Mysteries of the Unknown Ser.). 144p. 14.95 (*0-8094-6533-7*) Time-Life.

Search for Infinity: Solving the Mysteries of the Universe. Inge Sellevag et al. LC 94-29113. (Illus.). 144p. 1995. 22.95 (*0-8160-3250-5*) Facts on File.

***Search for Inner-Peace.** Steven Herberts. LC 97-17837. (J). 1997. pap. write for info. (*0-7734-2836-4*) E Mellen.

Search for Intimacy. Elaine Storkey. LC 95-52267. 268p. 1996. pap. text ed. 15.00 (*0-8028-4216-X*) Eerdmans.

Search for Isadora: The Legend & Legacy of Isadora Duncan. Lillian Loewenthal. 240p. 1993. 9.95 (*0-87127-179-6*) Princeton Bk Co.

Search for Ithaka. Sheridan Fonda. 20p. (Orig.). 1995. pap. write for info. (*1-885206-21-6*, Iliad Pr) Cader Pubng.

Search for Jesus: Modern Scholarship Looks at the Gospels. John D. Crossan et al. LC 94-70539. 152p. (Orig.). (C). 1994. audio 32.95 (*1-880317-15-X*, 7HC3) Biblical Arch Soc.

Search for Jesus: Modern Scholarship Looks at the Gospels. John D. Crossan et al. LC 94-70539. 152p. (Orig.). (C). 1994. pap. text ed. 11.95 (*1-880317-14-1*, 7H44) Biblical Arch Soc.

Search for John Bartlam at Cain Hoy: America's First Creamware Potter, 2 vols. Stanley South. (Research Manuscript Ser.). 300p. 1993. pap. text ed. 30.00 (*1-884616-00-3*) U SC Inst Archaeol.

***Search for Justice.** Arthur Bryant. Date not set. write for info. (*0-688-04292-9*) Morrow.

Search for Justice. Norbert Schlegel. 536p. 1995. mass mkt. 6.99 (*1-896329-56-X*, Pub. by Comnwlth Pub CN) Partners Pubs Grp.

Search for Justice: A Defense Attorney's Brief on the O. J. Simpson Case. Robert L. Shapiro & Larkin Warren. 384p. 1996. 24.95 (*0-446-52081-0*) Warner Bks.

Search for Justice: A Woman's Path to Renewed Self-Esteem from the Fear, Shame, & Anger of Sexual Harassment & Employment Discrimination. Charmaine Wellington & B. J. Holcombe. 240p. 1992. pap. 11.95 (*0-913299-86-3*) Stillpoint.

Search for Kate Duval. Page Edwards, Jr. 208p. (Orig.). 1996. pap. 14.95 (*0-7145-3000-X*) M Boyars Pubs.

Search for King Arthur. David Day. LC 95-24119. (Illus.). 176p. (YA). 1995. 24.95 (*0-8160-3370-6*) Facts on File.

Search for Labour Market Flexibility: The European Economies in Transition. Ed. by Robert Boyers. (Illus.). 328p. 1988. 75.00 (*0-19-828560-4*) OUP.

Search for Leadership. Allen E. Roberts. 236p. 1987. 18.00 (*0-935633-05-7*) Anchor Comm.

Search for Lee Harvey Oswald. Robert J. Groden. (Illus.). 1995. 29.95 (*0-614-15423-5*) Studio Bks.

Search for Lee Harvey Oswald: A Comprehensive Photographic Record. Robert J. Groden. 256R256p. 1995. pap. 29.95 (*0-670-85867-6*, Viking) Viking Penguin.

Search for Legitimate Social Development Education & Practice Models for Africa. Kwaku Osei-Hwedie. LC 95-9138. (Studies in African Economic & Social Development: Vol. 7). 288p. 1996. text ed. 89.95 (*0-7734-8887-1*, Mellen Biblical Pr) E Mellen.

Search for Liberty: From Reconstruction to Reagan, Vol. 1. Edmond Wright. (History of the United States of America Ser.). (Illus.). 352p. (C). 1995. 32.95 (*1-55786-588-4*) Blackwell Pubs.

Search for Life. Kim Unsong. LC 87-60116. 303p. 1987. 20.00 (*0-942049-01-2*) One Mind Pr.

Search for Life in the Universe. 2nd ed. Donald Goldsmith & Tobias Owen. (Illus.). 464p. (C). 1992. pap. text ed. 35.50 (*0-201-56949-3*) Addison-Wesley.

Search for Life's Origins: Progress & Future Directions in Planetary Biology & Chemical Evolution. National Research Council Staff. 160p. 1990. pap. text ed. 16.00 (*0-309-04246-1*) Natl Acad Pr.

Search for Lopez: Utah's Greatest Manhunt. Lynn R. Bailey. (Great West & Indian Ser.: Vol. 54). (Illus.). 1990. 24.95 (*0-87026-073-1*) Westernlore.

***Search for Lost Cities.** Nicola Barber. LC 96-40495. (Treasure Hunters Ser.). (J). 1998. write for info. (*0-8172-4840-4*) Raintree Steck-V.

Search for Lost Fathering: Rebuilding Your Father Relationship. James L. Schaller. LC 94-37752. 192p. (gr. 10). 1995. pap. 9.99 (*0-8007-5552-9*) Revell.

Search for Love. Nora Roberts. (NR Flowers Ser.: No. 11). 1992. mass mkt. 3.59 (*0-373-51011-X*) Harlequin Bks.

Search for Man's Sanity. Trigant Burrow. Ed. by Gerald N. Grob. LC 78-22553. (Historical Issues in Mental Health Ser.). 1980. reprint ed. lib. bdg. 50.95 (*0-405-11907-0*) Ayer.

Search for Meaning. Richard R. Erickson. LC 91-7144. 176p. (Orig.). (C). 1990. pap. 7.95 (*0-9628808-0-9*) Gentle Begin.

Search for Meaning. Antonio R. Gualtieri. 209p. 1991. pap. 16.00 (*0-920717-61-6*) SPD-Small Pr Dist.

Search for Meaning. William H. Willimon et al. LC 93-23618. 224p. 1994. 9.48 (*0-687-02586-9*) Abingdon.

***Search for Meaning.** William H. Willimon et al. 16p. 1997. pap. 39.95 incl. vhs (*0-687-02587-7*) Abingdon.

Search for Meaning: Exploring Religions of the World. Antonio R. Gualtieri. Date not set. write for info. (*0-614-17988-2*) Guernica Editions.

Search for Meaning: Insights Through Literature, History & Art. large type ed. Richard F. Hettlinger & Grace Worth. Ed. by National Council on the Aging Staff. (Large Print Inspirational Ser.). (Illus.). 1988. pap. 14.95 (*0-8027-2628-3*) Walker & Co.

***Search for Meaning: Leaders Guide.** pap. 5.95 (*0-687-11665-1*) Abingdon.

Search for Meaning: Towards a New Psychology of Fulfillment. Alan Garner. LC 88-81434. 160p. (Orig.). 1989. pap. 9.95 (*0-941404-85-4*) New Falcon Pubns.

Search for Meaning in the Workplace. Thomas H. Naylor et al. LC 96-21841. 1996. pap. 12.95 (*0-687-01548-0*) Abingdon.

Search for Meaning Workbook. Thomas H. Naylor et al. 88p. (Orig.). 1994. pap. 4.48 (*0-687-00440-3*) Abingdon.

Search for Messiah: Discovering the Identity of the True Messiah! 2nd expanded rev. ed. Chuck Smith & Mark Eastman. 288p. (Orig.). 1996. per. 10.00 (*0-936728-50-7*, ME001) Joy Pub SJC.

Search for MIAs. Garry L. Smith. Ed. by Ed Y. Hall. (Illus.). 176p. (Orig.). 1992. pap. 12.95 (*0-9622166-3-1*) Honoribus Pr.

Search for Mind: A New Foundation for Cognitive Science. Sean O. Nuallain. (Computational Science Ser.). 360p. 1995. pap. 39.50 (*1-56750-139-7*); text ed. 78.50 (*1-56750-138-9*) Ablex Pub.

Search for Miri. Libby Lazewnik. 273p. 1991. 15.95 (*0-944070-35-3*); pap. 12.95 (*0-944070-36-1*) Targum Pr.

Search for Missing Friends Vol. 1: 1831-1850: Irish Immigrant Advertisements Placed in the Boston Pilot. Ed. by Ruth-Ann Harris & Donald M. Jacobs. 748p. 1989. 45.00 (*0-88082-022-5*, S2-62561) New Eng Hist.

Search for Missing Friends, Vol. 2: 1851-53: Irish Immigrant Advertisements Placed in the Boston Pilot. Ed. by Ruth-Ann Harris & B. Emer O'Keeffe. 1991. 45.00 (*0-88082-029-2*, S2-62562) New Eng Hist.

Search for Modern China. Jonathan D. Spence. (C). 1988. pap. 28.95 (*0-393-30780-8*) Norton.

Search for Modern China. Jonathan D. Spence. 1990. 32.95 (*0-393-02708-2*) Norton.

Search for Modern Nationalism: Zhang Binglin & Revolutionary China, 1869-1936. Young-Tsu Wong. (East Asian Historical Monographs). 248p. 1989. 45.00 (*0-19-582740-6*) OUP.

Search for My Great Uncle's Head. Jonathan Latimer. LC 89-85718. 294p. reprint ed. pap. 7.95 (*1-55882-052-3*, Lib Crime Classics) Intl Polygonics.

Search for New Anticancer Drugs. Ed. by Michael J. Waring & B. A. Ponder. LC 92-49744. (Cancer Biology & Medicine Ser.: Vol. 3). (C). 1992. lib. bdg. 147.00 (*0-7923-8959-X*) Kluwer Ac.

Search for New Arts. Charles Biederman. LC 79-90835. 1979. 25.00 (*0-9605614-0-4*); pap. 25.00 (*0-9605614-1-2*) Art History.

Search for New Drugs. Ed. by Alan A. Rubin. LC 74-187516. (Medicinal Research Ser.: No. 6). (Illus.). 464p. reprint ed. pap. 132.30 (*0-7837-0931-5*, 2041236) Bks Demand.

***Search for New Elementary Particles.** 450p. 1993. text ed. 49.00 (*981-02-1271-2*) World Scientific Pub.

Search for New Elementary Particles: Status & Prospect, Proceedings of the Trieste Workshop. G. Herten et al. 450p. 1993. text ed. 121.00 (*981-02-1236-4*) World Scientific Pub.

S

An Asterisk (*) at the beginning of an entry indicates that the title is appearing in BIP for the first time.

Search for New Insights in Librarianship: A Day of Comparative Studies - Proceedings of the Library School Commons Conference, University of Wisconsin, April 25, 1975. Library School Commons Conference Staff. Ed. by William L. Williamson. 106p. 1976. pap. 4.00 (*0-936442-04-2*) U Wis Sch Lib.

***Search for New Vaccines: The Effects of the Vaccines for Children Program.** Henry Grabowski & John Vernon. 100p. (Orig.). 1997. pap. 14.95 (*0-8447-4033-0*) Am Enterprise.

Search for Nina Fletcher: A Metaphysical Adventure. Stephen H. Martin. 288p. (Orig.). 1995. pap. 14.95 (*0-9646601-3-X*) Oaklea Pr.

Search for Nirvana: Korean Monks' Life. Kwan-Jo Lee. (Illus.). 128p. 1984. 24.00 (*0-8048-1417-1*, Pub. by Seoul Intl Tourist KO) C E Tuttle.

***Search for Normality: National Identity & Historical Consciousness in Germany since 1800.** Stefan Berger. LC 96-53355. 250p. 1997. 49.95 (*1-57181-863-4*) Berghahn Bks.

S

Search for Objectivity in Constitutional Law. George D. Braden. (Reprint Series in Social Sciences). (C). 1993. reprint ed. pap. text ed. 1.90 (*0-8290-3147-2*, PS-31) Irvington.

Search for Oil: Some Statistical Methods & Techniques. Ed. by Donald B. Owen. LC 75-25162. (Statistics, Textbooks & Monographs: No. 13). (Illus.). 208p. reprint ed. pap. 59.30 (*0-7837-0975-7*, 2041281) Bks Demand.

Search for OMM SETY: A Story of Eternal Love. Jonathan Cott. 288p. 1989. pap. 9.95 (*0-446-39040-2*) Warner Bks.

Search for Oneness. Lloyd H. Silverman et al. LC 82-4658. x, 306p. 1983. 45.00 (*0-8236-6013-3*) Intl Univs Pr.

Search for Order: 1877-1920. Robert H. Wiebe. LC 66-27609. (Making of America Ser.). 336p. 1966. reprint ed. pap. 10.95 (*0-8090-0104-7*) Hill & Wang.

Search for Order Vol. 1: Landmarks of World Civilization. Marc Meyer. LC 93-73093. 432p. (C). 1994. per. 14.95 (*1-56134-230-0*) Dushkin Pub.

Search for Order Vol. 2: Landmarks of World Civilization. Marc Meyer. LC 93-73095. 448p. (C). 1994. per. 14.95 (*1-56134-231-9*) Dushkin Pub.

Search for Oregon's Lost Blue-Bucket Mine: The Stephen Meek Wagon Train of 1845: An Oregon Documentary. Charles S. Hoffman & Bert Webber. LC 92-10098. (Illus.). 112p. (Orig.). 1992. pap. 12.95 (*0-936738-63-4*) Webb Research.

Search for Paleoliquefaction & Evidence Bearing on the Recurrence Behavior of the Great 1811-12 New Madrid Earthquakes. Kaye M. Shedlock. (Illus.). 42p. (Orig.). (C). 1995. pap. text ed. 25.00 (*0-7881-1946-X*) DIANE Pub.

Search for Peace: Release from the Torments of Toxic Unforgiveness. Robert S. McGee & Donald W. Sapaugh. 200p. (Orig.). 1996. pap. 12.99 (*0-89283-891-4*, Vine Bks) Servant.

Search for Peace: The Story of the United Nations. William J. Jacobs. LC 93-27149. (Illus.). 144p. (J). (gr. 5-8). 1994. lib. bdg. 14.95 (*0-684-19652-2*, C Scribner Sons Young) S&S Childrens.

Search for Peace & Unity in the Sudan. Francis M. Deng & Prosser Gifford. LC 87-50714. (Illus.). 208p. (Orig.). (C). 1987. pap. text ed. 17.50 (*0-943875-00-5*, Johns Hopkins); lib. bdg. 32.75 (*0-943875-01-3*, Johns Hopkins) W Wilson Ctr Pr.

Search for Peace in Afghanistan: From Buffer State to Failed State. Barnett R. Rubin. LC 95-15694. 1996. 25.00 (*0-300-06376-8*) Yale U Pr.

Search for Peace in Europe: Perspectives from NATO & Eastern Europe. 1995. lib. bdg. 260.95 (*0-8490-7412-6*) Gordon Pr.

Search for Peace in Europe: Perspectives from NATO & Eastern Europe. (Illus.). 359p. (Orig.). (C). 1995. pap. text ed. 45.00 (*0-7881-1628-2*) DIANE Pub.

Search for Peace in the Middle East, 1967-1988. LC 89-85581. 836p. reprint ed. lib. bdg. 58.00 (*0-89941-727-2*, 201940) W S Hein.

Search for Personal Freedom. Robert C. Lamm et al. 672p. (C). 1985. pap. write for info. (*0-697-00499-6*) Brown & Benchmark.

Search for Philip K. Dick, 1928-1982: A Memoir. Anne R. Dick. LC 95-8690. (Illus.). 396p. 1996. text ed. 99.95 (*0-7734-9137-6*) E Mellen.

Search for Political Community: American Activists Reinventing Commitment. Paul Lichterman. (Cambridge Cultural Social Studies). 304p. (C). 1996. pap. text ed. 19.95 (*0-521-48343-3*) Cambridge U Pr.

Search for Political Community: American Activists Reinventing Commitment. Paul Lichterman. (Cultural Social Studies). 304p. (C). 1996. text ed. 54.95 (*0-521-48286-0*) Cambridge U Pr.

***Search for Political Space: Globalization, Social Movements, & the Urban Political Experience.** Warren Magnusson. (Studies in Comparative Political Economy & Public Policy Ser.). 400p. 1996. 60.00 (*0-8020-5959-7*); pap. 19.95 (*0-8020-6889-8*) U of Toronto Pr.

***Search for Priam's Gold: The Extraordinary Story of a Plundered Legend.** Klaus Goldmann & Wolfgang Schneider. Tr. by Rosemary Dear. (Illus.). 176p. 1997. 24.95 (*0-285-63356-2*, Pub. by Souvenir UK) IPG Chicago.

Search for Psychic Power: ESP & Parapsychology Revisited. rev. ed. C. E. Hansel. 308p. 1989. 32.95 (*0-87975-516-4*); pap. 22.95 (*0-87975-533-4*) Prometheus Bks.

Search for Pure Food: A Sociology of Legislation in Britain. Ingleborg Paulus. (Law in Society Ser.). 144p. 1974. text ed. 8.50 (*0-85520-076-6*) Rothman.

Search for Purity: A Retrospective Policy Analysis of Decision to Chlorinate Cincinnati's Public Water Supply, 1890-1920. Coleen O'Toole. LC 90-13865. (Environment: Problems & Solutions Ser.: Vol. 26). 150p. 1990. text ed. 15.00 (*0-8240-9792-0*) Garland.

Search for Purpose. Arthur E. Morgan. LC 55-10426. 1957. 5.00 (*0-317-06070-8*) Comm Serv OH.

Search for Quality: Planning for Improvement & Managing Change. Marilyn Leask & Del Goddard. 160p. 1992. pap. 37.50 (*1-85396-190-6*, Pub. by P Chapman UK) Taylor & Francis.

Search for Quality Integrated Education: Policy & Research on Minority Students in School & College. Meyer Weinberg. LC 82-12016. (Contributions to the Study of Education Ser.: No. 7). (Illus.). xv, 354p. 1983. text ed. 55.00 (*0-313-23714-X*, WEI/) Greenwood.

Search for Rational Drug Control. Franklin E. Zimring & Gordon J. Hawkins. (Illus.). 224p. (C). 1992. text ed. 49.95 (*0-521-41668-X*) Cambridge U Pr.

Search for Rational Drug Control. Franklin E. Zimring & Gordon Hawkins. (Illus.). 224p. (C). 1995. pap. text ed. 16.95 (*0-521-55882-4*) Cambridge U Pr.

Search for Relevance: The Campus in Crisis. Joseph Axelrod et al. LC 72-75941. (Jossey-Bass Higher Education Ser.). 256p. reprint ed. 73.00 (*0-8357-9346-X*, 2013946) Bks Demand.

***Search for Riches.** Andrew Langley. LC 96-30797. (Remarkable World Ser.). (J). 1997. lib. bdg. 24.26 (*0-8172-4544-8*) Raintree Steck-V.

Search for Sam. Anthony Tallarico. (Illus.). 24p. (J). 1988. pap. 2.95 (*0-942025-67-9*) Kidsbks.

Search for Sam. Anthony Tallarico. (Where Are They? Ser.). (Illus.). 24p. (J). 1990. 9.95 (*0-942025-58-X*) Kidsbks.

Search for Sam. Anthony Tallarico. (Where Are They? Ser.). (Illus.). 24p. (J). (gr. 2-6). 1990. lib. bdg. 10.95 (*0-8167-1958-6*) Troll Communs.

Search for Sanctuary: Brigham Young & the White Mountain Expedition. Clifford L. Stott. LC 84-15250. (University of Utah Publications in the American West: No. 19). (Illus.). 311p. reprint ed. pap. 88.70 (*0-7837-5535-X*, 2045308) Bks Demand.

Search for Sanity: The Politics of Nuclear Weapons & Disarmament. Ed. by Paul Joseph & Simon Rosenblum. LC 83-51289. 600p. 1984. 40.00 (*0-89608-205-9*); pap. 16.00 (*0-89608-204-0*) South End Pr.

Search for Santa. Anthony Tallarico. (Where Are They? Ser.). (Illus.). 32p. (Orig.). (J). 1990. 10.95 (*0-942025-71-7*); pap. 3.95 (*0-942025-72-5*) Kidsbks.

Search for Santa's Helpers. Anthony Tallarico. 1991. 4.98 (*0-8317-7726-5*) Smithmark.

Search for Santa's Helpers. Tony Tallarico. (Illus.). 32p. (J). 1991. 10.95 (*1-56156-015-4*); pap. 3.95 (*1-56156-031-6*); pap. 3.95 (*1-56156-042-1*) Kidsbks.

Search for Sara Sanderson. Thomas McKean. 160p. (J). (gr. 3-7). 1987. pap. 2.50 (*0-380-75295-6*, Camelot) Avon.

Search for Sebastian. Judston Crown. LC 90-84909. (Orig.). 1991. pap. 9.95 (*0-9623497-6-3*) Los Hombres.

Search for Security. Margaret J. Field. 478p. 1962. 45.00 (*0-89771-009-6*) St Mut.

Search for Security: A Study in Baltic Diplomacy, 1920-1934. Hugh I. Rodgers. LC 74-16366. xi, 181p. (Orig.). (C). 1975. lib. bdg. 31.00 (*0-208-01478-0*, Archon Bks) Shoe String.

Search for Security: An Ethno-psychiatric Study of Rural Ghana. Margaret J. Field. LC 60-14408. (Northwestern University African Studies Ser.: No. 5). 471p. reprint ed. pap. 134.30 (*0-317-27793-6*, 2015294) Bks Demand.

Search for Security: Saudi Arabian Oil & American Foreign Policy, 1939-1949. Aaron D. Miller. xviii, 320p. 1991. pap. 14.95 (*0-8078-4324-5*) U of NC Pr.

Search for Security: Saudi Arabian Oil & American Foreign Policy, 1939-1949. Aaron D. Miller. LC 79-18144. 340p. 1980. reprint ed. pap. 96.90 (*0-608-00199-6*, 2060982) Bks Demand.

Search for Security: The Political Economy of Australia's Post War Foreign & Defense Policy. David Lee. 200p. 1996. pap. 24.95 (*1-86373-607-7*) Paul & Co Pubs.

Search for Security in Space. Ed. by Kenneth N. Luongo & W. Thomas Wander. LC 88-47928. (Cornell Studies in Security Affairs). 304p. 1989. 42.50 (*0-8014-2145-4*); pap. 15.95 (*0-8014-9482-6*) Cornell U Pr.

Search for Seismosaurus. J. Lynette Gillette. LC 92-28199. (Illus.). (J). 1994. pap. 14.99 (*0-8037-1358-4*) Dial Bks Young.

Search for Seismosaurus: The World's Longest Dinosaur. J. Lynette Gillette. LC 92-28199. (J). (gr. 4-7). 1994. 14.89 (*0-8037-1359-2*) Dial Bks Young.

Search for Self: The Experience of Access to Adoption Information. Shurlee Swain & Phillip A. Swain. 124p. 1992. pap. 35.00 (*1-86287-087-X*, Pub. by Federation Pr AU) Gaunt.

Search for Self-Sovereignty: The Oratory of Elizabeth Cady Stanton. Beth M. Waggenspack. LC 89-7519. (Great American Orators: Critical Studies, Speeches & Sources: No. 4). 224p. 1989. text ed. 55.00 (*0-313-25978-X*, WKS/, Greenwood Pr) Greenwood.

Search for Serenity: Encouragement for Your Weary Days. Gigi G. Tchividjian. LC 90-48174. 194p. (YA). (gr. 10). 1993. reprint ed. pap. 8.99 (*0-8010-8908-5*, Ravens Ridge) Baker Bks.

Search for Shelter. N. Richter Greer. (Illus.). 131p. 1986. 8.95 (*0-913962-82-1*) AIA Press.

***Search for Sideny's Smile.** Marc Kornblatt. (Illus.). 24p. (J). 3.98 (*0-8317-2370-X*) Smithmark.

Search for Sidney's Smile. Marc Kornblatt. LC 92-12824. (Illus.). (J). 1993. 13.00 (*0-671-76912-X*, S&S Bks Young Read) S&S Childrens.

Search for Significance. Dawson McAllister & Robert S. McGee. 1990. student ed., wbk. ed., pap. 10.99 (*0-923417-12-5*) Shepherd Minst.

***Search for Significance.** Dan McGee. 1992. pap. text ed. 12.95 (*0-8054-9990-3*) Broadman.

Search for Significance. Robert S. McGee. 189p. (Orig.). 1990. pap. 14.99 (*0-945276-11-7*) Word Pub.

Search for Significance. rev. ed. Robert S. McGee. 200p. 1990. pap. 9.99 (*0-685-62305-X*) Rapha Pub.

***Search for Significance Leaders Guide.** Dan McGee. 1992. pap. text ed. 5.95 (*0-8054-9989-X*) Broadman.

Search for Significance Small Group Leader's Guide. Robert S. McGee. 58p. 1990. pap. 5.00 (*0-945276-09-5*) Rapha Pub.

Search for Significance (With Workbook) rev. ed. Robert S. McGee. 502p. (Orig.). 1990. wbk. ed., pap. 16.99 (*0-945276-07-9*) Rapha Pub.

Search for Signs of Intelligent Life in the Universe: Now a Major Motion Picture Starring Lily Tomlin. Jane Wagner. LC 86-45435. (Illus.). 224p. 1991. reprint ed. pap. 13.00 (*0-06-092071-8*, PL) HarpC.

***Search for Silence.** J. A. Bradner. (Technical Papers). (Illus.). (Orig.). 1958. pap. text ed. 30.00 incl. audio compact disk (*1-55589-385-6*) AGMA.

Search for Simplicity: Essays in Parallel Programming. Per B. Hansen. LC 96-647. 544p. 1996. 38.00 (*0-8186-7566-7*) IEEE Comp Soc.

Search for Snout. Bruce Coville. (Bruce Coville's Alien Adventures Ser.). (J). (gr. 3-6). 1995. 14.00 (*0-671-89073-5*) PB.

Search for Snout: Bruce Coville's Alien Adventures. Bruce Coville. (J). (gr. 3-6). 1995. mass mkt. 3.99 (*0-671-79834-0*) PB.

Search for Social Peace: Reform Legislation in France, 1890-1914. Judith F. Stone. LC 84-20531. 260p. 1985. text ed. 64.50 (*0-88706-022-6*); pap. text ed. 21.95 (*0-88706-023-4*) State U NY Pr.

Search for Society: Quest for a Biosocial Science & Morality. Robin Fox. LC 88-21759. 275p. (C). 1989. pap. 16.95 (*0-8135-1488-6*); text ed. 45.00 (*0-8135-1464-9*) Rutgers U Pr.

Search for Solitude: Pursuing the Monk's True Life. Thomas Merton. Ed. by Lawrence S. Cunningham. LC 95-46821. (Journals of Thomas Merton: Vol. 3). 1996. pap. write for info. (*0-06-065479-1*) Harper SF.

Search for Solitude: Pursuing the Monk's True Life. Thomas Merton. Ed. by Lawrence S. Cunningham. LC 95-46821. (Journals of Thomas Merton: Vol. 3). 496p. 1996. 27.50 (*0-06-065478-3*) Harper SF.

Search for Solutions. Horace F. Judson. LC 87-2856. 288p. 1987. pap. 12.95 (*0-8018-3526-7*) Johns Hopkins.

Search for Solvency: Bretton Woods & the International Monetary System, 1941-1971. Alfred E. Eckes. LC 75-14433. 369p. reprint ed. pap. 105.20 (*0-8357-7738-3*, 2036095) Bks Demand.

Search for Sonny Skies: A Novel. large type ed. Mickey Rooney. LC 95-2631. 1995. lib. bdg. 22.95 (*0-7838-1254-X*, GK Hall) Thorndike Pr.

***Search for Stability in Russian & the Former Soviet Bloc.** Ed. by David Carlton & Paul Ingram. LC 97-2266. (Studies in Disarmament & Conflicts). 220p. 1997. 63.95 (*1-85521-897-6*, Pub. by Ashgate UK) Ashgate Pub Co.

Search for Strategies for Sustainable Dryland Cropping in Semi-Arid Eastern Kenya. M. E. Probert. 134p. (C). 1992. text ed. 104.00 (*1-86320-068-1*, Pub. by ACIAR) St Mut.

Search for Strategy: Politics & Strategic Vision. Ed. by Gary L. Guertner. LC 92-35916. (Contributions in Military Studies: No. 143). 360p. 1993. text ed. 65.00 (*0-313-28881-X*, GM8881) Greenwood.

Search for Structure: A Report on American Youth Today. Francis A. Ianni. 352p. 1989. 27.95 (*0-02-915360-3*, Free Press) Free Pr.

Search for Structure: Selected Essays on Science, Art & History. Cyril S. Smith. (Illus.). 410p. 1983. pap. 19.95 (*0-262-69082-9*) MIT Pr.

Search for Successful Secondary Schools: The First Three Years of the Secondary School Recognition Program. Thomas B. Corcoran & Bruce L. Wilson. 106p. 1986. pap. 21.95 (*1-56602-012-3*) Research Better.

***Search for Sunken Treasure.** Nicola Barber & Anita Ganeri. LC 97-5403. (Treasure Hunters Ser.). (J). 1998. write for info. (*0-8172-4838-2*) Raintree Steck-V.

Search for Sunken Treasure: Exploring the World's Great Shipwrecks. Robert F. Marx & Jenifer Marx. (Illus.). 196p. (Orig.). 1996. pap. 19.95 (*1-55013-788-3*, Pub. by Key Porter Bks CN) Firefly Bks Ltd.

Search for Sunny Skies: A Novel. Mickey Rooney. LC 93-44187. 1994. 19.95 (*1-55972-231-2*, Birch Ln Pr) Carol Pub Group.

Search for Susie. Anthony Tallarico. (Where Are They? Ser.). (Illus.). 24p. (Orig.). (J). 1990. 9.95 (*0-942025-97-0*) Kidsbks.

Search for Susie. Anthony Tallarico. (Where Are They? Ser.). (Illus.). 24p. (Orig.). (J). 1991. pap. 2.95 (*0-942025-78-4*) Kidsbks.

Search for Sybil. A. C. Peniston. Ed. by Judy Hilovsky. LC 89-316. 1990. 22.95 (*0-87949-291-0*) Ashley Bks.

Search for Sylvester. Tony Tallarico. (Where Are They? Ser.). (Illus.). 24p. (J). 1992. 9.95 (*1-56156-068-5*) Kidsbks.

Search for Synthesis in Economic Theory. Ching-Yao Hsieh & Stephen L. Mangum. LC 84-29816. 272p. (gr. 13). 1986. text ed. 67.95 (*0-87332-328-9*); pap. text ed. 28.95 (*0-87332-329-7*) M E Sharpe.

Search for Synthesis in Literature & Art: The Paradox of Space. Ann C. Colley. LC 89-27427. (Illus.). 186p. 1990. 40.00 (*0-8203-1216-9*) U of Ga Pr.

Search for Tax Principles in the European Economic Community. Clara K. Sullivan. LC 63-22649. (Illus.). 104p. (Orig.). 1963. pap. 4.50 (*0-915506-04-1*) Harvard Law Intl Tax.

Search for Temperance Moon. D. Jones. 416p. 1994. mass mkt. 4.50 (*0-06-100755-2*, Harp PBks) HarpC.

Search for Temperance Moon. Douglas C. Jones. 320p. 1991. 22.00 (*0-8050-1387-3*, D Hutter Bks) H Holt & Co.

Search for Temperance Moon. large type ed. Douglas C. Jones. LC 91-25764. 622p. 1991. reprint ed. lib. bdg. 22.95 (*1-56054-244-6*) Thorndike Pr.

Search for the American Right Wing: The Social Science Record, 1955-1987. William B. Hixson, Jr. 392p. 1992. text ed. 59.50 (*0-691-08623-0*) Princeton U Pr.

Search for the Ancestors & Descendants of Henry Brasater Drake of Coles County, Illinois. Michael E. Drake. (Illus.). 141p. (Orig.). 1996. pap. 17.00 (*0-7884-0423-7*, D611) Heritage Bk.

Search for the Ancient Novel. Ed. by James Tatum. LC 93-13210. 512p. (C). 1993. text ed. 65.00 (*0-8018-4619-6*); pap. text ed. 24.95 (*0-8018-4621-8*) Johns Hopkins.

Search for the Ark of the Covenant. Dean Guest. (Illus.). 110p. 1991. pap. 8.95 (*1-879667-03-7*) Dove Pr TX.

***Search for the Beloved.** Jean Houston. 272p. 1997. pap. 15.95 (*0-87477-871-9*, Tarcher Putnam) Putnam Pub Group.

***Search for the Beloved.** Jean Houston. 288p. (Orig.). pap. write for info. (*0-614-23699-1*, Tarcher Putnam); pap. write for info. (*0-614-23700-9*, Tarcher Putnam) Putnam Pub Group.

Search for the Beloved: Journeys in Mythology & Sacred Psychology. Jean Houston. 272p. 1989. pap. 14.95 (*0-87477-476-4*, Tarcher Putnam) Putnam Pub Group.

Search for the Causes of Schizophrenia. Ed. by H. Hafner et al. (Illus.). 420p. 1987. 167.00 (*0-387-17376-5*) Spr-Verlag.

Search for the Causes of Schizophrenia, Vol. 2. Ed. by H. Hafner & W. F. Gattaz. (Illus.). 472p. 1990. 102.00 (*0-387-51366-3*) Spr-Verlag.

Search for the Causes of Schizophrenia, Vol. III. Ed. by H. Hafner & W. F. Gattaz. (Illus.). 352p. 1995. 108.00 (*3-540-58751-9*) Spr-Verlag.

Search for the Christian Doctrine of God: The Arian Controversy, 318-381 AD. R. P. Hanson. 954p. 1988. 69.95 (*0-567-09485-5*, Pub. by T & T Clark UK) Bks Intl VA.

***Search for the Christmas Star.** Neil F. Michelsen. 23p. 1996. pap. 5.95 (*0-935127-07-0*) ACS Pubns.

Search for the "City of St. Maries" Henry M. Miller. (Archaeology Ser.: No. 1). (Illus.). 195p. 1983. pap. 16.00 (*1-878399-31-4*) Div Hist Cult Progs.

Search for the Consumer Interest. David A. Aaker. 1994. 25.00 (*0-02-900053-X*) S&S Trade.

Search for the Eighteenth Century Village at Michilimackinac: A Soil Resistivity Survey. J. Mark Williams & Gary Shapiro. LC 83-199521. (Archaeological Completion Report Ser.: No. 4). (Illus.). 79p. (Orig.). 1982. pap. 8.00 (*0-911872-43-4*) Mackinac St Hist Pks.

Search for the First Americans. David J. Meltzer. LC 93-29453. (Exploring the Ancient World Ser.). (Illus.). 176p. 1996. text ed. 19.95 (*0-89599-035-0*) Smithsonian.

Search for the Fox. large type ed. Stephen Overholser. LC 96-20902. 1996. pap. 20.00 (*0-7838-1850-5*, GK Hall) Thorndike Pr.

Search for the Gene. Bruce Wallace. LC 92-4174. (Comstock Bk.). (Illus.). 240p. 1992. 39.95 (*0-8014-2680-4*); pap. 15.95 (*0-8014-9967-4*) Cornell U Pr.

Search for the Grail. Graham Phillips. (Illus.). 182p. 1996. 24.95 (*0-7126-7533-7*, Pub. by Century UK) Trafalgar.

Search for the Great Turtle Mother. Jack Rudloe. LC 94-44849. (Illus.). 288p. 1995. 17.95 (*1-56164-072-7*) Pineapple Pr.

Search for the Great Valley. Adapted by Jim Razzi. (Illus.). 24p. (J). (ps-3). 1988. pap. 5.95 (*0-448-09353-7*, G&D) Putnam Pub Group.

Search for the Green River Killer. Carlton Smith & Tomas Guillen. 496p. 1991. pap. 5.99 (*0-451-40239-1*, Onyx) NAL-Dutton.

Search for the Happy Life. Robert C. Taylor. 1995. 12.95 (*0-533-11023-8*) Vantage.

Search for the Historical Jesus: From Apocryphal, Buddhist, Islamic & Sanskrit Sources. 2nd ed. Fida Hassnain. 224p. 1994. pap. 14.95 (*0-946551-99-5*, Pub. by Gateway Books UK) ACCESS Pubs Network.

Search for the Killer Asteroid. Gregory L. Vogt. LC 93-47328. (Illus.). 72p. (J). (gr. 4-6). 1994. lib. bdg. 17.90 (*1-56294-448-7*) Millbrook Pr.

Search for the King. Tommy O'Dell. (Adventures of Zor Ser.). 182p. (Orig.). 1992. pap. 9.99 (*1-56043-650-6*) Destiny Image.

Search for the King. Gore Vidal. 208p. 1986. mass mkt. 4.95 (*0-345-33272-5*) Ballantine.

***Search for the Liberal College: The Beginning of the St. John's Program.** J. Winfree Smith. (Illus.). 136p. 11.00 (*0-9603690-6-6*) SJC Annapolis.

Search for the "Manchurian Candidate" The CIA & Mind Control. John D. Marks. 228p. 1991. pap. 10.95 (*0-393-30794-8*) Norton.

Search for the Meaning of Life: Essays & Reflections on the Mystical Experience. Willigis Jager. LC 94-40337. 336p. 1995. pap. 14.95 (*0-89243-774-X*, Triumph Books) Liguori Pubns.

Search for the Mystery Planet: Space Math. Time-Life Books Editors. Ed. by Jean B. Crawford. (I Love Math Ser.). (Illus.). 64p. (J). (gr. k-2). 1993. lib. bdg. write for info. (*0-8094-9983-5*) Time-Life.

Search for the Mystery Planet: Space Math. Time-Life Books Editors. Ed. by Jean B. Crawford. (I Love Math Ser.). (Illus.). 64p. (J). (gr. 1-4). 1993. 16.95 (*0-8094-9982-7*) Time-Life.

Search for the Northwest Passage. Lucile McDonald. LC 58-11860. (Illus.). 142p. (gr. 4-9). 1958. 8.95 (*0-8323-0029-2*); pap. 6.95 (*0-8323-0253-8*) Binford Mort.

Search for the Origin of Birds. Lawrence M. Witmer. LC 95-14635. (Prehistoric Life Ser.). (Illus.). 64p. (J). (gr. 5-8). 1995. lib. bdg. 24.90 (*0-531-11232-2*) Watts.

Search for the Origins of Christian Worship: Sources & Methods for the Study of Early Liturgy. Paul F. Bradshaw. 224p. 1993. 48.00 (*0-19-508050-5*); pap. 18.95 (*0-19-508051-3*) OUP.

***Search for the Origins of Judaism: From Joshua to the Mishnah.** Etienne Nodet. Tr. by Ed Crowley from FRE. (JSOTS Ser.: Vol. 165). 338p. 1997. 65.00 (*1-85075-445-4*, Pub. by Sheffield Acad UK) CUP Services.

Search for the Passengers of the Mary & John 1630, Set, Vols. I-X. Burton W. Spear. (Illus.). 1440p. 1987. Set. pap. 145.50 (*0-941273-10-5*) M & J Clear Hse.

Search for the Passengers of the Mary & John, 1630 - Mary & John Tour III to England - 1990 Plus New Discoveries. Burton W. Spear. (Illus.). 106p. (Orig.). 1990. pap. 13.50 (*0-941273-15-6*) M & J Clear Hse.

Search for the Passengers of the Mary & John, 1630 - New Ancestral Discoveries, 1989. Burton W. Spear. (Illus.). 151p. (Orig.). 1989. pap. text ed. 13.50 (*0-941273-12-1*) M & J Clear Hse.

Search for the Passengers of the Mary & John 1630, Mary & John Tour II to England - 1988 Plus New Discoveries. Burton W. Spear. (Illus.). 152p. (Orig.). 1988. pap. 13.50 (*0-941273-11-3*) M & J Clear Hse.

Search for the Passengers of the Mary & John 1630, New Ancestral Discoveries - 1990. Burton W. Spear. (Illus.). 136p. (Orig.). 1990. pap. 14.00 (*0-941273-13-X*) M & J Clear Hse.

Search for the Passengers of the Mary & John, 1630 Supplement to Volume 14 - West Country Planters, 1620-1643. Burton W. Spear. 144p. (Orig.). 1991. pap. 16.50 (*0-941273-16-4*) M & J Clear Hse.

Search for the Passengers of the Mary & John 1630, Vol. I: Passengers & Their Children. Burton W. Spear. (Illus.). 82p. (Orig.). 1985. pap. 12.00 (*0-941273-00-8*) M & J Clear Hse.

Search for the Passengers of the Mary & John 1630, Vol. II: Return to the Ancestral Homes-1985. Burton W. Spear. (Illus.). 134p. (Orig.). 1986. pap. 12.50 (*0-941273-01-6*) M & J Clear Hse.

Search for the Passengers of the Mary & John 1630, Vol. III: Updated Ancestries. Burton W. Spear. 73p. 1987. pap. 13.50 (*0-941273-02-4*) M & J Clear Hse.

Search for the Passengers of the Mary & John 1630, Vol. IV: Allen Thru Fyler. Burton W. Spear. (Illus.). 156p. 1987. pap. 14.00 (*0-941273-03-2*) M & J Clear Hse.

Search for the Passengers of the Mary & John 1630, Vol. V: Gallop Thru Greenway. Burton W. Spear. (Illus.). 136p. 1987. pap. 13.50 (*0-941273-04-0*) M & J Clear Hse.

Search for the Passengers of the Mary & John 1630, Vol. VI: Hannum Thru Ludlow. Burton W. Spear. (Illus.). 154p. 1987. pap. 14.00 (*0-941273-05-9*) M & J Clear Hse.

Search for the Passengers of the Mary & John 1630, Vol. VII: Maverick Thru Stoughton. Burton W. Spear. (Illus.). 190p. 1987. pap. 14.50 (*0-941273-06-7*) M & J Clear Hse.

Search for the Passengers of the Mary & John 1630, Vol. VIII: Strong & Fyler. Burton W. Spear. (Illus.). 144p. 1987. pap. 13.50 (*0-941273-07-5*) M & J Clear Hse.

Search for the Passengers of the Mary & John 1630, Vol. VIIII: Terry Thru Wolcott. Burton W. Spear. (Illus.). 114p. 1987. pap. 13.00 (*0-941273-08-3*) M & J Clear Hse.

Search for the Passengers of the Mary & John 1630, Vol. X: Master Index Vol's. IV-VIIII. Burton W. Spear. 257p. 1987. pap. 25.00 (*0-941273-09-1*) M & J Clear Hse.

Search for the Passengers of the Mary & John, 1630 West Country Planters to New England, 1620-1643. Burton W. Spear. 136p. (Orig.). 1990. pap. 16.00 (*0-941273-14-8*) M & J Clear Hse.

Search for the Peanut Butter King. Jane Norman & Frank Beazley. (Adventures of Tick-i-ty Ted Ser.). 24p. (J). (ps-3). 1993. pap. write for info. (*1-883585-00-7*) Pixanne Ent.

Search for the Perfect Chocolate Chip Cookie. Gwen W. Steege. LC 93-42252. 1994. 7.99 (*0-517-10107-6*) Random Hse Value.

Search for the Perfect Chocolate Chip Cookie. Gwen W. Steege. LC 87-46082. (Illus.). 144p. 1988. pap. 12.95 (*0-88266-478-6*, Storey Pub) Storey Comm Inc.

Search for the Perfect Christmas Drama. Barbara Rowland. 40p. (Orig.). 1993. pap. 5.95 (*0-687-37095-7*) Abingdon.

***Search for the Perfect Dog.** Gary Shiebler. LC 97-16350. (Illus.). 160p. 1997. 16.00 (*0-7679-0026-X*) Broadway BDD.

Search for the Perfect Language. Umberto Eco. Ed. by Jacques Le Goff. Tr. by James Fentress from ITA. LC 94-29141. (Making of Europe Ser.). Orig. Title: Ricerca della Lingua Perfetta Nella Cultura Europea. xii, 385p. 1995. 49.95 (*0-631-17465-6*) Blackwell Pubs.

Search for the Perfect Swing: The Proven Scientific Approach to Fundamentally Improve Your Game. Alastair Cochran & John Stobbs. (Illus.). 256p. (Orig.). 1996. pap. 22.95 (*1-57243-109-1*) Triumph Bks.

Search for the Picturesque: Landscape Aesthetics & Tourism in Britain, 1760-1800. Malcolm Andrews. LC 68-63668. (Illus.). xviii, 269p. 1989. 59.50 (*0-8047-1402-9*); pap. 24.95 (*0-8047-1834-2*) Stanford U Pr.

Search for the Pink-headed Duck: A Journey into the Himalayas & down the Brahmaputra. Rory Nugent. (Illus.). 240p. 1993. pap. 11.95 (*0-395-66994-4*) HM.

Search for the Purebloods. 2nd ed. Charles B. Wilson. LC 88-39307. (Oklahoma Museum of Natural History Publication Ser.). (Illus.). 56p. 1989. reprint ed. pap. 12.95 (*0-8061-2191-2*) U of Okla Pr.

Search for the Rabbit. P. Luc Valloglise. 138p. (YA). (gr. 7 up). 1988. pap. 10.00 (*0-934852-55-3*) Lorien Hse.

Search for the Real. rev. ed. Hans Hofmann. Ed. by Bartlett H. Hayes & Sara T. Weeks. (Illus.). 82p. 1967. reprint ed. pap. 6.95 (*1-879886-10-3*) Addison Gallery.

Search for the Real & Other Essays. rev. ed. Ed. by Hans Hofmann et al. (Illus.). 1967. pap. 7.95 (*0-262-58008-X*) MIT Pr.

Search for the Real Jesus. David Winter. 160p. (Orig.). 1982. reprint ed. pap. 6.95 (*0-8192-1318-7*) Morehouse Pub.

Search for the Real Self: Unmasking the Personality Disorders of Our Age. James F. Masterson. 1990. pap. 12.95 (*0-02-920292-2*, Free Press) Free Pr.

Search for the Right Whale. Scott Kraus & Kenneth Mallory. LC 92-18091. (Face to Face Ser.). (Illus.). 36p. (J). (gr. 2-6). 1993. lib. bdg. 14.99 (*0-517-57845-X*, Focal) Buttrwrth-Heinemann.

Search for the Sea Treasure. Christopher Carrie. (Crayola Color & Activity Ser.). (Illus.). 40p. (J). (gr. k up). 1990. 1.59 (*0-86696-246-8*) Binney & Smith.

Search for the Self: Selected Writings of Heinz Kohut, Vol. 3. Ed. by Paul H. Ornstein. 400p. 1991. 62.50 (*0-8236-6017-6*) Intl Univs Pr.

Search for the Self: Selected Writings of Heinz Kohut, Vol. 4. Ed. by Paul H. Ornstein. 500p. 1991. 65.00 (*0-8236-6018-4*) Intl Univs Pr.

Search for the Self: Selected Writings of Heinz Kohut 1950-1978, 4 vols., 1. Ed. by Paul H. Ornstein. LC 77-90229. 1978. 65.00 (*0-8236-6015-X*) Intl Univs Pr.

Search for the Self: Selected Writings of Heinz Kohut 1950-1978, 4 vols., 2. Ed. by Paul H. Ornstein. LC 77-90229. 1978. 65.00 (*0-8236-6016-8*) Intl Univs Pr.

Search for the Seven Sisters: A Hidden-Picture Geography Book. Time-Life Books Editors. (Early Learning Program Ser.). (Illus.). 56p. (J). (ps-2). 1991. write for info. (*0-8094-9287-3*); lib. bdg. write for info. (*0-8094-9288-1*) Time-Life.

Search for the Shadowman. Joan L. Nixon. LC 96-5740. 160p. (YA). 1996. 15.95 (*0-385-32203-8*) Delacorte.

Search for the Silver Persian. Carolyn Keene. (Nancy Drew Ser.: No. 114). 160p. (Orig.). (J). (gr. 3-6). 1993. pap. 3.99 (*0-671-79300-4*, Minstrel Bks) PB.

Search for the Smell of Christmas. Richard Upton & Sharon Fair. (Illus.). 32p. (J). 1992. 14.95 (*0-9633348-0-8*) Aromatique.

Search for the Snow Leopard. Franklin W. Dixon. (Hardy Boys Ser.: No. 139). (YA). 1996. mass mkt. 3.99 (*0-671-50525-4*) PB.

Search for the Soul. (Mysteries of the Unknown Ser.). (Illus.). 144p. 1989. 14.95 (*0-8094-6384-9*); lib. bdg. 23.27 (*0-8094-6385-7*) Time-Life.

Search for the Soul: In Everyday Living. The Mother. LC 89-85343. 168p. (Orig.). (C). 1990. pap. 8.95 (*0-941524-57-4*) Lotus Light.

Search for the Sunken City. M. Oliver. (Puzzle Adventures Ser.). (Illus.). 48p. (J). 1989. pap. 5.50 (*0-7460-0304-8*); lib. bdg. 13.95 (*0-88110-409-4*) EDC.

Search for the Tall Ships. Frank O. Braynard. (Illus.). 144p. 1986. 20.00 (*0-317-39399-5*) F O Braynard.

Search for the Tourette Syndrome & Human Behavior Genes. David E. Comings. 1996. 34.00 (*1-878267-36-1*); pap. 29.95 (*1-878267-41-8*) Hope Pr CA.

Search for the Truth. Ruth Montgomery. 256p. (Orig.). 1985. mass mkt. 5.99 (*0-449-21085-5*, Crest) Fawcett.

Search for the Truth: The Workers' Words Exposed. Lloyd Fortt. 348p. (Orig.). 1994. pap. 9.45 (*0-9639419-2-5*) Res Info Servs.

Search for the Twelve Apostles. William S. McBirnie. 312p. 1979. mass mkt. 5.99 (*0-8423-5839-0*) Tyndale.

***Search for the Ultimate Sink: Urban Pollution iIn Historical Perspective.** Joel A. Tarr. LC 96-38383. (Technology & the Environment Ser.). 419p. 1996. pap. text ed. 24.95 (*1-884836-06-2*) U Akron Pr.

***Search for the Ultimate Sink: Urban Pollution in Historical Perspective.** Joel A. Tarr. LC 96-38383. (Technology & the Environment Ser.). 419p. 1996. text ed. 49.95 (*1-884836-05-4*) U Akron Pr.

Search for the Word: Over 65 Biblical Puzzles for all Ages. Trisha Ruppert. LC 91-77489. 96p. (Orig.). 1993. pap. 3.95 (*1-883654-00-9*) Bethlehem Star.

Search for Thomas F. Ward, Teacher of Frederick Delius. Don C. Gillespie. LC 95-44706. (Illus.). 192p. (C). 1996. lib. bdg. 29.95 (*0-8130-1398-4*) U Press Fla.

***Search for Tombs.** Anita Ganeri. LC 96-51660. (Treasure Hunters Ser.). (J). Date not set. write for info. (*0-8172-4839-0*) Raintree Steck-V.

Search for Total Health. Hugh Bassham. 96p. (Orig.). 1993. pap. 6.99 (*1-56043-752-9*) Destiny Image.

Search for Treasure, Vol. 2. Thomas P. Terry. (Illus.). 125p. (Orig.). 1977. pap. 4.95 (*0-939850-11-7*) Spec Pub.

Search for Treasure, Vol. 3. Thomas P. Terry. (Illus.). 125p. (Orig.). 1977. pap. 4.95 (*0-939850-12-5*) Spec Pub.

Search for Treasure, Vol. 4. Thomas P. Terry. (Illus.). 125p. (Orig.). 1980. pap. 4.95 (*0-939850-13-3*) Spec Pub.

Search for Treasure, Vol. 5. Thomas P. Terry. (Illus.). 125p. (Orig.). 1980. pap. 4.95 (*0-939850-14-1*) Spec Pub.

Search for True Discipleship in Church History, Pt. I: Quarter 3. Bill Patterson. (Growing Christian Disciples Ser.). 96p. 1989. student ed. 3.95 (*1-56794-018-8*, C2283); teacher ed. 4.95 (*1-56794-019-6*, C2283T) Star Bible.

Search for True Discipleship in Church History, Pt. II: Quarter 4. Bill Patterson. (Growing Christian Disciples Ser.). 96p. 1989. student ed. 3.95 (*1-56794-020-X*, C2284); teacher ed. 4.95 (*1-56794-021-8*, C2284T) Star Bible.

Search for True Discipleship in Church History, Pt. II: Quarter 4. abr. ed. Bill Patterson. (Growing Christian Disciples Ser.). 199p. 1989. 5.95 (*0-940999-39-0*, C2151) Star Bible.

Search for Truth. Anas Khalid. Ed. by Aliyah F. Abdal-aziz. LC 86-51061. 56p. 1986. pap. 4.00 (*0-9617422-0-8*) A Khalid.

Search for Truth. A. T. Ronk. LC 73-82191. 1973. pap. 0.75 (*0-934970-04-1*) Brethren Church.

Search for Truth: Poetry by Terry L. Tolbert. Terry L. Tolbert. 156p. (Orig.). 1995. pap. 9.95 (*1-57502-061-0*) Morris Pubng.

Search for Truth see Studies in the Foundations, Methodology & Philosophy of Science

Search for Understanding. Richard L. Franklin. (Revisioning Philosophy Ser.: Vol. 24). 224p. (C). 1995. text ed. 40.95 (*0-8204-2722-5*) P Lang Pubng.

Search for Understanding: Selected Writings of Scientists of the Carnegie Institution. Ed. by Caryl P. Haskins. (Illus.). 330p. 1967. 5.00 (*0-87279-954-9*) Carnegie Inst.

Search for Unity: Relations Between the Anglican & Roman Catholic Churches from the 1950's to the 1970's. William Purdy. 352p. (Orig.). 1995. pap. 26.95 (*0-225-66710-X*, Pub. by Geoffrey Chapman UK) Morehouse Pub.

Search for Value: Measuring the Company's Cost of Capital. Michael C. Ehrhardt. LC 93-21411. (Financial Management Association Survey & Synthesis Series, the International Investor Series in Finance). 256p. 1994. 35.00 (*0-87584-380-8*) Harvard Busn.

Search for Value: Measuring the Company's Cost of Capital. Michael C. Ehrhardt. 1994. text ed. 35.00 (*0-07-103586-9*) McGraw.

Search for Virginia Dare. William L. MacDougall. (Illus.). 40p. (C). 1995. text ed. 19.50 (*0-930329-95-3*) Kabel Pubs.

Search for Wallace Whipple. Donald Smurthwaite. LC 93-46245. 359p. (YA). (gr. 8-12). 1994. pap. 6.95 (*0-87579-830-6*) Deseret Bk.

Search for Wellness: How to Turn Back Your Biological Clock. Frank K. Mattson. LC 90-70585. (Illus.). 218p. 1990. 12.95 (*0-9625584-7-8*) Super G Pub Co.

Search for Wisdom & Spirit: Thomas Merton's Theology of the Self. Anne E. Carr. LC 87-40352. 176p. (C). 1989. pap. text ed. 11.50 (*0-268-01735-2*) U of Notre Dame Pr.

Search for World Order. Cornelius F. Murphy, Jr. 1985. lib. bdg. 101.00 (*90-247-3188-7*) Kluwer Ac.

Search in Artificial Intelligence. L. N. Kanal. 1988. 92.95 (*0-387-96750-8*) Spr-Verlag.

Search in Secret Egypt. rev. ed. Paul Brunton. LC 83-50399. 194p. (Orig.). 1973. reprint ed. pap. 14.95 (*0-87728-603-5*) Weiser.

Search in Secret India. Paul Brunton. LC 83-50400. (Illus.). 336p. (Orig.). 1984. reprint ed. pap. 14.95 (*0-87728-602-7*) Weiser.

Search Incident to Arrest. FBI Staff. 6p. 1994. pap. 10.00 (*0-930179-30-7*) Johns Enter.

Search Inform. 4th ed. Ed. by Jalerie MacLeod. 1990. 65.00 (*0-914604-00-7*) UMI Louisville.

Search Is an Emergency: Field Coordinator's Handbook. Robert C. Stoffel et al. (Illus.). 154p. pap. 9.00 (*0-913724-30-0*) Emerg Response Inst.

Search Is an Emergency: Text for Managing Search Operations. Robert C. Stoffel. (Illus.). 480p. 30.00 (*0-913724-28-9*); teacher ed. 40.00 (*0-913724-29-7*) Emerg Response Inst.

Search, Journey, Discovery. Cynthia E. Cowen. 1992. pap. 6.95 (*1-55673-571-5*, 9257) CSS OH.

Search Mechanisms for Large Files. Marie-Anne K. Neimat. LC 81-13036. (Computer Science: Distributed Database Systems Ser.: No. 11). 130p. reprint ed. pap. 37.10 (*0-685-20839-7*, 2070064) Bks Demand.

Search Methods for Artificial Intelligence. Leonard Bolc & Jerzy Cytowski. (Illus.). 242p. 1992. text ed. 56.00 (*0-12-111240-3*) Acad Pr.

Search Models & Applied Labor Economics. Nicholas M. Kiefer & George R. Neumann. (Illus.). 320p. (C). 1989. text ed. 80.00 (*0-521-36053-6*) Cambridge U Pr.

Search My Heart: A Novel. Sarah Birnhack. 308p. 1986. 14.00 (*0-940118-66-1*) Moznaim.

Search N Shade. Pat Cornell. Ed. by Alan Jacobs. (Illus.). (J). (gr. 4-9). 1979. pap. 8.95 (*0-918272-07-6*) Jacobs.

Search of Gravitational Waves: Proceedings of the Workshop Held in Bogota, Columbia, March 30-April 7, 1982. Ed. by E. Posada & Galileo Violini. (CIF Ser.: Vol. 2). 244p. 1983. 47.00 (*9971-950-78-2*) World Scientific Pub.

Search of the Soul: Finding Peace with God. Ed. by Sue Reck. (Discovery Ser.). 1995. teacher ed., pap. 10.99 (*0-7814-5201-5*, 29538) Cook.

Search of the Soul Journal: Finding Peace with God. Ed. by Sue Reck. (Discovery Ser.). (YA). 1995. pap. 9.99 (*0-7814-5202-3*, 29538) Cook.

***Search Out Science Bk. 1.** Horn & Orchard. 1989. pap. text ed. write for info. (*0-582-05286-6*, Pub. by Longman UK) Longman.

***Search Out Science Bk. 2.** Longman Publishing Staff. 1990. pap. text ed. write for info. (*0-582-06247-0*, Pub. by Longman UK) Longman.

Search Out the Land: The Jewish Contribution to Civil & Political Equality in Canada. Sheldon J. Godfre & Judith C. Godfrey. (McGill-Queen's Studies in Ethnic History). (Illus.). 376p. 1995. 34.95 (*0-7735-1201-2*, Pub. by McGill CN) U of Toronto Pr.

Search Party. Donald L. Campbell. LC 88-92667. 125p. (Orig.). 1989. pap. 10.95 (*0-916317-04-8*) Sylvan Bks.

Search Patterns: Poetry. Donald W. Baker. 48p. (Orig.). 1996. pap. 7.95 (*1-884482-08-2*) Stepnstone.

Search, Planning & Problem Solving. Carbonell. (Computer Science Ser.). Date not set. pap. 32.95 (*0-534-19680-2*) PWS Pubs.

Search Problems. Rudolf Ahlswede & Ingo Wegener. Tr. by Jean E. Wotschke. LC 87-8240. (Wiley-Interscience Series in Discrete Mathematics & Optimization). (Illus.). 296p. 1987. reprint ed. pap. 84.40 (*0-7837-9506-8*, 2060256) Bks Demand.

Search Procedures. Erin Moure. (Orig.). 1996. pap. 12.95 (*0-88784-575-4*, Pub. by Hse of Anansi Pr CN) Genl Dist Srvs.

Search PsycINFO: Instructor Guide. Ed. by Carolyn G. Gosling et al. 49p. 1989. pap. 15.00 (*1-55798-056-X*) Am Psychol.

Search PsycINFO: Student Workbook. Ed. by Carolyn G. Gosling et al. 62p. (C). 1989. pap. 15.00 (*1-55798-055-1*) Am Psychol.

Search Seizure & Privacy. Darien A. McWhirter. LC 94-27882. (Exploring the Constitution Ser.). 192p. 1994. 29.95 (*0-89774-854-9*) Oryx Pr.

Search Software. 3rd ed. Ed. by Ruth Koolish. 100p. 1995. write for info. (*0-943906-05-9*) Info Sources.

***Search Software.** 3rd ed. Ed. by Ruth Koolish. 100p. 1997. write for info. (*0-943906-08-3*) Info Sources.

Search Strategies in Mass Communication. 3rd ed. LC 96-33780. (C). 1997. pap. text ed. 38.95 (*0-8013-1755-X*) Longman.

Search Strategies in Mass Communications. 2nd ed. Jean Ward & Kathleen A. Hansen. LC 92-8468. 320p. (C). 1993. pap. text ed. 33.50 (*0-8013-1035-0*) Longman.

Search Sweet Country. B. Kojo Laing. 312p. 1988. reprint ed. pap. 9.95 (*0-571-12996-X*) Faber & Faber.

Search the Amazon! Doug Wilhelm. (Choose Your Own Adventure Ser.: No. 149). 128p. (J). (gr. 4-7). 1994. pap. 3.50 (*0-553-56392-0*) Bantam.

Search the Scriptures. rev. ed. Ed. by Alan M. Stibbs. 496p. 1976. pap. 16.99 (*0-87784-856-4*, 856) InterVarsity.

Search the Scriptures: How To Study the Bible for Yourself. Earl W. Morey. (Illus.). 333p. 1993. pap. 18.95 (*0-9634717-1-6*) A Minis VA.

***Search the Scriptures Vol. 13: Pastoral Epistles.** H. Ray Dunning. 1958. pap. 1.99 (*0-8341-0023-1*) Beacon Hill.

***Search the Scriptures, New Testament Vol. 1: Matthew.** Norman R. Oke. 1952. pap. 1.99 (*0-8341-0011-8*) Nazarene.

***Search the Scriptures, New Testament Vol. 2: Mark.** Norman R. Oke. 1953. pap. 1.99 (*0-8341-0012-6*) Nazarene.

***Search the Scriptures, New Testament Vol. 3: Luke.** Joseph D. Gray. 1953. pap. 1.99 (*0-8341-0013-4*) Beacon Hill.

***Search the Scriptures, New Testament Vol. 4: John.** Joseph D. Gray. 1953. pap. 1.99 (*0-8341-0014-2*) Beacon Hill.

***Search the Scriptures, New Testament Vol. 5: Acts.** William M. Greathouse. 1954. pap. 1.99 (*0-8341-0015-0*) Beacon Hill.

***Search the Scriptures, New Testament Vol. 6: Romans.** William M. Greathouse. 1955. pap. 1.99 (*0-8341-0016-9*) Beacon Hill.

***Search the Scriptures, New Testament Vol. 7: I Corinthians.** Willard H. Taylor. 1956. pap. 1.99 (*0-8341-0017-7*) Beacon Hill.

***Search the Scriptures, New Testament Vol. 8: II Corinthians.** Willard H. Taylor. 1961. pap. 1.99 (*0-8341-0018-5*) Beacon Hill.

***Search the Scriptures, New Testament Vol. 9: Galatians.** Norman R. Oke. 1962. pap. 1.99 (*0-8341-0019-3*) Beacon Hill.

***Search the Scriptures, New Testament Vol. 10: Ephesians.** William M. Greathouse. 1958. pap. 1.99 (*0-8341-0020-7*) Beacon Hill.

***Search the Scriptures, New Testament Vol. 11: Prison Epistles.** William M. Greathouse. 52p. 1963. pap. 1.99 (*0-8341-0021-5*) Beacon Hill.

***Search the Scriptures, New Testament Vol. 12: I & II Thessalonians.** Ralph Earle. 1962. pap. 1.99 (*0-8341-0022-3*) Beacon Hill.

***Search the Scriptures, New Testament Vol. 14: Hebrews.** Harvey Finley. 1958. pap. 1.99 (*0-8341-0024-X*) Beacon Hill.

***Search the Scriptures, New Testament Vol. 15: James, Peter, John, Jude.** H. Ray Dunning. 1960. pap. 1.99 (*0-8341-0025-8*) Beacon Hill.

***Search the Scriptures, New Testament Vol. 16: Revelation.** Ralph Earle. 48p. 1960. pap. 1.99 (*0-8341-0026-6*) Beacon Hill.

***Search the Scriptures, Old Testament Vol. 1: Genesis.** W. T. Purkiser. 1969. pap. 1.99 (*0-8341-0028-2*) Beacon Hill.

***Search the Scriptures, Old Testament Vol. 2: Exodus.** Earl C. Wolf. 54p. 1967. pap. 1.99 (*0-8341-0029-0*) Beacon Hill.

***Search the Scriptures, Old Testament Vol. 3: Leviticus, Numbers.** Lauriston J. Du Bois. 1970. pap. 1.99 (*0-8341-0030-4*) Beacon Hill.

***Search the Scriptures, Old Testament Vol. 4: Deuteronomy.** A. R. Deasley. 1970. pap. 1.99 (*0-8341-0031-2*) Beacon Hill.

***Search the Scriptures, Old Testament Vol. 5: Joshua.** Chester O. Mulder. 1965. pap. 1.99 (*0-8341-0032-0*) Beacon Hill.

***Search the Scriptures, Old Testament Vol. 6: Judges, Ruth.** R. Clyde Ridall. 1965. pap. 1.99 (*0-8341-0033-9*) Beacon Hill.

***Search the Scriptures, Old Testament Vol. 7: I & II Samuel.** W. T. Purkiser. 1965. pap. 1.99 (*0-8341-0034-7*) Beacon Hill.

An Asterisk (*) at the beginning of an entry indicates that the title is appearing in BIP for the first time.

*__Search the Scriptures, Old Testament Vol. 8: I & II Kings.__ Harvey Finley. 1967. pap. 1.99 (*0-8341-0035-5*) Beacon Hill.

*__Search the Scriptures, Old Testament Vol. 9: I & II Chronicles.__ Robert Sawyer. 1966. pap. 1.99 (*0-8341-0036-3*) Beacon Hill.

*__Search the Scriptures, Old Testament Vol. 10: Ezra, Nehemiah, Esther.__ C. E. Demaray. 1967. pap. 1.99 (*0-8341-0037-1*) Beacon Hill.

*__Search the Scriptures, Old Testament Vol. 11: Job.__ Bennett Dudney. 1971. pap. 1.99 (*0-8341-0038-X*) Beacon Hill.

*__Search the Scriptures, Old Testament Vol. 12: Psalms.__ W. T. Purkiser. 1969. pap. 1.99 (*0-8341-0039-8*) Beacon Hill.

*__Search the Scriptures, Old Testament Vol. 13: Proverbs, Ecclesiastes, Song of Solomon.__ Earl C. Wolf & A. F. Harper. 1968. pap. 1.99 (*0-8341-0040-1*) Beacon Hill.

*__Search the Scriptures, Old Testament Vol. 14: Isaiah.__ Ross E. Price. 1969. pap. 1.99 (*0-8341-0041-X*) Beacon Hill.

*__Search the Scriptures, Old Testament Vol. 15: Jeremiah, Lamentation.__ C. Paul Gray. 1969. pap. 1.99 (*0-8341-0042-8*) Beacon Hill.

*__Search the Scriptures, Old Testament Vol. 16: Ezekiel, Daniel.__ J. Kenneth Grider. 1966. pap. 1.99 (*0-8341-0043-6*) Beacon Hill.

*__Search the Scriptures, Old Testament Vol. 17: Hosea, Joel, Amos.__ Oscar F. Reed. 1967. pap. 1.99 (*0-8341-0044-4*) Beacon Hill.

*__Search the Scriptures, Old Testament Vol. 18: Obadiah, Jonah, Micah.__ Ralph Earle. 112p. 1967. pap. 1.99 (*0-8341-0045-2*) Beacon Hill.

*__Search the Scriptures, Old Testament Vol. 19: Nahum, Haggai.__ H. Ray Dunning. 1967. pap. 1.99 (*0-8341-0046-0*) Beacon Hill.

*__Search the Scriptures, Old Testament Vol. 20: Zechariah, Malachi.__ William M. Greathouse. 1969. pap. 1.99 (*0-8341-0047-9*) Beacon Hill.

Search the Shadows. Barbara Michaels. 1988. mass mkt. 6.99 (*0-425-11183-0*, Berkley Trade) Berkley Pub.

*__Search the Shadows.__ Barbara Michaels. 400p. 1997. mass mkt. 5.50 (*0-06-101009-X*, Harp PBks) HarpC.

Search the Solar System: The Role of Unmanned Interplanetary Probes. James Strong. (Illus.). 1973. 19.95 (*0-8464-0827-9*) Beekman Pubs.

Search Theory: Some Recent Developments. Chudnovsky. (Lecture Notes in Pure & Applied Mathematics Ser.: Vol. 112). 176p. 1988. 125.00 (*0-8247-8000-0*) Dekker.

Search Warrant Law Deskbook, Vol. 1. John M. Burkoff. LC 86-26336. (Criminal Law Ser.). 1987. ring bd. 125.00 (*0-87632-530-4*) Clark Boardman Callaghan.

Search Without Idols. William Horosz. (Martinus Nijhoff Philosophy Library: No. 17). 408p. 1987. lib. bdg. 208.50 (*90-247-3327-8*, Pub. by M Nijhoff NE) Kluwer Ac.

Searchers. Gustaf Stromberg. 256p. 1967. pap. 8.95 (*0-911336-16-8*) Sci of Mind.

*__Searchers: A True Story.__ Ron Felber. Date not set. lib. bdg. 21.95 (*0-8488-1650-1*) Amereon Ltd.

Searchers: Collected Poetry. Tomas Rivera. Ed. by Julian Olivares. 1990. pap. 7.00 (*1-55885-018-X*) Arte Publico.

Searcher's Notebook & Guide. 3rd ed. Vance. 1993. pap. text ed. write for info. (*0-07-066874-4*) McGraw.

Searcher's Path: A Composer's Ways. Roger Reynolds. LC 87-82698. (I.S.A.M. Monographs: No. 25). 74p. (Orig.). 1988. audio 12.00 (*0-914678-28-0*) Inst Am Music.

Searches & Enquiries - a Conveyancer's Guide. 2nd ed. Frances Silverman. 440p. 1992. U.K. pap. 70.00 (*0-406-11555-9*) MICHIE.

Searches & Seizures: Three Novellas. Stanley Elkin. LC 78-58499. 304p. 1978. reprint ed. pap. 10.95 (*0-87923-253-6*) Godine.

Searches & Seizures, Arrests & Confessions, 3 vols., Set. 2nd ed. William E. Ringel & Mark Pellis. LC 79-22482. (Criminal Law Ser.). 1980. ring bd. 375.00 (*0-87632-079-5*) Clark Boardman Callaghan.

Searches for an Imaginary Kingdom: The Legend of the Kingdom of Prester John. L. N. Gumilev. Tr. by R. E. Smith. (Past & Present Publications). (Illus.). 420p. 1988. 79.95 (*0-521-32214-6*) Cambridge U Pr.

Searches into the History of the Gillman or Gilman Family. A. W. Gilman. (Illus.). 360p. 1989. reprint ed. pap. 54.00 (*0-8328-0598-X*); reprint ed. lib. bdg. 62.00 (*0-8328-0597-1*) Higginson Bk Co.

*__Searches of Students, Lockers & Automobiles.__ John H. Dise, Jr. et al. LC 96-86552. 110p. (Orig.). 1996. pap. 29.95 (*0-9630262-2-4*) Educ Risk.

Searchin' for Love. Ed. by Milton Okun. 128p. (YA). 1995. pap. 14.95 (*0-89524-979-0*) Cherry Lane.

Searchin' Safari: Natures Hidden Wonders. Jeff O'Hare. LC 91-72974. (Illus.). 32p. (J). (ps-3). 1992. 8.95 (*1-56397-016-3*) Boyds Mills Pr.

Searching. Nawal El-Saadawi. (C). 1991. pap. 7.95 (*1-85649-009-2*, Pub. by Zed Bks Ltd UK); text ed. 15.00 (*1-85649-008-4*, Pub. by Zed Bks Ltd UK) Humanities.

Searching. O. B. Rozell. (Illus.). 26p. (Orig.). 1980. pap. 3.00 (*0-88680-171-0*) I E Clark.

Searching Algorithms. J. Wiedermann. 124p. (C). 1987. 50.00 (*0-685-46650-7*, Pub. by Collets) St Mut.

Searching & Sharing: The Fourth & Fifth Steps for Teens. Laura Stamper. 30p. (J). 1991. pap. 1.75 (*0-925190-19-5*, F911124 C) Fairview Press.

Searching & the Delta Squared Magnetometer. Murphy L. Dalton, Jr. (Illus.). 121p. 1993. pap. text ed. 29.00 (*0-9613740-8-X*) M L Dalton Res.

Searching Behaviour: The Behavioural Ecology of Finding Resources. W. J. Bell. (Animal Behaviour Ser.). 400p. (gr. 13). 1991. text ed. 80.95 (*0-412-29210-6*, A1597) Chapman & Hall.

Searching Between the Stars. Lyman Spitzer. LC 81-13138. (Mrs. Hepsa Ely Silliman Memorial Lectures: No. 46). 196p. reprint ed. pap. 55.90 (*0-7837-3329-1*, 2057735) Bks Demand.

*__Searching Electronic Resources.__ Marjorie Pappas et al. LC 96-30809. (Professional Growth Ser.). 117p. 1996. spiral bd. 24.95 (*0-938865-52-8*) Linworth Pub.

Searching, Exploring, Pondering. Kenneth E. Sibley. LC 87-92046. (Illus.). 41p. (Orig.). 1988. pap. 5.95 (*0-9619934-0-5*) K E Sibley.

Searching for a Better Way. Monroe E. Hawley. 1981. pap. 7.95 (*0-89137-525-2*) Quality Pubns.

Searching for a New You. Denise Richards. Tr. by Media-Siegel Graphics. LC 85-61014. (Illus.). 109p. 1985. pap. 7.95 (*0-9614714-0-9*) Pavillion Fashion.

Searching for a Past: The Adopted Adult's Unique Process of Finding Identity. Jayne Schooler. LC 94-49057. 199p. (Orig.). 1995. pap. 14.00 (*0-89109-868-2*) Pinon Press.

Searching for a Slave Cemetery in Barbados, West Indies: A Bioarchaeological & Ethnohistorical Investigation. Jerome S. Handler et al. LC 89-62149. (Center for Archaeological Investigations Research Paper Ser.: No. 59). (Illus.). xviii, 125p. (Orig.). 1989. pap. 8.00 (*0-88104-071-1*) Center Archaeol.

Searching for Aboriginal Languages: Memoirs of a Field Worker. R. M. Dixon. LC 89-34383. (Illus.). 348p. 1989. reprint ed. pap. text ed. 18.95 (*0-226-15430-0*) U Ch Pr.

Searching for Agrarian Reform in Latin America: Thematic Studies in Latin America. William C. Thiesenhusen. 496p. 1988. text ed. 70.00 (*0-04-497017-X*) Routledge Chapman & Hall.

Searching for Alternatives: Alternative Energy Sources. Darrin D. Gitisetan & Gary L. Parsons. LC 92-31983. (CPL Bibliographies Ser.: No. 286). 52p. 1992. pap. 10.00 (*0-86602-286-4*, Sage Prdcls Pr) Sage.

Searching for Alternatives: Drug-Control Policy in the United States. Ed. by Melvyn B. Krauss & Edward P. Lazear. 454p. 1993. pap. 24.95 (*0-8179-9142-5*) Hoover Inst Pr.

*__Searching for Ancient Egypt: Art, Architecture, & Artifacts from the University of Pennsylvania Museum.__ David Silverman et al. (Illus.). 300p. 1997. 60.00 (*0-8014-3482-3*) Cornell U Pr.

*__Searching for Ancient Egypt: Art, Architecture, & Artifacts from the University of Pennsylvania Museum.__ Davis Silverman et al. (Illus.). 300p. (Orig.). 1997. 60.00 (*0-936227-20-6*) Dallas Mus.

*__Searching for Ancient Egypt: Art, Architecture, & Artifacts from the University of Pennsylvania Museum.__ Davis Silverman et al. (Illus.). 300p. (Orig.). 1997. pap. 35.00 (*0-936227-21-4*) Dallas Mus.

Searching for Answers: Annual Evaluation Report on Drugs & Crime (1992) (Illus.). 142p. (Orig.). (C). 1994. pap. text ed. 30.00 (*0-7881-0580-9*) DIANE Pub.

Searching for Atticus. Marino. LC 96-53146. (J). 1997. 16.00 (*0-689-80066-5*, S&S Bks Young Read) S&S Childrens.

Searching for Bobby Fischer. Fred Waitzkin. 1993. pap. 11.95 (*0-14-023038-6*, Penguin Bks) Viking Penguin.

Searching for Bobby Fischer: The Father of a Prodigy Observes the World of Chess. Fred Waitzkin. 242p. 1993. pap. 8.00 (*0-14-012657-0*, Penguin Bks) Viking Penguin.

Searching for Bobby Fischer: The World of Chess Observed by the Father of a Child Prodigy. Fred Waitzkin. LC 88-42657. 1988. 17.95 (*0-394-54455-2*) Random.

*__Searching for Caleb.__ Anne Tyler. 1996. pap. 12.00 (*0-449-91174-8*) Fawcett.

Searching for Camelot. Edith Thomas. Ed. by R. Charles & Elizabeth Pasco. (Illus.). 100p. (Orig.). 1996. pap. 12.95 (*1-887472-08-8*) Sunstar Pubng.

*__Searching for Candlestick Park.__ Peg Kehret. LC 97-11222. (J). 1997. pap. 14.99 (*0-525-65256-6*) Dutton Child Bks.

Searching for Causes of Work-Related Diseases: An Introduction to Epidemiology at the Work Site. Jorn Olsen. 100p. 1991. pap. 19.95 (*0-19-261819-9*) OUP.

Searching for Christ: The Spirituality of Dorothy Day. Brigid O. Merriman. LC 93-23827. (Studies in American Catholicism: Vol. 13). (C). 1994. text ed. 34.50 (*0-268-01750-6*) U of Notre Dame Pr.

Searching for Courtship: The Smart Woman's Guide to Finding a Good Husband. Winnifred B. Cutler. 352p. 1996. write for info. (*0-9651753-1-6*) Athena Inst.

*__Searching for Cyber-Roots: A Step-by-Step Guide to Genealogy on the World Wide Web.__ Laurie Bonner & Steve Bonner. LC 97-15558. 1997. pap. write for info. (*0-916489-78-7*) Ancestry.

Searching for Design: With Fibonacci & Phi. Dan Harwell. Ed. by Patty Hundley. (Illus.). 128p. (C). 1995. 49.95 (*0-9648677-0-2*) Gldn Spiral.

Searching for Dragons. Patricia C. Wrede. 240p. (J). (gr. 3-7). 1991. 17.00 (*0-15-200898-5*, J Yolen Bks) HarBrace.

Searching for Dragons. Patricia C. Wrede. 224p. (YA). 1992. 3.25 (*0-590-45721-7*, 071, Point) Scholastic Inc.

Searching for Everardo: A Story of Love, War, & the CIA in Guatemala. Jennifer K. Harbury. LC 96-42028. 352p. 1997. 24.00 (*0-446-52036-5*) Warner Bks.

*__Searching for Everardo: A Story of Love, War, & the CIA in Guatemala.__ Jennifer K. Harbury. 352p. 1998. pap. 13.99 (*0-446-67362-5*) Warner Bks.

Searching for Fifth Mesa. Juana Foust. LC 78-31284. (Orig.). 1979. pap. 4.95 (*0-913270-81-4*) Sunstone Pr.

*__Searching for Food.__ (Longman Biology Topics Ser.). Date not set. pap. text ed. write for info. (*0-582-32299-5*, Pub. by Longman UK) Longman.

Searching for Footsteps to the Past: Surface Finds Along the Kaskaskia River. James A. Smith. LC 92-61983. (Illus.). 182p. 1992. pap. 29.95 (*1-878044-03-6*) Mayhaven Pub.

Searching for God. Basil Hume. LC 92-34240. 239p. 1992. reprint ed. pap. 9.95 (*0-932506-92-5*) St Bedes Pubns.

Searching for God: Campus Faith. Francis L. Gross, Jr. LC 89-61928. 144p. (Orig.). 1989. pap. 8.95 (*1-55612-274-8*) Sheed & Ward MO.

Searching for God in America. Hugh Hewitt. (Illus.). 432p. 1996. 27.99 (*0-8499-1308-X*) Word Pub.

*__Searching for God on the Internet.__ Jon Katz. 1998. write for info. (*0-679-45678-3*) Random.

*__Searching for God with Our Fingertips: The Body As Spiritual Guide.__ Edwin M. McMahon & Peter A. Campbell. 12p. 1996. 1.25 (*1-55612-508-9*, LL1508) Sheed & Ward MO.

Searching for Health. Robert J. Peshek. 1982. 15.95 (*0-9605902-4-2*) Color Coded Charting.

Searching for Health Information: The Cancer Information Service Model. Vicki S. Freimuth et al. LC 88-38116. (Illus.). 264p. (C). 1989. text ed. 62.95 (*0-8122-8123-3*); pap. text ed. 24.95 (*0-8122-1272-X*) U of Pa Pr.

Searching for Heroes Vol. 1: The Quest of a Yankee Batboy. Joseph R. Carrieri. (Illus.). 214p. 1996. 22.00 (*0-9644701-0-1*) J R Carrieri.

Searching for Home. Laurelynn Martin. LC 96-21539. 180p. (Orig.). 1996. pap. 11.95 (*0-9620507-5-X*) Cosmic Concepts Pr.

Searching for Home: Three Families from the Orphan Trains, a True Story. Martha N. Vogt & Christina Vogt. (Illus.). 240p. (Orig.). 1979. pap. 11.95 (*0-931515-00-9*) Triumph Pr.

Searching for Kenny: Searching for God. Bob Miller. 352p. 1996. 15.00 (*0-9650373-0-4*) Lewis Creek.

Searching for Land Tenure Security in Africa. World Bank, International Bank for Reconstruction & Development Staff. 296p. 1994. per., pap. text ed. 32.95 (*0-8403-9508-6*) Kendall-Hunt.

Searching for Laura Ingalls: A Reader's Journal. Kathryn Lasky & Meribah Knight. LC 92-26188. (Illus.). 48p. (J). (gr. 2-6). 1993. lib. bdg. 15.95 (*0-02-751666-0*, Mac Bks Young Read) S&S Childrens.

Searching for Light: Michael's Information for a Time of Change. Carol Heideman. Ed. by Nancy W. McCarthy. 256p. (Orig.). 1994. pap. 12.95 (*0-9643455-0-1*) Twelve Star.

Searching for Lost Coins: Explorations in Christianity & Feminism. Ann Loades. LC 88-1056. (Princeton Theological Monographs: No. 14). 128p. (Orig.). 1988. reprint ed. pap. 12.00 (*1-55635-000-7*) Pickwick.

Searching for Magic Bullets: Orphan Drugs, Consumer Activism, & Pharmaceutical Development. Lisa R. Basara & Michael Montagne. LC 93-35534. (Illus.). 276p. 1994. pap. 14.95 (*1-56024-859-9*); lib. bdg. 39.95 (*1-56024-858-0*) Haworth Pr.

Searching for Memory: The Brain, the Mind, & the Past. Daniel L. Schacter. LC 96-19521. (Illus.). 398p. 1997. pap. 27.00 (*0-465-02502-1*) Basic.

*__Searching for Memory: The Brain, the Mind & the Past.__ Daniel L. Schacter. 1997. pap. text ed. 14.00 (*0-465-07552-5*) Basic.

*__Searching for Memory: The Brain, the Mind, & the Past.__ Daniel S. Schacter. 1997. pap. 14.00 (*0-614-27590-3*) Basic.

Searching for Mercy Street: My Journey Back to My Mother, Anne Sexton. Linda G. Sexton. LC 94-8889. 1994. 22.95 (*0-316-78207-6*) Little.

Searching For Mercy Street Vol. 1: My Journey Back to My Mother, Anne Sexton. Linda G. Sexton. 1996. pap. 12.95 (*0-316-78208-4*) Little.

Searching for Panama: The U. S.-Panama Relationship & Democratization. Mark Falcoff & Richard L. Millett. LC 93-7445. (Significant Issues Ser.: Vol. 15, No. 6). 52p. (Orig.). (C). 1993. pap. 8.50 (*0-89206-216-9*) CSI Studies.

*__Searching for Real Christianity.__ Ted Cline. 96p. (Orig.). 1988. pap. 2.50 (*0-933672-73-X*, C-2021) Star Bible.

Searching for Recognition: The Promotion of Latin American Literature in the United States. Irene Rostagno. LC 96-22008. (Contributions to the Study of World Literature Ser.: No. 72). 176p. 1997. text ed. 55.00 (*0-313-29869-6*, Greenwood Pr) Greenwood.

Searching for Riches: The California Gold Rush. Cecil K. Byrd. (Illus.). 95p. 1991. pap. 7.50 (*1-879598-02-7*) IN Univ Lilly Library.

Searching for Robert Johnson. Peter Guralnick. 1989. pap. 15.00 (*0-525-24801-3*, Obelisk) NAL-Dutton.

Searching for Rural Development: Labor Migration & Employment in Mexico. Merilee S. Grindle. LC 87-47970. (Illus.). 216p. 1988. 37.50 (*0-8014-2109-8*) Cornell U Pr.

Searching for Safety. Aaron Wildavsky. 356p. 1988. 44.95 (*0-88738-192-8*); pap. 24.95 (*0-88738-714-4*) Transaction Pubs.

Searching for Saleem: An Afghan Woman's Odyssey. Farooka Gauhari. LC 96-3453. (Illus.). xxv, 267p. 1996. text ed. 35.00 (*0-8032-2156-8*) U of Nebr Pr.

Searching for Sara. Shelley Singer. (Barrett Lake Mystery Ser.: No. 3). 256p. (Orig.). 1994. pap. 4.50 (*0-451-17985-4*, Sig) NAL-Dutton.

*__Searching for Satisfaction: Rock's Search for Faith & Meaning.__ John Smith & Alan L. Harvey. 112p. (Orig.). 1997. pap. 18.95 (*1-86407-146-X*, Pub. by JBCE AT) Morehouse Pub.

Searching for Scottish Ancestors. A. Maxim Coppage. 1983. 28.35 (*0-318-03039-X*); pap. 28.25 (*0-318-03040-3*) A M Coppage.

Searching for Security: Women's Responses to Economic Transformations. I. S. Baud & Ines Smyth. LC 96-21815. (Routledge Studies in Development & Society). 176p. (C). 1996. text ed. write for info. (*0-415-14227-X*) Routledge.

Searching for Shalom: Reasons for Creative Worship. Ann Weems. 192p. (Orig.). 1991. pap. 12.00 (*0-664-25223-0*) Westminster John Knox.

Searching for Sixty-Six. Tom Teague. 246p. (Orig.). 1991. pap. 10.00 (*0-940859-09-2*) Snd Dollar Pub.

*__Searching for Solace: A Biography of Abdullah Yusuf Ali, Interpreter of the Quran.__ Mohammad A. Sherif. 314p. 1996. pap. 14.95 (*0-614-21717-2*, 1384) Kazi Pubns.

Searching for Someone. Jim Wortham. LC 76-47781. 1976. pap. 2.95 (*0-915216-11-6*) Marathon Intl Bk.

Searching for Structure. rev. ed. John A. Sonquist et al. LC 73-620236. 236p. 1974. 15.00 (*0-87944-110-0*); pap. 10.00 (*0-87944-109-7*) Inst Soc Res.

*__Searching for Success.__ Ed. by Monica Crews & Louise McLaughlin. 200p. (Orig.). 1996. pap. 15.00 (*0-9653446-0-6*) Results Pr.

Searching for the Accorn. Deborah Latzke. (Illus.). 72p. (Orig.). Date not set. pap. 12.95 (*0-9643956-2-2*) Legacy of Love.

Searching for the Causes of Schizophrenia. Eve C. Johnstone. LC 93-42493. (Oxford Psychiatry Ser.: No. 2). (Illus.). 172p. 1994. 45.00 (*0-19-262296-X*) OUP.

Searching for the Disadvantaged among Gifted/Talented Students see Reaching for the Stars Series: A Minicourse for Education of Gifted Students

Searching for the Figure in the Carpet in the Tales of Henry James: Reflections of an Ordinary Reader. Benjamin Newman. (American University Studies: English Language & Literature: Ser. IV, Vol. 49). 194p. (C). 1987. text ed. 39.00 (*0-8204-0442-X*) P Lang Pubng.

Searching for the Handicapped among Gifted/Talented Students see Reaching for the Stars Series: A Minicourse for Education of Gifted Students

Searching for the Invisible Man: Slaves & Plantation Life in Jamaica. Michael M. Craton. LC 76-48281. 448p. 1978. 45.00 (*0-674-79629-2*) HUP.

Searching for the New France. Ed. by James F. Hollifield & George Ross. 320p. (C). 1991. pap. 17.95 (*0-415-90250-9*, A4547, Routledge NY) Routledge.

Searching for the Perfect Pumpkin. Frank Fiorello. (Illus.). 40p. (Orig.). (J). (ps-6). 1995. pap. 7.95 (*0-9646300-0-1*) Fiorellos Pumpkin Patch.

Searching for the Promised Land: An African-American's Optimistic Odyssey. Gary Franks. LC 96-10714. 240p. 1996. 24.00 (*0-06-039156-1*) HarpC.

*__Searching for the Promised Land: An African American's Optimistic Odyssey.__ Gary Franks. 240p. 1997. pap. 13.00 (*0-06-098717-0*, ReganBooks) HarpC.

Searching for the Sunbelt: Historical Perspectives on a Region. Ed. by Raymond A. Mohl. LC 89-77169. 288p. 1990. text ed. 36.00 (*0-87049-640-9*) U of Tenn Pr.

*__Searching for the Sunbelt: Historical Perspectives on a Region.__ Ed. by Raymond A. Mohl. LC 89-77169. 264p. pap. 75.30 (*0-608-05197-7*, 2065734) Bks Demand.

Searching for the Sunbelt: Historical Perspectives on a Region. Ed. by Raymond A. Mohl. LC 89-77169. 272p. 1993. reprint ed. pap. 18.00 (*0-8203-1579-6*) U of Ga Pr.

Searching for Treasure: A Guide to Wisdom & Character Development. Marty Elwell. 147p. (J). 1993. pap. text ed. 19.95 (*0-923463-84-4*) Noble Pub Assocs.

Searching for Treasure Coloring Book. Marty Elwell. (Illus.). (J). 1992. 4.95 (*0-923463-85-2*) Noble Pub Assocs.

*__Searching for Truth: Lenten Meditations on Science & Faith.__ John Polkinghorne. LC 96-45191. 160p. 1996. pap. 12.95 (*0-8245-1655-9*) Crossroad NY.

Searching for Velociraptor. Lowell Dingus & Mark A. Norell. LC 95-22238. (Illus.). 32p. (J). (gr. 2 up). 1996. 15.95 (*0-06-025893-4*); lib. bdg. 15.89 (*0-06-025894-2*) HarpC Child Bks.

Searching for World Security. Curt Gasteyger. LC 85-14375. 260p. 1985. text ed. 35.00 (*0-312-70823-8*) St Martin.

*__Searching for Yellowstone.__ Paul D. Schullery. 1997. 25.00 (*0-395-84174-7*) HM.

Searching for Your Ancestors: The How & Why of Genealogy. 6th rev. ed. Gilbert H. Doane & James B. Bell. (Illus.). 352p. (C). 1992. pap. 17.95 (*0-8166-1990-5*) U of Minn Pr.

Searching for Yourself: A Journey to Discover Values. rev. ed. Center for Learning Network Staff. (Values Ser.). 212p. 1992. teacher ed., spiral bd. 30.00 (*1-56077-152-6*) Ctr Learning.

Searching Hearts. Dorothy Garlock. 400p. 1997. mass mkt. 5.99 (*0-446-36526-2*, Warner Vision) Warner Bks.

Searching in Florida: A Reference Guide to Public & Private Records. Diane C. Robie. (ISC State Search Bks.: No. 2). (Orig.). 1982. 10.95 (*0-942916-01-8*) ISC Pubns.

Searching in Illinois: A Reference Guide to Public & Private Records. Gayle Beckstead & Mary L. Kozub. LC 84-80217. (ISC State Search Bks.: No. 3). 210p. (Orig.). 1984. pap. text ed. 12.95 (*0-942916-05-0*) ISC Pubns.

Searching in Indiana: A Reference Guide to Public & Private Records. Mickey D. Carty. LC 85-60284. (ISC State Search Bks.: No. 4). 278p. (Orig.). 1985. pap. text ed. 14.95 (*0-942916-06-9*) ISC Pubns.

Searching in New York: A Reference Guide to Public & Private Records. Kate Burke. (ISC State Search Bks.: No. 5). 270p. (Orig.). 1987. pap. text ed. 15.95 (*0-942916-10-7*) ISC Pubns.

An Asterisk (*) at the beginning of an entry indicates that the title is appearing in BIP for the first time.

Searching in the Syntax of Things: Experiments in the Study of Religion. Text by Maurice S. Friedman & T. Patrick Burke. LC 70-171494. 160p. reprint ed. pap. 45. 60 (0-685-16047-5, 2026864) Bks Demand.

Searching Land Titles in South Carolina. Edward D. Barnhill et al. 1991. pap. 25.00 (0-943856-31-0, 502) SC Bar CLE.

*__Searching Multimedia Databases by Content.__ Christos Faloutsos. LC 96-27161. (International Series on Advances in Database Systems). 168p. (C). 1996. lib. bdg. 97.50 (0-7923-9777-0) Kluwer Ac.

Searching on Location: Planning a Research Trip. Anne R. Balhuizen. LC 92-3207. 112p. 1993. pap. 8.95 (0-916489-43-4) Ancestry.

Searching Out the Best: A Tribute to the Morris Gallery of the Pennsylvania Academy of the Fine Arts. PennsylvaniaAcademy of Fine Arts Staff. (Illus.). 212p. (Orig.). 1988. pap. 19.95 (0-943836-09-3) Penn Acad Art.

Searching Out the Headwaters: Change & Rediscovery in Western Water Policy. Sarah F. Bates et al. LC 93-4637. 230p. 1993. pap. 17.95 (1-55963-218-6); text ed. 35.00 (1-55963-217-8) Island Pr.

Searching Suburban Skies. Richard W. Stern. 70p. (Orig.). (YA). 1995. pap. write for info. (1-57502-002-5) Morris Pub.

Searching, Teaching & Writing - What Fun. Alfred Burger. (Illus.). 167p. (Orig.). 1988. pap. 9.95 (0-9621746-0-2) A Burger.

Searching the Drowned Man: Poems. Sydney Lea. LC 79-26565. 86p. 1980. 9.95 (0-252-00798-0); text ed. 14.95 (0-252-00796-4) U of Ill Pr.

Searching the Drowned Man: Poems. fac. ed. Sydney Lea. LC 79-26565. 84p. 1980. reprint ed. pap. 25.00 (0-7837-8075-3, 2047828) Bks Demand.

Searching the Heart: Women, Men, & Romantic Love in Nineteenth-Century America. Karen Lystra. 352p. 1992. pap. 18.95 (0-19-507476-9) OUP.

Searching the Law. Edward J. Bander et al. 260p. 1987. lib. bdg. 45.50 (0-941320-27-8) Transnatl Pubs.

Searching the Law, Supp. No. 1. Edward J. Bander. 141p. 1989. pap. 25.00 (0-941320-57-X) Transnatl Pubs.

Searching the Law, Suppl. No. 2. Francis R. Doyle. pap. 25.00 (0-941320-60-X) Transnatl Pubs.

Searching the Law: The States. 2nd ed. Francis R. Doyle. LC 94-8319. 1994. 125.00 (0-941320-88-X) Transnatl Pubs.

*__Searching the Law: The States.__ 2nd ed. Francis R. Doyle. LC 94-8319. 1996. suppl. ed. 95.00 (1-57105-042-6) Transnatl Pubs.

Searching "The Philosopher's Index" Database on Dialog: A Tutorial Manual. Ed. by Richard H. Lineback. 63p. 1988. pap. 15.00 (0-912632-50-X) Philos Document.

*__Searching the Scriptures.__ Gene R. Cook. LC 97-13603. 1997. write for info. (1-57345-247-5) Deseret Bk.

Searching the Scriptures: A History of the Society of Biblical Literature 1880-1980. Ernest W. Saunders. LC 82-10818. (Society of Biblical Literature Biblical Scholarship in North America Ser.). 128p. 1982. 22.95 (0-89130-591-2, 06-11-08) Scholars Pr GA.

Searching the Scriptures, Vol. II: A Feminist Commentary. Elisabeth S. Fiorenza. 450p. 1994. pap. 49.50 (0-8245-1424-6) Crossroad NY.

Searching the Scriptures, Vol. 1: A Feminist Introduction. Elizabeth S. Fiorenza. 288p. 1993. 29.95 (0-8245-1381-9) Crossroad NY.

Searching the Shadows. Ella Blanche. (Contemporary Poets Ser.: No. 1). 48p. (Orig.). 1983. pap. 2.95 (0-916982-26-2, RL226) CCR Pubns.

Searching with Probabilities. Andrew J. Palay. (Research Notes in Artificial Intelligence Ser.). 1985. 29.95 (0-273-08664-2) Morgan Kaufmann.

Searchlight Remembered. Arda M. Haenszel. (Illus.). 111p. 1988. 12.50 (0-914224-15-8) Tales Mojave Rd.

Searchlights on Delinquency. Ed. by K. R. Eissler. 1967. 62.50 (0-8236-6020-6) Intl Univs Pr.

Searchworks: Your Job Search Planner & Organizer. 150p. 1993. student ed. 49.95 (0-9637210-4-6) Markpro Pub.

Searcy County Arkansas Marriages, Vol. III. Ruby Lacy. 53p. (Orig.). 1987. pap. write for info. (0-942977-25-4) Lacy Pubs.

Searle: Collection of Historical Memorials Relating to the Searle Families of Great Britain & America. Stannard Warne. (Illus.). 73p. 1995. reprint ed. pap. 15.00 (0-8328-4834-4); reprint ed. lib. bdg. 25.00 (0-8328-4833-6) Higginson Bk Co.

Searoom Handbook with Radar Anti-Collision Tables. E. S. Quilter. LC 76-240. 177p. 1976. text ed., spiral bd. 15.00 (0-87033-221-X) Cornell Maritime.

*__Sear's Anatomy & Physiology for Nurses.__ 6th ed. write for info. (0-7131-4463-7, Pub. by E Arnold UK) Routledge Chapman & Hall.

Sears & Roebuck C1910 Ammunition Catalog: Chicago, Ill. (Illus.). pap. 2.00 (0-686-20760-2) Sand Pond.

Sears Financial Network Guide to Personal Financial Planning. Bob Storall. (Orig.). 1986. pap. write for info. (0-671-60095-8) PB.

Sears Genealogical Catalogue. Ed. & Illus. by L. Ray Sears, III. 800p. (C). 1992. 48.00 (1-878333-00-3) Advncd Bus Syst.

Sears List of Subject Headings. 14th ed. LC 86-7734. 734p. 1991. 45.00 (0-8242-0803-X) Wilson.

Sears List of Subject Headings. 15th ed. Ed. by Joseph Miller. LC 94-16705. 758p. 1994. lib. bdg. 49.00 (0-8242-0858-7) Wilson.

Sears List of Subject Headings, Canadian Companion. 5th ed. 97p. 1995. 24.00 (0-8242-0879-X) Wilson.

Sears, Roebuck Catalog of Houses, 1926. Dover Publications Staff. 1991. pap. 11.95 (0-486-26709-1) Dover.

Sears, Roebuck Catalog, 1897. Ed. by Fred L. Israel. (Illus.). 1993. 39.95 (0-87754-045-4); pap. 19.95 (0-7910-1945-4) Chelsea Hse.

Sears Roebuck Home Builders Catalog. Sears Roebuck & Co. Staff. 1990. pap. 10.95 (0-486-26320-7) Dover.

Sears Tower. Katherine M. Doherty & Craig A. Doherty. Ed. by Bruce Glassman. LC 94-40642. (Building America Ser.). (Illus.). 48p. (J). (gr. 3-7). 1995. lib. bdg. 15.95 (1-56711-109-2) Blackbirch.

Seas. Jenny Tyler. (World Geography Ser.). (J). (gr. 3-6). 1976. pap. 6.95 (0-86020-064-7, Usborne) EDC.

Seas & Oceans. Nicola Barber. (Alpha Bks.). (Illus.). 45p. (J). (gr. 5-8). 1996. 19.95 (0-237-51685-3, Pub. by Evans Bros Ltd UK) Trafalgar.

Seas & Oceans. Felicity Brooks. (Understanding Geography Ser.). (Illus.). 32p. (J). (gr. 5-9). 1994. pap. 6.95 (0-7460-0986-0, Usborne); lib. bdg. 14.95 (0-88110-593-7, Usborne) EDC.

Seas & Oceans. David Lambert. LC 93-6352. (New View Ser.). (J). 1994. lib. bdg. 22.83 (0-8114-9245-1) Raintree Steck-V.

Seas & Oceans. David Lambert. (Our World Ser.). (Illus.). 48p. (J). (gr. 5-8). 1987. lib. bdg. 12.95 (0-382-09503-0) Silver Burdett Pr.

Seas & Oceans. Donna Lambert. (New View Ser.). (J). 1995. pap. text ed. 6.95 (0-8114-6448-2) Raintree Steck-V.

Seas & Oceans. Clint Twist. LC 91-18086. (Ecology Watch Ser.). (Illus.). 48p. (J). (gr. 4-6). 1991. lib. bdg. 13.95 (0-87518-491-X, Dillon Silver Burdett) Silver Burdett Pr.

*__Sea's Furthest End.__ Damien Broderick. 192p. (Orig.). pap. 10.00 (1-875346-07-4, Pub. by Aphelion AT) Firebird Dist.

Sea's Many Color. Elaine Lonergan. (Shamu's Little Library). (Illus.). 12p. (J). (ps). 1994. 5.95 (1-884506-01-1) Third Story.

Seas of Language. Michael Dummet. 504p. 1996. pap. 19.95 (0-19-823621-2) OUP.

*__Seas of Life.__ Diana Lyons. (Illus.). 106p. 1997. per. 9.95 (0-8087-7549-9) Burgess MN Intl.

Seasalt's Hidden Powers. 2nd ed. Jacques De Langre. (Illus.). 101p. 1993. 8.00 (0-916508-42-0) Happiness Pr.

Seascape. Edward Albee. 1975. pap. 5.25 (0-8222-1004-5) Dramatists Play.

Seascape. Peggy Darty. 262p. 1996. pap. 8.99 (0-88070-927-8, Palisades OR) Multnomah Pubs.

Seascape. large type ed. Anne Weale. (Harlequin Romance Ser.). 1995. 19.95 (0-263-14291-4, Pub. by Mills & Boon UK) Thorndike Pr.

Seascape with Dead Figures. large type ed. Roy Hart. 1989. 25.99 (0-7089-2105-1) Ulverscroft.

Seascapes. Jerry Hutchins. Ed. by Anne Hutchins. LC 85-82006. (Illus.). 56p. 1985. pap. 7.50 (0-9615989-0-5) J Hutchins.

Seascapes. Peggy Roalf. LC 91-73828. (Looking at Paintings Ser.). (Illus.). 48p. (J). (gr. 3-7). 1992. pap. 6.95 (1-56282-093-1) Hyprn Child.

Seascapes. Judith Shepard. 24.95 (0-8488-0627-1) Amereon Ltd.

Seascapes. Judith Shepard. LC 78-58642. (Illus.). 68p. 1984. 22.00 (0-932966-01-2); pap. 16.00 (0-932966-56-X) Permanent Pr.

Seascapes. Hans Van de Waarsenburgh. Ed. by Stanley H. Barkan. Tr. by Claire N. White. (Review Dutch Writers Chapbook Ser.: No. 1). (DUT & ENG.). 1991. 15.00 (0-89304-180-7); pap. 5.00 (0-89304-181-5) Cross-Cultrl NY.

Seascapes: A Collection of Photographs of the Jersey Shore. Joseph Paduano. LC 83-91284. (Illus.). 48p. (Orig.). 1983. pap. 9.95 (0-9612590-0-0, TR 24.N5) J Paduano.

Seascapes: Mini. Hans Van de Waarsenburgh. Ed. by Stanley H. Barkan. Tr. by Claire N. White. (Review Dutch Writers Chapbook Ser.: No. 1). (DUT & ENG.). 1991. 15.00 (0-89304-182-3); pap. 5.00 (0-89304-183-1) Cross-Cultrl NY.

Seascapes & Landscapes in Acrylics. Maurice Harvey. (How to Draw & Paint Ser.). (Illus.). 32p. (Orig.). 1989. pap. 6.95 (0-929261-65-8, HT148) W Foster Pub.

Seascapes & Landscapes in Oils. Vernon Kerr. (How to Draw & Paint Ser.). (Illus.). 32p. (Orig.). 1989. pap. 6.95 (0-929261-68-2, HT183) W Foster Pub.

Seascapes in Watercolor. Frank Germain. (How to Draw & Paint Ser.). (Illus.). 32p. (Orig.). 1990. pap. 6.95 (1-56010-066-4, HT229) W Foster Pub.

*__Seascapes of Prince Edward Island.__ Daphne Ross. (Island Pathways Ser.). (Illus.). 152p. 1992. spiral bd. 14.95 (0-614-21761-X, Pub. by Gynergy-Ragweed CN) LPC InBook.

*__Seascapes of Prince Edward Island.__ Daphne Ross. 92p. 14.95 (0-921556-26-8, Pub. by Gynergy-Ragweed CN) LPC InBook.

Seashell Magic. (Illus.). (J). (ps-2). 1991. pap. 5.10 (0-8136-5691-5); lib. bdg. 7.95 (0-8136-5191-3) Modern Curr.

Seashells. (American Nature Guide Ser.). 1992. 9.98 (0-8317-6967-X) Smithmark.

Seashells. (Golden Science Close-up Ser.). (Illus.). 24p. (J). (gr. k-5). 1991. 6.50 (0-307-12854-7, Golden Pr) Western Pub.

Seashells. (J). 1996. write for info. (0-679-87934-X) Random Bks Yng Read.

*__Seashells.__ (Portrait of the Animal World Ser.). 1996. 10.98 (0-7651-9967-X) Smithmark.

Seashells. R. Tucker Abbot. Ed. by Theodore Rowland-Entwistle. LC 93-46147. (Science Nature Guides Ser.). (Illus.). 80p. (J). (gr. 3-6). 1994. 12.95 (1-85028-264-1) Thunder Bay CA.

Seashells. Robert L. Buyer & Martha M. Towers. LC 96-13623. (Carving Sea Life Ser.). (Illus.). 40p. 1996. pap. 7.95 (0-8117-2469-7) Stackpole.

Seashells. Ruth Heller. (Designs for Coloring Ser.). (Illus.). 64p. (J). 1992. pap. 3.95 (0-448-03144-2, G&D) Putnam Pub Group.

Seashells. Barbara J. Zitwer. (Magic of the Ocean Ser.). (Illus.). 60p. 1995. write for info. (0-446-51882-4) Warner Bks.

Seashells: The Natural Treasures Collector's Kit. Greg H. Quinn. 32p. (gr. 4-6). 1995. pap. 4.95 (0-590-48486-9) Scholastic Inc.

Seashells: Treasures from the Sea. N. R. Gordon. LC 94-7780. (Illus.). 144p. 1994. pap. 12.95 (1-56799-106-8, Friedman-Fairfax) M Friedman Pub Grp Inc.

Seashells & Sunsets. Nan Chalat. Ed. by Don Weller & David Hampshire. LC 86-50559. (Illus.). 72p. 1986. write for info. (0-916873-51-X); pap. write for info. (0-916873-52-8) Weller Inst.

Seashells, Crabs, & Sea Stars. Christiane K. Tibbitts. LC 95-24501. (Take-Along Guide Ser.). (Illus.). 48p. (J). (gr. 3-7). 1996. 9.95 (1-55971-542-1) NorthWord.

Seashells in My Pocket: A Child's Nature Guide to Exploring the Atlantic Coast from Maine to Florida. 2nd ed. Judith Hansen. LC 92-24397. (Illus.). 160p. (J). (gr. 6 up). 1992. pap. 10.95 (1-878239-15-5) AMC Books.

Seashells of North America. R. Tucker Abbott. Ed. by Herbert S. Zim. (Golden Field Guide Ser.). (Illus.). 360p. (YA). (gr. 9 up). 1969. pap. 11.95 (0-307-13657-4) Western Pub.

Seashells of Oman. Donald Bosch & Eloise Bosch. LC 81-14236. (Illus.). 1982. text ed. 35.00 (0-582-78309-7) Longman.

Seashells of the Northeast Coast. Julius Gordon & Townsend E. Weeks. 64p. 1982. pap. 5.95 (0-88839-080-7) Hancock House.

Seashells of the World. rev. ed. R. Tucker Abbott. Ed. by Herbert S. Zim. (Golden Guide Ser.). (Illus.). 160p. (YA). (gr. 9 up). 1985. pap. 5.50 (0-307-24410-5) Western Pub.

*__Seashore.__ LC 97-5708. (Illus.). 48p. (J). (gr. 1-4). 1997. pap. text ed. 10.95 (0-07-057928-8) McGraw.

Seashore. David Burnie. LC 93-31075. (Eyewitness Explorers Ser.). (Illus.). 64p. (J). (gr. 3 up). 1994. 9.95 (1-56458-323-6) DK Pub Inc.

Seashore. Ed. by Elisabeth Cohat. LC 94-25896. (First Discovery Bks.). (Illus.). 24p. (J). (ps-2). 1995. 11.95 (0-590-20303-7, Cartwheel) Scholastic Inc.

*__Seashore.__ Dorling Kindersley Staff. (Eyewitness Explorers Ser.). (Illus.). 64p. (J). 1997. pap. 5.95 (0-7894-1681-6) DK Pub Inc.

*__Seashore.__ Cathie Felstead. (What Am I? Ser.). (J). 1997. 6.95 (0-7641-5025-1) Barron.

*__Seashore.__ John Feltwell. (Eyewitness Explorers Ser.). (Illus.). (J). (gr. 1 up). 1997. pap. 5.95 (0-614-28714-6) DK Pub Inc.

Seashore. Julie Lacome. LC 94-14877. (Fingerwiggle Board Bks.). (J). (ps). 1995. bds. 5.95 (1-56402-479-2) Candlewick Pr.

Seashore. Steve Parker. LC 88-27173. (Eyewitness Bks.). (Illus.). 64p. (J). (gr. 5 up). 1989. 19.00 (0-394-82254-4) Knopf Bks Yng Read.

Seashore. Steve Parker. LC 88-27173. (Eyewitness Bks.). (Illus.). 64p. (J). (gr. 5 up). 1989. lib. bdg. 18.99 (0-394-92254-9) Knopf Bks Yng Read.

Seashore. Steve Parker. (Illus.). 48p. (J). (gr. 7-9). 1992. pap. 7.95 (0-563-34411-3, BBC-Parkwest) Parkwest Pubns.

Seashore. Henry Pluckrose. LC 93-44698. (Walkabout Ser.). (Illus.). 32p. (J). (ps-3). 1994. lib. bdg. 17.60 (0-516-08120-9) Childrens.

Seashore. Henry Pluckrose. LC 93-44698. (Walkabout Ser.). 32p. (J). (ps-3). 1994. pap. 4.95 (0-516-40120-3) Childrens.

*__Seashore.__ Sayre. 1996. write for info. (0-8050-5260-7) H Holt & Co.

Seashore. April P. Sayre. LC 96-2420. (Exploring Earth's Biomes Ser.). (J). 1996. write for info. (0-8050-4085-4) TFC Bks NY.

Seashore. Jane Walker. (Fascinating Facts Ser.). (Illus.). 32p. (J). (gr. 2-4). 1995. pap. 5.95 (1-56294-897-0) Millbrook Pr.

Seashore. Jane Walker & David Marshall. (Fascinating Facts Ser.). (Illus.). 32p. (J). (gr. 2-4). 1995. lib. bdg. 14. 90 (1-56294-607-2) Millbrook Pr.

Seashore & Wading Birds of Florida. rev. ed. Patricia Pope. LC 75-2036. (Illus.). 44p. (Orig.). 1975. pap. 4.95 (0-8200-0903-2) Great Outdoors.

Seashore Animals of the Southeast. Edward E. Ruppert & Richard S. Fox. (Illus.). 429p. 1988. pap. text ed. 35.95 (0-87249-535-3) U of SC Pr.

*__Seashore Babies.__ Kathy Darling. LC 96-26951. (Illus.). 32p. (J). (ps-3). 1997. 15.95 (0-8027-8476-3); lib. bdg. 16.85 (0-8027-8477-1) Walker & Co.

Seashore Biology Notes: A New Guide to the Common Animals in the Northern Gulf of California Tidepools. Diana Warr & Albert Collier. (Illus.). (Orig.). 1982. 7.95 (0-938372-02-5) Winter Pub Co.

Seashore Book. Charlotte Zolotow. LC 91-22783. (Illus.). 32p. (J). (ps-3). 1992. 15.00 (0-06-020213-0) HarpC Child Bks.

*__Seashore Chronicles: Three Centuries of the Virginia Barrier Islands.__ Brooks M. Barnes & Barry R. Truitt. LC 97-2489. 1997. 24.95 (0-8139-1748-4) U Pr of Va.

*__Seashore Gardening with Native Plants.__ R. Marilyn Schmidt. (Illus.). 128p. (Orig.). 1997. pap. 12.95 (0-937996-32-7) Pine Barrens Pr.

Seashore Life. Christine Lazier. Tr. by Vicki Bogard from FRE. LC 90-50781. (Young Discovery Library). (Illus.). 38p. (J). (gr. k-5). 1991. 5.95 (0-944589-39-1, 391) Young Discovery Lib.

Seashore Life Between the Tides. William Crowder. Orig. Title: Between the Tides. (Illus.). 512p. reprint ed. pap. 10.95 (0-486-26817-9) Dover.

Seashore Life of Florida & the Caribbean. rev. ed. Gilbert L. Voss. LC 80-20172. (Illus.). 199p. 1980. pap. 9.95 (0-916224-58-9) Banyan Bks.

Seashore Life of Southern California. enl. rev. ed. Sam Hinton. (California Natural History Guides Ser.: No. 26). (Illus.). 256p. 1987. pap. 12.00 (0-520-05924-7) U CA Pr.

Seashore Life of the Northern Pacific Coast: An Illustrated Guide to Northern California, Oregon, Washington, & British Columbia. Eugene N. Kozloff. LC 83-1130. (Illus.). 378p. 1983. pap. 31.95 (0-295-96084-1) U of Wash Pr.

Seashore Life on Rocky Coasts. Judith Connor. (Natural History Ser.). (Illus.). 64p. (Orig.). 1993. pap. 9.95 (1-878244-05-1) Monterey Bay Aquarium.

Seashore Plants of California. E. Yale Dawson & Michael S. Foster. LC 81-19690. (California Natural History Guides Ser.: No. 47). (Illus.). 226p. 1982. pap. 9.95 (0-520-04139-9) U CA Pr.

Seashore Plants of South Florida & the Caribbean. David W. Nellis. LC 93-40713. (Illus.). 160p. 1994. 27.95 (1-56164-026-3); pap. 19.95 (1-56164-056-5) Pineapple Pr.

S

Seashore Stained Glass Coloring Book. John Green. (Illus.). (J). (gr. k-3). 1991. pap. 1.00 (0-486-26500-5) Dover.

Seashore State Park: A Walking Guide. Leonard M. Adkins. LC 89-49140. (Illus.). 64p. (Orig.). 1990. pap. 3.75 (0-87033-406-9, Tidewtr Pubs) Cornell Maritime.

*__Seashore Sticker Book.__ Graham Saunders. (Spotter's Guide Sticker Bks.). (Illus.). 32p. (J). (gr. 2 up). 1997. pap. 6.95 (0-7460-2998-5, Usborne) EDC.

*__Seashore Style: Decorative Ideas Inspired by the Spirit of the Seashore.__ Andrea Spencer. (Illus.). 160p. 1997. 27. 50 (1-85967-378-3, Lorenz Bks) Anness Pub.

Seashore Surprises. Rose Wyler. (Outdoor Science Ser.). (Illus.). 32p. (J). (gr. k-3). 1991. pap. 4.95 (0-671-69167-8, Julian Messner) Silver Burdett Pr.

Seashores. Joyce Pope. LC 89-20318. (Nature Club Ser.). (Illus.). 32p. (J). (gr. 3-6). 1990. pap. 4.95 (0-8167-1966-7); lib. bdg. 12.95 (0-8167-1965-9) Troll Communs.

Seashores. L. Stone. (Ecozones Ser.). (Illus.). 48p. (J). (gr. 4-8). 1989. 11.95 (0-685-58575-1); lib. bdg. 15.94 (0-86592-435-X) Rourke Corp.

Seashores. Herbert S. Zim & Lester Ingle. (Golden Guide Ser.). (Illus.). 160p. (YA). (gr. 5 up). 1955. pap. 5.50 (0-307-24496-2, Golden Pr) Western Pub.

Seashores: A Beachcomber's Guide. A. J. Underwood & M. G. Chapman. (Illus.). 124p. 1993. pap. 17.95 (0-86840-173-0, Pub. by New South Wales Univ Pr AT) Intl Spec Bk.

Seaside. Steven Brooke. LC 94-20911. (Illus.). 128p. 1995. 29.95 (0-88289-996-1); pap. 19.95 (0-88289-997-X) Pelican.

Seaside. Maria Rius & J. M. Parramon. (Let's Discover Ser.). (J). (ps). 1986. 6.95 (0-8120-5747-3); pap. 6.95 (0-8120-3699-9) Barron.

Seaside: Making a Town in America. David Mohney & Keller Easterling. (Illus.). 272p. (Orig.). 1991. pap. 29.95 (0-910413-26-6) Princeton Arch.

Seaside Fables & Other Incites. Roy P. Fairfield. 72p. (Orig.). 1994. pap. 7.95 (0-9621921-5-5) Bastille Bks.

Seaside Fashions 1860-1939. Avril Lansdell. 1989. pap. 25. 00 (0-7478-0066-9, Pub. by Shire UK) St Mut.

Seaside Gardening. Theodore James, Jr. LC 94-32138. (Illus.). 160p. 1995. 29.95 (0-8109-4451-0) Abrams.

Seaside Naturalist: A Guide to Study at the Seashore. Deborah A. Coulombe. (Illus.). 256p. 1990. pap. 15.00 (0-671-76503-5, Fireside) S&S Trade.

Seaside Pastels & Pickets. Seaside Town Council Staff. LC 94-72067. 1994. 21.95 (0-87197-410-X) Favorite Recipes.

Seaside Resorts. Stallibrass. (Progress in Planning Ser.). 1980. pap. 18.50 (0-08-026109-4, Pergamon Pr) Elsevier.

Seaside Sparrow, Its Biology & Management. Ed. by Thomas L. Quay et al. (Occasional Papers of the North Carolina Biological Survey). (Illus.). 174p. 1983. pap. 15. 00 (0-917134-05-2) NC Natl Sci.

Seaside Studies in Natural History: Marine Animals of Massachusetts Bay. Elizabeth Agassiz & Alexander Agassiz. LC 75-125726. (American Environmental Studies). (Illus.). 1975. reprint ed. 25.95 (0-405-02651-X) Ayer.

Seaside with the Savior. 1995. teacher ed., pap. 39.95 (0-7814-5175-2) Cook.

Seaskin Trousers. large type ed. Eric Linklater. (Illus.). 200p. 1991. 22.95 (1-85290-021-0, Pub. by ISIS UK) Transaction Pubs.

Season. Tom Kelly. LC 96-2789. 1996. 22.95 (1-55821-489-5) Lyons & Burford.

Season: A Candid Look at Broadway. rev. ed. William Goldman. LC 84-4409. 448p. 1984. reprint ed. pap. 17. 95 (0-87910-023-0) Limelight Edns.

Season & Strategy: The Changing Organization of the Rural Water Sector in Botswana. Emery Roe & Louise Fortmann. (Special Series on Resource Management: No. 1). 257p. (Orig.). (C). 1982. pap. text ed. 10.00 (0-86731-082-0) Cornell CIS RDC.

Season at Coole. Michael Stephens. LC 84-21373. 176p. 1984. reprint ed. 20.00 (0-916583-02-3); reprint ed. pap. 7.95 (0-916583-03-1) Dalkey Arch.

Season at the Point: A Birder's Journal of Cape May. Jack Connor. LC 91-9048. 320p. 1992. pap. 11.95 (0-87113-475-6, Atlntc Mnthly) Grove-Atltic.

*__Season for Butterflies.__ Laurie Paige. 1998. mass mkt. 4.50 (0-373-81035-0, 1-81035-7) Harlequin Bks.

Season for Change. Amy Roth. 24p. 1990. pap. 2.95 (*0-87227-147-1*, RBP5178) Reg Baptist.

Season for Change: Praying the Gospels of Lent. Philip St. Romain. LC 94-79994. 64p. (Orig.). 1994. pap. 2.95 (*0-89243-789-8*) Liguori Pubns.

Season for Dreams. Kevin J. Reed. LC 89-90670. (Illus.). 152p. (J). (gr. 5-7). 1989. pap. 5.95 (*0-9614546-3-6*) Chowder Pr.

Season for Goodbye. Lurlene McDaniel. (One Last Wish Ser.: No. 11). 151p. (J). (gr. 7 up). 1995. mass mkt. 3.99 (*0-553-56265-7*) Bantam.

Season for Love/Quiet Walks the Tiger, 2 bks. in 1. Heather X. Graham. 368p. 1994. mass mkt., pap. text ed. 4.99 (*0-505-51955-0*, Love Spell) Dorchester Pub Co.

***Season for Miracles.** Marilyn Pappano. 416p. (Orig.). 1997. mass mkt. 6.50 (*0-446-60356-2*) Warner Bks.

Season for Murder. Ann Granger. 256p. 1993. mass mkt. 4.99 (*0-380-71997-5*) Avon.

Season for Singles: Selected Meditations. Ed. by Rebecca England & Peggy A. Haymes. 128p. 1996. pap. text ed. 12.95 (*1-57312-048-0*, Peake Road) Smyth & Helwys.

Season for Slaughter. David Gerrold. (War Against the Chtorr Ser.: Bk. 4). 560p. 1993. mass mkt. 5.99 (*0-553-28976-4*, Spectra) Bantam.

Season for Tenure. John Thomchick. LC 83-90278. 1984. 15.00 (*0-87212-176-3*) Libra.

Season for the Spirit: Readings for the Days of Lent. Martin L. Smith. LC 90-48723. 167p. 1991. pap. 9.95 (*1-56101-026-X*) Cowley Pubns.

Season for War. P. F. Kluge. 244p. 1984. 15.95 (*0-88191-017-1*) Freundlich.

Season for Wilderness. Michael Furtman. 1991. pap. 9.95 (*1-55971-110-8*) NorthWord.

Season for Wilderness. Mike Furtman. (Illus.). 224p. 1989. 16.95 (*1-55971-005-5*) NorthWord.

Season in Grastorp. 155p. (Orig.). 1996. lib. bdg., mass mkt., pap. 13.00 (*0-9651224-0-9*) HAV Books.

Season in Hell. Jack Higgins. 1990. mass mkt. 6.99 (*0-671-72531-9*) PB.

***Season in Hell.** Arthur Rimbaud et al. 206p. 1994. 29.95 (*0-85646-219-5*, Pub. by Anvil Press UK); pap. 16.95 (*0-85646-220-9*, Pub. by Anvil Press UK) Dufour.

Season in Hell. Arthur Rimbaud. Tr. by Enid R. Peschel. Bd. with Illuminations. Illus.). 192p. (ENG & FRE.). 1974. Set pap. 9.95 (*0-19-501760-9*) OUP.

Season in Hell. large type ed. Jack Higgins. (General Ser.). 381p. 1990. pap. 13.95 (*0-8161-4841-4*, GK Hall) Thorndike Pr.

Season in Hell: The Life of Arthur Rimbaud. Jean M. Carre. Tr. by Hannah Josephson & Matthew Josephson from FRE. LC 77-10254. reprint ed. 38.00 (*0-404-16309-2*) AMS Pr.

Season in Hell & Illuminations: Bi-Lingual Edition. Arthur Rimbaud. Tr. by Bertrand Mathieu. 300p. (ENG & FRE.). 1991. 25.00 (*0-918526-88-4*); pap. 12.50 (*0-918526-89-2*) BOA Edns.

***Season in New South Wales.** George B. Perkins. 231p. (Orig.). 1997. mass mkt. 4.99 (*1-55237-086-0*, Pub. by Comnwlth Pub CN) Partners Pubs Grp.

***Season in Paradise.** Breytenbac. (J). 1996. pap. write for info. (*0-15-600374-0*, HB Juv Bks) HarBrace.

Season in Paradise. Breyten Breytenbach. Tr. by Rike Vaughan from AFR. LC 94-20364. (J). 1994. pap. 12.95 (*0-15-600133-0*, Harvest Bks) HarBrace.

Season in Purgatory. Dominick Dunne. LC 92-42352. 1993. 22.00 (*0-517-58386-0*, Crown) Crown Pub Group.

Season in Purgatory. Dominick Dunne. 464p. 1994. mass mkt. 6.99 (*0-553-29076-2*) Bantam.

Season in Purgatory. Thomas Keneally. LC 76-24458. 216p. 1985. pap. 8.95 (*0-15-679850-6*, Harvest Bks) HarBrace.

Season in Purgatory. large type ed. Dominick Dunne. LC 93-20379. 1993. 24.00 (*0-679-42539-X*) Random Hse Lrg Prnt.

Season in Rihata. Maryse Conde. Tr. by Richard Philcox. (Caribbean Writers Ser.). 192p. (Orig.). (C). 1988. pap. 9.95 (*0-435-98832-8*, 98832) Heinemann.

***Season in the Life of Emmanuel.** Marie-Claire Blais. 1996. pap. text ed. 6.95 (*0-7710-9880-4*) McCland & Stewart.

Season in the West. large type ed. Piers P. Read. (General Fiction Ser.). 496p. 1992. 25.99 (*0-7089-2632-0*) Ulverscroft.

Season in Turmoil: Lance Armstrong Replaces Greg LeMond As U. S. Cycling's Superstar. Samuel Abt. (Illus.). 176p. 1995. pap. 14.95 (*1-884737-09-9*) VeloPress.

Season, It Was Winter: Scenes from the Life of an American Jew, Vol. 5. John Sanford. LC 91-230. 302p. (Orig.). 1991. 30.00 (*0-87685-826-4*); pap. 15.00 (*0-87685-825-6*) Black Sparrow.

Season, It Was Winter: Scenes from the Life of an American Jew, Vol. 5, signed ed. deluxe ed. John Sanford. LC 91-230. 302p. (Orig.). 1991. 35.00 (*0-87685-827-2*) Black Sparrow.

Season Mystery Kit: Animal Coat Change. Diane D. Darneille. (Season Science Ser.). (Illus.). 32p. (Orig.). (J). (gr. k-3). 1994. boxed, pap. text ed. 14.95 (*0-9634246-0-2*) Sci Passport.

***Season of Adventure.** George Lamming. (C). 1997. pap. 14.95 (*0-472-06655-2*) U of Mich Pr.

***Season of Adventure.** George Lamming. (C). 1997. text ed. 39.50 (*0-472-09655-9*) U of Mich Pr.

Season of Adventure: Traveling Tales & Outdoor Journeys of Women Over 50. Ed. by Jean Gould. LC 96-24635. 304p. (Orig.). 1996. pap. 15.95 (*1-878067-81-8*) Seal Pr WA.

Season of Angels. Debbie Macomber. 336p. 1993. mass mkt. 5.99 (*0-06-108184-1*, Harp PBks) HarpC.

***Season of Blood: A Rwandan Journey.** Feargal Keane. 1997. pap. 11.95 (*0-14-024760-2*) Viking Penguin.

Season of Blood: A Rwandan Journey. Fergal Keane. 198p. 1996. pap. 21.95 (*0-670-86205-3*) Viking Penguin.

Season of Blood: A Suite of Poems. Henry Beissel. 64p. 1995. lib. bdg. 27.00 (*0-8095-4581-0*) Borgo Pr.

Season of Change. Lois L. Hodge. LC 87-18945. 108p. (Orig.). (YA). (gr. 7-12). 1987. pap. 2.95 (*0-930323-27-0*, Pub. by K Green Pubns) Gallaudet Univ Pr.

***Season of Change.** Marciniak. pap. 14.00 (*0-06-251459-8*) HarpC.

Season of Comebacks. Kathy Mackel. LC 96-6882. (J). 1997. 15.95 (*0-399-23026-2*, Putnam) Putnam Pub Group.

Season of Dead Water: A Response in Prose & Poetry to the Oil Spill in Prince William Sound. Ed. by Helen Frost. LC 90-1560. 130p. (Orig.). 1990. 19.95 (*0-932576-82-6*); pap. 9.95 (*0-932576-83-4*) Breitenbush Bks.

Season of Death. large type ed. Lee F. Gregson. (Linford Western Library). 1995. pap. 15.99 (*0-7089-7753-7*, Linford) Ulverscroft.

Season of Dorland-Bell: History of an Appalachian Mission School. Jacqueline B. Painter. LC 87-62800. (Illus.). 304p. 1987. reprint ed. 23.95 (*0-614-09745-2*); reprint ed. pap. 17.95 (*0-614-09746-0*) Appalach Consortium.

Season of Emmanuel: Daily Reflections for Advent, Christmas, & Epiphany. Kay Murdy. LC 96-31499. 160p. (Orig.). 1996. pap. 8.95 (*0-89390-389-2*) Resource Pubns.

***Season of Evil.** Bonnie Vincent. 1997. mass mkt. 4.99 (*1-55197-341-3*, Pub. by Comnwlth Pub CN) Partners Pubs Grp.

Season of Fire: The Confederate Strike on Washington. Joseph R. Judge. LC 94-15046. (Illus.). 325p. 1994. 30.00 (*1-883522-00-5*) Rockbridge Pub.

Season of Fire, Season of Faith. William H. Firmage. LC 82-24388. 336p. 1983. 22.95 (*0-87949-233-3*) Ashley Bks.

Season of Flesh. Byron H. Reece. LC 85-21333. 96p. 1985. reprint ed. 14.95 (*0-87797-104-8*) Cherokee.

Season of Giants 1492-1508: Michelangelo, Leonardo, Raphael. Vincenzo Labella. (Illus.). 1990. 45.00 (*0-316-85646-0*) Little.

Season of Goodwill. Elizabeth Walter. 256p. 1988. pap. 3.95 (*0-380-70501-X*) Avon.

Season of Growth. Sonia Murray. Ed. by Sherri York. LC 87-42911. 290p. 1990. pap. 3.95 (*1-55523-114-4*) Winston-Derek.

Season of High Adventure: Edgar Snow in China. S. Bernard Thomas. LC 95-21157. (Illus.). 587p. (C). 1996. 34.95 (*0-520-20276-7*) U CA Pr.

Season of Innocence. large type ed. Clare F. Holmes. (Historical Romance Ser.). 336p. 1993. 25.99 (*0-7089-2987-7*) Ulverscroft.

Season of Innocence: The Munroes at the Barnacle in Early Coconut Grove. Deborah A. Coulombe & Herbert L. Hiller. (Illus.). 128p. 1988. 22.95 (*0-940495-16-3*); pap. 12.95 (*0-940495-15-5*) Pickering Pr.

Season of Inquiry: The Senate Intelligence Investigation. Loch K. Johnson. LC 84-22106. (Illus.). 328p. 1985. 35.00 (*0-8131-1535-3*) U Pr of Ky.

Season of Inspiration One. Susie S. Piper. (Orig.). 1985. pap. write for info. (*0-9618280-1-3*) S S Piper.

Season of Knives: A Sir Robert Carey Mystery. P. F. Chisholm. (Sir Robert Carey Mystery Ser.). 240p. 1996. 19.95 (*0-8027-3276-3*) Walker & Co.

Season of Letters. S. Deal. write for info. (*0-943216-01-X*) MoonsQuilt Pr.

Season of Letting Go. Norval Rindfleisch. 144p. (Orig.). 1995. pap. 10.50 (*0-9645843-7-9*) Claritas Imprints.

***Season of Light: Daily Prayer for the Lighting of the Advent Wreath.** Jay Cormier. LC 97-13969. 96p. (Orig.). 1997. pap. 4.95 (*0-8146-2468-5*) Liturgical Pr.

Season of Loss. Jim Barnes. LC 85-3634. (Illus.). 84p. (Orig.). 1985. pap. 5.50 (*0-911198-75-X*) Purdue U Pr.

Season of Loving. Shirley Larson. 400p. 1988. mass mkt. 3.95 (*0-373-97058-7*) Harlequin Bks.

Season of Migration to the North. Tayeb Salih. (African Writers Ser.). 169p. (C). 1970. pap. 9.95 (*0-435-90066-8*, 90066) Heinemann.

Season of Migration to the North. Tayeb Salih. Tr. by Denys Johnson-Davies from ARA. LC 89-2423. 170p. 1989. 16.95 (*0-935576-29-0*) Kesend Pub Ltd.

Season of Migration to the North. Tayeb Salih. Tr. by Denys Johnson-Davies from ARA. 168p. 1996. reprint ed. 11.00 (*0-89410-199-4*, Three Contnts) Lynne Rienner.

***Season of Mists.** Harry Costello. 1996. mass mkt. 4.99 (*1-55197-052-X*, Pub. by Comnwlth Pub CN) Partners Pubs Grp.

Season of New Beginnings. Mitch Finley. (Orig.). 1996. pap. 4.50 (*1-878718-32-0*) Resurrection.

Season of Passage. Christopher Pike. 480p. 1993. mass mkt. 4.99 (*0-8125-1048-8*) Tor Bks.

Season of Passion. Danielle Steel. 352p. 1980. mass mkt. 6.50 (*0-440-17704-9*) Dell.

Season of Pause. Marian F. Park. (Illus.). 44p. (Orig.). 1994. 5.95 (*1-878116-46-0*) JVC Bks.

Season of Promise: Wild Plants in Winter, Northeastern United States. June C. Roberts. (Illus.). 336p. (C). 1992. 49.95 (*0-8214-1022-9*); pap. 24.95 (*0-8214-1023-7*) Ohio U Pr.

Season of Promises: Advent Reflections. Mitch Finley. (Spirit Life Ser.). 64p. 1995. pap. 4.50 (*1-878718-31-2*) Resurrection.

***Season of Reckoning, Vol. 3.** Cameron Judd. (Mountain War Ser.). 1997. mass mkt. 5.99 (*0-553-57390-X*) Bantam.

Season of Shadows. Ellen Foxxe. 1995. pap. 4.99 (*0-88677-620-1*) DAW Bks.

Season of Snows & Sins. Patricia Moyes. LC 74-155526. 224p. 1988. pap. 5.95 (*0-8050-0849-7*, Owl) H Holt & Co.

***Season of Sorcery: On Becoming a Wise Woman.** Poppy Palin. (Orig.). 1997. pap. 23.95 (*1-898307-96-2*, Pub. by Capall Bann Pubng UK) Holmes Pub.

Season of Storms. Ellen Foxxe. 1996. pap. 5.99 (*0-88677-692-9*) DAW Bks.

Season of Strength: New Visions of Adult Christian Maturing. Evelyn E. Whitehead & James D. Whitehead. Ed. by Carl Koch. 212p. 1994. pap. 11.95 (*0-88489-357-X*) St Marys.

Season of Swans, Vol. 3. Celeste De Blasis. 1990. pap. 5.95 (*0-685-47608-1*) Bantam.

***Season of the Christ-Mass.** John T. Ferrier. 24p. Date not set. pap. text ed. 5.00 (*0-900235-64-0*) Order Of The Cross.

***Season of the Eel.** Karen Radell. 1999. mass mkt. 4.99 (*1-55197-177-1*, Pub. by Comnwlth Pub CN) Partners Pubs Grp.

Season of the Elk. Dean Krakel, II. LC 75-42982. (Illus.). 117p. 1976. 22.95 (*0-685-11617-4*) Natl Cowboy Hall of Fame.

Season of the Heart. Virginia T. McAfee. (Illus.). 96p. (Orig.). 1995. pap. 12.95 (*0-9647323-0-0*) Home Place Bks.

Season of the Machete. James Patterson. 352p. 1995. mass mkt. 6.99 (*0-446-60047-4*) Warner Bks.

Season of the Monsoon. Paul Mann. 1995. mass mkt. 5.99 (*0-8041-1259-2*) Ivy Books.

***Season of the Senses.** Anne Worboys. 192p. 1996. 22.00 (*0-7278-4989-1*) Severn Hse.

Season of the Sun. Catherine Coulter. 384p. (Orig.). 1991. pap. 6.99 (*0-451-40262-6*, Onyx) NAL-Dutton.

***Season of the Swan.** Evan Maxwell. LC 96-38199. 1997. write for info. (*0-06-017529-X*) HarpC.

Season of the Tigers: A Novel of Pre-Pearl Harbor Espionage & Counterespionage. James O'Diear, pseud. Ed. by Susie McDonald & Terrie Ball. LC 95-958. (Illus.). 319p. (Orig.). 1995. pap. 14.99 (*1-57090-015-9*) Alexander Bks.

Season of the Vigilante Bk. I: The Bloody Season. Kirby Jonas. LC 93-43549. 178p. (Orig.). 1994. pap. 8.95 (*0-9624209-3-X*) Landmark ID.

***Season of the Vigilante Bk. II: Season's End.** Kirby Jonas. LC 93-43549. 225p. 1995. pap. 9.95 (*0-9624209-4-8*) Landmark ID.

Season of the Witch. Jean Stine. 1994. reprint ed. mass mkt. 6.95 (*1-56333-268-X*, Rhinoceros) Masquerade.

Season of the Witch: Border Lines, Marginal Notes. Gail B. Griffin. LC 95-20499. 288p. (Orig.). 1995. pap. 16.95 (*0-9623879-5-9*) Trilogy Bks.

Season of Valor: Gettysburg. Al Lacy. (Battles of Destiny Ser.: No. 6). 1996. pap. 9.99 (*0-88070-865-4*, Multnomah Bks) Multnomah Pubs.

Season of Yellow Leaf. Douglas C. Jones. 400p. 1995. mass mkt. 4.50 (*0-06-100851-6*, Harp PBks) HarpC.

Season of Youth: The American Revolution & the Historical Imagination. Michael G. Kammen. LC 88-47775. (Illus.). 432p. 1988. reprint ed. pap. 17.95 (*0-8014-9526-1*) Cornell U Pr.

Season of Youth: The Bildungsroman from Dickens to Golding. Jerome H. Buckley. LC 73-85887. 352p. 1974. 37.00 (*0-674-79640-3*) HUP.

Season on the Brink: A Year with Bob Knight & the Indiana Hoosiers. John Feinstein. 350p. 1989. pap. 12.00 (*0-671-68877-4*, Fireside) S&S Trade.

Season on the Earth: Selected Poems of Nirala. Tr. by David G. Rubin. LC 76-40026. 1976. text ed. 43.00 (*0-231-04160-8*) Col U Pr.

Season on the Earth: Selected Poems of Nirala. Tr. by David G. Rubin. LC 76-40026. 1977. pap. text ed. 16.50 (*0-231-04161-6*) Col U Pr.

***Season on the Trail.** Lynn Setzer. LC 97-9758. (Illus.). 192p. 1997. pap. 14.95 (*0-89732-234-7*) Menasha Ridge.

Season Science 1: Seasonal Mystery of Animal Coat Change. Diane D. Darneille. (Season Science Ser.). (Illus.). 32p. (Orig.). (J). (gr. k-3). 1992. pap. 13.95 (*0-9634246-1-0*) Sci Passport.

Season Songs. Ted Hughes. LC 74-18280. 77p. 1975. 20.00 (*0-670-62725-9*) Ultramarine Pub.

***Season Tickets: Christmas.** 1997. 8.99 (*0-8341-9315-9*) Lillenas.

Season Till Spring. J. B. Perry. 120p. 1991. pap. 7.99 (*0-8341-1393-7*) Beacon Hill.

Season to Heal: Help & Hope for Those Working Through Post-Abortion Stress. rev. ed. Luci Freed & Penny Salazar. LC 96-30778. 192p. 1996. pap. 10.95 (*1-888952-10-5*) Cumberland Hse.

Season to Taste: Low Salt-No Salt. Carol E. Goodkind & Abby L. Sproul. (Illus.). 64p. (Orig.). 1986. pap. 5.95 (*0-9610600-1-8*) Sea to Sea.

***Season Wild: 43 Selected Poems.** Lana E. Wolkonsky. 1997. 19.93 (*0-9653306-3-X*) L E Wolkonsky.

Season with Eagles. Scott Nielsen. (Illus.). 96p. 1991. 21.95 (*0-89658-148-9*) Voyageur Pr.

Season with Eagles. Scott Nielson. LC 90-25444. (Illus.). 96p. 1994. pap. 16.95 (*0-89658-247-7*) Voyageur Pr.

Season with Love. Compiled by Kay W. Wilder. 288p. 1985. kivar 12.99 (*0-8341-1061-X*) Beacon Hill.

Season Within. Marion Lineaweaver. 1967. 5.95 (*0-87233-836-3*) Bauhan.

Seasonal Activities. (Illus.). 208p. (J). (gr. 1-5). 1994. pap. text ed. 14.95 (*1-55799-273-8*, EMC 103) Evan-Moor Corp.

Seasonal Activities. 1984. pap. 14.95 (*0-590-70831-7*, Scholastic Hardcover) Scholastic Inc.

Seasonal Activities Vol. 1: A Learning Center Approach: September, October, November. Sandra Hillstrom-Svercek. (Illus.). 124p. 1985. pap. 12.95 (*0-932967-04-3*) Pacific Shoreline.

Seasonal Activities Vol. 2: A Learning Center Approach: December, January, February. Sandra Hillstrom-Svercek. (Illus.). 110p. 1985. pap. text ed. 12.95 (*0-932967-05-1*) Pacific Shoreline.

Seasonal Activities Vol. 3: A Learning Center Approach: March, April, May. Sandra Hillstrom-Svercek. (Illus.). 110p. 1986. pap. text ed. 12.95 (*0-932967-06-X*) Pacific Shoreline.

Seasonal Adaptations of Insects. Maurice J. Tauber et al. (Illus.). 428p. 1985. 55.00 (*0-19-503635-2*) OUP.

Seasonal Adjustments. Adib Khan. 240p. 1995. pap. 11.95 (*1-86373-652-2*) Paul & Co Pubs.

Seasonal Adjustments as a Practical Problem. F. A. Den Buttea & M. M. G. Fase. 226p. 1991. 131.50 (*0-444-88994-9*) Elsevier.

Seasonal Adjustments by Electronic Computer Methods. Julius Shiskin & Harry Eisenpress. (Technical Papers: No. 12). 40p. 1958. reprint ed. 20.00 (*0-87014-418-9*) Natl Bur Econ Res.

Seasonal Affective Disorder: Winter Depression: Who Gets It, What Causes It, How to Cure It. Angela Smyth & Chris Thompson. (Illus.). 1992. pap. 10.00 (*0-7225-2569-9*) Thorsons SF.

Seasonal Affective Disorders & Phototherapy. Ed. by Norman E. Rosenthal & Mary C. Blehar. LC 88-24402. 386p. 1989. lib. bdg. 55.00 (*0-89862-741-9*) Guilford Pr.

Seasonal Agricultural Circulation & Residential Mobility: A Prehistoric Example from the Pajarito Plateau, New Mexico. Robert W. Preucel, Jr. LC 90-21476. (Evolution of North American Indians Ser.). 261p. 1991. reprint ed. text ed. 20.00 (*0-8240-2511-3*) Garland.

Seasonal Agricultural Labor Markets in the United States. Ed. by Robert D. Emerson. LC 83-140. (Illus.). 584p. 1984. reprint ed. pap. 166.50 (*0-608-00103-1*, 2060868) Bks Demand.

Seasonal Analysis of Economic Time Series. Ed. by Arnold Zellner. (Other Conferences Ser.: No. 15). 498p. 1979. 124.50 (*0-317-37234-3*) Natl Bur Econ Res.

Seasonal Analysis of Economic Time Series. National Bureau of Economic Research, Bureau of the Census: Conference on the Seasonal Analysis of Economic Time Series (1976: Washington DC). Ed. by Arnold Zellner. LC 78-606108. (Economic Research Report Ser.: No. ER-1). 498p. reprint ed. pap. 142.00 (*0-317-55579-0*, 2056369) Bks Demand.

Seasonal & Holiday Springboards & Starters. Linda Milliken. (Illus.). 144p. (J). (gr. k-6). 1993. Grades k-6. pap. text ed. 12.95 (*1-56472-011-X*) Edupress.

Seasonal & Interannual Variability of the Western Mediterranean Sea. Ed. by Paul E. LaViolette. LC 94-34453. (Coastal & Estuarine Studies: Vol. 46). 370p. 1994. 57.00 (*0-87590-260-X*) Am Geophysical.

Seasonal & Sanctoral Cycle: Advent, Christmas, Lent & Easter & all Obligatory Memorials see Daily Homilies

Seasonal Arts & Crafts Activities for Early Childhood. Lorraine Clancy. (Illus.). 280p. 1988. pap. text ed. 24.95 (*0-13-796806-X*, Parker Publishing Co) P-H.

Seasonal Assistant. Jack Rudman. (Career Examination Ser.: C-704). 1994. pap. 23.95 (*0-8373-0704-X*) Nat Learn.

Seasonal Bulbs. Ann Lovejoy. (Cascadia Gardening Ser.). (Illus.). 96p. (Orig.). 1995. pap. 10.95 (*1-57061-027-4*) Sasquatch Bks.

Seasonal Bulletin Boards. Joy Evans & Jo E. Moore. (Illus.). 88p. (J). (gr. k-6). 1988. teacher ed., pap. 9.95 (*1-55799-122-7*, EMC 178) Evan-Moor Corp.

***Seasonal Campaign Graphics.** Ed. by P.I.E. Books Editorial Staff. (Illus.). 220p. 1996. 79.95 (*4-89444-019-9*, Pub. by PIE Bks JA) Bks Nippan.

Seasonal Celebrations. Corinne Sanders & Judith Bisignano. LC 85-62996. 104p. (Orig.). 1987. pap. 9.95 (*0-934134-56-1*) Sheed & Ward MO.

***Seasonal Celebrations.** Burillier Vongerichten. Date not set. write for info. (*0-688-07636-X*) Morrow.

Seasonal Charts for Futures Traders: A Source Book. Courtney D. Smith. 357p. 1987. text ed. 110.00 (*0-471-84888-3*) Wiley.

Seasonal Climatic Responses in the Quaternary: Proceedings of the American Quaternary Association, 8th Biennial Meeting. 148p. 1984. 10.00 (*0-318-32904-2*) Am Quaternary Assn.

Seasonal Clip Art. Gary Shipman. (Illus.). 48p. (J). (gr. k-6). 1989. teacher ed., pap. 5.95 (*1-55799-149-9*, EMC 193) Evan-Moor Corp.

***Seasonal Crafts.** Gillian Chapman. LC 97-4061. (J). 1998. write for info. (*0-8172-4870-6*); pap. write for info. (*0-8172-4871-4*) Raintree Steck-V.

Seasonal Creativity in the Classroom: A Teacher's Guide to Creating a Stimulating Classroom Environment. Patricia VanderGriend. (Illus.). 254p. (Orig.). (C). 1990. pap. text ed. 19.95 (*0-9627912-0-2*) Wndmill Pub WA.

Seasonal Cycles: A Study of Social Change & Continuity in a Sri Lankan Village. Victor C. De Munch. (C). 1993. text ed. 19.50 (*81-206-0816-X*, Pub. by Asian Educ Servs II) S Asia.

Seasonal Dance: How to Celebrate the Pagan Year. Janice Broch & Veronica MacLer. LC 93-10003. 186p. 1993. pap. 11.95 (*0-87728-774-0*) Weiser.

Seasonal Dating by Growth-Line Counting of the Clam, Meretrix Lusoria. Hiroko Koike. 104p. 1980. 37.50 (*0-86008-277-6*, Pub. by U of Tokyo JA) Col U Pr.

Seasonal Dimensions to Rural Poverty. Ed. by Robert Chambers et al. LC 81-2838. 276p. 1981. text ed. 50.00 (*0-86598-057-8*, R3835) Rowman.

Seasonal Drift: Adirondack Hunts & Wilderness Tales. Peter R. Schoonmaker. LC 94-17245. 136p. 1994. pap. 15.00 (*0-925168-31-9*) North Country.

***Seasonal Effects on Reproduction, Infection & Psychoses.** Ed. by T. Miura. (Progress in Biometeorology: Vol. 5). (Illus.). xii, 223p. 1987. 75.00 (*90-5103-005-3*, Pub. by SPB Acad Pub NE) Balogh.

An Asterisk (*) at the beginning of an entry indicates that the title is appearing in BIP for the first time.

Seasonal Entertaining. Sheridan Rogers. (Illus.). 144p. 1993. 30.00 (*0-207-17716-3*, Pub. by Angus & Robertson AT) HarpC.

Seasonal Favorites from the Herbfarm. Ron Zimmerman & Jerry Traunfeld. (Illus.). 28p. 1992. text ed. 5.95 (*0-912365-60-9*) Sasquatch Bks.

Seasonal Feasts & Festivals. Edwin O. James. LC 93-8917. 336p. 1993. reprint ed. lib. bdg. 38.00 (*0-7808-0001-X*) Omnigraphics Inc.

Seasonal Fluctuations in Employment in the Women's Clothing Industry in New York. Gertrud B. Greig. LC 74-76656. (Columbia University. Studies in the Social Sciences: No. 554). 1969. reprint ed. 20.00 (*0-404-51554-1*) AMS Pr.

***Seasonal Food Medicine.** Timothy Yeh et al. (Illus.). 300p. (Orig.). 1996. pap. text ed. 49.95 (*0-9652967-0-9*) Pearl Ctr Nat Med.

Seasonal Guide to Indoor Gardening. Jack Kramer. 224p. 1992. pap. 14.95 (*1-55821-198-5*) Lyons & Burford.

Seasonal Guide to the Natural Year: Colorado, New Mexico, Arizona & Utah. Ben Guterson. (Guidebook to Nature Ser.: No. 4). (Illus.). 360p. (Orig.). 1994. pap. 15.95 (*1-55591-153-6*) Fulcrum Pub.

Seasonal Guide to the Natural Year: Florida with Georgia & Alabama Coasts. M. Timothy O'Keefe. (Seasonal Guides to the Natural Year Ser.). (Illus.). 360p. (Orig.). 1996. pap. 16.95 (*1-55591-269-9*) Fulcrum Pub.

Seasonal Guide to the Natural Year: Illinois, Missouri & Arkansas. Barbara P. Lawton. (Illus.). 320p. (Orig.). 1994. pap. 16.95 (*1-55591-156-0*) Fulcrum Pub.

***Seasonal Guide to the Natural Year: Minnesota, Michigan & Wisconsin.** John Bates. LC 96-48511. (Illus.). 360p. (Orig.). 1997. pap. 16.95 (*1-55591-273-7*) Fulcrum Pub.

Seasonal Guide to the Natural Year: New England & New York. Scott Weidensaul. (Seasonal Guides to the Natural Year Ser.). (Illus.). 328p. (Orig.). 1993. pap. 15.95 (*1-55591-135-8*) Fulcrum Pub.

Seasonal Guide to the Natural Year: North Carolina, South Carolina & Tennessee. John Rucker. (Seasonal Guides to the Natural Year Ser.). (Illus.). 360p. (Orig.). 1996. pap. 16.95 (*1-55591-270-2*) Fulcrum Pub.

Seasonal Guide to the Natural Year: Northern California. Bill McMillon. (Illus.). 360p. 1995. pap. 15.95 (*1-55591-157-9*) Fulcrum Pub.

Seasonal Guide to the Natural Year: Oregon, Washington & British Columbia. James L. Davis. (Seasonal Guides to the Natural Year Ser.). (Illus.). 360p. (Orig.). 1996. pap. 16.95 (*1-55591-197-8*) Fulcrum Pub.

Seasonal Guide to the Natural Year: Pennsylvania, New Jersey, Maryland, Delaware, Virginia, West Virginia & Washington, D. C. Scott Weidensaul. LC 91-58483. (Illus.). 340p. (Orig.). 1992. pap. 16.95 (*1-55591-105-6*) Fulcrum Pub.

***Seasonal Guide to the Natural Year: Southern California & Baja, California.** Judy Wade. LC 96-37240. (Seasonal Guide to the Natural Year Ser.). (Illus.). 360p. (Orig.). 1997. pap. 16.95 (*1-55591-271-0*) Fulcrum Pub.

Seasonal Guide to the Natural Year: Texas. Steve Price. (Seasonal Guides to the Natural Year Ser.). (Illus.). 360p. (Orig.). 1996. pap. 16.95 (*1-55591-272-9*) Fulcrum Pub.

Seasonal Ideas & Activities. Robyn Spizman. 64p. (J). (gr. k-6). teacher ed. 6.99 (*0-86653-218-8*, GA568) Good Apple.

Seasonal Illustrations for Preaching & Teaching. Donald L. Deffner. LC 92-20122. (Illus.). 208p. (Orig.). (C). 1992. pap. 11.95 (*0-89390-234-9*) Resource Pubns.

Seasonal Journal: With Pleasures, Plans, & Projects for Home & Garden. Notes by Lauren Jarrett. (Illus.). 128p. 1987. 16.95 (*0-8109-7638-2*) Abrams.

Seasonal Learning Activities. Learning Exchange Staff. 112p. (J). (gr. 2-6). 1988. student ed. 6.99 (*0-86653-435-0*, GA1045) Good Apple.

Seasonal Math Motivators: Grades 1-3. Avaril Wedemeyer & Joyce Cejka. 1988. pap. 5.95 (*0-89108-189-5*, 8816) Love Pub Co.

Seasonal Movements of Exchange Rates & Interest Rates under the Pre-World War I Gold Standard. Ellen L. Foster. LC 94-10896. (Financial Sector of the American Economy Ser.). 240p. 1994. text ed. 64.00 (*0-8153-1722-0*) Garland.

Seasonal Parkman. Jack Rudman. (Career Examination Ser.: C-705). 1994. pap. 23.95 (*0-8373-0705-8*) Nat Learn.

Seasonal Patterns in Business & Everyday Life. W. T. Thorneycroft. 224p. 1987. text ed. 77.95 (*0-566-02699-6*, Pub. by Gower UK) Ashgate Pub Co.

Seasonal Performances: A Michigan Quarterly Review Reader. Ed. by Laurence Goldstein. (Illus.). 448p. (C). 1991. pap. 16.95 (*0-472-08147-0*) U of Mich Pr.

Seasonal Phonics Fun: Grades K-3. Rogene N. Penny & Patricia A. Vaughn. 1989. pap. 5.95 (*0-89108-209-3*, 8905) Love Pub Co.

Seasonal Prayer Services for Teenagers. Greg Dues. LC 90-71818. 80p. (Orig.). (gr. 7-12). 1991. pap. 9.95 (*0-89622-473-2*, C53) Twenty-Third.

Seasonal Quilting: A Year in Stitches. Cheryl Fall. (Illus.). 144p. 1995. pap. 14.95 (*0-8069-8659-X*) Sterling.

Seasonal Rain & Other Stories. Robert Flynn. LC 86-70716. 190p. 1986. pap. 7.95 (*0-931722-60-8*) Corona Pub.

Seasonal Reproduction in Higher Vertebrates. Ed. by B. K. Follett & Russell J. Reiter. (Progress in Reproductive Biology & Medicine Ser.: Vol. 5). (Illus.). vi, 222p. 1980. 124.00 (*3-8055-0246-X*) S Karger.

Seasonal Romance: Louis Hemon's Maria Chapdelaine. Patricia Demers. (Canadian Fiction Studies: No. 18). (C). 1993. pap. text ed. 14.95 (*1-55022-111-6*, Pub. by ECW Press CN) Genl Dist Srvs.

Seasonal Samplings. American Cancer Society Staff. 192p. 1981. pap. 6.00 (*0-686-31482-4*) Am Cancer Mich.

Seasonal Snowpacks: Processes of Compositional Change. Ed. by T. D. Davies et al. (NATO ASI Series G: Ecological Sciences: Vol. 28). (Illus.). 488p. 1991. 230.95 (*0-387-51760-X*) Spr-Verlag.

Seasonal Spermatogenesis in the Mute Swan (Cygnus Olor) H. Breucker. (Advances in Anatomy, Embryology & Cell Biology Ser.: Vol. 72). (Illus.). 104p. 1982. 39.95 (*0-387-11326-6*) Spr-Verlag.

Seasonal Stories for Family Festivals. Armandine Kelly. LC 86-62627. 136p. 1987. pap. 7.95 (*0-89390-096-6*) Resource Pubns.

Seasonal Subjects. Buford Johnson. 1981. pap. 3.95 (*0-934942-25-0*) White Wing Pub.

Seasonal Transitions of Richard Earl Thompson. Norton, R. W., Art Gallery Staff. LC 82-12437. (Illus.). 76p. 1982. pap. 10.00 (*0-913060-20-8*) Norton Art.

Seasonal Variability in Third World Agriculture: The Consequences for Food Security. Ed. by David E. Sahn. LC 89-32232. 320p. 1989. text ed. 44.50 (*0-8018-3829-0*) Johns Hopkins.

Seasonal Variation in Health & Diseases: With Sections on Effects of Weather & Temperature; a Bibliography. T. M. Allan & A. S. Douglas. LC 94-14865. 496p. 1995. 130.00 (*0-7201-2211-2*, Mansell Pub) Cassell.

Seasonal Variation of Interest Rates. Stanley Diller. (Occasional Papers: No. 108). 128p. 1970. reprint ed. 33.30 (*0-685-61350-X*) Natl Bur Econ Res.

Seasonal Variations in Industry & Trade. Simon Kuznets. LC 75-19723. (National Bureau of Economic Research Ser.). (Illus.). 1975. reprint ed. 40.95 (*0-405-07602-9*) Ayer.

Seasonal Variations in Industry & Trade. Simon Kuznets. (General Ser.: No. 22). 479p. 1933. reprint ed. 124.60 (*0-87014-021-3*) Natl Bur Econ Res.

Seasonal Variations in the Relative Demand for Money & Capital in the United States. Edwin W. Kemmerer. Ed. by Stuart Bruchey. LC 80-1154. (Rise of Commercial Banking Ser.). (Illus.). 1981. reprint ed. lib. bdg. 49.95 (*0-405-13660-9*) Ayer.

Seasonality: Practitioners' Suggestions for Managing Work Load Compression. LC 93-4149. 1993. 29.50 (*0-87051-134-3*) Am Inst CPA.

Seasonality & Agriculture in the Developing World: A Problem of the Poor & the Powerless. Gerard J. Gill. (Illus.). 250p. (C). 1991. text ed. 105.00 (*0-521-38257-2*) Cambridge U Pr.

Seasonality & Human Ecology. Ed. by Stanley J. Ulijaszek & S. S. Strickland. LC 92-43449. (Society for the Study of Human Biology Symposium Ser.: Vol. 35). (Illus.). 350p. (C). 1993. text ed. 65.00 (*0-521-43147-6*) Cambridge U Pr.

Seasonality in Human Mortality: A Medico-Geographical Study. Masako S. Momiyama. LC 78-315223. 201p. 1977. pap. 57.30 (*0-608-01246-7*, 2061934) Bks Demand.

***Seasonality of Birth.** Ed. by T. Miura. (Progress in Biometeorology: Vol. 6). (Illus.). xiii, 231p. 1987. 75.00 (*90-5103-006-1*, Pub. by SPB Acad Pub NE) Balogh.

Seasonality of Freshwater Phytoplankton. Ed. by M. Munawar & J. F. Talling. (Developments in Hydrobiology Ser.). 1986. lib. bdg. 184.00 (*90-6193-577-6*) Kluwer Ac.

Seasonally Dry Tropical Forests. Ed. by Ernesto Medina et al. (Illus.). 512p. (C). 1995. 95.00 (*0-521-43514-5*) Cambridge U Pr.

Seasoned Authors for a New Season: The Search for Standards in Popular Writing. Ed. by Louis Filler. LC 79-90128. 1980. 16.95 (*0-87972-143-X*) Bowling Green Univ Popular Press.

Seasoned by Salt: A Historical Album of the Outer Banks. Rodney Barfield. LC 95-9914. (Illus.). 206p. (C). 1995. 34.95 (*0-8078-2231-0*); pap. 18.95 (*0-8078-4537-X*) U of NC Pr.

Seasoned by the Sea: Delicious Fish from the Waters off Cape Cod, Nantucket & Martha's Vineyard. Cecy Ahern & Bob Ahern. LC 94-66787. 148p. 1994. pap. 11.95 (*1-883684-04-8*) Peninsula MA.

Seasoned Couple. Kamalini Sengupta. (C). 1994. pap. 8.50 (*81-7167-242-6*, Pub. by Rupa II) S Asia.

Seasoned in Texas: The Adolphus Cookbook. Kevin Garvin. Ed. by Betsy Field & David Davis. (Illus.). 160p. 1992. 24.95 (*0-9634101-0-5*) Adolphus.

Seasoned Judgments: Constitutional Rights & American History. Leonard W. Levy. 410p. (C). 1994. 44.95 (*1-56000-170-4*) Transaction Pubs.

Seasoned Judgments: The American Constitution, Rights, & History. Marion Levy. 468p. 1996. pap. text ed. 25.95 (*1-56000-925-X*) Transaction Pubs.

Seasoned Psychotherapist: Triumph over Adversity. Carl Goldberg. LC 92-16191. 200p. (C). 1992. 24.95 (*0-393-70146-8*) Norton.

Seasoned Schemer. Daniel P. Friedman & Matthias Felleisen. LC 95-25459. (Illus.). 224p. 1996. 18.50 (*0-262-56100-X*) MIT Pr.

Seasoned Timber. Dorothy C. Fisher. Ed. by Mark J. Madigan. LC 95-42558. (Hardscrabble Classics Ser.). (Illus.). 513p. 1996. pap. 16.95 (*0-87451-753-2*) U Pr of New Eng.

Seasoned Traveler. Marcia Schnedler. LC 91-77863. 208p. (Orig.). 1992. pap. 10.95 (*1-56626-001-9*) Country Rds.

Seasoned Traveler's Guide to Northern California. Victoria Sheridan. LC 92-81829. 120p. (Orig.). 1993. pap. 10.95 (*1-56626-011-6*) Country Rds.

Seasoned with Grace: My Generation of Shaker Cooking. Eldress B. Boswell. Ed. by Mary R. Boswell. LC 87-19933. (Illus.). 192p. (Orig.). 1987. pap. 14.00 (*0-88150-099-2*) Countryman.

Seasoned with Love: A Collection of Poems. Roberta Obert. LC 95-96239. 54p. 1996. pap. 10.95 (*0-9649582-2-8*) Brook Pubng.

Seasoned with Love: Southern Cousins' Favorite Recipes. Marjorie T. Donnelly. Ed. by Fundcraft Staff. (Illus.). 98p. 1990. 6.95 (*0-9626892-0-3*) T Donnelly.

Seasoned with Quilts. Retta Warehime. Ed. by Laura M. Reinstatler. (Illus.). 88p. (Orig.). 1995. pap. 19.95 (*1-56477-078-8*, B204) That Patchwork.

Seasoned with Sun: Recipes from the Corner of Texas & Old Mexico. rev. ed. Leon C. Metz. (Illus.). 272p. 1989. 16.95 (*0-9607974-1-6*) Jr League El Paso.

***Seasoned with Sunlight.** 52p. (Orig.). 1995. pap. 5.95 (*0-9607974-2-4*) Jr League Eugene.

Seasoning & Condiment Markets. Market Intelligence Staff. 319p. 1993. 1,200.00 (*1-56753-552-6*) Frost & Sullivan.

Seasoning Spoon. rev. ed. Loris Troup. 192p. 1990. reprint ed. pap. 8.95 (*0-916638-19-7*) Meyerbooks.

Seasoning the Fox Valley, Vol. 1. Friends of the Hesed House Pads Staff. LC 96-68053. (Illus.). 176p. (Orig.). 1996. pap. write for info. (*0-942495-57-8*) Amherst Pr.

Seasonings. Cora E. Cypser. (Illus.). 86p. (Orig.). 1992. pap. 7.95 (*0-9625774-5-6*) Kim Pathways.

Seasonings. Roz Levine. 366p. (Orig.). 1993. pap. 8.95 (*1-56245-075-1*) Great Quotations.

Seasons. (Shorewood Art Programs for Education Ser.). 1974. teacher ed. 107.00 (*0-88185-003-9*); 143.00 (*0-685-07204-5*) Shorewood Fine Art.

Seasons. Candy D. Boyd. 144p. (J). (gr. 3-7). 1994. pap. 3.99 (*0-14-036583-4*) Puffin Bks.

Seasons. Sherri M. Butterfield. (Science Mini Units Ser.). (Illus.). 48p. (J). (gr. 2-5). 1990. 6.95 (*0-88160-190-X*, LW 149) Learning Wks.

Seasons. Judith B. Cohen. LC 83-63240. 224p. 1984. 22.00 (*0-932966-38-1*) Permanent Pr.

Seasons. Rebecca Forster. 1996. pap. 4.99 (*0-8217-5313-4*) NAL-Dutton.

Seasons. Peggy Gavan. LC 94-26891. (First-Start Science Ser.). (Illus.). 32p. (J). (ps-2). 1994. lib. bdg. 9.79 (*0-8167-3605-7*) Troll Communs.

Seasons. Ed. by Peggy Gaven. LC 94-26891. (First Start Science Ser.). 32p. (J). (ps-2). 1996. pap. 2.95 (*0-8167-3606-5*) Troll Communs.

Seasons. Florence J. Goodman & Shelley Adler. 79p. 1980. pap. 10.00 (*0-917232-28-3*) Gee Tee Bee.

Seasons. Lisa Gregory. 1991. 20.00 (*0-7278-4248-X*) Severn Hse.

Seasons. Kathy Holler. (Science Ser.). 24p. (gr. 3-6). 1982. student ed. 5.00 (*0-8209-0163-6*, S-25) ESP.

Seasons. Debbie MacKinnon. (Illus.). 32p. (J). (ps) 1995. 12.95 (*0-8120-6422-4*) Barron.

Seasons. Constance O'Day-Flannery. 416p. (Orig.). 1995. mass mkt. 6.50 (*0-446-60107-1*) Warner Bks.

Seasons. Photos by Stephen Oliver. LC 89-63094. (My First Look At Ser.). (Illus.). 24p. (J). (ps). 1990. 7.00 (*0-679-80621-0*) Random Bks Yng Read.

Seasons. Illa Podendorf. LC 81-7751. (New True Bks.). (Illus.). 48p. (J). (gr. k-4). 1981. pap. 5.50 (*0-516-41647-2*); lib. bdg. 19.00 (*0-516-01647-4*) Childrens.

Seasons. Andres L. Ruiz. (Sequences of Earth & Space Ser.). (Illus.). 32p. (J). 1996. 12.95 (*0-8069-9335-9*) Sterling.

Seasons. Smithmark Staff. pap. 4.98 (*0-8317-7333-2*) Smithmark.

Seasons. Louise F. Underhill. 48p. (Orig.). 1993. pap. 12.50 (*0-9616734-5-1*) Underhill Ent.

Seasons. Brian Wildsmith. (Illus.). 32p. (J). (ps-3). 1981. 11.95 (*0-19-279730-1*) OUP.

Seasons. Brian Wildsmith. (Illus.). 32p. (J). (ps up). 1991. reprint ed. pap. 9.95 (*0-19-272175-5*, 12409) OUP.

Seasons: A Baby's First Photo Album. Illus. by Megan Montaguelash. 160p. Date not set. spiral bd. 24.95 (*1-55670-516-6*) Stewart Tabori & Chang.

Seasons: A Collection of Poems. unabridged ed. LC 96-85850. 52p. (Orig.). 1996. pap. 8.95 (*0-9653017-0-2*) Bywater Bks.

***Seasons: Cross-Curriculum Units for Theme Teaching.** Patricia O'Brien. Ed. by Judy Mitchell. (Illus.). 112p. (Orig.). 1997. teacher ed., pap. 10.95 (*1-57310-075-7*) Teachng & Lrning Co.

Seasons: Death & Transfiguration. Jo Sinclair. 288p. 1992. 35.00 (*1-55861-056-1*); pap. 12.95 (*1-55861-057-X*) Feminist Pr.

Seasons: Kalidasa's Ritusamhara. John T. Roberts. LC 89-82402. (Monograph Ser.: No. 25). 180p. 1990. pap. 10.00 (*0-939252-22-8*) ASU Ctr Asian.

Seasons: Violin, Flute, Viola, Harp. Smirnov. 1991. pap. 35.00 (*0-7935-0449-X*) H Leonard.

Seasons - A Thematic Unit. Ireta S. Graube. (Thematic Units Ser.). (Illus.). 80p. (J). (ps-1). 1990. student ed. 9.95 (*1-55734-251-2*) Tchr Create Mat.

Seasons along the Tiadaghton: An Environmental History of the Pine Creek Gorge. Steven E. Owlett. 104p. 1993. 39.95 (*0-9635905-0-2*); pap. 23.95 (*0-9635905-1-0*) S E Owlett.

Seasons & Celebrations. Rosalie F. Gaziano. LC 84-4226. 144p. 1984. reprint ed. pap. 11.95 (*0-88289-443-9*) Pelican.

Seasons & Feasts of the Church Year: An Introduction. Michael D. Whalen. LC 92-24215. 192p. 1993. pap. 9.95 (*0-8091-3346-6*) Paulist Pr.

Seasons & Holidays. Virginia Satkowski. Ed. by Susan Evento. (Macmillan Early Skills Program - Conversion Ser.). 64p. (J). (ps-2). 1995. pap. 9.95 (*1-56784-508-8*) Newbridge Comms.

Seasons & Holidays. Walt Disney Productions Staff. (Walt Disney's Fun-to-Learn Library Ser.: Vol. 13). (Illus.). 44p. (J). (gr. 1-6). 1983. reprint ed. 3.49 (*1-885222-04-1*) Advance Pubs.

Seasons & Its Weather, Variations & Mood Psychology: Index of New Information. Louise B. Millian. 150p. 1994. 44.50 (*0-7883-0052-0*); pap. 39.50 (*0-7883-0053-9*) ABBE Pubs Assn.

Seasons & Love. Faith T. Allum. (Illus.). 44p. (Orig.). 1984. pap. 3.00 (*0-9613349-1-6*) F T Allum.

Seasons & Nutrition at the Kenya Coast. Jan Hoorweg et al. (African Studies Center Leiden). 156p. 1996. pap. 38.95 (*1-85628-914-1*, Pub. by Avebury Pub UK) Ashgate Pub Co.

Seasons & Saints see Give Us This Day: Reflections for Each Day of the Liturgical Year

Seasons & Seasonings Vol. II: Recipes from Yesterday, for Today & for Tomorrow: All Pieces of a Legacy. 2nd ed. Ed. by Carol O'Hara et al. (Illus.). 156p. (Orig.). 1997. pap. 15.00 (*0-9625725-5-1*) Cat Tale Pr.

Seasons & Someone. Virginia L. Kroll. LC 93-11123. (Illus.). 32p. (J). (ps-3). 1994. 15.00 (*0-15-271233-X*) HarBrace.

Seasons & Spice. Rebecca Bowles. 180p. (Orig.). 1995. pap. 8.95 (*1-57532-021-5*) Press-Tige Pub.

***Seasons & Weather.** David Evans & Claudette Williams. (Let's Explore Science Ser.). (Illus.). (J). 12.95 (*0-590-74592-1*) Scholastic Inc.

Seasons at Eagle Pond. Donald Hall. (Illus.). 96p. 1987. 20.00 (*0-89919-542-3*) Ticknor & Fields.

***Seasons at Our House.** Nancy Twinem. (J). 1997. pap. text ed. 11.95 (*1-56189-400-1*) Amer Educ Pub.

***Seasons Change: Smocked Insert Jumper & Jumpsuit for 17"-18" Dolls.** Darcy A. Fechner. (Illus.). 16p. (Orig.). 1997. pap. 14.00 (*0-9658004-0-7*) Sara Fay.

Season's Edge. Edith Hodgkinson. 1980. pap. 4.00 (*0-914610-22-8*) Hanging Loose.

Seasons End. 3.98 (*0-8317-5691-8*) Smithmark.

Season's End: A Novel. Tom Grimes. LC 96-7732. vii, 319p. 1996. pap. 14.00 (*0-8032-7067-4*, Bison Books) U of Nebr Pr.

Seasons' Enigma. Naomi Y. Brown. (Illus.). 80p. (Orig.). (C). 1989. pap. 6.50 (*0-685-29144-8*) Yucca Bks.

Seasons for Celebration: A Contemporary Guide to the Joys, Practices, & Traditions of the Jewish Holidays. Karen L. Fox & Phyllis Z. Miller. (Illus.). 160p. 1992. pap. 15.95 (*0-399-51764-2*, Perigee Bks) Berkley Pub.

Season's Greetings. Ed. by Helen Exley. (So-Much-More-Than-a-Card Ser.). (Illus.). 28p. (Orig.). 1995. pap. 2.99 (*1-85015-655-7*) Exley Giftbooks.

Season's Greetings! Charles M. Schulz. LC 96-16594. (Festive Peanuts Bks.). (Illus.). 32p. 1996. 4.95 (*0-00-225024-1*) Collins SF.

Seasons Greetings: Cooking & Entertaining for Thanksgiving, Christmas, & New Year's. Marlene Sorosky. LC 85-30559. (Illus.). 144p. 1989. pap. 14.00 (*0-06-096054-X*, PL) HarpC.

***Season's Greetings: Cooking & Entertaining for Thanksgiving, Christmas, & New Year's.** Marlene Sorosky. LC 97-3733. 1997. pap. 19.95 (*0-8118-1668-0*) Chronicle Bks.

***Season's Greetings from the White House.** Mary E. Seeley. (Illus.). 192p. 1996. 39.95 (*1-57101-070-X*) MasterMedia Pub.

***Season's Greetings from the White House: The Collection of Presidential Christmas Cards, Messages & Gifts.** 2nd ed. Mary E. Seeley. Ed. by Virginia K. Hunt. (Illus.). 224p. 1996. reprint ed. 39.95 (*0-9657684-0-6*) Prsdntl Christmas.

Seasons in a Country Garden. Freda Cox. (Illus.). 160p. 1995. 27.95 (*1-55591-233-8*) Fulcrum Pub.

Seasons in Fern Hollow. John Patience. (Illus.). 64p. (J). (ps-1). 2.98 (*0-517-45857-8*) Random Hse Value.

Seasons in Full Score. Joseph Haydn. 1986. pap. 12.95 (*0-486-25022-9*) Dover.

Seasons in God's World. Beverly Beckmann. (In God's World Ser.). (Illus.). 24p. (J). (gr. 2-5). 1985. 6.99 (*0-570-04127-9*, 56-1538) Concordia.

***Seasons in Hell.** Mike Shropshire. 1997. mass mkt. 5.99 (*0-380-73023-5*) Avon.

Seasons in Hell: With Billy Martin, Whitey Herzog & "The Worst Baseball Team in History", the 1973-75 Texas Rangers. Mike Shropshire. 288p. 1996. pap. 23.95 (*1-55611-495-8*) D I Fine.

Seasons in Life. Bonnie Gear. Ed. by Mosazelle N. White. LC 82-62324. 61p. (Orig.). 1983. pap. 6.95 (*0-936026-19-7*) R&M Pub Co.

***Seasons in Mahakvya Literature.** Danielle Feller. (C). 1995. 24.00 (*81-86339-24-8*, Pub. by Eastern Bk Linkers II) S Asia.

***Seasons in Spirituality: Reflections on Vincentian Spirituality in Today's World.** Robert P. Maloney. 1997. pap. 9.95 (*1-56548-095-3*) New City.

***Seasons in Stained Glass.** Terra Parma. (Illus.). 52p. 1996. 11.95 (*0-936459-36-0*) Stained Glass.

***Seasons in the Desert: A Naturalist's Notebook.** Susan J. Tweit. LC 97-11384. 1998. write for info. (*0-8118-1685-0*) Chronicle Bks.

Seasons in the Heart. Donna L. DeSantis. (Orig.). 1996. pap. write for info. (*1-57553-168-2*) Watermrk Pr.

Seasons in the Sun. Ragna Dahl & Mary E. Gilliland. LC 86-71400. 173p. 1986. 9.95 (*0-9603624-4-4*) Alpenrose Pr.

Seasons in the Wild. John Daniels. 1994. 21.95 (*0-533-11127-7*) Vantage.

Seasons in the Year: Poems, Prayers, Praise, & Prose. J. Timothy Allen. LC 93-18733. 186p. 1993. pap. 11.95 (*1-880837-22-6*) Smyth & Helwys.

Seasons in Thunder Valley. Joann M. Everett. Ed. by Lucille Cychowski. (Illus.). 72p. (Orig.). 1986. pap. 5.95 (*0-930069-07-2*) Jasmine Pr.

Seasons Observed: Photographs. Evelyn Lauder. LC 94-8418. 1994. 24.95 (*0-8109-4455-3*) Abrams.

Seasons of a Farm Family: A Time to Celebrate Life on the Farm with Recipes & Stories. Kari F. Brandt. Ed. by David Brandt. LC 96-76030. (Illus.). 192p. (Orig.). 1996. pap. 15.95 (*0-942495-55-1*) Amherst Pr.

S

An Asterisk (*) at the beginning of an entry indicates that the title is appearing in BIP for the first time.

Seasons of a Lifetime: A Treasury of Meditations. Gerhard Frost. LC 89-36045. 160p. 1989. pap. 10.99 (*0-8066-2452-3*, 9-2452) Augsburg Fortress.

Seasons of a Man's Life. Daniel J. Levinson et al. LC 77-20978. 1978. 24.95 (*0-394-40694-X*) Knopf.

Seasons of a Man's Life. Daniel J. Levinson et al. 1986. pap. 14.00 (*0-345-33901-0*, Ballantine Trade) Ballantine.

Seasons of a Marriage. Sally Robinson. LC 93-24559. 190p. (Orig.). 1993. pap. 8.95 (*1-882185-12-9*) Crnrstone Pub.

Seasons of a Red Fox. Susan Saunders. LC 91-61145. (Smithsonian Wild Heritage Collection). (Illus.). 32p. (J). (gr. k-3). 1991. 11.95 (*0-924483-25-3*); 16.95 incl. audio (*0-924483-26-1*); audio write for info. (*0-924483-28-8*) Soundprints.

Seasons of a Red Fox. Susan Saunders. (Smithsonian Wild Heritage Collection). (Illus.). 32p. (J). (gr. k-3). 1995. pap. 4.95 (*1-56899-139-8*) Soundprints.

Seasons of a Red Fox, Incl. toy. Susan Saunders. LC 91-61145. (Smithsonian Wild Heritage Collection). (Illus.). 32p. (J). (gr. k-3). 1991. 25.95 incl. digital audio (*0-924483-40-7*) Soundprints.

Seasons of a Red Fox: Including 8" Stuffed Toy. Susan Saunders. (Smithsonian Wild Heritage Collection). (Illus.). 32p. (J). (gr. k-3). 1995. pap. 14.95 (*1-56899-145-2*) Soundprints.

Seasons of a Woman's Life. Normajean Hinders. 248p. 1994. 16.99 (*0-8054-6142-6*, 4261-42) Broadman.

Seasons of a Woman's Life. Daniel J. Levinson. 448p. 1996. 27.50 (*0-394-53235-X*) Random.

Seasons of a Woman's Life. Daniel J. Levinson & Judy D. Levinson. LC 95-20893. 438p. 1996. 27.50 (*0-614-09477-1*) Knopf.

Seasons of Arnold's Apple Tree. Gail Gibbons. LC 84-4484. (Illus.). 32p. (J). (ps-3). 1984. 15.00 (*0-15-271246-1*, HB Juv Bks) HarBrace.

Seasons of Arnold's Apple Tree. Gail Gibbons. LC 84-484. (Illus.). 32p. (J). (ps-3). 1988. pap. 5.00 (*0-15-271245-3*, HB Juv Bks) HarBrace.

***Seasons of Beento Blackbird.** Busia. 1997. pap. 12.00 (*0-671-01409-9*) PB.

Seasons of Beento Blackbird: A Novel. Akosua Busia. LC 96-2071. 368p. 1996. 22.95 (*0-316-11495-2*) Little.

***Seasons of Business.** Sarah E. Hutchinson & Glen Coulthard. 1992. per. 29.95 (*0-07-413183-4*) Irwin.

Seasons of Business: The Marketer's Guide to Consumer Behavior. Judith Waldrop. LC 91-58812. 269p. (C). 1992. 34.95 (*0-936889-12-8*); pap. 29.95 (*0-936889-13-6*) American Demo.

Seasons of Captivity: The Inner World of POW's. Amia Lieblich. 240p. (C). 1994. 40.00 (*0-8147-5079-6*) NYU Pr.

Seasons of Captivity: The Inner World of POW's. Amia Lieblich. 240p. (C). 1995. pap. 17.50 (*0-8147-5095-8*) NYU Pr.

Seasons of Celebration. Judy Miller. 146p. 1994. 6.95 (*0-614-04220-8*) Dawn Pubns TX.

Seasons of Celebrations: Prayers, Plays & Projects for the Church Year. Patricia Mathson. LC 95-77475. (Illus.). 168p. (Orig.). (J). (ps-10). 1995. teacher ed., pap. 9.95 (*0-87793-566-1*) Ave Maria.

***Seasons of Change: Baseball in America.** Richard L. Sartore. (Illus.). 157p. 1997. pap. 16.95 (*1-56072-464-1*) Nova Sci Pubs.

Seasons of Change: Growing Through Pregnancy & Birth. Suzanne Arms. (Illus.). 184p. (Orig.). 1994. pap. 14.95 (*1-882308-58-1*) Kivaki Pr.

Seasons of Change: Reflections of a Half Century at St. Louis University. Paul C. Reinert & Paul Shore. 186p. 1997. 29.95 (*0-9652929-0-8*) St Louis Univ.

Seasons of Communion: A Planning Workbook for Sharing the Lord's Table Through the Christian Year. Paul L. Escamilla. LC 93-73816. 96p. 1994. pap. 9.95 (*0-88177-130-9*, DR130) Discipleship Res.

Seasons of Death. M. K. Wren. 192p. 1990. mass mkt. 4.99 (*0-345-35003-0*) Ballantine.

***Seasons of Dust.** Ifeona Fulani. 224p. 22.00 (*0-86316-248-7*) Writers & Readers.

Seasons of Endearment. Emily Williams-Wheeler. 1993. pap. 5.95 (*0-934860-06-8*) Adventure Pubns.

Seasons of Erotic Love. Barbara Herrera. LC 92-61207. 130p. (Orig.). 1992. pap. 8.95 (*0-9628595-4-0*) Paradigm San Diego.

Seasons of Faith & Conscience: Kairos, Confession, Liturgy. Bill W. Kellermann. LC 91-7262. 1991. pap. 13.50 (*0-88344-726-6*) Orbis Bks.

Seasons of Friendship: Naomi & Ruth As a Pattern. Marjory Z. Bankson. LC 87-32528. 144p. (Orig.). 1987. pap. 12.95 (*0-931055-41-5*) Innisfree Pr.

Seasons of Giving. (Illus.). 160p. 1997. 19.96 (*1-57367-047-2*) Needlecrft Shop.

Seasons of Glory: Grant Teaff & the Baylor Bears, the Pictorial History 1972-1992. Grant Teaff. Ed. by Mike Towle. (Illus.). 200p. 1993. 34.95 (*1-56530-016-5*) Summit TX.

Seasons of Glory: Grant Teaff & the Baylor Bears, the Pictorial History 1972-1992. limited ed. Grant Teaff. Ed. by Mike Towle. (Illus.). 200p. 1993. 149.95 (*1-56530-043-2*) Summit TX.

Seasons of God's Love: The Church Year. Jeanne S. Fogle. Ed. by Mary J. Duckert & Ben Lane. LC 88-6414. (Illus.). 32p. (J). 1988. pap. 10.00 (*0-664-25032-7*, Geneva Pr) Westminster John Knox.

Seasons of Gold. Stef A. Holm. Ed. by Carolyn Tolley. 320p. (Orig.). 1992. mass mkt. 5.50 (*0-671-74126-8*) PB.

***Seasons of Grace.** Mark A. Noll. LC 97-19619. 96p. 1997. pap. 10.99 (*0-8010-5777-9*) Baker Bks.

Seasons of Grace: A History of the Catholic Archdiocese of Detroit. Leslie W. Tentler. LC 89-34282. (Great Lakes Bks.). (Illus.). 610p. (Orig.). (C). 1992. 45.00 (*0-8143-2105-4*, Great Lks Bks); pap. 17.95 (*0-8143-2106-2*, Great Lks Bks) Wayne St U Pr.

Seasons of Grace: Reflections from the Christian Year. James A. Kay. 112p. (Orig.). 1994. pap. 10.00 (*0-8028-0783-6*) Eerdmans.

Seasons of Grief & Grace: A Sister's Story of AIDS. Susan F. Wiltshire. LC 94-26440. (Illus.). 216p. (C). 1994. 24.95 (*0-8265-1261-5*) Vanderbilt U Pr.

Seasons of Grief & Grace: A Sister's Story of AIDS. Susan F. Wiltshire. LC 94-26440. (Illus.). 176p. 1995. reprint ed. pap. 14.95 (*0-8265-1271-2*) Vanderbilt U Pr.

***Seasons of Happiness.** (Illus.). 32p. 1997. 4.99 (*0-8007-7170-2*) Revell.

Seasons of Her Life. Fern Michaels. 1994. mass mkt. 5.99 (*0-345-36591-7*) Ballantine.

Seasons of Heron Pond: Wildlings of Air, Earth, & Water. Mary Leister. LC 81-9408. (Illus.). 192p. 1981. 14.95 (*0-916144-84-4*) Stemmer Hse.

Seasons of Inspiration Two. Susie S. Piper. (Orig.). 1986. pap. 3.50 (*0-9618280-2-1*) S S Piper.

Seasons of Jesse Stuart: An Autobiography in Poetry 1907-1976. Jesse H. Stuart. LC 76-49171. (Illus.). 1976. 200.00 (*0-89097-007-6*) Archer Edns.

***Seasons of Laughter for Teachers.** Janet C. Teitsort. 96p. (YA). (gr. 10). 1997. 11.99 (*0-8010-1135-3*) Baker Bks.

Seasons of Life. Frank G. Harrington. 55p. 1986. 9.95 (*0-9616001-0-1*) Pr Peachtree.

Seasons of Life. E. James Rohn & Ronald L. Reynolds. LC 81-66145. (Illus.). 117p. 1981. text ed. 9.95 (*0-939490-00-5*) Total Impact.

Seasons of Life: Our Dramatic Journey from Birth to Death. John Kotre & Elizabeth Hall. 1990. write for info. (*0-318-68139-0*) Little.

Seasons of Life: Self Help Reflections. Barbara Peterson. Ed. by Sharill Halstead. (Illus.). 206p. (Orig.). 1995. pap. 10.95 (*0-9650347-0-4*) Caritas Fnd.

***Seasons of Life: Separation-Individuation Perspectives.** Salman Akhtar & Selma Kramer. LC 96-39583. 208p. 1997. 35.00 (*0-7657-0055-7*) Aronson.

***Seasons of Life Study Guide: To Accompany the Developing Person Through the Life Span.** 3rd ed. R. Straub. (C). 1997. pap. text ed. 12.95 (*1-57259-349-0*) Worth.

***Seasons of Love.** Tony Evans & Lois Evans. 372p. 1997. 17.99 (*0-8499-1412-4*) Word Pub.

Seasons of Love. Edward Leone. LC 92-7373. 80p. 1992. 9.95 (*0-87319-035-1*) Hallberg Pub Corp.

Seasons of Love. rev. ed. George Betts & Donni Betts. LC 86-11733. (Illus.). 80p. (Orig.). 1986. pap. 5.95 (*0-89087-477-8*) Celestial Arts.

Seasons of Love: An American Romance Anthology. Elaine Barbieri. 368p. 1995. mass mkt. 5.50 (*0-06-108286-4*, Harp PBks) HarpC.

Seasons of Mind. Roger Bower. LC 82-90178. (Illus.). 73p. 1982. 8.95 (*0-9608748-0-1*) Marcourt Pr.

Seasons of Motherhood. Ruth Tucker. 240p. 1996. 16.99 (*1-56476-537-7*, 6-3537, Victor Bks) Chariot Victor.

Seasons of My Life. large type ed. Hannah Hauxwell & B. Cockcroft. 1990. 25.99 (*0-7089-2306-2*) Ulverscroft.

Seasons of Myself. Toni McAndrew. (Illus.). 21p. (Orig.). 1990. pap. 5.00 (*0-910147-86-8*) World Poetry Pr.

Seasons of Our Joy: A Modern Guide to the Jewish Holidays. Arthur I. Waskow. LC 90-651. (Illus.). 272p. (Orig.). 1991. pap. 15.00 (*0-8070-3611-0*) Beacon Pr.

***Seasons of Our Lives.** Shirley A. Krauss. (Illus.). 101p. (Orig.). 1997. pap. 16.75 (*0-9656441-0-3*) HrthFelt Express.

Seasons of Paradise: A Portrait of Crested Butte, Colorado, & the Gunnison High Country. Sandy Fails. (Illus.). 112p. 1993. per. 16.95 (*0-614-04389-1*) Crested Butte Pub.

Seasons of Passion *see* **Danielle Steel**

Seasons of Plenty. Colin Greenland. 432p. (Orig.). 1996. mass mkt. 5.50 (*0-380-77468-2*, AvoNova) Avon.

Seasons of Plenty: Amana Communal Cooking. Ed. by Emilie Hoppe. LC 94-21238. (Illus.). 246p. 1994. 24.95 (*0-8138-2242-4*) Iowa St U Pr.

***Seasons of Praise.** Rebecca H. Bauer. 239p. (J). 1996. 18.99 (*1-56476-582-2*, 6-3582, Victor Bks) Chariot Victor.

Seasons of Prayer: Resources for Worship. Lisa Withrow. 128p. 1995. pap. 16.95 (*0-687-85002-9*, Pub. by Society Promot Chrst Know UK) Abingdon.

Seasons of Preaching: 160 Best Sermons from the Preaching Resource Word & Witness. Ed. by John M. Rottman & Paul S. Wilson. 270p. (Orig.). 1996. pap. 20.00 (*0-940169-12-6*) Liturgical Pubns.

Seasons of Refreshing: Evangelism & Revivals in America. Keith J. Hardman. LC 93-30833. (Illus.). 304p. (C). 1994. pap. 16.99 (*0-8010-4389-1*) Baker Bks.

***Seasons of Revival: Understanding the Appointed Times of Spiritual Refreshing, Bk. 1.** Frank Damazio. (Strategic Impact Ser.). (Illus.). 1996. 18.95 (*1-886849-03-X*); pap. write for info. (*1-886849-04-8*) BT Pub.

Seasons of Rome: A Journal. Paul Hofmann. (Illus.). 272p. 1997. 25.00 (*0-8050-3890-6*) H Holt & Co.

Seasons of Sacred Lust. Kazuko Shiraishi. Ed. by Kenneth Rexroth. LC 77-14936. 1978. pap. 7.95 (*0-8112-0678-5*, NDP453) New Directions.

Seasons of Sentire. Anthony V. Santa-Maria. LC 95-19121. 80p. 1996. 12.95 (*0-944957-80-3*) Rivercross Pub.

Seasons of Sin. James R. Adams. (Illus.). 200p. 9.95 (*0-9618060-8-7*) Sheer Joy Pr.

Seasons of Splendor. Madhur Jaffrey. (Illus.). (J). (ps up). reprint ed. pap. 7.95 (*0-317-62172-6*, Puffin) Puffin Bks.

Seasons of Splendour. Madhur Jaffrey. (J). 1987. pap. 4.99 (*0-14-034699-6*, Puffin) NAL-Dutton.

Seasons of Splendour. Madhur Jaffrey. 1987. pap. 7.95 (*0-14-031854-2*, Puffin) Puffin Bks.

Seasons of Swans. Smithmark Staff. 4.98 (*0-8317-6217-9*) Smithmark.

Seasons of Swans. Monica Wellington. Date not set. pap. write for info. (*0-14-055289-8*) NAL-Dutton.

Seasons of the Crane. Dale Stahleker & Martin Frentzel. (Illus.). 64p. (Orig.). 1986. 6.95 (*0-910467-07-2*) Heritage Assocs.

Seasons of the Cranes. Peter Roop & Connie Roop. (Illus.). 32p. (J). (gr. 4-7). 1989. 14.95 (*0-8027-6859-8*); lib. bdg. 15.85 (*0-8027-6860-1*) Walker & Co.

Seasons of the Divine, Cycle C: Christian Feminist Prayers for the Liturgical Cycle, Year C. Mary K. Schmitt. 126p. (Orig.). 1994. pap. 13.95 (*0-8245-1443-2*) Crossroad NY.

***Seasons of the Elk.** Michael Furtman. LC 96-37141. (Wildlife Ser.). (Illus.). 144p. (Orig.). 1997. pap. write for info. (*1-55971-586-3*) NorthWord.

Seasons of the Family: An Introduction to Marriage & Family Life. William R. Garrett. LC 81-7240. 532p. (C). 1982. text ed. 46.75 (*0-03-057281-9*) HB Coll Pubs.

Seasons of the Farm Bureau. Ed. by William Strode. (Illus.). 136p. (C). 75.00 (*1-56469-018-0*) Harmony Hse Pub.

Seasons of the Feminine Divine, Cycle A. Mary K. Schmitt. 144p. 1995. pap. 13.95 (*0-8245-1515-3*) Crossroad NY.

Seasons of the Feminine Divine: Christian Feminist Prayers for the Liturgical Year. Kathleen S. Schmitt. 128p. (Orig.). 1993. pap. 11.95 (*0-8245-1279-0*) Crossroad NY.

***Seasons of the Heart.** Jackie Calhoun. LC 96-45489. 256p. (Orig.). 1997. pap. 11.95 (*1-56280-167-8*) Naiad Pr.

Seasons of the Heart. Susan C. Feldhake. (Enduring Faith Ser.: Vol. 2). 208p. 1993. pap. 8.99 (*0-310-48121-X*) Zondervan.

Seasons of the Heart. Judy Miller. 126p. 1984. 6.95 (*0-89225-272-3*) Dawn Pubns TX.

Seasons of the Heart. Janette Oke. 1993. 10.98 (*0-88486-088-4*) Arrowood Pr.

Seasons of the Heart. Alexandra Thorne. 416p. 1996. mass mkt. 4.99 (*0-7860-0301-4*, Pinncle Kensgtn) Kensgtn Pub Corp.

Seasons of the Heart. Evelyn M. Wallace. (Illus.). 76p. (Orig.). 1988. pap. 9.95 (*0-929919-00-9*) Saxifrage Bks.

Seasons of the Heart: A Book of Sensuous Meditations. Moi Tayler. Ed. by Annemarie S. Annerl. 64p. (Orig.). 1995. pap. 12.95 (*0-9646250-0-8*) Heathchris Bks.

Seasons of the Heart: A Quest in Faith. Sara H. Hay. Ed. by Agnes D. Kinard. LC 89-16088. (Princeton Theological Monographs: No. 21). xiv, 122p. (Orig.). 1989. pap. 10.00 (*1-55635-002-3*) Pickwick.

Seasons of the Heart: A Selection of Sermons by Canon Edward Nason West. Ed. by William B. Green. 168p. (Orig.). 1994. pap. 6.95 (*0-88028-154-5*, 1282) Forward Movement.

Seasons of the Hearts. Jane Garrard. 1995. mass mkt. 5.99 (*1-887298-13-4*) Penthse Images.

Seasons of the Italian Kitchen. Diane Darrow & Tom Maresca. 480p. 1996. pap. 14.00 (*0-87113-657-0*, Atlntc Mnthly) Grove-Atltic.

Seasons of the Kachina: Proceedings of the California State University Hayward Conferences on the Western Pueblos, 1987-1988. Ed. by Lowell J. Bean. LC 89-6953. (Anthropological Papers: No. 34). (Illus.). 185p. (Orig.). 1989. pap. 21.95 (*0-87919-114-7*) Ballena Pr.

Seasons of the Leelanau: A Traveler's Guide. Sandra G. Bradshaw. 104p. 1992. pap. 9.95 (*1-878005-71-5*) Northmont Pub.

Seasons of the Mind. Arlene Zekowski. LC 69-20441. (Archives of Post-Modern Literature Ser.). (Illus.). 1969. pap. 20.00 (*0-913844-06-3*) Am Canadian.

Seasons of the Moose. Jennie Promack. (Illus.). 128p. (Orig.). 1992. pap. 17.95 (*0-87905-455-7*, Peregrine Smith) Gibbs Smith Pub.

Seasons of the River. Dan Jaffe. LC 86-71748. 64p. (Orig.). 1987. 14.95 (*0-933532-58-X*) BkMk.

Seasons of the Salt Marsh. David A. Gates. LC 74-27956. (Illus.). 128p. 1975. 14.95 (*0-85699-121-X*) Chatham Pr.

***Seasons of the Seal.** Fred Bruemmer. 1997. pap. text ed. 24.95 (*1-55209-142-2*) Firefly Bks Ltd.

Seasons of the Seal. Fred Bruemmer & Brian Davies. (Illus.). 159p. 1991. 17.99 (*0-517-05372-1*) Random Hse Value.

Seasons of the Self. Max Coots. 1994. pap. 7.00 (*1-55896-285-9*, Skinner Hse Bks) Unitarian Univ.

***Seasons of the Senses.** large type ed. Anne Worboys. (Ulverscroft Large Print Ser.). 400p. 1997. 27.50 (*0-7089-3784-5*) Ulverscroft.

Seasons of the Soul. Sherry H. Steiger. (Illus.). 1995. pap. 7.95 (*1-880090-22-8*) Galde Pr.

Seasons of the Southwest: Country Cooking with Herbs. Susan G. Stephens. (Illus.). 304p. (Orig.). 1994. pap. 19.95 (*1-879560-33-X*) Harbor Hse West.

Seasons of the Spirit: Daily Mediations for Adults in Mid-Life & Beyond. Sally Coleman. 1992. pap. 10.00 (*1-56838-060-7*) Hazelden.

Seasons of the Spirit: Exploring Contemporary Spirituality. Clyde Crews. 96p. (Orig.). 1992. pap. text ed. 5.95 (*0-8146-2081-7*) Liturgical Pr.

Seasons of the Spirit: Meditations of a Jogging Nun. Illus. by Lorca Morella. LC 94-15813. 48p. (Orig.). 1994. pap. 14.95 (*0-8192-1571-6*) Morehouse Pub.

Seasons of the Spirit: The Archbishop of Canterbury at Home & Abroad. Robert A. Runcie. LC 83-1734. 272p. reprint ed. pap. 77.60 (*0-317-30160-8*, 2025342) Bks Demand.

***Seasons of the Spirit Dancing.** Demitra A. Syrtis. 34p. 1994. pap. text ed. 7.00 (*1-886352-09-7*) Crow Feather.

Seasons of the Sun: Celebrations, Festivals & Observances. Patricia Telesco. (Illus.). 288p. (Orig.). 1996. pap. 15.95 (*0-87728-872-0*) Weiser.

Seasons of the Vineyard: A Year of Celebration & Recipes from the Robert Mondavi Winery. Robert Mondavi et al. (Illus.). 224p. 1996. 40.00 (*0-684-80758-0*, S&S) S&S Trade.

***Seasons of the Whitetail.** John J. Ozoga. (Illus.). 608p. 1997. 99.50 (*1-57223-125-4*, 1254) Willow Creek Pr.

Seasons of the Wild: A Journey Through Our National Wildlife Refuges with John & Karen Hollingsworth. John Hollingsworth & Karen Hollingsworth. LC 94-61032. (Illus.). 64p. (Orig.). 1994. pap. 19.95 (*0-9636562-5-2*) Worm Pr.

Seasons of the Wild: A Year of Nature's Magic & Mysteries. Sy Montgomery. Ed. by Sandy Taylor. (Curious Naturalist Ser.). (Illus.). 152p. 1995. pap. 12.95 (*1-881527-90-5*) Chapters Pub.

Seasons of the Witch. Patricia Monaghan. (Illus.). 234p. (Orig.). 1992. pap. 11.95 (*1-878980-09-2*) Delphi IL.

Seasons of the Year: Poems. Frank Ebersole. 64p. 1983. pap. 5.00 (*0-941452-15-8*) Acheron Pr.

Seasons of Thomas Tebo. John Nagenda. (African Writers Ser.). 156p. (Orig.). (C). 1986. pap. 8.95 (*0-435-90824-3*, 90824) Heinemann.

Seasons of War: The Ordeal of a Confederate Community, 1861-1865. Daniel E. Sutherland. LC 95-18357. (Illus.). 400p. 1995. 30.00 (*0-02-874043-2*) Free Pr.

***Seasons of Womans Life.** Daniel Levinson. 1997. pap. 14.00 (*0-345-31174-4*) Ballantine.

Seasons of Women: An Anthology. Ed. by Gloria Norris. 480p. 1995. 27.50 (*0-393-03860-2*) Norton.

Seasons of Your Heart: Prayers & Reflections. Macrina Wiederkehr. LC 90-55776. 1991. pap. 11.00 (*0-06-069300-2*) Harper SF.

Seasons on the Farm. Ann L. Hansen. LC 96-11090. (Farm Ser.). (J). 1996. lib. bdg. 13.98 (*1-56239-624-2*) Abdo & Dghtrs.

Seasons on Whidbey: A Sampler of Recipes Celebrating Fall Winter Spring & Summer. Laura Moore & Deborah Skinner. LC 95-68281. (Illus.). 1995. pap. 13.95 (*0-9628766-1-5*) Saratoga Pubs.

Season's Premiere. Theatre Guild Members Staff. (Illus.). 456p. (Orig.). 1986. pap. 15.00 (*0-9614424-0-9*) Theatre Guild.

Seasons Remembered. Leisure Arts Staff. 1995. 24.95 (*0-942237-40-4*) Leisure AR.

Seasons Remembered, 4 vols., Set. Linda Shands. (Orig.). 1996. pap. 37.01 (*0-8308-8044-5*, 1930) InterVarsity.

Seasons Sewn: A Year in Patchwork. Ann W. Paul. LC 94-35358. (Illus.). 40p. (J). (gr. 3-6). 1996. 16.00 (*0-15-276918-8*, Browndeer Pr) HarBrace.

***Seasons to Be Cheerful: British Ice Hockey's Arena Era.** Liam Sluyter. (Illus.). 192p. 1997. 34.95 (*1-85158-817-5*, Pub. by Mnstream UK) Trafalgar.

Seasons to Celebrate: God's Children Celebrate the Church Year. Mary Albing. 64p. 1994. pap. 9.99 (*0-8066-2722-0*, 10-27220, Augsburg) Augsburg Fortress.

Seasons to Come. Ed. by Caroline Sullivan. 755p. 1995. 69.95 (*1-56167-261-0*) Nat Lib Poetry.

Seasons to Remember. C. Gowdy. pap. 5.98 (*0-8317-0043-2*) Smithmark.

***Seasons' Virtues.** Christine Tarantino. 24p. 1996. 4.95 (*1-887480-26-9*) Wrds Lght Intl.

Seaspeak Reference Manual: Recommendations for Maritime Communication, Principally by VHF Radio. Ed. by P. Weeks. (Essential English for Maritime Use Ser.). 160p. 1984. text ed. 39.00 (*0-08-031056-7*, Pergamon Pr) Elsevier.

Seaspeak Training Manual. Ed. by F. Weeks et al. (Essential English for Maritime Use Ser.). (Illus.). 180p. 1987. text ed. 19.50 (*0-08-031071-0*, Pub. by PPL UK); pap. text ed. 16.00 (*0-08-031555-0*, Pub. by PPL UK) Elsevier.

***Seaspell.** Bronwyn Williams. 1997. mass mkt. 5.99 (*0-451-40750-4*, Onyx) NAL-Dutton.

Seaspring. Gabriela Lobos. (Illus.). 112p. (Orig.). (J). (gr. 4-6). 1996. pap. 9.95 (*1-880284-19-7*) J Daniel.

Seaswept. Laura Halford. 416p. (Orig.). 1990. pap. 3.95 (*0-380-75736-2*) Avon.

Seat at the Table: An Insider's Guide for America's New Women Leaders. Patricia Harrison. LC 94-44759. 222p. 1995. 19.95 (*1-57101-013-0*) MasterMedia Pub.

Seat at the Table: An Insiders Guide for Americas New Women Leaders. Patricia Harrison. 1996. pap. 11.95 (*1-57101-042-4*) MasterMedia Pub.

Seat Behind the Coachman: Travellers in Ireland from 1800-1900. Diarmaid O. Muirithe. (Illus.). 209p. 1995. reprint ed. pap. 13.95 (*1-86079-000-3*, Pub. by R Wholesale Bks IE) Irish Bks Media.

Seat Belt Laws. Amoco Pathfinder Staff. 1992. pap. 2.25 (*0-671-84031-2*) S&S Trade.

Seat Belts: Index of Modern Information. Lynn P. Chenn. LC 88-47990. 150p. 1990. 44.50 (*1-55914-056-9*); pap. 39.50 (*1-55914-057-7*) ABBE Pubs Assn.

***Seat Belts & Other Devices to Reduce Injuries from Traffic Accidents: Report on a WHO Technical Group.** (Euro Reports & Studies Ser.: No. 40). 53p. 1981. pap. text ed. 4.00 (*92-890-1206-4*) World Health.

Seat in a Wild Place. Erik Brown. LC 81-15017. (Illus.). 128p. 1993. 8.95 (*0-87233-059-1*) Bauhan.

Seat of Soul. Gary Zukav. 1990. pap. 15.95 (*1-55927-091-8*) St Martin.

Seat of the Soul. Gary Zukav. 256p. 1990. pap. 12.00 (*0-671-69507-X*, Fireside) S&S Trade.

Seat System Comfort & Safety: Twenty-five Papers. 202p. 1993. 79.00 (*1-56091-348-7*, SP-963) Soc Auto Engineers.

Seat Weaving. C. Perry. 1940. pap. 6.00 (*0-02-665670-1*) Glencoe.

Seat Yourself: A Complete Guide to Twin Cities Arenas, Auditoriums & Theaters. 2nd ed. Marlys Mickelson. (Illus.). 76p. 1990. reprint ed. pap. 8.95 (*0-934860-75-0*) Adventure Pubns.

Seated in Hevenly Places. Richard Booker. 154p. 1992. 8.99 (*0-914903-73-X*) Destiny Image.

An Asterisk (*) at the beginning of an entry indicates that the title is appearing in BIP for the first time.

Seated Liberty Dollars, 1985. W. White. pap. 10.00 (0-685-10800-7) S J Durst.

Seated Liberty Dollars, 1985. limited ed. W. White. lib. bdg. 18.00 (0-942666-42-9) S J Durst.

Seating & Moving Through the Decades: A Literature Review of Seating & Mobility through 1992. 2nd ed. Jean A. Zollars. (C). 1993. pap. text ed. 29.95 (1-882632-03-6) PAX Pr.

SEATO: The Failure of an Alliance Strategy. Leszek Buszynski. 276p. 1983. 44.50 (9971-69-060-8, Pub. by Sgapore Univ SI) Coronet Bks.

Seaton Family, with Genealogy & Biography. O. A. Seaton. (Illus.). 441p. 1989. reprint ed. pap. 66.00 (0-8328-1055-X); reprint ed. lib. bdg. 74.00 (0-8328-1054-1) Higginson Bk Co.

Seats & Votes: The Effects & Determinants of Electoral Systems. Rein Taagepera & Matthew Shugart. LC 88-26088. 288p. (C). 1989. text ed. 40.00 (0-300-04319-8) Yale U Pr.

Seats & Votes: The Effects & Determinants of Electoral Systems. Rein Taagepera & Matthew S. Shugart. 310p. (C). 1991. reprint ed. pap. text ed. 19.00 (0-300-05077-1) Yale U Pr.

Seats of the Mighty. Gilbert Parker. 1976. lib. bdg. 16.75 (0-89968-077-1, Lghtyr Pr) Buccaneer Bks.

Seattle. Gousha, H. M., Editors. 1995. pap. 2.95 (0-671-55356-9, H M Gousha) P-H Gen Ref & Trav.

Seattle. Nancy Loewen. (Great Cities of the U. S. A. Ser.). (Illus.). (YA). (gr. 5 up). 1989. 11.95 (0-685-58592-1); lib. bdg. 15.94 (0-86592-545-3) Rourke Corp.

Seattle. Karin Snelson. LC 91-38232. (Downtown America Ser.). (Illus.). 64p. (J). (gr. 4 up). 1992. lib. bdg. 13.95 (0-87518-509-6, Dillon Silver Burdett) Silver Burdett Pr.

*Seattle. 3rd ed. Access Guides Staff. (Access Travel Guides Ser.). 224p. 1997. pap. 18.50 (0-06-277198-1, Access NY) HarpC.

*Seattle: Pacific Gem. Jim French & Teresa Taylor. LC 97-26166. (Urban Tapestry Ser.). (Illus.). 1997. 44.95 (1-881096-45-9) Towery Pub.

Seattle - Tacoma, WA. (Streetfinder Ser.). (Illus.). 1995. pap. 25.95 (0-528-91374-3) Rand McNally.

Seattle & Eastside Private School Guide. Ed. by Marie Bonfils. 480p. 1995. pap. 29.95 (0-9631102-3-3) Cap Hill WA.

Seattle & Its People. Pace International Research, Inc. Staff. (AAA Video Ser.). (Illus.). 135p. 1984. text ed. 8.95 (0-89209-048-0); pap. text ed. 4.25 (0-89209-078-2); audio 3.25 (0-89209-079-0); vhs 60.00 (0-89209-045-6) Pace Intl Res.

*Seattle Area Sport Climbs. Jeff Smoot. (Classic Rock Climbs Ser.). (Illus.). (Orig.). 1997. pap. 10.95 (1-57540-045-6) Chockstone Pr.

Seattle Art Museum Downtown. Seattle Art Museum Staff. (Illus.). 16p. (Orig.). 1992. pap. 4.95 (0-932216-39-0) Seattle Art.

Seattle Best Places: The Most Discriminating Guide to Seattle's Restaurants, Shops, Hotels, Nightlife, Arts, Sights, & Outings. 7th rev. ed. Ed. by Nancy Leson & Stephanie Irving. LC 95-22919. (Best Places Guidebooks Ser.). 448p. 1996. pap. 16.95 (1-57061-055-X) Sasquatch Bks.

Seattle Center. Loralie Cecotti. (Color-A-Story Ser.). (Illus.). 24p. (Orig.). (J). (gr. 1-4). 1983. pap. 2.75 (0-933992-30-0) Coffee Break.

Seattle Cheap Eats: Three Hundred Terrific Bargain Eateries. 5th rev. ed. Ed. by Kathryn Robinson & Stephanie Irving. (Illus.). 208p. 1993. pap. 9.95 (0-912365-72-2) Sasquatch Bks.

Seattle Children's Theatre: Six Plays for Young Actors. Ed. by Marisa Smith. LC 96-18740. (Young Actors Ser.). 256p. 1996. 16.95 (1-57525-008-X) Smith & Kraus.

*Seattle Citizens Against Freeways, 1968-1980: Fighting Fiercely & Winning Sometimes. Margaret C. Tunks. LC 96-90929. (Illus.). 278p. (Orig.). 1997. pap. write for info. (1-57502-387-3, P01223) Morris Pubng.

*Seattle, City by the Sound. L. E. Bragg. (Illus.). 32p. (J). (gr. k-6). 1997. 15.95 (0-9656755-0-5) East Seattle Pub.

Seattle Classic Cookbook. Seattle Junior League Staff. 320p. 1989. pap. 15.95 (0-89815-342-5) Ten Speed Pr.

Seattle Cookbook. John Owen. (Illus.). 105p. 1993. pap. 14.95 (0-9624559-1-1) Seattle Post.

Seattle Dog Lover's Companion: The Inside Scoop on Where to Take Your Dog in the Seattle Area, Including Victoria & Vancouver. Steve Giordano. (Dog Lover's Companion Ser.). (Illus.). 256p. (Orig.). 1996. pap. 17.95 (1-57354-002-1) Foghorn Pr.

Seattle Emergency Espresso: The Insider's Guide to Neighborhood Coffee Spots. Heather D. Barbieri. LC 92-20627. (Illus.). 180p. (Orig.). 1992. pap. 9.95 (0-88240-399-0) Alaska Northwest.

Seattle Engagement Calendar, 1991. (Illus.). 12p. (Orig.). 1991. pap. 3.50 (1-878395-11-4) Smith-Western.

Seattle Guidebook. 9th ed. Archie Satterfield. LC 93-43214. (Illus.). 256p. 1994. pap. 12.95 (1-56440-402-1) Globe Pequot.

*Seattle Guidebook. 10th rev. ed. Archie Satterfield. LC 97-2140. (Illus.). 256p. 1997. pap. 12.95 (0-7627-0074-2) Globe Pequot.

Seattle in the Eighteen Eighties. David Buerge & Stuart R. Grover. (Illus.). 128p. (Orig.). 1986. pap. 11.95 (0-939806-06-1) Hist Soc Seattle.

Seattle JOA & Newspaper Preservation. Tim A. Pilgrim. LC 97-15997. (Illus.). 288p. 1997. pap. 39.50 (1-56750-050-1); text ed. 78.50 (0-89391-886-5) Ablex Pub.

*Seattle Jobbank. Date not set. pap. 16.95 (1-55850-791-4) Adams Media.

Seattle Jobbank, 1996. Adams Publishing Staff. 1995. pap. text ed. 15.95 (1-55850-570-9) Adams Media.

Seattle Jobbank, 1997. Adams Publishing Staff. 1996. pap. text ed. 15.95 (1-55850-683-7) Adams Media.

Seattle Joke Book III. Elliot Maxx. (Illus.). 128p. (Orig.). 1995. pap. 8.95 (0-935735-06-2) Fiasco Productions.

Seattle Laughs: Cartoonists Look at Seattle. Ed. by Shary Flenniken. (Illus.). 112p. (Orig.). 1994. pap. 11.95 (0-930180-13-5) Homestead Bk.

Seattle Leschi Diary. Wade C. Vaughan. (Illus.). 281p. (Orig.). pap. write for info. (0-9608254-0-1) Leschi Improve.

Seattle Lite: Lite Recipes from Seattle's Top Restaurants. Catherine G. Crabtree. Ed. by Michael Grady. (Cookbook Ser.). (Illus.). 150p. (Orig.). 1992. pap. 12.95 (0-937070-11-4) Crabtree.

Seattle Mariners. Michael E. Goodman. (Baseball: The Great American Game Ser.). 48p. (J). (gr. 4-10). 1992. lib. bdg. 14.95 (0-88682-452-4) Creative Ed.

*Seattle Mariners. Michael E. Goodman. LC 97-6342. (Baseball Ser.). (Illus.). 32p. (YA). (gr. 4 up). 1998. lib. bdg. 15.95 (0-88682-925-9) Creative Ed.

Seattle Mariners. Paul Joseph. (America's Game Ser.). (J). 1997. lib. bdg. 15.95 (1-56239-680-3) Abdo & Dghtrs.

Seattle Menu Guide 1993-94 Edition: Menues from Puget Sounds Finest Restaurants Also Includes Banquet Facilities, Caterers, Bed & Breakfast Inns. Ed. by Michael Hablutzel. 180p. (Orig.). 1993. per. 9.95 (0-9636848-0-9) Sndgraphics.

*Seattle Metro Business Directory 1997. rev. ed. American Business Directories Staff. 3904p. 1997. boxed 450.00 (1-56105-979-X) Am Busn Direct.

Seattle Now & Then. Paul Dorpat. (Illus.). 288p. (Orig.). 1984. 25.00 (0-9614357-0-4); pap. 12.95 (0-9614357-1-2) Tartu Pubns.

Seattle Now & Then, Vol. 2. Paul Dorpat. 240p. (Orig.). 1987. 19.95 (0-9614357-3-9); pap. 12.95 (0-9614357-2-0) Tartu Pubns.

Seattle on Film. Randy Hodgins & Steve McLellan. (Illus.). 144p. (Orig.). 1995. pap. 12.95 (0-9648184-1-8) TNPP.

Seattle Pacific University: A Growing Vision. Donald McNichols. LC 89-10574. (Illus.). 288p. 1989. pap. text ed. 19.95 (0-9602642-3-X); lib. bdg. 19.95 (0-9602642-2-1) Seattle Pac Univ.

Seattle, Past to Present. Roger Sale. LC 76-7798. (Illus.). 294p. 1976. pap. 18.95 (0-295-95615-1) U of Wash Pr.

Seattle Picnics: Favorite Sites, Seasonal Menus, & 100 Recipes. Barbara H. Sullivan. LC 91-8398. 304p. (Orig.). 1991. pap. 10.95 (0-88240-408-3) Alaska Northwest.

Seattle Pilots Story. Carson Van Lindt. (Illus.). 220p. (Orig.). 1993. pap. text ed. 12.95 (0-9632595-5-5) Marabou Pub.

*Seattle Poems. J. Glenn Evans. Ed. by Kay Stewart. (Illus.). 28p. (Orig.). 1996. pap. 6.95 (1-877882-21-6) SCW Pubns.

*Seattle Psychotherapy Language Analysis Schema. Peter E. Maxim. 66p. 1986. ring bd., pap. 24.95 (0-295-96459-6) U of Wash Pr.

*Seattle Sacred Spaces & other Places to Heal the Earth. B. Lees. 1996. pap. 11.95 (0-89716-668-X) P B Pubng.

Seattle Scene: With Notes & Tablature. 80p. 1994. otabind 18.95 (0-7935-2087-8, 00694870) H Leonard.

Seattle Seahawks. Bob Italia. LC 95-40361. (Inside the NFL Ser.). (J). 1996. lib. bdg. 15.98 (1-56239-531-9) Abdo & Dghtrs.

Seattle Seahawks. Richard Rambeck. (NFL Today Ser.). (J). (gr. 4 up). 1991. lib. bdg. 14.95 (0-88682-384-6) Creative Ed.

Seattle Seahawks. 2nd rev. ed. Michael Goodman. (NFL Today Ser.). (Illus.). 32p. (J). (gr. 4-8). 1996. lib. bdg. 14.95 (0-88682-805-8) Creative Ed.

Seattle Sidewalk: The Restaurant Finder: An Offline Companion to www.seattle.sidewalk.com. LC 97-10082. 288p. (Orig.). 1997. pap. 12.95 (1-57061-080-0) Sasquatch Bks.

Seattle Sourcebook: A Shadowrun Sourcebook. FASA Staff. (Shadowrun Ser.). (Illus.). 128p. 1989. pap. 18.00 (1-55560-111-1, 7201) FASA Corp.

Seattle Space Needle. Craig A. Doherty & Katherine M. Doherty. Ed. by Nicole Bowman. LC 95-39085. (Building America Ser.). (Illus.). 48p. (J). (gr. 3-7). 1996. lib. bdg. 15.95 (1-56711-114-9) Blackbirch.

Seattle Sport Source, 1988-1989. Ed. by Stan Shermer et al. (Illus.). 288p. (Orig.). 1988. pap. 10.00 (0-685-44315-9) Sport Source.

Seattle Style Guide: Cultural Imperatives of the Hot Seattle Scene. Jeffrey Rands. 125p. (Orig.). 1993. pap. 9.95 (0-9636753-0-3) J Rands.

Seattle Subtext. Paul Berger. LC 83-26047. (Illus.). 52p. 1984. pap. 15.00 (0-941104-09-5) Real Comet.

Seattle Subtext. Paul Berger. (Artist's Bks.). 52p. 1984. 30.00 (0-89822-037-8) Visual Studies.

*Seattle SuperSonics. Michael E. Goodman. LC 96-52963. (NBA Today Ser.). (J). 1997. lib. bdg. 15.95 (0-88682-891-0) Creative Ed.

*Seattle Supersonics. Bob Italia. LC 96-52412. (Inside the NBA Ser.). (J). 1997. write for info. (1-56239-774-5) Abdo & Dghtrs.

Seattle Supersonics. rev. ed. Michael E. Goodman. (NBA Today Ser.). (Illus.). 32p. (J). (gr. 4 up). 1993. lib. bdg. 14.95 (0-88682-543-1) Creative Ed.

Seattle Survival Guide II: The Essential Handbook for City Living. 2nd rev. ed. Theresa Morrow. (Illus.). 420p. 1993. pap. 17.95 (0-912365-84-6) Sasquatch Bks.

Seattle Survival Guide III: The Essential Handbook for Urban Living. 3rd ed. Theresa Morrow. LC 96-19980. (Illus.). 384p. (Orig.). 1996. reprint ed. pap. 19.95 (1-57061-089-4) Sasquatch Bks.

Seattle, Tacoma & the Puget Sound Region. Cindy McIntyre. (Illus.). 128p. 1988. write for info. (0-942381-00-9) Sammamish Pr.

Seattle-Tacoma Health Care Choices: The Families U. S. A. Guide to Quality & Cost. Marc S. Miller. (Illus.). 240p. (Orig.). 1996. pap. 10.95 (0-9617893-1-X) Fam USA Found.

Seattle, the City We're In: A Citizen's Guide to Seattle City Government. League of Women Voters of Seattle Staff. 70p. 1996. pap. text ed. 9.00 (0-9648851-1-5) LOWVS.

Seattle Uncovered. JoAnn Roe. LC 95-20834. 304p. 1995. pap. 16.95 (1-55622-394-3, Seaside Pr) Wordware Pub.

Seattle University, a Century of Jesuit Education. Walt Crowley. (Illus.). 128p. 1991. 19.91 (0-9630691-0-1) Seattle Univ.

Seattle, WA. (Streetfinder Ser.). (Illus.). 1995. pap. 15.95 (0-528-91370-0) Rand McNally.

Seattle Women: A Legacy of Community Development. Mildred Andrews. LC 84-60808. 64p. 1984. pap. 4.50 (0-9615533-0-8) YWCA WA.

Seattle, 1900-1920: From Boomtown, Urban Turbulence, to Restoration. Richard C. Berner. LC 91-74159. (Seattle in the Twentieth Century Ser.: Vol. 1). (Illus.). 398p. (Orig.). 1991. pap. 24.95 (0-9629889-0-1) Charles Pr.

Seattle, 1921-1940: From Boom to Bust. Richard C. Berner. (Seattle in the Twentieth Century Ser.: Vol. 2). 576p. (Orig.). 1992. pap. 25.95 (0-9629889-1-X) Charles Pr.

Seattle's Black Victorians: Eighteen Fifty-Two to Nineteen One. Esther H. Mumford. (Illus.). 253p. (Orig.). 1980. pap. 7.95 (0-9605670-0-3) Ananse Pr.

Seattle's Gastronomic Shopper. Luise Brame. (Illus.). 179p. (Orig.). 1981. pap. 6.95 (0-932998-02-X) Reynard Hse.

*Seattle's Public Places Named for Black People. Mary Henry. (Illus.). 96p. (Orig.). 1997. pap. write for info. (0-89716-762-7) P B Pubng.

Seatwork Relief: Board Activities for Primary Teachers. Bonita S. Marciniak. 122p. 1991. pap. 15.95 (0-9630787-0-4) Scal-Mar.

Seaver Family - Genealogy of Robert Seaver of Roxbury, MA, & Some Descendants. Wm. B. Trask. 52p. 1995. reprint ed. pap. 11.00 (0-8328-4564-7); reprint ed. lib. bdg. 21.00 (0-8328-4563-9) Higginson Bk Co.

Seaview. Toby Olson. LC 88-22359. 288p. 1982. 9.95 (0-8112-0828-1) New Directions.

*Seaview Review. Cindy Iutzi. (Illus.). 16p. (Orig.). (J). 1996. pap. 15.95 (1-56490-014-2) G Grimm Assocs.

Seavy Seagull & the Friendship Sloop Race. 2nd ed. Rosemary S. Kelley. (Illus.). 39p. (J). (ps). 1985. pap. 5.95 (0-9616905-0-X) R S Kelley.

Seaward. Betty Coon. 36p. (Orig.). 1978. pap. 5.95 (0-917658-08-6) BPW & P.

Seaward. Susan Cooper. LC 83-7055. 180p. (YA). (gr. 5 up). 1983. lib. bdg. 16.00 (0-689-50275-3, McElderry) S&S Childrens.

Seaward. Brad Leithauser. LC 92-31047. 1993. 25.00 (0-685-61666-5) Knopf.

Seaward. Brad Leithauser. LC 92-31047. (Borzoi Reader Ser). 1993. 23.00 (0-394-58587-9) Knopf.

Seaward. Susan Cooper. LC 86-23234. 180p. (YA). (gr. 5 up). 1987. reprint ed. pap. 3.95 (0-02-042190-7) Macmillan.

Seaward: An Elegy. Richard Hovey. (Notable American Authors Ser.). 1992. reprint ed. lib. bdg. 75.00 (0-7812-3190-6) Rprt Serv.

Seawater. Open University Team Staff. (Open University Oceanography Ser.). 1989. pap. text ed. 11.75 (0-08-036931-6, Pergamon Pr) Elsevier.

Seawater: Its Composition, Properties & Behavior. 2nd ed. Open University Team Staff. (Illus.). 166p. 1995. pap. 34.95 (0-08-042518-6, Prgamon Press) Buttrwrth-Heinemann.

Seawater Aquariums. Stephen H. Spotte. LC 79-11038. 413p. 1979. text ed. 89.95 (0-471-05665-0) Wiley.

*Seaway Era Shipwrecks. Skip Gillham. (Great Lakes Marine History Ser.). (Illus.). 130p. 1994. pap. 16.95 (0-9697606-0-4, Pub. by Riverbank Trade CN) Partners Pubs Grp.

*Seaway Trail Guidebook to the War of 1812. Patrick Wilder. (Illus.). 96p. 1987. pap. 4.95 (0-614-26394-8) Purple Mnt Pr.

*Seaway Trail Lighthouses. 76p. pap. 2.95 (0-614-26448-0) Purple Mnt Pr.

*Seaway Trail Rocks & Landscapes. (Illus.). 76p. pap. 4.95 (0-614-26446-4) Purple Mnt Pr.

*Seaway Trail Wildguide to Natural History. Donald D. Cox. Ed. by Kara L. Dunn. LC 96-69011. (Illus.). 178p. (Orig.). 1996. pap. 7.95 (0-943689-04-X) Seaway Trail Inc.

Seaweed & Plant Growth. T. L. Senn. (Illus.). 192p. (Orig.). 1987. pap. write for info. (0-939241-01-3) Faith Print.

Seaweed Biogeography & Ecophysiology. Klaus Luning et al. LC 89-22633. 527p. 1990. text ed. 120.00 (0-471-62434-9) Wiley.

Seaweed Book: How to Find & Have Fun with Seaweed. Rose Treat. LC 95-34391. (Illus.). (J). (gr. 3-7). 1995. pap. 5.95 (1-887734-00-7) Star Brght Bks.

Seaweed Ecology & Physiology. Christopher S. Lobban & Paul J. Harrison. LC 93-21306. (Illus.). 416p. (C). 1994. text ed. 75.00 (0-521-40334-0) Cambridge U Pr.

Seaweed Flora of the Maritimes: One: Rhodophyta - the Red Algae. C. J. Bird & J. L. McLachlan. (Illus.). 177p. 1992. 90.00 (0-948737-18-2, Pub. by Biopress UK) Balogh.

Seaweed in Agriculture & Horticulture. 3rd ed. W. A. Stephenson. Ed. by Bargyla & Gylver Rateaver. LC 74-12812. (Conservation Gardening & Farming Ser.: Ser. C). (C). 1974. reprint ed. pap. 20.00 (0-9600698-3-6) Rateavers.

Seaweed Soup. Merridy C. Shinn. 40p. 1993. 20.00 (0-9637440-0-3) Hedgehog WA.

Seaweeds. 2nd ed. Isabella A. Abbott et al. (Pictured Key Nature Ser.). 152p. (C). 1978. spiral bd. write for info. (0-697-04892-6) Wm C Brown Pubs.

Seaweeds: A Color-Coded, Illustrated Guide to Common Marine Plants of the East Coast of the United States. Charles J. Hillson. LC 76-42192. (Keystone Bks.). 1977. 30.00 (0-271-01239-0); pap. 14.95 (0-271-01247-1) Pa St U Pr.

Seaweeds: A Story Samphlet & Activity Pages. Story Time Stories That Rhyme Staff. (Story Samphlet Edition Ser.). (Illus.). 17p. (J). (gr. 4-7). 1992. 9.95 (1-56820-007-2) Story Time.

Seaweeds of Cape Cod & the Islands. John M. Kingsbury. LC 69-15903. (Illus.). 1969. 24.50 (0-85699-009-4) Chatham Pr.

*Seaweeds of New Zealand: An Illustrated Guide. Nancy M. Adams. (Illus.). 360p. (C). 1994. 79.95 (0-908812-21-3, Pub. by Canterbury Univ NZ) Aubrey Bks.

Seaweeds of Singapore. Teo L. Wei & Wee Y. Chin. 130p. (Orig.). 1983. pap. 24.00 (9971-69-075-6, Pub. by Sgapore Univ SI) Coronet Bks.

Seaweeds of the Southeastern United States: Cape Hatteras to Cape Canaveral. Craig W. Schneider & Richard B. Searles. LC 90-42415. (Illus.). 569p. 1991. text ed. 49.95 (0-8223-1101-1) Duke.

Seawoman's Handbook. Shirley Herd. LC 89-35465. (Illus.). 1989. 21.95 (0-930006-03-8) S Deal Assoc.

Sebaceous Glands see Advances in Biology of Skin

Sebago Lakes Region, ME. J. Barnes & D. Barnes. (Images of America Ser.). 1996. pap. 16.99 (0-7524-0248-X, Arcdia) Chalford.

Sebastian. Vanessa Julian-Ottie. (Illus.). 28p. (J). 1995. 12.95 (0-7892-0069-4, Abbeville Kids) Abbeville Pr.

Sebastian Brant's "the Ship of Fools" in Critical Perspective 1800-1991. John Van Cleve. LC 92-45624. (LCGERM Ser.). x, 118p. 1993. 45.00 (1-879751-40-2) Camden Hse.

Sebastian Coe - Born to Run: A Life in Athletics. David Miller. (Illus.). 272p. 1993. pap. 19.95 (1-85793-091-6, Pub. by Pavilion UK) Trafalgar.

Sebastian (from the Little Mermaid) (Piano-Vocal Ser.). 64p. (Orig.). 1991. pap. 7.95 (0-7935-0422-8, 00490559) H Leonard.

Sebastian Lives in a Hat. Thelma Catterwell. (Illus.). 32p. (J). (ps-1). 1990. 13.95 (0-916291-30-8) Kane-Miller Bk.

Sebastian (Super Sleuth) & the Baffling Bigfoot. Mary B. Christian. LC 89-13049. (Sebastian Super Sleuth Ser.). (Illus.). 64p. (J). (gr. 2-6). 1990. lib. bdg. 11.95 (0-02-718215-0, Mac Bks Young Read) S&S Childrens.

Sebastian (Super Sleuth) & the Bone to Pick Mystery. Mary B. Christian. LC 83-5406. (Sebastian Barth Super Sleuth Mystery Ser.). (Illus.). 64p. (J). (gr. 2-5). 1983. lib. bdg. 12.00 (0-02-718440-4, Mac Bks Young Read) S&S Childrens.

Sebastian (Super Sleuth) & the Copycat Crime. Mary B. Christian. LC 93-7038. (Sebastian Super Sleuth Ser.). (Illus.). 64p. (J). (gr. 2-6). 1993. lib. bdg. 13.00 (0-02-718211-8, Mac Bks Young Read) S&S Childrens.

Sebastian (Super Sleuth) & the Crummy Yummies Caper. large type ed. Mary B. Christian. (Illus.). 1993. 17.50 (0-614-09853-X, L-34094-00) Am Printing Hse.

Sebastian (Super Sleuth) & the Flying Elephant. Mary B. Christian. LC 94-14434. (Sebastian, Super-Sleuth Ser.). (Illus.). (J). 1994. text ed. 13.00 (0-02-718252-5) Macmillan.

Sebastian (Super Sleuth) & the Impossible Crime. Mary B. Christian. LC 91-28633. (Sebastian Super Sleuth Ser.). (Illus.). 64p. (J). (gr. 2-6). 1992. lib. bdg. 11.95 (0-02-718435-8, Mac Bks Young Read) S&S Childrens.

Sebastian (Super Sleuth) & the Time Capsule Caper. Mary B. Christian. LC 88-29295. (Sebastian Super Sleuth Ser.). (Illus.). 64p. (J). (gr. 2-6). 1989. lib. bdg. 10.95 (0-02-718570-2, Mac Bks Young Read) S&S Childrens.

Sebastian the Star. Diane Ampeliotis. LC 94-90268. (Illus.). 64p. (Orig.). (J). 1996. pap. 6.00 (1-56002-483-6, Univ Edtns) Aegina Pr.

Sebastian Virdung: Musica Getutscht 1511 see Publikation Aelterer Praktischer und Theoretischer Musikwerke

*Sebastiano Serlio on Architecture. Sebastiano Serlio. Ed. by Vaughan Hart & Peter Hicks. Tr. by Peter Hicks. (Illus.). 528p. 1996. 55.00 (0-300-06286-9) Yale U Pr.

*Sebastian's Good Idea. (Ready Readers Stage 2 Ser.). (Illus.). 32p. (J). (gr. 2-4). 1995. pap. write for info. (1-56144-749-8, Honey Bear Bks) Modern Pub NYC.

Sebastian's Story: Disney's The Little Mermaid. J. Colby. (Golden Super Shape Bks.). (Illus.). 24p. (J). (ps-3). 1992. 1.95 (0-307-10020-0, 10020, Golden Books) Western Pub.

Sebastian's Trumpet. Miko Imai. LC 94-47191. (J). (ps up). 1995. 15.99 (1-56402-359-1) Candlewick Pr.

Sebastien Live Cat Chat Vive. Coco Gordon & Claude Maillard. (Intimate Ser.: No. 6). (Illus.). 60p. (Orig.). 1987. 125.00 (0-943375-05-3) W Space.

Sebastien Mercier. Leon Beclard. x, 810p. 1982. reprint ed. 130.00 (3-487-07262-9) G Olms Pubs.

Sebastopol Sketches. Leo Tolstoy. Tr. by David McDuff. (Classics Ser.). 176p. 1986. pap. 8.95 (0-14-044468-8, Penguin Classics) Viking Penguin.

Sebec Lake, ME. D. Blanchard. (Images of America Ser.). 128p. 1997. pap. 16.99 (0-7524-0273-0, Arcdia) Chalford.

Sebian Patericon, Vol. 1: Saints of the Serbian Orthodox Church. Daniel Rogich. Ed. by Abbot Herman. LC 94-64911. (Illus.). 330p. (Orig.). 1994. pap. 15.00 (0-938635-75-1) St Herman Pr.

Sebnitzer Kunsstblume: Die Geschichte Eines Handwerks im Zeichen der Mode. Manfred Schober. 64p. (GER.). 1994. pap. text ed. 12.00 (3-364-00302-5) Gordon & Breach.

*Sebring: The Official History of America's Great Sports Car Race. Ken Breslauer. Ed. by Dan Gurney. (Illus.). 288p. 1996. 79.95 (0-9649722-0-4) D Bull.

An Asterisk (*) at the beginning of an entry indicates that the title is appearing in BIP for the first time.

Sebring 12-Hour Race 1970 Photo Archive. Ed. by Robert C. Auten. LC 94-77482. (Photo Archive Ser.). (Illus.). 144p. 1994. pap. 29.95 (*1-882256-20-4*) Iconografix.

Sebugugugu the Glutton: A Bantu Tale from Ruanda, Africa. Verna Aardema & Nancy Clouse. (Illus.). 32p. (J). (gr. 2-4). 1993. 14.95 (*0-86543-377-1*) Africa World.

SEC Accounting & Reporting Manual, 2 vols. Robert F. Richter. ring bd. 340.00 (*0-685-69600-6*, SAPM) Warren Gorham & Lamont.

SEC Accounting & Reporting Update Service. Allan B. Afterman. 330.00 (*0-685-69603-0*, SARU) Warren Gorham & Lamont.

SEC Accounting Report. 215.00 (*0-685-69602-2*, SECR) Warren Gorham & Lamont.

SEC & Capital Market Regulation: The Politics of Expertise. Anne M. Khademian. LC 92-11577. (Series in Policy & Institutional Studies). 240p. (C). 1992. text ed. 49.95 (*0-8229-3725-5*) U of Pittsburgh Pr.

SEC & Social Policy Shareholder Resolutions in the 1990s. Carolyn Mathiasen. 100p. (Orig.). 1994. pap. 25.00 (*1-879775-22-0*) IRRC Inc DC.

SEC & the Future of Finance. Joel Seligman. LC 84-18017. 396p. 1985. text ed. 65.00 (*0-275-91757-6*, C1757, Praeger Pubs) Greenwood.

SEC Financial Reporting: Annual Reports to Shareholders. 2nd ed. Robert K. Herdman & Robert D. Neary. LC 82-177383. (Form 10-K Quarterly Financial Reporting Ser.). 1983. Updates. ring bd. write for info. (*0-8205-1625-2*) Bender.

SEC Guide, 1991, Vol. I. 97th ed. Earl C. Keller & Jerry L. Arnold. 1800p. 1997. pap. text ed. 50.00 (*0-15-602360-1*, Miller Acct Pubns) HarBrace.

SEC Guide, 1991, Vol. II. 97th ed. Earl C. Keller & Jerry L. Arnold. 1200p. 1997. pap. text ed. 50.00 (*0-15-602361-X*, Miller Acct Pubns) HarBrace.

SEC Guidelines: Rules & Regulations. 1993. pap. 80.00 (*0-685-69601-4*, SECG) Warren Gorham & Lamont.

SEC Guidelines, Rules & Regulations. Prentice Hall Editorial Staff. 590p. 1989. pap. text ed. 22.95 (*0-685-21947-X*, Busn) P-H.

***SEC Handbook: Rules & Forms for Financial Statements & Related Disclosures.** CCH Editorial Staff. Ed. by Carlos Tavares. 1048p. 1996. pap. text ed. 42.00 (*0-8080-0132-9*) Commerce.

SEC Handbook: Rules & Forms for Financial Statements & Related Disclosures. 3rd ed. 936p. 1992. pap. 35.00 (*0-685-67029-5*, 5499) Commerce.

***SEC Handbook, As of November 1996 - Rules & Forms for Financial Statements & Related Disclosures.** 7th ed. 1024p. 1996. pap. 42.00 (*0-614-26814-1*, 13196BLS02) Commerce.

SEC Register, Vol. 8. 3rd ed. Loss. 1991. 147.50 (*0-316-53380-7*) Little.

SEC Register, Vol. 9. 3rd ed. Loss. 1992. 147.50 (*0-316-53401-3*) Little.

SEC Register, Vol. 10. Loss. 1993. 147.50 (*0-316-53407-2*) Little.

SEC Register, Vol. 11. Loss. 1993. 147.50 (*0-316-53408-0*) Little.

SEC Regulation of Public Companies. Allan B. Afterman. LC 94-11319. 1994. pap. text ed. 29.80 (*0-13-037185-8*) P-H Gen Ref & Trav.

SEC Section Sixteen Rules. 427p. 1991. pap. text ed. 17.50 (*0-685-49915-4*, B4-6971) PLI.

SEC Section Sixteen Rules: An Update. (Corporate Law & Practice Ser.). 410p. 1991. pap. text ed. 17.50 (*0-685-56885-7*, B4-6987) PLI.

SEC Speaks in 1995, 3 vols., Set. (Corporate Law & Practice Course Handbook, 1985-86 Ser.). 2264p. 1995. pap. 198.00 (*0-685-56896-2*, B4-7080) PLI.

SEC Speaks in 1996, 3 vols., Set. (Corporate Law & Practice Course Handbook, 1985-86 Ser.). Date not set. pap. 198.00 (*0-614-17207-1*, B4-7126) PLI.

***SEC Telephone Interpretation Manual.** Jim Hamilton & Andrew Turner. 280p. (Orig.). 1997. pap. text ed. 85.00 (*0-8080-0177-9*) Commerce.

S.E.C. Trading Suspensions. John S. Howe. LC 92-33005. (Government & the Economy Ser.). 136p. 1993. text ed. 15.00 (*0-8153-1227-X*) Garland.

***Secada.** Jeannette DeLisa. (Illus.). 56p. (Orig.). (YA). 1997. pap. text ed. 19.95 (*1-57623-986-1*, PF9717) Warner Brothers.

***Secada!** Himilce Novas. 1997. pap. 5.99 (*0-451-19083-1*, Sig) NAL-Dutton.

SECD Microprocessor: A Verification Case Study. Brian T. Graham. LC 92-12620. (Kluwer International Series in Engineering & Computer Science). 192p. (C). 1992. lib. bdg. 80.50 (*0-7923-9245-0*) Kluwer Ac.

Seceders. J. H. Philpot. 1970. pap. 4.50 (*0-85151-132-5*) Banner of Truth.

Secession: The Disruption of the American Republic, 1844-1861. James A. Rawley. LC 89-2505. (Anvil Ser.). 276p. (Orig.). 1990. pap. 14.50 (*0-89464-249-9*) Krieger.

Secession: The Legitimacy of Self-Determination. Lee C. Buchheit. LC 77-20687. (Illus.). 272p. reprint ed. pap. 77.60 (*0-8357-3741-1*, 2036467) Bks Demand.

Secession: The Morality of Political Divorce from Fort Sumter to Lithuania & Quebec. Allen Buchanan. 174p. (C). 1991. pap. text ed. 19.95 (*0-8133-1133-0*) Westview.

Secession & Reconstruction of Tennessee. James W. Fertig. LC 71-168019. reprint ed. 29.50 (*0-404-00046-0*) AMS Pr.

Secession, Coercion, & Civil War. John B. Jones. (Notable American Authors Ser.). 1992. reprint ed. lib. bdg. 75.00 (*0-7812-3523-5*) Rprt Serv.

Secession Debated: Georgia's Showdown in 1860. Ed. by William W. Freehling & Craig M. Simpson. 224p. 1992. pap. 11.95 (*0-19-507945-0*) OUP.

Secession, Doleantie, & Union: 1834-1892. Hendrik Bouma. Tr. by Theodore Plantinga from DUT. LC 95-31943. 302p. (Orig.). 1995. pap. 13.90 (*0-921100-36-1*) Inhtce Pubns.

Secession Movement in Alabama. Clarence P. Denman. LC 79-170695. (Black Heritage Library Collection). 1977. reprint ed. 22.95 (*0-8369-8885-X*) Ayer.

Secession Movement in the Middle Atlantic States. William C. Wright. LC 72-424. 274p. 1973. 36.50 (*0-8386-1152-4*) Fairleigh Dickinson.

Secession Movement in Virginia Eighteen Forty-Seven to Eighteen Sixty-One. Henry T. Shanks. LC 77-155611. reprint ed. 45.00 (*0-404-00211-0*) AMS Pr.

Secession of Quebec & the Future of Canada. Robert A. Young. 304p. 1995. 42.95 (*0-7735-1315-9*, Pub. by McGill CN); pap. 17.95 (*0-7735-1316-7*, Pub. by McGill CN) U of Toronto Pr.

***Secession of Quebec & the Future of Canada.** 2nd ed. Robert A. Young. 408p. 1997. pap. 22.95 (*0-7735-1530-5*, Pub. by McGill CN) U of Toronto Pr.

Secessionist Impulse: Alabama & Mississippi in 1860. William L. Barney. LC 73-16769. 388p. reprint ed. pap. 110.60 (*0-7837-1411-4*, 2041765) Bks Demand.

Sechs Stucke Nach Stucken: Zu den Bearbeitungen von Peter Hacks. Margo R. Bosker. LC 93-468. (Studies in Modern German Literature: Vol. 55). 176p. (GER.). (C). 1994. text ed. 46.95 (*0-8204-2059-X*) P Lang Pubng.

Sechzig Chansons zu vier Stimmen aus der ersten Haelfte des 16. Jahrhunderts. Ed. by Robert Eitner. (Publikation aelterer praktischer und theoretischer Musikwerke Ser.: Vol. XXIII). (FRE & GER.). 1966. reprint ed. lib. bdg. 75.00 (*0-8450-1723-3*) Broude.

***Secluded Scholars: Women's Education & Muslim Social Reform in Colonial India.** Gail Minault. (Illus.). 368p. 1997. 35.00 (*0-19-564190-6*) OUP.

Seclusion & Mental Health. A. Alty & T. Mason. 208p. 1994. 35.95 (*1-56593-303-6*, 0627) Singular Publishing.

***Secme Siirler: Selected Poems.** Fazil H. Daglarca. Tr. by Talat S. Halman. LC 69-12329. (Pitt Poetry Ser.). 200p. pap. 57.00 (*0-608-05086-5*, 2065640) Bks Demand.

Secolo di Attivita. Giuseppe Prezzolini. 160p. 1982. write for info. (*0-614-10136-0*) Am Inst Ital Stud.

Second. Kirby Clements. 63p. 1989. mass mkt. 3.95 (*0-917595-29-7*) Kingdom Pubs.

Second. L. E. Romaine. 48p. (Orig.). 1996. pap. 3.50 (*0-936728-64-7*) Word for Today.

Second. rev. ed. Kirby Clements. 100p. (C). pap. 7.95 (*0-917595-43-2*) Kingdom Pubs.

***Second Act.** Barrie. LC 97-11993. 1997. 23.00 (*0-684-83587-8*) S&S Trade.

***Second Act.** Collins. LC 97-2547. 1997. 24.95 (*0-312-16997-3*) St Martin.

Second Advent (6) Ed. by Chung H. Kwak. (Home Study Course). 50p. (Orig.). (C). 1980. pap. 4.00 (*0-910621-15-2*) HSA Pubns.

Second Afghan War: Casualty Roll, 1878-1880. Ed. by Anthony Farrington. 190p. (C). 1987. 175.00 (*0-317-90443-4*, Pub. by Picton UK) St Mut.

Second American Revolution. Whitehead. 1982. pap. text ed. 10.95 (*0-89191-572-9*) Cook.

Second American Revolution. 2nd ed. John W. Whitehead. LC 85-71894. (Illus.). 260p. 1985. pap. 11.99 (*0-89107-367-1*) Crossway Bks.

Second American Revolution: And Other Essays, 1976-1982. Gore Vidal. 1982. 15.00 (*0-394-52265-6*) Random.

***Second American Revolution: First Shots Fired.** Marc Ridenour. 170p. (Orig.). Date not set. pap. 7.95 (*0-929408-19-5*) Amer Eagle Pubns Inc.

Second & Third Epistles of John. Judith Lieu. 280p. 1987. 44.95 (*0-567-09443-X*, Pub. by T & T Clark UK) Bks Intl VA.

Second Anglo-Boer War. Edwin Herbert. (Wargaming in History Ser.). (Illus.). 96p. (C). 1990. reprint ed. lib. bdg. 27.00 (*0-8095-7578-7*) Borgo Pr.

Second Annual ADR - Alternative Dispute Resolution Directory. 1991. 30.00 (*0-685-49173-0*) Graduate Group.

Second Annual Adults with Disabilities: Information Directory. 1995. 27.50 (*0-614-01205-8*) Graduate Group.

Second Annual Bar Examination Fact Book. 1992. 27.50 (*0-685-39158-2*) Graduate Group.

Second Annual Binding Private Arbitration Panel (BPAP) Directory of Registered Arbitrators. 1991. 30.00 (*0-685-39166-3*) Graduate Group.

Second Annual Conference on Astronomical Data Analysis Software & Systems. Ed. by R. J. Hanisch et al. (ASP Conference Series Proceedings: Vol. 52). 622p. 1993. 28.00 (*0-937707-71-6*) Astron Soc Pacific.

Second Annual Digest of ADR Organizations in the United States, 1991. 1991. 30.00 (*0-685-45339-1*) Graduate Group.

Second Annual Digest of Law School Joint Degree Programs. 1995. 27.50 (*0-685-72044-6*) Graduate Group.

Second Annual Digest of Law School Transfer Policies, 1991. 1991. 27.50 (*0-685-45333-2*) Graduate Group.

Second Annual Digest of Transfer Policies at Major Colleges & Universities, 1990. 1990. 27.50 (*0-685-45334-0*) Graduate Group.

Second Annual Directory of Graduate Programs in Medicine. 1996. 27.50 (*0-685-68807-0*) Graduate Group.

Second Annual Directory of Programs for Gifted Children. 1996. 27.50 (*0-685-72040-3*) Graduate Group.

Second Annual Directory of Programs for the Gifted Child. 1996. 27.50 (*0-685-71249-4*) Graduate Group.

Second Annual Directory of Services for the Gifted Child. 1996. 27.50 (*0-685-54626-8*) Graduate Group.

Second Annual Directory of Summer School Programs at Home & Abroad for High School & College Students. 1996. 27.50 (*0-614-01204-X*) Graduate Group.

Second Annual Global Directory of Schools of Law. 1994. 27.50 (*0-685-68809-7*) Graduate Group.

Second Annual Interim Report on the Archaeological Investigations at the Miller Site (45FR5) on Strawberry Island (1977), a Late Prehistoric Village Near Burbank, Washington. fac. ed. Ed. by Gregory C. Cleveland. (Washington Archaeological Research Center Project Reports: No. 72). (Illus.). 183p. (C). 1978. reprint ed. pap. text ed. 16.25 (*1-55567-502-6*) Coyote Press.

Second Annual Internships for Law Students. 1997. 27.50 (*0-685-72042-X*) Graduate Group.

Second Annual Internships in Congress. 125p. (C). 1990. pap. 27.50 (*0-317-58993-8*) Graduate Group.

Second Annual Joint Degree Programs at Law Schools in the U. S. 1996. 27.50 (*0-614-03510-4*) Graduate Group.

Second Annual Judicial Clerkship Opportunities. 1994. 27.50 (*0-685-67191-7*) Graduate Group.

Second Annual Labor & Employment Law Institute: New Directions in the Labor & Employment Field. Ed. by William F. Dolson. viii, 424p. 1986. text ed. 57.50 (*0-8377-0550-9*) Rothman.

Second Annual Law School Summer School Programs at Home & Abroad, 1990. 1990. 27.50 (*0-685-45337-5*) Graduate Group.

Second Annual Law School Transfer Policies. 1991. 27.50 (*0-685-49178-1*) Graduate Group.

Second Annual National Elderly Explanatory Directory of Services (NEEDS) 1992. 27.50 (*0-685-54628-4*) Graduate Group.

***Second Annual Nicholas E. Davies CPR Recognition Symposium Proceedings.** Ed. by Elaine B. Steen. (Illus.). 123p. (Orig.). 1997. pap. 24.00 (*0-9649285-1-5*, D596-5) Comp-based Patient Rec.

Second Annual No Cost - Low Cost Directory of Law School Legal Clinics. 1995. 27.50 (*0-685-67193-3*) Graduate Group.

Second Annual No Cost & Low Cost Legal Services Offered by Law School Legal Clinics Directory. 1995. 27.50 (*0-685-72045-4*) Graduate Group.

Second Annual Opportunities for Minority Students at Law Schools in the U. S. 1996. 27.50 (*0-614-03509-0*) Graduate Group.

Second Annual Opportunities for Minority Students at Law Schools in the United States. 1995. 27.50 (*0-685-72046-2*) Graduate Group.

Second Annual Outstanding Resumes of Two-Year College & College Graduates. 125p. (C). 1990. pap. 27.50 (*0-317-58983-0*) Graduate Group.

Second Annual Report of the Ayacucho Project. Antoinette Nelken-Turner et al. (Reports of the Ayacucho Archaeological-Botanical Project Ser.). 1970. pap. text ed. 4.00 (*0-939312-16-6*) Peabody Found.

Second Annual Report of the Defense Secretaries, 1988: Advice to the Next Administration. 1990. 5.00 (*0-685-34505-X*) Southern Ctr Intl Stud.

Second Annual Resumes of Two Year College Students. 1991. 27.50 (*0-685-49172-2*) Graduate Group.

Second Annual State-by-State Digest of Alcohol & Drug Rehabilitation Programs. 1992. 27.50 (*0-685-54627-6*) Graduate Group.

Second Annual Technology Advancement Contractor Review Meeting Proceedings (Sept. 19-20, 1994) Compiled by South Coast Air Quality Management District Staff. (Electric Vehicle Information Ser.: Vol. 17). (Illus.). 404p. 1996. pap. 95.00 (*0-89934-273-6*, BT044); lib. bdg. 145.00 (*0-89934-274-4*, BT944) Bus Tech Bks.

Second Annual Transfer Policies of Major Colleges & Universities. 1992. 27.50 (*0-685-54629-2*) Graduate Group.

Second Annual Vacations with a Purpose. 1995. 27.50 (*0-614-01206-6*) Graduate Group.

Second Anthology of Atheism & Rationalism. Ed. by Gordon Stein. 442p. 1988. 31.95 (*0-87975-415-X*) Prometheus Bks.

Second Arkansas Union Cavalry. Desmond W. Allen. (Arkansas Union Regiment Ser.). 122p. 1987. pap. 15.00 (*0-941765-17-2*) Arkansas Res.

Second Arkansas Union Infantry. Desmond W. Allen. (Arkansas Union Regiment Ser.). 81p. 1987. pap. 15.00 (*0-941765-21-0*) Arkansas Res.

Second Armored Division Association. Turner Publishing Company Staff. LC 91-75223. (Illus.). 128p. 1991. 48.00 (*1-56311-035-0*) Turner Pub KY.

Second Asia Pacific Physics Conference: Proceedings, Bangalore, India, January 13-17, 1986, 2 vols., Set. Ed. by S. Chandrasekhar. 1232p. 1987. text ed. 156.00 (*9971-5-0268-2*) World Scientific Pub.

***Second Asian Fisheries Forum.** Ed. by R. Hirano & I. Hanyu. 991p. 1989. write for info. (*971-10-2279-6*, Pub. by ICLARM PH) Intl Spec Bk.

Second Asian Regional Workshop on Injectable Contraceptives. Ed. by Edwin B. McDaniel. (Illus.). 93p. 1982. pap. 5.00 (*0-942716-04-3*) World Neigh.

Second Assassination of Maurice Bishop. Steve Clark. 272p. 1989. reprint ed. pap. 10.00 (*0-87348-641-2*) Pathfinder NY.

Second Assault: Rape & Public Attitudes. Joyce E. Williams & Karen A. Holmes. LC 81-339. (Contributions in Women's Studies: No. 27). (Illus.). 256p. 1981. text ed. 59.95 (*0-313-22542-7*, WIA/, Greenwood Pr) Greenwood.

Second Assembling. Ed. by Richard Kostelanetz & Henry J. Korn. (Illus.). 180p. (Orig.). 1971. pap. 16.00 (*0-915066-01-7*) Assembling Pr.

Second Avenue Elevated in Manhattan. (Illus.). 72p. 29.95 (*0-934088-33-0*) NJ Intl Inc.

Second Avenue Rag. Allan Knee. (Phoenix Theatre Ser.). 1980. pap. 2.95 (*0-912262-71-0*) Proscenium.

Second Baldwin Government & the United States, 1924-1929: Attitudes & Diplomacy. B. J. McKercher. (International Studies). 272p. 1984. text ed. 69.95 (*0-521-25802-2*) Cambridge U Pr.

Second Banking Directive. 1991. pap. 170.00 (*0-406-00271-1*, U.K.) MICHIE.

Second Bar-Ilan Conference on the Physics of Disordered Systems: Special Issue of Philosophical Magazine, Pt. B, Vol. 56, No. 6. Ed. by Cyril M. Domb & C. Domb. 414p. 1988. pap. 34.00 (*0-85066-907-3*) Taylor & Francis.

Second Battle of Manassas. A. Wilson Greene. (Civil War Ser.). (Illus.). 56p. (Orig.). 1995. pap. 4.95 (*0-915992-85-X*) Eastern Acorn.

Second Battle of New Orleans: The Hundred-Year Struggle to Integrate the Schools. Liva Baker. LC 96-4158. (Illus.). 576p. 1996. 32.00 (*0-06-016808-0*, HarpT) HarpC.

Second Battle of Winchester. Charles S. Grunder & Brandon H. Beck. (Virginia Civil War Battles & Leaders Ser.). (Illus.). 108p. 1989. 19.95 (*0-930919-90-4*) H E Howard.

Second Ben Wicks Treasury. Ben Wicks. (Illus.). 208p. 1987. pap. 9.95 (*0-458-81150-5*) Genl Dist Srvs.

Second Bend in the River. Ann Rinaldi. LC 96-25938. (J). 1997. 15.95 (*0-590-74258-2*) Scholastic Inc.

Second Berkshire Authology, 2 vols., Set. Ed. by Dana Collins & Mark Canner. LC 74-78475. (Illus.). 230p. 1975. Boxed set. pap. 20.00 (*0-912846-10-0*) Bookstore Pr.

Second Berlin Crisis, 1958-1959. Kim I. Moermond & Jack Snyder. (Pew Case Studies in International Affairs). 50p. (C). 1988. pap. text ed. 3.50 (*1-56927-441-X*) Geo U Inst Dplmcy.

Second Best. Francine Pascal. (Sweet Valley Twins Ser.: No. 16). 112p. (J). 1988. pap. 3.25 (*0-553-15665-9*) Bantam.

Second Best Bed. Tim Kelly. 1970. pap. 3.25 (*0-8222-1005-3*) Dramatists Play.

Second Best Bed: Shakespeare's Will in a New Light. Joyce Rogers. LC 92-33763. (Contributions to the Study of World Literature Ser.: No. 48). 160p. 1993. text ed. 47.95 (*0-313-28831-3*, GM8831, Greenwood Pr) Greenwood.

***Second-Best Bride.** 1997. write for info. (*0-8341-1628-6*) Beacon Hill.

Second-Best Bride. Sara Wood. 1996. mass mkt. 3.50 (*0-373-11817-1*, 1-11817-3) Harlequin Bks.

Second-Best Bride. large type ed. Sara Wood. 288p. 1995. 21.50 (*0-263-14362-7*, Pub. by M & B UK) Ulverscroft.

Second-Best Friend. Beverly Lewis. (Holly's Heart Ser.: Vol. 6). 160p. (J). (gr. 6-9). 1994. pap. 6.99 (*0-310-43331-2*) Zondervan.

Second Best Girl. large type ed. Nina Tinsley. LC 93-14407. 1993. lib. bdg. 15.95 (*0-8161-5840-1*, GK Hall) Thorndike Pr.

Second-Best Husband. Penny Jordon. (Presents Ser.). 1993. pap. 2.89 (*0-373-11552-0*, 1-11552-6) Harlequin Bks.

***Second Best Moments in Chinese History: Second Best Moments in Chinese History.** Frank Kuppner. 144p. 1997. pap. 16.95 (*1-85754-310-6*, Pub. by Carcanet Pr UK) Paul & Co Pubs.

(Second) Best of Everything. David Reid & John Jerald. 1987. 14.95 (*0-15-179950-4*, Harvest Bks); pap. 6.95 (*0-685-19152-4*, Harvest Bks) HarBrace.

***Second-Best Wife.** Rebecca Winters. (Romance Ser.: No. 3460). 1997. mass mkt. 3.25 (*0-373-03460-1*, 1-03460-2) Harlequin Bks.

***Second-Best Wife.** large type ed. Rebecca Winters. (Mills & Boon Large Print Ser.). 288p. 1997. 22.50 (*0-263-15048-8*) Ulverscroft.

Second Bibliographic Guide to the History of Computing, Computers, & the Information Processing Industry. Compiled by James W. Cortada. LC 95-20889. (Bibliographies & Indexes in Science & Technology Ser.: Vol. 9). 440p. 1996. text ed. 89.50 (*0-313-29542-5*) Greenwood.

***Second Biennial Tire Recycling Conference: Conference Proceedings.** (Illus.). 250p. (Orig.). 1997. pap. text ed. 50.00 (*0-7881-3749-2*) DIANE Pub.

***Second Big Book of Hell.** Matt Groening. 1997. pap. 17.95 (*0-14-026310-1*) Viking Penguin.

Second Big Book of Pencil Pastimes. James F. Minter. 1993. pap. 6.95 (*0-88486-075-2*, Bristol Park Bks) Arrowood Pr.

Second Big Dot to Dot. K. Bryant-Mole. (Dot to Dot Ser.). (Illus.). 96p. (J). (gr. k-4). 1993. pap. 11.95 (*0-7460-1377-9*, Usborne) EDC.

Second Biology Course. P. T. Bunyan. 348p. (C). 1985. text ed. 75.00 (*0-85950-190-6*, Pub. by S Thornes Pubs UK) St Mut.

Second Birth. Omraam M. Aivanhov. (Complete Works of O. M. Aivanhov: Vol. 1). 210p. 1981. reprint ed. pap. 13.95 (*0-87516-418-8*) DeVorss.

Second Birth: The Goal of Life. Gail Radley. 28p. 1984. pap. 6.50 (*0-900125-55-1*) Bahai.

Second Black Lizard Anthology of Crime Fiction. Ed. by Edward Gorman. LC 87-72695. 656p. (Orig.). 1988. pap. 15.95 (*0-88739-094-3*, Black Mask) Creat Arts Bk.

Second Black Renaissance: Essays in Black Literature. C. W. Bigsby. LC 79-7723. (Contributions in Afro-American & African Studies: No. 50). 332p. 1980. text ed. 42.95 (*0-313-21304-6*, BNB/, Greenwood Pr) Greenwood.

Second Blackstaff Book of Short Stories. Michael Carragher et al. 236p. (Orig.). 1991. pap. 14.95 (*0-85640-473-X*, Pub. by Blackstaff Pr IE) Dufour.

Second Book in English. Robert J. Dixson. 128p. 1987. pap. text ed. 6.50 (*0-13-797283-0*, 21179) Prentice ESL.

S

An Asterisk (*) at the beginning of an entry indicates that the title is appearing in BIP for the first time.

Second Book of Danish Verse. Tr. by Charles W. Stork. LC 68-57067. (Granger Index Reprint Ser.). 1977. 19.95 (0-8369-6044-0) Ayer.

Second Book of Danish Verse. Charles W. Stork. 1973. 69.75 (0-8490-1008-X) Gordon Pr.

Second Book of Discipline. James Kirk. 328p. (C). 1988. text ed. 59.00 (0-7152-0439-4) St Mut.

Second Book of Go. Richard Bozulich. 1987. pap. 8.95 (4-87187-031-6, G31) Ishi Pr Intl.

Second Book of Kingdoms: The Unsuper. Angus Wells. 384p. 1990. mass mkt. 5.99 (0-553-28566-1, Spectra) Bantam.

Second Book of Kings. Ed. by J. Robinson. LC 75-39371. (Cambridge Bible Commentary on the New English Bible, New Testament Ser.). (Illus.). 288p. 1976. pap. text ed. 24.95 (0-521-09774-6) Cambridge U Pr.

Second Book of Lost Swords: Sightblinder's Story. Fred Saberhagen. 256p. 1995. 4.50 (0-8125-3656-8) Tor Bks.

Second Book of Mathematical Bafflers. Angela Dunn. (Puzzles, Amusements, Recreations Ser.). (Illus.). 192p. (Orig.). 1983. pap. 5.95 (0-486-24352-4) Dover.

Second Book of Modern Lace Knitting. Marianne Kinzel. (Illus.). 1990. 8.75 (0-8446-4763-2) Peter Smith.

Second Book of Modern Lace Knitting. rev. ed. Marianne Kinzel. LC 72-86064. (Illus.). 128p. 1973. reprint ed. pap. 5.95 (0-486-22905-X) Dover.

Second Book of Modern Verse. Ed. by Jessie B. Rittenhouse. LC 75-149113. (Granger Index Reprint Ser.). 1977. 18.95 (0-8369-6238-9) Ayer.

Second Book of Operas, Their Histories, Their Plots & Their Music. Henry E. Krehbiel. LC 80-2280. reprint ed. 36.50 (0-404-18852-4) AMS Pr.

Second Book of Poems. Harland Sleight. 93p. 1986. 32.00 (0-7223-2037-X, Pub. by A H S Ltd UK) St Mut.

Second Book of Russian Verse. Ed. by Cecil M. Bowra. LC 73-114472. xvii, 153p. 1971. reprint ed. text ed. 49.75 (0-8371-4814-6, BORW, Greenwood Pr) Greenwood.

Second Book of Spinechillers. Paul Stewart & Phil Roxbee-Cox. (Spinechillers Ser.). (Illus.). 144p. (J). (gr. 3 up). 1996. pap. 11.95 (0-7460-2069-4, Usborne) EDC.

Second Book of Swords. Fred Saberhagen. 320p. 1995. 4.50 (0-8125-1934-5) Tor Bks.

Second Book of Tales. Eugene Field. (Notable American Authors Ser.). 1992. reprint ed. lib. bdg. 75.00 (0-685-49853-0) Rprt Serv.

Second Book of the Bible: Exodus. Walter Jacob. 1983. 79.50 (0-88125-028-7) Ktav.

Second Book of the Lamb. Peter C. Stone. 233p. 1987. 22.00 (0-934469-02-4) Gabriel Pr CA.

Second Book of the Rhymers Club. William Butler Yeats et al. 1987. pap. 12.95 (0-89979-033-X) British Am Bks.

Second Book of the Strange. World Almanac Editors & Laurence D. Gadd. LC 81-82644. (Science & the Paranormal Ser.). (Illus.). 341p. 1981. 26.95 (0-87975-170-3) Prometheus Bks.

Second Book of the Travels of Nicander Nucius, of Corcyra. Nicander Nucius. Tr. by J. A. Cramer. (Camden Society, London. Publications, First Ser.: No. 17). reprint ed. 38.50 (0-404-50117-6) AMS Pr.

Second Book of Verse. Eugene Field. (Notable American Authors Ser.). (J). 1992. reprint ed. lib. bdg. 75.00 (0-7812-2644-9) Rprt Serv.

Second Book of Whimsey: Word Paintings, Political Grotesqueries, & Other Things. Roberta Mendel. (Books for Browsers Ser.). (Illus.). 24p. (Orig.). 1994. pap. 9.00 (0-936424-01-X) Pin Prick.

***Second Bride.** George. 1997. mass mkt. 3.25 (0-373-15695-2) Harlequin Bks.

***Second Bride.** Catherine George. (Romance Ser.). 1997. mass mkt. 3.50 (0-373-03449-0, 1-03449-5) Harlequin Bks.

Second Bridegroom. Rodney Hall. 1991. 19.95 (0-374-25668-3) FS&G.

Second British Empire: Trade, Philanthropy, & Good Government, 1820-1890. John P. Halstead. LC 82-20965. (Contributions in Comparative Colonial Studies: No. 14). (Illus.). xiii, 261p. 1983. text ed. 59.95 (0-313-23519-8, HBE/, Greenwood Pr) Greenwood.

***Second Bull Run Campaign, July-August 1862.** David G. Martin. LC 96-3426. (Great Campaigns Ser.). 1996. 24.95 (0-938289-80-2) Combined Pub.

2nd CAD-Based Vision Workshop, 1994: Proceedings. LC 93-80368. 320p. 1994. pap. 60.00 (0-8186-5310-8, 5310) IEEE Comp Soc.

Second Career Vocations. E. Leger et al. Tr. by F. O'Hara & F. Lescoe from FRE. 20p. (C). 1986. pap. 1.50 (0-910919-02-X) Mariel Pubns.

Second Careers: New Ways to Work after Fifty. Caroline Bird. 1992. pap. 15.95 (0-316-09599-0) Little.

Second Carrot from the End. Frederick Beck. (American Autobiography Ser.). 160p. 1995. reprint ed. lib. bdg. 69.00 (0-7812-8455-4) Rprt Serv.

Second Catalogue of Variable Stars in Globular Clusters, Comprising 1,421 Entries. Helen B. Sawyer. (University of Toronto, David Dunlap Observatory Ser.: Vol. 2, No. 2). 61p. reprint ed. pap. 25.00 (0-685-15446-7, 2026544) Bks Demand.

Second Census of Kentucky: 1800. G. Glenn Clift. LC 66-19191. 333p. 1993. reprint ed. 25.00 (0-8063-0077-9) Genealog Pub.

Second Century of New & Rare Indian Plants, Vol. IX, Pt. 1. Royal Botanic Garden, Calcutta Staff et al. (Illus.). 80p. 1972. reprint ed. 50.00 (0-88065-012-5, Messers Today & Tomorrow) Scholarly Pubns.

Second Century of the Skyscraper. Council on Tall Buildings & Urban Habitats Staff. (Illus.). 1056p. (gr. 13). 1988. text ed. 133.95 (0-442-22116-9) Chapman & Hall.

Second Chambers. John A. Marriott. LC 78-102250. (Select Bibliographies Reprint Ser.). 1977. 29.95 (0-8369-5135-2) Ayer.

Second Chance. Judy Baer. (Cedar River Daydreams Ser.: Vol.14). 144p. (Orig.). (YA). (gr. 7-10). 1991. mass mkt. 4.99 (1-55661-217-6) Bethany Hse.

Second Chance. Jackie Calhoun. 256p. (Orig.). 1991. pap. 9.95 (0-941483-93-2) Naiad Pr.

Second Chance. Lori Handeland. 400p. (Orig.). 1994. mass mkt., pap. text ed. 4.99 (0-505-51966-6) Dorchester Pub Co.

Second Chance. Ralph Harper. LC 93-1237. 96p. 1993. pap. 11.00 (1-56338-059-5) TPI PA.

***Second Chance.** Robert E. Harrison. 140p. (Orig.). 1996. pap. write for info. (1-57502-324-5) Morris Pubng.

Second Chance. Steven Kroll. (Hit & Run Gang Ser.: No. 7). 80p. (Orig.). (J). 1994. pap. 3.50 (0-380-77368-6, Camelot Young) Avon.

Second Chance. Ed. by Werner E. Mosse et al. xii, 654p. 1991. 115.00 (3-16-145741-2, Pub. by J C B Mohr GW) Coronet Bks.

***Second Chance.** Daniel Ovist. (Orig.). 1997. pap. write for info. (0-9655772-0-1) D Ovist.

Second Chance. Francine Pascal. (Sweet Valley High Ser.: No. 53). 144p. (J). (ps-1). 1989. pap. 2.95 (0-553-27771-5) Bantam.

Second Chance. Ed. by John B. Whitton. LC 77-111874. (Essay Index Reprint Ser.). 1977. 21.95 (0-8369-1735-9) Ayer.

Second Chance. Jerome D. Wright. 288p. 1987. mass mkt. 3.50 (0-87067-834-5, BH834-5) Holloway.

Second Chance. large type ed. Francine Pascal. (Sweet Valley High Ser.: No. 53). 133p. (J). (gr. 5-8). 1989. reprint ed. 9.50 (1-55905-008-X, Gareth Stevens Inc); reprint ed. lib. bdg. 10.50 (1-55905-018-7, Gareth Stevens Inc) Grey Castle.

Second Chance. 2nd ed. Syd Banks. 91p. 1989. reprint ed. pap. 6.95 (0-937713-04-X) Duval-Bibb.

Second Chance. 2nd ed. Syd Banks. 91p. 1990. reprint ed. 10.95 (0-937713-01-5) Duval-Bibb.

Second Chance: A Guide to Post-Secondary Options for Young Adults with Severe Learning Disabilities. Riverview School Staff. 224p. 1993. 15.95 (0-9635773-0-1) Riverview Sch.

Second Chance: A True Story of Tragedy Turned to Triumph. Dean Nester. 283p. (Orig.). 1995. pap. 9.95 (0-9647710-0-4) Sable Pubng.

Second Chance: Living with a Rescued Dog. Judy Elsden & Larry Elsden. (Illus.). 96p. 1995. 12.95 (0-948955-14-7) Seven Hills Bk.

Second Chance: Proceedings of 1994 IWRC Conference. Ed. by Julia Hagen. (Illus.). 128p. (Orig.). 1995. pap. 20.00 (1-884196-04-7) IWRC.

Second Chance: The Evangelical Triumph in Central America. Joseph A. Yacaginsky. (Christian Universities Press Ser.). 216p. 1997. 39.95 (1-57309-091-3); pap. 29.95 (1-57309-090-5) Intl Scholars.

Second Chance: The Story of a Near-Death Experience. Ajamila. 208p. 1991. 9.95 (0-89213-271-X) Bhaktivedanta.

Second Chance: The United Nations in the 1990s. Max Jakobson. 194p. Date not set. 19.95 (92-1-157185-5, E.93.III.K.FS36) UN.

Second Chance: Training for Jobs. Sar A. Levitan & Frank Gallo. LC 87-37266. 220p. 1988. text ed. 26.00 (0-88099-057-0); pap. text ed. 16.00 (0-88099-056-2) W E Upjohn.

Second Chance: White Pastor - Black Church. Alan J. Davis. LC 90-62236. (Illus.). 184p. (Orig.). 1990. pap. 10.00 (0-913428-70-1) Landfall Pr.

Second Chance Activity Worksheets. Lucy Collingwood. 64p. 1991. pap. text ed. 10.00 (0-87879-909-5) High Noon Bks.

Second Chance at Life. Marilyn Birkley. 1996. 10.95 (0-533-11684-8) Vantage.

Second Chance at Life. William Pew. 1993. pap. 4.99 (1-56399-013-X) NewLife Pubns.

Second Chance at Marriage. Pamela Dalton. (Romance Ser.). 1995. mass mkt. 2.99 (0-373-19100-6, 1-19100-6) Silhouette.

***Second Chance Dad.** Benson. 1997. mass mkt. 3.99 (0-373-24146-1) Harlequin Bks.

Second Chance Family. Laura Anthony. 1995. mass mkt. 2.99 (0-373-19119-7, 1-19119-6) Silhouette.

Second Chance in Centerville. Thomas A. Baker. 96p. (J). (gr. 3-9). 1991. pap. 11.00 (0-87879-908-7) High Noon Bks.

Second Chance in Education. D. E. Inbar. 1990. 75.00 (1-85000-668-7, Falmer Pr); pap. 35.00 (1-85000-669-5, Falmer Pr) Taylor & Francis.

Second-Chance Nurse. large type ed. Jane Converse. 1991. 25.99 (0-7089-2387-9) Ulverscroft.

Second Chance to Dance. Miriam Leader. (Illus.). 50p. (Orig.). 1991. pap. text ed. 10.00 (0-9620092-6-1) Pine Isl Pr.

Second Chance to Live. Freddie L. Sirmans. 70p. 1995. 9.95 (1-887197-00-1) Zaporia Pr.

Second Chance to Live: The Suicide Syndrome. George Alpert et al. LC 75-20452. (Photography Ser.). (Illus.). 90p. 1976. pap. 6.95 (0-306-80023-3) Da Capo.

Second Chances. Gilbert Allen. LC 90-48742. 80p. (Orig.). 1991. pap. 10.00 (0-914061-20-8) Orchises Pr.

Second Chances. Constance O'Day-Flannery. 400p. 1992. mass mkt. 5.99 (0-8217-3950-6, Zebra Kensgtn) Kensgtn Pub Corp.

Second Chances. Cynthia Patterson. 232p. 1995. mass mkt. 4.99 (1-896329-88-8, Pub. by Comnwlth Pub CN) Partners Pubs Grp.

Second Chances. Denis F. Ratcliffe. 280p. 1996. pap. 16.95 (1-85411-151-5, Pub. by Seren Bks UK) Dufour.

Second Chances. Sharon Sala. 304p. 1996. mass mkt. 4.99 (0-06-108327-5, Harp PBks) HarpC.

Second Chances: Men, Women & Children a Decade After Divorce. Judith S. Wallerstein & Sandra Blakeslee. 352p. 1996. pap. 12.95 (0-395-73533-5) HM.

Second Characters or the Language of Forms. Anthony A. Shaftesbury. Ed. by Benjamin Rand. LC 69-14078. 182p. 1970. reprint ed. text ed. 35.00 (0-8371-2357-7, SHSC, Greenwood Pr) Greenwood.

***Second Characters or the Language of Forms: 1914 Editions.** Ed. by Benjamin Rand. 210p. 1996. reprint ed. write for info. (1-85506-426-X) Bks Intl VA.

Second Checklist of French Political Pamphlets, 1560-1653. Ed. by Doris V. Welsh. 1955. pap. 5.00 (0-911028-22-6) Newberry.

Second Chicago School? The Development of a Post-War American Sociology. Ed. by Gary A. Fine. LC 94-46877. 436p. 1995. lib. bdg. 70.00 (0-226-24938-7) U Ch Pr.

Second Chicago School? The Development of a Postwar Sociology. Fine. (C). 1995. pap. text ed. 22.50 (0-226-24939-5) U Ch Pr.

Second Child. John Saul. 384p. 1991. mass mkt. 6.50 (0-553-28730-3) Bantam.

Second Child: Family Transition & Adjustment. Robert B. Stewart, Jr. (New Perspectives on Family Ser.). 256p. (C). 1990. text ed. 48.00 (0-8039-3519-6); pap. text ed. 22.95 (0-8039-3520-X) Sage.

Second Choice: Growing up Adopted. Robert Andersen. LC 92-90502. (Illus.). 176p. (Orig.). (C). 1993. pap. 10.00 (0-9632648-4-2) Badger Hill.

2 Chronicles. Raymond B. Dillard. (Biblical Commentary Ser.: Vol. 15). 1988. 29.99 (0-8499-0214-2) Word Pub.

2 Chronicles: An Introduction & Commentary. Martin J. Selman. LC 94-3579. (Tyndale Old Testament Commentary Ser.: Vol. 10b). 288p. 1994. 18.99 (0-8308-1432-9, 1432); pap. 11.99 (0-87784-246-9, 246) InterVarsity.

Second Church of Elizabeth City Parish 1623-1698, No. 13. Eleanor S. Holt. 212p. 1985. pap. 22.00 (1-884626-04-1) Archeolog Soc.

Second-Class Citizen. Buchi Emecheta. LC 82-24355. 175p. 1983. reprint ed. pap. 8.95 (0-8076-1066-6) Braziller.

Second Class Suburbanites: White Blue-Collar Suburbs & Black White-Collar Suburbs, No. 739. Marcelion Cox. 1975. 6.00 (0-686-20337-2, Sage Prdcls Pr) Sage.

Second Class Township Code. Pennsylvania State Legislature Staff. 176p. (Orig.). 1995. text ed. 2.25 (0-8182-0001-4) Commonweal PA.

***Second Collection: Bernard Lonergan.** Ed. by William F. Ryan & Bernard J. Tyrrell. 320p. 1996. pap. 22.95 (0-8020-7943-1) U of Toronto Pr.

Second Colloquium in Biological Sciences. Ed. by Craig D. Burrell & Fleur L. Strand. (Annals Ser.: Vol. 463). 422p. 1986. text ed. 106.00 (0-89766-321-7); pap. text ed. 106.00 (0-89766-322-5) NY Acad Sci.

***Second Coming.** David L. Anderson. 467p. (Orig.). 1997. mass mkt. 5.99 (1-55197-809-1, Pub. by Comnwlth Pub CN) Partners Pubs Grp.

***Second Coming.** Cookie F. Kelley. 88p. (Orig.). 1996. pap. 11.95 (1-883893-77-1) WinePress Pub.

Second Coming. William Kelly. 375p. 7.25 (0-88172-108-5) Believers Bkshelf.

Second Coming. Kirk Nelson. (Orig.). 1986. pap. 8.95 (0-9617119-0-6) Wright Pub VA.

Second Coming. Walker Percy. 336p. 1990. mass mkt. 5.99 (0-8041-0542-1) Ivy Books.

Second Coming. Jim Wills. LC 95-96142. 207p. (Orig.). 1997. pap. 12.95 (0-9650569-0-2) Donnee Bks.

Second Coming: A Leatherdyke Reader. Pat Califia. Ed. by Robin Sweeney. 256p. (Orig.). 1996. pap. text ed. 12.95 (1-55583-281-4) Alyson Pubns.

Second Coming: A Wesleyan Approach to the Doctrine of Last Things. Ed. by H. Ray Dunning. 276p. (Orig.). 1995. kivar 21.99 (0-8341-1525-5) Beacon Hill.

Second Coming: Journey into the Great Incarnation of Christ. DeEtta C. Cunningham. (Illus.). 224p. 1996. pap. 14.00 (0-8059-3914-8) Dorrance.

Second Coming: The New Christian Right in Virginia Politics. Mark J. Rozell & Clyde Wilcox. LC 95-44562. 304p. (C). 1996. 32.95 (0-8018-5297-8) Johns Hopkins.

Second Coming: The Strange Odyssey of Michael Jordan, from Courtside to Home Plate & Back. Sam Smith. LC 95-37153. 256p. 1995. 23.00 (0-06-017502-8, HarpT) HarpC.

***Second Coming: The Strange Odyssey of Michael Jordon; From Courtside to Home Plate & Back...** Sam Smith. 400p. 1996. mass mkt. 5.99 (0-06-109455-2, Harp PBks) HarpC.

Second Coming: Tough Questions Answered. Kenneth B. MacDonald & Agnes MacDonald. 300p. (Orig.). (YA). 1991. pap. 9.95 (0-9626490-0-7) Revivals & Missions.

Second Coming Anthology: Ten Years in Retrospect. Ed. by A. D. Winans. (Illus.). 240p. 1984. pap. 10.00 (0-915016-33-8); lib. bdg. 15.00 (0-915016-32-X) Second Coming.

***Second Coming Attractions.** Prill. Date not set. write for info. (0-312-18173-6) St Martin.

Second Coming of Christ. Gordon Lindsay. (Literature Crusade Ser.). 1965. pap. 0.95 (0-89985-358-7) Christ for the Nations.

Second Coming of Christ. Gordon Lindsay. 1967. 1.95 (0-89985-061-8) Christ for the Nations.

***Second Coming of Christ.** Charles H. Spurgeon. 188p. 1996. mass mkt. 4.99 (0-88368-380-6) Whitaker Hse.

Second Coming of Christ, Vol. I. Paramahansa Yogananda. LC 79-50352. 240p. 1979. pap. 20.95 (0-937134-00-7) Amrita Found.

Second Coming of Christ, Vol. II. Paramahansa Yogananda. LC 79-50352. 226p. 1984. pap. 18.95 (0-937134-05-8) Amrita Found.

Second Coming of Christ, Vol. III. Paramahansa Yogananda. LC 79-50352. 180p. 1986. pap. 18.95 (0-937134-13-9) Amrita Found.

Second Coming of Christ: An Esoteric Interpretation. Tom Sage. LC 95-90539. (Illus.). 56p. 1995. 8.00 (0-9647409-9-0) Eleleth.

***Second Coming of Christ: Or the New Avatar.** John T. Ferrier. 48p. Date not set. pap. text ed. 6.00 (0-900235-04-7) Order Of The Cross.

Second Coming of Christ (La Segunda Venida De Cristo) Gordon Lindsay. (Literature Crusade Ser.). (SPA.). 1965. pap. 0.95 (0-89985-371-4) Christ for the Nations.

***Second Coming of Jesus.** M. R. De Haan. LC 96-32046. (M. R. De Haan Classic Library). 1997. pap. 9.99 (0-8254-2483-6) Kregel.

Second Coming of Jesus: Meditation & Commentary on the Book of Revelation see Our Sunday Visitor's Popular Bible Study Series

Second Coming of Joan of Arc & Other Plays by Carolyn Gage. Carolyn Gage. (Illus.). 160p. (Orig.). 1994. pap. 10.00 (0-939821-06-0) HerBooks.

Second Coming of Reb Yhshwh: The Rabbi Called Jesus Christ. Carlo Suares. LC 94-18308. 194p. (Orig.). 1994. pap. 12.95 (0-87728-818-6) Weiser.

Second Coming of Science: An Intimate Report on the New Science. Brian O'Leary. LC 92-29954. (Orig.). 1993. pap. 12.95 (1-55643-152-X) North Atlantic.

***Second Coming of the Church.** George Barna. 224p. 1997. 18.99 (0-8499-1490-6) Word Pub.

Second Common Reader. annot. ed. Virginia Woolf. 1986. pap. 7.95 (0-15-619808-8) HarBrace.

Second Complete Autocad Databook. A. E. Hill & Pilkington. 320p. 1992. pap. text ed. 43.00 (0-13-796988-0) P-H.

Second Compton Symposium. Ed. by Neil Gehrels et al. LC 94-70742. (AIP Conference Proceedings Ser.: No. 304). 812p. 1993. text ed. 783.00 (1-56396-261-6) Am Inst Physics.

Second Concerto in G Minor: Opus 22 2 Pianos 4 Hands. C. Sanit-Saens. 84p. 1986. pap. 12.95 (0-7935-3887-4, 50259010) H Leonard.

Second Conference on Ballistics Simulation. Ed. by Michael J. Chinni. 72p. 1991. pap. 32.00 (0-911801-90-1, EMC91-1) Soc Computer Sim.

Second Conference on Faint Blue Stars. D. S. Hayes & J. Liebert. Ed. by A. G. Davis Philip. (IAU Colloquium Ser.: No. 95). 700p. 1987. 47.00 (0-933485-07-7); pap. 37.00 (0-933485-06-9) L Davis Pr.

***Second Conference on NDE Applied to Process Control of Composite Fabrication.** Ed. by Donald D. Palmer & George A. Matzkanin. (Illus.). VIII, 259p. (Orig.). 1997. pap. 50.00 (1-890596-04-3) TX Res Inst.

Second Conference on Recent Advances in Active Control of Sound & Vibration. Ed. by R. A. Burdisso & C. R. Fuller. LC 93-60248. 1100p. 1993. text ed. 199.95 (1-56676-038-0) Technomic.

Second Conference on Tall Buildings in Seismic Regions, Proceedings. Council on Tall Buildings & Urban Habitat Staff. (Illus.). 436p. 1991. text ed. 55.00 (0-939493-07-1, 903.409) Coun Tall Bldg.

Second Conference on the Reliability of Transmission & Distribution Equipment. 225p. 1995. pap. 98.00 (0-85296-628-8, IC406) Inst Elect Eng.

Second Confession. Rex Stout. 256p. 1995. mass mkt. 4.99 (0-553-24594-5) Bantam.

Second Confession. large type ed. Rex Stout. (Nightingale Series Large Print Bks.). 311p. 1992. pap. 15.95 (0-8161-5202-0, GK Hall) Thorndike Pr.

Second Congress of Polish American Scholars & Scientists: Program & Abstracts of Papers. Ed. by Damian Wandycz. 100p. 1971. 5.00 (0-940962-37-3) Polish Inst Art & Sci.

Second Conquest. (Storytrails Ser.). 96p. (YA). (gr. 6-9). 1985. pap. text ed. 8.95 (0-521-31705-3) Cambridge U Pr.

***Second Conquest of Latin America: Coffee, Henequen, & Oil During the Export Boom, 1850-1930.** Ed. by Steven C. Topik & Allen Wells. (Illus.). 200p. 1998. pap. 13.95 (0-292-78153-9) U of Tex Pr.

***Second Conquest of Latin America: Coffee, Henequen, & Oil During the Export Boom, 1850-1930.** Ed. by Steven C. Topik & Allen Wells. (Illus.). 200p. 1998. 25.00 (0-292-78157-1) U of Tex Pr.

Second Contact. Mike Resnick. 1990. pap. 3.95 (0-8125-1113-1) Tor Bks.

Second Contact. G. Harry Stine. (Starsea Invaders Ser.: No. 2). 304p. (Orig.). 1994. pap. 4.99 (0-451-45344-1, ROC) NAL-Dutton.

Second Continuation see Continuations of the Old French Perceval of Chretien de Troyes

Second Cooperative Sports & Game Book. Terry Orlick. 288p. 1996. per., pap. text ed. 17.00 (0-7872-1929-0) Kendall-Hunt.

Second Cooperative Sports & Games Book: Over 200 Brand-New Noncompetitive Games for Kids & Adults Both. Terry Orlick. 255p. 1982. pap. 17.00 (0-394-74813-1) NASCO.

2 Corinthians. (Life Application Bible Study Guide Ser.). 96p. 1992. pap. 5.99 (0-8423-2882-3, 02-2882-3, Tyndale Christian) Tyndale.

Second Corinthians. J. Agar Beet. 1989. pap. 12.99 (0-88019-242-9) Schmul Pub Co.

Second Corinthians. Ernest Best. LC 86-45404. (Interpretation: A Bible Commentary for Teaching & Preaching Ser.). 156p. 1987. 20.00 (0-8042-3135-4, John Knox) Westminster John Knox.

II Corinthians. Intro. by Victor P. Furnish. LC 83-2056. (Anchor Bible Ser.: Vol. 32A). (Illus.). 648p. 1984. 42.50 (0-385-11199-1) Doubleday.

S

Second Corinthians. Geoffrey Grogan. (Focus on the Bible Commentary Ser.). 224p. (Orig.). 1996. pap. 10.99 (*1-85792-220-4*, Pub. by Christian Focus UK) Spring Arbor Dist.

2 Corinthians. Ed. by Daniel J. Harrington. (Sacra Pagina Ser.: No. 8). Date not set. write for info. (*0-8146-5810-5*, M Glazier) Liturgical Pr.

2 Corinthians. Charles Hodge. LC 95-24322. (Crossway Classic Commentaries Ser.). 240p. (Orig.). 1995. pap. 13.99 (*0-89107-868-1*) Crossway Bks.

2 Corinthians. Philip E. Hughes. (New International Commentary on the New Testament Ser.). 544p. 1995. 30.00 (*0-8028-2508-7*) Eerdmans.

Second Corinthians. Robert B. Hughes. (Everyman's Bible Commentary Ser.). 1983. pap. 9.99 (*0-8024-0241-0*) Moody.

II Corinthians. Henry A. Ironside. 292p. 1939. 14.99 (*0-87213-355-9*) Loizeaux.

***Second Corinthians.** Simon J. Kispemaker. (New Testament Commentaries). 512p. 1997. 34.99 (*0-8010-2105-7*) Baker Bks.

Second Corinthians. Larry Kreitzer. (NTG Ser.). 96p. 1996. pap. 9.95 (*1-85075-789-5*, Pub. by Sheffield Acad UK) CUP Services.

Second Corinthians. Colin Kruse. (Tyndale New Testament Commentaries Ser.). 224p. 1987. pap. 13.00 (*0-8028-0318-0*) Eerdmans.

2 Corinthians. Ralph P. Martin. (Biblical Commentary Ser.: Vol. 40). 1985. 29.99 (*0-8499-0239-8*) Word Pub.

Second Corinthians. Handley C. Moule. 1979. pap. 5.95 (*0-87508-359-5*) Chr Lit.

Second Corinthians. Navigators Staff. (Life Change Ser.). 176p. (Orig.). 1996. pap. 7.00 (*0-89109-951-4*) NavPress.

2 Corinthians. Paul Stevens. (LifeGuide Bible Studies). 64p. (Orig.). 1990. wbk. ed., pap. 4.99 (*0-8308-1010-2*, 1010) InterVarsity.

Second Corinthians. David J. Valleskey. (People's Bible Commentary Ser.). 260p. (Orig.). 1992. pap. 10.99 (*0-570-04600-9*, 12-8014) Concordia.

II Corinthians. David J. Valleskey. LC 91-66835. (People's Bible Ser.). 252p. (Orig.). 1992. pap. 10.99 (*0-8100-0419-4*, 15N0495) Northwest Pub.

Second Corinthians. Geoffrey B. Wilson. 1979. pap. 9.99 (*0-85151-295-X*) Banner of Truth.

Second Corinthians: Keys to Triumphant Living. Edgar C. James. (Teach Yourself the Bible Ser.). 1964. pap. 5.99 (*0-8024-7680-5*) Moody.

Second Corinthians: Ministry: God's Work in Me for the Good of Others. Paul F. Bubna. LC 93-72165. (Deeper Life Pulpit Commentary Ser.). 237p. (Orig.). 1993. pap. 10.99 (*0-87509-538-0*) Chr Pubns.

***2 Corinthians: Torrance Edition.** John Calvin. (Calvin's New Testament Commentaries Ser.: Vol. 10). 1996. pap. 20.00 (*0-8028-0810-7*) Eerdmans.

Second Corinthians: Where Life Endures. Roy L. Laurin. LC 85-8154. 248p. 1985. pap. 10.99 (*0-8254-3129-8*) Kregel.

Second Corinthians Eight & Nine: A Commentary on Two Administrative Letters of the Apostle Paul. Hans D. Betz. LC 84-48904. (Hermeneia: A Critical & Historical Commentary on the Bible Ser.). 184p. (C). 1985. 28.00 (*0-8006-6014-5*, 1-6014, Fortress Pr) Augsburg Fortress.

***2 Corinthians, 1 & 2 Timothy, Titus.** Thomas Nelson Publishers Staff. (Spirit-Filled Life Study Guide Ser.: Vol. 20). 160p. 1997. pap. 6.99 (*0-7852-1204-3*) Nelson.

Second Courante of Newes from the East India in Two Letters. LC 74-28849. (English Experience Ser.: No. 730). 1975. reprint ed. 10.00 (*90-221-0730-2*) Walter J Johnson.

Second Course in Calculus. John M. Olmsted. LC 68-14041. (Century Mathematics Ser.). (Illus.). 336p. (C). 1968. 39.50 (*0-89197-395-8*) Irvington.

Second Course in Computer Science with Pascal. Daniel D. McCracken. LC 86-32586. (Illus.). 432p. (C). 1987. Net. text ed. 41.00 (*0-471-01062-6*) Wiley.

Second Course in Elementary Differential Equations. Paul Waltman. 1985. text ed. 45.00 (*0-12-733910-8*) Acad Pr.

Second Course in Linear Algebra. William C. Brown. LC 87-23117. 264p. 1988. text ed. 98.95 (*0-471-62602-3*) Wiley.

Second Course in Ordinary Differential Equations for Scientists & Engineers. W. B. Miller, Jr. & M. Huni. (Illus.). xi, 441p. 1987. 65.95 (*0-387-96676-5*) Spr-Verlag.

Second Course in Statistics. 5th ed. Mendenhall & Terry Sincich. 1996. student ed., pap. text ed. 25.00 (*0-13-456468-5*) P-H.

Second Course in Statistics. 5th ed. William Mendenhall & Terry Sincich. 899p. (C). 1996. text ed. 80.00 (*0-13-396821-9*) P-H.

Second Course in Stochastic Processes. Samuel Karlin & Howard M. Taylor. LC 80-533. 1981. text ed. 63.00 (*0-12-398650-8*) Acad Pr.

Second Course on Computer Science with MODULA 2. Daniel D. McCracken & William I. Salmon. LC 87-14230. 496p. (C). 1987. Net. pap. text ed. 41.00 (*0-471-63111-6*) Wiley.

Second Court That Works: Judicial Implementation of Permanency Planning Reforms. Mark Hardin et al. LC 95-46820. 1995. lib. bdg., pap. write for info. (*1-57073-259-0*) Amer Bar Assn.

Second Creation. Richard L. Baucom. (Orig.). 1996. pap. write for info. (*1-57553-130-5*) Watermrk Pr.

Second Creation: Makers of the Revolution in Twentieth-Century Physics. Robert P. Crease & Charles C. Mann. 491p. 1995. pap. text ed. 21.95 (*0-8135-2177-7*) Rutgers U Pr.

Second Crop: Poems. John S. Harris. LC 96-10029. (BYU Studies Monographs). 1996. write for info. (*0-8425-2335-9*) Frnds of the Libry.

Second Crossing. N. A. Diaman. LC 82-7564. (Illus.). 240p. (Orig.). 1982. pap. 9.95 (*0-931906-03-2*, Persona Pr) Persona Prod.

Second Crucifixion. Allen. 24p. 1952. pap. 1.00 (*0-88053-018-9*, M067) Macoy Pub.

Second Crusade & the Cistercians. Ed. by Michael Gervers. 270p. 1992. text ed. 45.00 (*0-312-05607-9*) St Martin.

Second Cryptographic Shakespeare. rev. ed. Penn Leary. (Illus.). 313p. 1990. pap. 15.00 (*0-9617917-1-3*) Westchester Hse.

2nd Culprit. (WWL Mystery Ser.). 1995. mass mkt. 5.99 (*0-373-15280-9*, 1-15280-0) Harlequin Bks.

Second Cup of Coffee Daybreak. 1994. 7.99 (*0-310-96210-2*) Zondervan.

Second Curtain. Roy Fuller. 192p. 1986. reprint ed. pap. 5.95 (*0-89733-197-4*) Academy Chi Pubs.

***Second Curve.** I. Morrison & G. Scmid. 1997. pap. 14.00 (*0-345-40788-1*) Ballantine.

Second Curve. I. Morrison & G. Schmid. Date not set. write for info. (*0-449-91262-0*) Fawcett.

Second Curve: Managing the Velocity of Change. Ian Morrison. 288p. 1996. 25.00 (*0-614-96347-8*) Ballantine.

Second Curve: Managing the Velocity of Change. Ian Morrison & G. Schmid. 240p. 1996. 25.00 (*0-345-40541-2*) Ballantine.

Second Daffodil Poetry Book. Ed. by Ethel L. Fowler. LC 75-123389. (Granger Index Reprint Ser.). 1977. 19.95 (*0-8369-6177-3*) Ayer.

Second Daughter: The Story of a Slave Girl. Mildred P. Walter. LC 95-4691. 176p. (YA). (gr. 7 up). 1996. 15.95 (*0-590-48282-3*) Scholastic Inc.

Second Day at Gettysburg: Essays on Confederate & Union Leadership. Ed. by Gary W. Gallagher. LC 93-16146. (Illus.). 224p. 1993. pap. 14.00 (*0-87338-482-2*) Kent St U Pr.

Second Deadly Sin. Lawrence Sanders. 448p. 1990. mass mkt. 6.99 (*0-425-12519-X*) Berkley Pub.

Second Death. Michael Zuroy. 250p. 1992. 19.95 (*0-8027-1181-2*) Walker & Co.

Second Death of Laissez-Faire. James K. Galbraith. (Working Paper Ser.: No. 58). 53p. 1990. pap. 5.50 (*0-89940-539-8*) LBJ Sch Pub Aff.

Second Death of Tom Pender. LC 91-62187. 162p. (Orig.). 1991. pap. 6.95 (*0-9629335-1-1*) Loganhill Pr.

Second Decade of AIDS: A Mental Health Practice Handbook. Ed. by Walt Odets & Michael Shernoff. LC 94-40679. 320p. 1995. 29.95 (*1-886330-00-X*) Hatherleigh.

Second Decade of AIDS: A Mental Health Practice Handbook. Ed. by Walt Odets & Michael Shernoff. LC 94-40679. 320p. (Orig.). 1995. pap. 19.95 (*1-886330-01-8*) Hatherleigh.

Second Decade of Love: Finding a Renaissance in Marriage Before the Kids Leave Home. Greg Johnson & Mike Yorkey. LC 94-12492. 256p. 1994. 16.99 (*0-8423-5919-2*) Tyndale.

Second Declaration of Havana. 2nd ed. LC 95-130876. 45p. 1995. pap. 4.50 (*0-87348-798-2*) Pathfinder NY.

Second Dedalus Book of Decadence: The Black Feast. Brian M. Stableford. 1992. pap. 14.95 (*0-7818-0110-9*) Hippocrene Bks.

Second Dedalus Book of Decadence: The Black Feast. Brian M. Stableford. 337p. pap. 14.95 (*0-946626-80-4*, Pub. by Dedalus Bks UK) Hippocrene Bks.

Second Deeds of Trust: How to Make Money Safely. Barney G. Glaser & David J. Crabtree. 154p. 1969. pap. 22.00 (*1-884156-02-9*) Sociology Pr.

Second Deluge. Garrett P. Serviss. 1976. lib. bdg. 12.95 (*0-89968-172-7*, Lghtyr Pr) Buccaneer Bks.

Second Digest of Investigations in the Teaching of Science. Francis D. Curtis. LC 74-153694. 446p. reprint ed. pap. 127.20 (*0-317-42010-0*, 2026001) Bks Demand.

Second Dinosaur Action Set. Malcolm Whyte. (Action Sets Ser.). (Illus.). 24p. (J). (gr. 1 up). 1987. pap. 5.95 (*0-8431-1951-9*, Troubador) Price Stern Sloan.

Second Division, American Expeditionary Force in France, 1917-1919. Ed. by Second Division Historical Committee Staff. (Great War Ser.: No. 3). (Illus.). 412p. 1990. reprint ed. 34.95 (*0-89839-142-3*) Battery Pr.

Second Duma: A Study of the Social-Democratic Party & the Russian Constitutional Experiment. 2nd ed. Alfred Levin. LC 66-13342. xii, 422p. (C). 1966. lib. bdg. 43.50 (*0-208-00539-0*, Archon Bks) Shoe String.

Second Economy in Tanzania. T. L. Maliyamkono & Mboya S. Bagachwa. LC 89-27398. 224p. 1990. lib. bdg. 29.95 (*0-8214-0949-2*) Ohio U Pr.

Second Edition see Kentucky, a History of the State

Second Edition of The General Theory, Vol. 1. Ed. by G. C. Harcourt & P. A. Riach. LC 96-3293. 496p. (C). 1997. text ed. 75.00 (*0-415-14942-8*) Routledge.

Second Edition of The General Theory, Vol. 2. Ed. by G. C. Harcourt & P. A. Riach. LC 96-3293. 456p. (C). 1997. text ed. 75.00 (*0-415-14943-6*) Routledge.

Second Empire & Commune: France 1848-1871. 2nd ed. William H. Smith. (Seminar Studies in History). 120p. (C). 1996. pap. text ed. 12.50 (*0-582-28705-7*, Pub. by Longman UK) Longman.

Second Empire & Its Downfall. Napoleon, 3rd. Tr. by Herbert Wilson. LC 74-126266. (Select Bibliographies Reprint Ser.). 1977. reprint ed. 18.95 (*0-8369-5464-5*) Ayer.

Second Empire Opera. T. J. Walsh. (History of Opera Ser.). (Illus.). 1981. 35.00 (*0-7145-3659-8*) Riverrun NY.

Second Empire Revisited: A Study in French Historiography. Stuart L. Campbell. LC 77-20247. 246p. reprint ed. pap. 70.20 (*0-7837-5660-7*, 2059086) Bks Demand.

Second Encore II. Ed. by Alice Briley. (Illus.). 128p. 1985. pap. 6.95 (*0-910042-54-3*) Allegheny.

Second Enlargement of the EEC: The Integration of Unequal Partners. Ed. by Dudley Seers et al. LC 81-8750. 312p. 1982. text ed. 39.95 (*0-312-70830-0*) St Martin.

Second Enlargement of the European Community: Adjustments Requirements & Challenges for Policy Reform. Juegen B. Donges et al. 263p. 1982. lib. bdg. 62.50 (*3-16-344571-3*, Pub. by J C B Mohr GW) Coronet Bks.

Second Epistle Peter & Jude. M. Green. (Tyndale New Testament Commentaries Ser.: Vol. 18). 1987. pap. 13.00 (*0-8028-0078-5*) Eerdmans.

***Second Epistle to the Corinthians.** Paul Barnett. LC 96-49755. (New International Commentary on the New Testament Ser.). 696p. 1997. 45.00 (*0-8028-2300-9*) Eerdmans.

Second Epistle to the Corinthians. C. K. Barrett. (Black's New Testament Commentary Ser.). 416p. 1993. 24.95 (*1-56563-021-1*) Hendrickson MA.

Second Epistle to the Corinthians. Nigel Watson. (Epworth Commentary Ser.). 192p. (Orig.). (C). 1993. pap. 13.00 (*0-7162-0487-8*, Epworth Pr) TPI PA.

Second Epistle to the Corinthians: First-Seventh. Margaret E. Thrall. (International Critical Commentary Ser.). 544p. 1994. text ed. 59.95 (*0-567-09655-6*, Pub. by T & T Clark UK) Bks Intl VA.

2 Esdras. Bruce W. Longenecker. (Guides to Apocrypha & Pseudepigrapha Ser.: No. 1). 128p. pap. 12.50 (*1-85075-726-7*, Pub. by Sheffield Acad UK) CUP Services.

Second Essays on Literature. Edward B. Shanks. LC 68-20334. (Essay Index Reprint Ser.). 1977. 19.95 (*0-8369-0869-4*) Ayer.

Second European Conference on Architecture, 1989: Science & Technology at the Service of Architecture. Ed. by Theo C. Steemers & Wolfgang Palz. (C). 1990. lib. bdg. 291.00 (*0-7923-0732-1*) Kluwer Ac.

Second European Glacoma Symposium Helsinki, May 1984. Ed. by Erik L. Greve & C. Raitta. (Documenta Ophthalmologica Proceedings Ser.). 1985. lib. bdg. 204.50 (*90-6193-526-1*) Kluwer Ac.

Second European Ironmaking Congress. 441p. 1991. 100.00 (*0-901716-23-5*, Pub. by Inst Materials UK) Ashgate Pub Co.

Second Evil. R. L. Stine. Ed. by Patricia MacDonald. (Fear Street Cheerleaders Ser.). 176p. (Orig.). (YA). (gr. 7 up). mass mkt. 3.99 (*0-671-75118-2*, Archway) PB.

Second Ewings: A Facsimile of the Manuscript. John O'Hara. 1977. boxed 60.00 (*0-89723-012-4*) Bruccoli.

Second Exodus: The Full Story of the Jewish Illegal Immigration into Palestine, 1945-1948. Ze'ev V. Hadari. (Illus.). 309p. 1991. text ed. 29.50 (*0-85303-219-X*, Pub. by Vallentine Mitchell UK) Intl Spec Bk.

Second Father. Sally T. Hayes. 1996. pap. 3.99 (*0-373-07753-X*, 1-07753-6) Silhouette.

Second Feature: The Best of the "B" Films. John Cocchi. 1990. pap. 15.95 (*0-8065-1186-9*, Citadel Pr) Carol Pub Group.

Second Federal Issue 1801 - 1802: U. S. Embossed Revenue Stamped Paper. W. V. Combs. (Illus.). xvi, 142p. 1989. 20.00 (*0-945735-00-6*) Amer Revenue Assn.

Second Federalist: Congress Creates a Government. Ed. by Charles S. Hyneman & George W. Carey. LC 66-27380. (Orig.). 1966. pap. text ed. 9.95 (*0-89197-510-1*) Irvington.

***Second Female G-Spot Vol. 2: Advanced Techniques for Liberated Lovers.** (Sex Masters Collection). (Illus.). 94p. (Orig.). 1997. pap. write for info. (*1-890677-01-9*) Delphi Pr.

Second Fiber Optics & Communications Exposition: FOC '79, Chicago, Ill. 300p. 1979. 50.00 (*1-56851-021-7*, 133F02) Info Gatekeepers.

***Second Fiddle.** Kate Calloway. 1997. pap. 11.95 (*0-614-27304-8*) Naiad Pr.

Second Fiddle. Ronald Kidd. 176p. (J). (gr. 4-7). 1992. pap. 2.95 (*0-8167-1823-7*) Troll Communs.

Second Fiddle. Mary Wesley. 192p. 1990. pap. 7.95 (*0-14-011947-7*, Penguin Bks) Viking Penguin.

***Second Fiddle: A Cassidy James Mystery.** Kate Calloway. LC 96-47130. 224p. (Orig.). 1996. pap. 11.95 (*1-56280-161-9*) Naiad Pr.

Second Fiddle: A Historical Romance. Lester Mitchell. 280p. (Orig.). 1996. pap. 9.95 (*1-56002-524-7*) Aegina Pr.

Second Fifteen Years in Space. Ed. by S. Ferdman. (Science & Technology Ser.: Vol. 31). 1973. lib. bdg. 25.00 (*0-87703-064-2*) Univelt Inc.

Second Fifty Years: A Reference Manual for Senior Citizens. Walter J. Cheney et al. (Illus.). 445p. (Orig.). reprint ed. pap. 21.95 (*0-9641660-0-3*) Writers Consort.

Second Fifty Years: Promoting Health & Preventing Disability. Institute of Medicine Staff. Ed. by Robert L. Berg & J. S. Cassells. 344p. 1992. pap. 19.95 (*0-309-04681-5*) Natl Acad Pr.

Second Fifty Years - 1941-1991. Averill D. Geus. Ed. by Edward T. Chase. LC 91-20512. (Illus.). 260p. 1991. 100.00 (*0-914659-53-7*) Phoenix Pub.

Second Five-Year Annotated Index to Media Report to Women, 1977-1981. 48p. 1982. 5.00 (*0-930470-09-5*) Womens Inst Free Press.

Second Flood. John W. Stevenson. 112p. 1990. pap. 7.99 (*1-56043-057-5*) Destiny Image.

Second Florida Artificial Intelligence Research Symposium: Proceedings. Ed. by Mark B. Fishman. 400p. (Orig.). (C). 1989. pap. text ed. 25.00 (*0-9620173-1-0*) FL AI Research.

Second Flowering. Ruth Turk. LC 93-26742. 160p. 1993. 15.95 (*0-8329-0506-2*) New Win Pub.

Second Folio of Shakespeare. Archival Facsimles Ltd., Staff & William Shakespeare. (Books of the Monarchs of England). 920p. (C). 1989. reprint ed. 810.00 (*1-85297-011-1*, Pub. by Archival Facs UK) St Mut.

Second Forty Years. Edward J. Stiegliz. Ed. by Robert J. Kastenbaum. LC 78-22218. (Aging & Old Age Ser.). (Illus.). 1979. reprint ed. lib. bdg. 28.95 (*0-405-11831-7*) Ayer.

Second Foundation. Isaac Asimov. (Foundation Ser.: Bk. 3). 304p. 1986. mass mkt. 5.95 (*0-345-33629-1*, Del Rey) Ballantine.

Second Foundation. Isaac Asimov. 304p. 1991. mass mkt. 6.99 (*0-553-29336-2*) Bantam.

Second Four Books of Poems. W. S. Merwin. LC 92-39320. 400p. (Orig.). 1993. pap. 15.00 (*1-55659-054-7*) Copper Canyon.

Second Front: Censorship & Propaganda in the Gulf War. John R. MacArthur. 224p. 1992. 20.00 (*0-8090-8517-8*) Hill & Wang.

Second Front: Censorship & Propaganda in the Gulf War. John R. MacArthur. LC 93-19604. 1993. reprint ed. 12.00 (*0-520-08398-9*) U CA Pr.

Second Frutes. John Florio. LC 53-11448. 1977. reprint ed. 50.00 (*0-8201-1222-4*) Schol Facsimiles.

Second Furrow: Sequel to Too Wet to Plow (Americana & Homespun Philosophy) Frank Fuis, Jr. (Illus.). 400p. 1992. 18.95 (*0-9632006-0-7*) Norris World.

Second Garfield Treasury. Jim Davis. 112p. 1985. pap. 12.00 (*0-345-33276-8*, Ballantine Trade) Ballantine.

Second Gates of Paradise. Alberto Manguel. 704p. (Orig.). 1994. pap. 21.95 (*0-921912-77-3*, Pub. by Macfarlane Walter & Ross CN) Genl Dist Srvs.

***Second General Hospital Vol. 1: An Account of the Army Affiliated Unit of the Presbyterian Hospital of New York City in the European Theater of Operations, World War II, 1942-1945.** Albert R. Lamb, Jr. (Illus.). xiii, 193p. 1996. lib. bdg. write for info. (*0-9654040-0-5*) Col U Ofc Univ Publns.

Second Generation. Sheryl Aumack. 70p. (Orig.). (C). 1990. pap. 5.00 (*0-9625180-2-6*) Sea-Maid Pr.

***Second Generation.** Fast. Date not set. pap. write for info. (*0-15-600513-1*) HarBrace.

Second Generation. Esther McCoy. LC 83-14898. (Illus.). 200p. 1984. 27.50 (*0-87905-119-1*) Hennessey.

Second Generation. David C. Phillips. (Collected Works of David G. Phillips). 1988. reprint ed. lib. bdg. 59.00 (*0-7812-1333-9*) Rprt Serv.

Second Generation. David G. Phillips. (American Author Ser.). 1981. reprint ed. lib. bdg. 49.00 (*0-686-71943-3*) Scholarly.

Second Generation: Continuity & Change in the Kibbutz. Menachem Rosner et al. LC 90-3905. (Kibbutz Study Ser.: No. 2). 480p. 1990. text ed. 69.50 (*0-313-27287-5*, RSG/, Greenwood Pr) Greenwood.

Second Generation Automated Library Systems. Edwin Cortez & Tom Smorch. LC 92-30039. (Library Management Collection). 248p. 1993. text ed. 55.00 (*0-313-28361-3*, CSZ/, Greenwood Pr) Greenwood.

Second Generation Client - Server Computing. D. Travis Dewire. LC 96-35817. 448p. 1997. text ed. 49.95 (*0-07-016736-2*) McGraw.

Second Generation Expert Systems. Ed. by Jean M. David et al. LC 93-19194. 1993. 119.95 (*0-387-56192-7*) Spr-Verlag.

Second-Generation Japanese Problem. Edward K. Strong, Jr. LC 73-129415. (American Immigration Collection. Series 2). 1976. reprint ed. 24.95 (*0-405-00569-5*) Ayer.

Second-Generation Japanese Problem. Edward K. Strong, Jr. 120p. reprint ed. pap. 30.00 (*0-317-29833-X*, 2051956) Bks Demand.

Second Generation of Calcium Antagonists. W. G. Nayler. (Illus.). xiii, 226p. 1991. 103.00 (*0-387-54215-9*) Spr-Verlag.

Second Generation of Multivariate Analysis: Measurement & Evaluation, 2 Vols. Fornell. LC 82-11273. 444p. 1982. text ed. 125.00 (*0-275-90794-5*, C07940, Praeger Pubs) Greenwood.

Second Generation of Multivariate Analysis: Measurement & Evaluation, 2 Vols., 1. Fornell. LC 82-11273. 444p. 1982. text ed. 75.00 (*0-275-90792-9*, C07921, Praeger Pubs) Greenwood.

Second Generation of Multivariate Analysis: Measurement & Evaluation, 2 Vols., Vol. 2. Fornell. LC 82-11273. 444p. 1982. text ed. 75.00 (*0-275-90793-7*, C07932, Praeger Pubs) Greenwood.

Second Generation Subsea Production Systems, Vol. 20. (C). Ed. by Society for Underwater Technology Staff. (C). 1990. lib. bdg. 195.00 (*1-85333-302-6*, Pub. by Graham & Trotman UK) Kluwer Ac.

Second Generation United Nations: For Peace & Freedom in the 21st Century. Guido De Marco & Michael Bartolo. LC 96-8014. 152p. 1996. 76.50 (*0-7103-0558-3*, Pub. by Kegan Paul Intl UK) Col U Pr.

Second Generation WB Site Development Managing, Vol. I. Gene K. Landy. 1996. pap. 29.99 (*1-56884-806-4*) IDG Bks.

Second Gift. Edward Yarnold. (C). 1988. 50.00 (*0-85439-103-7*, Pub. by St Paul Pubns UK) St Mut.

Second Glances. Bruce L. Marcoon. (Illus.). 128p. 1994. pap. 8.50 (*0-8059-3705-6*) Dorrance.

Second Gold Rush: Oakland & the East Bay in World War II. Marilynn S. Johnson. LC 92-41889. (Illus.). 328p. (C). 1994. 35.00 (*0-520-08191-9*) U CA Pr.

Second Gold Rush: Oakland & the East Bay in World War II. Marilynn S. Johnson. (Illus.). 328p. 1996. pap. 16.95 (*0-520-20701-7*) U CA Pr.

Second Good News - Bad News Joke Book. Jeff Robin. 176p. (Orig.). 1994. pap. 3.99 (*0-451-17986-2*, Sig) NAL-Dutton.

An Asterisk (*) at the beginning of an entry indicates that the title is appearing in BIP for the first time.

Second Good News - Bad News Joke Book. Jeff Rovin. Date not set. pap. 3.99 (*0-451-17760-6*, Sig) NAL-Dutton.

Second Grade. B. K. Hixson. (Utah Core-Science Ser.). 75p. 1990. pap. text ed. 19.99 (*1-57156-013-0*) Wild Goose UT.

***Second Grade Ape.** Daniel Pinkwater. LC 97-13717. (Hello Reader! Ser.: Lvl. 4). (Illus.). (J). 1997. write for info. (*0-590-37261-0*) Scholastic Inc.

Second Grade Baby. Ann M. Martin. (Kids in Ms. Coleman's Class Ser.: No. 4). (J). (PS-3). 1996. pap. 2.99 (*0-590-69200-3*) Scholastic Inc.

Second-Grade Book. Grace Burton et al. Ed. by Miriam A. Leiva. LC 92-16408. (Curriculum & Evaluation Standards for School Mathematics Addenda Ser.: Grades K-6). (Illus.). 32p. (Orig.). 1992. pap. 9.50 (*0-87353-312-7*) NCTM.

Second Grade Dictionary Activity Book. Kaye Furlong. 1989. pap. 0.94 (*0-394-83405-4*) Random.

Second Grade Friends. Miriam Cohen. (J). 1993. pap. 2.99 (*0-590-47463-4*) Scholastic Inc.

Second Grade Friends . . . Again! Miriam Cohen. (J). (ps-3). 1994. pap. 2.95 (*0-590-45906-6*) Scholastic Inc.

Second Grade Grammar. Frank Schaffer Publications, Inc. Staff. (Skill Builders Ser.). (Illus.). 128p. 1996. wbk. ed. 10.95 (*0-7647-0007-3*, FS-32076) Schaffer Pubns.

Second Grade Ideas & Whole Language Activities. Barbara Gruber. (Instant Idea Bks.). (Illus.). 64p. 1990. 7.95 (*0-86734-083-5*, FS-8321) Schaffer Pubns.

Second Grade Math Review. Frank Schaffer Publications, Inc. Staff. (Skill Builders Ser.). (Illus.). 128p. 1996. wbk. ed. 10.95 (*0-7647-0003-0*, FS-32069) Schaffer Pubns.

Second Grade Math TAAS Instructional Packet. Patricia Enselek & Susan Griffin. (TAAS Instructional Packets (TIPs) Ser.). 127p. 1990. 26.95 (*1-883396-01-8*) Educ Etc.

Second-Grade Pig Pals. Kirby Larson. LC 93-16061. (Illus.). 96p. (J). (gr. 1-5). 1994. 14.95 (*0-8234-1107-9*) Holiday.

Second-Grade Pig Pals. Kirby Larson. (Illus.). 96p. (J). (gr. 1-4). 1996. pap. 3.50 (*0-440-41104-1*, YB BDD) BDD Bks Young Read.

Second Grade Reading & Writing TAAS Instructional Packet. Patricia Enselek & Susan Griffin. (TAAS Master Ser.). 134p. 1990. 26.95 (*1-883396-00-X*) Educ Etc.

Second Grade Review. Frank Schaffer Publications, Inc. Staff. (Skill Builders Ser.). (Illus.). 128p. 1996. wbk. ed. 10.95 (*0-86734-913-1*, FS-32057) Schaffer Pubns.

Second-Grade Star. Nancy Alberts. (J). 1996. pap. 3.50 (*0-590-25234-8*) Scholastic Inc.

Second Grade Teacher's Month-by-Month Activities Program. Elizabeth C. Stull. 356p. 1992. 29.95 (*0-87628-808-5*) Ctr Appl Res.

Second Great Brinks Robbery. Nelson H. White. LC 88-51272. 108p. (Orig.). 1988. pap. 25.00 (*0-939856-89-1*) Tech Group.

Second Greates Commandment see Nouveau Commandement

Second Greatest Commandment see O Segundo Grande Mandamento

Second Greatest Story Ever Told. Gorman Bechard. 1991. 17.95 (*0-8065-1263-6*, Citadel Pr) Carol Pub Group.

Second Greek Reader. G. Constantopoulos. (Illus.). 96p. (GRE.). 4.70 (*0-686-79627-6*) Divry.

Second Growth. Wallace Stegner. LC 85-8540. xii, 240p. 1985. pap. 10.00 (*0-8032-9157-4*, Bison Books) U of Nebr Pr.

Second Growth. Wallace Stegner. LC 85-8540. xii, 240p. 1985. text ed. 25.00 (*0-8032-4162-3*) U of Nebr Pr.

Second Guess: Second Amanda Valentine Mystery. Rose Beecham. 208p. 1994. pap. 9.95 (*1-56280-069-8*) Naiad Pr.

Second Half of Marriage: Facing the Eight Challenges of Every Long-Term Marriage. David Arp & Claudia Arp. LC 96-18553. 240p. 1996. 17.99 (*0-310-20714-2*) Zondervan.

Second Hand. N. T. Late. 11p. (Orig.). (C). 1994. pap. write for info. (*0-9641448-3-2*) N Late Pub.

Second Hand: An Exhibition of Contemporary Found Object Art. Contrib. by Joanne Cubbs. (Illus.). 16p. 1989. pap. 5.00 (*0-932718-27-2*) Kohler Arts.

Second-Hand Coat. Ruth Stone. 131p. 1991. reprint ed. pap. 10.95 (*0-938756-33-8*) Yellow Moon.

Second-Hand Dog: How to Turn Yours into a First-Rate Pet. Carol L. Benjamin. LC 88-748. (Illus.). 96p. 1988. pap. 6.95 (*0-87605-735-0*) Howell Bk.

Second-Hand Dreams. Louis R. Nobleman. (Illus.). (J). (gr. k-6). 1993. pap. 9.95 (*1-56883-010-6*) Colonial Pr AL.

Second Hand Kid. Craig Sodaro. 1992. pap. 5.00 (*0-87129-189-4*, S35) Dramatic Pub.

Second-Hand Knowledge: An Inquiry into Cognitive Authority. Patrick Wilson. LC 82-21069. (Contributions in Librarianship & Information Science Ser.: No. 44). vii, 211p. 1983. text ed. 37.50 (*0-313-23763-8*, WWK/, Greenwood Pr) Greenwood.

Second-Hand Markets for Consumer Durables. Natasha E. Stroeker. 340p. 1995. pap. 29.00 (*90-5170-349-X*, Pub. by Thesis Pubs NE) IBD Ltd.

***Second Hand Star.** Maryann MacDonald. (J). (gr. 2-3). 1997. pap. 3.95 (*0-7868-1168-4*) Hyprn Ppbks.

Second Hand Success: How to Turn Discards into Dollars. Jordan L. Cooper. LC 94-79873. 208p. (Orig.). (C). 1994. pap. 14.95 (*1-55950-122-7*, 64167) Loompanics.

Second Handbook of Anglo-Saxon Food & Drink: Production & Distribution. Ann Hagen. 432p. 1995. pap. 28.95 (*1-898281-12-2*) Paul & Co Pubs.

Second Handbook of Minority Student Services. Ed. by Charles A. Taylor. 1990. 44.00 (*0-935483-13-6*) Praxis Madison.

Second Handbook of Psychological & Social Instruments. D. M. Pestonjee. (C). 1990. 56.00 (*81-7022-193-5*, Pub. by Concept II) S Asia.

Second Handbook on Parent Education: Contemporary Perspectives. Ed. by Marvin J. Fine. (Educational Psychology Ser.). 651p. 1988. text ed. 69.00 (*0-12-256482-0*) Acad Pr.

Second Harmonic Generation - Sum Frequency Generation at Surfaces. Ed. by G. L. Richmond. (Studies in Surface Science & Catalysis). 1996. text ed. write for info. (*0-444-88893-4*) Elsevier.

Second Harvest. Denis Rogers. Ed. by Owen Davis. LC 81-84333. 196p. (Orig.). 1981. 12.95 (*0-935400-07-9*); pap. 7.95 (*0-935400-08-7*) News & Observer.

Second Harvest: More Life Stories of the Twentieth Century. Ed. by Ann Davidson et al. 352p. (Orig.). 1988. pap. 8.00 (*0-945131-00-3*) Terrace Pr.

2nd Helping of Chicken Soup for the Soul: 101 More Stories to Open the Heart & Rekindle the Spirit. Jack Canfield & Mark V. Hansen. (Chicken Soup for the Soul Ser.). 350p. (Orig.). 1995. 24.00 (*1-55874-332-4*, 3324); pap. 12.95 (*1-55874-331-6*, 3316) Health Comm.

2nd Helping of Chicken Soup for the Soul: 101 More Stories to Open the Heart & Rekindle the Spirit. large type ed. Jack Canfield & Mark V. Hansen. (Chicken Soup for the Soul Ser.). 420p. (Orig.). 1996. pap. 16.95 (*1-55874-382-0*, 3820) Health Comm.

Second Helpings: Books & Activities about Food. Robin Currie. Ed. by Jan Irving. (Peddler's Pack Ser.). (Illus.). 145p. 1994. pap. text ed. 18.50 (*1-56308-073-7*) Teacher Ideas Pr.

***Second Helpings: More Eating in Nebraska.** Katherine Endacott. 1996. pap. 12.95 (*0-9627861-1-X*) Pleasant Dale Pr.

Second Helpings: More Stories from the Pancake Man. Richard Speight. LC 93-15270. 144p. (Orig.). 1993. pap. 10.00 (*0-687-33632-5*) Dimen for Liv.

Second Helpings: Timeless Recipes Fondly Remembered. unabridged ed. Gretchen Markham. (Illus.). 100p. (Orig.). 1996. pap. 5.00 (*1-887146-18-0*) Ark Works.

Second Helpings of Cream & Bread. Janet L. Martin & Allen Todnem. Ed. by Eunice W. Pearson. (Illus.). (Orig.). 1986. pap. 7.95 (*0-9613437-1-0*) Redbird Prods.

Second Herman Treasury. Jim Unger. LC 80-67423. (Illus.). 192p. 1980. pap. 9.95 (*0-8362-1155-3*) Andrews & McMeel.

Second HGH Symposium, Amsterdam, June 1991. Ed. by J. Girard & J. S. Christiansen. (Journal: Hormone Research: Vol. 36, Suppl. 1, 1991). (Illus.). iv, 84p. 1991. pap. 38.50 (*3-8055-5552-0*) S Karger.

Second Hoeing. Hope W. Sykes & Timothy J. Kloberdanz. LC 82-8424. xviii, 309p. 1982. reprint ed. pap. 13.95 (*0-8032-9129-9*, Bison Books) U of Nebr Pr.

Second Hoeing. Hope W. Sykes. LC 82-8424. xviii, 309p. 1982. reprint ed. text ed. 30.00 (*0-8032-4136-4*) U of Nebr Pr.

***Second Home: Life in a Boarding School.** Ed. by Tim Hillman & Craig Thorn, IV. 166p. 1996. pap. 14.95 (*1-890765-00-7*) Avocus Pub.

***Second Home: Orphan Asylums & Poor Families in America.** Timothy A. Hacsi. 1997. 39.95 (*0-674-79644-6*) HUP.

Second Homes: Curse or Blessing. Ed. by J. T. Coppock. 1977. 105.00 (*0-08-021371-5*, Pub. by Pergamon Repr UK) Franklin.

Second Honeymoon. Sandra Field. (Presents Ser.). 1996. mass mkt. 3.50 (*0-373-11830-9*, 1-11830-6) Harlequin Bks.

***Second Honeymoon.** large type ed. Sandra Field. (Mills & Boon Large Print Ser.). 288p. 1996. 21.50 (*0-263-14574-3*, Pub. by M & B UK) Ulverscroft.

Second Honeymoon. large type ed. Vivien Young. (Linford Romance Library). 192p. 1992. pap. 15.99 (*0-7089-7296-9*, Linford) Ulverscroft.

Second Horror. R. L. Stine. Ed. by Patricia MacDonald. (Ninety-Nine Fear Street: The House of Evil Ser.). 176p. (Orig.). (YA). (gr. 7 up). 1994. mass mkt. 3.99 (*0-671-88563-4*, Archway) PB.

Second How-to Handbook for Jewish Living. Kerry M. Olitzky & Ronald H. Isaacs. LC 95-46769. 216p. 1996. 24.95 (*0-88125-534-3*); pap. 13.95 (*0-88125-550-5*) Ktav.

Second Hulbert Financial Digest Almanac. Mark J. Hulbert. 400p. (Orig.). 1988. pap. text ed. 24.95 (*0-9620125-0-5*) Minerva Bks.

Second Hundred Years of Hancock, New Hampshire. Ed. by Hancock History Committee. LC 79-14026. (Illus.). 1979. 15.00 (*0-914016-61-X*) Phoenix Pub.

Second Hundred Years War, Sixteen Eighty-Nine to Eighteen Fifteen. Arthur H. Buffinton. LC 75-14080. 114p. 1975. reprint ed. text ed. 45.00 (*0-8371-8204-2*, BUSYW, Greenwood Pr) Greenwood.

Second Husband. large type ed. Sheila Bishop. 1991. 25.99 (*0-7089-2424-7*) Ulverscroft.

2nd IEEE Symposium on High-Performance Computer Architecture. LC 95-81683. 352p. 1996. pap. 80.00 (*0-8186-7237-4*, PRO7237) IEEE Comp Soc.

Second IEEE Workshop on Interactive Voice Technology for Telecommunications Applications, 1994. IEEE, Communications Society Staff. LC 94-77698. 200p. 1994. pap. write for info. (*0-7803-2074-3*, 94TH0695-7) Inst Electrical.

Second Impression: Rural Life with a Rare Bookman. Barbara Kaye. LC 94-12220. 1995. 35.00 (*1-884718-04-3*) Oak Knoll.

Second Impressions: Modern Prints & Printmakers Reconsidered. Ed. by Clinton Adams. (Tamarind Papers). (Illus.). 120p. (C). 1996. pap. 29.95 (*0-8263-1672-7*) U of NM Pr.

***Second in the Realm.** Robert Cassler. 65p. (Orig.). 1996. pap. 4.00 (*1-57514-183-3*, 1164) Encore Perform Pub.

Second Incarnation: A Theology for the Twenty-First Century Church. Rubel Shelly & Randall J. Harris. 272p. (Orig.). 1992. pap. 12.99 (*1-878990-21-7*) Howard Pub LA.

Second India Revisited: Population, Poverty, & Environmental Stress over Two Decades. Robert C. Repetto. 95p. 1994. pap. 14.95 (*0-915825-96-1*, RESIP) World Resources Inst.

Second Industrial Divide: Possibilities for Prosperity. Michael J. Piore & Charles F. Sabel. LC 83-46080. 366p. 1985. pap. 20.00 (*0-465-07561-4*) Basic.

***Second Industrial Revolution: Reinventing Your Business on the Internet.** John J. Donovan. 240p. 1997. pap. text ed. 19.95 (*0-13-745621-2*) P-H.

Second Infantry Division. Turner Publishing Company Staff. LC 89-51929. 144p. 1990. 48.00 (*0-938021-79-6*) Turner Pub KY.

Second Infinity. Michael D. Weaver. 256p. (Orig.). 1996. mass mkt. 5.99 (*0-380-76101-7*, AvoNova) Avon.

Second Interim Report of the Interagency Commission on Alternative Motor Fuels. (Illus.). 75p. (Orig.). (C). 1993. pap. text ed. 25.00 (*1-56806-388-1*) DIANE Pub.

Second International Aphasia Rehabilitation Congress: Proceedings of the Conference, Goteborg, Sweden, June 1986. Ed. by Chris Code & Dave J. Muller. (Aphasiology Special Issue Ser.: Vol. 1, No. 3, May-June 1987). 116p. 1987. pap. 25.00 (*0-85066-913-8*) Taylor & Francis.

Second International Applied Statistics in Industry Conference Proceedings, 1994. Ed. by Bradley J. Brown. (Illus.). 480p. (Orig.). 1994. pap. 29.95 (*0-9642033-0-8*) ACG Pr.

Second International Conference on Algebra. Ed. by L. A. Bokut et al. LC 94-47104. (Contemporary Mathematics Ser.: Vol. 184). 1995. pap. 65.00 (*0-8218-0295-X*, CONM/184) Am Math.

Second International Conference on Austempered Duchle Iron. Sharon Schaefers. 428p. 1986. 60.00 (*0-317-67962-7*) ASME Gear Res.

2nd International Conference on Beam Processing of Advanced Materials. Ed. by J. Singh et al. 280p. 1995. pap. 109.00 (*0-87170-563-X*, 9201) ASM.

Second International Conference on Frontal Lobe Degeneration of Non-Alzheimer Type, Lund, Sweden, September 1992. Ed. by Victoria E. Chan-Palay. (Journal: Dementia: Vol. 4, No. 3-4, 1993). (Illus.). 116p. 1993. pap. 45.25 (*3-8055-5824-4*) S Karger.

***Second International Conference on Low Temperature Chemistry: Proceedings of the Second International Conference on Low Temperature Chemistry: 4-9 August 1996, University of Missouri-Kansas City, Kansas City, Missouri.** James R. Durig & Kenneth J. Klabunde. LC 96-31007. 1996. pap. 10.00 (*1-886157-11-1*) BkMk.

Second International Conference on River Flood Hydraulics, Vol. 2. Ed. by W. R. White & Jacqueline Watts. 604p. 1994. text ed. 150.00 (*0-471-95019-X*) Wiley.

***Second International Conference on the Recycling of Metals.** Bernard Cina. 443p. 1994. 70.00 (*0-614-24009-3*, 6449) ASM.

Second International Conference on Universal Personal Communications, 1993. IEEE, Communications Society Staff. Ed. by IEEE Staff. LC 93-79358. 100p. 1993. pap. write for info. (*0-7803-1396-8*, 93TH0573-6); fiche write for info. (*0-7803-1397-6*) Inst Electrical.

Second International Congress of Neuroendocrinology Abstracts, Bordeaux, June 1990: Journal: Neuroendocrinology, Vol. 52, Suppl. 1. Ed. by J. D. Vincent & D. A. Poulain. (Illus.). iv, 178p. 1990. pap. 56.75 (*3-8055-5252-1*) S Karger.

Second International Congress on Advances in Non-Impact Printing Technologies, Arlington, Virginia, 1984: Advance Printing of Paper Summaries. International Congress on Advances in Non-Impact Printing Technology Staff. 310p. reprint ed. pap. 88.40 (*0-317-29115-7*, 2025037) Bks Demand.

Second International Congress on Ethics in Medicine, 1987: Proceedings. Intro. by Elliot Leiter. 224p. 1988. 30.00 (*0-685-22943-2*) BIMC.

***2nd International Crop Science Congress.** Ed. by V. L. Cropra. 950p. (C). 1997. 295.00 (*1-57808-004-5*) Science Pubs.

Second International Exhibition of Holography. Tung H. Jeong. LC 85-80923. (Illus.). 24p. 1985. pap. text ed. 12.00 (*0-910535-03-5*) Lake Forest.

2nd International GABAg Symposium, Vol. 2, No. 1 & 2. Norman Bowery. 180p. 1992. pap. text ed. 150.00 (*3-7186-5352-4*, Harwood Acad Pubs) Gordon & Breach.

Second International Oat Conference - Proceedings: World Corps, Production, Utilization & Description. Ed. by D. A. Lawes & H. Thomas. 1986. lib. bdg. 116.00 (*90-247-3335-9*) Kluwer Ac.

***Second International Ocean Pollution Symposium, Beijing, China, 4-8 October, 1993.** Ed. by I. W. Duedall. 1995. pap. text ed. 45.00 (*2-88449-050-7*); pap. text ed. 45.00 (*2-88449-053-1*); pap. text ed. 90.00 (*90-5699-017-9*) Gordon & Breach.

Second International Round Table Conference on Historical Lexicography: Proceedings. Ed. by W. Pynenburg & F. De Tollenaere. viii, 353p. 1980. pap. 75.00 (*90-70176-21-1*) Mouton.

***Second International Sakharov Conference on Physics.** 900p. 1997. lib. bdg. 106.00 (*981-02-2861-9*) World Scientific Pub.

2nd International Symposium on Advanced Research in Asynchronous Circuits & Systems: ASYNC '96. LC 96-81680. 280p. 1996. 60.00 (*0-8186-7298-6*, PRO7298) IEEE Comp Soc.

Second International Symposium on Contamination Control: Proceedings. 75.00 (*0-685-63218-0*) Inst Environ Sci.

Second International Symposium on Environmental Geotechnology (May 15-18, 1989) Proceedings: May 15-18, 1989 Proceedings, Vol. 1. Ed. by Hsai-Yang Fang & Sibel Pamukcu. LC 89-80286. 550p. 1989. pap. 65.00 (*0-932871-17-8*) Envo Pub Co.

Second International Symposium on Environmental Geotechnology (May 15-18, 1989), Vol. 2: Proceedings: 15-18, 1989. Sibel Pamukcu. Ed. by Hsai-Yang Fang. LC 89-80286. 375p. 1991. pap. 55.00 (*0-932871-18-6*) Envo Pub Co.

***Second International Symposium on Extraction & Processing for the Treatment & Minimization of Wastes.** Ed. by V. Ramachandran & C. C. Nesbitt. (Illus.). 866p. 1996. 148.00 (*0-87339-369-4*, 3694) Minerals Metals.

***Second International Symposium on Fusion Nuclear Technology.** K. Herschbach et al. l, 1394p. 1991. 1,079.50 (*0-444-89382-2*, North Holland) Elsevier.

Second International Symposium on Magnetic Materials, Processes, & Devices. Ed. by L. T. Romankiw & D. A. Herman, Jr. LC 92-71336. (Proceedings Ser.: Vol. 92-10). 600p. 1992. 60.00 (*1-56677-010-6*) Electrochem Soc.

Second International Symposium on Memory. Peter Sebel. write for info. (*0-13-055055-8*) P-H.

Second International Symposium on Tilapia in Aquaculture. Ed. by Roger S. Pullin et al. 1990. 58.00 (*971-10-2260-5*, Pub. by ICLARM PH); pap. text ed. 45.00 (*971-10-2258-3*, Pub. by ICLARM PH) Intl Spec Bk.

Second International Workshop on Database Programming Languages, 1989. Ed. by Richard Hull et al. 450p. (Orig.). (C). 1989. pap. text ed. 39.95 (*1-55860-072-8*) Morgan Kaufmann.

Second Isaiah's Idol-Fabrication Passages. Knut Holter. (Beitr Age Zur Biblischen Exegese und Theologie Ser.: Vol. 28). 286p. 1995. pap. 54.95 (*0-8204-2934-1*) P Lang Pubng.

Second Jewish Book of Why. Alfred J. Kolatch. LC 84-21477. 432p. 1985. 18.95 (*0-8246-0305-2*) Jonathan David.

Second Jewish Catalog: Sources & Resources. Ed. by Michael Strassfeld & Sharon Strassfeld. LC 73-11759. (Illus.). 400p. 1976. pap. 17.95 (*0-8276-0084-4*) JPS Phila.

Second Jewish Trivia & Information Book. Ian Shapolsky. 400p. 1986. pap. 6.95 (*0-933503-45-8*) Sure Seller.

Second John McPhee Reader. John McPhee. Ed. & Selected by Patricia Strachan. 416p. 1996. pap. 14.00 (*0-374-52463-7*) FS&G.

Second John McPhee Reader. Ed. & Selected by Patricia Strachan. 1996. 27.50 (*0-374-25686-1*) FS&G.

***II Joshua: The Battle for Life.** Merrily Bittler. (Orig.). 1996. pap. text ed. 12.95 (*1-884687-05-9*) N Horzns Pub.

Second Journey: Spiritual Awareness & the Midlife Crisis. Gerals O'Collins. 120p. (Orig.). 1996. pap. 9.95 (*0-85244-321-8*, Pub. by Gracewing UK) Morehouse Pub.

Second Jumbo Book of Hidden Pictures. Highlights for Children Editors. LC 92-71869. 96p. (J). (ps-3). 1993. pap. 5.95 (*1-56397-185-2*) Boyds Mills Pr.

Second Jungle Book. Rudyard Kipling. 22.95 (*0-8488-0092-3*) Amereon Ltd.

Second Jungle Book. Rudyard Kipling. (J). (gr. 5 up). reprint ed. pap. 2.25 (*0-317-62282-X*, Puffin) Puffin Bks.

2 Kings. T. R. Hobbs. (Biblical Commentary Ser.: Vol. 13). 1986. 29.99 (*0-8499-0212-6*) Word Pub.

Second Kings. Burke O. Long. (Forms of the Old Testament Literature Ser.). xiv, 324p. 1991. pap. 25.00 (*0-8028-0535-3*) Eerdmans.

Second Kings. H. Rossier. 11.50 (*0-88172-182-4*) Believers Bkshelf.

Second Kings, Vol. 11. Mordechai Cogan. 408p. 1988. 20.00 (*0-385-02388-X*) Doubleday.

Second Kings & Chronicles. rev. ed. Ed. by Irving L. Jensen. (Bible Self-Study Ser.). (Illus.). (Orig.). 1968. pap. 6.99 (*0-8024-4485-7*) Moody.

Second Krishnamurti Reader. 317p. 1996. 12.75 (*0-14-019243-3*) Viking Penguin.

Second Language Acquisiition - Foreign Language Learning. Ed. by Bill VanPatten & Lee. (Multilingual Matters Ser.: No. 58). 266p. 1990. 89.00 (*1-85359-054-1*, Pub. by Multilingual Matters UK); pap. 36.00 (*1-85359-053-3*, Pub. by Multilingual Matters UK) Taylor & Francis.

Second Language Acquisition. Wolfgang Klein. (Cambridge Textbooks in Linguistics Ser.). 200p. (C). 1986. pap. text ed. 18.95 (*0-521-31702-9*) Cambridge U Pr.

Second Language Acquisition: An Introductory Course. Susan Gass & Larry Selinker. (Topics in Applied Psycholinguistics Ser.). 368p. (C). 1994. pap. 34.50 (*0-8058-0494-3*); text ed. 79.95 (*0-8058-0493-5*) L Erlbaum Assocs.

Second Language Acquisition: Socio-Cultural & Linguistic Aspects of English in India. Ed. by R. K. Agnihotri & A. L. Khanna. (Research in Applied Linguistics Ser.: Vol. 1). 404p. 1994. 39.95 (*0-8039-9178-9*) Sage.

Second Language Acquisition & Foreign Language Teaching. Ed. by Rosario C. Gingras. LC 78-74014. 117p. reprint ed. pap. 33.40 (*0-8357-3347-5*, 2039580) Bks Demand.

Second Language Acquisition & Language Pedagogy. Rod Ellis. (Multilingual Matters Ser.: No. 79). 282p. 1991. 99.00 (*1-85359-136-X*, Pub. by Multilingual Matters UK); pap. 34.90 (*1-85359-135-1*, Pub. by Multilingual Matters UK) Taylor & Francis.

S

Second Language Acquisition & Linguistic Variation. Ed. by Robert Bayley & Dennis R. Preston. LC 96-14699. (Studies in Bilingualism: Vol. 10). xviii, 317p. 1996. lib. bdg. 79.00 (*1-55619-544-3*) Benjamins North Am.

Second Language Acquisition in a Study Abroad Context. Ed. by Barbara F. Freed. LC 95-8924. (Studies in Bilingualism: No. 9). xiv, 345p. 1995. 79.00 (*1-55619-542-7*) Benjamins North Am.

Second Language Acquisition in Childhood, 2 vols. 2nd ed. Barry McLaughlin. 280p. (C). 1987. Vol. 1: Preschool Children, 256p. pap. text ed. 32.50 (*0-8058-0095-6*); Vol. 2: School Age Children, 304p. pap. text ed. 32.50 (*0-8058-0096-4*) L Erlbaum Assocs.

Second Language Acquisition in Childhood, 2 vols., Set. 2nd ed. Barry McLaughlin. (C). 1987. pap. text ed. 65.00 (*0-8058-0097-2*) L Erlbaum Assocs.

Second Language Acquisition in Childhood: School-Age Children. Ed. by Barry McLaughlin. 280p. 1984. 59.95 (*0-89859-378-6*) L Erlbaum Assocs.

Second Language Acquisition in Childhood: School-Age Children. Ed. by Barry McLaughlin. (Child Psychology Ser.). 304p. 1985. 59.95 (*0-89859-565-7*) L Erlbaum Assocs.

Second Language Acquisition Theory & Pedagogy. Ed. by Fred Eckman et al. 344p. 1995. text ed. 69.95 (*0-8058-1687-9*) L Erlbaum Assocs.

Second-Language Classroom Interaction. Ann C. Wintergerst. (Toronto Studies in Education). 108p. 1994. 35.00 (*0-8020-2994-9*) U of Toronto Pr.

Second Language Classrooms: Research on Teaching & Learning. Craig Chaudron. (Cambridge Applied Linguistics Ser.). (Illus.). 224p. 1988. pap. text ed. 19.95 (*0-521-33980-4*) Cambridge U Pr.

Second Language Curriculum. Ed. by Robert K. Johnson. (Cambridge Applied Linguistics Ser.). 336p. (C). 1989. pap. text ed. 30.95 (*0-521-36961-4*) Cambridge U Pr.

Second Language Curriculum. Ed. by Robert K. Johnson. (Cambridge Applied Linguistics Ser.). (C). 1989. 49.95 (*0-521-36156-7*) Cambridge U Pr.

2nd Language Discourse - A Textbook of Current Research. Jonathan Fine. Ed. by Roy O. Freedle. LC 87-19702. (Advances in Discourse Processes Ser.: Vol. 25). 208p. 1988. text ed. 78.50 (*0-89391-413-4*) Ablex Pub.

Second Language Grammer. Rutherford. (C). 1987. pap. text ed. 37.50 (*0-582-55375-X*) Addison-Wesley.

Second Language Learners & Middle School Reform. Julia Laro. 48p. (Orig.). 1995. pap. 6.00 (*1-884037-10-0*) Coun Chief St Schl Offs.

***Second Language Learning.** Gonzalez. 1997. pap. text ed. 30.00 (*0-205-26170-1*) P-H.

Second Language Learning: Contrastive Analysis, Error Analysis & Related Aspects. Jacquelyn Schachter. 432p. 1983. pap. text ed. 18.95 (*0-472-08033-4*) U of Mich Pr.

Second Language Learning: Theoretical Foundations. M. A. Smith. LC 93-33640. (Applied Linguistics & Language Ser.). pap. write for info. (*0-05-822186-7*, 76280) Longman.

Second Language Learning: Theoretical Foundations. Michael S. Smith. 1994. pap. text ed. 26.73 (*0-582-21886-1*, Pub. by Longman UK) Longman.

Second Language Learning & Language Teaching. Vivian Cook. 176p. 1995. text ed. 16.95 (*0-340-52626-2*, A5878, Pub. by E Arnld UK) St Martin.

Second Language Learning & Language Teaching. 2nd ed. Vivian Cook. LC 95-36369. 192p. 1996. text ed. 17.95 (*0-340-65202-0*, Pub. by E Arnld UK) St Martin.

Second Language Learning Data Analysis. Antonella Sorace et al. (Topics in Applied Psycholinguistics Ser.). 256p. 1994. pap. 24.95 (*0-8058-1863-4*) L Erlbaum Assocs.

Second Language Learning Through Cooperative Learning. Julie High. (Illus.). 77p. 1993. pap. text ed. 17.00 (*1-879097-18-4*) Kagan Cooperative.

Second Language Pedagogy. 1987. 14.95 (*0-19-437084-4*) OUP.

Second Language. Poems. Lisel Mueller. LC 86-7246. 72p. 1986. pap. 8.95 (*0-8071-1337-9*) La State U Pr.

Second Language Practice: Classroom Strategies for Deveoping Communicative Competence. Ed. by Georges Duquette. LC 95-30458. 200p. 1995. 79.00 (*1-85359-306-0*, Pub. by Multilingual Matters UK); pap. 29.95 (*1-85359-305-2*, Pub. by Multilingual Matters UK) Taylor & Francis.

Second Language Proficiency, Foreign Language Aptitude, & Intelligence Vol. 6: Quantitative & Qualitative Analyses. Miyuki Sasaki. (Theoretical Studies in Second Language Acquisition). 176p. (C). 1996. text ed. 40.95 (*0-8204-2497-8*) P Lang Pubng.

Second Language Reading & Vocabulary Learning. Ed. by Thomas Huckin et al. LC 92-10616. (Thematic Studies in 2nd Language Learning Acquisition & Learning). 320p. (C). 1993. pap. 39.50 (*0-89391-906-3*); text ed. 73.25 (*0-89391-850-4*) Ablex Pub.

Second Language Research Methods. Herbert W. Seliger & Elena Shohamy. (Language Education Ser.). 276p. 1990. 32.95 (*0-19-437009-7*); pap. text ed. 16.95 (*0-19-437067-4*) OUP.

Second Language Rhetorics in Process: A Comparison of Arabic, Chinese, & Spanish. Alexandra Rowe Henry. LC 93-383. (Theoretical Studies in Second Language Acquisition: Vol. 5). 158p. (C). 1994. text ed. 43.95 (*0-8204-2050-6*) P Lang Pubng.

***Second-Language Speech: Structure & Process.** Ed. by Allan James & Jonathan Leather. LC 96-43944. (Studies on Language Acquisition: Vol. 13). vii, 348p. (C). 1997. lib. bdg. 135.00 (*3-11-014126-4*) Mouton.

Second Language Teacher Education. Ed. by Jack C. Richards & David Nunan. (Cambridge Language Teaching Library). (Illus.). 336p. (C). 1990. pap. text ed. 20.95 (*0-521-38779-5*) Cambridge U Pr.

***Second Language Vocabulary Acquisition: A Rationale for Pedagogy.** Ed. by James Coady & Thomas Huckin. (Applied Linguistics Ser.). (Illus.). 336p. (C). 1996. text ed. 52.95 (*0-521-56132-9*); pap. text ed. 22.95 (*0-521-56764-5*) Cambridge U Pr.

Second Language Writing: Research Insights for the Classroom. Ed. by Barbara Kroll. (Cambridge Applied Linguistics Ser.). (Illus.). 224p. (C). 1990. text ed. 49.95 (*0-521-38383-8*); pap. text ed. 19.95 (*0-521-38778-7*) Cambridge U Pr.

Second Large Print Song Book. large type ed. Ulverscroft Editors. 1987. pap. 7.95 (*0-7089-1678-3*) Ulverscroft.

Second Large Print Song Book-Music Edition. large type ed. Ulverscroft Editors. 1987. pap. 15.95 (*0-7089-1736-4*) Ulverscroft.

Second Latin. Cora C. Scanlon & Charles L. Scanlon. LC 48-748. 1976. reprint ed. pap. 12.00 (*0-89555-003-2*) TAN Bks Pubs.

Second Law. P. W. Atkins. LC 84-5377. 230p. 1995. pap. text ed. write for info. (*0-7167-5005-8*) W H Freeman.

Second Law. Elizabeth Willis. LC 92-73493. (Orig.). (C). 1993. pap. text ed. 8.95 (*0-939691-08-6*) Avenue B.

Second Law. deluxe ed. Elizabeth Willis. LC 92-73493. (Orig.). (C). 1993. pap. text ed. 18.00 (*0-685-63393-4*) Avenue B.

Second Law: Energy, Chaos & Form. Peter Atkins. (C). 1995. pap. text ed. 19.95 (*0-7167-6006-1*) W H Freeman.

Second Legacy. Caroline Harvey. 540p. 1996. pap. 8.99 (*0-552-13917-3*) Bantam.

Second Legacy. large type ed. Caroline Harvey. (Charnwood Large Print Ser.). 624p. 1996. 27.99 (*0-7089-8890-3*, Charnwood) Ulverscroft.

Second Leicester International Dance Festival, Vol. 3, Part 1. Ed. by Val Bourne. 110p. 1992. pap. text ed. 23.00 (*3-7186-5320-6*, Harwood Acad Pubs) Gordon & Breach.

Second Lessons for Guitar Vol. 2: English Text. J. S. Sagreras. 36p. 1994. pap. 6.95 (*0-7935-3586-7*) H Leonard.

Second Letter of Paul to the Corinthians. James Thompson. 1970. 12.95 (*0-915547-28-7*) Abilene Christ U.

Second-Level Basic Electronics. U. S. Navy, Bureau of Naval Personnel Staff. Orig. Title: Basic Electronics Vol. 2. (Illus.). 352p. 1971. pap. text ed. 9.95 (*0-486-22841-X*) Dover.

Second Life: A West Bank Memoir. Janet V. Gunn. (Illus.). 216p. 1995. 19.95 (*0-8166-2530-1*) U of Minn Pr.

Second Life of Art: Selected Essays. Eugenio Montale. Ed. by Jonathan Galassi. LC 81-9861. 375p. 1982. 17.50 (*0-912946-84-9*) Ecco Pr.

Second-Line Agents in the Treatment of Arthritis. Ed. by Jonathan S. Dixon & D. E. Furst. (Inflammatory Disease & Therapy Ser.: Vol. 9). 640p. 1991. 235.00 (*0-8247-8541-X*) Dekker.

Second Line Assessment of APL. IPM Staff. (Assessment of NVQs & SVQs Ser.: No. 4). (C). 1994. 62.25 (*0-08-042119-9*, Pub. by IPM Hse UK) St Mut.

***Second Linguistic Turn: Chomsky & the Philosophy of Language.** Amitabha Das Gupta. xi, 220p. 1996. pap. 44.95 (*3-631-49866-7*) P Lang Pubng.

***Second Linguistic Turn: Chomsky & the Philosophy of Language.** Amitabha D. Gupta. xi, 220p. 1996. pap. 44.95 (*0-8204-2982-1*) P Lang Pubng.

Second Linin' Jazzmen of Southwest Louisiana, 1900-1950. Austin Sonnier, Jr. (Louisiana Life Ser.). (Illus.). 62p. (Orig.). 1989. pap. 5.00 (*0-940984-50-4*) U of SW LA Ctr LA Studies.

***Second Lining: Poems.** Norman Leer. LC 97-11765. (Illus.). 80p. 1997. pap. 12.95 (*0-7734-2824-0*, Mellen Poetry Pr) E Mellen.

***Second Lives: A Novel of the Gilded Age.** Richard S. Wheeler. LC 96-53275. 1997. 24.95 (*0-312-86333-0*) St Martin.

Second Lives: A Survey of Architectural Artifact Collections in the U. S. Emogene A. Bevitt. (Illus.). 100p. (Orig.). (C). 1995. pap. text ed. 30.00 (*0-7881-1829-3*) DIANE Pub.

Second Livre. Ed. by Albert Seay. (Transcriptions Ser.: No. 3). ii, 64p. 1980. pap. 4.00 (*0-933894-05-8*, Attaingnant) Colo Coll Music.

Second Livre d'Airs Des Plus Excelants Musiciens De Nostre Tems: Reduiz a Quatre Parties. Par M. Di. Le Blanc (Paris, 1579) Airs De Court. Mis En Musique a 4. E 5. Parties. De Plusieurs Autheurs (Paris, 1597) Ed. by Jane A. Bernstein. LC 95-5010. (Sixteenth-Century Chanson Ser.: Vol. 3). 208p. 1995. text ed. 85.00 (*0-8240-3102-4*) Garland.

Second Livre de Jungle. Rudyard Kipling. (FRE.). 1973. pap. 10.95 (*0-7859-2303-9*, 2070363252) Fr & Eur.

Second Livre des Amours. Pierre D. Ronsard. 227p. (FRE.). 1951. pap. 14.95 (*0-7859-5473-2*) Fr & Eur.

Second livre des Amours de Pierre de Ronsard see Monuments de la musique francaise au temps de la Renaissance

Second Look: The Reconstruction of Personal History in Psychiatry & Psychoanalysis. Samuel Novey. Ed. by Chicago Institute for Psychoanalysis Staff. LC 85-10884. (Classics in Psychoanalysis Monograph: No. 3). xiv, 162p. 1986. reprint ed. 30.00 (*0-8236-6022-2*, 06022) Intl Univs Pr.

Second Look at Agathis. M. R. Bowmen & T. C. Whitmore. 1980. 40.00 (*0-85074-053-3*) St Mut.

Second Look at America. Emilio Aguinaldo & Vicente A. Pacis. 9.95 (*0-8315-0051-4*) Speller.

Second Look at Calgary's Public Art. Barbara Kwasny & Elaine Peake. (Illus.). 208p. (Orig.). 1992. pap. 14.95 (*1-55059-041-3*) Temeron Bks.

Second Look at Harmony. Tibor Serly. 20.00 (*0-317-40588-8*, Modus Assoc) Tritone Music.

Second Look at Saint Bernard. Jean Leclercq. Tr. by Marie-Bernard Said from FRE. (Cistercian Studies: No. 105). 150p. 1991. 35.95 (*0-87907-605-4*); pap. 19.95 (*0-87907-405-1*) Cistercian Pubns.

Second Look in the Rearview Mirror: Further Autobiographical Reflections of a Philosopher at Large. Mortimer J. Adler. LC 92-9169. 1994. pap. 10.00 (*0-02-016030-5*) Macmillan.

Second Love. large type ed. Mary Munro. 352p. 1986. 25.99 (*0-7089-1464-0*) Ulverscroft.

Second Loves: A Guide for Women Involved with Divorced Men. Gerald A. Silver & Myrna Silver. LC 84-16018. 192p. 1984. text ed. 45.00 (*0-275-91748-7*, C1748, Praeger Pubs) Greenwood.

II Maccabees: A New Translation with Introduction & Commentary. Jonathan A. Goldstein. LC 82-45200. (Anchor Bible Ser.: Vol. 41-A). (Illus.). 624p. (C). 1983. 29.00 (*0-385-04864-5*) Doubleday.

Second Maiden's Tragedy. Ed. by David Hoeniger et al. LC 77-4604. (Revels Plays Ser.). 1978. text ed. 46.50 (*0-8018-2011-1*) Johns Hopkins.

Second Malaysian Family Life Survey: Codebook. Christine E. Peterson et al. LC 93-18801. 1993. pap. 9.00 (*0-8330-1352-1*, MR-108-NICHNIA) Rand Corp.

Second Malaysian Family Life Survey: Overview & Technical Report. John Haaga et al. LC 93-17339. 1993. pap. 9.00 (*0-8330-1372-6*, MR-106-NICHD/NI) Rand Corp.

Second Malaysian Family Life Survey: Quality of Retrospective Data for the New Sample. Jeffrey Sine & Christine E. Peterson. LC 93-45999. 1993. pap. 9.00 (*0-8330-1496-X*, MR-110-NICHD) Rand Corp.

Second Malaysian Family Life Survey: User's Guide. Christine E. Peterson. LC 93-25706. 1993. pap. 9.00 (*0-8330-1357-2*, MR-109-NICHNIA) Rand Corp.

Second Man: Monster, Myth, or Minister. Blaine Hughes. 20p. 1976. pap. text ed. 1.95 (*0-89265-110-5*) Randall Hse.

Second Man, & Other Poems. Louis O. Coxe. LC 55-9369. 72p. reprint ed. pap. 25.00 (*0-317-27945-9*, 2055851) Bks Demand.

Second Manassas. Ed. by Time-Life Books Editors. LC 94-48737. (Voices of the Civil War Ser.). (Illus.). 168p. 22.95 (*0-7835-4701-3*) Time-Life.

Second Manassas Battlefield Map Study. John Nennessy. (Virginia Civil War Battles & Leaders Ser.). (Illus.). 504p. 1991. 39.95 (*1-56190-009-5*) H E Howard.

Second Manual for the Calligraphic Arts. Ed. by M. Jane Van Milligen. (Illus.). 156p. 1987. pap. 14.95 (*0-9617137-1-2*) Ctr Calig KS.

Second Manual for the Calligraphic Arts. 2nd ed. M. Jane Van Milligen et al. (Illus.). 154p. 1992. pap. text ed. 16.95 (*0-9617137-4-7*) Ctr Calig KS.

Second Map of Days. Ed. by Nadine L. Smith et al. (Orig.). 1988. pap. 6.95 (*0-9617772-1-4*) Scottsdale Cmnty Coll.

Second Marriage. Frederick Barthelme. LC 95-22802. 224p. 1995. pap. 11.00 (*0-8021-3436-X*, Grove) Grove-Atltic.

Second Marriage: Make it Happy! Make it Last! Richard B. Stuart & Barbara Jacobson. 1985. 15.95 (*0-393-01910-1*) Norton.

Second Marriage Guidebook. George W. Knight. 96p. (Orig.). 1984. pap. 7.95 (*0-939298-23-6*, 236) J M Prods.

Second Martin: The Life & Theology of Martin Chemnitz. J. A. Preus. LC 94-15925. 336p. (Orig.). (C). 1994. pap. 34.95 (*0-570-04645-9*, 53-3227) Concordia.

Second Marxian Invasion: The Fiction of the Strugatsky Brothers. Stephen W. Potts. LC 84-309. (Milford Series: Popular Writers of Today: Vol. 50). 104p. (C). 1991. pap. 17.00 (*0-89370-279-X*); lib. bdg. 27.00 (*0-89370-179-3*) Borgo Pr.

Second Match. Emma Lange. 224p. 1993. pap. 3.99 (*0-451-17737-1*, Sig) NAL-Dutton.

Second Mate. Philip McCutchan. 192p. 1996. 19.95 (*0-312-14410-5*) St Martin.

***Second Mayflower: How Christian Ethics Can Restore Our Freedom.** Kevin Swanson. LC 95-82253. 224p. (Orig.). 1997. pap. 14.99 (*1-56384-116-9*) Huntington Hse.

Second Media Age. Mark Poster. LC 95-14498. 192p. 1995. text ed. 55.95 (*0-7456-1395-0*, Pub. by Polity Pr UK); pap. text ed. 24.95 (*0-7456-1396-9*, Pub. by Polity Pr UK) Blackwell Pubs.

Second Mencken Chrestomathy. H. L. Mencken. Ed. by Terry Teachout. LC 94-12087. 1995. 30.00 (*0-679-42829-1*) Knopf.

Second Mencken Chrestomathy: Selected, Revised, & Annotated by the Author. Mencken H. L. 1995. pap. 16.00 (*0-679-76407-0*, Vin) Random.

Second Mercury Story Book. London Mercury Staff. LC 79-37553. (Short Story Index Reprint Ser.). 1977. reprint ed. 25.95 (*0-8369-4112-8*) Ayer.

Second Message of Islam. Mahmoud M. Taha. Tr. by Abdullahi Ahmid-An-Na'im from ARA. (Contemporary Issues in the Middle East Ser.). 192p. 1987. text ed. 34.95 (*0-8156-2407-7*) Syracuse U Pr.

Second Messengers. Robert McNamara. LC 89-32935. (Wesleyan New Poets Ser.). 64p. 1990. pap. 11.95 (*0-8195-1184-6*, Wesleyan Univ Pr); text ed. 25.00 (*0-8195-2182-5*, Wesleyan Univ Pr) U Pr of New Eng.

Second Metabolism. 2nd ed. Mann. 390p. 1987. 75.00 (*0-19-855530-X*) OUP.

Second Metabolism. 2nd ed. J. Mann. 390p. 1987. pap. 39.95 (*0-19-855529-6*) OUP.

Second Middle Age: Looking Differently at Life Beyond Fifty. Ed. by Ronald J. Manheimer. LC 95-7303. (Illus.). 500p. 1995. 17.95 (*0-7876-0481-X*) Visible Ink Pr.

Second Mile. Roger Prescott. 1985. 5.25 (*0-89536-739-4*, 5823) CSS OH.

Second Mile. Erwin A. Thompson. 250p. (Orig.). 1994. pap. 8.50 (*0-9640561-0-0*) Julia Thompson.

Second Mile. Sarah H. Terry. viii, 88p. 1994. reprint ed. pap. 5.00 (*0-88053-322-6*, S-305) Macoy Pub.

Second Mile People. Isobel Kuhn. 155p. 1990. reprint ed. pap. 5.99 (*981-3009-00-4*) OMF Bks.

Second Miracle: Our Fundamental Call to Connection & Belonging. Richard M. Moss. LC 95-17541. 236p. 1995. pap. 12.95 (*0-89087-765-3*) Celestial Arts.

Second MNMA Conference Proceedings, 1991: With Test Drive the New Notation Systems. Ed. by Thomas S. Reed. LC 93-86922. 180p. (C). 1994. pap. 27.00 (*0-9638849-0-5*) Music Notation.

***Second Mrs. Adams.** Sandra Martin. (Harlequin Romance Ser.). 1997. 20.95 (*0-263-15045-3*, Pub. by Mills & Boon UK) Thorndike Pr.

***Second Mrs. Adams.** Sandra Marton. 1997. pap. 3.50 (*0-373-11899-6*, 1-11899-1) Harlequin Bks.

Second Mrs. Giaconda. E. L. Konigsburg. LC 75-6946. (Illus.). 144p. (J). (gr. 5-9). 1978. pap. 5.95 (*0-689-70450-X*, Aladdin Paperbacks) S&S Childrens.

Second Mrs. Hardy. Robert Gittings & Jo Manton. LC 79-63567. (Illus.). 1979. 20.00 (*0-295-95668-2*) U of Wash Pr.

***Second Mrs. Malone.** Amanda Stevens. 1997. pap. 3.75 (*0-373-22430-3*, 1-22430-2) Harlequin Bks.

***Second Mrs. Tanqueray.** Arthur W. Pinero. Ed. by William-Alan Landes. LC 96-37918. 70p. (Orig.). 1997. pap. 7.00 (*0-88734-719-3*) Players Pr.

Second Naivete: Barth, Ricoeur, & the New Yale Theology. Mark I. Wallace. LC 90-32249. (Studies in American Biblical Hermeneutics: No. 6). 136p. (C). 1995. pap. text ed. 16.95 (*0-86554-380-1*, MUP/P089) Mercer Univ Pr.

Second National Conference on Thermal Spray: 31 October-2 November, 1984, Hyatt Regency Long Beach, Long Beach, California. National Conference on Thermal Spray, Second, Long Beach, CA Staff. LC 85-71832. (Illus.). 152p. pap. 43.40 (*0-7837-1864-0*, 2042065) Bks Demand.

***Second National Roundtable on Outcome Measures in Child Welfare Services: Summary of Proceedings.** Ed. by American Humane Association, Children's Division Staff. (Illus.). vi, 130p. 1995. pap. text ed. write for info. (*0-930915-04-6*, COM02) Am Humane Assn.

Second Nature. James Aitchison. 100p. 1990. pap. text ed. 13.00 (*0-08-037986-9*, Pub. by Aberdeen U Pr) Macmillan.

Second Nature. Alice Hoffman. 304p. (Orig.). 1995. mass mkt. 6.50 (*0-425-14681-2*) Berkley Pub.

***Second Nature.** Alice Hoffman. 1998. pap. write for info. (*0-425-16163-3*, Berkley Trade) Berkley Pub.

Second Nature. Nora Roberts. (Language of Love Ser.: No. 30). 1993. mass mkt. 3.59 (*0-373-51030-6*, 5-51030-0) Silhouette.

Second Nature. large type ed. Alice Hoffman. LC 93-47474. 1994. lib. bdg. 23.95 (*0-7862-0177-0*) Thorndike Pr.

Second Nature. large type ed. Alice Hoffman. LC 93-47474. 1995. lib. bdg. 15.95 (*0-7862-0178-9*) Thorndike Pr.

Second Nature: A Gardener's Education. Michael Pollan. 320p. 1997. pap. 12.95 (*0-385-31266-0*, Delta) Dell.

***Second Nature: Environmental Enrichment for Captive Animals.** Ed. by David J. Shepherdson et al. (Zoo & Aquarium Biology & Conservation Ser.). (Illus.). 336p. 1997. text ed. 32.50 (*1-56098-745-6*) Smithsonian.

Second Nature: Forty Six Poems. Boris Pasternak. Tr. by A. Navrozov. LC 90-80796. 128p. 9000. 34.00 (*0-7206-0751-5*) Dufour.

Second Nature of Things. Will Curtis. LC 92-16806. 1992. 24.95 (*0-88001-285-4*) Ecco Pr.

Second Nature of Things. Will Curtis. LC 95-10569. (Illus.). 1995. pap. 14.00 (*0-88001-383-4*) Ecco Pr.

Second Navy Reader. Ed. by William H. Fetridge. LC 71-142627. (Essay Index Reprint Ser.). 1977. 32.95 (*0-8369-2156-9*) Ayer.

Second Noah. Laura O'Neil. (J). 1996. pap. text ed. 3.99 (*0-590-93710-3*) Scholastic Inc.

Second NREL Conference on Thermophotovoltaic Generation of Electricity: Golden, Colorado, July 16-20, 1995. John P. Benner et al. (CP Ser.: No. 358). (Illus.). 544p. 1996. boxed 140.00 (*1-56396-509-7*) Am Inst Physics.

Second Nuclear Era: A New Start for Nuclear Power. Alvin M. Weinberg et al. LC 85-12613. 460p. 1985. text ed. 65.00 (*0-275-90183-1*, C0183, Praeger Pubs) Greenwood.

Second Official Handbook of Practical Jokes. Peter Van der Linden. 1991. pap. 3.50 (*0-317-03030-2*, Sig) NAL-Dutton.

Second Oldest Profession: Spies & Spying in the Twentieth Century. Phillip Knightley. (Illus.). 436p. 1987. 19.95 (*0-393-02386-9*) Norton.

***II Olympiad, Paris 1900.** (Olympic Century Ser.). (Illus.). 1997. 21.95 (*1-888383-03-8*, Wrld Spt) Wld Sport Resch.

Second Opinion. H. J. Hirschfield. (Illus.). 64p. (Orig.). 1994. pap. 9.95 (*1-879260-33-6*) Evanston Pub.

Second Opinion. Francis Roe. 416p. 1995. mass mkt. 5.99 (*0-451-18506-4*, Sig) NAL-Dutton.

Second Opinion. Isadore Rosenfeld. 432p. 1991. mass mkt. 5.99 (*0-553-20562-5*) Bantam.

***Second Opinion.** large type ed. Claire Rayner. (Charnwood Large Print Ser.). 528p. 1996. 27.99 (*0-7089-8897-0*) Ulverscroft.

Second Opinion: A Holistic Approach to Treating Adults with A. D. D. Richard C. Bennett. 110p. 1994. pap. text ed. 19.95 (*1-885988-00-1*) Add Resources.

Second Opinion Elective Surgery. Eugene McCarthy et al. LC 81-3471. 193p. 1981. text ed. 55.00 (*0-86569-079-0*, Auburn Hse) Greenwood.

An Asterisk (*) at the beginning of an entry indicates that the title is appearing in BIP for the first time.

***Second Opinions: Americans' Changing Views on Healthcare Reform.** John Immerwahr & Jean Johnson. 40p. (Orig.). 1994. pap. 15.00 (*1-889483-26-5*) Public Agenda.

Second Opinion's Practical Guide to Home Remedies. Steven E. Kroening. 350p. 1996. pap. 19.95 (*1-885236-10-7*) Second Opinion.

***Second-Order Methods for Neural Networks: Fast & Reliable Training Methods for Multi-Layer Perceptrons.** Adrian J. Shepherd. LC 96-35297. (Perspectives in Neural Computing Ser.). 1997. write for info. (*3-540-76100-4*) Spr-Verlag.

***Second Order Parabolic Differential Equations.** 450p. 1996. lib. bdg. 54.00 (*981-02-2883-X*) World Scientific Pub.

Second-Order Sturm-Liouville Difference Equations & Orthogonal Polynomials. Alouf Jirari. LC 94-35341. (Memoirs Ser.: No. 542). 1995. pap. 37.00 (*0-8218-0359-X*, MEMO/113/542) Am Math.

Second Oswald. Richard H. Popkin. 17.95 (*0-8488-0888-6*) Amereon Ltd.

***Second Oswald.** Richard H. Popkin. 19.95 (*1-56723-086-5*) Yestermorrow.

Second Overseas Highway to Key West Florida. Rod Bethel. (Orig.). 1989. write for info. (*0-9614702-5-9*) Slumbering.

Second Paris Cosmology Colloquim. H. J. De Vega & N. Sanchez. 560p. 1995. text ed. 136.00 (*981-02-2172-X*) World Scientific Pub.

Second Part of King Henry IV. William Shakespeare. Ed. by Giorgio Melchiori. (New Cambridge Shakespeare Ser.). (Illus.). 260p. (C). 1989. text ed. 39.95 (*0-521-25695-X*); pap. text ed. 10.95 (*0-521-27652-7*) Cambridge U Pr.

Second Part of King Henry Sixth. William Shakespeare. Ed. by Michael Hattaway. (New Cambridge Shakespeare Ser.). (Illus.). 200p. (C). 1991. text ed. 39.95 (*0-521-37330-1*); pap. text ed. 10.95 (*0-521-37704-8*) Cambridge U Pr.

Second Part of the Booke of Battailes, Fought in Our Age. John Polemon. LC 78-38219. (English Experience Ser.: No. 483). 196p. 1972. reprint ed. 20.00 (*90-221-0483-4*) Walter J Johnson.

Second Part of the Institutes of the Laws on England, 4 vols. Edwardo Coke. Ed. by Bernard D. Reams, Jr. LC 86-62937. (Historical Writings in Law & Jurisprudence Ser.: No. 5B). 1992. reprint ed. Set. 240.00 (*0-89941-520-2*, 304560) W S Hein.

Second Part of the Popular Errors. Tr. & Anno. by Gregory D. De Rocher. LC 94-4708. 336p. 1995. text ed. 49.95 (*0-8173-0758-3*) U of Ala Pr.

Second Part of the Secretes of Maister Alexis of Piemont. Piemontese Alessio. Tr. by W. Ward. LC 77-6843. (English Experience Ser.: No. 839). 1977. reprint ed. lib. bdg. 20.00 (*90-221-0839-2*) Walter J Johnson.

Second Parting. Oral Bullard. 80p. (Orig.). 1980. pap. 4.95 (*0-918688-04-3*) Touchstone Oregon.

Second Partition of Poland. Robert H. Lord. LC 73-101268. 1970. reprint ed. 38.45 (*0-404-04009-8*) AMS Pr.

Second Pearl Harbor: America's Response to the Japan that Can Say No. T. Boone Pickens. 160p. 1991. 19.95 (*0-915765-94-2*) Krantz Co.

Second Period of Quakerism (to about 1725) Sessions, William Ltd., Staff. (C). 1989. pap. 37.00 (*0-900657-49-9*, Pub. by W Sessions UK) St Mut.

Second Person Rural: More Essays of a Sometime Farmer. Noel Perrin. LC 80-66193. 152p. 1990. reprint ed. pap. 9.95 (*0-87923-834-8*) Godine.

Second Person Singular, & Other Essays. Alice C. Meynell. LC 68-55851. (Essay Index Reprint Ser.). 1977. 17.95 (*0-8369-0706-X*) Ayer.

Second Peter. D. Martyn Lloyd-Jones. 1983. 23.99 (*0-85151-379-4*) Banner of Truth.

2 Peter & Jude. Jonathon Knight. (New Testament Guide Ser.). 100p. 1995. pap. 9.95 (*1-85075-744-5*) CUP Services.

Second Peter & Jude. William MacDonald. 1988. pap. 6.00 (*0-937396-77-X*) Walterick Pubs.

Second Peter & Jude: An Expositional Commentary. D. Edmond Hiebert. Ed. by David Waehr. 336p. (Orig.). 1989. pap. 21.95 (*0-89084-466-6*, 042952) Bob Jones Univ Pr.

Second Peter, Jude: A New Translation with Introduction & Commentary. Jerome H. Neyrey. LC 92-21142. (Anchor Bible Ser.: Vol. 37C). 304p. 1993. 28.00 (*0-385-41362-9*, Anchor NY) Doubleday.

Second Peter Principle. Richard A. Hamilton. 88p. 1991. 9.98 (*0-88290-428-0*) Horizon Utah.

2 Peter/Jude. Douglas J. Moo. LC 96-35833. (NIV Application Commentary Ser.). 256p. 1996. 19.99 (*0-310-20104-7*) Zondervan.

***2 Peter/Jude.** NavPress Staff. (Lifechange Ser.). 1996. pap. text ed. 7.00 (*0-89109-994-8*) NavPress.

Second Philippic Against Anthony see Selected Works

Second Philippic Oration. Marcus Tullius Cicero. Ed. by Lacey. (Classical Texts Ser.). 1986. 49.95 (*0-85668-254-3*, Pub. by Aris & Phillips UK); pap. 24.95 (*0-85668-255-1*, Pub. by Aris & Phillips UK) David Brown.

Second Piano Accompaniments for Students & Teachers, Vol. A. Ray Landers. 64p. 1982. pap. text ed. 8.95 (*0-87487-922-1*) Summy-Birchard.

Second Piano Accompaniments for Students & Teachers, Vol. B. Ray Landers. 72p. 1985. pap. text ed. 8.95 (*0-87487-923-X*) Summy-Birchard.

Second Picture Dictionary. (Picture Dictionaries Ser.: No. 642-2). (Illus.). (J). (ps-2). 3.50 (*0-7214-0618-1*, Ladybrd) Penguin.

Second Plague of Europe: AIDS Prevention & Sexual Transmission among Men in Western Europe. Michael Pollak. LC 92-18354. 1993. pap. 9.95 (*1-56023-020-7*) Harrington Pk.

Second Plague of Europe: AIDS Prevention & Sexual Transmission among Men in Western Europe. Michael Pollak. LC 92-18354. (Illus.). 104p. 1993. 24.95 (*1-56024-306-6*) Haworth Pr.

Second Poetry Book. John Foster et al. (Illus.). 128p. (J). (gr. 4-6). 1987. pap. 8.00 (*0-19-918136-5*) OUP.

Second Pond. Ray Smith. (Illus.). 1979. pap. 3.00 (*0-686-02398-6*) Kirk Pr.

Second Position Clitic & Related Phemonena. Ed. by Aaron L. Halpern & Arnold M. Zwicky. (Lecture Notes Ser.). 425p. 1996. pap. text ed. 22.95 (*1-57586-014-7*) CSLI.

Second Position Clitic & Related Phemonena. Ed. by Aaron L. Halpern & Arnold M. Zwicky. (Lecture Notes Ser.). 425p. (C). 1996. text ed. 69.95 (*1-57586-015-5*) CSLI.

Second Practice of Nineteenth Century Tonality. Ed. by William Kinderman & Harald Krebs. LC 95-16160. ix, 281p. 1996. text ed. 70.00 (*0-8032-2724-8*) U of Nebr Pr.

Second Prehistoric America Series No. 7. W. Michael Gear & Kathleen O'Neal Gear. 1995. 23.95 (*0-614-03847-2*) Forge NYC.

Second Princess. Hiawyn Oram. LC 94-1658. (Illus.). 32p. (J). (ps-3). 1994. 13.95 (*0-307-17513-8*, Golden Books) Western Pub.

***Second Principles: Survey of the Old Testament.** Kip McKean. 32p. (Orig.). 1996. wbk. ed., pap. 4.99 (*1-57782-000-2*) Discipleshp.

Second Prize: Two Months in Leningrad. Trish Johnson. 1984. pap. 5.25 (*0-8222-1006-1*) Dramatists Play.

Second Quantized Approach to Quantum Chemistry. Peter R. Surjan. (Illus.). 200p. 1989. 123.95 (*0-387-51137-7*) Spr-Verlag.

Second Quiltmaker's Handbook: Creative Approaches to Contemporary Quilt Design. Michael James. (Illus.). 192p. 1993. reprint ed. pap. text ed. 14.95 (*0-942786-40-8*) Leone Pubns.

***Second Quiltmaker's Handbook: Creative Approaches to Contemporary Quilt Design.** Michael James. (Illus.). 192p. reprint ed. pap. text ed. 7.95 (*0-486-29464-1*) Dover.

Second R: Writing Instruction for the Nineties & Beyond. John Brereton. 1994. pap. 10.00 (*0-8090-1572-2*); pap. text ed. 20.00 (*0-8090-8515-1*) Hill & Wang.

Second Rainbow Book of Adventures. Ed. by Charles L. Springer. (Illus.). 333p. (Orig.). 1985. pap. 13.95 (*0-932471-03-X*) Falsoft.

Second Rainbow Book of Simulations. Ed. by Tamara Dunn. (Illus.). 200p. (Orig.). 1986. pap. 9.95 (*0-932471-06-4*) Falsoft.

Second Ralliement: The Rapprochement Between Church & State in France in the Twentieth Century. Harry W. Paul. LC 67-14435. 246p. reprint ed. pap. 70.20 (*0-685-17841-2*, 2029503) Bks Demand.

Second Rape: Society's Continued Betrayal of the Victim. Lee Madigan & Nancy Gamble. 153p. 19.95 (*0-669-27189-6*) Free Pr.

Second Reader see McGuffey's Revised Eclectic Readers

Second Reader for Deaf Children. National Association for Teaching of the Deaf Staff. 1973. 59.95 (*0-8490-1009-8*) Gordon Pr.

Second Reference Catalogue of Bright Galaxies. Gerard H. De Vaucouleurs & Antoinette De Vaucouleurs. LC 75-44009. (Texas University Monographs in Astronomy: No. 2). 404p. reprint ed. pap. 115.20 (*0-317-08632-4*, 2021153) Bks Demand.

Second Reflections. Royal Satterlee. 210p. 1990. 9.95 (*1-879227-00-2*) Royal Ideas.

***Second Reformation: Reshaping the Church for the 21st Century.** William A. Beckham. (Illus.). 253p. (Orig.). 1995. pap. 12.95 (*1-880828-90-1*) Touch Pubns.

Second Regional Plan: A Draft for Discussion. (Illus.). 103p. 1968. 3.00 (*0-318-16384-5*, 110) Regional Plan Assn.

Second Reich. William Simpson. (Topics in History Ser.). (Illus.). 144p. (C). 1995. pap. text ed. 15.95 (*0-521-45909-5*) Cambridge U Pr.

Second Report on Dialectal Work see English Dialect Society Publications: Miscellanies

***Second Republic: Politics in Israel.** Alan Arian. LC 97-5247. 1997. write for info. (*1-56643-052-6*) Chatham Hse Pubs.

Second Republic & Napoleon Third. Rene Arnaud. LC 70-158271. reprint ed. 57.50 (*0-404-50799-9*) AMS Pr.

Second Ring of Power. Carlos Castaneda. (gr. 10-12). 1991. pap. 14.00 (*0-671-73247-1*) PB.

Second Round, Tea-Time at the Masters. Junior League of Augusta, Georgia, Inc. Staff. (Illus.). 360p. 1988. 8.95 (*0-9621062-0-8*) JL Augusta.

Second Row, Piano Side: With Humor, Heartache, & Hope: Chonda Pierce Tells Her Story. Chonda Pierce. LC 96-11035. 120p. (Orig.). 1996. pap. 9.99 (*0-8341-1589-1*) Beacon Hill.

Second Rumpole Omnibus. John Mortimer. 672p. 1988. pap. 14.95 (*0-14-008958-6*, Penguin Bks) Viking Penguin.

2 Samuel. Arnold A. Anderson. (Biblical Commentary Ser.: Vol. 11). 1989. 29.99 (*0-8499-0210-X*) Word Pub.

Second Sandoz Symposium on the Treatment of Parkinson's Disease, Tokyo, October 1993. Ed. by I. Goto. (Journal: European Neurology: Vol. 34, Suppl. 3, 1994). (Illus.). iv, 40p. 1994. pap. 19.25 (*3-8055-6058-3*) S Karger.

Second Scientific American Book of Mathematical Puzzles & Diversions. Martin Gardner. LC 87-10760. (Illus.). 256p. 1987. reprint ed. pap. 14.95 (*0-226-28253-8*) U Ch Pr.

Second Scramble for Africa: A Response & a Critical Analysis of the Challenges Facing Contemporary Sub-Saharan Africa. Ed. by Kivuto Ndeti & Kenneth R. Gray. 417p. 1992. pap. text ed. 19.95 (*9966-835-73-3*) Prof World Peace.

***Second Scroll.** A. M. Klein. 1996. pap. text ed. 6.95 (*0-7710-3452-0*) McCland & Stewart.

Second Scroll. A. M. Klein. LC 85-61442. 1985. reprint ed. pap. 8.95 (*0-910395-15-2*) Marlboro Pr.

Second Season. Therese Alderton. 1992. mass mkt. 3.99 (*0-8217-3640-X*, Zebra Kensgtn) Kensgtn Pub Corp.

Second Season. Pauline D. Marrs. 1979. mass mkt. 1.75 (*0-449-50012-8*, Coventry) Fawcett.

Second Season: Lent, Easter, Ascension. Wayne Saffen. LC 72-87064. 96p. reprint ed. pap. 27.40 (*0-685-16004-1*, 2026827) Bks Demand.

Second Seasonal Political Palate. Bloodroot Collective Staff. LC 84-52064. 200p. 1984. pap. 12.95 (*0-9605210-2-X*) Sanguinaria.

Second Secret: A Shraga Morgenstern - Pinny Katz Mystery Trilogy. Libby Lazewark. 178p. (J). (gr. k-4). 1995. 11.95 (*1-56871-088-7*) Targum Pr.

Second Semester Chemistry Experiments. Keith Symcox. (Orig.). (C). 1995. pap. text ed. 11.00 (*1-56870-214-0*) RonJon Pub.

Second Sequence in Maurice Sceve's Delie: A Study of Numerological Composition in the Renaissance. Christine Raffini. LC 88-61803. (Illus.). 167p. (ENG & FRE.). 1989. lib. bdg. 24.95 (*0-917786-62-9*) Summa Pubns.

Second Series see Tudor Translations

Second Series see Writings of the Nicene & Post-Nicene Fathers

Second Session of the Permanent Migration Committee. Bd. with Training Problems in the Far East. (I.L.O. Studies & Reports New Ser.: No. 10). 1974. reprint ed. 51.00 (*0-8115-3334-4*) Periodicals Srv.

Second Session of the Second National People's Congress of the People's Republic of China (Documents), 1949. Chuan Kuo Jne Min Tai Piao Ta Hui. LC 79-38053. (China Classic & Contemporary Works in Reprint Ser.). 1995. reprint ed. 34.50 (*0-404-56907-2*) AMS Pr.

Second Settlement, Eighteen Seventy-Five to Nineteen Twenty-Five: A Case Study in the Development of Victorian Boston. Douglass S. Tucci. (Illus.). 165p. 1974. pap. 10.00 (*0-686-12061-2*) St Margarets.

Second Sex. Simone De Beauvoir. LC 92-54303. 1993. 20.00 (*0-679-42016-9*, Everymans Lib) Knopf.

Second Sex. Simone De Beauvoir. 1990. pap. 16.00 (*0-679-72451-6*, Vin) Random.

Second Shadow. Aimee Thurlo & David Thurlo. 1995. mass mkt. 5.99 (*0-8125-2381-4*) Forge NYC.

Second Shanghai Symposium on Marine Geotechnology & Nearshore - Offshore Structures. Ed. by Hu Zhong-xiong & Liu Ji-ping. LC 86-80399. (Shanghai Symposium Proceedings 1985 Ser.: No. 2). 334p. 1985. pap. 35.00 (*0-932871-11-9*) Envo Pub Co.

Second Shepherd's Play. Ed. by Lisl Beer. (Silver Mosque Ser.). 1997. pap. 3.95 (*0-8283-1246-X*) Branden Pub Co.

Second Shift. Arlie Hochschild & Anne Machung. 368p. 1990. pap. 13.00 (*0-380-71157-5*) Avon.

Second Siberian Winter School "Algebra & Analysis" Proceedings of the Second Siberian School, Tomsk State University, Tomsk, 1989. Ed. by L. Bokut. LC 92-15960. (Translations Ser.: Series 2, Vol. 151). 145p. 1992. 130.00 (*0-8218-3142-9*, TRANS2/151) Am Math.

Second Sickle. large type ed. Ursula Curtiss. (Linford Mystery Library). 352p. 1989. pap. 15.99 (*0-7089-6732-9*, Linford) Ulverscroft.

***Second Sight.** Rickey G. Diamond. LC 97-15218. 275p. (Orig.). 1997. pap. 14.95 (*0-934971-55-2*) Calyx Bks.

***Second Sight.** Rickey G. Diamond. LC 97-15218. 275p. (Orig.). 1997. 28.95 (*0-934971-56-0*) Calyx Bks.

Second Sight. Robert V. Hine. LC 92-31096. 1993. pap. 22.50 (*0-520-08195-1*) U CA Pr.

***Second Sight.** Robert V. Hine. LC 92-31096. (Illus.). 1997. pap. 12.95 (*0-520-20891-9*) U CA Pr.

Second Sight. Judith Orloff. 1997. mass mkt. write for info. (*0-446-60422-4*) Warner Bks.

***Second Sight.** M. Judith Orloff. 1997. pap. text ed. 13.99 (*0-446-67335-8*) Warner Bks.

Second Sight. A. K. Ramanujan. 72p. 1986. pap. 11.95 (*0-19-561874-2*) OUP.

Second Sight. A. Sepharial. 96p. 1992. pap. 8.50 (*0-89540-205-X*, SB-205) Sun Pub.

Second Sight. Sinclair Smith. (J). 1996. pap. 3.99 (*0-590-60287-X*) Scholastic Inc.

***Second Sight.** Lindsay Welsh. (Orig.). 1997. mass mkt. 6.50 (*1-56333-507-7*, Rosebud) Masquerade.

Second Sight. large type ed. Robert V. Hine. LC 94-12083. 197p. 1994. lib. bdg. 20.95 (*0-7862-0237-8*) Thorndike Pr.

Second Sight: A Study of Natural & Induced Clairvoyance. A. Sepharial. 96p. 1996. pap. 13.95 (*1-56459-688-5*) Kessinger Pub.

Second Sight: A Study of Natural & Induced Clairvoyance. A. Sepharial. 96p. 1972. reprint ed. spiral bd. 2.75 (*0-7873-0765-3*) Hlth Research.

Second Sight: Biennial, No. IV. Graham W. Beal. LC 86-17839. (Illus.). 76p. 1986. pap. 14.95 (*0-918471-08-7*) San Fran MOMA.

Second Sight: Poems for Paintings by Carroll Cloar. Dabney Stuart. (Illus.). 80p. (C). 1996. pap. 29.95 (*0-8262-1018-X*) U of Mo Pr.

***Second Sight: Printmaking in Chicago, 1935-1995.** James Yood et al. LC 96-3403. 1996. write for info. (*0-941680-17-7*) M&L Block.

Second Sighting. Engle & Barnes. (Strange Matter Ser.: Vol. 23). 140p. (Orig.). (J). (gr. 4 up). 1996. pap. 3.99 (*1-56714-066-1*) Montage Bks.

Second Skin. John Hawkes. LC 64-10674. 1964. pap. 10.95 (*0-8112-0067-1*, NDP146) New Directions.

***Second Skin.** William Michaels. 1997. mass mkt. 6.99 (*1-55197-314-6*, Pub. by Comnwlth Pub CN) Partners Pubs Grp.

Second Skin. Eric Van Lustbader. 1996. mass mkt., pap. 6.50 (*0-671-70349-8*) PB.

2nd Skin. Eric Van Lustbader. 1995. pap. 24.95 (*0-7871-0397-7*, Dove Bks) Dove Audio.

Second Skin: A Nicholas Linnear Novel. Eric Van Lustbader. Ed. by Claire Zion. 464p. 1995. 22.00 (*0-671-86810-1*) PB.

Second Slump: A Marxist Analysis of Recession in the Seventies. Ernest Mandel. 226p. 1985. pap. 15.95 (*0-86091-728-2*) Routledge Chapman & Hall.

Second Soil Residue Analysis Workshop. J. Tarradellas. 232p. 1992. text ed. 686.00 (*2-88124-861-6*) Gordon & Breach.

Second Solo Book for Piano: New Edition. Diller & Quail. 40p. 1986. pap. 5.95 (*0-7935-2856-9*, 50333260) H Leonard.

Second Son. Charles Sailor. 1979. pap. 3.95 (*0-380-45567-6*) Avon.

Second Son. Stephen Stark. Ed. by Jane Rosenman. 432p. 1994. reprint ed. pap. 12.00 (*0-671-87119-6*, WSP) PB.

Second Sophistic: A Cultural Phenomenon in the Roman Empire. Graham Anderson. LC 92-47085. 272p. (C). (gr. 13). 1993. text ed. 62.95 (*0-415-09988-9*) Routledge.

Second Special Conference Issue. Ed. by Peter J. McEwan. 144p. 1983. pap. 22.00 (*0-08-027937-6*, Pergamon Pr) Elsevier.

Second Spring. William R. Miller. LC 92-80529. 109p. 1992. 8.95 (*1-55523-511-5*) Winston-Derek.

***Second Spring.** large type ed. Barbara Best. (Large Print Ser.). 464p. 1996. 25.99 (*0-7089-3549-4*) Ulverscroft.

Second SPSE International Conference on Photographic Papers: July 22-25, 1984, the Westin Bayshore Hotel, Vancouver, BC, Canada: Advanced Printing of Paper Summaries. SPSE International Conference on Photographic Papers Staff. (Illus.). 47p. reprint ed. pap. 25.00 (*0-8357-8649-8*, 2035090) Bks Demand.

Second St. Poems. Beverly Silva. LC 83-70276. 88p. 1983. pap. 9.00 (*0-916950-39-5*) Biling Rev-Pr.

***Second Stage Lensmen.** E. E. Smith. LC 96-3453. (History of Civilization Ser.). 1997. pap. 15.00 (*1-882968-13-1*) Old Earth Bks.

Second Stain. Arthur Conan Doyle. (Sherlock Holmes Ser.). 27p. (Orig.). 1996. pap. 2.50 (*1-57514-262-7*, 3070) Encore Perform Pub.

Second Star. Dana Stabenow. 208p. 1991. mass mkt. 4.50 (*0-441-75722-7*) Ace Bks.

Second Start. Jacqueline F. O'Neil. LC 96-38045. 1997. 16.95 (*0-87605-729-6*) Howell Bk.

***Second Step: Releasing Abuse, Abusers & Stalkers.** Heather Fisher. 64p. (Orig.). 1997. pap. write for info. (*0-614-30107-6*) Crossquarter.

Second Stephen King Quiz Book. Stephen J. Spignesi. 1992. pap. 3.99 (*0-451-17306-6*, Sig) NAL-Dutton.

Second Steps in Ballet: Basic Center Exercises. Thalia Mara. LC 75-37101. (Illus.). 64p. (J). (gr. 4-6). 1987. reprint ed. pap. 6.95 (*0-916622-54-1*) Princeton Bk Co.

Second Steps in Sociology: Use & Misuse of Sociological Concepts. Marcel Fredericks & Steven Miller. LC 89-14039. 280p. (C). 1990. text ed. 56.95 (*0-8204-1213-9*) P Lang Pubng.

Second Stitches: Recycle As You Sew. Susan D. Parker. (Illus.). 144p. 1993. pap. 18.95 (*0-8019-8476-9*) Chilton.

Second Stories: The Politics of Language, Form, & Gender in Early American Fictions. Cynthia S. Jordan. LC 88-27661. (Gender & American Culture Ser.). xvii, 242p. (C). 1989. 34.95 (*0-8078-1839-9*) U of NC Pr.

Second Story Theatre & Two Encores. James Brown. 181p. pap. 16.95 (*0-934257-49-3*) Story Line.

Second Street Gardens. Jacqueline B. Martin. LC 94-10869. (Illus.). (J). 1995. text ed. 16.00 (*0-02-762460-9*, S&S Bks Young Read) S&S Childrens.

Second-String Heroes; First-Class Saints: Character Studies in the Book of Acts. Harold Bonner. 96p. (Orig.). 1990. pap. 6.99 (*0-8341-1333-3*) Beacon Hill.

Second Sunrise. Marjorie Eatock. 1995. pap. 4.99 (*0-8217-4972-2*) NAL-Dutton.

Second Supplement to "A Comprehensive Bibliography of Yugoslav Literature in English" 1986-1990. Vasa D. Mihailovich. 301p. (Orig.). 1992. pap. 22.95 (*0-89357-230-6*) Slavica.

Second Supplementary Catalogue of Hebrew Books Acquired 1893-1960, 2 vols., Set. Diana R. Smith & David Goldstein. (Catalogues of the British Library Collections). 1994. 445.00 (*0-7123-0241-7*, Pub. by Brit Library UK) U of Toronto Pr.

Second Supplements to the Second Edition of Rodd's Chemistry of Carbon Compounds Vol. 1, Pt. A & B: Alphatic Compounds: Hydrocarbons; Halogen Derivatives; Monohydric Alcohols, Their Ethers & Esters; Sulphur Analogues; Nitrogen Derivatives; Organometallic Compounds. Ed. by M. Sainsbury. 620p. 1991. 455.75 (*0-444-88157-3*) Elsevier.

***Second Supplements to the 2nd Edition of Rodd's Chemistry of Carbon Compounds Pt. C: Monocarbonyl Derivatives of Aliphatic Hydrocarbons, Their Analogues & Derivatives.** M. Sainsbury. 388p. 1992. 253.25 (*0-444-89758-5*) Elsevier.

***Second Supplements to the 2nd Edition of Rodd's Chemistry of Carbon Compounds Pt. E, F, GE: Trihydric Alcohols, Their Oxidation Products & Derivatives. F: Penta- & Higher Polyhydric Alcohols, Their Oxidation Products & Derivatives; Saccharides. G: Tetrahydric Alcohols, Their Oxidation Products & Derivatives.** M. Sainsbury. 550p. 1993. 378.50 (*0-444-89873-5*) Elsevier.

Second Supplements to the 2nd Edition of Rodd's Chemistry of Carbon Compounds Vol. 1, Pt. D: Aliphatic Compounds: Dihydric Alcohols: Their Oxidation Products & Derivatives. Ed. by M. Sainsbury. 384p. 1993. 266.75 (*0-444-81517-1*) Elsevier.

***Second Supplements to the 2nd Edition of Rodd's Chemistry of Carbon Compounds Vol. II: Alicyclic Compounds, Pt. A & B. Pt. A: Monocarbocyclic Compounds to & Including Five Ring Atoms. Pt. B: Six- & Higher-Membered Monocarbocyclic Compounds (Partial: Chapt. 5 in This Vol.)** M. Sainsbury. 522p. 1992. 357.50 (*0-444-89844-1*) Elsevier.

***Second Supplements to the 2nd Edition of Rodd's Chemistry of Carbon Compounds Vol. III: Aromatic Compounds.** 544p. 1996. 350.00 (*0-444-82552-5*) Elsevier.

Second Supplements to the 2nd Edition of Rodd's Chemistry of Carbon Compounds, Vol. II: Alicyclic Compounds, Part B (partial), C, D & E. Ed. by M. Sainsbury. 666p. 1994. 432.25 (*0-444-81483-3*) Elsevier.

Second Survey. 6th ed. 1989. student ed. 42.00 (*1-56200-141-8*, 22924) Amer Safe Vid Pubs.

***Second Suspect: A Novel.** Heather Lewis. LC 97-22567. 1997. write for info. (*0-385-48747-9*, N A Talese) Doubleday.

Second Symposium by the Eight Winners of the Grants from Sandoz Foundation for Gerontological Research: Annual Meeting of the Japan Gerontological Society, Kochi-Japan, November 1990 - Journal: Gerontology, Vol. 37, Suppl. 1, 1991. Ed. by H. Orimo. (Illus.). iv, 64p. 1991. pap. 21.00 (*3-8055-5473-7*) S Karger.

Second Symposium on Integrated Environmental Controls for Coal Fired Power Plants. Ed. by H. E. Hesketh. 139p. 1983. pap. text ed. 8.00 (*0-317-02646-1*, H00252) ASME.

Second Temple Studies: 1. Persian Period. P. R. Davies. (Journal for the Study of the Old Testament Supplement Ser.: No. 117). 192p. (C). 1991. 33.50 (*1-85075-315-6*, Pub. by Sheffield Acad UK) CUP Services.

Second Temple Studies: 2. Temple & Community in the Persian Period. Ed. by T. C. Eskenazi & K. H. Richards. (Journal for the Study of the Old Testament Supplement Ser.: Vol. 175). 313p. 55.00 (*1-85075-472-1*, Pub. by Sheffield Acad UK) CUP Services.

2nd Ten Commandments: Your Guide to Success in the Consciousness Age. Orion M. Kopelman & Marc Lehrer. (Illus.). 196p. 1996. 19.95 (*1-885261-02-0*) Global Brain.

Second Ten Years of the World Health Organization, 1958-1967. 1968. text ed. 29.00 (*92-4-156015-0*, 1150139) World Health.

***Second Texas Infantry: From Shloh to Vicksburg.** Joseph E. Chance. (Illus.). 140p. 1984. pap. 16.95 (*1-57168-021-7*) Sunbelt Media.

Second Text Retrieval Conference (TRE C-2) Proceedings. D. K. Harman. (Illus.). 486p. (Orig.). (C). 1995. pap. text ed. 90.00 (*0-7881-0998-7*) DIANE Pub.

***Second Text Retrieval Conference (TREC-2), 2 vols.** (Illus.). 492p. 1994. pap. text ed. 75.00 (*1-57979-208-1*) BPI Info Servs.

***2 Thessalonians.** (LifeChange Ser.). 1996. pap. text ed. 7.00 (*0-89109-992-1*) NavPress.

Second Thessalonians: Facing the End with Sobriety. Maarten J. Menken. LC 93-33187. (New Testament Readings Ser.). 176p. (C). 1994. pap. 15.95 (*0-415-09505-0*, B3956, Routledge NY); text ed. 49.95 (*0-415-09504-2*, B3952, Routledge NY) Routledge.

***2 Thessalonians - Revelation, Vol. 5.** Charles Swindoll. (God's Masterwork Bible Study Guides Ser.). 1997. pap. 6.99 (*0-8499-8742-3*) Word Pub.

Second Thing I Remember: A Collection of Poems. Judith Hougen. LC 92-64071. (Minnesota Voices Project Ser.: Vol. 56). 72p. (Orig.). 1993. pap. 7.95 (*0-89823-143-4*) New Rivers Pr.

Second, Third & Fourth American Chess Congress, 3 vols. in 1. (Tschaturanga Ser.: Vol. 65). 419p. reprint ed. 55.00 (*3-283-00089-1*, Pub. by Edition Olms GW) Lubrecht & Cramer.

Second Thought. Michael J. Cormier. LC 91-41619. (Publish-a-Book Contest Ser.). (Illus.). 32p. (J). (gr. 2-6). 1992. lib. bdg. 22.83 (*0-8114-3578-4*) Raintree Steck-V.

Second Thought. Michael J. Cormier. 1993. pap. text ed. 3.95 (*0-8114-4306-X*) Raintree Steck-V.

Second Thoughts. Dana Lindsey. (Temptation Ser.: No. 398). 1992. mass mkt. 2.99 (*0-373-25498-9*, 1-25498-6) Harlequin Bks.

***Second Thoughts.** Paul Simpson. LC 96-48196. 252p. (Orig.). 1997. pap. 12.99 (*0-7852-7418-9*) Nelson.

Second Thoughts. Katie F. Wiebe. LC 81-80122. 201p. (Orig.). 1981. pap. 2.50 (*0-937364-01-0*) Kindred Prods.

Second Thoughts. large type ed. Caroline Anderson. 1995. 25.99 (*0-7505-0816-7*, Pub. by Magna Print Bks UK) Ulverscroft.

Second Thoughts: ...On Life & the Four Most Powerful Words. John W. Hartman. LC 94-72555. 250p. 1994. pap. 0.95 (*1-885884-00-1*, M Wheeler Pr) Cormorant Pr.

Second Thoughts: Critical Thinking from a Multicultural Perspective. Wanda Treys. LC 95-34125. (Illus.). 484p. (Orig.). (C). 1996. pap. text ed. 36.95 (*1-55934-479-2*, 1479) Mayfield Pub.

Second Thoughts: Former Radicals Look Back at the Sixties. Peter Collier & David Horowitz. LC 88-13427. 288p. 1989. 22.95 (*0-8191-7147-6*); pap. 12.95 (*0-8191-7148-4*) Madison Bks UPA.

Second Thoughts: More Poems. Mildred P. Richards. (Illus.). (Orig.). 1995. pap. 5.00 (*0-9637521-3-8*) Arlington Pl.

Second Thoughts: Myths & Morals of U. S. Economic History. Ed. by Donald N. McCloskey. 224p. 1995. pap. 15.95 (*0-19-510118-9*) OUP.

Second Thoughts: Reflections on Literature & on Life. Francois Mauriac. LC 72-13201. (Essay Index Reprint Ser.). 1977. reprint ed. 15.95 (*0-8369-8169-3*) Ayer.

Second Thoughts: Selected Papers on Psycho-Analysis. Wilfred R. Bion. LC 77-11747. 200p. 1993. reprint ed. 25.00 (*0-87668-330-8*) Aronson.

Second Thoughts: The Uses of Economic History. Ed. by Donald N. McCloskey. 256p. 1993. 35.00 (*0-19-506633-2*) OUP.

Second Thoughts about Race in America. Ed. by Peter Collier & David Horowitz. 175p. 1991. 17.95 (*0-8191-8243-5*) Madison Bks UPA.

Second Thoughts Instructor's Manual: Critical Thinking from a Multicultural Perspective. Wanda Teays. 183p. (Orig.). (C). 1996. pap. text ed. write for info. (*1-55934-480-6*, 1480) Mayfield Pub.

Second Thoughts on the Theory & Practice of the Milan Approach to Therapy. David Campbell et al. 96p. 1992. pap. text ed. 21.95 (*1-85575-014-7*, Pub. by Karnac Bks UK) Brunner-Mazel.

Second Thoughts on Work. Sar A. Levitan & Clifford M. Johnson. LC 82-13532. 241p. 1982. text ed. 24.00 (*0-88099-000-7*); pap. text ed. 14.00 (*0-88099-001-5*) W E Upjohn.

Second Thunder: Seeking the Black Ishayas. 2nd ed. MSI Staff. Ed. by Dharani Ishaya. LC 95-61426. (Illus.). 387p. (Orig.). 1995. reprint ed. pap. 17.95 (*0-931783-08-9*) SFA Pubns.

Second Time. Janet Dailey. 1994. mass mkt. 4.99 (*0-671-87513-2*) PB.

***Second Time.** Thomas Sprain. 1996. mass mkt. 4.99 (*1-55197-135-6*, Pub. by Comnwlth Pub CN) Partners Pubs Grp.

2nd Time Around. James E. Hardy. 288p. (Orig.). 1996. pap. 11.95 (*1-55583-372-1*) Alyson Pubns.

***Second Time Around.** Anna Larence. 256p. 1997. mass mkt. 4.99 (*0-7860-0433-9*, Pinncle Kensgtn) Kensgtn Pub Corp.

***Second Time Around, No. 2.** Sally Sauermilch. 66p. 1995. pap. 9.50 (*1-56770-318-6*) S Scheewe Pubns.

Second Time Around: Second Marriages & Their Spiritual Issues. Patty Sleem. LC 94-66481. 336p. 1995. 25.00 (*1-885288-00-X*); pap. 17.00 (*1-885288-05-0*) PREP Pubng.

Second Time Around: Why Some Second Marriages Fail While Others Succeed. Louis Janda & Ellen MacCormack. 352p. 1991. 18.95 (*0-8184-0557-0*, L Stuart) Carol Pub Group.

Second Time As Farce. Edgar. (C). 1988. pap. 17.50 (*0-85315-698-0*, Pub. by Lawrence & Wishart UK) NYU Pr.

Second Time As Farce: Reflections on the Drama of Mean Times. Edgar. (C). 1988. text ed. 29.95 (*0-85315-697-2*, Pub. by Lawrence & Wishart UK) NYU Pr.

***Second-Time Bride.** Lynne Graham. (Presents Ser.: No. 1888). 1997. mass mkt. 3.50 (*0-373-11888-0*, 1-11888-4) Harlequin Bks.

Second Time Loving. Penny Jordan. (Presents Ser.: No. 1476). 1992. pap. 2.89 (*0-373-11476-1*) Harlequin Bks.

Second Time Loving. large type ed. Penny Jordan. 1991. reprint ed. lib. bdg. 18.95 (*0-263-12677-3*) Thorndike Pr.

***2 Timothy.** (LifeChange Ser.). 1996. pap. text ed. 7.00 (*0-89109-995-6*) NavPress.

Second Timothy. D. Edmond Hiebert. (Everyman's Bible Commentary Ser). (C). 1958. pap. 9.99 (*0-8024-2055-9*) Moody.

Second Timothy. John J. MacArthur, Jr. (MacArthur New Testament Commentary Ser.). 1995. 19.99 (*0-8024-0757-9*) Moody.

Second Timothy & Titus. Donald L. Norbie. 1992. pap. 7.00 (*0-937396-90-7*) Walterick Pubs.

Second to Home. Ryne Sandberg & Barry Rozner. (Illus.). 313p. 1995. 22.95 (*1-56625-040-4*) Bonus Books.

Second to None. Garfield. Date not set. 4.98 (*0-8317-1240-6*) Smithmark.

Second to None: A Vision of the New California High School. California Department of Education Staff. (Illus.). 56p. 1992. pap. 9.50 (*0-8011-1040-8*) Calif Education.

Second to None: How Our Smartest Companies Put People First. Charles Garfield. 430p. 1991. text ed. 27.50 (*1-55623-360-4*) Irwin Prof Pubng.

Second to None: The Productive Power of Putting People First. Charles Garfield. 480p. 1995. pap. 12.50 (*0-380-72360-3*) Avon.

Second to None: The Story of the Second Maine Volunteer Infantry. James H. Mundy. (Illus.). 1992. 34.95 (*0-9626389-2-7*) Harp Pubns.

Second to None: A Documentary History of American Women Vol. 1: From the Sixteenth Century to 1865. Ed. by Ruth B. Moynihan et al. LC 93-14347. (Illus.). xx, 404p. 1994. pap. text ed. 22.50 (*0-8032-8199-4*, Bison Books) U of Nebr Pr.

Second to None: A Documentary History of American Women Vol. 2: From 1865 to the Present. Ed. by Ruth B. Moynihan et al. LC 93-14347. (Illus.). xxii, 474p. (C). 1994. pap. text ed. 22.50 (*0-8032-8204-4*, Bison Books) U of Nebr Pr.

Second to None Facilitator's Guide. Charles Garfield & Jeanine Drew. 88p. 1992. text ed. 20.00 (*1-55623-595-X*) Irwin Prof Pubng.

Second Touch. Lindsey M. Bowen. 32p. (Orig.). 1990. pap. 3.00 (*1-881048-00-4*) Paladin Contemp.

Second Touch - Chinese Edition. Keith Miller. Tr. by Samuel E. Kao. 202p. (CHI.). 1985. pap. 4.00 (*1-56582-090-8*) Christ Renew Min.

Second Treasure Chest of Tales. Paul Stroyer. (Illus.). (J). (gr. 3 up). 1960. 12.95 (*0-8392-3032-X*) Astor-Honor.

Second Treasury of Kahlil Gibran. Kahlil Gibran. pap. 12.95 (*0-8065-0411-0*, Citadel Pr) Carol Pub Group.

Second Treasury of the Familiar. Ralph L. Woods. (J). 1993. reprint ed. lib. bdg. 29.95 (*1-56849-105-0*) Buccaneer Bks.

Second Treatise of Government. John Locke. Ed. by C. B. Macpherson. LC 80-15052. (HPC Classics Ser.). 148p. (C). 1980. pap. text ed. 4.95 (*0-915144-86-7*); lib. bdg. 24.95 (*0-915144-93-X*) Hackett Pub.

Second Treatise of Government. John Locke. Ed. by Richard H. Cox. LC 82-25160. (Crofts Classics Ser.). 200p. 1982. pap. text ed. write for info. (*0-88295-125-4*) Harlan Davidson.

Second Treatise of Government: Locke. Ed. by Thomas P. Peardon. 168p. (C). 1952. pap. text ed. 5.67 (*0-02-393300-3*, Macmillan Coll) P-H.

Second Treatise on Civil Government. John Locke. (Great Books in Philosophy). 132p. 1986. pap. 4.95 (*0-87975-337-4*) Prometheus Bks.

Second Tree from the Corner. E. B. White. LC 84-47609. 272p. 1989. reprint ed. pap. 13.00 (*0-06-091516-1*, PL 1516, PL) HarpC.

2nd Tribute to Teddy Bear Artists. 2nd ed. L. Mullins. (Illus.). 160p. 1995. pap. 29.95 (*0-87588-456-3*) Hobby Hse.

Second Trimester Abortion. Ed. by G. Berger et al. 1981. lib. bdg. 135.00 (*90-247-2487-2*) Kluwer Ac.

Second Trip. Robert Silverberg. 192p. 1981. pap. 2.95 (*0-380-54874-7*) Avon.

Second Twelve Months of Life. Ed. by Frank Caplan. 448p. 1982. mass mkt. 6.50 (*0-553-26438-9*) Bantam.

Second Twelve Months of Life. Frank Caplan. LC 77-78748. (Illus.). 1983. reprint ed. pap. 15.95 (*0-399-50776-0*, Perigee Bks) Berkley Pub.

Second U. S. - Japan Science & Technology Exchange Symposium: Patterns of Interdependence. 1987. write for info. (*0-318-61730-7*) Japan-Am Soc.

***Second U. S. A. Civil War: America Erups in Turmoil.** Sharrieff Omar. 72p. (Orig.). 1997. pap. 7.00 (*1-56411-165-2*) Untd Bros & Sis.

***Second UJNR Tsunami Workshop (1990) Proceedings.** Ed. by Ann M. Brennan & James F. Lander. (Illus.). 260p. (C). 1997. reprint ed. pap. text ed. 50.00 (*0-7881-3935-5*) DIANE Pub.

2nd Ultimate Unauthorized Star Trek Quiz Book. Robert W. Bly. 192p. (Orig.). 1995. pap. 10.00 (*0-06-273384-2*, PL) HarpC.

Second United Order among the Mormons. Edward J. Allen. LC 73-38483. (Columbia University. Studies in the Social Sciences: No. 419). reprint ed. 20.00 (*0-404-51419-7*) AMS Pr.

Second United States Infantry Division in Korea, 1950-1951. Clark C. Munroe. (Divisional Ser.: No. 40). (Illus.). 256p. reprint ed. 39.95 (*0-89839-171-7*) Battery Pr.

Second United States Infantry Division in Korea, 1951-1952. Division Staff. (Divisional Ser.: No. 41). (Illus.). 232p. reprint ed. 39.95 (*0-89839-173-3*) Battery Pr.

Second United States Infantry Division in Korea, 1953. Division Staff. (Divisional Ser.: No. 43). (Illus.). 248p. reprint ed. 39.95 (*0-89839-177-6*) Battery Pr.

***Second Usborne Book of Solve It Yourself Mysteries.** P. Roxbee Cox & R. Heath. (Solve It Yourself Ser.). 66p. (Orig.). (J). 1997. pap. 15.95 (*0-7460-2701-X*, Usborne) EDC.

Second USENIX Conference on Object-Oriented Technologies & Systems (COOTS), Toronto, Canada. (Illus.). 264p. (Orig.). 1996. pap. text ed. 30.00 (*1-880446-77-4*) USENIX Assn.

2nd USENIX Symposium on Mobile & Location-Independent Computing Proceedings: Ann Arbor, MI. Intro. by Jim Rees. 132p. (Orig.). 1995. pap. text ed. 24.00 (*1-880446-69-3*) USENIX Assn.

***Second USENIX Workshop on Electronic Commerce Proceedings.** Ed. by Doug Tygar. 328p. (Orig.). 1996. pap. 26.00 (*1-880446-83-9*) USENIX Assn.

Second Vatican Council: Studies by Eight Anglican Observers. Bernard C. Pawley. 1990. 12.50 (*0-8446-2713-5*) Peter Smith.

***Second Vindication of Mr. Locke: 1738 Edition.** Vincent Perronet. 158p. 1996. reprint ed. write for info. (*1-85506-118-X*) Bks Intl VA.

Second Virginia Cavalry. Robert J. Driver & H. E. Howard. (Virginia Regimental Histories Ser.). (Illus.). 302p. 1995. 25.00 (*1-56190-084-2*) H E Howard.

Second Virginia Infantry. Dennis E. Frye. (Virginia Regimental Histories Ser.). (Illus.). 146p. 1984. 19.95 (*0-930919-06-8*) H E Howard.

***Second Vision.** Ralph Vallone, Jr. 456p. 4.98 (*0-8317-4531-2*) Smithmark.

Second Vision. Ralph Vallone. Date not set. pap. 10.95 (*0-452-27460-5*, Plume) NAL-Dutton.

Second Visit to North America, 2 vols., Set. Charles B. Lyell. 1855. 79.00 (*0-403-00357-1*) Scholarly.

Second Visit to North America, 2 vols., Set. Charles Lyell. (BCL1 - U. S. History Ser.). 1991. reprint ed. lib. bdg. 150.00 (*0-7812-6012-4*) Rprt Serv.

Second Vocation: Educating Emigre Professionals for Social Work. 1974. 3.30 (*0-318-35329-6*) Coun Soc Wk Ed.

Second Voice. Diane Sherrill. LC 95-61832. 286p. 1995. 24.95 (*0-9643126-2-X*) Woodburner Pr.

Second Volume de Bouvard et Pecuchet. Gustave Flaubert. 8.95 (*0-686-55989-4*) Fr & Eur.

Second Voyage. rev. ed. Eilean N. Chuillenain. LC 90-72091. 72p. (C). 1991. pap. 8.95 (*0-916390-45-4*) Wake Forest.

Second War, 6 vols. Winston S. Churchill. 1985. write for info. (*0-318-60284-9*) HM.

Second Wave: Feminist Theoretical Writings. Linda Nicholson. 416p. 1997. pap. 22.95 (*0-415-91761-1*) Routledge.

Second Wave: Feminist Theoretical Writings. Linda Nicholson. 416p. (C). 1997. text ed. 65.00 (*0-415-91760-3*) Routledge.

Second Wave: Hispanic Ministry & the Evangelization of Cultures. Allan F. Deck. 1989. pap. 9.95 (*0-8091-3042-4*) Paulist Pr.

Second Wave: Japan's Global Attack on Financial Services. Richard W. Wright & Gunter A. Pauli. 148p. 1987. 26.00 (*0-08-033090-8*, Waterlow) Macmillan.

Second Wave: Pinay & Pinoy. Caridad C. Vallangca. Ed. by Jody B. Larson. LC 87-10198. (Illus.). 288p. (Orig.). 1987. pap. 9.95 (*0-89407-043-6*) Strawberry Hill.

Second Wind. David Graham. LC 89-20388. 1990. 15.00 (*0-89672-210-4*); pap. 8.50 (*0-89672-211-2*) Tex Tech Univ Pr.

Second Wind. Neil B. Shulman. 240p. (Orig.). 1995. pap. 7.95 (*0-9639002-6-9*) N Shulman.

Second Wind. Lauraine Snelling. (Golden Filly Ser.: No. 8). (YA). (gr. 7-10). 1994. pap. 5.99 (*1-55661-401-2*) Bethany Hse.

Second Wind. Charles R. Swindoll. 1995. 4.99 (*0-310-96296-X*) Zondervan.

Second Wind: For Those Struggling to Get up Again. Charles R. Swindoll. LC 94-2809. 80p. 1995. pap. 8.99 (*0-310-42081-4*) Zondervan.

Second Wind: Selected Poems, 1968-1986. Phil Weidman & Kirk Robertson. LC 87-70383. (Windriver Ser.). 192p. (Orig.). 1987. pap. 14.00 (*0-916918-34-3*) Duck Down.

Second Wind: Selected Poems, 1968-1986. deluxe limited ed. Phil Weidman & Kirk Robertson. LC 87-70383. (Windriver Ser.). 192p. (Orig.). 1987. 25.00 (*0-916918-35-1*) Duck Down.

Second Woodcarvers Workbook: More Animal Carving with Mary Duke Guldan. 2nd ed. Mary D. Guldan. (Illus.). 96p. 1994. pap. 14.95 (*1-56523-037-X*) Fox Chapel Pub.

Second Wooing of Salina Sue & Other Stories. Ruth M. Stuart. 1972. reprint ed. lib. bdg. 24.00 (*0-8422-8114-2*) Irvington.

Second Wooing of Salina Sue & Other Stories. Ruth M. Stuart. 1986. reprint ed. pap. text ed. 6.95 (*0-8290-2018-7*) Irvington.

***II Workshop on Cybernetic Vision.** 350p. 1997. pap. 60.00 (*0-8186-8058-X*) IEEE Comp Soc.

Second Workshop on Finite Element Methods in Electromagnetic Wave Problems. Ed. by P. Silvester et al. (Illus.). 194p. (Orig.). (C). 1994. pap. text ed. 75.00 (*1-873936-31-1*, Pub. by J & J Sci Pubs UK) Bks Intl VA.

Second Workshop on Measurement of Microbial Activity in the Carbon Cycle of Aquatic Ecosystems: Proceedings. Ed. by Jurgen Overbeck et al. (Advances in Limnology Ser.: No. 19). (Illus.). 328p. 1984. pap. text ed. 110.00 (*3-510-47017-6*, Pub. by Schweitzerbartsche GW) Lubrecht & Cramer.

Second World & Green World: Studies in Renaissance Fiction-Making. Harry Berger, Jr. (Illus.). 542p. 1988. pap. 19.95 (*0-520-07181-6*) U CA Pr.

Second World Conference on Adult Education (UNESCO) (Education Studies & Documents: No. 46). 1974. reprint ed. pap. 25.00 (*0-8115-1370-X*) Periodicals Srv.

Second World Conference on Detergents: Proceedings. Ed. by A. R. Baldwin. 302p. 1987. 95.00 (*0-935315-14-4*) AOCS Pr.

Second World Congress on Land Policy, 1983. World Congress on Land Policy Staff. Ed. by Matthew Cullen & Sharon Woolery. LC 85-10455. (Lincoln Institute of Land Policy Book Ser.). 314p. reprint ed. pap. 89.50 (*0-7837-3262-7*, 2043281) Bks Demand.

Second World Congress on Superconductivity. Ed. by C. G. Burnham. 400p. (C). 1992. text ed. 114.00 (*981-02-0618-6*) World Scientific Pub.

***Second World War.** Date not set. 14.95 (*0-559-35028-7*) Putnam Pub Group.

Second World War, 6 vols. Winston S. Churchill. Incl. Gathering Storm. 1948. 35.00 (*0-395-07537-8*); Their Finest Hour. 1949. 35.00 (*0-395-07536-X*); Grand Alliance. 1950. 35.00 (*0-395-07538-6*); Hinge of Fate. 1960. 35.00 (*0-395-07539-4*); Closing the Ring. 1987. 35.00 (*0-395-07535-1*); Triumph & Tragedy. 1953. 35.00 (*0-395-07540-8*); 1975. write for info. (*0-318-53417-7*) HM.

Second World War. John Keegan. (Illus.). 608p. 1990. pap. 19.95 (*0-14-011341-X*, Penguin Bks) Viking Penguin.

Second World War, 6 Vols., Set Vols. I-VI. Winston S. Churchill. 1986. pap. 87.70 (*0-395-41685-X*) HM.

Second World War, Vol. I. Liliane Funcken & Fred Funcken. write for info. (*0-318-58182-5*) P-H.

Second World War: A Complete History. Martin Gilbert. (Illus.). 864p. 1991. pap. 19.95 (*0-8050-1788-7*, Owl) H Holt & Co.

Second World War: A Select Bibliography of Books in English since 1975. Compiled by Arthur L. Funk. LC 85-143644. 200p. (C). 1985. lib. bdg. 27.95 (*0-941690-15-6*) Regina Bks.

***Second World War: A Short History.** Alastair Parker. (Illus.). 344p. 1997. pap. 13.95 (*0-19-289285-1*) OUP.

Second World War: Asia & the Pacific. Ed. by Thomas E. Greiss. (The West Point Military History Ser.). (Illus.). 350p. (Orig.). pap. 19.95 (*0-89529-243-2*) Avery Pub.

Second World War: Asia & the Pacific. Ed. by Thomas E. Griess. (West Point Military History Ser.). (Illus.). 350p. (Orig.). 25.00 (*0-89529-313-7*) Avery Pub.

 An Asterisk (*) at the beginning of an entry indicates that the title is appearing in BIP for the first time.

Second World War: Conflict & Cooperation. Sean Lang. (History Programme Ser.). 96p. (C). 1993. pap. text ed. 12.95 (*0-521-43826-8*) Cambridge U Pr.

Second World War: Conflict & Cooperation. Sean Lang. (History Programme Ser.). 96p. (C). 1994. pap. text ed. 18.95 (*0-521-43827-6*) Cambridge U Pr.

Second World War: Essays in Military & Political History. Ed. by Walter Laqueur. LC 81-86067. (Sage Readers in 20th Century History Ser.: No. 4). 413p. reprint ed. pap. 117.80 (*0-8357-8444-4*, 2034708) Bks Demand.

Second World War: Europe & the Mediterranean. Ed. by Thomas E. Griess. (West Point Military History Ser.). 448p. (Orig.). 25.00 (*0-89529-314-5*); pap. 21.95 (*0-89529-242-4*) Avery Pub.

Second World War Airplane Coloring Book. Illus. by Richard King. 44p. (Orig.). 1996. pap. 5.95 (*1-882663-09-8*) Plymouth MI.

Second World War Airplane Coloring Book, Incl. crayons. Illus. by Richard King. 44p. (Orig.). 1996. pap. 6.95 (*1-882663-08-X*) Plymouth MI.

Second World War & the Atomic Age, 1940-1973. David Cronon. LC 74-28589. (Goldentree Bibliographies Series in American History). (C). 1975. pap. text ed. write for info. (*0-88295-538-1*) Harlan Davidson.

Second World War in History, Biography, Diary, Poetry, Literature, & Film: A Bibliography. Jill M. Phillips. 1983. lib. bdg. 250.00 (*0-8490-3231-8*) Gordon Pr.

Second World War, 1939-45: A Strategical & Tactical History. J. F. Fuller. LC 92-36812. (Illus.). 431p. 1993. reprint ed. pap. 14.95 (*0-306-80506-5*) Da Capo.

Second Writers Workshop Literary Reader: An Anthology. Ed. by P. Lal. 72p. 1975. 15.00 (*0-88253-624-9*); pap. text ed. 6.75 (*0-88253-623-0*) Ind-US Inc.

Second Year: The Emergence of Self-Awareness. Jerome Kagan. LC 81-4214. (Illus.). 171p. (C). 1981. 24.95 (*0-674-79662-4*) HUP.

Second Year: The Emergence of Self-Awareness. Jerome Kagan. 171p. 1986. pap. 11.95 (*0-674-79663-2*) HUP.

Second Year Calculus: From Celestial Mechanics to Special Relativity. D. M. Bressoud. (Undergraduate Texts in Mathematics Ser.). (Illus.). xi, 386p. 1996. reprint ed. 32. 95 (*0-387-97606-X*) Spr-Verlag.

Second Year Evaluation of the Florida Public Guardianship Pilot Program. K. Miller et al. 1984. write for info. (*0-318-58137-X*) FSU CSP.

Second Year Readings for Intermodal Course. Compiled by Linda Kleine. 158p. (Orig.). (C). 1996. pap. text ed. write for info. (*1-57790-009-X*) Book Tech.

Second-Year Spanish. Shirley Williams. 352p. (SPA.). (C). 1984. pap. text ed. write for info. (*0-07-554489-X*) McGraw.

Second-Year Spanish. Shirley Williams. 352p. (SPA.). (C). 1984. pap. text ed. 13.96 (*0-07-554490-3*) McGraw.

Second-Year Spanish. Shirley Williams. 352p. (SPA.). (C). 1985. 10.22 (*0-07-554492-X*) McGraw.

Second Youth. Vernice Gabriel & Jeanne Molli. (Illus.). 400p. 1995. 29.98 (*0-941683-32-X*) Instant Improve.

Second Zechariah & the Deuteronomic School. Raymond F. Person. 50.00 (*1-85075-455-1*, Pub. by Sheffield Acad UK) CUP Services.

Second Zen Reader: The Tiger's Cave & Translations of other Zen Writings. Trevor P. Leggett. LC 87-50163. (Illus.). 196p. (Orig.). 1988. pap. 9.95 (*0-8048-1525-9*) C E Tuttle.

Secondary Action Information Message, Set. Joseph S. Renzulli. 1987. pap. 24.95 (*0-936386-48-7*) Creative Learning.

Secondary Adjustments & Related Aspects of Transfer Pricing Corrections: Proceedings of a Seminar Held in Toronto, Canada, in 1994 During the 48th Congress of the International Fiscal Association. LC 95-45763. (IFA Congress Seminar Ser.: No. 19b). 1996. pap. 56.00 (*90-411-0158-6*) Kluwer Law Tax Pubs.

Secondary Analysis of Survey Data. K. Jill Kiecolt & Laura E. Nathan. (Quantitative Applications in the Social Sciences Ser.: Vol. 53). 96p. 1985. pap. text ed. 9.95 (*0-8039-2302-3*) Sage.

Secondary & Middle School Teaching. Allan C. Ornstein. (C). 1992. text ed. 49.50 (*0-06-044928-4*) Addson-Wesley Educ.

Secondary & Middle School Teaching Methods. 7th ed. Leonard Clark & Irving S. Starr. (Illus.). 512p. (C). 1995. pap. text ed. 47.00 (*0-02-322871-7*, Macmillan Coll) P-H.

Secondary Annotated Bibliography of John Winthrop, 1588-1649. Geoffrey Carpenter. LC 91-11030. (Studies in the Seventeenth Century: No. 5). 1991. 49.50 (*0-404-61725-5*) AMS Pr.

Secondary Art Education: An Anthology of Issues. Ed. by Bruce E. Little. 252p. (C). 1990. pap. text ed. 22.00 (*0-937652-53-9*) Natl Art Ed.

Secondary Cities in Developing Countries: Policies for Diffusing Urbanization. Dennis A. Rondinelli. LC 82-23165. (Sage Library of Social Research: No. 145). 288p. reprint ed. pap. 82.10 (*0-8357-4851-0*, 2037782) Bks Demand.

Secondary Cities of Argentina: The Social History of Corrientes, Salta, & Mendoza, 1850-1910. James R. Scobie. Ed. by Samuel L. Baily. LC 87-18093. (Illus.). 312p. 1988. 47.50 (*0-8047-1419-3*) Stanford U Pr.

Secondary Classroom Management: Lessons from Research & Practice. Carol S. Weinstein. LC 95-37068. 1997. pap. text ed. write for info. (*0-07-069156-8*) McGraw.

Secondary Colors: Three Essays. Alexander Theroux. 256p. 1996. 19.95 (*0-8050-4458-2*) H Holt & Co.

***Secondary Colors: Three Essays.** Alexander Theroux. 1997. pap. 12.00 (*0-8050-5326-3*, Owl) H Holt & Co.

Secondary Containment Systems. Richard K. Miller & Marcia E. Rupnow. (Survey on Technology & Markets Ser.: No. 157). 50p. 1991. 200.00 (*1-55865-227-2*) Future Tech Surveys.

Secondary Detachment of the Retina: Proceedings of the Collogue du Club Jules Gonin, 7th & the Assemblee de la Societe Suisse d'Ophthalmologie, 63rd, Lausanne, 1970. Colloque du Club Jules Gonin Staff & Assemblee de la Societe Suisse d'Ophthalmologie Staff. Ed. by R. Dufour. (Modern Problems in Ophthalmology Ser.: Vol. 10). (Illus.). 1972. 128.00 (*3-8055-1300-3*) S Karger.

Secondary Diabetes: The Spectrum of the Diabetic Syndromes. fac. ed. Ed. by Stephen Podolsky & M. Viswanathan. LC 79-62976. (Illus.). 624p. pap. 177.90 (*0-7837-7267-X*, 2047038) Bks Demand.

Secondary Education. H. S. Bhatta. (C). 1990. 56.00 (*81-7024-340-8*, Pub. by Ashish II) S Asia.

Secondary Education. Maureen O'Connor. Ed. by C. E. Wragg. (Education Matters Ser.). 112p. 1990. text ed. 50.00 (*0-304-31951-1*); pap. text ed. 17.95 (*0-304-31956-2*) Cassell.

Secondary Education: An Introduction. 3rd ed. David G. Armstrong et al. 624p. (C). 1993. pap. text ed. 51.00 (*0-02-304093-9*, Macmillan Coll) P-H.

Secondary Education & Beyond: Providing Opportunities Students with Learning Disabilities. 279p. (C). 1997. pap. 15.00 (*0-614-08299-4*) Lrn Dis Assn Am.

Secondary Education for All. R. H. Tawney. Ed. by J. R. Brooks. 160p. 1988. text ed. 40.00 (*0-907628-99-0*) Hambledon Press.

Secondary Education in China after Mao: Reform & Social Conflict. Stig Thogersen. 180p. (Orig.). (C). 1990. pap. 25.00 (*87-7288-219-0*, Pub. by Aarhus Univ Pr DK) David Brown.

Secondary Education in England, 1870-1902: Public Activity & Private Enterprise. John Roach. 320p. (C). (gr. 13). 1991. text ed. 99.95 (*0-415-03572-4*, A5695) Routledge.

Secondary Education in France. OECD Staff. (PEB Papers). 64p. (Orig.). 1995. pap. 18.00 (*92-64-14548-6*, Pub. by Org for Econ FR) OECD.

Secondary Education in Nepal. Kedar N. Shrestha. 39p. 1981. pap. 4.00 (*0-318-23180-8*) Am-Nepal Ed.

Secondary Education in the Nineteenth Century. R. L. Archer. 363p. 1966. reprint ed. 30.00 (*0-7146-1446-7*, BHA-01446, Pub. by F Cass Pubs UK) Intl Spec Bk.

Secondary Education in the South. Ed. by J. M. Gwynn et al. LC 70-134132. (Essay Index Reprint Ser.). 1977. reprint ed. 23.95 (*0-8369-2519-X*) Ayer.

Secondary Electron Spectra from Charged Particle Interactions. LC 96-7606. (Report Ser.: Vol. 55). 114p. (Orig.). 1996. pap. 65.00 (*0-913394-54-8*) Intl Comm Rad Meas.

Secondary Emission & Structural Properties of Solids. Ed. by Ubai A. Arifov. Tr. by Geoffrey C. Archard from RUS. LC 78-157931. 154p. reprint ed. pap. 43.90 (*0-317-08295-7*, 2020683) Bks Demand.

Secondary Fiber Recycling. Ed. by Richard J. Spangenberg. (Illus.). 304p. 1993. 116.00 (*0-89852-267-6*, 0101R201) TAPPI.

Secondary Fibers & Nonwood Pulping, Vol. 3. Ed. by Michael J. Kocurek et al. (Pulp & Paper Manufacture Ser.). 266p. 1987. pap. 58.00 (*0-919893-37-6*, 0202MS03) TAPPI.

Secondary Head: Roles, Responsibilities & Reflections. Peter Morimore & Jo Mortimore. 176p. 1991. pap. 27.00 (*1-85396-141-8*, Pub. by P Chapman Pub UK) Taylor & Francis.

Secondary Hyperlipoproteinemias. Eleazar Shafrir & George Steiner. 1991. text ed. 55.00 (*0-07-056383-7*) McGraw.

Secondary Hypertension. Ed. by H. Vetter. (Journal: Cardiology: Vol. 72, Suppl. 1, 1985). (Illus.). iv, 196p. 1985. pap. 47.25 (*3-8055-4079-5*) S Karger.

Secondary Information Service Statistics. Ed. by Wendy Schipper & Betty Unruh. (Report Series, 1990: No. 2). 140p. (Orig.). 1990. pap. text ed. 185.00 (*0-942308-26-3*) NFAIS.

Secondary Instructional Methods. Kenneth D. Moore & Cheri L. Quinn. 512p. (C). 1993. per. write for info. (*0-697-11792-8*) Brown & Benchmark.

Secondary Ion Mass Spectrometry: A Practical Handbook for Depth Profiling & Bulk Impurity Analysis. R. G. Wilson et al. LC 89-22460. 384p. 1989. text ed. 149.00 (*0-471-51945-6*) Wiley.

Secondary Ion Mass Spectrometry: Basic Concepts, Instrumental Aspects, Applications & Trends. A. Benninghoven et al. LC 86-11014. (Monographs on Analytical Chemistry & Its Applications). 1227p. 1987. text ed. 299.00 (*0-471-01056-1*) Wiley.

Secondary Ion Mass Spectrometry: Principles & Applications. Ed. by John C. Vickerman et al. (International Series of Monographs on Chemistry: No. 17). (Illus.). 360p. 1990. 95.00 (*0-19-855625-X*) OUP.

Secondary Ion Mass Spectrometry: Proceedings of the Sixth International Conference on Secondary Ion Mass Spectrometry (SIMS VI), Palais des Congres, Versailles, Paris, France, September 13-18th, 1987. International Conference on Secondary Ion Mass Spectrometry Staff. Ed. by A. Benninghove et al. LC 88-22757. (Illus.). 1108p. reprint ed. pap. 180.00 (*0-7837-1884-5*, 2042085) Bks Demand.

Secondary Ion Mass Spectrometry: Sims IX. R. Shimizu et al. 983p. 1995. text ed. 225.00 (*0-471-94218-9*) Wiley.

Secondary Ion Mass Spectrometry: SIMS V. Ed. by R. J. Colton et al. (Chemical Physics Ser.: Vol. 44). (Illus.). 590p. 1986. 87.00 (*0-387-16263-1*) Spr-Verlag.

Secondary Ion Mass Spectrometry SIMS-II: Proceedings of the International Conference on Secondary Ion Mass Spectrometry. Ed. by A. Benninghoven et al. LC 79-23997. (Chemical Physics Ser.: Vol. 9). (Illus.). 298p. 1979. 51.00 (*3-540-09843-7*) Spr-Verlag.

Secondary Ion Mass Spectrometry SIMS III: Proceedings. Ed. by A. Benninghoven et al. (Chemical Physics Ser.: Vol. 19). (Illus.). 444p. 1982. 64.95 (*0-387-11372-X*) Spr-Verlag.

Secondary Ion Mass Spectroscopy of Solid Surfaces. V. T. Cherepin. viii, 138p. 1987. lib. bdg. 110.00 (*90-6764-078-6*, Pub. by VSP NE) Coronet Bks.

Secondary Manufacturing in the Glass Industry. Alexis G. Pincus & S. H. Chang. LC 78-55369. (Processing in the Glass Industry Ser.). 314p. 1978. 34.95 (*0-911993-14-2*) Ashlee Pub Co.

Secondary Market Prices of LDC Debt. M. J. Dicks & S. Singh. LC 92-24302. (Bank of England Discussion Papers, Technical Ser.: Vol. 48). 48p. 1991. reprint ed. pap. 25.00 (*0-608-00542-8*, 2061421) Bks Demand.

Secondary Mathematics & Special Educational Needs. Harry Daniels & Julia Anghileri. (Special Needs in Ordinary Schools Ser.). 160p. 1995. 55.00 (*0-304-32800-6*); pap. 17.95 (*0-304-32798-0*) Cassell.

Secondary Mathematics Instruction: An Integrated Approach. rev. ed. Margaret A. Farrell & Walter A. Farmer. LC 88-28231. Orig. Title: Systematic Instruction in Mathematics for the Middle & High School Years. (Illus.). 380p. (Orig.). (C). 1988. pap. text ed. 29.95 (*0-939765-26-8*, G115) Janson Pubns.

Secondary Mathematics Methods. Douglas K. Brumbaugh et al. LC 96-25872. 400p. 1996. pap. text ed. 37.00 (*0-8058-8037-2*) L Erlbaum Assocs.

Secondary Mathematics Methods. Douglas K. Brumbaugh et al. 500p. 1996. text ed. 100.00 (*0-8058-8036-4*) L Erlbaum Assocs.

Secondary Metabolism & Differentiation in Fungi. Bennett & Ciegler. (Mycology Ser.: Vol. 5). 496p. 1983. 210.00 (*0-8247-1819-4*) Dekker.

Secondary Metabolism in Microorganisms, Plants & Animals. M. Luckner. 400p. 1990. 129.00 (*0-387-50287-4*) Spr-Verlag.

Secondary Metabolism in Microorganisms, Plants & Animals. 2nd rev. ed. M. Luckner. (Illus.). 570p. 1984. 93.50 (*0-387-12771-2*) Spr-Verlag.

Secondary-Metabolite Biosynthesis & Metabolism. Ed. by Richard J. Petroski & Susan P. McCormick. LC 92-49318. (Environmental Science Research Ser.: Vol. 44). (Illus.). 358p. (C). 1992. 95.00 (*0-306-44309-0*, Plenum Pr) Plenum.

Secondary Metabolites: Their Function & Evolution. CIBA Foundation Staff. (CIBA Foundation Symposium Ser.: Vol. 171). 318p. 1993. text ed. 84.95 (*0-471-93447-X*) Wiley.

Secondary Metabolites - Plant Cell & Tissue Cultures. Dicosmo. 1996. 272.00 (*0-8493-5135-9*, CRC Reprint) Franklin.

Secondary Moderns: Mimesis, History, & Revolution in Lezama Lima's "American Expression" Brett Levinson. LC 95-50475. 208p. (C). 1996. 33.50 (*0-8387-5300-0*) Bucknell U Pr.

Secondary Mortgage Market: Strategies for Surviving & Thriving in Today's Challenging Markets. rev. ed. Jess Lederman. 675p. 1992. text ed. 70.00 (*1-55738-288-3*) Irwin Prof Pubng.

Secondary Mortgage Market Basics. K. Darcy Matthews. 40p. (Orig.). (C). 1995. pap. text ed. 20.00 (*0-945359-96-9*) Mortgage Bankers.

***Secondary Mortgage Market Guide.** C. L. Edson. 800p. 195.00 (*0-614-31049-0*) Juris Pubng.

Secondary Operations: Preprint of a Seminar Held at the 1988 International Powder Metallurgy Conference, Orlando, Florida, June 6, 1988, Seminar Chairman: Reynold Sansoucy. Metal Powder Industries Federation Staff. 66p. reprint ed. pap. 25.00 (*0-7837-2212-5*, 2057274) Bks Demand.

Secondary Operations, Quality, & Standards, Vol. 4. 512p. 1992. 125.00 (*1-878954-23-7*) Metal Powder.

Secondary Plant Products. Ed. by E. A. Bell & Barry V. Charlwood. LC 79-16289. (Encyclopedia of Plant Physiology Ser.: Vol. 8). (Illus.). 1980. 248.95 (*0-387-09461-X*) Spr-Verlag.

Secondary Pollen Presentation: Form, Function, & Evolution. P. F. Yeo. (Plant Systematics & Evolution Ser.: Suppl. 6). (Illus.). 180p. 1993. 161.95 (*0-387-82448-0*) Spr-Verlag.

Secondary Prevention in Coronary Artery Disease & Myocardial Infarction. Ed. by P. Mathes. (Developments in Cardiovascular Medicine Ser.). 1985. lib. bdg. 223.50 (*0-89838-736-1*) Kluwer Ac.

Secondary Prevention of Colorectal Cancer. Ed. by P. Rozen & S. J. Winawer. (Frontiers of Gastrointestinal Research Ser.: Vol. 10). (Illus.). xiv, 274p. 1986. 158.50 (*3-8055-4252-6*) S Karger.

***Secondary Principal's Survival Guide.** Robert D. Ramsey. 1996. spiral bd. 34.95 (*0-13-799388-9*) P-H.

Secondary Products of Metabolism. Rose. 1979. text ed. 99.00 (*0-12-596553-2*) Acad Pr.

Secondary Progressions: Time to Remember. Nancy Hastings. LC 84-50243. 324p. 1984. pap. 14.95 (*0-87728-599-3*) Weiser.

Secondary Progressions in Eidetic Analysis. Laurie Purcell. 121p. 1993. pap. 11.00 (*0-913412-69-4*) Brandon Hse.

Secondary Reading, Writing, & Learning. Marian J. Tonjes. 400p. 1991. text ed. 64.00 (*0-205-12401-1*, H24011) Allyn.

Secondary Recycling Plastics Business, No. P-125. Business Communications Co., Inc. Staff. 245p. 1991. 2, 650.00 (*0-89336-842-3*) BCC.

Secondary Research: Information Sources & Methods. 2nd ed. David W. Stewart & Michael A. Kamins. (Applied Social Research Methods Ser.: Vol. 4). (Illus.). 160p. (C). 1993. text ed. 39.95 (*0-8039-5036-5*); pap. text ed. 17.95 (*0-8039-5037-3*) Sage.

Secondary Rhinoplasty & Nasal Reconstruction. Rod J. Rohrich et al. Ed. by James C. Grotting. (Illus.). 200p. 1995. 100.00 (*0-942219-80-5*) Quality Med Pub.

Secondary School Admissions Test/H. S. Entrance Exams (SSAT) Jack Rudman. (Admission Test Ser.: ATS-80). 1994. pap. 23.95 (*0-8373-5080-8*) Nat Learn.

Secondary School Evaluative Criteria. 186p. 8.00 (*0-318-17479-0*) Mid St Coll & Schl.

Secondary School Examinations: International Comparative Perspectives on Policies & Practice. Max A. Eckstein & Harold J. Noah. LC 92-38889. 304p. (C). 1993. text ed. 35.00 (*0-300-05393-2*) Yale U Pr.

Secondary School Journalism. Judith A. Isaacs. 245p. 1994. teacher ed. 85.00 (*0-9629645-1-4*) Butterfly Bear.

Secondary School Journalism. 2nd ed. Judith A. Isaacs. 208p. 1994. pap. text ed. 17.95 (*0-9629645-0-6*) Butterfly Bear.

Secondary School Librarian's Almanac: Month-by-Month Activities, Displays, & Procedures for the Entire School Year. Jane E. Streiff. 272p. 1989. text ed. 32.95 (*0-87628-783-6*) Ctr Appl Res.

Secondary School Librarian's Survival Guide. Jane E. Streiff. LC 94-34295. 1994. text ed. 32.95 (*0-87628-875-1*) Ctr Appl Res.

Secondary School Library Management Manual. 3rd rev. ed. 1992. pap. 50.00 (*0-943932-29-7*) Petervin Pr.

Secondary School Management Today. Stanley Thornes. (C). 1989. 110.00 (*0-09-165561-7*, Pub. by S Thornes Pubs UK) St Mut.

Secondary School Mathematics Curriculum: 1985 Yearbook. Ed. by Christian R. Hirsch. LC 84-29622. (Illus.). 250p. 1985. 22.00 (*0-87353-217-1*, 342E1) NCTM.

Secondary School Reading Exam, 5 Vols. Roe. (C). Date not set. text ed. write for info. (*0-395-71900-3*) HM.

***Secondary School Reading Instruction: The Content Areas, 5 Vols.** 5th ed. Betty D. Roe et al. 592p. (C). 1994. text ed. 58.36 (*0-395-70868-0*) HM.

***Secondary School Reading Instruction: The Content Areas, 5 Vols.** 5th ed. Betty D. Roe et al. (C). 1995. teacher ed., text ed. 11.96 (*0-395-71663-2*) HM.

Secondary Schools & Beyond: Transition of Individuals with Mild Disabilities. Anna Gajar et al. LC 92-27482. 480p. (C). 1993. pap. text ed. 44.00 (*0-675-21373-8*, Merrill Coll) P-H.

Secondary Schools & Cooperative Learning: Theories, Models & Strategies. Jon E. Pedersen & Annette D. Digby. LC 94-15326. (Source Books on Education: Vol. 40). 488p. 1995. text ed. 69.00 (*0-8153-0421-8*, SS788) Garland.

Secondary Schools at the Turn of the Century. Theodore R. Sizer. LC 76-43028. 304p. 1976. reprint ed. text ed. 59.75 (*0-8371-8972-1*, SISS, Greenwood Pr) Greenwood.

Secondary Schools for All? 2nd ed. John Sayer. (Special Needs in Ordinary Schools Ser.). (Illus.). 192p. 1994. pap. 22.50 (*0-304-32476-0*) Cassell.

Secondary Science: Contemporary Issues & Practical Approaches. Jerry Wellington. LC 93-31553. 296p. (C). 1994. pap. 22.95 (*0-415-09844-0*, Routledge NY) Routledge.

Secondary Science: Contemporary Issues & Practical Approaches. Jerry Wellington. LC 93-31553. 296p. (C). (gr. 13). 1994. text ed. 65.00 (*0-415-09843-2*, Routledge NY) Routledge.

Secondary Science Instruction: An Integrated Approach. rev. ed. Walter A. Farmer et al. Orig. Title: Systematic Instruction in Science for the Middle & High School Years. (Illus.). 376p. (Orig.). (C). 1991. pap. text ed. 29. 95 (*0-939765-53-5*, G147) Janson Pubns.

Secondary Social Science Workbook. Satish K. Bajaj. (Illus.). 236p. 1981. pap. text ed. 7.95 (*0-86131-271-6*, Pub. by Orient Longman Ltd II) Apt Bks.

Secondary Social Studies Curriculum, Activities, & Materials. James L. Barth. 342p. (Orig.). (C). 1984. pap. text ed. 28.00 (*0-8191-3797-9*) U Pr of Amer.

Secondary Social Studies Introduction, Curriculum, Evaluation. John U. Michaelis & J. Nelson. (Illus.). 1980. text ed. write for info. (*0-13-797753-0*) P-H.

Secondary Steelmaking for Product Improvement. 256p. 1985. pap. text ed. 52.50 (*0-904357-73-2*, Pub. by Inst Materials UK) Ashgate Pub Co.

Secondary Surveillance Radar. Michael C. Stevens. LC 88-3301. (Artech Radar Library). (Illus.). 315p. reprint ed. pap. 89.80 (*0-7837-4375-0*, 2044115) Bks Demand.

Secondary Teachers at Work. Jim Campbell & S. R. Neill. LC 93-44327. (Teaching As Work Project Ser.). 192p. (C). 1994. pap. text ed. 22.95 (*0-415-08865-8*, B3935, Routledge NY) Routledge.

Secondary Teachers at Work. Jim Campbell & S. R. Neill. LC 93-44327. (Teaching As Work Project Ser.). 224p. (C). (gr. 13). 1994. text ed. 74.95 (*0-415-08864-X*, B3931, Routledge NY) Routledge.

Secondary Teaching Techniques. Fred Stopsky. 1996. pap. text ed. write for info. (*0-205-17569-4*) Allyn.

Secondary Technical & Vocational Education in Underdeveloped Countries (UNESCO) (Education Studies & Documents: No. 33). 1974. reprint ed. pap. 25.00 (*0-8115-1357-2*) Periodicals Srv.

Secondary Technical School: A Usable Past? Gary McCulloch. (Studies in Curriculum History Ser.). 230p. 1989. 70.00 (*1-85000-496-X*, Falmer Pr); pap. 35.00 (*1-85000-497-8*, Falmer Pr) Taylor & Francis.

Secondary Textbook Review: Biology & Life Science, Grades 9-12. California Department of Education Staff. 418p. 1989. pap. 13.50 (*0-8011-0803-9*) Calif Education.

Secondary Textbook Review: English, Grades 9-12. California Department of Education Staff. 176p. 1988. pap. 9.75 (*0-8011-0738-5*) Calif Education.

S

An Asterisk (*) at the beginning of an entry indicates that the title is appearing in BIP for the first time.

Secondary Textbook Review: General Mathematics, Grades 9-12. California Department of Education Staff. 152p. 1987. pap. 7.00 (*0-8011-0677-X*) Calif Education.

Secondary Textbook Review: Mathematical Analysis. California Department of Education Staff. 210p. 1993. pap. 12.50 (*0-8011-1087-4*) Calif Education.

Secondary Traumatic Stress: Self-Care Issues for Clinicians, Researchers, & Educators. Ed. by B. Hudnall Stamm. LC 95-37421. xxiii, 279p. (Orig.). 1996. pap. 18.95 (*0-9629164-9-8*) Sidran Pr.

Secondary Triad Model: A Practical Plan for Implementing Gifted Programs at the Junior & Senior High School Levels. Sally M. Reis & Joseph S. Renzulli. 1985. pap. 16.95 (*0-936386-33-9*) Creative Learning.

Secondary Vocational Education. Rosemary Kolde. 16p. 1986. 3.00 (*0-318-22196-9*, OC119) Ctr Educ Trng Employ.

Secondary Vocational Education: Imperative for Excellence. Ruth P. Hughes. 36p. 1984. 4.95 (*0-318-22197-7*, IN277) Ctr Educ Trng Employ.

Secondary Worlds: Literature Teaching & Visual Arts. Michael J. Benton. (English, Language & Education Ser.). 192p. 1992. pap. 32.00 (*0-335-09797-9*, Open Univ Pr) Taylor & Francis.

Seconde. Sidonie-Gabrielle Colette. (FRE.). 1955. pap. 10.95 (*0-8288-9162-1*, F97311) Fr & Eur.

***Secondhand Basenji Handbook: The Guide to Adopting & Living with a "Rescued" Basenji.** Maria W. Cotter & Patrick J. Cotter. (Illus.). xii, 218p. 1996. spiral bd. 12.00 (*0-9658488-0-9*) Windigo.

Secondhand Bride. Roseanne Williams. (Temptation Ser.). 1995. pap. 3.25 (*0-373-25631-0*, 1-25631-2) Harlequin Bks.

Secondhand Husband. Dallas Schulze. (Intimate Moments Ser.). 1993. mass mkt. 3.50 (*0-373-07500-6*, 5-07500-7) Silhouette.

Secondhand Shopping in Washington, D. C., & Suburban Maryland. Linda C. White. (Illus.). 40p. (Orig.). 1983. pap. 3.75 (*0-915499-01-0*) Prudent Pubs.

***Secondhand Star.** Maryann MacDonald. LC 93-31812. 1997. 19.50 (*0-7868-2316-X*) Hyperion.

Secondhand Star. Maryann MacDonald. LC 93-31812. (Lots of O'Learys Ser.). (Illus.). 64p. (J). (gr. 2-5). 1994. 11.95 (*1-56282-616-6*); lib. bdg. 11.89 (*1-56282-617-4*) Hyprn Child.

Seconds. David Ely. 1993. reprint ed. lib. bdg. 18.95 (*0-89968-426-2*, Lghtyr Pr) Buccaneer Bks.

***Seconds of a Pinch of This & a Handful of That.** Daughters of the Republic of TX District VIII Staff. 192p. 1994. 15.95 (*0-89015-970-X*) Sunbelt Media.

***Secrecy.** Belva Plain. LC 96-49489. 1997. 24.95 (*0-385-31686-0*) Doubleday.

Secrecy: African Art That Conceals & Reveals. Ed. by Mary H. Nooter et al. LC 92-38495. (Illus.). 256p. 1995. 70.00 (*3-7913-1230-8*, Pub. by Prestel GW) te Neues.

Secrecy & Concealment: Studies in the History of Mediterranean & Near Eastern Religions. Ed. by Hans G. Kippenberg & Guy G. Stroumsa. LC 95-2085. (Studies in the History of Religions: Vol. 65). 406p. (ENG & GER.). 1995. 119.00 (*90-04-10235-3*) E J Brill.

Secrecy & Deceit: The Lives of Crypto-Jews. David M. Gitlitz. LC 95-43074. 662p. 1996. 51.95 (*0-8276-0562-5*) JPS Phila.

Secrecy & Democracy. Steven Cohen. 125p. (Orig.). 1990. pap. text ed. 15.00 (*0-942349-03-2*) Eductrs Soc Respons.

Secrecy & Fieldwork. Richard G. Mitchell, Jr. (Qualitative Research Methods Ser.: Vol. 29). (Illus.). 96p. (C). 1993. text ed. 22.95 (*0-8039-4384-9*); pap. text ed. 9.95 (*0-8039-4385-7*) Sage.

Secrecy & Power: The Life of J. Edgar Hoover. Richard G. Powers. (Illus.). 656p. 1988. pap. 18.95 (*0-02-925061-7*, Free Press) Free Pr.

***Secrecy & Power in the British State: A History of British Official Secrets Act, 1911-1989.** Ann Rogers. LC 96-53336. 1997. write for info. (*0-7453-1093-1*, Pub. by Pluto Pr UK) LPC InBook.

***Secrecy & Power in the British State: A History of the Official Secrets Act.** Ann Rogers. 1997. pap. text ed. 16.95 (*0-7453-1092-3*, Pub. by Pluto Pr UK) LPC InBook.

Secrecy & the Arms Race: A Theory of the Accumulation of Strategic Weapons & How Secrecy Affects It. Martin C. McGuire. LC 65-22062. (Economic Studies: No. 125). (Illus.). 1990. 16.50 (*0-674-79665-9*) HUP.

Secresy: Eliza Fenwick. Ed. by Isobel Grundy. 360p. 1994. pap. 12.95 (*1-55111-014-8*) Broadview Pr.

Secresy: Or, The Ruin of the Rock. Eliza Fenwick. (Mothers of the Novel Ser.). 500p. 1989. reprint ed. pap. 18.95 (*0-86358-307-5*) Routledge Chapman & Hall.

***Secret.** (Megamorphs Ser.: No. 9). 1997. 3.99 (*0-590-99729-7*) Scholastic Inc.

Secret. Bill Bright. LC 93-10169. 1993. pap. 8.99 (*0-8407-4435-8*) Nelson.

Secret. Julie Garwood. Ed. by Linda Marrow. 384p. (Orig.). 1992. mass mkt. 6.99 (*0-671-74421-6*) PB.

Secret. Jennifer Lemon. (Illus.). 11p. (J). (ps-2). 1994. pap. 4.95 (*0-909991-80-4*) Bahai.

Secret. Nancy N. Rue. LC 95-25700. (The Christian Heritage Ser.: Vol. 6). (Orig.). (J). 1996. pap. 5.99 (*1-56179-443-0*) Focus Family.

Secret. R. L. Stine. Ed. by Patricia MacDonald. (Fear Street Ser.: No. 2). 176p. (Orig.). (J). (gr. 7 up). 1993. mass mkt. 3.99 (*0-671-86832-2*, Archway) PB.

Secret. Diana Whitney. 1994. mass mkt. 3.50 (*0-373-09874-X*, 5-09874-4) Silhouette.

Secret. large type ed. Julie Garwood. LC 92-20071. 582p. (Orig.). 1992. reprint ed. lib. bdg. 20.95 (*1-56054-492-9*) Thorndike Pr.

Secret: A Child's Story of Sex Abuse, Ages 7-10. Diana L. McCoy. 32p. (Orig.). (J). (gr. 2-5). 1986. pap. text ed. 6.00 (*0-9619250-1-9*) Magic Lantrn.

Secret Activity. Mark Teague. 1996. pap. write for info. (*0-590-94834-2*, Scholastic Hardcover) Scholastic Inc.

Secret Admirer. Donna Guthrie. LC 95-9985. (Illus.). 32p. (J). (ps-3). 1996. 14.95 (*1-57102-045-4*, Ideals Child) Hambleton-Hill.

Secret Admirer. Patricia MacDonald. 384p. 1997. mass mkt. 6.50 (*0-446-60368-6*) Warner Bks.

Secret Admirer. Susan Napier. (Presents Ser.). 1993. pap. 2.89 (*0-373-11554-7*, 1-11554-2) Harlequin Bks.

Secret Admirer. R. L. Stine. (Fear Street Ser.: No. 36). (YA). (gr. 7 up). 1996. pap. 3.99 (*0-671-89429-3*, Archway) PB.

Secret Admirer. large type ed. Patricia MacDonald. (Large Print Ser.). 456p. 1996. lib. bdg. 23.95 (*1-57490-039-0*, Beeler LP Bks) T T Beeler.

Secret Admirer & Other Short Stories. Donald Deffner. 1995. pap. 4.99 (*0-570-09530-1*, 20-2621) Concordia.

Secret Adventures Books Episode 1: Spin. Dave Jackson & Neta Jackson. 120p. (J). 1994. pap. 4.99 (*0-8054-4004-6*, 4240-04) Broadman.

Secret Adventures Books Episode 2: Snap. Dave Jackson & Neta Jackson. 100p. (J). 1994. pap. 4.99 (*0-8054-4005-4*, 4240-05) Broadman.

Secret Adventures Books Episode 3: Smash. Dave Jackson & Neta Jackson. 136p. 1994. pap. 4.99 (*0-8054-4006-2*, 4240-06) Broadman.

Secret Adventures Books Episode 5: Snag. Dave Jackson & Neta Jackson. (Secret Adventures Ser.: Vol. 5). 112p. 1994. 4.99 (*0-8054-4007-0*, 4240-07) Broadman.

Secret Adversary: A Tommy & Tuppence Mystery. Agatha Christie. 240p. 1991. pap. text ed. 5.50 (*0-425-13027-4*) Berkley Pub.

***Secret Affair.** Barbara Bradford. 1997. mass mkt. write for info. (*0-06-101228-9*, Harp PBks) HarpC.

Secret Affair. Barbara Taylor Bradford. 224p. 1996. 16.00 (*0-06-018650-X*) HarpC.

***Secret Affair.** Barbara Taylor Bradford. LC 96-43455. 1997. pap. 24.95 (*0-7862-0927-5*) Thorndike Pr.

***Secret Affair.** large type ed. Barbara Taylor Bradford. LC 96-43455. (Basic Ser.). 200p. 1997. lib. bdg. 26.95 (*0-7862-0926-7*) Thorndike Pr.

Secret Affairs. Larry Hancock & Michael Cherkas. (Silent Invasion Ser.: No. 1). 80p. (Orig.). 1988. pap. 8.95 (*0-918348-50-1*) NBM.

Secret Affairs: Franklin Roosevelt, Cordell Hull, & Sumner Welles. Irwin F. Gellman. (Illus.). 384p. 1995. 35.00 (*0-8018-5083-5*) Johns Hopkins.

Secret Affairs of Mildred Wild. Paul Zindel. 1973. pap. 5.25 (*0-8222-1007-X*) Dramatists Play.

Secret Affinities. Terence Hoagwood. 36p. (Orig.). 1989. pap. 4.00 (*0-916155-10-2*) Trout Creek.

Secret Agencies: U. S. Intelligence in a Hostile World. Loch K. Johnson. LC 96-8610. (Illus.). 336p. 1996. 30.00 (*0-300-06611-2*) Yale U Pr.

***Secret Agenda: One Man's Fight Against Terrorists & Their Weapons - From the Genetical Bio-Engineered to the New Nuclears.** Howard H. Schack. 1996. pap. 12.95 (*1-56171-956-0*, S P I Bks) Sure Seller.

Secret Agent. Joseph Conrad. LC 92-52924. 352p. 1992. 17.00 (*0-679-41723-0*, Everymans Lib) Knopf.

Secret Agent. Joseph Conrad. 1988. lib. bdg. 25.95 (*0-89966-058-4*) Buccaneer Bks.

Secret Agent. Joseph Conrad. Ed. by Bruce Harkness & S. W. Reid. (Cambridge Edition of the Works of Joseph Conrad). (Illus.). 416p. (C). 1990. text ed. 85.00 (*0-521-34135-3*) Cambridge U Pr.

Secret Agent. Joseph Conrad & John K. Snyder, III. (Classics Illustrated Ser.). (Illus.). 52p. (YA). pap. 4.95 (*1-57209-017-0*) Classics Int Ent.

Secret Agent. Joseph Conrad. (Illus.). (J). (gr. k up). 1991. pap. 3.95 (*0-425-12524-6*) First Classics.

Secret Agent. Joseph Conrad. 240p. 1983. pap. 4.95 (*0-451-52416-0*, Sig Classics) NAL-Dutton.

Secret Agent. Joseph Conrad. 1989. pap. 2.50 (*0-451-51804-7*) NAL-Dutton.

Secret Agent. Joseph Conrad. Ed. by Martin Seymour-Smith. (English Library). 272p. 1985. pap. 2.50 (*0-14-043228-0*, Penguin Classics) Viking Penguin.

Secret Agent. Joseph Conrad. 21.95 (*0-8488-0462-7*) Amereon Ltd.

Secret Agent. Joseph Conrad. Ed. & Intro. by Martin S. Smith. 272p. 1990. pap. 9.95 (*0-14-018096-6*, Penguin Classics) Viking Penguin.

Secret Agent. Joseph Conrad. Ed. by Roger Tennant. (World's Classics Ser.). 368p. (C). 1996. pap. 5.95 (*0-19-281627-6*) OUP.

Secret Agent. Joseph Conrad & Seymore. 1996. pap. 9.95 (*0-14-026058-7*) Viking Penguin.

***Secret Agent & Heart of Darkness.** Joseph Conrad. LC 97-24381. 448p. 1996. 18.50 (*0-385-48728-2*) Doubleday.

***Secret Agent & Nostromo.** Christopher Hampton. (Illus.). (Orig.). 1997. pap. 15.95 (*0-571-19026-X*) Faber & Faber.

***Secret Agent Fun Files.** Henderson. (J). 1996. pap. 4.95 (*0-7894-1788-X*) DK Pub Inc.

***Secret Agent Grandma, Vol. 16.** R. L. Stine. (Give Yourself Goosebumps Ser.). 1997. pap. 3.99 (*0-590-84775-9*, Apple Paperbacks) Scholastic Inc.

Secret Agent Man: (Man of the Month) Diana Palmer. (Desire Ser.). 1994. mass mkt. 2.99 (*0-373-05829-2*, 5-05829-2) Silhouette.

***Secret Agent Number One.** large type ed. Frederick Frost. (Ulverscroft Large Print Ser.). 464p. 1996. 25.99 (*0-7089-3551-6*) Ulverscroft.

Secret Agent on Flight 101. Franklin W. Dixon. (Hardy Boys Ser.: Vol. 46). 180p. (J). (gr. 5-9). 1967. 5.95 (*0-448-08946-7*, G&D) Putnam Pub Group.

Secret Agents: The Rosenberg Case, McCarthyism & Fifties America. Ed. by Margorie Garber & Rebecca Walkowitz. (Culture Work). 256p. (gr. 13). 1995. pap. 17.95 (*0-415-91120-6*, B4843, Routledge NY) Routledge.

Secret Agents: The Rosenberg Case, McCarthyism & Fifties America. Ed. by Marjorie Garber & Rebecca Walkowitz. (Culture Work). 256p. (C). (gr. 13). 1995. text ed. 59.95 (*0-415-91119-2*, B4839, Routledge NY) Routledge.

Secret Alliance: The Extraordinary Story of the Rescue of the Jews Since World War II. Tad Szulc. (Illus.). 304p. 1991. 24.95 (*0-374-24946-6*) FS&G.

Secret among the Ruins. Jean A. McConochie. (Readers Ser.). 1984. pap. text ed. 2.25 (*0-88345-575-7*) Prentice ESL.

Secret & a Bridal Pledge: (This Time, Forever) Andrea Edwards. (Special Edition Ser.). 1995. pap. 3.75 (*0-373-09956-8*, 1-09956-3) Silhouette.

***Secret & Sacred: The Diaries of James Henry Hammond, a Southern Slaveholder.** Ed. by Carol Bleser. (Illus.). 372p. 1997. reprint ed. pap. 16.95 (*1-57003-222-X*) U of SC Pr.

Secret & Sanctioned. Stephen Knott. 1996. write for info. (*0-449-91037-7*) Fawcett.

Secret & Sanctioned: Covert Operations & the American Presidency. Stephen F. Knott. 272p. 1996. 27.50 (*0-19-510098-0*) OUP.

Secret & Suppressed: Banned Ideas & Hidden History. Jim Keith. 1993. pap. 12.95 (*0-922915-14-8*) Feral Hse.

Secret & Survival Radio Frequencies & Methods. John J. Williams. Ed. by Laurie Williams. (Illus.). 35p. (Orig.). 1990. pap. 24.00 (*0-934274-23-1*) Consumertronics.

Secret & Urgent: The Story of Codes & Ciphers. Fletcher Pratt. (Cryptographic Ser.: Vol. 72). (Illus.). 282p. 1996. reprint ed. pap. 28.80 (*0-89412-261-4*, C-72) Aegean Park Pr.

***Secret Armies: The Full Story of the SAS, Delta Force & Spetsnaz.** James Adams. (Illus.). 453p. (Orig.). 1988. pap. 19.95 (*0-330-30661-8*, Pub. by Pan Books UK) Trans-Atl Phila.

Secret Army. Tadeusz Bor-Komorowski. (Allied Forces Ser.: No. 2). (Illus.). 408p. 1984. reprint ed. 32.50 (*0-89839-082-6*) Battery Pr.

Secret Army: The I. R. A. Bowyer Bell. LC 96-3011. 600p. (Orig.). 1996. pap. text ed. 26.95 (*1-56000-901-2*) Transaction Pubs.

Secret Army: The IRA 1916-1979. rev. ed. Frwd. by J. Bowyer Bell. LC 89-85273. 481p. 1989. pap. 19.95 (*1-85371-027-X*, Pub. by Poolbeg Pr IE) Dufour.

Secret Army & the Premier: Conservative Paramilitary Organizations in NSW 1930-32. Andrew Moore. 312p. 1990. pap. 24.95 (*0-86840-283-4*, Pub. by New South Wales Univ Pr AT) Intl Spec Bk.

Secret Army, Secret War: Washington's Tragic Spy Operation in North Vietnam. Sedgwick D. Tourison. Ed. by Mark Gatlin. LC 95-17380. (Naval Institute Special Warfare Ser.). (Illus.). 320p. 1995. 31.95 (*1-55750-818-6*) Naval Inst Pr.

Secret Arsenal. 1994. mass mkt. 4.99 (*0-373-61894-8*) Harlequin Bks.

***Secret Art of Antonin Artaud.** Jacques Derrida. 1997. 25.00 (*0-262-04165-0*) MIT Pr.

Secret Art of Dr. Seuss. Dr. Seuss, pseud. LC 95-19024. (Illus.). (J). 1995. 30.00 (*0-679-43448-8*) Random.

Secret Ascension. Michael Bishop. 1989. mass mkt. 4.50 (*0-8125-3157-4*) Tor Bks.

***Secret at Bay Run.** Barbara Jellison. LC 96-90435. 64p. (Orig.). (YA). 1997. pap. 8.95 (*1-56002-680-4*, Univ Edtns) Aegina Pr.

Secret at Mossy Root Mansion. Barbara Davoll. (Molehole Mystery Ser.). (Illus.). (J). (gr. 2-7). 1992. pap. 6.99 (*0-8024-2701-4*) Moody.

Secret at Pheasant Cottage. Patricia M. St. John. LC 78-24384. (Patricia St. John Bks.). (J). (gr. 6-8). 1979. mass mkt., pap. 5.99 (*0-8024-7683-X*) Moody.

Secret at Robert's Roost. Mary Tallent. 161p. (Orig.). (J). (gr. 4-8). 1988. pap. 3.95 (*0-941711-05-6*) Wyrick & Co.

Secret at Seven Rocks, No. 99. Carolyn Keene. Ed. by Ann Greenberg. (Nancy Drew Ser.). 160p. (J). (gr. 3-6). pap. 3.99 (*0-671-69285-2*, Minstrel Bks) PB.

Secret at Shadow Ranch. Carolyn Keene. (Nancy Drew Ser.: Vol. 5). 180p. (J). (gr. 4-7). 1980. 5.95 (*0-448-09505-X*, G&D) Putnam Pub Group.

Secret at Shadow Ranch. Carolyn Keene. LC 94-9296. (Nancy Drew Mystery Stories Ser.: No. 5). 210p. (J). 1994. reprint ed. 12.95 (*1-55709-159-5*) Applewood.

Secret at Solaire. Carolyn Keene. Ed. by Ellen Winkler. (Nancy Drew Ser.: No. 111). 160p. (Orig.). (J). (gr. 3-6). 1993. pap. 3.99 (*0-671-79297-0*, Minstrel Bks) PB.

Secret at the Polk Street School. Patricia R. Giff. (Polka Dot Private Eye Ser.: No. 3). 80p. (Orig.). (J). (gr. k-6). 1987. pap. 3.50 (*0-440-47696-8*, YB BDD) BDD Bks Young Read.

Secret Attachments: Exposing the Roots of Addictions & Compulsions. Peter Michaelson. LC 92-83750. 208p. 1993. pap. 14.95 (*1-882631-26-9*) Prospect NM.

Secret Baby. Amy Frazier. (Special Edition Ser.). 1995. mass mkt. 3.75 (*0-373-09954-1*, 1-09954-8) Silhouette.

***Secret Baby.** Day Leclaire. (Baby Boom Ser.). 1997. mass mkt. 3.25 (*0-373-03457-1*, 1-03457-8) Harlequin Bks.

***Secret Baby.** Day Leclaire. (Baby Boom Ser.). 1997. mass mkt. 3.25 (*0-373-15703-7*, 1-15703-1) Harlequin Bks.

Secret Beauty: Insider Information to Transform You. Diane Irons. LC 96-94027. (Illus.). 256p. (Orig.). 1996. pap. 15.95 (*0-9639394-1-6*) Intl Image.

Secret Bedroom. R. L. Stine. Ed. by Patricia MacDonald. (Fear Street Ser.). 176p. (Orig.). (J). (gr. 7 up). mass mkt. 3.99 (*0-671-72483-5*, Archway) PB.

Secret Birthday Message. Eric Carle. LC 75-168726. (Illus.). 26p. (J). (ps-3). 1972. 15.00 (*0-690-72347-4*, Crowell Jr Bks); lib. bdg. 14.89 (*0-690-72348-2*, Crowell Jr Bks) HarpC Child Bks.

Secret Birthday Message. Eric Carle. LC 85-45403. (Trophy Picture Bk.). (Illus.). 26p. (J). (ps-3). 1986. pap. 5.95 (*0-06-443099-5*, Trophy) HarpC Child Bks.

Secret Book, Vol. 1. Edmund L. Pearson. LC 72-3419. (Short Story Index Reprint Ser.). 1977. reprint ed. 20.95 (*0-8369-4159-4*) Ayer.

Secret Book of Artephius. Ed. by Francis Barrett. 1984. reprint ed. pap. 4.95 (*0-916411-28-1*) Holmes Pub.

***Secret Book of Grazia Dei Ross.** Park. LC 97-3218. 1997. 25.00 (*0-684-81603-2*) S&S Trade.

***Secret Book of John.** Marvin Meyer. 128p. Date not set. 15.00 (*1-56975-083-1*) Ulysses Pr.

Secret Books of the Egyptian Gnostics. Jean Doresse. (Illus.). 446p. 1986. pap. 18.95 (*0-89281-107-2*) Inner Tradit.

Secret Books of the Egyptian Gnostics. Jean Doresse. LC 79-153316. reprint ed. 27.50 (*0-404-04646-0*) AMS Pr.

***Secret Books of the Egyptian Gnostics.** Jean Doresse. (Illus.). 446p. 1997. reprint ed. 8.98 (*1-56731-227-6*, MJF Bks) Fine Comms.

***Secret Box.** Gayle Pearson. LC 96-30459. (J). 1997. 15.00 (*0-689-81379-1*, Atheneum S&S) S&S Trade.

Secret Box, Vol. 2. Hilda Stahl. (Elizabeth Gail Ser.: Vol. 2). 128p. (YA). (gr. 5 up). 1988. pap. 5.99 (*0-8423-0740-0*) Tyndale.

Secret Brother & Other Poems. Elizabeth Jennings. LC 69-14765. (Illus.). (J). (gr. 1-5). 6600. 15.95 (*0-8023-1194-6*) Dufour.

Secret Buddhism: Vajrayana Practices. Kalu Rinpoche. Tr. by Christiane Buchet from FRE. (Illus.). 200p. (Orig.). 1995. pap. text ed. 15.95 (*0-9630371-6-1*) ClearPoint.

Secret Buddies. Mike Newman. 250p. (Orig.). 1992. pap. 11.95 (*1-879194-09-0*) GLB Pubs.

***Secret Camelot: The Lost Legends of King Arthur.** John Matthews. 1997. 29.95 (*0-7137-2646-6*, Pub. by Blandford Pr UK) Sterling.

Secret Camera: Issues in Doubt. Terence S. Kirk. Ed. by Pauline Jones. LC 87-62825. (Illus.). 248p. 1988. 17.95 (*0-944531-00-8*) Owl Wise Pub.

Secret Case of the Disgusting Sneakers. Donald J. Sobol. (Encyclopedia Brown Ser.: No. 18). 112p. (J). (gr. 4-7). 1991. mass mkt. 3.99 (*0-553-15851-1*) Bantam.

Secret Cause: A Discussion of Tragedy. Normand Berlin. LC 81-4089. 208p. 1983. pap. text ed. 15.95 (*0-87023-398-X*) U of Mass Pr.

***Secret Cave.** (J). 1998. 16.95 (*0-7868-0374-6*) Hyprn Child.

Secret Cave of Robinwood. Paul McCusker. (Adventures in Odyssey Ser.: No. 3). (J). (gr. 4-7). 1991. pap. 5.99 (*1-56179-102-4*) Focus Family.

Secret Ceremonies. Deborah Laake. 384p. 1994. mass mkt. 5.99 (*0-440-21780-6*) Dell.

Secret Chain: Evolution & Ethics. Michael Bradie. LC 93-47679. (SUNY Series in Philosophy & Biology). 198p. (C). 1994. text ed. 44.50 (*0-7914-2105-8*); pap. text ed. 14.95 (*0-7914-2106-6*) State U NY Pr.

***Secret Channels: The Inside Story of Arab-Israeli Peace Negotiations.** Muhamed Heikal. 576p. 1997. pap. 16.00 (*0-00-638337-8*) HarperColl Wrld.

Secret Charm Bracelet. Vivian Hamburg. (Illus.). 14p. (Orig.). (J). (gr. k-4). 1995. pap. 5.95 (*1-57532-005-3*) Press-Tige Pub.

Secret Child. Jamie A. Denton. 1995. mass mkt. 3.75 (*0-373-70663-4*, 1-70663-9) Harlequin Bks.

Secret Choices: How to Settle Little Issues Before They Become Big Problems. 2nd abr. rev. ed. Ed Wheat & Gloria O. Perkins. 224p. 1989. reprint ed. pap. 10.99 (*0-310-42501-8*) Zondervan.

Secret Chronicles of Sherlock Holmes. large type ed. June Thomson. LC 94-20458. 312p. 1994. pap. 17.95 (*0-7862-0275-0*) Thorndike Pr.

Secret Chronicles of Sherlock Holmes. June Thomson. 208p. 1994. reprint ed. 20.00 (*1-883402-37-9*) S&S Trade.

Secret Church. Louise A. Vernon. LC 67-15988. (Illus.). 128p. (J). (gr. 3-8). 1967. pap. 6.99 (*0-8361-1783-2*) Herald Pr.

Secret Cipher of the UFOnauts. Allen H. Greenfield. LC 94-31644. (Illus.). 120p. 1994. pap. 9.95 (*1-881532-04-6*) IllumiNet Pr.

Secret Ciphers of the Eighteen Seventy-Six Presidential Election. D. Beaird Glover. 155p. (Orig.). 1992. pap. 24.80 (*0-89412-175-8*) Aegean Park Pr.

Secret Circle: The Initiation, Vol. 1. L. J. Smith. 320p. (YA). 1992. mass mkt. 3.99 (*0-06-106712-1*, Harp PBks) HarpC.

***Secret Circle Booklet.** L. J. Smith. 32p. Date not set. mass mkt. write for info. (*0-06-106700-8*, Harp PBks) HarpC.

Secret Citizen: Poems. Arthur Gregor. LC 88-32701. 66p. (Orig.). 1989. pap. 10.95 (*0-935296-78-6*) Sheep Meadow.

Secret City. Andrew Brown. Ed. by Robert Bixby. 18p. 1994. pap. text ed. 6.00 (*1-882983-12-2*) March Street Pr.

***Secret Club Handbook.** Anne Civardi & Ruth Thomson. LC 96-27139. (Clubhouse Crew Ser.). (Illus.). (J). 1997. pap. 7.95 (*0-8118-1639-7*) Chronicle Bks.

Secret Code. Mercer Mayer. (LC & the Critter Kids Mini-Novels Ser.). (Illus.). 72p. (J). (ps-3). 1994. pap. (*0-307-15983-3*, Golden Books) Western Pub.

***Secret Code.** Dana M. Rau. LC 97-18797. (Illus.). (J). 1998. write for info. (*0-516-20700-8*) Childrens.

Secret Code: The Lost & Hidden Language of the Bible, Vol. 1. Thierry Gaudin. LC 85-70031. 300p. (Orig.). 1985. pap. 13.50 (*0-933357-05-2*) Bret Pubns.

An Asterisk (*) at the beginning of an entry indicates that the title is appearing in BIP for the first time.

Secret Code & Other Stories. Gershon Kranzler. (Illus.). 108p. (YA). reprint ed. 10.00 (*0-8266-0344-0*, Merkos LInyonei Chinuch) Kehot Pubn Soc.

Secret Code Book. Kenneth N. Carlson. 112p. (Orig.). 1994. pap. 9.95 (*0-938428-13-6*) Rain Belt.

Secret Code Book. Helen Huckle. LC 94-30019. (Illus.). 64p. (J). 1995. pap. 14.99 (*0-8037-1725-3*) Dial Bks Young.

***Secret Code Breaker: A Crtptanalysis Handbook.** Robert Reynard. (Illus.). 96p. 1996. pap. 12.95 incl. disk (*1-889668-00-1*) S & D.

Secret Code of DNA. Mary Razzell. (Illus.). 36p. (J). (ps-8). 1986. 7.95 (*0-920806-83-X*, Pub. by Penumbra Pr CN) U of Toronto Pr.

***Secret Codes.** Nancy Cook. Ed. by Joan Gideon. (Real-World Mathematics Through Science Ser.). (Illus.). 136p. (Orig.). (J). (gr. 6-8). 1996. pap. text ed. 18.95 (*0-201-49607-0*, 22733) Seymour Pubns.

***Secret Codes.** Eileen O'Brien & Diana Riddell. Ed. by Lisa Miles. (How to Make Ser.). (Illus.). 32p. (Orig.). (J). (gr. 3-7). 1997. pap. 5.95 (*0-7460-2329-4*, Usborne) EDC.

***Secret Codes: Science Action Book.** Robert Jackson. (Illus.). (J). 1996. pap. 19.95 (*1-56138-782-7*) Running Pr.

Secret Codes & Ciphers. 1986. lib. bdg. 79.95 (*0-8490-3529-5*) Gordon Pr.

***Secret Codes & Hidden Messages.** Jeff O'Hare. LC 96-86534. (Illus.). 48p. (J). (gr. 3-7). 1997. pap. 4.95 (*1-56397-652-8*) Boyds Mills Pr.

Secret Codes & Other Word Games. Elvira Gamiello. (Illus.). (Orig.). (J). (gr. 4-6). 1988. pap. 1.95 (*0-942025-45-8*) Kidsbks.

***Secret Codes for Nintendo 64.** Fitzpatrick & Owen. 128p. 1997. 7.99 (*1-56686-692-8*) Brady Pub.

Secret Codes for Sega Genesis. Bradygames Staff. 112p. 1996. pap. text ed. 7.99 (*1-56686-590-5*) Brady Pub.

Secret Codes for SNES. Bradygames Staff. 112p. 1996. 7.99 (*1-56686-574-3*) Brady Pub.

Secret Codes for the Playstation. Bradygames Staff. 96p. 1996. pap. text ed. 7.99 (*1-56686-598-0*) Brady Pub.

***Secret Codes for the Playstation, Vol. 2.** Brady Publishing Staff. 128p. 1997. 7.99 (*1-56686-684-7*) Brady Pub.

Secret Combinations Today: A Voice of Warning. Robert E. Hales. 1996. 18.98 (*0-88290-569-4*) Horizon Utah.

Secret Conan Doyle Correspondence. Ed. by Leslie V. Harper. Orig. Title: The Secret Holmes-Doyle Correspondence. 212p. (Orig.). 1986. pap. 19.95 (*0-935927-77-8*) Hascom Pubs.

Secret Congress Broadcasts & Storming Railway Tracks During Quit India Movement. Ed. by Syamalendu Sengupta & Gautam Chatterjee. (C). 1988. 44.00 (*81-7013-050-6*, Pub. by Navrang) S Asia.

Secret Connexion: Causation, Realism, & David Hume. Galen Strawson. (Illus.). 312p. 1989. 70.00 (*0-19-824853-9*) OUP.

Secret Connexion: Causation, Realism, & David Hume. Galen Strawson. 336p. 1992. pap. 29.95 (*0-19-824038-4*) OUP.

Secret Constitution & the Need for Constitutional Change. Arthur S. Miller. LC 87-235. (Contributions in American Studies: No. 90). 189p. 1987. text ed. 49.95 (*0-313-25745-0*, MCG/, Greenwood Pr) Greenwood.

***Secret Constitutional Teachings.** Max. 50p. (Orig.). 1997. pap. 30.00 (*0-922070-86-5*) M Tecton Pub.

Secret Corners of the World. Ed. by Donald J. Crump. LC 81-48073. (Special Publications Series 17: No. 1). 200p. 1982. 12.95 (*0-87044-412-3*) Natl Geog.

Secret Craft: The Journalism of Edward Farrer. Carman Cumming. (Illus.). 400p. 1992. 45.00 (*0-8020-2846-2*) U of Toronto Pr.

Secret Crush. Christie Wells. LC 88-16941. (Cranberry Cousins Ser.). 128p. (J). (gr. 5-8). 1989. pap. text ed. 2.95 (*0-8167-1499-1*) Troll Communs.

Secret Cuban Missile Crisis Documents. CIA Staff. 414p. 1994. 38.00 (*0-02-881082-1*); pap. 21.00 (*0-02-881083-X*) Brasseys Inc.

Secret Cult of the Order. Anthony C. Sutton. 140p. (Orig.). 1984. pap. text ed. 9.95 (*0-914981-09-9*) Res Pubns AZ.

Secret Dakini Oracle. Nik Douglas & Penny Slinger. (Illus.). 224p. 1979. pap. 12.95 (*0-89281-005-X*, Destiny Bks) Inner Tradit.

Secret Danger. rev. ed. John Preston. (Mission of Alex Kane Ser.). (Orig.). 1993. mass mkt. 4.95 (*1-56333-111-X*, Badboy) Masquerade.

***Secret d'Awa.** Francois Pratte. (Novels in the Premier Roman Ser.). 64p. (FRE.). (J). (gr. 2-5). 1996. pap. 7.95 (*2-89021-125-8*, Pub. by Les Editions CN) Firefly Bks Ltd.

Secret Dawn. Edith N. Chase. (Illus.). 32p. (J). (gr. k-3). 1996. 12.95 (*1-55209-028-0*) Firefly Bks Ltd.

Secret de la Licorne. Herge. (Illus.). (FRE.). (J). (gr. 7-9). 19.95 (*0-8288-5065-8*) Fr & Eur.

***Secret de Magali.** large type ed. Jean-Michel Thibaux. 276p. 1996. pap. 25.99 (*2-84011-154-3*) Ulverscroft.

Secret de Maitre Cornille. Alphonse Daudet. (Illus.). 32p. (FRE.). 1964. 14.95 (*0-8288-9187-7*, F60050) Fr & Eur.

***Secret de Wilhelm Storitz.** Jules Verne. 325p. (FRE.). 1997. pap. 25.99 (*2-84011-191-8*) Ulverscroft.

Secret de Wilhelm Stroritz. Jules Verne. (Illus.). 172p. (FRE.). 1985. pap. 49.95 (*0-7859-5525-9*) Fr & Eur.

Secret Democracy: Civil Liberties vs. the National Security State. Ed. by Gary E. McCuen. (Ideas in Conflict Ser.). (Illus.). 167p. 1990. 12.95 (*0-86596-074-7*) G E M.

Secret Destinations. Charles Causley. LC 87-46301. 1989. 9.95 (*0-87923-739-2*) Godine.

Secret Destiny of America. Manly P. Hall. pap. 12.95 (*0-89314-388-X*) Philos Res.

Secret Diary. Sukey S. Gross. (Girls of Riukah Gross Academy Ser.). (Illus.). (J). (gr. 5-8). 1989. 10.95 (*0-935063-67-6*); pap. 7.95 (*0-935063-68-4*) CIS Comm.

***Secret Diary.** Elizabeth Koda-Callan. LC 97-15923. (Magic Charm Bks.). 1997. write for info. (*0-7611-0108-X*) Workman Pub.

Secret Diary of a Satan Worshipper. Joel French. LC 91-62034. 192p. (Orig.). 1991. pap. 7.95 (*0-89221-210-1*) New Leaf.

Secret Diary of Adrian Mole, Aged 13 Three Quarters - The Play. Sue Townsend. 65p. (C). 1988. pap. 8.95 (*0-413-59250-2*, A0259, Pub. by Methuen UK) Heinemann.

Secret Diary of Adrian Mole, Aged 13 3-4. Sue Townsend. 208p. (J). (gr. 8 up). 1984. mass mkt. 4.99 (*0-380-86876-8*, Flare) Avon.

***Secret Diary of Adrian Mole, Aged 13 3/4: The Growing Pains of Adrian Mole.** Sue Townsend. (The Adrian Mole Diaries Ser.). 1997. pap. text ed. 12.00 (*0-380-73044-8*) Avon.

***Secret Diary of Anne Boleyn: A Novel.** Robin Maxwell. 1997. 23.95 (*1-55970-375-X*) Arcade Pub Inc.

Secret Diary of Harold L. Ickes, 3 vols., Set. Harold L. Ickes. LC 73-21721. (FDR & the Era of the New Deal Ser.). 1974. reprint ed. lib. bdg. 175.00 (*0-306-70626-1*) Da Capo.

Secret Diary of Harold L. Ickes, 3 vols., Vol. 1. Harold L. Ickes. LC 73-21721. (FDR & the Era of the New Deal Ser.). 1974. reprint ed. lib. bdg. 79.50 (*0-306-70627-X*) Da Capo.

Secret Diary of Harold L. Ickes, 3 vols., Vol. 2. Harold L. Ickes. LC 73-21721. (FDR & the Era of the New Deal Ser.). 1974. reprint ed. lib. bdg. 79.50 (*0-306-70628-8*) Da Capo.

Secret Diary of Harold L. Ickes, 3 vols., Vol. 3. Harold L. Ickes. LC 73-21721. (FDR & the Era of the New Deal Ser.). 1974. reprint ed. lib. bdg. 79.50 (*0-306-70629-6*) Da Capo.

Secret Diary of Mikhail Gorbachev. Frye Gaillard. Ed. by Jerry Bledsoe. LC 90-62193. 175p. (Orig.). 1990. pap. 9.95 (*0-9624255-6-7*, Imprimatur Bks) Down Home NC.

Secret Diary of William Byrd of Westover. William Byrd. 49.95 (*0-8488-0235-7*) Amereon Ltd.

Secret Diary of William Byrd of Westover 1709-1712. William Byrd. LC 72-141097. 1972. reprint ed. 42.95 (*0-405-03304-4*) Arno Press.

Secret Diplomacy of the Vietnam War: The Negotiating Volumes of the Pentagon Papers. Ed. by George C. Herring. 915p. 1983. text ed. 55.00 (*0-292-77573-3*) U of Tex Pr.

Secret Doctors: Ethnomedicine of African-Americans. Wonda L. Fontenot. LC 93-40560. 192p. 1994. text ed. 52.95 (*0-89789-354-9*, Bergin & Garvey) Greenwood.

Secret Doctrine, 3 vols. Helena P. Blavatsky. LC 92-51049. 2310p. 1993. pap. 49.95 (*0-8356-0238-9*, Quest) Theos Pub Hse.

Secret Doctrine, 2 vols. Helena P. Blavatsky. LC 92-51049. 1972. 500.00 (*0-8490-1010-1*) Gordon Pr.

Secret Doctrine, 2 vols., Set. fac. ed. Helena P. Blavatsky. LC 74-76603. 1571p. 1988. reprint ed. pap. 21.00 (*1-55700-002-6*) Theos U Pr.

Secret Doctrine: The Synthesis of Science, Religion & Philosophy. H. P. Blavatsky. (Occultism (1897) Ser.: Vol. 3). 610p. 1993. reprint ed. pap. 49.95 (*1-56459-415-7*) Kessinger Pub.

Secret Doctrine: The Synthesis of Science, Religion, & Philosophy, 2 vols. in 1. Helena P. Blavatsky. xci, 1474p. 1925. reprint ed. 18.50 (*0-938998-00-5*) Theosophy.

Secret Doctrine Commentary--Stanzas I-IV: Transactions of the Blavatsky Lodge. fac. ed. H. P. Blavatsky. LC 94-7279. 120p. 1994. reprint ed. 12.00 (*1-55700-027-1*); reprint ed. pap. 7.00 (*1-55700-028-X*) Theos U Pr.

Secret Doctrine in Israel: A Study of the Zohar & Its Connections. Arthur E. Waite. 350p. 1993. pap. 24.95 (*1-56459-403-3*) Kessinger Pub.

Secret Doctrine of H. P. Blavatsky: First International Symposium, July 1984. Ed. by Richard I. Robb. 112p. 1984. pap. 6.00 (*0-913510-52-1*) Wizards.

Secret Doctrine of Israel. Arthur E. Waite. 330p. 1976. reprint ed. spiral bd. 14.00 (*0-7873-0922-2*) Hlth Research.

Secret Doctrine of Jehovah's Witnesses. Duane Magnani. 1983. 4.95 (*1-883858-20-8*) Witness CA.

Secret Doctrine of the Rosicrucians. Magnus Incognito. 13.50 (*0-911662-30-8*) Yoga.

Secret Doctrine of the Rosicrucians. 252p. 1967. reprint ed. spiral bd. 8.50 (*0-7873-0581-2*) Hlth Research.

Secret Doctrine of the Rosicrucians Illustrated with the Secret Rosicrucian Symbols. Magus Incognito. (Illus.). 256p. 1992. pap. 19.95 (*1-56459-187-5*) Kessinger Pub.

Secret Doctrines of Jesus. H. Spencer Lewis. LC 37-22922. 237p. 1937. pap. 17.95 (*0-912057-91-2*, 501610) RO AMORC.

Secret Documents of America. Mark McCloskey. 1976. pap. 1.50 (*0-88031-032-4*) Invisible-Red Hill.

Secret Door Number Two. Julie A. Waterman. 7p. (Orig.). 1982. Secret Door Number Two. pap. 1.25 (*0-943334-04-7*) Carmonelle Pubns.

Secret Door to Success. Florence S. Shinn. 7.95 (*0-685-70721-0*) Wehman.

Secret Door to Success. Florence S. Shinn. 1978. reprint ed. pap. 5.95 (*0-87516-258-4*) DeVorss.

Secret Doors & Treasure. Robert L. Newbury. LC 90-71968. 64p. (J). 1993. pap. 6.95 (*1-56002-029-6*, Univ Edtns) Aegina Pr.

Secret Drama of Shakspeare's Sonnets Unfolded. 2nd enl. ed. Gerald Massey. LC 74-172854. reprint ed. 55.00 (*0-404-04237-6*) AMS Pr.

Secret Dream Formula. Darcy Altaville. (Illus.). 10p. (Orig.). (J). (gr. k-4). 1996. pap. 6.95 (*1-57532-010-X*) Press-Tige Pub.

Secret Dreams. Keith Korman. LC 94-43026. 400p. 1995. 23.95 (*1-55970-288-5*) Arcade Pub Inc.

***Secret du Bison Blanc.** Carrie J. Taylor. (Illus.). (FRE.). (J). (ps up). 1997. reprint ed. pap. 6.95 (*0-614-29140-2*) Tundra Bks.

Secret du Masque de Fer. Marcel Pagnol. (Illus.). 416p. (FRE.). 1978. 27.95 (*0-7859-4880-5*) Fr & Eur.

Secret Empire: How Twenty-Five Multi-Nationals Rule the World. Janet Lowe. 335p. 1992. text ed. 27.50 (*1-55623-513-5*) Irwin Prof Pubng.

Secret Enemy: Austria-Hungary & the German Alliance, 1914-1918. Gary W. Shanafelt. 272p. 1985. 75.50 (*0-88033-080-5*) East Eur Monographs.

Secret Everyone Knows. Cathleen Brooks. 40p. (YA). (gr. 5-10). 1989. pap. 3.25 (*0-89486-483-1*, 5165B) Hazelden.

Secret Exhibition: Six California Artists. Rebecca Solnit. (Illus.). 224p. (Orig.). 1990. pap. 17.95 (*0-87286-254-2*) City Lights.

Secret Eye: The Journal of Ella Gertrude Clanton Thomas, 1848-1889. Ed. by Virginia I. Burr. LC 89-37188. (Gender & American Culture Ser.). (Illus.). xxiv, 470p. (C). 1990. 39.95 (*0-8078-1897-6*); pap. 16.95 (*0-8078-4273-7*) U of NC Pr.

***Secret Fairy Handbook.** Penny Dann. (J). 1997. 14.95 (*0-689-81458-5*, Litl Simon S&S) S&S Childrens.

***Secret Family.** Bodanis. LC 97-14809. 1997. 27.50 (*0-684-81019-0*) S&S Trade.

Secret Family. T. Noel Stern. (Illus.). 197p. (Orig.). 1988. pap. 15.00 (*0-9619733-0-7*) T N Stern.

Secret Fast Food Recipes: The Fast Food Cookbook. rev. ed. Gloria Pitzer. (Illus.). 120p. 1995. reprint ed. pap. 8.75 (*1-886161-38-0*) G Pitzers.

***Secret Fighting Arts of the Warrior Race Vol. 1: betleH yIqel.** HetaQ. LC 96-71970. (Illus.). 176p. (Orig.). 1997. pap. 16.00 (*1-890065-00-5*) Pacific Warriors.

Secret Fighting Arts of the World. John F. Gilbey. 148p. 1989. pap. 12.95 (*0-8048-1608-5*) C E Tuttle.

Secret Fighting Arts of World. John F. Gilbey. 10.95 (*0-685-63779-4*) Wehman.

Secret Files. Eleanor Cooke. 58p. 1995. pap. 15.95 (*0-224-03893-1*, Pub. by Jonathan Cape UK) Trafalgar.

Secret Files of Lisa Weiss. Tehila Peterseil. (J). 1990. 11.95 (*0-87306-549-2*); pap. 9.95 (*0-87306-550-6*) Feldheim.

Secret Files of Sherlock Holmes. June Thomson. 224p. 1994. 20.00 (*1-883402-36-0*) S&S Trade.

Secret Fire. Johanna Lindsey. 416p. 1987. mass mkt. 6.99 (*0-380-75087-2*) Avon.

Secret Fire. large type ed. Johanna Lindsey. 517p. 1996. lib. bdg. 25.95 (*0-7862-0725-6*, Thorndike Lrg Prnt) Thorndike Pr.

Secret Fire. E. J. Garsten. 120p. 1992. reprint ed. pap. 17.95 (*0-922802-20-3*) Kessinger Pub.

***Secret Fire: The 1913-14 South African Journal of Pauline Smith.** Pauline Smith. Ed. by Harold Scheub. (Illus.). 448p. 1997. pap. 44.95 (*0-86980-930-X*, Pub. by Univ Natal Pr SA) Intl Spec Bk.

***Secret Firearms: An Illustrated History of Miniature & Concealed Handguns.** John D. Walter. (Illus.). 144p. 1997. 27.95 (*1-85409-230-8*, Pub. by Arms & Armour UK) Sterling.

***Secret Flowers: Mourning & the Adaptation to Loss.** Mary Jones. 96p. 1997. pap. 13.95 (*0-7043-4505-6*, Pub. by Womens Press UK) Trafalgar.

Secret for a Nightingale. Victoria Holt. 408p. 1987. mass mkt. 3.50 (*0-449-21296-3*, Crest) Fawcett.

Secret for Winning the Weight Control Game: The Almost-Too-Good-to-Be-True Cure for Obesity (after Which, You Can't Stay Fat) John A. Van Koevering. 100p. (Orig.). 1991. pap. 35.00 (*0-9601346-1-1*) Caballero Pr.

Secret Forces. Bruce A. Perreault. 7p. 1988. reprint ed. spiral bd. 5.50 (*0-7873-0667-3*) Hlth Research.

Secret Forces: The Technique of Underground Movements. Ferdinand O. Miksche. LC 73-110273. (Illus.). 181p. 1971. reprint ed. text ed. 49.75 (*0-8371-4499-X*, MISF, Greenwood Pr) Greenwood.

Secret Forces of the Pyramids. Warren Smith. 220p. 1975. mass mkt. 1.75 (*0-89083-114-9*, Zebra Kensgtn) Kensgtn Pub Corp.

Secret Forces of World War II. Philip Warner. LC 85-40239. (Illus.). 244p. 1992. 22.95 (*0-8128-3060-1*, Scrbrough Hse) Madison Bks UPA.

***Secret Forest.** Photos by Jack W. Dykinga. LC 92-34880. (Illus.). 154p. 1993. reprint ed. pap. 43.90 (*0-608-04140-8*, 2064873) Bks Demand.

Secret Forest: A Lift-the-Flap Nature Book. Time-Life Books Editors. Ed. by Neil Kagan. (Early Learning Program Ser.). (Illus.). 20p. (J). (gr. 3-7). 1991. write for info. (*0-8094-9275-X*); lib. bdg. write for info. (*0-8094-9276-8*) Time-Life.

Secret Forest of Dean. Fay Godwin. 128p. 1988. 50.00 (*0-948265-65-5*, Pub. by Redcliffe Pr Ltd) St Mut.

Secret Forests: A Collection of Hidden Creepy Crawly Bugs & Insects. Michael Gaffney. (Illus.). 32p. (J). 1994. 14.95 (*0-307-17505-7*) Western Pub.

Secret Formula. Frederick Allen. 544p. 1995. pap. 15.00 (*0-88730-751-5*) Harper Busn.

***Secret Formulas.** Rebecca Tilley & Carolyn Willard. Ed. by Lincoln Bergman et al. (Great Explorations in Math & Science (GEMS) Ser.). (Illus.). 160p. (Orig.). (J). (gr. 1-3). 1996. teacher ed., pap. 16.00 (*0-912511-96-6*) Lawrence Science.

Secret Friend. Sharon Porath. 320p. 1992. mass mkt. 4.50 (*0-8217-3906-9*, Zebra Kensgtn) Kensgtn Pub Corp.

Secret Friend, Level 3. Marcia Vaughan. (Let Me Read Ser.). (J). 1996. 2.95 (*0-673-36341-4*, GoodYrBooks) Addson-Wesley Educ.

Secret Funeral of Slim Jim the Snake. Elvira Woodruff. LC 92-54419. 144p. (J). (gr. 3-7). 1993. 15.95 (*0-8234-1014-5*) Holiday.

Secret Funeral of Slim Jim the Snake. Elvira Woodruff. 176p. (J). (gr. 4-7). 1994. pap. 3.99 (*0-440-40945-4*) Dell.

Secret Games of the Gods: Ancient Ritual Systems in Board Games. Nigel Pennick. LC 88-27786. (Illus.). 194p. 1992. pap. 12.95 (*0-87728-752-X*) Weiser.

Secret Garden. (Little Brown Notebook Ser.). (Illus.). 256p. 1995. 6.95 (*0-8069-3974-5*) Sterling.

Secret Garden. (J). 9.95 (*1-56156-312-9*) Kidsbks.

Secret Garden. Bixler. LC 96-20031. 1996. 23.95 (*0-8057-8814-X*, Twayne) Scribnrs Ref.

Secret Garden. Phyllis Bixler. 144p. 1996. 13.95 (*0-8057-8815-8*, Twayne) Scribnrs Ref.

***Secret Garden.** Frances H. Burnett. Ed. by Joshua Hanft. (Great Illustrated Classics Ser.: Vol. 38). (Illus.). 240p. (J). (gr. 3-6). 1994. 9.95 (*0-86611-989-2*) Playmore Inc.

Secret Garden. Frances Hodgson Burnett. (J). 1993. 14.95 (*0-679-42309-5*, Everymans Lib) Knopf.

Secret Garden. Frances Hodgson Burnett. (Classics Ser.). 256p. (J). 1987. mass mkt. 3.50 (*0-553-21201-X*, Bantam Classics) Bantam.

Secret Garden. Frances Hodgson Burnett. (Classics for Young Readers Ser.). 64p. (J). 1994. 5.98 (*0-86112-982-2*) Brimax Bks.

Secret Garden. Frances Hodgson Burnett. LC 86-45534. (Illus.). 224p. (YA). (gr. 5 up). 1987. 18.95 (*0-87923-649-3*) Godine.

Secret Garden. Frances Hodgson Burnett. 288p. (J). 1987. pap. 3.99 (*0-440-40055-4*) Dell.

Secret Garden. Frances Hodgson Burnett. (Illus.). 96p. (J). (gr. 4-7). 1994. pap. 1.00 (*0-486-28024-1*) Dover.

Secret Garden. Frances Hodgson Burnett. (Illus.). 200p. (J). 1993. 25.00 (*0-88363-202-0*) H L Levin.

Secret Garden. Frances Hodgson Burnett. (J). 1987. pap. 2.95 (*0-451-52417-9*, Sig Classics) NAL-Dutton.

Secret Garden. Frances Hodgson Burnett. (J). (gr. 5 up). 1989. pap. 2.50 (*0-451-52080-7*) NAL-Dutton.

Secret Garden. Frances Hodgson Burnett. (World's Classics Ser.). 360p. (J). 1987. pap. 5.95 (*0-19-281772-8*) OUP.

Secret Garden. Frances Hodgson Burnett. (Classics Ser.). (Illus.). 52p. (J). 1994. 3.50 (*0-7214-1657-8*, Ladybrd) Penguin.

Secret Garden. Frances Hodgson Burnett. (Classics Ser.). (J). (gr. 4-6). 1987. pap. 2.95 (*0-14-035004-7*, Puffin) Puffin Bks.

Secret Garden. Frances Hodgson Burnett. (Classics Ser.). 298p. (J). (gr. 5 up). 1994. pap. 3.99 (*0-14-036666-0*) Puffin Bks.

Secret Garden. Frances Hodgson Burnett. LC 86-17788. (Illus.). 72p. (J). (gr. k-5). 1987. 15.00 (*0-394-86467-0*) Random Bks Yng Read.

Secret Garden. Frances Hodgson Burnett. LC 93-18509. (Bullseye Step into Classics Ser.). (Illus.). 128p. (J). (gr. 2-6). 1993. pap. 3.99 (*0-679-84751-0*, Bullseye Bks) Random Bks Yng Read.

Secret Garden. Frances Hodgson Burnett. (Children's Classics Ser.). (Illus.). 288p. (J). (gr. k-6). 1988. 12.99 (*0-517-63225-X*) Random Hse Value.

Secret Garden. Frances Hodgson Burnett. 304p. (J). (gr. 4-7). 1987. pap. 3.50 (*0-590-43346-6*) Scholastic Inc.

Secret Garden. Frances Hodgson Burnett. (YA). 1991. mass mkt. 3.99 (*0-8125-1910-8*) Tor Bks.

Secret Garden. Frances Hodgson Burnett. LC 87-15490. (Illustrated Classics Ser.). (Illus.). (J). (gr. 3-6). 1988. lib. bdg. 12.89 (*0-8167-1203-4*) Troll Communs.

Secret Garden. Frances Hodgson Burnett. (Deluxe Watermill Classic Ser.). 288p. (YA). 1992. 9.49 (*0-8167-2558-6*); pap. 3.95 (*0-8167-2559-4*) Troll Communs.

Secret Garden. Frances Hodgson Burnett. LC 87-15490. (Illustrated Classics Ser.). (Illus.). (J). (gr. 3-6). 1996. pap. 4.95 (*0-8167-1204-2*) Troll Communs.

Secret Garden. Frances Hodgson Burnett. (Silver Elm Classic Ser.). 288p. (J). (gr. 5-8). 1991. pap. 2.99 (*0-87406-575-5*) Willowisp Pr.

Secret Garden. Frances Hodgson Burnett. (Signet Classics Ser.). (YA). 1993. mass mkt. 3.95 (*0-451-52581-7*, Sig Classics) NAL-Dutton.

Secret Garden. Frances Hodgson Burnett. (Illustrated Junior Library). (Illus.). 320p. (YA). 1996. 15.95 (*0-448-41250-0*, G&D) Putnam Pub Group.

Secret Garden. Frances Hodgson Burnett. (Illus.). 56p. (J). (gr. 2-4). 1996. pap. 2.99 (*0-7214-5611-1*, Ladybrd) Penguin.

Secret Garden. Frances Hodgson Burnett. (Illustrated Classics Ser.). (Illus.). 240p. (J). (ps-6). Date not set. text ed. 9.95 (*1-56987-392-5*); pap. text ed. 2.95 (*1-56987-408-5*); pap. text ed. 3.95 (*1-56987-411-5*) Landoll.

Secret Garden. Frances Hodgson Burnett. 288p. (J). (gr. k-6). 1990. pap. 3.50 (*0-440-47709-3*) Dell.

Secret Garden. Frances Hodgson Burnett. 288p. (J). (gr. k-6). 1989. mass mkt. 3.99 (*0-440-97709-6*, Dell Trade Pbks) Dell.

Secret Garden. Frances Hodgson Burnett. 1977. 21.95 (*0-89967-001-6*) Harmony Raine.

Secret Garden. Frances Hodgson Burnett. 288p. (J). 1990. pap. 2.50 (*0-8125-0501-8*) Tor Bks.

Secret Garden. Frances Hodgson Burnett. (J). 22.95 (*0-8488-0692-1*) Amereon Ltd.

Secret Garden. Frances Hodgson Burnett & Constance B. Burnett. (Literary Classics Ser.). 272p. (J). 1996. 5.98 (*1-56138-713-4*) Courage Bks.

***Secret Garden.** Frances Hodgson Burnett. (Illus.). (J). 22.95 (*0-590-24077-3*) Scholastic Inc.

***Secret Garden.** Francis H. Burnett. LC 97-20757. (J). 1998. write for info. (*0-06-027853-6*) HarpC.

Secret Garden. Jan Carr. (Illus.). 104p. (J). (ps-3). 1993. pap. 3.25 (*0-590-47172-4*) Scholastic Inc.

Secret Garden. Kathryn Cristaldi. (Illus.). 32p. (J). (ps-3). 1993. pap. 2.95 (*0-590-47170-8*) Scholastic Inc.

***Secret Garden.** Peter Glassman. (J). Date not set. write for info. (*0-688-14582-5*, Morrow Junior) Morrow.

S

Secret Garden. Adapted by R. Eugene Jackson. (Illus.). 51p. (Orig.). 1993. pap. 4.50 (*0-88680-380-2*); 15.00 (*0-88680-381-0*) I E Clark.

Secret Garden. Marsha Norman. LC 92-2562. 120p. 1992. 22.95 (*1-55936-048-8*); pap. 9.95 (*1-55936-047-X*) Theatre Comm.

Secret Garden. Random House - Value Publication Staff. (J). 1995. 1.10 (*0-517-14143-4*) Crown Pub Group.

Secret Garden. C. Warren Robertson. 60p. 1996. pap. 4.00 (*1-57514-173-6*, 1073) Encore Perform Pub.

Secret Garden. large type ed. Frances Hodgson Burnett. 380p. 1996. reprint ed. lib. bdg. 24.00 (*0-939495-02-3*) North Bks.

Secret Garden. Frances Hodgson Burnett. 302p. (J). 1981. reprint ed. lib. bdg. 21.95 (*0-89966-326-5*) Buccaneer Bks.

Secret Garden. Frances Hodgson Burnett. LC 62-17457. (Trophy Bk.). (Illus.). 256p. (J). (gr. 4-8). 1987. reprint ed. pap. 3.50 (*0-06-440188-X*, Trophy) HarpC Child Bks.

Secret Garden, 2 cassettes, Set. (Read-Along Ser.). (YA). 1994. student ed., pap. 34.95 incl. audio (*0-88432-968-2*, S23948) Audio-Forum.

Secret Garden: A Literature Unit. Concetta D. Ryan. (Literature Units Ser.). (Illus.). 48p. (Orig.). 1992. student ed. 7.95 (*1-55734-414-0*) Tchr Create Mat.

Secret Garden: A Musical. Froml Cohen. 30p. (J). (gr. 5-9). 1995. pap. 4.00 (*1-57514-145-0*, 0023) Encore Perform Pub.

Secret Garden: A Study Guide. Norma Marsh. (Novel-Ties Ser.). 1989. student ed., teacher ed., pap. text ed. 15.95 (*0-88122-057-4*) Lrn Links.

Secret Garden: A Young Reader's Edition of the Classic Story. abr. ed. Frances Hodgson Burnett. LC 90-80198. (Children's Classics Ser.). (Illus.). 56p. (J). (gr. 1 up). 1990. 9.98 (*0-89471-860-6*) Courage Bks.

***Secret Garden: An Anthology in the Kabbalah.** David Meltzer. 1998. pap. text ed. 16.95 (*1-886449-53-8*) Barrytown Ltd.

Secret Garden: Dawn to Dusk in the Astonishing Hidden World of the Garden. David Bodanis. (Illus.). 192p. 1992. 25.00 (*0-671-66353-4*) S&S Trade.

***Secret Garden: Musical.** Frances H. Burnett. 107p. (J). (gr. 1 up). 1997. pap. 5.50 (*0-87129-652-7*, S34) Dramatic Pub.

Secret Garden: Photographers of the Imagination. David D. Duncan. (Illus.). 80p. 19.95 (*0-9633849-1-0*) D D Duncan.

Secret Garden: Playscript. Helen P. Avery. (Orig.). (J). (gr. k-3). 1987. pap. 5.50 (*0-87602-271-9*) Anchorage.

Secret Garden: Vocal Score. Ed. by Carol Cuellar. (Illus.). 356p. (Orig.). (C). 1993. pap. text ed. 100.00 (*0-89724-112-6*, VF2084) Warner Brothers.

Secret Garden: Vocal Selections. Ed. by Carol Cuellar. 78p. (Orig.). (C). 1992. pap. text ed. 18.95 (*0-943351-68-5*, VF1792) Warner Brothers.

Secret Garden - One Hundred Floral Radiographs. Albert G. Richards. (Illus.). 114p. 1991. 40.00 (*0-9628791-0-X*) Almar MI.

Secret Garden - The Play - with Optional Underscoring. Pamela Sterling. 80p. 1991. pap. 5.50 (*0-87129-152-5*, S24) Dramatic Pub.

***Secret Garden; A Little Princess; Little Lord Fauntleroy.** Frances Hodgson Burnett. LC 95-14138. (J). 1995. 11.99 (*0-517-14748-3*, Pub. by Gramercy) Random Hse Value.

***Secret Garden Activity Book: 15 Gardening & Nature Projects Based on the Classic Story.** Frances H. Burnett. LC 97-4024. (Illus.). (J). 1997. write for info. (*1-57145-326-1*) Thunder Bay CA.

***Secret Garden Activity Kit.** Jo A. Padgett. 1997. 19.95 (*1-57145-325-3*) Advan Mktg Servs.

Secret Garden Coloring Book. Frances Hodgson Burnett. (Illus.). (J). (gr. 4-7). 1993. pap. 2.95 (*0-486-27680-5*) Dover.

Secret Garden Notebook. Graham Rust. (J). (gr. 4-7). 1991. 12.95 (*0-87923-890-9*) Godine.

Secret Garden of Mahumud Shabistari. Tr. by Johnson Pasha. 86p. 1969. 17.00 (*0-900860-38-3*, Pub. by Octagon Pr UK) ISHK.

Secret Garden, with Charm, Key-Shaped. Diane Molleson. (Illus.). (J). (ps-3). 1993. pap. 12.95 (*0-590-47173-2*) Scholastic Inc.

Secret Gardens. Billy Sims. Date not set. pap. 14.89 (*0-8037-1807-1*) Dial Bks Young.

***Secret Gardens.** Toogood. 1991. 14.95 (*0-7063-7008-2*, Pub. by Ward Lock UK) Sterling.

Secret Gardens: Revealed by Their Owners. Rosemary Verey. (Illus.). 208p. 1994. 45.00 (*0-8212-2074-8*) Bulfinch Pr.

Secret Gardens: The Golden Age of Children's Literature. Humphrey Carpenter. (Illus.). 272p. 1991. pap. 9.95 (*0-395-57374-2*) HM.

Secret Gardens in Venice. Cristiana Moldi-Ravenna et al. (Illus.). 168p. 1996. 50.00 (*88-7743-169-5*, Pub. by Arsenale Editrice IT) Antique Collect.

Secret Gardens of Georgetown: Behind the Walls of Washington's Most Historic Neighborhood. Adrian Higgins. LC 93-6334. 1994. 40.00 (*0-316-36084-8*) Little.

Secret Gardens of Marijuana. 1991. lib. bdg. 68.95 (*0-8490-4715-3*) Gordon Pr.

***Secret Gardens of Santa Fe.** Leblanc. LC 97-11858. 1997. 45.00 (*0-8478-2034-3*) Rizzoli Intl.

Secret Gift: Discovering God's Grace. Nancy Johnson & Shirley Wooldridge. LC 96-92260. (Illus.). 173p. (Orig.). 1996. pap. 12.00 (*0-9651920-0-8*) Johnson Wldrdg.

Secret Go the Wolves. R. D. Lawrence. 240p. 1985. mass mkt. 5.99 (*0-345-33200-8*) Ballantine.

Secret Gospels: A Harmony of Apocryphal Jesus Traditions. Ed. by R. Joseph Hoffman. (Westminster College - Oxford Ser.). 196p. 1996. 32.95 (*1-57392-069-X*) Prometheus Bks.

Secret Government: The Constitution in Crisis. 2nd ed. Bill Moyers. Ed. by Calvin Kytle. LC 89-70131. 131p. 1990. 16.95 (*0-932020-61-5*) Seven Locks Pr.

Secret Government: The Constitution in Crisis. 2nd ed. Bill Moyers. Ed. by Calvin Kytle. LC 89-70131. 131p. 1990. pap. 9.95 (*0-932020-60-7*) Seven Locks Pr.

Secret Grimoire of Turiel: Being a System of Ceremonial Magic of the Sixteenth Century. (Kabbalistic-Grimoire Ser.: No. 1). (Illus.). 1993. reprint ed. pap. 9.95 (*1-55818-233-0*, Sure Fire) Holmes Pub.

***Secret Groom.** Myrna Mackenzie. (Surprise Brides Ser.). 1997. mass mkt. 3.25 (*0-373-19225-8*, 1-19225-1) Silhouette.

Secret Grove. Barbara Cohen. (Illus.). 32p. (J). (gr. 4-6). 1985. 7.95 (*0-8074-0301-6*, 101065) UAHC.

Secret Grove. Cheri E. Silver. (Illus.). 32p. (J). (gr. 4-6). 1986. teacher ed., pap. 5.00 (*0-8074-0318-0*, 208027) UAHC.

Secret Grove. large type ed. Barbara Cohen. (Illus.). 1993. 9.50 (*0-614-09854-8*, L-34125-00) Am Printing Hse.

***Secret Guide to Computers.** 23th ed. Russ Walter. (Illus.). 639p. 1997. pap. 15.00 (*0-939151-23-5*, 23E) Russ Walter.

Secret Happiness of Marilyn Monroe. James E. Dougherty. (Illus.). 166p. 1992. reprint ed. lib. bdg. 16.95 (*0-89966-908-5*) Buccaneer Bks.

Secret Harmonies. Andrea Barrett. Ed. by Jane Rosenman. 256p. 1991. reprint ed. pap. 12.00 (*0-671-73137-8*, WSP) PB.

Secret Heart. 160p. (YA). 1993. pap. 3.50 (*0-553-29986-7*) Bantam.

Secret Heart of Numbers. Dirk Wales. LC 95-30441. (Illus.). 112p. 1995. 16.95 (*1-57071-053-8*) Sourcebks.

Secret Heart of the Clock: Notes, Aphorisms, Fragments. Elias Canetti. Tr. by Joel Agee from GER. 158p. 1989. 19.95 (*0-374-25694-2*) FS&G.

Secret Hedgehog. Paul Adshead. LC 91-38897. (J). (gr. 4 up). 1991. 7.99 (*0-85953-510-X*) Childs Play.

***Secret Heresy of Hieronymus Bosch.** Lynda Harris. 1996. 61.95 (*0-86315-198-1*, Pub. by Floris Bks UK) Gryphon Hse.

Secret Heritage. Papp. 1994. 22.95 (*0-02-923845-5*) S&S Trade.

Secret Hideout. Paul Hutchens. (Sugar Creek Gang Ser.: Vol. 5). (J). (gr. 3-7). 1968. mass mkt., pap. 3.99 (*0-8024-4806-2*) Moody.

***Secret Hideout.** Paul Hutchens. (Sugar Creek Gang Ser.: No. 6). 112p. (J). 1997. mass mkt. 4.99 (*0-8024-7010-6*) Moody.

Secret Hiding Places. Michael Hodgetts. 250p. 1989. pap. 39.00 (*1-85390-079-6*, Pub. by Veritas IE) St Mut.

Secret High Degree Rituals of the Masonic Rite of Memphis. John Yarker. 80p. 1993. pap. 16.95 (*1-56459-331-2*) Kessinger Pub.

Secret Historical Facts: Events of October 15, 1944; Record of Evidence of Interrogations at Sopronkohida, Hungary. Hungarian Historical Research Society Staff. LC 77-95241. Orig. Title: Titkos Tortenelmi Adatok Az 1944 Oktober 15.-I Esemenyek Sopronkohidai Kihallhatasok. 422p. 1978. pap. 15.95 (*0-935484-02-7*) Universe Pub Co.

Secret History. Procopius. Tr. & Intro. by G. Williamson. (Classics Ser.). 208p. 1982. pap. 10.95 (*0-14-044182-4*, Penguin Classics) Viking Penguin.

Secret History. Procopius. Tr. by Richard Atwater. 1960. pap. 9.95 (*0-472-08728-2*, Ann Arbor Bks) U of Mich Pr.

***Secret History.** Donna Tart. 1996. pap. 12.95 (*0-449-91151-9*) Fawcett.

Secret History. Donna Tartt. 512p. 1993. mass mkt. 6.99 (*0-8041-1135-9*) Ivy Books.

Secret History. LC 73-161273. (Black Heritage Library Collection). 1977. reprint ed. 24.95 (*0-8369-8832-9*) Ayer.

Secret History of Alcoholism. James Graham. 272p. 1996. pap. 13.95 (*1-85230-891-5*) Element MA.

***Secret History of Bill Clinton.** Ambrose Evans-Pritchard. 250p. 1997. 24.95 (*0-89526-408-0*, Gateway Editions) Regnery Pub.

Secret History of Gender: Women, Men, & Power in Late Colonial Mexico. Steve J. Stern. LC 94-39349. 1995. text ed. 29.95 (*0-8078-2217-5*) U of NC Pr.

***Secret History of Gender: Women, Men, & Power in Late Colonial Mexico.** Steve J. Stern. LC 94-39349. (Illus.). 496p. (C). 1997. pap. 18.95 (*0-8078-4643-0*) U of NC Pr.

Secret History of Henrietta, Princess of England: First Wife of Philippe, Duc D'Orleans; Together with, Memoirs of the Court of France for the Years 1688-1689. Madame De la Fayette. Tr. & Intro. by J. M. Shelmerdine. LC 92-29820. 1993. lib. bdg. 40.00 (*0-86527-409-6*) Fertig.

Secret History of Kate Bush. Fred Vermorel. (Illus.). 96p. 1983. pap. 15.95 (*0-7119-0152-X*, OP42035) Omnibus NY.

Secret History of the American Revolution: An Account of the Conspiracies of Benedict Arnold & Numerous Others. Carl Van Doren. LC 76-122062. (Illus.). xvi, 534p. 1973. reprint ed. 45.00 (*0-678-03176-2*) Kelley.

Secret History of the Convict Colony. Robert J. King. 192p. 1991. text ed. 29.95 (*0-04-610020-2*, Pub. by Allen Unwin AT) Paul & Co Pubs.

***Secret History of the Hittites, Philistines, Greeks, Hebrews, Galalians & Nazzarians.** Max. 50p. (Orig.). 1997. pap. 30.00 (*0-922070-82-2*) M Tecton Pub.

Secret History of the Jesuits. rev. ed. Edmond Paris. 208p. 1982. reprint ed. pap. 7.50 (*0-937958-10-7*) Chick Pubns.

Secret History of the Lord of Musashi & Arrowroot. Junichiro Tanizaki. Tr. by Anthony H. Chambers from JPN. 210p. (Orig.). 1991. reprint ed. pap. 10.95 (*0-86547-470-2*, North Pt Pr) FS&G.

Secret History of the Mongols. Ed. & Tr. by Francis W. Cleaves from MON. (Harvard-Yenching Institute Publications). 344p. 1982. 22.50 (*0-674-79670-5*) HUP.

Secret History of the Oxford Movement. Walter Walsh. 1977. lib. bdg. 59.95 (*0-8490-2583-4*) Gordon Pr.

Secret History of the Oxford Movement. Walter Walsh. LC 73-101915. reprint ed. 49.50 (*0-404-06819-7*) AMS Pr.

***Secret History of Water.** Silvia Curbelo. (Florida Poetry Ser.: No. 1). 96p. (Orig.). 1997. pap. 10.00 (*0-938078-52-6*) Anhinga Pr.

***Secret History of Water.** Silvia Curbelo. (Florida Poetry Ser.: No. 1). 96p. 1997. 18.95 (*0-938078-53-4*) Anhinga Pr.

Secret Holmes-Doyle Correspondence see Secret Conan Doyle Correspondence

Secret Holy War of Santiago de Chile. Marco A. De la Parra. LC 93-19641. (Emerging Voices: New International Fiction Ser.). 1994. 29.95 (*1-56656-127-2*); pap. 12.95 (*1-56656-123-X*) Interlink Pub.

Secret House of Death. Ruth Rendell. 240p. 1987. mass mkt. 5.99 (*0-345-34950-4*) Ballantine.

Secret Identity of the Beloved Disciple. Joseph A. Grassi. 1992. pap. 7.95 (*0-8091-3121-8*) Paulist Pr.

Secret in the Bird. Camarin Grae. 384p. 1988. pap. 8.95 (*0-941483-05-3*) Naiad Pr.

Secret in the Dark. Carolyn Keene. Ed. by Anne Greenberg. (Nancy Drew Ser.: No. 102). 160p. (J). (gr. 3-6). pap. 3.99 (*0-671-69279-8*, Minstrel Bks) PB.

Secret in the Dorm Attic. Jean F. Andrews. LC 90-2972. 104p. (Orig.). (J). (gr. 3-6). 1990. pap. 4.95 (*0-930323-66-1*, Pub. by K Green Pubns) Gallaudet Univ Pr.

Secret in the Kitchen. Lissa H. Johnson. (China Tate Ser.: No. 2). 1994. pap. 5.99 (*1-56179-282-9*) Focus Family.

Secret in the Lake. Lorraine Avery. LC 89-5119. (Apple Park Adventures Ser.). (Illus.). 96p. (J). (gr. 4-6). 1997. pap. 2.95 (*0-8167-1711-7*) Troll Communs.

Secret in the Matchbox. Val Willis. 1990. pap. 4.95 (*0-374-46593-2*) FS&G.

Secret in the Moonlight: Welcome Inn. E. L. Flood. LC 93-50936. (Welcome Inn Ser.). (Illus.). 144p. (J). (gr. 3-6). 1996. pap. 2.95 (*0-8167-3427-5*) Troll Communs.

Secret in the Old Model T. Lenora B. Caldwell. LC 94-90735. 120p. (Orig.). (J). 1995. pap. 8.00 (*1-56002-540-9*, Univ Edtns) Aegina Pr.

***Secret in the Rose Room.** 187p. (Orig.). 1997. pap. 5.99 (*1-56315-076-X*) Sterling Hse.

***Secret in the Swamp, 5.** Mary C. Reid. LC 97-21038. (Backpack Mystery Ser.). 1997. pap. 3.99 (*1-55661-719-4*) Bethany Hse.

Secret in the Toy Room. Pat Zawadsky. 28p. (Orig.). (J). (gr. 2-7). 1984. pap. 3.50 (*0-88680-225-3*); 7.50 (*0-88680-226-1*) I E Clark.

Secret in the Willows. Beverly Lewis. (Summerhill Secrets Ser.: Bk. 2). 144p. (J). (gr. 6-9). 1995. pap. 5.99 (*1-55661-477-2*) Bethany Hse.

Secret Incomes of the Soviet State Budget. Igor Birman. 330p. 1981. lib. bdg. 183.00 (*90-247-2550-X*) Kluwer Ac.

***Secret Indian Legends.** Snowbird & Sabbeleu. (Illus.). vi, 122p. (Orig.). 1996. 19.95 (*0-9653990-0-1*) Whispering Willows.

Secret Infatuation. Betty A. Neels. (Romance Ser.). 1995. mass mkt. 2.99 (*0-373-03363-X*, 1-03363-8) Harlequin Bks.

Secret Ingredient. Sarah H. Phillips & Mary H. Williams. (Illus.). 179p. 1987. 10.00 (*0-9619306-0-8*) M H Williams.

Secret Initiation. Herdt. 1994. 24.95 (*0-226-32750-7*) U Ch Pr.

Secret Inner Order Rituals of the Golden Dawn. Patrick Zalewski. Ed. by Christopher S. Hyatt & Joseph Lisiewski. LC 88-80072. (Illus.). 200p. (Orig.). 1988. pap. 14.95 (*1-56184-115-3*) New Falcon Pubns.

Secret Instructions of the Society of Jesus: The Jesuits. 1991. lib. bdg. 67.95 (*0-8490-4413-8*) Gordon Pr.

Secret Instructions of the Society of Jesus (Jesuit Priests) (1882) 1996. pap. 9.95 (*1-56459-912-4*) Kessinger Pub.

Secret Instructions to Probators of an Esoteric Occult School. Helena P. Blavatsky. 122p. 1969. reprint ed. spiral bd. 25.00 (*0-7873-1218-5*) Hlth Research.

Secret Instructions to the Society of Jesus: The Jesuits. 1992. lib. bdg. 250.00 (*0-8490-8832-1*) Gordon Pr.

Secret Intelligence & Public Policy: A Dilemma of Democracy. Pat M. Holt. LC 94-32202. 269p. 1994. pap. text ed. 19.95 (*0-87187-683-3*) Congr Quarterly.

Secret Iron of the Heart. Arvia McKaye-Ege. 192p. 1982. 18.00 (*0-932776-05-1*); pap. 15.00 (*0-932776-06-X*) Adonis Pr.

Secret Is in the Rainbow. Ruth Berger. LC 86-50045. 186p. 1986. reprint ed. pap. 7.95 (*0-87728-638-8*) Weiser.

Secret Is Out. Teri Martini. 144p. (J). (gr. 5). 1992. pap. 2.99 (*0-380-71465-5*, Camelot) Avon.

Secret Island of Oz. Eric Shanower. (Oz Ser.). (Illus.). 48p. (Orig.). (J). 1993. pap. 8.95 (*0-915419-08-4*) Dark Horse Comics.

***Secret Jealousy.** Misty A. Henson. (Kid Detectives Ser.). (Illus.). 84p. (J). (gr. 4-7). 1997. pap. 3.50 (*1-885744-09-9*) Otter Creek.

Secret Jokes & Hidden Riddles Activity & Fun Book. Elvira Gamiello. (Illus.). (Orig.). (J). (gr. 4-6). 1989. pap. 1.95 (*0-942025-25-3*) Kidsbks.

Secret Journal & Other Writings. Pierre Drieu La Rochelle. Tr. by Alastair Hamilton from FRE. 1974. 35.00 (*0-86527-300-6*) Fertig.

Secret Journal & Other Writings. Pierre Drieu La Rochelle. Tr. by Alastair Hamilton from FRE. 112p. 1980. 9.95 (*0-903747-02-2*) Writers & Readers.

Secret Journal, 1836-1837. 2nd ed. Aleksandr Pushkin. Tr. & Intro. by Mikhail Armalinsky. 91p. 1991. reprint ed. pap. 7.00 (*0-916201-07-4*) M I P Co.

Secret Journals of Sherlock Holmes. Thomson. 1995. 20.00 (*1-883402-38-7*) S&S Trade.

***Secret Journey.** Debra Polirer. (Orig.). 1997. pap. write for info. (*0-614-30139-4*) Watermrk Pr.

Secret Journeys: Theory & Practice in Reading Dickens. Nicholas Morgan. LC 91-55022. (Illus.). 152p. 1992. 29.50 (*0-8386-3447-8*) Fairleigh Dickinson.

Secret Judgments of God: Old World Disease in Colonial Spanish America. Ed. by Noble D. Cook & W. George Lovell. LC 91-50301. (Civilization of the American Indian Ser.: Vol. 205). (Illus.). 256p. 1992. 29.95 (*0-8061-2372-9*) U of Okla Pr.

Secret Justice. Dick Stivers. 1992. mass mkt. 4.99 (*0-373-62406-9*, 1-62406-3) Harlequin Bks.

Secret Keeper. Shirley Eskapa. 220p. 1985. pap. 5.95 (*0-89733-126-5*) Academy Chi Pubs.

Secret Keys. (Orig.). (J). 1993. pap. 5.99 (*0-8280-0724-1*) Review & Herald.

Secret Kingdom. (*0-8317-3496-5*) Smithmark.

Secret Kingdom. Pat Robertson. 1994. mass mkt. 5.99 (*0-8499-3567-9*) Word Pub.

Secret Kingdom. large type ed. Pat Robertson. (Large Print Inspirational Ser.). 352p. 1986. pap. 14.95 (*0-8027-2534-1*) Walker & Co.

Secret Laboratory Journal of Dr. Victor Frankenstein. Jeremy Kay. (Illus.). 208p. 1996. 29.95 (*0-87951-511-2*) Overlook Pr.

Secret Land of the Past. Miriam Schlein. (J). (gr. 4-7). 1992. pap. 2.75 (*0-590-45701-2*) Scholastic Inc.

***Secret Language.** Molly Barker. LC 97-4108. (Illus.). 200p. 1997. boxed 11.95 (*0-87286-328-X*) City Lights.

Secret Language. Ursula Nordstrom. LC 60-7701. (Illus.). 192p. (J). (gr. 3-5). 1960. lib. bdg. 12.89 (*0-06-024576-X*) HarpC Child Bks.

Secret Language. Ursula Nordstrom. LC 60-7701. (Trophy Bk.). (Illus.). 192p. (J). (gr. 3-5). 1972. pap. 3.95 (*0-06-440022-0*, Trophy) HarpC Child Bks.

Secret Language: A Novel. Monica Wood. 276p. 1993. 22.95 (*0-571-12948-X*) Faber & Faber.

Secret Language: Pheromones in the Animal World. Rebecca L. Johnson. (Discovery! Ser.). (Illus.). 64p. (J). (gr. 5 up). 1989. lib. bdg. 21.50 (*0-8225-1586-5*, Lerner Publctns) Lerner Group.

Secret Language of Birthdays: Personality Profiles for Each Day of the Year. Gary Goldschneider & Joost Elffers. (Illus.). 832p. 1994. pap. 34.95 (*0-670-85857-9*) Penguin.

***Secret Language of Crime.** George W. Matsell. LC 97-60412. 212p. 1997. pap. 12.95 (*0-87243-228-9*) Templegate.

Secret Language of Dreams. David Fontana. LC 93-48583. (Illus.). 192p. 1994. 29.95 (*0-8118-0791-6*); pap. 19.95 (*0-8118-0728-2*) Chronicle Bks.

***Secret Language of Eating Disorders: The Revolutionary New Approach to Curing Anorexia & Bulimia.** Peggy Claude-Pierre. LC 97-11899. 288p. 1997. 25.00 (*0-8129-2842-3*, Times Bks) Random.

Secret Language of Love. Megan Tresidder. LC 96-10958. (Illus.). 176p. 1997. 29.95 (*0-8118-1409-2*); pap. 19.95 (*0-8118-1433-5*) Chronicle Bks.

Secret Language of Men. Sherrie Weaver. 168p. (Orig.). 1995. pap. 5.95 (*1-56245-191-X*) Great Quotations.

***Secret Language of Relationships.** Gary Goldschneider. 1997. pap. 34.95 (*0-670-87527-9*) Viking Penguin.

Secret Language of Signs: How to Interpret the Coincidences & Symbols in Your Life. Denise Linn. 352p. 1996. pap. 12.00 (*0-345-40693-1*, Del Rey) Ballantine.

Secret Language of Success: Using Body Language to Get What You Want. David Lewis. (Illus.). 252p. 1990. pap. 11.95 (*0-88184-644-9*) Carroll & Graf.

Secret Language of Symbols: A Visual Key to Symbols & Their Meanings. David Fontana. LC 93-10297. (Illus.). 192p. 1994. 29.95 (*0-8118-0489-5*); pap. 19.95 (*0-8118-0462-3*) Chronicle Bks.

Secret Language of the Mind: A Visual Inquiry into the Mysteries of Consciousness. David Cohen. LC 96-10435. (Illus.). 192p. 1996. 29.95 (*0-8118-1407-6*); pap. 19.95 (*0-8118-1431-9*) Chronicle Bks.

***Secret Language of the Soul: A Visual Exploration of the Spiritual World.** Jane Hope. LC 97-2307. 1997. 29.95 (*0-8118-1862-4*); pap. 19.95 (*0-8118-1861-6*) Chronicle Bks.

Secret Language of the Stars & Planets: A Visual Key to the Heavens. Paul Devereux & Geoffrey Cornelius. LC 95-23316. 176p. 1996. 29.95 (*0-8118-1225-1*); pap. 19.95 (*0-8118-1200-6*) Chronicle Bks.

Secret Language of Waking Dreams. Mike Avery. 137p. 1992. pap. 11.00 (*1-57043-060-8*) ECKANKAR.

Secret Language of Women: A Humorous Guide to Understanding Women. Sherrie Weaver. 168p. (Orig.). 1995. pap. 5.95 (*1-56245-224-X*) Great Quotations.

Secret Languages of Ireland. Robert A. MacAlister. LC 78-72637. (Celtic Language & Literature). reprint ed. 29.50 (*0-404-17566-X*) AMS Pr.

Secret Languages of Success. David Lewis. 1995. 7.98 (*0-88365-894-1*) Galahad Bks.

Secret Leaves: The Novels of Walter Scott. Judith Wilt. LC 85-8615. x, 242p. 1985. pap. text ed. 14.50 (*0-226-90161-0*) U Ch Pr.

Secret Lessons. Don W. Weber & Charles Bosworth, Jr. 368p. (Orig.). 1994. pap. 5.99 (*0-451-40480-7*, Onyx) NAL-Dutton.

An Asterisk (*) at the beginning of an entry indicates that the title is appearing in BIP for the first time.

Secret Letters of Mama Cat. Jody Sorenson. LC 87-25333. 122p. (J). (gr. 5-8). 1988. 12.95 (0-8027-6779-6); lib. bdg. 13.85 (0-8027-6791-5) Walker & Co.

Secret Life. (Orig.). 1992. mass mkt. 4.95 (1-56333-017-2, Badboy) Masquerade.

Secret Life. Carol W. Lundberg. LC 93-33743. 68p. 1993. pap. 12.95 (0-7734-2801-1, Mellen Poetry Pr) E Mellen.

Secret Life. Michael Ryan. 1996. pap. 14.00 (0-679-76776-2, Vin) Random.

Secret Life. Claire Tomalin. 1989. pap. 13.95 (0-318-41610-7) St Martin.

Secret Life: An Autobiography. Michael Ryan. LC 94-43814. 368p. 1995. 25.00 (0-679-40775-8) Pantheon.

Secret Life: Firsthand, Documented Accounts of UFO Abductions. David M. Jacobs. 336p. 1993. pap. 12.00 (0-671-79720-4, Fireside) S&S Trade.

Secret Life: Natural Products & Marine Life. Francesco Pietra. 300p. 1990. 109.50 (0-8176-2346-9) Birkhauser.

Secret Life of a Satanist: The Authorized Biography of Anton LaVey. Blanche Barton. 1992. pap. 12.95 (0-922915-12-1) Feral Hse.

***Secret Life of American.** Dalma Heyn. Date not set. write for info. (0-688-09072-9) Morrow.

***Secret Life of Aphra Behn.** Janet Todd. LC 97-15584. (Illus.). 550p. 1997. 40.00 (0-8135-2455-5) Rutgers U Pr.

Secret Life of Beer: Legends, Lore, & Little-Known Facts. Alan D. Eames. LC 95-11077. (Illus.). 176p. 1995. pap. 9.95 (0-88266-807-2, Garden Way Pub) Storey Comm Inc.

Secret Life of Billie's Uncle Myron. Len Jenkin & Emily Jenkins. LC 96-3820. 144p. (J). (gr. 5-8). 1996. 15.95 (0-8050-4395-0, B Martin BYR) H Holt & Co.

Secret Life of Bob Hope. Arthur Marx. LC 92-35525. (Illus.). 480p. 1993. 21.99 (0-942637-74-7) Barricade Bks.

Secret Life of Buildings: An American Mythology for Modern Architecture. Gavin Macrae-Gibson. (Graham Foundation Architecture Ser.). 223p. 1985. 35.00 (0-262-13203-6) MIT Pr.

Secret Life of Cats. Robert De Laroche & Jean-Michel Labat. (Illus.). 120p. 1995. 18.95 (0-8120-6513-1) Barron.

***Secret Life of Cats: Mini-Edition.** Robert Delaroche. 1997. 5.95 (0-7641-5034-0) Barron.

Secret Life of Central Park. Marie Winn. 1997. write for info. (0-679-43997-8) Pantheon.

***Secret Life of Central Park.** Marie Winn. 1998. pap. write for info. (0-679-75846-1) Pantheon.

***Secret Life of Colonel Tom Parker.** Dickerson. 1998. 24. 95 (0-02-864871-4) S&S Trade.

***Secret Life of Compost: A "How-to" & "Why" Guide to Composting-Lawn, Garden, Feedlot or Farm.** Malcolm Beck. (Illus.). 140p. (Orig.). 1997. pap. 19.00 (0-911311-52-1); text ed. 25.00 (0-911311-53-X) Acres USA.

Secret Life of Cosmetics: A Science Experiment Book. Vicki Cobb. LC 85-40097. (Illus.). 128p. (J). (gr. 5-9). 1985. lib. bdg. 14.89 (0-397-32122-8, Lipp Jr Bks) HarpC Child Bks.

Secret Life of Dagmar Schultz. Lynn Hall. LC 87-28499. 96p. (J). (gr. 5-8). 1988. lib. bdg. 13.95 (0-684-18915-1, C Scribner Sons Young) S&S Childrens.

Secret Life of Dogs. David Sipress. 1990. mass mkt. 5.95 (0-452-29494-0) NAL-Dutton.

Secret Life of Jesse James. Arthur W. Knight. 166p. (Orig.). 1996. pap. 9.95 (0-9645655-2-8) BurnhillWolf.

Secret Life of Jesus the Essene. Raymond W. Bernard. (Essene-Jesus-Apollonius Ser.: Vol. 2). 56p. 1966. reprint ed. spiral bd. 7.00 (0-7873-1210-X) Hlth Research.

***Secret Life of John C. Van Dyke: Selected Letters.** John C. VanDyke. Ed. by David W. Teague & Peter Wild. LC 96-49496. (Western Literature Ser.). (Illus.). 200p. 1997. 35.00 (0-87417-294-2) U of Nev Pr.

Secret Life of Laszlo, Count Dracula. Roderick Anscombe. LC 93-49438. 416p. 1994. 22.95 (0-7868-6040-5) Hyperion.

Secret Life of Laszlo, Count Dracula. Roderick Anscombe. 480p. 1995. mass mkt. 6.50 (0-06-100943-1, Harp PBks) HarpC.

Secret Life of Moles. P. V. LeForge. LC 91-78124. 72p. (Orig.). (C). 1992. pap. 8.00 (0-938078-35-6) Anhinga Pr.

Secret Life of Money: How Money Can Be Food for the Soul. Tad Crawford. LC 96-84662. Orig. Title: The Secret Life of Money: Teaching Tales of Spending, Receiving, Saving, & Owing. 304p. 1996. reprint ed. pap. 14.95 (1-880559-51-X) Allworth Pr.

Secret Life of Money: Teaching Tales of Spending, Receiving, Saving, & Owing see Secret Life of Money: How Money Can Be Food for the Soul

Secret Life of Ms. X. Sheila Black. 192p. (Orig.). (J). 1996. mass mkt. 3.99 (0-06-106371-1, Harp PBks) HarpC.

Secret Life of Nature. Tompkin. LC 96-39647. 22.00 (0-06-250847-4, HarpT) Harper SF.

Secret Life of Nature. Tompkins. LC 96-39647. 1997. pap. 11.00 (0-06-250877-6, HarpT) HarpC.

Secret Life of Plants: A Fascinating Account of the Physical, Emotional, & Spiritual Relations Between Plants & Man. Peter Tompkins & Christopher Bird. LC 72-9160. 402p. 1989. reprint ed. pap. 16.00 (0-06-091587-0, PL 1587, PL) HarpC.

Secret Life of Quanta. M. Y. Han. 1990. 17.95 (0-8306-3397-9) McGraw-Hill Prof.

Secret Life of Quanta. M. Y. Han. 1990. text ed. 17.95 (0-07-156404-7) McGraw.

Secret Life of Quanta. M. Y. Han. 1992. pap. text ed. 12.95 (0-07-025969-0) McGraw.

Secret Life of Quanta. M. Y. Han. 200p. 1991. pap. 12.95 (0-8306-3889-X) McGraw-Hill Prof.

Secret Life of Saeed the Pessoptimist. Emile Habiby. Tr. by Salma K. Jayyusi & Trevor Le Gassick from ARA. 170p. 1989. pap. 9.95 (0-930523-08-3) Readers Intl.

Secret Life of Salvador Dali. Salvador Dali. Tr. by Haakon M. Chevalier from FRE. LC 92-36763. (Illus.). 432p. 1993. reprint ed. pap. 9.95 (0-486-27454-3) Dover.

Secret Life of Santa Claus. Gregoire Solotareff. LC 96-7455. (Illus.). 320p. 1996. 17.95 (0-8118-1453-X) Chronicle Bks.

***Secret Life of the American Male.** Doug Stanton. 256p. 1997. 22.00 (0-06-017388-2) HarpC.

***Secret Life of the Expectant Mother: Nine Months of Mysterious Intuitions & Heightened Perception.** Carl Jones. LC 97-22322. 1997. pap. text ed. 14.95 (0-8065-1938-X, Citadel Pr) Carol Pub Group.

Secret Life of the Seine. Mort Rosenblum. LC 93-42107. 1994. 21.00 (0-201-62461-3) Addison-Wesley.

Secret Life of the Seine. Mort Rosenblum. 304p. 1995. pap. 12.00 (0-201-48941-4) Addison-Wesley.

***Secret Life of the Soul.** J. Keith Miller. LC 97-26017. 1997. 19.99 (0-8054-6375-5) Broadman.

Secret Life of the Underwear Champ. Betty Miles. LC 80-15651. (Books for Young Readers Ser.). (Illus.). 128p. (J). (gr. 3-7). 1981. pap. 3.99 (0-394-84563-3, Silver Creek) Random Bks Yng Read.

Secret Life of Unborn Child. 256p. 1982. pap. 12.95 (0-440-50565-8, Dell Trade Pbks) Dell.

Secret Life of Victorian Houses. Elan Zingman-Leith & Susan Zingman-Leith. LC 93-12129. (Illus.). 144p. 1993. 36.00 (1-880216-10-8, Elliott Clark) Black Belt Comm.

Secret Life of Vulnerable Children. Ed. by Ved P. Varma. (Illus.). 256p. (C). 1991. pap. text ed. 22.95 (0-415-05982-8, A6374) Routledge.

Secret Life of Walter Mitty. James Thurber. LC 83-71786. (Creative Classic Ser.). 32p. (J). (gr. 4 up). 1983. lib. bdg. 13.95 (0-87191-961-3) Creative Ed.

Secret Life of Wilkie Collins. William M. Clarke. (Illus.). 256p. 1991. text ed. 24.95 (0-929587-51-0) I R Dee.

***Secret Life of Wilkie Collins.** William M. Clarke. (Illus.). 256p. pap. 17.95 (0-7509-1208-1, Pub. by Sutton Pubng UK) Bks Intl VA.

***Secret Life of William Butler Yeats.** Brenda Maddox. 432p. Date not set. 30.00 (0-06-017494-3, G Carr Bks) HarpC.

Secret Life of Your Cells. Robert S. Stone. LC 89-50767. 196p. 1989. 9.95 (0-914918-96-6, Whitford Pr) Schiffer.

Secret Lives. 256p. 1983. pap. 3.95 (0-88184-052-1) Carroll & Graf.

Secret Lives. Regan Forest. (Temptation Ser.: No. 399). 1992. mass mkt. 2.99 (0-373-25499-7, 1-25499-4) Harlequin Bks.

Secret Lives. Patrick Gale. 1994. pap. 12.99 (1-85242-215-7) Serpents Tail.

Secret Lives. Caroline MacDonald. 133p. (J). (gr. 7-10). 1995. 15.00 (0-671-51081-9, S&S Bks Young Read) S&S Childrens.

Secret Lives. Ngugi W. Thiong'o. 144p. (C). 1992. pap. 8.95 (0-435-90150-8, 90150) Heinemann.

Secret Lives: Women with Two Lives--& Loves. Sonya Friedman & Sondra Forsyth. LC 93-22143. 1994. 20.00 (0-517-59052-2) Crown Pub Group.

***Secret Lives of Birds.** Pierre Gingras. (Illus.). 224p. (Orig.). 1997. pap. 17.95 (1-55209-120-1) Firefly Bks Ltd.

Secret Lives of Cats. Val Lindahn & Ron Lindahn. (Illus.). 1996. 14.95 (1-56352-281-0) Longstreet Pr Inc.

Secret Lives of Fishes. rev. ed. Bernard L. Gordon. LC 76-575. (Illus.). 305p. 1994. pap. text ed. 20.00 (0-910258-12-0) Book & Tackle.

Secret Lives of Hummingbirds. David W. Lazaroff. (Illus.). 24p. (Orig.). 1995. pap. 4.95 (1-886679-00-2) Ariz-Sonora Des Mus.

***Secret Lives of Sgt. John Wilson: A True Story of Love & Murder.** Lois Simmie. (Illus.). 224p. 1997. 17.95 (1-55054-442-X) Orca Bk Pubs.

Secret Lives of Teddy Bears: Stories of Teddies & People Who Love Them. Rosalie Upton. (Illus.). 132p. 1996. pap. 23.00 (0-207-18743-6) HarperColl Wrld.

Secret Logic of Successful Discipline. Richard M. Greene, Jr. (Illus.). 66p. 1989. spiral bd. 5.95 (0-934487-22-7) R M Greene.

Secret Logic of Successful Discipline: Behavior Control. Richard M. Greene, Jr. (Illus.). 1989. pap. 10.95 (0-934487-58-8) R M Greene.

Secret Longings of the Heart: A Discussion Guide on Overcoming Deep Disappointment & Unfulfilled Expectations. Carol Kent. 96p. (Orig.). 1991. pap. 6.00 (0-89109-614-0) NavPress.

Secret Longings of the Heart: Overcoming Deep Disappointment and Unfulfilled Expectations. Carol Kent. LC 90-60917. 224p. 1990. pap. 12.00 (0-89109-698-1) NavPress.

Secret Lore of Gardening. Jackson Graham. (Patterns of Male Intimacy Ser.). pap. 16.00 (0-919123-53-8, Pub. by Inner City CN) BookWorld Dist.

Secret Lore of Magic. Idries Shah. 1970. pap. 3.95 (0-8065-0004-2, Citadel Pr) Carol Pub Group.

Secret Lore of the Cat. Fred Gettings. (Illus.). 288p. 1989. 19.95 (0-8184-0510-4) Carol Pub Group.

Secret Lost at Sea. Carolyn Keene. Ed. by Ellen Winkler. (Nancy Drew Ser.: No. 113). 160p. (Orig.). (J). (gr. 3-6). 1993. pap. 3.99 (0-671-79299-7, Minstrel Bks) PB.

Secret Love. Betsy Ryan. LC 90-24058. (Hampstead High Ser.). 128p. (J). (gr. 5-9). 1991. pap. text ed. 2.95 (0-8167-1913-6) Troll Communs.

Secret Love, Vol.16. Hilda Stahl. (Elizabeth Gail Ser.: Vol. 16). 128p. (J). 1989. pap. 5.99 (0-8423-0809-1) Tyndale.

Secret Love of Nurse Wilson. large type ed. Ivy Preston. (Linford Romance Library). 1988. pap. 10.95 (0-7089-6480-X, Linford) Ulverscroft.

***Secret Love of Sons.** Nicholas Weinstock. 224p. 1997. 21. 95 (1-57322-050-7, Riverhead Books) Putnam Pub Group.

Secret Lovers. Luann Linquist. 221p. pap. 16.95 (0-669-27666-9, Lexington) Jossey-Bass.

Secret Magic. Zeno Zeplin. (Illus.). 56p. (J). (gr. 3-6). 1990. pap. text ed. 6.95 (1-877740-04-7); boxed 11.95 (1-877740-03-9) Nel-Mar Pub.

Secret Magick Revealed. 2nd ed. Nelson H. White. LC 95-61240. (Illus.). 95p. (Orig.). (C). 1995. pap. 45.00 (1-877884-18-9) Tech Group.

Secret Malady: Venereal Disease in Eighteenth-Century Britain & France. Ed. by Linda E. Merians. LC 96-20580. (Illus.). 280p. 1997. pap. 19.95 (0-8131-0888-8); text ed. 39.95 (0-8131-1989-8) U Pr of Ky.

***Secret Man.** Frank Dux. 368p. 1997. mass mkt. 5.99 (0-06-109587-7, Harp PBks) HarpC.

Secret Man: An American Warrior's Uncensored Story. Frank Dux. 336p. 1996. 23.00 (0-06-039152-9) HarpC.

Secret Marriage of Sherlock Holmes & Other Eccentric Readings. Michael Atkinson. LC 96-10299. (C). 1995. 29.95 (0-472-10710-0) U of Mich Pr.

Secret Meaning of Money: How It Binds Together Families in Love, Envy, Compassion, or Anger. Cloe Madanes & Claudio Madanes. (Social Behavioral Sciences Ser.). 205p. 25.00 (1-55542-701-4) Jossey-Bass.

Secret Meaning of Things. Lawrence Ferlinghetti. LC 69-17826. 1969. pap. 7.95 (0-8112-0045-0, NDP268) New Directions.

Secret Medicine of the Pharoahs: Ancient Egyptian Medicine. Cornelius Stetter. LC 92-48470. 196p. (ENG & GER.). 1993. pap. 19.95 (0-86715-265-6) Quint Pub Co.

Secret Meeting: A Kwanzaa Singing School. Kwelismith. (Illus.). 150p. 1994. pap. text ed. write for info. (0-9624092-2-7) Anacostia Rep.

Secret Melody: And Man Created the Universe. Trinh X. Thuan. Tr. by Storm Dunlop. LC 94-17572. (Illus.). 305p. 1995. 25.00 (0-19-507370-3) OUP.

Secret Memoirs of Count Tadasu Hayashi. Tadasu Hayashi. Ed. by A. M. Pooley. LC 72-93536. reprint ed. 42.50 (0-404-03159-5) AMS Pr.

Secret Memoirs of the Court of Petersburg: Particularly Towards the End of the Reign of Catherine II & the Commencement of That of Paul I. Charles F. Masson. LC 75-115563. (Russia Observed, Series I). 1970. reprint ed. 20.95 (0-405-03049-5) Ayer.

***Secret Mesa: Inside Los Alamos National Laboratory.** Jo A. Shroyer. LC 97-9517. 320p. 1997. 24.95 (0-471-04063-0) Wiley.

Secret Messages: A Collection of Puzzles Using Codes & Ciphers. Jeff Hawtin. 48p. (J). 1991. 6.95 (0-906212-78-2, Pub. by Tarquin UK) Parkwest Pubns.

Secret Messages: Add.-Subt. Fred Justus. (Puzzles Ser.). 24p. (gr. 3-5). 1980. student ed. 5.00 (0-8209-0301-9, PU-15) ESP.

Secret Messages: Mult.-Div. Fred Justus. (Puzzles Ser.). 24p. (gr. 3-5). 1980. student ed. 5.00 (0-8209-0302-7, PU-16) ESP.

Secret Messages - Training a Happy Dog. Mary Shields. (Happy Dog Trilogy from Alaska Ser.). (Illus.). 32p. (Orig.). (J). (gr. k-3). 1993. pap. 12.00 (0-9618348-6-2) Pyrola Pub.

Secret Messengers: How Governments Correspond. William H. Bruce. 312p. (Orig.). 1995. pap. 14.95 (0-9644967-1-2) Bruce Intl.

Secret Messerschmitt Projects. Willy Radinger & Walter Schick. (Illus.). 208p. (ENG & GER.). (C). (gr. 13). 1996. 35.00 (0-88740-926-1) Schiffer.

Secret Mirror: Literary Form & History in Tocqueville's Recollections. fac. ed. Larry E. Shiner. LC 88-3679. 245p. 1988. reprint ed. pap. 69.90 (0-608-01019-7, 2061877) Bks Demand.

Secret Mission to Melbourne: November 1941. Sky Phillips. (Illus.). 296p. (Orig.). 1992. pap. 18.95 (0-89745-148-1) Sunflower U Pr.

Secret Missions. Michael Gannon. 400p. 1995. mass mkt. 5.50 (0-06-109239-8) HarpC.

Secret Missions of the Civil War. Philip V. Stern. 1990. 8.99 (0-517-00002-4) Random Hse Value.

Secret Missions of the Civil War. Phillip V. Stern. LC 74-9399. (Illus.). 320p. 1975. reprint ed. text ed. 55.00 (0-8371-7657-3, STSM, Greenwood Pr) Greenwood.

Secret Money: The Art & Science of Cloaking Assets. 1992. lib. bdg. 350.00 (0-8490-8884-4) Gordon Pr.

Secret Moose. Houghton Mifflin Company Staff. (Literature Experience 1991 Ser.). (J). (gr. 4). 1990. pap. 9.16 (0-395-55161-7) HM.

***Secret Muses: The life of Frederick Ashton.** Julie Kavanagh. LC 96-29524. (Illus.). 647p. 1997. 35.00 (0-679-44269-3) Pantheon.

Secret Museum: Pornography in Modern Culture. Walter Kendrick. LC 96-8107. 298p. 1996. pap. 13.95 (0-520-20729-7) U CA Pr.

Secret Music. Odie Hawkins. (Orig.). 1988. mass mkt. 2.95 (0-87067-265-7) Holloway.

Secret Mysteries Dingbats Book. Carole Marsh. (Carole Marsh Dingbats Bks.). (Illus.). (J). (gr. 3-12). 1994. pap. 19.95 (0-7933-5384-X); lib. bdg. 29.95 (0-7933-5383-1); disk 29.95 (0-7933-5385-8) Gallopade Pub Group.

Secret Nabob. Martha Kirkland. 224p. 1996. mass mkt., pap. 4.50 (0-451-18737-7, Sig) NAL-Dutton.

Secret Name of Ra. Illus. by Donald Harley. (Myths & Legends Ser.). (J). 1996. lib. bdg. write for info. (1-57572-016-7) Rigby Interact Libr.

Secret Names: Poems. Michael Burns. 64p. 1994. pap. 12. 95 (0-8262-0947-5) U of Mo Pr.

Secret Native American Pathways: A Guide to Inner Peace. Thomas E. Mails. LC 88-70671. 1988. audio 24.95 (0-571-78003-2) Coun Oak Bks.

Secret Native American Pathways: A Guide to Inner Peace. Thomas E. Mails. LC 88-70671. (Illus.). 312p. 1995. pap. 17.95 (0-933031-15-7) Coun Oak Bks.

Secret Native American Pathways: A Guide to Inner Peace. Thomas E. Mails. 1994. 24.95 (1-57178-003-3) Coun Oak Bks.

Secret Nature of the Channel Shore. Andrew Cooper. (Illus.). 224p. (Orig.). 1994. pap. 17.95 (0-563-36906-X, BBC-Parkwest) Parkwest Pubns.

Secret Nazi Plans of World War II. Ihor Kamenetsky. 1961. pap. 16.95 (0-8084-0273-0) NCUP.

Secret Nidan Techniques of Hakkoryu Jujutsu. Dennis G. Palumbo. (Illus.). 136p. 1988. pap. 14.00 (0-87364-455-7) Paladin Pr.

Secret Nights. Anita Mills. 384p. (Orig.). 1994. pap. 4.99 (0-451-40481-5, Topaz) NAL-Dutton.

***Secret Obsession.** Charlene Berry. 1997. pap. text ed. 10. 95 (1-885478-20-8) Genesis Press.

Secret Obsession. Charlotte Lamb. (Top Author/Sins Ser.). 1996. mass mkt. 3.50 (0-373-11816-3, 1-11816-5) Harlequin Bks.

Secret Obsession. large type ed. Charlotte Lamb. (Harlequin Romance Ser.). 1995. 20.95 (0-263-14262-0, Pub. by Mills & Boon UK) Thorndike Pr.

Secret Oceans. Betty Ballantine. LC 94-9448. (Illus.). 160p. 1994. 29.95 (0-553-09660-5) Bantam.

Secret of a Happy Wedded Life. W. G. Heslop. 1987. pap. 5.99 (0-88019-224-0) Schmul Pub Co.

Secret of Achievement. Orison S. Marden. 301p. 1997. pap. 27.00 (0-89540-337-4, SB-337) Sun Pub.

Secret of Adoration. Andrew Murray. (Secret Ser.). 1992. pap. 2.50 (0-87508-384-6) Chr Lit.

Secret of Adoration. Andrew Murray. 65p. pap. text ed. write for info. (0-614-02760-8) Christ Stewards.

Secret of Ajidamo. Alicia Schramm. (Illus.). 1995. 7.95 (0-533-11371-7) Vantage.

Secret of Annexe Three. Colin Dexter. 224p. 1988. reprint ed. pap. 5.99 (0-553-27549-6) Bantam.

Secret of Believing Prayer. Andrew Murray. LC 80-69320. 80p. 1980. pap. 6.99 (0-87123-590-0) Bethany Hse.

Secret of Better Baking. Mary D. Chambers. (Illus.). 1975. pap. 2.00 (0-89166-007-0) Cobblesmith.

Secret of Blackbeard's Treasure: A Pony's Tale. Mary Maden. LC 95-92332. (Outer Banks Animal Ser.). (Illus.). 20p. (Orig.). (J). (gr. 1-4). 1995. pap. 5.95 (0-9646970-1-7) Dog & Pony Enter.

Secret of Bone Hill. Lenard Lekofka. 1981. 5.50 (0-394-51425-4) Random.

Secret of Bowling Strikes. Dawson Taylor. 1972. pap. 5.00 (0-87980-132-8) Wilshire.

Secret of Brain Energy. 1992. lib. bdg. 248.95 (0-8490-8828-3) Gordon Pr.

Secret of Brain Energy. Frank C. Haddock. 59p. 1988. reprint ed. spiral bd. 7.00 (0-7873-1285-1) Hlth Research.

Secret of Brain Energy: Scientific Methods in Using Your Powers for Personal & Financial Success & Building a Better Brain. F. C. Haddock. 1991. lib. bdg. 79.95 (0-8490-4301-8) Gordon Pr.

Secret of Brotherly Love. Andrew Murray. (Secret Ser.). 1992. pap. 2.50 (0-87508-390-0) Chr Lit.

***Secret of Candlelight Inn.** Keene. (Nancy Drew Ser.: No. 139). (J). 1997. pap. 3.99 (0-671-00052-7) PB.

Secret of Cartwheels: Short Stories. Patricia Henley. LC 92-14989. 224p. 1992. pap. 11.00 (1-55597-168-7) Graywolf.

Secret of Chapultepec Castle. Henrietta Bell. 1980. pap. 4.95 (0-89741-013-0) Gila River.

Secret of Charisma. Doe Lang. 370p. reprint ed. pap. 12.95 (0-934297-00-2) New Choices.

Secret of Childhood. Maria Montessori. 416p. 1982. mass mkt. 5.99 (0-345-30583-3) Ballantine.

Secret of Childhood: A Book for All Parents & Teachers. Maria Montessori. Tr. by Barbara B. Carter from ITA. viii, 239p. (C). 1983. text ed. 14.95 (0-86131-375-5, Pub. by Kalakshetra Pubns II) N Montessori.

Secret of Chimneys. Agatha Christie. 224p. (Orig.). 1984. pap. text ed. 5.50 (0-425-06802-1) Berkley Pub.

Secret of Chinese Pulse Diagnosis. Bob Flaws. LC 95-80457. 160p. (Orig.). 1995. 29.95 (0-936185-67-8) Blue Poppy Pr.

Secret of Christ Our Life. Andrew Murray. (Secret Ser.). 1992. pap. 2.50 (0-87508-385-4) Chr Lit.

Secret of Church Growth. Timothy Lin. Tr. by Ruth W. Taniguchi. 118p. (Orig.). 1992. pap. write for info. (0-945304-01-3) FCBC.

Secret of Communion with God. Matthew Henry. LC 90-28623. 128p. 1991. pap. 7.99 (0-8254-2837-8, Kregel Class) Kregel.

Secret of Confession Including the Wonders of Confession. Paul O'Sullivan. LC 92-61255. 96p. 1992. reprint ed. pap. 5.00 (0-89555-459-3) TAN Bks Pubs.

Secret of Costa Brava. Giulio Mondello. 120p. pap. 9.95 (0-9630779-0-2) PPC Bks.

Secret of Creating Your Future. Tad James. LC 89-61422. (Illus.). 128p. (Orig.). 1989. pap. 9.95 (0-9623272-0-4) Advan Neuro Dynamics.

Secret of Cycles: Kali's Life Cycles Kalendar, 1987. Kali Sichen. (Illus.). 110p. 1986. 7.95 (0-916299-00-7) North Scale Co.

Secret of Daniel's Strength. Harry Foster. Tr. by Carl Fang from ENG. 97p. (CHI.). 1983. pap. write for info. (0-941598-05-5) Living Spring Pubns.

Secret of Devil Mountain. Beverly Van Hook. Ed. by Andrea Nelken. (Supergranny Ser.: No. 4). (Illus.). 112p. (Orig.). (J). (gr. 3-6). 1988. pap. 3.25 (0-916761-04-5); lib. bdg. 9.95 (0-916761-05-3) Holderby & Bierce.

Secret of Dickens. W. Walter Crotch. LC 72-3292. (Studies in Dickens: No. 52). 1972. reprint ed. lib. bdg. 59.95 (0-8383-1501-1) M S G Haskell Hse.

S

An Asterisk (*) at the beginning of an entry indicates that the title is appearing in BIP for the first time.

Secret of Divine Civilization. Abdu'l-Baha. Tr. by Marzieh Gail & Ali-Kuli Khan from PER. 126p. 1990. pap. 3.00 (*0-87743-219-8*) Bahai.

Secret of Dr. Kildare. large type ed. Max Brand. LC 96-20903. (Nightingale Ser.). 1996. 17.95 (*0-7838-1846-7*, GK Hall) Thorndike Pr.

Secret of Dr. Kildare. Max Brand. 180p. reprint ed. lib. bdg. 19.95 (*0-88411-530-5*, Rivercity Pr) Amereon Ltd.

*__Secret of Enneagrams: Mapping the Personality.__ Klausbernd Vollmar. 192p. 1997. pap. 15.95 (*1-85230-968-7*) Element MA.

Secret of Eureka Springs. Delores C. Stouffer. 50p. (Orig.). (J). (gr. 8-9). 1994. pap. 10.00 (*0-938041-24-X*) Arc Pr AR.

Secret of Everlasting Life. R. Bertschinger. 1994. pap. 24.95 (*1-85230-568-1*) Element MA.

Secret of Evermore: Authorized Power Play Guide. Prima Creative Services Staff & Simon Hill. 160p. 1995. pap. 12.95 (*0-7615-0394-3*) Prima Pub.

Secret of Evermore Strategy Guide. Bradygames Staff. (Illus.). 190p. (Orig.). 1995. 12.99 (*1-56686-328-7*) Brady Pub.

Secret of Excellence in Ancient Chinese Silks: Factors Contributing to the Extraordinary Development of Textile Design & Technology Achieved in Ancient China. Maryta M. Laumann. 1984. 35.00 (*0-89986-357-4*) Oriental Bk Store.

Secret Of Experiencing Christ. Witness Lee. 125p. per. 4.75 (*0-87083-227-1*, 07016001) Living Stream Ministry.

Secret of Facial Rejuvenation. James M. Piwonka. 15p. 1994. reprint ed. spiral bd. 3.50 (*0-7873-1052-2*) Hlth Research.

Secret of Fantasy Forest. Francine Pascal. (Sweet Valley Kids Ser.: No. 67). 96p. (J). 1996. pap. 3.50 (*0-553-48332-3*) BDD Bks Young Read.

Secret of Father Brown. Gilbert K. Chesterton. 20.95 (*0-89190-337-2*) Amereon Ltd.

Secret of Fatima Fact & Legend. Joaquin M. Alonso. Tr. by Dominican Nuns of the Perpetual Rosary from SPA. LC 79-13182. (Illus.). 1990. reprint ed. 11.95 (*0-911218-14-9*); reprint ed. pap. 5.95 (*0-911218-15-7*) Ravengate Pr.

Secret of Fellowship. Andrew Murray. (Secret Ser.). 1990. pap. 2.50 (*0-87508-388-9*) Chr Lit.

Secret of Finding Big Winners in the Stock Market. F. R. Margolius. 150p. 1995. text ed. 18.00 (*1-55738-281-6*) Irwin Prof Pubng.

Secret of Foghorn Island. Geoffrey Hayes. LC 87-16095. (Step into Reading Bks.). (Illus.). 48p. (Orig.). (J). (gr. 2-3). 1988. pap. 3.99 (*0-394-89614-9*); lib. bdg. 7.99 (*0-394-99614-3*) Random Bks Yng Read.

Secret of Getting Better Grades: Study Smarter, Not Harder. Brian Marshall & Wendy Ford. (Illus.). 168p. (Orig.). 1994. pap. 12.95 (*1-57112-061-0*, PA5027, Park Avenue) JIST Works.

Secret of Getting Straight A's: Learn More in Less Time with Little Effort. Brian Marshall. LC 92-72740. (Illus.). 169p. (Orig.). (YA). (gr. 6 up). 1993. pap. 12.95 (*0-9633357-9-0*) Hathaway Intl.

Secret of Giving.. Kimberly R. Rinehart. Ed. by Georgia M. Rettmer. (Illus.). 1990. pap. 3.95 (*0-942865-08-1*) It Takes Two.

Secret of GorBee Grotto. Scott E. Sutton. (Wizard Tells a Story Ser.: Bk. 3). (Illus.). 60p. (J). (gr. 2-4). 1987. 13.95 (*0-9617199-3-1*) Sutton Pubns.

Secret of Guidance. F. B. Meyer. Tr. by Ruth W. Taniguchi from ENG. (CHI.). 1984. pap. write for info. (*0-941598-07-1*) Living Spring Pubns.

*__Secret of Guidance.__ F. B. Meyer. (Classics Ser.). 128p. 1997. mass mkt. 4.99 (*0-8024-6398-3*) Moody.

Secret of Guidance. F. B. Meyer. 1987. pap. 0.40 (*9971-972-07-7*) OMF Bks.

*__Secret of Gumbo Grove.__ Eleanora E. Tate. 208p. (J). 1988. mass mkt. 4.50 (*0-440-22716-X*) BDD Bks Young Read.

Secret of Gumbo Grove. Eleanora E. Tate. 208p. (YA). (gr. 7 up). 1988. mass mkt. 4.50 (*0-553-27226-8*, Starfire BDD) BDD Bks Young Read.

Secret of Gumbo Grove. Eleanora E. Tate. 208p. (J). 1996. pap. 3.99 (*0-440-41273-0*) Dell.

Secret of Halloween. Robert T. Stout. (Illus.). 24p. (Orig.). (J). (ps-6). 1982. pap. 3.50 (*0-911049-02-9*) Yuletide Intl.

Secret of Happiness. Billy Graham. 200p. 1985. pap. 10.99 (*0-8499-3034-0*) Word Pub.

*__Secret of Happiness.__ Billy Graham. 1997. 16.99 (*0-8499-1478-7*) Word Pub.

Secret of Healing. Jack E. Addington. 204p. 1979. pap. 10.95 (*0-911336-80-X*) Sci of Mind.

Secret of Healing: The Healing Powers of Ze'ev Kolman - a True Story. Hans Holzer. 216p. 1996. 21.95 (*1-885223-20-X*) Beyond Words Pub.

Secret of Health. rev. ed. Richard Lynch. 1989. 6.95 (*0-87159-143-X*) Unity Bks.

Secret of Hegel: Being the Hegelian System in Origin Principle Form & Matter. 2nd rev. ed. J. H. Stirling. (Reprints in Philosophy Ser.). reprint ed. lib. bdg. 49.00 (*0-697-00058-3*) Irvington.

Secret of Heron Creek. Margaret Meacham. LC 90-50373. 136p. (Orig.). (J). (gr. 5-8). 1991. pap. 7.95 (*0-87033-414-X*, Tidewtr Pubs) Cornell Maritime.

Secret of High Tax Countries in Effective Tax Planning: The Secret... Lars-Erik Wenehed. 1995. 95.00 (*91-972352-4-5*, Pub. by Comtax SW) Intl Info Srvcs Inc.

Secret of High Wages. Bertram Austin, Jr. & W. Francis Lloyd. Ed. by Alfred D. Chandler. LC 79-7529. (History of Management Thought & Practice Ser.). 1980. reprint ed. lib. bdg. 15.95 (*0-405-12314-0*) Ayer.

Secret of Hilhouse: An Adult Book for Teens. P. J. Pokeberry. LC 93-60940. (Illus.). 96p. (Orig.). (J). (gr. 4 up). 1993. pap. 8.95 (*0-943962-02-1*) Viewpoint Pr.

Secret of Hind's Feet. Sue H. Boggs. 1982. 3.95 (*0-89137-537-6*) Quality Pubns.

Secret of How the Rich Create Wealth & Income Without Risk: The Junk Money Concept. Irving L. Blackman. 1995. pap. 29.00 (*0-916181-33-2*) Blackman Kallick Bartelstein.

Secret of Inspiration. Andrew Murray. (Secret Ser.). 1990. pap. 2.50 (*0-87508-386-2*) Chr Lit.

Secret of Instantaneous Healing. Harry D. Smith. 1986. 8.95 (*0-13-797951-7*, Reward); 5.95 (*0-13-797936-3*, Reward) P-H.

Secret of Intercession. Andrew Murray. (Secret Ser.). 1990. pap. 2.50 (*0-87508-391-9*) Chr Lit.

Secret of Intercession. Andrew Murray. 96p. 1985. mass mkt. 3.99 (*0-88368-289-3*) Whitaker Hse.

Secret of Intercession. Andrew Murray. 65p. pap. text ed. write for info. (*0-614-02759-4*) Christ Stewards.

Secret of Jewish Femininity: Insights into the Practice of Taharat Hamishpachah. Tehilla Abramov & Malka Touger. 176p. 1988. 12.95 (*0-944070-04-3*) Targum Pr.

Secret of Laughter. A. M. Ludovici. 1972. 79.95 (*0-8490-1011-X*) Gordon Pr.

Secret of Letting Go. Guy Finley. LC 90-45794. 240p. (Orig.). 1990. pap. 9.95 (*0-87542-223-3*) Llewellyn Pubns.

Secret of Life. Kaya. 208p. Date not set. pap. text ed. 12.95 (*0-87891-974-0*) Res & Educ.

Secret of Life. deluxe limited ed. Rudy Rocker. 250p. 1985. boxed 50.00 (*0-938075-55-1*) Ocean View Bks.

Secret of Life. Georges Lakhovsky. 213p. 1970. reprint ed. spiral bd. 12.00 (*0-7873-0522-7*) Hlth Research.

Secret of Life: Cosmic Rays & Radiations & Radiations of Living Beings & Electro-Magnetic Waves. G. Lakhovsky. (Alternative Energy Ser.). 1991. lib. bdg. 79.95 (*0-8490-4275-5*) Gordon Pr.

Secret of Life: Electricity, Radiation & Your Body. Georges Lakhovsky. Tr. by Mark Clement from FRE. (Illus.). 1988. reprint ed. pap. 9.95 (*0-939482-08-8*, Noontide Pr) Legion Survival.

Secret of Life: Redesigning the Living World. Joseph Levine & David Suzuki. LC 93-4817. (Illus.). 320p. 1993. 24.95 (*0-9636881-0-3*) WGBH.

Secret of Life & Death: Nineteen Sixty-Nine to Nineteen Eighty-Four, Vol. 1. Allen Ruppersberg. Ed. by Julia Brown. LC 84-63020. (Illus.). 127p. (C). 1985. pap. 50.00 (*0-914357-07-7*) Los Angeles Mus Contemp.

Secret of Light. Walter Russell. (Illus.). 288p. 1974. text ed. 23.00 (*1-879605-43-0*); pap. text ed. 17.00 (*1-879605-44-9*) U Sci & Philos.

Secret of Light. Walter Russell. (Illus.). 288p. 1974. reprint ed. text ed. 20.00 (*1-879605-10-4*) U Sci & Philos.

Secret of Lizard Island. Ernest Herndon. LC 93-5011. (Eric Sterling, Secret Agent Ser.: Vol. 1). 128p. (J). 1994. pap. 5.99 (*0-310-38251-3*) Zondervan.

Secret of Long Life: How to Live in Three Centuries. Goddard E. Diamond. 90p. 1960. reprint ed. spiral bd. 8.50 (*0-7873-0287-2*) Hlth Research.

Secret of Long Life: Or, How to Live in Three Centuries. G. E. Diamond. 1991. lib. bdg. 79.95 (*0-8700-952-X*) Revisionist Pr.

Secret of Love Bk. 14: The Mahanta Transcripts. Harold Klemp. LC 96-41518. (Illus.). 1997. pap. 14.00 (*1-57043-114-0*) ECKANKAR.

Secret of Loving. Josh McDowell. (Living Bks.). 333p. 1986. reprint ed. mass mkt. 5.99 (*0-8423-5845-5*) Tyndale.

Secret of Mana Official Game Secrets. Rusel DeMaria. 1993. pap. 15.99 (*1-55958-465-3*) Prima Pub.

Secret of Mind-Power & How to Use It. C. DeRadwan. 1991. lib. bdg. 79.95 (*0-8490-4961-X*) Gordon Pr.

Secret of Mind Power & How to Use It. C. De Radwan. 190p. 1972. reprint ed. spiral bd. 10.00 (*0-7873-0265-1*) Hlth Research.

Secret of Mirror Bay. Carolyn Keene. (Nancy Drew Ser.: Vol. 49). (Illus.). 180p. (J). (gr. 4-7). 1972. 5.95 (*0-448-09549-1*, G&D) Putnam Pub Group.

*__Secret of Misty Harbor.__ Courtney Taylor. LC 96-92089. (Illus.). 64p. (Orig.). (J). 1997. pap. 8.00 (*1-56002-672-3*, Univ Edtns) Aegina Pr.

Secret of Mojo: The Story of the Odessa, Texas, Permian High School Football Team. Regina W. McCally. Ed. by James Baldwin. LC 86-90445. 236p. 1986. 20.00 (*0-9619703-0-8*) R W McCally.

*__Secret of Monk's House.__ large type ed. Rachelle Edwards. (Linford Romance Library). 304p. 1997. pap. 16.99 (*0-7089-5029-9*) Ulverscroft.

Secret of Mystery Hill, No. 141. Doug Wilhelm. (Choose-Your-Own-Adventure Ser.). (YA). 1993. pap. 3.50 (*0-553-56001-8*) Bantam.

Secret of Nimh. Robert C. O'Brien. 256p. (J). (gr. 4-6). 1988. pap. 3.99 (*0-590-41708-8*) Scholastic Inc.

*__Secret of Old Zeb.__ Carmen A. Deedy. LC 97-12346. (Illus.). 40p. (J). (gr. 1-5). 1997. 16.95 (*1-56145-115-0*) Peachtree Pubs.

Secret of Papillote Cooking, No. 1: No Mess Gourmet Cooking. Gil Pique & Chantal Pique. (Illus.). 112p. text ed. 19.95 (*0-9633688-7-7*) Papillote.

Secret of Paul the Apostle. Joseph A. Grassi. LC 77-29045. 176p. reprint ed. pap. 50.20 (*0-8357-7015-X*, 2033537) Bks Demand.

Secret of Peace & the Environmental Crisis. John F. Gardner. 40p. 1978. reprint ed. pap. 1.50 (*0-913098-15-9*) Myrin Institute.

*__Secret of Personal Success.__ 35p. 1992. ring bd. 95.00 incl. audio (*1-58034-010-5*) IML Pubns.

Secret of Petroglyph Cave. Helen M. Swanson. 128p. (J). (gr. 3-6). 1995. pap. 6.95 (*1-880188-97-X*) Bess Pr.

Secret of Pirates' Hill. rev. ed. Franklin W. Dixon. (Hardy Boys Ser.: Vol. 36). (Illus.). 196p. (J). (gr. 5-9). 1957. 5.95 (*0-448-08936-X*, G&D) Putnam Pub Group.

Secret of Polk St. School. Patricia R. Giff. 80p. (J). 1990. pap. write for info. (*0-440-80077-3*) Dell.

Secret of Poplar Island. Beth Deemer. Ed. by Myrna Kemnitz. 126p. (Orig.). (J). (gr. 5-7). 1996. pap. 5.00 (*0-88092-129-3*) Royal Fireworks.

Secret of Power from on High. Andrew Murray. (Secret Ser.). 1992. pap. 2.50 (*0-87508-392-7*) Chr Lit.

Secret of Quarry House. large type ed. Claire Lorrimer. 1991. 25.99 (*0-7089-2539-1*) Ulverscroft.

Secret of Quarry House. Claire Lorrimer. 1994. reprint ed. lib. bdg. 19.00 (*0-7278-4649-3*) Severn Hse.

Secret of Red Gate Farm. Carolyn Keene. (Nancy Drew Ser.: Vol. 6). 180p. (J). (gr. 4-7). 1931. 5.95 (*0-448-09506-8*, G&D) Putnam Pub Group.

Secret of Red Gate Farm. Carolyn Keene. LC 94-41449. (Nancy Drew Mystery Stories Ser.: No. 6). (Illus.). 228p. (J). (gr. 2-8). 1995. reprint ed. 12.95 (*1-55709-160-9*) Applewood.

Secret of Regeneration. Hilton Hotema. Orig. Title: The Science of Human Regeneration (Postgraduate Orthopathy). 300p. 1963. reprint ed. spiral bd. 41.50 (*0-7873-0429-8*) Hlth Research.

Secret of Rejuvenation: Prof. Brown Sequard's Great Discovery of the Fountain of Youth. Raymond W. Bernard. 1956. spiral bd. 7.00 (*0-7873-0998-2*) Hlth Research.

Secret of Richmond Manor. Gilbert Morris. (Bonnets & Bugles Ser.: No. 3). (J). (gr. 5-9). 1995. pap. 5.99 (*0-8024-0913-X*) Moody.

Secret of Right Activity. 4th ed. Swami Paramananda. 1964. 4.95 (*0-911564-12-8*) Vedanta Ctr.

Secret of Rock Island. Matt Christopher. (J). (gr. 3-7). 1995. 14.00 (*0-922242-90-9*) Bepuzzled.

Secret of Room 401. Judith A. Green. (Adult Basic Learner Ser.). (Illus.). 223p. (Orig.). 1981. pap. text ed. 8.98 (*0-89061-210-2*, 204) Jamestown Pubs.

Secret of Salvation. E. E. Byrum. 264p. pap. 2.50 (*0-686-29166-2*) Faith Pub Hse.

Secret of Sambatyon. Gershon Winkler. Ed. by Bonnie Goldman. 132p. (J). (gr. 4 up). 1987. 7.95 (*0-910818-68-1*); pap. 6.95 (*0-910818-69-X*) Judaica Pr.

Secret of San Saba. Jack Jackson. Ed. by Dave Schreiner. (Illus.). 152p. 1989. 25.00 (*0-87816-080-9*) Kitchen Sink.

Secret of Sanctuary Island. A. M. Monson. Ed. by ALC Staff. LC 90-6479. 176p. (J). (gr. 5 up). 1992. pap. 4.95 (*0-688-11693-0*) Morrow.

Secret of Sandhills. large type ed. Una Rothwell. 320p. 1987. 25.99 (*0-7089-1732-1*) Ulverscroft.

Secret of Santa Claus: Flower Blue & Snowie Elves Help Santa Meet His Brothers. Bev Stone. (Illus.). 64p. (J). (gr. k-6). 1987. pap. 12.95 (*0-9619791-0-0*) Stone Studios.

Secret of Santa Vittoria. Robert Crichton. 416p. 1986. pap. 3.95 (*0-88184-267-2*) Carroll & Graf.

Secret of Santa Vittoria. Robert Crichton. 1993. reprint ed. lib. bdg. 21.95 (*1-56849-149-2*) Buccaneer Bks.

*__Secret of Santiago: A Novel of Medieval Spain.__ Bernard Reilly. LC 96-3251. 256p. Date not set. 24.95 (*0-938289-60-8*, Combined Bks) Combined Pub.

Secret of Sarah Revere. Ann Rinaldi. LC 95-5570. 352p. (YA). (gr. 7 up). 1995. 11.00 (*0-15-200393-2*, Gulliver Bks); pap. 6.00 (*0-15-200392-4*, Gulliver Bks) HarBrace.

Secret of Scotty's Castle Set. Carole Marsh. (Carole Marsh Mysteries Ser.). 1994. 125.00 (*0-7933-6964-9*) Gallopade Pub Group.

Secret of Seaside. Linda Barr. 144p. (J). (gr. 5-8). 1995. pap. 2.99 (*0-87406-746-4*) Willowisp Pr.

Secret of Secrets. Hadrat'Abd A. Al-Jilani. Tr. & Intro. by Tosun Bayrak. (Golden Palm Ser.). 138p. (Orig.). 1992. pap. 18.95 (*0-946621-29-2*, Pub. by Islamic Texts UK) Intl Spec Bk.

Secret of Secrets. Uell S. Andersen. 318p. 1976. pap. 10.00 (*0-87980-134-4*) Wilshire.

Secret of Secrets: Spiritual Discourses. 3rd ed. Darshan Singh. LC 78-69930. (Illus.). 1982. reprint ed. pap. 10.00 (*0-918224-06-3*) S K Pubns.

Secret of Secrets: The Unwritten Mysteries of Esoteric Qabbalah. Michael-Albion Macdonald. LC 86-81789. (Illus.). 92p. 1986. 20.00 (*0-935214-08-9*) Heptangle.

Secret of Selecting Stocks for Immediate & Substantial Gains. Larry Williams. 1986. 25.00 (*0-930233-05-0*) Windsor.

Secret of Self-Realization. I. K. Taimni. 1990. 13.50 (*81-7059-127-9*) Theos Pub Hse.

Secret of Self-Transformation: A Synthesis of Tantra & Yoga. Rohit Mehta. (C). 1987. 21.00 (*81-208-0381-7*, Pub. by Motilal Banarsidass II); pap. text ed. 10.00 (*81-208-0402-3*, Pub. by Motilal Banarsidass II) S Asia.

Secret of Selling Inventions. 2nd ed. Richard C. Levy. Ed. by Sheryl Levy. 200p. (Orig.). 1986. 49.50 (*0-931347-00-9*) Ricsher Pub Ltd.

*__Secret of Sentinel Rock.__ Judith Silverthorne. (J). 1997. pap. 6.95 (*1-55050-103-8*, Pub. by Coteau CN) Genl Dist Srvs.

Secret of Shady Glen. Carolyn Keene. Ed. by Ann Greenberg. (Nancy Drew Ser.: No. 85). 160p. (J). (gr. 3-6). pap. 3.99 (*0-671-63416-X*, Minstrel Bks) PB.

Secret of Shakespeare. Martin Lings. 144p. (Orig.). 1984. pap. 8.95 (*0-89281-059-9*) Inner Tradit.

Secret of Shakespeare. rev. ed. Martin Lings. 200p. (Orig.). 1996. pap. 11.95 (*1-870196-14-7*, Pub. by Islamic Texts UK) Intl Spec Bk.

Secret of Shangrila: An Inquiry into the Love, Legend & Culture of Nepal. N. Shrestha. (C). 1991. text ed. 70.00 (*0-7855-0154-1*, Pub. by Ratna Pustak Bhandar) St Mut.

Secret of Sherlock Holmes. Jeremy Paul. 60p. (Orig.). 1991. pap. 11.00 (*86025-438-0*, Pub. by Ian Henry Pubns UK) Empire Pub Srvs.

*__Secret of Sherlock Holmes.__ Jeremy Paul. LC 96-36105. 55p. (Orig.). 1996. pap. 11.00 (*0-88734-708-8*) Players Pr.

Secret of Sherwood Forest: Oil Production in England During World War Two. Guy H. Woodward & Grace S. Woodward. LC 72-12546. (Illus.). 284p. reprint ed. 81.00 (*0-8357-9741-4*, 2016280) Bks Demand.

Secret of Sigma Seven. Franklin W. Dixon. (Hardy Boys Ser.: No. 110). 160p. (Orig.). (J). (gr. 3-6). pap. 3.99 (*0-671-72717-6*, Minstrel Bks) PB.

*__Secret of Skeleton Reef.__ Franklin W. Dixon. (Hardy Boys Mystery Stories Ser.: No. 144). (J). (gr. 3-6). 1997. pap. 3.99 (*0-671-00056-X*, Archway) PB.

Secret of Skull Mountain. Franklin W. Dixon. (Hardy Boys Ser.: Vol. 27). 180p. (J). (gr. 5-9). 1948. 5.95 (*0-448-08927-0*, G&D) Putnam Pub Group.

Secret of Slavers Stockade. Harold Johnson. 1981. 5.50 (*0-394-51421-1*) Random.

Secret of Snake Canyon. Terrell L. Bowers. LC 93-9756. 168p. 1993. 19.95 (*0-8027-1264-9*) Walker & Co.

Secret of Somerset Place. Carole Marsh. (History Mystery Ser.). (Illus.). (Orig.). (gr. 3-9). 1994. pap. 19.95 (*0-935326-02-2*) Gallopade Pub Group.

Secret of Somerset Place S. P. A. R. K. Kit. Carole Marsh. (S. P. A. R. K. Ser.). (Illus.). (Orig.). (J). (gr. 3-9). 1994. pap. 19.95 (*0-935326-20-0*) Gallopade Pub Group.

Secret of Somerset Place Set. Carole Marsh. (Carole Marsh Mysteries Ser.). 1994. teacher ed. 125.00 (*0-7933-6946-0*) Gallopade Pub Group.

Secret of Soul Winning. Stephen F. Olford. 126p. (Orig.). 1994. pap. 5.95 (*1-56043-800-2*) Destiny Image.

Secret of Squaw Rock. Charles Mills. LC 92-1660. 1992. 5.99 (*0-8280-0700-4*) Review & Herald.

Secret of Staying Together. John P. Zahody. LC 85-82014. 116p. 1985. 12.00 (*0-9615911-0-2*) HeartLight Pubns.

Secret of Success. William W. Atkinson. 92p. 1972. spiral bd. 6.50 (*0-7873-0049-7*) Hlth Research.

Secret of Success. Ed. by Nissan Mindel. (Illus.). 64p. (YA). 1973. reprint ed. 10.00 (*0-8266-0346-7*, Merkos LInyonei Chinuch) Kehot Pubn Soc.

Secret of Success: A Course of Nine Lessons on the Subject of the Application of the Latent Powers of the Individual Toward Attainment of Success in Life. William W. Atkinson. 92p. 1996. pap. 14.95 (*1-56459-647-8*) Kessinger Pub.

Secret of Success in Wall Street. Tumbridge & Co. Staff. LC 87-80247. (Illus.). 48p. 1987. reprint ed. pap. 8.00 (*0-87034-083-2*) Fraser Pub Co.

Secret of Sugarbush Hollow. Spencer Douglas. LC 95-60395. (Spencer Douglas Presents Ser.). (Illus.). (J). (gr. 3-6). 1995. pap. 5.95 (*0-9645152-0-2*) Applchn Pub.

Secret of Swedenborg: Being an Elucidation of His Doctrine of the Divine Humanity. Henry James, Sr. LC 72-914. (Selected Works of Henry James, Sr.: Vol. 7). 1983. reprint ed. 39.50 (*0-404-10087-2*) AMS Pr.

*__Secret of Teaching Science & Math Through Music.__ Madeline Frank. (How Music Can Make Your Child Brighter Ser.). (Illus.). 65p. (Orig.). 1997. teacher ed., pap. 20.00 (*0-9658583-0-8*) M Frank.

Secret of Telfair Inn. Idella F. Bodie. LC 79-177909. (Illus.). 98p. (J). (gr. 5-7). 1983. pap. 6.95 (*0-87844-050-X*) Sandlapper Pub Co.

Secret of the Abiding Presence. Andrew Murray. (Secret Ser.). 1990. pap. 2.50 (*0-87508-382-X*) Chr Lit.

Secret of the Ages. rev. ed. Robert Collier. 1984. 17.95 (*0-912576-12-X*); pap. 11.45 (*0-912576-11-1*) R Collier.

Secret of the Andes. Ann N. Clark. (Storybooks Ser.). (Illus.). (J). (gr. 3-7). 1976. pap. 4.99 (*0-14-030926-8*, Puffin) Puffin Bks.

Secret of the Attic. Sheri C. Sinykin. (Magic Attic Club Ser.). (Illus.). 80p. (Orig.). (J). (gr. 2-6). 1995. 12.95 (*1-57513-000-9*) Magic Attic.

Secret of the Attic see Magic Attic Club Series

Secret of the Barbican, & Other Stories. Joseph S. Fletcher. LC 79-121543. (Short Story Index Reprint Ser.). 1977. 21.95 (*0-8369-3499-7*) Ayer.

Secret of the Big Thicket. Earlynne Webber. (J). 1994. pap. 7.95 (*0-89015-958-0*) Sunbelt Media.

Secret of the Black Chrysanthemum. Charles Stein. LC 85-14781. (Illus.). 232p. (Orig.). (C). 1987. 27.50 (*0-88268-017-X*, Clinamen Studies) Station Hill Pr.

Secret of the Black Chrysanthemum: The Poetic Cosmology of Charles Olson & His Use of the Writings of C. G. Jung. Charles Stein. 1996. pap. text ed. 19.95 (*1-886449-30-9*) Barrytown Ltd.

*__Secret of the Bulls.__ Bernardo. 1997. pap. 12.00 (*0-684-83137-6*, Scribners PB Fict) S&S Trade.

Secret of the Bulls: A Novel. Jose R. Bernardo. LC 95-38281. 336p. 1996. 22.00 (*0-684-81817-5*) S&S Trade.

*__Secret of the Bulls Reading Group Guide.__ Bernardo. 1997. pap. write for info. (*0-684-00255-8*, Scribners PB Fict) S&S Trade.

*__Secret of the Cards.__ Sonia Craddock. (J). pap. 4.99 (*0-590-73662-0*) Scholastic Inc.

Secret of the Caves. rev. ed. Franklin W. Dixon. (Hardy Boys Ser.: Vol. 7). 180p. (J). (gr. 5-9). 1929. 5.95 (*0-448-08907-6*, G&D) Putnam Pub Group.

*__Secret of the Cellar.__ Jacqueline Stem. (J). (gr. 3-7). 1997. 12.95 (*0-614-28728-6*, Eakin Pr) Sunbelt Media.

Secret of the Chateau. large type ed. D. M. Carlisle. (Linford Romance Library). 304p. 1987. pap. 8.95 (*0-7089-6434-6*, Linford) Ulverscroft.

Secret of the Cibolo. Billie P. Matthews & A. Lee Chichester. Ed. by Melissa Roberts. (Illus.). 104p. (J). (gr. 4-7). 1988. 9.95 (*0-89015-638-7*) Sunbelt Media.

Secret of the Crater. Duffield Osborn. 1979. reprint ed. 8.50 (*0-686-65259-2*) Bookfinger.

Secret of the Creative Vacuum. John Davidson. 432p. (Orig.). pap. 35.95 (*0-8464-4287-6*) Beekman Pubs.

Secret of the Creative Vacuum. John Davidson. 189p. 1989. pap. 25.95 (*0-85207-202-3*, Pub. by C W Daniel UK) Natl Bk Netwk.

Secret of the Cross. Andrew Murray. (Secret Ser.). 1990. pap. 2.50 (*0-87508-389-7*) Chr Lit.

Secret of the Cure d'Ars. Francis J. Sheed. viii, 248p. 1995. text ed. 15.95 (*0-912141-18-2*) Roman Cath Bks.

***Secret of the Desert: The Rock Art of the Messak Sattafet & Messak Mellet, Libya.** Rudiger Lutz. (Illus.). xxii, 177p. 1995. 60.00 (*3-900773-10-6*) Cities in Color.

Secret of the Desert Stone. Frank E. Peretti. LC 96-1919. (Cooper Kids Adventure Ser.: No. 5). 160p. (J). 1996. pap. 4.99 (*0-8499-3643-8*) Word Pub.

Secret of the Dolphins. Edward Packard. (Choose Your Own Adventure Ser.: No. 134). 128p. (J). (gr. 4-7). 1993. pap. 3.50 (*0-553-29300-1*) Bantam.

Secret of the Doo Dah House. Adam Aba. LC 91-89270. (Illus.). 192p. (J). (gr. 4-7). 1997. pap. 16.95 (*1-878756-51-6*) YCP Pubns.

Secret of the Dragon Mark. Jeanette Windle. (Twin Pursuits Ser.: No. 2). 128p. 1996. pap. 4.99 (*0-88070-905-7*, Multnomah Bks) Multnomah Pubs.

***Secret of the Eagle Feathers.** Maura E. McKinley. LC 96-44250. (Publish-a-Book Ser.). (Illus.). (J). 1997. lib. bdg. 22.83 (*0-8172-4436-0*) Raintree Steck-V.

Secret of the Earth. Charles W. Beale. LC 74-15950. (Science Fiction Ser.). 256p. 1975. reprint ed. 23.95 (*0-405-06276-1*) Ayer.

***Secret of the Elm.** Ann Stepp. 160p. (Orig.). 1997. mass mkt. 4.99 (*1-55197-670-6*, Pub. by Comnwlth Pub CN) Partners Pubs Grp.

Secret of the Emerald Tablet of Hermes. Gottlieb Latz. Ed. by J. D. Holmes. Tr. by D. William Hauck from GER. 1993. pap. 8.95 (*1-55818-203-9*) Holmes Pub.

Secret of the Faith Life. Andrew Murray. (Secret Ser.). 1990. pap. 2.50 (*0-87508-387-0*) Chr Lit.

Secret of the Faith Life. Andrew Murray. 65p. pap. text ed. write for info. (*0-614-02758-6*) Christ Stewards.

Secret of the Floating Phantom. Norma Lehr. LC 94-3004. 192p. (J). (gr. 3-6). 1994. lib. bdg. 18.95 (*0-8225-0736-6*, Lerner Publctns) Lerner Group.

Secret of the Forgotten Cave. Carolyn Keene. (Nancy Drew Ser.: No. 134). (J). 1996. pap. 3.99 (*0-671-50516-5*, PB Trade Paper) PB.

Secret of the Forgotten City. Carolyn Keene. LC 74-10461. (Nancy Drew Ser.: Vol. 52). (Illus.). 180p. (J). (gr. 4-7). 1975. 5.95 (*0-448-09552-1*, G&D) Putnam Pub Group.

Secret of the Ghost Piano. Elizabeth Bolton. LC 84-8745. (Illus.). 48p. (J). (gr. 2-4). 1985. pap. 3.50 (*0-8167-0411-2*) Troll Communs.

Secret of the Gold Charm, Vol. 21. Hilda Stahl. (Elizabeth Gail Ser.: Vol. 21). (J). (gr. 4-7). 1992. pap. 5.99 (*0-8423-0817-2*) Tyndale.

Secret of the Golden Cowrie. Gloria Repp. Ed. by Suzette Jordan. (Light Line Ser.). (Illus.). 192p. (Orig.). (J). (gr. 4-6). 1988. pap. 6.49 (*0-89084-459-3*, 042887) Bob Jones Univ Pr.

Secret of the Golden Flower. Tr. by Thomas Cleary. LC 90-55796. 160p. 1993. reprint ed. pap. 12.00 (*0-06-250193-3*) Harper SF.

Secret of the Golden Flower: A Chinese Book of Life. Richard Wilhelm & Carl G. Jung. LC 62-10499. (Illus.). 149p. 1970. reprint ed. pap. 9.00 (*0-15-679980-4*, Harvest Bks) HarBrace.

Secret of the Golden Hours. Ed. by Regency Press, Ltd. Staff. 112p. 1984. 40.00 (*0-7212-0656-5*, Pub. by Regency Press UK) St Mut.

Secret of the Golden Pavilion. Carolyn Keene. (Nancy Drew Ser.: Vol. 36). (Illus.). 180p. (J). (gr. 4-7). 1959. 5.95 (*0-448-09536-X*, G&D) Putnam Pub Group.

Secret of the Harvest: Mobilizing for Team Evangelism. Warren L. Hoffman. 256p. 1988. pap. 7.95 (*0-916035-25-5*) Evangel Indiana.

Secret of the Haunted Chimney. Adrian Robert. LC 84-8763. (Illus.). 48p. (J). (gr. 2-4). 1996. pap. 3.50 (*0-8167-0409-0*) Troll Communs.

Secret of the Hawaiian Rainbow: A Hawaiian Story about Colors. Stacey S. Kaopuiki. Ed. by Cindy R. Despins. LC 91-72018. (Peter Panini Keiki Reader Ser.). (Illus.). 32p. (J). (ps-3). 1991. 12.95 (*1-878498-02-9*) Hawaiian Isl Concepts.

***Secret of the Healing Treasures.** Dharma Publishing Staff. LC 96-48214. (King Gesar Ser.). 1996. write for info. (*0-89800-217-6*) Dharma Pub.

Secret of the Healing Treasures. Ed. by Zara Wallace. Tr. by Sylvia Gretchen from TIB. LC 96-48214. (King Gesar Ser.: Vol. 2). (Illus.). 32p. (Orig.). (J). (gr. 2-7). 1996. pap. 7.95 (*0-89800-216-8*) Dharma Pub.

Secret of the Heart: A Theological Study of Catherine of Siena's Teaching on the Heart of Jesus. Mary Jeremiah. 210p. 1995. pap. 12.95 (*0-931888-62-X*) Christendom Pr.

Secret of the Hotel DelaRosa: A Bina Gold Mystery. Ruchama Feuerman. Ed. by Shirley Kaufman. (Bina Gold Mystery Ser.). 150p. (Orig.). 1996. pap. 9.95 (*0-911643-21-4*) Aura Bklyn.

Secret of the Howling Cave. Lee Roddy. (American Adventure Ser.: Vol. 4). 192p. (Orig.). (J). (gr. 4-10). 1990. pap. 5.99 (*1-55661-094-7*) Bethany Hse.

Secret of the Immortal Liquor Called Alkahest. Eirenaeus Philalethes. 1984. reprint ed. pap. 3.95 (*0-916411-40-0*) Holmes Pub.

Secret of the Incas. William Sullivan. 1997. pap. 18.00 (*0-517-88851-3*, Crown) Crown Pub Group.

Secret of the Incas: Myth, Astronomy, & the War Against Time. William Sullivan. LC 95-34627. 1996. 35.00 (*0-517-59468-4*) Crown Pub Group.

Secret of the Indian. Lynne Reid Banks. (Indian in the Cupboard Ser.). 160p. (J). 1990. pap. 3.99 (*0-380-71040-4*, Camelot) Avon.

Secret of the Indian. Lynne Reid Banks. 160p. (YA). (gr. 5 up). 1989. 15.95 (*0-385-26292-2*) Doubleday.

Secret of the Indian. large type ed. Lynne Reid Banks. 208p. (J). (gr. 4-8). 1995. lib. bdg. 16.95 (*1-885885-14-8*, Cornerstone FL) Pages Inc FL.

Secret of the Indian. Lynne Reid Banks. (Indian in the Cupboard Ser.). 176p. (J). 1995. reprint ed. mass mkt. 3.99 (*0-380-72594-0*, Flare) Avon.

***Secret of the Island.** Jules Verne. lib. bdg. 22.95 (*0-8488-2044-4*) Amereon Ltd.

Secret of the Kara Sea. Eric Collenette. 1987. 16.95 (*0-8027-0990-7*) Walker & Co.

***Secret of the Kellermans.** Ken Follett. (J). Date not set. lib. bdg. write for info. (*0-688-08722-1*, Morrow Junior) Morrow.

Secret of the Kingdom. Mika Waltari. 1994. lib. bdg. 29.95 (*1-56849-487-4*) Buccaneer Bks.

Secret of the League: The Story of a Social War. Ernest Bramah. Ed. & Intro. by Daniel Jencka. (Capitalist Fiction Ser.). 300p. 1995. reprint ed. pap. 15.95 (*1-887207-00-7*) Specular Pr.

Secret of the Leaves. E. Van Handel. (Middos Ser.). (J). 1991. 7.99 (*0-89906-507-4*) Mesorah Pubns.

Secret of the Lion's Head. Beverly B. Hall. LC 95-30202. 155p. (Orig.). (J). (gr. 4-7). 1995. pap. 7.95 (*0-942597-92-3*, WM Kids) White Mane Pub.

Secret of the Lizard People. Michael J. Friedman. Ed. by Lisa Clancy. (Starfleet Academy Ser.: No. 7). 128p. (Orig.). (J). (gr. 3-6). 1995. mass mkt. 3.99 (*0-671-50109-7*, Minstrel Bks) PB.

***Secret of the Locked Trunk.** Janet H. McHenry. LC 96-49818. (Annie Shepard Mysteries Ser.). (J). 1997. write for info. (*1-56476-567-9*) SP Pubns.

Secret of the Lost Colony. Rebecca P. Janney. (Impossible Dreamers Ser.: Vol. 1). 128p. (J). (gr. 4-7). 1997. pap. 5.99 (*1-57673-018-2*) Multnomah Pubs.

***Secret of the Lost Kingdom.** Michael Bolton. LC 96-46838. (Illus.). 48p. (J). 1997. pap. 15.95 (*0-7868-0286-3*) Hyprn Child.

Secret of the Lost Tunnel. rev. ed. Franklin W. Dixon. (Hardy Boys Ser.: Vol. 29). (Illus.). 180p. (J). (gr. 5-9). 1950. 5.95 (*0-448-08929-7*, G&D) Putnam Pub Group.

Secret of the Magic Pen. Francine Pascal. (Sweet Valley Twins Super Chiller Ser.: No. 8). 192p. (J). (gr. 4-7). 1995. pap. 3.99 (*0-553-48282-3*) Bantam.

Secret of the Mask. Brian Wyant & Eric Wyant. (Illus.). 64p. 1997. pap. 7.50 (*1-883788-19-6*) Event Horzn.

Secret of the Mountains. Brian O'Malley. 40p. (J). (gr. 1-6). 1993. 14.95 (*0-9634446-0-3*) Spirit of Advent.

Secret of the Night. Gaston Leroux. 1975. lib. bdg. 16.70 (*0-89966-139-4*) Buccaneer Bks.

Secret of the Ninja, Vol. 66. large type ed. Jay Liebold. LC 95-22334. (Choose Your Own Adventure Ser.: Vol. 66). (Illus.). 128p. (J). (gr. 4 up). 1995. lib. bdg. 15.93 (*0-8368-1405-3*) Gareth Stevens Inc.

Secret of the Old Barn. Adrian Robert. LC 84-8743. (Illus.). 48p. (J). (gr. 2-4). 1985. lib. bdg. 11.50 (*0-8167-0412-0*) Troll Communs.

Secret of the Old Clock. Carolyn Keene. (Nancy Drew Ser.: Vol. 1). 180p. (J). (gr. 4-7). 1930. 5.95 (*0-448-09501-7*, G&D) Putnam Pub Group.

Secret of the Old Clock: The Secret of the Old Clock. Carolyn Keene. LC 91-46735. (Nancy Drew Mystery Stories Ser.: No. 1). (J). 1991. reprint ed. 12.95 (*1-55709-155-2*) Applewood.

Secret of the Old Graveyard. Susan K. Wright. LC 92-26679. (Dead-End Road Mysteries Ser.: No. 1). 184p. (Orig.). (J). (gr. 4-8). 1996. pap. 6.99 (*0-8361-3627-6*) Herald Pr.

Secret of the Old Mill. Franklin W. Dixon. LC 91-46349. (Hardy Boys Ser.: No. 3). 212p. (J). 1991. 12.95 (*1-55709-146-3*) Applewood.

Secret of the Old Mill. Franklin W. Dixon. (Hardy Boys Ser.: Vol. 3). 180p. (J). (gr. 5-9). 1927. 5.95 (*0-448-08903-3*, G&D) Putnam Pub Group.

Secret of the Old Patio. C. Arthur Bundrant. 118p. (Orig.). (J). (gr. 2-5). 1995. pap. write for info. (*1-885591-74-8*) Morris Pubng.

***Secret of the Old Rifle.** Stephen A. Bly. LC 96-40081. (Lewis & Clark Squad Adventure Ser.: 2). 160p. (Orig.). (J). (gr. 4-9). 1997. pap. 4.99 (*0-89107-940-8*) Crossway Bks.

Secret of the Old Well. Eric Wiggin. (Hannah's Island Ser.: Bk. 5). 150p. (Orig.). (J). (gr. 3-7). 1996. pap. 5.99 (*1-883002-28-1*) Emerald WA.

Secret of the Orient: Dwarf Rhapis Excelsa. Lynn McKamey. LC 85-50589. (Illus.). 52p. (Orig.). 1983. pap. 6.00 (*0-9612130-0-0*) Rhapis Gardens.

Secret of the Pacific: Origins of the Toltecs, Aztecs, Mayas, & Incas. C. Reginald Enock. 1977. lib. bdg. 59.95 (*0-8490-2584-2*) Gordon Pr.

Secret of the Peaceful Warrior. Dan Millman. Ed. by Robert San Souci. LC 90-52636. (Illus.). 32p. 1991. 14. 95 (*0-915811-23-5*, Starseed) H J Kramer Inc.

Secret of the Peruvian Quipus, 2 pts. in 1 vol. Erland Nordenskiold. LC 75-46059. (Comparative Ethnographical Studies: Vol. 6). reprint ed. 55.00 (*0-404-15146-9*) AMS Pr.

Secret of the Pit. large type ed. Laurence Meynell. 336p. 1985. 25.99 (*0-7089-1328-8*) Ulverscroft.

Secret of the Plant That Ate Dirty Socks. Nancy McArthur. 128p. (Orig.). (J). 1993. pap. 3.99 (*0-380-76757-0*, Camelot) Avon.

Secret of the Power: A Healing Journey into Self & Soul. Gail G. Cook. 136p. (Orig.). pap. 9.95 (*0-9638414-0-8*) Educ Remodeling.

Secret of the Pros: How to Become a Baseball Card Dealer. Mel Cohen. 176p. (Orig.). (YA). (gr. 8 up). 1991. pap. 12.95 (*0-9631104-1-1*) M Cohen.

Secret of the Rapture. Kingdom Quotes Staff. pap. write for info. (*0-930179-14-5*) Johns Enter.

***Secret of the Raven.** 64p. 1997. 3.70 (*0-8341-1647-2*) Nazarene.

Secret of the Red Silk Pouch. Les Simon. (YA). (gr. 7 up). 1997. pap. 5.00 (*0-88092-362-8*) Royal Fireworks.

Secret of the Ring in the Offering. Jennifer P. Schneider. (Really Reading! Bks.). (Illus.). 48p. (Orig.). (J). (gr. 1-3). 1993. pap. 4.49 (*0-7847-0094-X*, 03944) Standard Pub.

Secret of the Ring Muscles: Healing Yourself Through Sphincter Exercise. Paula Garbourg. LC 97-7770. 124p. 1997. pap. 9.95 (*0-89529-762-0*) Avery Pub.

Secret of the Rosary. St. Louis De Montfort. pap. 2.00 (*0-910984-04-2*) Montfort Pubns.

Secret of the Rosary. St. Louis De Monfort. Tr. by Mary Barbour from FRE. 1976. reprint ed. pap. 3.00 (*0-89555-056-3*) TAN Bks Pubs.

Secret of the Rothschilds. M. Hobart. 1972. 69.95 (*0-8490-1012-8*) Gordon Pr.

Secret of the Ruby Ring. Yvonne MacGrory. LC 93-35950. (Illus.). 192p. (Orig.). (J). (gr. 4-7). 1994. reprint ed. pap. 6.95 (*0-915943-92-1*) Milkweed Ed.

Secret of the Runes. Ed. & Tr. by Stephen E. Flowers. 196p. 1988. pap. 9.95 (*0-89281-207-9*) Inner Tradit.

Secret of the S. S. Crimson. Diane Woo. (Hidden Picture Hunt Ser.). 64p. (Orig.). (J). (gr. 2-6). 1992. pap. 3.95 (*1-56288-218-X*) Checkerboard.

***Secret of the Sand Castle.** Margaret Sutton. Date not set. lib. bdg. 21.95 (*0-8488-1816-4*) Amereon Ltd.

Secret of the Sands. Catherine West. (Illus.). 60p. (Orig.). 1987. pap. 6.95 (*0-944153-00-3*) Crosing Pub.

Secret of the Scarlet Hand. Carolyn Keene. Ed. by Anne Greenberg. (Nancy Drew Ser.: No. 124). 160p. (Orig.). (J). (gr. 3-6). 1995. pap. 3.99 (*0-671-87207-9*, Minstrel Bks) PB.

Secret of the Sea: Violetta Books' Fourth Annual Poetry Anthology. Ed. by Kathleen Gilbert. 45p. (Orig.). 1989. pap. 4.00 (*0-915913-10-0*) Violetta Bks.

Secret of the Sea & C. Brander Matthews. LC 74-160942. (Short Story Index Reprint Ser.). 1977. reprint ed. 19.95 (*0-8369-3921-2*) Ayer.

Secret of the Seal. Deborah Davis. (Illus.). (J). (gr. 2 up). 1988. 15.00 (*0-517-56725-3*) Crown Bks Yng Read.

Secret of the Seal. Deborah Davis. (Illus.). 64p. (J). (gr. 2 up). 1994. pap. 3.25 (*0-679-86566-7*, Bullseye Bks) Random Bks Yng Read.

Secret of the Seashell. C. Halperin. 1993. 12.99 (*0-89906-144-3*); 9.99 (*0-89906-145-1*) Mesorah Pubns.

***Secret of the Secrets.** Shaykh A. Gilani. Tr. by Shaykh T. Al-Halveti. 124p. 1996. pap. 17.95 (*0-614-21341-X*, 1117) Kazi Pubns.

Secret of the Seraphims & Other Poems. J. Noel. (Illus.). 28p. pap. 4.95 (*0-930422-16-3*) Dennis-Landman.

Secret of the Seven Thunders. (Illus.). 128p. (Orig.). 1994. pap. 12.00 (*0-930351-04-5*) Spirit Prophecy.

Secret of the Seven Willows. Thomas McKean. LC 91-4447. 160p. (J). 1991. pap. 12.95 (*0-671-72997-7*) S&S Trade.

Secret of the Shark Pit. Lee Roddy. (Ladd Family Adventure Ser.: Vol. 1). 136p. (Orig.). (J). (gr. 3-6). 1989. pap. 5.99 (*0-929608-63-1*) Focus Family.

Secret of the Sheep. Le Rap. (Nursery Rhymes Ser.). 15p. (J). (gr. k-2). 1991. pap. text ed. 23.00 (*1-56843-037-X*); pap. text ed. 4.50 (*1-56843-084-1*) BGR Pub.

Secret of the Siddhas. Swami Muktananda. LC 80-53590. 264p. 1980. pap. 12.95 (*0-914602-52-7*) SYDA Found.

***Secret of the Silver Sea.** Jenny Reid. (J). 1996. pap. 6.95 (*1-85594-182-1*, Pub. by Attic Press IE) Intl Spec Bk.

Secret of the Silver Shell. Terry Page. (Illus.). 24p. (J). (gr. 2-6). 1997. pap. text ed. 4.00 (*1-887864-64-4*); lib. bdg. 7.00 (*1-887864-28-8*) Boo Bks.

Secret of the Silver Shell Coloring Book. Terry Page. (Illus.). 32p. (J). (ps-5). 1997. pap. 3.00 (*1-887864-29-6*) Boo Bks.

Secret of the Snows. large type ed. Katrina Wright. (Linford Romance Library). 240p. 1995. pap. 15.99 (*0-7089-7741-3*, Linford) Ulverscroft.

Secret of the Space Scrolls & Cholent. Gideon Marc. (Illus.). 144p. (Orig.). (J). (gr. 4-7). 1994. pap. 6.95 (*965-483-001-9*) Pitspopany.

***Secret of the Stairs.** Wade Taylor. 168p. (Orig.). 1996. pap. 8.99 (*1-884369-35-9*, EBED Pubns) McDougal Pubng.

Secret of the Stallion. Bonnie Bryant. (Saddle Club Super Ser.: No. 2). (J). (gr. 4-7). 1995. mass mkt. 4.50 (*0-553-48152-5*) Bantam.

Secret of the Stone. Barbara Delinsky. 1992. mass mkt. 4.50 (*0-373-83251-6*, 1-83251-8) Harlequin Bks.

Secret of the Sunken Sub. Lee Roddy. (Ladd Family Adventure Ser.: Vol. 5). 160p. (Orig.). (J). (gr. 3-6). 1990. pap. 5.99 (*1-929608-63-1*) Focus Family.

Secret of the Swan: Seeing Yourself Through God's Eyes. Gloria Chisholm. LC 93-22406. 152p. 1993. pap. 9.99 (*0-8066-2671-2*, 9-2671, Augsburg) Augsburg Fortress.

Secret of the Three Cities: An Introduction to Hindu Sakta Tantrism. Douglas R. Brooks. (Illus.). 328p. 1990. pap. text ed. 19.95 (*0-226-07570-2*); lib. bdg. 57.00 (*0-226-07569-9*) U Ch Pr.

Secret of the Throne of Grace. Andrew Murray. (Secret Ser.). 1992. pap. 2.50 (*0-87508-393-5*) Chr Lit.

Secret of the Tibetan Treasure. Carolyn Keene. Ed. by Ellen Winkler. (Nancy Drew Ser.: No. 108). 160p. (Orig.). (YA). (gr. 3-6). 1992. pap. 3.99 (*0-671-73054-1*, Minstrel Bks) PB.

Secret of the Time Capsule. Joan L. Nixon. LC 95-83601. (Disney Adventures Casebusters Ser.: No. 6). 96p. (J). (gr. 2-6). 1996. pap. 3.95 (*0-7868-4079-X*) Disney Pr.

Secret of the Torah: A Translation of Abraham Ibn Ezra's Sefer Yesod Mora Ve-Sod Ha-Torah. annot. ed. Abraham I. Ezra. Tr. & Anno. by H. Norman Strickman. LC 94-22071. 232p. 1995. 25.00 (*1-56821-296-8*) Aronson.

Secret of the Totem. Andrew Lang. LC 70-115094. 1970. reprint ed. 34.50 (*0-404-03866-2*) AMS Pr.

Secret of the Underground Room. John Bellairs. (Illus.). 160p. (J). (ps-3). 1990. pap. 14.00 (*0-8037-0863-7*); lib. bdg. 13.89 (*0-8037-0864-5*) Dial Bks Young.

Secret of the Underground Room. John Bellairs. LC 92-17304. 128p. (J). (gr. 5 up). 1992. pap. 3.99 (*0-14-034932-4*, Puffin) Puffin Bks.

Secret of the Unicorn. Herge. (Illus.). 62p. (J). 19.95 (*0-8288-5066-6*) Fr & Eur.

Secret of the Unicorn. Herge. LC 73-21250. (Adventures of Tintin Ser.). (Illus.). 64p. (J). (gr. k up). 1974. reprint ed. pap. 8.95 (*0-316-35832-0*, Joy St Bks) Little.

Secret of the Universe. Isaac Asimov. 256p. 1992. reprint ed. mass mkt. 4.50 (*1-55817-658-6*, Pinncle Kensgtn) Kensgtn Pub Corp.

Secret of the Untroubled Mind. Manly P. Hall. pap. 4.95 (*0-89314-352-9*) Philos Res.

Secret of the Veda. Sri Aurobindo. (ENG & SAN.). 1979. 16.00 (*0-89744-975-4*, Pub. by Sri Aurob Ashram Trust II); pap. 12.00 (*0-685-00596-8*, Pub. by Sri Aurob Ashram Trust II) Auromere.

Secret of the Veda. Sri Aurobindo. 581p. 1982. 16.50 (*0-89071-303-0*, Pub. by SAA II); pap. 12.50 (*0-89071-302-2*, Pub. by SAA II) Aurobindo Assn.

***Secret of the Viking Dagger.** Scarlett R. Foster. Ed. by James D. Qualben. LC 96-51184. 1997. pap. 7.95 (*1-880292-55-6*, North Sea); lib. bdg. 15.95 (*1-880292-56-4*, North Sea) LangMarc.

Secret of the Villa Mimosa. Elizabeth Adler. 400p. 1995. mass mkt. 6.50 (*0-440-21748-2*) Dell.

Secret of the Villa Mimosa. large type ed. Elizabeth Adler. LC 94-22937. 603p. 1995. lib. bdg. 24.95 (*0-7862-0324-2*) Thorndike Pr.

Secret of the Villa Mimosa. large type ed. Elizabeth Adler. LC 94-22937. 603p. 1996. pap. 18.95 (*0-7862-0325-0*) Thorndike Pr.

Secret of the Vineyard. large type ed. Monica Heath. 256p. 1995. 23.95 (*0-7089-3364-5*) Ulverscroft.

***Secret of the White Buffalo.** C. J. Taylor. (Native Peoples Ser.). 24p. (YA). (gr. 3 up). 1994. lib. bdg. 18.90 (*0-516-08172-1*) Childrens.

Secret of the White Buffalo. C. J. Taylor. LC 93-60551. (Native Dwellings Ser.). (Illus.). 24p. (J). (gr. 3 up). 1993. 13.95 (*0-88776-321-9*) Tundra Bks.

***Secret of the White Buffalo.** Carrie J. Taylor. (Illus.). (J). (ps up). 1997. reprint ed. pap. 6.95 (*0-614-29139-9*) Tundra Bks.

***Secret of the White Buffalo: An Oglala Sioux Legend.** C. J. Taylor. (Illus.). 1997. pap. text ed. 6.95 (*0-88776-399-5*) Tundra Bks.

Secret of the Wooden Lady. Carolyn Keene. (Nancy Drew Ser.: Vol. 27). 180p. (J). (gr. 4-7). 1950. 5.95 (*0-448-09527-0*, G&D) Putnam Pub Group.

Secret of the Zodiac. N. H. Webster. 1979. lib. bdg. 250.00 (*0-8490-3004-8*) Gordon Pr.

Secret of the 2 Bar 4 Ranch. Leona D. Cox. LC 93-81079. (Illus.). 153p. (J). (gr. 4-12). 1994. pap. 11.95 (*0-9627680-6-5*) Inkwell CA.

Secret of Theatrical Space. Josef Svoboda. 224p. 1993. 49. 95 (*1-55783-137-8*) Applause Theatre Bk Pubs.

Secret of Theatrical Space: The Memoirs of Josef Svoboda. Ed. & Tr. by J. M. Burian from CZE. (Illus.). 144p. 1995. pap. 29.95 (*1-55783-216-1*) Applause Theatre Bk Pubs.

Secret of Thut Mouse III: Or Basil Beaudesert's Revenge. Mansfield Kirby. LC 85-47588. (Illus.). 64p. (J). (ps up). 1985. 14.00 (*0-374-36677-2*) FS&G.

Secret of Two Brothers. Irene B. Hernandez. LC 95-9844. 182p. (YA). (gr. 6 up). 1995. 14.95 (*1-55885-141-0*, Pinata Bks); pap. 7.95 (*1-55885-142-9*, Pinata Bks) Arte Publico.

Secret of Unicorn. Herge. 1986. 7.95 (*0-416-92530-8*) Routledge Chapman & Hall.

Secret of United Prayer. Andrew Murray. (Secret Ser.). 1979. pap. 2.50 (*0-87508-394-3*) Chr Lit.

Secret of Unlimited Prosperity. Catherine Ponder. 60p. 1981. pap. 5.95 (*0-87516-419-6*) DeVorss.

Secret of Vatican Hill. Charles A. Berry. (Illus.). 296p. (Orig.). 1987. pap. 10.00 (*0-943625-00-9*) Allen & Nurri.

Secret of Villa Mimosa. Elizabeth Adler. 1995. mass mkt. 6.50 (*0-614-15543-6*) Dell.

***Secret of Weeping Wood.** large type ed. Robert Swindells. (J). 1996. 16.95 (*0-7451-4956-1*, Galaxy Child Lrg Print) Chivers N Amer.

***Secret of Whispering Woods: The Journeys of Jessie Land.** Jerry Jerman. 132p. (J). (gr. 3-7). 1996. mass mkt. 5.99 (*1-56476-552-0*, Victor Bks) Chariot Victor.

Secret of Wildcat Swamp. Franklin W. Dixon. (Hardy Boys Ser.: Vol. 31). 180p. (J). (gr. 5-9). 1952. 5.95 (*0-448-08931-9*, G&D) Putnam Pub Group.

***Secret of Wilhelm Storitz.** Jules Verne. lib. bdg. 22.95 (*0-8488-2061-4*) Amereon Ltd.

***Secret of Youth.** Gayle Olinekova. (Illus.). 200p. (Orig.). 1997. pap. 14.95 (*1-56025-123-9*) Thunders Mouth.

Secret on Volcano Hill. Peggy Samet. LC 89-51672. 44p. (J). (ps). 1989. pap. 5.95 (*1-55523-269-8*) Winston-Derek.

Secret Oral Teachings in Tibetan Buddhist Sects. Alexandra David-Neel. 1967. pap. 8.95 (*0-87286-012-4*) City Lights.

Secret Oral Teachings on Generating the Deity. Gyutrul Rinpoche. Tr. by Sangye Khandro. (Illus.). 164p. 1992. pap. 25.00 (*957-638-105-3*, PRE015, Pub. by SMC Pub CC) Oriental Bk Store.

***Secret Pal.** Williams. (J). 1998. pap. 3.95 (*0-7868-1219-2*); lib. bdg. 13.89 (*0-7868-2270-8*) Hyprn Child.

Secret Panel. rev. ed. Franklin W. Dixon. LC 74-86693. (Hardy Boys Ser.: Vol. 25). (Illus.). 180p. (J). (gr. 5-9). 1946. 5.95 (*0-448-08925-4*, G&D) Putnam Pub Group.

***Secret Passages.** Preuss. Date not set. 23.95 (*0-312-86346-2*) St Martin.

S

Secret Passions. Dianne V. Mayhew. 150p. 1993. mass mkt. 3.79 (*0-9634431-0-0*) C Y Pub Grp.

Secret Past. Dokmaisot. Tr. by Ted Strehlow from THA. (Southeast Asia Program Ser.: No. 9). 72p. 1992. pap. text ed. 10.00 (*0-87727-126-7*) Cornell SE Asia.

Secret Path. Nick Butterworth. (Illus.). (J). (ps-3). 1995. 14.95 (*0-316-11914-8*) Little.

Secret Path. Christopher Pike. (Spooksville Ser.: No. 1). (J). 1995. pap. 3.50 (*0-671-53725-3*) PB.

Secret Path. Paul Brunton. LC 85-50917. 187p. 1985. reprint ed. pap. 6.95 (*0-87728-652-3*) Weiser.

***Secret Path: A Collection of Mystical & Romantic Poetry & Thoughts.** Micah Sadigh. 78p. (Orig.). 1997. pap. write for info. (*1-57502-394-6*, P01231) Morris Pubng.

Secret Paths: Women in the New Midlife. Terri Apter. 320p. 1995. 25.00 (*0-393-03766-5*) Norton.

Secret Paths: Women in the New Midlife. Terri Apter. 352p. 1997. pap. 15.00 (*0-393-31500-2*) Norton.

Secret Pet see Homeplay: Joyful Learning for Children & Adults, Series I

Secret Pilgrim. John Le Carre. 1991. 27.50 (*0-394-58842-8*) Knopf.

Secret Pilgrim. John Le Carre. 1992. mass mkt. 5.99 (*0-345-37476-2*) Ballantine.

***Secret Pilgrim.** John Le Carre. 1997. pap. 12.00 (*0-345-41832-8*) Ballantine.

Secret Place. Eve Bunting. LC 95-20466. (Illus.). 32p. (J). (ps-3). 1996. 14.95 (*0-395-64367-8*, Clarion Bks) HM.

Secret Place. Richard McKenzie. 4.95 (*0-913343-21-8*) Inst Psych Inc.

Secret Place. Judy Romero-Oak. 97p. 1994. pap. 14.95 (*0-9644174-0-5*) Writing Designs.

Secret Place. L. W. Stevenson. (Illus.). 144p. 1979. 10.00 (*0-89733-043-9*) Academy Chi Pubs.

Secret Place. L. W. Stevenson. (Illus.). 144p. 1981. pap. 5.00 (*0-89733-042-0*) Academy Chi Pubs.

Secret Place of Strength. Marie Chapian. (Heart for God Devotional Ser.: Bk. 5). 176p. (Orig.). 1991. 11.99 (*1-55661-219-2*) Bethany Hse.

Secret Place of the Most High. Frank E. Stranges. 12p. 1985. pap. text ed. 2.00 (*0-933470-09-6*) Intl Evang.

Secret Place of Thunder. Lynn Morris & Gilbert Morris. (Cheney Duvall M. D. Ser.: No. 5). 336p. 1996. pap. 9.99 (*1-55661-426-8*) Bethany Hse.

Secret Places. Illus. by Lindsay B. George. LC 92-29014. 32p. (J). (ps up). 1993. 15.00 (*0-688-11669-8*); lib. bdg. 14.93 (*0-688-11670-1*) Greenwillow.

Secret Places. Bruce Kershner. 128p. 1995. per. 14.95 (*0-8403-9123-4*) Kendall-Hunt.

Secret Places: The Story of a Child's Adventure with Grief. James A. Campbell. (Illus.). 45p. (Orig.). (J). (gr. 4-9). 1992. pap. 3.50 (*1-56123-051-0*) Centering Corp.

Secret Places: The Winter of My Life. Donna K. Shuman. (Illus.). 55p. (Orig.). 1986. pap. 5.95 (*0-9616669-0-0*) Shades Blue Pubns.

Secret Places ... Sacred Paths: Understanding Prayer in Our World Today. Madeline Duckett. 64p. (Orig.). 1992. pap. 6.95 (*0-8146-2236-4*) Liturgical Pr.

Secret Places of Donegal. John M. Feehan. 1988. pap. 11.95 (*0-946645-07-8*) Dufour.

Secret Places of the Goddess: Contacting the Earth Spirit. Philip Heselton. (Illus.). 208p. (Orig.). 1995. pap. 21.95 (*1-898307-40-7*) Holmes Pub.

Secret Places of the Lion: Alien Influences on Earth's Destiny. George H. Williamson. 240p. 1983. reprint ed. pap. 14.95 (*0-89281-601-5*, Destiny Bks) Inner Tradit.

Secret Plague: Venereal Disease in Canada, 1838-1939. Jay Cassel. 35.00 (*0-8020-2593-5*); pap. 17.95 (*0-8020-6617-8*) U of Toronto Pr.

Secret Plan of Canberra. Peter Proudfoot. 160p. 1994. 29.95 (*0-86840-030-0*, Pub. by New South Wales Univ Pr AT) Intl Spec Bk.

Secret Plan to Uproot the U. S. Constitution. 1992. lib. bdg. 74.95 (*0-8490-5258-0*) Gordon Pr.

Secret Pleasures. Thea Devine. 1995. pap. 4.99 (*0-8217-4995-1*) NAL-Dutton.

***Secret Poems by John Berry.** 42p. (Orig.). 1996. pap. 6.95 (*0-614-19352-4*) Soft Pallette.

Secret Police: Inside the New York City Department of Investigation. Peter Benjaminson. LC 96-24933. 256p. 1997. 22.00 (*1-56980-090-1*) Barricade Bks.

***Secret Politics of Our Desires: Nation, Culture, & Gender in Indian Popular Cinema.** Ashis Nandy. LC 97-24677. 1997. write for info. (*1-85649-515-9*); pap. write for info. (*1-85649-516-7*) Humanities.

Secret Pony Club: A Mystery Jigsaw Puzzle Thriller. Nancy Butcher. (Spider Tales Ser.). (Orig.). (J). (gr. 3-7). 1996. pap. 13.50 (*1-57561-009-4*, 00807SPC) Bepuzzled.

***Secret Power.** D. L. Moody. 146p. (Orig.). 1997. mass mkt. 3.99 (*0-88368-302-4*) Whitaker Hse.

Secret Power. rev. ed. Dwight L. Moody. LC 87-9533. 166p. 1987. reprint ed. pap. 9.99 (*0-8307-1219-4*, 5419181) Regal.

Secret Power. Marie Corelli. 342p. 1971. reprint ed. spiral bd. 12.00 (*0-7873-0218-X*) Hlth Research.

Secret Power of Dreams: A New Approach to Unlocking Their Hidden Potential. David Fontana. LC 95-12180. 1995. pap. 10.95 (*1-85230-697-1*) Element MA.

Secret Power of Music: The Transformation of Self & Society Through Musical Energy. David Tame. 304p. (Orig.). 1984. pap. 14.95 (*0-89281-056-4*, Destiny Bks) Inner Tradit.

Secret Power of Pyramids. Bill D. Schul & Ed Pettit. 1987. mass mkt. 5.99 (*0-449-13266-8*, GM) Fawcett.

***Secret Power of Tantrik Breathing.** Swami Sivapriyananda. 1996. 12.00 (*81-7017-340-X*, Pub. by Abhinav II) S Asia.

Secret Power of Tantrik Breathing. Swami Sivapriyananda. (C). 1983. 12.75 (*0-8364-2405-0*, Pub. by Abhinav II) S Asia.

Secret Power of the Pyramids. U. S. Andersen. 266p. 1977. pap. 7.00 (*0-87980-343-6*) Wilshire.

Secret Power of Words. Roy Masters. Ed. by Dorothy Baker. LC 88-81474. 213p. (Orig.). 1988. pap. text ed. 15.95 (*0-933900-14-7*) Foun Human Under.

Secret Power Source. Frederick Drummond. 96p. (Orig.). 1994. pap. 5.95 (*1-56043-798-7*) Destiny Image.

***Secret Power Within: Zen Solutions to Real Problems.** Chuck Norris. LC 96-31801. 288p. 1997. pap. 12.00 (*0-553-06908-X*) Broadway BDD.

Secret Power Within: Zen Solutions to Real Problems, Vol. 1. Chuck Norris. LC 95-45630. 1996. 20.95 (*0-316-58350-2*) Little.

Secret Power (1921) Marie Corelli. 342p. 1996. pap. 24.95 (*1-56459-739-3*) Kessinger Pub.

Secret Powers Behind the Revolution. Leon V. DePoncins. 1973. 59.95 (*0-8490-1013-6*) Gordon Pr.

Secret Powers of Karma: Revenge & Reconciliation in the Sexual Revolution. Karma Phoenix. 1996. pap. 6.00 (*0-945516-01-0*) Merit Prods.

Secret Prize in Every Box. David L. Cannon. (Appleseed Books for Children). (Illus.). 70p. (J). (gr. 3-4). 1993. 9.95 (*0-9631028-1-8*) Comm Just Foun TX.

Secret Proceedings & Debates of the Constitutional Convention of 1787. 1995. lib. bdg. 255.75 (*0-8490-6691-3*) Gordon Pr.

Secret Proceedings & Debates of the Convention to Form the U. S. Constitution Philadelphia 1787. Robert Yates. Ed. by George R. Stewart. LC 87-80615. 344p. (C). 1987. reprint ed. pap. 17.50 (*0-942301-01-3*); reprint ed. lib. bdg. 35.00 (*0-942301-00-5*) Birm Pub Lib.

Secret Prophecies of Nostradamus. Ed. by Cynthia Sternau & Martin H. Greenberg. 320p. (Orig.). 1995. pap. 4.99 (*0-88677-646-5*) DAW Bks.

***Secret Prophecies of Nostradamus.** Ed. by Cynthia Sternau & Martin H. Greenberg. 1997. 7.98 (*1-56731-180-6*, MJF Bks) Fine Comms.

Secret Proximity of Everywhere. Leo L. Marcello. 32p. (C). 1994. pap. 8.00 (*1-884725-01-5*) Blue Heron LA.

Secret Pulse: A Channeled Work. Meredith Standiford. 153p. (Orig.). 1994. pap. 9.95 (*0-9640021-0-8*) Sublight Pubns.

Secret Radio Message. Date not set. pap. 2.50 (*0-590-03319-0*) Scholastic Inc.

Secret Rapture. David Hare. LC 89-7447. 96p. 1989. pap. 9.95 (*0-8021-3175-1*, Grove) Grove-Atltic.

Secret Rapture: Is It Scriptural? Ralph E. Woodrow. (Illus.). 64p. 1989. pap. 5.00 (*0-916938-09-3*) R Woodrow.

Secret Raven. Sharp. 1995. pap. 15.00 (*0-919123-00-7*, Pub. by Inner City CN) BookWorld Dist.

Secret Reader: 501 Sonnets. Willis Barnstone. LC 95-17105. 440p. (C). 1996. pap. 21.95 (*0-87451-660-9*) U Pr of New Eng.

Secret Rebellion. Anne Mather. (Presents Ser.). 1994. mass mkt. 2.99 (*0-373-11663-2*, 1-11663-1) Harlequin Bks.

Secret Rebellion. large type ed. Anne Mather. (Harlequin Romance Ser.). 1994. lib. bdg. 19.95 (*0-263-13822-4*) Thorndike Pr.

***Secret Recipes of the Karate Masters.** George Krat. 1996. 33.95 (*1-889149-01-2*) C Scott Pub.

Secret Record: Modern Erotic Literature. Michael Perkins. (Orig.). 1993. reprint ed. mass mkt. 6.95 (*1-56333-039-3*, Rhinoceros) Masquerade.

Secret Relationship Between Blacks & Jews, Vol. 1. Nation of Islam Staff. 334p. 1991. pap. text ed. 19.95 (*0-9636877-0-0*) Hist Res Dept.

Secret Rendezvous: A Novel. Kobo Abe. Ed. by Paul De Angelis & Helena Franklin. Tr. by Juliet W. Carpenter. 192p. 1993. pap. 12.00 (*1-56836-003-7*) Kodansha.

Secret Revealed: A Shraga Morgenstern - Pinny Kate Mystery Trilogy. Perel Shreiber. 169p. 1995. 11.95 (*1-56871-081-X*) Targum Pr.

Secret Revelations Manuscript. A. B. Abe. 55p. (Orig.). 1993. pap. 12.00 (*0-9637922-1-0*) Cherry Stne Bks.

Secret Rites & Secret Writing: Royalist Literature, 1641-1660. Lois Potter. (Illus.). 264p. (C). 1990. text ed. 69.95 (*0-521-25512-0*) Cambridge U Pr.

Secret Ritual & Manhood in Victorian America. Mark C. Carnes. 240p. (C). 1989. text ed. 37.50 (*0-300-04424-0*) Yale U Pr.

Secret Ritual & Manhood in Victorian America. Mark C. Carnes. 296p. (C). 1991. reprint ed. pap. text ed. 18.00 (*0-300-05146-8*) Yale U Pr.

Secret Ritual of the Pythian Knighthood. James R. Carnahan. 101p. 1993. pap. 16.95 (*1-56459-383-5*) Kessinger Pub.

Secret Rituals of the Adonhiramite of Freemasonry. Tr. by Louis Guilleman. 160p. 1993. pap. 18.95 (*1-56459-332-0*) Kessinger Pub.

Secret Rituals of the Adoptive Rite of Freemasonry (Masonic Rituals for Women) Tr. by John Yarker. 100p. 1993. pap. 16.95 (*1-56459-333-9*) Kessinger Pub.

Secret Rituals of the Thirty-Third & Last Degree of Scottish Rite Freemasonry. 1993. pap. 12.00 (*1-56459-326-6*) Kessinger Pub.

Secret Roan Inish Photo Book. Amanda Stephens. (Movie Tie-in Ser.). (Illus.). 32p. (J). (gr. k-3). pap. 4.95 (*0-7868-1064-5*) Hyprn Ppbks.

Secret Room. Jennifer J. Mook. LC 91-67102. 148p. 1992. pap. 7.95 (*1-55523-487-9*) Winston-Derek.

Secret Room. Andy Rector. (Really Reading! Bks.). (Illus.). 48p. (Orig.). (J). (ps-3). 1994. pap. 4.49 (*0-7847-0179-2*, 03939) Standard Pub.

Secret Room. Uri Shulevitz. (J). 1993. 15.00 (*0-374-34169-9*) FS&G.

Secret Room. Uri Shulevitz. 32p. (J). 1996. pap. 5.95 (*0-374-46596-7*, Sunburst Bks) FS&G.

Secret Room: Poems. James Laughlin. LC 96-26188. 192p. 1997. 22.95 (*0-8112-1343-9*); pap. 14.95 (*0-8112-1344-7*, NDP837) New Directions.

***Secret Room & Other Stories: Prepared to Accompany the Bible Answer Card "The Creation"** large type ed. Vivian D. Gunderson. (Illus.). 128p. (Orig.). (J). (gr. 5-8). 1994. pap. 5.00 (*0-614-24109-X*) Rapids Christian.

Secret Room Downstairs. Ruth Willock. Ed. by Ruth Ashby. 112p. (Orig.). 1992. pap. 2.99 (*0-671-72324-3*, Minstrel Bks) PB.

Secret Rose Garden. Mahmud Shabistari. Tr. by Florence Lederer. 80p. 1985. pap. 8.50 (*1-56744-380-X*) Kazi Pubns.

Secret Rules. Carolyn Keene. (Nancy Drew on Campus Ser.: No. 5). (J). (gr. 8 up). 1996. mass mkt. 3.99 (*0-671-52746-0*, Pocket Books) PB.

***Secret, Sacred, Symbolic Story Revealing Hidden Meanings of Our Journey Through This Life & the Rest of Eternity.** Calvin Cottam. 44p. 1996. pap. 10.00 (*0-917628-14-4*) Coraco.

Secret Saga of Five-Sack. Henry L. Reimers. 25p. 1975. pap. 4.95 (*0-87770-145-8*) Ye Galleon.

Secret Santa. Carolyn Keene. Ed. by Anne Greenberg. (Nancy Drew Notebooks Ser.: No. 3). 80p. (Orig.). (YA). (gr. 2-4). 1994. pap. 3.99 (*0-671-87947-2*, Minstrel Bks) PB.

Secret Santa. Ann M. Martin. LC 93-48981. (Baby-Sitters Club Ser.). 40p. (J). (gr. 4-6). 1994. 14.95 (*0-590-48295-5*) Scholastic Inc.

***Secret Santa: Special Edition.** Laura E. Williams. (Let's Have a Party Ser.: No. 7). (Illus.). (J). 1997. pap. 3.99 (*0-380-79258-3*) Avon.

***Secret School.** Whitley Strieber. mass mkt. 6.99 (*0-06-109618-0*, Harp PBks) HarpC.

***Secret School: Preparation for Contact.** Whitley Strieber. LC 96-30230. 288p. 1997. 24.00 (*0-06-018731-X*) HarpC.

Secret Science: Federal Control of American Science & Technology. Herbert N. Foerstel. LC 92-23453. 256p. 1993. text ed. 35.00 (*0-275-94447-6*, C4447, Praeger Pubs) Greenwood.

Secret Science: For the Physical & Spiritual Transformation of Man. 2nd ed. John Baines. Tr. by Evelyne Brown from SPA. LC 93-91617. (Hermetic Philosophy Ser.: Bk. 1). (Illus.). 240p. 1994. pap. 7.95 (*1-882692-01-2*) J Baines Inst.

Secret Science at Work. Max F. Long. 1953. pap. 15.95 (*0-87516-046-8*) DeVorss.

Secret Science Behind Miracles. Max F. Long. 416p. 1948. pap. 15.95 (*0-87516-047-6*) DeVorss.

Secret Science of Covert Inks. Samuel Rubin. LC 86-82957. 138p. (Orig.). 1987. pap. 14.95 (*0-915179-44-X*) Loompanics.

Secret Sciences in the Light of Our Time: Genesis, Golgotha's Mystery, Occultism, Philosopher's Stone, Rudolf Steiner. Hans Liebstoeckl. 1972. 59.95 (*0-8490-1014-4*) Gordon Pr.

Secret Sea. Burt Jones & Maurine Shimlock. LC 95-61625. (Illus.). 164p. 1995. 85.00 (*0-9642736-7-5*) Fourth Day Pub.

Secret Seas: Stories & Essays. Carlos Eyles. 159p. 12.95 (*0-922769-23-0*) Watersport Pub.

Secret Seed: Stories & Poems. Sidney Sulkin. 1983. pap. 9.95 (*0-931848-47-4*) Dryad Pr.

Secret Self: Short Stories by Women. Ed. by Hermione Lee. 384p. 1993. pap. 6.95 (*0-460-87348-2*, Everyman's Classic Lib) C E Tuttle.

Secret Service. Wendy Walker. (Sun & Moon Classics Ser.: No. 20). 464p. 1989. pap. 13.95 (*1-55713-084-1*) Sun & Moon CA.

Secret Service: The Field, the Dungeon, & the Escape. Albert D. Richardson. LC 77-173119. 1972. reprint ed. 39.95 (*0-405-08888-4*, Pub. by Blom Pubns UK) Ayer.

Secret Service Agent (Uniformed) Jack Rudman. (Career Examination Ser.: C-3255). 1994. pap. 27.95 (*0-8373-3255-9*) Nat Learn.

Secret Service of the Post Office Department. P. H. Woodward. (Illus.). 1978. reprint ed. lib. bdg. 35.00 (*0-915262-23-1*) S J Durst.

Secret Service, the Field, the Dungeon, & the Escape. Albert D. Richardson. LC 70-37315. (Black Heritage Library Collection). 1977. reprint ed. 39.95 (*0-8369-8952-X*) Ayer.

Secret Services: Is There a Case for Greater Openness? Ed. by Michael Mates. (C). 1990. 40.00 (*0-907967-07-8*, Pub. by Inst Euro Def & Strat UK) St Mut.

***Secret Sexual Positions: Ancient Techniques for Modern Lovers.** Kenneth R. Stubbs. 128p. 1997. pap. 16.95 (*0-939263-15-7*) Secret Garden.

Secret Shadows of Ravensfall. Vivien F. Wake. 304p. 1992. mass mkt. 3.99 (*0-8217-3856-9*, Zebra Kensgtn) Kensgtn Pub Corp.

Secret Shapes. (Changing Picture Bks.). (Illus.). 20p. (J). (ps-1). 1995. 6.95 (*1-56458-962-5*) DK Pub Inc.

***Secret Shapes.** (Illus.). (J). 9.99 (*0-590-24644-5*) Scholastic Inc.

Secret Sharer. Conrad. 1997. text ed. 35.00 (*0-312-16291-X*) St Martin.

***Secret Sharer.** Conrad. Date not set. pap. 12.95 (*0-312-15465-8*) St Martin.

Secret Sharer. Schwarz. 1997. pap. text ed. 8.00 (*0-312-11224-6*) St Martin.

Secret Sharer & Other Great Stories. Abraham H. Lass. Ed. by N. Trasman. (Orig.). 1989. pap. 4.50 (*0-451-62540-4*) NAL-Dutton.

***Secret Sharer & Other Sea Stories.** Conrad. 1992. pap. text ed. write for info. (*0-17-556426-4*) Addison-Wesley.

Secret Sharer & Other Stories. Joseph Conrad. LC 92-36764. (Thrift Editions Ser.). 128p. 1993. reprint ed. pap. 1.00 (*0-486-27546-9*) Dover.

Secret Sharers: Studies in Contemporary Fictions. Bruce Bassoff. LC 82-20766. (Ars Poetica Ser.: No. 1). (Illus.). 152p. 1983. 34.50 (*0-404-62501-0*) AMS Pr.

Secret Sharers in Italian Comedy: From Machiavelli to Goldoni. Jackson I. Cope. LC 95-49319. 232p. 1996. text ed. 39.95 (*0-8223-1760-5*) Duke.

Secret Shore. large type ed. Jennifer Hyde. (Dales Large Print Ser.). 235p. 1995. pap. 17.99 (*1-85389-543-1*, Dales) Ulverscroft.

Secret Shortcut. Mark Teague. 32p. (J). (ps up). 1996. 14.95 (*0-590-67714-4*) Scholastic Inc.

Secret Shortcut. Mark Teague. (J). 1996. pap. write for info. (*0-590-67715-2*) Scholastic Inc.

Secret Side of History: Mystery Babylon & the New World Order. Dee Zahner. LC 95-90310. 1996. reprint ed. pap. 10.00 (*1-887017-01-1*) LTAA Commun.

Secret Side of Money: A History of Manipulation. Dee Zahner. LC 95-90956. 155p. (Orig.). 1996. pap. 10.00 (*1-887017-02-X*) LTAA Commun.

Secret Signals: The Euronumbers Mystery. Simon Mason. 60p. 1991. pap. 12.95 (*0-936653-28-0*) Tiare Pubns.

***Secret Signs: Along the Underground Railroad.** Anita Riggio. LC 95-80777. (Illus.). 32p. (J). (ps-3). 1997. 15.95 (*1-56397-555-6*) Boyds Mills Pr.

Secret Silent Screams. Joan L. Nixon. 192p. (J). (gr. k-8). 1990. pap. 3.99 (*0-440-20539-5*, LLL BDD) BDD Bks Young Read.

Secret Sin. Michael J. Wota. LC 95-91050. 1996. 18.95 (*0-533-11834-4*) Vantage.

***Secret Sins.** Jasmine Cresswell. (Mira Bks.). 1997. 5.99 (*1-55166-261-2*, 1-66261-8, Mira Bks) Harlequin Bks.

***Secret Sins.** Tina Leonard. (Scarlet Ser.). (Orig.). 1997. mass mkt. 3.99 (*1-85487-955-3*, Pub. by Scarlet Bks UK) London Brdge.

***Secret Sins: Sex, Violence & Society in Carmarthenshire 1870-1920.** Russell Davies. 334p. 1997. pap. 29.95 (*0-7083-1367-1*, Pub. by Univ Wales Pr UK) Paul & Co Pubs.

Secret Sites of Historic Trivia: Explore San Diego. William Carroll. (Explore San Diego County Ser.). (Illus.). 160p. (Orig.). 1994. pap. 10.00 (*0-910390-39-8*, Coda Pubns) Auto Bk.

Secret Six. Otto Scott. (Sacred Fool Quartet Ser.: Vol. 3). (Illus.). 375p. 1989. reprint ed. 30.00 (*0-685-28039-X*) Fndtn Amer Ed.

Secret Six: John Brown & the Abolitionists. Otto Scott. 375p. 1993. pap. 17.95 (*0-9638381-0-5*) Uncommon Bks.

Secret Six: The True Tale of the Men Who Conspired with John Brown. Edward J. Renehan, Jr. 1995. 25.00 (*0-517-59028-X*, Crown) Crown Pub Group.

***Secret Six: The True Tale of the Men Who Conspired with John Brown.** Edward J. Renehan, Jr. LC 96-47366. (Illus.). 318p. 1997. reprint ed. 16.95 (*1-57003-181-9*) U of SC Pr.

***Secret Skater: A Winner Family Sports Mystery.** Robin Aran. LC 96-35659. (Winning Readers Ser.). (J). 1996. write for info. (*1-879852-52-7*) Univ Tampa.

Secret Societies. Stewart Ross. (Fact or Fiction Ser.). (Illus.). 48p. (YA). (gr. 5 up). 1996. 6.95 (*0-7613-0510-6*, Copper Beech Bks); lib. bdg. 18.50 (*0-7613-0533-5*, Copper Beech Bks) Millbrook Pr.

Secret Societies: Can a Christian Belong to Them & Still Honor Christ? George L. Hunt. LC 86-21476. 1902. pap. 14.95 (*0-87213-559-4*); pap. 2.99 (*0-87213-338-9*) Loizeaux.

Secret Societies: Sourcebook of Occult Organizations for the Nephilim Gamemaster. Kenneth Hite. Ed. by Sam Shirley. (Nephilim Role Playing Game Ser.). (Illus.). 96p. (Orig.). 1995. pap. 16.95 (*1-56882-036-4*, 3103) Chaosium.

Secret Societies & Subversive Movements. Nesta H. Webster. 419p. 1924. reprint ed. pap. 14.95 (*0-945001-04-5*) GSG & Assocs.

Secret Societies & the French Revolution. Una Birch. 1976. lib. bdg. 59.95 (*0-8490-2585-0*) Gordon Pr.

Secret Societies of All Ages & Countries. Charles W. Heckethorn. 760p. 1992. pap. 45.00 (*1-56459-296-0*) Kessinger Pub.

Secret Societies Reconsidered: Perspectives on the Social History of Early Modern South China & Southeast Asia. Ed. by David Ownby & Mary S. Heidhues. LC 93-26121. (Studies on Modern China). (Illus.). 272p. (C). (gr. 13). 1993. text ed. 72.95 (*1-56324-198-6*, East Gate Bk); pap. text ed. 27.95 (*1-56324-199-4*, East Gate Bk) M E Sharpe.

Secret Society of the Left Hand. Dandi D. Mackall. LC 96-14503. (Cinnamon Lake Mysteries Ser.: Vol. 1). 80p. (J). 1996. pap. 4.99 (*0-570-04792-7*, 56-1812) Concordia.

***Secret Soldier.** Muki Betzer & Robert Rosenberg. mass mkt. write for info. (*0-06-109259-2*, Harp PBks) HarpC.

Secret Soldier. Anne Spencer. Ed. by J. Friedland & R. Kessler. (Novel-Ties Ser.). 1992. student ed., pap. text ed. 15.95 (*0-88122-719-6*) Lrn Links.

Secret Soldier: The Story of Deborah Sampson. Ann McGovern. 64p. (J). (gr. 4-6). 1990. pap. 2.99 (*0-590-43052-1*) Scholastic Inc.

Secret Soldier: The True Life Story of Israel's Greatest Commando. Muki Betzer & Robert Rosenberg. (Illus.). 296p. 1996. 23.00 (*0-87113-637-6*, Atlntc Mnthly) Grove-Atltic.

Secret Song. Catherine Coulter. 1991. pap. 6.99 (*0-451-40234-0*, Onyx) NAL-Dutton.

***Secret Songs of Sara.** Elaine S. Brown. 231p. 1997. pap. 12.95 (*1-878647-37-7*) Duncan & Duncan.

Secret Speeches of Chairman Mao: From the Hundred Flowers to the Great Leap Forward. Ed. by Roderick MacFarquhar et al. (Contemporary China Ser.: No. 6). 400p. 1989. pap. 18.00 (*0-674-79673-X*) HUP.

Secret Splendor. Sandra Brown. (Mira Bks.). 1996. mass mkt. 5.99 (*1-55166-095-4*, 1-66095-0, Mira Bks) Harlequin Bks.

***Secret Splendor.** Charles E. Essert. LC 97-3908. 1997. reprint ed. pap. 13.95 (*1-889051-13-6*, I Lvl) Acrpls Bks CO.

An Asterisk (*) at the beginning of an entry indicates that the title is appearing in BIP for the first time.

Secret Spot. Michael E. Degregorio. LC TXU-753-190. (Illus.). 160p. (Orig.). (J). (ps-12). 1996. pap. 14.95 (*0-9649417-6-7*) Degregorio.

Secret Squadron. large type ed. Bill Spence. 272p. 1995. 25.99 (*0-7089-3400-5*) Ulverscroft.

Secret Squadrons of the Eighth. Pat Carty. 1990. 24.95 (*0-933424-43-4*) Specialty Pr.

Secret Staircase. Bob Wright. Tr. by Phyllis Bourne & Eugenia Tusquets. (Tom & Ricky Spanish-English Readers Ser.). (Illus.). 96p. (ENG & SPA.). (J). (gr. 1-5). 1988. pap. 4.95 (*0-87879-659-2*) High Noon Bks.

Secret Star. Nancy Springer. LC 96-12091. 144p. (YA). (gr. 5-9). 1997. 15.95 (*0-399-23028-9*, Philomel Bks) Putnam Pub Group.

***Secret Stars.** Joseph Slate. LC 97-20624. (Illus.). (J). 1998. write for info. (*0-7614-5027-0*) Marshall Cavendish.

Secret State: British Internal Security in the Twentieth Century. Richard C. Thurlow. LC 94-6153. 288p. 1994. 50.95 (*0-631-16066-3*) Blackwell Pubs.

Secret Storm. Yvonne Lehman. (White Dove Romance Ser.: Vol. 2). 160p. (Orig.). (YA). (gr. 7 up). 1995. mass mkt. 4.99 (*1-55661-706-2*, Hampshire MN) Bethany Hse.

Secret Strategies from North America's Top Whitetail Hunters: Bow & Gun Hunters Share Their... Nick Sisley. LC 95-77311. (Illus.). 240p. 1995. pap. text ed. 14.95 (*0-87341-342-3*, GBT01) Krause Pubns.

Secret Strength: For Those Who Search. Joni E. Tada. 208p. 1994. 11.99 (*0-88070-590-6*); pap. 5.99 (*0-88070-700-3*) Multnomah Pubs.

***Secret Strength: For Those Who Search.** Joni E. Tada. 159p. 1996. pap. 9.99 (*0-88070-989-8*) Multnomah Pubs.

Secret Strength of Depression. rev. ed. Frederic F. Flach. 272p. 1995. pap. 14.95 (*1-886330-02-6*) Hatherleigh.

***Secret Summer.** large type ed. Helen McCabe. (Linford Romance Large Print Ser.). 208p. 1997. pap. 16.99 (*0-7089-5121-X*, Linford) Ulverscroft.

Secret Summer Dreams. Beverly Lewis. (Holly's Heart Ser.: Vol. 2). 160p. (J). (gr. 6-9). 1993. pap. 6.99 (*0-310-38061-8*) Zondervan.

Secret Super Power of Marco. Meredith S. Willis. LC 93-14491. 112p. (J). (gr. 3-7). 1994. lib. bdg. 13.89 (*0-06-023559-4*) HarpC Child Bks.

Secret Super Powers of Marco. Meredith S. Willis. LC 93-14491. 112p. (J). (gr. 3-7). 1995. pap. 3.95 (*0-06-440506-0*, Trophy) HarpC Child Bks.

***Secret Survivors.** Sue E. Blume. 1997. pap. 12.95 (*0-345-41945-6*) Ballantine.

Secret Survivors: Uncovering Incest & Its After Effects in Women. E. Sue Blume. LC 89-34113. 352p. 1990. text ed. 27.95 (*0-471-61843-8*) Wiley.

Secret Survivors: Uncovering Incest & Its Aftereffects in Women. E. Sue Blume. 352p. 1991. mass mkt. 5.99 (*0-345-36979-3*) Ballantine.

Secret Symbolism of the Tarot. Doris C. Doane. 112p. 1993. pap. 11.00 (*0-86690-430-1*) Am Fed Astrologers.

Secret Symbols of the Rosicrucians of the 16th & 17th Centuries. 2nd ed. 1967. pap. 24.50 (*0-912057-44-0*, 501470) RO AMORC.

Secret Table. Mark Mirsky. LC 74-24914. 167p. 1975. 15.95 (*0-914590-10-3*); pap. 6.95 (*0-914590-11-1*) Fiction Coll.

Secret Talents. Olga Tergora. 315p. 1996. mass mkt. 7.95 (*1-56201-038-7*) Blue Moon Bks.

Secret Teachings. Harold Klemp. (Mahanta Transcripts Ser.: Bk. 3). 315p. 1989. pap. 14.00 (*1-57043-005-5*) ECKANKAR.

Secret Teachings in the Art of Japanese Gardens: Design Principles - Aesthetic Values. David A. Slawson. (Illus.). 220p. 1991. reprint ed. pap. 30.00 (*4-7700-1541-0*) Kodansha.

Secret Teachings of All Ages: An Encyclopedic Outline of Masonic, Hermetic, Quabbalistic, & Rosicrucian Symbolical Philosophy. Manly P. Hall. (Illus.). 1978. pap. 39.95 (*0-89314-830-X*) Philos Res.

Secret Teachings of All Ages: An Encyclopedic Outline of Masonic, Hermetic, Quabbalistic, & Rosicrucian Symbolical Philosophy. Manly P. Hall. (Illus.). 1978. 165.00 (*0-89314-546-7*) Philos Res.

Secret Teachings of Jesus: Four Gnostic Gospels. Marvin Meyer. 1986. pap. 10.00 (*0-394-74433-0*, Vin) Random.

Secret Teachings of the Masonic Lodge. John Ankerberg & John Weldon. 1990. pap. 14.99 (*0-8024-7695-3*) Moody.

Secret Teachings of the Vedas: The Ancient Knowledge of the East. Sri Nanda-Nandana. LC 86-51209. 320p. (Orig.). 1987. pap. 14.95 (*0-9617410-0-7*) World Relief.

Secret Teachings of the Vedas: The Eastern Answers to the Mysteries of Life. rev. ed. Stephen Knapp. LC 90-71652. (Illus.). 325p. (C). 1991. pap. 14.95 (*0-9617410-1-5*) World Relief.

***Secret Teachings of Yeshua.** Ed. & Tr. by Jay G. Williams from GEC. 24p. (Orig.). 1997. pap. 4.00 (*0-9629662-4-X*) G Santes.

***Secret Techniques of Wing Chun Kung Fu Vol. I: Sil Lim Tao.** J. E. Weakland. 18.95 (*0-901764-35-3*, 93324, Pub. by P H Crompton UK) Talman.

***Secret Techniques of Wing Chun Kung Fu Vol. II: Chum Kil.** J. E. Weakland. 18.95 (*0-901764-49-3*, 93325, Pub. by P H Crompton UK) Talman.

***Secret Techniques of Wing Chun Kung Fu Vol. III: Bil Jee.** J. E. Weakland. 19.95 (*0-901764-62-0*, 93326, Pub. by P H Crompton UK) Talman.

Secret Temple of Adajy: Fantasy Game Adventure. Steve Johansson. 1996. pap. 10.95 (*1-889182-02-8*) Kenzer & Co.

Secret Texts: The Literature of Secret Societies. Ed. by Marie Roberts & Hugh Ormsby-Lennon. LC 91-13789. (Studies in Cultural History: No. 1). 1995. 55.00 (*0-404-64251-9*) AMS Pr.

Secret That's Never Been Told: Healing the Wounds of Childhood Sexual Abuse. Tracy Hansen. LC 92-80387. 120p. (Orig.). 1992. pap. 7.95 (*0-89622-513-5*) Twenty-Third.

Secret Thoughts of an Adoptive Mother. Jana Wolff. LC 96-26394. 160p. 1997. 16.95 (*0-8362-2186-9*) Andrews & McMeel.

Secret Thoughts of Men: Why Men Won't Talk. Jeff O'Den & John Sexton. 480p. 1992. pap. 19.95 (*0-9631291-0-4*) Intl Assn Men.

***Secret Thunder.** Patricia Ryan. 1997. mass mkt. 5.99 (*0-614-27798-1*, Topaz) NAL-Dutton.

Secret to a Million Dollar Night Club - Restaurant. James Virgil. Ed. by Millard Collier & Elizabeth Bryant. (Illus.). 226p. 1991. 59.95 (*0-9631121-0-4*) Lakewood Pub.

***Secret to a Satisfied Life.** E. Larsen. 1996. 29.95 incl. vhs (*0-89486-817-9*) Hazelden.

Secret to Be Buried: The Diary & Life of Emily Hawley Gillespie, 1858-1888. Judy N. Lensink. LC 88-38514. (Bur Oak Original Ser.). (Illus.). 472p. 1989. pap. 16.95 (*0-87745-237-7*); text ed. 42.95 (*0-87745-229-6*) U of Iowa Pr.

Secret to Conquering Fear. Mike Hernacki. LC 96-24881. 112p. 1996. pap. 7.95 (*1-56554-192-8*) Pelican.

Secret to Hunza Superior Health. Carl Classic. Ed. by Gordon F. Richiusa. 203p. (Orig.). 1991. reprint ed. pap. 7.95 (*0-9628298-7-0*) Ctr Human Natural Ntrtn.

Secret to Making Your Invention a Reality: The Workbook. Ed. by Cynthia F. Stephens. (Illus.). 183p. (Orig.). 1994. pap. text ed. 24.95 (*0-9639336-1-2*) VenturSource.

***Secret to Tender Pie.** Mindy Marin. 1997. 17.95 (*0-345-40985-X*) Ballantine.

Secret to the Christian Life: An Introduction to the Deeper Christian Life. Gene Edwards. LC 93-15361. (Illus.). 150p. 1993. reprint ed. pap. 8.99 (*0-8423-5916-8*) Tyndale.

***Secret to Wealth & Happiness.** Anthony Robbins. 1998. 24.00 (*0-684-80902-8*, S&S) S&S Trade.

Secret Tradition in Alchemy. Arthur E. Waite. 413p. 1992. reprint ed. pap. 33.00 (*0-922802-83-1*) Kessinger Pub.

Secret Tradition in Arthurian Legend. Gareth Knight. LC 96-3333. 55p. 1996. reprint ed. pap. 16.00 (*0-87728-861-5*) Weiser.

Secret Tradition in Freemasonry, 2 vols., Set. Arthur E. Waite. 870p. 1992. reprint ed. pap. 45.00 (*0-922802-98-X*) Kessinger Pub.

Secret Tradition in Freemasonry, 1937. Arthur E. Waite. 675p. 1993. pap. 45.00 (*1-56459-305-3*) Kessinger Pub.

***Secret Treasures.** Catherine Howell. (Illus.). (J). (ps-3). 1997. 16.00 (*0-614-28874-6*) Natl Geog.

Secret Treasures; Animal Acrobats, 2 vols. Illus. by John Buxton. LC 93-9767. (National Geographic Action Bk.). (J). 1993. 27.50 (*0-87044-956-7*) Natl Geog.

Secret Treasures of Coco Island. Ilona K. Stashko. 24p. (J). (ps-4). 1995. pap. 4.95 (*1-882651-00-6*) Come Alive Pubns.

Secret Treasures of Coco Island: Includes Pirate Hat, Necklace, Sword & Eye-Patch, Book. Ilona K. Stashko. (J). (ps-4). 1995. pap. 12.95 (*1-882651-03-0*) Come Alive Pubns.

Secret Trial of Imre Nagy. Alajos Dornbach. LC 94-16459. 216p. 1994. text ed. 59.95 (*0-275-94332-1*, Praeger Pubs) Greenwood.

Secret Trout Flies: The Book of Unrevealed Patterns. Theodore D. Naydan. (Illus.). 63p. 1989. pap. text ed. write for info. (*0-318-65818-6*) T D Naydan.

Secret Tunnel Mystery. 2nd ed. Hilda Stahl. LC 92-27202. (Best Friends Ser.: Vol. 16). 160p. (J). (gr. 4-7). 1994. pap. 4.99 (*0-89107-826-6*) Crossway Bks.

Secret Turning of the Earth. Anthony Libby. LC 94-33242. (Wick Poetry Chapbook Ser.: No. 5). 32p. (Orig.). 1995. pap. 4.75 (*0-87338-520-9*) Kent St U Pr.

***Secret under the Whirlpool.** Elaine B. Hammond. 176p. (J). (gr. 4-8). 1996. pap. 7.95 (*0-921556-61-6*, Pub. by Gynergy-Ragweed CN) LPC InBook.

Secret Valentine. Laura Damon. LC 87-13736. (Giant First Start Reader Ser.). (Illus.). 32p. (J). (gr. k-2). 1988. lib. bdg. 12.95 (*0-8167-1101-1*) Troll Communs.

Secret Valentine. Laura Damon. LC 87-13736. (Giant First Start Reader Ser.). (Illus.). 32p. (J). (gr. k-2). 1996. pap. 3.95 (*0-8167-1102-X*) Troll Communs.

Secret Valentine. Quin & Harkin. (TGIF Ser.: No. 6). (J). (gr. 3-6). 1996. pap. 3.50 (*0-671-51022-3*) PB.

Secret Valley. Clyde R. Bulla. LC 49-10917. (Trophy Bk.). (Illus.). 112p. (J). (gr. 2-5). 1993. pap. 3.95 (*0-06-440456-0*, Trophy) HarpC Child Bks.

Secret Vampire. L. J. Smith. (YA). (gr. 7 up). 1996. pap. 3.99 (*0-671-55133-7*) S&S Trade.

Secret Vice Exposed. LC 73-20648. (Sex, Marriage & Society Ser.). 470p. 1974. reprint ed. 39.95 (*0-405-05816-0*) Ayer.

Secret Vietnam War: The United States Air Force in Thailand, 1961-1975. Jeffrey D. Glasser. LC 95-10731. (Illus.). 287p. 1995. lib. bdg. 48.00 (*0-7864-0084-6*) McFarland & Co.

***Secret Voice.** Gaetan Brulotte. 96p. 1990. pap. 8.95 (*0-88984-097-0*, Pub. by Porcupines Quill CN) Genl Dist Srvs.

***Secret Vow.** Kathy Cecala. 1997. pap. 19.95 (*0-525-94290-4*) NAL-Dutton.

Secret Vows. Denise R. Twiggs & Bert Twiggs. 304p. (Orig.). 1995. mass mkt. 5.50 (*0-425-14685-5*) Berkley Pub.

Secret War. Robert J. Lamphere. 1994. 16.95 (*0-533-10552-8*) Vantage.

Secret War. Doris B. Smith. (J). 1999. pap. 14.99 (*0-670-84930-8*) Viking Penguin.

Secret War. Russell J. Smith. 224p. 1986. 19.95 (*0-89754-051-4*); pap. 9.95 (*0-89754-050-6*) Dan River Pr.

Secret War: CIA Covert Operations Against Cuba, 1959-1962. Fabian Escalante. Ed. by Mirta Muniz. Tr. by Maxine Shaw from SPA. (Illus.). 200p. (Orig.). 1995. pap. 15.95 (*1-875284-86-9*) Ocean Pr NY.

Secret War: Espionage in World War II. James T. Rogers. (World Espionage Ser.). (Illus.). 128p. (YA). (gr. 7-10). 1991. lib. bdg. 16.95 (*0-8160-2395-6*) Facts on File.

Secret War: The Office of Strategic Services in World War II. Ed. by George C. Chalou. (Illus.). 376p. 1995. 55.00 (*0-7881-2598-2*) DIANE Pub.

***Secret War Against the Jews.** John Loftus. 1997. pap. 16.95 (*0-312-15648-0*) St Martin.

Secret War Against the Jews. John Loftus. 1994. 26.95 (*0-312-11057-X*) St Martin.

Secret War for the Union: The Untold Story of Military Intelligence in the Civil War. Edwin C. Fishel. 1996. write for info. (*0-03-957428-8*) HM.

Secret War for the Union: The Untold Story of Military Intelligence in the Civil War. Edwin C. Fishel. 752p. 1996. 35.00 (*0-395-74281-1*) HM.

Secret War in Central America: Sandinista Assault on World Order. John N. Moore. LC 86-28092. 204p. 1987. text ed. 47.95 (*0-313-27041-4*, U7041, Greenwood Pr) Greenwood.

Secret War of Independence. Helen Augur. LC 75-25250. 381p. 1976. reprint ed. text ed. 45.00 (*0-8371-8380-4*, AUSW, Greenwood Pr) Greenwood.

Secret Warning. Franklin W. Dixon. (Hardy Boys Ser.: Vol. 17). 180p. (J). (gr. 5-9). 1938. 5.95 (*0-448-08917-3*, G&D) Putnam Pub Group.

Secret Wars. Mike Zeck et al. 336p. 1992. 19.95 (*0-87135-903-0*) Marvel Entmnt.

Secret Wars: A Guide to Sources in English, 3 vols., Set. Myron J. Smith, Jr. 29.95 (*0-87436-407-8*) Regina Bks.

Secret Wars: Covert Operations in Vietnam. (Vietnam Experience Ser.). (Illus.). 192p. 1988. 16.30 (*0-201-11944-7*) Addison-Wesley.

Secret Wars: The Shadowy World of Spies & Killers. Arun Kumar. (C). 1994. text ed. 27.00 (*81-241-0236-8*, Pub. by Har-Anand Pubns II) S Asia.

Secret Water. Arthur Ransome. LC 95-24644. (Godine Storyteller Ser.). 376p. (J). (gr. 5-8). 1996. pap. 14.95 (*1-56792-064-0*) Godine.

***Secret Waters.** Linda C. Brown. (Women's Poetry Ser.). 68p. (Orig.). 1997. pap. 10.00 (*0-911287-24-8*) Blue Begonia.

Secret Way of Wonder: Insights from the Silence. Guy Finley. LC 92-2920. 192p. 1992. pap. 9.95 (*0-87542-221-7*) Llewellyn Pubns.

Secret Ways. Alistair MacLean. 1976. 22.95 (*0-89190-172-8*) Amereon Ltd.

Secret Weapon: Men Overcoming Chaos. Dave Winecott. 226p. (Orig.). 1996. pap. 9.95 (*1-883893-37-2*) WinePress Pub.

Secret Weapon: U. S. High-Frequency Direction Finding in the Battle of the Atlantic. Kathleen B. Williams. LC 96-14583. (Illus.). 312p. 1996. 35.00 (*1-55750-935-2*) Naval Inst Pr.

Secret Weapons. Zilpha K. Snyder. (Castle Court Kids Ser.: Vol. 4). 128p. (J). (gr. 4-6). 1995. pap. 3.99 (*0-440-40988-8*, YB BDD) BDD Bks Young Read.

Secret Web. (Red Stripe Ser.). 1988. pap. 4.50 (*0-8216-5059-9*, Univ Books) Carol Pub Group.

***Secret Wife.** Susan Mallery. 1997. mass mkt. 3.99 (*0-373-24123-2*, 1-24123-1) Silhouette.

Secret Wing. Nancy Chalker-Tennant. (Illus.). 12p. 1991. pap. 10.00 (*0-89822-068-8*) Visual Studies.

***Secret Wires: Codes & Telegraphers of the Civil War.** Frederick W. Chesson. (Illus.). 1997. write for info. (*1-883522-16-1*) Rockbridge Pub.

Secret Wisdom of Qabalah. J. F. C. Fuller. 1976. reprint ed. 13.50 (*0-911662-63-4*) Yoga.

Secret Wisdom of the Great Initiates. Earlyne C. Chaney. LC 92-74029. 169p. 1993. per. 15.95 (*0-918936-25-X*) Astara.

Secret Wish. Leslie Miller. 35p. (J). (ps-3). 1996. pap. text ed. 1.95 (*1-56763-167-3*) Ozark Pub.

Secret Wish of Nannerl Mozart. Barbara Nickel. 1996. pap. 6.95 (*0-929005-89-9*, Pub. by Second Story Pr CN) LPC InBook.

Secret Wishes. Lou Kassem. 144p. (J). (gr. 3-7). 1989. pap. 2.95 (*0-380-75544-0*, Camelot) Avon.

Secret Woman. Victoria Holt. 352p. 1985. mass mkt. 5.99 (*0-449-20878-8*, Crest) Fawcett.

Secret Wonder Weapons of the Third Reich: German Missiles 1934-1945. J. Miranda & P. Mercado. (Illus.). 144p. 1996. 35.00 (*0-7643-0086-5*) Schiffer.

Secret Word. Molana S. Ali. LC 88-39008. 75p. (Orig.). (ENG & PER.). 1989. pap. 12.00 (*0-8191-7331-2*) U Pr of Amer.

Secret Word. Molana S. Angha. LC 88-39006. 75p. (Orig.). 1989. lib. bdg. 29.00 (*0-8191-7330-4*) U Pr of Amer.

Secret Words. Jonathan Strong. LC 91-66473. 232p. 1992. 18.95 (*0-944072-19-4*) Zoland Bks.

Secret Words. Jonathan Strong. LC 91-66473. 232p. 1993. pap. 9.95 (*0-944072-11-9*) Zoland Bks.

Secret World: Sexuality & the Search for Celibacy. A. W. Sipe. LC 90-32435. 336p. 1990. text ed. 38.95 (*0-87630-585-0*) Brunner-Mazel.

Secret World Government: Or, the Hidden Hand of the Unrevealed in History. Count Cherep-Spriridovich. 1977. lib. bdg. 250.00 (*0-8490-2586-9*) Gordon Pr.

***Secret World of Alex Mack: Milady Alex!** Diana G. Gallagher. (Orig.). (J). 1997. pap. 3.99 (*0-671-00684-3*) PB.

Secret World of American Communism. Harvey E. Klehr. 386p. 1996. pap. 16.00 (*0-300-06855-7*) Yale U Pr.

Secret World of American Communism: Documents from the Soviet Archives. Harvey E. Klehr et al. LC 94-3596. (Documents of Communism Ser.). 1995. 30.00 (*0-300-06183-8*) Yale U Pr.

***Secret World of Angels: Revelations from Another Dimension.** Daphne S. Reed. (Illus.). ix, 240p. (Orig.). 1997. spiral bd. 39.95 (*0-9655978-1-4*, 9655978-1) Owl Pubs.

Secret World of Animals. Ed. by Donald J. Crump. (Books for World Explorers Series 7: No. 3). (Illus.). 104p. 1986. lib. bdg. 12.50 (*0-87044-580-4*) Natl Geog.

Secret World of Animals. Ed. by Donald J. Crump. (Books for World Explorers Series 7: No. 3). (Illus.). 104p. 1995. 12.50 (*0-87044-575-8*) Natl Geog.

Secret World of Animals - Below & Above the Ground. Canadian Museum of Nature Staff. 1992. 9.95 (*0-660-13062-9*) U Ch Pr.

Secret World of Animals - In the Air. Canadian Museum of Nature Staff. 1992. 9.95 (*0-660-13059-9*) U Ch Pr.

Secret World of Animals - On the Earth. Canadian Museum of Nature Staff. 1992. 9.95 (*0-660-13061-0*) U Ch Pr.

Secret World of Animals - Under the Water. Canadian Museum of Nature Staff. 1992. 9.95 (*0-660-13060-2*) U Ch Pr.

Secret World of Drawings: Healing Through Art. Gregg M. Furth. (Illus.). 150p. (Orig.). (C). 1989. 27.50 (*0-938434-47-0*); pap. 18.95 (*0-938434-46-2*) Sigo Pr.

***Secret World of Gardens.** Mia Amato. 1997. pap. 12.95 (*0-614-27231-9*) H Holt & Co.

***Secret World of Money.** Andrew Gause. 144p. 1996. pap. write for info. (*0-9656589-0-2*) SDL.

***Secret World of Og.** Pierre Berton. (Illus.). 60p. (Orig.). (J). (gr. k-4). pap. 12.99 (*0-7710-1399-X*) McCland & Stewart.

Secret World of Polly Flint. Helen Cresswell. 1994. 18.00 (*0-8446-6760-9*) Peter Smith.

Secret World of the Irish Male. Joseph O'Connor. Date not set. pap. 6.99 (*0-7493-2108-3*) Heinemann.

Secret World of Your Dreams. Julia Parker & Derek Parker. 240p. 1991. reprint ed. pap. 11.00 (*0-399-51700-6*, Perigee Bks) Berkley Pub.

Secret Worlds of Colin Fletcher. Colin Fletcher. LC 89-40551. 1990. pap. 12.00 (*0-679-72554-7*, Vin) Random.

Secret Wounds & Silent Cries. rev. ed. Dewey Bertolini. LC 93-18867. Orig. Title: Sometimes I Really Hate You!. 156p. (J). 1993. pap. 9.99 (*1-56476-116-9*, 6-3116, Victor Bks) Chariot Victor.

Secret Writing: An Introduction to Cryptograms, Ciphers, & Codes. Henry Lysing, pseud. LC 74-75261. 128p. 1974. reprint ed. pap. 3.95 (*0-486-23062-7*) Dover.

Secret Writing: Keys to the Mysteries of Reading & Writing. Peter Sears. 180p. (J). 1986. pap. 12.95 (*0-915924-86-2*) Tchrs & Writers Coll.

Secret Yearning. Debra Cowan. 384p. 1996. mass mkt. 5.50 (*0-440-22195-1*) Dell.

Secret Years: (Showcase) Margot Dalton. (Superromance Ser.). 1995. mass mkt. 3.75 (*0-373-70638-3*, 1-70638-1) Harlequin Bks.

Secreta: Three Methods of Laying Gold Leaf. Joyce Grafe. LC 89-26593. (Illus.). 112p. 1990. reprint ed. pap. 12.95 (*0-87595-225-9*) Oregon Hist.

Secreta Secretorum. Aristotle. Tr. by Robert Copland. LC 71-26095. (English Experience Ser.: No. 220). 72p. 1970. reprint ed. 20.00 (*90-221-0220-3*) Walter J Johnson.

Secretarial Administration & Management. Daniel R. Boyd & Stephen D. Lewis. (Illus.). 550p. (C). 1985. student ed. 8.95 (*0-13-798315-8*) P-H.

Secretarial & Administrative Procedures. 3rd ed. Lucy M. Jennings. 576p. (C). 1989. text ed. 60.00 (*0-13-798349-2*) P-H.

Secretarial Assistant. Jack Rudman. (Career Examination Ser.: C-1464). 1994. pap. 19.95 (*0-8373-1464-X*) Nat Learn.

Secretarial Dental Assistant. Douglas. (Dental Assisting Procedures Ser.). 1976. teacher ed. 9.00 (*0-8273-0350-5*) Delmar.

Secretarial Duties. 9th ed. John Harrison. 384p. (Orig.). 1992. pap. 33.50 (*0-273-03828-1*, Pub. by Pitman Pub Ltd UK) Trans-Atl Phila.

***Secretarial Duties.** 10th ed. Harrison. 1996. pap. text ed. write for info. (*0-582-27844-9*, Pub. by Longman UK) Longman.

Secretarial English. Donald A. Sheff. (YA). (gr. 9-12). 1987. pap. text ed. 11.10 (*0-13-797770-0*, 17512) Prentice ESL.

Secretarial Handbook, 4 vols. rev. ed. Teena Sandstrom et al. (Speaking from Experience Ser.). 48p. 1981. Working Better Together: A Human Relations Guidebook for Office Professionals, 48p. pap. 7.50 (*1-877948-00-4*); Faster, Easier, Cheaper: A Quick Guide to Secretarial Efficiency, 48p. pap. 7.50 (*1-877948-01-2*); Working Smarter: A Time Management Guidebook for Secretaries, 48p. pap. 7.50 (*1-877948-02-0*); Be Yourself: A Guide to Self-Development, 47p. pap. 7.50 (*1-877948-03-9*) Prof Train TX.

Secretarial Handbook, 4 vols., Set. rev. ed. Teena Sandstrom et al. (Speaking from Experience Ser.). 1981. pap. 20.00 (*1-877948-04-7*) Prof Train TX.

Secretarial Office Procedures. Dorothy E. Lee et al. (Illus.). 400p. 1988. pap. text ed. 23.00 (*0-07-037050-8*) McGraw.

Secretarial Office Procedures. 2nd ed. Dorothy E. Lee, Jr. & Walter A. Brower. (Illus.). 416p. 1981. text ed. 29.95 (*0-07-037037-0*) McGraw.

Secretarial Office Procedures Supplement. 10th ed. Oliverio. (KM - Office Procedures Ser.). 1982. wbk. ed., pap. 18.95 (*0-538-11341-3*) S-W Pub.

Secretarial Practice: Syllabus. 2nd ed. Carl Salser et al. 1977. pap. text ed. 7.95 (*0-89420-044-5*, 218505) Natl Book.

Secretarial Practice: Syllabus. 2nd ed. Carl W. Salser & Charlotte A. Butsch. 1977. audio 101.00 (*0-89420-183-2*, 186700) Natl Book.

Secretarial Procedure & Administrative Work Assignments. 9th ed. Jackson & Rita S. Tilton. (KU - Office Procedures Ser.). 1987. pap. 24.95 (0-538-11791-5) S-W Pub.

Secretarial Procedures. Ed. by Stanley Thornes. (C). 1990. 90.00 (0-7487-0172-9, Pub. by Stanley Thornes UK) Trans-Atl Phila.

Secretarial Procedures: Theory & Applications. 2nd ed. Helen Harding. 208p. 1990. pap. 27.50 (0-273-03086-8, Pub. by Pitman Pub Ltd UK) Trans-Atl Phila.

Secretarial Procedures for the Automated Office. Dalton E. McFarland & Kitterman. (C). 1985. teacher ed. write for info. (0-8359-6598-8, Reston) P-H.

Secretarial Stenographer. Jack Rudman. (Career Examination Ser.: C-1465). 1994. pap. 23.95 (0-8373-1465-8) Nat Learn.

Secretarial Word Finder. Ed. by Linnea L. Ochs & Susan Van Der Reyden. LC 83-8640. 540p. 1983. 19.95 (0-13-798157-0, Busn) P-H.

Secretariat: The Making of a Champion. William Nack. (Quality Paperbacks Ser.). 342p. 1988. reprint ed. pap. 13.95 (0-306-80317-8) Da Capo.

Secretariat Making of a Champ. Nack. 1989. pap. text ed. 10.95 (0-306-88317-1) Da Capo.

Secretariat of the United Nations, Vol. 11. Sydney D. Bailey. LC 78-2880. (Carnegie Endowment for International Peace, United Nations Studies: No. 11). 132p. 1978. reprint ed. text ed. 45.00 (0-313-20338-5, BASU, Greenwood Pr) Greenwood.

***Secretaries of God: Women Prophets in Late Medieval & Early Modern England.** Diane Watt. 192p. (Orig.). 1997. 63.00 (0-85991-524-7) Boydell & Brewer.

Secretaries of State in Conference, 1985: Foreign Policy Options Available to the Newly Elected Administration. 1990. 5.00 (0-685-34499-1) Southern Ctr Intl Stud.

Secretaries of State, 1681-1782. Mark A. Thomson. 206p. 1968. reprint ed. 35.00 (0-7146-1521-8, BHA-01521, Pub. by F Cass Pubs UK) Intl Spec Bk.

Secretaries of the Moon: The Letters of Wallace Stevens & Jose Rodriguez Feo. Ed. by Beverly Coyle & Alan Filreis. LC 86-16835. x, 202p. 1986. text ed. 29.95 (0-8223-0670-0) Duke.

Secretaries Study: Directions for the Inditing of Letters. Thomas Gainsford. LC 74-80177. (English Experience Ser.: No. 658). 1974. reprint ed. 20.00 (90-221-0658-6) Walter J Johnson.

Secretary. Jack Rudman. (Career Examination Ser.: C-1466). 1994. pap. 19.95 (0-8373-1466-6) Nat Learn.

Secretary: A Manual of Writing Style & Handbook of Business English for Education Secretaries. Audrey Fatooh & Barbara R. Mauk. LC 96-3331. 1996. 23.95 (0-88280-129-5) ETC Pubns.

***Secretary: An Office Job Simulation.** 3rd ed. McIntosh. 1989. 57.95 (0-538-60083-7) S-W Pub.

Secretary - General & Satellite Diplomacy. Thomas E. Boudreau. 1984. pap. write for info. (0-87641-311-4) Carnegie Ethics & Intl Affairs.

Secretary & a Cook: Challenging Women's Wages in the Courts of the United States & Great Britain. Steven Willborn. 224p. 1989. 35.00 (0-87546-157-3, ILR Press); pap. 14.95 (0-87546-158-1, ILR Press) Cornell U Pr.

Secretary I. Jack Rudman. (Career Examination Ser.: C-3577). 1994. pap. 23.95 (0-8373-3577-9) Nat Learn.

Secretary II. Jack Rudman. (Career Examination Ser.: C-3578). 1994. pap. 27.95 (0-8373-3578-7) Nat Learn.

Secretary in the Letters to Paul. E. Randolph Richards. (WissUNT Neuen Testament Ser.). 280p. (Orig.). 1990. pap. 77.50 (3-16-145575-4, Pub. by J C B Mohr GW) Coronet Bks.

Secretary of Defense. Douglas Kinnard. LC 80-5178. 264p. 1981. 29.00 (0-8131-1434-9) U Pr of Ky.

Secretary of Defense Through Les Aspin. Bob Italia. Ed. by Rosemary Wallner. LC 93-28145. (All the President's Men & Women Ser.). 1993. lib. bdg. write for info. (1-56239-252-2) Abdo & Dghtrs.

Secretary of State. American Assembly Staff. LC 73-133511. (Select Bibliographies Reprint Ser.). 1977. 19.95 (0-8369-5543-9) Ayer.

Secretary of State. David Kynaston. (Illus.). 1988. 120.00 (0-900963-80-8, Pub. by T Dalton UK) St Mut.

Secretary of State. Ed. by Don K. Price. LC 60-53378. 1960. 3.50 (0-317-02964-9, 79749-C) Am Assembly.

Secretary of State: The Office & Duties. 3rd ed. Council of State Governments Staff. 105p. 1991. pap. 30.00 (0-87292-964-7, D-009-91) Coun State Govts.

Secretary of State Through Warren Christopher. John Hamilton. LC 93-22623. (All the President's Men & Women Ser.). 1993. lib. bdg. 14.98 (1-56239-250-6) Abdo & Dghtrs.

Secretary of the Interior's Standards for Rehabilitation & Guidelines for Rehabilitating Historic Buildings. 59p. 1990. pap. 3.00 (0-16-021067-4, S/N 024-005-01061-1) USGPO.

***Secretary of the Interior's Standards for the Treatment of Historic Properties: With Guidelines for the Treatment of Cultural Landscapes.** Charles A. Birnbaum et al. LC 96-37575. 1996. per., pap. 16.00 (0-16-048700-5, 024-005-01171-4) USGPO.

Secretary of the Interior's Standards for the Treatment of Historic Properties with Guidelines for Preserving Rehabilitating Restoring & Reconstructing Historic Buildings. Compiled by Kay D. Weeks & Anne E. Grimmer. 1995. 12.00 (0-16-048061-2, 024-005-01157-9) USGPO.

Secretary of the Treasury Through Lloyd Bentsen. John Hamilton. LC 93-11214. (All the President's Men & Women Ser.). (J). 1993. lib. bdg. 14.98 (1-56239-254-9) Abdo & Dghtrs.

Secretary on the Job. 3rd ed. Mary Witherow. 1983. text ed. 16.88 (0-07-071187-9) McGraw.

Secretary Parables. Nancy Lagomarsino. LC 91-16373. 72p. (Orig.). 1991. pap. 9.95 (0-914086-92-8) Alicejamesbooks.

Secretary (Stenography) GS5. Jack Rudman. (Career Examination Ser.: C-706). 1994. pap. 23.95 (0-8373-0706-6) Nat Learn.

Secretary to Paralegal: A Career Manual & Guide. Lesley J. Prendergast. LC 84-6641. 272p. 1984. 24.95 (0-87624-510-6, Inst Busn Plan) P-H.

Secretary to the Delegation: A Filmplay. Thomas J. Cox. 119p. (Orig.). 1991. pap. 14.50 (1-879710-01-3) Riverside FL.

Secretary to the Spirits. Ishmael Reed. (Poets Ser.). (Illus.). 42p. 1977. 11.95 (0-88357-057-2); pap. 4.95 (0-88357-058-0) NOK Pubs.

Secretary's Complete Self-Training Manual. Bureau of Business Practice Staff. LC 92-19850. 1992. pap. text ed. 19.95 (0-13-799529-6) P-H.

Secretary's Factomatic. Ayesha Chopra. 1991. pap. text ed. 39.95 (0-13-799313-7, Busn) P-H.

Secretary's Friend: The Office Management Manual. Anne Morton. LC 86-45541. 256p. 1986. 14.95 (0-933051-16-6) Lowen Pub.

Secretary's Friend: The Office Management Manual. 2nd rev. ed. Anne Morton. 256p. 1987. pap. 9.95 (0-933051-33-6) Lowen Pub.

Secretary's Guide to Modern English Usage. 2nd rev. ed. Jean C. Vermes & Carol M. Barnum. 288p. 1991. text ed. 29.95 (0-13-796921-X, 180701) P-H.

Secretary's Handbook. 10th ed. Sarah A. Taintor & Kate M. Monro. Ed. by Margaret D. Shertzer. 608p. 1988. 19.95 (0-02-610211-0) Macmillan.

Secretary's Index to English. Jean C. Vermes. 1966. 17.50 (0-13-797472-8, Parker Publishing Co) P-H.

Secretary's International Dictionary: English-Spanish-French. B. Lapeyre. 165p. (ENG, FRE & SPA.). 1992. 24.95 (0-7859-7512-8, 8428319456) Fr & Eur.

Secretary's New Guide to Dealing with People. Helen N. Saputo & Nancy G. Rutherford. (Illus.). 252p. 1986. 21.95 (0-13-797382-9) P-H.

Secretary's Portable Answer Book. Peggy J. Grillot & Lynda R. Abegg. LC 93-47896. 1994. text ed. 27.95 (0-13-042466-8); pap. text ed. 14.95 (0-13-042458-7) P-H.

***Secretary's Portfolio of Instant Letters.** Anne Wayman. 280p. 24.95 (0-13-798521-5) P-H.

Secretary's Quick Reference Handbook. 3rd ed. Sheryl Lindsell-Roberts. (Illus.). 304p. 1992. pap. 8.00 (0-13-799396-X, Arco) Macmillan Gen Ref.

Secretary's Quick Reference Handbook. 4th ed. Lindsell Roberts. 1995. pap. 8.00 (0-671-89918-X) S&S Trade.

Secretary's Secret Weapon: Arm Yourself for Success with 7 Essential Communication Skills. Bobbi Linkemer. Ed. by Mary Glenn. LC 96-18069. 192p. (Orig.). 1996. pap. 17.95 (0-8144-7895-6) AMACOM.

Secretary's Standard Reference Manual & Guide. Mary A. DeVries. (Illus.). 1986. 19.95 (0-13-797712-3, Parker Publishing Co) P-H.

***Secretary's Survival Manual.** 2nd ed. Sandra Tomkins. (Careers & Testing Ser.). 1991. pap. 14.95 (0-7494-0432-9) Kogan Page Ltd.

Secrete Correspondences of the Leaders of Governments in the Year Nineteen Forty-Four & Earlier Years. Hungarian Historical Research Society Staff. LC 80-65046. Orig. Title: Allamvezetok Titkos Levelei Az 1944 Ev Elotti Es Az 1944 Evbol. 110p. 1980. pap. 7.95 (0-935484-04-3) Universe Pub Co.

Secreti Lisistrata. Vremya Temnoti: Secrets of Lisistrata, Times of Darkness. Roman Gershgorin. (Illus.). 254p. (Orig.). (RUS.). 1992. pap. 3.00 (1-881910-03-2) Adventure NY.

Secretin, Cholecystokinin-Pancreozymin & Gastrin. Ed. by T. E. Jorpes & Viktor Mutt. (Handbook of Experimental Pharmacology Ser.: Vol. 34). (Illus.). 350p. 1973. 144.00 (0-387-05952-0) Spr-Verlag.

Secretion & Action of Gonadotropins. Ed. by B. Runnebaum et al. (Illus.). 105p. 1984. 47.95 (0-387-13854-4) Spr-Verlag.

Secretion & Its Control. Ed. by Gerry S. Oxford & Clay Armstrong. 347p. 1989. 50.00 (0-87470-045-0) Rockefeller.

Secreto de Amar & de Ser Amado. Josh McDowell. Tr. by Juan S. Araujo from ENG. 272p. (SPA.). (C). 1988. pap. 5.95 (0-88113-271-3) Edit Betania.

Secreto de Awa. Francois Pratte. (Coleccion Rosa Ser.). (Illus.). 60p. (SPA.). (J). (gr. 5 up). 1994. pap. 5.95 (958-07-0069-9) Firefly Bks Ltd.

Secreto de la Felicidad. enl. rev. ed. Billy Graham. 172p. (SPA.). 1987. pap. 10.50 (0-311-46108-5) Casa Bautista.

***Secreto de la Hermana Mayor, el Maria - The Big Sister's Secret.** Mackenzie. (SPA.). (J). write for info. (1-56063-700-5) Editorial Unilit.

Secreto de la Llama - the Llama's Secret: Una Leyenda Peruana. Argentina Palacios. LC 93-21436. (J). (gr. 4-7). 1993. lib. bdg. 13.95 (0-8167-3123-3) Troll Communs.

Secreto de la Llama - the Llama's Secret: Una Leyenda Peruana. Argentina Palacios. LC 93-21436. (J). (gr. 4-7). 1997. pap. 4.95 (0-8167-3072-5) Troll Communs.

Secreto de la Oracion Diaria. Basilea Schlink. 96p. 2.95 (0-88113-201-2) Edit Betania.

Secreto de la Oracion Tenaz. John Bisagno. Tr. by Rhode Flores from ENG. 172p. (SPA.). 1988. pap. 6.99 (0-311-40049-3) Casa Bautista.

Secreto de la Vida Cristiana. Juan C. Ryle. 252p. (SPA.). 1988. reprint ed. pap. 7.99 (0-85151-412-X) Banner of Truth.

Secreto de los Quince Segundos. Larry Jones. 149p. (SPA.). 1991. pap. 5.99 (1-56063-192-9, 498408) Editorial Unilit.

Secreto de los Secretos: A Castilian Version. Ed. by Philip Jones. ix, 111p. 1995. 59.50 (1-882528-12-3) Scripta.

***Secreto de los Toros.** Bernardo. (SPA.). 1997. pap. 12.00 (0-684-83299-2, Simon Aguilar) S&S Trade.

Secreto de los Toros. Jose Raul Bernardo. 336p. (SPA.). 1996. 22.00 (0-684-82353-5, Simon Aguilar) S&S Trade.

Secreto de Selena. Arraras. 1997. pap. 12.00 (0-684-83135-X) S&S Trade.

Secreto del Amor. Carlos Gonzalez. 1982. write for info. (1-56491-001-6) Imagine Pubs.

Secreto del Unicornio. Herge. (Illus.). 62p. (SPA.). (J). 19.95 (0-8288-5067-4) Fr & Eur.

Secreto en la Caja de Fostoros: The Secret in the Matchbox. Val Willis. (J). (ps-3). 1993. 16.00 (0-374-36701-9, Mirasol) FS&G.

Secreto en la Mujer. Andres De Claramonte. Ed. by Alfredo R. Lopez-Vasquez. (Textos B Ser.: No. 35). 238p. (SPA.). (C). 1991. 35.00 (1-85566-009-1, Pub. by Tamesis Bks Ltd UK) Boydell & Brewer.

Secreto Espiritual de Hudson Taylor. H. G. Taylor. 256p. (SPA.). 1988. mass mkt. 5.99 (0-8254-1703-1, Edit Portavoz) Kregel.

***Secreto Mas Grande del Mundo.** Og Mandino. 186p. (Orig.). (ENG & SPA.). 1997. pap. 14.95 (0-8119-0864-X) LIFETIME.

***Secreto Mas Raro.** Earl Nightingale & Diana Nightingale. Tr. by Fred De Rosset from ENG. (Earl Nightingale's Library of Little Gems: Vol. 1). 78p. (Orig.). (SPA.). Date not set. pap. 7.95 (0-9655760-2-7) Keys Co Inc.

***Secreto Mas Raro.** Earl Nightingale & Diana Nightingale. Tr. by Fred De Rosset. (Earl Nightingale's Library of Little Gems). 78p. (ENG & SPA.). Date not set. pap. write for info. incl. audio (0-9655760-6-X) Keys Co Inc.

Secreto Para Cambiar Su Familia y Su Mundo. Victor Ricardo. 26p. 1992. pap. text ed. 1.00 (1-885630-09-3) HLM Producciones.

Secreto Para Vencer el Temor. Don Gosset. 78p. (SPA.). 1994. pap. write for info. (0-938127-18-7) Gospel Pr FL.

Secreto Trimetrico. Marvin Pietruszka. 320p. (Orig.). (SPA.). 1989. pap. 7.95 (0-934290-42-3) Quail Valley.

Secretory Immune System. Ed. by Jerry R. McGhee & Jiri Mestecky. 1983. 175.00 (0-89766-210-5); pap. 175.00 (0-89766-211-3, VOL. 409) NY Acad Sci.

Secretory Otitis Media & Its Sequelae. Jacob Sade. LC 79-13663. (Monographs in Clinical Otolaryngology: No. 1). (Illus.). 333p. reprint ed. pap. 95.00 (0-7837-2572-8, 2042731) Bks Demand.

Secretory Tumors of the Pituitary Gland. Ed. by Peter M. Black et al. LC 84-15991. (Progress in Endocrine Research & Therapy Ser.: No. 1). (Illus.). 416p. 1984. reprint ed. pap. 118.60 (0-7837-9565-3, 2060314) Bks Demand.

Secretos De Como Triunfar En la Vida: Su Guia Personal. George Gascon & Mariann Gascon. (Illus.). 115p. (Orig.). (SPA.). 1993. pap. 20.00 (0-9635655-0-8) Most Ent.

***Secretos de la Alegria: Una Tesoreria de Sabiduria.** Running Press Staff. (SPA.). 1997. 4.95 (0-7624-0045-5) Running Pr.

Secretos de la Oracion. F. J. Huegel. Orig. Title: Secrets of Prayer. 128p. (SPA.). 1980. mass mkt. 4.50 (0-8254-1323-0, Edit Portavoz) Kregel.

Secretos de la Santeria. Agun Efunde. LC 78-60113. (Coleccion Ebano y Canela). (Illus.). 117p. (SPA.). 1996. reprint ed. pap. 12.00 (0-89729-204-9) Ediciones.

Secretos de la Uncion. Nahum Rosario. 120p. (Orig.). 1993. pap. 7.00 (0-9634761-1-4) Pub Maranatha.

Secretos De las Plantas. Eyewitness Staff. 1995. 18.95 (84-372-3719-X) Santillana.

Secretos de Sus Manos: La Clave del Exito y de la Felicidad. Editorial America, S. A. Staff. Ed. by Maria E. Del Real. (Illus.). 296p. (Orig.). (SPA.). 1987. pap. 4.75 (0-944499-27-9) Editorial Amer.

Secretos en las Lineas de Sus Manos. Indira Shankar. (Illus.). 112p. (Orig.). (SPA.). 1985. pap. 2.95 (0-939193-02-7) Edit Concepts.

Secrets. (Sweet Valley High Ser.: No. 2). 118p. (J). (gr. 6 up). 1984. 3.99 (0-553-27578-X) Bantam.

Secrets. (Brookville Chese Committee Ser. - Tamar Bks.: Vol. IV). 1993. pap. 7.99 (0-89906-139-7) Mesorah Pubns.

Secrets. (J). pap. 1.95 (0-590-31346-0) Scholastic Inc.

Secrets. Alane Ferguson. LC 96-38782. (J). 1997. 16.00 (0-689-80313-3, S&S Bks Young Read) S&S Childrens.

***Secrets.** Robin J. Gunn. 263p. (Orig.). 1994. pap. 8.99 (0-614-31006-7, Palisades OR) Multnomah Pubs.

Secrets. Douglas Huebler. 1977. pap. 6.50 (0-89439-801-6) Printed Matter.

Secrets. Kelvin C. James. 1994. pap. 10.00 (0-679-75546-2, Vin) Random.

Secrets. Brenda Joyce. 416p. (Orig.). 1993. mass mkt. 6.50 (0-380-77139-X) Avon.

Secrets. Angus Mackenzie. LC 96-22685. 1997. 26.00 (0-520-20020-9) U CA Pr.

Secrets. Katharine Marlowe. 400p. 1993. mass mkt., pap. text ed. 4.99 (0-8439-3415-8) Dorchester Pub Co.

Secrets. Leslea Newman. LC 90-31303. 206p. (Orig.). 1990. pap. 8.95 (0-934678-24-3) New Victoria Pubs.

Secrets. Sunny Oaks & Blaine M. Yorgason. LC 92-33959. 504p. 1992. 15.95 (0-87579-657-5) Deseret Bk.

***Secrets.** Luis Royo. (Illus.). 80p. 1996. pap. 16.95 (1-56163-162-0) NBM.

Secrets. Ellen B. Senisi. LC 94-39763. (J). (gr. k-2). 1995. pap. 13.99 (0-525-45393-8) Dutton Child Bks.

Secrets. Danielle Steel. 336p. 1985. 19.95 (0-385-29418-2) Delacorte.

Secrets. Danielle Steel. 448p. 1986. mass mkt. 6.50 (0-440-17648-4) Dell.

Secrets. Ed. by Linny Stovall. (Left Bank Books Ser.: No. 9). (Illus.). 160p. (Orig.). 1995. pap. 11.95 (0-936085-33-9) Blue Heron OR.

***Secrets.** Jan E. Wallace. 213p. (Orig.). 1998. mass mkt. 4.99 (1-55237-381-9, Pub. by Comnwlth Pub CN) Partners Pubs Grp.

Secrets. Frances Wilshire. 1941. pap. 4.95 (0-87516-318-1) DeVorss.

Secrets. large type ed. Francine Pascal. (Sweet Valley High Ser.: No. 2). 118p. (J). (gr. 5-8). 1989. reprint ed. 9.50 (1-55905-001-2, Gareth Stevens Inc); reprint ed. lib. bdg. 10.50 (1-55905-011-X, Gareth Stevens Inc) Grey Castle.

Secrets, Bk. 1. Robin J. Gunn. 263p. (Orig.). 1994. pap. 8.99 (0-88070-721-6, Palisades OR) Multnomah Pubs.

Secrets: A Collection of Short Stories. Bo Yang. Tr. by David Deterding. 175p. (CHI.). 1985. 12.95 (0-88727-037-9); pap. 8.95 (0-88727-051-4) Cheng & Tsui.

Secrets: A Drama in One Act. Source Teen Theatre Staff & Planned Parenthood Assoc. of Southwest Florida, Inc., Staff. (Young Adult Awareness Plays Ser.). (Illus.). 30p. (Orig.). (YA). (gr. 6-12). 1995. pap. 4.00 (0-88680-402-7, 402-7) I E Clark.

Secrets: A Practical Guide to Undreamed-of Possibilities. Christina Thomas. (Illus.). 220p. (Orig.). 1989. pap. 9.95 (0-9622119-0-7) Chela Pubns.

***Secrets: A Writer in the Cold War.** Paul Brodeur. LC 96-43622. 1997. 24.95 (0-571-19907-0) Faber & Faber.

Secrets: Boyhood in a Jewish Hotel, 1932-1954. Ronald Hayman. LC 86-82060. (Illus.). 224p. 8500. 25.00 (0-7206-0642-X, Pub. by P Owen Ltd UK) Dufour.

Secrets: On the Ethics of Concealment & Revelation. Sissela Bok. 1989. pap. 13.00 (0-679-72473-7, Vin) Random.

Secrets: Therapy for Adults Molested As Children. Bobbi Hobbs. Ed. by F. Beard. 150p. 1988. 23.95 (0-941819-16-7) Windrose Pubs CA.

Secrets Vol. 1: The Best in Women's Sensual Fiction, Vol. 1. Alice Gaines et al. Ed. by Alexandria Kendall. 214p. (Orig.). 1995. pap. 12.99 (0-9648942-0-3) Red Sage.

***Secrets Vol. 2: The Best in Women's Sensual Fiction. Bonnie Hamre et al. 210p. (Orig.). 1996. pap. 12.99 (0-9648942-1-1) Red Sage.**
In SECRETS VOLUME 2 readers will find the same daring, adventurous, have your deepest desires fulfilled stories, as they did in SECRETS VOLUME 1. Readers embraced these stories for their liberated plots. "Wonderful entertaining escapism! It's delightful having erotica written by women & for women," & "Finally erotic romantic fiction in the USA." Bonnie Hamre's new intriguing Regency tale is titled SNOWBOUND, a marriage-shy, devilishly handsome, Earl is teased & tortured with his own desires by a woman who can equal his overpowering sensuality. In Mexico 1865, Susan Paul, creates SAVAGE GARDEN, where a dark, sexy hero is truly dangerous to a French beauty as they fight a sensual war. Reach for the stars in Angela Knight's ROARKE'S PRISONER. A science fiction swashbuckling fantasy, ultra sexy captive/captor tale. There are things that can be done in zero gravity that I never thought possible! Doreen DeSalvo's SURROGATE LOVER, is a contemporary tale about a man who thinks he has all the answers, well he is a surrogate sex partner,... that is, until he meets Sarah. Read with lots of chocolate & a nice romance cover model at all times. Not responsible for singed fingers. *Publisher Provided Annotation.*

Secrets about Men Every Woman Should Know. Barbara De Angelis. 400p. 1991. mass mkt. 6.99 (0-440-20841-6) Dell.

Secrets about Men Every Woman Should Know. Barbara De Angelis. 304p. 1992. pap. 10.95 (0-440-50538-0, Dell Trade Pbks) Dell.

***Secrets & Benefits of Internal Qigong Cultivation: Lectures by Qigong Master Dr. Yan Xin.** write for info. (0-614-28577-1) Amber Leaf.

Secrets & Lies. Marilyn Kaye. (Video High Ser.: No. 8). 224p. 1995. mass mkt. 3.99 (0-8217-4915-3, Zebra Kensgtn) Kensgtn Pub Corp.

***Secrets & Lies.** Mike Leigh. 1997. pap. text ed. 13.95 (0-571-19291-2) Faber & Faber.

Secrets & Mysteries of Hawaii. Pila of Hawaii. 244p. 1995. pap. 10.95 (1-55874-362-6, 3626) Health Comm.

***Secrets & Scents.** 496p. 1997. mass mkt. 6.95 (0-7867-0499-3) Carroll & Graf.

Secrets & Surprises. Ann Beattie. 1991. pap. 11.00 (0-679-73193-8) McKay.

Secrets & Sympathy: Forms of Disclosure in Hawthorne's Novels. Gordon Hutner. LC 87-20583. 232p. 1988. 35.00 (0-8203-0992-3) U of Ga Pr.

Secrets Aren't (Always) for Keeps: Featuring Jennifer Hauser. Barbara Aiello & Jeffrey Shulman. (Kids on the Block Bks.). (Illus.). 48p. (J). (gr. 5-8). 1991. lib. bdg. 13.98 (0-8050-3069-7) TFC Bks NY.

***Secrets at Hidden Valley.** Willo D. Roberts. (J). (gr. 4-8). 1997. 16.00 (0-614-29094-5, Atheneum Bks Young) S&S Childrens.

Secrets Can Kill. Carolyn Keene. (Nancy Drew Files Ser.: Vol. 1). (YA). 1986. mass mkt. 3.99 (0-671-74674-X) PB.

Secrets Can Kill. large type ed. Carolyn Keene. (Nancy Drew Files Ser.). (J). (gr. 5-10). 1988. 9.50 (0-942545-22-2); lib. bdg. 10.50 (0-942545-27-3) Grey Castle.

An Asterisk (*) at the beginning of an entry indicates that the title is appearing in BIP for the first time.

Secrets of Consulting: A Guide to Giving & Getting Advice Successfully. Virginia M. Satir. LC 85-72964. (Illus.). 248p. (Orig.). 1985. pap. 28.00 (0-932633-01-3) Dorset Hse Pub Co.

Secrets of Cooking: Armenian, Lebanese, Persian. Ed. by Linda Chirinian. (Cookbook Ser.). (Illus.). 264p. 29.95 (0-9617033-0-X) Lionhart Inc Pub.

Secrets of Corvette Detailing. Michael Antonick. (Illus.). 96p. (Orig.). 1988. pap. text ed. 14.95 (0-933534-28-0) M Bruce Assocs.

Secrets of Cranberry Beach. Ted M. Murphy. LC 95-21033. (Belltown Mystery Ser.: No. 2). (J). 1996. pap. 4.95 (0-382-39303-1) Silver Burdett Pr.

Secrets of Cromwell Crossing. large type ed. Daoma Winston. 336p. 1986. 25.99 (0-7089-1452-7) Ulverscroft.

Secrets of Cruising: North to Alaska. Hugo Anderson. 256p. 1993. pap. 16.95 (0-945989-23-7) Anderson WA.

***Secrets of Cruising British Columbia Coast.** H. Anderson. 1996. pap. 16.95 (0-945989-25-3) Anderson WA.

Secrets of Cuban Entertaining: A Menu Cookbook. Piedad Robertson et al. 133p. 5.95 (0-941072-00-2) Southern Herit.

Secrets of Deciding Wisely: How Our Choices Change Our Lives. Ron Kincaid. LC 94-412. 180p. (Orig.). 1994. pap. 9.99 (0-8308-1633-X, 1633, Saltshaker Bk) InterVarsity.

S

Secrets of Delphi 2 No. 2: Exposing Undocumented Features & the VCL. Ray Lischner et al. (Illus.). 890p. 1996. 59.99 (1-57169-026-3, Waite Grp Pr) Mac Comp Pub.

Secrets of Doctor John Dee: Being His Alchemical, Astrological, Qabalistic & Rosicrucian Arcana: Together with the Trees of the Planets. Ed. by Gordon James & J. D. Holmes. (Illus.). 184p. 1995. pap. 19.95 (1-55818-317-5) Holmes Pub.

Secrets of Dr. Taverner. Dion Fortune. 1989. pap. 10.95 (0-89804-137-6) Ariel GA.

Secrets of Dynamic Communication: Preparing & Delivering Powerful Speeches. Ken Davis. 160p. 1991. pap. 10.99 (0-310-53461-5) Zondervan.

Secrets of Earth & Sea. Edwin R. Lankester. LC 76-93352. (Essay Index Reprint Ser.). 1977. 21.95 (0-8369-1301-9) Ayer.

***Secrets of Echo Moon.** large type ed. Jill Giencke. LC 97-21452. 1997. write for info. (0-7862-1188-1) Thorndike Pr.

Secrets of Effective GUI Design. Mark Minasi. LC 93-87704. 225p. 1994. pap. 19.99 (0-7821-1495-4) Sybex.

Secrets of Effective Leadership - A Practical Guide to Success. 2nd rev. ed. Fred A. Manske, Jr. (Illus.). 210p. 1990. 19.95 (0-943703-03-4) Leader Educ Dev.

Secrets of El Dorado: Colombia. German Arciniegas et al. (Illus.). 240p. 1992. 65.00 (0-252-01914-8) U of Ill Pr.

Secrets of Electricity, Magnetism & Gravity Series, 4 Bks. Charles R. Storey. Incl. Grand Unified Theory Made Easy. 93p. 1993. student ed., pap. 19.95 (0-9638766-2-7); Grand Unified Theory Made Easy. 93p. 1993. 29.95 (0-9638766-1-9); Electricity, Magnetism, Gravity, & the Big Bang. (Illus.). 120p. 29.95 (0-9638766-3-5); Electricity, Magnetism, Gravity, & the Big Bang. (Illus.). 120p. student ed. 19.95 (0-9638766-4-3); 89.80 (0-9638766-6-X) Am Sci Innovat.

Secrets of Emotional Healing. J. Donald Walters. 72p. 1995. 5.95 (1-56589-044-2) Crystal Clarity.

Secrets of Entrepreneurial Leadership: Building Top Performance Through Trust & Teamwork. Ted Nicholas. Orig. Title: Management for Entrepreneurs. 149p. 1992. 19.95 (0-7931-0493-9, 5615-6101) Dearborn Finan.

Secrets of Eternal Youth. Victor G. Rocine. (Orig.). reprint ed. spiral bd. 10.50 (0-7873-0733-5) Hlth Research.

Secrets of Eternal Youth: Why Diet Should Be Based upon Bio-Chemical Food Analysis for Health & Long Life. Victor G. Rocine. (Longevity Ser.). 1991. lib. bdg. 79.95 (0-8490-4103-1) Gordon Pr.

Secrets of Eternity. Annalee Skarin. 287p. 1960. pap. 6.95 (0-87516-092-1) DeVorss.

Secrets of Farand Isle. Patricia Robinson. LC 96-96142. 192p. 1996. 19.95 (0-8034-9174-3) Bouregy.

Secrets of Fat-Free Baking: Over 130 Low-Fat & Fat-Free Recipes for Scrumptious & Simple-to-Make Cakes, Cookies, Brownies, Muffins, Pies, Breads, Plus Many Other Tasty Goodies. Sandra Woodruff. LC 94-21307. (Illus.). 208p. pap. 13.95 (0-89529-630-6) Avery Pub.

Secrets of Fat-Free Chinese Cooking: Over 130 Fat-Free & Low-Fat Traditional Chinese Recipes - From Egg Rolls to Almond Cookies. Ying Chang Compestine. LC 96-49697. (Illus.). 153p. Date not set. pap. 14.95 (0-89529-735-3) Avery Pub.

Secrets of Fat-Free Cooking: Over 150 Fat-Free & Low-Fat Recipes from Breakfast to Dinner - Appetizers to Desserts. Sandra Woodruff. LC 94-21307. (Illus.). 192p. Date not set. pap. 13.95 (0-89529-668-3) Avery Pub.

***Secrets of Fat-Free Indian Cooking: Over 150 Low-Fat & Fat-Free, Traditional & Contemporary.** Priya Kulkarni. 1997. pap. 14.95 (0-89529-805-8) Avery Group Inc.

Secrets of Fat-Free Italian Cooking: Over 130 Low-Fat & Fat-Free, Traditional & Contemporary Recipes - from Antipasto to Ziti. Sandra Woodruff. (Illus.). 240p. 1996. pap. 14.95 (0-89529-748-5) Avery Pub.

***Secrets of Fat-Free Kosher Cooking: Over 150 Low-Fat & Fat-Free, Traditional & Contemporary.** Deborah Bernstein. 1997. pap. 14.95 (0-89529-806-6) Avery Group Inc.

Secrets of Finding Unclaimed Money. Richard S. Johnson. LC 96-439. 192p. 1996. 11.95 (1-877639-40-0, MIE Pub) Military Information.

***Secrets of Freemasonry.** Elijah Muhammad. 64p. 1994. pap. text ed. 6.95 (1-884855-05-9) Secretarius.

Secrets of Friendship. J. Donald Walters. (Illus.). 66p. (Orig.). 1989. pap. 4.95 (0-916124-60-6, CCP21) Crystal Clarity.

Secrets of Friendship. J. Donald Walters. (Illus.). 66p. (Orig.). 1993. 5.95 (1-56589-026-4) Crystal Clarity.

Secrets of Glader: Minnesota's Oldest Swedish Cemetery. Robert B. Porter. (Illus.). 230p. 1989. pap. 12.95 (0-933565-06-2) Porter Pub Co.

***Secrets of God's Mystical Oneness: Asrar al-Towhid.** Muhammab I. Munawwar. 665p. 1996. pap. 28.00 (0-614-21342-8, 1401) Kazi Pubns.

Secrets of God's Mystical Oneness (Asrar al-Towhid) The Spiritual Stations of Shaikh Abu-Sa'id. Mohammad E. Monavvar. Tr. by John O'Kane from PER. (Persian Heritage Ser.: No. 38). 670p. (C). 1992. pap. text ed. 28.00 (0-939214-88-1); lib. bdg. 55.00 (0-939214-87-3) Mazda Pubs.

***Secrets of Golgotha: The Lost History of Jesus' Crucifixion.** 2nd rev. ed. Ernst L. Martin. (Illus.). 466p. 1996. pap. 18.95 (0-945657-86-2) Acad Scriptural Knowledge.

Secrets of Good French Cooking. Pierre Paillon. (Illus.). 192p. 1996. text ed. 55.00 (0-471-16062-8) Wiley.

Secret(s) of Good Patient Care: Thoughts on Medicine in the 21st Century. William C. Felch. LC 95-25334. 208p. 1996. text ed. 52.95 (0-275-95448-X, Praeger Pubs) Greenwood.

***Secrets of Grandmaster Chess.** 2nd rev. ed. John Nunn. (New American Batsford Chess Library). 288p. 1997. pap. 26.95 (1-879479-54-0) ICE WA.

***Secrets of Gravity & Motion.** Henry H. Gwillim. (Illus.). ii, 126p. (Orig.). 1996. pap. text ed. 12.95 (0-9653134-0-9) H H Gwillim.

Secrets of Green-Sand Casting. 1983. reprint ed. pap. 9.95 (0-917914-08-2) Lindsay Pubns.

Secrets of Gypsy Dream Reading. Raymond Buckland. LC 90-39288. (New Age Ser.). (Illus.). 224p. (Orig.). 1990. mass mkt. 3.95 (0-87542-086-9) Llewellyn Pubns.

Secrets of Gypsy Fortunetelling. Raymond Buckland. LC 88-45196. (New Age Ser.). (Illus.). 240p. 1988. mass mkt. 4.99 (0-87542-051-6) Llewellyn Pubns.

Secrets of Gypsy Love Magick. Raymond Buckland. LC 89-77239. (New Age Ser.). (Illus.). 176p. (Orig.). 1990. mass mkt. 4.99 (0-87542-053-2) Llewellyn Pubns.

Secrets of Hakkoryu Jujutsu: Shodan Tactics. Dennis G. Palumbo. (Illus.). 144p. 1987. pap. 12.50 (0-87364-422-0) Paladin Pr.

Secrets of Happiness. J. Donald Walters. (Illus.). 68p. (Orig.). 1987. pap. 4.95 (0-916124-39-8, CCP14) Crystal Clarity.

Secrets of Happiness. J. Donald Walters. (Illus.). 68p. (Orig.). 1993. 5.95 (1-56589-025-6) Crystal Clarity.

Secrets of Happy People: Learning How to Be Happy & Enthusiastic. Michael P. Wilens. (Orig.). 1995. pap. 10.00 (0-9642914-0-1) Toby Pubng.

Secrets of Harry Bright. Joseph Wambaugh. 320p. 1986. mass mkt. 6.50 (0-553-27430-9) Bantam.

***Secrets of Hatha Vidya: As Disclosed by Svatmarama in Hathapradipika.** Ed. & Tr. by Vijayendra Pratap from SAN. LC 96-68803. (Illus.). 160p. (Orig.). 1996. mass mkt. 9.25 (0-944731-02-3) Sky Fnd.

Secrets of Health & Beauty: How to Make Yourself Over. Linda A. Clark. 1969. 12.95 (0-8159-6807-8) Devin.

Secrets of Hebrew Words. Benjamin Blech. LC 90-48735. 248p. 1993. 30.00 (0-87668-610-2) Aronson.

Secrets of Hebrew Words. Benjamin Blech. LC 90-48735. 248p. 1997. pap. 20.00 (1-56821-918-0) Aronson.

Secrets of Hiding. Albert. (J). Date not set. pap. 4.95 (0-02-041130-8) S&S Childrens.

Secrets of Highly Effective Meetings. Maria M. Shelton & Laurie K. Bauer. Ed. by Jerry L. Herman & Janice L. Herman. (Road Maps to Success Ser.). 64p. 1994. pap. 11.95 (0-8039-6133-2) Corwin Pr.

Secrets of Hollywood Special Effects. Robert E. McCarthy. 708p. 1992. 44.95 (0-240-80108-3, Focal) Buttrwrth-Heinemann.

Secrets of Home Theater & High Fidelity. John E. Johnson, Jr. 32p. 1994. pap. 3.95 (0-9643759-0-7) Sci Design.

Secrets of Hoshis Island: Unauthorized Pocket Guide to Super Mario World 2 for SNES. Bradygames Staff & Christine Watson. 1995. 7.99 (1-56686-518-2) Brady Pub.

Secrets of Houdini. J. Cannell. 7.95 (0-685-47573-5) Wehman.

Secrets of Houdini. J. C. Cannell. LC 72-93609. (Illus.). 288p. 1973. reprint ed. pap. 7.95 (0-486-22913-0) Dover.

Secrets of How to Advertise in the Yellow Pages: Without the Walking Fingers Walking All over You. Arri. Ed. by Robert Mecham. (Illus.). 125p. student ed. 29.95 (0-9638138-0-3) Ad Response.

Secrets of Hypnotism. Sydney J. Van Pelt. 1970. pap. 5.00 (0-87980-135-2) Wilshire.

Secrets of Inner Peace. J. Donald Walters. (Illus.). 66p. (Orig.). 1990. pap. 4.95 (0-916124-61-4, CCP22) Crystal Clarity.

Secrets of Inner Peace. J. Donald Walters. (Illus.). 66p. (Orig.). 1993. 5.95 (1-56589-027-2) Crystal Clarity.

Secrets of Inspired Cold Calling. James D. Gamble. Ed. by Barbara Gaenzler. 106p. (Orig.). 1996. pap. 9.95 (0-9617220-1-0) Tanro Co.

Secrets of International Identity Change: New I. D. in Canada, England, Australia & New Zealand. Tony Newborn. (Illus.). 120p. 1985. pap. 17.95 (0-87364-532-4) Paladin Pr.

Secrets of Investigating Discrimination Complaints. 2nd ed. William H. Truesdell. 170p. (Orig.). 1995. pap. text ed. 89.95 (1-879876-28-0) Mgmt Advantage.

Secrets of Japanese Astrology: The Science of Kigaku. Takeo Mori & Dragen Milenkovic. Tr. by Patricia Robinson from CZE. LC 92-46664. (Illus.). 144p. (ENG & JPN.). 1993. pap. 9.95 (0-8348-0290-2, Tengu Bks) Weatherhill.

Secrets of Jesuit Breadmaking: Recipes & Traditions from Jesuit Bakers Around the World. Rick Curry. 1995. pap. 16.50 (0-06-095118-4, PL) HarpC.

Secrets of Journalism in Russia: Mass Media under Gorbachev & Yeltsin. George N. Vachnadze. 427p. 1992. lib. bdg. 79.00 (1-56072-081-6) Nova Sci Pubs.

Secrets of Joy: A Treasury of Wisdom. (Miniature Editions Ser.). (Illus.). 128p. 1995. 4.95 (1-56138-516-6, Running Pr Mini Edtns) Running Pr.

Secrets of Judo. Jiichi Watanabe & Lindy Avakian. LC 59-14089. (Illus.). 192p. 1959. 19.95 (0-8048-0516-4) C E Tuttle.

Secrets of Judo. Jilchi Watanabe & Lindy Avakian. LC 59-14089. (Illus.). 192p. 1989. pap. 12.95 (0-8048-1631-X) C E Tuttle.

Secrets of Kaidara. Hyacinthe Vulliez. Tr. by Gwen Marsh from FRE. (Tales of Heaven & Earth Ser.). (Illus.). 40p. (J). (gr. 5 up). 1997. lib. bdg. 14.95 (0-88682-823-6) Creative Ed.

Secrets of Lactose-Free Cooking: Over 150 Easy-to-Make & Delicious Dairy-Free Recipes - From Breakfast to Dinner. Arlene Burlant. LC 95-50595. 192p. 1996. pap. 13.95 (0-89529-724-8) Avery Pub.

Secrets of Lake Success. Janet Quin-Harkin. 1993. mass mkt. 4.99 (0-87086-014-3) Tor Bks.

Secrets of Leadership. Sue Vineyard & Rick Lynch. 1991. pap. 11.00 (0-911029-31-1) Heritage Arts.

Secrets of Leadership. J. Donald Walters. 68p. 1993. 5.95 (1-56589-034-5) Crystal Clarity.

Secrets of Life. Stuart Wilde. 280p. (Orig.). pap. 9.95 (1-56170-164-5, 191) Hay House.

Secrets of Life. Stuart Wilde. (Illus.). 400p. (Orig.). 1990. pap. 9.95 (0-930603-03-6) White Dove NM.

***Secrets of Life & Death.** Renate Siebert. 333p. (C). Date not set. pap. text ed. 20.00 (1-85984-023-X, Pub. by Verso UK) Routledge Chapman & Hall.

***Secrets of Life & Death: Women & the Mafia.** Renate Siebert. 352p. (C). Date not set. text ed. 65.00 (1-85984-903-2) Routledge Chapman & Hall.

Secrets of Life Every Teen Needs to Know. Terry L. Paulson & Sean D. Paulson. LC 90-63405. (Illus.). 160p. (Orig.). (YA). (gr. 7-12). 1990. pap. 6.95 (0-939513-42-0) Joy Pub SJC.

Secrets of Life Extension: Anti-Oxidants, the Immune System, Vitamins & Supplements & the Longevity Diet. (Life Extension Ser.). 1993. lib. bdg. 255.95 (0-8490-9014-8) Gordon Pr.

Secrets of Life, Secrets of Death: Essays on Language, Gender & Science. Evelyn F. Keller. LC 92-28013. 288p. (C). (gr. 13). 1992. pap. 16.95 (0-415-90525-7, A6763, Routledge NY) Routledge.

Secrets of Life Telecourse. Wgbh Educational Foundation Staff. 1993. student ed., pap. text ed. write for info. (0-07-032769-6) McGraw.

Secrets of Life Telecourse. Wgbh Educational Foundation Staff. 1993. teacher ed., pap. text ed. write for info. (0-07-032770-X) McGraw.

Secrets of Lighting on Location: A Photographer's Guide to Professional Lighting Techniques. Bob Krist. 1996. pap. text ed. 24.95 (0-8174-5823-9) Watsn-Guptill.

***Secrets of Living Fat-Free: Hints, Tips, Recipes, & Strategies for Losing Weight & Feeling Great.** Sandra Woodruff. LC 97-6065. 208p. Date not set. pap. 9.95 (0-89529-787-6) Avery Pub.

Secrets of Lock Picking. Steven M. Hampton. (Illus.). 72p. 1987. pap. 17.00 (0-87364-423-9) Paladin Pr.

***Secrets of Lost Empires: Reconstructing the Glories of Ages Past.** Michael Barnes. LC 96-39795. 1997. write for info. (0-8069-9584-X) Sterling Pubng.

Secrets of Love. J. Donald Walters. 68p. 1993. 5.95 (1-56589-035-3) Crystal Clarity.

***Secrets of Love: The Erotic Arts Through the Ages.** Nigel Cawthorne. 1997. pap. text ed. 22.50 (0-06-251362-1) Harper SF.

Secrets of Love Magick. Gerina Dunwich. (Illus.). 192p. 1992. pap. 7.95 (0-8065-1365-9, Citadel Pr) Carol Pub Group.

Secrets of Loving Touch. Franz Benedikter. (Illus.). 144p. (Orig.). 1996. pap. 12.95 (0-941524-90-6) Lotus Light.

Secrets of Low Fat Cooking: 100 Techniques & 200 Recipes for Great Healthy Food. Food & Health Magazine Editors. LC 96-41794. 1997. pap. text ed. 17.95 (1-884943-12-8) Eat Well Bks.

Secrets of Lysistrata, Times of Darkness. Roman Gershgorin. (Illus.). 214p. (Orig.). 1992. pap. 3.00 (1-881910-02-4) Adventure NY.

Secrets of Magical Seals. Anna Riva. (Illus.). 64p. 1975. pap. 4.50 (0-943832-04-7) Intl Imports.

Secrets of Major Gift Fund Raising. Charles F. Mai. LC 87-25568. 170p. 1987. 25.95 (0-914756-39-7) Taft Group.

Secrets of Making & Breaking Codes. Hamilton Nickels. LC 94-18198. 1994. 6.95 (0-8065-1563-5, Citadel Pr) Carol Pub Group.

Secrets of Making A's the Easy Speedlearning Way. Marsha A. Murphy. LC 92-75555. (Illus.). 300p. 1995. pap. 19.95 (0-9635508-2-9) DataQuest VA.

Secrets of Making A's the Easy SpeedLearning Way: The Learning Kit, Set. Marsha A. Murphy. LC 92-75555. (Illus.). 300p. (Orig.). 1995. Incl. audio tape. pap. 39.95 incl. audio (0-9635508-0-2) DataQuest VA.

Secrets of Mariko. Elisabeth Bumiller. 1996. pap. 13.00 (0-679-77262-6) McKay.

***Secrets of Mariko: A Year in the Life of a Japanese Woman & Her Family.** Elisabeth Bumiller. Date not set. pap. 13.00 (0-614-25848-0, Vin) Random.

Secrets of Masonic Mind Control. 1991. lib. bdg. 79.95 (0-8490-4616-5) Gordon Pr.

Secrets of Mayan Science - Religion. Hunbatz Men. LC 89-6637. (Illus.). 156p. (Orig.). 1989. pap. 12.00 (0-939680-63-7) Bear & Co.

Secrets of Meditation. J. Donald Walters. (Illus.). 66p. (Orig.). 1989. pap. 4.95 (0-916124-64-9, CCP23) Crystal Clarity.

Secrets of Mental Supremacy. W. R. Latson. 138p. 1968. reprint ed. spiral bd. 6.50 (0-7873-1047-6) Hlth Research.

Secrets of Mental Supremacy: How to Cultivate Mind, Memory, Perspective, Imagination & Ideas. W. R. Latson. 1991. lib. bdg. 75.00 (0-8490-4185-6) Gordon Pr.

Secrets of Mental Supremacy (1913) W. R. Latson. 138p. 1996. pap. 16.95 (1-56459-864-0) Kessinger Pub.

Secrets of Metals. Wilhelm Pelikan. Tr. by Charlotte Lebensart from GER. 189p. reprint ed. pap. 10.95 (0-88010-257-8) Anthroposophic.

***Secrets of Methamphetamine.** 1997. pap. text ed. 24.95 (1-55950-144-8) Loompanics.

Secrets of Methamphetamine Manufacture. 4th rev. ed. Uncle Fester. (Illus.). 202p. (C). 1996. pap. 24.95 (0-614-14877-4, 85177) Loompanics.

Secrets of Midnight. Mirian Minger. 352p. (Orig.). 1995. pap. 5.50 (0-515-11726-9) Jove Pubns.

Secrets of Mind Power. rev. ed. Harry Lorayne. 240p. 1995. 17.95 (0-8119-0756-2) LIFETIME.

Secrets of Miyama Ryu Combat: Combat Ju-Jutsu - The Lost Art. 2nd ed. D'Arcy Rahming. Orig. Title: Combat Ju-Jutsu - The Lost Art. 182p. 1995. pap. 18.95 (1-886219-00-1) Mdrn Bu-Jutsu.

Secrets of Modern Knife Fighting. David E. Steele. (Illus.). 149p. (C). 1989. pap. text ed. 11.95 (0-317-94037-6) Survival Larder.

Secrets of Modern Soccer. Ljubo Zaja. (Illus.). 104p. 1994. pap. text ed. 13.95 (0-9640054-0-9) Adriatic Prods.

***Secrets of Monet's Garden.** Derek Fell. LC 97-8124. 1997. write for info. (1-56799-463-6, Friedman-Fairfax) M Friedman Pub Grp Inc.

***Secrets of More Powerful Personal Prayer: Gaining Assurance Through Greater Faith.** Paul L. Morris. 174p. 1996. pap. 1.95 (0-9645356-3-7) Morris-Lee Pub.

Secrets of Motivation: How to Get & Keep Volunteers & Paid Staff. Sue Vineyard. (Short 'n Sweet Bk.). (Illus.). 36p. (Orig.). 1991. pap. text ed. 11.00 (0-911029-32-X) Heritage Arts.

Secrets of Natural Healing with Food: Wellness & Body Chemistry. Nancy Appleton. Ed. by Aurelia Navarro. 160p. (Orig.). 1994. pap. 10.95 (0-915801-49-3) Rudra Pr.

***Secrets of Natural Health.** Shyam Singha. LC 96-48639. 288p. 1997. pap. 14.95 (1-85230-938-5) Element MA.

Secrets of Naturally Youthful Health & Vitality. Samuel Homola. LC 70-152523. (Illus.). 1971. 14.95 (0-13-797514-7, Parker Publishing Co) P-H.

Secrets of Nature: Big Book Collection. Ron Cole et al. Ed. by Donna Schaffer & Lauren Weidenman. (Ranger Rick Science Spectacular Ser.). (Illus.). 16p. (J). (gr. 2-4). 1996. pap. write for info. (1-56784-288-7) Newbridge Comms.

Secrets of Nature Set. Ron Cole & Darlyne Murawski. Ed. by Donna Schaffer et al. (Ranger Rick Science Spectacular Ser.). (Illus.). 16p. (J). (gr. 2-4). 1996. pap. write for info. (1-56784-287-9) Newbridge Comms.

***Secrets of Nostradamus: The Medieval Code of the Master Revealed in the Age of Computer Science.** David Ovason. (Illus.). 512p. 1997. 29.95 (0-7126-7710-0, Pub. by Century UK) Trafalgar.

Secrets of Nostradamus Exposed: Undisclosed Secrets of the World's Greatest Prophet. Ray Comfort. (Illus.). 198p. (Orig.). 1996. pap. 5.95 (1-878859-18-8) Living Wat CA.

Secrets of Numerology: How to Read Character & Destiny. Ravindra Kumar. 240p. (Orig.). (C). 1992. pap. 10.00 (81-207-1363-X, Pub. by Sterling Pubs II) Apt Bks.

Secrets of Occult Sciences. L. R. Chawdhri. (C). 1993. 6.50 (81-207-1067-3, Pub. by Sterling Plns Pvt II) S Asia.

Secrets of Occult Sciences: How to Read Omens, Moles, Dreams & Handwriting. L. R. Chawdhri. 152p. 1990. text ed. 22.50 (81-207-1066-5, Pub. by Sterling Pubs II) Apt Bks.

Secrets of One Hundred Twenty-Three Classic Science Tricks & Experiments. Edi Lanners. (Illus.). 196p. (Orig.). 1987. pap. 8.95 (0-8306-2821-5) McGraw-Hill Prof.

Secrets of Oriental Physicians. Paul M. Kourenoff. 146p. 1951. reprint ed. spiral bd. 13.50 (0-7873-0512-X) Hlth Research.

Secrets of Oriental Physicians: Two Hundred Natural Healing Formulas for Nearly Every Ailment. (Alternative Medicine Ser.). 1991. lib. bdg. 79.95 (0-8490-4307-7) Gordon Pr.

***Secrets of Origami: The Japanese Art of Paper Folding.** Robert Harbin. LC 97-139. 256p. 1997. pap. 10.95 (0-486-29707-1) Dover.

Secrets of Overcoming Harmful Emotions. J. Donald Walters. (Illus.). 66p. (Orig.). 1990. pap. 4.95 (0-916124-04-5, CCP24) Crystal Clarity.

Secrets of Personal Marketing Power. Don Price. 208p. (Orig.). 1995. pap. text ed. 19.95 (0-8403-9392-X) Kendall-Hunt.

Secrets of Personal Persuasion. William Turner. 1986. 19.95 (0-13-798687-4) P-H.

***Secrets of Piano Technique & Tone.** Albert DeVito. LC 96-94778. 80p. 1996. pap. 14.95 (0-934286-70-1) Kenyon.

Secrets of Pilgrim Pond. Ted M. Murphy. LC 96-26014. (A Belltown Mystery Ser.: Vol. 4). (J). (gr. 5-8). 1998. pap. 4.95 (0-382-39776-2) Silver Burdett Pr.

An Asterisk (*) at the beginning of an entry indicates that the title is appearing in BIP for the first time.

Secrets of Pistoulet. Jana Kolpen. (Illus.). 72p. 1996. 18.95 (*1-55670-440-2*) Stewart Tabori & Chang.

Secrets of Plant Propagation: Starting Your Own Flowers, Vegetables, Fruits, Berries, Shrubs, Trees, & Houseplants. Lewis Hill. LC 84-47788. (Illus.). 168p. 1985. pap. 16.95 (*0-88266-370-4*, Garden Way Pub) Storey Comm Inc.

***Secrets of Police Aikido: Controlling Tactics Used by Law Enforcement Professionals.** Bill Sosa. 1997. pap. text ed. 14.95 (*0-8065-1932-0*, Citadel Pr) Carol Pub Group.

Secrets of Potfishing. Edward R. Ricciuti. (Illus.). 74p. pap. 3.50 (*0-88839-085-8*) Hancock House.

Secrets of Power Persuasion: Everything You'll Ever Need to Get Anything You'll Ever Want. Roger Dawson. 1992. text ed. 27.95 (*0-13-799354-4*, Busn) P-H.

Secrets of Power Persuasion: Everything You'll Ever Need to Get Anything You'll Ever Want. Roger Dawson. 1992. pap. 12.95 (*0-13-799362-5*, Busn) P-H.

Secrets of Power Presentations. Peter U. Bender. (Illus.). 212p. 1995. pap. 12.95 (*1-895565-57-X*) Firefly Bks Ltd.

Secrets of Power Presentations. William Hendricks et al. 263p. (Orig.). 1996. pap. 16.99 (*1-56414-242-6*) Career Pr Inc.

Secrets of Prayer see Secretos de la Oracion

Secrets of Prophecy. P. Kuhlmann & J. Paton. (Christian Classics Ser.). 1995. pap. 3.49 (*1-56570-015-5*) Meridian MI.

Secrets of Prosperity. J. Donald Walters. 68p. 1993. 5.95 (*1-56589-037-X*) Crystal Clarity.

Secrets of Radiant Health & Well-Being. J. Donald Walters. 72p. 1995. 5.95 (*1-56589-038-8*) Crystal Clarity.

Secrets of Real Lace: Is It Handmade or Machine? Elizabeth M. Kurella. (Lace Unveiled Ser.). 70p. 1994. pap. 16.95 (*0-9642871-0-2*) Lace Merchant.

Secrets of Relaxation: A Three Way Program That Really Works. Mariane Kohler. (Illus.). 128p. (Orig.). 1982. pap. 8.95 (*0-8128-6071-3*, Scrbrough Hse) Madison Bks UPA.

Secrets of Rennes-Le-Chateau. Lionel Fanthorpe & Patricia Fanthorpe. LC 91-43311. 256p. (Orig.). 1992. pap. 14.95 (*0-87728-744-9*) Weiser.

Secrets of Revival. R. Edward Miller. (Illus.). 270p. (Orig.). (YA). (gr. 10). 1996. pap. 9.95 (*0-945818-10-6*) Peniel Pubns.

Secrets of RF Circuit Design. Joseph J. Carr. (Illus.). 416p. 1991. 32.95 (*0-8306-8710-6*, 3710); pap. 19.95 (*0-8306-3710-9*) McGraw-Hill Prof.

Secrets of Rf Circuit Design. Joseph J. Carr. 1991. text ed. 32.95 (*0-07-010095-0*) McGraw.

***Secrets of RF Circuit Design.** 2nd ed. Joseph J. Carr. 1996. text ed. 49.95 (*0-07-912943-9*); pap. text ed. 24.95 (*0-07-912944-7*) McGraw.

Secrets of RF Circuit Design. 2nd ed. Joseph J. Carr. LC 96-30966. (Illus.). 464p. 1996. text ed. 49.95 (*0-07-011672-5*); pap. text ed. 24.95 (*0-07-011673-3*) McGraw.

Secrets of River Angling. Eric Carlisle. 176p. 1995. pap. 14.95 (*0-88839-299-0*) Hancock House.

Secrets of River Fishing. Jerry E. Sneath. LC 95-71834. (Illus.). 88p. (Orig.). 1995. pap. 8.95 (*0-9651239-0-1*) Catlett Pubng.

Secrets of Salt-Free Cooking. 2nd ed. Jeanne Jones. (One Hundred One Productions Ser.). 1991. pap. 11.95 (*1-56426-504-8*, One Hund One Prods) Cole Group.

Secrets of Samurai. A. Westbrook. 21.00 (*0-685-47575-1*) Wehman.

Secrets of Santa. Annie Civardi. LC 91-130. (Illus.). 32p. (J). (ps-1). 1991. pap. 13.95 (*0-671-74270-1*, S&S Bks Young Read) S&S Childrens.

Secrets of Savvy Networking: How to Make the Best Connections for Business & Personal Success. Susan RoAne. 224p. (Orig.). 1993. 12.99 (*0-446-39410-6*) Warner Bks.

Secrets of Science Series: Group One, 4 vols., Set. Robin Kerrod. (Illus.). (J). (gr. 3-8). 1991. lib. bdg. 41.61 (*1-85435-268-7*) Marshall Cavendish.

Secrets of Science Series: Group Two, 6 vols. Robin Kerrod. (Illus.). (J). (gr. 3-8). 1990. lib. bdg. 62.42 (*1-85435-151-6*) Marshall Cavendish.

Secrets of Sebastian Beaumont. Carrie Peterson. (Shadows Ser.). 1993. mass mkt. 3.50 (*0-373-27022-4*, 5-27022-8) Silhouette.

Secrets of Seduction. Brenda Venus. Date not set. pap. 5.99 (*0-451-18289-8*, Sig) NAL-Dutton.

Secrets of Seduction: How to Be the Best Lover Your Woman Ever Had. Brenda Venus. 192p. 1996. pap. 10.95 (*0-452-27364-1*, Plume) NAL-Dutton.

Secrets of Seduction for Women. Brenda Venus. 1996. pap. 18.95 (*0-525-94103-7*, Dutton) NAL-Dutton.

Secrets of Seduction for Women. Brenda Venus. 1997. pap. 9.95 (*0-452-27794-9*, Plume) NAL-Dutton.

Secrets of Self Acceptance. J. Donald Walters. 68p. 1993. 5.95 (*1-56589-043-4*) Crystal Clarity.

Secrets of Self-Employment: Surviving & Thriving on the Ups & Downs at Being Your Own Boss. rev. ed. Paul Edwards & Sarah Edwards. LC 96-12715. (Working from Home Ser.). Orig. Title: Making It on Your Own. 304p. (Orig.). 1996. pap. 13.95 (*0-87477-837-9*, Tarcher Putnam) Putnam Pub Group.

Secrets of Self-Esteem: A New Approach for Everyone. Patricia Cleghorn. 1996. pap. 10.95 (*1-85230-777-3*) Element MA.

***Secrets of Self-Hypnosis: Making it Work for You.** Bruce Goldberg. LC 96-35449. 1997. 12.95 (*0-8069-9620-X*) Sterling.

Secrets of Selling by Using Spiritual Powers. Roger A. Kessinger. (Illus.). 100p. (Orig.). 1988. pap. 5.00 (*0-922802-00-9*) Kessinger Pub.

Secrets of Sensual Love. Tom Leonardi. Date not set. pap. 9.95 (*0-452-27457-5*, Plume) NAL-Dutton.

Secrets of Sensual Lovemaking: How to Give Her the Ultimate Pleasure. Tom Leonardi. LC 94-47136. 1995. pap. 15.95 (*0-525-93983-0*, Dutton) NAL-Dutton.

Secrets of Serenity: A Treasury of Inspiration. (Miniature Editions Ser.). (Illus.). 128p. 1996. 4.95 (*1-56138-690-1*, Running Pr Mini Edtns) Running Pr.

Secrets of Serotonin Vol. 1: The Natural Plan for Mood Enhancement, Appetite Control, & Higher Energy. Carol Hart. 1996. mass mkt. 5.99 (*0-312-96087-5*) St Martin.

Secrets of Sewing with Plaid. Patricia Andres. 80p. (Orig.). 1985. pap. text ed. 6.00 (*0-9618825-0-6*) Value Pubns.

Secrets of Sex Appeal from Head to Heel. W. Gary Boss. (Illus.). 68p. (Orig.). Date not set. pap. 15.00 (*0-9623763-0-2*) Boss Enterprises.

Secrets of Sex Magick: A Practical Handbook for Men & Women. 2nd rev. ed. U. D. Frater. Tr. by Ingrid Fischer from GER. LC 91-7285. (Tantra & Sexual Arts Ser.). (Illus.). 256p. 1991. pap. 17.95 (*0-87542-773-1*) Llewellyn Pubns.

Secrets of Sexual Body Language. Martin Lloyd-Elliot. LC 95-62401. 144p. (Orig.). 1996. pap. 16.95 (*1-56975-060-2*) Ulysses Pr.

Secrets of Sexual Ecstasy: Pathways to Erotic Pleasure. Carlo De Paoli. (Illus.). 119p. (Orig.). 1996. pap. 15.95 (*1-56924-768-4*) Marlowe & Co.

Secrets of Shamanism: Tapping the Spirit Power Within You. Jose Stevens & Lena S. Stevens. 249p. 1988. mass mkt. 6.50 (*0-380-75607-2*) Avon.

Secrets of Shangri-La: An Enquiry into the Lore Legend & Culture of Nepal. N. Sharma. (C). 1992. 60.00 (*0-7855-0215-7*, Pub. by Ratna Pustak Bhandar) St Mut.

Secrets of Shangri-La: An Enquiry into the Lore, Legend & Culture of Nepal. Nagendra Sharma. 292p. 1992. 20.00 (*0-685-72917-6*, Pub. by Nirala Pubns II) Nataraj Bks.

Secrets of Shaolin Temple Boxing. Robert W. Smith. LC 64-22002. (Illus.). 1989. pap. 9.95 (*0-8048-1630-1*) C E Tuttle.

Secrets of Shellfishing. Edward R. Ricciuti. (Illus.). 70p. pap. 3.50 (*0-88839-140-4*) Hancock House.

Secrets of Shuffleboard Strategy. 2nd enl. ed. Omero C. Catan. LC 72-91761. (Illus.). 224p. 1973. lib. bdg. 6.00 (*0-9600618-1-9*) Catan.

Secrets of Silver Heart. Hope Goodwin. 1994. 17.95 (*0-8034-9078-X*, 094432) Bouregy.

Secrets of Silver Valley. 2nd ed. Zeno Zeplin. (Illus.). 130p. (Orig.). 1987. 16.95 (*0-9615760-4-9*) Nel-Mar Pub.

Secrets of Silver Valley. 2nd ed. Zeno Zeplin. (Illus.). 130p. (Orig.). (J). 1987. pap. 9.95 (*0-9615760-5-7*) Nel-Mar Pub.

Secrets of Singing: Female Edition. Jeffrey L. Allen. Ed. by Sandy Feldstein. (Illus.). 388p. (Orig.). (C). 1994. 44.95 incl. disk (*0-910957-77-0*, EL03806FCD) Warner Brothers.

Secrets of Singing Male Voice. Jeffrey Allen. 1994. pap. text ed. 44.95 incl. audio compact disk (*0-910957-76-2*, EL03806MCD) Warner Brothers.

***Secrets of Skating.** Baiul. Date not set. 29.95 (*0-7893-0104-0*) Universe.

Secrets of Sleep. Alexander Borbely. LC 85-83887. (Illus.). 240p. 1988. pap. 17.00 (*0-465-07593-2*) Basic.

Secrets of Small Business Success. rev. ed. Malcolm Newell. 126p. 1995. pap. 14.95 (*0-949142-24-7*, Pub. by Stirling Pr AT) Intl Spec Bk.

Secrets of Software Quality Forty Innovations from IBM. Craig Kaplan. 1994. text ed. 49.00 (*0-07-911795-3*) McGraw.

Secrets of Solo Racing: Expert Techniques for Autocross & Time Trials. Henry Watts. LC 89-92254. (Illus.). 192p. 1989. pap. 14.95 (*0-9620573-1-2*) Loki Pub Co.

Secrets of Sorcery Spells & Pleasure Cults of India. P. Thomas. (Illus.). 284p. 1983. reprint ed. text ed. 45.00 (*0-86590-237-2*, Pub. by Taraporevala II) Apt Bks.

***Secrets of Space, 3 vols.** lib. bdg. 50.94 (*0-8050-5022-1*) TFC Bks NY.

***Secrets of Space Series, 7 vols.** Incl. Exploring the Origins of the Universe. Stuart A. Kallen. (Illus.). 64p. (J). (gr. 5-8). 1997. lib. bdg. 16.98 (*0-8050-4478-7*); Space Travel & Exploration. Rebecca Clay. LC 96-30070. (Illus.). 64p. (J). (gr. 5-8). 1997. lib. bdg. 16.98 (*0-8050-4474-4*); Stars & Galaxies. Rebecca Clay. (Illus.). 64p. (J). (gr. 5-8). 1997. lib. bdg. 16.98 (*0-8050-4476-0*); Black Holes & Supernovae. David E. Newton. LC 96-48188. (Illus.). 64p. (J). (gr. 5-8). 1997. lib. bdg. 16.98 (*0-8050-4477-9*); Asteroids, Comets & Meteors. Carole Marsh. (Illus.). 64p. (J). (gr. 5-8). 1996. lib. bdg. 16.98 (*0-8050-4473-6*); The Sun & the Solar System. Franklyn M. Branley. (Illus.). 64p. (J). (gr. 5-8). 1996. lib. bdg. 16.98 (*0-8050-4475-2*); Unidentified Flying Objects & Extraterrestrial Life. Carole Marsh. (Illus.). 64p. (J). (gr. 5-8). 1996. lib. bdg. 16.98 (*0-8050-4472-8*); 95.08 (*0-8050-5382-4*) TFC Bks NY.

Secrets of Spiritual Stamina: Healthy Habits for a Lasting Faith. Stuart Briscoe. LC 94-2438. 208p. 1994. pap. 8.99 (*0-87788-757-8*) Shaw Pubs.

Secrets of Spirulina. Ed. by C. Hills. LC 80-22087. 218p. 1980. pap. 13.95 (*0-916438-38-4*) Dr Hills Technol.

Secrets of Star Wars: Shadows of the Empire. Mark C. Vaz. (Illus.). 304p. (Orig.). 1996. pap. 15.00 (*0-345-40236-7*, Del Rey) Ballantine.

***Secrets of Staying in Love.** John Powell. (Illus.). 168p. 1995. reprint ed. pap. 9.50 (*0-88347-299-6*) Res Christian Liv.

Secrets of Street Survival - Israeli Style: Staying Alive in a Civilian War Zone. Eugene Sockut. (Illus.). 400p. 1995. pap. 25.00 (*0-87364-819-6*) Paladin Pr.

Secrets of Striped Bass Fishing. D. W. Bennett. (Illus.). 80p. pap. 3.50 (*0-88839-103-X*) Hancock House.

Secrets of Studio Still Life Photography. Gary Perweiler. (Illus.). 144p. 1984. pap. 22.50 (*0-8174-5898-0*, Amphoto) Watsn-Guptill.

Secrets of Style. Doris Pooser. Ed. by Michael G. Crisp. LC 92-10401. (Illus.). 107p. (Orig.). 1994. pap. 12.95 (*1-56052-152-X*) Crisp Pubns.

Secrets of Success. Lloyd K. Ulery. 96p. 1986. 6.95 (*0-930984-04-8*) Psychic Bks.

Secrets of Success. J. Donald Walters. (Illus.). 67p. (Orig.). 1989. pap. 4.95 (*0-916124-58-4*, CCP19) Crystal Clarity.

Secrets of Success. J. Donald Walters. 68p. (Orig.). 1993. 5.95 (*1-56589-031-0*) Crystal Clarity.

Secrets of Success & Happiness. Og Mandino. 1996. mass mkt. 5.99 (*0-449-14799-1*) Fawcett.

Secrets of Success for Today's Interior Designers & Decorators: Easily Sell the Job, Plan It Correctly & Keep the Customer Coming Back for Repeat Sales. 3rd rev. ed. Linda M. Ramsay. Ed. by Faren Bachelis. LC 91-91011. (Illus.). 336p. 1996. reprint ed. pap. text ed. 39.99 (*0-9629918-3-X*, Baker & Taylor) Touch Design.

Secrets of Success in Your Own Business. James L. Silvester. 288p. (C). 1986. 20.00 (*0-8184-0418-3*) Carol Pub Group.

Secrets of Successful Brides: Brides Share Wedding Wisdom on How They Did It. Suzanne Kresse. 160p. (Orig.). 1994. pap. 9.95 (*0-312-10538-X*) St Martin.

Secrets of Successful Christian Living: Studies in the Life of Daniel. rev. ed. Thomas P. Hill. 1992. pap. text ed. 4.95 (*0-941251-01-2*) Master Prods.

Secrets of Successful Direct Mail. Richard V. Benson. 208p. 1994. 29.95 (*0-8442-3178-9*, NTC Busn Bks) NTC Pub Grp.

Secrets of Successful Direct Mail. Richard V. Benson. 208p. 1994. pap. 16.95 (*0-8442-3294-7*, NTC Busn Bks) NTC Pub Grp.

Secrets of Successful Fiction Writing: A Guide to Techniques & Approaches the Professionals Take for Granted. Shelly Lowenkopf. (Santa Barbara Writers Conference Shop Talk Ser.: Bk. I). 152p. (Orig.). (C). 1991. pap. text ed. 9.95 (*1-880093-00-6*) Charters W.

***Secrets of Successful Grantsmanship: A Guerrilla Guide to Raising Money.** Susan L. Golden. LC 96-45858. (The Jossey-Bass Nonprofit Sector Ser.). 1997. write for info. (*0-7879-0306-X*) Jossey-Bass.

Secrets of Successful Hiring & Firing. Goodworth. 1990. pap. 29.95 (*0-434-90704-9*) Buttrwrth-Heinemann.

Secrets of Successful Insurance Sales. Hill, Napoleon, Foundation Staff et al. 250p. 1988. 19.95 (*0-396-09329-9*) WC Stone PMA.

Secrets of Successful Job Hunting: Surefire Tactics for Finding Hidden Jobs, Writing Effective Resumes, Handling Tough Interviews, & Beating Chemical & Psychological Tests. Tony Lesce. (Illus.). 104p. 1994. pap. 14.00 (*0-87364-776-9*) Paladin Pr.

Secrets of Successful Low-Budget Advertising. Quinn. 242p. 1988. pap. 31.95 (*0-434-91614-5*) Buttrwrth-Heinemann.

Secrets of Successful Marriages. Matthew N. Sadiku. Ed. by Steve Dunham. (Illus.). 374p. (Orig.). 1991. 19.95 (*1-879420-00-7*); pap. 11.95 (*1-879420-01-5*) Covenant Pubs.

Secrets of Successful Public Relations. Charles S. Phillips. LC 85-6426. 315p. 1985. 49.95 (*0-317-39230-1*) P-H.

Secrets of Successful QSL'ing. 2nd ed. Gerry L. Dexter. 120p. 1992. pap. 14.95 (*0-936653-36-1*) Tiare Pubns.

Secrets of Successful Rail-Trails: An Acquisition & Organizing Manual for Converting Rails into Trails. Ed. by Karen-Lee Ryan & Julie Winicerich. (Illus.). 192p. (Orig.). 1990. 19.95 (*0-925794-05-8*) Rails Trails.

***Secrets of Successful Selling.** Peter Prospere. LC 96-94758. 64p. (Orig.). 1996. pap. text ed. 8.95 (*0-9654374-1-8*) Integrated Mktg Sys.

Secrets of Successful Speakers: How You Can Motivate, Captivate, & Persuade. Lillet Walters. LC 92-46321. 1993. text ed. 21.95 (*0-07-068033-7*); pap. text ed. 14.95 (*0-07-068034-5*) McGraw.

Secrets of Successful Students: What it Takes to Succeed . . . For Today's High School & College Students. James L. Warner. LC 91-92866. 48p. 1991. write for info. incl. audio (*0-9630611-0-0*) Stud Success.

***Secrets of Successful Subscription Marketing: How, Why, & What to Test.** Donald L. Nicholas. (Illus.). 300p. 1997. pap. 39.95 (*0-85013-294-0*) Dartnell Corp.

Secrets of Successful Telephone Selling. Robert W. Bly. 224p. 1997. pap. 14.95 (*0-8050-4098-6*, Owl) H Holt & Co.

Secrets of Successful Video Training: The Training with Video Casebook. Steve R. Cartwright. 149p. 1990. 42.95 (*0-86729-281-4*, Focal) Buttrwrth-Heinemann.

***Secrets of Successful Web Sites.** David Siegel. 320p. 1997. 49.99 (*1-56830-382-3*) Hayden.

Secrets of Superselling: How to Program Your Subconscious for Success. Lynea Corson. 1991. pap. 12.00 (*0-425-12661-7*, Berkley Trade) Berkley Pub.

Secrets of Surf Fishing at Night. William A. Muller. 140p. (Orig.). 1993. pap. 11.95 (*0-9625187-6-X*) Wavecrest Comns.

Secrets of Surveillance: A Professional's Guide to Tailing Subjects by Vehicle, Foot, Airplane, & Public Transportation. ACM IV Security Services Staff. (Illus.). 248p. 1993. pap. 25.00 (*0-87364-722-X*) Paladin Pr.

***Secrets of Taking Any Test in 20 Minutes a Day.** Judith Meyers. Ed. by Jim Gish. LC 97-21550. (Basics Made Easy Ser.). 192p. 1997. pap. 13.95 (*1-57685-071-4*) LrningExprss.

Secrets of Taming the Wild Food Bill. Joe Urshan. 72p. 1983. pap. 6.95 (*0-318-00153-5*) PDQ Printers.

***Secrets of Telephone Selling.** Neil Johnson. (Marketing & Sales Ser.). 1994. pap. 15.95 (*0-7494-1219-4*) Kogan Page Ltd.

Secrets of the ABCs. D. Dowdell. LC 65-22301. (Illus.). 64p. (J). (gr. 2 up). 1968. lib. bdg. 10.95 (*0-87783-035-5*) Oddo.

Secrets of the Alchemists. Time-Life Books Editors. (Mysteries of the Unknown Ser.). (Illus.). 144p. 1990. 14.95 (*0-8094-6500-0*); lib. bdg. write for info. (*0-8094-6501-9*) Time-Life.

Secrets of the Amazing Kreskin: The World's Foremost Mentalist Reveals How You Can Expand Your Powers. A. Kreskin. 166p. 1991. pap. 16.95 (*0-87975-676-4*) Prometheus Bks.

Secrets of the Anointing. Nahum Rosario. Tr. by Efren Toledo from SPA. 112p. (Orig.). 1994. pap. 7.00 (*0-9634761-5-7*) Pub Maranatha.

Secrets of the Astonishing Executive. Bill Herz & Paul Harris. 160p. (Orig.). 1991. pap. 9.00 (*0-380-76244-7*) Avon.

Secrets of the Bible People. Kamal Salibi. LC 87-21920. (Illus.). 210p. 1988. 16.95 (*0-940793-16-4*) Interlink Pub.

Secrets of the Biblical Story of Creation. Rudolf Steiner. (Series Twenty-Four). 88p. 1971. reprint ed. spiral bd. 10.50 (*0-7873-1046-8*) Hlth Research.

Secrets of the Biblical Story of Creation (1910) Rudolph Steiner. 93p. 1996. pap. 14.95 (*1-56459-779-2*) Kessinger Pub.

Secrets of the Blessed Man. rev. ed. Paul N. Tassell. LC 78-22065. 123p. 1996. pap. 3.50 (*0-87227-033-5*, RBP5005) Reg Baptist.

Secrets of the C Plus Plus Masters. Jeff Alger. LC 94-44469. (Illus.). 388p. 1995. pap. text ed., pap. 39.95 incl. disk (*0-12-049940-1*, AP Prof) Acad Pr.

Secrets of the Camera Obscura. David Knowles. LC 93-30339. 144p. 1994. 10.95 (*0-8118-0655-3*) Chronicle Bks.

Secrets of the Car Buying Game. Sky Stargel. (Illus.). 77p. (Orig.). 1989. pap. 5.95 (*1-878455-00-1*) Markas Pub.

Secrets of the Cat: Its Lore, Legends, & Lives. Barbara Holland. 224p. 1994. mass mkt. 5.99 (*0-8041-1276-2*) Ivy Books.

Secrets of the Children of Og. Rikki. (Story of Og & Man Ser.: Part 1). (Illus.). 220p. (Orig.). 1982. pap. 10.00 (*0-910149-01-1*) Msng Link AZ.

Secrets of the Chinese Drama. Cecilia S. Zung. LC 63-23194. (Illus.). 1972. 30.95 (*0-405-09112-5*) Ayer.

Secrets of the Chinese Drama: A Complete Explanatory Guide. Cecilia S. Zung. 1972. 250.00 (*0-8490-1016-0*) Gordon Pr.

Secrets of the Chinese Herbalists. rev. ed. Richard M. Lucas. 252p. 1986. reprint ed. pap. text ed. 10.95 (*0-13-798174-0*) P-H.

Secrets of the Chinese Herbalists. rev. ed. Richard M. Lucas. 252p. 1987. reprint ed. 21.95 (*0-13-797879-0*) P-H.

Secrets of the Congdon Mansion. Joe Kimball. (Illus.). 64p. 1985. pap. 5.95 (*0-9613778-1-X*) Jaykay Pub Inc.

Secrets of the Dark Cedars. Seth Thompson. 142p. (Orig.). pap. 7.95 (*0-614-07916-0*) LGG.

***Secrets of the Dead Lands.** TSR Inc. Staff. (Dark Sun Game World Ser.). 1997. 20.00 (*0-7869-0667-7*) TSR Inc.

Secrets of the Dead Sea Scrolls: The Controversy & Intrigue Behind the... Randall Price. 350p. (Orig.). 1996. pap. 12.99 (*1-56507-454-8*) Harvest Hse.

Secrets of the Dolls' House Makers. Jean Nisbett. (Illus.). 200p. 1995. pap. 21.95 (*0-946819-54-8*) Sterling.

***Secrets of the Eucharist.** Michael H. Brown. LC 96-85387. 96p. 1996. pap. 5.50 (*1-880033-23-2*) Faith Pub OH.

Secrets of the Flute: The Physics, Math, & Design of Non-Mechanical Folk Flutes. Lew P. Price. (Illus.). 80p. (Orig.). (C). 1991. pap. 12.00 (*0-917578-08-2*) L Paxton Price.

Secrets of the Flying Saucers from Khabaram Khoom. D. C. Lucchesi. 75p. 1985. reprint ed. spiral bd. 18.00 (*0-7873-0572-3*) Hlth Research.

Secrets of the Forest. Muriel S. Lipp. LC 94-47033. (Illus.). 32p. (J). (gr. 3-8). 1995. 11.95 (*1-55971-456-5*) NorthWord.

Secrets of the Forest: Playscript. Olive Evans. (J). (gr. 3-12). 1985. reprint ed. pap. 6.00 (*0-88734-502-6*) Players Pr.

Secrets of the Gaelic Harp: A Method for Clairseach Based on Remnants of the Gaelic Oral Tradition, Including the First Tunes Taught Student Harpers. Ann Heymann. (Illus.). 128p. (Orig.). (C). 1989. 50.00 (*0-9621867-2-4*) Clairseach Pubns.

***Secrets of the Garden: Creating Beauty from Nature's Gifts.** Emilie Barnes. (Illus.). 48p. (Orig.). 1997. pap. 7.99 (*1-56507-564-1*) Harvest Hse.

Secrets of the Gathering Darkness. Barbara Scott & Carrie Younce. LC 95-21111. 288p. 1996. pap. 11.99 (*0-7852-7776-5*) Nelson.

Secrets of the Great Pyramid. Peter Tompkins. 1996. 16.98 (*0-88365-957-3*) Galahad Bks.

Secrets of the Haggadah. Matityahu Glazerson. 1989. 14.95 (*0-685-25973-0*) Feldheim.

Secrets of the Haggadah. Matityahu Glazerson. LC 95-43076. 192p. 1996. reprint ed. pap. 20.00 (*1-56821-936-9*) Aronson.

***Secrets of the Harem.** Carla Coco. LC 97-13595. 1997. write for info. (*0-86565-996-6*) Vendome.

Secrets of the Heart. Jennifer Blake et al. (Topaz Man Ser.). 384p. (Orig.). 1994. pap. 4.99 (*0-451-40552-8*, Topaz) NAL-Dutton.

Secrets of the Heart. Charlene Bowen. 1995. 17.95 (*0-8034-9096-8*, 094624) Bouregy.

***Secrets of the Heart.** Joan L. Matthews. 352p. 1998. mass mkt. 4.99 (*0-8217-5845-4*, Zebra Kensgtn) Kensgtn Pub Corp.

Secrets of the Heart. Kasey Michaels. Ed. by Claire Zion. 384p. (Orig.). 1995. mass mkt. 5.99 (*0-671-79341-1*) PB.

Secrets of the Heart. Kahlil Gibran. Tr. by Anthony R. Ferris from ARA. 1978. reprint ed. pap. 12.95 (*0-8065-0062-X*, Citadel Pr) Carol Pub Group.

S

An Asterisk (*) at the beginning of an entry indicates that the title is appearing in BIP for the first time.

Secrets of the Heart: Finding the Key to a Joyous Heart, Vol. 1. Richard W. Dortch. 192p. 1996. pap. text ed. 11.95 (*0-89221-299-3*) New Leaf.

Secrets of the Himalaya Mountain Masters. Yogi Wassan. 414p. 1973. reprint ed. spiral bd. 17.50 (*0-7873-0935-4*) Hlth Research.

Secrets of the Himalayan Mountain Masters. Yogi Wassan. (Longevity Ser.). 1991. lib. bdg. 79.95 (*0-8490-4177-5*) Gordon Pr.

*__Secrets of the Hopewell Box.__ James D. Squires. 1997. 4.99 (*0-517-17339-5*) Random Hse Value.

Secrets of the Hopewell Box: Stolen Elections, Southern Politics, & a City's Coming of Age. James D. Squires. 1996. 25.00 (*0-614-96814-3*, Times Bks) Random.

Secrets of the Hunting Pros. LC 92-83733. (Hunter's Information Ser.). 232p. 1993. write for info. (*0-914697-54-4*) N Amer Outdoor Grp.

Secrets of the I Ching. Joseph Murphy. 1989. pap. text ed. 9.95 (*0-13-798083-3*) P-H.

Secrets of the Ice Age: A Reappraisal of Prehistoric Man. Evans Hadingham. 342p. 1981. pap. 9.95 (*0-8027-7192-0*) Walker & Co.

Secrets of The Illuminati. Alan H. Peterson. Ed. by Doc Marquis et al. (American Focus on Satanic Crime Ser.: Vol. 5). (Illus.). 390p. 1994. pap. 44.00 (*1-877858-66-8*) Amer Focus Pub.

Secrets of the Inner Circle. 3rd ed. Harry C. Pellow. 450p. 1983. per. 29.95 (*0-941210-06-5*) HCP Res.

Secrets of the Inner Mind. Ed. by Robert Somerville. (Journey Through the Mind & Body Ser.). (Illus.). 144p. 1993. 17.95 (*0-7835-1036-5*); lib. bdg. 16.99 (*0-7835-1037-3*) Time-Life.

Secrets of the Interior Life. Luis M. Matinez. Tr. by H. J. Beutler. 207p. 1996. reprint ed. 25.95 (*0-912141-44-1*) Roman Cath Bks.

Secrets of the Jennivine Restaurant Cookbook. Jennifer Messina. 202p. 1992. pap. 12.95 (*0-9636478-0-6*) Jennivine.

Secrets of the Jews. Stuart E. Rosenberg. 220p. 1995. lib. bdg. 47.00 (*0-8095-4901-8*) Borgo Pr.

Secrets of the Jews. Stuart E. Rosenberg. 220p. 1994. pap. 18.95 (*0-88962-548-4*) Mosaic.

Secrets of the Jungle: Lessons in Survival & Success in Today's Organizations. Shirley Peddy. 1996. 14.95 (*0-9651376-0-0*) lrningconnections.

*__Secrets of the Jungle: Lessons on Survival & Success in Today's Organizations.__ Shirley Peddg. 1996. boxed, pap. 29.95 incl. audio (*0-9651376-2-7*) lrningconnections.

*__Secrets of the Karate Masters.__ J. Allen Queen. 1996. write for info. (*0-8069-8136-9*) Sterling.

Secrets of the Kingdom. R. Edward Miller. 180p. (Orig.). (YA). (gr. 10). 1989. pap. 7.95 (*0-945818-08-4*) Peniel Pubns.

Secrets of the Kingdom: British Radicals from the Popish Plot to the Revolution of 1688-89. Richard L. Greaves. LC 91-44781. 488p. (C). 1992. 55.00 (*0-8047-2052-5*) Stanford U Pr.

*__Secrets of the Lost Empires: Reconstructing the Glories of Ages Past.__ Narrated by Michael Barnes. 1997. 24.95 (*0-614-27833-3*) Sterling.

Secrets of the Lost Races. Rene Noorbergen. LC 77-76883. (Illus.). 1977. write for info. (*0-672-52289-6*) Macmillan.

*__Secrets of the M*A*S*H Mess: The Lost Recipes of Private Igor.__ Jeff Maxwell. (Illus.). 272p. (Orig.). 1997. pap. 16.95 (*1-888952-41-5*) Cumberland Hse.

*__Secrets of the M.A.S.H Mess: The Lost Recipes of Private Igor.__ Jeff Maxwell. 1997. pap. text ed. 101.70 (*1-888952-62-8*) Cumberland Hse.

*__Secrets of the Master: The Best of Bobby Jones.__ Bobby Jones. Ed. by Sidney L. Matthew. LC 96-35338. 160p. 1996. 22.00 (*1-886947-07-4*) Sleepng Bear.

Secrets of the Master Sales Managers. Compiled by Porter Henry, Jr. LC 93-13755. 176p. 1993. 19.95 (*0-8144-0221-6*) AMACOM.

Secrets of the Mayan Ruins. P. J. Stray. (Passport to Mystery Ser.). 144p. (J). (gr. 5-9). 1995. pap. 4.95 (*0-382-24705-1*); lib. bdg. 13.95 (*0-382-24704-3*) Silver Burdett Pr.

*__Secrets of the Maze.__ Adrian Fisher. 1997. 24.95 (*0-7641-5053-7*) Barron.

Secrets of the Millionaires. 1987. lib. bdg. 69.95 (*0-8490-3881-2*) Gordon Pr.

Secrets of the Millionaires. George Sterne et al. Ed. by Russ Von Hoelscher. 138p. 1981. write for info. (*0-940398-02-8*); pap. write for info. (*0-940398-20-6*) Profit Ideas.

Secrets of the Morning. V. C. Andrews. Ed. by Linda Marrow. 416p. 1991. pap. 6.99 (*0-671-69512-6*) PB.

Secrets of the Morning. large type ed. V. C. Andrews. (General Ser.). 487p. 1992. pap. 17.95 (*0-8161-5386-8*, GK Hall); lib. bdg. 20.95 (*0-8161-5385-X*, GK Hall) Thorndike Pr.

Secrets of the Most Holy Place. Donald F. Nori. 182p. (Orig.). 1992. pap. 8.99 (*1-56043-076-1*) Destiny Image.

Secrets of the Nest: The Family Life of North American Birds. Joan Dunning. (Illus.). 228p. 1996. pap. 15.95 (*0-395-71820-1*) HM.

Secrets of the New Age, 4 vols. in 1. Moore et al. (Illus.). 395p. 1989. 7.99 (*0-517-68020-3*) Random Hse Value.

Secrets of the New Age. Kenneth R. Wade. Ed. by Richard W. Coffen. 160p. 1989. pap. 4.99 (*0-8280-0520-6*) Review & Herald.

*__Secrets of the Night.__ Bob Berman. Date not set. pap. write for info. (*0-688-12728-2*, Quill) Morrow.

Secrets of the Night Sky: The Most Amazing Things in the Universe You Can See with the Naked Eye. Bob Berman. LC 94-21604. (Illus.). 320p. 1995. 23.00 (*0-688-12727-4*) Morrow.

Secrets of the Night Sky: The Most Amazing Things in the Universe You Can See with the Naked Eye. Bob Berman. LC 95-46182. (Illus.). 512p. 1996. pap. 14.00 (*0-06-097687-X*) HarpC.

Secrets of the Nile. Carolyn Keene. (Nancy Drew & Hardy Boys Supermystery Ser.: No. 25). (J). 1995. mass mkt. 3.99 (*0-671-50290-5*) PB.

*__Secrets of the Nile.__ Deidre S. Laiken. 320p. mass mkt. write for info. (*0-06-106196-4*, Harp PBks) HarpC.

Secrets of the Ninja. Ashida Kim. 152p. 1983. pap. 7.95 (*0-8065-0866-3*, Citadel Pr) Carol Pub Group.

Secrets of the Ninja. Ashida Kim. (Illus.). 168p. 1981. 16.95 (*0-87364-234-1*) Paladin Pr.

*__Secrets of the Ocean Realm.__ Howard Hall & Michele Hall. (Illus.). 176p. 1997. 39.95 (*0-7867-0453-5*) Carroll & Graf.

*__Secrets of the Original Don's Seafood & Steakhouse.__ Ed. by Ashby D. Landry, Jr. & Brenda Landry. (Illus.). 82p. 1996. 11.95 (*0-9654883-0-6*) Dons Seafood.

Secrets of the OS-2 Warp Masters. Martin Sullivan. LC 95-50549. 1996. pap. text ed. 44.95 (*0-471-13171-7*) Wiley.

Secrets of the P. V. B. Confessions of an Ex-Judge. Andrew Kone. Ed. by Richard Fireman. (Orig.). 1994. pap. write for info. (*0-931579-30-9*) J F Caroll Pub.

Secrets of the Parables: How to Use Them to Reach Life Goals Told in Modern & Contemporary Story Form. Culver Wold. LC 96-68084. 352p. (Orig.). 1996. pap. 24.95 (*0-9651482-0-3*) Quest for Vision.

Secrets of the Past. large type ed. Rose Boucheron. (Magna Large Print Ser.). 463p. 1996. 25.99 (*0-7505-0875-2*, Pub. by Magna Print Bks UK) Ulverscroft.

*__Secrets of the Pulse: The Ancient Art of Ayurvedic Pulse Diagnosis.__ Vasant D. Lad & Margaret S. Peet. LC 96-86347. (Illus.). 232p. (Orig.). 1996. pap. 21.95 (*1-883725-03-8*) Ayurvedic Pr.

Secrets of the Research Paper: An Easy Guide to Success. William Russo. (C). 1980. pap. 2.95 (*0-931660-03-3*) R Oman Pub.

Secrets of the Roses: A Novel. Lila Peiffer. LC 93-42076. 1994. pap. 10.99 (*0-7852-8192-4*) Nelson.

Secrets of the Rosicrucian Brotherhood, 4 vols. Jan Van Rijckenborgh. Incl. Vol. 2. Confession of the Brotherhood of the Rosycross (Confessio Fraternitatis R.C.). 1989. 21.00 (*90-6732-037-4*); Vol. 3. Alchemical Wedding of Christian Rosycross (Chymische Hochzeit Christiani Rosencreutz, Anno 1459, Part I). 1991. 28.00 (*90-70053-15-2*); Vol. 4. Alchemical Wedding of Christian Rosycross (Chymische Hochzeit Christiani Rosencreutz, Anno 1459, Part II). 1991. 28.00 (*90-70053-16-0*); Vol. 1. Call of the Brotherhood of the Rosycross: Esoteric Analysis of the Fama Fraternitatis R. C of 1615. 1989. 27.00 (*90-6732-028-5*); 1991. 31.00 (*0-685-17567-7*) Rosycross Pr.

*__Secrets of the Russian Chess Masters Vol. 1: Fundamentals of the Game, 2 vols., Vols. 1 & 2.__ Lev Alburt & Larry Parr. (Illus.). 224p. (C). 1997. 25.00 (*0-393-04115-8*) Norton.

*__Secrets of the Russian Chess Masters Vol. 2: Beyond the Basics, 2 vols., Vol. 2.__ Lev Albutt & Larry Parr. (Illus.). 224p. (C). 1997. 25.00 (*0-393-04116-6*) Norton.

Secrets of the Saints. Francis J. Sheed. viii, 406p. 1995. text ed. 17.95 (*0-912141-14-X*) Roman Cath Bks.

*__Secrets of the Saltwater Fly.__ F-Stop Fitzgerald. 1997. 24.95 (*0-614-28166-0*) Little.

*__Secrets of the Saltwater Fly: Tips & Tales from the World's Great Angles.__ F. S. Fitzgerald. 1997. 24.95 (*0-8212-2308-9*) Bulfinch Pr.

Secrets of the Samurai: The Martial Arts of Feudal Japan. Oscar Ratti & Adele Westbrook. LC 72-91551. (Illus.). 483p. 1991. pap. 21.95 (*0-8048-1684-0*) C E Tuttle.

*__Secrets of the Sea.__ Penny King & Clare Roundhill. LC 96-53245. (Making Pictures Ser.). (J). 1997. write for info. (*1-57572-193-7*) Rigby Educ.

*__Secrets of the Sea.__ Penny King & Clare Roundhill. LC 96-40519. (Making Pictures Ser.). (J). 1997. write for info. (*1-57572-194-5*) Rigby Interact Libr.

Secrets of the Seeds: Guide to Science Anytime 1995. annuals 95th ed. 1995. pap. text ed. 9.00 (*0-15-306070-0*) HarBrace.

Secrets of the Self. Muhammad Iqbal. 148p. (Orig.). 1985. 7.50 (*1-56744-381-8*) Kazi Pubns.

Secrets of the Sexually Alive Woman. Adelaide Bry. 1976. pap. 4.50 (*0-451-15967-5*, Sig) NAL-Dutton.

Secrets of the Shaman. Gini G. Scott. LC 91-60063. 192p. (Orig.). 1991. pap. 12.95 (*1-56184-023-8*) New Falcon Pubns.

Secrets of the Shopping Mall. Richard Peck. 192p. (J). (gr. k-6). 1980. mass mkt. 3.99 (*0-440-98099-2*) Dell.

Secrets of the Skeleton: Form in Metamorphosis. L. F. Mees. Ed. by Ellen Bohr & David Adams. (Illus.). 108p. (Orig.). 1984. pap. 16.95 (*0-88010-087-7*) Anthroposophic.

Secrets of the Soviet Skaters: Off-Ice Training Methods. Tamara Moskuina. Ed. by L. Copley-Graves. (Illus.). 1995. pap. 40.00 (*1-882849-03-5*) Platoro Pr.

Secrets of the Sphinx: Mysteries of the Ages Revealed. Andrew Raymond. (Illus.). 160p. (Orig.). 1995. pap. 12.95 (*0-9646954-6-4*) UNI Prods.

*__Secrets of the Squaw Bay Caves.__ Mike Savage. (Illus.). 24p. (Orig.). 1997. pap. 6.95 (*1-886028-25-7*) Savage Pr.

Secrets of the SS. Glenn B Infield. 288p. 1990. mass mkt. 5.50 (*0-515-10246-6*) Jove Pubns.

Secrets of the Stones. John Michell. (Illus.). 128p. 1989. pap. 10.95 (*0-89281-337-7*, Destiny Bks) Inner Tradit.

*__Secrets of the Stork: A Workbook for Expecting Mothers & Their Families.__ Linda R. Yerger & Susan O. Diket. Ed. by John P. Yerger. (Illus.). 110p. 1996. wbk. ed., spiral bd. 14.95 (*0-9655414-0-1*) L Y A N Pub.

Secrets of the Street: The Dark Side of Making Money. Gene Marcial. 256p. 1996. pap. text ed. 10.95 (*0-07-040256-6*) McGraw.

Secrets of the Super Net Searchers: The Reflections, Revelations & Hard-Won Wisdom of 35 of the World's Top Internet Researchers. Reva Basch. Ed. by Mary E. Bates. (Cyber Age Bks.). 274p. (Orig.). 1996. pap. 29.95 (*0-910965-22-6*, Pembrtn Pr Bks) Online.

Secrets of the Super Searchers: The Accumulated Wisdom of 23 of the World's Top Online Searchers. Reva Basch. 238p. 1993. pap. 39.95 (*0-910965-12-9*) Online.

Secrets of the Supernatural: Investigating the World's Occult Mysteries. Joe Nickell & John F. Fischer. (Illus.). 199p. 1991. 25.95 (*0-87975-461-3*); pap. 17.95 (*0-87975-685-3*) Prometheus Bks.

Secrets of the Superstars: Excellence in Selling New Homes. Bonnie Alfriend. (Illus.). 319p. (Orig.). 1993. pap. text ed. 24.95 (*0-9639500-0-2*) Alfriend & Assocs.

*__Secrets of the Sword.__ Baron Bazancourt. Ed. by Lance C. Lobo. (Illus.). 208p. 1997. reprint ed. pap. 19.95 (*1-884528-18-X*) Laureate Pr.

Secrets of the Tarot: Origins, History, & Symbolism. Barbara G. Walker. LC 84-47737. (Illus.). 256p. (Orig.). 1984. pap. 18.00 (*0-06-250927-6*, CN 4102) Harper SF.

Secrets of the Temple: How the Federal Reserve Runs the Country. William Greider. 800p. 1989. pap. 17.00 (*0-671-67556-7*, Touchstone Bks) S&S Trade.

Secrets of the Threshold. Rudolf Steiner. Tr. by Ruth Pusch from GER. 157p. 1988. 20.00 (*0-88010-196-2*) Anthroposophic.

Secrets of the Times: Myth & History in Biblical Chronology. Jeremy Hughes. (Journal for the Study of the Old Testament Supplement Ser.: Vol. 66). 315p. 60.00 (*1-85075-178-1*, Pub. by Sheffield Acad UK) CUP Services.

Secrets of the Twenty-Five Year Happy Marriage. Sherman N. Miller & Gwynelle W. Miller. (Illus.). 110p. (Orig.). 1992. pap. text ed. write for info. (*0-9635708-0-3*, TXU534-407) Royal Pub DE.

Secrets of the UFO. Don Elkins & Carla L. Rueckert. 104p. (Orig.). (C). 1977. pap. 6.95 (*0-945007-00-0*) L-L Resrch.

Secrets of the Universe: Scenes from the Journey Home. Scott R. Sanders. LC 91-10219. 256p. 1992. pap. 12.95 (*0-8070-6331-2*) Beacon Pr.

Secrets of the Visual Basic 3.0 Masters. 3rd ed. 1998. 45.00 (*0-672-30780-4*) Sams.

Secrets of the Visual C++ Masters. 2nd ed. 1998. 45.00 (*0-672-30805-3*) Sams.

Secrets of the Webmasters. Charles Deemer. (Illus.). 240p. 1996. pap. 18.95 (*0-945264-20-8*) Resolution Busn Pr.

Secrets of the World's Top Sales Performers. Christine Harvey. 156p. 1990. pap. 6.95 (*1-55850-852-X*) Adams Media.

*__Secrets of the Yellow Brick Road: A Map for the Modern Spiritual Journey.__ Jesse Stewart. LC 96-71662. (Illus.). 150p. (Orig.). 1997. pap. 16.00 (*1-888604-03-4*) SunShine CO.

Secrets of Tut's Tomb. Stephanie A. Reiff. LC 77-22770. (Great Unsolved Mysteries Ser.). (Illus.). (J). (gr. 4 up). 1983. reprint ed. lib. bdg. 24.26 (*0-8172-1051-2*) Raintree Steck-V.

Secrets of Tyrone. Regan Forest. (Men Made in America Ser.). 1994. mass mkt. 3.59 (*0-373-45177-6*, 1-45177-2) Harlequin Bks.

Secrets of Uechi Ryu Karate: And the Mysteries of Okinawa. Alan Dollar. Ed. by Alice Dollar & Robert Davidson. Tr. by Kiyohide Shinjo. (Illus.). 512p. (Orig.). 1996. pap. 44.95 (*0-9651671-1-9*) Cherokee Pubng.

Secrets of Underground Organization & Operations. U. S. Army, Special Research Office Staff. LC 74-25006. 1974. reprint ed. pap. 8.95 (*0-685-16395-4*) Omega Grp.

Secrets of User-Seductive Documents. (Guide Ser.). 1991. per. 30.00 (*0-914548-60-3*, 136-91) Soc Tech Comm.

Secrets of Venus: A Lover's Guide to Charms, Potions & Aphrodisiacs. Vera Lee. (Illus.). 200p. 1995. pap. 14.95 (*0-9635257-6-X*) Mt Ivy Pr.

Secrets of Voodoo. Milo Rigaud. Tr. by Robert B. Cross from FRE. (Illus.). 256p. 1985. reprint ed. pap. 14.95 (*0-87286-171-6*) City Lights.

*__Secrets of Walden Rising.__ Allan Baillie. (J). 1997. pap. 13.99 (*0-670-87351-9*) Viking Child Bks.

Secrets of Warmth: Never Be Cold Again! 2nd enl. rev. ed. Hal Weiss. (Illus.). 160p. 1992. pap. 11.95 (*0-938567-32-2*) Cloudcap.

Secrets of Warmth: Warmth for Comfort or Survival. Hal Weiss. Ed. by Rita Fishman. (Illus.). (Orig.). 1988. pap. 8.95 (*0-9620771-0-0*) Vibe Pubns.

Secrets of Western Tantra: The Sexuality of the Middle Path. 2nd ed. Christopher S. Hyatt. LC 89-81556. (Illus.). 192p. (Orig.). 1989. pap. 14.95 (*1-56184-113-7*) New Falcon Pubns.

Secrets of Whole-Hearted Thinking: 100 Sayings, Ideas, & Paradoxes That Can Make Your Life Fuller, Happier, & Less Complicated. Evan T. Pritchard. LC 93-33283. 1993. 8.95 (*0-88268-160-5*) Station Hill Pr.

Secrets of Winning at Casino Roulette. Lawrence Lowrey. 32p. 1988. pap. 7.95 (*0-934650-15-2*) Sunnyside.

Secrets of Winning at Video Poker. Hugh McKenna. 32p. (Orig.). 1990. pap. 7.95 (*0-934650-18-7*) Sunnyside.

Secrets of Winning Bridge. Jeff Rubens. 241p. 1981. reprint ed. pap. 5.95 (*0-486-24076-2*) Dover.

Secrets of Winning Men. Helen Andelin. Orig. Title: The Fascinating Girl. 262p. 1994. pap. 12.00 (*0-911094-19-9*) Pacific Santa Barbara.

Secrets of Winning People to Your Ideas. J. Donald Walters. (Illus.). 66p. (Orig.). 1989. pap. 4.95 (*0-916124-59-2*, CCP20) Crystal Clarity.

Secrets of Winning People to Your Ideas. J. Donald Walters. 68p. (Orig.). 1993. 5.95 (*1-56589-030-2*) Crystal Clarity.

Secrets of Winning Poker: Outplaying the Best of 'Em! Tex Sheahan & Shane Smith. 200p. 1993. pap. 19.95 (*1-884466-02-8*) Poker Plus.

Secrets of Wise Men, Chemists & Great Physicians. William K. David. 125p. 1993. reprint ed. spiral bd. 9.00 (*0-7873-0238-4*) Hlth Research.

Secrets of Wise Men, Chemists & Great Physicians: A Book of Rare Formulas, Recipes & Prescriptions. W. K. David. (Alternative Medicine Ser.). 1991. lib. bdg. 79.95 (*0-8490-4306-9*) Gordon Pr.

Secrets of Wise Men, Chemists & Great Physicians: Formulas, Recipes & Prescriptions. W. K. David. 1991. lib. bdg. 250.00 (*0-87700-994-5*) Revisionist Pr.

Secrets of Wise Men, Chemists & Great Physicians (1889) William K. David. 130p. 1996. pap. 16.95 (*1-56459-757-1*) Kessinger Pub.

Secrets of Women. 256p. (Orig.). 1993. mass mkt. 6.99 (*0-515-11191-0*) Jove Pubns.

Secrets of World Class Lovers: Erotic Tips & Sensual Stories for a Lifetime of Sexual Fulfillment. Jaid Barrymore. Ed. by Sarah Pirch. LC 95-76107. 256p. 1995. 19.95 (*1-881649-55-5*) Genl Pub Grp.

Secrets of Yantra, Mantra & Tantra. L. R. Chawdhri. 200p. 1992. pap. 10.00 (*81-207-1351-6*, Pub. by Sterling Pubs II) Apt Bks.

Secrets of Yashir. Lisa Carolle. 168p. 1995. mass mkt. 4.99 (*1-896329-22-5*, Pub. by Comnwlth Pub CN) Partners Pubs Grp.

Secrets of Your Family Tree: Healing for Adult Children of Dsyfunctional Famlies. Dave Carder et al. 1995. pap. 14.99 (*0-8024-7749-6*) Moody.

Secrets of Youthing. Leonard D. Orr. 1994. 22.00 (*0-945793-16-2*) Inspir Univ.

Secrets of 123 Classic Science Tricks & Experiments. Edi Lanners. 1987. pap. text ed. 12.95 (*0-07-157345-3*) McGraw.

Secret's Out. Kate Kimball. (Full House Ser.: No. 6). (YA). (gr. 3-6). 1994. mass mkt. 3.99 (*0-671-89859-0*, Minstrel Bks) PB.

*__Secrets Reveal'd; or, An Open Entrance to the Shut Palace of the King: A New Edition.__ Eirenaeus Philalethes. Ed. by William Cooper. (Alchemical Studies Ser.: No. 8). (Orig.). 1997. pap. 9.95 (*1-55818-363-9*, Alchemical) Holmes Pub.

Secret's Shadow: The First Cassidy McCabe Mystery. Alex Matthews. Ed. by Lee Ellison. LC 95-80820. 296p. 1996. 22.50 (*0-9643161-3-7*) Columb Pub.

Secrets Stored in Ecstasy. Carol Bridges. 192p. (Orig.). 1991. pap. 12.95 (*0-945111-07-X*) Earth Nation.

Secrets That Hurt. Jim Boulden & Joan Boulden. (Illus.). 32p. (Orig.). (J). (gr. 1-6). 1993. pap. 5.95 (*1-878076-28-0*) Boulden Pub.

*__Secrets to a Beautiful Garden.__ Sara Godwin. Ed. by Marianne Lipanovich. (Illus.). 96p. (Orig.). 1998. pap. 9.95 (*0-89721-340-8*) Ortho Info.

Secrets to a Better Sex Life. 1992. lib. bdg. 75.00 (*0-8490-8713-9*) Gordon Pr.

Secrets to a Very Good Marriage. Sherry Cohen. 1995. 3.99 (*0-517-15706-3*) Random Hse Value.

Secrets to Auditioning for Commercials. Iris Acker. LC 90-20427. (Illus.). 128p. 1991. pap. 9.95 (*0-942963-04-0*) Distinctive Pub.

Secrets to Beautiful Translucents. Donna M. Stevens. 44p. 1993. reprint ed. pap. 5.95 (*0-916809-67-6*) Scott Pubns MI.

*__Secrets to Buying & Selling a Business.__ 2nd ed. Ira N. Nottonsom. Ed. by Erin Wait. LC 97-1939. 1997. pap. text ed. 24.95 (*1-55571-398-X*) Oasis Pr OR.

Secrets to Debt-Free Home Ownership. Edison R. Guzman. (Illus.). 106p. (Orig.). 1994. pap. 19.95 (*0-9642963-0-6*) ERG Concepts.

Secrets to Decorating & Moving to Florida. Ron Renner. LC 91-91378. (Orig.). 1991. pap. 14.95 (*0-9631435-0-6*) Renner FL.

Secrets to Enliven Learning: How to Develop Extraordinary Self-Directed Training Materials. Ann Petit. LC 94-65592. 176p. 1994. pap. 29.95 (*0-88390-416-0*, Pfiffr & Co) Jossey-Bass.

Secrets to Fast, Natural Healing of Major Health Problems. Andrew Kim. (Illus.). 240p. (Orig.). 1988. 20.95 (*0-317-92303-X*); pap. 15.95 (*0-317-92304-8*) Kims Pub.

Secrets to Financial Success in Marriage. John C. Shimer et al. Ed. by David Harner. LC 92-91090. (Illus.). 450p. (Orig.). 1992. pap. text ed. 22.95 (*0-9633044-3-7*) Success Finan Plan.

*__Secrets to Happiness, Inner Peace & Health: Complete Guide to Optimal Wellness of Body, Mind & Spirit.__ Charles R. Attwood et al. (Illus.). 320p. (Orig.). 1997. pap. 15.95 (*0-9654904-0-8*) Hlth Unltd.

Secrets to Increasing Your Power, Wealth, & Happiness: How to Unleash the Champion Hidden Within You. Alan C. Walter. Ed. by Beverly Miles. (Illus.). 121p. (Orig.). 1995. pap. 27.77 (*1-57569-000-4*) Wisdom Pubng.

Secrets to Keep. large type ed. Josie Metcalfe. 288p. 1995. 21.50 (*0-263-14625-1*, Pub. by M & B UK) Ulverscroft.

Secrets to Keeping Your Faith Strong. Norvel Hayes. 80p. (Orig.). 1989. pap. 4.99 (*0-89274-709-9*, HH709) Harrison Hse.

Secrets to Making Love Happen: Using Handwriting Analysis to Improve Relationships, Vol. 3. 2nd ed. Bart A. Baggett. (Illus.). 304p. (Orig.). 1997. reprint ed. pap. 15.95 (*1-882929-24-1*) Empresse.

***Secrets to Managing Your Energy: The Ki to Life. unabridged ed. Tae Yun Kim. 192p. (Orig.). 1997. pap. 14.95 (*0-9656959-0-5*) NorthStar CA. In this revolutionary book, Grandmaster Kim teaches readers how to become consciously aware**

An Asterisk (*) at the beginning of an entry indicates that the title is appearing in BIP for the first time.

of their energy & how to direct it to achieve far more than ever thought possible - in business & family. Through specific exercises, Kim explains how Ki energy is the key to: 1. staying healthy & feeling young, strong & well-balanced - physically, emotionally, mentally & spiritually 2. forming healthy, fulfilling relationships with unconditional love, no dependency, less conflict & more individuality. 3. transforming & taking charge of one's life. 4. feeling full of life - vibrant, expressive & powerful 5. radiating positive energy to reduce stress & discord & promote peace & harmony. Grandmaster Kim is our nation's foremost energy training specialist, having studied Ki energy since the age of seven. Today she is CEO of Lighthouse Worldwide Solutions (a highly successful cleanroom monitoring systems company), an internationally recognized author & public speaker & a prominent member of our community. She excels in helping others achieve their dreams through the teachings of Ki energy. ***Publisher Provided Annotation.***

---

*__Secrets to Preparing for the LAPD Process: The Leading LAPD Test Preparation Book.__ abr. ed. Rodger A. Sanchez. (Orig.). 1997. pap. text ed. 34.95 (*0-9657685-9-7*) RAS Ventures.

Secrets to Running a Successful Business: How to Have Fun Getting More Business. Jeanette L. Rosenberg. 120p. 1994. student ed. 19.95 (*0-9639304-0-0*) JLR Pub.

*__Secrets to Scheduling the Executive Level Sales Call: How to Win over the Million-Dollar Decision Maker.__ Leslie Buterin. Ed. by Jill St. John. (Illus.). 1997. pap. 24.95 (*0-9658697-0-9*) Lead Edge.

Secrets to School Success: Guiding Your Child Through a Joyous Learning Experience. Brandi Roth & Fay Van Der Kar-Levinson. 250p. Date not set. pap. write for info. (*0-9647119-1-5*) Assoc of Ideas.

Secrets to Staying Happily Married. Murray Mead. (Illus.). 60p. (Orig.). 1994. pap. text ed. 19.95 (*0-9642629-9-1*) Murray Pubng.

*__Secrets to Success in Law School: A Professor's Strategies for Straight A's.__ Theodore Silver. 1997. pap. 16.95 (*1-56171-969-2*) Spi Bks.

Secrets to Tell. Ann Gabhart. 176p. (Orig.). 1994. pap. 3.50 (*0-380-76610-8*, Flare) Avon.

Secrets to Tell, Secrets to Keep: How to Best Handle Your Hidden Thoughts & Feelings & Move Beyond Therapy to a Truly Joyous, Creative & Fulfilling Life. Karen Paine-Gernee & Larry Rothstein. Ed. by Terry Hunt. 240p. (Orig.). 1994. pap. 10.99 (*0-446-39479-3*) Warner Bks.

*__Secrets to Tender Pie.__ Mindy Martin. 1997. 17.95 (*0-614-27968-2*) Ballantine.

*__Secrets to the Game of Golf & Life.__ Leonard Finkel. (Illus.). 112p. 1997. 24.95 (*1-880461-41-2*) Celebrat Excell.

Secrets to the Magic of Oil Painting. William Alexander. (How to Draw & Paint Ser.). (Illus.). 32p. (Orig.). 1989. pap. 6.95 (*0-929261-60-7*, HT208) W Foster Pub.

Secrets to the Tai Chi Circle: Journey to Enlightenment. Luke Chan. (Illus.). 144p. (Orig.). 1993. pap. 10.00 (*0-9637341-0-5*) Benefactor.

Secrets to Writing Killer Metal Songs. 1993. pap. 17.95 incl. cd-rom (*0-7935-2085-1*, 00696510) H Leonard.

Secrets to Writing Killer Metal Songs. 1993. pap. 14.95 incl. audio (*0-7935-2086-X*, 00696511) H Leonard.

Secrets Told by Children of Alcoholics. Donald G. Jorgensen, Jr. & June A. Jorgensen. (Illus.). 144p. 1989. pap. 12.95 (*0-8306-5008-3*) TAB Bks.

Secrets under the Bridge. Overton Shelmire. (Illus.). 245p. 1994. 24.95 (*0-9641720-0-3*) Beran & Shelmire.

Secrets War: The Office of Strategic Services in World War II. Ed. by George C. Chalou. LC 91-45158. (Illus.). 376p. (C). 1992. text ed. 25.00 (*0-911333-91-6*, 100021) National Archives & Recs.

Secrets White Racists Would Never Want Blacks to Know. Timothy D. Williams, Jr. & Herbert Schraufnagel. 110p. (Orig.). 1994. pap. 12.95 (*0-9649959-0-5*) Vociferous Voice.

*__Secrets Within.__ Emma Darcy. 1997. mass mkt. 5.99 (*1-55166-294-9*, Mira Bks) Harlequin Bks.

Secret/Secret. George J. Lamneck. 56p. 1995. pap. 5.25 (*0-8059-3791-9*) Dorrance.

Secretum Secretorum. Ed. by Robert Steele. (EETS, ES Ser.: No. 66). 1974. reprint ed. 35.00 (*0-527-00270-4*) Periodicals Srv.

Secretum Secretorum: The Gouernaunce of Kynges & Prynces. LC 57-5948. 1978. reprint ed. 50.00 (*0-8201-1241-0*) Schol Facsimiles.

Secretum Secretorum: Three Prose Versions. Ed. by Robert Steele. (EETS, ES Ser.: No. 74). 1974. reprint ed. 50.00 (*0-527-00276-3*) Periodicals Srv.

*__Secret...Your Beliefs Create Your Reality: 15-Minutes That Could Change Your Life.__ unabridged ed. Joseph H. Dalconzo. Ed. & Des. by Lisa Gilbert. iv, 76p. (Orig.). 1996. pap. 5.95 (*0-9656207-0-0*) Renaiss Ent.

Sect Ideologies & Social Status. Gary Schwartz. LC 72-120598. 270p. 1970. lib. bdg. 22.00 (*0-226-74216-4*) U Ch Pr.

Sectarian: Or, the Church & the Meeting-House, 3 vols. in 2, 2. Andrew Picken. LC 79-8189. reprint ed. write for info. (*0-404-62096-5*) AMS Pr.

Sectarian Against His Will: Gerrit Roelof Polman & the Birth of Pentecostalism in the Netherlands. Cornelis Van der Laan. LC 91-18217. (Studies in Evangelicalism). (Illus.). 382p. 1991. 45.00 (*0-8108-2412-4*) Scarecrow.

Sectarian Childrearing: The Dunkers 1708-1900. Alvin E. Conner. (Illus.). 259p. 1987. 19.95 (*0-943429-00-5*) Brethren Heritage Pr.

Sectarian Law in the Dead Sea Scrolls: Courts, Testimony & the Penal Code. Lawrence H. Schiffman. LC 82-837. (Brown Judaic Studies). 278p. (C). 1983. pap. 29.50 (*0-89130-569-6*, 14 00 33) Scholars Pr GA.

Sectarian Violence: The Liverpool Experience, 1819-1914: An Aspect of Anglo-Irish History. Frank Neal. LC 87-26030. 284p. 1991. text ed. 24.95 (*0-7190-2348-3*, Pub. by Manchester Univ Pr UK) St Martin.

Sectarianism in Southern Myasaland. R. L. Wishlade. LC 65-5669. 170p. reprint ed. pap. 48.50 (*0-317-28620-X*, 2055391) Bks Demand.

Sectarismo o Cristianismo? Rodrigo Archilla. (SPA.). 1990. 4.50 (*0-685-74982-7*, 498476) Editorial Unilit.

Sectarismo o Cristianismo. Rogelio Archilla. (SPA.). 1991. pap. 5.99 (*1-56063-122-8*, 498417) Editorial Unilit.

*__Sectas Falsa.__ S. Cory. (SPA.). 1.50 (*0-8297-0404-3*) Life Pubs Intl.

Sectas, Tomo I: Adventistas del Septimo Dia. Jorge R. Catalan. (SPA.). 1981. 4.25 (*1-55955-103-8*) CRC Wrld Lit.

Sectas, Tomo II: Los Testigos de Jehova. Jorge R. Catalan. (SPA.). 1981. 5.25 (*1-55955-104-6*) CRC Wrld Lit.

Sectas, Tomo III: Los Mormones. Jorge R. Catalan. (SPA.). 1981. 6.75 (*1-55955-105-4*) CRC Wrld Lit.

*__Sectet of the Stairs.__ Wade Taylor. 165p. pap. 8.00 (*0-9639416-1-5*) Pinecrest Bible.

*__Secteur Informel & les Institutions de Microfinancement en Afrique de l'Ouest.__ (Technical Paper Ser.: No. 342F). 362p. (FRE.). 1996. 30.00 (*0-8213-3805-6*, 13805) World Bank.

Section & Party: A Political Geography of American Presidential Elections from Andrew Jackson to Ronald Reagan. J. Clark Archer & Peter J. Taylor. LC 81-182752. (Geographical Research Studies: No. 4). (Illus.). 285p. reprint ed. pap. 81.30 (*0-8357-3529-X*, 2034211) Bks Demand.

Section Complanata of the Genus Lycopodium. J. H. Wilce. (Illus.). 1965. pap. 48.00 (*3-7682-5419-4*) Lubrecht & Cramer.

Section Eighty-Nine Companion. Ed. by Ari Cowan & Lee T. Paterson. (Orig.). 1989. pap. 38.00 (*0-932823-01-7*) Am Somerset.

Section Five Hundred Fifty-Eight: or The Fatal Letter: From the Diary of Inspector Byrnes. Julian Hawthorne. LC 73-164563. (American Fiction Reprint Ser.). 1977. reprint ed. 23.95 (*0-8369-7040-3*) Ayer.

Section Maintenance Supervisor. (Career Examination Ser.: C-3320). 1994. pap. 29.95 (*0-8373-3320-2*) Nat Learn.

Section Nineteen Eighty-Three Civil Rights Litigation & Attorney's Fees: Current Developments 1991, 2 vols., Set. (Litigation & Administrative Practice Ser.). 1212p. 1991. pap. text ed. 80.00 (*0-685-56916-0*, H4-5110) PLI.

Section Nineteen Eighty-Three Litigation in State Courts, 2 vols. Steven H. Steinglass. LC 87-14596. (Civil Rights Ser.). 1987. ring bd. 225.00 (*0-87632-553-3*) Clark Boardman Callaghan.

Section Nineteen Eighty-Three, Sword & Shield: Civil Rights Violations & the Liability of Urban, State, & Local Government. Robert H. Freilich & Richard G. Carlisle. LC 83-71848. 478p. 1983. 35.00 (*0-89707-110-7*, 5330012) Amer Bar Assn.

Section of Corporation, Banking & Business Law: Proceedings, 1939-1950. American Bar Association Staff. mic. film write for info. (*0-318-57396-2*) Rothman.

Section of Corporation, Banking & Business Law: Proceedings, 1939-1950, Set. American Bar Association Staff. 110.00 (*0-686-89499-5*) Rothman.

Section of Criminal Law: Proceedings, 1955-1963, Set. American Bar Association Staff. 95.00 (*0-686-89500-2*) Rothman.

Section of Criminal Law: Program & Committee Reports, 1932-1955, Set. American Bar Association Staff. 42.50 (*0-8377-9015-8*) Rothman.

Section of International & Comparative Law: Proceedings, 1942-1965, 23 vols. American Bar Association Staff. mic. film write for info. (*0-318-57398-9*) Rothman.

Section of International & Comparative Law: Proceedings, 1942-1965, 23 vols., Set. American Bar Association Staff. 350.00 (*0-8377-9006-9*) Rothman.

Section of Municipal Law: Proceedings, 1935, Set. American Bar Association Staff. 25.00 (*0-8377-9201-0*) Rothman.

Section of Patent, Trademark & Copyright Law: Committee Reports, 1961-1990, Set. American Bar Association Staff. 700.00 (*0-8377-9008-5*) Rothman.

Section of Patent, Trademark & Copyright Law: Proceedings, 1935-1990, 48 vols., Set. American Bar Association Staff. 665.00 (*0-8377-9007-7*) Rothman.

Section of Public Utility Law: Program & Committee Reports, 1933, Set. American Bar Association Staff. 25.00 (*0-685-42623-8*) Rothman.

Section of Real Property Probate & Trust Law: Proceedings, 1938-1965, 28 vols., Set. American Bar Association Staff. 525.00 (*0-686-89519-3*) Rothman.

Section of Taxation: Proceedings, 1940-1946, 7 vols., Set. American Bar Association Staff. ring bd. 25.00 (*0-8377-9215-0*) Rothman.

*__Section Pentanthera, Vol. 50, No. 3.__ K. A. Kron. (Revision of Rhododendron Ser.). 1993. 46.00 (*0-11-495213-2*, Pub. by Royal Botanic Edinburgh UK) Balogh.

Section Reviews for Modern Chemistry 1990. Tzimopoulo. 1990. student ed., pap. 15.25 (*0-03-021878-0*) H Holt & Co.

Section 608 Certification Test Preparatory Manual. ESCO Institute Staff. LC 95-10202. 1995. pap. 8.00 (*0-8273-7365-1*) Delmar.

Section Twenty-Eight: A Practical Guide to the Law & Its Implications. Madeleine Calvin. (C). 1988. 21.00 (*0-946088-32-2*, Pub. by NCCL UK) St Mut.

Section 16 of the Securities Exchange Act, 2 vols. Arnold S. Jacobs. LC 89-7148. (Securities Law Ser.). 1989. ring bd. 250.00 (*0-87632-649-1*) Clark Boardman Callaghan.

Section 1983 Civil Rights Anthology. Ed. by Sheldon H. Nahmod. LC 93-19309. 303p. 1993. pap. 27.95 (*0-87084-135-1*) Anderson Pub Co.

Section 1983 Civil Rights Litigation & Attorney's Fees, 2 vols., Set. (Litigation & Administrative Practice Course Handbook, 1983-84 Ser.). 1760p. 1994. 149.00 (*0-614-17253-5*, H4-5201) PLI.

Section 1983 Civil Rights Litigation & Attorney's Fees, 1989: A Course Handbook, 2 vols., Set. 1146p. 1989. 30.00 (*0-685-69490-9*) PLI.

Section 1983 Civil Rights Litigation & Attorneys' Fees 1995, 2 vols., Set. (Litigation & Administrative Practice Course Handbook, 1983-84 Ser.). 1995. pap. 149.00 (*0-685-65526-1*, H4-5216) PLI.

*__Section 1983 Litigation, Vol. 1.__ 3rd ed. Martin A. Schwartz & John E. Kirklin. (Civil Rights Library). text ed. write for info. (*0-471-11759-5*) Wiley.

*__Section 1983 Litigation: Claims & Defenses, Vol. 1.__ 3rd ed. Martin A. Schwartz & John E. Kirklin. (Civil Rights Library). text ed. 360.00 (*0-471-11761-7*) Wiley.

*__Section 1983 Litigation: Claims, Defenses & Fees, Vol. 1.__ 2nd ed. Martin A. Schwartz & John E. Kirklin. LC 90-28397. (Trial Practice Library Ser.). 1991. text ed. 120.00 (*0-471-51583-3*) Wiley.

*__Section 1983 Litigation: Claims, Defenses & Fees, Vol. 2.__ 2nd ed. Martin A. Schwartz & John E. Kirklin. LC 90-28397. (Trial Practice Library Ser.). 1991. text ed. 120.00 (*0-471-51584-1*) Wiley.

Section 1983 Litigation: Claims, Defenses & Fees, Vol. 3. 2nd ed. Schwartz. (Trial Practice Library). 560p. 1994. text ed. 120.00 (*0-471-60902-1*, Pub. by Wiley Law Pubns) Wiley.

*__Section 1983 Litigation: Federal Evidence - 1997 Cumulative Supplement No. 1, Vol. 3.__ 2nd ed. Martin A. Schwartz. pap. text ed. write for info. (*0-471-17895-0*) Wiley.

*__Section 1983 Litigation: Statutory Attorney's Fees, Vol. 2.__ 3rd ed. Martin A. Schwartz & John E. Kirklin. (Civil Rights Library). text ed. 125.00 (*0-471-11758-7*) Wiley.

Section 1983 Litigation: 1996 Cumulative Supplement, Vol. 3. 2nd ed. John W. Witt et al. 1996. pap. text ed. 65.00 (*0-471-15965-4*, Wiley-Liss) Wiley.

*__Section 1983 Litigation No. 1: 1996 Cumulative Supplement, 3 vols., Vol. 3.__ 2nd ed. Martin A. Schwartz & John E. Kirklin. LC 90-28397. 1048p. 1995. suppl. ed., pap. text ed. 99.00 (*0-471-14646-3*, LA20) Wiley.

Section 1983 Litigation No. 2: 1996 Supplement, 2 vols., Vol. 2. 2nd ed. Martin A. Schwartz & John E. Kirklin. LC 90-28397. 1996. pap. text ed. 59.00 (*0-471-16316-3*, Wiley-Liss) Wiley.

Section 1983 Litigation Forms: Claims, Defenses, Fees, Vol. 3. 2nd ed. John W. Witt et al. (Civil Rights Library). 360p. 1994. text ed. 130.00 (*0-471-30631-2*) Wiley.

Section 2: Maritime Ports & Seaways see Inland & Maritime Waterways & Ports: Proceedings of the XXV Congress of the Permanent International Association of Navigation Congresses, (PIANC) Edinburgh, Scotland

Section 401(k)...Everybody Wins, Employer & Employee. Irving L. Blackman & Andrew J. Bedsole, III. (Special Report Ser.: No. 22). 62p. 1991. pap. 25.00 (*0-916181-25-1*) Blackman Kallick Bartelstein.

Section 403(b) Manual. 9th ed. Arvid L. Mortensen. 420p. 1994. pap. 39.95 (*0-7931-0943-4*, 56050209) Dearborn Finan.

Section 504 & the Schools Includes Supplement for 1994. Perry A. Zirkel. LC 93-28807. 470p. 1993. ring bd. 74.50 (*0-934753-95-4*) LRP Pubns.

Section 8 Rental Voucher & Rental Certificate Utilization Study: Final Report. Stephen D. Kennedy & Meryl Finkel. (Illus.). 130p. (Orig.). (C). 1996. pap. text ed. 30.00 (*0-7881-2655-5*) DIANE Pub.

Section 89 Compliance Manual: The Complete Guide to the New Non-Discrimination Rules for Employee Benefit Plans. LC 88-37270. 1988. 250.00 (*1-55871-029-9*) BNA Plus.

Sectional Anatomy. Kelley & Petersen. 192p. (gr. 13). 1997. student ed., pap. text ed. 19.95 (*0-8151-8667-3*) Mosby Yr Bk.

Sectional Anatomy by MRI. 2nd ed. Georges Y. El-Khoury et al. (Illus.). 776p. 1994. 250.00 (*0-443-08890-X*) Churchill.

Sectional Anatomy by MRI-CT. Georges Y. El-Khoury et al. (Illus.). 732p. 1990. text ed. 195.00 (*0-443-08543-9*) Churchill.

Sectional Anatomy for Imaging Professionals. Kelley & Petersen. 304p. (gr. 13). 1996. text ed. 52.00 (*0-8151-8665-7*) Mosby Yr Bk.

Sectional Anatomy for Imaging Professionals. Kelley & Peterson. (gr. 13). 1997. teacher ed., pap. text ed. write for info. (*0-8151-4933-6*) Mosby Yr Bk.

*__Sectional Anatomy Learning System: Concepts & Applications.__ Edith J. Applegate. (Illus.). 1991. teacher ed. write for info. (*0-7216-3240-8*) Saunders.

Sectional Anatomy Learning System: Concepts & Applications, 2 vols., Set. Applegate. (Illus.). 1991. text ed. 58.50 (*0-7216-3269-6*) Saunders.

Sectional Anatomy of the Head & Neck: A Detailed Atlas. John H. Lillie & Brent A. Bauer. (Illus.). 224p. 1994. 57.95 (*0-19-504297-2*) OUP.

Sectional Anatomy of the Head & Neck with Correlative Radiology. Lynn J. Romrell et al. LC 92-49088. (Illus.). 230p. 1994. text ed. 125.00 (*0-8121-1673-9*) Williams & Wilkins.

Sectional Crisis & Southern Constitutionalism. Don E. Fehrenbacher. LC 95-44022. 208p. (C). 1996. pap. text ed. 12.95 (*0-8071-2036-7*) La State U Pr.

Sectional Fetal Anatomy in Ultrasound. Ed. by A. Staudach. (Illus.). 180p. 1987. 137.00 (*0-387-18213-6*) Spr-Verlag.

Sectional Human Anatomy: Correlated with CT & MRI. 3rd ed. Man-Chung Han & Chu-Wan Kim. (Illus.). 325p. 1995. 95.00 (*0-89640-279-7*) Igaku-Shoin.

Sectional Stress & Party Strength: A Study of Roll-Call Voting Patterns in the United States House of Representatives, 1836-1860. Thomas B. Alexander. LC 67-21652. (Illus.). 326p. reprint ed. pap. 93.00 (*0-8357-3198-7*, 2039469) Bks Demand.

Sectional Title Handbook. 2nd ed. G. J. Paddock. 216p. 1990. pap. write for info. (*0-7021-2346-3*, Pub. by Juta SA) Gaunt.

Sectional Warping Made Easy. (Illus.). 1988. reprint ed. pap. 8.00 (*1-56659-017-5*) Robin & Russ.

Sectionalism & American Political Development, 1880-1980. Richard Bensel. LC 84-40145. (Illus.). 520p. (C). 1984. reprint ed. text ed. 35.00 (*0-299-09830-3*) U of Wis Pr.

Sectionalism & American Political Development, 1880-1980. Richard Bensel. LC 84-40145. (Illus.). 520p. (C). 1987. reprint ed. pap. text ed. 16.95 (*0-299-09834-6*) U of Wis Pr.

Sectionalism & Representation in South Carolina. W. A. Schaper. LC 68-31582. (American Scene Ser.). (Illus.). 1968. reprint ed. lib. bdg. 29.50 (*0-306-71158-3*) Da Capo.

Sectionalism in American Politics, 1774-1787. Joseph L. Davis. LC 76-11310. reprint ed. pap. 71.60 (*0-608-01964-X*, 2062619) Bks Demand.

Sectioning & Cryosectioning for Electron Microscopy. A. M. Glauert et al. (Practical Methods in Electron Microscopy Ser.: Vol. 13). 322p. 1991. 229.25 (*0-444-81191-5*); pap. 66.75 (*0-444-81190-7*) Elsevier.

Sections & Politics: Selected Essays by William B. Hesseltine. Ed. by Richard N. Current. LC 68-65095. 150p. 1968. 7.50 (*0-87020-027-5*) State Hist Soc Wis.

Sections of Orange. Doris Walker. (Illus.). 1989. 45.00 (*0-9606476-5-1*) To-the-Point.

Sections (1-5) (Basic & Clinical Science Course (1989-90) Ser.). (C). 1989. pap. text ed. 180.00 (*0-685-26056-9*) Am Acad Ophthal.

Sections (6-11) (Basic & Clinical Science Course (1989-90) Ser.). (C). 1989. pap. text ed. 200.00 (*0-685-26057-7*) Am Acad Ophthal.

Sector Adjustment Lending & the Inter-American Development Bank. Stanley Please. 22p. 1989. pap. text ed. write for info. (*0-940602-29-6*) IADB.

Sector Participation Decisions in Labor Supply Models. Menno Pradhan. LC 94-41478. (LSMS Working Papers: No. 113). 44p. 1995. 6.95 (*0-8213-3124-8*, 13124) World Bank.

Sectoral Aggregation Error in Regional Input-Output Models: A Simulation Study. Benjamin H. Stevens & Michael L. Lahr. (Discussion Paper Ser.: No. 134). 1993. pap. 10.00 (*1-55869-141-3*) Regional Sci Res Inst.

Sectoral Aggregation Error in Regional Input-Output Models: An Empirical Investigation. rev. ed. Benjamin H. Stevens & Michael L. Lahr. (Discussion Paper Ser.: No. 130). 30p. 1990. pap. 10.00 (*1-55869-140-5*) Regional Sci Res Inst.

Sectoral Foundations of China's Development. Ed. by Shahid J. Burki & Shahid Yusuf. (Discussion Paper Ser.: No. 148). 128p. 1992. 7.95 (*0-8213-2000-9*, 12000) World Bank.

Sectoral Growth in Chile, 1962-82. Juan E. Coeymans & Yair Mundlak. LC 93-30465. 1993. write for info. (*0-89629-098-0*) Intl Food Policy.

Sectoral Labor Effects of North American Free Trade. Ed. by Sidney Weintraub et al. (Special Publications: No. 1). 389p. 1993. pap. 20.00 (*0-89940-318-2*) LBJ Sch Pub Aff.

Sectoral Study of Transnational Enterprises in Latin America: The Automotive Industry. 41p. 1974. 5.00 (*0-8270-3295-1*) OAS.

Sectoral Study of Transnational Enterprises in Latin America: The Banana Industry. Organization of American States Staff. 1978. reprint ed. pap. text ed. 5.00 (*0-685-03624-3*); reprint ed. Span. Ed. write for info. (*0-8270-3310-9*) OAS.

Sectors of Mutual Benefit in U. S.-Soviet Relations. Ed. by Nish Jamgotch, Jr. LC 85-1576. (Duke Press Policy Studies). xxii, 254p. (C). 1985. text ed. 46.95 (*0-8223-0606-9*) Duke.

Sects & New Religious Movements: An Anthology of Texts from the Catholic Church, 1986-1994. New Working Group On New Religious Movments Editors. 78p. (Orig.). 1995. pap. 7.95 (*1-57455-023-3*) US Catholic.

Sects & Scrolls: Essays on Qumran & Related Topics. Philip R. Davies. (South Florida Studies in the History of Judaism: Vol. 134). 198p. 1996. 74.95 (*0-7885-0213-1*) Scholars Pr GA.

Sects & Society: A Sociological Study of Three Religious Groups in Britain. Bryan R. Wilson. LC 78-5993. 397p. 1978. reprint ed. text ed. 99.75 (*0-313-20439-X*, WISA, Greenwood Pr) Greenwood.

*__Sects, Cults & Alternative Religions: A World Survey & Sourcebook.__ David V. Barrett. (Illus.). 272p. 1997. 24.95 (*0-7137-2567-2*, Pub. by Blandford Pr UK) Sterling.

Secuencia Ceramica de la Region de Coba, Quintana Roo. Jose F. Robles. 278p. 1990. pap. 11.00 (*968-6068-75-9*, IN028) UPLAAP.

S

S

Secular & Christian Leadership in Corinth: A Socio-Historical & Exegetical Study of 1 Corinthians 1-6. Andrew D. Clarke. LC 93-10139. (Arbeiten zur Geschichte des Antiken Judentums & des Urchristentums Ser.: Vol. 18). (Illus.). xi, 188p. 1993. 78.75 (90-04-09862-3) E J Brill.

***Secular & Sacred: Photographs of Mexico.** Van D. Coke. LC 92-15219. (Illus.). 181p. 1992. reprint ed. pap. 51.60 (0-608-04141-6, 2064874) Bks Demand.

Secular Ark: Studies in the History of Biogeography. Janet Browne. LC 82-17497. (Illus.). 273p. 1983. text ed. 47.50 (0-300-02460-6) Yale U Pr.

Secular Bioethics in Theological Perspective. Ed. by Earl E. Shelp. LC 95-20651. (Theology & Medicine Ser.: Vol. 8). 236p. (C). 1996. lib. bdg. 133.00 (0-7923-3735-2) Kluwer Ac.

***Secular Buildings in the Crusader Kingdom of Jerusalem: An Archaeological Gazetteer.** Denys Pringle. (Illus.). 250p. (C). 1997. text ed. 70.00 (0-521-46010-7) Cambridge U Pr.

Secular Choral Music in Print, 2 vols. 2nd ed. Ed. by Susan H. Simon & F. Mark Daugherty. LC 87-24749. (Music in Print Ser.: Vol. 2). 1179p. 1987. lib. bdg. 220.00 (0-88478-020-1) Musicdata.

Secular Choral Music in Print: Arranger Index. 2nd ed. LC 87-24033. (Music in Print Ser.: Vol. 2C). 128p. 1987. lib. bdg. 35.00 (0-88478-021-X) Musicdata.

Secular Choral Music in Print: Master Index 1993. LC 93-42281. (Music-in-Print Ser.: Vol. 2). 1993. 95.00 (0-88478-032-5) Musicdata.

***Secular Choral Music in Print: Master Index 1996.** LC 87-24749. (Music-in-Print Ser.: Vol. 2x). 390p. 1996. lib. bdg. 95.00 (0-88478-042-2) Musicdata.

Secular Choral Music in Print: 1991 Supplement. Ed. by F. Mark Daugherty & Susan H. Simon. LC 91-15287. (Music-in-Print Ser.: Vol. 2S). 200p. 1991. 95.00 (0-88478-027-9) Musicdata.

Secular Choral Music in Print: 1993 Supplement. Ed. by F. Mark Daugherty & Susan H. Simon. LC 93-28494. (Music-in-Print Ser.: Vol. 2). 210p. 1993. 95.00 (0-88478-031-7) Musicdata.

***Secular Choral Music in Print: 1996 Supplement.** Ed. by Robert W. Cho et al. LC 87-24749. (Music-in-Print Ser.: Vol. 2u). 165p. 1996. lib. bdg. 95.00 (0-88478-041-4) Musicdata.

Secular City: Studies in the Enlightenment. Ed. by Hemming et al. 256p. 1995. text ed. 49.95 (0-85989-416-9, Pub. by Univ Exeter Pr UK) Northwestern U Pr.

Secular Crown on Fire: The Kashmir Problem. Ed. by Asghar A. Engineer. (C). 1991. 36.00 (0-685-49095-5, Pub. by Ajanta II) S Asia.

Secular Darkness: Religious Right Involvement in Texas Public Education, 1963-1989. James R. Durham. LC 94-11507. (American University Studies: Vol. 167). 136p. (C). 1995. text ed. 33.95 (0-8204-2543-5) P Lang Pubng.

Secular Education in Philo of Alexandria. Alan Mendelson. (Monographs of the Hebrew Union College: No. 7). 128p. 1981. 20.00 (0-87820-406-7) Hebrew Union Coll Pr.

***Secular Experience of God.** Kenneth Cragg. (Christian Mission & Modern Culture Ser.). 80p. (Orig.). 1998. pap. 8.00 (1-56338-223-7) TPI PA.

Secular Franciscan Companion. rev. ed. Marion A. Habig. 294p. 1987. pap. 7.50 (0-8199-0910-6, Frncscn Herld) Franciscan Pr.

***Secular Goldsmiths' Work in Medieval France: A History.** R. W. Lightbown. (Illus.). 230p. 1978. 19.98 (0-85431-224-2, Pub. by Soc Antiquaries UK) David Brown.

Secular Humanism: An Orthodox Perspective. John F. Bockman. LC 90-63251. 85p. (Orig.). 1991. pap. 8.00 (0-913026-73-5) St Nectarios.

Secular Humanist Declaration. Paul Kurtz. 29p. 1981. pap. 4.95 (0-87975-149-5) Prometheus Bks.

Secular India: A Historical Quest. Sanjeev Tare. (C). 1991. 24.00 (0-685-59774-1, Pub. by Anmol II) S Asia.

Secular Is Sacred. Collins. 1974. lib. bdg. 82.50 (90-247-1588-1, Pub. by M Nijhoff NE) Kluwer Ac.

Secular Lyric in Middle English. Arthur K. Moore. LC 71-100170. 255p. 1970. reprint ed. text ed. 35.00 (0-8371-2973-7, MOME, Greenwood Pr) Greenwood.

Secular Madrigals of Filippo Di Monte, 1521- 1603. Brian Mann. LC 83-1061. (Studies in Musicology: No. 64). 497p. reprint ed. pap. 141.70 (0-8357-1402-0, 2070483) Bks Demand.

Secular Magi: Marx, Freud, & Nietzsche on Religion. William L. Newell. 240p. (C). 1994. pap. text ed. 21.50 (0-8191-9588-X) U Pr of Amer.

Secular Medieval Latin Song: An Anthology. Bryan Gillingham. (Wissenschaftliche Abhandlungen-Musicological Studies: Vol. LC-1). xvi, 475p. 1993. lib. bdg. 160.00 (0-931902-81-9) Inst Mediaeval Mus.

Secular Mind: Transformations of Faith in Modern Europe. Ed. by W. Warren Wagar. LC 81-20019. 275p. 1982. 45.00 (0-8419-0766-8) Holmes & Meier.

Secular Miracle: Religion, Politics & Economic Policy in Iran. Ali Rahnema & Farhad Nomani. LC 90-46689. 432p. (C). 1990. pap. 25.00 (0-86232-939-6, Pub. by Zed Bks Ltd UK); text ed. 60.00 (0-86232-938-8, Pub. by Zed Bks Ltd UK) Humanities.

Secular Movements in Production & Prices: Their Nature & Bearing upon Cyclical Fluctuations. Simon Kuznets. LC 67-16341. (Reprints of Economic Classics Ser.). xxiv, 536p. 1967. reprint ed. 57.50 (0-678-00318-1) Kelley.

Secular Music in Colonial Annapolis: The Tuesday Club, 1745-56. John B. Talley. LC 86-24992. (Music in American Life Ser.). 336p. 1988. text ed. 29.95 (0-252-01402-2) U of Ill Pr.

Secular Poems of Henry Vaughan. Ed. by E. L. Marilla. (Essays & Studies on English Language & Literature: Vol. 21). 1974. reprint ed. pap. 40.00 (0-8115-0219-8) Periodicals Srv.

***Secular Psalms, Vol. 28.** Bradford Morrow. 1997. pap. text ed. 12.00 (0-941964-44-2) Conjunctions.

Secular Saints: Two Hundred Fifty Canonized & Beatified Lay Men, Women & Children. Joan C. Cruz. LC 89-50830. (Illus.). 800p. 1989. 40.00 (0-89555-383-X) TAN Bks Pubs.

Secular Sanctity. rev. ed. Edward Hays. LC 84-81954. (Illus.). 176p. 1984. reprint ed. pap. 8.95 (0-939516-05-5) Forest Peace.

Secular Scripture: A Study of the Structure of Romance. Northrop Frye. (Charles Eliot Norton Lectures). 200p. 1978. pap. 11.95 (0-674-79676-4, HP 127) HUP.

Secular Socialists: The CCF-NDP in Ontario: a Biography. John T. Morley. LC 85-160769. (Illus.). 283p. reprint ed. pap. 80.70 (0-7837-6906-7, 2046736) Bks Demand.

Secular Solar & Geomagnetic Variations in the Last 10,000 Years. Ed. by F. Richard Stephenson & Arnold W. Wolfendale. (C). 1988. lib. bdg. 216.00 (90-277-2755-4) Kluwer Ac.

Secular Squeeze: Reclaiming Christian Depth in a Shallow World. John F. Alexander. LC 93-18086. 307p. (Orig.). 1993. pap. 12.99 (0-8308-1341-1, 1341) InterVarsity.

Secular Values for Secular India. P. C. Chatterji. (C). 1995. 40.00 (81-7304-004-4, Pub. by Manohar II) S Asia.

Secular Vocations: Intellectuals, Professionalism, Culture. Bruce Robbins. 256p. (C). 1993. pap. text ed. 19.00 (0-86091-630-8, B0530, Pub. by Vrso UK) Norton.

Secular Vocations: Intellectuals, Professionalism, Culture. Bruce Robbins. 256p. (C). (gr. 13). 1993. text ed. 60.00 (0-86091-430-5, B0526, Pub. by Vrso UK) Norton.

Secular Wizard: Book IV of a Wizard in Rhyme. Christopher Stasheff. 1995. mass mkt. 5.99 (0-345-38854-2, Del Rey) Ballantine.

Secular Word Is Full-Time Service Study Guide. Larry Peabody. 1976. pap. 1.50 (0-87508-449-4) Chr Lit.

Secular Work Is Full Time Service. Larry Peabody. 1974. pap. 4.95 (0-87508-448-6) Chr Lit.

Secularism & Development: The Indian Experience. P. C. Joshi. (C). 1995. 28.00 (0-7069-8370-X, Pub. by Vikas II) S Asia.

Secularism, Art & Freedom. David Nash. 224p. 1992. text ed. 54.00 (0-7185-1417-3) St Martin.

Secularism, Art & Freedom, Vol. 1. Nash. (C). 1994. pap. text ed. 19.00 (0-7185-2084-X, Pub. by Leicester Univ Pr) Bks Intl VA.

Secularism in India: A Reappraisal. Saral Jhingram. (C). 1995. 32.00 (81-241-0246-5, Pub. by Har-Anand Pubns II) S Asia.

Secularism in India: Dilemmas & Challenges. M. M. Sankhdher. (C). 1992. 38.00 (81-7100-409-1, Pub. by Deep II) S Asia.

Secularism in Indian Art. K. V. Rajan. (C). 1988. 48.50 (81-7017-245-4, Pub. by Abhinav II) S Asia.

Secularism versus Biblical Secularity. Ed. by Marianne Postiglione & Robert A. Brungs. 272p. (Orig.). (C). 1994. pap. 15.95 (1-885583-00-1) ITEST Faith.

Secularist: Poems by Claudia Keelan. Claudia Keelan. LC 95-36584. (Contemporary Poetry Ser.). 1997. pap. 15.95 (0-8203-1802-7) U of Ga Pr.

***Secularization & Mission: A Theological Essay.** Bert Hoedemaker. (Christian Mission & Modern Culture Ser.). 96p. (Orig.). 1998. pap. 8.00 (1-56338-224-5) TPI PA.

Secularization of American Education As Shown by State Legislation, State Constitutional Provisions & State Supreme Court Decisions. S. W. Brown. LC 70-176600. (Columbia University. Teachers College. Contributions to Education Ser.: No. 49). reprint ed. 37.50 (0-404-55049-5) AMS Pr.

Secularization of Philosophy. Gianni Vattimo. (Contemporary Studies in Philosophy & the Human Sciences Ser.). (C). 1996. text ed. write for info. (0-391-03900-8) Humanities.

Secularization of the Academy. Ed. by George M. Marsden & Bradley J. Longfield. (Religion in America Ser.). 288p. (C). 1992. pap. text ed. 19.95 (0-19-507352-5) OUP.

Secularization of the California Missions (1810-1846) Gerald J. Geary. LC 73-3572. (Catholic University of America. Studies in Romance Languages & Literatures: No. 17). reprint ed. 39.50 (0-404-57767-9) AMS Pr.

Secularization of the European Mind in the Nineteenth Century. Owen Chadwick. (Canto Book Ser.). 292p. (C). 1990. pap. text ed. 11.95 (0-521-39829-0) Cambridge U Pr.

Secularization, Rationalism, & Sectarianism: Essays in Honour of Bryan R. Wilson. Ed. by Eileen Barker. LC 92-41458. (Illus.). 344p. 1993. 59.00 (0-19-827721-0, Old Oregon Bk Store) OUP.

Secularization 1995, Vol. 2. Frankel. 1995. 82.50 (0-316-29137-4) Little.

Secularizing the Faith: Canadian Protestant Clergy & the Crisis of Belief, 1850-1940. David B. Marshall. (Illus.). 288p. 1992. 55.00 (0-8020-5938-4); pap. 19.95 (0-8020-6879-0) U of Toronto Pr.

***Secundum/Tertium Adiacens Vicissitudes of a Logical Distinction.** Ed. by G. Nuchelmans. (Verhandelingen der Koninklijke Nederlandse Akademie van Wetenschappen, Afd. Letterkunde, Nieuwe Reeks Ser.). 56p. 1992. pap. text ed. 20.00 (0-444-85762-1) Elsevier.

Secure Accommodation in the Child Care System: "Between Hospital & Prison or Thereabouts?" Robert Harris & Noel Timms. LC 92-38923. 224p. 1993. pap. write for info. (0-415-06282-9, Tavistock) Routledge.

Secure Accommodation in the Child Care System: "Between Hospital & Prison or Thereabouts?" Robert Harris & Noel Timms. LC 92-38923. 224p. (C). (gr. 13). 1993. text ed. 69.95 (0-415-06281-0, B0247, Tavistock) Routledge.

Secure & Rejoicing. George E. Failing. 1980. pap. 0.95 (0-937296-03-1, 223-A) Presence Inc.

Secure Base. John Bowlby. 224p. 1990. pap. 16.00 (0-465-07597-5) Basic.

***Secure Commerce on the Internet.** Vijay Ahuja. LC 96-30881. (Illus.). 298p. 1996. pap. text ed. 29.95 (0-12-045597-8, AP Prof) Acad Pr.

Secure Computing: Threats & Safeguards. Rita C. Summers. LC 96-45108. (Illus.). 448p. 1996. pap. text ed. 59.95 (0-07-069419-2) McGraw.

Secure Data Networking. Michael Purser. LC 93-7161. 1993. text ed. 69.00 (0-89006-692-2) Artech Hse.

Secure Digital Communications. Ed. by G. Longo. (CISM International Centre for Mechanical Sciences Ser.: No. 279). (Illus.). v, 332p. 1984. 54.95 (0-387-81784-0) Spr-Verlag.

Secure Electronic Commerce. Ford & Baum. LC 97-7695. (C). 1997. pap. text ed. 48.00 (0-13-476342-4) P-H.

***Secure Electronic Transactions.** Loeb. (ITCP-US Computer Science Ser.). 1997. pap. 34.99 incl. cd-rom (1-85032-901-X) ITCP.

Secure from Crime: How to Be Your Own Bodyguard. Craig F. Huber & Don Paul. LC 92-81773. (Illus.). 150p. (Orig.). 1993. pap. 14.95 (0-938263-16-1) Path Finder.

Secure from Crime: How to Be Your Own Bodyguard. 2nd expanded rev. ed. Ed. by Craig F. Huber & Don Paul. LC 92-81773. (Illus.). 180p. 1995. pap. 14.95 (0-938263-18-8) Path Finder.

Secure Information Transfer - PC Encryption. Jackson. 1990. 61.00 (0-8493-7711-0, QA76) CRC Pr.

Secure Networking: Standards Protocols & Algorithms. Charles Kaufman. (C). 1995. text ed. 53.00 (0-13-061466-1) P-H.

***Secure Old Age: Approaches to Long-Term Care Financing.** Ed. by Kathleen H. Wilber et al. LC 96-36294. (Illus.). 200p. 1996. 39.95 (0-8261-9431-1) Springer Pub.

Secure Passage at Sea. Ed. by Ray S. Cline & William M. Carpenter. LC 91-65338. 248p. (Orig.). (C). 1991. pap. text ed. 12.50 (0-943057-03-5) US Global Strat.

Secure People: A Report on Corporate Personnel Security. Jack Smith. 96p. (C). 1990. 490.00 (1-85271-094-2, Pub. by IBC Tech Srvs UK) St Mut.

Secure Speech Communications: A Monograph. Henry J. Beker & F. C. Piper. (Microelectronics & Signal Processing Ser.). 1985. text ed. 119.00 (0-12-084780-9) Acad Pr.

Secure the Shadow: Death & Photography in America. Jay Ruby. LC 94-23118. (Illus.). 220p. 1995. 39.95 (0-262-18164-9) MIT Pr.

Secure UNIX. Samuel Samalin. LC 96-35315. 202p. 1996. pap. text ed. 34.95 (0-07-054554-5) McGraw.

Secure Your Child's Future: Financial Strategies to Safeguard Your Child's College Education. Price Waterhouse Staff. 1996. pap. 16.00 (0-614-12583-9) Irwin Prof Pubng.

Secure Your Child's Future: Financial Strategies to Safeguard Your Child's College Education. Price Waterhouse. 125p. 1996. pap. 15.95 (0-7863-1003-0) Irwin Prof Pubng.

***Secure Your Future.** Price Waterhouse Staff. 1996. pap. text ed. 16.95 (0-7863-1049-9) Irwin Prof Pubng.

Secure Your Future: Financial Planning at Any Age. Chuck Tellalian & Walter Rosen. (Successful Business Library). 206p. 1994. pap. 19.95 (1-55571-335-1); ring bd. 39.95 (1-55571-334-3) Oasis Pr OR.

Secure Your Future: Your Personal Companion for Understanding Lifestyle & Financial Aspects... Price Waterhouse LLP Staff. 352p. 1995. per. 16.95 (0-7863-0526-6) Irwin Prof Pubng.

Secured Credit. Lynn M. LoPucki. 1995. 52.00 (0-316-53219-3) Little.

Secured Creditors & Lessors under the Bank Reform Act of 1989. 534p. 1989. 17.50 (0-317-99802-1, A4-4279) PLI.

Secured Creditors & Lessors under the Bankruptcy Reform Act of 1988. (Commercial Law & Practice Course Handbook Ser.). 558p. 1988. 15.00 (0-685-69491-7) PLI.

Secured Transaction under the Uniform Commercial Code, 5 vols., Vol. 1, 1a, 1b, 1c & 1d. Peter Coogan & William E. Hogan. (Bender's Uniform Commercial Code Service Ser.). 1963. Updates. ring bd. write for info. (0-8205-1615-5) Bender.

Secured Transactions. Dolan. 1995. 20.95 (0-316-18910-3) Little.

Secured Transactions. Steven Emanuel. 180p. 1988. pap. text ed. 12.95 (1-56542-060-8) E Pub Corp.

Secured Transactions. Lloyd. 1988. teacher ed. write for info. (0-318-67319-3) Bender.

Secured Transactions. 3rd ed. Whaley. 1993. 41.00 (0-316-93242-6) Little.

Secured Transactions: Suitable for Use with Whaley. Richard G. Bell. (Cambridge Ser.). 188p. 1989. pap. text ed. 14.50 (0-685-54295-5, Chicago Law Bk) Cambridge Law.

Secured Transactions: Teaching Materials. 5th ed. Richard E. Speidel et al. (American Casebook Ser.). 67p. 1993. student ed., teacher ed., pap. text ed. 30.00 (0-314-03032-8) West Pub.

Secured Transactions Casenotes Law Outlines. Donald B. King. Ed. by Norman S. Goldenberg et al. (Law Outlines Ser.). (Orig.). (C). 1995. pap. text ed. write for info. (0-87457-190-1, 5710) Casenotes Pub.

Secured Transactions in a Nutshell. 3rd ed. Henry J. Bailey, III & Richard B. Hagedorn. (Nutshell Ser.). 390p. 1988. pap. text ed. 17.00 (0-314-41445-2) West Pub.

Secured Transactions in Arizona: A Lawyer's Guide to Article Nine of the UCC. William E. Boyd. 106p. 1984. ring bd. 18.20 (0-910039-10-0) AZ Law Inst.

Secured Transactions in California Commercial Law Practice. John D. Ayer et al. 363p. 1986. text ed. 100.00 (0-88124-142-3, BU-32310) Cont Ed Bar-CA.

Secured Transactions in Florida. 2nd ed. Florida Bar Staff. LC 81-71838. 1991. ring bd. 70.00 (0-910373-51-5, 239) FL Bar Legal Ed.

Secured Transactions in Personal Property. Brian N. Siegel. 1979. pap. 26.50 (0-89074-067-4) Lega Bks.

Secured Transactions in Personal Property. 3rd ed. Robert L. Jordan & William D. Warren. (University Casebook Ser.). 1992. text ed. 37.00 (0-88277-986-9) Foundation Pr.

***Secured Transactions in Personal Property.** 4th ed. Robert L. Jordan & William D. Warren. (University Casebook Ser.). 683p. 1997. pap. text ed. write for info. (1-56662-549-1) Foundation Pr.

Secured Transactions, Teaching Materials. 5th ed. Richard E. Speidel et al. (American Casebook Ser.). 456p. 1993. teacher ed., pap. text ed. 32.00 (0-314-02620-7) West Pub.

Secured Transactions under the Revised Uniform Commercial Code, 1989. 3rd ed. William A. Dreier et al. LC 86-104417. 228p. ring bd. 65.00 (0-685-65979-8) NJ Inst CLE.

Secured Transactions under the Uniform Commercial Code. 2nd ed. Ray D. Henson. LC 78-26098. (Hornbook Ser.). 504p. 1979. text ed. 31.50 (0-8299-2023-4) West Pub.

Securing America's Pension Promise: How to Avoid the Threats to Funding a Secure Retirement. James H. Smalhout. LC 95-47695. 1996. write for info. (1-78630-794-4) Irwin Prof Pubng.

Securing & Using Medical Evidence in Personal Injury & Healthcare Cases. Robert C. Strodel. 340p. 1988. text ed. 49.95 (0-13-050303-7, Busn) P-H.

***Securing Best Practice: An Induction Manual for Residential Staff in Secure Accomodation.** Precencia Gabbidon & Barry Goldson. 306p. 1997. pap. 60.00 (1-900990-10-5, Pub. by Natl Childrens Bur UK) Paul & Co Pubs.

Securing Client/Server Networks. Peter Davis. (McGraw-Hill Computer Communications Series). 1996. text ed. 50.00 (0-07-015841-X) McGraw.

Securing Command of the Sea: NATO Naval Planning, 1948-1954. Sean M. Maloney. (Illus.). 256p. 1994. 45.00 (1-55750-562-4) Naval Inst Pr.

Securing Compliance: Seven Case Studies. Ed. by Martin L. Friedland. 432p. 1990. 60.00 (0-8020-2710-5) U of Toronto Pr.

Securing Employer-Based Pensions: An International Perspective. Ed. by Zvi Bodie et al. (Illus.). 388p. 1996. text ed. 44.95 (0-8122-3334-4) U of Pa Pr.

Securing Europe. Richard H. Ullman. 200p. 1991. text ed. 29.95 (0-691-07891-2) Princeton U Pr.

Securing Europe's Future: Changing Elements of European Security. Ed. by Stephen J. Flanagan & Fen O. Hampson. LC 86-10879. 334p. 1986. text ed. 59.95 (0-86569-135-5, Auburn Hse) Greenwood.

Securing Goods on Semi-Trailer. ICHCA Staff. (C). 1988. 70.00 (0-685-46491-1, Pub. by ICHCA UK) St Mut.

Securing Goods on Semi-Trailer: Guidelines for Securing Goods Conveyed in Combined Modes of Transport. ICHCA Staff. (C). 1987. 90.00 (91-86944-05-3, Pub. by ICHCA UK) St Mut.

Securing Home & Business: A Guide to the Electronic Security Industry. Simon Hakim & Erwin A. Blackstone. LC 96-41451. (Illus.). 300p. 1996. pap. 39.95 (0-7506-9629-X) Buttrwrth-Heinemann.

Securing Minnesota's Financial Future: Fiscal Arrangements in Other States. Mark B. Dayton. (Illus.). 94p. (Orig.). (C). 1995. pap. text ed. 30.00 (0-7881-0996-0) DIANE Pub.

Securing Minnesota's Financial Future: Property Tax Reform in the 1990s. Mark B. Dayton. (Illus.). 206p. (Orig.). (C). 1995. pap. text ed. 40.00 (0-7881-0997-9) DIANE Pub.

***Securing Nonqualified Arrangements: An Approach to Choosing a Funding Mechanism for Executive Deferral & Retirement Plan.** David M. Sugar & Robert A. Romanchek. (Building Blocks Ser.: Vol. 18). (Illus.). 20p. (Orig.). 1994. pap. 24.95 (1-57963-021-9, A0038) Am Compensation.

Securing of ISO Containers: Theory & Practice. Anthony R. Cole. 95p. (C). 1981. 220.00 (0-906297-19-2, Pub. by ICHCA UK) St Mut.

Securing Open Spaces for Urban America: Conservation Easements. William H. Whyte. LC 60-4745. (Urban Land Institute, Technical Bulletin Ser.: No. 36). 67p. reprint ed. pap. 25.00 (0-317-20032-1, 2023240) Bks Demand.

Securing Our Future: The Importance of Quality Education for Minorities. Robert Glover & Ray Marshall. (Policy Research Project Report: No. 96). 348p. 1992. pap. 14.50 (0-89940-704-8) LBJ Sch Pub Aff.

Securing Peace in Europe, 1945-62: Thoughts for the 1990s. Ed. by Beatrice Heuser & Robert O'Neill. LC 91-8154. 315p. 1991. text ed. 69.95 (0-312-06217-6) St Martin.

Securing Peace in the Middle East: Project on Economic Transition. Stanley Fischer et al. 150p. 1994. 20.00 (0-262-06168-6) MIT Pr.

Securing Peace in the New Era: Politics in the Former Soviet Union & the Challenge to American Security. 190p. 1994. pap. 9.95 (0-89843-159-X) Brookings.

Securing Religious Liberty: Principles for Judicial Interpretation of the Religion Clauses. Jesse H. Choper. LC 94-36239. 212p. 1995. 24.95 (0-226-10445-1) U Ch Pr.

***Securing South Africa's Democracy.** Cawthra. LC 96-46508. 1997. text ed. 65.00 (0-312-17419-5) St Martin.

An Asterisk (*) at the beginning of an entry indicates that the title is appearing in BIP for the first time.

Securing Stability & Growth in Latin America: Policy Issues & Prospects for Shock-Prone Economies. Ed. by Ricardo Hausmann & Helmut Reisen. 304p. (Orig.). (ENG & FRE.). 1996. pap. 65.00 (*92-64-14799-3*, Pub. by Org for Econ FR) OECD.

Securing the Covenant: The United States - Israeli Relations after the Cold War. Bernard Reich. LC 94-37881. (Contibutions in Political Science Ser.: Vol. 351). 184p. 1995. pap. text ed. 15.95 (*0-275-95121-9*, Praeger Pubs) Greenwood.

Securing the Covenant: United States - Israeli Relations after the Cold War. Bernard Reich. LC 94-37881. (Contributions in Political Science Ser.: Vol. 351). 192p. 1995. text ed. 57.95 (*0-313-29540-9*, Greenwood Pr) Greenwood.

Securing the Enactment of Civil Rights Legislation: Civil Rights Act of 1964. Ed. by Michal R. Belknap. LC 91-3615. (Civil Rights, White House & Justice Dept. Ser.: Vol. 13). 184p. 1991. text ed. 63.00 (*0-8240-3382-5*) Garland.

Securing the Enactment of Civil Rights Legislation, 1946-1960. Ed. by Michal R. Belknap. LC 91-3616. (Civil Rights, White House & Justice Dept. Ser.: Vol. 12). 488p. 1991. text ed. 138.00 (*0-8240-3381-7*) Garland.

Securing the Enactment of Civil Rights Legislation, 1965-1968. Ed. by Michal R. Belknap. LC 91-3614. (Civil Rights, White House & Justice Dept. Ser.: Vol. 14). 464p. 1991. text ed. 115.00 (*0-8240-3383-3*) Garland.

*__Securing the Enterprise Network.__ Computer Technology Research Corp. Staff. LC 96-50426. (Illus.). 210p. (Orig.). 1997. pap. 280.00 (*1-56607-984-5*) Comput Tech Res.

Securing the Euro-Atlantic Bridge: The Council of Europe & the United States. Ed. by Diana Pinto-Moisi et al. LC 93-1208. 1993. 14.85 (*0-8133-8785-X*) Westview.

*__Securing the Perimeter.__ 1996. 17.75 (*0-8307-1777-3*) Regal.

Securing the Planet: How to Succeed When Threats Are Too Risky & There's Really No Defense. Ed. by Don Carlson & Craig Comstock. 368p. 1986. pap. 11.95 (*0-87477-407-1*, Tarcher Putnam) Putnam Pub Group.

Securing the Right to Employment: Social Welfare Policy & the Unemployment in the United States. Philip Harvey. 160p. (C). 1989. text ed. 39.50 (*0-691-04244-6*) Princeton U Pr.

Securing Your Assets: A Guide to Financial Planning. Linda Ginsberg. (Illus.). (Orig.). (C). 1991. text ed. 49.95 (*1-878487-21-3*) Practice Mgmt Info.

Securing Your Assets: A Physician's Guide to Financial Planning. Linda G. Ginsberg. (Practice & Financial Management Ser.). (Illus.). 288p. 1990. text ed. 45.00 (*0-87489-569-3*) Med Econ.

Securing Your Child's Future: A Financial & Legal Planner for Parents. Winifred Conkling. 256p. (Orig.). 1995. pap. 12.95 (*0-449-90876-3*) Fawcett.

Securing Your Future: A Lifetime Guide to an Active, Worry-Free Retirement. Robert Busch. 224p. (Orig.). 1997. pap. 17.95 (*1-57488-103-5*) Brasseys Inc.

Securing Your Organization's Future: A Complete Guide to Fundraising Strategies. Michael Seltzer. LC 86-31843. 514p. 1987. 24.95 (*0-87954-190-3*) Foundation Ctr.

Securitech. FMJ Intl. Publ. Ltd. Staff. 300p. (C). 1989. 325.00 (*0-685-36822-X*, Pub. by Fuel Metallurgical Jrnl UK) St Mut.

Securitech. Portcullis Press Ltd. Staff. 300p. 1989. 400.00 (*0-317-54376-8*) St Mut.

Securities, 2 vols., 1. Frankel. 1991. 165.00 (*0-316-29209-5*) Little.

Securities, 2 vols., 2. Frankel. 1991. 165.00 (*0-316-29211-7*) Little.

Securities, 2 vols., Set. Frankel. 1991. 325.00 (*0-316-29213-3*) Little.

Securities: Buying & Selling Discipline. Earl J. Weinreb. LC 86-61264. 221p. 1986. 24.95 (*0-9616896-0-9*) Multi Strategy Pubs.

Securities: Public & Private Offerings, 2 vols. William A. Prifti. LC 82-24495. (Securities Law Ser.). 1983. ring bd. 250.00 (*0-317-11924-9*) Clark Boardman Callaghan.

Securities: Public & Private Offerings. William M. Prifti. write for info. (*0-318-57517-5*) West Pub.

Securities: Public & Private Offerings. 2nd ed. William M. Prifti. LC 95-39401. 1995. write for info. (*0-87632-745-5*) Clark Boardman Callaghan.

Securities: Public & Private Offerings, 2 vols., Set. 2nd ed. William M. Prifti. (Securities Ser.). 1995. ring bd. write for info. (*0-614-06274-8*) Clark Boardman Callaghan.

Securities: 1994. Frankel. 1994. suppl. ed. 75.00 (*0-316-29155-2*) Little.

*__Securities Act Handbook.__ Ed. by Bowne Publishing Division Staff & Barbara E. Sanders-Harris. 2300p. 1997. ring bd. 250.00 (*1-886100-02-0*, A-1) Bowne Pubng.

Securities Against Misrule & Other Constitutional Writings for Tripoli & Greece. Jeremy Bentham. Ed. by Philip Schofield. (Collected Works of Jeremy Bentham). 382p. 1991. 110.00 (*0-19-822725-6*) OUP.

Securities Analysis: A Personal Seminar. New York Institute of Finance Staff. 240p. 1989. pap. 21.95 (*0-13-658204-4*) NY Inst Finance.

Securities & Banking Law of the Republic Kazakhstan. Tr. & Compiled by W. E. Butler. 202p. 1995. pap. 55.00 (*1-898029-21-0*, Pub. by Simmonds & Hill Pubng UK) Gaunt.

Securities & Exchange Commission: A Case Study in the Use of Accounting As an Instrument of Public Policy. Charles W. Lamden. Ed. by Richard P. Brief. LC 77-87302. (Development of Contemporary Accounting Thought Ser.). 1978. lib. bdg. 37.95 (*0-405-10941-5*) Ayer.

Securities & Exchange Commission Docket: Cumulative Index. U. S. Securities & Exchange Commission. LC 73-643813. 1983. reprint ed. Index v.1-20, 1973-1980 with 1983 supplement. lib. bdg. 55.00 (*0-89941-193-2*, 201550) W S Hein.

Securities & Federal Corporate Law, 6 vols., Set. Harold S. Bloomenthal. LC 72-90956. (Securities Law Ser.). 1972. ring bd. 795.00 (*0-87632-086-8*) Clark Boardman Callaghan.

Securities & Futures Markets: Cross-Border Information Sharing. 76p. (Orig.). (C). 1993. pap. text ed. 25.00 (*1-56806-326-1*) DIANE Pub.

Securities Arbitration: How Investors Fare. (Illus.). 114p. (Orig.). (C). 1993. pap. text ed. 25.00 (*1-56806-968-5*) DIANE Pub.

Securities Arbitration: Law & Procedure. Marilyn B. Cane. LC 91-22848. 583p. 1991. reprint ed. pap. 166.20 (*0-608-00705-6*, 2061477) Bks Demand.

Securities Arbitration: Practice & Forms, Vol. 1. Djinis & Post. 1991. write for info. (*0-8205-1696-1*) Bender.

Securities Arbitration for Brokers, Attorneys & Investors. J. Kirkland Grant. LC 94-2992. 496p. 1994. text ed. 69.50 (*0-89930-682-9*, Quorum Bks) Greenwood.

Securities Arbitration Procedure Manual. David E. Robbins. 300p. 1994. ring bd. 125.00 (*0-614-05963-1*) MICHIE.

*__Securities Arbitration Procedure Manual.__ 2nd ed. David E. Robbins. 1990. spiral bd. 110.00 (*1-55834-266-4*, 82378) MICHIE.

Securities Arbitration Procedure Manual, 1990-1993. David E. Robbins. 300p. 1990. ring bd. 125.00 (*0-88063-345-X*) MICHIE.

Securities Arbitration Procedure Manual, 1990-1993. David E. Robbins. 1994. suppl. ed., ring bd. 63.00 (*0-614-03168-0*) MICHIE.

Securities Arbitration, 1992, 2 vols., Set. (Corporate Law & Practice Course Handbook, 1985-86 Ser.). 1387p. 1992. pap. 80.00 (*0-685-69492-5*) PLI.

Securities Arbitration 1995, 2 vols., Set. (Corporate Law & Practice Course Handbook, 1985-86 Ser.). 1296p. 1995. pap. 149.00 (*0-685-69724-X*, B4-7107) PLI.

Securities Broker Home Study Course. 884p. 1996. pap. 175.00 (*0-915513-63-3*) Ctr Futures Ed.

Securities Compliance Handbook: 1994 Edition. Price. 1994. per. 60.00 (*1-55738-706-0*) Irwin Prof Pubng.

Securities Compliance Handbook: 1995 Edition. 3rd ed. Price Waterhouse Staff. 136p. (C). 1995. per. 65.00 (*1-55738-766-4*) Irwin Prof Pubng.

Securities Counseling for New and Developing Companies, 1 vol. Stuart R. Cohn. (Corporate Law Ser.). 1993. 130.00 (*0-685-68840-2*) Clark Boardman Callaghan.

Securities Credit Regulation. Charles F. Rechlin. LC 93-44704. (Securities Law Ser.). 1994. ring bd. 145.00 (*0-87632-984-9*) Clark Boardman Callaghan.

Securities Crimes, 1 vol. Marvin G. Pickholz. LC 93-14817. (Securities Law Ser.). 1993. ring bd. 145.00 (*0-87632-971-7*) Clark Boardman Callaghan.

Securities Disclosure of Contingent Environmental Liabilities, 2 vols., Vol. 2. Elizabeth G. Geltman. Incl. Vol. 1. Securities Disclosure of Contingent Environmental Liabilites. LC 95-31642. 1995. text ed. 120.00 (*0-471-13293-4*); Vol. 2. Securities Disclosure of Contingent Environmental Liabilites. LC 95-31642. 1995. text ed. 120.00 (*0-471-13292-6*); LC 95-31642. (Environmental Law Library). 1995. Set text ed. 240.00 (*0-471-11571-1*) Wiley.

Securities Disclosure of Contingent Environmental Liabilites see Securities Disclosure of Contingent Environmental Liabilities

*__Securities Enforcement Manual.__ Roger M. Adelman & Richard M. Phillips. LC 97-11812. 1997. write for info. (*1-57073-423-2*) Amer Bar Assn.

Securities Exchange Act of 1934: Analyzed & Explained. Charles H. Meyer. 251p. 1994. reprint ed. lib. bdg. 35.00 (*0-8377-2447-3*) Rothman.

Securities Filings: Review & Update 1989. LC 80-83161. (Corporate Law & Practice Course Handbook, 1985-86 Ser.). 782p. 1989. 17.50 (*0-685-69493-3*) PLI.

Securities Filings, 1991: Review & Update. (Corporate Law & Practice Ser.). 778p. 1991. 17.50 (*0-685-51871-X*, B4-6984) PLI.

Securities Filings 1994: Review & Update. (Corporate Law & Practice Course Handbook, 1985-86 Ser.). 800p. 1994. pap. 99.00 (*0-685-65497-4*, B4-7073) PLI.

Securities Filings 1995. (Commercial Law & Practice Course Handbook Ser.). Date not set. pap. 99.00 (*0-614-17160-1*, A4-4493) PLI.

Securities Firms: Assessing the Need to Regulate Additional Financial Activities. (Illus.). 93p. (Orig.). (C). 1993. pap. text ed. 30.00 (*1-56806-329-6*) DIANE Pub.

Securities Fraud: Litigating under Rule 10b-5. Thomas E. Patton & Terry R. Saunders. 1993. suppl. ed., ring bd. 75.00 (*0-685-74475-2*) MICHIE.

Securities Fraud: Litigating under Rule 10b-5. Thomas E. Patton & Terry R. Saunders. 1994. spiral bd. 125.00 (*0-8342-0130-5*) MICHIE.

Securities Fraud & Commodities Fraud, 7 vols. Alan R. Bromberg & Lewis D. Lowenfels. (Securities Law Publications). 5027p. 1980. text ed. 420.00 (*0-07-008016-X*) Shepards.

Securities Handbook. Martin Torosian. 1986. 53.00 (*0-9603592-2-2*) MTA Financial Servs.

Securities in Movables in German Law: An Outline. Rolf Serick et al. Tr. by Tony Weir from GER. 120p. 1990. pap. 72.00 (*90-6544-481-5*) Kluwer Law Tax Pubs.

Securities Industry Glossary. 216p. (Orig.). 1985. pap. text ed. 14.95 (*0-13-798836-2*) NY Inst Finance.

Securities Industry Glossary. 2nd ed. New York Institute of Finance Staff. 1988. pap. 12.95 (*0-13-798778-1*) P-H.

Securities Industry Law. 4th ed. R. Baxt. 384p. 1993. pap. 71.00 (*0-409-30647-9*, Austral) MICHIE.

Securities Industry Yearbook, 1995-96. 1995. 125.00 (*0-614-04614-9*) Securities Industry.

Securities Law Compliance: A Guide for Brokers, Dealers & Investors. Allan H. Pessin. 320p. 1989. text ed. 70.00 (*1-55623-228-4*) Irwin Prof Pubng.

Securities Law Considerations Affecting Employee Benefits Plans. Simon M. Lorne. (Corporate Practice Ser.: No. 44). 1995. 92.00 (*1-55871-299-2*) BNA Books.

Securities Law Digest. Warren Gorham. Ed. by Ralph S. Janvey. 1200p. 1994. 140.00 (*0-7913-1916-4*) Warren Gorham & Lamont.

*__Securities Law Handbook for the Wisconsin Practitioner.__ Jeffrey B. Bartell et al. 1000p. 1994. ring bd. 95.00 (*0-945574-30-4*) State Bar WI CLE Bk Div.

Securities Law of Public Finance. Robert A. Fippinger. 800p. 1993. ring bd. 145.00 (*0-318-41231-4*, B1-1340) PLI.

Securities Law Techniques, 5 vols., Set. A. A. Sommer. 1985. ring bd. write for info. (*0-8205-1636-8*) Bender.

*__Securities Lending & Repurchase Agreements.__ Ed. by Frank J. Fabozzi. 266p. 1997. 85.00 (*1-883249-16-3*) F J Fabozzi.

Securities Litigation: Damages. Michael Kaufman. LC 89-15789. (Securities Law Ser.). 1990. ring bd. 145.00 (*0-318-41454-6*) Clark Boardman Callaghan.

Securities Litigation: Forms & Analysis, 2 vols. Scott E. Richter et al. 1989. ring bd. 250.00 (*0-685-44956-4*) Clark Boardman Callaghan.

Securities Litigation 1994. (Litigation & Administrative Practice Course Handbook, 1983-84 Ser.). 656p. 1994. Set. pap. 99.00 (*0-685-65522-9*, H4-5196) PLI.

Securities Litigation 1995. (Litigation & Administrative Practice Course Handbook, 1983-84 Ser.). 1995. pap. 99.00 (*0-685-51872-8*, H4-5233) PLI.

Securities Litigation, 1995. (Corporate Law & Practice Course Handbook, 1995-96 Ser.). 1995. pap. 99.00 (*0-685-69494-1*, B4-7112) PLI.

Securities Markets. K. Garbade. (Finance Ser.). 1982. text ed. write for info. (*0-07-022780-2*) McGraw.

Securities Markets: Actions Needed to Better Protect Investors Against Unscrupulous Brokers. (Illus.). 47p. (Orig.). (C). 1995. pap. text ed. 20.00 (*0-7881-1858-7*) DIANE Pub.

Securities Markets: Challenges to Harmonizing International Capital Standards Remain. (Illus.). 68p. (Orig.). (C). 1993. pap. text ed. 20.00 (*1-56806-566-3*) DIANE Pub.

Securities Markets in OECD Countries: Organisaton & Regulation. OECD Staff. 104p. (Orig.). 1995. pap. 22.00 (*92-64-14632-6*, Pub. by Org for Econ FR) OECD.

*__Securities Markets in the 1980s: The New Regime 1979-1984, Vol. 1.__ Barrie A. Wigmore. (Illus.). 400p. 1997. text ed. 45.00 (*0-19-510632-6*) OUP.

Securities Operations: A Guide to Operations & Information Systems in the Securities Industry. Michael T. Reddy. 1990. 75.00 (*0-13-799123-1*) NY Inst Finance.

Securities Operations: A Guide to Operations & Information Systems in the Securities Industry. Michael T. Reddy. 1995. 75.00 (*0-13-161044-9*) P-H.

Securities over Personality. Ed. by Michael Gillooly. 320p. 1994. pap. 79.00 (*1-86287-129-9*) Gaunt.

Securities Practice: Federal & State Enforcement. Marc I. Steinberg & Ralph C. Ferrara. LC 85-25526. (Securities Law Ser.). 1990. ring bd. 250.00 (*0-685-12019-8*) Clark Boardman Callaghan.

Securities Practice Handbook. 5th ed. Robert E. Shields & Robert H. Strouse. 350p. 1987. 77.00 (*0-8318-0460-2*, B460) Am Law Inst.

Securities Processing. 2nd rev. ed. American Bankers Association Staff. Ed. by Allyn C. Buzzell. (Illus.). 651p. (C). 1989. text ed. 70.00 (*0-89982-359-9*) Am Bankers.

*__Securities Processing.__ 3rd ed. William Imhot. 475p. (C). 1995. 92.00 (*0-89982-434-X*) Am Bankers.

Securities Reforms of Nineteen Ninety. 256p. 1990. pap. 25.00 (*0-685-67030-9*, 4960) Commerce.

Securities Register, Vol. 2. 3rd ed. Louis Loss. 1988. 147.50 (*0-316-53338-6*) Little.

Securities Register, Vol. 4. 3rd ed. Louis Loss. 1989. 147.50 (*0-316-53347-5*) Little.

Securities Register, Vol. 5. 3rd ed. Louis Loss. 1990. 147.50 (*0-316-53348-3*) Little.

Securities Register, Vol. 6. 3rd ed. Louis Loss. 1990. 147.50 (*0-316-53360-2*) Little.

Securities Register, Vol. 7. 3rd ed. Louis Loss. 1991. 147.50 (*0-316-53375-0*) Little.

Securities Regulation. Steinberg. 1986. write for info. (*0-8205-0371-1*, 648); teacher ed. write for info. (*0-8205-0372-X*) Bender.

Securities Regulation. Steinberg. 1990. Supplement 1990. suppl. ed. write for info. (*0-8205-0374-6*) Bender.

Securities Regulation. Steinberg. 1991. Supplement 1991 (June). suppl. ed. write for info. (*0-8205-0375-4*) Bender.

Securities Regulation, 6 vols. 2nd ed. Louis Loss. Incl. 1969 Supplement. , 3 vols. 2053p. 1969. 325.00 (*0-316-53320-3*); 2199p. 1961. write for info. (*0-318-54101-7*) Little.

Securities Regulation. 3rd ed. Larry D. Soderquist. LC 93-49781. (University Casebook Ser.). 786p. 1994. text ed. 41.00 (*1-56662-142-9*); teacher ed., pap. text ed. write for info. (*1-56662-168-2*) Foundation Pr.

Securities Regulation, 3 vols., Set. 3rd ed. Louis Loss & Joel Seligman. 1800p. 1988. 240.00 (*0-316-36123-X*) Little.

Securities Regulation, Vol. 1. 3rd ed. Louis Loss. 1988. 147.50 (*0-316-53337-8*) Little.

Securities Regulation, Vol. 3. 3rd ed. Louis Loss. 1988. 147.50 (*0-316-53339-4*) Little.

Securities Regulation: Adaptable to Courses Utilizing Cox, Hillman & Langevoort's Casebook on Securities Regulation. Casenotes Publishing Co., Inc. Staff et al. (Legal Briefs Ser.). (Orig.). 1994. pap. text ed. write for info. (*0-87457-206-1*, 1272) Casenotes Pub.

Securities Regulation: Adaptable to Courses Utilizing Ratner's Casebook on Securities Regulation. Casenotes Publishing Co., Inc. Staff. Ed. by Norman S. Goldenberg et al. (Legal Briefs Ser.). 1986. pap. write for info. (*0-87457-124-3*, 1271) Casenotes Pub.

Securities Regulation: Cases & Materials. Cox & Hill. 1991. 57.00 (*0-316-15865-8*) Little.

Securities Regulation: Cases & Materials. 5th ed. David L. Ratner & Thomas L. Hazen. 991p. 1996. text ed. write for info. (*0-314-06655-1*) West Pub.

Securities Regulation: Cases & Materials Containing Problems & New Cases & Materials, 1994 Supplement. 4th ed. David L. Ratner & Thomas L. Mazen. (American Casebook Ser.). 62p. 1993. pap. text ed. 8.00 (*0-314-03030-1*) West Pub.

Securities Regulation: Cases & Materials, 1994 Supplement. 7th ed. Joel Seligman et al. (University Casebook Ser.). 328p. 1994. pap. text ed. 11.95 (*1-56662-193-3*) Foundation Pr.

Securities Regulation: Liabilities & Remedies. Marc I. Steinberg. 800p. 1984. ring bd. 110.00 (*0-317-05393-0*, 00582) NY Law Pub.

Securities Regulation: Materials for a Basic Course On. 4th ed. David L. Ratner & Thomas L. Hazen. (American Casebook Ser.). 1062p. (C). 1990. text ed. 52.00 (*0-314-79326-7*) West Pub.

Securities Regulation: Treatise on the Law of Securities Regulation, Pocket Parts, 1993. 2nd ed. Thomas L. Hazen. Vols. 1 & 2. 1992. pap. text ed. write for info. (*0-318-69677-0*) West Pub.

Securities Regulation & the New Deal. Michael E. Parrish. LC 70-118735. (Yale Historical Publications: Miscellany: No. 93). 282p. reprint ed. pap. 80.40 (*0-317-09459-9*, 2022027) Bks Demand.

Securities Regulation, Cases & Materials. 7th ed. John C. Coffee, Jr. et al. (University Casebook Ser.). 1992. text ed. 48.95 (*0-88277-967-2*) Foundation Pr.

Securities Regulation, Cases & Materials: 1996 Supplement (Containing Selected Cases, Releases & Other Materials under the Federal Securities Laws) to. 7th ed. Joel Seligman et al. (University Casebook Ser.). 450p. (C). 1996. pap. text ed. write for info. (*1-56662-354-5*) Foundation Pr.

*__Securities Regulation, Cases & Materials, 1996 Supplement To.__ David L. Ratner. Ed. by Thomas L. Hayen. (American Casebook Ser.). 70p. 1996. pap. text ed. write for info. (*0-314-20470-9*) West Pub.

Securities Regulation Complete Set. 3rd ed. Louis Loss. 1989. 1,495.00 (*0-316-53343-2*) Little.

Securities Regulation Forms, 3 vols., Set. Denis T. Rice & Charles P. Ortmeyer. LC 88-17561. 1988. ring bd. 395.00 (*0-87632-606-8*) Clark Boardman Callaghan.

Securities Regulation Forms, 3 vols., Set with forms on disk. Denis T. Rice & Charles P. Ortmeyer. (Securities Law Ser.). 1988. 495.00 incl. disk (*0-614-07308-1*) Clark Boardman Callaghan.

Securities Regulation in a Nutshell. 4th ed. David L. Ratner. LC 92-18886. (Nutshell Ser.). 326p. (C). 1992. pap. text ed. 17.00 (*0-314-00930-2*) West Pub.

Securities Regulation in a Nutshell. 5th ed. David L. Ratner. (Nutshell Ser.). 300p. 1996. pap. 17.50 (*0-314-06591-1*) West Pub.

Securities Regulation in Australia & New Zealand. Ed. by Gordon Walker & Brent Fisse. 800p. 1995. pap. 165.00 (*0-19-558290-X*) OUP.

*__Securities Regulation in Cyberspace.__ Howard M. Friedman. Ed. by Susan F. Koffman & Bruce S. Brumberg. (Illus.). 600p. 1997. 175.00 (*1-886100-03-9*, SLC) Bowne Pubng.

Securities Regulation in Japan. Misao Tatsuta. LC 77-165013. 141p. 1972. 40.00 (*0-295-95166-4*) U of Wash Pr.

Securities Regulation in the Netherlands. N. Van de Vijver. LC 93-43435. (Loeff Legal Ser.: Vol. 1). 1993. write for info. (*90-6544-801-2*) Kluwer Law Tax Pubs.

Securities Regulation Law Journal. Ed. by Marc I. Steinberg. 180.00 (*0-685-69646-4*, SRLJ) Warren Gorham & Lamont.

Securities Regulation Law Journal: 1973-1996/97, Vols. 1-24. Bound set. 2,400.00 (*0-8377-9141-3*) Rothman.

Securities Regulation, Selected Statutes, Rules & Forms: 1995 Edition. David L. Ratner. Ed. by Thomas L. Hazen. 1246p. 1994. 26.00 (*0-314-04766-2*) West Pub.

Securities Regulation, Selected Statutes, Rules & Forms: 1996 Edition. Ed. by David L. Ratner & Thomas L. Hazen. 1315p. 1996. pap. 28.50 (*0-314-07699-9*) West Pub.

*__Securities Regulation, Selected Statutes, Rules & Forms: 1997 Edition.__ David L. Ratner & Thomas L. Hazen. 1280p. (C). 1996. pap. text ed. write for info. (*0-314-21221-3*) West Pub.

Securities Regulation Series, 10 vols., Set. Incl. Vol. 1. Introduction. John T. Marlin & Peter F. Rousmaniere. 36p. 1980. (*0-318-51453-2*); Vol. 2. Certain Legal Considerations. Chadbourne et al. 129p. 1980. (*0-916450-09-0*); Vol. 4. Summary of Publications & Hearings. Chadbourne et al. 264p. 1980. (*0-318-51454-0*); Vol. 5. Federal Legislative Background. Chadbourne et al. 1980. (*0-318-51455-9*); Vol. 6. Four Legal Memoranda. Chadbourne et al. 1980. (*0-318-51456-7*); Vol. 7. Municipal Disclosure Standards Sourcebook. Kay Anderson. 199p. (*0-318-51457-5*); Vol. 8. State Laws. Chadbourne et al. 204p. 1980. (*0-318-51458-3*); State Level Disclosure Guidelines. Peter F. Rousmaniere. 233p. 1980. (*0-318-51459-1*); 1980. 100.00 (*0-686-70181-X*) Nat Civic League.

S

Securities Regulation, the Law of 1994 Pocket Part. 2nd ed. Thomas L. Hazen. (Hornbook Ser.). 200p. 1994. pap. text ed. 12.50 (*0-314-04202-4*) West Pub.

Securities Regulation, 1995: Supplement To. 3rd ed. Larry D. Soderquist. (Universith Casebook Ser.). 57p. (C). 1995. pap. text ed. 4.95 (*1-56662-313-8*) Foundation Pr.

Securities Regulations: Adaptable to Courses Utilizing Jennings, Marsh & Coffee's Casebook on Securities Regulation. Casenotes Publishing Co., Inc. Staff. Ed. by Norman S. Goldenberg & Peter Tenen. (Legal Briefs Ser.). 1992. pap. write for info. (*0-87457-123-5*, 1270) Casenotes Pub.

Securities Regulations, Cases & Materials. 4th ed. David L. Ratner & Thomas L. Hazen. (American Casebook Ser.). 41p. (C). 1991. pap. text ed. write for info. (*0-314-92863-4*) West Pub.

Securities Regulations in Korea: Problems & Recommendations for Feasible Reforms. Young M. Shin. LC 82-4918. (Asian Law Ser.: No. 8). 522p. (C). 1983. 50.00 (*0-295-95937-1*) U of Wash Pr.

Securities Regulaton: Liabilities & Remedies. Marc I. Steinberg. 500p. 1984. ring bd. 75.00 (*0-318-20271-9*, 00582) NY Law Pub.

***Securities Regulatory Handbook, 1996-1997.** 4th ed. 168p. (C). 1996. per. 65.00 (*0-7863-0953-9*) Irwin.

Securities Sales Planning Guide: A Manual for Achieving Success in Your First Year. Robert M. Cohn. 320p. 1988. 24.95 (*0-13-798935-0*) P-H.

Securities Transaction Taxes: False Hopes & Unintended Consequences. Ed. by Catalyst Institute Staff. LC 94-18464. 204p. 1994. text ed. 75.00 (*0-7863-0354-9*) Irwin Prof Pubng.

Securities Transfer: Principles & Procedures. Martin Torosian. (Illus.). 400p. 1988. 44.95 (*0-13-799081-2*, Busn) P-H.

Securities Transfer: Principles & Procedures. 4th ed. Martin Torosian. LC 82-14245. 368p. 1982. 29.95 (*0-13-799072-3*) NY Inst Finance.

Securitisation. Ed. by David Bonsall. 335p. 1990. boxed 170.00 (*0-406-11722-5*, UK) MICHIE.

Securitisation. An International Perspective. OECD Staff. 140p. (Orig.). 1995. pap. 45.00 (*92-64-14565-6*, Pub. by Org for Econ FR) OECD.

Securitisation-Training Manual. Z. Shaw. 1996. 250.00 (*1-85564-488-6*, Pub. by Euromoney UK) Am Educ Systs.

Securitization. John Henderson & Jonathan Scott. 1988. 49.95 (*0-13-799008-1*) NY Inst Finance.

Securitization: Asset-Backed & Mortgaged-Backed Securities. Ronald S. Borod. 590p. 1994. spiral bd. 125.00 (*0-88063-281-X*) MICHIE.

Securitization: Redefining the Bank. Paul W. Feeney. LC 94-35591. 1995. text ed. 75.00 (*0-312-12515-1*) St Martin.

Securitization of Credit: Inside the New Technology of Finance. James Rosenthal & Juan Ocampo. 266p. 1988. text ed. 99.95 (*0-471-61368-1*) Wiley.

Securitization 1995, Vol. 1. Frankel. 1995. 82.50 (*0-316-29136-6*) Little.

Security. (Open Learning for Supervisory Management). 1990. pap. text ed. 19.50 (*0-08-070178-7*, Pergamon Pr) Elsevier.

Security. 2nd ed. (Open Learning Super Ser.). 1991. pap. text ed. 26.00 (*0-08-041638-1*, Pergamon Pr) Elsevier.

Security: A Guide to Security System Design & Equipment Selection & Installation. 2nd ed. Neil Cumming. 338p. 1992. reprint ed. pap. 52.95 (*0-7506-9624-9*) Buttrwrth-Heinemann.

Security: A Management Perspective. Harvey Burstein. LC 95-9241. 1995. text ed. 55.00 (*0-13-150657-9*) P-H.

***Security: A New Framework for Analysis.** Barry Buzan et al. LC 97-21300. 272p. 1997. 55.00 (*1-55587-603-X*); pap. 19.95 (*1-55587-784-2*) Lynne Rienner.

Security: Everything You Need to Know about Household Alarm Systems. Tom Lewin. LC 82-61141. (Illus.). 99p. 1982. 16.95 (*0-9609362-0-3*); pap. 7.95 (*0-9609362-1-1*) Park Lane Ent.

***Security: Survey Results.** Urban Libs. Council Staff. (Frequent Fast Facts Ser.). pap. 45.00 (*1-885251-02-5*) Urban Libraries.

Security: The False & the Truth. W. T. Purkiser. 64p. 1974. pap. 5.99 (*0-8341-0048-7*) Beacon Hill.

Security Abstracts: Article Summaries from Security Management 1989-1994. Ed. by American Society for Industrial Security Staff. (Reference Ser.). (Orig.). 1995. pap. write for info. (*1-887056-03-3*) Am Soc Indus Secur.

Security Administration: A Practical Systems Approach. Donald C. Becker. (Illus.). 224p. (C). 1985. 38.95 (*0-398-05064-3*) C C Thomas.

Security Administration: An Introduction to the Protective Services. 4th ed. Richard S. Post et al. (Illus.). 256p. 1990. 39.95 (*0-409-90096-6*) Buttrwrth-Heinemann.

Security Affiliates of National Bank. William N. Peach. LC 75-2660. (Wall Street & the Security Market Ser.). 1975. reprint ed. 19.95 (*0-405-06984-7*) Ayer.

Security Affiliates of National Banks. William N. Peach. LC 78-64180. (Johns Hopkins University. Studies in the Social Sciences. Thirtieth Ser. 1912: 3). 192p. 1983. reprint ed. 34.50 (*0-404-61288-1*) AMS Pr.

Security Against Sickness: A Study of Health Insurance. Isidore Sydney Falk. LC 79-38822. (FDR & the Era of the New Deal Ser.). 424p. 1972. reprint ed. lib. bdg. 49.50 (*0-306-70447-1*) Da Capo.

Security Alarm Systems: Updated. 130p. 1985. 1,250.00 (*0-89336-111-9*, G-046N) BCC.

***Security Analysis.** Edelen. 1997. pap. text ed. write for info. (*0-07-021978-8*) McGraw.

Security Analysis. 5th ed. S. Cottle et al. 640p. 1988. text ed. 59.95 (*0-07-013235-6*) McGraw.

Security Analysis: The Original 1934 Edition. Benjamin Graham & David Dodd. (Illus.). 735p. 1996. text ed. 150.00 (*0-07-024497-9*) McGraw.

Security Analysis: The Original 1934 Edition. Benjamin Graham & David Dodd. (Illus.). 735p. 1996. text ed. 50.00 (*0-07-024496-0*) McGraw.

Security Analysis & Portfolio Management. C. F. Lee et al. (C). 1990. text ed. 76.00 (*0-673-38635-X*) Addson-Wesley Educ.

Security Analysis & Portfolio Management. 6th ed. Donald E. Fischer & Ronald L. Jordan. LC 94-19435. 1995. text ed. 80.00 (*0-13-157256-3*) P-H.

Security Analysis for Portfolio Construction & Management. Boyet Wayne. 136p. (C). 1989. pap. text ed. 34.00 (*0-03-029449-5*) Dryden Pr.

Security Analyst Multi-Year Earnings Forecasts & the Capital Market, Vol. 21. Philip Brown et al. (Studies in Accounting Research). 172p. 1985. 12.00 (*0-86539-049-5*) Am Accounting.

Security & Arms, 2 vols. Edward A. Kolodziej. 1989. text ed. 150.00 (*0-313-26819-3*, KNT/, Greenwood Pr) Greenwood.

Security & Arms Control: A Guide to International Policymaking, Vol. 2. Ed. by Edward A. Kolodziej & Patrick A. Morgan. LC 88-7224. 431p. 1989. text ed. 85.00 (*0-313-25258-0*, KNT02, Greenwood Pr) Greenwood.

Security & Arms Control in Post-Confrontation Europe. Jenonne Walker. LC 93-49447. (SIPRI Strategic Issue Papers). 160p. 1994. 35.00 (*0-19-829176-0*) OUP.

Security & Arms Control, Vol. 1: A Guide to National Policymaking. Ed. by Edward A. Kolodziej & Patrick M. Morgan. LC 88-7224. 322p. 1989. text ed. 75.00 (*0-313-25257-2*, KNT01, Greenwood Pr) Greenwood.

Security & Co-Operation in Europe: The Human Dimension, 1972-1992. Alexis Heraclides. LC 92-19256. 217p. 1993. text ed. 45.00 (*0-7146-3484-0*, Pub. by F Cass Pubs UK) Intl Spec Bk.

Security & Control of Information Technology in Society: Proceedings of the IFIP TC9 - WG9.6 Working Conference on Security & Control of Information Technology in Society on Board M-S Ilich & Ashore at St. Peterburg, Russia, 12- 17 August 1993. Ed. by Richard Sizer et al. LC 93-27819. (IFIP Transactions A: Computer Science & Technology Ser.). 242p. 1994. 110.50 (*0-444-81831-6*, North Holland) Elsevier.

Security & Crime Prevention. 2nd ed. Robert L. O'Block et al. 439p. 1991. 42.95 (*0-7506-9007-0*) Buttrwrth-Heinemann.

Security & Crime Prevention in Libraries. Alan F. MacDougall & Michael Chaney. 250p. 1992. 59.95 (*1-85742-014-4*, Pub. by Gower UK) Ashgate Pub Co.

Security & Defence: Pacific & Global Perspectives. Ed. by Desmond Ball & Cathy Downs. 512p. 1991. pap. text ed. 24.95 (*0-04-442161-3*, Pub. by Allen Unwin AT) Paul & Co Pubs.

Security & Defence in South West England Before 1800. Ed. by Higham. 110p. 1987. pap. text ed. 13.95 (*0-85989-209-3*, Pub. by Univ Exeter Pr UK) Northwestern U Pr.

Security & Detente. Helga Haftendorn. LC 84-26305. 336p. 1985. text ed. 65.00 (*0-275-90113-0*, C0113, Praeger Pubs) Greenwood.

Security & Economics in the Asia-Pacific Region. Ed. by Gerrit W. Gong & Richard L. Grant. (Significant Issues Ser.). 128p. (Orig.). 1991. pap. text ed. 9.95 (*0-89206-176-6*) CSI Studies.

***Security & Economy in the Third World.** Nicole Ball. LC 88-9875. (Illus.). 459p. (Orig.). 1988. reprint ed. pap. 130.90 (*0-608-02584-4*, 2063230) Bks Demand.

Security & Emergency Procedures. Stevenson. 52p. 1990. per. 15.00 (*1-55520-175-X*) Irwin Prof Pubng.

Security & Intelligence in a Changing World: New Perspectives for the 1990s. Ed. by A. Stuart Farson et al. (Studies in Intelligence). 1991. text ed. 37.50 (*0-7146-3395-X*, Pub. by F Cass Pubs UK) Intl Spec Bk.

Security & Loss Prevention. 3rd ed. Philip P. Purpura. Date not set. write for info. (*0-7506-9642-7*) Buttrwrth-Heinemann.

Security & Loss Prevention: An Introduction. 2nd ed. Philip P. Purpura. LC 83-10044. 384p. 1990. 39.95 (*0-409-90203-9*) Buttrwrth-Heinemann.

Security & Loss Prevention Management. Raymond C. Ellis, Jr. & AH & MA Security Committee. (Illus.). 279p. 1995. pap. write for info. (*0-86612-110-2*) Educ Inst Am Hotel.

***Security & Peace in the Middle East: An American Agenda.** Washington Institute for Near East Policy Staff & Robert B. Satloff. LC 97-6298. 1997. write for info. (*0-944029-69-8*) Wash Inst NEP.

Security & Politics in the Nordic Area. John Fitzmaurice. Orig. Title: The Politics of Security in the Nordic Area. 200p. 1987. text ed. 53.95 (*0-566-05035-8*, Pub. by Dartmth Pub UK) Ashgate Pub Co.

Security & Portfolio Analysis: Concepts & Management. Daniel French. 576p. (C). 1989. write for info. (*0-675-20810-6*, Merrill Coll) P-H.

Security & Privacy in Computer Systems. Lance J. Hoffman. LC 73-6744. (Information Sciences Ser.). 431p. reprint ed. pap. 122.90 (*0-317-26258-0*, 2055715) Bks Demand.

Security & Privacy, 1995 IEEE Symposium on. LC 10-816011. 272p. 1995. pap. text ed. 60.00 (*0-8186-7015-0*) IEEE Comp Soc.

Security & Privacy, 1996 IEEE Symposium On. IEEE Staff. LC 10-816011. 233p. 1996. pap. 60.00 (*0-8186-7417-2*) IEEE Comp Soc.

***Security & Privacy, 1997.** LC 10-816011. 250p. 1997. pap. 60.00 (*0-8186-7828-3*) IEEE Comp Soc.

Security & Privacy,1994 Symposium On Research In. LC 10-637109. 256p. 1994. pap. 60.00 (*0-8186-5675-1*, 5675) IEEE Comp Soc.

Security & Sacrifice: Isolation, Intervention, & American Foreign Policy. Elliott Abrams. 150p. (Orig.). 1995. pap. 19.95 (*1-55813-049-7*) Hudson Instit IN.

Security & Safety: Issues & Ideas for Shopping Center Professionals. 179p. (Orig.). 1989. pap. 69.95 (*0-913598-88-7*, 861) Intl Coun Shop.

Security & Services for Children: An Original Anthology, Vol. 24. Ed. by Robert H. Bremner. LC 74-1703. (Children & Youth Ser.). 1974. 19.95 (*0-405-05980-9*) Ayer.

Security & Society: Reflections on Law, Order & Politics. R. N. Berki. LC 86-6661. 1986. text ed. 32.50 (*0-312-70920-X*) St Martin.

Security & Strategy in the New Europe. Ed. by Colin J. McInnes. LC 92-9285. 256p. (C). 1992. pap. text ed. 17.95 (*0-415-08303-6*, A7659) Routledge.

Security & Strategy in the New Europe. Ed. by Colin J. McInnes. LC 92-9285. 256p. (C). (gr. 13). 1992. text ed. 85.00 (*0-415-07120-8*, A7655) Routledge.

Security & the CSCE Process: The Stockholm Conference & Beyond. John Freeman. LC 91-3334. (RUSI Defence Studies). 240p. 1991. text ed. 69.95 (*0-312-06558-2*) St Martin.

Security Applications in Industry & Institutions. Ed. by Lawrence J. Fennelly. 336p. 1992. 39.95 (*0-7506-9389-4*) Buttrwrth-Heinemann.

Security Architecture for Open Distributed Systems. Sead Muftic, Jr. et al. (Communication & Distributed Systems Ser.). 281p. 1993. text ed. 90.00 (*0-471-93472-0*) Wiley.

Security, Arms Control, & Conflict Reduction in East Asia & the Pacific. Compiled by Andrew McClean. LC 93-18142. (Bibliographies & Indexes in Law & Political Science Ser.: No. 19). 576p. 1993. text ed. 105.00 (*0-313-27539-4*, MNB, Greenwood Pr) Greenwood.

Security Arrangements in the Gulf. Caspar W. Weinberger. 76p. (Orig.). 1988. pap. 5.00 (*0-685-38597-3*) Natl Coun Arab.

Security Assistance: Need for Improved Reporting on Excess Defense Article Transfers. (Illus.). 57p. (Orig.). (C). 1995. pap. text ed. 25.00 (*0-7881-1734-3*) DIANE Pub.

Security at a Lower Level of Armament: A Perspective from the United States of America. 50p. 4.50 (*92-9045-010-X*) UN.

Security at Sea: Naval Forces & Arms Control. Ed. by Richard Fieldhouse. (SIPRI Publication). 320p. 1990. 59.00 (*0-19-829130-2*) OUP.

Security, Audit & Control of Databases. R. Clark. Ed. by S. R. Holloway & W. List. 170p. 1991. text ed. 55.95 (*1-85628-168-X*, Pub. by Avebury Pub UK) Ashgate Pub Co.

Security Awareness in the 1980s: Featured Articles from the Security Awareness Bulletin, 1981-1989. (Illus.). 205p. (Orig.). (C). 1992. pap. text ed. 40.00 (*0-941375-50-1*) DIANE Pub.

Security Awareness Overseas: An Overview. 52p. (Orig.). (C). 1992. pap. text ed. 20.00 (*1-56806-047-5*) DIANE Pub.

Security Challenges for Japan & Europe in a Post-Cold War World. Seizaburo Sato. 1993. pap. text ed. 15.95 (*0-905031-65-2*, Pub. by Royal Inst Intl Affairs UK) Brookings.

Security Challenges in the Mediterranean Region. Ed. by Roberto Aliboni et al. LC 95-51117. 208p. 1996. 39.50 (*0-7146-4686-5*, Pub. by F Cass Pubs UK); pap. 21.00 (*0-7146-4220-7*, Pub. by F Cass Pubs UK) Intl Spec Bk.

Security Closed Circuit Television Handbook: Applications & Technical. Thomas G. Kyle & James Aldridge. (Illus.). 228p. 1992. pap. 29.95 (*0-398-06219-6*) C C Thomas.

Security Closed Circuit Television Handbook: Applications & Technical. Thomas G. Kyle & James Aldridge. (Illus.). 228p. (C). 1992. text ed. 41.95 (*0-398-05805-9*) C C Thomas.

Security Commitments & Capabilities: Elements of an American Global Strategy. Ed. by Uri Ra'anan & Robert L. Pfaltzgraff, Jr. LC 85-13339. xii, 204p. (C). 1985. lib. bdg. 33.50 (*0-208-02095-0*, Archon Bks) Shoe String.

Security Consulting. 2nd ed. Charles A. Sennewald. LC 95-19952. 168p. 1996. pap. 29.95 (*0-7506-9643-5*) Buttrwrth-Heinemann.

***Security Control of Air Traffic.** 1997. lib. bdg. 251.99 (*0-8490-8158-0*) Gordon Pr.

Security Cooperation in the Asia Pacific Region. Desmond Ball et al. (Significant Issues Ser.). 50p. (Orig.). (C). 1993. pap. text ed. 8.50 (*0-89206-219-3*) CSI Studies.

Security Council: A Study in Adolescence. Richard Hiscocks. LC 73-18457. 1974. 12.95 (*0-02-914760-3*, Free Press) Free Pr.

Security Dealers of North America, 2 vols., Set. 1988. 375.00 (*0-686-10240-1*) Standard Poors.

Security, Democracy, & Development in U. S. - Latin American Relations: Task Force on Democratization. Ed. by William C. Smith et al. LC 94-7502. 304p. (C). 1994. pap. 22.95 (*1-56000-760-5*) U Miami N-S Ctr.

Security Deposit Protection Kit. Steven C. Thomas. (Illus.). 64p. (Orig.). 1991. student ed., pap. 9.95 (*0-9630232-0-9*) Nevets Pub.

***Security Dilemma & End of Cold.** Collins. Date not set. text ed. 59.95 (*0-312-17672-4*) St Martin.

Security Dilemma of a Small State, Pt. 2. Ed. by Mahinda Werake & P. V. Jayasekera. (C). 1995. 28.00 (*81-7003-185-0*, Pub. by S Asia Pubs II) S Asia.

Security, Disarmament & Confidence-Building in the CIS Context. (Disarmament Topical Papers: No. 19). 154p. Date not set. pap. 13.50 (*92-1-142210-8*, E.94.IX.10) UN.

***Security Electronics Circuits Manual.** R. M. Marston. (Illus.). 192p. 1997. pap. 28.95 (*0-7506-3007-8*, Newnes) Buttrwrth-Heinemann.

Security Fire Alarm Systems Design, Installation, & Maintenance: Design, Installation, Maintenance. 2nd ed. John E. Traister. LC 95-35183. 1995. text ed. 45.00 (*0-07-065296-1*) McGraw.

Security First Bank: A Banking Customer Simulation. 3rd ed. Sargent. (HM - Consumer Education Ser.). 1992. 17.95 (*0-538-60861-7*) S-W Pub.

Security for a New Europe: The Vienna Negotiations on Confidence & Security-Building Measures, 1989 & Beyond. John Borawski. (Illus.). 255p. 1992. 58.00 (*1-85753-040-3*, Pub. by Brasseys UK) Brasseys Inc.

Security for America's Children: Proceedings of the Fourth Annual Conference of NASI. NASI Staff. 176p. 1992. pap. text ed. 34.95 (*0-8403-8250-2*) Kendall-Hunt.

Security for Children: Protecting Youngsters. David Y. Coverston. (Illus.). 1990. 8.95 (*0-936101-07-5*); pap. 6.95 (*0-936101-06-7*) Security Seminars.

Security for Computer Networks: An Introduction to Data Security in Teleprocessing & Electronic Funds Transfer. 2nd ed. D. W. Davies & W. L. Price. LC 89-14760. 377p. 1989. text ed. 98.00 (*0-471-92137-8*) Wiley.

Security for Costs. Jim Delany. xvii, 215p. 1989. 45.50 (*0-455-20780-1*, Pub. by Law Bk Co AT) Gaunt.

Security for Credit: Law & Practice in Hong Kong. Betty M. Ho. 540p. 1992. boxed 122.00 (*0-409-99632-7*, SI) MICHIE.

Security for Dial-up Lines. Eugene F. Troy. (Illus.). 71p. (Orig.). (C). 1992. pap. text ed. 30.00 (*1-56806-134-X*) DIANE Pub.

***Security for Distributed Computing.** Rob Dempsey & Glen Bruce. 1996. 38.00 (*0-614-20317-1*) P-H.

Security for Hotels, Motels, & Restaurants. Bruce H. Axler. 1974. pap. 3.95 (*0-672-96123-7*, Bobbs) Macmillan.

Security for Object-Oriented Systems: Proceedings of the OOPSLA '93 Conference Workshop on Security for Object-Oriented Systems, Washington, D. C., U. S. A., 26 September 1993. Ed. by R. Sandhu et al. LC 94-15683. (Workshops in Computing Ser.). 1994. 61.95 (*0-387-19877-6*) Spr-Verlag.

Security for Open Systems. David Bonyun. (C). 1995. text ed. write for info. (*0-201-54875-5*) Addison-Wesley.

Security for Senior Citizens: "Making the Golden Years Safer Years" David Y. Coverston. LC 87-12885. (Illus.). 1988. 22.00 (*0-936101-03-2*); pap. 10.00 (*0-936101-02-4*) Security Seminars.

***Security for Small Computer Systems.** T. Saddington. 120p. 1988. 81.00 (*0-946395-35-7*, Pub. by Elsvr Adv Tech UK) Elsevier.

Security for Women: Safety for Females. David Y. Coverston. (Illus.). 100p. 1990. 12.00 (*0-936101-09-1*); pap. 10.00 (*0-936101-08-3*) Security Seminars.

Security Forces in Northern Ireland 1969-92. Tom Ripley. (Elite Ser.: No. 44). (Illus.). 64p. pap. 12.95 (*1-85532-278-1*, 9459, Pub. by Osprey UK) Stackpole.

Security Gamble: Deterrence Dilemmas in the Nuclear Age. Ed. by Douglas MacLean. 1984. pap. 22.75 (*0-317-05231-4*) IPPP.

Security Guarantees in a Middle East Settlement. Nathan A. Pelcovits. LC 76-2219. (Foreign Policy Papers: Vol. 2, No. 5). 76p. reprint ed. pap. 25.00 (*0-7837-1987-6*, 2042261) Bks Demand.

Security Guard. Jack Rudman. (Career Examination Ser.: C-1999). 1994. pap. 23.95 (*0-8373-1999-4*) Nat Learn.

Security Guard: A Guidebook for Guards, Officers, Managers of Agency & In-House Security Forces. David Y. Coverston. LC 85-30430. (Illus.). 208p. (C). 1986. 22.00 (*0-936101-01-6*); pap. 20.00 (*0-936101-00-8*) Security Seminars.

Security Guarding Services: A Guide to Buying. Paul Elliott. 1991. 75.00 (*1-85609-029-9*, Pub. by Witherby & Co UK) St Mut.

Security Guide. 272p. 1989. 29.95 (*0-13-972142-8*) P-H.

Security Guide for Executives. 1991. lib. bdg. 88.95 (*0-8490-4607-6*) Gordon Pr.

Security Guidelines for American Enterprises Abroad. rev. ed. 66p. (C). 1993. pap. 25.00 (*1-56806-547-7*) DIANE Pub.

Security Guidelines for American Families Living Abroad. rev. ed. 59p. (C). 1993. pap. text ed. 25.00 (*1-56806-546-9*) DIANE Pub.

Security Handbook. Philip P. Purpura. 288p. 1991. pap. 37.75 (*0-8273-3825-2*) Delmar.

Security Handbook. Philip P. Purpura. 288p. 1991. teacher ed., pap. 11.95 (*0-8273-3826-0*) Delmar.

***Security Handbook: How to Keep You & Your Family Safe, Secure, & Happy.** Alan W. Foust. LC 96-77643. 94p. (Orig.). 1996. pap. 9.95 (*0-9653960-3-7*) Harmny Hse.

Security Hospital Treatment Assistant. Jack Rudman. (Career Examination Ser.: C-1615). 1994. pap. 23.95 (*0-8373-1615-4*) Nat Learn.

Security Hospital Treatment Assistant (Adolescent) Jack Rudman. (Career Examination Ser.: C-1616). 1994. pap. 27.95 (*0-8373-1616-2*) Nat Learn.

Security, Identity & Nation Building: Cyprus & the EU in Comparative Perspective. Demetrios Theophylactou. 192p. 1995. 51.95 (*1-85972-175-3*, Pub. by Avebury Pub UK) Ashgate Pub Co.

Security in Computing. 2nd ed. Charles P. Pfleeger. 550p. (C). 1996. text ed. 52.00 (*0-13-337486-6*) P-H.

***Security in Cyberspace: Challenges for Society: Proceedings of an International Conference.** Ed. by Robert Anderson et al. 72p. (Orig.). 1996. pap. 9.00 (*0-8330-2470-1*, CF-128-RC) Rand Corp.

Security in Disarmament. Ed. by Richard J. Barnet & Richard A. Falk. LC 65-12989. 451p. reprint ed. pap. 128.60 (*0-8357-7016-8*, 2033404) Bks Demand.

Security in East Asia. Ed. by Robert O'Neill. LC 83-40156. (Adelphi Library). 208p. 1984. text ed. 29.95 (*0-312-70916-1*) St Martin.

S

An Asterisk (*) at the beginning of an entry indicates that the title is appearing in BIP for the first time.

Security in Europe: A Crisis of Confidence. Bernard A. Goetze. LC 84-16008. 240p. 1984. text ed. 49.95 (0-275-91174-8, C1174, Praeger Pubs) Greenwood.

Security in Europe: The Role of NATO after the Cold War. Ed. by Walter Goldstein. LC 94-21295. 1994. 59.95 (1-85753-195-7, Pub. by Brasseys UK) Brasseys Inc.

Security in North Africa: Internal & External Challenges. Ian O. Lesser. 90p. 1993. pap. 15.00 (0-8330-1380-7, MR-203) Rand Corp.

***Security in Our Time: Four Essays on the Future of Europe.** Ed. by Ann-Sofie Dahl. 93p. 1996. reprint ed. pap. 25.00 (0-7881-3350-0) DIANE Pub.

Security in South-East Asia & the South-West Pacific: Challenges of the 1990's. Ed. by International Peace Academy Staff. (C). 1988. lib. bdg. 77.50 (90-247-3756-7) Kluwer Ac.

***Security in Southeastern European & the U. S. - Greek Relationship.** Ed. by Robert L. Pfaltzgraff & Dimitris Keridis. (Institute for Foreign Policy Analysis Special Report). 225p. (Orig.). 1997. pap. 11.95 (1-57488-133-7) Brasseys Inc.

Security in the Eastern Mediterranean: Re-Thinking American Policy. Joseph J. Wolf. 19p. (C). 1978. pap. 12.95 (0-87855-739-3) Transaction Pubs.

Security in the New World Order. Suresh A. Sinha. (C). 1993. 17.50 (81-7001-091-8, Pub. by Chanakya II) S Asia.

Security in the Nuclear Age: Developing U. S. Strategic Arms Policy. Jerome H. Kahan. LC 75-20145. 361p. 1975. pap. 10.95 (0-8157-4817-5) Brookings.

Security in the Year 2000 & Beyond. Louis A. Tyska & Lawrence J. Fennelly. (Illus.). 276p. 1987. 23.95 (0-88280-117-1) ETC Pubns.

Security Industry Markets: Products & Services. 203p. 1993. 1,950.00 (0-945235-69-0) Lead Edge Reports.

Security Interests in Personal Property, 2 Vols. Grant Gilmore. 1508p. 1965. 160.00 (0-316-31374-2) Little.

Security Interests in Personal Property: Cases & Materials On. 2nd ed. John O. Honnold & Steven L. Harris. Ed. by Charles W. Mooney, Jr. (University Casebook Ser.). 475p. 1992. text ed. 42.95 (1-56662-008-2) Foundation Pr.

Security Interests in Personal Property: Cases, Problems & Materials. 2nd ed. Douglas G. Baird & Thomas J. Jackson. (University Casebook Ser.). 889p. 1990. reprint ed. text ed. 39.50 (0-88277-549-9) Foundation Pr.

Security Interests in Personal Property: Cases, Problems & Materials. Douglas G. Baird & Thomas J. Jackson. (University Casebook Ser.). 889p. 1990. reprint ed. pap. text ed. write for info. (0-88277-604-5) Foundation Pr.

Security Interests in Personal Property, Manual for Teachers to Accompany Cases, Problems & Materials On. 2nd ed. John O. Honnold et al. (University Casebook Ser.). 230p. (C). 1992. pap. text ed. write for info. (1-56662-038-4) Foundation Pr.

Security Investigator's Handbook. Paul Q. Fugua & Jerry V. Wilson. LC 78-62615. 240p. reprint ed. pap. 68.40 (0-685-23763-X, 2032839) Bks Demand.

Security Investments. David L. Scott. (Quality Paperback Ser.: No. 352). (Illus.). 220p. (Orig.). 1981. pap. 9.95 (0-8226-0352-7) Littlefield.

Security Investments. David L. Scott. LC 80-27005. (Illus.). 104p. (Orig.). 1981. 38.50 (0-8476-6971-8) Rowman.

Security Is a Thumb & a Blanket. Charles M. Schulz. LC 82-70029. (Illus.). (J). 1982. 6.95 (0-915696-53-3) Determined Prods.

Security Is a Thumb & Blanket. Charles M. Schulz. (Illus.). 1983. pap. 4.95 (0-915696-79-7) Determined Prods.

Security Issues & the Law of the Sea. David L. Larson. LC 93-20257. 396p. (C). 1994. lib. bdg. 55.00 (0-8191-9089-6) U Pr of Amer.

Security Issues for the Internet & the World Wide Web. Computer Technology Research Corporation Staff. (Illus.). 218p. (Orig.). 1996. 290.00 (1-56607-973-X) Comput Tech Res.

Security Issues in the Database Language SQL. (Illus.). 53p. (Orig.). (C). 1994. pap. text ed. 25.00 (0-7881-1136-1) DIANE Pub.

Security Issues in the Post-Cold War World. Ed. by M. Jane Davis. LC 95-39638. 256p. 1996. 70.00 (1-85898-334-7) E Elgar.

Security Law. Gilmere. Date not set. write for info. (0-7506-9465-3) Buttrwrth-Heinemann.

***Security Letter Source Book: A Reference Directory of Leading Services.** 6th ed. Ed. by Robert D. McCrie. (Orig.). 1997. pap. write for info. (0-614-30062-2) Security Let.

Security Letter Source Book, 1993. Robert D. McCrie. 450p. 1992. pap. 79.95 (0-9609820-4-3) Buttrwrth-Heinemann.

Security Letter Source Book, 1993. abr. ed. Ed. by Robert D. McCrie. 416p. 1990. pap. 75.00 (0-9609820-3-5) Security Let.

Security Man. Dixie Browning. 1995. mass mkt. 3.99 (0-373-45183-0, 1-45183-0) Harlequin Bks.

Security Management: Business Strategies for Success. Dennis Dalton. 328p. 1994. 34.95 (0-7506-9492-0) Buttrwrth-Heinemann.

Security Manager's Desk Reference. David A. Schachtsiek. 466p. 1986. 59.95 (0-409-90014-1) Buttrwrth-Heinemann.

Security Manager's Directory of A-V Training Materials. Ed. by Information Resources Center Staff & American Society for Industrial Security Staff. (Orig.). 1995. pap. write for info. (1-887056-04-1) Am Soc Indus Secur.

Security Manual. 6th ed. Eric Oliver & John Wilson. (Illus.). 250p. (Orig.). 1994. pap. 15.95 (0-566-07443-5, Pub. by Gower UK) Ashgate Pub Co.

***Security Market Imperfections in World Wide Equity Markets.** Ed. by Donald B. Keim & William T. Ziemba. (Publications of the Newton Institute: No. 9). 320p. (C). Date not set. text ed. 49.95 (0-521-57138-3) Cambridge U Pr.

Security Markets: Findings & Recommendations of a Special Staff of the Twentieth Century Fund. Twentieth Century Fund Staff. LC 75-2675. (Wall Street & the Security Market Ser.). 1975. reprint ed. 72.95 (0-405-07237-6) Ayer.

Security Markets: Stochastic Models. J. Darrell Duffie. (Economic Theory, Econometrics & Mathematical Economics Ser.). 358p. 1988. text ed. 42.00 (0-12-223345-X) Acad Pr.

Security Measures - for Professionals, Patients, Hospitals & Data Protection: Index of New Information. Jeff M. Davidson. 160p. 1994. 47.50 (0-7883-0214-0); pap. 44.50 (0-7883-0215-9) ABBE Pubs Assn.

Security Metaphors: Cold War Discourse from Containment to Common House. Paul A. Chilton. (Conflict & Consciousness: Studies in War, Peace & Social Thought: Vol. 2). 480p. (C). 1996. text ed. 39.95 (0-8204-2178-2) P Lang Pubng.

Security of Infants. Betty M. Flint. LC 59-40393. (Illus.). 144p. reprint ed. pap. 41.10 (0-317-08106-3, 2014209) Bks Demand.

Security of Personal Computer Systems: A Management Guide. 1986. lib. bdg. 79.95 (0-8490-3741-7) Gordon Pr.

Security of South Asia: American & Asian Perspectives. Ed. by Stephen P. Cohen. LC 87-10772. 304p. 1987. text ed. 29.95 (0-252-01394-8) U of Ill Pr.

Security of Southwest Asia. Zalmay Khalilzad et al. LC 83-13837. 425p. 1984. text ed. 45.00 (0-312-70914-5) St Martin.

Security of Tenure & Land Registration in Africa: Literature Review & Synthesis. Carol W. Dickerman et al. (LTC Papers: No. 141). 316p. (Orig.). 1987. 12.00 (0-614-14633-X) U of Wis Land.

Security of Tenure & Land Registration in Africa: Literature Review & Synthesis. Carol W. Dickerman et al. (LTC Research Papes: No. 137). 316p. (Orig.). 1989. pap. 12.00 (0-685-45512-2) U of Wis Land.

Security of Third World Countries. Jasjit Singh & Thomas Bernauer. (UNIDIR Ser.). 168p. 1993. 59.95 (1-85521-356-7, Pub. by Dartmth Pub UK) Ashgate Pub Co.

Security Officer. Jack Rudman. (Career Examination Ser.: C-1467). 1994. pap. 23.95 (0-8373-1467-4) Nat Learn.

Security Officer Training. Training Consultants Inc. Staff. 1975. pap. 37.95 (0-614-05764-7) Abbott Langer Assocs.

Security Officers: The Practice of Professional Security. David A. Kanne. 139p. 1994. pap. text ed. 35.00 (0-9642514-0-X); disk 22.50 (0-9642514-1-8) Safe Hse Pubng.

Security Officers Handbook. 2nd ed. John A. Gillen. (Illus.). 152p. 1991. pap. text ed. 7.95 (1-879563-01-0) Lexicon CA.

Security Officer's Handbook: Orientation. 1994. pap. 9.95 (0-9640460-2-4) Coleman Pubng.

Security Officer's Handbook: Standard Operating Procedure. Edward P. Kehoe. LC 93-32709. (Illus.). 272p. 1994. pap. 49.95 (0-7506-9474-2) Buttrwrth-Heinemann.

Security Officer's Manual. Bill Clede. LC 92-85104. (Illus.). 160p. (Orig.). 1993. pap. 16.95 (0-9630016-1-2) Lakeland Pub.

Security Officer's Training Manual. Robert D. Heitert. 176p. 1992. pap. text ed. 19.20 (0-13-799420-6) P-H.

Security on Virginia's Campuses. (Illus.). 66p. (Orig.). (C). 1995. pap. text ed. 20.00 (0-7881-2343-2) DIANE Pub.

Security One Information & "How To" Personal Pocket Manual. D'Andre Collins. Tr. by Maricella. 75p. (Orig.). (SPA.). 1993. pap. text ed. write for info. (0-9636273-1-7) DAndre Collins.

Security Options Strategy. Albert I. Bookbinder. LC 76-46120. 201p. 1976. 15.00 (0-916106-01-2) Prog Pr.

Security Planning Guidebook: Safeguarding Your Tenants & Property. 69p. (Orig.). 1995. pap. 140.00 (0-943130-16-6) Build Own & Man.

Security Policy: Dilemmas of Using & Controlling Military Power. Robert Harkavy & Edward A. Kolodziej. (C). 1979. pap. 15.00 (0-918592-34-8) Pol Studies.

Security Practices at Soviet Scientific Research Facilities. Irina Dunskaya. Ed. by Barbara Dash. 143p. (Orig.). 1983. pap. text ed. 75.00 (1-55831-007-X) Delphic Associates.

Security Problems: An African Predicament. Francis Deng. LC 81-71701. (Hans Wolff Memorial Lecture Ser.). 1982. pap. text ed. 5.00 (0-941934-36-5) Indiana Africa.

Security Problems & Policies in the Post-Cold War Caribbean. Ed. by Jorge R. Beruff & Humberto G. Muniz. LC 95-34284. (International Political Economy Ser.). 230p. 1996. text ed. 59.95 (0-312-12828-2) St Martin.

Security Program Design & Management: A Guide for Security-Conscious Managers. Donald B. Tweedy. LC 88-38102. 309p. 1989. text ed. 65.00 (0-89930-424-9, TWY, Quorum Bks) Greenwood.

Security Regulations in Hong Kong, Nineteen Seventy-Two to Nineteen Seventy-Seven. M. F. Higgins. 192p. 1978. lib. bdg. 59.50 (90-286-0948-2) Kluwer Ac.

Security Requirements for ADP Systems. 500p. (Orig.). (C). 1994. pap. text ed. 60.00 (0-941375-89-7) DIANE Pub.

Security Services Assistant. Jack Rudman. (Career Examination Ser.: C-2204). 1994. pap. 23.95 (0-8373-2204-9) Nat Learn.

Security Services, Security Science. Frank J. MacHovec. 154p. 1992. pap. 21.95 (0-398-06259-5) C C Thomas.

Security Services, Security Science. Frank J. MacHovec. 154p. (C). 1992. text ed. 35.95 (0-398-05811-3) C C Thomas.

Security Strategy & Missile Defense. Ed. by Robert L. Pfaltzgraff, Jr. (Institute for Foreign Policy Analysis Special Report). 138p. (Orig.). 1995. pap. 11.95 (1-57488-084-5) Brasseys Inc.

Security, Strategy, & Policy Responses in the Pacific Rim. rev. ed. Ed. by Young W. Kihl & Lawrence E. Grinter. LC 88-30611. 272p. 1989. lib. bdg. 38.50 (1-55587-131-3) Lynne Rienner.

Security Studies for the 1990s. Ed. by Richard Shultz et al. (Intelligence & National Security Library). 432p. 1993. 45.00 (0-02-881072-4) Brasseys Inc.

Security Studies for the 21st Century. Ed. by Richard Schultz et al. LC 97-24344. 448p. 1997. 49.95 (1-57488-066-7) Brasseys Inc.

Security Supervisor Training Manual. Ronald R. Minion & Sandi J. Davies. Ed. by Sandi J. Davies et al. 192p. 1995. pap. 34.95 (0-7506-9632-X) Buttrwrth-Heinemann.

Security Supervisor's Handbook: A Guide for the Private Security Primary Manager. John L. Coleman. (Illus.). 122p. 1987. pap. 24.95 (0-398-06068-1) C C Thomas.

Security Supervisor's Handbook: A Guide for the Private Security Primary Manager. John L. Coleman. (Illus.). 122p. (C). 1987. 36.95 (0-398-05291-3) C C Thomas.

Security Syndicate Operations: Organization, Management & Accounting. enl. rev. ed. Arthur Galston. LC 75-2634. (Wall Street & the Security Market Ser.). 1975. reprint ed. 23.95 (0-405-06959-6) Ayer.

Security Systems: A Guide to Buying. Paul E. Fii. 86p. 1990. 54.00 (1-85609-045-0, Pub. by Witherby & Co UK) St Mut.

Security Systems & Intruder Alarms. Vivian Capel. (Illus.). 268p. 1989. 39.95 (0-7506-0799-8) Buttrwrth-Heinemann.

Security Systems for Your Home & Automobile. Gordon McComb. (Illus.). 130p. 1994. pap. 16.95 (0-7906-1054-X) H W Sams.

Security Systems Simplified: Protecting Your Home, Business, & Car with State-of-the-Art Burglar Alarms. Steven M. Hampton. (Illus.). 128p. 1992. pap. 14.00 (0-87364-654-1) Paladin Pr.

Security Systems Technicians: Start & Run a Money-Making Business. R. Dodge Woodson. 1995. pap. text ed. 19.95 (0-07-071775-3) McGraw.

Security Threatened: Surveying Israeli Opinion on Peace & War. Asher Arian. (Studies in Political Psychology & Public Opinion). (Illus.). 353p. (C). 1995. text ed. 64.95 (0-521-48314-X) Cambridge U Pr.

Security Threatened: Surveying Israeli Opinion on Peace & War. Asher Arian. (Studies in Political Psychology & Public Opinion). (Illus.). 353p. (C). 1995. pap. text ed. 22.95 (0-521-49925-9) Cambridge U Pr.

Security Through Science & Engineering: Proceedings. International Carnahan Conference Staff. Ed. by J. S. Jackson & R. William De Vore. LC 82-646157. (Illus.). 278p. (Orig.). 1983. pap. 10.00 (0-89779-057-X, UKY BU 132) OES Pubns.

Security Through Science & Engineering: Proceedings, Third International Conference. Ed. by R. William De Vore & J. S. Jackson. LC 80-83300. (Illus.). 313p. 1980. pap. 10.00 (0-89779-042-1, UKYBU122) OES Pubns.

Security to the North: Canada - U. S. Defense Relations in the 1990s. Joseph T. Jockel. LC 91-52910. 250p. (C). 1991. 26.00 (0-87013-293-8) Mich St U Pr.

Security Training: Readings from Security Management Magazine. Shari M. Gallery. (Illus.). 291p. 1989. pap. 32.95 (0-409-90122-9) Buttrwrth-Heinemann.

Security Training & Education: A Handbook with Questions & Answers. David Y. Coverston & Sam S. Coverston. (Illus.). 1990. 12.00 (0-936101-05-9); pap. 10.00 (0-936101-04-0) Security Seminars.

Security Transactions, 1993. 32p. 1993. pap. 3.50 (0-685-67031-7, 4364) Commerce.

Security Watershed: Disarmament & Security Yearbook, 1991-1992. Ed. by Alexei G. Arbatov. (Science & Global Security Monograph Ser.: Vol. 2). 664p. 1993. text ed. 75.00 (2-88124-551-X) Gordon & Breach.

Security Within the Pacific Rim. Douglas Stuart. 250p. 1987. text ed. 53.95 (0-566-05246-6, Pub. by Dartmth Pub UK) Ashgate Pub Co.

Security Without Nuclear Weapons? Different Perspectives on Non-Nuclear Security. Ed. by Regina C. Karp. (SIPRI Publication). 416p. 1993. 59.00 (0-19-829143-4) OUP.

Security Without Nuclear Weapons - Indo-Soviet Dialogue. K. Subrahmanyam & Jasjit Singh. 218p. 1986. 26.00 (81-7062-012-0, Pub. by Lancer II) S Asia.

Security Without Starwars: Verifying a Ban on Ballistic Missle Defense. Betty G. Lall. 106p. 1987. pap. 6.00 (0-87871-052-3) CEP.

Security Yearbook. FMJ Intl. Publ. Ltd. Staff. (C). 1990. 325.00 (0-685-36823-8, Pub. by Fuel Metallurgical Jrnl UK) St Mut.

Security (3 Sermons) Charles H. Spurgeon. 1976. pap. 3.00 (1-56186-408-0) Pilgrim Pubns.

Securityland's Safety. Karl Kratz. Ed. by Cal Lum & Sherrey Bussey. (Illus.). 150p. (Orig.). 1987. 19.95 (0-941201-00-7); pap. 9.95 (0-941201-01-5) INNPRO.

***Sed & Awk.** 2nd ed. Arnold D. Robbins. Ed. by Gigi Estabrook. (Illus.). 450p. 1997. pap. 29.95 (1-56592-225-5) OReilly & Assocs.

Sed de Realidad. George Verwer. (SPA.). 1991. pap. 3.50 (1-56063-014-0, 498461) Editorial Unilit.

Sedad Eldem. Sibel Bozdogan et al. (Illus.). 175p. 1987. reprint ed. 57.95 (0-408-50042-5) Buttrwrth-Heinemann.

Sedation: A Guide to Patient Management. 3rd ed. Stanley F. Malamed. LC 94-32507. 641p. (C). (gr. 13). 1994. pap. text ed. 52.00 (0-8151-5736-3) Mosby Yr Bk.

Sedation & Analgesia. Park. 1993. pap. text ed. 69.00 (0-7020-1568-7) HarBrace.

Sedation & Analgesia in the Critically Ill. G. R. Park et al. (Illus.). 250p. 1995. 75.00 (0-86542-905-7) Blackwell Sci.

Sedem Sviatkov Izraela. 2nd ed. Vladimir Uhri. 38p. (Orig.). (SLO.). 1995. pap. 1.80 (1-56983-036-3) New Creat WI.

Sedeq & Sedaqah in the Hebrew Bible. Ahuva Ho. LC 90-19404. (American University Studies: Theology & Religion: Ser. VII, Vol. 78). 224p. (C). 1990. text ed. 36.95 (0-8204-1349-6) P Lang Pubng.

Seder for Tu B'Shevat. Harlene Appleman & Jane Shapiro. (Illus.). 32p. (J). (ps up). 1984. pap. 3.95 (0-930494-39-3) Kar-Ben.

Seder in Herlin & Other Stories. Gershon Kranzler. (Illus.). 108p. (YA). reprint ed. 10.00 (0-8266-0343-2, Merkos LInyonei Chinuch) Kehot Pubn Soc.

***Seder Kodashim: Arachin.** Comment by Yad Avraham. (Mishnah Ser.). pap. 15.99 (0-89906-311-X) Mesorah Pubns.

***Seder Kodashim: Bechoros.** Comment by Yad Avraham. (Mishnah Ser.). 22.99 (0-89906-307-1, K2BH) Mesorah Pubns.

***Seder Kodashim: Kereisos.** Comment by Yad Avraham. (Mishnah Ser.). 19.99 (0-89906-309-8, K3CH) Mesorah Pubns.

***Seder Kodashim: Kereisos.** Comment by Yad Avraham. (Mishnah Ser.). pap. 13.99 (0-89906-310-1) Mesorah Pubns.

Seder R. Armram Gaon: The Order of the Sabbath Prayer. Tryggve Kronholm. 238p. (Orig.). 1974. pap. 41.00 (91-22-00979-5) Coronet Bks.

***Seder Tohoros: Mikvaos.** Comment by Yad Avraham. (Mishnah Ser.). 22.99 (0-89906-330-6, T4BH) Mesorah Pubns.

Seder Tu Bishevat: The Festival of Trees. Adam Fisher. LC 89-25212. 98p. (Orig.). 1989. pap. text ed. 6.95 (0-88123-008-1) Central Conf.

Seder with the Animals. Howard I. Bogot & Mary K. Bogot. (J). 1995. 16.95 (0-88123-066-9); pap. 10.95 (0-88123-067-7) Central Conf.

***Seder Zeraim: Kilayim.** Comment by Yad Avraham. (Mishnah Ser.). 22.99 (0-89906-332-2, R3AH) Mesorah Pubns.

***Seder Zeraim: Peah.** Comment by Yad Avraham. (Mishnah Ser.). 22.99 (0-89906-328-4) Mesorah Pubns.

Sedge Moths of North America. John B. Heppner. LC 85-13087. (Handbook Ser.: No. 1). (Illus.). vii, 254p. (Orig.). 1985. pap. 49.95 (0-916846-32-6) Sandhill Crane.

Sedgemoor, 1685. John Whiles. (Illus.). 277p. (C). 1990. pap. 27.00 (0-948251-00-X, Pub. by Picton UK) St Mut.

Sedgemoor 1685: From Monmouth's Invasion to the Bloody Assizes. Text by David Chandler. (Illus.). 248p. 1995. 34.95 (1-873376-42-1) Howell Pr VA.

Sedgewick County, Colorado, Vol. II. Jean Williamson. Ed. by Fort Sedgwick Historical Society Staff. (Illus.). 482p. 1985. 50.00 (0-88107-037-8) Curtis Media.

***Sedgewick Gravestone Inscriptions to 1892.** Compiled by Grace M. Limeburner. (Illus.). 85p. 1997. reprint ed. pap. 15.50 (0-8328-5912-5) Higginson Bk Co.

***Sedgewick, Incorporated January 12, 1789: All Vital Statistics...(1789 to 1809)** Compiled by Grace M. Limeburner. (Illus.). 84p. 1997. reprint ed. pap. 15.00 (0-8328-5913-3) Higginson Bk Co.

Sediment - Water Interactions: Proceedings of the Fourth International Symposium. Ed. by Peter G. Sly & B. T. Hart. (C). 1989. lib. bdg. 375.00 (0-7923-0259-1) Kluwer Ac.

Sediment Acoustics. Robert D. Stoll. (Lecture Notes in Earth Sciences Ser.: Vol. 26). (Illus.). v, 155p. 1989. 37.95 (0-387-97191-2) Spr-Verlag.

Sediment & Water Quality in River Catchments. Ed. by Ian Foster et al. LC 95-3054. 400p. 1995. text ed. 155.00 (0-471-95728-3) Wiley.

Sediment Diagenesis. Parker. 1983. lib. bdg. 165.00 (90-277-1677-3) Kluwer Ac.

Sediment Dynamics on the Changjiang Estuary & the Adjacent East China Sea: A Selection of Edited Papers from the International Symposium Held in Hangzhou, People's Republic of China, April 1983. Ed. by John D. Milliman & J. Qingming. 236p. 1985. pap. 44.00 (0-08-030257-2, Pergamon Pr) Elsevier.

Sediment-Freshwater Interaction. Peter G. Sly. 1982. lib. bdg. 340.50 (90-6193-760-4) Kluwer Ac.

Sediment-Hosted Zn-Pb Ores. Ed. by L. Fontbote & M. Boni. LC 93-43690. (Special Publications of the Society for General Microbiology: Vol. 10). (Illus.). 430p. 1994. 216.95 (0-387-56551-5) Spr-Verlag.

Sediment in Streams: Sources, Biological Effects, & Control. Thomas F. Waters. (Monograph Ser.: No. 7). 251p. 1995. pap. 34.00 (0-913235-97-0) Am Fisheries Soc.

Sediment Microbiology. Ed. by D. B. Nedwell & C. M. Brown. (Society for General Microbiology Special Publications: No. 7). 1982. text ed. 99.00 (0-12-515380-5) Acad Pr.

Sediment Oxygen Demand: Processes, Modeling & Measurement. Ed. by Kathryn J. Hatcher. LC 85-82274. (Illus.). 448p. (Orig.). 1986. pap. write for info. (0-935835-00-8) Univ GA Nat Res.

***Sediment Records of Biomass Burning & Global Change.** LC 96-29756. (NATO ASI Series I: Global Environmental Change). 1997. 197.00 (3-540-62434-1) Spr-Verlag.

Sediment Toxicity Assessment. Burton. 480p. 1992. 89.95 (0-87371-450-4, L450) Lewis Pubs.

S

Sediment Transport: Theory & Practice. Chia T. Yang. LC 95-37208. (Series in Water Resources & Environmental Engineering Ser.). (Illus.). 480p. 1996. text ed. 45.00 (*0-07-072309-5*) McGraw.

Sediment Transport: Theory & Practice. Chih T. Yang. LC 95-37208. (Series in Water Resources & Environmental Engineering Ser.). 1995. pap. write for info. (*0-07-072310-9*) McGraw.

Sediment Transport & Depositional Processes. Ed. by Kenneth Pye. LC 93-17446. 330p. 1994. pap. 59.95 (*0-632-03112-3*) Blackwell Sci.

Sediment Transport in Alluvial Streams. John L. Bogardi. 826p. (C). 1978. 150.00 (*963-05-1826-0*, Pub. by Akad Kiado HU) St Mut.

Sediment Transport in Gravel-Bed Rivers. Ed. by C. R. Thorne et al. LC 86-15954. 995p. 1987. text ed. 505.00 (*0-471-90914-9*) Wiley.

Sediment Transport in the Near-Shore Zone. Ed. by William F. Tanner. 147p. 1974. pap. 20.00 (*0-686-83994-3*) FSU Geology.

Sediment Transport Mechanisms in Coastal Environments & Rivers. M. Belorgey et al. 400p. 1994. text ed. 112.00 (*981-02-1854-0*) World Scientific Pub.

Sediment Transport Technology - Water & Sediment Dynamics. Daryl B. Simons. 919p. 1992. text ed. 129.00 (*0-918334-66-7*) WRP.

Sediment Transport Technology, Solution Manual. Daryl B. Simons. 287p. 1992. pap. text ed. 55.00 (*0-918334-67-5*) WRP.

Sediment-Water Interactions: Proceedings of the Fifth International Symposium. Ed. by B. T. Hart & Peter G. Sly. LC 92-17637. (Developments in Hydrobiology Ser.: Vol. 75). 768p. (C). 1992. lib. bdg. 412.00 (*0-7923-1812-9*) Kluwer Ac.

Sedimentary & Diagonetic Mineral Deposits: A Basin Analysis Approach to Exploration, Vol. 5. (Reviews in Economic Geology Ser.). (Illus.). 216p. (C). pap. text ed. write for info. (*0-9613074-4-7*) Soc Econ Geol.

***Sedimentary & Tectonic Evolution of Rift Basins: The Red Sea, Gulf of Aden.** Ed. by Bosence & Ann Purser. (Illus.). 512p. 1997. text ed. 1.19 (*0-412-73490-7*, Chap & Hall NY) Chapman & Hall.

Sedimentary Basins: Evolution, Facies, & Sediment Budget. G. Einsele. (Illus.). x, 628p. 1992. 99.95 (*0-387-54743-6*) Spr-Verlag.

Sedimentary Cover - North American Craton: U. S. Ed. by L. L. Sloss. (DNAG, Geology of North America Ser.: Vol. D2). (Illus.). 520p. 1988. 49.50 (*0-8137-5205-1*) Geol Soc.

Sedimentary Cover of the Craton in Canada. Ed. by D. F. Stott. (Geology of Canada Ser.: No. 5). 826p. 1993. 91.00 (*0-660-13133-1*, Pub. by Canada Commun Grp CN) Accents Pubns.

***Sedimentary Deposition in Rift & Foreland Basins in France & Spain (Paleogene & Lower Neogene)** Georges Busson & B. Charlotte Schreiber. LC 96-32223. 1997. write for info. (*0-231-06786-0*) Col U Pr.

Sedimentary Environments: Processes, Facies, & Stratigraphy. 2nd ed. Harold G. Reading. (Illus.). 680p. 1986. pap. text ed. 59.95 (*0-632-01223-4*) Blackwell Sci.

Sedimentary Facies Analysis: A Tribute to the Research & Teaching of Harold G. Reading. Guy A. Plint. LC 94-30445. 1995. 89.95 (*0-86542-898-0*) Blackwell Sci.

Sedimentary Geologists' Guide to Helping K-12 Earth Science Teachers. Ed. by K-12 Earth Science Committee. (K-Twelve Curriculum Ser.: No. 50). (Illus.). 92p. 1990. pap. 5.00 (*0-918985-86-2*) SEPM.

Sedimentary Geology. Donald R. Prothero. (C). 1996. text ed. write for info. (*0-7167-2726-9*) W H Freeman.

Sedimentary Geology of the Himalaya. Ed. by R. A. Srivastava. (Current Trends in Geology Ser.: Vol. 5). xii, 250p. 1985. 50.00 (*1-55528-051-X*, Pub. by Today & Tomorrows P & P II) Scholarly Pubns.

Sedimentary Gradients in a High Energy Carbonate Lagoon, Snow Bay, San Salvador, Bahamas. C. B. Anderson & Mark R. Boardman. (Occasional Papers: No. 1). 25p. 1987. pap. text ed. 4.00 (*0-935909-25-7*) Bahamian.

***Sedimentary Organic Matter: Organic Facies & Palynofacies.** Tyson. (Illus.). 640p. (C). (gr. 13 up). 1994. text ed. 178.95 (*0-412-36350-X*, Chap & Hall NY) Chapman & Hall.

Sedimentary Petrology. 2nd ed. Harvey Blatt. LC 91-24385. 514p. (C). 1995. text ed. write for info. (*0-7167-2273-9*) W H Freeman.

Sedimentary Petrology, Vol. II. Loren A. Raymond. 320p. (C). 1994. per. write for info. (*0-697-23691-9*) Wm C Brown Pubs.

Sedimentary Petrology & History of the Haymond Formation (Pennsylvanian), Marathon Basin, Texas. Earle F. McBride. (Report of Investigations Ser.: RI 57). 101p. 1966. pap. 2.50 (*0-686-29339-8*) Bur Econ Geology.

Sedimentary Processes: Depositional Processes in Ancient Carbonates. Society of Economic Paleontologists & Mineralogists Staff. (Society of Economic Paleontologists & Mineralogists, Special Publication Ser.: No. 7). (Illus.). 239p. reprint ed. pap. 68.20 (*0-317-58121-X*, 2029674) Bks Demand.

Sedimentary Processes: Diagenesis. Doris M. Curtis. (Society of Economic Paleontologists & Mineralogists, Special Publication Ser.: No. 1). 222p. reprint ed. pap. 63.30 (*0-317-27145-8*, 2024747) Bks Demand.

Sedimentary Processes, Carbonate Sedimentology: Selected Papers Reprinted from Journal of Sedimentary Petrology. Clif Jordon. LC 79-116635. (Society of Economic Paleontologists & Mineralogists, Special Publication Ser.: No. 5). 242p. reprint ed. pap. 69.00 (*0-685-15783-0*, 2026654) Bks Demand.

Sedimentary Processes on the Amazon Continental Shelf. Ed. by C. A. Nittrouer & D. J. Demaster. (Illus.). 336p. 1987. 39.50 (*0-08-033928-X*, Pergamon Pr) Elsevier.

Sedimentary Rocks in the Field. 2nd ed. Maurice E. Tucker. (Geological Field Guide Ser.). 150p. 1996. pap. text ed. 26.95 (*0-471-96215-5*) Wiley.

***Sedimentary Structures.** 2nd ed. Collinson & Thompson. (Illus.). 208p. (Orig.). (C). (gr. 13 up). 1989. pap. text ed. 36.95 (*0-412-44560-3*, Chap & Hall NY) Chapman & Hall.

Sedimentary Structures. 2nd ed. J. D. Collinson & D. B. Thompson. (Illus.). 240p. 1987. text ed. 80.00 (*0-04-445171-7*); pap. text ed. 29.95 (*0-04-445172-5*) Routledge Chapman & Hall.

Sedimentary Structures & Early Diagenetic Features of Shallow Marine Carbonate Deposits. Robert V. Demicco & Lawrence A. Hardie. (SEPM Atlas Ser.: No. 1). (Illus.). 272p. 1995. text ed. 93.00 (*1-56576-013-1*) SEPM.

Sedimentary Structures & Facies Analysis of Shallow Marine Carbonates. H. U. Schwarz. (Contributions to Sedimentology Ser.: No. 3). (Illus.). 100p. 1975. pap. text ed. 45.00 (*3-510-57003-0*) Lubrecht & Cramer.

Sedimentary Structures in Dunes of the Namib Desert, South West Africa. Edwin D. McKee. LC 81-20155. (Geological Society of America, Special Paper Ser.: No. 188). (Illus.). 68p. reprint ed. pap. 25.00 (*0-8357-6842-2*, 2035530) Bks Demand.

Sedimentation: Exclusion & Removal of Sediment from Diverted Water. Arved J. Raudkivi. (Hydraulic Structures Design Manual Ser.: No. 6). (Illus.). 176p. 1993. text ed. 85.00 (*90-5410-132-6*, Pub. by A A Balkema NE) Ashgate Pub Co.

Sedimentation & Mineral Deposits in the Southwestern Pacific Ocean. Ed. by David S. Cronan. (Ocean Science, Resources & Technology Ser.). 1986. text ed. 140.00 (*0-12-195870-1*) Acad Pr.

Sedimentation & Tectonics in Coastal Southern California, No. T110. Ed. by Abbott. (IGC Field Trip Guidebooks Ser.). 64p. 1989. 21.00 (*0-87590-609-5*) Am Geophysical.

Sedimentation & Tectonics of the Welsh Basin. Ed. by W. R. Fitches & N. H. Woodcock. LC 87-23439. (Geological Journal, Spring Thematic Issues - Conference Papers: Vol. 22). (Illus.). 224p. reprint ed. pap. 63.90 (*0-8357-3077-8*, 2039334) Bks Demand.

Sedimentation Engineering. Ed. by Vito A. Vanoni. (Manual & Report on Engineering Practice Ser.: No. 54). 761p. 1975. 39.00 (*0-87262-001-8*) Am Soc Civil Eng.

Sedimentation in the Mississippi River Between Davenport, Iowa, & Cairo, Illinois. Alvin L. Lugn. LC 28-14418. (Augustana College Library Publications: No. 11). 104p. 1927. pap. 1.00 (*0-910182-08-6*) Augustana Coll.

Sedimentation in the World Ocean with Emphasis on the Nature, Distribution & Behavior of Marine Suspensions. Alexander P. Lisitzin. Ed. by Kelvin S. Rodolfo. LC 72-172081. (Society of Economic Paleontologists & Mineralogists, Special Publication Ser.: No. 17). 232p. reprint ed. pap. 66.20 (*0-317-27149-0*, 2024744) Bks Demand.

Sedimentation in Volcanic Settings. Ed. by Richard V. Fisher & Gary A. Smith. (Special Publications: No. 45). (Illus.). 264p. 1991. 68.50 (*0-918985-89-7*) SEPM.

Sedimentation of Organic Particles. Ed. by Alfred Traverse. LC 92-39221. (Illus.). 512p. (C). 1994. text ed. 145.00 (*0-521-38436-2*) Cambridge U Pr.

Sedimentation of Small Particles in a Viscous Fluid. Ed. by E. M. Tory. LC 95-70468. (Advances in Fluid Mechanics Ser.: Vol. 7). 304p. 1996. 132.00 (*1-56252-280-9*, 3579) Computational Mech MA.

Sedimentation, Tectonics & Eustasy. D. Macdonald. 1991. pap. 125.00 (*0-632-03017-8*) Blackwell Sci.

Sedimente und Sedimentgesteine. 4th ed. Ed. by Hans Fuechtbauer. (Illus.). 1141p. (GER.). 1988. lib. bdg. 138.95 (*3-510-65138-3*, Pub. by Schweitzerbartsche GW) Lubrecht & Cramer.

Sedimentographica: Photographic Atlas of Sedimentary Structures. 2nd ed. Franco R. Lucci. LC 94-24952. 280p. 1995. 45.00 (*0-231-10018-3*) Col U Pr.

Sedimentologic Analysis of Cores from the Upper Triassic Chinle Formation & the Lower Periman Cutler Formation, Lisbon Valley, Utah. Russell F. Dubiel & Janet L. Brown. Ch. E. write for info. (*0-318-71685-2*) US Geol Survey.

Sedimentologic Consequences of Convulsive Geologic Events. Ed. by H. E. Clifton. (Special Papers: No. 229). 150p. 1988. pap. 5.00 (*0-8137-2229-2*) Geol Soc.

***Sedimentologie und Tektonik des Ruhr-Beckens: Sequenzstratigraphische Interpretation und Modellierung eines Vorlandsbeckens der Varisciden.** M. Peter Suess. (Bonner Geowissen Schaftliche Schriften Ser.: Band 20). (Illus.). 158p. 1996. pap. 70.00 (*3-931251-11-X*, Pub. by Martina Galunder GW) Balogh.

Sedimentology. H. Chamley. (Illus.). 288p. 1990. 42.95 (*0-387-52376-6*) Spr-Verlag.

Sedimentology. Michael McLane. (Illus.). 512p. (C). 1995. text ed. 59.95 (*0-19-507868-3*) OUP.

Sedimentology: Proceedings of the 27th International Geological Congress, Vol. 4. International Geological Congress Staff. 262p. 1984. lib. bdg. 90.00 (*90-6764-013-1*, Pub. by VSP NE) Coronet Bks.

Sedimentology: Process & Product. M. R. Leeder. (Illus.). 528p. (C). 1982. pap. text ed. 34.95 (*0-04-551054-7*) Routledge Chapman & Hall.

Sedimentology: Process & Product. M. R. Leeder. 362p. (gr. 13). 1988. pap. text ed. 42.95 (*0-412-53300-6*) Chapman & Hall.

Sedimentology & Coal Resources of the Early Oligocene Australian Creek Formation Near Quesnel, British Columbia. D. G. Long. (GSC Paper Ser.: No. 92-11). 73p. (Orig.). 1993. pap. 10.70 (*0-660-14551-0*, Pub. by Canada Commun Grp CN) Accents Pubns.

Sedimentology & Geochemistry of Dolostones. Ed. by Vijai Shukla & Paul A. Baker. (Special Publications: No. 43). 268p. 1988. text ed. 47.50 (*0-918985-77-3*) SEPM.

Sedimentology & Geochemistry of Modern & Ancient Saline Lakes. Ed. by R. W. Renaut & W. M. Last. (SEPM Special Publications: No. 50). (Illus.). 348p. 1994. text ed. 90.00 (*1-56576-014-X*) SEPM.

Sedimentology & Paleontology of Eocene Rocks in the Sespe Creek Area, Ventura County, California. Ed. by A. E. Fritsche. (Illus.). 106p. (Orig.). 1994. pap. 13.00 (*1-878861-67-0*) Pac Section SEPM.

Sedimentology & Petroleum Geology. K. O. Bjorlykke. (Illus.). 310p. 1989. 70.95 (*0-387-17691-8*) Spr-Verlag.

Sedimentology & Sequence Stratigraphy of Reefs & Carbonate Platforms: A Short Course. Wolfgang Schlager. (Continuing Education Course Note Ser.: No. 34). (Illus.). 71p. (Orig.). 1992. pap. 5.00 (*0-89181-183-4*, 567) AAPG.

Sedimentology & Thermal-Mechanical History of Basins in the Central Appalachian Orogen, No. T152. Ed. by Slingerland. (IGC Field Trip Guidebooks Ser.). 88p. 1989. 21.00 (*0-87590-615-X*) Am Geophysical.

Sedimentology of Chalk. H. Zijlstra. LC 94-45979. (Lecture Notes in Earth Sciences Ser.: Vol. 54). 1995. write for info. (*0-387-58948-1*) Spr-Verlag.

Sedimentology of Chalk. H. Zijlstra. LC 94-45979. (Lecture Notes in Earth Sciences Ser.: Vol. 54). (Illus.). ix, 194p. 1995. 75.95 (*3-540-58948-1*) Spr-Verlag.

Sedimentology of Coal & Coal-Bearing Sequences. Ed. by Ray A. Rahmani & Romeo M. Flores. 396p. 1985. pap. 75.00 (*0-632-01286-2*) Blackwell Sci.

Sedimentology of Shale: Study Guide & Reference Source. P. E. Potter et al. (Illus.). 316p. 1984. pap. 72.00 (*0-387-90430-1*) Spr-Verlag.

Sedimentology Review, No. 1. V. P. Wright. (Illus.). 160p. 1993. pap. 85.00 (*0-632-03102-6*) Blackwell Sci.

Sediments: Chemistry & Toxicity of In-Place Pollutants. Ed. by John P. Giesy et al. 424p. 1990. 99.95 (*0-87371-252-8*, L252) Lewis Pubs.

Sediments & Environmental Geochemistry. Ed. by D. Heling et al. (Illus.). 384p. 1990. 153.95 (*0-387-51735-9*) Spr-Verlag.

Sediments & Sedimentary Rocks 1. Hans Fuechtbauer. (Sedimentary Petrology Ser.: Pt. 2). (Illus.). 464p. 1974. lib. bdg. 67.50 (*3-510-65007-7*) Lubrecht & Cramer.

Sediments & Toxic Substances: Environmental Effects & Ecotoxicity. Ed. by W. Cahnano et al. (Environmental Science Ser.). (Illus.). 350p. 1996. 115.00 (*3-540-60051-5*) Spr-Verlag.

Sediments & Toxic Substances: Environmental Effects & Ecotoxity. Ed. by W. Calmano & U. Forstner. LC 95-52310. (Environmental Science Ser.: No. 3234). 1996. write for info. (*0-387-60051-5*) Spr-Verlag.

Sediments & Water Interactions. Ed. by Peter G. Sly. (Illus.). 575p. 1986. 173.00 (*0-387-96293-X*) Spr-Verlag.

***Sediments of Time: Environment & Society in Chinese History.** Ed. by Mark Elvin & Liu Ts'ui-jung. (Studies in Environment & History). (Illus.). 450p. (C). 1997. text ed. 84.95 (*0-521-56381-X*) Cambridge U Pr.

Sedition Case of Nineteen Forty-Four. Lutheran Research Society Staff. 1979. lib. bdg. 59.95 (*0-8490-3005-6*) Gordon Pr.

***Seditions: Heidegger & the Limit of Modernity.** Heribert Boeder. Ed. & Tr. by Marcus Brainard from GER. LC 97-12835. (SUNY Series in Contemporary Continental Philosophy). 359p. (C). 1997. text ed. 59.50 (*0-7914-3531-8*); pap. text ed. 19.95 (*0-7914-3532-6*) State U NY Pr.

Seditious Mandibles: Surrealist Drawings & Poems. Robert Green. (Illus.). 24p. 1981. pap. 7.00 (*0-941194-13-2*) Black Swan Pr.

Sedjenane: The Pay-off Battle. Henry G. Phillips. (Illus.). 150p. (Orig.). 1993. pap. 11.25 (*0-9637444-0-2*) H G Phillips.

Sed'Maia Zhena. Igor Efimov, pseud. LC 90-3368. 444p. (Orig.). (RUS.). 1990. pap. 14.00 (*1-55779-027-2*) Hermitage.

Sedona: Arizona's Red Rock Community. Robert H. Brown. (Illus.). (Orig.). 1993. pap. write for info. (*0-9639209-1-X*) Bronze Age.

Sedona: Deutsche Ausgabe. Lance Yaste. 20p. 1993. 9.95 (*0-9637513-0-1*) Vortex Pub.

Sedona: Psychic Energy Vortexes. Dick Sutphen. (Illus.). 228p. 1993. pap. 9.98 (*0-87554-557-2*, B922) Valley Sun.

Sedona: Red Rock Country. Bob Bradshaw. LC 94-78579. (Illus.). 64p. pap. text ed. write for info. (*0-9629319-1-8*) Bradshaw Color.

Sedona - Beyond the Vortex: The Power of the Vortex, Sacred Geometry & the Merkba. Richard Dannelley. (Sedona Ser.: Bk. 3). (Illus.). 128p. (Orig.). 1995. pap. 12.00 (*0-9629453-7-4*) Vortex Society.

Sedona Cook Book: Recipes from Red Rock Country. Susan K. Bollin. LC 94-12950. 1994. pap. 7.95 (*0-914846-98-1*) Golden West Pub.

Sedona Guide: Day Hiking & Sightseeing Arizona's Redrock Country. Steve Krause & Teresa Henkle. (Illus.). 128p. 1991. pap. 8.95 (*0-910973-02-4*) Arrowhead AZ.

Sedona Hikes: One Hundred Twenty-One Day Hikes, Five Vortex Sites Around Sedona, Arizona. 2nd rev. ed. Richard K. Mangum & Sherry G. Mangum. (Illus.). 256p. 1994. reprint ed. pap. 14.95 (*0-9632265-6-8*) Hexagon Pr.

***Sedona Hikes: 121 Day Hikes, 5 Vortex Sites Around Sedona, Arizona.** 3rd rev. ed. Richard K. Mangum. (Illus.). 256p. 1997. pap. 14.95 (*0-9632265-8-4*) Hexagon Pr.

***Sedona Magic: Science Looks at Sedona's Healing Power.** Clifford Williams. (Illus.). 20p. (Orig.). 1996. pap. 15.95 (*0-934274-51-7*) Consumertronics.

Sedona Mountain Bike Guide. Armor Todd. (Illus.). 32p. (Orig.). 1993. pap. 5.95 (*0-9623537-3-6*) A Todd.

Sedona Power Spot, Vortex & Medicine Wheel Guide. Richard Dannelley. (Illus.). 112p. 1991. pap. 11.00 (*0-9629453-2-3*) Vortex Society.

Sedona, Responding to the Call. Sharon Marer & Shirley Piwonski. (Illus.). 200p. (Orig.). 1994. pap. 12.95 (*1-885782-89-6*) Sources of Light.

Sedona-Sacred Earth: Ancient Lore, Modern Myths - A Guide to the Red Rock Country. rev. ed. Nicholas R. Mann. Ed. by Margaret Thompson & Nancy Dye. (Illus.). 108p. 1990. pap. 12.95 (*0-914732-36-6*) Bro Life Inc.

Sedona Starseed: A Galactic Initiation. Raymond Mardyks. (Illus.). 145p. (Orig.). 1995. pap. 14.95 (*0-9644180-0-2*) Star Heart.

Sedona Storm. LC 93-30667. 1993. 10.99 (*0-7852-8266-1*) Nelson.

Sedona Through Time: Geology of the Red Rocks. Wayne Ranney. (Illus.). 97p. 1993. pap. 12.95 (*0-9611678-9-0*) Red Lake Bks.

Sedona Trilogy, Bk. 2: Doorways Between the Worlds. Heather Hughes-Calero. LC 85-89057. 140p. (Orig.). 1985. pap. 9.95 (*0-932927-01-7*) Higher Consciousness.

Sedona Visual. John Hoffman. 1987. pap. 7.95 (*0-934148-05-8*) Wstrn Rec Pubns.

Sedona Vortex Experience: Finding Your Personal Power Place. Gayle Johansen & Shinan N. Barclay. (Illus.). 24p. (Orig.). 1988. pap. 4.95 (*0-945086-00-8*) Sunlight Prodns.

Sedona Vortex Guide Book. 236p. (Orig.). 1991. pap. 14.95 (*0-929385-25-X*) Light Tech Comns Servs.

Sedra Scenes: Skits for Every Torah Portion. Stan J. Beiner. LC 82-71282. 225p. (Orig.). (J). (gr. 6-12). 1982. pap. text ed. 10.50 (*0-86705-007-1*) A R E Pub.

Sedrah Study for Everybody: A Guide to the Weekly Reading. Leonard I. Wanetik. 266p. (Orig.). 1995. pap. 25.00 (*0-9648758-0-2*) L I Wanetik.

Seduccion de la Cristiandad. David Hunt & T. A. McMahon. Orig. Title: The Seduction of Christianity. 240p. (SPA.). 1988. pap. 8.99 (*0-8254-1325-7*, Edit Portavoz) Kregel.

***Seduccion de Nuestros Hijos.** Neil T. Anderson. 217p. (SPA.). write for info. (*1-56063-916-4*) Editorial Unilit.

Seduccion Salvaje - Savage Courtship. Susan Napier. (Harlequin Bianca - Harlequin Presents Ser.: Vol. 359). (ENG & SPA.). 1996. mass mkt. 3.50 (*0-373-33359-5*) Harlequin Bks.

***Seduced.** Nelson George. 1997. pap. 12.00 (*0-345-41266-4*) Ballantine.

Seduced. Virginia Henley. 544p. 1994. mass mkt. 5.99 (*0-440-21135-2*) Dell.

Seduced. Metsy Hingle. (Desire Ser.). 1994. mass mkt. 2.99 (*0-373-05900-0*, 1-05900-5) Silhouette.

Seduced. Catherine Lanigan. 400p. (Orig.). 1996. mass mkt., pap. text ed. 5.50 (*0-8439-3942-7*) Dorchester Pub Co.

Seduced. Sam Shepard. 1978. pap. 5.25 (*0-8222-1008-8*) Dramatists Play.

Seduced. Marcus Van Heller. 1995. mass mkt. 5.95 (*0-7867-0295-8*) Carroll & Graf.

Seduced: The Life & Times of a One-Hit Wonder. Nelson George. 352p. 1996. 23.95 (*0-399-14169-3*, Putnam) Putnam Pub Group.

Seduced & Abandoned: Essays on Gay Men & Popular Music. Richard Smith. (Lesbian & Gay Studies). 288p. Date not set. write for info. (*0-304-33343-3*); pap. write for info. (*0-304-33347-6*) Cassell.

Seduced & Betrayed (Bachelor Arms) Candace Schuler. 1995. mass mkt. 3.25 (*0-373-25653-1*) Harlequin Bks.

***Seduced by a Stranger.** Morgan Hayes. 1997. pap. 3.50 (*0-373-25745-7*, 1-25745-0) Harlequin Bks.

Seduced by Death: Doctors, Patients, & the Dutch Cure. Herbert Hendin. 256p. 1996. 27.50 (*0-393-04003-8*) Norton.

Seduced by Innocence. Lucy Gordon. (Special Edition Ser.). 1994. mass mkt. 3.50 (*0-373-09902-9*, 1-09902-7) Harlequin Bks.

Seduced by Innocence. large type ed. Lucy Gordon. (Silhouette Romance Ser.). 1995. 19.95 (*0-373-59627-8*) Harlequin Bks.

Seducer. Linda Turner. (Desire Ser.). 1993. mass mkt. 2.99 (*0-373-05802-0*, 5-05802-9) Silhouette.

Seducer: It Is Hard to Die in Dieppe. Henrik Strangerup. Tr. by Sean Martin. 1990. 22.95 (*0-7145-2894-3*) M Boyars Pubs.

Seducer: It's Hard to Die in Dieppe. Henrik Stangerup. Tr. by Sean Martin from DAN. 320p. 1996. pap. 13.95 (*0-7145-2986-9*) M Boyars Pubs.

Seducers. Martin Shepard. LC 80-80408. 260p. 1981. reprint ed. 22.00 (*0-932966-12-8*) Permanent Pr.

***Seducer's Diary.** Sren Kierkegaard et al. LC 97-10671. 1997. pap. write for info. (*0-691-01737-9*) Princeton U Pr.

Seducers in Ecuador & the Heir. large type ed. Vita Sackville-West. LC 95-12777. 1995. pap. 19.95 (*0-7862-0484-2*) Thorndike Pr.

***Seducing America: Is Gambling a Good Bet?** Rex M. Rogers. 176p. (Orig.). 1997. pap. 10.99 (*0-8010-5759-0*) Baker Bks.

Seducing Hunter. Cathie Linz. (Desire Ser.). 1996. mass mkt. 3.50 (*0-373-76029-9*, 1-76029-7) Silhouette.

***Seducing Santa.** Henderson. 1997. mass mkt. 3.50 (*0-373-52058-1*) Harlequin Bks.

An Asterisk (*) at the beginning of an entry indicates that the title is appearing in BIP for the first time.

Seducing Spencer. Nikki Rivers. (American Romance Ser.). 1994. mass mkt. 3.50 (*0-373-16550-1*, 1-16550-5) Harlequin Bks.

Seducing Spirits & Doctrines of Demons. Rick Renner. (Orig.). 1995. pap. text ed. 7.99 (*1-880089-07-6*) Albury Pub.

Seducing Spirits & Doctrines of Demons. Rick Renner. Ed. by Phyllis MacKall. (Orig.). 1988. 6.95 (*0-9621436-0-X*) R Renner Minst.

Seducing Sydney. Kathy Marks. (Yours Truly Ser.). 1996. mass mkt. 3.50 (*0-373-52018-2*, 1-52018-8) Silhouette.

***Seducing the Enemy.** Emma Darcy. 1997. mass mkt. 3.50 (*0-373-11906-2*, 1-11906-4) Harlequin Bks.

Seducing the French: The Dilemma of Americanization. Richard F. Kuisel. LC 92-26548. 1993. 35.00 (*0-520-07962-0*) U CA Pr.

Seducing the French: The Dilemma of Americanization. Richard F. Kuisel. 293p. 1996. pap. 15.95 (*0-520-20698-3*) U CA Pr.

***Seducing the Samaritan: How Government Contracts Are Reshaping Social Service.** Joseph Loconte. LC 97-21676. (Pioneer Paper Ser.). 1997. write for info. (*0-929930-18-5*) Pioneer Inst.

Seduction. Jean Baudrillard. Ed. by Arthur Kroker & Marilouise Kroker. Tr. by Brian Singer from FRE. (Culture Texts Ser.). 187p. 1991. pap. 13.95 (*0-312-05294-4*) St Martin.

Seduction. Cynthia Blair. (Dark Moon Legacy Ser.: No. 2). 320p. 1993. mass mkt. 3.99 (*0-06-106151-4*, Harp PBks) HarpC.

Seduction. Robert Evans. 1996. pap. 22.95 (*0-7871-0885-5*, Dove Bks) Dove Audio.

***Seduction.** Laura Guhrke. 432p. 1997. mass mkt. 5.50 (*0-06-108403-4*) HarpC.

Seduction. Felicia Mason. 320p. 1996. mass mkt. 4.99 (*0-7860-0297-2*, Pinncle Kensgtn) Kensgtn Pub Corp.

Seduction. Amanda Quick. 352p. 1990. pap. 6.50 (*0-553-28354-5*) Bantam.

***Seduction.** Marilyn Wallace. 432p. 31.50 (*0-7089-3692-X*) Ulverscroft.

Seduction. large type ed. Amanda Quick. LC 94-12082. 1994. lib. bdg. 23.95 (*0-7862-0259-9*) Thorndike Pr.

Seduction: A Book of Stories. Tony Peake. 224p. (Orig.). 1995. pap. 11.99 (*1-85242-314-5*) Serpents Tail.

Seduction & Betrayal: Women & Literature. Elizabeth Hardwick. 1990. pap. 8.95 (*0-679-72427-3*, Vin) Random.

Seduction & Repetition in Ovid's Ars Amatoria II. Alison Sharrock. 336p. 1994. 58.00 (*0-19-814959-X*) OUP.

Seduction & Sacrifice. Miranda Lee. (Presents Ser.). 1995. mass mkt. 3.25 (*0-373-11754-X*, 1-11754-8) Harlequin Bks.

Seduction & Theory: Readings of Gender, Representation, & Rhetoric. Ed. by Dianne Hunter. LC 88-37602. 264p. 1989. text ed. 27.50 (*0-252-01626-2*); pap. text ed. 11.95 (*0-252-06063-6*) U of Ill Pr.

Seduction by the Stars: An Astrological Guide to All Stages of a Relationship. Geraldine Soadhi & Ren Lexander. LC 94-17150. 272p. 1995. pap. 12.95 (*0-553-37451-6*) Bantam.

Seduction Lines Heard 'Round the World & Answers You Can Give: A World Book of Lines. Sol Gordon. (Illus.). 176p. 1988. pap. 15.95 (*0-87975-405-2*) Prometheus Bks.

***Seduction Mystique.** Ginie P. Sayles. LC 96-46401. 272p. 1997. pap. 12.00 (*0-380-78365-7*) Avon.

***Seduction of a New Age Cult.** Mark Sprague. 195p. (Orig.). 1998. mass mkt. 4.99 (*1-55237-448-3*, Pub. by Comnwlth Pub CN) Partners Pubs Grp.

***Seduction of Black Criminality: A Psychopolitical Analysis of Black Crime in America.** Gene A. Jones. LC 96-85172. vi, 144p. (Orig.). 1996. pap. 13.95 (*0-9650505-0-5*) CGS Communs.

Seduction of Christianity. Dave Hunt & T. A. McMahon. LC 84-81211. 242p. 1985. pap. 9.99 (*0-89081-441-4*) Harvest Hse.

Seduction of Christianity see Seduccion de la Cristiandad

***Seduction of Hillary Rodham.** David Brock. 432p. 1996. 26.00 (*0-684-83451-0*) Free Pr.

***Seduction of Hillary Rodham.** David Brock. 1997. pap. 14.00 (*0-684-83770-6*) Free Pr.

Seduction of Jake Tallman: Man of the Month. Cait London. (Desire Ser.). 1993. mass mkt. 2.99 (*0-373-05811-X*, 5-05811-0) Silhouette.

Seduction of Keira. Emma Darcy. (Presents Ser.: No. 1472). 1992. pap. 2.89 (*0-373-11472-9*) Harlequin Bks.

Seduction of Keira. large type ed. Emma Darcy. 203p. 1995. 21.95 (*0-7838-1242-6*, GK Hall) Thorndike Pr.

Seduction of Lady Carroll. Joy Reed. 224p. 1996. mass mkt. 4.50 (*0-8217-5382-7*, Zebra Kensgtn) Kensgtn Pub Corp.

Seduction of Our Children: Protecting Our Kids Against Satanism, New Age, & the Occult. Neil T. Anderson & Steve Russo. 224p. (Orig.). 1991. pap. 8.99 (*0-89081-888-6*) Harvest Hse.

Seduction of Peter S. Lawrence Sanders. 400p. 1990. reprint ed. mass mkt. 6.99 (*0-425-12462-2*) Berkley Pub.

Seduction of Samantha Kincade. Maggie Osborne. 384p. (Orig.). 1995. mass mkt. 5.99 (*0-446-60093-8*) Warner Bks.

***Seduction of the Innocent.** Fredric Wertham. Date not set. lib. bdg. 27.95 (*0-8488-1657-9*) Amereon Ltd.

Seduction of the Mediterranean: Writing, Art & Homosexual Fantasy. Robert Aldrich. LC 92-40812. 1993. XRoutledge NY. write for info. (*0-415-03277-6*, Routledge NY) Routledge.

Seduction of the Mediterranean: Writing, Art & Homosexual Fantasy. Robert Aldrich. LC 92-40812. 288p. (C). (gr. 13). 1993. pap. 16.95 (*0-415-09312-0*) Routledge.

Seduction of the Mediterranean: Writing, Art & Homosexual Fantasy. Robert Aldrich. LC 91-40812. (Illus.). 288p. (C). (gr. 13). 1993. text ed. 49.95 (*0-415-03227-X*, Routledge NY) Routledge.

Seduction of the Minotaur. Anais Nin. LC 61-66834. 146p. (Orig.). 1961. pap. 8.95 (*0-8040-0268-1*) Swallow.

***Seduction of Time.** William J. Russell. 57p. (Orig.). 1997. mass mkt. 5.99 (*1-55197-597-1*, Pub. by Comnwlth Pub CN) Partners Pubs Grp.

***Seduction, Prostitution & Moral Reform in New York, 1830-1860.** Larry Whiteaker. LC 97-20132. (Garland Studies in American Popular History & Culture). 1997. write for info. (*0-8153-2873-7*) Garland.

Seduction Stakes. Lindsay Armstrong. (Presents Ser.). 1994. mass mkt. 2.99 (*0-373-11626-8*, 1-11626-8) Harlequin Bks.

Seduction Subliminally Via the Media, 3 vols., Set. 1991. lib. bdg. 79.95 (*0-8490-4648-3*) Gordon Pr.

Seduction Theory. Thomas Beller. 208p. 1996. pap. 11.99 (*0-446-67252-1*) Warner Bks.

Seduction Theory: Stories. Thomas Beller. LC 94-36704. 224p. 1995. 21.00 (*0-393-03767-3*) Norton.

Seductions. Penn. pap. 12.00 (*0-06-095029-3*) HarpC.

Seductions: Studies in Reading & Culture. Jane Miller. (Convergences Ser.). 194p. (C). 1991. 24.95 (*0-674-79679-9*) HUP.

Seductions Exposed: The Spiritual Dynamics of Relationships. Gary L. Greenwald. LC 88-82484. 192p. (Orig.). 1989. pap. 7.95 (*0-929748-00-X*) Eagles Nest Pubns.

Seductions of Biography. Ed. by David Suchoff & Mary Rheil. 256p. 1996. pap. 16.95 (*0-415-91090-0*) Routledge.

Seductions of Biography. Ed. by David Suchoff & Mary Rheil. (Culture Work). 256p. (C). 1996. text ed. 55.00 (*0-415-91089-7*, Routledge NY) Routledge.

Seductions of Crime. Jack Katz. 384p. 1990. pap. 16.00 (*0-465-07616-5*) Basic.

Seductions of Emily Dickinson. Robert M. Smith. LC 95-12591. 232p. 1996. text ed. 34.95 (*0-8173-0806-7*) U of Ala Pr.

Seductions of Psychoanalysis: Freud, Lacan & Derrida. John Forrester. (Cambridge Studies in French: No. 26). 300p. (C). 1991. pap. text ed. 21.95 (*0-521-42466-6*) Cambridge U Pr.

Seductions-Relationships. Richard Kostelanetz. 68p. 1983. 10.00 (*0-932360-46-7*) Archae Edns.

***Seductive & Scandalous.** Kirkland et al. 288p. 1997. mass mkt. 4.99 (*0-8217-5713-X*, Zebra Kensgtn) Kensgtn Pub Corp.

Seductive Art of Astrology: Meet Your Dream Lover Through the Stars. Carole Golder. (Illus.). 192p. 1989. pap. 8.95 (*0-8050-1025-4*, Owl) H Holt & Co.

Seductive Beauty of Great Salt Lake: Images of a Lake Unknown. Ella Sorensen. LC 95-44989. (Illus.). 96p. (Orig.). 1998. pap. 21.95 (*0-87905-703-3*, Peregrine Smith) Gibbs Smith Pub.

Seductive Cinema. James Card. LC 93-15431. 1994. 35.00 (*0-394-57218-1*) Knopf.

Seductive Mirage: An Exploration of the Work of Sigmund Freud. Allen Esterson. LC 93-994. 280p. 1993. 52.95 (*0-8126-9230-6*); pap. 18.95 (*0-8126-9231-4*) Open Court.

Seductive Reasoning: Pluralism as the Problematic of Contemporary Literary Theory. Ellen Rooney. LC 88-47917. 288p. 1989. 37.50 (*0-8014-2192-6*) Cornell U Pr.

***Seductive Selling.** Kit Sadgrove. (Marketing & Sales Ser.). 1994. pap. 15.95 (*0-7494-1214-3*) Kogan Page Ltd.

***Seductive Smuggler.** Donna Davidson. 256p. 1997. mass mkt. 4.99 (*0-8217-5689-3*, Zebra Kensgtn) Kensgtn Pub Corp.

***Seductive Solutions.** Toni Elder. Ed. by Kelly O'Donnell. 1998. pap. 10.95 (*1-57532-154-8*) Press-Tige Pub.

Seductive Spectres. Ed. by Amarantha Knight. (Orig.). 1996. mass mkt. 6.95 (*1-56333-464-X*, Rhinoceros) Masquerade.

Seductive Wager. Leigh Greenwood. 1990. mass mkt. 4.25 (*0-8217-2996-9*, Zebra Kensgtn) Kensgtn Pub Corp.

***Seductiveness of Jewish Myth: Challenge or Response?** Ed. by S. Daniel Breslauer. LC 97-7430. (SUNY Series in Judaica). 317p. (C). 1997. text ed. 59.50 (*0-7914-3601-2*) State Univ of New York.

***Seductiveness of Jewish Myth: Challenge or Response?** Ed. by S. Daniel Breslauer. LC 97-7430. (SUNY Series in Judaica). 317p. (C). 1997. pap. text ed. 19.95 (*0-7914-3602-0*) State Univ of New York.

Seductress. Vivienne Lafay. (Black Lace Ser.). 1995. mass mkt. 5.95 (*0-352-32997-1*, Pub. by Virgin Pub UK) London Brdge.

Sedulius - Concordantia in Sedulium. Ed. by Manfred Wacht. (Alpha-Omega, Reihe A Ser.: Bd. CXXVII). 243p. (GER.). 1992. write for info. (*3-487-09600-5*) G Olms Pubs.

Sedulius Scottus: On Christian Rulers & The Poems. Tr. by Edward G. Doyle. LC 83-14174. (Medieval & Renaissance Texts & Studies: Vol. 17). 208p. 1983. 25.00 (*0-86698-024-5*, MR17) MRTS.

Sedum: Cultivated Stonecrops. Ray Stephenson. LC 93-683. (Illus.). 372p. 1994. 49.95 (*0-88192-238-2*) Timber.

Sedum of North America North of the Mexican Plateau. Ed. by Robert T. Clausen. LC 75-6084. (Comstock Bk.). (Illus.). 784p. 1975. 110.00 (*0-8014-0950-0*) Cornell U Pr.

See: A Journal, Vol. 2. Ed. by Andy Grundberg. (Illus.). 72p. 1997. pap. 18.95 (*0-262-56106-9*) MIT Pr.

See: A Journal of Visual Culture, Vol. 2, Issue 1. (Illus.). 72p. (Orig.). 1996. pap. 18.95 (*0-614-96738-4*) Frnds Photography.

See: A Journal of Visual Culture, Vol. 2, Issue 1. Andy Grundberg. 1996. pap. 18.95 (*0-262-56101-8*) MIT Pr.

See: A Journal of Visual Culture, Vol. 2, Issue 2. (Illus.). 72p. (Orig.). 1996. pap. 18.95 (*0-614-96741-4*) Frnds Photography.

See: A Journal of Visual Culture, Vol. 2, Issue 2. Andy Grundberg. 1996. pap. 18.95 (*0-262-56102-6*) MIT Pr.

See: A Journal of Visual Culture, Vol. 2, Issue 3. (Illus.). 72p. (Orig.). 1996. pap. 18.95 (*0-614-96739-2*) Frnds Photography.

See: A Journal of Visual Culture, Vol. 2, Issue 4. (Illus.). 72p. (Orig.). 1996. pap. 18.95 (*0-614-96740-6*) Frnds Photography.

See Primer Issue: A Journal of Visual Culture. Ed. by Andy Grundberg. (Illus.). 80p. 1994. pap. 18.95 (*0-262-56084-4*) MIT Pr.

See Vol. 1: A Journal of Visual Culture, Vol. 1, Issue 1. Ed. by Andy Grundberg. (Illus.). 72p. 1995. pap. 18.95 (*0-262-56087-9*) MIT Pr.

See Vol. 2: A Journal of Visual Culture, Vol. 1, Issue 2. Ed. by Andy Grundberg. (Illus.). 72p. 1995. pap. 18.95 (*0-262-56088-7*) MIT Pr.

See Vol. 2, Issue 3: A Journal of Visual Culture, Vol. 2, Issue 4. Ed. by Andy Grundberg. (Illus.). 72p. 1996. pap. 18.95 (*0-262-56105-0*) MIT Pr.

See - A Journal of Visual Culture, Vol. 1, Issue 3. Ed. by Andy Grundberg. (Journal of Visual Culture Ser.: Vol. 1). (Illus.). 72p. (C). 1995. pap. 18.95 (*0-262-56089-5*) MIT Pr.

See - A Journal of Visual Culture, Vol. 1, Issue 4. Andy Grundberg. (Journal of Visual Culture Ser.: Vol. 1). (Illus.). 72p. (C). 1996. pap. 18.95 (*0-262-56090-9*) MIT Pr.

***See a Grown Man Cry/Now Watch Him Die.** Henry Rollins. 352p. 1997. pap. 17.00 (*1-880985-37-3*) Two Thirteen Sixty-one.

***See Amber.** large type ed. Norma A. Callender. (Beginning Reader Comprehension Ser.: Vol. 2). (Illus.). 12p. (Orig.). (J). (ps-2). 1997. pap. 4.95 (*1-890274-02-X*) BATA Bks.

See & Avoid. Fred G. DeLaceroa. (Illus.). 86p. (Orig.). (C). 1989. pap. text ed. 6.00 (*0-9623197-0-8*) Delta Aviation.

See & Do. George B. Eager. (Illus.). 128p. (J). (gr. k-3). 1993. pap. 5.95 (*1-879224-14-3*) Mailbox.

See & Draw. Karl V. Larsen. LC 91-73904. (Illus.). 152p. 1993. 26.50 (*0-87192-242-8*) Davis Mass.

See & Feel the Inside Move the Outside. 2nd ed. Michael Hebron. (Illus.). 151p. 1988. pap. text ed. 14.95 (*0-9620214-0-7*) Smithtown Landing CC.

See & Know. Lois Whitaker. 87p. (Orig.). 1980. pap. text ed. 3.95 (*0-931097-02-9*) Sentinel Pub.

See & Paint: Gods & Goddesses. 18p. (J). (ps-5). 2.95 (*81-7120-136-9*) Vedanta Pr.

See & Say: A Book of First Words. Illus. by Page E. O'Rourke. (Teddy Board Bks.). 10p. (J). (ps). 1993. bds. 4.95 (*0-448-40540-7*, G&D) Putnam Pub Group.

See & Seem Blind: or A Critical Dissertation on the Publick Diversions, & c. of Persons & Things, & Things & Persons, & What Not. Intro. by Robert D. Hume. LC 92-22034. (Augustan Reprints Ser.: No. 235). 1986. reprint ed. 14.50 (*0-404-70235-X*, PN2596) AMS Pr.

***See Bob Run & Wild Abandon.** Daniel MacIvor. LC 90-175665. 1997. pap. text ed. 10.95 (*0-88754-486-X*, Pub. by Playwrights CN Pr CN) Theatre Comm.

See Britain by Train. Automobile Association Staff. (Illus.). 128p. (Orig.). 1989. pap. 15.95 (*0-86145-760-9*) Hunter NJ.

See Charlie Run. Brian Freemantle. (Orig.). 1989. pap. 4.50 (*0-317-99639-8*) Bantam.

See Dick & Jane Start a Homebased Business. V. Jeanne Gormick. 64p. 1995. pap. 8.95 (*0-9623816-7-5*) Gormicks All Amer.

***See for Yourself.** Carol Sussman-Skalka. 1995. 50.00 incl. vhs (*0-9603444-3-8*, P180) Lighthouse NYC.

See Hear: A Book about Sound & Light. Jill C. Wheeler. (Kid Physics Ser.). (J). 1997. lib. bdg. 13.98 (*1-56239-629-3*) Abdo & Dghtrs.

See Hear! Playing with Light & Sound. Milan Tytla. (Illus.). 120p. (J). (gr. 4-8). 1994. pap. 9.95 (*1-55037-988-7*, Pub. by Annick CN) Firefly Bks Ltd.

See, Hear, Interact: Beginning Developments in Two-Way Television. Maxine Holmes Jones. LC 84-10715. 165p. 1985. 20.00 (*0-8108-1720-9*) Scarecrow.

See, Hear Play! Kids Discover Music! Hands-On Activities for Preschoolers. Kay Jones & Carol Kranowitz. (Melody Bells Ser.). (Illus.). 98p. 1989. teacher ed. 14.95 (*0-913500-27-5*, S-4TE) Peg Hoenack MusicWorks.

See, Hear, Touch, Taste, Smell. Melvin Berger. Ed. by Natalie Lunis. (Early Science Big Bks.). (Illus.). 16p. (J). (ps-2). 1993. pap. 14.95 (*1-56784-009-4*) Newbridge Comms.

See, Hear, Touch, Taste, Smell: Mini Book. Melvin Berger. Ed. by Natalie Lunis. (Early Science Big Bks.). (Illus.). 16p. (J). (ps-2). 1994. pap. 2.95 (*1-56784-034-5*) Newbridge Comms.

See, Hear, Touch, Taste, Smell Theme Pack. Melvin Berger. Ed. by Susan Evento. (Macmillan Early Science Big Bks.). (Illus.). (J). (ps-2). 1995. pap. write for info. (*1-56784-141-4*) Newbridge Comms.

See Here, Private Hargrove. Marion Hargrove. LC 83-46021. (Classics of Modern American Humor Ser.). reprint ed. 29.00 (*0-404-19933-X*) AMS Pr.

See Here, Private Hargrove. Marion Hargrove. LC 83-46021. 1994. reprint ed. lib. bdg. 24.95 (*1-56849-554-4*) Buccaneer Bks.

See How I Grow. Angela Wilkes. LC 93-27039. (Illus.). 32p. (J). (ps). 1994. 13.95 (*1-56458-464-X*) DK Pub Inc.

See How I Love You: Meditating on the Way of the Cross with Julian of Norwich. Elizabeth R. Obbard. (Illus.). 112p. (Orig.). 1996. pap. 8.95 (*1-85311-141-4*, Pub. by Canterbury Press Norwich UK) Morehouse Pub.

See How It Flies: Perceptions, Procedures, & Principles of Flight. John S. Denker. 400p. 1995. pap. text ed. 34.95 (*0-07-016405-3*) McGraw.

See How It Grows. (Emergent Reader Big Bks.). 8p. (J). (gr. k-2). 1995. 7.98 (*0-916119-72-6*) Creat Teach Pr.

See How it Grows. Kimberlee Graves. (Spanish Emergent Reader Bks.). (Illus.). 8p. (Orig.). (SPA.). (J). (gr. k-2). 1995. pap. 1.59 (*1-57471-036-2*) Creat Teach Pr.

See How It Grows, Level 1. Kimberlee Graves. (Emergent Reader Science Ser.). 8p. 1994. 1.59 (*0-916119-27-0*, 3503) Creat Teach Pr.

See How the Earth Works. Geoff Williams. 1994. 13.95 (*0-312-85493-5*) Forge NYC.

***See How They Grow: A Parent's Guide to Normal & Abnormal Physical Growth from Birth Through Adolescence.** Robert S. Siffert. LC 84-43194. (Illus.). reprint ed. pap. 63.90 (*0-608-04683-3*, 2065404) Bks Demand.

See How They Grow: Duck. Photos by Barrie Watts. (Illus.). 24p. (J). (gr. k-3). 1991. pap. 6.95 (*0-525-67346-6*, Lodestar Bks) Dutton Child Bks.

See How They Grow: The Early Childhood Years. Dorothy Dixon. LC 93-60400. 96p. (Orig.). 1993. pap. 7.95 (*0-89622-567-4*) Twenty-Third.

See How They Ran: The Changing Role of the Presidential Candidate. Gil Troy. 400p. 1991. text ed. 29.95 (*0-02-933035-1*, Free Press) Free Pr.

See How They Ran: The Changing Role of the Presidential Candidate. Gil Troy. (Illus.). 400p. 1996. pap. 16.95 (*0-674-79680-2*) HUP.

See How They Run. Bethany Campbell. 352p. 1996. mass mkt. 5.50 (*0-553-56972-4*) Bantam.

See How They Run. Marilyn Campbell. 1996. pap. 5.99 (*0-451-40691-5*, Onyx) NAL-Dutton.

See How They Run. Marilyn Campbell. 1996. pap. 5.99 (*0-614-98079-8*, Onyx) NAL-Dutton.

See How They Run. James Patterson. 336p. 1997. pap. 6.99 (*0-446-60392-9*, Warner Vision) Warner Bks.

***See How They Run: Elections of 1996.** Larry J. Sabato. 1997. 29.95 (*0-205-27151-0*) P-H.

See How You Grow. Patricia Pearse. LC 87-33268. (Illus.). 32p. (J). (gr. 1-4). 1988. 14.95 (*0-8120-5936-0*) Barron.

See, I Told You So. large type ed. Rush H. Limbaugh, III. LC 94-1662. 1994. lib. bdg. 25.95 (*0-8161-7427-X*, GK Hall) Thorndike Pr.

See, I Told You So. large type ed. Rush H. Limbaugh, III. LC 94-1662. 1995. pap. 18.95 (*0-8161-7428-8*, GK Hall) Thorndike Pr.

See, I Told You So. Rush H. Limbaugh. 1994. reprint ed. pap. 6.99 (*0-671-87121-8*, Pocket Star Bks) PB.

See It & Say It in French. Margarita Madrigal & Colette Dulac. 1963. pap. 5.99 (*0-451-16347-8*) NAL-Dutton.

See It & Say It in German. Margarita Madrigal & Inge Halpert. (Orig.). 1962. pap. 4.50 (*0-451-15698-6*, AE2929, Sig); mass mkt. 5.99 (*0-451-16678-7*) NAL-Dutton.

See It & Say It in Italian. Margarita Madrigal & Giuseppina Salvadori. (Orig.). 1961. pap. 3.95 (*0-451-15532-7*, AJ1327, Sig) NAL-Dutton.

See It & Say It in Itallian. M. Madrigal & Salvatore Ramondinl. 1961. mass mkt. 5.99 (*0-451-16821-6*) NAL-Dutton.

See It & Say It in Spanish. Margarita Madrigal. (Orig.). 1961. pap. 5.99 (*0-451-16837-2*, Sig) NAL-Dutton.

***See It & Sink It: Mastering Putting Through Peak Visual Performance.** Craig L. Farnsworth. LC 97-1540. 1997. write for info. (*0-06-270203-3*) HarpC.

***See It, Hear It!** Thomas-Cochran. (What a Wonderful World Intro Ser.). 1993. pap. text ed. write for info. (*0-582-91081-1*, Pub. by Longman UK) Longman.

See It Now Confronts McCarthyism: Television Documentary & the Politics of Representation. Thomas Rosteck. LC 93-4780. (Studies in Rhetoric & Communication). 264p. (C). 1994. text ed. 29.95 (*0-8173-0705-2*) U of Ala Pr.

See It-Say It: Red Bag Irregular Verbs. 2nd ed. Jacot Yves. 1977. text ed. 118.75 (*0-201-11290-6*) Addison-Wesley.

See It-Say It: Regular Verbs. Yves Jacob. 1981. pap. text ed. 118.75 (*0-201-03608-8*) Addison-Wesley.

See Jane Run. Joy Fielding. 416p. 1992. reprint ed. mass mkt. 6.50 (*0-380-71152-4*) Avon.

See Life Through Words. Valjeanne White. (Illus.). 54p. 1993. pap. text ed. write for info. (*0-9639766-0-5*) Just Me Pubng.

See Me after School: Identifying & Helping Children with Emotional & Behavioral Problems. Daphne Lennox. 144p. (Orig.). 1991. pap. 34.95 (*0-8464-1496-1*) Beekman Pubs.

See Me after School: Identifying & Helping Children with Emotional & Behavioral Problems. Daphne Lennox. 144p. (Orig.). 1991. pap. 29.95 (*1-85346-163-6*, Pub. by D Fulton UK) Taylor & Francis.

See Me Grow, Head to Toe. Nanette Mellage. (J). 1996. pap. text ed. 2.95 (*0-307-10036-7*, Golden Books) Western Pub.

***See Me Grow Head to Toe.** Nanette Mellage. (Illus.). (J). (gr. 2-5). 1996. pap. 2.69 (*0-614-25371-3*, Golden Books) Western Pub.

See Me in Your Dreams. Patricia Rosemoor. (Intrigue Ser.). 1996. mass mkt. 3.75 (*0-373-22382-X*, 1-22382-5) Harlequin Bks.

See Me Read. Betty G. Price & Claude Caujolle. (Illus.). (J). (ps). 1985. pap. 19.95 (*0-9614374-0-5*) Prof Reading Serv.

***See Me with the Heart: How to Receive the Blessing of Adi Da Samraj & What to Do in His Physical Company.** 78p. pap. 2.95 (*0-614-24031-X*) Dawn Horse Pr.

S

An Asterisk (*) at the beginning of an entry indicates that the title is appearing in BIP for the first time.

S

See More Love, Hear More Love, Feel More Love: Discover Your Love Style & Live More Love. Elizabeth A. Ely. LC 89-92028. (Illus.). 160p. (Orig.). 1990. pap. 7.95 (*0-9623797-0-0*) Land Es Pubns.

See-More's Stories: A Series of Six Read-Aloud Books & Read-Along/Move-Along Tapes. Sandra Robbins. (See-More's Stories Ser.). (Illus.). 32p. (Orig.). (J). (ps-4). 1993. pap. 54.95 incl. audio (*1-882601-22-X*) See-Mores Wrkshop.

***See My Brightness Face to Face.** Adi Da. 1997. pap. 19.95 (*1-57097-038-6*) Dawn Horse Pr.

***See My Giant Activity.** Playskool Staff. 1996. pap. 25.00 (*0-525-45725-9*, Playskool Bks) Dutton Child Bks.

See My Message & Come Home. Ed. by Mark Vinz. (Illus.). 88p. (Orig.). 1978. pap. 4.00 (*0-927663-13-9*) COMPAS.

See Naples: A Memoir of Love, Peace & War in Italy. Douglas Allanbrook. LC 95-21202. (Illus.). 270p. 1995. 22.95 (*0-395-74585-3*, P Davison Bk) HM.

See Naples & Die: A World War II Memoir of a United States Army Ski Trooper in the Mountains of Italy. Robert B. Ellis. LC 96-22230. (Illus.). 263p. 1996. lib. bdg. 29.50 (*0-7864-0199-0*) McFarland & Co.

See No Evil. Franklin W. Dixon. (Hardy Boys Casefiles Ser.: No. 8). (YA). (gr. 6 up). 1991. pap. 3.50 (*0-671-73673-6*, Archway) PB.

See No Evil. Marjorie Eatock. (Judy Sullivan Romance Ser.). 192p. 1985. 14.95 (*0-8027-0862-5*) Walker & Co.

See No Evil. Jay Finkelstein. 288p. 1996. mass mkt. 5.50 (*0-440-22293-1*) Dell.

See No Evil. Morgan Hayes. 1997. mass mkt. 3.99 (*0-373-70722-3*, 1-70722-3) Silhouette.

See No Evil. Barbara Shapiro. 304p. (Orig.). 1996. mass mkt. 5.99 (*0-380-77421-6*) Avon.

See No Evil: Blind Devotion & Bloodshed in David Koresh's Holy War. Tim Madigan. (Illus.). 300p. (Orig.). 1993. pap. 11.95 (*1-56530-063-7*) Summit TX.

See No Evil: Casefiles Eight. large type ed. Franklin W. Dixon. (Hardy Boys Ser.). 152p. (J). (gr. 5-10). 1988. reprint ed. 9.50 (*0-942545-49-4*); reprint ed. lib. bdg. 10.50 (*0-942545-59-1*) Grey Castle.

***See No Evil: The Strange Case of Christine Lamont & David Spencer.** Isabel Vincent. LC 95-158582. 1997. pap. text ed. 16.95 (*0-433-39619-9*) Buttrwrth-Heinemann.

***See No Weevil.** Kenyon Morr. (King's Quest Ser.). 1996. mass mkt. 5.99 (*1-57297-174-6*) Blvd Books.

See of Peter. James T. Shotwell & Louise R. Loomis. (Records of Western Civilization Ser.). 737p. 1991. text ed. 85.00 (*0-231-00394-3*); pap. text ed. 19.50 (*0-231-09635-6*) Col U Pr.

See Ouarzazate & Die Travels Through Morocco. Sylvia Kennedy. 1995. pap. text ed. 13.95 (*0-316-48923-9*) Little.

See Rock City: A Story Journey Through Appalachia. Donald Davis. 1996. 22.95 (*0-87483-448-1*); pap. text ed. 12.95 (*0-87483-456-2*) August Hse.

***See Rock City Barns Vol. 1: A Tennessee Tradition.** Anita A. Capps. LC 96-70305. (Illus.). 112p. 1997. 26.95 (*0-9654815-0-6*) See Rock City.

See the Circus. H. A. Rey. (Illus.). (J). (gr. k-3). 1956. pap. 3.50 (*0-395-07068-6*, Sandpiper) HM.

See the Dinosaurs. Roma Bishop. 1994. pap. 3.95 (*0-671-88308-9*, Litl Simon S&S) S&S Childrens.

See the Loud Feeling. Kurt Brecht. 88p. (Orig.). (C). 1990. pap. 4.00 (*1-879188-02-3*) Dirty Rotten Pr.

See the Ocean. Estelle Condra. LC 94-4234. (Illus.). 32p. (J). (gr. k-3). 1994. 14.95 (*1-57102-005-5*, Ideals Child) Hambleton-Hill.

See the Paintings: A Handbook for Art Appreciation in the Classroom. Susan W. Brooks & Susan M. Senatori. 95p. (Orig.). 1988. pap. 12.95 (*0-935493-13-1*, RRB 369) Modern Learn Pr.

***See the USA.** (My First Backseat Bks.). (Illus.). (J). (ps-2). 1997. pap. 3.95 (*0-614-28916-5*) Rand McNally.

See the Wind, Mommy: Sensing God's Presence Through the Life of Your Children. Marsha Crockett. LC 95-52262. (Illus.). 128p. (gr. 10). 1996. 13.99 (*0-8010-1100-0*) Baker Bks.

See the World Passport. Camaro Editors. 1988. pap. 4.95 (*0-913290-70-X*) Camaro Pub.

See Them Die. Ed McBain. 1989. pap. 2.95 (*0-451-14596-8*) NAL-Dutton.

***See Them Go.** Max Grover. 1997. 12.95 (*0-15-201513-2*) HarBrace.

See-Through Years: Creation & Destruction in Texas Architecture, 1981-1991. Joel W. Barna. LC 92-5336. (Illus.). 300p. 1992. 27.50 (*0-89263-316-6*) Tex A&M Univ Pr.

See Under: Love. David Grossman. Tr. by Betsy Rosenberg. 458p. 1989. 22.95 (*0-374-25731-0*) FS&G.

***See Under: Love.** David Grossman. 1997. pap. text ed. 14.00 (*0-374-52519-6*) FS&G.

See Us Hear Us: Voices of Breast Cancer. Ed. by Kana Riley. 128p. (Orig.). 1994. pap. 5.00 (*0-9644254-0-8*) NH Breast Cancer.

See What Baby Can Do! Denise L. Patrick. (J). 1996. 3.95 (*0-307-12208-5*, Golden Books) Western Pub.

***See What I Can Do!** Denise L. Patrick. (Illus.). (J). (ps). 1996. bds. 3.49 (*0-614-25369-1*, Golden Books) Western Pub.

See What I Can Do Today: A Year's Worth of Fascinating Fun for Your Pre-Schooler. Margaret Joslin. 366p. (Orig.). (J). (ps). 1992. spiral bd. 8.50 (*1-882835-07-7*) STA-Kris.

See What I Mean? An Introduction to Visual Communication. 2nd ed. John Morgan & Peter Welton. 160p. 1995. text ed. 16.95 (*0-340-55781-8*, A7066, Pub. by E Arnld UK) St Martin.

See with Your Ears: The Creative Music Book. Don Kaplan. LC 82-81463. (Illus.). 128p. (Orig.). (J). (gr. 1-7). 1982. pap. 6.95 (*0-938530-09-7*, 09-7) Lexikos.

See Ya, Simon. David Hill. LC 93-39870. 120p. (J). 1994. pap. 14.99 (*0-525-45247-8*) Dutton Child Bks.

See Ya, Simon. David Hill. 160p. (J). (gr. 5-9). 1996. pap. 3.99 (*0-14-037056-0*) Puffin Bks.

See You Around, Sam! Lois Lowry. LC 96-1213. (J). 1996. write for info. (*0-614-13120-0*) HM.

See You Around, Sam! Lois Lowry. (Illus.). 144p. (J). (gr. 2-7). 1996. 14.95 (*0-395-81664-5*) HM.

See You at the Top. Zig Ziglar. LC 77-670008. Orig. Title: Biscuits, Fleas, & Pump Handles. (Illus.). 382p. 1984. reprint ed. 20.95 (*0-88289-126-X*) Pelican.

See You in Heaven. Mary Z. Holmes. LC 91-37283. (History's Children Ser.). (Illus.). 48p. (J). (gr. 4-5). 1992. lib. bdg. 21.36 (*0-8114-3502-4*) Raintree Steck-V.

See You in Second Grade! Miriam Cohen. 32p. (J). 1996. pap. 4.99 (*0-440-41168-8*) Dell.

See You in September. Katherine Applegate et al. 125p. (Orig.). (J). (gr. 7-10). 1995. mass mkt. 3.99 (*0-380-78088-7*, Flare) Avon.

See You Later. Christopher Pike. Ed. by Patricia MacDonald. 240p. (YA). (gr. 8 up). reprint ed. pap. 3.99 (*0-671-74390-2*, Archway) PB.

See You Later, Alligator! Laura M. Kvasnosky. LC 94-74409. (Illus.). 24p. (J). (ps). 1995. 9.00 (*0-15-200301-0*, Red Wagon Bks) HarBrace.

See You Later, Alligator. Bobette McCarthy. (Illus.). (J). (ps-1). 1995. 15.00 (*0-02-765447-8*, Mac Bks Young Read) S&S Childrens.

***See You Later, Alligator.** William F. Buckley, Jr. LC 97-13298. 320p. 1997. reprint ed. pap. 10.95 (*1-888952-51-2*) Cumberland Hse.

See You Later Escalator: Mall Math. Time-Life Books Editors. Ed. by Patricia Daniels et al. LC 93-6494. (I Love Math Ser.). (Illus.). 64p. (J). (gr. k-2). 1993. lib. bdg. write for info. (*0-8094-9975-4*) Time-Life.

See You Later Escalator: Mall Math. Time-Life Books Editors. Ed. by Patricia Daniels et al. LC 93-6494. (I Love Math Ser.). (Illus.). 64p. (J). (gr. 1-4). 1993. 16.95 (*0-8094-9974-6*) Time-Life.

See You Later, Litigator! Charles M. Schulz. LC 96-19376. (Peanuts at Work & Play Bks.). (Illus.). 144p. (Orig.). 1996. 10.95 (*0-00-225198-1*) Collins SF.

See You Later Mashed Potater. Anna Dickson. (J). (ps). 1990. write for info. (*0-307-12042-2*) Western Pub.

See You Sunday! Sixty-Two Pastor's Letters to Children. Larry McCaw. 1992. pap. 3.95 (*1-55673-512-X*, 9304) CSS OH.

***See You Thursday.** Ure. (Sky Bks.). 1991. pap. text ed. write for info. (*0-582-05810-4*, Pub. by Longman UK) Longman.

***See You Tomorrow, Charles.** Miriam Cohen. 1997. pap. 4.99 (*0-440-41151-3*); pap. 4.99 (*0-440-91192-3*) Dell.

See Your Way to Self-Esteem: An In-Depth Study of the Causes & Cures of Low Self-Esteem. Peter Michaelson. LC 92-62627. 210p. (Orig.). 1993. pap. 14.95 (*1-882631-25-0*) Prospect NM.

Seeable Signs: The Iconography of the Seven Sacraments, 1350-1544. Ann E. Nichols. (Illus.). 496p. (C). 1996. 89.00 (*0-85115-342-9*) Boydell & Brewer.

Seeburg BMC1 "Background Music Compact-1" of 1960: Installation, Operation, Maintenance, Service & Parts Manual. rev. ed. Seeburg Company Staff. Ed. by Frank Adams. 30p. 1986. reprint ed. spiral bd. 17.50 (*0-913599-89-1*, R-349) A M C Corp.

Seeburg Coon Hunt Ray-O-Lite Rifle Range Model G-5 & Coon Whiner Kit Type CWA-1: Installation & Operation Manual, Parts List & Schematics. rev. ed. Ed. by Frank Adams. (Illus.). 26p. 1992. reprint ed. spiral bd. 17.50 (*1-56642-003-2*, R-4) A M C Corp.

Seeburg Library Unit Model 200LU-3 of 1957 Installation & Service Manual. rev. ed. Seeburg Company Staff. Ed. by Frank Adams. 82p. 1986. reprint ed. 32.50 (*0-939971-11-9*, R-369) A M C Corp.

Seeburg Library Unit Model 200LU1 of 1952 Installation & Service Manual. Seeburg Company Staff. Ed. by Frank Adams. 102p. 1986. reprint ed. 35.00 (*0-939971-10-0*, R-368) A M C Corp.

Seeburg Model HSC1, HSC2, HSC3, API, & AP2 Home Stereo Service Manual. rev. ed. Ed. by Frank Adams. (Illus.). 104p. 1992. reprint ed. spiral bd. 35.00 (*0-939971-46-1*, R-449) A M C Corp.

Seeburg Model HSC1, HSC2, HSC3, AP1, AP2 Home Stereo Installation & Operation Manual & Parts Catalog. rev. ed. Ed. by Frank Adams. (Illus.). 50p. 1992. reprint ed. 27.50 (*0-939971-47-X*, R-452) A M C Corp.

Seeburg Model SABMC1 Automatic Background Music Center: Installation & Operation Manual. rev. ed. Ed. by Frank Adams. (Illus.). 17p. 1992. reprint ed. 12.95 (*1-56642-174-8*, R-62) A M C Corp.

Seeburg Model 6000, 6001, 6002 Home Stereo Parts Catalog. rev. ed. Ed. by Frank Adams. (Illus.). 34p. 1991. reprint ed. 24.50 (*0-939971-49-6*, R-454) A M C Corp.

Seeburg Model 6000, 6001, 6002 Home Stereo Service Manual. rev. ed. Ed. by Frank Adams. (Illus.). 100p. 1991. reprint ed. 35.00 (*0-939971-48-8*, R-453) A M C Corp.

Seeburg Multi Rayolite Rifle Range Model G-1 of 1939 Service Manual & Parts List. rev. ed. Ed. by Frank Adams. (Illus.). 64p. 1991. reprint ed. 29.50 (*0-939971-51-8*, R-527) A M C Corp.

Seeburg Shoot the Bear, Ray-O-Lite Rifle Range Model G-4: Installation & Operation, Parts List & Schematic. rev. ed. Ed. by Frank Adams. (Illus.). 10p. 1992. reprint ed. spiral bd. 15.00 (*1-56642-010-5*, R-10) A M C Corp.

Seeburg S.I.C.M. Service Manual, 1948-1951. rev. ed. Ed. by Frank Adams. (Illus.). 180p. 1991. reprint ed. spiral bd. 35.00 (*1-56642-153-5*, R-10) A M C Corp.

Seeburg Stereo Consolette, Type SC1 & Type SC2 & Consolette Tercom Master, Type CIM-1: Installation, Operation, Adjustments, Service & Parts Manual. Seeburg Company Staff. Ed. by Frank Adams. 48p. 1986. reprint ed. 24.50 (*0-913599-75-1*, R-317) A M C Corp.

Seeburg "1000" Series Background Music Systems & Accessory Equipment for Models BSM2, BMCA1, BMC1, & BMU10: Service & Parts Manual. rev. ed. Ed. by Frank Adams. (Illus.). 142p. 1990. reprint ed. 35.00 (*1-56642-063-6*, R-390) A M C Corp.

Seed. David Richard. 40p. (Orig.). 1996. pap. 5.95 (*0-9637547-8-5*) Arbor Hill Pr.

Seed Aging: Implications for Seed Storage & Persistence in the Soil. David A. Priestly. LC 85-21334. (Comstock Bk.). (Illus.). 304p. (C). 1986. 45.00 (*0-8014-1865-8*) Cornell U Pr.

Seed Analysis. Ed. by H. F. Linskens & J. F. Jackson. (Modern Methods of Plant Analysis Ser.: Vol. 14). (Illus.). 384p. 1992. 294.95 (*0-387-52737-0*) Spr-Verlag.

Seed & the Root. Paulinus Redmond. 272p. 1995. 39.95 (*1-899163-08-5*, Pub. by Quiller Pr UK) St Mut.

Seed & the Soil: Gender & Cosmology in Turkish Village Society. Carol Delaney. LC 90-28545. (Comparative Studies on Muslim Societies: No. 11). (Illus.). 393p. 1991. 48.00 (*0-520-07314-2*); pap. 16.95 (*0-520-07550-1*) U CA Pr.

Seed & the Sower. Laurens Van Der Post. 256p. 1990. reprint ed. lib. bdg. 29.95 (*0-89966-657-4*) Buccaneer Bks.

Seed & the Tree: Reflections on Nonviolence. Daniel A. Seeger. LC 86-62180. (Orig.). 1986. pap. 3.00 (*0-87574-269-6*) Pendle Hill.

Seed Bearers. Irene Coates. (C). 1989. text ed. 49.00 (*1-85821-040-2*, Pub. by Pentland Pr UK) St Mut.

Seed Bunny. Jennifer Selby. (J). 1997. 14.00 (*0-15-201397-0*) HarBrace.

Seed Corn & Other Short Stories. Anna Blair. 192p. 1981. pap. 7.95 (*0-85683-118-2*, Pub. by Shepheard-Walwyn Pubs UK) Paul & Co Pubs.

***Seed Corn of the Confederacy: The Virginia Military Institute at New Market.** James Gindlesperger. LC 97-6747. (Illus.). 240p. Date not set. 24.95 (*1-57249-056-X*, Burd St Pr) White Mane Pub.

Seed Development & Germination. Ed. by Jaime Kigel & Gad Galili. LC 94-24927. (Books in Soils, Plants & the Environment: Vol. 41). 872p. 1995. 195.00 (*0-8247-9229-7*) Dekker.

Seed Dispersal. Ed. by David Murray. LC 86-72353. 322p. 1987. text ed. 89.00 (*0-12-511900-3*) Acad Pr.

Seed Dormancy in Grasses. G. M. Simpson. (Illus.). 300p. (C). 1990. text ed. 69.95 (*0-521-37288-7*) Cambridge U Pr.

Seed Ecology. Micheal Fenner. (Outline Studies in Ecology). 150p. (gr. 13). 1985. pap. text ed. 29.95 (*0-412-25930-3*, 9639) Chapman & Hall.

Seed Ecophysiology of Temperate & Boreal Zone Forest Trees. Robert E. Farmer. (Illus.). 250p. 1996. 49.95 (*1-57444-054-3*) St Lucie Pr.

Seed, Flower a Minute, an Hour. Joan W. Blos. LC 91-4992. (J). (ps-3). 1994. pap. 4.95 (*0-671-88632-0*, Half Moon Paper) S&S Childrens.

Seed from Madagascar. Duncan C. Heyward. LC 92-21426. (Southern Classics Ser.). (Illus.). 311p. (C). 1993. reprint ed. pap. text ed. 14.95 (*0-87249-894-8*) U of SC Pr.

Seed Germination in Desert Plants. Y. Gutterman. (Adaptations of Desert Organisms Ser.). (Illus.). 240p. 1993. write for info. (*3-540-52562-9*) Spr-Verlag.

Seed Germination in Desert Plants. Y. Gutterman. LC 93-29023. (Adaptations of Desert Organisms Ser.). 1993. 174.95 (*0-387-52562-9*) Spr-Verlag.

Seed Gift Greetings to Duplicate & Use. Greetings Etc. by Alfreda Staff. 1992. ring bd. 29.95 (*0-318-04378-5*) Prosperity & Profits.

Seed Grower's List of Vegetable Varieties Grown in the United States in 1906, with Descriptions & Synonyms. Charles Johnson. 45p. (Orig.). 1986. pap. 6.00 (*0-933421-07-9*) Redwood Seed.

***Seed Grows: My First Look at a Plant's Life Cycle.** unabridged ed. Pamela Hickman. (Illus.). 20p. (J). (ps-4). 1997. 6.95 (*1-55074-200-0*, Pub. by Kids Can Pr CN) Genl Dist Srvs.

Seed in the Wind: The Story of Commissioner George Scott Railton & the Work of the Salvation Army in St. Louis, Missouri. Marlene J. Chase & John D. Waldron. 1995. pap. 9.95 (*0-9648347-0-7*) Salvtn Army.

Seed Is a Promise. Claire Merrill. 32p. (J). 1990. pap. 2.50 (*0-590-43454-3*) Scholastic Inc.

Seed Is Mine: The Life of Kas Maine, a South African Sharecropper, 1894-1985. Charles Van Onselen. 1996. 27.50 (*0-8090-9603-X*) FS&G.

Seed Is Mine: The Life of Kas Maine, a South African Sharecropper, 1894-1985. Charles Van Onselen. 672p. 1997. pap. 16.00 (*0-8090-1594-3*) Hill & Wang.

Seed Moisture. P. C. Stanwood & M. B. McDonald. 136p. 1989. 18.00 (*0-89118-525-9*) Am Soc Agron.

Seed Money in Action. Jon P. Speller. 130p. 1989. pap. 4.00 (*0-9622881-0-1*) Morning NY.

***Seed Money in Action.** Jon P. Speller. 1965. pap. 5.00 (*0-8315-0007-7*) Speller.

Seed of a Woman. Ruth Geller. LC 79-53219. 314p. (Orig.). 1979. pap. 5.95 (*0-9603008-0-5*) Imp Pr.

Seed of Abraham: Jews & Arabs in Contact & Conflict. Raphael Patai. LC 85-29453. 408p. 1986. pap. 116.30 (*0-7837-8560-7*, 2049375) Bks Demand.

Seed of Calamity. Ted Markey. 376p. 1995. mass mkt. 4.99 (*1-896329-52-7*, Pub. by Comnwlth Pub CN) Partners Pubs Grp.

***Seed of Darkness.** Mayfair Games Staff. 1994. 4.99 (*0-923763-78-3*) Mayfair Games.

Seed of Madness A: Constitution, Environment, & Fantasy in the Organization of the Psychotic Core. Vamik D. Volkan & Salman Akhtar. LC 96-25084. 1997. 35.00 (*0-8236-6023-0*) Intl Univs Pr.

Seed of Sally Good'n: A Black Family of Arkansas 1833-1953. Ruth P. Patterson. (Illus.). 200p. 1996. pap. 14.95 (*0-8131-0876-4*) U Pr of Ky.

Seed of Sarah: Memoirs of a Survivor. 2nd ed. Judith M. Isaacson. (Illus.). 208p. 1991. 12.95 (*0-252-06219-1*) U of Ill Pr.

Seed of the Divine Fruit. Enrico Rihaldi. LC 86-91340. 1987. 18.95 (*0-87212-200-X*) Libra.

***Seed of the Fire.** Virginia W. Brodine. 310p. 1996. 18.95 (*0-7178-0721-5*); pap. 9.95 (*0-7178-0722-3*) Intl Pubs Co.

Seed of the Fire Lily. Angela Devine. (Presents Ser.). 1994. mass mkt. 2.99 (*0-373-11621-7*, 1-11621-9) Harlequin Bks.

Seed of the Fire Lily. large type ed. Angela Devine. (Harlequin Ser.). 1993. reprint ed. lib. bdg. 18.95 (*0-263-13273-0*, Pub. by Mills & Boon UK) Thorndike Pr.

***Seed of the Princess.** Peter Ferrell. 217p. (Orig.). 1996. pap. write for info. (*1-57579-017-3*) Pine Hill Pr.

Seed of the Sun. Wallace Irwin. Ed. by Roger Daniels. LC 78-54342. (Asian Experience in North America Ser.). 1979. reprint ed. lib. bdg. 26.95 (*0-405-11308-0*) Ayer.

***Seed of the Vine.** Beverly Y. Yarbrough. (YA). (gr. 7 up). 1997. pap. 15.50 (*0-9656873-1-7*) B Yvonne Entrprise.

Seed of the Woman. Arthur C. Custance. 604p. 1980. 34.95 (*0-919857-00-0*, Pub. by Doorway Pubns CN) Doorway USA.

Seed of Vengeance. Elizabeth Power. (Presents Ser.: No. 445). 1992. pap. 2.89 (*0-373-11445-1*, 1-11445-3) Harlequin Bks.

***Seed of Virtue.** C. J. Santangleo. 1997. mass mkt. 5.99 (*1-55197-316-2*, Pub. by Comnwlth Pub CN) Partners Pubs Grp.

Seed of Wisdom: Essays in Honour of T. J. Meek. Ed. by W. S. McCullough. 212p. reprint ed. pap. 60.50 (*0-317-11296-1*, 2014302) Bks Demand.

Seed Oils for the Future. Ed. by Samuel L. MacKenzie & David C. Taylor. LC 93-7118. 190p. 1993. 60.00 (*0-935315-46-2*) AOCS Pr.

Seed Pathology. D. Suryanarayana. 111p. 1978. 12.95 (*0-7069-0676-4*) Asia Bk Corp.

Seed Plants. Arthur Cronquist et al. (Pictured Key Nature Ser.). 250p. (C). 1979. spiral bd. write for info. (*0-697-04761-X*) Wm C Brown Pubs.

Seed Plants of the High Andes of Ecuador: A Checklist. Peter M. Jorgensen & Carmen U. Ulloa. Ed. by Henrik Balslev. (AAU Reports: No. 34). 443p. (C). 1995. pap. 12.95 (*87-87600-60-9*, Pub. by Aarhus Univ Pr DK) David Brown.

Seed Poems. Compiled by John Foster. (Pocket Poetry Ser.). (Illus.). 16p. (J). (gr. 1 up). 1992. pap. 3.95 (*0-19-916426-6*) OUP.

Seed Portions. J. Daussant. LC 82-71240. 1983. text ed. 139.00 (*0-12-204380-4*) Acad Pr.

Seed Preservation & Longevity. L. V. Barton. 216p. 1992. pap. 175.00 (*0-7855-0390-0*, Pub. by Intl Bks & Periodicals II) St Mut.

Seed Production: Principles & Practices. M. B. McDonald & L. O. Copeland. 576p. (gr. 13). 1996. text ed. 69.95 (*0-412-07551-2*) Chapman & Hall.

Seed-Propagated & Regal Geraniums. 2nd ed. Allan Armitage & Mark Kaczperski. LC 91-43172. (Growers Handbook Ser.: Vol. 1). (Illus.). 142p. 1992. pap. 12.95 (*0-88192-217-X*) Timber.

Seed Propagation of Native California Plants. Dara E. Emery. LC 87-12903. 1988. pap. 12.95 (*0-916436-11-X*) Santa Barb Botanic.

Seed Proteins. Gottschalk. 1983. lib. bdg. 294.50 (*90-247-2789-8*, Pub. by M Nijhoff NE) Kluwer Ac.

Seed Quality: Basic Mechanisms & Agricultural Implications. Ed. by Amarjit S. Basra. LC 93-6092. 440p. 1995. 69.95 (*1-56022-850-4*) Haworth Jrnl Co-Edits.

Seed Regeneration in Cross-Pollinated Species: Proceedings of the C. E. C. - Eucarpia Seminar, Nyborg, Denmark, 15-17 July 1981. Ed. by E. Porceddu & G. Jenkins. 302p. (C). 1982. text ed. 85.00 (*90-6191-244-X*, Pub. by A A Balkema NE) Ashgate Pub Co.

Seed Royale. Guy BonGiovanni. 21p. 1988. pap. 2.00 (*0-912981-19-9*) Hse BonGiovanni.

Seed Savers Exchange: The First Ten Years. Ed. by Kent Whealy & Arllys Adelmann. LC 86-61687. (Orig.). 1986. pap. 16.00 (*0-9613977-2-1*) Seed Savers.

***Seed Science & Technology for Plant Breeding & Genetics.** Roberts. (Plant Breeding Ser.). 592p. (C). (gr. 13 up). 1997. text ed. 165.00 (*0-412-47400-X*, Chap & Hall NY) Chapman & Hall.

Seed Science & Technology Laboratory Manual. M. B. McDonald & L. O. Copeland. LC 88-83562. (Illus.). 240p. (C). 1989. pap. text ed. 26.95 (*0-8138-0190-7*) Iowa St U Pr.

Seed Science & Technology Laboratory Manual. M. B. McDonald & L. O. Copeland. (C). 1992. text ed. 225.00 (*81-7233-038-3*, Pub. by Scientific Pubs II) St Mut.

Seed Song. Judy Saksie. (Emergent Reader Big Bks.). 16p. (J). (gr. k-2). 1995. 11.98 (*0-916119-79-3*) Creat Teach Pr.

Seed Song, Level II. Judy Saksie. (Emergent Reader Science Ser.). 16p. 1994. 2.49 (*0-916119-38-6*, 3528) Creat Teach Pr.

Seed Sown: Themes & Reflections on the Sunday Readings. Jay Cormier. 280p. (Orig.). 1996. pap. 29.95 (*1-55612-801-0*) Sheed & Ward MO.

An Asterisk (*) at the beginning of an entry indicates that the title is appearing in BIP for the first time.

Seed Storage Compounds: Biosynthesis, Interactions & Manipulations. Ed. by Peter R. Shrewry & Keith Stobart. (Proceedings of the Phytochemical Society of Europe Ser.: No. 35). (Illus.). 350p. 1994. 98.00 (*0-19-857768-0*) OUP.

Seed Systems in Sub-Saharan Africa: Issues & Options. V. Venkatesan. LC 94-36170. (Discussion Papers, Africa Technical Department Ser.: Vol. 266). 1994. 8.95 (*0-8213-3086-1*, 13086) World Bank.

Seed Testing Handbook. Craig C. Dremann. 1995. pap. write for info. (*0-933421-22-2*) Redwood Seed.

Seed Thoughts for a Change for the Better. Caldwell Van Roden. 46p. (Orig.). 1988. spiral bd. 5.00 (*0-940844-67-2*) Wellspring.

Seed Thoughts in Prose & Verse. Norman M. Bowman. LC 92-22155. 100p. (Orig.). 1992. pap. 9.95 (*0-926487-12-4*) Rowan Mtn Pr.

Seed-Time & Harvest of Ragged Schools: Three Pleas for Ragged Schools. Thomas Guthrie. LC 75-172569. (Criminology, Law Enforcement, & Social Problems Ser.: No. 150). 1973. reprint ed. lib. bdg. 15.00 (*0-87585-150-9*) Patterson Smith.

Seed Time, Harvest Time: A Book of Poems. Jim Thomas. 1990. 25.00 (*0-943549-10-8*) TJU Pr.

Seed to Civilization: The Story of Food. Charles B. Heiser, Jr. (Illus.). 228p. 1990. 36.50 (*0-674-79681-0*); pap. 12.95 (*0-674-79682-9*) HUP.

Seed to Peanut. Oliver S. Owen. LC 95-10523. (Lifewatch Ser.). (J). (gr. 3-4). 1996. lib. bdg. 14.98 (*1-56239-489-4*) Abdo & Dghtrs.

***Seed to Plant.** Arthur Morton. (Illus.). (J). (gr. k-3). 1992. write for info. (*1-57842-073-3*) Delmas Creat.

***Seed to Plant.** Tr. by Manny Phantha. (LAO.). (J). (gr. k-3). 1994. write for info. (*1-57842-076-8*) Delmas Creat.

***Seed to Plant.** Tr. by Suon Thach. (CAM.). (J). (gr. k-3). 1994. write for info. (*1-57842-077-6*) Delmas Creat.

Seed to Seed: Seed Saving Techniques for the Vegetable Gardener. Suzanne Ashworth. LC 90-62386. (Illus.). 224p. (Orig.). 1995. pap. 20.00 (*0-9613977-7-2*) Seed Savers.

Seed upon the Wind. Carole N. Douglas. 320p. 1994. mass mkt. 4.99 (*0-8125-1249-9*) Tor Bks.

Seedbed of Protest: Social Structure & Radical Politics in Ettlingen, Grand Duchy of Baden, 1815-1850. John R. Wilson. LC 92-837. (Modern European History Ser.). 248p. 1992. text ed. 20.00 (*0-8153-0665-2*) Garland.

Seedbeds of Virtue: Sources of Competence, Character, & Citizenship in American Society. Ed. by Mary A. Glendon & David Blankenhorn. 320p. (C). 1995. 27.95 (*1-56833-046-4*) Madison Bks UPA.

Seedborne Diseases & Their Control. R. B. Maude. (A CAB International Publication). 304p. 1996. 75.00 (*0-85198-922-5*) CAB Intl.

Seedfolks. Paul Fleischman. LC 96-26696. (Joanna Cotler Bks.). (Illus.). 80p. (YA). (gr. 5 up). 1997. 13.95 (*0-06-027471-9*); lib. bdg. 13.89 (*0-06-027472-7*) HarpC Child Bks.

Seeding Program for Fertilizer Marketing. Lewis B. Williams. Ed. by E. N. Roth & M. K. Thompson. (Special Publications: No. SP-4). (Illus.). (Orig.). 1984. pap. text ed. 4.00 (*0-88090-054-7*) Intl Fertilizer.

Seedings & Other Poems. Jerome Rothenberg. LC 96-14180. 128p. (Orig.). 1996. pap. 10.95 (*0-8112-1331-5*, NDP828) New Directions.

Seedling. James Axler. (Deathlands Ser.: No. 13). 1991. mass mkt. 4.95 (*0-373-62513-8*) Harlequin Bks.

Seedling of Some Tropical Trees & Shrubs Mainly of South-East Asia. H. D. Burger. 399p. 1989. pap. 375.00 (*81-7089-107-8*, Pub. by Intl Bk Distr II) St Mut.

Seedling Physiology & Reforestation Success. Ed. by Mary L. Duryea & Gregory N. Brown. (Forestry Sciences Ser.). 1984. lib. bdg. 128.00 (*90-247-2949-1*) Kluwer Ac.

Seedling Spruce. Katy Gilmore. (Alaska Christmas Ser.: No. III). (Illus.). 17p. 1993. pap. 20.00 (*1-884236-02-2*) Limner Pr.

Seedling Spruce. deluxe limited ed. Katy Gilmore. (Alaska Christmas Ser.: No. III). (Illus.). 17p. 1993. 50.00 (*1-884236-01-4*) Limner Pr.

Seedlings. Shirley Klein. 41p. 1993. 3.75 (*0-941092-27-5*) Mtn St Pr.

Seedling's Journey. Janet Pfeiffer. 1994. pap. 3.95 (*1-55673-591-X*, 7990) CSS OH.

Seedlings of Some Tropical Trees & Shrubs Mainly of South East Asia 1989. Hzn D. Burger. 1989. 230.00 (*81-7089-110-8*, Pub. by Intl Bk Distr II) St Mut.

Seedlings of the North-Western European Lowland. F. M. Muller. 1978. lib. bdg. 184.00 (*90-6193-588-1*) Kluwer Ac.

Seeds. George Shannon. LC 92-40738. (Illus.). (J). 1994. 13.95 (*0-395-66990-1*) HM.

Seeds: A Collection of Sayings & Things. 2nd ed. Jay Frankston. (Illus.). 96p. 1993. pap. 9.95 (*0-9629754-5-1*) Whole Loaf.

Seeds: Index of New Information & Research Bible. Jonathon J. Krull. 160p. 1994. 44.50 (*0-7883-0208-6*); pap. 39.50 (*0-7883-0209-4*) ABBE Pubs Assn.

Seeds: Physiology of Development & Germination. J. D. Bewley & M. Black. (Illus.). 420p. (C). 1994. pap. text ed. 39.50 (*0-306-44748-7*, Plenum Pr) Plenum.

Seeds: Physiology of Development & Germination. 2nd ed. J. D. Bewley & M. Black. (Illus.). 420p. (C). 1994. text ed. 75.00 (*0-306-44747-9*, Plenum Pr) Plenum.

Seeds: Some Good Ways to Improve Our Schools. Cynthia Parsons. LC 84-29160. 224p. (Orig.). 1992. pap. 12.95 (*0-88007-200-8*) Woodbridge Pr.

Seeds: Supporting Women's Work in the Third World. Ed. by Ann Leonard. LC 89-23329. (Illus.). 256p. 1989. 35.00 (*0-935312-92-7*); pap. 12.95 (*0-935312-93-5*) Feminist Pr.

Seeds: The Definitive Guide to Growing, History, & Lore. Peter H. Loewer. LC 95-35876. 256p. 1996. pap. 25.00 (*0-02-574042-3*) Macmillan Info.

Seeds: The Ecology of Regeneration in Plant Communities. Ed. by Michael Fenner. 384p. 1992. 110.00 (*0-85198-726-5*) CAB Intl.

***Seeds & Deep Seasons: Poems.** Marie-Ange Somdah. LC 96-27262. 76p. 1997. pap. 12.95 (*0-7734-2677-9*, Mellen Poetry Pr) E Mellen.

Seeds & Plants. Doris Roettger. 1991. 8.99 (*0-86653-982-4*) Fearon Teach Aids.

***Seeds & Propagation.** Susan McClure. 1997. pap. 10.95 (*0-614-27259-9*) Workman Pub.

Seeds & Seedlings. Elaine Pascoe. Ed. by Nicole Bowman. LC 95-25178. (Nature Close Up Ser.). (Illus.). 48p. (J). (gr. 3-7). 1996. lib. bdg. 16.95 (*1-56711-178-5*) Blackbirch.

Seeds & Seeds & Seeds. Ralph F. Parkison. Ed. by Marion O. Withrow. (Illus.). 65p. (Orig.). (J). (gr. 2-8). 1988. pap. write for info. (*0-318-64001-5*) Little Wood Bks.

Seeds & Sovereignty: Debate over the Use & Control of Plant Genetic Resources. Ed. by Jack R. Kloppenburg, Jr. LC 88-3760. (Illus.). 368p. (C). 1988. text ed. 54.95 (*0-8223-0756-1*) Duke.

Seeds & their Uses. C. M. Duffus & J. C. Slaughter. LC 80-40283. 164p. reprint ed. pap. 46.80 (*0-685-15404-1*, 2026674) Bks Demand.

Seeds As Food Use: A Workbook, 1. Alpha Pyramis Research Division Staff. 1984. ring bd. 25.95 (*0-913597-70-8*) Prosperity & Profits.

Seeds Beneath the Snow: Vignettes from the South. Arthenia J. Bates. LC 69-18851. 146p. 1975. 14.95 (*0-88258-046-9*) Howard U Pr.

***Seeds by the Millions.** Thomas-Cochran. (What a Wonderful World Intro Ser.). 1993. pap. text ed. write for info. (*0-582-91085-4*, Pub. by Longman UK) Longman.

Seeds, etc.... Carl Tant. LC 91-76151. (Illus.). 160p. (YA). (gr. 6-9). 1992. pap. 13.95 (*1-880319-01-2*) Biotech.

Seeds, Flowers, & Trees: Science in Art, Song, & Play. Rhonda Vansant & Barbara L. Dondiego. 1996. pap. text ed. 12.95 (*0-07-017909-3*) McGraw.

Seeds for African Peasants: Peasants' Needs & Agricultural Research: The Case of Zimbabwe. Esbern Friis-Hansen. (Scandinavian Institute of African Studies: No. 9). (Illus.). 228p. (Orig.). 1995. pap. 46.50 (*91-7106-365-X*) Coronet Bks.

Seeds from a Birch Tree: Writing Haiku & the Spiritual Journey. Clark Strand. LC 96-25621. 208p. 1997. 19.95 (*0-7868-6242-4*) Hyperion.

***Seeds from a Secret Garden.** Gertrude Hyde. (Keepsakes Ser.). (Illus.). 56p. 1997. 7.99 (*0-88088-890-3*) Peter Pauper.

Seeds Get Around. Melvin Berger. Ed. by Natalie Lunis. (Early Science Big Bks.). (Illus.). 16p. (J). (ps-2). 1993. pap. 14.95 (*1-56784-006-X*) Newbridge Comms.

Seeds Get Around: Mini Book. Nancy White. Ed. by Natalie Lunis. (Early Science Big Bks.). (Illus.). 16p. (J). (ps-2). 1993. pap. 2.95 (*1-56784-031-0*) Newbridge Comms.

Seeds Get Around Theme Pack. Melvin Berger. Ed. by Susan Evento. (Macmillan Early Science Big Bks.). (Illus.). (J). (ps-2). 1995. pap. write for info. (*1-56784-138-4*) Newbridge Comms.

***Seeds Handbook.** Desai et al. (Books in Soils, Plants & the Environment: Vol. 55). 640p. 1996. 185.00 (*0-8247-0042-2*) Dekker.

Seeds in the Heart: Japanese Literature from Earliest Times to the Late Sixteenth Century. Donald Keene. 1995. pap. 40.00 (*0-8050-4364-0*) H Holt & Co.

Seeds in the Palm of Your Hand. Edward K. Uku. LC 93-45272. 1994. 30.00 (*0-942615-17-4*) U Wis African Stud.

Seeds in the Passes. Robert Summers. LC 78-59774. (Scene Award Ser.). 86p. (Orig.). 1979. pap. 5.00 (*1-882986-09-1*) Smith.

Seeds in the Wilderness. Marty Gervais. 1995. pap. 14.95 (*1-55082-110-5*) LPC InBook.

Seeds Of. 0.46 (*0-685-74983-5*, 490049) Editorial Unilit.

Seeds of a New Partnership: Indigenous Peoples & the United Nations. 74p. Date not set. pap. 9.95 (*92-1-100535-3*, E>94.I.16) UN.

Seeds of Another Summer. 1999. pap. 29.95 (*0-670-86786-1*) Viking Penguin.

Seeds of Change: A Quincentennial Commemoration. Ed. by Herman J. Viola & Carolyn J. Margolis. LC 90-10289. (Illus.). 280p. (C). 1991. 45.00 (*1-56098-035-4*) Smithsonian.

Seeds of Change: Five Plants That Transformed Mankind. Henry Hobhouse. LC 86-45114. 1987. pap. 13.00 (*0-06-091440-8*, PL) HarpC.

Seeds of Change: Stories of IDB Innovation in Latin America. Frank Meissner. 132p. (Orig.). (C). 1991. pap. text ed. 15.95 (*0-940602-39-3*) IADB.

Seeds of Change: The Spiritual Quest of Kerry Livgren. 2nd rev. ed. Kenneth Boa & Kerry Livgren. 230p. reprint ed. pap. 9.95 (*0-917143-03-5*) Sparrow TN.

Seeds of Change Student Edition. J. Davis Hawke. 1993. pap. 13.50 (*0-201-29419-2*) Addison-Wesley.

Seeds of Conflict, Vol. S. 10: Economic Depression & Political Expansion. Europe & Japan Between the Wars, 8 vols., Set. 1990. reprint ed. 720.00 (*0-8115-3517-7*) Periodicals Srv.

Seeds of Conflict, Vol. S. 2: Palestine, Zionism & the Levant, 1912-1945, 9 vols., Set. 1990. reprint ed. 630.00 (*0-8115-3509-6*) Periodicals Srv.

Seeds of Conflict, Vol. S. 3: The Spanish Civil War, 1936-1939, 5 vols., Set. 1990. reprint ed. 400.00 (*0-8115-3510-X*) Periodicals Srv.

Seeds of Conflict, Vol. S. 4: The Russian Revolution. From the October Revolution to the Moscow Trials, 1917-1936, 10 vols., Set. 1990. reprint ed. 700.00 (*0-8115-3511-8*) Periodicals Srv.

Seeds of Conflict, Vol. S. 5: Germany, 1900-1930. From World War to Weimar, Fall of the Empire - Rise of the Republic, 13 vols., Set. 1990. reprint ed. 975.00 (*0-8115-3512-6*) Periodicals Srv.

Seeds of Conflict, Vol. S. 6: Pandora's Treaties. Minority Settlements in Central Europe after World War I, 17 vols., Set. 1990. reprint ed. 1,130.00 (*0-8115-3513-4*) Periodicals Srv.

Seeds of Conflict, Vol. S. 7: Palestine. The Twice-Promised Land, 5 vols., Set. 1990. reprint ed. 400.00 (*0-8115-3514-2*) Periodicals Srv.

Seeds of Conflict, Vol. S. 8: Danzig & the Polish Corridor - Threshold to War, 5 vols., Set. 1990. reprint ed. 400.00 (*0-8115-3515-0*) Periodicals Srv.

Seeds of Conflict, Vol. S. 9: The Sino-Japanese Conflict, 1931-1941. Prelude to Pearl Harbor, 10 vols., Set. 1990. reprint ed. 950.00 (*0-8115-3516-9*) Periodicals Srv.

Seeds of Consciousness: The Wisdom of Sri Nisargadatta Maharaj. Nisargadatta Maharaj. Ed. by Jean Dunn. LC 89-81146. 215p. 1997. reprint ed. pap. 14.95 (*0-89386-025-5*) Acorn NC.

Seeds of Consistency, Fruits of Life: An Historio-Philosophical Narrative. Kiarri T-H. Cheatwood. LC 89-63844. 556p. (Orig.). 1990. 21.95 (*0-9625169-1-0*); pap. 15.95 (*0-9625169-0-2*) Native Sun Pubs.

Seeds of Continental United States Legumes (Fabaceae) Richard J. Delorit & Charles R. Gunn. (Illus.). 140p. (C). 1986. 32.00 (*0-9616847-0-4*); pap. 28.00 (*0-9616847-1-2*) Agronomy Pubns.

Seeds of Crisis: Public Schooling in Milwaukee since 1920. Ed. by John L. Rury & Frank A. Cassell. LC 93-18827. (Illus.). 389p. (Orig.). (C). 1993. pap. text ed. 17.95 (*0-299-13814-3*); lib. bdg. 50.00 (*0-299-13810-0*) U of Wis Pr.

Seeds of Decadence in the Late Nineteenth-Century Novel. Suzanne Nalbantian. 1984. pap. 15.95 (*0-333-47400-7*, Pub. by Macm UK) St Martin.

Seeds of Desire. Robert Spooner. Ed. by M. L. Jones. LC 94-76891. 295p. (Orig.). 1994. pap. 9.95 (*1-882270-18-5*) Old Rugged Cross.

***Seeds of Destiny: Restoring Purpose to Everyday Life.** Arthur F. Miller & William Hendricks. 288p. 1997. 19.99 (*0-7852-7896-6*) Nelson.

Seeds of Destruction: Nationalist China in War & Revolution, 1937-1949. Lloyd E. Eastman. LC 82-42861. 328p. 1984. 42.50 (*0-8047-1191-7*) Stanford U Pr.

Seeds of Disaster: The Development of French Army Doctrine, 1919-1939. Robert A. Doughty. LC 85-20473. 232p. (C). 1985. lib. bdg. 35.00 (*0-208-02096-9*, Archon Bks) Shoe String.

Seeds of Discord: De Gaulle, Free France, & the Allies. Dorothy S. White. LC 64-16922. (Illus.). 1964. 39.95 (*0-8156-0038-0*) Syracuse U Pr.

***Seeds of Discord: How to Discern, Expose & Destroy Divisive & Disloyal Spirits.** John Tetsola. 132p. (Orig.). 1996. pap. 9.99 (*1-889389-02-1*) End-Time Wave.

Seeds of Disquiet: One Deaf Woman's Experience. Cheryl M. Heppner. LC 92-9693. 200p. 1992. 17.95 (*1-56368-016-5*) Gallaudet Univ Pr.

Seeds of Evil. Margaret Bingley. 245p. 1990. pap. 3.95 (*0-88184-618-X*) Carroll & Graf.

Seeds of Evil. Micki Geyer. 225p. 1997. pap. 10.95 (*1-57532-015-0*) Press-Tige Pub.

***Seeds of Evil, Vol. 1.** Smith. 1997. mass mkt. 5.99 (*0-312-96285-1*) St Martin.

Seeds of Extinction: Jeffersonian Philanthropy & the American Indian. Bernard W. Sheehan. LC 72-85403. 313p. 1973. reprint ed. pap. 89.30 (*0-7837-9021-X*, 2049773) Bks Demand.

Seeds of Extinction: Jeffersonian Philanthropy & the American Indian. Bernard W. Sheehan. 320p. 1974. reprint ed. pap. 9.95 (*0-393-00716-2*) Norton.

Seeds of Faith. Randall K. Mehew. (Personal Enrichment Ser.). 132p. (Orig.). 1991. pap. write for info. (*0-929985-75-3*) Jackman Pubng.

Seeds of Faith, Vol. I. R. Paul Caudill. (Illus.). 175p. (Orig.). 1987. pap. 3.00 (*0-317-65700-3*) Blue Ridge.

Seeds of Faith, Vol. II. R. Paul Caudill. (Illus.). 210p. (Orig.). 1988. pap. 3.00 (*0-938980-07-6*) Blue Ridge.

Seeds of Faith, Vol. 11. Clarence M. Wagner. 100p. 1981. pap. 4.00 (*0-937498-02-5*) Tru-Faith.

Seeds of Famine: Ecological Destruction & the Development Dilemma in the West African Sahel. Richard Franke & Barbara Chasin. LC 79-52471. 284p. 1980. pap. 24.00 (*0-86598-053-5*, R7020) Rowman.

Seeds of Fear. Jeff Gelb. (Illus.). (J). 1995. mass mkt. 5.50 (*0-671-89846-9*) PB.

Seeds of Gold. Institute for Science in Society Staff. 1995. text ed. 14.95 (*0-07-057168-6*) McGraw.

Seeds of Greatness: Best-Kept Secrets of Total Success. Denis E. Waitley. LC 83-4550. 224p. 1984. 14.99 (*0-8007-1361-3*) Revell.

Seeds of Greatness: The Ten Best Kept Secrets of Total Success. Denis E. Waitley. 1988. mass mkt. 6.50 (*0-671-67432-3*) PB.

Seeds of Happiness. Omraam M. Aivanhov. (Izvor Collection: Vol. 231). 203p. (Orig.). 1992. pap. 8.95 (*2-85566-522-1*, Pub. by Prosveta FR) Prosveta USA.

Seeds of Heaven. Barbara B. Taylor. 80p. 1990. pap. 2.95 (*0-88028-111-1*, 1078) Forward Movement.

Seeds of Hope: A Faith Journey. Phil Grout. LC 89-286. 82p. 1989. reprint ed. pap. 25.00 (*0-608-02163-6*, 2062832) Bks Demand.

***Seeds of Hope: A Henri Nouwen Reader.** Ed. by Robert Durback. 284p. 1996. pap. 11.00 (*0-385-49049-6*, Image Bks) Doubleday.

Seeds of Jealousy. large type ed. Hilda Durman. (Linford Romance Library). 1991. pap. 15.99 (*0-7089-7049-4*) Ulverscroft.

Seeds of Kindness: Garden Thoughts for the Heart. Ed. by Caroline Burns. (Cherished Moments Ser.). (Illus.). 64p. 1996. 9.99 (*1-57051-108-X*) Brownlow Pub Co.

Seeds of Liberty: The Genesis of the American Mind. Max Savelle. (History - United States Ser.). 587p. 1993. reprint ed. lib. bdg. 99.00 (*0-7812-4844-2*) Rprt Serv.

Seeds of Life. John Langdon-Davies. 1955. 12.95 (*0-8159-6808-6*) Devin.

Seeds of Light. Sivananda Radha. LC 90-49580. (Illus.). 116p. 1991. pap. 9.95 (*0-931454-22-0*) Timeless Bks.

***Seeds of Light: Healing Meditations for Body & Soul.** Elizabeth K. Stratton. LC 96-54827. 1997. 22.00 (*0-684-83094-9*) S&S Trade.

***Seeds of Love: For Brothers & Sisters of International Adoption.** Mary E. Petertyl. LC 96-61921. (Illus.). 32p. (J). (ps-4). 1997. 15.95 (*0-9655753-1-4*) Folio One.

Seeds of Magick: An Expose of Modern Occult Practices. Catherine Summers & Julian Vayne. LC 91-10203. 192p. 1991. reprint ed. pap. 9.95 (*0-87542-865-7*) Llewellyn Pubns.

Seeds of Man: An Experience Lived & Dreamed. Woody Guthrie. LC 95-10934. 401p. 1995. pap. 15.00 (*0-8032-7053-4*, Bison Books) U of Nebr Pr.

Seeds of Modern Drama. Ed. by Norris Houghton. 420p. 1986. reprint ed. pap. 12.95 (*0-936839-15-5*) Applause Theatre Bk Pubs.

Seeds of Modern Public Law in Ancient Indian Jurisprudence. Rama Jois. (C). 1990. text ed. 125.00 (*0-89771-503-9*) St Mut.

Seeds of Murder. large type ed. Michael Underwood. (Mystery Ser.). 416p. 1993. 25.99 (*0-7089-2979-6*) Ulverscroft.

Seeds of Nonviolence. John Dear. 500p. (Orig.). 1992. pap. 19.95 (*1-879175-11-8*) Fortkamp.

***Seeds of Our Soul.** Mallika Chopra. 1998. pap. write for info. (*0-609-80125-2*, Harmony) Crown Pub Group.

Seeds of Peace: A Buddhist Vision for Renewing Society. Sulak Sivaraksa. LC 91-45201. 132p. (Orig.). 1992. pap. 12.00 (*0-938077-78-3*) Parallax Pr.

Seeds of Peace: Contemplation & Non-Violence. William H. Shannon. 192p. 1996. 20.95 (*0-8245-1557-9*) Crossroad NY.

Seeds of Peace: Reflections on Contemplation & Non-Violence. William H. Shannon. 192p. 1996. pap. 14.95 (*0-8245-1548-X*) Crossroad NY.

Seeds of Power. Christopher Nicole. 224p. 1995. lib. bdg. 20.00 (*0-7278-4691-4*) Severn Hse.

Seeds of Progress. Leonard E. Read. 128p. 1980. pap. 8.95 (*0-910614-66-0*) Foun Econ Ed.

Seeds of Promise: The Prophetic Church in Central America. Guillermo Melendez. 1990. pap. 6.95 (*0-377-00204-6*) Friendship Pr.

Seeds of Promise: World Consultation on Frontier Missions, Edinburgh '80. Ed. by Allan Starling. LC 81-69488. (Illus.). 258p. (Orig.). 1981. pap. 9.95 (*0-87808-186-0*) William Carey Lib.

Seeds of Reconciliation. Ed. by Katharine T. Hargrove. LC 96-14426. 1996. pap. 15.95 (*0-941037-40-1*) BIBAL Pr.

Seeds of Reflection: Panetic Word Clusters. R. G. Siu. LC 93-61386. 341p. 1994. pap. write for info. (*1-884437-03-6*) Intl Soc Panetics.

Seeds of Sensitivity: Deepening Your Spiritual Life. Robert J. Wicks. LC 94-79007. 160p. (Orig.). 1995. pap. 7.95 (*0-87793-541-6*) Ave Maria.

Seeds of Speech: Language Origin & Evolution. Jean Aitchison. (Approaches to Linguistics Ser.). 270p. (C). 1996. text ed. 49.95 (*0-521-46246-0*); pap. text ed. 17.95 (*0-521-46793-4*) Cambridge U Pr.

Seeds of Stillness: Opening to the Self. Marian A. McClellan. (Illus.). 64p. (Orig.). 1994. pap. 8.50 (*1-56474-074-9*) Fithian Pr.

***Seeds of Success: Original Insights on Business from America's Heartland.** Peter Reese. (Home-Grown Wisdom Collection). 84p. (Orig.). 1997. spiral bd. 8.99 (*1-881830-49-7*, DS18476) Garborgs.

Seeds of Suspicion. John McGreevey. 1952. pap. 3.00 (*0-87129-195-9*, S23) Dramatic Pub.

Seeds of the Sixties. Andrew Jamison & Ron Eyerman. LC 93-9092. 250p. 1994. 25.00 (*0-520-08516-7*) U CA Pr.

Seeds of the Sixties. Andrew Jamison & Ron Eyerman. 248p. 1995. pap. 12.95 (*0-520-20341-0*) U CA Pr.

Seeds of the Spirit: Wisdom of the Twentieth Century. Ed. by Richard H. Bell & Barbara Battin. LC 94-48631. 200p. (Orig.). 1995. pap. 16.00 (*0-664-25465-9*) Westminster John Knox.

Seeds of the Sun. large type ed. Vicky Martin. 479p. 1981. 25.99 (*0-7089-0635-4*) Ulverscroft.

Seeds of Thought. 2nd ed. Debbie Gallagher & Sharon Willen. (Illus.). 50p. 1991. reprint ed. pap. 4.95 (*1-878131-03-6*) Brght Ideas Make Diff.

Seeds of Time. Fredric Jameson. LC 94-8735. (Wellek Library Lectures at the University of California Ser.). 192p. 1994. 22.95 (*0-231-08058-1*) Col U Pr.

Seeds of Time. Fredric Jameson. 240p. 1996. pap. 16.50 (*0-231-08059-X*) Col U Pr.

***Seeds of Time.** Kay L. Kenyon. 1997. mass mkt. 5.99 (*0-553-57681-X*, Spectra) Bantam.

***Seeds of Victory: Psychological Warfare & Propaganda.** Richard D. Johnson. 200p. 1997. write for info. (*0-7643-0349-X*) Schiffer.

Seeds of Violence. large type ed. Miriam Sharman. 1989. 25.99 (*0-7089-2185-X*) Ulverscroft.

***Seeds of Virtue & Knowledge.** Maryanne C. Horowitz. LC 97-18580. 1997. write for info. (*0-691-04463-5*) Princeton U Pr.

Seeds of Yesterday. V. C. Andrews. 416p. 1987. pap. 4.95 (*0-317-63632-4*) NAL-Dutton.

An Asterisk (*) at the beginning of an entry indicates that the title is appearing in BIP for the first time.

Seeds of Yesterday. V. C. Andrews. Ed. by Linda Marrow. 1990. pap. 6.99 (*0-671-72948-9*) PB.

Seeds of Yesterday. V. C. Andrews. 1983. write for info. (*0-671-44328-3*) S&S Trade.

Seeds of Yesterday see Flowers in the Attic

Seeds on Good Soil. Bettie W. Story. LC 89-6654. 80p. 1989. pap. 6.95 (*0-687-37150-3*) Abingdon.

Seeds on the Wind. Jean B. Mosley. 220p. 1994. text ed. 25.00 (*0-9642039-0-1*) Concord Prnting.

Seeds, Poetry for Positive Blackmen. Avonne S. Abnathya-Arnold. 50p. (Orig.). pap. 6.95 (*0-9631147-2-7*) A S Abrathyn-Arnold.

***Seeds That Grew & Grew.** Arch Books Staff. 1997. 1.99 (*0-570-07539-4*) Concordia.

Seeds That Grew to Be a Hundred: Matthew 13:1-17. V. Mann. LC 59-1209. (Arch Bks.). (Illus.). 24p. 1973. pap. 1.99 (*0-570-06091-5*, 59-1209) Concordia.

Seeds 2. Ed. by Ann Leonard. 200p. (Orig.). 1995. lib. bdg. 35.00 (*1-55861-107-X*) Feminist Pr.

Seeds 2: Supporting Women's Work Around the World. Ed. by Ann Leonard. 227p. (Orig.). 1995. pap. 12.95 (*1-55861-106-1*) Feminist Pr.

***Seedsaving Tips: A Starting Guide.** Deborah A. Murphy. (Sound-Off Ser.). 16p. 1996. pap. 2.95 (*0-9646811-1-0*) Stardust PA.

Seedtime. Phillipe Jaccottet. Tr. by Andre Lefevere & Michael Hamburger from FRE. LC 76-45640. 1977. 9.00 (*0-8112-0636-X*); pap. 3.25 (*0-8112-0637-8*, NDP428) New Directions.

Seedtime & Harvest. Peggy Bailer. 80p. (Orig.). 1993. pap. 7.50 (*1-879260-08-5*) Evanston Pub.

Seedtime & Harvest. Neville. 160p. 1985. reprint ed. pap. 7.95 (*0-87516-557-5*) DeVorss.

Seedtime & Harvest: Minibook. Charles Capps. 39p. (Orig.). 1986. pap. 0.99 (*0-89274-397-2*) Harrison Hse.

***Seedtime for Fascism: The Disintegration of Austrian Political Culture, 1867-1918.** George V. Strong. 264p. (C). (gr. 13). 1997. text ed. 64.95 (*0-7656-0189-3*); pap. text ed. 23.95 (*0-7656-0190-7*) M E Sharpe.

Seedtime for the Modern Civil Rights Movement: The President's Committee on Fair Employment Practice, 1941-1946. Merl E. Reed. LC 90-39656. 344p. 1991. text ed. 42.50 (*0-8071-1617-3*); pap. text ed. 17.95 (*0-8071-1688-2*) La State U Pr.

Seedtime of Reform: American Social Service & Social Action, 1918 to 1933. Clarke A. Chambers. LC 80-36788. xviii, 326p. 1980. reprint ed. text ed. 65.00 (*0-313-22666-0*, CHRE, Greenwood Pr) Greenwood.

Seedtime of Reform: American Social Service & Social Action, 1918-1933. Clarke A. Chambers. LC 63-23058. 346p. reprint ed. pap. 98.70 (*0-317-29390-7*, 2055847) Bks Demand.

Seedtime on the Cumberland. Harriette S. Arnow. LC 95-34152. (Illus.). xxiv, 451p. 1995. pap. 16.95 (*0-8032-5926-3*, Bison Books) U of Nebr Pr.

Seedtime Stories: Bedtime Stories with Poems & Devotionals. Beverly C. Burgess. (Illus.). (Orig.). (J). (gr. 2-6). 1991. pap. 4.98 (*1-879470-01-2*) Burgess Pub.

Seege of Troy: The "Seege or Batayle of Troye" (EETS, OS Ser.: No. 172). 1974. reprint ed. 63.00 (*0-527-00169-4*) Periodicals Srv.

Seege of Troye: A Study in the Intertextual Relations of the Middle English Romance the "Seege or Batayle of Troye" (Lund Studies in English: Vol. 4). 1974. reprint ed. pap. 30.00 (*0-8115-0547-2*) Periodicals Srv.

Seeing. Lesley Sims. (What about...? Ser.). (J). 1995. pap. text ed. 4.95 (*0-8114-7996-X*) Raintree Steck-V.

Seeing. Kathie B. Smith & Victoria Crenson. LC 87-5862. (Question Bks.). (Illus.). 24p. (J). (gr. k-3). 1988. lib. bdg. 11.89 (*0-8167-1008-2*) Troll Communs.

Seeing. Brenda Walpole. LC 96-11076. (See for Yourself Ser.). (Illus.). (J). 1997. lib. bdg. 21.40 (*0-8172-4218-X*) Raintree Steck-V.

Seeing. Lillian Wright. LC 94-10720. (What about...? Ser.). (Illus.). 32p. (J). (gr. 2-4). 1994. lib. bdg. 21.40 (*0-8114-5515-7*) Raintree Steck-V.

***Seeing a Large Cat.** Elizabeth Peters. LC 96-37998. 400p. 1997. 24.00 (*0-446-51834-4*) Warner Bks.

***Seeing a Large Cat.** Elizabeth Peters. 1998. mass mkt. write for info. (*0-446-60557-3*) Warner Bks.

***Seeing a Large Cat: Volume Nine of the Journals of Amelia Peabody.** Elizabeth Peters. LC 97-14525. 1997. write for info. (*0-7838-8211-4*) G K Hall.

Seeing America & Its Great Men: The Journal & Letters of Count Francesco Dal Verme, 1783-1784. Francesco Dal Verme. Ed. by Elizabeth Cometti. LC 69-17333. (Illus.). 196p. reprint ed. 55.90 (*0-8357-9818-6*, 2011164) Bks Demand.

Seeing America First. Nathaniel Tarn. LC 89-26124. 118p. (Orig.). 1989. pap. 8.95 (*0-918273-53-6*) Coffee Hse.

Seeing American Foreign Policy Whole. Brewster C. Denny. LC 84-16390. 208p. 1985. text ed. 19.95 (*0-252-01181-3*) U of Ill Pr.

Seeing & Believing: Images of the Christian Faith. Paul Philibert & Frank Kacarcik. 224p. (Orig.). 1995. 49.95 (*0-8146-6126-2*, Pueblo Bks) Liturgical Pr.

Seeing & Believing: Religion & Values in the Movies. Margaret R. Miles. LC 95-24927. 240p. 1996. 25.00 (*0-8070-1030-8*) Beacon Pr.

***Seeing & Believing: Religion & Values in the Movies.** Margaret R. Miles. LC 95-24927. 272p. 1997. reprint ed. pap. 15.00 (*0-8070-1031-6*) Beacon Pr.

Seeing & Believing: The Influence of Television. Greg Philo. 240p. (C). 1990. pap. text ed. 19.95 (*0-415-03621-6*, A4240) Routledge.

Seeing & Believing, Instructor's Manual. Arthur A. Berger. (C). 1989. teacher ed., pap. text ed. write for info. (*0-87484-887-3*, 887) Mayfield Pub.

Seeing & Consciousness: Marxism, Gender, & Representation. Gen Doy. LC 94-33342. 1995. 45.95 (*0-85496-960-8*); pap. 19.95 (*1-85973-017-5*) Berg Pubs.

Seeing & Feeling the Church. Bill Freeman. 125p. (Orig.). 1992. pap. 3.50 (*0-914271-39-3*) Mnstry Wrd.

Seeing & Hearing God with the Psalms: The Prophetic Liturgy of the Second Temple in Jerusalem. Raymond J. Tournay. Tr. by Crowley. (JSOT Supplement Ser.: No. 118). 300p. (C). 1991. 60.00 (*1-85075-313-X*, Pub. by Sheffield Acad UK) CUP Services.

Seeing & Observing: Rousseau's Rhetoric of Perception. John C. O'Neal. (Stanford French & Italian Studies: Vol. 41). 160p. 1985. pap. 46.50 (*0-915838-55-9*) Anma Libri.

Seeing & Painting the Colors of Nature: An Impressionist's View. Joseph Dawley & Gloria Dawley. (Illus.). 144p. 1993. pap. 18.95 (*0-8230-4762-8*, Watsn-Guptill) Watsn-Guptill.

Seeing & Remembering. Christian Matras. Tr. by George Johnston. 48p. 1988. 7.95 (*0-921254-09-1*, Pub. by Penumbra Pr CN) U of Toronto Pr.

Seeing & Unseeing Social Structure: Sociology's Essential Insights. Lynn M. Mulkey. LC 94-49567. 1995. pap. text ed. 17.00 (*0-205-14881-6*) Allyn.

Seeing Anew: Teachers Theories of Action. Jennifer Nias. (C). 1995. pap. 28.00 (*0-7300-0448-1*, Pub. by Deakin Univ AT) St Mut.

Seeing Behind the Mask. Jim Toombs. 256p. 1995. pap. 9.99 (*0-88070-676-7*, Multnomah Bks) Multnomah Pubs.

Seeing Berger: A Revaluation of "Ways of Seeing" Peter Fuller. (Art Ser.). 50p. (Orig.). 1981. pap. 1.95 (*0-906495-48-2*) Writers & Readers.

Seeing Between the Pixels: Pictures in Interactive Systems. Thomas Strothotte & C. Strothotte. LC 96-40255. 256p. 1997. 49.50 (*3-540-59417-5*) Spr-Verlag.

Seeing Beyond St. Louis. Barringer Fifield. 1991. pap. 10.95 (*0-9623809-1-1*) WA Univ Campus.

Seeing Beyond 20-20 see Seeing Without Glasses: Improving Your Vision Naturally

Seeing Beyond 20-20 see Seeing Without Glasses: Improving Your Eyesight Naturally

Seeing Both Sides: Classic Controversies in Abnormal Psychology. Scott O. Lilienfeld. LC 94-18083. 512p. 1995. pap. 31.95 (*0-534-25134-X*) Brooks-Cole.

Seeing Calvin Coolidge in a Dream. John Derbyshire. 272p. 1996. 22.95 (*0-312-14044-4*) St Martin.

***Seeing Calvin Coolidge in a Dream: A Novel.** John Derbyshire. 1997. pap. 11.95 (*0-312-15649-9*, Griffin) St Martin.

Seeing Christ: Windows on His Saving Grace. Calvin B. Rock. LC 93-40955. 1994. 9.99 (*0-8280-0794-2*) Review & Herald.

Seeing Christ in the Tabernacle: He's Typified in Every Piece. Ervin N. Hershberger. Ed. by Richard Polzyn. (Illus.). 100p. (Orig.). 1995. pap. write for info. (*0-940883-07-4*) Calvary Pubns.

Seeing Circle: A Parable for Children Over & Under 21. Jim Ballard. LC 75-25393. (Mandala Series in Education). 1975. pap. 3.50 (*0-916250-07-5*) Irvington.

Seeing Contour & Colour: Proceedings of the Third International Symposium of the Northern Eye Institute, Manchester, UK, 9-13 August 1987. Ed. by J. Kulkikowski et al. LC 89-2988. (Vision & Visual Health Care Ser.: Vol. 3). (Illus.). 775p. 1989. 365.00 (*0-08-036136-6*, Pub. by Pergamon Repr UK) Franklin.

Seeing Curriculum in a New Light: Essays from Science Education. Ed. by Hugh Munby et al. 190p. 1984. reprint ed. pap. text ed. 20.50 (*0-8191-4238-7*) U Pr of Amer.

Seeing Dell. Carol Guess. LC 95-43309. 174p. 1996. pap. 12.95 (*1-57344-023-X*); lib. bdg. 24.95 (*1-57344-024-8*) Cleis Pr.

Seeing Differences. Marilyn Hayes. (Early Education Ser.). 24p. (gr. k). 1982. student ed. 5.00 (*0-8209-0210-1*, K-12) ESP.

***Seeing Differently: Insights on Innovation.** Ed. by John S. Brown. (Business Review Bks.). 288p. 1997. 29.95 (*0-87584-755-2*) Harvard Busn.

***Seeing Differently: Insights on Innovation.** Harvard Business School Press Staff. 1997. text ed. 29.95 (*0-07-103867-1*) McGraw.

Seeing Double: Revisioning Edwardian & Modernist Literature. Carola M. Kaplan & Anne B. Simpson. LC 96-34457. 266p. 1996. text ed. 39.95 (*0-312-15896-3*) St Martin.

Seeing Double, the Autopen Guide. Marvin B. Blatt & Norman Schwab. 80p. (Orig.). 1986. pap. 7.95 (*0-937991-00-7*) La La Ltd.

***Seeing Ear, 7 cass.** audio 60.00 (*0-614-25227-X*, Pub. by Univ of West Aust Pr AT) Intl Spec Bk.

***Seeing Ear.** Rupert Thackray. 268p. teacher ed., pap. 28.00 (*0-86422-401-X*, Pub. by Univ of West Aust Pr AT); student ed., pap. 22.00 (*0-86422-402-8*, Pub. by Univ of West Aust Pr AT) Intl Spec Bk.

Seeing Earth: Literary Responses to Space Exploration. Ronald Weber. LC 84-16567. xiv, 138p. 1985. text ed. 21.95 (*0-8214-0791-0*) Ohio U Pr.

Seeing Earth from Space. Patricia Lauber. LC 89-77523. (Illus.). 80p. (YA). (gr. 5 up). 1990. 21.95 (*0-531-05902-2*); lib. bdg. 22.99 (*0-531-08502-3*) Orchard Bks Watts.

Seeing Earth from Space. Patricia Lauber. LC 89-77523. (Illus.). 80p. (YA). (gr. 5 up). 1994. pap. 9.95 (*0-531-07057-3*) Orchard Bks Watts.

Seeing England from the Fifty-Yard Line: A Rewarding Season Spent Coaching American Football & Touring the Land of Cricket & Rugby. George H. Baldwin. (Illus.). 150p. 1996. 14.95 (*0-930753-20-8*) Spect Ln Pr.

Seeing Europe Again: Secrets from a First World Traveler. Elaine Kendall. 160p. (Orig.). 1995. lib. bdg. 33.00 (*0-8095-4133-5*) Borgo Pr.

Seeing Europe Again: Secrets from a First World Traveler. Elaine Kendall. 125p. (Orig.). 1995. pap. 11.95 (*0-88496-384-5*) Capra Pr.

Seeing Eye. Comment by Clare Jordan. LC 84-62371. (Illus.). 80p. 1984. pap. 15.00 (*0-914155-01-6*) Mingei Intl Mus.

Seeing Eye: An Artist's Perception. Clare Jordan. LC 84-62371. (Illus.). 80p. 1984. pap. 15.00 (*0-295-96277-1*) U of Wash Pr.

Seeing Eye: Short Stories. Michael Martone. LC 95-22744. 192p. 1995. 20.95 (*0-944072-51-8*) Zoland Bks.

Seeing Eye & Other Selected Essays from Christian Reflections. C. S. Lewis. 256p. 1986. mass mkt. 5.99 (*0-345-32866-3*) Ballantine.

Seeing Eye to Eye. large type ed. Josie Metcalfe. 288p. 1996. 21.50 (*0-263-14520-4*, Pub. by M & B UK) Ulverscroft.

Seeing Eye Wife. Bayla Winters. 32p. (Orig.). 1996. pap. 8.00 (*1-887853-06-5*) Radiolarian.

Seeing-Eye Willie. Gottlieb. 1994. 4.99 (*0-517-13530-2*) Random Hse Value.

Seeing Female: Social Roles & Personal Lives. Ed. by Sharon S. Brehm. LC 87-15039. (Contributions in Women's Studies: No. 88). 232p. 1988. text ed. 42.95 (*0-313-25589-X*, BWN/, Greenwood Pr) Greenwood.

Seeing Fernandina: A Guide to the City & Its Industries. Federal Writers' Project, Florida. LC 73-3604. (American Guide Ser.). reprint ed. 20.00 (*0-404-57908-6*) AMS Pr.

Seeing Films Politically. Mas'ud Zavarzadeh. LC 90-9688. (SUNY Series in Radical, Social & Political Theory). 269p. (C). 1991. pap. text ed. 18.95 (*0-7914-0527-3*) State U NY Pr.

Seeing Films Politically. Mas'ud Zavarzadeh. LC 90-9688. (SUNY Series in Radical, Social & Political Theory). 269p. (C). 1991. text ed. 57.50 (*0-7914-0526-5*) State U NY Pr.

***Seeing Fireworks, Vol. 1.** Barrett. 1997. mass mkt. 5.99 (*0-312-96258-4*) St Martin.

Seeing for Ourselves: Case-Study Research by Teachers of Writing. Ed. by Glenda L. Bissex & Richard Bullock. LC 86-27153. 228p. 1987. pap. text ed. 25.00 (*0-435-08436-4*, 08436) Heinemann.

Seeing for Yourself: Research Handbook for Girls' Education in Africa. Eileen Kane. (EDI Learning Resources Ser.). 344p. 1996. 20.95 (*0-8213-3453-0*, 13453) World Bank.

Seeing for Yourself: Techniques & Projects for Beginning Photographers. Roger Gleason. LC 92-18867. (Illus.). 200p. (YA). (gr. 7-12). 1992. pap. 14.95 (*1-55652-159-6*) Chicago Review.

Seeing Fractions: A Unit for the Upper Elementary Grades. California Department of Education Staff. (Illus.). 130p. 1990. pap. 10.25 (*0-8011-0926-4*) Calif Education.

Seeing from an Unprotected Perspective. Steve Emma. 1991. 7.95 (*0-533-09127-6*) Vantage.

***Seeing Glass: A Memoir.** Jacqueline Gorman. LC 96-53345. 288p. 1997. 22.95 (*1-57322-061-2*, Riverhead Books) Putnam Pub Group.

Seeing God: Twelve Reliable Signs of True Spirituality. Gerald R. McDermott. LC 95-25286. 288p. (Orig.). 1995. pap. 11.99 (*0-8308-1616-X*, 1616) InterVarsity.

Seeing God Everywhere: A Practical Guide to Spiritual Living. Swami Shraddhananda. Ed. & Pref. by Pravrajika Vrajaprana. LC 96-9304. 232p. (Orig.). 1996. pap. text ed. 12.95 (*0-87481-052-3*) Vedanta Pr.

***Seeing Hands.** 81p. (Orig.). 1997. pap. 6.00 (*0-9653700-2-X*) B L Pubng.

Seeing, Hearing. Eugene M. Schwartz. 1990. pap. 10.95 (*0-945803-04-4*) R Steiner Col Pubns.

Seeing Historic Alabama: Fifteen Guided Tours. rev. ed. Virginia V. Hamilton & Jacqueline A. Matte. LC 95-50431. (Illus.). 256p. 1996. pap. 19.95 (*0-8173-0790-7*) U of Ala Pr.

Seeing in the Dark: A Compendium of Cinemagoing. Ian Breakwell. LC 90-60283. 1991. pap. 15.95 (*1-85242-166-5*) Serpents Tail.

Seeing in the Dark: Poems. Matthew Brennan. 56p. 1993. pap. 8.00 (*0-9635631-1-4*) Hawkhead Pr.

Seeing in the Dark: Reflections on Dreams & Dreaming. Bert O. States. LC 96-20997. 1997. write for info. (*0-300-06910-3*) Yale U Pr.

***Seeing in the Dark: The Poetry of Phyllis Webb.** Pauline Butling. xiv, 184p. 1997. pap. 24.95 (*0-88920-271-0*) W Laurier Pr.

***Seeing in the Dark No. 35: Margaret Atwood's Cat's Eye.** Arnold E. Davidson. (Canadian Fiction Studies). pap. 14.95 (*1-55022-312-7*, Pub. by ECW Press CN) Genl Dist Srvs.

***Seeing into the Earth: Noninvasive Charaterization of the Shallow Subsurface.** 180p. 1997. 37.95 (*0-309-06359-0*) Natl Acad Pr.

***Seeing into the Life of Things: Essays on Religion in Literature.** Ed. by John L. Mahoney. 1997. pap. 17.00 (*0-8232-1733-7*) Fordham.

***Seeing into the Life of Things: Essays on Religion in Literature.** Ed. by John L. Mahoney. (C). 1997. 35.00 (*0-8232-1732-9*) Fordham.

Seeing Is Above All: Sant Darshan Singh's First Indian Tour. Ed. by H. C. Chadda. (Illus.). 117p. 1977. pap. 5.00 (*0-918224-04-7*) S K Pubns.

Seeing Is Believing. Elizabeth Shub. LC 78-12378. (Illus.). 64p. (J). 1994. 14.00 (*0-688-13647-8*) Greenwillow.

Seeing Is Believing. Charles Tomlinson. 1958. 10.95 (*0-8392-1097-3*) Astor-Honor.

Seeing Is Believing: A Christmas Gift. Mark Bishop. 24.95 (*1-883755-10-7*) Lost Riv Pr.

Seeing Is Believing: Activities to Show You How People Think & See. Patrick Green. (Amazing Brain Ser.). 1996. pap. 9.95 (*0-382-39606-5*, Julian Messner); lib. bdg. 15.95 (*0-382-39605-7*, Julian Messner) Silver Burdett Pr.

Seeing Is Believing: An Introduction to Visual Communication. Arthur A. Berger. LC 88-26627. (Illus.). 189p. (C). 1989. pap. text ed. 22.95 (*0-87484-873-3*, 873) Mayfield Pub.

***Seeing Is Believing: An Introduction to Visual Communication.** Arthur A. Berger. LC 97-10862. 1997. write for info. (*1-55934-909-3*) Mayfield Pub.

Seeing Is Believing? Haunted Shacks, Mystery Spots, & Other Delightful Phenomena. rev. ed. Christopher C. Banta. LC 95-92322. (Illus.). 224p. (Orig.). 1996. pap. 21.95 (*0-942742-14-1*) Funhouse Pr.

Seeing Is Believing: Moving Statues in Ireland. Ed. by Colm Toibin. 1982. pap. 8.95 (*0-685-20032-9*, Pub. by Colin Smythe Ltd UK) Dufour.

***Seeing Is Believing: Murals in Derry.** Oona Woods. (Illus.). 56p. (Orig.). 1996. pap. 11.95 (*0-946451-31-1*, Pub. by Guildhall Pr IE) Irish Bks Media.

***Seeing is Deceiving.** Sarah J. Mason. 208p. 1997. mass mkt. 5.99 (*0-425-15901-9*, Prime Crime) Berkley Pub.

***Seeing Is Deceiving: A Phoebe Fairfax Mystery.** Suzanne North. 1996. 25.99 (*0-7710-6805-0*) McCland & Stewart.

Seeing Is Forgetting the Name of the Thing One Sees: A Life of Contemporary Artist Robert Irwin. Lawrence Weschler. LC 81-16176. (Illus.). 215p. 1982. 30.00 (*0-520-04595-5*); pap. 13.95 (*0-520-04920-9*) U CA Pr.

***Seeing Islam As Others Saw It: A Survey & Evaluation of Christian, Jewish & Zoroastrian Writings on Early Islam.** Robert G. Hoyland. LC 97-19196. (Studies in Late Antiquity & Early Islam: No. 13). 740p. 1997. lib. bdg. 49.95 (*0-87850-125-8*) Darwin Pr.

Seeing It Was So. Anthony Piccone. 87p. 1986. 18.00 (*0-918526-50-7*); pap. 10.00 (*0-918526-51-5*) BOA Edns.

Seeing Japan. (Illus.). 30p. 1994. 12.95 (*4-89684-232-4*, Pub. by Yohan Pubns JA) Weatherhill.

***Seeing Jazz: Artists & Writers on Jazz.** Smithsonian Institution Travel Staff. 1997. 35.00 (*0-8118-1180-8*); pap. text ed. 22.95 (*0-8118-1732-6*) Chronicle Bks.

Seeing Jesus: The Case Against Pictures of Our Lord Jesus Christ. 14p. 1990. pap. 1.25 (*0-85151-580-0*) Banner of Truth.

Seeing Jesus: 1-2 Peter, 1-3 John. Linda R. McGinn. (Women in the Word Ser.). 96p. (Orig.). (YA). (gr. 10). 1994. pap. 3.99 (*0-8010-3877-4*) Baker Bks.

Seeing Jesus Leader's Guide: 1-2 Peter, 1-3 John. Linda R. McGinn. (Women in the Word Ser.). 110p. (Orig.). (YA). (gr. 10). 1994. teacher ed., pap. 7.99 (*0-8010-5244-0*) Baker Bks.

Seeing Kyoto. (Illus.). 30p. 1994. 12.95 (*4-89684-233-2*, Pub. by Yohan Pubns JA) Weatherhill.

Seeing Language in Sign: The Work of William C. Stokoe. Jane Maher. LC 95-46906. 216p. 1996. 24.95 (*1-56368-053-X*) Gallaudet Univ Pr.

Seeing London. E. M. Newman. 1972. 59.95 (*0-8490-1017-9*) Gordon Pr.

Seeing Mary Plain. Fran Kiernan. Date not set. write for info. (*0-393-03801-7*) Norton.

Seeing Mathematical Relationships, Unit 1. Albert Bennett et al. (Math & the Mind's Eye Ser.). (Illus.). 29p. (C). 1988. teacher ed., ring bd. 5.50 (*1-886131-13-9*, ME1) Math Lrning.

Seeing Mona Naked. Thomas F. Averill. 172p. 1989. pap. 9.75 (*0-922820-01-5*) Watermrk Pr.

Seeing Myself, Seeing the World: A Woman's Journey Around the World on a Bicycle. 2nd rev. ed. Sally Vantress. Ed. by Martin Kreig & Larry Pearson. (Illus.). 284p. (Orig.). 1991. reprint ed. pap. 11.95 (*1-880101-07-6*) SMSW Pub.

Seeing New Worlds: Henry David Thoreau & Nineteenth-Century Natural Science. Laura D. Walls. LC 95-7401. 316p. 1995. 42.00 (*0-299-14740-1*); pap. 22.95 (*0-299-14744-4*) U of Wis Pr.

Seeing New York: History Walks for Armchair & Footloose Travelers. Hope Cooke. (Critical Perspectives on the Past Ser.). (Illus.). 440p. (Orig.). (C). 1995. pap. 18.95 (*1-56639-289-6*); lib. bdg. 59.95 (*1-56639-288-8*) Temple U Pr.

***Seeing off Uncle Jack.** large type ed. Bernard Ashley. (J). 1997. 16.95 (*0-7451-6907-4*, Galaxy Child Lrg Print) Chivers N Amer.

Seeing Organizational Patterns: A New Theory & Language of Organizational Design. Robert W. Keidel. LC 94-47065. (Illus.). 220p. 1995. 29.95 (*1-881052-65-6*) Berrett-Koehler.

***Seeing Ourselves.** 4th ed. Macionis & Benokraitis. LC 97-14965. 1997. pap. text ed. 26.00 (*0-13-610684-6*) P-H.

Seeing Ourselves: Classic, Contemporary, & Cross-Cultural Readings in Sociology. 3rd ed. Ed. by John J. Macionis. LC 94-6822. 476p. 1994. pap. text ed. 28.67 (*0-13-101130-8*) P-H.

Seeing Paris. E. M. Newman. 1972. 59.95 (*0-8490-1018-7*) Gordon Pr.

Seeing Pittsburgh. Barringer Fifield. LC 96-10111. (Illus.). 288p. (C). 1996. 29.95 (*0-8229-3859-6*); pap. 16.95 (*0-8229-5542-3*) U of Pittsburgh Pr.

Seeing, Reaching, Touching: The Relations Between Vision & Touch in Infancy. Arlette Streri. Tr. by Tim Pownall & Susan Kingerlee from FRE. LC 93-11782. (Illus.). 232p. 1993. 29.95 (*0-262-19343-4*) MIT Pr.

***Seeing Red.** Sarah Garland. (Illus.). 32p. (J). 1996. 12.95 (*0-916291-64-2*) Kane-Miller Bk.

Seeing Red. Roseanne Williams. 1993. mass mkt. 2.99 (*0-373-25531-4*, 1-25531-4) Harlequin Bks.

Seeing Red: The Red Auerbach Story. Dan Shaughnessy. LC 95-36951. 1995. pap. 10.95 (*1-55850-548-2*) Adams Media.

Seeing Seattle. Roger Sale. LC 94-5715. (Illus.). 256p. 1994. pap. 17.50 (*0-295-97359-5*) U of Wash Pr.

Seeing Shapes. (Illus.). 14p. (J). 1995. pap. 5.99 (*0-525-45476-4*) Dutton Child Bks.

An Asterisk (*) at the beginning of an entry indicates that the title is appearing in BIP for the first time.

Seeing Society: Perspectives on Social Life. 2nd ed. Ed. by Paul B. Brezina et al. LC 93-9936. 1993. pap. text ed. 35.00 (*0-205-14348-2*) Allyn.

Seeing Solids & Silhouettes: 3-D Geometry. Michael T. Battista & Douglas H. Clements. Ed. by Priscilla C. Samii & Beverly Cory. (Investigations in Number, Data, & Space Ser.). (Illus.). 112p. (Orig.). 1994. teacher ed., pap. 22.95 (*0-86651-797-9*, DS21237) Seymour Pubns.

***Seeing Solids & Silhouettes: 3-D Geometry.** rev. ed. Michael T. Battista & Douglas H. Clements. Ed. by Catherine Anderson & Beverly Cory. (Investigations in Number, Data, & Space Ser.). (Illus.). 116p. (YA). (gr. 4 up). 1997. pap. text ed. 22.95 (*1-57232-745-6*, 43892) Seymour Pubns.

Seeing Souderton: The Borough's Story in Photographs, 1887-1987. Phil J. Ruth. (Illus.). 192p. (C). 1987. 29.95 (*0-9619350-1-4*) P J Ruth.

***Seeing Southeastern Geology Through Chattanooga: Over 500 Million Years of Rock Formation, Deformation, & Erosion.** (Illus.). vii, 164p. (Orig.). 1997. pap. 24.95 (*0-9656186-0-9*) HGC.

Seeing St. Augustine. Federal Writers' Project, Florida. LC 73-3605. (American Guide Ser.). reprint ed. 37.50 (*0-404-57909-4*) AMS Pr.

Seeing St. Louis. Barringer Fifield. 198p. (Orig.). 1989. pap. 9.95 (*0-685-27215-X*) WA Univ Campus.

Seeing St. Louis. 2nd ed. Barringer Fifield. (Orig.). 1991. pap. 9.95 (*0-9623809-0-3*) WA Univ Campus.

Seeing Stars. Sharleen Collicott. LC 93-49846. (Illus.). 32p. (J). (ps-2). 1996. pap. 14.99 (*0-8037-1522-6*); pap. 14.89 (*0-8037-1523-4*) Dial Bks Young.

Seeing Stars. Institute for Science in Society Staff. 1996. text ed. 14.95 (*0-07-057166-X*) McGraw.

***Seeing Stars.** James Muirden. (SuperSmarts Ser.). (Illus.). 24p. (J). 1997. 11.99 (*0-7636-0373-2*) Candlewick Pr.

Seeing Stars. Charles L. Wagner. Ed. by Andrew Farkas. LC 76-29976. (Opera Biographies Ser.). (Illus.). 1977. reprint ed. lib. bdg. 35.95 (*0-405-09714-X*) Ayer.

Seeing Stars: A Book & Poster about the Constellations. Barbara Seiger. LC 92-43199. (Illus.). 24p. (J). (gr. 2-6). 1993. pap. 8.95 (*0-448-40198-3*, G&D) Putnam Pub Group.

***Seeing Stars: The McDonald Observatory & Its Astronomers.** LC 96-50011. (J). 1997. 15.95 (*1-57168-117-5*, Eakin Pr) Sunbelt Media.

***Seeing Statistics.** McClelland. (Career Education Ser.). Date not set. 43.95 (*0-534-34982-X*) Brooks-Cole.

Seeing Stick. Jane Yolen. LC 75-6946. (Illus.). 32p. (J). (gr. k up). 1975. lib. bdg. 14.89 (*0-690-00596-2*, Crowell Jr Bks) HarpC Child Bks.

Seeing Symmetry: Unit X. Michael J. Arcidiacono et al. (Math & the Mind's Eye Ser.). (Illus.). 81p. (C). 1996. teacher ed., text ed. 14.50 (*1-886131-22-8*, ME10) Math Lrning.

Seeing Systems: Unlocking the Mysteries of Organizational Life. Barry Oshry. LC 95-33582. (Illus.). 228p. 1996. reprint ed. pap. 22.95 (*1-881052-99-0*) Berrett-Koehler.

Seeing the Blossom: Two Interviews & a Lecture. Dennis Potter. 1994. pap. 11.95 (*0-571-17436-1*) Faber & Faber.

Seeing the Crab: A Memoir Before Dying. Christina Middlebrook. LC 95-49471. 224p. 1996. 22.00 (*0-465-07493-6*) Basic.

***Seeing the Crab: A Memoir of Dying Before I Do.** Christina Middlebrook. LC 97-26082. 224p. 1998. pap. 12.95 (*0-385-48865-3*, Anchor NY) Doubleday.

Seeing the Deep Sky: Telescopic Astronomy Projects Beyond the Solar System. Fred Schaaf. LC 91-33119. (Science Editions Ser.: No. 1800). 224p. 1992. text ed. 29.95 (*0-471-53068-9*); pap. text ed. 14.95 (*0-471-53069-7*) Wiley.

Seeing the Elephant: Raw Recruits at the Battle of Shiloh. Joseph A. Frank & George A. Reaves. LC 88-34823. (Contributions in Military Studies: No. 88). 215p. 1989. text ed. 49.95 (*0-313-26692-1*, FSH/, Greenwood Pr) Greenwood.

Seeing the Figure Now. unabridged ed. Dennis Adrian. (Illus.). 64p. (Orig.). 1996. pap. 12.95 (*0-9637817-4-X*) Schl Art Inst.

Seeing the Forest among the Trees: The Case for Wholistic Forest Use. Herb Hammond. (Illus.). 312p. (Orig.). 1991. pap. 39.95 (*0-919591-58-2*, Pub. by Polestar Bk Pubs CN) Orca Bk Pubs.

Seeing the Gawain-Poet. Sarah Stanbury. LC 91-27295. (Middle Ages Ser.). 178p. (C). 1992. text ed. 25.95 (*0-8122-3109-0*) U of Pa Pr.

Seeing the Insane. Sander L. Gilman. LC 96-10208. xvi, 253p. 1996. reprint ed. pap. 30.00 (*0-8032-7064-X*, Bison Books) U of Nebr Pr.

***Seeing the Inside: Bark Painting in Western Arnhem Land.** Luke Taylor. (Oxford Studies in Social & Cultural Anthropology). (Illus.). 1997. 68.00 (*0-19-827390-8*); pap. 29.95 (*0-19-823354-X*) OUP.

***Seeing the Invisible: New Writing from America, the Pacific, & Asia.** Ed. by Frank Stewart & Bruce Fulton. (Illus.). 240p. (Orig.). 1997. pap. 15.00 (*0-8248-1906-3*) UH Pr.

Seeing the Invisible: The Art of Spiritual Perception. A. B. Simpson. 190p. 1994. pap. 8.99 (*0-87509-565-8*) Chr Pubns.

Seeing the Light: Optics in Nature, Photography, Color, Vision, & Holography. David R. Falk et al. 480p. 1985. Net. text ed. 70.95 (*0-471-60385-6*) Wiley.

***Seeing the Light: Personal Encounters with the Middle East & Islam.** Ed. by Richard H. Curtiss & Janet McMahon. (Illus.). 280p. (Orig.). 1997. pap. 18.95 (*0-937165-06-9*) Am Educ Trust.

Seeing the Light: The Art of Becoming Beautiful. John Pepper. LC 93-36316. 1994. pap. 11.95 (*1-85230-445-6*) Element MA.

Seeing the Lions. Robert F. Walton. LC 88-90471. (Illus.). 56p. (Orig.). 1989. pap. text ed. 7.95 (*0-9622073-0-6*) Phoenix Irvine.

Seeing the Lord: Resurrection & Early Christian Practices. Marianne Sawicki. LC 93-40947. 1994. pap. 26.00 (*0-8006-2709-1*, 1-2709, Fortress Pr) Augsburg Fortress.

Seeing the Multitudes Delayed. Lissa McLaughlin. (Burning Deck Fiction Ser.). (Illus.). 1979. 15.00 (*0-930900-75-8*); pap. 4.00 (*0-930900-76-6*) Burning Deck.

Seeing the Newspaper. Kevin G. Barnhurst. LC 92-62727. 1994. 23.95 (*0-312-10800-1*); pap. 12.00 (*0-685-71199-4*) St Martin.

Seeing the Newspaper. Kevin G. Barnhurst. 240p. 1993. pap. text ed. 18.00 (*0-312-06149-8*) St Martin.

Seeing the Raven: A Narrative of Renewal. Peter M. Leschak. LC 93-27943. 1994. 16.95 (*0-8166-2429-1*) U of Minn Pr.

***Seeing the River.** Raymond Friel. 1995. 12.00 (*0-7486-6195-6*, Pub. by Polygon UK) Subterranean Co.

Seeing the Sky: One Hundred Projects, Activities & Explorations in Astronomy. Fred Schaaf. (Science Editions Ser.). 212p. 1990. pap. text ed. 18.95 (*0-471-51067-X*) Wiley.

Seeing the Solar System: Telescopic Projects, Activities & Explorations in Astronomy. Fred Schaaf. (Science Editions Ser.: No. 1800). 224p. 1991. text ed. 29.95 (*0-471-53070-0*); pap. text ed. 14.95 (*0-471-53071-9*) Wiley.

Seeing the Story of the Bible. Myer Pearlman. 128p. 1930. pap. 4.95 (*0-88243-581-7*, 02-0581) Gospel Pub.

Seeing the Unseen. Carl R. Green & William R. Sanford. LC 92-44677. (Illus.). 48p. (J). (gr. 4-10). 1993. lib. bdg. 14.95 (*0-89490-454-X*) Enslow Pubs.

Seeing the Unseen: A Hand Book for Spiritual Warfare. Joe Beam. 334p. 1994. pap. 11.99 (*1-878990-27-6*) Howard Pub LA.

Seeing the Unseen: A Hand Book for Spiritual Warfare. Joe Beam. 1994. audio 14.99 (*1-878990-37-3*) Howard Pub LA.

Seeing the Unseen: Dr. Harold E. Edgerton & the Wonders of Strobe Alley. Douglas Collins. (Illus.). 106p. 1994. spiral bd. 35.00 (*0-935398-21-X*) G Eastman Hse.

Seeing the Unseen: Dr. Harold E. Edgerton & the Wonders of Strobe Alley. Douglas Collins & Joyce Bedi. Ed. by Roger R. Bruce. (Illus.). 100p. 1994. 39.95 (*0-262-02387-3*) MIT Pr.

Seeing the White Buffalo. Robert B. Pickering. LC 97-7411. (Illus.). 160p. 1997. 24.95 (*1-55566-181-5*); pap. 16.95 (*1-55566-182-3*) Johnson Bks.

Seeing the Whole Through Social Studies. Tarry Lindquist. LC 94-48190. 206p. 1995. pap. text ed. 21.00 (*0-435-08902-1*, 08902) Heinemann.

***Seeing the Win.** Vince Lombardi. (Illus.). 125p. 1997. pap. 14.95 (*0-85013-308-4*) Dartnell Corp.

***Seeing the World.** Dick Davis. 56p. 1980. pap. 13.95 (*0-85646-061-3*, Pub. by Anvil Press UK) Dufour.

***Seeing the World Through Women's Eyes.** Ed. by Naima Richmond & Marilyn M. Cuneo. (Illus.). 183p. (Orig.). 1996. pap. 11.95 (*0-9655569-0-5*) Womens Intl Leag.

Seeing Things. Allan Fowler. LC 90-22527. (Rookie Read-about Science Ser.). (Illus.). 32p. (J). (ps-2). 1991. pap. 3.95 (*0-516-44910-9*); lib. bdg. 17.30 (*0-516-04910-0*) Childrens.

Seeing Things. Herbst. (J). 1997. 16.00 (*0-689-31652-6*, Atheneum Bks Young) S&S Childrens.

Seeing Things. Robin Klein. 200p. (J). (gr. 7 up). 1994. pap. 12.50 (*0-670-85282-1*) Viking Child Bks.

Seeing Things. John M. Brown. LC 75-138209. viii, 341p. 1971. reprint ed. text ed. 38.50 (*0-8371-5564-9*, BRST, Greenwood Pr) Greenwood.

Seeing Things: A Chronicle of Surprises. Richard A. Hawley. 1987. 17.95 (*0-8027-0987-7*) Walker & Co.

Seeing Things: Poems. Seamus Heaney. 112p. 1991. 19.00 (*0-374-25776-0*) FS&G.

Seeing Things: Poems. Seamus Heaney. 112p. 1993. pap. 10.00 (*0-374-52389-4*, Noonday) FS&G.

Seeing Things Big Book. Allan Fowler. (Rookie Read-about Science Big Bks.). (Illus.). 32p. (J). (ps-2). 1991. pap. 32. 40 (*0-516-49470-8*) Childrens.

Seeing Things Differently. Philip D. Zimmerman. LC 92-10345. (Illus.). 80p. 1992. pap. 12.95 (*0-912724-23-4*) Winterthur.

Seeing Things Simply: Color. Jeremy Galton. 1994. 6.98 (*0-7858-0125-1*) Bk Sales Inc.

Seeing Things Simply: Composition & Perspective. James Horton. 1994. 6.98 (*0-7858-0066-2*) Bk Sales Inc.

Seeing Through: Shining God's Light in an Age Gone Mad. David Roper. 256p. 1995. pap. text ed. 10.99 (*0-88070-735-6*, Multnomah Bks) Multnomah Pubs.

Seeing Through Broccoli. Penny Minkler. (Illus.). 1993. 5.00 (*0-9619744-8-6*) Blue Light Pr.

Seeing Through Clothes. Anne Hollander. LC 92-34151. (C). 1993. pap. 18.00 (*0-520-08231-1*) U CA Pr.

Seeing Through Language: A Guide to Styles of English Language. Ronald Carter & Walter Nash. (Language Library). 240p. (C). 1990. pap. text ed. 20.95 (*0-631-15135-4*) Blackwell Pubs.

Seeing Through Movies. Ed. by Mark C. Miller. 266p. 1990. pap. 10.36 (*0-679-72367-6*) Pantheon.

Seeing Through "Paradise" Artists & the Terezin Concentration Camp. Terezin Committee, Exhibitions Department Staff. 1991. pap. 15.00 (*0-614-03711-5*) MA Collge Art.

Seeing Through Shuck. Ed. by Richard Kostelanetz. 1978. reprint ed. pap. 100.00 (*0-932360-14-9*) Archae Edns.

Seeing Through Statistics. Jessica M. Utts. LC 95-22554. 464p. (C). 1996. pap. 41.95 (*0-534-25776-3*) Wadsworth Pub.

Seeing Through Texts: Doing Theology among the Srivaisnavas of South India. Francis X. Clooney. LC 95-35858. (SUNY Series, Toward a Comparative Philosophy of Religions). 351p. 1996. text ed. 73.50 (*0-7914-2995-4*); pap. text ed. 24.95 (*0-7914-2996-2*) State U NY Pr.

Seeing Through the Eighties: Television & Reaganism. Jane Feuer. LC 95-6221. (Console-ing Passions Ser.). (Illus.). 184p. 1995. text ed. 45.95 (*0-8223-1675-7*); pap. text ed. 14.95 (*0-8223-1687-0*) Duke.

Seeing Through the Eyes of Love: How We See Life Is How We Experience Life. Christie L. Jones. 72p. 1992. pap. 10.99 (*0-9633852-0-8*) C L Jones.

Seeing Through the Heart. Donna J. Bauman. (Illus.). 100p. 1994. pap. text ed. 18.00 (*0-9631696-1-0*) Wrld Peace Inst.

***Seeing Through the Media: A Religious View of Communications & Cultural Analysis.** Michael Warren. Orig. Title: Communications & Cultural Analysis: A Religious View. 224p. 1997. reprint ed. pap. 17.00 (*1-56338-211-3*) TPI PA.

Seeing Through the Media: The Persian Gulf War. Ed. by Susan Jeffords & Lauren Rabinovitz. LC 93-25725. (Media, Culture, & Communication Ser.). (Illus.). 280p. (C). 1994. text ed. 45.00 (*0-8135-2041-X*); pap. text ed. 16.00 (*0-8135-2042-8*) Rutgers U Pr.

Seeing Through the Mother Goose Tales: Visual Turns in the Writings of Charles Perrault. Philip Lewis. LC 95-18795. 312p. 1996. 39.50 (*0-8047-2410-5*) Stanford U Pr.

Seeing through the Sun. Linda Hogan. LC 84-28019. 88p. 1985. pap. 9.95 (*0-87023-472-2*) U of Mass Pr.

Seeing Through Words: The Scope of Late Renaissance Poetry. Elizabeth Cook. LC 85-29502. 192p. 1986. 25. 00 (*0-300-03675-2*) Yale U Pr.

Seeing Together: Friendship Between the Sexes in English Writing from Mill to Woolf. Victor Luftig. 320p. 1995. pap. 15.95 (*0-8047-2591-8*) Stanford U Pr.

Seeing Together: Friendship Between the Sexes in English Writing from Mill to Woolf. Victor Luftig. LC 92-44199. 320p. (C). 1995. 45.00 (*0-8047-2168-8*) Stanford U Pr.

Seeing Tokyo. (Illus.). 30p. 1994. 12.95 (*4-89684-234-0*, Pub. by Yohan Pubns JA) Weatherhill.

Seeing Voices: A Journey into the World of the Deaf. Oliver Sacks. 1989. 22.00 (*0-520-06083-0*) U CA Pr.

Seeing Voices: A Journey into the World of the Deaf. Oliver Sacks. LC 89-46487. 224p. 1990. reprint ed. pap. 11.00 (*0-06-097347-1*, PL) HarpC.

Seeing Well Again Without Your Glasses. Christopher Markert. (Illus.). 128p. 17.95 (*0-8464-4288-4*) Beekman Pubs.

Seeing What I Like & Liking What I See. Charles Colbert. LC 91-90374. (Illus.). 204p. 1991. 49.50 (*0-944853-04-8*) Pendaya Pubns.

Seeing with a Native Eye: Contributions to the Study of Native American Religion. Ed. by Walter H. Capps. LC 76-9980. 1976. pap. 6.95 (*0-06-061312-2*, RD-177) Harper SF.

Seeing with an Eye of Faith. Grant Von Harrison. 73p. (Orig.). 1991. write for info. (*0-318-68388-1*) Jackman Pubng.

Seeing with Magic Glasses: A Teacher's View from the Front Line of the Learning Revolution. Launa Ellison. LC 93-29173. (Illus.). 195p. (Orig.). 1993. pap. 14.95 (*0-915556-22-7*) Great Ocean.

Seeing with Music: The Lives of Three Blind African Musicians. Simon Ottenberg. LC 95-49962. (Illus.). 232p. 1996. text ed. 35.00 (*0-295-97525-3*) U of Wash Pr.

Seeing with the Eyes of Love: Eknath Easwaran on the Imitation of Christ. Eknath Easwaran. LC 91-27913. (Classics of Christian Inspiration Ser.). 288p. 1996. 22.00 (*0-915132-88-5*); pap. 12.95 (*0-915132-87-7*) Nilgiri Pr.

Seeing with the Heart: How to Be Spiritual in an Unspiritual World. Johnnie W. Skinner, Sr. Ed. by Denis Gates. 160p. (Orig.). 1996. teacher ed., pap. 6.95 (*0-940955-33-4*) Urban Ministries.

Seeing with the Heart: How to Be Spiritual in an Unspiritual World. Johnnie W. Skinner, Sr. Ed. by Denise Gates. (Leadership Training Bks.). 176p. (Orig.). 1996. pap. text ed. 7.95 (*0-940955-32-6*) Urban Ministries.

Seeing with the Mind's Eye. Mike Samuels & Nancy H. Samuels. 1975. pap. 19.95 (*0-394-73113-1*) Random.

***Seeing with the Soul.** Shepherd. 13.35 (*0-687-61025-7*) Abingdon.

Seeing Without Glasses: Improving Your Eyesight Naturally. 2nd rev. ed. Robert M. Kaplan. LC 94-21957. Orig. Title: Seeing Beyond 20-20. (Illus.). 178p. 1994. 19.95 (*1-885223-02-1*) Beyond Words Pub.

Seeing Without Glasses: Improving Your Vision Naturally. 2nd rev. ed. Robert M. Kaplan. LC 94-21957. Orig. Title: Seeing Beyond 20-20. 177p. 1994. pap. 12.95 (*0-941831-97-3*) Beyond Words Pub.

Seeing Young Children. 3rd ed. Bentzen. (Early Childhood Education Ser.). 1997. 10.50 (*0-8273-7666-9*) Delmar.

Seeing Young Children: A Guide for Observing & Recording Behavior. Warren R. Bentzen. LC 85-1564. 272p. (C). 1985. pap. 27.00 (*0-8273-2329-8*) Delmar.

Seeing Young Children: A Guide to Observing & Recording Behavior. 2nd ed. Warren R. Bentzen. 269p. 1991. pap. 28.50 (*0-8273-4477-5*) Delmar.

Seeing Young Children: A Guide to Observing & Recording Behavior. 2nd ed. Warren R. Bentzen. 269p. 1991. teacher ed., pap. 9.50 (*0-8273-4478-3*) Delmar.

Seeing Young Children: A Guide to Observing & Recording Behavior. 3rd ed. Warren R. Bentzen. (Illus.). 384p. 1996. pap. 29.95 (*0-8273-7665-0*) Delmar.

Seeing Your Future: A Modern Look at Prophecy & Prediction. John E. Ronner. (Illus.). 190p. (Orig.). 1990. pap. 10.95 (*0-932945-38-4*) Mamre Pr.

Seeing Yourself As a Teacher: Conversations with Five New Teachers in a University Writing Program. Elizabeth Rankin. 137p. 1994. 12.95 (*0-8141-4298-2*) NCTE.

Seek & Destroy. Alan Evans. 256p. 1986. 15.95 (*0-8027-0928-1*) Walker & Co.

Seek & Destroy: A Personal View of WWII. Douglas F. DeGroote. LC 95-83610. 212p. 1996. pap. 12.95 (*1-885487-17-7*) Brownell & Carroll.

Seek & Find. C. MacKenzie. 2.99 (*0-906731-78-X*, Pub. by Christian Focus UK) Spring Arbor Dist.

Seek & Ye Shall Find New Testament. Michael Berry & Nora Berry. (J). (ps-3). 1992. 12.99 (*0-929216-74-1*) KindrVision.

Seek & Ye Shall Find Old Testament. Michael Berry & Nora Berry. (J). (ps-3). 1992. 12.99 (*0-929216-78-4*) KindrVision.

***Seek First the Kingdom.** Date not set. pap. 1.20 (*0-8341-9230-6*) Lillenas.

Seek Knowledge: Thought & Travel in the House of Islam. Ian R. Netton. 176p. (C). 1996. 75.00 (*0-7007-0339-X*, Pub. by Curzon Pr UK); pap. 25.00 (*0-7007-0340-3*, Pub. by Curzon Pr UK) Paul & Co Pubs.

Seek My Face: Prayer as Personal Relationship in Scripture. William A. Barry. LC 88-30534. 112p. 1989. pap. 4.95 (*0-8091-3025-4*) Paulist Pr.

Seek My Face, Speak My Name: A Contemporary Jewish Theology. Arthur Green. LC 91-23082. 296p. 1997. pap. 20.00 (*1-56821-213-5*) Aronson.

***Seek n' Peek Mummy.** Ladybird Staff. (Seek n' Peek Ser.). (J). Date not set. pap. 7.99 (*0-7214-5737-1*, Ladybrd) Penguin.

***Seek n' Peek Tyrannosaurus Rex.** Ladybird Staff. (Seek n' Peek Ser.). (J). Date not set. pap. 7.99 (*0-7214-5738-X*, Ladybrd) Penguin.

Seek out & Destroy. large type ed. Alan Evans. 512p. 1985. 25.99 (*0-7089-1361-X*) Ulverscroft.

Seek Peace & Pursue It: Proceedings from the 1988 International Baptist Peace Conference. Ed. by H. Wayne Pipkin. 222p. (Orig.). 1989. pap. 15.00 (*0-9622896-0-4*) Baptist Peace.

Seek, Strike, Destroy: The History of the 894th Tank Destroyer Battalion in World War II. Patrick J. Chase. LC 95-75464. (Illus.). 240p. 1995. 35.00 (*0-9645659-0-0*) P J Chase.

Seek That Which Is Above. Cardinal J. Ratzinger. Tr. by Graham Harrison from GER. LC 86-81553. 133p. 1986. 9.95 (*0-89870-101-5*) Ignatius Pr.

Seek the Happy Life. Paul H. Dunn. 1985. 9.95 (*0-88494-553-7*) Bookcraft Inc.

Seek the Peace of the City: Reflections on Urban Ministry. Eldin Villafane. 160p. 1995. pap. 13.00 (*0-8028-0729-1*) Eerdmans.

***Seek the Way.** C. Hsu. 270p. 1996. pap. 7.00 (*1-879771-16-0*) World Scientific Pub.

Seek the Welfare of the City: Christians As Benefactors & Citizens. Bruce W. Winter. 230p. 1994. pap. 19.00 (*0-8028-4091-4*) Eerdmans.

Seek to See Him: Ascent & Vision Mysticism in the Gospel of Thomas. April D. De Conick. (Supplements to Vigiliae Christianae Ser.: Vol. 33). 200p. 1996. 80.75 (*90-04-10401-1*) E J Brill.

Seek Ye First. William MacDonald. 1972. pap. 3.00 (*0-937396-38-9*) Walterick Pubs.

Seek Ye First. Elva Martin. 1973. pap. 2.50 (*0-915374-32-3*, 32-3) Rapids Christian.

Seeker. 42p. (Orig.). 1995. pap. 5.00 (*0-934852-41-3*) Lorien Hse.

Seeker. Elizabeth August. (Romance Ser.). 1994. pap. 2.75 (*0-373-08989-9*, 5-08989-1) Silhouette.

Seeker. Simon Hawke. (Dark Sun, Tribe of One Ser.: No. 2). 320p. (Orig.). 1994. pap. 4.95 (*1-56076-701-4*) TSR Inc.

Seeker. Slightly Off Center Writers Group Staff. (J). (gr. 6-11). 1995. 7.95 (*1-56721-106-2*) Twnty-Fifth Cent Pr.

Seeker: D. S. Merezhkovskiy. C. Harold Bedford. LC 74-28496. x, 222p. 1975. 27.50 (*0-7006-0131-7*) U Pr of KS.

Seeker after Truth. Idries Shah. 1982. 25.00 (*0-900860-91-X*, Pub. by Octagon Pr UK) ISHK.

Seeker & Servant: Reflections on Religious Leadership. Robert K. Greenleaf. Ed. by Anne T. Fraker & Larry C. Spears. (Nonprofit Sector Ser.). 330p. Date not set. 29. 95 (*0-7879-0229-2*) Jossey-Bass.

Seeker of Dreams. large type ed. Jean Innes. 1989. 25.99 (*0-7089-2075-6*) Ulverscroft.

Seeker, Reaper. Saltire Society Staff. 1989. 80.00 (*0-85411-041-0*, Pub. by Saltire Soc) St Mut.

Seekers, 2 vols. in 1. 100p. 1994. pap. 8.00 (*1-886134-00-6*) Miraculous Fngerprnt.

Seekers. Paul A. Hawkins. 352p. (Orig.). 1994. pap. 4.50 (*0-451-17880-7*, Sig) NAL-Dutton.

Seekers. El Krueger. 151p. 16.95 (*1-878096-25-7*) Best E TX Pubs.

Seeker's Catechism: The Basics of Catholicism. Michael F. Pennock. LC 94-71886. 132p. (Orig.). 1994. pap. 3.95 (*0-87793-539-4*) Ave Maria.

Seekers Guide. David R. Furford. 112p. 1985. pap. write for info. (*0-9641207-0-4*) D R Furford.

***Seeker's Guide to Being Catholic.** Mitch Finley. LC 96-47164. 150p. 1997. pap. 10.95 (*0-8294-0934-3*) Loyola Pr.

***Seekers of His Face: Two Companies.** Cynthia Duggan. 140p. (Orig.). 1997. pap. 7.99 (*1-884369-58-8*, EBED Pubns) McDougal Pubng.

Seekers of the Healing Energy: Reich Cayce the Kahunas & Other Masters of the Vital Force. Mary Coddington. 1991. pap. 9.95 (*0-89281-313-X*) Inner Tradit.

S

An Asterisk (*) at the beginning of an entry indicates that the title is appearing in BIP for the first time.

S

Seekers of Truth: The Story of the Philalethes Society. Allen E. Roberts. (History of the Philalethes Society Ser.). (Illus.). 269p. 1988. 18.00 (*0-935633-06-5*) Anchor Comm.

Seeker's Path: Myth, Maturity & the Baha'i Teachings. David Langness. 240p. (Orig.). 1996. pap. 18.99 (*1-85168-041-1*) Onewrld Pubns.

Seeking. D. Smith Nath. 50p. 1994. pap. 5.95 (*1-886134-01-4*) Miraculous Fngerprnt.

Seeking a Center: My Life as a "Great Bookie" Otto A. Bird. LC 91-71555. 145p. (Orig.). 1991. pap. 9.95 (*0-89870-370-0*) Ignatius Pr.

Seeking a Faith for a New Age: Essays on the Interdependence of Religion, Science & Philosophy. Henry N. Wieman. Ed. & Intro. by Cedric L. Hepler. 313p. 1988. reprint ed. 14.95 (*0-913029-18-1*) Stevens Bk Pr.

Seeking a New Canadian Partnership: Asymmetrical & Confederal Options. F. Leslie Seidle. 231p. 1995. pap. 15.95 (*0-88645-163-9*, Pub. by Inst Res Pub CN) Ashgate Pub Co.

Seeking Air. Barbara Guest. (Sun & Moon Classics Ser.: No. 120). 188p. (Orig.). 1996. pap. 12.95 (*1-55713-260-7*) Sun & Moon CA.

***Seeking Alternatives: American Women in Progressive Era 1900-1920.** Levine. Date not set. 26.95 (*0-8057-1633-5*) Mac Lib Ref.

Seeking & Finding Manual. 1970. pap. 7.95 (*0-913308-03-X*) Fordham Pub.

Seeking & Finding Workbook. 1970. pap. 18.95 (*0-913308-02-1*) Fordham Pub.

Seeking & Keeping Customers with Field Guide to Marketing. Benson P. Shapiro. 1994. 49.95 (*0-87584-442-1*) Harvard Busn.

Seeking Asylum: Comparative Law & Practice in Selected European Countries. Helene Kambert. LC 94-35316. (International Studies in Human Rights: Vol. 37). 232p. (C). 1995. lib. bdg. 93.00 (*0-7923-3152-4*, Pub. by M Nijhoff NE) Kluwer Ac.

Seeking Awareness in American Nature Writing: Henry Thoreau, Annie Dillard, Edward Abbey, Wendell Berry, & Barry Lopez. Scott Slovic. LC 91-24313. 216p. (Orig.). (C). 1992. pap. 17.95 (*0-87480-362-4*) U of Utah Pr.

***Seeking Christ: Men.** Stoop. Date not set. pap. 12.99 (*0-8407-6736-6*) Nelson.

***Seeking Christ: Women.** Stromm. Date not set. pap. 12.99 (*0-8407-6737-4*) Nelson.

Seeking Common Ground: Canada-U. S. Trade Dispute Settlement Policies for the Nineties. Andrew D. Anderson. 313p. (C). 1994. text ed. 71.50 (*0-8133-8752-3*) Westview.

Seeking Common Ground: Multidisciplinary Studies of Immigrant Women in the United States. Ed. by Donna R. Gabaccia. LC 92-9327. (Contributions in Women's Studies: No. 129). 272p. 1992. text ed. 59.95 (*0-313-27483-5*, GIF, Greenwood Pr); pap. text ed. 19.95 (*0-275-94387-9*, B4387, Greenwood Pr) Greenwood.

Seeking Compliance: The Production of Interpersonal Influence Messages. James P. Dillard. 200p. (Orig.). (C). 1990. pap. text ed. 29.95 (*0-89787-340-8*) Gorsuch Scarisbrick.

Seeking Connections in Psychotherapy. Barbara F. Okun. LC 90-4738. (Social & Behavioral Science Ser.). 475p. 36.95 (*1-55542-261-6*) Jossey-Bass.

Seeking Customers: A Harvard Business Review Book. Ed. by Benson P. Shapiro & John J. Sviokla. 368p. (C). 1992. 29.95 (*0-87584-332-8*) Harvard Busn.

Seeking Customers: A Harvard Business Review Book. Benson P. Shapiro & John J. Sviokla. 1993. text ed. 32.00 (*0-07-103379-3*) McGraw.

Seeking Customers, Keeping Customers, & Field Guide to Marketing. Ed. by Benson P. Shapiro & John J. Sviokla. 1994. text ed. 49.95 (*0-07-103611-3*) McGraw.

Seeking Diversity: Language Arts with Adolescents. Linda Rief. LC 91-34800. 299p. (Orig.). 1991. pap. text ed. 24.00 (*0-435-08598-0*, 08598) Heinemann.

Seeking Diversity: Language Arts with Adolescents. Linda Rief. LC 91-34800. 300p. (Orig.). 1992. 28.95 (*0-435-08724-X*, 08724) Heinemann.

Seeking Effective Schools for African American Children. Bunyan Bryant & Alan H. Jones. LC 92-73154. 88p. (Orig.). 1993. pap. 11.95 (*1-880192-01-2*) Caddo Gap Pr.

Seeking Employment in Criminal Justice & Related Professions. 2nd ed. J. Scott Harr & Karen M. Hess. 200p. 1996. pap. text ed. 24.50 (*0-314-07146-6*) West Pub.

Seeking Employment in Law Enforcement, Private Security, & Related Fields. J. Scott Harr & Karen M. Hess. Ed. by Jucha. 244p. (C). 1992. pap. text ed. 23.25 (*0-314-93444-8*) West Pub.

***Seeking Excellence Through Independence: Liberating Colleges & Universities from State Regulations.** Terrence J. Mactaggart. 1997. 29.95 (*0-7879-0922-X*) Jossey-Bass.

Seeking Ezekial: Text & Psychology. David J. Halperin. LC 92-33568. 264p. 1993. 35.00 (*0-271-00947-0*); pap. 16.95 (*0-271-00948-9*) Pa St U Pr.

Seeking Fair Treatment: From the AIDS Epidemic to National Health Care Reform. Norman Daniels. 208p. 1995. 25.00 (*0-19-505712-0*) OUP.

Seeking for the Kingdom of God: Origins of the Bruderhof Communities. Eberhard Arnold & Emmy Arnold. LC 74-6317. 308p. 1974. 3.00 (*0-87486-133-0*) Plough.

Seeking Foreign Trouble. Ralph Townsend. 1984. lib. bdg. 79.95 (*0-87700-609-1*) Revisionist Pr.

Seeking God: The Recovery of Religious Identity in Orthodox Russia, Ukraine, & Georgia. Ed. by Stephen K. Batalden. LC 93-16553. 295p. (C). 1993. lib. bdg. 32.00 (*0-87580-178-1*) N Ill U Pr.

Seeking God: The Way of St. Benedict. Esther De Waal. 160p. 1985. pap. 5.95 (*0-8146-1388-8*) Liturgical Pr.

Seeking God in Story. John Navone. 250p. 1990. pap. text ed. 11.95 (*0-8146-1919-3*) Liturgical Pr.

***Seeking God Together: Spiritual Intimacy in Marriage.** LC 96-39777. 1996. pap. 10.99 (*0-8423-5855-2*) Tyndale.

Seeking God's Face. Cardinal R. Joseph. 104p. 1982. 6.00 (*0-8199-0774-X*, Frncscn Herld) Franciscan Pr.

Seeking God's Face: A Prayer Journal. 80p. 1995. pap. text ed. 4.99 (*0-8066-2771-9*) Augsburg Fortress.

Seeking God's Will Through Faith, Hope & Charity. Philip Schuster. LC 93-83258. 144p. (Orig.). 1994. pap. 9.95 (*0-87973-534-1*, 534) Our Sunday Visitor.

Seeking God's Wisdom about Christian Homosexuality. Robert Alexander. 31p. 1993. write for info. (*1-888258-00-4*) Evangel Concern Wstrn.

Seeking Good, Speaking Peace: Collected Essays of Rabbi Marc D. Angel. Ed. by Hayyim J. Angel. LC 94-10452. 1994. 25.00 (*0-88125-241-7*) Ktav.

Seeking Heart. Fenelon. LC 92-81562. Orig. Title: Fenelon's Spiritual Letters. 221p. 1992. pap. 8.95 (*0-940232-49-9*) Seedsowers.

Seeking His Choice. Horatio Alger, Jr. (Works of Horatio Alger Jr.). 1989. reprint ed. lib. bdg. 79.00 (*0-685-27558-2*) Rprt Serv.

Seeking Home: An Immigrant's Realization. Jayant Patel. 181p. 1991. write for info. (*0-9631583-0-9*) J C Patel.

Seeking Identity: Individualism vs. Community in an Ethnic Context. Raymond A. Belliotti. LC 95-31444. 280p. (C). 1995. 35.00 (*0-7006-0729-3*); pap. 17.95 (*0-7006-0730-7*) U Pr of KS.

Seeking Inner Peace: The Art of Facing Your Emotions. John D. Powers. LC 87-50839. 112p. (Orig.). 1987. pap. 8.95 (*0-89622-344-2*) Twenty-Third.

Seeking Jesus in Contemplation & Discernment. Robert Faricy. LC 83-81843. 111p. 1987. reprint ed. pap. 7.95 (*0-87061-142-9*) Chr Classics.

Seeking Justice. Lynn Neu. (Discovering Program Ser.). (Illus.). 64p. (Orig.). 1990. 2.80 (*0-88489-208-5*); teacher ed. 6.00 (*0-88489-209-3*) St Marys.

Seeking Light in the Darkness of the Unconscious. John R. Yungblut. LC 77-71933. (Orig.). 1977. pap. 3.00 (*0-87574-211-4*) Pendle Hill.

Seeking Major Gifts: How Fifty-Seven Institutions Do It. Compiled by Anne W. Altizer. 166p. 1992. pap. 32.00 (*0-89964-287-X*, 28402) Coun Adv & Supp Ed.

Seeking Many Inventions: The Idea of Community in America. Philip Abbott. LC 86-11338. 224p. 1987. text ed. 27.00 (*0-87049-514-3*) U of Tenn Pr.

Seeking Meaning: A Process Approach to Library & Information Services. Carol C. Kuhlthau. LC 92-40770. (Information Management, Policies & Services Ser.). 232p. 1993. pap. 39.50 (*1-56750-019-6*); text ed. 73.25 (*0-89391-968-3*) Ablex Pub.

Seeking Mr. Hyde: Studies in Robert Louis Stevenson Symbolism, Myth, & the Pre-Modern. Tom Hubbard. LC 95-35952. (Scottish Studies: Vol. 18). 155p. 1995. pap. 29.95 (*0-8204-2922-8*) P Lang Pubng.

Seeking New Horizons: A Perceptual Approach to Geographic Education. Henry W. Castner. 240p. (C). 1990. 49.95 (*0-7735-0728-0*, Pub. by McGill CN) U of Toronto Pr.

Seeking Our Brothers in the Light: A Plea for Reformed Ecumenicity. Theodore Plantinga. 142p. (Orig.). 1992. pap. 4.50 (*0-921100-48-5*) Inhtce Pubns.

Seeking Peace. Titus Peachey & Linda G. Peachey. LC 91-74053. 238p. 1991. pap. 11.95 (*1-56148-049-5*) Good Bks PA.

Seeking Peace from Chaos: Humanitarian Intervention in Somalia. Samuel M. Makinda. LC 93-20731. (International Peace Academy Occasional Paper Ser.). 96p. 1993. pap. text ed. 8.95 (*1-55587-477-0*) Lynne Rienner.

Seeking Pleasure in the Old West. David Dary. 400p. 1995. 30.00 (*0-394-56178-3*) Knopf.

***Seeking Pleasure in the Old West.** David Dary. 364p. 1997. reprint ed. 14.95 (*0-7006-0828-1*) U Pr of KS.

Seeking Promethean Woman in the New Poetry: Stein, Vallejo, Artaud, Rimbaud, Eliot, Jacob. Doris T. Wight. (American University Studies: General Literature: Ser. XIX, Vol. 11). 200p. (C). 1988. text ed. 32.50 (*0-8204-0618-X*) P Lang Pubng.

Seeking Prospective, Weaving Spirituality & Psychology in Search of Clarity. Robert J. Wicks. 96p. 1991. pap. 4.95 (*0-8091-3234-6*) Paulist Pr.

Seeking Security & Development: The Impact of Military Spending & Arms Transfers. Ed. by Norman A. Graham. LC 93-41148. 295p. 1994. lib. bdg. 43.00 (*1-55587-416-9*) Lynne Rienner.

Seeking Shelter: Cambodian Refugees in Thailand. Lawyers Committee for Human Rights. (Orig.). 1986. pap. 7.00 (*0-934143-14-5*) Lawyers Comm Human.

Seeking Solid Ground: Anchoring Your Life in Godly Character. John Trent & Rick Hicks. LC 95-12524. 1995. 16.99 (*1-56179-364-7*) Focus Family.

Seeking Solutions: Case Leader's Guide. fac. ed. Ed. by Charles K. Mann et al. LC 90-35169. (Kumarian Press Library of Management for Development). 199p. 1990. pap. 56.80 (*0-7837-7583-0*, 2047336) Bks Demand.

Seeking Spiritual Direction: How to Grow the Divine Life Within. Thomas Dubay. LC 93-26747. 300p. 1994. pap. 11.99 (*0-89283-810-8*, Charis) Servant.

Seeking Spiritual Meaning: The World of Vedanta. Joseph D. Damrell. LC 77-9145. (Sociological Observations Ser.: No. 2). 252p. reprint ed. pap. 71.90 (*0-317-08760-6*, 2021885) Bks Demand.

Seeking Stability in Space: Anti-Satelite Weapons & the Evolving Space Regime. Ed. by Joseph S. Nye, Jr. & James A. Shear. LC 87-21619. (Illus.). 184p. (Orig.). (C). 1988. pap. text ed. 19.50 (*0-8191-6422-4*) U Pr of Amer.

Seeking Strategic Advantage Through Health Policy Analysis. Beaufort B. Longest, Jr. LC 96-26898. (Orig.). 1996. pap. 36.00 (*1-56793-047-6*) Health Admin Pr.

Seeking Structure from Nature: The Organic Architecture of Hungary. Jeffrey Cook. 191p. 1996. 66.00 (*0-8176-5178-0*); 66.00 (*3-7643-5178-0*) Birkhauser.

Seeking Synergy: Creating a Museum Collaborative That Works. Victoria Coats. 48p. 1994. pap. text ed. 24.95 (*0-9617645-1-1*) Oreg Mus Sci & Indus.

Seeking the Best. Otis M. Shackelford. LC 73-18606. reprint ed. 32.50 (*0-404-11416-4*) AMS Pr.

Seeking the Common Ground: Protestant Christianity, the Three-Self Movement & China's United Front. Philip Wickeri. LC 88-17486. 400p. 1989. 35.00 (*0-88344-441-0*) Orbis Bks.

Seeking the Face of God. William H. Shannon. 192p. 1990. pap. 11.95 (*0-8245-0985-4*) Crossroad NY.

Seeking the Face of God. Gary L. Thomas. LC 94-17530. 1994. 15.99 (*0-7852-8277-7*) Nelson.

Seeking the Heart of Wisdom: The Path of Insight Meditation. Joseph Goldstein & Jack Kornfield. LC 87-9710. (Dragon Editions Ser.). 195p. (Orig.). 1987. pap. 13.00 (*0-87773-327-9*) Shambhala Pubns.

Seeking the Highest Good: Social Service & Gender at the University of Toronto, 1888-1937. Sara Z. Burke. (Studies in Gender & History). (Illus.). 200p. 1996. 55.00 (*0-8020-0782-1*); pap. 17.95 (*0-8020-7146-5*) U of Toronto Pr.

Seeking the Hills. Lee Perron. 64p. 1992. pap. 10.00 (*0-9620634-3-6*); lib. bdg. 25.00 (*0-9620634-5-2*) Sun Moon Bear Pr.

Seeking the Hills. limited ed. Lee Perron. (Illus.). 64p. 1992. 50.00 (*0-9620634-4-4*) Sun Moon Bear Pr.

Seeking the Humanity of God: Practices, Doctrines, & Catholic Theology. James J. Buckley. (Theology & Life Ser.: Vol. 36). 240p. (Orig.). 1992. pap. text ed. 14.95 (*0-8146-5718-4*) Liturgical Pr.

Seeking the Kingdom: Devotions for the Daily Journey of Faith. Richard J. Foster. 144p. 1995. pap. 10.00 (*0-06-062686-0*) Harper SF.

***Seeking the Light.** James R. Lewis. 1997. 24.00 (*0-914829-42-4*) Mandeville LA.

***Seeking the Light: Essays in Quaker History in Honor of Edwin E. Bronner.** Ed. by J. William Frost & John M. Moore. 1996. pap. 16.00 (*0-87574-909-7*) Pendle Hill.

Seeking the Lord, the Real Key to Success. T. Crank. 1995. pap. 6.00 (*0-927936-56-9*) Vincom Inc.

Seeking the Meaning of the Management of "Relationships" Joel W. Weaver. 115p. (Orig.). (YA). (gr. 11 up). 1994. pap. 18.00 (*0-938919-31-8*) Six Lights.

Seeking the Path to Life: Theological Meditations on God & the Nature of People, Love, Life, & Death. Ira F. Stone. LC 92-12090. 132p. 1993. 19.95 (*1-879045-17-6*) Jewish Lights.

Seeking the Path to Life: Theological Meditations on God & the Nature of People, Love, Life, & Death. Ira F. Stone. LC 92-12090. 132p. 1995. pap. 14.95 (*1-879045-47-8*) Jewish Lights.

Seeking the Perfect Game: Baseball in American Literature. Cordelia Candelaria. LC 89-2157. (Contributions to the Study of Popular Culture Ser.: No. 24). 175p. 1989. text ed. 45.00 (*0-313-25465-6*, CBA, Greenwood Pr) Greenwood.

Seeking the Sublime: Neo-Romanticism in Landscape Photography. Valerie A. Leeds. (Illus.). 24p. 1995. pap. text ed. 12.00 (*1-887040-13-7*) SE Mus Photo.

Seeking the Wilderness: A Spiritual Journey. Tim Lehman. LC 93-71663. 240p. (Orig.). 1993. pap. 12.95 (*0-87303-205-5*) Faith & Life.

Seeking the Woman in Late Medieval & Renaissance Writings: Essays in Feminist Contextual Criticism. Sheila Fisher & Janet E. Halley. LC 82-22802. 288p. 1989. text ed. 31.00 (*0-87049-591-7*) U of Tenn Pr.

***Seeking to Improve Your Business: A Guide for Owner-Managers & Business Advisers.** abr. ed. Ron Flavel. LC 95-13841. (Managing the Small Business Ser.: No. 49). 46p. 1996. pap. 8.95 (*0-644-46268-X*, Pub. by AGPS Pr AT) Intl Spec Bk.

Seeking Wealth. Blaine M. Yorgason & Brenton Yorgason. (Gospel Power Ser.). 59p. (Orig.). (C). 1990. pap. text ed. 3.95 (*0-929985-19-2*) Jackman Pubng.

Seeking Western Waters: The Lewis & Clark Trail from the Rockies to the Pacific. Emory Strong & Ruth Strong. (Illus.). 250p. 1995. pap. 16.95 (*0-87595-245-3*) Oregon Hist.

Seeking Wholeness: Healing & Spirituality for Women. Karen B. Werth. 105p. 1995. spiral bd. 16.95 (*0-9647695-0-6*) Neshamah Pubng.

Seeking Wisdom. N. Sri Ram. 1969. 14.95 (*81-7059-070-1*) Theos Pub Hse.

Seeking Wisdom: Collected Essays on the Human Condition. Aaron Arouin. (Illus.). 103p. 1995. pap. 20.00 (*1-57074-291-X*) Greyden Pr.

Seeking Wisdom: The Sufi Path. Stuart Litvak. LC 82-60163. 194p. (Orig.). 1985. pap. 6.95 (*0-87728-543-8*) Weiser.

Seeking World Order: The United States & International Organization to 1920. Warren F. Kuehl. LC 69-19952. 1969. 22.95 (*0-8265-1137-6*) Vanderbilt U Pr.

Seeking Your Healthy Balance: A Do-It-Yourself Guide to Whole Person Wellness. Donald A. Tubesing & Nancy L. Tubesing. LC 91-65787. 216p. (Orig.). 1991. pap. 14.95 (*0-938586-45-9*) Whole Person.

Seekrieg 1939-1945 see Sea War: Nineteen Thirty-Nine to Nineteen Forty-Five

Seelenleben des Kruppels: Kruppelseelen Kundliche Erziehung und das Gesetz Betr. Hans Wurtz. Ed. by William R. Phillips & Janet Rosenberg. LC 79-6007. (Physically Handicapped in Society Ser.). (GER.). 1980. reprint ed. lib. bdg. 15.95 (*0-405-13138-0*) Ayer.

Seeley, A&P, No. 2: LM. Jay M. Templin. 736p. 1992. spiral bd. 29.95 (*0-8016-6653-8*) Mosby Yr Bk.

Seeley, A&P, No. 2: Study Guide. Tate. 624p. 1991. pap. 19.95 (*0-8016-4803-3*) Mosby Yr Bk.

Seeley Swan Day Hikes: A Guide for the Casual Traveler. Suzanne M. Vernon. 62p. (Orig.). 1989. pap. text ed. 6.95 (*0-9620902-0-4*) Vernon Print & Pub.

Seemaennisches Woerterbuch. Wolfram Claviez. (GER.). 1973. 75.00 (*0-8288-6329-6*, M-7620) Fr & Eur.

***Seeming: Selected Shorter Poems.** John Guenther. 72p. (Orig.). 1996. pap. 10.00 (*0-938266-03-9*) Purchase Pr.

Seemingly Unrelated Regression Equations Models Estimation & Inference. Srivastava & Giles. (Statistics: Textbooks & Monographs: Vol. 80). 392p. 1987. 125.00 (*0-8247-7610-0*) Dekker.

Seems Like Old Times: The Big Bands of the Midwest. Loren Belker. (Illus.). 131p. (Orig.). 1992. pap. 16.95 (*0-934904-30-8*) J & L Lee.

Seems Like Time. Kevin Urick. LC 76-62813. (Illus.). 1977. pap. 3.00 (*0-917976-00-2*, White Ewe Pr) Thunder Baas Pr.

Seems Like Yesterday: A Surgeon's Odyssey. Charles C. Kissinger. Ed. by Anna M. Nesmith. LC 88-81078. (Illus.). 254p. (Orig.). 1988. pap. 14.95 (*0-9620330-0-6*) Henderson Pr.

***Seen: The Guide to Nightlife - New YOrk/Los Angeles/Miami.** Ed. by Zachary Soreff. (Illus.). 96p. 1997. pap. 5.95 (*0-9640926-6-2*) Seen Pubng.

Seen & Heard. Ed. by David Merritt. 1992. pap. 6.95 (*0-85819-593-3*, Pub. by JBCE AT) Morehouse Pub.

Seen & Not Heard: Memories of Childhood in the Early 20th Century. Geoffrey K. Nelson. LC 93-33708. 1994. 30.00 (*0-7509-0460-7*, Pub. by Sutton Pubng UK) Bks Intl VA.

Seen & the Unseen: Shamanism, Mediumship, & Possession in Borneo. Intro. by Robert L. Winzeler. LC 93-72413. (Monograph Ser.). (Illus.). xxxiii, 320p. 25.00 (*0-9629568-1-3*) Borneo Res.

Seen & Unseen. Marta Berg. 42p. 1991. pap. 5.95 (*1-55523-355-4*) Winston-Derek.

Seen & Unseen: A Biologist Views the Universe. Ed. by Edward McCrady, III. 1990. pap. 14.95 (*0-918769-16-7*) Univ South Pr.

Seen but Not Heard - Coordinating Community Child Health & Social Services for Children in Need. 90p. 1994. pap. 25.00 (*0-11-886113-1*, HM61131, Pub. by Stationery Ofc UK) Bernan Associates.

Seen from the South. Ed. by Peter K. Kresl. LC 89-7133. 238p. (Orig.). 1989. pap. 15.00 (*0-912575-09-3*) D M Kennedy Ctr Brigham.

Seen on Halloween: Elementary Piano Solos. K. Beard. 16p. 1991. pap. 5.95 (*0-7935-0601-8*, 00290306) H Leonard.

Seen That, Now What? The Ultimate Guideto Finding the Video You Really Want to Watch. Andrea Shaw. 512p. 1996. pap. 15.95 (*0-684-80011-X*, Fireside) S&S Trade.

Seepage & Groundwater Flow: Numerical Analysis by Analog & Digital Methods. K. R. Rushton & S. C. Redshaw. LC 78-23359. (Wiley Series in Geotechnical Engineering). 351p. reprint ed. pap. 100.10 (*0-8357-7017-6*, 2033622) Bks Demand.

Seepage & Leakage from Dams & Impoundments: Proceedings of a Symposium Sponsored by the Geotechnical Engineering Division. Ed. by Richard L. Volpe & William E. Kelly. 317p. 1985. 33.00 (*0-87262-448-X*) Am Soc Civil Eng.

***Seepage, Drainage & Flow Nets.** 3rd ed. pap. text ed. write for info. (*0-471-18053-X*) Wiley.

Seepage, Drainage & Flow Nets. 3rd ed. Harry R. Cedergren. LC 88-18670. 465p. 1989. text ed. 79.95 (*0-471-61178-6*) Wiley.

Seepages. Simon Cutts. 1990. 20.00 (*0-912330-68-6*) Jargon Soc.

Seeping into - out of the Well. Stan Cohen. (Steam Press Ser.). (Illus.). 72p. 1991. pap. 16.00 (*0-9627440-3-4*) LAD Publishing.

Seeping into - out of the Well. limited ed. Stan Cohen. (Steam Press Ser.). (Illus.). 72p. 1991. 725.00 (*0-9627440-2-6*) LAD Publishing.

Seer. Orson Pratt. 320p. (C). 1994. 24.95 (*0-910523-18-5*) Grandin Bk Co.

Seer: Joseph Smith. Ron Jackson. Orig. Title: Joseph Smith: the Seer. 1977. 6.95 (*0-89036-088-X*) Hawkes Pub Inc.

Seer & Other Norwegian Tales. Jonas L. Lie. Tr. by Brian Morton & Richard Trevor from NOR. 160p. (Orig.). 9000. pap. 19.95 (*0-948259-65-5*, Pub. by Forest Bks UK) Dufour.

Seer King. Chris Bunch. LC 96-22487. 528p. (Orig.). 1997. pap. 13.99 (*0-446-67282-3*, Aspect) Warner Bks.

***Seer Out of Season: The Life of Edgar Casey, Vol. 1.** Harmon H. Bro. 1996. mass mkt. 6.99 (*0-312-95988-5*) St Martin.

Seerat-un-Nabi: 2 Vols-Shibli Numani. M. T. Badauni. 29.95 (*0-933511-51-5*) Kazi Pubns.

Seerecht: Terminologie des Seerechtsuebereinkommens. Ed. by Foreign Office of the Federal Republic of Germany, Language Services Division Staff. (Terminologische Schriftenreihe Ser.: Bd. 5). xii, 202p. (Orig.). (ENG, FRE & GER.). (C). 1992. pap. text ed. 52.35 (*3-11-013564-7*) De Gruyter.

Seeress of Kell. David Eddings. (Mallorean Ser.: Bk. 5). 384p. 1992. mass mkt. 6.99 (*0-345-37759-1*, Del Rey) Ballantine.

***Seeress of Kell.** David Eddings. 1997. pap. 12.95 (*0-345-41922-7*, Del Rey) Ballantine.

Seers & Scientists: Can the Future Be Predicted? Ann E. Weiss. (Illus.). 128p. (YA). (gr. 7 up). 1986. 14.00 (*0-15-272850-3*, HB Juv Bks) HarBrace.

Seers of God: Puritan Providentialism in the Restoration & Early Enlightenment. Michael P. Winship. (Early America). 240p. 1996. text ed. 39.95 (*0-8018-5137-8*) Johns Hopkins.

***Seer's Stone.** (FunFax Horror Ser.). (Illus.). 144p. (J). (gr. 3-9). 1996. pap. 2.95 (*0-7894-1152-0*) DK Pub Inc.

Seership. Swami Bhakta Vishita. 13.50 (*0-911662-33-2*) Yoga.

Seership: Soul Sight. Paschal B. Randolph. reprint ed. spiral bd. 7.00 (*0-7873-0697-5*) Hlth Research.

Sees & Bishops in the Holy Eastern Church. 1995. reprint ed. pap. 1.95 (*0-89981-157-4*) Eastern Orthodox.

Sees Behind Trees. Michael Dorris. LC 96-15859. (Illus.). 128p. (J). (gr. 3 up). 1996. 14.95 (*0-7868-0224-3*); lib. bdg. 14.89 (*0-7868-2215-5*) Hyprn Child.

***Sees Thru the Invisible Man.** Seymou Simon. (J). Date not set. lib. bdg. write for info. (*0-688-14448-9*, Morrow Junior) Morrow.

***Sees Thru the Invisible Man.** Seymour Simon. (J). Date not set. write for info. (*0-688-14447-0*, Morrow Junior) Morrow.

Seesaw. David Drew. LC 92-21394. (Illus.). (J). (gr. 2 up). 1993. 2.50 (*0-685-69191-8*) SRA McGraw.

***Seesaw: Vocal Selections.** Ed. by Carol Cuellar. 60p. (Orig.). (C). 1992. pap. text ed. 12.95 (*0-7692-0917-3*, VF1896) Warner Brothers.

Seesaw Log: A Chronicle of the Stage Production with the Text of Two for the Seesaw. William Gibson. 288p. 1984. reprint ed. pap. 7.95 (*0-87910-008-7*) Limelight Edns.

Seesaws, Nutcrackers, Brooms: Simple Machines That Are Really Levers. Christopher Lampton. (Gateway Simple Machines Ser.). (Illus.). 32p. (J). (gr. 2-4). 1991. pap. 4.95 (*1-878841-43-2*); lib. bdg. 14.40 (*1-878841-22-X*) Millbrook Pr.

Seethu: A Novel. Shanta R. Rao. 160p. 1980. pap. text ed. 3.95 (*0-86131-178-7*, Pub. by Orient Longman Ltd II) Apt Bks.

Sefas Emes Haggadah. Tr. by Simcha L. Grossbard. 218p. 1995. 15.95 (*1-56871-077-1*) Targum Pr.

***Sefer Chamesh haPekudim - Bemidbar - the Scroll of Numbers: Chapter 26: 1-65, 15 vols., Set.** Shmuel Wahli. Ed. by Bora E. Finton. (Bet HaShem Midrash Torah Light Notes Ser.). 1996. ring bd. write for info. (*1-883517-03-6*) Alef Bet Comns.

Sefer Chasidism. Yehudah HeChasid. LC 96-2944. 448p. 1997. 40.00 (*1-56821-920-2*) Aronson.

Sefer Ha-Aggadah Vol. 1: Bible Legends: The Book of Legends for Young Readers. Seymour Rossel. LC 96-8558. (Illus.). 90p. (Orig.). (J). (gr. 3-7). 1996. pap. 14.00 (*0-8074-0603-1*, 104031) UAHC.

Sefer ha-Bahir see Bahir

Sefer Hachinuch, the Book of Education, Vol. 5: Devorim, Pt. 2. 1989. 20.95 (*0-87306-497-6*) Feldheim.

Sefer Ha'hinnuch: The Book of Education, Vols. 2 & 3. Leviticus. 1985. 33.95 (*0-87306-145-4*) Feldheim.

Sefer Ha'hinnuch, the Book of Education: Genesis-Exodus, 1. Tr. by Charles Wengrov from HEB. 1978. 20.95 (*0-87306-179-9*) Feldheim.

Sefer Hahinnuch, Vol. 4: Numbers & Part I. of Deuteronomy. 500p. (ENG & HEB.). 1988. 20.95 (*0-87306-457-7*) Feldheim.

***Sefer Hahishtatchus.** 178p. (HEB.). 1996. 13.00 (*0-8266-0244-4*) Kehot Pubn Soc.

Sefer Hamaamorim. Joseph I. Schneersohn. 351p. (HEB.). reprint ed. 17.00 (*0-8266-5682-X*, 5680-1); reprint ed. 17.00 (*0-8266-5683-8*, 5682-3); reprint ed. 17.00 (*0-8266-5684-6*, 5684); reprint ed. 17.00 (*0-8266-5685-4*, 5685); reprint ed. 17.00 (*0-8266-5686-2*, 5686); reprint ed. 17.00 (*0-8266-5687-0*, 5687-8); reprint ed. 17.00 (*0-8266-5689-7*, 5689); reprint ed. 17.00 (*0-8266-5698-6*, 5698); reprint ed. 17.00 (*0-8266-5701-X*, 5699-5700); reprint ed. 17.00 (*0-8266-5702-8*, 5701-3); reprint ed. 17.00 (*0-8266-5703-6*, 5704-7); reprint ed. 17.00 (*0-8266-5704-4*, 5708-9); reprint ed. 17.00 (*0-8266-5705-2*, 5710-11) Kehot Pubn Soc.

Sefer Hamaamorim. Shalom D. Schneersohn. 330p. (HEB.). reprint ed. 17.00 (*0-8266-5643-9*, 5643-4); reprint ed. 17.00 (*0-8266-5645-5*, 5646-50); reprint ed. 17.00 (*0-8266-5651-X*, 5651); reprint ed. 17.00 (*0-8266-5652-8*, 5652); reprint ed. 17.00 (*0-8266-5659-5*, 5659); reprint ed. 17.00 (*0-8266-5655-2*, 5655); reprint ed. 17.00 (*0-8266-5658-7*, 5658); reprint ed. 17.00 (*0-8266-5660-9*, 5660-2); reprint ed. 17.00 (*0-8266-6663-9*, 5663); reprint ed. 17.00 (*0-8266-5665-X*, 5665); reprint ed. 17.00 (*0-8266-5666-8*, 5666); reprint ed. 17.00 (*0-8266-5668-4*, 5668); reprint ed. 17.00 (*0-8266-5669-2*, 5669); reprint ed. 17.00 (*0-8266-5670-6*, 5670); reprint ed. 17.00 (*0-8266-5671-4*, 5671); reprint ed. 17.00 (*0-8266-5661-7*, 5672-6); reprint ed. 17.00 (*0-8266-5677-3*, 5677); reprint ed. 17.00 (*0-8266-5678-1*, 5678); reprint ed. 17.00 (*0-8266-5679-X*, 5679); reprint ed. 17.00 (*0-8266-5680-3*, 5680) Kehot Pubn Soc.

***Sefer Hamaamorim: 5654.** 2nd ed. Dov B. Schneersohn. LC 86-21049. 410p. (HEB.). 1982. reprint ed. 17.00 (*0-8266-5654-4*) Kehot Pubn Soc.

***Sefer Hamaamorim: 5664.** Shalom D. Schneersohn. LC 85-45438. 356p. (HEB.). 1993. 17.00 (*0-8266-6664-7*) Kehot Pubn Soc.

***Sefer Hamaamorim: 5696-97.** Joseph I. Schneersohn. LC 86-220154. 334p. (HEB.). 1988. 17.00 (*0-8266-5697-8*) Kehot Pubn Soc.

***Sefer Hamaamorim: 5740.** Menachem M. Schneerson. 252p. (HEB.). 1988. 10.00 (*0-8266-1871-5*) Kehot Pubn Soc.

***Sefer Hamaamorim: 5748.** Menachem M. Schneerson. 224p. (HEB.). 1988. 10.00 (*0-8266-1879-0*) Kehot Pubn Soc.

Sefer Ha'Maamorim Bosi Lgani. Menachem M. Schneerson. 380p. (HEB.). reprint ed. 15.00 (*0-8266-5716-8*) Kehot Pubn Soc.

Sefer Hamaamorim Melukat Vol. 2. Shalom D. Schneersohn. LC 86-21049. 342p. (HEB.). 1992. reprint ed. 17.00 (*0-8266-5453-3*) Kehot Pubn Soc.

***Sefer Hamaamorim 5745.** Menachem M. Schneerson. (HEB.). 1985. 10.00 (*0-8266-1876-6*) Kehot Pubn Soc.

Sefer Hamaftach Hamafteichos Lisifrei Admur Hozoken Vol. 1. 348p. (HEB.). 1980. reprint ed. 14.00 (*0-8266-5301-4*) Kehot Pubn Soc.

***Sefer Hamafteichos L'Sifrei Admor Hazoken, Vol. 2.** Yitchok Cansbourg. 92p. (Orig.). (HEB.). 1981. pap. 3.00 (*0-8266-5302-2*) Kehot Pubn Soc.

Sefer Hamafteichos L'Sifrei Harayatz. 352p. (HEB.). reprint ed. 8.00 (*0-8266-5330-8*) Kehot Pubn Soc.

Sefer Hamaamorim Kuntraisim, Vol. 1. 5th ed. Joseph I. Schneersohn. LC 85-23700. 558p. (HEB.). 1962. reprint ed. 17.00 (*0-8266-5411-8*) Kehot Pubn Soc.

Sefer Hamaamorim Kuntraisim, Vol. 2. 5th ed. Joseph I. Schneersohn. LC 85-23700. 456p. (HEB.). 1962. reprint ed. 17.00 (*0-8266-5412-6*) Kehot Pubn Soc.

Sefer Hamaamorim Kuntraisim, Vol. 3. 2nd ed. Joseph I. Schneersohn. LC 85-23700. 218p. (HEB.). 1977. reprint ed. 10.00 (*0-8266-5413-4*) Kehot Pubn Soc.

Sefer Ha'Mamorim Melukat, Vol. 1. Menachem M. Schneerson. 396p. reprint ed. 15.00 (*0-8266-5747-8*) Kehot Pubn Soc.

Sefer Ha'Mamorim Melukat, Vol. 3. Menachem M. Schneerson. 399p. reprint ed. 15.00 (*0-8266-5758-3*) Kehot Pubn Soc.

Sefer Ha'Mamorim Melukat, Vol. 4. Menachem M. Schneerson. 463p. reprint ed. 15.00 (*0-8266-5759-1*) Kehot Pubn Soc.

Sefer Ha'Mamorim Melukat, Vol. 5. Menachem M. Schneerson. 411p. reprint ed. 15.00 (*0-8266-5760-5*) Kehot Pubn Soc.

Sefer Ha'Mamorim Melukat, Vol. 6. Menachem M. Schneerson. 323p. reprint ed. 15.00 (*0-8266-5773-7*) Kehot Pubn Soc.

Sefer Hamfteichos L'Sifrei Haemtzoi. 301p. (HEB.). 1982. 10.00 (*0-8266-5315-4*) Kehot Pubn Soc.

Sefer Haminhagim: The Book of Chabad-Lubavitch Customs. Menachem M. Schneerson. Tr. by Uri Kaploun. 1991. reprint ed. 17.00 (*0-8266-0555-9*) Kehot Pubn Soc.

Sefer Hamitzvot for Youth, Vols. 1 & 2. Malka Touger. (YA). (gr. 7-10). 1988. 20.00 (*0-940118-26-2*) Moznaim.

Sefer Hamitzvoth I: Book of Mitzvoth Positive Commandments. Tr. by Shraga Silverstein from HEB. (Book of Mitzvoth Maimonidies Ser.). 241p. 1993. 13.00 (*0-940118-91-2*) Moznaim.

Sefer Hamitzvoth II: Book of Mitzvoth Negative Commandments. Tr. by Shraga Silverstein from HEB. (Book of Mitzvoth Maimonidies). 252p. 1993. 13.00 (*0-940118-92-0*) Moznaim.

Sefer Harkim, Vol. 5. 377p. (HEB.). 20.00 (*0-8266-5105-4*) Kehot Pubn Soc.

Sefer Harkim Vol. 2. 368p. (HEB.). 20.00 (*0-8266-5102-X*) Kehot Pubn Soc.

Sefer Harkim Chabad, Vol. 1. 418p. (HEB.). 20.00 (*0-8266-5101-1*) Kehot Pubn Soc.

Sefer Harkim Chabad, Vol. 3. 646p. (HEB.). 20.00 (*0-8266-5103-8*) Kehot Pubn Soc.

Sefer Harkim Chabad, Vol. 4. 334p. (HEB.). 20.00 (*0-8266-5104-6*) Kehot Pubn Soc.

Sefer Harkim Chabad, Vol. 6. 279p. (HEB.). 20.00 (*0-8266-5106-2*) Kehot Pubn Soc.

Sefer Hashliches. Menachem M. Schneerson. 631p. (HEB.). 1991. 15.00 (*0-8266-5450-9*) Kehot Pubn Soc.

Sefer Hashluchim, Set. 1991. 160.00 (*0-8266-0391-2*) Kehot Pubn Soc.

***Sefer Hashluchim, 4 vols., Vol. 1.** (Illus.). 1991. 40.00 (*0-8266-0392-0*) Kehot Pubn Soc.

Sefer Hashluchim, Vol. 2. 1991. 40.00 (*0-8266-0393-9*) Kehot Pubn Soc.

Sefer Hashluchim, Vol. 3. 1991. 40.00 (*0-8266-0394-7*) Kehot Pubn Soc.

Sefer Hashluchim, Vol. 4. 1992. 40.00 (*0-8266-0395-5*) Kehot Pubn Soc.

Sefer Hasichos. Joseph I. Schneersohn. 315p. (HEB & YID.). reprint ed. 17.00 (*0-8266-5404-5*, 5680-7); reprint ed. 17.00 (*0-8266-5402-9*, 5703-5) Kehot Pubn Soc.

Sefer Hasichos, No. 574. Menachem M. Schneerson. Date not set. 14.00 (*0-614-10934-5*) Kehot Pubn Soc.

Sefer Hasichos, Vol. 1. Menachem M. Schneerson. 420p. (HEB.). 1990. 14.00 (*0-614-11042-4*, 5749) Kehot Pubn Soc.

Sefer Hasichos, Vol. 2. Menachem M. Schneerson. 475p. (HEB.). 1991. 14.00 (*0-8266-5764-8*, 5750) Kehot Pubn Soc.

***Sefer Hasichos: 5688-5691.** Joseph I. Schneersohn. LC 85-45949. 360p. (HEB.). 1995. 17.00 (*0-8266-5405-3*) Kehot Pubn Soc.

***Sefer Hasichos: 5749, Vol. 1.** Menachem M. Schneerson. 420p. (HEB.). 1990. 15.00 (*0-8266-5761-3*) Kehot Pubn Soc.

***Sefer Hasichos: 5752, Vol. 1.** Menachem M. Schneerson. LC 89-15266. 344p. (HEB.). 1993. 15.00 (*0-8266-5772-9*) Kehot Pubn Soc.

***Sefer Hasichos: 5752, Vol. 2.** Menachem M. Schneerson. LC 89-15226. 312p. (HEB.). 1993. 15.00 (*0-8266-5774-5*) Kehot Pubn Soc.

Sefer Hasichos Vol. 1. Menachem M. Schneerson. 383p. (HEB.). 1989. 14.00 (*0-8266-5756-7*, 5748) Kehot Pubn Soc.

Sefer Hasichos Vol. 1. Menachem M. Schneerson. 405p. (HEB.). 1991. 14.00 (*0-8266-5763-X*, 5750) Kehot Pubn Soc.

Sefer Hasichos Vol. 1. Menachem M. Schneerson. 455p. (HEB.). 1992. 14.00 (*0-8266-5770-2*, 5751) Kehot Pubn Soc.

Sefer Hasichos Vol. 1, Vol. 2. Menachem M. Schneerson. 414p. (HEB.). 1989. 17.00 (*0-8266-5757-5*) Kehot Pubn Soc.

Sefer Hasichos Vol. 2. Menachem M. Schneerson. 590p. (HEB.). 1992. 14.00 (*0-8266-5771-0*, 5751) Kehot Pubn Soc.

Sefer Hasichos Vol. 2. Menachem M. Schneerson. 465p. (HEB.). 1990. 15.00 (*0-8266-5762-1*, 5749) Kehot Pubn Soc.

***Sefer Hasichos 5746, Vol. 1.** Menachem M. Schneerson. LC 86-1532. 816p. (HEB.). 1986. 10.00 (*0-8266-1950-9*) Kehot Pubn Soc.

Sefer HaToda'ah see Book of Our Heritage

***Sefer Hazichronos: Memoirs of Rabbi Joseph I. Schneersohn.** 3rd ed. D. L. Mekler. LC 85-23288. (YID.). 1988. reprint ed. write for info. (*0-8266-5420-7*) Kehot Pubn Soc.

***Sefer Hazichronos: Memoirs of Rabbi Joseph I. Schneersohn, Vol. 1.** 3rd ed. D. L. Mekler. LC 85-23288. (YID.). 1988. reprint ed. 12.00 (*0-8266-5418-5*) Kehot Pubn Soc.

***Sefer Hazichronos: Memoirs of Rabbi Joseph I. Schneersohn, Vol. 2.** 3rd ed. D. L. Mekler. LC 85-23288. (YID.). 1988. reprint ed. 12.00 (*0-8266-5419-3*) Kehot Pubn Soc.

Sefer Hisichos. Joseph I. Schneersohn. 542p. (HEB & YID.). reprint ed. 17.00 (*0-8266-5401-0*, 5700) Kehot Pubn Soc.

***Sefer Kovetz Raza"sh.** Ed. by D. Lipskier et al. 270p. (HEB.). 1987. 12.00 (*0-8266-5428-2*) Kehot Pubn Soc.

Sefer lekarth tov: Perush le-megilat Ester, Tsfat, 1577. Yom-Tov B. Zahalon. 1978. 34.95 (*0-405-11952-6*) Ayer.

***Sefer Mafteach Inyonim Lesichos Kodesh: 5701-5724, Vol. 1.** Michael A. Zeligson. LC 94-32901. 676p. (HEB.). 1994. 25.00 (*0-8266-5324-3*) Kehot Pubn Soc.

***Sefer Siyumei Horambam.** (Illus.). 240p. (HEB.). 1989. 30.00 (*0-8266-0382-3*, Merkos LInyonei Chinuch) Kehot Pubn Soc.

Sefer Tesubah: Book on Repentance. Ed. by Moshe Lazar & Robert Dilligan. LC 93-85953. (Sephardic Classical Library). 304p. (LAD.). (C). 1993. text ed. 65.00 (*0-911437-62-2*) Labyrinthos.

***Sefer Thilim.** 224p. (HEB.). 1995. reprint ed. 5.00 (*0-8266-0280-0*) Kehot Pubn Soc.

***Sefer Tochen Kotzer Mesichos 5749.** Menachem M. Schneerson. 1102p. (HEB.). 1989. 10.00 (*0-8266-1975-4*) Kehot Pubn Soc.

***Sefer Tochen Kozer Mesichos 5750, 2 vols., Vol. 1.** Menachem M. Schneerson. 414p. (HEB.). 1990. 10.00 (*0-8266-1976-2*) Kehot Pubn Soc.

***Sefer Tohorat Mayim.** Nissan Telushkin. LC 90-4800. 390p. (HEB.). 1990. 15.00 (*0-8266-5429-0*) Kehot Pubn Soc.

Sefer Yehoshua. Ariel Asa. Ed. by Yaakov Fruchter. (Illus.). 88p. 1996. wbk. ed. 6.00 (*1-878895-17-6*, A375) Torah Umesorah.

Sefer Yetzirah. 1990. 26.00 (*0-924457-12-0*) Res Ctr Kabbalah.

Sefer Yetzirah: The Book of Creation. Tr. & Comment by Aryeh Kaplan. LC 94-49637. 416p. (ENG & HEB.). 1995. 30.00 (*1-56821-503-7*) Aronson.

***Sefer Yetzirah: The Book of Creation: In Theory & Practice.** Aryeh Kaplan. LC 96-49121. (Illus.). 448p. (ENG & HEB.). 1997. pap. 22.95 (*0-87728-855-0*) Weiser.

Sefirat Haomer see Mitzvah of the Month

Sefirot: Ten Emanations of Divine Power. Y. David Shulman. LC 96-33833. 280p. 1996. 30.00 (*1-56821-929-6*) Aronson.

SEG, 1983: Supplementum Epigraphicum Graecum. Ed. by H. W. Pleket & R. S. Stroud. xx, 532p. (C). 1986. 130.00 (*90-70265-57-5*, Pub. by Gieben NE) Benjamins North Am.

Sega Genesis & Sega CD Secrets, Vol. 5. Rusel DeMaria & Jeronimo Barrera. (Illus.). 416p. (Orig.). 1993. pap. 12.95 (*1-55958-379-7*) Prima Pub.

Sega Genesis Games Secrets, Vol. 2. Rusel DeMaria & Zach Meston. (Secrets of the Games Ser.). (Illus.). 288p. (Orig.). 1991. pap. 9.95 (*1-55958-125-5*) Prima Pub.

Sega Genesis Games Secrets Greatest Tips. 2nd ed. Gamepro Magazine Editors. (Illus.). 288p. (Orig.). 1994. pap. 12.95 (*1-55958-401-7*) Prima Pub.

Sega Genesis Games Secrets Greatest Tips: Over 1000 Tips, Strategies, Passwords, & Other Secrets. Gamepro Magazine Editors. (Secrets of the Games Ser.). (Illus.). 240p. (Orig.). 1992. pap. 9.99 (*1-55958-261-8*) Prima Pub.

Sega Genesis Secrets. Rusel DeMaria & Zach Meston. (Secrets of the Games Ser.: Vol. 3). (Illus.). 304p. (Orig.). 1992. pap. 9.99 (*1-55958-189-1*) Prima Pub.

Sega Genesis Secrets, Vol. 4. Andrew Eddy. (Illus.). 416p. (Orig.). 1993. pap. 12.99 (*1-55958-250-2*) Prima Pub.

Sega Genesis Secrets, Vol. 6. Rusel DeMaria. (Orig.). 1994. pap. 12.95 (*1-55958-453-X*) Prima Pub.

Sega Genesis Secrets: The Power User's Guide. Rusel DeMaria. (Secrets of the Games Ser.). 272p. (Orig.). 1990. pap. 9.95 (*1-55958-063-1*) Prima Pub.

Sega Saturn Game Secrets: The Unauthorized Edition. PCS Staff. 352p. 1996. per. 14.99 (*0-7615-0313-7*) Prima Pub.

***Sega Saturn Pocket Power Guide: Unauthorized.** PCS Staff. 128p. 1996. pap. 7.99 (*0-7615-0972-0*) Prima Pub.

***Sega Saturn Pocket Power Guide: Unauthorized, Vol. 2.** Prima Publishing Staff. 1997. pap. 7.99 (*0-7615-1122-9*) Prima Pub.

Segar a los Muertos. M. M. Huidobro. LC 79-51343. (Coleccion Caniqui). (Illus.). 82p. (Orig.). (SPA.). 1980. pap. 5.95 (*0-89729-227-8*) Ediciones.

***Segeu: Business Unit Strategy.** Eli Segeu. LC 97-9282. text ed. 55.00 (*0-471-97164-2*) Wiley.

Segmental Concrete MSE Walls, Geogrid Reinforcements, & Soil Nailing (TRR 1414) Ed. by Susan Brown. (Transportation Research Record Ser.). (Illus.). 80p. 1994. pap. text ed. 23.00 (*0-309-05562-8*) Natl Res Coun.

Segmental Functions, Text & Tables. rev. ed. C. K. Smoley. Ed. by E. R. Smoley & N. G. Smoley. 616p. 1974. 41.95 (*0-911390-04-9*, QA) Smoley.

Segmental Idiopathic Necrosis of the Femoral Head, Vol. 5. Ed. by U. H. Weil. (Progress in Orthopedic Surgery Ser.). (Illus.). 130p. 1981. 55.95 (*0-387-10718-5*) Spr-Verlag.

Segmental Motor System. Ed. by Marc D. Binder & Lorne M. Mendell. (Illus.). 416p. 1989. 68.00 (*0-19-505484-9*) OUP.

Segmentation & Positioning for Strategic Marketing Decisions. James H. Meyers. LC 96-16461. 1996. 49.95 (*0-87757-259-3*) Am Mktg.

Segmentation & Unionization: Working Class Stratification & the Demand for Unionization in the United States. Hyunhee Kim. LC 96-19558. (Garland Studies in the History of American Labor). 205p. 1997. text ed. 55.00 (*0-8153-2402-2*) Garland.

Segmented Box Girders for the High Level West Seattle Bridge. (PCI Journal Reprints Ser.). 17p. 1984. pap. 12.00 (*0-318-19810-X*, JR301) P-PCI.

Segmented Labor, Fractured Politics: Labor Politics in American Life. William H. Form. LC 95-21046. (Plenum Studies in Work & Industry). 379p. (C). 1995. 42.50 (*0-306-45031-3*, Plenum Pr) Plenum.

Segmenting the Mature Market: Identifying, Targeting & Reaching America's Diverse, Booming Senior Markets. Carol M. Morgan & Doran J. Levy. 300p. 1993. text ed. 32.50 (*1-55738-448-7*) Irwin Prof Pubng.

Segmenting the Mature Market: Identifying, Targeting, & Reaching America's Diverse, Booming, Senior Markets. Carol M. Morgan & Doran J. Levy. (Illus.). 363p. 1996. reprint ed. pap. 32.50 (*0-936889-41-1*) American Demo.

Segmenting the Women's Market: Using Niche Marketing to Understand & Meet the Divers Needs. E. Janice Leeming & Cynthia F. Tripp. 1994. text ed. 32.50 (*1-55738-561-0*) Irwin Prof Pubng.

Sego Dektria, La. 2nd ed. George Wagner. 24p. (ESP.). 1993. pap. 3.00 (*1-882251-02-4*) Eldonejo Bero.

Segonzac: Provence. Francois Fosca. (Rhythem & Color Two Ser.). 1970. 9.95 (*0-8288-9519-8*) Fr & Eur.

Segou: Les Murailles de Terre, 2 vols., 1. Maryse Conde. 1987. pap. 12.95 (*0-7859-3125-2*) Fr & Eur.

Segou: Les Murailles de Terre, 2 vols., 2. Maryse Conde. 1987. pap. 12.95 (*0-7859-3126-0*) Fr & Eur.

Segou, Vol. 3: La Terre en Mietes. Maryse Conde. (FRE.). 1987. pap. 16.95 (*0-7859-3137-6*) Fr & Eur.

Segovia-Ponce Letters. Andres Segovia. Ed. by Miguel Alcazar. Tr. by Peter Segal from SPA. LC 89-23764. 304p. (Orig.). 1989. pap. 29.00 (*0-936186-29-1*, RTFT-8) Edit Orphee.

***Segovia Technique.** Vladimir Bobri. (Illus.). 1997. 17.95 (*0-933224-41-9*, T038) Bold Strummer Ltd.

Segovia Technique. 2nd ed. Vladimir Bobri et al. (Illus.). 98p. 1990. reprint ed. pap. 17.95 (*0-933224-49-4*) Bold Strummer Ltd.

Segra & Stargull see Lost Prince

Segregated Sisterhood: Racism & the Politics of American Feminism. Nancie Caraway. LC 91-2528. 296p. (C). 1991. 42.50 (*0-87049-719-7*); pap. text ed. 19.95 (*0-87049-720-0*) U of Tenn Pr.

Segregated Skies: All-Black Combat Squadrons of World War II. Stanley Sandler. LC 91-39452. (History of Aviation Ser.). (Illus.). 240p. 1992. 24.95 (*1-56098-154-7*) Smithsonian.

Segregation: The Inner Conflict in the South. Robert Penn Warren. LC 94-7292. (Brown Thrasher Bks.). 88p. 1994. reprint ed. pap. 9.95 (*0-8203-1670-9*) U of Ga Pr.

Segregation & Apartheid in Twentieth Century South Africa. William Beinart & Saul Dubow. LC 94-36134. (Rewriting Histories Ser.). 256p. (C). (gr. 13). 1995. text ed. 62.95 (*0-415-10356-8*, B4358, Routledge NY) Routledge.

Segregation & Apartheid in Twentieth Century South Africa. Ed. by William Beinart & Saul Dubow. (Rewriting Histories Ser.). 256p. (C). 1995. pap. 17.95 (*0-415-10357-6*, B4362) Routledge.

Segregation & Desegregation, a Digest of Recent Research. Melvin M. Tumin. LC 74-73. 112p. 1975. reprint ed. text ed. 49.75 (*0-8371-7365-5*, TUSD, Greenwood Pr) Greenwood.

Segregation & Opportunity in the Region's Housing. 56p. 7.00 (*0-318-16386-1*, 104) Regional Plan Assn.

Segregation in Copper Alloys. University of Pittsburgh Staff. 91p. 1972. 13.65 (*0-317-34544-3*, 137) Intl Copper.

***Segregation in Federally Subsidized Low-Income Housing in the United States.** Modibo D. Coulibaly & Rodney Green. LC 97-23347. (Praeger Series in Political Economy). 1998. text ed. write for info. (*0-275-94820-X*, Praeger Pubs) Greenwood.

***Segregation, Poverty, & Morality in Urban African Americans.** Anthony P. Polednak. (Illus.). 192p. 1997. text ed. 39.95 (*0-19-511165-6*) OUP.

Segreto del Liocorno. Herge. (Illus.). 62p. (ITA.). (J). pap. 19.95 (*0-8288-5068-2*) Fr & Eur.

Segu. Maryse Conde. 508p. 1988. pap. 14.50 (*0-345-35306-4*, Ballantine Trade) Ballantine.

Segu. Maryse Conde. 512p. 1996. pap. 14.95 (*0-14-025949-X*) Viking Penguin.

Seguimiento de Cristo see Following Jesus

Seguiremos Siendo Amigos: Amber Brown Is Not a Crayon. Paula Danziger. 1995. pap. text ed. 9.95 (*84-204-4857-5*) Santillana.

Segun las Horas. Jorge Guillen. 49p. (SPA.). (C). 1962. 1.50 (*0-8477-3203-7*); pap. 1.25 (*0-8477-3204-5*) U of PR Pr.

Segunda Antologia Poetica. Juan R. Jimenez. 294p. (SPA.). 1983. 12.95 (*0-8288-7137-X*, 8423920062) Fr & Eur.

Segunda Antologia Poetica (1889-1918) Juan R. Jimenez. Ed. by Jorge Urrutia. (Nueva Austral Ser.: Vol. 243). (SPA.). 1991. pap. text ed. 19.95 (*84-239-7243-7*) Elliots Bks.

Segunda Epistola a los Corintos. Pablo Wickham. 320p. (SPA.). 1985. pap. 9.99 (*0-8254-1870-4*, Edit Portavoz) Kregel.

Segunda Epistola de Pablo a los Corintios. Charles Erdman. 143p. (SPA.). 1987. reprint ed. pap. 5.95 (*0-939125-23-4*) Evangelical Lit.

Segunda Hija. Olga Nolla. 94p. 1993. 11.95 (*0-8477-0176-X*) U of PR Pr.

***Segunda Parte de Lazarillo de Tormes, 1555.** Ed. by Manuel Ferrer-Chivite. xvi, 273p. 1993. 35.00 (*0-940639-94-7*) Hispanic Seminary.

Segundo. Jane Tilton & Lynn Tilton. 1994. pap. 7.95 (*0-88494-959-1*) Bookcraft Inc.

***Seguridad Siempre Llama dos Veces... Y los Orichas Tambien.** Ricardo Menendez. (SPA.). Date not set. pap. write for info. (*0-89729-817-9*) Ediciones.

Seguro Social En Venezuela. Gustavo Marguez. 56p. 1992. write for info. (*0-940602-54-7*) IADB.

Seguy's Decorative Butterflies & Insects in Full Color. E. A. Seguy. LC 77-83361. (Illus.). (Orig.). 1977. pap. 8.95 (*0-486-23552-1*) Dover.

***Segwagwanyana: Ein Beitung zur Afrikanischen Ethnoherpetologie.** Ronald D. Auerbach. 248p. (Orig.). (GER.). 1995. pap. 32.95 (*3-930612-00-3*, Pub. by Edition Chimaira GW) Bibliomania.

Sehen und Verstehen: Arbeit mit Filmen. Inge Schwerdtfeger. 192p. 1989. 26.95 (*3-468-49438-6*) Langenscheidt.

Sehende Liebe. Marcel Muller-Wieland. (Illus.). xiv, 230p. (GER.). 1992. write for info. (*3-487-09502-5*) G Olms Pubs.

Seher. Rene De Goscinny & M. Uderzo. (Illus.). (GER.). (J). 19.95 (*0-8288-5125-5*) Fr & Eur.

***Sehnsucht und Distanz: Theologische Aspekte in den Wortgebundenen Religiosen Kompositionen von Johannes Brahms.** Hanns C. Stekel. (Europaische Hochschulschriften Ser.: Reihe 23, Bd. 592). 316p. (GER.). 1997. 57.95 (*3-631-30416-1*) P Lang Pubng.

Sei Whale: Population Biology, Ecology & Management. J. W. Horwood. (Illus.). 400p. 1987. lib. bdg. 63.00 (*0-7099-4786-0*, Pub. by Croom Helm UK) Routledge Chapman & Hall.

Seianus His Fall. Ben Jonson. LC 76-25852. (English Experience Ser.: No. 265). 92p. 1970. reprint ed. 25.00 (*90-221-0265-3*) Walter J Johnson.

Seibei: A Study in Cultural Adaptation. Walter Goldschmidt. 250p. (C). 1987. pap. text ed. 13.50 (*0-03-008922-0*) HB Coll Pubs.

Seiberg-Witten Equations & Applications to the Topology of Smooth Four-Manifolds. John W. Morgan. LC 95-43748. (Mathematical Notes Ser.: Vol. 44). 130p. 1996. pap. text ed. 19.95 (*0-691-02597-5*) Princeton U Pr.

Seichu Gishi Den see Bushido of the 47 Samurai

Seidell's Solubilities: Inorganic & Metal-Organic Compounds, 2 vols. 4th ed. Ed. by William F. Linke. Incl. A-J. 1486p. 1958. 39.95 (*0-8412-0097-1*); K-Z. 1914p. 1966. 49.95 (*0-8412-0098-X*); write for info. (*0-318-50483-9*) Am Chemical.

Seidman's Legislative History of Excess Profit Tax Laws: 1917-1946. J. Seidman. 1959. 20.00 (*0-686-70813-X*) P-H.

Seidman's Legislative History of Federal Income & Excess Profits Tax Laws: 1939-1953, 2 vols. J. Seidman. 1959. 60.00 (*0-13-799742-6*) P-H.

Seidman's Legislative History of Federal Income Tax Laws: 1851-1938. J. Seidman. 30.00 (*0-13-799767-1*) P-H.

Seidmentation as a Three-Component System: Organic Carbon, Carbonate, Noncarbonate. Werner Ricken. LC 93-34945. (Lecture Notes in Earth Sciences Ser.: Vol. 51). 1993. 65.95 (*0-387-57386-0*) Spr-Verlag.

***Seif Bin Ziyazin: Desert Fox.** Denys Johnson-Davies. (Illus.). 64p. (Orig.). (J). (gr. 2-6). 1996. pap. 8.95 (*977-5325-40-4*, Pub. by Hoopoe Bks UA) AMIDEAST.

Seifert Fibered Spaces in Three-Manifolds. William H. Jaco & P. B. Shalen. LC 79-18160. (Memoirs Ser.: No. 21/220). 192p. 1991. reprint ed. pap. 19.00 (*0-8218-2220-9*, MEMO/21/220) Am Math.

Seiffener Spielzeug. H. Flade. 48p. 1992. pap. text ed. 12.00 (*3-364-00262-2*) Gordon & Breach.

Seig the Magnificent. Ann Gilbert. Ed. by Jan Martin. LC 93-74001. (Illus.). 110p. (Orig.). (YA). (gr. 6-12). 1994. pap. 13.75 (*0-944875-32-7*) Doral Pub.

***Seige of Gresham.** Ray Murphy. 1997. pap. text ed. 10.00 (*1-873176-05-8*) AK Pr Dist.

Seigneur Apprenez-Nous a Prier. Paul Claudel. 128p. (FRE.). 1943. 10.95 (*0-7859-1118-9*, 2070215083) Fr & Eur.

Seigneurial System in Early Canada: A Geographical Study. R. Cole Harris. 270p. (C). 1984. reprint ed. 49.95 (*0-7735-0431-1*, Pub. by McGill CN); reprint ed. pap. text ed. 24.95 (*0-7735-0434-6*, Pub. by McGill CN) U of Toronto Pr.

Seignorial Regime in Canada. Dorothy A. Heneker. LC 79-13329. 439p. 1980. reprint ed. lib. bdg. 49.50 (*0-87991-130-1*) Porcupine Pr.

***Seiji Ozawa.** LC 96-48640. (Contemporary Asian Americans Ser.). (J). 1997. lib. bdg. write for info. (*0-8172-3993-6*) Raintree Steck-V.

Seiji Ozawa: Symphony Conductor. Charnan Simon. LC 91-36741. (Picture-Story Biographies Ser.). (Illus.). 32p. (J). (gr. 2-5). 1992. lib. bdg. 17.50 (*0-516-04182-7*) Childrens.

Sein. Philip Roth. (FRE.). 1984. pap. 10.95 (*0-7859-4215-7*) Fr & Eur.

***Sein, Reflexion, Freiheit: Aspecte der Philosophie Johann Gottlieb Fichtes.** Christoph Asmuth. LC 97-1982. (Bochumer Studien zur Philosophie: Vol. 25). 309p. (GER.). 1997. lib. bdg. 89.00 (*90-6032-349-1*) Benjamins North Am.

Sein und Gnade: Die Ontologie in Karl Barths Kirchlicher Dogmatik. Wilfried Haerle. (Theologische Bibliothek Toepelmann Ser.: Vol. 27). 428p. (GER.). (C). 1975. 115.40 (*3-11-005706-9*) De Gruyter.

Sein und Sprache. Historische Grundlegung einer Ontologie der Sprache. T. Kobusch. (Studien zur Problemgeschichte der Antiken und Mittelalterlichen Philosophie: Vol. 11). 680p. 1987. 139.50 (*90-04-07562-3*) E J Brill.

Sein und Zeit. Martin Heidegger. (GER.). 1993. 45.95 (*3-484-70122-6*) Adlers Foreign Bks.

Seinfeld Aptitude Test: Hundreds of Spectacular Questions on Minute Details from TV's Greatest Show about Absolutely Nothing. Beth B. Golub. LC 94-20348. 1994. pap. 8.95 (*0-8065-1583-X*, Citadel Pr) Carol Pub Group.

"Seinfeld" Universe: An Unauthorized Fan's Eye View of the Entire Domain. Greg Gattuso. LC 95-48055. (Illus.). 160p. 1996. pap. 9.95 (*0-8065-1744-1*, Citadel Pr) Carol Pub Group.

Seining the Air for Sparrows. Cecil J. Mullins. LC 88-31434. (Illus.). 52p. (Orig.). 1988. pap. 5.95 (*0-936015-15-2*) Pocahontas Pr.

SeinLanguage. Jerry Seinfeld. 192p. 1993. 19.95 (*0-553-09606-0*) Bantam.

SeinLanguage. Jerry Seinfeld. 160p. 1995. mass mkt. 5.99 (*0-553-56915-5*) Bantam.

Seinswahrheit und Lebenswirklichkeit see Platon

Seinte Marherete. Ed. by Frances Mack. (EETS, OS Ser.: Vol. 193). 1974. reprint ed. 40.00 (*0-8115-3381-6*) Periodicals Srv.

Seis Actitudes para Vencer. Norman Vincent Peale. (SPA.). 1989. pap. 2.49 (*1-56063-001-9*, 498050) Editorial Unilit.

Seis Aproximaciones a la Poesia de Sergio Manejias. Orlando Gomez-Gil. LC 91-65816. 112p. 1991. 12.00 (*0-89729-610-9*) Ediciones.

Seis Cachorros RevoHosos. (SPA.). 1995. pap. 2.98 (*1-85854-315-0*) Brimax Bks.

***Seis Chaves para Recrutar, Orientar e Envolver Membros Do Conselho Diretor de Organizacoes Sem Fins Lucrativos.** Judith G. Nelson. 61p. (Orig.). (POR.). 1996. pap. write for info. (*0-925299-64-2*) Natl Ctr Nonprofit.

Seis Deseos de la Jirafa (Big Book) Alma F. Ada. (Rimas y Risas Green Ser.). (Illus.). 16p. (Orig.). (SPA.). (J). (gr. k-3). 1988. pap. text ed. 29.95 (*0-917837-02-9*) Hampton-Brown.

Seis Deseos de la Jirafa (Small Book) Alma F. Ada. (Rimas y Risas Green Ser.). (Illus.). 16p. (Orig.). (SPA.). (J). (gr. k-3). 1992. pap. text ed. 6.00 (*1-56334-078-X*) Hampton-Brown.

Seis Dias de Noviembre: El Fusilamiento de los Estudiantes de Medicina. Byron Miguel. LC 90-84963. (Coleccion Cuba y Sus Jueces). (Illus.). 96p. (Orig.). (SPA.). 1990. pap. 9.95 (*0-89729-586-2*) Ediciones.

Seis Dias y un Dia. Marvin Byers. (Orig.). 1996. pap. 11.95 (*0-9647871-1-3*, Hope of Israel) Hebron Minist.

Seis Grandes Errores de Marti. Daniel Roman. LC 93-70879. (Coleccion Cuba y Sus Jueces). 181p. (Orig.). (SPA.). 1993. pap. 18.00 (*0-89729-679-6*) Ediciones.

Seismic Activity in Western Europe: With Particular Consideration to the Liege Earthquake of November 8, 1983. Ed. by Paul Melchior. 1984. lib. bdg. 171.00 (*90-277-1889-X*) Kluwer Ac.

Seismic Analysis of Power Plant Systems & Components. Ed. by C. Lin & M. K. Au-Yang. (PVP Ser.: Vol. 73). 200p. 1983. pap. text ed. 12.00 (*0-317-02647-X*, H00259) ASME.

Seismic Analysis of the Duval County Ranch Area, South Texas: Assessment of Exploration Potential in the Wilcox, Queen City & Jackson-Yegua Plays. J. C. Fiduk & D. S. Hamilton. (Geological Circular Ser.: No. 95-4). (Illus.). 43p. (Orig.). 1995. pap. 8.00 (*0-614-11617-1*) Bur Econ Geology.

Seismic & Acoustic Velocities in Reservoir Rocks, Vol. 1: Experimental Studies. Ed. by Amos Nur & Zhijing Wang. (Geophysics Reprint Ser.: No. 10). 420p. (Orig.). 1989. pap. 45.00 (*0-931830-70-2*, 470) Soc Expl Geophys.

Seismic & Acoustic Velocities in Reservoir Rocks, Vol. 2: Theoretical & Model Studies. Ed. by Zhijing Wang & Amos Nur. 450p. 1992. pap. 80.00 (*1-56080-056-9*, 475) Soc Expl Geophys.

***Seismic & Dynamic Analysis & Design Considerations for High Level Nuclear Waste Repositories.** J. Carl Stepp & Structural Engineering Institute Staff. LC 96-47913. 1996. write for info. (*0-7844-0215-9*) Am Soc Civil Eng.

Seismic & Wind Loads in Architectural Design. 2nd ed. Stanley W. Crawley & Delbert B. Ward. 308p. pap. 50.00 (*1-55835-030-6*) AIA Press.

***Seismic Anisotropy.** Ed. by Erling Fjoer et al. (Illus.). 763p. (Orig.). 1997. pap. text ed. 72.00 (*0-614-30646-9*, 762) Soc Expl Geophys.

Seismic Anisotropy in the Earth. V. Babuska & M. Cara. (C). 1991. lib. bdg. 88.50 (*0-7923-1321-6*) Kluwer Ac.

Seismic Applications of Acoustic Reciprocity. J. T. Fokkema & P. M. Van Den Berg. LC 92-44403. 350p. 1993. 176.00 (*0-444-89044-0*) Elsevier.

***Seismic Coal Exploration.** Anton Ziolkowski. (Handbook of Geophysical Exploration: Vol. 16). 1995. write for info. (*0-08-037222-8*, Pergamon Pr) Elsevier.

Seismic Coal Exploration, Part B: In-Seam Seismics. L. Dresen & Horst Ruter. (Handbook of Geophysical Exploration Ser.: Vol. 16). 446p. 1994. 145.25 (*0-08-037226-0*) Elsevier.

Seismic Data Processing. Les Hatton et al. 1986. pap. 65.00 (*0-632-01374-5*) Blackwell Sci.

Seismic Data Processing. Ozdogan Yilmaz. (Investigations in Geophysics Ser.: No. 2). (Illus.). 536p. 1987. reprint ed. 81.00 (*0-931830-40-0*, 442) Soc Expl Geophys.

Seismic Data Processing & Interpretation: A Bibliography, Vol. 1. G. N. Tripathi. 1983p. (C). 1981. 60.00 (*0-685-21815-5*, Pub. by Intl Bk Distr II) St Mut.

Seismic Data Processing & Interpretation: A Bibliography, 1975-1980, Vol. 1. G. N. Tripathi. (C). 1983. text ed. 70.00 (*0-89771-671-X*, Pub. by Intl Bk Distr II) St Mut.

Seismic Design & Construction of Complex Civil Engineering Systems. Ed. by Michael A. Cassaro & James D. Cooper. 112p. 1988. 19.00 (*0-87262-678-4*) Am Soc Civil Eng.

Seismic Design & Qualification for Nuclear Power Plants: A Safety Guide. (Safety Ser.: No. 50-SG-Di5). 77p. 1992. pap. 35.00 (*92-0-103592-6*, STI/PUB/917, Pub. by IAEA AU) Bernan Associates.

Seismic Design & Retrofit of Bridges. M. J. Priestley et al. LC 95-35406. (Illus.). 500p. 1996. text ed. 84.95 (*0-471-57998-X*) Wiley.

Seismic Design Codes & Procedures. Glen V. Berg. 140p. 1983. 25.00 (*0-943198-25-9*) Earthquake Eng.

Seismic Design Criteria for Multistory Precast Prestressed Buildings. (PCI Journal Reprints Ser.). 27p. 1979. pap. 14.00 (*0-686-40115-8*, JR207) P-PCI.

Seismic Design Fast, Set 3. 2nd ed. Theodore Zsutty. (Engineering Reference Manual Ser.). 88p. 1993. audio 54.95 (*0-912045-59-0*) Prof Pubns CA.

Seismic Design for Buildings: A Manual, 2 vols. 1995. lib. bdg. 600.99 (*0-8490-8371-0*) Gordon Pr.

Seismic Design Fundamentals: Civil License Examination. Frank Talania. (Illus.). 200p. 1995. pap. 23.50 (*0-929176-18-9*) Burdick & Landreth Co.

Seismic Design Guide for Natural Gas Distributors. Ed. by Peter W. McDonough. (Monograph Ser.: No. 9). 104p. 1995. 24.00 (*0-7844-0105-5*) Am Soc Civil Eng.

***Seismic Design Handbook.** Ed. by Farzad Naeim. (Illus.). 450p. (C). (gr. 13 up). 1989. text ed. 102.95 (*0-412-07891-0*) Chapman & Hall.

Seismic Design Handbook. Ed. by Farzed Naeim. (Illus.). 576p. 1989. text ed. 95.00 (*0-442-26922-6*) Chapman & Hall.

Seismic Design of Building Structures: A Professional's Introduction to Earthquake Forces & Design Details. 7th ed. Michael R. Lindeburg. LC 96-11575. 208p. 1996. pap. 26.95 (*0-912045-91-4*) Prof Pubns CA.

Seismic Design of Buildings. James E. Ambrose & Dimitry Vergun. LC 90-26564. 304p. (C). 1993. reprint ed. lib. bdg. 48.50 (*0-89464-583-8*) Krieger.

Seismic Design of Buildings & Structures. Alan Williams. (Illus.). 437p. (C). 1995. 41.50 (*0-910554-04-8*, 048) Engineering.

Seismic Design of Concrete Structures: Part I--The CEB Model Code for the Seismic Design of Concrete Structures & Part II--Numerical Applications & Trial Calculations. Comite Euro-International du Beton (C. E. B.) Staff. 300p. 1987. text ed. 114.50 (*0-291-39737-9*, Pub. by Gower UK) Ashgate Pub Co.

Seismic Design of Frame-Panel Buildings & Their Structural Members. M. A. Mardzhanishvili. Tr. by K. S. Dhillon from RUS. 131p. (C). 1984. text ed. 90.00 (*90-6191-424-8*, Pub. by A A Balkema NE) Ashgate Pub Co.

Seismic Design of Reinforced Concrete & Masonry Buildings. Tom Paulay & M. J. Priestley. LC 91-34862. 768p. 1992. text ed. 110.00 (*0-471-54915-0*) Wiley.

Seismic Design of Timber Building Structures. Frank Talania. (Illus.). 280p. 1995. pap. 32.95 (*0-929176-17-0*) Burdick & Landreth Co.

Seismic Design of 24-Story Building with Precast Elements. (PCI Journal Reprints Ser.). 17p. 1972. pap. 12.00 (*0-686-40047-X*, JR117) P-PCI.

Seismic Design Problems & Solutions: For the Civil Engineering License Examination. Frank Talania. Ed. by Frank Landreth. LC 93-73751. (Illus.). 200p. 1993. pap. 25.00 (*0-929176-11-1*) Burdick & Landreth Co.

Seismic Design Review Manual: For Civil Engineering License Examination. 2nd ed. Franquintin Talania. Ed. by Frank Landreth. LC 93-73309. (Illus.). 320p. 1993. pap. 35.00 (*0-929176-10-3*) Burdick & Landreth Co.

Seismic Design Technology for Breeder Reactor Structures: Special Topics in Earthquake Ground Motion, Vol. 1. Ed. by D. P. Reddy. LC 83-50358. 277p. 1983. pap. 36.50 (*0-87079-542-2*, DOE/SF/01011-T25, VOL. 1, DE84004808); fiche 9.00 (*0-87079-543-0*, DOE/SF/01011-T25, VOL. 1, DE84004808) DOE.

Seismic Design Technology for Breeder Reactor Structures: Special Topics in Piping & Equipment, Vol. 4. Ed. by D. P. Reddy. 215p. 1983. pap. 36.50 (*0-87079-548-1*, DOE/SF/01011-T25, VOL. 4, DE84004811); fiche 9.00 (*0-87079-549-X*, DOE/SF/01011-T25, VOL. 4, DE84004811) DOE.

Seismic Design Technology for Breeder Reactor Structures: Special Topics in Reactor Structures, Vol. 3. Ed. by D. P. Reddy. 167p. 1983. pap. 36.50 (*0-87079-546-5*, DOE/SF/01011-T25, VOL. 3, DE84004810); fiche 9.00 (*0-87079-547-3*, DOE/SF/01011-T25, VOL. 3, DE84004810) DOE.

Seismic Design Technology for Breeder Reactor Structures: Special Topics in Soil Structure Interaction Analyses, Vol. 2. Ed. by D. P. Reddy. LC 83-50358. 134p. 1983. pap. 27.00 (*0-87079-544-9*, DOE/SF/01011-T25, VOL. 2, DE84004309); fiche 9.00 (*0-87079-545-7*, DOE/SF/01011-T25, VOL. 2, DE84004309) DOE.

Seismic Effects of Blasting in Rock. A. A. Kuzmenko et al. Tr. by S. Shridhar from RUS. (Russian Translation Ser.: Vol. 103). (Illus.). 177p. (ENG.). 1993. text ed. 70.00 (*90-5410-214-4*, Pub. by A A Balkema NE) Ashgate Pub Co.

Seismic Effects on Structures. E. Juhasova. (Developments in Geotechnical Engineering Ser.: Vol. 67). 1991. 177.50 (*0-444-98743-6*, DGE 67) Elsevier.

***Seismic Engineering.** Ed. by M. A. Saleem & M. L. Aggarwal. 365p. 1996. pap. text ed. 120.00 (*0-7918-1787-3*, TS283) ASME Pr.

Seismic Engineering - 1993, Vol. 1. Ed. by Y. K. Tang. (PVP Ser.: Vol. 256-1). 300p. 1993. 60.00 (*0-7918-0983-8*, H0815A) ASME.

Seismic Engineering - 1993, Vol. 2. Ed. by Y. K. Tang. 244p. 1993. 55.00 (*0-685-71175-7*, H0815B) ASME.

Seismic Engineering - 1995. Ed. by D. C. Ma et al. LC 88-71134. (Proceedings of the 1995 ASME/JSME Pressure Vessels & Piping Conference Ser.: PVP-Vol. 312). 472p. 1995. 140.00 (*0-7918-1343-6*, H00975) ASME.

Seismic Engineering 1994: Proceedings of the Pressure Vessels & Piping Conference, 2 vol. Ed. by S. L. MacCabe. LC 88-71134. (PVP Ser.: Vol. 275-1,275-2). 382p. 1994. pap. 115.00 (*0-7918-1198-0*) ASME.

Seismic Evaluation of Existing Buildings: Supporting Documentation. 160p. (Orig.). (C). 1993. pap. text ed. 35.00 (*1-56806-992-8*) DIANE Pub.

Seismic Evaluation of Lifeline System - Case Studies. Ed. by Leon R. L. Wang & Robert V. Whitman. (Sessions Proceedings Ser.). 88p. 1986. 13.00 (*0-87262-563-X*) Am Soc Civil Eng.

Seismic Experience Data-Nuclear & Other Plants: Proceedings of a Session Sponsored by the Structural Division. Ed. by Yogindra N. Anand. 85p. 1985. 14.00 (*0-87262-501-X*) Am Soc Civil Eng.

Seismic Exploration Fundamentals. 2nd ed. J. A. Coffeen. 360p. 1986. 79.95 (*0-87814-295-9*) PennWell Bks.

Seismic Expression of Structural Styles: A Picture & Work Atlas, Vol. 3. Ed. by A. W. Bally. (Studies in Geology: No. 15). (Illus.). ix, 388p. 1996. ring bd. 44.00 (*0-614-00768-2*) Fodors Travel.

Seismic Facies & Sedimentary Processes of Submarine Fans & Turbidite Systems. Ed. by P. Weimer et al. (Frontiers in Sedimentary Geology Ser.). (Illus.). 456p. 1991. 130.95 (*0-387-97469-5*) Spr-Verlag.

Seismic Filtering. Ed. by R. Van Nostrand. Tr. by Nathan Rothenburg. 235p. 1971. 12.00 (*0-931830-04-4*, 522) Soc Expl Geophys.

Seismic Hazard in Mediterranean Regions. Ed. by J. Bonnin et al. (C). 1988. lib. bdg. 175.00 (*90-277-2779-1*) Kluwer Ac.

Seismic Images of Modern Convergent Margin Tectonic Structure. Ed. by Roland E. Von Huene. LC 86-20551. (AAPG Studies in Geology: No. 26). (Illus.). 62p. 1986. reprint ed. pap. 25.00 (*0-7837-1743-1*, 2057276) Bks Demand.

Seismic Instrumentation. M. Pieuchot. (Handbook of Geophysical Exploration Ser.). 375p. 1984. 129.25 (*0-08-036944-8*, Pergamon Pr) Elsevier.

Seismic Interpretation. Nigel A. Anstey. 563p. 1988. text ed. 58.67 (*0-13-799792-2*) P-H.

Seismic Interpretation: The Physical Aspects. Nigel A. Anstey. LC 77-86312. (Illus.). 625p. 1977. text ed. 31.00 (*0-934634-01-7*); pap. text ed. 18.00 (*0-934634-18-1*) Intl Human Res.

Seismic Interpretation Series, Vol. 1. 70p. (Orig.). 1989. pap. 19.00 (*0-931830-92-3*, 581) Soc Expl Geophys.

Seismic Loss Estimates for a Hypothetical Water System: A Demonstration Project. Ed. by Craig E. Taylor. LC 91-25815. (Technical Council on Lifeline Earthquake Engineering, Monographs: No. 2). 160p. 1991. pap. text ed. 17.00 (*0-87262-843-4*) Am Soc Civil Eng.

Seismic Methods. Michel Lavergne. (C). 1989. lib. bdg. 116.50 (*1-85333-224-0*, Pub. by Graham & Trotman UK) Kluwer Ac.

Seismic Methods. Michel Lavergne. (Illus.). 192p. (C). 1989. 375.00 (*2-7108-0552-9*, Pub. by Edits Technip FR) St Mut.

Seismic Migration: Imaging of Acoustic Energy by Wave Field Extrapolation, Part A: Theoretical Aspects. A. J. Berkhout. (Developments in Solid Earth Geophysics Ser.: No. 14A). 446p. 1985. 85.00 (*0-444-42547-0*) Elsevier.

Seismic Migration Vol. 5: Theory & Practice. R. H. Stolt. (Handbook of Geophysical Exploration Ser.). 1986. 178.00 (*0-946631-05-0*, Pub. by Pergamon Repr UK) Franklin.

Seismic Modal Analysis & System Interaction. Ed. by C. W. Lin. (PVP Ser.: Vol. 249). 156p. 1993. 45.00 (*0-7918-0976-5*, H00808) ASME.

Seismic Modeling of Geologic Structures. Ed. by Stuart W. Fagin. (Geophysical Developments Ser.: No. 2). (Illus.). 288p. (C). 1991. text ed. 58.00 (*1-56080-050-X*, 452) Soc Expl Geophys.

Seismic Modelling & Pattern Recognition in Oil Exploration. Amita Sinvhal & Harsha Sinvhal. (C). 1992. lib. bdg. 141.50 (*0-7923-1487-5*) Kluwer Ac.

Seismic Models of Sandstone Stratigraphic Traps in Rocky Mountain Basins. Robert T. Ryder et al. LC 81-52315. (Methods in Exploration Ser.). 124p. reprint ed. pap. 35.40 (*0-7837-3972-9*, 2043801) Bks Demand.

***Seismic Monitoring in Mines.** Ed. by Mendecki. 256p. 1997. text ed. write for info. (*0-412-75300-6*, Chap & Hall NY) Chapman & Hall.

An Asterisk (*) at the beginning of an entry indicates that the title is appearing in BIP for the first time.

Seismic Noise Attenuation. Ernest R. Kanasewich & K. Helbig. (Handbook of Geophysical Exploration Ser.: Vol. 7). 244p. 1990. 114.00 (*0-08-037219-8*, Pub. by Pergamon Repr UK) Franklin.

Seismic on Screen: An Introduction to Interactive Interpretation. James A. Coffeen. 306p. 1990. 25.00 (*0-87814-364-5*) PennWell Bks.

Seismic Pavement Analyzer Operations Manual with Technical Specifications. Mark R. Baker et al. 61p. (Orig.). (C). 1993. pap. text ed. 10.00 (*0-309-05752-3*, SHRP-H-374) SHRP.

Seismic Performance of Low Rise Buildings: State-of-the-Art & Research Needs. Ed. by Ajaya K. Gupta & A. K. Gupta. LC 81-6930. 221p. 1981. pap. 23.00 (*0-87262-283-5*) Am Soc Civil Eng.

Seismic Physical Modeling. Ed. by Daniel A. Ebrom & John A. McDonald. LC 94-34763. (Geophysics Reprint Ser.: No. 15). 519p. 1994. pap. 98.00 (*1-56080-072-0*, 476) Soc Expl Geophys.

Seismic Pressure of Water on Hydraulic Structures. 2nd rev. ed. Ed. by S. G. Shul'man. Tr. by C. Natarajan from RUS. 197p. (C). 1987. text ed. 90.00 (*90-6191-480-9*, Pub. by A A Balkema NE) Ashgate Pub Co.

***Seismic Principles Practice Exams for the California Special Civil Engineer Examination.** Majid Baradar. LC 97-12536. 88p. (Orig.). 1997. pap. 19.95 (*1-888577-10-X*) Prof Pubns CA.

Seismic Prospecting for Oil. Dix. 422p. 1988. text ed. 54. 20 (*0-13-799800-7*) P-H.

Seismic Prospecting for Sedimentary Formations. G. N. Gogonenkov. (Russian Translation Ser.: No. 76). 228p. (C). 1990. text ed. 85.00 (*90-6191-930-4*, Pub. by A A Balkema NE) Ashgate Pub Co.

Seismic Prospecting Instruments: Instrument Performance & Testing, Vol. 2. 2nd enl. ed. B. S. Evenden & M. Pieuchot. (Geoexploration Monographs: No. 3). (Illus.). 158p. 1984. text ed. 48.00 (*3-443-13014-3*) Lubrecht & Cramer.

Seismic Prospecting Instruments Vol. 1: Signal Characteristics & Instrument Specifications. 2nd ed. Nigel A. Anstey. (Geoexploration Monographs: No. 3). (Illus.). 154p. 1981. lib. bdg. 40.00 (*3-443-13303-7*) Lubrecht & Cramer.

***Seismic Protection.** Richard K. Miller et al. (Market Research Survey Ser.: No. 234). 50p. 1996. 200.00 (*1-55865-265-5*) Future Tech Surveys.

Seismic Provisions for Structural Steel - Load & Resistance Factor Design. 1992. 10.00 (*1-56424-039-8*, S341) Am Inst Steel Construct.

Seismic Reflection Interpretation. 2nd rev. ed. M. K. Jenyon & A. A. Fitch. (Geoexploration Monographs: Ser. 1, No. 8). (Illus.). 318p. 1985. lib. bdg. 68.95 (*3-443-13015-1*) Lubrecht & Cramer.

Seismic Reflection Profiles in the Western Pacific, 1965-74. Sadanori Murauchi & Toshioo Asanuma. LC 80-499022. 232p. 1977. reprint ed. pap. 66.20 (*0-608-01250-5*, 2061938) Bks Demand.

Seismic Rehabilitation of Buildings-Phase 1: Issues Identification & Resolution. 150p. (Orig.). (C). 1993. pap. text ed. 35.00 (*1-56806-994-4*) DIANE Pub.

Seismic Response Analysis of Nuclear Power Plant Systems. Ed. by Folker H. Wittmann. (Structural Mechanics in Reactor Technology Ser.: Vol. K1). 608p. (C). 1987. text ed. 130.00 (*90-6191-771-9*, Pub. by A A Balkema NE) Ashgate Pub Co.

Seismic Response Analysis of Nuclear Power Plant Systems. Ed. by Folker H. Wittmann. (Structural Mechanics in Reactor Technology Ser.: Vol. K2). 670p. (C). 1987. text ed. 130.00 (*90-6191-772-7*, Pub. by A A Balkema NE) Ashgate Pub Co.

Seismic Response of Buried Pipes & Structural Components. ASCE Committee on Seismic Analysis. 58p. 1983. pap. 13.00 (*0-87262-368-8*) Am Soc Civil Eng.

***Seismic Risk in the San Diego Region: Special Focus on the Rose Canyon Fault Systems: Workshop Proceedings.** Ed. by Glenn Roquemore. (Illus.). 99p. (C). 1997. reprint ed. pap. text ed. 45.00 (*0-7881-4262-3*) DIANE Pub.

Seismic Risk Management for Countries of the Asia Pacific Region: Proceedings of the WSSI Workshop. Ed. by K. Megurd & T. Katayama. (Illus.). 192p. (Orig.). (C). 1995. pap. text ed. 45.00 (*0-7881-2588-5*) DIANE Pub.

Seismic Safety Standards for Library Shelving: Manual of Recommended Practice - California State Library. John A. Shelton. 45p. 1990. pap. text ed. 10.00 (*0-929722-39-6*) CA State Library Fndtn.

Seismic Sequence Stratigraphy. P. K. Trabant. 1996. 59.00 (*3-540-60490-1*) Spr-Verlag.

Seismic Shear Waves Vol. 15, Pt. A: Theory. G. Dohr & K. Helbig. (Handbook of Geophysical Exploration Ser.). 1985. 166.00 (*0-946631-15-8*, Pub. by Pergamon Repr UK) Franklin.

Seismic Shear Waves Vol. 15, Pt. B: Applications. G. Dohr & K. Helbig. (Handbook of Geophysical Exploration Ser.). 1985. 131.00 (*0-946631-29-8*, Pub. by Pergamon Repr UK) Franklin.

Seismic, Shock, & Vibration Isolation. Ed. by G. C. Mok et al. (Proceedings of the 1995 ASME/JSME Pressure Vessels & Piping Conference Ser.: PVP-Vol. 319). 332p. 1995. 130.00 (*0-7918-1325-8*, H00957) ASME.

***Seismic, Shock & Vibration Isolation, 1996.** Ed. by H. H. Chung & M. A. Saleem. 139p. 1996. pap. 70.00 (*0-7918-1788-1*) ASME Pr.

***Seismic Source Signature Estimation & Measurement.** Ed. by Osman M. Osman & Enders A. Robinson. LC 96-38275. (Geophysics Reprints Ser.: Vol. 18). (Illus.). 742p. (Orig.). 1996. pap. text ed. 84.00 (*1-56080-040-2*, 479) Soc Expl Geophys.

Seismic Stratigraphy. B. A. Hardage. (Handbook of Geophysical Exploration Ser.). 428p. 1985. 129.25 (*0-08-036953-7*, Pergamon Pr) Elsevier.

Seismic Stratigraphy. Robert E. Sheriff. LC 80-83974. (Illus.). 227p. 1980. text ed. 32.00 (*0-934634-08-4*) Intl Human Res.

***Seismic Stratigraphy: Applications to Hydrocarbon Exploration.** Ed. by Charles E. Payton. LC 77-91023. (American Association of Petroleum Geologists. Memoir Ser.: No. 26). (Illus.). 523p. 1977. reprint ed. pap. 149.10 (*0-608-02951-3*, 2063416) Bks Demand.

***Seismic Stratigraphy No. II: An Integrated Approach to Hydrocarbon Exploration.** Ed. by Orville R. Berg & Donald G. Woolverton. LC 85-18652. (American Association of Petroleum Geologists. Memoir Ser.: No. 39). (Illus.). 422p. 1985. reprint ed. pap. 120.30 (*0-608-02744-8*, 2063409) Bks Demand.

Seismic Stratigraphy & Hydrocarbon Traps: Louisiana Offshore & Onshore. Allen Lowrie. LC 94-35381. (Course Notes Ser.). 224p. 1994. 30.00 (*1-56080-025-9*, 460) Soc Expl Geophys.

Seismic Surface Waves in a Laterally Inhomogeneous Earth. Ed. by V. I. Keilis-Borok. (C). 1989. lib. bdg. 171.50 (*0-7923-0044-0*) Kluwer Ac.

Seismic Tomography. Stewart. (Handbook of Geophysical Exploration Ser.). Date not set. write for info. (*0-08-037242-2*, Pergamon Pr) Elsevier.

***Seismic Tomography: Theory And Practice.** Ed. by H. M. Iyer & K. Hirahara. (Illus.). 864p. (C). (gr. 13 up). 1993. text ed. 275.95 (*0-412-37190-1*) Chapman & Hall.

Seismic Tomography: With Applications in Global Seismology & Exploration Geophysics. Ed. by Guust Nolet. (C). 1987. lib. bdg. 156.50 (*90-277-2521-7*) Kluwer Ac.

***Seismic Tomography& Mantle Circulation.** 151p. 1990. text ed. 80.00 (*0-521-38575-X*) Cambridge U Pr.

Seismic Traveltime Inversion. S. V. Goldin. Ed. by Peter Hubral. Tr. by Alfred J. Hermont from RUS. (Investigations in Geophysics Ser.: No. 1). (Illus.). 378p. 1986. text ed. 89.00 (*0-931830-38-9*, 441) Soc Expl Geophys.

Seismic Velocity Analysis. Diebold. (Handbook of Geophysical Exploration Ser.). Date not set. write for info. (*0-08-037218-X*, Pergamon Pr) Elsevier.

Seismic Velocity & the Convolutional Model. Robinson. 290p. 1988. text ed. 55.00 (*0-13-799826-0*) P-H.

Seismic Verification of Nuclear Testing Treaties. 1991. lib. bdg. 75.95 (*0-8490-4921-0*) Gordon Pr.

***Seismic Vulnerability & Impact of Disruption of Lifelines in the Conterminous U. S.** Charles Scawthorn et al. (Illus.). 439p. (C). 1996. reprint ed. pap. 75.00 (*0-7881-3419-1*) DIANE Pub.

Seismic Wave Attenuation. Ed. by D. H. Johnston & Nafi M. Toksoz. LC 81-50381. (Geophysics Reprint Ser.: No. 2). (Illus.). 465p. 1981. pap. 20.00 (*0-931830-16-8*, 462) Soc Expl Geophys.

Seismic Wave Propagation in the Earth. Ed. by A. Hanyga. (Physics & Evolution of the Earth's Interior Ser.: Vol. 2). 488p. 1985. 214.50 (*0-444-99611-7*) Elsevier.

Seismic Wavefield Sampling. G. J. Vermeer. (Geophysical References Ser.: No. 4). 120p. 1990. text ed. 61.00 (*1-56080-010-0*, 434) Soc Expl Geophys.

Seismic Waves & Sources. A. Ben-Menahem & S. Singh. (Illus.). 1000p. 1981. 215.95 (*0-387-90506-5*) Spr-Verlag.

***Seismic Waves in Laterally Inhomogeneous Media.** I. Psencik et al. LC 96-48399. (Pageoph Topical Ser.). 1996. write for info. (*0-8176-5648-0*) Birkhauser.

***Seismic Waves in Laterally Inhomogeneous Media, Pt. I.** Vlastislav Cerveny et al. LC 96-48399. (Pageoph Topical Volumes Ser.: Vol. 148, Nos. 1 & 2, 1996). 342p. 1997. pap. 34.50 (*3-7643-5648-0*) Birkhauser.

***Seismic Waves in Laterally Inhomogeneous Media, Pt. II.** I. Psencik et al. (Pageoph Topical Volumes Ser.: Vol. 148, Nos. 3 & 4, 1996). 370p. 1996. pap. 34.50 (*3-7643-5651-0*) Birkhauser.

Seismic Well Surveying. Jean-Luc Mari & Francoise Coppens. 128p. (C). 1991. 255.00 (*2-7108-0605-3*, Pub. by Edits Technip FR) St Mut.

Seismicity in Mines. S. J. Gibowicz. 404p. 1989. 34.50 (*0-8176-2273-X*) Birkhauser.

Seismicity of Egypt, Arabia & the Red Sea: A Historical Review. N. N. Ambraseys et al. (Illus.). 320p. (C). 1995. text ed. 100.00 (*0-521-39120-2*) Cambridge U Pr.

Seismicity of the European Area, Pt. 1. V. Karnik. 364p. 1971. lib. bdg. 126.00 (*90-277-0121-0*) Kluwer Ac.

Seismicity of the European Area, Pt. 2. V. Karnik. LC 78-468652. (Illus.). 218p. 1971. lib. bdg. 152.00 (*90-277-0179-2*) Kluwer Ac.

Seismicity of the United States, 1568-1989. C. W. Stover & J. L. Coffman. (Illus.). 418p. (Orig.). (C). 1994. pap. text ed. 75.00 (*0-7881-0353-9*) DIANE Pub.

Seismo & Ellie. 2nd ed. Pat Foley. (Illus.). 14p. (J). (gr. k-1). 1990. reprint ed. pap. 6.00 (*0-9624315-1-6*) Pajari Pr.

Seismological Algorithms: Computational Methods & Computer Programs. Ed. by Durk J. Doornbos. 469p. 1988. text ed. 131.00 (*0-12-220770-X*) Acad Pr.

***Seismological Research Requirement for a Comprehensive Test-Ban Monitoring System.** 94p. 1995. pap. text ed. 29.00 (*0-309-05332-3*) Natl Acad Pr.

Seismology. Hugh A. Doyle. LC 95-9101. 260p. 1996. pap. text ed. 56.95 (*0-471-94869-1*) Wiley.

Seismology & Plate Tectonics. David Gubbins. (Illus.). 300p. (C). 1990. text ed. 80.00 (*0-521-37141-4*); pap. text ed. 34.95 (*0-521-37995-4*) Cambridge U Pr.

Seismology of the Sun & the Distant Stars. Ed. by D. O. Gough. (NATO Advanced Science Institutes Series C: Mathematical & Physical Sciences). 1986. lib. bdg. 182. 50 (*90-277-2196-3*) Kluwer Ac.

Seismology, 1989-1992: Nuclear Test-Ban Verification (in Sweden) Compiled by Eva Johannisson et al. (Illus.). 57p. (Orig.). (C). 1994. pap. text ed. 25.00 (*0-7881-1393-3*) DIANE Pub.

Seismosaurus: The Earth-Shaker. David D. Gillette. LC 93-40318. (Illus.). 1994. 39.95 (*0-231-07874-9*) Col U Pr.

Seismosaurus: The Longest Dinosaur. Don Lessem. LC 95-36473. (Illus.). (J). (gr. 2-5). 1996. lib. bdg. 14.96 (*0-87614-987-5*, Carolrhoda) Lerner Group.

***Seismotectonics of North-Central Utah & Southwestern Wyoming.** Michael W. West. (Special Study of the Utah Geological Survey Ser.: Vol. 82, No. 4). (Illus.). 93p. (Orig.). 1994. pap. 15.00 (*1-55791-201-7*, SS82) Utah Geological Survey.

Seismotectonics of the Central California Coast Ranges, 292. Ed. by Ina B. Alterman et al. LC 94-28189. (Special Papers: Vol. 292). 1994. pap. 50.25 (*0-8137-2292-6*) Geol Soc.

Seismosaurus: The Longest Dinosaur. Elizabeth Sandell. Ed. by Marjorie Oelerich & Howard Schroeder. LC 88-963. (Dinosaur Discovery Era Ser.). (Illus.). 32p. (J). (gr. k-5). 1988. pap. 5.95 (*0-944280-09-9*); lib. bdg. 12.95 (*0-944280-03-X*) Bancroft-Sage.

Seitseman Retkea Itaan see Seven Journeys Eastward Eighteen Ninety-Eight to Nineteen Twelve

Seiyu Roku: Oil Manufacturing in Japan in 1836. Nagatsune Okura. Tr. by Eiko Ariga. LC 74-6761. (Illus.). 79p. 1974. 25.00 (*0-917526-01-5*) Olearius Edns.

Seizando's New English-Japanese Dictionary of Sea Terms. H. Shinomiya. 372p. (ENG & JPN.). 1980. 125.00 (*0-8288-0422-2*, M9348) Fr & Eur.

Seize a Passing Stranger. large type ed. Cyril A. Joyce. (Linford Mystery Library). 288p. 1992. pap. 15.99 (*0-7089-7226-8*, Linford) Ulverscroft.

Seize the Day. Saul Bellow. 120p. 1984. pap. 10.95 (*0-14-007285-3*, Penguin Bks) Viking Penguin.

Seize the Day. Saul Bellow. 144p. 1996. pap. 10.95 (*0-14-018937-8*, Penguin Classics) Viking Penguin.

***Seize the Day: A Declaration of the Coming Revival.** Burt McDaniel. 165p. (Orig.). 1996. pap. 10.00 (*1-57502-289-3*, PO998) Morris Pubng.

Seize the Day: How to Achieve Excellence in a World of Mediocrity...Every Day. John Hoover & Danny Cox. 253p. 1994. 21.95 (*1-56414-134-9*) Career Pr Inc.

Seize the Day! How to Best Use What Can't Be Replaced - Time. Michael F. Woolery. LC 91-67673. (Illus.). 148p. (Orig.). Date not set. mass mkt. 8.95 (*0-9631378-0-8*) TimeLink.

Seize the Day: Your Church Can Survive Thrive! Ed. by Keith Drury. (Illus.). 112p. (Orig.). 1992. wbk. ed., spiral bd. 14.95 (*0-89827-102-9*, BKR79) Wesleyan Pub Hse.

Seize the Day: Your Church Can Survive Thrive! H. C. Wilson. 152p. (Orig.). 1992. pap. 9.95 (*0-89827-096-0*, BKZ18) Wesleyan Pub Hse.

Seize the Day for People over 49. Dana Hornig et al. LC 94-78026. (Illus.). 360p. (Orig.). 1994. pap. 14.95 (*1-57281-002-5*, CBK901) US Games Syst.

Seize the Day for People over 49 Card Pack. Dana Hornig et al. (Illus.). 360p. 1994. pap. 17.95 (*0-88079-708-8*) US Games Syst.

Seize the Fire. Laura Kinsale. 1989. mass mkt. 4.50 (*0-380-75399-5*) Avon.

Seize the Moment. Hilliard Arrington, Sr. Ed. by Janet Berres. 150p. (Orig.). (C). 1995. reprint ed. pap. 9.95 (*0-9647346-1-3*) CNA Pubng.

***Seize the Moment, Not Your Teen: The Art of Opportunity Parenting.** Bill Sanders. LC 96-48808. 1997. pap. 9.99 (*0-8423-6936-8*) Tyndale.

Seize the Moment, Share the Message: And God Will Change Lives. Roberta Kuhne. LC 95-44405. 180p. 1995. pap. 9.99 (*0-88070-661-9*, Multnomah Bks) Multnomah Pubs.

Seize the Sky. Terry C. Johnston. (Son of the Plains Ser.: No. 2). 432p. 1991. 6.50 (*0-553-28910-1*) Bantam.

Seize the Time: The Story of the Black Panther Party & Huey P. Newton. Bobby Seale. LC 91-70097. 429p. 1991. reprint ed. pap. 14.95 (*0-933121-30-X*) Black Classic.

***Seized: My Life with Epilepsy.** Teresa McLean. 174p. 1996. pap. 16.95 (*1-86066-013-4*, Pub. by R Cohen Bks UK) Trafalgar.

Seized by Love. Susan Johnson. 304p. 1994. mass mkt. 5.50 (*0-553-56327-0*) Bantam.

Seized, Surplus, Repos & Rentals: How to Get the Car of Your Dreams...Without Ever Hasseling with a Salesman. Dunk Chen. 1989. pap. 10.00 (*0-9612732-64-4*) Duane Shinn.

Seizieme Siecle see Histoire de la Langue Francaise des Origines a nos Jours

Seizieme Siecle see Collection Litteraire

Seizing Control: Live with Epilepsy. Betts. Date not set. text ed. write for info. (*0-7190-3813-8*, Pub. by Manchester Univ Pr UK); text ed. write for info. (*0-7190-3814-6*, Pub. by Manchester Univ Pr UK) St Martin.

***Seizing Control: The International Market Power of Cooperatives.** Lee Egerstrom et al. LC 96-78130. Orig. Title: Internationale Marktmacht van Cooperaties. (Illus.). 210p. 1996. 29.95 (*1-883477-14-X*) Lone Oak MN.

Seizing of Yankee Green Mall. Ridley Pearson. 304p. 1988. pap. 4.50 (*0-373-97076-5*) Harlequin Bks.

***Seizing the Airwaves: A Culture Jammers' Handbook.** Ron Sakolsky. 1997. pap. text ed. 12.95 (*1-873176-99-6*) AK Pr Dist.

Seizing the Future. Michael G. Zey. 1994. 24.00 (*0-671-74948-X*) S&S Trade.

Seizing the Growth Initiative: Assessing the Effects of Ballot Box Planning. 19p. 1989. 10.00 (*0-317-05663-8*, P88001PAF) Assn Bay Area.

Seizing the Media. (Immediast Underground Ser.). 26p. 1994. 3.50 (*1-884519-02-4*) Open Media.

Seizing the Moments. James W. Moore. 1992. pap. 9.95 (*0-687-37151-1*) Abingdon.

Seizing the Word: History, Art, & Self in the Work of W. E. B. Du Bois. Keith E. Byerman. LC 93-30368. 256p. 1994. 40.00 (*0-8203-1624-5*) U of Ga Pr.

Seizure of State Power. M. Velli. (Illus.). 126p. (Orig.). 1992. pap. 9.95 (*0-948984-23-6*, Pub. by Phoenix Pr UK) AK Pr Dist.

Seizure Recognition & Observation: A Guide for Allied Health Professionals. Epilepsy Foundation of America Staff. 12p. 1992. pap. 2.95 (*0-916570-17-7*) Epilepsy Foundation of America.

Seizure Recognition & Treatment. Richard Lechtenberg. (Illus.). 204p. 1990. text ed. 59.95 (*0-443-08701-6*) Churchill.

Seizures. Judy Sublette. 200p. 1995. write for info. (*1-888558-00-8*) Public Res.

Seizures & Convulsions in Infants, Children & Adolescents: Practical Informative Guide for Parents, Teachers & Paramedical Personnel. Leonardo Garcia-Mendez. LC 93-80704. (Pediatric Neurology Ser.). (Illus.). 364p. (Orig.). (C). 1994. pap. text ed. 16.99 (*0-9639269-0-X*) Lemar Pubs.

Seizures & Epilepsy. Jerome Engel, Jr. (Contemporary Neurology Ser.: No. 31). (Illus.). 536p. (C). 1989. pap. text ed. 49.00 (*0-8036-3202-9*) Davis Co.

Seizures & Epilepsy. Jerome Engel, Jr. LC 89-7930. (Contemporary Neurology Ser.: Vol. 31). (Illus.). 536p. (C). 1989. text ed. 99.00 (*0-8036-3201-0*) Davis Co.

***Seizures & Epilepsy in Childhood: A Guide for Parents.** 2nd ed. John M. Freeman et al. LC 96-31617. (Health Bks.). (Illus.). 352p. 1997. pap. 16.95 (*0-8018-5498-9*); text ed. 39.95 (*0-8018-5497-0*) Johns Hopkins.

Seizures & Epilepsy in Childhood: A Guide for Parents. John M. Freeman et al. (Illus.). 312p. 1993. reprint ed. pap. 16.95 (*0-8018-4649-8*) Johns Hopkins.

Seizures & Epilepsy in the Elderly. A. James Rowan. LC 96-28927. 320p. 1996. text ed. 85.00 (*0-7506-9622-2*) Buttrwrth-Heinemann.

***Seizures & Overindebtedness in the European Union - Les Saisies et le Surendettement dans l'Union Europ Eenne.** Georges De Leval. LC 96-52726. (Civil Procedure in Europe Ser.). 1997. write for info. (*90-411-0152-7*) Kluwer Law Tax Pubs.

Seizures of the Sun: First Poems. Meschach McLachlan. (Stewardship Ser.: No. 6). 40p. (Orig.). 1996. pap. 6.00 (*1-883197-11-2*) New Native Pr.

Seizures of the Will in Early Modern English Drama. Frank Whigham. (Studies in Renaissance Literature & Culture: No. 11). 312p. (C). 1996. pap. text ed. 19.95 (*0-521-56449-2*) Cambridge U Pr.

Seizures of the Will in Early Modern English Drama. Frank Whigham. (Studies in Renaissance Literature & Culture: No. 11). 312p. (C). 1996. text ed. 54.95 (*0-521-41877-1*) Cambridge U Pr.

Sejanus. Ben Jonson. Ed. by Jonas A. Barish. LC 65-11173. (Yale Ben Jonson Ser.). 224p. reprint ed. pap. 63.90 (*0-8357-8317-0*, 2033776) Bks Demand.

Sejanus: The Secret Ruler of Rome. John W. Graham. (Golden Age of Rome Ser.). 1978. mass mkt. 2.50 (*0-89083-353-2*, Zebra Kensgtn) Kensgtn Pub Corp.

Sejarah Melayu or Malay Annals. Tr. by C. C. Brown. (Oxford in Asia Historical Reprints Ser.). 1970. 10.50 (*0-19-638106-1*) OUP.

Sejatel. Claudia Loukashevitch. (Illus.). 462p. 1966. 20.00 (*0-317-30416-X*); pap. 15.00 (*0-317-30417-8*) Holy Trinity.

Sejba Slova. Vladimir Uhri. 32p. (Orig.). (SLO.). 1996. pap. 1.60 (*1-56983-049-5*) New Creat WI.

Sejour: Parisian Playwright from Louisiana. Charles E. O'Neill. LC 95-83199. 164p. 1996. 25.00 (*1-887366-00-8*) U of SW LA Ctr LA Studies.

Sek Says. M. Seklemian. Ed. by Carole A. Miller. 1979. 15. 95 (*0-934590-00-1*) Retail Report.

Sekai No Naka No Nihon Bijutsu see Japanese Art in World Perspective

Sekha-Sen Ren-A: May They Mention My Name. Mai T. Angaza. 50p. (Orig.). (C). 1991. pap. text ed. 6.95 (*0-9628211-0-1*) Angaza Pubns.

Seki-nin (Duty Bound) George Nakagawa. 1989. 19.95 (*0-930046-10-2*) CSUF Oral Hist.

Sekigahara 1600. Anthony J. Bryant. (Campaign Ser.). (Illus.). 96p. 1995. pap. 14.95 (*1-85532-395-8*, Pub. by Osprey UK) Stackpole.

Sekiyu Tooshi No Kagi. John Orban, III. Tr. by Japan Connection of Oklahoma City Staff from ENG. (Illus.). 168p. (Orig.). (JPN.). 1988. pap. 50.00 (*0-9615776-4-9*) Meridian Oklahoma.

Sekoto: The Art of Gerard Sekoto. Barbara Lindop. (Illus.). 64p. 1995. 27.50 (*1-85793-461-X*, Pub. by Pavilion UK) Trafalgar.

***Sekrety Giekdowe.** unabridged ed. Michael A. Hamil. 256p. (Orig.). (POL.). 1997. pap. 25.00 (*0-9658109-0-9*) M A Hamil.

***Sektor.** Artists' Services Staff. (Illus.). 256p. (Orig.). Date not set. 39.00 (*3-931126-07-2*, Pub. by Die Gestalten GW); pap. 32.99 (*3-931126-08-0*, Pub. by Die Gestalten GW) Consort Bk Sales.

Selamat Jalan, Mate: Poems from a Short Trip. Des. by Marek Lugowski. (Illus.). 36p. (Orig.). 1996. pap. 3.00 (*1-888431-07-5*) Small Garlic.

Selberg Trace Formula & Related Topics. Ed. by D. Hejhal et al. LC 86-3512. (Contemporary Mathematics Ser.: Vol. 53). 554p. 1986. pap. text ed. 55.00 (*0-8218-5058-X*, CONM/53) Am Math.

Selberg Trace Formula for PSL Vol. 2: 2, IR. D. A. Hejhal. (Lecture Notes in Mathematics Ser.: Vol. 1001). 806p. 1983. 75.95 (*0-387-12323-7*) Spr-Verlag.

Selberg Trace Formula for PSL(R) Sub 2 Super N. I. Efrat. LC 86-28808. (Memoirs of the American Mathematical Society Ser.: Vol. 65/359). 111p. 1987. pap. text ed. 22.00 (0-8218-2424-4, MEMO/65/359) Am Math.

Selberg Trace Formula III: Inner Product Formulae (Initial Considerations) M. Scott Osborne & G. Warner. LC 83-3918. (Memoirs of the American Mathematical Society Ser.: No. 44/283). 209p. 1983. pap. 26.00 (0-8218-2283-7, MEMO/44/283) Am Math.

Selberg Trace Formulae & Equidistribution Theorems for Closed Geodesics & Laplace Eigenfunctions: Finite Area Surfaces. Morris Zelditch. LC 91-44875. (Memoirs Ser.: Vol. 465). 102p. 1992. pap. 25.00 (0-8218-2526-7, MEMO/96/465) Am Math.

Selberg Zeta & Theta Functions: A Differential Operator Approach. Ulrich Bunke & Martin Olbrich. LC 95-4564. (Mathematical Research Ser.: Vol. 83). 168p. 1995. pap. 60.00 (3-05-501690-4, Pub. by Akademie Verlag GW) Wiley.

Selberg's Zeta-, L-, & Eisensteinseries. U. Christian. (Lecture Notes in Mathematics Ser.: Vol. 1030). 196p. 1983. 35.95 (0-387-12701-1) Spr-Verlag.

***Selbstbestimmt Leben - Handlungsfelder Einer Offensiven Behindertenpadagogik.** Udo Wilken. (Hildesheimer Schriftenreihe Zur Sozialpadagogik und Sozialarbeit Ser.: Vol. 1). 152p. (GER.). 1992. write for info. (3-487-09527-0) G Olms Pubs.

***Selbstbewusstsein und Selbstanschauung: Eine Reflexion Ueber Einheit und Entzweiung des Subjekts in Kants "Opus Postumum"** So-In Choi. (Kantstudien Ergaenzungsheft Ser.: Vol. 130). xii, 154p. (GER.). (C). 1996. lib. bdg. 72.60 (3-11-015264-9, 120/96) De Gruyter.

Selbstbewusstsein und Unbewusstes: Studien Zu Freud und Heidegger. Martin Bartels. (Quellen und Studien zur Philosophie Ser.: Vol. 10). (C). 1976. 92.30 (3-11-005778-6) De Gruyter.

Selbsthilfe und Krise der Wohlfahrtsgesellschaft. Ernst Von Kardorff & Hubert Oppl. (Soziokulturelle Herausforderungen-Sozialpolitische Aufgaben: Aspekte Moderner Sozialarbeit Ser.). 196p. (GER.). 1989. pap. text ed. 20.00 (3-597-10683-8) K G Saur.

Selbstmord als Sociale Massenerscheinung der Modernen Civilisation. Thomas G. Masaryk. Ed. & Intro. by J. C. Nyiri. (Philosophia Resources Library). xvi, 245p. (GER.). 1982. lib. bdg. 66.00 (3-88405-014-1) Philosophia Pr.

Selbstverstandnis der Judischen Diaspora in der Hellenistisch-Romischen Zeit. Willem C. Van Unnik & Pieter W. Van der Horst. LC 92-34556. (Arbeiten zur Geschichte des Antiken Judentums & des Urchristentums Ser.: Vol. 17). 1992. 78.75 (90-04-09693-0) E J Brill.

Selbstverwirklichung/Selbstverneinung Vol. 15: Rollenkonflikte im Werk von Hebbel, Ibsen und Strindberg. Herlinde N. Ayers. (Studies on Themes & Motifs in Literature). 184p. (GER.). (C). 1995. text ed. 45.95 (0-8204-2668-7) P Lang Pubng.

Selbstzitat Bei Thomas Mann: Untersuchungen Zum Verhaltnis von Fiktion und Autobiographie in Seinem Werk. Gert Bruhn. LC 92-21920. (American University Studies: Germanic Languages & Literature: Ser. I, Vol. 98). 203p. (C). 1993. text ed. 39.95 (0-8204-1810-2) P Lang Pubng.

Selby: The Secret Adventures of a Talking Dog. Duncan Ball. LC 96-20730. (Illus.). 112p. (J). (gr. 3-6). 1997. pap. 4.50 (0-06-440673-3, Trophy) HarpC Child Bks.

***Selby Speaks: More Adventures of Talking Dogs.** Duncan Ball. LC 96-38247. (Illus.). 128p. (J). (gr. 3-6). 1997. pap. 4.50 (0-06-440676-8, Trophy) HarpC Child Bks.

Selchie's Seed. Shulamith L. Oppenheim. LC 96-2279. (Illus.). (J). 1996. pap. 7.00 (0-15-201412-8) HarBrace.

Selden & Kindred of Virginia. E. M. Selden. (Illus.). 224p. 1993. reprint ed. pap. 35.00 (0-8328-3747-4); reprint ed. lib. bdg. 45.00 (0-8328-3746-6) Higginson Bk Co.

Selden Society, 106 vols., Set. Date not set. write for info. (1-57588-128-4, 308800) W S Hein.

Selden Society Supplementary Series, 11 vols., Set. 635.00 (0-614-13135-9) Gaunt.

Selden Society Supplementary Series, Vols. 1-10: 1965-1993, Set. 585.00 (0-685-70591-9, Pub. by Selden Soc UK) Gaunt.

Seldens of Virginia & Allied Families, 2 vols. in 1. M. Kennedy. (Illus.). 1363p. 1989. reprint ed. pap. 198.00 (0-8328-1057-6); reprint ed. lib. bdg. 206.00 (0-8328-1056-8) Higginson Bk Co.

Seldin, Donald W. Festschrift: Journal: Mineral & Electrolyte Metabolism, Vol. 11, No. 4, 1985. Ed. by N. A. Kurtzman. (Illus.). 76p. 1985. pap. 25.75 (3-8055-4063-9) S Karger.

Seldom Remembered Now. Ben A. Clements. (Illus.). 79p. (Orig.). 1989. pap. 9.95 (0-943487-21-8) Sevgo Pr.

Seldom Sung Songs. Ray Locke. LC 83-63200. 192p. 1984. 13.95 (0-915677-02-4) Roundtable Pub.

Seldwyla Folks: Three Singular Tales by the Swiss Poet. Gottfried Keller. Tr. by Wolf Von Schierbrand from GER. LC 70-150545. (Short Story Index Reprint Ser.). 1977. reprint ed. 19.95 (0-8369-3842-9) Ayer.

Seleccion de Personal en el Servicio Publico de Puerto Rico. Irma G. De Serrano. 3112p. 1969. 4.50 (0-8477-2204-X); pap. 3.50 (0-8477-2205-8) U of PR Pr.

Seleccion de Prosa Lirica. Juan R. Jimenez. Ed. by Francisco J. Blasco Pascual. (Nueva Austral Ser.: Vol. 158). (SPA.). 1991. pap. text ed. 24.95 (84-239-1958-7) Elliots Bks.

Seleccion de Romances. (SPA.). 9.95 (84-241-5619-6) E Torres & Sons.

Seleccion Poetica - Selected Poems. Luis Bemitez. Ed. & Tr. by Veronica Miranda. (Carpeta de Poesia Luz Bilingue Ser.: No. 1). 40p. (Orig.). (ENG & SPA.). 1996. 6.00 (0-9634009-2-4) Luz Bilingual.

Selecciones de Aliento Cotidiano. Marfa Cabrera. 385p. (SPA.). 1990. pap. 6.99 (1-56063-101-5, 498409) Editorial Unilit.

Selecciones de "Mi Camino a Rotary" Paul Harris. 58p. (SPA.). 1984. 3.00 (0-915062-21-6) Rotary Intl.

Selecciones Espanolas. (C). 1987. pap. text ed. write for info. (0-13-087545-7) P-H.

Select. F. Paul Wilson. 400p. 1995. mass mkt. 6.50 (0-440-21866-7) Dell.

Select. large type ed. F. Paul Wilson. LC 94-19118. 1994. 24.95 (1-56895-112-4) Wheeler Pub.

S.E.L.E.C.T. Creative-Innovative Approaches. John G. Young. 110p. (Orig.). 1986. pap. 14.95 (0-943456-13-4) Bearly Ltd.

***Select: Internet Guideposts.** Lorilee Sadler. Ed. by James Rigney. 256p. (C). 1997. pap. text ed. 22.95 (0-201-30422-8) Addison-Wesley.

***Select: Netscape Navigator 3.0.** Gillian Hall. 208p. (Orig.). (C). 1997. pap. text ed. 22.95 (0-201-30419-8) Addison-Wesley.

***Select: Students Speak Out on the Realities of Life & Learning in America's Elite Colleges.** Howard Greene. 1997. 26.00 (0-06-017815-9) HarpC.

Select a Story. L. Schwartz. (Creative Writing Ser.). 40p. (J). (gr. 3-6). 1993. 6.95 (0-88160-259-0, LW249B) Learning Wks.

***Select Access 2.0 for Windows.** H. L. Capron. (C). 1995. pap. text ed. 22.95 (0-8053-2950-1) Addison-Wesley.

Select Annotated Bibliography: A Philosophy for Planners. Huw Thomas. (C). 1982. 35.00 (0-685-30283-0, Pub. by Oxford Polytechnic UK) St Mut.

Select Bibliography: 1990 Edition, Vol. 2. (Law of the Sea Ser.). 73p. 1991. 15.00 (92-1-033067-6, E.91.V.2) UN.

Select Bibliography: 1991 Edition, Vol. 6. (Law of the Sea Ser.). 64p. 1992. pap. 15.00 (92-1-133427-6, E.92.V.6) UN.

Select Bibliography: 1992 Edition, Vol. 12. (Law of the Sea Ser.). 61p. 1993. 15.00 (92-1-133451-9, E.93.V.12) UN.

Select Bibliography: 1993 Edition, Vol. 10. (Law of the Sea Ser.): 64p. 1993. pap. 15.00 (92-1-133470-5, E.94.V.10) UN.

Select Bibliography: 1994 Edition, Vol. 11. (Law of the Sea Ser.). 72p. 1995. 15.00 (92-1-033073-0, M.95.V.11) UN.

Select Bibliography of Adult Continuing Education. John Davies & J. E. Thomas. 300p. (C). 1988. 125.00 (0-900559-78-0, Pub. by Natl Inst Adult Continuing Educ UK) St Mut.

Select Bibliography of Books on World War Two: Published in the United States 1966-1975. Compiled by A. L. Funk. 33p. 1975. pap. text ed. 25.95 (0-89126-074-9) MA-AH Pub.

Select Bibliography of European Folk Music. Ed. by Karel Vetterl. 144p. 1966. 8.00 (0-318-17463-4) Intl Coun Trad.

Select Bibliography of Journal Articles on Philosophy Religion, Science & Related Aspects of Indian Culture. Ed. by Debiprasad Chattopadhyaya. (C). 1989. 8.00 (0-685-30851-0, Pub. by Munshiram Manoharial II) S Asia.

Select Bibliography of Music in Africa. International African Institute Staff & L. J. Gaskin. LC 66-36908. (Africa Bibliography Ser.: No. 8). 95p. reprint ed. pap. 27.10 (0-317-10104-8, 2007644) Bks Demand.

Select Bibliography of Revisionist Books. rev. ed. Harry E. Barnes. 1971. 250.00 (0-685-26300-2) Revisionist Pr.

Select Bibliography of the Principal Modern Presses, Public & Private, in Great Britain & Ireland. G. S. Tomkinson. LC 75-2752. (Illus.). 1975. reprint ed. 40.00 (0-915346-00-1) A Wofsy Fine Arts.

Select Bibliography on Women in India. 131p. 1978. 7.95 (0-318-37049-2) Asia Bk Corp.

Select Body: The Gay Dance Party Subculture & the HIV/AIDS Pandemic. Lynette Lewis & Michael Ross. (AIDS Awareness Ser.). 256p. Date not set. write for info. (0-304-33510-X); pap. write for info. (0-304-33511-8) Cassell.

Select British Documents of the Canadian War of 1812, Vol. 13. Ed. by William C. Wood. LC 68-28604. 678p. 1969. reprint ed. text ed. 85.00 (0-8371-5051-5, WOBA, Greenwood Pr) Greenwood.

Select British Documents of the Canadian War of 1812, Vol. 14. Ed. by William C. Wood. LC 68-28604. 517p. 1969. reprint ed. text ed. 75.00 (0-8371-5052-3, WOBB, Greenwood Pr) Greenwood.

Select British Documents of the Canadian War of 1812, Vol. 15. Ed. by William C. Wood. LC 68-28604. 539p. 1969. reprint ed. text ed. 75.00 (0-8371-5053-1, WOBC, Greenwood Pr) Greenwood.

Select British Documents of the Canadian War of 1812, Vol. 17. Ed. by William C. Wood. LC 68-28604. 517p. 1969. reprint ed. text ed. 75.00 (0-8371-5054-X, WOBD, Greenwood Pr) Greenwood.

Select Catalog of Language Universals. Ed. by Gyula Decsy. (Bibliotheca Nostratica Ser.: Vol. 8). 141p. 1988. pap. 26.00 (0-931922-29-1) Eurolingua.

Select Charters & Other Documents Illustrative of American History, 1606-1775. William MacDonald. (Illus.). ix, 401p. 1992. reprint ed. 45.00 (0-8377-2443-0) Rothman.

Select Charters & Other Illustrations of English Constitutional History from the Earliest Times to the Reign of Edward the First. 9th ed. William Stubbs. LC 85-28220. xix, 528p. 1985. reprint ed. lib. bdg. 47.50 (0-8377-2609-3) Rothman.

***Select Charters & Other Illustrations of English Constitutional History from the Earliest Times to the Reign of Edward the First.** 9th rev. ed. Ed. by William Stubbs. 528p. 1997. 165.00 (1-56169-257-3) Gaunt.

Select Collection of Old English Plays, 15 vols. in 7, 1. rev. ed. Ed. by Robert Dodsley. LC 64-14702. 1972. 35.95 (0-405-08453-6, Pub. by Blom Pubns UK) Ayer.

Select Collection of Old English Plays, 15 vols. in 7, 2. Ed. by Robert Dodsley. LC 64-14702. 1972. reprint ed. 35. 95 (0-405-08454-4, Pub. by Blom Pubns UK) Ayer.

Select Collection of Old English Plays, 15 vols. in 7, 3. rev. ed. Ed. by Robert Dodsley. LC 64-14702. 1972. 35.95 (0-405-08455-2, Pub. by Blom Pubns UK) Ayer.

Select Collection of Old English Plays, 15 vols. in 7, 4. Ed. by Robert Dodsley. LC 64-14702. 1972. reprint ed. 35. 95 (0-405-08456-0, Pub. by Blom Pubns UK) Ayer.

Select Collection of Old English Plays, 15 vols. in 7, 5. Ed. by Robert Dodsley. LC 64-14702. 1972. reprint ed. 35. 95 (0-405-08457-9, Pub. by Blom Pubns UK) Ayer.

Select Collection of Old English Plays, 15 vols. in 7, Set. Ed. by Robert Dodsley. LC 64-14702. reprint ed. 247.95 (0-405-08452-8, Pub. by Blom Pubns UK) Ayer.

Select Collection of Old English Plays, 15 vols. in 7, Vol. 6. Ed. by Robert Dodsley. LC 64-14702. 1972. reprint ed. 35.95 (0-405-08458-7, Pub. by Blom Pubns UK) Ayer.

Select Collection of Old English Plays, 15 vols. in 7, Vol. 7. Ed. by Robert Dodsley. LC 64-14702. 1972. reprint ed. 35.95 (0-405-08459-5, Pub. by Blom Pubns UK) Ayer.

Select Collection of Old Plays, 12 vols., Set. Robert Dodsley. (BCL1-PR English Literature Ser.). 1992. reprint ed. lib. bdg. 900.00 (0-7812-7149-5) Rprt Serv.

Select Collection of Poems, with Notes Biographical & Historical, 8 vols. Ed. by John Nichols. LC 11-29585. reprint ed. 380.00 (0-404-04750-5) AMS Pr.

Select Collection of Poems, with Notes Biographical & Historical, 8 vols., Set. Ed. by John Nichols. 1974. reprint ed. 480.00 (0-527-67180-0) Periodicals Srv.

Select Committee on Small Business: Hearings 89th Congress, 1st Session. U. S. Congress Staff. LC 66-62486. 1982. reprint ed. lib. bdg. 195.00 (0-89941-232-7, 201480) W S Hein.

***Select Despatches from the British Foreign Office Archives.** J. H. Rose. (Camden Third Ser.). 54.00 (0-86193-007-X) David Brown.

Select Discourses. John Smith. Ed. by C. A. Patrides. LC 79-15690. 1979. reprint ed. 75.00 (0-8201-1335-2) Schol Facsimiles.

Select Dissertations from the Amoenitates Academicae: Supplement to Mr. Stillingfleet's Tracts, Relating Natural History. Carl Linnaeus. Ed. by Frank N. Egerton, 3rd. Tr. by F. J. Brand. LC 77-74238. (History of Ecology Ser.). 1978. reprint ed. lib. bdg. 42.95 (0-405-10407-3) Ayer.

Select Documents for Queen Anne's Reign Down to the Union with Scotland, 1702-07. Ed. by George M. Trevelyan & Gerald M. Straka. LC 72-83173. (English Studies). 1972. reprint ed. lib. bdg. 23.00 (0-8420-1429-2) Scholarly Res Inc.

Select Documents Illustrating the Four Voyages of Columbus No. I: The First & Second Voyages. Ed. by Cecil Jane. (Hakluyt Society Second Ser.: Vol. 65). (Illus.). 344p. 1996. 63.00 (0-85115-983-4, Pub. by Hakluyt Soc UK) Boydell & Brewer.

Select Documents Illustrating the Four Voyages of Columbus No. II: The Third & Fourth Voyages. (Hakluyt Society Second Ser.: Vol. 70). (Illus.). 253p. 1996. 45.00 (0-85115-984-2, Pub. by Hakluyt Soc UK) Boydell & Brewer.

Select Documents in Canadian Economic History, 2 vols., Set. Ed. by Harold A. Innis & A. R. Lower. LC 77-8258. 1977. reprint ed. lib. bdg. 125.00 (0-87991-132-8) Porcupine Pr.

Select Documents in Canadian Economic History, 2 vols., Vol. 1 1497-1783. Ed. by Harold A. Innis & A. R. Lower. LC 77-8258. 581p. 1977. reprint ed. Vol. 1. lib. bdg. 57.50 (0-87991-133-6) Porcupine Pr.

Select Documents in Canadian Economic History, 2 vols., Vol. 2 1783-1885. Ed. by Harold A. Innis & A. R. Lower. LC 77-8258. 846p. 1977. reprint ed. Vol. 2. lib. bdg. 75.00 (0-87991-134-4) Porcupine Pr.

***Select Documents of the English Lands of the Abbey of Bec.** Marjorie Chibnall. (Camden Third Ser.). 63.00 (0-86193-073-8) David Brown.

Select Documents Relating to the Unification of South Africa. Ed. by A. P. Newton. 574p. 1968. reprint ed. 59.50 (0-7146-1777-6, Pub. by F Cass Pubs UK) Intl Spec Bk.

Select Easy Piano Classics. Charles Bateman. 80p. (Orig.). 1995. pap. 11.95 (1-56922-098-0, 07-2038) Creat Cncpts.

Select English Songs & Dialogues of the 16th & 17th Centuries, 2 vols. in 1. Ed. by A. Dolmetsch. LC 74-24070. reprint ed. 45.00 (0-404-12897-1) AMS Pr.

Select Epigrams of Martial. Donald C. Goertz. LC 74-127795. 128p. 1971. 5.95 (0-8216-0150-4, Univ Bks) Carol Pub Group.

Select Essays in Anglo-American Legal History, 3 vols. Ed. by Association of American Law Schools Staff. LC 91-77977. 2532p. 1992. reprint ed. lib. bdg. 195.00 (0-9630106-1-1) Lawbk Exchange.

Select Extra Tropical Plants. B. F. Von Mueller. (C). 1988. text ed. 50.00 (0-685-22104-0, Pub. by Scientific UK) St Mut.

Select Fables of Esop & Other Fabulists. Aesop. Ed. by Robert Dodsley. LC 70-161796. (Augustan Translators Ser.). reprint ed. 49.50 (0-404-54101-1) AMS Pr.

Select Fire: (The Arms Trilogy) (Executioner Ser.). 1995. mass mkt. 3.50 (0-373-61195-1, 1-61195-3) Harlequin Bks.

Select from the Black. Ed. by Jamestown Publishers Staff. 1989. pap. 15.53 (0-8092-0082-1) Jamestown Pubs.

Select Guide to California Catholic History. Francis J. Weber. 22.00 (0-87026-001-4) Westernlore.

Select Guide to Human Resource Executives: 1994 Edition, Vol. 1. Hunt. 1994. pap. text ed. 99.25 (0-9631920-4-3) Hunt-Scanlon.

Select Historical Documents of the Middle Ages. Ed. by Ernest F. Henderson. LC 65-15247. 1992. 30.00 (0-8196-0149-7) Biblo.

Select Historical Documents of the Middle Ages. Ed. by Ernest F. Henderson. LC 68-57867. (Bohn's Antiquarian Library). 1968. reprint ed. 47.00 (0-404-50016-1) AMS Pr.

***Select Internet Explorer.** Paul Thurrot. (Select Ser.). 208p. (Orig.). (C). 1997. pap. text ed. 22.95 (0-201-30362-0) Addison-Wesley.

***Select Letters.** 244p. 1980. text ed. 65.00 (0-521-22492-6) Cambridge U Pr.

Select Letters. Augustine, Saint. (Loeb Classical Library: No. 239). 590p. 1930. 18.95 (0-674-99264-4) HUP.

Select Letters. Marcus T. Cicero. Ed. by D. R. Bailey. LC 78-67430. (Cambridge Greek & Latin Classics Ser.). 250p. 1980. pap. text ed. 22.95 (0-521-29524-6) Cambridge U Pr.

Select Letters. Jerome. (Loeb Classical Library: No. 262). 536p. 1933. 18.95 (0-674-99288-1) HUP.

Select Letters. Augustinus Aurelius. Tr. by James H. Baxter. LC 75-41012. reprint ed. 37.50 (0-404-14502-7) AMS Pr.

Select Letters of Major Jack Downing. Seba Smith. LC 77-104567. (Illus.). 223p. reprint ed. lib. bdg. 26.50 (0-8398-1868-8) Irvington.

Select Letters of Major Jack Downing. Seba Smith. 223p. (C). 1986. reprint ed. pap. text ed. 6.95 (0-8290-2393-3) Irvington.

Select Letters of Seneca. Lucius A. Seneca. (College Classical Ser.). vii, 380p. (C). 1983. reprint ed. pap. text ed. 22.50 (0-89241-385-9) Caratzas.

***Select Lotus 1.2.3 REL 4 for Windows.** H. L. Capron. (C). 1995. pap. text ed. 22.95 (0-8053-2933-1) Addison-Wesley.

***Select Lotus 1.2.3 Release 2.2 for DOS.** H. L. Capron. (C). 1992. pap. text ed. 22.95 (0-8053-0836-9) Addison-Wesley.

***Select Lotus 1.2.3 Release 5.0 for Windows 95.** Gary Brent. (C). 1997. pap. text ed. 21.25 (0-8053-1630-2) Addison-Wesley.

Select Material in Macroeconomics. 3rd ed. Gary Walton et al. (C). 1994. 27.95 (0-256-19145-X) Irwin.

Select Medieval Documents & Other Material Illustrative in the History of Church & Empire, 754 A.D.-1254 A.D. Shailer Mathews. LC 70-178566. (LAT.). reprint ed. 34. 50 (0-404-56628-6) AMS Pr.

***Select Microsoft Access 97.** Pam Toliver. (C). 1997. pap. text ed. 22.95 (0-201-31527-0) Addison-Wesley.

***Select Microsoft Excel 97.** Pamela Toliver. (C). 1997. pap. text ed. 22.95 (0-201-31119-4) Addison-Wesley.

***Select Microsoft Windows 95.** (C). 1996. pap. text ed. 22. 95 (0-8053-5793-9) Addison-Wesley.

Select Microsoft Word 7 Projects for Windows 95. 2nd ed. James A. Folts. (C). 1997. pap. text ed. 22.95 (0-8053-1701-5) Addison-Wesley.

***Select Microsoft Works 3.0 DOS.** Carl Scharpf. (C). 1994. pap. text ed. 33.50 (0-8053-4255-9) Addison-Wesley.

***Select Microsoft Works 4 Projects for Windows 95.** 2nd ed. Carl A. Scharpf. (C). 1997. pap. text ed. 33.50 (0-8053-7260-1) Addison-Wesley.

Select Mod Microsoft Access 7 Projects for Windows 95. Marianne B. Fox. (C). 1997. pap. text ed. 22.95 (0-8053-1693-0) Addison-Wesley.

Select Mod Microsoft Excel 7 Projects for Windows 95. 2nd ed. Gary R. Brent. (C). 1996. pap. text ed. 22.95 (0-8053-1617-5) Addison-Wesley.

Select Mod Microsoft Powerpoint 7 Projects for Windows 95. 2nd ed. Marianne B. Fox. (C). 1997. pap. text ed. 22.95 (0-8053-1692-2) Addison-Wesley.

Select Mod Netscape 2.0 Projects for the Internet Stand Alone. Gillian Hall. (C). 1997. pap. text ed. 22.95 (0-8053-2283-3) Addison-Wesley.

***Select Mod Quattro Pro 7 Projects for Windows 95 Standalone.** James T. Perry. (C). 1997. pap. text ed. 22. 95 (0-8053-6772-1) Benjamin-Cummings.

***Select Mod Wordperfect 7 Projects for Windows 95 Standalone.** Eugene J. Rathswohl. (C). 1997. pap. text ed. 22.95 (0-8053-6773-X) Addison-Wesley.

Select Module Paradox, 7 Projects for Windows 95. 2nd ed. Ahmer S. Karim. (C). 1997. pap. text ed. 22.95 (0-8053-2702-9) Addison-Wesley.

Select Module World 6.0 for Windows: Custom Book. H. L. Capron. (C). 1995. pap. text ed. 22.95 (0-8053-2873-4) Benjamin-Cummings.

***Select Modules: Quattro Pro 6 for Windows.** (C). 1996. pap. text ed. 22.95 (0-8053-5758-0) Benjamin-Cummings.

***Select Modules: Wordperfect 6.1 for Windows.** Capron. (C). 1996. pap. text ed. 22.95 (0-8053-3890-X) Benjamin-Cummings.

***Select MS Excel 4.0 for Windows.** H. L. Capron. (C). 1994. pap. text ed. 22.95 (0-8053-2910-2) Addison-Wesley.

***Select Netscape Communicator 4.0 Plus.** Gillian Hall. (C). 1997. pap. text ed. 31.50 (0-201-31566-1) Addison-Wesley.

***Select Nonsense of Sukumar Ray.** Sukumar Ray. Tr. by Sukanta Chaudhuri. (Illus.). 80p. (Orig.). 1997. pap. 8.95 (0-19-563039-4) OUP.

Select Passages Illustrating Neoplatonism. E. R. Dodds. 128p. 1980. pap. 15.00 (0-89005-302-2) Ares.

Select Philosophical Methodical Papers. Paul E. Meehl. 512p. (C). 1991. text ed. 39.95 (0-8166-1855-0) U of Minn Pr.

An Asterisk (*) at the beginning of an entry indicates that the title is appearing in BIP for the first time.

Select Plays. Francis Beaumont & John Beaumont. reprint ed. 49.00 (*0-403-04257-7*) Somerset Pub.

*****Select Plus: Internet.** Linda Ericksen. (C). 1998. pap. text ed. write for info. (*0-201-33615-4*) Addison-Wesley.

*****Select Powerpoint 4.0 for Windows.** H. L. Capron. (C). 1996. pap. text ed. 22.95 (*0-8053-3881-0*) Addison-Wesley.

Select Private Orations of Demosthenes, 2 Vols., Pts. I & II. Demosthenes. Ed. by W. R. Connor. LC 78-18601. (Greek Texts & Commentaries Ser.). (Illus.). 1979. reprint ed. lib. bdg. 61.95 (*0-405-11442-7*) Ayer.

Select Problems in Historical Interpretation, 2 vols., Set. David M. Potter. (History - United States Ser.). 1993. reprint ed. lib. bdg. 150.00 (*0-7812-4840-X*) Rprt Serv.

Select Prose of Christina Ross. Stanwood. Date not set. text ed. write for info. (*0-312-15903-X*) St Martin.

*****Select Readings in Forest Biometrics.** Bell. 12.95 (*0-88246-125-7*) Oreg St U Bkstrs.

Select Scientific Developments in Romania: The Physical Chemistry of Molten Salts: A Case Study. Ludmila Popescu. Ed. by Melissa Dawson. (Illus.). 109p. (Orig.). 1989. pap. text ed. 75.00 (*1-55831-097-5*) Delphic Associates.

Select Scottish Ballads, 2 vols, Set. 2nd enl. ed. Ed. by John Pinkerton. LC 72-144529. reprint ed. 20.00 (*0-404-08674-8*) AMS Pr.

Select Sermons of Benjamin Whichcote. Benjamin Whichcote. LC 77-16025. 1977. reprint ed. 50.00 (*0-8201-1306-9*) Schol Facsimiles.

Select Sermons of George Whitefield. George Whitefield. 200p. 1985. reprint ed. pap. 6.50 (*0-85151-454-5*) Banner of Truth.

Select Soccer Drills. Ed. by J. Malcolm Simon & John A. Reeves. LC 90-38919. (Illus.). 152p. (Orig.). 1991. pap. 14.95 (*0-88011-408-8*, PREE0408) Human Kinetics.

Select Solutions - Principles. Raymond A. Serway. (C). 1994. teacher ed. 245.50 (*0-03-003258-X*) HB Coll Pubs.

Select Speeches for Declamation. Ed. by John H. Bechtel. LC 75-103083. (Granger Index Reprint Ser.). 1977. 19.95 (*0-8369-6098-X*) Ayer.

Select Statutes & Other Constitutional Documents Illustrative of the Reigns of Elizabeth & James I. 4th ed. Ed. by George W. Prothero. LC 83-1740. cxxv, 490p. 1983. reprint ed. text ed. 150.00 (*0-313-23973-8*, PRSE, Greenwood Pr) Greenwood.

Select Statutes, Documents & Reports Relating to British Banking: 1832-1928, 2 vols., Set. Ed. by Theodore Gregory. (Illus.). 1964. reprint ed. 85.00 (*0-7146-1225-1*, BHA-01225, Pub. by F Cass Pubs UK) Intl Spec Bk.

Select Statutes, Documents & Reports Relating to British Banking, 1832-1928, 2 vols. Ed. by Theodore E. Gregory. LC 67-93658. (Reprints of Economic Classics Ser.). 1964. reprint ed. 95.00 (*0-678-05169-0*) Kelley.

Select Texts in Stone Age Ertakasenti. Ed. & Intro. by Dibinga W. Said. LC 95-967259. 150p. (Orig.). (C). 1995. pap. text ed. 15.00 (*0-943324-63-7*) Omenana.

Select Titles from the Digest of Justinian. Ed. by Thomas E. Holland & Charles L. Shadwell. x, 466p. 1992. reprint ed. 47.50 (*0-8377-2175-X*) Rothman.

Select Tracts & Documents Illustrative of English Monetary History 1626-1730. William A. Shaw. LC 67-19743. (Library of Money & Banking History). x, 214p. 1967. reprint ed. 37.50 (*0-678-00251-7*) Kelley.

Select Translations from Old English Poetry. rev. ed. Ed. by Albert S. Cook & Chauncey B. Tinker. LC 68-59036. 195p. (C). 1968. reprint ed. 40.00 (*0-87752-024-0*) Gordian.

Select Translations from Old English Poetry. Albert S. Cook. (BCL1-PR English Literature Ser.). 195p. 1992. reprint ed. lib. bdg. 69.00 (*0-7812-7157-6*) Rprt Serv.

Select Translations from Old English Prose. Ed. by Albert S. Cook & Chauncey B. Tinker. LC 68-57700. 304p. (C). 1968. reprint ed. 40.00 (*0-87752-025-9*) Gordian.

Select Translations from Old English Prose. Albert S. Cook. (BCL1-PR English Literature Ser.). 296p. 1992. reprint ed. lib. bdg. 79.00 (*0-7812-7158-4*) Rprt Serv.

Select Treatises of St. Athanasius in Controversy with the Arians, 2 vols., Set. 5th ed. Athanasius. Tr. by John H. Newman. LC 77-84694. (Heresies of the Early Christian & Medieval Era Ser.). reprint ed. 125.00 (*0-404-16100-6*) AMS Pr.

Select View: American Paintings from the Columbus Museum. Anne Timpano. 32p. 1987. pap. 10.00 (*1-882650-04-2*) Colmbs Mus GA.

*****Select Visual Basic 3.0 for Windows.** H. L. Capron. (C). 1996. pap. text ed. 22.95 (*0-8053-3874-8*) Addison-Wesley.

*****Select Visual Basic 4.0 for Windows 95.** 2nd ed. Paul B. Thurrott. (C). 1997. pap. text ed. 22.95 (*0-8053-1619-1*) Addison-Wesley.

*****Select Visual Basic 5 for Windows 95 Plus Instructor's Manual.** Stephen Solosky. (C). 1997. pap. text ed. 14.95 (*0-201-31555-6*) Addison-Wesley.

Select Visual Field Guide for Microsoft Access 7 Projects for Windows 95. Marianne B. Fox. (C). 1997. pap. text ed. write for info. (*0-8053-1307-9*) Addison-Wesley.

Select Visual Field Guide for Microsoft Word 7 Projects for Windows 95. 2nd ed. James A. Folts. (C). 1997. pap. text ed. write for info. (*0-8053-1608-6*) Addison-Wesley.

Select Visual Field Guide Microsoft Excel 7 Projects for Windows 95. Gary R. Brent. (C). 1997. pap. text ed. write for info. (*0-8053-1615-9*) Addison-Wesley.

*****Select Wordperfect 5.1 for Dos.** H. L. Capron. (C). 1992. pap. text ed. 22.95 (*0-8053-0837-7*) Addison-Wesley.

*****Select Wordperfect 6.0 for Windows.** H. L. Capron. (C). 1995. pap. text ed. 22.95 (*0-8053-2924-2*) Addison-Wesley.

Select Works of Antony Van Leeuwenhoek: His Microscopical Discoveries in Many Works of Nature, 2 vols in 1. Anthony Van Leeuwenhoek, 3rd. Ed. by Frank N. Egerton. Tr. by Samuel Hoole. LC 77-74236. (History of Ecology Ser.). (Illus.). 1978. reprint ed. lib. bdg. 59.95 (*0-405-10405-7*) Ayer.

Select Works of Plotinus. Ed. by G. R. Mead. Tr. by Thomas Taylor. 421p. 1994. pap. 37.00 (*1-56459-429-7*) Kessinger Pub.

Select Works of Porphyry. Tr. by Thomas Taylor. (Thomas Taylor Ser.: No. 2). 1994. 28.00 (*1-898910-01-4*) Minerva CA.

Select Works of Robert Crowley, Printer, Archdeacon of Hereford, Vicar of St. Lawrence, Jewry. Robert Crowley. Ed. by J. M. Cowper. (EETS, ES Ser.: No. 15). 1974. reprint ed. 55.00 (*0-527-00230-5*) Periodicals Srv.

Select Works of Thomas Case. Thomas Case. 432p. 1993. reprint ed. 26.95 (*1-877611-58-1*) Soli Deo Gloria.

*****Select Writings of John Edward Bruce: Militant Black Journalist.** John E. Bruce. 182p. 1971. 11.95 (*0-405-01982-3*) Arno Press.

Select Your Own Tree & Shrubbery Locations with a Tree & Shrubbery Care Information Locator Guide: A How to Find or Locate Workbook. Center for Self-Sufficiency, Research Division Staff. 50p. 1984. ring bd. 21.95 (*0-910811-58-X*) Ctr Self Suff.

Selecta. E. Hlawka. 550p. 1990. 151.95 (*0-387-50623-3*) Spr-Verlag.

Selecta: Expository Writing, Vol. 2. P. R. Halmos. (Illus.). 256p. 1983. 43.00 (*0-387-90756-4*) Spr-Verlag.

Selecta: Research Contributions, Vol. 1. P. R. Halmos. (Illus.). 458p. 1982. 66.00 (*0-387-90755-6*) Spr-Verlag.

Selecta: Selected Papers of D. C. Spencer, 3 vols., 1. D. C. Spencer. 1800p. 1985. text ed. 258.00 (*9971-978-02-4*) World Scientific Pub.

Selecta: Selected Papers of D. C. Spencer, 3 vols., 2. D. C. Spencer. 1800p. 1985. text ed. write for info. (*9971-978-03-2*) World Scientific Pub.

Selecta: Selected Papers of D. C. Spencer, 3 vols., 3. D. C. Spencer. 1800p. 1985. text ed. write for info. (*9971-978-04-0*) World Scientific Pub.

Selected. Thomas Traherne. Ed. by Alan Bradford. 416p. 1992. pap. 12.95 (*0-14-044543-9*, Penguin Classics) Viking Penguin.

Selected Abstracts on Structural Applications of Plastics. (ASCE Manual & Report on Engineering Practice: No. 47). 80p. 1967. pap. 4.00 (*0-87262-221-5*) Am Soc Civil Eng.

Selected Addresses & Essays. Richard B. Haldane. LC 71-107704. (Essay Index Reprint Ser.). 1977. 20.95 (*0-8369-1507-0*) Ayer.

Selected Addresses of a Southern Lawyer. Aubrey L. Brooks. ix, 165p. 1954. 19.95 (*0-8078-0657-9*) U of NC Pr.

*****Selected Adventures of Sherlock Holmes.** abr. ed. Arthur Conan Doyle. Ed. by Michael J. Marshall. (Core Classics Ser.: Vol. 5). (Illus.). 160p. (J). (gr. 4-6). 1997. pap. 5.95 (*1-890517-08-9*); lib. bdg. write for info. (*1-890517-09-7*) Core Knowledge.

Selected Adventures of Sherlock Holmes. large type ed. Arthur Conan Doyle. 12.00 (*0-85456-589-2*) Ulverscroft.

Selected African American Writing from 1760 to 1910. Authur P. Davis. 320p. 1995. 5.95 (*0-553-21435-7*, Bantam Classics) Bantam.

Selected American Indian Artifacts: Teachers Guide. Intro. by Leilani L. Duke. (Multicultural Art Print Series: No. II). (Illus.). 36p. 1991. teacher ed. write for info. (*1-56290-062-5*, 6017) Crystal.

Selected Analytes in Clinical Chemistry. Ed. by Jocelyn M. Hicks & K. Michael Parker. LC 84-71707. 218p. 1984. 20.00 (*0-915274-25-6*) Am Assn Clinical Chem.

Selected & Annotated Bibliography of American Naval History. Compiled by Paolo E. Coletta. 548p. (C). 1988. lib. bdg. 66.50 (*0-8191-7111-5*) U Pr of Amer.

Selected & Annotated Bibliography of Books & Periodicals in Western Languages Dealing with the Near & Middle East, with Special Emphasis on Medieval & Modern Times. Richard Ettinghausen. LC 70-180337. reprint ed. 42.50 (*0-404-56249-3*) AMS Pr.

*****Selected & Annotated Bibliography of Chicano Studies.** Charles M. Tatum. 121p. (Orig.). 12.00 (*0-614-24973-2*) Society Sp & Sp-Am.

*****Selected & Annotated Bibliography of Chicano Studies.** 2nd ed. Charles M. Tatum. LC 79-64044. 121p. (Orig.). 1979. pap. 12.00 (*0-614-25186-9*) Society Sp & Sp-Am.

Selected & Annotated Bibliography of Economic Literature in the Arabic Countries of the Middle East, 2 vols., Vol. 1. pap. 10.00 (*0-8156-6020-0*, Am U Beirut) Syracuse U Pr.

Selected & Annotated Bibliography of Economic Literature in the Arabic Countries of the Middle East, 2 vols., Vol. 2. pap. 14.95 (*0-685-57787-2*, Am U Beirut) Syracuse U Pr.

Selected & Annotated Bibliography of the Republic of China, 1958-59, & 1959-60, 2 vols. in 1. Tai-Pei National Central Library. Chung-Yang T'u-Shu Kuan Staff. LC 75-38403. (China Classic & Contemporary Works in Reprint Ser.). reprint ed. 64.50 (*0-404-56921-8*) AMS Pr.

Selected & Annotated Bibliography on Business Archives & Records Management. Compiled by Karen M. Benedict. 248p. 1992. pap. 25.00 (*0-931828-86-4*) Soc Am Archivists.

Selected & Last Poems. Paul Zweig. Ed. & Intro. by C. K. Williams. LC 89-5417. (Wesleyan Poetry Ser.). 111p. 1989. pap. 12.95 (*0-8195-1159-5*, Wesleyan Univ Pr) U Pr of New Eng.

Selected & New Poems. Norman Dubie. LC 83-42686. 160p. 1983. pap. 5.95 (*0-393-30140-0*) Norton.

Selected & New Poems, 1980-1990. Kathleen Iddings. 160p. (Orig.). (C). 1990. pap. 10.00 (*0-942424-13-1*) W Anglia Pubns.

Selected, Annotated Bibliography of Completed Research on Management Theory & Practice in Physical Education & Athletics to 1972: Including a Background Essay. Earle F. Zeigler. (Monograph Series on Sport & Physical Education Management). 54p. (C). 1995. pap. text ed. 5.00 (*0-87563-555-5*) Stipes.

Selected Annotated Bibliography of Ohio Raptors. Jeffery R. Stenzel. Ed. by Veda M. Cafazzo. (Informative Circular Ser.: No. 13). 11p. 1984. 2.00 (*0-86727-097-7*) Ohio Bio Survey.

Selected Annotated Bibliography of the Physician Assistant Profession. 2nd ed. Ed. by Susan M. Anderson. 119p. 1980. pap. 20.00 (*0-318-13477-2*) Assn Phys Asst Prog.

Selected Annotated Bibliography of the Physician Assistant Profession. 3rd ed. Ed. by Susan M. Anderson. 155p. 1984. pap. 15.00 (*0-318-50054-X*) Assn Phys Asst Prog.

Selected Annotated Bibliography of Vocational Education: Planning & Implementaion in Developing Countries, with Special Reference to Nepal. Lekh Belbase et al. 49p. 1982. 8.00 (*0-318-04180-4*, 48) Am-Nepal Ed.

Selected Annotated Bibliography on Italian Serial Composers. Harvey J. Stokes. LC 89-13877. (Studies in the History & Interpretation of Music: Vol. 27). 80p. 1990. lib. bdg. 49.95 (*0-88946-577-0*) E Mellen.

*****Selected Annotated Readings on Outcome Measures in Child Welfare Services.** Ed. by American Humane Association, Children's Division Staff. (Illus.). ii, 35p. 1993. pap. text ed. write for info. (*0-930915-11-9*, COM01A) Am Humane Assn.

Selected Annual Reviews of the Analytical Sciences, Vol. 1. Royal Society of Chemistry Staff. 1989. 24.00 (*0-85990-201-3*) CRC Pr.

Selected Annual Reviews of the Analytical Sciences, Vol. 2. Royal Society of Chemistry Staff. 1989. 24.00 (*0-85990-202-1*) CRC Pr.

Selected Annual Reviews of the Analytical Sciences, Vol. 3. Royal Society of Chemistry Staff. 1989. 28.00 (*0-85990-203-X*) CRC Pr.

Selected Annual Reviews on the Analytical Sciences, Vol. 4. Royal Society of Chemistry Staff. 1989. 40.00 (*0-85990-204-8*) CRC Pr.

Selected Anthropological Papers: 1928-1949. Franz Weidenreich. LC 78-72708. reprint ed. 57.50 (*0-404-18279-8*) AMS Pr.

Selected Antitrust Cases: Landmark Decisions. 7th ed. Irwin M. Stelzer & Howard Kitt. (C). 1985. pap. text ed. 29.95 (*0-256-03222-X*) Irwin.

Selected Applications of Geometry to Low Dimensional Topology. M. Freedman & F. Luo. LC 89-18287. (University Lectures: Vol. 1). 104p. 1989. pap. 19.00 (*0-8218-7000-9*, ULECT/1) Am Math.

Selected Applications of Modern FT-IR Techniques. Koichi Nishikida et al. 1995. text ed. 100.00 (*2-88449-073-6*) Gordon & Breach.

Selected Archaeological Papers of Frederic Ward Putnam. Frederic W. Putnam. LC 76-178419. (Harvard University. Peabody Museum of Archaeology & Ethnology. Antiquities of the New World Ser.: No. 5). (Illus.). reprint ed. 110.00 (*0-404-57305-3*) AMS Pr.

Selected Articles. Incl. 1976-1977. 78p. 2.00 (*0-89567-010-0*); 1977-1978. Sam Marcy. 72p. 2.00 (*0-89567-029-1*); 1978-1979. 62p. 2.00 (*0-89567-032-1*); 1979-1980. 73p. 2.00 (*0-685-11763-4*); 1980-1981. 64p. 2.00 (*0-89567-004-6*); 1982-1983. 111p. 2.50 (*0-685-11764-2*); write for info. (*0-318-60117-6*) World View Forum.

Selected Articles: 1981-82. Sam Marcy. 89p. 1982. pap. 2.50 (*0-89567-078-X*) World View Forum.

Selected Articles & Program Reviews from Computers & Mining, Vol. 2: 1989-1991. Ed. by Betty L. Gibbs. 114p. 1992. pap. 20.00 (*0-943909-07-4*) Gibbs Assocs.

Selected Articles & Program Reviews from Computers & Mining, Vols. 1-4: 1985-1989. Ed. by Betty L. Gibbs. 93p. 1989. pap. 20.00 (*0-943909-04-X*) Gibbs Assocs.

Selected Articles by Harry Gunnison Brown: The Case for Land Value Taxation. Harry G. Brown. LC 80-25662. 245p. 1980. 6.00 (*0-911312-50-1*) Schalkenbach.

Selected Articles from the TESOL Newsletter, 1966-1983. Ed. by John F. Haskell. LC 86-50889. 272p. (Orig.). (C). 1986. pap. 16.50 (*0-939791-29-3*) Tchrs Eng Spkrs.

Selected Articles in Social Ecology. Ed. by James S. Wittman. LC 73-609. 295p. 1973. text ed. 39.50 (*0-8422-5086-7*); pap. text ed. 14.50 (*0-8422-0293-5*) Irvington.

Selected Articles on Censorship of Speech & the Press. Compiled by Lamar T. Beman. LC 76-98813. 507p. 1971. reprint ed. text ed. 35.00 (*0-8371-3073-5*, BECE, Greenwood Pr) Greenwood.

Selected Articles on Censorship of the Theater & Moving Pictures. Ed. by Lamar T. Beman. LC 78-160229. (Moving Pictures Ser.). 385p. 1971. reprint ed. lib. bdg. 42.95 (*0-89198-030-X*) Ozer.

*****Selected Articles on the Pact of Paris, Officially the General Pact for the Renunciation of War.** James T. Gerould. 287p. 1972. 18.95 (*0-8369-6934-0*) Ayer.

Selected Aspects of Nursing. Searle. 1989. pap. 21.50 (*0-409-10008-0*) Buttrwrth-Heinemann.

Selected Aspects of Potential Legal Liabilities of Independent Information Professionals. 2nd ed. T. R. Halvorson. 40p. 1995. pap. text ed. 39.50 (*0-938519-13-1*) Burwell Ent.

Selected ASTM General Use Standards on Water. 106p. 1988. pap. 26.00 (*0-8031-1172-X*, 03-419088-16) ASTM.

Selected ASTM Standards for Fence Materials & Products. 4th ed. American Society for Testing & Materials Staff. LC 88-22152. 178p. 1988. reprint ed. pap. 50.80 (*0-8357-2582-0*, 2040276) Bks Demand.

Selected ASTM Standards for Fence Materials & Products. 6th ed. LC 94-34831. 1994. 43.00 (*0-8031-1801-5*, 03-614094-02) ASTM.

*****Selected ASTM Standards for Fence Materials & Products.** 7th ed. LC 96-45393. 1996. write for info. (*0-8031-1828-7*) ASTM.

Selected ASTM Standards for the Purchasing Community. 2nd ed. ASTM Staff. LC 89-28297. 760p. 1989. pap. 72.00 (*0-8031-1222-X*, 03-080090-47) ASTM.

Selected ASTM Standards on Fastener-Related Materials & Testing. LC 96-13348. 1996. 28.00 (*0-8031-1820-1*) ASTM.

Selected ASTM Standards on Packaging. 2nd ed. American Society for Testing & Materials Staff. (Illus.). 223p. 1987. reprint ed. pap. 63.60 (*0-8357-3058-1*, 2039314) Bks Demand.

Selected ASTM Standards on Packaging. 4th ed. ASTM Committee D-10 on Packaging Staff. LC 94-17264. (Pack Ser.: Vol. 94). 1994. 59.00 (*0-8031-1792-2*, 03-410094-11) ASTM.

Selected ASTM Standards on Packaging. American Society for Testing & Materials Staff. (Illus.). 239p. 1984. reprint ed. pap. 68.20 (*0-317-58777-3*, 2029660) Bks Demand.

Selected Atlases of Bone Scintigraphy. Ed. by Douglas Van Nostrand et al. LC 92-2321. (Atlases of Clinical Nuclear Medicine Ser.). (Illus.). 168p. 1992. 104.00 (*0-387-97823-2*) Spr-Verlag.

Selected Atlases of Cardiovascular Nuclear Medicine. Ed. by Douglas Van Nostrand. LC 93-10234. (Atlases of Clinical Nuclear Medicine Ser.). (Illus.). 168p. 1993. 108.00 (*0-387-94045-6*) Spr-Verlag.

Selected Atlases of Gastrointestinal Scintigraphy. Ed. by Harvey A. Ziessman & Douglas Van Nostrand. (Atlases of Clinical Nuclear Medicine Ser.). (Illus.). xi, 173p. 1991. 104.00 (*0-387-97618-3*) Spr-Verlag.

Selected Attempts at Stereoscopic Moving Pictures & Their Relationship to the Motion Picture Technology, 1852-1903. H. Mark Gosser. 1977. 24.95 (*0-405-09890-1*, 11485) Ayer.

Selected Austrian Short Stories. Tr. by Marie Busch. LC 70-37260. (Short Story Index Reprint Ser.). 1977. reprint ed. 20.95 (*0-8369-4071-7*) Ayer.

Selected Basic Agreements & Joint Declarations on Labour-Management Relations. (Labour-Management Relations Ser.: No. 63). iv, 299p. 1983. pap. 22.50 (*92-2-103460-7*) Intl Labour Office.

Selected Bible Readings. 1962. pap. 3.95 (*0-686-24354-4*); spiral bd. 4.95 (*0-686-24355-2*); 5.95 (*0-686-28567-0*) Divine Sci Fed.

Selected Bibliographies of Hydrothermal & Magmatic Mineral Deposits. John D. Ridge. LC 59-1279. (Geological Society of America, Memoir Ser.: No. 75). 209p. reprint ed. pap. 59.60 (*0-317-10309-1*, 2004397) Bks Demand.

Selected Bibliography: Illinois, Chicago & Environs. Federal Writers Project (WPA) Staff. 60p. 1990. reprint ed. pap. 15.00 (*0-924772-13-1*) CH Bookworks.

Selected Bibliography for Chicano Studies. Juan Gomez-Quinones & Albert Camarillo. (Bibliographic & Reference Ser: No. 3). 1977. pap. 2.50 (*0-89551-009-X*) UCLA Chicano Studies.

Selected Bibliography for Washington & Descriptions of Major Local Collections. Fisher & Linda J. Lear. 1981. 6.00 (*0-318-21777-5*) G Washington Univ.

Selected Bibliography for Washington & Descriptions of Major Local Collections, Vol. M8. Perry G. Fisher & Linda J. Lear. 1981. 6.00 (*1-888028-06-8*) GWU Ctr WAS.

Selected Bibliography of Alkaline Ingneous Rocks & Related Mineral Deposits, with an Emphasis on Western North America. Ed. by F. E. Mutschler et al. 222p. (Orig.). (C). 1996. pap. text ed. 50.00 (*0-7881-2729-2*) DIANE Pub.

Selected Bibliography of Applied Ethics in the Professions, 1950-1970: A Working Sourcebook with Annotations & Indexes. Daniel L. Gothie. LC 73-80627. 198p. reprint ed. pap. 56.50 (*0-8357-2709-2*, 2039822) Bks Demand.

Selected Bibliography of Books & Articles on Censorship (1950-1983) Compiled by Denise Rogers. LC 83-204879. (Washington University Law Library Bibliography Ser.: No. 4). vi, 22p. (Orig.). 1983. pap. text ed. 8.00 (*0-317-00753-X*) Wash U Law Lib.

Selected Bibliography of County, City & Town History & Related Published Records in the South Carolina Archives Reference Library. Robert H. Mackintosh, Jr. 43p. 1994. pap. text ed. 2.00 (*1-880067-27-7*) SC Dept of Arch & Hist.

Selected Bibliography of Missouri Archaeology. Randy L. Cottier et al. Ed. by W. Raymond Wood. LC 72-619659. (Research Ser.: No. 10). (Illus.). 34p. (Orig.). 1973. pap. 2.00 (*0-943414-11-3*) MO Arch Soc.

Selected Bibliography of Modern Historiography. Ed. by Attila Pok. LC 91-46699. (Bibliographies & Indexes in World History Ser.: No. 24). 304p. 1992. text ed. 59.95 (*0-313-27231-X*, PBM, Greenwood Pr) Greenwood.

Selected Bibliography of Music Librarianship. Don Phillips. (Illinois University Graduate School of Library Science Occasional Papers: No.113). 48p. reprint ed. pap. 25.00 (*0-317-10108-0*, 2007257) Bks Demand.

*****Selected Bibliography of Pediatric Orthopaedics.** 4th ed. Ed. by James H. Beaty & Charles T. Price. 400p. 1996. pap. 30.00 (*0-89203-158-1*) Amer Acad Ortho Surg.

Selected Bibliography of Pediatric Orthopaedics with Commentary. 3rd ed. Ed. by Walter B. Greene & Eric T. Jones. LC 90-62232. 250p. 1990. pap. 30.00 (*0-89203-038-0*) Amer Acad Ortho Surg.

Selected Bibliography of Slavic Linguistics, 2 Vols, 1. Ed. by Edward Stankiewicz & Dean S. Worth. (Slavistic Printings & Reprintings Ser.: No. 2). 1966. text ed. 111.55 (*3-11-000135-7*) Mouton.

S

Selected Bibliography of Slavic Linguistics, 2 Vols, 2. Ed. by Edward Stankiewicz & Dean S. Worth. (Slavistic Printings & Reprintings Ser.: No. 2). 1966. text ed. 116.95 (*3-11-000109-8*) Mouton.

Selected Bibliography of the Foot & Ankle with Commentary. Ed. by Glen Pfeffer & Mark S. Mizel. 321p. 1992. pap. 25.00 (*0-89203-061-5*) Amer Acad Ortho Surg.

Selected Bibliography of Twentieth Century GeoScience: Mariana Island Arc. H. Galt Siegrist. (Bibliography Ser.: No. 4). 105p. (C). 1992. 9.95 (*1-878453-13-0*); 9.95 (*0-685-59579-X*) Univ Guam MAR Ctr.

Selected Bibliography of Utah Archaeology. Alan R. Schroedl. (Anthropological Papers: No. 102). (Orig.). 1979. pap. text ed. 10.00 (*0-87480-141-9*) U of Utah Pr.

Selected Bibliography of Virginia, 1607-1699. John M. Jennings et al. (Illus.). 80p. 1994. pap. 10.00 (*0-614-00900-6*, 9452) Clearfield Co.

Selected Bibliography on Detection of Dependence-Producing Drugs in Body Fluids. T. L. Chruscie & M. Chrusciel. (Offset Publication Ser.: No. 17). 1975. pap. text ed. 15.00 (*92-4-052004-X*, 1120017) World Health.

Selected Bibliography on Legal & Related Matters Affecting Business in Latin America. Ed. by Raoul Gordon. 1976. lib. bdg. 59.95 (*0-8490-2587-7*) Gordon Pr.

Selected Bibliography on the American Jail with Special Emphasis on Illinois Jails, No. 821. Hans W. Mattick. 1975. 8.50 (*0-686-20357-7*, Sage Prdcls Pr) Sage.

Selected Books for Social Workers. rev. ed. 1982. pap. 6.00 (*0-942644-10-7*) Univ Bk Serv.

Selected by see Adventure Stories

Selected Byzantine Hymns. 2nd ed. Holy Transfiguration Monastery Staff. LC 86-83031. 120p. (Orig.). 1987. pap. 10.00 (*0-913026-59-X*) St Nectarios.

***Selected Canadian Spinning Wheels in Perspective: An Analytical Approach.** Judith Buxton. (Mercury Ser.: No. 30). (Illus.). 340p. 1992. pap. 24.95 (*0-660-14000-4*, Pub. by Can Mus Civil CN) U of Wash Pr.

Selected Canterbury Tales. Geoffrey Chaucer. LC 94-35008. (Thrift Editions Ser.). 128p. (Orig.). 1994. pap. text ed. 1.00 (*0-486-28241-4*) Dover.

Selected Cantos. Ezra Pound. LC 75-11446. 1970. pap. text ed. 7.95 (*0-8112-0160-0*, NDP304) New Directions.

Selected Case Studies in Powder Metallurgy. Ed. by Ivor Jenkins & John Wood. 152p. 1991. 73.50 (*0-901462-80-2*, Pub. by Inst Materials UK) Ashgate Pub Co.

Selected Cases in Fashion Marketing, 2 vols. 3rd ed. Nathan Axelrod. 1968. pap. write for info. (*0-318-51118-5*) Macmillan.

Selected Cases in Fashion Marketing, 2 vols., 2. 3rd ed. Nathan Axelrod. 1968. pap. write for info. (*0-672-96038-9*) Macmillan.

Selected Cases in General & Systemic Pathology. American Registry of Pathology Staff & Armed Forces Institute of Pathology Staff. (C). 1991. 250.00 incl. disk (*1-56815-000-8*) Mosby Yr Bk.

Selected Cases in Labor Relations: An Experiential Approach. Finston & Porter. (C). 1983. teacher ed. write for info. (*0-8359-6982-7*, Reston) P-H.

Selected Cases in Strategic Management. 3rd ed. Samuel C. Certo. Ed. by J. Paul Peter. LC 94-36522. (C). 1994. 53.95 (*0-256-18172-1*) Irwin.

Selected Chapters - Business One Irwin. 2nd ed. AIMR Staff et al. 1991. per. write for info. (*1-55623-765-0*) Irwin Prof Pubng.

Selected Chapters from Finite Mathematics & Its Applications. 2nd ed. Stanley J. Farlow. 1994. pap. text ed. write for info. (*0-07-021282-1*) McGraw.

Selected Chapters from Finite Mathematics with Its Applications. Farlow. 1993. pap. text ed. write for info. (*0-07-021204-X*) McGraw.

Selected Chapters from the Elements of Logic. 5th ed. Stephen Barker. 1994. pap. text ed. write for info. (*0-07-005229-8*) McGraw.

Selected Chapters from the Writings of the Maya Indians. Ed. by Yuri V. Knorozov & Tatiana Proskouriakoff. Tr. by Sophie Coe. LC 70-38502. (Harvard University. Peabody Museum of Archaeology & Ethnology. Antiquities of the New World Ser.: No. 4). reprint ed. 47.50 (*0-404-52647-0*) AMS Pr.

Selected Chapters from Understanding Chemistry: A Preparatory Course. Herron. 1994. pap. text ed. write for info. (*0-07-028394-X*) McGraw.

Selected Characteristics of Occupations Defined in the Dictionary Occupational Titles. 1993. pap. 40.00 (*0-16-038202-5*) Claitors.

***Selected Characteristics of Occupations Defined in the Dictionary Occupational Titles.** 1993. pap. 40.00 (*0-87511-484-9*) Claitors.

***Selected Characteristics of Occupations Defined in the Revised Dictionary of Occupational Titles, 2 vols.** 1997. lib. bdg. 605.75 (*0-8490-7665-X*) Gordon Pr.

Selected Characteristics of Occupations Defined in the Revised Dictionary of Occupational Titles, 2 vols., Set. 1994. lib. bdg. 600.00 (*0-8490-8512-8*) Gordon Pr.

Selected Chinese-English & English-Chinese Dictionary. Wen-Hwa Zhang. (CHI & ENG.). pap. 12.95 (*7-100-00589-2*, Pub. by China Intl Bk CH) Distribks Inc.

Selected Chinese Texts in the Classical & Colloquial Styles. Ed. by Lien-Sheng Yang. LC 53-5949. (Harvard-Yenching Institute Publications). 210p. 1953. pap. 6.95 (*0-674-79710-8*) HUP.

Selected Christian Hebraists. William McKane. 256p. (C). 1989. text ed. 80.00 (*0-521-35507-9*) Cambridge U Pr.

***Selected Civil War Bibliography.** Patrick McCawley. (Illus.). 44p. 1997. pap. text ed. 2.00 (*1-880067-42-0*) SC Dept of Arch & Hist.

Selected Clarinet Solos, EFS43. (Illus.). 192p. pap. 14.95 (*0-8256-2043-0*, AM40221) Music Sales.

***Selected Classical Papers.** D. R. Bailey. LC 97-3789. (C). 1997. 42.50 (*0-472-10816-6*) U of Mich Pr.

Selected Classical Papers of Basil Lanneau Gildersleeve. Ed. by Ward W. Briggs, Jr. LC 92-35986. (American Philological Association, American Classical Studies: No. 30). 355p. 1992. 59.95 (*1-55540-806-0*, 40 04 30); pap. 39.95 (*1-55540-807-9*, 400430) Scholars Pr GA.

Selected Climatic Data for a Global Set of Standard Stations for Vegetation Science. Manfred J. Muller. 1982. lib. bdg. 234.00 (*90-6193-945-3*) Kluwer Ac.

Selected Climbs in the Cascades. Peter Potterfield & Jim Nelson. (Illus.). 240p. 1993. pap. 22.95 (*0-89886-368-6*) Mountaineers.

Selected Comedies: Elizabeth Inchbald. Intro. by Roger Manvell. (Illus.). 372p. (Orig.). (C). 1988. lib. bdg. 49.00 (*0-8191-6635-9*) U Pr of Amer.

Selected Commercial Statutes. 1900p. (C). 1993. pap. text ed. 24.00 (*0-314-02445-X*) West Pub.

Selected Commercial Statutes: Pamphlet. 1995. 25.00 (*0-314-06840-6*) West Pub.

Selected Commercial Statutes, 1996 Edition. 1725p. 1996. pap. text ed. write for info. (*0-314-09770-8*) West Pub.

***Selected Commerical Statutes.** 1725p. 1997. pap. text ed. write for info. (*0-314-21222-1*) West Pub.

Selected Concepts from Educational Psychology & Adult Education for Extension & Continuing Educators. J. Paul Leagans et al. LC 74-171881. (Notes & Essays Ser.: No. 71). 1971. pap. text ed. 3.50 (*0-87060-046-X*, NES 71) Syracuse U Cont Ed.

Selected Concrete Poems. Michael J. Phillips. (Cambric Poetry Ser.). 108p. (Orig.). 1986. pap. 11.95 (*0-918342-25-2*) Cambric.

Selected Conjurations from the Lemegeton & Other Rituals. 2nd ed. Ed. by Nelson H. White. 30p. (Orig.). (C). 1995. pap. 15.00 (*1-877884-19-7*) Tech Group.

Selected Constants Optical Rotary Power: IA Steroids. Jean P. Mathieu & J. Jacques. (Tables of Constants & Numerical Data Ser.: Vol. 14). 453.00 (*0-08-010982-9*, Pub. by Pergamon Repr UK) Franklin.

Selected Constants Optical Rotatory Power: Alkaloids. Jean P. Mathieu & M. Janot. (Tables of Constants & Numerical Data Ser.). 1959. 104.00 (*0-08-009312-4*, Pub. by Pergamon Repr UK) Franklin.

Selected Constants Optical Rotatory Power: Amino Acids. Jean P. Mathieu & P. Desnuelle. (Tables of Constants & Numerical Data Ser.: Vol. 10). 1959. 35.00 (*0-08-009202-0*, Pub. by Pergamon Repr UK) Franklin.

Selected Contemporary Work Force Reports: A Synthesis & Critique. James M. Weber. 67p. (Orig.). (C). 1994. pap. text ed. 25.00 (*0-7881-0799-2*) DIANE Pub.

Selected Contributions of Ukrainian Scholars to Economics. Ed. by Iwan S. Koropeckyj. LC 84-80076. (Sources & Documents Ser.). 244p. 1990. 7.50 (*0-916458-10-5*) Harvard Ukrainian.

Selected Contributions to Ground-Water Hydrology by C. V. Theis, & a Review of His Life & Work. Ed. by Alfred Clebsch. Vol. 2415. 1994. write for info. (*0-318-72588-6*) US Geol Survey.

Selected Coolwater Fishes of North America. Ed. by R. L. Kendall. LC 78-72983. (Special Publication Ser.: No. 11). 437p. 1978. 21.00 (*0-913235-08-3*) Am Fisheries Soc.

Selected Corporation & Partnership, Statutes, Rules & Forms. Lewis D. Solomon et al. 1014p. 1994. pap. text ed. 18.00 (*0-314-04266-0*) West Pub.

Selected Correspondence: Eighteen Forty-Six to Eighteen Ninety-Five. Karl Marx & Friedric Engels. LC 75-25261. 551p. 1975. reprint ed. text ed. 38.50 (*0-8371-8385-5*, MAKMF, Greenwood Pr) Greenwood.

Selected Correspondence of Bernard Shaw: Bernard Shaw & H. G. Wells. Ed. by J. Percy Smith. 256p. 1995. 40.00 (*0-8020-3001-7*) U of Toronto Pr.

Selected Correspondence of Bernard Shaw: Theatrics, 1889-1950. Ed. by Dan H. Laurence. 256p. 1995. 40.00 (*0-8020-3000-9*) U of Toronto Pr.

Selected Correspondence of Dr. Karl A. Menninger, 1919-1945. Howard J. Faulkner & Virginia D. Pruitt. LC 88-5502. (C). 1989. text ed. 40.00 (*0-300-03978-6*) Yale U Pr.

Selected Correspondence of Fryderyk Chopin. Ed. by Arthur Hedley. LC 79-17655. (Music Reprint Ser.). 1980. reprint ed. 45.00 (*0-306-79579-5*) Da Capo.

Selected Correspondence of Karl A. Menninger, 1919-1945. Ed. by Howard J. Faulkner & Virginia D. Pruitt. (Illus.). 488p. 1995. pap. 29.95 (*0-8262-1013-9*) U of Mo Pr.

Selected Correspondence of Karl A. Menninger, 1945-1965. Ed. by Howard J. Faulkner & Virginia D. Pruitt. (Illus.). 294p. 1995. pap. 29.95 (*0-8262-0998-X*) U of Mo Pr.

Selected Correspondence of Kenneth Burke & Malcolm Cowley, 1915-1981. Ed. by Paul Jay. 1990. pap. 13.95 (*0-520-06899-8*) U CA Pr.

Selected County Government Bibliography with Annotations, Nos. 1233- 1234. Cortus T. Koehler. 1977. 9.00 (*0-686-19691-0*, Sage Prdcls Pr) Sage.

Selected Critical Essays. William Wordsworth & Samuel Taylor Coleridge. Ed. by Thomas M. Raysor. (Crofts Classics Ser.). 128p. 1958. pap. text ed. write for info. (*0-88295-104-1*) Harlan Davidson.

Selected Critical Studies of Baudelaire. Charles Baudelaire. Ed. by D. Parmee. LC 76-29452. reprint ed. 45.00 (*0-404-15300-3*) AMS Pr.

Selected Critical Writings. George Eliot. (World's Classics Ser.). 400p. 1993. pap. 11.95 (*0-19-282886-X*) OUP.

Selected Critical Writings of George Santayana, Vol. 1. George Santayana. Ed. by Norman Henfrey. LC 68-21394. 348p. reprint ed. pap. 99.20 (*0-317-28141-0*, 2022470) Bks Demand.

Selected Critical Writings of George Santayana, Vol. 2. George Santayana. Ed. by Norman Henfrey. LC 68-21394. 257p. reprint ed. pap. 73.30 (*0-317-26410-9*, 2024466) Bks Demand.

Selected Criticism. Nicolas Boileau-Despreaux. Tr. by Ernest Dilworth from FRE. LC 65-26530. 1965. pap. text ed. 8.95 (*0-672-60471-X*) Irvington.

Selected Criticism, Nineteen Sixteen to Nineteen Fifty-Seven. John M. Murry. LC 86-18339. 320p. 1986. reprint ed. text ed. 69.50 (*0-313-25219-X*, MUSE, Greenwood Pr) Greenwood.

Selected Cronicas. Clarice Lispector. Tr. by Giovanni Pontiero from POR. LC 96-23768. 212p. (Orig.). 1996. pap. 12.95 (*0-8112-1340-4*, NDP834) New Directions.

Selected Czech Tales. Marie Busch & Otto Pick. LC 73-13412. (Short Story Index Reprint Ser.). 1977. reprint ed. 18.95 (*0-8369-3669-8*) Ayer.

Selected Dances for Piano (Tanzweisen fuer Klavier), 6 vols in 2. Josef Strauss. Ed. by Carl Pfleger. (Selected Dances for the Piano Ser.). 372p. (GER.). 1973. reprint ed. lib. bdg. 125.00 (*0-8450-1009-3*) Broude.

***Selected Data on Federal Funds for Research & Development - Fiscal Years 1993, 1994, & 1995.** Ronald L. Meeks. (Illus.). 35p. (C). 1996. reprint ed. pap. 25.00 (*0-7881-3406-X*) DIANE Pub.

Selected Data on Graduate Students & Postdoctorates in Science & Engineering. 53p. (Orig.). (C). 1993. pap. text ed. 25.00 (*1-56806-472-1*) DIANE Pub.

Selected Data on Science & Engineering Doctorate Awards (1993) Susan T. Hill. 79p. (Orig.). (C). 1995. pap. text ed. 25.00 (*0-7881-2183-9*) DIANE Pub.

Selected Decisions of the Human Rights Committee under the Optional Protocol, Vol. 2. 246p. 1989. 45.00 (*92-1-154074-7*, 89.XIV.1) UN.

Selected Declarations of Dependence. Harry Mathews. (Sun & Moon Classics Ser.: No. 128). (Illus.). 200p. (Orig.). 1995. pap. 10.95 (*1-55713-234-8*) Sun & Moon CA.

Selected Developments in Soviet Airborne Computer Technology, 1958-1977. Andrew A. Michta. 76p. (Orig.). 1986. pap. text ed. 100.00 (*1-55831-065-7*) Delphic Associates.

Selected Developments in Soviet Mathematical Cybernetics. Boris Trakhtenbrot. Ed. by Rebecca Krafft. (Illus.). 125p. (Orig.). 1986. pap. text ed. 75.00 (*1-55831-051-7*) Delphic Associates.

Selected Dickinson Lectures in Accounting, 1936-1952: Original Anthology. Ed. by Stephen A. Zeff. LC 77-87323. (Contemporary Accounting Thought Ser.). 1978. lib. bdg. 37.95 (*0-405-10935-0*) Ayer.

Selected Directory of Audio Visual Materials on Puerto Rico & the Puerto Ricans. Ed. by Luis A. Cardona. 70p. (Orig.). 1984. pap. text ed. 8.95 (*0-914199-02-1*) Carreta Pr.

Selected Discography of Solo Song: Supplement 1971-1974. Dorothy Stahl. LC 76-12132. (Detroit Studies in Music Bibliography: No. 34). 99p. 1976. 18.00 (*0-911772-80-4*) Info Coord.

Selected Doctrines from Indian Philosophy. V. R. Rao. (C). 1987. 21.50 (*81-7099-000-9*, Pub. by Mittal II) S Asia.

Selected Documentation on Criminology see New Towns: A Selected Annotated Bibliography

Selected Documents Dealing with the Organization of the First Congregations & the First Conferences of the Augustana Synod & Their Growth until 1860, Pt. 1. Ed. by I. O. Nothstein. (Augustana Historical Society Publications: No. 10). 195p. 1944. pap. 3.00 (*0-910184-10-0*) Augustana.

Selected Documents Dealing with the Organization of the First Congregations & the First Conferences of the Augustana Synod & Their Growth until 1860, Pt. 2. Ed. by I. O. Nothstein. (Augustana Historical Society Publications: Vol. 11). 167p. 1946. pap. 3.00 (*0-910184-11-9*) Augustana.

Selected Documents of Lala Lajpat Rai, 5 vols., Set. Ravindra Kumar. (C). 1992. 150.00 (*81-7041-648-5*, Pub. by Anmol II) S Asia.

Selected Documents of Lokamanya Bal Gangadhar Tilak, 4 vols., Set. Ravindra Kumar. (C). 1992. 120.00 (*81-7041-603-5*, Pub. by Anmol II) S Asia.

Selected Documents of the International Petroleum Industry: 1966-1978 (with Pre-1966 Reports), 15 bks., Set. Organization of the Petroleum Exporting Countries (OPEC) Staff. 1983. reprint ed. 465.00 (*0-89941-291-2*, 201610) W S Hein.

Selected Drawings Nineteen Seventy-Five to Nineteen Eighty-One. Illus. by Michael Hafftka. 112p. 1981. pap. 12.50 (*0-941062-00-7*) Begos & Rosenberg.

Selected Drawings Nineteen Seventy-Five to Nineteen Eighty-One. deluxe ed. Illus. by Michael Hafftka. 112p. 1981. 85.00 (*0-941062-01-5*) Begos & Rosenberg.

Selected Earthquake Engineering Papers of George W. Housner: Civil Engineering Classics. LC 90-987. 783p. 1990. pap. text ed. 70.00 (*0-87262-766-7*) Am Soc Civil Eng.

Selected Economic Writings. Sukhamoy Chakravarty. 600p. (C). 1993. 39.95 (*0-19-562803-9*, 5966) OUP.

Selected Economic Writings of Abba P. Lerner. Ed. by David C. Colander. (Selected Economic Writings Ser.). 752p. (C). 1983. text ed. 84.00 (*0-8147-1385-8*) NYU Pr.

Selected Economic Writings of Oskar Morgenstern. Ed. by Andre R. Schottter. LC 75-27380. 539p. (C). 1978. text ed. 84.00 (*0-8147-7771-6*) NYU Pr.

Selected Elementary Reactions see Comprehensive Chemical Kinetics

Selected English Short Stores (XIX & XX Centuries) - Second Series. (BCL1-PR English Literature Ser.). 483p. 1992. reprint ed. lib. bdg. 99.00 (*0-7812-7154-1*) Rprt Serv.

Selected English Short Stores, XIX & XX Centuries - Third Series. (BCL1-PR English Literature Ser.). 507p. 1992. reprint ed. lib. bdg. 99.00 (*0-7812-7155-X*) Rprt Serv.

Selected English Writings of Yone Noguchi: An East-West Literary Assimilation, Vol. 1: Poetry. Ed. by Yoshinobu Hakutani. LC 88-46180. (Illus.). 216p. 1990. 39.50 (*0-8386-3356-0*) Fairleigh Dickinson.

Selected English Writings of Yone Noguchi - an East-West Literary Assimilation: Prose, Vol. 2. Ed. by Yoshinobu Hakutani. LC 88-46180. (Illus.). 352p. 1992. 49.50 (*0-8386-3422-2*) Fairleigh Dickinson.

Selected Environmental Law Statutes, 1995-96: Educational Edition. 1300p. (C). 1995. pap. text ed. 20.00 (*0-314-06876-7*) West Pub.

Selected Environmental Law Statutes, 1996-97: Educational Edition. 1300p. 1996. pap. text ed. write for info. (*0-614-14191-5*) West Pub.

***Selected Environmental Law Statutes, 1996-97 Educational Edition.** 1300p. 1996. pap. text ed. write for info. (*0-314-09977-8*) West Pub.

Selected Epigrams. Richard O'Connell. 1990. pap. 10.00 (*0-685-38407-1*) Atlantis Edns.

Selected Errors: Writings on Art & Politics, 1981-90. John Roberts. 292p. (C). 66.50 (*0-7453-0498-2*, Pub. by Pluto Pr UK); pap. 18.95 (*0-7453-0497-4*, Pub. by Pluto Pr UK) LPC InBook.

Selected Essays. Anne C. Allinson. LC 68-55836. (Essay Index Reprint Ser.). 1977. 20.95 (*0-8369-0146-0*) Ayer.

***Selected Essays.** Broch. 1993. lib. bdg. 34.95 (*0-226-07517-6*) U Ch Pr.

Selected Essays. John B. Bury. Ed. by Harold W. Temperley. LC 68-30177. (Essay Index Reprint Ser.). 1977. 20.95 (*0-8369-0267-X*) Ayer.

Selected Essays. Hayden Carruth. LC 95-4425. (Writing Re). 450p. 1995. pap. 18.00 (*1-55659-107-1*) Copper Canyon.

Selected Essays. Ralph Waldo Emerson. Ed. & Intro. by Larzer Ziff. (Classics Ser.). 360p. 1982. pap. 10.95 (*0-14-039013-8*, Penguin Classics) Viking Penguin.

Selected Essays. William C. Hazlitt. Ed. by John R. Nabholtz. (Crofts Classics Ser.). 160p. 1970. pap. text ed. write for info. (*0-88295-042-8*) Harlan Davidson.

Selected Essays. David Hume. LC 92-44092. (World's Classics Ser.). 448p. 1993. 11.95 (*0-19-283072-4*) OUP.

Selected Essays. Laurance Labadie. LC 78-78149. (Libertarian Broadsides Ser.: No. 7). (Illus.). 1978. pap. 1.50 (*0-87926-022-X*) R Myles.

Selected Essays. Frederic W. Maitland. Ed. by H. D. Hazeltine et al. LC 68-20316. (Essay Index Reprint Ser.). 1977. 20.95 (*0-8369-0670-5*) Ayer.

Selected Essays. Rich Mangelsdorff. (American Dust Ser.: No. 8). 1977. pap. 2.95 (*0-913218-50-2*) Dustbooks.

Selected Essays. Karl Marx. Tr. by H. J. Stenning. LC 68-16955. (Essay Index Reprint Ser.). 1977. 18.95 (*0-8369-0687-X*) Ayer.

Selected Essays. Michel de Montaigne. LC 95-49132. (Thrift Editions Ser.). 96p. (Orig.). 1996. pap. text ed. 1.50 (*0-486-29109-X*) Dover.

***Selected Essays.** Rav S. Schwab. LC 94-69579. 190p. (C). Date not set. 15.95 (*1-56062-292-X*) CIS Comm.

Selected Essays. August Strindberg. 275p. (C). 1996. text ed. 54.95 (*0-521-56375-5*) Cambridge U Pr.

Selected Essays. F. Lyman Windolph. LC 72-186116. 1972. 7.50 (*0-685-36105-5*) Franklin & Marshall.

Selected Essays. rev. ed. Swami Muktananda. Ed. by Paul Zweig. LC 95-47165. 216p. 1995. pap. 12.95 (*0-911307-37-0*) SYDA Found.

Selected Essays. James Darmesteter. Ed. by Morris Jastrow, Jr. LC 70-37149. (Essay Index Reprint Ser.). 1977. reprint ed. 23.95 (*0-8369-2492-4*) Ayer.

Selected Essays. Havelock Ellis. LC 83-45750. reprint ed. 32.50 (*0-404-20088-5*) AMS Pr.

Selected Essays. Ed. by Claude M. Fuess. LC 72-134078. (Essay Index Reprint Ser.). 1977. reprint ed. 20.95 (*0-8369-2394-4*) Ayer.

Selected Essays. A. D. Gordon. LC 73-2201. (Jewish People; History, Religion, Literature Ser.). 1973. reprint ed. 28.95 (*0-405-05266-9*) Ayer.

Selected Essays. Ludvig Holberg. LC 76-16842. 166p. 1976. reprint ed. text ed. 49.75 (*0-8371-8970-5*, HOSES, Greenwood Pr) Greenwood.

Selected Essays. Charles-Augustin Sainte-Beuve. Ed. by Francis Steegmuller & Norbert Guterman. Tr. by Norbert Guterman. LC 76-167409. (Essay Index Reprint Ser.). 1977. reprint ed. 21.95 (*0-8369-2919-5*) Ayer.

Selected Essays. William C. Williams. LC 54-7815. 352p. 1969. reprint ed. pap. 10.95 (*0-8112-0235-6*, NDP273) New Directions.

Selected Essays: Nineteen Sixty-Three to Nineteen Seventy-Five. Carl O. Sauer. Ed. & Intro. by Bob Callahan. 391p. 1981. 19.95 (*0-913666-45-9*) Turtle Isl Foun.

Selected Essays: Poems & Others Writings. George Eliot. Ed. by A. S. Byatt & N. D. Warren. 544p. 1991. pap. 12.95 (*0-14-043148-9*, Penguin Classics) Viking Penguin.

Selected Essays: World Bank, ICSID, & Other Subjects of Public & Private International Law. Aaron Broches. LC 94-19430. 563p. (C). 1995. lib. bdg. 165.00 (*0-7923-2906-6*) Kluwer Ac.

Selected Essays see Psychological Methods of Testing Intelligence

Selected Essays & Critical Writings. Denis Saurat. LC 67-30225. (Essay Index Reprint Ser.). 1977. 19.95 (*0-8369-0754-X*) Ayer.

Selected Essays & Dialogues. Plutarch. LC 92-18159. (World's Classics Ser.). 464p. 1993. 10.95 (*0-19-283094-5*) OUP.

Selected Essays & Reviews, 1948-1968. Richard F. Goldman. Ed. by Dorothy Klotzman. LC 79-56152. (I.S. A.M. Monographs: No. 13). 262p. 1980. pap. 10.00 (*0-914678-13-2*) Inst Am Music.

S

An Asterisk (*) at the beginning of an entry indicates that the title is appearing in BIP for the first time.

Selected Essays by Teochew Chinese in Singapore & Malaysia. Phua-Xing Nong. 208p. 1993. pap. text ed. 9.00 (*1-879771-05-5*) Global Pub NJ.

Selected Essays, First Series. Edmund W. Gosse. LC 68-29210. (Essay Index Reprint Ser.). 1977. 19.95 (*0-8369-0487-7*) Ayer.

Selected Essays from the Fiftieth Anniversary Congress of the Polish Institute of Arts & Sciences in America. Ed. by James S. Pula & M. B. Biskupski. 755p. 1994. 99.00 (*0-88033-287-5*) East Eur Monographs.

Selected Essays from the International Conference on Myth & Fantasy 1991. Joseph Tyler et al. (Orig.). 1994. per. write for info. (*1-883199-02-6*) W GA College.

Selected Essays from the International Conference on Surrealism & the Oneiric Process. Anna Balakian et al. 202p. 1993. per. 13.00 (*1-883199-00-X*) W GA College.

Selected Essays from the Rambler, Adventurer & Idler. Samuel Johnson. Ed. by Walter Jackson Bate. LC 68-27747. (Works of Samuel Johnson Ser). 1968. 65.00 (*0-300-00364-1*); pap. 17.00 (*0-300-00016-2*, Y207) Yale U Pr.

Selected Essays from the Tatler, the Spectator, & the Guardian. Joseph Addison & Richard Steele. Ed. by Daniel L. McDonald. LC 73-179472. (Library of Literature: No. 15). 1973. pap. 5.95 (*0-672-60990-8*, Bobbs) Macmillan.

Selected Essays of Assar Lindbeck, 2 vols. Assar Lindbeck. (Economists of the Twentieth Century Ser.). 680p. 1993. Set. 160.00 (*1-85278-603-5*) E Elgar.

***Selected Essays of Catherine V. Chvany.** Catherine V. Chvany. Ed. by Olga T. Yokoyama & Emily Klenin. 391p. 1997. pap. 24.95 (*0-89357-269-1*) Slavica.

Selected Essays of Cyril Connolly. Cyril Connolly. Ed. by Peter Quennell. 312p. (C). 1984. 17.95 (*0-89255-072-4*) Persea Bks.

Selected Essays of Edward P. J. Corbett. Edward P. J. Corbett. Ed. by Robert J. Connors. LC 87-42940. (SMU Studies in Composition & Rhetoric). 384p. 1989. 26.95 (*0-87074-264-7*); pap. 14.95 (*0-87074-271-X*) SMU Press.

Selected Essays of Gottfried Haberler. Gottfried Haberler. Ed. by Anthony Y. Koo. 672p. 1986. 80.00 (*0-262-11105-5*) MIT Pr.

Selected Essays of John Crowe Ransom. fac. ed. John C. Ransom. Ed. by Thomas D. Young & John Hindle. LC 83-12041. (Southern Literary Studies). 368p. 1984. reprint ed. pap. 104.90 (*0-7837-7816-3*, 2047572) Bks Demand.

Selected Essays of John Gould Fletcher. J. G. Fletcher. Ed. by Lucas Carpenter. LC 88-35336. 290p. 1989. 28.00 (*1-55728-078-9*) U of Ark Pr.

Selected Essays of R. P. Blackmur. Richard P. Blackmur. Ed. by Denis Donoghue. 350p. (C). 1988. pap. 10.50 (*0-88001-103-3*) Ecco Pr.

Selected Essays of T. Harry Williams. fac. ed. Thomas H. Williams. LC 82-18646. 284p. reprint ed. pap. 81.00 (*0-7837-7750-7*, 2047506) Bks Demand.

Selected Essays on Atheism. Percy Bysshe Shelley. LC 72-161341. (Atheist Viewpoint Ser.). 100p. 1976. reprint ed. 16.95 (*0-405-03794-5*) Ayer.

Selected Essays on Economic Planning. Michal Kalecki. Ed. & Tr. by Jan Toporowski. (Illus.). 150p. 1987. 49.95 (*0-521-30837-2*) Cambridge U Pr.

Selected Essays on Employment & Growth. Richard F. Kahn. LC 78-187079. 240p. 1972. 59.95 (*0-521-08493-8*) Cambridge U Pr.

Selected Essays on English Usage. Thomas Pyles. Ed. by John Algeo. LC 78-18833. 237p. 1983. reprint ed. pap. 81.00 (*0-7837-4904-X*, 2044569) Bks Demand.

Selected Essays on Food & Agriculture in the Virgin Islands. Darshan S. Padda. (Illus.). 700p. (Orig.). 1991. pap. text ed. write for info. (*0-9628909-0-1*) U VI CES.

Selected Essays on German Literature. Hermann Boeschenstein. Ed. by Rodney Symington. (Canadian Studies in German Language & Literature: Vol. 34). 163p. 1986. pap. 20.05 (*0-8204-0326-1*) P Lang Pubng.

Selected Essays on German Literature. Barker Fairley. Ed. by Rodney Symington. LC 83-49517. (Canadian Studies in German Language & Literature: Vol. 29). 378p. (Orig.). (C). 1984. pap. text ed. 35.80 (*0-8204-0107-2*) P Lang Pubng.

Selected Essays on Language, Mythology & Religion, 2 vols., Set. Friedrich M. Mueller. LC 73-18814. reprint ed. 145.00 (*0-404-11456-3*) AMS Pr.

Selected Essays on Music. Vladimir Stasov. Tr. by Florence Jonas. LC 80-11294. (Music Reprint Ser.). (Illus.). 200p. 1980. reprint ed. lib. bdg. 29.50 (*0-306-76033-9*) Da Capo.

Selected Essays on Music: Berlioz, Liszt, & Schumann. Vladimir Stasov. Tr. by Florene Jonas from RUS. 1968. 24.95 (*0-8464-0832-5*) Beekman Pubs.

Selected Essays on Political Economy. Frederic Bastiat. Tr. by Seymour Cain. 352p. (FRE.). 1995. reprint ed. pap. 14.95 (*0-910614-15-6*) Foun Econ Ed.

Selected Essays on Scottish Language & Literature: A Festschrift in Honor of Allan H. MacLaine. Ed. by Steven R. McKenna. LC 92-24194. (Illus.). 284p. 1992. text ed. 89.95 (*0-7734-9597-5*) E Mellen.

Selected Essays on the Conflict of Laws. Brainerd Currie. LC 63-17326. 771p. reprint ed. pap. 180.00 (*0-317-28857-1*, 2017896) Bks Demand.

Selected Essays on the Conflict of Laws. Ed. by Brainerd Currie. LC 63-17326. 774p. 1990. reprint ed. lib. bdg. 60.00 (*0-89941-700-0*, 305980) W S Hein.

Selected Essays on the Dynamics of the Capitalist Economy, 1933-1970. Michal Kalecki. LC 78-123667. (Illus.). 206p. 1971. text ed. 59.95 (*0-521-07983-7*) Cambridge U Pr.

Selected Essays on the History of Letter-Forms in Manuscript & Print, 2 vols., Set. Stanley Morison. Ed. by David McKitterick. LC 78-54718. (Illus.). 543p. 1981. 350.00 (*0-521-22338-5*) Cambridge U Pr.

Selected Essays, 1963-1975. Sauer. 1990. pap. 12.95 (*0-913666-46-7*) Turtle Isl Foun.

Selected Essays, 1965-1985. Thomas D. Young. LC 89-13692. (Southern Literary Studies). 184p. 1990. text ed. 27.50 (*0-8071-1559-2*) La State U Pr.

Selected Essays, 2nd Series. Edmund W. Gosse. LC 68-8464. (Essay Index Reprint Ser.). 1977. 19.95 (*0-8369-0488-5*) Ayer.

Selected Etchings of James A. McN. Whistler. James A. Whistler. LC 73-86438. (Illus.). 160p. (Orig.). 1975. pap. 12.95 (*0-486-23194-1*) Dover.

Selected Ethics & Protocols in Chiropractic. Edward L. Maurer. 288p. 1991. 57.00 (*0-8342-0277-8*) Aspen Pub.

Selected Examples of Indian Art. Ananda K. Coomaraswamy. vii, 20p. 1971. 25.00 (*0-88065-045-1*, Pub. by Today & Tomorrows P & P II) Scholarly Pubns.

Selected Examples of the Plant Kingdom. Obermire. 1980. pap. 14.75 (*0-88246-059-5*) Oreg St U Bkstrs.

Selected Exercises for Developing Competency in Basic Music Skills. 4th ed. Ian Polster. 43p. (C). 1994. pap. text ed. 25.00 (*1-887964-02-9*) Prescript Music.

Selected Exercises from Microbes in Action: A Laboratory Manual of Microbiology. Harry W. Seeley, Jr. (Illus.). 272p. (C). 1995. pap. text ed. write for info. (*0-7167-2111-2*) W H Freeman.

Selected Experiments in College Chemistry: Some Basic Concepts & Techniques. Donald E. Rice & Joseph Fisher. 288p. 1994. spiral bd. 20.95 (*0-8403-7907-2*) Kendall-Hunt.

Selected Experiments in General Chemistry & Qualitative Analysis. Esther Rodriguez & Joanna Kirvatis. 1994. spiral bd. 20.65 (*0-88252-163-2*) Paladin Hse.

Selected Fables. Jean De La Fontaine. 1976. 19.95 (*0-8488-0556-9*) Amereon Ltd.

Selected Fables. Jean De la Fontaine. Ed. by Maya Slater. Tr. by Christopher Wood. (World's Classics Ser.). 368p. 1995. pap. 8.95 (*0-19-282440-6*) OUP.

Selected Fables. Jean de La Fontaine & Alexander Calder. Tr. by Eunice Clark. (Illus.). 86p. pap. 4.50 (*0-486-21878-3*) Dover.

Selected Fables: Selected Fables. Jean De La Fontaine. Tr. by James Michie from FRE. 176p. 1982. pap. 10.95 (*0-14-044376-2*, Penguin Classics) Viking Penguin.

***Selected Fables/Fables Choisies: A Dual-Language Book.** Jean De La Fontaine & Stanley Appelbaum. LC 96-35538. 224p. (Orig.). (ENG & FRE.). 1997. pap. text ed. 8.95 (*0-486-29574-5*) Dover.

Selected Fairy Tales. Barbara L. Picard. (Illus.). 190p. (YA). (gr. 7 up). 1995. 12.95 (*0-19-274162-4*) OUP.

Selected Families of Plants Study Guide. David J. Keil. 60p. 1986. ring bd. 149.00 incl. fiche (*0-88736-087-4*) Chadwyck-Healey.

Selected Fault Testing of Electronic Isolation Devices Used in Nuclear Power Plant Operations. (Illus.). 124p. (Orig.). (C). 1995. pap. text ed. 35.00 (*0-7881-1620-7*) DIANE Pub.

***Selected Federal & State Administrative & Regulatory Laws.** William F. Funk et al. (Miscellaneous Ser.). 200p. 1997. pap. text ed. write for info. (*0-314-22466-1*) West Pub.

Selected Federal & State Publications of Interest to Planning Librarians: List No. 4, No. 1151. Jean MacLaury. 1976. 5.50 (*0-686-20413-1*, Sage Prdcls Pr) Sage.

Selected Federal & State Publications of Interest to Planning Librarians: No. 8. Jean MacLaury. 1977. 2.50 (*0-686-19123-4*, 1246, Sage Prdcls Pr) Sage.

Selected Federal & State Publications of Interest to Planning Librarians: No. 9. Jean MacLaury. 1977. 2.50 (*0-686-19104-8*, 1268, Sage Prdcls Pr) Sage.

Selected Federal & State Publications of Interest to Planning Librarians, No. 1, No. 1092. Jean MacLaury. 1976. 7.00 (*0-686-20404-2*, Sage Prdcls Pr) Sage.

Selected Federal & State Publications of Interest to Planning Librarians, No. 2, No. 1115. Jean MacLaury. 1976. 5.00 (*0-686-20405-0*, Sage Prdcls Pr) Sage.

Selected Federal & State Publications of Interest to Planning Librarians, No. 5, No. 1174. Jean MacLaury. 1976. 6.00 (*0-686-20417-4*, Sage Prdcls Pr) Sage.

***Selected Federal Taxation, Statutes & Regulations.** Michael D. Rose. 1759p. 1997. pap. text ed. write for info. (*0-314-21224-8*) West Pub.

Selected Federal Taxation, Statutes & Regulations: 1996 Edition. Michael D. Rose. 1664p. (C). 1995. pap. text ed. 25.00 (*0-314-06723-X*) West Pub.

Selected Federal Taxation Statutes & Regulations: 1997 Edition. Ed. & Selected by Michael D. Rose. 1650p. 1997. write for info. (*0-314-06637-3*) West Pub.

Selected Federal Taxation Statutes & Regulations: 1997 Edition. Michael D. Rose. 908p. (C). 1996. pap. text ed. write for info. (*0-314-09751-1*) West Pub.

Selected Fiction of M. Kianush. M. Kianush. 1988. write for info. (*0-911323-10-4*) Concourse Pr.

Selected Figural Works, Vol. 1. Ed. by Andrea Ross. (Illus.). 32p. 1989. pap. text ed. write for info. (*0-318-66432-1*) A Ross Gallery.

Selected Film Criticism: Eighteen Ninety-Six to Nineteen Hundred Eleven. Ed. by Anthony Slide. LC 82-10623. 134p. 1982. 18.50 (*0-8108-1575-3*) Scarecrow.

Selected Film Criticism: Foreign Films 1930-1950. Ed. by Anthony Slide. LC 81-23344. 219p. 1984. 22.50 (*0-8108-1673-3*) Scarecrow.

Selected Film Criticism: Nineteen Forty-One to Nineteen Hundred Fifty. Ed. by Anthony Slide. LC 81-23344. 280p. 1983. 24.00 (*0-8108-1593-1*) Scarecrow.

Selected Film Criticism: Nineteen Thirty-One to Nineteen Hundred Forty. Ed. by Anthony Slide. LC 82-10642. 292p. 1982. 24.00 (*0-8108-1570-2*) Scarecrow.

Selected Film Criticism: Nineteen Twelve to Nineteen Hundred Twenty, Vol. 2. Ed. by Anthony Slide. LC 81-23344. 325p. 1982. 26.00 (*0-8108-1525-7*) Scarecrow.

Selected Film Criticism: Nineteen Twenty-One to Nineteen Hundred Thirty. Ed. by Anthony Slide. LC 81-23344. 335p. 1982. 26.00 (*0-8108-1551-6*) Scarecrow.

Selected Film Criticism, 1951-1960, Vol. 7. Ed. by Anthony Slide. LC 81-23344. 198p. 1985. 20.00 (*0-8108-1763-2*) Scarecrow.

Selected Financial Aid Opportunities to Help You Achieve Your Educational Goals. Joseph H. Horton. 275p. (Orig.). (YA). (gr. 7 up). 1992. pap. 24.95 (*0-9652418-1-5*) Horton Pubng.

Selected Flowers of Evil. rev. ed. Charles P. Baudelaire. Ed. by Marthiel Mathews & Jackson Mathews. LC 58-9276. 1946. pap. 8.95 (*0-8112-0006-X*, NDP71) New Directions.

Selected Flute Discography: Long-Playing & Compact Disk Classical Recordings, 1948-1990. Peter Middleton. 2000p. 1995. 25.00 (*0-9627940-0-7*) Cornell Pr.

Selected Flute Solos, EFS101. (Illus.). 160p. pap. 14.95 (*0-8256-2101-1*, AM40403) Music Sales.

Selected from A Different Kind of Christmas. abr. ed. Alex Haley. (Writers' Voices Ser.). 64p. (Orig.). 1991. pap. text ed. 3.95 (*0-929631-26-9*, Signal Hill) New Readers.

Selected from Bless Me, Ultima. abr. ed. Suppl. by Literacy Volunteers of New York City Staff. (Writers' Voices Ser.). (Illus.). 64p. (Orig.). 1989. pap. text ed. 3.95 (*0-929631-06-4*, Signal Hill) New Readers.

Selected from Borrowed Time: An AIDS Memoir. abr. ed. Paul Monette. Ed. by Literacy Volunteers of New York City Staff & Patricia Fogarty. (Writers' Voices Ser.). 64p. (Orig.). 1992. pap. text ed. 3.95 (*0-929631-56-0*, Signal Hill) New Readers.

Selected from Carrie. abr. ed. Stephen King. Ed. by Literacy Volunteers of New York City Staff & George Ochoa. (Writers' Voices Ser.). 64p. (Orig.). 1992. pap. 3.95 (*0-929631-55-2*, Signal Hill) New Readers.

Selected from China Men & The Woman Warrior. abr. ed. Maxine H. Kingston. Ed. by Literacy Volunteers of New York City Staff. (Writers' Voices Ser.). 64p. (Orig.). 1990. pap. text ed. 3.95 (*0-929631-12-9*, Signal Hill) New Readers.

Selected from Coal Miner's Daughter. abr. ed. Loretta Lynn. Ed. by Literacy Volunteers of New York City Staff & George Vecsey. (Writers' Voices Ser.). 64p. (Orig.). 1990. pap. text ed. 3.95 (*0-929631-11-0*, Signal Hill) New Readers.

Selected from Contemporary American Plays, Vol. 2. abr. ed. Beth Henley et al. Ed. by Literacy Volunteers of New York City Staff. (Writers' Voices Ser.). 64p. (Orig.). 1992. pap. text ed. 3.95 (*0-929631-62-5*, Signal Hill) New Readers.

Selected from Contemporary American Plays: An Anthology. abr. ed. Jules Feiffer et al. Ed. by Literacy Volunteers of New York City Staff. (Writers' Voices Ser.). 64p. (Orig.). 1990. pap. text ed. 3.95 (*0-929631-15-3*, Signal Hill) New Readers.

Selected from Cosmos. Reader's Digest Editors & Carl Sagan. (Our World Ser.). (Illus.). 64p. (Orig.). 1993. pap. text ed. 3.95 (*1-56853-000-5*, Signal Hill) New Readers.

Selected from Dark They Were, & Golden-Eyed. abr. ed. Ray Bradbury. (Writers' Voices Ser.). 64p. (Orig.). 1991. pap. text ed. 3.95 (*0-929631-24-2*, Signal Hill) New Readers.

Selected from Dazzle. abr. ed. Judith Krantz. Ed. by Literacy Volunteers of New York City Staff & Edward Lavitt. (Writers' Voices Ser.). 64p. (Orig.). 1992. pap. text ed. 3.95 (*0-929631-60-9*, Signal Hill) New Readers.

Selected from Elvis & Me. abr. ed. Priscilla B. Presley. (Writers' Voices Ser.). 64p. (Orig.). 1991. pap. text ed. 3.95 (*0-929631-27-7*, Signal Hill) New Readers.

Selected from Fatherhood & Time Flies. abr. ed. Bill Cosby. (Writers' Voices Ser.). (Illus.). 64p. (Orig.). 1989. pap. text ed. 3.95 (*0-929631-00-5*, Signal Hill) New Readers.

Selected from Giant Steps: The Autobiography of Kareem Abdul-Jabbar. abr. ed. Peter Knobler & Kareem Abdul-Jabbar. Ed. by Literacy Volunteers of New York City Staff. (Writers' Voices Ser.). 64p. (Orig.). 1990. pap. text ed. 3.95 (*0-929631-10-2*, Signal Hill) New Readers.

Selected from I Know Why the Caged Bird Sings & The Heart of a Woman. abr. ed. Maya Angelou. (Writers' Voices Ser.). (Illus.). 64p. 1989. pap. text ed. 3.95 (*0-929631-04-8*, Signal Hill) New Readers.

Selected from In the Shadow of Man. abr. ed. Jane Goodall. Ed. by Literacy Volunteers of New York City Staff & Edward Lavitt. (Writers' Voices Ser.). 64p. (Orig.). 1992. pap. text ed. 3.50 (*0-929631-52-8*, Signal Hill) New Readers.

Selected from It Was on Fire When I Lay Down On It. abr. ed. Robert Fulghum. Ed. by Literacy Volunteers of New York City Staff & Melinda Corey. (Writers' Voices Ser.). 64p. (Orig.). 1992. pap. text ed. 3.50 (*0-929631-54-4*, Signal Hill) New Readers.

Selected from Jaws. abr. ed. Peter Benchley. Ed. by Literacy Volunteers of New York City Staff. (Writers' Voices Ser.). 64p. (Orig.). 1990. pap. text ed. 3.95 (*0-929631-14-5*, Signal Hill) New Readers.

Selected from Kaffir Boy. abr. ed. Mark Mathabane. (Writers' Voices Ser.). 64p. (Orig.). 1991. pap. text ed. 3.95 (*0-929631-28-5*, Signal Hill) New Readers.

Selected from "Kon-Tiki" Reader's Digest Editors & Thor Heyerdahl. (Our World Ser.). (Illus.). 64p. (Orig.). 1993. pap. text ed. 3.95 (*1-56853-001-3*, Signal Hill) New Readers.

Selected from Kramer vs. Kramer. abr. ed. Avery Corman. (Writers' Voices Ser.). (Illus.). 64p. 1989. pap. text ed. 3.95 (*0-929631-01-3*, Signal Hill) New Readers.

Selected from "Life on Earth" Reader's Digest Editors & David Attenborough. (Our World Ser.). (Illus.). 64p. (Orig.). 1993. pap. text ed. 3.95 (*1-56853-002-1*, Signal Hill) New Readers.

Selected from Lonesome Dove. abr. ed. Larry McMurtry. Ed. by Literacy Volunteers of New York City Staff & Seth Margolis. (Writers' Voices Ser.). 64p. (Orig.). 1992. pap. text ed. 3.95 (*0-929631-58-7*, Signal Hill) New Readers.

Selected from Love Medicine. abr. ed. Louise Erdrich. (Writers' Voices Ser.). (Illus.). 64p. 1989. pap. text ed. 3.95 (*0-929631-02-1*, Signal Hill) New Readers.

Selected from My Family, The Jacksons. abr. ed. Katherine Jackson & Richard Wiseman. Ed. by Literacy Volunteers of New York City Staff & Alan S. Gintzler. (Writers' Voices Ser.). 64p. (Orig.). 1992. pap. text ed. 3.95 (*0-929631-61-7*, Signal Hill) New Readers.

Selected from My Turn at Bat: The Story of My Life. abr. ed. John Underwood & Ted Williams. Ed. by Literacy Volunteers of New York City Staff et al. (Writers' Voices Ser.). 64p. (Orig.). 1992. pap. text ed. 3.95 (*0-929631-57-9*, Signal Hill) New Readers.

Selected from One More Time: A Memoir. abr. ed. Carol Burnett. (Writers' Voices Ser.). (Illus.). 64p. 1989. pap. text ed. 3.95 (*0-929631-03-X*, Signal Hill) New Readers.

Selected from Rashad: Mikes, Vikes & Something on the Backside. abr. ed. Ahmad Rashad. (Writers' Voices Ser.). 64p. (Orig.). 1991. pap. text ed. 3.95 (*0-929631-30-7*, Signal Hill) New Readers.

Selected from The Accidental Tourist. abr. ed. Anne Tyler. (Writers' Voices Ser.). 64p. (Orig.). 1991. pap. text ed. 3.95 (*0-929631-23-4*, Signal Hill) New Readers.

Selected from The Best of Dear Abby. abr. ed. Abigail Van Buren. (Writers' Voices Ser.). 64p. (Orig.). 1991. pap. text ed. 3.95 (*0-929631-25-0*, Signal Hill) New Readers.

Selected from The Godfather. abr. ed. Mario Puzo. (Writers' Voices Ser.). 64p. (Orig.). 1991. pap. text ed. 3.95 (*0-929631-22-6*, Signal Hill) New Readers.

Selected from The Joy Luck Club. abr. ed. Amy Tan. Ed. by Literacy Volunteers of New York City Staff & Melinda Corey. (Writers' Voices Ser.). 64p. (Orig.). 1992. pap. text ed. 3.95 (*0-929631-51-X*, Signal Hill) New Readers.

Selected from The Lost Angel. abr. ed. Mary Higgins Clark. Ed. by Literacy Volunteers of New York City Staff. (Writers' Voices Ser.). 64p. (Orig.). 1990. pap. text ed. 3.95 (*0-929631-13-7*, Signal Hill) New Readers.

Selected from The Mambo Kings Play Songs of Love. abr. ed. Oscar Hijuelos. Ed. by Literacy Volunteers of New York City Staff & Seth Margolis. (Writers' Voices Ser.). 64p. (Orig.). 1992. pap. text ed. 3.95 (*0-929631-53-6*, Signal Hill) New Readers.

Selected from The Right Stuff. abr. ed. Tom Wolfe. (Writers' Voices Ser.). 64p. (Orig.). 1991. pap. text ed. 3.95 (*0-929631-31-5*, Signal Hill) New Readers.

Selected from The Temple of My Familiar. abr. ed. Alice Walker. Ed. by Literacy Volunteers of New York City Staff & Patricia Fogarty. (Writers' Voices Ser.). 64p. (Orig.). 1992. pap. text ed. 3.95 (*0-929631-59-5*, Signal Hill) New Readers.

Selected from The Women of Brewster Place. abr. ed. Gloria R. Naylor. (Writers' Voices Ser.). 64p. (Orig.). 1991. pap. text ed. 3.95 (*0-929631-33-1*, Signal Hill) New Readers.

Selected from Twentieth-Century American Poetry: An Anthology. William C. Williams et al. (Writers' Voices Ser.). 64p. (Orig.). 1991. pap. text ed. 3.95 (*0-929631-29-3*, Signal Hill) New Readers.

Selected from Windmills of the Gods. abr. ed. Sidney Sheldon. (Writers' Voices Ser.). 64p. (Orig.). 1991. pap. text ed. 3.95 (*0-929631-32-3*, Signal Hill) New Readers.

Selected Games. Vasily V. Smyslov. LC 81-23466. (Russian Chess Ser.). 250p. 1983. 29.90 (*0-08-026912-5*, Pergamon Pr) Elsevier.

Selected Games Nineteen Sixty-Seven to Nineteen Seventy. Mikhael M. Botvinnik. Tr. by Kenneth P. Neat. (Russian Chess Ser.). (Illus.). 318p. 1981. 29.95 (*0-08-024124-7*, Pergamon Pr); pap. 17.95 (*0-08-024123-9*, Pergamon Pr) Elsevier.

Selected Garlands. Phillipa Jones. 160p. 1987. pap. 35.00 (*0-317-62100-9*) St Mut.

Selected Gems, Poetry, Comedy, Drama & Sara Wooden: African-American Women Writers by Gilbert. Gates. LC 96-31490. 1996. 25.00 (*0-7838-1428-3*, Hall Reference) Macmillan.

Selected Genetic Papers of J. B. S. Haldane. Ed. by Krishna R. Dronamraju. LC 90-14125. 568p. 1991. text ed. 40.00 (*0-8240-0473-6*) Garland.

***Selected Guidance from the Quran.** 3rd ed. Mazhar U. Kazi. 112p. 1996. pap. write for info. (*0-9642101-4-2*) Al-Huda Prnting.

Selected Guidelines for Ethnobotanical Research: A Field Manual. Ed. by Miguel N. Alexiades & Jennie W. Sheldon. (Advances in Economic Botany Ser.: No. 10). 306p. 1996. pap. text ed. 22.95 (*0-89327-404-6*, AEB 10) NY Botanical.

Selected Historical & Genealogical Records of Scott County, Arkansas. 399p. 1993. 43.50 (*1-884683-01-0*); pap. 27.50 (*1-884683-00-2*) Historian AR.

Selected Historical Essays of F. W. Maitland. Frederic W. Maitland, pseud. LC 85-12552. xxx, 278p. 1985. reprint ed. text ed. 65.00 (*0-313-24954-7*, MSHE, Greenwood Pr) Greenwood.

Selected Hospital Waste Streams: Guides to Pollution Prevention. (Illus.). 45p. (Orig.). (C). 1993. pap. text ed. 30.00 (*1-56806-664-3*) DIANE Pub.

S

An Asterisk (*) at the beginning of an entry indicates that the title is appearing in BIP for the first time.

Selected Imaginary Conversations of Literary Men & Statesmen. Walter S. Landor. Ed. by Charles L. Proudfit. LC 69-10272. 302p. reprint ed. pap. 86.10 (0-7837-6030-2, 2045842) Bks Demand.

Selected Indices of Industrial Characteristics for U. S. SMSA. Robert C. Douglas. (Discussion Paper Ser.: No. 20). 1967. pap. 10.00 (1-55869-111-1) Regional Sci Res Inst.

Selected Information Resources on Scholarships, Fellowships & Grants. 1992. lib. bdg. 75.00 (0-8490-8769-4) Gordon Pr.

Selected Intellectual Property & Unfair Competition Statutes, Regulations & Treaties. 730p. 1993. pap. text ed. 16.00 (0-314-02549-9) West Pub.

Selected Intellectual Property & Unfair Competition Statutes, Regulations & Treatise. Roger E. Schechter. 800p. 1995. pap. text ed. 17.00 (0-314-06877-5) West Pub.

***Selected International Human Rights Instruments & Bibliography for Research on International Human Rights Law.** 2nd ed. Frank C. Newman & David Weissbrodt. 304p. (C). 1996. pap. 16.00 (0-87084-362-1) Anderson Pub Co.

Selected Interview & Essays. C. N. Yang. 249p. 1988. text ed. 22.00 (962-362-001-2); pap. text ed. 9.00 (962-362-002-0) World Scientific Pub.

***Selected Interviews.** Charlie Reilly. 227p. (Orig.). (C). 1995. pap. 23.00 (0-9638132-1-8) Clydewater Pubs.

Selected Issues in Mathematics Education. Ed. by Mary M. Lindquist. LC 80-82903. (National Society for the Education Series on Contemporary Education Issues). 276p. (C). 1981. 28.90 (0-8211-1114-0) McCutchan.

Selected John Hewitt. John Hewitt. 128p. 8100. pap. 12.95 (0-85640-244-3, Pub. by Blackstaff Pr IE) Dufour.

Selected John Locke. Paul E. Sigmund. (Critical Edition Ser.). (C). Date not set. pap. text ed. write for info. (0-393-96451-5, Norton Paperbks) Norton.

Selected Journalism. Stendhal. Tr. by Geoffrey Strickland from FRE. 341p. (Orig.). pap. 13.95 (0-7145-0519-6) Riverrun NY.

Selected Journals of L. M. Montgomery, Vol. 2: 1910-1921. Ed. by Mary Rubio & Elizabeth Waterston. 464p. 1988. 35.00 (0-19-540586-2) OUP.

Selected Journals of L. M. Montgomery: 1889-1910, Vol. 1. Ed. by Lucy Maud Montgomery et al. (Illus.). 424p. 1986. 35.00 (0-19-540503-X) OUP.

Selected Journals of L. M. Montgomery: 1921-1929, Vol. 3. Lucy Maud Montgomery. Ed. by Mary Rubio & Elizabeth Waterston. (Illus.). 464p. 1993. 30.00 (0-19-540936-1) OUP.

Selected Judgments of the Supreme Court of Israel: Special Volume. Asher F. Landau. 191p. 1971. 39.95 (0-87855-175-1) Transaction Pubs.

Selected Later Poems of Marie Luise Kaschnitz. Mary L. Kaschnitz. Tr. by Lisel Mueller from GER. LC 80-7537. (Lockert Library of Poetry in Translation). 128p. 1980. pap. 9.95 (0-691-01374-8); text ed. 23.95 (0-691-06442-3) Princeton U Pr.

***Selected Latin American One-Act Plays.** Tr. by Francesca Colecchia & Julio Matas. LC 72-92696. 224p. pap. 63.90 (0-608-05090-3, 2065644) Bks Demand.

Selected Lectures of Rudolf Wittkower: The Impact of Non-European Civilization on the Art of the West. Rudolf Wittkower. Ed. by Donald M. Reynolds. (Illus.). 208p. (C). 1989. text ed. 85.00 (0-521-30508-X) Cambridge U Pr.

Selected Legal Documents of the People's Republic of China, Vol. 2. Ed. by Joseph E. Wang. LC 76-5167. (Studies in Chinese Government & Law). 564p. 1979. text ed. 95.00 (0-313-26923-8, U6923, Greenwood Pr) Greenwood.

Selected Legal Papers, 3 vols. 1985. write for info. (0-318-60835-9) Am IPLA.

Selected Legal Papers, 3 vols., Vol. 1, No. 1. 1985. 25.00 (0-317-05985-8, P-3) Am IPLA.

Selected Legal Papers, 3 vols., Vol. 1, No. 2. 1985. 25.00 (0-317-05986-6, P-4) Am IPLA.

Selected Legal Papers, 3 vols., Vol. 2, No. 1. 1985. 25.00 (0-317-05987-4, P-5) Am IPLA.

Selected Legal Papers, 3 vols., Vol. 2, No. 2. 1985. 25.00 (0-317-05988-2, P-6) Am IPLA.

Selected Legal Papers, 3 vols., Vol. 3, No. 1. 1985. 25.00 (0-318-60836-7, P-7) Am IPLA.

Selected Lessons of Professor Didymous: Cartoons for the Wry of Mind. Lloyd S. Kaplan & William K. Bottorff. (Illus.). 184p. 1995. pap. 11.95 (0-940139-34-0) Consortium RI.

Selected Letters. Marcus Tullius Cicero. Tr. & Intro. by D. S. Bailey. (Classics Ser.). 288p. 1986. pap. 10.95 (0-14-044458-0, Penguin Classics) Viking Penguin.

Selected Letters. Marquis DeSade. 186p. 9200. pap. 18.95 (0-7206-0860-0, Pub. by P Owen Ltd UK) Dufour.

Selected Letters. Federico Garcia Lorca. Tr. by O'Conell & Graham-Lujan from SPA. LC 47-11626. 212p. 1947. pap. 6.95 (0-8112-0873-7, NDP52) New Directions.

Selected Letters. Federico Garcia Lorca. Tr. by David Gershator from SPA. LC 47-11626. 172p. 1984. 15.00 (0-8112-0872-9) New Directions.

***Selected Letters.** Maksim Gorky. Ed. by Andrew Barratt & Barry P. Scherr. Tr. by Barry P. Scherr. 424p. 1997. 65.00 (0-19-815175-6) OUP.

Selected Letters. Thomas Hardy. Ed. by Michael Millgate. (Illus.). 464p. 1990. 70.00 (0-19-818546-4) OUP.

Selected Letters. D. H. Lawrence. Ed. by Richard Aldington. 1996. pap. 12.95 (0-14-018950-5) Viking Penguin.

Selected Letters. Thomas B. Macaulay. Ed. by Thomas Pinney. LC 81-10016. 350p. 1983. text ed. 69.95 (0-521-24009-3) Cambridge U Pr.

Selected Letters. Edward Thomas. 248p. 1996. 59.00 (0-19-818562-6) OUP.

Selected Letters. Carl F. Walther. (Selected Writings of C. F. W. Walther Ser.). 192p. 1981. 17.99 (0-570-08279-X, 15-2737) Concordia.

Selected Letters. Sherwood Anderson. Ed. by Charles E. Modlin. LC 83-6530. 279p. 1984. reprint ed. pap. 77.60 (0-608-01432-X, 2062194) Bks Demand.

Selected Letters. Gustave Flaubert. Tr. by Francis Steegmuller. LC 78-160919. (Biography Index Reprint Ser.). 1977. reprint ed. 20.95 (0-8369-8082-4) Ayer.

Selected Letters. Friedrich W. Nietzsche. Ed. by Oscar Levy. Tr. by A. N. Ludovici from GER. 364p. 1985. reprint ed. pap. 16.95 (0-948166-01-0, Pub. by Soho Bk Co UK) Dufour.

Selected Letters: 1940-1985. Philip Larkin. Ed. by Anthony Thwaite. 1993. 40.00 (0-374-25829-5) FS&G.

***Selected Letters Vol. III: 1929-1931.** H. P. Lovecraft. 1998. 19.95 (0-87054-032-7, Arkham Hse) Arkham.

Selected Letters Five. H. P. Lovecraft. Ed. by August Derleth & James Turner. LC 75-44847. (Illus.). 400p. 1976. 19.95 (0-87054-036-X) Arkham.

Selected Letters Four. H. P. Lovecraft. Ed. by August Derleth & James Turner. LC 75-44847. (Illus.). 424p. 1976. 19.95 (0-87054-035-1) Arkham.

***Selected Letters II: 1898-1952.** Knut Hamsun et al. 384p. 1997. pap. 35.00 (1-870041-33-X, Pub. by Norvik Pr UK) Dufour.

Selected Letters Nineteen Twenty-four to Nineteen Fifty. Cesare Pavese. Tr. by A. E. Murch from ITA. 1969. 30.00 (0-7206-1520-8) Dufour.

Selected Letters, Nineteen Twenty-Three to Nineteen Thirty. Robert E. Howard. Ed. by Glenn Lord et al. vi, 84p. (Orig.). 1989. pap. 9.95 (0-940884-26-7) Necronomicon.

***Selected Letters o Rabindranath Tagore.** Ed. by Krishna Dutta & Andrew Robinson. (University of Cambridge Oriental Publications: No. 53). (Illus.). 500p. (C). 1997. text ed. 95.00 (0-521-59018-3) Cambridge U Pr.

Selected Letters of Albert Jay Nock. Albert J. Nock. 1986. lib. bdg. 79.95 (0-8490-3848-0) Gordon Pr.

Selected Letters of Alessandra Strozzi: Bilingual Edition. Alessandra Strozzi. Tr. & Intro. by Heather Gregory. (Biblioteca Italiana Ser.: Vol. 9). 293p. (C). 1997. 40.00 (0-520-20389-5); pap. 16.00 (0-520-20390-9) U CA Pr.

Selected Letters of Anton Chekhov. Anton P. Chekhov. Ed. by Lillian Hellman. 1994. pap. 13.00 (0-88001-352-4) Ecco Pr.

***Selected Letters of Bayard Taylor.** Bayard Taylor & Paul C. Wermuth. LC 97-13091. 1997. write for info. (0-8387-5363-9) Bucknell U Pr.

***Selected Letters of Berlioz.** Ed. by Hugh MacDonald. Tr. by Roger Nichols. LC 96-47015. 496p. (C). 1996. 35.00 (0-393-04062-3) Norton.

Selected Letters of Bret Harte. Bret Harte. Ed. by Gary Scharnhorst. LC 96-18191. (Literature of the American West Ser.: Vol. 1). (Illus.). 480p. 1997. 34.95 (0-8061-2897-6) U of Okla Pr.

Selected Letters of Charles Baudelaire: The Conquest of Solitude. Charles Baudelaire. Ed. & Tr. by Rosemary Lloyd from FRE. LC 85-16461. xxxii, 296p. 1986. 29.95 (0-226-03928-5) U Ch Pr.

***Selected Letters of Charles Reznikoff 1917-1976.** Charles Renkikoff. Ed. by Milton Hindus. LC 97-25367. 350p. 1997. 27.50 (1-57423-035-2); pap. 17.50 (1-57423-034-4) Black Sparrow.

***Selected Letters of Charles Reznikoff 1917-1976.** deluxe ed. Charles Renkikoff. Ed. by Milton Hindus. LC 97-25367. 350p. 1997. 35.00 (1-57423-036-0) Black Sparrow.

Selected Letters of Charles Sumner, Set, Vols. 1 & 2. Beverly W. Palmer. (Illus.). 1504p. 1990. Set. text ed. 200.00 (1-55553-078-8) NE U Pr.

Selected Letters of Conrad Aiken. Conrad Aiken. Ed. by Joseph R. Killorin. LC 77-20620. (Illus.). 396p. reprint ed. pap. 112.90 (0-8357-3749-7, 2036475) Bks Demand.

Selected Letters of Cotton Mather. Cotton Mather. Ed. by Kenneth Silverman. LC 78-142338. 472p. reprint ed. pap. 134.60 (0-317-29860-7, 2019565) Bks Demand.

***Selected Letters of D. H. Lawrence.** D. H. Lawrence. Ed. by James T. Boulton. (Cambridge Edition of the Letters of D. H. Lawrence Ser.). (Illus.). 576p. (C). 1997. text ed. 39.95 (0-521-40115-1) Cambridge U Pr.

Selected Letters of E. M. Forster: 1879-1920, Vol. 1. E. M. Forster. Ed. by Mary M. Lago & P. N. Furbank. LC 83-4376. (Illus.). 352p. (C). 1983. text ed. 35.00 (0-674-79825-2) HUP.

Selected Letters of E. M. Forster: 1921-1970, Vol. 2. E. M. Forster. Ed. by Mary M. Lago & P. N. Furbank. (Illus.). 352p. 1985. text ed. 35.00 (0-674-79827-9) HUP.

Selected Letters of E. T. A. Hoffmann. E. T. Hoffmann. Tr. by Johanna C. Sahlin & Leonard J. Kent from GER. LC 76-8096. 368p. 1978. reprint ed. 28.50 (0-226-34790-7) U Ch Pr.

Selected Letters of Edmund Burke. Edmund E. Burke. Ed. by Harvey C. Mansfield, Jr. LC 83-18138. 508p. 1984. 42.00 (0-226-08068-4) U Ch Pr.

Selected Letters of Edwin Arlington Robinson. Edwin Arlington Robinson & Ridgely Torrence. LC 79-15514. (Illus.). 191p. 1980. reprint ed. text ed. 39.75 (0-313-21266-X, ROSL, Greenwood Pr) Greenwood.

Selected Letters of Eugene O'Neill. Eugene O'Neill. Ed. by Travis Bogard & Jackson Bryer. (Illus.). (C). 1988. 50.00 (0-300-04374-0) Yale U Pr.

Selected Letters of Eugene O'Neill. Ed. by Travis Bogard & Jackson R. Bryer. LC 94-28978. (Illus.). 614p. 1994. reprint ed. pap. 18.95 (0-87910-181-4) Limelight Edns.

Selected Letters of Ezra Pound to John Quinn, 1915-1924. Ed. by Timothy Materer. LC 90-23613. 252p. 1991. text ed. 39.95 (0-8223-1132-1) Duke.

Selected Letters of Frederick Manfred, 1932-1954. Frederick Manfred. Ed. by Arthur R. Huseboe & Nancy O. Nelson. LC 88-4798. (Illus.). viii, 421p. 1989. text ed. 40.00 (0-8032-2344-7) U of Nebr Pr.

***Selected Letters of Friedrich Nietzsche.** Friedrich W. Nietzsche. LC 96-46577. 388p. 1996. reprint ed. pap. text ed. 18.95 (0-87220-358-1); reprint ed. lib. bdg. 37.95 (0-87220-359-X) Hackett Pub.

Selected Letters of Fyodor Dostoyevsky. Ed. by Joseph Frank & David I. Goldstein. 533p. (C). 1987. 50.00 (0-8135-1185-2) Rutgers U Pr.

Selected Letters of Fyodor Dostoyevsky. Ed. by Joseph Frank & David I. Goldstein. Tr. by Andrew R. MacAndrew. 543p. (C). 1990. pap. 17.95 (0-8135-1453-3) Rutgers U Pr.

Selected Letters of George Edward Woodberry. George E. Woodberry. (American Biography Ser.). 282p. 1991. reprint ed. lib. bdg. 69.00 (0-7812-8426-0) Rprt Serv.

Selected Letters of George Meredith. Ed. by Mohammed Shaheen. 350p. 1997. text ed. 45.00 (0-312-16045-3) St Martin.

Selected Letters of George Oppen. Ed. by Rachel B. DuPlessis. LC 89-23772. (Illus.). 471p. (Orig.). (C). 1990. text ed. 42.95 (0-8223-1017-1); pap. text ed. 21.95 (0-8223-1024-4) Duke.

***Selected Letters of Hamlin Garland.** Hamlin Garland et al. LC 97-15356. 1998. write for info. (0-8032-2160-6) U of Nebr Pr.

Selected Letters of Henry James to Edmund Gosse, 1882-1915: Literary Friendship. fac. ed. Henry James. Ed. by Rayburn S. Moore. LC 88-1392. 342p. 1988. reprint ed. pap. 97.50 (0-7837-7810-4, 2047566) Bks Demand.

Selected Letters of Horace Walpole. Horace Walpole. Ed. by W. S. Lewis. LC 72-91300. 344p. reprint ed. pap. 98.10 (0-317-29273-0, 2022013) Bks Demand.

Selected Letters of John Ciardi. Ed. by Edward Cifelli. 497p. 1991. 40.00 (1-55728-171-8) U of Ark Pr.

Selected Letters of John Gould Fletcher. Ed. by Leighton Rudolph et al. LC 95-39410. (John Gould Fletcher Ser.: Vol. 7). 384p. 1996. 50.00 (1-55728-329-X) U of Ark Pr.

Selected Letters of Leslie Stephen, Vol. 1. Ed. by John W. Bicknell. 320p. 1996. 65.00 (0-8142-0690-5) Ohio St U Pr.

Selected Letters of Leslie Stephen, Vol. 2. Ed. by John W. Bicknell. LC 96-1738. 296p. 1996. 65.00 (0-8142-0691-3) Ohio St U Pr.

Selected Letters of Lidian Jackson Emerson. Delores B. Carpenter. LC 86-16102. 384p. 1987. text ed. 42.00 (0-8262-0610-7, 83-36240) U of Mo Pr.

Selected Letters of Louisa May Alcott. Ed. by Joel Myerson & Daniel Shealy. LC 95-8400. 1995. pap. 19.95 (0-8203-1740-3) U of Ga Pr.

***Selected Letters of Marianne Moore.** Bonnie Costello. LC 96-52200. 1997. 35.00 (0-679-43909-9) Knopf.

Selected Letters of Marjorie Kinnan Rawlings. Ed. by Gordon E. Bigelow & Laura V. Monti. LC 82-2674. (Illus.). vi, 414p. 1983. pap. 19.95 (0-8130-0899-9) U Press Fla.

Selected Letters of Mark Van Doren. Mark Van Doren. Ed. by George Hendrick. LC 86-7456. x, 280p. 1986. text ed. 35.00 (0-8071-1317-4) La State U Pr.

Selected Letters of Mary Moody Emerson. Ed. by Nancy C. Simmons. LC 92-5076. (Illus.). 800p. 1993. 65.00 (0-8203-1462-5) U of Ga Pr.

Selected Letters of Mary Wollstonecraft Shelley. Ed. by Betty T. Bennett. LC 94-9815. 480p. 1995. pap. 19.95 (0-8018-4886-5); text ed. 49.95 (0-8018-4885-7) Johns Hopkins.

Selected Letters of Matthew Arnold. Ed. by Forrest D. Burt & Clinton Machann. LC 92-16553. 270p. (C). 1992. text ed. 44.50 (0-472-10224-9) U of Mich Pr.

Selected Letters of P. T. Barnum. Arthur H. Saxon. LC 82-12843. (Illus.). 360p. 1983. text ed. 39.50 (0-231-05412-2) Col U Pr.

Selected Letters of Paul Hindemith. Ed. & Tr. by Geoffrey Skelton from GER. LC 95-17335. 1995. 30.00 (0-300-06451-9) Yale U Pr.

Selected Letters of Philip K. Dick - 1974. Philip K. Dick. 310p. 1991. 39.95 (0-88733-104-1) Underwood Bks.

Selected Letters of Philip K. Dick - 1974. deluxe limited ed. Philip K. Dick. 310p. 1991. boxed 60.00 (0-88733-105-X) Underwood Bks.

***Selected Letters of Philip K. Dick, 1938-1971, 1.** Philip K. Dick. 350p. 1994. 39.95 (1-887424-20-2) Underwood Bks.

Selected Letters of Philip K. Dick 1938-1971, Vol. 5. Philip K. Dick. 350p. 1994. 39.95 (0-88733-169-6) Underwood Bks.

Selected Letters of Philip K. Dick 1972-1973, Vol. 2. Philip K. Dick. 360p. 1993. 39.95 (0-88733-161-0) Underwood Bks.

Selected Letters of Philip K. Dick, 1975-1976, 6 vols., Vol. 4. Philip K. Dick. 384p. 1992. 39.95 (0-88733-111-4) Underwood Bks.

Selected Letters of Philip K. Dick, 1975-1976, 6 vols., Vol. 4. deluxe limited ed. Philip K. Dick. 384p. 1992. Ltd. signed ed. boxed 60.00 (0-88733-112-2) Underwood Bks.

Selected Letters of Philip K. Dick, 1977-79, 6 vols., Vol. 5. Philip K. Dick. 296p. 1992. 39.95 (0-88733-120-3) Underwood Bks.

Selected Letters of Philip K. Dick, 1977-79, 6 vols., Vol. 5. deluxe limited ed. Philip K. Dick. 296p. 1992. boxed 60.00 (0-88733-121-1) Underwood Bks.

***Selected Letters of Ralph Waldo Emerson.** Ralph Waldo Emerson & Joel Myerson. LC 97-15060. 1997. write for info. (0-231-10282-8) Col U Pr.

Selected Letters of Raymond Chandler. Ed. by Frank MacShane. LC 81-4852. 616p. 1981. text ed. 49.50 (0-231-05080-1) Col U Pr.

Selected Letters of Robert Bridges, 2 vols., 1. Ed. by Donald E. Stanford. LC 80-54789. (Illus.). 960p. 1983. 85.00 (0-87413-177-4) U Delaware Pr.

Selected Letters of Robert Bridges, 2 vols., 2. Ed. by Donald E. Stanford. LC 80-54789. (Illus.). 960p. 1984. 85.00 (0-87413-204-5) U Delaware Pr.

Selected Letters of Roger Ascham. Alvin Vos. Tr. by Maurice Hatch from LAT. 322p. (C). 1989. 52.95 (0-318-41571-2) P Lang Pubng.

Selected Letters of Samuel Johnson. Samuel Johnson. LC 76-29446. reprint ed. 45.00 (0-404-15312-7) AMS Pr.

Selected Letters of Stephane Mallarme. Stephane Mallarme. Ed. & Tr. by Rosemary Lloyd. 262p. 1988. 33.00 (0-226-48841-1) U Ch Pr.

Selected Letters of Walt Whitman. Ed. by Edwin H. Miller. LC 89-20478. (Illus.). 340p. (Orig.). (C). 1990. pap. 19.95 (0-87745-267-9) U of Iowa Pr.

Selected Letters of William Carlos Williams. William C. Williams. 1957. 19.95 (0-8392-1098-1) Astor-Honor.

Selected Letters of William Carlos Williams. William C. Williams. LC 84-20550. 352p. 1985. pap. 9.95 (0-8112-0934-2, NDP589) New Directions.

Selected Letters of William Makepeace Thackeray. William M. Thackery. Ed. by Edgar F. Harden. LC 96-21335. (Illus.). 416p. (C). 1996. 60.00 (0-8147-3546-0) NYU Pr.

Selected Letters of William Michael Rossetti. Roger W. Peattie. LC 89-3838. 704p. 1990. lib. bdg. 65.00 (0-271-00678-1) Pa St U Pr.

Selected Letters on Politics & Society. Alexis De Tocqueville. Ed. by Roger Boesche. Tr. by James Toupin from FRE. LC 84-2524. 288p. 1985. pap. 15.00 (0-520-05751-1) U CA Pr.

Selected Letters, Seventeen Ninety-Six to Eighteen Seventeen. Jane Austen. Ed. by R. W. Chapman. 240p. 1985. pap. 11.95 (0-19-281485-0) OUP.

Selected Letters, 1932-1981. John Fante. Ed. & Intro. by Seamus Cooney. LC 91-12456. (Illus.). 356p. (Orig.). 1991. 25.00 (0-87685-832-9); pap. 15.00 (0-87685-831-0) Black Sparrow.

Selected List of Books & Articles on Japan in English, French & German. enl. rev. ed. Ed. by Hugh Borton et al. LC 53-5055. (Harvard-Yenching Institute Publications). 286p. 1954. 18.50 (0-674-79800-7) HUP.

Selected List of Choruses for Women's Voices. 2nd ed. Arthur W. Locke. 253p. 1993. reprint ed. lib. bdg. 79.00 (0-7812-9691-9) Rprt Serv.

Selected List of Compounds from Present-Day Reading; On the Interpretation of Occasional Spellings; The Stressed Vowels of Yiddish-American English. Margaret M. Bryant et al. (Publications of the American Dialect Society Ser.: No. 48). 59p. 1967. pap. text ed. 5.90 (0-8173-0648-X) U of Ala Pr.

Selected List of Fellowship & Other Support Organizations for Advanced Education for U. S. Citizens & Foreign Nationals. 77p. (Orig.). (C). 1994. pap. text ed. 30.00 (0-7881-0629-5) DIANE Pub.

Selected Literary Criticism. Henry James. Ed. by Morris Shapira. LC 80-49685. 350p. 1981. pap. 29.95 (0-521-28365-5) Cambridge U Pr.

Selected Literary Essays. C. S. Lewis. Ed. by Walter Hooper. LC 74-85724. 1979. pap. 24.95 (0-521-29680-3) Cambridge U Pr.

Selected Lives from the Lives of the Noble Grecians & Romans, 1. Plutarch. Ed. by Paul Turner. reprint ed. pap. 92.50 (0-317-28721-4, 2051320) Bks Demand.

Selected Lives from the Lives of the Noble Grecians & Romans, 2. Plutarch. Ed. by Paul Turner. reprint ed. pap. 70.30 (0-317-28722-2) Bks Demand.

Selected Logic Papers. enl. ed. Willard V. Quine. LC 94-28372. 320p. 1995. text ed. 45.00 (0-674-79836-8, QUISEL); pap. text ed. 16.95 (0-674-79837-6, QUISEY) HUP.

Selected Magazine Articles of Theodore Dreiser. Ed. by Yoshinobu Hakutani. LC 82-49316. (Illus.). 288p. 1985. 45.00 (0-8386-3174-6) Fairleigh Dickinson.

Selected Magazine Articles of Theodore Dreiser: Life & Art in the American 1890s, Vol. 2. Theodore Dreiser. Ed. by Yoshinobu Hakutani. LC 82-49316. (Illus.). 1987. 35.00 (0-8386-3294-7) Fairleigh Dickinson.

Selected Mark Twain-Howells Letters, 1872-1910. Mark Twain. Ed. by Frederick Anderson et al. LC 67-13251. 467p. reprint ed. pap. 133.10 (0-7837-2335-0, 2057423) Bks Demand.

Selected Marxist Writings of Paul Lafargue. Paul Lafargue. Ed. by Richard Broadhead. 530p. (C). 1984. pap. 10.50 (0-916695-05-0) Ctr Social Hist.

Selected Masterpieces Vol. 2: Centennial Edition. R. Schumann. 184p. 1994. 10.95 (0-7935-3066-0) H Leonard.

Selected Mathematical Papers. Su Buchin. 412p. 1983. text ed. 226.00 (0-677-31300-4) Gordon & Breach.

Selected Measurement Methods for Plutonium & Uranium in the Nuclear Fuel Cycle. 2nd ed. AEC Technical Information Center Staff. Ed. by Clement J. Rodden. LC 72-600015. 416p. 1972. pap. 52.00 (0-87079-354-3, TID-7029); fiche 9.00 (0-87079-355-1, TID-7029) DOE.

***Selected Medicinal Plants.** 99p. 1984. 12.00 (92-5-101481-7, Pub. by FAO IT) Bernan Associates.

Selected Melanie Klein: The Essential Writings. Ed. by Juliet Mitchell. 256p. (Orig.). 1987. pap. 14.95 (0-02-921481-5, Free Press) Free Pr.

Selected Messages, Vol. III. Ellen G. White. 1980. Christian Home Library Ed. 12.99 (0-8280-0055-7, 19275-7) Review & Herald.

Selected Methods for the Small Clinical Chemistry Laboratory, Vol. 9. Ed. by Willard R. Faulkner & Samuel Meites. LC 80-66258. 330p. 1982. 30.00 (0-915274-13-2) Am Assn Clinical Chem.

An Asterisk (*) at the beginning of an entry indicates that the title is appearing in BIP for the first time.

Selected Methods of Clinical Chemistry, Vol. 8. Gerald Cooper. LC 53-7099. 209p. 1977. 25.00 (*0-915274-05-1*) Am Assn Clinical Chem.

Selected Methods of Clinical Chemistry, Vol. 10. Ed. by Gerald R. Cooper. LC 53-7099. 234p. 1983. 25.00 (*0-915274-21-3*) Am Assn Clinical Chem.

Selected Methods of Emergency Toxicology: Selected Methods of Clinical Chemistry, Vol. 11. Ed. by Christopher Frings & Willard R. Faulkner. LC 53-7099. 100p. 1986. 25.00 (*0-915274-31-0*) Am Assn Clinical Chem.

Selected Methods of Trace Metal Analysis: Biological & Environmental Samples. Jon C. Van Loon. LC 85-3279. (Chemical Analysis Ser.). 357p. 1985. text ed. 142.00 (*0-471-89634-9*) Wiley.

Selected Models of Anxiety, Depression & Psychosis. Ed. by P. Simon et al. (Animal Models of Psychiatric Disorders Ser.: Vol. 1). (Illus.). vi, 198p. 1988. 143.25 (*3-8055-4667-X*) S Karger.

Selected Models of Practice in Geriatric Psychiatry: A Task Force Report of the American Psychiatric Association. APA Task Force on Models of Practice in Geriatric Psychiatry Staff. LC 92-48940. 82p. 1993. text ed. 28.50 (*0-89042-239-7*, 2239) Am Psychiatric.

Selected Modern English Essays. Ed. by Humphrey S. Milford. LC 80-29398. (World's Classics, Second Ser.). x, 342p. 1981. reprint ed. text ed. 65.00 (*0-313-22763-2*, MISE, Greenwood Pr) Greenwood.

***Selected Multilateral Treaties in the Field of the Environment, Vol. 1.** 535p. 1993. pap. text ed. 100.00 (*0-521-46310-6*) Cambridge U Pr.

***Selected Multilateral Treaties in the Field of the Environment, Vol. 2.** 537p. 1993. pap. text ed. 100.00 (*0-521-46337-8*) Cambridge U Pr.

***Selected Multilateral Treaties in the Field of the Environment: 2-Volume Set, Set.** 1072p. 1994. pap. text ed. 150.00 (*0-521-46988-0*) Cambridge U Pr.

Selected Mycotoxins: Ochratoxins, Trichothecenes, Ergot. (Environmental Health Criteria Ser.: No. 105). 263p. 1990. pap. text ed. 46.00 (*92-4-157105-5*, 1160105) World Health.

Selected New York City Public School Data, 1993-1994. 9th ed. Suzanne DeCamp. 116p. 1994. 9.00 (*0-88156-168-1*) Comm Serv Soc NY.

Selected Nineteenth Century Essays. Ed. by Clyde Hyder & John E. Hankins. LC 72-90648. (Essay Index Reprint Ser.). 1977. 36.95 (*0-8369-1662-X*) Ayer.

Selected Non-Dramatic Writings of Bernard Shaw. George Bernard Shaw. Ed. by Dan H. Laurence. LC 65-4708. (C). 1965. pap. 11.56 (*0-395-05166-5*, Hill Stead Mus) HM.

***Selected North Carolina Statutes Relating to Civil Duties of Sheriffs.** Compiled by Joan G. Brannon. 66p. (Orig.). 1997. pap. 12.00 (*1-56011-310-3*, 97.07) Institute Government.

Selected Notebooks: 1960-67. James G. Cozzens. Ed. by Matthew J. Bruccoli. 1984. 25.00 (*0-89723-042-6*) Bruccoli.

Selected Notes Upon Shakespeare's Comedy of the Tempest. James O. Halliwell-Phillipps. LC 70-168230. reprint ed. 29.50 (*0-404-03085-8*) AMS Pr.

Selected Numismatic Studies. Paul Z. Bedoukian. 570p. (ARM & ENG.). 1981. boxed 35.00 (*0-9606842-0-4*) ANS.

Selected Odes of Pablo Neruda. Pablo Neruda. Tr. by Margaret S. Peden. LC 90-10707. 388p. 1990. pap. 13.95 (*0-520-07172-7*) U CA Pr.

Selected Old Testament Themes As in Literature. Deborah Dineen. (YA). (gr. 9-12). 1985. teacher ed. 13.50 (*1-881678-14-8*); student ed. 9.00 (*1-881678-15-6*) CRIS.

Selected One-Act Plays of Horton Foote. Horton Foote. Ed. & Intro. by Gerald C. Wood. LC 88-42635. 538p. 1989. pap. 16.95 (*0-87074-275-2*) SMU Press.

Selected Operas & Plays of Gertrude Stein. Ed. by John M. Brinnin. LC 70-101196. 336p. (C). reprint ed. pap. text ed. 16.95 (*0-8229-5501-6*) U of Pittsburgh Pr.

Selected Options for Expanding Health Insurance Coverage. Jack Rodgers. (Illus.). 79p. (Orig.). (C). 1994. pap. text ed. 30.00 (*0-7881-0418-7*) DIANE Pub.

Selected Orations, 2 vols., I. Libanius. Ed. by E. H. Warmington. (Loeb Classical Library: No. 451, 452). 590p. (ENG & GRE.). 1969. text ed. 18.95 (*0-674-99496-5*) HUP.

Selected Orations, 2 vols., II. Libanius. Ed. by E. H. Warmington. (Loeb Classical Library: No. 451, 452). 556p. (ENG & GRE.). 1969. 18.95 (*0-674-99497-3*) HUP.

Selected Orchestral Works, 11 vols. Karl D. Von Dittersdorf. Ed. by Joseph Liebeskind. LC 79-87694. (Music Ser.). 1971. reprint ed. lib. bdg. 65.00 (*0-306-71698-4*) Da Capo.

Selected Organic Syntheses: A Guidebook for Organic Chemists. Ian Fleming. LC 72-615. 235p. reprint ed. pap. 67.00 (*0-8357-6304-8*, 2035577) Bks Demand.

Selected Paintings, Drawings, & Rare Books. Yale Center for British Art Staff. LC 77-71659. (Illus.). 100p. (Orig.). 1977. pap. 5.95 (*0-685-59699-0*) Yale Ctr Brit Art.

Selected Paintings of Anthony Terenzio. Intro. by Peter Devine. LC 10-6949. (Illus.). 32p. Date not set. 3.00 (*0-614-10421-1*) W Benton Mus.

Selected Paper on Columbus & His Time. Intro. by Anne A. Paolucci. 80p. 15.00 (*0-918680-40-9*) Bagehot Council.

Selected Papers. Shiing-Shen Chern. (Illus.). 1978. 87.95 (*0-387-90339-9*) Spr-Verlag.

Selected Papers. C. C. Elgot. (Illus.). 456p. 1982. 97.95 (*0-387-90698-3*) Spr-Verlag.

Selected Papers. H. Grauert. 500p. 1995. 275.00 (*0-387-57107-8*) Spr-Verlag.

Selected Papers. L. K. Hua. (Illus.). 888p. 1982. 144.95 (*0-387-90744-0*) Spr-Verlag.

Selected Papers. Kiyoshi Ito. Ed. by S. R. Varadhan & Daniel W. Stroock. 625p. 1986. 107.95 (*0-387-96326-X*) Spr-Verlag.

Selected Papers. Ludwig Jekels. LC 72-117815. (Essay Index Reprint Ser.). 1977. 20.95 (*0-8369-1963-7*) Ayer.

Selected Papers. Solomon Lefschetz. LC 73-113137. 639p. (C). 1990. text ed. 59.50 (*0-8284-0234-5*, 234) Chelsea Pub.

Selected Papers. Marjorie J. Morse. (Illus.). 882p. 1981. 118.95 (*0-387-90532-4*) Spr-Verlag.

Selected Papers. E. S. Pearson. 327p. 1966. lib. bdg. 35.00 (*0-521-05926-7*) Lubrecht & Cramer.

Selected Papers. J. Wolfowitz. 642p. 1980. 118.95 (*0-387-90463-8*) Spr-Verlag.

Selected Papers, 2 vols., Vol. 1. Richard Von Mises. Ed. by P. Frank. LC 63-18572. pap. 160.00 (*0-317-11105-1*, 2011307) Bks Demand.

Selected Papers, Vol. II. Shiing-Shen Chern. (Illus.). 465p. 1989. 79.95 (*0-387-96816-4*) Spr-Verlag.

Selected Papers, 2 vols., Vol. 2. Richard Von Mises. Ed. by P. Frank. LC 63-18572. pap. 144.00 (*0-317-11106-X*) Bks Demand.

Selected Papers, Vol. III. Shiing-Shen Chern. (Illus.). 520p. 1989. 87.95 (*0-387-96817-2*) Spr-Verlag.

Selected Papers, Vol. IV. Shiing-Shen Chern. (Illus.). 385p. 1989. 79.95 (*0-387-96820-2*) Spr-Verlag.

Selected Papers: Psychoanalysis & Group Analysis. S. H. Foulkes. 360p. 1990. pap. text ed. 39.95 (*0-946439-56-7*, Pub. by Karnac Bks UK) Brunner-Mazel.

Selected Papers: Saunders MacLane. Saunders MacLane. Ed. by Irving Kaplansky. LC 79-10105. 1979. 107.95 (*0-387-90394-1*) Spr-Verlag.

Selected Papers: The Non-Radial Oscillations of Stars in General Relativity & Other Writings, Vol. 7. S. Chandrasekhar. LC 96-17573. 275p. 1997. pap. text ed. 45.00 (*0-226-10104-5*); lib. bdg. 99.00 (*0-226-10103-7*) U Ch Pr.

Selected Papers & Discussion from the Second Annual Meeting of the SISE June 2-3, 1989, Geneva, Switzerland. Ed. by D. J. Leaper. (Surgical Research Communications Ser.). 138, iip. 1990. pap. text ed. 107.00 (*3-7186-5023-1*) Gordon & Breach.

Selected Papers & Other Writings. Irving Kaplansky. LC 94-38704. 1995. 59.95 (*0-387-94406-0*) Spr-Verlag.

Selected Papers by Alfred M. Freudenthal: Civil Engineering Classics. 813p. 1981. pap. 59.00 (*0-87262-263-0*) Am Soc Civil Eng.

Selected Papers by G. U. Yule, 1871-1951. George U. Yule. Ed. by A. Stuart & M. G. Kendall. 447p. 1971. lib. bdg. 40.00 (*0-85264-201-6*) Lubrecht & Cramer.

Selected Papers by Nathan M. Newmark. Nathan M. Newmark. LC 76-25684. (Civil Engineering Classics Ser.). (Illus.). 897p. reprint ed. pap. 180.00 (*0-317-08325-2*, 2019537) Bks Demand.

Selected Papers Fourth International Conference on Malignant Lymphoma, June 6-9, 1990, Iugano. Ed. by J. E. Ultmann. (C). 1993. pap. text ed. 88.50 (*0-7923-1116-7*) Kluwer Ac.

Selected Papers from Chinese Journals of Structural Engineering. Ed. by Robert C. Young. 232p. 1989. 35.00 (*0-87262-690-3*) Am Soc Civil Eng.

Selected Papers from the "American Anthropologist" 1888-1920. Ed. by Frederica De Laguna. 930p. 1976. pap. 10.00 (*0-685-10026-X*); text ed. 15.00 (*0-913167-04-5*) Am Anthro Assn.

Selected Papers from the "American Anthropologist" 1921-1945. Ed. by George W. Stocking. 485p. 1976. pap. 6.00 (*0-685-10028-6*); text ed. 10.00 (*0-913167-05-3*) Am Anthro Assn.

Selected Papers from the "American Anthropologist" 1946-1970. Ed. by Robert F. Murphy. 424p. 1976. pap. 5.00 (*0-685-10030-8*); text ed. 9.00 (*0-913167-06-1*) Am Anthro Assn.

Selected Papers from the Charles Waldo Haskins Accounting History Series. Ed. by James F. Gaertner. (Monograph Series of the Academy of Accounting Historians: Monograph 4). 172p. 1983. pap. 10.00 (*1-879750-02-3*) Acad Acct Hist.

Selected Papers from the Chinese Journal of Geotechnical Engineering. Ed. by Yang H. Huang. 208p. 1987. 23.00 (*0-87262-621-0*) Am Soc Civil Eng.

Selected Papers from the English Institute. Incl. Critical Approaches to Medieval Literature. Ed. by Dorothy Bethurum. reprint ed. 19.50 (*0-404-52219-X*); Presence of Walt Whitman. Ed. by R. W. Lewis. reprint ed. 19.50 (*0-404-52221-1*); Ideas in the Drama. Ed. by John Gassner. reprint ed. 19.50 (*0-404-52224-6*); Lyric & Dramatic Milton. Ed. & Frwd. by Joseph H. Summers. reprint ed. 19.50 (*0-404-52225-4*); Northrop Frye in Modern Criticism. Ed. & Intro. by Murray Krieger. reprint ed. 19.50 (*0-404-52226-2*); Literary Criticism & Historical Understanding. Ed. & Intro. by Phillip Damon. reprint ed. 19.50 (*0-404-52227-0*); Experience in the Novel. Ed. & Intro. by Roy H. Pearce. reprint ed. 19.50 (*0-318-50713-7*); write for info. (*0-404-52228-9*) AMS Pr.

Selected Papers from the First Meeting of the SISE. Ed. by D. J. Leaper. (Surgical Research Communications Ser.). 94p. 1989. pap. text ed. 61.00 (*3-7186-4894-6*) Gordon & Breach.

Selected Papers from the International Symposium on Mast Cell, October 29, 1990, Hiroshima, Japan & the 7th Annual Symposium of the Skin Pharmacology Society on Immunopharmacology & Carcinogenesis, October 30, 1990, Hiroshima, Japan: Journal: Skin Pharmacology, Vol. 4, Suppl. 1, 1991. Ed. by S. Yamamoto. (Illus.). iv, 100p. 1991. pap. 31.50 (*3-8055-5497-4*) S Karger.

Selected Papers from the Proceedings of the Conference on Ethics, Higher Education, & Social Responsibility: Howard University, Washington, DC, April 8, 1994. Ed. by Segun Gbadegesin & Joyce A. Ladner. LC 95-26808. (C). 1996. 17.95 (*0-88258-151-1*) Howard U Pr.

Selected Papers from the Second Conference on Parallel Processing for Scientific Computing. Ed. by C. W. Gear & Robert G. Voigt. LC 87-60435. (Miscellaneous Bks.: No. 16). iv, 287p. 1987. pap. text ed. 20.00 (*0-89871-216-5*) Soc Indus-Appl Math.

Selected Papers from the XIIIth Linguistic Symposium on Romance Languages: Chapel Hill, N. C., March 24-26, 1983. Ed. by Larry D. King & Catherine A. Maley. LC 84-27994. (Current Issues in Linguistic Theory Ser.: No. 36). x, 440p. 1985. 91.00 (*90-272-3525-2*) Benjamins North Am.

Selected Papers from the 1995 Telecommunications Policy Research Conference. Ed. by Gerald W. Brock & Gregory L. Rosston. LC 96-23166. (Telecommunications Ser.). 328p. 1996. 69.95 (*0-8058-2418-9*); pap. 29.95 (*0-8058-2419-7*) L Erlbaum Assocs.

***Selected Papers from the 1996 Telecommunications Policy Research Conference, Vol. 3.** Ed. by Gregory L. Rosston & David Waterman. LC 97-22934. 330p. 1997. write for info. (*0-8058-2847-8*) L Erlbaum Assocs.

***Selected Papers from the 1996 Telecommunications Policy Research Conference, Vol. 3.** Ed. by Gregory L. Rosston & David Waterman. LC 97-22934. 330p. 1997. pap. write for info. (*0-8058-2848-6*) L Erlbaum Assocs.

***Selected Papers in Combinatorics.** B. D. McKay et al. (Topics in Discrete Mathematics Ser.: Vol. 2). viii, 452p. 1992. 197.00 (*0-444-89383-0*, North Holland) Elsevier.

Selected Papers in Genius & Creativity. Dean K. Simonton. (Publications in Creativity Research). (Illus.). 305p. 1997. pap. 42.50 (*1-56750-257-1*); text ed. 78.50 (*1-56750-256-3*) Ablex Pub.

***Selected Papers in Greek & Near Eastern History.** David M. Lewis. Ed. by P. J. Rhodes. (Illus.). 440p. (C). 1997. text ed. 89.95 (*0-521-46564-8*) Cambridge U Pr.

Selected Papers in Illinois History, 1980. Illinois State Historical Society Staff. LC 85-14310. 1982. pap. 7.50 (*0-912226-13-7*) Ill St Hist Soc.

Selected Papers in Illinois History, 1981. Ed. by Bruce D. Cody. LC 85-14310. 1982. pap. 7.50 (*0-912226-14-5*) Ill St Hist Soc.

Selected Papers in Illinois History, 1982. Ed. by Robert W. McCluggage. LC 85-14310. 1984. pap. 7.50 (*0-912226-15-3*) Ill St Hist Soc.

Selected Papers in Illinois History, 1983. Ed. by Robert W. McCluggage. LC 86-116885. 1985. pap. 7.50 (*0-912226-17-X*) Ill St Hist Soc.

Selected Papers in K-Theory. LC 92-18202. (Translations Ser.: Series 2, Vol. 154). 195p. 1992. 83.00 (*0-8218-7504-3*, TRANS2/154) Am Math.

Selected Papers in Logic & Foundations, Didactics, & Economics. Karl Menger. (Vienna Circle Collection: No. 10). 354p. 1979. pap. text ed. 76.00 (*90-277-0321-3*, D Reidel); lib. bdg. 146.00 (*90-277-0320-5*, D Reidel) Kluwer Ac.

Selected Papers in Mother Tongue Education. Ed. by G. Gagne et al. vi, 201p. 1987. pap. 46.15 (*90-6765-333-0*) Mouton.

Selected Papers in Multidimensional Digital Signal Processing. Ed. by IEEE Acoustics, Speech & Signal Processing Society, MDSP Committee Staff. LC 86-10669. 496p. 1986. 59.95 (*0-87942-202-5*, PC01990) Inst Electrical.

***Selected Papers in Proof Theory.** G. E. Mints. (Studies in Proof Theory: Vol. 3). 294p. 1992. 147.00 (*0-444-89619-8*, North Holland) Elsevier.

Selected Papers in Statistics & Probability. Abraham Wald. ix, 702p. 1955. 72.50 (*0-8047-0493-7*) Stanford U Pr.

Selected Papers in Structural Linguistics: Contributions to English & General Linguistics Written in the Years 1928-1978. Bohumil Trnka. (Janua Linguarum, Series Major: No. 88). 1982. text ed. 96.95 (*90-279-3148-8*) Mouton.

Selected Papers Nineteen Forty-Five to Nineteen Eighty with Commentary. Chen N. Yang. LC 82-13599. 596p. (C). 1995. pap. text ed. write for info. (*0-7167-1407-8*) W H Freeman.

Selected Papers of Abdus Salam. Ed. by E. Ali et al. (Series on Twentieth Century Physics). 696p. 1994. pap. text ed. 53.00 (*981-02-1663-7*) World Scientific Pub.

Selected Papers of Abdus Salam. Ed. by C. J. Isham & T. Kibble. (Series on Twentieth Century Physics). 696p. 1994. text ed. 109.00 (*981-02-1662-9*) World Scientific Pub.

Selected Papers of Antoni Zygmund, 3 vols., Set, Vols. 1-3. Ed. by A. Hulanicki et al. (C). 1989. Set. lib. bdg. 613.00 (*0-7923-0474-8*) Kluwer Ac.

Selected Papers of Boulton & Watt: Vol. I: the Engine Partnership, 1775-1825. Ed. by Jennifer Tann. (Illus.). 448p. 1981. 75.00 (*0-262-02167-6*) MIT Pr.

Selected Papers of C. C. Lin with Commentary, Vols. 1 & 2. Ed. by Chi Yuan. 1044p. 1987. Vol 1, Fluid Mechanics; Vol. 2, Astrophysics. text ed. 213.00 (*9971-5-0318-2*) World Scientific Pub.

Selected Papers of C. R. Rao, Vol. 1. Ed. by S. Gupta et al. 506p. 1994. text ed. 40.95 (*0-470-22091-0*) Halsted Pr.

Selected Papers of C. R. Rao, Vol. 2. Ed. by S. Gupta et al. 504p. 1994. text ed. 40.95 (*0-470-22092-9*) Halsted Pr.

Selected Papers of C. R. Rao, Vol. 3. Ed. by S. Gupta et al. 500p. 1996. text ed. 34.95 (*0-470-22093-7*) Halsted Pr.

Selected Papers of C. R. Rao, Vol. 4. Ed. by S. Gupta et al. 500p. 1996. text ed. 34.95 (*0-470-22094-5*) Halsted Pr.

Selected Papers of C. R. Rao, Vol. 5. Ed. by S. Gupta et al. 500p. 1996. text ed. 34.95 (*0-470-22095-3*); Set. text ed. 140.00 (*0-470-22096-1*) Halsted Pr.

Selected Papers of Charles Willson Peale & His Family, Vol. 3: The Belfield Farm Years, 1810-1820. Charles W. Peale. Ed. by Lillian B. Miller et al. 832p. (C). 1992. text ed. 135.00 (*0-300-04930-7*) Yale U Pr.

***Selected Papers of Charles Wilson Peale & His Family.** Ed. by Lillian B. Miller et al. (Illus.). 576p. 1997. 100.00 (*0-300-06180-3*) Yale U Pr.

Selected Papers of Charles Wilson Peale & His Family: Charles Wilson Peale: Artist in Revolutionary America, 1735 to 1791, Vol. 1. Charles W. Peale. Ed. by Lillian B. Miller & Sidney Hart. LC 82-20155. (Illus.). 676p. 1983. text ed. 80.00 (*0-300-02576-9*) Yale U Pr.

Selected Papers of Chia-Shun Yih, 2 vols. S. P. Lin & W. Michael Lai. (Advanced Series on Fluid Mechanics). 1064p. (C). 1991. text ed. 193.00 (*981-02-0543-0*) World Scientific Pub.

Selected Papers of Earle C. King. Alfred R. Roberts. Ed. by Richard P. Brief. LC 80-1464. (Dimensions of Accounting Theory & Practice Ser.). 1980. lib. bdg. 25.95 (*0-405-13486-X*) Ayer.

***Selected Papers of Elizabeth Cady Stanton & Susan B. Anthony Vol. 1: In the School of Anti-Slavery, 1840-1866.** Ed. by Ann D. Gordon. LC 97-5666. (Illus.). 600p. (C). 1997. text ed. 60.00 (*0-8135-2317-6*) Rutgers U Pr.

Selected Papers of Ernst Kris. Ernst Kris. LC 74-29725. 547p. reprint ed. pap. 155.90 (*0-8357-3750-0*, 2036476) Bks Demand.

Selected Papers of Errett Bishop. Errett Bishop. 440p. 1986. text ed. 79.00 (*9971-5-0127-9*) World Scientific Pub.

Selected Papers of Frederick Sanger with Commentaries. Ed. by Frederick Sanger & Margaret Dowding. LC 96-33754. (Series in Twentieth Century Biology). 650p. 1996. text ed. 86.00 (*981-02-2430-3*, BcCBd-BR2902) World Scientific Pub.

Selected Papers of Freeman Dyson: With Commentary. Freeman Dyson. LC 96-6211. (Collected Works Ser.: Vol. 5). (Illus.). 1996. 59.00 (*0-8218-0561-4*, CWORKS/5) Am Math.

Selected Papers of Homer Cummings. Ed. by Carl B. Swisher. LC 79-168392. (FDR & the Era of the New Deal Ser.). (Illus.). 1972. reprint ed. lib. bdg. 37.50 (*0-306-70329-7*) Da Capo.

Selected Papers of Homer Cummings: Attorney General of the United States. Ed. by Carl B. Swisher. xxvi, 316p. 1996. reprint ed. 82.00 (*1-56169-212-3*) Gaunt.

Selected Papers of J. L. Koszul. (Pure Mathematics Ser.). 296p. 1994. text ed. 86.00 (*981-02-1395-6*) World Scientific Pub.

Selected Papers of J. M. Burgers. Ed. by F. T. Nieuwstadt & J. A. Steketee. LC 94-39288. 650p. 1994. lib. bdg. 332.00 (*0-7923-3265-2*) Kluwer Ac.

Selected Papers of Julian Schwinger. C. Fronsdal et al. (Mathematical Physics & Applied Mathematics Ser: No. 4). 1979. pap. text ed. 62.00 (*90-277-0975-0*); lib. bdg. 101.50 (*90-277-0974-2*) Kluwer Ac.

***Selected Papers of Lawrence R. Klein: Theoretical Reflections & Econometric Applications.** Kanta Marwah. LC 97-18837. 1997. 86.00 (*981-02-2600-4*) World Scientific Pub.

***Selected Papers of Linus Pauling.** (World Scientific Ser.). 750p. 1997. lib. bdg. 90.00 (*981-02-2939-9*) World Scientific Pub.

***Selected Papers of Linus Pauling.** (World Scientific Ser.: Vol. 2). 750p. 1997. lib. bdg. 90.00 (*981-02-2940-2*) World Scientific Pub.

Selected Papers of Ludwig Jekels. Ludwig Jekels. 1970. reprint ed. pap. 24.95 (*0-8236-8305-2*, 26025) Intl Univs Pr.

Selected Papers of Morikazu Toda. M. Wadati. (Pure Matematics Ser.). 328p. 1993. text ed. 95.00 (*981-02-1469-3*) World Scientific Pub.

Selected Papers of Morris B. Bender: Memorial Volume. fac. ed. Morris B. Bender. Ed. by Robert P. Friedland. LC 83-2851. (Illus.). 463p. pap. 125.10 (*0-7837-7280-7*) Bks Demand.

Selected Papers of Robert S. Mulliken. Robert S. Mulliken. Ed. by J. Hinze & D. A. Ramsay. LC 74-11633. xvi, 1120p. 1975. lib. bdg. 66.00 (*0-226-54847-3*) U Ch Pr.

Selected Papers of T. H. R. Skyrme with Commentaries. G. E. Brown. (Series on Twentieth Century Physics). 456p. 1994. text ed. 86.00 (*981-02-1646-7*) World Scientific Pub.

Selected Papers of the Academy for Youth Leaders. Ed. by Susan R. Edginton & Christopher R. Edginton. (Youth Development Professionals Monographs: No. 6). 180p. (C). 1995. pap. text ed. 15.00 (*1-881516-05-9*) U of NI Inst Youth Lead.

Selected Papers of the International Migraine-Headache Symposium: Proceedings of the International Symposium, Florence, 1970. International Migraine-Headache Symposium Staff. Ed. by F. Sicuteri. (Pain & Headache Ser.: Vol. 3). 1972. 112.00 (*3-8055-1295-3*) S Karger.

Selected Papers of Theodore S. Motzkin. Ed. by D. Cantor et al. 1983. 122.00 (*0-8176-3087-2*) Birkhauser.

Selected Papers of Turner Alfrey. Turner Alfrey. Ed. by Raymond F. Boyer & Herman F. Mark. LC 85-29344. (Illus.). 591p. reprint ed. pap. 168.50 (*0-7837-0603-0*, 2040951) Bks Demand.

Selected Papers of Walter Isard, 2 vols. Ed. by Christine Smith. 288p. (C). 1990. Vol. 1: Location Analysis & General Theory. 80.00 (*0-8147-7900-X*) NYU Pr.

Selected Papers of Walter Isard, 2 vols., Set. Ed. by Christine Smith. 288p. (C). 1990. 150.00 (*0-8147-7899-2*) NYU Pr.

Selected Papers of Walter Isard, 2 vols., Vol. 2. Ed. by Christine Smith. 288p. (C). 1990. 75.00 (*0-8147-7901-8*) NYU Pr.

Selected Papers of Wilhelm P. A. Klingenberg. 548p. (C). 1991. text ed. 97.00 (*981-02-0764-6*) World Scientific Pub.

Selected Papers of William Clayton. William Clayton. Ed. by Frederick J. Dobney. LC 70-164565. 320p. reprint ed. pap. 91.20 (*0-317-19877-7*, 2023093) Bks Demand.

Selected Papers of Wolfgang Kohler. Wolfgang Kohler. Ed. by Solomon E. Asch & Mary Henle. (C). 1971. text ed. 15.95 (*0-87140-505-9*) Liveright.

Selected Papers of Yu. I. Manin. Yu I. Manin. LC 96-18705. (World Scientific Series in 20th Century Mathematics). 612p. 1996. write for info. (*981-02-2498-2*) World Scientific Pub.

Selected Papers on Acousto-Optics. Ed. by Adrian Korpel. 640p. 1990. pap. 91.00 (*0-8194-0438-1*, VOL. MS16) SPIE.

Selected Papers on Adaptive Optics & Speckle Imaging. Ed. by Devon G. Crowe. LC 93-48071. (Milestone Ser.: Vol. MS93). 1994. 35.00 (*0-8194-1557-X*); pap. 35.00 (*0-8194-1556-1*) SPIE.

Selected Papers on Adaptive Optics for Atmospheric Compensation. Ed. by James E. Pearson. LC 93-46626. (Milestone Ser.: Vol. MS 92). 1994. pap. 45.00 (*0-8194-1509-X*) SPIE.

Selected Papers on Adaptive Optics for Atmospheric Compensation. Ed. by James E. Pearson. LC 93-46626. (Milestone Ser.: Vol. MS 92/HC). 1994. 55.00 (*0-8194-1510-3*) SPIE.

Selected Papers on Agricultural Chemicals in Water Resources of the Midcontinental U. S. Ed. by D. A. Goolsby. (Illus.). 89p. (Orig.). (YA). (gr. 12 up). 1994. pap. text ed. 30.00 (*0-7881-0844-1*) DIANE Pub.

Selected Papers on Analysis, Probability & Statistics. Ed. by Katsumi Nomizu. LC 94-23002. (American Mathematical Society translations ser.: Series 2, Vol. 161). 151p. 1994. 75.00 (*0-8218-7512-4*, TRANS2/161) Am Math.

Selected Papers on Anthropology, Travel & Exploration. Richard Burton. LC 72-80499. 240p. 1972. reprint ed. 24.95 (*0-405-08335-1*, Pub. by Blom Pubns UK) Ayer.

Selected Papers on Apodization - Coherent Optical Systems. Ed. by James P. Mills & Brian J. Thompson. (SPIE Milestone Ser.: Vol. MS 119). 1996. 100.00 (*0-8194-2150-2*) SPIE.

Selected Papers on Applications of Polarized Light. Ed. by Bruce H. Billings. LC 92-19413. (Milestone Ser.: Vol. 57). 1992. pap. 35.00 (*0-8194-0990-1*) SPIE.

Selected Papers on Applications of Polarized Light. Ed. by Bruce H. Billings. LC 92-19413. (Milestone Ser.: Vol. MS 57/HC). 1992. 45.00 (*0-8194-0989-8*) SPIE.

Selected Papers on Architectural Lighting. Ed. by Mark S. Rea. LC 92-19412. (Milestone Ser.: Vol. 58). 1992. pap. 45.00 (*0-8194-0992-8*) SPIE.

Selected Papers on Architectural Lighting. Ed. by Mark S. Rea. LC 92-19412. (Milestone Ser.: Vol. MS 58/HC). 1992. 55.00 (*0-8194-0991-X*) SPIE.

Selected Papers on Astronomical Optics. Ed. by Daniel J. Schroeder. (Milestone Ser.: Vol. 73). 1993. pap. 45.00 (*0-8194-1124-8*, MS73) SPIE.

Selected Papers on Atmospheric Optics. Vladimir E. Zuev. (SPIE Milestone Ser.: Vol. MS 112). 1995. 110.00 (*0-8194-1940-0*) SPIE.

Selected Papers on Automath. R. P. Nederpelt et al. LC 94-34022. (Studies in Logic & the Foundations of Mathematics: Vol. 133). 1044p. 1994. 243.25 (*0-444-89822-0*) Elsevier.

Selected Papers on Characterization of Optical Coatings. Michael J. Jacobson. LC 92-31684. (Milestone Ser.: Vol. MS 63). 1992. pap. 35.00 (*0-8194-1052-7*) SPIE.

Selected Papers on Characterization of Optical Coatings. Michael J. Jacobson. LC 92-31684. (Milestone Ser.: Vol. MS 63/HC). 1992. 45.00 (*0-8194-1053-5*) SPIE.

Selected Papers on Coherence & Fluctuations of Light (1850-1966), MS19. Ed. by L. Mandel & E. Wolf. 976p. 1990. pap. 35.00 (*0-8194-0440-3*) SPIE.

Selected Papers on Coherence & Fluctuations of Light (1850-1966), MS19/HC. Ed. by L. Mandel & E. Wolf. 976p. 1990. 45.00 (*0-8194-0439-X*) SPIE.

Selected Papers on Coherence & Radiometry. Ed. by Ari T. Friberg. LC 92-34885. (Milestone Ser.: Vol. MS 69). 1993. pap. 45.00 (*0-8194-1128-0*) SPIE.

Selected Papers on Coherence & Radiometry. Ed. by Ari T. Friberg. LC 92-34885. (Milestone Ser.: Vol. MS 69/HC). 1993. 55.00 (*0-8194-1127-2*) SPIE.

Selected Papers on Coherent Optical Processing. Ed. by Francis T. Yu & Shizhuo Yin. LC 92-14136. (Milestone Ser.: Vol. 52). 1992. pap. 55.00 (*0-8194-0957-X*) SPIE.

Selected Papers on Coherent Optical Processing. Ed. by Francis T. Yu & Shizhuo Yin. LC 92-14136. (Milestone Ser.: Vol. MS 52/HC). 1992. 45.00 (*0-8194-0956-1*) SPIE.

Selected Papers on Colorimetry-Fundamentals. Ed. by David L. MacAdam. LC 93-10037. (Milestone Ser.: Vol. MS 77). 1993. pap. 45.00 (*0-8194-1295-3*) SPIE.

Selected Papers on Colorimetry-Fundamentals. Ed. by David L. MacAdam. LC 93-10037. (Milestone Ser.: Vol. MS 77/HC). 1993. 55.00 (*0-8194-1296-1*) SPIE.

Selected Papers on Comparative Tai Studies. William J. Gedney. Ed. by Robert J. Bickner et al. LC 85-48239. (Michigan Papers on South & Southeast Asia: No. 29). 544p. 1989. 39.95 (*0-89148-037-4*); pap. 19.95 (*0-89148-038-2*) Ctr S&SE Asian.

Selected Papers on Computer-Controlled Optical Surfacing. Ed. by Robert A. Jones. (Milestone Ser.: Vol. MS 40/HC). 416p. 1991. 55.00 (*0-8194-0740-2*) SPIE.

Selected Papers on Computer-Controlled Optical Surfacing. Ed. by Robert A. Jones. (Milestone Ser.: Vol. MS40). 416p. 1991. pap. 45.00 (*0-8194-0741-0*) SPIE.

Selected Papers on Computer Science. Donald E. Knuth. (Illus.). 169p. (C). 1996. text ed. 49.95 (*1-881526-92-5*); pap. text ed. 22.95 (*1-881526-91-7*) CSLI.

***Selected Papers on Confocal Microscopy.** Barry R. Masters. LC 96-41849. (SPIE Milestone Ser.). 1996. write for info. (*0-8194-2372-6*) SPIE.

Selected Papers on Coupled-Mode Theory in Guided-Wave Optics. Ed. by Dennis G. Hall. LC 93-27725. (Milestone Ser.: Vol. MS 84/HC). 1993. 55.00 (*0-8194-1373-9*) SPIE.

Selected Papers on Coupled-Mode Theory in Guided-Wave Optics. Ed. by Dennis G. Hall. LC 93-27725. (Milestone Ser.: Vol. MS84). 1993. pap. 45.00 (*0-8194-1372-0*) SPIE.

Selected Papers on CO2 Lasers, MS22. Ed. by J. D. Evans. 560p. 1990. pap. 35.00 (*0-8194-0493-4*) SPIE.

Selected Papers on CO2 Lasers, MS22/HC. Ed. by J. D. Evans. 560p. 1990. 45.00 (*0-8194-0492-6*) SPIE.

***Selected Papers on Crack Tip Stress Fields.** Rober J. Sanford. LC 97-20468. (SPIE Milestone Ser.). 1997. write for info. (*0-912053-56-9*) SPIE.

***Selected Papers on Crack Tip Stress Fields.** Robert J. Sanford. LC 97-20468. (SPIE Milestone Ser.). 1997. write for info. (*0-8194-2621-0*) SPIE.

Selected Papers on Cryogenic Optical Systems. Ed. by Gerald R. Pruitt. LC 94-11392. (Milestone Ser.: Vol. MS 98). 1994. pap. 45.00 (*0-8194-1632-0*) SPIE.

Selected Papers on Cryogenic Optical Systems. Ed. by Gerald R. Pruitt. LC 94-11392. (Milestone Ser.: Vol. MS 98/HC). 1994. 55.00 (*0-8194-1633-9*) SPIE.

Selected Papers on Deposition of Optical Coatings. Ed. by Michael R. Jacobson. (Milestone Ser.: Vol. MS 6). 665p. 1989. pap. 50.00 (*0-8194-0239-7*) SPIE.

Selected Papers on Deposition of Optical Coatings. Ed. by Michael R. Jacobson. (Milestone Ser.: Vol. MS 6/HC). 665p. 1989. 50.00 (*0-8194-0285-0*) SPIE.

Selected Papers on Desalination & Ocean Technology. S. N. Levine. (Illus.). 1990. 11.75 (*0-8446-2459-4*) Peter Smith.

Selected Papers on Design of Optical Coatings. Ed. by M. R. Jacobson. 720p. 1990. 50.00 (*0-8194-0568-X*, VOL. MS26/HC); pap. 50.00 (*0-8194-0569-8*, VOL. MS26) SPIE.

Selected Papers on Diffraction Gratings. Ed. by Daniel Maystre. LC 93-27724. (Milestone Ser.: Vol. MS 83/HC). 1993. 55.00 (*0-8194-1371-2*) SPIE.

Selected Papers on Diffraction Gratings. Ed. by Daniel Maystre. LC 93-27724. (Milestone Ser.: Vol. MS83). 1993. pap. 45.00 (*0-8194-1370-4*) SPIE.

Selected Papers on Digital Image Processing. Ed. by M. M. Trivedi. 736p. 1990. 50.00 (*0-8194-0473-X*, VOL. MS17/HC); pap. 50.00 (*0-8194-0474-8*, VOL. MS17) SPIE.

Selected Papers on Digital Typography. Donald Knuth. (CSLI Lecture Notes). 400p. 1996. 55.95 (*1-57586-011-2*); pap. 24.95 (*1-57586-010-4*) CSLI.

Selected Papers on Dye Lasers. Ed. by Frank J. Duarte. 682p. 1992. 55.00 (*0-8194-0884-0*, MS45/HC) SPIE.

Selected Papers on Economic Theory. Knut Wicksell. Ed. by Erik Lindhal. LC 68-58667. (Reprints of Economic Classics Ser.). (Illus.). 292p. 1969. reprint ed. 39.50 (*0-678-00493-5*) Kelley.

Selected Papers on Effects of Aberrations in Optical Imaging. Ed. by Virendra N. Mahajan. LC 92-46455. (Milestone Ser.: Vol. MS 74). 1993. 55.00 (*0-8194-1215-5*, MS74/HC) SPIE.

Selected Papers on Effects of Aberrations in Optical Imaging. Ed. by Virendra N. Mahajan. LC 92-46455. (Milestone Ser.: Vol. MS74). 1993. pap. 45.00 (*0-8194-1214-7*) SPIE.

Selected Papers on Electron Optics. Ed. by Peter W. Hawkes. LC 94-7556. (Milestone Ser.: Vol. MS 94). 1994. pap. 45.00 (*0-8194-1572-3*) SPIE.

Selected Papers on Electron Optics. Ed. by Peter W. Hawkes. LC 94-7556. (Milestone Ser.: Vol. MS 94/HC). 1994. 55.00 (*0-8194-1573-1*) SPIE.

***Selected Papers on Electronic Speckle Pattern Interferometry: Principles & Practice.** K. D. Hinsch et al. LC 96-36820. (Milestone Ser.). 1996. write for info. (*0-8194-2376-9*) SPIE.

Selected Papers on Ellipsometry. Ed. by R. M. Azzan. 736p. 1991. pap. 50.00 (*0-8194-0571-X*, VOL. MS27) SPIE.

Selected Papers on Fiber Optic Communications. Ed. by Lynn D. Hutcheson & Stephen C. Mettler. LC 93-32188. (Milestone Ser.: Vol. MS 88). 1993. pap. 35.00 (*0-8194-1400-X*) SPIE.

Selected Papers on Fiber Optic Communications. Ed. by Lynn D. Hutcheson & Stephen C. Mettler. LC 93-32188. (Milestone Ser.: Vol. MS 88/HC). 1993. 45.00 (*0-8194-1401-8*) SPIE.

Selected Papers on Fiber Optic Gyroscopes. Ed. by R. B. Smith. (Milestone Ser.). 638p. 1989. pap. 50.00 (*0-8194-0329-6*, MS08) SPIE.

Selected Papers on Fiber Optic Local Area Networks. Ed. by Eric G. Rawson. LC 93-42627. (Milestone Ser.: Vol. 91). 1994. pap. 45.00 (*0-8194-1502-2*) SPIE.

Selected Papers on Fiber Optic Local Area Networks. Ed. by Eric G. Rawson. LC 93-42627. (Milestone Ser.: Vol. 91/HC). 1994. 45.00 (*0-8194-1503-0*) SPIE.

Selected Papers on Fiber Optic Sensors. Ed. by Reinhardt Willsch & Ralf T. Kersten. LC 94-45981. (Milestone Ser.: Vol. 108S). 1995. 50.00 (*0-8194-1814-5*) SPIE.

Selected Papers on Folklore. Carl W. Von Sydow. Ed. by Richard M. Dorson. LC 77-70623. (International Folklore Ser.). 1977. lib. bdg. 25.95 (*0-405-10125-2*) Ayer.

***Selected Papers on Foundations of Linear Elastic Fracture Mechanics.** Robert J. Sanford. LC 97-20467. (SPIE Milestone Ser.). 1997. write for info. (*0-8194-2620-2*) SPIE.

Selected Papers on Fourier Optics. Ed. by Mustafa A. Abushagur & H. John Caulfield. LC 94-40115. (Milestone Ser.: Vol. 105). 1994. 50.00 (*0-8194-1772-6*) SPIE.

Selected Papers on Free-Space Laser Communications II. David L. Begley. LC 94-11393. (Milestone Ser.: Vol. MS 100). 1994. pap. 45.00 (*0-8194-1636-3*) SPIE.

Selected Papers on Free-Space Laser Communications II. David L. Begley. LC 94-11393. (Milestone Ser.: Vol. MS 100/HC). 1994. 55.00 (*0-8194-1637-1*) SPIE.

Selected Papers on Fundamentals of Lasers. Ed. by William T. Silfvast. (Milestone Ser.: Vol. 70). 1993. pap. 35.00 (*0-8194-1211-2*) SPIE.

Selected Papers on Fundamentals of Lasers. Ed. by William T. Silfvast. (Milestone Ser.: Vol. 70/HC). 1993. 45.00 (*0-8194-1212-0*) SPIE.

Selected Papers on Fundamentals of Optoelectronics. Ed. by Gordon Little. LC 93-38813. 1993. 45.00 (*0-8194-1498-0*, MS 90/HC); pap. 35.00 (*0-8194-1497-2*, MS 90) SPIE.

Selected Papers on Fundamentals of Quantum Optics. Ed. by Girish S. Agarwal. LC 94-36850. (Milestone Ser.). 1994. 50.00 (*0-8194-1717-3*, MS103) SPIE.

Selected Papers on Gaussian Beam Mode Optics for Millimeter Wave & Terahertz Systems. Ed. by James C. Lesurf. LC 92-31312. (Milestone Ser.: Vol. 68). 1992. pap. 45.00 (*0-8194-1060-8*) SPIE.

Selected Papers on Gaussian Beam Mode Optics for Millimeter Wave & Terahertz Systems. Ed. by James C. Lesurf. LC 92-31312. (Milestone Ser.: Vol. 68/HC). 1992. 55.00 (*0-8194-1061-6*) SPIE.

Selected Papers on Geometrical Aspects of Scattering. Ed. by Philip L. Marston. LC 93-34227. (Milestone Ser.: Vol. MS 89/HC). 1993. 55.00 (*0-8194-1405-0*) SPIE.

Selected Papers on Geometrical Aspects of Scattering. Ed. by Philip L. Marston. LC 93-34227. (Milestone Ser.: Vol. MS89). 1993. pap. 45.00 (*0-8194-1404-2*) SPIE.

Selected Papers on Geometry. Ed. by Anne Stehney & Tilla Milnor. LC 79-65512. (Raymond W. Brink Selected Mathematical Papers). 347p. 1979. 12.00 (*0-88385-204-7*, BSP-04) Math Assn.

Selected Papers on Gradient-Index Optics. Ed. by Duncan T. Moore. LC 92-34884. (Milestone Ser.: Vol. MS 67). 1992. pap. 35.00 (*0-8194-1058-6*) SPIE.

Selected Papers on Gradient-Index Optics. Ed. by Duncan T. Moore. LC 92-34884. (Milestone Ser.: Vol. MS 67/HC). 1992. 45.00 (*0-8194-1059-4*) SPIE.

Selected Papers on High Power Lasers. Ed. by John M. Soures. (Milestone Ser.: Vol. MS43). 726p. 1991. pap. 35.00 (*0-8194-0800-X*) SPIE.

Selected Papers on High Power Lasers. Ed. by John M. Soures. (Milestone Ser.: Vol. MS 43/HC). 726p. 1992. 45.00 (*0-8194-0799-2*) SPIE.

Selected Papers on History of Sciences by C. N. Yang. C. N. Yang. 368p. 1994. pap. text ed. 15.00 (*1-879771-04-7*) Global Pub NJ.

Selected Papers on History of Sciences by C. N. Yang. C. N. Yang. 368p. 1994. text ed. 24.00 (*0-9625118-7-0*) World Scientific Pub.

Selected Papers on Holographic & Diffractive Lenses & Mirrors. Ed. by T. W. Stone & B. J. Thompson. 1991. pap. 50.00 (*0-8194-0637-6*, VOL. MS34) SPIE.

Selected Papers on Holographic Particle Diagnostics. Ed. by C. S. Vileran. 610p. 1990. 45.00 (*0-8194-0490-X*, VOL. MS21/HC); pap. 35.00 (*0-8194-0491-8*, VOL. MS21) SPIE.

***Selected Papers on Holographic Recording Materials.** Hans I. Bjelkhagen. LC 96-35808. (SPIE Milestone Ser.). 1996. write for info. (*0-8194-2371-8*) SPIE.

Selected Papers on Holographic Storage. Ed. by Glenn T. Sincerbox. LC 94-7897. (SPIE Milestone Ser.: Vol. MS 95/HC). 1994. 55.00 (*0-8194-1576-6*) SPIE.

Selected Papers on Image Coding & Compression. Ed. by Majid Rabbani. LC 92-5748. (Milestone Ser.: Vol. 48). 1992. pap. 35.00 (*0-8194-0889-1*) SPIE.

Selected Papers on Image Coding & Compression. Ed. by Majid Rabbani. LC 92-5748. (Milestone Ser.: Vol. 48/HC). 1992. 45.00 (*0-8194-0888-3*) SPIE.

Selected Papers on Image Tubes. Ed. by I. P. Csorba. 736p. 1990. 45.00 (*0-8194-0475-6*, VOL. MS20/HC); pap. 35.00 (*0-8194-0476-4*, VOL. MS20) SPIE.

Selected Papers on Industrial Machine Vision Systems. Ed. by Bruce G. Batchelor. LC 94-7899. (Milestone Ser.: Vol. MS 97). 1994. pap. 45.00 (*0-8194-1579-0*) SPIE.

Selected Papers on Industrial Machine Vision Systems. Ed. by Bruce G. Batchelor. LC 94-7899. (Milestone Ser.: Vol. MS 97/HC). 1994. 55.00 (*0-8194-1580-4*) SPIE.

Selected Papers on Infrared Design. Ed. by R. B. Johnson & W. L. Wolfe. 1032p. 1985. 50.00 (*0-89252-548-7*, 513) SPIE.

Selected Papers on Infrared Fiber Optics. Ed. by James A. Harrington. (Milestone Ser.: Vol. MS 9). 603p. 1990. pap. 35.00 (*0-8194-0331-8*) SPIE.

Selected Papers on Instrumentation in Astronomy. Ed. by William Livingston. LC 93-23374. (Milestone Ser.: Vol. MS 87). 1993. pap. 35.00 (*0-8194-1395-X*) SPIE.

Selected Papers on Instrumentation in Astronomy. Ed. by William Livingston. LC 93-23374. (Milestone Ser.: Vol. MS 87/HC). 1993. 45.00 (*0-8194-1396-8*) SPIE.

Selected Papers on Interference, Interferometry, & Interferometric Metrology. Ed. by P. Hariharan & Daniel Malacara. LC 95-16763. (SPIE Milestone Ser.). 1995. 50.00 (*0-8194-1936-2*, MS110) SPIE.

Selected Papers on Interferometry. Ed. by P. Hariharan. 1991. pap. 50.00 (*0-8194-0573-6*, VOL. MS28) SPIE.

Selected Papers on Laser Beam Diagnostics. Robert N. Hindy & Jeffrey H. Hunt. LC 96-26559. (Milestone Ser.). 1996. 110.00 (*0-8194-2283-5*, MS126) SPIE.

Selected Papers on Laser Damage in Optical Materials. Ed. by R. M. Wood. 512p. 1990. 45.00 (*0-8194-0542-6*, MS24/HC); pap. 35.00 (*0-8194-0543-4*, VOL. MS24) SPIE.

Selected Papers on Laser Distance Measurements. Ed. by Thierry Bosch & Marc Lescure. (SPIE Milestone Ser.: Vol. MS 115). 1995. 118.00 (*0-8194-2010-7*) SPIE.

Selected Papers on Laser Doppler Velocimetry. Ed. by R. J. Adrian. LC 93-10185. (Milestone Ser.: Vol. MS 78/HC). 1993. 55.00 (*0-8194-1298-8*) SPIE.

Selected Papers on Laser Doppler Velocimetry. Ed. by R. J. Adrian. LC 93-10185. (Milestone Ser.: Vol. MS78). 1993. pap. 45.00 (*0-8194-1297-X*) SPIE.

Selected Papers on Laser Isotope Separation: Science & Technology. Ed. by Jeff W. Eerkens. LC 95-30340. (Milestone Ser.: Vol. MS 113). 1995. 118.00 (*0-8194-1998-2*) SPIE.

***Selected Papers on Laser Radar.** Gary W. Kamerman. LC 96-50395. (Spie Milestone Ser.). 1997. write for info. (*0-8194-2467-6*) SPIE.

Selected Papers on Laser Safety. Ed. by David H. Sliney & Brian J. Thompson. LC 95-20693. (SPIE Milestone Ser.: Vol. MS 117). 1995. 118.00 (*0-8194-2014-X*) SPIE.

Selected Papers on Laser Scanning & Recording. Ed. by Leo Beiser. 504p. 1985. 35.00 (*0-89252-413-8*, 378) SPIE.

Selected Papers on Laser System Design. Ed. by H. Weichel. 1991. pap. 50.00 (*0-8194-0625-2*, VOL. MS29) SPIE.

Selected Papers on Light Scattering, Vol. 951. Ed. by Milton Kerker. (Milestone Ser.). 1016p. 1988. 50.00 (*0-89252-986-5*) SPIE.

Selected Papers on Linear Optical Composite Materials. Ed. by Akhlesh Lakhtakia. LC 95-53169. (SPIE Milestone Ser.: Vol. MS120). 1996. 118.00 (*0-8194-2152-9*) SPIE.

Selected Papers on Lovecraft. S. T. Joshi. vi, 75p. (Orig.). 1989. pap. 9.95 (*0-940884-23-2*) Necronomicon.

Selected Papers on Microdensitometry. Ed. by Brian J. Thompson & Richard E. Swing. 1995. 95.00 (*0-8194-1939-7*, MS111) SPIE.

Selected Papers on Model-Based Vision. Ed. by Hatem N. Nasr. LC 92-42878. (Milestone Ser.: Vol. MS 72). 1993. pap. 45.00 (*0-8194-1165-5*) SPIE.

Selected Papers on Model-Based Vision. Ed. by Hatem N. Nasr. LC 92-42878. (Milestone Ser.: Vol. MS 72/HC). 1993. 55.00 (*0-8194-1164-7*) SPIE.

Selected Papers on Morphological Image Processing: Principles & Optoelectronic Implementations. LC 96-9400. (SPIE Milestone Ser.). 1996. 110.00 (*0-8194-2284-3*, MS127) SPIE.

Selected Papers on Multiple Scattering in Plane Parallel Atmospheres & Oceans: Methods. Ed. by George W. Kattawar. (Milestone Ser.: Vol. MS42). 656p. 1991. 55.00 (*0-8194-0797-6*); pap. 45.00 (*0-8194-0798-4*) SPIE.

Selected Papers on National Income. M. Mukherjee. (C). 1995. 34.00 (*81-7074-150-5*, Pub. by KP Bagchi II) S Asia.

Selected Papers on Natural & Artificial Compound Eye Sensors. Ed. by Jeffrey S. Sanders. (Milestone Ser.: MS 122). 1996. 118.00 (*0-8194-2183-9*) SPIE.

Selected Papers on Natural Optical Activity. Ed. by A. Lakhakia. 624p. 1990. pap. 35.00 (*0-8194-0436-5*, VOL. MS15) SPIE.

Selected Papers on Nonimaging Optics. Ed. by Roland Winston. LC 94-42849. (Milestone Ser.: Vol. 106). 1995. 50.00 (*0-8194-1799-8*) SPIE.

Selected Papers on Nonlinear Optics. H. E. Brandt. 1991. pap. 45.00 (*0-8194-0631-7*, VOL. MS32) SPIE.

Selected Papers on Number Theory, Algebraic Geometry & Differential Equations. Katsumi Nomizu. LC 94-26691. (Translations Ser.: Series 2, Vol. 160). 154p. 1994. 75.00 (*0-8218-7511-6*, TRANS2/160) Am Math.

Selected Papers on Number Theory & Algebraic Geometry. Ed. by Katsumi Nomizu. LC 95-39031. (American Mathematical Society Translations Ser.: Series 2, Vol. 172). 91p. 1996. 42.00 (*0-8218-0445-6*, TRANS2/172) Am Math.

Selected Papers on Optical Chaos. Ed. by F. T. Arecchi & R. G. Harison. LC 92-46456. (Milestone Ser.: Vol. MS 75/HC). 1993. 45.00 (*0-8194-1217-1*) SPIE.

Selected Papers on Optical Computing, Vol. 1142. Ed. by H. John Caulfield & Gregory Gheen. (Milestone Series of Selected Reprints). (Illus.). 636p. 1989. pap. text ed. 50.00 (*0-8194-0178-1*) SPIE.

Selected Papers on Optical Correlators. Ed. by Suganda Jutamulia. LC 93-10036. (Milestone Ser.: Vol. MS 76). 1993. pap. 35.00 (*0-8194-1293-7*) SPIE.

Selected Papers on Optical Correlators. Ed. by Suganda Jutamulia. LC 93-10036. (Milestone Ser.: Vol. MS 76/HC). 1993. 45.00 (*0-8194-1294-5*) SPIE.

Selected Papers on Optical Fibers in Medicine. Ed. by A. Katzir. (Milestone Ser.). 736p. 1990. 45.00 (*0-8194-0368-7*, VOL. MS11(H)); pap. 35.00 (*0-8194-0369-5*, VOL. MS11(S)) SPIE.

***Selected Papers on Optical Methods in Surface Metrology.** D. J. Whitehouse. LC 96-30857. (Milestone Ser.). 1996. 110.00 (*0-8194-2347-5*, MS129) SPIE.

Selected Papers on Optical Microlithography. Ed. by Harry L. Stover. LC 92-19421. (Milestone Ser.: Vol. 55). 1992. pap. 45.00 (*0-8194-0986-3*) SPIE.

Selected Papers on Optical Microlithography. Ed. by Harry L. Stover. LC 92-19421. (Milestone Ser.: Vol. MS 55/HC). 1992. 55.00 (*0-8194-0985-5*) SPIE.

Selected Papers on Optical Moire & Applications, Vol. MS 64. Ed. by Guy Indebetouw & Robert Czarnek. LC 92-29546. 1992. pap. 45.00 (*0-8194-1054-3*) SPIE.

Selected Papers on Optical Neural Networks. Ed. by Suganda Jutamulia. LC 94-7898. (SPIE Milestone Ser.: Vol. MS 96/HC). 1994. 55.00 (*0-8194-1578-2*) SPIE.

***Selected Papers on Optical Remote Sensing Theory & Measurements.** James Smith. LC 97-5753. (Milestone Ser.). 1997. write for info. (*0-8194-2524-9*) SPIE.

Selected Papers on Optical Shop Metrology. Ed. by D. Malacara. 720p. 1990. pap. 50.00 (*0-8194-0479-9*, VOL. MS18) SPIE.

***Selected Papers on Optical Techniques for Industrial Inspection.** Paolo G. Cielo. LC 97-3031. (Milestone Ser.). 1997. write for info. (*0-8194-2531-1*) SPIE.

Selected Papers on Optical Tolerancing. Ed. by G. E. Wiese. 1991. pap. 50.00 (*0-8194-0641-4*, VOL. MS36) SPIE.

Selected Papers on Optical Transfer Function - Foundation & Theory. Ed. by Lionel Baker. LC 92-19409. (Milestone Ser.: Vol. 59). 1992. pap. 45.00 (*0-8194-0994-4*) SPIE.

Selected Papers on Optical Transfer Function - Foundation & Theory. Ed. by Lionel Baker. LC 92-19409. (Milestone Ser.: Vol. MS 59/HC). 1992. 55.00 (*0-8194-0993-6*) SPIE.

Selected Papers on Optical Transfer Function - Measurement. Ed. by Lionel Baker. LC 92-19408. (Milestone Ser.: Vol. 60). 1992. pap. 45.00 (*0-8194-0996-0*) SPIE.

Selected Papers on Optometry. Ed. by William M. Rosenblum & William J. Benjamin. LC 92-29543. (Milestone Ser.: Vol. MS 62). 1992. pap. 45.00 (*0-8194-1050-0*) SPIE.

Selected Papers on Particle Image Velocimetry. Ed. by Ian Grant. LC 94-11391. (Milestone Ser.: Vol. MS 99). 1994. pap. 45.00 (*0-8194-1634-7*) SPIE.

Selected Papers on Particle Image Velocimetry. Ed. by Ian Grant. LC 94-11391. (Milestone Ser.: Vol. MS 99/HC). 1994. 55.00 (*0-8194-1635-5*) SPIE.

Selected Papers on Performance Evaluation of Signal & Image Processing Systems. Ed. by Firooz A. Sadjadi. LC 93-13658. (Milestone Ser.: Vol. MS 79). 1993. pap. 45.00 (*0-8194-1316-X*) SPIE.

Selected Papers on Performance Evaluation of Signal & Image Processing Systems. Ed. by Firooz A. Sadjadi. LC 93-13658. (Milestone Ser.: Vol. MS 79/HC). 1993. 55.00 (*0-8194-1317-8*) SPIE.

Selected Papers on Photochemistry. Ed. by Douglas C. Neckers. LC 92-29753. (Milestone Ser.: Vol. MS 65). 1992. pap. 45.00 (*0-8194-1056-X*) SPIE.

Selected Papers on Photochemistry. Ed. by Douglas C. Neckers. LC 92-29753. (Milestone Ser.: Vol. MS 65/HC). 1992. 55.00 (*0-8194-1057-8*) SPIE.

Selected Papers on Photoconductivity. Ed. by N. V. Joshi. LC 92-19410. (Milestone Ser.: Vol. 56). 1992. 45.00 (*0-8194-0987-1*); pap. 35.00 (*0-8194-0988-X*) SPIE.

Selected Papers on Photodynamic Therapy. Ed. by David Kessel. LC 93-5236. (Milestone Ser.: Vol. MS 82/HC). 1993. 55.00 (*0-8194-1368-2*) SPIE.

Selected Papers on Photodynamic Therapy. Ed. by David Kessel. LC 93-5236. (Milestone Ser.: Vol. MS82). 1993. pap. 45.00 (*0-8194-1367-4*) SPIE.

Selected Papers on Photon Statistics & Coherence in Nonlinear Optics. Ed. by Jan Perina. (Milestone Ser.: Vol. MS39). 512p. 1991. pap. 35.00 (*0-8194-0739-9*) SPIE.

Selected Papers on Photon Statistics & Coherence in Nonlinear Optics. Ed. by Jan Perina. (Milestone Ser.: Vol. MS 39/HC). 512p. 1991. 45.00 (*0-8194-0738-0*) SPIE.

***Selected Papers on Photonic Control Systems for Phased Array Antennas.** Nebeel A. Riza. LC 97-3308. (SPIE Milestone Ser.). 1997. write for info. (*0-8194-2613-X*) SPIE.

Selected Papers on Photonic Switching, Vol. MS 121. Ed. by Abdellatif Marrakchi. (Milestone Ser.: Vol. 121). 1996. 95.00 (*0-8194-2163-4*) SPIE.

Selected Papers on Photopolymers: Physics, Chemistry, & Applications, Vol. MS 114. Ed. by Roger A. Lessard & Gurusamy Manivannan. LC 95-23392. (SPIE Milestone Ser.). 1995. text ed. 110.00 (*0-8194-2000-X*) SPIE.

Selected Papers on Photorefractive Materials. Ed. by Frederic M. Davidson. LC 93-34008. (Milestone Ser.: Vol. MS 86). 1993. pap. 45.00 (*0-8194-1393-3*) SPIE.

Selected Papers on Photorefractive Materials. Ed. by Frederic M. Davidson. LC 93-34008. (Milestone Ser.: Vol. MS 86/HC). 1993. 55.00 (*0-8194-1394-1*) SPIE.

Selected Papers on Polarization. Ed. by B. H. Billings. 736p. 1990. pap. 35.00 (*0-8194-0495-0*, VOL. MS23) SPIE.

Selected Papers on Precalculus. Ed. by Tom M. Apostol. (Raymond W. Brink Selected Mathematical Papers: Vol. 1). 469p. 1977. 12.00 (*0-88385-202-0*, BSP-01) Math Assn.

Selected Papers on Precision Stabilization & Tracking Systems for Acquisition, Pointing, & Control Applications. Ed. by Michael K. Masten & Larry A. Stockum. LC 96-844. (Milestone Ser.: Vol. MS 123). 1996. 118.00 (*0-8194-2259-2*) SPIE.

Selected Papers on Prisms & Mirrors: Design & Fabrications. Ed. by R. Hradaynath. LC 93-23182. (Milestone Ser.: Vol. 81). 1993. pap. 35.00 (*0-8194-1354-2*) SPIE.

Selected Papers on Prisms & Mirrors: Design & Fabrications. Ed. by R. Hradaynath. LC 93-23182. (Milestone Ser.: Vol. MS 81/HC). 1993. 45.00 (*0-8194-1355-0*) SPIE.

Selected Papers on Quantum Electrodynamics. Ed. by Julian Schwinger. 1958. pap. text ed. 10.95 (*0-486-60444-6*) Dover.

Selected Papers on Quasielastic Light Scattering by Nacromolecular, Supramolecular, & Fluid Systems. Ed. by B. Chu. 736p. 1990. 45.00 (*0-8194-0374-1*, VOL. MS12/HC); pap. 35.00 (*0-8194-0375-X*, VOL. MS12) SPIE.

Selected Papers on Radiometry. Irving J. Spiro. 704p. 1990. 50.00 (*0-8194-0378-4*, VOL. MS14/HC); pap. 50.00 (*0-8194-0379-2*, VOL. MS14) SPIE.

Selected Papers on Refugee Issues, Vol. II. Ed. by MaryCarol Hopkins & Nancy D. Donnelly. LC 93-33088. 1993. write for info. (*0-913167-58-4*) Am Anthro Assn.

Selected Papers on Refugee Issues, 1992. Ed. by Pamela DeVoe. LC 92-38436. 1992. write for info. (*0-913167-54-1*) Am Anthro Assn.

Selected Papers on Resonant & Collective Phenomena in Quantum Optics. Ed. by Girish S. Agarwal. LC 94-37447. (SPIE Milestone Ser.: Vol. MS 104). 1994. 50.00 (*0-8194-1718-1*) SPIE.

Selected Papers on Scanning Acoustic Microscopy. Ed. by Butrus T. Khuri-Yakub & Calvin F. Quate. LC 92-18872. (Milestone Ser.: Vol. MS 53). 1992. pap. 45.00 (*0-8194-0982-0*) SPIE.

Selected Papers on Scanning Acoustic Microscopy. Ed. by Butrus T. Khuri-Yakub & Calvin F. Quate. LC 92-18872. (Milestone Ser.: Vol. MS 53/HC). 1992. 55.00 (*0-8194-0981-2*) SPIE.

Selected Papers on Scanning Prove Microscopes: Design & Applications. Ed. by Yves Martin. LC 94-42035. (Milestone Ser.: No. 107). 1995. 50.00 (*0-8194-1804-8*, MS107) SPIE.

Selected Papers on Scattering in the Atmosphere. Ed. by Craig F. Bohren. (Milestone Ser.). 648p. 1989. 50.00 (*0-8194-0283-4*, VOL. MS07(H)); pap. 50.00 (*0-8194-0240-0*, VOL. MS07(S)) SPIE.

Selected Papers on Schlieren Optics. Ed. by Jurgen R. Meyer-Arendt. LC 92-29545. (Milestone Ser.: Vol. MS 61). 1992. pap. 45.00 (*0-8194-1048-9*) SPIE.

Selected Papers on Schlieren Optics. Ed. by Jurgen R. Meyer-Arendt. LC 92-29545. (Milestone Ser.: Vol. MS 61/HC). 1992. 55.00 (*0-8194-1049-7*) SPIE.

Selected Papers on Scientific & Engineering High-Speed Photography: Technology, Systems, & Applications. Ed. by Dennis Paisley. LC 95-1595. (Milestone Ser.: Vol. MS 109). 1995. text ed. 50.00 (*0-8194-1854-4*) SPIE.

Selected Papers on Semiconductor Infrared Detectors. Ed. by Antoni Rogalski. LC 92-31686. (Milestone Ser.: Vol. MS 66). 1993. pap. 45.00 (*0-8194-1064-0*) SPIE.

Selected Papers on Semiconductor Infrared Detectors. Ed. by Antoni Rogalski. LC 92-31686. (Milestone Ser.: Vol. MS 66/HC). 1993. 55.00 (*0-8194-1063-2*) SPIE.

Selected Papers on Sensor & Data Fusion. Firooz A. Sadjadi. LC 96-19938. (SPIE Milestone Ser.). 1996. 110.00 (*0-8194-2265-7*, MS124) SPIE.

Selected Papers on Silica Integrated Optical Circuits. Herman M. Presby. LC 96-22981. (Milestone Ser.). 1996. 100.00 (*0-8194-2269-X*, MS125) SPIE.

Selected Papers on Single Mode Optical Fibers: Characteristics & Applications of Standard Birefringent Fibers, MS 101. Ed. by A. Brozeit et al. LC 94-28411. (Milestone Ser.). 1994. pap. text ed. 50.00 (*0-8194-1693-2*) SPIE.

Selected Papers on Solar Radiation & Solar Thermal Systems. Ed. by Donald E. Osborn. LC 92-19411. (Milestone Ser.: Vol. 54). 1992. pap. 45.00 (*0-8194-0984-7*) SPIE.

Selected Papers on Solar Radiation & Solar Thermal Systems. Ed. by Donald E. Osborn. LC 92-19411. (Milestone Ser.: Vol. MS 54/HC). 1992. 55.00 (*0-8194-0983-9*) SPIE.

Selected Papers on Solid State Lasers, MS31. Ed. by R. C. Powell. 1991. pap. 35.00 (*0-8194-0629-5*) SPIE.

Selected Papers on Solid State Lasers, MS31/HC. Ed. by R. C. Powell. 1991. 45.00 (*0-8194-0628-7*) SPIE.

Selected Papers on Speckle Metrology. Rajpal S. Sirohi. 1991. pap. 35.00 (*0-8194-0639-2*, VOL. MS35) SPIE.

Selected Papers on Speckle Metrology. Rajpal S. Sirohi. 1991. 45.00 (*0-8194-0638-4*, VOL. MS35/HC) SPIE.

Selected Papers on Surface-Enhanced Raman Scattering. Ed. by Milton Kerker. (Milestone Ser.). 696p. 1990. pap. 35.00 (*0-8194-0367-9*, VOL. MS10(S)) SPIE.

Selected Papers on Temperature Sensing -- Optical Methods, Vol. MS 116. Ed. by Ronald D. Lucier. LC 95-32740. (Milestone Ser.). 1995. 110.00 (*0-8194-2011-5*) SPIE.

Selected Papers on the History of Psychology. Robert Watson. Ed. by Josef Brozek & Rand B. Evans. LC 76-11675. 347p. reprint ed. pap. 98.90 (*0-317-39648-X*, 2023235) Bks Demand.

Selected Papers on the Microbiology & Engineering of Sterilization Processes. 5th ed. I. J. Pflug. 298p. (C). 1988. pap. text ed. write for info. (*0-929340-05-1*) Environ Sterilization Lab.

Selected Papers on the Pathogenic Rickettsiae. Ed. by Nicholas Hahon. LC 68-17625. (Illus.). 382p. 1968. 38.50 (*0-674-79890-2*) HUP.

Selected Papers on the Teaching of Mathematics As a Service Subject. R. R. Clements et al. (CISM Ser.: Vol. 305). (Illus.). vi, 181p. 1988. 58.95 (*0-387-82056-6*) Spr-Verlag.

Selected Papers on Tissue Optics: Applications in Medical Diagnostics & Therapy. Ed. by Valery V. Turchin. LC 94-28511. (Milestone Ser.: MS. 102). 1994. 50.00 (*0-8194-1695-9*) SPIE.

Selected Papers on Turbulence in a Refractive Medium. Ed. by E. L. Andreas. 720p. 1990. pap. 35.00 (*0-8194-0545-0*, VOL. MS25) SPIE.

Selected Papers on Ultrafast Laser Technology. Ed. by Timothy R. Gosnell & Antoinette J. Taylor. (Milestone Ser.: Vol. MS 44/HC). 700p. 1991. 45.00 (*0-8194-0830-1*) SPIE.

Selected Papers on Ultrafast Laser Technology. Ed. by Timothy R. Gosnell & Antoinette J. Taylor. (Milestone Ser.: Vol. MS44). 700p. 1991. pap. 35.00 (*0-8194-0831-X*) SPIE.

Selected Papers on Ultraviolet Optics & Technology. Ed. by Robert E. Huffman. LC 93-13654. (Milestone Ser.: Vol. MS 80). 1993. pap. 45.00 (*0-8194-1318-6*) SPIE.

Selected Papers on Ultraviolet Optics & Technology. Ed. by Robert E. Huffman. LC 93-13654. (Milestone Ser.: Vol. MS 80/HC). 1993. 55.00 (*0-8194-1319-4*) SPIE.

Selected Papers on Underwater Optics. Ed. by Frank M. Caimi. LC 95-45446. (Milestone Ser.: Vol. MS118). 1996. 118.00 (*0-8194-2098-0*) SPIE.

Selected Papers on UV, VUV, & X-Ray Lasers. Ronald W. Waynant & Marwood N. Ediger. LC 92-33721. (Milestone Ser.: Vol. MS 71). 1993. pap. 45.00 (*0-8194-1126-4*) SPIE.

Selected Papers on UV, VUV, & X-Ray Lasers. Ronald W. Waynant & Marwood N. Ediger. LC 92-33721. (Milestone Ser.: Vol. MS 71/HC). 1993. 55.00 (*0-8194-1125-6*) SPIE.

Selected Papers on Visual Communication: Technology & Applications. Ed. by T. R. Hsing & A. G. Tescher. 662p. 1990. 45.00 (*0-8194-0376-8*, VOL. MS13/HC); pap. 35.00 (*0-8194-0377-6*, VOL. MS13) SPIE.

Selected Papers on X-Ray & EUV Optics. Ed. by R. B. Hoover. 1992. 55.00 (*0-8194-0634-1*, MS33/HC); pap. 45.00 (*0-8194-0635-X*, MS33) SPIE.

***Selected Papers on Zone Plates.** Jorge Ojeda-Castaneda & Carlos Gomez-Reino. LC 96-9781. (SPIE Milestone Ser.). 1996. 100.00 (*0-8194-2302-5*, MS128) SPIE.

Selected Papers on Zoom Lenses. Ed. by Allen Mann. LC 93-32573. (Milestone Ser.: Vol. MS 85). 1993. pap. 45.00 (*0-8194-1388-7*) SPIE.

Selected Papers on Zoom Lenses. Ed. by Allen Mann. LC 93-32573. (Milestone Ser.: Vol. MS 85/HC). 1993. 55.00 (*0-8194-1389-5*) SPIE.

Selected Papers, Vol. 1: Stellar Structure & Stellar Atmospheres. S. Chandrasekhar. LC 88-26110. 536p. 1989. pap. text ed. 36.00 (*0-226-10090-1*); lib. bdg. 90.00 (*0-226-10089-8*) U Ch Pr.

Selected Papers, Vol. 2: Radiative Transfer & Negative Ion of Hydrogen. S. Chandrasekhar. LC 88-26111. (Illus.). 640p. 1989. pap. text ed. 36.00 (*0-226-10093-6*) U Ch Pr.

Selected Papers, Vol. 2: Radiative Transfer & Negative Ion of Hydrogen. S. Chandrasekhar. LC 88-26111. (Illus.). 640p. 1989. lib. bdg. 90.00 (*0-226-10092-8*) U Ch Pr.

Selected Papers, Vol. 3: Stochastic, Statistical, & Hydromagnetic Problems in Physics & Astronomy. S. Chandrasekhar. LC 89-4883. (Illus.). 656p. 1989. reprint ed. pap. text ed. 36.00 (*0-226-10095-2*); reprint ed. lib. bdg. 96.00 (*0-226-10094-4*) U Ch Pr.

Selected Papers, Vol. 4: Plasma Physics, Hydrodynamic & Hydromagnetic Stability, & Applications of the Tensor-Virial Theorem. S. Chandrasekhar. 600p. 1989. pap. text ed. 36.00 (*0-226-10097-9*); lib. bdg. 96.00 (*0-226-10096-0*) U Ch Pr.

Selected Papers, Vol. 5: Relativistic Astrophysics. S. Chandrasekhar. LC 89-20400. (Illus.). 608p. 1990. pap. text ed. 36.00 (*0-226-10099-5*); lib. bdg. 96.00 (*0-226-10098-7*) U Ch Pr.

Selected Papers, Vol. 6: The Mathematical Theory of Black Holes & of Colliding Plane Waves. S. Chandrasekhar. LC 90-11149. (Illus.). 768p. 1991. pap. text ed. 42.00 (*0-226-10101-0*); lib. bdg. 96.00 (*0-226-10100-2*) U Ch Pr.

Selected Passages from Correspondence with Friends. Nikolai Gogol. Tr. by Jesse Zeldin. LC 69-14661. 300p. 1969. reprint ed. pap. 85.50 (*0-7837-9883-0*, 2060609) Bks Demand.

***Selected Passages from Sai Baba's Teachings.** Frances Reeves. Date not set. pap. 2.75 (*0-614-19088-6*, BW-175) Sathya Sai Bk Ctr.

***Selected Peak Marking Features in the Gospel of John.** Steve Booth. (American University Studies: Series 7, Vol. 178). xiii, 183p. 1996. 39.95 (*0-8204-2474-9*) P Lang Pubng.

Selected Peak Marking Features in the Gospel of John, Vol. 178. Steven C. Booth. (American University Studies: Ser. VII). 200p. (C). 1996. text ed. 39.95 (*0-8204-2749-7*) P Lang Pubng.

Selected Personal & Social Issues see Handbook of Sexology

***Selected Petroleum Products.** (Environmental Health Criteria Ser.: No. 20). 139p. 1982. pap. text ed. 20.00 (*92-4-154080-X*, 1160020) World Health.

Selected Philosophical Essays. Max F. Scheler. LC 70-186550. (Studies in Phenomenology & Existential Philosophy). 359p. (C). 1973. pap. 19.95 (*0-8101-0619-1*) Northwestern U Pr.

Selected Philosophical Papers of Robert Boyle. rev. ed. Robert Boyle. LC 91-25480. (HPC Classics Ser.). (Illus.). 288p. (C). 1991. reprint ed. pap. text ed. 18.95 (*0-87220-122-8*); reprint ed. lib. bdg. 37.95 (*0-87220-123-6*) Hackett Pub.

Selected Philosophical Writings. Rene Descartes. Ed. by John Cottingham et al. 150p. 1988. text ed. 39.95 (*0-521-35264-9*) Cambridge U Pr.

Selected Philosophical Writings. Rene Descartes. Ed. by John Cottingham et al. 150p. 1993. pap. text ed. 16.95 (*0-521-35812-4*) Cambridge U Pr.

Selected Philosophical Writings. St. Thomas Aquinas. Tr. & Selected by Timothy McDermott. LC 92-45583. (World's Classics Ser.). 496p. 1993. 13.95 (*0-19-282946-7*) OUP.

Selected Philosophical Writings. Denis Diderot. Ed. by J. Lough. LC 86-25774. 232p. 1987. reprint ed. text ed. 55.00 (*0-313-25228-9*, DISE, Greenwood Pr) Greenwood.

Selected Physical & Chemical Standard Methods for Students. 676p. 1990. pap. 60.00 (*0-87553-171-7*, 10060) Am Pub Health.

Selected Physical & Chemical Standard Methods for Students. American Public Health Association Staff et al. 674p. 1990. 60.00 (*0-87553-144-X*) Am Pub Health.

Selected Piano Compositions. Cesar Franck. Ed. by Vincent D'Indy. 1990. 10.75 (*0-8446-5457-4*) Peter Smith.

Selected Piano Compositions. Cesar Franck. Ed. by Vincent D'Indy. LC 75-27672. 192p. 1976. reprint ed. pap. 9.95 (*0-486-23269-7*) Dover.

Selected Piano Music. 10.95 (*0-7935-4621-4*, 50482405) H Leonard.

Selected Piano Works for Four Hands. Franz Schubert. 273p. 1977. pap. 10.95 (*0-486-23529-7*) Dover.

Selected Pieces for Harp & Flute. Shawna L. Sellin. LC 90-91479. (Illus.). 1991. spiral bd. write for info. (*0-9626187-1-3*) Coast Ridge Pubns.

Selected Piping Problems. S. D. Bowman. 1980. pap. 6.25 (*0-87511-009-6*) Claitors.

Selected Plays. Incl. Importance of Being Earnest. Oscar Wilde. 1986. pap. (*0-318-55088-1*); Ideal Husband. Oscar Wilde. 1986. pap. (*0-318-55089-X*); Lady Windermere's Fan. (*0-318-55090-3*); Woman of No Importance. Oscar Wilde. 1986. pap. (*0-318-55091-1*); Salome. (*0-318-55092-X*); (Plays Ser.). 352p. 1986. pap. 7.95 (*0-14-048209-1*, Penguin Bks) Viking Penguin.

Selected Plays. Dion Boucicault. Ed. by Andrew Parkin. LC 85-31345. (Irish Drama Selections Ser.: No. 4). 407p. 1987. 34.95 (*0-8132-0616-2*); pap. 16.95 (*0-8132-0617-0*) Cath U Pr.

Selected Plays. Christopher Fry. 368p. 1985. pap. 19.95 (*0-19-281873-2*) OUP.

Selected Plays. Denis Johnston. Ed. by Joseph Ronsley. LC 82-9443. (Irish Drama Selections Ser.: No. 2). 411p. (C). 1983. 33.50 (*0-8132-0576-X*); pap. 16.95 (*0-8132-0577-8*) Cath U Pr.

Selected Plays. Lennox Robinson. Ed. by Christopher Murray. LC 82-71455. (Irish Drama Selections Ser.: No. 1). (Illus.). 296p. (C). 1982. 27.95 (*0-8132-0574-3*); pap. 16.95 (*0-8132-0575-1*) Cath U Pr.

Selected Plays. unabridged ed. N. Richard Nash. 525p. 1996. 27.95 (*1-888825-01-4*) Greenhse & Kirby.

Selected Plays, Vol. 1. Ben Jonson. Ed. by Johanna Procter. (Plays by Renaissance & Restoration Dramatists Ser.). (Illus.). 464p. (C). 1989. text ed. 85.00 (*0-521-21747-4*); pap. text ed. 30.95 (*0-521-29248-4*) Cambridge U Pr.

Selected Plays, Vol. 1. unabridged ed. N. Richard Nash. 525p. 1996. pap. 12.95 (*1-888825-02-2*) Greenhse & Kirby.

Selected Plays, Vol. 2. Ben Jonson. Ed. by Martin Butler. (Plays by Renaissance & Restoration Dramatists Ser.). (Illus.). 560p. (C). 1989. text ed. 85.00 (*0-521-26738-2*); pap. text ed. 30.95 (*0-521-31842-4*) Cambridge U Pr.

Selected Plays: The Broken Heart, 'Tis Pity She's a Whore, Perkin Warbeck. John Ford. Ed. by C. Gibson. (Plays by Renaissance & Restoration Dramatists Ser.). (Illus.). 352p. 1986. 74.95 (*0-521-22543-4*) Cambridge U Pr.

Selected Plays: The Post-Inferno Period. August Strindberg. Tr. by Evert Sprinchorn from SWE. LC 85-8742. (Selected Plays Ser.: Vol. 2). (Orig.). (C). 1986. pap. 14.95 (*0-8166-1339-7*) U of Minn Pr.

Selected Plays: The Pre-Inferno Period. August Strindberg. Tr. by Evert Sprinchorn from SWE. LC 85-8742. (Selected Plays Ser.: Vol. 1). (Orig.). 1986. pap. text ed. 14.95 (*0-8166-1338-9*) U of Minn Pr.

Selected Plays & Poems. Cale Y. Rice. LC 27-16490. xviii, 786p. 1972. reprint ed. 79.00 (*0-403-01174-4*) Scholarly.

Selected Plays from Bell's British Theatre, 16 vols., Set. Ed. by John Bell. LC 76-44553. (Illus.). reprint ed. 920.00 (*0-404-00840-2*) AMS Pr.

Selected Plays of Brian Friel. Brian Friel. LC 85-31340. (Irish Drama Selections Ser.: No. 6). 455p. 1986. 33.50 (*0-8132-0626-X*); pap. 16.95 (*0-8132-0627-8*) Cath U Pr.

Selected Plays of Douglas Hyde. Douglas Hyde. Ed. by Gareth W. Dunleavy & Janet E. Dunleavy. LC 88-23712. (Irish Drama Selections Ser.: No. 7). 192p. (C). 1991. pap. 16.95 (*0-8132-0683-9*); text ed. 39.95 (*0-8132-0682-0*) Cath U Pr.

Selected Plays of Edward Albee. Edward Albee. 480p. 1994. 16.99 (*1-56865-107-4*, GuildAmerica) Dblday Direct.

***Selected Plays of George Bernard Shaw.** George Bernard Shaw. (Vintage Classics Ser.). Date not set. write for info. (*0-679-72749-3*, Vin) Random.

Selected Plays of George Moore & Edward Martyn. David B. Eakin & Michael Case. LC 94-22021. 362p. 1996. 49.95 (*0-8132-0822-X*); pap. 16.95 (*0-8132-0823-8*) Cath U Pr.

Selected Plays of Hugh Leonard. Hugh Leonard. LC 91-25924. (Irish Drama Selections Ser.). 464p. 1992. pap. 16.95 (*0-8132-0760-6*); text ed. 49.95 (*0-8132-0759-2*) Cath U Pr.

Selected Plays of Jerome Lawrence & Robert E. Lee. Jerome Lawrence & Robert E. Lee. Ed. by Alan Woods. LC 94-15894. (Illus.). 576p. 1995. text ed. 39.50 (*0-8142-0646-8*) Ohio St U Pr.

Selected Plays of Lady Gregory. Ed. by Mary FitzGerald. LC 82-22013. (Irish Drama Selections Ser.: No. 3). 377p. (C). 1983. 29.95 (*0-8132-0582-4*); pap. 16.95 (*0-8132-0583-2*) Cath U Pr.

Selected Plays of Louis MacNeice. Louis MacNeice. Ed. by Alan Heuser & Peter McDonald. 430p. 1994. 58.00 (*0-19-811245-9*) OUP.

***Selected Plays of Michael MacLiammoir.** Michael MacLiammoir & John Barrett. LC 96-37909. (Irish Drama Selections Ser.). 319p. 1997. pap. 16.95 (*0-8132-0889-0*); text ed. 39.95 (*0-8132-0888-2*) Cath U Pr.

Selected Plays of Padraic Colum. Padraic Colum. Ed. by Sanford Sternlicht. (Irish Studies). (Illus.). 128p. 1986. text ed. 22.50 (*0-8156-2386-0*) Syracuse U Pr.

Selected Plays of Severino Montano, Vol. 1. Severino Montano. (Illus.). 234p. (Orig.). 1982. pap. 12.50 (*0-686-37565-3*, Pub. by New Day Pub PH) Cellar.

S

Selected Plays of Severino Montano, Vol. 2. Severino Montano. (Illus.). 319p. (Orig.). 1982. pap. 15.00 (*0-686-37566-1*, Pub. by New Day Pub PH) Cellar.
Selected Plays of Severino Montano, Vol. 3. Severino Montano. (Illus.). 64p. (Orig.). 1983. pap. 7.50 (*971-10-0046-6*, Pub. by New Day Pub PH) Cellar.
Selected Plays of St. John Ervine. Ed. by John Cronin. LC 85-31343. (Irish Drama Selections Ser.: No. 5). 387p. 1988. 39.95 (*0-8132-0628-6*); pap. 16.95 (*0-8132-0629-4*) Cath U Pr.
Selected Poems. Anna Akhmatova. Tr. by D. M. Thomas. 160p. 1989. pap. 7.95 (*0-14-058558-3*, Penguin Bks) Viking Penguin.
Selected Poems. Anna Akhmatova. Tr. & Intro. by D. M. Thomas. 160p. 1992. pap. 11.95 (*0-14-018617-4*, Penguin Classics) Viking Penguin.
Selected Poems. A. R. Ammons. 1987. pap. 10.95 (*0-393-30396-9*) Norton.
Selected Poems. Michael Anania. 224p. 1994. pap. 14.95 (*1-55921-113-X*) Moyer Bell.
***Selected Poems.** Guillaume Apollinaire & Oliver Bernard. 158p. 1994. pap. 18.95 (*0-85646-155-5*, Pub. by Anvil Press UK) Dufour.
Selected Poems. Ed. by Matthew Arnold. 256p. 1995. pap. 9.95 (*0-14-042376-1*, Penguin Classics) Viking Penguin.
Selected Poems. John Ashbery. 386p. 1986. pap. 16.95 (*0-14-058553-2*, Penguin Bks) Viking Penguin.
Selected Poems. Werner Aspenstrom. Tr. by Robin Fulton. (QRL Poetry Bks.: Vol. XXXIV). 1995. 20.00 (*0-614-06460-0*) Quarterly Rev.
Selected Poems. W. H. Auden. 1979. pap. 8.95 (*0-394-72506-9*) Random.
Selected Poems. George Barker. 1995. pap. 14.95 (*0-571-17285-7*) Faber & Faber.
Selected Poems. Charles P. Baudelaire. Tr. by Carol Clark. 1996. pap. 12.95 (*0-14-044624-9*) Viking Penguin.
Selected Poems. Attilio Bertolucci. Tr. by Charles Tomlinson from ITA. 160p. 9400. pap. 18.95 (*1-85224-242-6*, Pub. by Bloodaxe Bks UK) Dufour.
Selected Poems. Ruth Bidgood. 138p. 1993. pap. 17.95 (*1-85411-069-1*, Pub. by Seren Bks UK) Dufour.
Selected Poems. William Blake. Ed. by P. H. Butter. 256p. 1993. pap. 7.95 (*0-460-87309-1*, Everyman's Classic Lib) C E Tuttle.
Selected Poems. William Blake. LC 94-23674. 1995. 7.99 (*0-517-12367-3*) Random Hse Value.
Selected Poems. William Blake. Ed. by David Stevens. (Literature Ser.). (Illus.). 144p. (C). 1995. pap. text ed. 7.95 (*0-521-48546-0*) Cambridge U Pr.
Selected Poems. Robert Bly. LC 84-47556. 224p. 1991. pap. 12.00 (*0-06-096048-5*, PL) HarpC.
Selected Poems. William Bronk. Ed. & Intro. by Henry Weinfield. LC 95-290. 96p. (Orig.). 1995. pap. 8.95 (*0-8112-1314-5*, NDP816) New Directions.
Selected Poems. Brontes. Ed. by Juliet R. Barker. 182p. 1993. pap. 6.95 (*0-460-87282-6*, Everyman's Classic Lib) C E Tuttle.
Selected Poems. Gwendolyn Brooks. 1982. pap. 11.00 (*0-06-090989-7*, PL) HarpC.
Selected Poems. Elizabeth Barrett Browning. 250p. 1994. 7.50 (*0-460-87425-X*, Everyman's Classic Lib) C E Tuttle.
Selected Poems. Robert Browning. Ed. by William C. DeVane. (Crofts Classics Ser.). 128p. 1949. pap. text ed. write for info. (*0-88295-019-3*) Harlan Davidson.
Selected Poems. Robert Browning. Ed. & Intro. by Daniel Karlin. 352p. 1990. pap. 10.95 (*0-14-058615-6*, Penguin Bks) Viking Penguin.
Selected Poems. Robert Burns. Ed. by Carol McGuirk. 368p. 1994. pap. 11.95 (*0-14-042382-6*, Penguin Classics) Viking Penguin.
Selected Poems. Witter Bynner. Ed. by Richard Wilbur. 384p. 1978. 30.00 (*0-374-25863-5*) FS&G.
Selected Poems. George Gordon Byron. Ed. by Susan J. Wolfson. 1996. pap. 13.95 (*0-14-042381-8*) Viking Penguin.
Selected Poems. Austin Clarke. Ed. & Intro. by Hugh Maxton. 288p. 1993. pap. 11.95 (*0-14-018649-2*, Penguin Classics) Viking Penguin.
Selected Poems. Austin Clarke. Ed. by Hugh Maxton. LC 91-65935. 288p. (C). 1991. 20.00 (*0-916390-50-0*) Wake Forest.
Selected Poems. Jack Clemo. LC 88-70228. 160p. (Orig.). 9300. pap. 15.95 (*1-85224-052-0*, Pub. by Bloodaxe Bks UK) Dufour.
Selected Poems. Arthur H. Clough. Ed. by Jim McCue. 272p. 1991. pap. 10.95 (*0-14-042374-5*, Penguin Classics) Viking Penguin.
Selected Poems. Brian Coffey. (Belacqua Ser.). 68p. 1971. pap. 14.95 (*0-906897-61-0*) Dufour.
Selected Poems. Samuel Taylor Coleridge. LC 94-13081. 1994. 9.95 (*0-312-11250-5*) St Martin.
Selected Poems. David Constantine. 160p. (Orig.). 9200. pap. 18.95 (*1-85224-166-7*, Pub. by Bloodaxe Bks UK) Dufour.
***Selected Poems.** Frances Cornford & Jane Dowson. 74p. 9700. pap. 19.95 (*1-870612-87-6*, Pub. by Enitha Pr UK) Dufour.
Selected Poems. Robert Creeley. 300p. 1991. 35.00 (*0-520-06935-8*) U CA Pr.
Selected Poems. Robert Creeley. LC 91-7152. 366p. (C). 1996. pap. 14.95 (*0-520-06936-6*) U CA Pr.
Selected Poems. I. Crichton-Smith. LC 74-135657. 7000. 14.95 (*0-8023-1160-1*) Dufour.
Selected Poems. e. e. Cummings. 224p. 1994. 25.00 (*0-87140-153-3*); pap. 9.95 (*0-87140-154-1*) Liveright.
***Selected Poems.** De La Mere. (York Notes Ser.). 1992. pap. text ed. write for info. (*0-582-79289-4*, Pub. by Longman UK) Longman.
***Selected Poems.** Seamus Deane. 78p. 1988. pap. 12.95 (*1-85235-028-8*) Dufour.
Selected Poems. Diana Der-Hovanessian. LC 94-1260. 96p. (Orig.). 1994. pap. 12.95 (*1-878818-27-9*) Sheep Meadow.
Selected Poems. Bishnu Dey. Ed. by Samir Dasgupta. (Writers Workshop Saffronbird Ser.). 1975. 12.00 (*0-88253-626-5*); pap. text ed. 4.80 (*0-88253-625-7*) Ind-US Inc.
Selected Poems. Emily Dickinson. 64p. 1990. pap. 1.00 (*0-486-26466-1*) Dover.
Selected Poems. John Donne. Ed. by Matthias A. Shaaber. (Crofts Classics Ser.). 128p. 1958. pap. text ed. write for info. (*0-88295-032-0*) Harlan Davidson.
Selected Poems. Hilda Doolittle. LC 88-1460. 224p. 1988. 10.95 (*0-8112-1065-0*) New Directions.
Selected Poems. Edward Dorn. Ed. by Donald Allen. LC 78-2925. 108p. 1978. pap. 3.50 (*0-912516-32-1*) Grey Fox.
Selected Poems. John Dryden. 320p. 1993. pap. 7.95 (*0-460-87230-3*, Everyman's Classic Lib) C E Tuttle.
Selected Poems. Robert Duncan. Ed. by Robert J. Bertholf. LC 92-35812. 160p. 1993. 22.95 (*0-8112-1227-0*) New Directions.
Selected Poems. Jacques Dupin. Ed. by Germaine Bree. Tr. by Paul Auster et al. from FRE. LC 92-53715. (French Poetry in Translation Ser.). 191p. (Orig.). 1992. pap. 11.95 (*0-916390-52-7*) Wake Forest.
Selected Poems. Jean Earle. 148p. 1990. pap. 16.95 (*1-85411-030-6*, Pub. by Seren Bks UK) Dufour.
Selected Poems. Gunter Eich. Tr. by Teo Savory. LC 69-13015. (German Ser.: Vol. 3). (ENG & GER.). 1975. pap. 9.95 (*0-87775-090-4*) Unicorn Pr.
Selected Poems. Larry Eigner. 1972. 6.00 (*0-685-29871-X*); pap. 2.50 (*0-685-29872-8*) Oyez.
Selected Poems. T. S. Eliot. LC 67-23064. 127p. (J). (gr. 7-12). 1967. pap. 8.00 (*0-15-680647-9*, Harvest Bks) HarBrace.
***Selected Poems.** Odysseus Elytis et al. 114p. 1981. pap. 17.95 (*0-85646-229-2*, Pub. by Anvil Press UK) Dufour.
***Selected Poems.** John Ennis. 224p. 9600. 21.95 (*1-873790-93-7*); pap. 15.95 (*1-873790-92-9*) Dufour.
***Selected Poems.** Hans M. Enzensberger. 255p. 9400. pap. 18.95 (*1-85224-291-4*, Pub. by Bloodaxe Bks UK) Dufour.
Selected Poems. Hans M. Enzensberger. Tr. by Michael Hamburger from GER. 256p. (ENG & GER.). 9500. 40.00 (*1-85224-290-6*) Dufour.
Selected Poems. Dave Etter. 240p. 1987. 14.95 (*0-933180-91-8*) Spoon Riv Poetry.
Selected Poems. Vincent Ferrini. Ed. & Intro. by George F. Butterick. LC 76-463360. (Orig.). 1976. pap. 3.95 (*0-917590-00-7*) Univ Conn Lib.
Selected Poems. Luisa Futoransky. Tr. by Jason Weiss. 96p. (Orig.). (ENG & SPA.). 1997. pap. 11.00 (*1-881523-07-1*) Junction CA.
Selected Poems. Federico Garcia Lorca. Ed. by Christopher Maurer. 343p. (ENG & SPA.). pap. 16.00 (*0-374-52352-5*) FS&G.
Selected Poems. Federico Garcia Lorca. Ed. by Donald M. Allen. (ENG & SPA.). 1962. pap. 9.95 (*0-8112-0091-4*, NDP114) New Directions.
Selected Poems. David Gascoyne. 253p. 9500. pap. 18.95 (*1-870612-34-5*, Pub. by Enitha Pr UK) Dufour.
Selected Poems. M. Ghose. 8.00 (*0-89253-546-6*); text ed. 4.00 (*0-89253-547-4*) Ind-US Inc.
Selected Poems. Zulfikar Ghose. 136p. 1992. 24.95 (*0-19-577408-6*) OUP.
Selected Poems. Madeleine Gleason. LC 73-186603. (Living Poets' Library). pap. 2.50 (*0-686-02574-1*) Dragons Teeth.
Selected Poems. Yvan Goll. Tr. by Rainer Schulte & Michael Bullock from ENG. 110p. (ENG & GER.). 1981. pap. 8.00 (*0-939378-02-7*) Mundus Artium.
Selected Poems. Lorna Goodison. 160p. (C). 1992. pap. 13.95 (*0-472-06493-2*) U of Mich Pr.
Selected Poems. W. S. Graham. LC 80-11534. 128p. 1980. 12.95 (*0-912946-73-3*) Ecco Pr.
Selected Poems. W. S. Graham. Ed. by Daniel Halpern. LC 80-11534. 112p. 1981. pap. 6.95 (*0-912946-74-1*) Ecco Pr.
Selected Poems. W. S. Graham. 128p. (Orig.). 1996. pap. text ed. 15.95 (*0-571-17659-3*) Faber & Faber.
Selected Poems. Steve Griffiths. 128p. 1994. pap. 16.95 (*1-85411-088-8*, Pub. by Seren Bks UK) Dufour.
Selected Poems. Barbara Guest. 200p. 1995. 22.95 (*1-55713-200-3*) Sun & Moon CA.
Selected Poems. Eugene Guillevic. Tr. by Denise Levertov. LC 74-88726. (Orig.). (ENG & FRE.). 1969. 5.95 (*0-8112-0283-6*) New Directions.
Selected Poems. Daniel Halpern. LC 93-33368. 1994. 23.00 (*0-679-42986-7*) Knopf.
Selected Poems. Daniel Halpern. 272p. 1996. pap. 15.00 (*0-679-76565-4*) McKay.
Selected Poems. Josef Hanzlik. Tr. by Ewald Osers et al. from CZE. 157p. 1993. pap. 19.95 (*0-685-68157-2*, Pub. by Bloodaxe Bks UK) Dufour.
Selected Poems. Josef Hanzlik. Tr. by Jarmila Milner et al. 157p. 1993. pap. 19.95 (*1-85224-124-1*, Pub. by Bloodaxe Bks UK) Dufour.
Selected Poems. Michael Hartnett. 112p. 1994. pap. 9.95 (*0-916390-62-4*) Wake Forest.
Selected Poems. Friedrich Holderlin. LC 90-80809. 80p. 1989. pap. 13.95 (*1-85224-064-4*, Pub. by Bloodaxe Bks UK) Dufour.
***Selected Poems.** Pearse Hutchinson. 92p. 8200. pap. 12.95 (*0-904011-28-3*) Dufour.
Selected Poems. Philippe Jaccottet. Tr. by Derek Mahon from FRE. (French Poetry in Translation Ser.). 160p. (Orig.). 1988. pap. 11.95 (*0-916390-31-4*) Wake Forest.
Selected Poems. Randall Jarrell. Ed. by William H. Pritchard. 1990. 17.95 (*0-374-25867-8*) FS&G.
Selected Poems. Randall Jarrell. 1991. pap. 10.95 (*0-374-52290-1*, Noonday) FS&G.
Selected Poems. Robinson Jeffers. 114p. 1965. pap. 8.00 (*0-394-70295-6*, Vin) Random.
Selected Poems. Stephen Jonas. 250p. (Orig.). 1994. pap. 16.95 (*1-883689-06-6*); lib. bdg. 37.95 (*1-883689-07-4*) Talisman Hse.
Selected Poems. Jenny Joseph. 157p. 9300. pap. 18.95 (*1-85224-095-4*) Dufour.
Selected Poems. John Keats. Ed. by George H. Ford. (Crofts Classics Ser.). 128p. 1950. pap. text ed. write for info. (*0-88295-050-9*) Harlan Davidson.
Selected Poems. John Keats. 256p. 1989. pap. 9.95 (*0-14-058598-2*, Penguin Bks) Viking Penguin.
Selected Poems. John Keats. Ed. by Nicholas Roe. 1995. pap. 6.95 (*0-460-87459-4*, Everyman's Classic Lib) C E Tuttle.
Selected Poems. Galway Kinnell. 160p. 1983. pap. 12.95 (*0-395-32046-1*) HM.
Selected Poems. Joseph Langland. LC 90-24604. 128p. 1991. lib. bdg. 20.00 (*0-87023-747-0*) U of Mass Pr.
Selected Poems. Joseph Langland. LC 90-24604. 1992. pap. 10.95 (*0-87023-800-0*) U of Mass Pr.
Selected Poems. Marianne Larsen. LC 82-5083. 50p. 1982. pap. 7.95 (*0-915306-29-8*) Curbstone.
Selected Poems. D. H. Lawrence. (Poets Ser.). 1980. pap. 3.95 (*0-14-042281-1*, Penguin Bks) Viking Penguin.
Selected Poems. D. H. Lawrence. 272p. 1989. pap. 10.95 (*0-14-058540-0*, Penguin Bks) Viking Penguin.
Selected Poems. Henry Wadsworth Longfellow. Ed. by Anthony Thwaite. 384p. 1993. pap. 12.95 (*0-460-87229-X*, Everyman's Classic Lib) C E Tuttle.
Selected Poems. Henry Wadsworth Longfellow. Ed. & Intro. by Laurence Buell. 240p. 1988. pap. 11.95 (*0-14-039064-2*, Penguin Classics) Viking Penguin.
Selected Poems. Robert Lowell. LC 76-2000. 320p. 1977. pap. 14.00 (*0-374-51400-3*) FS&G.
Selected Poems. Malcolm Lowry. (Pocket Poets Ser.: No. 17). (Orig.). 1962. pap. 6.95 (*0-87286-030-2*, PP17) City Lights.
Selected Poems. Jayanta Mahapatra. 80p. 1989. pap. 8.95 (*0-19-562051-8*) OUP.
Selected Poems. Derek Mahon. LC 93-2221. 198p. 1993. pap. 12.00 (*0-14-058704-7*, Penguin Bks) Viking Penguin.
Selected Poems. Stephane Mallarme. Tr. by C. F. MacIntyre. (C). 1957. pap. 10.95 (*0-520-00801-4*) U CA Pr.
Selected Poems. Dennis Maloney. 100p. 1990. 17.50 (*0-87775-232-X*); pap. 7.95 (*0-87775-231-1*) Unicorn Pr.
***Selected Poems.** Osip Mandelstam. Tr. by James Green. 144p. 1992. pap. 10.95 (*0-14-018474-0*, Penguin Classics) Viking Penguin.
Selected Poems. Michael McClure. LC 85-21477. 128p. 1986. 8.95 (*0-8112-0950-4*) New Directions.
***Selected Poems.** Medbh McGuckian. 96p. (Orig.). 1997. pap. 14.95 (*0-916390-77-2*) Wake Forest.
***Selected Poems.** Medbh McGuckian. 96p. 1997. 8.95 (*0-916390-78-0*) Wake Forest.
***Selected Poems.** Eugenio Montale. Ed. by Glauco Camson. LC 65-15669. 192p. 1966. pap. 9.95 (*0-8112-0119-8*) New Directions.
Selected Poems. Intro. by Andrew Motion. 240p. 1994. 7.50 (*0-460-87458-6*, Everyman's Classic Lib) C E Tuttle.
Selected Poems. Emile Nelligan. Tr. by P. F. Widdows from FRE. (Essential Poets Ser.: No. 73). 96p. 1995. 10.00 (*1-55071-034-6*) Guernica Editions.
Selected Poems. Pablo Neruda. Ed. & Tr. by Ben Belitt from SPA. LC 61-11772. 320p. (ENG & SPA.). 1989. Bilingual ed. pap. 12.00 (*0-8021-5102-7*, Grove) Grove-Atltic.
Selected Poems. John F. Nims. LC 81-19820. (Phoenix Ser.). xii, 160p. 1982. pap. 8.95 (*0-226-58118-7*) U Ch Pr.
Selected Poems. Frank O'Hara. Ed. by Donald Allen. 1974. pap. 17.00 (*0-394-71973-5*, V-973, Vin) Random.
Selected Poems. John Oldham. Ed. by Ken Robinson. 88p. 8000. pap. 10.95 (*0-906427-12-6*, Pub. by Bloodaxe Bks UK) Dufour.
Selected Poems. Douglas Oliver. 120p. 1996. 30.50 (*1-883689-35-X*); pap. 10.50 (*1-883689-34-1*) Talisman Hse.
Selected Poems. Charles Olson. Ed. by Robert Creeley. LC 92-23838. 1993. 25.00 (*0-520-07528-5*) U CA Pr.
***Selected Poems.** Charles Olson. 1997. pap. text ed. 14.95 (*0-520-21232-0*) U CA Pr.
Selected Poems. Niyi Osundare. (African Writers Ser.). 116p. (C). 1992. pap. 8.95 (*0-435-91195-3*, 91195) Heinemann.
Selected Poems. Jose E. Pacheco. Ed. by George McWhirter. Tr. by Thomas Hoeksema et al. from SPA. LC 86-31075. 224p. 1987. 23.95 (*0-8112-1021-9*); pap. 11.95 (*0-8112-1022-7*, NDP638) New Directions.
Selected Poems. Boris Pasternak. Tr. by Peter France & Jon Stallworthy. (Twentieth-Century Classics Ser.). 160p. 1992. pap. 9.95 (*0-14-018466-X*, Penguin Classics) Viking Penguin.
Selected Poems. Kenneth Patchen. LC 58-590. 1964. pap. 10.95 (*0-8112-0146-5*, NDP160) New Directions.
Selected Poems. Saint-John Perse. Ed. by Mary A. Caws. Tr. by T. S. Eliot et al. from FRE. LC 82-8305. 160p. (Orig.). (C). 1982. pap. 9.95 (*0-8112-0855-9*, NDP547) New Directions.
Selected Poems. Simon Pettet. 120p. (Orig.). 1995. pap. 9.95 (*1-883689-30-9*) Talisman Hse.
Selected Poems. Heinz Piontek. Tr. by Ewald Osers from GER. LC 93-71942. 80p. 1994. pap. 14.95 (*1-85610-033-2*, Pub. by Forest Bks UK) Dufour.
Selected Poems. Francis Ponge. Tr. by C. K. Williams et al. LC 93-61394. (French Poetry in Translation Ser.). 232p. 1994. 18.95 (*0-916390-59-4*); pap. 12.95 (*0-916390-58-6*) Wake Forest.
Selected Poems. Ezra Pound. LC 57-8603. 1957. pap. 8.95 (*0-8112-0162-7*, NDP66) New Directions.
Selected Poems. Sheenagh Pugh. 148p. 1990. pap. 15.95 (*1-85411-029-2*, Pub. by Seren Bks UK) Dufour.
Selected Poems. Shamsur Rahman. Tr. by Kabir Chowdhury from BEN. (Writers Workshop Redbird Ser.). 61p. 1975. 9.00 (*0-89253-621-7*); text ed. 4.80 (*0-89253-622-5*) Ind-US Inc.
Selected Poems. Kathleen Raine. 160p. 1988. pap. 12.95 (*0-940262-19-3*) Lindisfarne Bks.
Selected Poems. Pierre Reverdy. Tr. by Kenneth Rexroth. LC 68-25548. 1969. 4.95 (*0-8112-0373-5*) New Directions.
Selected Poems. Pierre Reverdy. Ed. by Germaine Bree. Tr. by John Ashbery et al. from FRE. LC 90-72092. (French Poetry in Translation Ser.). 179p. 1991. 18.95 (*0-916390-47-0*); pap. 12.95 (*0-916390-46-2*) Wake Forest.
Selected Poems. Kenneth Rexroth. Ed. by Bradford Morrow. LC 84-9972. (Illus.). 160p. 1984. pap. 9.95 (*0-8112-0917-2*, NDP581) New Directions.
Selected Poems. Rainer M. Rilke. Tr. by C. F. MacIntyre. (C). 1940. pap. 8.95 (*0-520-01070-1*) U CA Pr.
Selected Poems. Norman Rosten. LC 79-52399. 171p. 1979. 10.00 (*0-8076-0930-7*); pap. 4.95 (*0-8076-0938-2*) Braziller.
Selected Poems. Tomaz Salamun. Tr. by Robert Hass & Charles Simic from SLV. 1988. pap. 12.95 (*0-88001-161-0*) Ecco Pr.
Selected Poems. Intro. by Ricardo Sanchez & Nicolas Kanellos. LC 83-72573. 120p. (C). 1985. pap. 7.50 (*0-934770-35-2*) Arte Publico.
Selected Poems. Carl Sandburg. Ed. by George Hendrick & Willene Hendrick. LC 95-50686. 350p. 1996. pap. 15.00 (*0-15-600396-1*) HarBrace.
Selected Poems. Carl Sandburg. Ed. by George Hendrick & Willene Hendrick. 1996. pap. 15.00 (*0-614-97705-3*, Harvest Bks) HarBrace.
Selected Poems. Siegfried Sassoon. 94p. 1968. pap. 10.95 (*0-571-08540-7*) Faber & Faber.
Selected Poems. James Schuyler. 320p. 1988. 25.00 (*0-374-25878-3*) FS&G.
Selected Poems. James Schuyler. 292p. 1989. pap. 12.95 (*0-374-52166-2*, Noonday) FS&G.
***Selected Poems.** Vittorio Sereni et al. 158p. 1990. pap. 19.95 (*0-85646-204-7*, Pub. by Anvil Press UK) Dufour.
Selected Poems. Shu Ting. Ed. & Tr. by Eva Hung. 135p. 1994. pap. 14.95 (*962-7255-14-9*) Cheng & Tsui.
Selected Poems. Philip Sidney. Ed. & Intro. by Catherine Bates. 224p. 1994. pap. 9.95 (*0-14-042378-8*, Penguin Classics) Viking Penguin.
***Selected Poems.** Angelos Sikelianos. Date not set. pap. 14.95 (*0-85646-128-8*, Pub. by Anvil Press UK) Dufour.
Selected Poems. Sam Simichovitch. 96p. 1995. lib. bdg. 35.00 (*0-8095-4878-X*) Borgo Pr.
Selected Poems. C. H. Sisson. LC 95-47599. 96p. (Orig.). 1996. pap. 9.95 (*0-8112-1327-7*) New Directions.
Selected Poems. Christopher Smart. Ed. by Marcus Walsh & Katrina Williamson. 400p. 1991. pap. 10.95 (*0-14-042367-2*, Penguin Classics) Viking Penguin.
Selected Poems. Stephen Spender. 1964. pap. 8.95 (*0-394-40445-9*) Random.
Selected Poems. Gaspara Stampa. Ed. by Laura A. Stortoni & Mary P. Lillie. Tr. by Mary P. Lillie from ITA. LC 94-30764. 272p. (Orig.). 1994. pap. 15.00 (*0-934977-37-2*) Italica Pr.
Selected Poems. C. J. Stevens. LC 95-60291. 180p. 1995. pap. text ed. 10.00 (*1-882425-05-7*) J Wade.
Selected Poems. C. J. Stevens. LC 95-60291. 180p. 1995. 18.00 (*1-882425-04-9*) J Wade.
Selected Poems. Mark Strand. 1990. pap. 15.00 (*0-679-73301-9*) Knopf.
Selected Poems. Mark Strand. LC 80-66013. 1980. 10.95 (*0-689-11088-X*, Atheneum S&S) S&S Trade.
Selected Poems. Lucien Stryk. LC 76-18007. 137p. 1976. pap. 9.95 (*0-8040-0741-1*) Swallow.
Selected Poems. Wislawa Szymborska. Tr. by S. Olds et al. (QRL Poetry Bks.: Vol. XXIII). (POL.). 1982. 20.00 (*0-614-06402-3*) Quarterly Rev.
Selected Poems. Rabindranath Tagore. Ed. by William Radice. (Modern Classics Ser.). 224p. 1985. mass mkt. 6.95 (*0-14-007985-8*, Penguin Bks) Viking Penguin.
Selected Poems. Rabindranath Tagore. Ed. & Tr. by William Radice. 224p. 1990. pap. 10.95 (*0-14-018366-3*, Penguin Classics) Viking Penguin.
Selected Poems. Miyoko Tanahashi. Ed. by Raymond P. Tripp, Jr. 1971. pap. 2.00 (*0-685-32558-X*) Soc New Lang Study.
Selected Poems. James Tate. LC 90-50918. (Wesleyan Poetry Ser.). 250p. 1991. pap. 15.95 (*0-8195-1192-7*, Wesleyan Univ Pr) U Pr of New Eng.
Selected Poems. Alfred Tennyson. Ed. by Aidan Day. 400p. 1992. pap. 11.95 (*0-14-044545-5*, Penguin Classics) Viking Penguin.
Selected Poems. William I. Thompson. 96p. (Orig.). 1989. pap. 7.95 (*0-940262-29-0*) Lindisfarne Bks.
***Selected Poems.** Charles Tomlinson. 1997. pap. 11.95 (*0-614-29431-2*, NDP855) New Directions.
***Selected Poems.** Georg Trakl. 112p. 1997. pap. 17.95 (*0-85646-285-3*, Pub. by Anvil Press UK) Dufour.
Selected Poems. John Tripp. LC 89-50984. 191p. 1989. pap. 12.95 (*0-685-31957-1*) Dufour.
Selected Poems. Marina Tsvetaeva. Tr. by David McDuff from RUS. LC 87-73046. 160p. (Orig.). 1988. pap. 18.95 (*1-85224-025-3*, Pub. by Bloodaxe Bks UK) Dufour.
Selected Poems. Marina I. Tsvetaeva. 160p. 1994. pap. 11.95 (*0-14-018759-6*, Penguin Classics) Viking Penguin.

An Asterisk (*) at the beginning of an entry indicates that the title is appearing in BIP for the first time.

Selected Poems. Marie Uguay. 1990. pap. 6.00 (*0-920717-46-2*) Guernica Editions.
Selected Poems. Paul Verlaine. Tr. by C. F. MacIntyre. (C). 1948. pap. 12.95 (*0-520-01298-4*) U CA Pr.
Selected Poems. Francois Villon. Tr. by Peter Dale. 240p. 1993. pap. 10.95 (*0-14-042218-8*, Penguin Classics) Viking Penguin.
Selected Poems. Johann W. Von Goethe. Ed. by Christopher Middleton. LC 93-27617. (Goethe: The Collected Works: Vol. 1). 328p. (C). 1994. pap. 15.95 (*0-691-03658-6*) Princeton U Pr.
Selected Poems. Vernon Watkins. LC 66-23889. (Orig.). 1967. pap. 2.25 (*0-8112-0214-3*, NDP221) New Directions.
Selected Poems. Theodore Weiss. LC 95-1841. 1995. 49.95 (*0-8101-5037-9*); pap. 15.95 (*0-8101-5040-9*) Northwestern U Pr.
Selected Poems. Lew Welch. Ed. by Donald Allen & Gary Snyder. LC 75-44269. 102p. (Orig.). 1976. pap. 4.95 (*0-912516-20-8*) Grey Fox.
Selected Poems. Walt Whitman. (Thrift Editions Ser.). 128p. (Orig.). 1991. pap. 1.00 (*0-486-26878-0*) Dover.
Selected Poems. C. K. Williams. 290p. 12.00 (*0-374-52455-6*) FS&G.
Selected Poems. William C. Williams. LC 94-14359. 1994. 22.00 (*0-374-25881-3*) FS&G.
Selected Poems. William C. Williams. LC 85-8874. 320p. 1985. pap. 9.95 (*0-8112-0958-X*, NDP602) New Directions.
***Selected Poems.** MacDara Woods. 1996. 21.95 (*1-873790-89-9*) Dufour.
***Selected Poems.** MacDara Woods. 194p. 9700. pap. 15.95 (*1-873790-88-0*) Dufour.
Selected Poems. William Wordsworth. Ed. by George W. Meyer. LC 50-8748. (Crofts Classics Ser.). 128p. (C). 1950. pap. text ed. write for info. (*0-88295-103-3*) Harlan Davidson.
Selected Poems. William Wordsworth. LC 93-7890. (Great Poets Ser.). 1993. 7.99 (*0-517-09325-1*, Pub. by Gramercy) Random Hse Value.
Selected Poems. William Wordsworth. Ed. by John O. Hayden. 624p. 1994. pap. 10.95 (*0-14-042375-3*, Penguin Classics) Viking Penguin.
Selected Poems. William Wordsworth. Ed. by Damian Walford. 280p. 1994. 6.50 (*0-460-87318-0*, Everyman's Classic Lib) C E Tuttle.
Selected Poems. Ivan Zhdanov. Tr. by John High & Patrick Henry. LC 96-37829. 60p. 1996. pap. 8.95 (*1-883689-43-0*) Talisman Hse.
***Selected Poems.** Ivan Zhdanov. Tr. by John High & Patrick Henry. LC 96-37829. 60p. 1996. 21.95 (*1-883689-44-9*) Talisman Hse.
Selected Poems. enl. ed. Thomas Merton. LC 67-23488. 1967. pap. 9.95 (*0-8112-0100-7*, NDP85) New Directions.
***Selected Poems.** enl. rev. ed. Robert E. Duncan. Ed. by Robert J. Bertholf. LC 96-43881. (New Directions Paperbook Ser.). 192p. 1997. pap. 9.95 (*0-8112-1345-5*, NDP838) New Directions.
***Selected Poems.** 2nd ed. Friedrich Holderlin & David Constantine. 112p. 1996. pap. 16.95 (*1-85224-378-3*, Pub. by Bloodaxe Bks UK) Dufour.
Selected Poems. 2nd ed. Henrik Nordbrandt. Tr. by Alexander Taylor. LC 78-1047. (Illus.). 88p. 1978. pap. 9.95 (*0-915306-33-6*) Curbstone.
Selected Poems. 3rd ed. John C. Ransom. 1991. 22.00 (*0-679-40257-8*) Knopf.
Selected Poems. Anna Akhmatova. Tr. by Richard McKane from RUS. LC 88-51306. 256p. 8800. reprint ed. pap. 21.00 (*1-85224-063-6*, Pub. by Bloodaxe Bks UK) Dufour.
***Selected Poems.** Benny Andersen. LC 74-27873. (Lockert Library of Poetry in Translation). reprint ed. pap. 27.40 (*0-608-04632-9*, 2065319) Bks Demand.
Selected Poems. George Gordon Byron. LC 93-1522. 112p. 1993. reprint ed. pap. text ed. 1.00 (*0-486-27784-4*) Dover.
Selected Poems. Emily Dickinson. (BCL1-PS American Literature Ser.). 231p. 1993. reprint ed. lib. bdg. 79.00 (*0-7812-6957-1*) Rprt Serv.
Selected Poems. Laurence Housman. (BCL1-PR English Literature Ser.). 125p. 1992. reprint ed. lib. bdg. 69.00 (*0-7812-7567-9*) Rprt Serv.
Selected Poems. Sidney Lanier. LC 83-48838. reprint ed. 34.50 (*0-404-20151-2*) AMS Pr.
Selected Poems. Amy Lowell. 1988. reprint ed. lib. bdg. 49.00 (*0-7812-0518-2*) Rprt Serv.
Selected Poems. Amy Lowell. 1971. reprint ed. 49.00 (*0-403-00657-0*) Scholarly.
Selected Poems. George Meredith. Ed. by Graham G. Hough. LC 79-2564. 95p. 1980. reprint ed. text ed. 42.50 (*0-313-22034-4*, MESP, Greenwood Pr) Greenwood.
Selected Poems. Czeslaw Milosz. 128p. 1996. reprint ed. pap. 13.00 (*0-88001-455-5*) Ecco Pr.
Selected Poems. John Milton. LC 92-29792. (Thrift Editions Ser.). 128p. 1993. reprint ed. pap. 1.00 (*0-486-27554-X*) Dover.
Selected Poems. Lizette W. Reese. (BCL1-PS American Literature Ser.). 187p. 1992. reprint ed. lib. bdg. 69.00 (*0-7812-6839-7*) Rprt Serv.
Selected Poems. Percy Bysshe Shelley. LC 92-29780. (Thrift Editions Ser.). 128p. 1993. reprint ed. pap. 1.00 (*0-486-27558-2*) Dover.
Selected Poems. Sacheverell Sitwell. LC 75-41255. reprint ed. 34.00 (*0-404-14605-8*) AMS Pr.
Selected Poems. George Sterling. reprint ed. lib. bdg. 50.00 (*0-7812-0782-7*) Rprt Serv.
Selected Poems. George Sterling. LC 74-131840. 1971. reprint ed. 59.00 (*0-403-00727-5*) Scholarly.
Selected Poems. Algernon C. Swinburne. LC 80-19421. 339p. 1980. reprint ed. text ed. 45.50 (*0-313-22649-0*, SWSP, Greenwood Pr) Greenwood.
Selected Poems. Alfred Tennyson. 112p. 1992. reprint ed. pap. text ed. 1.00 (*0-486-27282-6*) Dover.
Selected Poems. Alfred Tennyson. Ed. by Michael Millgate. (New Oxford English Ser.). 218p. 1973. reprint ed. pap. text ed. 12.95 (*0-19-911056-5*) OUP.
Selected Poems: African-American Women Writers 1910-1940 by Gertrude Fisher & Moody. Gates. LC 96-48714. 1996. 30.00 (*0-7838-1431-3*, Hall Reference) Macmillan.
Selected Poems: Beyond Even Faithful. Bissett. 1993. pap. 11.95 (*0-88922-172-3*) Genl Dist Srvs.
Selected Poems: In Five Sets. Laura J. Riding. 96p. 1993. reprint ed. pap. 9.95 (*0-89255-189-5*) Persea Bks.
Selected Poems: Jean Garrigue. Jean Garrigue. 224p. 1992. 12.95 (*0-252-06224-8*); text ed. 27.50 (*0-252-01859-1*) U of Ill Pr.
Selected Poems: John Donne. John Donne. LC 93-21800. (Thrift Editions Ser.). 96p. 1993. reprint ed. pap. 1.00 (*0-486-27788-7*) Dover.
***Selected Poems: Loki Is Buried at Smoky Creek.** Fred Wah. 13.95 (*0-88922-177-4*, Pub. by Talonbooks CN) Genl Dist Srvs.
Selected Poems: Nineteen Fifty-Eight to Nineteen Eighty. Gilbert Sorrentino. LC 81-1094. 271p. (Orig.). (C). 1981. pap. 12.50 (*0-87685-501-X*) Black Sparrow.
Selected Poems: Nineteen Fifty-Eight to Nineteen Eighty-Four. John Wieners. Ed. by Raymond Foye. LC 86-1046. 322p. (Orig.). 1986. pap. 13.50 (*0-87685-661-X*) Black Sparrow.
Selected Poems: One Hundred Poems Translated from the Noewegian with Eight Poems in the Original Nynorsk. Tarjei Vesaas. Tr. by Anthony Barnett. 128p. (Orig.). (ENG & NOR.). 1988. pap. 15.00 (*0-907954-12-X*, Pub. by Allardyce Barnett UK) SPD-Small Pr Dist.
Selected Poems: Rogha Danta, 1968-1984. Michael Davitt. 143p. 8700. pap. 12.95 (*1-85186-029-0*) Dufour.
Selected Poems: Selected Poems. Clive Wilmer. 128p. 1996. pap. 16.96 (*1-85754-134-0*, Pub. by Carcanet Pr UK) Paul & Co Pubs.
Selected Poems: Selected Poems. Thomas Wyatt. Ed. by Hardiman Scott. 128p. 1996. pap. 14.95 (*1-85754-229-0*, Pub. by Carcanet Pr UK) Paul & Co Pubs.
Selected Poems: Selected Poems. rev. ed. Charles P. Baudelaire. Tr. & Intro. by Joanna Richardson. (Poets Ser.). 256p. 1975. pap. 10.95 (*0-14-042188-2*, Penguin Classics) Viking Penguin.
Selected Poems: Six Sets, 1951-1983. Howard Hart. LC 84-70011. 88p. 1984. 12.50 (*0-933944-05-5*); pap. 6.95 (*0-933944-06-3*) City Miner Bks.
Selected Poems: Six Sets, 1951-1983. deluxe ed. Howard Hart. LC 84-70011. 88p. 1984. 25.00 (*0-933944-19-5*) City Miner Bks.
Selected Poems: Summer Knowledge. Delmore Schwartz. LC 59-10689. 1967. pap. 9.95 (*0-8112-0191-0*, NDP241) New Directions.
***Selected Poems: The Arches.** Frank Davey. 13.95 (*0-88922-174-X*, Pub. by Talonbooks CN) Genl Dist Srvs.
***Selected Poems: The Vision Tree.** Phyllis Webb. 14.95 (*0-88922-202-9*, Pub. by Talonbooks CN) Genl Dist Srvs.
***Selected Poems: 1947-1995.** Allen Ginsberg. 1997. pap. text ed. 16.00 (*0-06-092854-9*, PL) HarpC.
Selected Poems: 1958-1988. Horst Bienek. Tr. by Ruth Mead et al. from GER. 200p. 1989. 20.00 (*0-87775-206-0*); pap. 12.50 (*0-87775-207-9*) Unicorn Pr.
Selected Poems: 1960-1985. rev. ed. Andrew Taylor. LC 87-30207. 205p. 1989. pap. text ed. 19.95 (*0-7022-2124-4*, Pub. by Univ Queensland Pr AT) Intl Spec Bk.
***Selected Poems: 1960-1990.** Maxine Kumin. LC 96-42433. 320p. (C). 1997. 27.50 (*0-393-04073-9*) Norton.
Selected Poems: 1963-1973. David Antin. (Sun & Moon Classics Ser.: No. 10). 440p. (Orig.). 1990. pap. 13.95 (*1-55713-058-2*) Sun & Moon CA.
Selected Poems: 1965-1990. Marilyn Hacker. 272p. 1995. pap. 13.00 (*0-393-31349-2*) Norton.
Selected Poems: 1972-1986. Manfred Jurgensen. (C). 1990. 85.00 (*0-9587713-0-8*, Pub. by Pascoe Pub AT) St Mut.
Selected Poems: 1973-1992. Gary Catalano. 158p. 1993. pap. 19.95 (*0-7022-2542-8*, Pub. by Univ Queensland Pr AT) Intl Spec Bk.
Selected Poems see Early Poems, Nineteen Thirty-Five to Nineteen Fifty-Five
Selected Poems - Rogha Danta. Nuala Ni Dhomhnaill. Tr. & Intro. by Michael Hartnett. LC 88-51546. 159p. (Orig.). (ENG & IRI.). 8800. pap. 14.95 (*1-85186-027-4*) Dufour.
Selected Poems a Collection. Jocelyn Hollis: Russian Language Edition with Poems in English on Facing Pages. Nora Faynberg & Jocelyn Hollis. LC 90-43202. 80p. (RUS.). 1991. 19.95 (*0-930933-15-X*); pap. 12.95 (*0-930933-17-6*); lib. bdg. 19.95 (*0-930933-16-8*) Am Poetry & Lit.
Selected Poems & Ballads. Helen Adam. LC 74-77378. (Publication Ser.: No. 5b). (Illus.). 60p. 1975. 10.00 (*0-914496-04-2*) Helikon NY.
Selected Poems & Four Plays. 4th ed. William Butler Yeats. 1996. 16.00 (*0-684-82646-1*) S&S Trade.
Selected Poems & Letters. John Keats. Ed. by Douglas Bush. LC 59-3635. (YA). (gr. 9 up). 1959. pap. 11.56 (*0-395-05140-1*, RivEd) HM.
Selected Poems & Letters of Emily Dickinson. Emily Dickinson. LC 59-12052. 343p. 1959. pap. 8.95 (*0-385-09423-X*, Anchor NY) Doubleday.
Selected Poems & New. James B. Allen. 76p. (Orig.). 1993. pap. 12.00 (*0-9635033-0-8*) Salt Creek Pr.
Selected Poems & Prefaces. William Wordsworth. Ed. by Jack Stillinger. LC 65-8540. (C). 1965. pap. 11.56 (*0-395-05179-7*, Hill Stead Mus) HM.
Selected Poems & Prose. Matthew Arnold. Ed. by Miriam Allott. 296p. 1993. pap. 7.95 (*0-460-87392-X*, Everyman's Classic Lib) C E Tuttle.
Selected Poems & Prose of John Davidson. John Davidson. Ed. by John Sloan. 240p. 1995. 55.00 (*0-19-818335-6*) OUP.
Selected Poems & Related Prose. Filippo T. Marinetti. Tr. by Elizabeth R. Napier & Barbara R. Studholme from FRE. LC 96-11140. 1997. 35.00 (*0-300-04103-9*) Yale U Pr.
Selected Poems & Three Plays of William Butler Yeats. 3rd rev. ed. William Butler Yeats. Ed. by Macha L. Rosenthal. 248p. 1987. pap. 14.00 (*0-02-071560-9*) Macmillan.
Selected Poems & Translations, 1969-1991. William Matthews. 224p. 1993. pap. 15.00 (*0-395-66993-6*) HM.
Selected Poems & Verse Fables, Seventeen Eighty-Four to Seventeen Ninety-Two. William H. Brown. Ed. by Richard Walser. LC 82-2660. 94p. 1982. 23.50 (*0-87413-223-1*) U Delaware Pr.
***Selected Poems by James Hearst.** James Hearst. (Illus.). (Orig.). 1994. pap. 10.50 (*0-9656482-0-6*) J&M Hearst.
Selected Poems by Jay Wright. Ed. by Robert B. Stepto. LC 86-43128. 218p. 1987. pap. 13.95 (*0-691-01435-3*) Princeton U Pr.
Selected Poems by Judita Vaiciunaite in Lithuanian & English: Fire Put Out by Fire. Judita Vaiciunaite. Tr. by Viktoria Skrupskelis & Stuart Friebert. LC 96-11058. 236p. 1996. 89.95 (*0-7734-8797-2*) E Mellen.
Selected Poems by Kim Namjo. Tr. by David R. McCann & Hyunjae Y. Sallee from KOR. (East Asia Papers: No. 63). (C). 1993. 18.00 (*0-939657-05-8*, 63); pap. 12.00 (*0-939657-63-5*, 63) Cornell East Asia Pgm.
Selected Poems by Laurence Housman. Laurence Housman. LC 75-41142. reprint ed. 27.50 (*0-404-14672-4*) AMS Pr.
Selected Poems from "Flowers of Evil" unabridged ed. Charles Baudelaire. (Thrift Editions Ser.). 64p. 1995. pap. text ed. 1.00 (*0-486-28450-6*) Dover.
Selected Poems from the Divani Shamsi Tabriz. Ed. & Tr. by Reynold A. Nicholson. 432p. (C). 1994. text ed. 68.00 (*0-7007-0277-6*, Pub. by Curzon Pr UK) Paul & Co Pubs.
Selected Poems from the Divani Shamsi Tabriz. Ed. & Tr. by Reynold A. Nicholson. 432p. 1996. pap. 29.95 (*0-7007-0462-0*, Pub. by Curzon Pr UK) Paul & Co Pubs.
Selected Poems II: Poems Selected & New, Nineteen Seventy-Six to Nineteen Eighty-Six. Margaret Atwood. 160p. 1987. pap. 13.95 (*0-395-45406-9*) HM.
Selected Poems, June 1988. Charles Doria. 24p. 1990. pap. 9.00 (*0-916258-23-8*) Left Hand Bks.
Selected Poems, Nineteen Fifty-Seven to Nineteen Eighty-Seven. 3rd rev. ed. Ed. by D. M. Shin. 270p. 1988. pap. text ed. 21.00 (*0-9621052-0-1*) UCLA CIRID.
Selected Poems, Nineteen Fifty to Nineteen Eighty-Two. Kenneth Koch. 1985. 9.95 (*0-394-73771-7*, Vin) Random.
Selected Poems, Nineteen Seventy to Nineteen Eighty-Three. Lance Henson. LC 85-70355. 64p. (Orig.). 1985. pap. 5.00 (*0-912678-62-3*, Greenfld Rev Pr) Greenfld Rev Lit.
Selected Poems, Nineteen Sixty-Nine to Nineteen Eighty-One. Richard Shelton. LC 82-2680. (Poetry Ser.). 221p. 1982. 24.95 (*0-8229-3470-1*) U of Pittsburgh Pr.
Selected Poems, Nineteen Sixty-Three to Nineteen Eighty-Three. enl. rev. ed. Charles Simic. LC 89-25129. 240p. (Orig.). 1990. pap. 12.95 (*0-8076-1240-5*) Braziller.
Selected Poems Nineteen Sixty to Nineteen Seventy-Five. Paul Mariah. 1978. 8.95 (*0-686-18930-2*) Man-Root.
Selected Poems Nineteen Thirty-Eight to Nineteen Eighty-Eight. Thomas McGrath. Ed. by Sam Hamill. LC 87-172648. 208p. 1988. pap. 10.00 (*1-55659-012-1*) Copper Canyon.
Selected Poems, Nineteen Thirty-Three to Nineteen Eighty-Eight. Gavin Ewart. LC 87-26873. 128p. 1988. 18.95 (*0-8112-1054-5*); pap. 8.95 (*0-8112-1055-3*, NDP655) New Directions.
Selected Poems, Nineteen Twenty-Three to Nineteen Seventy-Five. Robert Penn Warren. 1976. 17.95 (*0-394-40531-5*) Random.
***Selected Poems of Albert Steffen, Vol. 1.** Albert Steffen. Tr. by Daisy Alden. 1968. 9.95 (*0-913152-38-2*) Folder Edns.
Selected Poems of Alfonsina Storni. Alfonsina Storni. Tr. by Crow et al. 1988. pap. 8.00 (*0-934834-16-4*) White Pine.
Selected Poems of Alice Notley. Alice Notley. LC 93-30099. 144p. (Orig.). 1993. pap. 11.95 (*1-883689-02-3*); lib. bdg. 32.95 (*1-883689-03-1*) Talisman Hse.
Selected Poems of Andree Chedid. Ed. & Tr. by Judy Cochran from FRE. LC 95-21917. (Studies in French Literature: Vol. 21). (Illus.). 224p. 1996. text ed. 89.95 (*0-7734-2908-5*) E Mellen.
Selected Poems of Anghel Dumbraveanu in Romanian & English: Love & Winter. Tr. by Adam J. Sorkin & Irina G. Pana from ENG. LC 92-26690. 232p. 1992. text ed. 89.95 (*0-7734-9172-4*) E Mellen.
Selected Poems of Anne Sexton. Anne Sexton. Ed. by Diane W. Middlebrook & Diana H. George. LC 87-34253. 320p. 1988. pap. 15.00 (*0-395-47782-4*) HM.
Selected Poems of Barnabe Googe. Barnabe Googe. Ed. by Alan Stephens. LC 80-29155. (Books of the Renaissance). 60p. 1981. reprint ed. text ed. 45.00 (*0-313-22830-2*, GOSEP, Greenwood Pr) Greenwood.
Selected Poems of Ben Jonson. Ed. by Ted-Larry Pebworth & Claude J. Summers. LC 95-8284. 112p. 1995. pap. 7.95 (*0-86698-178-0*, P31) Pegasus Pr.
Selected Poems of Carl Sandburg. Carl Sandburg. (Great Poets Ser.). 192p. 1992. 7.99 (*0-517-07244-0*, Pub. by Gramercy) Random Hse Value.
Selected Poems of Cesar Vallejo. Cesar Vallejo. Tr. by H. R. Hays from SPA. LC 81-159. 122p. (C). 1993. reprint ed. 13.50 (*0-937584-01-0*); reprint ed. pap. 9.95 (*0-937584-02-9*) Sachem Pr.
Selected Poems of Christina Rossetti. Christina Rossetti. (Bloomsbury Classic Poetry Ser.). 128p. 1995. 9.95 (*0-312-13437-1*) St Martin.
Selected Poems of Desmond Egan. Desmond Egan. LC 92-73298. (Illus.). x, 183p. (Orig.). (C). 1993. pap. 17.50 (*1-881871-03-7*) Creighton U Pr.
Selected Poems of Emily Bronte. Emily Bronte. (Bloomsbury Classic Poetry Ser.). 128p. 1995. 9.95 (*0-312-13438-X*) St Martin.
Selected Poems of Emily Dickinson. 1996. 14.50 (*0-679-60201-1*) Random.
Selected Poems of Emily Dickinson. Emily Dickinson. LC 96-10466. 1996. write for info. (*0-614-13397-1*, Modern Lib) Random.
Selected Poems of George Faludy. George Faludy. Ed. & Tr. by Robin Skelton from HUN. LC 85-16397. 224p. 1985. pap. 14.95 (*0-8203-0814-5*) U of Ga Pr.
Selected Poems of Gerard Manley Hopkins with Modern English Paraphrases. Donald Walhout. LC 95-2974. 80p. 1995. text ed. 49.95 (*0-7734-8932-0*) E Mellen.
Selected Poems of Gunnar Ekelof. Gunnar Ekelof. Tr. by Muriel Rukeyser & Leif Sjoberg from SWE. LC 66-16109. (Library of Scandinavian Literature). 1971. lib. bdg. 26.50 (*0-8057-5852-6*) Irvington.
Selected Poems of H. L. Davis. 2nd ed. H. L. Davis. Ed. by O. Burmaster. LC 77-83226. (Ahsahta Press Modern & Contemporary Poets of the West Ser.). 72p. 1978. pap. 6.95 (*0-916272-07-9*) Ahsahta Pr.
Selected Poems of Halldis Moren Vesaas. Tr. by Wakefield & Thompson. 1990. 8.00 (*0-934834-21-0*) White Pine.
***Selected Poems of Hayyim Nahman Bialik.** Hayyim N. Bialik. Ed. by I. Efros. 1965. 19.95 (*0-8197-0060-6*) Bloch.
Selected Poems of Henry Vaughan. Henry Vaughan. LC 75-43096. 79p. pap. 3.50 (*0-317-61301-4*) Dufour.
Selected Poems of Henry Wadsworth Longfellow. Henry Wadsworth Longfellow. 1992. 7.99 (*0-517-08246-2*) Random Hse Value.
Selected Poems of Herman Melville. Hennig Cohen. LC 91-55378. xviii, 259p. 1991. reprint ed. pap. 13.50 (*0-8232-1336-6*) Fordham.
Selected Poems of Irving Layton. Irving Layton. LC 76-54704. 1977. 8.50 (*0-8112-0641-6*); pap. 2.25 (*0-8112-0642-4*, NDP431) New Directions.
***Selected Poems of Ivor Gurney.** Ivor Gurney. Ed. by P. J. Kavanagh. 180p. 1997. pap. 17.95 (*0-19-288065-9*) OUP.
Selected Poems of Jacob Glatstein. Jacob Glatstein. Tr. by Ruth Whitman. 1973. 9.50 (*0-8079-0176-8*); pap. 5.95 (*0-8079-0175-X*) October.
Selected Poems of Jehudah Halevi. Judah Halevi. 1972. 59.95 (*0-8490-1019-5*) Gordon Pr.
Selected Poems of Jehudah Halevi. Jehudah Halevi. LC 73-2203. (Jewish People; History, Religion, Literature Ser.). 1973. reprint ed. 35.95 (*0-405-05268-5*) Ayer.
Selected Poems of John Knoepfle. John Knoepfle. LC 85-70735. (Selected Poems Ser.). 96p. (Orig.). 1985. pap. 6.50 (*0-933532-53-9*) BkMk.
Selected Poems of John Oxenham. John Oxenham. Ed. by Charles L. Wallis. LC 71-179735. (Biography Index Reprint Ser.). 1977. reprint ed. 18.95 (*0-8369-8103-0*) Ayer.
Selected Poems of John Tutchin. John Tutchin. LC 92-23646. (Augustan Reprints Ser.: No. 110). 1964. reprint ed. 14.50 (*0-404-70110-8*, PR3736) AMS Pr.
Selected Poems of Langston Hughes. Langston Hughes. (Illus.). 1959. 25.00 (*0-394-40438-6*) Knopf.
Selected Poems of Langston Hughes. Langston Hughes. LC 90-50179. (Vintage Classics Ser.). 320p. 1990. pap. 12.00 (*0-679-72818-X*, Vin) Random.
Selected Poems of Leah Goldberg. Leah Goldberg. Tr. by Robert Friend. 64p. 1977. pap. 6.00 (*0-915572-27-3*) Panjandrum.
Selected Poems of Li Po. Li Po. Tr. by David Hinton from CHI. LC 96-5139. 160p. (Orig.). 1996. pap. 11.95 (*0-8112-1323-4*, NDP823) New Directions.
Selected Poems of Lord Byron. William H. Marshall. (C). 1977. pap. text ed. 16.00 (*0-8147-5418-X*) NYU Pr.
Selected Poems of Louis MacNeice. Intro. by Michael Longley. LC 89-51504. 160p. 1990. 15.95 (*0-916390-39-X*); pap. 9.95 (*0-916390-38-1*) Wake Forest.
Selected Poems of May Sarton. Ed. by May Sarton et al. 1978. pap. 10.95 (*0-393-04512-9*) Norton.
Selected Poems of Mbembe. Milton Smith. LC 85-70737. 120p. (Orig.). 1986. pap. 8.95 (*0-933532-50-4*) BkMk.
Selected Poems of Miguel Hernandez. Miguel Hernandez. Tr. by Bly et al. 1989. pap. 10.00 (*0-934834-93-8*) White Pine.
Selected Poems of Miltos Sahtouris. Miltos Sahtouris. Tr. by Kimon Friar from GRE. LC 81-21374. 125p. 1982. 13.50 (*0-937584-03-7*); pap. 6.95 (*0-937584-04-5*) Sachem Pr.
Selected Poems of Nikki Giovanni. Nikki Giovanni. 224p. 1996. 20.00 (*0-688-14047-5*) Morrow.
Selected Poems of Norman Macleod. 3rd ed. Norman W. Macleod. Ed. by Tom Trusky. LC 75-21690. (Ahsahta Press Modern & Contemporary Poets of the West Ser.). 60p. 1975. pap. 6.95 (*0-916272-00-1*) Ahsahta Pr.
Selected Poems of Octavio Paz. Octavio Paz. Tr. by G. Aroul et al. from SPA. LC 84-9856. 160p. 1984. pap. 9.95 (*0-8112-0899-0*, NDP574) New Directions.

S

Selected Poems of Ogden Nash: Eight Hundred & Eight Light-Hearted Verses. Ogden Nash. 704p. 1995. 12.98 (*1-884822-30-4*) Blck Dog & Leventhal.
Selected Poems of Olav Hauge. Tr. by Robin Fulton. 1990. pap. 9.00 (*1-877727-03-2*) White Pine.
Selected Poems of Padraic Colum. Padraic Colum. Ed. by Sanford Sternlicht. (Irish Studies). (Illus.). 120p. 1989. text ed. 22.50 (*0-8156-2458-1*) Syracuse U Pr.
Selected Poems of Pak Mogwol. Mog-wol Pak. Tr. & Intro. by Uchang Kim. LC 90-39264. 214p. reprint ed. pap. 61.00 (*0-7837-5212-1*, 2044943) Bks Demand.
Selected Poems of Patrick Galvin. Ed. & Intro. by Greg Delanty. 128p. 1996. 40.00 (*1-85918-079-5*, Pub. by Cork Univ IE); pap. 19.95 (*1-85918-091-4*, Pub. by Cork Univ IE) Intl Spec Bk.
Selected Poems of Paul Blackburn. Paul Blackburn. Ed. & Intro. by Edith Jarolim. (Lamplighter Ser.). 286p. (Orig.). 1989. pap. 14.95 (*0-89255-123-2*) Persea Bks.
Selected Poems of Phillips Kloss. Phillips Kloss. LC 82-19131. 120p. 1983. 10.95 (*0-86534-014-5*) Sunstone Pr.
Selected Poems of Rainer Maria Rilke. Rainer M. Rilke. 1981. pap. 14.00 (*0-06-090727-4*, PL) HarpC.
Selected Poems of Rene Char. Rene Char. Tr. by Mary A. Caws & Tina Jolas from FRE. LC 92-6351. 160p. 1992. 19.95 (*0-8112-1191-6*); pap. 10.95 (*0-8112-1192-4*, NDP734) New Directions.
Selected Poems of Richard A. Seffron. Richard A. Seffron. Ed. by Leonard J. Cirino. (Illus.). 72p. 1996. per., pap. 9.00 (*0-944550-40-1*) Pygmy Forest Pr.
Selected Poems of Richard Hugo. Richard Hugo. 1979. pap. 10.95 (*0-393-00936-X*) Norton.
Selected Poems of Rita Dove. Rita Dove. 1993. pap. 12.00 (*0-679-75080-0*, Vin) Random.
Selected Poems of Robert Desnos. Robert Desnos. Tr. by Carolyn Forche & William Kulik from FRE. (Modern European Poets Ser.). 192p. 1991. 24.95 (*0-88001-261-7*) Ecco Pr.
Selected Poems of Robert Frost. Robert Frost. Ed. by Robert Graves. 326p. (C). 1963. pap. text ed. 23.75 (*0-03-012060-8*) HB Coll Pubs.
Selected Poems of Robert Frost. Robert Frost. (Great Poets Ser.). 288p. 1992. 7.99 (*0-517-07245-9*, Pub. by Gramercy) Random Hse Value.
Selected Poems of Rosemary Thomas. Rosemary Thomas. LC 67-25189. 161p. 1968. 19.50 (*0-8290-0204-9*) Irvington.
Selected Poems of Salvador Espriu. Salvador Espriu. Tr. by Magda Bogin from CAT. 1989. 15.95 (*0-393-02608-6*) Norton.
Selected Poems of Sandor Csoori. Sandor Csoori. Tr. & Intro. by Len Roberts. LC 92-6972. 128p. (Orig.). 1992. pap. 11.00 (*1-55659-047-4*) Copper Canyon.
Selected Poems of Shmuel HaNagid. Tr. by Peter Cole. (Lockert Library of Poetry in Translation). 312p. 1996. text ed. 39.95 (*0-691-01121-4*) Princeton U Pr.
Selected Poems of Shmuel HaNagid. Peter Cole. 312p. (C). 1996. pap. 14.95 (*0-691-01120-6*) Princeton U Pr.
Selected Poems of So Chongju. So Chongju. Tr. by David R. McCann from KOR. (Modern Asian Literature Ser.). 160p. 1989. text ed. 42.00 (*0-231-06794-1*) Col U Pr.
Selected Poems of Su Tung-Po. Su Tung-Po. Tr. & Intro. by Burton Watson. LC 93-28332. 160p. (Orig.). 1994. pap. 12.00 (*1-55659-064-4*) Copper Canyon.
Selected Poems of T'ao Ch'ien. T'ao Ch'ien. Tr. & Intro. by David Hinton. LC 93-1635. 96p. (Orig.). 1993. pap. 11.00 (*1-55659-056-3*) Copper Canyon.
Selected Poems of Theo. Marzials. Ed. by John M. Munro. 1973. 10.00 (*0-8156-6040-5*, Am U Beirut) Syracuse U Pr.
Selected Poems of Thomas Hood. Thomas Hood. Ed. by John Clubbe. LC 72-95924. 423p. 1970. reprint ed. pap. 120.30 (*0-7837-4109-X*, 2057932) Bks Demand.
Selected Poems of Tomas Transtromer, 1954-1986. Tomas Transtromer. Ed. by Robert Hass. Tr. by May Swenson et al. from SWE. (Modern European Poets Ser.). 1989. pap. 13.00 (*0-88001-403-2*) Ecco Pr.
Selected Poems of Tu Fu. Tu Fu. Tr. & Intro. by David Hinton. LC 88-38041. 224p. 1989. 10.95 (*0-8112-1099-5*) New Directions.
Selected Poems of Vern Rutsala. Vern Rutsala. LC 90-52857. 281p. 21.95 (*0-934257-52-3*); pap. 16.95 (*0-934257-61-2*) Story Line.
Selected Poems of W. H. Auden. Ed. by Edward Mendelson. 240p. 1990. pap. 13.00 (*0-679-72483-4*, Vin) Random.
Selected Poems of Walt Whitman. Walt Whitman. (Great Poets Ser.). 224p. 1992. 7.99 (*0-517-07397-8*, Pub. by Gramercy) Random Hse Value.
Selected Poems of Walt Whitman: Anthology. Ed. by George McMichael. 1993. pap. text ed. 2.20 (*0-02-379609-X*, Macmillan Coll) P-H.
Selected Poems of Walter Von der Vogel Weide. Ed. by W. A. Phillips. 69.95 (*0-8490-1020-9*) Gordon Pr.
Selected Poems of William Butler Yeats: W. B. Yeats. William Butler Yeats. (Great Poets Ser.). 256p. 1992. 7.99 (*0-517-07396-X*, Pub. by Gramercy) Random Hse Value.
Selected Poems of William Gilmore Simms. William G. Simms, Jr. Ed. by James E. Kibler, Jr. LC 89-5128. 432p. 1990. 50.00 (*0-8203-1188-X*) U of Ga Pr.
Selected Poems of Yankev Glatshteyn. Richard Fein. 256p. 1988. 24.95 (*0-8276-0299-5*) JPS Phila.
Selected Poems of Zareh Khrakhouni. Zareh Khrakhouni. Tr. by A. J. Hacikyan & Arsene Mamourian from ARM. LC 90-49606. (Mellen Poetry Ser.: Vol. 13). 144p. 1990. lib. bdg. 39.95 (*0-88946-745-5*) E Mellen.
Selected Poems, Old & New. Osbert Sitwell. LC 75-41253. reprint ed. 24.50 (*0-404-14603-1*) AMS Pr.
Selected Poems, Pettet. Simon Pettet. 120p. (Orig.). 1995. 29.95 (*1-883689-31-7*) Talisman Hse.

***Selected Poems 1913-1956.** Bertolt Brecht. 1998. 14.95 (*1-55970-417-9*) Arcade Pub Inc.
Selected Poems, 1946-1985. James Merrill. 1993. pap. 15.00 (*0-679-74731-1*) Knopf.
Selected Poems (1947-1980) Robert Stock. LC 94-94207. 368p. 1994. 15.95 (*0-9640977-0-2*) Crane & Hopper.
Selected Poems, 1947-1995. Allen Ginsberg. LC 96-33824. 1996. 27.50 (*0-06-016457-3*) HarpC.
Selected Poems, 1954-1992. George Mackay Brown. LC 96-60408. 144p. 1996. pap. 12.95 (*0-87745-555-4*) U of Iowa Pr.
***Selected Poems, 1954-1994.** Gennadi I. Aigi & Peter France. LC 96-40076. 1997. write for info. (*0-8101-1540-9*) Northwestern U Pr.
***Selected Poems, 1956-1996.** Anthony Thwaite. 144p. 1997. pap. 19.95 (*1-900564-55-6*, Pub. by Enitha Pr UK) Dufour.
Selected Poems, 1957-1987. W. D. Snodgrass. LC 87-9463. 270p. 1987. 19.95 (*0-939149-04-4*) Soho Press.
Selected Poems, 1957-1987. W. D. Snodgrass. LC 87-9463. 270p. 1991. pap. 15.95 (*0-939149-61-3*) Soho Press.
***Selected Poems, 1961-1978.** David Holbrook. Date not set. pap. 22.95 (*0-85646-066-4*, Pub. by Anvil Press UK) Dufour.
Selected Poems 1965-1973. Marin Sorescu. 8300. pap. 17.95 (*0-906427-48-7*, Pub. by Bloodaxe Bks UK) Dufour.
Selected Poems, 1965-1975. Margaret Atwood. 1987. pap. 14.00 (*0-395-40422-3*) HM.
Selected Poems 1965-1990. Marilyn Hacker. 288p. 1994. 22.00 (*0-393-03675-8*) Norton.
***Selected Poems, 1965-1995.** Michael D. Browne. 128p. 1997. 20.95 (*0-88748-243-0*) Carnegie-Mellon.
***Selected Poems, 1965-1995.** Michael D. Browne. 128p. 1997. pap. 11.95 (*0-88748-244-9*) Carnegie-Mellon.
Selected Poems, 1965-1995. Hugh Seidman. LC 94-42464. (Poetry Ser.). 231p. 1995. 20.95 (*1-881163-10-5*); pap. 14.95 (*1-881163-11-3*) Miami Univ Pr.
Selected Poems 1966-1987. Seamus Heaney. 276p. 1991. pap. 15.00 (*0-374-52280-4*, Noonday) FS&G.
Selected Poems, 1966-1987. Seamus Heaney. 260p. 1990. 30.00 (*0-374-25868-6*) FS&G.
Selected Poems, 1968-1986. Paul Muldoon. 128p. 1987. 16.50 (*0-88001-154-8*) Ecco Pr.
Selected Poems, 1968-1986. Paul Muldoon. 153p. 1993. pap. 12.00 (*0-374-52374-6*, Noonday) FS&G.
Selected Poems 1976-1996. George Szirtes. 128p. (C). 1996. pap. 15.95 (*0-19-283223-9*) OUP.
Selected Poems, 1981-1984. Malcolm S. MacKenzie. 103p. 1984. 4.95 (*0-89697-180-5*) Intl Univ Pr.
Selected Poetry. William Blake. LC 93-40488. 320p. 1989. pap. 8.95 (*0-14-058596-0*) OUP.
***Selected Poetry.** William Blake. Ed. by Michael Mason. (The World's Classics Ser.). 336p. 1996. pap. 8.95 (*0-19-283272-7*) OUP.
Selected Poetry. Martin Camaj. (Studies in Near Eastern Civilization: No. 14). 220p. (C). 1990. text ed. 32.00 (*0-8147-1444-7*) NYU Pr.
***Selected Poetry.** Samuel Taylor Coleridge. Ed. & Intro. by Heather Jackson. (The World's Classics Ser.). 240p. 1997. pap. 7.95 (*0-19-283278-6*) OUP.
Selected Poetry. John Donne. Ed. by John Carey. (Oxford Poetry Library). 288p. (C). 1996. pap. 8.95 (*0-19-282499-6*) OUP.
Selected Poetry. Charles Ede. 86p. 1993. pap. 7.95 (*1-880365-02-2*) Prof Pr NC.
***Selected Poetry.** Thomas Hardy. Ed. by Samuel Hynes. (The World's Classics Ser.). 304p. 1996. pap. 8.95 (*0-19-283273-5*) OUP.
***Selected Poetry.** Gerard M. Hopkins. Ed. & Intro. by Catherine Phillips. (The World's Classics Ser.). 286p. 1997. pap. 8.95 (*0-19-283274-3*) OUP.
Selected Poetry. Robinson Jeffers. 1938. 24.95 (*0-394-40442-4*) Random.
***Selected Poetry.** John Keats. Ed. by Elizabeth Cook. (World's Classics Ser.). 288p. 1996. pap. 7.95 (*0-19-283275-1*) OUP.
***Selected Poetry.** Lord Byron. Ed. by Jerome J. McGann. (The World's Classics Ser.). 256p. 1997. pap. 8.95 (*0-19-283277-8*) OUP.
Selected Poetry. Hugh MacDiarmid. Ed. by Alan Riach & Michael Grieve. LC 93-5312. 320p. 1993. 23.95 (*0-8112-1248-3*) New Directions.
***Selected Poetry.** John Milton. Ed. by Jonathan Goldberg & Stephen Orgel. (The World's Classics Ser.). 352p. 1997. pap. 9.95 (*0-19-283279-4*) OUP.
Selected Poetry. Edmund Spenser. Ed. by A. Kent Hieatt & Constance Hieatt. LC 76-91402. (Crofts Classics Ser.). 176p. (C). 1970. pap. text ed. write for info. (*0-88295-095-9*) Harlan Davidson.
Selected Poetry. Alfred Tennyson. Ed. by Douglas Bush. (Modern Library College Editions). 1951. pap. text ed. write for info. (*0-07-553643-9*, T60) McGraw.
Selected Poetry. Alfred Tennyson. LC 94-48827. (English Texts Ser.). 240p. (C). 1995. pap. 18.95 (*0-415-07724-9*) Routledge.
Selected Poetry. William Wordsworth. Ed. by Mark Van Doren. (Modern Library College Editions). 1950. pap. text ed. write for info. (*0-07-553635-8*, T41) McGraw.
***Selected Poetry.** William Wordsworth. Ed. by Stephen Gill & Duncan Wu. (The World's Classics Ser.). 272p. 1997. pap. text ed. 8.95 (*0-19-283280-8*) OUP.
Selected Poetry: Hollander. John Hollander. LC 92-54789. 1995. pap. 15.00 (*0-679-76198-5*) Knopf.
Selected Poetry: Twenty Contemporary Voices from Latin America. Ed. by Ludwig Zeller. Tr. by Beatriz Zeller. 200p. 1995. lib. bdg. 43.00 (*0-8095-4891-7*) Borgo Pr.
Selected Poetry: Twenty Contemporary Voices from Latin America. Ed. by Ludwig Zeller. Tr. by Beatriz Zeller. 200p. 1995. pap. 16.95 (*0-88962-546-8*) Mosaic.
***Selected Poetry: 1966-1996.** Donald Lashley. 32p. 1997. pap. 7.00 (*0-8059-4149-5*) Dorrance.

Selected Poetry & Critical Prose. Charles G. Roberts. LC 73-91558. (Literature of Canada, Poetry & Prose in Reprint Ser.: No. 9). 366p. reprint ed. pap. 104.40 (*0-317-27000-1*, 2023662) Bks Demand.
Selected Poetry & Prose. William Blake. Ed. by Northrop Frye. (Modern Library College Editions). (C). 1966. pap. text ed. write for info. (*0-07-553661-7*, T86) McGraw.
Selected Poetry & Prose. Samuel Taylor Coleridge. Ed. by Donald Stauffer. (Modern Library College Editions). (C). 1951. pap. text ed. write for info. (*0-07-553638-2*, T52) McGraw.
Selected Poetry & Prose. John Dryden. LC 69-17414. (Modern Library College Editions). (C). 1970. pap. text ed. write for info. (*0-07-553553-X*) McGraw.
Selected Poetry & Prose. Stephane Mallarme. Ed. & Intro. by Mary A. Caws. LC 81-18899. 128p. 1982. pap. 9.95 (*0-8112-0823-0*, NDP529) New Directions.
Selected Poetry & Prose. Edgar Allan Poe. Ed. by Thomas O. Mabbott. (Modern Library College Editions). 1951. pap. text ed. write for info. (*0-07-553641-2*) McGraw.
Selected Poetry & Prose. 2nd ed. Pope. 514p. (C). 1972. pap. text ed. 26.75 (*0-03-083262-4*) HB Coll Pubs.
Selected Poetry & Prose of Helga Novak. Allen H. Chappel. LC 88-28686. (American University Studies: Germanic Languages & Literature: Ser. I, Vol. 79). 202p. (C). 1989. text ed. 34.95 (*0-8204-1042-X*) P Lang Pubng.
Selected Poetry of Andrea Zanzotto. Andrea Zanzotto. Ed. by Ruth Feldman & Brian Swann. LC 75-2990. (Lockert Library of Poetry in Translation). 368p. 1975. reprint ed. pap. 104.90 (*0-7837-9335-9*, 2060076) Bks Demand.
Selected Poetry of Dan Pagis. Dan Pagis. Tr. by Stephen Mitchell from HEB. LC 96-14395. (Literature of the Middle East Ser.: Vol. 7). 160p. (C). 1996. pap. 14.95 (*0-520-20539-1*) U CA Pr.
Selected Poetry of Del "Irish" Meader, "King of the Road" Del I. Meader. LC 95-90691. (Orig.). 1996. pap. 14.95 (*0-533-11686-4*) Vantage.
***Selected Poetry of Erich Kastner.** Erich Kastner. Tr. by Ruth Booley & Ted Booley from GER. 96p. (Orig.). 1996. pap. 9.95 (*1-881168-07-7*) Red Danceflr.
Selected Poetry of F. S. Hermann. F. S. Hermann. 1988. write for info. (*0-911323-11-2*) Concourse Pr.
Selected Poetry of Jessica Powers. Ed. by Regina Siegfried & Robert Morneau. LC 88-63849. 244p. (Orig.). (C). 1989. pap. 14.95 (*1-55612-248-9*) Sheed & Ward MO.
Selected Poetry of Lina Kostenko: Wanderings of the Heart. Lina Kostenko. Ed. by James J. Wilhelm. Tr. by Michael Nayden from UKR. LC 90-3020. (Library of World Literature in Translation: Vol. 13). 150p. 1990. text ed. 25.00 (*0-8240-2999-2*) Garland.
Selected Poetry of M. Kianush. M. Kianush. 1988. write for info. (*0-911323-09-0*) Concourse Pr.
Selected Poetry of Rainer Maria Rilke. Rainer M. Rilke. Ed. by Stephen Mitchell. (Illus.). 315p. 1982. 25.00 (*0-394-52434-9*) Random.
Selected Poetry of Rainer Maria Rilke. Rainer M. Rilke. Tr. by Stephen Mitchell. (International Ser.). 1989. pap. 13.00 (*0-679-72201-7*, Vin) Random.
Selected Poetry of Vicente Huidobro. Vicente Huidobro. Ed. by David M. Guss. Tr. by Stephen Fredman et al. from SPA. LC 81-4305. (Illus.). 288p. 1981. 18.95 (*0-8112-0804-4*); pap. 6.95 (*0-8112-0805-2*, NDP520) New Directions.
Selected Poetry of Yehuda Amichai. expanded rev. ed. Yehuda Amichai. Tr. by Chana Bloch & Stephen Mitchell from HEB. (Literature of the Middle East Ser.: Vol. 6). 192p. 1996. pap. 14.95 (*0-520-20538-3*) U CA Pr.
Selected Poetry, 1937-1990. Joao Cabral de Melo Neto. Ed. by Djelal Kadir. Tr. by Elizabeth Bishop et al. LC 94-17252. (Wesleyan Poetry Ser.). 214p. 1994. text ed. 30.00 (*0-8195-2217-1*, Wesleyan Univ Pr) U Pr of New Eng.
Selected Poetry, 1937-1990. Joao Cabral De Melo Neto. Ed. by Djelal Kadir. Tr. by Elizabeth Bishop et al. LC 94-17252. 214p. (ENG & POR.). 1996. pap. 14.95 (*0-8195-2231-7*, Wesleyan Univ Pr) U Pr of New Eng.
Selected Poisonous Plants from the Tribal Areas of India. K. Thothothri et al. (Illus.). 82p. 1985. pap. text ed. 15.00 (*0-945345-48-8*, Pub. by Mahendra Pal Singh II) Lubrecht & Cramer.
Selected Policies for the Management of Long-Term Financial Assets of Colleges & Universities. LC 92-32829. 146p. 1992. 44.95 (*0-915164-87-6*) NACUBO.
Selected Political Speeches. Marcus Tullius Cicero. Tr. by Michael Grant. (Classics Ser.). 336p. 1977. pap. 11.95 (*0-14-044214-6*, Penguin Classics) Viking Penguin.
Selected Political Writings. Mahatma Gandhi. Ed. by Dennis Dalton. LC 95-47532. 148p. (C). 1996. pap. text ed. 8.95 (*0-87220-330-1*); lib. bdg. 32.95 (*0-87220-331-X*) Hackett Pub.
Selected Political Writings. Niccolo Machiavelli. Ed. by David Wootton et al. LC 94-21202. (Hackett Classics Ser.). 272p. (Orig.). (C). 1994. pap. text ed. 7.95 (*0-87220-247-X*) Hackett Pub.
Selected Political Writings. Niccolo Machiavelli. Ed. by David Wootton et al. LC 94-21202. (Hackett Classics Ser.). 272p. (Orig.). (C). 1994. lib. bdg. 34.95 (*0-87220-248-8*) Hackett Pub.
Selected Political Writings. rev. ed. Montesquieu. Tr. & Intro. by Melvin Richter. LC 89-29578. 299p. (C). 1990. reprint ed. pap. text ed. 11.95 (*0-87220-090-6*); reprint ed. lib. bdg. 34.95 (*0-87220-091-4*) Hackett Pub.
Selected Popular Writings of E. U. Condon. Asim O. Barut. Ed. by Alwyn Van Der Merwe. (Illus.). 304p. 1991. 54.95 (*0-387-97421-0*) Spr-Verlag.
Selected Post-War Lithuanian Poetry. Ed. by Jonas Zdanys. (Illus.). 1978. 12.00 (*0-87141-056-7*) Manyland.

Selected Practical Problems in Health & Social Research. Ed. by Thomas E. Dinero. LC 96-30652. (Journal of Health & Social Policy: Vol. 8, No. 1). 107p. (C). 1996. 29.95 (*1-56024-832-7*) Haworth Pr.
Selected Prayers. Jamal A. Badawi. 78p. (Orig.). 1979. pap. 2.50 (*0-89259-092-0*) Am Trust Pubns.
Selected Prefaces & Introductions. W. Somerset Maugham. LC 75-25375. (Works of W. Somerset Maugham). 1977. reprint ed. 23.95 (*0-405-07828-5*) Ayer.
Selected Private Speeches. Demosthenes. Ed. by Christopher Carey & R. A. Reid. (Cambridge Greek & Latin Classics Ser.). 250p. 1985. text ed. 65.00 (*0-521-23960-5*); pap. text ed. 22.95 (*0-521-28373-6*) Cambridge U Pr.
Selected Problems & Questions in Strength of Materials. V. I. Feodosyev. 429p. 1977. 22.50 (*0-8464-1436-8*) Beekman Pubs.
Selected Problems in Real Analysis. B. M. Makarov et al. LC 92-15594. (Translations of Mathematical Monographs, 0065-9282: Vol. 107). 392p. 1992. 49.00 (*0-8218-4559-4*, MMONO/107) Am Math.
Selected Problems in Theoretical Physics (with Solutions) A. Di Giacomo et al. 408p. 1994. text ed. 99.00 (*981-02-1614-9*); pap. text ed. 48.00 (*981-02-1615-7*) World Scientific Pub.
Selected Problems of Adolescence: With Emphasis on Group Formation. Helene Deutsch. LC 67-28587. (Psychoanalytic Study of the Child Monographs: No. 3). 246p. (Orig.). 1967. 27.50 (*0-8236-6040-0*) Intl Univs Pr.
Selected Problems of Weighted Approximation & Spectral Analysis: Proceedings. Ed. by N. K. Nikol'skii. LC 76-46375. (Proceeding of the Steklov Institute of Mathematics Ser.: No. 120). 276p. 1976. pap. 92.00 (*0-8218-3020-1*, STEKLO/120) Am Math.
Selected Procedures in Teaching Biology. E. Irene Hollenbeck & Elmo N. Stevenson. LC 50-62687. (Oregon State Monographs. Studies in Education & Guidance: No. 3). 58p. reprint ed. pap. 25.00 (*0-7837-1077-1*, 2041607) Bks Demand.
Selected Proceedings from the First & Second Delft Pain Symposia: Journal: Applied Neurophysiology, Vol. 47, No. 4-6. Ed. by Janine M. Pernak et al. (Illus.). 112p. 1986. pap. 59.25 (*3-8055-4044-2*) S Karger.
Selected Proceedings of the Annual Meeting of the American Society of Pediatric Neurosurgeons, San Juan, Puerto Rico, January 1991. Ed. by A. E. Marlin. (Journal of Pediatric Neurosurgery: Vol. 18, Nos. 5-6, 1992). (Illus.). iv, 108p. 1992. pap. 96.75 (*3-8055-5711-6*) S Karger.
Selected Proceedings of the Mid-America Conference on Hispanic Literature. Ed. by Luis T. Gonzalez-del-Valle & Catherine Nickel. LC 85-61851. 189p. 1986. pap. 30.00 (*0-89295-039-0*) Society Sp & Sp-Am.
Selected Proceedings of the Mountain Interstate Foreign Conference, 32nd. Ed. by Gregorio C. Martin. 415p. (Orig.). 1984. pap. text ed. write for info. (*0-918401-00-3*) U Wake Forest.
Selected Proceedings of the Sheffield Symposium on Applied Probability. Ed. by I. V. Basawa & R. L. Taylor. LC 91-77908. (IMS Lecture Notes - Monograph Ser.: Vol. 18). x, 278p. 1991. pap. 15.00 (*0-940600-25-0*) Inst Math.
Selected Proceedings of the Singularidad y Trascendencia Conference. Ed. by Nora De Marval-McNair. LC 89-64458. 150p. 1990. pap. 40.00 (*0-89295-059-5*) Society Sp & Sp-Am.
Selected Prose. Matthew Arnold. Ed. & Intro. by J. P. Keating. (Classics Ser.). 480p. 1971. pap. 12.95 (*0-14-043058-X*, Penguin Classics) Viking Penguin.
Selected Prose. John Donne. Ed. & Intro. by Neil Rhodes. 552p. 1987. pap. 11.95 (*0-14-043239-6*, Penguin Classics) Viking Penguin.
Selected Prose. Robert Duncan. Ed. by Robert J. Bertholf. LC 94-12983. 208p. 1995. 24.95 (*0-8112-1278-5*) New Directions.
Selected Prose. Nissim Ezekiel. 184p. (C). 1993. 19.95 (*0-19-562866-7*, 14373) OUP.
Selected Prose. Heinrich Heine. Ed. & Tr. by Ritchie Robertson. 368p. 1993. pap. 13.95 (*0-14-044555-2*, Penguin Classics) Viking Penguin.
Selected Prose. John H. Reynolds. Ed. by Leonidas M. Jones. LC 66-15653. (Illus.). 502p. 1966. 45.00 (*0-674-79935-6*) HUP.
***Selected Prose & Drama.** Ingeborg Bachmann & Christa Wolf. Ed. by Patricia A. Herminghouse. (The German Library). 324p. 1997. 29.50 (*0-8264-0956-3*); pap. text ed. 19.95 (*0-8264-0957-1*) Continuum.
Selected Prose & Poetry. 2nd ed. Ralph Waldo Emerson. 568p. (C). 1969. pap. text ed. 27.75 (*0-03-077140-4*) HB Coll Pubs.
Selected Prose Fiction of Charles Brockden Brown. Charles B. Brown. Ed. by Philip Barnard. (Masterworks of Literature Ser.). 1995. pap. 16.95 (*0-8084-0487-3*) NCUP.
Selected Prose of John Gray. Intro. by Jerusha H. McCormack. LC 92-81206. (British Authors, 1880-1920 Ser.). 316p. 1992. lib. bdg. 30.00 (*0-944318-06-1*) ELT Pr.
Selected Prose of Su Qing. Su Qing. (CHI.). pap. 12.95 (*7-5339-0772-8*, Pub. by China Intl Bk CH) Distribks Inc.
Selected Prose of T. S. Eliot. Ed. by Frank Kermode. 313p. 1975. reprint ed. pap. 11.00 (*0-15-680654-1*, Harvest Bks) HarBrace.
Selected Prose Works: Commentary on Genesis, Letter to Publius, Homily on Our Lord. St. Ephrem the Syrian. Ed. by Kathleen McVey. Tr. by Edward G. Mathews, Jr. & Joseph P. Amar. LC 94-7480. (Fathers of the Church Ser.: Vol. 91). 393p. 1994. text ed. 39.95 (*0-8132-0091-1*) Cath U Pr.

An Asterisk (*) at the beginning of an entry indicates that the title is appearing in BIP for the first time.

Selected Prose Writings. William Wordsworth. Ed. & Intro. by John O. Hayden. 528p. 1988. pap. 10.95 (*0-14-043292-2*, Penguin Classics) Viking Penguin.

Selected Prose 1909-1965. Ezra Pound. Ed. by William Cookson. LC 72-93978. 480p. 1975. pap. 15.95 (*0-8112-0574-6*, NDP396) New Directions.

Selected Publications of the United Nations Department of International Economic & Social Affairs, 1985-1989. 25p. 1989. 7.50 (*92-1-104323-9*, 89.II.A.16) UN.

***Selected Pyrotechnic Publications of K. L. & B. J. Kosanke, Set.** Kenneth L. Kosanke & Bonnie J. Kosanke. (Illus.). (Orig.). Date not set. pap. write for info. (*1-889526-04-5*) Jrnl of Pyrotechnics.

***Selected Pyrotechnic Publications of K. L. & B. J. Kosanke Pt. 1: 1981 Through 1989.** Kenneth L. Kosanke & Bonnie J. Kosanke. (Pyrotechnic Literature Ser.). (Illus.). 127p. (Orig.). 1995. pap. 30.00 (*1-889526-05-3*) Jrnl of Pyrotechnics.

***Selected Pyrotechnic Publications of K. L. & B. J. Kosanke Pt. 2: 1990 Through 1992.** Kenneth L. Kosanke & Bonnie J. Kosanke. (Pyrotechnic Literature Ser.). (Illus.). 96p. (Orig.). 1995. pap. 25.00 (*1-889526-06-1*) Jrnl of Pyrotechnics.

***Selected Pyrotechnic Publications of K. L. & B. J. Kosanke Pt. 3: 1993 & 1994.** Kenneth L. Kosanke & Bonnie J. Kosanke. (Pyrotechnic Literature Ser.). (Illus.). 93p. (Orig.). 1996. pap. 25.00 (*1-889526-07-X*) Jrnl of Pyrotechnics.

Selected Questions in Cross-Examination in Criminal Trials. Ed. by S. K. Shanglo. (C). 1990. 60.00 (*0-89771-167-X*) St Mut.

Selected Radio & Television Criticism. Ed. by Anthony Slide. LC 86-27891. 213p. 1987. 20.00 (*0-8108-1942-2*) Scarecrow.

***Selected Radionuclides, Tritium, Carbon-14, Krypton-85, Strontium-90, Iodine, Caesium-137, Radon & Plutonium.** (Environmental Health Criteria Ser.: No. 25). 237p. 1983. pap. text ed. 29.00 (*92-4-154085-0*, 1160025) World Health.

Selected Readings. Noam Chomsky. Ed. by J. P. Allen & Paul M. Van Buren. (Language & Language Learning Ser.). (C). 1971. text ed. 16.95 (*0-19-437046-1*) OUP.

Selected Readings: Military. USMA Cornell Staff. 480p. (C). 1995. per., pap. text ed. 27.05 (*0-7872-1550-3*) Kendall-Hunt.

Selected Readings see Computer Security, Auditing & Controls, Text & Readings

Selected Readings for CPAs in Industry: July-December 1989, Vol. 1. American Institute of Certified Public Accountants Staff. LC 91-641527. 169p. pap. 45.70 (*0-7837-0074-1*, 2040323) Bks Demand.

Selected Readings for CPAs in Industry: July-December 1989, Vol. 2. American Institute of Certified Public Accountants Staff. LC 91-641527. 174p. pap. 49.60 (*0-7837-0075-X*) Bks Demand.

Selected Readings for CPAs in Industry, January-June 1990, Vol. 1. American Institute of Certified Public Accountants Staff. LC 91-641527. 155p. reprint ed. pap. 44.20 (*0-7837-6631-9*, 2046222) Bks Demand.

Selected Readings for CPAs in Industry, January-June 1990, Vol. 2. American Institute of Certified Public Accountants Staff. LC 91-641527. 159p. reprint ed. pap. 45.40 (*0-7837-6632-7*, 2046222) Bks Demand.

Selected Readings in Advanced Estate Planning. CFFP Staff. 376p. 1987. per. 37.15 (*1-55623-013-3*) Irwin Prof Pubng.

Selected Readings in Business. Myra Shulman. Ed. by John Swales. (English for Special Purposes Ser.). 372p. (C). 1991. teacher ed. 6.95 (*0-472-08137-3*); pap. text ed. 39.50 (*0-472-08134-9*) U of Mich Pr.

Selected Readings in Business & Office Occupations, 1967. (Yearbook Ser.). 351p. 5.00 (*0-933964-05-6*) Natl Busn Ed Assoc.

Selected Readings in Chinese Communist Literature. rev. ed. Compiled by Tien-Yi Li. 1954. 11.95 (*0-88710-080-5*); audio write for info. (*0-88710-081-3*) Yale Far Eastern Pubns.

Selected Readings in Financial Planning for the Retired. CFFP Staff. 608p. 1987. per. 41.18 (*1-55623-012-5*) Irwin Prof Pubng.

Selected Readings in International Business. Ed. by Khosrow Fatemi. (International Business & Trade Ser.). 256p. 1991. 34.00 (*0-8448-1694-9*, Pub. by Tay Francis Ltd UK) Taylor & Francis.

Selected Readings in Investment Strategies & Portfolio Management. CFFP Staff. 304p. 1987. per. 35.20 (*1-55623-014-1*) Irwin Prof Pubng.

Selected Readings in Scholasticism & Education. Ed. by Vincent J. Colimore. 115p. (C). 1971. pap. text ed. 9.95 (*0-8422-0142-4*) Irvington.

Selected Readings in Scripture & Morals: Twelve Canonical Scriptures Considered As Sources of True Propositions about the Morality of Eating Meat & of Drinking Alcohol, of Making War & of Making Love. Richard H. Lampkin. 327p. reprint ed. pap. 93.20 (*0-7837-2031-9*, AU00418) Bks Demand.

Selected References in Elective Orthopaedics. A. H. Ratliff et al. xviii, 204p. 1991. pap. 39.00 (*0-387-19682-X*) Spr-Verlag.

Selected References in Orthopaedic Trauma. A. H. Ratliff et al. xvii, 124p. 1989. 40.95 (*0-387-19556-4*) Spr-Verlag.

Selected References on Reliability Growth. LC 62-38584. 414p. (Orig.). 1988. pap. text ed. 100.00 (*0-915414-40-6*) Inst Environ Sci.

Selected References on the Geology & Coal Resources of the Central & Western Colorado Coal Fields & Regions. Peter Rushworth et al. (Information Ser.: No. 25). 141p. (Orig.). 1989. pap. 8.00 (*1-884216-20-X*) Colo Geol Survey.

Selected References Related to Coalbed Methane in the Greater Green River, Piceance, Powder River, Raton, & San Juan Basins. Robert Tyler et al. (Information Ser.: No. 35). 77p. (Orig.). 1992. pap. 10.00 incl. disk (*1-884216-24-2*) Colo Geol Survey.

Selected Religious Poems of Solomon Ibn Gabiro. Solomon I. Gabirol. LC 73-2210. (Jewish People; History, Religion, Literature Ser.). 1973. reprint ed. 35.95 (*0-405-05274-X*) Ayer.

Selected Reports in Ethnomusicology, Vol. II, No. 2. Ed. by David Morton. LC 75-24270. (Illus.). xii, 259p. (Orig.). 1975. pap. text ed. 9.50 (*0-88287-005-X*) UCLA Dept Ethnom.

Selected Reports in Ethnomusicology: Studies in African Music, Vol. V. Ed. by J. H. Nketia & Jacqueline C. Dje Dje. LC 76-640181. (Illus.). xx, 387p. (Orig.). 1984. pap. text ed. 18.95 incl. audio (*0-88287-017-3*) UCLA Dept Ethnom.

Selected Reports in Ethnomusicology, Vol. 2, No. 1: The Melograph. Ed. by Peter Crossley-Holland. LC 73-620035. vii, 125p. (Orig.). 1974. pap. text ed. 7.50 (*0-88287-004-1*) UCLA Dept Ethnom.

Selected Reports in Ethnomusicology, Vol. 3, No. 1: The Traditional Music of Europeans in America. Ed. by James Porter. LC 76-640181. (Illus.). vii, 260p. 1978. pap. text ed. 11.95 (*0-88287-011-4*) UCLA Dept Ethnom.

Selected Reports in Ethnomusicology, Vol. 3, No. 2: Music of the American Indians. Ed. by Charlotte Heth. LC 76-640181. (Illus.). xii, 202p. 1980. pap. text ed. 11.95 (*0-88287-012-2*) UCLA Dept Ethnom.

Selected Reports in Ethnomusicology, Vol. 8: Issues in Organology. Ed. by Sue C. DeVale. 297p. 1990. 30.00 (*0-88287-024-6*) UCLA Dept Ethnom.

Selected Research on Work Team Diversity. Marian N. Ruderman et al. LC 95-34408. 183p. 1996. pap. text ed. 24.95 (*1-882197-08-9*) Ctr Creat Leader.

Selected Resources on Sibling Abuse: An Annotated Bibliography for Researchers, Educators, & Consumers. Billie H. Frazier & Kathleen C. Hayes. 31p. (C). 1995. pap. text ed. 20.00 (*0-7881-2002-6*) DIANE Pub.

Selected Revisionist Pamphlets: An Original Arno Press Compilation. Harry E. Barnes. LC 72-172205. (Right Wing Individualist Tradition in America Ser.). 1972. reprint ed. 21.95 (*0-405-00415-X*) Ayer.

***Selected Richard McKeon, 1.** McKeon. LC 97-10782. 1996. 49.95 (*0-226-56036-8*) U Ch Pr.

***Selected Safety Aspects of WWER-440 Mode L213 Nuclear Power Plants.** 444p. 1996. pap. 155.00 (*92-0-101196-2*, STI/PUB/1012, Pub. by IAEA AU) Bernan Associates.

***Selected SAS Documentation: Applied Regression Analysis.** 266p. (C). 1997. pap. 33.00 (*1-55544-967-0*) SAS Inst.

Selected Scientific Papers of Alfred Lande. Ed. by Asim O. Barut & Alwyn Van Der Merwe. (C). 1987. lib. bdg. 222.00 (*90-277-2594-2*) Kluwer Ac.

Selected Scientific Papers of E. U. Condon. Ed. by Asim O. Barut et al. (Illus.). 632p. 1991. 131.95 (*0-387-97420-2*) Spr-Verlag.

***Selected Scientific Papers of Sir Rudolf Peierls.** Rudolf Peierls. LC 96-32743. 850p. 1997. lib. bdg. 104.00 (*981-02-2692-6*); lib. bdg. 53.00 (*981-02-2693-4*) World Scientific Pub.

***Selected Scientific Works of Hans Christian Orsted.** Hans C. Orsted et al. LC 97-6179. 1997. write for info. (*0-691-04334-5*) Princeton U Pr.

Selected Sensory Methods Problems & Approaches to Measuring Hedonics - STP 773. Ed. by Kuznicki & Rutkiewic. 113p. 1982. pap. 18.00 (*0-8031-0782-X*, 04-773000-36) ASTM.

Selected Sermons. Phillips Brooks. Ed. by William Scarlett. LC 79-142610. (Essay Index Reprint Ser.). 1977. 22.95 (*0-8369-2146-1*) Ayer.

Selected Sermons. Carl F. Walther. (Selected Writings of C. F. W. Walther Ser.). 192p. 1981. 17.99 (*0-570-08276-5*, 15-2734) Concordia.

***Selected Sermons: Selected Sermons of the Martyr, Young Hie Paik.** Tr. by Samuel L. Choi from KOR. 360p. (Orig.). 1997. pap. 10.00 (*0-9655790-2-6*) Young Hie Paik.

Selected Sermons for Christian Students on Campus. Ed. by David Brodie & Rachel McConnell. LC 93-12553. 248p. 1993. text ed. 89.95 (*0-7734-9247-X*) E Mellen.

Selected Sermons of Hugh Latimer. Hugh Latimer. Ed. by Allan G. Chester. (Documents Ser.). 1978. 29.50 (*0-918016-43-6*) Folger Bks.

Selected Sermons of Zachary Boyd. Ed. by David W. Atkinson. (STS Ser.). 335p. 1989. text ed. 45.00 (*0-08-037000-4*, Pub. by Aberdeen U Pr) Macmillan.

Selected Shelburne Essays. Paul E. More. reprint ed. 39.00 (*0-403-07240-9*) Somerset Pub.

Selected Short Fiction. Charles Dickens. Ed. by Deborah A. Thomas. (English Library). 368p. 1976. pap. 8.95 (*0-14-043103-9*, Penguin Classics) Viking Penguin.

Selected Short Plays. George Bernard Shaw. 384p. 1988. pap. 11.95 (*0-14-045024-6*, Penguin Bks) Viking Penguin.

Selected Short Stories. E. J. Arnold. Ed. by A. W. Hornsey. 1964. 3.35 (*0-08-010714-1*, Pergamon Pr); pap. 3.45 (*0-08-010713-3*, Pergamon Pr) Elsevier.

Selected Short Stories. Honore De Balzac. 22.95 (*0-8488-0422-8*) Amereon Ltd.

Selected Short Stories. Guy De Maupassant. Tr. by Roger Colet. (Classics Ser.). 368p. 1971. pap. 9.95 (*0-14-044243-X*, Penguin Classics) Viking Penguin.

Selected Short Stories. Maxim Gorky. 410p. (C). 1975. 16.95 (*0-8464-0834-1*) Beekman Pubs.

Selected Short Stories. Franz Kafka. Tr. by Wilma Muir. 378p. 1993. 15.50 (*0-679-60061-2*, Modern Lib) Random.

Selected Short Stories. Rabindranath Tagore. Tr. & Intro. by William Radice. (Twentieth-Century Classics Ser.). (Illus.). 336p. pap. 9.95 (*0-14-018425-2*, Penguin Classics) Viking Penguin.

Selected Short Stories. Rabindranath Tagore. 1995. pap. 10.95 (*0-14-018854-1*) Viking Penguin.

Selected Short Stories. Robert Treu. (Juniper Bks.: Vol. 62). 48p. (Orig.). 1996. pap. 8.00 (*1-55780-146-0*) Juniper Pr WI.

Selected Short Stories. H. G. Wells. 352p. 1988. mass mkt. 4.95 (*0-14-008247-6*, Penguin Bks) Viking Penguin.

Selected Short Stories. H. G. Wells. 352p. 1990. pap. 9.95 (*0-14-018188-1*, Penguin Classics) Viking Penguin.

Selected Short Stories. Per Hallstrom. Tr. by F. J. Fielden from SWE. LC 77-144155. (Short Story Index Reprint Ser.). 1977. reprint ed. 15.95 (*0-8369-3770-8*) Ayer.

Selected Short Stories. D. H. Lawrence. 128p. 1993. reprint ed. pap. text ed. 1.00 (*0-486-27794-1*) Dover.

Selected Short Stories of Edith Wharton: Introduced & Edited by R. W. B. Lewis. Intro. by R. W. Lewis. 416p. 1991. 24.95 (*0-684-19304-3*) S&S Trade.

Selected Short Stories of Franz Kafka. Franz Kafka. Tr. by Willa Muir & Edwin Muir. LC 52-9771. 1977. 11.95 (*0-394-60422-9*, Modern Lib) Random.

Selected Short Stories of Franz Kafka. Franz Kafka. Tr. by Willa Muir & Edwin Muir from GER. LC 93-14747. (ENG.). 1993. write for info. (*0-679-42790-2*, Modern Lib) Random.

Selected Short Stories of Mulk Raj Anand. Ed. by M. K. Naik. 296p. 1984. 12.00 (*0-86578-233-4*) Ind-US Inc.

Selected Short Stories of Nathaniel Hawthorne. Nathaniel Hawthorne. 1976. 22.95 (*0-8488-0165-2*) Amereon Ltd.

Selected Short Stories of Nathaniel Hawthorne. Nathaniel Hawthorne. 256p. 1983. mass mkt. 5.99 (*0-449-30012-9*, Prem) Fawcett.

Selected Short Stories of Padraic Colum. Ed. by Sanford Sternlicht. LC 84-20522. (Irish Studies). (Illus.). 160p. 1985. text ed. 34.95 (*0-8156-2327-5*) Syracuse U Pr.

Selected Short Stories of Padraic Colum. Ed. by Sanford Sternlicht. LC 84-20522. (Irish Studies). (Illus.). 160p. 1986. pap. 16.95 (*0-8156-0202-2*) Syracuse U Pr.

Selected Short Stories of Sinclair Lewis. Sinclair Lewis. 456p. 1990. pap. 12.95 (*0-929587-22-7*, Elephant Paperbacks) I R Dee.

Selected Short Stories of William Bankier. William Bankier. 250p. 1995. pap. 16.95 (*0-88962-553-0*) Mosaic.

Selected Short Stories of William Bankier. Ed. by Peter Sellers. 250p. 1995. lib. bdg. 43.00 (*0-8095-4839-9*) Borgo Pr.

***Selected Short Stories of William Dean Howells.** William D. Howells. Ed. by Ruth Bardon. LC 97-14161. 280p. 1997. text ed. 39.95 (*0-8214-1193-4*); pap. text ed. 21.95 (*0-8214-1194-2*) Ohio U Pr.

Selected Short Stories of William Faulkner. William Faulkner. LC 62-9690. 306p. 1978. 11.95 (*0-394-60456-3*, Modern Lib) Random.

Selected Short Stories of William Faulkner. William Faulkner. LC 92-51072. 1993. 15.50 (*0-679-42478-4*, Modern Lib) Random.

Selected Short Works for Piano Solo: Centennial Edition. Claude Debussy. 152p. 1993. 10.95 (*0-7935-2966-2*) H Leonard.

***Selected Shorter Poems.** Luis De Gongora & Michael Smith. 166p. 1995. pap. 16.95 (*0-85646-250-0*, Pub. by Anvil Press UK) Dufour.

Selected Shorter Poems. Edmund Spenser. Ed. by Douglas Brooks-Davies. LC 94-22616. (Annotated Texts Ser.). (C). 1995. text ed. 64.95 (*0-582-08912-3*, Pub. by Longman UK) Longman.

Selected Shorter Poems. Edmund Spenser. Ed. by Douglas Brooks-Davies. LC 94-22616. (Annotated Texts Ser.). (C). 1996. pap. text ed. 29.50 (*0-582-08910-7*, Pub. by Longman UK) Longman.

Selected Shorter Writings of Mark Twain. Mark Twain. Ed. by Walter Blair. LC 62-51467. (YA). (gr. 9 up). 1974. pap. 11.56 (*0-395-05155-X*, RivEd) HM.

***Selected Sijo by Korean Poets in China.** Kim Unsong. LC 96-72153. 120p. (ENG & KOR.). 1997. pap. 15.00 (*0-942049-07-1*) One Mind Pr.

Selected Small Homes...Keyed to the Times. rev. ed. Ed. by National Plan Service, Inc. Staff. (Illus.). 32p. reprint ed. pap. 3.95 (*0-934039-11-9*, A37) Natl Plan Serv.

Selected Social Safety Net Programs in the Philippines: Targetting, Cost-Effectiveness, & Options for Reform. Kalanidhi Subbarao et al. (Discussion Papers: Vol. 317). 88p. 1996. 7.95 (*0-8213-3543-X*, 13543) World Bank.

Selected Sonatinas Bk. 1: For the Elementary Piano. 36p. 1986. pap. 7.95 (*0-7935-5194-3*, 50260370) H Leonard.

Selected Songs. Josephine Lang. LC 82-2435. (Women Composers Ser.). 1982. 29.50 (*0-306-76097-5*) Da Capo.

***Selected Songs.** Modest P. Moussorgsky. (Orig.). pap. 9.95 (*0-486-28089-6*) Dover.

Selected Songs. Jeanne Singer. LC 82-71820. (Living Composers' Library: No. 3). 1982. pap. 12.50 (*0-934218-26-9*) Dragons Teeth.

Selected Songs for Solo Voice & Piano. Robert A. Schumann. Tr. by Stanley Appelbaum. 256p. 1981. pap. 10.95 (*0-486-24202-1*) Dover.

Selected Songs of Eliakum Zunser. Eliakum Zunser. LC 74-29534. (Modern Jewish Experience Ser.). 1975. reprint ed. 26.95 (*0-405-06757-7*) Ayer.

Selected Sonnets. Peter Russell. 72p. (Orig.). 1996. pap. 10.00 (*0-944920-16-0*) Bellowing Ark Pr.

Selected Sonnets, Odes, & Letters. Francesco Petrarch. Ed. by Thomas G. Bergin. (Crofts Classics Ser.). 160p. 1966. pap. text ed. write for info. (*0-88295-066-5*) Harlan Davidson.

Selected Sonnets of Khawju of Kirman. Khawju of Kirman. Tr. by Mehdi K. Nakosteen. LC 78-65312. 118p. 1979. 25.00 (*0-936347-43-0*) Iran Bks.

Selected Speeches. Lysias. Ed. by Christopher Carey. (Cambridge Greek & Latin Classics Ser.). 232p. (C). 1990. text ed. 65.00 (*0-521-26435-9*); pap. text ed. 22.95 (*0-521-26988-1*) Cambridge U Pr.

Selected Speeches. Shimon Schwab. 250p. (C). 1991. 15.95 (*1-56062-058-7*) CIS Comm.

Selected Speeches & Statements of General of the Army George C. Marshall. George C. Marshall. Ed. by H. A. DeWeerd. LC 72-10365. (FDR & the Era of the New Deal Ser.). 1973. reprint ed. lib. bdg. 37.50 (*0-306-70556-7*) Da Capo.

Selected Speeches & Writings. Abraham Lincoln. LC 91-50227. (Vintage Books - the Library of America). 608p. 1992. pap. 15.00 (*0-679-73731-6*, Vin) Random.

Selected Speeches & Writings by Fang Lizhi, Vol. 1. Fang Lizhi. 176p. 1989. text ed. 18.00 (*962-362-003-9*); pap. text ed. 9.00 (*962-362-004-7*) World Scientific Pub.

Selected Speeches & Writings by Fang Lizhi, Vol. 2. Lizhi Fang. 267p. 1989. text ed. 22.00 (*962-362-005-5*) World Scientific Pub.

Selected Speeches & Writings by Fang Lizhi, Vol. 2. Fang Lizhi. 267p. 1989. pap. text ed. 11.00 (*962-362-006-3*) World Scientific Pub.

Selected Speeches & Writings by Fang Lizhi, Vol. 3. Lizhi Fang. 248p. 1989. text ed. 22.00 (*962-362-007-1*); pap. text ed. 11.00 (*962-362-008-X*) World Scientific Pub.

Selected Speeches & Writings by Fang Lizhi, Vol. 4. Lizhi Fang. 272p. 1989. text ed. 22.00 (*962-362-009-8*); pap. text ed. 11.00 (*962-362-010-1*) World Scientific Pub.

Selected Speeches of Fidel Castro. 2nd ed. Fidel Castro. (Illus.). 134p. 1992. pap. 14.00 (*0-87348-700-1*) Pathfinder NY.

Selected Speeches of Mason Gross. Ed. by Richard P. McCormick & Richard Schlatter. 160p. 1980. 34.95 (*0-87855-388-6*) Transaction Pubs.

Selected Speeches of W. E. B. Du Bois. W. E. B. Dubois. 1996. pap. 1.99 (*0-679-77199-9*) Random.

Selected Speeches on Adult Education by A. A. Liveright, 1958-1968. Ed. by Dennis W. Dressler & Ben Newsom. LC 92-10798. 224p. 1992. 89.95 (*0-7734-9556-8*) E Mellen.

Selected Speeches, Sermons & Writings of Adam Clayton Powell Jr., 1935-1971. Mwalimu I. Mwadilifu. LC 89-81785. 150p. pap. 10.95 (*0-938818-17-1*) ECA Assoc.

Selected Speeches to the United Nations. S. E. Pheko. LC 94-65534. 200p. 1994. 17.00 (*1-884921-14-0*) Pheko & Assocs.

Selected Standards & Policy Statements of Special Interest to Women Workers Adopted under the Auspices of International Labour Office. v, 132p. (Orig.). 1980. pap. 11.25 (*92-2-102441-5*); pap. 20.25 (*92-2-102418-0*) Intl Labour Office.

Selected Standards on Professional Responsibility, Including California Rules, 1994. 5th ed. Thomas D. Morgan & Ronald D. Rotunda. 607p. 1991. pap. text ed. 16.00 (*1-56662-141-0*) Foundation Pr.

Selected Statistical Tables on the Economy of the Occupied Palestinian Territory (West Bank & Gaza Strip) 14p. 1992. 6.00 (*92-1-112275-9*) UN.

Selected Statistics on the Office of Attorney General. 86p. 1979. 4.50 (*0-318-15227-4*) Natl Attys General.

***Selected Statutes & International Agreements on Unfair Competition, Trademark, Copyright & Patent.** Paul Goldstein et al. 475p. 1997. pap. text ed. write for info. (*1-56662-492-4*) Foundation Pr.

Selected Statutes & International Agreements on Unfair Competition, Trademark, Copyright & Patent: 1995 Edition. Ed. by Paul Goldstein et al. 445p. 1995. pap. text ed. 17.95 (*1-56662-272-7*) Foundation Pr.

Selected Statutes & International Agreements on Unfair Competition, Trademark, Copyright & Patent, 1994. Paul Goldstein et al. 466p. 1994. pap. text ed. 16.95 (*1-56662-187-9*) Foundation Pr.

***Selected Statutes & International Agreements on Unfair Competition, Trademark, Copyright & Patent 1996.** Paul Goldstein et al. 464p. 1996. pap. text ed. write for info. (*1-56662-399-5*) Foundation Pr.

Selected Statutes on Trusts & Estates. John H. Langbein & Lawrence W. Waggoner. 851p. 1993. pap. text ed. 21.95 (*1-56662-144-5*) Foundation Pr.

Selected Statutes on Trusts & Estates, 1995. John H. Langbein & Laurence W. Waggoner. 908p. 1994. pap. text ed. 21.95 (*1-56662-237-9*) Foundation Pr.

Selected Statutes, Rules & Standards on the Legal Profession: 1994 Edition. John S. Dzienkowski. 1050p. 1994. pap. text ed. 18.00 (*0-314-04331-4*) West Pub.

Selected Stories. Benny Andersen. LC 82-23459. 96p. 1983. pap. 7.95 (*0-915306-25-5*) Curbstone.

***Selected Stories.** Russell Banks. 448p. Date not set. 27.50 (*0-06-017396-3*) HarpC.

Selected Stories. Adolfo Bioy Casares. LC 96-6744. (Illus.). 176p. (SPA.). 1994. 21.95 (*0-8112-1275-0*) New Directions.

Selected Stories. Anton P. Chekhov. 256p. 1994. 12.50 (*0-460-87472-1*, Everyman's Classic Lib) C E Tuttle.

Selected Stories. Guy De Maupassant. Tr. by Andrew R. MacAndrew. 288p. 1984. mass mkt. 4.95 (*0-452-00686-4*, Mer) NAL-Dutton.

Selected Stories. Andre Dubus. 1989. pap. 13.00 (*0-679-72533-4*, Publishers Media) Random.

Selected Stories. Andre Dubus. 496p. 1996. pap. 14.00 (*0-679-76730-4*) Random.

***Selected Stories.** Brian Friel. 126p. 1996. pap. 14.95 (*1-85235-149-7*) Dufour.

Selected Stories. Nadine Gordimer. 448p. 1983. pap. 12.95 (*0-14-006737-X*, Penguin Bks) Viking Penguin.

Selected Stories. O. Henry. Ed. & Intro. by Guy Davenport. LC 92-39604. 384p. 1993. pap. 12.95 (*0-14-018688-3*, Penguin Classics) Viking Penguin.

S

An Asterisk (*) at the beginning of an entry indicates that the title is appearing in BIP for the first time.

Selected Stories. Siegfried Lenz. Ed. & Tr. by Breon Mitchell. LC 89-13120. 1989. 19.95 (0-8112-1105-3) New Directions.
Selected Stories. Alice Munro. LC 96-4145. 544p. 1996. 30.00 (0-679-44627-3) Knopf.
Selected Stories. Vintage Contemporaries Staff. 1997. pap. 16.00 (0-679-76674-X) Random.
Selected Stories. Eudora Welty. LC 83-5466. 1978. 12.95 (0-394-60445-8, Modern Lib) Random.
Selected Stories. Elizabeth Bowen. LC 83-45415. reprint ed. 20.00 (0-404-20037-0) AMS Pr.
Selected Stories & Poems. Thomas Hardy. Ed. by James Gibson. 224p. 1993. pap. 6.95 (0-460-87386-5, Everyman's Classic Lib) C E Tuttle.
Selected Stories & Poems. Edgar Allan Poe. Ed. by Richard Gray. 320p. 1993. pap. 6.95 (0-460-87261-3, Everyman's Classic Lib) C E Tuttle.
Selected Stories & Sketches. Francis B. Harte. Ed. by David Wyatt. (World's Classics Ser.). 336p. 1995. pap. 8.95 (0-19-282354-X) OUP.
Selected Stories from the Southern Review, 1965-1985. Ed. by Lewis P. Simpson et al. LC 87-21383. 384p. 1988. 24.95 (0-8071-1443-X); pap. 14.95 (0-8071-1490-1) La State U Pr.
Selected Stories-Izbrannie Rasskazy: Eight Stories & Fables by Sologub, A Lampoon by Gorky, Papers on Sologub. Fedor Sologub & Maxim Gorky. Ed. & Tr. by Vassar W. Smith. Tr. by Murl G. Barker et al. LC 94-61420. (Illus.). 308p. (ENG & RUS.). (C). (gr. 13). 1994. pap. text ed. 24.95 (1-880964-09-0) Zapizdat Pubns.
Selected Stories of Eudora Welty. Eudora Welty. LC 92-50232. 448p. 1992. 15.50 (0-679-60002-7, Modern Lib) Random.
Selected Stories of Freeman. Marjorie Pryse. (C). 1991. pap. text ed. 9.95 (0-393-30106-0, Norton Paperbks) Norton.
Selected Stories of Hawthorne. large type ed. Nathaniel Hawthorne. 600p. 1996. reprint ed. lib. bdg. 24.00 (0-939495-03-1) North Bks.
Selected Stories of Lu Hsun. 3rd ed. Lu Hsun. Tr. by Gladys Yang & Hsien-Yi Yang from CHI. (Illus.). 255p. (C). 1989. pap. 11.95 (0-917056-71-X, Pub. by Foreign Lang Pr CH) Cheng & Tsui.
Selected Stories of Poe. large type ed. Edgar Allan Poe. (Large Print Ser.). 600p. 1993. reprint ed. lib. bdg. 24.00 (0-939495-47-3) North Bks.
Selected Stories of Richard Bausch. Richard Bausch. LC 95-38614. 288p. 1996. 14.50 (0-679-60189-9, Modern Lib) Random.
Selected Stories of Siegfried Lenz. Siegfried Lenz. Ed. by Breon Mitchell. LC 95-36430. 232p. (C). 1995. pap. 51.00 (0-8101-1314-7) Northwestern U Pr.
Selected Stories of V. S. Pritchett. V. S. Pritchett. 1978. 11.95 (0-394-50128-4) Random.
Selected Strategic Minerals: The Impending Crisis. Marc D. Lax. 356p. (C). 1991. lib. bdg. 57.50 (0-8191-8300-8) U Pr of Amer.
Selected Studies. Ernst H. Kantorowicz. LC 65-25431. 38.00 (0-685-71745-3) J J Augustin.
Selected Studies: Presented to the Author by the Department of Indology, Utrecht University, 2 pts., Set. Jan Gonda. 1991. 391.75 (90-04-09446-6) E J Brill.
Selected Studies in Bibliography. George T. Tanselle. LC 79-12476. 595p. reprint ed. pap. 169.60 (0-7837-1243-X, 2041380) Bks Demand.
Selected Studies in Highway Law, 4 vols., Set, ls. I & II. 1037p. 1976. Set, Vols. I & II, 1037 pgs., 1976. 145.00 (0-309-02434-X) Transport Res Bd.
Selected Studies in Pseudepigrapha & Apocrypha. With Special Reference to the Armenian Tradition. M. E. Stone. LC 90-21919. (Studia in Veteris Testamenti Pseudepigrapha Ser.: No. 9). (Illus.). x, 473p. 1991. 143.00 (90-04-09343-5) E J Brill.
Selected Studies of Archean Gneisses & Lower Proterozoic Rocks, Southern Canadian Shield. Ed. by G. B. Morey & Gilbert N. Hanson. LC 80-67113. (Geological Society of America, Special Paper Ser.: No. 182). (Illus.). 181p. (Orig.). reprint ed. pap. 51.60 (0-8357-3147-2, 2039410) Bks Demand.
Selected Studies on Prophetic Interpretation, 7 vols. rev. ed. William H. Shea. Ed. by Frank B. Holbrook. LC 90-39036. (Daniel & Revelation Committee Ser.: Vol. 1). (Illus.). 174p. (Orig.). 1992. pap. 6.95 (0-925675-11-3) BRI DC.
Selected Subaltern Studies. Ed. by Ranajit Guha & Gayatri C. Spivak. 416p. 1988. pap. 18.95 (0-19-505289-7) OUP.
Selected Subjects. Wallace Stevens. 44p. 1990. pap. 8.95 (0-912159-04-9) Center Pr CA.
Selected Supplications: Prayers & Salutations. 1990. pap. 6.00 (0-685-67784-2, 158) Tahrike Tarsile Quran.
Selected Syndromes & Therapy see Handbook of Sexology
Selected Synthetic Organic Fibres. Ed. by World Health Organization Staff. (Environmental Health Criteria Ser.: No. 151). 100p. (ENG, FRE & SPA.). 1993. pap. text ed. 26.00 (92-4-157151-9, 1160151) World Health.
***Selected Tables in Mathematical Statistics, Vol. 3.** Bernard Harris et al. Ed. by Institute of Mathematical Statistics Staff. 419p. 1975. reprint ed. 55.00 (0-8218-1903-8, TABLES-3) Am Math.
***Selected Tables in Mathematical Statistics, Vol. 5.** LC 75-17091. 263p. 1977. 38.00 (0-8218-1905-4, TABLES-5) Am Math.
Selected Takes: Film Editors on Editing. Vincent LoBrutto. LC 90-24262. 264p. 1991. text ed. 59.95 (0-275-93378-4, C3378, Praeger Pubs); pap. text ed. 19.95 (0-275-93395-4, B3395, Praeger Pubs) Greenwood.
Selected Tales. Jacob W. Grimm & Wilhelm K. Grimm. 432p. 1983. pap. 10.95 (0-14-044401-7, Penguin Classics) Viking Penguin.
Selected Tales. Peter B. Messent. 456p. 1993. pap. 10.95 (0-460-87209-5, Everyman's Classic Lib) C E Tuttle.
Selected Tales. Edgar Allan Poe. Ed. by Julian Symons. (World's Classics Paperback Ser.). 330p. 1980. pap. 5.95 (0-19-281522-9) OUP.
Selected Tales & Sketches. Nathaniel Hawthorne. 484p. 1987. pap. 10.95 (0-14-039057-X, Penguin Classics) Viking Penguin.
Selected Tales of Edgar Allan Poe. Edgar Allan Poe. LC 90-50620. 436p. 1991. pap. 14.00 (0-679-72524-5, Vin) Random.
Selected Tales of Grim & Grue from the Horror Pulps. Ed. by Sheldon Jaffery. LC 87-72859. 186p. 1987. 32.95 (0-87972-391-2); pap. 16.95 (0-87972-392-0) Bowling Green Univ Popular Press.
Selected Tales of Jacques Ferron. Jacques Ferron. Tr. by Betty Bednarski from FRE. 245p. (Orig.). 1984. reprint ed. pap. 9.95 (0-88784-140-6, Pub. by Hse of Anansi Pr CN) Genl Dist Srvs.
Selected Temple Documents of the Ur Dynasty. Clarence E. Keiser. LC 78-63533. (Yale Oriental Series: Babylonian Texts: No. 4). (Illus.). 240p. reprint ed. 42.50 (0-404-60254-1) AMS Pr.
Selected Terms in Fish Culture. FAO Staff. (Terminology Bulletins Ser.: No. 19-IT). 204p. 1993. pap. 17.00 (92-5-003248-X, F3248X, Pub. by FAO IT) Bernan Associates.
***Selected Terms on Bananas.** 81p. (ENG, FRE & SPA.). 1985. 12.00 (92-5-000786-8, Pub. by FAO IT) Bernan Associates.
Selected Texts on Prayer. Nilus of Sinai. pap. 0.50 (0-89981-090-X) Eastern Orthodox.
Selected Theatre Criticism, Vol. 2: Nineteen Twenty to Nineteen Thirty. Ed. by Anthony Slide. LC 85-2266. 1985. 24.00 (0-8108-1844-2) Scarecrow.
Selected Theatre Criticism: Volume 3: Nineteen Thirty-One to Nineteen Fifty. Ed. by Anthony Slide. LC 85-2266. 297p. 1986. 24.00 (0-8108-1846-9) Scarecrow.
Selected Theatre Criticism, Vol 1: Nineteen Hundred to Nineteen-Nineteen. Ed. by Anthony Slide. LC 85-2266. 395p. 1985. 32.50 (0-8108-1811-6) Scarecrow.
Selected Theories of Music Perception. Harold E. Fiske. LC 95-46932. (Studies in the History & Interpretation of Music: Vol. 49). 176p. 1996. text ed. 79.95 (0-7734-9771-4) E Mellen.
Selected Theses & Dissertations on the Washington, D. C. Region, Vol. CA. Compiled by Rita A. Calvan. 1982. 4.00 (1-888028-27-0) GWU Ctr WAS.
Selected Theses & Dissertations on the Washington, D.C. Region. Calvan. 1982. 4.00 (0-318-21783-X) G Washington Univ.
Selected Titles in Chemistry. 4th ed. 1977. pap. 1.25 (0-8412-0413-6) Am Chemical.
Selected to Live. Johanna Dobschiner. pap. 5.99 (0-7208-0212-1) Zondervan.
Selected Tooling Treasures. R. C. Womack. 250p. (C). 1995. pap. text ed. 16.95 (0-943719-03-8) Womack Educ Pubns.
Selected Topics: Intermediate Listening Comprehension. Ellen Kisslinger. LC 93-21020. (Lecture Ser.). 1994. text ed. 22.65 (0-8013-0967-0); audio 66.00 (0-8013-0968-9) Longman.
Selected Topics from Molecular Cell Biology. 3rd ed. H. Lodish. (C). Date not set. write for info. (0-7167-2949-0) W H Freeman.
Selected Topics in Algebra. Ionel Bucur. LC 83-24609. 1984. lib. bdg. 206.00 (90-277-1671-4) Kluwer Ac.
Selected Topics in Algebraic Geometry, 2 Vols in 1. 2nd ed. Virgil Snyder et al. LC 78-113149. 1970. text ed. 24.95 (0-8284-0189-6) Chelsea Pub.
Selected Topics in Approximation & Computation. Marek Kowalski et al. (International Series of Monographs on Computer Science). (Illus.). 320p. 1995. 65.00 (0-19-508059-9) OUP.
***Selected Topics in Bond Portfolio Management.** Ed. by Frank J. Fabozzi. (Illus.). 216p. 1997. pap. 45.00 (1-883249-28-7) F J Fabozzi.
Selected Topics in Cataloging Asian Art. Eleanor Mannikka. 1989. 20.00 (0-685-46055-X) Visual Resources Assn.
Selected Topics in Clinical Enzymology: Proceedings of the Third International Congress of Clinical Enzymology, Salzburg, Austria, September 6-9, 1981. Ed. by D. M. Goldberg & M. Werner. 362p. 1983. 123.10 (3-11-009688-9) De Gruyter.
Selected Topics in Clinical Enzymology: Vol. 2, Proceedings (Selected) of the 4th International Congress on Clinical Enzymology, Washington, D.C., July 30 - August 2, 1983. Ed. by M. Werner & D. M. Goldberg. (Illus.). xxii, 667p. 1985. 200.00 (3-11-010233-1) De Gruyter.
Selected Topics in Discrete Mathematics: Proceedings of the Moscow Discrete Mathematics Seminar, 1972-1990. Ed. by A. K. Kelmans. LC 93-48534. (American Mathematical Society Translations Ser. 2: Vol. 158). 248p. 1994. 79.00 (0-8218-7509-4, TRANS2/158) Am Math.
Selected Topics in Electroweak Interactions: Proceedings of the 2nd Lake Louise Winter Institute on New Frontiers in Particle Physics. Ed. by Abdul N. Kamal et al. 600p. (C). 1987. pap. 54.00 (9971-5-0303-4); text ed. 138.00 (9971-5-0302-6) World Scientific Pub.
***Selected Topics in Field Theory, High Energy & Astroparticle Physics.** 400p. 1996. lib. bdg. 60.00 (981-02-2800-7) World Scientific Pub.
Selected Topics in Graph Theory, Vol. 2. Lowell W. Beineke & Robin J. Wilson. 1983. text ed. 138.00 (0-12-086202-6) Acad Pr.
Selected Topics in Group IV & II-Vi Semiconductors: Proceedings of Symposium L - 6th International Symposium on Silicon Molecular Beam Epitazy, & Symposium D on Purification, Doping & Defects in II-VI Materials of the 1995 E-MRS Spring Conference, Strasbourg, France, May 22-26, 1995. Ed. by Erich Kasper et al. (European Materials Research Society Symposia Proceedings Ser.: Vol. 54). 770p. 1996. 349.00 (0-444-82411-1, North Holland) Elsevier.
Selected Topics in Harmonic Maps. James Eells & Luc Lemaire. LC 82-25526. (CBMS Regional Conference Series in Mathematics: No. 50). 85p. 1983. pap. 25.00 (0-8218-0700-5, CBMS/50) Am Math.
Selected Topics in High Temperature Chemistry: Defect Chemistry of Solids. D. Johannesen & A. Anderson. (Studies in Inorganic Chemistry: Vol. 9). 1990. 222.50 (0-444-88534-X, SIC 9) Elsevier.
Selected Topics in Identification, Modelling & Control, 5 vols., Set. Ed. by O. H. Bosgra & P. M. Van Den Hof. 426p. (Orig.). 1990. pap. 150.00 (90-6275-834-7, Pub. by Delft U Pr NE) Coronet Bks.
Selected Topics in Indeterministic Systems. Aron I. Katsenelinboigen. 350p. 1989. pap. text ed. 15.95 (0-914105-47-7) Intersystems Pubns.
Selected Topics in Magnetism. L. C. Gupta & M. S. Multani. LC 92-42308. (Frontiers in Solid State Sciences Ser.: Vol. 2). 460p. 1993. pap. write for info. (981-02-1213-5); text ed. 105.00 (981-02-1212-7) World Scientific Pub.
Selected Topics in Medical Artificial Intelligence. Ed. by P. L. Miller. (Computers & Medicine Ser.). (Illus.). 220p. 1988. 74.00 (0-387-96701-X) Spr-Verlag.
Selected Topics in Mineral Processing. A. Ghosh & P. K. Kumar. 1995. write for info. (81-224-0745-5, Pub. by Wiley Estrn II) Franklin.
***Selected Topics in Non-Perturbative Qcd.** Ed. by A. Di Giacomo & D. Diakonov. LC 96-78119. (International School of Physics Enrico Fermi Ser.: Vol. 130). 504p. (YA). (gr. 12 up). 1997. 170.00 (90-5199-293-9, 293-9) IOS Press.
***Selected Topics in Philosophy.** John L. Bowman. 200p. (Orig.). 1997. pap. 19.95 (0-9650797-1-6) J L Bowman.
Selected Topics in Physics: Astrophysics & Biophysics, Proceedings of the Latin School of Physics, 14th, Caracas, Venezuela, July 10-28, 1972. Latin School of Physics Staff. Ed. by E. Abecassis De Laredo & N. K. Jurisic. LC 73-83563. 420p. 1973. lib. bdg. 175.00 (90-277-0367-1) Kluwer Ac.
Selected Topics in Quantum Field Theory & Mathematical Physics. J. Niederle & J. Fischer. 468p. (C). 1990. text ed. 144.00 (981-02-0116-8) World Scientific Pub.
Selected Topics in Shock Wave Physics & Equation of State Modeling. G. Roger Gathers. 280p. 1994. text ed. 61.00 (981-02-1691-2) World Scientific Pub.
Selected Topics in Statistical Mechanics. John G. Kirkwood. Ed. by R. W. Zwanzig. LC 68-6792. (Documents on Modern Physics Ser.). (Illus.). xx, 266p. 1967. text ed. 266.00 (0-677-00330-7) Gordon & Breach.
Selected Topics in Statistical Mechanics. A. A. Logunov, Jr. et al. 556p. (C). 1990. text ed. 130.00 (981-02-0118-4) World Scientific Pub.
Selected Topics in Superconductivity. M. S. Multani & L. C. Gupta. LC 92-43565. (Frontiers in Solid State Sciences Ser.). 676p. 1993. pap. write for info. (981-02-1202-X); text ed. 135.00 (981-02-1201-1) World Scientific Pub.
Selected Topics in the Biochemistry Part IV. Personal Recollections. Ed. by E. C. Slater. (Comprehensive Biochemistry Ser.: Vol. 38). 506p. 1994. 207.50 (0-444-81942-8) Elsevier.
Selected Topics on Data Analysis in Astronomy. L. Scarsi et al. 180p. 1987. text ed. 54.00 (9971-5-0262-3) World Scientific Pub.
***Selected Topics on Electron Physics: Proceedings of the Peter Farago Symposium on Electron Physics Held As a Satellite Symposium to the Fifth European Conference on Atomic & Molecular Physics, March 31-April 1, 1995, Edinburgh, Scotland.** Hans Kleinpoppen. Ed. by D. Murray Campbell. LC 96-43717. (Physics of Atoms & Molecules Ser.). 470p. 1996. 129.50 (0-306-45484-X) Plenum.
Selected Topics on Stochastic Modeling. R. Gutierrez & M. J. V. Bonnet. 300p. 1994. text ed. 93.00 (981-02-1804-4) World Scientific Pub.
Selected Topics on the General Properties of Quantum Field Theory. F. Strocchi. 188p. 1993. text ed. 61.00 (981-02-1143-0); pap. text ed. 30.00 (981-02-1149-X) World Scientific Pub.
Selected Tragedies of A. P. Sumarokov. A. P. Sumarokov. Tr. by Richard Fortune & Raymond Fortune. LC 72-129498. (Publications of Eighteenth-Century Russian Literature Ser.). 246p. reprint ed. pap. 70.20 (0-685-07753-5, 2010271) Bks Demand.
Selected Trumpet Solos, EFS42. Jay Arnold. (Illus.). 128p. 1960. pap. 14.95 (0-8256-2042-2, AM40213) Music Sales.
Selected Tutorial Notes. 405p. (Orig.). 1993. pap. text ed. 35.00 (1-880083-07-8) Wolfram Research.
Selected U. S. Government Series: A Guide for Public & Academic Libraries. Nancy P. Van Zant. LC 77-10337. 186p. reprint ed. pap. 53.10 (0-7837-5960-6, 2045760) Bks Demand.
Selected Values of the Thermodynamic Properties of the Elements. Ralph Hultgren & Pramod D. Desai. LC 73-76587. 646p. reprint ed. pap. 180.00 (0-317-08976-5, 2019486) Bks Demand.
Selected Values of Thermodynamic Properties of Binary Alloys. Ralph Hultgren & Pramod D. Desai. LC 73-76588. 1445p. reprint ed. pap. 180.00 (0-317-08922-6, 2019487) Bks Demand.
Selected Vaudeville Criticism. Ed. by Anthony Slide. LC 87-28553. 318p. 1988. 29.50 (0-8108-2052-8) Scarecrow.
***Selected Verse.** Friedrich Holderlin & Michael Hamburger. 270p. 1996. 32.95 (0-85646-147-4, Pub. by Anvil Press UK) Dufour.
Selected Verse: Selected Verse. Heinrich Heine. Tr. & Intro. by Peter Branscombe. (Classics Ser.). 294p. 1987. pap. 11.95 (0-14-042098-3, Penguin Classics) Viking Penguin.
Selected Verse: Selected Verse. Johann W. Von Goethe. Tr. by David Luke. 368p. 1982. pap. 11.95 (0-14-042074-6, Penguin Classics) Viking Penguin.

Selected Verse by an Ozark Maverick. 2nd ed. Burr E. Fancher. (Illus.). 117p. (YA). (gr. 6 up). 1995. reprint ed. pap. 6.00 (1-887335-02-1) Fancher & Assocs.
SELECTED VERSE BY AN OZARK MAVERICK is a collection of verse by Burr Fancher, Ph.D., reflecting on fifty years of roaming across the United States & other parts of the world. The book is organized into four sections: "Ozarkia, My Roots, My Love" are reflections on a childhood environment in the Ozark Mountains; "My Family" includes verse about various family members & a brief family history; "Good Old USA" is a travelogue of experiences in various places with interesting people met along the way; & "Thoughts of an Ozark Maverick" is a philosophy of life acquired through a maverick existence. This is a second printing of a book first published in 1978. Burr has been invited into many classrooms to share his poetry & story telling. Order information: Ada Fancher, Fancher Publications, 5890 N.W. Primrose, Albany, OR 97321. Tel. (503) 926-3125, FAX: (503) 926-0980. ISBN 1-887335-02-1. Cost $6.00 plus postage. Grade Level 6-adult.
Publisher Provided Annotation.

Selected Video & Pulse Circuitry. Richard S. Hughes. LC 74-136725. 153p. 1969. 19.00 (0-403-04506-1) Scholarly.
Selected Vitamins, Minerals & Functional Consequences of Maternal Malnutrition. Ed. by Artemis P. Simopoulos. (World Review of Nutrition & Dietetics Ser.: Vol. 64). (Illus.). x, 180p. 1991. 170.50 (3-8055-5168-1) S Karger.
***Selected vs. Translations.** David Gascoyne & Alan Clodd. 168p. 9700. pap. 21.00 (1-870612-33-7, Pub. by Enitha Pr UK) Dufour.
Selected Walks, 1969-1989. Hamish Fulton & Michael Auping. 107p. 1990. 85.00 (0-914782-72-X) Buffalo Fine-Albrght-Knox.
Selected Water Management Issues in Latin American Agriculture. Ed. by Pierre R. Crosson et al. LC 77-10193. (Resources for the Future Ser.). (Illus.). 1978. text ed. 16.50 (0-8018-2047-2) Johns Hopkins.
Selected Water Management Issues in Latin American Agriculture. Ed. by Pierre R. Crosson et al. LC 77-10193. (Illus.). 208p. reprint ed. pap. 59.30 (0-685-20402-2, 2030198) Bks Demand.
Selected Water Problems in Islands & Coastal Waters: Proceedings, Malta, 1978. United Nations Economic Commission for Europe. (ECE Seminars & Symposia Ser.). (Illus.). 1979. 228.00 (0-08-024447-5, Pub. by Pergamon Repr UK) Franklin.
Selected Women of the Scriptures of Stamina & Courage. Dolores S. Gilliland. (Illus.). 1978. pap. 3.95 (0-931446-02-3) Honor Bks.
Selected Works. Incl. Against Verres. Marcus Tullius Cicero. Tr. by Michael Grant. 1960. pap. (0-318-55093-8); Twenty Three Letters. Marcus Tullius Cicero. Tr. by Michael Grant. 1960. pap. (0-318-55094-6); Second Philippic Against Anthony. Marcus Tullius Cicero. Tr. by Michael Grant. 1960. pap. (0-318-55095-4); On Duties. Marcus T. Cicero. Tr. by Michael Grant. 1960. pap. (0-318-55096-2); Old Age. Marcus T. Cicero. Tr. by Michael Grant. 1960. pap. (0-318-55097-0); (Classics Ser.). 272p. (Orig.). (gr. 9 up). 1960. pap. 11.95 (0-14-044099-2, Penguin Classics) Viking Penguin.
Selected Works, 2 vols. J. Frank Adams. Ed. by J. Peter May & Charles B. Thomas. (Illus.). 400p. (C). 1991. write for info. (0-318-68319-9) Cambridge U Pr.
Selected Works. Konrad Bayer. 1986. pap. 13.99 (0-947757-06-6, Pub. by Atlas Pr UK) Serpents Tail.
Selected Works. Giordano Bruno. 1972. 75.00 (0-8490-1021-7) Gordon Pr.
Selected Works. Fulgentius. Tr. by Robert B. Eno. LC 96-19713. (Fathers of the Church Ser.: Vol. 95). 500p. 1997. text ed. 36.95 (0-8132-0095-4) Cath U Pr.
***Selected Works.** Galen. Tr. & Intro. by Peter Singer. (The World's Classics Ser.). 352p. 1997. pap. 12.95 (0-19-282450-3) OUP.
***Selected Works.** Philip Gurlik. LC 96-60573. (Illus.). 42p. (Orig.). 1996. pap. 10.00 (1-889027-01-4) Tafford Pub.
Selected Works. Rudyard Kipling. LC 94-24680. 1995. 12.99 (0-517-11827-0, Pub. by Gramercy) Random Hse Value.
Selected Works. Lucian. Tr. by B. P. Reardon. LC 64-16706. (Orig.). 1965. pap. 5.65 (0-672-60385-3, LLA161, Bobbs) Macmillan.
Selected Works. Sissy Thomas. (Illus.). 52p. (Orig.). 1990. 17.50 (0-942779-04-5) Greenberg Voin Doren.
Selected Works. I. M. Vinogradov. Ed. by L. D. Fadeev et al. Tr. by N. Psv from RUS. (Illus.). 410p. 1985. 235.00 (0-387-12788-7) Spr-Verlag.

S

An Asterisk (*) at the beginning of an entry indicates that the title is appearing in BIP for the first time.

Selected Works. Edmund E. Burke. Ed. by Walter Jackson Bate. LC 75-9946. 536p. 1975. reprint ed. text ed. 35.00 (*0-8371-8122-4*, BUSEW, Greenwood Pr) Greenwood.

Selected Works. Voltairine De Cleyre. Ed. by H. Havel. (Notable American Authors Ser.). 1992. reprint ed. lib. bdg. 75.00 (*0-7812-2625-2*) Rprt Serv.

Selected Works. Ulrich Zwingli. Ed. by Samuel M. Jackson. Tr. by Lawrence A. McLouth et al. from GER. LC 72-80383. (Pennsylvania Paperback Ser.: No. 49). 288p. reprint ed. pap. 82.10 (*0-8357-3327-0*, 2039551) Bks Demand.

Selected Works: Articles on General Linguistics. E. D. Polivanov. Tr. by Daniel Armstrong from RUS. LC 73-83930. (Janua Linguarum, Ser. Major: No. 72). (Illus.). 386p. 1974. text ed. 109.25 (*90-279-2693-X*) Mouton.

Selected Works: Centennial Edition. R. Schumann. 160p. 1994. 10.96 (*0-7935-3067-9*) H Leonard.

Selected Works: Seattle Art Museum. Ed. by Helen Abbott. LC 91-9704. (Illus.). 208p. (Orig.). 1991. pap. 9.95 (*0-932216-35-8*) Seattle Art.

Selected Works: Three Volumes in One. Israel Zangwill. LC 72-38728. (Short Story Index Reprint Ser.). 1977. reprint ed. 63.95 (*0-8369-4141-1*) Ayer.

Selected Works: Tragic Sense of Life in Men & Nations, Vol. 4. Miguel De Unamuno. Ed. by Anthony Kerrigan. (Bollingen Ser.: Vol. 85). 574p. 1973. pap. text ed. 21.95 (*0-691-01820-0*) Princeton U Pr.

Selected Works: Volume 5: Poetry & Experience. Wilhelm Dilthey. Ed. by Rudolf A. Makkreel & Rodi Frithjof. LC 84-4200. 416p. 1985. text ed. 59.50 (*0-691-07297-3*) Princeton U Pr.

Selected Works by Edythe Mae Gordon: African-American Women Writers 1910-1940. Gates. LC 96-5811. 1996. 25.00 (*0-7838-1420-8*, Hall Reference) Macmillan.

Selected Works by Eighteenth Century Naturalists & Travelers. LC 73-17840. (Natural Sciences in America Ser.). 266p. 1974. reprint ed. 21.95 (*0-405-05762-8*) Ayer.

Selected Works from the Collection of Samuel Gallu: Exhibition Catalogue. Jeanne C. Porter. (Illus.). 68p. 1981. pap. 5.00 (*0-911209-21-2*) Palmer Mus Art.

Selected Works from the Frederick R. Weisman Art Foundation. Ed. by Nora H. Brougher & Andrea P. Belloli. (Illus.). 50p. (Orig.). 1988. write for info. (*0-9614537-2-9*) F R Weisman Collect.

Selected Works in Applied Mechanics & Mathematics. Eric Reissner. (Math Ser.). 656p. 1995. 75.00 (*0-86720-968-2*) Jones & Bartlett.

Selected Works in Nineteenth Century North American Paleontology. LC 73-17841. (Natural Sciences in America Ser.). 482p. 1974. reprint ed. 33.95 (*0-405-05763-6*) Ayer.

Selected Works in the High Museum. Donald C. Peirce et al. LC 87-80790. (Illus.). 86p. (Orig.). 1987. 25.00 (*0-685-18200-2*) High Mus Art.

Selected Works Nineteen Seventy-Six to Nineteen Eighty-Two. Guy Williams. 1982. pap. 10.00 (*0-935724-11-7*) Figures.

Selected Works of A. M. Kolmogorov: Mathematics & Mechanics, Vol. 1. Ed. by Vladimir M. Tikhomirov. (Mathematics & Its Applications, Soviet Ser.: Vol. 1). 576p. 1991. lib. bdg. 282.50 (*90-277-2796-1*) Kluwer Ac.

Selected Works of A. N. Kolmogorov: Information Theory & the Theory of Algorithms. Andrei N. Kolmogorov. (Mathematics & Its Applications, Soviet Ser.: Vol. 3). 304p. (C). 1992. 271.00 (*90-277-2798-8*) Kluwer Ac.

Selected Works of A. N. Kolmogorov: Probability Theory & Mathematical Statistics. Ed. by A. N. Shiryayev. (Mathematics & Its Applications, Soviet Ser.: Vol. 2). (C). 1992. lib. bdg. 282.50 (*90-277-2797-X*) Kluwer Ac.

Selected Works of Angelina Weld Grimke. Angela W. Grimke. Ed. by Carolivia Herron. (Schomburg Library of Nineteenth-Century Black Women Writers). 496p. 1991. 42.00 (*0-19-506199-3*) OUP.

Selected Works of Anthony Trollope Ser., 62 Vols., Set. Anthony Trollope. Ed. by N. John Hall. 1981. reprint ed. lib. bdg. 1,994.00 (*0-405-14114-9*) Ayer.

Selected Works of Anthony Trollope Series. Anthony Trollope. Ed. by N. John Hall. 80-1890. 1981. reprint ed. lib. bdg. 24.95 (*0-405-14157-2*) Ayer.

Selected Works of Artemus Ward. Artemus Ward, pseud. Ed. by Albert J. Nock. LC 79-177846. reprint ed. 47.50 (*0-404-06835-9*) AMS Pr.

Selected Works of Artemus Ward. Artemus Ward & Bro Ward. 1988. reprint ed. lib. bdg. 49.00 (*0-7812-0528-X*) Rprt Serv.

Selected Works of Artemus Ward. Artemus Ward & Charles F. Browne. Ed. by Albert J. Nock. LC 73-144907. 1971. reprint ed. 22.00 (*0-403-00845-X*) Scholarly.

Selected Works of Benjamin Aaron. Ed. by George H. Hildebrand & Frederic Meyers. (Monograph & Research Ser.: No. 18). 427p. 1977. 8.50 (*0-89215-076-9*) U Cal LA Indus Rel.

Selected Works of Clinton Hart Merriam. Ed. by Keir B. Sterling. LC 73-17842. (Natural Sciences in America Ser.). 893p. 1974. reprint ed. 69.95 (*0-405-05764-4*) Ayer.

Selected Works of David Jones. Ed. by John Matthias. (Poetry & Literature Ser.). 237p. 1993. pap. 12.00 (*0-943373-19-0*) Natl Poet Foun.

Selected Works of David Jones. Ed. by John Matthias. (Poetry & Literature Ser.). 237p. 1993. 18.00 (*0-943373-18-2*) Natl Poet Foun.

Selected Works of George A. Kennedy. Ed. by Tien-Yi Li. 1964. 25.95 (*0-88710-082-1*) Yale Far Eastern Pubns.

Selected Works of George McCready Price. Ed. by Ronald L. Numbers. LC 94-45071. (Creationism in Twentieth-Century America Ser.: Vol. 7). 512p. 1995. text ed. 80.00 (*0-8153-1808-1*) Garland.

Selected Works of Georgia Douglas Johnson: African American Writer, 1910-1940. Gates. LC 96-23997. 1996. 30.00 (*0-7838-0038-X*) G K Hall.

***Selected Works of Govind Ballabh Pant, 8.** Govind B. Pant. Ed. by B. R. Nanda. 510p. 1997. 24.95 (*0-19-563954-5*) OUP.

***Selected Works of Govind Ballabh Pant, 9.** Govind B. Pant. Ed. by B. R. Nanda. 462p. 1997. 25.00 (*0-19-564117-5*) OUP.

Selected Works of Govind Ballabh Pant, Vol. I. Govind B. Pant. Ed. by B. R. Nanda. (Illus.). 356p. 1994. 27.00 (*0-19-563150-1*) OUP.

Selected Works of Govind Ballabh Pant, Vol. 2. Ed. by B. R. Nanda. 392p. 1994. 26.00 (*0-19-563463-2*) OUP.

Selected Works of Govind Ballabh Pant, Vol. 3. Ed. by B. R. Nanda. 400p. 1995. 26.00 (*0-19-563464-0*) OUP.

Selected Works of Govind Ballabh Pant, Vol. 4. Govind B. Pant. Ed. by B. R. Nanda. (Illus.). 422p. 1995. 24.95 (*0-19-563674-0*) OUP.

Selected Works of Govind Ballabh Pant, Vol. 5. Govind B. Pant. Ed. by B. R. Nanda. (Illus.). 546p. 1996. 22.00 (*0-19-563675-9*) OUP.

***Selected Works of Govind Ballabh Pant, Vol. 6.** Govind B. Pant. Ed. by B. R. Nanda. 440p. 1997. text ed. 25.00 (*0-19-563952-9*) OUP.

***Selected Works of Hans A. Bethe.** 500p. 1997. lib. bdg. 49.00 (*981-02-2876-7*) World Scientific Pub.

Selected Works of Henry James, Sr., 10 vols, Set. Henry James, Sr. reprint ed. 426.00 (*0-404-10080-5*) AMS Pr.

Selected Works of I. L. Peretz: I. L. Perets (in English Translation) Ed. by Marvin Zuckerman & Marion Herbst. (Three Great Classic Writers of Modern Yiddish Literature Ser.: Vol. III). (Illus.). 512p. 1996. 37.50 (*0-934710-25-2*) J Simon.

Selected Works of Ida B. Wells-Barnett. Ida B. Wells-Barnett. (Schomburg Library of Nineteenth-Century Black Women Writers). (Illus.). 352p. 1991. 42.00 (*0-19-506202-7*) OUP.

Selected Works of Ion Creanga & Mihai Eminescu. Ed. by Ana Cartianu & R. C. Johnston. Tr. by R. C. Johnston from RUM. LC 91-72148. (Classics of Romanian Literature Ser.: Vol. 1). 307p. 1993. text ed. 46.50 (*0-88033-224-7*) Col U Pr.

Selected Works of Irving Bernstein. Ed. by George H. Hildebrand & Frederic Meyers. (Monograph & Research Ser.: No. 17). 233p. 1977. 7.00 (*0-89215-075-0*) U Cal LA Indus Rel.

Selected Works of J. Frank Adams, Vol. 1. Ed. by J. Peter May & Charles B. Thomas. 552p. 1992. text ed. 85.00 (*0-521-41063-0*) Cambridge U Pr.

***Selected Works of J. Frank Adams, Vol. 2.** 545p. 1992. text ed. 85.00 (*0-521-41065-7*) Cambridge U Pr.

Selected Works of Jamaharlal Nehru, Vol. 16, Pt. II. Jawaharlal Nehru. Ed. by S. Gopal. (Illus.). 800p. 1995. 16.95 (*0-19-563681-3*) OUP.

Selected Works of James Marsh, 3 vols. Intro. by James Marsh. LC 76-42199. 2400p. 1976. lib. bdg. 200.00 (*0-8201-1275-5*) Schol Facsimiles.

Selected Works of Jawaharlal Nehru, 7. Jawaharlal Nehru. Ed. by S. Gopal. LC 72-900197. 1975. 14.00 (*0-685-40473-0*) S Asia.

Selected Works of Jawaharlal Nehru, 8. S. Gopal & Jawaharlal Nehru. 1976. 15.00 (*0-88386-376-6*) S Asia.

Selected Works of Jawaharlal Nehru, 9. S. Gopal & Jawaharlal Nehru. 1977. 15.00 (*0-685-66727-8*) S Asia.

Selected Works of Jawaharlal Nehru, 10. S. Gopal & Jawaharlal Nehru. 1977. 15.00 (*0-8364-0344-4*) S Asia.

Selected Works of Jawaharlal Nehru, 11. S. Gopal & Jawaharlal Nehru. 1978. 16.00 (*0-8364-0345-2*) S Asia.

***Selected Works of Jawaharlal Nehru, 19.** Jawaharlal Nehru. Ed. by S. Gopal. (Illus.). 814p. 1997. 29.95 (*0-19-564193-0*) OUP.

Selected Works of Jawaharlal Nehru, Vol. 14. Jawaharlal Nehru. Ed. by Sarvepalli Gopal. (Illus.). 644p. 1993. 24.00 (*0-19-563096-3*) OUP.

Selected Works of Jawaharlal Nehru, Vol. 15. 1983. 38.00 (*0-8364-0966-3*) S Asia.

Selected Works of Jawaharlal Nehru, Vol. 15, Pt. I. 2nd ed. Jawaharlal Nehru. Ed. by S. Gopal. 593p. write for info. (*0-318-72311-5*) OUP.

Selected Works of Jawaharlal Nehru, Vols. 1-4. Jawaharlal Nehru. Ed. by S. Gopal. 1973. 12.75 (*0-318-55754-1*) S Asia.

Selected Works of Jawaharlal Nehru, Vols. 5-6. Jawaharlal Nehru. Ed. by S. Gopal. 1973. 13.75 (*0-318-55755-X*) S Asia.

Selected Works of Jawaharlal Nehru: Second Series, Vol. 3. Jawaharlal Nehru. Ed. by Sarvepalli Gopal. (Illus.). 554p. 1987. 36.00 (*0-19-561849-1*) OUP.

Selected Works of Jawaharlal Nehru: Second Series, Vol. 8. Jawaharlal Nehru. Ed. by Sarvepalli Gopal. 514p. 1990. 32.00 (*0-19-562513-7*) OUP.

Selected Works of Jawaharlal Nehru: Second Series, Vol. 9. Jawaharlal Nehru. Ed. by Sarvepalli Gopal. (Illus.). 560p. 1992. 32.00 (*0-19-562654-0*) OUP.

Selected Works of Jawaharlal Nehru: Second Series, Vol. 10. Jawaharlal Nehru. Ed. by Sarvepalli Gopal. (Illus.). 588p. 1991. 26.00 (*0-19-562838-1*) OUP.

Selected Works of Jawaharlal Nehru: Second Series, Vol. 12. Jawaharlal Nehru. Ed. by Sarvepalli Gopal. (Illus.). 524p. 1992. 26.00 (*0-19-562964-7*) OUP.

Selected Works of Jawaharlal Nehru: Second Series, Vol. 14, Pt. II. Jawaharlal Nehru. Ed. by S. Gopal. 530p. 1995. 14.95 (*0-19-563309-1*) OUP.

Selected Works of Jawaharlal Nehru Vol. 16, Pt. 1: (One March 1951 - Thirty June 1951) Jawaharlal Nehru. Ed. by S. Gopal. (Illus.). 718p. 1996. 10.95 (*0-19-563478-0*) OUP.

Selected Works of Jawaharlal Nehru Vol. 17: Second Series, Vol. 17. Jawaharlal Nehru. (Illus.). 722p. (C). 1996. 36.00 (*0-19-563745-3*) OUP.

Selected Works of Jawaharlal Nehru, Vol. 15, Pt. 2: Second Series. Ed. by S. Gopal. 697p. 1994. 16.95 (*0-19-563477-2*) OUP.

Selected Works of Joel Asaph Allen. LC 73-17843. (Natural Sciences in America Ser.). (Illus.). 976p. 1974. reprint ed. 71.95 (*0-405-05765-2*) Ayer.

Selected Works of J.S. Bach. William F. Buckley. 1992. pap. 18.25 (*0-943748-49-6*) Ekay Music.

Selected Works of La Fontaine. Ed. by Philip A. Wadsworth. 1990. 7.25 (*0-8446-3127-2*) Peter Smith.

Selected Works of Louis Neel. Tr. by N. Kurti. 467p. 1984. 208.00 (*0-677-30980-5*) Gordon & Breach.

Selected Works of Louis Neel. Ed. by N. Kurti. 467p. 1988. text ed. 364.00 (*2-88124-300-2*) Gordon & Breach.

***Selected Works of M. N. Roy: 1932-1936, Vol. IV.** M. N. Roy. Ed. by Sibnarayan Ray. (Illus.). 700p. 1997. 35.00 (*0-19-563768-2*) OUP.

Selected Works of M. N. Roy 1927-1932, Vol. III. M. N. Roy. Ed. by Sibnarayan Ray. (Illus.). 664p. 1991. 35.00 (*0-19-562640-0*) OUP.

Selected Works of Mao Tse-Tung, 5 vols., Set. Mao Tse-Tung. 931.00 (*0-08-022262-5*, Pub. by Pergamon Repr UK) Franklin.

Selected Works of Maulana Abul Kalam Azad, 3 vols., 1. Ed. by Ravindra Kumar. (C). 1991. 30.00 (*0-685-74416-7*, Pub. by Manohar II) S Asia.

Selected Works of Maulana Abul Kalam Azad, 3 vols., 2. Ed. by Ravindra Kumar. (C). 1991. 30.00 (*0-8364-2747-5*, Pub. by Manohar II) S Asia.

Selected Works of Maulana Abul Kalam Azad, 3 vols., 3. Ed. by Ravindra Kumar. (C). 1991. 30.00 (*0-8364-2748-3*, Pub. by Manohar II) S Asia.

Selected Works of Motilal Nehru: Volume 5: 1926-1928. Ed. by Ravindar Kumar & H. D. Sharma. 1993. 75.00 (*0-7069-6379-2*, Pub. by Vikas II) S Asia.

Selected Works of Paul J. Flory, 3 vols., Set. Paul J. Flory. Ed. by Leo Mandelkern et al. LC 84-51712. 2664p. 1985. 229.50 (*0-8047-1277-8*) Stanford U Pr.

Selected Works of Ramon Llull, 2 vols. Ed. by Anthony Bonner. (Illus.). 1330p. 1985. text ed. 225.00 (*0-691-07288-4*) Princeton U Pr.

Selected Works of Robert Owen, 4 vols., Set. Robert Owen. Ed. by Gregory Claeys. 1577p. 1993. 395.00 (*1-85196-088-0*, Pub. by Pickering & Chatto UK) Ashgate Pub Co.

Selected Works of Sholem-Aleykhem. Sholem-Aleykhem. Ed. by Marvin Zuckerman & Marion Herbst. LC 94-582. (Three Great Classic Writers of Modern Yiddish Literature Ser.: Vol. II). (Illus.). 512p. (C). 1994. 37.50 (*0-934710-24-4*) J Simon.

Selected Works of Subhas Chandra Bose, 3 vols., Set. Ravindra Kumar. (C). 1992. 72.00 (*81-7156-320-1*, Pub. by UBS Pubs Dist II) S Asia.

Selected Works of Voltairine De Cleyre. Voltairine De Cleyre. Ed. by Alexander Berkman & H. Havel. (Great Women Ser.). 484p. 1972. reprint ed. lib. bdg. 250.00 (*0-87700-191-X*) Revisionist Pr.

Selected Works of W. A. Mozart. William F. Buckley. 1993. pap. 12.98 (*0-943748-54-2*) Ekay Music.

Selected Works of Washington Irving. Washington Irving. Ed. by William Kelly. (Modern Library College Editions). 680p. (C). 1983. pap. text ed. write for info. (*0-07-554394-X*) McGraw.

***Selected Works of Yakov Borisovich Zeldovich, 2 vols.** Ed. by Jeremiah P. Ostriker. 1996. 150.00 (*0-691-08743-1*) Princeton U Pr.

***Selected Works of Yakov Borisovich Zeldovich Vol. I: Chemical Physics & Hydrodynamics.** Ed. by Jeremiah P. Ostriker. 500p. 1996. 75.00 (*0-691-08594-3*) Princeton U Pr.

Selected Works of Yakow Borisovich Zeldovich, Vol. II: Particles, Nuclei, & the Universe. Ed. by Jeremiah P. Ostriker & A. Granik. Tr. by A. Granik & E. Jackson. 644p. 1993. text ed. 99.50 (*0-691-08742-3*) Princeton U Pr.

Selected Works of Zinaida Hippius. Zinaida N. Hippius. Ed. by Temira Pachmuss. LC 72-188447. 327p. reprint ed. pap. 93.20 (*0-317-29016-9*, 2020253) Bks Demand.

***Selected Works on Biomechanics & Aeroelasticity.** Y. C. Fung. LC 97-12963. (Advanced Series in Biomechanics). 1997. pap. text ed. write for info. (*981-02-3987-4*); pap. text ed. write for info. (*981-02-3988-2*) World Scientific Pub.

Selected Works, 1764-1767: Early Addresses, Essays, & Drafts; Fragments on Recent German Literature. Johann G. Herder. Ed. by Ernest A. Menze & Karl Menges. Tr. by Michael Palma. 368p. 1992. 40.00 (*0-271-00712-5*) Pa St U Pr.

Selected Worldwide Marine Weather Broadcasts. (Illus.). 200p. (Orig.). (C). 1995. pap. text ed. 40.00 (*0-7881-2255-X*) DIANE Pub.

Selected Writing of Madame de Villedieu, Vol. 18. Ed. by Nancy D. Klein. (Writing about Women Ser.). 160p. (FRE.). (C). 1995. text ed. 39.95 (*0-8204-2714-4*) P Lang Pubng.

Selected Writings. John M. Addey. LC 76-46204. 232p. 1976. 11.00 (*0-86690-057-8*, A1011-014) Am Fed Astrologers.

Selected Writings. Christopher A. Anderson. LC 88-71661. (Illus.). 287p. (Orig.). 1988. pap. text ed. 14.00 (*0-931353-15-7*) Andersons Pubns.

Selected Writings. Joe Brainard. pap. 3.50 (*0-686-09752-1*) Kulchur Foun.

Selected Writings. Thomas Carlyle. Ed. by Alan Shelston. (English Library). 400p. 1980. pap. 12.95 (*0-14-043065-2*, Penguin Classics) Viking Penguin.

Selected Writings. Lama Dalai. 1973. lib. bdg. 250.00 (*0-87968-508-5*) Krishna Pr.

Selected Writings. Emile Durkheim. Ed. by Anthony Giddens. 288p. 1972. pap. text ed. 18.95 (*0-521-09712-6*) Cambridge U Pr.

Selected Writings. Meister Eckhart. Ed. & Tr. by Oliver Davies. 336p. 1995. pap. 11.95 (*0-14-043343-0*, Penguin Classics) Viking Penguin.

Selected Writings. Ralph Waldo Emerson. 1981. pap. 4.00 (*0-685-03399-6*, T14, Modern Lib) Random.

Selected Writings. Ralph Waldo Emerson. Ed. by Donald McQuade. LC 80-27210. (Modern Library College Editions). 911p. (C). 1981. pap. text ed. write for info. (*0-07-554265-X*) McGraw.

Selected Writings. F. Erdei. Ed. by T. Huszar. 406p. (C). 1989. 92.00 (*963-05-4779-1*, Pub. by Akad Kiado HU) St Mut.

Selected Writings. Lady Gregory. Ed. by Lucy McDiarmid & Maureen Waters. (Illus.). 624p. 1996. pap. 13.95 (*0-14-018955-6*) Penguin.

Selected Writings. William C. Hazlitt. Ed. by Jon Cook. (World's Classics Ser.). 472p. 1991. pap. 10.95 (*0-19-281734-5*) OUP.

Selected Writings. William C. Hazlitt. Ed. & Intro. by Ronald Blythe. (Classics Ser.). 512p. 1982. pap. 12.95 (*0-14-043050-4*, Penguin Classics) Viking Penguin.

Selected Writings. William James. Ed. by Graham Bird. 1995. pap. 7.50 (*0-460-87557-4*, Everyman's Classic Lib) C E Tuttle.

Selected Writings. Thomas Jefferson. Ed. by Harvey C. Mansfield, Jr. LC 77-86039. (Crofts Classics Ser.). 144p. (C). 1979. pap. text ed. write for info. (*0-88295-120-3*) Harlan Davidson.

Selected Writings. Samuel Johnson. Ed. & Intro. by Patrick Crutwell. 576p. 1982. pap. 12.95 (*0-14-043033-4*, Penguin Classics) Viking Penguin.

Selected Writings. Raj Krishna. Ed. by Vijay Krishna. (Illus.). 480p. 1995. 39.95 (*0-19-563433-0*) OUP.

Selected Writings. Ernst Kurth. Ed. by Lee A. Rothfarb. (Studies in Music Theory & Analysis: No. 2). (Illus.). 275p. (C). 1991. text ed. 69.95 (*0-521-35522-2*) Cambridge U Pr.

Selected Writings. Karl Marx. Ed. by Lawrence H. Simon. 384p. (Orig.). (C). 1994. pap. text ed. 9.95 (*0-87220-218-6*); lib. bdg. 34.95 (*0-87220-219-4*) Hackett Pub.

Selected Writings. Vadim Mesyats. Tr. by Tanya Beylin et al. 112p. 1996. pap. 10.50 (*1-883689-45-7*) Talisman Hse.

***Selected Writings.** Vadim Mesyats. Tr. by Tanya Beylin et al. 112p. 1996. 30.50 (*1-883689-46-5*) Talisman Hse.

Selected Writings. Robert Musil. (German Library: Vol. 72). 320p. 1986. 29.50 (*0-8264-0305-0*); pap. text ed. 16.95 (*0-8264-0304-2*) Continuum.

Selected Writings. Charles Olson. Ed. by Robert Creeley. LC 66-27613. (Orig.). 1967. pap. 12.95 (*0-8112-0128-7*, NDP231) New Directions.

Selected Writings. Franz Oppenheimer. 1973. 300.00 (*0-8490-1022-5*) Gordon Pr.

Selected Writings. Josiah Royce. 1972. 59.95 (*0-8490-1023-3*) Gordon Pr.

Selected Writings. John Ruskin. Ed. by Kenneth Clark. 384p. 1992. pap. 12.95 (*0-14-043355-4*, Penguin Classics) Viking Penguin.

Selected Writings. John Ruskin. Ed. by Philip Davis. 360p. (Orig.). 1995. pap. 8.50 (*0-460-87460-8*, Everyman's Classic Lib) C E Tuttle.

***Selected Writings.** Rav S. Schwab. 330p. (C). Date not set. 17.95 (*0-935063-49-8*) CIS Comm.

Selected Writings. Jules Supervielle. LC 66-11415. (Orig.). (ENG & FRE.). 1967. 4.95 (*0-8112-0389-1*) New Directions.

Selected Writings. Henry David Thoreau. Ed. by Lewis Leary. (Crofts Classics Ser.). 160p. 1958. pap. text ed. write for info. (*0-88295-099-1*) Harlan Davidson.

Selected Writings. Mirjam Tuominen et al. Tr. by David McDuff from SWE. 160p. 9500. pap. 18.95 (*1-85224-218-3*, Pub. by Bloodaxe Bks UK) Dufour.

Selected Writings. Paul Valery. LC 50-7546. (ENG & FRE.). (C). 1964. pap. 12.95 (*0-8112-0213-5*, NDP184) New Directions.

Selected Writings. Voltaire. Ed. by Christopher Thacker. (Everyman Paperback Classics Ser.). 228p. (Orig.). (C). 1995. pap. 6.50 (*0-460-87624-4*, Everyman's Classic Lib) C E Tuttle.

Selected Writings, 8 vols. Roman Jakobson. Incl. Vol. 1. Phonological Studies. 2nd ed. 1971. 94.00 (*0-89925-072-6*); Vol. 2. Word & Language. 1971. 91.00 (*0-89925-073-4*); Vol. 4. Slavic Epic Studies. 1966. 91.00 (*0-89925-075-0*); Vol. 3. Poetry of Grammar & Grammar of Poetry. 1982. 178.00 (*0-89925-074-2*); Vol. 5. On Verse, Its Masters & Explorers. 1980. 118.00 (*0-89925-076-9*); 157.35 (*0-685-03448-8*) Mouton.

Selected Writings. Marquis DeSade. Tr. by L. St. Ives. 306p. 1954. reprint ed. pap. 25.00 (*0-87556-698-7*) Saifer.

Selected Writings. Marquis DeSade. Ed. by Gilbert Lely. 185p. 1954. reprint ed. pap. 25.00 (*0-87556-045-8*) Saifer.

Selected Writings. Robert Louis Stevenson. Ed. by Saxe Commins. LC 70-37157. (Essay Index Reprint Ser.). 1977. reprint ed. 46.95 (*0-8369-2523-8*) Ayer.

Selected Writings, Vol. 2. Christopher A. Anderson. LC 88-71661. (Illus.). 391p. (Orig.). 1991. pap. text ed. 15.50 (*0-931353-26-2*) Andersons Pubns.

Selected Writings: Aquinas. Robert P. Goodwin. 192p. (C). 1965. pap. text ed. 13.00 (*0-02-345050-9*, Macmillan Coll) P-H.

Selected Writings: Early Slavic Paths & Crossroads, Vol. 6, Pt. 1. Roman Jakobson. xxvi, 401p. 1985. Pt. I: Comparative Slavic Studies-The Cyrillo-Methodian Tradition (xxvi, 401 pg.). lib. bdg. 121.55 (*3-11-010605-1*) Mouton.

Selected Writings: Early Slavic Paths & Crossroads, Vol. 6, Pt. 2: Medieval Slavic Studies. Roman Jakobson. viii, 541p. 1985. Pt. 2: Medieval Slavic Studies (viii, 541 pg.). lib. bdg. 129.25 (*3-11-010606-X*) Mouton.

Selected Writings: Including Scarlet Letter. Nathaniel Hawthorne. Ed. by Gordon Roper. 480p. 1949. 12.95 (*0-87532-112-7*) Hendricks House.

Selected Writings & Correspondence Vol. I: Virginia's Agent During the American Revolution. Philip Mazzei. xlviii, 585p. Date not set. write for info. (*0-614-10128-X*) Am Inst Ital Stud.

Selected Writings & Correspondence Vol. II: Agent for the King of Poland During the French Revolution. Philip Mazzei. 802p. 1983. write for info. (*0-614-10129-8*) Am Inst Ital Stud.

Selected Writings & Correspondence Vol. III: World Citizen. Philip Mazzei. 623p. 1983. pap. write for info. (*0-614-10130-1*) Am Inst Ital Stud.

***Selected Writings & Prayers of Saint Alphonsus Liguori.** Alphonsus Liguori. LC 97-71961. 192p. (Orig.). 1997. pap. 6.95 (*0-7648-0025-6*) Liguori Pubns.

Selected Writings & Speeches. Edmund E. Burke. Ed. by J. Peter Stanlis. 1990. 21.75 (*0-8446-1094-1*) Peter Smith.

Selected Writings & Speeches. Abraham Lincoln. Ed. by T. Harry Williams. (University Classics Ser.). 334p. 1980. pap. 12.95 (*0-87532-136-4*) Hendricks House.

Selected Writings & Speeches of Alexander Hamilton. Ed. by Morton J. Frisch. 524p. 1985. write for info. (*0-8447-3553-1*); pap. 12.95 (*0-8447-3551-5*) Am Enterprise.

Selected Writings Eighteen Seventy-Seven to Nineteen Thirty. D'Arcy Power. LC 78-95632. (Illus.). x, 368p. 1970. reprint ed. 45.00 (*0-678-03750-7*) Kelley.

Selected Writings from a Connectionist's Psychology. Edward L. Thorndike. LC 76-94621. 370p. 1969. reprint ed. text ed. 59.75 (*0-8371-2570-7*, THWP, Greenwood Pr) Greenwood.

Selected Writings, George Herbert Mead. George H. Mead. Ed. by Andrew J. Reck. LC 80-27048. lxxii, 488p. (C). 1981. pap. text ed. 12.95 (*0-226-51671-7*) U Ch Pr.

Selected Writings in English & General Linguistics. Josef Vachek. (Janua Linguarum, Series Major: No. 92). 451p. 1976. text ed. 103.10 (*90-279-3024-4*) Mouton.

***Selected Writings in Medical Sociological Research.** Ed. by Michael Bloor. (Cardiff Papers in Qualitative Research). 222p. 1997. text ed. 55.95 (*1-85972-676-3*, Pub. by Ashgate UK) Ashgate Pub Co.

Selected Writings in Sociology & Social Philosophy. Karl Marx. 1963. pap. text ed. write for info. (*0-07-040672-3*) McGraw.

***Selected Writings of Andres Bello.** Andres Bello. (Library of Latin America). 400p. 1997. 25.00 (*0-19-510545-1*) OUP.

Selected Writings of Apollinaire. rev. ed. Guillaume Apollinaire. Tr. by Roger Shattuck from FRE. LC 72-145928. 1971. pap. 12.95 (*0-8112-0003-5*, NDP310) New Directions.

Selected Writings of Bertram D. Lewin, M. D. Ed. & Intro. by Jacob A. Arlow. LC 72-94802. (Illus.). 608p. 1973. 25.00 (*0-911194-02-9*) Psych Qtly.

Selected Writings of Blaise Cendrars. Blaise Cendrars. Ed. by Walter Albert. LC 78-14223. 273p. 1978. reprint ed. text ed. 35.00 (*0-313-21020-9*, CESW, Greenwood Pr) Greenwood.

Selected Writings of C. L. James. C. L. James. 1977. lib. bdg. 59.95 (*0-8490-2588-5*) Gordon Pr.

Selected Writings of Caroline Norton. Caroline S. Norton. LC 78-18828. 1978. 100.00 (*0-8201-1312-3*) Schol Facsimiles.

Selected Writings of Christine de Pizan: New Translations, Criticism. Ed. & Tr. by Renate Blumenfeld-Kosinski. LC 96-12764. (C). 1996. pap. text ed. 12.95 (*0-393-97010-8*) Norton.

Selected Writings of Cunningham Graham. Ed. by Cedric P. Watts. LC 80-70682. 140p. 1981. 28.50 (*0-8386-3087-1*) Fairleigh Dickinson.

Selected Writings of Edgar Allan Poe. Edgar Allan Poe. Ed. by E. H. Davidson. LC 56-13895. (C). 1956. pap. 11.56 (*0-395-05110-X*, Hill Stead Mus) HM.

Selected Writings of Eduard Bernstein, 1900-1921. Eduard Bernstein. Ed. & Tr. by Manfred Steger. LC 95-30963. 240p. (C). 1996. text ed. 49.95 (*0-391-03919-9*) Humanities.

Selected Writings of Edward S. Curtis. 3rd ed. Edward S. Curtis. Ed. by Barry Gifford. LC 76-7891. (Illus.). 192p. 1976. pap. 6.95 (*0-916870-00-6*) Creat Arts Bk.

Selected Writings of Edward Sapir in Language, Culture, & Personality. Edward Sapir. Ed. by David G. Mandelbaum. 1949. reprint ed. pap. 17.95 (*0-520-05594-2*) U CA Pr.

Selected Writings of Gertrude Stein. Gertrude Stein. 1992. 25.50 (*0-8446-6633-5*) Peter Smith.

Selected Writings of Gertrude Stein. Gertrude Stein. LC 74-19117. 768p. 1990. pap. 18.00 (*0-679-72464-8*, Vin) Random.

Selected Writings of Gyula Laziczius. Ed. by Thomas A. Sebeok. (Janua Linguarum, Series Minor: No. 55). 1966. pap. 49.25 (*90-279-0603-3*) Mouton.

Selected Writings of Hannah More. Ed. by Robert Hole. LC 95-21348. (Women's Classics Ser.). 304p. 1996. text ed. 39.95 (*1-85196-266-2*, Pub. by Pickering & Chatto UK) Ashgate Pub Co.

Selected Writings of Hans Denck. Ed. & Tr. by E. J. Furcha. LC 76-7057. (Pittsburgh Original Texts & Translations Ser.: No. 1). 1976. 5.50 (*0-915138-15-8*) Pickwick.

Selected Writings of Hans Denck 1500-1527. Hans Denck. Tr. by Edward J. Furcha. LC 89-28426. (Texts & Studies in Religion: Vol. 14). 563p. 1989. lib. bdg. 119.95 (*0-88946-833-8*) E Mellen.

Selected Writings of Henri Michaux. Henri Michaux. Tr. by Richard Ellmann. LC 68-25545. (ENG & FRE.). 1968. 10.95 (*0-8112-0105-8*, NDP264) New Directions.

Selected Writings of Hiram Bingham - Missionary to the Hawaiian Islands, 1814-1869: To Raise the Lord's Banner. Char Miller. LC 88-11790. (Studies in American Religion: Vol. 31). 550p. 1988. lib. bdg. 119.95 (*0-88946-675-0*) E Mellen.

Selected Writings of Holbrook Working. Chicago Board of Trade, Education Department Staff. (Readings in Futures Markets Ser.: Bk. 1). 1977. pap. 10.00 (*0-317-46965-7*, 52-35) Chicago Bd Trade.

Selected Writings of Isaac Mayer Wise. Ed. by David Phillipson & Louis Grossman. LC 71-83433. (Religion in America, Ser. 1). 1975. reprint ed. 31.95 (*0-405-00258-0*) Ayer.

Selected Writings of J. Potapenko, 3 vols., Set. J. Potapenko. 1976. lib. bdg. 350.00 (*0-8490-2589-3*) Gordon Pr.

Selected Writings of James Hayden Tufts. Intro. by James Campbell. LC 91-3193. 496p. (C). 1992. 45.00 (*0-8093-1714-1*) S Ill U Pr.

Selected Writings of James Weldon Johnson Vol. I: New York Age Editorials (1914-1923) Ed. by Sondra K. Wilson. 336p. 1995. 49.95 (*0-19-507644-3*) OUP.

Selected Writings of James Weldon Johnson Vol. II: Social, Political, & Literary Essays. Ed. by Sondra K. Wilson. 384p. 1995. 52.00 (*0-19-507645-1*) OUP.

Selected Writings of Jean Genet. Jean Genet. Ed. by Edmund White. (Ecco Companions Ser.). 1993. pap. 17.00 (*0-88001-420-2*) Ecco Pr.

Selected Writings of Jean Genet. Edmund White. LC 93-2408. (Ecco Companions Ser.). 1993. 27.50 (*0-88001-331-1*) Ecco Pr.

Selected Writings of Jeremy Bentham & John Austin see Utilitarianism

Selected Writings of Joaquin Miller. Joaquin Miller. Ed. by Alan Rosenus. LC 73-88918. (Primary Source Bks.). (Illus.). 1976. 18.95 (*0-913522-05-8*); pap. 12.95 (*0-913522-06-6*) Urion Pr CA.

Selected Writings of Joel Augustus Rogers. Joel A. Rogers. Ed. by Kinya Kiongozi. 100p. (Orig.). 1989. write for info. (*0-939841-04-5*); pap. write for info. (*0-939841-03-7*) Pyramid MD.

Selected Writings of John Marin. John Marin. (American Biography Ser.). 241p. 1991. reprint ed. lib. bdg. 69.00 (*0-7812-8267-5*) Rprt Serv.

Selected Writings of John Witherspoon. Ed. by Thomas P. Miller. LC 89-29994. 320p. (C). 1990. 29.95 (*0-8093-1469-X*) S Ill U Pr.

Selected Writings of Jonathan Edwards. rev. ed. Harold P. Simonson. 200p. (C). 1992. reprint ed. pap. text ed. 9.95 (*0-88133-718-8*) Waveland Pr.

Selected Writings of Judith Sargent Murray. Judith S. Murray. Ed. by Sharon M. Harris. (Women Writers in English 1350-1850 Ser.). 320p. 1995. 39.95 (*0-19-507883-7*); pap. 17.95 (*0-19-510038-7*) OUP.

Selected Writings of Julius Guttmann: An Original Anthology. Ed. by Steven Katz. LC 79-7175. (Jewish Philosophy, Mysticism & History of Ideas Ser.). 1980. lib. bdg. 37.95 (*0-405-12232-2*) Ayer.

Selected Writings of Lafcadio Hearn. Lafcadio Hearn. 576p. (C). 1988. reprint ed. pap. 12.95 (*0-8065-1107-9*, Citadel Pr) Carol Pub Group.

Selected Writings of Lu Xun, 4 vols. Lu Xun. (Studies in Chinese Literature). 1990. lib. bdg. 750.00 (*0-8490-4058-2*) Gordon Pr.

Selected Writings of Maurice Moonlitz, 2 vols., Set. Maurice Moonlitz. (Accounting History & Thought Ser.). 540p. 1990. reprint ed. text ed. 35.00 (*0-8240-3322-1*) Garland.

Selected Writings of Nichiren. Nichiren Daishonin. Tr. by Burton Watson from JPN. (Translations from the Oriental Classics Ser.). 508p. 1990. text ed. 49.50 (*0-231-07260-0*) Col U Pr.

Selected Writings of Ralph Waldo Emerson. 1965. pap. 5.95 (*0-451-52404-7*) NAL-Dutton.

Selected Writings of Ralph Waldo Emerson. Ed. by Brooks Atkinson. LC 92-50234. 880p. 1992. 22.00 (*0-679-60018-3*, Modern Lib) Random.

Selected Writings of Ralph Waldo Emerson. Ralph Waldo Emerson. Ed. by Brooks Atkinson. LC 83-42942. 930p. 1977. 14.95 (*0-394-60418-0*, Modern Lib) Random.

Selected Writings of Rosemary Ellis: In Search of the Meaning of Nursing Science. Ed. by Joyce J. Fitzpatrick & Ida Martinson. 152p. 1996. 44.95 (*0-8261-9400-1*) Springer Pub.

Selected Writings of Samuel Johnson. Samuel Johnson. LC 77-25885. 1977. 50.00 (*0-8201-1305-0*) Schol Facsimiles.

Selected Writings of Selma Fraiberg. Selma Fraiberg. Ed. by Louis Fraiberg. LC 86-23454. 728p. 1987. pap. text ed. 36.00 (*0-8142-0427-9*) Ohio St U Pr.

Selected Writings of Shoghi Effendi. rev. ed. Shoghi Effendi. 202p. 1975. pap. 1.00 (*0-87743-079-9*, 308-043) Bahai.

Selected Writings of Sidney H. Morse. Sidney H. Morse. 1977. lib. bdg. 59.95 (*0-8490-2590-7*) Gordon Pr.

Selected Writings of Sophronia Robinson Menke. Sophronia R. Menke. LC 93-80370. 97p. 1993. Incl. My Childhood Memories; Reflections from the Past--also written by Veronica Voss & William F. A. spiral bd. 20.00 (*0-317-05608-5*) J R Menke.

Selected Writings of Truman Capote. Truman Capote. 1963. 16.95 (*0-394-44467-1*) Random.

Selected Writings of Vahram Mavian, 1926-1983: A Unique Voice in Armenian Diaspora Literature. Vahram Mavian. Ed. & Tr. by Agop J. Hacikyan from ARM. Tr. by Arsene Mamourian from ARM. LC 92-21428. 296p. 1992. text ed. 89.95 (*0-7734-9198-8*) E Mellen.

Selected Writings of Walter Pater. Ed. by Harold Bloom. LC 81-17099. (Morningside Bk.). 304p. 1982. reprint ed. pap. text ed. 19.50 (*0-231-05481-5*) Col U Pr.

Selected Writings of William C. Owen. William C. Owen. 1977. lib. bdg. 69.95 (*0-8490-2591-5*) Gordon Pr.

Selected Writings of William Dwight Whitney. William D. Whitney. Ed. by Michael Silverstein. 1971. text ed. 35.00 (*0-262-19087-7*) MIT Pr.

Selected Writings on Agricultural Policy & Economic Analysis. Ed. by Frederick V. Waugh et al. LC 83-6963. 483p. 1984. reprint ed. pap. 137.70 (*0-7837-2908-1*, 2057546) Bks Demand.

Selected Writings on Art & Literature. Charles P. Baudelaire. Tr. & Intro. by P. E. Charret. 464p. 1993. pap. 14.95 (*0-14-044606-0*, Penguin Classics) Viking Penguin.

Selected Writings on Art & Literature. Denis Diderot. Tr. & Intro. by Geoffrey Bremner. 432p. 1994. pap. 12.95 (*0-14-044588-9*, Penguin Classics) Viking Penguin.

Selected Writings on Art & Literature. Denis Diderot. Tr. & Intro. by Geoffrey Bremner. 1995. 22.50 (*0-8446-6824-9*) Peter Smith.

Selected Writings on Asian Law. Chin Kim. xiv, 572p. 1982. lib. bdg. 37.50 (*0-8377-0741-2*) Rothman.

Selected Writings on Comparative & Private International Law. Chin Kim. LC 95-21620. xxxiii, 521p. 65.00 (*0-8377-0782-X*) Rothman.

Selected Writings on Computing: A Personal Perspective. Edsger W. Dijkstra. (Texts & Monographs in Computer Science). (Illus.). 272p. 1982. 83.95 (*0-387-90652-5*) Spr-Verlag.

Selected Writings on Femenism & Socialism. Lilly Braun. LC 86-45942. 256p. 1987. 12.95 (*0-253-35101-4*) Ind U Pr.

Selected Writings on Futures Markets: Basic Research in Commodity Markets. Chicago Board of Trade, Education Department Staff. (Readings in Futures Markets Ser.: Bk. 2). 1977. pap. 10.00 (*0-317-46966-5*, 52-36) Chicago Bd Trade.

Selected Writings on Futures Markets: Explorations in Financial Futures Markets. Chicago Board of Trade, Education Department Staff. (Readings in Futures Markets Ser.: Bk. 5). 1978. pap. 10.00 (*0-317-46970-3*, 52-86) Chicago Bd Trade.

Selected Writings on Futures Markets: Interrelations among Futures, Options, & Futures Option Markets. Ed. by Patrick J. Catania & Robert E. Whaley. (Readings in Futures Markets Ser.: Bk. VI). 416p. (C). 1992. 15.00 (*0-917456-03-3*) Chicago Bd Trade.

Selected Writings on Futures Markets: Research Directions in Commodity Markets, 1970-1980. Chicago Board of Trade, Education Department Staff. (Readings in Futures Markets Ser.: Bk. 4). 1984. pap. 10.00 (*0-317-46968-1*, 52-14) Chicago Bd Trade.

Selected Writings on Philosophy & Adult Education. 2nd ed. Ed. by Sharan B. Merriam. LC 95-24355. 332p. (C). 1995. pap. 29.50 (*0-89464-887-X*) Krieger.

Selected Writings on Religion & Society. Edward Bellamy. Ed. by Joseph Schiffman. LC 74-40. (American Heritage Ser.: No. 11). 139p. 1974. reprint ed. text ed. 45.00 (*0-8371-7359-0*, BEWR, Greenwood Pr) Greenwood.

Selected Writings on Soviet Law & Marxism. Piotr I. Stuchka. Ed. by Robert Sharlet & P. Beirne. LC 87-36773. 288p. (C). (gr. 13). 1988. text ed. 79.95 (*0-87332-473-0*) M E Sharpe.

Selected Writings on the State & the Transition to Socialism. Nikolai I. Bukharin. Ed. & Tr. by Richard B. Day from RUS. LC 82-851. 416p. (gr. 13). 1982. text ed. 74.95 (*0-87332-190-1*) M E Sharpe.

Selected Writings, 1909-1953, Vol. I. H. Reichenbach. Ed. by Maria Reichenbach & Robert S. Cohen. Tr. by Elizabeth H. Schneewind. (Vienna Circle Collection: No. 4a). 518p. 1978. lib. bdg. 187.00 (*90-277-0291-8*) Kluwer Ac.

Selected Writings, 1909-1953, Vol. II. H. Reichenbach. Ed. by Maria Reichenbach & Robert S. Cohen. Tr. by Elizabeth H. Schneewind. (Vienna Circle Collection: No. 4b). 446p. 1978. lib. bdg. 171.00 (*90-277-0909-2*) Kluwer Ac.

Selected Writings, 1950-1990. Irving Howe. 512p. 1990. 34.95 (*0-15-180390-0*) HarBrace.

Selected Writings, 1950-1990. Irving Howe. 1992. pap. 14.95 (*0-15-680636-3*, Harvest Bks) HarBrace.

Selecting a Basal Reading Program: Making the Right Choice. Douglas P. Barnard & Robert W. Hetzel. LC 88-51816. 103p. 1989. pap. 24.95 (*0-87762-633-2*) Technomic.

Selecting a Developer. David Nutter. Ed. by Mary McClean. 20p. (Orig.). 1983. pap. 13.00 (*0-317-04834-1*) Natl Coun Econ Dev.

Selecting a High-Performance Embedded Microprocessor. Jim Turley. 500p. 1995. 1,995.00 (*1-885330-05-7*) MicroDes Res.

Selecting a Pediatric Residency: An Employment Guide. American Academy of Pediatrics Staff. 110p. 1993. pap. 20.00 (*0-910761-47-7*) Am Acad Pediat.

Selecting a Proprietary Severity-of-Illness System. Edward C. Geehr. Ed. by Wesley Curry. 37p. (Orig.). (C). 1989. pap. text ed. 19.95 (*0-924674-03-2*) Am Coll Phys Execs.

Selecting a Superintendent. (Superintendent Career Development Ser.). 1979. 3.50 (*0-87652-047-6*, 021-00817) Am Assn Sch Admin.

Selecting a Thinking Skills Program. Joyce R. Banks. LC 90-72123. 120p. 1991. 24.95 (*0-87762-788-6*) Technomic.

Selecting Access Systems for Individuals with Physical Disabilities. Kathy S. Lee & Debra J. Thomas. 310p. 1990. pap. 50.00 (*0-8020-6695-X*) U of Toronto Pr.

Selecting an Ada Compilation System. Ed. by J. Dawes et al. (Ada Companion Ser.). 183p. (C). 1991. text ed. 57.95 (*0-521-40498-3*) Cambridge U Pr.

Selecting an Auditor. John S. Ostrom. Ed. by Deirdre M. Greene. LC 92-23093. 184p. 1992. 60.00 (*0-915164-86-8*) NACUBO.

Selecting an On-Site Manager, GAP19. 2nd ed. Thomas Burgess. 32p. (C). 1996. pap. 17.50 (*0-944715-46-X*) CAI.

Selecting & Appraising Archives & Manuscripts. F. Gerald Ham. (Archival Fundamentals Ser.). 106p. 1993. 25.00 (*0-931828-84-8*) Soc Am Archivists.

***Selecting & Evaluating a Referral Laboratory: Tentative Guideline (1991)** Contrib. by Robert R. Rickert. 1991. 75.00 (*1-56238-139-3*, GP9-T) Natl Comm Clin Lab Stds.

Selecting & Evaluating an Investment Manager. William T. Spitz. Ed. by Deirdre M. Greene. LC 92-17931. (Financial Management Guidebook Ser.: Vol. 1). 94p. 1992. 60.00 (*0-915164-85-X*) NACUBO.

Selecting & Installing Software Packages: New Methodology for Corporate Implementation. Jud Breslin. LC 86-12403. 260p. 1986. text ed. 55.00 (*0-89930-158-4*, BSG/, Quorum Bks) Greenwood.

***Selecting & Managing an Outsourcing Provider.** Lane S. Caruso. (Innovations Ser.: Vol. 3). (Illus.). 36p. (Orig.). 1996. pap. 39.95 (*1-57963-001-4*, A0103) Am Compensation.

Selecting & Storing Fuels & Lubricants. (Illus.). 55p. 1983. 7.00 (*0-89606-123-X*, 102) Am Assn Voc Materials.

Selecting & Using a Core-Reference Collection. 2nd ed. Margaret I. Nichols. 67p. (Orig.). (C). 1995. pap. text ed. 20.00 (*0-7881-2358-0*) DIANE Pub.

***Selecting & Working with a School Attorney: A Guide for School Boards.** NSBA Council of School Attorneys Staff. 142p. 1997. pap. text ed. 35.00 (*0-88364-209-3*, 06-162) Natl Sch Boards.

Selecting Benefits: A New Dimension to Sales Success. Vincent W Kafka. 10p. 1990. 7.95 (*0-913261-22-X*) Effect Learn Sys.

Selecting Business Partners for Success. Keith O. Nyman. LC 91-65740. 96p. (Orig.). 1991. pap. text ed. 12.95 (*0-9605826-1-4*) Staff Recrters.

Selecting College & University Personnel: The Quest & the Questions. Richard A. Kaplowitz. LC 86-70537. (ASHE-ERIC Higher Education Reports: No. 86-8). 113p. (Orig.). 1987. pap. 18.75 (*0-913317-35-7*) GWU Grad Schl E&HD.

Selecting Contract Types. rev. ed. Barbara Bowen & Tom Reid. Ed. by Anne M. Gibbs & Margaret G. Rumbaugh. 128p. 1990. pap. 37.45 (*0-940343-01-0*, TYPE) Natl Contract Mgmt.

Selecting, Designing, & Using Speech Recognizers. Wayne A. Lea. (Speech Technology Ser.). (Illus.). 400p. 1982. 74.00 (*0-686-37644-7*); student ed. 49.00 (*0-686-37645-5*) Speech Science.

Selecting Development Projects for the World Bank. Jean Baneth. LC 96-16613. (Discussion Papers: Vol. 322). 1996. 7.95 (*0-8213-3625-8*) World Bank.

Selecting Educational Equipment & Materials for School & Home. Association for Childhood Education International. Ed. by Joan Moyer. 1995. 15.00 (*0-87173-134-7*) ACEI.

Selecting Effective Insurance Agents. Didactic Systems Staff. (Simulation Game Ser.). 1973. pap. 26.25 (*0-89401-090-5*); pap. 35.00 (*0-89401-091-3*) Didactic Syst.

Selecting Effective People. Didactic Systems Staff. (Simulation Game Ser.). 1970. pap. 26.25 (*0-89401-087-5*); pap. 35.00 (*0-89401-089-1*) Didactic Syst.

Selecting Effective Treatments: A Comprehensive, Systematic Guide to Treating Adult Mental Disorders. Linda Seligman. LC 89-26975. (Social & Behavioral Science Ser.). 430p. 33.95 (*1-55542-232-2*) Jossey-Bass.

Selecting Electromechanical Drive Systems. A. Horodecki. (Studies in Production & Engineering Economics: No. 10). 140p. 1991. 131.25 (*0-444-98776-2*) Elsevier.

Selecting Ethnographic Informants. Jeffrey C. Johnson. (Qualitative Research Methods Ser.: Vol. 22). 96p. (C). 1990. text ed. 22.95 (*0-8039-3586-2*); pap. text ed. 9.95 (*0-8039-3587-0*) Sage.

Selecting Financial Services for Government. Government Finance, Officers Association Staff & Girard Miller. LC 84-80555. ix, 115p. write for info. (*0-89125-084-0*) Municipal.

Selecting Foster Parents: The Ideal & the Reality. Martin Wolins. LC 63-19855. 237p. reprint ed. pap. 67.60 (*0-685-20376-X*, 2029831) Bks Demand.

Selecting Investments for Your Retirement Account. 3rd rev. ed. Richard D. Glass. (Illus.). 109p. 1994. pap. 10.95 (*0-9638029-2-5*) Invest Horizons.

Selecting Library Materials. 3rd rev. ed. Arthur W. Swarthout. LC 74-10504. (Guide Ser.: No. 4). 16p. 1986. pap. 4.75 (*0-915324-07-5*) CSLA.

Selecting Managers: How British Industry Recruits. Ed. by Deirdre Gill. (C). 1980. 65.00 (*0-85292-272-8*, Pub. by IPM Hse UK) St Mut.

Selecting, Managing & Marketing Technologies. Jamieson A. McKenzie. Ed. by Jerry J. Herman & Janice L. Herman. LC 93-22349. (Road Maps to Success Ser.). 72p. 1993. pap. 11.95 (*0-8039-6054-9*) Corwin Pr.

Selecting Materials for Children & Young Adults: A Bibliography of Bibliographies & Review Sources. Association for Library Service to Children Staff. LC 80-12374. 80p. reprint ed. pap. 25.00 (*0-7837-5957-6*, 2045757) Bks Demand.

***Selecting Materials for School Library Media Centers.** Ed. & Compiled by Dona J. Helmer. 111p. 1993. 22.00 (*0-8389-7693-X*) ALA.

An Asterisk (*) at the beginning of an entry indicates that the title is appearing in BIP for the first time.

Selecting Media for Learning. 96p. 1974. pap. 10.95 (0-89240-022-6, 906); pap. 8.95 (0-685-00549-6) Assn Ed Comm Tech.

Selecting Models from Data: AI & Statistics IV. Ed. by P. Cheeseman & R. W. Oldford. (Lecture Notes in Statistics Ser.: Vol. 89). xvii, 485p. 1994. 59.95 (0-387-94281-5) Spr-Verlag.

Selecting, Preparing, & Developing the School District Superintendent. Ed. by David A. Carter et al. 176p. 1993. 75.00 (0-7507-0170-6, Falmer Pr); pap. 26.00 (0-7507-0171-4, Falmer Pr) Taylor & Francis.

Selecting Prison Sites: State Processes, Site-Selection Criteria, & Local Initiatives. David N. Ammons et al. LC 92-23147. 96p. 1992. pap. 14.95 (0-89854-158-1, HV8815.A44) U of GA Inst Govt.

Selecting Process Equipment. Donald Woods. 350p. 1994. text ed. 90.00 (0-13-805755-9) P-H.

Selecting Product Development Projects: Pioneering Versus Incremental Innovation Strategies. (Illus.). 31p. (Orig.). (C). 1993. pap. text ed. 20.00 (1-56806-685-6) DIANE Pub.

Selecting School Administrators. Donald F. Musella. LC 83-191790. (Informal Ser.: No. 54). 181p. reprint ed. pap. 51.60 (0-7837-0554-9, 2040895) Bks Demand.

***Selecting Software for Non-Profit Organizations & Trade Associations.** Sheldon Needle & June R. Jewell. 321p. (Orig.). 1995. pap. 99.00 (0-917429-17-6) CTS.

***Selecting Students for Training in Health Care: A Practical Guide to Improving Selection Procedures.** M. Bennet & R. Wakeford. (WHO Offset Publications: No. 74). 38p. 1983. 7.00 (92-4-170074-2) World Health.

Selecting Technologies for Sustainable Agriculture. Robert E. Hudgens. (Development Studies Paper). (Illus.). (Orig.). 1992. pap. 6.00 (0-933595-70-0) Winrock Intl.

***Selecting the Best Dog for You.** Chris Nelson. (Illus.). 64p. 1997. 12.95 (0-7938-0144-3) TFH Pubns.

Selecting the College Student in America: A Study of Theory & Practice. Habib A. Kurani. LC 79-176936. (Columbia University. Teachers College. Contributions to Education Ser.: No. 503). reprint ed. 37.50 (0-404-55503-9) AMS Pr.

Selecting the Form of a Small Business Entity. Harry J. Haynsworth, IV. 203p. 1988. suppl. ed. 92.00 (0-8318-0472-6, B472/B577) Am Law Inst.

Selecting the Form of a Small Business Entity, 1988 Supplement. Harry J. Haynsworth. 114p. (Orig.). 1988. pap. 39.00 (0-8318-0577-3, B577) Am Law Inst.

Selecting the Landscape Maintenance Contractor: Selecting the Landscape Maintenance Contractor. 3rd ed. James B. Cranford. (GAP Report Ser.: Vol. 12). (C). 1996. pap. 17.50 (0-944715-26-5) CAI.

Selecting the President: From Washington to Bush. 300p. 1992. 24.95 (0-87187-688-4) Congr Quarterly.

***Selecting the President: From 1789 to 1996.** Congressional Quarterly, Inc. Staff. LC 97-6398. 1997. write for info. (1-56802-312-X) Congr Quarterly.

***Selecting the Right Cat for You.** Dennis Kelsey-Wood & Eve Kelsey-Wood. (Illus.). 64p. 1997. 12.95 (0-7938-0207-5, RE-406) TFH Pubns.

Selecting the Right Form of Business: The Comprehensive Decision-Making Guide for the Business Advisor. Bruce Bernard. 384p. 1996. text ed. 55.00 (0-7863-1056-1) Irwin Prof Pubng.

Selecting the Right PC. Edmond Hong. Ed. by Susan P. Hagen. LC 92-73081. (Mastering Personal Computers Ser.: Vol. 1). 120p. 1992. pap. 12.95 (1-881994-00-7) East Comput Lab.

Selecting the Right Products & Service. Allan Sutherlin. 160p. 1992. pap. 19.95 (0-8442-3577-6) NTC Pub Grp.

***Selecting Thermoplastics in Engineering.** 2nd ed. MacDermott & Shenoy. LC 97-4020. (Plastics Engineering Ser.: Vol. 42). 328p. 1997. 125.00 (0-8247-9845-7) Dekker.

Selecting Traffic Signal Control at Individual Intersections. (National Cooperative Highway Research Program Report Ser.: No. 233). 133p. 1981. 9.20 (0-309-03158-3) Transport Res Bd.

Selecting Treatment Interventions: A Casebook for Clinical Practice in Child & Adolescent Managed Mental Health. John B. Mordock. 250p. (Orig.). Date not set. pap. 49.95 (1-884937-38-1) Manisses Communs.

***Selecting Wines for Food.** Ric Dunseth. 160p. (Orig.). 1997. pap. 12.95 (1-56550-064-4) Vis Bks Intl.

Selecting Your Accountant. Paul F. Rice. 8p. (Orig.). 1988. 3.95 (0-9620188-2-1) Lifestyle Group.

Selecting Your Financial Advisors: Keys to Choosing a Good Accountant, Lawyer, Securities Broker, Financial Planner & Other Sources of Financial Advice. Paul F. Rice. 52p. (Orig.). 1988. pap. 7.95 (0-318-23895-0) Lifestyle Group.

Selecting Your First Telescope. Sheldon Harrington. (Illus.). 16p. 1982. 4.00 (0-937707-06-6, IP 300) Astron Soc Pacific.

Selecting Your Lawyer. Paul F. Rice. 8p. (Orig.). 1988. 3.95 (0-9620188-1-3) Lifestyle Group.

Selecting Your Psychic, Vol. I: From Main Street to Wall Street. Victoria Weston. Ed. by Suzzane Bentz. 169p. (Orig.). 1989. per. 10.95 (0-9623198-0-5) O Dey Pub Inc.

Selecting Your Securities Broker & Financial Planner. Paul F. Rice. 8p. (Orig.). 1988. 3.95 (0-9620188-3-X) Lifestyle Group.

***Selectins: Initiators of Leukocyte Endothelial Adhesion.** Ed. by Dietmar Vestweber. 240p. 1997. text ed. 90.00 (90-5702-074-2, ECU75, Harwood Acad Pubs) Gordon & Breach.

Selection. Lucian. Ed. by M. C. McLeod. (Classical Texts Ser.). 320p. (C). 1991. text ed. 49.95 (0-85668-415-5, Pub. by Aris & Phillips UK); pap. text ed. 28.00 (0-85668-416-3, Pub. by Aris & Phillips UK) David Brown.

***Selection: Plant Resources of South-East Asia.** E. Westphal & P. C. Jansen. (PROSEA Ser.). (Illus.). 322p. 1989. 1,250.00 (90-220-0985-8, Pub. by Backhuys Pubs NE) Balogh.

Selection: The Mechanism of Evolution. Graham Bell. LC 95-17458. 688p. (gr. 13). 1996. text ed. 75.00 (0-412-05521-X); pap. text ed. 37.50 (0-412-05531-7) Chapman & Hall.

Selection Among Alternates in Language Standardization: The Case of Albanian. Janet Byron. (Contributions to the Sociology of Language Ser.: No. 12). 1976. pap. text ed. 35.40 (90-279-7542-6) Mouton.

Selection & Appointment of School Heads. 3rd ed. Eileen R. Driscoll. 1982. pap. 16.00 (0-934338-47-7) NAIS.

Selection & Breeding to Improve Some Tropical Conifers, 2 Vols., 1. J. Burley & D. C. Nikles. 1972. 110.00 (0-85074-026-6) St Mut.

Selection & Breeding to Improve Some Tropical Conifers, 2 Vols., 2. J. Burley & D. C. Nikles. 1972. 110.00 (0-85074-027-4) St Mut.

Selection & Care of Cleaning Equipment. American Institute of Maintenance Staff, Jr. 86p. 1982. pap. 9.95 (0-9609052-3-5) Clean Mgmt Inst.

***Selection & Design of Gear Generating Tools.** W. H. Bookmiller. (Technical Papers: Vol. 129.02). 1950. pap. text ed. 30.00 (1-55589-153-5) AGMA.

Selection & Design of Mixing Processes for Coagulation. (Illus.). 172p. 1994. pap. 62.00 (0-89867-737-8, 90641) Am Water Wks Assn.

Selection & Election. Ali Shariati. Tr. by Ali Asghar Ghasemy from PER. 12p. 1980. pap. 2.00 (0-941722-13-9) Book Dist Ctr.

Selection & Evaluation of Advanced Manufacturing Technologies. Ed. by M. J. Liberatore. (Illus.). vi, 324p. 1990. 95.95 (0-387-52656-0) Spr-Verlag.

Selection & Evaluation of Electronic Resources. Gail K. Dickinson. xi, 103p. 1994. pap. text ed. 21.00 (1-56308-098-2) Libs Unl.

Selection & Evaluation of Teachers. Dale Bolton. LC 72-10648. 234p. 1973. 31.00 (0-8211-0123-4) McCutchan.

Selection & Installation of Well Screens & Gravel Packs: Anthology. 96p. 1982. 6.25 (1-56034-042-8, K069) Natl Grnd Water.

Selection & Tenure of Judges. Evan Haynes. xix, 308p. 1981. reprint ed. lib. bdg. 30.00 (0-8377-0636-X) Rothman.

Selection & Use of Chemical Indicators for Steam Sterilization Monitoring in Health Care Facilities. 49p. 1988. pap. 90.00 (0-910275-87-4, TIR3-209) Assn Adv Med Instrn.

Selection & Use of Engineering Materials. 2nd ed. Charles. 251p. 1989. pap. 52.95 (0-7506-1549-4) Buttrwrth-Heinemann.

Selection & Use of Personal Sampling Pumps. R. M. Wagg et al. (C). 1992. 102.00 (0-905927-86-9, Pub. by H&H Sci Cnslts UK) St Mut.

Selection & Use of Preservative-Treated Wood. 104p. 1995. 24.95 (0-935018-75-1, 7299) Forest Prod.

Selection & Use of Wear Tests for Ceramics, STP 1010. Ed. by C. S. Yust & Raymond G. Bayer. LC 88-22170. (Special Technical Publication (STP) Ser.). (Illus.). 100p. 1988. pap. text ed. 29.00 (0-8031-1182-7, 04-010100-29) ASTM.

Selection & Use of Wear Tests for Coatings - STP 769. Ed. by Raymond G. Bayer. 179p. 1982. 21.00 (0-8031-0710-2, 04-769000-29) ASTM.

Selection & Use of Wear Tests for Metals - STP 615. Ed. by Raymond G. Bayer. 111p. 1977. pap. 10.75 (0-8031-0563-0, 04-615000-23) ASTM.

***Selection at the Top: An Annotated Bibliography.** Valerie I. Sessa & Richard J. Campbell. LC 97-8113. 1997. write for info. (1-882197-29-1) Ctr Creat Leader.

Selection Criteria & Ecological Consequences of Importing Natural Enemies. W. Kauffman. (Thomas Say Monographs). 117p. 1992. 22.00 (0-938522-42-6, TSP1) Entomol Soc.

Selection for Community Service Orders. Liz Hoggarth. 237p. 1991. text ed. 63.95 (1-85628-209-0, Pub. by Avebury Pub UK) Ashgate Pub Co.

Selection for Parole. Lloyd E. Ohlin. (Russell Sage Foundation Reprint Ser.). reprint ed. lib. bdg. 34.50 (0-697-00207-1) Irvington.

Selection for Secondary Education. Peter Gordon. 270p. 1980. text ed. 29.50 (0-7130-0157-7, Pub. by Woburn Pr UK) Intl Spec Bk.

Selection from Our Shelves: Books, Manuscripts & Drawings from the Rosenbach Foundation Museum. Clive E. Driver. (Illus.). 140p. 1973. pap. 13.25 (0-939084-08-2) R Mus & Lib.

Selection from the Best English Essays, Illustrative of the History of English Prose Style. Ed. by Sherwin Cody. LC 68-8448. (Essay Index Reprint Ser.). 1977. 23.95 (0-8369-0320-X) Ayer.

Selection from the Great English Poets. Ed. by Sherwin Cody. LC 76-128152. (Granger Index Reprint Ser.). 1977. 35.95 (0-8369-6179-X) Ayer.

Selection from the Great English Poets. Ed. by Sherwin Cody. LC 76-128152. (Granger Index Reprint Ser.). 576p. reprint ed. lib. bdg. 17.50 (0-8290-0516-1) Irvington.

Selection from the Menil Collection. 26p. 1971. pap. 5.00 (0-939594-43-9) Menil Collect.

Selection from the Writings of Joseph Needham. Joseph Needham. Ed. by Mansel Davies. LC 93-31507. 487p. 1994. lib. bdg. 48.50 (0-89950-903-7) McFarland & Co.

Selection I: American Drawings & Watercolors from the Museum Collection. 76p. 1972. pap. 3.50 (0-911517-33-2) Mus of Art RI.

Selection II: British Watercolors & Drawings from the Museum's Collection. Malcolm Cormack. LC 72-78344. 188p. 1972. pap. 6.50 (0-685-65902-X) Mus of Art RI.

Selection III: Contemporary Graphics from the Museum's Collection. Diana L. Johnson. LC 73-76521. 67p. 1973. pap. 5.00 (0-911517-35-9) Mus of Art RI.

***Selection in Natural Populations.** Jeffry B. Mitton. (Illus.). 272p. 1997. 65.00 (0-19-506352-X) OUP.

Selection in One-&-Two-Locus Systems. T. Nagylaki. (Lecture Notes in Biomathematics Ser.: Vol. 15). 1977. 35.95 (0-387-08247-6) Spr-Verlag.

Selection Index & Introduction to Mixed Model Methods. L. Dale Van Vleck. 512p. 1993. 69.95 (0-685-67836-9, SF105) CRC Pr.

***Selection Indices & Prediction & Genetic Merit in Animal Breeding.** N. D. Cameron. 200p. 1997. 40.00 (0-85199-169-6, Pub. by CAB Intntl UK) OUP.

Selection Indices in Plant Breeding. Robert J. Baker. 240p. 1986. 132.00 (0-8493-6377-2, SB123, CRC Reprint) Franklin.

Selection Interview: Some Reasons for Optimis see IPMA Assessment Council Monograph Series, Vol. I

Selection Interviewing for the 1990's. Drake Beam Morin, Inc. Staff. 57p. (Orig.). 1993. pap. 10.95 (1-880030-03-9) DBM Pub.

Selection Interviews. Robert Dipboye. (C). 1992. pap. 34.95 (0-538-80647-8, GJ64AA) S-W Pub.

Selection IV: Glass from the Museum's Collection. Hedy B. Landman. LC 73-94132. (Illus.). 144p. 1974. pap. 6.50 (0-911517-36-7) Mus of Art RI.

***Selection Mechanisms Controlling Biomass Distribution.** L. R. Mur et al. (Water Science & Technology Ser.: Vol. 32). 222p. 1995. 109.25 (0-08-042880-0, Pergamon Pr) Elsevier.

***Selection Methods in Plant Breeding.** Bos & Caligari. (Plant Breeding Ser.). (Illus.). 360p. 1995. text ed. 78.00 (0-412-55330-9, Chap & Hall NY) Chapman & Hall.

Selection of African Poetry. 2nd ed. Ed. by K. E. Senanu & T. Vincent. 320p. (C). 1990. pap. text ed. 6.36 (0-582-01683-5, 78584) Longman.

Selection of Air-to-Air Heat Recovery Systems. Ed. by G. Hamilton. (C). 1986. 105.00 (0-86022-183-0, Pub. by Build Servs Info Assn UK) St Mut.

Selection of American Art: The Skowhegan School. Bernard B. Shan. (Illus.). 1976. 5.00 (0-910663-11-4) ICA Inc.

Selection of Automatic Control Valves. EEMUA Staff. 1969. 125.00 (0-85931-087-6, Pub. by EEMUA UK) St Mut.

***Selection of Bearings for Gear Drives.** S. L. Crawshaw. (Technical Papers). (Illus.). (Orig.). 1940. pap. text ed. 30.00 incl. audio compact disk (1-55589-364-3) AGMA.

Selection of Behavior: The Operant Behaviorism of B. F. Skinner: Comments & Consequences. Ed. by A. Charles Catania & Stevan Harnad. (Illus.). 640p. 1988. pap. text ed. 39.95 (0-521-34861-7) Cambridge U Pr.

Selection of British Paintings. Sara Cannon et al. 32p. 1988. 6.00 (0-945192-00-2) USC Fisher Gallery.

Selection of College & University Presidents. Joseph F. Kauffman. LC 74-18134. 86p. reprint ed. pap. 25.00 (0-7837-1648-6, 2041942) Bks Demand.

Selection of Control Valves & Other Final Control Devices: Instructor's Guide. Les Driskell. LC 81-80514. (Instructional Resource Package Ser.). (Illus.). 54p. reprint ed. pap. 25.00 (0-7837-5151-6, 2044880) Bks Demand.

Selection of Current Najdi-Arabic Proverbs. Muhammad Al Sudais. 301p. (ARA.). 1993. 29.95 (0-86685-643-9, LDL6609, Pub. by Librairie du Liban FR) Intl Bk Ctr.

***Selection of Dazzling Scarves.** R. M. Vaughan. 96p. 1996. pap. 12.00 (1-55022-286-4, Pub. by ECW Press CN) Genl Dist Srvs.

Selection of Doses in Chronic Toxicity-Carcinogenicity Studies. Ed. by Harold C. Grice. (Current Issues in Toxicology Ser.). (Illus.). 130p. 1983. 37.95 (0-387-12845-X) Spr-Verlag.

Selection of Early Music from the Repertoire of the Society for Old Music (Musical Scores) Ed. by Matthew Steel & Nicholas Batch. Tr. by Audrey E. Davidson. 1993. pap. 20.00 (1-879288-40-0) Medieval Inst.

Selection of Emblems. Intro. by William A. McQueen. LC 92-22032. (Augustan Reprints Ser.: No. 155-156). 1972. reprint ed. 21.50 (0-404-70155-8, PR1209) AMS Pr.

Selection of English Carols. Ed. by Richard L. Greene. LC 77-13760. 279p. 1978. reprint ed. text ed. 59.75 (0-313-20002-5, GREC, Greenwood Pr) Greenwood.

Selection of European Folk Dances, 5 vols., 1. J. F. Richardson. 1965. pap. text ed. 4.20 (0-08-010833-4, Ed Skills Dallas) Elsevier.

Selection of European Folk Dances, 5 vols., 2. J. F. Richardson. 1966. pap. text ed. 4.20 (0-08-010842-3) Elsevier.

Selection of European Folk Dances, 5 vols., 3. J. F. Richardson. 1966. pap. text ed. 4.20 (0-08-011926-3) Elsevier.

Selection of European Folk Dances, 5 vols., 4. J. F. Richardson. 1971. pap. text ed. 4.20 (0-08-016190-1) Elsevier.

Selection of European Folk Dances, 5 vols., Vol. 5. J. F. Richardson. 1978. pap. text ed. 4.20 (0-08-021589-0, Pergamon Pr) Elsevier.

Selection of Folk Dances. Richardson. 1981. pap. 18.25 (0-08-026281-3, Pergamon Pr) Elsevier.

Selection of Greek Historical Inscriptions to the End of the Fifth Century B.C. rev. ed. Ed. by Russell Meiggs & David M. Lewis. 344p. 1989. pap. 35.00 (0-19-814487-3) OUP.

Selection of Hebrew Melodies, Ancient & Modern by Isaac Nathan & Lord Byron. Ed. by Frederick Burwick & Paul Douglass. LC 87-750758. (Illus.). 256p. 1988. 51.90 incl. digital audio (0-8173-0406-1); text ed. 39.95 (0-8173-0373-1); audio 11.95 (0-8173-0405-3) U of Ala Pr.

Selection of Historic American Papers on Concrete, 1876-1926. Ed. by Howard Newlon, Jr. LC 76-47294. (American Concrete Institute Publication Ser.: SP-52). 342p. reprint ed. pap. 97.50 (0-317-27231-4, 2025081) Bks Demand.

Selection of International Penmanship Systems. Katherine M. Koppenhaver & William Koppenhaver. (Illus.). 90p. (Orig.). 1992. pap. text ed. 10.00 (0-9632206-2-4) Foren Pubs Joppa.

Selection of Isadora Duncan Dances: The Schubert Selection, Written in Sutton Dance Writing. Sylvia Gold. Ed. by Valerie J. Sutton. 100p. (Orig.). 1996. 45.00 (0-914336-20-7) Ctr Sutton Movement.

Selection of Japan's Emergency Legislation. Tr. by William J. Sebald. LC 78-78384. (Studies in Japanese Law & Government). 177p. 1979. reprint ed. text ed. 59.95 (0-313-27036-8, U7036, Greenwood Pr) Greenwood.

Selection of Laboratory Aging Procedures for Asphalt-Aggregate Mixtures. Don Sosnovske et al. 89p. (Orig.). (C). 1994. pap. text ed. 15.00 (0-309-05762-0, SHRP-A-393) SHRP.

Selection of Library Materials for Area Studies, Pt. I: Asia, Iberia, the Caribbean & Latin America, Eastern Europe & the Soviet Union & the South Pacific. Ed. by Cecily Johns. LC 89-18502. 510p. 1990. 25.00 (0-8389-5328-X) ALA.

Selection of Library Materials for Area Studies, Pt. 2: Australia, Canada & New Zealand. Ed. by Cecily Johns. LC 89-18502. 110p. (Orig.). 1994. pap. text ed. 25.00 (0-8389-0631-1) ALA.

Selection of Library Materials in the Humanities, Social Sciences, & Sciences. Ed. by Patricia A. McClung. LC 85-20084. 1985. 22.00 (0-8389-3305-X) ALA.

Selection of Manuscripts Through the Ages-Un Choix de Manuscrits Parcourant les Siecles. Sandra Hindman. 164p. 1995. pap. 35.00 (0-9634255-3-6) Les Enluminures.

Selection of Memorable Objects in the Walters Art Gallery: A Picture Book. (Illus.). 1964. pap. 1.25 (0-911886-18-4) Walters Art.

Selection of Nineteenth Century Paintings in the Walters Art Gallery: A Picture Book. LC 66-58391. (Illus.). 1965. pap. 1.25 (0-911886-19-2) Walters Art.

Selection of Oils for High-Btu Oil Gas. H. R. Linden & E. S. Pettyjohn. (Research Bulletin Ser.: No. 12). iv, 48p. 1952. 5.00 (0-317-56810-8); suppl. ed. 1.50 (0-317-56811-6) Inst Gas Tech.

Selection of Oxidants in Synthesis: Oxidation at the Carbon Atom. Leland J. Chinn. LC 71-134781. (Oxidation in Organic Chemistry Ser.). 203p. reprint ed. pap. 57.90 (0-8357-3530-3, 2034521) Bks Demand.

Selection of Paintings from the Gerald Peters Collection. Gayle Maxon. LC 83-62810. (Illus.). 98p. 1983. pap. 25.00 (0-935037-05-5) G Peters Gallery.

Selection of Papers from Info II, 3 vols., Vol. 1. Ed. by Nicolaos S. Tzannes & Demetrios G. Lainiotis. 530p. 1980. lib. bdg. 133.00 (90-277-1140-2) Kluwer Ac.

Selection of Papers from Info II, 3 vols., Vol. 2. Ed. by Nicolaos S. Tzannes & Demetrios G. Lainiotis. 600p. 1980. lib. bdg. 133.00 (90-277-1129-1) Kluwer Ac.

Selection of Papers from Info II, 3 vols., Vol. 3. Ed. by Nicolaos S. Tzannes & Demetrios G. Lainiotis. 530p. 1980. lib. bdg. 133.00 (90-277-1143-7) Kluwer Ac.

Selection of Personnel for Clandestine Operations: Assessment of Men. rev. ed. Donald W. Fiske et al. (Illus.). 556p. 1993. reprint ed. pap. 38.80 (0-89412-202-9) Aegean Park Pr.

***Selection of Poems.** John Birtwhistle. 40p. 1989. pap. 9.95 (0-85646-215-2, Pub. by Anvil Press UK) Dufour.

***Selection of Poems of Laura Riding.** Laura Riding. Ed. & Intro. by Robert Nye. 1997. pap. 12.95 (0-614-29443-6) Penguin.

Selection of Poetry of the Afghans. H. G. Raverty. (C). 1988. 135.00 (1-85077-197-9, Pub. by Darf Pubs Ltd UK) St Mut.

Selection of Primary Sources for the History of Pharmacy in the United States: Books & Trade Catalogs from the Colonial Period to 1940. Nydia M. King. 123p. (Orig.). 1987. pap. 11.00 (0-931292-16-6) Am Inst Hist Pharm.

Selection of Production Processes for the Manufacturing Subsidiaries of U. S. - Based Multinational Corporations. Wayne A. Yeoman. Ed. by Stuart Bruchey & Eleanor Bruchey. LC 76-5044. (American Business Abroad Ser.). (Illus.). 1976. 19.95 (0-405-09309-8) Ayer.

***Selection of Representative TPH Fractions Based on Fate & Transport Considerations.** Ed. by John H. Gustafson et al. (TPH Working Group Ser.: Vol. 3). (Illus.). 80p. 1997. pap. 19.95 (1-884940-12-9) Amherst Sci Pubs.

Selection of Secondary School Headteachers. Colin Morgan et al. 192p. 1983. pap. 32.00 (0-335-10410-X, Open Univ Pr) Taylor & Francis.

Selection of Selves. Mimi Holmes. (Illus.). 55p. (Orig.). 1991. pap. 3.00 (0-926935-51-8) Runaway Spoon.

Selection of Spanish Masterworks from the Meadows Museum. Marcus Burke et al. LC 86-62402. (Illus.). 16p. (Orig.). 1986. pap. 4.00 (0-935937-01-3) Meadows Mus.

Selection of Surgical Gowns & Drapes in Health Care Facilities. AAMI Staff. (AAMI Technical Information Report Ser.). (Illus.). 43p. (Orig.). 1994. pap. 90.00 (1-57020-024-6, TIR11-209) Assn Adv Med Instrn.

Selection of Teachers in Large City School Systems. John Coulbourn. LC 72-176673. (Columbia University. Teachers College. Contributions to Education Ser.: No. 740). reprint ed. 37.50 (0-404-55740-6) AMS Pr.

Selection of Telegu Proverbs: Translated & Explained. M. W. Carr. 1986. 9.00 (0-8364-1874-3, Pub. by Usha II) S Asia.

S

Selection of the Correspondence of Linnaeus & Other Naturalists: From Original Manuscripts, 2 Vols., Set. James E. Smith. Ed. by Keir B. Sterling. LC 77-81132. (Biologists & Their World Ser.). (Illus.). 1978. reprint ed. lib. bdg. 108.95 (*0-405-10730-7*) Ayer.

Selection of the Correspondence of Linnaeus & Other Naturalists: From Original Manuscripts, 2 Vols., Vol. 1. James E. Smith. Ed. by Keir B. Sterling. LC 77-81132. (Biologists & Their World Ser.). (Illus.). 1978. reprint ed. lib. bdg. 54.95 (*0-405-10731-5*) Ayer.

Selection of the Correspondence of Linnaeus & Other Naturalists: From Original Manuscripts, 2 Vols., Vol. 2. James E. Smith. Ed. by Keir B. Sterling. LC 77-81132. (Biologists & Their World Ser.). (Illus.). 1978. reprint ed. lib. bdg. 54.95 (*0-405-10732-3*) Ayer.

Selection of the Poems of Laura Riding. Laura R. Jackson. Ed. & Intro. by Robert Nye. 164p. (Orig.). 1996. pap. 12.95 (*0-89255-221-2*) Persea Bks.

Selection of the Poetry of Sir Constantijn Huygens (1596-1687) Ed. by Peter Davidson & Adriaan Van der Weel. (Orig.). (C). 1995. pap. 39.50 (*90-5356-180-3*, Pub. by Amsterdam U Pr NE) U of Mich Pr.

Selection of the Political Pamphlets of Charles Bradlaugh 1865-1891. Charles Bradlaugh. LC 77-104611. 662p. 1970. lib. bdg. 57.50 (*0-678-00604-0*) Kelley.

Selection of the Social & Political Pamphlets of Annie Besant 1874-1890. Annie Besant. LC 78-114024. 526p. 1970. 57.50 (*0-678-00638-5*) Kelley.

Selection of the University Librarian. Ruth J. Person & G. C. Newman. 1988. pap. 25.00 (*0-918006-56-2*, OP#13) ARL.

Selection of Thomas Twining's Letters, 1734-1804: A Record of a Tranquil Life, 2 vols., Set. Ed. by Ralph S. Walker. LC 91-15414. (Studies in British History: Vol. 25). (Illus.). 880p. 1991. lib. bdg. 139.95 (*0-7734-9789-7*) E Mellen.

Selection of Treatment for Alcoholics. Ed. by E. Mansell Pattison. LC 79-620007. (NIAAA-RUCAS Alcoholism Treatment Ser.: No. 1). 1982. pap. 22.50 (*0-911290-47-8*) Rutgers Ctr Alcohol.

Selection of 16th & 17th-Century Woodcuts from Gesner & Topsell's Natural Histories see Curious Woodcuts of Fanciful & Real Beasts

Selection Principles for the Genetic Improvement of Animals. L. Dale Van Vleck. 512p. 1993. 80.95 (*0-8493-8762-0*) CRC Pr.

Selection Process for Capital Projects. Hans J. Lang & Donald N. Merino. LC 92-40500. (Engineering & Technology Management Ser.). 720p. 1993. text ed. 89.95 (*0-471-63425-5*) Wiley.

Selection Process for the National Endowment for the Arts Theatre Program: An Historical - Critical Study. Stephen M. Ayers. LC 91-4343. (American University Studies: General Literature: Ser. XIX, Vol. 26). 224p. (C). 1992. text ed. 38.95 (*0-8204-1510-3*) P Lang Pubng.

Selection, Social Origins, Education & Training of East Central European Office Corps. Ed. by Bela K. Kiraly & Scott W. Dillard. write for info. (*0-318-60324-1*) Brooklyn Coll Pr.

Selection, Social Origins, Education, & Training of the East Central European Officers Corps & Their Affects on Politics. Ed. by Bela K. Kiraly & Walter S. Dillard. (East Central European Militarism Ser.). 241p. 1988. text ed. 59.00 (*0-88033-138-0*) East Eur Monographs.

Selection Solution: Solving the Mystery of Matching People to Jobs. William C. Byham & Steven M. Krauzer. (Illus.). 216p. 1996. 17.95 (*0-9623483-3-3*) Dev Dimensions.

Selections. Lucretius. Ed. by G.E. Benfield & R. C. Reeves. 200p. 1967. 14.95 (*0-19-831768-9*) OUP.

Selections. Junior League of Huntsville Staff. 300p. 1988. reprint ed. boxed 15.00 (*0-9618113-1-5*) J L Huntsville.

Selections: Poems from Khayam, Rumi, Hafez, Shah Maghsoud. Tr. by Nahid Angha. 1991. pap. 14.95 (*0-918437-04-0*) Intl Sufism.

Selections: Selections. Aristotle. Tr. by Gail Fine & Terence H. Irwin. LC 95-31470. 650p. (C). 1995. pap. text ed. 19.95 (*0-915145-67-7*) Hackett Pub.

Selections: Selections. Aristotle. Tr. by Gail Fine & Terence H. Irwin. LC 95-31470. 650p. (C). 1995. lib. bdg. 47.95 (*0-915145-68-5*) Hackett Pub.

***Selections: Virginia Museum of Fine Arts.** Anne B. Barriault. Ed. by Rosalie A. West. Tr. by Kay M. Davidson. (Illus.). 132p. pap. 19.95 (*0-917046-47-1*) Va Mus Arts.

Selections & Essays. John Ruskin. 1988. reprint ed. lib. bdg. 69.00 (*0-7812-0370-8*) Rprt Serv.

Selections & Essays. John Ruskin. Ed. by Frederick W. Roe. LC 77-145274. 1971. reprint ed. 69.00 (*0-403-01189-2*) Scholarly.

Selections for Contracts - Statutes, Restatement Second, Forms. E. Allan Farnsworth, Jr. & William F. Young. 200p. 1992. pap. text ed. 13.95 (*1-56662-006-6*) Foundation Pr.

Selections from a Van Rensselaer Family Library, 1536-1799. Joyce Jackson & Melissa Perlman. 17p. 1979. pap. 2.50 (*0-943366-03-8*) Hist Cherry Hill.

Selections from American Authors. Samuel Eliot. (Notable American Authors Ser.). 1992. reprint ed. lib. bdg. 75.00 (*0-7812-2789-5*) Rprt Serv.

Selections from Ancient Irish Poetry. Tr. by Kuno Meyer. LC 75-28829. reprint ed. 27.50 (*0-404-13819-5*) AMS Pr.

Selections from Arthur D. Graeff's Scholla. Ed. by Larry M. Neff. LC 79-166008. (Pennsylvania German Folklore Ser.: Vol. 5). 1971. 15.00 (*0-911122-27-3*) Penn German Soc.

***Selections from Augustine.** pap. 2.00 (*0-8358-0053-9*) Upper Room Bks.

Selections from Barbour's Bruce, Set, Pts. 1 & 4. John Barbour. Ed. by Walter W. Skeat. (EETS, ES Ser.: No. 11). 1974. reprint ed. Set. 30.00 (*0-527-00225-9*) Periodicals Srv.

Selections from Berkeley. George Berkeley. LC 72-4216. (Select Bibliographies Reprint Ser.). 1977. reprint ed. 24.95 (*0-8369-6873-5*) Ayer.

Selections From Black, Set. Ed. by Jamestown Publishers Staff. 1989. pap. 38.00 (*0-8092-0008-2*) Jamestown Pubs.

Selections from Boiardo's Orlando Innamorato. Mark Staebler. (American University Studies: Romance Languages & Literature: Ser. II, Vol. 101). 485p. (C). 1989. text ed. 68.50 (*0-8204-0842-5*) P Lang Pubng.

Selections from Bologna, Civico Museo Bibliografico Musicale MS Q19 (Rusconi Codex), Pt. 1. Ed. by Richard Sherr. LC 88-753792. (Sixteenth-Century Motet Ser.: Vol. 6). 890303p. 1989. text ed. 95.00 (*0-8240-7906-X*) Garland.

Selections from Bologna, Civico Museo Bibliografico Musicale MS Q20. Ed. by Richard Sherr. LC 90-754886. (Sixteenth-Century Motet Ser.: Vol. 8). 280p. 1990. text ed. 95.00 (*0-8240-7908-6*) Garland.

Selections from Bologna, Civico Museo Bibliografico Musicalems Q19, Pt. 2. LC 88-753792. (Sixteenth-Century Motet Ser.: Vol. 7). 248p. 1989. text ed. 90.00 (*0-8240-7907-8*) Garland.

Selections from British Poets. Fitz-Greene Halleck. (Notable American Authors Ser.). 1992. reprint ed. lib. bdg. 75.00 (*0-7812-2990-1*) Rprt Serv.

***Selections from Brother Lawrence's the Practice of the Presence of God.** Lawrence. pap. 2.00 (*0-8358-0051-2*) Upper Room Bks.

Selections from Catullus. Gaius V. Catullus. Ed. by R. O. Lyne. (Cambridge Latin Texts Ser.). 48p. 1973. pap. text ed. 8.50 (*0-521-20267-1*) Cambridge U Pr.

Selections from Certain of His Books. Raymond Roussel. 1991. pap. 14.95 (*0-947757-26-0*) Serpents Tail.

Selections from Cultural Writings. Antonio Gramsci. Ed. by David Forgacs & Geoffrey Nowell-Smith. Tr. by William Boelhower from ITA. 464p. 1985. 32.00 (*0-674-79985-2*) HUP.

Selections from Cultural Writings. Antonio Gramsci. Ed. by Geoffrey Nowell-Smith. Tr. by William Boelhower. 464p. (C). 1991. pap. 17.95 (*0-674-79986-0*) HUP.

***Selections from Diwan of Rusafi.** (Arab Translation Ser.: Vol. 146). (Illus.). 150p. (Orig.). 1997. pap. 6.50 (*0-940307-52-9*) Wormhoudt.

Selections from Encyclopaedia of Accounting, 1903: Original Anthology. Ed. by George Lisle & Richard P. Brief. LC 77-87310. (Contemporary Accounting Thought Ser.). 1978. lib. bdg. 41.95 (*0-405-10923-7*) Ayer.

Selections from Erasmus...Principally from His Epistles. Desiderius Erasmus. Ed. by P. S. Allen. (College Classical Ser.). 610p. 1983. 25.00 (*0-89241-361-1*); pap. 12.50 (*0-89241-116-3*) Caratzas.

Selections from Five Roman Authors. H. Gould & J. Whiteley. (Latin Texts Ser.). 1972. 15.95 (*0-17-438518-8*) Focus Pub-R Pullins.

Selections from Five Roman Poets. H. Gould & J. Whiteley. (Latin Texts Ser.). 15.95 (*0-333-03329-9*) Focus Pub-R Pullins.

Selections from Fornander's Hawaiian Antiquities & Folk-Lore. Ed. by Samuel H. Elbert. (Illus.). 298p. 1959. pap. text ed. 12.00 (*0-87022-213-9*) UH Pr.

Selections from Free America & Other Works. Bolton Hall. 200p. 1987. pap. 8.95 (*0-915179-65-2*) Loompanics.

Selections from Ghalib & Iqbal. Tr. by K. N. Sud from URD. 106p. 1978. pap. 2.50 (*0-86578-220-2*) Ind-US Inc.

Selections from Goethe's Letters to Frau von Stein 1776-1789. Johann W. Von Goethe. Ed. & Tr. by Robert M. Browning from GER. (GERM Ser.: Vol. 48). (Illus.). viii, 308p. 1990. 47.00 (*0-938100-74-2*) Camden Hse.

Selections from Greek & Roman Historians. Ed. by Robinson. 341p. (C). 1957. pap. text ed. 25.00 (*0-03-009425-9*) HB Coll Pubs.

Selections from Greek Historians. Xenophon et al. Ed. by O. M. Fernald. (College Classical Ser.). viii, 407p. (C). 1983. reprint ed. lib. bdg. 32.50 (*0-89241-362-X*); reprint ed. pap. text ed. 17.50 (*0-89241-109-0*) Caratzas.

Selections from Hegel's Phenomenology of Spirit: Selections. Ed. by Howard P. Kainz. LC 93-9648. 200p. (C). 1994. 32.50 (*0-271-01075-4*); pap. 16.95 (*0-271-01076-2*) Pa St U Pr.

Selections from Hellenistic Philosophy. Ed. by Gordon H. Clark. LC 40-31306. 1964. pap. text ed. 11.95 (*0-89197-396-6*) Irvington.

***Selections from Hellenistic Philosophy.** 2nd rev. ed. Gordon H. Clark. (Trinity Papers: Vol. 52). 200p. 1997. pap. text ed. 16.95 (*0-940931-52-4*) Trinity Found.

Selections from Herodotus. Ed. by Amy L. Barbour. (Illus.). 1977. reprint ed. pap. 18.95 (*0-8061-1427-4*) U of Okla Pr.

Selections from His Historie of the World, His Letters, Etc. Walter Raleigh. (BCL1-PR English Literature Ser.). 212p. 1992. reprint ed. lib. bdg. 79.00 (*0-7812-7218-1*) Rprt Serv.

***Selections from "Home Alone"** Ed. by Carol Cuellar. 20p. (Orig.). (C). 1990. pap. text ed. 10.95 (*0-7692-0757-X*, VF1695) Warner Brothers.

Selections from Homer's Iliad. Homer. Ed. by Allen R. Benner. (Illus.). 522p. (GRE.). 1976. reprint ed. text ed. 37.95 (*0-89197-636-1*) Irvington.

Selections from Immortal Beloved. Ed. by Jeanette DeLisa & Dale Tucker. 44p. (Orig.). (YA). 1995. pap. text ed. 17.95 (*0-89724-666-7*, PF9517) Warner Brothers.

***Selections from John Wool.** (Great Devotional Classics Ser.). pap. 1.49 (*0-687-61038-9*) Abingdon.

Selections from Juan Montalvo. Tr. by Frank M. Spindler & Nancy C. Brooks from SPA. LC 84-23229. (Special Studies: No. 23). 123p. 1985. pap. 8.00 (*0-87918-056-0*) ASU Lat Am St.

Selections from Julius Caesar's Gallic War. John C. Sang. 96p. (Orig.). (C). 1991. pap. text ed. 18.50 (*0-8191-8043-2*) U Pr of Amer.

Selections from Les Miserables: Alto Sax. 4.95 (*0-7935-4898-5*, 00849018) H Leonard.

Selections from Les Miserables: Clarinet. 4.95 (*0-7935-4897-7*, 00849017) H Leonard.

Selections from Les Miserables: Flute. 4.95 (*0-7935-4893-4*, 00849016) H Leonard.

Selections from Les Miserables: Trombone. 4.95 (*0-7935-4900-0*, 00849020) H Leonard.

Selections from Les Miserables: Trumpet. 4.95 (*0-7935-4899-3*, 00849019) H Leonard.

Selections from Les Miserables: Violin. 4.95 (*0-7935-4901-9*, 00849021) H Leonard.

Selections from Lush Life & So near, So Far. 19.95 (*0-7935-3656-1*, 00673252) H Leonard.

Selections from Lyndon H. LaRouche, Jr. Lyndon H. LaRouche, Jr. Ed. & Tr. by Ray Wei. Tr. by Andy Chu. LC 92-62931. 140p. (Orig.). (CHI.). 1992. pap. 7.00 (*0-9621095-9-2*) Schiller Inst.

Selections from Managing the Human Climate. Philip Lesly. 178p. (Orig.). 1979. pap. 9.00 (*0-9602866-0-8*) Lesly Co.

Selections from Messiah, No. 348. George F. Handel. 64p. 1992. pap. 6.95 (*0-7935-1508-4*, 00102239) H Leonard.

Selections from Motetti C: (Venice, 1504) Ed. by Richard Sherr. LC 90-754886. (Sixteenth-Century Motet Ser.: Vol. 2). 320p. 1991. text ed. 90.00 (*0-8240-7902-7*) Garland.

Selections from Motetti De La Corona: Libro Secondo (Fossombre, 1519); Motetti de La Corona, Libro Tertio (Fossombre, 1519); Motetti de La Corona, Libro Quarto (Fossombre, 1519) Ed. by Richard Sherr. LC 92-29070. (Sixteenth-Century Motet Ser.: Vol. 5). 256p. 1992. text ed. 85.00 (*0-8240-7905-1*) Garland.

Selections from Motetti de la Corona Libro Primo: (Fossombrone, 1514) Ed. by Richard Sherr. LC 91-756727. (Sixteenth-Century Motet Ser.: Vol. 4). 160p. 1992. text ed. 65.00 (*0-8240-7904-3*) Garland.

Selections from Motetti Libro Quarto: (Venice, 1505) Ed. by Richard Sherr. LC 90-754886. (Sixteenth-Century Motet Ser.: Vol. 3). 302p. 1991. text ed. 90.00 (*0-8240-7903-5*) Garland.

Selections from "My Road to Rotary" Paul Harris. 58p. 1984. 3.00 (*0-915062-18-6*); 3.00 (*0-915062-19-4*) Rotary Intl.

Selections from Ovid's Metamorphoses. William S. Anderson & Mary P. Frederick. 1987. pap. text ed. 10.47 (*0-582-36748-4*, 72524) Longman.

Selections from Pindar. Gordon M. Kirkwood. LC 80-23801. 362p. (C). 1982. 28.00 (*0-89130-430-4*, 400307) Scholars Pr GA.

Selections from Pliny's Letters. Pliny. Ed. by M. B. Fisher & M. R. Griffen. LC 73-80489. (Latin Texts Ser.). (Illus.). 64p. 1973. pap. text ed. 11.95 (*0-521-20298-1*) Cambridge U Pr.

Selections from Political Writings 1921-1926. Ed. & Intro. by Quintin Hoare. 544p. write for info. (*0-85315-120-2*, Pub. by Lawrence & Wishart UK); pap. write for info. (*0-85315-421-X*, Pub. by Lawrence & Wishart UK) NYU Pr.

Selections from Public Health in Reports and Papers: American Public Health Association (1873-1883) Ed. by Barbara G. Rosenkrantz. LC 76-4065. (Public Health in America Ser.). 1977. reprint ed. lib. bdg. 34.95 (*0-405-09838-3*) Ayer.

Selections from Public Health Reports & Papers Presented at the Meetings of the American Public Health Association (1884-1907) An Original Anthology. Ed. by Barbara G. Rosenkrantz. LC 76-40657. (Public Health in America Ser.). 1977. reprint ed. lib. bdg. 21.95 (*0-405-09883-9*) Ayer.

Selections from "Pure Country" 32p. (Orig.). 1993. pap. 10.95 (*0-89724-029-4*, VF1998) Warner Brothers.

Selections from Quran & Hadith. Abdul H. Siddiqui. pap. 18.50 (*0-933511-52-3*) Kazi Pubns.

Selections from Ralph Waldo Emerson. Stephen E. Whicher. LC 61-16166. (YA). (gr. 9 up). 1972. pap. 11.56 (*0-395-05112-6*, RivEd) HM.

Selections from Recollections of a Lifetime. abr. ed. Ed. by Calvert W. Tazewell. LC 92-81592. 64p. 1993. reprint ed. pap. 8.00 (*1-878515-93-4*) W S Dawson.

Selections from Robert Landor see Robert Eyres Landor: A Biographical & Critical Sketch

***Selections from Romeo & Juliet.** Ed. by Jeannette DeLisa & Sy Feldman. (Illus.). 60p. (Orig.). (YA). 1997. pap. text ed. 18.95 (*0-7692-0019-2*) Warner Brothers.

Selections from Rousseau (1920) Christian Gauss. 232p. reprint ed. 12.00 (*0-911858-15-6*) Appel.

Selections from Science & Sanity. Alfred Kurzygski. Ed. by G. E. Janssen. 306p. (C). 1976. reprint ed. 10.95 (*0-937298-02-6*) Inst Gen Seman.

Selections from Sharing the Season, Vol. 2. Lorie Line. Ed. by Paul Maybery. (Illus.). 36p. (YA). 1993. pap. text ed. 9.95 (*0-9638000-0-0*) Time Line Prods.

Selections from Swami Vivekananda. Swami Vivekananda. pap. 5.95 (*0-87481-174-0*, Pub. by Advaita Ashrama II) Vedanta Pr.

Selections from Tennyson. Alfred Tennyson. Ed. by William C. DeVane & M. P. DeVane. 1940. 47.50 (*0-89197-398-2*) Irvington.

Selections from the American Art Collection of the New Jersey State Museum. (Illus.). 160p. (Orig.). 1983. pap. 15.00 (*0-938766-59-7*) NJ State Mus.

Selections from the Attic Orators: Antiphon, Andocides, Lysias, Isocrates & Isaeus. Ed. by Richard C. Jebb. 1981. 32.50 (*0-89241-360-3*) Caratzas.

Selections from the Autobiography of Elizabeth Oakes Smith. Elizabeth O. Smith. Ed. by Annette K. Baxter. LC 79-8815. (Signal Lives Ser.). (Illus.). 1980. reprint ed. lib. bdg. 23.95 (*0-405-12869-X*) Ayer.

Selections from the Black, Bks. 1-4. rev. ed. (College Reading Skills Ser.). 1989. pap. text ed. write for info. (*0-89061-538-1*) Jamestown Pubs.

Selections from the Black Bk. 1, 4 Bks., Bk. 1. rev. ed. (College Reading Skills Ser.). 1989. pap. text ed. 14.56 (*0-89061-482-2*) Jamestown Pubs.

Selections from the Black Bk. 2, 4 Bks. rev. ed. (College Reading Skills Ser.). 1989. pap. text ed. 14.56 (*0-89061-483-0*) Jamestown Pubs.

Selections from the Black Bk. 3, 4 Bks. rev. ed. (College Reading Skills Ser.). 1989. pap. text ed. 14.56 (*0-89061-484-9*) Jamestown Pubs.

Selections from the Black Bk. 4, 4 Bks., Bk. 4. rev. ed. (College Reading Skill Ser.). (C). 1989. pap. text ed. 14.56 (*0-89061-485-7*) Jamestown Pubs.

Selections from the Canzoniere & Other Works. Francesco Petrarch. Ed. & Tr. by Mark Musa from ITA. (World's Classics Ser.). 128p. 1986. pap. 7.95 (*0-19-281707-8*) OUP.

***Selections from the Cloud of Unknowing.** pap. 2.00 (*0-8358-0145-4*) Upper Room Bks.

Selections from the Collection of the Carolina Art Association. (Illus.). 127p. 1977. 4.50 (*0-910326-09-6*) Carolina Art.

Selections from the Correspondence of Theodore Roosevelt & Henry Cabot Lodge, 1884-1918. Theodore Roosevelt. (American Biography Ser.). 72p. 1991. reprint ed. lib. bdg. 59.00 (*0-7812-8327-2*) Rprt Serv.

Selections from the Correspondence of Theodore Roosevelt & Henry Cabot Lodge, 1884-1918, 2 Vols, Set. Ed. by Henry C. Lodge & C. F. Redmond. LC 72-146156. (American Public Figures Ser.). 1971. reprint ed. lib. bdg. 125.00 (*0-306-70129-4*) Da Capo.

Selections from the Correspondence of Theodore Roosevelt & Henry Cabot Lodge, 1884-1918, 2 vols., Set. Theodore Roosevelt. (History - United States Ser.). 1992. reprint ed. lib. bdg. 150.00 (*0-7812-6221-6*) Rprt Serv.

Selections from the Court Reports Originally Published in the Boston Morning Post from 1834 to 1837. Ed. by Robert M. Fogelson. LC 74-3850. (Criminal Justice in America Ser.). 1974. reprint ed. 23.95 (*0-405-06166-8*) Ayer.

Selections from the Critical Writings of Edgar Allan Poe. Ed. by Frederick C. Prescott. 425p. (C). 1981. reprint ed. 50.00 (*0-87752-182-4*) Gordian.

Selections from the Decorative Arts in the J. Paul Getty Museum. Gillian Wilson. LC 82-681807. (Illus.). 116p. 1983. pap. 29.95 (*0-89236-050-X*, J P Getty Museum) J P Getty Trust.

Selections from the Distribution & Abundance of Animals. Herbert G. Andrewartha & L. C. Birch. LC 82-6948. (Illus.). 288p. (C). 1982. pap. text ed. 14.95 (*0-226-02032-0*); lib. bdg. 30.00 (*0-226-02031-2*) U Ch Pr.

Selections from "The Eagle & the Serpent" & "Nationality" J. B. Barnhill & John E. McCall. (Men & Movements in the History & Philosophy of Anarchism Ser.). 1979. lib. bdg. 34.50 (*0-87700-286-X*) Revisionist Pr.

Selections from the Economic History of the United States 1765-1860: With Introductory Essays. Guy S. Callender. LC 65-19646. (Reprints of Economic Classics Ser.). xviii, 809p. 1965. reprint ed. 57.50 (*0-678-00080-8*) Kelley.

Selections from the Edward Albee Collection. Edward Albee & David S. Rubin. LC 88-82766. (Illus.). 28p. (Orig.). 1988. pap. text ed. 8.00 (*0-941972-07-0*) Freedman.

Selections from the Edward-Dean Museum of Decorative Arts. Ed. by Julius Kaplan & Janice R. Holmlund. (Illus.). 63p. 1984. per. 7.00 (*0-945486-02-2*) CSU SBRVFAM.

Selections from the Essays. Thomas H. Huxley. Ed. by Alburey Castell. (Crofts Classics Ser.). 128p. 1948. pap. text ed. write for info. (*0-88295-043-6*) Harlan Davidson.

Selections from the Essays. Michel de Montaigne. Ed. & Tr. by Donald M. Frame. (Crofts Classics Ser.). 144p. 1943. pap. text ed. write for info. (*0-88295-105-X*) Harlan Davidson.

Selections from the Estate of Jozef Gabryel Bakos: (1891-1977) Ed. by Agnes Tatarka. LC 92-62202. (Illus.). 48p. 1992. pap. 15.00 (*0-935037-48-9*) G Peters Gallery.

Selections from the Family Papers Preserved at Caldwell, 2 pts. in 3 vols., Set. William Mure. LC 70-173006. (Maitland Club, Glasgow. Publications: No. 71). reprint ed. 105.00 (*0-404-53091-5*) AMS Pr.

Selections from the Federalist. Alexander Hamilton et al. Ed. by Henry S. Commager. (Crofts Classics Ser.). 160p. 1949. pap. text ed. write for info. (*0-88295-041-X*) Harlan Davidson.

Selections from the Fiddler on the Roof: Alto Sax. Ed. by Carol Cuellar. 20p. (Orig.). 1995. pap. text ed. 4.95 (*0-89724-677-2*, IF9523) Warner Brothers.

Selections from the Fiddler on the Roof: Clarinet. Ed. by Carol Cuellar. 20p. (Orig.). 1995. pap. text ed. 4.95 (*0-89724-675-6*, IF9521) Warner Brothers.

Selections from the Fiddler on the Roof: Piano Accompaniment. Ed. by Carol Cuellar. 40p. (Orig.). 1995. pap. text ed. 6.95 (*0-89724-673-X*, MF9535) Warner Brothers.

Selections from the Fiddler on the Roof: Trombone. Ed. by Carol Cuellar. 20p. (Orig.). 1995. pap. text ed. 4.95 (*0-89724-679-9*, IF9525) Warner Brothers.

An Asterisk (*) at the beginning of an entry indicates that the title is appearing in BIP for the first time.

Selections from the Frederick Weisman Co. Collection of Southern California. Museum Studies Class of Nineteen Seventy-Eight Staff. (Illus.). 64p. (Orig.). (C). 1978. pap. text ed. 35.00 (*0-936270-11-X*) CA St U LB Art.

Selections from the Greek Lyric Poets. Ed. by Henry M. Tyler. 1983. 32.50 (*0-89241-363-8*); pap. 17.00 (*0-89241-120-1*) Caratzas.

Selections from the Greek Papyri. Ed. & Tr. by George Milligan. LC 76-103654. (Select Bibliographies Reprint Ser.). 1977. 21.95 (*0-8369-5154-9*) Ayer.

Selections from the Gutter: Portraits from the Jazz Record. Ed. by Art Hodes & Chadwick Hansen. LC 75-7193. 1977. pap. 14.00 (*0-520-03719-7*) U CA Pr.

Selections from the Health-Education Series: An Original Anthology. Ed. by Barbara G. Rosenkrantz. LC 76-40664. (Public Health in America Ser.). 1977. reprint ed. lib. bdg. 17.95 (*0-405-09873-1*) Ayer.

Selections from the Himalaya: Aspects of Change. Ed. by J. S. Lall. (Oxford India Paperbacks Ser.). (Illus.). 220p. 1995. pap. 14.95 (*0-19-563263-X*) OUP.

Selections from the Histories. Tacitus. Ed. by P. V. Jones. (Cambridge Latin Texts Ser.). (Illus.). 48p. 1974. pap. 7.95 (*0-521-20435-6*) Cambridge U Pr.

Selections from the Husia: Sacred Wisdom from Ancient Egypt. Maulana Karenga. 125p. 1984. 19.95 (*0-943412-05-6*); pap. 9.95 (*0-943412-06-4*) Univ Sankore Pr.

Selections from the Irvine Museum. Jean Stern et al. LC 92-75559. 35.00 (*0-9635468-0-5*); pap. 17.50 (*0-9635468-1-3*) Irvine Mus.

Selections from the Joseph L. Schulman Collection. (Illus.). 47p. 1975. pap. 5.00 (*0-317-13581-3*) Wadsworth Atheneum.

***Selections from the Journal & Letters of George Fox.** pap. 2.00 (*0-8358-0058-X*) Upper Room Bks.

***Selections from the Journal & Letters of Henry Martyn.** pap. 2.00 (*0-8358-0121-7*) Upper Room Bks.

***Selections from the Journal of Francis Asbury.** pap. 2.00 (*0-8358-0067-9*) Upper Room Bks.

***Selections from the Journal of John Wesley.** pap. 2.00 (*0-8358-0225-6*) Upper Room Bks.

***Selections from the Journal of John Woolman.** pap. 2.00 (*0-8358-0100-4*) Upper Room Bks.

Selections from the Journal of the Massachusetts Association of Boards of Health, 1891-1904: An Original Anthology. Ed. by Barbara G. Rosenkrantz. LC 76-40669. (Public Health in America Ser.). 1977. lib. bdg. 41.95 (*0-405-09878-2*) Ayer.

Selections from the Journals. Dorothy Wordsworth. Ed. by Paul Hamilton. LC 92-28495. (Women's Classics Ser.). (C). 1992. 55.00 (*0-8147-9259-6*) NYU Pr.

Selections from the Journals. Henry David Thoreau. Ed. by Walter Harding. LC 95-12191. (Thrift Editions Ser.). 128p. (Orig.). 1995. reprint ed. pap. text ed. 1.00 (*0-486-28760-2*) Dover.

Selections from the Journeys - Selecciones de las Jornadas. 3rd ed. Nelson A. Ossorio. (Illus.). 140p. (Orig.). (ENG & SPA.). 1994. 14.95 (*1-56721-088-0*) Twenty-Fifth Cent Pr.

Selections from the Julian & Irma Brody Collection. Christopher D. Roy. LC 88-70384. (Illus.). 40p. (Orig.). 1988. pap. 10.00 (*0-9614615-3-5*) Edmundson.

Selections from the Koran. Sirdar Ikbal Ali Shah. 1980. 19.00 (*0-900860-85-5*, Pub. by Octagon Pr UK) ISHK.

***Selections from the Letters of John Wesley.** pap. 2.00 (*0-8358-0060-1*) Upper Room Bks.

Selections from the Letters of Robert Southey, 4 Vols, Set. Robert Southey. Ed. by John W. Warter. LC 77-175992. reprint ed. 306.00 (*0-404-07760-9*) AMS Pr.

Selections from the Letters of Thomas Sergeant Perry. Thomas S. Perry. (American Biography Ser.). 255p. 1991. reprint ed. lib. bdg. 69.00 (*0-7812-8312-4*) Rprt Serv.

Selections from the Letters of Thomas Sergeant Perry. Thomas S. Perry. (BCL1-PS American Literature Ser.). 255p. 1992. reprint ed. lib. bdg. 79.00 (*0-7812-6830-3*) Rprt Serv.

Selections from the Letters of Thomas Sergeant Perry. Thomas S. Perry. Ed. by Edwin Arlington Robinson. LC 78-131797. 1971. reprint ed. 25.00 (*0-403-00684-8*) Scholarly.

Selections from the Literature of American Biogeography. LC 73-17844. (Natural Sciences in America Ser.). (Illus.). 512p. 1974. 35.95 (*0-405-05766-0*) Ayer.

Selections from the M. & M. Karolik Collection of American Painting, 1815-1865. Lucretia H. Giese & Laura C. Luckey. LC 75-39918. (Illus.). 1976. pap. 3.50 (*0-87846-095-0*) Mus Fine Arts Boston.

Selections from the Major Writings on Scepticism, Man, & God: Selections from the Major Writings on Scepticism, Man, & God. rev. ed. Sextus Empiricus. Ed. by Phillip P. Hallie. Tr. by Sanford G. Etheridge from GRE. LC 85-27059. (HPC Classics Ser.). 256p. (C). 1985. reprint ed. pap. 7.95 (*0-87220-006-X*); reprint ed. lib. bdg. 32.95 (*0-87220-007-8*) Hackett Pub.

Selections from the New Testament in Chinese. John W. Chu. 1966. 9.95 (*0-88710-083-X*); audio write for info. (*0-88710-084-8*) Yale Far Eastern Pubns.

Selections from the Observator. Roger L'Estrange. LC 92-24819. (Augustan Reprints Ser.: No. 141). 1970. reprint ed. 14.50 (*0-404-70141-8*, DA452) AMS Pr.

Selections from the Permanent Collection of the Arkansas Arts Center Foundation. Irma B. Jaffe & Yvonne Korshak. 176p. 1983. pap. 22.00 (*0-9612750-0-6*) Arkansas Art Ctr.

Selections from the Permanent Collection of the San Diego Museum of Contemporary Art. Pref. by Hugh Davies. LC 90-61679. (Illus.). 120p. (C). 1990. text ed. 35.00 (*0-934418-36-5*) Mus Contemp Art.

Selections from the Permanent Collection of the Springfield Art Museum. Edgar A. Albin et al. Ed. by William C. Landwehr. LC 80-53333. 100p. (Orig.). 1980. pap. text ed. 9.95 (*0-934306-03-6*) Springfield.

Selections from the Piano Teacher, 1958-1963: A Collection of Articles from the Piano Teacher's First Five Years. Piano Teacher Staff. Ed. by Roberta Savler. LC 64-57578. 136p. reprint ed. pap. 38.80 (*0-317-10057-2*, 2005327) Bks Demand.

Selections from the Poems of John Greenleaf Whittier: Fifty-Four of His Poems with Notes & Biographical Sketch. Ed. by Wilbert F. Barrett. 142p. 1983. reprint ed. pap. 6.00 (*1-878651-04-8*) HPL Pr.

Selections from the Poems of Sir Walter Scott. Walter Scott. (BCL1-PR English Literature Ser.). 196p. 1992. reprint ed. lib. bdg. 69.00 (*0-7812-7640-3*) Rprt Serv.

Selections from the Poetical Literature of the West. Ed. by William D. Gallagher. LC 68-29083. 1968. reprint ed. 50.00 (*0-8201-1019-1*) Schol Facsimiles.

***Selections from the Print Collection of John Huseby.** Deborah Leveton. (Illus.). 26p. 1995. pap. 7.00 (*0-614-31047-4*) Edmundson.

Selections from the Prison Notebooks. Ed. by Quintin Hoare & Geoffrey N. Smith. 580p. pap. write for info. (*0-85315-280-2*, Pub. by Lawrence & Wishart UK) NYU Pr.

Selections from the Qur'an. O. P. Ghai. 88p. 1992. 13.95 (*81-207-1379-6*) Apt Bks.

Selections from the Report on the Scientific Results of the Voyage of H.M.S. Challenger During the Years 1872-76. John Murray. Ed. by Frank N. Egerton, 3rd. LC 77-74242. (History of Ecology Ser.). (Illus.). 1978. reprint ed. lib. bdg. 21.95 (*0-405-10411-1*) Ayer.

Selections from the Second International Interdisciplinary Congress on Women. Ed. by R. Duelli Klein et al. (Illus.). 100p. 1988. 25.00 (*0-08-031815-0*, Pub. by PPL UK) Elsevier.

Selections from the Septuagint. Ed. by F. C. Conybeare & George Stock. (College Classical Ser.). vi, 313p. (C). 1981. reprint ed. pap. 17.00 (*0-89241-114-7*); reprint ed. lib. bdg. 32.50 (*0-89241-366-2*) Caratzas.

Selections from the Shui-Hu Chuan. Ed. by James I. Crump, Jr. 1947. audio write for info. (*0-88710-086-4*) Yale Far Eastern Pubns.

Selections from the Sound of Music. Richard Rodgers & Oscar Hammerstein. 16p. 1981. pap. 5.95 (*0-7935-0887-8*, 00301932) H Leonard.

Selections from the Spira Collection: An Exhibition at George Eastman House Sept. 26, 1980 - Jan. 11, 1981. Philip L. Condax. (Illus.). 24p. (Orig.). 1981. pap. 4.00 (*0-935398-04-X*) G Eastman Hse.

Selections from the Symbolical Poems of William Blake. William Blake. Ed. by F. E. Pierce. 1915. 49.50 (*0-686-51308-8*) Elliots Bks.

Selections from the Tatler & the Spectator. Ed. by Angus Ross. 1988. pap. 7.95 (*0-14-043298-1*, Penguin Classics) Viking Penguin.

Selections from "The Tatler" & "The Spectator" 2nd ed. Steele Addison. Ed. by Robert J. Allen. 452p. (C). 1970. pap. text ed. 23.75 (*0-03-080790-5*) HB Coll Pubs.

Selections from The Thoughts. Blaise Pascal. Ed. & Tr. by Arthur H. Beattie. (Crofts Classics Ser.). 144p. 1965. pap. text ed. write for info. (*0-88295-065-7*) Harlan Davidson.

Selections from the Unpublished Writings of Jonathan Edwards. Ed. by Alexander Grosart. 209p. 1992. reprint ed. 20.95 (*1-877611-43-3*) Soli Deo Gloria.

Selections from the Upanishads & the Tao Te King. Tr. by Charles Johnston & Lionel Giles. 142p. 1951. 4.00 (*0-938998-15-3*) Theosophy.

Selections from the Upanishads & The Tao Te King. Tr. by Charles Johnston & Lionel Giles. 142p. 1951. reprint ed. 3.00 (*0-317-00027-6*) Cunningham Pr.

Selections from the Wealth of Nations. Adam Smith. Ed. by George J. Stigler. (Crofts Classics Ser.). 128p. 1957. pap. text ed. write for info. (*0-88295-093-2*) Harlan Davidson.

Selections from the William Faulkner Collection of Louis Daniel Brodsky: A Descriptive Catalogue. Robert W. Hamblin & Louis D. Brodsky. LC 79-15031. 191p. reprint ed. pap. 54.50 (*0-317-28911-X*, 2020270) Bks Demand.

Selections from the Wizard of Oz: Alto Sax. Ed. by Carol Cuellar. (Illus.). 16p. (Orig.). 1995. pap. text ed. 4.95 (*0-89724-684-5*, IF9529) Warner Brothers.

Selections from the Wizard of Oz: Clarinet. Ed. by Carol Cuellar. (Illus.). 16p. (Orig.). 1995. pap. text ed. 4.95 (*0-89724-682-9*, IF9527) Warner Brothers.

Selections from the Wizard of Oz: Flute. Ed. by Carol Cuellar. (Illus.). 16p. (Orig.). 1995. pap. text ed. 4.95 (*0-89724-681-0*, IF9526) Warner Brothers.

Selections from the Wizard of Oz: Piano Accompaniment. Ed. by Carol Cuellar. (Illus.). 28p. (Orig.). 1995. pap. text ed. 6.95 (*0-89724-680-2*, MF9536) Warner Brothers.

Selections from the Wizard of Oz: Tenor Sax. Ed. by Carol Cuellar. (Illus.). 16p. (Orig.). 1995. pap. text ed. 4.95 (*0-89724-685-3*, IF9530) Warner Brothers.

Selections from the Wizard of Oz: Trombone. Ed. by Carol Cuellar. (Illus.). 16p. (Orig.). 1995. pap. text ed. 4.95 (*0-89724-686-1*, IF9531) Warner Brothers.

Selections from the Wizard of Oz: Trumpet. Ed. by Carol Cuellar. (Illus.). 16p. (Orig.). 1995. pap. text ed. 4.95 (*0-89724-683-7*, IF9528) Warner Brothers.

Selections from "The Woman Question in Europe" Ed. by Theodore Stanton. LC 73-22232. 1974. text ed. 27.50 (*0-8422-5158-8*); pap. text ed. 6.95 (*0-8422-0387-7*) Irvington.

Selections from the Works of Fourier. C. Fourier & C. Gide. 1972. 250.00 (*0-87968-023-7*) Gordon Pr.

Selections from the Works of Su-Tung-P'o (A. D. 1036-1101) Su Shih. Tr. by Cyril D. Clark. (Illus.). reprint ed. 34.50 (*0-404-56961-7*) AMS Pr.

***Selections from the World's Greatest Short Stories.** Sherwin Cody. 412p. 1970. 23.95 (*0-8369-3304-4*) Ayer.

***Selections from the Writings of Abdul-Baha.** Abdul-Baha & Universal House of Justice Staff. LC 96-29279. 1996. write for info. (*0-87743-251-1*) Bahai.

***Selections from the Writings of Bernard of Clairvaux.** pap. 2.00 (*0-8358-0142-X*) Upper Room Bks.

***Selections from the Writings of Dietrich Bonhoeffer.** pap. 2.00 (*0-8358-0222-1*) Upper Room Bks.

Selections from the Writings of E. G. Browne on the Babi & Baha'i Religions. Moojan Momen. 528p. 1987. 36.50 (*0-85398-246-5*); pap. 19.95 (*0-85398-247-3*) G Ronald Pub.

***Selections from the Writings of Evelyn Underhill.** pap. 2.00 (*0-8358-0144-6*) Upper Room Bks.

***Selections from the Writings of Francois Fenelon.** pap. 2.00 (*0-8358-0160-8*) Upper Room Bks.

***Selections from the Writings of Jeremy Taylor.** pap. 2.00 (*0-8358-0147-0*) Upper Room Bks.

***Selections from the Writings of John Bunyan.** pap. 2.00 (*0-8358-0057-1*) Upper Room Bks.

***Selections from the Writings of John Calvin.** pap. 2.00 (*0-8358-0108-X*) Upper Room Bks.

***Selections from the Writings of John Knox.** pap. 2.00 (*0-8358-0104-7*) Upper Room Bks.

***Selections from the Writings of Soren Kierkegaard.** pap. 2.00 (*0-8358-0062-8*) Upper Room Bks.

***Selections from the Writings of St. Francis of Assisi.** pap. 2.00 (*0-8358-0065-2*) Upper Room Bks.

Selections from the Writings of the Bab. Bab. LC 79-670141. 223p. 1977. 12.95 (*0-85398-066-7*, 105-050) Bahai.

***Selections from the Writings of Thomas Coke.** pap. 2.00 (*0-8358-0213-2*) Upper Room Bks.

***Selections from the Writings of William Temple.** pap. 2.00 (*0-8358-0227-2*) Upper Room Bks.

***Selections from Theo. Germ.** (Great Devotional Classics Ser.). pap. 1.85 (*0-687-61036-2*) Abingdon.

***Selections from Three Works of Francisco Suarez, Vol. 2.** Francisco Suarez. LC 95-77184. (Classics in International Law Reprint Ser.: No. 29). (LAT.). 1995. reprint ed. 150.00 (*1-57588-263-9*, 310390) W S Hein.

Selections from Understanding Human Sexuality. Janet S. Hyde. 1994. pap. text ed. write for info. (*0-07-031779-8*) McGraw.

Selections from Unpublished Manuscripts in the College of Arms & the British Museum. Ed. by Joseph Stevenson. LC 74-176443. (Maitland Club, Glasgow. Publications: No. 41). reprint ed. 37.50 (*0-404-53017-6*) AMS Pr.

Selections from Vergil's Aeneid, Bks. I, IV, VI. Jane H. Hall & Alexander G. McKay. 1988. pap. text ed. 13.96 (*0-582-36749-2*, 72525) Longman.

Selections in Translation: Selections in Translation. Max Weber. Ed. by Walter G. Runciman. Tr. by Eric Matthews. LC 77-80846. 416p. 1978. pap. text ed. 22.95 (*0-521-29268-9*) Cambridge U Pr.

Selections in Two Keys. K. Srinivasan. 10.00 (*0-89253-548-2*) Ind-US Inc.

***Selections McGuffy Readers, Vol. 1.** Gorn. Date not set. pap. text ed. write for info. (*0-312-13398-7*) St Martin.

Selections, No. 5: The International Polaroid Collection. Afterword by Barbara Hitchcock. 96p. (ENG, FRE, GER & SPA.). 1990. 28.95 (*0-9616459-3-8*); pap. 17.50 (*0-685-35765-1*) Polaroid Corp.

Selections of the Elements of Jurisprudence. William A. Keener. LC 95-76362. vi, 220p. 1995. reprint ed. 50.00 (*0-89941-936-4*, 308710) W S Hein.

Selections, 1993: Alexander Pope. Alexander Pope. Ed. by Pat Rogers. LC 92-23197. (Oxford Authors Ser.). 768p. 1993. 75.00 (*0-19-254182-X*); pap. 22.00 (*0-19-281346-3*) OUP.

Selective Activation of Drugs by Redox Processes. Ed. by G. E. Adams et al. LC 90-14335. (NATO ASI, Series A: Life Sciences: Vol. 198). (Illus.). 360p. 1990. 110.00 (*0-306-43735-X*, Plenum Pr) Plenum.

Selective Admissions in Higher Education: Public Policy & Academic Policy, the Pursuit of Fairness in Admissions to Higher Education, the Status of Selective Admissions. Carnegie Council on Policy Studies in Higher Education Staff. LC 77-88501. 272p. reprint ed. pap. 77.60 (*0-317-27211-X*, 2023874) Bks Demand.

Selective Annotated Bibliography of Shakespeare's "Timon of Athens" Compiled by W. R. Elton & E. A. Rauchut. LC 90-19306. (Studies in Renaissance Literature: Vol. 11). 100p. 1991. lib. bdg. 59.95 (*0-88946-372-7*) E Mellen.

Selective Application of Materials for Products & Energy: 23rd National SAMPE Symposium & Exhibition, Disneyland Hotel, Anaheim, California, May 2-4, 1978. National SAMPE Symposium & Exhibition Staff. LC 78-105428. (Science of Advanced Materials & Process Enginnering Ser.: No. 23). 1260p. reprint ed. pap. 180.00 (*0-7837-1277-4*, 2041418) Bks Demand.

Selective Arteriography of the Spinal Cord. John L. Doppman et al. LC 68-58106. (Illus.). 157p. 1969. 12.30 (*0-87527-006-9*) Green.

Selective Attention & the Control of Binocular Rivalry. Leon C. Lack. (Psychological Studies: No. II). 1978. pap. text ed. 66.15 (*90-279-7644-9*) Mouton.

Selective Attention in Vision. A. H. Van der Heijden. LC 90-24543. (International Library of Psychology). (Illus.). 310p. (C). (gr. 13). 1991. text ed. 69.95 (*0-415-06105-9*, A5773) Routledge.

Selective Awareness. Virginia M. Satir. 197p. (C). 1984. pap. 8.95 (*0-930298-07-1*) Westwood Pub Co.

Selective Awareness: The New Mind-Body Answer to Self Healing. rev. ed. Virginia M. Satir. 156p. 1987. pap. 7.95 (*0-914629-50-6*, St Martin) Prima Pub.

Selective Bibliography of American Literature 1775-1900. B. M. Fullerton. LC 89-9208. xiv, 327p. 1989. reprint ed. 55.00 (*0-918024-06-4*) Ox Bow.

Selective Bibliography of California Labor History. Mitchell Slobodek. 265p. 1964. 8.00 (*0-89215-045-9*) U Cal LA Indus Rel.

Selective Bibliography of Shakespeare: Editions, Textual Studies, Commentary. James G. McManaway & Jeanne A. Roberts. (Special Publications Ser.). 1978. 30.00 (*0-918016-02-9*); pap. 12.95 (*0-918016-03-7*) Folger Bks.

Selective Bibliography on the Conservation of Research Library Materials. Paul N. Banks. (Orig.). 1981. pap. 5.00 (*0-911028-26-9*) Newberry.

Selective Biocatalysis: A Synthetic Approach. Laszlo Poppe & Lajos Novak. LC 92-9284. 319p. 1993. 126.00 (*3-527-28372-2*, VCH) Wiley.

Selective Character of American Secondary Education. George S. Counts. LC 75-89166. (American Education: Its Men, Institutions, & Ideas. Series 1). 1975. reprint ed. 17.95 (*0-405-01404-X*) Ayer.

Selective Check Lists of Bibliographical Scholarship, 1956-1962, Series B. University of Virginia, Bibliographical Society Staff. Ed. by Howell J. Heaney & Rudolf Hirsch. LC 66-63536. 255p. reprint ed. pap. 72.70 (*0-8357-2727-0*, 2039837) Bks Demand.

Selective Check Lists of Press Books. Will Ransom. 420p. 1992. 75.00 (*1-882860-03-9*) J Cummins Bksell.

Selective Checklist of the Published Work of Aubrey Beardsley. Mark S. Lasner. 1994. text ed. 75.00 (*0-9644734-0-2*) T G Boss.

Selective Computation. Richard E. Bellman. (Series in Modern Applied Mathematics: Vol. 4). 250p. (C). 1985. text ed. 46.00 (*9971-966-86-7*) World Scientific Pub.

Selective Detectors: Environmental, Industrial, & Biomedical Applications. Ed. by Robert E. Sievers. LC 94-44366. (Chemical Analysis: A Series of Monographs on Analy). 200p. 1995. text ed. 69.95 (*0-471-01343-9*) Wiley.

Selective English Old-French Glossary As a Basis for Studies in Old French Onomatology & Synonymics. Joseph P. Murray. LC 77-128932. (Catholic University of America. Studies in Romance Languages & Literature: No. 40). (ENG & FRE.). reprint ed. 37.50 (*0-404-50340-3*) AMS Pr.

***Selective Epitaxial Growth for Smart Silicon Sensor Applications.** Marian Bartek. (Illus.). x, 147p. (Orig.). 1995. pap. 59.50 (*90-407-1178-X*, Pub. by Delft U Pr NE) Coronet Bks.

Selective Exposure to Communication. Ed. by Dolf Zillmann & Jennings Bryant. (Communication Ser.). 264p. (C). 1985. text ed. 49.95 (*0-89859-585-1*) L Erlbaum Assocs.

Selective Feeding Programmes: Oxfam Practical Health Guide no. 1, No. 1. Tim Lusty. (Oxfam Practical Guide: 1). (Illus.). 96p. (C). 1984. pap. 9.95 (*0-85598-097-4*, Pub. by Oxfam UK) Humanities.

Selective Guide to Chinese Literature, 1900- 1949, Vol. 3: The Poem. Ed. by Lloyd Haft. LC 87-17871. xii, 301p. 1989. 96.50 (*90-04-08960-8*) E J Brill.

Selective Guide to Chinese Literature, 1900-1940, Vol. 4: The Drama. Ed. by Bernd Eberstein. LC 90-38656. xi, 347p. 1990. 107.00 (*90-04-09098-3*) E J Brill.

Selective Guide to the Pressure Systems & Transportable GA's Containers Regulations. EEMUA Staff. 1994. 125.00 (*0-85931-065-5*, Pub. by EEMUA UK) St Mut.

Selective Guide to Women-Related Records in the North Carolina State Archives. Catherine E. Thompson. 77p. 1977. pap. 3.00 (*0-86526-167-9*) NC Archives.

***Selective History of the Crego Family.** Roy Crego. LC 92-76117. ix, 127p. 1993. 29.95 (*0-9657133-0-X*) Crego Pubng.

Selective Hydrocarbon Activation: Principles & Progress. Ed. by Julian A. Davies et al. 568p. 1990. 155.00 (*0-89573-713-2*, VCH) Wiley.

Selective Immunosuppression: Basic Concepts & Clinical Applications. Ed. by L. Adorini. (Chemical Immunology Ser.: Vol. 60). (Illus.). x, 166p. 1994. 151.50 (*3-8055-6034-6*) S Karger.

Selective Incapacitation & the Serious Offender. R. A. Haapanen. (Research in Criminology Ser.). (Illus.). 168p. 1989. 89.95 (*0-387-97051-7*) Spr-Verlag.

Selective Incapacitation Revisited: Why the High Rate Offenders are Hard to Predict. Peter W. Greenwood & Susan Turner. LC 86-33845. 1987. pap. 7.50 (*0-8330-0782-3*, R-3397-NIJ) Rand Corp.

Selective Inhibitors of Viral Functions. Ed. by W. A. Carter. LC 73-81479. (Uniscience Ser.). 377p. 1973. 70.50 (*0-87819-027-9*, CRC Reprint) Franklin.

Selective Judicial Competence: The Cirebon-Priangan Legal Administration, 1680-1792. Mason C. Hoadley. (Studies on Southeast Asia: No. 15). (Orig.). 1994. pap. text ed. 16.00 (*0-87727-714-1*) Cornell SE Asia.

Selective Laser Spectroscopy of Activated Crystals & Glasses. Ed. by V. V. Osiko. (Proceedings of the Institute of General Physics of the Academy of Sciences of the U. S. S. R. Ser.: Vol. 9). 220p. (RUS.). 1990. text ed. 125.00 (*0-941743-31-4*) Nova Sci Pubs.

Selective Laser Spectroscopy of Activated Crystals & Glasses. Ed. by V. V. Osiko. (Proceedings of the Institute of General Physics of the Academy of Sciences of the U. S. S. R. Ser.: Vol. 9). 220p. (C). 1990. text ed. 125.00 (*0-941743-92-6*) Nova Sci Pubs.

Selective Linear-Phase Switched-Capacitor & Digital Filters. Hussein Baher. LC 92-34564. (Kluwer International Series in Engineering & Computer Science). 160p. (C). 1993. lib. bdg. 83.00 (*0-7923-9298-1*) Kluwer Ac.

Selective Music Bibliography from the Period 1663-1763. James Pruett & Lee Rigsby. (Illus.). vii, 53p. 1962. pap. 2.00 (*0-86526-109-1*) NC Archives.

S

An Asterisk (*) at the beginning of an entry indicates that the title is appearing in BIP for the first time.

Selective Mutism: Implications for Research & Treatment. Thomas R. Kratochwill. LC 80-18631. 208p. 1981. text ed. 39.95 (*0-89859-064-7*) L Erlbaum Assocs.

Selective Mutism in Children. Tony Cline. 168p. (Orig.). (C). 1994. pap. text ed. 34.95 (*1-56593-257-9*, 0546) Singular Publishing.

Selective Narrative Poems in Lambent Line. Robert E. Paxton. (Orig.). 1996. pap. write for info. (*1-57553-204-2*) Watermrk Pr.

Selective Neurotoxicity. Ed. by H. Herken et al. (Handbook of Experimental Pharmacology Ser.: Vol. 107). (Illus.). 888p. 1992. 398.00 (*0-387-54654-5*) Spr-Verlag.

Selective Neurotoxity. Ed. by H. Herken & F. Hucho. LC 94-7806. 1994. 158.00 (*3-540-57815-3*) Spr-Verlag.

Selective Neurotoxity. Ed. by H. Herken & F. Hucho. LC 94-7806. 1994. 139.95 (*0-387-57815-3*) Spr-Verlag.

Selective Nontreatment of Handicapped Newborns: Moral Dilemmas in Neonatal Medicine. Robert F. Weir. LC 83-19376. 292p. 1986. pap. 19.95 (*0-19-504881-4*) OUP.

Selective Optical Surfaces for Solar Energy Converters. M. M. Koltun. Ed. by D. P. Siddons. Tr. by S. Chomet from RUS. LC 81-69401. vi, 239p. 1981. 42.50 (*0-89864-003-2*) Allerton Pr.

Selective Practice Typing Drills. Alan C. Lloyd et al. 1974. text ed. 10.88 (*0-07-038147-X*) McGraw.

Selective Reactions of Metal-Activated Molecules. Ed. by Helmut Werner & Axel G. Griesbeck. x, 235p. (C). 1992. 70.00 (*3-528-06450-1*, Pub. by Vieweg & Sohn GW) Informatica.

Selective Safeguard Measures in Multilateral Trade Relations. M. C. Bronckers. 306p. 1985. 106.00 (*90-6544-222-7*) Kluwer Law Tax Pubs.

Selective Sample Handling & Detection in High Performance Liquid Chromatography. R. W. Frei & K. Zech. (JCL Ser.: Vol. 39, No. 1). 458p. 1987. 203.25 (*0-444-42881-X*) Elsevier.

Selective Sample Handling & Detection in High-Performance Liquid Chromatography, Part B. Ed. by K. Zech & R. W. Frei. (Journal of Chromatography Library: No. 39B). 394p. 1989. 203.25 (*0-444-88327-4*) Elsevier.

Selective Serotonin Re-Uptake Inhibitors. J. P. Feighner. LC 90-13134. (Progress in Psychiatry Ser.). 168p. 1991. text ed. 98.00 (*0-471-92890-9*) Wiley.

Selective Serotonin Re-Uptake Inhibitors: Advances in Basic Research & Clinical Practice. 2nd ed. Ed. by J. P. Feighner & W. F. Boyer. LC 95-39512. (Perspectives in Psychiatry Ser.: Vol. 5). 1996. text ed. 89.95 (*0-471-95600-7*) Wiley.

Selective Studies in Health & Social Services. Ed. by A. G. McDonald. (OMEGA Special Issue Ser.: Vol. 9, No. 5). 104p. 1981. pap. 35.00 (*0-08-023620-0*, Pergamon Pr) Elsevier.

Selective Survey of English Language Studies on Scandinavian Law. Ruth B. Ginsburg. vi, 53p. (Orig.). 1970. pap. text ed. 4.50 (*0-8377-0600-9*) Rothman.

Selective Trout. Doug Swisher & Carl Richards. (Illus.). 128p. 1988. pap. 19.95 (*0-941130-72-X*) Lyons & Burford.

Selective Voet Being the Commentary on the Pandects, 7 vols., Set. P. C. Gane. 5600p. 1989. boxed 1,520.00 (*0-409-00800-1*) MICHIE.

***Selective Writings by Nissim Koen.** Nissim Koen. Ed. by Judi Thompson. (Illus.). 95p. 1996. pap. 7.00 (*0-9651708-7-X*) N Koen.

Selective 5-HT Reuptake Inhibitors: Novel or Commonplace Agents? Ed. by M. Gastpar & Jennifers S. Wakelin. (Advances in Biological Psychiatry Ser.: Vol. 17). (Illus.). viii, 108p. 1988. 78.50 (*3-8055-4776-5*) S Karger.

Selectivities in Lewis Acid Promoted Reactions. Ed. by Dieter Schinzer. (C). 1989. lib. bdg. 167.50 (*0-7923-0452-7*) Kluwer Ac.

Selectivity & Detectability Optimazations in HPLC. Ahuja. LC 88-38315. (Chemical Analysis Ser.). 604p. 1989. text ed. 150.00 (*0-471-62645-7*) Wiley.

Selectivity in Catalysis. Ed. by Mark E. Davis & Steven L. Suib. LC 92-42872. (Symposium Ser.: No. 517). 420p. 1993. 99.95 (*0-8412-2519-2*) Am Chemical.

Selectivity in Chemical Reactions. Ed. by J. C. Whitehead. (C). 1988. lib. bdg. 234.00 (*90-277-2791-0*) Kluwer Ac.

Selectivity in Information Systems: Survival of the Fittest. Kenneth S. Warren. LC 84-11607. 188p. 1985. text ed. 45.00 (*0-275-90180-7*, C0180, Praeger Pubs) Greenwood.

Selectivity in Lewis Acid Promoted Reactions. M. Santelli & J. M. Pons. (Organic & Bio-Organic Chemistry Ser.). 352p. 1995. 89.95 (*0-8493-7866-4*, 7866) CRC Pr.

SELECT...SQL: The Relational Database Language. Larry R. Newcomer. 446p. (C). 1991. pap. text ed. 51.00 (*0-02-386693-4*, Macmillan Coll) P-H.

***Selena.** Barbara Marvis. LC 97-21960. (Real Life Reader Biographies Ser.). (Illus.). 24p. (J). (gr. k-4). 1997. lib. bdg. 15.95 (*1-883845-47-5*) M Lane Pubs.

Selena. Gordon R. Willey. LC 92-44855. 208p. 1993. 19.95 (*0-8027-3227-5*) Walker & Co.

Selena. Gordon R. Willey. (Mystery Ser.). 1996. mass mkt. 3.99 (*0-373-26190-X*, 1-26190-8) Harlequin Bks.

Selena: Como la Flor. Joe N. Patoski. 304p. 1996. 22.95 (*0-316-69378-2*) Little.

***Selena: Como la Flor.** Joe N. Patoski. 368p. 1997. reprint ed. mass mkt. 6.50 (*1-57297-246-7*) Blvd Books.

Selena: The Last Song. Geraldo Ruiz. 1995. mass mkt. 5.99 (*1-887599-01-0*) El Diario Bks.

Selena: The Phenomenal Life & Tragic Death of the Tejano Music Queen. Clint Richmond. 1995. mass mkt. 5.99 (*0-671-54522-1*) PB.

***Selena Perez: Queen of Tejano Music.** Maritza Romero. LC 97-6730. (Great Hispanics of Our Time Ser.). (J). 1997. write for info. (*0-8239-5086-7*, PowerKids) Rosen Group.

Selena, the Queen of Tejano. Jill C. Wheeler. LC 95-30175. (J). 1995. lib. bdg. 13.98 (*1-56239-523-8*) Abdo & Dghtrs.

Selena's Secret. Arraras. 1997. pap. 12.00 (*0-684-83193-7*) S&S Trade.

Selenium. (Environmental Health Criteria Ser.: No. 58). 276p. 1987. pap. text ed. 38.00 (*92-4-154258-6*, 1160058) World Health.

Selenium. Ralph Zingaro & Charles W. Cooper. LC 74-1246. 856p. 1974. 64.50 (*0-442-29575-8*) Krieger.

Selenium: Index of New Information & Research Bible. Sidney K. Winnans. LC 96-12483. 1996. 44.50 (*0-7883-0800-9*); pap. 44.50 (*0-7883-0801-7*) ABBE Pubs Assn.

***Selenium & Cancer.** Richard A. Passwater. (Good Health Guides Ser.). Date not set. reprint ed. pap. 17.50 (*0-87983-784-5*) Keats.

Selenium As Food & Medicine. Richard A. Passwater. LC 80-82325. 200p. 1981. 10.95 (*0-87983-237-1*); pap. 2.95 (*0-87983-229-0*) Keats.

Selenium Contamination. David W. Felder. 48p. 1996. pap. text ed. 8.95 (*0-910959-70-6*, B&G 14A) Wellington Pr.

Selenium in Agriculture & the Environment. Ed. by L. W. Jacobs. 233p. 1989. 24.00 (*0-89118-789-8*) Soil Sci Soc Am.

Selenium in Biology & Human Health. Ed. by Raymond F. Burk. LC 93-4691. 1993. 79.95 (*0-387-94080-4*) Spr-Verlag.

Selenium in Biology & Medicine. Ed. by A. Wendel. (Illus.). 335p. 1989. 152.95 (*0-387-50755-8*) Spr-Verlag.

Selenium in Medicine & Biology: Proceedings of the Second International Congress on Trace Elements in Medicine & Biology. Ed. by Jean Neve & Alain Favier. xx, 428p. (C). 1989. lib. bdg. 234.65 (*3-11-011770-3*) De Gruyter.

Selenium in the Environment. Ed. by Frankenberger & Benson. (Books in Soils, Plants & the Environment: Vol. 34). 480p. 1994. 165.00 (*0-8247-8993-8*) Dekker.

***Selenium 1988: Present Status & Perspectives in Biology & Medicine.** Ed. by Gerhard N. Schrauzer. 316p. 1988. pap. 95.00 (*0-89603-154-3*) Humana.

Seleucid Archival Texts in the Harvard Semitic Museum. Ronald Wallenfels. 1996. write for info. (*0-614-96306-0*, Pub. by Styx NE) Eisenbrauns.

Seleucid Army. Bezalal Bar-Kochva. (Cambridge Classical Studies). 318p. 1976. text ed. 59.95 (*0-521-20667-7*) Cambridge U Pr.

***Seleucid Coins of Bactria.** Brian Krittt. Ed. by Kerry K. Wetterstrom. LC 96-85763. (Classical Numismatic Studies: No. I). (Illus.). 80p. 1996. 35.00 (*0-9636738-2-3*) Classical Numismatic Grp.

Seleucid Mint of Antioch. Edward T. Newell. (Illus.). 1978. 50.00 (*0-916710-38-6*) Obol Intl.

***Seleukid Prosopography & Gazetteer.** John D. Grainger. (Mnemosyne, Suppplements Ser.: Vol. 172). (Illus.). 576p. 1997. 206.25 (*90-04-10799-1*) E J Brill.

Seleukos Nikator: Constructing a Hellenistic Kingdom. John D. Grainger. 224p. (C). (gr. 13). 1990. text ed. 62.95 (*0-415-04701-3*, A4254) Routledge.

Selevac: A Neolithic Village in Yugoslavia. Ed. by Ruth Tringham & Dusan Krstic. LC 90-4514. (Monumenta Archaeologica Ser.: No. 15). (Illus.). 702p. (C). 1990. text ed. 48.00 (*0-917956-68-0*) UCLA Arch.

***Self.** Jonathan D. Brown. LC 97-1298. 1997. write for info. (*0-07-008306-1*) McGraw.

Self. Buss. 1995. pap. text ed. write for info. (*0-205-16365-3*) Allyn.

Self. Shirley Greenslade. 38p. 1985. pap. write for info. (*1-886799-01-6*) Agape Word.

Self. Anthony Kenny. LC 88-60191. (Aquinas Lectures). 33p. 1988. 15.00 (*0-87462-155-0*) Marquette.

Self. Osborne. 1996. pap. text ed. 32.00 (*0-205-20021-4*) Allyn.

Self. Strube. 1996. pap. text ed. write for info. (*0-205-17392-6*) Allyn.

Self: Definitional & Methodological Issues. Ed. by Thomas M. Brinthaupt & Richard P. Lipka. LC 91-13139. (SUNY Series, Studying the Self). 351p. 1992. text ed. 64.50 (*0-7914-0987-2*); pap. text ed. 21.95 (*0-7914-0988-0*) State U NY Pr.

Self: Interdisciplinary Approaches (Second G. Stanley Hall Symposium) Ed. by J. Strauss & G. R. Geothals. (Illus.). xii, 278p. 1991. 71.95 (*0-387-97536-5*) Spr-Verlag.

Self - Power - Other: Political Theory & Dialogical Ethics. Romand Coles. LC 91-55546. 224p. 1992. 37.50 (*0-8014-2609-X*) Cornell U Pr.

Self - Talk Solution. Shad Helmstetter. 1990. pap. 6.99 (*0-671-72757-5*, PB Trade Paper) PB.

Self - Yours, Mine, or Ours? A Dialectic View. Anne-lise Lovlie. 153p. (Orig.). 1982. pap. 23.00 (*82-00-05946-4*) Scandnvan Univ Pr.

Self-Abandonment to Divine Providence: Abandonment to Divine Providence. Jean-Pierre De Caussade. Tr. by Algar Thorold from FRE. LC 86-51602. 450p. 1993. reprint ed. pap. 18.00 (*0-89555-312-0*) TAN Bks Pubs.

Self Access. 1989. 12.95 (*0-19-437099-2*) OUP.

***Self Across Psychology: Self Recognition, Self-Awareness, & the Self Concept.** Ed. by Joan G. Snodgrass & Robert L. Thompson. LC 97-20571. 1997. write for info. (*1-57331-034-4*) NY Acad Sci.

***Self Across Psychology: Self-Recognition, Self-Awareness, & the Self Concept.** Joan Gay Snodgrass et al. LC 97-20571. (Annals of the New York Academy of Sciences Ser.). 1997. pap. write for info. (*1-57331-035-2*) NY Acad Sci.

Self Actualization. Torkom Saraydarian. LC 90-90137. 200p. pap. write for info. (*0-929874-17-X*) TSG Pub Found.

Self-Actualization: Theory & Technology. Joseph Sassoon. 300p. 1988. 24.95 (*0-9693115-0-8*) Humanica Pr.

Self-Actuated Healing: The Alternative to Doctors & Drugs Is Within You. Lonny Brown. 176p. (Orig.). 1988. pap. 8.95 (*0-87961-185-5*) Naturegraph.

Self-Administered Patient Education Audit for Family Practices. Ed. by John H. Renner. 19p. 1990. 10.00 (*0-9626145-1-3*) Health Facts Pub.

Self-Advocacy Movement by People with Developmental Disabilities: A Demographic Study & Directory of Self-Advocacy Groups in the United States. Nancy A. Longhurst. LC 93-48121. 1994. 21.95 (*0-940898-32-2*) Am Assn Mental.

Self-Analysis. Karen Horney. 1994. pap. 8.95 (*0-393-31165-1*) Norton.

***Self Analysis.** L. Ron Hubbard. Date not set. pap. 12.95 (*1-57318-041-6*) Bridge Pubns Inc.

Self Analysis. L. Ron Hubbard. 324p. 1990. 35.00 (*0-88404-449-1*) Bridge Pubns Inc.

Self Analysis. L. Ron Hubbard. 312p. 1995. mass mkt. 5.99 (*0-88404-264-2*) Bridge Pubns Inc.

Self-Analysis: Critical Inquiries, Personal Visions. Ed. by James W. Barron. LC 93-15733. 320p. 1993. text ed. 45.00 (*0-88163-143-4*) Analytic Pr.

Self Analysis: The Book about Life. James J. Carter. (Illus.). (Orig.). 1979. pap. 4.95 (*0-937004-00-6*) Unicorn PA.

Self-Analysis in Literary Study: Exploring Hidden Agendas. Ed. by Daniel Rancour-Laferriere. (Literature & Psychoanalysis Ser.). 240p. (C). 1994. 45.00 (*0-8147-7439-3*) NYU Pr.

Self-Analyzers: A Workbook. Jean Kirkpatrick. 40p. 7.95 (*0-317-05940-8*) WFS.

Self & Colonial Desire: Travel Writings of V. S. Naipaul. Wimal Dissanayake & Carmen Wickramagamage. LC 92-43638. (Studies of World Literature in English: Vol. 2). 160p. (C). 1993. text ed. 45.95 (*0-8204-1975-3*) P Lang Pubng.

Self & Community in the Fiction of Elizabeth Spencer. Terry Roberts. LC 93-26078. (Southern Literary Studies). 176p. 1994. text ed. 30.00 (*0-8071-1879-6*) La State U Pr.

Self & Consciousness: Multiple Perspectives. Ed. by Frank Kessel et al. 136p. 1992. text ed. 29.95 (*0-8058-0532-X*) L Erlbaum Assocs.

Self & Deception: A Cross-Cultural Philosophical Enquiry. Ed. by Roger T. Ames & Wimal Dissanayake. LC 96-1329. 373p. 1996. text ed. 74.50 (*0-7914-3031-6*); pap. text ed. 24.95 (*0-7914-3032-4*) State U NY Pr.

***Self & Existence: J.M.R. Lenz's Subjective Point of View.** Brigitte O'Regan. (Studies in Modern German Literature: No. 73). 168p. (C). 1997. text ed. 39.95 (*0-8204-2524-9*) P Lang Pubng.

Self & Form in Modern Narrative. Vincent P. Pecora. LC 88-46067. 336p. 1989. text ed. 49.95 (*0-8018-3768-5*) Johns Hopkins.

Self & Identity. Daniel Kolak. 1990. 18.00 (*0-685-38325-3*) Macmillan.

Self & Identity. Daniel Kolak. 1990. pap. text ed. 29.80 (*0-02-365710-3*, Macmillan Coll) P-H.

***Self & Identity: Fundamental Issues.** Ed. by Richard D. Ashmore & Lee Jussim. (Rutgers Series on Self & Social Identity). (Illus.). 256p. 1997. text ed. 65.00 (*0-19-509826-9*) OUP.

***Self & Identity: Fundamental Issues.** Ed. by Richard D. Ashmore & Lee Jussim. (Rutgers Series on Self & Social Identity: Vol. 1). (Illus.). 256p. 1997. pap. text ed. 28.00 (*0-19-509827-7*) OUP.

Self & Identity: Perspectives across the Lifespan. T. Honess & K. M. Yardley. (International Library of Psychology). 416p. 1987. lib. bdg. 67.50 (*0-7102-0829-4*, RKP) Routledge.

***Self & It's Body in Hegel's Phenomenology of Spirit.** John Russon. (Toronto Studies in Philosophy). 192p. 1996. 65.00 (*0-8020-0919-0*) U of Toronto Pr.

Self & Its Brain. Karl R. Popper. 400p. (C). 1984. pap. 22.50 (*0-415-05898-8*) Routledge.

Self & Its Brain. rev. ed. Karl R. Popper & John C. Eccles. (Illus.). 597p. 1985. 86.95 (*0-387-08307-3*) Spr-Verlag.

Self & Its Brain: An Argument for Interactionism. Karl R. Popper & John C. Eccles. 616p. 1984. reprint ed. pap. 16.95 (*0-7100-9584-8*, RKP) Routledge.

Self & Its Pleasures: Bataille, Lacan, & the History of the Decentered Subject. Carolyn J. Dean. LC 92-52748. (Illus.). 288p. 1992. 42.50 (*0-8014-2660-X*); pap. 16.95 (*0-8014-9954-2*) Cornell U Pr.

Self & Its Problems: The Blavatsky Lecture for 1919. H. P. Blavatsky. Ed. by Charlotte E. Woods. 190p. 1992. pap. 19.95 (*1-56459-264-2*) Kessinger Pub.

Self & Its States: A States of Consciousness Doctrine in Advaita Vedanta. Andrew O. Fort. 1990. 32.50 (*81-208-0633-6*, Pub. by Motilal Banarsidass II) S Asia.

Self & Liberation: The Jung - Buddhism Dialogue. Robert L. Moore. Ed. by Daniel J. Meckel. LC 91-40818. (Jung & Spirituality Ser.). 352p. 1992. pap. 19.95 (*0-8091-3301-6*) Paulist Pr.

Self & Motivational Systems: Toward a Theory of Psychoanalytic Technique. Joseph D. Lichtenberg et al. (Psychoanalytic Inquiry Bk.: Vol. 13). 272p. 1992. 39.95 (*0-88163-154-X*) Analytic Pr.

Self & Nature. De Witt Parker. LC 75-3306. reprint ed. 32.50 (*0-404-59291-0*) AMS Pr.

Self & Nature in Kant's Philosophy. Ed. by Allen W. Wood. LC 84-7678. 240p. 1984. pap. 15.95 (*0-8014-9268-8*) Cornell U Pr.

Self & Non-Self: The Drigdrisyaviveka Attributed to Sankara. Raphael. 140p. 1990. 35.00 (*0-7103-0377-7*, A4515) Routledge Chapman & Hall.

Self & Non-Self in Early Buddhism. Joacquin Perez-Ramon. (Religion & Society Ser.: No. 17). 1980. 84.65 (*90-279-7987-1*) Mouton.

Self & Object Constancy: Clinical & Theoretical Perspectives. Ed. by Ruth F. Lax et al. LC 85-27365. (Guilford Psychiatry Ser.). 355p. 1985. lib. bdg. 47.00 (*0-89862-226-3*) Guilford Pr.

Self & Other. Ed. by David Hershberg. (Perspectives on Contemporary Literature Ser.: No. 12). 112p. 1986. pap. 7.50 (*0-8131-0712-1*) U Pr of Ky.

Self & Other: Object Relations in Psychoanalysis & Literature. Robert Rogers. (Psychoanalytic Crosscurrents Ser.). 228p. (C). 1991. 45.00 (*0-8147-7418-0*) NYU Pr.

Self & Other: Object Relations in Psychoanalysis & Literature. Robert Rogers. (Psychoanalytic Crosscurrents Ser.). 228p. (C). 1993. pap. 17.50 (*0-8147-7443-1*) NYU Pr.

Self & Others. R. D. Laing. 1972. mass mkt. 5.95 (*0-14-021376-7*, Penguin Bks) Viking Penguin.

Self & Others. R. D. Laing. 1991. pap. 9.95 (*0-14-013467-0*) Viking Penguin.

Self & Others: A Study of Ethical Egoism. Jan Osterberg. 266p. (C). 1988. lib. bdg. 122.00 (*90-277-2648-5*, Pub. by Klwr Acad Pubs NE) Kluwer Ac.

Self & Others: Object Relations Theory in Practice. N. Gregory Hamilton. LC 87-19479. 352p. 1992. reprint ed. pap. 30.00 (*0-87668-544-0*) Aronson.

Self & Others: Object Relations Theory in Practice. N. Gregory Hamilton. LC 87-19479. 352p. 1991. 35.00 (*0-87668-961-6*) Aronson.

Self & Process: Brain States & the Conscious Present. J. W. Brown. (Illus.). xiii, 201p. 1991. 57.95 (*0-387-97514-4*) Spr-Verlag.

Self & Savagery on the California Frontier: A Study of the Digger Stereotype. Allan Lonnberg. (Illus.). 98p. 1980. reprint ed. pap. text ed. 10.00 (*1-55567-048-2*) Coyote Press.

Self & School Success: Voices & Lore of Inner-City Students. Edwin Farrell. LC 93-10229. (SUNY Series, Studying the Self & Student Lore). 173p. (C). 1994. pap. text ed. 19.95 (*0-7914-1846-4*) State U NY Pr.

Self & School Success: Voices & Lore of Inner-City Students. Edwin Farrell. LC 93-10229. (SUNY Series, Studying the Self & Student Lore). 173p. (C). 1994. text ed. 59.50 (*0-7914-1845-6*) State U NY Pr.

Self & Self-Management. Arnold Bennett. LC 74-16345. (Collected Works of Arnold Bennett: Vol. 73). 1977. reprint ed. 19.95 (*0-518-19154-0*) Ayer.

Self & Sequence: The Poetry of D. H. Lawrence. Holly A. Laird. LC 87-23047. 228p. 1988. text ed. 19.50 (*0-8139-1147-8*) U Pr of Va.

Self & Social Context. Ray F. Holland. LC 77-27530. 1978. text ed. 32.50 (*0-312-71229-4*) St Martin.

Self & Society. HarperCollins Staff & Josephine K. Tarvers. LC 92-26732. (C). 1993. text ed. 9.50 (*0-06-501127-9*) Addson-Wesley Educ.

Self & Society: A Study of Gandhian Thought. Ramashray Roy. 205p. 1985. text ed. 25.00 (*0-8039-9484-2*) Sage.

Self & Society: A Symbolic Interactionist Social Psychology. 7th ed. John P. Hewitt. LC 96-835. 263p. 1996. pap. 36.00 (*0-205-19140-1*) Allyn.

Self & Society: Narcissism, Collectivism, & the Development of Morals. Drew Westen. LC 84-28478. 430p. 1985. text ed. 80.00 (*0-521-30171-8*); pap. text ed. 35.95 (*0-521-31770-3*) Cambridge U Pr.

Self & Society in Medieval France: The Memories of Abbot Guibert of Nogent. Ed. by John F. Benton. (Medieval Academy Reprints for Teaching Ser.: No. 15). 260p. (C). 1984. reprint ed. pap. text ed. 12.95 (*0-8020-6550-3*) U of Toronto Pr.

Self & Society in Ming Thought. William T. Debary. LC 78-101229. (Studies in Oriental Culture: No. 4). 566p. reprint ed. pap. 161.40 (*0-685-18177-4*, 2029702) Bks Demand.

Self & Society in the Poetry of Nicolas Guillen. Lorna V. Williams. LC 81-8404. (Johns Hopkins Studies in Atlantic History & Culture Ser.). 189p. reprint ed. pap. 53.90 (*0-8357-6629-2*, 2035275) Bks Demand.

***Self & Soul: A Woman's Guide to Enhancing Self Esteem Through Spirituality.** Adele Wilcox. LC 97-724. 192p. 1997. 19.95 (*0-87596-446-X*, Daybrk) Rodale Pr Inc.

Self & Symbolism in the Poetry of Michelangelo, John Donne & Agrippa d'Aubigne. A. B. Altizer. (Archives Internationales D'Histoire des Idees Ser.: No. 10). 117p. 1973. pap. text ed. 47.00 (*90-247-1551-2*, Pub. by M Nijhoff NE) Kluwer Ac.

Self & the Ego in Psychotherapy: A New Approach to Object Relations Theory & Therapy. N. Gregory Hamilton. LC 95-39263. 200p. 1996. 40.00 (*1-56821-659-9*) Aronson.

Self & the Object World. Edith Jacobson. LC 64-15489. (Journal of the American Psychoanalytic Association Monograph Ser.: No. 2). 250p. 1964. 37.50 (*0-8236-6060-5*) Intl Univs Pr.

***Self & the Other.** Ed. by Ismail Serageldin & Afaf M. Mahfouz. (Environmentally Sustainable Development Occasional Papers: No. 13). 76p. 1996. 7.95 (*0-8213-3714-9*, 13714) World Bank.

Self & the Other: Personhood & Images among the Baule, Cote d'Ivoire. Philip L. Ravenhill. (Monograph Ser.: No. 28). (Illus.). 48p. 1994. pap. 15.00 (*0-930741-39-0*) UCLA Fowler Mus.

Self & the Political Order. Ed. by Tracy B. Strong. (Readings in Social & Political Theory Ser.: Vol. 10). 352p. (C). 1991. 45.00 (*0-8147-7925-5*); pap. 18.50 (*0-8147-7926-3*) NYU Pr.

***Self & World.** Quassim Cassam. 216p. 1997. 49.95 (*0-19-823540-2*) OUP.

An Asterisk (*) at the beginning of an entry indicates that the title is appearing in BIP for the first time.

Self & World: An Explanation of Aesthetic Realism. Eli Siegel. LC 75-44647. 427p. 1981. pap. 12.00 (*0-910492-28-X*) Definition.

Self & World: Readings in Philosophy. 2nd ed. James A. Ogilvy. 507p. (C). 1981. pap. text ed. 22.75 (*0-15-579628-3*) HB Coll Pubs.

Self-Apparent Word: Fiction as Language-Language as Fiction. Jerome Klinkowitz. LC 83-20071. 163p. 1984. 19.95 (*0-8093-1164-X*) S Ill U Pr.

Self-Appropriation of Inferiority: A Foundation for Psychology. William R. Eidle. LC 89-36365. (American University Studies: Psychology: Ser. VIII, Vol. 18). 226p. 1990. text ed. 45.95 (*0-8204-0996-0*) P Lang Pubng.

Self As Agent. John Macmurray. LC 91-21419. 232p. (C). 1991. pap. 17.50 (*0-391-03715-3*) Humanities.

Self As Body in Asian Theory & Practice. Ed. by Thomas P. Kasulis et al. LC 91-26009. (SUNY Series, The Body in Culture, History, & Religion). 383p. (C). 1992. pap. text ed. 21.95 (*0-7914-1080-3*) State U NY Pr.

Self As Body in Asian Theory & Practice. Ed. by Thomas P. Kasulis et al. LC 91-26009. (SUNY Series, The Body in Culture, History, & Religion). 383p. (C). 1993. text ed. 64.50 (*0-7914-1079-X*) State U NY Pr.

Self As Fighter. Shlomo Kalo. 160p. (C). 1990. 35.00 (*0-85439-369-2*, Pub. by St Paul Pubns UK) St Mut.

Self As Mind: Vision & Identity in Wordsworth, Coleridge, & Keats. Charles J. Rzepka. 298p. 1986. 34.50 (*0-674-80085-0*) HUP.

Self As Narrative: Subjectivity & Community in Contemporary Fiction. Kim L. Worthington. (Oxford English Monographs). 344p. (C). 1996. 75.00 (*0-19-818364-X*) OUP.

Self As Person in Asian Theory & Practice. Ed. by Roger T. Ames et al. LC 93-9297. 392p. 1994. pap. text ed. 21.95 (*0-7914-1724-7*) State U NY Pr.

Self As Person in Asian Theory & Practice. Ed. by Roger T. Ames et al. LC 93-9297. 392p. 1994. text ed. 63.50 (*0-7914-1723-9*) State U NY Pr.

Self-Assembling Architecture. Ed. by Joseph E. Varner. 288p. 1988. text ed. 164.95 (*0-471-50509-9*) Wiley.

Self-Assembly Furniture Market In Europe 1986. 1986. 130.00 (*0-317-43734-8*) St Mut.

Self-Assertion for Women. Pamela E. Butler. LC 90-84723. 288p. (Orig.). 1992. reprint ed. pap. 14.00 (*0-06-250125-9*) Harper SF.

Self-Assessment & Career Development. 3rd ed. James G. Clawson et al. 480p. (C). 1991. pap. text ed. 58.00 (*0-13-803180-0*) P-H.

Self-Assessment Atlas of Gastroenterology. Ed. by Tadataka Yamada et al. (Illus.). 200p. 1994. 49.95 (*0-397-51367-4*) Lppncott-Raven.

***Self-Assessment Color Review of Cardiology.** Stuart D. Rosen et al. 192p. 1997. pap. text ed. 24.95 (*0-316-75813-2*) Lppncott-Raven.

***Self-Assessment Color Review of Cardiothoracic Critical Care.** Karmy-Jones. 160p. 1997. pap. text ed. 24.95 (*0-316-74755-6*) Lppncott-Raven.

***Self-Assessment Color Review of Clinical Haematology.** Mehta. 1995. pap. text ed. 25.95 (*0-316-56557-1*) Lppncott-Raven.

***Self-Assessment Color Review of Equine Internal Medicine.** Tim S. Mair. 1997. pap. text ed. 34.95 (*0-8138-2864-3*) Iowa St U Pr.

***Self-Assessment Color Review of Equine Orthopedics & Rheumatology.** Stephen C. Maay. 1997. pap. text ed. 34.95 (*0-8138-2137-1*) Iowa St U Pr.

***Self-Assessment Color Review of Equine Reproduction & Stud Medicine.** Jonathan F. Pycock. (Illus.). 224p. 1997. pap. 34.95 (*0-8138-2303-X*) Iowa St U Pr.

***Self-Assessment Color Review of Renal Medicine.** Timothy H. J. Goodship & Bradley J. Maroni. 192p. 1997. pap. text ed. 24.95 (*0-316-83932-9*) Lppncott-Raven.

Self-Assessment Color Review of Reptiles & Amphibians. Fredric L. Frye. 192p. 1995. pap. text ed. 34.95 (*0-8138-2990-9*, Pub. by Manson Pubng UK) Iowa St U Pr.

***Self-Assessment Color Review of Respiratory Medicine.** Spiro. 192p. 1997. pap. text ed. 24.95 (*0-316-80697-8*) Lppncott-Raven.

Self-Assessment Color Review of Small Animal Neurology. Simon J. Wheeler. 152p. 1996. pap. text ed. 34.95 (*0-8138-2217-3*, Pub. by Manson Pubng UK) Iowa St U Pr.

***Self-Assessment Color Review of Small Mammals.** Ed. by Susan A. Brown & Karen Rosenthal. (Illus.). 192p. 1997. pap. 29.95 (*0-8138-2092-8*) Iowa St U Pr.

Self-Assessment Exercises in Surgery. W. E. Thomas. (Illus.). 208p. (C). 1987. pap. 50.00 (*0-407-00419-X*) Buttrwrth-Heinemann.

Self Assessment for Business Excellence. David Lascelles & Roy Peacock. LC 95-39122. (Quality in Action Ser.). 1996. pap. write for info. (*0-07-709186-8*) McGraw.

Self Assessment for Managers of Health Care: How Can I Be a Better Manager. (Offset Publication Ser.: No. 97). 60p. 1987. pap. text ed. 10.00 (*92-4-170097-1*, 1120097) World Health.

Self Assessment for MRCP: Part I. 4th ed. C. F. Corke. LC 95-32582. 1995. 29.95 (*0-86542-937-5*) Blackwell Sci.

Self Assessment for Nonprofit Governing Boards. Larry H. Slesinger. (Nonprofit Governance Ser.: No. 47). 60p. (C). 1991. pap. 149.00 (*0-925299-45-6*) Natl Ctr Nonprofit.

***Self-Assessment for Teachers of Health Workers: How to Be a Better Teacher.** A. Rotem & F. Abbatt. (WHO Offset Publications: No. 68). 59p. 1982. 8.00 (*92-4-170068-8*) World Health.

***Self Assessment for the Diploma in Child Health.** Wai-Ching Leung & Adrian Minford. LC 97-20459. (Self-Assessment Ser.). 1997. write for info. (*0-340-67720-1*, Pub. by E Arnld UK) St Martin.

Self-Assessment Guide to Hematology. Holmes. (C). (gr. 13). 1994. 29.95 (*0-8151-4626-4*, Yr Bk Med Pubs) Mosby Yr Bk.

Self Assessment Handbook: For Measuring Corporate Excellence. C. Hakes. 1994. 34.95 (*0-412-58660-6*) Chapman & Hall.

Self-Assessment in Accident & Emergency Medicine. Ian Greaves et al. (Illus.). 232p. 1996. pap. 40.00 (*0-7506-2215-6*, Focal) Buttrwrth-Heinemann.

Self-Assessment in Chest Medicine. Ronald B. George et al. LC 95-35114. 196p. 1995. 39.95 (*0-683-03460-X*) Williams & Wilkins.

Self Assessment in Clinical Cardiology, Vol. 1. Teaching Conference in Clinical Cardiology Staff. Ed. by Michael S. Gordon. LC 74-77256. (Illus.). 259p. reprint ed. pap. 73.90 (*0-8357-6759-0*, 2035420) Bks Demand.

Self Assessment in Clinical Cardiology, Vol. 2. Teaching Conference in Clinical Cardiology Staff. Ed. by Michael S. Gordon. LC 74-77256. (Illus.). 349p. reprint ed. pap. 99.50 (*0-8357-7954-8*, 2057029) Bks Demand.

***Self-Assessment in Endocrinology.** John Laycock & Peter Wise. (Illus.). 320p. 1997. pap. 29.50 (*0-19-262846-1*) OUP.

***Self-Assessment in Haematology.** 200p. 1997. pap. text ed. 19.00 (*1-86094-068-4*) World Scientific Pub.

Self-Assessment in Hematology. Christopher J. Pallister. (Illus.). 192p. 1991. pap. 40.00 (*0-7506-1216-9*) Buttrwrth-Heinemann.

Self-Assessment in Histology: Questions & Quiz Micrographs. Paul R. Wheater & H. George Burkitt. (Illus.). 176p. 1981. pap. text ed. 19.95 (*0-443-02109-0*) Churchill.

Self Assessment in Immediate Medical Care. Richard M. Hodgetts. 1990. text ed. 19.00 (*0-7020-1510-5*) Saunders.

Self Assessment in Multidisciplinary Critical Care: A Comprehensive Review. Ed. by Phillip Dellinger & Robert Taylor. LC 86-60806. 1986. write for info. (*0-936145-25-0*) SCCM Fullerton.

Self-Assessment in Nephrology. Sanford E. Warren et al. LC 86-30559. 270p. 1987. 65.00 (*0-306-42342-1*, Plenum Med Bk) Plenum.

Self-Assessment in Physiology & Pharmacology. T. Bennett et al. (Self-Assessment Ser.). (Illus.). 372p. 1984. pap. write for info. (*0-632-01161-0*) Blackwell Sci.

Self-Assessment Manual 1992-93. rev. ed. 100p. 1991. student ed. write for info. (*0-932915-06-X*) Accredit Assn Ambulatory.

Self-Assessment of Adult Physical Rehabilitation Skills: RIC-SAPhyRes. Kathleen H. Culler. 1993. student ed. write for info. (*0-910317-99-2*) Am Occup Therapy.

Self Assessment Picture Tests in Dentistry. Glyn & Jones. 144p. (C). (gr. 13). 1993. pap. text ed. 31.00 (*0-8151-4023-1*, Yr Bk Med Pubs) Mosby Yr Bk.

Self Assessment Picture Tests in Dentistry. Shaw. 144p. (C). (gr. 13). 1993. pap. text ed. 31.00 (*0-8151-7664-3*, Yr Bk Med Pubs) Mosby Yr Bk.

Self Assessment Picture Tests in Dentistry. Winstanley. 144p. (C). (gr. 13). 1994. pap. text ed. 31.00 (*0-8151-9336-X*, Yr Bk Med Pubs) Mosby Yr Bk.

Self-Assessment Picture Tests in Dentistry: Pedodontics. Linda Shaw. LC 93-8372. 1993. write for info. (*0-7234-1929-9*, Pub. by Wolfe Pub UK) Mosby Yr Bk.

Self Assessment Picture Tests in Dentistry - Endod... Walker. 000144p. (C). (gr. 13). 1994. 31.00 (*0-8151-9148-0*, Yr Bk Med Pubs) Mosby Yr Bk.

Self Assessment Picture Tests in Dentistry - Period... Glenwright. 144p. (C). (gr. 13). 1993. pap. text ed. 31.00 (*0-8151-3505-X*, Yr Bk Med Pubs) Mosby Yr Bk.

Self Assessment Picture Tests in Medicine: Pediatr. Milner. 176p. (C). (gr. 13). 1994. pap. text ed. 25.00 (*0-8151-5916-1*, Yr Bk Med Pubs) Mosby Yr Bk.

Self-Assessment Picture Tests in Rheumatology Medicine. Michael Doherty & Emmanuel George. (Illus.). 144p. (gr. 13). 1995. 21.00 (*0-7234-1968-X*) Mosby Yr Bk.

Self Assessment Picture Tests in Veterinary Medicine: Equine Practice. Dyson. 294p. (gr. 13). 1992. pap. text ed. 41.95 (*0-7234-1744-X*) Mosby Yr Bk.

Self Assessment Picture Tests in Veterinary Medicine: Farm Animals. Taylor & Blowey. 180p. (gr. 13). 1992. pap. text ed. 27.95 (*0-7234-1743-1*) Mosby Yr Bk.

Self-Assessment Picture Tests in Veterinary Medicine: Small Animal. Long. (Illus.). 198p. (gr. 13). 1992. pap. text ed. 29.95 (*0-7234-1745-8*) Mosby Yr Bk.

Self Assessment Picture Tests Veterinary Medicine: Small Animal Dermatology. Kummel. 144p. 1994. 31.95 (*0-7234-1705-9*) Mosby Yr Bk.

Self-Assessment Questions & Answers for Dental Assistants. 2nd ed. P. L. Erridge. 262p. 1988. student ed., pap. text ed. 32.50 (*0-7236-0963-2*) Buttrwrth-Heinemann.

Self-Assessment Questions & Answers for Equine Practitioners. James Pratt. 1993. 36.95 (*0-939674-47-5*) Am Vet Pubns.

Self-Assessment Questions & Answers for Food Animal Practitioners. James Pratt. 484p. 1993. pap. text ed. 36.95 (*0-939674-48-3*) Am Vet Pubns.

Self-Assessment Questions & Answers for Small Animal Practitioners, vol. 1. James Pratt. 540p. 1993. pap. text ed. 36.95 (*0-939674-45-9*) Am Vet Pubns.

Self-Assessment Questions & Answers for Small Animal Practitioners, Vol. 2. James Pratt. 536p. 1993. pap. text ed. 36.95 (*0-939674-46-7*) Am Vet Pubns.

***Self at Liberty: Political Argument & the Arts of Government.** Duncan Ivison. LC 97-508. (Contestations Ser.). 256p. 1996. 39.95 (*0-8014-3293-6*) Cornell U Pr.

Self-Avoiding Walk. Neal Madras & Gordon Slade. LC 92-28276. (Probability & Its Applications Ser.). xiv, 425p. 1992. 68.00 (*0-8176-3589-0*) Birkhauser.

***Self-Avoiding Walk.** Neal Madras & G. Slade. (Illus.). 448p. 1996. pap. 36.50 (*0-8176-3891-1*) Birkhauser.

***Self-Aware Image: An Insight into Early Modern Meta-Painting.** Victor I. Stoichita. Tr. by Anne-Marie Glasheen. LC 96-46977. (Studies in New Art History & Criticism). (Illus.). 368p. (C). 1997. text ed. 75.00 (*0-521-43393-2*) Cambridge U Pr.

Self-Aware Universe: How Consciousness Creates the Material World. Amit Goswami. 1995. pap. text ed. 14.95 (*0-87477-798-4*, Tarcher Putnam) Putnam Pub Group.

Self-Awareness. Dennis E. Coates & Meredith M. Bell. 42p. 1995. pap. text ed. 10.00 (*1-886713-07-3*) Perform Support Systs.

Self-Awareness: A Semantical Inquiry. Harald Delius. 276p. 1987. 87.00 (*3-406-07945-8*) Philosophia Pr.

Self-Awareness & Drug Abuse & Drug Control. L. Pickens. Ed. by Therese A. Zak. (Lifeworks Ser.). (Illus.). 128p. 1981. text ed. 13.96 (*0-07-049910-1*) McGraw.

Self-Awareness Growth Experiences (SAGE) Strategies That Promote Positive Self-Esteem at the Secondary Grade Level. rev. ed. V. Alex Kehayan. Ed. by Janet Lovelady. LC 89-84063. (Creative Teaching Ser.). (Illus.). 224p. 1989. reprint ed. pap. 16.95 (*0-915190-61-3*, JP9061-3) Jalmar Pr.

Self-Awareness in Animals & Humans: Developmental Perspectives. Ed. by Sue T. Parker et al. (Illus.). 450p. (C). 1994. text ed. 64.95 (*0-521-44108-0*) Cambridge U Pr.

Self-Awareness in Domesticated Animals. 1981. 40.00 (*0-317-43807-7*) St Mut.

Self-Begetting Novel. Steven G. Kellman. LC 70-15700. 1980. text ed. 49.50 (*0-231-04782-7*) Col U Pr.

Self-Begetting, Self-Devouring: Jungian Archetypes in the Fiction of Robert A. Heinlein. Robin Usher. LC 95-3912. (Milford Ser. : Popular Writers of Today: Vol. 70). 1996. pap. write for info. (*0-89370-973-5*); lib. bdg. write for info. (*0-89370-972-7*) Borgo Pr.

Self Between: From Freud to the New Social Psychology of France. Eugene Webb. LC 92-46472. 264p. (C). 1993. 35.00 (*0-295-97226-2*) U of Wash Pr.

Self Beyond Self: Judaism's Dynamic Ascent to the Infinite. Y. S. Hurwitz. LC 94-28449. 1994. 18.95 (*0-87306-674-X*) Feldheim.

Self Bows & Other Archery Tackle from Tomb of Tutankhamun. McLeod. (Tutankhamuns Tomb Ser.: Vol. 4). 1982. 50.00 (*0-900416-33-5*, Pub. by Aris & Phillips UK) David Brown.

Self-Build Book: How to Enjoy Designing & Building Your Own Home. rev. ed. Jon Broome & Brian Richardson. (Illus.). 271p. (Orig.). 1996. pap. 30.00 (*1-900322-00-5*) Chelsea Green Pub.

Self-Calmed Baby. William A. Sammons. 1991. mass mkt. 4.99 (*0-312-92468-2*) St Martin.

Self-Calmed Baby: A Liberating New Approach to Parenting Your Infant. William A. Sammons. 1989. 17.95 (*0-318-41367-1*) Little.

***Self-Care: A Theology of Personal Empowerment & Spiritual Healing.** (Illus.). 280p. 1995. pap. 16.99 (*0-8010-5743-4*, Bridgept Bks) Baker Bks.

Self-Care: Lay Initiatives in Health. Lowell S. Levin et al. LC 76-29361. 1976. pap. 7.95 (*0-88202-111-7*) Watson Pub Intl.

Self-Care: Your Family Guide to Symptoms & How to Treat Them. Don R. Powell. (Illus.). 288p. 1996. 21.95 (*1-882606-24-8*); pap. 14.95 (*1-882606-50-7*) Peoples Med Soc.

Self Care Acupressure Kit. David G. Williams. 26p. 1992. pap. 15.95 incl. vhs (*0-944649-13-0*) Mtn Home Pub.

Self-Care Advisor. Health Publishing Group Editors. (Illus.). 336p. (Orig.). 1996. pap. write for info. (*0-9644119-1-1*) Time Inc Health.

***Self-Care Advisor: The Essential Home Health Guide for You & Your Family.** 2nd ed. Time Inc. Health Editors. (Illus.). 352p. 1996. pap. write for info. (*0-9644119-2-X*) Time Inc Health.

Self-Care & Health in Old Age: Health & Behaviour Implications for Policy & Practice. Ed. by Kathryn Dean et al. LC 85-28015. 368p. 1986. 59.50 (*0-7099-0881-4*, Pub. by Croom Helm UK) Routledge Chapman & Hall.

Self-Care & Self-Help Groups for the Elderly. 1991. lib. bdg. 69.95 (*0-8490-4487-1*) Gordon Pr.

Self Care Deficit Nursing Theory: In Practice. Dennis. 176p. (C). (gr. 13). 1996. pap. text ed. 27.00 (*0-8151-2426-0*) Mosby Yr Bk.

Self Care Deficit Theory of Nursing. Joan Munley. 128p. (C). 1984. pap. text ed. write for info. (*0-910973-03-2*) Arrowhead AZ.

Self Care for Every Day: Reflections on Healthy, Spiritual Living. Robert J. Wicks. LC 91-77633. pap. 5.95 (*0-87029-238-2*) Abbey.

Self-Care In & Out of Bed. Yetta Bernhard. 1975. pap. 12.00 (*0-930017-00-5*) Sci & Behavior.

Self-Care Nursing in a Multicultural Context. Juliene Lipson & Nancy Steiger. LC 96-4508. 352p. 1996. 46.00 (*0-8039-7054-4*); pap. 24.95 (*0-8039-7055-2*) Sage.

Self Care Versus Medical Care. 1992. lib. bdg. 69.99 (*0-8490-8793-7*) Gordon Pr.

Self Caring Nursing. 2nd ed. Hill & Smith. 1989. pap. text ed. 38.95 (*0-8385-8528-0*) P-H.

***Self Catering Guide to Southern Ireland 1997.** SITB Staff. (Southern Ireland Tourist Board Ser.). 200p. (Orig.). 1997. pap. 8.95 (*0-9528915-0-6*, Pub. by Jarrold Pub UK) Seven Hills Bk.

***Self-Catering Holiday Homes in England 1998.** 23th ed. English Tourist Board Staff. (Where to Stay Ser.). (Illus.). 304p. 1998. pap. 10.95 (*0-86143-203-7*, Pub. by Jarrold Pub UK) Seven Hills Bk.

Self-Centering Manual: How to Align Your Outward Behavior with Your Inner Belief. Rob Sanford. (Illus.). 102p. 1995. pap. 16.95 (*1-57077-998-8*) TitleWaves.

Self Change: Social Psychological & Clinical Perspectives. Ed. by Y. Klar et al. (Illus.). x, 285p. 1992. 62.95 (*0-387-97811-9*) Spr-Verlag.

***Self Coached Reading.** Dennis Matthies. (C). 1996. spiral bd. write for info. (*1-887981-07-1*) Stanford Bookstore.

Self, Collective Behavior & Society Vol. 12: Essays Honoring the Contributions of Ralph H. Turner. Ed. by Gerald M. Platt & Chad Gordon. 413p. 1994. 73.25 (*0-614-11071-8*) Jai Pr.

Self-Complementary Antennas: Principle of Self-Complementarity for Constant Impedance. Yasuto Mushaike. LC 95-25745. (Illus.). 150p. 1996. 79.00 (*3-540-76002-4*) Spr-Verlag.

Self-Completion: Keys to the Meaningful Life. Robert S. De Ropp. LC 87-82943. (Illus.). 210p. 1988. 15.95 (*0-89556-053-4*) Gateways Bks & Tapes.

Self Concept. John Hattie. 320p. 1992. text ed. 59.95 (*0-89859-629-7*) L Erlbaum Assocs.

Self Concept: A Critical Survey of Pertinent Research Literature. Ruth C. Wylie. LC 61-8377. 405p. reprint ed. pap. 115.50 (*0-317-10559-0*, 2004728) Bks Demand.

Self-Concept: European Perspectives on Its Development, Aspects, & Applications. Ed. by L. Oppenheimer. (Recent Research in Psychology Ser.). (Illus.). viii, 160p. 1990. 42.95 (*0-387-52371-5*) Spr-Verlag.

Self-Concept Vol. 1: A Review of Methodological Considerations & Measuring Instruments. rev. ed. Ruth C. Wylie. LC 72-97165. xx, 433p. 1974. text ed. 45.00 (*0-8032-0830-8*) U of Nebr Pr.

Self-Concept Vol. 2: Theory & Research on Selected Topics. rev. ed. Ruth C. Wylie et al. LC 72-97165. xvi, 825p. 1979. text ed. 55.00 (*0-8032-4701-X*) U of Nebr Pr.

Self-Concept in the Young Child: An Anthology. Ed. by Thomas D. Yawkey. LC 80-13812. 256p. (Orig.). 1980. pap. text ed. 12.95 (*0-8425-1815-0*) Frnds of the Libry.

Self-Concept of Exceptional Learners: Current Perspectives for Educators. Festus E. Obiakor. 240p. (C). 1994. per. 41.94 (*0-8403-9545-0*) Kendall-Hunt.

Self-Concept, Self-Esteem, & the Curriculum. James A. Beane & Richard P. Lipka. 272p. (C). 1986. pap. text ed. 19.95 (*0-8077-2839-X*) Tchrs Coll.

Self Concept Sourcebook: Ideas & Activities for Building Self Esteem. Ed. by Dov P. Elkins. LC 79-88300. 1979. pap. 19.00 (*0-918834-09-0*) Growth Assoc.

Self Condemned. Wyndham Lewis. LC 83-2836. (Illus.). 440p. (Orig.). 1983. 25.00 (*0-87685-576-1*); pap. 15.00 (*0-87685-575-3*) Black Sparrow.

Self-Confident Child. Jean Yoder & William Proctor. 224p. 1990. mass mkt. 4.50 (*0-380-70842-6*) Avon.

Self-Confident Child. Jean Yoder & William Proctor. 192p. 1988. 22.95 (*0-8160-1270-9*) Facts on File.

***Self-Confident Child.** Jean Yoder & William Proctor. LC 87-28068. 184p. 1988. reprint ed. pap. 52.50 (*0-608-02822-3*, 2063889) Bks Demand.

Self-Conflict & Self Healing. John King-Farlow & Sean O'Connell. LC 87-31735. 276p. (Orig.). (C). 1988. pap. text ed. 24.00 (*0-8191-6795-9*) U Pr of Amer.

Self-Confrontation: A Manual for In-Depth Discipleship. John C. Broger. 1994. pap. 24.99 (*0-7852-8246-7*) Nelson.

Self-Confrontation: Syllabus for Biblical Counseling Training Program, Course I. 2nd ed. John C. Broger. 1992. pap. text ed. 24.95 (*1-878114-01-8*) Biblical Counseling.

Self-Congruity: Toward a Theory of Personality & Cybernetics. M. Joseph Sirgy. LC 86-8583. 246p. 1986. text ed. 55.00 (*0-275-92192-1*, C2192, Praeger Pubs) Greenwood.

Self-Conscious Art: A Tribute to John W. Kronik. Ed. by Susan L. Fischer. LC 55-58217. (Bucknell Review Ser.). (Illus.). 184p. 1995. 22.00 (*0-8387-5324-8*) Bucknell U Pr.

Self-Conscious Emotions: The Psychology of Shame, Guilt, Embarrassment, & Pride. Ed. by June P. Tangney & Kurt W. Fischer. 1995. lib. bdg. 46.95 (*0-89862-264-6*, 2264) Guilford Pr.

Self-Conscious Novel: Artifice in Fiction from Joyce to Pynchon. Brian Stonehill. LC 87-30784. (Pennsylvania Studies in Contemporary American Fiction). (Illus.). 232p. 1988. pap. 18.95 (*0-8122-1304-1*) U of Pa Pr.

Self-Conscious Structure: A Study of the British Theatre from Buchingham Through Fielding & Sheridan. C. N. Ramachandran. 210p. 1987. 17.50 (*81-202-0183-3*, Pub. by Ajanta II) S Asia.

Self Consciousness: An Alternative Anthropology of Identity. Anthony P. Cohen. LC 94-344. 244p. (C). 1994. pap. 16.95 (*0-415-08324-9*, B4363) Routledge.

Self-Consciousness: Memoirs. John Updike. 1989. 18.95 (*0-394-57222-X*) Knopf.

Self-Consciousness: Memoirs. John Updike. 288p. 1990. mass mkt. 5.95 (*0-449-21821-X*, Expression) Fawcett.

Self-Consciousness: The Spiritual Human Being, Vol. 24. Rudolf Steiner. Ed. by Bernard J. Garber. LC 82-82477. 328p. 1985. lib. bdg. 19.00 (*0-89345-020-0*, Spir Sci Lib) Garber Comm.

Self-Consciousness & Selfreference: An Interpretation of Wittgenstein's Tractatus. B. A. Worthington. 189p. 1988. text ed. 63.95 (*0-566-05554-6*, Pub. by Avebury Pub UK) Ashgate Pub Co.

Self-Consistency: A Theory of Personality. Prescott Lecky. LC 82-82238. 144p. 1982. pap. 6.95 (*0-87208-221-0*) Shoeless Pub.

S

Self-Consistency: A Theory of Personality. rev. ed. Rolfe F. Schell. LC 93-81260. 176p. (C). 1994. pap. 12.95 (*0-87208-310-1*) Shoeless Pub.

Self Consuming Paper Cartridges for the Percussion Revolver. W. J. Kirst. 1986. 3.95 (*0-913150-51-7*) Pioneer Pr.

Self-Contained Breathing Apparatus. 2nd ed. IFSTA Committee. Ed. by Lynne C. Murnane. LC 91-71902. (Illus.). 360p. 1991. pap. text ed. 30.00 (*0-87939-093-X*) IFSTA.

Self-Contained Breathing Apparatus for Fire Fighters. National Fire Protection Association Staff. 1992. 20.25 (*0-317-63573-5*, 1981-92) Natl Fire Prot.

Self-Contradictions of the Bible. William H. Burr. 96p. 1988. 23.95 (*0-87975-416-8*) Prometheus Bks.

Self-Control. Henrietta Gambill. LC 82-1201. (Values to Live By Ser.). (Illus.). 32p. (J). (ps-2). 1982. lib. bdg. 21.36 (*0-89565-225-0*) Childs World.

Self Control. Jack Kuhatschek. (Fruit of the Spirit Bible Studies). 48p. 1991. pap. 4.99 (*0-310-53731-2*) Zondervan.

Self Control, Reading Level 2. Elaine Goley. (Learn the Value Ser.: Set II). (Illus.). 32p. (J). (gr. 1-4). 1989. 11.95 (*0-685-58790-8*); lib. bdg. 15.94 (*0-86592-397-3*) Rourke Corp.

Self-Control: Waiting Until Tomorrow for What You Want Today. Alexandra W. Logue. LC 94-5478. 224p. 1994. pap. text ed. 21.80 (*0-13-803750-7*) P-H.

Self-Control & Man's Will see Lay Counseling Series

Self-Control & Mastery in Early Childhood Education: Helping Young Children Grow. Erna Furman. 160p. 1997. pap. 24.95 (*0-8236-8063-0*, BN 26055) Intl Univs Pr.

Self-Control & Self-Modification of Emotional Behavior. Ed. by Kirk R. Blankstein et al. (Advances in the Study of Communication & Affect Ser.: Vol. 7). 216p. 1982. 42.50 (*0-306-40945-3*, Plenum Pr) Plenum.

Self-Control Classroom: Understanding & Managing the Disruptive Behavior of All Students Including Students with ADHD. James Levin & John Shanken-Kaye. 182p. 1996. pap. text ed. 27.00 (*0-7872-1299-7*) Kendall-Hunt.

Self Control Not Gun Control. J. Neil Schulman. LC 95-74682. 312p. 1995. 24.95 (*1-882639-05-7*) Synapse Cent.

***Self-Control Patrol Workbook.** Terry Trower. (Illus.). 63p. (J). (gr. 2-6). 1995. pap. 16.95 (*1-882732-38-3*) Ctr Applied Psy.

Self, Cosmos, God. Daniel Kolak & Raymond Martin. 775p. (C). 1993. text ed. 42.75 (*0-03-054197-2*) HB Coll Pubs.

Self Creation. George Weinberg. 1989. mass mkt. 4.50 (*0-312-91627-2*) St Martin.

Self-Creation & History: Collingwood & Nietzsche. Michael Hinz. 252p. (Orig.). (C). 1994. pap. text ed. 26.50 (*0-8191-9344-5*); lib. bdg. 58.00 (*0-8191-9343-7*) U Pr of Amer.

Self-Crowned Laureates: Spenser, Jonson, Milton, & the Literary System. Richard Helgerson. LC 82-8496. 330p. 1983. 42.50 (*0-520-04808-3*) U CA Pr.

Self-Culture. William E. Channing. LC 74-89163. (Essay Index Reprint Ser.). 1977. reprint ed. 13.95 (*0-405-01401-5*) Ayer.

Self-Deceit. Frederick Faber. (C). 1949. pap. 3.00 (*0-87574-050-2*) Pendle Hill.

Self-Deception & Morality. Mike W. Martin. LC 86-5467. x, 182p. 1986. 19.95 (*0-7006-0297-6*); pap. 9.95 (*0-7006-0353-0*) U Pr of KS.

Self-Deception & Self-Understanding: New Essays in Philosophy & Psychology. Ed. by Mike W. Martin. LC 84-27013. x, 310p. 1985. pap. 12.95 (*0-7006-0396-4*) U Pr of KS.

Self-Defeating Behaviors: Experimental Research, Clinical Impressions, & Practical Implications. Ed. by R. C. Curtis. (Social - Clinical Psychology Ser.). (Illus.). 398p. 1989. 59.50 (*0-306-43129-7*, Plenum Pr) Plenum.

Self-Defeating Behaviors: Free Yourself from the Habits, Compulsions, Feelings, & Attitudes That Hold You Back. Milton R. Cudney & Robert E. Hardy. LC 90-84903. 256p. 1993. reprint ed. pap. 12.00 (*0-06-250197-6*) Harper SF.

Self Defeating Organization. Alexander J. Matejko. LC 85-9524. 425p. 1986. text ed. 65.00 (*0-275-90026-6*, C0026, Praeger Pubs) Greenwood.

Self-Defeating Organization: How Smart Companies Can Stop Outsmarting Themselves. Robert E. Hardy & Randy Schwartz. 288p. 1996. 25.00 (*0-201-48313-0*) Addison-Wesley.

***Self-Defeating Organizations.** Robert Hardy. 1997. pap. 13.00 (*0-201-15486-2*) Addison-Wesley.

Self Defense. Susan L. Peterson. (Illus.). 128p. (Orig.). (C). 1988. pap. text ed. 15.95 (*0-89582-185-0*) Morton Pub.

Self-Defense. large type ed. Jonathan Kellerman. LC 95-2021. (Large Print Bks.). 1995. 26.95 (*1-56895-206-6*) Wheeler Pub.

Self-Defense. 2nd ed. Connie H. Lavergne. 102p. (C). 1995. pap. text ed. 11.95 (*0-89641-244-X*) American Pr.

Self-Defense. Jonathan Kellerman. 464p. 1995. reprint ed. mass mkt., pap. 6.99 (*0-553-57220-2*) Bantam.

Self-Defense: Steps to Success. Joan M. Nelson. LC 90-25460. (Steps to Success Activity Ser.). (Illus.). 160p. (Orig.). 1991. pap. 14.95 (*0-88011-430-4*, PNEL0430) Human Kinetics.

Self Defense: The Womanly Art of Self-Care, Intuition & Choice. Debbie Leung. LC 91-61404. (Illus.). 176p. 1991. pap. 12.95 (*0-929838-08-4*) R & M Pr WA.

Self-Defense Against the Use of Force in International Law. LC 96-28524. (Developments in International Law Ser.). 1996. 185.00 (*90-411-0247-7*) Kluwer Law Tax Pubs.

Self-Defense & Assault Prevention for Girls & Women. Bruce Tegner & Alice McGrath. (Illus.). 128p. 1977. pap. 8.00 (*0-87407-026-0*, T-26) Thor.

Self-Defense Finance: For Small Businesses. Wilbur M. Yegge. LC 95-11737. 256p. 1995. pap. text ed. 17.95 (*0-471-12295-5*) Wiley.

Self-Defense Finance: For Small Businesses. 2nd rev. ed. Wilbur M. Yegge et al. LC 95-11737. 649p. 1995. text ed. 55.00 (*0-471-12294-7*) Wiley.

Self-Defense for Criminal Justice. E. Leslie Knight & Chuck Reaume. Ed. by Katharine Corbin. write for info. (*0-929736-10-9*) ISC Div Wellness.

Self-Defense for Everybody: A Primer in Applied Karate. Bernd W. Weiss & Hilda O. Weiss. LC 87-82033. (Illus.). 150p. (C). 1992. text ed. 15.00 (*0-931373-02-6*) Hiles & Hardin Pubs.

Self Defense for Today. Paul Crompton. pap. 13.95 (*0-901764-99-X*, 93164) Talman.

Self-Defense for Wimps: The "ART of Oneupmanship. Sid Campbell. 1989. 29.95 (*0-682-87114-1*) Gong Prods.

***Self-Defense for Women.** Willy Cahill. LC 96-72480. Orig. Title: Kick & Run. (Illus.). 96p. 1997. pap. 10.95 (*0-89750-061-X*, 209) Ohara Pubns.

Self-Defense for Women. Eva Shaw. 275p. 1996. pap. 12.95 (*1-888197-00-5*) E Dalton Bks.

Self Defense for Your Child. Bruce Tegner. 1986. lib. bdg. 79.95 (*0-8490-3816-2*) Gordon Pr.

Self-Defense for Your Child: Practical Defenses & Assault-Prevention. Bruce Tegner & Alice McGrath. LC 76-1856. (Illus.). 128p. (Orig.). (J). (gr. k-6). 1976. pap. 7.00 (*0-87407-024-4*, T-24) Thor.

Self-Defense in Intern Law. McCormack. LC 96-22889. 1996. text ed. 49.95 (*0-312-16279-0*) St Martin.

***Self Defense in Kata Vol. I: Shotokan Forms Applications.** Bernd W. Weiss. 85p. (Orig.). (YA). 1997. pap. 15.00 (*0-931373-06-9*) Hiles & Hardin Pubs.

Self-Defense Laws & Violent Crime Rates in the United States. John F. Ross. 16p. (C). 1996. pap. text ed. 5.00 (*1-888118-03-2*) Accurate Pr.

Self-Defense Mechanisms: Role of Macrophage. D. Mizuno et al. 344p. 1983. 137.50 (*0-444-80460-9*) Elsevier.

Self-Defense Nerve Centers & Pressure Points for Karate, Jujitsu & Atemi-Waza. enl. rev. ed. Bruce Tegner. LC 78-18169. (Illus.). 1968. pap. 8.00 (*0-87407-029-5*, T-29) Thor.

Self Defense One Hundred: One-Step Sparring. B. Y. Kwak. 160p. 1992. 19.95 (*0-9632784-0-1*) B Y Kwak.

Self-Definition & Self-Discovery in Early Christianity: A Study in Changing Horizons. Ed. by David J. Hawkin & Tom Robinson. LC 90-49660. (Studies in the Bible & Early Christianity: Vol. 26). 276p. 1990. lib. bdg. 89.95 (*0-88946-374-3*) E Mellen.

Self-Delight in a Harsh World: The Main Stories of Individual, Marital, & Family Psychotherapy. James P. Gustafson. 200p. (C). 1992. 22.95 (*0-393-70136-0*) Norton.

Self-Designing Organizations: Learning How to Create High Performance. Susan A. Mohrman & Thomas G. Cummings. (Organization Development Ser.). (Illus.). 200p. (C). 1989. pap. text ed. 26.95 (*0-201-14603-7*) Addison-Wesley.

Self-Destruction in the Promised Land: A Psychocultural History. Howard I. Kushner. 280p. 1989. 24.95 (*0-8135-1377-4*) Rutgers U Pr.

Self-Determination: An Examination of the Question & its Application to African-American People. 2nd ed. James Forman. LC 81-82611. (Illus.). 116p. (C). 1984. 18.95 (*0-940880-09-1*); pap. 8.95 (*0-940880-08-3*) Open Hand.

Self Determination: International Perspectives. Ed. by Donald Clark & Robert Williamson. 432p. 1996. text ed. 75.00 (*0-312-16171-9*) St Martin.

Self-Determination Across the Life Span: Independence & Choice for People with Disabilities. Ed. by Deanna J. Sands & Michael L. Wehmeyer. LC 96-6837. 1996. 35.00 (*1-55766-238-X*) P H Brookes.

***Self-Determination & National Minorities.** Thomas D. Musgrave. LC 96-40030. (Oxford Monographes in International Law). 400p. 1997. 95.00 (*0-19-826058-X*) OUP.

***Self-Determination & Self-Administration: A Sourcebook.** Ed. by Wolfgang Danspeckgruber & Arthur Watts. 500p. 1997. 110.00 (*1-55587-786-9*) Lynne Rienner.

Self-Determination & the Social Education of Native Americans. Guy B. Senese. LC 90-20011. 248p. 1991. text ed. 49.95 (*0-275-93776-3*, C3776, Praeger Pubs) Greenwood.

Self-Determination in a Western Democracies: Aboriginal Politics in a Comparative Perspective. Guntram F. Werther. LC 92-9576. (Contributions in Political Science Ser.: No. 302). 160p. 1992. text ed. 47.95 (*0-313-28432-6*, WAK, Greenwood Pr) Greenwood.

Self-Determination in the Commonwealth. W. J. Macartney. 128p. 1988. pap. text ed. 25.90 (*0-08-034525-5*, Pergamon Pr) Elsevier.

Self-Determination in the Middle East. Yosef Gotlieb. LC 82-13239. 190p. 1982. text ed. 55.00 (*0-275-90808-9*, C0808, Praeger Pubs) Greenwood.

Self-Determination in the New World Order: Guidelines for U. S. Policy. Morton H. Halperin et al. LC 92-23015. 1992. 21.95 (*0-87003-018-3*); pap. 8.95 (*0-87003-019-1*) Carnegie Endow.

Self Determination of Minorities in International Politics. Alexis Heraclides. 1992. pap. 20.00 (*0-7146-4082-4*, Pub. by F Cass Pubs UK); pap. text ed. 39.50 (*0-7146-3384-4*, Pub. by F Cass Pubs UK) Intl Spec Bk.

Self-Determination of Peoples: A Legal Reappraisal. A. Cassese. (Hersch Lauterpacht Memorial Lectures: No. 12). 432p. (C). 1995. text ed. 90.00 (*0-521-48187-2*) Cambridge U Pr.

Self-Determination, Terrorism, & the International Humanitarian Law of Armed Conflict. rev. ed. E. Chadwick. LC 96-2672. 1996. text ed. 95.00 (*90-411-0122-5*, Pub. by M Nijhoff NE) Kluwer Ac.

Self-Determined Kids: Helping Children Succeed. Dennis E. Mithaug. 228p. pap. 24.95 (*0-669-27140-3*, Lexington) Jossey-Bass.

Self Development Skills see Career Skills Library

Self-Development Skills see Productive Supervisor: A Program of Practical Managerial Skills

Self Development Test Study Guide. Wilson L. Walker. 1993. pap. 14.95 (*0-942710-97-5*) Impact VA.

Self Development Through Meditative Practice. Donald Melcer. 1983. pap. 4.50 (*0-916786-70-6*, Saint George Pubns) R Steiner Col Pubns.

Self-Development Through Self-Defense: A Course in Personal Security. John Roseberry. (Illus.). 58p. (Orig.). 1994. student ed., pap. 19.95 (*0-9639936-0-7*) J Samuel Pubng.

Self Development with Astrology. Sheila Geddes. 160p. 1995. pap. 9.95 (*0-572-01534-8*, Pub. by Foulsham UK) Assoc Pubs Grp.

Self-Development with the I Ching: A New Interpretation. Paul Sneddon. 160p. (Orig.). 1995. pap. 9.95 (*0-572-01529-1*, Pub. by Foulsham UK) Assoc Pubs Grp.

Self Development with the Tarot. Catherine Summers & Julian Vayne. 151p. (Orig.). 1992. pap. 9.95 (*0-572-01788-X*, Pub. by W Foulsham UK) Trans-Atl Phila.

Self Development with the Zodiac Oracle. Foulsham Editors. 160p. 1995. pap. 9.95 (*0-572-01652-2*, Pub. by Foulsham UK) Assoc Pubs Grp.

Self-Diagnostic Approach to Understanding Organizational & Personal Stressors: The C-O-P-E Model for Stress Reduction. Bernadette H. Schell. LC 96-9048. 320p. 1997. text ed. 59.95 (*0-89930-938-0*, Quorum Bks) Greenwood.

Self-Directed Behavior. 6th ed. Roland G. Tharp. 354p. (C). 1993. text ed. 34.00 (*0-534-18978-4*) Brooks-Cole.

Self-Directed Behavior: Self-Modification for Personal Adjustment. 6th ed. David L. Watson & Roland G. Tharp. 1996. teacher ed. write for info. (*0-534-18979-2*) Brooks-Cole.

Self-Directed Behavior: Self-Modification for Personal Adjustment. 7th ed. David L. Watson & Roland G. Tharp. (Psychology Ser.). 402p. (C). 1997. text ed. 28.95 (*0-534-34481-X*) Brooks-Cole.

Self-Directed Career Counseling Approach: Holland's Exploratory View. Rod Kennedy. LC 91-90480. 85p. (Orig.). 1991. pap. 15.00 (*0-9629869-0-9*) Kenner Pub.

Self Directed Career Planning Workbook. Gibaldi & McCarthy. 1993. pap. text ed. write for info. (*0-07-023155-9*) McGraw.

Self-Directed Groupwork: Users Take Action for Empowerment. Audrey Mullender & Dave Ward. 194p. 1992. pap. text ed. 17.95 (*1-871177-11-1*, Pub. by Whiting & Birch UK) Paul & Co Pubs.

Self-Directed Growth. Douglas L. Robertson. LC 87-72746. xxiv, 213p. (C). 1988. pap. text ed. 19.95 (*0-915202-75-1*) Accel Devel.

***Self-Directed IEP.** 2nd ed. James E. Martin et al. (ChoiceMaker Self-Determination Curriculum Ser.). (Illus.). 152p. 1996. teacher ed., wbk. ed., pap. text ed. 95.00 incl. vhs (*1-57035-105-8*, C88DIR) Sopris.

***Self-Directed IEP: Student Workbook.** 2nd ed. James E. Martin et al. (ChoiceMaker Self-Determination Curriculum Ser.). 32p. 1996. student ed., wbk. ed., pap. 29.00 (*1-57035-107-4*, 88STU) Sopris.

Self Directed Learning. C. Caffarella & O. O'Donnell. (C). 1989. pap. 32.00 (*1-85041-029-1*, Pub. by Univ Nottingham UK) St Mut.

Self-Directed Learning: A Guide for Learners & Teachers. Malcolm S. Knowles. 144p. (C). 1988. text ed. 15.00 (*0-8428-2215-1*) Cambridge Bk.

Self-Directed Learning: A Practical Guide to Design, Development & Implementation. George M. Piskurich. LC 93-12369. (Management Ser.). 379p. text ed. 35.95 (*1-55542-532-1*) Jossey-Bass.

Self-Directed Learning: Application & Research. Long, Huey B., & Assoc. Staff. 400p. (Orig.). 1992. pap. text ed. 25.95 (*0-9622488-7-8*) U OK PMC.

Self-Directed Learning: Consensus & Conflict. Huey B. Long et al. 300p. (Orig.). (C). 1991. pap. 25.95 (*0-9622488-3-5*) U OK PMC.

Self-Directed Learning: Emerging Theory & Practice. Long, Huey B., & Associates Staff. LC 89-611107. 144p. (Orig.). (C). 1989. pap. text ed. 24.95 (*0-9622488-0-0*) U OK PMC.

Self-Directed Learning: From Theory to Practice. Ed. by Stephen D. Brookfield. LC 84-82368. (New Directions for Adult & Continuing Education Ser.: No. 25). (Orig.). 1985. pap. 19.00 (*0-87589-743-6*) Jossey-Bass.

Self-Directed Learning Dissertation Abstracts 1966-1991. Huey B. Long & Terrence R. Reddy. 1991. pap. 24.95 (*0-9622488-4-3*) U OK PMC.

Self-Directed Learning in Counsellor Training. Mary Charleton. Ed. by Windy Dryden. LC 96-500. (Counselor Trainer & Supervisor Ser.). (Illus.). 128p. 1996. pap. 16.95 (*0-304-32943-6*); text ed. 60.00 (*0-304-32941-X*) Cassell.

Self-Directed Problem Solving: Idea Production in Mathematics. Ann Dirkes. 132p. (Orig.). (C). 1993. pap. text ed. 19.50 (*0-8191-9130-2*) U Pr of Amer.

Self-Directed School: Empowering the Stakeholders. Ronald G. McIntire & John T. Fessenden. LC 93-34345. 1995. 29.95 (*0-590-49267-5*, 28063m35 1994) Scholastic Inc.

Self-Directed Search (SDS) in Business & Industry: A Resource Guide. Ed. by Michael Shahnasarian. LC 96-8242. 1996. 23.95 (*0-911907-23-8*) Psych Assess.

Self-Directed Teacher: Managing the Learning Process. David Nunan & Clarice Lamb. (Language Education Ser.). (Illus.). 320p. (C). 1996. text ed. 47.95 (*0-521-49716-7*); pap. text ed. 18.95 (*0-521-49773-6*) Cambridge U Pr.

Self-Directed Work Teams: A Concise Guide to Understanding & Implementing Self-Directed Work Teams. rev. ed. Glenn H. Varney. 1997. pap. 12.50 (*0-614-04325-5*) Mgmt Advisory Assoc Inc.

Self-Directed Work Teams: A Primer. Cresencio Torres & Jerry Spiegel. LC 91-42. (Illus.). 100p. (Orig.). 1990. pap. 19.95 (*0-88390-057-2*, Pfffr & Co) Jossey-Bass.

Self-Directed Work Teams: The New American Challenge. Jack D. Orsburn et al. 353p. 1990. text ed. 40.00 (*1-55623-341-8*) Irwin Prof Pubng.

Self-Directed Work Teams Implementation Guide. rev. ed. Glenn H. Varney. 1997. pap. 14.50 (*0-614-04324-7*) Mgmt Advisory Assoc Inc.

Self-Directedness: Causes & Effects Throughout the Life Course. Ed. by Judith Rodin et al. 280p. 1990. 59.95 (*0-8058-0562-1*) L Erlbaum Assocs.

Self-Direction for Lifelong Learning: A Comprehensive Guide to Theory & Practice. Philip C. Candy. LC 90-47291. (Higher & Adult Education Ser.). 600p. text ed. 45.00 (*1-55542-303-5*) Jossey-Bass.

Self-Direction in Adult Learning: Perspective on Theory, Research & Practice. Ralph G. Brockett & Roger Hiemstra. 364p. (C). 1994. pap. 24.95 (*0-415-90912-0*) Routledge.

***Self-Discipline & Loyalty.** Shelagh Canning. (Adventures from the Book of Virtues Ser.). (Illus.). (J). (ps-2). 1997. pap. 3.25 (*0-614-29076-7*, Aladdin Paperbacks) S&S Childrens.

Self-Disclosure. Valerian J. Derlega et al. (Series on Close Relationships: Vol. 5). (Illus.). 160p. (C). 1993. text ed. 38.00 (*0-8039-3954-X*); pap. text ed. 16.95 (*0-8039-3955-8*) Sage.

Self-Disclosure: Origins, Patterns & Implications of Openness in Interpersonal Relationships. Gordon J. Chelune et al. LC 79-88766. (Jossey-Bass Social & Behavioral Science Ser.). 416p. reprint ed. pap. 118.60 (*0-8357-4972-X*, 2037905) Bks Demand.

Self-Disclosure: Theory, Research, & Therapy. Ed. by V. J. Derlega & J. H. Berg. LC 87-18654. (Perspectives in Social Psychology Ser.). (Illus.). 380p. 1987. 62.50 (*0-306-42635-8*, Plenum Pr) Plenum.

Self-Disclosure in the Therapeutic Relationship. George Stricker. LC 90-6740. (Illus.). 309p. 1990. 54.50 (*0-306-43448-2*, Plenum Pr) Plenum.

***Self-Disclosure of God: Principles of Ibn al-'Arabi's Cosmology.** William C. Chittick. (SUNY Series in Islam). 544p. (C). 1997. text ed. 74.50 (*0-7914-3403-6*); pap. text ed. 24.95 (*0-7914-3404-4*) State U NY Pr.

Self Discovery & Authority in Afro-American Narrative. Valerie Smith. 192p. (C). 1991. pap. 12.95 (*0-674-80088-5*) HUP.

Self Discovery & Manifestation. Jane K. Burke. (Orig.). 1995. pap. 9.95 (*0-929377-00-1*) Burke-Srour Pubns Inc.

Self Discovery Notebook. Lisa Engelhardt. 1993. pap. text ed. 6.95 (*0-87029-265-X*) Abbey.

Self-Discovery the Jungian Way: The Watchword Technique. Michael Daniels. (Illus.). 176p. (Orig.). (C). 1991. pap. 14.95 (*0-415-06755-3*, A6904) Routledge.

Self-Dual Chern-Simons Theories, Vol. X. Gerald Dunne. Ed. by W. Beiglbock et al. (Lecture Notes in Physics Ser.: No. M 36). 217p. 1995. 49.95 (*3-540-60257-7*) Spr-Verlag.

***Self, Earth & Society: Alienation & Trinitarian Transformation.** Thomas N. Finger. 424p. 1997. pap. 27.99 (*0-8308-1893-6*, 1893) InterVarsity.

Self-Editing for Fiction Writers: How to Edit Yourself into Print. Renni Browne & Dave King. LC 92-11229. (Illus.). 240p. 1994. pap. 12.00 (*0-06-272046-5*, Harper Ref) HarpC.

Self-Education/Self-Assessment in Thoracic Surgery (SESATS) Syllabus, No. VI. CCCETS Staff. 320p. 1996. 225.00 (*0-7872-2076-0*) Kendall-Hunt.

Self Efficacy: The Exercise of Control. Albert Bandura. Date not set. text ed. write for info. (*0-7167-2626-2*); pap. text ed. write for info. (*0-7167-2850-8*) W H Freeman.

Self-Efficacy: Thought Control of Action. Ed. by Ralf Schwarzer. 425p. 1992. 44.95 (*1-56032-269-1*) Hemisp Pub.

Self-Efficacy, Adaptation, & Adjustment: Theory, Research, & Application. Ed. by James E. Maddux. LC 95-3668. (Plenum Series in Social-Clinical Psychology). 395p. (C). 1995. 54.50 (*0-306-44875-0*, Plenum Pr) Plenum.

***Self-Efficacy in Changing Societies.** 352p. 1997. pap. text ed. 21.95 (*0-521-58696-8*) Cambridge U Pr.

Self-Efficacy in Changing Societies. Ed. by Albert Bandura. (Illus.). 368p. (C). 1995. text ed. 52.95 (*0-521-47467-1*) Cambridge U Pr.

Self, Ego, & Identity. Ed. by D. K. Lapsley & F. Clark Power. (Illus.). 280p. 1988. 71.95 (*0-387-96588-2*) Spr-Verlag.

Self-Embodiment of God. Thomas J. Altizer. LC 87-13365. (Brown Classics in Judaica Ser.). 114p. 1987. reprint ed. pap. text ed. 18.00 (*0-8191-6467-4*) U Pr of Amer.

Self Emloyment Initiatives: How to Promote & Finance Micro-Enterprises. Kenneth Poole. Ed. by Jenny Murphy. 64p. (Orig.). 1988. pap. 20.00 (*0-317-04901-1*) Natl Coun Econ Dev.

Self Employed Woman (R) Jeanette R. Scollard. 1989. pap. 7.95 (*0-671-68407-8*) S&S Trade.

Self Employment: A Labor Market Perspective. Robert L. Aronson. (Cornell Studies in Industrial & Labor Relations: No. 24). 168p. (Orig.). 1991. 29.95 (*0-87546-175-1*, ILR Press); pap. 12.95 (*0-87546-176-X*, ILR Press) Cornell U Pr.

***Self Employment: From Dream to Reality.** Gilkerson & Pauwee. 1997. pap. 16.95 (*1-57112-083-1*) JIST Works.

***Self Employment: From Dream to Reality.** Linda Gilkerson & Theresia Pauwee. 144p. 1997. pap. 16.95 (*1-56370-443-9*, Park Avenue) JIST Works.

S

An Asterisk (*) at the beginning of an entry indicates that the title is appearing in BIP for the first time.

Self-Employment for Disabled People: Experiences from Africa & Asia. Malcolm Harper & Willi Momm. (Illus.). viii, 85p. (Orig.). 1992. pap. 13.50 (*92-2-106457-3*) Intl Labour Office.

Self-Employment for Low Income People. Steven Balkin. LC 88-35735. 258p. 1989. text ed. 55.00 (*0-275-92807-1*, C2807, Praeger Pubs) Greenwood.

Self-Employment for the Unemployed: Experience in OECD & Transitional Economies. Sandra Wilson & Arvil V. Adams. LC 94-33787. (World Bank Discussion Papers). 1994. 6.95 (*0-8213-3027-6*, 13027) World Bank.

Self Employment Opportunities: Career Alternatives for the 1990s. Walt Sonneville. 278p. (Orig.). 1993. pap. 59.50 (*0-9635855-0-9*) Sonneville Assocs.

Self-Employment Pattern of Scheduled Castes. Devendra Thakur. (C). 1992. 24.00 (*81-7100-355-9*, Pub. by Deep II) S Asia.

Self-Employment Programme in India. P. N. Pande. (C). 1988. 17.50 (*81-7024-213-4*, Pub. by Ashish II) S Asia.

Self-Employment Resource Guide: Your Key to Money-Making Info. Arthur A. Hawkins, 2nd. 120p. (Orig.). (C). 1996. pap. 24.97 (*1-881297-15-2*) Info Res Lab.

Self Employment, Self Starter, & Start Your Own: A How to Get Started Possibilities Workbook. Center For Self Sufficiency, Research Division Staff. LC 83-90708. 200p. 1983. ring bd. 39.95 (*0-910811-12-1*) Ctr Self Suff.

Self Employment Survival Manual: How to Start & Operate a One-Person Business Successfully. A. William Benitez. Ed. by Barbara Frances. 120p. (Orig.). 1993. pap. 18.95 (*0-9636035-0-7*) A W Benitez.

Self-Empowerment: Break Through in Stress Management, Common Sense Strategies. Doc L. Childre. LC RA785. C45. 141p. 1992. pap. text ed. 13.95 (*1-879052-16-4*) Planetary Pubns.

Self-Empowerment: Getting What You Want from Life. Sam Lloyd & Christine Berthelot. Ed. by Kay Keppler. LC 91-76251. (Fifty-Minute Ser.). 90p. (Orig.). 1992. pap. 10.95 (*1-56052-128-7*) Crisp Pubns.

Self-Empowerment: Strategies for Success. Joe H. Sate. 1992. pap. 24.95 (*0-938991-66-3*) Colonial Pr AL.

Self Empowerment: The Heart Approach to Stress Management. Doc L. Childre. 152p. 1993. lib. bdg. 37.00 (*0-8095-5811-4*) Borgo Pr.

Self Empowerment: The Heart Approach to Stress Management: Common Sense Strategies. Doc L. Childre. Ed. by Deborah A. Rozman & Bruce Cryer. LC RA785.C45. 141p. (Orig.). 1992. 22.95 (*1-879052-34-2*) Planetary Pubns.

Self-Envy: Therapy & the Divided Internal World. Raphael E. Lopez-Corvo. LC 94-7733. 248p. 1995. 30.00 (*1-56821-252-6*) Aronson.

Self-Esteem. (Looking Good Ser.: Set 2). (Illus.). 32p. (J). (gr. 5 up). 1989. 11.95 (*0-685-58600-6*); lib. bdg. 15.94 (*0-86625-288-6*) Rourke Corp.

Self-Esteem. (YouthTalk Ser.). 32p. (YA). 1994. teacher ed., pap. 4.95 (*0-8066-0258-9*, 15-5213) Augsburg Fortress.

Self-Esteem. (YouthTalk Ser.). 48p. (YA). 1997. pap. 5.25 (*0-8066-0257-0*, 15-5212) Augsburg Fortress.

***Self-Esteem.** Gael Lindenfield. 240p. 1997. mass mkt. 5.99 (*0-06-101105-3*, Harp PBks) HarpC.

Self-Esteem. Matthew McKay & Fanning. 1987. mass mkt. 5.99 (*0-312-90443-6*) St Martin.

Self Esteem. Matthew McKay & Patrick Fanning. 1994. 7.98 (*1-56731-003-6*, MJF Bks) Fine Comms.

Self-Esteem. Shelly Nielsen. Ed. by Rosemary Wallner. LC 91-73047. (Values Matter Ser.). (J). 1992. lib. bdg. 14.98 (*1-56239-061-9*) Abdo & Dghtrs.

Self Esteem. Ellen Rosenberg. Date not set. pap. 12.99 (*0-670-86573-7*) Viking Penguin.

Self-Esteem. Anita Russell. Ed. by William Schulz. (Options Ser.). 88p. (Orig.). (gr. 1-8). 1989. teacher ed., pap. 8.00 (*0-920541-51-8*) Peguis Pubs Ltd.

Self Esteem. Virginia M. Satir. LC 75-9447. (Illus.). 64p. 1995. pap. 6.95 (*0-89087-109-4*) Celestial Arts.

Self-Esteem. Dale Zevin. (Comprehensive Health for Middle Grades Ser.). (J). (gr. 6-9). 1996. 24.00 (*1-56071-460-3*, H562) ETR Assocs.

Self Esteem. rev. ed. Constance H. Dembrowsky. 242p. (Orig.). 1989. spiral bd. 10.95 (*0-924609-01-X*); spiral bd. 133.00 (*0-924609-00-1*); spiral bd. 6.95 (*0-924609-03-6*) Inst Affect Skill.

Self-Esteem. rev. ed. Constance H. Dembrowsky. 177p. 1989. pap. write for info. (*0-924609-08-7*) Inst Affect Skill.

Self-Esteem. rev. ed. Constance H. Dembrowsky. 150p. 1989. spiral bd. 59.95 (*0-924609-02-8*) Inst Affect Skill.

Self-Esteem, 5 Vols., Set. rev. ed. Constance H. Dembrowsky. (J). (gr. 6-8). 1989. spiral bd. 229.00 (*0-924609-18-4*) Inst Affect Skill.

***Self-Esteem: A Classroom Affair.** GoodYear Books Staff. 1996. pap. text ed. 14.00 (*0-673-36117-9*, GoodYrBooks) Addson-Wesley Educ.

Self-Esteem: A Classroom Affair, Vol. 1. Michele Borba & Craig Borba. LC 92-24209. 140p. 1984. pap. 16.00 (*0-86683-612-8*, AY8939) Harper SF.

Self-Esteem: A Classroom Affair,, Vol. 2. Michele Borba & Craig Borba. LC 92-24209. 144p. (Orig.). 1985. pap. 16.00 (*0-86683-675-6*, AY8210) Harper SF.

***Self Esteem: A Classroom Affair, Vol. 2.** GoodYear Books Staff. 1996. pap. text ed. 14.00 (*0-673-36118-7*, GoodYrBooks) Addson-Wesley Educ.

Self-Esteem: A Family Affair. Jean I. Clarke. 280p. 1985. pap. 15.00 (*0-86683-615-2*) Harper SF.

***Self Esteem: A Program Designed for Students with a Variety of Handicapping Conditions.** Doris Robinson & Wendy Mopsik. (Illus.). 28p. (Orig.). (J). (gr. k-6). 1990. pap. 7.95 (*1-57543-007-X*) Mar Co Prods.

Self-Esteem: A Proven Program of Cognitive Techniques for Assessing & Improving. 2nd ed. Matthew McKay & Patrick Fanning. 288p. 1993. pap. 13.95 (*1-879237-44-X*) New Harbinger.

Self-Esteem: A Workbook. Jean Kirkpatrick. 42p. 7.95 (*0-317-05942-4*) WFS.

***Self-Esteem: Concepts for Activities, Discussion & Insights.** Greta B. Lipson. Ed. by Judy Mitchell. (Illus.). 96p. (Orig.). 1997. pap. 9.95 (*1-57310-080-3*) Teachng & Lrning Co.

Self-Esteem: Encouraging Self & Others. Eddie J. Pelkey & Irene Getz. (Intersections: Small Group Ser.). 1995. pap. 5.25 (*0-8066-0137-X*) Augsburg Fortress.

Self Esteem: Giving Children from Birth to Six the Freedom to Grow. rev. ed. Angie Rose & Lynn Weiss. LC 83-81434. 170p. (Orig.). 1984. pap. 16.95 (*0-89334-046-4*) Humanics Ltd.

***Self-Esteem: How to Feel Better about Yourself.** David C. Rainham. (Illus.). 8p. (Orig.). 1995. pap. 2.50 (*1-884241-58-1*, EHO600) Energeia Pub.

Self-Esteem: Key to Happiness. Russell M. Abata. LC 93-79878. 64p. (Orig.). 1994. pap. 3.95 (*0-89243-535-6*) Liguori Pubns.

Self-Esteem: Loving Yourself at Every Age. Jerry Aldridge. LC 93-11765. 152p. (Orig.). 1993. pap. 12.95 (*0-9637034-0-4*) Religious Educ.

Self-Esteem: Paradoxes & Innovations in Clinical Theory & Practice. 2nd ed. Richard L. Bednar & Scott R. Peterson. LC 95-16098. 433p. 1995. pap. text ed. 24.95 (*1-55798-290-2*) Am Psychol.

Self-Esteem: Paradoxes & Innovations in Clinical Theory & Practice. 2nd ed. Richard L. Bednar & Scott R. Peterson. 433p. 1995. text ed. 39.95 (*1-55798-305-4*) Am Psychol.

Self-Esteem: Research, Theory, & Practice. Chris Mruk. (Illus.). 240p. 1994. 35.95 (*0-8261-8750-1*) Springer Pub.

***Self-Esteem: Road to Happiness.** Chris Fife. 11p. (Orig.). 1996. pap. 4.00 (*1-890143-06-5*) Kinetic Aesthetics.

Self-Esteem: Seeing Ourselves As God Sees Us. Jack Kuhatschek. (LifeGuide Bible Studies). 62p. (Orig.). 1990. wbk. ed., pap. 4.99 (*0-8308-1065-X*, 1065) InterVarsity.

Self Esteem: Stories, Poetry & Activity Pages. Story Rhyme Staff. (Illus.). 28p. (YA). (gr. 4-9). Date not set. ring bd. 19.95 (*1-56820-107-9*) Story Time.

Self-Esteem: The Necessary Ingredient for Success: A Student-Centered Approach to Restructuring Education. Sandi Redenbach. Ed. by Carol S. Cole. LC 91-90017. (Illus.). 135p. (Orig.). 1991. pap. 14.00 (*0-9632112-0-X*) Esteem Sem.

Self Esteem: The Power to Be Your Best. 69p. (Orig.). Date not set. pap. 9.95 (*1-55852-152-6*) Natl Pr Pubns.

Self-Esteem: The Power to Be Your Best. Marc Towers. LC 94-74366. (AMI How-to Ser.). 70p. (Orig.). 1996. pap. text ed. 12.95 (*1-884926-29-0*) Amer Media.

Self-Esteem: The Puzzle of Low Self-Regard. Ed. by Roy F. Baumeister. LC 93-7043. (Social - Clinical Psychology Ser.). (Illus.). 275p. (C). 1993. 42.50 (*0-306-44373-2*, Plenum Pr) Plenum.

Self-Esteem: Tools for Recovery. Lindsey Hall & Leigh Cohn. LC 89-11852. 128p. 1991. reprint ed. pap. 10.95 (*0-936077-08-5*) Gurze Bks.

Self-Esteem see IVP Booklets

Self-Esteem - A Thematic Unit. Diane Williams. (Thematic Units Ser.). (Illus.). 80p. (J). (gr. 1-3). 1990. student ed. 9.95 (*1-55734-269-5*) Tchr Create Mat.

Self-Esteem - Empower Kidz: Through Over 100 Hands-on Activities. Allison Wonders & Jami Edelheit. 1992. pap. write for info. (*1-881497-02-X*) Global Pr Wks.

Self Esteem Activities: Giving Children from Birth to Six the Freedom to Grow. Angie Rose & Lynn Weiss. LC 83-81434. (Illus.). 192p. (Orig.). 1995. lib. bdg. 26.95 (*0-89334-238-6*, 2246X09) Humanics Ltd.

Self-Esteem & Adjusting with Blindness: The Process of Responding to Life's Demands. 2nd ed. Dean W. Tuttle & Naomi R. Tuttle. (Illus.). 308p. 1996. 54.95 (*0-398-06597-7*); pap. 37.95 (*0-398-06598-5*) C C Thomas.

Self-Esteem & Getting Ahead. Braham. (Adult Education Ser.). 1992. pap. 9.95 (*0-538-70572-8*) S-W Pub.

Self Esteem & Loneliness. Dawson McAllister. (Illus.). (J). (gr. 5-12). 1989. pap. 3.95 (*0-923417-02-8*) Shepherd Minst.

Self-Esteem & Meaning: A Life Historical Investigation. Michael R. Jackson. LC 83-18248. 228p. 1985. text ed. 67.50 (*0-87395-852-7*); pap. text ed. 24.95 (*0-87395-853-5*) State U NY Pr.

Self-Esteem & Mental Health: Health Facts. Nora J. Krantzler & Kathleen R. Miner. LC 93-43820. 1994. 12.95 (*1-56071-181-7*, H301) ETR Assocs.

Self-Esteem & the Six-Second Secret. Connie Podesta. 96p. 1990. pap. 15.00 (*0-8039-6037-9*) Corwin Pr.

Self-Esteem & You. Frederick Sion. Ed. by Tim Beauchemin et al. 150p. (Orig.). 1992. pap. text ed. 8.50 (*1-884332-03-X*) Netwrk Pr TX.

Self-Esteem Builders, Quick & Easy. rev. ed. Bertie Ryan Synowiec. (Self Esteem Builders Ser.). 60p. 1997. pap. 9.97 (*1-885335-00-8*) Positive Support.

Self-Esteem Comes in All Sizes. Carol Johnson. LC 94-49095. 352p. 1995. 18.95 (*0-385-47565-9*) Doubleday.

Self-Esteem Comes in All Sizes. Carol Johnson. 352p. 1996. pap. 10.95 (*0-385-47569-1*) Doubleday.

Self-Esteem Enhancement. Pope. (C). 1988. pap. text ed. 31.50 (*0-205-14455-1*, H4455) Allyn.

Self-Esteem Family & Friends: Sharing & Caring. rev. ed. Irene Handberg. 112p. 1995. write for info. (*1-56831-110-9*); teacher ed. write for info. (*1-56831-112-5*) Lrning Connect.

Self-Esteem for Children: A Parent's Gift That Lasts Forever. Dale R. Olen. (Life Skills Parenting Ser.). (Illus.). 195p. (Orig.). 1996. pap. 9.95 (*1-56583-016-4*) JODA.

Self Esteem for Tots to Teens. Eugene Anderson et al. 1991. pap. 8.95 (*1-879276-00-3*) Parent Tching Pubns.

***Self-Esteem for Women: A Practical Guide to Love, Intimacy & Success.** Lynda Field. LC 96-37030. 160p. 1997. pap. 10.95 (*1-85230-936-9*) Element MA.

Self-Esteem Guidebook: Learning to Embrace Your Imperfect Self. Kenneth A. Beavers. 339p. (Orig.). 1992. pap. 17.95 (*1-883660-23-8*) Galloway Pr.

Self-Esteem Guidebook: Learning to Embrace Your Imperfect Self. Kenneth A. Beavers. LC 91-90244. (Illus.). 346p. (Orig.). 1992. pap. 24.95 (*1-880025-16-7*) Psych-Care Pub.

Self-Esteem in Children with Special Educational Needs. Peter W. Gurney. 160p. 1988. text ed. 35.00 (*0-415-00599-X*) Routledge.

Self-Esteem in the Classroom: A Curriculum Guide. Ellen Fleischmann et al. 397p. 1986. teacher ed. 65.00 (*1-880082-00-4*) S-E Seminars.

Self-Esteem Is Just an Idea We Have about Ourselves: Simultaneous English & Spanish Text. Marsha Sinetar. 80p. (ENG & SPA.). 1990. pap. 6.95 (*0-8091-3229-X*) Paulist Pr.

Self Esteem, Mood & Evolutionary Fitness: A Synthesis. Eric A. Stone. (Illus.). 12p. (C). 1992. pap. 9.95 (*0-9631937-0-8*) BioPsych Pr.

Self-Esteem Passport. Michael Krawetz. 32p. 1984. pap. 3.95 (*0-8050-0218-9*, Owl) H Holt & Co.

Self-Esteem Passport II. Michael Krawetz. LC 89-36686. 32p. 1990. pap. 3.95 (*0-8050-1238-9*, Owl) H Holt & Co.

Self-Esteem Problems of Children: Psychodynamics & Psychotherapy. Richard A. Gardner. LC 92-9573. 584p. 1992. text ed. 40.00 (*0-933812-26-4*) Creative Therapeutics.

Self-Esteem Repair & Maintenance Manual. B. David Brooks & Rex K. Dalby. Ed. by Paula J. Hunter. LC 89-36692. (Illus.). 122p. (Orig.). 1990. pap. 9.95 (*0-943793-27-0*) Kincaid Hse.

Self Esteem Repair & Maintenance Manual. B. David Brooks & Rex K. Dalby. 123p. 1990. pap. text ed. 9.95 (*0-9635491-0-3*) Reda Pr.

Self-Esteem Revolutions in Children: Understanding & Managing the Critical Transitions in Your Child's Life. Thomas W. Phelan. (Illus.). 172p. (Orig.). 1996. pap. 12.95 (*1-889140-01-5*) Child Mgmt.

Self-Esteem Study Group Package. 2nd rev. ed. Lilburn S. Barksdale. (Illus.). 1989. Incl. Building Self-Esteem 2nd ed., Study Guide for Building Self-Esteem, 2nd ed., 1 audio cassette. pap. 21.95 (*0-918588-17-0*, 116) Barksdale Foun.

Self-Esteem Therapy. R. A. Steffenhagen. LC 89-49159. 208p. 1990. text ed. 55.00 (*0-275-93193-5*, Praeger Pubs) Greenwood.

Self-Esteem Workbook. Lynda Field. 1995. pap. 15.95 (*1-85230-645-9*) Element MA.

***Self-Esteem 101: The Self-Healing Manual: Awaken the Power Within.** Magdalene Valentin. (Illus.). 210p. (Orig.). 1997. pap. 14.95 (*0-9651657-3-6*) NWI.

Self-Evaluation. S. L. Groves & D. L. Groves. 20p. 1978. pap. text ed. 4.00 (*0-940414-01-5*) Appalach Assoc.

Self-Evaluation: Ideas for Participatory Evaluation of Rural Community Development Projects. Jim Rugh. (Illus.). 43p. (Orig.). 1986. pap. 5.00 (*0-942716-05-1*) World Neigh.

Self-Evaluation for BMET Certification. 1994. 100.00 incl. disk (*0-685-65448-6*, SG3-209); pap. 50.00 (*1-57020-040-8*, SG1-209); disk 70.00 (*0-685-65449-4*, SG2-209) Assn Adv Med Instrn.

Self-Evaluation in Young Children. Deborah J. Stipek et al. (Child Development Research & Social Policy Ser.). (Illus.). 142p. 1992. pap. text ed. 15.00 (*0-226-77487-2*) U Ch Pr.

Self Evidence. Ed. by Larry Rinder & Jerry Estrin. (Illus.). (C). 1989. pap. 8.00 (*0-937335-05-3*) LA Contemp Exhib.

***Self-Evident Truths: Youths Living with HIV.** G. Cajetan Luna. 1997. pap. 14.95 (*0-614-27658-6*) Haworth Pr.

***Self-Evident Truths: Youths Living with HIV.** G. Cajetan Luna. 1997. 39.95 (*0-614-27659-4*) Haworth Pr.

Self-Excellence: Key to Preventive Stress Management & Goal-Oriented Living. S. A. Swami. (Illus.). 198p. 1987. 19.95 (*0-941553-00-0*) Minibook Pub.

Self-Exploration Inventories: Sixteen Reproducible Self-Scoring Instruments. 2nd ed. James L. Lee & Charles J. Pulvino. 32p. 1993. pap. text ed. 12.95 (*0-932796-58-3*) Ed Media Corp.

Self-Explorations: Diarists in England & America, 1641-1962. Lola L. Szladits. (Illus.). 12p. 1988. pap. 3.00 (*0-685-65651-9*) NY Pub Lib.

Self Expressions: Mind, Morals, & the Meaning of Life. Owen Flanagan. (Illus.). 240p. 1996. 24.95 (*0-19-509696-7*) OUP.

Self-Focusing: Experimental & Theory see Progress in Quantum Electronics

***Self-Forgiveness Handbook: A Practical & Empowering Guide.** Thom Rutledge. 176p. (Orig.). 1997. pap. 12.95 (*1-57224-083-0*) New Harbinger.

Self-Fulfilling Prophecies: Social, Psychological, & Physiological Effects of Expectancies. Russell A. Jones. 288p. (C). 1977. text ed. 49.95 (*0-89859-126-0*) L Erlbaum Assocs.

***Self-Fulfilling Prophecy: A Practical Guide to Its Use in Education.** Robert T. Tauber. LC 96-33192. 200p. 1997. text ed. 55.00 (*0-275-95502-8*, Praeger Pubs); pap. text ed. 18.95 (*0-275-95503-6*, Praeger Pubs) Greenwood.

Self-Fulfilling Prophecy: Exile & Return in the History of Judaism. Jacob Neusner. (Studies in History of Judaism). 260p. 1990. 64.95 (*1-55540-494-4*, 24 00 03) Scholars Pr GA.

Self Fulfillment: A Starting Point. Helen C. Stassen. (Orig.). 1992. pap. text ed. write for info. (*0-9633809-5-8*) Mara Pubns.

Self-Fulfillment: Thoughts on Success, Happiness, & a Meaningful Life. Don Kasparek. LC 92-62340. 406p. (Orig.). 1993. pap. 15.95 (*0-9634624-7-4*) Timberlake Pr.

Self-Fulfillment Through Zionism: A Study in Jewish Adjustment. Ed. by Shlomo Bardin. LC 70-142605. (Biography Index Reprint Ser.). 1977. reprint ed. 19.95 (*0-8369-8076-X*) Ayer.

Self Funding of Health Care Benefits. 3rd ed. Carlton Harker. Ed. by Mary Brennan. LC 92-75625. 827p. 1993. pap. 84.00 (*0-89154-446-1*) Intl Found Employ.

Self-Funding Your Employee Medical Benefits: A Survival Guide & How-To-Do-It Book. Thomas R. Young. Ed. by Gulf Coast Offset, Inc. Staff. (Orig.). (C). 1985. pap. write for info. (*0-9614151-1-8*); lib. bdg. write for info. (*0-9614151-0-X*) Young.

***Self-Generation: Biology, Philosophy & Literature Around 1800.** Helmut Muller-Sievers. LC 96-31973. 1997. write for info. (*0-8047-2779-1*) Stanford U Pr.

Self, Global Issues, & Ethics. Howard L. Parsons. 209p. (Orig.). 1980. pap. 27.00 (*90-6032-178-2*, Pub. by B R Gruener NE) Benjamins North Am.

Self-Governing Socialism, Vol. I. Ed. by Branko Horvat et al. 497p. (C). (gr. 13). 1975. text ed. 90.95 (*0-87332-050-6*) M E Sharpe.

Self-Governing Socialism: A Reader, Vol. 2. Ed. by Branko Horvat et al. 330p. (gr. 13). 1975. text ed. 90.95 (*0-87332-061-1*) M E Sharpe.

Self-Government at the King's Command. Albert B. White. LC 74-5927. 130p. 1974. reprint ed. text ed. 65.00 (*0-8371-7526-7*, WHKC, Greenwood Pr) Greenwood.

Self-Government in Industry. George D. Cole. LC 71-152979. (Select Bibliographies Reprint Ser.). 1977. reprint ed. 23.95 (*0-8369-5731-8*) Ayer.

Self-Government in Modernizing Nations. Ed. by James R. Pennock. LC 77-167401. (Essay Index Reprint Ser.). 1977. reprint ed. 18.95 (*0-8369-2517-3*) Ayer.

Self-Guided Architectural Tours of Cape May, NJ. Marsha Cudworth. LC 84-81044. (Illus.). 1985. pap. 6.95 (*0-9608554-2-4*) Lady Raspbrry.

Self Guided Architectural Tours of Cape May, N.J. An Illustrated Guide to Cape Mays Rich Architectural Heritage - 2 Walking Tours & 1 Auto Tour Featuring over 100 Historical Sights. Marsha Cudworth. LC 84-81044. 82p. 1987. pap. 8.95 (*0-317-01463-3*) Bric-A-Brac.

Self-Guided Exploration. 3rd ed. Jeffrey A. Kottler. (Counseling Ser.). 78p. 1996. wbk. ed., pap. 19.95 (*0-534-34042-3*) Brooks-Cole.

Self-Guided Exploration for Beginning Counseling Students. 2nd ed. Jeffrey A. Kottler. 72p. (C). 1992. pap. 17.95 (*0-534-17287-3*) Brooks-Cole.

Self-Handicapping: The Paradox That Isn't. Ed. by R. L. Higgins et al. (Social-Clinical Psychology Ser.). (Illus.). 312p. 1990. 45.00 (*0-306-43540-3*, Plenum Pr) Plenum.

***Self Healing.** Louis Proto. 1998. mass mkt. write for info. (*0-425-16192-7*) Berkley Pub.

Self Healing. Meir Schneider. 1988. pap. 10.95 (*0-14-019127-5*, Penguin Bks) Viking Penguin.

Self Healing. Henry H. Brown. 61p. 1973. reprint ed. spiral bd. 6.00 (*0-7873-0122-1*) Hlth Research.

Self Healing: The Secret of the Ring Muscles. Paula Garbourg. 184p. 1992. pap. write for info. (*0-86689-032-7*) Balaban Intl Sci Serv.

Self-Healing: Use Your Mind to Heal Your Body. Louis Proto. LC 91-8690. (Illus.). 194p. (Orig.). 1991. pap. 10.95 (*0-87728-732-5*) Weiser.

Self-Healing Body: Craniosacral Therapy & Sonato-Emotional Release. Carol J. Manheim & Diane K. Lavett. LC 89-42578. 250p. (Orig.). 1989. pap. text ed. 32.00 (*1-55642-250-4*) SLACK Inc.

***Self Healing Book.** Zoilita Grant & Neal Rohr. 175p. 1997. per. 14.95 (*1-890575-00-3*) Mstr Key.

Self Healing by Thought Force. W. W. Atkinson. 1991. lib. bdg. 75.00 (*0-87700-973-2*) Revisionist Pr.

Self Healing by Thought Force. William W. Atkinson. 92p. 1997. pap. 8.00 (*0-89540-286-6*, SB-286) Sun Pub.

Self-Healing by Thought Force. William W. Atkinson. 91p. 1996. pap. 14.95 (*1-56459-646-X*) Kessinger Pub.

Self Healing by Thought Force. William W. Atkinson. 91p. 1971. reprint ed. spiral bd. 5.50 (*0-7873-0048-9*) Hlth Research.

Self Healing Chronic Illness. J. Elias & Katherine Ketcham. 1997. write for info. (*0-517-70487-0*) Random.

Self-Healing Cookbook: A Macrobiotic Primer for Healing Body, Mind & Moods with Whole, Natural Foods. 6th rev. ed. Kristina Turner. (Illus.). 216p. (Orig.). 1996. reprint ed. pap. 16.50 (*0-945668-10-4*) Earthtones Pr.

Self-Healing Dynamics for Cancer & Other Illnesses. Jan K. Garverick. 96p. (Orig.). 1991. pap. text ed. 7.95 (*0-9630177-0-5*) Morgana Pubns.

Self-Healing for Women: Let America's Top Doctors, Therapists, & Health Experts Solve Women's Unique Health Problems. Ed. by Prevention Magazine Health Book Editors. LC 94-24203. (Family Home Remedies Collection). 1995. pap. 6.95 (*0-87596-265-3*) Rodale Pr Inc.

Self-Healing Handbook: Nutrition & the Harston Method of Deep Muscle Therapy. Anna W. Harston. LC 93-78404. (Illus.). 248p. 1993. pap. 12.95 (*0-9636998-0-6*) LHC Pubns.

Self-Healing Pocket Guide, No. 1. Walter L. Weston. (Illus.). 200p. (Orig.). 1996. pap. 9.95 (*1-884537-07-3*) Transit Press.

S

Self-Healing Power & Therapy: Old Teachings from Africa. Kimbwadiende K. Kiau. 1991. 8.95 (*0-533-08863-1*) Vantage.

Self-Healing Technology: A Powerful Educational Option. Nick Ortiz. (Orig.). 1996. pap. 14.95 (*0-533-11616-3*) Vantage.

Self Healing Through Autosuggestion. Charles F. Winbigler. 122p. 1970. reprint ed. spiral bd. 8.00 (*0-7873-1055-7*) Hlth Research.

Self Healing Through Autosuggestion: The Self-Treatment of Nervousness, Insomnia, Indecision, Etc. C. F. Winbigler. 1991. lib. bdg. 75.00 (*0-87700-947-3*) Revisionist Pr.

Self Healing Workbook: Ninety Days to Optimal Health. C. Norman Shealy. (Home Library of Alternative Medicine). (Illus.). 160p. 1993. pap. 14.95 (*1-85230-429-4*) Element MA.

Self Healing Yoga & Destiny. 100p. 1983. 5.95 (*0-943358-06-X*) Aurora Press.

Self-Health Guide: A Personal Program for Holistic Living. Kripalu Center for Holistic Health Staff. LC 80-82166. (Illus.). 207p. (Orig.). 1980. pap. 9.95 (*0-940258-00-5*) Kripalu Pubns.

***Self-Health Self-Cure.** Max. 50p. (Orig.). 1997. pap. 25.00 (*0-922070-54-7*) M Tecton Pub.

Self Heating: Evaluation & Controlling the Hazards. P. C. Bowes. 1984. 210.75 (*0-444-99624-9*, I-099-84) Elsevier.

Self-Help: Concepts & Applications. Ed. by Alfred H. Katz et al. LC 91-28890. 336p. (Orig.). 1992. pap. 24.95 (*0-914783-56-4*) Charles.

Self Help: Your Strategy for Living with COPD. American Lung Association of South Western Pennsylvania Staff. 1992. 5.95 (*0-923521-20-8*) Bull Pub.

Self-Help a Hundred Years Ago. 3rd ed. George J. Holyoake. LC 76-47881. reprint ed. 29.50 (*0-404-60084-0*) AMS Pr.

Self-Help Accounting: A Guide for the Volunteer Treasurer. John P. Dalsimer. Ed. by Susan J. Ellis. LC 88-83599. (Volunteer Energy Ser.). (Illus.). 104p. (Orig.). 1989. pap. 14.75 (*0-940576-08-2*) Energize.

Self-Help Among the Elderly: Formal & Informal Support Systems. Bessie Wright. LC 93-48665. (Studies on the Elderly in America). 184p. 1994. text ed. 55.00 (*0-8153-1613-5*) Garland.

Self-Help & Mutual Aid Groups: International & Multicultural Perspectives. Ed. by Francine Lavoie et al. LC 94-44762. (Prevention in Human Services Ser.). 363p. 1995. 49.95 (*1-56024-716-9*) Haworth Pr.

***Self-Help & Support Groups: A Handbook for Practitioners.** Linda F. Kurtz. LC 96-35630. (Sage Human Services Guides Ser.). 1997. 55.00 (*0-8039-7098-6*) Sage.

***Self-Help & Support Groups: A Handbook for Practitioners.** Linda F. Kurtz. LC 96-35630. (Human Services Guides Ser.: Vol. 72). 416p. 1997. pap. 26.95 (*0-8039-7099-4*) Sage.

***Self Help Approach to Living Well with Fibromyalgia.** Arthritis Foundation Staff. 1997. pap. 14.95 (*1-56352-382-5*) Longstreet Pr Inc.

Self-Help Book Display: Seventy-Two Best-Selling Legal Books in a Floor Display. pap. text ed. 2.95 (*1-880398-12-5*) SJT Enterprises.

Self-Help by the People: The History of the Rochdale Pioneers, 1844-1892. 10th enl. rev. ed. George J. Holyoake. LC 76-47882. reprint ed. 36.00 (*0-404-60085-9*) AMS Pr.

***Self-Help Directory: A Guide to Connecticut & National Groups 1996-1997.** 8th rev. ed. Connecticut Self-Help Network Staff. 348p. 1996. pap. 20.00 (*0-9647301-1-1*) CT Self-Help Netwrk.

Self-Help Directory: A Sourcebook to Self-Help in the United States & Canada. Joe Donovan. LC 93-12074. 176p. 1993. 29.95 (*0-8160-2621-1*) Facts on File.

Self-Help for Kids: Improving Performance & Building Self-Esteem in School Home & Sports, Learning Blocks, Repetitive Muscle Stress, Environmental Sensitivity. 2nd ed. Elizabeth Barhydt & Hamilton Barhydt. (Illus.). 64p. 1992. pap. 10.00 (*0-9605346-2-8*) Loving Life.

***Self-Help for PMS.** rev. ed. Michelle Harrison. 1998. pap. write for info. (*0-679-77800-4*) Random.

Self-Help for Premenstrual Syndrome. rev. ed. Michelle Harrison. LC 84-23723. 169p. 1985. pap. 12.00 (*0-394-73502-1*) Random.

Self-Help for Stress & Pain: Simple Energy Balancing Exercises for Home, School, Office, & Athletics, Repetitive Muscle Stress, Learning Blocks, Environmental Sensitivity. 5th ed. Elizabeth Barhydt & Hamilton Barhydt. (Illus.). 64p. 1990. pap. 10.00 (*0-9605346-1-X*) Loving Life.

***Self-Help for Stress & Pain Plus Learning Blocks: Simple Energy Balancing Exercises for Home, School, Office & Athletics.** expanded ed. Elizabeth Barhydt & Hamilton Barhydt. (Illus.). 80p. (Orig.). 1997. pap. 15.00 (*0-9605346-4-4*) Loving Life.

***Self-Help for Your Anxiety: The Proven Anxiety Antidote Method.** Robert Sharpe. 1997. pap. 12.95 (*0-285-62986-7*, Pub. by Souvenir UK) IPG Chicago.

Self-Help Group Directory. 13th rev. ed. New Jersey Self-Help Clearinghouse Staff. Ed. by Karen Fehre & Barbara J. White. 542p. (Orig.). 1995. pap. 25.00 (*0-9634322-5-7*) NW Covenant Med.

Self-Help Groups: Index of Modern Information with Bibliography. Judy G. Whitefield. LC 88-47792. 150p. (Orig.). 1988. 37.50 (*0-88164-892-2*); pap. 34.50 (*0-88164-893-0*) ABBE Pubs Assn.

Self-Help Groups & Human Service Agencies: How They Work Together. Daniel Remine et al. LC 83-48645. 109p. (Orig.). (C). 1984. pap. text ed. 6.95 (*0-87304-204-2*) Families Intl.

Self-Help Groups & Voluntary Action: International Perspectives. Alfred H. Katz & David H. Smith. 250p. text ed. write for info. (*0-8290-1274-5*) Irvington.

Self-Help Groups for Coping with Crisis: Origins, Members, Processes, & Impact. Morton A. Lieberman et al. LC 79-88772. (Jossey-Bass Social & Behavioral Science Ser.). 480p. reprint ed. pap. 136.80 (*0-8357-4903-7*, 2037833) Bks Demand.

Self-Help Guide. Arthur A. Hawkins, II. 210p. 1992. pap. 27.00 (*1-881297-57-8*); pap. text ed. 27.00 (*1-881297-58-6*) Info Res Lab.

***Self-Help Guide: A Directory of Self-Help Organizations in the United Kingdom.** S. Knight & R. Gann. (Illus.). 128p. (Orig.). (C). (gr. 13 up). 1988. pap. text ed. 32.95 (*0-412-29370-6*) Chapman & Hall.

Self-Help Guide to Managing Depression. Barker. 78p. 1993. pap. 16.00 (*1-56593-216-1*, 0575) Singular Publishing.

***Self-Help Guide to Succcessful Living. Leopoldo Lozano. Tr. by David A. Botta from SPA. (Illus.). 109p. (Orig.). 1996. pap. 14.99 (*0-9653530-0-1*) Intnl O Ctr.**
THE SELF-HELP GUIDE TO SUCCESSFUL LIVING by Leopoldo Lozano is a fresh, light-hearted approach to good manners & social etiquette. The book is aimed at a general audience & falls under the subject heading of self-actualization/self-help. Indeed, this book teaches us how to improve the quality of our individual lives & the quality of our society through good manners. It highlights how the bonds we share with others are strengthened when we infuse into them a sense of mindfulness or a touch of kindness. For centuries, the rules of good manners were developed by the noble classes. Many of these norms are today considered archaic & obsolete. Times have changed. New realities, new technologies, & new philosophies have changed the ways human beings interact. Yet certain facets of human relationships are timeless. How we treat one another, how we express our bonds with each other, how we conduct our interactions, these are the constants. This book is an effective guide to daily rituals that celebrate these constants; in turn, these rituals form the basis of a successful life. For more information or to place an order, please call Leopoldo Lozano at (305) 365-9736/ FAX (305) 365-9526. ***Publisher Provided Annotation.***

Self-Help Handbook: For Small Town Water & Wastewater Projects. Jane W. Schwartz & Christopher M. Conway. LC 94-80130. (Illus.). 300p. 1995. pap. 21.95 (*0-9629798-4-8*) Rensselaerville Inst.

Self-Help Housing, the Poor, & the State in the Caribbean. Ed. by Robert B. Potter & Dennis Conway. LC 96-25220. (Illus.). 320p. 1997. 26.00 (*0-87049-963-7*) U of Tenn Pr.

Self Help in Health & Social Welfare. Ed. by Stephen Humble & Judith Unell. 160p. 1988. text ed. 39.95 (*0-415-00611-2*) Routledge.

Self Help in Soweto. Julian Y. Kramer. (Bergen Studies in Social Anthropology: No. 12). 172p. (Orig.). 1985. pap. text ed. 13.95 (*0-936508-55-8*, Pub. by Bergen Univ Dept Social Anthro NO) Barber Pr.

Self-Help in the Human Services. Alan Gartner & Frank Riessman. LC 77-79483. (Jossey-Bass Behavioral Science Ser.). 224p. reprint ed. pap. 63.90 (*0-8357-4885-5*, 2037817) Bks Demand.

Self-Help Job Search: Ten Easy Steps to Your Future. Donald L. Wilkes & Viola Hamilton-Wilkes. Ed. by Nancy Teppler. (Illus.). 116p. (C). 1992. pap. 12.95 (*0-9628787-0-7*) JEM Job Educ.

Self-Help or Self-Destruction? Chris Thurman. 256p. 1996. 16.99 (*0-7852-7787-0*) Nelson.

Self-Help Organizations & Professional Practice. Thomas J. Powell. LC 86-21761. 367p. 1987. 23.95 (*0-87101-133-6*) Natl Assn Soc Wkrs.

Self-Help Revolution. Ed. by Alan Gartner & Frank Riessman. (Community Psychology Ser.: Vol. X). 304p. 1984. 42.95 (*0-89885-070-3*) Human Sci Pr.

Self-Help Sourcebook: The Comprehensive Reference of Self-Help Group Resources. 5th rev. ed. American Self-Help Clearinghouse Staff. Ed. by Barbara J. White & Edward J. Madara. LC 95-68450. 272p. (Orig.). 1995. pap. 9.00 (*0-9634322-3-0*) NW Covenant Med.

***Self-Help Support Groups for Older Women: Rebuilding Elder Networks Through Personal Empowerment.** Lenard W. Kaye. LC 97-6368. 1997. write for info. (*1-56032-461-9*); pap. write for info. (*1-56032-462-7*) Hemisp Pub.

***Self-Help Without the Hype.** LC 82-61868. (Illus.). 195p. 1997. pap. 14.95 (*0-937100-00-5*) Perf Manage.

Self-Hypnosis. C. F. Freimuth. 12p. 1979. pap. 5.00 (*0-933992-07-6*) Coffee Break.

Self Hypnosis. Leandro Katz. (Viper's Tongue Bks.). 1975. 8.00 (*0-931106-11-7*, Printed Matter) TVRT.

Self-Hypnosis: A Conditioned-Response Technique. Laurence Sparks. 1976. pap. 7.00 (*0-87980-139-5*) Wilshire.

Self Hypnosis: A Method of Improving your Life. 140p. (Orig.). 1984. 6.95 (*0-9610480-1-8*) Park West.

Self-Hypnosis: A Safe Self-Help Guide. Valerie Austin. 1995. pap. 10.00 (*0-7225-2924-4*) Thorsons SF.

Self-Hypnosis: Creating Your Own Destiny. Henry L. Bolduc. 165p. 1993. pap. 9.95 (*0-9601302-2-5*) Adventures Time.

***Self-Hypnosis: Effective Techniques for Everyday Problems.** Elaine Sheehan. (Health Essentials Ser.). 1997. pap. 9.95 (*1-86204-095-8*) Element MA.

Self-Hypnosis: Its Theory, Technique & Application. Melvin Powers. 1975. pap. 7.00 (*0-87980-138-7*) Wilshire.

Self-Hypnosis: The Chicago Paradigm. Erika Fromm & Stephen Kahn. LC 90-3167. (Guilford Clinical & Self Hypnosis Ser.). 254p. 1990. lib. bdg. 31.50 (*0-89862-341-3*) Guilford Pr.

Self-Hypnosis: The Complete Manual for Health & Self-Change. 2nd ed. Brian M. Alman & Peter Lambrou. LC 91-29007. (Illus.). 304p. 1991. pap. 22.95 (*0-87630-650-4*) Brunner-Mazel.

Self-Hypnosis: The Key to Athletic Success. John G. Kappas. 168p. 1984. write for info. (*0-13-803321-8*); pap. 6.95 (*0-13-803313-7*) Panorama Van Nuys.

Self-Hypnosis: The Key to Athletic Success. John G. Kappas. write for info. (*0-318-58216-3*) P-H.

Self Hypnosis & Other Mind Expanding Techniques. rev. ed. Gil Boyne. 160p. 1987. pap. 9.95 (*0-914629-41-7*) Prima Pub.

Self-Hypnosis & Other Mind Expanding Techniques. 2nd ed. Charles Tebbetts. 141p. (C). 1977. pap. 7.95 (*0-930298-18-7*) Westwood Pub Co.

Self Hypnosis Can Change Your Life. 3.00 (*0-686-40896-9*, SR1) Transitions.

Self Hypnosis Dynamics. Hyman Lewis. 1962. pap. 3.00 (*0-87505-334-3*) Borden.

***Self-Hypnosis for a Better Life: Use the Power of Your Own Voice to Stop Smoking & Reduce Stress.** William W. Hewitt. LC 97-25587. 1997. pap. 9.95 (*1-56718-358-1*) Llewellyn Pubns.

Self-Hypnosis in Two Days. Freda Morris. 1975. pap. 7.95 (*0-525-48364-0*, Dutton) NAL-Dutton.

Self-Hypnosis Kit: Discover the Power of Hypnotherapy to Improve Your Life. Cherith Powell & Greg Forde. (Illus.). 128p. 1996. pap. 22.95 (*0-670-86530-3*) Viking Penguin.

***Self-Hypnosis Step by Step: The 30 Essential Techniques.** J. P. Guyonnaud & Giovanni Sciuto. (Illus.). 208p. 1996. pap. text ed. 12.95 (*0-285-63324-4*, Pub. by Souvenir UK) IPG Chicago.

Self Hypnotism: The Technique & Its Use in Daily Living. Leslie M. LeCron. 1970. pap. 5.99 (*0-451-15984-5*, Sig) NAL-Dutton.

Self-Hypnotism: The Technique & Its Use in Daily Living. Leslie M. Lecron. pap. 4.95 (*0-13-803486-9*, Reward) P-H.

Self Image & Learning Disabilities. Jill Smith & Howard Diller. LC 96-24663. 81p. 1996. pap. text ed. 24.00 (*0-9630539-5-7*) Apodixis.

Self-Image Is the Key. Joyce Duco. LC 86-90983. 71p. 1986. pap. 5.95 (*0-9612896-1-9*) J Duco.

Self-Image of Primary School Teachers: A Cross Cultural Study of their Role & Status in Twelve Cities. Marion L. Edman. LC 68-19683. 339p. reprint ed. 96.70 (*0-685-16240-0*, 2027604) Bks Demand.

Self Images: 100 Women. Andre Rival. 152p. 1995. 49.95 (*3-905514-45-1*, Pub. by Edit Stemmle SZ) Dist Art Pubs.

Self Imagined: Philosophical Reflections on the Social Character of Psyche. Karen Hanson. 160p. 1986. 27.50 (*0-7102-0559-7*, 05597, RKP) Routledge.

Self-Imitation in the Eighteenth-Century Novel. Marie-Paule Laden. 196p. 1987. text ed. 35.00 (*0-691-06705-8*) Princeton U Pr.

***Self-Imitation of Myself: Fictions False & Falser: Stories.** Gordon Lish. LC 97-13200. 224p. 1997. 22.00 (*1-56858-098-3*) FWEW.

***Self Improvement? - I'm Jewish!** Abraham J. Twerski. 14.99 (*0-89906-583-X*, SELH); pap. 11.99 (*0-89906-584-8*, SELP) Mesorah Pubns.

Self in Early Childhood. Joel Ryce-Menuhin. (Free Association Bks.). 288p. 1988. 55.00 (*1-85343-002-1*) St Martin.

Self in Emotional Distress: Cognitive & Psychodynamic Perspectives. Ed. by Zindel V. Segal & Sidney J. Blatt. LC 92-49988. 400p. 1993. lib. bdg. 44.00 (*0-89862-256-5*) Guilford Pr.

Self in European & North American Culture: Development & Processes: Proceedings of the NATO Advanced Research Workshop, Chersonnisos, Crete, Greece, January 10-14, 1994. Ed. by Annerieke Oosterwegel & Robert A. Wicklund. LC 95-34233. (NATO Advanced Science Institutes Ser.: Series D, Vol. 84). 408p. (C). 1995. lib. bdg. 199.00 (*0-7923-3672-0*) Kluwer Ac.

Self in Indian Philosophy. K. P. Sinha. (C). 1991. 21.00 (*81-85094-46-2*, Pub. by Punthi Pus II) S Asia.

Self in Infancy: Theory & Research. Ed. by Philippe Rochat. LC 95-35838. (Advances in Psychology Ser.: Vol.112). 496p. Date not set. 154.50 (*0-444-81925-8*) Elsevier.

Self in Its Worlds: East & West. Troy W. Organ. LC 87-42799. 256p. 1988. 36.50 (*0-941664-88-0*) Susquehanna U Pr.

Self in Process: Toward a Post-Rationalist Cognitive Therapy. Vittorio F. Guidano. LC 90-14129. 237p. 1991. lib. bdg. 35.00 (*0-89862-447-9*) Guilford Pr.

***Self in Social Inquiry: Researching Methods.** Ed. by David N. Berg & Kenwyn K. Smith. LC 88-11320. 400p. pap. 114.00 (*0-608-04805-4*, 2052582) Bks Demand.

Self in Social Theory: A Psychoanalytic Account of Its Construction in Plato, Hobbes, Locke, Rawls, & Rousseau. C. Fred Alford. 272p. (C). 1991. text ed. 35.00 (*0-300-04922-6*) Yale U Pr.

Self in the Family: A Classification of Personality, Criminality, & Psychopathology. Luciano L'Abate & Margaret Baggett. LC 96-19639. (Wiley Series in Couples & Family Dynamics & Treatment). 1997. text ed. 45.00 (*0-471-12247-5*) Wiley.

Self in the System: Expanding the Limits of Family Therapy. Michael P. Nichols. LC 87-13773. 328p. 1987. text ed. 40.95 (*0-87630-472-2*) Brunner-Mazel.

***Self in Time: Retrieving Existential Theology & Freud.** Charles E. Brown. LC 96-42212. 328p. 1996. 44.00 (*0-7618-0516-8*) U Pr of Amer.

Self in Transition: Infancy to Childhood. Ed. by Dante Cicchetti & Marjorie Beeghly. LC 90-35059. (John D. & Catherine T. MacArthur Foundation Series on Mental Health & Development). (Illus.). 412p. 1990. 41.95 (*0-226-10662-4*) U Ch Pr.

Self-Incrimination in Jewish Law. Aaron Kirschenbaum. 1970. 8.00 (*0-8381-3111-5*) USCJE.

Self-Induced Oscillations of Rotors. Mikhail Y. Kushulb. LC 64-19440. 132p. reprint ed. pap. 37.70 (*0-317-28008-2*, 2055802) Bks Demand.

Self-Inference Processes: The Ontario Symposium, Vol. 6. Ed. by James M. Olson & Mark P. Zanna. 336p. (C). 1990. text ed. 69.95 (*0-8058-0551-6*) L Erlbaum Assocs.

Self-Inflicted Wound: Southern Politics in the Nineteenth Century. Robert F. Durden. LC 84-29173. (New Perspectives on the South Ser.). 160p. 1985. 18.00 (*0-8131-0307-X*) U Pr of Ky.

Self-Initiation into the Golden Dawn Tradition: A Complete Curriculum of Study for Both the Solitary Magician & the Working Magical Group. Chic Cicero et al. LC 95-1118. (New Age Tarot Ser.). (Illus.). 784p. 1995. pap. 29.95 (*1-56718-136-8*) Llewellyn Pubns.

Self-Injurious Behavior. Favell. 1982. pap. 53.00 (*0-08-028824-3*) Elsevier.

Self-Injurious Behavior: A Somatosensory Treatment Approach. Haru Hirama. 38p. (C). 1989. pap. text ed. 11.50 (*0-935273-01-8*) Chess Pub.

Self-Injurious Behavior: Analysis, Assessment & Treatment. Ed. by J. K. Luiselli et al. (Disorders of Human Learning, Behavior, & Communication Ser.). (Illus.). x, 393p. 1991. 87.95 (*0-387-97580-2*) Spr-Verlag.

Self-Injurious Behaviors: Diagnosis & Treatment. William I. Gardner & Robert Sovner. 200p. 1994. pap. 20.00 (*1-884442-00-5*) Vida Pubng.

***Self Inquiry.** M. Robert Gardner. 136p. 1989. pap. 17.50 (*0-88163-104-3*) Analytic Pr.

Self-Instruction for IFSTA Chief Officer. Rhonda Wiley-Jones. Ed. & Intro. by Gene P. Carlson. LC 86-80302. (Illus.). 142p. (Orig.). 1986. pap. text ed. 16.50 (*0-87939-060-3*) IFSTA.

Self-Instruction Guide Through Brethren History. fac. ed. Donald E. Miller. (Church of the Brethren, Heritage Learning Program Ser.). 108p. 1976. pap. 30.80 (*0-7837-7346-3*, 2047299) Bks Demand.

Self Instruction in Language Learning. Leslie Dickinson. (New Directions in Language Teaching Ser.). 192p. 1987. pap. text ed. 18.95 (*0-521-31967-6*) Cambridge U Pr.

Self Instruction in Language Learning. Leslie Dickinson. (New Directions in Language Teaching Ser.). 192p. 1987. 39.95 (*0-521-26600-9*) Cambridge U Pr.

Self-Instruction Manual for Filing Catalog Cards. Diane F. Carothers. LC 81-3606. 127p. reprint ed. pap. 36.20 (*0-7837-5916-9*, 2045715) Bks Demand.

Self Instruction Workbook for Emergencies. 6th ed. Bergeron. 1994. wbk. ed., pap. 18.25 (*0-89303-159-3*, Medical Exam) Appleton & Lange.

Self Instructional Module Regarding the Effects of Abused Drugs. Richard G. Cavasina. Ed. by Robert D. Reed. LC 81-83632. (Illus.). 125p. (C). 1982. pap. 9.95 (*0-88247-607-6*) R & E Pubs.

Self-Instructional Modules in English As a Second Language for Spanish-Speaking Students, 2 vols., I. Antonio J. Martinez. (Orig.). (C). 1989. 8.95 (*0-8477-3323-8*) U of PR Pr.

Self-Instructional Modules in English As a Second Language for Spanish-Speaking Students, 2 vols., Set. Antonio J. Martinez. (Orig.). (C). 1989. write for info. (*0-8477-3330-0*) U of PR Pr.

Self-Instructional Modules in English As a Second Language for Spanish-Speaking Students, 2 vols., Vol. II. Antonio J. Martinez. 88p. (Orig.). (C). 1989. 5.00 (*0-8477-3329-7*) U of PR Pr.

***Self Instrument.** Guy De Furia. (Interpersonal Trust Surveys Ser.). 1997. pap. 5.95 (*0-7879-0897-5*, Pfffr & Co) Jossey-Bass.

Self-Insurance Decision. Joseph M. Conder & Gilbert N. Hopkins. 119p. 1981. pap. 20.00 (*0-86641-002-3*, 81124) Inst Mgmt Account.

Self, Interaction, & Natural Environment: Refocusing Our Eyesight. Andrew J. Weigert. LC 96-32486. 218p. 1997. text ed. 54.50 (*0-7914-3259-9*); pap. text ed. 17.95 (*0-7914-3260-2*) State U NY Pr.

***Self-interest: Anthology of Philosophical Perspectives from Antiquity to the Present.** Kelly Rogers. LC 96-48798. 320p. (C). 1997. pap. 18.95 (*0-415-91252-0*, Routledge NY); text ed. 59.95 (*0-415-91251-2*, Routledge NY) Routledge.

Self Interest & Public Interest in Western Politics. Leif Lewin. Tr. by Donald S. Lavery. (Comparative European Politics Ser.). (Illus.). 160p. 1991. 55.00 (*0-19-827726-1*, 11906); pap. 18.95 (*0-19-827725-3*) OUP.

Self-Interest & Universal Health Care: Why Well-Insured Americans Should Support Coverage for Everyone. Larry Churchill. 124p. 1994. text ed. 19.95 (*0-674-80092-3*, CHUSEL) HUP.

Self-Interest (L'Interesse) Nicolo Secchi. Ed. by Helen A. Kaufman. Tr. by William Reymes. LC 53-13162. (Illus.). 136p. 1953. pap. 5.50 (*0-295-73930-4*) U of Wash Pr.

An Asterisk (*) at the beginning of an entry indicates that the title is appearing in BIP for the first time.

Self-Interviews. James Dickey. LC 83-24416. 190p. 1984. reprint ed. pap. text ed. 11.95 (*0-8071-1141-4*) La State U Pr.

Self Is Already Attained. Swami Muktananda. 40p. 1981. pap. 4.75 (*0-914602-77-5*) SYDA Found.

Self, Its Body & Freedom. William E. Hocking. LC 75-3189. reprint ed. 27.50 (*0-404-59191-4*) AMS Pr.

Self-Knower: A Hero Under Control. R. A. Wicklund et al. (Social-Clinical Psychology Ser.). (Illus.). 170p. 1992. 34.50 (*0-306-43988-3*, Plenum Pr) Plenum.

Self-Knowledge. Quassim Cassam. (Oxford Readings in Philosophy Ser.). 240p. 1994. 55.00 (*0-19-875115-X*); pap. 18.95 (*0-19-875116-8*) OUP.

Self Knowledge: Atma-Bodhi. Sri Sankaracharya. Tr. by T. M. Mahadevan. pap. text ed. 3.00 (*0-89253-044-8*); lib. bdg. 8.50 (*0-89253-043-X*) Ind-US Inc.

Self-Knowledge: Sankara's "Atmabodha" Tr. by Swami Nikhilananda. LC 50-36440. 248p. (C). 1946. 12.95 (*0-911206-11-6*) Ramakrishna.

Self-Knowledge & Self-Discipline. B. W. Maturin. vi, 276p. 1995. text ed. 18.95 (*0-912141-16-6*) Roman Cath Bks.

Self Knowledge & Spiritual Yearning. Abdul Fattah Rashid Hamid. Ed. by Hamid Quinlan. LC 82-70348. (Illus.). 116p. 1993. pap. 5.00 (*0-89259-127-7*) Am Trust Pubns.

Self-Knowledge in Plato's Phaedrus. Charles L. Griswold, Jr. LC 96-41249. 328p. 1996. pap. 18.95 (*0-271-01618-3*) Pa St U Pr.

Self-Knowledge in Plato's Phaedrus. Charles L. Griswold, Jr. LC 86-5506. 328p. 1986. text ed. 18.00 (*0-300-03594-2*) Yale U Pr.

***Self-Knowledge in the Age of Theory.** Ann Hartle. LC 96-35269. 192p. 1996. 52.50 (*0-8476-8417-2*); pap. 21.95 (*0-8476-8418-0*) Rowman.

Self-Knowledge Through Handwriting Analysis. Joseph Zmuda. (Illus.). 44p. (Orig.). 1985. pap. text ed. 20.00 (*0-941572-03-X*) Z Graphic Pubns.

Self-Leader. Mark Hamilton. 142p. 1993. pap. 39.95 (*0-911752-69-2*) Neo-Tech Pub.

***Self-Learning Materials & Modules for Health Workers: A Guide for Their Development, Utilization & Evaluation.** (SEARO Technical Publications Ser.: No. 6). 18p. 1985. pap. text ed. 3.00 (*92-9022-145-3*) World Health.

Self Liberation. rev. ed. L. A. Ammann. Tr. by Paul Tooby from SPA. (Illus.). 225p. 1992. pap. 15.95 (*1-878977-14-8*) Latitude Pr.

Self Liberation Through Seeing Everything in Its Nakedness. John Reynolds. 1989. 29.95 (*0-88268-058-7*) Station Hill Pr.

Self-Liberation Through Seeing with Naked Awareness: An introduction to the Nature of One's Own Mind in the Tibetan Dzogchen Tradition. Padmasambhava. Ed. by George Quasha. Tr. by John M. Reynolds from TIB. (Illus.). 240p. (C). 1989. 14.95 (*0-88268-050-1*) Station Hill Pr.

Self-Life & the Christ-Life see Christ in You: The Self-Life & the Christ Life

***Self Love.** Schuller. mass mkt. write for info. (*0-06-109255-X*, Harp PBks) HarpC.

Self Love. R. Schuller. 20.00 (*0-06-017761-6*, HarpT) HarpC.

Self-Love. Robert H. Schuller. 160p. 1986. mass mkt. 4.99 (*0-515-08986-9*) Jove Pubns.

***Self-Love.** W. G. Shepherd. 48p. 1983. pap. 11.95 (*0-85646-097-4*, Pub. by Anvil Press UK) Dufour.

Self Love: Developing & Maintaining Self-Esteem for the Black Woman. Rosenna Bakari. LC 94-78294. 90p. 1995. pap. text ed. 6.95 (*0-9642744-3-4*) Karibu Pubng.

Self-Made Americans: Interviews with Dreamers, Visionaries & Entrepreneurs. Margery Mandell. Ed. by Alexia Dorszynski. 310p. 1996. 24.00 (*0-9634249-9-8*) Gift Future Two Thous.

Self-Made & Blues-Rich. Spencer. 130p. Date not set. pap. 11.95 (*0-86543-503-0*) Africa World.

***Self-Made & Blues-Rich.** Jon M. Spencer. 130p. 1996. 32.95 (*0-86543-502-2*) Africa World.

Self Made in America: Plain Talk for Plain People about Extraordinary Success. John Mccormack. 1990. 19.95 (*0-201-55099-7*) Addison-Wesley.

Self-Made in America: Plain Talk for Plain People about the Meaning of Success. John McCormack & David R. Legge. (Illus.). 240p. 1992. pap. 12.00 (*0-201-60823-5*) Addison-Wesley.

Self-Made Man. Carole Halston. (Special Edition Ser.). 1995. mass mkt. 3.75 (*0-373-09950-9*, 1-09950-6) Silhouette.

***Self-Made Man.** Paul Hewitt & Jane Warren. (Illus.). 352p. 1997. pap. 13.95 (*0-7472-4998-9*, Pub. by Headline UK) Trafalgar.

Self-Made Man: Human Evolution from Eden to Extinction? Jonathan Kingdon. 384p. 1993. text ed. 27.95 (*0-471-30538-3*) Wiley.

Self Made Man: The Story of Human Evolution. Jonathan Kingdon. 384p. 1996. pap. text ed. 16.95 (*0-471-15960-3*) Wiley.

Self-Made Map: Cartographic Writing in Early Modern France. Tom Conley. (Illus.). 448p. (C). 1996. text ed. 34.95 (*0-8166-2700-2*) U of Minn Pr.

Self Made Miracles: Using Your Intuition. Patricia Holmes. (Illus.). 100p. (Orig.). 1996. pap. 12.95 (*0-9648237-0-5*) Hgher Self.

***Self-Made Worlds: Visionary Folk Art Environments.** Roger Manley et al. (Illus.). 144p. 1997. 40.00 (*0-89381-732-5*) Aperture.

Self-Managed Teamworking. Graham Wilson. (Financial Times Management Ser.). 224p. 1995. 25.00 (*0-273-60714-6*) Pitman Publng.

Self-Managed Work Teams in Health Care Organizations. Elizabeth D. Becker-Reems. LC 94-1253. 246p. 1994. pap. 49.00 (*1-55648-122-5*, 169109) AHPI.

Self-Management: Strategies for Personal Success. Albert Ellis & Gina Vega. 56p. (Orig.). 1990. pap. 3.00 (*0-917476-21-2*) A Ellis Institute.

Self-Management for Adolescents: A Skills Training Program. Thomas A. Brigham. LC 88-19031. (Treatment Manuals for Practitioners Ser.). 161p. 1988. pap. text ed. 27.95 (*0-89862-202-6*) Guilford Pr.

Self-Management for College Students: The ABC Approach. rev. ed. Edward J. O'Keefe & Donna S. Berger. LC 93-85780. (Illus.). (C). 1993. pap. 22.95 (*0-9637801-0-7*) Partridge Hill.

A holistic approach to self-management provides a comprehensive framework for attaining academic & personal goals. Students learn to manage time, motivation, study habits, procrastination, assertiveness, & self-esteem by managing their Affect, Behavior & Cognition. Seemingly disparate skills are integrated through common ABC principles & methods. The central role of the ABCs to developing & applying skills in all of these areas transforms otherwise complex topics such as motivation & self-esteem into skills that students can understand & manage. Basic feelings, behaviors, & thoughts that help or hinder achievement are discussed along with methods for change & improvement. These principles are then applied to each of the topic areas. A useful self-help book for high school seniors or college-bound students, its focus on life skills is relevant to everyone. With plenty of exercises that can be done independently or in a classroom setting, the book is an excellent resource for student success courses, freshman seminars, or any program emphasizing self-reliance. The foreword by John Gardner, Director of the University of South Carolina's Freshman Year Experience, urges students to read carefully its "all-powerful message." Teacher's guide is also available. Contact Partridge Hill Publishers, FAX/Phone: 914-229-6672. Price $22.95. ***Publisher Provided Annotation.***

Self Management in Organizations: The Dynamics of Interaction. M. DeWaele et al. 220p. 1993. text ed. 26.95 (*0-88937-079-6*) Hogrefe & Huber Pubs.

Self-Management in Yugoslavia & the Developing World. Hans D. Seibel & Ukandi G. Damachi. LC 81-21214. 1982. text ed. 39.95 (*0-312-71237-5*) St Martin.

Self-Management on Trial: Yugoslavia's Attempt to Establish a Society. Milojko Drulovic. 346p. 1978. 44.50 (*0-85124-231-6*, Pub. by Spokesman Bks UK) Coronet Bks.

Self-Management Strategies: Theory, Curriculum & Teaching Procedures. Michael B. Medland. LC 90-31211. 320p. 1990. text ed. 65.00 (*0-275-93519-1*, C3519, Praeger Pubs) Greenwood.

Self-Management Tactics. Fowler. 1985. pap. 21.00 (*0-08-032381-2*, Pergamon Pr) Elsevier.

Self-Management Therapy for Borderline Personality Disorder: A Therapist-Guided Approach. Michael H. Langley. LC 93-34656. 216p. 1993. 29.95 (*0-8261-8300-X*) Springer Pub.

Self Manager Program, 11 booklets, Set. Gene Bedley. 1985. pap. 40.00 (*1-888353-06-6*) People-Wise.

Self-Managing Environment. Alan Roberts. 189p. 1980. 29.00 (*0-8476-6211-X*) Rowman.

Self-Managing School. Brian J. Caldwell & Jim M. Spinks. 260p. 1988. 80.00 (*1-85000-330-0*, Falmer Pr); pap. 40.00 (*1-85000-331-9*, Falmer Pr) Taylor & Francis.

***Self-Managing Teams.** Robert F. Hicks & Diane Bone. (Better Management Skills Ser.). 1991. pap. 12.95 (*0-7494-0527-9*) Kogan Page Ltd.

Self-Managing Teams: Creating & Maintaining Self-Managed Work Groups. Robert Hicks & Diane Bone. LC 89-81520. (Fifty-Minute Ser.). (Illus.). 91p. (Orig.). 1990. pap. 10.95 (*1-56052-000-0*) Crisp Pubns.

Self-Managing Teams: Understanding Your Role As a Member Or a Leader. Robert E. Ripley & Marie J. Ripley. LC 93-70695. (Illus.). 100p. 1993. pap. 12.95 (*0-9621133-5-2*, WB011) Carefree Pr.

Self Massage: A Complete Fifteen-Minutes-a-Day Massage System for Health & Healing. Jacqueline C. Young. (Illus.). 1992. pap. 16.00 (*0-7225-2510-9*) Thorsons SF.

Self Mastery. 5th ed. Swami Paramananda. 1961. pap. 3.95 (*0-911564-08-X*) Vedanta Ctr.

***Self-Mastery: Making the Most of What You've Got.** Michael S. Haro. 159p. (Orig.). 1997. mass mkt. 4.99 (*1-55237-250-2*, Pub. by Comnwlth Pub CN) Partners Pubs Grp.

Self Mastery & Fate with the Cycles of Life. H. Spencer Lewis. LC 55-16785. (Illus.). 253p. 1929. pap. 14.95 (*0-912057-45-9*, 501970) RO AMORC.

Self Mastery Through Conscious Autosuggestion. Emile Coue. 93p. 1981. pap. 10.00 (*0-89540-095-2*, SB-095) Sun Pub.

Self Mastery Through Conscious Autosuggestion. Emile Coue. 94p. 1970. reprint ed. spiral bd. 7.00 (*0-7873-0226-0*) Hlth Research.

Self Mastery Through Conscious Autosuggestion (1922) Emile Coue. 93p. 1996. pap. 14.95 (*1-56459-721-0*) Kessinger Pub.

Self-Mastery Through Self-Hypnosis. Roger Bernhardt & David Martin. 1989. pap. 3.95 (*0-451-14989-0*) NAL-Dutton.

Self-Ministry Through Self-Understanding: A Guide to Christian Introspection. Robert J. Wicks. 112p. (Orig.). 1990. pap. 8.95 (*0-8294-0692-1*) Loyola Pr.

Self-Modifying Systems in Biology & Cognitive Science: A New Framework for Dynamics, Information & Complexity. George Kampis. (IFSR International Series on Systems Science). (Illus.). 565p. 1991. 142.00 (*0-08-036979-0*, Pergamon Pr) Elsevier.

***Self Monitoring Primary School.** Pearl White & Cyril Poster. (Educational Management Ser.). 160p. (C). 1997. pap. text ed. 18.95 (*0-415-14817-0*) Routledge.

Self-Motion: From Aristotle to Newton. Ed. by Mary L. Gill & James G. Lennox. LC 88-5154... 400p. 1994. text ed. 47.50 (*0-691-03235-1*) Princeton U Pr.

***Self-Motivation for the Self-Employed: The 5 Step Action Plan to Keep Your Passion Alive & Achieve Your Goals.** Martin Edic. 256p. 1997. per. 14.00 (*0-7615-1174-1*) Prima Pub.

Self-Mutilation: Theory, Research, & Treatment. Barent W. Walsh & Paul M. Rosen. LC 88-5154. 273p. 1988. lib. bdg. 36.95 (*0-89862-731-1*) Guilford Pr.

Self-Narratives: The Emergence of Meaning. Hubert J. Hermans & Els Herman-Jansen. (Culture & Human Developmen Ser.). 1995. lib. bdg. 35.00 (*0-89862-878-4*, C2878) Guilford Pr.

Self-Neglecting Elders: A Clinical Dilemma. Ed. by Eloise Rathbone-McCuan & Dorothy R. Fabian. LC 91-36343. 216p. 1992. text ed. 47.95 (*0-86569-047-2*, T047, Auburn Hse) Greenwood.

Self Observed: Swift, Johnson, Wordsworth. Morris Golden. LC 70-179137. 199p. 1972. 23.00 (*0-8018-1289-5*) Johns Hopkins.

Self on the Shelf: Recovery Books & the Good Life. Gary Greenberg. LC 93-38024. 287p. (C). 1994. pap. 19.95 (*0-7914-2046-9*); text ed. 59.50 (*0-7914-2045-0*) State U NY Pr.

Self-Order & Form in Polymeric Materials. Ed. by A. Keller et al. 181p. (gr. 13). 1995. text ed. 79.95 (*0-412-62450-8*) Chapman & Hall.

Self-Organization. Ed. by V. I. Krinsky. (Synergetics Ser.: Vol. 28). (Illus.). xi, 263p. 1985. 85.95 (*0-387-15080-3*) Spr-Verlag.

Self-Organization & Associative Memory. Teuvo Kohonen. (Information Sciences Ser.: Vol. 8). (Illus.). 328p. 1989. pap. 44.00 (*0-387-51387-6*) Spr-Verlag.

Self-Organization & Associative Memory. 2nd ed. Teuvo Kohonen. (Information Sciences Ser.: Vol. 8). (Illus.). 320p. 1988. 39.50 (*0-387-18314-0*) Spr-Verlag.

Self-Organization & Dissipative Structures: Applications in the Physical & Social Sciences. W. C. Schieve. (Illus.). 373p. 1982. text ed. 50.00 (*0-292-70354-6*) U of Tex Pr.

Self-Organization & Management of Social Systems. Ed. by H. Ulrich & G. J. Probst. (Synergetics Ser.: Vol. 26). (Illus.). 170p. 1984. 78.95 (*0-387-13459-X*) Spr-Verlag.

Self-Organization & Psychotherapy. Ed. by A. L. Goudsmit. (Recent Research in Psychology Ser.). vii, 189p. 1990. 47.95 (*0-387-52161-5*) Spr-Verlag.

***Self-Organization, Computational Maps, & Motor Control, Vol. 119.** P. Morasso & Vittorio Sanguineti. LC 97-36. (Advances in Psychology Ser.). 656p. 1997. 168.75 (*0-444-82323-9*) Elsevier.

Self-Organization, Emerging Properties & Learning. Ed. by A. Babloyantz. (NATO ASI Series B, Physics: Vol. 260). (Illus.). 306p. 1991. 85.00 (*0-306-43930-1*, Plenum Pr) Plenum.

Self-Organization in Non-Equilibrium Systems: From Dissipative Structures to Order Through Fluctuations. G. Nicolis & Ilya Prigogine. 491p. 1977. text ed. 175.00 (*0-471-02401-5*, Wiley-Interscience) Wiley.

Self-Organization in Optical Systems & Applications in Information Technology. Ed. by M. A. Vorontsov et al. (Springer Series in Synergetics: Vol. 66). (Illus.). xvi, 247p. 1995. 99.95 (*0-387-57086-1*) Spr-Verlag.

Self-Organization in Optical Systems & Applications in Information Technology. Ed. by Mikhail A. Vorontsov & Walter B. Miller. LC 95-10517. (Synergetics Ser.: Vol. 66). 1954. write for info. (*3-540-57086-1*) Spr-Verlag.

***Self-Organization of Complex Structures: From Individual to Collective Dynamics.** Ed. by Frank Schweitzer. 622p. 1997. text ed. 180.00 (*90-5699-027-6*) Gordon & Breach.

Self-Organizing Control of Stochastic Systems. George N. Saridis. LC 75-40645. (Control & Systems Theory Ser.: Vol. 4). 512p. reprint ed. pap. 146.00 (*0-685-16275-3*, 2027116) Bks Demand.

Self Organizing Economy. Paul R. Krugman. 1995. pap. 18.95 (*1-55786-699-6*) Blackwell Pubs.

Self-Organizing Maps. Teuvo Kohonen. LC 95-4098. (Information Sciences Ser.: Vol. 30). 362p. 1995. 49.50 (*3-540-58600-8*) Spr-Verlag.

***Self-Organizing Maps.** 2nd ed. Teuvo Kohonen. LC 96-53987. (Series in Information Sciences). 1997. pap. write for info. (*3-540-62017-6*) Spr-Verlag.

Self-Organizing Methods in Modeling: GMDH Type Algorithms. Farlow. (Statistics: Textbooks & Monographs: Vol. 54). 368p. 1984. 140.00 (*0-8247-7161-3*) Dekker.

Self-Organizing Systems. A. M. Andrew. x, 244p. 1989. pap. text ed. 134.00 (*2-88124-686-9*) Gordon & Breach.

Self-Organizing Systems. Atlan. 1995. write for info. (*0-8493-6953-3*) CRC Pr.

Self Organizing Systems: Proceedings of an Interdisciplinary Conference, May 1959. M. Yovits & S. Cameron. LC 60-12574. (International Tracts Computer Science & Technology & Their Application Ser.: Vol. 2). 1960. 151.00 (*0-08-009303-5*, Pub. by Pergamon Repr UK) Franklin.

Self-Organizing Systems: The Emergence of Order. Ed. by F. E. Yates. LC 87-10151. (Life Science Monographs). (Illus.). 684p. 1988. 135.00 (*0-306-42145-3*, Plenum Pr) Plenum.

Self-Overcoming of Nihilism. Keiji Nishitani. Tr. by Graham Parkes & Setsuko Aihara from JPN. LC 90-31631. (SUNY Series in Modern Japanese Philosophy). 240p. 1990. text ed. 69.50 (*0-7914-0437-4*); pap. text ed. 23.95 (*0-7914-0438-2*) State U NY Pr.

Self-Ownership, Freedom, & Equality. G. A. Cohen. (Studies in Marxism & Social Theory). 320p. (C). 1995. pap. text ed. 18.95 (*0-521-47751-4*) Cambridge U Pr.

Self-Ownership, Freedom, & Equality. G. A. Cohen. (Studies in Marxism & Social Theory). 320p. (C). 1995. text ed. 59.95 (*0-521-47174-5*) Cambridge U Pr.

Self-Paced Instructor Training Modules, 5 modules. (Illus.). 66.00 (*0-87683-936-7*) GP Courseware.

Self-Paced Phonics: A Text for Education. G. Thomas Baer. 160p. (C). 1990. pap. text ed. 21.00 (*0-675-21246-4*, Merrill Coll) P-H.

Self-Paced Study Guide & Laboratory Exercise in Astronomy. 7th ed. John L. Safko. 528p. (C). 1995. ring bd. 35.64 (*0-8403-9105-6*) Kendall-Hunt.

Self-Paced/Introduction to Mathematics. C. J. Stokoe. (Australian National University Press Ser.). 1986. pap. text ed. 22.00 (*0-08-032985-3*, Pergamon Pr) Elsevier.

Self, Person, World: The Interplay of Conscious & Unconscious in Human Life. Donald McIntosh. LC 94-47481. (Psychosocial Issues Ser.). 1995. 59.95 (*0-8101-1233-7*); pap. 19.95 (*0-8101-1217-5*) Northwestern U Pr.

Self-Perspectives Across the Life Span. Ed. by Richard P. Lipka & Thomas M. Brinthaupt. LC 91-16383. (SUNY Series, Studying the Self). 282p. (C). 1992. text ed. 64.50 (*0-7914-1003-X*); pap. text ed. 21.95 (*0-7914-1004-8*) State U NY Pr.

Self Portrait. (Illus.). 16p. 1980. 2.00 (*0-916746-50-X*) Springfield Lib & Mus.

Self Portrait. John Perlman. 1976. pap. 8.00 (*0-685-79204-8*) Elizabeth Pr.

Self-Portrait: Ceaselessly into the Past. Ross Macdonald. Ed. by Ralph B. Sipper. LC 95-1610. (Brownstone Mystery Guides Ser.: Vol. 13). iv, 131p. (Orig.). 1995. pap. 19.00 (*0-941028-26-7*, Brownstone Bks); lib. bdg. 29.00 (*0-941028-25-9*, Brownstone Bks) Borgo Pr.

Self-Portrait: 12 Poems for the Road. Irving Stettner. 26p. 1991. pap. 4.95 (*0-941543-03-X*) Sun Dog Pr.

Self-Portrait in a Convex Mirror. John Ashbery. (Poets Ser.). 1976. mass mkt. 6.95 (*0-14-042201-3*, Penguin Bks) Viking Penguin.

Self-Portrait in a Convex Mirror. John Ashbery. 96p. 1990. reprint ed. pap. 12.95 (*0-14-058668-7*, Penguin Bks) Viking Penguin.

***Self-Portrait in Tyvek Windbreaker.** James Merrill. 32p. 9500. pap. 10.95 (*1-873790-79-1*) Dufour.

Self-Portrait in Words: Collected Writings & Statements, 1903-1950. Max Beckmann & Barbara C. Buenger. LC 96-23422. 1996. 34.95 (*0-226-04136-0*) U Ch Pr.

Self-Portrait in Words: Collected Writings & Statements, 1903-1950. Max Beckmann. Ed. by Barbara C. Buenger. Tr. by Reinhold Heller & David Britt. (Illus.). 496p. (C). 1997. 34.95 (*0-226-04135-2*) U Ch Pr.

Self-Portrait of a Literary Biographer. Joan Givner. LC 92-44772. 192p. 1993. 24.95 (*0-8203-1552-4*) U of Ga Pr.

***Self Portrait of Someone.** Vincent Eaton. Date not set. pap. 7.95 (*0-14-011521-8*) Viking Penguin.

Self-Portrait of the Other: A Memoir. Heberto Padilla. Tr. by Alexander Coleman from SPA. 220p. 1990. 19.95 (*0-374-26086-9*) FS&G.

Self-Portrait with an Unwilling Landscape. Laurie Blauner. 1990. pap. 9.00 (*0-937669-39-3*) Owl Creek Pr.

Self-Portrait, with Birds: Some Semi-Ornithological Recollections. John Graves. 48p. 1991. bond lthr., boxed 600.00 (*0-9626336-4-X*) Chama Pr.

Self-Portrait, with Birds: Some Semi-Ornithological Recollections. limited ed. John Graves. 48p. 1991. boxed 195.00 (*0-9626336-3-1*) Chama Pr.

Self-Portrait with Hand Microscope. Lucille Day. 52p. 1982. pap. 5.95 (*0-917658-18-3*) BPW & P.

***Self-Portrait with Woman: A Novel.** Andrzej Szczypiorski. Tr. by Bill Johnston from POL. 256p. 1997. reprint ed. pap. 12.00 (*0-8021-3488-2*, Grove) Grove-Atltic.

Self-Portraits. Peggy Roalf. LC 92-72042. (Looking at Paintings Ser.). (Illus.). 48p. (J). (gr. 3-7). 1993. pap. 6.95 (*1-56282-356-6*) Hyprn Child.

Self Portraits: Tales from the Life of Japan's Great Decadent Romantic. Osamu Dazai. Ed. by Pockell. (Illus.). 208p. 1993. reprint ed. pap. 8.00 (*4-7700-1689-1*) Kodansha.

Self Portraits of Great Artists. Ed. by Stephen Longstreet. (Master Draughtsman Ser.). (Illus.). 1973. pap. 4.95 (*0-87505-201-0*) Borden.

Self-Portraits, the Gide-Valery Letters, 1890-1942. Andre Gide. Ed. by Robert Mallet. Tr. by June Guicharnaud. LC 65-25125. 346p. reprint ed. pap. 98.70 (*0-317-26503-2*, 2024041) Bks Demand.

Self Possession. Marion Halligan. 1988. pap. 16.95 (*0-7022-2097-3*, Pub. by Univ Queensland Pr AT) Intl Spec Bk.

***Self Power.** Eldon Taylor. Ed. by Tony Markham. (Illus.). 278p. 1997. pap. 12.95 (*1-55978-783-X*) R K Bks.

Self-Presentation. Ed. by S. L. Zelen. (Recent Research in Psychology Ser.). 180p. 1988. 63.95 (*0-387-96862-8*) Spr-Verlag.

Self-Presentation: Impression Management & Interpersonal Behavior. Mark Leary. 264p. (C). 1994. pap. text ed. write for info. (*0-697-14796-7*) Brown & Benchmark.

Self-Presentation: Impression Management & Interpersonal Behavior. Mark R. Leary. LC 96-1276. (Social Psychology Ser.). (C). 1996. pap. text ed. 21.00 (*0-8133-3004-1*) Westview.

***Self-Preservation.** Anita Hallman. LC 97-2130. 1997. pap. write for info. (*1-57345-230-0*) Deseret Bk.

Self Process & Development: The Minnesota Symposia on Child Psychology, Vol. 23. L. Alan Sroufe. 280p. (C). 1990. text ed. 69.95 (*0-8058-0695-4*) L Erlbaum Assocs.

Self-Producing Systems: Implications & Applications of Autopoiesis. John Mingers. LC 94-43375. (Contemporary Systems Thinking Ser.). 240p. 1995. 49. 50 (*0-306-44797-5*, Plenum Pr) Plenum.

Self-Production of Society. Alain Touraine. Tr. by Derek Coltman from FRE. LC 76-611. (Illus.). 408p. 1977. lib. bdg. 13.50 (*0-226-80858-0*) U Ch Pr.

Self-Production of Supramolecular Structures from Synthetic Structures to Models of Minimal Living Systems: Proceedings of the NATO Advanced Research Workshop, Acquafredda di Maratea, Italy, September 12-16, 1993. Ed. by Gail R. Fleischaker et al. LC 94-32554. (NATO ASI Series C: Vol. 446). 336p. (C). 1994. lib. bdg. 169.00 (*0-7923-3163-X*, Pub. by Klwr Acad Pubs NE) Kluwer Ac.

Self Profile: A Guide for Positive Interpersonal Communication. (Illus.). 99p. 1995. pap. 9.95 (*1-55852-150-X*) Natl Pr Pubns.

Self Programer: The Psychology of Destiny Making: An Evo-Revolution in Psychology of Being, Bk. 8. Rose A. Parvin. LC 95-35694. 288p. 1995. write for info. (*1-885917-07-4*) Univrsl Pubng.

Self-Protection Complete: The A.S.P. System: A Complete System of Holistic Body-Mind Self-Protection, for Mental & Physical Fitness, for Self-Defense & Prevention for Sport. deluxe ed. Evan S. Baltazzi. Ed. by Nellie D. Baltazzi. (Illus.). 334p. (C). (gr. 13 up). 1991. text ed. 37.00 (*0-918948-04-5*) Evanel.

Self-Protective Measures to Enhance Airlift Operations in Hostile Environments. 1990. lib. bdg. 79.00 (*0-8490-4011-6*) Gordon Pr.

Self Psychology. Goldstein. Date not set. 27.95 (*0-02-912325-9*, Free Press) Free Pr.

Self Psychology: Comparisons & Contrasts. Ed. by Douglas W. Detrick & Susan P. Detrick. 512p. 1989. text ed. 49. 95 (*0-88163-077-2*) Analytic Pr.

Self Psychology in Clinical Social Work. Miriam Elson. (Professional Bks.). (C). 1988. pap. text ed. 13.95 (*0-393-95797-7*) Norton.

Self Publish to Success: Make Money Publishing. Shami Maxwell & Kathryn Maxwell. (Illus.). 128p. (Orig.). 1988. pap. 9.95 (*0-940649-03-9*) Parnell Pub.

Self-Publish Your Book. Garbo. 54p. 1993. student ed. 19. 95 (*1-881152-06-5*) Big Breakfast.

Self-Published Cook: How to Write, Publish & Sell Your Own Cookbook. Marilyn M. Moore. (Illus.). 142p. (Orig.). 1995. pap. 14.95 (*0-9603788-1-2*) Wooden Spoon.

***Self Publisher's Guide: Your Personal Consultant Through the Self Publishing Process.** Judy A. Miller. Ed. by Barry Bernard & David Linder. LC 97-91795. x, 116p. (Orig.). 1997. per. write for info. (*0-9631327-1-7*) Cascade Spec.

Self Publishers Guide to Marketing & Promotion. rev. ed. Alisa M. Hoffman. 32p. (Orig.). 1995. pap. 8.95 (*1-56167-072-3*) Am Literary Pr.

Self-Publishers Handbook of Contacts & Sources. 2nd ed. Thomas A. Williams. 96p. 1996. ring bd. 19.95 (*1-878853-52-X*) Venture Pr FL.

Self-Publishing: The Art of Turning Words into Cash. Jerry E. Moffett. LC 94-96309. 150p. (Orig.). pap. 19.95 (*0-9642508-1-0*) Jerett Pubng.

Self Publishing by the Seat of Your Pants! Carole Marsh. (ProPub Ser.). 1994. pap. text ed. 19.95 (*1-55609-963-0*); lib. bdg. 29.95 (*1-55609-962-2*); ring bd. 29.95 (*1-55609-964-9*); disk 29.95 (*1-55609-965-7*) Gallopade Pub Group.

Self-Publishing Can Be Profitable & Immensely Rewarding. Ruth R. Moen. Ed. by Paul Cocke. (Kathleen O'Shaghnessy Mystery Ser.). 138p. (Orig.). (C). 1995. pap. 17.49 (*0-9635653-4-6*) Flying Swan.

Self-Publishing Directory Guide of Choice: How to Write, Print & Sell Your Own Book. Maria Valentin. LC 96-69213. 464p. (Orig.). 1997. pap. 14.95 (*0-9651657-9-5*) NWI.

Self-Publishing for Genealogy & Local History Researchers, Seminar Teaching Guide: Everything You Need to Conduct This Seminar... Even If You Have Never Given a Seminar Before. Dina C. Carson. LC 91-73443. (Illus.). 150p. (Orig.). 1992. teacher ed. 89.95 (*1-879579-30-8*) Iron Gate Pub.

Self-Publishing Made Simple: Step-by-Step Guide No Thinking Required. Lori A. Patterson. LC 94-65050. 320p. (Orig.). 1998. 29.95 (*1-884573-04-5*); pap. 19.95 (*1-884573-15-0*) S-By-S Pubns.

Self-Publishing Manual: How to Write, Print, & Sell Your Own Book. 9th ed. Dan Poynter. LC 95-33712. 464p. 1996. pap. 19.95 (*1-56860-018-6*) Para Pub.

Self-Publishing Seminar Resource Manual & Workbook: Exhibits, Exercises & Examples. (Illus.). 100p. (Orig.). 1992. wbk. ed. 10.00 (*1-879579-31-6*) Iron Gate Pub.

Self Publishing Success Story. Jim Muckle. Ed. by Shari Conradson. (Illus.). 50p. (Orig.). 1990. pap. 5.00 (*0-9620445-4-7*) KSJ Publishing.

***Self-Publishing Your Book (on a Budget)** John M. Denney. (Illus.). 52p. (Orig.). 1996. pap. 7.95 (*0-9654698-2-4*) Denney Literary.

Self-Purification. Jaina Sutra. (Illus.). 8.75 (*0-88695-020-1*) Concord Grove.

Self-Realization. Satguru S. Keshavadas. (Illus.). 131p. (Orig.). 1976. pap. 8.00 (*0-942508-10-6*) Vishwa.

Self-Realization - the Knowledge of the Absolute. Al Drucker. (Wisdom Teachings Ser.). 54p. 1994. pap. 4.50 (*0-9638449-1-1*) ATMA Pr.

Self Realization in Kashmir Shaivism: The Oral Teachings of Swami Lakshmanjoo. John Hughes. LC 94-29842. 139p. (C). 1994. pap. 16.95 (*0-7914-2180-5*); text ed. 49. 50 (*0-7914-2179-1*) State U NY Pr.

Self-Realization of Noble Wisdom. Lankavatara-Sutra. Ed. by Dwight Goddard. Tr. by D. T. Suzuki. LC 78-72461. reprint ed. 37.50 (*0-404-17333-0*) AMS Pr.

Self-Realization of Noble Wisdom: The Lankavatara Sutra. D. T. Suzuki. 166p. 1983. pap. 9.95 (*0-913922-79-X*) Dawn Horse Pr.

Self-Realization, Success, & Adjustment. Ed. by Edgar Krau. LC 88-30747. 179p. 1989. text ed. 55.00 (*0-275-93210-9*, C3210, Praeger Pubs) Greenwood.

Self-Realization Through Love. I. K. Taimni. 1981. 4.75 (*0-8356-7522-X*) Theos Pub Hse.

Self-Recovery: Treating Addictions Using Transcendental Meditation & Maharishi Ayur-Veda. Ed. by Charles N. Alexander. LC 94-3952. (Alcoholism Treatment Quarterly Ser.). (Illus.). 341p. 1995. pap. 14.95 (*1-56023-044-4*) Haworth Pr.

Self-Recovery: Treating Addictions Using Transcendental Meditation & Maharishi Ayur-Veda. Ed. by Charles N. Alexander. LC 94-3952. (Alcoholism Treatment Quarterly Ser.). (Illus.). 341p. 1995. lib. bdg. 59.95 (*1-56024-454-2*) Haworth Pr.

Self-Reference & Modal Logic. C. Smorynski. (Universitext Ser.). xii, 333p. 1985. 71.95 (*0-387-96209-3*) Spr-Verlag.

Self Reflections. Tr. by Gabriela Sanchez-Diaz from SPA. (Illus.). 80p. (Orig.). (ENG.). 1987. pap. 10.00 (*0-942607-01-5*) Hispanic Anglo Pubns.

Self-Reform of the Criminal Herschell Dudley Walker. Jim Walker. Ed. by Clara Baker & John Pritchard. LC 94-781169. 310p. (Orig.). 1994. pap. 9.95 (*0-914207-06-7*) Cornucopia Pubns.

Self-Regulation in Higher Education: A Multi-National Perspective on Collaborative Systems of Quality Assurance & Control. H. R. Kells. (Higher Education Policy Ser.: No. 15). 180p. 1992. 62.50 (*1-85302-528-3*) Taylor & Francis.

***Self-Regulation of Environmental Management: An Analysis of Guidelines Set by World Industry Associations for Their Member Firms.** United Nations Conference on Trade & Development Staff. 158p. 1996. pap. 35.00 (*92-1-104458-8*, K3585) UN.

Self-Regulation of Learning & Performance: Issues & Educational Applications. Ed. by Dale H. Schunk & Barry J. Zimmerman. 344p. 1994. pap. 36.00 (*0-8058-1335-7*); text ed. 79.95 (*0-8058-1334-9*) L Erlbaum Assocs.

Self-Regulation Test for Children: Computer-Assisted Test of Resistance to Distraction & Temptation. J. Kuhl & K. Kraska. 60p. pap. text ed. 495.00 (*0-88937-125-3*) Hogrefe & Huber Pubs.

***Self-Regulation Theory: Applying Theory to Your Practice.** Jean E. Johnson et al. (Illus.). 130p. (Orig.). 1997. pap. text ed., spiral bd. 29.50 (*1-890504-02-5*) Oncology Nursing.

Self-Regulation Theory: How Optimal Adjustment Maximizes Gain. Dennis E. Mithaug. LC 92-17812. 256p. 1993. text ed. 49.95 (*0-275-94422-0*, C4422, Praeger Pubs) Greenwood.

Self-Regulatory Behavior & Risk Taking: Causes & Consequences. Ed. by Lewis P. Lipsitt & Leonard L. Mitnick. 432p. (C). 1991. text ed. 82.50 (*0-89391-818-0*) Ablex Pub.

Self-Related Cognitions in Anxiety & Motivation. Ed. by Ralf Schwarzer. 360p. (C). 1985. text ed. 69.95 (*0-89859-513-4*) L Erlbaum Assocs.

Self Relaxation: Comfort in Times of Tension. Harley D. Christiansen. LC 81-2595. (Illus.). 96p. (Orig.). 1981. pap. 15.95 (*0-915456-02-8*) P Juul Pr.

Self-Reliance. Michael Brownstein. LC 93-23690. 296p. (Orig.). 1994. pap. 12.95 (*1-56689-018-7*) Coffee Hse.

Self Reliance. 2nd ed. Ralph Waldo Emerson. Ed. by Gene Dekovic. LC 75-12544. (Illus.). 96p. 1983. reprint ed. 15.00 (*0-937088-07-2*) Illum Pr.

Self Reliance: Reforming Welfare in Advanced Societies. Ed. by David Marsland. LC 95-18147. 134p. 1995. 32. 95 (*1-56000-211-5*) Transaction Pubs.

Self Reliance: The Key to Business Success. Sidney A. Weltmer. 49p. 1959. reprint ed. spiral bd. 7.00 (*0-7873-0946-X*) Hlth Research.

Self-Reliance: The Wisdom of Ralph Waldo Emerson as Inspiration for Daily Living. Intro. by Richard Whelan. 212p. 1991. pap. 11.00 (*0-517-58512-X*, Bell Tower) Crown Pub Group.

Self-Reliance & Constructive Change: The Declaration of Spiritual Independence. Hua-Ching Ni. LC 95-10463. (Course for Total Health Ser.). 1995. pap. 7.00 (*0-937064-85-8*) SevenStar Comm.

Self Reliance & Foreign Policy in Tanzania. Okwudiba Nnoli. LC 73-91415. (Studies in East African Society & History). 1977. text ed. 21.50 (*0-88357-014-9*); pap. text ed. 8.95 (*0-88357-039-4*) NOK Pubs.

Self-Reliance, & Other Essays. Ralph Waldo Emerson. LC 93-16611. (Thrift Editions Ser.). 128p. 1993. reprint ed. pap. 1.00 (*0-486-27790-9*) Dover.

Self-Reliance vs. Power Politics: American & Indian Experiences in Building Nation - States. J. Ann Tickner. LC 86-12989. (Political Economy of International Change Ser.). 282p. 1987. text ed. 52.50 (*0-231-06272-9*) Col U Pr.

Self-Reliant Cities: Energy & the Transformation of Urban America. David Morris. LC 81-18301. (Illus.). 256p. 1982. pap. 8.95 (*0-87156-309-6*) Sierra.

Self-Reliant Defense Without Bankruptcy or War. Gene Sharp. 72p. (Orig.). 1992. 4.00 (*1-880813-05-X*) A Einstein Inst.

Self Reliant Development in Europe. E. Brugger & B. Stuckey. 300p. 1986. text ed. 53.95 (*0-566-05095-1*, Pub. by Dartmth Pub UK) Ashgate Pub Co.

Self-Reliant Living. James McKeever. 420p. (C). pap. text ed. 25.00 (*0-86694-126-6*) Omega Pubns OR.

Self-Reliant Potter: Clay & Raw Materials. Henrik Norsker. Ed. by Deutsches Zentrum fur Entwicklungstechnologien GATE In: Deutsche Gesellschaft fur Technische Zusammenarbeit (GTZ) GmbH Staff. (Illus.). 98p. 1990. pap. 17.50 (*3-528-02057-1*, Pub. by Vieweg & Sohn GW) Informatica.

Self-Reliant Potter Refractories & Kilns. Henrik Norsker. (GATE Ser.). 134p. (Orig.). 1987. pap. 17.50 (*3-528-02031-8*, Pub. by Vieweg & Sohn GW) Informatica.

Self-Remembering. rev. ed. Robert E. Burton. LC 95-16125. 175p. 1995. reprint ed. pap. text ed. 12.95 (*0-87728-844-5*) Weiser.

Self-Renewal. Dennis Jaffe & Cynthia D. Scott. Ed. by Philip Gerould. LC 93-72971. 177p. (Orig.). 1994. pap. 15.95 (*1-56052-265-8*) Crisp Pubns.

Self-Renewal: The Individual & the Innovative Society. John W. Gardner. 176p. 1995. pap. 9.95 (*0-393-31295-X*, Norton Paperbks) Norton.

Self-Renewing School. Bruce Joyce et al. LC 93-5130. 97p. (Orig.). 1993. pap. 17.95 (*0-87120-210-7*, 611-93145) Assn Supervision.

Self-Renewing Society: The Role of Television & Communications Technology. N. D. Batra. 194p. (Orig.). (C). 1990. pap. text ed. 23.00 (*0-8191-7949-3*); lib. bdg. 43.50 (*0-8191-7948-5*) U Pr of Amer.

Self-Representation: Life Narrative Studies in Identity & Ideology. Gary S. Gregg. LC 91-7227. (Contributions in Psychology Ser.: No. 18). 248p. 1991. text ed. 55.00 (*0-313-27862-8*, GGA/, Greenwood Pr) Greenwood.

Self Rescue. David Fasulo. (How to Rock Climb Ser.). (Illus.). 100p. 1996. pap. 12.95 (*0-934641-97-8*) Chockstone Pr.

Self Rescue. John C. Kiley. 228p. 1992. pap. 10.95 (*0-929923-64-2*) Lowell Hse.

Self-Respect & Sexual Assault. Jeanette Mauro-Cochrane. LC 92-38938. 1993. pap. 12.60 (*0-8306-4289-7*) McGraw-Hill Prof.

Self Respecting Child. Alison Stallibrass. 1989. pap. 10.95 (*0-201-19340-X*) Addison-Wesley.

Self Righteous, Arrogant & Untouchable. Jack B. Harvey. Ed. by Gayle Martinez. LC 96-83878. 176p. (Orig.). 1996. 16.95 (*0-9651647-0-5*) Crystal Lake.

Self-Righting Lamp: Selected Poetry of Maruyama Kaoru. Ed. by Thomas Fitzsimmons. Tr. & Intro. by Robert Epp. (Asian Poetry in Translation: Japan Ser.: No. 12). 128p. (C). 1990. pap. 12.95 (*0-942668-24-3*) Katydid Bks.

Self-Rule: A Cultural History of American Democracy. Robert H. Wiebe. x, 322p. 1996. pap. text ed. 15.95 (*0-226-89563-7*) U Ch Pr.

Self-Rule: American Democracy. Robert H. Wiebe. 332p. 1995. 25.95 (*0-226-89562-9*) U Ch Pr.

Self Rule-Shared Rule: Federal Solutions to the Middle East Conflict. A Colloquium. Ed. by Daniel J. Elazar. 276p. 1985. pap. text ed. 24.00 (*0-8191-4355-3*, Pub. by Jerusalem Ctr Public) U Pr of Amer.

Self-Run, Self-Supported Houses for More Effective Recovery from Alcohol & Drug Addiction. 1995. lib. bdg. 251.95 (*0-8490-6820-7*) Gordon Pr.

Self-Run, Self-Supported Houses for More Effective Recovery from Alcohol & Drug Addiction: A Technical Assistance Manual. J. Paul Molloy. (Illus.). 124p. (Orig.). (C). 1994. pap. text ed. 30.00 (*0-7881-0307-5*) DIANE Pub.

Self-Sabotage: How to Stop it & Soar to Success. Martha Baldwin. 160p. 1990. pap. 11.99 (*0-446-39108-5*) Warner Bks.

Self-Sabotage: Solve It! Alyce P. Cornyn-Selby. 80p. 1989. pap. 8.95 (*0-941383-09-1*) Beynch Pr.

Self-Sabotage Syndrome: Adult Children in the Workplace. Janet G. Woititz. 1989. 8.95 (*1-55874-050-3*) Health Comm.

Self Scoring I. Q. Test. Dan Pape. (Illus.). 32p. (Orig.). (C). 1993. pap. text ed. write for info. (*1-882330-13-7*) Magni Co.

Self-Scoring I.Q. Test. Alfred W. Munzert. Ed. by Karen K. Elskamp. 1977. pap. 1.95 (*0-917292-00-6*) H-U Public.

***Self-Seeking & the Pursuit of Justice.** David P. Levine. (Avebury Series in Philosophy). 130p. 1997. text ed. 55. 95 (*1-84014-113-1*, Pub. by Ashgate UK) Ashgate Pub Co.

Self-Selected Essays. J. B. Priestley. (Essay Index Reprint Ser.). 1977. 20.95 (*0-8369-0801-5*) Ayer.

Self-Serve Brewery: Open & Operate Your Own Brew-on-Premise. Victoria Thomas & Diana Shellenberger. 120p. 1996. pap. 19.95 (*0-943289-02-5*) Passport Adventure.

Self-Service Storage: The Handbook for Investors & Managers. rev. ed. Richard E. Cornwell & Buzz Victor. LC 81-86050. (Series on Specific Property Types). (Illus.). 208p. 1983. pap. 34.95 (*0-912104-54-6*, 853) Inst Real Estate.

Self, Sex & Gender in Cross-Cultural Fieldwork. Ed. by Tony L. Whitehead & Mary E. Conaway. LC 85-8597. 328p. 1986. reprint ed. pap. 93.50 (*0-8357-3531-1*, 2034467) Bks Demand.

Self-Shiatsu Handbook. Pamela Ferguson. LC 94-23816. 160p. (Orig.). 1995. pap. 12.00 (*0-399-51949-1*, Perigee Bks) Berkley Pub.

Self-Shielded Arc Welding. Tad Boniszewski. (Illus.). 232p. 1992. 125.00 (*1-85573-063-4*, Pub. by Woodhead Pubng UK) Am Educ Systs.

Self, Sign, & Symbol. Ed. by Mark Nueman & Michael Payne. LC 86-47606. (Bucknell Review Ser.: Vol. 30, No. 2). 184p. 1987. 22.00 (*0-8387-5108-3*) Bucknell U Pr.

***Self-Similar Melodies.** unabridged ed. Tom Johnson. (Illus.). 292p. 1996. pap. 24.00 (*2-907200-01-1*) Two Eighteen.

Self, Situations, & Social Behavior. Ed. by Phillip R. Shaver. (Review of Personality & Social Psychology Ser.: No. 6). (Illus.). 311p. reprint ed. pap. 88.70 (*0-7837-1117-4*, 2041647) Bks Demand.

Self, Society, & Personal Choice. Diana T. Meyers. 452p. 1989. text ed. 49.50 (*0-231-06418-7*) Col U Pr.

Self, Society, & Womankind: The Dialectic of Liberation. Kathy E. Ferguson. LC 79-6831. (Contributions in Women's Studies: No. 17). xii, 200p. 1980. text ed. 49. 95 (*0-313-22245-2*, FSS/, Greenwood Pr) Greenwood.

Self-Society Dynamic: Cognition, Emotion, & Action. Ed. by Judith A. Howard & Peter J. Callero. (Illus.). 330p. (C). 1991. text ed. 57.95 (*0-521-38433-8*) Cambridge U Pr.

Self, Society, Existence: Human Nature & Dialogue in the Thought of George Herbert Mead & Martin Buber. Paul Pfuetze. LC 72-11743. 400p. 1973. reprint ed. text ed. 65.00 (*0-8371-6708-6*, PFSS, Greenwood Pr) Greenwood.

***Self-Speaking in Medieval & Early Modern English Drama: Subjectivity, Discourse & the Stage.** Richard Hillman. LC 97-6895. 1997. write for info. (*0-312-17552-3*) St Martin.

Self-Splitting Atom: A History of the Rutherford-Soddy Collaboration. Thaddeus J. Trenn. 176p. 1977. 42.00 (*0-85066-109-9*) Taylor & Francis.

Self-Starvation: From Individual to Family Therapy in the Treatment of Anorexia Nervosa. Mara S. Palazzoli. LC 78-60671. 320p. 1985. 40.00 (*0-87668-757-5*) Aronson.

Self-Starvation: From Individual to Family Therapy in the Treatment of Anorexia Nervosa. Mara P. Selvini. LC 84-45722. 312p. 1996. pap. 40.00 (*1-56821-822-2*) Aronson.

Self-Steering & Cognition in Complex Systems, Vol. 22. Ed. by F. Heylighen et al. xvi, 432p. 1990. pap. text ed. 101.00 (*2-88124-729-6*) Gordon & Breach.

***Self Storage: And Other Stories.** Mary H. Stefaniak. (Illus.). 300p. (Orig.). 1997. pap. 14.95 (*0-89823-183-3*) New Rivers Pr.

Self Storage Units or Warehouses: An International Directory. Alpha Pyramis Research Division Staff. 300p. 1983. ring bd. 52.95 (*0-913597-12-0*) Prosperity & Profits.

Self, Struggle & Change: Family Conflict Stories in Genesis & Their Healing Insights. Norman J. Cohen. LC 94-39880. 244p. 1996. pap. 16.95 (*1-879045-66-4*) Jewish Lights.

Self, Struggle & Change: Family Conflict Stories in Genesis & Their Healing Insights for Our Lives. Norman J. Cohen. LC 94-39880. 224p. 1995. 21.95 (*1-879045-19-2*) Jewish Lights.

Self Studies: On the Psychology of Self & Identity. Karl E. Scheibe. LC 94-40037. 240p. 1995. text ed. 59.95 (*0-275-94538-3*, Praeger Pubs) Greenwood.

Self Study Bible Course. Derek Prince. 1969. pap. 5.95 (*0-934920-08-7*, B-90) Derek Prince.

***Self Study Bible Course Workbook.** Derek Prince. 61p. 1996. pap. 5.99 (*0-88368-421-7*) Whitaker Hse.

Self-Study Course for Optometric Assisting. 2nd ed. AOA Staff. Ed. by Mary Jameson. LC 96-30878. (Illus.). 358p. 1996. 250.00 (*0-7506-9473-4*) Buttrwrth-Heinemann.

Self-Study Course for the Interest Rate Options Examination 5. Wall Street Training Staff. 1985. text ed. 75.00 (*0-87094-635-8*) Irwin Prof Pubng.

Self-Study Guide for Catholic High Schools. 98p. 7.50 (*0-318-17481-2*) Mid St Coll & Schl.

Self-Study Processes: A Guide for Postsecondary & Similar Service-Oriented Institutions & Programs. 4th ed. H. R. Kells. LC 95-18729. (American Council on Education-Oryx Press Series on Higher Education). (Illus.). 208p. 1995. pap. 34.95 (*0-89774-903-0*, ACE-Oryx) Oryx Pr.

Self-Study Processes: A Guide for Postsecondary Institutions. 2nd ed. 156p. 1983. 15.95 (*0-318-17484-7*) Mid St Coll & Schl.

Self Sufficiency Continuing Education Alternatives: A Self Paced Approach to Possibilities. rev. ed. Center for Self-Sufficiency, Research Division Staff. 200p. 1996. ring bd. 24.95 (*0-910811-73-3*) Ctr Self Suff.

Self-Sufficiency Encyclopaedia. Center for Self-Sufficiency, Research Division Staff. LC 83-90715. 75p. 1983. ring bd. 34.95 (*0-910811-00-8*) Ctr Self Suff.

Self-Sufficiency for Poor Families: Opportunities & Disincentives on the Road to Economic Independence. (Illus.). 81p. (Orig.). (C). 1994. pap. text ed. 25.00 (*0-7881-0217-6*) DIANE Pub.

Self-Sufficiency Gardening: Financial, Physical & Emotional Security from Your Own Backyard. Martin P. Waterman. LC 95-78038. (Illus.). 120p. 1995. pap. 13.95 (*1-55950-135-9*) Loompanics.

Self-Sufficient Homestead: Site Selection. Randy Kidd. (Illus.). 69p. (Orig.). 1981. spiral bd. 5.00 (*0-936352-05-1*) U of KS Cont Ed.

Self-Sufficient Sailor. Lin Pardey & Larry Pardey. 312p. 30.00 (*0-393-03269-8*) Paradise Cay Pubns.

***Self-Sufficient Sailor.** rev. ed. Larry Pardey & Lin Pardey. (Illus.). 320p. 1997. write for info. (*0-9646036-7-5*) Pardey Prods.

***Self Sufficient Woman: Things Every Woman Must Know but Men Won't Tell You.** 2nd rev. ed. Larry Perry. 150p. 1997. pap. 19.95 (*0-942442-00-8*) Perry Pubns.

Self-Suggestion & Its Influence on the Human Organism. A. S. Romen. Tr. by A. J. Lewis & Valentina Forsky. LC 80-28703. Orig. Title: Samovnushenie I Ego Vliianie Na Organizm Cheloveka. (Illus.). 235p. reprint ed. pap. 67. 00 (*0-685-23745-1*, 2032786) Bks Demand.

***Self, Supervenience & Personal Identity.** Ronald G. Alexander. (Avebury Series in Philosophy). 180p. 1997. text ed. 59.95 (*1-85972-603-8*, Pub. by Ashgate UK) Ashgate Pub Co.

An Asterisk (*) at the beginning of an entry indicates that the title is appearing in BIP for the first time.

Self-Supporting City: How to Improve Urban Life by Cutting Taxes, Stabilizing Finances & Housing People Better, the People vs. the Speculators. 1992. lib. bdg. 75.00 (*0-8490-8760-0*) Gordon Pr.

Self-Supporting Scenery for Children's Theatre & Grown-Ups' Too: A Scenic Workbook for the Open Stage. 5th rev. ed. James H. Miller. Ed. by Arthur L. Zapel. LC 81-84402. (Illus.). 128p. (C). 1993. reprint ed. pap. 14.95 (*0-916260-91-7*, B105) Meriwether Pub.

Self-Sustaining Mechanisms of Wall Turbulence. Ed. by R. Punton. (Advances in Fluid Mechanics Ser.). 300p. 1997. 129.00 (*1-85312-453-2*, 4532) Computational Mech MA.

***Self, Symptoms, & Psychotherapy.** Ed. by Neil Cheshire & Helmut Thomae. LC 86-32565. (Wiley Series on Methods in Psychotherapy). (Illus.). 316p. reprint ed. pap. 90.10 (*0-608-05261-2*, 2065799) Bks Demand.

Self-System: Developmental Changes Between & Within Self-Concepts. Annerieke Oosterwegel & Louis Oppenheimer. 208p. 1993. text ed. 39.95 (*0-8058-1216-4*) L Erlbaum Assocs.

Self-Talk: Key to Personal Growth. 2nd ed. David Stoop. LC 95-47526. 200p. (YA). (gr. 10). 1996. pap. 9.99 (*0-8007-5593-6*) Revell.

Self-Talk for Teachers & Students: Metacognitive Strategies for Personal & Classroom Use. Brenda H. Manning & Beverly D. Payne. LC 95-32106. 1996. pap. text ed. 30.50 (*0-205-15948-6*) Allyn.

Self-Talk for Weight Loss. Shad Helmstetter. 1994. 22.95 (*0-942540-10-7*) Breakthru Pub.

Self-Talk, Imagery & Prayer in Counseling. Norman Wright. (Resources for Christian Counseling Ser.: Vol. 3). 205p. 1986. 18.99 (*0-8499-0585-0*) Word Pub.

Self-Talk, Imagery & Prayer in Counseling. Norman Wright. (Resources for Christian Counseling Ser.). 1994. pap. 10.99 (*0-8499-3621-7*) Word Pub.

Self Taught Gardener. Sydney Eddison. LC 96-36151. 1997. pap. 24.95 (*0-670-86071-9*) Viking Penguin.

***Self Taught Gardener.** Sydney Eddison. 1998. pap. 14.95 (*0-14-024555-3*) Viking Penguin.

***Self-Taught Gardener.** Sydney Eddison. 1997. 24.95 (*0-614-27256-4*) Viking Penguin.

Self Taught-Self Help. Rachel Rowlson & Dusty Staub. Ed. by Tim Williams. 75p. (Orig.). 1984. pap. 7.95 (*0-9614201-0-3*) Dragonlord Pr.

Self-Taught Sparrow. Angus L. Jamieson. 29p. 1986. 30.00 (*0-7223-1925-8*, Pub. by A H S Ltd UK) St Mut.

***Self Teaching: Techniques for Mastering Difficult Abstract Concepts.** Dennis Matthies. (Illus.). 250p. (C). 1996. spiral bd. 18.00 (*1-887981-06-3*) Stanford Bookstore.

Self Teaching Manual for the Text Economic Evaluation & Investment Decision Methods. 9th ed. Franklin J. Stermole & John M. Stermole. LC 96-75183. 89p. 1996. spiral bd. 15.00 (*1-878740-08-3*) Invest Eval.

Self Teaching New Testament. Benny B. Bristow. 506p. 1996. 29.95 (*0-89137-213-X*) Quality Pubns.

Self-Teaching Study Guide & Workbook for "The Sensation of Being Somebody" 3rd ed. Maurice E. Wagner. 148p. 1985. 10.00 (*0-940445-00-X*) Christ Growth Pubs.

Self-Teaching Study Guide & Workbook for "The Sensation of Being Somebody" 4th enl. ed. Maurice E. Wagner. 148p. 1986. pap. 10.95 (*0-940445-02-6*) Christ Growth Pubs.

Self-Test Nutrition Guide: How to Improve Your Health & Nutritional Status Through Personalized Tests. Cass Igram & Judy K. Gray. (Literary Visions Publications). 280p. 29.95 (*0-614-17780-4*) Knowledge Hse.

Self-Test Nutrition Guide: How to Improve Your Health & Nutritional Status Through Personalized Tests. Cass Igram & Judy K. Gray. (Literary Visions Publications). 280p. 1993. pap. 17.95 (*0-911119-50-7*) Knowledge Hse.

***Self-Testing Made Easy.** Danton H. O'Day. (Illus.). 8p. (Orig.). 1997. pap. 2.50 (*0-9626591-4-2*, SPS0340) Energeia Pub.

Self-Testing VLSI Design. V. N. Yarmolik & I. V. Kachan. LC 92-46538. 346p. 1993. 163.75 (*0-444-89640-6*) Elsevier.

***Self, Text, & Romantic Irony: The Example of Byron.** Frederick Garber. LC 87-38494. reprint ed. pap. 96.70 (*0-608-04638-8*, 2065325) Bks Demand.

Self-Therapy for the Stutterer. Malcolm Fraser. 1985. pap. 3.00 (*0-87980-415-7*) Wilshire.

Self Therapy for the Stutterer, No. 12. 8th ed. Malcolm Fraser. LC 86-63599. 192p. 1993. pap. 3.00 (*0-933388-32-2*) Stuttering Fnd Am.

Self-Timed Control of Concurrent Processes: The Design of Aperiodic Logical Circuits in Computers & Discrete Systems. Ed. by Victor I. Varshavsky. (C). 1990. lib. bdg. 247.00 (*0-7923-0525-6*) Kluwer Ac.

Self to the Self. Dora Wilson. (C). 1947. pap. 3.00 (*0-87574-035-9*) Pendle Hill.

Self-Tormenter see Lady of Andros

Self-Tormentor. Terence. Ed. by Brothers. (Classical Texts Ser.). 1988. 49.95 (*0-85668-302-7*, Pub. by Aris & Phillips UK); pap. 24.95 (*0-85668-303-5*, Pub. by Aris & Phillips UK) David Brown.

Self Torture & Strenuous Exercise: Selected Plays. Harry Kondoleon. LC 91-22125. 260p. 1991. 24.95 (*1-55936-037-2*); pap. 13.95 (*1-55936-036-4*) Theatre Comm.

Self Transformation. Rudolf Steiner. Ed. & Intro. by Stefan Leber. 250p. (Orig.). 1995. pap. 19.95 (*1-85584-019-7*, Pub. by R Steiner Pr UK) Anthroposophic.

Self-Transformation Through Music. Joanne Crandall. (Illus.). 165p. (Orig.). 1986. pap. 7.50 (*0-8356-0608-2*, Quest) Theos Pub Hse.

Self-Trapped Excitons. A. K. Song & R. T. Williams. LC 92-27022. (Solid-State Sciences Ser.: Vol. 105). 1993. 135.95 (*0-387-55906-X*) Spr-Verlag.

Self-Trapped Excitons. 2nd rev. ed. Ed. by M. Cardona et al. 424p. 1996. pap. 69.00 (*3-540-60446-4*) Spr-Verlag.

Self-Traps: The Elusive Quest for Higher Self-Esteem. William B. Swann. 256p. (C). 1996. text ed. 23.95 (*0-7167-2898-2*) W H Freeman.

Self Treatment for AIDS: Oxygen Therapy. rev. ed. Betsy Russell-Manning. 1989. per. 16.95 (*0-930165-12-8*) Greensward Pr.

***Self-Trust: A Study of Reason, Knowledge, & Autonomy.** Keith Lehrer. (Illus.). 216p. 1997. 58.00 (*0-19-823665-4*); pap. 14.95 (*0-19-823694-8*) OUP.

Self-Tuning & Adaptive Control: Theory & Applications. rev. ed. C. J. Harris & S. A. Billings. (IEE Control Engineering Ser.). 352p. 1985. pap. 85.00 (*0-86341-036-7*, CE015) Inst Elect Eng.

Self-tuning Control for Two-Dimensional Processes. William P. Heath. LC 94-7741. (UNIST Control Systems Centre Ser.). 260p. 1994. text ed. 105.00 (*0-471-95135-8*) Wiley.

Self Tuning Control Systems. Allidina & Hughes. 53.33 (*0-13-803677-2*) P-H.

Self-Understanding in Childhood & Adolescence. William Damon & Daniel Hart. (Cambridge Studies in Social & Emotional Development). (Illus.). 280p. 1988. 39.95 (*0-521-30791-0*) Cambridge U Pr.

Self-Understanding in Childhood & Adolescence. William Damon & Daniel Hart. (Cambridge Studies in Social & Emotional Development). (Illus.). 224p. (C). 1991. pap. 16.95 (*0-521-42499-2*) Cambridge U Pr.

Self-Unfoldment. Manly P. Hall. pap. 15.95 (*0-89314-524-6*) Philos Res.

Self-Unfoldment. Swami Chinmayananda. 280p. 1992. 12. 00 (*1-880687-04-6*) Chinmaya Pubns.

Self-University: The Price of Tuition Is the Desire to Learn, Your Degree Is a Better Life. Charles D. Hayes. LC 89-80280. (Illus.). 280p. (C). 1989. 24.95 (*0-9621979-0-4*) Autodidactic Pr.

Self-Views in Historical Perspective in Egypt & Israel. Ed. by Shimon Shamir. (Books from the American University of Beirut Press). 132p. (Orig.). (C). 1988. pap. text ed. 9.45 (*0-8156-7053-2*) Syracuse U Pr.

***Self Wealth: Financial Independence in One Year.** Mark Yarnell. 224p. 1997. 23.95 (*1-879706-74-1*) Paper Chase.

Self-Winding Circle: A Study of Hegel's System. Mitchell Aboulafia. LC 82-210652. 124p. (C). 1982. 14.75 (*0-87527-307-6*) Green.

Self Winding Clocks. 1986. pap. 5.95 (*0-930476-18-2*) Am Clock & Watch.

Self-Working Card Tricks: Seventy-Two Foolproof Card Miracles for the Amateur Magician. Karl Fulves. (Illus.). 113p. (Orig.). 1976. pap. 4.95 (*0-486-23334-0*) Dover.

Self-Working Close-up Card Magic: 53 Foolproof Tricks. Karl Fulves. LC 94-16898. (Illus.). 128p. (Orig.). 1994. pap. 5.95 (*0-486-28124-8*) Dover.

Self-Working Coin Magic. Karl Fulves. 160p. 1990. pap. 3.95 (*0-486-26179-4*) Dover.

Self-Working Handkerchief Magic: Sixty-One Foolproof Tricks. Karl Fulves. (Illus.). 192p. (Orig.). 1988. pap. 5.95 (*0-486-25694-4*) Dover.

Self-Working Mental Magic: Sixty-Seven Foolproof Mind-Reading Tricks. Karl Fulves. LC 79-50010. (Illus.). 128p. 1979. pap. 4.95 (*0-486-23806-7*) Dover.

Self Working Number Magic. Karl Fulves. (Magic Ser.). (Illus.). 128p. (Orig.). pap. 4.95 (*0-486-24391-5*) Dover.

Self-Working Paper Magic: Eighty-One Foolproof Tricks. Karl Fulves. (Magic, Legerdemain Ser.). 144p. 1985. pap. 3.95 (*0-486-24847-X*) Dover.

Self Working Rope Magic: Seventy Foolproof Tricks. Karl Fulves. 1990. pap. 4.95 (*0-486-26541-2*) Dover.

Self-Working Table Magic: Ninety-Seven Foolproof Tricks with Everyday Objects. Karl Fulves. (Illus.). 128p. (Orig.). (J). 1981. pap. 5.95 (*0-486-24116-5*) Dover.

Self-Worth Without Self-Worship: The Bible-Based Approach to Self-Acceptance. Kenneth A. Beavers. LC 94-76801. 256p. (Orig.). 1995. pap. 9.95 (*1-883660-39-4*) Galloway Pr.

Selfadjoint & Nonselfadjoint Operator Algebras & Operator Theory: (Proceedings of th Cbms Regional Conference Held May 19-26, 1990 at Texas christ) Ed. by Robert S. Doran. LC 91-19767. (Contemporary Mathematics Ser.: Vol. 120). 215p. 1991. pap. text ed. 51.00 (*0-8218-5127-6*, CONM/120) Am Math.

Selfadjoint Operators in Spaces of Functions of Infinitely Many Variables. Yu. Berezanskii. Tr. by H. H. McFaden. LC 85-30841. (Translations of Mathematical Monographs: Vol. 63). 438p. 1986. 136.00 (*0-8218-4515-2*, MMONO/63) Am Math.

Selfhood & Redemption in Blakes's Songs. Harold Pagliaro. LC 86-43162. (Illus.). 176p. 1987. 27.50 (*0-271-00603-X*) Pa St U Pr.

Selfhood As Thinking Thought in the Work of Gabriel Marcel: A New Interpretation. Francisco L. Peccorini. LC 86-28549. (Problems in Contemporary Philosophy Ser.: Vol. 3). 200p. 1987. lib. bdg. 79.95 (*0-88946-329-8*) E Mellen.

Selfhood of the Human Person. John F. Crosby. LC 96-30424. 313p. (C). 1996. text ed. 34.95 (*0-8132-0864-5*); pap. text ed. 19.95 (*0-8132-0865-3*) Cath U Pr.

Selfish see It's Your Choice

Selfish Brain: Learning from Addiction. Robert L. DuPont. 589p. 1997. 29.95 (*0-88048-686-4*, 8686) Am Psychiatric.

Selfish Gene. 2nd ed. Richard Dawkins. (Illus.). 368p. 1989. 30.00 (*0-19-217773-7*) OUP.

Selfish Gene. 2nd ed. Richard Dawkins. (Illus.). 368p. 1990. pap. 12.95 (*0-19-286092-5*) OUP.

Selfish Gene Pool: An Evolutionary Stable System. D. M. Wonderly. 262p. 1996. pap. text ed. 36.00 (*0-7618-0383-1*); lib. bdg. 56.00 (*0-7618-0382-3*) U Pr of Amer.

Selfish Generations? The Ageing of the Welfare State. David Thomson. 300p. 1994. 59.95 (*1-874267-06-5*, Pub. by White Horse Pr UK); pap. 24.95 (*1-874267-07-3*, Pub. by White Horse Pr UK) Paul & Co Pubs.

Selfish Giant. Oscar Wilde. LC 93-10393. (Illus.). 32p. (J). 1995. 15.95 (*0-399-22448-3*, Putnam) Putnam Pub Group.

Selfish Giant. Oscar Wilde. (Illus.). 24p. (J). 1991. pap. 4.95 (*0-590-44460-3*) Scholastic Inc.

Selfish Giant. Oscar Wilde. LC 83-24930. (Illus.). 28p. (J). (gr. 1 up). 1991. pap. 16.00 (*0-907234-30-5*, Picture Book Studio) S&S Childrens.

Selfish Giant. Oscar Wilde. (Illus.). (J). 1986. pap. 10.95 (*0-671-66847-1*) S&S Trade.

Selfish Giant: (Gigante Egoista) (SPA.). (J). (gr. 1-6). 19.95 (*84-372-6602-5*) Santillana.

Selfish Giant by Oscar Wilde. Carol J. Cincereli. (Integrating Literature, Language & the Arts Ser.). 96p. (J). (gr. 1-6). teacher ed. 6.99 (*0-86653-537-3*, GA1158) Good Apple.

***Selfish Hoopoe.** abr. large type ed. Kambiz-Azordegan. (Tootee's Magical Stories Ser.: Vol. 12). (Illus.). 34p. (J). (gr. 1-3). 1998. write for info. (*1-890571-36-9*) Parrot Prod.

Selfishness, Altruism & Rationality: A Theory of Social Choice. Howard Margolis. LC 84-2620. xii, 206p. 1984. pap. text ed. 15.00 (*0-226-50524-3*) U Ch Pr.

Selfishness System. Margaret H. Goldstein. LC 94-96204. 100p. (Orig.). 1994. pap. 4.75 (*0-9642049-0-8*) M H Goldstein.

Selfless Mind: Personality, Consciousness & Nirvana in Early Buddhism. Peter Harvey. 304p. (C). 1995. text ed. 47.00 (*0-7007-0337-3*, Pub. by Curzon Press UK); pap. text ed. 21.95 (*0-7007-0338-1*, Pub. by Curzon Press UK) UH Pr.

Selfless Persons: Imagery & Thought in Theravada Buddhism. Steven Collins. 326p. (C). 1990. pap. text ed. 24.95 (*0-521-39726-X*) Cambridge U Pr.

***SELFOC Handbook.** (Fiber Optics User's Manual & Design Ser.: Vol. VI). 87p. 1979. 75.00 (*0-614-18462-2*, 152U06) Info Gatekeepers.

Selforganization. Ed. by S. Fox. (Illus.). 250p. 1986. text ed. 40.00 (*0-940030-13-6*) Adenine Pr.

Selforganization by Nonlinear Irreversible Processes. Ed. by W. Ebeling & H. Ulbricht. (Synergetics Ser.: Vol. 33). (Illus.). ix, 221p. 1986. 93.95 (*0-387-16255-0*) Spr-Verlag.

Selichos: Ashkenaz Lita. 1992. 19.99 (*0-89906-886-3*) Mesorah Pubns.

***Selichos: Minhag Polin - Sefard.** 19.99 (*0-89906-919-3*, SLSH) Mesorah Pubns.

Selichot - A Family Service. Judith Z. Abrams. LC 90-4863. (Illus.). 24p. (J). (ps-4). 1990. pap. 3.95 (*0-929371-15-1*) Kar-Ben.

Selichot for the Whole Year. Tr. by Abraham Rosenfeld. 832p. (ENG & HEB.). 1956. 17.95 (*0-910818-10-X*) Judaica Pr.

Selichot Reader. pap. 0.75 (*0-686-96114-5*) USCJE.

Selig Perlman's Lectures on Capitalism & Socialism. Selig Perlman. LC 74-27312. 203p. reprint ed. pap. 57.90 (*0-8357-6791-4*, 2035468) Bks Demand.

Selihot. Philip Birnbaum. 63p. pap. 3.50 (*0-88482-344-X*) Hebrew Pub.

Selihot Service. rev. ed. Morris Silverman & Max Arzt. pap. 3.95 (*0-87677-066-9*) Prayer Bk.

Selihoth of the Sepharadim: Hebrew Text & Ladino Translation of the Vienna 1865 Alschech Edition. Isaac Jerusalmi & Josef Alschech. (Ladino Bks.: No. 3). (Illus.). 223p. (ENG, HEB & LAD.). (C). 1990. text ed. 22.00 (*1-878191-02-0*) Ladino Bks.

Selina & the Bear Paw Quilt. Barbara Smucker. 32p. (J). (gr. 1-5). 1996. lib. bdg. 17.99 (*0-517-70910-4*) Crown Pub Group.

Selina & the Bear Paw Quilt. Barbara Smucker. LC 95-12964. (Illus.). 32p. (J). (gr. 1-5). 1996. 16.00 (*0-517-70904-X*, Crown) Crown Pub Group.

***Selinsgrove Chronology Vol. I: 1700-1850.** Compiled by William M. Schnure. (Illus.). 150p. 1997. reprint ed. pap. 19.50 (*0-8328-6449-8*) Higginson Bk Co.

Selish or Flat-Head Grammar. Gregory Mengarini. LC 10-30201. (Library of American Linguistics: No. 2). reprint ed. 42.75 (*0-404-50982-7*) AMS Pr.

Seljuks of Anatolia: Local Muslim Sources for Their History & Culture. Mehmed F. Koprulu. Ed. & Tr. by Gary Leiser from TUR. LC 92-53611. 140p. 1992. 25.00 (*0-87480-403-5*) U of Utah Pr.

***Selkie.** Laurie B. Gollobin. 47p. (Orig.). (J). 1997. pap. 5.50 (*0-87602-353-7*) Anchorage.

Selkie Girl. Susan Cooper. LC 86-70147. (Illus.). 32p. (J). (gr. k-4). 1986. lib. bdg. 14.95 (*0-689-50390-3*, McElderry) S&S Childrens.

Selkie Girl. Illus. by Warwick Hutton. LC 90-39982. 32p. (J). 1991. reprint ed. pap. 4.95 (*0-689-71467-X*, Aladdin Paperbacks) S&S Childrens.

Selkies. Mary Rosenblum. pap. write for info. (*0-345-39525-5*) Ballantine.

Selkup Texts: With Phonetic Introduction & Vocabulary. Laszlo Szabo. LC 66-64929. (Uralic & Altaic Ser.: Vol. 75). 62p. 1967. pap. text ed. 9.00 (*0-87750-026-6*) Res Inst Inner Asian Studies.

Sell & Grow Rich: The Ten Habits of Highly Successful Salespeople. Joe Gandolfo & Donald J. Korn. 201p. 1993. 19.95 (*0-7931-0512-9*, 2401-4901) Dearborn Finan.

***Sell & Re-Sell Your Photos.** 4th ed. Rohn Engh. LC 97-9074. (Illus.). 400p. 1997. pap. 16.99 (*0-89879-774-8*, Wrtrs Digest Bks) F & W Pubns Inc.

***Sell & Resell Your Magazine Articles.** Gordon Burgett. 1997. pap. text ed. 17.99 (*0-89879-799-3*, Wrtrs Digest Bks) F & W Pubns Inc.

Sell Don't Tell Approach to Leadership. Paul Nevels. 1995. pap. 5.95 (*0-533-11495-0*) Vantage.

***Sell Like a Pro: The Seven Steps to Sales Success.** Jerry Griffith. 144p. 1989. pap. 4.50 (*0-85013-161-8*) Dartnell Corp.

Sell More - Lease More: Proven Tactics for Selling & Leasing Residential Real Estate. Gloria Tibbs. 128p. (C). 1994. per. 14.95 (*0-8403-9427-6*) Kendall-Hunt.

Sell Out. large type ed. Henriette Charles. 1991. 25.99 (*0-7089-2426-3*) Ulverscroft.

Sell-Publish Your Own Best Seller! Complete Production & Marketing for Success & Profits. Laurence Leichman. 1995. pap. 14.95 (*0-9636867-2-0*) Leichman Assocs.

Sell! Sell! Sell! Robert Conklin. 1995. pap. text ed. 11.95 (*0-8087-7253-8*) Burgess MN Intl.

Sell, Sell, Sell: How to Market Your Painting Company & Increase Sales. Lynn H. Fife. Ed. by Lafferty & Assoc. Staff. 160p. (C). 1993. ring bd. 19.95 (*1-882947-75-4*) Evergreen Tech.

***Sell up & Sail: Taking the Ulysses Option.** 2nd ed. Bill Cooper & Laurel Cooper. 1996. pap. text ed. 29.95 (*0-07-021529-4*) McGraw.

Sell up & Sail: Taking the Ulysses Option. 2nd ed. Bill Cooper & Laurel Cooper. (Illus.). 317p. 1990. pap. 29.95 (*0-7136-3948-2*) Sheridan.

Sell What You Sow! The Grower's Guide to Successful Produce Marketing. Eric L. Gibson. LC 92-90951. (Illus.). 304p. (Orig.). 1994. pap. 22.50 (*0-9632814-0-2*) N Wrld CA.

Sell Wise: Automate Your Retail, Repair or Mail Order Business. 2nd ed. Chuck Atkinson. 148p. 1994. pap. text ed. 14.95 (*0-917081-29-3*) CAP Automation.

***Sell Your Knowledge.** Monica Nicou & Christine Ribbing. (Marketing & Sales Ser.). 1994. pap. 27.95 (*0-7494-1366-2*) Kogan Page Ltd.

***Sell-Your-Novel Tool Kit: Queries, Synopses, & Strategies to Market Your Novel.** Elizabeth Lyon. 352p. (Orig.). 1997. pap. 17.95 (*0-936085-40-1*) Blue Heron OR.

Sell Your Own Home. Thomas V. Tamanny. 136p. 1982. 12.95 (*0-89182-049-3*); pap. 7.95 (*0-89182-058-2*) Charles River Bks.

Sell Your Photographs: The Complete Marketing Strategy for the Freelancer. Natalie Canavor. 1982. pap. 7.95 (*0-452-25638-0*, Plume) NAL-Dutton.

Sell Your Property Fast: How to Take Back a Mortgage Without Being Taken. Bill Broadbent & George Rosenberg. 176p. 1993. pap. 25.00 (*0-9637838-0-7*) Whos Who Creat.

Sell Your Short Stories & Poetry. Jaye L. Montgomery. 88p. 1988. pap. 15.95 (*0-86617-038-3*) Multi Media TX.

Sell Yourself: A Unique & Effective Approach to Selling Products, Services & Ideas. William M. Saleebey. 158p. 1994. pap. 15.95 (*0-9640821-8-7*) Mentor Pubng.

Sell Yourself: Persuasive Tactics to Boost Your Image. Polly Bird. (Institute of Management Ser.). 192p. (Orig.). 1994. pap. 39.50 (*0-273-60331-0*, Pub. by Pitman Pub Ltd UK) Trans-Atl Phila.

Sell Yourself to Science: The Complete Guide to Selling Your Organs, Body Fluids, Bodily Functions & Being a Human Guinea Pig. Jim Hogshire. LC 92-81803. (Illus.). 166p. (Orig.). 1992. pap. 16.95 (*1-55950-084-0*, 94129) Loompanics.

Sellabration of Jesus. R. Hugh McLean. Ed. by A. Eldredge. 32p. (Orig.). 1995. pap. 4.00 (*1-885857-10-1*) Four Wnds Pubng.

Selleck & Peck Genealogy. Wm. E. Peck. (Illus.). 74p. 1994. reprint ed. pap. 15.00 (*0-8328-4379-2*); reprint ed. lib. bdg. 25.00 (*0-8328-4378-4*) Higginson Bk Co.

Seller of Talismans. J. C. Hronsky. Tr. by J. J. Kester from SLO. LC 78-20357. 1979. pap. 2.50 (*0-9602084-0-2*) J J Kester.

Sellers: A Genealogy of the Descendants of Heinrich Sellers in America, 1738 to Present. Frank M. Sellers. 96p. 1984. 35.00 (*0-9608122-1-0*) F Sellers.

Sellers & Servants: Working Women in Lima, Peru. Ximena B. Bunster & Elsa M. Chaney. LC 85-6529. 200p. 1985. text ed. 59.95 (*0-275-90067-3*, C0067, Praeger Pubs) Greenwood.

Sellers & Servants: Working Women in Lima, Peru. Ximena B. Bunster & Elsa M. Chaney. LC 88-10356. 276p. (C). 1988. pap. text ed. 18.95 (*0-89789-171-6*, Bergin & Garvey) Greenwood.

Seller's Credit Guide, Vol. 1. Wayne H. Lazarus & Marion B. Stokes. (Illus.). 250p. 1996. 29.95 (*0-9651931-0-1*) Busn Pathways.

Seller's Guide to Government Purchasing 1991-1992: Federal, State, & Local Contacts & Key Publications & Resources. Ed. by Kenneth Estell. 750p. 1990. 140.00 (*0-8103-7733-0*) Gale.

Sellie & Dee: A Friendship. Estelle Leontief. LC 93-29920. (Crimson Edge Chapbook Ser.). 1993. 7.95 (*0-9619111-6-6*) Chicory Blue.

Selling. Lloyd Allard. LC 91-12319. 176p. 1991. 15.95 (*0-88289-849-3*) Pelican.

Selling. Peter Allen. 168p. (C). 1991. pap. 36.00 (*0-273-03629-7*, Pub. by Pitman Pubng UK) St Mut.

Selling. Ditzenberger. (SB - Marketing Education Ser.). 1984. text ed. 19.95 (*0-538-19160-0*) S-W Pub.

Selling: Building Customer Partnerships in a Competitive Marketplace. Phillip F. Farris. 250p. 1995. pap. 19.95 (*0-87425-267-9*) HRD Press.

Selling: Building Partnerships. 2nd ed. Barton A. Weitz et al. 576p. (C). 1994. text ed. 66.95 (*0-256-13675-0*) Irwin.

***Selling: Building Partnerships.** 3rd ed. Barton A. Weitz et al. LC 97-21684. (Irwin Series in Marketing). 1997. write for info. (*0-256-22826-4*) Irwin Prof Pubng.

***Selling: Effective Techniques for Getting & Keeping Customers.** R. Stephen Payseur. LC 97-91461. ix, 220p. Date not set. pap. 12.95 (*0-9656697-1-8*) Creekside Pub.

S

Selling: Helping Customers Buy. 2nd ed. Ditzenberger. (SB - Marketing Education Ser.). 1986. wbk. ed., pap. 14.95 (0-538-19201-1) S-W Pub.
Selling: Helping Customers Buy. 2nd ed. Ditzenberger. (SB - Marketing Education Ser.). 1986. 3.95 (0-538-19203-8) S-W Pub.
Selling: Helping Customers Buy. 2nd ed. Ditzenberger. (SB - Marketing Education Ser.). 1990. text ed. 19.95 (0-538-60416-6) S-W Pub.
Selling: Helping Customers Buy. 3rd ed. Ditzenberger. (SB - Marketing Education Ser.). 1992. text ed. 37.95 (0-538-60531-6) S-W Pub.
Selling: Helping Customers Buy. 3rd ed. Ditzenberger. (SB - Marketing Education Ser.). 1992. wbk. ed., pap. 20.95 (0-538-60532-4) S-W Pub.
Selling: Marketing Personified. Ronald D. Balsley & Patricia E. Birsner. 560p. (C). 1986. 50.00 (0-03-070628-9) Dryden Pr.
Selling: Principles & Practices. 13th ed. Richard H. Buskirk & Bruce D. Buskirk. 1992. text ed. write for info. (0-07-009356-3) McGraw.
Selling - the Danielle Kennedy Way. Danielle Kennedy. 1991. 18.95 (0-13-803727-2, Busn) P-H.
Selling - When You Hate to Sell: Getting in Gear When You Fear Selling. Lawrence Schulz. (Illus.). 102p. (Orig.). 1994. pap. 11.99 (0-9621072-0-4) CA Entrprnr Pub.
Selling--Recruiting--Managing: An Accelerated Path to Health, Wealth & Fulfillment. Randy J. Ward. LC 87-72722. (Illus.). 244p. (Orig.). 1989. pap. 12.95 (0-9613958-2-6) Prosperity OK.
Selling a Screenplay: The Screenwriter's Guide to Hollywood. Syd Field. 304p. 1989. pap. 12.95 (0-440-50244-6, Dell Trade Pbks) Dell.
Selling Adventure Travel: Marketing Today's Travel. Jerry J. Mallett et al. Ed. by Adventure Travel Society Staff. (Illus.). (Orig.). pap. 29.95 (1-885789-04-1) Advent Trvl Soc.
Selling & Building Sales Skills: A Resource Kit. Stephen B. Castleberry & John F. Tanner. 336p. (C). 1991. per. 21.50 (0-256-10356-9) Irwin.
Selling & Designing Party Flowers. Redbook Florist Services Educational Advisory Committee. LC 92-64275. (Encycloflora Ser.). (Illus.). 404p. (Orig.). 1992. pap. text ed. 34.95 (1-56963-021-6) Redbk Florist.
Selling & Designing Sympathy Flowers. Redbook Florist Services Educational Advisory Committee. LC 92-60503. (Encycloflora Ser.). (Illus.). 222p. (Orig.). 1992. pap. text ed. 34.95 (1-56963-023-2) Redbk Florist.
Selling & Designing Wedding Flowers. Redbook Florist Services Educational Advisory Committee. LC 91-60000. (Encycloflora Ser.). (Illus.). 304p. (Orig.). 1991. pap. text ed. 34.95 (1-56963-022-4) Redbk Florist.
Selling & Sales Management. Robert D. Hisrich & Ralph W. Jackson. (Barron's Business Library). 1993. pap. 16.95 (0-8120-4693-5) Barron.
*Selling & Sales Management. 4th ed. David Jobber & Geoff Lancaster. (Illus.). 427p. (Orig.). 1997. pap. 52.50 (0-273-62592-6, Pub. by Pitman Pub Ltd UK) Trans-Atl Phila.
Selling Antiques & Collectibles: Fifty Ways to Improve Your Business. Don Johnson & Elizabeth A. Garland. LC 92-50675. 176p. 1993. pap. 17.95 (0-87069-685-8) Chilton.
Selling Art with a Higher Mind or No More Art Sharks. Barbara G. Scott. LC 90-83247. (Illus.). 158p. (Orig.). 1990. pap. 19.95 (0-9626478-4-5) ICHOR.
Selling Arts & Crafts By Mail Order. Allan Smith. (Illus.). 60p. (Orig.). 1990. pap. 7.00 (0-931113-34-2) Success Publ.
Selling at Mach 1: Motivational Acceleration. Steve Sullivan. 192p. 1994. pap. 11.95 (0-9641053-0-6) Motivat Resources.
*Selling at Mach 1: Motivational Acceleration. Steve Sullivan. Ed. by Amy J. Pecora. (Illus.). 192p. 1995. 16.95 (0-9641053-3-0) Motivat Resources.
Selling Benefits: A Self Study Course for Perceptive Sales People. T. J. King. 39p. 1984. pap. 7.95 (0-913261-01-7) Effect Learn Sys.
Selling Benefits: Bank Services Edition. T. J. King. 39p. 1986. pap. 7.95 (0-913261-08-4) Effect Learn Sys.
Selling Benefits Effectively. T. J. King. 24p. 1986. pap. 6.95 (0-913261-09-2) Effect Learn Sys.
Selling Benefits Retail. T. J. King. 74p. 1986. pap. 9.95 (0-913261-10-6) Effect Learn Sys.
Selling Bible: For People in the Business of Selling. John F. Lawhon. Ed. by Sherwood Harris. LC 94-79522. (Illus.). 496p. (C). 1995. text ed. 36.95 (1-57178-007-6) J Franklin.

***Selling Bible: For People in the Business of Selling. 2nd ed. John F. Lawhon. Ed. by Sherwood Harris. LC 94-79522. (Illus.). 490p. 1996. 36.95 (0-9616736-3-X) J Franklin.**
THE SELLING BIBLE defines the profession of selling for the first time, shows how selling skills can be accurately measured, offers a plan that guarantees measurable improvement in selling competence. "In the first few paragraphs, salesman, business owner & trainer Lawhon debunks the idea that owning your own business means being your own boss--the great American dream. The government will impose regulations, & the customer will be the absolute authority in your company. Therefore, the only goal that will guarantee success & bottom-line profit is turning prospective customers into satisfied customers. 'Either you are in the business of selling or you are not in business.' From that premise, Lawhon gives entrepreneurs sound advice on how to achieve this goal. From the five basic groups of knowledge to the skills of selling & trade secrets, he teaches readers how to sell & thus how to succeed... "...buy this title..."--LIBRARY JOURNAL, July, 1995. THE SELLING BIBLE, named in top five "Best Selling Books on General Sales" by SELLING magazine, 10/95, gives readers a renewed sense of integrity & pride in the profession of selling. Used as a text in colleges & universities, Lawhon's book, SELLING RETAIL, 1986, now in its thirteenth printing, & the basis of sales education in over 15,000 companies. To order: 1-800-234-9384.
Publisher Provided Annotation.

Selling Big Charity: The CARE Story. Harold Gauer. (Illus.). 352p. 1990. pap. 19.95 (1-877831-02-6) Prec Process.
Selling Black History for Carter G. Woodson: A Diary, 1930-1933. Lorenzo J. Greene. Ed. & Intro. by Arvarh E. Strickland. LC 96-8542. (Illus.). 424p. (C). 1996. pap. 24.95 (0-8262-1069-4); text ed. 49.95 (0-8262-1068-6) U of Mo Pr.
*Selling Books As Premiums & Incentives: How to Make Big Bucks, Be Paid Promptly, Trim Printing Costs, Boost Your PR, & Never Have Another Return. Marilyn Ross & Tom Ross. (Orig.). 1997. pap. 25.00 (0-918880-40-8) Comm Creat.
Selling by Objectives. Anthony J. Alessandra. 1982. pap. 9.95 (0-8359-6988-6, Reston); text ed. 15.00 (0-8359-6989-4, Reston) P-H.
Selling by Phone: How to Reach & Sell to Customers. Linda Richardson. 1995. pap. text ed. 14.95 (0-07-052376-2) McGraw.
*Selling by Telephone. 2nd ed. Chris De Winter. (Small Business Ser.). 1995. pap. 14.95 (0-7494-1393-X) Kogan Page Ltd.
*Selling Cars, Insurance, & over the Counter Products: Differential Selling in the Real World. James S. Payne. 145p. (Orig.). 1996. pap. 14.95 (1-57171-004-3) Lincoln-Rembrandt.
Selling Circles. spiral bd. 9.95 (0-317-69753-6) IAQC Pr.
Selling Cities: Attracting Homebuyers Through Schools & Housing Programs. David P. Varady & Jeffrey A. Raffel. LC 94-23443. (SUNY Series in Urban Public Policy). 367p. 1995. text ed. 59.50 (0-7914-2557-6); pap. text ed. 19.95 (0-7914-2558-4) State U NY Pr.
Selling Consulting Engineering & Architecture Services to the U. S. Government. Ed. by Elizabeth J. Sherfy. 149p. 1995. ring bd. 105.00 (1-56726-031-4, B595) Holbrook & Kellogg.
Selling Covered Calls: The Safest Game on the Option Market. Charles J. Caes. 1990. 24.95 (0-07-155815-2) McGraw.
Selling Covered Calls: The Safest Game on the Options Market. Charles J. Caes. (Illus.). 220p. (Orig.). 1989. 24.95 (0-8306-3038-4, Liberty Hse) TAB Bks.
Selling Culture: Magazines, Markets, & the Class at the Turn of the Century. Richard M. Ohmann. (Haymarket Ser.). 416p. 1996. 29.00 (1-85984-974-1, Pub. by Vrso UK) Norton.
Selling Destinations: Geography for the Travel Professional. 2nd ed. Marc Mancini. LC 94-13909. 1995. pap. 39.20 (0-538-63450-2) S-W Pub.
Selling Destinations: Geography Travel. Mancini. (Hospitality, Travel & Tourism Ser.). 1992. teacher ed. 54.95 (0-538-70403-9); pap. 35.95 (0-538-70402-0) S-W Pub.
Selling DSM-III: The Rhetoric of Science in Psychiatry. Stuart A. Kirk & Herb Kutchins. (Social Problems & Social Issues Ser.). 280p. 1992. pap. text ed. 23.95 (0-202-30432-9) Aldine de Gruyter.
Selling Edge: Winning over Today's Business Customers. Michael Levokove. LC 92-75676. 200p. 1993. 18.95 (0-944435-21-1) Glenbridge Pub.
*Selling 'Em by the Sack. Hogan. LC 97-21076. 1998. 24.95 (0-8147-3566-5) NYU Pr.
Selling Equipment Leasing. Michael Berke. LC 93-49660. 350p. 1994. 59.95 (0-8144-5122-5) AMACOM.
Selling Europe to the Emerging Markets of Asia: Long Term Strategies for Effective Partnership. Corrado G. Letta. 1996. text ed. 90.00 (0-471-96091-8) Wiley.
*Selling Fear - Conspiracy Theories & End-Times Paranoia. Gregory S. Camp. 1997. pap. 15.99 (0-614-28114-8) Baker Bks.
Selling Financial Services: A Professional Approach. Derek Waterworth. 192p. 1995. 89.95 (1-85573-158-4, Pub. by Woodhead Pubng UK) Am Educ Systs.
Selling for Dummies. Tom Hopkins. 400p. 1995. pap. 16.99 (1-56884-389-5) IDG Bks.
Selling for People Who Hate to Sell: Successful Selling Skills for the Rest of Us. Brigid Massie. 208p. 1996. per., pap. 12.00 (0-7615-0665-9) Prima Pub.
Selling for Results: The Health Club's Guide to Professional Selling. Brenda Abdilla. 1996. 19.00 (1-878956-65-5) CBM Bks.
Selling Free Enterprise: The Business Assault on Labor & Liberalism, 1945-60. Elizabeth Fones-Wolf. LC 94-10785. (History of Communication Ser.). 352p. 1994. text ed. 49.95 (0-252-02118-5); pap. text ed. 16.95 (0-252-06439-9) U of Ill Pr.
Selling-From-Home Sourcebook: A Guide to Home-Based Business Opportunities in the Selling Industry. Kathryn Caputo. 272p. 1996. pap. 17.99 (1-55870-405-1, Betrwy Bks) F & W Pubns Inc.
Selling Garment Graphics: Sales & Marketing for Textile Screen Printers. Mark Goodridge. 54p. 1995. pap. 14.95 (0-944094-06-6) ST Pubns.
Selling Genius: Achieving Extraordinary Sales Results with Ordinary People. Stephen M. Riddell. LC 94-60402. viii, 182p. 1994. write for info. (0-936840-17-X) Tech Marketing.
Selling God: American Religion in the Marketplace of American Culture. R. Laurence Moore. 288p. 1994. 27.50 (0-19-508228-1) OUP.
Selling God: American Religion in the Marketplace of Culture. R. Laurence Moore. 334p. 1995. pap. 12.95 (0-19-509838-2) OUP.
Selling Graphic Design. Don Sparkman. LC 95-76688. 256p. 1995. pap. 18.95 (1-880559-29-3) Allworth Pr.
Selling High Tech High Ticket: Using Relationship Management Techniques to Sell & Service. John Katsaros. 1993. text ed. 24.95 (1-55738-511-4) Irwin Prof Pubng.
Selling High-Tech Products & Services. Ira S. Kalb. (Illus.). 244p. 1990. 42.95 (0-924050-04-7) K & A Pr.
Selling Hope: State Lotteries in America. Charles T. Clotfelter & Philip J. Cook. 336p. 1991. pap. 17.95 (0-674-80098-2) HUP.
Selling in Agribusiness. Larry Miller. Ed. by Jasper S. Lee. (Career Preparation for Agriculture-Agribusiness Ser.). (Illus.). 1979. text ed. 16.96 (0-07-041962-0) McGraw.
Selling in Banking: Today's Reality, Tomorrow's Opportunity. Leonard L. Berry & Donna M. Kantek. 66p. (Orig.). 1989. 30.00 (1-55695-003-9) Bank Mktg Assn.
*Selling in Craft Malls: Everything You Need to Know about Selecting the Right Stores & Making a Profit. 2nd rev. ed. Patricia Krauss. 58p. 1996. spiral bd. 7.95 (0-9653727-3-1) Showpl Mktg.
Selling in Japan. 291p. 1985. pap. 55.00 (4-8224-0317-3, Pub. by Japan External Trade JA) Intl Pubns Serv.
Selling in the Financial Sector, Set. 145p. 140.00 (1-871682-33-9, Pub. by Euromoney UK) Am Educ Systs.
Selling in the Nineteen Nineties: What All Sales Super Stars Share in Common. Gary Winokur. (Illus.). 112p. (Orig.). 1990. 9.95 (0-9624623-0-6) Win Enterprises.
Selling in the Nineteen Nineties: What All Sales Superstars Share in Common. Gary Winokur. 112p. (Orig.). 1989. pap. 9.95 (0-685-29330-0) Win Enterprises.
Selling in the Nineties. H. Wayne White. (Illus.). 211p. (Orig.). 1988. pap. 14.95 (0-945229-00-3) Delta Enterprises.
Selling in the Nineties. H. Wayne White. (Illus.). 211p. (Orig.). 1988. pap. 4.95 (0-945229-01-1) Delta Enterprises.
Selling in the Nineties: The Fundamentals of Selling Success. Gregg DeVita & Franks Editing. 240p. (C). 1991. pap. text ed. 18.00 (0-9628645-5-2) PST Lrn Systs.
Selling in the Quality Era. George Peeler. (C). 1995. pap. text ed. 20.95 (1-55786-666-X) Blackwell Pubs.
Selling Internationally - Without a Product: How to Be a Broker & Link Buyers & Sellers Together...for Profit. W. Kelsea Wilber. Ed. by Jennifer Friedland. 210p. (Orig.). pap. 14.95 (0-9644778-0-7) Intl Trade Ctr.
Selling Investment Products: A Sourcebook for the Securities Sales Executive. LeRoy Gross. 1988. ring bd. 95.00 (0-13-805482-7) NY Inst Finance.
Selling Is a Personal Affair. H. Gordon Bethards. 190p. (Orig.). (C). 1984. pap. 16.95 (0-930264-53-3) Century Comm.
Selling Is a Woman's Game: Fifteen Powerful Reasons Why Women Can Outsell Men. Nicki Joy. LC 94-6825. 192p. (Orig.). 1994. pap. 11.00 (0-380-77416-X) Avon.
Selling It. Joan Irving. 264p. 1995. pap. 19.95 (0-385-25515-2) Doubleday.
Selling Jesus: What's Wrong with Marketing the Church. Douglas D. Webster. LC 92-34516. (Illus.). 165p. (Orig.). 1993. pap. 9.99 (0-8308-1317-9, 1317) InterVarsity.
Selling Lucky. Art Fettig. LC 77-89820. (Illus.). 128p. 1984. pap. 9.95 (0-9601334-6-1) Growth Unltd.
Selling Machine: How to Focus Every Member of Your Company on the Vital Business. Sanchez. LC 96-46736. 1997. 25.00 (0-8129-2717-6, Times Bks) Random.
*Selling Manhattan. Carol A. Duffy. Date not set. pap. 14.95 (0-85646-194-6, Pub. by Anvil Press UK) Dufour.
*Selling Microsoft. Doug Dayton. Date not set. 20.00 (1-55850-821-X) Adams Media.
*Selling Microsoft. Doug Dayton. 1997. pap. 20.00 (0-614-28440-6) Adams Media.
Selling Nature Photographs. Norbert Wu. LC 96-35313. (How to Photograph Ser.). (Illus.). 128p. 1997. pap. 16.95 (0-8117-2459-X) Stackpole.
Selling New Homes. Charles Clark & David Parker. LC 89-34605. 160p. 1989. pap. 22.00 (0-86718-336-5) Home Builder.
Selling of Contraception: The Dalkon Shield Case, Sexuality, & Women's Autonomy. Nicole J. Grant. (Women & Health Ser.). 240p. 1992. 35.00 (0-8142-0572-0); pap. 16.95 (0-8142-0615-8) Ohio St U Pr.
Selling of DSM III: The Rhetoric of Science in Psychiatry. Stuart A. Kirk & Herb Kutchins. (Social Problems & Social Issues Ser.). 280p. 1992. lib. bdg. 46.95 (0-202-30431-0) Aldine de Gruyter.
Selling of Fidel Castro: The Media & the Cuban Revolution. William E. Ratliff et al. 193p. 1986. 34.95 (0-88738-104-9); pap. 21.95 (0-88738-649-0) Transaction Pubs.
Selling of General Electric. James R. Burnside. LC 89-51860. 224p. (Orig.). 1990. pap. 14.95 (0-9624923-0-2) High Peaks Pr.
Selling of Joseph: A Memorial. Samuel Sewall. Ed. by Sidney Kaplan. LC 74-87832. 68p. 1969. reprint ed. pap. 9.95 (0-87023-051-4) U of Mass Pr.
Selling of Joseph see Dialogue Concerning the Slavery of the Africans
Selling of Mary Davies: And Other Writings. Simon Jenkins. (Illus.). 192p. 1994. 34.95 (0-7195-5298-2, Pub. by John Murray UK) Trafalgar.
Selling of Supreme Court Nominees. John A. Maltese. LC 95-3536. (Interpreting American Politics Ser.). 232p. 1995. 26.95 (0-8018-5102-5) Johns Hopkins.
Selling of the Constitutional Convention: A History of News Coverage. John K. Alexander. 240p. (C). 1990. 27.95 (0-945612-15-X) Madison Hse.
Selling of the Empire: British & French Imperialist Propaganda, 1890-1940. Thomas G. August. LC 84-25233. (Contributions in Comparative Colonial Studies: No. 19). (Illus.). xiv, 234p. 1985. text ed. 59.95 (0-313-24722-6, AUA/, Greenwood Pr) Greenwood.
Selling of the President. Joe McGinniss. 288p. 1988. pap. 13.95 (0-14-011240-5, Penguin Bks) Viking Penguin.
Selling of the South: The Southern Crusade for Industrial Development, 1936 - 1980. 2nd ed. James C. Cobb. LC 92-30045. 328p. (C). 1993. reprint ed. text ed. 32.50 (0-252-01770-6); reprint ed. pap. text ed. 13.95 (0-252-06162-4) U of Ill Pr.
Selling on Line with First Virtual. Peter Loshin. (Illus.). 400p. (Orig.). 1996. pap. 32.95 (1-886801-41-X) Chrles River Media.
*Selling on Paper. Joy Van Skiver. LC 96-29434. 1996. pap. write for info. (0-9643824-1-5) WREXpress.
Selling on the Fast Track: How to Become a Sales Athlete. Kathy Aaronson. 224p. 1989. 18.95 (0-399-13460-3, Putnam) Putnam Pub Group.
Selling on the Internet: How to Open an Electronic Storefront & Have Millions of Customers. James C. Gonyea & Wayne M. Gonyea. 1996. pap. text ed. 24.95 (0-07-024187-2) McGraw.
Selling on the Net: The Complete Guide. Herschell G. Lewis & Robert D. Lewis. LC 96-23087. 224p. 1996. 39.95 (0-8442-3233-5); pap. write for info. (0-8442-3234-3) NTC Pub Grp.
Selling on the Phone see Teleselling: A Self-Teaching Guide
Selling or Buying a Medical Practice. Gary R. Schaub. 192p. 1988. 34.95 (0-87489-487-5) Med Econ.
Selling Out: If Famous Authors Wrote Advertising. Joey Green. 128p. 1996. 12.95 (0-02-860843-7) Macmillan.
Selling Out America's Children: How America Puts Profits Before Values & What Parents Can Do. David Walsh. 160p. 1994. 16.95 (0-925190-27-6) Fairview Press.
Selling Out America's Children: How America Puts Profits Before Values-& What Parents Can Do. David Walsh. 184p. 1995. pap. 11.95 (0-925190-47-0) Fairview Press.
*Selling Out the Church: The Dangers of Church Marketing. Philip D. Kenneson & James L. Street. LC 96-53658. 160p. 1997. pap. 12.95 (0-687-01044-6) Abingdon.
Selling Outerspace: Kennedy, the Media, & Funding for Project Apollo, 1961-1963. James L. Kauffman. LC 94-4653. (Studies in Rhetoric & Communication). 208p. 1994. text ed. 34.95 (0-8173-0747-8) U of Ala Pr.
*Selling Packages. Rockport Publishers Editorial Staff. Date not set. write for info. (0-688-08376-5) Morrow.
Selling Performance & Contentment in Relation to School Background. Albert C. Mossin. LC 79-177093. (Columbia University. Teachers College. Contributions to Education Ser.: No. 952). reprint ed. 37.50 (0-404-55952-2) AMS Pr.
Selling Places. Gerry Kearns. 316p. 1993. pap. 87.95 (0-08-041384-6, Prgamon Press) Buttrwrth-Heinemann.
*Selling Places. Ward. (Studies in History, Planning & the Environment). (Illus.). 240p. 1997. text ed. write for info. (0-419-20610-8, E & FN Spon) Routledge Chapman & Hall.
Selling Principles & Practices. 5th ed. John W. Ernest & Richard D. Ashmun. LC 79-17748. (Illus.). 1980. text ed. 23.24 (0-07-019620-6) McGraw.
Selling Professional Services: A Handbook for Professionals. J. Nicholls. (C). 1994. 150.00 (0-946655-56-1, Pub. by Stanley Thornes UK) Trans-Atl Phila.
*Selling Professionally. Rebecca L. Morgan. (Better Management Skills Ser.). 1991. pap. 12.95 (0-7494-0586-4) Kogan Page Ltd.
Selling Radio: The Commercialization of American Broadcasting, 1920-1934. Susan Smulyan. LC 93-12833. (Illus.). 240p. 1994. text ed. 24.95 (1-56098-312-4) Smithsonian.
Selling Radio: The Commercialization of American Broadcasting, 1920-1934. Susan Smulyan. (Illus.). 224p. 1996. pap. text ed. 14.95 (1-56098-686-7) Smithsonian.
Selling Radio Direct. Michael C. Keith. (Electronic Media Guide Ser.). (Illus.). 128p. 1992. pap. 19.95 (0-240-80091-5, Focal) Buttrwrth-Heinemann.
Selling Real Estate: How to Succeed in the Real World. Phil Hoover. LC 88-90127. (Orig.). 1989. pap. 14.95 (0-9620536-0-0) Word Gets Around.
Selling Remodeling: Nine Steps to Sales Success. Victoria L. Downing. LC 92-33760. (Illus.). 107p. 1992. pap. 22.50 (0-86718-381-0) Home Builder.

Selling Retail: All the Secrets of Many of the Highest Paid Retail Salespeople in America. John F. Lawhon & Catherine D. Lawhon. LC 86-80853. (Illus.). 360p. 1986. 29.95 (0-9616736-0-5) J Franklin.
SELLING RETAIL by John F. Lawhon is now in its 13th printing. The book is used in over 15,000 companies as the basis of sales education. A primer for salespeople, SELLING RETAIL

An Asterisk (*) at the beginning of an entry indicates that the title is appearing in BIP for the first time.

includes Book I (everything you need to know before you start to sell) & Book II (selling skills). Includes psychology of selling "revelations." Auxiliary support & aids available from publisher. Currently not available in bookstores except by special order from the publisher. Mr. Lawhon's THE SELLING BIBLE FOR PEOPLE IN THE BUSINESS OF SELLING (May 1995; 2nd Edition, 1996) is distributed nationwide to bookstores through J. Franklin 1-800-234-9384. ***Publisher Provided Annotation.***

---

*Selling Rights. 2nd ed. (Blueprint Ser.). 264p. (C). 1994. text ed. 55.00 (*0-415-13664-4*, Routledge NY) Routledge.

Selling Rights. 2nd ed. Lynette Owen. 244p. 1994. 39.95 (*1-85713-007-3*) Chapman & Hall.

***Selling Rights.** 3rd ed. Lynette Owen. LC 97-9444. 1997. write for info. (*0-415-16854-6*) Routledge.

Selling Satan: The Evangelical Media & the Mike Warnke Scandal. Jon Trott & Michael Hertenstein. LC 93-13756. 472p. 1993. pap. 15.95 (*0-940895-07-2*) Cornerstone IL.

Selling Science: How the Press Covers Science & Technology. 2nd rev. ed. Dorothy Nelkin. 217p. 1995. pap. text ed. 15.95 (*0-7167-2595-9*) W H Freeman.

Selling Serenity: Life among the Recovery Stars. Andrew Meacham. 1996. 14.95 (*0-89777-136-2*) Sirs Inc.

Selling Services & Products: A Pictorial Guide for Managers. Malcolm H. McDonald & Morris. 96p. 1994. pap. text ed. 29.95 (*0-7506-1958-9*) Buttrwrth-Heinemann.

Selling Short: Risks, Rewards, & Strategies for Short Selling Stocks, Options, & Futures. Joseph A. Walker. LC 90-24800. (Finance Editions Ser.: No. 1935). 224p. 1991. text ed. 45.00 (*0-471-53464-1*) Wiley.

Selling Sin: The Marketing of Socially Unacceptable Products. D. Kirk Davidson. LC 96-3621. 232p. 1996. text ed. 59.95 (*0-89930-994-1*, Quorum Bks) Greenwood.

Selling Skills for the Nonsalesperson: For People Who Hate to Sell but Love to Succeed. Gary S. Goodman. 144p. 1984. pap. 10.00 (*0-671-76506-X*) S&S Trade.

Selling Smart: Great Ideas for Salespeople. LC 93-81266. 167p. (C). 1994. pap. text ed. 9.95 (*0-944448-09-7*) Motivation Pr.

Selling Smart: How the Magazine Pros Sell Advertising. Ira Ellenthal. Ed. by Folio Staff. 1982. 59.95 (*0-918110-06-8*) Cowles Busn Media.

Selling Smoke. Kenneth E. Warner. LC 86-25875. 120p. 1988. 17.50 (*0-87553-145-8*) Am Pub Health.

Selling Songs Successfully. Henry Boye. LC 94-30255. 1994. pap. 14.95 (*0-8119-0798-8*) LIFETIME.

Selling Spelling to Kids: Motivating Games & Activities to Reinforce Spelling Skills. Imogene Forte & Mary A. Pangle. (Illus.). 96p. (Orig.). (J). (gr. 4-6). 1985. pap. text ed. 9.95 (*0-86530-060-7*, IP 607) Incentive Pubns.

Selling Starts When the Customer Says No: The 12 Toughest Sells - & How to Overcome Them. Richard S. Seelye & O. William Moody. 250p. 1993. text ed. 22.95 (*1-55738-446-0*) Irwin Prof Pubng.

Selling Strategic Defense: Interests, Ideologies & the Arms Race. Erik K. Pratt. LC 89-24351. 180p. 1990. lib. bdg. 32.00 (*1-55587-190-9*) Lynne Rienner.

Selling Students Short: Classroom Bargains & Academic Reform in the American High School. Michael Sedlak et al. 240p. (C). 1986. pap. text ed. 18.95 (*0-8077-2817-9*) Tchrs Coll.

Selling, Tests: Helping Customers Buy. 3rd ed. Ditzenberger. (SB - Marketing Education Ser.). 1992. 3.95 (*0-538-60533-2*) S-W Pub.

Selling the Air: A Critique of the Policy of Commerical Broadcasting in the United States. Thomas Streeter. LC 95-35028. 352p. 1996. pap. text ed. 16.95 (*0-226-77722-7*); lib. bdg. 52.50 (*0-226-77721-9*) U Ch Pr.

***Selling the All-American Wonder: The World II Consumer Advertising of Willys-Overland Motors, Inc.** Frederic L. Coldwell. (Illus.). 104p. 1997. pap. 30.00 (*0-910667-25-X*) USM.

***Selling the Big Ticket: How to Manage the Multiple Approval Sale.** 2nd unabridged ed. Buck Blessing. (Illus.). v, 187p. (Orig.). 1994. pap. 23.95 (*0-9656474-0-4*) Buck Blessing.

Selling the City. G. J. Ashworth & H. Voogd. 177p. 1992. text ed. 59.95 (*0-470-21875-4*) Halsted Pr.

Selling the City: Marketing Approaches in Public Sector Urban Planning. G. J. Ashworth & H. Voogd. 177p. 1993. text ed. 80.00 (*0-471-94470-X*) Wiley.

Selling the Dream: How to Promote Your Product, Company, or Ideas - & Make a Difference - Using Everyday Evangelism. Guy Kawasaki. LC 90-56378. 352p. 1992. pap. 12.00 (*0-88730-600-4*) Harper Busn.

Selling the Dream: The Gulf American Corporation & the Building of Cape Coral, Florida. David E. Dodrill. LC 92-39732. 328p. 1993. text ed. 39.95 (*0-8173-0597-1*) U of Ala Pr.

Selling-the How & Why: A Comprehensive Introduction to Salesmanship. James S. Norris. (Illus.). 304p. (C). 1982. pap. text ed. write for info. (*0-13-805986-1*) P-H.

Selling the Invisible: A Field Guide to Modern Marketing. Harry Beckwith. 272p. 1997. 15.00 (*0-446-52094-2*) Warner Bks.

Selling the Invisible: A Field Guide to Modern Marketing. Harry Beckwith. 272p. 1998. pap. 12.00 (*0-446-67231-9*) Warner Bks.

Selling the Lite of Heaven. Suzanne S. Shea. 288p. pap. 10.00 (*0-671-79865-0*, WSP) PB.

Selling the Lite of Heaven. Suzanne Strempek-Shea. Ed. by Jane Rosenman. LC 93-49359. 288p. 1994. 20.00 (*0-671-79864-2*) PB.

Selling, the Mother of All Enterprise. William H. Blades. 152p. 1994. pap. 12.95 (*0-9624798-7-X*) Mktg Methods Pr.

Selling the New Ford 1927-1931. 2nd rev. ed. Jim Schild. LC 96-84414. (Illus.). 184p. 1996. pap. 14.95 (*0-9624958-3-2*) Auto Review Pub.

Selling the People's Cadillac: The Edsel & Corporate Responsibility. Jan G. Deutsch. LC 75-37292. 300p. 1976. 55.00 (*0-300-01950-5*) Yale U Pr.

***Selling the Right Way.** Quigg & Wisner. 1997. pap. text ed. 45.33 (*0-13-613654-0*) P-H.

Selling the Sea: An Inside Look at the Cruise Industry. Robert H. Dickinson & Andrew Vladimir. LC 96-20420. 1996. text ed. 44.95 (*0-471-12001-4*) Wiley.

Selling the Sixties: The Pirates & Pop Music Radio. Robert Chapman. 256p. 1992. 39.95 (*0-04-445881-9*, A8204) Routledge Chapman & Hall.

***Selling the Story.** Sarah E. Hutchinson & Stacey Sawyer. 1992. per. 29.95 (*0-07-413184-2*) Irwin.

Selling the Story: The Layman's Guide to Collecting & Communicating Demographic Information. William Dunn. LC 91-58811. 245p. (C). 1992. 24.95 (*0-936889-14-4*); pap. 29.95 (*0-936889-15-2*) American Demo.

Selling the Top Brass. Robert K. Weill. 1977. 59.50 (*0-13-806000-2*) Exec Reports.

Selling the Way Your Customer Buys: Understand Your Prospects' Unspoken Needs & Close Every Sale. 2nd ed. M. C. Sadovsky & J. Caswell. LC 94-45494. 176p. 1996. pap. 16.95 (*0-8144-7889-1*) AMACOM.

***Selling Things.** Orison S. Marden. 276p. 1997. pap. 25.00 (*0-89540-339-0*) Sun Pub.

Selling Through Independent Reps. 2nd ed. Harold J. Novick. LC 93-20716. 372p. 1993. 69.95 (*0-8144-5146-2*) AMACOM.

Selling Through Negotiation: The Handbook of Sales Negotiation. Homer B. Smith. 192p. (Orig.). 1988. pap. 14.95 (*0-9621285-1-1*) Mktg Educ Assocs.

Selling to a Segmented Market: The Lifestyle Approach. Chester A. Swenson. LC 89-49432. 192p. 1990. text ed. 55.00 (*0-89930-446-X*, SMV/, Greenwood Pr) Greenwood.

Selling to a Segmented Market: The Lifestyle Approach. Chester A. Swenson. 192p. 1992. pap. 24.95 (*0-8442-3459-1*, NTC Busn Bks) NTC Pub Grp.

Selling to an ESOP. Ed. by Scott Rodrick. (Illus.). viii, 154p. (Orig.). 1996. text ed. 35.00 (*0-926902-29-6*) NCEO.

***Selling to an ESOP: Legal Structures, Valuation Issues, Financing Strategies, Feasibility Assessment, & Tax-Deferral Mechanisms for Employee Stock Ownership Plans.** 2nd ed. Ed. by Scott Rodrick. (Illus.). 138p. 1997. pap. text ed. 35.00 (*0-926902-35-0*) NCEO.

Selling to Catalog Houses. 1987. lib. bdg. 69.95 (*0-8490-3888-X*) Gordon Pr.

Selling to Consumers: Complete Training Book. Zack Right. 350p. (Orig.). (C). 1984. pap. 9.95 (*0-9604554-1-8*) Talmud Pr.

Selling to Corporate America. N.M.B.C. (Pisula) Staff. 272p. 1996. per., pap. text ed. 155.00 (*0-7872-1831-6*) Kendall-Hunt.

Selling to Humans: A New Approach to Exchange. David N. Plotkin. 268p. 1995. pap. 14.00 (*0-9643549-4-2*) Influence Trning.

***Selling to India's Consumer Market.** Douglas Bullis. LC 97-1704. 1997. text ed. write for info. (*1-56720-105-9*, Quorum Bks) Greenwood.

Selling to NASA. (Illus.). 53p. (Orig.). (C). 1994. pap. text ed. 25.00 (*0-7881-0358-X*) DIANE Pub.

***Selling to the Affluent.** Thomas J. Stanley. 1997. pap. 24.95 (*0-07-061049-5*) McGraw.

Selling to the Affluent: The Professional's Guide to Closing the Sales That Count. Thomas J. Stanley. 492p. 1990. text ed. 55.00 (*1-55623-418-X*) Irwin Prof Pubng.

Selling to the Giants: How to Become a Key Supplier to Large Corporations. Jeffrey P. Davidson. 1991. text ed. 27.95 (*0-07-157618-5*) McGraw.

Selling to the Giants: How to Become a Key Supplier to Large Corporations. Jeffrey P. Davidson. 210p. 1991. 27.95 (*0-8306-7586-8*, 3586); pap. 14.95 (*0-8306-3586-6*, Liberty Hall Pr) TAB Bks.

Selling to the Military. (Illus.). 129p. (C). 1993. pap. text ed. 30.00 (*1-56806-322-9*) DIANE Pub.

***Selling to the Military.** (Illus.). 143p. (Orig.). (C). 1997. pap. 35.00 (*0-7881-3756-5*) DIANE Pub.

***Selling to the Military.** (Illus.). 158p. 1996. reprint ed. pap. 35.00 (*0-7881-3381-0*) DIANE Pub.

Selling to the Top: David Peoples' Executive Selling Skills. David A. Peoples. 256p. 1993. pap. text ed. 17.95 (*0-471-58105-4*) Wiley.

Selling to the Top: David Peoples' Executive Selling Skills. David A. Peoples. LC 93-526. 256p. 1993. text ed. 49.95 (*0-471-58104-6*) Wiley.

Selling to the U. S. Government. Ed. by Holbrook & Kellogg Staff. 144p. Date not set. lib. bdg. 49.00 (*1-56726-028-4*, B590) Holbrook & Kellogg.

Selling to the World: Your Fast & Easy Guide to Exporting & Importing. L. Fargo Wells. (Illus.). 352p. 1996. pap. text ed. 16.95 (*0-07-069302-1*) McGraw.

Selling to Vito: The Very Important Top Officer. Anthony Parinello. 1994. pap. 10.95 (*1-55850-386-2*) Adams Media.

***Selling to Win.** Richard Denny. (Marketing & Sales Ser.). 1989. 24.95 (*1-85091-626-8*) Kogan Page Ltd.

Selling Today. 6th ed. Gerald L. Manning & Barry L. Reece. LC 94-35214. (C). 1995. text ed. 77.00 (*0-205-16446-3*) P-H.

Selling Today: A Personal Approach. 4th ed. Gerald L. Manning & Barry L. Reece. 570p. 1989. text ed. 48.00 (*0-205-12102-0*, H21025) Allyn.

Selling Today: A Personal Approach. 4th ed. Gerald L. Manning & Barry L. Reece. 570p. 1989. teacher ed. write for info. (*0-318-66325-2*, H27253); write for info. (*0-318-66326-0*, H21041); vhs write for info. (*0-318-66327-9*, H21066) P-H.

***Selling Today: Building Quality Partnerships.** 7th ed. Gerald L. Manning & Barry L. Reece. LC 97-11434. 1997. 68.00 (*0-13-613837-3*) P-H.

Selling Used Books by Mail: A Grass-Roots Guide for the Homeworker. 2nd ed. A. G. Gersdorf. LC 89-92249. (Illus.). 151p. 1990. pap. 9.50 (*0-9621860-2-3*) Loup Garou Pr Inc.

Selling Venus: Futuristic Tales of the Age Old Tradition of Exchanging Sex for Money. Ed. by Cecilia Tan. 152p. (Orig.). 1997. pap. 7.95 (*1-885865-05-8*) Circlet Pr.

Selling War: The British Propaganda Campaign Against American "Neutrality" in World War II. Nicholas J. Cull. (Illus.). 304p. 1996. reprint ed. pap. 16.95 (*0-19-511150-8*) OUP.

***Selling What You Make.** Lea L. Oldham. 72p. (Orig.). 1997. pap. 5.95 (*0-942923-03-0*) NETWIC.

Selling What You Make: Profit from Your Handcrafts. James E. Seitz. 1992. pap. text ed. 14.95 (*0-07-056130-3*) McGraw.

Selling What You Make: Profit from Your Handcrafts. James E. Seitz. (Illus.). 240p. 1992. pap. 12.95 (*0-8306-4144-0*, 4235) McGraw-Hill Prof.

Selling with Excellence: A Quality Approach for Sales Professionals. Larry A. McCloskey. LC 94-37982. 140p. 1994. pap. 16.00 (*0-87389-322-0*, H0873) ASQC Qual Pr.

***Selling with Honor: Strategies for Selling without Selling Your Soul.** Lawrence M. Kohn & Joel Saltzman. 128p. 1997. pap. 11.00 (*0-425-15704-0*, Berkley Trade) Berkley Pub.

***Selling with Integrity: Reinventing Sales Through Collaboration, Respect, & Serving.** Sharon Drew Morgen. (Illus.). 225p. 1997. 24.95 (*1-57675-017-5*) Berrett-Koehler.

Selling with Magic: How to Turn Your Presentations into Dollars! Michael Jeffreys. (Illus.). 200p. (Orig.). 1989. pap. 24.95 (*1-878407-00-7*) Powerful Magic Pub.

***Selling with Silk Gloves, Not Brass Knuckles: A Guide to Winning Relationships.** Norman Levine. 300p. 1997. pap. 12.95 (*1-55874-466-5*) Health Comm.

Selling Without Confrontation. Jack Greening. LC 92-21789. (Illus.). 128p. (Orig.). 1993. 29.95 (*1-56024-326-0*); 12.95 (*1-56024-327-9*) Haworth Pr.

***Selling Words.** Wright. LC 97-4899. 1997. 30.00 (*0-8147-9315-0*) NYU Pr.

Selling Your Book: The Writer's Guide to Publishing & Marketing. Dorothy Kavka. LC 91-168950. (Illus.). 128p. (Orig.). 1991. pap. 9.95 (*1-879260-01-8*) Evanston Pub.

***Selling Your Business: Goodwill & Intangibles - Paths to Maximum Gain.** 2nd rev. ed. Holmes F. Crouch. Ed. by Irma J. Crouch. LC 97-70093. (Four Hundred Tax Guides: Owners & Sellers Ser.: Vol. 405). (Illus.). 224p. 1997. pap. 18.95 (*0-944817-35-1*, T/G 405) Allyear Tax.

Selling Your Business: How to Make the Best Deal. John W. Hartman. LC 95-69881. 160p. (Orig.). (C). 1996. pap. 16.95 (*1-885884-88-5*) Cormorant Pr.

Selling Your Business Without Selling Yourself Short. Gary Viner. 140p. 1991. student ed. 99.95 (*0-9631182-1-8*) G Viner.

Selling Your Church in the Nineties: A Public Relations Guide for Clergy & Laity. Boyce A. Bowdon. 112p. (Orig.). 1992. pap. 8.95 (*0-9632495-0-9*) Koinonia Pr.

Selling Your Crafts at Craft Shows: The Basics for Beginners. Madelaine Gray. LC 96-8194. (Bulletin Ser.). 1996. pap. 2.95 (*0-88266-476-X*) Storey Comm Inc.

***Selling Your Dolls & Teddy Bears.** Carol-Lynn R. Waugh & Barbara L. Giguere. LC 96-42196. (Illus.). 160p. 1997. pap. 18.99 (*1-55870-439-6*, Betrwy Bks) F & W Pubns Inc.

Selling Your Film: A Guide to the Contemporary Marketplace. Eric Sherman. 192p. (Orig.). (C). 1990. pap. 15.95 (*0-918226-27-9*) Acrobat.

Selling Your Graphic Design & Illustration. Tad Crawford & Arie Kopelman. 272p. 1981. 19.95 (*0-312-71252-9*) St Martin.

Selling Your Home. Carolyn Janik. 1980. 8.95 (*0-02-558920-2*) Macmillan.

***Selling Your Home: The $125,000 Exclusion - When & How to Claim It.** 2nd rev. ed. Holmes F. Crouch. Ed. by Irma J. Crouch. LC 97-70094. (Series 400: Vol. 403). (Illus.). 224p. 1997. pap. 18.95 (*0-944817-36-X*, T/G 403) Allyear Tax.

Selling Your Home in the Washington, D.C. Metropolitan Area. David G. Rathgeber. 134p. 1995. pap. 9.95 (*0-9635337-4-6*) Realty Res.

Selling Your Idea or Invention: The Birthplace to Marketplace Guide. Sonny Bloch & Gary Ahlert. LC 94-19043. 1994. 19.95 (*1-55972-244-4*, Birch Ln Pr) Carol Pub Group.

Selling Your Own Real Estate: Secrets from a Realtor. Thomas L. Loveless. LC 92-81723. 194p. (Orig.). 1992. pap. 28.95 (*0-9633103-0-5*) TRuth Pub.

Selling Your Screenplay: A Successful Hollywood Screenwriter Tells You How to Break into the Business ... & Stay There. Cynthia Whitcomb. 224p. 1988. pap. 11.95 (*0-517-57008-4*, Crown) Crown Pub Group.

Selling Your Services: Proven Strategies for Getting Clients to Hire You (Or Your Firm) Robert W. Bly. 368p. 1992. pap. 14.95 (*0-8050-2041-1*, Owl) H Holt & Co.

Selling Your Valuables: From Tiddleywinks to Diamonds. Jeanne Siegel. (Illus.). 106p. 1996. pap. 12.95 (*1-56625-055-2*) Bonus Books.

Selling Yourself: How to Be the Competent Confident Person You Really Are. Kathy Thebo. 1993. pap. 12.95 (*0-942361-80-6*) MasterMedia Pub.

Selling Yourself on You: Discovering God's Will for Your Life. Mary A. Diorio. LC 88-70291. 214p. (Orig.). 1988. pap. 14.95 (*0-930037-02-2*) Daystar Comm.

Selling 101: A Course for Business Owners & Non-Sales People: Includes Finding Leads, Cold Calling, Handling Objections, Closing Sales, Growing Sales. Michael T. McGaulley. (An Adams Business Advisor Ser.). 1995. pap. 12.95 (*1-55850-545-8*) Adams Media.

***Selling 101: Essential Selling Skills For Business Owners And Non-Sales People.** Michael T. McGaulley. 1997. pap. text ed. 9.95 (*1-55850-705-1*) Adams Media.

Selling's My Game: Riley's the Name. Corwin E. Riley. (Illus.). 96p. 1988. 6.95 (*0-9621048-0-9*) Corray Pub Co.

Sellout. Jeff Putnam. Ed. by Sam Chase. 338p. 1995. 22.00 (*1-880909-35-9*) Baskerville.

Sell's British Exporters 1987. 1987. pap. 75.00 (*0-85499-553-6*) Taylor & Francis.

Sell's Directory. 1000p. 1992. 620.00 (*0-85499-519-6*) St Mut.

Selma: Queen City of the Blackbelt. Alston Fitts, III. Ed. by Sarah E. Sims. (Illus.). 230p. (Orig.). 1989. pap. 10.00 (*0-9623319-3-7*) Clairmont Pr.

Selma: The Gospel at Work. F. Wilbur Helmbold. 1983. 12.50 (*0-685-09687-4*); pap. 8.50 (*0-685-09688-2*) Banner Pr AL.

Selma Burke, Artist. Garnet N. Jackson. (Illus.). (J). (gr. 1-4). 1994. pap. 4.95 (*0-8136-5246-4*); lib. bdg. 9.95 (*0-8136-5240-5*) Modern Curr.

Selma Erving Collection: Modern Illustrated Books. Intro. by Ruth Mortimer. 60p. 1977. pap. 7.00 (*0-87391-037-0*) Smith Coll Mus Art.

Selma Erving Collection: Nineteenth & Twentieth Century Prints. Ed. by N. Sojka & C. Swenson. LC 85-80045. 140p. 1985. pap. 12.00 (*0-87391-036-2*) Smith Coll Mus Art.

***Selma Lagerlof: Great Short Stories from Around the World I.** Illus. by James McConnell. LC 94-75343. (Classic Short Stories Ser.). 80p. 1994. pap. 5.95 (*0-7854-0651-4*, 40064) Am Guidance.

Selma, Lord, Selma: Girlhood Memories of the Civil-Rights Days. Sheyann Webb & Rachel W. Nelson. LC 79-19327. (Illus.). 168p. 1980. 17.95 (*0-8173-0031-7*) U of Ala Pr.

Selmo Comes Home & Other Stories. Benjamin M. Pascual. 138p. (Orig.). (C). 1989. pap. 10.75 (*971-10-0351-1*, Pub. by New Day Pub PH) Cellar.

Selsey Gold. large type ed. Howard C. Davis. (Linford Mystery Library). 1991. pap. 15.99 (*0-7089-7066-4*) Ulverscroft.

Seltene Augenblicke: Interpretations of Poems by Hugo von Hofmannsthal. Ed. by Margit Resch. LC 88-62942. (Studies in German Literature, Linguistics & Culture: Vol. 40). (Illus.). 224p. 1989. 34.00 (*0-938100-63-7*) Camden Hse.

Seltold Life. Ernst Barlach. Tr. by Naomi J. Groves from GER. (Illus.). 104p. 1990. pap. 15.95 (*0-921254-07-5*, Pub. by Penumbra Pr CN) U of Toronto Pr.

Seltzer Man. Ken Rush. LC 91-40905. (Illus.). 32p. (J). (ps-3). 1993. lib. bdg. 14.95 (*0-02-777917-3*, Mac Bks Young Read) S&S Childrens.

***Seltzer Man.** Ken Rush. (Illus.). (J). 3.98 (*0-7651-0096-7*) Smithmark.

Seltzer's New Jersey Law with Forms, 9 vols., Set. D. E. Jennings. 9000p. 795.00 (*0-8205-1620-1*) Juris Pubng.

Selu: Seeking the Corn-Mother's Wisdom. Marilou Awiakta. (Illus.). 224p. 1993. 19.95 (*1-55591-144-7*) Fulcrum Pub.

Selu: Seeking the Corn-Mother's Wisdom. Marilou Awiakta. (Illus.). 352p. 1994. pap. 14.95 (*1-55591-206-0*) Fulcrum Pub.

***Selu & Kana'Ti: Cherokee Corn Mother & Lucky Hunter.** Nadema Agard. LC 96-52311. (Mondo Folktales ser.). (J). 1997. pap. write for info. (*1-57255-167-4*); lib. bdg. write for info. (*1-57255-169-0*) Mondo Pubng.

Selu's Song. Wade Blevins. 53p. (J). (gr. 4-7). 1995. pap. text ed. 2.95 (*1-56763-134-7*) Ozark Pub.

***Selva.** (Eyewitness Bks.). (SPA.). (J). 1997. 19.99 (*84-372-3789-0*) Random.

Selva: Ecology & Natural History of a Neotropical Rainforest. Lucinda A. McDade et al. LC 93-1776. (Illus.). 498p. 1994. pap. text ed. 28.95 (*0-226-03952-8*); lib. bdg. 90.00 (*0-226-03950-1*) U Ch Pr.

***Selva Humanizada: Ecologia Alternativa en el Tropico Humedo Colombiano.** Ed. by Francois Correa. 232p. (SPA.). 1989. pap. 12.00 (*958-612-024-4*, IC001) UPLAAP.

Selvages & Biases: The Fabric of History in American Culture. Michael G. Kammen. LC 87-5285. (Illus.). 352p. (C). 1987. 45.00 (*0-8014-1924-7*) Cornell U Pr.

Selvages & Biases: The Fabric of History in American Culture. Michael G Kammen. LC 87-5285. (Illus.). 352p. (C). 1987. pap. 17.95 (*0-8014-9404-4*) Cornell U Pr.

Selves. Philip Booth. 96p. 1991. pap. 9.95 (*0-14-058646-6*) Viking Penguin.

Selves at Risk: Patterns of Quest in Contemporary American Letters. Ihab Hassan. LC 89-36082. (Wisconsin Project on American Writers Ser.). 246p. 1989. 22.95 (*0-299-12370-7*) U of Wis Pr.

Selves in Discord & Resolve: Essays in Kierkegaard's Moralreligious Psychology from Either/Or to Sickness unto Death. Edward Mooney. 140p. (C). 1996. pap. 17.95 (*0-415-91370-5*, Routledge NY); text ed. 59.95 (*0-415-91369-1*, Routledge NY) Routledge.

S

An Asterisk (*) at the beginning of an entry indicates that the title is appearing in BIP for the first time.

S

***Selves in Time & Place: Identities, Experience, & History in Nepal.** Ed. by Debra Skinner et al. 375p. 1997. 65.00 (*0-8476-8598-5*) Rowman.

***Selves in Time & Place: Identities, Experience, & History in Nepal.** Ed. by Debra Skinner et al. 375p. 1997. pap. 26.95 (*0-8476-8599-3*) Rowman.

Selves, People, & Persons: What Does It Mean to Be a Self?, Vol. 13. Ed. by Leroy S. Rouner. LC 92-53748. (Boston University Studies in Philosophy & Religion: Vol. 13). (C). 1992. text ed. 37.00 (*0-268-01747-6*) U of Notre Dame Pr.

Selwym Image, Previously Unpublished Poems. Selwyn Image. 1987. pap. 5.00 (*0-89979-050-X*) British Am Bks.

Selznick. Bob Thomas. LC 82-49237. (Cinema Classics Ser.). 381p. 1985. lib. bdg. 16.00 (*0-8240-5780-5*) Garland.

***Selznick's Vision: Gone with the Wind & Hollywood Filmmaking.** LC 96-53554. (Texas Film Studies). 1997. write for info. (*0-292-78728-6*) U of Tex Pr.

***Selznick's Vision: Gone with the Wind & Hollywood Filmmaking.** Alan D. Vertrees. LC 96-53554. (Texas Film Studies Ser.). (Illus.). 256p. 1997. pap. 30.00 (*0-292-78729-4*) U of Tex Pr.

SEM: A User's Manual for Materials Science. Barbara L. Gabriel. (Illus.). 198p. 1985. 101.00 (*0-87170-202-9*, 6144) ASM.

Sem, Erotics: Theorizing Lesbian: Writing. Elizabeth A. Meese. (Cutting Edge: Lesbian Life & Literature Ser.). 304p. (C). 1992. 45.00 (*0-8147-5469-4*); pap. 15.00 (*0-8147-5470-8*) NYU Pr.

SEM Microcharacterization of Semiconductors. Ed. by D. B. Holt & David C. Joy. 452p. 1989. text ed. 142.00 (*0-12-353855-6*) Acad Pr.

***SEM V Workbook.** 1996. 50.00 (*0-614-23454-9*, 9923) Am Assn Coll Registrars.

Sema-Kanda: Threshold Memories. Coulson Turnbull. 254p. 1994. pap. 20.00 (*0-89540-131-2*, SB-131) Sun Pub.

Sema-Kanda: Threshold Memories, a Mystic's Story. Coulson Turnbull. 254p. 1971. reprint ed. spiral bd. 12.00 (*0-7873-1045-X*) Hlth Research.

Sema-Kanda - Threshold Memories: A Mystic's Story. Coulson Turnbull. 257p. 1996. pap. 18.95 (*1-56459-692-3*) Kessinger Pub.

Semai: A Nonviolent People of Malaya, Fieldwork Edition. Dentan. 128p. (C). 1979. pap. text ed. 13.50 (*0-03-045376-3*) HB Coll Pubs.

Semaine De Bonte: A Surrealistic Novel in Collage. 2nd ed. Max Ernst. LC 75-17362. (Illus.). 224p. 1976. reprint ed. pap. 8.95 (*0-486-23252-2*) Dover.

Semaine De Mai. Camille Pelletan. LC 75-173941. (FRE.). reprint ed. 54.00 (*0-404-07163-5*) AMS Pr.

Semana de la Pasion, Muerte y Resurreccion. Ed. by Laura Disselkoen. 75p. 1988. reprint ed. pap. 5.99 (*0-311-08501-6*) Casa Bautista.

Semana Santa en Tierra Santa-bL-Alumno. Pablo Canche. (SPA.). 1989. 1.00 (*1-55955-010-4*) CRC Wrld Lit.

Semana Santa En Tierra Santa-bL-Maestro. Pablo Canche. (SPA.). 1990. 1.00 (*1-55955-011-2*) CRC Wrld Lit.

Semana Santa en Tierra Santa-C-Alumno. Pablo Canche. (SPA.). 1989. 1.00 (*1-55955-006-6*) CRC Wrld Lit.

Semana Santa en Tierra Santa-C-Maestro. Pablo Canche. (SPA.). 1990. 1.00 (*1-55955-007-4*) CRC Wrld Lit.

Semana Santa en Tierra Santa-Db-Alumno. Pablo Canche. (SPA.). 1989. 1.00 (*1-55955-008-2*) CRC Wrld Lit.

Semana Santa En Tierra Santa-Db-Maestro. Pablo Canche. (SPA.). 1990. 1.00 (*1-55955-009-0*) CRC Wrld Lit.

Semantic Ambiguity & Underspecification. Stanley Peters. Ed. by Kees Van Deemter. 294p. (Orig.). (C). 1996. 69.95 (*1-57586-029-5*); pap. 24.95 (*1-57586-028-7*) CSLI.

Semantic Analysis of Literary Texts: To Honour Jan Van Der Eng on the Occasion of His 65th Birthday. Willem G. Westseijn et al. 1990. 213.75 (*0-444-88892-6*) Elsevier.

Semantic Analysis of the Old Russian Finite Preterite System. C. H. Van Schooneveld. 1959. text ed. 40.00 (*90-279-0164-3*) Mouton.

Semantic & Conceptual Development: An Ontological Perspective. Frank C. Keil. LC 79-10491. 229p. 1979. 25.00 (*0-674-80100-8*) HUP.

Semantic & Lexical Universals: Theory & Empirical Findings. Ed. by Cliff Goddard & Anna Wierzbicka. LC 94-4253. (Studies in Language Companion: Vol. 25). viii, 510p. 1994. lib. bdg. 95.00 (*1-55619-377-7*) Benjamins North Am.

Semantic & Pragmatic Language Disorder: Assessment & Intervention. 2nd ed. Ellyn Arwood. LC 91-15139. 272p. 1991. 56.00 (*0-8342-0272-7*) Aspen Pub.

***Semantic & Pragmatic Model of Lexical & Grammatical Aspect.** Mari B. Olsen. (Outstanding Dissertations in Linguistics Ser.). 340p. 1997. 67.00 (*0-8153-2849-4*) Garland.

Semantic Basis of Argument Structure: A Study of the Relation Between Word Meaning & Syntax. Stephen Wechsler. (Dissertations in Linguistics Ser.). 178p. (Orig.). 1995. text ed. 45.00 (*1-881526-69-0*); pap. text ed. 22.95 (*1-881526-68-2*) CSLI.

Semantic Behavior & Decision Making. William J. Williams. LC 78-23923. 165p. reprint ed. pap. 47.10 (*0-317-10025-4*, 2022587) Bks Demand.

Semantic Conception of Theories & Scientific Realism. Frederick Suppe. LC 88-27878. 496p. 1989. text ed. 34.95 (*0-252-01605-X*) U of Ill Pr.

Semantic Data Modelling. J. H. Ter Bekke. 300p. 1992. pap. text ed. 51.00 (*0-13-806050-9*) P-H.

Semantic Database Systems: A Functional Introduction. C. S. Prabhu. 1993. text ed. 25.00 (*0-86311-346-X*, Pub. by Universities Pr II) Apt Bks.

Semantic Development of Words for "Eating" & "Drinking" in Germanic. Henry O. Schwabe. LC 70-173195. (Chicago. University. Linguistic Studies in Germanic: No. 1). reprint ed. 29.50 (*0-404-50281-4*) AMS Pr.

Semantic Development of Words for Walk, Run in the Germanic Languages, No. 4. Roscoe M. Ihrig. LC 71-170058. (Chicago. University. Linguistic Studies in Germanic). reprint ed. 32.50 (*0-404-50284-9*) AMS Pr.

Semantic Divergence in Anglo-French Cognates: A Synchronic Study in Contrastive Lexicography. Jean-Luc Garneau. (Edward Sapir Monograph Ser. in Language, Culture & Cognition: No. 14). x, 128p. (Orig.). 1985. pap. 20.00 (*0-933104-20-0*) Jupiter Pr.

Semantic Feature Analysis: Classroom Application. Susan D. Pittelman et al. 66p. 1991. pap. 8.95 (*0-87207-235-5*) Intl Reading.

Semantic Foundations of Logic: Propositional Logics. 2nd ed. Richard L. Epstein & Rodger D. Maddux. 512p. (C). 1995. 75.00 (*0-19-508761-5*) OUP.

Semantic Indexicality. M. J. Cresswell. LC 95-52126. (Studies in Linguistics & Philosophy: Vol. 60). 228p. (C). 1996. lib. bdg. 98.00 (*0-7923-3914-2*) Kluwer Ac.

Semantic Information Processing. Ed. by Marvin L. Minsky. LC 68-18239. 440p. 1969. 42.50 (*0-262-13044-0*) MIT Pr.

Semantic Interpretation & the Resolution of Ambiguity. Graeme Hirst. (Studies in Natural Language Processing). (Illus.). 275p. (C). 1992. pap. text ed. 27.95 (*0-521-42898-X*) Cambridge U Pr.

Semantic Language & Metacognition of Children with Hearing Loss: Beyond the Great Debate. Christine Yoshinaga-Itano. 350p. 1997. 45.00 (*1-56593-271-4*, 0593) Singular Publishing.

Semantic Mapping: Classroom Applications. Joan E. Heimlich & Susan D. Pittelman. 48p. 1986. pap. 8.95 (*0-87207-230-4*) Intl Reading.

***Semantic Modeling for the Acquisition of Topographic Information from Images & Maps: SMATI 97.** W. Forstner & Lutz Plumer. LC 97-19724. 1997. write for info. (*3-7643-5758-4*); write for info. (*0-8176-5758-4*) Birkhauser.

Semantic Networks: An Evidential Formalization & Its Connectionist Realization. Lokenda Shastri. LC 86-34409. (Research Notes in Artificial Intelligence Ser.). (Illus.). 222p. (Orig.). 1988. pap. text ed. 29.95 (*0-934613-39-7*) Morgan Kaufmann.

Semantic Networks: An Evidential Formalization & Its Connectionist Realization. Ed. by Lokendra Shastri. 250p. (Orig.). (C). 1988. pap. text ed. 180.00 (*0-273-08779-7*, Pub. by Pitman Pubng UK) St Mut.

***Semantic Networks for Understanding Scenes.** Gerhard Sagerer & Heinrich Niemann. LC 97-21740. (Advances in Archaeological & Museum Science Ser.). 1997. write for info. (*0-306-45704-0*) Plenum.

***Semantic Networks in Artificial Intelligence.** F. Lehmann. (International Series in Modern Applied Mathematics: Vol. 24). 768p. 1992. 125.00 (*0-08-042012-5*, Pergamon Pr) Elsevier.

Semantic Problems of Translated Subject Headings. Gertrude Soonja Lee Koh. 1979. 20.00 (*0-686-25169-5*) Chinese Cult Serv.

Semantic Processing for Finite Domains. Martha S. Palmer. (Studies in Natural Language Processing). 248p. (C). 1990. text ed. 65.00 (*0-521-36226-1*) Cambridge U Pr.

Semantic Structure & Word Formation: Verb-Particle Constructions in Contemporary English. Leonard Lipka. 1973. bds. 47.75 (*3-7705-0947-1*) Adlers Foreign Bks.

Semantic Structure of Spanish: Meaning & Grammatical Form. Larry D. King. LC 92-17858. (Current Issues in Linguistic Theory Ser.: Vol. 90). xii, 287p. 1992. 74.00 (*1-55619-147-2*) Benjamins North Am.

Semantic Structures. Ray S. Jackendoff. Ed. by Samuel J. Keyser. (Current Studies in Linguistics: No. 18). 344p. 1990. 37.50 (*0-262-10043-6*) MIT Pr.

Semantic Structures. Ray S. Jackendoff. (Illus.). 336p. 1992. pap. 21.00 (*0-262-60020-X*) MIT Pr.

Semantic Structures: Advances in Natural Language Processing. David Waltz. 240p. (C). 1989. text ed. 49.95 (*0-89859-817-6*) L Erlbaum Assocs.

Semantic Structures in Spanish: A Proposal for Instructional Materials. Frances M. Aid. LC 72-96297. 152p. reprint ed. pap. 43.40 (*0-7837-6454-5*, 2046454) Bks Demand.

Semantic Syntax. Pietes A. Seuren. 400p. Date not set. 59.95 (*0-631-16005-1*) Blackwell Pubs.

Semantic Syntax. Pietes A. Seuren. 400p. Date not set. pap. 29.95 (*0-631-16006-X*) Blackwell Pubs.

Semantic Theories & Language Teaching. Ed. by V. Prakashan. (C). 1986. 17.50 (*81-7023-080-2*, Pub. by Allied II) S Asia.

Semantic Theories in Europe, 1830-1930: From Etymology to Contextuality. Brigitte Nerlich. LC 91-42523. (Studies in the History of the Language Sciences: No. 59). xii, 346p. 1992. 74.00 (*1-55619-354-8*) Benjamins North Am.

Semantic Theory of Evolution. M. Barbieri. Ed. by R. Hahn et al. (Models of Scientific Thought Ser.: Vol. 2). 188p. 1985. pap. text ed. 44.00 (*3-7186-0397-7*) Gordon & Breach.

Semantic Theory of Evolution. Marcello Barbieri. (Models of Scientific Thought Ser.: Vol. 2). 188p. 1985. text ed. 79.00 (*3-7186-0243-1*) Gordon & Breach.

Semantic Tradition from Kant to Carnap: To the Vienna Station. J. Alberto Coffa. Ed. by Linda Wessels. 455p. (C). 1993. pap. text ed. 21.95 (*0-521-44707-0*) Cambridge U Pr.

Semantic Universals & Universal Semantics. Ed. by Dietmar Zaefferer. LC 91-33618. (Groningen-Amsterdam Studies in Semantics: No. 12). viii, 242p. (Orig.). (C). 1992. reprint ed. pap. text ed. 86.15 (*3-11-013391-1*) Mouton.

Semantic Variability of Absolute Constructions. Gregory T. Stump. (C). 1984. lib. bdg. 143.50 (*90-277-1895-4*) Kluwer Ac.

Semantics. John I. Saeed. LC 96-18295. (Introducing Linguistics). 368p. (C). 1997. text ed. 54.95 (*0-631-20034-7*); pap. text ed. 24.95 (*0-631-20035-5*) Blackwell Pubs.

Semantics: A Bibliography Nineteen Sixty-Five to Nineteen Seventy-Eight. W. Terrence Gordon. LC 79-24719. 321p. 1980. 32.50 (*0-8108-1300-9*) Scarecrow.

Semantics: A Bibliography, 1979-1985. W. Terrence Gordon. LC 87-16344. 304p. 1987. 27.50 (*0-8108-2055-2*) Scarecrow.

Semantics: A Bibliography, 1986-1991. W. Terrence Gordon. LC 92-27597. 291p. 1992. 29.50 (*0-8108-2598-8*) Scarecrow.

Semantics: A Coursebook. James R. Hurford & Brendan Heasley. LC 82-22005. (Illus.). 256p. 1983. pap. text ed. 19.95 (*0-521-28949-1*) Cambridge U Pr.

Semantics: An Interdisciplinary Reader in Philosophy, Linguistics & Psychology. Ed. by Danny D. Steinberg & Leon A. Jakobovits. LC 78-123675. 615p. reprint ed. pap. 175.30 (*0-317-20822-5*, 2024539) Bks Demand.

Semantics: Arriving at Meaning. Richard Ambacher. 400p. (C). 1993. pap. text ed. 42.99 (*0-8403-8206-5*) Kendall-Hunt.

Semantics: Defining the Discipline. Robert A. Hipkiss. 136p. 1995. text ed. 29.95 (*0-8058-2026-4*) L Erlbaum Assocs.

Semantics: Defining the Discipline. enl. ed. Robert A. Hipkiss. 136p. 1995. pap. 17.50 (*0-8058-1593-7*) L Erlbaum Assocs.

Semantics: Foundations & Applications: REX Workshop, Beekbergen, the Netherlands, June 1-4, 1992: Proceedings. Ed. by J. W. De Bakker et al. LC 93-16725. (Lecture Notes in Computer Science Ser.: Vol. 666). 1993. 93.95 (*0-387-56596-5*) Spr-Verlag.

Semantics: Primes & Universals. Wierzbicka. 512p. 1996. 105.00 (*0-19-870002-4*) OUP.

Semantics: Primes & Universals. Anna Wierzbicka. 512p. 1996. pap. 29.95 (*0-19-870003-2*) OUP.

Semantics: Studies in the Science of Meaning. Michel J. Breal. 1977. lib. bdg. 69.95 (*0-8490-2592-3*) Gordon Pr.

Semantics: The Nature of Words & Their Meanings. Hugh R. Walpole. LC 84-541. 264p. 1984. reprint ed. text ed. 59.75 (*0-313-24430-8*, WALS, Greenwood Pr) Greenwood.

Semantics: Theories of Meaning in Generative Grammar. Janet D. Fodor. (Language & Thought Ser.). 236p. 1980. pap. 14.95 (*0-674-80134-2*) HUP.

Semantics: Theory & Application: Proceedings. fac. ed. Georgetown University Round Table on Languages & Linguistics Staff. Ed. by Clea Rameh. LC 58-31607. (Illus.). 295p. 1976. reprint ed. pap. 84.10 (*0-7837-7793-0*, 2047549) Bks Demand.

Semantics & Cognition. Ray S. Jackendoff. Ed. by Joan Bresnan et al. (Current Studies in Linguistics). (Illus.). 304p. (C). 1985. pap. 14.95 (*0-262-60013-7*) MIT Pr.

Semantics & Communications. 3rd ed. John C. Condon, Jr. 160p. (C). 1985. pap. text ed. 46.00 (*0-02-324200-0*, Macmillan Coll) P-H.

Semantics & Comprehension. Herbert H. Clark. (Janua Linguarum, Series Minor: No. 187). 148p. 1976. pap. text ed. 32.35 (*90-279-3384-7*) Mouton.

Semantics & Contextual Expression. R. Bartsch et al. (Groningen-Amsterdam Studies in Semantics). 336p. (Orig.). (C). 1990. pap. 75.40 (*90-6765-443-4*) Mouton.

Semantics & Experience: Universal Metaphors of Time in English, Mandarin, Hindi, & Sesotho. Hoyt Alverson. LC 93-40748. (Parallax). 1994. 27.50 (*0-8018-4811-3*) Johns Hopkins.

Semantics & Language Analysis. Robert L. Benjamin. 128p. 1970. pap. text ed. 9.95 (*0-8290-0330-4*) Irvington.

Semantics & Language Analysis. Robert L. Benjamin. LC 77-75141. (Speech Communication Ser.). (C). 1970. pap. write for info. (*0-672-61085-X*, SC15, Bobbs) Macmillan.

***Semantics & Logics of Computation.** Ed. by A. Pitts & P. Dybjer. LC 96-50390. (Publications of the Newton Institute: No. 14). 350p. (C). 1997. text ed. 54.95 (*0-521-58057-9*) Cambridge U Pr.

Semantics & Philosophy. Ed. by Milton K. Munitz & Peter K. Unger. (C). 1980. pap. text ed. 16.00 (*0-8147-5376-0*) NYU Pr.

Semantics & Pragmatics of Verbal Categories in Bulgarian. Grace E. Fielder. LC 93-28605. 456p. 1993. text ed. 109.95 (*0-7734-9313-1*) E Mellen.

Semantics & Syntactic Regularity. Georgia M. Green. LC 74-9947. 251p. 1974. reprint ed. pap. 71.60 (*0-7837-3708-4*, 2057886) Bks Demand.

Semantics & the Lexicon. Ed. by James Pustejovsky. 416p. (C). 1993. pap. text ed. 39.00 (*0-7923-2386-6*) Kluwer Ac.

Semantics & the Lexicon. Ed. by James Pustejovsky. LC 92-28758. (Studies in Linguistics & Philosophy: Vol. 49). 416p. (C). 1993. lib. bdg. 158.50 (*0-7923-1963-X*) Kluwer Ac.

Semantics & the Philosophy of Language. 2nd ed. Ed. by Leonard Linsky. LC 52-10465. 304p. 1952. reprint ed. pap. text ed. 12.95 (*0-252-00093-5*) U of Ill Pr.

Semantics & the Social Sciences. Graham MacDonald & Philip Pettit. 224p. (C). 1981. pap. 13.95 (*0-7100-0784-1*, RKP) Routledge.

Semantics, Culture, & Cognition: Universal Human Concepts in Culture-Specific Configurations. Anna Wierzbicka. (Illus.). 512p. 1992. pap. 35.00 (*0-19-507326-6*) OUP.

Semantics for Concurrency: Proceedings of the International BCS-FACS Workshop Sponsored by Logic for IT (S.E.R.C.), 23-25 July 1990, University of Leicester UK. Ed. by M. Z. Kwiatkowska et al. (Workshops in Computing Ser.). viii, 346p. 1990. 59.00 (*0-387-19625-0*) Spr-Verlag.

Semantics for Groups & Events. Peter Lasersohn. (Linguistics Ser.: No. 3). 160p. 1991. text ed. 15.00 (*0-8153-0153-7*) Garland.

Semantics for the English Existential Construction. rev. ed. Louise McNally. Ed. by Laurence Horn. LC 96-46189. (Outstanding Dissertations in Linguistics Ser.). 237p. 1996. text ed. 62.00 (*0-8153-2557-6*) Garland.

Semantics Foundations of Logic: Predicate Logic. Richard L. Epstein. (Illus.). 412p. 1994. 70.00 (*0-19-508760-7*) OUP.

Semantics from Different Points of View. Ed. by R. Bauerie et al. (Language & Communication Ser.: Vol. 6). (Illus.). 1979. 54.95 (*0-387-09676-0*) Spr-Verlag.

***Semantics in Generative Grammar.** Irene Heim & Angelika Kratzer. (Textbooks in Linguistics Ser.: Vol. 13). 412p. (C). 1998. text ed. 64.95 (*0-631-19712-5*) Blackwell Pubs.

***Semantics in Generative Grammar.** Irene Heim & Angelika Kratzer. (Textbooks in Linguistics Ser.: Vol. 13). 412p. (C). 1998. pap. text ed. 29.95 (*0-631-19713-3*) Blackwell Pubs.

Semantics of Air Passenger Transportation. Edward MacNeal. LC 80-85432. (Illus.). 132p. 1981. 19.95 (*0-9605682-0-4*) Norfolk Port.

***Semantics of Aspect & Modality: Evidence from English & Biblical Hebrew.** Galia Hatav. LC 97-6117. (Studies in Language Companion Ser.: Vol. 34). 250p. 1997. lib. bdg. 85.00 (*1-55619-845-0*) Holland Pubng.

Semantics of Choice & Chance. Jorma Suokko. (Janua Linguarum, Ser. Minor: No. 131). 1972. pap. text ed. 13.85 (*3-10-800270-8*) Mouton.

Semantics of Coordination. Ewald Lang. LC 84-14541. (Studies in Language Companion: No. 9). 300p. 1984. 91.00 (*90-272-3008-0*) Benjamins North Am.

Semantics of Desire: Changing Models of Identity from Dickens to Joyce. Philip M. Weinstein. LC 83-43098. 325p. 1984. reprint ed. pap. 92.70 (*0-7837-9475-4*, 2060217) Bks Demand.

Semantics of Destructive Lisp. Ian A. Mason. LC 86-72170. (Center for the Study of Language & Information-Lecture Notes Ser.: No. 5). 290p. 1986. 39.95 (*0-937073-05-9*); pap. 17.95 (*0-937073-06-7*) CSLI.

Semantics of Digital Circuits. C. Delgado Kloos. (Lecture Notes in Computer Science Ser.: Vol. 285). ix, 124p. 1987. pap. 24.40 (*0-387-18540-2*) Spr-Verlag.

Semantics of English: Aspectual Complementation. Alice Freed. 1979. pap. text ed. 39.00 (*90-277-1011-2*); lib. bdg. 74.00 (*90-277-1010-4*) Kluwer Ac.

Semantics of Form in Arabic in the Mirror of European Languages. David Justice. LC 87-13180. (Studies in Language Campanion: No. 15). iv, 417p. (C). 1987. 130.00 (*90-272-3016-1*) Benjamins North Am.

Semantics of Grammar. Anna Wierzbicka. LC 88-19772. (Studies in Language Companion: Vol. 18). 617p. (C). 1989. 124.00 (*90-272-3019-6*); pap. 32.95 (*90-272-3022-6*) Benjamins North Am.

Semantics of John Stuart Mill. Willem R. De Jong. (Synthese Historical Library: No. 23). 382p. 1982. lib. bdg. 135.00 (*90-277-1408-8*) Kluwer Ac.

Semantics of Literature. Trevor Eaton. (De Proprietatibus Litterarum, Ser. Minor: No. 1). (Orig.). 1966. pap. text ed. 14.65 (*90-279-0084-1*) Mouton.

***Semantics of Media.** Jeff Ross. LC 96-52724. (Studies in Linguistics & Philosophy). 148p. (C). 1997. lib. bdg. 77.00 (*0-7923-4389-1*) Kluwer Ac.

Semantics of Metaphor. Samuel R. Levin. LC 77-4550. 176p. reprint ed. pap. 50.20 (*0-317-41827-0*, 2025626) Bks Demand.

Semantics of Natural Language. 2nd ed. Ed. by D. Davidson & G. Harman. LC 73-76427. (Synthese Library: No. 40). 779p. 1973. lib. bdg. 177.50 (*90-277-0304-3*, D Reidel) Kluwer Ac.

Semantics of New Testament Greek. J. P. Louw. (Semeia Studies). 166p. 1982. pap. 19.95 (*0-89130-693-5*, 06 06 11) Scholars Pr GA.

***Semantics of Parallelism: Non-Interleaving Representation of Behaviour.** M. W. Shields. LC 96-51077. 1997. pap. write for info. (*3-540-76059-8*) Spr-Verlag.

Semantics of Prepositions: From Mental Processing to Natural Language Processing. Ed. by Cornelia Zelinsky-Wibbelt. LC 93-30213. (Natural Language Processing Ser.: No. 3). (Illus.). viii, 526p. (C). 1993. lib. bdg. 198.50 (*3-11-013634-1*) Mouton.

Semantics of Programming Languages. Bjorn Kirkerud. (ITCP-UK Computer Science Ser.). 1997. pap. 39.95 (*1-85032-273-2*) ITCP.

Semantics of Programming Languages: An Elementary Introduction Using Structural Operational Semantics. Mathew Hennessy. LC 90-40979. 169p. reprint ed. pap. 48.20 (*0-7837-6381-6*, 2046094) Bks Demand.

Semantics of Programming Languages: Structures & Techniques. Carl A. Gunter. (Foundations of Computing Ser.). (Illus.). 375p. 1992. 45.00 (*0-262-07143-6*) MIT Pr.

Semantics of Programming Languages & Model Theory, Vol. 5. Ed. by Manfred Droste & Yuri Gurevich. LC 93-18657. (Algebra, Logic & Applications Ser.: Vol. 5). 416p. 1993. text ed. 99.00 (*2-88124-935-3*) Gordon & Breach.

Semantics of Sequential & Parallel Programs. Eike Best. 1996. pap. 49.00 (*0-13-460643-4*) P-H.

Semantics of Specification Langauges (SoSL) Proceedings of the International Workshop on Semantics of Specification Languages, Utrecht, the Netherlands, October 1993. D. J. Andrews et al. LC 94-2518. (Workshops in Computing Ser.). 1994. 78.95 (*0-387-19854-7*) Spr-Verlag.

Semantics of Syntactic Change: Aspects of the Evolution of "Do" in English. Dieter Stein. (Trends in Linguistics, Studies & Monographs: No. 47). xiv, 444p. (C). 1990. lib. bdg. 144.65 (*3-11-011283-3*) Mouton.

Semantics of Syntax: A Minimalist Approach to Grammar. Denis Bouchard. LC 95-8405. 540p. 1995. pap. text ed. 35.95 (*0-226-06733-5*) U Ch Pr.

Semantics of Syntax: A Minimalist Approach to Grammar. Denis Bouchard. LC 95-8405. 540p. 1995. lib. bdg. 95.00 (*0-226-06732-7*) U Ch Pr.

Semantics of Systems of Concurrent Processes: Proceedings of the LITP Spring School on Theoretical Computer Science La Roche Posay, France, April 23-27, 1990. Ed. by Irene Guessarian. (Lecture Notes in Computer Science Ser.: Vol. 469). v, 456p. 1990. 49.00 (*0-387-53479-2*) Spr-Verlag.

Semantics of the Modal Auxiliaries in Contemporary German. Lowell Bouma. (Janua Linguarum, Series Practica: No. 146). 1973. pap. text ed. 40.80 (*90-279-2390-6*) Mouton.

Semantics of Time: Aspectual Categorization in Koyukon Athabaskan. Melissa Axelrod. LC 92-42719. (Studies in the Anthropology of North American Indians). xii, 200p. 1993. text ed. 45.00 (*0-8032-1032-9*) U of Nebr Pr.

Semantics of Type Theory: Correctness, Completeness & Independence Results. T. Streicher. (Progress in Theoretical Computer Science Ser.). xii, 298p. 1991. 85.00 (*0-8176-3594-7*) Birkhauser.

Semantics One. John Lyons. LC 76-40838. (Illus.). 384p. 1977. pap. text ed. 29.95 (*0-521-29165-8*) Cambridge U Pr.

Semantics Two. John Lyons. LC 76-40838. (Illus.). 460p. 1977. text ed. 85.00 (*0-521-21560-9*); pap. text ed. 29.95 (*0-521-29186-0*) Cambridge U Pr.

Semantik-Semantics: Ein Internationales Handbuch der Zeitgenossichen Forschung. Ed. by Arnim Von Stechow & Dieter Wunderlich. (Handbooks of Linguistics & Communication Science: Bd. 6). xiii, 922p. (GER.). (C). 1991. lib. bdg. 484.65 (*3-11-012696-6*) De Gruyter.

Semantik und Lexikographie: Untersuchungen zur lexikalischen Kodifikation der deutschen Sprache. Helmut Henne. (Studia Linguistica Germanica: Vol. 7). 144p. (C). 1972. 89.25 (*3-11-003528-6*) De Gruyter.

Semantique et Poetique. Maurice Molho. (Coll. Ducros, Ser.). 9.95 (*0-685-36656-1*) Fr & Eur.

Semantische Strukturen im Bereich der alt und mittelhochdeutschen Schallwoerter. Andreas Loetscher. (Quellen und Forschungen zur Sprach und Kulturgeschichte der Germanischen Voelker Ser.: NF 53). (C). 1973. 86.15 (*3-11-003870-6*) De Gruyter.

Semantography. Jonathon J. Thompson, Jr. (Illus.). 60p. (YA). (gr. 7-12). 1992. write for info. (*0-933479-13-1*) Thompson.

Sematech's Technological Progress & Proposed R & D Program. (Illus.). 51p. (Orig.). (C). 1994. pap. text ed. 25.00 (*0-7881-0369-5*) DIANE Pub.

***Semblance of Subjectivity: Essays in Adorno's Aesthetic Theory.** Ed. by Tom Huhn & Lambert Zuidervaart. LC 96-37741. (Studies in Contemporary German Social Thought Ser.). (Illus.). 352p. 1997. 35.00 (*0-262-08257-8*) MIT Pr.

Semblances (1962-1971) Vincent B. Price. 1976. pap. 4.95 (*0-913270-64-4*) Sunstone Pr.

Semblanza y Circunstancia de Manuel Gonzalez Prada. Catherine Rovira. LC 93-72951. (Coleccion Polymita). 142p. (Orig.). (SPA.). 1993. pap. 19.00 (*0-89729-704-0*) Ediciones.

Sembrando Amor. (Serie Sembrando - Seeds of...Ser.). 24p. (SPA.). 1977. pap. 1.50 (*0-8423-6329-7*, 490464) Editorial Unilit.

Sembrando Confianza. (Serie Sembrando - Seeds of...Ser.). 24p. (SPA.). 1977. pap. 1.50 (*0-8423-6332-7*, 490467) Editorial Unilit.

Sembrando Consuelo. (Serie Sembrando - Seeds of...Ser.). 24p. (SPA.). 1977. pap. 1.50 (*0-8423-6331-9*, 490466) Editorial Unilit.

Sembrando Esperanza. (Serie Sembrando - Seeds of...Ser.). 24p. (SPA.). 1977. pap. 1.50 (*0-8423-6333-5*, 490468) Editorial Unilit.

Sembrando Gozo. (Serie Sembrando - Seeds of...Ser.). 24p. (SPA.). 1977. pap. 1.50 (*0-8423-6326-2*, 490461) Editorial Unilit.

Sembrando Gratitud. (Serie Sembrando - Seeds of...Ser.). 24p. (SPA.). 1977. pap. 1.50 (*0-8423-6327-0*, 490462) Editorial Unilit.

***Sembrando Gratitud.** (Serie Sembrando - Seeds of...Ser.). 26p. (SPA.). 1986. pap. write for info. (*0-614-27138-X*) Editorial Unilit.

Sembrando Paz. (Serie Sembrando - Seeds of...Ser.). 24p. (SPA.). 1977. pap. 1.50 (*0-8423-6330-0*, 490465) Editorial Unilit.

Sembrando Seguridad. (Serie Sembrando - Seeds of...Ser.). 24p. (SPA.). 1977. pap. 1.50 (*0-8423-6328-9*, 490463) Editorial Unilit.

***Sembrando y Sanando en Puerto Rico: Tradiciones y Visiones para un Futuro Verde.** Maria Benedetti. (Illus.). 360p. (Orig.). (ENG & SPA.). 1996. pap. 23.00 (*0-9633440-0-5*) Verde Luz.

Sembrar en Tierra Buena. Lope De Vega. 228p. (SPA.). 1968. 10.95 (*0-8288-7152-3*, S18402) Fr & Eur.

Sembrar Sopa de Verduras. Lois Ehlert. Tr. by Alma F. Ada & F. Isabel Campoy. (Illus.). 32p. (SPA.). (J). (ps-3). 1996. pap. 6.00 (*0-15-201202-X*, Voyager Bks) HarBrace.

Sembraron la No Siembra: Los Cosecheros de Tabaco Puertorriquenos Frente a las Corporaciones Tabacaleras, 1920-1934. Juan J. Baldrich. LC 88-81126. (Coleccion Semilla). 194p. (SPA.). 1988. pap. 7.50 (*0-940238-08-X*) Ediciones Huracan.

Seme: Aleksandr Pushkin. 176p. 1982. 35.00 (*0-317-40661-2*) St Mut.

Seme: The Founder of the ANC. Richard Rive & Tim Couzens. LC 91-78313. 100p. 1992. 29.95 (*0-86543-312-7*); pap. 9.95 (*0-86543-313-5*) Africa World.

Semeiosis of Poetic Metaphor. Michael C. Haley. LC 87-46087. (Peirce Studies: No. 4). (Illus.). 192p. 1989. 10.95 (*0-253-35179-0*) Ind U Pr.

Semeiotike: Recherche pour une Semanalyse. Julia Kristeva. (FRE.). 1978. pap. 16.95 (*0-7859-2675-5*) Fr & Eur.

Semelai Culture & Resin Technology. Rosemary Gianno. (Memoirs of the Connecticut Academy of Arts & Sciences Ser.: Vol. 22). (Illus.). 238p. 1990. 50.00 (*1-878508-00-8*) CT Acad Arts & Sciences.

Semen Analysis. A. M. Jequier & J. P. Crich. (Illus.). 160p. 1986. 85.00 (*0-632-01591-8*) Blackwell Sci.

Semences de la Colere. Anthony Lespes. (B. E. Ser.: No. 49). (FRE.). 1949. 35.00 (*0-8115-3000-0*) Periodicals Srv.

Semi-Automatic Pistol in Police Service & Self Defense. Massad F. Ayoob. 1987. pap. 9.95 (*0-936279-07-9*) Police Bkshelf.

Semi-Automatic Welding Processes. Henry L. Jackson. 75p. (C). 1996. pap. text ed. 28.00 (*1-881870-01-4*) BJ Pubns.

***Semi-Centenarians of Butler Grove Township, Montgomery Co. Illinois: Also a Brief History of the Village of Butler.** T. E. Spilman. (Illus.). 143p. 1997. reprint ed. pap. 19.00 (*0-8328-5718-1*) Higginson Bk Co.

Semi-Centenary & the Retrospection of the African Methodist Episcopal Church. Daniel A. Payne. LC 76-37598. (Black Heritage Library Collection). 1977. reprint ed. 25.95 (*0-8369-8974-0*) Ayer.

Semi-Centenary Discourse. William T. Catto. LC 78-154073. (Black Heritage Library Collection). 1977. 19.95 (*0-8369-8784-5*) Ayer.

Semi-Centennial Anniversary of the National Academy of Sciences: And a History of the First Half-Century of the National Academy of Sciences, 2 Vols., Set. Ed. by Frederick W. True & I. Bernard Cohen. LC 79-7977. (Three Centuries of Science in America Ser.). (Illus.). 1980. reprint ed. lib. bdg. 53.95 (*0-405-12560-7*) Ayer.

Semi-centennial of the Public Career of W. H. Gibson, Sr., from the Year 1847 to 1897 see History of the United Brothers of Friendship, & Sisters of the Mysterious Ten

Semi-Classical Analysis for the Schrodinger Operator & Applications. B. Helffer. (Lecture Notes in Mathematics Ser.: Vol. 1336). v, 107p. 1988. 30.95 (*0-387-50076-6*) Spr-Verlag.

Semi-Classical Methods for Nucleus-Nucleus Scattering. D. M. Brink. (Cambridge Monographs on Mathematical Physics). 300p. 1986. text ed. 49.95 (*0-521-23940-0*) Cambridge U Pr.

Semi Closed Openings in Action. Anatoly Karpov. Tr. by Ian White from RUS. (Illus.). 144p. (Orig.). 1990. pap. 14.95 (*0-02-021805-2*) Macmillan.

Semi-Conductor Devices: Testing & Evaluation. Charles E. Jowett. 1974. 28.00 (*0-8464-0835-X*) Beekman Pubs.

Semi-Constructs of the Secretaire De Registre. Carl D. Clark & Loris Essary. 1980. pap. 2.00 (*0-918406-07-2*) Future Pr.

Semi-Custom IC Design & VLSI. Ed. by P. J. Hicks et al. (Digital Electronics, Computing & Software Engineering Ser.). 218p. 1984. boxed 69.00 (*0-86341-011-1*, CM001) Inst Elect Eng.

Semi-Deep Thoughts. Merrit Malloy. 1996. mass mkt. 5.99 (*0-7860-0278-6*, Pinncle Kensgtn) Kensgtn Pub Corp.

Semi-Detached: Manuscript Edition. David Turner. 1971. pap. 13.00 (*0-8222-1009-6*) Dramatists Play.

Semi-Detached Teachers: Building Advisory & Support Relationships in Classrooms. Colin Biott. 1990. 55.00 (*1-85000-442-0*, Falmer Pr); pap. 27.00 (*1-85000-443-9*, Falmer Pr) Taylor & Francis.

Semi-Empirical Self-Consistent-Field Molecular Orbital Theory of Molecules. John N. Murrell & A. J. Harget. LC 71-172470. (Illus.). 190p. reprint ed. pap. 54.20 (*0-685-20751-X*, 2030392) Bks Demand.

***Semi-Football: Love Stories of the National Amateur Football League.** Matt Schroeder. LC 96-92688. (Illus.). 133p. (Orig.). 1996. pap. 11.95 (*0-9654453-0-5*) Spaldings Revenge.

Semi-Infinite Programming: Proceedings. Ed. by R. Hettich. (Lecture Notes in Control & Information Sciences Ser.: Vol. 15). (Illus.). 1979. pap. 19.00 (*0-387-09479-2*) Spr-Verlag.

Semi-Infinite Programming & Applications. Ed. by Anthony V. Fiacco & K. O. Kortanek. (Lecture Notes in Economics & Mathematical Systems Ser.: Vol. 215). 322p. 1983. 41.00 (*0-387-12304-0*) Spr-Verlag.

Semi-Insulating III-V Materials: Nottingham 1980. Ed. by P. R. Jay et al. 360p. 1980. 37.95 (*0-906812-05-4*) Birkhauser.

Semi-Insulating III-V Materials: Proceedings of the 8th Conference. M. Godlewski. 380p. 1995. text ed. 86.00 (*981-02-2008-1*) World Scientific Pub.

Semi-Insulating III-V Materials, Ixtapa, Mexico, 1992: Proceedings of the 7th Conference on Semi-Insulating III-V Materials, Ixtapa, Mexico, 21-24 April 1992. Ed. by C. J. Miner et al. (Illus.). 360p. 1993. 146.00 (*0-7503-0242-9*) IOP Pub.

Semi-Insulating III-V Materials, Toronto, 1990. Ed. by A. Milnes & C. J. Miner. (Illus.). 480p. 1991. 132.00 (*0-7503-0066-3*) IOP Pub.

Semi-Insulating Three-Four Materials: Evian 1982. Ed. by S. Makram-Ebeid & B. Tuck. 420p. 1980. 62.95 (*0-906812-22-4*) Birkhauser.

Semi-Linear Hyperbolic Problems in Bounded Domains, Vol. 3. A. Haraux. Ed. by J. Dieudonne. (Mathematical Reports: Vol. 3, No. 1). 284p. 1987. pap. text ed. 198.00 (*3-7186-0460-4*) Gordon & Breach.

Semi-Markov Models: Theory & Applications. Ed. by Jacques Janssen. 598p. 1986. 125.00 (*0-306-42362-6*, Plenum Pr) Plenum.

Semi-Markov Random Evolutions. Vladimir S. Korolyuk. Ed. by A. Swishchuk. (Mathematics & Its Applications Ser.: No. 308). x, 310p. (C). 1994. lib. bdg. 158.50 (*0-7923-3150-8*) Kluwer Ac.

Semi-Open Game in Action. Anatoly Karpov. 1989. pap. 14.95 (*0-02-021801-X*) Macmillan.

Semi-Open Games, Vol. 2 see Comprehensive Chess Openings

Semi-Professions & Their Organization: Teachers, Nurses, Social Workers. Amitai Etzioni. LC 69-10481. 350p. reprint ed. pap. 99.80 (*0-317-29974-3*, 2051760) Bks Demand.

Semi-Riemannian Geometry: With Applications to Relativity. Barrett O'Neill. (Pure & Applied Mathematics Ser.). 1983. text ed. 94.00 (*0-12-526740-1*) Acad Pr.

Semi-Rigid Connections in Steel Frames. Wai-Fah Chen. 320p. 1993. text ed. 39.00 (*0-07-012535-X*) McGraw.

Semi-Simple Lie Algebras & their Representations. Robert N. Cahn. (Frontiers in Physics Ser.). 300p. (C). 1984. text ed. 23.96 (*0-8053-1600-0*, 31600, Adv Bk Prog) Addison-Wesley.

***Semi-Simple Zeta Function of Quaternionic Shimura Varieties.** Harry Reimann. LC 97-6505. (Lecture Notes in Mathematics Ser.: Vol. 165). 1997. pap. write for info. (*3-540-62645-X*) Spr-Verlag.

Semi-Solid Processing. K. P. Young. (Illus.). 224p. 1997. 73.95 (*0-412-61980-6*) Chapman & Hall.

***Semi-Solid Processing of Alloys & Composites: Proceedings of the Second International Conference: Massachusetts Institute of Technology, Cambridge, Massachusetts, June 10-12, 1992.** International Conference on the Semi-Solid Processing of Alloys & Composites Staff. Ed. by Stuart B. Brown & Merton C. Flemings. LC 93-79601. (Illus.). 479p. 1993. reprint ed. pap. 136.60 (*0-608-02491-0*, 2063135) Bks Demand.

Semi-Sovereign People. Schattschneider. 143p. (C). 1975. pap. text ed. 20.00 (*0-03-013366-1*) HB Coll Pubs.

Semi-Transparent Envelope: Women Writing - Feminism & Fiction. Nicole W. Jouve et al. 208p. (Orig.). 1995. pap. 16.95 (*0-7145-2967-2*) M Boyars Pubs.

***Semi Trucks in Action.** Robert Genat. (Enthusiast Color Ser.). (Illus.). 96p. 1997. pap. 12.95 (*0-7603-0345-2*) Motorbooks Intl.

Semialignment & Western Security. Ed. by Nils Orvik. LC 85-26274. 320p. 1986. text ed. 39.95 (*0-312-71274-X*) St Martin.

Semiaquatic & Aquatic Hemiptera of California: Heteroptera: Hemiptera. Ed. by Arnold S. Menke. LC 77-91755. (Bulletin of the California Insect Survey Ser.: Vol. 21). 178p. reprint ed. pap. 50.80 (*0-317-30426-7*, 2024935) Bks Demand.

Semiarid Lands & Deserts: Soil Resource & Reclamation. Ed. by J. Skujins. (Books in Soils, Plants & the Environment: Vol. 19). 648p. 1991. 235.00 (*0-8247-8388-3*) Dekker.

Semiarid Soil & Water Conservation. Herman J. Finkel. LC 85-29157. 136p. 1986. 83.00 (*0-8493-6112-5*) CRC Pr.

Semicentennial Addresses of the American Mathematical Society, Vol. 2. 316p. 1988. reprint ed. 49.00 (*0-8218-0119-8*, PROCSEMI) Am Math.

Semicentennial History of the American Mathematical Society: Eighteen Hundred Eighty-Eight to Nineteen Hundred Thirty-Eight; with Biographies & Bibliographies Odents, 2 Vols., Set. Raymond C. Archibald. Ed. by I. Bernard Cohen. LC 79-7947. (Three Centuries of Science in America Ser.). (Illus.). 1980. reprint ed. lib. bdg. 60.95 (*0-405-12528-3*) Ayer.

Semicentennial History of the American Mathematical Society (1888-1938), Set. R. Archibald. (Procsemi Ser.: Vol. 1). 262p. 1988. reprint ed. pap. text ed. 90.00 (*0-8218-0128-7*, SEMISET) Am Math.

Semicentennial History of the American Mathematical Society, 1888-1938, Vol. 1. Raymond C. Archibald. 1980. 30.95 (*0-405-12618-2*) Ayer.

Semicentennial History of the American Mathematical Society (1888-1938), Vol. 1. R. Archibald. 262p. 1988. reprint ed. text ed. 52.00 (*0-8218-0118-X*, HMREPRINT) Am Math.

Semiclassical Mechanics with Molecular Applications. M. S. Child. (International Series of Monographs on Chemistry: No. 25). (Illus.). 432p. 1991. 105.00 (*0-19-855654-3*) OUP.

Semiclassical Methods in Mean-Field Systems. Bhaduri. (C). 1997. 55.95 (*0-201-48351-3*) Addison-Wesley.

Semiclassical Methods in Molecular Scattering & Spectroscopy: Proceedings of the NATO Advanced Study Institute, Cambridge, England, September, 1979. NATO Advanced Study Institute Staff. Ed. by M. S. Child. (NATO Advanced Study Institutes Series C, Mathematical & Physical Sciences: No. 53). 344p. 1980. lib. bdg. 112.00 (*90-277-1082-1*) Kluwer Ac.

Semiclassical Theories of Molecular Scattering. Byung C. Eu. (Chemical Physics Ser.: Vol. 26). (Illus.). 240p. 1983. 56.95 (*0-387-12410-1*) Spr-Verlag.

Semiclassical Theory of Atoms. B. G. Englert. (Lecture Notes in Physics Ser.: Vol. 300). vii, 401p. 1988. 47.95 (*0-387-19204-2*) Spr-Verlag.

Semiclassical Theory of Shape Resonances in Quantum Mechanics. P. Hislop & I. Sigal. LC 89-182. (Memoirs Ser.: Vol. 78/399). 123p. 1989. pap. 19.00 (*0-8218-2462-7*, MEMO/78/399) Am Math.

Semiclassical Theory of the Gas Laser see Progress in Quantum Electronics

Semiconducting Lead Chalcogenides. Uri I. Ravich et al. Ed. by L. S. Stillbans & Albin Tybulewicz. LC 77-107542. (Monographs in Semiconductor Physics: Vol. 5). 393p. reprint ed. pap. 112.10 (*0-685-15851-9*, 2026308) Bks Demand.

Semiconducting Transparent Thin Films. H. L. Hartnagel et al. LC 95-30589. (Illus.). 358p. 1995. 180.00 (*0-7503-0322-0*) IOP Pub.

Semiconductor & Integrated Circuit Technology: Beijing, China, October 19-26 1986. Ed. by X. Y. Wang & B. X. Mo. 872p. 1986. text ed. 148.00 (*9971-5-0196-1*) World Scientific Pub.

Semiconductor & Metal Binary Systems: Phase Equilibria & Chemical Thermodynamics. V. M. Glazov & L. M. Pavlova. Tr. by E. A. White from RUS. (Illus.). 320p. 1989. 105.00 (*0-306-11025-3*, Consultants) Plenum.

Semiconductor & Microprocesor Technology 1979: Proceedings of the Seminex Technical Seminar & Exhibition, London, England, March 26-30, 1979. SEMINEX Staff. Ed. by Geoffrey W. Dummer. (Illus.). 252p. 1980. pap. 61.00 (*0-08-026134-5*, Pergamon Pr) Elsevier.

Semiconductor & Microprocessor Technology 1980: Selected Papers Presented at the Annual SEMINEX Technical Seminar & Exhibition, London, U. K. Ed. by Geoffrey W. Dummer & Malvern Wells. 190p. 1981. pap. 48.00 (*0-08-028674-7*, Pergamon Pr) Elsevier.

Semiconductor & Microprocessor Technology 1981: Selected Papers Presented at the 1981 Annual Seminex Technical Seminar & Exhibition, London, U. K. Ed. by Geoffrey W. Dummer. 144p. 1982. pap. 47.00 (*0-08-028722-0*, Pergamon Pr) Elsevier.

S

Semiconductor-Based Heterostructures: Interfacial Structure & Stability: Proceedings of the Northeast Regional Meeting of the Metallurgical Society, Sponsored by the New Jersey Chapter & the Materials Research Society, Held at AT & T Bell Laboratories, Murray Hill, New Jersey, May 1-2, 1986. Metallurgical Society Of Aime Staff. LC 86-23799. (Illus.). 474p. reprint ed. pap. 135.10 (*0-7837-4076-X*, 2052473) Bks Demand.

Semiconductor Ceramics: Grain Boundary Effects. Leszek Hozer. 160p. 1994. text ed. 79.00 (*0-13-808049-6*) P-H.

Semiconductor Characterization: Present Status & Future Needs: Gaithersburg, MD, January 30-February 2, 1995. W. Murray Bullis. Ed. by D. G. Seiler & A. C. Diebold. (Illus.). 730p. 1996. text ed. 78.00 (*1-56396-503-8*) Am Inst Physics.

Semiconductor Characterization Techniques: Proceedings of the Topical Conference on Characterization Techniques for Semi-Conductor Materials & Devices, Seattle, 1978. Topical Conference on Characterization Techniques for Semi-Conductor Materials & Devices Staff. Ed. by George A. Rozgonyi et al. LC 78-67994. (Electrochemical Society Proceedings Ser.: Vol. 78-3). (Illus.). 544p. reprint ed. pap. 155.10 (*0-317-09572-2*, 2051951) Bks Demand.

Semiconductor Chip Protection Act of 1984: Analysis, History & Practical Applications, 2 vols. Computer Law Reporter Editors. 140.00 (*0-318-04464-1*) Comp Law Rep.

Semiconductor Circuit Approximations: An Introduction to Transistors & Integrated Circuits; Experiments for Semiconductor Circuit Approximations. 4th ed. Albert P. Malvino. 128p. 1985. text ed. 42.95 (*0-07-039898-4*); 17.95 (*0-07-039899-2*) McGraw.

Semiconductor Cleaning Technology - 1991. Ed. by R. E. Novak & Jerzy Ruzyllo. LC 92-71447. (Proceedings Ser.: Vol. 92-12). 500p. 1992. 53.00 (*1-56677-012-2*) Electrochem Soc.

Semiconductor Cleaning Technology, 1989: Proceedings of the First International Symposium on Cleaning Technology in Semiconductor Device Manufacturing. International Symposium on Cleaning Technology in Semiconductor Device Manufacturing Staff. Ed. by Jerzy Ruzyllo & Richard E. Novak. LC 90-81371. (Electrochemical Society Proceedings Ser.: No. 90-9). (Illus.). 409p. 1990. reprint ed. pap. 116.60 (*0-7837-9643-9*, 2059276) Bks Demand.

Semiconductor Competition & National Security. Daniel I. Okimoto et al. (Special Report of the Northeast Asia-United States Forum on International Policy, Stanford University Ser.). 87p. (Orig.). 1987. pap. 12.00 (*0-935371-16-8*) CFISAC.

Semiconductor Compounds, II-VI. M. Jain. 604p. 1993. text ed. 121.00 (*981-02-1074-4*) World Scientific Pub.

Semiconductor Contacts: An Approach to Ideas & Models. Heinz K. Henisch. (International Series of Monographs on Physics: No. 70). (Illus.). 400p. 1989. reprint ed. pap. 45.00 (*0-19-852035-2*) OUP.

***Semiconductor Cross Reference Book.** 4th rev. ed. Howard W. Sams & Company Engineering Staff. 688p. 1996. pap. 24.95 (*0-7906-1080-9*) Prompt Publns.

Semiconductor Detectors. (Advanced Health Physics Training Ser.). (Illus.). 106p. 1983. ring bd. 69.50 (*0-87683-198-6*) GP Courseware.

Semiconductor Device. Christou. 1990. lib. bdg. 251.50 (*0-7923-0536-1*) Kluwer Ac.

Semiconductor-Device Electronics. R. M. Warner, Jr. & B. L. Grung. (Oxford Series in Electrical & Computer Engineering). (Illus.). 958p. (C). 1995. text ed. 73.00 (*0-03-009559-X*); Solutions manual. pap. text ed. write for info. (*0-03-009562-X*) OUP.

Semiconductor Device Fundamentals. Robert F. Pierret. Ed. by Katherine Harutunian. LC 95-17387. 800p. (C). 1996. text ed. 72.95 (*0-201-54393-1*) Addison-Wesley.

Semiconductor Device Modeling for VLSI. Michael Shur et al. 450p. 1993. text ed. 52.60 (*0-13-805656-0*) P-H.

Semiconductor Device Modeling with Spice. 2nd ed. Paolo Antognetti. LC 93-9726. 1993. text ed. 60.00 (*0-07-002469-3*) McGraw.

Semiconductor Device Modelling. C. M. Snowden. (Materials & Devices Ser.: No. 5). 224p. 1988. text ed. 92.00 (*0-86341-130-4*, ED005) Inst Elect Eng.

Semiconductor Device Modelling. Ed. by C. M. Snowden. (Illus.). 285p. 1989. 68.95 (*0-387-19545-9*) Spr-Verlag.

Semiconductor Device Processing: Technology Trends in the VLSI Era. Robert N. Castellano. LC 91-36127. 234p. 1992. text ed. 59.00 (*2-88124-516-1*) Gordon & Breach.

Semiconductor Devices. Heath Company Staff. (Fundamental Electronics Ser.). (Illus.). 365p. (C). 1978. teacher ed. 9.95 (*0-87119-006-0*); student ed. 10.95 (*0-87119-005-2*); pap. text ed. 19.95 (*0-87119-004-4*) Heathkit-Zenith Ed.

***Semiconductor Devices.** Kano. LC 97-13152. 1997. text ed. 84.00 (*0-02-361938-4*) P-H.

Semiconductor Devices. Simon M. Sze. LC 85-3217. 523p. 1985. Net. text ed. 54.50 (*0-471-87424-8*) Wiley.

Semiconductor Devices. Mauro Zambuto. 448p. 1989. text ed. write for info. (*0-07-072700-7*) McGraw.

Semiconductor Devices. rev. ed. Heath Company Staff. (Fundamental Electronics Ser.). (Illus.). 476p. (C). 1982. ring bd. 54.95 (*0-87119-003-6*, EE-3103A) Heathkit-Zenith Ed.

Semiconductor Devices. 2nd ed. J. J. Sparkles. (Tutorial Guides in Electronic Engineering Ser.: 12). 224p. (gr. 13). 1994. pap. text ed. 28.95 (*0-412-58770-X*) Chapman & Hall.

***Semiconductor Devices: A Simulation Approach.** Kramer & Hitchon. (C). 1997. text ed. 45.00 (*0-13-614330-X*) P-H.

S

Semiconductor Devices: An Introduction. Jasprit Singh. 1994. text ed. write for info. (*0-07-057625-4*) McGraw.

Semiconductor Devices: Pioneering Papers. Ed. by Simon M. Sze. 1028p. (C). 1991. text ed. 141.00 (*981-02-0209-1*); pap. text ed. 61.00 (*981-02-0210-5*) World Scientific Pub.

Semiconductor Devices, Circuits & Systems. Albrecht Moschwitzer. (Monographs in Electrical & Electronic Engineering). (Illus.). 368p. 1991. 85.00 (*0-19-859374-0*) OUP.

Semiconductor Devices for Electronic Tuners, Vol. 3. S. Watanabe. (Japanese Technology Reviews Ser.: Sec. A). 142p. 1991. text ed. 103.00 (*2-88124-475-0*) Gordon & Breach.

Semiconductor Devices for Optical Communication. 2nd ed. Ed. by H. Kressel. (Topics in Applied Physics Ser.: Vol. 39). (Illus.). 325p. 1990. 71.95 (*0-387-11348-7*) Spr-Verlag.

Semiconductor Devices Using Electronic Workbench. John P. Borris. LC 95-18949. 150p. 1995. pap. text ed. 48.00 (*0-13-409814-5*) P-H.

Semiconductor Electrodes. Ed. by H. O. Finklea. (Studies in Physical & Theoretical Chemistry: Vol. 55). 520p. 1988. 273.25 (*0-444-42926-3*) Elsevier.

Semiconductor Electronic Devices. G. Sanders. 1991. text ed. write for info. (*0-442-00621-7*) Van Nos Reinhold.

Semiconductor Equations. P. A. Markowich. (Illus.). 250p. 1990. 86.95 (*0-387-82157-0*) Spr-Verlag.

Semiconductor Essentials: For Hobbyists, Technicians & Engineers. Stephen Kamichik. (Illus.). 112p. 1995. pap. 16.95 (*0-7906-1071-X*) Prompt Publns.

Semiconductor Fabrication: Technology & Metrology. Ed. by Dinesh C. Gupta. (Special Technical Publication Ser.: No. STP 990). (Illus.). 470p. 1989. text ed. 55.00 (*0-8031-1273-4*, 04-990000-46) ASTM.

Semiconductor Fundamentals. Buck Engineering Staff. Ed. by Buck Engineering Tech. Writers. (F. A. C. E. T. Ser.: Vol. 5). (Illus.). 60p. 1988. teacher ed., pap. text ed. 11.00 (*0-86657-017-9*); ring bd. 13.00 (*0-86657-016-0*) Lab-Volt.

Semiconductor Fundamentals. 2nd ed. Robert F. Pierret. (Modular Series on Solid State Devices). (Illus.). 128p. (C). 1988. pap. text ed. 18.25 (*0-201-12295-2*) Addison-Wesley.

***Semiconductor Gas Sensors.** INSPEC Staff. 85.00 (*0-614-18495-9*, 135P34) Info Gatekeepers.

***Semiconductor Growth, Surfaces & Interfaces.** Ed. by Davies & Williams. (Illus.). 176p. 1994. text ed. 52.95 (*0-412-57730-5*, Chap & Hall NY) Chapman & Hall.

Semiconductor Heteroepitaxy: Growth Characterization & Device Applications, Montpellier, France 4 - 7 July 1995. Ed. by B. Gil & R. L. Aulombard. 700p. 1995. text ed. 112.00 (*981-02-2479-6*, PcdE-P2950) World Scientific Pub.

Semiconductor Heterostructure Devices, Vol. 2. Masayuki Abe & Naoki Yokoyama. Ed. by Toshiaki Ikoma. (Japanese Technology Reviews Ser.: Vol. 8). 98p. 1989. pap. text ed. 120.00 (*2-88124-338-X*) Gordon & Breach.

Semiconductor Heterostructures. Alferov. 1990. 104.00 (*0-8493-7120-1*, TK) CRC Pr.

Semiconductor Heterostructures for Photonic & Electronic Applications. Ed. by D. C. Houghton et al. (Materials Research Society Symposium Proceedings Ser.: Vol. 281). 833p. 1993. text ed. 67.00 (*1-55899-176-X*) Materials Res.

Semiconductor Industrial Hygiene Handbook: Monitoring, Ventilation, Equipment, & Ergonomics. Michael E. Williams et al. LC 94-31248. (Illus.). 348p. 1995. 64.00 (*0-8155-1369-0*) Noyes.

Semiconductor Industry. Ed. by Peter Allen. 310p. 1984. pap. 295.00 (*0-931634-40-7*) FIND-SVP.

***Semiconductor Industry: Devices, Materials, Equipment, FABs - Forecasts to 2001.** (Report Ser.: No. GB-188). 161p. 1996. 3,000.00 (*1-56965-233-3*) BCC.

Semiconductor Industry in Southeast Asia: Organization, Location, & the International Division of Labor. Allen J. Scott. 57p. 1993. reprint ed. 7.00 (*0-685-62445-5*) U Cal LA Indus Rel.

Semiconductor Integrated Circuit Processing Technology. Walter R. Runyan & Kenneth E. Bean. (Electrical Engineering Ser.). (Illus.). 592p. (C). 1990. text ed. 75.25 (*0-201-10831-3*) Addison-Wesley.

Semiconductor Interfaces: Formation & Properties. G. Le Lay et al. (Proceedings in Physics Ser.: Vol. 22). (Illus.). 420p. 1987. 75.00 (*0-387-18328-0*) Spr-Verlag.

Semiconductor Interfaces & Microstructures. Ed. by Zhe C. Feng. LC 92-11298. 400p. 1992. 82.00 (*981-02-0988-6*); text ed. 95.00 (*981-02-0864-2*) World Scientific Pub.

Semiconductor Interfaces at the Sub-Nanometer Scale: Proceedings of the NATO Advanced Research Workshop on the Physical Properties, Riva del Garda, Italy, 31 August-2 September 1992. Ed. by H. W. Salemink & M. D. Pashley. LC 93-5134. (NATO Advanced Study Institutes Series E, Applied Sciences: Vol. 243). 268p. (C). 1993. lib. bdg. 144.00 (*0-7923-2397-1*) Kluwer Ac.

Semiconductor Interfaces, Microstructures & Devices: Properties & Applications. Ed. by Zhe C. Feng. (Illus.). 308p. 1993. 154.00 (*0-7503-0180-5*) IOP Pub.

Semiconductor Laser Diodes: A User's Handbook. M. E. Fabian. 1981. 200.00 (*0-686-71789-9*) St Mut.

Semiconductor-Laser Physics. W. W. Chow et al. LC 93-46745. (Illus.). xii, 497p. 1994. 54.95 (*0-387-57614-2*) Spr-Verlag.

Semiconductor Lasers. 2nd ed. Govind P. Agrawal & Niloy K. Dutta. LC 92-46782. 1993. text ed. 89.95 (*0-442-01102-4*) Van Nos Reinhold.

Semiconductor Lasers: Advanced Devices & Applications. LC 95-68687. (Nineteen Ninety-Five Technical Digest Ser.: Vol. 20). 221p. (Orig.). 1995. pap. 75.00 (*1-55752-410-6*) Optical Soc.

Semiconductor Lasers: Past, Present, & Future. Govind Agrawal. (Theoretical & Applied Optics Ser.). 360p. 1995. text ed. 75.00 (*1-56396-211-X*) Am Inst Physics.

Semiconductor Liquid-Junction Solar Cells: Proceedings of a Conference on the Electrochemistry & Physics of Semiconductor Liquid Interfaces under Illumination Held at Airlie, VA, May 3-5, 1977. Conference on the Electrochemistry & Physics of Semiconductor Liquid Interfaces under Illumination. LC 77-79771. (Electrochemical Society. Proceedings Ser.: Vol. 77-3). (Illus.). 339p. 1977. pap. 96.70 (*0-7837-8993-9*, 2059258) Bks Demand.

Semiconductor Lithography: Principles, Practices, & Materials. W. M. Moreau. LC 87-29077. (Microdevices: Physics & Fabrication Technologies Ser.). (Illus.). 952p. 1988. 149.50 (*0-306-42185-2*, Plenum Pr) Plenum.

Semiconductor Master Selection Guide. Texas Instruments Engineering Staff. 506p. 1990. 9.95 (*0-685-62522-2*, SSYC005B) Tex Instr Inc.

Semiconductor Material & Device Characterization. Dieter K. Schroder. LC 89-24881. 624p. 1990. text ed. 89.95 (*0-471-51104-8*) Wiley.

Semiconductor Materials. L. I. Berger. LC 96-41739. (Illus.). 464p. 1996. 99.95 (*0-8493-8912-7*) CRC Pr.

Semiconductor Materials Analysis & Fabrication Process Control. Ed. by G. M. Crean et al. (European Materials Research Society Symposia Proceedings Ser.: Vol. 34). xii, 338p. 1993. 215.75 (*0-444-89908-1*) Elsevier.

Semiconductor Materials & Process Technology Handbook: For Very Large Scale Integration (VLSI) & Ultra Large Scale Integration (ULSI) Ed. by Gary E. McGuire. LC 87-31529. (Illus.). 675p. 1988. 92.00 (*0-8155-1150-7*) Noyes.

Semiconductor Materials for Optoelectronics & LTMBE Materials. Ed. by J. P. Hirtz et al. 368p. 1993. 204.50 (*0-444-81769-7*, North Holland) Elsevier.

Semiconductor Measurement Technology: A Collection of Computer Programs for Two-Probe & Four-Probe Resistance. (Illus.). 110p. (Orig.). (C). 1994. pap. text ed. 95.00 (*0-7881-1124-8*) DIANE Pub.

***Semiconductor Measurements & Instrumentation.** 2nd ed. W. R. Runyan & T. J. Shaffner. 1997. text ed. 70.00 (*0-07-057697-1*) McGraw.

Semiconductor Memories. 2nd ed. Betty Prince. LC 91-6943. 500p. 1992. text ed. 110.00 (*0-471-92465-2*) Wiley.

Semiconductor Memories: A Handbook of Design Manufacturing & Application. 2nd ed. Betty Prince. 1996. pap. text ed. 69.95 (*0-471-94295-2*) Wiley.

Semiconductor Memories: Technology, Testing, & Reliability. Ashok K. Sharma. LC 96-6824. 480p. 1996. 99.95 (*0-7803-1000-4*, PC 3491) Inst Electrical.

***Semiconductor Memories: Testing & Reliability.** Rochit Rajusuman. 400p. 1997. pap. 45.00 (*0-8186-7797-X*, BP07797) IEEE Comp Soc.

Semiconductor Microdevices & Materials. David H. Navon. (Illus.). 80p. (C). 1995. Solutions manual. pap. text ed. write for info. (*0-03-063984-0*) OUP.

***Semiconductor Micromachining.** S. A. Campbell & H. J. Lewerenz. LC 97-26052. 1998. write for info. (*0-471-96681-9*) Wiley.

***Semiconductor Nanoclusters - Physical, Chemical, & Catalytic Aspects.** Prashant V. Kamat & Dan Meisel. LC 96-46447. (Studies in Surface Science & Catalysis). 484p. 1996. 272.00 (*0-444-82064-7*) Elsevier.

Semiconductor-On-Insulator & Thin Film Transistor Technology, Vol. 53. Ed. by Alpha C. Chiang et al. (Materials Research Society Symposium Proceedings Ser.). 1986. text ed. 17.50 (*0-931837-18-9*) Materials Res.

Semiconductor Optics. C. F. Klingshirn. LC 95-1801. 1995. write for info. (*3-540-58312-2*) Spr-Verlag.

***Semiconductor Optics.** C. F. Klingshirn. LC 96-46128. 1997. pap. 49.95 (*3-540-61687-X*) Spr-Verlag.

Semiconductor Optics. C. F. Klingshirn. (Illus.). 509p. 1995. 59.95 (*0-387-58312-2*) Spr-Verlag.

***Semiconductor Optics & Transport Phenomena: From Fundamentals to Current Physics.** Martin Wegener. 1997. 69.00 (*3-540-61614-4*) Spr-Verlag.

Semiconductor Opto-Electronics. Trevor S. Moss et al. LC 73-167813. 453p. reprint ed. pap. 129.20 (*0-317-41852-1*, 2025735) Bks Demand.

Semiconductor Optoelectronic: Physics & Technology. Jasprit Singh. 1994. text ed. 49.25 (*0-07-057637-8*) McGraw.

Semiconductor Optoelectronic Devices. 2nd ed. Pallab Bhattacharya. LC 96-35109. 613p. (C). 1996. text ed. 94.67 (*0-13-495656-7*) P-H.

***Semiconductor Packaging: A Multidisciplinary Approach.** Michael Hanneman et al. (Professional Paperback Ser.). 864p. 1997. pap. 49.95 (*0-471-18123-4*, EM15) Wiley.

Semiconductor Particle Detectors. James M. Taylor. LC 64-9673. (Semiconductor Monographs). 196p. reprint ed. pap. 55.90 (*0-317-09005-4*, 2051333) Bks Demand.

Semiconductor Photoelectrochemistry. Yu V. Pleskov & Y. Y. Gurevich. Tr. by P. N. Bartlett from RUS. LC 85-17411. 448p. 1985. 125.00 (*0-306-10983-2*, Consultants) Plenum.

Semiconductor Physical Electronics. Ed. by S. S. Li. (Microdevices: Physics & Fabrication Technologies Ser.). (Illus.). 565p. 1992. 65.00 (*0-306-44157-8*, Plenum Pr) Plenum.

Semiconductor Physics. Ed. by V. M. Tuchkevich & V. Ya. Frenkel. LC 86-18760. 562p. 1986. 145.00 (*0-306-10987-5*, Consultants) Plenum.

Semiconductor Physics. 3rd rev. ed. Karlheinz Seeger. (Solid-State Sciences Ser.: Vol. 40). (Illus.). 490p. 1985. 39.95 (*0-387-15578-3*) Spr-Verlag.

Semiconductor Physics. 4th ed. Karlheinz Seeger. (Solid-State Sciences Ser.: Vol. 40). (Illus.). xiv, 480p. 1989. pap. 45.00 (*0-387-19410-X*) Spr-Verlag.

Semiconductor Physics: An Introduction. 5th ed. Karlheinz Seeger. Ed. by H. J. Queisser et al. (Solid-State Sciences Ser.: Vol. 40). (Illus.). xiv, 502p. 1991. 77.95 (*0-387-53809-7*) Spr-Verlag.

Semiconductor Physics: Proceedings of the Third Brazilian School. Ed. by C. E. Goncalves da Silva et al. 328p. 1987. pap. 64.00 (*9971-5-0332-8*); text ed. 138.00 (*9971-5-0331-X*) World Scientific Pub.

Semiconductor Physics: Proceedings of the 4th Brazilian School. Ed. by A. S. Chaves et al. 472p. (C). 1990. text ed. 147.00 (*9971-5-0968-7*) World Scientific Pub.

Semiconductor Physics: Proceedings of the 5th Brazilian School. Ed. by J. R. Leite et al. 450p. (C). 1992. text ed. 127.00 (*981-02-0613-5*) World Scientific Pub.

***Semiconductor Physics Vol. XII: An Introduction.** 6th ed. Karlheinz Seeger. LC 96-42132. (Springer Series in Solid-State Sciences: Vol. 40). (Illus.). 515p. 1997. pap. 89.50 (*3-540-61507-5*) Spr-Verlag.

Semiconductor Physics & Devices. Donald A. Neamen. 550p. (C). 1992. text ed. 76.95 (*0-256-08405-X*) Irwin.

Semiconductor Physics Device: Basic Principles. 2nd ed. Donald A. Neamen. LC 96-44284. 800p. (C). 1996. 78.75 (*0-256-20869-7*) Irwin.

***Semiconductor Picture Dictionary.** 2nd ed. Howard K. Dicken. 1996. cd-rom 195.00 (*0-614-30074-6*) DM Data.

Semiconductor Picture Dictionary. 2nd ed. Ed. by Howard K. Dicken. (Illus.). 186p. 1996. student ed. 245.00 (*1-878266-03-9*) DM Data.

Semiconductor Power Electronics. Richard G. Hoft. 336p. (C). 1991. reprint ed. lib. bdg. 49.50 (*0-89464-568-4*) Krieger.

Semiconductor Processing - STP 850. Ed. by D. C. Gupta. 700p. 1984. 60.00 (*0-8031-0403-0*, 04-850000-46) ASTM.

Semiconductor Quantum Wells & Superlattices for Long-Wavelength Infrared Detectors. M. O. Manasreh. LC 92-32246. (Materials Ser.). 265p. (C). 1992. text ed. 85.00 (*0-89006-603-5*) Artech Hse.

Semiconductor Quatum Dots. L. Banyai & Stephan W. Koch. (Atomic, Molecular & Optical Ser.). 256p. 1993. text ed. 48.00 (*981-02-1390-5*) World Scientific Pub.

Semiconductor Raman Laser. Ken Suto & Junichi Nishizawa. LC 94-21067. 1994. 89.00 (*0-89006-667-1*) Artech Hse.

Semiconductor Science. Tudor E. Jenkins. LC 94-5370. (C). 1995. pap. text ed. 44.00 (*0-13-805771-0*) P-H.

Semiconductor Sensors. Ed. by Simon M. Sze. 560p. 1994. text ed. 79.95 (*0-471-54609-7*) Wiley.

Semiconductor Sensors in Physico-Chemical Studies. Ed. by L. Yu Kupriyanov. LC 96-5829. (Handbook of Sensors & Actuators Ser.: Vol. 4). 412p. 1996. text ed. 185.25 (*0-444-82261-5*) Elsevier.

Semiconductor Silicon. Ed. by G. C. Harbeke et al. (Materials Science Ser.: Vol. 13). (Illus.). 360p. 1989. 83.95 (*0-387-51073-7*) Spr-Verlag.

Semiconductor Silicon: Proceedings of the International Symposium on Silicon Materials, Science & Technology, 2nd, Chicago, 1973. International Symposium on Silicon Materials, Science & Technology Staff. Ed. by Howard R. Huff & Ronald R. Burgess. (Illus.). 936p. reprint ed. pap. 180.00 (*0-317-08778-9*, 2051088) Bks Demand.

Semiconductor Silicon, 1977. International Symposium on Silicon Materials, Science & Technology Staff. Ed. by Howard R. Huff & Erhard Sirtl. LC 77-76669. (Proceedings Ser.: Vol. 77-2). 1118p. reprint ed. pap. 180.00 (*0-7837-5646-1*, 2052498) Bks Demand.

Semiconductor Silicon, 1981: Proceedings of the 4th International Symposium on Silicon Materials Science & Technology. International Symposium on Silicon Materials, Science & Technology Staff. Ed. by Howard R. Huff et al. LC 69-17607. (Illus.). 1063p. reprint ed. pap. 180.00 (*0-7837-6108-2*, 2059154) Bks Demand.

Semiconductor Statistics. J. S. Blakemore. 416p. 1987. reprint ed. pap. text ed. 10.95 (*0-486-65362-5*) Dover.

Semiconductor Superlattices: Growth & Electronic Properties. H. Grahn. 268p. 1995. text ed. 74.00 (*981-02-2061-8*) World Scientific Pub.

Semiconductor Superlattices & Interfaces: Varenna on Lake Como, Villa Monsatero, 25 June-5 July 1991. Ed. by A. Stella & L. Miglio. LC 93-28288. 492p. 1993. 248.25 (*0-444-81643-7*, North Holland) Elsevier.

Semiconductor Surfaces & Interfaces. Winfried Monch. LC 93-9523. (Surface Sciences Ser.: Vol. 26). 1993. 79.00 (*0-387-54423-2*) Spr-Verlag.

Semiconductor Surfaces & Interfaces. 2nd ed. Winfried Monch. LC 95-1412. (Series in Surface Sciences: Vol. 26). 1995. write for info. (*0-358-67533-2*) Spr-Verlag.

Semiconductor Surfaces & Interfaces. 2nd ed. Winfried Monch. (Surface Sciences Ser.: Vol. 26). 432p. 1995. 49.95 (*3-540-58625-3*) Spr-Verlag.

Semiconductor Technologies 1982 see Japan Annual Reviews in Electronics, Computers & Telecommunications, 1982

***Semiconductor Technology: Processing & Novel Fabrication Techniques.** Mikhail Levinshtein & Michael Schur. 320p. 1997. 74.95 (*0-471-12792-2*) Wiley.

Semiconductor Technology 1975. Geoffrey W. Dummer. 1976. pap. 35.00 (*0-08-019976-3*, Pergamon Pr) Elsevier.

Semiconductor Technology 1976. Ed. by Geoffrey W. Dummer. 1977. pap. 35.00 (*0-08-020983-1*, Pergamon Pr) Elsevier.

Semiconductor Technology 1977. Geoffrey W. Dummer. 1977. pap. 43.00 (*0-08-022148-3*, Pergamon Pr) Elsevier.

Semiconductor Technology 1978. Geoffrey W. Dummer. 1979. pap. 57.00 (*0-08-024205-7*, Pergamon Pr) Elsevier.

***Semiconductor Terminology: Graphic Glossary of Terms.** 2nd ed. Beverly Griggs et al. Ed. by Kerry Lopez. (Illus.). 119p. (C). 1996. pap. 25.00 (*1-887574-00-X*) Semiconductor.

Semiconductor Wafer Bonding: Science, Technology & Applications: Third International Symposium. C. E. Hunt et al. 1995. 65.00 (*1-56677-101-3*, PV 95-7) Electrochem Soc.

***Semiconductor Water Bonding IV: Science, Technology, & Applications.** Ed. by U. Goesele et al. Date not set. 92.00 (*1-56677-189-7*, PV97-36) Electrochem Soc.

Semiconductors. David K. Ferry. 1991. write for info. (*0-02-337130-7*, Macmillan Coll) P-H.

Semiconductors. 2nd ed. OAS, General Secretariat, Department of Scientific & Technological Affairs Staff. (Serie de Fisica (Monograph on Physics): No. 6). 63p. (C). 1980. reprint ed. text ed. 3.50 (*0-8270-1068-0*) OAS.

Semiconductors. Helmut F. Wolf. LC 77-159286. (Illus.). 572p. reprint ed. pap. 163.10 (*0-317-09131-X*, 2055668) Bks Demand.

Semiconductors: Group IV-Elements & III-V-Compounds. Ed. by O. Madeling. (Data in Science & Technology Ser.). 200p. 1991. pap. 49.50 (*0-387-53150-5*) Spr-Verlag.

Semiconductors: Index of New Information & Research Bible of Current Reviews. Dean D. Dankovich. 150p. 1994. 44.50 (*0-7883-0028-8*); pap. 39.50 (*0-7883-0029-6*) ABBE Pubs Assn.

Semiconductors: Industry & Trade Summary. Andrew F. Malison. (Illus.). 53p. (Orig.). (C). 1994. pap. text ed. 30.00 (*0-7881-0320-2*) DIANE Pub.

Semiconductors: Others Than Group IV Elements & III-V Compounds. Ed. by Otfried Madelung & R. Poerschke. LC 92-8630. (Data in Science & Technology Ser.). vii, 153p. 1992. Berlin. write for info. (*3-540-55373-8*); New York. 64.95 (*0-387-55373-8*) Spr-Verlag.

Semiconductors & Electronic Devices. 3rd ed. Adir Bar-Lev. LC 92-30166. 480p. 1993. pap. text ed. 62.00 (*0-13-825209-2*) P-H.

Semiconductors & Insulators: Optical & Spectroscopic Research. Ed. by Yu I. Koptev. 385p. (C). 1993. lib. bdg. 140.00 (*1-56072-088-3*) Nova Sci Pubs.

Semiconductors & Rare Earth Based Materials. Ed. by Nguyen Van Hieu. 400p. (C). 1991. text ed. 104.00 (*981-02-0779-4*) World Scientific Pub.

Semiconductors & Semimetals: Spectroscopy of Semiconductors, Vol. 36. D. G. Seiler. (Illus.). 435p. 1992. text ed. 117.00 (*0-12-752136-4*) Acad Pr.

Semiconductors & Semimetals Vol. 42: Oxygen in Silicon. Ed. by Fumio Shimura. (Illus.). 679p. 1994. text ed. 178.00 (*0-12-752142-9*) Acad Pr.

Semiconductors & Semimetals Vol. 43: Semiconductors for Room Temperature Nuclear Detector Applications. T. E. Schlesinger & R. B. Jones. (Illus.). 606p. 1995. text ed. 140.00 (*0-12-752143-7*) Acad Pr.

***Semiconductors & Semimetals Vol. 44: II-VI Semiconductor Blue - Green Light Emitters.** Robert K. Willardson. (Illus.). 338p. 1997. boxed 119.00 (*0-12-752144-5*, AP Prof) Acad Pr.

***Semiconductors & Semimetals Vol. 45: Effect of Disorder & Defects in Ion-Implanted Semiconductors: Electrical & Physicochemical Characterization.** Ed. by Albert Beer et al. (Illus.). 300p. 1997. boxed 130.00 (*0-12-752145-3*, AP Prof) Acad Pr.

***Semiconductors & Semimetals Vol. 46: Effect of Disorder & Defects in Ion-Implanted Semiconductors: Optical & Photo-Thermal Characterization.** Ed. by Constantinos Christofides & Gerard Chibaudo. (Illus.). 316p. 1997. boxed 125.00 (*0-12-752146-1*, AP Prof) Acad Pr.

Semiconductors & Semimetals, Vol. 33: Strained-Layer Superlattices: Materials Science & Technology. Ed. by Thomas P. Pearsall. 431p. 1990. text ed. 131.00 (*0-12-752133-X*) Acad Pr.

Semiconductors & Semimetals, Vol. 34: Hydrogen in Semiconductors. Ed. by Robert K. Willardson et al. (Illus.). 629p. 1991. text ed. 194.00 (*0-12-752134-8*) Acad Pr.

Semiconductors & Semimetals, Vol. 35: Nanostructured Systems. Ed. by Robert K. Willardson et al. (Illus.). 387p. 1992. text ed. 100.00 (*0-12-752135-6*) Acad Pr.

An Asterisk (*) at the beginning of an entry indicates that the title is appearing in BIP for the first time.

Semiconductors & Semimetals, Vol. 40: Epitaxial Microstructures. Ed. by Arthur C. Gossard. (Illus.). 426p. 1994. text ed. 125.00 (*0-12-752140-2*) Acad Pr.

Semiconductors & Semimetals, Vol. 41: High Speed Heterostructure Devices. Ed. by Richard A. Kiehl & Gerhard Sollner. (Illus.). 454p. 1994. text ed. 125.00 (*0-12-752141-0*) Acad Pr.

Semiconductors Explained. Kathleen Barton. Ed. by Kelly Gorham. (Electricity & Electronics Ser.). 28p. (YA). (gr. 10 up). 1994. student ed. 7.00 (*0-8064-0015-3*, E30); audio, vhs 299.00 (*0-8064-0014-5*) Bergwall.

Semiconductors for Room-Temperature Radiation Detector Applications. Ed. by R. B. James et al. (Symposium Proceedings Ser.: Vol. 302). 609p. 1993. text ed. 67.00 (*1-55899-198-0*) Materials Res.

Semiconductors for Solar Cells. Hans J. Moller. LC 92-40718. (Optoelectronics Library). 275p. 1993. text ed. 69.00 (*0-89006-574-8*) Artech Hse.

Semiconductors, Part I. Ed. by W. M. Coughran, Jr. et al. LC 93-50622. (IMA Volumes in Mathematics & Its Applications Ser.: Vol. 58). (Illus.). xxiv, 154p. 1994. 59.95 (*0-387-94250-5*) Spr-Verlag.

Semiconductors, Part II. Ed. by W. M. Coughran, Jr. et al. LC 93-50622. (IMA Volumes in Mathematics & Its Applications Ser.: Vol. 59). (Illus.). xxii, 408p. 1994. 83.95 (*0-387-94251-3*) Spr-Verlag.

Semiconductors: Physics of Group IV Elements & IL-V Compounds see Crystal & Solid State Physics: Group III

Semiconductors, Subvol. B, Physics of II-VI & I-VII Compounds, Semimagnetic Conductors see Crystal & Solid State Physics: Group III

Semiconductors, Subvol. E, Physics of Non-Tetrahodrally Bonded Elements & Binary Compounds I see Crystal & Solid State Physics: Group III

Semidynamical Systems in Infinite Dimensional Spaces. S. H. Saperstone. (Applied Mathematical Sciences Ser.: Vol. 37). 474p. 1981. 83.95 (*0-387-90643-6*) Spr-Verlag.

Semiempirical Life. Michael J. Dewar. Ed. by Jeffrey I. Seeman. LC 90-911. (Profiles, Pathways, & Dreams Ser.). (Illus.). 202p. 1992. 34.95 (*0-8412-1771-8*) Am Chemical.

Semiempirical Wave-Mechanical Calculations Polyatomic Molecules: A Current Review. Raymond Daudel & Camille Sandorfy. LC 74-140525. (Yale Series in the Sciences). (Illus.). 147p. reprint ed. pap. 41.90 (*0-317-13001-3*, 2016797) Bks Demand.

Semigroup Algebras. Ed. by Jan Okninski. (Pure & Applied Mathematics Ser.: Vol. 138). 376p. 1990. 145.00 (*0-8247-8356-5*) Dekker.

Semigroup Theory. T. E. Hall et al. 352p. 1991. text ed. 101.00 (*981-02-0491-4*) World Scientific Pub.

Semigroup Theory & Applications. Clement et al. (Lecture Notes in Pure & Applied Mathematics Ser.: Vol. 116). 472p. 1989. 175.00 (*0-8247-8088-4*) Dekker.

Semigroup Theory & Evolution Equations: The Second International Conference. Ed. by Philippe Clement et al. (Lecture Notes in Pure & Applied Mathematics Ser.: Vol. 135). 544p. 1991. 199.00 (*0-8247-8545-2*) Dekker.

Semigroup Theory & Its Applications: Proceedings of the 1994 Conference Commemorating the Work of Alfred H. Clifford. Ed. by Karl H. Hofman & Michael W. Mislove. (London Mathematical Society Lecture Note Ser.: No. 231). (Illus.). 150p. (C). 1996. pap. text ed. 30.95 (*0-521-57669-5*) Cambridge U Pr.

***Semigroup Theory with Applications to Systems & Control.** Nasir U. Ahmed. LC 90-49350. (Pitman Research Notes in Mathematics Ser.: Vol. 246). 298p. 1991. reprint ed. pap. 85.00 (*0-608-03600-5*, 2064423) Bks Demand.

***Semigroups.** Kantorovitz. 1995. pap. 37.95 (*0-582-27778-7*, Pub. by Longman UK) Longman.

Semigroups. Ed. by J. Szep et al. 121p. (C). 1991. pap. 69.00 (*963-05-6046-1*, Pub. by Akad Kiado HU) St Mut.

Semigroups. 4th ed. E. S. Ljapin. Tr. by A. Brown et al. LC 63-15659. (Translations of Mathematical Monographs: Vol. 3). 519p. 1975. reprint ed. pap. 62.00 (*0-8218-1553-9*, MMONO/3) Am Math.

Semigroups: An Introduction to the Structure Theory. P. A. Grillet. LC 95-23322. (Monographs & Textbooks in Pure & Applied Mathematics: Vol. 193). 406p. 1995. 150.00 (*0-8247-9662-4*) Dekker.

Semigroups - Algebraic Theory & Applications to Formal Languages & Codes. C. Bonzini et al. 348p. 1993. text ed. 109.00 (*981-02-1521-5*) World Scientific Pub.

***Semigroups & Their Subsemigroup Lattices.** L. N. Shevrin & A. J. Ovsyannikov. LC 96-3329. (Mathematics & Its Applications Ser.). 392p. (C). 1996. lib. bdg. 173.00 (*0-7923-4221-6*) Kluwer Ac.

***Semigroups, Automata & Languages.** 250p. 1996. 41.00 (*981-02-2515-6*) World Scientific Pub.

Semigroups, Formal Languages, & Groups: Proceedings of the NATO ASI, University of York, U. K., 7-21 August 1993. Ed. by John Fountain. LC 95-17491. (NATO ASI Series C: Vol. 466). 440p. (C). 1995. lib. bdg. 199.00 (*0-7923-3540-6*) Kluwer Ac.

Semigroups in Algebra, Geometry, & Analysis. Ed. by Karl H. Hofmann et al. LC 95-14934. (Expositions in Mathematics Ser.: No. 20). xii, 370p. (C). 1995. lib. bdg. 98.95 (*3-11-014319-4*) De Gruyter.

Semigroups of Linear & Nonlinear Operations & Applications: Proceedings of the Curacao Conference, August 1992. Jerome A. Goldstein. Ed. by Gisele R. Goldstein. LC 93-43034. 1993. lib. bdg. 144.00 (*0-7923-2560-5*) Kluwer Ac.

Semigroups of Linear Operators & Applications. Jerome A. Goldstein. (Oxford Mathematical Monographs). 256p. 1985. 60.00 (*0-19-503540-2*) OUP.

Semigroups of Linear Operators & Applications to Partial Differential Equations. A. Pazy. Ed. by F. John et al. (Applied Mathematical Sciences Ser.: Vol. 44). viii, 279p. 1996. 59.00 (*0-387-90845-5*) Spr-Verlag.

Semigroups Theory & Applications. Ed. by H. Jurgensen et al. (Lecture Notes in Mathematics Ser.: Vol. 1320). 416p. 1988. 57.95 (*0-387-19347-2*) Spr-Verlag.

Semigroups with Applications: Proceedings of the Conference. W. D. Munn et al. 276p. 1992. text ed. 81.00 (*981-02-1121-X*) World Scientific Pub.

Semilla de Zanahoria. (J). 1989. 25.20 (*0-590-65739-9*) Scholastic Inc.

Semilla de Zanahoria. Ruth Krauss. 24p. (SPA.). (J). 1991. pap. 2.95 (*0-590-45092-1*) Scholastic Inc.

Semilla Nada Mas (Big Book) Alma F. Ada. (Rimas y Risas Red Ser.). (Illus.). 16p. (Orig.). (SPA.). (J). (gr. k-3). 1990. pap. text ed. 29.95 (*0-917837-56-8*) Hampton-Brown.

Semilla Nada Mas (Small Book) Alma F. Ada. (Rimas y Risas Red Ser.). (Illus.). 16p. (Orig.). (SPA.). (J). (gr. k-3). 1992. pap. text ed. 6.00 (*1-56334-083-6*) Hampton-Brown.

Semimagnetic Semiconductors & Diluted Magnetic Semiconductors. Ed. by M. Averous & M. Balkanski. (Ettore Majorana International Science Series, Life Sciences: Vol. 55). (Illus.). 274p. 1991. 85.00 (*0-306-43931-X*, Plenum Pr) Plenum.

Semimartingales: A Course on Stochastic Processes. Michel Metivier. (Studies in Mathematics). 287p. 1982. 79.95 (*3-11-008674-3*) De Gruyter.

Semimartingales & Stochastic Calculus. 1992. 84.00 (*0-8493-7715-3*, QA274) CRC Pr.

Seminaire d'Algebre Paul Dubreil et Marie-Paule Malliavin. Ed. by M. P. Malliavin. (Lecture Notes in Mathematics Ser.: Vol. 1029). 339p. 1983. 42.95 (*0-387-12699-6*) Spr-Verlag.

Seminaire d'Algebre Paul Dubreil et Marie-Paule Malliavin. M. P. Malliavin. (Lecture Notes in Mathematics Ser.: Vol. 1146). iv, 420p. (ENG & FRE.). 1985. 54.95 (*0-387-15686-0*) Spr-Verlag.

Seminaire d'Algebre Paule Dubreil et Marie-Paul Malliavin. Ed. by M. P. Malliavin. (Lecture Notes in Mathematics Ser.: Vol. 1404). ix, 410p. 1989. pap. 51.30 (*0-387-51812-6*) Spr-Verlag.

Seminaire d'Analyse. Ed. by P. Lelong et al. (Lecture Notes in Mathematics Ser.: Vol. 1198). x, 260p. 1986. 38.95 (*0-387-16762-5*) Spr-Verlag.

Seminaire de Proabilites, XXVII: Lecture Notes in Mathematics Ser. Ed. by J. Azema & P. A. Meyer. (Vol. 1557). vi, 327p. 1993. 60.95 (*0-387-57282-1*) Spr-Verlag.

Seminaire de Probabilites, Vol. 1583. Ed. by J. Azema et al. (Lecture Notes in Mathematics). 334p. 1994. 59.95 (*0-387-58331-9*) Spr-Verlag.

Seminaire de Probabilites Twenty-Five. Ed. by J. Azema et al. (Lecture Notes in Mathematics Ser.: Vol. 1485). viii, 440p. 1991. 75.95 (*0-387-54616-2*) Spr-Verlag.

Seminaire de Probabilites XIX 1983-84. Ed. by J. Azema & M. Yor. (Lecture Notes in Mathematics Ser.: Vol. 1123). iv, 504p. (ENG & FRE.). 1985. 64.95 (*0-387-15230-X*) Spr-Verlag.

Seminaire de Probabilites XXIX, Vol. VI. Ed. by J. Azema et al. (Lecture Notes in Mathematics Ser.: Vol. 1613). 326p. 1995. pap. 62.95 (*3-540-60219-4*) Spr-Verlag.

Seminaire de Probabilites XXVI. Ed. by J. Azema et al. (Lecture Notes in Mathematics Ser.: Vol. 1526). x, 633p. 1992. 114.95 (*0-387-56021-1*) Spr-Verlag.

***Seminaire de Probabilites XXX.** Ed. by J. Azema et al. VIII, 382p. 1996. pap. 68.00 (*3-540-61336-6*) Spr-Verlag.

Seminaire de Probabilites 1988-1989, No. XXIV. Ed. by J. Azema et al. (Lecture Notes in Mathematics Ser.: Vol. 1426). (Illus.). v, 490p. 1990. 79.95 (*0-387-52694-3*) Spr-Verlag.

Seminaire de Probabilities XX 1984-85. Ed. by J. Azema & M. Yor. (Lecture Notes in Mathematics Ser.: Vol. 1204). v, 639p. 1986. 85.95 (*0-387-16779-X*) Spr-Verlag.

Seminaire de Theorie des Nombres: Nineteen Eighty-Two to Nineteen Eighty-Three. Ed. by Marie-Jose Bertin & Catherine Goldstein. (Progress in Mathematics Ser.: No. 51). 312p. 1985. 69.00 (*0-8176-3261-1*) Birkhauser.

Seminaire de Theorie des Nombres, Paris 1980-1981, Vol. 22. Ed. by Marie-Jose Bertin. (Progress in Mathematics Ser.). 360p. 1983. 64.00 (*0-8176-3066-X*) Birkhauser.

Seminaire de Theorie des Nombres, Paris 1984-85. Ed. by Catherine Goldstein. (Progress in Mathematics Ser.: Vol. 63). 252p. 1986. 69.00 (*0-8176-3347-2*) Birkhauser.

Seminaire de Theorie des Nombres, Paris 1985-86. Ed. by Catherine Goldstein. (Progress in Mathematics Ser.: No. 71). 224p. 1987. 69.00 (*0-8176-3369-3*) Birkhauser.

Seminaire de Theorie des Nombres, Paris 1986-87. Ed. by Catherine Goldstein. (Progress in Mathematics Ser.: Vol. 75). 480p. 1988. 69.00 (*0-8176-3414-2*) Spr-Verlag.

Seminaire de Theorie des Nombres, Paris 1987-88. Catherine Goldstein. (Progress in Mathematics Ser.: No. 81). 368p. 1989. 69.00 (*0-8176-3458-4*) Birkhauser.

Seminaire de Theorie des Nombres, Paris, 1988-89. Ed. by Catherine Goldstein. (Progress in Mathematics Ser.: Vol. 91). x, 252p. 1990. 63.50 (*0-8176-3493-2*) Birkhauser.

Seminaire de Theorie des Nombres, Paris, 1990-1991. Ed. by S. David. (Progress in Mathematics Ser.: Vol. 108). vii, 279p. 1992. 92.00 (*0-8176-3684-6*) Birkhauser.

Seminaire de Theorie des Nombres, Paris, 1991-1992. Ed. by S. David. (Progress in Mathematics Ser.: Vol. 116). (Illus.). vii, 302p. 1993. 103.50 (*0-8176-3741-9*) Spr-Verlag.

Seminaire de Theorie du Potentiel, Paris, No. 8. Ed. by F. Hirsch & G. Mokobodzki. (Lecture Notes in Mathematics Ser.: Vol. 1235). iii, 209p. 1987. pap. 34.50 (*0-387-17210-6*) Spr-Verlag.

Seminaire, Vol. 11: Les Quatre Concepts Fodaementaux de la Psychanalyse. Jacques Lacan. (FRE.). 1990. pap. 19.95 (*0-7859-2719-0*) Fr & Eur.

Seminal Research Papers, Vol. 11. Charles E. Spearman et al. LC 77-72191. (Contributions to the History of Psychology Ser.: No. 11, Pt. A, Orientations). 532p. 1977. reprint ed. text ed. 75.00 (*0-313-26935-1*, U6935, Greenwood Pr) Greenwood.

Seminal Vesicles & Fertility. Ed. by C. G. Bollack & A. Clavert. (Progress in Reproductive Biology & Medicine Ser.: Vol. 12). (Illus.). x, 182p. 1984. 119.25 (*3-8055-3907-X*) S Karger.

Seminal Zinc As a Screening Instrument for the Preliminary Identification of Semen Traces. P. Hooft. No. 55. 133p. (Orig.). 1992. pap. 39.50 (*90-6186-519-0*, Pub. by Leuven Univ BE) Coronet Bks.

Seminar Analysis System (Kit) rev. ed. Edward E. Hubbard. 56p. 1992. pap. 99.95 (*1-883733-07-3*) Global Insghts.

Seminar at Sea: Second International Hemex Symposium on the Duromedics Bileaflet Valve. Ed. & Illus. by Silent Partners, Inc. Staff. 144p. 1986. pap. write for info. (*1-878353-06-3*) Silent Partners.

Seminar in Evil. large type ed. Daoma Winston. LC 95-11463. 244p. 1995. pap. 20.95 (*0-7862-0470-2*) Thorndike Pr.

Seminar in Evil. Daoma Winston. 208p. 1994. reprint ed. 19.00 (*0-7278-4542-X*) Severn Hse.

Seminar Instructor's Guide to Essentials for Child Development Associates. Ed. by Carol B. Phillips. (Illus.). 135p. (Orig.). 1991. pap. text ed. 12.50 (*1-879891-02-6*) Council Early Child.

Seminar Material for Real Estate Tax Appeals. Saul A. Wolfe. LC 86-206170. 341p. 1993. 42.00 (*0-685-67539-4*) NJ Inst CLE.

Seminar of Jacques Lacan: The Ethics of Psychoanalysis, 1959-1960, Bk. 7. Jacques-Alain Miller. Tr. & Notes by Dennis Porter. 352p. 1992. 35.00 (*0-393-03357-0*) Norton.

Seminar of Jacques Lacan: The Psychoses 1955-1956, Bk. 3. Jacques Lacan. Ed. by Jacques-Alain Miller. Tr. by Russell Grigg. LC 92-28360. 352p. 1993. 35.00 (*0-393-03467-4*) Norton.

***Seminar of Jacques Lacan Bk. III: The Psychoses, 1955-1956, Bk. 3.** Jacques Lacan. Ed. by Jacques-Alain Miller. 352p. (C). 1997. pap. 18.95 (*0-393-31612-2*) Norton.

***Seminar of Jacques Lacan Bk. VII: The Ethics of Psychoanalysis, 1959-1960.** Jacques Lacan. Ed. by Jacques-Alain Miller. 352p. (C). 1997. pap. 18.95 (*0-393-31613-0*) Norton.

Seminar of Jacques Lacan, Bk. 1: Freud's Papers on Technique, 1953-1954. Ed. by Jacques-Alain Miller. Tr. & Notes by John Forrester. 1991. pap. 14.95 (*0-393-30697-6*) Norton.

Seminar of Jacques Lacan, Bk. 2: The Ego in Freud's Theory & in the Technique of Psychoanalyis, 1954-1955. Ed. by Jacques-Alain Miller. Tr. by Sylvana Tomaselli. 1988. 24.95 (*0-393-01897-0*) Norton.

Seminar of Jacques Lacan, Bk. 2: The Ego in Freud's Theory & in the Technique of Psychoanalyis, 1954-1955. Ed. by Jacques-Alain Miller. Tr. by Sylvana Tomaselli. 1991. pap. 15.95 (*0-393-30709-3*) Norton.

Seminar on Ambulatory Pediatrics: Journal: Paediatrician, Vol. 5, No. 3. Ed. by George D. Maragos. (Illus.). 1977. 24.00 (*3-8055-2433-1*) S Karger.

Seminar on Bibliographic Records. Ed. by Marie-France Plassard. 147p. 1992. 55.00 (*3-598-11085-5*) K G Saur.

Seminar on Bibliotherapy: Proceedings of Sessions on Bibliotherapy Madison, Wisconsin, June 21-23, 1978. Ed. by Margaret E. Monroe. 180p. 1978. pap. 6.00 (*0-936442-07-7*) U Wis Sch Lib.

Seminar on Children at Risk. Ed. by O. Wasz-Hoeckert. (Journal: Paediatrician: Vol. 8, No. 4). (Illus.). 1979. pap. 26.50 (*3-8055-3073-0*) S Karger.

Seminar on Concurrrency, Vol. 197. Ed. by Stephen D. Brookes et al. (Lecture Notes in Computer Science Ser.: Vol. 197). xi, 523p. 1985. 49.00 (*0-387-15670-4*) Spr-Verlag.

Seminar on Deformations. Ed. by Julian Lawrynowicz. (Lecture Notes in Mathematics Ser.: Vol. 1165). ix, 331p. 1985. 46.95 (*0-387-16050-7*) Spr-Verlag.

Seminar on Delivery of Child Health Care. Ed. by O. P. Petersson. (Journal: Paediatrician: Vol. 9, No 1, 1980). 52p. 1979. pap. 26.50 (*3-8055-0800-X*) S Karger.

Seminar on Designing Electronic Equipment for Random Vibration Environments: Proceedings, March 1982, Los Angeles, CA. 98p. 50.00 (*0-915414-68-6*) Inst Environ Sci.

Seminar on Dynamical Systems: Euler International Mathematical Institute, St. Petersburg, 1991. Ed. by S. Kuksin et al. LC 93-41381. (Progress in Nonlinear Differential Equations & Their Applications Ser.: Vol. 12). 1993. 93.50 (*0-8176-2980-7*) Birkhauser.

Seminar on East-West Energy Trade: Proceedings Vienna, 3-4 October 1991. OECD Staff. 308p. (Orig.). 1992. pap. 50.00 (*92-64-13621-5*) OECD.

Seminar on Empirical Processes. P. Gaenssler & W. Stute. (DMV Seminar Ser.: No. 9). 114p. 1987. 35.00 (*0-8176-1921-6*) Birkhauser.

Seminar on Environmental Pharmacology. Ed. by Ryuta Ito. (Journal: Paediatrician: Vol. 6, No. 1). (Illus.). 1977. 25.00 (*3-8055-2794-2*) S Karger.

Seminar on Geographical Pediatrics. Ed. by George D. Maragos. (Journal: Paediatrician: Vol. 6, No. 2). (Illus.). 1977. 25.00 (*3-8055-2795-0*) S Karger.

Seminar on Haematology & Oncology. Ed. by H. Ekert. (Journal: Paediatrician: Vol. 9, No. 2). (Illus.). 88p. 1980. pap. 26.50 (*3-8055-1302-X*) S Karger.

Seminar on Harmonic Analysis, 1980. Ed. by C. Herz & R. Rigelhof. LC 81-19116. (Canadian Mathematical Society Conference Proceedings Ser.: No. 1). 313p. 1982. reprint ed. pap. 24.00 (*0-8218-6000-3*, CMSAMS/1) Am Math.

Seminar on Human Genetics. Ed. by George D. Maragos. (Journal: Paediatrician: Vol. 6, No. 6). (Illus.). 1978. 25.00 (*3-8055-2909-0*) S Karger.

Seminar on Immunological Aspects of Kidney Diseases in Children. Ed. by George D. Maragos. (Journal: Paediatrician: Vol. 10, No. 5-6). (Illus.). 164p. 1981. pap. 56.00 (*3-8055-3488-4*) S Karger.

Seminar on Infectious Diseases in Childhood. Ed. by George D. Maragos. (Journal: Paediatrician: Vol. 8, No. 1-2). (Illus.). 1979. pap. 53.00 (*3-8055-3027-7*) S Karger.

Seminar on Intelligence, Command, & Control: Guest Presentations, Spring 1991, No. I-93-1. C. Kenneth Allard et al. Ed. by John McLaughlin. (Illus.). 208p. (Orig.). 1993. pap. text ed. write for info. (*1-879716-03-8*) Ctr Info Policy.

Seminar on Intelligence, Command, & Control: Guest Presentations, Spring 1992. Frank B. Horton et al. Ed. by Anthony G. Oettinger. (Illus.). 186p. (Orig.). 1994. pap. text ed. write for info. (*1-879716-16-X*, I-94-4) Ctr Info Policy.

Seminar on Intelligence, Command, & Control: Guest Presentations, Spring 1993. Michelle K. Van Cleave, pseud. et al. (Illus.). 164p. (Orig.). 1994. pap. text ed. write for info. (*1-879716-12-7*, I-94-5) Ctr Info Policy.

Seminar on Intelligence, Command, & Control: Guest Presentations, Spring 1994, Vol. I-95-3. unabridged ed. Thomas P. Quinn et al. (Illus.). 267p. (Orig.). 1995. pap. text ed. write for info. (*1-879716-23-2*) Ctr Info Policy.

Seminar on Intelligence, Command, & Control: Guest Presentations, Spring 1995, Vol. I-96-2. unabridged ed. Michael L. Brown et al. (Illus.). 232p. (Orig.). 1996. pap. text ed. write for info. (*1-879716-29-1*) Ctr Info Policy.

S

Seminar on Jewish Art: Proceedings. Ed. by Vivian B. Mann & Gordon Tucker. 37p. (Orig.). 1985. pap. 6.00 (*0-87334-029-9*) Jewish Sem.

Seminar on Kidney Diseases in Children. Ed. by F. Mota-Hernandez. (Journal: Paediatrician: Vol. 8, No. 5-6, 1979). 1979. pap. 53.00 (*3-8055-0344-X*) S Karger.

Seminar on Micro-Local Analysis. Victor Guillemin et al. LC 78-70609. (Annals of Mathematics Studies: No. 93). 152p. 1979. pap. text ed. 16.95 (*0-691-08232-4*) Princeton U Pr.

Seminar on Minimal Submanifolds. Enrico Bombieri. LC 82-61356. (Annals of Mathematics Studies: No. 103). 500p. 1983. pap. text ed. 35.00 (*0-691-08319-3*) Princeton U Pr.

Seminar on Neonatology. Ed. by George D. Maragos. (Journal: Paediatrician: Vol. 5, No. 5). (Illus.). 1977. 24.00 (*3-8055-2702-0*) S Karger.

Seminar on New Results in Nonlinear Partial Differential Equations: A Publication of the Max-Planck-Institut fur Mathematik. Anthony J. Tromba. (Aspects of Mathematics Ser.: Vol. 10). vi, 198p. 1987. pap. 30.00 (*3-528-08975-X*, Pub. by Vieweg & Sohn GW) Informatica.

Seminar on Nonlinear Partial, & Differential Equations. Ed. by S. S. Cherm. (Mathematical Sciences Research Institute Publications: Vol. 2). (Illus.). 373p. 1984. 59.95 (*0-387-96079-1*) Spr-Verlag.

Seminar on Office Pediatrics, Part II. Ed. by George D. Maragos. (Journal: Paediatrician: Vol. 8, No. 3). (Illus.). 1979. pap. 26.50 (*3-8055-3074-9*) S Karger.

Seminar on Pediatric Allergy. Ed. by George D. Maragos. (Journal: Paediatrician: Vol. 5, No. 4). (Illus.). 80p. 1977. 24.00 (*3-8055-2648-2*) S Karger.

Seminar on Pediatric Cardiology. Ed. by George D. Maragos. (Journal: Paediatrician: Vol. 7, No. 1-3). (Illus.). 1978. pap. 74.50 (*3-8055-2912-0*) S Karger.

Seminar on Pediatric Cardiology. Ed. by J. G. Shakibi. (Journal: Paediatrician: Vol. 10, No. 1-3). (Illus.). 180p. 1981. pap. 84.00 (*3-8055-2675-X*) S Karger.

Seminar on Phosphate Rock for Direct Application. Ed. by M. Thompson. (Special Publications: No. SP-1). (Illus.). 472p. (Orig.). 1979. pap. 10.00 (*0-88090-022-9*) Intl Fertilizer.

Seminar on Public Health, Pt. I. Ed. by George D. Maragos. (Journal: Paediatrician: Vol. II, No. 1-2, 1982). (Illus.). iv, 120p. 1982. pap. 56.50 (*3-8055-3533-3*) S Karger.

Seminar on Public Health, Pt. 2. Ed. by George D. Maragos. (Journal: Paediatrician: Vol. II, No. 3-4). (Illus.). 126p. 1982. pap. 61.75 (*3-8055-3532-5*) S Karger.

Seminar on Reliability Growth, Management, Testing & Modeling: Proceedings. LC 62-38584. (Illus.). 1978. pap. text ed. 50.00 (*0-915414-57-0*) Inst Environ Sci.

Seminar on Spinal Cord Stimulation for the Control of Pain & other Neurological Disorders. Ed. by Philip L. Gildenberg & D. M. Long. (Journal: Applied Neurophysiology: Vol. 44, No. 4). (Illus.). vi, 84p. 1982. pap. 39.25 (*3-8055-3531-7*) S Karger.

Seminar on Stochastic Processes. 1987. 69.00 (*0-8176-3353-7*) Birkhauser.

Seminar on Stochastic Processes: Proceedings from 12th Seminar on Stochastic Processes, 1992, University of Washington. Erhan Cinlar et al. Ed. by Kai L. Chung & M. J. Sharpe. LC 93-22016. (Progress in Probability Ser.: Vol. 33). vii, 276p. 1993. 90.50 (*0-8176-3649-8*) Birkhauser.

Seminar on Stochastic Processes: 1987. Ed. by Erhan Cinlar et al. (Progress in Probability & Statistics Ser.: No. 15). 250p. 1988. 69.00 (*0-8176-3381-2*) Birkhauser.

Seminar on Stochastic Processes, 1985. Ed. by Erhan Cinlar. (Progress in Probability & Statistics Ser.: Vol. 12). 336p. 1986. 69.00 (*0-8176-3331-6*) Birkhauser.

An Asterisk (*) at the beginning of an entry indicates that the title is appearing in BIP for the first time.

Seminar on Stochastic Processes, 1988. Ed. by Erhan Cinlar et al. (Progress in Probability Ser.: No. 17). 250p. 1989. 69.00 (*0-8176-3422-3*) Birkhauser.
Seminar on Stochastic Processes, 1989. Ed. by Erhan Cinlar et al. (Progress in Probability Ser.: No. 18). 224p. 1989. 69.00 (*0-8176-3457-6*) Birkhauser.
Seminar on Stochastic Processes, 1991. Ed. by Erhan Cinlar & M. J. Sharpe. (Progress in Probability Ser.: Vol. 29). viii, 247p. 1992. 90.50 (*0-8176-3628-5*) Birkhauser.
***Seminar on the Atiyah-Singer Index Theorem.** Ed. by Richard S. Palais. LC 65-17157. (Annals of Mathematics Studies: Vol. 57). 376p. reprint ed. pap. 107.20 (*0-608-04524-1*, 2065269) Bks Demand.
Seminar on Time. A. G. Blake. LC 79-52756. 1980. 5.95 (*0-934254-00-1*) Claymont Comm.
***Seminar on Tourism Statistics in the Countries of Central & Eastern Europe.** 247p. 1997. pap. 25.00 (*92-844-0091-0*, WTO0001, Pub. by Wrld Tourism Org SP) Bernan Associates.
Seminar on Tubal Physiology & Biochemistry. Ed. by Carl J. Pauerstein. (Journal: Gynecologic Investigation: Vol. 6, Nos. 3-4). iv, 160p. 1975. reprint ed. 45.00 (*3-8055-2252-5*) S Karger.
Seminar Selling: The Ultimate Resource Guide for Marketing Financial Services. Paul Karasik. 208p. 1994. text ed. 40.00 (*0-7863-0351-4*) Irwin Prof Pubng.
***Seminar Selling on the Internet.** Joseph Sinclair. 1996. pap. write for info. (*0-679-77092-5*) Random.
Seminar Studies in History: Austro-Hungarian Empire. (C). 1985. pap. text ed. 13.50 (*0-582-35393-9*, 72214) Longman.
Seminar Studies in History: Emperor Charles V. (C). 1988. pap. text ed. 13.50 (*0-582-35475-7*, 78075) Longman.
Seminar Studies in History: Restoration England: The Reign of Charles II. 1985. pap. text ed. 10.23 (*0-582-35396-3*, 72216) Longman.
Seminar Studies in History: Stalin & Stalinism. (C). 1989. pap. text ed. 12.50 (*0-582-35266-5*, 72162) Longman.
Seminar Studies in History: The Eastern Question. (C). 1989. pap. text ed. 12.50 (*0-582-35602-4*, 78423) Longman.
Seminar Studies in History: The English Republic 1649-1660. (C). 1987. pap. text ed. 13.50 (*0-582-35231-2*, 72148) Longman.
Seminar Studies in History: The French Wars of Religion. (C). 1989. pap. text ed. 12.50 (*0-582-35456-0*, 78425) Longman.
Seminar Studies in History: The Origins of the First World War. (C). 1987. pap. text ed. 12.50 (*0-582-22382-2*, 70931) Longman.
Seminar Studies in History: The Origins of the Second World War. (C). 1987. pap. text ed. 13.50 (*0-582-35378-5*, 72209) Longman.
Seminar Studies in History: The Pre-Reformation Church in England. (C). 1989. pap. text ed. 13.50 (*0-582-35555-9*, 78422) Longman.
Seminar Studies in History: The Russian Revolution. 2nd ed. (C). 1986. pap. text ed. 13.50 (*0-582-35559-1*, 72240) Longman.
Seminar Studies in History: The Thirty-Years War. (C). 1984. pap. text ed. 13.50 (*0-582-35373-4*, 72206) Longman.
Seminar Studies in History: War in Europe 1939-45. (C). 1987. pap. text ed. 12.50 (*0-582-35455-2*, 72227) Longman.
Seminarians in Theology: A National Profile. Eugene F. Hemrick et al. 128p. 1985. pap. 8.95 (*1-55586-978-5*) US Catholic.
Seminarians of the Eighties: A National Survey. Raymond H. Potvin. 64p. 1986. 5.65 (*0-318-20579-3*) Natl Cath Educ.
Seminario De Religion Yoruba: Santeria. Miguel W. Ramos. 54p. (Orig.). (SPA.). (C). 1988. pap. 16.99 (*1-877845-05-1*) M W Ramos.
Seminarkit: Supplementary Material. Irene Kleiman & Carol Shulman. 41p. (C). 1995. student ed., ring bd. 12.95 (*0-9638804-3-8*) Dynamic Lrning.
***Seminars - The Emotional Dynamic: Advanced Presentation Techniques for Financial Professionals.** Frank Maselli. 230p. (Orig.). 1997. pap. 24.99 (*1-57502-412-8*, PO1276) Morris Pubng.
Seminars Directory. 2nd ed. 1000p. 1990. 130.00 (*0-8103-5049-1*) Gale.
Seminars Directory, 1989. 1000p. 1988. 125.00 (*0-8103-2842-9*) Gale.
Seminars in Organic Synthesis. Abbotto. 1992. 109.00 (*88-85104-44-4*) CRC Pr.
Seminars in Organic Synthesis, June 1992, Vol. II. Italian Chemistry Society Staff. 1993. 116.00 (*88-86162-00-6*) CRC Pr.
Seminars in Organic Systhesis, Vol. 3. Royal Society of Chemistry Staff. 1993. 121.00 (*88-86208-09-X*) CRC Pr.
Seminars in Training. Gloria Walker. LC 94-73396. 109p. (C). 1995. lib. bdg. 92.00 (*0-9637115-4-7*) AmeriTrain.
Seminars of Jacques Lacan: Freud's Writings on Technique 1953-1954. Jacques Lacan. Ed. by Jacques-Alain Miller. Tr. by John Forrester & Sylvana Tomaselli from FRE. (Lacan's Series of Seminars: Bk. 1). 1988. 24.95 (*0-393-01895-4*) Norton.
Seminary. 2nd ed. Alanson E. Russell & Joan M. Russell. 128p. (Orig.). (C). 1987. pap. 12.95 (*0-9619115-0-6*) Seminary Pubn.
Seminary Addresses. Solomon Schechter. 1959. pap. 2.45 (*0-8381-2109-8*) USCJE.
Seminary Addresses & Other Papers. Solomon Schechter. LC 79-83435. (Religion in America, Ser. 1). 1975. reprint ed. 21.95 (*0-405-00262-2*) Ayer.
***Seminary Development News: The First Ten Years.** Ed. by David L. Heetland. 256p. (Orig.). 1996. pap. text ed. write for info. (*0-9654902-0-3*) Garrett-Evang.
Seminary in the City: A Study of New York Theological Seminary. Robert W. Pazmino. LC 88-17250. 146p. (Orig.). (C). 1988. pap. text ed. 16.50 (*0-8191-7074-7*); lib. bdg. 35.50 (*0-8191-7073-9*) U Pr of Amer.
Seminary Libraries & University Extension. Herbert B. Adams. (Works of Herbert B. Adams). 33p. 1985. reprint ed. lib. bdg. 39.00 (*0-318-03785-8*) Rprt Serv.
Seminary Notes on Recent Historical Literature. Herbert B. Adams. (Principle Works of Herbert Baxter Adams). 1989. reprint ed. lib. bdg. 79.00 (*0-7812-1475-0*) Rprt Serv.
Seminary or University? The Genevan Academy & Reformed Higher Education, 1560-1620. Karin Maag. LC 95-24368. (St. Andrews Studies in Reformation History). 224p. 1996. 69.95 (*1-85928-166-4*, Pub. by Scolar Pr UK) Ashgate Pub Co.
Seminary Poems. Diane Di Prima. (Orig.). 1991. pap. 6.00 (*0-912449-34-9*) Floating Island.
Seminary Priests - a Dictionary of the Secular Clergy of England & Wales, 1558-1850 Vol. 1: Elizabeth, 1558-1603. Godfrey Anstruthor. 448p. 1968. 18.50 (*0-87921-059-1*) Attic Pr.
Seminary Priests - a Dictionary of the Secular Clergy of England & Wales, 1558-1850 Vol. 2: Early Stuarts, 1603-1659. Godfrey Anstruthor. 1975. 18.50 (*0-85597-082-0*) Attic Pr.
Seminary Priests - a Dictionary of the Secular Clergy of England & Wales, 1558-1850 Vol. 3: 660-1715. Godfrey Anstruthor. 1976. pap. 18.50 (*0-85597-116-9*) Attic Pr.
Seminary Priests - a Dictionary of the Secular Clergy of England & Wales, 1558-1850 Vol. 4: 1716-1800. Godfrey Anstruthor. LC 76-441910. 367p. 1977. pap. 18.50 (*0-85597-118-5*) Attic Pr.
Seminary Townhouses Stay: The History of a Unique Community Preservation Process in Chicago. Elizabeth K. Ware. (Illus.). 48p. (Orig.). 1994. 8.50 (*0-9633717-2-X*) DePaul Univ.
Seminole. B. Brooks. (Native American People Ser.). (Illus.). 32p. (J). (gr. 5-8). 1989. 11.95 (*0-685-58584-0*); lib. bdg. 15.94 (*0-86625-377-7*) Rourke Corp.
Seminole. rev. ed. Emilie U. Lepthien. LC 84-23141. (New True Bks.). (Illus.). 48p. (J). (gr. k-4). 1992. pap. 5.50 (*0-516-41941-2*); lib. bdg. 19.00 (*0-516-01941-4*) Childrens.
Seminole see Indians of North America
Seminole & Miccosukee Tribes: A Critical Bibliography. Harry A. Kersey, Jr. LC 85-30545. 116p. (C). 1987. pap. 4.95 (*0-253-30662-0*) Ind U Pr.
Seminole Burning: A Story of Racial Vengeance. Daniel L. Littlefield, Jr. LC 96-16413. 240p. 1996. 26.00 (*0-87805-923-7*) U Pr of Miss.
Seminole Diary: Remembrances of a Slave. Dolores Johnson. LC 94-4240. (Illus.). 32p. (J). 1994. text ed. 16.00 (*0-02-747848-3*) Macmillan.
Seminole Gold: Fifty Years of Sports at Florida State. Philip L. Ben. (Illus.). 160p. 1996. 39.95 (*1-56352-332-9*) Longstreet Pr Inc.
Seminole Indian Recipes. Marina Polvay. 29p. 1996. 5.95 (*0-942084-35-7*) SeaSide Pub.
***Seminole Indians.** Bill Lund. LC 96-39764. (Native Peoples Ser.). (J). 1997. write for info. (*1-56065-482-1*) Capstone Pr.
***Seminole Indians.** Bill Lund. (Native Peoples Ser.). (J). 1997. 13.25 (*0-516-20526-9*) Childrens.
Seminole Indians see Junior Library of American Indians
Seminole Indians of Florida 1850-1874. Raymond C. Lantz. 415p. (Orig.). 1994. pap. text ed. 30.00 (*0-7884-0034-7*) Heritage Bk.
Seminole Indians of Florida 1875-1879. Raymond C. Lantz. 436p. 1995. pap. 31.00 (*0-7884-0333-8*) Heritage Bk.
Seminole Music. Frances Densmore. (Bureau of American Ethnology Bulletins Ser.). 223p. 1995. lib. bdg. 89.00 (*0-7812-4161-8*) Rprt Serv.
***Seminole Song.** Munn. LC 96-44497. 1997. 23.95 (*0-312-85896-5*) St Martin.
Seminole Vengeance. J. R. Roberts. (Gunsmith Ser.: No. 157). 192p. (Orig.). 1995. mass mkt. 3.99 (*0-515-11530-4*) Jove Pubns.
Seminole Wind, an Eaglet Hatchling Story. Barbara Birenbaum. LC 93-17659. (Illus.). 24p. (Orig.). 1997. write for info. (*0-935343-50-4*); pap. write for info. (*0-935343-51-2*) Peartree.
Seminoles. Martin Lee. LC 89-8900. (First Bks.). (Illus.). 64p. (J). (gr. 4-7). 1989. lib. bdg. 21.00 (*0-531-10752-3*) Watts.
Seminoles. Martin Lee. (First Bks.). (Illus.). 64p. (J). (gr. 5-8). 1991. pap. 6.95 (*0-531-15604-4*) Watts.
Seminoles. Virginia D. Sneve. LC 93-14316. (First American Bk.). 32p. (J). (gr. 2-6). 1994. lib. bdg. 15.95 (*0-8234-1112-5*) Holiday.
Seminoles. Edwin C. McReynolds. LC 57-11198. (Civilization of the American Indian Ser.: No. 47). (Illus.). 1975. reprint ed. pap. 14.95 (*0-8061-1255-7*) U of Okla Pr.
Seminoles: People of the Southeast. Tricia Andryszewski. LC 94-21819. (Native Americans Ser.). (Illus.). 64p. (J). (gr. 4-6). 1995. lib. bdg. 16.40 (*1-56294-530-0*) Millbrook Pr.
Seminoles - Days of Long Ago. 2nd rev. ed. Kenneth W. Mulder. Ed. by Sandra Mulder. (Illus.). 32p. 1996. 5.00 (*1-889034-01-0*) Mulder Ent.
Seminoles of Florida. James W. Covington. LC 92-40978. (Illus.). 416p. 1993. pap. 18.95 (*0-8130-1204-X*); lib. bdg. 49.95 (*0-8130-1196-5*) U Press Fla.
Seminoles! The First Forty Years. Bill McGrotha. LC 87-51238. (Illus.). 256p. 1987. 20.95 (*0-9613040-1-4*) Talla Dem.
SEMINT: Seamless Model Integration. Jed Marti et al. LC 94-27715. 1994. pap. text ed. 7.50 (*0-8330-1567-2*, MR-403-OSD/A) Rand Corp.
Semio-Esthetique. Dominique Fournier. 272p. (FRE.). 1981. pap. 32.95 (*1-55725-032-4*, 6201, Pub. by Abbey St Peter Solesmes FR) Paraclete MA.
Semio Physics: A Sketch. Rene Thom. Tr. by Vendla Meyer. (Illus.). 256p. (C). 1990. 44.95 (*0-201-50060-4*, Adv Bk Prog) Addison-Wesley.
Semiochemistry - Flavors & Pheromones: Proceedings of American Chemical Society Symposium, Washington, D.C. August 1983. David M. Soderlund. (Illus.). x, 289p. 1985. 130.80 (*3-11-010120-3*) De Gruyter.
Semiological Reductionism: A Critique of the Deconstructionist Movement in Postmodern Thought. M. C. Dillon. LC 94-13720. 241p. 1995. text ed. 59.50 (*0-7914-2375-1*); pap. text ed. 19.95 (*0-7914-2376-X*) State U NY Pr.
***Semiology.** Pierre Guiraud. 115p. (C). 1975. pap. text ed. 18.95 (*0-415-09070-9*, Routledge NY) Routledge.
Semiology of Graphics: Diagrams, Networks, Maps. Jacques Bertin. Tr. by William J. Berg. LC 83-47755. (Illus.). 429p. reprint ed. pap. 122.30 (*0-8357-3532-X*, 2034270) Bks Demand.
***Semiorders Properties, Representations, Applications.** Date not set. text ed. 160.00 (*0-7923-4617-3*) Kluwer Ac.
Semiosis: Semiotics & the History of Culture. Ed. by Merris Halle et al. (Michigan Slavic Contributions Ser.: No. 10). 1984. pap. 15.00 (*0-930042-55-7*) Mich Slavic Pubns.
Semiosis in the Postmodern Age. Floyd Merrell. LC 94-21557. (Illus.). 360p. 1995. 37.95 (*1-55753-055-6*) Purdue U Pr.
Semiotext(e) Architecture. Ed. by Hraztan Zeitlian. 160p. Date not set. 15.00 (*0-936756-84-5*, Semiotexte) Autonomedia.
Semiotext(e) Canadas. Ed. by Jordan Zinovich. 320p. Date not set. 12.00 (*1-57027-013-9*, Semiotexte) Autonomedia.
Semiotext(e)SF. Ed. by Rudy Rucker et al. 384p. Date not set. 12.00 (*0-936756-43-8*, Semiotexte) Autonomedia.
Semiotic Analysis of Genesis 2-3: A Semiotic Theory & Method of Analysis Applied to the Story of the Garden of Eden. E. J. Van Wolde. (Studia Semitica Neerlandica Ser.: Vol. 25). 252p. 1989. pap. text ed. 30.00 (*90-232-2433-7*, Pub. by Van Gorcum NE) Eisenbrauns.
Semiotic Analysis of Guillaume Apollinaire's Mythology in Alcools, Vol. 17. Nathalie G. Cornelius. (Berkeley Insights in Linguistics & Semiotics Ser.). 192p. (C). 1995. text ed. 45.95 (*0-8204-2834-5*) P Lang Pubng.
Semiotic & Psychoanalytic Interpretation of Herman Melville's Fiction. Zan D. Robinson. LC 91-30813. 220p. 1991. lib. bdg. 89.95 (*0-7734-9957-1*) E Mellen.
Semiotic & Significs: The Correspondence Between Charles S. Peirce & Lady Victoria Welby. Ed. by Charles S. Hardwick. LC 76-12369. (Illus.). 235p. reprint ed. pap. 68.20 (*0-8357-3955-4*, 2057051) Bks Demand.
Semiotic & Structuralist Analyses of Fiction: An Introduction & a Survey of Applications. Leonard D. Orr. LC 86-50685. 224p. 1986. 30.00 (*0-87875-331-1*) Whitston Pub.
Semiotic Approaches to Human Relations. Jurgen Ruesch. 1972. 141.55 (*90-279-2299-3*) Mouton.
Semiotic Approaches to Psychiatry. Harley C. Shands. (Approaches to Semiotics Ser.: No. 2). 1970. text ed. 64.65 (*90-279-0506-1*) Mouton.
Semiotic Bridge: Trends from California. Ed. by Irmengard Rauch & Gerald F. Carr. (Approaches to Semiotics Ser.: No. 86). x, 428p. (C). 1989. lib. bdg. 142.35 (*0-89925-626-0*) Mouton.
Semiotic Challenge. Roland Barthes. Tr. by Richard Howard from FRE. LC 94-7124. 1994. pap. 15.00 (*0-520-08784-4*) U CA Pr.
Semiotic Foundations: Steps Toward An Epistemology of Written Texts. Floyd Merrell. LC 81-48631. (Illus.). 191p. 1982. pap. 54.50 (*0-7837-3718-1*, 2057896) Bks Demand.
Semiotic Foundations of Drug Therapy: The Placebo Problem in a New Perspective. Klaus Schonauer. LC 93-36818. (Approaches to Semiotics Ser.: Vol. 112). (Illus.). x, 258p. (C). 1994. lib. bdg. 121.55 (*3-11-013532-9*) Mouton.
***Semiotic Grammar.** William B. McGregor. (Illus.). 448p. 1997. 115.00 (*0-19-823688-3*) OUP.
Semiotic Investigations: Towards an Effective Semiotics. Alec McHoul. LC 95-43854. (Stages Ser.). (Illus.). xxiii, 250p. 1996. text ed. 35.00 (*0-8032-3191-1*) U of Nebr Pr.
Semiotic Landscape-Panorama Semiotique. Ed. by Seymour B. Chatman et al. (Approaches to Semiotics Ser.: No. 29). (FRE.). 1979. text ed. 192.35 (*90-279-7928-6*) Mouton.
Semiotic of Myth: A Critical Study of the Symbol. James J. Liszka. LC 88-45500. (Advances in Semiotics Ser.). (Illus.). 256p. 1990. 35.00 (*0-253-33513-2*) Ind U Pr.
Semiotic Perspectives. Sandor Hervey. 304p. 1982. text ed. 18.95 (*0-04-400026-X*) Routledge Chapman & Hall.
Semiotic Perspectives on Clinical Theory & Practice: Medicine, Neuropsychiatry & Psychoanalysis. Ed. by Bonnie E. Litowitz & Phillip S. Epstein. (Approaches to Semiotics Ser.: No. 98). (Illus.). xii, 206p. (C). 1991. lib. bdg. 90.80 (*3-11-012632-X*, 140-91) Mouton.
Semiotic Phenomenology of Rhetoric: Eidetic Practice in Henry Grattan's Discourse on Tolerance. Richard L. Lanigan. (Current Continental Research Ser.: No. 203). (Illus.). 248p. (Orig.). 1984. 52.00 (*0-8191-4294-8*, Ctr Adv Res); pap. 23.00 (*0-8191-4295-6*, Ctr Adv Res) U Pr of Amer.
Semiotic Praxis: Studies in Pertinence & in the Means of Expression & Communication. Georges Mounin. Tr. by Catherine Tihanyi. (Topics in Contemporary Semiotics Ser.). 226p. 1985. 59.50 (*0-306-41767-7*, Plenum Pr) Plenum.
Semiotic Principles in Semantic Theory. Neal R. Norrick. (Current Issues in Linguistic Theory Ser.: No. 20). xiii, 252p. 1981. 59.00 (*90-272-3513-9*) Benjamins North Am.
Semiotic Reconstruction of Ryle's Critique of Cartesianism. B. Narahari Rao. LC 94-31008. (Quellen Und Studien Zur Philosophie: Bd. 38). xiv, 165p. (C). 1994. lib. bdg. 96.35 (*3-11-014156-6*) De Gruyter.
Semiotic Self. Norbert Wiley. 264p. 1994. pap. text ed. 19.95 (*0-226-89816-4*); lib. bdg. 39.95 (*0-226-89815-6*) U Ch Pr.
Semiotic Sphere. Ed. by Thomas A. Sebeok & Jean Umiker-Sebeok. (Topics in Contemporary Semiotics Ser.). 618p. 1986. 135.00 (*0-306-41765-0*, Plenum Pr) Plenum.
Semiotic Stage: Prague School Theatre Theory. Michael L. Quinn. LC 92-37227. (Pittsburgh Studies in Theatre & Culture: Vol. 1). 176p. (C). 1995. text ed. 42.95 (*0-8204-1877-3*) P Lang Pubng.
Semiotic Study of Three Plays by Plinio Marcos. Elzbieta Szoka. LC 94-901. (Berkeley Insights in Linguistics & Semiotics Ser.: Vol. 13). 160p. (C). 1995. text ed. 39.95 (*0-8204-2463-3*) P Lang Pubng.
Semiotic Theory & Practice: Proceedings of the 3rd International Congress of the IASS Palermo, 1984, 2 vols., Set. Ed. by Michael Herzfeld & Lucio Melazzo. xxxiv, 1304p. (C). 1988. lib. bdg. 376.95 (*0-89925-530-2*) Mouton.
Semiotic Theory of Language. Sebastian K. Shaumyan. LC 85-46033. (Advances in Semiotics Ser.). 368p. 1987. 24.50 (*0-253-30472-5*) Ind U Pr.
Semiotic Theory of Texts. Floyd Merrell. (Approaches to Semiotics Ser.: No. 70). x, 234p. 1985. 93.85 (*0-89925-035-1*) Mouton.
Semiotic Web. Ed. by Thomas A. Sebeok & Jean Umiker-Sebeok. (Approaches to Semiotics Ser.). 732p. (C). 1987. lib. bdg. 226.95 (*0-89925-215-X*) Mouton.
Semiotic Web, 1987. Ed. by Thomas A. Sebeok & Jean Umiker-Sebeok. (Approaches to Semiotics Ser.: No. 81). xii, 853p. (C). 1988. lib. bdg. 230.80 (*0-89925-484-5*) Mouton.
Semiotic Web, 1988. Ed. by Thomas A. Sebeok & Jean Umiker-Sebeok. (Approaches to Semiotics Ser.: No. 85). x, 430p. (C). 1989. lib. bdg. 161.55 (*0-89925-617-1*) Mouton.
Semiotic Web, 1989. Ed. by Thomas A. Sebeok & Jean Umiker-Sebeok. (Approaches to Semiotics Ser.: No. 92). (Illus.). xii, 797p. (C). 1990. lib. bdg. 334.65 (*3-11-012350-9*) Mouton.
Semiotica: Diccionario Razonado de la Teoria del Lenguaje, 2 vols., Set. A. J. Greimas & J. Courtes. 800p. (SPA.). 1993. pap. 150.00 (*0-614-00135-8*) Elliots Bks.
Semiotica: Diccionario Razonado de la Teoria del Lenguaje, 2 vols., Set. A. J. Greimas & J. Courtes. 800p. (SPA.). 1993. pap. 150.00 (*0-614-00240-0*) Elliots Bks.
Semiotica: Diccionario Razonado de la Teoria del Lenguaje, Vol. 1. A. J. Greimas & J. Courtes. (SPA.). 1993. pap. write for info. (*84-249-0851-1*) Elliots Bks.
Semiotica: Diccionario Razonado de la Teoria del Lenguaje, Vol. 2. A. J. Greimas & J. Courtes. (SPA.). 1993. pap. write for info. (*84-249-1459-7*) Elliots Bks.
Semiotics: An Introductory Anthology. Ed. by Robert E. Innis. LC 84-47700. (Advances in Semiotics Ser.). (Illus.). 352p. 1995. pap. 13.95 (*0-253-20344-9*, MB-344) Ind U Pr.
***Semiotics & Church Architecture: Applying the Semiotics of A. J. Greimas & the Paris School to the Analysis of Church Buildings.** Gerard Lukken & Mark Searle. (Liturgia Condenda Ser.: Vol. 1). 136p. 1993. pap. 37.50 (*90-390-0063-8*, Pub. by KOK Pharos NE) Eisenbrauns.
Semiotics & Communication: Signs, Codes, & Cultures. Wendy Leeds-Hurwitz. (Communication Ser.). 232p. (C). 1993. pap. 24.50 (*0-8058-1140-0*); text ed. 49.95 (*0-8058-1139-7*) L Erlbaum Assocs.
Semiotics & Dialectics: Ideology & the Text. Ed. by Peter V. Zima. (Linguistic & Literary Studies in Eastern Europe: Vol. 5). vi, 573p. 1981. 124.00 (*90-272-1505-7*) Benjamins North Am.
Semiotics & Fieldwork. Peter K. Manning. (Qualitative Research Methods Ser.: Vol. 7). 96p. (C). 1987. text ed. 22.95 (*0-8039-2761-4*); pap. text ed. 9.95 (*0-8039-2640-5*) Sage.
Semiotics & Human Sign Languages. William C. Stokoe, Jr. LC 71-173380. (Approaches to Semiotics Ser.: No. 21). (Illus.). 177p. 1972. text ed. 43.10 (*90-279-2096-6*) Mouton.
Semiotics & International Scholarship: Towards a Language of Theory. Ed. by Jonathan D. Evans. 1986. lib. bdg. 139.00 (*90-247-3391-X*) Kluwer Ac.
Semiotics & Interpretation. Robert Scholes. LC 81-15971. 1982. 30.00 (*0-300-02798-2*) Yale U Pr.
Semiotics & Interpretation. Robert Scholes. LC 81-15971. 1983. pap. 12.00 (*0-300-03093-2*, Y-465) Yale U Pr.
Semiotics & Language: An Analytical Dictionary. Algirdas J. Greimas & J. Courtes. Tr. by Larry Crist et al. LC 81-47828. (Advances in Semiotics Ser.). (Illus.). 432p. 1983. 57.50 (*0-253-35169-3*) Ind U Pr.
Semiotics & Legal Theory. Bernard S. Jackson. 350p. 1987. pap. 17.95 (*0-7102-1214-3*, RKP) Routledge.
Semiotics & Lighting: A Study of Six Modern French Cameramen. Sharon A. Russell. LC 81-3377. (Studies in Photography & Cinematography: No. 2). 185p. reprint ed. pap. 52.80 (*0-685-20881-8*, 2070215) Bks Demand.
Semiotics & Linguistic Structure: A Primer of Philosophic Logic. Richard M. Martin. LC 78-6873. 321p. (C). 1978. text ed. 29.50 (*0-87395-381-9*) State U NY Pr.

An Asterisk (*) at the beginning of an entry indicates that the title is appearing in BIP for the first time.

Semiotics & Linguistics. Yishai Tobin. (Linguistics Library). 336p. (Orig.). (C). 1990. pap. text ed. 22.95 (*0-582-01670-3*) Longman.

*__Semiotics & Linguistics.__ Yishai Tobin. LC 89-13490. (Longman Linguistics Library). 303p. 1990. reprint ed. pap. 86.40 (*0-608-03621-8*, 2064448) Bks Demand.

Semiotics & Linguistics in Alice's World. Ed. by Rachel Fordyce & Carla Marello. (Research in Text Theory Ser.: No. 19). viii, 277p. (C). 1994. lib. bdg. 130.80 (*3-11-013894-8*, 99-94) De Gruyter.

Semiotics & Literary Criticism. Cesare Segre. 1973. text ed. 26.95 (*90-279-2620-4*) Mouton.

Semiotics & Pragmatics: An Evaluative Comparison of Conceptual Frameworks. Herman Parret. (Pragmatics & Beyond Ser.: Vol. IV, No. 7). xii, 136p. (Orig.). 1983. pap. 44.00 (*90-272-2532-X*) Benjamins North Am.

Semiotics & Pragmatics: Proceedings of the Perpignan Symposium, 1983. Ed. by Gerard Deledalle. LC 89-229. (Foundations of Semiotics Ser.: No. 18). xii, 476p. 1989. 133.00 (*90-272-3290-3*) Benjamins North Am.

Semiotics & Second Language Pedogogy. James W. Brown. LC 90-13287. (American University Studies: Linguistics: Ser. XIII, Vol. 16). 232p. (C). 1990. text ed. 43.95 (*0-8204-1233-3*) P Lang Pubng.

Semiotics & the History of Culture in Honor of Jurij Lotman: Studies in Russian. Ed. by Morris Halle et al. (UCLA Slavic Studies: Vol. 17). 437p. (RUS.). 1989. 29.95 (*0-89357-195-4*) Slavica.

Semiotics & the Philosophy of Language. Umberto Eco. LC 82-49016. (Advances in Semiotics Ser.). (Illus.). 254p. 1984. 31.50 (*0-253-35168-5*) Ind U Pr.

Semiotics & the Philosophy of Language. Umberto Eco. LC 82-49016. (Advances in Semiotics Ser.). (Illus.). 254p. 1986. pap. 13.95 (*0-253-20398-8*, MB-398) Ind U Pr.

Semiotics from Peirce to Barthes: A Conceptual Introduction to the Study of Communication, Interpretation & Expression. V. Tejera. ix, 201p. 1988. 35.50 (*90-04-08597-1*) E J Brill.

Semiotics in Poland, 1894-1969. Ed. by Jerzy Pelc. Tr. by Oligierd A. Wojtasiewicz from POL. (Synthese Library: No. 119). 526p. 1978. lib. bdg. 141.50 (*90-277-0811-8*, D Reidel) Kluwer Ac.

Semiotics in the United States. Thomas A. Sebeok. LC 90-25040. (Advances in Semiotics Ser.). 184p. 1991. 12.95 (*0-253-35134-0*); pap. 5.95 (*0-253-20654-5*, MB-654) Ind U Pr.

*__Semiotics of a Bourgeois Society: An Analysis of the Aguafuertes Porte Nas by Roberto Arlt, Vol. 132.__ Victoria J. Martinez & Roberto Arlt. LC 97-9900. (Humanistica Ser.). 1997. write for info. (*1-882528-22-0*) Scripta.

Semiotics of Art: Prague School Contributions. Ed. by Ladislav Matejka & Irwin R. Titunik. 1984. reprint ed. pap. 14.95 (*0-262-63065-6*) MIT Pr.

Semiotics of Cellular Communication in the Immune System. Ed. by N. Avrion Mitchison et al. (NATO ASI Series H: Vol. 23). (Illus.). xiii, 335p. 1988. 133.00 (*0-387-18552-6*) Spr-Verlag.

Semiotics of Cities, Selves & Cultures: Explorations in Semiotic Anthropology. Milton B. Singer. LC 91-22332. (Approaches to Semiotics Ser.: No. 102). xiv, 380p. 1991. lib. bdg. 144.65 (*3-11-012601-X*) Mouton.

Semiotics of Consumption: Interpreting Symbolic Consumer Behavior in Popular Culture & Works of Art. Morris B. Holbrook & Elizabeth C. Hirschman. LC 92-47431. (Approaches to Semiotics Ser.: Vol. 110). xii, 365p. (C). 1993. 144.65 (*3-11-013491-8*) Mouton.

Semiotics of Culture & Language, Vol. 1. Fawcett. (C). 1992. text ed. 55.00 (*0-86187-295-9*) St Martin.

Semiotics of Culture & Language, Vol. 2. Fawcett. (C). 1992. text ed. 55.00 (*0-86187-469-2*) St Martin.

Semiotics of Deceit: Language, Drama, & Culture in Maistre Pierre Pathelin. Donald Maddox. LC 82-74491. (Illus.). 232p. 1984. 35.00 (*0-8387-5040-0*) Bucknell U Pr.

Semiotics of Drama & the Style of Eugene O'Neill. Mark Kobernick. LC 89-220. (Foundations of Semiotics Ser.: Vol. 19). xiii, 159p. 1989. 53.00 (*90-272-3291-1*) Benjamins North Am.

Semiotics of Fortune Telling. Edna Aphek & Yishai Tobin. LC 89-35950. (Foundations of Semiotics Ser.: No. 22). vii, 216p. 1989. 74.00 (*90-272-3294-6*); pap. 27.95 (*1-55619-091-3*) Benjamins North Am.

Semiotics of French Gestures. Genevieve Calbris. LC 88-46027. (Advances in Semiotics Ser.). (Illus.). 256p. 1990. 14.95 (*0-253-31297-3*) Ind U Pr.

Semiotics of Misogyny Through the Humor of Chekhov & Maugham. Anna Makolkin. LC 92-18419. 260p. 1992. text ed. 89.95 (*0-7734-9570-3*) E Mellen.

Semiotics of Narration in Film & Prose Fiction: Case Studies of Scarecrow & My Friend Ivan Lapshin. Benjamin A. Rifkin. LC 92-25032. (Russian & East European Studies in Aesthetics & the Philosophy of Culture: Vol. 2). (Illus.). 250p. (C). 1994. text ed. 59.95 (*0-8204-1995-8*) P Lang Pubng.

Semiotics of Passion: From States of Affair to States of Feeling. Algirdas J. Greimas & Jacques Fontanille. Tr. by Frank Collins & Paul J. Perron from FRE. 272p. (C). 1992. text ed. 49.95 (*0-8166-2104-7*); pap. text ed. 19.95 (*0-8166-2105-5*) U of Minn Pr.

Semiotics of Performance. Marco De Marinis. Tr. by Aine O'Healy. LC 92-38671. (Advances in Semiotics Ser.). 1993. 39.95 (*0-253-31686-3*) Ind U Pr.

Semiotics of Poetry. Michael Riffaterre. LC 78-3245. (Advances in Semiotics Ser.). 224p. 1984. pap. 15.95 (*0-253-20332-5*, MB-332) Ind U Pr.

*__Semiotics of Poetry.__ Michael Riffaterre. LC 78-3245. (Advances in Semiotics Ser.). 223p. pap. 63.60 (*0-608-05039-3*, 2059700) Bks Demand.

Semiotics of Russian Culture. Ju M. Lotman & B. A. Uspenskij. Ed. by Ann Shukman. (Michigan Slavic Contributions Ser.: No. 11). 356p. 1984. pap. 15.00 (*0-930042-56-5*) Mich Slavic Pubns.

Semiotics of Subtext in Modern Drama. Joanne E. Horwood. LC 95-36532. (Berkeley Insights in Linguistics & Semiotics Ser.: Vol. 18). 1996. write for info. (*0-8204-2842-6*) P Lang Pubng.

Semiotics of the Built Environment: An Introduction to Architectonic Analysis. Donald Preziosi. LC 78-20404. (Advances in Semiotics Ser.). 126p. pap. 36.50 (*0-8357-3956-2*, 2057052) Bks Demand.

Semiotics of the Dramatic Text. Susan Melrose. LC 93-17914. (New Directions in Theatre Ser.). 1994. text ed. 45.00 (*0-312-10086-8*) St Martin.

*__Semiotics of the Media.__ LC 97-16398. 1997. write for info. (*3-11-015537-0*) De Gruyter.

Semiotics of the Passion Narratives. Louis Marin. Tr. by Alfred M. Johnson, Jr. LC 80-18199. (Pittsburgh Theological Monographs: No. 25). 1980. 12.95 (*0-915138-23-9*) Pickwick.

Semiotics of Theatre. Erika Fischer-Lichte. Tr. by Jeremy Gaines & Doris L. Jones. LC 91-24781. (Advances in Semiotics Ser.). (Illus.). 356p. 1992. text ed. 49.95 (*0-253-32237-5*) Ind U Pr.

Semiotics of Theatre & Drama. Kier Elam. 224p. (C). 1980. pap. 13.95 (*0-415-03984-3*, NO. 6392) Routledge Chapman & Hall.

Semiotics of Visual Language. Fernande Saint-Martin. LC 89-45920. (Advances in Semiotics Ser.). (Illus.). 270p. 1990. 35.00 (*0-253-35057-3*) Ind U Pr.

Semiotics of World Literature. Michael E. Moriarty. LC 96-25764. (Studies in Comparative Literature: Vol. 21). 340p. 1997. text ed. 99.95 (*0-7734-8776-X*) E Mellen.

Semiotics, Romanticism & the Scriptures. Jacques M. Chevalier. (Approaches to Semiotics Ser.: No. 88). viii, 368p. (C). 1990. lib. bdg. 121.55 (*0-89925-619-8*) Mouton.

Semiotics, Self & Society. Ed. by Benjamin Lee & Greg Urban. (Approaches to Semiotics Ser.: No. 84). xviii, 311p. (C). 1989. lib. bdg. 95.40 (*0-89925-560-4*) Mouton.

Semiotics Unfolding, 3 vols., Set. Ed. by Tasso Borbe. LC 83-13439. (Approaches to Semiotics Ser.: No. 68). 1983. 323.10 (*3-11-009779-6*) Mouton.

Semiotics with "Symbolicity" 1990: Proceedings of the Fifteenth Annual Meeting of the Semiotic Society of America. Ed. by Jeff Bernard et al. 704p. (Orig.). (C). 1993. lib. bdg. 95.00 (*0-8191-8868-9*, Semiotic Society of America) U Pr of Amer.

Semiotics, 1982. Ed. by John Deely & Jonathan Evans. (Sources in Semiotics Ser.). 682p. (C). 1987. lib. bdg. 98.50 (*0-8191-5107-6*, Semiotic Society of America) U Pr of Amer.

Semiotics, 1983. Ed. by Jonathan Evans & John Deely. (Sources in Semiotics Ser.). 712p. (C). 1987. lib. bdg. 96.00 (*0-8191-5352-4*, Semiotic Society of America) U Pr of Amer.

Semiotics, 1984: Proceedings of the Ninth Annual Meeting of the Semiotic Society of America, 11-14 October 1984, Bloomington, Indiana. Ed. by John Deely. LC 84-640162. (Illus.). 754p. (Orig.). 1985. pap. text ed. 55.50 (*0-8191-4880-6*); lib. bdg. 91.00 (*0-8191-4879-2*) U Pr of Amer.

Semiotics, 1986. Ed. by John Deely & Jonathan Evans. LC 84-640162. (Sources in Semiotics Ser.). (Illus.). 472p. (C). 1988. lib. bdg. 72.50 (*0-8191-6672-3*, Semiotic Society of America) U Pr of Amer.

Semiotics, 1987. Ed. by John Deely. LC 84-640162. 510p. (C). 1988. lib. bdg. 85.50 (*0-8191-7163-8*, Semiotic Society of America) U Pr of Amer.

Semiotics, 1988. Ed. by Terry J. Prewitt et al. LC 84-640162. (Illus.). 612p. (C). 1989. lib. bdg. 103.00 (*0-8191-7478-5*) U Pr of Amer.

Semiotics, 1989. Ed. by John Deely et al. LC 84-640162. (Proceedings of the 14th Annual Meeting of the Semiotic Society of America Staff Ser.). 454p. (C). 1990. lib. bdg. 65.00 (*0-8191-7840-3*) U Pr of Amer.

Semiotics, 1991: Proceedings of the Sixteenth Annual Meeting of the Semiotic Society of America. Ed. by John Deely & Terry J. Prewitt. 404p. (C). lib. bdg. 85.00 (*0-8191-8870-0*) U Pr of Amer.

Semiotics 1993. Ed. by John Deely. (Proceedings of the 18th Annual Meeting of the Semiotic Society of America Ser.). 624p. (C). 1995. 74.95 (*0-614-08642-6*) P Lang Pubng.

Semiotics 1994. Ed. by John Deely. (Proceedings of the Semiotic Society of America, 20-23 Oct. '94). 512p. (C). 1995. text ed. 69.95 (*0-8204-2876-0*) P Lang Pubng.

Semiotics 1995: Proceedings of the Twentieth Annual Meeting of the Semiotic Society of America. John Deely. 440p. (C). 1996. text ed. 59.95 (*0-614-17854-1*) P Lang Pubng.

*__Semiotik - Semiotics: Ein Handbuch Zu Den Zeichentheoretischen Grundlagen von Natur und Kultur - A Handbook on the Sign-Theoretic Foundations of Nature & Culture.__ Ed. by Roland Posner et al. LC 96-49024. (Handbooks of Linguistics & Communication Sciencchaft Ser.: Vol. 13.1). (Illus.). xxxiv, 1198p. (ENG & GER.). (C). 1996. lib. bdg. 712.85 (*3-11-009584-X*) De Gruyter.

Semiotique Vol. 1: Dictionnaire Raisonne de la Theorie du Langage. Algirdas J. Greimas. 424p. (FRE.). 1979. 69.95 (*0-7859-7601-9*, 2010052218) Fr & Eur.

Semiotique Vol. 2: Dictionnaire Raisonne de la Theorie du Langage. Algirdas J. Greimas. 270p. (FRE.). 1986. 69.95 (*0-7859-7603-5*, 2010113632) Fr & Eur.

Semiotique et philosophie. Georges Kalinowski. (Actes Semiotiques Ser.: No. 3). 293p. (FRE.). 1985. pap. 65.00 (*90-272-2263-0*) Benjamins North Am.

*__Semiotisches Denken und Kulturanthropologische Forschungen Bei Claude Levi-Strauss.__ Manfred Hainzl. (Europaische Hochschulschriften Ser.: Reihe 20, Bd. 522). 168p. (GER.). 1997. 35.95 (*3-631-30911-2*) P Lang Pubng.

Semiparametric & Nonparametric Econometrics. Ed. by Aman Ullah. (Studies in Empirical Economics: Vol. 1). 294p. 1989. 95.95 (*0-387-91350-5*) Spr-Verlag.

Semiperipheral Development: The Politics of Southern Europe in the Twentieth Century. Giovanni Arrighi. LC 85-2411. (Explorations in the World-Economy Ser.: Vol. 5). 279p. 1985. reprint ed. pap. 79.60 (*0-608-00817-6*, 2061605) Bks Demand.

Semiperipheral States in the World-Economy. Ed. by William G. Martin. LC 90-36779. (Contributions in Economics & Economic History Ser.: No. 113). 248p. 1990. text ed. 55.00 (*0-313-27489-4*, MGP, Greenwood Pr) Greenwood.

Semirings, Automata & Languages. W. Kuich & Arto Salomaa. (EATCS Monographs on Theoretical Computer Science: Vol. 5). (Illus.). 490p. 1985. 107.95 (*0-387-13716-5*) Spr-Verlag.

Semisimple Lie Algebras. Goto & Grosshans. (Lecture Notes in Pure & Applied Mathematics Ser.: Vol. 38). 496p. 1978. 165.00 (*0-8247-6744-6*) Dekker.

Semistability of Amalgamated Products & HNN-Extensions. Mihalik & Tschantz. (Memoirs Ser.: No. 471). 86p. 1992. 24.00 (*0-8218-2531-3*, MEMO/98/471) Am Math.

Semisynthetic Proteins. Robin E. Offord. LC 79-40521. (Illus.). 247p. reprint ed. pap. 70.40 (*0-685-20601-7*, 2030535) Bks Demand.

Semites & Stereotypes: Characteristics of Jewish Humor. Ed. by Avner Ziv & Anat Zajdman. LC 92-28979. (Contributions in Ethnic Studies: No. 31). 224p. 1993. text ed. 52.95 (*0-313-26135-0*, ZSM/, Greenwood Pr) Greenwood.

Semites, Iranians, Greeks, & Romans: Studies in Their Interactions. Jonathan A. Goldstein. (Brown Judaic Studies). 274p. 1990. 59.95 (*1-55540-512-6*, 14 02 17) Scholars Pr GA.

Semitic Alphabets see Alphabet: An Account of the Origin & Development of Letters

Semitic & Indo-European: The Principal Etymologies: With Observations on Afro-Asiatic. Saul Levin. LC 95-19984. (Current Issues in Linguistic Theory Ser.: No. 129). xxii, 514p. 1995. student ed., lib. bdg. 97.00 (*1-55619-583-4*) Benjamins North Am.

Semitic & Oriental Studies: A Volume Presented to William Popper, on the Occasion of His 75th Birthday, October 29, 1949. Ed. by Walter J. Fischel. LC 51-9375. (University of California Publications in Social Welfare: Vol. 11). 476p. reprint ed. pap. 135.70 (*0-317-29578-0*, 2021490) Bks Demand.

*__Semitic Background of the New Testament.__ Joseph A. Fitzmyer. LC 97-10581. (Biblical Resource Ser.). 872p. 1997. pap. text ed. 35.00 (*0-8028-4344-1*) Eerdmans.

Semitic Influence in Hellenic Mythology. Robert Brown. 1977. 25.95 (*0-405-10084-1*, 14709) Ayer.

Semitic Interference in Marcan Syntax. Elliott C. Maloney. LC 80-13016. (Society of Biblical Literature Dissertation Ser.: No. 51). 311p. 1981. pap. 22.95 (*0-89130-406-1*, 06-01-51) Scholars Pr GA.

*__Semitic Languages.__ Robert Hetzron. LC 96-45373. 552p. (C). 1997. text ed. write for info. (*0-415-05767-1*) Routledge.

Semitic Magic: Its Origins & Development. Reginald C. Thompson. LC 73-18858. reprint ed. 36.50 (*0-404-11361-3*) AMS Pr.

Semitic Religious Thought & Sikhism. Bhagat S. Hira. xii, 376p. 1992. 20.00 (*81-7116-127-8*, Pub. by National Bk Shop II) Nataraj Bks.

Semitic Words in Egyptian Texts of the New Kingdom & Third Intermediate Period. James E. Hoch. LC 94-9976. 600p. 1994. text ed. 69.50 (*0-691-03761-2*) Princeton U Pr.

Semitischen Personennamen in Den Alt- und Reichsamaischen Inschriften Aus Vorderasien. Mohammed Maraqten. (Texte und Studien Zur Orientalistik Ser.: Vol. 5). vi, 250p. 1988. write for info. (*3-487-09042-2*) G Olms Pubs.

Semja Pravoslavnago Khristjanina. 569p. 1958. reprint ed. 15.00 (*0-317-30248-5*) Holy Trinity.

Semmelweis. Jens Bjorneboe. Tr. & Intro. by Joe Martin. (Classics Ser.: No. 133). 120p. (Orig.). 1997. pap. 10.95 (*1-55713-350-6*) Sun & Moon CA.

Semmelweis Krankheit. I. Benedek. 112p. (C). 1983. 24.00 (*963-05-3428-2*, Pub. by Akad Kiado HU) St Mut.

Semmes America. Anderson Humphreys & Curt Guenther. (Illus.). 736p. 1989. 40.00 (*0-9621835-0-4*) Humphreys Ink.

Semone: Broken & Poured Out: A Korean's Journey with Jesus. Ki Dong Kim. 266p. (Orig.). 1996. pap. 9.99 (*1-56043-266-7*) Destiny Image.

Sempe - On Holiday. Pref. by Jacques Reda et al. (Illus.). 88p. 1995. pap. 19.95 (*3-7913-1099-2*, Pub. by Prestel GW) te Neues.

Semper Fi. Michael Brady. 1988. pap. 5.95 (*0-88145-062-6*) Broadway Play.

Semper Fi, Mac: Living Memories of the U. S. Marines in World War II. Henry Berry. 374p. 1996. pap. 12.00 (*0-688-14956-1*) Morrow.

*__Semper Fi, Vietnam: From Da Nang to the DMZ: Marine Corps Campaigns, 1965-1972.__ Edward F. Murphy. LC 97-7246. 1997. 24.95 (*0-89141-562-9*) Presidio Pr.

Semper Fidelis: The History of the United States Marine Corps. enl. rev. ed. Allan R. Millett. 800p. 1991. pap. 21.95 (*0-02-921596-X*, Free Press); text ed. 40.00 (*0-02-921595-1*, Free Press) Free Pr.

Semper Fidelis in Peace & War. Albert C. Smith, Jr. Ed. by Laura T. Smith. LC 94-93957. (Illus.). 208p. (Orig.). 1995. 9.95 (*0-933086-11-3*) Cromwell-Smith.

Sempiternal Season: Studies in Seventeenth-Century Devotional Writing. Paul G. Stanwood. LC 91-36045. (Seventeenth-Century Texts & Studies: Vol. 3). 185p. (C). 1992. text ed. 42.95 (*0-8204-1778-5*) P Lang Pubng.

Semple Math, Level 1. 245p. 1985. Tchr's. manual, 245p. teacher ed. 19.95 (*0-941112-26-8*) Stevnson Lrn.

Semple Math, Level 2. 382p. 1990. Tchr's. manual, 382p. teacher ed. 22.95 (*0-941112-31-4*) Stevnson Lrn.

Semple Math, Wkbk. C, Level 1. 92p. 1986. Wkbk. C, 92p., 1986. student ed. 4.50 (*0-941112-27-6*) Stevnson Lrn.

Semple Math, Wkbk. C, Level 2. 92p. 1990. Wkbk. C, 92p. student ed. 4.50 (*0-941112-34-9*) Stevnson Lrn.

Semple Math, Wkbk. A, Level 1. 92p. 1985. Wkbk. A, 92p. student ed. 4.50 (*0-941112-24-1*) Stevnson Lrn.

Semple Math, Wkbk. A, Level 2. 92p. 1990. Wkbk. A, 92p. student ed. 4.50 (*0-941112-32-2*) Stevnson Lrn.

Semple Math, Wkbk. B, Level 1. 92p. 1985. Wkbk. B, 92p. student ed. 4.50 (*0-941112-25-X*) Stevnson Lrn.

Semple Math, Wkbk. B, Level 2. 92p. 1990. Wkbk. B, 92p. student ed. 4.50 (*0-941112-33-0*) Stevnson Lrn.

Sempre Adelante. Cubillos. (College Spanish Ser.). (SPA.). 1996. wbk. ed., pap. 30.95 (*0-8384-6489-0*) Heinle & Heinle.

Sempre Adelante. Johnson. (College Spanish Ser.). (SPA.). 1996. suppl. ed., pap. 21.95 (*0-8384-6487-4*) Heinle & Heinle.

Sempre Adelante. Mccone & Cubillos. (College Spanish Ser.). (SPA.). 1996. pap. 34.95 (*0-8384-6522-6*) Heinle & Heinle.

Sempre Adelante. annot. ed. Cubillos. (College Spanish Ser.). (SPA.). 1996. teacher ed., text ed. 36.95 (*0-8384-6488-2*) Heinle & Heinle.

Semrad: The Heart of a Therapist. Ed. by Susan Rako & Harvey Mazer. LC 84-45091. 208p. 1983. 30.00 (*0-87668-684-6*) Aronson.

*__Senal - The Sign: Profecia Biblica Acerca/Ultimos Tiempos - Bible Prophecy Concerning the End Times.__ Van Kampen. 542p. (SPA.). 1996. write for info. (*0-7899-0191-9*) Editorial Unilit.

Senal Que Se Espera. A. Buero Vallejo. 75p. (SPA.). 1966. 1.00 (*0-8288-7033-0*) Fr & Eur.

Senales de Los Apostoles: Observaciones Sobre el Pentecostalismo Antiguo Y Moderno. Chantry J. Chantry. Tr. by Jorge E. Zamora from ENG. 157p. (Orig.). (SPA.). 1990. pap. 6.99 (*0-85151-573-8*) Banner of Truth.

Senales de Su Venida. Yiye Avila. 110p. (SPA.). 1995. pap. 5.99 (*1-56063-433-2*, 550035) Editorial Unilit.

Senat De la Republique Romaine: Sa Composition et Ses Attributions, 3 Vols., Set. Pierre Willems. LC 75-7350. (Roman History Ser.). (FRE.). 1975. reprint ed. 134.95 (*0-405-07071-3*) Ayer.

Senat De la Republique Romaine: Sa Composition et Ses Attributions, 3 Vols., Vol. 1. Pierre Willems. LC 75-7350. (Roman History Ser.). (FRE.). 1975. reprint ed. 67.95 (*0-405-07072-1*) Ayer.

Senat De la Republique Romaine: Sa Composition et Ses Attributions, 3 Vols., Vol. 2. Pierre Willems. LC 75-7350. (Roman History Ser.). (FRE.). 1975. reprint ed. 67.95 (*0-405-07073-X*) Ayer.

Senate & the Versailles Mandate System. Rayford W. Logan. LC 74-14357. 112p. 1975. reprint ed. text ed. 55.00 (*0-8371-7798-7*, LOVM, Greenwood Pr) Greenwood.

Senate & Treaties, Seventeen Eighty-Nine to Eighteen Seventeen. Ralston Hayden. LC 73-127295. (Law, Politics & History Ser.). 1970. reprint ed. lib. bdg. 32.50 (*0-306-71164-8*) Da Capo.

Senate & U. S. Troops in Europe. Phil Williams. LC 84-22851. 224p. 1985. text ed. 39.95 (*0-312-71300-2*) St Martin.

Senate Documents, Treaties, Conventions, International Acts, Protocols, & Agreements Between the United States of America & Other Powers, 4 vols., Set. William M. Malloy. reprint ed. lib. bdg. 395.00 (*0-403-00246-X*) Scholarly.

Senate Elections. Alan I. Abramowitz & Jeffrey A. Segal. LC 92-20733. (Illus.). 280p. (C). 1992. text ed. 52.50 (*0-472-10345-8*); pap. text ed. 19.95 (*0-472-08192-6*) U of Mich Pr.

Senate Elections & Campaign Intensity. Mark C. Westlye. LC 90-46421. 304p. 1991. text ed. 48.50 (*0-8018-4102-X*) Johns Hopkins.

Senate Establishment. Joseph S. Clark et al. LC 83-26395. 138p. 1984. reprint ed. text ed. 49.75 (*0-313-24285-2*, CLSE, Greenwood Pr) Greenwood.

Senate Executive Journal & Related Documents, 3 vols., Vol. 2. Ed. by Linda G. De Pauw. 592p. 1974. 65.00 (*0-8018-1572-X*) Johns Hopkins.

Senate Journal, Nineteen Forty-Three to Nineteen Forty-Five. Allen Drury. LC 76-38824. (FDR & the Era of the New Deal Ser.). 1972. reprint ed. lib. bdg. 59.50 (*0-306-70448-X*) Da Capo.

Senate Legislative Journal, 3 vols., Vol. 3. Ed. by Linda G. De Pauw. 800p. 1972. 65.00 (*0-8018-1280-1*) Johns Hopkins.

*__Senate Munitions Inquiry of the 1930s: Beyond the Merchants of Death.__ Matthew W. Coulter. LC 97-1692. (Contributions in American History: Vol. 177). 1997. text ed. write for info. (*0-313-30394-0*, Greenwood Pr) Greenwood.

Senate Nobody Knows. Bernard Asbell. LC 80-8928. 480p. (C). 1981. reprint ed. pap. text ed. 16.95 (*0-8018-2620-9*) Johns Hopkins.

Senate of Imperial Rome. Richard J. Talbert. LC 83-42580. (Illus.). 606p. 1983. pap. text ed. 32.50 (*0-691-10238-4*) Princeton U Pr.

S

An Asterisk (*) at the beginning of an entry indicates that the title is appearing in BIP for the first time.

Senate of the Roman Republic: Addresses on the History of Roman Constitutionalism. 1996. lib. bdg. 251.95 (0-8490-6873-8) Gordon Pr.

Senate of the United States. Richard A. Baker. LC 87-3740. (Anvil Ser.). 272p. 1987. pap. 15.00 (0-89874-865-8, (K)) Krieger.

Senate, One Hundredth Congress. Robert S. Smith. LC 86-62570. 200p. 1987. 29.95 (0-940441-00-4) Madison Pub AL.

***Senate Prayers of Peter Marshall. Peter Marshall. Ed. by Lloyd J. Ogilvie. 128p. 1997. 16.95 (0-939218-11-9) Chapman Billies.**
Each day, the United States Senate opens with a prayer from its Chaplain. Over the years, none has performed this task with greater impact on the Senate & on the nation than the Reverend Peter Marshall. His daily prayers spoke so pungently to current topic that they were widely quoted in the press & were so helpful to senators that they began seeking him out as their "pastor." This book contains much of the text of the Memorial Edition of his prayers published by the Senate after his death in 1949. The current Chaplain, the Reverend Lloyd Ogilvie, has added some new words that will help introduce Dr. Marshall to today's readers. Catherine Marshall, Peter Marshall's widow, wrote a bestselling biography, A MAN CALLED PETER, which is still in print. Their son, Peter, is also a Presbyterian minister & an author with national recognition. ***Publisher Provided Annotation.***

Senate, Treaties & National Security, 1945-1974. Bernard T. Pitsvada. 252p. (C). 1991. pap. text ed. 29.50 (0-8191-8199-4); lib. bdg. 52.50 (0-8191-8198-6) U Pr of Amer.

Senate vs. Governor, Alabama, 1971: Referents for Opposition in a One-Party Legislature. Harold W. Stanley. LC 74-23369. 128p. 1975. pap. 36.50 (0-7837-8407-4, 2059218) Bks Demand.

Senate, 1983 (Annual) see Porter's Guide to Congressional Roll Call Votes

Senate, 1984 (Serial & Annual) see Porter's Guide to Congressional Roll Call Votes

Senate, 1985 (Serial & Annual) see Porter's Guide to Congressional Roll Call Votes

Senator. Richard Bowker. 432p. 1995. mass mkt. 5.99 (0-380-72056-6) Avon.

Senator: In the Company of Connie Mack, U.S. Senator from Florida. Richard Sobol. LC 94-33076. (Government in Action Ser.). (Illus.). 30p. (J). (gr. 3-7). 1995. pap. 14.99 (0-525-65197-7, Cobblehill Bks) Dutton Child Bks.

Senator Alan Bible & the Politics of the New West. Gary E. Elliott. LC 94-9701. (Wilbur S. Shepperson Series in History & Humanities: No. 36). 1994. 34.95 (0-87417-240-3) U of Nev Pr.

Senator Allen Ellender of Louisiana: A Biography. Thomas A. Becnel. LC 95-35101. (Southern Biography Ser.). (Illus.). 344p. (C). 1995. text ed. 30.00 (0-8071-1978-4) La State U Pr.

***Senator & the Sharecropper's Son: Exoneration of the Brownsville Soldiers.** John D. Weaver. LC 96-29637. (Illus.). 264p. (C). 1997. text ed. 29.95 (0-89096-748-2) Tex A&M Univ Pr.

Senator Bob Packwood's Secret Diary. Bob Packwood. 1994. pap. 4.99 (1-56171-315-5, S P I Bks) Sure Seller.

Senator for Sale. Stanley Hilton. 1996. mass mkt. 6.99 (0-312-95925-7) St Martin.

Senator for Sale: An Unauthorized Biography of Senator Bob Dole. Stanley Hilton. 320p. 1995. 22.95 (0-312-13600-5) St Martin.

***Senator from Slaughter County.** Harry M. Caudill. (Illus.). 1997. reprint ed. 24.00 (0-945084-66-8) J Stuart Found.

***Senator James Murray Mason: Defender of the Old South.** Robert W. Young. LC 97-21073. 1998. write for info. (0-87049-998-X) U of Tenn Pr.

Senator Joe McCarthy. Richard H. Rovere. LC 95-40975. 285p. (Orig.). (C). 1996. pap. 12.95 (0-520-20472-7) U CA Pr.

Senator John Sherman Cooper: Consummate Statesman. Clarice J. Mitchner. 1981. 38.95 (0-405-14099-1) Ayer.

Senator Josiah William Bailey of North Carolina: A Political Biography. John R. Moore. LC 68-24639. 271p. reprint ed. 77.30 (0-8357-9118-1, 2017914) Bks Demand.

Senator Love. Warren Adler. 256p. 1992. reprint ed. mass mkt. 3.99 (0-8217-3998-0, Zebra Kensgtn) Kensgtn Pub Corp.

***Senator Mitchell's Last Stand.** Peter J. Ferrara. 25p. 1994. pap. 5.00 (1-56808-023-9, BG134) Natl Ctr Pol.

Senator Must Die. Robert D. Morrow. LC 88-61816. (Illus.). 368p. 1988. 22.95 (0-915677-39-3) Roundtable Pub.

Senator North. Gertrude F. Atherton. LC 67-29258. (Americans in Fiction Ser.). 367p. reprint ed. lib. bdg. 29.00 (0-8398-0068-1) Irvington.

Senator North. Gertrude F. Atherton. (Americans in Fiction Ser.). 367p. 1986. reprint ed. pap. text ed. 7.95 (0-8290-2021-7) Irvington.

Senator Pothole: The Unauthorized Biography of Al D'Amato. Leonard Lurie. LC 93-47232. 1994. 21.95 (1-55972-227-4, Birch Ln Pr) Carol Pub Group.

***Senator Proxmire's Golden Fleece Award: A History & Appreciation.** (Orig.). 1996. pap. 5.00 (1-888415-02-9) Taxpyrs Common Sense.

Senator Sorghum's Primer of Politics. Philander C. Johnson. LC 78-104499. reprint ed. lib. bdg. 14.00 (0-8398-0955-7) Irvington.

Senator Sorghum's Primer of Politics. Philander C. Johnson. (C). 1986. reprint ed. pap. text ed. 4.95 (0-8290-2022-5) Irvington.

Senatorial Career of Fred T. Dubois of Idaho, 1890-1907. Leo W. Graff. LC 88-10272. (Modern American History Ser.). 616p. 1988. 35.00 (0-8240-4330-8) Garland.

***Senatorial Career of Harley Martin Kilgore.** rev. ed. Robert F. Maddox. (Illus.). 351p. (C). 1996. reprint ed. pap. text ed. 16.95 (0-943025-81-8) Cummngs & Hath.

***Senatorial Privilege.** Gorman. LC 97-13324. 1997. 23.95 (0-312-85778-0) St Martin.

Senatorial Privilege: The Chappaquiddick Coverup. Leo Damore. LC 88-11535. (Illus.). 496p. 1988. 21.95 (0-89526-564-8) Regnery Pub.

Senator's Agenda. Bob Larson. LC 94-49019. 288p. 1995. 16.99 (0-7852-7879-6) Nelson.

Senator's Bride. Janet Peart. (Brides of Montclair Ser.: Vol. 12). 224p. 1994. pap. 8.99 (0-310-67151-5) Zondervan.

***Senator's Daughter.** Victoria Gotti. LC 96-53195. 1997. 23.95 (0-312-86323-3) St Martin.

***Senator's Daughter.** large type ed. Victoria Gotti. LC 97-9303. (Core Ser.). 464p. 1997. 26.95 (0-7838-8196-7, GK Hall) Thorndike Pr.

Senators on the Campaign Trail: The Politics of Representation. Richard F. Fenno, Jr. LC 95-42282. (Julian J. Rothbaum Distinguished Lectures: Vol. 6). (Illus.). 448p. 1996. 24.95 (0-8061-2827-5) U of Okla Pr.

Senato. s Son & Other Stories. Steven Porter. LC 90-61762. 154p. (Orig.). 1994. pap. write for info. (0-9625372-1-7) Phantom Pubns.

Senator's Whore. Cindy Kallmer & Leo Guild. 224p. 1990. mass mkt. 3.95 (0-87067-355-6) Holloway.

***SENCO Handbook: Working Within a Whole-School Approach.** Elizabeth Cowne. 160p. 1996. pap. 24.95 (1-85346-413-9) Taylor & Francis.

Send a Baby: Birth of John the Baptist. Mary M. Simon. (Hear Me Read Ser.). (Illus.). 24p. (Orig.). (J). (ps-1). 1992. pap. 2.49 (0-570-04706-4, 56-1665) Concordia.

Send a Gunboat. Douglas Reeman. 256p. 1986. reprint ed. lib. bdg. 19.95 (0-89966-557-8) Buccaneer Bks.

Send Fresh Horses. Bob Budd. (Illus.). 128p. 1987. 12.95 (0-943255-00-7); pap. 8.95 (0-943255-01-5) Portfolio Pub.

***Send Guns & Money: Security Assistance & U. S. Foreign Policy.** Duncan L. Clarke & Daniel D. O'Connor. LC 97-5885. 1997. text ed. write for info. (0-275-95991-0, Praeger Pubs); pap. text ed. write for info. (0-275-95992-9, Praeger Pubs) Greenwood.

***Send in the Stunt Man: A Committed Collection.** Michael Fry. (Illus.). 128p. (Orig.). 1997. pap. 9.95 (0-8362-3663-7) Andrews & McMeel.

***Send Mail Quick Reference.** Bryan Costales & Eric Allman. Ed. by Gigi Estabrook. (Illus.). 40p. (Orig.). 1997. pap. 6.95 (1-56592-278-6) OReilly & Assocs.

Send Me a Letter: A Basic Guide to Letter Writing. Sol Gonshack & Joanna McKenzie. (Illus.). 224p. (C). 1982. pap. text ed. write for info. (0-13-806604-3) P-H.

Send Me a Memo: A Handbook of Model Memos. Dianna Booher. 224p. 1984. 19.95 (0-87196-906-8) Facts on File.

Send Me down a Miracle. Han Nolan. LC 95-38169. 256p. (YA). (gr. 7 up). 1996. 12.00 (0-15-200979-5) HarBrace.

Send Me Down a Miracle. Han Nolan. 256p. (YA). (gr. 7 up). 1996. pap. 6.00 (0-15-200978-7) HarBrace.

Send Me? The Itineracy in Crisis. Ed. by Donald E. Messer. 208p. (Orig.). 1991. pap. 12.95 (0-687-37155-4) Abingdon.

Send My Roots Rain. Ibis Gomez-Vega. LC 91-37831. 224p. (Orig.). 1991. pap. 9.95 (1-879960-04-4) Aunt Lute Bks.

Send No Blessings. Phyllis R. Naylor. 240p. (YA). (gr. 5 up). 1992. pap. 3.99 (0-14-034859-X) Puffin Bks.

Send No Blessings. Phyllis R. Naylor. LC 89-28024. 240p. (YA). (gr. 7 up). 1990. lib. bdg. 16.00 (0-689-31582-1, Atheneum Bks Young) S&S Childrens.

Send Out the Dove. limited ed. Stanley Mason. (New Poetic Drama Ser.). 1986. pap. 5.00 (0-934218-37-4) Dragons Teeth.

Send These to Me: Immigrants in Urban America. rev. ed. John Higham. LC 84-47960. (C). 1984. reprint ed. pap. text ed. 14.95 (0-8018-2438-9) Johns Hopkins.

Send This Jerk the Bedbug Letter: How Companies, Politicians, & the Mass Media Deal with Complaints & how to be a more effective complainer. John Bear. 224p. (Orig.). 1996. pap. 11.95 (0-89815-811-7) Ten Speed Pr.

Send Us a Lady Physician: Women Doctors in America, 1835-1920. Ruth Abram. LC 85-13856. (Illus.). 1986. pap. 12.95 (0-393-30278-4) Norton.

Senda De Vida: El Expositor. Gospel Press Corp. Staff. (SPA.). 1993. pap. write for info. (0-938127-04-7) Gospel Pr FL.

Sendak at the Rosenbach. Maurice Sendak. Ed. by Vincent Giroud & Maurice Sendak. LC 95-68402. (Illus.). 48p. (Orig.). 1995. pap. 15.00 (0-939084-27-9) R Mus & Lib.

***Sendak in Asia.** Ed. by Justine G. Schiller. (Illus.). 52p. (Orig.). 1996. pap. 20.00 (0-9627110-1-2) Battledore Ltd.

Sendas Literarias. Ruth A. Barraza & Aida W. Lier. LC 94-11182. 1995. text ed. 46.95 (0-8384-5126-8) Heinle & Heinle.

Sendas Literarias. Walqui. (Secondary Spanish Ser.). (SPA.). 1995. teacher ed., text ed. 25.95 (0-8384-5132-2) Heinle & Heinle.

Sendas Literarias. Walqui. (Secondary Spanish Ser.). (SPA.). 1996. text ed. 46.95 (0-8384-5135-7) Heinle & Heinle.

Sendas Literarias. Walqui. (Secondary Spanish Ser.). (SPA.). 1996. teacher ed., text ed. 25.95 (0-8384-5136-5) Heinle & Heinle.

Sendas Literarias: Hispanoamerica. Edward J. Mullen & David H. Darst. 256p. (C). 1988. pap. text ed. write for info. (0-07-554129-7) McGraw.

Sendero Luminoso: An Annotated Bibliography of the Shining Path Guerrilla Movement, 1980-1993. Peter A. Stern. xxv, 363p. (Orig.). 1995. pap. 56.95 (0-917617-43-6) SALALM.

Sendero Luminoso: Evolucion de una Secta Estalinista. Martin Koppel. Orig. Title: Sitting Still. 1994. pap. 3.50 (0-87348-782-6) Pathfinder NY.

Sendero Luminoso & the Threat of Narcoterrorism. Gabriela Tarazona-Sevillano. LC 90-37058. (Washington Papers: No. 144). 184p. 1990. text ed. 49.95 (0-275-93642-2, C3642, Praeger Pubs); pap. text ed. 17.95 (0-275-93643-0, B3643, Praeger Pubs) Greenwood.

Senderos de mi Destino. Pedro J. Ruiz. 80p. (SPA.). 1984. pap. 5.00 (0-685-08592-9) SLUSA.

Senderos de Paz. Norman Warren. 48p. (SPA.). 1989. pap. 1.50 (0-945792-21-2, 490251) Editorial Unilit.

Sendi Lee Mason & the Big Mistake. Hilda Stahl. LC 90-23026. (Growing up Adventure Ser.). 128p. (Orig.). (J). (gr. 1-4). 1991. pap. 4.99 (0-89107-613-1) Crossway Bks.

Sendi Lee Mason & the Great Crusade. Hilda Stahl. (Sandi Lee Mason - Growing up Adventure Ser.). 128p. (J). (gr. 2-5). 1991. pap. 4.99 (0-89107-632-8) Crossway Bks.

Sending. Robert Hawks. 160p. (Orig.). (YA). (gr. 7 up). 1996. pap. 3.99 (0-380-78158-1, Flare) Avon.

Sending My Heart Back Across the Years: Tradition & Innovation in Native American Autobiography. Hertha D. Wong. (Illus.). 256p. 1992. 45.00 (0-19-506912-9) OUP.

Sending of Dragons. Jane Yolen. LC 96-8457. 1997. pap. 6.00 (0-15-200864-0) HarBrace.

***Sending Workers Abroad.** Manolo Abella. 120p. 1997. pap. 18.00 (92-2-108525-2) Intl Labour Office.

***Sendmail.** 2nd ed. Bryan Costales & Eric Allman. Ed. by Gigi Estabrook. (Illus.). 900p. 1997. pap. 39.95 (1-56592-222-0) OReilly & Assocs.

Sendmail: Theory & Practice. Frederick M. Avolio & Paul Vixie. 220p. (C). 1995. pap. 31.95 (1-55558-127-7, Digital DEC) Buttrwrth-Heinemann.

Sendschreiben Uber Seine Glaubenslehre an Lucke see On the Glaubenslehre: Two Letters to Dr. Lucke

***Seneca.** Karen Baker. (J). Date not set. lib. bdg. write for info. (0-688-14031-9) Greenwillow.

Seneca. Karen L. Baker. LC 95-35846. (J). (ps up). 1997. 15.00 (0-688-14030-0) Greenwillow.

Seneca. Jill Duvall. LC 90-21150. (New True Bks.). (Illus.). 48p. (J). (gr. k-4). 1991. pap. 5.50 (0-516-41119-5); lib. bdg. 19.00 (0-516-01119-7) Childrens.

Seneca. Francis Holland. LC 72-102246. (Select Bibliographies Reprint Ser.). 1977. 26.95 (0-8369-5131-X) Ayer.

Seneca. large type ed. Donald C. Porter. LC 93-27951. (White Indian Ser.). (Orig.). 1994. lib. bdg. 22.95 (0-8161-5847-9, GK Hall) Thorndike Pr.

Seneca: A Critical Bibliography, 1900-1980: Scholarship on His Life, Thought, Prose, & Influence. Ed. by Anna L. Motto & John R. Clark. 372p. (Orig.). 1989. pap. 98.00 (90-256-0959-7, Pub. by A M Hakkert NE) Benjamins North Am.

Seneca: A Philosopher in Politics. Ed. by Miriam Griffin. 520p. 1992. pap. 39.95 (0-19-814774-0) OUP.

Seneca: Four Dialogues. Ed. by Costa. 1995. 49.95 (0-85668-560-7, Pub. by Aris & Phillips UK); pap. 24.95 (0-85668-561-5, Pub. by Aris & Phillips UK) David Brown.

Seneca: Hercules Furens: The Madness of Hercules. Jo-Ann Shelton. 113p. 1990. 12.50 (0-87291-201-9) Coronado Pr.

Seneca: Select Letters. Walter C. Summers. 500p. (LAT.). 1983. pap. 32.95 (0-86292-120-1, Pub. by Brstl Class Pr UK) Focus Pub-R Pullins.

Seneca: Seventeen Letters. Ed. by Costa. (Classical Texts Ser.). 1988. 49.95 (0-85668-354-X, Pub. by Aris & Phillips UK); pap. 24.95 (0-85668-355-8, Pub. by Aris & Phillips UK) David Brown.

***Seneca: Suasoriae.** Ed. by W. Edward. 208p. (Orig.). 1996. pap. text ed. 26.95 (1-85399-504-5, Pub. by Brstl Class Pr UK) Focus Pub-R Pullins.

Seneca: The Climber's Guide. Tony Barnes. 169p. 1995. pap. 19.95 (0-9643698-1-8) Earthbnd Spts.

Seneca: The Humanist at the Court of Nero. Villy Sorenson. Tr. by W. Glyn Jones. LC 84-18. 352p. 1984. 30.00 (0-226-76827-9) U Ch Pr.

Seneca & Celestina. Louise Fothergill-Payne. (Cambridge Iberian & Latin American Studies). (Illus.). 192p. 1988. text ed. 59.95 (0-521-32212-X) Cambridge U Pr.

Seneca & Elizabethan Tragedy. E. F. Lucas. 1973. 250.00 (0-87968-047-4) Gordon Pr.

Seneca & Elizabethan Tragedy. F. L. Lucas. LC 68-1142. (Studies in Comparative Literature: No. 35). 1969. reprint ed. lib. bdg. 75.00 (0-8383-0668-3) M S G Haskell Hse.

Seneca & Tuscarora Indians: An Annotated Bibliography. Marilyn L. Haas. LC 94-4415. (Native American Bibliography Ser.: Vol. 17). 465p. 1994. 55.00 (0-8108-2740-9) Scarecrow.

Seneca Apocolocyntosis. Paul Roth. (Latin Commentaries Ser.). 54p. (Orig.). (C). 1988. pap. text ed. 6.00 (0-929524-51-9) Bryn Mawr Commentaries.

***Seneca by Candlelight & Other Stories of Renaissance Drama.** Lorraine R. Helms. LC 97-15557. 1997. write for info. (0-8122-3413-8) U of Pa Pr.

Seneca Falls Inheritance. Miriam G. Monfredo. 304p. 1994. mass mkt. 5.99 (0-425-14465-8, Prime Crime) Berkley Pub.

Seneca, His Tenne Tragedies, 2 Vols, Set. Lucius A. Seneca. LC 31-16192. (Tudor Translations, Second Ser: Nos. 11-12). reprint ed. 115.00 (0-404-52000-6) AMS Pr.

Seneca Indian in the Union Army: The Civil War Letters of Sergeant Isaac Newton Parker, 1861-1865. Ed. by Laurence M. Hauptman. LC 95-9179. (Civil War Heritage Ser.: Vol. V). (Illus.). 112p. (Orig.). (C). 1995. pap. 12.00 (0-942597-57-5, Burd St Pr) White Mane Pub.

Seneca Indian Myths. Jeremiah Curtin. (Works of Jeremiah Curtin Ser.). 1990. reprint ed. lib. bdg. 79.00 (0-685-44787-1) Rprt Serv.

Seneca Indian Stories. Leo Cooper. 1995. pap. 9.95 (0-912678-89-5) Greenfld Rev Lit.

***Seneca Lake: Past, Present & Future.** Carol U. Sisler. (Illus.). 144p. 1995. pap. 18.95 (0-614-26431-6) Purple Mnt Pr.

Seneca, Lucius Annaeus: Tragoediae, Index Verborum, Releves Lexicaux et Grammaticaux. Ed. by Joseph Denooz. (Alpha-Omega, Reihe A Ser.: Bd. XL). xiv, 628p. 1980. write for info. (3-487-06962-8) G Olms Pubs.

Seneca Myths & Folk Tales. Arthur C. Parker. LC 89-4869. (Illus.). xxxiv, 483p. 1989. pap. 15.00 (0-8032-8723-2, Bison Books) U of Nebr Pr.

Seneca Myths & Folk Tales. Arthur C. Parker. LC 76-43803. (Buffalo Historical Society, Publication Ser.: Vol. 27). reprint ed. 74.50 (0-404-15659-2) AMS Pr.

Seneca Myths & Folktales. A. C. Parker. 465p. 1993. reprint ed. lib. bdg. 99.00 (0-7812-5162-1) Rprt Serv.

Seneca O el Beneficio de la Duda. Antonio Gala. (Nueva Austral Ser.: Vol. 4). (SPA.). 1991. pap. text ed. 24.95 (84-239-1804-1) Elliots Bks.

Seneca Thanksgiving Rituala. Wallace L. Chafe. 1988. reprint ed. lib. bdg. 75.00 (0-7812-0079-2) Rprt Serv.

Seneca Thanksgiving Rituals No. 25. L. Chafe. (Bureau of American Ethnology Bulletins Ser.). 302p. 1995. lib. bdg. 99.00 (0-7812-4183-9) Rprt Serv.

Seneca the Elder. Janet Fairweather. (Cambridge Classical Studies). 384p. 1981. text ed. 69.95 (0-521-23101-9) Cambridge U Pr.

Seneca the Philosopher & His Modern Message. Richard M. Gummere. 1976. lib. bdg. 59.95 (0-8490-2593-1) Gordon Pr.

Seneca, the Philosopher & His Modern Message. Richard M. Gummere. LC 63-10274. (Our Debt to Greece & Rome Ser.). 145p. 1963. reprint ed. lib. bdg. 50.50 (0-8154-0098-5) Cooper Sq.

Seneca Tragodien: Sprachliche Und Stilistische Untersuchungen. M. Billerbeck. LC 88-4114. (Supplements to Mnemosyne Biblioteca Classica Batava Ser.: Vol. 105). vi, 219p. (Orig.). (GER.). 1988. pap. 53.75 (90-04-08631-5) E J Brill.

Seneca Unmasqued: Aphra Behn's Translation of la Rochefoucauld's Maxims. Ed. by Irwin Primer. (Studies in the Eighteenth Century: No. 29). 1995. reprint ed. write for info. (0-404-63529-6) AMS Pr.

Seneca Unmasqued & Other Prose Translations. Aphra A. Behn. Ed. by Janet Todd. (Complete Works of Aphra Behn: Vol. IV). 434p. 1994. text ed. 72.50 (0-8142-0627-1) Ohio St U Pr.

Seneca, Vol. 1: The Tragedies. Tr. by David R. Slavitt from LAT. 208p. 1992. pap. 12.95 (0-8018-4309-X); text ed. 38.50 (0-8018-4308-1) Johns Hopkins.

Seneca, Vol. 2: The Tragedies. Tr. by David R. Slavitt from LAT. (Complete Roman Drama in Translation Ser.). 296p. 1995. pap. 15.95 (0-8018-4932-2); text ed. 45.00 (0-8018-4931-4) Johns Hopkins.

Senecae libri duo de clementia commentariis illustrati (1532) John Calvin. Ed. by Ford L. Battles & Andre M. Hugo. No. 3. 1969. write for info. (0-318-59381-5) Renaiss Society Am.

Senecan Drama & Stoic Cosmology. Thomas G. Rosenmeyer. 1989. 42.00 (0-520-06445-3) U CA Pr.

Senecan Tragedy. Anna L. Motto & John R. Clark. 367p. 1988. 128.00 (90-256-0920-1, Pub. by A M Hakkert NE) Benjamins North Am.

***Senecan Tragedy: An Essay in the Theatrical Tradition.** LC 96-52766. 272p. (C). 1997. text ed. write for info. (0-415-12495-6) Routledge.

Seneca's Anapaests: Metre, Colometry, Text & Artistry in the Anapaests of Seneca's Tragedies. John G. Fitch. LC 87-20466. (American Classical Studies). 103p. 1987. 23.95 (1-55540-162-7, 40-04-17); pap. 15.95 (1-55540-214-3) Scholars Pr GA.

Seneca's Drama. Norman T. Pratt. LC 82-23791. viii, 230p. 1983. 37.50 (0-8078-1555-1) U of NC Pr.

Seneca's "Hercules Furens" A Critical Text with Introduction & Commentary. Lucius A. Seneca. LC 86-11582. (Cornell Studies in Classical Philology). 496p. (C). 1987. 65.00 (0-8014-1876-3) Cornell U Pr.

Seneca's Hercules Furens: A Critical Text with Introduction & Commentary. Lucius Annaeus Seneca. LC 86-11582. (Cornell Studies in Classical Philology: Vol. 45). 491p. 1987. reprint ed. pap. 140.00 (0-608-01694-2, 2062349) Bks Demand.

Seneca's Phoenissae: Introduction & Commentary. Marica Frank. 296p. 1994. 83.50 (90-04-09776-7) E J Brill.

Seneca's Thyestes. R. J. Tarrant. (American Philological Association Textbook Ser.). 269p. (C). 1985. pap. 19.00 (0-89130-871-7, 40-03-11) Scholars Pr GA.

Senefer: A Young Genius in Old Egypt. Beatrice Lumpkin. LC 92-71026. (Young Reader's Ser.). (Illus.). 32p. (J). (gr. 2-5). 1992. 16.95 (0-86543-244-9); pap. 6.95 (0-86543-245-7) Africa World.

Senefer & Hatshepsut. Beatrice Lumpkin. LC 91-75349. (Young Reader's Ser.). (Illus.). 64p. 1995. reprint ed. 24.95 (0-86543-272-4); reprint ed. pap. 9.95 (0-86543-273-2) Africa World.

An Asterisk (*) at the beginning of an entry indicates that the title is appearing in BIP for the first time.

***Senegal.** Margaret Beaton. LC 96-51578. (Enchantment of the World Ser.). (J). 1997. lib. bdg. 30.00 (*0-516-20304-5*) Childrens.

Senegal. Alison Brownlie. LC 95-26778. (Worldfocus Ser.). (J). 1996. write for info. (*1-57572-076-0*) Rigby Interact Libr.

Senegal. J. S. Eades. (World Bibliographical Ser.: Vol. 166). 284p. 1994. lib. bdg. 76.00 (*1-85109-156-4*) ABC-CLIO.

Senegal. Christa Mang. (Bradt Country Guides Ser.). 96p. (Orig.). 1994. pap. 15.95 (*1-56440-555-9*, Pub. by Bradt Pubns UK) Globe Pequot.

Senegal. Jasmin Saidi. LC 95-18027. 1996. 22.00 (*0-929851-48-X*) Am Assn Coll Registrars.

Senegal: A Country & Its People. Akihiro Yamamura. 1995. 35.00 (*1-883489-12-1*) Takarajima.

Senegal: A State of Change; Oxfam Country Profiles. Robin Sharp. (Oxfam Country Profiles). (Illus.). 64p. (C). 1994. pap. 9.95 (*0-85598-283-7*, Pub. by Oxfam UK) Humanities.

Senegal: La France dans l'Afrique Occidentale. Le General Faidherbe. (B. E. Ser.: No. 170). (FRE.). 1889. 45.00 (*0-8115-3082-5*) Periodicals Srv.

Senegal: Narrative Paintings. Maurice Dedieu. Tr. by Diana Barry & Jacques Henry. (Illus.). 100p. (Orig.). (ENG & FRE.). 1986. pap. 15.00 (*0-936819-02-2*) USL Art Museum.

Senegal behind Glass: Images of Religious & Daily Life. Anne-Marie Bouttiaux-Ndiaye et al. (Illus.). 168p. 1995. 60.00 (*3-7913-1424-6*, Pub. by Prestel GW) te Neues.

Senegal in Pictures. Department of Geography, Lerner Publications. (Visual Geography Ser.). (Illus.). 64p. (YA). (gr. 5 up). 1988. lib. bdg. 19.95 (*0-8225-1827-9*, Lerner Publctns) Lerner Group.

Senegalese Novel by Women: Through Their Own Eyes, Vol. 7. Susan Stringer. LC 94-34709. (Francophone Cultures & Literatures Ser.: Vol. 7). 400p. (C). 1995. 48. 95 (*0-8204-2664-4*) P Lang Pubng.

Senegambia: Land of the Lion. Philip Koslow. (Kingdoms of Africa Ser.). (Illus.). 64p. (J). (gr. 3 up). 1995. lib. bdg. 17.95 (*0-7910-3135-7*) Chelsea Hse.

Senegambia: Land of the Lion. Philip Koslow. LC 96-32297. (Kingdoms of Africa Ser.). (Illus.). 64p. (J). (gr. 3 up). 1996. pap. 8.95 (*0-7910-3136-5*) Chelsea Hse.

Senescence & Rejuvenescence. Charles M. Child. Ed. by Robert J. Kastenbaum. LC 78-22192. (Aging & Old Age Ser.). (Illus.). 1979. reprint ed. lib. bdg. 37.95 (*0-405-11809-0*) Ayer.

Senescence in Plants. Kenneth V. Thimann. 288p. 1980. 129.95 (*0-8493-5803-5*, QK762, CRC Reprint) Franklin.

Senescence, the Last Half of Life. Granville S. Hall. LC 73-169385. (Family in America Ser.). 530p. 1979. reprint ed. 31.95 (*0-405-03860-7*) Ayer.

Senghennydd: The Universal Pit Village 1890-1930. Michael Lieven. 387p. 1994. 53.00 (*1-85902-043-7*, Pub. by Gomer Pr UK) St Mut.

Senhora: Profile of a Woman. Jose M. De Alencar. Tr. by Catarina F. Edinger from POR. LC 93-791. (Texas Pan American Ser.). 225p. (C). 1994. pap. 12.95 (*0-292-70450-X*); text ed. 30.00 (*0-292-70449-6*) U of Tex Pr.

Senia Gharana: Its Contribution to Indian Classical Music. Sunita Dhar. (C). 1989. 23.50 (*0-685-33358-2*, Pub. by Reliance Pub Hse II) S Asia.

Senile Dementia: Policy & Services. Bernard Ineichen. 180p. 1989. 47.50 (*0-412-33790-8*) Chapman & Hall.

Senile Macular Degeneration. Jan E. Lovie-Kitchin & Kenneth J. Bowman. (Illus.). 144p. 1985. 37.95 (*0-409-90007-9*) Buttrwrth-Heinemann.

Senior Account Clerk. Jack Rudman. (Career Examination Ser.: C-1874). 1994. pap. 27.95 (*0-8373-1874-2*) Nat Learn.

Senior Account Clerk-Stenographer. Jack Rudman. (Career Examination Ser.: C-3470). 1994. pap. 27.95 (*0-8373-3470-5*) Nat Learn.

Senior Account Clerk-Typist. Jack Rudman. (Career Examination Ser.: C-3471). 1994. pap. 27.95 (*0-8373-3471-3*) Nat Learn.

Senior Accountant. Jack Rudman. (Career Examination Ser.: C-992). 1994. pap. 34.95 (*0-8373-0992-1*) Nat Learn.

Senior Accounting Machine Operator. Jack Rudman. (Career Examination Ser.: C-2203). 1994. pap. 27.95 (*0-8373-2203-0*) Nat Learn.

Senior Actuarial Clerk. Jack Rudman. (Career Examination Ser.: C-2418). 1994. pap. 29.95 (*0-8373-2418-1*) Nat Learn.

Senior Actuary. Jack Rudman. (Career Examination Ser.: C-993). 1994. pap. 44.95 (*0-8373-0993-X*) Nat Learn.

Senior Addiction Specialist. Jack Rudman. (Career Examination Ser.: C-1810). 1994. pap. 34.95 (*0-8373-1810-6*) Nat Learn.

Senior Administrative Analyst. Jack Rudman. (Career Examination Ser.: C-2709). 1994. pap. 34.95 (*0-8373-2709-1*) Nat Learn.

Senior Administrative Assistant. Jack Rudman. (Career Examination Ser.: C-1468). 1994. pap. 29.95 (*0-8373-1468-2*) Nat Learn.

Senior Administrative Associate. Jack Rudman. (Career Examination Ser.: C-2393). 1994. pap. 29.95 (*0-8373-2393-2*) Nat Learn.

Senior Administrative Services Clerk. Jack Rudman. (Career Examination Ser.: C-2870). 1994. pap. 29.95 (*0-8373-2870-5*) Nat Learn.

Senior Admitting Clerk. Jack Rudman. (Career Examination Ser.: C-994). 1994. pap. 27.95 (*0-8373-0994-8*) Nat Learn.

Senior Adult Camping. Constance H. Armstrong. Ed. by Glenn T. Job. (Illus.). 46p. 1979. pap. 5.95 (*0-87603-042-8*) Am Camping.

***Senior Adult Ministries with Brother Sam.** 128p. 1974. 5.99 (*0-8341-0133-5*) Nazarene.

Senior Adult Ministry: How-To Guide for the Local Church. LC 94-28208. (Service Ser.). 93p. 1994. 4.95 (*0-87227-184-6*, RBP5221) Reg Baptist.

Senior Adult Peer Advocacy. Telesis Corp. Staff. 1991. teacher ed. 125.00 (*1-56117-031-3*) Telesis CA.

Senior Adult Peer Advocacy. Telesis Corp. Staff. 1992. student ed. 9.95 (*1-56117-018-6*) Telesis CA.

Senior Adult Program Builder, No. 1. Compiled by Paul M. Miller. 1984. 5.50 (*0-685-68743-0*, MP-627) Lillenas.

Senior Adult Program Builder, No. 2. Compiled by Paul M. Miller. 1992. 5.50 (*0-685-68742-2*, MP-502) Lillenas.

Senior Air Pollution Inspector. Jack Rudman. (Career Examination Ser.: C-1469). 1994. pap. 34.95 (*0-8373-1469-0*) Nat Learn.

Senior Airport Attendant. Jack Rudman. (Career Examination Ser.: C-307). 1994. pap. 27.95 (*0-8373-0307-9*) Nat Learn.

Senior Airport Security Guard. Jack Rudman. (Career Examination Ser.: C-457). 1994. pap. 27.95 (*0-8373-0457-1*) Nat Learn.

Senior Alcoholism Counselor. (Career Examination Ser.: C-3745). 1994. pap. 34.95 (*0-8373-3745-3*) Nat Learn.

Senior Analytical Chemist. Jack Rudman. (Career Examination Ser.: C-3193). 1994. pap. 34.95 (*0-8373-3193-5*) Nat Learn.

Senior Animal Shelter Officer. Jack Rudman. (Career Examination Ser.: C-2362). 1994. pap. 27.95 (*0-8373-2362-2*) Nat Learn.

Senior Appraiser. Jack Rudman. (Career Examination Ser.: C-1470). 1994. pap. 27.95 (*0-8373-1470-4*) Nat Learn.

Senior Architect. Jack Rudman. (Career Examination Ser.: C-1326). 1994. pap. 34.95 (*0-8373-1326-0*) Nat Learn.

Senior Architectural Draftsman. Jack Rudman. (Career Examination Ser.: C-2365). 1994. pap. 29.95 (*0-8373-2365-7*) Nat Learn.

Senior Assessment Assistant. Jack Rudman. (Career Examination Ser.: C-2183). 1994. pap. 27.95 (*0-8373-2183-2*) Nat Learn.

Senior Assessment Clerk. Jack Rudman. (Career Examination Ser.: C-2921). 1994. pap. 27.95 (*0-8373-2921-3*) Nat Learn.

Senior Assessor. Jack Rudman. (Career Examination Ser.: C-995). 1994. pap. 27.95 (*0-8373-0995-6*) Nat Learn.

Senior Assets Analyst. Jack Rudman. (Career Examination Ser.: C-3498). 1994. pap. 29.95 (*0-8373-3498-5*) Nat Learn.

Senior Attorney. Jack Rudman. (Career Examination Ser.: C-996). 1994. pap. 44.95 (*0-8373-0996-4*) Nat Learn.

Senior Attorney (Realty) Jack Rudman. (Career Examination Ser.: C-568). 1994. pap. 49.95 (*0-8373-0568-3*) Nat Learn.

Senior Audio-Visual Aid Technician. Jack Rudman. (Career Examination Ser.: C-1471). 1994. pap. 27.95 (*0-8373-1471-2*) Nat Learn.

Senior Auditor. Jack Rudman. (Career Examination Ser.: C-2059). 1994. reprint ed. pap. 34.95 (*0-8373-2059-3*) Nat Learn.

Senior Auto Glass Technician Manual. National Glass Association Staff. (Illus.). 120p. 1990. pap. 29.95 (*1-56393-002-1*) National Glass Assn.

Senior Automotive Facilities Inspector. Jack Rudman. (Career Examination Ser.: C-2214). 1994. pap. 34.95 (*0-8373-2214-6*) Nat Learn.

Senior Automotive Mechanic. Jack Rudman. (Career Examination Ser.: C-3472). 1994. pap. 29.95 (*0-8373-3472-1*) Nat Learn.

Senior Automotive Serviceman. Jack Rudman. (Career Examination Ser.: C-1869). 1994. pap. 29.95 (*0-8373-1869-6*) Nat Learn.

Senior Balancing Rep. 1970. 7.24 (*0-07-521224-2*) McGraw.

Senior Bay Constable. Jack Rudman. (Career Examination Ser.: C-2525). 1994. pap. 34.95 (*0-8373-2525-0*) Nat Learn.

Senior Beverage Control Investigator. Jack Rudman. (Career Examination Ser.: C-2823). 1994. pap. 29.95 (*0-8373-2823-3*) Nat Learn.

Senior Boiler Inspector. Jack Rudman. (Career Examination Ser.: C-1629). 1994. pap. 34.95 (*0-8373-1629-4*) Nat Learn.

Senior Bookkeeper. Jack Rudman. (Career Examination Ser.: C-1751). 1994. pap. 27.95 (*0-8373-1751-7*) Nat Learn.

Senior Bookkeeping Machine Operator. Jack Rudman. (Career Examination Ser.: C-3097). 1994. pap. 27.95 (*0-8373-3097-1*) Nat Learn.

Senior Bridge & Tunnel Maintainer. Jack Rudman. (Career Examination Ser.: C-1472). 1997. pap. 29.95 (*0-8373-1472-0*) Nat Learn.

Senior Budget Analyst. Jack Rudman. (Career Examination Ser.: C-2415). 1994. pap. 39.95 (*0-8373-2415-7*) Nat Learn.

Senior Budget Examiner. Jack Rudman. (Career Examination Ser.: C-2528). 1994. pap. 34.95 (*0-8373-2528-5*) Nat Learn.

Senior Budget Officer. Jack Rudman. (Career Examination Ser.: C-2683). 1994. pap. 34.95 (*0-8373-2683-4*) Nat Learn.

Senior Building Construction Engineer. Jack Rudman. (Career Examination Ser.: C-3171). 1994. pap. 39.95 (*0-8373-3171-4*) Nat Learn.

Senior Building Custodian. Jack Rudman. (Career Examination Ser.: C-997). 1994. pap. 27.95 (*0-8373-0997-2*) Nat Learn.

Senior Building Electrical Engineer. Jack Rudman. (Career Examination Ser.: C-1916). 1994. pap. 39.95 (*0-8373-1916-1*) Nat Learn.

Senior Building Guard. Jack Rudman. (Career Examination Ser.: C-2529). 1994. pap. 27.95 (*0-8373-2529-3*) Nat Learn.

Senior Building Inspector. Jack Rudman. (Career Examination Ser.: C-2113). 1994. reprint ed. pap. 34.95 (*0-8373-2113-1*) Nat Learn.

Senior Building Mechanical Engineer. Jack Rudman. (Career Examination Ser.: C-2572). 1994. pap. 39.95 (*0-8373-2572-2*) Nat Learn.

Senior Building Rehabilitation Specialist. Jack Rudman. (Career Examination Ser.: C-1933). 1994. pap. 39.95 (*0-8373-1933-1*) Nat Learn.

Senior Building Structural Engineer. Jack Rudman. (Career Examination Ser.: C-2569). 1994. pap. 39.95 (*0-8373-2569-2*) Nat Learn.

Senior Business Consultant. Jack Rudman. (Career Examination Ser.: C-1983). 1994. pap. 39.95 (*0-8373-1983-8*) Nat Learn.

Senior Business Machine Operator. Jack Rudman. (Career Examination Ser.: C-1896). 1994. pap. 27.95 (*0-8373-1896-3*) Nat Learn.

Senior Business Manager. Jack Rudman. (Career Examination Ser.: C-2359). 1994. pap. 39.95 (*0-8373-2359-2*) Nat Learn.

Senior Buyer. Jack Rudman. (Career Examination Ser.: C-2254). 1994. reprint ed. pap. 29.95 (*0-8373-2254-5*) Nat Learn.

Senior Campus Security Officer. Jack Rudman. (Career Examination Ser.: C-2265). 1994. reprint ed. pap. 27.95 (*0-8373-2265-0*) Nat Learn.

Senior Capital Police Officer. Jack Rudman. (Career Examination Ser.: C-2070). 1994. reprint ed. pap. 29.95 (*0-8373-2070-4*) Nat Learn.

Senior Caseworker. Jack Rudman. (Career Examination Ser.: C-2931). 1994. pap. 27.95 (*0-8373-2931-0*) Nat Learn.

Senior Cashier. Jack Rudman. (Career Examination Ser.: C-860). 1994. pap. 23.95 (*0-8373-0860-7*) Nat Learn.

Senior Center Evaluation: A Technical Assistance Guide for Providers of Services to the Aging. 27p. 1993. pap. 8.00 (*0-910883-72-6*, 859) Natl Coun Aging.

Senior Center Facility Design: A Technical Assistance Guide for Providers of Services to the Aging. 45p. 1993. pap. 8.00 (*0-910883-71-8*, 857) Natl Coun Aging.

Senior Center Fund-Raising: A Technical Assistance Guide for Providers of Services to the Aging. 32p. 1993. pap. 8.00 (*0-910883-70-X*, 858) Natl Coun Aging.

Senior Center Programming for At-Risk Older Persons: A Technical Assistance Guide for Providers of Services to the Aging. 37p. 1994. pap. 8.00 (*0-910883-74-2*, 860) Natl Coun Aging.

Senior Center Standards & Self-Assessment Trainer's Guide. 80p. 1991. 15.00 (*0-910883-59-9*, 856) Natl Coun Aging.

Senior Center Standards & Self-Assessment Workbook: Guidelines for Practice 1990 Edition. National Institute of Senior Centers Staff. Ed. by Helen Ericson. 150p. 1990. ring bd. 25.00 (*0-910883-56-4*, 855) Natl Coun Aging.

Senior Center Studies & Program Evaluations: Outcomes of the Challenge Grants Initiative of the National Eldercare Institute on Multipurpose Senior Centers & Community Focal Points. Compiled by Debra Schollenberger. 61p. 1995. pap. text ed. 10.00 (*0-910883-82-3*, 863) Natl Coun Aging.

Senior Centers in America. John A. Krout. LC 89-11993. (Contributions to the Study of Aging Ser.: No. 14). 175p. 1989. text ed. 45.00 (*0-313-26058-3*, KSR/, Greenwood Pr) Greenwood.

Senior Centers in America: A Blueprint for the Future. Contrib. by NCOA's National Eldercare Institute on Multipurpose Senior Centers & Community Focal Points Staff. 54p. 1995. pap. 17.00 (*0-910883-83-1*, 864) Natl Coun Aging.

Senior Chemist. Jack Rudman. (Career Examination Ser.: C-2402). 1994. pap. 29.95 (*0-8373-2402-5*) Nat Learn.

Senior Children's Counselor. Jack Rudman. (Career Examination Ser.: C-1601). 1994. reprint ed. pap. 34.95 (*0-8373-1601-4*) Nat Learn.

Senior Citizen: A Musical Comedy in Two Acts. B. L. Holmes. LC 91-66369. 72p. (Orig.). 1991. pap. 8.95 (*0-941300-22-6*) Mother Courage.

Senior Citizen Aide. Jack Rudman. (Career Examination Ser.: C-1473). 1994. pap. 23.95 (*0-8373-1473-9*) Nat Learn.

Senior Citizen Alert! Enjoy Your Financial Future Without Fear! 2nd rev. ed. W. V. Montgomery, Jr. 229p. 1995. pap. 19.95 (*0-9630975-1-2*) Mont Assocs.

***Senior Citizen Alert! Enjoy Your Financial Future Without Fear!** 3rd rev. ed. W. V. Montgomery, Jr. 229p. 1997. pap. 19.95 (*0-9630975-2-0*) Mont Assocs.

Senior Citizen Directory of Queens, 1996/1997 Edition. 324p. (Orig.). 1996. pap. 14.95 (*1-889263-00-1*) Queens Senior.

Senior Citizen Education Programs: Opportunities on College Campuses in the Southeast. Diane Sudak & Phyllis Kozokoff. LC 87-20789. (Illus.). 300p. 1988. 35. 00 (*0-8108-2063-3*) Scarecrow.

Senior Citizen Handbook: A Self-Help & Resource Guide. Marjorie Stokell & Bonnie Kennedy. LC 84-22353. 260p. 1986. 22.95 (*0-13-806522-5*, Busn) P-H.

Senior Citizen School Volunteer Program: A Manual for Program Implementation. Cynthia Kramer & Sally Newman. LC 86-9575. 1986. 10.95 (*0-937829-01-3*) Ctr Study Aging.

Senior Citizen Services, 4 Vols., Vol. 4. Charles B. Montney. 1992. 100.00 (*0-8103-8319-5*) Gale.

Senior Citizen Services: Midwest, Vol. 3. Charles B. Montney. 1992. 40.00 (*0-8103-8322-5*) Gale.

Senior Citizen Services: Northeast, Vol. 1. Charles B. Montney. 1992. 40.00 (*0-8103-8320-9*) Gale.

Senior Citizen Services: Southeast, Vol. 2. Charles B. Montney. 1992. 40.00 (*0-8103-8321-7*) Gale.

Senior Citizen Services: West, Vol. 4. Charles B. Montney. 1992. 40.00 (*0-8103-8323-3*) Gale.

Senior Citizen Sourcebook: A Complete Guide to Services, Organizations, Opportunities & Ideas for Your Retirement Years. Marjorie Stokell & Bonnie Kennedy. write for info. (*0-318-58213-9*) P-H.

Senior Citizens' Activities Specialist. Jack Rudman. (Career Examination Ser.: C-900). 1994. pap. 23.95 (*0-8373-0900-X*) Nat Learn.

Senior Citizens & the Law. 5th ed. 176p. 1989. 10.00 (*0-932622-29-1*) Ctr Public Rep.

Senior Citizens' Club Leader. Jack Rudman. (Career Examination Ser.: C-2745). 1994. pap. 23.95 (*0-8373-2745-8*) Nat Learn.

Senior Citizen's Guide to Budget Travel in Europe. rev. ed. Paige Palmer. LC 82-441. 62p. 1993. pap. 5.95 (*0-87576-173-9*) Pilot Bks.

Senior Citizen's Guide to Budget Travel in the United States & Canada. rev. ed. Paige Palmer. LC 83-3949. 61p. 1994. pap. 5.95 (*0-87576-184-4*) Pilot Bks.

Senior Citizen's Guide to Starting a Part-Time, Home-Based Business. Judy Kerr. LC 92-21690. 1992. 5.95 (*0-87576-160-7*) Pilot Bks.

Senior Citizens' Information & Referral Specialist. Jack Rudman. (Career Examination Ser.: C-2814). 1994. pap. 27.95 (*0-8373-2814-4*) Nat Learn.

Senior Citizens' Nutrition Center Manager. (Career Examination Ser.: C-3356). 1994. pap. 34.95 (*0-8373-3356-3*) Nat Learn.

Senior Citizens on Stage. John J. Murray. 1980. pap. 3.00 (*0-686-30558-2*) Eldridge Pub.

Senior Citizens' Program Coordinator. Jack Rudman. (Career Examination Ser.: C-2811). 1994. pap. 29.95 (*0-8373-2811-X*) Nat Learn.

Senior Citizens' Program Supervisor. Jack Rudman. (Career Examination Ser.: C-2360). 1994. pap. 29.95 (*0-8373-2360-6*) Nat Learn.

Senior Citizens' Services Coordinator. Jack Rudman. (Career Examination Ser.: C-2117). 1994. reprint ed. pap. 29.95 (*0-8373-2117-4*) Nat Learn.

***Senior Citizens' Survival Guide.** Bob Feigel & Malcolm Walker. (Illus.). 95p. (Orig.). 1997. pap. 9.95 (*0-908697-73-2*) Seven Hills Bk.

Senior Civil Engineer. Jack Rudman. (Career Examination Ser.: C-998). 1994. pap. 29.95 (*0-8373-0998-0*) Nat Learn.

Senior Civil Engineer (Structures) Jack Rudman. (Career Examination Ser.: C-1917). 1994. pap. 34.95 (*0-8373-1917-X*) Nat Learn.

Senior Claim Examiner. Jack Rudman. (Career Examination Ser.: C-1716). 1994. pap. 29.95 (*0-8373-1716-9*) Nat Learn.

Senior Clerical Examinations. 3rd ed. Harry W. Koch. 1976. 6.00 (*0-913164-62-3*) Ken-Bks.

Senior Clerical Examinations. 4th ed. Harry W. Koch. 1985. 8.00 (*0-910553-02-5*) Ken-Bks.

Senior Clerical Series. Jack Rudman. (Career Examination Ser.: C-3473). 1994. pap. 23.95 (*0-8373-3473-X*) Nat Learn.

Senior Clerk. Jack Rudman. (Career Examination Ser.: C-707). 1994. pap. 23.95 (*0-8373-0707-4*) Nat Learn.

Senior Clerk-Stenographer. Jack Rudman. (Career Examination Ser.: C-2633). 1994. pap. 23.95 (*0-8373-2633-8*) Nat Learn.

Senior Clerk (Surrogate) Jack Rudman. (Career Examination Ser.: C-2128). 1994. reprint ed. pap. 29.95 (*0-8373-2128-X*) Nat Learn.

Senior Clerk-Typist. Jack Rudman. (Career Examination Ser.: C-1936). 1994. pap. 23.95 (*0-8373-1936-6*) Nat Learn.

Senior Clinical Psychologist. Jack Rudman. (Career Examination Ser.: C-1906). 1994. pap. 39.95 (*0-8373-1906-4*) Nat Learn.

Senior Code Enforcement Officer. Jack Rudman. (Career Examination Ser.: C-3602). 1994. pap. 39.95 (*0-8373-3602-3*) Nat Learn.

Senior Colleges see Directory of Computer Education & Research

Senior Commissary Clerk. Jack Rudman. (Career Examination Ser.: C-2050). 1994. pap. 27.95 (*0-8373-2050-X*) Nat Learn.

Senior Communications Technician. Jack Rudman. (Career Examination Ser.: C-2412). 1994. pap. 29.95 (*0-8373-2412-2*) Nat Learn.

Senior Community Liaison Worker. Jack Rudman. (Career Examination Ser.: C-2995). 1994. pap. 27.95 (*0-8373-2995-7*) Nat Learn.

Senior Community Narcotic Education Representative. Jack Rudman. (Career Examination Ser.: C-1942). 1994. pap. 34.95 (*0-8373-1942-0*) Nat Learn.

Senior Community Organization Specialist (Urban Renewal) (Career Examination Ser.: C-1474). pap. 34. 95 (*0-8373-1474-7*) Nat Learn.

Senior Community Service Worker. Jack Rudman. (Career Examination Ser.: C-2676). 1994. pap. 27.95 (*0-8373-2676-1*) Nat Learn.

Senior Compensation Claims Auditor. Jack Rudman. (Career Examination Ser.: C-2127). 1994. reprint ed. pap. 34.95 (*0-8373-2127-1*) Nat Learn.

Senior Compensation Claims Clerk. Jack Rudman. (Career Examination Ser.: C-867). 1994. pap. 27.95 (*0-8373-0867-4*) Nat Learn.

Senior Compensation Claims Examiner. Jack Rudman. (Career Examination Ser.: C-1702). 1994. pap. 29.95 (*0-8373-1702-9*) Nat Learn.

Senior Compensation Claims Investigator. Jack Rudman. (Career Examination Ser.: C-2613). 1994. pap. 29.95 (*0-8373-2613-3*) Nat Learn.

Senior Compensation Investigator. Jack Rudman. (Career Examination Ser.: C-2609). 1994. pap. 29.95 (*0-8373-2609-5*) Nat Learn.

Senior Compliance Investigator. Jack Rudman. (Career Examination Ser.: C-2422). 1994. pap. 29.95 (0-8373-2422-X) Nat Learn.

Senior Computer Operator. Jack Rudman. (Career Examination Ser.: C-708). 1994. pap. 27.95 (0-8373-0708-2) Nat Learn.

Senior Computer Programmer. Jack Rudman. (Career Examination Ser.: C-1630). 1994. pap. 29.95 (0-8373-1630-8) Nat Learn.

Senior Computer Programmer-Analyst. Jack Rudman. (Career Examination Ser.: C-1030). 1994. pap. 29.95 (0-8373-1030-X) Nat Learn.

Senior Computer Systems Analyst. Jack Rudman. (Career Examination Ser.: C-999). 1994. pap. 29.95 (0-8373-0999-9) Nat Learn.

Senior Construction Inspector. Jack Rudman. (Career Examination Ser.: C-709). 1994. pap. 34.95 (0-8373-0709-0) Nat Learn.

Senior Consumer Affairs Inspector. Jack Rudman. (Career Examination Ser.: C-1656). 1994. pap. 29.95 (0-8373-1656-1) Nat Learn.

Senior Consumer Affairs Investigator. Jack Rudman. (Career Examination Ser.: C-2376). 1994. pap. 29.95 (0-8373-2376-2) Nat Learn.

Senior Consumer Frauds Representative. Jack Rudman. (Career Examination Ser.: C-877). 1994. pap. 29.95 (0-8373-0877-1) Nat Learn.

Senior Contracts Examiner. Jack Rudman. (Career Examination Ser.: C-3536). 1994. pap. 29.95 (0-8373-3536-1) Nat Learn.

Senior Correction Counselor. Jack Rudman. (Career Examination Ser.: C-3263). 1994. pap. 34.95 (0-8373-3263-X) Nat Learn.

Senior Counsel: Legal & Financial Strategies for Age 50 & Beyond. Carl W. Battle. LC 92-75526. 256p. 1993. pap. 16.95 (1-880559-06-4) Allworth Pr.

Senior Court Clerk. Jack Rudman. (Career Examination Ser.: C-2704). 1994. pap. 29.95 (0-8373-2704-0) Nat Learn.

Senior Court Officer. Jack Rudman. (Career Examination Ser.: C-710). 1994. pap. 27.95 (0-8373-0710-4) Nat Learn.

Senior Court Reporter. Jack Rudman. (Career Examination Ser.: C-3543). 1994. pap. 27.95 (0-8373-3543-4) Nat Learn.

Senior Custodial Assistant. Jack Rudman. (Career Examination Ser.: Vol. C-1001). 1994. pap. 23.95 (0-8373-1001-6) Nat Learn.

Senior Custodial Foreman. Jack Rudman. (Career Examination Ser.: C-2271). 1994. reprint ed. pap. 29.95 (0-8373-2271-5) Nat Learn.

Senior Data Entry Clerk. Jack Rudman. (Career Examination Ser.: C-3506). 1994. pap. 27.95 (0-8373-3506-X) Nat Learn.

Senior Data Entry Machine Operator. Jack Rudman. (Career Examination Ser.: C-3063). 1994. pap. 27.95 (0-8373-3063-7) Nat Learn.

Senior Data Processing Control Clerk. Jack Rudman. (Career Examination Ser.: C-2484). 1994. pap. 27.95 (0-8373-2484-X) Nat Learn.

Senior Data Processing Equipment Operator. Jack Rudman. (Career Examination Ser.: C-2302). 1994. reprint ed. pap. 27.95 (0-8373-2302-9) Nat Learn.

Senior Demolition Inspector. Jack Rudman. (Career Examination Ser.: C-1475). 1994. pap. 34.95 (0-8373-1475-5) Nat Learn.

Senior Dental Hygienist. Jack Rudman. (Career Examination Ser.: C-2855). 1994. pap. 34.95 (0-8373-2855-1) Nat Learn.

Senior Dentist. Jack Rudman. (Career Examination Ser.: C-711). 1994. pap. 54.95 (0-8373-0711-2) Nat Learn.

Senior Deputy Sheriff. Jack Rudman. (Career Examination Ser.: C-1665). 1994. pap. 27.95 (0-8373-1665-0) Nat Learn.

Senior Detective Investigator. Jack Rudman. (Career Examination Ser.: C-2038). 1994. pap. 39.95 (0-8373-2038-0) Nat Learn.

Senior Dietitian. Jack Rudman. (Career Examination Ser.: C-1985). 1994. pap. 29.95 (0-8373-1985-4) Nat Learn.

Senior Dog Warden. Jack Rudman. (Career Examination Ser.: C-2646). 1994. pap. 27.95 (0-8373-2646-X) Nat Learn.

Senior Drafting Technician. Jack Rudman. (Career Examination Ser.: C-2679). 1994. pap. 27.95 (0-8373-2679-6) Nat Learn.

Senior Draftsman. Jack Rudman. (Career Examination Ser.: C-1575). 1994. pap. 27.95 (0-8373-1575-1) Nat Learn.

Senior Drug Abuse Educator. Jack Rudman. (Career Examination Ser.: C-2520). 1994. pap. 34.95 (0-8373-2520-X) Nat Learn.

Senior Drug Abuse Rehabilitation Counselor. Jack Rudman. (Career Examination Ser.: C-2928). 1994. pap. 34.95 (0-8373-2928-0) Nat Learn.

Senior Drug & Alcohol Counselor. Jack Rudman. (Career Examination Ser.: C-2742). 1994. pap. 34.95 (0-8373-2742-3) Nat Learn.

Senior Duplicating Machine Operator. Jack Rudman. (Career Examination Ser.: C-1899). 1994. pap. 23.95 (0-8373-1899-8) Nat Learn.

Senior Economist. Jack Rudman. (Career Examination Ser.: C-3252). 1994. pap. 34.95 (0-8373-3252-4) Nat Learn.

Senior Edition: The Complete Guide for the Guitar. Cathy Ellis. 74p. 1992. student ed. 15.95 (1-879542-06-4); teacher ed. 18.95 (1-879542-18-8); audio 8.95 (1-879542-23-4) Ellis Family Mus.

Senior Editorial Clerk. Jack Rudman. (Career Examination Ser.: C-2565). 1994. pap. 27.95 (0-8373-2565-X) Nat Learn.

Senior Electrical Engineer. Jack Rudman. (Career Examination Ser.: C-1631). 1994. pap. 39.95 (0-8373-1631-6) Nat Learn.

Senior Electrical Inspector. Jack Rudman. (Career Examination Ser.: C-712). 1994. pap. 34.95 (0-8373-0712-0) Nat Learn.

Senior Electronic Computer Operator. Jack Rudman. (Career Examination Ser.: C-1002). 1994. pap. 27.95 (0-8373-1002-4) Nat Learn.

Senior Elevator Inspector. Jack Rudman. (Career Examination Ser.: C-1717). 1994. pap. 34.95 (0-8373-1717-7) Nat Learn.

Senior Employment Counselor. Jack Rudman. (Career Examination Ser.: C-1003). 1994. pap. 34.95 (0-8373-1003-2) Nat Learn.

Senior Employment Interviewer. Jack Rudman. (Career Examination Ser.: C-2284). 1994. reprint ed. pap. 34.95 (0-8373-2284-7) Nat Learn.

Senior Employment Security Clerk. Jack Rudman. (Career Examination Ser.: C-2351). 1994. pap. 27.95 (0-8373-2351-7) Nat Learn.

Senior Engineer. Jack Rudman. (Career Examination Ser.: C-1476). 1994. pap. 44.95 (0-8373-1476-3) Nat Learn.

Senior Engineering Aide. Jack Rudman. (Career Examination Ser.: C-1560). 1994. pap. 27.95 (0-8373-1560-3) Nat Learn.

Senior Engineering Inspector. Jack Rudman. (Career Examination Ser.: C-2808). 1994. pap. 44.95 (0-8373-2808-X) Nat Learn.

Senior Engineering Materials Technician. Jack Rudman. (Career Examination Ser.: C-316). 1994. pap. 29.95 (0-8373-0316-8) Nat Learn.

Senior Engineering Technician. Jack Rudman. (Career Examination Ser.: C-1004). 1994. pap. 27.95 (0-8373-1004-0) Nat Learn.

Senior Engineering Technician (Drafting) Jack Rudman. (Career Examination Ser.: C-1005). 1994. pap. 27.95 (0-8373-1005-9) Nat Learn.

Senior Engineering Technician (Environmental Quality) Jack Rudman. (Career Examination Ser.: C-3238). 1994. pap. 29.95 (0-8373-3238-9) Nat Learn.

Senior Environmental Analyst. Jack Rudman. (Career Examination Ser.: C-2660). 1994. pap. 39.95 (0-8373-2660-5) Nat Learn.

Senior Environmental Control Technician. Jack Rudman. (Career Examination Ser.: C-3363). 1994. pap. 34.95 (0-8373-3363-6) Nat Learn.

Senior Environmental Planner. Jack Rudman. (Career Examination Ser.: C-2663). 1994. pap. 39.95 (0-8373-2663-X) Nat Learn.

Senior Environmentalist. Jack Rudman. (Career Examination Ser.: C-1585). 1994. pap. 34.95 (0-8373-1585-9) Nat Learn.

Senior Estimator (Construction) (Career Examination Ser.: C-3689). pap. 39.95 (0-8373-3689-9) Nat Learn.

Senior Evidence Technician. Jack Rudman. (Career Examination Ser.: C-2749). 1994. pap. 34.95 (0-8373-2749-0) Nat Learn.

Senior Examiner, Social Services. Jack Rudman. (Career Examination Ser.: C-2139). 1994. reprint ed. pap. 27.95 (0-8373-2139-5) Nat Learn.

Senior Excise Tax Investigator. Jack Rudman. (Career Examination Ser.: C-2419). 1994. pap. 29.95 (0-8373-2419-X) Nat Learn.

Senior Executive Officer. Jack Rudman. (Career Examination Ser.: C-2826). 1994. pap. 39.95 (0-8373-2826-8) Nat Learn.

Senior Executive Service: Opinions about the Federal Work Environment. (Illus.). 107p. (Orig.). (C). 1993. pap. text ed. 35.00 (1-56806-919-7) DIANE Pub.

Senior Field Accountant. Jack Rudman. (Career Examination Ser.: C-1569). 1994. pap. 34.95 (0-8373-1569-7) Nat Learn.

Senior Field Representative (Human Rights) Jack Rudman. (Career Examination Ser.: C-2563). 1994. pap. 29.95 (0-8373-2563-3) Nat Learn.

Senior File Clerk. Jack Rudman. (Career Examination Ser.: C-713). 1940. pap. 23.95 (0-8373-0713-9) Nat Learn.

Senior Financial Analyst. Jack Rudman. (Career Examination Ser.: C-2643). 1994. pap. 39.95 (0-8373-2643-5) Nat Learn.

Senior Fingerprint Technician. Jack Rudman. (Career Examination Ser.: C-2073). 1994. reprint ed. pap. 29.95 (0-8373-2073-9) Nat Learn.

Senior Fire Prevention Inspector. Jack Rudman. (Career Examination Ser.: C-1765). 1994. reprint ed. pap. 34.95 (0-8373-1765-7) Nat Learn.

Senior Food Inspector. Jack Rudman. (Career Examination Ser.: C-2051). 1994. pap. 34.95 (0-8373-2051-8) Nat Learn.

Senior Forestry Technician. Jack Rudman. (Career Examination Ser.: C-2715). 1994. pap. 29.95 (0-8373-2715-6) Nat Learn.

Senior Functional Health Screen. (C). 1991. student ed. 99.00 (0-933948-40-9, 2892) Ctr Res Ambulatory.

Senior Geologist. Jack Rudman. (Career Examination Ser.: C-1006). 1994. pap. 29.95 (0-8373-1006-7) Nat Learn.

***Senior Golfers: A Powerful Part of the Golfing Population.** unabridged ed. (NGF Info Pacs Ser.). (Illus.). 111p. (Orig.). 1996. pap. 45.00 (1-57701-032-9) Natl Golf.

Senior Grants Analyst. Jack Rudman. (Career Examination Ser.: C-2833). 1994. pap. 39.95 (0-8373-2833-0) Nat Learn.

Senior Groundskeeper. Jack Rudman. (Career Examination Ser.: C-1572). 1994. pap. 29.95 (0-8373-1572-7) Nat Learn.

Senior Harbormaster. Jack Rudman. (Career Examination Ser.: C-3474). 1994. pap. 34.95 (0-8373-3474-8) Nat Learn.

Senior Health Planner. Jack Rudman. (Career Examination Ser.: C-3028). 1994. pap. 39.95 (0-8373-3028-9) Nat Learn.

Senior Heating & Ventilating Engineer. Jack Rudman. (Career Examination Ser.: C-1918). 1994. pap. 34.95 (0-8373-1918-8) Nat Learn.

Senior Hi Artist. Henry J. Filson. (Draw-Sketch Practice Ser.). (Illus.). 44p. (gr. 12 up). 1978. spiral bd. 3.75 (0-918554-02-0) Old Violin.

Senior High Computer Connection. Mindy Pantiel & Becky Petersen. LC 85-3660. (Illus.). 272p. 1985. pap. 22.95 (0-13-806530-6) P-H.

Senior High Retreats. Center for Learning Network Staff. 150p. 1992. reprint ed. teacher ed., spiral bd. 15.95 (1-56077-216-6) Ctr Learning.

Senior High School. Jack Rudman. (Teachers Lesson Plan Bk.: S-1). 1994. pap. 6.95 (0-8373-7954-7) Nat Learn.

Senior High School Library Catalog. 14th ed. Ed. by Brenda Smith & Juliette Yaakov. 1464p. 1992. 115.00 (0-8242-0831-5) Wilson.

Senior Highway Engineer. Jack Rudman. (Career Examination Ser.: C-2522). 1994. pap. 39.95 (0-8373-2522-6) Nat Learn.

Senior Highway Maintenance Supervisor. Jack Rudman. (Career Examination Ser.: C-2631). 1994. pap. 34.95 (0-8373-2631-1) Nat Learn.

Senior Highway Transportation Specialist. Jack Rudman. (Career Examination Ser.: C-1477). 1994. pap. 34.95 (0-8373-1477-1) Nat Learn.

Senior Hospital Administration Consultant. Jack Rudman. (Career Examination Ser.: C-2769). 1994. pap. 44.95 (0-8373-2769-5) Nat Learn.

Senior Hospital Care Investigator. Jack Rudman. (Career Examination Ser.: C-715). 1994. pap. 29.95 (0-8373-0715-5) Nat Learn.

Senior Hospital Case Investigator. Jack Rudman. (Career Examination Ser.: C-1888). 1994. reprint ed. pap. 29.95 (0-8373-1888-2) Nat Learn.

Senior Housekeeper. Jack Rudman. (Career Examination Ser.: C-1007). 1994. pap. 29.95 (0-8373-1007-5) Nat Learn.

Senior Housing Inspector. Jack Rudman. (Career Examination Ser.: C-792). 1994. pap. 34.95 (0-8373-0792-9) Nat Learn.

Senior Housing Management Assistant. Jack Rudman. (Career Examination Ser.: C-2538). 1994. pap. 29.95 (0-8373-2538-2) Nat Learn.

Senior Housing Management Representative. Jack Rudman. (Career Examination Ser.: C-2540). 1994. pap. 34.95 (0-8373-2540-4) Nat Learn.

Senior Housing Rehabilitation Specialist. (Career Examination Ser.: C-3648). pap. 39.95 (0-8373-3648-1) Nat Learn.

Senior Housing Teller. Jack Rudman. (Career Examination Ser.: C-714). 1994. pap. 27.95 (0-8373-0714-7) Nat Learn.

Senior Human Relations Representative. Jack Rudman. (Career Examination Ser.: C-2584). 1994. pap. 29.95 (0-8373-2584-6) Nat Learn.

Senior Human Resources Specialist. Jack Rudman. (Career Examination Ser.: C-1064). 1994. pap. 29.95 (0-8373-1064-4) Nat Learn.

Senior Human Resources Technician. Jack Rudman. (Career Examination Ser.: C-1478). 1994. pap. 29.95 (0-8373-1478-X) Nat Learn.

Senior Human Rights Investigator. Jack Rudman. (Career Examination Ser.: C-1417). 1994. pap. 29.95 (0-8373-1417-8) Nat Learn.

Senior Identification Clerk. Jack Rudman. (Career Examination Ser.: C-2293). 1994. pap. 27.95 (0-8373-2293-6) Nat Learn.

Senior Identification Officer. Jack Rudman. (Career Examination Ser.: C-1987). 1994. pap. 34.95 (0-8373-1987-0) Nat Learn.

Senior Identification Specialist. Jack Rudman. (Career Examination Ser.: C-2512). 1994. pap. 34.95 (0-8373-2512-9) Nat Learn.

Senior Illustrator. Jack Rudman. (Career Examination Ser.: C-1008). 1994. pap. 34.95 (0-8373-1008-3) Nat Learn.

Senior Incinerator Stationary Engineer. Jack Rudman. (Career Examination Ser.: C-2637). 1994. pap. 34.95 (0-8373-2637-0) Nat Learn.

Senior Industrial Hygienist. Jack Rudman. (Career Examination Ser.: C-3036). 1994. pap. 44.95 (0-8373-3036-X) Nat Learn.

Senior Inspector Meat & Poultry. Jack Rudman. (Career Examination Ser.: C-1771). 1994. pap. 34.95 (0-8373-1771-1) Nat Learn.

Senior Inspector of Fire Alarm Boxes. Jack Rudman. (Career Examination Ser.: C-2516). 1994. pap. 34.95 (0-8373-2516-1) Nat Learn.

Senior Inspector of Low Pressure Boilers. Jack Rudman. (Career Examination Ser.: C-2272). 1994. reprint ed. pap. 34.95 (0-8373-2272-3) Nat Learn.

Senior Inspector of Markets, Weights & Measures. Jack Rudman. (Career Examination Ser.: C-716). 1994. pap. 29.95 (0-8373-0716-3) Nat Learn.

Senior Institution Safety Officer. Jack Rudman. (Career Examination Ser.: C-2119). 1994. reprint ed. pap. 34.95 (0-8373-2119-0) Nat Learn.

Senior Instrumentation Technician. Jack Rudman. (Career Examination Ser.: C-3256). 1994. pap. 34.95 (0-8373-3256-7) Nat Learn.

Senior Insurance Examiner. Jack Rudman. (Career Examination Ser.: C-2685). 1994. pap. 34.95 (0-8373-2695-8) Nat Learn.

Senior Internal Auditor. Jack Rudman. (Career Examination Ser.: C-1009). 1994. pap. 34.95 (0-8373-1009-1) Nat Learn.

Senior Investigator. Jack Rudman. (Career Examination Ser.: C-1010). 1994. pap. 29.95 (0-8373-1010-5) Nat Learn.

Senior Investment Analyst. Jack Rudman. (Career Examination Ser.: C-1623). 1994. pap. 44.95 (0-8373-1623-5) Nat Learn.

Senior Justice Court Clerk. Jack Rudman. (Career Examination Ser.: C-3615). 1994. pap. 29.95 (0-8373-3615-5) Nat Learn.

Senior Juvenile Counselor. Jack Rudman. (Career Examination Ser.: C-421). 1994. pap. 34.95 (0-8373-0421-0) Nat Learn.

Senior Key Punch Operator. Jack Rudman. (Career Examination Ser.: C-717). 1994. pap. 27.95 (0-8373-0717-1) Nat Learn.

Senior Kisses. Diane Namm. LC 94-25436. (Kisses Ser.: No. 3). 224p. (YA). (gr. 6 up). 1997. pap. 3.50 (0-8167-3442-9, WestWind) Troll Communs.

Senior Labor-Management Practices Adjuster. Jack Rudman. (Career Examination Ser.: C-718). 1994. pap. 44.95 (0-8373-0718-X) Nat Learn.

Senior Labor Relations Analyst. (Career Examination Ser.: C-3746). 1994. pap. 44.95 (0-8373-3746-1) Nat Learn.

Senior Labor Specialist. Jack Rudman. (Career Examination Ser.: C-2381). 1994. pap. 34.95 (0-8373-2381-9) Nat Learn.

Senior Laboratory Animal Caretaker. (Career Examination Ser.). 1997. pap. 27.95 (0-8373-3793-3, C3793) Nat Learn.

Senior Laboratory Technician. Jack Rudman. (Career Examination Ser.: C-1693). 1994. pap. 29.95 (0-8373-1693-6) Nat Learn.

Senior Laboratory Technician (Biochemistry) Jack Rudman. (Career Examination Ser.: C-3081). 1994. pap. 34.95 (0-8373-3081-5) Nat Learn.

Senior Laboratory Technician (Chemistry) Jack Rudman. (Career Examination Ser.: C-3082). 1994. pap. 34.95 (0-8373-3082-3) Nat Learn.

Senior Laboratory Technician (Food Chemistry) Jack Rudman. (Career Examination Ser.: C-3253). 1994. pap. 34.95 (0-8373-3253-2) Nat Learn.

Senior Laboratory Technician (Microbiology) Jack Rudman. (Career Examination Ser.: C-3083). 1994. pap. 34.95 (0-8373-3083-1) Nat Learn.

Senior Land Management Specialist. Jack Rudman. (Career Examination Ser.: C-2619). 1994. pap. 34.95 (0-8373-2619-2) Nat Learn.

Senior Landscape Architect. Jack Rudman. (Career Examination Ser.: C-1479). 1994. pap. 34.95 (0-8373-1479-8) Nat Learn.

Senior Laundry Supervisor. Jack Rudman. (Career Examination Ser.: C-2220). 1994. pap. 34.95 (0-8373-2220-0) Nat Learn.

Senior Laundry Worker. Jack Rudman. (Career Examination Ser.: C-719). 1994. pap. 27.95 (0-8373-0719-8) Nat Learn.

Senior Leasing Agent. Jack Rudman. (Career Examination Ser.: C-2494). 1994. pap. 34.95 (0-8373-2494-7) Nat Learn.

Senior Legal Stenographer. Jack Rudman. (Career Examination Ser.: C-2634). 1994. pap. 29.95 (0-8373-2634-6) Nat Learn.

Senior Level Positions. Jack Rudman. (Career Examination Ser.: C-720). 1994. pap. 29.95 (0-8373-0720-1) Nat Learn.

Senior Librarian. Jack Rudman. (Career Examination Ser.: C-1011). 1994. pap. 29.95 (0-8373-1011-3) Nat Learn.

Senior Librarian I. Jack Rudman. (Career Examination Ser.: C-1821). 1994. pap. 29.95 (0-8373-1821-1) Nat Learn.

Senior Library Clerk. Jack Rudman. (Career Examination Ser.: C-1930). 1994. pap. 27.95 (0-8373-1930-7) Nat Learn.

Senior License Investigator. Jack Rudman. (Career Examination Ser.: C-2530). 1994. pap. 27.95 (0-8373-2530-7) Nat Learn.

Senior Licensed Practical Nurse. Jack Rudman. (Career Examination Ser.: C-3500). 1994. pap. 29.95 (0-8373-3500-0) Nat Learn.

Senior Mail Clerk. Jack Rudman. (Career Examination Ser.: C-1053). 1994. pap. 23.95 (0-8373-1053-9) Nat Learn.

Senior Maintenance Supervisor. Jack Rudman. (Career Examination Ser.: C-2052). 1994. pap. 29.95 (0-8373-2052-6) Nat Learn.

Senior Management: The Dynamics of Effectiveness. Sushila Singhal. LC 94-15770. 216p. 1994. 35.00 (0-8039-9180-0) Sage.

Senior Management Analyst. Jack Rudman. (Career Examination Ser.: C-1782). 1994. pap. 39.95 (0-8373-1782-7) Nat Learn.

Senior Management Service for Texas State Government. Terrell Blodgett. (Special Project Report). 103p. 1989. pap. 7.00 (0-89940-862-1) LBJ Sch Pub Aff.

Senior Management Technician. Jack Rudman. (Career Examination Ser.: C-2752). 1994. pap. 29.95 (0-8373-2752-0) Nat Learn.

***Senior Managers & Their Effectiveness.** Farhad Analoui. 176p. 1997. text ed. 55.95 (1-85972-041-2, Pub. by Avebury Pub UK) Ashgate Pub Co.

Senior Manpower Counselor. Jack Rudman. (Career Examination Ser.: C-2436). 1994. pap. 39.95 (0-8373-2436-X) Nat Learn.

Senior Marketing Representative. Jack Rudman. (Career Examination Ser.: C-2053). 1994. reprint ed. pap. 34.95 (0-8373-2053-4) Nat Learn.

Senior Mathematician. Jack Rudman. (Career Examination Ser.: C-2078). 1994. reprint ed. pap. 34.95 (0-8373-2078-X) Nat Learn.

Senior Meat Cutter. Jack Rudman. (Career Examination Ser.: C-1012). 1994. pap. 29.95 (0-8373-1012-1) Nat Learn.

An Asterisk (*) at the beginning of an entry indicates that the title is appearing in BIP for the first time.

Senior Meat Inspector. Jack Rudman. (Career Examination Ser.: C-2054). 1994. pap. 29.95 (*0-8373-2054-2*) Nat Learn.

Senior Mechanical Engineer. Jack Rudman. (Career Examination Ser.: C-1648). 1994. reprint ed. pap. 34.95 (*0-8373-1648-0*) Nat Learn.

Senior Mechanical Estimator. (Career Examination Ser.: C-3592). 1994. pap. 34.95 (*0-8373-3592-2*) Nat Learn.

Senior Mechanical Stores Clerk. Jack Rudman. (Career Examination Ser.: C-3060). 1994. pap. 27.95 (*0-8373-3060-2*) Nat Learn.

***Senior Media Directory 1997.** rev. ed. Gene E. Malott. 1997. lib. bdg. 99.00 (*0-9629034-7-7*) GEM Pub Group.

Senior Medicaid Claims Examiner. Jack Rudman. (Career Examination Ser.: C-2692). 1994. pap. 29.95 (*0-8373-2692-3*) Nat Learn.

Senior Medical Conduct Investigator. Jack Rudman. (Career Examination Ser.: C-2610). 1994. pap. 29.95 (*0-8373-2610-9*) Nat Learn.

Senior Medical Emergency Dispatcher. Jack Rudman. (Career Examination Ser.: C-2332). 1994. pap. 29.95 (*0-8373-2332-0*) Nat Learn.

Senior Medical Laboratory Technician. Jack Rudman. (Career Examination Ser.: C-2496). 1994. pap. 29.95 (*0-8373-2496-3*) Nat Learn.

Senior Medical Records Clerk. Jack Rudman. (Career Examination Ser.: C-2310). 1994. reprint ed. pap. 29.95 (*0-8373-2310-X*) Nat Learn.

Senior Medical Records Librarian. Jack Rudman. (Career Examination Ser.: C-1013). 1994. pap. 29.95 (*0-8373-1013-X*) Nat Learn.

Senior Medical Services Specialist. Jack Rudman. (Career Examination Ser.: C-2747). 1994. pap. 39.95 (*0-8373-2747-4*) Nat Learn.

Senior Medical Social Worker. Jack Rudman. (Career Examination Ser.: C-2629). 1994. pap. 34.95 (*0-8373-2629-X*) Nat Learn.

Senior Medical Stenographer. Jack Rudman. (Career Examination Ser.: C-2940). 1994. pap. 27.95 (*0-8373-2940-X*) Nat Learn.

Senior Menagerie Keeper. Jack Rudman. (Career Examination Ser.: C-1971). 1994. pap. 27.95 (*0-8373-1971-4*) Nat Learn.

Senior Mental Health Worker. Jack Rudman. (Career Examination Ser.: C-1925). 1994. pap. 29.95 (*0-8373-1925-0*) Nat Learn.

Senior Meteorologist. Jack Rudman. (Career Examination Ser.: C-2201). 1994. pap. 34.95 (*0-8373-2201-4*) Nat Learn.

Senior Methods Analyst. Jack Rudman. (Career Examination Ser.: C-1014). 1994. pap. 39.95 (*0-8373-1014-8*) Nat Learn.

Senior Microbiologist. Jack Rudman. (Career Examination Ser.: C-1945). 1994. pap. 34.95 (*0-8373-1945-5*) Nat Learn.

Senior Micrographics Operator. Jack Rudman. (Career Examination Ser.: C-2760). 1994. pap. 27.95 (*0-8373-2760-1*) Nat Learn.

Senior Micrographics Technician. Jack Rudman. (Career Examination Ser.: C-2762). 1994. pap. 27.95 (*0-8373-2762-8*) Nat Learn.

Senior Minister. Lyle E. Schaller. LC 87-28997. 192p. 1988. pap. 5.18 (*0-687-37180-5*) Abingdon.

Senior Mortuary Caretaker. Jack Rudman. (Career Examination Ser.: C-721). 1994. pap. 27.95 (*0-8373-0721-X*) Nat Learn.

Senior Motor Vehicle License Clerk. Jack Rudman. (Career Examination Ser.: C-2611). 1994. pap. 27.95 (*0-8373-2611-7*) Nat Learn.

Senior Motor Vehicle License Examiner. (Career Examination Ser.: C-3589). 1994. pap. 27.95 (*0-8373-3589-2*) Nat Learn.

Senior Motor Vehicle Referee. (Career Examination Ser.: C-3581). 1994. pap. 39.95 (*0-8373-3581-7*) Nat Learn.

Senior Motor Vehicle Supervisor. Jack Rudman. (Career Examination Ser.: C-3527). 1994. pap. 34.95 (*0-8373-3527-2*) Nat Learn.

Senior Movement: References & Resources. Steven P. Wallace & John B. Williamson. (Reference Ser.). 250p. 1992. 45.00 (*0-8161-1841-8*, Hall Reference) Macmillan.

Senior Multiple Residence Inspector. Jack Rudman. (Career Examination Ser.: C-2843). 1994. pap. 34.95 (*0-8373-2843-8*) Nat Learn.

Senior Museum Curator. Jack Rudman. (Career Examination Ser.: C-2374). 1994. pap. 29.95 (*0-8373-2374-6*) Nat Learn.

Senior Museum Instructor. Jack Rudman. (Career Examination Ser.: C-1016). 1994. pap. 29.95 (*0-8373-1016-4*) Nat Learn.

Senior Narcotics Investigator. Jack Rudman. (Career Examination Ser.: C-2531). 1994. pap. 39.95 (*0-8373-2531-5*) Nat Learn.

Senior Neighborhood Aide. Jack Rudman. (Career Examination Ser.: C-2911). 1994. pap. 27.95 (*0-8373-2911-6*) Nat Learn.

***Senior Net's Official Guide to the Web.** Eugenia Johnson & Kathleen McFadden. 426p. 1997. 29.99 (*0-7897-1069-2*) Mac Comp Pub.

Senior Nutritionist. Jack Rudman. (Career Examination Ser.: C-1419). 1994. pap. 29.95 (*0-8373-1419-4*) Nat Learn.

Senior Occupational Analyst. Jack Rudman. (Career Examination Ser.: C-2549). 1994. pap. 34.95 (*0-8373-2549-8*) Nat Learn.

Senior Occupational Therapist. Jack Rudman. (Career Examination Ser.: C-2174). 1994. pap. 34.95 (*0-8373-2174-3*) Nat Learn.

Senior Office Appliance Operator. Jack Rudman. (Career Examination Ser.: C-1677). 1994. pap. 27.95 (*0-8373-1677-4*) Nat Learn.

Senior Office Assistant. Jack Rudman. (Career Examination Ser.: C-2594). 1994. pap. 23.95 (*0-8373-2594-3*) Nat Learn.

Senior Office Machine Operator. Jack Rudman. (Career Examination Ser.: C-1480). 1994. pap. 27.95 (*0-8373-1480-1*) Nat Learn.

Senior Office Manager. Jack Rudman. (Career Examination Ser.: C-2399). 1994. pap. 34.95 (*0-8373-2399-1*) Nat Learn.

Senior Office Stenographer. Jack Rudman. (Career Examination Ser.: C-3376). 1994. pap. 23.95 (*0-8373-3376-8*) Nat Learn.

Senior Office Typist. Jack Rudman. (Career Examination Ser.: C-3374). 1994. pap. 23.95 (*0-8373-3374-1*) Nat Learn.

Senior Office Worker. Jack Rudman. (Career Examination Ser.: C-2519). 1994. pap. 23.95 (*0-8373-2519-6*) Nat Learn.

Senior Offset Printing Machine Operator. Jack Rudman. (Career Examination Ser.: C-3334). 1994. pap. 27.95 (*0-8373-3334-2*) Nat Learn.

Senior Olympics, Preventive Medicine, & Findings Pertaining to Health & Longevity. C. Antonio Provost & Worth Blaney. 1981. 6.00 (*0-686-32025-5*) Provost.

Senior Operations Review Specialist. Jack Rudman. (Career Examination Ser.: C-3261). 1994. pap. 39.95 (*0-8373-3261-3*) Nat Learn.

Senior Park Attendant. Jack Rudman. (Career Examination Ser.: C-1542). 1994. pap. 27.95 (*0-8373-1542-5*) Nat Learn.

Senior Park Engineer. Jack Rudman. (Career Examination Ser.: C-3192). 1994. pap. 39.95 (*0-8373-3192-7*) Nat Learn.

Senior Park Foreman. Jack Rudman. (Career Examination Ser.: C-1562). 1994. pap. 29.95 (*0-8373-1562-X*) Nat Learn.

Senior Park Supervisor. Jack Rudman. (Career Examination Ser.: C-2356). 1994. pap. 29.95 (*0-8373-2356-8*) Nat Learn.

Senior Parking Enforcement Agent. Jack Rudman. (Career Examination Ser.: C-793). 1994. pap. 27.95 (*0-8373-0793-7*) Nat Learn.

Senior Parole Officer. Jack Rudman. (Career Examination Ser.: C-2466). 1994. pap. 29.95 (*0-8373-2466-1*) Nat Learn.

Senior Payroll Audit Clerk. Jack Rudman. (Career Examination Ser.: C-2085). 1994. reprint ed. pap. 27.95 (*0-8373-2085-2*) Nat Learn.

Senior Personnel Administrator. Jack Rudman. (Career Examination Ser.: C-2410). 1994. pap. 44.95 (*0-8373-2410-6*) Nat Learn.

Senior Personnel Analyst. Jack Rudman. (Career Examination Ser.: C-2345). 1994. pap. 39.95 (*0-8373-2345-2*) Nat Learn.

Senior Personnel Clerk. Jack Rudman. (Career Examination Ser.: C-2867). 1994. pap. 27.95 (*0-8373-2867-5*) Nat Learn.

Senior Personnel Examiner. Jack Rudman. (Career Examination Ser.: C-1017). 1994. pap. 34.95 (*0-8373-1017-2*, C-1017) Nat Learn.

Senior Pesticide Control Inspector. Jack Rudman. (Career Examination Ser.: C-2562). 1994. pap. 34.95 (*0-8373-2562-5*) Nat Learn.

Senior Pharmacist. Jack Rudman. (Career Examination Ser.: C-722). 1994. pap. 34.95 (*0-8373-0722-8*) Nat Learn.

Senior Pharmacy Inspector. Jack Rudman. (Career Examination Ser.: C-2532). 1994. pap. 39.95 (*0-8373-2532-3*) Nat Learn.

Senior Photographic Machine Operator. Jack Rudman. (Career Examination Ser.: C-2882). 1994. pap. 23.95 (*0-8373-2882-9*) Nat Learn.

Senior Physical Therapist. Jack Rudman. (Career Examination Ser.: C-1018). 1994. pap. 29.95 (*0-8373-1018-0*) Nat Learn.

Senior Plan Examiner. Jack Rudman. (Career Examination Ser.: C-1481). 1994. pap. 34.95 (*0-8373-1481-X*) Nat Learn.

Senior Planner. Jack Rudman. (Career Examination Ser.: C-1019). 1994. pap. 34.95 (*0-8373-1019-9*) Nat Learn.

Senior Plumbing Inspector. Jack Rudman. (Career Examination Ser.: C-1740). 1994. pap. 34.95 (*0-8373-1740-1*) Nat Learn.

Senior Police Administrative Aide. Jack Rudman. (Career Examination Ser.: C-1020). 1994. pap. 27.95 (*0-8373-1020-2*) Nat Learn.

Senior Police Operations Aide. (Career Examination Ser.). Date not set. pap. 27.95 (*0-8373-3796-8*, C3796) Nat Learn.

Senior Probation Officer. Jack Rudman. (Career Examination Ser.: C-1594). 1994. pap. 29.95 (*0-8373-1594-8*) Nat Learn.

Senior Professional Conduct Investigator. Jack Rudman. (Career Examination Ser.: C-2298). 1994. reprint ed. pap. 29.95 (*0-8373-2298-7*) Nat Learn.

Senior Program Evaluation Specialist. Jack Rudman. (Career Examination Ser.: C-2700). 1994. pap. 39.95 (*0-8373-2700-8*) Nat Learn.

Senior Program Examiner. Jack Rudman. (Career Examination Ser.: C-2755). 1994. pap. 39.95 (*0-8373-2755-5*) Nat Learn.

Senior Program Research Analyst. Jack Rudman. (Career Examination Ser.: C-2219). 1994. reprint ed. pap. 39.95 (*0-8373-2219-7*) Nat Learn.

Senior Program Specialist. Jack Rudman. (Career Examination Ser.: C-2862). 1994. pap. 39.95 (*0-8373-2862-4*) Nat Learn.

Senior Program Specialist (Correction) Jack Rudman. (Career Examination Ser.: C-1998). 1994. pap. 39.95 (*0-8373-1998-6*) Nat Learn.

Senior Programmer. Jack Rudman. (Career Examination Ser.: C-2580). 1994. pap. 34.95 (*0-8373-2580-3*) Nat Learn.

Senior Project Coordinator. Jack Rudman. (Career Examination Ser.: C-1482). 1994. pap. 34.95 (*0-8373-1482-8*) Nat Learn.

Senior Project Development Coordinator. Jack Rudman. (Career Examination Ser.: C-2898). 1994. pap. 34.95 (*0-8373-2898-5*) Nat Learn.

Senior Project Services Specialist. Jack Rudman. (Career Examination Ser.: C-1662). 1994. pap. 34.95 (*0-8373-1662-6*) Nat Learn.

Senior Psychiatric Social Worker. Jack Rudman. (Career Examination Ser.: C-2487). 1994. pap. 34.95 (*0-8373-2487-4*) Nat Learn.

Senior Psychologist. Jack Rudman. (Career Examination Ser.: C-2173). 1994. pap. 39.95 (*0-8373-2173-5*) Nat Learn.

Senior Public Health Adviser. Jack Rudman. (Career Examination Ser.: C-3175). 1994. pap. 29.95 (*0-8373-3175-7*) Nat Learn.

Senior Public Health Educator. Jack Rudman. (Career Examination Ser.: C-3475). 1994. pap. 34.95 (*0-8373-3475-6*) Nat Learn.

Senior Public Health Engineer. Jack Rudman. (Career Examination Ser.: C-3346). 1994. pap. 34.95 (*0-8373-3346-6*) Nat Learn.

Senior Public Health Nutritionist. Jack Rudman. (Career Examination Ser.: C-1592). 1994. pap. 29.95 (*0-8373-1592-1*) Nat Learn.

Senior Public Health Representative. Jack Rudman. (Career Examination Ser.: C-2385). 1994. pap. 29.95 (*0-8373-2385-1*) Nat Learn.

Senior Public Health Sanitarian. Jack Rudman. (Career Examination Ser.: C-2002). 1994. pap. 29.95 (*0-8373-2002-X*) Nat Learn.

Senior Public Information Assistant. Jack Rudman. (Career Examination Ser.: C-2957). 1994. pap. 29.95 (*0-8373-2957-4*) Nat Learn.

Senior Pump Operator. Jack Rudman. (Career Examination Ser.: C-2951). 1994. pap. 29.95 (*0-8373-2951-5*) Nat Learn.

Senior Purchase Inspector. Jack Rudman. (Career Examination Ser.: C-1483). 1994. pap. 29.95 (*0-8373-1483-6*) Nat Learn.

Senior Pursuits: Making the Golden Years Worth the Wait. Roberta Sandler. (Illus.). 192p. 1993. 19.95 (*0-9633461-2-1*) Valiant Pr.

Senior Quantitative Analyst. Jack Rudman. (Career Examination Ser.: C-1718). 1994. pap. 34.95 (*0-8373-1718-5*) Nat Learn.

Senior Radio Operator. Jack Rudman. (Career Examination Ser.: C-2551). 1994. pap. 29.95 (*0-8373-2551-X*) Nat Learn.

Senior Radiologic Technologist. Jack Rudman. (Career Examination Ser.: C-1545). 1994. pap. 34.95 (*0-8373-1545-X*) Nat Learn.

Senior Real Estate Agent. Jack Rudman. (Career Examination Ser.: C-1941). 1994. pap. 27.95 (*0-8373-1941-2*) Nat Learn.

Senior Real Estate Appraiser. Jack Rudman. (Career Examination Ser.: C-569). 1994. pap. 27.95 (*0-8373-0569-1*) Nat Learn.

Senior Real Estate Manager. Jack Rudman. (Career Examination Ser.: C-1021). 1994. pap. 34.95 (*0-8373-1021-0*) Nat Learn.

Senior Real Property Recorder. Jack Rudman. (Career Examination Ser.: C-3103). 1994. pap. 29.95 (*0-8373-3103-X*) Nat Learn.

Senior Records Center Assistant. Jack Rudman. (Career Examination Ser.: C-1919). 1994. pap. 27.95 (*0-8373-1919-6*) Nat Learn.

Senior Recreation Leader. Jack Rudman. (Career Examination Ser.: C-1938). 1994. pap. 29.95 (*0-8373-1938-2*) Nat Learn.

Senior Recreation Therapist. Jack Rudman. (Career Examination Ser.: C-2974). 1994. pap. 29.95 (*0-8373-2974-4*) Nat Learn.

Senior Rehabilitation Counselor. Jack Rudman. (Career Examination Ser.: C-1952). 1994. pap. 34.95 (*0-8373-1952-8*) Nat Learn.

Senior Rent Examiner. Jack Rudman. (Career Examination Ser.: C-1022). 1994. pap. 27.95 (*0-8373-1022-9*) Nat Learn.

Senior Rent Inspector. Jack Rudman. (Career Examination Ser.: C-2721). 1994. pap. 27.95 (*0-8373-2721-0*) Nat Learn.

Senior Rent Research Associate. Jack Rudman. (Career Examination Ser.: C-1023). 1994. pap. 34.95 (*0-8373-1023-7*) Nat Learn.

Senior Research Analyst. Jack Rudman. (Career Examination Ser.: C-1543). 1994. pap. 39.95 (*0-8373-1543-3*) Nat Learn.

Senior Research Assistant. Jack Rudman. (Career Examination Ser.: C-2717). 1994. pap. 34.95 (*0-8373-2717-2*) Nat Learn.

Senior Right-of-Way Agent. (Career Examination Ser.: C-3626). pap. 29.95 (*0-8373-3626-0*) Nat Learn.

Senior Right-of-Way Aide. Jack Rudman. (Career Examination Ser.: C-2736). 1994. pap. 29.95 (*0-8373-2736-9*) Nat Learn.

Senior Rights Movement. Powell. 1995. pap. 14.95 (*0-8057-9746-7*, Twayne) Scribnrs Ref.

Senior Rights Movement. Powell. 1996. 28.95 (*0-8057-9710-6*, Twayne) Scribnrs Ref.

Senior Safety & Health Engineer. Jack Rudman. (Career Examination Ser.: C-3204). 1994. pap. 39.95 (*0-8373-3204-4*) Nat Learn.

Senior Safety Coordinator. Jack Rudman. (Career Examination Ser.: C-2668). 1994. pap. 39.95 (*0-8373-2668-0*) Nat Learn.

Senior Saints: Growing Older in God's Family. Jim Reapsome & Martha Reapsome. (Fisherman Bible Studyguide Ser.). 80p. (Orig.). 1993. pap. text ed. 4.99 (*0-87788-746-2*) Shaw Pubs.

Senior Sanitarian. Jack Rudman. (Career Examination Ser.: C-2430). 1994. pap. 29.95 (*0-8373-2430-0*) Nat Learn.

Senior Sanitary Engineer. Jack Rudman. (Career Examination Ser.: C-2446). 1994. pap. 34.95 (*0-8373-2446-7*) Nat Learn.

***Senior Savvy: Simple Strategies & Advanced Techniques to Control, Preserve & Maximize Your Life Savings.** 3rd ed. Kenneth A. Stern. 1996. pap. 19.95 (*0-9652268-0-8*) Asset Planning.

Senior Security Hospital Treatment Assistant. Jack Rudman. (Career Examination Ser.: C-1617). 1994. pap. 27.95 (*0-8373-1617-0*) Nat Learn.

Senior Security Officer. Jack Rudman. (Career Examination Ser.: C-2449). 1994. pap. 27.95 (*0-8373-2449-1*) Nat Learn.

Senior Sense & Nonsense. Caldwell Van Roden. 32p. (Orig.). 1987. spiral bd. 5.00 (*0-940844-65-6*) Wellspring.

Senior Services Resource Directory. Ed. by Margaret Monsour. 53p. (Orig.). 1989. spiral bd. (*0-9623088-0-3*) Eureka St Pubns.

Senior Settlers: Social Integration in Retirement Communities. Ed. by Nancy J. Osgood. LC 82-13352. 304p. 1982. text ed. 55.00 (*0-275-90873-9*, C0873, Praeger Pubs) Greenwood.

Senior, Seventy-Five Years of the Wianno Senior Class. Joseph D. Hukle & Donald F. Law. Ed. by W. B. Peale. 70p. (Orig.). 1989. pap. text ed. 20.00 (*0-685-27214-1*) Wianno Sr Class.

Senior Sewage Treatment Plant Operator. Jack Rudman. (Career Examination Ser.: C-1556). 1994. pap. 29.95 (*0-8373-1556-5*) Nat Learn.

Senior Sewage Treatment Worker. Jack Rudman. (Career Examination Ser.: C-791). 1994. pap. 29.95 (*0-8373-0791-0*) Nat Learn.

Senior Shorthand Reporter. Jack Rudman. (Career Examination Ser.: C-724). 1994. pap. 27.95 (*0-8373-0724-4*) Nat Learn.

Senior Sleuths. Cynthia Manson. 288p. (Orig.). 1996. mass mkt. 5.99 (*0-425-15258-8*) Berkley Pub.

Senior Social Case Worker. Jack Rudman. (Career Examination Ser.: C-1555). 1994. pap. 27.95 (*0-8373-1555-7*) Nat Learn.

Senior Social Investigator. (Career Examination Ser.: C-3649). pap. 29.95 (*0-8373-3649-X*) Nat Learn.

Senior Social Services Employment Specialist. Jack Rudman. (Career Examination Ser.: C-2817). 1994. pap. 34.95 (*0-8373-2817-9*) Nat Learn.

Senior Social Services Management Specialist. Jack Rudman. (Career Examination Ser.: C-2579). 1994. pap. 39.95 (*0-8373-2579-X*) Nat Learn.

Senior Social Services Medical Assistance Specialist. Jack Rudman. (Career Examination Ser.: C-2432). 1994. pap. 39.95 (*0-8373-2432-7*) Nat Learn.

Senior Social Services Program Specialist. Jack Rudman. (Career Examination Ser.: C-2236). 1994. pap. 39.95 (*0-8373-2236-7*) Nat Learn.

Senior Social Welfare Examiner. Jack Rudman. (Career Examination Ser.: C-2320). 1994. pap. 27.95 (*0-8373-2320-7*) Nat Learn.

Senior Social Welfare Examiner (Spanish Speaking) Jack Rudman. (Career Examination Ser.: C-2321). 1994. pap. 29.95 (*0-8373-2321-5*) Nat Learn.

Senior Social Worker. Jack Rudman. (Career Examination Ser.: C-2488). 1994. pap. 27.95 (*0-8373-2488-2*) Nat Learn.

Senior Special Investigator. Jack Rudman. (Career Examination Ser.: C-1589). 1994. pap. 34.95 (*0-8373-1589-1*) Nat Learn.

Senior Special Officer. Jack Rudman. (Career Examination Ser.: C-725). 1994. pap. 27.95 (*0-8373-0725-2*) Nat Learn.

Senior Speech & Hearing Therapist. Jack Rudman. (Career Examination Ser.: C-2273). 1994. reprint ed. pap. 34.95 (*0-8373-2273-1*) Nat Learn.

Senior Square: Thirteen Lives in Search of the Twelfth Grade. Twelve Monologues & a Rap. John-Michael Williams. 72p. (Orig.). 1987. pap. 6.95 (*0-936839-81-3*) Applause Theatre Bk Pubs.

Senior Staff Development Specialist. Jack Rudman. (Career Examination Ser.: C-2702). 1994. pap. 39.95 (*0-8373-2702-4*) Nat Learn.

Senior Stationary Engineer. Jack Rudman. (Career Examination Ser.: C-1024). 1994. pap. 29.95 (*0-8373-1024-5*) Nat Learn.

Senior Stationary Engineer (Electric) Jack Rudman. (Career Examination Ser.: C-2433). 1994. pap. 29.95 (*0-8373-2433-5*) Nat Learn.

Senior Statistician. Jack Rudman. (Career Examination Ser.: C-1025). 1994. pap. 34.95 (*0-8373-1025-3*) Nat Learn.

Senior Stenographer. Jack Rudman. (Career Examination Ser.: C-726). 1994. pap. 23.95 (*0-8373-0726-0*) Nat Learn.

Senior Storekeeper. Jack Rudman. (Career Examination Ser.: C-3009). 1994. pap. 27.95 (*0-8373-3009-2*) Nat Learn.

Senior Stores Clerk. Jack Rudman. (Career Examination Ser.: C-2383). 1994. pap. 27.95 (*0-8373-2383-5*) Nat Learn.

Senior Street Club Worker. Jack Rudman. (Career Examination Ser.: C-727). 1994. pap. 29.95 (*0-8373-0727-9*) Nat Learn.

Senior Superintendent (Department of Sanitation) Jack Rudman. (Career Examination Ser.: C-1026). 1994. pap. 39.95 (*0-8373-1026-1*) Nat Learn.

S

Senior Superintendent of Construction. Jack Rudman. (Career Examination Ser.: C-541). 1994. pap. 39.95 (*0-8373-0541-1*) Nat Learn.

Senior Supervisor of Mechanical Installations. Jack Rudman. (Career Examination Ser.: C-1679). 1994. pap. 34.95 (*0-8373-1679-0*) Nat Learn.

Senior Supervisor of Park Operations. Jack Rudman. (Career Examination Ser.: C-1694). 1994. pap. 34.95 (*0-8373-1694-4*) Nat Learn.

Senior Support Collector. Jack Rudman. (Career Examination Ser.: C-3211). 1994. pap. 27.95 (*0-8373-3211-7*) Nat Learn.

Senior Surface Line Dispatcher. Jack Rudman. (Career Examination Ser.: C-728). 1994. pap. 27.95 (*0-8373-0728-7*) Nat Learn.

Senior Systems Analyst. Jack Rudman. (Career Examination Ser.: C-2389). 1994. pap. 34.95 (*0-8373-2389-4*) Nat Learn.

Senior Tabulator Operator. Jack Rudman. (Career Examination Ser.: C-1678). 1994. pap. 27.95 (*0-8373-1678-2*) Nat Learn.

Senior Tax Cashier. Jack Rudman. (Career Examination Ser.: C-2095). 1994. pap. 23.95 (*0-8373-2095-X*) Nat Learn.

Senior Tax Compliance Agent. Jack Rudman. (Career Examination Ser.: C-2953). 1994. pap. 29.95 (*0-8373-2953-1*) Nat Learn.

Senior Tax Valuation Engineer. Jack Rudman. (Career Examination Ser.: C-3197). 1994. pap. 29.95 (*0-8373-3197-8*) Nat Learn.

Senior Taxi & Limousine Inspector. Jack Rudman. (Career Examination Ser.: C-2553). 1994. pap. 27.95 (*0-8373-2553-6*) Nat Learn.

Senior Telephone Inspector. Jack Rudman. (Career Examination Ser.: C-2217). 1994. reprint ed. pap. 29.95 (*0-8373-2217-0*) Nat Learn.

Senior Telephone Operator. Jack Rudman. (Career Examination Ser.: C-1027). 1994. pap. 23.95 (*0-8373-1027-X*) Nat Learn.

Senior Tenant Supervisor. Jack Rudman. (Career Examination Ser.: C-544). 1994. pap. 34.95 (*0-8373-0544-6*) Nat Learn.

Senior Texan Legal Guide. 18.95 (*0-685-52377-2*, B11) Sterling TX.

Senior Title Examiner. Jack Rudman. (Career Examination Ser.: C-2250). 1994. pap. 27.95 (*0-8373-2250-2*) Nat Learn.

Senior Title Searcher. Jack Rudman. (Career Examination Ser.: C-2086). 1994. reprint ed. pap. 27.95 (*0-8373-2086-0*) Nat Learn.

Senior Traffic Control Inspector. Jack Rudman. (Career Examination Ser.: C-729). 1994. pap. 29.95 (*0-8373-0729-5*) Nat Learn.

Senior Traffic Supervisor. Jack Rudman. (Career Examination Ser.: C-2628). 1994. pap. 34.95 (*0-8373-2628-1*) Nat Learn.

Senior Training Officer. Jack Rudman. (Career Examination Ser.: C-1485). 1994. pap. 39.95 (*0-8373-1485-2*) Nat Learn.

Senior Training Technician. Jack Rudman. (Career Examination Ser.: C-1486). 1994. pap. 39.95 (*0-8373-1486-0*) Nat Learn.

Senior Training Technician (Code Compliance) (Career Examination Ser.: C-3355). 1994. pap. 44.95 (*0-8373-3355-5*) Nat Learn.

Senior Training Technician (Police) Jack Rudman. (Career Examination Ser.: C-418). 1994. pap. 44.95 (*0-8373-0418-0*) Nat Learn.

Senior Transportation Analyst. Jack Rudman. (Career Examination Ser.: C-3202). 1994. pap. 34.95 (*0-8373-3202-8*) Nat Learn.

Senior Transportation Inspector. Jack Rudman. (Career Examination Ser.: C-1487). 1994. pap. 34.95 (*0-8373-1487-9*) Nat Learn.

Senior Typist. Jack Rudman. (Career Examination Ser.: C-730). 1994. pap. 23.95 (*0-8373-0730-9*) Nat Learn.

Senior Underwriting Clerk. Jack Rudman. (Career Examination Ser.: C-2987). 1994. pap. 27.95 (*0-8373-2987-6*) Nat Learn.

Senior Unemployment Insurance Claims Examiner. Jack Rudman. (Career Examination Ser.: C-2285). 1994. reprint ed. pap. 29.95 (*0-8373-2285-5*) Nat Learn.

Senior Unemployment Insurance Hearing Representative. Jack Rudman. (Career Examination Ser.: C-2729). 1994. pap. 34.95 (*0-8373-2729-6*) Nat Learn.

Senior Unemployment Insurance Investigator. Jack Rudman. (Career Examination Ser.: C-2830). 1994. pap. 34.95 (*0-8373-2830-6*) Nat Learn.

Senior Vocational Counselor. Jack Rudman. (Career Examination Ser.: C-2438). 1994. pap. 34.95 (*0-8373-2438-6*) Nat Learn.

Senior Vocational Rehabilitation Counselor. (Career Examination Ser.: C-1054). 1994. pap. 34.95 (*0-8373-1054-7*) Nat Learn.

Senior Water Plant Operator. Jack Rudman. (Career Examination Ser.: C-1638). 1994. pap. 29.95 (*0-8373-1638-3*) Nat Learn.

Senior Water Plant Supervisor. Jack Rudman. (Career Examination Ser.: C-2959). 1994. pap. 34.95 (*0-8373-2959-0*) Nat Learn.

Senior Water Use Inspector. Jack Rudman. (Career Examination Ser.: C-1639). 1994. pap. 27.95 (*0-8373-1639-1*) Nat Learn.

Senior Women: How to Make the Extra Money You Need. Helen Hunt & Paula Sanderson. LC 84-1130. 205p. 1983. 17.95 (*0-13-806570-5*, Busn); pap. 5.95 (*0-13-806562-4*, Busn) P-H.

Senior X-Ray Technician. Jack Rudman. (Career Examination Ser.: C-731). 1994. pap. 27.95 (*0-8373-0731-7*) Nat Learn.

***Senior Year Experience: Facilitating Integration, Reflection, Closure, & Transition.** John N. Gardner & Gretchen Van Der Veer. LC 97-18833. (Higher & Adult Education Ser.). 1997. write for info. (*0-7879-0927-0*) Jossey-Bass.

Senior Youth Division Counselor. Jack Rudman. (Career Examination Ser.: C-2500). 1994. pap. 34.95 (*0-8373-2500-5*) Nat Learn.

Senior Youth Group Worker. Jack Rudman. (Career Examination Ser.: C-2585). 1994. pap. 29.95 (*0-8373-2585-4*) Nat Learn.

Senior Zoning Inspector. Jack Rudman. (Career Examination Ser.: C-2341). 1994. pap. 34.95 (*0-8373-2341-X*) Nat Learn.

Senior, 75 Years of the Wianno Senior Class. Joseph D. Hinkle & Donald F. Law. Ed. by W. B. Peale. 70p. (Orig.). 1989. pap. 20.00 (*0-9623811-0-1*) Wianno Sr Class.

Seniorcise: A Simple Guide to Fitness for the Elderly & Disabled. Janie Clark. LC 88-25062. (Illus.). 160p. 1988. 14.95 (*0-910923-55-8*) Pineapple Pr.

Seniority System in Congress. Barbara Hinckley. LC 70-138414. (Midland Bks.: No.151). 156p. reprint ed. 44.50 (*0-8357-9240-4*, 2015820) Bks Demand.

Seniority Wage System in the Far East: Confucian Influence over Japan & South Korea. Byung W. Kim. 222p. 1992. 68.95 (*1-85628-293-7*, Pub. by Avebury Pub UK) Ashgate Pub Co.

***SeniorNet Official Guide to the Web 1997.** K. McFadden & SeniorNet Staff. 1997. pap. 29.99 (*0-614-28474-0*, Lycos Pr) Que.

Seniorobics: The Fitness Guide for People 55 Plus. Ellen Coven. LC 92-70482. (Illus.). 96p. (Orig.). 1992. pap. 14.95 (*0-9631945-7-7*) FitWise Progs.

Seniorplots: A Book Talk Guide for Use with Readers Ages 15-18. John T. Gillespie & Corinne J. Naden. 386p. 1989. 43.00 (*0-8352-2513-5*) Bowker.

Seniors Acting Up: Humorous New One-Act Plays & Skits for Older Adults. Ed. by Ted Fuller. (Illus.). 160p. (Orig.). 1996. pap. 17.95 (*0-9649776-0-5*) Plesnt Hill.

Seniors Arise: Cast off the Twin Yokes of Congress & AARP. Frank A. Fleck. 48p. (Orig.). 1989. pap. 10.00 (*0-918826-04-7*) Time-Wise.

Seniors' Guide to Healthy Travel. Donald Sullivan. 144p. (Orig.). 1994. pap. 14.95 (*1-56414-126-8*) Career Pr Inc.

Seniors' Guide to the Best Deals, Bargains, & Steals! Ed. by Freebies Magazine Editors. (Illus.). 144p. 1996. pap. 12.00 (*1-56565-452-8*) Lowell Hse.

Seniors Housing: A Development & Management Handbook. National Association of Home Builders Staff. LC 87-62642. (Illus.). 121p. 1987. pap. 40.00 (*0-86718-275-X*) Home Builder.

Seniors Living It up on a Budget: California Edition. Ruth Callarman. 212p. (Orig.). 1983. pap. 10.00 (*0-9613087-0-2*) Potter Pubns.

Seniors on Stage: The Impact of Applying Theatre Techniques on the Elderly. Patricia A. Clark & Nancy J. Osgood. LC 85-9347. 224p. 1985. text ed. 49.95 (*0-275-90198-X*, C0198, Praeger Pubs) Greenwood.

Seniors on the Move. Renate Rikkers. LC 85-24846. (Illus.). 256p. 1986. spiral bd. 27.00 (*0-87322-040-4*, BRIK0040) Human Kinetics.

Senior's Piggy Bank: Make Your Money Last As Long As You Do. John A. Stone. (Illus.). 96p. 1992. student ed. 14.95 (*0-9633203-0-0*) Pinewood Pub.

***Seniors' Tennis Quiz.** Jerry Cooper. 24p. (Orig.). 1996. pap. 3.95 (*1-889419-04-4*) J Cooper.

Senna: The Best. Paolo D'Alessio. (Illus.). 48p. (Orig.). 1996. pap. 39.95 (*88-7911-153-1*, Pub. by Giorgio Nada Editore IT) Howell Pr VA.

Senna & Its Rational Use. Ed. by Elke Leng-Peschlow. (Journal: Pharmacology: Vol. 44, Suppl. 1, 1992). (Illus.). iv, 52p. 1992. pap. 17.50 (*3-8055-5574-1*) S Karger.

Sennacherib's Aqueduct at Jerwan. Thorkild Jacobsen & Seton Lloyd. LC 36-20583. (Oriental Institute Publications: No. 24). (Illus.). 52p. 1935. lib. bdg. 24.00 (*0-226-62120-0*, OIP24) U Ch Pr.

Sennacherib's Invasion of Palestine. Leo L. Honor. LC 26-20926. (Columbia University. Contributions to Oriental History & Philology Ser.: No. 12). reprint ed. 27.50 (*0-404-50542-2*) AMS Pr.

Sennacherib's "Palace Without Rival" at Nineveh. John M. Russell. (Illus.). 358p. 1991. 51.95 (*0-226-73175-8*) U Ch Pr.

Senner's Gold. Helen M. Corbin. Ed. by Christina Edelblut. LC 93-73213. (Illus.). 200p. (Orig.). 1993. pap. 12.95 (*1-879029-02-2*, 578.32) Fox West.

Senology: Proceedings of the Seventh International Congress on Senology, Island of Rhodes, Greece, 3-7 May 1992. Ed. by Lydia Ioannidou-Mouzaka et al. LC 92-48837. (International Congress Ser.: No. 1005). 1992. 197.00 (*0-444-89681-3*, Excerpta Medica) Elsevier.

Senor Cat's Romance. Illus. by Lulu DeLacre. LC 95-34144. (J). 1997. 17.95 (*0-590-48537-7*) Scholastic Inc.

Senor Conejo y el Hermosa Regalo. Charlotte Zolotow. Tr. by Maria A. Fiol. LC 94-78492. (Illus.). 32p. (SPA.). (J). (ps-3). 1995. 13.95 (*0-06-025326-6*, HpArco Iris) HarpC Child Bks.

Senor Conejo y el Hermosa Regalo. Charlotte Zotolow. Tr. by Maria A. Fiol from ENG. LC 94-78492. (Illus.). 32p. (SPA.). (J). (ps-3). 1995. pap. 4.95 (*0-06-443404-4*, HpArco Iris) HarpC Child Bks.

Senor de los Pobres. Abraao De Almeida. 208p. (SPA.). 1991. pap. 1.50 (*0-8297-0368-3*) Life Pubs Intl.

Senor Dominguito Tenia una Perrita. Jane B. Moncure. (Castillo Magico Ser.). (Illus.). 32p. (SPA.). (J). (ps-2). 1987. lib. bdg. 21.36 (*0-89565-910-7*) Childs World.

***Senor Esename a Orar en 28 Diaz.** K. Arthur. (SPA.). 7.95 (*0-8297-0460-4*) Life Pubs Intl.

Senor, Guiame Hacia Mi Vocacion. Arnoldo Canclini. (Soy Joven, y Ahora Que Hago? Ser.). 64p. (Orig.). (SPA.). 1989. pap. 2.99 (*0-311-12338-4*) Casa Bautista.

***Senor, Hazme Llorar.** C. Rodriguez. (SPA.). pap. 5.95 (*0-8297-0597-X*) Life Pubs Intl.

Senor Necesito Un Milagro. Benny Hinn. (SPA.). pap. 7.99 (*0-88113-171-7*) Edit Betania.

***Senor Quiero Conocerte.** K. Arthur. (SPA.). 9.95 (*0-8297-0507-4*) Life Pubs Intl.

***Senor, Sana Mis Heridas.** K. Arthur. (SPA.). 10.95 (*0-8297-1984-9*) Life Pubs Intl.

Senor Scrooge: Charles Dickens' A Christmas Carol adapted for the Bilingual Stage. Charles Dickens. Tr. by Betty Alderete. (Illus.). 32p. (Orig.). 1995. pap. 3.25 (*0-88680-404-3*, 404-3) I E Clark.

Senor Sol y el Senor Mar. Andrea Butler. Tr. by Alma F. Ada. (Dejame Leer Ser.). (Illus.). 16p. (SPA.). (J). (ps-2). 1995. 2.95 (*0-673-36302-3*, GoodYrBooks) Addison-Wesley Educ.

Senor, Te Consagro Mi Vida. Ed. by David F. Garces. (Soy Joven, y Ahora Que Hago? Ser.). 64p. (Orig.). (SPA.). 1988. pap. 2.99 (*0-311-12336-8*) Casa Bautista.

***Senor, Tengo un Problema.** B. Ferguson. (SPA.). pap. 1.50 (*0-8297-1415-4*) Life Pubs Intl.

Senor, Usare los Dones Que Me Diste. Carlos G. Sanchez. (Soy Joven, y Ahora Que Hago? Ser.). 64p. (Orig.). (SPA.). 1989. pap. 3.50 (*0-311-12337-6*) Casa Bautista.

***Senor Vivo.** Louis De Bernieres. 1998. pap. write for info. (*0-375-70014-5*, Vin) Random.

Senor y lo Demas, Son Cuentos. Leopoldo A. Clarin. (Nueva Austral Ser.: Vol. 43). (SPA.). 1991. pap. text ed. 24.95 (*84-239-1843-2*) Elliots Bks.

Senora Ama: La Malquerida. Jacinto Benavente. Ed. by Mariano D. Paco. (Nueva Austral Ser.: No. 191). (SPA.). 1991. pap. text ed. 24.95 (*84-239-1991-9*) Elliots Bks.

Senora de la Miel. Fanny Buitrago. LC 95-44610. 240p. 1996. pap. 10.00 (*0-06-095159-1*) HarpC.

***Senora de los Suenos: The Lady of Dreams.** Sara Sotchovich. 1997. pap. 14.95 (*0-679-77658-3*, Vin) Random.

Senora Honeycomb. Fanny Buitrago. Tr. by Margaret S. Peden. LC 95-44609. 232p. 1996. 18.00 (*0-06-017365-3*) HarpC.

***Senora Honeycomb: A Novel.** Margaret S. Peden. 240p. 1997. pap. 11.00 (*0-06-092800-X*, PL) HarpC.

***Senora Rodriguez & Other Worlds.** Martha Cerda. Tr. by Sylvia Jimenez-Anderson from SPA. LC 96-33336. (Latin America in Translation Ser.). 128p. 1997. pap. 12.95 (*0-8223-1890-3*); lib. bdg. 35.00 (*0-8223-1886-5*) Duke.

Senorita Mexican Restaurant's Favorite South of the Border Recipes. Ken Kleinrichert. (Illus.). 160p. 1995. pap. 12.95 (*0-9646333-0-2*) La Senorita Pubns.

Senorita Monstruo ayuda see Monstruo

Senorita Rumfio: Miss Rumphius. Barbara Cooney. (Illus.). 32p. (SPA.). (J). (ps-3). 1996. pap. 14.99 (*0-670-86831-0*) Viking Penguin.

***Senorita Rumfio.** Barbara Cooney. 1997. pap. 4.99 (*0-14-056231-1*) Penguin.

Senorita Sin. Pleasant Gehman. (Illus.). 110p. (Orig.). 1994. pap. 11.00 (*0-9627013-9-4*) Incommcdo San Diego.

Senoufo Phonology, Discourse to Syllable: A Prosodic Approach. Elizabeth Mills. LC 81-51057. (Publications in Linguistics: No. 72). 217p. 1984. fiche 12.00 (*0-88312-434-3*) Summer Instit Ling.

Senryu: Japanese Satirical Verses. Reginald H. Blyth. LC 72-98820. 230p. 1971. reprint ed. text ed. 35.00 (*0-8371-2958-3*, BLSE, Greenwood Pr) Greenwood.

Senryu: Poems of the People. J. C. Brown. (Illus.). 96p. 1991. text ed. 15.95 (*0-8048-1664-6*) C E Tuttle.

Sens a la Vie. Antoine de Saint-Exupery. pap. 10.50 (*0-685-37090-9*) Fr & Eur.

Sens du Mal. M. Auge & C. Herzlich. 278p. 1984. pap. text ed. 242.00 (*2-903928-06-1*) Gordon & Breach.

Sens du Non-Sens. 3rd ed. Florentin Smarandache. Ed. by Xiquan Publishing House Staff. 76p. (FRE.). (C). 1991. reprint ed. pap. 7.99 (*1-879585-14-6*) Erhus Univ Pr.

Sens Interdit. Armand Salacrou. 9.95 (*0-686-55439-6*) Fr & Eur.

Sensabout Bow Tuning. Emery J. Loiselle. (Illus.). 20p. (Orig.). 1971. pap. 3.00 (*0-9613281-1-8*) E J Loiselle.

***Sensaciones Peligrosas - Dangerous Feelings.** Alison Kelly. (SPA.). 1997. mass mkt. 3.50 (*0-373-33424-9*, 1-33424-2) Harlequin Bks.

Sensate Culture: Reversing America's Decline into Cultural Chaos. Harold O. Brown. LC 96-24595. 272p. 1996. 17.99 (*0-8499-1313-6*) Word Pub.

Sensation. Shelby Lewis. 224p. 1997. mass mkt. 4.99 (*0-7860-0351-0*, Pinncle Kensgtn) Kensgtn Pub Corp.

Sensation: Intelligibility in Sensibility. Alphonso Lingis. LC 95-21456. (Contemporary Studies in Philosophy & the Human Sciences). (Illus.). 136p. (C). 1996. 35.00 (*0-391-03899-0*) Humanities.

Sensation & Judgment: Complementarity Theory of Psychophysics. John C. Baird. LC 96-26481. (Scientific Psychology Ser.). 352p. 1997. 79.95 (*0-8058-1830-8*) L Erlbaum Assocs.

Sensation & Measurement: Papers in Honor of S. S. Stevens. Ed. by H. R. Moskowitz et al. LC 74-77966. 550p. 1974. lib. bdg. 187.00 (*90-277-0474-0*) Kluwer Ac.

Sensation & Perception. Ed. by Richard L. Gregory & Andrew M. Colman. LC 95-18103. (Essential Psychology Ser.). (Illus.). 135p. (C). 1995. pap. text ed. 11.95 (*0-582-27811-2*, Pub. by Longman UK) Longman.

Sensation & Perception. 2nd ed. Margaret W. Matlin. 550p. (C). 1988. pap. text ed. 49.33 (*0-205-11125-4*, H11257) Allyn.

Sensation & Perception. 3rd ed. Stanley Coren & Lawrence M. Ward. 612p. (C). 1989. text ed. 46.75 (*0-15-579647-X*) HB Coll Pubs.

Sensation & Perception. 3rd ed. E. Bruce Goldstein. 598p. (C). 1989. text ed. 53.95 (*0-534-09672-7*) Brooks-Cole.

Sensation & Perception. 3rd ed. Margaret W. Matlin. LC 91-26132. 533p. 1992. 55.00 (*0-205-13519-6*) Allyn.

Sensation & Perception. 4th ed. Coren. (C). 1994. teacher ed., text ed. 35.00 (*0-15-500773-4*) HB Coll Pubs.

Sensation & Perception. 4th ed. Stanley Coren et al. (Illus.). (C). 1993. text ed. write for info. (*0-15-500103-5*) HB Coll Pubs.

Sensation & Perception. 4th ed. Bruce E. Goldstein. 1996. text ed. 66.95 (*0-534-26622-3*) Brooks-Cole.

Sensation & Perception. 4th ed. Margaret W. Matlin. LC 96-38560. 1996. text ed. 69.00 (*0-205-26382-8*) Allyn.

Sensation & Perception: An Integrated Approach. 4th ed. Harvey R. Schiffman. LC 95-21053. 592p. 1995. text ed. 44.50 (*0-471-58620-X*) Wiley.

Sensation Novel. Lyn Pykett. (Writers & Their Work Ser.). 95p. (Orig.). 1996. pap. text ed. 15.00 (*0-7463-0725-X*, Pub. by Nrthcote House UK) U Pr of Miss.

Sensation of Being Somebody. Maurice E. Wagner. 352p. 1991. mass mkt. 4.99 (*0-06-104015-0*, Harp PBks) HarpC.

Sensational Beauty, Vol. 1: Universal Controversy. Kevin Dounuts. Ed. by Saralyn Daiell. LC 92-82046. (Illus.). 50p. (Orig.). (YA). (gr. 7 up). 1993. pap. 4.95 (*0-9636006-2-1*) Old Ctry Bks.

Sensational Chocolate. Faye Levy. (Illus.). 192p. 1992. pap. 14.95 (*1-55788-049-2*, HP Books) Berkley Pub.

Sensational Designs: The Cultural Work of American Fiction, 1790-1860. Jane P. Tompkins. 265p. 1986. pap. 18.95 (*0-19-504119-4*) OUP.

Sensational Desserts. Judi Olstein. 93p. 1994. write for info. (*1-57215-001-7*) World Pubns.

Sensational Dutch. David Pelham. 1995. student ed., pap. write for info. (*0-525-45731-3*) NAL-Dutton.

Sensational Fashions & Crafts. Arthur Hettich et al. 1947. 12.95 (*0-405-12052-4*) Ayer.

Sensational French. David Pelham. 1995. student ed., pap. write for info. (*0-525-45730-5*) NAL-Dutton.

Sensational German. David Pelham. 1995. student ed., pap. write for info. (*0-525-45729-1*) NAL-Dutton.

Sensational Ladies: A Handbook for Women Who Want More. George Cappannelli. 90p. 1989. 14.95 (*0-685-29401-3*) Onlife Pub.

Sensational Learning Centers. 64p. 1994. pap. 9.99 (*0-8066-2721-2*, 10-27212, Augsburg) Augsburg Fortress.

***Sensational Music Club Murder, Vol. 1.** Landrum. 1997. mass mkt. 5.99 (*0-312-96261-4*) St Martin.

Sensational Music Club Mystery tc. large type ed. Graham Landrum. LC 95-2758. 250p. 1995. lib. bdg. 21.95 (*0-7838-1278-7*, GK Hall) Thorndike Pr.

Sensational Preserves. Hilaire Walden. LC 95-25974. (Illus.). 144p. 1996. 24.95 (*0-89577-840-8*) RD Assn.

Sensational Restoration. Ed. by J. James Jensen. LC 96-1727. (Indiana Masterpiece Editions Ser.). 512p. 1996. pap. 24.95 (*0-253-21059-3*) Ind U Pr.

Sensational Restoration. Ed. by J. James Jensen. LC 96-1727. (Indiana Masterpiece Editions Ser.). 512p. (C). 1996. text ed. 49.95 (*0-253-33049-1*) Ind U Pr.

***Sensational Sachets: Sewing Scented Treasures.** Stephanie Valley. LC 96-39315. (Great Sewing Projects Ser.). 1997. 27.95 (*0-8069-9810-5*) Sterling.

***Sensational Salads.** (Collector's Ser.: Vol. 41). (Illus.). 64p. Date not set. pap. write for info. (*0-942320-53-0*) Am Cooking.

Sensational Salads. Leila Daly. 93p. 1994. write for info. (*1-57215-003-3*) World Pubns.

Sensational Samburger. Illus. by David Pelham. 10p. (J). (ps). 1995. pap. 12.99 (*0-525-45426-8*) Dutton Child Bks.

Sensational Scarfs. Carol Straley. 1996. pap. 5.99 (*0-517-88616-2*) Random Hse Value.

Sensational Scarfs: Forty-Four Ways to Turn a Scarf into a Fabulous Fashion Look. Carole Straley. (Illus.). 64p. 1984. pap. 3.95 (*0-517-55575-1*, Crown) Crown Pub Group.

Sensational Scarves: Favulous Ideas for Twisting, Tying, Draping & Folding. Carol E. Sterbenz. (Illus.). 72p. 1993. 9.98 (*0-8317-7701-X*) Smithmark.

Sensational Scrap Quilts. Darra D. Williamson. 160p. 1992. pap. 24.95 (*0-89145-983-9*) Collector Bks.

Sensational Search-a-Words. (Little Simon Activity Bks.). (Illus.). 64p. (J). (gr. 2-5). 1990. pap. 1.99 (*0-671-72334-0*, Litl Simon S&S) S&S Childrens.

Sensational Seasons. Junior League Staff. 1993. 16.95 (*0-9634847-0-2*) Ft Smith Jr Leag.

Sensational Settings: Over Eighty Ways to Arrange Quilt Blocks. Joan Hanson. Ed. by Barbara Weiland. LC 92-35396. (Joy of Quilting Ser.). (Illus.). 52p. (Orig.). 1993. pap. 12.95 (*1-56477-018-4*, B146) That Patchwork.

***Sensational Sex: A Pocket Guide.** Jane Hertford. LC 97-22801. (Illus.). 96p. 1997. 9.95 (*0-7867-0411-X*) Carroll & Graf.

Sensational She-Hulk. John Byrne et al. (Illus.). 64p. 1985. 9.95 (*0-87135-084-X*) Marvel Entmnt.

Sensational Silk. Gail Brown. LC 82-80827. 128p. (Orig.). 1982. pap. 6.95 (*0-935278-07-9*) Palmer-Pletsch.

Sensational Sixties. John Gunnell. LC 93-80694. (Illus.). 304p. 1994. pap. 16.95 (*0-87341-294-X*, SX01) Krause Pubns.

***Sensational '60's: A Doll Album with Price Guide.** Glenn A. Mandeville. (Illus.). 112p. 1996. 29.95 (*0-87588-469-5*, 5233) Hobby Hse.

Sensational Suncatchers. Janet Schrader. (Illus.). 56p. 1987. pap. 16.95 (*0-935133-09-7*) CKE Pubns.

Sensational TV: Trash or Journalism? Nancy Day. LC 95-35675. (Issues in Focus Ser.). (Illus.). 112p. (YA). (gr. 6 up). 1996. lib. bdg. 18.95 (*0-89490-733-6*) Enslow Pubs.

Sensations. Jessica March. 432p. (Orig.). 1993. pap. 5.99 (*0-451-40356-8*, Onyx) NAL-Dutton.

An Asterisk (*) at the beginning of an entry indicates that the title is appearing in BIP for the first time.

Sensations. Tuppy Owens. (Orig.). 1993. mass mkt. 6.95 (*1-56333-081-4*, Rhinoceros) Masquerade.

Sensations: A Defense of Type Materialism. Christopher S. Hill. (Cambridge Studies in Philosophy). 256p. (C). 1991. text ed. 69.95 (*0-521-39423-6*); pap. text ed. 21.95 (*0-521-39737-5*) Cambridge U Pr.

Sensations & Phenomenology. Harmon M. Chapman. LC 66-22443. 173p. reprint ed. pap. 49.40 (*0-317-08107-1*, 2050043) Bks Demand.

Sensations "As If -" Herbert A. Roberts. 1976. 9.95 (*0-685-76571-7*) Formur Intl.

Sensations, Memories & the Flow of Time: A Theory of Subjective States - Reductive Materialism Using a Spacetime Analysis. James T. Culbertson. LC 75-30170. (Illus.). 1976. 12.00 (*0-916298-01-9*) Cromwel.

Sensations Novels. Lyn Pykett. 1990. 40.00 (*0-7463-0720-9*, Pub. by Northcote UK); pap. 21.00 (*0-7463-0752-7*, Pub. by Northcote UK) St Mut.

Sense-able Science. (J). (gr. k-1). 1994. 16.95 (*1-881431-42-8*, 1107) AIMS Educ Fnd.

Sense & Absence: Structure & Suspension in the Ending of Mark's Gospel. J. Lee Magness. (Semeia Studies). 136p. (C). 1986. text ed. 16.95 (*1-55540-006-X*, 06-06-15) Scholars Pr GA.

Sense & Absence: Structure & Suspension in the Ending of Mark's Gospel. Lee Magness. (Semeia Studies). 136p. (C). 1986. pap. 15.95 (*1-55540-007-8*) Scholars Pr GA.

Sense & Contradiction: A Study in Aristotle. R. M. Dancy. LC 75-2184. (Synthese Historical Library: No. 14). 196p. 1975. lib. bdg. 93.00 (*90-277-0565-8*, D Reidel) Kluwer Ac.

Sense & Contradiction: A Study in Aristotle. R. M. Dancy. (Synthese Historical Library). 196p. 1980. pap. text ed. 40.00 (*90-277-1189-5*) Kluwer Ac.

Sense & Non-Sense. Maurice Merleau-Ponty. Tr. by Herbert L. Dreyfus & Patrica A Dreyfus from FRE. (Studies in Phenomenology & Existential Philosophy). 193p. 1964. 32.95 (*0-8101-0167-X*); pap. 16.95 (*0-8101-0166-1*) Northwestern U Pr.

Sense & Nonsense. Don M. Cornwell. Ed. by Glenna Holiday & Tom Roby. (Orig.). 1995. pap. 10.00 (*0-9646734-0-1*) D M Cornwell.

Sense & Nonsense. John Patrick. 200p. 1990. write for info. (*0-573-64232-X*) French.

Sense & Nonsense. Jerome K. Jerome. (Jerome K. Jerome Ser.). 208p. (J). (gr. 7-8). 1991. reprint ed. pap. 8.00 (*0-86299-922-7*, Pub. by Sutton Pubng UK) Bks Intl VA.

Sense & Nonsense: A Study in Human Communication. Alfred Fleishman. LC 77-156304. 1971. pap. 6.00 (*0-918970-07-5*) Intl Gen Semantics.

Sense & Nonsense: Original Limericks by Laurence Perrine. Laurence Perrine. LC 93-42068. 64p. (Orig.). 1994. pap. 10.00 (*0-914061-41-0*) Orchises Pr.

***Sense & Nonsense: Uplifting Humor, Vol. 1.** large type ed. Edward Postel. (Illus.). 334p. (Orig.). 1996. pap. 9.95 (*0-9654967-0-8*) Post-n-Tell.

Sense & Nonsense about Crime: A Policy Guide. 2nd ed. Samuel Walker. LC 88-8120. 276p. (C). 1989. pap. 19.95 (*0-534-09120-2*) Wadsworth Pub.

Sense & Nonsense about Crime & Drugs: A Policy Guide. 3rd ed. Samuel Walker. 300p. 1994. pap. 26.95 (*0-534-18966-0*) Wadsworth Pub.

***Sense & Nonsense about Crime & Drugs: A Policy Guide.** 4th ed. Samuel Walker. (Criminal Justice Ser.). (C). 1997. pap. text ed. 24.95 (*0-534-50867-7*) Wadsworth Pub.

Sense & Nonsense about IQ: The Case for Uniqueness. Charles Locurto. LC 90-23133. 224p. 1991. text ed. 55.00 (*0-275-93803-4*, C3803, Praeger Pubs); pap. text ed. 18.95 (*0-275-93911-1*, B3911, Praeger Pubs) Greenwood.

Sense & Nonsense about Prayer. Lehman Strauss. 1976. pap. 9.99 (*0-8024-7702-X*) Moody.

Sense & Nonsense in Corporate Finance: An Antidote to Conventional Thinking about LOBs Capital Budgeting Dividend Policy & Creating Shareholder Value. Louis Lowenstein. (Illus.). 272p. 1992. pap. 14.00 (*0-201-63223-3*) Addison-Wesley.

Sense & Nonsense of Statistical Inference: Controversy, Misuse, & Subtlety. Chamont Wang. (Popular Statistics Ser.: Vol. 6). 256p. 1992. 39.75 (*0-8247-8798-6*) Dekker.

Sense & Nonsense of Weld Defects. 2nd ed. Helmut Thielsch. (Monticello Bks.). 56p. 1982. 5.50 (*0-686-28905-6*) Jefferson Pubns.

Sense & Reference in Frege's Philosophy. Ed. by Hans Sluga. LC 92-36021. (Philosophy of Frege Ser.: Vol. 4). 384p. 1993. text ed. 66.00 (*0-8153-1040-4*) Garland.

***Sense & Senility: The Neuropathology of the Aged Human Brain.** David M. Mann. (Neuroscience Intelligence Unit Ser.). 198p. 1997. 89.95 (*0-412-13431-4*) Chapman & Hall.

***Sense & Senility: The Neuropathy of the Aged Human Brain.** D. M. Mann. LC 96-29707. (Neuroscience Intelligence Unit Ser.). 206p. 1997. 89.95 (*1-57059-422-8*) R G Landes.

Sense & Sensibilia. John L. Austin. Ed. by Geoffrey J. Warnock. 156p. 1964. pap. 12.95 (*0-19-500307-1*) OUP.

Sense & Sensibility. Jane Austen. 352p. (YA). (gr. 9-12). 1983. mass mkt. 3.95 (*0-553-21334-2*, Bantam Classics) Bantam.

Sense & Sensibility. Jane Austen. 352p. 1996. 7.98 (*1-56138-705-3*) Courage Bks.

Sense & Sensibility. Jane Austen. 1992. 15.95 (*0-679-40987-4*) McKay.

Sense & Sensibility. Jane Austen. 1961. pap. 3.95 (*0-451-52419-5*, CE1826, Sig Classics) NAL-Dutton.

Sense & Sensibility. Jane Austen. 1989. pap. 2.95 (*0-451-52185-4*) NAL-Dutton.

Sense & Sensibility. Jane Austen. 1995. mass mkt. 5.99 (*0-451-18790-3*, Sig) NAL-Dutton.

Sense & Sensibility. Jane Austen. Ed. by James Kinsley. (World's Classics Ser.). 400p. 1990. pap. 4.95 (*0-19-282761-8*) OUP.

Sense & Sensibility. Jane Austen. 1995. 14.50 (*0-679-60195-3*, Modern Lib) Random.

Sense & Sensibility. Jane Austen. 380p. 1996. 17.00 (*0-676-50808-1*) Random.

Sense & Sensibility. Jane Austen. 1995. mass mkt. 2.99 (*0-8125-4312-2*) Tor Bks.

Sense & Sensibility. Jane Austen. Ed. by Tony Tanner. (English Library). 374p. pap. 4.95 (*0-14-043047-4*, Penguin Classics) Viking Penguin.

Sense & Sensibility. Jane Austen. Ed. & Intro. by Ros Ballaster. 268p. 1996. pap. 6.95 (*0-14-043425-9*) Viking Penguin.

Sense & Sensibility. Jane Austen. 1997. pap. 4.95 (*0-451-52589-2*, Sig Classics) NAL-Dutton.

Sense & Sensibility. Jane Austin. (Classics Ser.). (YA). (gr. 10 up). 1965. mass mkt. 2.50 (*0-8049-0058-2*, CL-58) Airmont.

Sense & Sensibility. abr. ed. Jane Austen. 336p. (J). 1996. pap. text ed. 3.99 (*0-14-037850-2*) Moonbeam Pubns.

Sense & Sensibility. large type ed. Jane Austen. 501p. 1985. 23.95 (*0-7089-8246-8*, Charnwood) Ulverscroft.

***Sense & Sensibility.** large type ed. Jane Austen. 465p. 1997. reprint ed. lib. bdg. 24.00 (*0-939495-09-0*) North Bks.

Sense & Sensibility. unabridged ed. Jane Austen. LC 95-49594. (Thrift Editions Ser.). 272p. 1996. reprint ed. pap. text ed. 2.00 (*0-486-29049-2*) Dover.

Sense & Sensibility. Jane Austen. 544p. (C). 1981. reprint ed. lib. bdg. 18.95 (*0-89966-287-0*) Buccaneer Bks.

Sense & Sensibility: Women Artists & Minimalism in the Nineties. Lynn Zelevansky. 1994. pap. 16.95 (*0-8109-6131-8*) Abrams.

Sense & Sensibility: Women Artists & Minimalism in the Nineties. Lynn Zelevansky. (Illus.). 64p. 1994. pap. 16.95 (*0-87070-120-7*, 0-8109-6131-8) Mus of Modern Art.

Sense & Sensibility see Oxford Illustrated Jane Austen

Sense & Sensibility & Pride & Prejudice - Jane Austen. Jane Austen. Ed. by Robert Clark. LC 94-20728. 1994. text ed. 49.95 (*0-312-12307-8*) St Martin.

***Sense & Sensibility in Health Care.** Ed. by Marshall Marinker. 296p. (Orig.). (C). Date not set. pap. text ed. 48.00 (*0-7279-1111-2*, Pub. by BMJ Pubng Grp UK) Amer Coll Phys.

Sense & Sensibility in Modern Poetry. William O'Connor. (BCL1-PS American Literature Ser.). 278p. 1993. reprint ed. lib. bdg. 79.00 (*0-7812-6586-X*) Rprt Serv.

Sense & Sensibility in Modern Poetry. William Van O'Connor. LC 71-180986. 291p. 1973. reprint ed. text ed. 45.00 (*0-87752-157-3*) Gordian.

Sense & Sensibility in Twentieth Century Writing: A Gathering in Memory of William Van O'Conner. Ed. by Brom Weber. LC 75-112395. (Crosscurrents-Modern Critiques Ser.). 191p. 1970. 12.95 (*0-8093-0448-1*) S Ill U Pr.

Sense & Sensibility Screenplay & Diaries. expanded ed. Emma Thompson. (Illus.). 288p. 1996. pap. 15.95 (*1-55704-292-6*) Newmarket.

Sense & Sensibility Screenplay & Diaries: Bringing Jane Austen's Novel to Film. Emma Thompson. (Illus.). 288p. 1995. 24.95 (*1-55704-260-8*) Newmarket.

Sense & Subjectivity: A Study of Wittgenstein & Merleau-Ponty. Philip Dwyer. LC 89-37713. (Studies in Epistemology, Psychology & Psychiatry: Vol. 2). xii, 223p. 1990. 71.50 (*90-04-09205-6*) E J Brill.

***Sense & Transcendence: Essays in Honour of Herman Servotte.** Ed. by Ortwin De Graef et al. (Symbolae; Facultatis Litterarum Lovaniensis Series A: Vol. 17). 325p. (Orig.). 1995. pap. 87.50 (*90-6186-667-7*, Pub. by Leuven Univ BE) Coronet Bks.

Sense, Antisense, Nonsense. Robert Champigny. LC 83-26007. (University of Florida Humanities Monographs: No. 57). 128p. 1986. pap. 19.95 (*0-8130-0791-7*) U Press Fla.

Sense Dominance. Aza Baxter. (Illus.). 90p. 1995. pap. text ed. 11.95 (*0-9643205-6-8*) Intuitive Psy.

Sense Dominance & Enneagram. Aza Baxter. (Sense Dominance Ser.: No. 2). (Orig.). 1996. pap. write for info. (*0-614-13946-5*) Intuitive Psy.

Sense Dominance in Therapy. Aza Baxter. (Sense Dominance Ser.: No. 3). Date not set. pap. write for info. (*0-614-13947-3*) Intuitive Psy.

Sense Dominance Tarot. (Sense Dominance Ser.: No. 4). (Orig.). 1996. wbk. ed., pap. write for info. (*0-614-13943-0*) Intuitive Psy.

Sense Dominance Tarot Cards, No. 2. Aza Baxter. (Sense Dominance Ser.). (Illus.). 1994. 12.95 (*0-9643205-1-7*) Intuitive Psy.

Sense Dominance Tarot Workbook. Aza Baxter. (Illus.). 1995. disk 29.95 (*0-9643205-7-6*) Intuitive Psy.

Sense Dominance Tarot Workbook, No. 1. 2nd ed. Aza Baxter. 90p. 1996. pap. text ed. 14.95 (*0-9643205-9-2*) Intuitive Psy.

Sense It! Hear It! Wren & Maile. (Keikis First Bks.). (Illus.). 10p. (J). 1994. bds. 4.95 (*1-880188-86-4*) Bess Pr.

Sense It! See It! Wren & Maile. (Keikis First Bks.). (Illus.). 10p. (J). 1994. bds. 4.95 (*1-880188-84-8*) Bess Pr.

Sense It! Smell It! Wren & Maile. (Keikis First Bks. Ser.). (Illus.). 10p. (J). 1994. bds. 4.95 (*1-880188-85-6*) Bess Pr.

Sense It! Taste It! Wren & Maile. (Keikis First Bks. Ser.). (Illus.). 10p. (J). 1994. bds. 4.95 (*1-880188-87-2*) Bess Pr.

Sense It! Touch It! Wren & Maile. (Keikis First Bks. Ser.). (Illus.). 10p. (J). 1994. bds. 4.95 (*1-880188-88-0*) Bess Pr.

***Sense Making in Science: Professional Development Resources.** (Sense Making in Science Ser.). 1996. text ed. 250.00 (*0-435-07117-3*, 07117) Heinemann.

Sense, Nonsense, & the National Curriculum. Ed. by Michael Barber & Duncan Graham. LC 92-39724. 1993. 75.00 (*0-7507-0160-9*, Falmer Pr); pap. 27.50 (*0-7507-0161-7*, Falmer Pr) Taylor & Francis.

Sense of a People: Toward a Church for the Human Future. Lewis S. Mudge. LC 92-7926. 272p. 1992. pap. 17.95 (*1-56338-040-4*) TPI PA.

Sense of Adharma. Ariel Glucklich. (Illus.). 256p. (C). 1994. 55.00 (*0-19-508341-5*, 4700) OUP.

Sense of an Ending: Studies in the Theory of Fiction. Frank Kermode. 334p. 1968. reprint ed. pap. 10.95 (*0-19-500770-0*) OUP.

Sense of Animals. E. T. Burtt. (Wykeham Science Ser.: No. 26). 128p. 1974. pap. 18.00 (*0-85109-370-1*) Taylor & Francis.

Sense of Appropriateness: Application Discourses in Morality & Law. Klaus Gunther. Tr. by John Farrell. LC 92-31385. (SUNY Series in Social & Political Thought). 353p. (C). 1993. text ed. 74.50 (*0-7914-1551-1*); pap. text ed. 24.95 (*0-7914-1552-X*) State U NY Pr.

Sense of Art. Ralph A. Smith. 250p. (C). 1989. 35.00 (*0-415-90089-1*, A1701, Routledge NY) Routledge.

Sense of Asher. Richard Asher. (Illus.). 112p. 1984. pap. 18.00 (*0-7279-0136-2*, Pub. by Brit Med Assn UK) Amer Coll Phys.

Sense of Audience in Written Communication. Ed. by Gesa E. Kirsch & Duane H. Roen. (Written Communication Annual Ser.: Vol. 5). (Illus.). 320p. (C). 1990. 55.00 (*0-8039-3654-0*); pap. 24.95 (*0-8039-3655-9*) Sage.

Sense of Beauty. George Santayana. 1896. pap. text ed. 4.95 (*0-486-20238-0*) Dover.

Sense of Beauty: Critical Edition. George Santayana. Ed. by Herman J. Saatkamp, Jr. & William G. Holzberger. (Complete Works of George Santayana). 250p. 1988. 37.50 (*0-262-19271-3*, Bradford Bks) MIT Pr.

Sense of Belonging. Margaret T. Davis. 352p. 1994. 25.95 (*0-7126-9847-7*, Pub. by Century UK) Trafalgar.

Sense of Belonging. large type ed. Margaret T. Davis. 578p. 1995. 25.99 (*0-7505-0676-8*) Ulverscroft.

Sense of Change: Language as History. Michael Shapiro. LC 90-39422. (Advances in Semiotics Ser.). 160p. 1991. 12.95 (*0-253-35203-7*) Ind U Pr.

Sense of Coherence & Resiliency: Stress, Coping, & Health. Ed. by Hamilton I. McCubbin et al. (Resiliency & Families Ser.). 300p. (Orig.). (C). 1994. pap. write for info. (*0-9639334-0-X*) U of Wis CEFM.

Sense of Common Ground. 96p. 1995. 39.95 (*1-881616-51-7*, Pub. by Scalo Pubs) Dist Art Pubs.

Sense of Dance: Exploring Your Movement Potential. Constance A. Schrader. LC 95-26221. (Illus.). 192p. 1996. pap. text ed. 24.95 (*0-87322-476-0*, BSCH0476) Human Kinetics.

Sense of Deity: The Republican Spirituality of Dr. Benjamin Rush. John M. Kloos, Jr. LC 91-25222. (Chicago Studies in the History of American Religion Ser.: Vol. 10). 200p. 1991. 50.00 (*0-926019-47-3*) Carlson Pub.

Sense of Destiny. Patricia Wilson. (Romance Ser.). 1995. mass mkt. 2.99 (*0-373-03372-9*, 1-03372-9) Harlequin Bks.

Sense of Destiny. large type ed. Patricia Wilson. 18.95 (*0-263-14043-1*) Thorndike Pr.

Sense of Direction. Karen Swenson. 88p. 1989. 16.95 (*0-912292-85-7*) Smith.

Sense of Direction: Some Obervations on the Art of Directing. William Ball. LC 84-8104. 196p. (C). 1984. pap. 16.95 (*0-89676-082-0*, Drama Pubs) QSMG Ltd.

Sense of Entitlement. Cheryl Mildenhall. (Black Lace Ser.). 272p. (Orig.). 1996. mass mkt. 5.95 (*0-352-33053-8*, Pub. by Virgin Pub UK) London Brdge.

***Sense of Exile: Essays in the Literature of the Asia-Pacific Region.** Ed. by Bruce Bennett & Susan Miller. pap. 12.95 (*0-86422-072-3*, Pub. by Univ of West Aust Pr AT) Intl Spec Bk.

Sense of Form in Art. Heinrich Woelfflin. LC 57-12877. (Illus.). (Orig.). pap. 7.50 (*0-8284-0153-5*) Chelsea Pub.

Sense of Glory: Essays in Criticism. Herbert E. Read. LC 67-26773. (Essay Index Reprint Ser.). 1977. 19.95 (*0-8369-0814-7*) Ayer.

Sense of God. John Bowker. 237p. 1995. pap. 14.95 (*1-85168-093-4*) Onewrld Pubns.

***Sense of Grammar: Language As Semeiotic.** Michael Shapiro. LC 82-49244. (Illus.). 247p. pap. 70.40 (*0-608-05043-1*, 2059704) Bks Demand.

Sense of Grammar: Language As Semiotic. Michael Shapiro. LC 82-49244. (Advances in Semiotics Ser.). (Illus.). 256p. 1983. 31.50 (*0-253-35173-1*) Ind U Pr.

Sense of His Presence. David R. Mains. 196p. (Orig.). 1995. pap. 8.99 (*1-56043-162-8*) Destiny Image.

Sense of History. Peter P. Passman. 360p. 1995. mass mkt. 4.99 (*1-896329-37-3*, Pub. by Comnwlth Pub CN) Partners Pubs Grp.

Sense of History: A Collection of Poems. John Hatcher. (Illus.). 224p. 1990. 21.95 (*0-85398-312-7*); pap. 11.95 (*0-85398-313-5*) G Ronald Pub.

Sense of History: The Best Writing from the Pages of American Heritage. American Heritage Staff. 1995. 14.98 (*0-8317-1368-2*) Smithmark.

Sense of Honor: A Novel. James Webb. (Bluejacket Paperback Ser.). 320p. 1995. pap. 15.95 (*1-55750-917-4*) Naval Inst Pr.

Sense of Injustice: A Social Psychological Perspective. Ed. by Robert G. Folger. LC 84-2068. (Critical Issues in Social Justice Ser.). 1984. 54.50 (*0-306-41459-7*, Plenum Pr) Plenum.

Sense of Irony: An Examination of the Tragedies of Franz Grillparzer, Vol. 4. Bruce Thompson. (Literaturwissenschaftliche Texte Ser.). x, 213p. 1976. pap. 40.10 (*3-261-01775-9*) P Lang Pubng.

Sense of Justice: Biological Foundations of Law. Ed. by Roger D. Masters & Margaret Gruter. (Focus Editions Ser.: Vol. 136). 288p. (C). 1992. text ed. 54.00 (*0-8039-4397-0*); pap. text ed. 24.95 (*0-8039-4398-9*) Sage.

Sense of Learning. Ann E. Berthoff. LC 89-295087. 171p. (Orig.). (C). 1990. pap. text ed. 22.00 (*0-86709-201-7*, 0201) Boynton Cook Pubs.

Sense of Living. Mildred Tonge. (C). 1954. pap. 3.00 (*0-87574-079-0*) Pendle Hill.

Sense of Love. Andrew M. Greeley. LC 92-74851. 96p. 1992. pap. 10.00 (*0-912592-33-8*) Ashland Poetry.

Sense of Mission. Andrew Campbell et al. 240p. 1990. 75.00 (*0-273-60534-8*, Pub. by Pitman Pubng UK) St Mut.

Sense of Mission: Defining Direction for the Large Corporation. Andrew Campbell et al. LC 92-21088. 288p. 1992. 29.95 (*0-201-60800-6*) Addison-Wesley.

Sense of Mission: Historic Churches of the Southwest. Thomas A. Drain. LC 93-5122. (Illus.). 144p. 1994. pap. 19.95 (*0-8118-0404-6*) Chronicle Bks.

Sense of Mission: Historic Churches of the Southwest. Photos by David Wakely. LC 93-5122. (Illus.). 144p. 1994. 35.00 (*0-8118-0632-4*) Chronicle Bks.

Sense of Music. Stephen Brown. 395p. (C). 1988. text ed. 33.25 (*0-15-579637-2*) HB Coll Pubs.

Sense of Music. Victor Zuckerkandl. LC 57-8670. 299p. reprint ed. pap. 85.30 (*0-7837-0246-9*, 2040555) Bks Demand.

Sense of Ocean & Old Trees: Collections of Poems by Writers in Maryland, Virginia, & the District of Columbia. Compiled & Pref. by Joseph D. Adams. (Poet's Domain Ser.: Vol. 5). xii, 68p. (Orig.). 1992. pap. 6.95 (*1-880016-08-7*) Road Pubs.

Sense of Order: A Study in the Psychology of Decorative Art. Ernest H. Gombrich. LC 77-83898. (Wrightsman Lectures). (Illus.). 422p. 1979. 65.00 (*0-8014-1143-2*) Cornell U Pr.

Sense of Order: A Study in the Psychology of Decorative Art. rev. ed. Ernest H. Gombrich. (Illus.). 432p. (C). 1995. pap. 29.95 (*0-7148-2259-0*, Pub. by Phaidon Press UK) Chronicle Bks.

Sense of Place. R. Cobb. pap. 18.95 (*0-7156-1287-5*, Pub. by Duckworth UK) Focus Pub-R Pullins.

Sense of Place. Ed. by Robert McDonald. 24p. (Orig.). 1987. 15.00 (*0-9602974-8-0*) USC Fisher Gallery.

Sense of Place: American Regional Cultures. Ed. by Barbara Allen & Thomas J. Schlereth. (Illus.). 224p. 1990. reprint ed. pap. text ed. 15.00 (*0-8131-0817-9*) U Pr of Ky.

Sense of Place: Essays on the Ozarks. W. C. Jameson. LC 91-91187. 97p. (Orig.). 1992. pap. 7.95 (*0-9630829-0-6*) Seven Oaks Pub.

Sense of Place: In Centerville & Washington Township. Ed. by Howard R. Houser. (Illus.). 240p. 1986. 20.00 (*0-913428-59-0*) Landfall Pr.

Sense of Place: Listening to Americans. large type ed. David Lamb. LC 93-24125. 1993. lib. bdg. 22.95 (*0-7862-0005-7*) Thorndike Pr.

***Sense of Place: The Artist & the American Land.** Alan Gussow. 159p. 1997. text ed. 50.00 (*1-55963-568-1*, Shearwater Bks) Island Pr.

Sense of Place: The Life & Work of Forrest Shreve. Janice E. Bowers. LC 88-14014. 195p. 1988. 22.50 (*0-8165-1072-5*) U of Ariz Pr.

Sense of Place - Tu Barrio: Jamaica Plain People & Where They Live - La Gente de Jamaica Plain y Donde Ellos Viven. Janice Rogovin. Tr. by Yolanda Rivas. (Illus.). 48p. (Orig.). (ENG & SPA.). 1981. pap. text ed. 10.00 (*0-9621783-1-4*) Stonybrook Pr.

Sense of Place, a Sense of Time. John B. Jackson. (Illus.). 176p. 1994. 25.00 (*0-300-06002-5*) Yale U Pr.

Sense of Place, a Sense of Time. John B. Jackson. (Illus.). 1996. pap. 12.00 (*0-300-06397-0*) Yale U Pr.

Sense of Place, a Sense of Time. John B. Jackson. (C). 1996. pap. 13.00 (*0-614-12543-X*) Yale U Pr.

Sense of Place in the New Literatures in English. Ed. by Peggy Nightingale. 252p. 1986. text ed. 29.95 (*0-7022-1849-9*, Pub. by Univ Queensland Pr AT) Intl Spec Bk.

***Sense of Place: Michigan's Upper Peninsula: Essays in Honor of the Career of William E. Vandament.** Ed. by Russell M. Magnaghi & Michael T. Marsden. (Illus.). 257p. 1997. 20.00 (*0-918616-20-4*) Northern Mich.

***Sense of Place: Michigan's Upper Peninsula: Essays in Honor of the Career of William E. Vandament.** Ed. by Russell M. Magnaghi & Michael T. Marsden. (Illus.). 257p. 1997. pap. 10.00 (*0-918616-21-2*) Northern Mich.

Sense of Place, Mississippi. Ed. by Peggy W. Prenshaw & Jesse O. McKee. LC 79-26098. (Illus.). 235p. reprint ed. pap. 67.00 (*0-7837-1074-7*, 2041598) Bks Demand.

Sense of Place Tsarskoe Selo & Its Poets: Papers from the Dartmouth Conference Dedicated to the Centennial of Anna Akhmatova, 1989. Ed. by Lev Loseff & Barry P. Scherr. (Illus.). 368p. (Orig.). 1993. pap. 22.95 (*0-89357-239-X*) Slavica.

Sense of Power: Studies in the Ideas of Canadian Imperialism, 1867-1914. Carl Berger. LC 79-470040. 289p. reprint ed. pap. 82.40 (*0-8357-6356-0*, 2035710) Bks Demand.

Sense of Precious: Human Nature's Missing Ingredient. Gary Hutchison. 1994. pap. write for info. incl. audio (*1-885631-08-1*) G F Hutchison.

***Sense of Precious: Mankinds Missing Ingredient?** Gary Hutchison. 40p. (Orig.). 1996. pap. 10.00 (*1-885631-34-0*, 34-0) G F Hutchison.

Sense of Presence. Edwin F. White. 98p. 1989. pap. 6.99 (*0-89225-357-6*) Gospel Advocate.

S

S

***Sense of Purpose: Great Australian Women of the 20th Century.** NCAS Staff. (Illus.). 240p. 1996. pap. write for info. (*1-86452-008-6*) D W Thorpe.

***Sense of Reality: Studies in Ideas & Their History.** Isaiah Berlin. LC 96-39829. 1997. 25.00 (*0-374-26092-3*) FS&G.

***Sense of Reference: Intentionality in Frege.** Gilead Bar-Elli. LC 96-32718. (Perspektiven der Analytischen Philosophie - Perspectives in Analytical Philosophy Ser.: Vol. 10). xxvi, 251p. 1996. lib. bdg. 124.50 (*3-11-015059-X*) De Gruyter.

Sense of Responsibility in Society. Torkom Saraydarian. LC 89-192450. 173p. (Orig.). 1989. pap. 12.00 (*0-929874-07-2*) TSG Pub Found.

Sense of Self. Camerawork Ltd. Staff. (C). 1990. 50.00 (*1-871103-01-0*, Pub. by Camerawork UK) St Mut.

Sense of Self: Listening to Homeschooled Adolescent Girls. Susannah Sheffer. LC 95-18160. 191p. 1995. 22.95 (*0-86709-357-9*, 0357) Boynton Cook Pubs.

Sense of Self: Listening to Homeschooled Adolescent Girls. Susannah Sheffer. LC 95-18160. 191p. 1997. pap. write for info. (*0-86709-405-2*, 0405) Boynton Cook Pubs.

Sense of Self: Research & Theory. Alan O. Ross. LC 91-868. 208p. (C). 1992. text ed. 32.95 (*0-8261-7430-2*) Springer Pub.

Sense of Sex: Feminist Perspectives on Hardy. Ed. by Margaret R. Higonnet. 280p. (C). 1993. text ed. 42.50 (*0-252-01940-7*); pap. text ed. 15.95 (*0-252-06260-4*) U of Ill Pr.

Sense of Sexuality: Christian Love & Intimacy. Evelyn E. Whitehead & James D. Whitehead. 336p. 1994. reprint ed. pap. 16.95 (*0-8245-1454-8*) Crossroad NY.

Sense of Shabbat. Faige Kobre. LC 89-40361. (Illus.). 32p. (J). 1990. 11.95 (*0-933873-44-1*) Torah Aura.

Sense of Shakespeare's Sonnets. Edward Hubler. LC 76-3790. 169p. 1976. reprint ed. text ed. 49.75 (*0-8371-8815-6*, HUSSS, Greenwood Pr) Greenwood.

Sense of Siege: The Geopolitic. Graham E. Fuller & Ian O. Lesser. (RAND Study Ser.). 193p. (C). 1995. pap. text ed. 19.95 (*0-8133-2149-2*) Westview.

Sense of Sight. John Berger. 1992. 22.50 (*0-8446-6612-2*) Peter Smith.

Sense of Sight: Writings. John Berger. LC 93-13120. 1993. reprint ed. pap. 14.00 (*0-679-73722-7*, Vin) Random.

Sense of Smell. Ed. by R. H. Wright. 248p. 1982. 141.00 (*0-8493-5232-0*, QP458, CRC Reprint) Franklin.

Sense of Society: A History of the American Novel of Manners. Gordon Milne. 305p. 1977. 35.00 (*0-8386-1927-4*) Fairleigh Dickinson.

Sense of Sociology. rev. ed. Lee Braude. LC 79-20785. 160p. 1981. reprint ed. pap. 10.50 (*0-89874-016-9*) Krieger.

Sense of Story: Essays on Contemporary Writers for Children. John R. Townsend. 216p. 1973. reprint ed. pap. 6.95 (*0-87675-276-8*) Horn Bk.

Sense of Style: Reading in English Prose. James Thorpe. LC 87-17498. vi, 185p. (C). 1987. lib. bdg. 29.50 (*0-208-02181-7*, Archon Bks) Shoe String.

Sense of Style: Studies in the Art of Fiction in English-Speaking Canada. W. J. Keith. 235p. (C). 1989. text ed. 26.00 (*1-55022-092-6*, Pub. by ECW Press CN) Genl Dist Srvs.

Sense of Survival. rev. ed. J. Allan South. 336p. 1985. pap. 14.95 (*0-935329-01-3*) Timpanogos Pub.

Sense of Text: The Art of Language in the Study of Biblical Literature. Stephen A. Geller et al. 113p. 1983. pap. text ed. 12.50 (*0-9602686-1-8*) Center Judaic Studies.

Sense of Text: The Art of Language in the Study of Biblical Literature. Stephen A. Geller. (Jewish Quarterly Review Supplement: 1982 Ser.). 113p. 1982. pap. 12.50 (*0-685-49420-9*, Ctr Judaic Studies) Eisenbrauns.

Sense of the Divine: The Natural Environment from a Theocentric Perspective. James Gustafson. LC 94-3890. 200p. 1994. 16.95 (*0-8298-1003-X*) Pilgrim OH.

***Sense of the Divine: The Natural Environment from a Theocentric Perspective.** James M. Gustafson. 200p. 1996. pap. 12.95 (*0-8298-1100-1*) Pilgrim OH.

***Sense of the Holy: An Introduction to the Thought of P. T. Forsyth.** Peter T. Forsyth. 265p. (Orig.). 1996. pap. 26.00 (*0-9653517-0-X*) Wipf & Stock.

Sense of the Meeting. Jack L. Willcuts. 179p. 1992. 16.95 (*0-913342-75-0*) Barclay Pr.

Sense of the Past. Henry James. (BCL1-PS American Literature Ser.). 358p. 1992. reprint ed. lib. bdg. 89.00 (*0-7812-6766-8*) Rprt Serv.

Sense of the People: Politics, Culture & Imperialism in England, 1715-1785. Kathleen Wilson. (Past & Present Publications). (Illus.). 464p. (C). 1995. text ed. 74.95 (*0-521-34072-1*) Cambridge U Pr.

***Sense of the Sacramental: Movement & Measure in Art & Music, Place & Time.** Ed. by David Brown & Ann Loades. 224p. 1995. pap. 22.95 (*0-687-06615-8*) Abingdon.

Sense of the Sacred: A Biography of Bede Griffiths. Kathryn Spink. LC 88-15270. 222p. reprint ed. pap. 63.30 (*0-8357-2692-4*, 2040228) Bks Demand.

***Sense of the Sacred: Finding Our Spiritual Lives.** Adele Getty. LC 97-8997. (Illus.). 208p. 1997. 19.95 (*0-87833-946-9*) Taylor Pub.

Sense of the Self: From Self-Portrait to Autobiography. Nina C. Sundell et al. LC 78-10863. (Illus.). 40p. 1978. 10.00 (*0-916365-06-9*) Ind Curators.

Sense of the Song of Roland. Robert F. Cook. LC 87-5407. 296p. (C). 1987. 45.00 (*0-8014-1930-1*) Cornell U Pr.

***Sense of the World.** LC 97-11889. 1997. write for info. (*0-8166-2610-3*); pap. write for info. (*0-8166-2611-1*) U of Minn Pr.

***Sense of Unity: The Sufi Tradition in Persian Architecture.** Laleh Bakhtiar & Nader Ardalan. 155p. 1996. pap. 29.95 (*0-614-21589-7*, 1121) Kazi Pubns.

Sense of Value: A Thematic Reader. Christopher J. Thaiss. LC 93-28683. 622p. (Orig.). (C). 1993. pap. text ed. 28.95 (*1-55934-203-X*, 1203) Mayfield Pub.

Sense of Value, Instructor's Manual. Christopher J. Thaiss. LC 93-28683. (Orig.). (C). 1993. teacher ed., pap. text ed. write for info. (*1-55934-204-8*, 1204) Mayfield Pub.

Sense of Vocation: A Study of Career & Life Development. Larry Cochran. LC 89-34226. 211p. 1990. text ed. 67.50 (*0-7914-0245-2*); pap. text ed. 24.95 (*0-7914-0246-0*) State U NY Pr.

Sense of Where You Are: A Profile of William Warren Bradley. John McPhee. (Illus.). 172p. 1978. pap. 10.00 (*0-374-51485-2*) FS&G.

Sense of Where You Are: A Profile of William Warren Bradley. 2nd ed. John McPhee. (Illus.). 206p. 1978. 19.95 (*0-374-26093-1*) FS&G.

Sense of Wonder. Edgar J. Saxon & John S. Collis. 64p. (C). 1980. pap. 7.50 (*0-8464-1048-6*) Beekman Pubs.

Sense of Wonder. Edgar J. Saxon. 66p. (Orig.). pap. 7.50 (*0-8464-4289-2*) Beekman Pubs.

Sense of Wonder: A Spiritual Guidebook. 2nd ed. Alison Davis. LC 84-81421. 96p. (Orig.). 1987. reprint ed. pap. 7.95 (*0-9619499-5-3*) Little River Pr.

Sense of Wonder: On Reading & Writing Books for Children. Katherine Paterson. 352p. 1995. pap. 12.95 (*0-452-27476-1*, Plume) NAL-Dutton.

Sense of Wonder Series, 6 bks., Set. Joan Gilbert. Ed. by Aline D. Wolf. 1994. 22.95 (*0-939195-13-5*) Parent-Child Pr.

Sense Perception in Dante's Commedia. Edward G. Miller. LC 96-6262. (Studies in Medieval Literature: No. 15). 376p. 1996. 99.95 (*0-7734-8795-6*) E Mellen.

Sense Relaxation. Bernard Gunther. 144p. 1986. reprint ed. pap. 9.95 (*0-87877-093-3*) Newcastle Pub.

Sense Suspense. Bruce McMillan. LC 93-30272. (Illus.). 40p. (J). 1994. 15.95 (*0-590-47904-0*) Scholastic Inc.

Sensei: The Ultra American. Harold E. Zaugg. (Illus.). 160p. 1995. pap. text ed. 16.95 (*0-89745-172-4*) Sunflower U Pr.

Senseless Acts of Beauty. George McKay. (Illus.). 224p. 1996. pap. 18.00 (*1-85984-028-0*, Pub. by Vrso UK) Norton.

Senseless Acts of Beauty. George McKay. (Illus.). 224p. (C). 1996. text ed. 60.00 (*1-85984-908-3*, Pub. by Vrso UK) Norton.

Senseless Secrets: The Failures of U. S. Military Intelligence from George Washington to the Present. Michael L. Lanning. LC 95-19249. (Illus.). 336p. 1995. 24.95 (*1-55972-322-X*, Birch Ln Pr) Carol Pub Group.

Sensem. Milena Burilova. (Illus.). 122p. (Orig.). (CZE.). (J). (gr. 3-9). 1992. text ed. 24.50 (*0-930329-62-7*) Kabel Pubs.

Sensem. Milena Burilova. (Illus.). 121p. (Orig.). (CZE.). (J). (gr. 3-9). 1994. pap. 24.50 (*0-685-71259-1*) Kabel Pubs.

Sensemaking in Organizations. Karl E. Weick. LC 95-8203. (Foundations for Organizational Science Ser.). (Illus.). 231p. 1995. 39.95 (*0-8039-7176-1*); pap. 18.95 (*0-8039-7177-X*) Sage.

Sensen-Ti Thef Black Dragon C'Hi Kung: Chi King Kofamitic Afrikan Beginnings. Cwolde Kyte. (Illus.). 155p. (Orig.). (YA). (gr. 9 up). 1985. pap. 14.90 (*0-936901-01-2*) Ctr Sacred Healing.

Senses. (Secrets of Science Ser.). (Illus.). 32p. (J). (gr. 3-8). 1991. lib. bdg. 10.95 (*1-85435-271-7*) Marshall Cavendish.

Senses. Ed. by H. B. Barlow & J. D. Mollon. LC 81-17007. (Cambridge Texts in the Physiological Sciences Ser.: No. 3). (Illus.). 400p. 1982. pap. 39.95 (*0-521-28714-6*) Cambridge U Pr.

Senses. David Drew. LC 92-34162. (Illus.). (J). 1993. 3.75 (*0-383-03651-8*) SRA McGraw.

Senses. Parramon Editorial Team Staff. (Discover My World Ser.). (Illus.). 96p. (J). (ps-1). 1994. 16.95 (*0-8120-6442-9*) Barron.

Senses. Angela Royston. LC 92-25715. (Illus.). 24p. (J). (ps-3). 1993. 13.95 (*0-8120-6272-8*) Barron.

Senses. Anna Sandeman. LC 95-13395. (Body Bks.). (Illus.). 32p. (J). (gr. k-2). 1995. lib. bdg. 14.40 (*1-56294-944-6*, Copper Beech Bks) Millbrook Pr.

Senses. Mary Talbot. (Encyclopedia of Health Ser.). (Illus.). 112p. (YA). (gr. 5 up). 1990. lib. bdg. 19.95 (*0-7910-0027-3*) Chelsea Hse.

***Senses: Cross-Curriculum Units for Theme Teaching.** Patricia O'Brien. Ed. by Judy Mitchell. (Illus.). 112p. (Orig.). 1997. teacher ed., pap. 10.95 (*1-57310-076-5*) Teachng & Lrning Co.

Senses & Sensibilities. Jilyn Smith. 230p. 1989. text ed. 18.95 (*0-471-50657-5*); pap. text ed. 9.95 (*0-471-61839-X*) Wiley.

Senses & the Intellect, Vol. 4. Alexander Bain. LC 77-72191. (Contributions to the History of Psychology Ser.: No. 4, Pt. A, Orientations). 496p. 1977. reprint ed. text ed. 95.00 (*0-313-26928-9*, U6928, Greenwood Pr) Greenwood.

Senses Considered As Perceptual Systems. James J. Gibson. LC 83-1716. (Illus.). xiv, 335p. (C). 1983. reprint ed. text ed. 79.50 (*0-313-23961-4*, GISE, Greenwood Pr) Greenwood.

Senses in God's World. Beverly Beckman. (Illus.). 24p. (J). (ps). 1986. 6.99 (*0-570-04150-3*, 56-1604) Concordia.

Senses of Animals. E. T. Burtt & A. Pringle. LC 73-77794. (Wykeham Science Ser.: No. 26). 168p. (C). 1974. 18.00 (*0-8448-1153-X*, Crane Russak) Taylor & Francis.

***Senses of Humor: Self & Laughter in Modern America.** Daniel Wickberg. 264p. 1997. 35.00 (*0-8014-3078-X*) Cornell U Pr.

***Senses of Mystery.** Bernard J. Verkamp. (C). 1997. 24.95 (*0-940866-60-9*); pap. 19.95 (*0-940866-63-3*) U Scranton Pr.

***Senses of Mystery: Religious & Non-Religious.** Bernard J. Verkamp. LC 96-49177. 1997. pap. write for info. (*0-940866-61-7*) U Scranton Pr.

Senses of Nonsense. Alison Rieke. LC 92-10292. 295p. 1992. text ed. 26.95 (*0-87745-384-5*) U of Iowa Pr.

***Senses of Place.** Ed. by Steven Feld & Keith H. Basso. (School of American Research - Advanced Seminar Ser.). (Illus.). 308p. 1997. 40.00 (*0-933452-94-2*); pap. 18.00 (*0-933452-95-0*) Schol Am Res.

Senses of Preaching. Thomas G. Long. LC 88-9148. 96p. 1988. pap. 12.00 (*0-8042-1570-7*) Westminster John Knox.

Senses of Responsibility. Charles Bernstein. 28p. 1990. pap. 4.00 (*0-945926-16-2*) Paradigm RI.

Senses of Stanley Cavell. Ed. by Richard Fleming & Michael Payne. LC 87-48004. (Bucknell Review Ser.: Vol. 32, No. 1). (Illus.). 336p. 1989. 22.00 (*0-8387-5146-6*) Bucknell U Pr.

Senses of Walden. Stanley Cavell. LC 91-35306. 168p. 1992. pap. 12.95 (*0-226-09813-3*) U Ch Pr.

Senses Still. C. Nadia Seremetakis. xii, 148p. 1996. pap. text ed. 13.95 (*0-226-74877-4*) U Ch Pr.

Senses' Tender: Recovering the Novel for the Reader. William K. Buckley. 250p. (C). 1989. text ed. 41.50 (*0-8204-0724-0*) P Lang Pubng.

***SenseSational Home.** (Daybreaks Ser.). 1996. 9.99 (*0-310-96330-3*) Zondervan.

***SenseSational Object Talks.** Bonnie Bruno. Ed. by Lise Caldwell. (Illus.). 48p. (Orig.). 1997. pap. 4.49 (*0-7847-0616-6*, 14-02835) Standard Pub.

Sensescapes. Werner Reichhold. (Illus.). 65p. (Orig.). 1991. pap. 8.00 (*0-944676-14-6*) AHA Bks.

Sensibility: An Introduction. Janet M. Todd. 120p. 1986. 37.50 (*0-416-37710-6*, 1023) Routledge Chapman & Hall.

Sensibility: An Introduction. Janet M. Todd. 120p. (C). 1986. pap. text ed. 12.95 (*0-416-37720-3*, 1037) Routledge Chapman & Hall.

Sensibility & English Song: Critical Studies of the Early Twentieth Century, 2 vol. set. Stephen Banfield. (Illus.). 656p. (C). 1989. pap. 36.95 (*0-521-37944-X*) Cambridge U Pr.

Sensibility & English Song: Critical Studies of the Early 20th Century, 2 vol. set, Vol. 2. Stephen Banfield. 320p. 1985. 69.95 (*0-521-30360-5*) Cambridge U Pr.

Sensibility & Sense. Richard Nelson. 96p. 1989. pap. 7.95 (*0-571-15329-1*) Faber & Faber.

Sensibility in Transformation: Creative Resistance to Sentiment from the Augustans to the Romantics; Essays in Honor of Jean H. Hagstrum. Ed. by Conger S. McMillen. LC 88-46055. (Illus.). 240p. 1990. 36.50 (*0-8386-3352-8*) Fairleigh Dickinson.

Sensible Book: A Celebration of Your Five Senses. rev. ed. Barbara K. Polland. (Illus.). 64p. (J). 1995. pap. 7.95 (*0-89087-707-6*) Celestial Arts.

Sensible Cook: Dutch Foodways in the Old & the New World. Peter G. Rose. LC 89-33457. (Illus.). 160p. 1989. 29.95 (*0-8156-0241-3*) Syracuse U Pr.

Sensible Cruising: The Thoreau Approach. Don Casey & Lew Hackler. (Illus.). 356p. 1990. pap. text ed. 17.95 (*0-87742-288-5*) Intl Marine.

Sensible Cruising: The Thoreau Approach, a Philosophic & a Practical Approach to Cruising. Don Casey & Lew Hackler. LC 86-60480. (Illus.). 364p. 1986. 24.95 (*0-931595-01-0*) Seascape Enters.

Sensible Cruising Designs. L. Francis Herreshoff. (Illus.). 208p. 1991. pap. 21.95 (*0-87742-298-2*, 60275P) Intl Marine.

Sensible Cruising Designs. L. Francis Herreshoff. 1991. pap. text ed. 22.95 (*0-07-028364-8*) McGraw.

***Sensible Justice.** David Anderson. Date not set. 25.00 (*1-56584-389-4*) New Press NY.

Sensible Life. Mary Wesley. 1995. pap. 9.95 (*0-552-99393-X*) Bantam.

Sensible Life. Mary Wesley. 368p. 1991. pap. 11.95 (*0-14-013436-0*, Penguin Bks) Viking Penguin.

Sensible Life. large type ed. Mary Wesley. (General Ser.). 350p. 1991. lib. bdg. 21.95 (*0-8161-5127-X*, GK Hall) Thorndike Pr.

Sensible Listening: The Key to Responsive Interaction. 3rd ed. Paul J. Kaufmann. 256p. (C). 1994. per., pap. text ed. 31.44 (*0-8403-9548-5*) Kendall-Hunt.

***Sensible Listening: The Key to Responsive Interaction.** 4th ed. Paul Kaufmann. 272p. (C). 1997. per. 31.95 (*0-7872-3644-6*) Kendall-Hunt.

Sensible Plainness. Bobbie L. Hawkins. Ed. by Anne Waldman. 112p. (Orig.). 1995. pap. 8.00 (*1-887625-00-3*) Bijou Bks.

Sensible Saver: A Commonsense Guide to Saving More While Still Living Well. Mark Miller. 1996. 14.95 (*0-02-861288-4*) Macmillan.

Sensible Self-Help: The First Road Map for the Healing Journey. David Grudermeyer et al. 429p. (Orig.). 1996. pap. 19.95 (*0-9648648-0-0*) Willingness Wrks.

Sensible Spirit: Walter Pater & the Modernist Paradigm. F. C. McGrath. LC 85-29503. 320p. 1986. 49.95 (*0-8130-0829-8*) U Press Fla.

Sensible Wife. Jessica Hart. 1994. mass mkt. 2.99 (*0-373-03334-6*, 1-03334-9) Harlequin Bks.

Sensible Words: Linguistic Practice in England, 1640-1785. Murray Cohen. LC 77-1856. (Illus.). 1977. text ed. 32.50 (*0-8018-1924-5*) Johns Hopkins.

Sensibly Thin Low-Fat Living & Cooking, Vol. I. Sandra S. Eukel. 175p. 1992. 12.00 (*0-9636350-0-X*) Sensibly Thin.

Sensibly Thin Lowfat Living & Cooking, Vol. II. 284p. 1994. 14.50 (*0-9636350-1-8*) Sensibly Thin.

Sensibly Thin Orientation Book. 48p. 1993. 8.00 (*0-9636350-3-4*) Sensibly Thin.

Sensim III. R. D. Wormald. (C). 1982. pap. text ed. 39.00 (*0-900269-21-9*, Pub. by Old Vicarage UK) St Mut.

Sensing & Controlling Motion: Vestibular & Sensorimotor Function. Ed. by Bernard Cohen et al. LC 92-13003. (Annals Ser.: Vol. 656). 1992. write for info. (*0-89766-733-6*); pap. write for info. (*0-89766-734-4*) NY Acad Sci.

Sensing Feeling & Action: The Experiential Anatomy of Body-Mind Centering. Bonnie B. Cohen. (Illus.). 171p. (Orig.). 1993. pap. 25.00 (*0-937645-03-6*) Contact Edit.

Sensing His Presence, Hearing the Voice: How to Cultivate Hearing the Voice of God. Carrol J. Shewmake. LC 94-22402. 1994. 7.99 (*0-8280-0829-9*) Review & Herald.

***Sensing, Modeling & Simulation in Emerging Electronic Packaging: Proceedings ASME International Mechanical Engineering Congress & Exposition, 1996, Atlanta, Georgia.** Ed. by Chao-Pin Yeh & Charles Ume. LC 96-78690. (EEP Ser.: Vol. 17). 125p. 1996. pap. text ed. 60.00 (*0-7918-1548-X*) ASME Pr.

***Sensing Semiosis.** Merril. Date not set. text ed. write for info. (*0-312-17693-7*) St Martin.

Sensing the World. Moreland Perkins. LC 83-10825. 352p. (C). 1983. text ed. 16.95 (*0-915145-75-8*); lib. bdg. 34.95 (*0-915145-74-X*) Hackett Pub.

Sensitivae Censitae: A Description of the Genus Mimosa (Mimosaceae) in the New World. Rupert C. Barneby. (Memoirs Ser.: No. 65). (Illus.). 835p. 1991. text ed. 130.00 (*0-89327-366-X*) NY Botanical.

Sensitive Chaos: The Creation of Flowing Forms in Water & Air. Theodor Schwenk. Tr. by J. Collins from GER. 288p. 1996. reprint ed. pap. 29.95 (*1-85584-055-3*, Pub. by R Steiner Pr UK) Anthroposophic.

Sensitive Child. Janet Poland et al. 1996. mass mkt. 5.99 (*0-312-95931-1*) St Martin.

Sensitive Crystallization Processes. Pfeiffer. LC 68-31125. 1975. pap. 16.00 (*0-910142-66-1*) Anthroposophic.

Sensitive Independence: Canadian Methodist Women Missionaries in Canada & the Orient, 1881-1925. Rosemary R. Gagan. (Illus.). 320p. 1992. 49.95 (*0-7735-0896-1*, Pub. by McGill CN) U of Toronto Pr.

Sensitive Issues: An Annotated Guide to Children's Literature K-6. Timothy V. Rasinski & Cindy Gillespie. LC 92-18682. 288p. 1992. pap. 29.95 (*0-89774-777-1*) Oryx Pr.

Sensitive Man: And It's OK to Be Feminine. Richard E. Petitti. (Self Realization Bks.: Bk. II). (Illus.). 150p. 1982. pap. 20.00 (*0-938582-03-8*) Sensitive Man.

Sensitive Midwifery. Caroline Flint. (Illus.). 240p. 1986. pap. 37.50 (*0-7506-0419-0*) Buttrwrth-Heinemann.

Sensitive Periods in Development: Interdisciplinary Perspectives. Ed. by Marc Bornstein. (Crosscurrents in Contemporary Psychology Ser.). 304p. 1987. text ed. 59.95 (*0-89859-696-3*) L Erlbaum Assocs.

Sensitive Plant. Percy Bysshe Shelley. LC 72-4547. (Studies in Shelley: No. 25). (Illus.). (C). 1972. reprint ed. lib. bdg. 29.95 (*0-8383-1612-3*) M S G Haskell Hse.

Sensitive Spots: Nine Drawings. Douglas C. Landies. (Illus.). 1978. pap. 4.00 (*0-935350-89-6*) Luna Bisonte.

Sensitividad de Corazon. Kenneth Copeland. Tr. by Copeland, Kenneth, Publications Staff. 27p. (Orig.). (SPA.). 1984. pap. 2.50 (*0-88114-722-2*) K Copeland Pubns.

Sensitivity Analyses for Selected Pavement Distress. Amy L. Simpson et al. 341p. (Orig.). (C). 1994. pap. text ed. 20.00 (*0-309-05771-X*, SHRP-P-393) SHRP.

Sensitivity Analysis in Linear Regression. Samprit Chatterjee & Ali S. Hadi. LC 87-28580. (Probability & Mathematical Statistics Ser.). 315p. 1988. text ed. 94.95 (*0-471-82216-7*) Wiley.

Sensitivity Analysis in Linear Systems. A. Deif. (Illus.). 260p. 1986. 123.95 (*0-387-16312-3*) Spr-Verlag.

Sensitivity & Awareness: A Guide for Developing Understanding among Children. rev. ed. Norma H. McPhee et al. (Illus.). 85p. 1996. pap. 10.95 (*0-944727-30-1*) Jason & Nordic Pubs.

Sensitivity in the Foreign Language Classroom. Incl. Individualization of Instruction. Ronald L. Gougher. 1973. (*0-318-54628-0*); Interraction in the Foreign Language Class. Gertrude Moskowitz. 1973. (*0-318-54629-9*); Teaching Spanish to the Native Spanish Speaker. Herman LaFontaine. 1973. (*0-318-54630-2*); 142p. 1973. pap. 10.95 (*0-915432-73-0*) NE Conf Teach Foreign.

Sensitivity of Functionals with Applications to Engineering Sciences. Ed. by Vadim Komkov. (Lecture Notes in Mathematics Ser.: Vol. 1086). v, 130p. 1984. 29.95 (*0-387-13871-4*) Spr-Verlag.

Sensitivity of Heart. Kenneth Copeland. 28p. 1983. pap. 2.50 (*0-88114-711-7*) K Copeland Pubns.

***Sensitivity to Change: Black Sea, Baltic Sea & North Sea.** 1997. lib. bdg. 245.00 (*0-7923-4535-5*) Kluwer Ac.

Sensitivity to Nonverbal Communication: The PONS Test. Robert Rosenthal et al. LC 78-17322. (Illus.). 432p. 1979. reprint ed. pap. 123.20 (*0-7837-1618-4*, 2041911) Bks Demand.

Sensitivity to People with Disabilities: Training Managers to Comply with the Americans with Disabilities Act. 48p. 1991. 40.00 (*1-55871-227-5*, BSP152) BNA Plus.

Sensitivity to Water Resources in the Delaware River Basin to Climate Variability & Change. Mark A. Ayers et al. No. 1098. write for info. (*0-318-71689-5*) US Geol Survey.

Sensitivity Training: Processes, Problems & Applications. Arthur Blumberg. LC 74-157409. (Notes & Essays Ser.: No. 68). 1971. pap. 2.50 (*0-87060-040-0*, NES 68) Syracuse U Cont Ed.

Sensitization of the Nervous System. Ed. by Charles Barnes & Peter W. Kaliuas. (Illus.). 300p. 1988. 45.00 (*0-936923-12-1*) Telford Pr.

SENSO: The Japanese Remember the Pacific War. Asahi Shinbun. Ed. by Frank B. Gibney. Tr. by Beth Cary. LC 95-34939. 344p. (C). 1995. pap. 19.95 (*1-56324-589-2*, East Gate Bk) M E Sharpe.

SENSO: The Japanese Remember the Pacific War. Asahi Shinbun. Ed. by Frank B. Gibney. Tr. by Beth Cary. LC 95-34939. 344p. (C). (gr. 13). 1995. 65.95 (*1-56324-588-4*, East Gate Bk) M E Sharpe.

Senso - Visconti's Film & Boito's Novella: A Case Study in the Relation Between Literature & Film. Colin Partridge. LC 91-38740. 124p. 1992. lib. bdg. 59.95 (*0-7734-9746-3*) E Mellen.

Sensor & Data Fusion Concepts & Applications. Lawrence A. Klein. LC 93-9503. (Tutorial Texts in Optical Engineering Ser.: Vol. TT 14). 1993. 20.00 (*0-8194-1227-9*) SPIE.

Sensor & Instrumentation Markets: 1992-1995. Ed. by Richard K. Miller & Terri C. Walker. (Orig.). 1992. pap. text ed. 485.00 (*1-881503-01-1*) R K Miller Assocs.

***Sensor & Transducer Selection Guide.** Harry N. Norton. 252p. 1990. 272.25 (*0-946395-80-2*, Pub. by Elsvr Adv Tech UK) Elsevier.

Sensor-Based Robots: Algorithms & Architectures. Ed. by C. S. Lee. (NATO ASI Series F: Computer & Systems Sciences, Special Programme AET: Vol. 66). x, 285p. 1991. 82.95 (*0-387-52298-0*) Spr-Verlag.

Sensor Devices & Systems for Robotics. Ed. by A. Casals. (NATO Asi Series F: Vol. 52). ix, 362p. 1989. 89.00 (*0-387-50885-6*) Spr-Verlag.

***Sensor Dynamics, 3 vols.** O. P. Skobolev. Incl. Vol. 1 Pressure Sensor Dynamics. 64p. (C). 1995. 152.00 incl. disk (*1-56252-348-1*, 4338); Vol. 2 Resistive Temperature Sensor Dynamics. 82p. (C). 1995. 152.00 incl. disk (*1-56252-349-X*, 4346); Vol. 3 Acceleration, Vibration & Shock Sensor Dynamics. 70p. (C). 1995. 152.00 incl. disk (*1-56252-350-3*, 4354); 368.00 (*1-56252-347-3*, 432X) Computational Mech MA.

***Sensor Fusion: Architecture, Algorithms & Applications.** Ed. by Belur V. Dasarathy. 27p. 1997. pap. 59.00 (*0-8194-2482-X*) SPIE.

Sensor Market 'Ninety-Four. Market Intelligence Staff. 244p. 1994. 545.00 (*1-56753-932-7*) Frost & Sullivan.

Sensor Markets 1991-95. Richard K. Miller & Terri C. Walker. 235p. 1991. 485.00 (*0-89671-115-3*) SEAI Tech Pubns.

Sensor Materials. Pat Mosley & John Crocker. LC 96-20098. (Sensors Ser.). (Illus.). 196p. 1996. 136.00 (*0-7503-0015-9*) IOP Pub.

***Sensor Science & Technology: Proceedings of the Symposium, Electronics Design Center, Case Western Reserve University, Cleveland, Ohio, April 6-8, 1987.** Symposium on Sensor Science & Technology Staff. Ed. by B. Schumm, Jr. et al. LC 87-83041. (Electrochemical Society, Proceedings Ser.: Vol. 87-15). reprint ed. pap. 69.30 (*0-608-04661-2*, 2052578) Bks Demand.

Sensor Technology & Devices. Ed. by Ljubisa Ristic. LC 94-2361. 524p. 1994. 99.00 (*0-89006-532-2*) Artech Hse.

Sensor Technology Sourcebook: Guide to Worldwide Research & Development. 2nd ed. 241p. 1995. spiral bd., vinyl bd. 695.00 (*1-56217-010-4*) Tech Insights.

Sensorimotor Impairment in the Elderly: Proceedings of the NATO Advanced Research Workshop, Bad Windsheim, Germany, September 11-13, 1992. Ed. by George E. Stelmach & Volker Homberg. LC 93-5120. (NATO Advanced Study Institutes Series D, Behavioural & Social Sciences: Vol. 75). 480p. (C). 1993. lib. bdg. 236.50 (*0-7923-2393-9*) Kluwer Ac.

Sensorimotor Integration. Ed. by Carl Gans & Philip S. Ulinski. (Biology of the Reptilia Ser.: Vol. 17, Neurology C). (Illus.). 790p. 1992. pap. text ed. 46.50 (*0-226-28119-1*) U Ch Pr.

Sensorimotor Integration. Ed. by Carl Gans & Philip S. Ulinski. (Biology of the Reptilia Ser.: Vol. 17, Neurology C). (Illus.). 790p. 1992. lib. bdg. 106.00 (*0-226-28118-3*) U Ch Pr.

Sensorimotor Integration for Developmentally Disabled Children: A Handbook. 2nd ed. Eileen W. Richter & Patricia C. Montgomery. LC 76-62660. 100p. 1991. pap. 65.00 (*0-87424-142-1*, W-142A) Western Psych.

Sensorimotor Performance Analysis. Eileen W. Richter & Patricia C. Montgomery. (Illus.). 135p. (C). 1989. pap. 30.00 (*0-685-27007-6*) PDP Pr.

Sensorless Control of AC Motor Drives: Speed & Position Sensorless Operation. Ed. by Kaushik Rajashekara et al. LC 95-47574. 512p. 1996. 99.95 (*0-7803-1046-2*, PC3996) Inst Electrical.

***Sensorn, Sensor Systems & Sensor Data Processing.** Ed. by Otmas Loffeld. 52p. 1997. pap. 89.00 (*0-8194-2520-6*) SPIE.

***Sensors: A Comprehensive Survey, 8 vols.** 1,975.00 (*1-56081-193-5*, VCH) Wiley.

***Sensors: A Comprehensive Survey, Vol. 6.** Kenneth I. Spenner. (Sensors Ser.). 1991. text ed. 300.00 (*3-527-26772-7*) Wiley.

Sensors: Principles & Applications. Peter Hauptmann. Tr. by Tim Pownall. LC 92-42438. 185p. 1993. pap. text ed. 39.95 (*0-13-805789-3*) P-H.

***Sensors & Actuators 1997.** 23p. 1997. 86.00 (*1-56091-932-9*) Soc Auto Engineers.

Sensors & Actuators (P-242), 1991. 260p. 1991. pap. 19.00 (*1-56091-111-5*) Soc Auto Engineers.

Sensors & Actuators, 1992. 192p. 1992. pap. 19.00 (*1-56091-220-0*, SP-903) Soc Auto Engineers.

Sensors & Actuators, 1993: Fifteen Papers. 124p. 1993. 19.00 (*1-56091-333-9*, SP-948) Soc Auto Engineers.

Sensors & Actuators, 1994: SAE International Congress & Exposition 1994, 12 papers. (Special Publications). 100p. 1994. pap. 36.00 (*1-56091-465-3*, SP-1013) Soc Auto Engineers.

Sensors & Actuators 1995: 1995 International Congress & Exposition Meeting. 90p. 1995. pap. 36.00 (*1-56091-616-8*, SP1066) Soc Auto Engineers.

Sensors & Actuators 1996: 1996 International Congress & Exposition. (Special Publications). 52p. 1996. pap. 30.00 (*1-56091-763-6*, SP-1133) Soc Auto Engineers.

Sensors & Circuits: Sensors, Transducers, & Supporting Circuits for Electronic Instrumentation, Measurement, & Control. Joseph J. Carr. LC 92-14958. 368p. 1993. text ed. 60.00 (*0-13-805631-5*) P-H.

***Sensors & Control Systems in Arc Welding.** Nomura. (Illus.). 448p. (C). (gr. 13 up). 1993. text ed. 131.95 (*0-412-47490-5*, Chap & Hall NY) Chapman & Hall.

Sensors & Control Systems in Manufacturing. Sabrie Soloman. 1994. text ed. 70.00 (*0-07-059626-3*) McGraw.

Sensors & Environmental Applications of Remote Sensing: Proceedings of the 14th EARSEL Symposium, Goteborg, Sweden, 6-8 June 1994. Ed. by Jan Askne. 500p. 1995. 130.00 (*90-5410-524-0*) Balkema RSA.

Sensors & Monitors for Water Pollution Control, No. E-068. 279p. 1993. 2,450.00 (*0-89336-996-9*) BCC.

Sensors & Sensory Systems for Advanced Robots. Ed. by P. Dario. (NATO Asi Series F: Vol. 43). xi, 597p. 1988. 143.95 (*0-387-19089-9*) Spr-Verlag.

Sensors & Signal Conditioning. Ramon Pallas-Avery et al. LC 91-2472. 416p. 1993. text ed. 80.95 (*0-471-54565-1*) Wiley.

Sensors & Signal Processing for Manufacturing. Ed. by S. Y. Liang & C. L. Wu. (PED Ser.: Vol. 55). 240p. 1992. 57.50 (*0-7918-0798-3*, G00692) ASME.

Sensors & Their Applications VII: Proceedings of the Seventh Conference, Held in Dublin, Ireland, 10-13 September 1995. Ed. by A. T. Augoisti. LC 95-33264. (Sensors Ser.). (Illus.). 447p. 1995. 190.00 (*0-7503-0331-X*) IOP Pub.

Sensors & Transducers: A Guide for Technicians. 2nd ed. Ian R. Sinclair. (Illus.). 208p. 1992. 52.95 (*0-7506-0415-8*) Buttrwrth-Heinemann.

Sensors for Domestic Applications: Proceedings of the 1st European School of Sensors (ESS '94) Arnaldo D'Amico & Giorgio Sberveglieri. 300p. 1995. text ed. 86.00 (*981-02-2246-7*) World Scientific Pub.

Sensors for Industrial Inspection. C. Loughlin. 1992. lib. bdg. 255.00 (*0-7923-2046-8*) Kluwer Ac.

Sensors for Mobile Robots. H. R. Everett. LC 95-17178. 544p. (C). 1995. text ed. 68.00 (*1-56881-048-2*) AK Peters.

Sensors in Bioprocess Control. Twork & Yacynych. (Bioprocess Technology Ser.: Vol. 6). 440p. 1990. 175.00 (*0-8247-8274-7*) Dekker.

Sensors in Electronic Packaging Vol. 3-14: Proceedings of the ASME International Mechanical Engineering Congress & Exposition, 1995, San Francisco, CA. Ed. by C. Ume & C. P. Yeh. LC 95-81274. (1995 ASME International Mechanical Engineering Congress & Exposition Ser.: MED-Vol. 3/EEP-Vol. 14). 132p. 1995. 56.00 (*0-7918-1740-7*, H01022) ASME.

***Sensors in Wastewater Technology: Selected Proceedings of the IAWQ Specialized Conference on Sensors & Wastewater Technology, Held in Copenhagen, Denmark, 25-27 October, 1995.** (Water Science & Technology 33 Ser.). 334p. 1995. pap. text ed. 207.00 (*0-08-042891-6*, Pergamon Pr) Elsevier.

***Sensors, Safety Systems, & Human Factors.** 1996. 30.00 (*1-56091-841-1*, SP-1190) Soc Auto Engineers.

***Sensors Update 2.** Ed. by H. Baltes et al. (Sensors Ser.). 1996. pap. text ed. 348.00 (*3-527-29432-5*) Wiley.

Sensors VI Technology, Systems, & Applications: Proceedings of the 6th Conference on Sensors & Their Applications Held 12-15 September 1993 in Manchester. Ed. by K. T. Grattan & A. T. Augousti. (Sensors Ser.). (Illus.). 480p. 1993. 196.00 (*0-7503-0316-6*) IOP Pub.

Sensors, Which Way Now? A. J. Martin. (C). 1988. 105.00 (*0-86022-211-X*, Pub. by Build Servs Info Assn UK) St Mut.

Sensory Abilities of Cetaceans: Laboratory & Field Evidence. Ed. by J. A. Thomas & Ronald A. Kastelein. (NATO ASI Series A, Life Sciences: Vol. 196). (Illus.). 710p. 1990. 149.50 (*0-306-43695-7*, Plenum Pr) Plenum.

Sensory Aids for the Hearing Impaired. Ed. by H. Levitt et al. LC 76-28875. 576p. 1980. pap. 39.95 (*0-685-55581-X*, PP01297) Inst Electrical.

Sensory Analysis. R. G. Laming. 1986. text ed. 145.00 (*0-12-435455-6*) Acad Pr.

Sensory Awareness: Rediscovery of Experiencing Through the Workshops & Classes of Charlotte Selver. Charles V. W. Brooks. (Illus.). 256p. 1986. reprint ed. pap. 12.95 (*0-9615659-2-6*) F Morrow.

Sensory Awareness & Music Focus. Katherine Clipp & Betty Cox. 60p. (C). 1994. pap. text ed. 12.00 (*0-935273-08-5*) Chess Pub.

Sensory Biology of Aquatic Animals. Ed. by Arthur N. Popper et al. (Proceedings in Life Sciences Ser.). (Illus.). 830p. 1987. 318.95 (*0-387-96373-1*) Spr-Verlag.

Sensory Coding in the Mammalian Nervous System. George Somien. LC 75-31519. 403p. reprint ed. pap. 114.90 (*0-317-26288-2*, 2055694) Bks Demand.

Sensory Deception: A Scientific Analysis of Hallucinations. Peter D. Slade & Richard Bentall. LC 88-45398. (Contemporary Medicine & Public Health Ser.). 300p. 1988. text ed. 55.00 (*0-8018-3760-X*) Johns Hopkins.

***Sensory Development Self-Study Course.** 2nd ed. David Longmire. (CIL Publications & Audiobooks). Date not set. write for info. incl. audio (*1-890786-00-4*) Visions-Srvs.

Sensory Ecology: How Organisms Acquire & Respond to Information. David B. Dusenbery. LC 92-2278. (C). 1995. text ed. 42.95 (*0-7167-2333-6*) W H Freeman.

Sensory Evaluation in Quality Control. Alejandra Munoz et al. (Illus.). 268p. (gr. 13). 1991. text ed. 67.95 (*0-442-00459-1*) Chapman & Hall.

Sensory Evaluation of Appearance of Materials - STP 545. 194p. 1973. 19.75 (*0-8031-0564-9*, 04-545000-36) ASTM.

***Sensory Evaluation of Food: Principles & Practices.** Hildegarde Heymann & Harry Lawless. LC 97-3311. 416p. 1997. 64.95 (*0-412-99441-0*) Chapman & Hall.

Sensory Evaluation of Food: Statistical Methods & Procedure. Michael O'Mahony. (Food Science & Technology Ser.: Vol. 16). 510p. 1986. 175.00 (*0-8247-7337-3*) Dekker.

Sensory Evaluation of Food: Theory & Practice. G. Jellinek. 429p. 1985. text ed. 100.00 (*3-527-26216-4*, VCH) Wiley.

Sensory Evaluation of Strabismus & Amblyopia in a Natural Environment. Ed. by Emilio C. Campos. (Documenta Ophthalmologica Proceedings Ser.). 1984. lib. bdg. 97.00 (*90-6193-508-3*) Kluwer Ac.

Sensory Evaluation Practices. 2nd ed. Herbert Stone & Joel L. Sidel. (Food Science & Technology Ser.). (Illus.). 338p. 1992. text ed. 65.00 (*0-12-672482-2*) Acad Pr.

Sensory Evaluation Techniques. Morten C. Meilgaard. 1987. 99.50 (*0-8493-5431-5*, TA418, CRC Reprint) Franklin.

Sensory Evaluation Techniques. 2nd rev. ed. Morten C. Meilgaard et al. 376p. 1991. 110.00 (*0-8493-4280-5*, TA418) CRC Pr.

Sensory Experience, Adaptation & Perception: Festschrift for Ivo Kohler. Ed. by Lothar Spillmann & Bill Wooten. 775p. (C). 1984. text ed. 160.00 (*0-89859-218-6*) L Erlbaum Assocs.

Sensory Hair Cells: Synaptic Transmission. G. N. Akoev & Y. N. Andrianov. LC 93-7183. 1993. 211.95 (*0-387-56186-2*) Spr-Verlag.

Sensory Inhibition. Georg Von Bekesy. LC 66-17713. 280p. 1967. pap. text ed. 16.95 (*0-691-02453-7*) Princeton U Pr.

Sensory Integration: Theory & Practice. Anne G. Fisher et al. LC 92-2139. (Illus.). 418p. 1991. text ed. 38.00 (*0-8036-3565-6*) Davis Co.

Sensory Integration & Learning Disorders. A. Jean Ayres. LC 72-91446. 294p. (C). 1973. 69.50 (*0-87424-303-3*, W-303) Western Psych.

Sensory Integration & the Child. A. Jean Ayres. LC 79-66987. 191p. 1979. pap. text ed. 23.50 (*0-87424-158-8*, W-158) Western Psych.

Sensory Integrative Approaches in Occupational Therapy. Zoe Mailloux. LC 87-2878. (Occupational Therapy in Health Care Ser.: Vol. 4, No. 2). 179p. 1987. 49.95 (*0-86656-665-1*) Haworth Pr.

Sensory Mechanisms of the Spinal Cord. 2nd ed. W. D. Willis, Jr. (Illus.). 580p. 1991. 99.50 (*0-306-43781-3*, Plenum Pr) Plenum.

Sensory Motor Handbook: A Guide for Implementing & Modifyinig Activities in the Classroom. Julie Bissell et al. LC 88-60760. (Illus.). 150p. (Orig.). 1988. pap. 18.00 (*1-882068-02-5*) Sensory Integration.

Sensory-Motor Integration: Implication for Neurological Disease. Ed. by A. Struppler et al. (Journal: Applied Neurophysiology: Vol. 49, No. 5, 1987). (Illus.). 48p. 1987. pap. 35.25 (*3-8055-4633-5*) S Karger.

Sensory Nerves & Neuropeptides in Gastroenterology: From Basic Science to Clinical Perspectives. Ed. by M. Costa et al. (Advances in Experimental Medicine & Biology Ser.). (Illus.). 306p. 1991. 89.50 (*0-306-43911-5*, Plenum Pr) Plenum.

Sensory Neural Networks: Lateral Inhibition. Bahram Nabet & Robert B. Pinter. 200p. 1991. 86.00 (*0-8493-4278-3*, QA) CRC Pr.

Sensory Neurons: Diversity, Development, & Plasticity. Sheryl A. Scott. (Illus.). 512p. 1992. 80.00 (*0-19-506676-6*) OUP.

Sensory Neuropathies. Ed. by Arthur K. Asbury et al. LC 94-47263. (Illus.). 220p. 1995. 86.95 (*3-211-82642-4*) Spr-Verlag.

Sensory Processing in the Brain: An Exercise in Neuroconnective Modeling. Dean E. Wooldridge. LC 78-24559. 390p. reprint ed. pap. 111.20 (*0-317-28071-6*, 2055767) Bks Demand.

Sensory Processing in the Mammalian Brain: Neural Substrates & Experimental Strategies. Jennifer S. Lund. (Illus.). 384p. 1988. 49.95 (*0-19-504554-8*) OUP.

Sensory Qualities. Austen Clark. (Clarendon Library of Logic & Philosophy). (Illus.). 224p. 1993. 49.95 (*0-19-824001-5*) OUP.

***Sensory Qualities.** Austen Clark. (Clarendon Library of Logic & Philosophy). (Illus.). 264p. 1996. reprint ed. pap. 19.95 (*0-19-823680-8*, Clarendon Pr) OUP.

Sensory Receptors & Signal Transduction. Ed. by John L. Spudich & Birgit H. Satir. (Modern Cell Biology Ser.: No. 1916). 282p. 1991. text ed. 151.00 (*0-471-56105-3*, Wiley-L) Wiley.

Sensory Research: Multimodal Perspectives. Ed. by Ronald T. Verrillo. 328p. 1993. 69.95 (*0-8058-1342-X*) L Erlbaum Assocs.

Sensory Robotics for the Handling of Limp Materials. Ed. by P. M. Taylor. (NATO ASI Series F: Computer & Systems Sciences, Special Programme AET: Vol. 64). ix, 343p. 1990. 94.95 (*0-387-52299-9*) Spr-Verlag.

Sensory Science Theory & Applications in Foods. Ed. by Harry T. Lawless & Barbara P. Klein. (IFT Basic Symposium Ser.: Vol. 6). 456p. 1991. 99.75 (*0-8247-8537-1*) Dekker.

Sensory Systems & Communication in Arthropods. Ed. by F. G. Gribakin et al. (Advances in Life Sciences Ser.). 448p. 1990. 99.00 (*0-8176-2360-4*) Birkhauser.

Sensory Systems of Arthropods. Ed. by K. Wiese et al. LC 93-22173. (Advances in Life Sciences Ser.). (Illus.). 696p. 1993. 147.00 (*0-8176-2795-2*) Birkhauser.

Sensory Systems One: Vision & Visual Systems. Richard Held. (Readings from the Encyclopedia of Neuroscience Ser.). 144p. 1988. 38.00 (*0-8176-3395-2*) Birkhauser.

Sensory Systems Two: Senses Other Than Vision. Jeremy Wolfe. (Readings from the Encyclopedia of Neuroscience Ser.). 192p. 1988. 38.00 (*0-8176-3396-0*) Birkhauser.

***Sensory Testing Methods.** 2nd ed. ASTM, Committee E-18 on Sensory Evaluation of Materials & Products Staff et al. LC 96-32386. (Manual Ser.). 1996. write for info. (*0-8031-2068-0*) ASTM.

Sensory to Motor Transformation: Pre-Motor Mechanisms. Ed. by B. Blum et al. (Journal: Brain, Behavior & Evolution: Vol. 33, Nos. 2-3, 1989). (Illus.). 136p. 1989. pap. 75.25 (*3-8055-5061-8*) S Karger.

Sensory Transduction. Ed. by A. Borsellino et al. LC 90-42555. (NATO ASI Series A, Life Sciences: Vol. 194). (Illus.). 290p. 1990. 89.50 (*0-306-43677-9*, Plenum Pr) Plenum.

***Sensual Atraccion - Sensual Attraction.** Patty Salier. (SPA.). 1997. mass mkt. 3.50 (*0-373-35204-2*, 1-35204-6) Harlequin Bks.

Sensual Ceremony: A Contemporary Guide to Sexual Intimacy, Vol. 2. Kenneth R. Stubbs. (Illus.). 111p. (Orig.). 1993. pap. 18.95 (*0-939263-10-6*) Secret Garden.

Sensual Dreaming: How to Understand & Interpret the Erotic Content of Your Dreams. Gayle Delaney. 288p. 1995. pap. 12.00 (*0-449-90974-3*) Fawcett.

Sensual Drugs. H. B. Jones & Helen C. Jones. LC 76-8154. (Illus.). 1977. 44.50 (*0-521-21247-2*) Cambridge U Pr.

Sensual Healing: An Elemental Guide to Feeling Good. Teresa Kennedy. LC 96-8368. 224p. (Orig.). 1996. pap. 12.95 (*0-87131-806-7*) M Evans.

Sensual Images. Pie Books Staff. (Illus.). 208p. 1994. pap. 49.95 (*4-938586-57-6*, Pub. by PIE Bks JA) Bks Nippan.

Sensual Lingerie: The Art of Silken Seduction. 1990. 14.99 (*0-517-05651-8*) Random Hse Value.

Sensual Massage. Nitya LaCroix. LC 90-4101. 128p. (Orig.). 1990. pap. 15.95 (*0-8050-1231-1*, Owl) H Holt & Co.

Sensual Math: Poems. Alice Fulton. LC 94-32191. 128p. 1995. 17.95 (*0-393-03750-9*) Norton.

Sensual Math: Poems. Alice Fulton. 128p. 1996. pap. 12.00 (*0-393-31445-6*, Norton Paperbks) Norton.

Sensual Mirror. Marco Vassi. 238p. 1993. pap. 16.95 (*0-933256-88-4*) Second Chance.

***Sensual Philosophy: Joyce & the Aesthetics of Mysticism.** Colleen Jaurretche. LC 97-15598. 176p. 1997. 27.95 (*0-299-15620-6*) U of Wis Pr.

Sensual Rhythms & Purple Bats. Esther K. Heggie & Virginia Rubino. 82p. (Orig.). 1986. pap. text ed. 6.00 (*0-938885-13-8*) Shu Pub.

Sensual Secrets. (Red Stripe Ser.). 1989. pap. 4.50 (*0-8216-5071-8*) Carol Pub Group.

Sensual Secrets. 224p. 1990. pap. 4.50 (*0-88184-661-9*) Carroll & Graf.

***Sensual Secrets.** 4.50 (*0-7867-0661-9*) Carroll & Graf.

Sensual Thread: A Novel. Beatrice Stone. LC 94-9299. 240p. (Orig.). 1994. pap. 10.95 (*1-879427-18-4*) Third Side Pr.

Sensual Touch. Glenn Wilson. 192p. 1996. pap. 17.95 (*0-7867-0274-5*) Carroll & Graf.

Sensualidad: Resistiendo el Encanto de Lujuria. Charles R. Swindoll. (Serie Realidades - Realities Ser.). 36p. (SPA.). 1989. pap. 1.79 (*0-945792-45-X*, 498102) Editorial Unilit.

Sensualistic Philosophy of the 19th Century. Robert L. Dabney. LC 75-3008. reprint ed. 32.50 (*0-404-59124-8*) AMS Pr.

Sensuality. Charles R. Swindoll. (Swindoll Booklets Ser.). 32p. 1995. pap. 3.99 (*0-310-20089-X*) Zondervan.

Sensuality Sex: To Understand Yourself & Choose to be Your Creative, Released, Sexual Self. Harold J. Brednel. 125p. 1987. pap. 5.95 (*0-943073-01-4*) Ctr Creat Lvg.

***Sensually Sensible Cooking: A Flavorful Feast.** Lisa Galus & Elizabeth B. Galus. Ed. by Sam Galus & Debra Duncan. LC 96-72161. 145p. (Orig.). 1996. spiral bd. 19.95 (*1-888347-35-X*, Gnosis TX) Donnchad.

Sensuous Animal: The Real Birds & the Bees Story. Melvin D. Saunders. LC 75-41839. (Illus.). 239p. reprint ed. pap. 68.20 (*0-8357-6287-4*, AU00387) Bks Demand.

Sensuous Burgundy. Barbara Delinsky. 272p. 1996. mass mkt. 5.99 (*0-06-101101-0*, Harp PBks) HarpC.

***Sensuous Burgundy.** large type ed. Barbara Delinsky. LC 96-45009. 1996. pap. 22.95 (*1-56895-393-3*) Wheeler Pub.

Sensuous Child. Hal M. Wells. LC 75-37842. 188p. pap. 3.95 (*0-8128-2472-5*, Scrbrough Hse) Madison Bks UPA.

***Sensuous Cinema of My Mind.** Roni. x, 91p. (Orig.). 1996. pap. 16.95 (*0-9654292-0-2*) Laugh Buddha Pr.

Sensuous Cooking. Steve Urevith. 160p. 1994. per. 19.95 (*0-8403-9479-9*) Kendall-Hunt.

Sensuous Couple. 2nd ed. Robert Chartham. 192p. 1987. mass mkt. 5.99 (*0-345-35188-6*) Ballantine.

Sensuous Debris: Selected Poems 1970-1995. deluxe limited ed. Bruce Boston. (Illus.). 96p. 1996. 50.00 (*0-938075-63-2*) Ocean View Bks.

Sensuous Debris: Selected Poems, 1979-1995. Bruce Boston. (Illus.). 96p. 1995. 40.00 (*0-9626708-8-X*) Talisman IN.

***Sensuous Garden.** Montagu Don. LC 97-17129. 1997. 32.50 (*0-684-83965-2*, S&S) S&S Trade.

Sensuous Geographies: Body, Sense, & Place. Paul Rodaway. LC 93-40331. 224p. (C). (gr. 13). 1994. text ed. 62.95 (*0-415-08829-1*, B0835) Routledge.

Sensuous Golfer. Mark Oman. LC 76-19347. (Illus.). 1976. pap. 7.95 (*0-917346-01-7*) Golfaholics Anon.

***Sensuous Gourmet: Exciting Vegetarian Cooking.** Joy K. Johnson. (Illus.). 150p. 1997. 24.95 (*0-9652214-0-7*) Joyous Health.

S

An Asterisk (*) at the beginning of an entry indicates that the title is appearing in BIP for the first time.

S

Sensuous Heart: Guidelines for Sex after a Heart Attack or Heart Surgery. Suzanne Cambre. Ed. by Faye Hoffman & Nancy Hull. LC 90-8192. (Illus.). 20p. (Orig.). 1990. pap. text ed. 5.75 (*0-939838-28-1*) Pritchett & Hull.

Sensuous in Art: Reflections on Indian Aesthetics. Rakha Jhanji. (C). 1989. 13.50 (*81-208-0617-4*, Pub. by Motilal Banarsidass II) S Asia.

Sensuous Living: Expand Your Sensory Awareness. Nancy Conger. LC 95-12263. (Llewellyn's Whole Life Ser.). (Illus.). 216p. 1995. pap. 12.95 (*1-56718-160-0*) Llewellyn Pubns.

***Sensuous Magic.** 2nd ed. Pat Califia. 1996. pap. 12.95 (*1-56333-458-5*, R Kasak Bks) Masquerade.

Sensuous Man. M. 6.00 (*0-8184-0076-5*) Carol Pub Group.

Sensuous Man. Murphy. 224p. 1972. mass mkt. 5.50 (*0-440-17916-5*) Dell.

Sensuous Muscle: The Women of Bodybuilding. Ed. by Jerry Kindela. 176p. (Orig.). 1995. pap. 4.95 (*0-945797-24-9*) Weider Health.

Sensuous Person: Critique & Corrections. Albert Ellis. 1973. 6.00 (*0-8184-0077-3*) Carol Pub Group.

***Sensuous Scholarship: Contemporary Ethnography.** Paul Stoller. LC 96-53514. (Contemporary Ethnography Ser.). (Illus.). 160p. 1997. text ed. 36.50 (*0-8122-3398-0*); pap. text ed. 16.50 (*0-8122-1615-6*) U of Pa Pr.

Sensuous Spirituality: Out from Fundamentalism. Virginia R. Mollenkott. 192p. 1992. pap. 12.95 (*0-8245-1168-9*) Crossroad NY.

***Sensuous Trekker: How to Enhance Your Relationship with a Star Trek Fan.** Samuel Ramer. 1997. pap. text ed. 10.95 (*0-8065-1919-3*, Citadel Pr) Carol Pub Group.

Sensuous Vegetarian Barbeque: A Hot & Healthful Collection of Recipes, Marinades, & Grilling Tips. Vicki R. Chelf & Dominique Biscotti. LC 94-13375. 224p. pap. 9.95 (*0-89529-613-6*) Avery Pub.

Sensuous Woman. J. 192p. 1971. mass mkt. 5.50 (*0-440-17859-2*) Dell.

Sensuous Woman. J. LC 70-105435. 1970. 6.00 (*0-8184-0078-1*) Carol Pub Group.

Sensus Communis: Vico, Rhetoric, & the Limits of Relativism. John D. Schaeffer. LC 89-23826. 192p. (C). 1990. text ed. 29.95 (*0-8223-1026-0*) Duke.

Sensus Fidelium: The Use of a Concept in the Post-Vatican II Era. Daniel J. Finucane. 728p. 1996. 79.95 (*1-57309-081-6*); pap. 59.95 (*1-57309-080-8*) Intl Scholars.

Sensus Spiritualis. Ohly. 1994. 39.00 (*0-226-62089-1*) U Ch Pr.

Sent As a Gift: Eight Correspondences from the Eighteenth Century. Ed. by Alan T. McKenzie. LC 92-6568. 256p. 1993. 40.00 (*0-8203-1466-8*) U of Ga Pr.

Sent Away: A Study of Young Offenders in Care. J. A. Walter. 193p. 1978. text ed. 59.95 (*0-566-00199-3*, Pub. by Avebury Pub UK) Ashgate Pub Co.

Sent by Jesus. D. B. Knox. 79p. 1992. 11.99 (*0-85151-625-4*) Banner of Truth.

Sent for You Yesterday. John Edgar Wideman. 1988. pap. 11.00 (*0-679-72029-4*, Vin) Random.

Sent from the Father: Meditations on the Fourth Gospel. Joseph Comblin. Tr. by Carl Kabat. LC 78-16750. Orig. Title: O Enviado do Pai. 128p. (Orig.). reprint ed. pap. 36.50 (*0-8357-4071-4*, 2036761) Bks Demand.

***Sent into Hiding.** Kathy Dahlstrom. (God News Club Ser.: Bk. 5). (J). (gr. 4 up). 1996. 4.99 (*1-55976-831-2*) CEF Press.

Sent to the River God Forgot. Jim Walton & Janice Walton. LC 95-6408. 240p. 1995. pap. 9.99 (*0-8423-5977-X*) Tyndale.

***Sentamental Hearts.** Sharon Buononato. Date not set. pap. text ed. 10.95 (*1-57377-005-1*) Easl Pubns.

Sentaos, Andad, Estad Firmes. T. S. Nee. Orig. Title: Sit, Walk, Stand. 80p. (SPA.). 1992. mass mkt. 3.50 (*0-8254-1505-5*, Edit Portavoz) Kregel.

Sentence. deluxe ed. Robert Kelly. 40p. pap. 10.00 (*0-930794-64-8*) Station Hill Pr.

Sentence Adverbials in a Functional Description. Eva Koktova. LC 86-26354. (Pragmatics & Beyond Ser.: Vol. VII, 2). viii, 96p. (Orig.). 1986. pap. 33.00 (*1-55619-001-8*) Benjamins North Am.

Sentence & Parole Handbook. Stuart J. Faber. 318p. 1986. pap. 27.50 (*0-89074-054-2*) Lega Bks.

Sentence Basics. Smith. 1993. teacher ed., pap. text ed. 22.50 (*0-312-09562-7*) St Martin.

Sentence Basics. Smith. 1994. teacher ed., pap. text ed. 5.00 (*0-312-09563-5*) St Martin.

Sentence Basics: Diction, Usage, & Mechanics. Elliott L. Smith & Blythe M. Smith. 464p. 1993. pap. text ed. 24.00 (*0-312-06560-4*) St Martin.

Sentence Book. 3rd ed. Lee A. Jacobus & Judith D. Miller. 341p. (C). 1989. pap. text ed. 18.75 (*0-15-579660-7*); pap. text ed. 4.00 (*0-15-579661-5*) HB Coll Pubs.

Sentence by Sentence: A Basic Rhetoric, Reader & Grammar. Madelyn T. Mihm. 375p. (C). 1989. pap. text ed. 18.75 (*0-15-579672-0*) HB Coll Pubs.

Sentence Combing & Paragraph Building. William Strong. (Illus.). 320p. (C). 1981. pap. text ed. write for info. (*0-07-553677-3*) McGraw.

Sentence Combining: A Composing Book. 3rd ed. William Strong. LC 93-20825. 1993. pap. text ed. write for info. (*0-07-062535-2*) McGraw.

Sentence Combining: A Rhetorical Perspective. Ed. by Donald A. Daiker et al. LC 84-14026. 408p. 1985. 19.95 (*0-8093-1191-7*) S Ill U Pr.

Sentence Combining: Improving Student Writing Without Formal Grammar Instruction. Frank O'Hare. LC 72-95432. (NCTE Research Reports: No. 15). 121p. 1973. reprint ed. pap. 34.50 (*0-608-00858-3*, 2061649) Bks Demand.

Sentence Combining Student Workbook with Exercises & Key. Robert McBaine. 135p. (Orig.). (YA). (gr. 8 up). 1984. pap. 8.90 (*0-89420-244-8*, 261000) Natl Book.

Sentence Composing: Teacher's Guide. Don Killgallon. 29p. (gr. 10-12). 1985. pap. text ed. 2.00 (*0-86709-161-4*, 6121) Boynton Cook Pubs.

Sentence Composing: The Complete Course. Don Killgallon. LC 86-14757. 160p. (Orig.). (YA). (gr. 10). 1986. pap. text ed. 18.50 (*0-86709-183-5*, 0183) Boynton Cook Pubs.

Sentence Composing Eleven. Don Killgallon. 142p. (YA). (gr. 11). 1984. pap. text ed. 13.50 (*0-86709-125-8*, 0125) Boynton Cook Pubs.

Sentence Construction. 2nd ed. Henrichsen. 1992. teacher ed. 5.00 (*0-8384-3016-3*) Heinle & Heinle.

Sentence Construction: Writing & Combining Standard English Sentence, Bk. I. 2nd ed. Alice C. Pack & Lynn E. Henrichsen. 176p. 1992. pap. 21.95 (*0-8384-3015-5*) Heinle & Heinle.

Sentence Dictionary. Eric Neal. 432p. (C). 1988. 45.00 (*0-7175-0194-9*, Pub. by S Thornes Pubs UK) St Mut.

Sentence Dynamics. 3rd ed. Constance Immel & Sacks. (C). 1991. pap. text ed. 41.50 (*0-673-46302-8*) Addson-Wesley Educ.

Sentence Extenders. Carole Gray. (J). (gr. 2-12). 1986. 22.95 (*0-937857-56-4*, 1221) Speech Bin.

Sentence Initial Devices, No. 75: Publications in Linguistics, Set 4. Ed. by Joseph E. Grimes. LC 83-51455. 350p. (Orig.). 1985. fiche 16.00 (*0-88312-724-5*) Summer Instit Ling.

Sentence Intonation of Contemporary Standard Russian As a Linguistic Structure. J. E. Buning & C. H. van Schooneveld. (Description & Analysis of Contemporary Standard Russian: No. 3). 1961. 43.10 (*3-11-000021-0*) Mouton.

Sentence Maker for Levels A-D: Beginner Sequence. Barbara D. DiBenedetto. (Linguistic Pattern Ser.). 10p. (Orig.). 1993. 10.00 (*1-56775-048-6*) ISM Teach Systs.

Sentence Making: A Writing Workbook in English As a Second Language. Robert G. Bander. 248p. (C). 1982. pap. text ed. 12.95 (*0-03-058072-2*) HB Coll Pubs.

Sentence Mastery, Level C. Edgar H. Schuster. Ed. by Hester E. Weeden. (Sentence Mastery Ser.). (Illus.). 160p. (gr. 7). 1982. Bk. C. 6.64 (*0-07-055623-7*) McGraw.

Sentence Mastery, Level A. Edgar H. Schuster. Ed. by Hester E. Weeden. (Sentence Mastery Ser.). (Illus.). 160p. (gr. 7). 1981. Bk. A. 6.64 (*0-07-055621-0*) McGraw.

Sentence Mastery, Level B. Edgar H. Schuster. Ed. by Hester E. Weeden. (Sentence Mastery Ser.). (Illus.). 160p. (gr. 7). 1981. Bk. B. 6.64 (*0-07-055622-9*) McGraw.

Sentence Matters: With Sentence Exercises, Proofreading Passages, Writing Assignments. R. Kent Smith. LC 93-31526. 356p. 1994. pap. text ed. 35.20 (*0-13-319039-0*) P-H.

Sentence Patterns of Indonesian. Soenjono Dardjowidjojo. LC 78-6687. (PALI Language Text Ser.). 448p. 1983. pap. text ed. 27.00 (*0-8248-0418-X*) UH Pr.

Sentence Patterns of Indonesian. Soenjono Dardjowidjojo. (PALI Language Text Ser.). 1994. audio 500.00 (*0-8248-1624-2*) UH Pr.

Sentence Power. Reynolds. (C). 1991. teacher ed., pap. text ed. 34.00 (*0-03-026334-4*) HB Coll Pubs.

Sentence Power. Jean Reynolds. (C). 1991. pap. text ed. 20.75 (*0-03-026333-6*) HB Coll Pubs.

Sentence Repetition Testing for Studies of Community Bilingualism. Carla Radloff. LC 91-68075. (Publications in Linguistics: No. 104). xvi, 214p. (Orig.). 1992. pap. 15.00 (*0-88312-667-2*) Summer Instit Ling.

Sentence Repetition Testing for Studies of Community Bilingualism, Set 4. Carla Radloff. LC 91-68075. (Publications in Linguistics: No. 104). xvi, 214p. (Orig.). 1992. fiche 16.00 (*0-88312-561-7*) Summer Instit Ling.

Sentence Sense. Farbman. (C). 1988. teacher ed., pap. 2.76 (*0-395-46473-0*) HM.

Sentence Sense: A Writer's Guide. Evelyn Farbman. LC 88-81329. 352p. (C). 1988. pap. 35.56 (*0-395-38004-9*) HM.

Sentence Skills: A Workbook for Writers. 5th ed. John Langan. LC 94-31072. (Langan Ser.). 1994. write for info. (*0-07-036424-9*) McGraw.

Sentence Skills: A Workbook for Writers : Form C. 5th ed. John Langan. LC 94-34371. 1995. pap. text ed. write for info. (*0-07-036423-0*) McGraw.

Sentence Skills: A Workbook for Writers, Form A. 3rd ed. John Langan. 496p. (C). 1986. pap. text ed. write for info. (*0-07-036305-6*) McGraw.

Sentence Skills: A Workbook for Writers: Form B. 5th ed. John Langan. LC 93-28530. 1994. pap. text ed. write for info. (*0-07-036410-9*) McGraw.

Sentence Skills: Form A. 5th ed. John Langan. 1993. pap. text ed. write for info. (*0-07-036396-X*) McGraw.

***Sentence Skills with Readings.** John Langan. 1996. pap. text ed. write for info. (*0-07-036506-7*) McGraw.

Sentence Structure. Lindell Bruce. 80p. (C). 1994. 7.30 (*0-8403-9699-6*) Kendall-Hunt.

Sentence Structure. Nigel Fabb. (Language Workbooks Ser.). (Illus.). 160p. (C). 1994. pap. 12.95 (*0-415-08569-1*, B4366) Routledge.

***Sentence Structure.** Sheehan. 1996. teacher ed., pap. text ed. 5.00 (*0-13-187881-6*) P-H.

***Sentence Structure: A Communicative Course Using Story Squares.** Thomas Sheehan. LC 96-36981. 176p. 1996. pap. 15.75 (*0-13-035510-0*) P-H.

Sentence Structure & Characterization in the Tragedies of Jean Racine: A Computer-Assisted Study. Mary L. Flowers. LC 76-50284. 223p. 1979. 33.50 (*0-8386-2056-6*) Fairleigh Dickinson.

Sentence Structure of Japanese: Viewed in the Light of Dialectology. Yoichi Fujiwara. Ed. by Noah S. Brannen & Scott J. Baird. LC 73-78976. 175p. reprint ed. pap. 49.90 (*0-317-10167-6*, 2020443) Bks Demand.

Sentence Style. Lindell Bruce. 84p. (C). 1994. 7.30 (*0-8403-9698-8*) Kendall-Hunt.

Sentence Suspended. large type ed. Cyril A. Joyce. 288p. 1992. pap. 15.99 (*0-7089-7217-9*) Ulverscroft.

Sentence Tracking. 48p. (J). (gr. 3 up). 1987. pap. 10.00 (*0-87879-748-3*, Ann Arbor Div); pap. 10.00 (*0-87879-749-1*, Ann Arbor Div); pap. 10.00 (*0-87879-750-5*, Ann Arbor Div) Acad Therapy.

Sentence Writing. Mary Spangler. (C). 1992. text ed. 39.50 (*0-06-047016-X*) Addson-Wesley Educ.

***Sentence Writing.** Werner. (C). Date not set. text ed. write for info. (*0-321-40624-9*) Addson-Wesley Educ.

Sentence Writing Simplified. Selby. (C). 1992. text ed. 8.95 (*0-06-501149-X*) Addson-Wesley Educ.

Sentence Writing Simplified. Norwood Selby. 178p. 1994. pap. text ed. 8.95 (*0-8230-4973-6*) Watsn-Guptill.

***Sentenced to Death: The American Novel & Capital Punishment.** David Guest. LC 96-30603. 1997. pap. write for info. (*0-87805-918-0*) U Pr of Miss.

Sentenced to Death: The American Novel & Capital Punishment. David Guest. 256p. (C). 1997. text ed. 40.00 (*0-87805-917-2*) U Pr of Miss.

Sentenced to Hospital: Offenders at Broadmoor. Susanne Dell & Graham Robertson. (Maudsley Monographs: No. 32). 180p. 1988. 55.00 (*0-19-712156-X*) OUP.

Sentenced to Life: Fifty Years of Missionary Life in Japan. Leone Cole. 288p. 1987. pap. write for info. (*0-9618026-1-8*) Natl Design Assocs.

Sentenced to Life in a Cell. Daniel Valone. (Illus.). 90p. 1975. pap. 1.50 (*0-942788-02-8*) Iris Visual.

Sentenced to Live. Cecilie Klein. 1989. 16.95 (*0-89604-097-6*, Holocaust Library); pap. 10.95 (*0-89604-128-X*, Holocaust Library) US Holocaust.

Sentenced to Remember: My Legacy of Life in Pre-1939 Poland & Sixty-Eight Months of Nazi Occupation. Williams Kornbluth. Ed. by Carl Calendar. LC 92-82976. 1994. 37.50 (*0-934223-30-0*) Lehigh Univ Pr.

***Sentenced to Servitude.** Paul Little. (Orig.). 1997. pap. 9.95 (*1-56333-565-4*) Masquerade.

Sentences. 1981. 3.00 (*0-939418-40-1*) Ferguson-Florissant.

Sentences. S. Harold Collins. (Straight Forward English Ser.). 34p. (Orig.). (J). (gr. 4-6). 1991. pap. 3.95 (*0-931993-41-5*, GP-041) Garlic Pr OR.

Sentences. Howard Nemerov. LC 80-17702. 96p. 1983. pap. 10.95 (*0-226-57262-5*) U Ch Pr.

Sentences & Complex Structures see Modern English: Exercises for Non Native Speakers

Sentences & Other Systems: A Language & Learning Curriculum for Hearing-Impaired Children. Peter M. Blackwell et al. LC 78-51922. 200p. reprint ed. pap. 57.00 (*0-7837-1254-5*, 2041391) Bks Demand.

Sentences & Paragraphs. Lee Brandon & Kelly Brandon. 448p. (C). 1993. pap. text ed. 34.36 (*0-669-27634-0*); Instr.'s ed. teacher ed. 34.36 (*0-669-27635-9*) HM College Div.

Sentences Children Use. Paula Menyuk. (Press Research Monographs: No. 52). 176p. 1972. pap. 8.95 (*0-262-63043-5*) MIT Pr.

Sentences for Dictation. Janet S. Edlich. (Angling for Words Ser.). 80p. pap. 10.00 (*0-87879-403-4*) Acad Therapy.

***Sentences, Paragraphs, & Beyond: With Culturally Diverse Readings, 2 Vols.** Lee Brandon & Kelly Brandon. (C). 1997. teacher ed., text ed. write for info. (*0-669-41846-3*) HM College Div.

***Sentences, Paragraphs, & Beyond: With Culturally Diverse Readings, 2 Vols.** 2nd annot. ed. Lee Brandon & Kelly Brandon. (C). 1997. teacher ed., text ed. write for info. (*0-669-41853-6*) HM College Div.

***Sentences, Paragraphs, & Beyond: With Culturally Diverse Readings.** 2nd ed. Lee Brandon & Kelly Brandon. 480p. (C). 1996. pap. text ed. 34.36 (*0-669-41597-9*) HM College Div.

Sentences Undecidable in Formalized Arithmetic: An Exposition of the Theory of Kurt Godel. Andrej Mostowski. LC 82-11886. (Studies in Logic & the Foundations of Mathematics). viii, 117p. 1982. reprint ed. text ed. 35.00 (*0-313-23151-6*, MOSU) Greenwood.

Sentencing. Miller. (Nutshell Ser.). Date not set. pap. text ed. write for info. (*0-314-06587-3*) West Pub.

Sentencing: Intermediate Sanctions in the Federal Criminal Justice System. (Illus.). 131p. (Orig.). (C). 1995. pap. text ed. 35.00 (*0-7881-1730-0*) DIANE Pub.

***Sentencing: Intermediate Sanctions in the Federal Criminal Justice System.** (Illus.). 132p. 1994. pap. text ed. 45.00 (*1-57979-088-7*) BPI Info Servs.

Sentencing - Theory, Law & Practice. Nigel Walker. 1985. U.K. 86.00 (*0-406-25263-7*) MICHIE.

Sentencing & Criminal Justice. Andrew Ashworth. (Law in Context Ser.). 408p. (C). 1994. text ed. 70.00 (*0-297-82044-3*); pap. text ed. 33.95 (*0-297-82045-1*) Northwestern U Pr.

Sentencing & Criminal Justice. 2nd ed. Ashworth. 1995. pap. text ed. 40.00 (*0-406-04538-0*) MICHIE.

Sentencing As a Human Process. John Hogarth. LC 73-151374. (Canadian Studies in Criminology: No. 1). 448p. reprint ed. pap. 127.70 (*0-317-27028-1*, 2023637) Bks Demand.

Sentencing Commission & Its Guidelines. Andrew Von Hirsch et al. 215p. 1987. text ed. 40.00 (*1-55553-009-5*) NE U Pr.

***Sentencing, Corrections & Prisoners' Rights, Cases & Materials on the Law Of.** 5th ed. Lynn S. Branham & Sheldon Krantz. LC 96-36925. (American Casebook Ser.). 657p. 1996. write for info. (*0-314-20469-5*) West Pub.

***Sentencing, Corrections & Prisoners' Rights, Teacher's Manual to Accompany Cases & Materials on the Law Of.** Lynn Branham & Sheldon Krantz. (American Casebook Ser.). 175p. 1997. pap. text ed. write for info. (*0-314-22431-9*) West Pub.

Sentencing Defense Manual: Advocacy-Practice-Procedure. Marcia G. Shein. LC 88-14474. (Criminal Law Ser.). 1988. ring bd. 140.00 (*0-87632-597-5*) Clark Boardman Callaghan.

Sentencing Dynamics Study: A Sourcebook of Sentencing Practices in Urban Texas in 1991. (Illus.). 80p. (Orig.). (C). 1994. pap. text ed. 30.00 (*0-7881-0453-5*) DIANE Pub.

Sentencing Guidelines for Chemically Dependent Criminal Offenders. Terence T. Gorski. 19p. (Orig.). 1995. pap. text ed. 4.00 (*0-8309-0703-3*, Indep Pr) Herald Hse.

Sentencing in Hong Kong. I. Grenville Cross & Patrick W. Cheung. xxxii,128p. 1994. text ed. write for info. (*0-409-99713-7*, ASIA) MICHIE.

Sentencing in South Africa. D. Van Der Merwe. 240p. 1991. ring bd. 52.00 (*0-7021-2551-2*, Pub. by Juta SA) Gaunt.

Sentencing in the Courts. Eric Stockdale. (Criminal Law Library). 352p. 1987. 80.00 (*0-08-039248-2*, Pergamon Pr); 64.80 (*0-08-033066-5*, Pergamon Pr) Elsevier.

Sentencing in the Federal Courts: Does Race Matter?: The Transition to Sentencing Guidelines, 1986-90. Douglas C. McDonald & Kenneth E. Carlson. (Illus.). 229p. (Orig.). (C). 1994. pap. text ed. 50.00 (*0-7881-1472-7*) DIANE Pub.

Sentencing Law in Tasmania. Kate Warner. 503p. 1991. pap. 78.00 (*1-86287-037-3*, Pub. by Federation Pr AU) Gaunt.

Sentencing Matters. Michael H. Tonry. (Studies in Crime & Public Policy). (Illus.). 256p. 1996. 29.95 (*0-19-509498-0*) OUP.

Sentencing Principles & Magistrates' Sentencing Behavior. Ralph J. Henham. 258p. 1990. text ed. 63.95 (*1-85628-000-4*, Pub. by Avebury Pub UK) Ashgate Pub Co.

***Sentencing Process.** Ed. by Martin Wasik. LC 96-43131. (International Library of Criminology, Criminal Justice & Penology). (Illus.). 528p. 1997. text ed. 127.95 (*1-85521-784-8*, Pub. by Dartmth Pub UK) Ashgate Pub Co.

Sentencing Reform: Experiments in Reducing Disparity. Ed. by Martin L. Forst. LC 82-10369. (Sage Criminal Justice System Annuals Ser.: No. 17). 247p. reprint ed. pap. 70.40 (*0-8357-8460-6*, 2034726) Bks Demand.

***Sentencing Reform in Overcrowded Times: A Comparative Perspective.** Ed. by Michael H. Tonry & Kathleen Haltestad. LC 96-8403. (Illus.). 304p. 1997. text ed. 45.00 (*0-19-510786-1*) OUP.

***Sentencing Reform in Overcrowded Times: A Comparative Perspective.** Ed. by Michael H. Tonry & Kathleen Hatlestad. LC 96-8403. (Illus.). 304p. 1997. pap. text ed. 19.95 (*0-19-510787-X*) OUP.

Sentencing Research in Texas: A Survey of Issues Relevant to Local Criminal Justice. Robert C. Rickards et al. (Special Project Report). 42p. 1991. pap. 9.50 (*0-89940-870-2*) LBJ Sch Pub Aff.

***Sentencing Robbers in New South Wales: Principles, Policy & Practice.** I. Potas. 201p. 1990. pap. 20.00 (*0-642-14487-7*, Pub. by Aust Inst Criminology) Willow Tree NY.

Sententiae. Publilius Syrus. (Illus.). 314p. 1964. reprint ed. write for info. (*0-318-71205-9*) G Olms Pubs.

Sentential Complementation & the Lexicon: Studies in Honour of Wim de Geest. Ed. by P. Seuren et al. xiv, 456p. (C). 1989. pap. 103.85 (*90-6765-415-9*) Mouton.

Sentential Complementation in Spanish: A Lexico-Grammatical Study of Three Classes of Verbs. Carlos Subirats-Ruggeberg. LC 86-26865. (Lingvisticae Investigationes Supplementa Ser.: No. 14). xii, 290p. 1987. 62.00 (*90-272-3123-0*) Benjamins North Am.

Sentential Probability Logic: Origins, Development, Current Status, & Technical Applications. Theodore Hailperin. LC 96-10867. 304p. 1996. 43.50 (*0-934223-45-9*) Lehigh Univ Pr.

Sententiousness & the Novel: Laying Down the Law in Eighteenth Century French Fiction. Geoffrey Bennington. (Cambridge Studies in French: No. 10). 280p. 1986. text ed. 59.95 (*0-521-30246-3*) Cambridge U Pr.

Sentido, Forma y Estilo de "Redentores" de Manuel Zeno Gandia. Rosa M. Palmer de Dueno. (UPREX, Estudios Literarios Ser.: No. 34). 124p. (C). 1974. pap. 1.50 (*0-8477-0034-8*) U of PR Pr.

Sentidos. Parramon Editorial Team Staff. (Discover My World Ser.). (Illus.). 96p. (J). (ps-1). 1994. 16.95 (*0-8120-6443-7*) Barron.

Sentience. Wallace I. Matson. (Illus.). 200p. 1976. pap. 11.95 (*0-520-04776-1*) U CA Pr.

***Sentient: The Official Strategy Guide.** 112p. 1997. per. 14.99 (*0-7615-1075-3*) Prima Pub.

Sentimen's Svr la Distinction des Diverses Manieres de Peinture... fac. ed. Abraham Bosse. (Documents of Art & Architectural History Ser.: Ser. II; Vol. 5). 142p. (FRE.). 1981. lib. bdg. 30.00 (*0-89371-205-1*) Broude Intl Edns.

***Sentimental Calendar, Being Twelve Funny Stories.** Frederic J. Stimson. (Illus.). 280p. 1969. 20.95 (*0-8369-3171-8*) Ayer.

Sentimental Comedy: Theory & Practice. Frank H. Ellis. (Cambridge Studies in Eighteenth-Century English Literature & Thought: No. 10). (Illus.). 260p. (C). 1991. text ed. 59.95 (*0-521-39431-7*) Cambridge U Pr.

Sentimental Economy: Commodity & Community in Rural Ireland. Carles Salazar. LC 96-33871. (New Directions in Anthropology Ser.: Vol. 2). 192p. 1996. 35.00 (*1-57181-887-1*) Berghahn Bks.

Sentimental Education. Gustave Flaubert. Tr. by Robert Baldick. (Classics Ser.). 432p. (Orig.). 1964. pap. 5.95 (*0-14-044141-7*, Penguin Classics) Viking Penguin.

Sentimental Education. Gustave Flaubert. 1987. mass mkt. 4.95 (*0-452-00852-2*, Mer) NAL-Dutton.

Sentimental Education. Carole Stone. 20p. 1981. 3.00 (*0-934714-14-2*) Swamp Pr.
Sentimental Education: Schooling, Popular Culture & the Regulation of Liberty. James Donald. 192p. (C). 1992. pap. 18.00 (*0-86091-555-7*, A6409, Pub. by Vrso UK) Norton.
Sentimental Education: The Story of a Young Man. Gustave Flaubert. Ed. & Tr. by Douglas Parmee. (World's Classics Ser.). (Illus.). 528p. 1990. pap. 5.95 (*0-19-281731-0*) OUP.
Sentimental Favorites. Carolyn Kyle. 36p. 1993. pap. 13.95 (*0-935133-48-8*) CKE Pubns.
Sentimental Imperialists. James C. Thomson, Jr. et al. LC 79-1689. 347p. 1985. pap. text ed. 14.00 (*0-06-131998-8*, TB 1998, Torch) HarpC.
Sentimental Journey. Janet Dailey. (Janet Dailey Americana Ser.). 1992. mass mkt. 3.59 (*0-373-89892-4*, 1-89892-3) Harlequin Bks.
Sentimental Journey. Laurence Sterne. Ed. by A. Alvarez & Graham Petrie. (English Library). 160p. 1967. pap. 5.95 (*0-14-043026-1*, Penguin Classics) Viking Penguin.
Sentimental Journey. Laurence Sterne. 282p. 5.50 (*0-460-87336-9*, Everyman's Classic Lib) C E Tuttle.
Sentimental Journey. Viktor Shklovsky. Tr. by Richard Sheldon from RUS. LC 71-87022. 352p. 1984. reprint ed. pap. 15.95 (*0-8014-9291-2*) Cornell U Pr.
Sentimental Journey: A Guide to Preserving the Architectural Heritage of Georgetown, Texas. Dan K. Utley et al. (Illus.). (Orig.). 1989. pap. text ed. 20.00 (*0-936149-03-5*) Georgetown Herit.
Sentimental Journey: Songs of the World War II Era. Friedman-Fairfax & Sony Music Group. (Life, Times & Music Book/CD Ser.). 1995. pap. 16.98 incl. audio compact disk (*1-56799-127-0*, Friedman-Fairfax) M Friedman Pub Grp Inc.
Sentimental Journey Through France & Italy. Laurence Sterne. Ed. by Ian Jack. Bd. with Journal to Eliza.; Political Romance. (World's Classics Paperback Ser.). 270p. 1984. pap. 4.95 (*0-19-281685-3*) OUP.
Sentimental Journeys. Christy Davis. 48p. 1994. text ed. 7.95 (*0-8059-3439-1*) Dorrance.
Sentimental Modernism: Women Writers & the Revolution of the Word. Suzanne Clark. LC 90-47556. 240p. 1991. 19.95 (*0-253-31374-0*); pap. 6.95 (*0-253-20640-5*) Ind U Pr.
Sentimental Narrative & the Social Order in France, 1760-1820. David J. Denby. (Cambridge Studies in French: No. 47). (Illus.). 314p. (C). 1994. text ed. 69.95 (*0-521-43086-0*) Cambridge U Pr.
Sentimental Notion. large type ed. Jan McDaniel. 185p. 1995. pap. 20.95 (*0-7838-1517-4*, GK Hall) Thorndike Pr.
Sentimental Novel in America, 1789-1860. Herbert Brown. (BCL1-PS American Literature Ser.). 407p. 1993. reprint ed. lib. bdg. 99.00 (*0-7812-6590-8*) Rprt Serv.
Sentimental Novel in America, 1789-1860. Herbert R. Brown. LC 75-107685. (Essay Index Reprint Ser.). 1977. reprint ed. 24.95 (*0-8369-1490-2*) Ayer.
Sentimental Songs: La Poesia Cursi. Felipe Alfau. Tr. & Intro. by Ilan Stavans. LC 91-33545. 96p. 1992. 15.95 (*0-916583-98-8*); pap. 9.95 (*0-916583-99-6*) Dalkey Arch.
***Sentimental Talk & An Unlikely Meeting.** Daniel Castelain. Tr. by Patrick Bowles from FRE. LC 79-131217. 128p. 1971. 4.95 (*0-87376-014-X*) Red Dust.
Sentimental Tommy. J. M. Barrie. 21.95 (*0-8488-0192-X*) Amereon Ltd.
Sentimental Tommy. James M. Barrie. (BCL1-PR English Literature Ser.). 503p. 1992. reprint ed. lib. bdg. 99.00 (*0-7812-7430-3*) Rprt Serv.
Sentimental Tommy see Works of J. M. Barrie. Peter Pan Edition
Sentimental Twain: Samuel Clemens in the Maze of Moral Philosophy. Gregg Camfield. LC 94-5007. (New Cultural Studies). 296p. (C). 1994. text ed. 36.50 (*0-8122-3285-2*) U of Pa Pr.
Sentimental Venture. E. I. Edwards. LC 76-21423. (Illus.). 71p. 1976. 10.00 (*0-914224-06-9*) Tales Mojave Rd.
Sentimental 20's. Warner Brothers Staff. 1996. pap. text ed. 16.95 (*1-57623-284-0*, MF9575) Warner Brothers.
Sentimental 30's. Warner Brothers Staff. 1996. pap. text ed. 16.95 (*1-57623-286-7*, MF9576) Warner Brothers.
Sentimental 40's. Warner Brothers Staff. 1996. pap. text ed. 16.95 (*1-57623-287-5*, MF9577) Warner Brothers.
Sentiments & Activities: Essays in Social Science. George C. Homans. 342p. (Orig.). 1988. pap. 24.95 (*0-88738-725-X*) Transaction Pubs.
Sentiments & Acts. Irwin Deutscher et al. LC 92-27887. (Communication & Social Order Ser.). 280p. 1993. pap. text ed. 23.95 (*0-202-30445-0*); lib. bdg. 44.95 (*0-202-30444-2*) Aldine de Gruyter.
Sentiments & D-Votions. Elsie M. Jackson. (Orig.). 1995. pap. write for info. (*1-57553-071-6*) Watermrk Pr.
Sentiments et Coutumes. Andre Maurois. pap. 17.50 (*0-685-36959-5*) Fr & Eur.
Sentiments Fabriques en Laboratoire. 2nd ed. Florentin Smarandache. Ed. by Xiquan Publishing House Staff. Tr. by Traian Nica from RUM. 120p. (FRE.). (C). 1993. reprint ed. pap. 8.99 (*1-879585-11-1*) Erhus Univ Pr.
Sentiments of Love. Intervisual Books Staff. (Illus.). 16p. 1995. 4.95 (*0-8362-0052-7*) Andrews & McMeel.
***Sentiments of the Heart: A Collection of Poems about the Experiences of Love.** Christopher Taylor. (Illus.). 100p. (Orig.). 1997. pap. 10.00 (*0-614-30280-3*, CT002) Costa Pubng.
Sentinel. Emerson Daggett. 12p. (Orig.). 1981. pap. 2.00 (*0-932942-01-6*) Pacific NW Labor.
Sentinel. Ed. by Kathleen L. Mendel. LC 90-70012. (Illus.). 146p. (Orig.). 1990. pap. 12.95 (*0-9624384-4-8*) Telstar FL.
***Sentinel: A "Nameless Detective" Mystery.** Bill Pronzini. LC 96-29613. 1996. lib. bdg. 23.95 (*1-57490-074-9*, Beeler LP Bks) T T Beeler.
Sentinel: And Other Poems. Robert Hunter. LC 93-12968. 128p. (Orig.). 1993. pap. 12.00 (*0-14-058698-9*, Penguin Bks) Viking Penguin.
***Sentinel: Central Africa.** 1996. 425.00 (*0-7106-1407-1*) Janes Info Group.
***Sentinel: Central America & the Caribbean.** (Illus.). 1996. 425.00 (*0-7106-1467-5*) Janes Info Group.
***Sentinel: Central Europe & the Baltic.** (Illus.). 1996. 425.00 (*0-7106-1249-4*) Janes Info Group.
***Sentinel: China & North-East Asia.** (Illus.). 1996. 425.00 (*0-7106-1328-8*) Janes Info Group.
***Sentinel: Commonwealth of Independent States.** 3rd ed. (Illus.). 1996. 425.00 (*0-7106-1461-6*) Janes Info Group.
***Sentinel: Eastern Mediterranean.** (Illus.). 1996. 425.00 (*0-7106-1248-6*) Janes Info Group.
***Sentinel: Gulf States - Economic Assessment.** (Illus.). 1996. 425.00 (*0-7106-1391-1*) Janes Info Group.
***Sentinel: Gulf States - Security Assessment.** 3rd ed. (Illus.). 1996. 425.00 (*0-7106-1323-7*) Janes Info Group.
***Sentinel: North Africa.** 2nd ed. (Illus.). 1995. 425.00 (*0-7106-1324-5*) Janes Info Group.
***Sentinel: South America.** (Illus.). 1995. 425.00 (*0-7106-1222-2*) Janes Info Group.
***Sentinel: South Asia & Indian Ocean.** (Illus.). 1996. 425.00 (*0-7106-1406-3*) Janes Info Group.
***Sentinel: South China Sea - Economic Assessment.** (Illus.). 1996. 425.00 (*0-7106-1408-X*) Janes Info Group.
***Sentinel: South China Sea - Security Assessment.** 3rd ed. (Illus.). 1996. 425.00 (*0-7106-1464-0*) Janes Info Group.
Sentinel: Southern Africa. 2nd ed. (Illus.). 200p. 1996. 425.00 (*0-7106-1466-7*) Janes Info Group.
***Sentinel: The Balkans.** 3rd ed. 1996. 425.00 (*0-7106-1462-4*) Janes Info Group.
Sentinel at Ellwood: The Barnsdall-Rio Grande Gasoline Station. Gary B. Coombs & Phyllis J. Olsen. (Illus.). 24p. 1985. pap. 2.50 (*0-911773-06-1*) Inst Am Res.
Sentinel For Health: A History of the Centers for Disease Ccontrol. Elizabeth W. Etheridge. LC 90-24679. (Illus.). 384p. 1991. 50.00 (*0-520-07107-7*) U CA Pr.
Sentinel HIV Seroprevalence Surveys. (Illus.). 103p. (Orig.). (C). 1995. pap. text ed. 25.00 (*0-7881-1914-1*) DIANE Pub.
***Sentinel II.** Sydney J. Mead. (Sentinelkodansha Ser.). (Illus.). 116p. (JPN.). 1987. per. 49.50 (*4-06-202322-9*) Oblagon.
***Sentinel Method & Its Application To Environmental Pollution Problems.** Jean P. Kernevez. LC 96-3457. (Mathematical Modelling Ser.). 204p. 1996. 69.95 (*0-8493-9630-1*) CRC Pr.
Sentinel of the East. Durlab Singh. LC 74-7099. (Studies in Asiatic Literature: No. 57). 1974. lib. bdg. 47.95 (*0-8383-1975-0*) M S G Haskell Hse.
Sentinel of the Southern Plains: Fort Richardson & the Northwest Texas Frontier, 1866-1878. Allen L. Hamilton. LC 87-17379. (Chisholm Trail Ser.: No. 5). (Illus.). 272p. (Orig.). 1988. pap. 14.95 (*0-87565-073-2*) Tex Christian.
***Sentinel under Siege: The Triumphs & Troubles of America's Free Press.** Stanley E. Flink Stanley. LC 97-20628. 1997. text ed. 25.00 (*0-8133-3344-X*) Westview.
***Sentinels.** Mayfair Games Staff. Date not set. 25.00 (*0-923763-79-1*) Mayfair Games.
Sentinels. Kevin Siembieda. Ed. by Alex Marciniszyn. (Robotech II Role-Playing Game Ser.). (Illus.). 160p. (Orig.). (YA). (gr. 8 up). 1987. pap. 15.95 (*0-916211-33-9*, 557) Palladium Bks.
Sentinels: A Nameless Detective Novel. Bill Pronzini. 288p. 1996. 20.00 (*0-7867-0311-3*) Carroll & Graf.
Sentinels, No. 4: World Killers. Jack McKinney. 224p. 1988. mass mkt. 5.99 (*0-345-35304-8*, Del Rey) Ballantine.
Sentinels, No. 5: Rubicon. Jack Mckinney. 224p. 1988. mass mkt. 5.99 (*0-345-35305-6*, Del Rey) Ballantine.
***Sentinels of Dawn.** Eric Mackenzie-Lamb. Date not set. write for info. (*0-688-05023-9*) Morrow.
Sentinels of Empire: The United States & Latin American Militarism. Jan K. Black. LC 85-21850. (Contributions in Political Science Ser.: No. 144). 249p. 1986. text ed. 55.00 (*0-313-25155-X*, BKS/, Greenwood Pr) Greenwood.
Sentinels of Love: Rural Churches of California. Jeanne Mord & Bette R. Millis. LC 89-38422. (Illus.). 224p. (Orig.). 1990. pap. 9.95 (*0-931832-39-X*) Fithian Pr.
Sentinels of Order: A Study of Social Control & the Minneapolis Settlement House Movement, 1915-1950. Howard J. Karger. LC 87-2208. 202p. (C). 1987. lib. bdg. 43.00 (*0-8191-6275-2*) U Pr of Amer.
Sentinels of Solitude: West Coast Lighthouses. rev. ed. Jim Gibbs. (Illus.). 88p. (Orig.). 1989. reprint ed. pap. 14.95 (*0-945092-06-7*) EZ Nature.
Sentinels of the Shore: Guide to Lighthouses & Lightships of New Jersey. Bill Gately. 1997. pap. write for info. (*0-945582-37-4*) Down the Shore Pub.
Sentinels on Stone: The Petroglyphs of Los Alamos. Illus. & Text by Dorothy Hoard. LC 95-49097. 75p. 1995. 14.95 (*0-941232-16-6*) Los Alamos Hist Soc.
Sentinels 3-in-1: The Devil's Hand; Dark Powers; Death Dance. Jack McKinney. 1995. mass mkt. 5.99 (*0-345-38901-8*) Ballantine.
Sentries. Ed McBain. 304p. 1988. pap. 3.50 (*0-380-70489-7*) Avon.
Sentries. Ed McBain. 304p. 1995. pap. 5.99 (*0-446-60145-4*) Warner Bks.
Sentries. Gary Paulsen. LC 85-26978. 160p. (YA). (gr. 7 up). 1986. lib. bdg. 17.00 (*0-02-770100-X*, Bradbury S&S) S&S Childrens.
Sentries. Gary Paulsen. (J). 1995. 3.95 (*0-689-80411-3*) S&S Childrens.
Sentries. Gary Paulsen. (J). (gr. 5-9). reprint ed. pap. 3.95 (*0-317-62279-X*, Puffin) Puffin Bks.

Sentry Towers. Maria L. Spaziani. Ed. & Tr. by Laura Stortoni from ITA. 102p. (Orig.). 1996. pap. 13.00 (*0-9641003-1-2*) Hesperia Pr.
This is the first English translation in the U.S. of a complete poetry book by Maria Luisa Spaziani, Italy's foremost living poet & candidate for the Nobel Prize for poetry. This dual language (Italian-English) volume features a cover by Lawrence Ferlinghetti & an introduction by Professor Natalia Costa-Zalessow. Spaziani's rich & sensuous poetry is a celebration of desire & memory, spoken with a powerful woman's voice within the symbolist & hermetic tradition. This book represents the poet's summation of her most moving life experiences (such as her relationship with Nobel Prize winning poet Montale), & is brilliantly & faithfully translated by Italian-born poet Laura Stortoni. The editor-translator has provided extensive biographical & bibliographical data, & Spaziani wrote the endnotes & a special message for the American reader. This bilingual book is suitable for poetry lovers & students of Italian, & is ideal for libraries. Can be ordered directly from Hesperia Press, P.O. Box 9246, Berkeley, CA 94709. Phone: (510) 644-8259, FAX: (510) 644-2109, or through Small Press Distribution, 1814 San Pablo Avenue, Berkeley, CA 94702. ***Publisher Provided Annotation.***

Senya. Senya Darklight. Ed. by Marty Campbell. LC 88-92537. (Illus.). 200p. 1989. pap. 9.00 (*0-929749-00-6*) Mar Crafs.
***SenZar.** Todd King. Ed. by Joseph Giacone, Jr. & Johnny Bruner. (Illus.). 256p. (Orig.). 1996. pap. 24.00 (*0-9656145-9-X*) Nova Eth Pub.
Seoul. J. Kim et al. LC 97-11185. 256p. 1993. text ed. 65.00 (*0-471-94936-1*) Wiley.
Seoul. Joochul Kim. (World Cities Ser.). 256p. 1994. text ed. 49.95 (*0-470-22006-6*) Halsted Pr.
Seoul. 2nd ed. Robert Storey. (Illus.). 288p. 1996. pap. 11.95 (*0-86442-385-3*) Lonely Planet.
Seoul: A Pictorial Guidebook. enl. ed. Suzanne C. Han. 86p. 1986. pap. 14.95 (*0-930878-52-3*) Hollym Intl.
Seoul Food Guide. Betsy O'Brien. 1994. 22.95 (*1-56591-039-7*) Hollym Intl.
Seoul Food Guide: A Selection of Restaurants. Betsy O'Brien. (Illus.). 280p. 1995. pap. 14.95 (*1-56591-040-0*, Pub. by Hollym Bks SK) Weatherhill.
Seoul Sketches: A Visual Sketch of the Yi Dynasty. Charlotte Rountree. (Illus.). 84p. 1985. 22.50 (*0-930878-43-4*) Hollym Intl.
Seoul Stirring: 5 Korean Directors. Tony Rayns. 1996. pap. text ed. 9.95 (*0-905263-79-0*, Pub. by British Film Inst UK) Ind U Pr.
SEP & SARSEP Answer Book. annuals Gary S. Lesser. 472p. 1995. 126.00 incl. disk (*1-56706-176-1*) Panel Pubs.
***SEP & SARSEP Answer Book.** 2nd ed. Lesser. 1996. 79.00 (*1-56706-359-4*) Aspen Pub.
Sepa Como Alimentarse. Linda Clark. Orig. Title: Know Your Nutrition. (Orig.). (SPA.). 1980. pap. 5.95 (*0-87983-174-X*) Keats.
Sepa Todo Sobre Addicciones. Editorial America, S. A. Staff. Ed. by Maria E. Del Real. (Illus.). 360p. (Orig.). (SPA.). 1990. pap. write for info. (*0-944499-90-2*) Editorial Amer.
Separability & Aggregation: The Collected Works of W. M. Gorman, Vol. 1. W. M. Gorman. Ed. by C. Blackorby & A. Shorrocks. (Illus.). 504p. 1996. 98.00 (*0-19-828521-3*) OUP.
Separable Algebroids. Barry Mitchell. LC 85-15092. (Memoirs of the American Mathematical Society Ser.: No. 333). 96p. 1985. pap. 18.00 (*0-8218-2334-5*, MEMO/57/333) Am Math.
Separable Galois Theory of Commutative Rings. Andy R. Magid. LC 74-80286. (Pure & Applied Mathematics Ser.: No. 27). 156p. reprint ed. pap. 44.50 (*0-7837-0872-6*, 2041180) Bks Demand.
Separable User Interface. Ed. by Ernest Edmonds. (Computers & People Ser.). (Illus.). 371p. 1992. text ed. 78.00 (*0-12-232150-2*) Acad Pr.
Separados por la Espuma. Lillian Bertot. LC 80-65223. (Coleccion Espejo de Paciencia). 46p. 1980. pap. 5.95 (*0-89729-250-2*) Ediciones.
Separate Actions (Playscript) rev. ed. Mary Steelsmith. LC 88-92712. 36p. 1989. pap. 6.00 (*0-88734-801-7*) Players Pr.
Separate & Equal Station: Hegel, America & the Nation-State System. Henry Paolucci. 1978. pap. 3.00 (*0-918680-05-0*) Bagehot Council.
Separate & Unequal: Black Americans & the U. S. Federal Government. Desmond King. (Illus.). 380p. 1995. 39.95 (*0-19-828016-5*) OUP.
***Separate & Unequal: Black Americans & the U. S. Federal Government.** Desmond King. (Illus.). 368p. 1997. reprint ed. pap. text ed. 19.95 (*0-19-829249-X*) OUP.
Separate Battle: Women & the Civil War. Ina Chang. (Young Readers' History of the Civil War Ser.). (Illus.). 112p. (J). (gr. 5-9). 1991. pap. 16.99 (*0-525-67365-2*, Lodestar Bks) Dutton Child Bks.
Separate Battle: Women & the Civil War. Ina Chang. 112p. (J). (gr. 5-12). 1996. pap. 6.99 (*0-14-038106-6*, Puffin) Puffin Bks.
Separate Beds. LaVyrle Spencer. 400p. (Orig.). 1986. mass mkt. 6.99 (*0-515-09037-9*) Jove Pubns.
Separate Beds. large type ed. LaVyrle Spencer. LC 93-31181. (Orig.). 1993. lib. bdg. 23.95 (*0-8161-5326-4*, GK Hall) Thorndike Pr.
Separate Beds. large type ed. LaVyrle Spencer. LC 93-31181. (Orig.). 1994. pap. 18.95 (*0-8161-5327-2*, GK Hall) Thorndike Pr.
***Separate but Equal? A-Levels & GNVQS.** A. D. Edwards. LC 97-12119. (Further Education Ser.). 1997. write for info. (*0-415-15297-6*); pap. write for info. (*0-415-15298-4*) Routledge.
Separate but Equal Branches: Congress & the Presidency. Charles O. Jones. LC 94-36362. (Illus.). 272p. (Orig.). (C). 1995. pap. text ed. 19.95 (*1-56643-015-1*) Chatham Hse Pubs.
***Separate, but Not Equal: The Dream & the Struggle.** James Haskins. LC 96-51507. (J). 1997. write for info. (*0-590-45910-4*) Scholastic Inc.
Separate Cabins. Janet Dailey. 1994. mass mkt. 4.99 (*0-671-87514-0*) PB.
***Separate Canaan: The Making of an Afro-Moravian World in North Carolina, 1763-1840.** Jon F. Sensbach. LC 97-17726. 1998. write for info. (*0-8078-2394-5*); pap. write for info. (*0-8078-4698-8*) U of NC Pr.
Separate Cases. Robert J. Randisi. 192p. 1990. 18.95 (*0-8027-5723-5*) Walker & Co.
Separate Cinema: Fifty Years of Black-Cast Posters. John Kisch & Edward Mapp. LC 92-15037. 1992. pap. 20.00 (*0-374-52360-6*) FS&G.
Separate City: Black Communities in the Urban South, 1940-1968. Christopher Silver & John V. Moeser. 232p. 1995. text ed. 29.95 (*0-8131-1911-1*) U Pr of Ky.
Separate Creation: The Search for the Biological Origins of Sexual Orientation. Chandler Burr. 288p. 1996. 24.95 (*0-7868-6081-2*) Hyperion.
***Separate Creation: The Search for the Biological Origins of Sexual Orientation.** Chandler Burr. 288p. 1997. pap. 12.95 (*0-7868-8240-9*) Hyperion.
Separate Flights. Andre Dubus. LC 74-25955. 206p. 1977. reprint ed. pap. 10.95 (*0-87923-123-8*) Godine.
Separate Hours. Jonathan Baumbach. Ed. by Curtis White. 204p. 1990. text ed. 18.95 (*0-932511-27-9*); pap. text ed. 8.95 (*0-932511-28-7*) Fiction Coll.
Separate Life. S. A. Padmanab. 9.00 (*0-89253-712-4*); text ed. 4.80 (*0-89253-713-2*) Ind-US Inc.
Separate Lifetimes. Irving Townsend. (Illus.). 176p. (Orig.). 1986. pap. 15.00 (*0-9617426-0-7*) J N Townsend.
Separate Notebooks. Czeslaw Milosz. Tr. by Robert Hass et al. 250p. 1986. 12.50 (*0-88001-116-5*) Ecco Pr.
Separate Pasts: Growing up White in the Segregated South. Melton A. McLaurin. LC 86-27283. (Brown Thrasher Bks.). 164p. 1987. 19.95 (*0-8203-0943-5*); pap. 9.95 (*0-8203-1044-1*) U of Ga Pr.
Separate Peace. Created by Harcourt Brace Staff. 1990. student ed., pap. 10.00 (*0-15-348524-8*) HR&W Schl Div.
Separate Peace. Created by Harcourt Brace Staff. 1990. student ed., teacher ed., pap. 22.75 (*0-15-348530-2*) HR&W Schl Div.
Separate Peace. Holt. 1989. student ed., pap. 10.00 (*0-03-023444-1*) HR&W Schl Div.
Separate Peace. John Knowles. 208p. (J). (gr. 7 up). 1985. mass mkt. 5.50 (*0-553-28041-4*) Bantam.
Separate Peace. John Knowles. LC 60-5312. (Hudson River Editions Ver.). 186p. (Orig.). 1987. 40.00 (*0-02-564850-0*) S&S Trade.
Separate Peace. John Knowles. 1997. 22.00 (*0-684-83366-2*) S&S Trade.
Separate Peace: A Novel. large type ed. John Knowles. LC 93-33483. 1994. lib. bdg. 21.95 (*0-8161-5895-9*, GK Hall) Thorndike Pr.
Separate Peace - Study Guide. Joyce Friedland & Rikki Kessler. (Novel-Ties Ser.). (YA). (gr. 7-10). 1993. pap. text ed. 15.95 (*0-88122-022-1*) Lrn Links.
Separate Peace (Knowles) Baldwin. (Book Notes Ser.). (C). 1984. pap. 3.95 (*0-8120-3441-4*) Barron.
Separate Peace Notes. Cary M. Roberts. 1965. pap. 3.75 (*0-8220-1183-2*) Cliffs.
Separate Plates of William Blake: A Catalogue. Robert N. Essick. LC 82-7588. (Illus.). 344p. 1983. text ed. 125.00 (*0-691-04011-7*) Princeton U Pr.
Separate Problem: Case Studies of Black Education in the North, 1900-1930. Judy J. Mohraz. LC 78-4026. (Contributions in Afro-American & African Studies: No. 42). xvi, 165p. 1979. text ed. 49.95 (*0-313-20411-X*, MSP/, Greenwood Pr) Greenwood.
Separate Reality. Carlos Castaneda. Ed. by Jane Rosenman. 272p. 1991. pap. 12.00 (*0-671-73249-8*, WSP) PB.
Separate Reality: Florida Eccentrics. Arthur F. Jones. Ed. by Ruth A. Matinko-Wald. 32p. (Orig.). 1987. pap. write for info. (*0-942461-00-2*) Mus Art Fl.
Separate Rooms. Pier V. Tondelli. (Masks Ser.). 1993. pap. 13.99 (*1-85242-223-8*) Serpents Tail.
Separate Rooms. large type ed. Diana Hamilton. (Harlequin Romance Ser.). 1994. lib. bdg. 19.95 (*0-263-13873-9*) Thorndike Pr.
Separate Rooms: (Secrets...) Diana Hamilton & Lee Wilkinson. (Presents Ser.). 1995. mass mkt. 3.25 (*0-373-11732-9*, 1-11732-4) Harlequin Bks.
Separate Rose. Pablo Neruda. Tr. by William O'Daly from SPA. LC 84-73338. 80p. (Orig.). 1985. pap. 9.00 (*0-914742-88-4*) Copper Canyon.
Separate Social Worlds of Siblings: The Impact of Nonshared Environment on Development. Ed. by E. Mavis Hetherington et al. (Advances in Family Research Ser.). 232p. 1993. text ed. 49.95 (*0-8058-1311-X*) L Erlbaum Assocs.

S

An Asterisk (*) at the beginning of an entry indicates that the title is appearing in BIP for the first time.

Separate Societies: Poverty & Inequality in U. S. Cities. William W. Goldsmith & Edward J. Blakely. (Conflicts in Urban & Regional Development Ser.). 280p. (C). 1992. pap. 19.95 (*0-87722-933-3*) Temple U Pr.

Separate Star. deluxe limited ed. Frank K. Freas. (Illus.). 128p. (Orig.). 1984. boxed 75.00 (*0-917431-00-6*) K Freas Studios.

Separate Trains. Elaine Erickson. 64p. 1989. pap. 5.95 (*0-932616-25-9*) Brick Hse Bks.

Separate, Unequal & Inequate: Educational Opportunities & Outcomes in New York City Public Schools. CSS's Dept. of Public Policy Unit Staff. 30p. 1995. 5.00 (*0-88156-167-3*) Comm Serv Soc NY.

Separate, Unequal, but More Autonomous. Ward Morehouse. 50p. 1981. pap. text ed. 14.95 (*0-685-54936-4*) Transaction Pubs.

Separate Vision: Case Studies of Four Contemporary Indian Artists. Linda B. Eaton. (Bulletin Ser.). 90p. 1990. pap. 14.95 (*0-89734-100-7*, BS-58) Mus Northern Ariz.

Separate Vision: Isolation in Contemporary Women's Poetry. Deborah Pope. LC 84-5735. 174p. 1984. text ed. 27.50 (*0-8071-1159-7*) La State U Pr.

S

***Separate Yet Sisters.** Susan Harkna. LC 97-90283. 1997. 12.95 (*0-533-12358-5*) Vantage.

Separated & Complex Flows - 1995. Ed. by M. V. Otugen et al. (1995 ASME/JSME Fluids Engineering Conference Ser.: FED-Vol. 217). 288p. 1995. 130.00 (*0-7918-1472-6*, G00967) ASME.

Separated & Divorced Women. Lynne C. Halem. LC 81-13178. (Contributions in Women's Studies: No. 32). xiv, 335p. 1982. text ed. 69.50 (*0-313-23160-5*, HDW/, Greenwood Pr) Greenwood.

Separated & Waiting. Jan Northington. LC 93-50869. 1994. pap. 9.99 (*0-8407-9193-3*) Nelson.

Separated Angels. Larry A. Fanning. Ed. by Leanne Pankoch. (Illus.). 210p. (Orig.). 1995. pap. 11.95 (*0-9646812-0-X*) Storybk Pr.

Separated at Death. Leo Axler. 272p. 1996. pap. text ed. 5.99 (*0-425-15257-X*) Berkley Pub.

Separated Brethren. rev. ed. William J. Whalen. LC 79-83874. 1979. pap. 7.95 (*0-87973-829-4*) Our Sunday Visitor.

Separated by War: An Oral History by Desert Storm Fighters & Their Families. Edward C. Herlik. LC 93-14695. 1993. write for info. (*0-8306-4481-4*, TAB-Aero) TAB Bks.

Separated by War: An Oral History by Desert Storm Fliers & Their Families. Edward C. Herlik. 1993. text ed. 24.95 (*0-07-028362-1*) McGraw.

Separated Flows & Jets: IUTAM - Symposium, Novosibirsk, U. S. S. R., July 9-13, 1990. Valery V. Kozlov. (Illus.). 912p. 1992. 287.95 (*0-387-53762-7*) Spr-Verlag.

Separated Flows 1993. Ed. by J. C. Dutton & L. P. Purtell. LC 93-71636. (FED Ser.: Vol. 149). 217p. 1993. pap. 45.00 (*0-7918-0957-9*, H00789) ASME.

Separated Ones: Jesus, the Pharisees, & Islam. Ruqaiyyah W. Maqsood. 192p. 1992. pap. 17.50 (*0-334-02498-6*, SCM Pr) TPI PA.

Separated People: A Look at Contemporary South Africa. Ely J. Kahn, Jr. 1968. 6.95 (*0-393-05351-2*) Norton.

***Separated Sisters.** Kaitlyn Gorton. (Special Edition Ser.). 1997. mass mkt. 3.99 (*0-373-24092-9*, 1-24092-8) Silhouette.

Separates General Chemistry in the Lab. 3rd ed. Roberts. (C). 1995. 2.95 (*0-7167-2259-3*) W H Freeman.

***Separating a Mixture of Biphenyl, Benzhydrol, & Benzophenone by Thin-Layer Chromatography.** Ronald J. Wikholm. Ed. by J. Jeffers. (Modular Laboratory Program in Chemistry Ser.). 12p. (C). 1997. pap. text ed. 1.75 (*0-87540-707-2*) Chem Educ Res.

***Separating Acids & Neutral Compounds by Solvent Extraction.** Jerry Manion. Ed. by J. Jeffers. (Modular Laboratory Program in Chemistry Ser.). 16p. (C). 1997. pap. text ed. 1.75 (*0-87540-705-6*) Chem Educ Res.

Separating & Determining the Mass of Calcium Ion in a Calcium-Enriched Tablet. H. Anthony Neidig & M. L. Gillette. (Modular Laboratory Program in Chemistry Ser.). 12p. (C). 1995. pap. text ed. 1.35 (*0-87540-455-3*, ANAL 455-3) Chem Educ Res.

***Separating & Identifying Food Dyes by Paper Chromatography.** Peter G. Markow. Ed. by C. L. Stanitski. (Modular Laboratory Program in Chemistry Ser.). 16p. (C). 1997. pap. text ed. 1.35 (*0-87540-492-8*) Chem Educ Res.

***Separating & Identifying Mixtures by Gas Chromatography.** L. G. Wade, Jr. Ed. by Joe Jeffers. (Modular Laboratory Program in Chemistry Ser.). 12p. (C). 1997. pap. text ed. 1.75 (*0-87540-709-9*) Chem Educ Res.

Separating & Identifying Some Food & Drug Dyes by Thin-Layer Chromatography. Harold T. McKone. Ed. by H. Anthony Neidig. (Modular Laboratory Program in Chemistry Ser.). 7p. (C). 1994. pap. text ed. 1.35 (*0-87540-445-6*, ANAL 445-6) Chem Educ Res.

Separating & Isolating the Components of a Binary System. Marcia L. Gillette & H. Anthony Neidig. (Modular Laboratory Program in Chemistry Ser.). 12p. (C). 1995. pap. text ed. 1.35 (*0-87540-460-X*, PROP 460-X) Chem Educ Res.

Separating & Isolating the Components of a Ternary System. Marcia L. Gillette & H. Anthony Neidig. (Modular Laboratory Program in Chemistry Ser.). 12p. (C). 1995. pap. text ed. 1.35 (*0-87540-461-8*, PROP 461-8) Chem Educ Res.

***Separating Camphor from Beta-Carotene by Sublimation.** Joseph W. LeFevre. Ed. by J. Jeffers. (Modular Laboratory Program in Chemistry Ser.). 12p. (C). 1997. pap. text ed. 1.75 (*0-87540-706-4*) Chem Educ Res.

***Separating Church & State: Roger Williams & Religious Liberty.** Timothy Hall. LC 97-4688. 1998. write for info. (*0-252-02360-9*); pap. write for info. (*0-252-06664-2*) U of Ill Pr.

***Separating Cyclohexane & Toluene by Distillation.** Jerry Manion. Ed. by J. Jeffers. (Modular Laboratory Program in Chemistry Ser.). 16p. (C). 1997. pap. text ed. 1.75 (*0-87540-704-8*) Chem Educ Res.

***Separating Ferrocene & Acetylferrocene by Adsorption Column Chromatography.** Joe Jeffers. (Modular Laboratory Program in Chemistry Ser.). 12p. (C). 1997. pap. text ed. 1.75 (*0-87540-708-0*) Chem Educ Res.

***Separating Powers: Essays on the Founding Period.** Gerhard Casper. LC 96-36353. 1996. write for info. (*0-674-80140-7*); pap. write for info. (*0-674-80141-5*) HUP.

Separating School & State: How to Liberate America's Families. Sheldon Richman. 150p. (Orig.). 1994. 22.95 (*0-9640447-1-4*); pap. 14.95 (*0-9640447-2-2*) Future of Freedom.

Separating the Components of a Binary Mixture. H. Anthony Neidig et al. (Modular Laboratory Program in Chemistry Ser.). 11p. (C). 1989. pap. text ed. 1.35 (*0-87540-374-3*, PROP 374-3) Chem Educ Res.

Separating the Components of a Ternary Mixture. H. Anthony Neidig et al. (Modular Laboratory Program in Chemistry Ser.). 12p. (C). 1989. pap. text ed. 1.35 (*0-87540-375-1*, PROP 375-1) Chem Educ Res.

Separation. Dan Franck. 1995. pap. 13.00 (*0-679-75444-X*, Vin) Random.

Separation. Multimedia Development Services Staff. (Plant Fundamentals Ser.: Vol. VII, Module II). (Illus.). 1995. teacher ed. 65.00 (*1-57431-062-3*); student ed. 30.00 (*1-57431-022-4*) Tech Trng Systs.

Separation: Anxiety & Anger. John Bowlby. LC 70-78464. (Attachment & Loss Ser.: Vol. 2). 476p. 1976. pap. text ed. 20.00 (*0-465-09716-2*) Basic.

Separation: Strategies for Helping Two to Four Year Olds. Ed. by Kathe Jervis. LC 89-62138. 52p. 1984. pap. 4.00 (*0-935989-29-3*, NAEYC #230) Natl Assn Child Ed.

Separation - Individuation: Theory & Application. 2nd ed. Joyce Edward et al. LC 92-31503. 385p. 1992. text ed. 47.95 (*0-87630-697-0*) Brunner-Mazel.

***Separation Agreement Kit for Ontario: Includes Do-It-Yourself Forms & Instruction Booklet.** Sandra Meyrick. (Ontario Legal Ser.). 20p. 1992. pap. 15.95 (*1-55180-077-2*) Self-Counsel Pr.

Separation Agreements & Ante-Nuptial Contracts, 3 vols. Alexancer Lindey. 1964. Updates. ring bd. write for info. (*0-8205-1360-1*) Bender.

Separation Agreements & Marital Contracts: With 1990 Cumulative Supplement, 2 vols., Set. Stephen W. Schlissel. 1986. 170.00 (*0-930273-18-4*) MICHIE.

Separation & Divorce in North Carolina: Answers to the Most Commonly Asked Questions about Your Legal Rights. Mary K. Nicholson. Ed. by Jerry Bledsoe. LC 92-72659. 68p. (Orig.). 1992. pap. 7.95 (*1-878086-16-2*) Down Home NC.

***Separation & Its Discontents: Toward an Evolutionary Theory of Anti-Semitism.** Kevin MacDonald. (Human Evolution, Behavior & Intelligence Ser.). 1998. text ed. write for info. (*0-275-94870-6*, Praeger Pubs) Greenwood.

***Separation & Purification by Crystallization, Vol. 667.** G. D. Botsaris & Ken Toyokura. LC 97-11250. (ACS Symposium Ser.). 1997. write for info. (*0-8412-3513-9*) Am Chemical.

Separation & Purification Methods, Vol. 3. Ed. by Edmond S. Perry et al. LC 73-77000. (Illus.). 479p. reprint ed. pap. 136.60 (*0-685-23648-X*, 2029008) Bks Demand.

Separation & Purification Techniques in Biotechnology. Frederick J. Dechow. LC 88-34502. (Illus.). 490p. 1989. 72.00 (*0-8155-1197-3*) Noyes.

Separation & Purification Technology. Ed. by Norman N. Li & Joseph M. Calo. LC 92-19323. 320p. 1992. 145.00 (*0-8247-8721-8*) Dekker.

Separation Anxiety & the Dread of Abandonment in Adult Males. Gwendolyn Stevens & Sheldon Gardner. LC 93-37884. 208p. 1994. text ed. 59.95 (*0-275-94609-6*, Praeger Pubs) Greenwood.

Separation Anxiety Disorder: Psychodynamics & Psychotherapy. Richard A. Gardner. LC 84-26348. ix, 180p. 1985. 22.50 (*0-933812-10-8*) Creative Therapeutics.

Separation in My Family: A Child's Workbook about Parental Separation & Divorce. Wendy Deaton. 32p. (J). 1994. 17.95 (*0-89793-154-8*); pap. 8.95 (*0-89793-151-3*) Hunter Hse.

Separation-Individuation: Essays in Honor of Margaret S. Mahler. Ed. by John B. McDevitt & Calvin F. Settlage. LC 78-143378. 520p. 1971. 75.00 (*0-8236-6065-6*) Intl Univs Pr.

Separation-Individuation Vol. 2: The Selected Papers of Margaret S. Mahler, Vol. 2. Margaret S. Mahler. LC 94-70014. 272p. 1995. reprint ed. pap. 35.00 (*1-56821-224-0*) Aronson.

Separation Methods for Nucleic Acids & Oligonucleotides. H. Could & H. R. Matthews. (Laboratory Techniques in Biochemistry & Molecular Biology Ser.: Vol. 4, Pt. 2). 1976. pap. 28.50 (*0-7204-4213-3*, North Holland) Elsevier.

Separation Methods in Chemical Analysis. James M. Miller. LC 74-13781. (Illus.). 319p. reprint ed. pap. 91.00 (*0-685-20442-1*, 2056454) Bks Demand.

Separation of Church & Child: The Constitution & Federal Aid to Religious Schools. Thomas Vitullo-Martin & Bruce Cooper. 126p. (Orig.). 1987. pap. 12.50 (*0-318-32469-5*) Hudson Instit IN.

Separation of Church & Freedom: A War Manual for Christian Soldiers. Kent Kelly et al. LC 80-80341. (Illus.). 308p. 1980. 7.95 (*0-9604138-0-4*) Calvary Pr.

Separation of Church & State. Darien A. McWhirter. LC 93-40703. (Exploring the Constitution Ser.). 208p. 1994. 29.95 (*0-89774-852-2*) Oryx Pr.

Separation of Church & State: Dina de-Malkhuta Dina in Jewish Law, 1750-1848. Gil Graff. LC 84-24061. (Judaic Studies Ser.). 236p. 1985. reprint ed. pap. 67.30 (*0-608-01668-3*, 2062324) Bks Demand.

Separation of Church & State: Historical Fact & Current Fiction. Robert L. Cord. LC 94-20242. 307p. 1995. 19.95 (*0-931186-03-X*) Lambeth Pr.

Separation of Church & State Defended: Selected Writings of James E. Wood, Jr. Ed. by Derek H. Davis. LC 95-75329. 375p. 1995. 24.95 (*0-929182-23-5*) Baylor U J M Dawson.

Separation of Church & State Defended: Selected Writings of James E. Wood, Jr. Ed. by Derek H. Davis. LC 95-75329. 375p. 1995. pap. 10.95 (*0-929182-24-3*) Baylor U J M Dawson.

Separation of Church & State in the United States. Alvin W. Johnson & Frank H. Yost. LC 79-92302. 279p. 1970. reprint ed. text ed. 59.75 (*0-8371-2436-0*, JOCS, Greenwood Pr) Greenwood.

Separation of Church & State in Virginia. Hamilton J. Eckenrode. LC 75-122164. (Civil Liberties in American History Ser.). 1971. reprint ed. lib. bdg. 22.50 (*0-306-71969-X*) Da Capo.

Separation of College & State: Columbia, Dartmouth, Harvard, & Yale, 1776-1876. John S. Whitehead. LC 73-77170. (Yale Publications in History: Miscellany: No. 97). 272p. 1973. pap. 77.60 (*0-7837-2993-6*, 2043190) Bks Demand.

Separation of Commercial & Investment Banking: The Glass-Steagall Act Revisited & Reconsidered. George J. Benston. 276p. 1990. 45.00 (*0-19-520830-7*) OUP.

Separation of Gases. W. H. Isalski. (Monographs on Cryogenics). (Illus.). 324p. 1989. 75.00 (*0-19-854811-7*) OUP.

Separation of Gases: BOC Priestley Conference, 5th, No. 80. Royal Society of Chemistry Staff. 1990. 131.00 (*0-85186-637-9*) CRC Pr.

Separation of Governmental Powers in History, in Theory, & in the Constitutions. William Bondy. LC 04-1845. (Columbia University. Studies in the Social Sciences: No. 14). reprint ed. 34.50 (*0-404-51014-0*) AMS Pr.

***Separation of Lubrication & Cooling in Oil-Jet Lubricated Gears.** J. Greiner & K. Langenbeck. (1991 Fall Technical Meeting Ser.: Vol. 13). 1991. pap. text ed. 30.00 (*1-55589-610-3*) AGMA.

Separation of Particles from Air & Gases, Vol. I. Akira Ogawa. 168p. 1984. 97.00 (*0-8493-5787-X*, TH7692, CRC Reprint) Franklin.

Separation of Particles from Air & Gases, Vol. II. Akira Ogawa. 200p. 1984. 111.00 (*0-8493-5788-8*, CRC Reprint) Franklin.

***Separation of Particles from Water.** J. Gregory. (Water Science & Technology Ser.: Vol. 27). 234p. 1993. 114.25 (*0-08-042338-8*, Pergamon Pr) Elsevier.

Separation of Powers: Does It Still Work? Ed. by Robert A. Goldwin & Art Kaufman. 193p. 1986. 26.75 (*0-8447-3606-6*); pap. 9.95 (*0-8447-3607-4*) Am Enterprise.

Separation of Powers & Good Government. Ed. by Bradford P. Wilson & Peter W. Schramm. LC 94-7185. (Ashbrook Series on Constitutional Politics). 300p. (C). 1994. pap. text ed. 23.95 (*0-8476-7900-4*); lib. bdg. 58.50 (*0-8476-7899-7*) Rowman.

Separation of Powers Law: Cases & Materials. Peter M. Shane & Harold H. Bruff. LC 95-83227. 1060p. 1996. boxed 85.00 (*0-89089-927-4*) Carolina Acad Pr.

***Separation of Runout from Elemental Inspection Data.** Irving Laskin & Ed Lawson. (1995 Fall Technical Meeting). 1995. pap. text ed. 30.00 (*1-55589-650-2*) AGMA.

Separation of Singapore from Malaysia. Nancy M. Fletcher. LC 76-7456. (Cornell University, Southeast Asia Program, Data Paper Ser.: No. 73). 122p. reprint ed. pap. 34.80 (*0-8357-3673-3*, 2036398) Bks Demand.

Separation of State & Local Revenues in the United States. Mabel Newcomer. LC 68-56675. (Columbia University. Studies in the Social Sciences: No. 180). reprint ed. 27.50 (*0-404-51180-5*) AMS Pr.

Separation of the Boron Isotopes. AEC Technical Information Center Staff. Ed. by George M. Murphy. (National Nuclear Energy Ser.: Div. III, Vol. 5). 459p. 1952. pap. 52.00 (*0-87079-349-7*, TID-5227); fiche 9.00 (*0-87079-350-0*, TID-5227) DOE.

Separation of the Monophysites. William A. Wigram. LC 77-84708. reprint ed. 37.50 (*0-404-16115-4*) AMS Pr.

Separation Poems. Winslow Durgin. 4.00 (*0-318-11911-0*) Great Raven Pr.

***Separation Process Technology.** Jimmy L. Humphrey & George E. Keller, II. LC 97-12. (Illus.). 300p. 1997. text ed. 55.00 (*0-07-031173-0*) McGraw.

Separation Processes. Ed. by J. M. Calo & E. J Henley. LC 80-25577. (AIChEMI Modular Instruction Series B: Stagewise & Mass Transfer Operations: No. 6). 134p. 1986. text ed. 44.00 (*0-8169-0426-X*, J-32) Am Inst Chem Eng.

Separation Processes. 2nd ed. Intro. by C. Judson King. (Chemical Engineering Ser.). (Illus.). 1980. text ed. write for info. (*0-07-034612-7*) McGraw.

Separation Processes - Heavy Metals, Ions & Minerals: Proceedings of the Symposium on Separation Processes. TMS Annual Meeting (1995: Las Vegas, Nevada) Ed. by Manoranjan Misra. (Illus.). 290p. 1995. 94.00 (*0-87339-279-5*, 2795) Minerals Metals.

Separation Processes in Biotechnology. Asenjo. (Bioprocess Technology Ser.: Vol. 9). 840p. 1990. 210.00 (*0-8247-8270-4*) Dekker.

***Separation Processes in the Sugar Industry.** Ed. & Intro. by Margaret A. Clarke. (Illus.). 307p. (Orig.). 1996. pap. 100.00 (*1-883326-04-4*) Sugar Process Res.

Separation Processes in Waste Minimization. Robert B. Long. LC 95-2944. (Environmental Science & Pollution Control Ser.: Vol. 16). 480p. 1995. 175.00 (*0-8247-9634-9*) Dekker.

Separation, Recovery, & Purification in Biotechnology: Recent Advances & Mathematical Modeling. Ed. by Juan A. Asenjo & Juan Hong. LC 86-10833. (ACS Symposium Ser.: No. 314). (Illus.). 226p. 1986. 60.95 (*0-8412-0978-2*) Am Chemical.

***Separation, Recovery, & Purification in Biotechnology: Recent Advances & Mathematical Modeling.** Ed. by Juan A. Asenjo & Juan Hong. LC 86-10833. (ACS Symposium Ser.: Vol. 314). 240p. 1986. reprint ed. pap. 68.40 (*0-608-03519-X*, 2064238) Bks Demand.

Separation Revisited: Adolescents in Foster Family Care. Celia Downes. 210p. 1992. pap. 55.95 (*1-85742-042-X*, Pub. by Arena UK) Ashgate Pub Co.

Separation Techniques in Chemistry & Biochemistry. Summer Symposium On Analytical Chemistry Staff. LC 67-24544. (Illus.). 429p. reprint ed. pap. 122.30 (*0-7837-0661-8*, 2040997) Bks Demand.

Separation Techniques in Nuclear Waste Management. Ed. by Thomas E. Carleson et al. 352p. 1995. 236.00 (*0-8493-4876-5*, 4876) CRC Pr.

Separation Technology: Proceedings of the Third International Symposium of Separation Technology, Amtwerp, Belgium, August 22-27. Ed. by E. F. Vansant. LC 94-1634. 994p. 1994. 458.25 (*0-444-89977-4*) Elsevier.

Separation Technology in Japan. Ed. by C. Judson King. (JTEC Panel Reports). xvi, 143p. 1993. pap. write for info. (*1-883712-01-7*, JTEC) Intl Tech Res.

Separation Throughout Church History. 4th rev. ed. William McGrath. 72p. 1990. pap. 2.00 (*0-935409-01-7*) Amish Mennonite.

Separation, Violence Towards Women & Other Outcomes: The Impact of Mediation & Lawyer Negotiations. Desmond Ellis & Noreen Stuckless. LC 96-10128. 160p. 1996. 42.00 (*0-7619-0502-2*); pap. 17.95 (*0-7619-0503-0*) Sage.

Separation, Will & Creativity: The Wisdom of Otto Ranks. Ed. by Esther Menaker & Claude Barbre. LC 95-50974. (Illus.). 264p. 1996. pap. 30.00 (*1-56821-802-8*) Aronson.

Separation Without Hope? Essays on the Relation Between the Church & the Poor During the Industrial Revolution & the Western Colonial Expansion. Ed. by Julio De Santa Ana. LC 80-12831. 106p. reprint ed. pap. 30.30 (*0-8357-7018-4*, 2033574) Bks Demand.

***Separation/Divorce & Your Child at School.** Greg Anderson. (Illus.). 8p. (Orig.). 1996. pap. 2.50 (*1-884241-73-5*, AN1020) Energeia Pub.

Separations. Tom Beckett. (Chapbook Ser.). 24p. 1988. pap. 5.00 (*0-945112-06-8*) Generator Pr.

***Separations.** Mary Jane Van Sant. 150p. 1997. pap. 14.95 (*0-13-082687-1*) P-H.

***Separations: Chromatography & Electrophoresis.** (Market Research Reports: No. 660). 90p. 1996. 995.00 (*0-614-20542-5*) Theta Corp.

***Separations: Novel.** Oakley Hall. LC 96-37263. (Western Literature Ser.). 272p. 1997. pap. 15.00 (*0-87417-292-6*) U of Nev Pr.

Separations for Biotechnology 2. D. L. Pyle. 1990. 146.00 (*1-85166-545-5*) Elsevier.

Separations for Biotechnology 3: Proceedings of the International Symposium, Reading, UK, 1994. Ed. by D. L. Pyle. 618p. 1994. 184.00 (*0-85186-724-3*, R6724) CRC Pr.

Separations Manual & Letters of Interpretation. 151p. 1988. 25.00 (*0-317-02702-6*) NARUC.

Separations of f Elements: Proceedings of an ACS Symposium of f Elements Separations Held in San Diego, California, March 13-17, 1994. Ed. by Kenneth L. Nash & Gregory R. Choppin. 270p. 1995. 95.00 (*0-306-45070-4*) Plenum.

Separations Systems for Commercial Biotechnology. 228p. 1995. 2,650.00 (*0-614-03467-1*, C073R) BCC.

Separations Technology: Pharmaceutical & Biotechnology Applications. Ed. by Wayne P. Olson. 505p. 1995. 169.00 (*0-935184-72-4*) Interpharm.

Separations Using Aqueous Phase Systems: Applications in Cell Biology & Biotechnology. Ed. by D. Fisher & I. A. Sutherland. (Illus.). 532p. 1989. 135.00 (*0-306-43227-7*, Plenum Pr) Plenum.

***Separatism: Democracy & Disintegration.** Ed. by Metta Spencer. 265p. 1997. 62.50 (*0-8476-8584-5*) Rowman.

***Separatism: Democracy & Disintegration.** Ed. by Metta Spencer. 265p. 1997. pap. 21.95 (*0-8476-8585-3*) Rowman.

Separatism among Indian Muslims: The Politics of the United Provinces' Muslims. Francis Robinson. 496p. 1993. reprint ed. pap. 18.95 (*0-19-563126-9*) OUP.

Separatism among Indian Muslims: The Politics of the United Provinces' Muslims, 1860-1923. Francis Robinson. LC 73-93393. (Cambridge South Asian Studies: No. 16). 487p. reprint ed. pap. 138.80 (*0-317-26379-X*, 2024521) Bks Demand.

Separatism & Subculture: Boston Catholicism, 1900-1920. Paula M. Kane. LC 93-32053. (Illus.). xiv, 416p. (C). 1994. 49.95 (*0-8078-2128-4*) U of NC Pr.

Separatism & Women's Community. Dana R. Shugar. LC 94-32900. xvii, 216p. 1995. text ed. 30.00 (*0-8032-4244-1*) U of Nebr Pr.

Separatist Society of Zoar: An Experiment in Communism - from Its Commencement to Its Conclusion. E. O. Randall. (Ohio History, Communism Ser.). (Illus.). 128p. 1990. reprint ed. pap. 14.80 (*1-56651-019-8*); reprint ed. lib. bdg. 31.80 (*1-56651-020-1*) A W McGraw.

An Asterisk (*) at the beginning of an entry indicates that the title is appearing in BIP for the first time.

Separatrix Surfaces & Invariant Manifolds of a Class of Integrable Hamiltonian Systems & Their Perturbations. Jaume Llibre & Ana Nunes. LC 93-39026. (Memoirs of the American Mathematical Society Ser.: No. 513). 208p. 1994. pap. 36.00 (*0-8218-2581-X*, MEMO/107/513) Am Math.

***Seperation of East Pakistan: The Rise & Realization of Bengali Muslim Nationalism.** Hasan Zaheer. (Illus.). 544p. 1997. reprint ed. pap. 21.00 (*0-19-577592-9*) OUP.

***Sepharad: The Embezzled Land.** Salamon Eskinazi. LC 97-15872. 488p. 1997. 29.95 (*1-882897-17-X*) Lost Coast.

Sephardi & Middle Eastern Jewries: History & Culture. Ed. by Harvey E. Goldberg. LC 95-31525. 360p. (C). 1996. 39.95 (*0-253-33013-0*); pap. 18.95 (*0-253-21041-0*) Ind U Pr.

Sephardi Haggadah & the Laws of Pesach & the Seder. Jonathan Cohen. 1988. 15.95 (*0-87306-460-7*); pap. 12.95 (*0-317-66554-5*) Feldheim.

Sephardi Story: A Celebration of Jewish History. Chaim Raphael. 1991. text ed. 27.50 (*0-85303-247-5*, Pub. by Vallentine Mitchell UK); pap. text ed. 15.00 (*0-85303-251-3*, Pub. by Vallentine Mitchell UK) Intl Spec Bk.

Sephardic American Voices: Two Hundred Years of a Literary Legacy. Ed. by Diane Matza. LC 96-25559. (Brandeis Series in American Jewish History, Culture, & Life). (Illus.). 377p. 1997. 50.00 (*0-87451-786-9*) U Pr of New Eng.

Sephardic Cookery: Traditional Recipes for a Joyful Table. Emilie De Vidas Levy. 150p. (Orig.). 1983. pap. 8.50 (*0-9611294-0-9*) Women's Div.

Sephardic Cooking: Six Hundred Recipes Created in Exotic Sephardic Kitchens from Morocco to India. Copeland Marks. LC 94-71112. 560p. 1994. pap. 17.95 (*1-55611-419-2*, Primus) D I Fine.

Sephardic Holiday Cooking: Recipes & Traditions. Gilda Angel. (Illus.). 1986. 19.95 (*0-915474-04-2*, Effective Learn) Decalogue Bks.

Sephardic Jewish Community of Los Angeles: A Study in Folklore & Ethnic Identity. Stephen Stern. Ed. by Richard M. Dorson. LC 80-734. (Folklore of the World Ser.). 1981. lib. bdg. 44.95 (*0-405-13324-3*) Ayer.

Sephardic Jews in the West Coast States Vol. 1: The San Francisco Grandees. Ed. by William M. Kramer. 300p. (Orig.). 1996. pap. text ed. 24.95 (*0-914615-18-1*) I Nathan Pub Co.

***Sephardic Jews in the West Coast States Vol. 2: The Los Angeles Sephardic Experience.** Ed. by William M. Kramer. 206p. 1996. pap. 24.95 (*0-914615-19-X*) I Nathan Pub Co.

***Sephardic Jews in the West Coast States Vol. 3: Seattle, Washington & Portland Oregon.** Ed. by William M. Kramer. 256p. 1996. pap. 24.95 (*0-914615-21-1*) I Nathan Pub Co.

Sephardic Journey: 1492-1992. Marc D. Angel et al. (Illus.). 500p. 1992. pap. text ed. write for info. (*0-945447-03-5*) Yesh Mus.

Sephardic Kitchen: The Healthy Food & Rich Culture of the Mediterranean Jews. Robert Sternberg. LC 96-5390. 384p. 1996. 30.00 (*0-06-017691-1*) HarpC.

Sephardic Passover Haggadah. Marc D. Angel. 1988. pap. 7.95 (*0-88125-143-7*) Ktav.

Sephardic Playwrights of the Seventeenth & Eighteenth Centuries in Amsterdam. Haydee Litovsky. 184p. (Orig.). (C). 1990. lib. bdg. 41.00 (*0-8191-7843-8*) U Pr of Amer.

Sephardic Recipes: Delicacies from Baghdad. David Rabeeya & Roni Rueveni. (Illus.). 52p. 1992. pap. 14.95 (*0-9631746-0-6*) Maimuna Pr.

Sephardic Religious Responses to Modernity. Norman A. Stillman. (The Sherman Lecture Ser). 150p. 1995. text ed. 18.00 (*3-7186-5699-X*, Harwood Acad Pubs) Gordon & Breach.

Sephardic Spain. Victor Laredo. (Illus.). 1978. pap. 8.00 (*84-399-8381-6*) Edit Mensaje.

Sephardic Studies in the University. Ed. by Jane S. Gerber & Michel Abitbol. LC 92-55113. 1995. 45.00 (*0-8386-3542-3*) Fairleigh Dickinson.

Sephardim. Meyer Kayserling. xii, 372p. 1972. reprint ed. write for info. (*3-487-04195-2*) G Olms Pubs.

Sephardim: The Jews from Spain. Paloma Dias-Mas. Ed. & Tr. by George K. Zucker. LC 92-15523. 250p. 1992. 32.50 (*0-226-14483-6*) U Ch Pr.

Sephardim: Their Glorious Tradition from the Babylonian Exile to the Present Day. Lucien Gubbay & Abraham Levy. (Illus.). 222p. 1992. write for info. (*1-85779-036-7*) Gefen Bks.

***Sephardim in the Americas: Studies in Culture & History.** Ed. by Martin A. Cohen & Abraham J. Peck. LC 93-20083. (Judaic Studies). 510p. 1993. reprint ed. pap. 145.40 (*0-608-03803-2*, 2064654) Bks Demand.

Sephardim in the Ottoman Empire. Avigdor Levy. LC 92-2992. (Illus.). 192p. (C). 1994. pap. 12.95 (*0-87850-089-8*) Darwin Pr.

Sephardim of England: History of the Spanish & Portugese Jewish Community, 1492-1951. Albert M. Hyamson. LC 77-87544. reprint ed. 32.50 (*0-404-16610-5*) AMS Pr.

Sepharial's Astrology: How to Make & How to Read Your Own Horoscope. A. Sepharial. 126p. 1986. reprint ed. spiral bd. 5.50 (*0-7873-0770-X*) Hlth Research.

Sepharial's Astrology: How to Make & Read Your Own Horoscope. A. Sepharial. 126p. 1996. pap. 16.95 (*1-56459-819-5*) Kessinger Pub.

Sepher Yetzirah: The Book of Formation & the 32 Paths of Wisdom. W. Wynn Westcott. 1992. pap. 4.95 (*1-56459-262-6*) Kessinger Pub.

Sepher Yetzirah: The Thirty-Two Paths of Wisdom; with the Complete Hebrew Text. W. Wynn Westcott. (Golden Dawn Studies: Vol. 3). 1995. reprint ed. pap. 8.95 (*1-55818-333-7*) Holmes Pub.

Sepher Yetzireh: Book of Formation. rev. ed. W. Wynn Westcott. (Secret Doctrine Reference Ser.). 50p. 1990. pap. 4.00 (*0-913510-59-9*) Wizards.

Sepher Yezirah. Isidor Kalisch. 1987. 20.00 (*0-935214-09-7*) Heptangle.

Sepher Yezirah. 2nd ed. Tr. by Isidor Kalisch. LC 45-41757. 60p. 1977. pap. 6.95 (*0-912057-19-X*, 501720) RO AMORC.

Sepia & Song. David Foxton. (Drama Anthologies Ser.). (Illus.). 148p. (Orig.). (YA). 1990. pap. 15.00 (*0-333-40923-X*, Pub. by Macmillan Ed UK) Players Pr.

Sepia Prints: Memoirs of a Missionary in India. Viola C. Wiebe & Marilyn S. Dodge. (Illus.). 174p. (Orig.). 1990. pap. 19.95 (*0-921788-03-7*) Kindred Prods.

Sepia Tones (7 Short Stories) 2nd ed. Rimo Publications Staff et al. 1986. 11.50 (*0-918680-32-8*) Bagehot Council.

Sepik Heritage: Tradition & Change in Papua New Guinea. Nancy Lutkehaus et al. LC 90-80282. (Illus.). 688p. 1990. lib. bdg. 75.00 (*0-89089-322-5*) Carolina Acad Pr.

SEPM Meeting Abstracts Volume (Portland, OR) (Abstract Ser.: No. 6). (Illus.). 39p. 1991. pap. 12.50 (*0-918985-93-5*) SEPM.

SEPM Midyear Meeting Abastracts: 21-24 August 1988, Columbus, Ohio. SEPM Midyear Meeting Staff. 71p. reprint ed. pap. 25.00 (*0-7837-5985-1*, 2045792) Bks Demand.

Sepoys & the Company: Tradition & Transition in Northern India 1770-1830. Seema Alavi. (Illus.). 340p. 1996. 22.00 (*0-19-563484-5*) OUP.

Seppala - Alaskan Dog Driver. deluxe ed. Elizabeth M. Ricker. 296p. 1995. 40.00 (*0-614-04553-3*) Donald R Hoflin.

Sepphoris. Eric M. Meyers et al. viii, 63p. 1992. pap. 14.95 (*0-9602686-9-3*, Ctr Judaic Studies) Eisenbrauns.

***Sepphoris in Galilee: Crosscurrents of Culture.** Ed. by Rebecca M. Nagy et al. (Illus.). 275p. 1996. 29.95 (*0-88259-971-2*) NCMA.

Sepsis. Ed. by K. Reinhardt & K. Eyrich. (Illus.). 410p. 1989. 122.95 (*0-387-17763-9*) Spr-Verlag.

Sepsis: Current Perspectives in Pathophysiology & Therapy. Ed. by K. Reinhart et al. LC 94-373. (Update in Intensive Care & Emergency Medicine Ser.: Vol. 18). 1994. 98.00 (*0-387-57349-6*) Spr-Verlag.

***Sepsis & Multiorgan Failure.** Alan Fein. LC 96-40538. 1997. write for info. (*0-683-03097-3*) Williams & Wilkins.

Sepsis unter besonderer Beruecksichtigung der Ernaehrungsprobleme. Ed. by J. Eckhart. (Beitraege zur Infusionstherapie, Contributions to Infusion Therapy Ser.: Vol. 10). (Illus.). viii, 208p. 1983. pap. 40.00 (*3-8055-3677-1*) S Karger.

Sept Boules de Cristal. Herge. (Illus.). (FRE.). (J). (gr. 7-9). 19.95 (*0-8288-5069-0*) Fr & Eur.

Sept Contes. Michel Tournier. (Folio - Junior Ser.: No. 497). (Illus.). 161p. (FRE.). (J). (gr. 5-10). 1990. pap. 9.95 (*2-07-033497-X*) Schoenhof.

Sept Cordes de la Lyre. George Sand, pseud. 192p. (FRE.). 1973. pap. 18.95 (*0-7859-1415-3*, 2080610058) Fr & Eur.

Sept Femmes. Guy Des Cars. 384p. (FRE.). 1985. pap. 11.95 (*0-7859-4799-X*) Fr & Eur.

Sept Femmes de la Barbe-Bleue. Anatole France. 224p. (FRE.). 1975. 10.95 (*0-7859-0093-4*, M3439) Fr & Eur.

Sept Jours en Inde see My Burning Heart

Sept Psaumes de la Penitence. Paul Claudel. (FRE.). 1945. 10.95 (*0-7859-1070-0*, 2020041235) Fr & Eur.

Sept. 22, 1852-May 28, 1853 see Germans to America: Lists of Passengers Arriving at U. S. Ports

***Septage Handling.** Water Environment Federation Staff. LC 97-834. (Manual of Practice Ser.). 1997. write for info. (*1-57278-060-6*) Water Environ.

Septem Quae Supersunt Tragoediae. Aeschylus. Ed. by Denys L. Page. (Oxford Classical Texts Ser.). 348p. 1973. 32.00 (*0-19-814570-5*) OUP.

September. Rosamunde Pilcher. 1990. 413.10 (*0-312-04467-4*) St Martin.

September. Rosamunde Pilcher. 1991. mass mkt. 7.99 (*0-312-92480-1*) St Martin.

September. Suzanne S. Zenkel. (Birthstone Petite Collection). (Illus.). 80p. 1995. 4.95 (*0-88088-983-7*) Peter Pauper.

September. large type ed. Rosamunde Pilcher. LC 90-11097. 874p. 1991. pap. 17.95 (*1-56054-089-3*) Thorndike Pr.

September - October. Barbara Gruber. (Instant Idea Bks.). (Illus.). 64p. 1988. 7.95 (*0-86734-098-3*, FS-8311) Schaffer Pubns.

September Blackberries. Michael McClure. LC 73-89482. 160p. 1974. pap. 3.25 (*0-8112-0524-X*, NDP370) New Directions.

***September Commando: Gestures of Futility & Frustration.** John Yates. (Illus.). 96p. 1996. pap. 11.95 (*1-873176-52-X*, AK Pr San Fran) AK Pr Dist.

September-December 96 Catalog. Dutton Catalog Staff. 1996. pap. write for info. (*0-525-94262-9*) NAL-Dutton.

***September Essentials: Idea Booklet & Pocket Folder Organizer.** Karen Sevaly. (Illus.). 16p. (J). (ps-6). 1997. teacher ed., wbk. ed., pap. 3.99 (*1-57882-008-1*, TF-1259) Teachers Friend Pubns.

September Idea Book: A Creative Idea Book for the Elementary Teacher, Ps-6. Karen Sevaly. (Illus.). 112p. (Orig.). 1986. pap. 9.95 (*0-943263-00-X*, TF-900) Teachers Friend Pubns.

September Monthly Activities. Sterling Nowlin. (Monthly Activities Ser.). (Illus.). 80p. (J). (gr. 1-3). 1996. wbk. ed., pap. 9.95 (*1-55734-151-6*) Tchr Create Mat.

September Monthly Activities. Rice. (Monthly Activities Ser.). 80p. (J). (ps-1). 1996. pap. 9.95 (*1-55734-860-X*) Tchr Create Mat.

September Moon. Constance O'Banyon. 1986. mass mkt. 3.95 (*0-8217-1838-X*, Zebra Kensgtn) Kensgtn Pub Corp.

September Morning. Diana Palmer. (Here Come the Grooms Ser.: No. 12). 1996. mass mkt. 3.99 (*0-373-30112-X*, 1-30112-6) Harlequin Bks.

***September Mourn.** Mary R. Daheim. (Bed & Breakfast Mystery Ser.). 320p. (Orig.). 1997. mass mkt. 5.99 (*0-380-78518-8*) Avon.

September Nineteenth, Seventeen Seventy-Seven to January Thirty First, Seventeen Seventy-Eight see Letters of Delegates to Congress, 1774-1789

September Patterns, Projects & Plans. Imogene Forte. 80p. (J). (ps-1). 1989. pap. text ed. 8.95 (*0-86530-125-5*, IP 166-7) Incentive Pubns.

September September. Shelby Foote. LC 90-50942. 320p. 1991. pap. 12.00 (*0-679-73543-7*, Publishers Media) Random.

***September Song: An Intimate Biography of Walter Huston.** John Weld. (Filmmakers Ser.: No. 60). (Illus.). 288p. 1998. 39.50 (*0-8108-3408-1*) Scarecrow.

September Strike. Ward M. Tanneberg. LC 94-4346. (Ward Tanneberg Ser.: No. 1). 1994. pap. 11.99 (*1-56476-339-0*, 6-3339, Victor Bks) Chariot Victor.

September Sun. Paul-Eerik Rummo. Ed. by Stanley H. Barkan. Tr. by Ritva Poom. (Review Chapbook Ser.: No. 16: Estonian Poetry 1). 16p. 1989. reprint ed. 15.00 (*0-89304-822-4*, CCC143); reprint ed. pap. 5.00 (*0-89304-815-1*); reprint ed. pap. 5.00 (*0-89304-824-0*) Cross-Cultrl NY.

September Sun: Mini. Paul-Eerik Rummo. Ed. by Stanley H. Barkan. Tr. by Ritva Poom. (Review Chapbook Ser.: No. 16: Estonian Poetry 1). 16p. 1989. reprint ed. 15.00 (*0-89304-823-2*) Cross-Cultrl NY.

September to April. Margaret Brechan. 167p. (Orig.). 1987. pap. write for info. (*0-9619900-2-3*) Fireplace Bks.

September to December Seventeen Seventy-Five see Letters of Delegates to Congress, 1774-1789

***September Valentine, Vol. 1.** Ashley. 1997. mass mkt. 5.99 (*0-312-96279-7*) St Martin.

September 1, 1780 to February 28, 1781 see Letters of Delegates to Congress, 1774-1789

September 1781 to July 31, 1782 see Letters of Delegates to Congress, 1774-1789

September, 1790-January, 1971 see Papers of Alexander Hamilton

September 1829 - February 1831 see Diary of Charles Francis Adams

September 1864 - April 1869 see Briefwechsel: Kritische Gesamtausgabe

September 1915. (Southern Historical Society Papers: Vol. XL). 337p. 1991. reprint ed. 40.00 (*1-56837-143-8*) Broadfoot.

September 1916. (Southern Historical Society Papers: Vol. XLI). (Illus.). 221p. 1991. reprint ed. 40.00 (*1-56837-144-6*) Broadfoot.

September 1917. (Southern Historical Society Papers: Vol. XLII). (Illus.). 237p. 1991. reprint ed. 40.00 (*1-56837-145-4*) Broadfoot.

September 1920. (Southern Historical Society Papers: Vol. XLIII). (Illus.). 295p. 1992. reprint ed. 40.00 (*1-56837-146-2*) Broadfoot.

September 2, 1992, ML 5.8 St. George Earthquake, Washington County, Utah. Ed. by Gary E. Christenson. (Circular of the Utah Geological Survey Ser.: No. 88). (Illus.). 41p. (Orig.). 1995. pap. 6.95 (*1-55791-367-6*, C-88) Utah Geological Survey.

September 3, 1965-August 27, 1968 see Philosophy in Process

September's Bonfire. Theodore Enslin. 32p. (Orig.). 1981. pap. 5.50 (*0-937013-05-6*) Potes Poets.

September's Child. Debbie B. Hefflinger. 170p. (Orig.). 1992. pap. 12.00 (*0-9638291-0-6*) D Hefflinger.

Septemlingual Dictionary of the Names of European Animals, 2 vols., Set. L. Gozmanny et al. 2137p. (ENG, FRE, GER, HUN, LAT, RUS & SPA.). 1980. 295.00 (*0-8288-7195-7*, M15542) Fr & Eur.

Septentrion. Louis Calaferte. 440p. (FRE.). 1990. pap. 16.95 (*0-7859-2137-0*, 2070382273) Fr & Eur.

***Septic Shock.** Dhainaut. 1997. text ed. write for info. (*0-7020-1773-6*) Saunders.

Septic Shock. Ed. by Richard K. Root & Merle A. Sande. (Contemporary Issues in Infectious Diseases Ser.: Vol. 4). (Illus.). 281p. 1985. text ed. 52.00 (*0-443-08397-5*) Churchill.

Septic Shock. Ed. by J. L. Vincent & L. G. Thijs. (Intensive Care & Emergency Medicine Ser.: Vol. 4). (Illus.). 335p. 1987. 85.95 (*0-387-17861-9*) Spr-Verlag.

Septic Systems Handbook. O. Benjamin Kaplan. LC 86-27339. (Illus.). 300p. 1987. 170.00 (*0-87371-095-9*, TD778) Franklin.

Septic Systems Handbook. O. Benjamin Kaplan. LC 86-27339. 456p. 1991. 79.95 (*0-87371-236-6*, L236) Lewis Pubs.

Septic Tank System Effects on Ground Water Quality. Larry W. Canter & R. C. Knox. (Illus.). 360p. 1985. 89.00 (*0-87371-012-6*, L012) Lewis Pubs.

***Septic Tanks.** Richard K. Miller & Christy H. Gunter. (Market Research Survey Ser.: No. 317). 50p. 1996. 200.00 (*1-55865-340-6*) Future Tech Surveys.

Septicaemia & Endocarditis: Clinical & Microbiological Aspects. Ed. by D. C. Shanson. (Illus.). 188p. 1989. 53.00 (*0-19-261507-6*) OUP.

Septieme Croix. Anna Seghers. (FRE.). 1985. pap. 18.95 (*0-7859-4237-8*) Fr & Eur.

Septimius Felton see Dolliver Romance

Septimo Curso de Derecho Internacional Organizado por el Comite Juridico Interamericano: Agosto 1980. (Conferencias e Informes Ser.: OEA/CJI-44). pap. text ed. 38.00 (*0-8270-1460-0*) OAS.

Septimus Bean & His Amazing Machine. (Parents Magazine Press Read-Aloud Library). (Illus.). 42p. (J). (ps-3). 1992. lib. bdg. 17.27 (*0-8368-0887-8*) Gareth Stevens Inc.

Septimus Bean & His Amazing Machine. Janet Quin-Harkin. LC 79-163. (Illus.). 48p. (J). (ps-3). 1980. 5.95 (*0-8193-0999-0*) Parents.

Septuagenarian Stew: Stories & Poems. Charles Bukowski. LC 90-316. 380p. 1996. reprint ed. 25.00 (*0-87685-795-0*); reprint ed. pap. 15.00 (*0-87685-794-2*) Black Sparrow.

Septuagint & Modern Study. Sidney Jellicoe. xix, 424p. 1993. reprint ed. 32.50 (*0-931464-00-5*) Eisenbrauns.

Septuagint of Jewish Worship. H. S. Thackeray. (British Academy, London, Schweich Lectures on Biblical Archaeology Series, 1930). 1974. reprint ed. pap. 25.00 (*0-8115-1262-2*) Periodicals Srv.

***Septuagint Quotations in the Context of the Petrine & Pauline Speeches of the Acta Apostolorum.** Gert J. Steyn. (Contributions to Biblical Exegesis & Theology Ser.: Vol. 12). 290p. 1995. pap. 39.00 (*90-390-0131-6*, Pub. by KOK Pharos NE) Eisenbrauns.

Septuagint, Scrolls & Cognate Writings: Papers Presented to the International Symposium on the Septuagint, Dead Sea Scrolls & Other Writings, Held at University of Manchester, July 30-August 2, 1990. Ed. by George J. Brooke & Barnabas Lindars. (Society of Biblical Literature Septuagint & Cognate Studies Ser.). 668p. (C). 1992. 44.95 (*1-55540-706-4*, 060433); pap. 29.95 (*1-55540-707-2*) Scholars Pr GA.

Septuagint Translation Technique in the Book of Job. Homer Heater, Jr. Ed. by Bruce Vawter. LC 81-10085. (Catholic Biblical Quarterly Monographs: No. 11). xiv, 152p. 1982. pap. 4.00 (*0-915170-10-8*) Catholic Bibl Assn.

Septuagint with Apocrypha: Greek & English. Lancelot C. Brenton. 1408p. 1986. 44.95 (*0-913573-44-2*) Hendrickson MA.

Sepulchers Are Whited. Russell R. Standish & Colin D. Standish. 301p. (Orig.). 1992. pap. 7.95 (*0-923309-02-0*) Hartland Pubns.

Sepulchral House. Richard J. Johnson. LC 94-90463. 392p. (Orig.). 1995. pap. 7.95 (*1-56002-488-7*, Univ Edtns) Aegina Pr.

Sepultura: Just the Riffs. 31p. (YA). pap. 9.95 (*0-89524-955-3*, 02506323) Cherry Lane.

Sepultura: Schizophrenia. 78p. (Orig.). (YA). 1995. pap. 19.95 (*0-89524-874-3*, 02501241) Cherry Lane.

Sepultura - Beneath the Remains. 85p. (Orig.). (YA). 1994. pap. 19.95 (*0-89524-870-0*, 02501240) Cherry Lane.

Sepultura - Chaos A.D. 58p. (Orig.). (YA). 1994. pap. 19.95 (*0-89524-850-6*, 02501238) Cherry Lane.

Sepultura Arise. Sepultura. 79p. (Orig.). (YA). 1994. pap. 19.95 (*0-89524-855-7*, 02501239) Cherry Lane.

Sequatchie: A Story of the Southern Cumberlands. J. Leonard Raulston & James W. Livingood. LC 73-17360. (Illus.). 313p. reprint ed. pap. 89.30 (*0-7837-5391-8*, 2045155) Bks Demand.

***Sequel.** Shirley Y. Campbell. (C). Date not set. pap. write for info. (*0-943461-02-2*) Hill & Valley Pub.

Sequel: A Handbook for the Critical Analysis of Literature. 3rd rev. ed. Richard C. Guches. ix, 304p. (C). 1991. pap. text ed. 19.95 (*0-917962-96-6*, 59SE) T H Peek.

Sequel of Appomattox: Chronicle of the Reunion of the States. Walter L. Fleming. (History - United States Ser.). 322p. 1992. reprint ed. lib. bdg. 89.00 (*0-7812-6203-8*) Rprt Serv.

Sequel to a Verdict. Phillip Dunning. 1962. pap. 5.25 (*0-8222-1010-X*) Dramatists Play.

Sequel to an Enquiry into the Nature of Certain Nineteenth Century Pamphlets. Nicolas Barker & John Collins. (Illus.). 394p. 1992. reprint ed. 55.00 (*0-938768-32-8*) Oak Knoll.

Sequel to Bretton Woods: A Proposal to Reform the World Monetary System. Lawrence B. Krause. LC 71-180726. (Brookings Institution Staff Paper Ser.). 60p. reprint ed. pap. 25.00 (*0-317-26729-9*, 2025386) Bks Demand.

***Sequel to Hero & Crown.** Robin McKinley. (J). Date not set. write for info. (*0-688-06384-5*) Greenwillow.

Sequel to History: Postmodernism & the Crisis of Representational Time. Elizabeth D. Ermarth. 257p. 1992. text ed. 45.00 (*0-691-06930-1*); pap. text ed. 16.95 (*0-691-01517-1*) Princeton U Pr.

Sequel to Riley's Narrative. W. Willshire Riley. 1979. reprint ed. lib. bdg. 49.00 (*0-403-00317-2*) Scholarly.

***Sequel to the Hour of the Hunter.** J. A. Jance. Date not set. write for info. (*0-688-10922-5*) Morrow.

Sequelae of Low Birthweight. Ed. by Henry G. Dunn. LC 65-80534. (Clinics in Developmental Medicine Ser.: No. 95-96). (Illus.). 306p. (C). 1991. text ed. 69.95 (*0-521-41215-3*, Pub. by Mc Keith Pr UK) Cambridge U Pr.

Sequellae to Atlantis 2, 3, 4, 5 & 1: Short Stories. 1992. 10.00 (*0-614-13543-5*) R C Rapier.

***Sequels: An Annotated Guide to Novels in Series.** 2nd annot. ed. Janet Husband & Jonathan F. Husband. LC 90-180. 585p. 1990. reprint ed. pap. 166.80 (*0-608-02966-1*, 2063431) Bks Demand.

***Sequels: An Annotated Guide to Novels in Series.** 3rd ed. Janet Husband & Jonathan F. Husband. LC 96-27296. 1997. 70.00 (*0-8389-0696-6*) ALA.

Sequels: An Annotated Guide to Novels in Series. Janet Husband. LC 82-16309. 371p. reprint ed. pap. 105.80 (*0-7837-5911-8*, 2045709) Bks Demand.

***Sequels in Children's Literature: An Annotated Bibliography of Books in Succession, K-6.** Vicki Anderson. 264p. 1997. pap. 35.00 (*0-7864-0285-7*) McFarland & Co.

Sequence. Karlyn Kamm & Gerald Chastain, Jr. (Solar Reading - Flight One Ser.). (J). (gr. 3). 70.00 incl. disk (*0-912899-11-5*) Lrning Multi-Systs.

Sequence. Karlyn Kamm & Gerald Chastain, Jr. (Solar Reading - Flight Two Ser.). (J). (gr. 5). 95.00 incl. disk (*0-912899-15-8*) Lrning Multi-Systs.

Sequence. 4th ed. Donnelly. (C). 1996. teacher ed., pap. text ed. write for info. (*0-15-503585-1*) HB Coll Pubs.

Sequence: A Basic Writing Course. 2nd ed. Rory D. Stephens. 352p. (C). 1986. pap. text ed. 22.00 (*0-03-001519-7*) HB Coll Pubs.

Sequence: A Basic Writing Course. 3rd ed. Rory Donnelly. (Illus.). 416p. (C). 1993. pap. text ed. 22.00 (*0-03-055134-X*) HB Coll Pubs.

Sequence: A Basic Writing Course. 4th ed. Donnelly. (C). 1996. pap. text ed. 29.00 (*0-15-501996-1*) HB Coll Pubs.

Sequence: A Basic Writing Course. 4th ed. Rory Donnelly. (C). 1996. teacher ed., pap. text ed. 28.00 (*0-15-503446-4*) HB Coll Pubs.

Sequence Dances. (Ballroom Dance Ser.). 1991. lib. bdg. 75.00 (*0-8490-5191-6*) Gordon Pr.

Sequence Dances of 1982, 1983, 1984: 128 from Rumba Amour to Zara Tango, Abbeydale Foxtrot to Wiclif Waltz & Saunter Adele to Wentworth Waltz. (Ballroom Dance Ser.). 1985. lib. bdg. 74.50 (*0-87700-716-0*) Revisionist Pr.

Sequence Dancing. (Ballroom Dance Ser.). 1991. lib. bdg. 75.00 (*0-8490-5189-4*) Gordon Pr.

Sequence Data Analysis Guidebook. Ed. by Simon Swindell. LC 96-44660. (Methods in Molecular Biology Ser.: Vol. 70). 336p. 1996. 69.50 (*0-89603-358-9*) Humana.

***Sequence Design for Communications Applications.** Pingzhi Fan & Mike Darnell. LC 96-2760. 1996. write for info. (*0-471-96557-X*) Wiley.

Sequence Detection for High-Density Storage Channels. Jaekyun Moon & L. Richard Carley. LC 92-2346. (International Series in Engineering & Computer Science, VLSI, Computer Architecture, & Digital Screen Processing: SECS 63). 176p. (C). 1992. lib. bdg. 81.00 (*0-7923-9264-7*) Kluwer Ac.

Sequence Hierarchy & Facies Architecture of a Carbonate-Ramp System: San Andres Formation of Algerita Escarpment & Western Guadalupe Mountains, West Texas & New Mexico. Charles Kerans & W. M. Fitchen. (Reports of Investigations: No. 235). (Illus.). 86p. (Orig.). 1995. pap. 9.50 (*0-614-11613-9*) Bur Econ Geology.

Sequence New York-New Jersey, 1990-1993. George Segal. 1994. 29.95 (*1-884167-00-4*) Umbra Edits.

Sequence of Chemical Reactions: Transforming Copper. Marcia L. Gillette & Guy B. Homman. Ed. by Conrad L. Stanitski. (Modular Laboratory Program in Chemistry Ser.). 8p. (C). 1996. pap. text ed. 1.35 (*0-87540-480-4*, REAC 480-4) Chem Educ Res.

Sequence of Events in the Old Testament: Diagramatic-Geographical-Chronological. Eliezer Shulman. Tr. by Sarah Lederhandler. 180p. 1995. 23.95 (*965-05-0268-8*, Pub. by Israel Ministry Def IS) Gefen Bks.

Sequence of Plumages & Moults of the Passerine Birds of New York, Vol. 13. Jonathan Dwight, Jr. (Annals Ser.). reprint ed. 10.00 (*0-89072-004-5*) NY Acad Sci.

Sequence Plus: Sequence Pictures with Vocabulary. Marilyn M. Toomey. (Illus.). 105p. 1992. write for info. (*0-923573-15-1*) Circuit Pubns.

Sequence Stratigraphy. Ed. by Dominic Emery & Keith Myers. (Orig.). 1996. pap. text ed. 55.00 (*0-632-03706-7*) Blackwell Sci.

Sequence Stratigraphy: Advances & Applications for Exploration & Production in Northwest Europe. Ed. by R. J. Steel. LC 94-25236. (Norwegian Petroleum Society Special Publications: No. 5). 620p. 1994. 218.00 (*0-444-81863-4*) Elsevier.

Sequence Stratigraphy & Depositional Response to Eustatic, Tectonic & Climatic Forcing. Ed. by Bilal U. Haq. (Coastal Systems & Continental Margins Ser.: Vol. 1). 400p. (C). 1995. lib. bdg. 185.00 (*0-7923-3780-8*) Kluwer Ac.

Sequence Stratigraphy & Facies Associations. Ed. by Henry W. Posamentier et al. LC 92-34625. (International Association of Sedimentologists Special Publication Ser.: No. 18). 1993. 110.00 (*0-632-03548-X*) Blackwell Sci.

Sequence Stratigraphy Applications to Shelf Sandstone Reservoirs: Outcrop to Subsurface Examples. D. R. Taylor et al. (Field Conference, September 21-38, 1991 Ser.). (Illus.). x, 267p. (Orig.). 1992. pap. 15.00 (*0-89181-815-4*, 547) AAPG.

Sequence Stratigraphy in British Geology. Ed. by S. P. & D. N. (Geological Society Special Publication: Vol. 103). (Illus.). vi, 284p. 1996. 93.00 (*1-897799-49-7*, 266, Pub. by Geol Soc Pub Hse UK) AAPG.

Sequence Stratigraphy in Fine-Grained Rocks: Examples from the Monterey Formation. J. R. Schwalbach & K. M. Bohacs. 80p. (Orig.). 1992. pap. 10.00 (*1-878861-63-8*) Pac Section SEPM.

Sequence Stratigraphy in Offshore South African Divergent Basins: An Atlas on Exploration for Cretaceous Lowstand Traps by Soekor (Pty.) Ltd. L. F. Brown, Jr. et al. (AAPG Studies in Geology: No. 41). (Illus.). vii, 184p. 1995. spiral bd. 89.00 (*0-89181-049-8*, 533) AAPG.

Sequence Stratigraphy of Foreland Basin Deposits: Outcrop & Subsurface Examples from the Cretaceous of North America. Ed. by J. C. Van Wagoner & G. T. Bertram. (Memoir Ser.: Vol. 64). (Illus.). xxi, 487p. 1995. 134.00 (*0-89181-343-8*, 532) AAPG.

Sequence Stratigraphy of the Mid-Continent. Ed. by Norman J. Hyne. (Illus.). 352p. (C). 1995. 79.00 (*0-945087-01-2*) Tulsa Geol Soc.

Sequence Transformations. J. P. Delahaye. (Computational Mathematics Ser.: Vol. 11). (Illus.). 250p. 1988. 127.95 (*0-387-15283-0*) Spr-Verlag.

Sequencer Secrets. Ian Waugh. (Illus.). 103p. 1995. pap. 13.95 (*1-870775-37-6*) Cimino Pub Grp.

Sequences. Ed. by Renato M. Capocelli. (Illus.). xii, 549p. 1989. 92.95 (*0-387-97186-6*) Spr-Verlag.

Sequences. Alan C. Walter. Ed. by Beverly Miles. 13p. (Orig.). 1996. pap. text ed. 7.77 (*1-57569-007-1*) Wisdom Pubng.

Sequences. H. Halberstam & K. Roth. 293p. 1983. reprint ed. 75.95 (*0-387-90801-3*) Spr-Verlag.

Sequences: Strategies for Shooting News in the Real World. John Hewitt. LC 91-22359. 176p. (C). 1992. pap. text ed. 35.95 incl. vhs (*0-87484-903-9*, 903) Mayfield Pub.

Sequences & Series in Banach Spaces. J. Diestel. (Graduate Texts in Mathematics Ser.: Vol. 92). 280p. 1984. 49.00 (*0-387-90859-5*) Spr-Verlag.

***Sequences, Discrepancies, & Applications, Vol. 165.** Michael Drmota & R. F. Tichy. LC 97-7675. (Lecture Notes in Mathematics Ser.). 1997. write for info. (*3-540-62606-9*) Spr-Verlag.

Sequences II: Methods in Communication, Security & Computer Science. Ed. by Renato M. Capocelli et al. LC 92-32461. 488p. 1992. 130.95 (*0-387-97940-9*) Spr-Verlag.

Sequences of Convergence for Series: Proceedings. S. B. Steckin et al. (Proceedings of the Steklov Institute of Mathematics Ser.: No. 86). 85p. 1967. pap. 36.00 (*0-8218-1886-4*, STEKLO/86) Am Math.

Sequences of Proteins of Immunological Interest, 3 vols., Set. 5th ed. Elvin A. Kabat. (Illus.). 2400p. (Orig.). (C). 1992. pap. text ed., pap. 145.00 (*0-941375-65-X*) DIANE Pub.

Sequencing. Joy Evans & Jo E. Moore. (Illus.). 20p. (J). (gr. k-1). 1988. teacher ed., pap. 4.95 (*1-55799-013-1*, EMC 124) Evan-Moor Corp.

***Sequencing.** Jo E. Moore. (Reading & Writing Ser.). (Illus.). 32p. (J). (ps-k). 1997. teacher ed., pap. 2.95 (*1-55799-403-X*, 4005) Evan-Moor Corp.

Sequencing. 2nd ed. Arlene R. Cardozo. 355p. 1996. reprint ed. pap. 13.95 (*0-9651238-0-4*) Brownstne Bks.

***Sequencing? Financial Strategies for Developing Countries.** Ed. by Alison Harwood & Bruce L. Smith. LC 96-48792. 200p. 1997. text ed. 38.95 (*0-8157-3498-0*); pap. text ed. 16.95 (*0-8157-3499-9*) Brookings.

Sequencing & Timing of Human Movement. Ed. by Arnold J. Thomassen et al. LC 92-12714. 1992. reprint ed. 108.25 (*0-444-89245-1*, North Holland) Elsevier.

Sequencing of Proteins & Peptides. 2nd ed. G. Allen. (Laboratory Techniques in Biochemistry & Molecular Biology Ser.: Vol. 9). 426p. 1989. 190.25 (*0-444-81022-6*); pap. 42.00 (*0-444-81021-8*) Elsevier.

Sequencing of Structural Adjustment & Stabilization. Sebastian Edwards. LC 92-30451. 1992. pap. 6.95 (*1-55815-235-0*) ICS Pr.

***Sequencing Simple Stories (Language)** Jo E. Moore. (Reading & Writing Ser.). (Illus.). 32p. (J). (gr. 1-2). 1996. teacher ed., pap. 2.95 (*1-55799-407-2*, 4009) Evan-Moor Corp.

Sequential Analysis. John Gottman & Anup K. Roy. (Illus.). 230p. (C). 1990. text ed. 36.95 (*0-521-34665-7*) Cambridge U Pr.

Sequential Analysis: Tests & Confidence Intervals. D. Siegmund. (Series in Statistics). (Illus.). xi, 272p. 1985. 64.95 (*0-387-96134-8*) Spr-Verlag.

Sequential Analysis & Optimal Design. Herman Chernoff. (CBMS-NSF Regional Conference Series in Applied Mathematics: No. 8). (Illus.). v, 119p. (Orig.). 1972. reprint ed. pap. text ed. 21.50 (*0-89871-006-5*) Soc Indus-Appl Math.

Sequential & Parallel Processing in Depth Search Machines. Adam Kapralski. 336p. 1994. text ed. 67.00 (*981-02-1716-1*) World Scientific Pub.

Sequential Binary Investment Decisions. W. Jammernegg. (Lecture Notes in Economics & Mathematical Systems Ser.: Vol. 313). vi, 156p. 1988. 47.90 (*0-387-50034-0*) Spr-Verlag.

Sequential Control with Incomplete Information. E. L. Presman & I. N. Sonon. (Economic Theory, Econometrics & Mathematical Economics Ser.). 266p. 1990. text ed. 125.00 (*0-12-564435-3*) Acad Pr.

Sequential Data in Biological Experiments: An Introduction for Research Workers. Ellis A. Roberts. (Illus.). 184p. (gr. 13). 1991. text ed. 84.95 (*0-412-41410-4*, A6307) Chapman & Hall.

***Sequential Estimation.** Malay Ghosh. LC 96-32001. (Wiley Series in Probability & Mathematical Statistics). 465p. 1996. text ed. 69.95 (*0-471-81271-4*) Wiley.

Sequential Gymnastics, No. Two: The Instructor's Guide. 3rd ed. Patty Hacker et al. 108p. 1992. pap. 13.00 (*1-885250-15-0*) USA Gymnastics.

Sequential Identification & Ranking Procedures: With Special Reference to Koopman-Darmois Populations. Robert E. Bechhofer et al. LC 67-28463. (Statistical Research Monographs: Vol. 3). 438p. reprint ed. pap. 124.90 (*0-317-09299-5*, 2019954) Bks Demand.

Sequential Logic Synthesis. Pranav Ashar et al. (C). 1991. lib. bdg. 88.00 (*0-7923-9187-X*) Kluwer Ac.

Sequential Logic Testing & Verification. Abhijit Ghosh et al. (C). 1991. lib. bdg. 88.00 (*0-7923-9188-8*) Kluwer Ac.

Sequential Machines & Automata Theory. Taylor L. Booth. LC 67-25924. (Illus.). 606p. reprint ed. pap. 173.30 (*0-7837-3431-X*, 2057752) Bks Demand.

Sequential Math 1: A Workbook. John Allasio et al. 148p. (YA). (gr. 8-12). 1988. pap. 8.95 (*0-937820-54-7*) WestSea Pub.

Sequential Math 1 Answer Key. John Allasio et al. 20p. (YA). (gr. 8-12). 1988. teacher ed., pap. 3.25 (*0-937820-55-5*) WestSea Pub.

Sequential Math 2: A Workbook. John Allasio et al. 141p. (YA). (gr. 9-12). 1990. pap. 8.95 (*0-937820-65-2*) WestSea Pub.

Sequential Math 2 Answer Key. John Allasio et al. 20p. (YA). (gr. 9-12). 1990. teacher ed., pap. 3.25 (*0-937820-66-0*) WestSea Pub.

Sequential Math 3: A Workbook. John Allasio et al. 156p. (YA). (gr. 10-12). 1993. pap. 8.95 (*0-937820-67-9*) WestSea Pub.

Sequential Math 3 Answer Key. John Allasio et al. 20p. (YA). (gr. 10-12). 1993. teacher ed., pap. 3.25 (*0-937820-68-7*) WestSea Pub.

***Sequential Mathematics, Course III.** 2nd ed. Lawrence S. Leff. LC 96-35975. (Barron's Review Course Ser.). 1997. pap. 9.95 (*0-8120-9917-6*) Barron.

***Sequential Mathematics Course 1, Vol. 1.** Barron's Educational Series Staff. (Barron's Regents Passware Computer Study Program Ser.). 1997. pap. 19.95 incl. disk (*0-7641-7003-1*) Barron.

***Sequential Mathematics Course 2 11, Vol. 2.** Barron's Educational Series Staff. (Barron's Regents Passware Computer Study Program Ser.). 1997. pap. 19.95 incl. disk (*0-7641-7005-8*) Barron.

Sequential Nonparametrics: Invariance Principles & Statistical Inference. Pranab K. Sen. LC 81-4432. (Probability & Mathematical Statistics Applied Prob). 440p. 1991. reprint ed. lib. bdg. 79.95 (*0-471-06013-5*) Krieger.

Sequential Optimization: Dynamic Programming, Maximum Principle & Extensions. Joseph Burstein. LC 85-61000. (Illus.). 74p. 1985. pap. 26.87 (*0-9607126-2-3*) Metrics Pr.

Sequential Simplex Optimization: A Technique for Improving Quality & Productivity in Research, Development, & Manufacturing. Frederick H. Walters et al. 352p. 1991. 64.95 (*0-8493-5894-9*, QH541) CRC Pr.

Sequential Sourcebook for Elementary School Music: A Curriculum Guide & Sourcebook Combined. 2nd ed. Laura Hochheimer. (Illus.). 92p. 1979. reprint ed. spiral bd. 13.50 (*0-918812-12-7*, SE 0039) MMB Music.

Sequential Spelling, Vol. VI. Don McCabe. 72p. (Orig.). 1992. pap. text ed. 9.95 (*1-56400-362-0*, 306) AVKO Educ Res.

Sequential Spelling, Vol. VII. Don McCabe. 72p. (Orig.). 1992. pap. text ed. 9.95 (*1-56400-370-1*, 307) AVKO Educ Res.

Sequential Spelling Examination Set. Don McCabe. 240p. 1992. pap. text ed. 49.95 (*1-56400-300-0*, 300) AVKO Educ Res.

Sequential Spelling I. Don McCabe. 36p. (Orig.). 1992. pap. text ed. 9.95 (*1-56400-311-6*, 301) AVKO Educ Res.

Sequential Spelling II. Don McCabe. 36p. 1992. pap. text ed. 9.95 (*1-56400-321-3*, 302) AVKO Educ Res.

Sequential Spelling III. Don McCabe. 36p. 1992. pap. text ed. 9.95 (*1-56400-331-0*, 303) AVKO Educ Res.

Sequential Spelling IV. Don McCabe. 36p. 1992. pap. text ed. 9.95 (*1-56400-341-8*, 304) AVKO Educ Res.

Sequential Spelling V. Don McCabe. 36p. 1992. pap. text ed. 9.95 (*1-56400-351-5*, 305) AVKO Educ Res.

Sequential Statistical Analysis of Hypothesis Testing, Point & Interval Estimation, & Decision Theory. Zakkula Govindarajulu. LC 80-68287. (American Sciences Press Series in Mathematical & Management Sciences: Vol. 5). 1987. text ed. 125.00 (*0-935950-17-6*) Am Sciences Pr.

Sequential Stochastic Optimization. R. Cairoli & Robert C. Dalang. LC 94-39134. (Probability & Mathematics Statistics Ser.). 1996. text ed. 59.95 (*0-471-57754-5*) Wiley.

Sequential Strategies for Math. Dee Burrow. (Primary Level Ser.). 336p. 1995. teacher ed., pap. text ed. 55.00 (*0-9641654-1-4*) G W Teal.

Sequential Traumatization in Children. Hans Keilson. 464p. (Orig.). 1993. pap. 30.00 (*965-223-806-6*) Gefen Bks.

Sequestered Soliloquies. Earl J. Perel. 96p. 1994. 10.00 (*0-932616-46-1*) Brick Hse Bks.

Sequestering Methods of Iron & Manganese Treatment. 322p. 1990. pap. 42.00 (*0-89867-510-3*, 90558) Am Water Wks Assn.

Sequestres d'Altona. Jean-Paul Sartre. (FRE.). 1991. pap. 11.95 (*0-8288-3779-1*, F125510) Fr & Eur.

Sequestres d'Altona. Jean-Paul Sartre. (Folio Ser.: No. 938). (FRE.). 1972. pap. 9.95 (*2-07-036938-2*) Schoenhof.

Sequim Bay see Fish Tales of Port Angeles

Sequins & Lace: Sacramento's Guide to Planning Weddings, Parties & Special Events. Sharon Havranek & Kathy Elyash. 80p. (Orig.). 1993. pap. text ed. 8.95 (*1-882826-00-0*) Inform Pub.

Sequins & Shades: The Michael Jackson Reference Guide. Carol Terry. (Rock & Roll Reference Ser.: No. 22). (Illus.). 542p. 1989. reprint ed. 45.00 (*1-56075-010-3*) Popular Culture.

Sequoia & His Miracle. William Roper. (J). (gr. 5-12). 1972. pap. 4.95 (*0-89992-056-X*) Coun India Ed.

Sequoia & Kings Canyon. Ed. by Jeff Nicholas. (Wish You Were Here Postcard Bks.). (Illus.). 32p. 1993. pap. 4.95 (*0-939365-25-1*) Sierra Pr CA.

***Sequoia & Kings Canyon: A Guide to Sequoia & Kings Canyon National Parks.** 1997. lib. bdg. 250.95 (*0-8490-6137-7*) Gordon Pr.

Sequoia & Kings Canyon: A Guide to Sequoia & Kings Canyon National Parks, California. National Park Service Staff. LC 91-37844. (Handbook Ser.: No. 145). (Illus.). 128p. (Orig.). 1992. pap. 4.50 (*0-912627-47-6*, 024-005-01095-9) Natl Park Serv.

***Sequoia & Kings Canyon: The Story Behind the Scenery.** 2nd rev. ed. William C. Tweed. LC 96-77756. (Illus.). 64p. 1997. pap. 7.95 (*0-88714-121-8*) KC Pubns.

Sequoia & Kings Canyon Discovery. Bobbi Salts. (Illus.). 36p. (Orig.). (J). (gr. 1-6). 1992. pap. 3.95 (*1-878441-05-1*) Sequoia Nat Hist Assn.

Sequoia & Kings Canyon National Parks. rev. ed. George Yago, 3rd. Ed. by Kristine Miller. 53p. 1995. pap. 5.95 (*1-56413-308-7*) Auto Club.

Sequoia Kings Canyon. Sally Moser et al. (Southern Sierra Rock Climbing Ser.). (Illus.). 312p. (Orig.). 1993. pap. 25.00 (*0-934641-51-X*) Chockstone Pr.

Sequoia-King's Canyon National Park, CA. rev. ed. Ed. by Trails Illustrated Staff. (Illus.). 1995. Folded topographical map. 8.99 (*0-925873-05-5*) Trails Illustrated.

Sequoia Scout. Brock Thoene & Bodie Thoene. (Saga of the Sierras Ser.: Bk. 4). 240p. (Orig.). 1991. pap. 7.99 (*1-55661-165-X*) Bethany Hse.

Sequoias. Michael George. (Images Ser.). (J). (gr. 5 up). 1992. lib. bdg. 16.95 (*0-88682-482-6*) Creative Ed.

Sequoias of Yosemite National Park. H. T. Harvey. (Illus.). 36p. 1978. pap. 3.50 (*0-939666-14-6*) Yosemite Assn.

Sequoyah. Robert Cwiklik. Ed. by Nancy Furstinger. (Alvin Josephy's Biography of the American Indians Ser.). (Illus.). 142p. (J). (gr. 5-7). 1989. pap. 7.95 (*0-382-09759-9*, Silver Pr NJ); lib. bdg. 12.95 (*0-382-09570-7*, Silver Pr NJ) Silver Burdett Pr.

Sequoyah. Grant Foreman. LC 38-27481. (Civilization of the American Indian Ser.: No. 16). (Illus.). 85p. 1938. pap. 8.95 (*0-8061-1056-2*) U of Okla Pr.

***Sequoyah: Inventor of the Cherokee Written Language.** Diane Shaughnessy & Jack Carpenter. LC 97-17643. (Famous Native Americans Ser.). 1997. write for info. (*0-8239-5110-3*) Rosen Group.

Sequoyah: Story Pak. L. Johnson. (Graphic Learning Literature Program Series: Folk Tales). (Illus.). (ENG & SPA.). 1992. 43.00 (*0-87746-253-4*) Graphic Learning.

Sequoyah: The Cherokee Genius. Stan Hoig. (Illus.). 160p. 1995. 19.95 (*0-941498-68-9*) OK Hist Soc.

Sequoyah, Cherokee Hero. Joanne F. Oppenheim. LC 78-60117. (Illus.). 48p. (J). (gr. 4-6). 1979. pap. 3.50 (*0-89375-149-9*); lib. bdg. 11.89 (*0-89375-159-6*) Troll Communs.

Sequoyah: Inventor of the Cherokee Alphabet see North American Indians of Achievement

Sequoyah's Gift: A Portrait of the Cherokee Leader. Janet Klausner. LC 92-24939. (Illus.). 128p. (J). (gr. 4 up). 1993. lib. bdg. 14.89 (*0-06-021236-5*) HarpC Child Bks.

Ser Algo: E. U. Cuba-Puerto Rico (Federalismo: Union para la Defensa para la Union) Jose R. Goldaras. LC 79-53923. 1979. pap. 7.00 (*0-89729-201-4*) Ediciones.

Ser Tu Misma: Meditaciones Para la Capacitacion y la Paz Mental. 2nd ed. Sue P. Thoele. Tr. by Jose M. Pomares from ENG. 200p. (SPA.). 1995. pap. 8.95 (*0-943233-96-8*) Conari Press.

Ser Tu Misma: Tecnicas y Meditaciones Para Aprender a Confiar Nen Nuestros Mismos. Sue P. Thoele. 200p. 1995. lib. bdg. 27.00 (*0-8095-5895-5*) Borgo Pr.

Ser y el Mesias see Being & the Messiah: The Message of St. John

Serach's Song. Yaffa L. Gottleib. Ed. by Ruth Zakutinsky. (E-Z Reader Ser.). (Illus.). 32p. (J). (gr. 3-4). 1995. 7.95 (*0-911643-20-6*) Aura Bklyn.

Seraffyn's Mediterranean Adventure. Lin Pardey & Larry Pardey. (Illus.). 256p. 1991. pap. 14.95 (*0-924486-15-5*) Sheridan.

Seraffyn's Oriental Adventure. 2nd ed. Lin Pardey & Larry Pardey. 2p. 1996. reprint ed. pap. 16.95 (*0-9646036-3-2*) Pardey Prods.

Serafin Estebanez Calderon: Bajo la Corteza de su Obra. Ronald J. Quirk. LC 91-42499. (American University Studies: Romance Languages & Literature: Ser. II, Vol. 187). 223p. (C). 1992. text ed. 38.95 (*0-8204-1748-3*) P Lang Pubng.

Serafina. large type ed. Sylvia Andrew. 350p. 1995. 21.50 (*0-263-14192-6*) Ulverscroft.

Serafina's Wild Horse. Margarita Engle. 1997. write for info. (*0-517-70500-1*) Random.

Serait un Fois. Didier Martin. (FRE.). 1979. pap. 10.95 (*0-7859-4116-9*) Fr & Eur.

***Seraph on the Suwanee.** Zora Neale Hurston. LC 97-7049. (Perennial Ser.). 519p. 1997. 24.95 (*0-7838-8126-6*) G K Hall.

Seraph on the Suwanee. Zora Neale Hurston. LC 90-55503. 320p. (C). 1991. reprint ed. lib. bdg. 35.00 (*0-8095-9032-8*) Borgo Pr.

Seraph on the Suwanee: A Novel. Zora Neale Hurston. LC 90-55503. 320p. 1991. reprint ed. pap. 13.50 (*0-06-097359-5*, PL) HarpC.

Seraphic Love: Some Motives & Incentives to the Love of God. Robert Boyle. 176p. 1992. reprint ed. pap. 16.95 (*1-56459-008-9*) Kessinger Pub.

Seraphim Kill: A Lt. Abe Rainfinch Mystery. P. B. Shaw. LC 93-37915. 224p. 1994. 21.95 (*0-8027-3181-3*) Walker & Co.

Seraphim of Sarov see St. Seraphim of Sarov

***Seraphim Rising.** Elisabeth Devos. 1997. mass mkt. 5.99 (*0-451-45655-6*, ROC) NAL-Dutton.

Seraphim's Seraphim: The Life of Pelagia Ivanovna Serebrenikova, Fool for Christ's Sake of the Seraphim-Diveyevo Convent. Tr. by Holy Transfiguration Monastery Staff from RUS. LC 79-90720. (Illus.). 184p. (Orig.). 1980. pap. 4.50 (*0-913026-08-5*) St Nectarios.

Seraphina. Jean Merrill. 224p. (Orig.). 1980. pap. 1.75 (*0-449-50124-8*, Coventry) Fawcett.

Seraphita. Honore De Balzac. LC 73-134961. (Short Story Index Reprint Ser.). 1980. 20.95 (*0-8369-3691-4*) Ayer.

Seraphita. Honore De Balzac. 172p. (FRE.). 1986. pap. 29.95 (*0-7859-4756-6*, M2149) Fr & Eur.

Serapion von Thmuis: Echte und Unechte Schriften Sowie die Zeugnisse des Athanasius und Anderer. Klaus Fitschen. (Patristische Texte und Studien: No. 37). xii, 220p. (GER.). (C). 1992. lib. bdg. 83.10 (3-11-012886-1) De Gruyter.

***Seras Lo Que Quieras Ser.** Robert Schuller. (SPA.). pap. 7.95 (0-8297-0514-7) Life Pubs Intl.

Seras Tu el Lider Que Dios Necesita? Guia de Bolsillo. Jorge A. Ovando. (Guia de Bolsillo Ser.). 120p. (SPA.). 1990. pap. 2.49 (1-56063-017-5, 498054) Editorial Unilit.

SERB Official Reporter. 1994. 379.00 (0-8322-0601-6) Banks-Baldwin.

SERB Official Reporter Full Set 1984-1994, Set. 1993. Full set (1984-1994). 1,100.00 (0-318-69421-2) Banks-Baldwin.

Serber Says: About Nuclear Physics. Robert Serber. (Lecture Notes in Physics Ser.: Vol. 10). 308p. 1987. text ed. 70.00 (9971-5-0158-9); pap. text ed. 37.00 (9971-5-0376-X) World Scientific Pub.

Serbia: The Rise & Fall of a Medieval Empire. Thomas Durham. 152p. (C). 1989. pap. 25.00 (1-85072-060-6, Pub. by W Sessions UK) St Mut.

Serbian-Croation-English Maritime Dictionary. B. Pricard. 285p. 1989. 42.25 (86-03-00362-9) IBD Ltd.

Serbian Diaries. Boris L. Davidovich. 1996. pap. 14.95 (0-85449-222-4, Pub. by Gay Mens Pr UK) LPC InBook.

***Serbian-English/English-Serbian Concise Dictionary.** LC 97-10030. 400p. 1997. pap. 14.95 (0-7818-0556-2, 326) Hippocrene Bks.

Serbian Folklore. Elodie L. Mijatovic. Ed. by W. Denton. LC 68-56477. 1972. reprint ed. 24.95 (0-405-08788-8, Pub. by Blom Pubns UK) Ayer.

Serbian Golgotha: Kosovo, 1389. Thomas A. Emmert. (East European Monographs). 240p. 1990. text ed. 60.00 (0-88033-175-5) Col U Pr.

Serbian Poetry from the Beginnings to the Present: An Historical Anthology. Milne Holton & Vasa D. Mihailovich. LC 88-50322. (Yale Russian & East European Publications: No. 11). 472p. 1989. 20.00 (0-936586-11-7) Yale Russian.

***Serbian Politics in Croatia: 1903-1914.** Nicholas J. Miller. LC 97-4821. (Series in Russian & East European Studies). (Illus.). 280p. 1997. text ed. 45.00 (0-8229-3989-4) U of Pittsburgh Pr.

Serbian Village in Historical Perspective. Joel M. Halpern & Barbara K. Halpern. (George & Louise Spindler Case Studies in Cultural Anthropology). (Illus.). 156p. (C). 1983. reprint ed. pap. text ed. 7.95 (0-8290-0585-4) Irvington.

Serbia's Historical Heritage, No. 347. Ed. by Alex N. Dragnich. 180p. 1994. text ed. 37.00 (0-88033-244-1) Col U Pr.

***Serbia's Secret War: Propaganda & the Deceit of History.** Philip J. Cohen. LC 95-46662. (Eastern European Studies: Vol. 2). (Illus.). 264p. (Orig.). (C). 1997. pap. 15.95 (0-89096-760-1) Tex A&M Univ Pr.

Serbo Croat. (Hugo's Phrasebks.). 128p. (Orig.). 1989. pap. 4.95 (0-85285-140-5) Hunter NJ.

Serbo-Croate Sans Peine: Serbo-Croatian for French Speakers. Assimil Staff. (FRE & SER.). 28.95 (0-8288-4377-5, F40076); audio 125.00 (0-685-53038-8) Fr & Eur.

Serbo-Croatian. (Handy Dictionaries Ser.). 120p. (Orig.). 1991. pap. 8.95 (0-87052-051-2) Hippocrene Bks.

Serbo-Croatian - English, English - Serbo-Croatian Dictionary. Nicholas Awde. 400p. (Orig.). (CRO, ENG & SER.). 1996. pap. 16.95 (0-7818-0445-0) Hippocrene Bks.

Serbo-Croatian Basic Course, Vol. I. Foreign Service Institute Staff. 633p. (CRO & SER.). 1980. pap. text ed. 195.00 incl. audio (0-88432-042-1, AFY601) Audio-Forum.

Serbo-Croatian Basic Course, Vol. II. Foreign Service Institute Staff. 677p. 1981. pap. text ed. 245.00 incl. audio (0-88432-101-0, AFY650) Audio-Forum.

Serbo-Croatian Dictionary of Business and Government. 3rd ed. V. Iver. 235p. (CRO, ENG & SER.). 1993. 37.95 (0-8288-7250-3, F75140) Fr & Eur.

Serbo-Croatian-English - English-Serbo-Croatian Dictionary of Naval Architecture, Mechanical Engineering & Nuclear Energy. L. Bartolic. 275p. 1987. 44.25 (0-88431-555-X) IBD Ltd.

Serbo-Croatian-English Dictionary of Maritime Terms. B. Pricard. 285p. (CRO, ENG & SER.). 1989. 29.95 (0-8288-7251-1, 8603992088) Fr & Eur.

Serbo-Croatian Heroic Songs: Bijelo Polje: Three Texts from Avdo Mededovic, Vol. 3. Ed. by Albert B. Lord & David E. Bynum. (Milman Parry Collection, Texts & Translation Ser.: No. 4). (Illus.). 383p. 1980. 25.00 (0-674-80166-0) HUP.

Serbo-Croatian-Hungarian Concise Dictionary. E. Levasics & M. Suranyi. 848p. 1988. 36.00 (963-205-216-1, Pub. by Akad Kiado HU) St Mut.

Serbo-Croatian Just For You. Biljana Sljivic-Simsic. (OSU Foreign Language Publications: No. 32). (Illus.). 665p. (Orig.). (CRO & SER.). (C). 1985. pap. text ed. 50.00 (0-87415-074-4) OSU Foreign Lang.

Serbo-Croation Heroic Poems from Bihac, Cazin, & Kulen Vakuf. Ed. by David E. Bynum. LC 93-16372. (Milman Parry Studies in Oral Tradition). (Illus.). 832p. 1993. Alk. paper. text ed. 40.00 (0-8153-1236-9) Garland.

Serbocroat-English Dictionary. Nikola Imperl. 280p. (CRO, ENG & SER.). 1991. pap. 49.95 (0-8288-7351-8) Fr & Eur.

Serbocroatian - English Dictionary: Hrvatsko Ili Srpsko-Engelski Rjecnik. Milan Drvodelic. 848p. (ENG & SER.). 1988. 49.95 (0-8288-0503-2, F36830) Fr & Eur.

Serbocroatian - Italian Dictionary: Hrvatsko Ili Srpsko-Talijanski Rjecnik. Deanovic-Jernej. 1068p. (ITA & SER.). 1988. write for info. (0-8288-1639-5, F79210) Fr & Eur.

***SerboCroatian Dictionaries, 2 vols., Set.** 1618p. 1990. text ed. 150.00 (0-521-40071-6) Cambridge U Pr.

Serbocroatian-English - English-Serbocroatian Dictionary. 1985. 42.50 (0-87557-074-7) Saphrograph.

Serbocroatian-English Business Dictionary: Privredno-Poslovni Recnik Srpskohrvatsko-Engleski. Landa Marija. 260p. (ENG & SER.). 1984. 29.95 (0-8288-4414-3, F110100); 24.95 (0-8288-0121-5, F18170) Fr & Eur.

Serbocroatian-English Dictionary. 2nd rev. ed. M. Benson. 769p. (C). 1986. 160.00 (0-685-54145-2, Pub. by Collets) St Mut.

Serbocroatian-English Dictionary. 2nd rev. ed. Morton Benson. 844p. (ENG & SER.). 1990. 125.00 (0-8288-0499-0, M9630) Fr & Eur.

SerboCroatian-English Dictionary. 3rd ed. Ed. by Morton Benson & Biljana Sljivic-Simsic. 844p. (C). 1990. text ed. 85.00 (0-521-38495-8) Cambridge U Pr.

Serbocroatian-English Dictionary: Srpskohrvatsko-Engelski Recnik. 2nd ed. Svetozar Brkic. 416p. (CRO, ENG & SER.). 1990. pap. 29.95 (0-8288-4714-2, M9631) Fr & Eur.

Serbocroatian-English Dictionary of Construction. Branko Vukicevic. 652p. (ENG & SER.). 1984. pap. 75.00 (0-8288-0215-7, F 36380) Fr & Eur.

Serbocroatian-English Dictionary of Mechanical Engineering. Jovan Milicivec. 250p. (ENG & SER.). 1986. 39.95 (0-8288-0656-X, F 14125) Fr & Eur.

Serbocroatian-English Encyclopedic Dictionary: Hrvatsko Ili Srpsko-Engleski Enciclopedijski Rjecnik, 2 vols. Zeljko Bujas. (ENG & SER.). 1983. 95.00 (0-8288-0500-8, F78460) Fr & Eur.

Serbocroatian for Foreigners, Bk. 1. S. Babic. 233p. (C). 1988. 125.00 (0-569-20342-2, Pub. by Collets) St Mut.

Serbocroatian-German Dictionary: Hrvatsko Srpsko-Njemacki Rjenik. Jacik-Hurm. 848p. (GER & SER.). 1984. 49.95 (0-8288-1050-8, F114900) Fr & Eur.

Serbocroatian Heroic Songs: Bihacka Krajina: Epics from Bihac, Cazin, & Kulen Vakuf, Vol. 4. Milman Parry. Ed. by David E. Bynum. (Milman Parry Collection, Texts & Translation Ser.). (Illus.). 529p. (C). 1980. 22.50 (0-674-80165-2) HUP.

Serbocroatian-Hungarian Concise Dictionary. 3rd ed. E. Levasics & M. Suranyi. 848p. (HUN & SER.). 1982. 39.95 (0-8288-1668-9, M 8578) Fr & Eur.

Serbocroatian-Macedonian Dictionary: Srpskohrvatsko-Makedonski Recnik. 446p. (MAC & SER.). 1984. 14.95 (0-8288-1140-7, F78590) Fr & Eur.

Serbocroation Heroic Songs, Vol III: Wedding of Smailagic Meho. Millman Parry. Ed. by Albert B. Lord & David E. Bynum. Tr. by David E. Bynum. 338p. 1974. 22.50 (0-674-80163-6) HUP.

Serbokraotischen Dialekte, Ihre Struktur und Entwicklung. Pavle Ivic. (S P R Ser: No. 18). 1958. text ed. 70.80 (3-10-80073X-5) Mouton.

***Serbs: History, Myth & the Destruction of Yugoslavia.** Tim Judah. LC 96-52212. 1997. write for info. (0-300-07113-2) Yale U Pr.

Serbs & Croats: The Struggle in Yugoslavia. Alex N. Dragnich. LC 92-19786. 1992. 22.95 (0-15-181073-7) HarBrace.

Serbs & Croats: The Struggle in Yugoslavia. Alex N. Dragnich. 1993. pap. 10.95 (0-15-680663-0) HarBrace.

***Serbs & Their Leaders in the Twentieth Century.** Ed. by Peter Radan & Aleksandar Pavkovic. LC 97-16726. 278p. 1997. text ed. 63.95 (1-85521-891-7, Pub. by Ashgate UK) Ashgate Pub Co.

Serbs in the United States & Canada: A Comprehensive Bibliography. 2nd enl. rev. ed. Ed. by Judith Rosenblatt. LC 92-71568. (Bibliography Ser.: No. 1). ix, 193p. 1992. pap. 20.00 (0-932833-12-8) Immig His Res.

***Serca2-Type Ca (2+)-Transport ATPases in the Pig (Sus Scrofa) Isoform Diversity & Regulation by Phospholamban.** Hilde Verboomen. (Acta Biomedica Lovaniensia Ser.: Vol. 106). (Illus.). 89p. (Orig.). 1995. pap. 34.00 (90-6186-666-9, Pub. by Leuven Univ BE) Coronet Bks.

Serce, Krzyz i Karabin (a Heart, a Cross, a Rifle) Stanislaw Dobkowski. 80p. (Orig.). (POL.). 1989. pap. text ed. 9.00 (0-930401-24-7) Artex Pub.

Serebrianyi Gost' O Liricheskom Geroe Bal'monta. Viktor A. Dmitriev. LC 92-4594. 192p. (Orig.). (RUS.). (C). 1992. pap. 15.00 (1-55779-047-7) Hermitage.

Serefina under the Circumstances. Theroux. (J). 1997. 16.00 (0-689-80450-4) S&S Childrens.

Serena Katz. Charlotte Pomerantz. LC 90-48672. (Illus.). 32p. (J). (gr. k-3). 1992. lib. bdg. 13.95 (0-02-774901-0, Mac Bks Young Read) S&S Childrens.

***Serena McKee's Back in Town.** Marie Ferrarella. 1997. mass mkt. 3.99 (0-373-07808-0, 1-07808-8) Silhouette.

Serenade. James M. Cain. 256p. (FRE.). 1983. pap. 11.95 (0-7859-1976-7, 2070374750) Fr & Eur.

Serenade. Bro Halff. 20p. 1989. pap. 25.00 (1-885238-06-1); audio 5.00 (1-885238-07-X) Simpler Gifts.

Serenade. Sandra Kitt. 288p. 1994. mass mkt. 4.99 (0-7860-0024-4, Pinncle Kensgtn) Kensgtn Pub Corp.

Serenade. Bernard Welt. Ed. by Kenward Elmslie. (Orig.). 1980. pap. 5.00 (0-915990-15-6) Z Pr.

***Serenade for Violin & Piano.** Mario Lombardo. Ed. by Thom Proctor. 20p. (Orig.). 1997. pap. text ed. 14.95 (0-7692-0091-5) Warner Brothers.

Serenade of Carols. M. Gould. 88p. 1994. pap. 9.95 (0-7935-3736-3) H Leonard.

Serenade of Fear. Noel Ross-Russell. 256p. 1995. pap. 12.95 (1-871871-21-2) Paul & Co Pubs.

Serenade to the Blue Lady: The Story of Bert Stiles. Robert F. Cooper. LC 92-82993. (Illus.). 256p. (Orig.). 1993. pap. 12.95 (1-879384-21-3) Cypress Hse.

Serenading Louie. Lanford Wilson. 1976. pap. 5.25 (0-8222-1011-8) Dramatists Play.

Serena's Secret. Bryan Strong & Christine DeVault. Ed. by Mary Nelson. (Illus.). (J). (gr. 5-8). 1988. pap. 3.95 (0-941816-32-X) ETR Assocs.

Serendipity. Stephen Cosgrove. LC 94-25575. (Serendipity Ser.). 32p. 1995. 3.95 (0-8431-3819-X) Price Stern Sloan.

Serendipity. Fern Michaels. LC 94-19693. 1994. 22.00 (0-345-39271-X) Ballantine.

Serendipity. Fern Michaels. 1997. mass mkt. 6.99 (0-449-14982-X) Fawcett.

Serendipity: Accidental Discoveries in Science. Royston M. Roberts. LC 88-33638. 270p. 1989. pap. text ed. 16.95 (0-471-60203-5) Wiley.

Serendipity & Synergy: Collection Development, Access & Research Opportunities at the American Antiquarian Society in the McCorison Era. Patricia C. Cohen et al. 61p. 1993. pap. 9.50 (0-944026-40-0) Am Antiquarian.

Serendipity Cookbook: The Best from New York's Incredible Dessert Emporium. Pat Miller et al. LC 94-20351. (Illus.). 1994. 14.95 (0-8065-1541-4, Citadel Pr) Carol Pub Group.

Serendipity Cooks. Marilyn Sparks. 199p. 1995. 16.98 (0-9647031-0-6) Tradits KY.

Serendipity New Testament for Groups: New International Version. rev. ed. Lyman Coleman. 494p. 1990. pap. 11.95 (0-8091-3260-5) Paulist Pr.

Serendipity Stories of Cats & Their People. Esther G. Johnson. LC 93-84614. (Illus.). 112p. (Orig.). 1993. pap. 11.95 (0-9629143-1-2) Skyehill Pubns.

Serene Compassion: A Christian Appreciation of Buddhist Holiness. Denise L. Carmody & John T. Carmody. 144p. 1996. 25.00 (0-19-509969-9) OUP.

Serene Life. A. Pupil. 1981. pap. 2.00 (0-911794-47-6) Aqua Educ.

Serene Reflection Meditation. 6th rev. ed. Order of Buddhist Contemplatives Monks Staff & P. T. Jiyu-Kennett. LC 96-67050. Orig. Title: Zen Meditation. (Illus.). 102p. (Orig.). 1996. pap. 6.00 (0-930066-16-2, B301) Shasta Abbey.

***Serengeti.** rev. ed. William Mulvihill. Ed. by D. Zebrowski. 138p. 1996. pap. 12.00 (0-9645875-4-8) Brickiln Pr.

Serengeti: Dynamics of an Ecosystem. Ed. by A. R. Sinclair & M. Norton-Griffiths. LC 79-10146. (Illus.). 389p. 1984. pap. text ed. 32.95 (0-226-76029-4) U Ch Pr.

Serengeti: Natural Order on the African Plain. Mitsuaki Iwago. LC 87-6393. (Illus.). 380p. 1987. pap. 22.95 (0-87701-432-9) Chronicle Bks.

Serengeti: Natural Order on the African Plain. Mitsuaki Iwago. LC 87-6393. (Illus.). 380p. 1996. 29.95 (0-87701-441-8) Chronicle Bks.

Serengeti II: Dynamics, Management & Conservation of an Ecosystem. Ed. by A. R. Sinclair & Peter Arcese. LC 94-45542. 678p. 1995. pap. text ed. 34.00 (0-226-76032-4); lib. bdg. 90.00 (0-226-76031-6) U Ch Pr.

Serengeti Lion: A Study of Predator-Prey Relations. George B. Schaller. LC 78-180043. (Wildlife Behavior & Ecology Ser.). (Illus.). 496p. 1976. pap. text ed. 27.50 (0-226-73640-7, P661) U Ch Pr.

Serengeti Migration. Lisa Lindblad. LC 93-26338. (Illus.). 40p. (J). (gr. 3-7). 1994. 15.95 (1-56282-668-9); lib. bdg. 15.89 (1-56282-669-7) Hyprn Child.

Serengeti Plain. Terri Willis. LC 94-3022. (Wonders of the World Ser.). 64p. (J). 1994. lib. bdg. 25.68 (0-8114-6368-0) Raintree Steck-V.

Serengeti Wind. Russ Thomas. LC 87-40252. 115p. (Orig.). 1987. pap. 7.95 (1-55523-093-8) Winston-Derek.

***Serenidad.** P. Keller. (SPA.). 5.95 (0-8297-1927-X) Life Pubs Intl.

Serenissima. Erica Jong. 1987. 17.95 (0-685-14254-X) HM.

Serenity. (Pocket Power Ser.). 16p. (Orig.). 1986. pap. 1.25 (0-89486-355-X, 5362B) Hazelden.

Serenity. 1994. pap. text ed. 7.95 (1-55674-149-9) Dugan Pubs Inc.

Serenity. Ariel Books Staff. (Illus.). 80p. 1994. 4.95 (0-8362-3081-7) Andrews & McMeel.

Serenity. Sandra A. Kolinofsky. 1993. 11.95 (0-533-10430-0) Vantage.

Serenity: A Storybook about a Little Native American Girl. Antoinette Saunders. (J). (gr. k-3). Date not set. write for info. (0-614-13813-2) Joy Pubng.

Serenity: Living with Equanimity, Zest, & Fulfilment by Applying the Wisdom of the World's Greatest Thinkers. William Gerber. 464p. (Orig.). 1986. pap. text ed. 36.00 (0-8191-5020-7); lib. bdg. 74.00 (0-8191-5019-3) U Pr of Amer.

***Serenity Book.** Jubilee Staff. 1996. pap. text ed. 5.95 (1-57727-018-5) Jubilee Pub Grp.

Serenity, Courage & Wisdom. Gale T. Richardson. 2p. (J). (ps). 1989. 3.50 (0-9614337-2-8) Poetry Unltd.

Serenity, Courage, & Wisdom: The Enduring Legacy of Reinhold Niebuhr. Henry Clark. LC 94-21482. (Illus.). 208p. (Orig.). 1994. pap. 14.95 (0-8298-1004-8) Pilgrim OH.

Serenity in Crisis: A Preface to Paul de Man, 1939-1960. Ortwin De Graef. LC 92-14721. (Texts & Contexts Ser.). xviii, 242p. 1993. text ed. 35.00 (0-8032-1694-7) U of Nebr Pr.

Serenity in the Storm. Susan Feldhake. (Enduring Faith Ser.: Bk. 7). 288p. 1996. pap. 8.99 (0-310-20261-2) Zondervan.

Serenity Prayer Book. William V. Pietsch. LC 89-46441. 160p. 1992. reprint ed. pap. 12.00 (0-06-250637-4) Harper SF.

Serenity Principle: Finding Inner Peace in Recovery. Joseph Bailey. LC 87-46195. 144p. 1990. pap. 12.00 (0-06-250039-2, PL 4286) Harper SF.

Serenity! Living the Serenity Prayer. Art Fettig. (Illus.). 96p. (Orig.). 1993. pap. 5.95 (0-916927-17-2) Growth Unltd.

***Serenity the Peaceful Dolphin: The Power of the Dream.** Heather L. Smith. (Illus.). 26p. (J). (ps-6). 1997. 24.95 (0-9658770-1-9, 1806) G S Properties.

Serenity to the End: A Collection of Photos & Verse. Christine M. Moyer. (Illus.). 50p. (Orig.). pap. 9.95 (1-886453-02-0) Candleberry Pr.

Serente. Curt Nimuendaju. Tr. by Robert H. Lowie. LC 76-44769. reprint ed. 37.50 (0-404-15873-0) AMS Pr.

Serente. Curt Nimuendaju. Ed. & Tr. by Robert H. Lowie. (Frederick Webb Hodge Publications: No. 4). (Illus.). xii, 106p. 1967. reprint ed. pap. 5.00 (0-916561-58-5) Southwest Mus.

Serf. Josef Winkler. Tr. & Afterword by Michael Mitchell. LC 95-47963. (Studies in Austrian Literature, Culture, & Thought). 306p. (Orig.). 1997. pap. 22.50 (1-57241-024-8) Ariadne CA.

Serf Actor: The Life & Art of Mikhail Shchepkin. Laurence Senelick. LC 83-12593. (Contributions in Drama & Theatre Studies: No. 9). xvi, 305p. 1984. text ed. 55.00 (0-313-22494-3, SSF/, Greenwood Pr) Greenwood.

Serf & State Peasant Agriculture: Kharkov Province, 1842-1861. Zack J. Deal, III. Ed. by Stuart Bruchey. LC 80-2803. (Dissertations in European Economic History Ser.). (Illus.). 1981. lib. bdg. 47.95 (0-405-13987-X) Ayer.

S

Serf Population in Russia: A Statistical Survey According to the Tenth National Census 1858. A. Troynitskii. Tr. by Elaine Herman. 160p. 1982. 21.00 (0-89250-061-1) Orient Res Partners.

Serf, Seigneur, & Sovereign: Agrarian Reform in Eighteenth-Century Bohemia. William E. Wright. LC 66-29653. 227p. reprint ed. pap. 64.70 (0-685-15922-1, 2056205) Bks Demand.

Serfdom & Slavery: Studies in Legal Bondage. Ed. by Michael Bush. 352p. (C). 1996. text ed. 51.95 (0-582-29186-0); pap. text ed. 19.50 (0-582-29185-2) Longman.

Serfdom & Social Control in Russia: Petrovskoe, a Village in Tambov. Stephen L. Hoch. LC 86-6915. (Illus.). x, 232p. (C). 1989. pap. text ed. 11.95 (0-226-34585-8) U Ch Pr.

***Serge Chaloff: A Musical Biography & Discography.** Vladimir Simosko. (Studies in Jazz: No. 29). (Illus.). 208p. 1998. 45.00 (0-8108-3396-4) Scarecrow.

Serge It in an Hour or Less. Cindy Cummins. LC 96-8945. 1996. pap. 14.95 (0-8019-8773-3) Chilton.

Serge Koussevitsky, the Boston Symphony Orchestra & the New American Music. Hugo Leichtentritt. LC 75-41172. reprint ed. 32.50 (0-404-14680-5) AMS Pr.

Serge Koussevitsky, the Boston Symphony Orchestra & the New American Music: Music Book Index. Hugo Leichentritt. 199p. 1993. reprint ed. lib. bdg. 69.00 (0-7812-9636-6) Rprt Serv.

Serge Tousignant: Phases Through Photography. Ed. by Pierre Dessureault. (Illus.). 84p. (C). 1993. pap. 35.00 (0-88884-561-8, Pub. by CN Mus Contemporary Photo CN) U Ch Pr.

Serge-Trotsky Papers: Correspondence & Other Writings. Serge Trotsky. Ed. by D. J. Cotterill. LC 93-51068. (FRE.). (C). 76.00 (0-7453-0515-6, Pub. by Pluto Pr UK) LPC InBook.

Sergeant & Sims on Stamp Duties, Capital Duty & Stamp Duty Reserve Tax. 10th ed. B. J. Sims et al. 1992. 390.00 (0-406-01195-8) MICHIE.

Sergeant & Sims on Stamp Duty. 10th ed. B. J. Sims & R. D. Fulton. 1993. 230.00 (0-406-01220-2) MICHIE.

Sergeant Bridge & Tunnel Authority. Jack Rudman. (Career Examination Ser.: C-732). 1994. pap. 29.95 (0-8373-0732-5) Nat Learn.

Sergeant Gringo. Jack Cummings. 1993. mass mkt. 3.50 (1-55817-744-2, Pinncle Kensgtn) Kensgtn Pub Corp.

Sergeant Gringo. large type ed. Jack Cummings. LC 93-7856. 1993. lib. bdg. 16.95 (1-56054-438-4) Thorndike Pr.

Sergeant Has Four Legs. Betty J. Taber. (Illus.). 104p. 1993. pap. 8.95 (0-932807-86-0) Overmountain Pr.

Sergeant Lamb's America. Robert Graves. 336p. 1995. reprint ed. pap. 13.95 (0-89733-213-X) Academy Chi Pubs.

Sergeant Major, U. S. Marine. Bruce H. Norton & Maurice J. Jacques. 1995. mass mkt. 5.99 (0-8041-1030-1) Ivy Books.

Sergeant Murphy's Busiest Day Ever. (Favorite Sound Story Bks.). (Illus.). 24p. (J). 1995. bds. 9.95 (0-307-70901-9, Golden Pr) Western Pub.

Sergeant Murphy's Busiest Day Ever: Richard Scarry. Richard Scarry. (Golden Sound Story Bks.). (Illus.). 20p. (J). (ps up). 1992. write for info. (0-307-74710-7, 64710, Golden Pr) Western Pub.

Sergeant Ola & His Followers. David Lan. 45p. (C). 1988. pap. 4.95 (0-413-47590-5, A0260, Pub. by Methuen UK) Heinemann.

Sergeant Pepper's Lonely Hearts Club Band: The Beatles. (Illus.). 72p. 1987. per. 14.95 (0-7935-0270-5, HL 00358168) H Leonard.

Sergeant Savage: The Adventures of John Savage: A Man Called Squad Leader. Tom Applegate. (Illus.). 166p. (Orig.). 1996. pap. 16.95 (1-887617-50-7); lib. bdg. 55.00 (1-887617-51-5) St Bart Pr Ltd.

Sergeant Shakespeare. Duff Cooper. LC 76-30696. (Studies in Shakespeare: No. 24). 1977. lib. bdg. 75.00 (0-8383-2152-6) M S G Haskell Hse.

Sergeant, Sheriff's Department. Jack Rudman. (Career Examination Ser.: C-874). 1994. pap. 29.95 (0-8373-0874-7) Nat Learn.

An Asterisk (*) at the beginning of an entry indicates that the title is appearing in BIP for the first time.

Sergeant York: An American Hero. David D. Lee. LC 84-10465. (Illus.). 184p. 1985. 20.00 (*0-8131-1517-5*) U Pr of Ky.

Sergeant/Police Department. Jack Rudman. (Career Examination Ser.: C-733). 1994. pap. 29.95 (*0-8373-0733-3*) Nat Learn.

Sergeant's Assessment Center: A Training Manual for Law Enforcement Officers, Vol. I. NBPA Staff & Armstead. 224p. 1993. per. 19.95 (*0-8403-8713-X*) Kendall-Hunt.

Sergeant's Assessment Center: A Training Manual for Law Enforcement Officers, Vol. II. NBPA Staff & Armstead. 176p. 1993. per. 19.95 (*0-8403-8714-8*) Kendall-Hunt.

Serged Garments in Minutes. Tammy Young & Naomi Baker. LC 92-53148. (New Ser.). (Illus.). 144p. 1992. pap. 16.95 (*0-8019-8354-1*) Chilton.

Sergei Kirov & the Struggle for Soviet Power in the Terek Region, 1917-1918. Richard D. King. (Modern European History Ser.). 430p. 1987. text ed. 15.00 (*0-8240-8056-4*) Garland.

Sergei Koussevitsky & His Epoch. Arthur Lourie. LC 78-121287. reprint ed. 27.50 (*0-404-04036-5*) AMS Pr.

Sergei Koussevitzky & His Epoch. Arthur Lourie. Tr. by S. W. Pring. LC 78-94276. (Select Bibliographies Reprint Ser.). 1977. 26.95 (*0-8369-5050-X*) Ayer.

Sergei M. Eisenstein's Potemkin: A Shot-by-Shot Presentation. David Mayer. (Quality Paperbacks Ser.). (Illus.). 256p. 1990. reprint ed. pap. 12.95 (*0-306-80388-7*) Da Capo.

***Sergei Rachmaninov.** Julian Haylock. (Classic FM Lifelines Ser.). 112p. 1997. 9.95 (*1-85793-944-1*, Pub. by Pavilion UK) Trafalgar.

Sergei Radlov: The Shakespearian Fate of a Soviet Director. David Zolotnitsky. (Russian Theatre Archive Ser.: Vol. 4). 336p. 1996. text ed. 93.00 (*3-7186-5586-1*, ECU72, Harwood Acad Pubs) Gordon & Breach.

Serger Idea Book. 2nd ed. Ann Price & Pati Palmer. (Illus.). 160p. 1991. pap. 19.95 (*0-935278-18-4*) Palmer-Pletsch.

Serger Patchwork Projects: Fast Patchwork Projects on the Serging Machine. rev. ed. Kaye Wood. (Illus.). 40p. pap. 9.95 (*0-944588-15-8*) K Wood.

***Sergio Leone: The Great American Dream of Legendary America.** Oreste De Cornare. (Illus.). 1997. 39.95 (*88-7301-094-6*, Pub. by Gremese Intl IT) Natl Bk Netwk.

Seri. A. L. Kroeber. (Illus.). 60p. 1964. reprint ed. pap. 3.50 (*0-916561-59-3*) Southwest Mus.

Seri. Alfred L. Kroeber. LC 76-43764. (Southwest Museum, Papers: No. 6). reprint ed. 27.50 (*0-404-15619-3*) AMS Pr.

Seri Indians of Sonora, Mexico. rev. ed. Bernice Johnston. 20p. 1980. reprint ed. pap. 25.00 (*0-7837-9234-4*, 2049985) Bks Demand.

Seri Prehistory: The Archaeology of the Central Coast of Sonora, Mexico. Thomas G. Bowen. LC 74-29360. (Anthropological Papers of the University of Arizona: No. 27). 120p. reprint ed. pap. 34.20 (*0-8357-7790-1*, 2036151) Bks Demand.

Serial Bibliographies & Abstracts in History: An Annotated Guide. Compiled by David P. Henige. LC 85-27178. (Bibliographies & Indexes in World History Ser.: No. 2). 234p. 1986. text ed. 55.00 (*0-313-25070-7*, HSE/, Greenwood Pr) Greenwood.

Serial Bibliographies in the Humanities & Social Sciences. Ed. by Richard A. Gray. LC 68-58895. 1969. 29.50 (*0-87650-004-1*) Pierian.

Serial Blood. Alexander Brinton. 320p. 1992. mass mkt. 4.50 (*0-8217-3939-5*, Zebra Kensgtn) Kensgtn Pub Corp.

Serial Changes in Subcutaneous Fat Thicknesses of Children & Adults. Alex F. Roche et al. (Monographs in Pediatrics: Vol. 17). (Illus.). x, 110p. 1982. pap. 63.25 (*3-8055-3496-5*) S Karger.

Serial Communications: A C++ Developer's Guide. Mark Nelson. 400p. (Orig.). 1992. pap. 44.95 incl. disk (*1-55851-281-0*, M&T Books) H Holt & Co.

Serial Composition. Reginald Smith-Brindle. 218p. (YA). (gr. 9 up). 1968. 26.95 (*0-19-311906-4*) OUP.

Serial Composition & Atonality: An Introduction to the Music of Schoenberg, Berg, & Webern. 6th rev. ed. George Perle. (Illus.). 178p. 1991. 35.00 (*0-520-07430-0*) U CA Pr.

Serial Connections: People, Information, & Communication. Ed. by Leigh A. Chatterton & Mary E. Clack. LC 86-32021. (Serials Librarian Ser.: Vol. 11, Nos. 3-4). 200p. 1987. text ed. 29.95 (*0-86656-654-6*) Haworth Pr.

Serial-Data Computation. Stewart G. Smith & Peter B. Denyer. 256p. (C). 1987. lib. bdg. 73.50 (*0-89838-253-X*) Kluwer Ac.

Serial Diversification of Eidetics. Elizabeth Earl. 1991. 8.88 (*0-913412-85-6*) Brandon Hse.

Serial Diversification of Eidetics. Elizabeth Earl. (C). 1991. text ed. 8.88 (*0-913412-60-0*) Brandon Hse.

Serial Holdings Statements at the Summary Level: Recommendations. Ed. by IFLA International Programme for UBC Staff. i, 56p. 1985. reprint ed. pap. 24.00 (*3-598-10965-2*) K G Saur.

Serial Issue Identification: Code & Symbol Guidelines. Joint Committee of the Book Industry Study Group & Book Industry Systems Advisory Committee. (Illus.). 72p. 1992. pap. 7.25 (*0-940016-36-2*) Bk Indus Study.

***Serial Item & Contribution Identifier (SICI)** LC 96-43631. (National Information Standards Ser.). 48p. (Orig.). 1996. pap. 49.00 (*1-880124-28-9*) NISO.

Serial Item & Contribution Identifier (SICI), Z39.56-1991. rev. ed. National Information Standards Organization Staff. LC 95-41627. (National Information Standards Ser.). 41p. 1995. reprint ed. 49.00 (*1-880124-15-7*, 1041-5653) NISO.

Serial Item & Contribution Identifier, 1991. National Information Standards Organization Staff. 1992. 40.00 (*0-88738-943-0*, Z39.56) Transaction Pubs.

Serial Killer Days. David Prill. 208p. 1996. 21.95 (*0-312-14411-3*) St Martin.

***Serial Killers.** Mark Seltzer. 1998. pap. 18.95 (*0-415-91481-7*, Routledge NY) Routledge.

***Serial Killers.** Mark Seltzer. (C). 1998. text ed. 65.00 (*0-415-91480-9*, Routledge NY) Routledge.

Serial Killers. Time-Life Books Editors. Ed. by Laura Foreman. (Illus.). 1992. 12.99 (*0-7835-0000-9*); lib. bdg. 12.99 (*0-7835-0001-7*) Time-Life.

Serial Killers. B. D. Wallace & M. J. Philippus. 145p. (YA). (gr. 7-12). 1991. pap. 6.95 (*1-57515-007-7*) PPI Pubng.

Serial Killers: The Growing Menace. Joel Norris. 272p. 1989. pap. 11.00 (*0-385-26328-7*, Anchor NY) Doubleday.

Serial Killers: The Insatiable Passion. Ed. by David Lester. LC 95-19309. 208p. (Orig.). 1995. pap. 18.95 (*0-914783-77-7*) Charles.

Serial Killers & Mass Murderers. Valarie Jones et al. (True Crime Ser.: Vol. 2). 1993. pap. 4.95 (*1-56060-172-8*) Eclipse Bks.

Serial Murder. Ronald M. Holmes & James DeBurger. (Studies in Crime, Law, & Justice: Vol. 2). 160p. (C). 1987. text ed. 49.95 (*0-8039-2840-8*); pap. text ed. 20.50 (*0-8039-2841-6*) Sage.

Serial Murder: An Elusive Phenomenon. Steven A. Egger. LC 89-70949. 256p. 1990. text ed. 55.00 (*0-275-92986-8*, C2986, Greenwood Pr) Greenwood.

Serial Murderers & Their Victims. 2nd ed. Eric W. Hickey. LC 96-21978. (Contemporary Issues in Crime & Justice Ser.). 299p. (C). 1997. pap. text ed. 25.95 (*0-534-50704-2*) Wadsworth Pub.

Serial Murders. Robert Dolan. LC 97-8598. (Crime, Justice, & Punishment Ser.). (YA). 1997. lib. bdg. 19.95 (*0-7910-4275-8*) Chelsea Hse.

Serial Music: A Classified Bibliography of Writings on 12 Tone & Electronic Music. Ann P. Basart. LC 75-45460. 151p. 1976. reprint ed. text ed. 49.75 (*0-8371-8753-2*, BASM, Greenwood Pr) Greenwood.

Serial Networked Field Instrumentation. J. R. Jordan. LC 95-934. (Measurement Science & Technology Ser.). 238p. 1996. text ed. 71.95 (*0-471-95326-1*) Wiley.

Serial Numbers of U. S. Martial Arms. Franklin B. Mallory. LC 82-63083. 112p. 1983. pap. 15.00 (*0-9603306-1-5*) Springfield Res Serv.

Serial Numbers of U. S. Martial Arms. Franklin B. Mallory. 208p. 1990. pap. 20.00 (*0-9603306-4-X*) Springfield Res Serv.

Serial Numbers of U. S. Martial Arms. Franklin B. Mallory. 320p. 1995. pap. 30.00 (*0-9603306-5-8*) Springfield Res Serv.

Serial Numbers of U. S. Martial Arms, Vol. 2. Franklin B. Mallory. 209p. 1986. pap. 20.00 (*0-9603306-3-1*) Springfield Res Serv.

Serial Publications Available by Exchange: Caribbean Area. Shelley Miller & Gabriela Sonntag-Grigera. (Bibliography & Reference Ser.: No. 36). 48p. (Orig.). 1994. pap. 19.50 (*0-917617-45-2*) SALALM.

Serial Publications Available by Exchange: Mexico, Central America & Panama. Compiled by Shelley Miller. (Bibliography & Reference Ser.: No. 29). vii, 86p. (Orig.). 1992. pap. 22.00 (*0-917617-28-2*) SALALM.

Serial Publications Available by Exchange: Spanish South America. Gabriela Sonntag. (Bibliography & Reference Ser.: No. 37). vii, 182p. (Orig.). 1995. pap. 22.00 (*0-917617-46-0*) SALALM.

Serial Publications Containing Medical Classics. 2nd ed. Lee Ash & Gertrude L. Annan. 1979. 35.00 (*0-9603990-0-3*) Antiquarium.

Serial Reactions Considered As Conditioned Reactions. William M. Lepley. Bd. with Classified Bibliography of Psychodietetics. M. F. Frtiz. ; Development of Alfred Binet's Psychology. E. J. Varon. ; Autistic Gestures, an Experimental Study in Symbolic Movement. M. H. Krout. ; Nightmare Dream. H. Cason. ; Studies in Psychology from Smith College. Ed. by J. J. Gibson. (Psychology Monographs General & Applied: Vol. 46). 1974. reprint ed. 55.00 (*0-8115-1445-5*) Periodicals Srv.

***Serial Sneak Thief.** E. W. Hildick. LC 97-8425. (Felicity Snell Mystery Ser.). (Illus.). 96p. (J). (gr. 3-7). 1997. write for info. (*0-7614-5011-4*) Marshall Cavendish.

Serial Verb Formation in the Dravidian Languages. Sanford B. Steever. 1987. 17.50 (*81-208-0378-7*, Pub. by Motilal Banarsidass II) S Asia.

Serial Verbs: Grammatical, Comparative & Cognitive Approaches. Ed. by Claire Lefebvre. LC 91-7128. (Studies in the Sciences of Language: No. 8). viii, 210p. 1991. pap. 50.00 (*1-55619-384-X*) Benjamins North Am.

***Serialitat in Den Medien.** Endlose Geschichten. (Germanistische Texte und Studien: Vol. 43). viii, 202p. (GER.). 1994. write for info. (*3-487-09799-0*) G Olms Pubs.

Serials & Reference Services. Ed. by Robin Kinder & Bill Katz. LC 90-4305. (Reference Librarian Ser.: Nos. 27 & 28). 457p. (C). 1990. text ed. 59.95 (*0-86656-810-7*) Haworth Pr.

Serials & Their Readers, 1620-1914. Ed. by Robin Myers & Michael Harris. 192p. 1993. 30.00 (*1-873040-20-2*) Oak Knoll.

Serials Automation for Acquisition & Inventory Control: Papers from the Institute, Milwaukee, September 4-5, 1980. American Library Association Staff. Ed. by William G. Potter & Arlene F. Sirkin. LC 81-10798. 191p. reprint ed. pap. 54.50 (*0-7837-5958-4*, 2045758) Bks Demand.

Serials Canada: Aspects of Serials Work in Canadian Libraries. Ed. by Wayne Jones. LC 95-36737. (Serials Librarian Ser.: Vol. 26, Nos. 3 & 4). 166p. 1995. 49.95 (*1-56024-779-7*) Haworth Pr.

Serials Cataloging: The State of the Art. Ed. by Jim E. Cole & Jackie Zajanc. LC 87-2877. (Serials Librarian Ser.: Vol. 12, Nos. 1-2). 184p. 1987. text ed. 49.95 (*0-86656-619-8*) Haworth Pr.

Serials Cataloging No. II: Modern Perspectives & International Developments. Ed. by Jim E. Cole & James W. Williams. LC 92-18492. (Serials Librarian Ser.: Vol. 22, Nos. 1-4). (Illus.). 415p. 1992. lib. bdg. 89.95 (*1-56024-281-7*) Haworth Pr.

Serials Cataloging Handbook: An Illustrative Guide to the Use of AACR2 & L C Rule Interpretations. Carol Leong. 320p. 1989. text ed. 55.00 (*0-8389-0501-3*) ALA.

Serials Collection: Organization & Administration. Ed. by Nancy J. Melin. LC 82-81133. (Current Issues in Serials Management Ser.: No. 1). 168p. 1982. 30.00 (*0-87650-140-4*) Pierian.

Serials Collection Development: Choices & Strategies. Ed. by Sul H. Lee. LC 81-84645. (Library Management Ser.: No. 5). 98p. 1981. 30.00 (*0-87650-136-6*) Pierian.

Serials Control, Vol. I. Ed. by James E. Rush. LC 83-9584. (Library Systems Evaluation Guides Ser.). (Illus.). 194p. 1983. ring bd. 59.50 (*0-912803-01-0*) Rush Assoc.

Serials Directory: An International Reference Book, 5 Vol. Set. 9th ed. Ed. by Leanne Wofford. 8751p. 1995. 339.00 (*0-913956-86-4*) EBSCO.

***Serials Directory: An International Reference Book, 5 vols.** Incl. Vol. I. . 11th ed. (C). 1997. Not sold separately (*1-888751-12-6*); Vol. II. . 11th ed. (C). 1997. Not sold separately (*1-888751-13-4*); Vol. III. . 11th ed. (C). 1997. Not sold separately (*1-888751-14-2*); Vol. IV. . 11th ed. (C). 1997. Not sold separately (*1-888751-15-0*); Vol. V. . 11th ed. (C). 1997. Not sold separately (*1-888751-16-9*); 339.00 (*1-888751-11-8*) EBSCO.

Serials Directory: An International Reference Book, 3 vols., 1. 6th ed. EBSCO Publishing Staff. 1992. write for info. (*0-913956-60-0*) EBSCO.

Serials Directory: An International Reference Book, 3 vols., 2. 6th ed. EBSCO Publishing Staff. 1992. write for info. (*0-913956-61-9*) EBSCO.

Serials Directory: An International Reference Book, 3 vols., 3. 6th ed. EBSCO Publishing Staff. 1992. write for info. (*0-913956-62-7*) EBSCO.

Serials Directory: An International Reference Book, 3 vols., Set. 6th ed. EBSCO Publishing Staff. 1992. 329.00 (*0-913956-59-7*) EBSCO.

Serials Directory: An International Reference Book, 3 vols., Set, Vols. 1-3. 8th rev. ed. Ed. by J. Leanne Wofford. 7790p. 1994. Set. write for info. (*0-913956-68-6*) EBSCO.

Serials Directory: An International Reference Book, Vol. 1. 8th rev. ed. Ed. by J. Leanne Wofford. 2482p. 1994. write for info. (*0-913956-65-1*) EBSCO.

Serials Directory: An International Reference Book, Vol. 2. 8th rev. ed. Ed. by J. Leanne Wofford. 2456p. 1994. write for info. (*0-913956-66-X*) EBSCO.

Serials Directory: An International Reference Book, Vol. 3. 8th rev. ed. Ed. by J. Leanne Wofford. 2161p. 1994. write for info. (*0-913956-67-8*) EBSCO.

Serials Directory Vol. I: An International Reference Book, 5 Vol. Set. Ed. by Leanne Wofford. 8751p. 1995. 339.00 (*0-913956-81-3*) EBSCO.

Serials Directory Vol. II: An International Reference Book, 5 Vol. Set. Ed. by Leanne Wofford. 8751p. 1995. 339.00 (*0-913956-82-1*) EBSCO.

Serials Directory Vol. III: An International Reference Book, 5 Vol. Set. Ed. by Leanne Wofford. 8751p. 1995. 339.00 (*0-913956-83-X*) EBSCO.

Serials Directory Vol. IV: An International Reference Book, 5 Vol. Set. Ed. by Leanne Wofford. 8751p. 1995. 339.00 (*0-913956-84-8*) EBSCO.

Serials Directory Vol. V: An International Reference Book, 5 Vol. Set. 9th ed. Ed. by Leanne Wofford. 8751p. 1995. 339.00 (*0-614-04087-6*) EBSCO.

Serials for Libraries: An Annotated Guide to Continuations, Annuals, Yearbooks, Almanacs, Transactions, Proceedings, Directories, Services. 2nd ed. Diane Sciattara. Ed. by John Ganly. LC 85-4997. 442p. 1985. lib. bdg. 85.00 (*0-918212-85-5*) Neal-Schuman.

Serials Guide to Ethnoart: A Guide to Serial Publications on Visual Arts of Africa, Oceania, & the Americas. Ed. by Eugene C. Burt. LC 90-40202. (Art Reference Collection: No. 11). 416p. 1990. text ed. 69.50 (*0-313-27332-4*, BEM, Greenwood Pr) Greenwood.

Serials in Psychology & Allied Fields. Margaret Tompkins & Norma Shirley. LC 75-38213. 475p. 1976. 22.50 (*0-87875-083-5*) Whitston Pub.

Serials Information Chain: Discussion, Debate, & Dialog. Ed. by Leigh A. Chatterton & Mary E. Clack. LC 87-31063. (Serials Librarian Ser.: Vol. 13, Nos. 2-3). (Illus.). 168p. 1988. text ed. 29.95 (*0-86656-744-5*) Haworth Pr.

Serials Information from Publisher to User: Practice, Programs & Progress Proceedings of the North American Serials Interest Group. Ed. by Leigh A. Chatterton & Mary E. Clack. LC 88-32871. (Serials Librarian Ser.: Vol. 15, Nos. 3-4). (Illus.). 187p. 1988. text ed. 29.95 (*0-86656-894-8*) Haworth Pr.

Serials Librarianship. Ed. by Ross Bourne. LC 81-129419. (Handbooks on Library Practice). 269p. 1980. reprint ed. pap. 76.70 (*0-7837-9275-1*, 2060013) Bks Demand.

Serials Librarianship as an Art: Essays in Honor of Andrew D. Osborn. Ed. by Peter Gellaty. (Serials Librarian Ser.: Vol. 6, Nos. 2-3). 158p. 1982. pap. 15.00 (*0-86656-165-X*) Haworth Pr.

Serials Librarianship in Transition: Issues & Developments. Ed. by Peter Gellatly. LC 85-16439. (Serials Librarian Ser.: Vol. 10, Nos. 1-2). 298p. 1986. text ed. 49.95 (*0-86656-497-7*) Haworth Pr.

Serials-ly Speaking: Essays on Cliffhangers. William C. Cline. LC 93-32499. (Illus.). 271p. 1994. lib. bdg. 32.50 (*0-89950-909-6*) McFarland & Co.

Serials Management: A Practical Guide. Chiou-sen D. Chen. LC 95-17986. (Frontiers of Access to Library Materials: 3). 186p. (Orig.). 1995. pap. 35.00 (*0-8389-0658-3*, 0658-3-2045) ALA.

***Serials Management in Academic Libraries: A Guide to Issues & Practices.** Jean W. Farrington. LC 96-37648. (Greenwood Library Management Collection). 192p. 1997. text ed. 59.95 (*0-313-27378-2*, Greenwood Pr) Greenwood.

Serials Management in Australia & New Zealand: Profile of Excellence. Ed. by Toby Burrows & Philip G. Kent. LC 93-13212. (Australian & New Zealand Journal of Serials Librarianship: Vol. 3, Nos. 3-4). (Illus.). 175p. 1993. lib. bdg. 29.95 (*1-56024-453-4*) Haworth Pr.

***Serials Management in the Electronic Era: Papers in Honor of Peter Gellatly, Founding Editor of The Serials Librarian.** Ed. by Jim E. Cole & James W. Williams. LC 96-38911. (Serials Librarian Ser.: Vol. 29, Nos. 3 & 4). 231p. (C). 1996. 39.95 (*0-7890-0021-0*) Haworth Pr.

Serials on Aging: An Analytical Guide. Compiled by Shirley B. Hesslein. LC 86-14969. (Annotated Bibliographies of Serials: A Subject Approach Ser.: No. 9). 197p. 1986. text ed. 49.95 (*0-313-24709-9*, HSA/, Greenwood Pr) Greenwood.

Serials on British Television. Ellen Baskin. 346p. 1996. 69.96 (*1-85928-015-3*, Pub. by Scolar Pr UK) Ashgate Pub Co.

Serials Partnership: Teamwork, Technology, & Trends. Ed. by Patricia O. Rice & Joyce L. Ogburn. LC 89-28050. (Serials Librarian Ser.: Vol. 17, Nos. 3-4). (Illus.). 208p. 1990. text ed. 29.95 (*0-86656-991-X*) Haworth Pr.

Serials Publishing & Acquisitions in Australia. Ed. by Alfred Gans. LC 94-1510. (Australian & New Zealand Journal of Serials Librarianship: Vol. 4, No. 2). (Illus.). 118p. 1994. 24.95 (*1-56024-660-X*) Haworth Pr.

Serials to the Tenth Power: Traditions, Technology & Transformation. Ed. by Mary A. Sheble & Beth Holley. LC 96-2320. (Serials Librarian Ser.: Vol. 28, Nos. 1-4). 408p. (C). 1996. 49.95 (*1-56024-840-8*) Haworth Pr.

Serian, Tequistlatecan, & Hokan. fac. ed. A. L. Kroeber. (University of California Publications in American Archaeology & Ethnology: Vol. 11: 4). 11p. (C). 1915. reprint ed. pap. text ed. 1.55 (*1-55567-197-7*) Coyote Press.

***Seribus Centura: Building Enterprise Applications with Centura Team Developer 2.0.** David Burke. Ed. by Mark Hunter. (Illus.). 644p. 1997. pap. text ed. 49.99 (*0-9657635-1-X*) Pro Pub WA.

Sericulture & Silk Production: A Handbook. Prabha Shekar & Martin Hardingham. (Small Scale Textiles Ser.). 55p. (Orig.). 1995. pap. 13.50 (*1-85339-317-7*, Pub. by Intermed Tech UK) Women Ink.

Sericulture in India. P. V. Narasaiah. (C). 1992. 34.00 (*81-7024-508-7*, Pub. by Ashish II) S Asia.

***Sericulture Training Manual.** 125p. 1990. 14.00 (*92-5-102904-0*, F9140, Pub. by FAO IT) Bernan Associates.

Serie Illustrada, "Now Age" Incl. Veinte Mille Leguas de Viaje Submarino. Jules Verne. Ed. by Teresa Agnes. Tr. by Rudolf Heller. Orig. Title: Twenty Thousand Leagues Under the Sea. (SPA., Illus.). 64p. 1979. pap. text ed. 3.95 (*0-88301-455-6*); Veinte Mille Leguas de Viaje Submarino. Jules Verne. Ed. by Teresa Agnes. Tr. by Rudolf Heller. Orig. Title: Twenty Thousand Leagues Under the Sea. (SPA., Illus.). 64p. 1979. 1.50 (*0-88301-575-7*); Viaje al Centro de la Tierra. Jules Verne. Ed. by Teresa Agnes. Tr. by Rudolf Heller. Orig. Title: Journey to the Center of the Earth. (SPA., Illus.). 64p. 1979. pap. text ed. 3.95 (*0-88301-456-4*); Viaje al Centro de la Tierra. Jules Verne. Ed. by Teresa Agnes. Tr. by Rudolf Heller. Orig. Title: Journey to the Center of the Earth. (SPA., Illus.). 64p. 1979. 1.50 (*0-88301-576-5*); Moby Dick. Herman Melville. Ed. by Teresa Agnes. Tr. by Rudolf Heller. (SPA., Illus.). 64p. 1979. pap. text ed. 3.95 (*0-88301-454-8*); Moby Dick. Herman Melville. Ed. by Teresa Agnes. Tr. by Rudolf Heller. (SPA., Illus.). 64p. 1979. student ed. 1.50 (*0-88301-574-9*); Isla del Tesoro. Robert Louis Stevenson. Ed. by Teresa Agnes. Tr. by Rudolf Heller. Orig. Title: Treasure Island. (SPA., Illus.). 64p. 1979. pap. text ed. 3.95 (*0-88301-451-3*); Isla del Tesoro. Robert Louis Stevenson. Ed. by Teresa Agnes. Tr. by Rudolf Heller. Orig. Title: Treasure Island. (SPA., Illus.). 64p. 1979. student ed. 1.50 (*0-88301-571-4*); Mejores Cuentos de O. Henry. William S. Porter. Ed. by Teresa Agnes. Tr. by Rudolf Heller. Orig. Title: The Best of O. Henry. (SPA., Illus.). 64p. 1979. pap. text ed. 3.95 (*0-88301-453-X*); Mejores Cuentos de O. Henry. William S. Porter. Ed. by Teresa Agnes. Tr. by Rudolf Heller. Orig. Title: The Best of O. Henry. (SPA., Illus.). 64p. 1979. student ed. 1.50 (*0-88301-573-0*); Huckleberry Finn. Ed. by Teresa Agnes. Tr. by Rudolf Heller. (SPA., Illus.). 64p. 1979. pap. text ed. 3.95 (*0-88301-450-5*); Huckleberry Finn. Ed. by Teresa Agnes. Tr. by Rudolf Heller. (SPA., Illus.). 64p. 1979. student ed. 1.50 (*0-88301-570-6*); Frankenstein. Mary Wollstonecraft Shelley. Ed. by Teresa Agnes. Tr. by Rudolf Heller. (SPA., Illus.). 64p. 1979. pap. text ed. 3.95 (*0-88301-448-3*); Frankenstein. Mary Wollstonecraft Shelley. Ed. by Teresa Agnes. Tr. by Rudolf Heller. (SPA., Illus.). 64p. 1979. student ed. 1.50 (*0-88301-568-4*); Llamado de la Selva. Jack London. Ed. by Teresa Agnes. Tr. by Rudolf Heller. Orig. Title: The Call of the Wild. (SPA., Illus.). 64p. 1979. pap. text ed. 3.95 (*0-88301-452-1*); Llamado de la Selva. Jack London. Ed. by Teresa Agnes. Tr. by Rudolf Heller. Orig. Title: The Call of the Wild. (SPA., Illus.). 64p. 1979. student ed. 1.50 (*0-88301-572-2*); Hombre Invisible. H. G. Wells. Ed. by Teresa Agnes. Tr. by Rudolf Heller. Orig. Title: The Invisible Man. (SPA.,

S

64p. 1979. pap. text ed. 3.95 (*0-88301-449-1*); Hombre Invisible. H. G. Wells. Ed. by Teresa Agnes. Tr. by Rudolf Heller. Orig. Title: The Invisible Man. (SPA., Illus.). 64p. 1979. student ed. 1.50 (*0-88301-569-2*); Extrano Casa de Dr. Jekyll y Mister Hyde. Robert Louis Stevenson. Ed. by Teresa Agnes. Tr. by Rudolf Heller. Orig. Title: Dr. Jekyll & Mr. Hyde. (SPA., Illus.). 64p. 1979. pap. text ed. 3.95 (*0-88301-447-5*); Extrano Casa de Dr. Jekyll y Mister Hyde. Robert Louis Stevenson. Ed. by Teresa Agnes. Tr. by Rudolf Heller. Orig. Title: Dr. Jekyll & Mr. Hyde. (SPA., Illus.). 64p. 1979. student ed. 1.50 (*0-88301-567-6*); Azabache. Anna Sewell. Ed. by Teresa Agnes. Tr. by Rudolf Heller. Orig. Title: Black Beauty. (SPA., Illus.). 64p. 1979. pap. text ed. 3.95 (*0-88301-445-9*); Azabache. Anna Sewell. Ed. by Teresa Agnes. Tr. by Rudolf Heller. Orig. Title: Black Beauty. (SPA., Illus.). 64p. 1979. student ed. 1.50 (*0-88301-565-X*); Dracula. Bram Stoker. Ed. by Teresa Agnes. Tr. by Rudolf Heller. LC 83-5471. (SPA., Illus.). 64p. (Orig.). 1979. pap. text ed. 3.95 (*0-88301-446-7*); Dracula.
Bram Stoker. Ed. by Teresa Agnes. Tr. by Rudolf Heller. LC 83-5471. (SPA., Illus.). 64p. (Orig.). 1979. student ed. 1.50 (*0-88301-566-8*); Illus.). 64p. (Orig.). (SPA.). 1979. Set pap. text ed. write for info. (*0-318-55006-7*) Pendulum Pr.

***Series, Vol. IV.** Ed. by Donna Witzleben. 1062p. (Orig.). 1996. pap. 395.00 (*1-888576-07-3*) North Am Pub Co.

Series & Approximation. N. K. Bari et al. (Translations Ser.: Series 1, Vol. 3). 391p. 1962. 35.00 (*0-8218-1603-9*, TRANS1/3) Am Math.

Series Approximation Methods in Statistics. John E. Kolassa. LC 94-3109. (Lecture Notes in Statistics Ser.: Vol. 88). (Illus.). 160p. 1994. pap. 39.00 (*0-387-94277-7*) Spr-Verlag.

***Series Approximation Methods in Statistics.** 2nd ed. J. E. Kolassa. LC 97-20556. (Lecture Notes in Statistics Ser.: Vol. 127). 172p. 1997. pap. 34.95 (*0-387-98224-8*) Spr-Verlag.

Series Books & the Media: or This Isn't All. David Farah & Ilana Nash. 404p. 1996. spiral bd. 67.95 (*0-9639949-7-2*) SynSine Pr.

Series Eighty Software Catalog. 4th ed. Hewlett-Packard Company Staff. 15.95 (*0-317-13082-X*) P-H.

Series Foundation Volume see Philosophy for Young Thinkers Program

Series I see Piano Music of Robert Schumann

***Series in Banach Spaces: Conditional & Unconditional Convergence.** M. I. Kadets & V. M. Kadets. LC 97-6600. (Operator Theory, Advances, & Applications Ser.). 1997. write for info. (*0-8176-5401-1*); write for info. (*3-7643-5401-1*) Birkhauser.

Series in Mathematics Modules, 5 Modules. Leon J. Ablon et al. 1981. pap. 9.75 (*0-685-42003-5*) Addison-Wesley.

Series in Mathematics Modules, 5 Modules, Module 1. Leon J. Ablon et al. 1981. pap. text ed. 8.95 (*0-8053-0131-3*) Addison-Wesley.

Series in Mathematics Modules, 5 Modules, Module 2. Leon J. Ablon et al. 1981. pap. text ed. 8.95 (*0-8053-0132-1*) Addison-Wesley.

Series in Mathematics Modules, 5 Modules, Module 3. Helen B. Siner et al. 1981. pap. text ed. 8.95 (*0-8053-0133-X*) Addison-Wesley.

Series in Mathematics Modules, 5 Modules, Module 4. Leon J. Ablon et al. 1981. pap. text ed. 8.95 (*0-8053-0134-8*) Addison-Wesley.

Series in Mathematics Modules, 5 Modules, Module 5. Leon J. Ablon et al. 1981. pap. text ed. 8.95 (*0-8053-0135-6*) Addison-Wesley.

Series in Medicinal Chemistry Handbook Chemotherapeutic Agents, No. 2. M. Verderame. LC 84-24410. reprint ed. 366.00 (*0-8493-3285-0*, CRC Reprint) Franklin.

Series in Radiation Meaurement & Protection, No. 2. A. Brodsky. LC 78-10558. 1982. reprint ed. 781.00 (*0-8493-3750-X*, CRC Reprint) Franklin.

Series Index, Vol. 1. Campbell. (C). 1995. 100.00 (*0-8147-1490-0*) NYU Pr.

Series Index, Vol. 2. Campbell. (C). 1995. 100.00 (*0-8147-1491-9*) NYU Pr.

Series Index see Encyclopedia of World Geography

***Series Master Reference.** (Olympic Century Ser.). (Illus.). 1997. 21.95 (*1-888383-24-0*, Wrld Spt) Wld Sport Resch.

Series of Etchings: Chiefly of Views in Scotland. John Clerk. Ed. by David Laing. LC 72-963. (Bannatyne Club, Edinburgh. Publications: No. 98). reprint ed. 110.00 (*0-404-52854-6*) AMS Pr.

Series of Irregular Observations. R. Azencott & D. Dacunha-Castelle. Tr. by D. McHale from FRE. (Applied Probability Ser.). 250p. 1986. 65.95 (*0-387-96263-8*) Spr-Verlag.

Series of Lectures on Social Justice. C. E. Coughlin. LC 71-173652. (FDR & the Era of the New Deal Ser.). 242p. 1971. reprint ed. lib. bdg. 32.50 (*0-306-70373-4*) Da Capo.

Series of Letters Between Mrs. Elizabeth Carter & Miss Catherine Talbot from the Year 1741 to 1770, 4 vols, Set. Elizabeth Carter. reprint ed. 295.00 (*0-404-56730-4*) AMS Pr.

Series of Old Welsh Texts, 11 vols. in 14, Set. Ed. by John Rhys & John G. Evans. reprint ed. 600.00 (*0-404-60580-X*) AMS Pr.

Series of Plays. Joanna Baillie. LC 90-36661. 424p. 1990. reprint ed. 65.00 (*1-85477-035-7*, Pub. by Woodstock Bks UK) Cassell.

Series of Public Issues, No. 3. Lawrence C. Wolken. Ed. by Pejovich Svetozar & Janet G. Joyce. Orig. Title: Japan: The Modernization of Ancient Culture. 1983. pap. 2.00 (*0-86599-012-3*) PERC.

***Series of Revisions of Apocynaceae, Vol. XVI-XVIII.** A. J. Leeuwenberg. (Wageningen Agricultural University Papers: No. 85-2). 83p. 1985. pap. 45.00 (*90-6754-064-1*, Pub. by Backhuys Pubs NE) Balogh.

***Series of Revisions of Apocynaceae Vol. XXIV: A Revision of the Tribe Ambelaniea (Apocynaceae-Plumerioldeae)** J. L. Zarucchi. (Wageningen Agricultural University Papers: No. 87-1). 106p. 1988. pap. 40.00 (*90-6754-100-1*, Pub. by Backhuys Pubs NE) Balogh.

***Series of Revisions of Apocynaceae Vol. XXVI: A Revision of Cleghornia Wight, Sindechites Oliv. & Epigynum Chinese Merr (Apocynaceae)** Xu Zhaoran. (Wageningen Agricultural University Papers: No. 88-6). 35p. 1988. pap. 15.00 (*90-6754-145-1*, Pub. by Backhuys Pubs NE) Balogh.

***Series of Revisions of Apocynaceae Vol. XXXIV: The African Species of Landolphia P. Beauv.** Ed. by J. G. Persoon et al. (Wageningen Agricultural University Papers: No. 92-2). 250p. 1992. 85.00 (*90-6754-234-2*, Pub. by Backhuys Pubs NE) Balogh.

***Series of Revisions of Apocynaceae Vols. XXXVII, XXXVIII: Pollination of Apocynaceae.** Ed. by A. J. Leeuwenberg. (Wageningen Agricultural University Papers: No. 94-3). (Illus.). 81p. 1994. pap. 32.00 (*90-6754-361-6*, Pub. by Backhuys Pubs NE) Balogh.

Series of Slides for the Atlas of Histopathology of the Cervix Uteri. Gisela Dallenbach-Hellweg & Hemming Poulsen. 1992. 224.00 incl. sl. (*0-387-92119-2*) Spr-Verlag.

Series on Environment & Development. Ed. by Dennis Conway & Victoria Cuffel. 579p. 1992. pap. 25.00 (*1-881157-15-6*) In Ctr Global.

Series on Nursing Administration, Vol. 3. Joyce Y. Johnson & McCloskey. Ed. by Debra Hunter. (C). 1990. text ed. write for info. (*0-201-12937-X*) Addison-Wesley.

Series on Public Issues, No. 2. S. Charles Maurice & Jane Hobson. Ed. by Svetozar Pejovich. Orig. Title: Minimum Wage Law: Who Benefits, Who Loses?. 1983. pap. 2.00 (*0-86599-009-3*) PERC.

Series One see Poet's Translation Series

Series Seven Made Ridiculously Simple. Martin Torosian. 1987. 150.00 (*0-9603592-3-0*) MTA Financial Servs.

Series Seven Typing Complete Course, Gregg Typing. Alan C. Lloyd et al. 496p. (gr. 11-12). 1982. text ed. 27.96 (*0-07-038280-8*) McGraw.

Series Showdown. Mark Freeman. (Rookies Ser.: No. 6). 144p. (J). 1989. mass mkt. 4.99 (*0-345-35907-0*) Ballantine.

Series Sixty-Two Exam Preparations. Eric L. Reiner. 184p. (Orig.). 1989. pap. text ed. 69.95 (*0-932889-10-7*) Examco Inc.

Series Summa Izbu. E. V. Leichty. LC 66-25697. 38.00 (*0-685-71732-1*) J J Augustin.

Series Two see Poet's Translation Series

Series 2 see Piano Music of Robert Schumann

Series 32000, Programmer's Reference Manual. National Semiconductor Staff. (Illus.). 323p. 1987. pap. 31.95 (*0-13-806936-0*) P-H.

Series/Parallel Circuits. Bergwall. (Electronics Technology Ser.). 1991. 95.00 (*0-8273-4819-3*) Van Nos Reinhold.

Serigamy of Stories. Kathryn T. Windham. LC 88-5461. (Muscadine Bk.). (Illus.). 130p. 1988. 16.95 (*0-87805-354-9*) U Pr of Miss.

***Serigraphs of Doug West.** Joseph Dispenza. Ed. by Camille Flores-Turney. (Artist Ser.). (Illus.). 67p. 1995. pap. text ed. 40.00 (*0-937206-41-5*) New Mexico Mag.

***Serigraphs of Doug West.** Joseph Dispenza. Ed. by Camille Flores-Turney. (Artist Ser.). (Illus.). 67p. 1995. text ed. 190.00 (*0-937206-42-3*) New Mexico Mag.

Serine Proteases & Their Serpin Inhibitors in the Nervous System: Regulation in Development & in Degenerative & Malignant Disease. Ed. by B. W. Festoff. (NATO ASI Series A, Life Sciences: Vol. 191). (Illus.). 384p. 1990. 120.00 (*0-306-43584-5*, Plenum Pr) Plenum.

Serine/Threonine Kinases & the Signal Transduction of Mitogenic, Cytotoxic & Chemotactic Factors. J. Van Lint. No. 86. 115p. (Orig.). 1994. pap. 33.50 (*90-6186-621-9*, Pub. by Leuven Univ BE) Coronet Bks.

Serious & Unstable Condition: Financing America's Health Care. Henry J. Aaron. 158p. 1991. 32.95 (*0-8157-0051-2*) Brookings.

Serious & Unstable Condition: Financing America's Health Care. Henry J. Aaron. 158p. 1992. pap. 12.95 (*0-8157-0050-4*) Brookings.

Serious Art. John Passmore. 302p. (C). 1991. 49.95 (*0-8126-9181-4*) Open Court.

Serious Breach of National Security As Occurred: Some Game!!! (Analysis Ser.: No. 9). 1982. pap. 10.00 (*0-686-42844-7*) Inst Analysis.

***Serious Business: The Art & Commerce of Animation in America.** Stefan Kanfer. LC 96-37819. 256p. 1997. 30.00 (*0-684-80079-9*, Scrbnr) Scribnrs Ref.

Serious Business of Growing Up: A Study of Children's Lives Outside School. Elliott A. Medrich et al. LC 81-7650. 412p. 1981. pap. 14.00 (*0-520-05071-1*) U CA Pr.

Serious Business of Growing Up: A Study of Children's Lives Outside School. Elliott A. Medrich et al. LC 81-7630. 419p. reprint ed. pap. 119.50 (*0-7837-4754-3*, 2044501) Bks Demand.

Serious Call to a Contemplative Lifestyle. rev. ed. E. Glenn Hinson. 98p. (C). 1993. pap. 9.95 (*1-880837-40-4*) Smyth & Helwys.

***Serious Call to a Devout.** (Great Devotional Classics Ser.). pap. 1.85 (*0-687-61045-1*) Abingdon.

***Serious Call to a Devout & Holy Life.** Law. pap. 2.00 (*0-8358-0061-X*) Upper Room Bks.

Serious Call to a Devout & Holy Life. William Law. LC 82-80470. (Treasures from the Spiritual Classics Ser.). 64p. 1982. reprint ed. pap. 3.95 (*0-8192-1306-3*) Morehouse Pub.

Serious Call to a Devout & Holy Life. William Law. Ed. by John Meister et al. LC 55-5330. 156p. 1968. reprint ed. pap. 10.00 (*0-664-24833-0*, Westminster) Westminster John Knox.

Serious Composer, Vol. 4: The Larger Forms of Musical Composition. rev. ed. Percy Goetschius. Ed. by Peter L. Alexander. (Illus.). 303p. (C). 1988. pap. text ed. 31.95 (*0-939067-71-4*) Alexander Pub.

Serious Concerns. Wendy Cope. 96p. 1993. pap. 8.95 (*0-571-16705-5*) Faber & Faber.

Serious Creativity: Using the Power of Lateral Thinking to Create New Ideas. Edward De Bono. LC 91-58498. (Illus.). 352p. 1993. pap. 14.00 (*0-88730-635-7*) Harper Busn.

***Serious Crime Community & the Underground Economy: A Postscript.** Alan A. Block. LC 97-20175. 1997. pap. write for info. (*1-56000-971-3*) Transaction Pubs.

Serious Crimes. Laurence Gough. Date not set. pap. write for info. (*0-670-83675-3*) Viking Penguin.

Serious Cycling. Edmund R. Burke. LC 94-17276. (Illus.). 272p. 1994. pap. 18.95 (*0-87322-759-X*, PBUR0759) Human Kinetics.

Serious Cycling for Beginners. 1977. pap. 4.95 (*0-02-499760-9*, Macmillan Coll) P-H.

Serious Daring from Within: Female Narrative Strategies in Eudora Welty's Novels. Franziska Gygax. LC 90-2732. (Contributions in Women's Studies: No. 114). 176p. 1990. text ed. 49.95 (*0-313-26865-7*, GFF/, Greenwood Pr) Greenwood.

Serious Disappointment: The Battle of Aubers Ridge, 1915, & the Subsequent Munitions Scandal. Adrian Bristow. 202p. 1995. 47.50 (*0-85052-462-8*, Pub. by L Cooper Bks UK) Trans-Atl Phila.

Serious Fraud: Investigation & Trial. David N. Kirk & Anthony J. Woodcock. 1992. 180.00 (*0-406-00366-1*) MICHIE.

Serious Fun. rev. ed. David R. Veerman. 252p. 1995. pap. 15.99 (*1-56476-498-2*, 6-3498, Victor Bks) Chariot Victor.

Serious Fun: A History of Spectator Sport in the U. S. S. R. Robert Edelman. LC 92-23762. 320p. 1993. 27.50 (*0-19-507948-5*) OUP.

Serious Fun: An Amazing Collection of Things Children Can Do & Try in Their Free Time. Amity K. Horowitz. LC 88-31064. (Metro Washington Edition Ser.). (Illus.). 203p. (Orig.). 1988. pap. 14.95 (*0-939009-15-3*) EPM Pubns.

Serious Games. Clark C. Abt. LC 86-34021. 196p. (C). 1987. pap. text ed. 21.50 (*0-8191-6148-9*); lib. bdg. 44.00 (*0-8191-6147-0*) U Pr of Amer.

***Serious Gardener: Reliable Roses.** New York Botanical Garden Staff. 1997. pap. 23.00 (*0-609-80086-8*, C P Pubs) Crown Pub Group.

***Serious Gardener: Rock Gardens.** New York Botanical Garden Staff. 1997. pap. 23.00 (*0-609-80087-6*, C P Pubs) Crown Pub Group.

Serious Gardner: Reliable Roses, Bk. 1. 1997. 23.00 (*0-517-59820-5*) Crown Pub Group.

Serious Gardner: Rock Gardens. 1997. 23.00 (*0-517-59822-1*) Crown Pub Group.

***Serious Humor of Harry Golden.** Clarence W. Thomas. LC 96-41173. 218p. 1996. 52.50 (*0-7618-0565-6*); pap. 29.50 (*0-7618-0566-4*) U Pr of Amer.

Serious Hysterics. Ed. by Alison Fell. 224p. (Orig.). 1992. pap. 12.99 (*1-85242-222-X*) Serpents Tail.

***Serious Illness in the Classroom: An Educator's Resource.** Andrea L. Mesec. LC 96-41965. 140p. 1997. pap. text ed. 22.50 (*1-56308-416-3*) Teacher Ideas Pr.

Serious Intent. Margaret Yorke. 272p. 1996. 21.95 (*0-89296-583-5*) Mysterious Pr.

Serious Intent. Margaret Yorke. 288p. 1997. mass mkt. 5.99 (*0-446-40514-0*, Mysterious Paperbk) Warner Bks.

Serious Intent. large type ed. Margaret Yorke. LC 96-5471. 431p. 1996. 22.95 (*0-7862-0690-X*) Thorndike Pr.

Serious Joy. Mark Anderson. LC 90-34156. 64p. (Orig.). 1990. pap. 10.00 (*0-914061-14-3*) Orchises Pr.

Serious Money. Caryl Churchill. (Royal Court Writers Ser.). 112p. (C). 1988. pap. 9.95 (*0-413-16660-0*, A0261, Pub. by Methuen UK) Heinemann.

Serious Money. Caryl Churchill. 114p. 1995. pap. 9.95 (*0-413-64190-2*, AO485, Pub. by Methuen UK) Heinemann.

Serious Money: Fundraising & Contributing in Presidential Nomination Campaigns. Clifford W. Brown, Jr. et al. (Illus.). 240p. (C). 1995. text ed. 54.95 (*0-521-44058-0*); pap. text ed. 19.95 (*0-521-49780-9*) Cambridge U Pr.

Serious Pig: An American Cook in Search of His Roots. John Thorne & Matt L. Thorne. LC 96-5564. 416p. 1996. 27.50 (*0-86547-502-4*, North Pt Pr) FS&G.

Serious Play. Martin Kimeldorf. 192p. 1994. pap. 11.95 (*0-89815-630-0*) Ten Speed Pr.

Serious Play: Creativity & Innovation in Social Work. Ed. by Harold H. Wiessman. LC 89-35206. 288p. 1990. 23.95 (*0-87101-171-9*) Natl Assn Soc Wkrs.

Serious Players in the Primary Classroom: Empowering the Young Child Through Active Learning Experiences. Selma Wassermann. (Early Childhood Education Ser.: No. 27). 264p. (C). 1990. pap. text ed. 18.95 (*0-8077-3030-0*) Tchrs Coll.

Serious Pleasure: Lesbian Erotic Stories & Poetry. Ed. by Sheba Collective Staff. 208p. 1991. reprint ed. 24.95 (*0-939416-46-8*); reprint ed. pap. 9.95 (*0-939416-45-X*) Cleis Pr.

Serious Proposal to the Ladies, Pts. I & II. Mary Astell. Ed. by Patricia Springborg. LC 95-21345. (Pickering Women's Classics Ser.). 240p. Date not set. 39.95 (*1-85196-268-9*, Pub. by Pickering & Chatto UK) Ashgate Pub Co.

Serious Red. Amy B. Sparks. (Cleveland Poets Ser.: Vol. 49). 30p. (Orig.). 1996. pap. 8.00 (*1-880834-24-3*) Cleveland St Univ Poetry Ctr.

Serious Reflections During the Life & Surprising Adventures of Robinson Crusoe, with His Vision of the Angelic World. Daniel Defoe. LC 74-13445. (Illus.). reprint ed. write for info. (*0-404-07913-X*) AMS Pr.

Serious Runner's Handbook. Tom Osler. 1978. pap. 5.95 (*0-02-499770-6*, Macmillan Coll) P-H.

***Serious Sadie.** (Little Monsters Ser.). (J). 1997. write for info. (*0-614-21785-7*, Pub. by Splash UK) Assoc Pubs Grp.

Serious Science. Janice L. Smith. LC 91-130824. (Trophy Chapter Bk.: Vo. 10). (Illus.). 96p. (J). (gr. 1-4). 1996. pap. 3.95 (*0-06-442008-6*, Trophy) HarpC Child Bks.

Serious Science: An Adam Joshua Story. Janice L. Smith. LC 91-30824. (Illus.). 80p. (J). (gr. 1-4). 1993. 12.95 (*0-06-020779-5*); lib. bdg. 12.89 (*0-06-020782-5*) HarpC Child Bks.

Serious Season: Daily Lenten Meldiations for Everyday Christians. Ed. by Roger A. Swenson. LC 86-25876. 116p. (Orig.). 1987. pap. 7.95 (*0-8189-0512-3*) Alba.

Serious Sides of Sex: Sex Medicine, Law, Ethics & Psychology Related to Sexual Behavior. Ed. by Neville Blakemore et al. LC 91-72213. (Illus.). 254p. (Orig.). 1991. pap. 14.95 (*0-9627611-1-7*) Nevbet.

Serious Sportsman Taxidermy for Beginners. Bob Williamson & Ken Edwards. (Illus.). 238p. (C). 1991. pap. text ed. 24.95 (*0-925245-30-5*) WASCO Manufact.

Serious Surveillance for the Private Investigator. Bob Bruno. (Illus.). 96p. 1992. pap. 20.00 (*0-87364-665-7*) Paladin Pr.

Serious Survival Strategies: For Victory. Rod Parsley. 229p. (Orig.). 1992. pap. 9.99 (*1-880244-08-X*) Wrld Harvest Church.

Serious Talk: Science & Religion in Dialogue. John Polkinghorne. LC 95-6976. 128p. 1995. pap. 13.50 (*1-56338-109-5*) TPI PA.

Serious Training for Endurance Athletes. 2nd rev. ed. Rob Sleamaker & Ray Browning. LC 96-6729. Orig. Title: Serious Training for Serious Athletes. (Illus.). 312p. (Orig.). 1996. pap. 15.95 (*0-87322-644-5*, PSLE0644) Human Kinetics.

Serious Training for Serious Athletes see Serious Training for Endurance Athletes

Serious Trouble. Stories. Paul Friedman. LC 85-28843. (Illinois Short Fiction Ser.). 168p. 1986. 14.95 (*0-252-01310-7*) U of Ill Pr.

***Serious Violence: Patterns of Homicide & Assault in America.** 2nd ed. Keith D. Harries. LC 96-31513. (Illus.). 244p. 1997. text ed. 49.95 (*0-398-06718-X*) C C Thomas.

***Serious Violence: Patterns of Homicide & Assault in America.** 2nd ed. Keith D. Harries. LC 96-31513. (Illus.). 244p. (Orig.). 1997. pap. text ed. 34.95 (*0-398-06719-8*) C C Thomas.

***Serious Violent Offenders: Sentencing, Psychiatry/Law Reform.** Ed. by Sally-Anne Gerull & W. Lucas. (Australian Institute Conference Proceedings Ser.: Vol. 19). 276p. 1993. pap. 35.00 (*0-642-19258-8*, Pub. by Aust Inst Criminology) Willow Tree NY.

Serious Whimsey. George J. Seidel. 1987. 35.70 (*0-926725-05-X*) Scaramouche.

Seriously Now... Bill Garner. (Editorial Cartoonists Ser.). (Illus.). 160p. 1995. pap. 8.95 (*1-56554-127-8*) Pelican.

***Seripada.** Irving Davidson. 152p. (Orig.). 1997. mass mkt. 4.99 (*1-55197-756-7*, Pub. by Comnwlth Pub CN) Partners Pubs Grp.

***Serlio on Domestic Architecture.** Sebastiano Serlio. LC 96-48301. (Illus.). 176p. 1996. reprint ed. pap. text ed. 12.95 (*0-486-29352-1*) Dover.

Sermo Lupi Ad Anglos. Ed. by Dorothy Whitelock. 83p. 1977. pap. text ed. 10.95 (*0-85989-071-6*, Pub. by Univ Exeter Pr UK) Northwestern U Pr.

Sermo Lupi Ad Anglos. Wulfstan. Ed. by Dorothy Whitelock. (Old English Ser.). 1967. pap. text ed. 4.95 (*0-89197-575-6*) Irvington.

***Sermon: Dancing the Edge of Mystery.** Eugene L. Lowry. LC 97-6707. 208p. 1997. 19.95 (*0-687-01543-X*) Abingdon.

Sermon a Day Keeps the Devil Away. Bob Jones, III. 208p. (Orig.). 1980. pap. 6.50 (*0-89084-114-4*, 009159) Bob Jones Univ Pr.

Sermon & the African American Literary Imagination. Dolan Hubbard. LC 94-9968. 192p. 1994. text ed. 29.95 (*0-8262-0961-0*) U of Mo Pr.

Sermon & the African American Literary Imagination. Dolan Hubbard. LC 94-9968. 192p. (C). 1994. pap. 14.95 (*0-8262-1087-2*) U of Mo Pr.

***Sermon As Symphony: Preaching the Literary Forms of the New Testament.** Mike Graves. LC 96-49361. 256p. (Orig.). 1997. pap. 18.00 (*0-8170-1257-5*) Judson.

***Sermon-Booster Dramas.** Timothy J. Kurth. 80p. 1997. pap. 15.99 (*0-7644-2016-X*) Group Pub.

Sermon-Conferences of St. Thomas Aquinas on the Apostles' Creed. Ed. by Nicholas R. Ayo. LC 87-40620. 176p. 1989. pap. text ed. 18.50 (*0-268-01729-8*) U of Notre Dame Pr.

Sermon del Monte. J. Dwight Pentecost. 256p. (SPA.). 1995. mass mkt. 5.99 (*0-8254-1555-1*, Edit Portavoz) Kregel.

***Sermon del Monte.** 4th rev. ed. Emmet Fox. LC 83-50247. 233p. (SPA.). 1997. pap. 10.95 (*0-87159-201-0*, 272) Unity Bks.

Sermon del Monte, 1. D. Martyn Lloyd-Jones. 1978. 10.99 (*0-85151-631-9*) Banner of Truth.

Sermon del Monte, 2. D. Martyn Lloyd-Jones. 1978. 7.99 (*0-85151-509-6*) Banner of Truth.

***Sermon del Monte - The Sermon on the Mount.** Illus. by Sixto Ramirez. (Serie Conozca Su Biblia - Know Your Bible Ser.). 149p. (SPA.). 1996. pap. text ed. 5.95 (*1-889505-02-1*) White Wing Pub.

Sermon Eficaz. James D. Crane. 308p. (SPA.). 1991. reprint ed. pap. 8.50 (*0-311-42032-X*) Casa Bautista.

S

***Sermon for Children.** Paul Adams. 1996. 12.95 (*1-55673-971-0*) CSS OH.

Sermon Guides for Preaching in Easter, Ascension, & Pentecost. Ed. by C. W. Burger et al. LC 88-3574. 292p. reprint ed. pap. 83.30 (*0-8357-4358-6*, 2037186) Bks Demand.

Sermon Notebook of Samuel Parris, 1689-1694. Ed. by Kenneth P. Minkema. (Publication: Vol. 66). (Illus.). 322p. (C). 1993. text ed. 50.00 (*0-9620737-1-7*) Colonial MA.

Sermon of a Cynic. William F. Bryant. LC 95-90442. 1996. 16.95 (*0-533-11567-1*) Vantage.

Sermon of Repentance. John Bradford. LC 74-28835. (English Experience Ser.: No. 716). 1975. reprint ed. 25.00 (*90-221-0716-7*) Walter J Johnson.

Sermon on the Decollation of St. John the Baptist, & on Herodias, & on Good & Evil Women. St. John Chrysostom. (Early Slavic Literatures, Studies, Texts, & Seminar Materials: Vol. 3). Orig. Title: V 29 den' mesiatsa avgusta slovo Ioanna Zlatoustogo na useknovenie glavy. 45p. (CHU & GRE.). 1982. reprint ed. pap. 4.00 (*0-933884-23-0*) Berkeley Slavic.

Sermon on the Mount. John Bligh. (C). 1988. 39.00 (*0-85439-118-5*, Pub. by St Paul Pubns UK) St Mut.

Sermon on the Mount. Robert C. Bowman. (Covenant Bible Study Ser.). 48p. (Orig.). 1988. pap. 4.95 (*0-87178-777-6*, 8776) Brethren.

Sermon on the Mount. William D. Davies. 172p. (Orig.). (C). 1966. pap. text ed. 18.95 (*0-521-09384-8*) Cambridge U Pr.

Sermon on the Mount. Robert Guelich. 1991. pap. 16.99 (*0-8499-3310-2*) Word Pub.

Sermon on the Mount. Manly P. Hall. pap. 4.95 (*0-89314-353-7*) Philos Res.

Sermon on the Mount. Clarence Jordan. 1970. pap. 10.00 (*0-8170-0501-3*) Judson.

Sermon on the Mount. John R. Stott. (LifeGuide Bible Studies). 64p. (Orig.). 1987. wbk. ed., pap. 4.99 (*0-8308-1036-6*, 1036) InterVarsity.

Sermon on the Mount. Georg Strecker. 1996. pap. 24.95 (*0-567-29152-9*) Bks Intl VA.

Sermon on the Mount. Carl G. Vaught. LC 86-14500. (SUNY Series in Religious Studies). 217p. (Orig.). (C). 1987. text ed. 16.50 (*0-88706-364-0*) State U NY Pr.

Sermon on the Mount. Ed. by Thomas B. Warren & Garland Elkins. 1982. 16.00 (*0-934916-00-4*) Natl Christian Pr.

Sermon on the Mount. Emmet Fox. 200p. 1991. reprint ed. lib. bdg. 29.95 (*0-89966-770-8*) Buccaneer Bks.

Sermon on the Mount: A Commentary on the Sermon on the Mount, Including the Sermon on the Plain (Matthew 5:3 - 7:27 & Luke 6:20-49) Hans D. Betz. Ed. by Adela Y. Collins. LC 95-5123. (Hermeneia: A Critical & Historical Commentary on the Bible Ser.). 768p. 1995. 79.00 (*0-8006-6031-5*, 1-6031, Fortress Pr) Augsburg Fortress.

Sermon on the Mount: A History of Interpretation & Bibliography. Warren S. Kissinger. LC 75-29031. (American Theological Library Association Monograph: No. 3). 309p. 1975. 32.50 (*0-8108-0843-9*) Scarecrow.

Sermon on the Mount: A Study Guide. T. C. Smith. 128p. (Orig.). 1992. pap. 6.95 (*1-880837-05-6*) Smyth & Helwys.

Sermon on the Mount: An Evangelical Exposition of Matthew 5-7. D. A. Carson. LC 77-93260. 160p. (C). 1990. pap. 8.99 (*0-8010-2480-3*) Baker Bks.

Sermon on the Mount: An Occult View. J. M. Pryse. 1991. lib. bdg. 66.95 (*0-8490-4548-7*) Gordon Pr.

Sermon on the Mount: Daring to Be Different. Stuart Briscoe. (Foundations of the Faith Ser.: No. 4). 192p. 1995. pap. 8.99 (*0-87788-758-6*) Shaw Pubs.

Sermon on the Mount: Kingdom Life in a Fallen World. Sinclair B. Ferguson. 171p. (Orig.). 1987. pap. 7.50 (*0-85151-519-3*) Banner of Truth.

Sermon on the Mount: Studies & Sermons. Ed. by Scott Nash. LC 92-42137. (Kerygma & Church Ser.). 192p. 1992. pap. 8.95 (*1-880837-06-4*) Smyth & Helwys.

Sermon on the Mount: The God Who Understands Me. Gladys Hunt. LC 75-181992. (Fisherman Bible Studyguide Ser.). 87p. 1971. 4.99 (*0-87788-316-5*) Shaw Pubs.

Sermon on the Mount: The Key to Success in Life. Emmet Fox. LC 89-45350. 1989. pap. 10.00 (*0-06-062862-6*, PL) HarpC.

Sermon on the Mount: Utopia or Program for Action? Pinchas Lapide. Tr. by Arlene Swidler from GER. LC 85-29810. 160p. (Orig.). reprint ed. pap. 45.60 (*0-8357-2681-9*, 2040217) Bks Demand.

Sermon on the Mount According to Vedanta. Swami Prabhavananda. 1972. pap. 4.50 (*0-451-62679-6*, Ment) NAL-Dutton.

Sermon on the Mount According to Vedanta. Swami Prabhavananda. LC 64-8660. 127p. 1963. 12.95 (*0-87481-002-7*) Vedanta Pr.

Sermon on the Mount According to Vedanta. Swami Prabhavananda. LC 64-8660. 127p. 1991. pap. 8.95 (*0-87481-050-7*) Vedanta Pr.

Sermon on the Mount & Other Extracts from the New Testament. James M. Pryse. 80p. 1984. reprint ed. spiral bd. 13.50 (*0-7873-0684-3*) Hlth Research.

Sermon on the Mount & Other Selections from the New Testament. Comment by James M. Pryse. 1994. pap. 8.50 (*0-913004-92-8*) Point Loma Pub.

Sermon on the Mount for Modern Living. Thomas L. Seals. 1989. pap. 6.50 (*0-89137-117-6*) Quality Pubns.

Sermon on the Mount, Interpreted by Paramhansa Yogananada. LC 79-91531. 122p. 1980. pap. 14.95 (*0-937134-01-5*) Amrita Found.

Sermon Outlines. W. A. Schultz. 3.95 (*0-88027-092-6*) Firm Foun Pub.

Sermon Outlines for Busy Pastors. Russell E. Spray. (Pulpit Library). 64p. 1989. pap. 4.99 (*0-8010-8294-3*) Baker Bks.

Sermon Outlines for Evangelism. H. Lee Mason. (Sermon Outline Ser.). 48p. (Orig.). (C). 1981. pap. 4.99 (*0-8010-6120-2*) Baker Bks.

Sermon Outlines for Evangelistic Occasions. Al Bryant. LC 91-21641. 64p. 1992. pap. 4.99 (*0-8254-2295-7*) Kregel.

Sermon Outlines for Funeral Services. Ed. by Charles R. Wood. 64p. 1970. pap. 4.99 (*0-8254-4007-6*) Kregel.

Sermon Outlines for Funerals. C. W. Keiningham. (Sermon Outline Ser.). 48p. (Orig.). (C). 1981. pap. 3.99 (*0-8010-5427-3*) Baker Bks.

Sermon Outlines for Funerals, No. 2. C. W. Keiningham. (Sermon Outline Ser.). 48p. (Orig.). 1988. pap. 3.99 (*0-8010-5493-1*) Baker Bks.

Sermon Outlines for Growing Christians. Stephen M. Hooks. Ed. by Sam E. Stone. (Sermon Starters Ser.). 64p. (Orig.). 1996. pap. text ed. 4.99 (*0-7847-0527-5*, 23007) Standard Pub.

Sermon Outlines for Lay Leaders. Al Bryant. LC 95-7843. 64p. 1995. pap. 4.99 (*0-8254-2271-X*) Kregel.

Sermon Outlines for Lent & Easter. Compiled by Charles R. Wood. LC 93-49095. 64p. 1994. pap. 4.99 (*0-8254-4056-4*) Kregel.

Sermon Outlines for Revival Preaching. James H. Bolick. (Pulpit Library). 64p. (C). 1980. pap. 4.99 (*0-8010-0922-7*) Baker Bks.

Sermon Outlines for Seekers. J. Michael Shannon. Ed. by Sam E. Stone. (Sermon Starters Ser.). 64p. (Orig.). 1996. pap. text ed. 4.99 (*0-7847-0525-9*, 23005) Standard Pub.

Sermon Outlines for Special Days. Croft M. Pentz. (Sermon Outline Ser.). 64p. 1986. pap. 3.99 (*0-8010-7046-5*) Baker Bks.

Sermon Outlines for Special Days & Occasions. Ed. by Charles R. Wood. LC 90-38561. 64p. 1970. pap. 4.99 (*0-8254-4006-8*) Kregel.

Sermon Outlines for Special Occasions. Al Bryant. LC 91-39389. 64p. 1992. pap. 4.99 (*0-8254-2195-0*) Kregel.

Sermon Outlines for Weddings & Funerals see Bosquejos de Sermones para Bodas y Funerales

Sermon Outlines for Worship Services. Al Bryant. LC 91-21653. 64p. 1992. pap. 4.99 (*0-8254-2298-1*) Kregel.

***Sermon Outlines from Exodus.** John Phillips. 1996. pap. 9.99 (*0-87213-573-X*) Loizeaux.

***Sermon Outlines from Jeremiah.** John Phillips. 1996. pap. 9.99 (*0-87213-574-8*) Loizeaux.

Sermon Outlines from Proverbs. Charles R. Wood. LC 83-25569. 88p. 1984. pap. 4.99 (*0-8254-4023-8*) Kregel.

Sermon Outlines from the Sermon on the Mount. Charles R. Wood. LC 85-23734. 64p. 1986. pap. 4.99 (*0-8254-4032-7*) Kregel.

Sermon Outlines from the Word. James H. Bolick. (Sermon Outline Ser.). 64p. (Orig.). (C). 1959. pap. 3.99 (*0-8010-0528-0*) Baker Bks.

Sermon Outlines on Bible Characters (New Testament) Al Bryant. LC 91-21655. 64p. 1992. pap. 4.99 (*0-8254-2297-3*) Kregel.

Sermon Outlines on Bible Characters (Old Testament) Al Bryant. LC 91-21654. 64p. 1992. pap. 4.99 (*0-8254-2296-5*) Kregel.

Sermon Outlines on Comfort & Assurance. Compiled by Charles R. Wood. LC 93-49093. 64p. 1994. pap. 4.99 (*0-8254-4059-9*) Kregel.

Sermon Outlines on Ephesians. Floyd Strater. Ed. by Sam E. Stone. (Sermon Starters Ser.). 64p. (Orig.). 1996. pap. text ed. 4.99 (*0-7847-0528-3*, 23008) Standard Pub.

Sermon Outlines on Faith, Hope, & Love. Al Bryant. 64p. 1996. pap. 4.99 (*0-8254-2154-3*) Kregel.

Sermon Outlines on Family & Home. Al Bryant. 64p. 1996. pap. 4.99 (*0-8254-2153-5*) Kregel.

Sermon Outlines on Great Doctrinal Themes. Compiled by Charles R. Wood. LC 93-49096. 64p. 1994. pap. 4.99 (*0-8254-4058-0*) Kregel.

Sermon Outlines on Great Doctrines of the Bible see Bosquejos de Sermones Sobre Temas Doctrinales

Sermon Outlines on Men of the Bible. Charles R. Wood. LC 90-38573. (Charles R. Wood Sermon Outline Ser.). 64p. 1990. pap. 4.99 (*0-8254-3988-4*) Kregel.

Sermon Outlines on Prayer. Al Bryant. LC 91-39390. 64p. 1992. pap. 4.99 (*0-8254-2194-2*) Kregel.

Sermon Outlines on Prayer. Compiled by Charles R. Wood. LC 93-49094. 64p. 1994. pap. 4.99 (*0-8254-4057-2*) Kregel.

Sermon Outlines on Prayer see Bosquejos de Sermones Sobre la Oracion

Sermon Outlines on Prophetic Themes. Compiled by Al Bryant. LC 92-23982. 64p. 1993. pap. 4.99 (*0-8254-2191-8*) Kregel.

Sermon Outlines on Romans. Marshall W. Hayden. Ed. by Sam E. Stone. (Sermon Starters Ser.). 64p. (Orig.). 1996. pap. 4.99 (*0-7847-0526-7*, 23006) Standard Pub.

Sermon Outlines on the Attributes of God. Compiled by Al Bryant. LC 92-23980. 64p. 1993. pap. 4.99 (*0-8254-2188-8*) Kregel.

***Sermon Outlines on the Cross.** Stephen F. Olford. 64p. 1997. pap. 5.99 (*0-8010-9045-8*) Baker Bks.

Sermon Outlines on the Cross of Christ. Compiled by Al Bryant. LC 92-23981. 64p. 1993. 4.99 (*0-8254-2189-6*) Kregel.

Sermon Outlines on the Deeper Life. Al Bryant. LC 91-39391. 64p. 1992. pap. 4.99 (*0-8254-2196-9*) Kregel.

***Sermon Outlines on the Fruit of the Spirit.** Al Bryant. LC 96-30472. 64p. 1996. pap. 4.99 (*0-8254-2155-1*) Kregel.

***Sermon Outlines on the Grace of God.** Al Bryant. LC 96-30470. 64p. 1996. pap. 4.99 (*0-8254-2156-X*) Kregel.

Sermon Outlines on the Great Themes of the Bible. Charles R. Wood. LC 91-27157. 64p. 1991. pap. 4.99 (*0-8254-3992-2*) Kregel.

Sermon Outlines on the Life of Christ. Compiled by Al Bryant. LC 92-26143. 64p. 1993. 4.99 (*0-8254-2186-1*) Kregel.

Sermon Outlines on the Names & Character of God. Charles R. Wood. LC 91-27156. 64p. 1991. pap. 4.99 (*0-8254-3990-6*) Kregel.

Sermon Outlines on the New Birth. Charles R. Wood. LC 91-27155. 64p. 1991. pap. 4.99 (*0-8254-3991-4*) Kregel.

Sermon Outlines on the Psalms. Charles R. Wood. LC 85-23735. 64p. 1986. pap. 4.99 (*0-8254-4033-5*) Kregel.

Sermon Outlines on the Psalms: Pastoral Aids. John Phillips. 1995. pap. 9.99 (*0-87213-677-9*) Loizeaux.

Sermon Outlines on Women of the Bible. Charles R. Wood. LC 90-37992. (Charles R. Wood Sermon Outline Ser.). 64p. 1990. pap. 4.99 (*0-8254-3989-2*) Kregel.

Sermon Preached at Pauls Crosse Touching the Supposed Apostasie of J. King, Late Bishop of London. Henry King. LC 76-57392. (English Experience Ser.: No. 809). 1977. reprint ed. lib. bdg. 15.00 (*90-221-0809-0*) Walter J Johnson.

Sermon Preached upon the Anniversary of the Gunpowder Treason. Jeremy Taylor. LC 78-25673. (English Experience Ser.: No. 354). 64p. 1971. reprint ed. 15.00 (*90-221-0354-4*) Walter J Johnson.

Sermon Starters & Chancel Teasers: Four Short Interludes. Ellen Larabee. (Christian Theatre Ser.). 33p. (Orig.). 1994. pap. 5.95 (*1-57514-132-9*, 1164) Encore Perform Pub.

Sermon Studies on the Epistle: Series C. Ed. by Richard D. Balge. LC 91-61108. 355p. 1991. 23.99 (*0-8100-0381-3*, 15N0530) Northwest Pub.

Sermon Studies on the Epistles: Series A. Ed. by Ernest H. Wendland. LC 86-60185. 400p. 1986. 23.99 (*0-8100-0239-6*, 15N0441) Northwest Pub.

Sermon Studies on the Epistles: Series B. Ed. by Richard D. Balge. LC 98-83035. 332p. 1993. 23.99 (*0-8100-0486-0*, 15N0552) Northwest Pub.

Sermon Studies on the Gospels. Ed. by Ernest H. Wendland. (Series C). 371p. 1982. 23.99 (*0-8100-0149-7*, 15NO378) Northwest Pub.

Sermon Studies on the Gospels: Series A. Ed. by Richard D. Balge. LC 89-60651. 380p. 1989. 23.99 (*0-8100-0312-0*, 15N0484) Northwest Pub.

Sermon Studies on the Gospels: Series B. Ed. by Ernst H. Wendland. LC 87-61580. 392p. 1987. 23.99 (*0-8100-0269-8*, 15N0450) Northwest Pub.

Sermon Studies on the Old Testament. Ed. by Ernest H. Wendland. (Series B). 411p. 1984. 23.99 (*0-8100-0192-6*, 15N0412) Northwest Pub.

Sermon Texts. Ed. by Ernest H. Wendland. 182p. 1984. 17.99 (*0-8100-0186-1*, 15N0409) Northwest Pub.

Sermones Catholici or Homilies of Aelfric: In the Original Anglo-Saxon with an English Version, 2 vols., Set. Benjamin Thorpe. 1983. reprint ed. 193.70 (*3-487-07318-8*) G Olms Pubs.

***Sermones del Ano de Avivamiento.** C. H. Spurgeon. 176p. (SPA.). 1996. reprint ed. pap. 5.50 (*0-85151-711-0*) Banner of Truth.

Sermones para Dias Especiales, Tomo I. Adolfo Robleto. 112p. (SPA.). 1989. reprint ed. 7.50 (*0-311-07009-4*) Casa Bautista.

Sermones para Dias Especiales, Tomo II. Adolfo Robleto. 96p. 1991. reprint ed. 7.50 (*0-311-07011-6*) Casa Bautista.

Sermones Sobre la Obra Salvadora de Cristo. John Calvin. Tr. by Guillermo Kratzig from ENG. 250p. (SPA.). 1988. 15.00 (*0-939125-11-0*) Evangelical Lit.

Sermonette. (Composer's Flute Choir Ser.). 1990. 10.00 (*0-685-32141-X*, 77192) Hansen Ed Mus.

Sermonic Pictures of a Preacher's Soul. 1981. pap. 4.95 (*0-933184-32-8*) Flame Intl.

Sermons. Catharine Berliner. Ed. by Lucille B. Smeeth. 48p. (Orig.). 1987. pap. 10.00 (*0-9612592-4-8*) StarRays Pubs.

Sermons. Ed. by John E. Rotelle. Tr. by Maria Boulding. LC 93-44267. (Augustinian Ser.: Vol. 20). (ENG & LAT.). 1994. 24.00 (*0-941491-60-9*); pap. 16.95 (*0-941491-59-5*) Augustinian Pr.

Sermons. St. Leo the Great. Tr. by Jane P. Freeland & Agnes J. Conway. LC 95-23000. (Fathers of the Church Ser.: Vol. 93). 436p. 1996. 36.95 (*0-8132-0093-8*) Cath U Pr.

Sermons. Hugh Latimer. LC 76-172301. reprint ed. 45.00 (*0-404-03886-7*) AMS Pr.

Sermons. Jonathan Mayhew. LC 76-83429. (Religion in America, Ser. 1). 1975. reprint ed. 21.95 (*0-405-00254-8*) Ayer.

Sermons, 2 vols., Set. Charles E. Coughlin. 1972. 250.00 (*0-8490-1025-X*) Gordon Pr.

Sermons, Vol I, Nos. 1-80. Caesarius of Arles, Saint. Tr. by Mary M. Mueller. LC 56-3628. (Fathers of the Church Ser.: Vol. 31). 375p. 1956. 36.95 (*0-8132-0031-8*) Cath U Pr.

Sermons, Vol. II, Nos. 81-186. Caesarius of Arles, Saint. Tr. by Mary M. Mueller. LC 56-3628. (Fathers of the Church Ser.: Vol. 47). 495p. 1964. 27.95 (*0-8132-0047-4*) Cath U Pr.

Sermons, Vol. III-8. St. Augustine. Ed. by John E. Rotelle. Tr. by Edmund Hill from LAT. (Works of St. Augustine). 348p. 1994. lib. bdg. 39.00 (*1-56548-060-0*) New City.

Sermons, Vol. III-9. St. Augustine. Ed. by John E. Rotelle. Tr. by Edmund Hill from LAT. (Works of St. Augustine). 348p. 1994. lib. bdg. 39.00 (*1-56548-068-6*) New City.

Sermons, Vol. III-10. St. Augustine. Ed. by John E. Rotelle. Tr. by Edmund Hill from LAT. (Works of St. Augustine). 520p. 1995. lib. bdg. 39.00 (*1-56548-028-7*) New City.

Sermons, Vol. III, Nos. 187-238. Caesarius of Arles, Saint. Tr. by Mary M. Mueller. LC 56-3628. (Fathers of the Church Ser.: Vol. 66). 312p. 1973. 19.95 (*0-8132-0066-0*) Cath U Pr.

Sermons, Vol. III/1. St. Augustine. Tr. by Edmund Hill & Matthew O'Connell from LAT. 400p. 1990. 39.00 (*0-911782-75-3*) New City.

Sermons, Vol. III/2. St. Augustine. Tr. by Edmund Hill. 385p. 1990. 39.00 (*0-911782-78-8*) New City.

Sermons, Vol. III/3. St. Augustine. Tr. by Edmund Hill. 520p. 1991. 39.00 (*0-911782-85-0*) New City.

Sermons, Vol. III/4. St. Augustine. Tr. by Edmund Hill. 480p. 1992. 39.00 (*1-56548-000-7*) New City.

Sermons, Vol. III/5. St. Augustine. Ed. by John E. Rotelle. Tr. by Edmund Hill from LAT. (Works of St. Augustine). 376p. 1992. 39.00 (*1-56548-007-4*) New City.

Sermons, Vol. III/6. St. Augustine. Ed. by John E. Rotelle. Tr. by Edmund Hill from LAT. (Works of St. Augustine). 384p. 1993. 39.00 (*1-56548-050-3*) New City.

Sermons, Vol. III/7. St. Augustine. Ed. by John E. Rotelle. Tr. by Edmund Hill from LAT. (Works of St. Augustine). 384p. 1993. 39.00 (*1-56548-059-7*) New City.

Sermons: Looking Toward Easter from Here. Ed. by Henry R. Rust. 54p. (Orig.). 1991. pap. 8.95 (*1-877871-10-9*) Ed Ministries.

Sermons: The Yale Edition of the Works of Samuel Johnson, Vol. 14. Samuel Johnson. Ed. by Jean H. Hagstrum & James Gray. LC 57-918. (Illus.). 1978. 60.00 (*0-300-02104-6*) Yale U Pr.

Sermons, Addresses & Reminiscences & Important Correspondence, with a Picture Gallery of Eminent Ministers & Scholars. Elias C. Morris. Ed. by Edwin S. Gaustad. LC 79-52598. (Baptist Tradition Ser.). (Illus.). 1980. reprint ed. lib. bdg. 30.95 (*0-405-12465-1*) Ayer.

Sermons, Advent. Ed. by John E. Rotelle. Tr. by Maria Boulding. (Augustinian Ser.). (ENG & LAT.). 1994. 24.00 (*0-941491-58-7*); pap. 16.95 (*0-941491-57-9*) Augustinian Pr.

Sermons Alive! 52 Short Dramatic Sketches for Sunday Worship. Paul N. Lessard. Ed. by Rhonda Wray. LC 92-44911. 208p. (Orig.). 1993. pap. 12.95 (*0-916260-95-X*, B132) Meriwether Pub.

Sermons & Addresses, 1853-1891. Daniel A. Payne. LC 70-38458. (Religion in America, Ser. 2). 1976. 21.95 (*0-405-04079-2*) Ayer.

Sermons & Battle Hymns. Ed. by Graham Walker & Tom Gallagher. 1991. text ed. 60.00 (*0-7486-0217-8*, Pub. by Edinburgh U Pr UK) Col U Pr.

Sermons & Cannonballs. LC 81-13594. (Sermon in America: 1620-1800). 1982. reprint ed. 75.00 (*0-8201-1370-0*) Schol Facsimiles.

***Sermons & Discourses, 1723-1729.** Jonathan Edwards & Kenneth P. Minkema. LC 96-28169. (Works of Jonathan Edwards Ser.). 1997. write for info. (*0-300-06841-7*) Yale U Pr.

Sermons & Epistles. Horace. Ed. by John C. Rolfe. (College Classical Ser.). 1977. 32.50 (*0-89241-025-6*) Caratzas.

Sermons & Homilies of the Christ of Elqui by Nicanor Parra. Nicanor Parra. Tr. by Sandra Reyes. LC 84-2187. 120p. 1984. text ed. 19.95 (*0-8262-0451-1*) U of Mo Pr.

Sermons & Illustrations for Every Occasion. Willie W. White. LC 88-71158. 164p. (Orig.). 1988. pap. 6.99 (*0-89900-306-0*) College Pr Pub.

Sermons & Memoirs of Christmas Evans. Christmas Evans. LC 86-7108. 304p. (C). 1986. pap. 12.99 (*0-8254-2522-0*, Kregel Class) Kregel.

Sermons & Rhetoric of Kievan Rus' Tr. by Simon Franklin. (Library of Early Ukrainian Literature: English Translations: Vol. 5). 1991. 17.00 (*0-916458-42-3*) Harvard Ukrainian.

Sermons & Soda Water. John O'Hara. 336p. 1986. pap. 4.95 (*0-88184-271-0*) Carroll & Graf.

Sermons & Soda-Water, 3 Vols, Set. John O'Hara. 1960. 12.50 (*0-394-44480-9*) Random.

Sermons & Speeches of Gerrit Smith. Gerrit Smith. LC 73-82222. (Anti-Slavery Crusade in America Ser.). 1978. reprint ed. 20.95 (*0-405-00660-8*) Ayer.

Sermons de Marcel Pagnol. Marcel Pagnol. Ed. by Calmels. 12.50 (*0-685-37009-7*) Fr & Eur.

Sermons, Easter. Ed. by John E. Rotelle. Tr. by Maria Boulding. (Augustinian Ser.). (ENG & LAT.). 1994. 24.00 (*0-941491-64-1*); pap. 16.95 (*0-941491-63-3*) Augustinian Pr.

***Sermons for Advent - Christmas - Epiphany Based on First Lesson Texts for Cycle C: Where Is God in All This?** Daryl S. Everett. LC 96-46511. (First Lesson Texts for Cycle C Ser.). 88p. (Orig.). 1997. pap. write for info. (*0-7880-1028-X*) CSS OH.

***Sermons for Advent - Christmas - Epiphany Based on Gospel Texts for Cycle C: Deep Joy for a Shallow World.** Richard Wing. LC 97-9973. (Sermons Based on the Gospel Ser.). 112p. (Orig.). 1997. pap. write for info. (*0-7880-1033-6*) CSS OH.

Sermons for All Seasons. Alexander Maclaren. 550p. 1995. reprint ed. 19.99 (*0-529-10481-4*, SFS) World Publng.

Sermons for All Seasons: A Year's Ministry. Alexander Maclaren. Ed. by Zodhiates. (Bible Sermon Ser.: Pulpit Legends Collection). 497p. 1995. 19.99 (*0-89957-207-3*) AMG Pubs.

***Sermons for Church Year Festivals.** Donald L. Deffner. LC 97-2350. 1997. 10.99 (*0-570-04975-X*) Concordia.

Sermons for Eighteen Special Occasions. LC 12-2963. 96p. 1982. pap. 7.95 (*0-570-03870-7*, 12-2963) Concordia.

An Asterisk (*) at the beginning of an entry indicates that the title is appearing in BIP for the first time.

*Sermons for Lent - Easter Based on First Lesson Texts for Cycle C: Returning to God. Douglas Deuel. LC 96-52620. (First Lesson Texts for Cycle C Ser.). 152p. (Orig.). 1997. pap. write for info. (0-7880-1029-8) CSS OH.

*Sermons for Lent - Easter Based on Gospel Texts for Cycle C: Taking the Risk Out of Dying. Lee Griess. LC 96-53601. (Gospel Texts for Cycle C Ser.). 104p. (Orig.). 1997. pap. write for info. (0-7880-1030-1) CSS OH.

*Sermons for Pentecost I Based on First Lesson Texts for Cycle C: How Long Will You Limp? Carlyle R. Stewart, III. LC 96-46505. (First Lesson Texts Ser.). 84p. (Orig.). 1997. pap. write for info. (0-7880-1050-6) CSS OH.

*Sermons for Pentecost I Based on Gospel Texts for Cycle C: Homing in on the Heart. Alexander H. Wales. LC 96-46496. (Sermons Based on the Gospel Texts Ser.). 59p. (Orig.). 1997. pap. write for info. (0-7880-1047-6) CSS OH.

*Sermons for Pentecost II Based on First Lesson Texts for Cycle C: Lord, Send the Wind. James McLemore. LC 96-46506. (First Lesson Texts Ser.). 60p. (Orig.). 1997. pap. write for info. (0-7880-1039-5) CSS OH.

*Sermons for Pentecost II Based on Gospel Texts for Cycle C: All Stirred Up. Richard W. Patt. LC 96-53192. (Sermons Based on the Gospel Texts Ser.). 94p. (Orig.). 1997. pap. write for info. (0-7880-1040-9) CSS OH.

*Sermons for Pentecost III Based on First Lesson Texts for Cycle C: Buying Swamp Land for God. Robert P. Hines. LC 96-46507. (First Lesson Texts for Cycle C Ser.). 76p. (Orig.). 1997. pap. write for info. (0-7880-1034-4) CSS OH.

*Sermons for Pentecost III Based on Gospel Texts for Cycle C: Good News among the Rubble. J. Will Ormond. LC 96-46498. (Sermons Based on the Gospel Text Ser.). 72p. (Orig.). 1997. pap. write for info. (0-7880-1038-7) CSS OH.

Sermons for Sermon Haters. Andre Papineau. LC 91-48019. 184p. (Orig.). 1992. pap. 10.95 (0-89390-229-2) Resource Pubns.

*Sermons for Special Days: Preaching for the Non-Liturgical Calendar. Ed. by Henry R. Rust. 67p. 1992. pap. 10.95 (1-877871-43-5, 3545) Ed Ministries.

*Sermons for Special Days & Occasions. Donald L. Deffner. LC 97-2362. 1997. 10.99 (0-570-04976-8) Concordia.

Sermons for Special Occasions. Charles H. Spurgeon. 256p. 1977. reprint ed. 8.50 (0-551-05573-1) Attic Pr.

Sermons for the Church Year. Anthony M. Coniaris. 1991. pap. 15.95 (0-937032-76-X) Light&Life Pub Co MN.

*Sermons for the City: Fourth Presbyterian Church - Chicago, Illinois. Elam Davies & John M. Buchanan. LC 96-69158. 112p. (Orig.). 1996. pap. 12.95 (1-57736-008-7) Providence Hse.

Sermons for the Seventies. Alfred J. Kolatch. LC 75-164518. 1971. 7.95 (0-8246-0122-X) Jonathan David.

Sermons from the Black Pulpit. Samuel D. Proctor & William D. Watley. 128p. 1984. pap. 11.00 (0-8170-1034-3) Judson.

Sermons from the Mystery Box: Object Lessons for Children. R. Douglas Reinard. 1991. pap. 8.95 (0-687-37534-7) Abingdon.

Sermons in a Monastery: Chapter Talks by Matthew Kelty Ocso, No. 59. Ed. by William O. Paulsell. (Cistercian Studies). 1983. pap. 9.95 (0-87907-958-4) Cistercian Pubns.

Sermons in Science Fiction: The Novels of S. Fowler Wright. Mary S. Weinkauf. Ed. by Michael Burgess. LC 94-36012. (Milford Series: Vol. 51). 128p. 1994. pap. 17.00 (0-89370-280-3); lib. bdg. 27.00 (0-89370-180-7) Borgo Pr.

Sermons in Stone. Susan Allport. 208p. 1994. pap. 12.95 (0-393-31202-X) Norton.

Sermons in Stone. Christopher Munford. (Illus.). 92p. (Orig.). 1993. pap. 8.95 (0-913559-22-9) Birch Brook Pr.

Sermons in Stones. Rajneesh Osho Staff. Ed. by Ma D. Sarito. LC 87-42569. (Mystery School Ser.). 900p. (Orig.). 1987. pap. 9.95 (3-907757-04-1) Osho America.

*Sermons in Stones. 2nd rev. ed. Ernest C. Pollard. LC 97-70354. (Illus.). 260p. 1997. pap. 12.00 (0-9627680-4-9) Inkwell CA.

Sermons in Stones: Science & People. Ernest C. Pollard. LC 92-91167. (Illus.). 218p. (Orig.). 1993. pap. 10.00 (0-9612798-6-9) Woodburn Pr.

Sermons in Stones: Science & People. 2nd rev. ed. Ernest C. Pollard. Ed. by Marjorie B. Giles. LC 97-70354. (Illus.). 260p. 1997. 25.00 (0-9627680-3-0) Inkwell CA.

*Sermons in Verse. Grace Woolsey. 299p. (Orig.). 1996. pap. 9.95 (1-57502-286-9, PO993) Morris Pubng.

Sermons, Lent. Ed. by John E. Rotelle. Tr. by Maria Boulding. (Augustinian Ser.). (ENG & LAT.). 1994. 28.00 (0-941491-62-5); pap. 21.95 (0-941491-61-7) Augustinian Pr.

Sermons of a Buddhist Abbot. Soyen Shaku. 1972. 250.00 (0-8490-1026-8) Gordon Pr.

Sermons of Evangelist Rolfe Barnard, Vol. 3. Compiled by Eulala Bullock. 1984. pap. 4.99 (1-56632-091-7) Revival Lit.

Sermons of Evangelist Rolfe Barnard, 1904-1969, Vol. 1. Charles H. Shofstahl. 52p. (C). 1985. pap. 4.99 (1-56632-086-0) Revival Lit.

Sermons of Evangelist Rolfe Barnard, 1904-1969, Vol. 2. Compiled by Eulala Bullock. 1984. pap. 4.99 (1-56632-087-9) Revival Lit.

Sermons of Henry King, Bishop of Chichester, 1592-1669. Comment & Intro. by Mary Hobbs. LC 89-46292. (Illus.). 336p. 1992. 85.00 (0-8386-3390-0) Fairleigh Dickinson.

Sermons of John Donne: In Ten Volumes, Set. John Donne. Ed. by Evelyn M. Simpson & George R. Potter. LC 52-7179. 4365p. (C). 1984. 495.00 (0-520-05255-2) U CA Pr.

Sermons of Lancelot Andrewes, Vol. 11: Pascal & Pentecost. Marianne Dorman. (C). 1989. text ed. 75.00 (1-85821-014-3, Pub. by Pentland Pr UK) St Mut.

Sermons of Lancelot Andrews, Vol. 1: Nativity, Lentan & Passion. Marianne Dorman. 275p. (C). 1989. text ed. 70.00 (1-872795-77-3, Pub. by Pentland Pr UK) St Mut.

Sermons of Laurence Sterne Vol. 4: The Text. Ed. by Melvyn New. (Florida Edition of the Works of Laurence Sterne: Vol. 4). 424p. (C). 1996. lib. bdg. 49.95 (0-8130-1385-2) U Press Fla.

Sermons of Laurence Sterne Vol. 5: The Notes. Laurence Sterne. Ed. by Melvyn New. (Florida Edition of the Works of Laurence Sterne: Vol. 4-5). (Illus.). 517p. (C). 1996. lib. bdg. 49.95 (0-8130-1386-0) U Press Fla.

Sermons of Liberation. Daniel M. Geslin. 192p. (Orig.). 1995. pap. 13.95 (0-9646547-7-6) Thumb Print.

Sermons of Martin Luther: The Church Postils, 4 vols. Martin Luther. Ed. by John N. Lenker. 3168p. (C). 1996. 120.00 (0-8010-2072-7) Baker Bks.

Sermons of Martin Luther Vol. 3: The House Postils. Martin Luther. Ed. by Eugene F. Klug. LC 96-12327. 1328p. (C). 1996. 100.00 (0-8010-2071-9) Baker Bks.

Sermons of Matthew Mead: Original Sermons on the Jews & Falling into the Hands of the Living God. Matthew Mead. 435p. 1991. reprint ed. 21.95 (1-877611-29-8) Soli Deo Gloria.

Sermons of Metropolitan Philaret of Moscow. pap. 3.95 (0-89981-091-8) Eastern Orthodox.

Sermons of R. M. M'Cheyne. R. M. M'Cheyne. 1985. reprint ed. pap. 7.50 (0-85151-165-1) Banner of Truth.

Sermons of Samuel Davies, 3 vols. Incl. Vol. 3. Sermons of Samuel Davies. Samuel Davies. 660p. 1995. 40.00 (1-57358-026-0); Vol. 1. . William B. Sprague. 667p. 1993. reprint ed. 40.00 (1-877611-67-0); Vol. 2. . Samuel Davies. 672p. 1996. reprint ed. 40.00 (1-877611-94-8); 1995. 120.00 (1-57358-029-5) Soli Deo Gloria.

Sermons of Samuel Davies see Sermons of Samuel Davies

Sermons of St. Alphonsus Liguori for All the Sundays of the Year. Alphonsus De Liguori. LC 82-50894. 408p. 1992. reprint ed. pap. 16.50 (0-89555-193-4) TAN Bks Pubs.

Sermons of St. Francis de Sales for Advent & Christmas. St. Francis de Sales. Ed. by Lewis S. Fiorelli. Tr. by Nuns of the Visitation Staff. LC 87-50748. 135p. 1993. pap. 7.00 (0-89555-261-2) TAN Bks Pubs.

Sermons of St. Francis de Sales for Lent Given in 1622. St. Francis de Sales. Ed. by Lewis S. Fiorelli. Tr. by Nuns of the Visitation Staff. LC 87-50084. 226p. (Orig.). 1990. pap. 12.00 (0-89555-260-4) TAN Bks Pubs.

Sermons of St. Francis de Sales on Our Lady. St. Francis of Sales. Ed. by Lewis S. Fiorelli. LC 85-51662. 197p. 1993. pap. 10.00 (0-89555-259-0) TAN Bks Pubs.

Sermons of St. Francis de Sales on Prayer. Francis De Sales. Ed. by Lewis S. Fiorelli. Tr. by Visitation Nuns. LC 84-52310. 51p. 1985. pap. 4.00 (0-89555-258-2) TAN Bks Pubs.

Sermons of St. Maximus of Turin. Tr. & Anno. by Boniface Ramsey. (Ancient Christian Writers Ser.: No. 50). 1989. 22.95 (0-8091-0423-7) Paulist Pr.

Sermons of the American Revolution see Millennium in America: From the Puritan Migration to the Civil War

Sermons of the Cure of Ars. Marie St. John-Baptist Vianney. 185p. 1995. pap. 12.50 (0-89555-524-7) TAN Bks Pubs.

Sermons of the Log College: Sermons by the Tennents & Their Contemporaries. Gilbert Tennent et al. Ed. by Archibald Alexander. 404p. 1993. reprint ed. 29.95 (1-877611-64-6) Soli Deo Gloria.

Sermons of Thomas Foxcroft of Boston: 1697-1769. Thomas Foxcroft. LC 82-10457. 1983. 50.00 (0-8201-1387-5) Schol Facsimiles.

Sermons of Thomas Watson. rev. ed. Thomas Watson. 745p. 1990. reprint ed. 29.95 (1-877611-23-9) Soli Deo Gloria.

Sermons on Conduct & Manners see Library of American Puritan Writings. The Seventeenth Century: The Seventeenth Century

Sermons on Deuteronomy. John Calvin. Tr. by Arthur Golding from FRE. (Sixteenth-Seventeenth Century Facsimile Editions Ser.). 1408p. 1987. 99.99 (0-85151-511-8) Banner of Truth.

Sermons on Ephesians. John Calvin. 1979. 34.99 (0-85151-170-8) Banner of Truth.

Sermons on Galatians. John Clavin. Tr. by Arthur Golding. 1000p. 49.95 (0-9632557-8-9) Old Paths Pubns.

Sermons on Jeremiah by Jean Calvin. Jean Calvin. Tr. by Blair Reynolds from FRE. LC 90-31837. (Texts & Studies in Religion: Vol. 46). 312p. 1990. lib. bdg. 99.95 (0-88946-835-4) E Mellen.

Sermons on Job. John Calvin. 752p. 1993. reprint ed. 69.99 (0-85151-644-0) Banner of Truth.

Sermons on Micah by Jean Calvin. Jean Calvin. Tr. by Blair Reynolds from FRE. LC 90-30841. (Texts & Studies in Religion: Vol. 47). 468p. 1990. lib. bdg. 109.95 (0-88946-839-7) E Mellen.

Sermons on Revival: Kelvedon. Charles H. Spurgeon. 256p. 1977. reprint ed. 8.50 (0-551-05575-8) Attic Pr.

Sermons on Second Samuel. John Calvin. Tr. by Douglas Kelly. (Illus.). 520p. 1992. 46.99 (0-85151-578-9) Banner of Truth.

Sermons on Shalom. Steve Clapp. 79p. (Orig.). 1982. pap. 8.00 (0-914527-37-1) C-Four Res.

Sermons on Sovereignty (19 Sermons) Charles H. Spurgeon. 256p. 1990. reprint ed. pap. 12.00 (1-56186-223-1) Pilgrim Pubns.

Sermons on Special Days: Preaching Through the Year in the Black Church. William D. Watley. 128p. 1987. pap. 11.00 (0-8170-1089-0) Judson.

*Sermons on the Be-Attitudes: Invitations to the Kingdom of Heaven. John A. Terry. LC 96-38666. 72p. (Orig.). 1997. pap. 8.00 (0-7880-0764-5) CSS OH.

Sermons on the Christian Household. Friedrich E. Schleiermacher. LC 89-49275. (Schleiermacher Studies & Translations: Vol. 3). 1991. lib. bdg. 89.95 (0-88946-360-3) E Mellen.

Sermons on the Final Verses of the Song of Songs, Vol. 2. John Of Ford. Tr. by Wendy M. Beckett from LAT. (Cistercian Fathers Ser.: No. 39). 1982. 21.95 (0-87907-639-9) Cistercian Pubns.

Sermons on the Final Verses of the Song of Songs, Vol. 3. (Cistercian Fathers Ser.: No. 43). 1982. 21.95 (0-87907-643-7) Cistercian Pubns.

Sermons on the Final Verses of the Song of Songs, Vol. 4. John of Ford. (Cistercian Fathers Ser.: No. 44). 1983. 24.95 (0-87907-644-5) Cistercian Pubns.

Sermons on the Final Verses of the Song of Songs, Vol. 5. John of Ford. (Cistercian Fathers Ser.: No. 45). 1983. 24.95 (0-87907-645-3) Cistercian Pubns.

Sermons on the Final Verses of the Song of Songs, Vol. 6. John of Ford. 1984. 26.95 (0-87907-646-1) Cistercian Pubns.

Sermons on the Liturgical Seasons, Saint Augustine. Augustine, Saint. Tr. by Mary S. Muldowney. (Fathers of the Church Ser.: Vol. 38). 471p. 1984. reprint ed. pap. 134.30 (0-7837-9200-X, 2049950) Bks Demand.

Sermons on the Major Holy Days of the Orthodox Church. Anthony M. Coniaris. 1978. pap. 15.95 (0-937032-03-4) Light&Life Pub Co MN.

Sermons on the Miracles. Charles H. Spurgeon. 256p. 1977. reprint ed. 8.50 (0-551-05576-6) Attic Pr.

Sermons on the Parables. Charles H. Spurgeon. 256p. 1977. reprint ed. 8.50 (0-551-05574-X) Attic Pr.

Sermons on the Song of Songs, Vol. 1. Bernard of Clairvaux. (Cistercian Fathers Ser.: No. 4). 1971. pap. 7.00 (0-87907-704-2) Cistercian Pubns.

Sermons on the Word. Edward S. Hyatt. 1970. pap. 12.50 (1-883270-06-5) Swedenborg Assn.

Sermons on Timothy & Titus. John Calvin. 1983. 56.99 (0-85151-374-3) Banner of Truth.

Sermons on United Methodist Beliefs. Kenneth Carder. (Orig.). 1991. pap. 8.95 (0-687-38002-2) Abingdon.

Sermons on Unusual Occasions (44 Short Sermons) Charles H. Spurgeon. 1978. pap. 12.00 (1-56186-213-4) Pilgrim Pubns.

Sermons Preached at the Church of St. Paul the Apostle, New York, During the Year, 1863. Church of St. Paul the Apostle, New York Staff. 1978. 35.95 (0-405-10851-6, 11854) Ayer.

Sermons Preached in the African Protestant Episcopal Church of St. Thomas' Philadelphia. William Douglass. LC 79-157366. (Black Heritage Library Collection). 1977. 24.95 (0-8369-8804-3) Ayer.

Sermons Preached on Plantations to Congregations of Negroes. Alexander Glennie. LC 75-161260. (Black Heritage Library Collection). 1977. reprint ed. 18.95 (0-8369-8819-1) Ayer.

Sermons Preached upon Various Occasions, 8 vols., Set. Robert South. LC 73-175991. reprint ed. 410.00 (0-404-06180-X) AMS Pr.

Sermons, Speeches, Letters on Slavery & Its War 1850-1868. Gilbert Haven. LC 74-82197. (Anti-Slavery Crusade in America Ser.). 1970. reprint ed. 43.95 (0-405-00637-3) Ayer.

Sermons That Demand a Decision. Edward Fudge. pap. 2.50 (0-686-12681-5) E Fudge.

Sermons That Save. Robert R. Taylor. 1984. 10.95 (0-317-16702-2) Firm Foun Pub.

Sermons That Strengthen. Edward Fudge. pap. 2.50 (0-686-12682-3) E Fudge.

Sermons That Work: Ten Prize-Winning Sermons. Contrib. by Robert N. Bellah. 80p. (Orig.). 1991. pap. 2.95 (0-88028-124-3, 1136) Forward Movement.

Sermons That Work, III: Prize Winning Sermons & Addresses, 1993. Pref. by Roger Alling. 136p. (Orig.). 1993. pap. 4.95 (0-88028-144-8, 1226) Forward Movement.

Sermons That Work IV. A. Gary Shilling. 128p. (Orig.). 1994. pap. 4.95 (0-88028-153-7, 1283) Forward Movement.

Sermons That Work V: Distinctive Dimensions in Anglican Preaching. Ed. by Roger Alling & David J. Schlafer. 128p. (Orig.). 1995. pap. 6.95 (0-88028-167-7) Forward Movement.

Sermons to Grow On. Edward Fudge. pap. 2.50 (0-686-12683-1) E Fudge.

Sermons to See & Hear. Benny B. Bristow. 1990. pap. 7.95 (0-89137-624-0) Quality Pubns.

Sermons Very Fruitfull, Godly, & Learned by Roger Edgeworth: Preaching in the Reformation, c. 1535 to c. 1553. Rodger Edgeworth. Ed. by Janet Wilson. 496p. (C). 1993. 117.00 (0-85991-336-8, DS Brewer) Boydell & Brewer.

Sermons Which Spiritually Interpret the Scriptures & Other Writings on Christian Science: A History of Pioneer Steps... Augusta E. Stetson. LC 91-76113. (Illus.). lxv, 1277p. 1992. reprint ed. 40.00 (1-879135-09-4) Emma Pub Soc.

Sermons with Life Sketch. B. H. Carroll. 1986. reprint ed. 19.50 (0-317-47643-2) Church History.

Sermons You Can Preach. W. Herschel Ford. (Simple Sermon Ser.). 384p. 1983. pap. 15.99 (0-310-46971-6, 9833P) Zondervan.

Sermons You Should Preach. J. J. Turner. 1984. pap. 5.95 (0-89137-547-3) Quality Pubns.

Sermons, 1550. Thomas Lever. Ed. by Edward Arber. 143p. 1990. pap. 15.00 (0-87556-200-0) Saifer.

Sermons 1824-1843, Vol. I: Sermons on the Liturgy & Sacraments & on Christ the Mediator. John H. Newman. Ed. by Placid Murray. 408p. 1992. 95.00 (0-19-920088-2) OUP.

Sermons 1824-1843, Vol. II: Sermons on Biblical History, Sin & Justification, the Christian Way of Life, & Biblical Theology. John H. Newman. Ed. by Vincent F. Blehl. 496p. 1994. 95.00 (0-19-920401-2) OUP.

Sero-Monitoring of Rinderpest Throughout Africa - Phase Two: Results for 1993. Ed. by M. H. Jeggo & R. Geiger. (Illus.). 239p. (Orig.). (C). 1995. pap. text ed. 50.00 (0-7881-1663-0) DIANE Pub.

Serologic Diagnosis of Celiac Diseases. Chorzelski. 216p. 1990. 121.00 (0-8493-5436-6, RC862, CRC Reprint) Franklin.

*Serologic Problem-Solving Strategies: A Systematic Approach. Ed. by Susan T. Johnson et al. (Illus.). 158p. 1996. pap. text ed. 60.00 (1-56395-066-9, PC97-960019) Am Assn Blood.

Serological Cancer Markers. Ed. by Stewart Sell. LC 92-1428. (Contemporary Biomedicine Ser.: Vol. 11). (Illus.). 552p. 1992. 125.00 (0-89603-209-4) Humana.

Serological Methods for Detection & Identification of Viral & Bacterial Plant Pathogens: A Laboratory Manual. Ed. by R. Hampton et al. LC 90-83302. (Illus.). 389p. (Orig.). 1990. student ed. 48.00 (0-89054-115-9) Am Phytopathol Soc.

Serological Tumour Markers: An Introduction. J. E. Roulston & R. C. Leonard. LC 92-49368. (Illus.). 192p. 1993. text ed. 71.00 (0-443-04511-9) Churchill.

Serology of Tuberculosis & BCG Vaccination. Ed. by W. Fox. (Advances in Tuberculosis Research Ser.: Vol. 21). (Illus.). viii, 192p. 1983. 132.00 (3-8055-3855-3) S Karger.

Serotonin: From Cell Biology to Pharmacology & Therapeutics. Ed. by Paul M. Vanhoutte & Rodolfo Paoletti. 688p. 1990. lib. bdg. 353.00 (0-7923-0531-0) Kluwer Ac.

Serotonin: From Cell Biology to Pharmacology & Therapeutics. Ed. by Paul M. Vanhoutte. LC 93-20892. (Medical Science Symposia Ser.). 445p. (C). 1993. lib. bdg. 166.50 (0-7923-2518-4) Kluwer Ac.

Serotonin: Molecular Biology, Receptors & Functional Effects. J. R. Fozard & P. R. Saxena. xi, 509p. 1991. 294.50 (0-8176-2607-7) Birkhauser.

Serotonin & Gastrointestinal Function. Ed. by Timothy S. Gaginella & James J. Galligan. 192p. 1995. 115.95 (0-8493-8387-0, 8387) CRC Pr.

Serotonin & Microcirculation. Ed. by R. S. Reneman & A. Bollinger. (Mikrozirkulation in Forschung und Klinik; Progress in Applied Microcirculation Ser.: Vol. 10). (Illus.). x, 92p. 1986. pap. 53.00 (3-8055-4163-5) S Karger.

Serotonin & Serotonin Antagonists: Journal: Clinical Physiology & Biochemistry, Vol. 8, Suppl. 3. Ed. by J. Rosenthal & Pieter A. Van Zwieten. (Illus.). iv, 128p. 1991. pap. 40.00 (3-8055-5456-7) S Karger.

Serotonin & 5-HT2-Receptor-Blockade (Ketanserin) in the Cardiovascular System. Gothert. (Progress in Pharmacology & Clinical Pharmacology Ser.: No. 7/4). (Illus.). (Orig.). 1990. pap. 60.00 (0-614-97053-9, Pub. by G Fischer Verlag GW) Lubrecht & Cramer.

*Serotonin, CNS Receptors & Brain Function. P. B. Bradley et al. (Advances in the Biosciences Ser.: Vol. 85). 430p. 1993. 181.50 (0-08-042051-6, Pergamon Pr) Elsevier.

Serotonin in Affective Disorders. Ed. by J. Menlewicz et al. (Advances in Biological Psychiatry Ser.: Vol. 14). (Illus.). vi, 90p. 1984. 43.25 (3-8055-3898-7) S Karger.

Serotonin in Antipsychotic Treatment. Ed. by Kane et al. (Medical Psychiatry Ser.: Vol. 3). 408p. 1996. 115.00 (0-8247-9302-1) Dekker.

Serotonin in Biological Psychiatry. Ed. by Beng T. Ho et al. LC 81-40611. (Advances in Biochemical Psychopharmacology Ser.: No. 34). (Illus.). 352p. 1982. reprint ed. pap. 100.40 (0-608-00638-6, 2061226) Bks Demand.

Serotonin in Major Psychiatric Disorders. Ed. by Emil F. Coccaro & Dennis L. Murphy. LC 89-18281. (Progress in Psychiatry Ser.: No. 21). 260p. 1990. text ed. 33.00 (0-88048-292-3, 8292) Am Psychiatric.

Serotonin in Mental Abnormalities. Ed. by David J. Boullin. LC 77-1828. 328p. reprint ed. pap. 93.50 (0-317-07778-3, 2019207) Bks Demand.

Serotonin in the Central Nervous System & Periphery: Proceedings of the Symposium on Serotoin in the Central Nervous System & Pheriphey, April 1-2, 1995, Nagoya, Japan. Ed. by Akikazu Takada & Gerald Curzon. LC 95-34967. (International Congress Ser.: Vol. 1088). 270p. 1995. 184.75 (0-444-81965-7) Elsevier.

Serotonin Neurotoxins. Ed. by J. H. Jacoby & L. D. Lytle. (Annals Ser.: Vol. 305). 702p. 1978. 68.00 (0-89072-061-4); pap. write for info. (0-89072-078-9) NY Acad Sci.

Serotonin Neurotransmission & Behavior. Ed. by Barry L. Jacobs & Alan Gelperin. 430p. 1981. 65.00 (0-262-10023-1) MIT Pr.

Serotonin Receptor Subtypes: Basic & Clinical Aspects. Ed. by Stephen J. Peroutka. LC 90-12804. (Receptor Biochemistry & Methodology Ser.: Vol. 15). 246p. 1990. text ed. 149.95 (0-471-56840-6) Wiley.

Serotonin Receptor Subtypes: Pharmacological Significance & Clinical Implications. Julien Mendlewicz. (International Academy for Biomedical & Drug Research Ser.: Vol. 1). (Illus.). x, 146p. 1992. 117.50 (3-8055-5550-4) S Karger.

Serotonin Receptors. Ed. by Elaine Sanders-Bush. LC 88-26646. (Receptors Ser.). 400p. 1989. 79.50 (0-89603-142-X) Humana.

S

***Serotonin Receptors & Their Ligands.** Berend Olivier et al. LC 97-24994. (Pharmacochemistry Library). 1997. write for info. (0-444-82041-8) Elsevier.

Serotonin, Sleep & Mental Disorder. Ed. by C. Idzikowski & P. J. Cowen. 312p. 1991. 95.00 (1-871816-06-8, Pub. by Wrightson Biomed UK) Taylor & Francis.

Serotonin Solution: The Powerful Substance That Can Help You Stop Bingeing, Lose Weight, & Feel Great. Susan Suffes & Judith J. Wurtman. 256p. 1996. 24.00 (0-449-91001-6) Fawcett.

***Serotonin Solutions.** Judith J. Wurtman & Susan Suffes. 1997. pap. 12.00 (0-449-91131-4) Fawcett.

Serotonin 1A Receptors in Depression & Anxiety. Stephen Stahl. 228p. 1992. pap. text ed. 40.00 (0-88167-900-3) Lppncott-Raven.

***Serotoninergic Neurons & 5-Ht Receptors in the C. N. S.** H. G. Baumgarten et al. LC 97-23528. (Handbook of Experimental Pharmacology Ser.). 1997. write for info. (3-540-62666-2) Springer Pub.

Serov, Valentin: 1865-1911. Dmitri V. Sarabianov. 272p. (C). 1987. 250.00 (0-685-34420-7, Pub. by Collets) St Mut.

Serowe: Village of the Rain-Wind. Bessie Head. (African Writers Ser.). 200p. (Orig.). (C). 1981. pap. 11.95 (0-435-90220-2, 90220) Heinemann.

Serpe d'Or. Rene De Goscinny. (J). (gr. 7-9). 1990. 19.95 (0-8288-5126-3, FC874) Fr & Eur.

Serpe d'Or. Rene De Goscinny & M. Uderzo. (Illus.). (FRE.). (J). 1990. 19.95 (0-8288-4904-8) Fr & Eur.

Serpent. Jean-Claude Van Itallie. 1971. pap. 5.25 (0-8222-1012-6) Dramatists Play.

Serpent. rev. ed. Nicholas Mosley. LC 89-35214. 190p. 1990. 19.95 (0-916583-49-X) Dalkey Arch.

Serpent & Lily: A Novella, with a Manifesto: The Sickness of the Age. Nikos Kazantzakis. Tr. by Theodora Vasils from GRE. LC 78-68832. 1980. 28.00 (0-520-03885-1) U CA Pr.

Serpent & the Bees: A KGB Chronicle. Edward Alexander. 298p. 1990. 21.95 (0-8191-7820-9) U Pr of Amer.

Serpent & the Goddess. Mary Condren. 1989. pap. 16.00 (0-06-250156-9, PL) HarpC.

***Serpent & the Rainbow.** Davis. 1997. pap. 13.00 (0-684-83929-6, Touchstone Bks) S&S Trade.

Serpent & the Rope. Raja Rao. LC 85-13628. 408p. 1986. 22.50 (0-87951-220-2) Overlook Pr.

Serpent & the Rope. Raja Rao. 408p. 1988. Tusk. pap. 9.95 (0-87951-243-1) Overlook Pr.

Serpent & the Rope. Raja Rao. 408p. 1968. reprint ed. pap. 6.00 (0-88253-766-0) Ind-US Inc.

***Serpent & the Staff.** Jeremy Brown. 465p. (Orig.). 1997. mass mkt. 5.99 (1-55237-224-3, Pub. by Comnwlth Pub CN) Partners Pubs Grp.

Serpent & the Wave: A Guide to Movement Meditation. Jalaja Bonheim. (Illus.). 320p. (Orig.). 1995. pap. 14.95 (0-89087-657-6) Celestial Arts.

Serpent at Her Breast. Alexander Lurkis. 376p. 1995. mass mkt. 4.99 (1-896329-61-6, Pub. by Comnwlth Pub CN) Partners Pubs Grp.

Serpent Beguiled. Betina Lindsey. Ed. by Carolyn Tolley. 256p. (Orig.). 1992. mass mkt. 4.99 (0-671-74467-4) PB.

Serpent de Mer. Jules Verne. 254p. 1976. 8.95 (0-686-55950-9) Fr & Eur.

Serpent d'Etoiles. Jean Giono. 192p. (FRE.). 1962. 10.95 (0-8288-9789-1, F103780) Fr & Eur.

Serpent Fire: Awakening Kundalini. Raymond W. Bernard. 98p. (Orig.). 1965. reprint ed. spiral bd. 12.00 (0-7873-1056-5) Hlth Research.

Serpent Garden. Judith M. Riley. LC 95-36067. (Illus.). 467p. 1996. pap. 24.95 (0-670-86661-X, Viking) Viking Penguin.

Serpent Garden. Judith M. Riley. 1997. pap. 12.95 (0-14-025880-9) Viking Penguin.

Serpent-Handling Believers. Thomas Burton. LC 92-30409. (Illus.). 344p. (Orig.). (C). 1993. pap. 21.95 (0-87049-788-X) U of Tenn Pr.

Serpent Imagery & Symbolism. Lura Pedrini & Duilio T. Pedrini. 1966. pap. 15.95 (0-8084-0274-9) NCUP.

Serpent in Eden: H. L. Mencken & the South. Fred Hobson. LC 73-15674. 242p. 1994. pap. text ed. 14.95 (0-8071-0455-8) La State U Pr.

***Serpent in Eden: H. L. Mencken & the South.** Fred C. Hobson. LC 73-15674. 1974. reprint ed. pap. 73.60 (0-608-02801-0, 2063868) Bks Demand.

***Serpent in Paradise: Among the People of the Bounty.** Dea Birkett. LC 97-10890. 1997. 23.95 (0-385-48870-X, Anchor NY) Doubleday.

***Serpent in the Cup: Temperance in American Literature.** Ed. by David S. Reynolds & Debra J. Rosenthal. 320p. 1997. pap. 17.95 (1-55849-082-5); text ed. 55.00 (1-55849-081-7) U of Mass Pr.

Serpent in the Mirror: A Collection of Poems. Fidel Fajardo-Acosta. LC 92-12070. 56p. 1992. pap. 12.95 (0-7734-0026-5) E Mellen.

***Serpent in the Night Sky.** Dianne Warren. LC 93-100607. 1997. pap. text ed. 10.95 (0-88754-477-0, Pub. by Playwrights CN Pr CN) Theatre Comm.

Serpent in the Sky: The High Wisdom of Ancient Egypt. rev. ed. John A. West. LC 92-56483. (Illus.). 286p. 1993. pap. 18.00 (0-8356-0691-0, Quest) Theos Pub Hse.

***Serpent Kills: Play.** Jim Millan. LC 95-130601. 1997. pap. text ed. 11.95 (0-88754-528-9, Pub. by Playwrights CN Pr CN) Theatre Comm.

Serpent Mage. Margaret Weis. (Death Gate Cycle Ser.: No. 4). 480p. 1993. mass mkt. 6.50 (0-553-56140-5) Bantam.

Serpent Moon: An Adventure Campaign for the Nephilum Role-Playing Game. Mark Angeli et al. Ed. by Sam Shirley. (Nephilim Roleplaying Game Ser.). (Illus.). 128p. (Orig.). 1995. pap. 19.95 (1-56882-037-2, 3104) Chaosium.

Serpent Mound. Anthony Masters. (J). 14.00 (0-671-79976-2, S&S Bks Young Read) S&S Childrens.

Serpent Mound - Adams County, Ohio: Mystery of the Mound & History of the Serpent. E. O. Randall. (Ohio History, Prehistoric Indians, Serpent Worship Ser.). (Illus.). 56p. (C). 1993. reprint ed. pap. 7.55 (1-56651-087-2); reprint ed. lib. bdg. 25.65 (1-56651-088-0) A W McGraw.

Serpent Mound of Ohio: Site Excavation & Park Construction. F. W. Putnam. (Ohio History, Archaeology, Prehistoric Indians Ser.). (Illus.). 8p. (C). 1994. reprint ed. lib. bdg. 2.80 (1-56651-091-0) A W McGraw.

Serpent Myth. W. W. Westcott. Ed. by Darcy Kuntz. (Golden Dawn Studies: Vol. 9). 1996. pap. 4.95 (1-55818-339-6) Holmes Pub.

Serpent Never Sleeps: A Novel of Jamestown & Pocahontas. Scott O'Dell. 192p. (YA). (gr. 8 up). 1989. mass mkt. 4.50 (0-449-70328-2, Juniper) Fawcett.

Serpent Never Sleeps: A Novel of Jamestown & Pocahontas. Scott O'Dell. (Illus.). 240p. (J). (gr. 5 up). 1987. 16.95 (0-395-44242-7) HM.

Serpent of Fire: A Modern View of Kundalini. Darrel Irving. LC 95-3720. (Illus.). 256p. (Orig.). 1995. pap. 14.95 (0-87728-830-5) Weiser.

Serpent of Paradise: The Incredible Story of How Satan's Rebellion Serves God's Purposes. Erwin W. Lutzer. 1996. pap. 10.99 (0-8024-2720-0) Moody.

***Serpent of the Nile.** Wendy Buonaventura. 1997. pap. text ed. 35.00 (1-56656-300-3) Interlink Pub.

Serpent of the Nile: Women & Dance in the Arab World. Wendy Buonaventura. LC 89-15393. (Illus.). 208p. 1994. pap. 35.00 (1-56656-117-5) Interlink Pub.

Serpent on the Rock. Kurt Eichenwald. LC 95-8945. (Illus.). 496p. 1995. 27.50 (0-88730-720-5) Harper Busn.

Serpent on the Rock. Kurt Eichenwald. 512p. 1996. pap. 15.00 (0-88730-803-1) Harper Busn.

Serpent on the Rock: A Personal View of Christianity. Alice Thomas Ellis. (Illus.). 224p. 1995. pap. 13.95 (0-340-68796-7, Pub. by H & S UK) Trafalgar.

Serpent Power: The Secrets of Tantric & Shaktic Yoga. Arthur Avalon. LC 74-75259. (Illus.). 543p. 1974. pap. 11.95 (0-486-23058-9) Dover.

***Serpent Power: The Yoga of Life Force Development for Spiritual Enlightenment.** unabridged ed. Abhaya A. Muata. (Illus.). 156p. (Orig.). 1997. pap. 14.99 (1-884564-19-4) Cruzian Mystic.

Serpent Power (Sat-Chakra-Nirupana & Paduka-Panchaka) Tr. by John Woodroffe from SAN. (Illus.). 512p. 1973. 24.00 (0-89744-117-6) Auromere.

Serpent River: An Earthdawn Sourcebook. (Earthdawn Ser.). (Illus.). 144p. (Orig.). 1996. suppl. ed., pap. 18.00 (1-55560-288-6, 6109) FASA Corp.

Serpent Shell. Margaret Greaves. (J). 1995. pap. text ed. 5.95 (0-8120-9271-6) Barron.

Serpent Slayer: And Other Stories of Strong Women. Illus. by Trina S. Hyman. (J). 1997. write for info. (0-316-38701-0) Little.

Serpent Slayers: A Southwestern Supernatural Thriller. Adam Niswander. LC 94-1284. (Shaman Cycle Ser.: Bk. 2). 320p. 1994. lib. bdg. 21.95 (0-9626148-2-3) Integra Pr.

Serpent, the Beast & the Golden Dawn: Secrets of a Western Master. Christopher S. Hyatt. LC 91-60061. 220p. (Orig.). 1997. pap. 12.95 (1-56184-020-3) New Falcon Pubns.

Serpent under It: A Novel. Edith Taylor. 256p. 1973. 5.95 (0-393-08673-9) Norton.

Serpent Underfoot. Frank Varela. LC 93-77185. 75p. 1993. pap. 7.95 (1-877636-11-8) March Abrazo.

Serpent Waltz. Jo Clayton. (Dancer Trilogy Ser.: Bk. 2). 368p. (Orig.). 1994. mass mkt. 4.99 (0-88677-597-3) DAW Bks.

***Serpent Within: Politics, Literature & American Individualism.** Joseph C. Bertolini. LC 96-40871. 1996. pap. write for info. (0-7618-0626-1) U Pr of Amer.

Serpent Worship in Africa - the Ovimbundu of Angola: Culture Areas of Nigeria. W. D. Hambly. (Chicago Field Museum of Natural History Fieldiana Anthropology Ser.). 1974. reprint ed. 60.00 (0-527-01881-3) Periodicals Srv.

Serpent Worship in Ancient India. B. C. Sinha. xvi, 87p. 1979. 16.00 (1-55528-052-8, Pub. by Today & Tomorrows P & P II) Scholarly Pubns.

Serpentes. Jean-Claude Rage. (Encyclopedia of Paleoherpetology Ser.: Pt. 11). (Illus.). 80p. 1984. pap. text ed. 77.00 (3-437-30448-8) Lubrecht & Cramer.

***Serpentine Cave.** Walsh. LC 97-23094. 1997. 20.95 (0-312-16999-X) St Martin.

Serpentine Lattice: The Douglas F. Cooley Memorial Art Gallery, Reed College. Helen M. Harrison & Newton Harrison. (Illus.). 28p. 1993. pap. 10.00 (0-685-67187-9) Feldman Fine Arts.

Serpentine Rouletted Stamps of Finland: Issues of 1860 & 1866. Leo Linder & D. A. Dromberg. Ed. by George B. Koplowitz. Tr. by Kauko Aro from FIN. (Illus.). 106p. (Orig.). 1983. pap. text ed. 17.50 (0-936493-00-3) Scand Philatelic.

Serpentine Rouletted Stamps of Finland: Issues of 1860 & 1866, Vol. 2. Mikka Ossa. Ed. by George B. Koplowitz. Tr. by Kauko I. Aro from FIN. (Illus.). 116p. (Orig.). 1985. pap. text ed. 18.50 (0-936493-08-9) Scand Philatelic.

Serpentinites: Recorders of Tectonic & Petrological History. David S. O'Hanley. (Oxford Monographs on Geology & Geophysics: No. 34). (Illus.). 296p. 1996. 95.00 (0-19-508254-0) OUP.

Serpents. Pierre Bourgeade. 271p. (FRE.). 1986. pap. 11.95 (0-7859-2025-0, 2070377040) Fr & Eur.

Serpent's Children. Laurence Yep. LC 82-48855. (Trophy Bk.). 288p. (YA). (gr. 7 up). 1996. pap. 5.95 (0-06-440645-8, Trophy) HarpC Child Bks.

Serpent's Coil. Farley Mowat. 224p. 1981. mass mkt. 4.95 (0-7704-2313-2) Bantam.

Serpent's Crown. John McKeon. 208p. 1991. 19.95 (0-8027-1146-4) Walker & Co.

Serpent's Egg: A Collection of Literature & Art. LC 79-84549. 1979. pap. 10.00 (0-931350-02-6) Moonlight Pubns.

Serpent's Gift. Helen E. Lee. 374p. 1994. 21.00 (0-689-12193-8, Scribners PB Fict) S&S Trade.

Serpent's Gift. Helen E. Lee. 1995. pap. 12.00 (0-684-80160-4, Scribners PB Fict) S&S Trade.

Serpent's Head. Alice N. Colcock. LC 95-90122. (Orig.). 1996. pap. 12.95 (0-533-11464-0) Vantage.

Serpents in the Manger: Overcoming Abusive Christianity. Jerry L. Harris & Melody J. Milam. 320p. 1994. 24.00 (1-56980-017-0) Barricade Bks.

Serpents in the Sand: Essays on the Nonlinear Nature of Politics & Human Destiny. Courtney Brown. LC 95-11859. (C). 1995. 37.50 (0-472-10643-0) U of Mich Pr.

Serpent's Mark. Robert L. Duncan. 1990. mass mkt. 4.95 (0-312-92365-1) St Martin.

Serpents of Paradise: A Reader. Edward Abbey. 12.95p. 1996. pap. 12.95 (0-8050-3133-2, Owl) H Holt & Co.

Serpents of the Sky, Dragons of the Earth. F. W. Holiday. LC 93-61063. (Illus.). 247p. 1993. reprint ed. pap. 13.95 (1-881852-07-5) Horus Hse Pr.

Serpent's Reach. C. J. Cherryh. 288p. 1980. mass mkt. 4.99 (0-88677-088-2) DAW Bks.

***Serpent's Shadow.** Timothy Boggs. (Hercules: The Legendary Journeys Ser.: No. 2). (J). 1996. mass mkt. 5.99 (1-57297-214-9) Blvd Books.

Serpent's Silver. Piers Anthony. 320p. 1989. mass mkt. 4.95 (0-8125-0257-4) Tor Bks.

Serpent's Tail. Martin Dillon. 326p. 1996. pap. 16.95 (1-86066-007-X, Pub. by R Cohen Bks UK) Trafalgar.

Serpent's Tongue: Prose Poetry, & Art of the New Mexican Pueblos. Ed. by Nancy Wood. 1997. pap. 30.00 (0-525-45514-0) NAL-Dutton.

Serpent's Tooth. Diana L. Paxson. 400p. 1993. mass mkt. 4.99 (0-380-75680-3, AvoNova) Avon.

***Serpent's Tooth.** large type ed. Margaret Bacon. (Magna Large Print Ser.). 545p. 1996. 25.99 (0-7505-0971-6, Pub. by Magna Print Bks UK) Ulverscroft.

***Serpent's Tooth: A Peter Decker/Rina Lazarus Novel.** Faye Kellerman. LC 97-10685. 416p. 1997. 24.00 (0-688-14368-7) Morrow.

Serpent's Tooth Mystery. Franklin W. Dixon. (Hardy Boys Mystery Stories Ser.: No. 93). (Orig.). (J). (gr. 3-6). pap. 3.99 (0-671-66310-0, Minstrel Bks) PB.

Serpent's Walk. Randolph D. Calverhall. 449p. (Orig.). 1991. pap. 6.95 (0-937944-05-X) Natl Vanguard.

***Serpico.** Peter Maas. 336p. 1997. mass mkt. 5.99 (0-06-101214-9, Harp PBks) HarpC.

Serpientes. Donna Bailey. LC 91-23778. (Animales Ser.). (Illus.). 32p. (SPA.). (J). (gr. 1-4). 1992. lib. bdg. 21.40 (0-8114-2657-2) Raintree Steck-V.

Serpientes. Norman S. Barrett. LC 90-70891. (Picture Library). (Illus.). 32p. (SPA.). (J). (gr. k-4). 1990. lib. bdg. 18.60 (0-531-07909-0) Watts.

Serpins: Structure, Function & Biology. Peter Gettins et al. (Molecular Biology Intelligence Unit Ser.). 215p. 1996. 89.95 (1-57059-324-8) R G Landes.

Serpins Structure, Function & Biology. Peter Gettins. (Medicine Ser). 1996. text ed. 69.95 (0-412-10351-6) Van Nos Reinhold.

Serr-ol Hajar: Secret of Hajar. Shah Maghsoud Sadegh Angha. LC 82-84673. 161p. (Orig.). (PER.). 1983. 75.00 (0-910735-43-3); pap. 35.00 (0-910735-42-5) MTO Printing & Pubn Ctr.

Serranilla Espanola. Nancy Marino. 153p. 1990. 29.50 (0-916379-45-0) Scripta.

Serrano Indians of Southern California. Francis J. Johnston. 1967. pap. 2.00 (0-939046-22-9) Malki Mus Pr.

Serrano Songs & Stories. Ed. by Guy Mount. 48p. 1993. 4.95 (0-9604462-7-3) Sweetlight.

Serra's San Diego: Father Junipero Serra & California's Beginnings. Iris H. Engstrand. (Illus.). 16p. 1982. 2.95 (0-918740-02-9) San Diego Hist.

Serrasine: L'Hermaphrodite. Honore De Balzac. (FRE.). 1989. pap. 11.95 (0-7859-2997-5) Fr & Eur.

Serre: Abelian One-Adic Representations & Elliptic Curves. (ABC Ser.). 1989. reprint ed. 26.95 (0-318-41399-X) Addison-Wesley.

***Serre: Somme.** Jack Horsfall. (Battleground Europe Ser.). 1996. pap. text ed. 14.95 (0-85052-508-X, Pub. by L Cooper Bks UK) Trans-Atl Phila.

Serres Chaudes, Quinze Chansond: La Princesse Maleine. Maurice Maeterlinck. 320p. (FRE.). 1983. pap. 16.95 (0-7859-4688-8) Fr & Eur.

Serres Chaudes. Quinze Chansons. La Princesse Maleine. Maurice Maeterlinck. (Poesie Ser.). 320p. (FRE.). 1983. pap. 13.95 (2-07-032245-9) Schoenhof.

Sertoli Cell. Ed. by Lonnie D. Russell & Micheal D. Griswold. (Illus.). 802p. (C). 1993. 137.50 (0-9627422-1-X) Cache River Pr.

Sertorius. Pierre Corneille. 160p. (FRE.). 1959. pap. 14.95 (0-7859-0692-4, F35960) Fr & Eur.

Sertorius. Adolf Schulten. LC 75-7340. (Roman History Ser.). (GER.). 1975. reprint ed. 23.95 (0-405-07061-6) Ayer.

Sertum Austro-Caledonicum. Jean J. De La Billardiere. (Illus.). 1968. reprint ed. 130.00 (3-7682-0541-X) Lubrecht & Cramer.

Serum Lipids & Lipoproteins of Hispanics, 1982-84: PHS 90-1690. (Vital & Health Statistics Ser. 11: Data from the National Health Survey: No. 240). 72p. 3.75 (0-685-61584-7, 017-022-01113-1) Natl Ctr Health Stats.

Serum of the Water. Dean Phelps. LC 78-12785. 1978. pap. 4.95 (0-914974-17-3) Holmgangers.

Servant. Ivy E. Harwell. 180p. (Orig.). (YA). (gr. 12 up). 1994. pap. 8.99 (1-882671-09-0) Wrds of Life.

Servant & Master: Building & Running the Grand Houses of Sydney, 1788-1850. Barrie Dyster. (Illus.). 260p. 1990. pap. 19.95 (0-86840-395-4, Pub. by New South Wales Univ Pr AT) Intl Spec Bk.

Servant Church: Diaconal Ministry & the Episcopal Church. John E. Booty. LC 82-81429. 108p. (Orig.). 1982. pap. 7.95 (0-8192-1316-0) Morehouse Pub.

***Servant Ethic in the New Testament.** Philippa Carter. (American University Studies VII: Vol. 196). 168p. (C). 1997. text ed. 35.95 (0-8204-3393-4) P Lang Pubng.

Servant Girl Question. Harriet E. Spofford. Ed. by Leon Stein. LC 77-70535. 1977. reprint ed. lib. bdg. 23.95 (0-405-10203-8) Ayer.

Servant Gladly: Essays in Honor of John W. Beardslee the Third. Ed. by Jack D. Klunder. 144p. (Orig.). (C). 1989. pap. 11.00 (0-8028-0466-7) Eerdmans.

Servant in God's Kingdom. 1995. 19.95 (0-87162-659-4, D1020H) Warner Pr.

Servant King. Clegg Dyson & Betty Dyson. (Kingdom Kids Ser.). 39p. (J). (gr. 3-7). 1994. wbk. ed., pap. 4.99 (1-884553-20-6) Discipleshp.

***Servant King.** Verne Nesbitt. 176p. (Orig.). 1996. mass mkt. 4.99 (0-88368-436-5) Whitaker Hse.

Servant Leaders of the People of God: An Ecclesial Spirituality for American Priests. Robert M. Schwartz. 1989. pap. 12.95 (0-8091-3106-4) Paulist Pr.

Servant Leaders, Servant Structures. Elizabeth O'Connor. (Illus.). 96p. (Orig.). 1991. pap. 7.95 (1-883639-03-4) Servant Ldrship.

Servant Leadership: A Journey into the Nature of Legitimate Power & Greatness. Robert K. Greenleaf. LC 76-45678. 338p. 1977. pap. 12.95 (0-8091-2527-7) Paulist Pr.

Servant of God Mother Mary Angeline Teresa, O. Carm: Daughter of Carmel, Mother to the Aged. Jude Mead. LC 90-32360. (Illus.). 256p. 1990. 12.95 (0-932506-81-X); pap. 9.95 (0-932506-79-8) St Bedes Pubns.

Servant of Jehovah. H. L. Ellison. 32p. pap. 2.95 (0-85365-254-6) Attic Pr.

Servant of Power: A Political Biography of Senator William M. Stewart. Russell R. Elliott. LC 83-6946. (History & Political Science Ser.: No. 18). (Illus.). 360p. (Orig.). 1983. pap. 14.95 (0-87417-076-1) U of Nev Pr.

Servant of the Bones. Anne O. Rice. LC 95-49357. 387p. 1996. 26.00 (0-679-42832-1) Knopf.

***Servant of the Bones.** Anne O. Rice. 1996. mass mkt. write for info. (0-676-52155-X) Ballantine.

Servant of the Bones. Anne O. Rice. 400p. 1996. 26.00 (0-679-43301-5) Random.

Servant of the Bones. large type ed. Anne O. Rice. 640p. 1996. pap. 26.00 (0-7838-1915-3) Random Hse Lrg Prnt.

***Servant of the Bones.** large type ed. Anne O. Rice. (Large Print Ser.). 1996. pap. 26.00 (0-679-75904-2) Random.

***Servant of the Bones.** limited ed. Anne Rice. 387p. 1996. 150.00 (0-9631925-6-6) B E Trice.

***Servant of the Bones Trade.** Anne O. Rice. 1997. pap. 14.00 (0-345-40966-3) Ballantine.

***Servant of the Dead.** Ashland Brown. Ed. by Carolyn S. Zagury. LC 96-61493. 328p. (Orig.). 1997. pap. 14.95 (1-880254-40-9) Vista.

Servant of the Empire. Raymond E. Feist. 704p. 1991. mass mkt. 6.50 (0-553-29245-5, Spectra) Bantam.

Servant of the Lord. N. A. Woychuk. (Service Adult Ser.: Memory Bk. 1). (Illus.). 232p. (Orig.). 1979. pap. 3.00 (1-880960-15-X) Script Memory Fl.

Servant of the Stuarts. Moyra Cimino. 1982. 32.00 (0-7223-1557-0, Pub. by A H S Ltd UK) St Mut.

Servant of Two Masters & Other Italian Classics. Ed. by Eric Bentley. (Eric Bentley's Dramatic Repertoire Ser.). 272p. (Orig.). (ITA.). 1986. pap. 10.95 (0-936839-20-1) Applause Theatre Bk Pubs.

***Servant Shoes.** Shirley M. Davis. 192p. (Orig.). 1996. pap. 10.95 (1-883893-46-1) WinePress Pub.

***Servant-Son: Jesus Then & Now.** Donald Coggan. 128p. 1995. pap. 5.95 (0-687-86162-4) Abingdon.

Servant Songs: Reflections on the History and Mission of Southeastern Baptist Theological Seminary, 1950-1988. W. Randall Lolley et al. Ed. by Thomas A. Bland, Jr. LC 94-4441. 264p. (Orig.). 1994. pap. 14.95 (1-880837-94-3) Smyth & Helwys.

Servant Warfare: How Kindness Conquers Spiritual Darkness. Steve Sjogren. LC 96-22396. 240p. (Orig.). 1996. pap. 10.99 (0-89283-964-3, Vine Bks) Servant.

***Servanthood: Leadership for the New Millennium.** Bennett J. Sims. LC 97-13336. 170p. 1997. 11.95 (1-56101-145-2) Cowley Pubns.

***Servanthood Leadership, Vol. 4.** Roger E. Dickson. (Biblical Research Library). 107p. (Orig.). 1996. pap. 5.95 (1-56794-127-3, C-2449) Star Bible.

***Servants: English Domestics in the Eighteenth Century.** Bridget Hill. 288p. 1996. 65.00 (0-19-820621-6) OUP.

Servants & Gentlewomen to the Golden Land: The Emigration of Single Women from Britain to Southern Africa, 1820-1939. Cecillie Swaisland. 200p. 1993. 36.95 (0-85496-745-1) Berg Pubs.

Servants & Gentlewomen to the Golden Land: The Emigration of Single Women from Britain to Southern Africa, 1820-1939. Cecillie Swaisland. (Illus.). 200p. (C). 1993. pap. text ed. 15.95 (0-85496-870-9) Berg Pubs.

***Servants & Gentlewomen to the Golden Land: The Emigration of Single Women from Britain to Southern Africa, 1820-1939.** Cecillie Swaisland. (Illus.). 200p. 1993. pap. write for info. (0-86980-883-4, Pub. by Univ Natal Pr SA) Intl Spec Bk.

Servant's Hall: The Domestic History of a Country House. Merlin Waterson. (Illus.). 240p. 1991. pap. 22.95 (0-7078-0126-5, Pub. by Natl Trust UK) Trafalgar.

An Asterisk (*) at the beginning of an entry indicates that the title is appearing in BIP for the first time.

Servant's Hand: English Fiction from Below. Bruce Robbins. LC 85-14955. 256p. 1986. text ed. 49.50 (*0-231-05966-3*) Col U Pr.

Servant's Hand: English Fiction from Below. Bruce Robbins. LC 93-7141. 280p. (C). 1993. pap. text ed. 15.95 (*0-8223-1397-9*) Duke.

Servants in Charge. Keith M. Bailey. 123p. 1979. pap. 8.99 (*0-87509-160-1*) Chr Pubns.

Servants in Husbandry in Early Modern England. Ann Kussmaul. (Interdisciplinary Perspectives on Modern History Ser.). (Illus.). 240p. 1981. 49.95 (*0-521-23566-9*) Cambridge U Pr.

Servants into Planters, the Origin of the American Image. Aaron M. Shatzman. (Outstanding Studies in Early American History). 350p. 1990. reprint ed. 15.00 (*0-8240-6197-7*) Garland.

Servants of All. Wilbert L. Walker. LC 82-81162. 244p. 1982. 12.00 (*0-935428-02-X*) Heritage Pr.

***Servants of Darkness.** TSR Inc. Staff. 1997. 12.95 (*0-7869-0659-6*) TSR Inc.

Servants of God: The Lives of the Ten Gurus of the Sikhs. Jon Engle. LC 79-63457. (Illus.). 192p. 1980. pap. 6.00 (*0-89142-035-5*) Sant Bani Ash.

Servants of Power. Charles A. Powell. LC 90-91860. 314p. 1990. 18.95 (*0-9627161-9-7*) QLP Phila PA.

Servants of Power. Loren Baritz. LC 73-17924. 273p. (C). 1974. reprint ed. text ed. 69.50 (*0-8371-7275-6*, BASP, Greenwood Pr) Greenwood.

Servants of Satan: The Age of the Witch Hunts. Joseph Klaits. LC 84-48252. (Illus.). 224p. 1985. 25.95 (*0-253-35182-0*) Ind U Pr.

Servants of Satan: The Age of the Witch Hunts. Joseph Klaits. LC 84-48252. (Illus.). 224p. 1987. pap. 12.95 (*0-253-20422-4*, MB-422) Ind U Pr.

Servants of the Banquet: Stories & Ideas about Fighting Hunger. Cathy Butler. Ed. by Becky Nelson. 100p. (Orig.). 1994. pap. text ed. 6.95 (*1-56309-101-1*, New Hope) Womans Mission Union.

Servants of the Buddha: Winter in a Himalayan Convent. Anna Grimshaw. LC 93-34019. (Illus.). 176p. 1994. reprint ed. pap. 12.95 (*0-8298-0963-5*) Pilgrim OH.

Servants of the Land: God, Family & Farm; The Trinity of Belgian-American Folkways in Southwest Minnesota. Joseph A. Amato. (Orig.). 1990. pap. 8.95 (*0-9614119-2-9*) Crossings Pr.

***Servants of the Lord.** Marian Baden et al. 1995. pap. text ed. 3.50 (*0-570-09531-X*, 20-2601) Concordia.

Servants of the People. Board of St. Paul Editorial Staff. (C). 1989. 75.00 (*0-85439-318-8*, Pub. by St Paul Pubns UK) St Mut.

***Servants of the People.** Williams. Date not set. pap. write for info. (*0-312-17684-8*) St Martin.

Servants of the People: The 1960s Legacy of African American Leadership. Lea E. Williams. LC 96-34384. 1996. text ed. 39.95 (*0-312-16372-X*) St Martin.

Servants of the State: The Contested Control of Teaching 1900-1930. Martin Lawn. 180p. 1987. 60.00 (*1-85000-257-6*, Falmer Pr); pap. 30.00 (*1-85000-258-4*, Falmer Pr) Taylor & Francis.

Servants of the Word: Ministry in the Believers' Church: Papers from a Study Conference Held at Bethany Theological Seminary, September 2-4, 1987. Ed. by David B. Eller. LC 91-107345. 282p. 1990. reprint ed. pap. 80.40 (*0-608-02157-1*, 2062826) Bks Demand.

Servants of Twilight. Dean R. Koontz. 432p. 1990. mass mkt. 7.50 (*0-425-12125-9*) Berkley Pub.

Servants or Friends? Another Look at God. Graham Maxwell. LC 92-15397. (Illus.). 224p. 1992. 15.95 (*1-56652-000-2*); 9.95 (*1-56652-001-0*); audio 15.95 (*1-56652-002-9*) Pine Knoll Pubns.

Servants, Shophands, & Laborers. Gary P. Leupp. 250p. 1992. pap. text ed. 17.95 (*0-691-02961-X*) Princeton U Pr.

Servants, Shophands, & Laborers in the Cities of Tokugawa Japan. Gary P. Leupp. (Illus.). 252p. 1992. text ed. 37.50 (*0-691-03139-8*) Princeton U Pr.

Servants, Sirdars & Settlers: Indians in Mauritius, 1834-1874. Ed. by Marina Carter. (Oxford University South Asian Studies Ser.). (Illus.). 250p. 1995. 29.95 (*0-19-563296-6*) OUP.

Servants Tale. Margaret Frazer. 1993. mass mkt. 5.50 (*0-425-14389-9*) Berkley Pub.

Serve God with Gladness: A Server's Manual. David Philippart. 80p. (Orig.). 1997. pap. 8.00 (*1-56854-151-1*, SERVER) Liturgy Tr Pubns.

Serve It Forth. M. F. K. Fisher. LC 88-37227. 148p. 1989. reprint ed. pap. 12.00 (*0-86547-369-2*, North Pt Pr) FS&G.

Serve It Forth: Cooking with Anne McCaffrey. Ed. by Anne McCaffrey & John G. Betancourt. (Illus.). 288p. (Orig.). 1996. pap. 12.99 (*0-446-67161-4*) Warner Bks.

Serve It Forth: Cooking with Anne McCaffrey. Ed. by Anne McCaffrey & John Betancourt. (Orig.). 1996. write for info. (*0-446-67141-X*) Warner Bks.

Serve It Up: Volleyball for Life. William Neville. LC 93-36096. (Illus.). 175p. (Orig.). (C). 1993. pap. 13.95 (*1-55934-110-6*, 1110) Mayfield Pub.

Serve Something Super for Your Kids. Cindy Cummins. 160p. 1995. pap. 19.95 (*0-8019-8607-9*) Chilton.

Serve the Lord with All Your Heart. Grant Von Harrison. (Missionary Success Ser.). 26p. (Orig.). 1991. pap. write for info. (*0-910558-07-8*) Ensign Pub.

Serve the Lord with Gladness. Monk of the Eastern Church Staff. Tr. by John Breck from FRE. LC 90-20916. 112p. (Orig.). 1990. pap. 7.95 (*0-88141-085-3*) St Vladimirs.

Serve with Honor: A Guide for Missionaries. Randy L. Bott. LC 95-35438. 1995. 10.95 (*0-87579-955-8*) Deseret Bk.

***Served Cold.** Ed Goldberg. 224p. 1997. mass mkt. 5.99 (*0-425-15943-4*, Prime Crime) Berkley Pub.

Served Cold. Ed Goldberg. 179p. 1994. pap. 9.00 (*1-883303-12-5*) W Coast Crime.

Server at the Lord's Table. Liturgical Commission Publishings Diocese of Lansing Staff. Ed. by Mary J. Gilliland. (Illus.). 28p. (Orig.). 1995. pap. text ed. 4.00 (*1-878268-00-7*) Lit Comm Pubs.

***Server-Side Java.** Troy Downing. 1997. pap. 39.99 (*0-7645-8046-9*) IDG Bks.

***Servers & Desktop Converters, 1994.** (VDT-2000 Ser.: Vol. 2). 1994. 2,995.00 (*0-614-18339-1*, IGIC-93) Info Gatekeepers.

Server's Art I: A Guide for the Serving Professional. Johanna C. Moline. (Illus.). 50p. (Orig.). (C). 1994. pap. text ed. 12.95 (*0-9644063-0-6*) Anvilcross.

Server's Art II: A Short Course for the Serving Professional. abr. ed. Johanna C. Moline. (Illus.). 16p. (C). 1995. pap. text ed. 4.25 (*0-9644063-1-4*) Anvilcross.

Serviani in Aeneidem Commentarii: Editio Harvardiana, Vol. 3 - Aeneid III-V. E. K. Rand et al. (American Philological Association Special Publications Ser.). 590p. 1974. 39.50 (*0-89130-718-4*, 40 05 01) Scholars Pr GA.

Service. Henry David Thoreau. 1976. 250.00 (*0-87968-441-0*) Gordon Pr.

***Service: A Strategy Not a Transaction.** Linda F. Fracassi. Ed. by Kris Yeaworth & Bob Prins. 60p. 1997. pap. 495.00 incl. vhs (*0-9657897-0-5*) Learning Essentials.

Service: A Trilogy on Colonization. Martha Rosler. 36p. 1978. pap. 5.00 (*0-89439-007-4*) Printed Matter.

Service: Ideal & Aspects. Bernard D. Hirsh & Donald P. Wilcox. 320p. (Orig.). 1994. pap. 5.95 (*81-7120-640-9*, Pub. by Ramakrishna Math II) Vedanta Pr.

Service: Managing the Guest Experience. David I. Smith. 180p. 1988. 36.95 (*0-86730-253-4*) Lebhar Friedman.

Service a la Clientele en Assurance: Perfectionnment, ACS 100. Richard Bailey et al. Ed. by Vivian Duisit. (Associate, Customer Service Program Ser.). (FRE.). 1994. pap. text ed. 36.00 (*0-939921-52-9*) Life Office.

Service a la Clientele en Assurance: Principes et Pratiques, ACS 100. Kenneth Huggins. Ed. by Joel V. Basarich. (Associate, Customer Service Program Ser.). (FRE.). 1994. text ed. 57.00 (*0-939921-53-7*) Life Office.

Service Advantage: How to Identify & Fulfill Customer Needs. Karl Albrecht & Lawrence Bradford. 200p. 1989. text ed. 32.00 (*1-55623-247-0*) Irwin Prof Pubng.

Service Agreement Dynamics. Steve Howard. LC 89-15880. 1989. 17.95 (*0-912524-49-9*) Busn News.

Service America: Doing Business in the New Economy. Karl Albrecht & Ron Zemke. 235p. 1985. text ed. 32.50 (*0-87094-659-5*) Irwin Prof Pubng.

Service America: Doing Business in the New Economy. Karl Albrecht & Ron Zemke. 1990. pap. 13.99 (*0-446-39092-5*) Warner Bks.

Service & Leadership: Best of the Grapevine. Valerie H. Briggs. (Illus.). 62p. (Orig.). 1993. pap. 7.95 (*1-888482-09-5*) CNH.

Service & Spirituality. Swami Swahananda. 211p. (Orig.). 1980. reprint ed. pap. 3.95 (*0-87481-500-2*, Pub. by Ramakrishna Math II) Vedanta Pr.

Service Area Representative Trainee. (Career Examination Ser.: C-3675). pap. 27.95 (*0-8373-3675-9*) Nat Learn.

Service Banking: All Purpose Bank. Derrick Hanson. 539p. (C). 1990. pap. 125.00 (*0-85297-200-8*, Pub. by Inst Bankers UK) St Mut.

Service Banking: The All Purpose Bank. D. G. Hanson. 1987. 100.00 (*0-85297-192-3*, Pub. by Inst Bankers UK) St Mut.

Service Banking: The Arrival of the All Purpose Bank. Derrek Hanson. 1985. 75.00 (*0-85297-066-8*, Pub. by Inst Bankers UK) St Mut.

Service Bay Handbook. Chilton Automotives Editorial Staff. 560p. 1993. pap. write for info. (*0-8019-8469-6*) Chilton.

Service Books of the Orthodox Church, 2 vols. 1984. Set. 16.00 (*1-878997-23-8*); Set. 24.00 (*1-878997-24-6*) St Tikhons Pr.

Service Books of the Royal Abbey of Saint-Denis: Images of Ritual & Music in the Middle Ages. Anne W. Robertson. (Oxford Monographs on Music). (Illus.). 608p. 1991. 150.00 (*0-19-315254-1*) OUP.

Service Breakthroughs: Changing the Rules of the Game. James Heskett. 320p. 1990. 35.00 (*0-02-914675-5*, Free Press) Free Pr.

Service Centers & Consumer Trips: Studies on the Philadelphia Metropolitan Fringe. John E. Brush & Howard L. Gauthier. LC 67-25274. (University of Chicago, Department of Geography, Research Paper Ser.: No. 113). 195p. reprint ed. pap. 55.60 (*0-7837-0393-7*, 2040714) Bks Demand.

Service Charges in Gas & Electric Rates. Hubert F. Havlik. LC 68-58590. (Columbia University. Studies in the Social Sciences: No. 435). reprint ed. 29.50 (*0-404-51435-9*) AMS Pr.

Service Charges in Leases: A Practical Guide. G. Sherriff. (Waterlow Practitioner's Library). 128p. 1989. pap. 19.95 (*0-08-036904-9*, Pergamon Pr) Elsevier.

Service City: State & Townsmen in Russia, 1600-1800. J. Michael Hittle. LC 79-10909. 309p. 1979. reprint ed. pap. 88.10 (*0-7837-4154-5*, 2059002) Bks Demand.

Service Clubs in American Society: Rotary, Kiwanis, & Lions. Jeffrey A. Charles. LC 93-9803. (Illus.). 240p. 1993. text ed. 32.50 (*0-252-02015-4*) U of Ill Pr.

Service Condition of Workmen in Banks with Supplement. A. Arora & S. Sachdeva. (C). 1990. 60.00 (*0-89771-292-7*) St Mut.

Service Contracting: A Local Government Guide. Donald F. Harney. LC 92-5846. (Municipal Management Ser.). 1992. 45.00 (*0-87326-063-5*) Intl City-Cnty Mgt.

***Service Coordination: An Orientation for Families & Professionals.** B. Wightman. 134p. 1993. pap. text ed. write for info. (*1-888557-30-3*, 100046) No Ariz Univ.

Service Coordination for Early Intervention: Parents & Professionals. I. N. Zipper et al. 110p. 1993. pap. text ed. 19.95 (*0-914797-91-3*) Brookline Bks.

***Service Counts: Lessons from the Field of Service & Higher Education.** 160p. 1995. pap. 20.00 (*0-614-30595-0*) Ed Comm States.

Service Delivery in Educational Settings. Goldsmith. Date not set. write for info. (*0-7506-9573-0*) Buttrwrth-Heinemann.

Service Delivery in the Nineties: Alternative Approaches for Local Governments. Lydia Manchester & Carl Valente. Ed. by Cheryl Farr. 189p. (Orig.). 1989. pap. text ed. 38.00 (*0-87326-926-8*) Intl City-Cnty Mgt.

***Service Delivery Tools.** 84p. 1996. pap. 80.00 (*0-11-330633-4*, HM06334, Pub. by Stationery Ofc UK) Bernan Associates.

Service Economy. Victor R. Fuchs & Irving Leveson. (General Ser.: No. 87). 308p. 1968. 80.60 (*0-87014-475-8*, 62); pap. 9.00 (*0-87014-476-6*) Natl Bur Econ Res.

Service Economy: A Geographical Approach. Sven Illeris. LC 96-5962. 1996. text ed. 85.00 (*0-471-96618-5*) Wiley.

Service Edge: One Hundred One Companies That Profit from Customer Care. Ron Zemke & Dick Schaaf. 1990. pap. 16.95 (*0-452-26493-6*, Plume) NAL-Dutton.

Service Etiquette. 4th ed. Oretha D. Swartz. (Illus.). 580p. 1997. 29.95 (*0-87021-620-1*) Naval Inst Pr.

Service Evangelism. Richard S. Armstrong. LC 78-26701. 198p. 1979. pap. 13.00 (*0-664-24252-9*, Westminster) Westminster John Knox.

Service Excellence! Price Pritchett. 31p. (Orig.). 1989. pap. 5.95 (*0-944002-02-1*) Pritchett Assocs.

***Service Experience & Design in Pressure Vessels & Piping Including high Pressure Technology.** Ed. by W. H. Bamford. 261p. 1996. pap. text ed. 110.00 (*0-7918-1782-2*, TS283) ASME Pr.

Service Experience & Life Management - Nuclear, Fossil, & Petrochemical Plants. Ed. by W. H. Bamford. (PVP Ser.: Vol. 261). 352p. 1993. 70.00 (*0-7918-0988-9*, H00820) ASME.

Service Experience & Reliability Improvement: Nuclear, Fossil & Petrochemical Plants: Proceedings of the Pressure Vessels & Piping Conference, Minneapolis, MN, 1994. Ed. by W. H. Bamford. LC 94-71758. (PVP Ser.: Vol. 288). 430p. 1994. pap. 70.00 (*0-7918-1361-4*) ASME.

Service Experience, Structural Integrity, Severe Accidents, & Erosion in Nuclear & Fossil Plants. Ed. by S. R. Paterson et al. (Proceedings of the 1995 ASME/JSME Pressure Vessels & Piping Conference Ser.: PVP-Vol. 303). 428p. 1995. 130.00 (*0-7918-1334-7*, H00966) ASME.

Service Factor: Leveraging Customer Satisfaction in Small Business. Borg. 1991. pap. 7.50 (*0-9631663-0-1*) W & A Pub.

Service Fatigue Loads Monitoring, Simulation, Analysis - STP 671. Ed. by P. R. Abelkis & J. M. Potter. 298p. 1979. 29.50 (*0-8031-0721-8*, 04-671000-30) ASTM.

Service for the Dead. Robert A. Anderson. 288p. 1987. pap. 3.95 (*0-380-89980-9*) Avon.

Service for the High Holy Days Adapted for Youth. Adapted by Hyman Chanover. LC 72-2058. 192p. (J). (gr. 8 up). 1972. pap. 4.95 (*0-87441-123-8*) Behrman.

Service for the Lord's Day: The Worship of God. LC 84-5220. (Supplemental Liturgical Resource Ser.: No. 1). 192p. (Orig.). 1984. pap. 15.00 (*0-664-24641-9*, Westminster) Westminster John Knox.

Service for Two. Kate Kingsbury. 208p. (Orig.). 1994. mass mkt. 4.99 (*0-425-14223-X*, Prime Crime) Berkley Pub.

Service Hub Concept in Human Services Planning, Vol. 42-3. Dear. (Progress in Planning Ser.). 120p. 1994. pap. 61.00 (*0-08-042543-7*, Pergamon Pr) Elsevier.

Service in Siberia. Ned E. Wick. LC 72-29500. 1975. 4.00 (*0-685-64827-3*) Honor Bks.

Service in the Church Life. Bill Freeman. 24p. (Orig.). 1991. pap. 1.00 (*0-914271-22-9*) Mnstry Wrd.

Service in the Space Between Darkness & Light: A Service for Holy Week. James D. Freeman & Debra C. Freeman. 20p. (Orig.). 1995. pap. 3.95 (*0-7880-0300-3*) CSS OH.

Service Industries: A Geographical Appraisal. Peter Daniels. 300p. (C). 1986. text ed. 57.50 (*0-416-34530-1*, 9793) Routledge Chapman & Hall.

Service Industries: A WEP Study. Yves Sabolo. xv, 238p. 1975. 31.50 (*92-2-101300-6*); pap. 22.50 (*92-2-101133-X*) Intl Labour Office.

Service Industries & Economic Development: Case Studies in Technology Transfer. Ronald K. Shelp et al. LC 84-8304. 192p. 1984. text ed. 49.95 (*0-275-91265-5*, C1265, Praeger Pubs) Greenwood.

Service Industries in Developing Countries. Ed. by Erdener Kaynak. 224p. 1986. 35.00 (*0-7146-3291-0*, Pub. by F Cass Pubs UK) Intl Spec Bk.

Service Industries in Regional Development. William J. Coffey & James J. McRae. 166p. 1990. pap. text ed. 29.95 (*0-88645-103-5*, Pub. by Inst Res Pub CN) Ashgate Pub Co.

Service Industries in the World Economy. P. W. Daniels. LC 92-43005. (IBG Studies in Geography). (Illus.). 204p. 1993. pap. 20.95 (*0-631-18132-6*) Blackwell Pubs.

Service Industries U. S. A. Stet & Julie E. Towell. 1991. 169.00 (*0-8103-8397-7*) Gale.

Service Industries USA. 2nd ed. Darnay-Towell. 1994. 200.00 (*0-8103-8571-6*) Gale.

Service Industries USA. 3rd ed. Darney & Hart. 1996. 210.00 (*0-8103-5644-9*) Gale.

Service Inspector. Jack Rudman. (Career Examination Ser.: C-3501). 1994. pap. 29.95 (*0-8373-3501-9*) Nat Learn.

Service Inutile. Henry De Montherlant. 9.95 (*0-685-36986-2*) Fr & Eur.

Service Inutile: A Study of the Tragic in the Theatre of Henry de Montherlant. John E. Golsan. LC 88-15785. (Romance Monographs: No. 47). 1988. 24.00 (*84-599-2404-1*) Romance.

***Service Is an Honorable Profession.** Ed Soloman. (Illus.). 170p. 1997. 14.95 (*1-886939-13-6*) Oak Hill Pr OH.

Service Is No Inheritance, or Rules to Servants According to the Rev. Dr. J. Swift. Jonathan Swift. Ed. by Simona Draghici. LC 87-15113. Orig. Title: Directions to Servants. (Illus.). 80p. (Orig.). 1987. pap. text ed. 4.95 (*0-943045-01-0*) Plutarch Pr DC.

Service Laws & Constitutional. A. K. Kulshrestha. (C). 1988. 250.00 (*0-685-36463-1*) St Mut.

Service Laws & Constitutional Remedies. S. Kulshreshtha. (C). 1988. 150.00 (*0-685-25681-2*) St Mut.

***Service Leaders Club: Dazzling Your Customers Through Service.** William C. Byham et al. (Illus.). 200p. 1997. 17.95 (*0-9623483-7-6*, BPSLCHB) Dev Dimensions.

***Service Learning.** Joan Schine. (National Society for the Study of Education Yearbook Ser.). 1997. 24.00 (*0-226-73838-8*) U Ch Pr.

***Service-Learning: Applications from the Research.** Ed. by Alan Waterman. LC 96-49391. 208p. 1997. 45.00 (*0-8058-2535-5*); pap. 22.50 (*0-8058-2536-3*) L Erlbaum Assocs.

Service-Learning in Higher Education: Concepts & Practices. Barbara C. Jacoby et al. LC 96-10047. (Higher & Adult Education Ser.). 1996. write for info. (*0-7879-0291-8*) Jossey-Bass.

***Service-Learning in the Disciplines, 18 vols.** Ed. by Edward Zlotkowski. 1997. pap. 405.00 (*1-56377-005-9*) Am Assn Higher Ed.

Service Learning in the Middle School: Building a Culture of Service. Carl I. Fertman et al. LC 96-15861. 1996. pap. write for info. (*1-56090-108-X*) Natl Middle Schl.

Service Learning in the Middle School Curriculum: A Resource Book. Ron Schukar et al. (Illus.). (Orig.). 1996. pap. text ed. 18.95 (*0-89994-387-X*) Soc Sci Ed.

Service Learning Planning & Resource Guide. 277p. 1994. pap. 15.00 (*1-884037-04-6*) Coun Chief St Schl Offs.

Service-Learning Reader: Reflections & Perspectives on Service. Ed. by Gail Albert. 375p. (Orig.). 1994. pap. text ed. 38.00 (*0-937883-13-1*) NSEE.

Service-Led Growth: The Role of the Service Sector in World Development. Dorothy I. Riddle. LC 85-16743. 304p. 1985. text ed. 79.50 (*0-275-92041-0*, C2041, Praeger Pubs) Greenwood.

Service Level Agreements: Measuring Cost & Quality in Service Relationships. Andrew Hiles. LC 93-18878. 144p. 1993. 59.00 (*0-412-54240-4*) Chapman & Hall.

Service Life of Rehabilitated Buildings. Ed. by Stephen J. Kelley & Philip C. Marshall. LC 90-891. (Special Technical Publication (STP) Ser.: STP 1098). (Illus.). 130p. 1990. text ed. 40.00 (*0-8031-1398-6*, 04-010980-10) ASTM.

Service Load in Teacher Training Institutions of the United States. Lynn B. McMullen. LC 73-177038. (Columbia University. Teachers College. Contributions to Education Ser.: No. 244). reprint ed. 37.50 (*0-404-55244-7*) AMS Pr.

Service Load of a Staff Nurse in One Official Public Health Agency. Marion Ferguson. LC 71-176768. (Columbia University. Teachers College. Contributions to Education Ser.: No. 915). reprint ed. 37.50 (*0-404-55915-8*) AMS Pr.

Service Management. Harvard Business Review Staff. 100p. 1991. pap. 19.95 (*0-87584-298-4*) Harvard Busn.

Service Management. Harvard Business School Press Staff. 1991. pap. text ed. 19.95 (*0-07-103358-0*) McGraw.

***Service Management: Operations, Strategy, & Information Technology.** 2nd ed. James A. Fitzsimmons & Mona J. Fitzsimmons. LC 97-8293. 1997. write for info. (*0-07-021760-2*) McGraw.

Service Management: Principles & Practices. 2nd ed. William H. Bleuel & Joseph D. Patton. LC 86-10682. 326p. 1986. reprint ed. pap. 93.00 (*0-7837-5131-1*, 2044859) Bks Demand.

Service Management: Strategy & Leadership in Service Business. 2nd ed. Richard Normann. LC 90-43731. 185p. 1991. text ed. 60.00 (*0-471-92885-2*) Wiley.

Service Management: The Automation of Services. David A. Collier. 183p. 1985. write for info. (*0-8359-6907-X*) P-H.

Service Management & Marketing: Managing the Moment of Truth in Service Competition. Christian Gronroos. (Issues in Organization & Management Ser.). 298p. 44.95 (*0-669-20035-2*, Lexington) Jossey-Bass.

Service Management Course: Cases & Readings. W. Earl Sasser, Jr. et al. 700p. 1991. 45.00 (*0-02-914091-9*, Free Press) Free Pr.

Service Management Effectiveness: Balancing Strategy, Organization & Human Resources, Operations, & Marketing. David E. Bowen et al. LC 90-4047. (Management Ser.). 444p. 39.95 (*1-55542-222-5*) Jossey-Bass.

Service Management for Competitive Advantage. James A. Fitzsimmons & Mona J. Fitzsimmons. LC 93-35762. (Series in Management). 1993. text ed. write for info. (*0-07-021217-1*) McGraw.

Service Management in Computing & Telecommunications. Richard Hallows. LC 94-36072. 1994. 49.00 (*0-89006-676-0*) Artech Hse.

Service Marketing. 3rd ed. Christopher H. Lovelock. 600p. 1996. text ed. 71.33 (*0-13-455841-3*) P-H.

Service Marketing: Quality & Financial Impact. (C). 1996. teacher ed. write for info. incl. disk (*0-673-55524-0*) Addson-Wesley Educ.

Service Marketing: Quality & Financial Impact. Roland T. Rust et al. LC 95-38909. 528p. (C). 1996. text ed. 70.50 (*0-673-99145-8*) Addson-Wesley Educ.

S

Service Marketing: Quality & Financial Impact Reader. Rust & Anthony J. Zahorik. 528p. (C). 1996. text ed. 68.95 (0-673-98309-9) Addson-Wesley Educ.

***Service Matters 1996: A Sourcebook for Community Service in Higher Education.** 180p. 1996. pap. 25.00 (0-614-30594-2) Ed Comm States.

Service Ministry of the Deacon. Timothy J. Shugrue. 125p. (Orig.). 1988. pap. 3.95 (1-55586-240-3) US Catholic.

Service Monographs of the United States Government, No. 1-66. Brookings Institution Staff. reprint ed. write for info. (0-404-57100-X) AMS Pr.

Service Needs of the Seriously Mentally Ill: Training Implications for Psychology. Ed. by Dale L. Johnson. LC 90-1229. 160p. (Orig.). 1991. pap. 24.00 (1-55798-102-7) Am Psychol.

Service Occupations, 6 vols., Set. 98.00 (0-685-23034-1, CG109S) Ready Ref Pr.

Service of All the Dead. Colin Dexter. 1996. mass mkt. 5.99 (0-8041-1485-4) Ivy Books.

Service of Caring, the Art of Caring: A History of Expanding Health Care in the Pecos Valley. Charles W. Sanford. LC 95-76625. 88p. 1995. write for info. (0-929690-26-5) Herit Pubs AZ.

***Service of Glory: The "Cathechism of the Catholic Church" on Worship, Ethics, Spirituality.** Aidan Nichols. 320p. 1997. pap. 29.95 (0-567-08555-4, Pub. by T & T Clark UK) Bks Intl VA.

Service of God in Man. Swami Akhandananda. 186p. 1979. pap. 2.95 (0-87481-503-7) Vedanta Pr.

Service of Humanity. Damodar K. Mavalankar. (Sangam Texts Ser.). 132p. 1986. pap. 8.75 (0-88695-025-2) Concord Grove.

Service of Process Abroad: Practical Handbook on the Operation of the Hague Convention of 15 November 1965 on the Service Abroad of Judicial & Extrajudicial Documents in Civil or Commercial Matters. 2nd ed. 173p. 1992. 57.00 (90-6215-330-5, Pub. by Maklu Uitgevers BE) Gaunt.

Service of Shadows. J. B. Quisenberry. 1991. pap. 3.25 (1-55673-390-9, 9208) CSS OH.

Service of Supplication Chanted in Time of Drought. Tr. by Isaac E. Lambertsen from SLA. 20p. (Orig.). 1991. pap. 2.00 (0-912927-45-3, D002) St John Kronstadt.

Service of the Cavalry in the Army of the Potomac: A Paper Read Before the Rhode Island Soldiers & Sailors Historical Society February 12, 1879. Edward P. Tobie. LC 88-39204. (Eyewitness Accounts of the Civil War Ser.). 65p. (C). 1989. reprint ed. pap. 10.00 (0-942301-13-7) Birm Pub Lib.

Service of the Heart. Evelyn Garfiel. 1975. pap. 10.00 (0-87980-140-9) Wilshire.

Service of the Heart: A Guide to the Jewish Prayer Book. Evelyn Garfiel. LC 88-7830. 254p. 1995. pap. 19.95 (1-56821-041-8) Aronson.

Service of the Lesser Sanctification of Water: Customarily Used on the 1st Day of August. Tr. by Isaac E. Lambertsen from SLA. 12p. (Orig.). 1992. pap. 3.00 (0-912927-48-8, D011) St John Kronstadt.

Service of the Sunday Vespers. Nomikos M. Vaporis. 108p. (Orig.). 1992. pap. write for info. (0-318-72220-8) Themely Pubns.

Service of the Word & Sacrament: An Explanation. Wayne Schulz. 17p. (Orig.). 1996. pap. 1.75 (0-614-16402-8, 18N0360) NW Pub Co WA.

Service Operations Management. Roger W. Schmenner. (Illus.). 576p. 1994. text ed. 86.00 (0-02-406811-X, Macmillan Coll) P-H.

Service Operations Supervisor. Jack Rudman. (Career Examination Ser.: C-1880). 1994. pap. 29.95 (0-8373-1880-7) Nat Learn.

Service Opportunities for Electric Utilities: Creating Differentiated Products. Ed. by Shmuel S. Oren & Stephen A. Smith. LC 92-44559. (Topics in Regulatory Economics & Policy Ser.). 352p. (C). 1993. lib. bdg. 99.00 (0-7923-9319-8) Kluwer Ac.

***Service Parts Handbook.** Joseph D. Patton & Herbert C. Feldmann. LC 96-35417. 1996. write for info. (0-934623-73-2) Solomon Pr.

Service Parts Management. Joseph D. Patton, Jr. LC 84-19163. 320p. 1984. text ed. 56.00 (0-87664-811-1, 1811-1) ISA.

Service Parts Management: Principles & Practices. William B. Lee & Earle Steinberg. LC 84-70976. 129p. 1984. pap. 20.00 (0-935406-47-6) Am Prod & Inventory.

Service Parts Management Reprints. Ed. by David C. Davis et al. LC 82-72118. 123p. 1982. pap. 10.00 (0-935406-19-0) Am Prod & Inventory.

***Service Parts Seminar Proceedings 1981.** 36p. (Orig.). 1987. pap. 3.00 (0-614-24996-1) Am Prod & Inventory.

Service Parts Seminar Proceedings, 1983. Ed. by American Production & Inventory Control Society Staff. LC 83-72512. 90p. 1983. pap. 5.00 (0-935406-31-X, 40631) Am Prod & Inventory.

Service Productivity & Quality Challenge. Ed. by Patrick T. Harker. LC 95-8278. (International Studies in the Service Economy: Vol. 5). 516p. (C). 1995. lib. bdg. 115.00 (0-7923-3447-7) Kluwer Ac.

Service Profession, a Service Commitment: A Festschrift in Honor of Charles D. Patterson. Ed. by Connie Van Fleet & Danny P. Wallace. (Illus.). 268p. 1992. 32.50 (0-8108-2640-2) Scarecrow.

***Service Profit Chain.** Herskett & Sasser. LC 96-44611. 1997. 30.00 (0-684-83256-9, Free Press) Free Pr.

Service Provision Under Stress: States & Voluntary Organizations in Kenya, Tanzania & Uganda. Joseph Semboja & Ole Therkildsen. LC 95-21488. 242p. 1996. 70.00 (0-435-08980-3, 08980); pap. 30.00 (0-435-08982-X, 08982) Heinemann.

Service Quality: A Profit Strategy for Financial Institutions. Leonard L. Berry et al. 300p. 1988. text ed. 45.00 (1-55623-094-X) Irwin Prof Pubng.

Service Quality: Multidisciplinary & Multinational Perspectives. Ed. by Stephen W. Brown et al. (Issues in Organization & Management Ser.). 49p. 49.00 (0-669-21152-4, Lexington) Jossey-Bass.

Service Quality: New Directions in Theory & Practice. Ed. by Roland T. Rust & Richard L. Oliver. (Illus.). 304p. (C). 1993. text ed. 49.95 (0-8039-4919-7); pap. text ed. 22.95 (0-8039-4920-0) Sage.

Service Quality Handbook. Ed. by Eberhard E. Scheuing & William F. Christopher. LC 93-26614. (Illus.). 600p. 1993. 75.00 (0-8144-0119-8) AMACOM.

Service Quality Improvement: The Customer Satisfaction Strategy for Health Care. Wendy Leebov & Gail Scott. LC 93-32889. 378p. 1993. pap. 52.00 (1-55648-110-1, 136107) AHPI.

Service Quality in Academic Libraries. Peter Hernon & Ellen Altman. LC 95-42989. (Information Management, Policy & Services Ser.). (Illus.). 187p. 1996. pap. 39.50 (1-56750-210-5); text ed. 73.25 (1-56750-209-1) Ablex Pub.

Service Quality Management. 180p. 1992. ring bd. 245.00 (0-89982-347-5, 125900) Am Bankers.

Service-Quality Solution: Using Service Management to Gain Competitive Advantage. David A. Collier. 324p. 1994. text ed. 40.00 (1-55623-753-7) Irwin Prof Pubng.

Service Recovery: Fixing Broken Customers. Ron Zemke. LC 95-12451. (Management Master Ser.). (Illus.). 88p. 1996. pap. 12.95 (1-56327-097-8) Prod Press.

Service Recovery: Fixing Broken Customers. Ron Zemke. LC 95-12451. (Management Master Ser.). (Illus.). 88p. 1995. 15.95 (1-56327-150-8) Prod Press.

Service Sector: Productivity & Growth. Ed. by E. Felli et al. (Contributions to Economics Ser.). (Illus.). viii, 355p. 1995. pap. 78.00 (3-7908-0875-X) Spr-Verlag.

Service Sector in Soviet Economic Growth: A Comparative Study. Gur Ofer. LC 72-87775. (Russian Research Center Studies, No. 71, Economic Studies: No. 141). (Illus.). 216p. 1973. 16.50 (0-674-80180-6) HUP.

Service Sector in the United States Eighteen Thirty-Nine Through Eighteen Ninety-Nine. Thomas J. Weiss. LC 75-2602. (Dissertations in American Economic History Ser.). (Illus.). 1975. 28.95 (0-405-07223-6) Ayer.

Service Selling: A Guide to Increasing Sales & Profits in Consumer Financial Services. Robert G. Stemper. 230p. 1991. text ed. 65.00 (0-471-54030-7) Wiley.

***Service, Service, Service.** Steven Albrecht. Date not set. pap. 9.95 (1-55850-758-2) Adams Media.

Service, Service, Service: The Competitive Edge. Marian Thomas. (Communication Ser.). (Illus.). 194p. (Orig.). pap. 19.95 (1-55852-090-2) Natl Pr Pubns.

Service, Service, Service: The Growing Business' Secret Weapons. Steven Albrecht. 1994. pap. 10.95 (1-55850-432-X) Adams Media.

Service, Service, Service ... the Key to Winning & Keeping Customers for Life. Marian Thomas. 1992. pap. 7.95 (1-55852-064-3) Natl Pr Pubns.

Service Shop School. Peter T. Kulak. (Illus.). 92p. (Orig.). 1985. pap. text ed. 27.95 (0-943876-02-8) Barks Pubns.

Service Station Collectibles. Rick Pease. LC 95-42727. 160p. (YA). (gr. 10). 1996. pap. 29.95 (0-88740-934-2) Schiffer.

Service Station Manager. (Career Examination Ser.: C-3650). pap. 34.95 (0-8373-3650-3) Nat Learn.

Service Station Recordkeeping: A Practice Set. N. Fritz. 1968. text ed. 19.20 (0-07-022474-9) McGraw.

Service Stations in Western Europe. Euromonitor Staff. 90p. 1988. 825.00 (0-86338-314-9, Pub. by Euromonitor Pubns UK) Gale.

Service, Stud. Clay Caldwell. 1995. mass mkt. 5.95 (1-56333-336-8, Badboy) Masquerade.

Service Success: Lessons from a Leader on How to Turn Around a Service Business. Daniel I. Kaplan & Carl Reiser. 262p. 1994. text ed. 24.95 (0-471-59129-7) Wiley.

Service That Sells: The Art of Profitable Hospitality. Jim Sullivan & Phil Roberts. 178p. (Orig.). 1991. pap. 16.95 (1-879239-00-0) Pencom.

Service to a Fool for Christ Sake. Orthodox Eastern Church Staff. pap. 0.75 (0-89981-093-4) Eastern Orthodox.

***Service to Our Blessed in Christ Saint Xenia.** Ed. by St. Xenia Skete Staff. (Illus.). 48p. 1992. 3.50 (0-614-30955-7) St Herman Pr.

Service to St. Tikhon of Kaluga. (CHU.). pap. 5.00 (0-89981-092-6) Eastern Orthodox.

Service to the Nation Through Photo-Optical Instrumentation: 13th Annual Technical Symposium. Society of Photo-Optical Instrumentation Engineers Staff. LC 79-8810. (SPIE Ser.: Vol. 1). (Illus.). 486p. reprint ed. pap. 138.60 (0-317-41788-6, 2025646) Bks Demand.

Service Velocity: The Art of Service & Reverse Service. Michael Harding. (Illus.). 165p. (Orig.). pap. write for info. (0-614-07021-X) Northwest Home.

Service Wisdom: Creating & Maintaining the Customer Service Edge. Ron Zemke & Chip R. Bell. 342p. 1989. 19.95 (0-943210-08-9) Lakewood Pubns.

Service with a Smile. Carolyn Andrews. (Temptation Ser.). 1995. pap. 3.25 (0-373-25628-0, 1-25628-8) Harlequin Bks.

Service with a Smile. Karen O'Conner. 80p. (J). (ps-3). 1994. pap. 4.99 (0-570-04772-2, 56-1791) Concordia.

Service with the Sixth Wisconsin Volunteers. Rufus R. Dawes. 367p. 1984. 35.00 (0-89029-079-2) Morningside Bkshop.

Service Within: Solving the Middle Management Leadership Crisis. Karl Albrecht. 200p. 1990. text ed. 35.00 (1-55623-353-1) Irwin Prof Pubng.

Serviceability & Durability of Construction Materials. Ed. by Bruce A. Suprenant. LC 90-41923. 1384p. 1990. pap. text ed. 127.00 (0-87262-777-2) Am Soc Civil Eng.

Serviceability-Based Design of Partially Prestressed Beams. (PCI Journal Reprints Ser.). 47p. 1979. pap. 18.00 (0-685-06910-9, JR209) P-PCI.

Serviceability Design Considerations for Low-Rise Buildings, 1990. Fisher & West. 1990. 16.00 (1-56424-030-4, D803) Am Inst Steel Construct.

Serviceability of Earth Retaining Structures: Proceedings of Sessions Sponsored by the Geotechnical Engineering Division of the American Society of Civil Engineers in Conjunction with the ASCE National Convention in Atlanta, Georgia, October 9-13,1994. American Society of Civil Engineers, Geotechnical Engineering Division Staff. Ed. by Richard J. Finno. LC 94-23244. (Geotechnical Special Publications: Vol. 42). 1994. 21.00 (0-7844-0051-2) Am Soc Civil Eng.

Servicemember's Legal Guide. 3rd ed. Jonathan P. Tomes. (Illus.). 256p. 1996. pap. 16.95 (0-8117-3089-1) Stackpole.

Servicemember's Legal Guide: Everything You & Your Family Need to Know About the Law. 2nd ed. Jonathan P. Tomes. LC 91-29279. (Illus.). 240p. 1992. pap. 16.95 (0-8117-3016-6) Stackpole.

Serviceroboter. 1995. 70.00 (3-540-59359-4) Spr-Verlag.

Services: Measuring Real Annual Value Added. Statistics Directorate Staff. 122p. (Orig.). (ENG & FRE.). 1996. pap. 39.00 (92-64-14786-1, Pub. by Org for Econ FR) OECD.

Services: Statistics on International Transactions 1970-1992. 220p. 1995. 65.00 (92-64-04350-0, Pub. by Org for Econ FR) OECD.

***Services: Statistics on International Transactions 1970-1994.** OECD Staff. 444p. (Orig.). 1996. pap. 71.00 (92-64-15333-0, 30-96-14-1, Pub. by Org for Econ FR) OECD.

***Services: Statistics on Value Added & Employment, 1996 Edition.** 320p. 1996. 77.00 (92-64-04851-0, Pub. by Org for Econ FR) OECD.

Services - Statistics on International Transactions: 1970-1993. OECD Staff. 500p. (Orig.). 1996. pap. 67.00 (92-64-04836-7, Pub. by Org for Econ FR) OECD.

***Services--The Export of the 21st Century: A Guidebook for U. S. Service Exporters.** Joe Reif et al. LC 96-33514. 1996. write for info. (1-885073-41-0) Wrld Trade Pr.

Services Agenda: Essay in International Economics. Rodney C. Grey. 200p. 1990. pap. text ed. 29.95 (0-88645-095-0, Pub. by Inst Res Pub CN) Ashgate Pub Co.

Services & Circuses: Community & the Welfare State. Frederic Lesemann. Tr. by Lorne Huston & Margaret Heap from FRE. Orig. Title: Du Pain et des Services. 276p. 1984. 29.95 (0-920057-06-3, Pub. by Black Rose Bks CN); pap. 12.95 (0-920057-05-5, Pub. by Black Rose Bks CN) Consort Bk Sales.

Services & Development: The Role of Foreign Direct Investment & Trade. 187p. 1989. 26.00 (92-1-104324-7, E.89.II.A.17) UN.

Services & Metropolitan Development: International Perspectives. Ed. by Peter W. Daniels. (Illus.). 336p. (C). (gr. 13). 1991. text ed. 120.00 (0-415-00852-2, A5630) Routledge.

Services & Regions in Europe. Sven Illeris. (Fast Programme of the Commission of the European Communities Ser.). 237p. 1989. text ed. 63.95 (0-566-05722-0, Pub. by Avebury Pub UK) Ashgate Pub Co.

Services & Security Inside the Legislature 1992 Edition. Kae M. Warnock. 74p. 1992. pap. text ed. 15.00 (1-55516-740-3, 7133) Natl Conf State Legis.

Services & Services Trade: A Theoretical Inquiry. Joachim J. Stibora & Albert De Vaal. (Tinbergen Institute Research Ser.: No. 97). 273p. 1995. pap. 27.50 (90-5170-339-2, Pub. by Thesis Pubs NE) IBD Ltd.

Services & Space: Aspects of Urban & Regional Development. J. N. Marshall. (C). 1995. pap. text ed. 43.95 (0-582-25162-1) Addison-Wesley.

Services & Uneven Development. Ed. by J. N. Marshall. (Illus.). 328p. 1988. 75.00 (0-19-823285-3) OUP.

Services Around the World, Vol. 7. Ed. by Wesley F. Craven & James L. Cate. (Army Air Forces in World War II Ser.). (Illus.). 667p. (C). 1983. reprint ed. 20.00 (0-912799-09-9) Off Air Force.

Services Challenge: Integrating for Competitive Advantage. Ed. by John A. Czepiel et al. LC 87-12543. (American Marketing Association, Proceedings Ser.). (Illus.). 114p. 1987. reprint ed. pap. 32.50 (0-7837-9763-X, 2060491) Bks Demand.

Services Challenge: Integrating for Competitive Advantage - Proceedings. Ed. by Carole Congram et al. LC 87-12543. (Illus.). 125p. 1987. pap. text ed. 18.00 (0-87757-188-0) Am Mktg.

Services de Communication des Archives au Public. (ICA Handbook Ser.: Vol. 9). 306p. 1994. pap. 75.00 (3-598-20281-4) K G Saur.

***Services de Consultants: Contrat a Remuneration Forfaitaire.** (FRE.). 1996. 7.95 (0-8213-3608-8, 13608) World Bank.

***Services de Consultants: Taches Complexes Renumerees Au Temps Passe.** (FRE.). 1996. 7.95 (0-8213-3609-6, 13609) World Bank.

Services for Cardiovascular Emergencies: Proceedings of the WHO Expert Committee, Geneva, 1974. WHO Staff. (Technical Report Ser.: No. 562). 1975. pap. text ed. 10.00 (92-4-120562-8, 1100562) World Health.

Services for Crime Victims. Laura Lein & Robert C. Rickards. (Policy Research Project Report: No. 92). 76p. 1991. pap. 9.50 (0-89940-700-5) LBJ Sch Pub Aff.

Services for Employees. (Personnel Policies Forum Surveys Ser.: No. 133). 58p. 1981. 30.00 (0-87179-973-1) BNA.

Services for Ministers & Workers see Ministers Manual Ser.

Services for Occasions of Pastoral Care. (Supplemental Liturgical Resource Ser.: No. 6). (Orig.). 1990. pap. 7.00 (0-664-25153-6) Westminster John Knox.

Services for People with Learning Disabilities. Nigel A. Malin. LC 94-5049. 256p. (C). 1994. pap. 24.95 (0-415-09938-2, B4669) Routledge.

Services for People with Learning Disabilities. Nigel A. Malin. LC 94-5049. 256p. (C). (gr. 13). 1994. text ed. 69.95 (0-415-09937-4, B4665) Routledge.

Services for Sale: Purchasing Health & Human Services. Ed. by Harold Demone, Jr. & Margaret Gibelman. LC 88-18443. 500p. (C). 1989. text ed. 50.00 (0-8135-1361-8); pap. text ed. 18.00 (0-8135-1362-6) Rutgers U Pr.

***Services for Special Days.** 8.90 (0-687-38096-0) Abingdon.

***Services for Special Holidays: A Collection of Five Creative Celebrations to Impact Lives.** Robert L. Kintigh. Ed. by Cindy G. Spear. 105p. 1996. ring bd. 49.95 (1-57052-061-5) Chrch Grwth VA.

Services for Special Occasions, Vol.1 see Ministers Manual Ser.

Services for the Chronically Mentally Ill: New Approaches for Mental Health Professionals, 2 vols., 1. Ed. by Joan P. Bowker. 1988. 10.00 (0-87293-021-1) Coun Soc Wk Ed.

Services for the Chronically Mentally Ill: New Approaches for Mental Health Professionals, 2 vols., 2. Ed. by Joan P. Bowker. 1988. write for info. (0-87293-022-X) Coun Soc Wk Ed.

Services for the Chronically Mentally Ill: New Approaches for Mental Health Professionals, 2 vols., Vols. 1 & 2. Ed. by Joan P. Bowker. 1988. 10.00 (0-685-74118-4) Coun Soc Wk Ed.

Services for the Elderly: Case Studies in Administration & Management. Milan J. Dluhy & Martha Pelaez. 128p. (C). 1992. text ed. 29.95 (0-8039-4409-8); pap. text ed. 14.50 (0-8039-4410-1) Sage.

***Services for the Prevention & Treatment of Dependence on Alcohol & Other Drugs: Fourteenth Report of the WHO Expert Committee on Mental Health.** (Technical Report Ser.: No. 363). 0045p. 1900. pap. text ed. 5.00 (92-4-120363-3, 1100363) World Health.

Services for the Seriously Mentally Ill in Texas: Facts & Issues. Mary A. Pisani. 39p. (Orig.). 1988. pap. 1.00 (0-915757-11-7) League Women Voters TX.

Services for the Urban Poor: A Select Bibliography. Richard Franceys & Andrew Cotton. 84p. (Orig.). 1993. pap. 30.50 (1-85339-188-3, Pub. by Intermed Tech UK) Women Ink.

Services for Weddings & Funerals, Vol.2 see Ministers Manual Ser.

***Services from the Book of Common Prayer with a Deacon As Officiant.** Ed. by Justus Van Houten. 136p. (Orig.). 1996. pap. 12.00 (1-886136-01-7) N Am Assn Diaconate.

Services in Asia & the Pacific: Selected Papers. 366p. 1991. write for info. (92-1-112301-1, 91.II.D.7) UN.

Services in Asia & the Pacific: Selected Papers, 2 Vols., Vol. I. 441p. 1992. 55.00 (0-685-74413-2) UN.

Services in Asia & the Pacific: Selected Papers, 2 Vols., Vol. II. 366p. 1992. 55.00 (0-685-74414-0) UN.

Services in Distributed & Networked Environments, 1st Workshop (SDNE '94) LC 94-75252. 200p. 1994. pap. text ed. 40.00 (0-8186-5835-5) IEEE Comp Soc.

Services in Distributed & Networked Environments, 2nd Workshop (SDNE '95) LC 95-75327. 184p. 1995. pap. 40.00 (0-8186-7092-4, PR07092) IEEE Comp Soc.

Services in Distributed & Networked Environments, 3rd Workshop (SDNE '96) LC 96-76640. 174p. 1996. pap. 50.00 (0-8186-7499-7) IEEE Comp Soc.

Services in Economic Thought: Three Centuries of Debate. Jean-Claude Delauney. (International Studies in the Service Economy). 144p. (C). 1992. lib. bdg. 94.00 (0-7923-9230-2) Kluwer Ac.

Services in Switzerland: Structure, Performance, & Implications of European Economic Integration. Ed. by Peter Zweifel. LC 93-38660. 1993. 72.95 (0-387-57286-4) Spr-Verlag.

Services in the Global Market. Jacques A. Nusbaumer. (C). 1987. lib. bdg. 79.00 (0-89838-198-3) Kluwer Ac.

Services in the Transition Economies: Business Options for Trade & Investment. Michel Kostecki & Andras Fehervary. LC 96-15080. (Series in International Business & Economics). 240p. 1996. text ed. 66.00 (0-08-042582-8, Pergamon Pr) Elsevier.

Services Management: New Directions & Perspectives. Colin G. Armistead & Richard Teare. (Illus.). 304p. Date not set. 95.00 (0-614-09379-1) Cassell.

***Services Marketing.** David L. Kurtz & Kenneth E. Clow. 592p. 1997. text ed. write for info. (0-471-18034-3) Wiley.

***Services Marketing.** Helen Woodruffe. 307p. (Orig.). 1995. pap. 42.50 (0-7121-1039-9, Pub. by Pitman Pub Ltd UK) Trans-Atl Phila.

Services Marketing. Valarie A. Zeithaml. LC 95-44395. 1995. text ed. write for info. (0-07-078250-4) McGraw.

***Services Marketing: A Strategic Approach.** Karen P. Goncalves. (C). 1997. pap. text ed. 25.00 (0-13-106527-0) P-H.

Services Marketing: An Annotating Bibliography. Ed. by Raymond P. Fisk & Patriya S. Tansuhaj. LC 84-3028. 256p. (Orig.). 1985. pap. text ed. 16.00 (0-87757-167-8) Am Mktg.

Services Marketing: Principles & Practice. Adrian Palmer & Catherine Cole. LC 94-36242. 389p. (C). 1995. text ed. 75.00 (0-02-390563-8, Macmillan Coll) P-H.

Services Marketing in a Changing Environment: Proceedings. Ed. by Thomas M. Bloch et al. LC 84-24307. (Illus.). 138p. (Orig.). (C). 1985. pap. text ed. 18.00 (0-87757-174-0) Am Mktg.

An Asterisk (*) at the beginning of an entry indicates that the title is appearing in BIP for the first time.

Services of Colored Americans in the Wars of 1776 & 1812. William C. Nell. LC 78-144663. reprint ed. 27.50 (*0-404-00202-1*) AMS Pr.
Services of Graduates in Indian Wars. pap. 12.00 (*0-685-71806-9*, J M C & Co) Amereon Ltd.
Services of Graduates of West Point in Indian Wars. Eben Swift. (Guidon Monographs). 1976. 25.50 (*0-8488-1184-4*, J M C & Co) Amereon Ltd.
Services of Holy Week & Easter Sunday. Tr. by Nomikos M. Vaporis. LC 92-46039. 1993. pap. 20.00 (*0-917651-75-8*) Holy Cross Orthodox.
Services of Our Lady. Ed. by Sten Von Krusenstierna. 70p. 1982. pap. text ed. 3.80 (*0-918980-11-9*) St Alban Pr.
Services of the Bengal Native Army. F. G. Cardew. 576p. 1990. 105.00 (*0-948251-69-7*, Pub. by Picton UK) St Mut.
Services Operations Management. Robert G. Murdick et al. 650p. 1990. text ed. 91.00 (*0-205-12250-7*, H2250-2) Allyn.
Services Operations Management. Robert G. Murdick et al. 650p. 1990. teacher ed. write for info. (*0-318-66339-2*, H22510) P-H.
Services to the Aging & Aged: Public Policies & Programs. Ed. by Paul K. Kim. LC 94-28668. (Issues in Aging Ser.: Vol. 3). 344p. 1994. text ed. 56.00 (*0-8153-0611-3*, SS802) Garland.
Services to the Aging & Aged: Public Policies & Programs. Ed. by Paul K. Kim. LC 94-28668. (Issues in Aging Ser.: Vol. 3). 344p. 1995. pap. text ed. 20.95 (*0-8153-2275-5*) Garland.
Services to the Orthopedically Handicapped. Louis Hoyer & Charles K. Hay. Ed. by William R. Phillips & Janet Rosenberg. LC 79-6906. (Physically Handicapped in Society Ser.). (Illus.). 1980. reprint ed. lib. bdg. 17.95 (*0-405-13115-1*) Ayer.
Services under the State. M. Rama Jois. (C). 1987. 250.00 (*0-685-27903-0*) St Mut.
***Servicescapes: The Concept of Place in Contemporary Markets.** John Sherry. 320p. 1997. 37.95 (*0-8442-3005-7*) NTC Pub Grp.
***ServiceSim: Managing Customer Satisfaction.** Stuart James et al. (Illus.). 45p. (Orig.). (C). 1997. pap. text ed. 40.00 incl. disk (*1-885837-22-4*) Interpret Sftware.
Serviceworks: A Customer Service Workbook for Water Utilities. (Illus.). 80p. 1993. pap. 33.00 (*0-89867-684-3*, 20304) Am Water Wks Assn.
ServiceWorks! (Kit) A Step-by-Step Approach for People Responsible for Customer Service. Edward E. Hubbard. 57p. 1990. pap. 149.95 (*1-883733-10-3*) Global Insghts.
Servicing & Supporting IBM PCs & Compatibles. Julian V. Moss. 358p. (Orig.). 1992. pap. 47.50 (*1-85058-243-2*, Pub. by Sigma Press UK) Coronet Bks.
Servicing Audio & Hi-Fi Equipment. 2nd ed. Nick Beer. LC 94-22230. (Illus.). 304p. 1995. 49.95 (*0-7506-2117-6*) Buttrwrth-Heinemann.
Servicing Commercial Refrigeration Systems. Raymond K. Schneider. 280p. 1991. 19.95 (*0-912524-67-7*) Busn News.
Servicing Electrical Appliances. Incl. Vol. 1. Electrical Fundamentals & Heat-Producing Items. Ed. by National Radio Institute Staff et al. 1972. text ed. 33.95 (*0-07-046128-7*); Vol. 2. Motor Theory & Motor-Driven Items. Ed. by National Radio Institute Staff et al. 1972. text ed. 33.95 (*0-07-046129-5*); (C). 1972. write for info. (*0-318-54175-0*) McGraw.
Servicing Electronic Systems, Vol. 2, Part 1. Ian R. Sinclair & Geoffrey E. Lewis. 200p. 1991. pap. 24.95 (*1-85628-167-1*, Pub. by Avebury Pub UK) Ashgate Pub Co.
Servicing Electronics Systems, Vol. 1. Geoff E. Lewis & Ian R. Sinclair. 256p. 1991. pap. text ed. 24.95 (*1-85628-171-X*, Pub. by Avebury Pub UK) Ashgate Pub Co.
Servicing Electronics Systems, Vol. 2, Pt. 2. Ian R. Sinclair. 208p. 1992. pap. 29.95 (*1-85628-810-2*, Pub. by Avebury Pub UK) Ashgate Pub Co.
Servicing International Markets: Competitive Strategies of Firms. Peter J. Buckley et al. 336p. (C). 1992. text ed. 66.95 (*0-631-18189-X*) Blackwell Pubs.
Servicing Personal Computers. Salsberb. 1985. 24.95 (*0-13-806951-4*) P-H.
Servicing Personal Computers. 2nd ed. Michael H. Tooley. 1988. 44.00 (*0-434-91975-6*) CRC Pr.
Servicing Personal Computers. 4th ed. Michael H. Tooley. LC 93-44369. 304p. 1994. 49.95 (*0-7506-1757-8*) Buttrwrth-Heinemann.
Servicing Portfolio Evaluation & Management. Tom Healy & Jeff Briggs. Ed. by Lynn S. Powell. (Illus.). 125p. (Orig.). 1992. pap. 40.00 (*0-945359-07-1*) Mortgage Bankers.
Servicing the Middle Classes: Class, Gender, & Waged Domestic Labour in Contemporary Britain. Nicky Gregson & Michelle Lowe. LC 93-38461. (International Studies of Women & Place). (Illus.). 352p. (C). 1994. pap. 24.95 (*0-415-08531-4*, B4167) Routledge.
Servicing the Middle Classes: Class, Gender, & Waged Domestic Labour in Contemporary Britain. Nicky Gregson & Michelle Lowe. LC 93-38461. (International Studies of Women & Place). (Illus.). 352p. (C). (gr. 13). 1994. text ed. 85.00 (*0-415-08530-6*, B4163) Routledge.
Servicing TV & Video Equipment. Eugene Trundle. (Illus.). 256p. 1989. 69.95 (*0-7506-0102-7*) Buttrwrth-Heinemann.
Servicing Videocassette Recorders. 4th ed. Steve Beeching. (Illus.). 250p. 1993. 54.95 (*0-7506-0935-4*) Buttrwrth-Heinemann.
Servicio De Anotaciones Provisionales. 1993. pap. 25.00 (*0-614-03767-0*) MICHIE.
Servicio de Notas (Advanced Digesto Case Service) Ed. by Butterworth Staff. 100p. 1993. pap. 25.00 (*0-250-44701-0*) MICHIE.
Servicio de Notas Provisionales (Advanced Digesto Case Service) Ed. by Butterworth Staff. 27p. 1994. pap. 25.00 (*0-250-44842-4*) MICHIE.
Servicio Que Vende! El Arte de la Hospitalidad Rentable. Jim Sullivan & Phil Roberts. Tr. by Marcela Mendoza. (Illus.). 208p. (Orig.). (SPA.). pap. 16.95 (*1-879239-06-X*) Pencom.
Servicios de Consultoria: Servicios Complejos en Base al Tiempo Trabajado. 64p. (SPA.). 1996. 7.95 (*0-8213-3623-1*, 13609) World Bank.
Servicios de Consultoria - Consultant's Services: Remuneracion Mediante Pago de una Suma Global - Lump Sum Remuneration. 64p. (SPA.). 1996. 7.95 (*0-8213-3624-X*, 13623) World Bank.
Servii Grammatici Qui Feruntur in Vergilii Carmina Commentarii, 3 vols. Georg Thilo & Hermann Hagen. 1850p. (GER.). 1986. reprint ed. Bd. I: Aeneidos Librorum I-V Commentarii. write for info. (*0-318-70520-6*); reprint ed. Bd. II: Aeneidos Librorum VI-XII Commentarii. write for info. (*0-318-70521-4*); reprint ed. Bd. III: In Vergilii Bucolica et Georgica Commentarii. write for info. (*0-318-70522-2*) G Olms Pubs.
Servii Grammatici Qui Feruntur in Vergilii Carmina Commentarii, 3 vols., Set. Georg Thilo & Hermann Hagen. 1850p. (GER.). 1986. reprint ed. write for info. (*3-487-07787-6*) G Olms Pubs.
Servile State. Hilaire Belloc. LC 77-2914. 1977. 14.00 (*0-913966-31-2*); pap. 6.00 (*0-913966-32-0*) Liberty Fund.
Servility & Service: The Life & Work of Sir John Coke. Michael B. Young. (Royal Historical Society: Studies in History: No. 45). 312p. 1986. 63.00 (*0-86193-202-1*) Boydell & Brewer.
Serving America: Prospects for the Volunteer Force - A Twentieth Century Fund Paper. Richard Halloran. 71p. 1988. 18.95 (*0-87078-243-6*); pap. 8.95 (*0-87078-242-8*) TCFP-PPP.
Serving & Saving. Glenn Rogers. LC 88-63244. 150p. (Orig.). 1989. pap. 6.99 (*0-89900-326-5*) College Pr Pub.
Serving & Surviving As a Human-Service Worker. 2nd ed. J. Robert Russo. 182p. (C). 1993. pap. text ed. 16.95 (*0-88133-691-2*) Waveland Pr.
Serving As Senders: How to Care for Your Missionaries While They Are Preparing to Go, While They Are on the Field, When They Return Home. Neal Pirolo. 207p. (Orig.). 1991. pap. 7.95 (*1-880185-00-8*) Emmaus Rd Intl.
Serving Banquets. Anthony J. Strianese. (Food & Hospitality Ser.). 1992. 140.00 (*0-8273-5217-4*) Van Nos Reinhold.
Serving Children with Disabilities: A Systematic Look at the Programmes. Laudan Aron et al. (Urban Institute Ser.). 201p. 1996. pap. 59.95 (*1-85972-352-7*, Pub. by Avebury Pub UK) Ashgate Pub Co.
Serving Children with Disabilities: A Systematic Look at the Programs. Laudan Y. Aron et al. 200p. (Orig.). 1995. pap. text ed. 22.95 (*0-87766-651-2*) Urban Inst.
Serving Children with Disabilities: A Systematic Look at the Programs. Laudan Y. Aron et al. LC 95-45762. 182p. (Orig.). 1996. lib. bdg. 52.50 (*0-87766-650-4*) Urban Inst.
Serving Children with HIV Infection in Child Day Care: A Guide for Center-Based & Family Day Care Providers. Child Welfare League of America Staff. 48p. 1991. 11.95 (*0-87868-439-5*) Child Welfare.
Serving Christ: A Family Affair. Terry L. Miethe & Beverly Miethe. LC 95-140. 1995. pap. 12.99 (*0-89900-730-9*) College Pr Pub.
Serving Church. 2nd ed. L. T. Johnson. LC 83-80609. (Enabling Ser.). (Illus.). 104p. (Orig.). 1984. pap. 3.95 (*0-935797-01-7*) Harvest IL.
Serving Culturally Diverse Populations. Ed. by Jovita M. Ross-Gordon et al. LC 85-644750. (New Directions for Adult & Continuing Education Ser.: No. ACE 48). 1990. 16.95 (*1-55542-801-0*) Jossey-Bass.
Serving End-Users in Sci-Tech Libraries. Ed. by Ellis Mount. LC 84-10789. (Science & Technology Libraries: Vol. 5, No. 1). 122p. 1984. text ed. 29.95 (*0-86656-327-X*) Haworth Pr.
Serving Families & Children Through Partnerships: A How-to-Do-It Manual for Librarians. Sandra Feinberg & Sari Feldman. LC 96-10177. (How-to-Do-It Manuals Ser.: No. 65). 266p. 1996. pap. 35.00 (*1-55570-227-9*) Neal-Schuman.
Serving Families, Building Partnerships. Geoffrey Link & Marjorie Beggs. Ed. by Ethel Seiderman & Lisa Lee. (Illus.). 72p. (Orig.). 1996. pap. 10.00 (*0-936434-97-X*, PSP-SF) SF Study Ctr.
Serving Fire: Food for Thought, Body, & Soul. Anne Scott. (Illus.). 160p. (Orig.). 1995. pap. 12.95 (*0-89087-739-4*) Celestial Arts.
Serving Food. Anthony J. Strianese. (Food & Hospitality Ser.). 1992. 210.00 (*0-8273-5215-8*) Van Nos Reinhold.
Serving Gay & Lesbian Youths: The Role of Child Welfare Agencies: Recommendations from a CWLA Colloquium. Child Welfare League of America Staff. 1991. 6.95 (*0-87868-495-6*) Child Welfare.
Serving Gifted & Talented Students: A Resource for School Personnel. Ed. by Judy L. Genshaft et al. LC 94-9263. (C). 1994. text ed. 41.00 (*0-89079-605-X*, 6804) PRO-ED.
Serving God: The Grand Essentials of Work & Worship. rev. ed. Ben Patterson. 192p. 1994. pap. 9.99 (*0-8308-1399-3*, 1399) InterVarsity.
Serving God & Mammon: William Juxon, 1582-1663. Thomas Mason. LC 83-40507. (Illus.). 208p. 1985. 35.00 (*0-87413-251-7*) U Delaware Pr.
Serving Grace. Michael Griffiths. 1986. pap. 4.95 (*9971-972-40-9*) OMF Bks.
Serving HIV-Infected Children, Youth, & Their Families: A Guide for Residential Group Care Providers. 1989. pap. 14.95 (*0-87868-367-4*) Child Welfare.
Serving Humanity: A Compilation. Alice A. Bailey. 1977. pap. 14.00 (*0-85330-133-6*) Lucis.
Serving in Silence. Margarethe Cammermeyer & Chris Fisher. (Illus.). 320p. 1995. pap. 11.95 (*0-14-023159-5*, Penguin Bks) Viking Penguin.
Serving Job Seekers & Career Changers: A Critical Bibliography for Public Libraries. Kathleen M. Savage. LC 92-46877. 52p. (C). 1993. pap. text ed. 10.00 (*0-8389-3427-7*) ALA.
Serving Job Seekers & Career Changers: A Planning Manual for Public Libraries. Kathleen M. Savage et al. LC 92-38870. (Public Library Development Ser.). (Illus.). 125p. (C). 1993. pap. text ed. 25.00 (*0-8389-3419-6*) ALA.
***Serving Latino Communities: A How-to-Do-It Manual for School & Public Librarians.** Camila Alive & Orlando Archibecque. 150p. 1997. pap. 32.50 (*1-55570-276-7*) Neal-Schuman.
Serving Learners at a Distance: A Guide to Program Practices. Charles E. Feasley. Ed. & Frwd. by Jonathan D. Fife. LC 84-160901. (ASHE-ERIC Higher Education Reports: No. 83-5). 80p. (Orig.). 1983. pap. 18.75 (*0-913317-04-7*) GWU Grad Schl E&HD.
Serving Life & Faith: Adult Religious Education & the American Catholic Community. Ed. by Neil A. Parent. 72p. 1986. pap. 9.95 (*1-55586-982-3*) US Catholic.
Serving Linguistically & Culturally Diverse Students: Strategies for the School Library Media Specialist. Melvina A. Dame. 175p. 1993. 29.95 (*1-55570-116-7*) Neal-Schuman.
***Serving Older Adults in Libraries: Strategies & Solutions.** Ed. by Virginia H. Mathews. 200p. 1997. pap. 29.95 (*1-55570-279-1*) Neal-Schuman.
Serving on Promotion & Tenure Committees: A Faculty Guide. Robert M. Diamond. 64p. (C). 1994. pap. text ed. 7.50 (*1-882982-02-9*) Anker Pub.
***Serving One Another.** 1984. write for info. (*0-88207-121-1*, Victor Bks) Chariot Victor.
Serving One Another. Gene A. Getz. 156p. 1984. pap. 1.80 (*0-88207-612-4*, Victor Bks) Chariot Victor.
Serving Others. rev. ed. Navigators Staff. (Studies in Christian Living: Bk. 6). 32p. 1981. pap. 3.00 (*0-89109-082-7*) NavPress.
***Serving Our Public: Standards for Illinois Public Libraries.** rev. ed. Ed. by Robert P. Doyle & Joan A. Grygel. LC 97-25790. 100p. 1997. pap. write for info. (*1-890249-01-7*) IL Lib Assn.
Serving Personal & Community Needs Through Adult Education. Ed. by Edgar J. Boone et al. LC 79-9664. (Jossey-Bass Series in Higher Education). 360p. reprint ed. pap. 102.60 (*0-8357-4836-7*, 2037773) Bks Demand.
Serving Planet Earth. John S. Haigh. 112p. 1986. reprint ed. pap. 7.95 (*0-87516-568-0*) DeVorss.
Serving Power: The Making of the Academic Social Science Expert. Edward T. Silva & Sheila A. Slaughter. LC 83-18518. (Contributions to the Study of Education Ser.: No. 11). xi, 346p. 1984. text ed. 55.00 (*0-313-24058-2*, SSG/, Greenwood Pr) Greenwood.
Serving Print Disabled Library Patrons: A Textbook for Facilitators of Library Service to People with Visual or Physical Impairments. Ed. by Bruce E. Massis. LC 96-12720. 190p. 1996. lib. bdg. 42.50 (*0-7864-0209-1*) McFarland & Co.
Serving Readers. Ed. by William T. Balcom. LC 96-38513. (Highsmith Press Handbook Ser.). 96p. (Orig.). 1997. pap. 15.00 (*0-917846-74-5*, 95643) Highsmith Pr.
Serving Safe Food. Education Foundation of NRA Staff. 208p. 1996. per., pap. text ed. 2.92 (*0-7872-0231-2*) Kendall-Hunt.
Serving Safe Food: A Guide for Foodservice Employees. Educational Foundation of the National Restaurant Association Staff. (ServSafe Ser.). (Illus.). 43p. (Orig.). (C). 1990. pap. text ed. 5.95 (*0-915452-56-1*) Educ Found.
Serving Special Needs Students in the School Library Media Center. Caren L. Wesson & Margaret J. Keefe. LC 94-39085. (Professional Guides in School Librarianship Ser.). 280p. 1995. text ed. 45.00 (*0-313-28697-3*) Greenwood.
Serving Survivors of Torture. Glenn R. Randall & Ellen L. Lutz. 218p. 1991. 18.00 (*0-87168-433-0*, 91-42S) AAAS.
***Serving the American Public: Best Practices in Resolving Customer Complaints.** 1997. lib. bdg. 251.95 (*0-8490-6123-7*) Gordon Pr.
***Serving the American Public: Best Practices in Telephone Service: Federal Consortium Benchmark Study Report.** Al Gore. 35p. (Orig.). (C). 1996. pap. text ed. 25.00 (*0-7881-2858-2*) DIANE Pub.
Serving the Chronically Mentally Ill in an Urban Setting: The Massachusetts Mental Health Center Experience. Ed. by Miles F. Shore & Jon E. Gudeman. LC 87-646993. (New Directions for Mental Health Services Ser.: No. MHS 39). 1988. 19.00 (*1-55542-892-4*) Jossey-Bass.
Serving the Difficult Customer: A How-to-Do-It Manual for Library Staff. Kitty Smith. LC 93-46452. (How-to-Do-It Manuals for Libraries Ser.: No. 39). 166p. 1994. pap. 42.50 (*1-55570-161-2*) Neal-Schuman.
Serving the Disabled: A How-to-Do-It Manual for Librarians. Kieth C. Wright & Judith F. Davie. (How-to-Do-It Ser.). 159p. 1991. 39.95 (*1-55570-085-3*) Neal-Schuman.
Serving the Elderly: Skills for Practice. Ed. by Paul K. Kim. (Modern Applications of Social Work Ser.). 350p. 1991. pap. text ed. 30.95 (*0-202-36074-1*); lib. bdg. 49.95 (*0-202-36073-3*) Aldine de Gruyter.
Serving the Geriatric Market. Business Communications Co., Inc. Staff. 427p. 1988. pap. 1,750.00 (*0-89336-530-0*, GB-096) BCC.
Serving the Gospel Feast: How God Invites You & All Peoples to Share His Varied Gifts. Arthur M. Vincent. 288p. (Orig.). 1989. pap. 8.95 (*0-9621882-0-4*) Adv Renewal.
***Serving the High-Risk Investor.** Fowler. Date not set. pap. text ed. 49.00 (*0-15-601942-6*) Profess Pubns.
***Serving the Internet with Windows NT.** Ed. by Robert J. Denn. (Illus.). (Orig.). 1997. pap. write for info. (*0-614-21752-0*) OReilly & Assocs.
***Serving the Internet with Windows NT.** R. Scott Starsman. 1997. pap. text ed. 34.95 (*1-56592-248-4*) OReilly & Assocs.
Serving the Jewish Family. Ed. by G. B. Bubis. 35.00 (*0-87068-439-6*) Ktav.
Serving the King. Albert B. Simpson. 1996. pap. 7.99 (*0-87509-593-3*) Chr Pubns.
Serving the King. Derek Thomas. 1989. pap. 3.99 (*0-85234-270-5*, Pub. by Evangelical Pr) Presby & Reformed.
***Serving the Net: Using the Microsoft Internet Information Server.** Robert Lee. 1996. pap. text ed. 34.95 incl. cd-rom (*0-13-492281-6*) P-H.
Serving the People: Social Services & Social Change. Ann Withorn. LC 84-3160. 272p. 1984. text ed. 45.00 (*0-231-05560-9*) Col U Pr.
Serving the Present Age: Revivalism, Progressivism, & the Methodist Tradition in Canada. Phyllis D. Airhart. 232p. 1992. 44.95 (*0-7735-0882-1*, Pub. by McGill CN) U of Toronto Pr.
Serving the Profession: Tax Executives Institute at Fifty. Tax Executives Institute, Inc. Staff. Ed. by Timothy J. McCormally. 40p. (Orig.). 1994. pap. text ed. 25.00 (*0-915128-04-7*) Tax Exec Inst.
Serving the Public - Building the Union: The Forerunners 1889-1928. Dix. (History of N U P E Ser.: Vol. 1). (C). 1987. pap. 19.95 (*0-85315-646-8*, Pub. by Lawrence & Wishart UK); text ed. 39.95 (*0-85315-645-X*, Pub. by Lawrence & Wishart UK) NYU Pr.
Serving the Republic: Memoirs of the Civil & Military Life of Nelson A. Miles. Nelson A. Miles. LC 74-147786. (Select Bibliographies Reprint Ser.). 1977. reprint ed. 28.95 (*0-8369-5632-X*) Ayer.
Serving the Seriously Mentally Ill: Public-Academic Linkages in Services, Research & Training. Ed. by Paul Wohlford et al. 275p. 1993. pap. 34.95 (*1-55798-216-3*) Am Psychol.
Serving the Silent Service: The Legend of Electric Boat. Jeffrey L. Rodengen. (Illus.). 144p. 39.95 (*0-945903-24-3*) Write Stuff Syndicate.
Serving the Underserved: Caring for People Who Are Both Old & Mentally Retarded. Ed. by Mary C. Howell et al. 508p. 1989. pap. 29.95 (*0-930958-08-X*) Excptnl Parent.
Serving the Underserved: Caring for People Who Are Both Old & Mentally Retarded, a Handbook for Caregivers. Mary C. Howell et al. LC 89-84088. 512p. 1989. text ed. 55.00 (*0-313-28382-6*) Greenwood.
Serving the Unemployed & Their Families. Robert Sunley & G. William Sheek. LC 86-6344. 128p. 1986. pap. 13.95 (*0-87304-218-2*) Families Intl.
Serving the University of Missouri: A Memoir of Campus & System Administration. James C. Olson. (Illus.). 232p. 1993. text ed. 34.95 (*0-8262-0924-6*) U of Mo Pr.
Serving the Urban Poor. David Fanshel et al. LC 91-44572. 368p. 1992. text ed. 55.00 (*0-275-94075-6*, C4075, Praeger Pubs) Greenwood.
Serving the Web. Robert Mudry. 1995. pap. 34.99 (*1-883577-30-6*) Coriolis Grp.
Serving Time Together. Sanders & Forrest. 1993. pap. 18.95 (*1-85230-340-9*) Element MA.
Serving to Learn, Learning to Serve: Civics & Service from A-Z. Cynthia Parsons. LC 95-21434. (Illus.). 112p. 1995. 40.00 (*0-8039-6364-5*); pap. 18.00 (*0-8039-6365-3*) Corwin Pr.
Serving Two Masters: The Law of Lawyer Disqualification. American Bar Association Staff. 54p. 1984. 7.95 (*0-89707-149-2*, 515-0022) Amer Bar Assn.
Serving with Christ: A Study of Jesus' Farewell Commission to His Disciples. R. Wade Paschal, Jr. LC 94-72242. 104p. 1994. pap. 8.95 (*0-88177-137-6*, DR137) Discipleship Res.
***Serving with the Poor in Africa: Cases in Holistic Ministry.** Ed. by T. Yamamori et al. 240p. 1996. pap. 15.95 (*0-912552-98-0*) MARC.
***Serving with the Poor in Asia: Cases in Holistic Ministry.** Ed. by T. Yamamori et al. 216p. 1995. pap. 15.95 (*0-912552-90-5*) MARC.
Serving Your Community: How to Meet the Needs of Small Business Customers & Comply with the CRA. Ed. by Charlotte Weisman. (Special Collection from the Journal of Commercial Bank Lending). 1994. pap. text ed. 45.00 (*1-57070-002-8*, 36050) Robt Morris Assocs.
Servitude & Grandeur of Arms. Alfred De Vigny. Tr. by Roger Gard. 1997. pap. 11.95 (*0-14-044663-X*) Viking Penguin.
Servitude et Grandeur Militaires. Alfred De Vigny. Ed. by Sylvie Germain. 1965. pap. 7.95 (*0-8288-9672-0*, F75920) Fr & Eur.
Servitude et Grandeur Militaires. A. Vigny. 361p. 1965. 39.95 (*0-8288-7419-0*) Fr & Eur.
Servitudes of International Law: A Study of Rights in Foreign Territory. 2nd ed. F. A. Vali. (Legal Reprint Ser.). xvi, 349p. 1986. reprint ed. lib. bdg. 40.00 (*0-8377-2703-0*) Rothman.
***Servius & Commentary on Virgil.** Peter K. Marshall. LC 97-23566. (Occasional Papers, Center for Medieval & Early Renaissance Studies). 1997. pap. write for info. (*1-889818-03-8*) Pegasus Pr.

An Asterisk (*) at the beginning of an entry indicates that the title is appearing in BIP for the first time.

S

*Servius & Commentary on Virgil. Peter K. Marshall. (Cemers Occasional Papers: Vol. 5). 44p. 1997. pap. 6.95 (0-86698-216-7, PCM5) Pegasus Pr.
Seryozha: Several Stories From the Life of a Very Small Boy. 3rd ed. Tr. by Nicholas Bierkoff. (Illus.). 110p. 1995. 16.50 (0-939074-10-9) Harvest Pubns.
S.E.S. Study Series: Student Text: Grade Kindergarten. rev. ed. Sensa Educational Systems, Inc. Staff. 1991. pap. text ed. 8.95 (0-941535-05-3) Sensa Educ Syst.
S.E.S. Study Series: Student Text: Grade 10. rev. ed. Sensa Educational Systems, Inc. Staff. 1991. pap. text ed. 8.95 (0-941535-15-0) Sensa Educ Syst.
S.E.S. Study Series: Student Text: Grade 11. rev. ed. Sensa Educational Systems, Inc. Staff. 1991. pap. text ed. 8.95 (0-941535-16-9) Sensa Educ Syst.
S.E.S. Study Series: Student Text: Grade 12. rev. ed. Sensa Educational Systems, Inc. Staff. 1991. pap. text ed. 8.95 (0-941535-17-7) Sensa Educ Syst.
S.E.S. Study Series: Student Text: Grade 2. rev. ed. Sensa Educational Systems, Inc. Staff. 1991. pap. text ed. 8.95 (0-941535-07-X) Sensa Educ Syst.
S.E.S. Study Series: Student Text: Grade 3. rev. ed. Sensa Educational Systems, Inc. Staff. 1991. pap. text ed. 8.95 (0-941535-08-8) Sensa Educ Syst.
S.E.S. Study Series: Student Text: Grade 4. rev. ed. Sensa Educational Systems, Inc. Staff. 1991. pap. text ed. 8.95 (0-941535-09-6) Sensa Educ Syst.
S.E.S. Study Series: Student Text: Grade 5. rev. ed. Sensa Educational Systems, Inc. Staff. 1991. pap. text ed. 8.95 (0-941535-10-X) Sensa Educ Syst.
S.E.S. Study Series: Student Text: Grade 6. rev. ed. Sensa Educational Systems, Inc. Staff. 1991. pap. text ed. 8.95 (0-941535-11-8) Sensa Educ Syst.
S.E.S. Study Series: Student Text: Grade 7. rev. ed. Sensa Educational Systems, Inc. Staff. 1991. pap. text ed. 8.95 (0-941535-12-6) Sensa Educ Syst.
S.E.S. Study Series: Student Text: Grade 8. rev. ed. Sensa Educational Systems, Inc. Staff. 1991. pap. text ed. 8.95 (0-941535-13-4) Sensa Educ Syst.
S.E.S. Study Series: Student Text: Grade 9. rev. ed. Sensa Educational Systems, Inc. Staff. 1991. pap. text ed. 8.95 (0-941535-14-2) Sensa Educ Syst.
S.E.S. Study Series Bk. 1: Grades K, 1, 2, 3. rev. ed. Sensa Educational Systems, Inc. Staff. 1991. teacher ed. 95.00 (0-941535-00-2) Sensa Educ Syst.
S.E.S. Study Series Bk. 2: Grades 4, 5, 6. rev. ed. Sensa Educational Systems, Inc. Staff. 1991. teacher ed. 95.00 (0-941535-01-0) Sensa Educ Syst.
S.E.S. Study Series Bk. 3: Grades 7 & 8. rev. ed. Sensa Educational Systems, Inc. Staff. 1991. teacher ed. 95.00 (0-941535-02-9) Sensa Educ Syst.
S.E.S. Study Series Bk. 4: Grades 9 & 10. rev. ed. Sensa Educational Systems, Inc. Staff. 1991. teacher ed. 95.00 (0-941535-03-7) Sensa Educ Syst.
S.E.S. Study Series Bk. 5: Grades 11 & 12. rev. ed. Sensa Educational Systems, Inc. Staff. 1991. teacher ed. 95.00 (0-941535-04-5) Sensa Educ Syst.
S.E.S. Study Series, Student Text: Grade 1. rev. ed. Sensa Educational Systems, Inc. Staff. 1991. pap. text ed. 8.95 (0-941535-06-1) Sensa Educ Syst.
Sesame. Betty Kamen. 1989. pap. 1.95 (0-87983-436-6) Keats.
Sesame. Jack Marshall. LC 93-26494. (Orig.). 1993. pap. 11.95 (1-56689-015-2) Coffee Hse.
Sesame & Lilies: The Two Paths & the King of the Golden River. John Ruskin. LC 70-145275. (Illus.). 1971. reprint ed. 69.00 (0-403-01190-6) Scholarly.
*Sesame Street. (Little Golden Bks.). (J). (gr. k up). 1996. boxed write for info. (0-307-35513-6, Golden Books) Western Pub.
Sesame Street: A Sesame Street Sing-Along. (Golden Lyric Book 'N' Tape, Sing-Along Ser.). (Illus.). 32p. (J). (ps-3). write for info. incl. audio (0-307-05336-9, 5336, Golden Books) Western Pub.
Sesame Street: Another Monster at the End of This Book. Jon Stone. (J). 1996. 2.50 (0-307-98769-8, Golden Books) Western Pub.
Sesame Street: At the Playground. Norman Gorbaty. (J). 1987. 1.10 (0-394-88503-1) Random Bks Yng Read.
Sesame Street: Big Bird Meets the Orchestra. (Golden Story Book 'n Tape, Learn about Music Ser.). (Illus.). 24p. (J). (ps-3). write for info. incl. audio (0-307-14426-7, 14426) Western Pub.
*Sesame Street: Color Surprise. Golden Books Staff. (Illus.). (J). 1997. pap. text ed. 2.99 (0-307-15280-4, Golden Books) Western Pub.
Sesame Street: Come to the Playground. Elisabeth Clasing. (Golden Touch & Feel Bks.). (Illus.). 12p. (J). (ps-3). 1992. write for info. (0-307-12003-1, 12003, Golden Books) Western Pub.
Sesame Street: Elmo's Favorite Sing-Alongs. (Golden Lyric Book 'N' Tape, Sing-Along Ser.). (Illus.). 32p. (J). (ps-3). write for info. incl. audio (0-307-05335-0, 5335, Golden Books) Western Pub.
*Sesame Street: Elmo's Noisy Day. Sarah Albee. Ed. by Betsy Loredo. (Magic Touch Talking Bks.). (Illus.). (J). (ps-2). 1997. 19.99 (1-888208-37-6) Hasbro.
Sesame Street: Little Ernie Loves Rubber Duckie. Illus. by Tom Brannon. (Baby's First Bks.). 12p. (J). (ps-3). 1992. write for info. (0-307-06064-0, 6064, Golden Books) Western Pub.
Sesame Street: Little Grover Takes a Walk. Illus. by Tom Brannon. (Deluxe Baby's First Bks.). (J). (ps). 1991. pap. write for info. (0-307-06062-4, Golden Pr) Western Pub.
Sesame Street: My Name Is Oscar the Grouch. Liza Alexander. (Illus.). 24p. (J). (ps-3). 1994. pap. 1.49 (0-307-11617-4, Golden Books) Western Pub.
Sesame Street: Playtime with Bigbird. Norman Gorbaty. (J). 1987. 1.10 (0-394-88507-4) Random Bks Yng Read.
Sesame Street: Rise & Shine! Constance Allen. (Golden Super Shape Bks.). (Illus.). (J). 1996. pap. 2.69 (0-614-15647-5, Golden Books) Western Pub.
Sesame Street: Scheherryzade & the Arabian Nights. (Golden Story Book 'n Tape, Learn about Music Ser.). (Illus.). 24p. (J). (ps-3). write for info. incl. audio (0-307-14425-9, 14425) Western Pub.
Sesame Street: The Twelve Days of Christmas Starring Elmo. Sarah Albee. (J). 1996. 2.50 (0-307-98787-6, Golden Books) Western Pub.
Sesame Street: Tubbie Time with Little Ernie. Norman Gorbaty. (J). 1987. 1.10 (0-394-88505-8) Random Bks Yng Read.
Sesame Street: Zip, Pop, Hop & Other Fun Words to Say. Michaela Muntean. (J). (ps-3). 1996. 1.50 (0-307-30310-1, Golden Pr) Western Pub.
*Sesame Street No. 2: 1, 2, 3, Go! (J). 1989. mass mkt. 1.86 (0-553-18381-8) Bantam.
*Sesame Street No. 3: Red, Yellow, Blue. (J). 1989. mass mkt. 1.86 (0-553-18382-6) Bantam.
*Sesame Street No. 4: Shape Up! (J). 1989. mass mkt. 1.86 (0-553-18385-0) Bantam.
*Sesame Street No. 5: Look & See. (J). 1989. mass mkt. 1.86 (0-553-18386-9) Bantam.
*Sesame Street No. 6: What Next? (J). 1989. mass mkt. 1.86 (0-553-18387-7) Bantam.
*Sesame Street No. 7: Animals, Animals. (J). 1989. mass mkt. 1.86 (0-553-18388-5) Bantam.
*Sesame Street No. 8: Sound It Out. (J). 1989. mass mkt. 1.86 (0-553-18389-3) Bantam.
*Sesame Street No. 9: One of These Things Is Not Like the Other. (J). 1989. mass mkt. 1.86 (0-553-18390-7) Bantam.
*Sesame Street No. 10: Big Little, Near Far. (J). 1989. mass mkt. 1.86 (0-553-18391-5) Bantam.
*Sesame Street - Easter: Super Coloring Books. (J). 2.29 (0-307-08544-9, 08544, Golden Books) Western Pub.
Sesame Street ABC Book of Words. Sesame Street Staff. LC 86-62405. (Illus.). 48p. (J). (ps). 1988. 11.00 (0-394-88880-4) Random Bks Yng Read.
Sesame Street Babies. (J). 23.70 (0-679-86351-6) Random Bks Yng Read.
Sesame Street Babies Busy Busy Day. (Illus.). (J). (ps-3). pap. 2.19 (0-307-07101-4, Golden Books) Western Pub.
Sesame Street Bert's Beautifil Sights. Constance Allen. (Golden Sturdy Shape Bks.). (J). (ps). 1990. bds. 3.95 (0-307-12318-9, Golden Books) Western Pub.
Sesame Street Big Bird's Animal Game. Illus. by Tom Cooke. (Golden Sturdy Shape Bks.). 14p. (J). (ps). 1993. bds. 3.95 (0-307-12395-2, 12395, Golden Books) Western Pub.
Sesame Street Big Bird's Busy Day. Little Golden Books Staff. (First Little Golden Bks). (Illus.). 24p. (J). (ps). 1995. bds. 1.19 (0-307-10157-6, Golden Books) Western Pub.
*Sesame Street Bunny Hop. Sarah Albee. (Sesame Street Ser.). (J). 1997. 1.99 (0-307-98791-4, Golden Books) Western Pub.
Sesame Street Cookie Monster's Good Time to Eat! Richard Brown. (Golden Sturdy Shape Bks.). (Illus.). 14p. (J). (ps). 1989. bds. 3.95 (0-307-12259-X, Golden Books) Western Pub.
Sesame Street Cookie Monster's Little Kitchen: A Chunky Book. Tom Cooke. LC 94-66510. 1995. 3.99 (0-679-85456-8) Random.
Sesame Street Count to Ten. Little Golden Books Staff. (First Little Golden Bks). (Illus.). 24p. (J). (ps). 1995. bds. 1.13 (0-307-10163-0, Golden Books) Western Pub.
Sesame Street Counting Book. Dina Anastasio. (J). 1985. 1.00 (0-307-02023-1) Western Pub.
Sesame Street Dictionary. Sesame Street Staff & Linda Hayward. LC 80-11644. (Illus.). 256p. (J). (ps-3). 1980. 18.00 (0-394-84007-0); lib. bdg. 17.99 (0-394-94007-5) Random Bks Yng Read.
Sesame Street Elmo's Guessing Game. Constance Allen. (Illus.). 14p. (J). (ps). 1993. bds. 3.95 (0-307-12398-7, Golden Books) Western Pub.
Sesame Street Farm Friends. Illus. by Pat Sustendal. (Cuddle Cloth Bks.). 12p. (J). (ps). 1985. 4.99 (0-394-87466-8) Random Bks Yng Read.
Sesame Street Favorites. (Boxed Bks.). (J). (ps-3). 1990. write for info. (0-307-15537-4) Western Pub.
Sesame Street Fire Trucks. Illus. by Joe Mathieu. (Wheel Bks.). 14p. (J). (ps). 1988. bds. 4.99 (0-394-89952-0) Random Bks Yng Read.
Sesame Street Golden Books, 10 vols., Set. Sesame Street Staff. (Illus.). (J). (ps). 1993. boxed 12.95 (0-307-95534-6, Golden Books) Western Pub.
Sesame Street Grouches on Parade. (Magic Corner Bks.). (Illus.). 14p. (J). 1995. bds. 9.95 (0-307-76032-4, Golden Pr) Western Pub.
Sesame Street Grover's Little Backpack: A Chunky Book. Tom Cooke. LC 94-66511. 1995. 3.25 (0-679-85454-1) Random.
Sesame Street Grover's Mommy. Little Golden Books Staff. (First Little Golden Bks). (Illus.). (J). (ps-3). 1.19 (0-307-30203-2, Golden Books) Western Pub.
*Sesame Street Growing up Grouchy. Golden Books Staff. (Sesame Street Ser.). (J). 1997. 1.99 (0-307-30368-3, Golden Books) Western Pub.
Sesame Street Happy Birthday Rosita. (Illus.). (J). (ps-3). pap. 1.59 (0-307-04012-7, Golden Books) Western Pub.
Sesame Street I Can Dress Myself. Little Golden Books Staff. (First Little Golden Bks). (Illus.). 24p. (J). (ps). 1983. bds. 1.09 (0-307-10140-1, Golden Books) Western Pub.
Sesame Street Little Elmo's Tay Box. Illus. by Tom Brannon. (J). (ps). 1990. bds. 1.95 (0-307-06038-1, Golden Books) Western Pub.
Sesame Street Little Theater. Stef De Reuver. (J). 1996. 4.99 (0-679-87185-3) Random Bks Yng Read.
Sesame Street Look at Me! C. W. Hood. (Golden Little Super Shape Bks.). (Illus.). 24p. (J). (ps). 1994. pap. 1.49 (0-307-10557-1, Golden Books) Western Pub.
Sesame Street Mother Grouch Nursery Rhymes. Michael J. Smollin. 1995. pap. 4.99 (0-679-85459-2) Random.
Sesame Street Musical Storybook: Big Bird's Tea Party. Jim Henson. (J). 1989. 12.99 (0-88704-096-9) Sight & Sound.
Sesame Street My Name Is, 6 bks., Set. (Sesame Street My Name Is...Ser.). (Illus.). 24p. (J). (ps-3). 1995. boxed 8.95 (0-307-16260-5, Golden Books) Western Pub.
Sesame Street No More Diapers! Emma Thompson. (Illus.). 24p. (J). (ps-3). 1995. pap. text ed. 1.95 (0-307-10010-3, Golden Books) Western Pub.
Sesame Street Numbers/Bedtime Big Book. (Illus.). (J). (ps-3). pap. 1.59 (0-307-01129-1, Golden Books) Western Pub.
Sesame Street Oscar's Grouchy Sounds. Constance Allen. (Golden Sturdy Shape Bks.). (Illus.). 14p. (J). (ps). 1990. bds. 3.95 (0-307-12319-7, Golden Books) Western Pub.
Sesame Street Peek-a-Boo! Constance Allen. (Golden Little Super Shape Bks.). (Illus.). 24p. (J). (ps). 1994. pap. 1.49 (0-307-10556-3, Golden Books) Western Pub.
Sesame Street Pet Parade. (Deluxe Golden Sound Story Bks.). (Illus.). 24p. (J). (ps-3). 1991. 9.95 (0-307-74007-2, Golden Books) Western Pub.
Sesame Street Pop-up Riddle Book. Sesame Street Staff. LC 77-70852. (Sesame Street Pop-up Ser.: No. 11). (Illus.). (J). (ps-3). 1977. bds. 8.99 (0-394-83546-8) Random Bks Yng Read.
Sesame Street Rainforest Adventure. Liza Alexander. (Golden Sound Story Bks.). (Illus.). 24p. (J). (ps-3). 1992. 9.95 (0-307-74021-8, 64021, Golden Books) Western Pub.
Sesame Street Revisited. Thomas D. Cook et al. LC 74-25853. 420p. 1975. 39.95 (0-87154-207-2) Russell Sage.
Sesame Street Shake a Leg. (Illus.). (J). (ps-3). 1.59 (0-307-10184-3, Golden Books) Western Pub.
Sesame Street Side Kick. (J). write for info. (0-676-73298-4) Random.
Sesame Street Sign Language ABC with Linda Bove. Linda Bove. LC 85-1845. (Pictureback Ser.). (Illus.). 32p. (J). (gr. 3-8). 1985. pap. 3.25 (0-394-87516-8) Random Bks Yng Read.
Sesame Street Songbook: Sixty Favorite Songs. 217p. (J). (ps-3). 1992. 25.00 (0-02-525141-4, Mac Bks Young Read) S&S Childrens.
Sesame Street Songbook: Sixty-Four Favorite Songs. Collier Books Staff. (J). 1994. pap. 20.00 (0-02-019201-0) Macmillan.
Sesame Street Stays up Late: Based on the Television Special by Lou Berger. Illus. by Joe Mathieu. LC 94-32232. (Pictureback Ser.). (J). (ps-3). 1995. pap. 3.25 (0-679-86743-0) Random.
Sesame Street Story Land. LC 86-80134. (Prestige Editions Ser.). (Illus.). 196p. (J). (ps-3). 1986. 12.95 (0-307-16530-2, Golden Books) Western Pub.
Sesame Street Storybook. Sesame Street Staff. (Illus.). (J). (ps-4). 1971. lib. bdg. 5.99 (0-394-92332-4) Random Bks Yng Read.
Sesame Street Talent Show. Sesame Street Staff. (J). 1997. pap. 5.99 (0-679-88401-7) Random.
Sesame Street Treasury: Featuring Jim Henson's Sesame Street Muppets. Liza Alexander et al. LC 93-8326. (Illus.). (J). write for info. (0-679-84655-7); lib. bdg. write for info. (0-679-94655-1) Random.
Sesame Street Whose Knees Are These? Anna Ross. (J). (ps). 1994. 4.99 (0-679-84742-1) Random Bks Yng Read.
Sesame Street Whose Who. (Illus.). (J). (ps-3). Date not set. pap. 2.99 (0-307-05573-6, Golden Books) Western Pub.
Sesame Street Word Book. Illus. by Tom Leigh. (Golden Bestsellers Ser.). 72p. (J). (ps-3). 1983. write for info. (0-307-15549-8, 15818, Golden Books) Western Pub.
Sesiidae (Lepidoptera) of Fennoscandia & Denmark. M. Fibiger & Niels P. Kristensen. (Fauna Entomologica Scandinavica Ser.: No. 2). (Illus.). 91p. 1974. pap. 20.00 (87-87491-02-8) Lubrecht & Cramer.
*SESOIL in Environmental Fate & Risk Modeling. Ed. by Marc Bonazountas et al. (Illus.). 686p. (C). 1997. text ed. 59.95 (1-884940-05-6) Amherst Sci Pubs.
Sesqui-Centennial International Exposition. E. L. Austin & Odell Hauser. LC 75-24109. (America in Two Centuries Ser.). 1976. reprint ed. 58.95 (0-405-07670-3) Ayer.
Sesquicentennial Chronological Tables of the Written Laws of the Republic of Singapore, 1834-1984. G. W. Bartholomew et al. cxii, 350p. 1987. 117.00 (9971-70-053-0) MICHIE.
Sesquicentennial History of Iowa, 14 vols. Donald L. Kimball. (Illus.). 1992. Set. write for info. (0-942698-19-3) Trends & Events.
Sesquicentennial History of the Connecticut Academy of Arts & Sciences. Rollin G. Osterweis. (Connecticut Academy of Arts & Sciences Ser., Trans.: Vol. 38, Pt. 2). 1949. pap. 29.50 (0-685-22901-7) Elliots Bks.
Sesquicentennial History of the First United Methodist Church, Nacogdoches, Texas 1837-1987. Carolyn Ericson. LC 87-81865. (Illus.). 200p. (Orig.). 1987. pap. text ed. 15.00 (0-911317-42-2) Ericson Bks.
Sesquicentennial History of the Town of Greene, Androscoggin Co., Me., 1775 to 1900, with Some Matter Extending to a Later Date. Walter L. Mower. (Illus.). 578p. 1995. reprint ed. lib. bdg. 58.00 (0-8328-4463-2) Higginson Bk Co.
Sesquicentennial History, Williamson County, Illinois. Williamson County, Illinois Sesquicentennial Committee Staff. LC 89-51691. 456p. 1990. 49.95 (0-938021-76-1) Turner Pub KY.
Sesquicentennial of Effingham County. Sandra Buechler. (Illus.). 808p. 1982. 75.00 (0-9609598-0-7) Banbury Pub Co.
Sesquicentennial Park: The Design Competition. Shawn McKinney et al. (Illus.). 70p. (Orig.). (C). 1987. pap. 35.00 (0-9618107-0-X) Cent Houst Civic.
Sesquicentennial Tribute to Galdos, 1843-1993. Ed. by Linda Willem. 395p. 1993. 24.50 (0-936388-57-9) Juan de la Cuesta.
Sesquipedalian Neologist's Lexicon. Thompson. 1995. pap. 5.00 (0-88092-174-9) Royal Fireworks.
Sesquiterpene Lactones: Chemistry, NMR & Plant Distribution. Hirosuke Yoshioka et al. LC 74-178545. 556p. 1973. reprint ed. pap. 158.50 (0-608-01568-7, 2061987) Bks Demand.
Sesshu's Long Scroll: A Zen Landscape Journey. Reiko Chiba. LC 54-14085. (Illus.). 1959. 19.95 (0-8048-0677-2) C E Tuttle.
Sessile Animals of the Sea Shore. Vernon Harris. (Illus.). 416p. (gr. 13). 1990. text ed. 90.95 (0-412-33760-6, A4377) Chapman & Hall.
Session Cats Sidekicks & Special Guests: Secret History of Rock Session Cats. Fredericksall. 1998. 27.00 (0-02-864720-3) Mac Lib Ref.
*Session Family - Short Stories & Poetry. Garry Session. (Illus.). 43p. (Orig.). 1997. 18.00 (0-9658006-0-1) Session Family.
*Session Family - Short Stories & Poetry. Garry Session. (Illus.). 43p. (Orig.). 1997. pap. 15.00 (0-9658006-1-X) Session Family.
Session Laws see Pimsleur's Checklists of Basic American Legal Publications
Session Matters: A Handbook for Elders. Tr. by Stewart Matthew. 88p. (C). 1989. 35.00 (0-685-60673-2, Pub. by St Andrew UK) St Mut.
Session Matters: A Handbook for Elders. Stewart Matthew. 88p. 1993. pap. 22.00 (0-7152-0644-3, Pub. by St Andrew UK) St Mut.
Session Plans. 217p. 1988. write for info. (0-318-64307-3) US HHS.
Session Plans. Robert C. Godfrey. Ed. by Danny G. Langdon. LC 77-25427. (Instructional Design Library). (Illus.). 96p. 1978. 27.95 (0-87778-120-6) Educ Tech Pubns.
Sessions. Eli Goldblatt. (Illus.). 80p. (Orig.). 1990. pap. 9.00 (0-925904-06-6) Chax Pr.
Sessions! Norman Seeff. Ed. by Paul Berry. (Illus.). 240p. 1994. 39.95 (0-9627095-5-7) WhaleSong.
Sessions: A Self-Help Guide Through Psychotherapy. Ann P. Wildemann. LC 95-51291. 192p. 1996. pap. text ed. 16.95 (0-8245-1559-5) Crossroad NY.
Sessions of York & Their Printing Forebears, 1985. Sessions, William Ltd., Staff. (C). 1985. 60.00 (0-685-37108-5, Pub. by W Sessions UK) St Mut.
Sessions of York & Their Printing Forebears, 1985. Sessions, William Ltd., Staff. (C). 1990. 70.00 (0-685-37375-4, Pub. by W Sessions UK) St Mut.
Sessions of York & Their Printing Forebears, 1985. Sessions, William, Ltd. Staff. (C). 1985. pap. 21.00 (0-685-67278-6, Pub. by W Sessions UK) St Mut.
Sessions on Remote Sensing 1980. Ed. by A. B. Kahle et al. (Advances in Space Research Ser.: Vol. 1, No. 10). (Illus.). 314p. 1981. pap. 48.00 (0-08-028388-8, Pergamon Pr) Elsevier.
Sessions Trial. 5th rev. ed. K. C. Mehrotra. (C). 1991. 95.00 (0-685-47800-9) St Mut.
Sesto libro de' madrigali a sei voci (1595) Luca Marenzio. Ed. by Patricia Myers. (Secular Works Ser.: Vol. 6). xxxv, 220p. (ITA.). 1983. pap. 50.00 (0-8450-7106-8) Broude.
*Set. Paul E. Secker. 325p. (Orig.). 1997. mass mkt. 4.99 (1-55237-182-4, Pub. by Comnwlth Pub CN) Partners Pubs Grp.
Set All Afire: A Novel of Saint Francis Xavier. 2nd rev. ed. Louis De Wohl. LC 90-85368. 280p. (YA). (gr. 8 up). 1991. reprint ed. pap. 12.95 (0-89870-351-4) Ignatius Pr.
*Set Apart to Serve. Mathews. 20.75 (0-687-38100-2) Abingdon.
*Set Aside Every Fear: Based on the Classic Spirituality of Catherine of Siena. John Kirvan. LC 97-19240. (Thirty Days with a Great Spiritual Teacher Ser.). 216p. (Orig.). 1997. pap. 6.95 (0-87793-624-2) Ave Maria.
Set Dances of Ireland: Tradition & Evolution. Larry Lynch. (Illus.). 316p. (Orig.). 1991. reprint ed. 25.00 (0-9623366-0-2) Seadna Bks.
Set Fair for Roanoke: Voyages & Colonies, 1584-1606. David B. Quinn. LC 84-2345. (Illus.). xxiv, 468p. 1985. pap. 16.95 (0-8078-4123-4) U of NC Pr.
Set for Edwin Honig. Hugo Leckey. (First Edition Ser.: Vol. 2, No. 3). (Illus.). (Orig.). 1973. pap. 1.50 (0-916912-07-8) Hellcoal Pr.
Set for Life: Eat More - Weigh Less - Feel Terrific! 2nd rev. ed. Jane P. Merrill & Karen M. Sunderland. (Illus.). 326p. 1995. pap. 18.95 (0-9621168-3-1) Sunrise Pubs.
Set for Life: The Only Complete Guide to Retirement Living in New Hampshire. Wilma L. Allen. LC 93-60807. 75p. 1993. pap. 9.95 (0-9637690-0-6) Wellington Allen Grp.
Set for the Donut Franchise: A Microcomputer Simulation for Business in Action. 2nd ed. Lester R. Bittel et al. 48p. 1985. TRS-Version. 150.00 (0-07-079411-1); Apple Version. 150.00 (0-07-079357-3) McGraw.
Set Free. Betty Tapscott. 1978. pap. 6.95 (0-917726-24-3) Hunter Bks.
Set Free! A Personal Message for Former & Non-attending Seventh-day Adventists. Don Hawley. 450p. (Orig.). 1989. pap. write for info. (0-318-65721-X) Better Living.
Set Free: A Woman's Victory over Eating Disorders. Linda McGrath. 112p. (Orig.). 1992. pap. 12.95 (0-87040-795-3) Japan Pubns USA.

***Set Free! Christianity Versus American Indians, Jews & Other Non-Christians.** 4th ed. Helen Smith. LC 97-20358. (Illus.). 1997. ring bd. 19.95 (*0-945437-23-4*) MacDonald-Sward.

Set Free: Leaving Negative Emotions Behind. rev. ed. Marilyn Kunz & Catherine Schell. 55p. 1995. pap. 4.99 (*1-880266-17-2*) Neighborhood Bible.

Set Free from Satan's Slavery. Peter Popoff. Ed. by Don Tanner. LC 82-83455. 64p. 1982. pap. 2.00 (*0-938544-17-9*) Faith Messenger.

Set Free from the Prison of Unforgiveness. Debra K. Moore. 1991. pap. write for info. (*1-56588-000-5*) Moore Educ.

Set Free in China: Sojourns on the Edge. Peter Heller. LC 91-40238. 180p. 1992. reprint ed. pap. 51.30 (*0-608-00548-7*, 2061427) Bks Demand.

SET, H. E. S. T-a Humanistic Endeavor & Surgent Train-Ascendance. Russell E. Mason. 1975. Incl: Guides for Groups & Communication; Broad Considerations; Ways of Train-Ascendance. pap. 10.00 (*0-89533-028-8*) F I Comm.

Set III Mini Sampler. 1995. write for info. (*0-13-515412-X*) P-H.

Set in Authority. Sarah J. Duncan. Ed. by Germaine Warkentin. 250p. 1995. pap. 12.95 (*1-55111-080-6*) Broadview Pr.

Set in L. A. Scenes of the City in Fiction. Sam Bluefarb. LC 86-18819. v, 87p. 1986. reprint ed. lib. bdg. 33.00 (*0-89370-573-X*) Borgo Pr.

Set in Motion. Valerie Martin. 224p. 1978. 8.95 (*0-374-26140-7*) FS&G.

Set in Motion. Valerie Martin. 224p. 1991. reprint ed. pap. 10.00 (*0-671-73687-6*, WSP) PB.

Set in Motion: Essays, Interviews, & Dialogues. A. R. Ammons. Ed. by Zofia Burr. (Poets on Poetry Ser.). (Orig.). 1996. pap. 13.95 (*0-472-06603-X*); text ed. 39.50 (*0-472-09603-6*) U of Mich Pr.

Set in Stone, Fixed in Glass: The Mormons, the West, & Their Photographers. 2nd ed. Nelson B. Wadsworth. LC 96-7281. (Illus.). xii, 388p. (Orig.). 1992. pap. 29.95 (*1-56085-106-6*) Signature Bks.

***Set It on Paper: Teaching Notes, No. 1.** Anja Fonck. 23p. 1994. teacher ed., pap. 19.95 (*90-5356-110-2*, Pub. by Amsterdam U Pr NE) U of Mich Pr.

Set It on Paper Vol. 1: Writing from a Communicative Perspective Dutch As a Second Language. Anja Fonck et al. (Orig.). (DUT & ENG.). (C). 1995. pap. 13.95 (*90-5356-079-3*, Pub. by Amsterdam U Pr NE) U of Mich Pr.

Set It on Paper Vol. 2: Writing from a Communicative Perspective Dutch As a Second Language. Anja Fonck et al. (Orig.). (DUT & ENG.). (C). 1995. pap. 13.95 (*90-5356-080-7*, Pub. by Amsterdam U Pr NE) U of Mich Pr.

***Set It on Paper Teaching Notes, Vol. 2.** Marijke Asscheman & Stephanie Kuijper. 34p. 1994. teacher ed., pap. 27.95 (*90-5356-113-7*, Pub. by Amsterdam U Pr NE) U of Mich Pr.

Set Lighting Technician's Handbook: Film Lighting Equipment, Practice, & Electrical Distribution. Harry C. Box. (Illus.). 376p. 1993. 36.95 (*0-240-80161-X*, Focal) Buttrwrth-Heinemann.

Set Lighting Technician's Handbook: Film Lighting Equipment, Practice, & Electrical Distribution. 2nd ed. Harry C. Box. LC 96-24075. (Illus.). 448p. 1996. pap. 39.95 (*0-240-80257-8*, Focal) Buttrwrth-Heinemann.

Set Me Free. large type ed. Denise Robins. 1993. 17.95 (*0-7505-0479-X*, Pub. by Magna Print Bks UK) Ulverscroft.

Set Model for Database & Information Systems. Mikhail Gilula. LC 93-49804. (C). 1994. text ed. 37.75 (*0-201-59379-3*) Addison-Wesley.

***Set My Daughter Free.** Mary N. Segalla. 90p. (Orig.). 1997. pap. 5.00 (*1-57502-432-2*, PO1317) Morris Pubng.

Set My Heart Free. Rita J. Carmack. 144p. 1984. pap. 5.00 (*0-88144-031-0*) Jewel Pr.

***Set My Spirit Free: Expressions of Pentecost.** large type ed. E. Myron Noble & Evelyn M. Taylor. Tr. & Intro. by Wardell J. Payne. 95p. (Orig.). 1995. pap. text ed. 9.95 (*1-877971-18-9*) Mid Atl Reg Pr.

Set No Limits: A Rebuttal to Daniel Callahan's Proposal to Limit Health Care for the Elderly. Ed. by Robert L. Barry & Gerard V. Bradley. 160p. 1991. text ed. 22.95 (*0-252-01860-5*) U of Ill Pr.

Set of Alphabets in Modern Use with Examples of Each Style: Letters, Cyphers, Figures, Monograms, Borders, Compasses & Flourishes. Frank S. Copley. 200p. 1989. pap. 15.00 (*0-87556-490-9*) Saifer.

Set of Directions for Putting (& Keeping) Yourself Together. Robert E. Wubbolding. (Illus.). 78p. (Orig.). 1990. pap. 8.00 (*0-9626410-0-6*) Real World OH.

Set of Four. Claire Gibeau. 4p. 1995. pap. 2.50 (*0-87487-907-8*) Summy-Birchard.

Set of Six. Joseph Conrad. 395p. 1983. lib. bdg. 18.95 (*0-89966-264-1*) Buccaneer Bks.

Set of the Sail. Aiden W. Tozer. Ed. by Harry Verploegh. LC 86-70772. 172p. (Orig.). 1986. pap. 8.99 (*0-87509-379-5*) Chr Pubns.

Set-Off. 2nd ed. Ed. by Rory Derham. 750p. 1996. 165.00 (*0-19-825907-7*) OUP.

Set Phasers on Stun: And Other True Tales of Design, Technology, & Human Error. Steven M. Casey. LC 93-70944. 221p. 1993. 24.95 (*0-9636178-7-7*) Aegean Pub.

Set Piece. Kate Orman. (Dr. Who New Adventures Ser.). 1995. pap. 5.95 (*0-426-20436-0*, Pub. by Virgin Pub UK) London Brdge.

Set Pieces: Being about Film Stills, Mostly. Daniel Meadows. (Illus.). 116p. (C). 1993. 52.95 (*0-85170-389-5*, Pub. by British Film Inst UK); pap. 22.95 (*0-85170-390-9*, Pub. by British Film Inst UK) Ind U Pr.

***Set Point of Happiness.** Elizabeth Berg. LC 97-25206. 1998. write for info. (*0-679-45722-4*) Random.

Set the Hook! Guide to Lone Star Lakes & Lunkers. Bobby Farquhar & Mark McDonald. 300p. 1991. pap. 19.95 (*0-9630964-0-0*) FarMac Bks.

Set the Stars Alight. large type ed. Denise Robins. 288p. 1995. 25.99 (*0-7089-3352-1*) Ulverscroft.

Set the Table: Recipes from Teens to Grandma. Marilyn Avery. (Illus.). 160p. (Orig.). 1986. pap. 8.95 (*0-9620775-0-X*, TX1-994-127) M Avery.

Set the Trumpet to Thy Mouth. David Wilkerson. 176p. 1993. mass mkt. 4.99 (*0-88368-318-0*) Whitaker Hse.

Set Theory. Ed. by Tomek Bartoszynski & Marion Scheepers. LC 95-34595. (Contemporary Mathematics Ser.: Vol. 192). 200p. 1995. pap. 45.00 (*0-8218-0306-9*, CONM/192) Am Math.

Set Theory. K. Kunen. (Studies in Logic & the Foundations of Mathematics: Vol. 102). 314p. 1984. pap. 74.75 (*0-444-86839-9*, I-013-84) Elsevier.

Set Theory. 2nd ed. Felix Hausdorff. LC 57-8493. 27.50 (*0-8284-0119-5*) Chelsea Pub.

***Set Theory.** 2nd ed. Thomas J. Jech. LC 97-17626. (Perspectives in Mathematical Logic Ser.). 1997. write for info. (*3-540-63048-1*) Springer Pub.

Set Theory: An Introduction. Robert L. Vaught. 1986. 45.95 (*0-8176-3238-7*) Birkhauser.

Set Theory: An Introduction. 2nd ed. Robert L. Vaught. LC 94-9544. 1994. 49.50 (*0-8176-3697-8*) Birkhauser.

***Set Theory: An Operational Approach.** Luis E. Sanchis. 279p. 1997. text ed. 69.00 (*90-5699-507-3*, QA248) Gordon & Breach.

Set Theory: On the Structure of the Real Line. Tomek Bartoszynski & Haim Judah. LC 95-34063. 560p. 1995. text ed. 78.00 (*1-56881-044-X*) AK Peters.

Set Theory & Its Applications. Ed. by S. Watson & J. Steprans. (Lecture Notes in Mathematics Ser.: Vol. 1401). vi, 219p. 1989. pap. 33.00 (*0-387-51730-8*) Spr-Verlag.

Set Theory & Its Logic. rev. ed. Willard V. Quine. LC 68-14271. 378p. 1969. pap. 14.95 (*0-674-80207-1*) Belknap Pr.

Set Theory & Linguistics. Alejandro Ortiz & Ernesto Zierer. (Janua Linguarum, Ser. Minor: No. 70). (Orig.). 1968. pap. text ed. 12.70 (*90-279-0597-5*) Mouton.

Set Theory & Logic. Robert R. Stoll. 474p. 1979. reprint ed. pap. 12.95 (*0-486-63829-4*) Dover.

Set Theory & Metric Spaces. 2nd ed. Irving Kaplansky. LC 77-7344. 1977. text ed. 13.95 (*0-8284-0298-1*) Chelsea Pub.

Set Theory & Related Topics. Seymour Lipschutz. (Orig.). (C). 1964. pap. text ed. 14.95 (*0-07-037986-6*) McGraw.

Set Theory & Syntactic Description. William S. Cooper. (Janua Linguarum, Ser. Minor: No. 34). 52p. 1974. pap. text ed. 53.85 (*90-279-2704-9*) Mouton.

***Set Theory & the Continuum Problem.** Raymond M. Smullyan & Melvin Fitting. (Oxford Logic Guides Ser.: No. 34). (Illus.). 304p. 1996. 75.00 (*0-19-852395-5*) OUP.

***Set Theory for the Working Mathematician.** Krzysztof Ciesielski. (London Mathematical Society Student Texts Ser.: Vol. 39). 240p. (C). 1997. text ed. 59.95 (*0-521-59441-3*) Cambridge U Pr.

***Set Theory for the Working Mathematician.** Krzysztof Ciesielski. (London Mathematical Society Student Texts Ser.: Vol. 39). 240p. (C). 1997. pap. text ed. 19.95 (*0-521-59465-0*) Cambridge U Pr.

Set Theory, Logic & Their Limitations. Moshe Machover. 256p. (C). 1996. pap. text ed. 24.95 (*0-521-47998-3*) Cambridge U Pr.

Set Theory, Logic & Their Limitations. Moshe Machover. 256p. (C). 1996. text ed. 65.00 (*0-521-47493-0*) Cambridge U Pr.

Set Theory Objects: Abstractions for Computer-Aided Design Analysis & Compostion of Serial & Atonal Music. Peter Castine. LC 94-33468. (European University Studies Series XXXVI: Vol. 121). 1994. write for info. (*3-631-47897-6*) P Lang Pubng.

Set Theory of the Continuum. Chiing-Chen Chern. Ed. by Winifrid Just et al. LC 92-28316. (Mathematical Sciences Research Institute Publications: Vol. 26). ix, 416p. 1992. 64.95 (*0-387-97874-7*) Spr-Verlag.

Set Theory of the Reals. Ed. by Haim Judah. (Israel Mathematical Conference Proceedings Ser.: Vol. 6). 654p. 1993. pap. 61.00 (*0-685-70693-1*, IMCP/6C, Bar-Ilan Univ) Am Math.

Set Theory with a Universal Set: Exploring an Untyped Universe. 2nd ed. T. E. Forster. (Oxford Logic Guides Ser.: Vol. 31). 176p. (C). 1995. 60.00 (*0-19-851477-8*) OUP.

Set Theory with Applications. You-Feng Lin & Shwu Yeng T. Lin. (Illus.). ix, 221p. 1985. reprint ed. pap. text ed. 29.50 (*0-931541-04-2*) Mancorp Pub.

Set This House on Fire. William Styron. 1960. 15.00 (*0-394-44482-5*) Random.

Set This House on Fire. William Styron. LC 91-50737. 1993. pap. 14.00 (*0-679-73674-3*) Random.

Set Three Voc. Game Cards. Steven Molinsky & Bill Bliss. 1994. 6.50 (*0-13-121153-6*) P-H.

Set Three Wall Charts. Steven Molinsky & Bill Bliss. 1994. pap. text ed. 74.25 (*0-13-121112-9*) P-H.

Set to Explode: A Sully Gomez Mystery. Mel Cebulash. LC 93-29069. 1993. 3.95 (*1-56420-004-3*); audio 9.95 (*1-56420-005-1*) New Readers.

Set to Kill. Arthur Marx. LC 92-33271. 1993. 17.95 (*0-942637-80-1*) Barricade Bks.

***Set to Music.** large type ed. Patricia Fawcett. (Ulverscroft Large Print Ser.). 592p. 1997. 27.50 (*0-7089-3753-5*) Ulverscroft.

***Set-Up.** Paul Erdman. 1997. 24.95 (*0-312-15110-1*) St Martin.

Set-Up. large type ed. William Newton. 1990. pap. 15.99 (*0-7089-6954-2*, Traittree Bookshop) Ulverscroft.

Set up & Sold Out: Find Out What Green Really Means. Holly Swanson. LC 95-70310. 322p. 1995. pap. 14.95 (*0-9645108-0-4*) CIN Pubng.

Set-up Reduction: Saving Dollars with Common Sense. Jerry W. Claunch & Philip D. Stang. LC 89-27627. (Illus.). 309p. 1990. text ed. 59.95 (*0-945456-04-2*) PT Pubns.

Set up Reduction...Workholding. Njit & Edward G. Hoffman. 242p. 1996. 39.95 (*0-8311-3067-9*) Indus Pr.

Set-Up Time Reduction: How to Increase Profits & Decrease Costs. Jerry C. Claunch. 224p. 1996. text ed. 45.00 (*0-7863-0863-X*) Irwin.

Set-Valued Analysis. Jean P. Aubin & H. Frankowska. (Systems & Control: Foundations & Applications Ser.: No. 2). 450p. 1990. 78.50 (*0-8176-3478-9*) Birkhauser.

Set-Valued Analysis & Differential Inclusions: A Collection of Papers Resulting from a Workshop Held in Pamporovo, Bulgaria, September 1990. Ed. by Alexander B. Kurzhanski & Vladimir M. Veliov. LC 93-20847. (Progress in Systems & Control Theory Ser.: Vol. 16). 1993. 98.00 (*0-8176-3733-8*) Birkhauser.

Set Visits: Interviews with 32 Horror & Science Fiction Filmmakers. Bill Warren. LC 96-27597. (Illus.). 319p. 1996. lib. bdg. 38.50 (*0-7864-0247-4*) McFarland & Co.

***Set Your Heart Free: The Practical Spirituality of Francis de Sales.** John Kirvan. LC 97-19250. (Thirty Days with a Great Spiritual Teacher Ser.). 216p. (Orig.). 1997. pap. 6.95 (*0-87793-627-7*) Ave Maria.

Set Your Hearts on the Greatest Gift: Living the Art of Christian Love. Morton Kelsey. LC 95-34531. 216p. 1996. pap. 10.95 (*1-56548-043-0*) New City.

Set Your Sights: A Guide to Handgun Basics. (Illus.). 1995. 1.95 (*0-916682-34-X*) Outdoor Empire.

Set Your Soul Free! How to Play Black Gospel, Bk. II. 2nd ed. Robert L. Jefferson. 80p. 1995. pap. 19.95 (*1-880549-05-0*) Pensacola Pubns.

Set Your Soul Free! How to Play Black Gospel see How to Play Black Gospel: Amazing Grace!

Set Your Soul Free! How to Play Soul Gospel, Tape 2. Robert L. Jefferson. 85p. 1992. audio 9.95 (*1-880549-03-4*) Pensacola Pubns.

Set Yourself Free. Mary Hellstern. 111p. 1993. pap. 9.95 (*0-7829-0391-6*) Tabor Pub.

***Set 1, 4 bks.** Kathleen Urmston & Karen Evans. Ed. by Kaeden Corp. Staff. Incl. Snowflakes. (Illus.). 12p. (Orig.). (J). (gr. k-2). 1991. pap. text ed. 4.25 (*1-879835-01-0*); Looking for Halloween. (Illus.). 10p. (Orig.). (J). (gr. k-2). 1991. pap. text ed. 4.25 (*1-879835-00-2*); Clown. (Illus.). 8p. (Orig.). (J). (gr. k-2). 1991. pap. text ed. 4.25 (*1-879835-06-1*); Marching Band. (Illus.). 8p. (Orig.). (J). (gr. k-2). 1991. pap. text ed. 4.25 (*1-879835-07-X*); 16.90 (*1-879835-08-8*) Kaeden Corp.

***Set 11, 4 bks.** Incl. Fun at the Amusement Park. large type ed. Marilyn K. Frankford. (Illus.). 16p. (Orig.). (J). (ps up). 1996. pap. 4.95 (*1-879835-82-7*); Best Friends. large type ed. Pamela Fitros. (Illus.). 12p. (J). (ps up). 1996. pap. 4.95 (*1-879835-83-5*); Mrs. Cook's Hats. large type ed. Jan Mader. (Illus.). 16p. (Orig.). (J). (ps up). 1996. pap. 4.95 (*1-879835-85-1*); Package. large type ed. Roger Bauer. (Illus.). 8p. (Orig.). (J). (ps up). 1996. pap. 4.95 (*1-879835-84-3*); 18.90 (*1-879835-81-9*) Kaeden Corp.

***Set 12: The Big Fish, Sammy Gets a Ride, Waiting for a Frog, Jungle Tiger Cat.** Joe Yukish et al. (Illus.). (Orig.). (J). (gr. k-2). 1997. pap. write for info. (*1-879835-91-6*) Kaeden Corp.

***Set 2, 4 bks.** Incl. To the Beach. Kathleen Urmston & Karen Evans. Ed. by Kaeden Corp. Staff. (Illus.). 8p. (Orig.). (J). (gr. k-2). 1991. pap. text ed. 4.50 (*1-879835-09-6*); Shopping at the Mall. Kathleen Urmston & Karen Evans. Ed. by Kaeden Corp. Staff. (Illus.). 16p. (Orig.). (J). (gr. k-2). 1991. pap. text ed. 4.50 (*1-879835-10-X*); Dressed up Sammy. Kathleen Urmston & Karen Evans. Ed. by Kaeden Corp. Staff. (Illus.). 12p. (Orig.). (J). (gr. k-2). 1991. pap. text ed. 4.50 (*1-879835-11-8*); Surprise for Mom. Kathleen Urmston & Karen Evans. Ed. by Kaeden Corp. Staff. (Illus.). 16p. (Orig.). (J). (gr. k-2). 1991. pap. text ed. 4.50 (*1-879835-12-6*); 16.90 (*1-879835-13-4*) Kaeden Corp.

Set 2 Voc. Game Cards. Steven Molinsky & Bill Bliss. 1994. 6.50 (*0-13-121146-3*) P-H.

***Set 3, 4 bks.** Incl. Fishing. Kate S. Palmer & Joseph Yukish. (Illus.). 16p. (J). (gr. k-2). 1992. pap. text ed. 4.50 (*1-879835-16-9*); Guess What Kind of Ball. Kathleen Urmston & Karen Evans. Ed. by Kaeden Corp. Staff. (Illus.). 16p. (Orig.). (J). (gr. k-2). 1992. pap. text ed. 4.50 (*1-879835-15-0*); Lunch. Kathleen Urmston & Karen Evans. Ed. by Kaeden Corp. Staff. (Illus.). 12p. (Orig.). (J). 1992. pap. text ed. 4.50 (*1-879835-14-2*); Our Garage. Kathleen Urmston. Ed. by Karen Evans & Kaeden Corp. Staff. (Illus.). 12p. (Orig.). (J). (gr. k-2). 1992. pap. text ed. 4.50 (*1-879835-17-7*); 16.90 (*1-879835-18-5*) Kaeden Corp.

***Set 4, 4 bks.** Incl. Swat It!. Roger Bauer. Ed. by Kaeden Corp. Staff. (Illus.). 12p. (J). (gr. k-2). 1992. pap. text ed. 4.50 (*1-879835-20-7*); Boots & Shoes. Ann Cooper. Ed. by Kaeden Corp. Staff. (Illus.). 12p. (J). (gr. k-2). 1992. pap. text ed. 4.50 (*1-879835-21-5*); Gifts for Dad. Karen Evans & Kathleen Urmston. Ed. by Kaeden Corp. Staff. (Illus.). 12p. (J). (gr. k-2). 1992. pap. text ed. 4.50 (*1-879835-22-3*); Grocery Shopping. Deborah Yannone. Ed. by Kaeden Corp. Staff. (Illus.). 12p. (Orig.). (J). (gr. k-2). 1992. pap. text ed. 4.50 (*1-879835-23-1*); 16.90 (*1-879835-24-X*) Kaeden Corp.

***Set 5, 4 bks.** Incl. My Doll. Joseph Yukish. Ed. by Kaeden Corp. Staff. (Illus.). 8p. (Orig.). (J). (gr. k-2). 1995. pap. text ed. 4.50 (*1-879835-02-9*); Sammy at the Farm. Kathleen Urmston & Karen Evans. Ed. by Kaeden Corp. Staff. (Illus.). 16p. (Orig.). (J). (gr. k-2). 1992. pap. text ed. 4.50 (*1-879835-51-7*); My Tiger Cat. Marilyn Frankford. Ed. by Kaeden Corp. Staff. (Illus.). 12p. (Orig.). (J). (gr. k-2). 1992. pap. text ed. 4.50 (*1-879835-52-5*); Carla's Ribbons. Leslie Harper. Ed. by Kaeden Corp. Staff. (Illus.). 16p. (Orig.). (J). (gr. k-2). 1992. pap. text ed. 4.50 (*1-879835-53-3*); 16.90 (*1-879835-54-1*) Kaeden Corp.

***Set 6, 4 bks.** Incl. Let's Play Basketball. Diane E. Geddes. Ed. by Kaeden Corp. Staff. (Illus.). 16p. (Orig.). (J). (gr. k-2). 1993. pap. text ed. 4.50 (*1-879835-55-X*); Fun. Deborah Yannone. Ed. by Kaeden Corp. Staff. (Illus.). 12p. (Orig.). (J). (gr. k-2). 1993. pap. text ed. 4.50 (*1-879835-56-8*); Thanksgiving. Karen Evans & Kathleen Urmston. Ed. by Kaeden Corp. Staff. (Illus.). 12p. (Orig.). (J). (gr. k-2). 1993. pap. text ed. 4.50 (*1-879835-57-6*); Carla's Breakfast. Leslie Harper. Ed. by Kaeden Corp. Staff. (Illus.). 16p. (Orig.). (J). (gr. k-2). 1993. pap. text ed. 4.50 (*1-879835-58-4*); 17.90 (*1-879835-59-2*) Kaeden Corp.

***Set 7, 4 bks.** Incl. Going to Grandpa's House. Marilyn Frankford. Ed. by Kaeden Corp. Staff. (Illus.). 12p. (Orig.). (J). (gr. k-2). 1993. pap. text ed. 4.50 (*1-879835-60-6*); Traffic Jam. Leslie Harper. Ed. by Kaeden Corp. Staff. (Illus.). 12p. (Orig.). (J). (gr. k-2). 1993. pap. text ed. 4.50 (*1-879835-61-4*); It's Football Time. Dianna E. Geddes. Ed. by Kaeden Corporation Staff. (Illus.). 12p. (Orig.). (J). (gr. k-2). 1993. pap. text ed. 4.50 (*1-879835-62-2*); Colors in the City. Karen Evans & Kathleen Urmston. Ed. by Kaeden Corp. Staff. (Illus.). 16p. (Orig.). (J). (gr. k-2). 1993. pap. text ed. 4.50 (*1-879835-63-0*); 17.90 (*1-879835-64-9*) Kaeden Corp.

***Set 8, 4 bks.** Incl. How to Make a Card. Karen Evans & Kathleen Urmston. Ed. by Kaeden Corp. Staff. (Illus.). 16p. (Orig.). (J). (gr. k-2). 1995. pap. text ed. 4.95 (*1-879835-65-7*); At the Zoo. Carol Kloes. Ed. by Kaeden Corp. Staff. (Illus.). (Orig.). (J). (gr. k-2). 1995. pap. text ed. 4.95 (*1-879835-66-5*); When It Rains. Marilyn Frankford. Ed. by Kaeden Corp. Staff. (Illus.). 16p. (Orig.). (J). (gr. k-2). 1995. pap. text ed. 4.95 (*1-879835-67-3*); Family Soccer. Diana Geddes. Ed. by Kaeden Corp. Staff. (Illus.). 16p. (Orig.). (J). (gr. k-2). 1995. pap. text ed. 4.95 (*1-879835-68-1*); 18.90 (*1-879835-69-X*) Kaeden Corp.

***Set 9, 4 bks.** Incl. Baseball Fun. Diana Geddes. Ed. by Kaeden Corp. Staff. (Illus.). 12p. (Orig.). (J). (gr. k-2). 1995. pap. text ed. 4.95 (*1-879835-72-X*); Bandages. Ellen Moskowitz. Ed. by Kaeden Corp. Staff. (Illus.). 16p. (Orig.). (J). (gr. k-2). 1995. pap. text ed. 4.95 (*1-879835-71-1*); Drummers. Carol Gould. Ed. by Kaeden Corp. Staff. (Illus.). 12p. (Orig.). (J). (gr. k-2). 1995. pap. text ed. 4.95 (*1-879835-73-8*); Late One Night. Jan Mader. Ed. by Kaeden Corp. Staff. (Illus.). 16p. (Orig.). (J). (gr. k-2). 1995. pap. text ed. 4.95 (*1-879835-70-3*); 18.90 (*1-879835-74-6*) Kaeden Corp.

Setas y Hongos (Mushrooms) J. Cooper. (Spanish Language Books, Set 3: Los Jardines de la Tierra (The Earth's Garden)). (J). 1991. 8.95 (*0-86592-499-6*) Rourke Enter.

Seth & Samona. Joanne Hyppolite. LC 94-36719. 128p. (J). 1995. 13.95 (*0-385-32093-0*) Delacorte.

Seth & Samona. Joanne Hyppolite. 128p. (J). 1997. pap. 3.99 (*0-440-41272-2*) Dell.

Seth Eastman: A Portfolio of North American Indians. Sarah E. Boehme et al. (Illus.). 168p. 1995. 75.00 (*0-9639338-4-1*) Afton Hist Soc.

Seth Eastman, Pictorial Historian of the Indian. John F. McDermott. LC 61-15145. (Illus.). 302p. reprint ed. pap. 86.10 (*0-685-09010-8*, 2005846) Bks Demand.

Seth Low. Benjamin R. Low. LC 70-137256. reprint ed. 20.00 (*0-404-04037-3*) AMS Pr.

Seth Low. Benjamin R. Low. (BCL1 - United States Local History Ser.). 92p. 1991. reprint ed. lib. bdg. 59.00 (*0-7812-6276-3*) Rprt Serv.

Seth Low: The Patrician As Social Reformer; the Patrician As Social Architect--a Biography. Gerald Kurland. LC 76-125816. 405p. 1971. reprint ed. 39.50 (*0-8290-0205-7*) Irvington.

Seth Material. Jane Roberts. 1993. reprint ed. lib. bdg. 29.95 (*1-56849-185-9*) Buccaneer Bks.

Seth Reader. Jane Roberts & Richard Roberts. 339p. (Orig.). 1993. pap. 15.95 (*0-942380-15-0*) Vernal Equinox.

Seth Speaks: The Eternal Validity of the Soul. Jane Roberts. (Seth Bk.). 480p. 1994. reprint ed. pap. 17.95 (*1-878424-07-6*) Amber-Allen Pub.

Seth Thomas Clock & Movements: 1996 Revised & Price up-Date. 2nd enl. ed. Tran D. Ly. (Illus.). 496p. (C). 1996. reprint ed. 49.50 (*0-9647406-0-5*) US Bks.

Seth Thomas Clock & Movements: 1996 Revised & Price up-Date. 2nd enl. rev. ed. Tran D. Ly. (Illus.). 496p. (C). 1996. pap. 39.50 (*0-9647406-1-3*) US Bks.

Seth Thomas Clocks & Movements: A Guide to Identification & Prices. Tran D. Ly. (Illus.). 260p. (Orig.). 1985. pap. 25.00 (*0-930163-26-5*) Arlington Bk.

Seth Thomas Clocks & Movements: Price Guide Up-Date, 1995. Tran D. Ly. 12p. 1995. pap. 5.00 (*0-9647406-2-1*) US Bks.

Seth Thomas Watches, 1855-1915. 1981. 6.00 (*0-930476-09-3*) Am Clock & Watch.

Seth's Brother's Wife. Harold Frederic. LC 68-23720. (Americans in Fiction Ser.). reprint ed. pap. text ed. 4.95 (*0-89197-934-4*); reprint ed. lib. bdg. 29.50 (*0-8398-0565-9*) Irvington.

S

Seth's Brother's Wife. Harold Frederic. (Collected Works of Harold Frederic). 1988. reprint ed. lib. bdg. 59.00 (*0-7812-1183-2*) Rprt Serv.

Seth's Brother's Wife see Collected Works of Harold Frederic

SETI Factor: How the Search for Extraterrestrial Intelligence is Changing Our View of the Universe & Ourselves. Frank White. 224p. 1990. 19.95 (*0-8027-1105-7*) Walker & Co.

***Seti League Technical Manual: How to Join the Search.** H. Paul Shuch. (Illus.). 64p. (Orig.). 1997. 10.00 (*0-9650707-2-7*) SETI League.

Seti (Pervaya Kniga Stikhov). 3rd ed. Mikhail A. Kuzmin. LC 78-68927. 1979. reprint ed. pap. 5.95 (*0-89830-003-7*) Russica Pubs.

SETI Pioneers: Scientists Talk about Their Search for Extraterrestrial Intelligence. David W. Swift. LC 89-20214. 434p. 1990. 45.95 (*0-8165-1119-5*) U of Ariz Pr.

SETI Pioneers: Scientists Talk about Their Search for Extraterrestrial Intelligence. David W. Swift. LC 89-20214. (Illus.). 434p. 1993. reprint ed. pap. 21.50 (*0-8165-1408-9*) U of Ariz Pr.

Seto & Mino Ceramics. Louise A. Cort. (Japanese Collections in the Freer Gallery of Art). (Illus.). 256p. 1992. text ed. 45.00 (*0-8248-1437-1*) Freer.

Seto & Mino Ceramics. Louise A. Cort. (Japanese Collections in the Freer Gallery of Art). (Illus.). 240p. 1992. pap. text ed. 25.00 (*0-8248-1436-3*) Freer.

Setons of Scotland & America: or An Old Family. M. Seton. (Illus.). 438p. 1989. reprint ed. pap. 65.50 (*0-8328-1059-2*); reprint ed. lib. bdg. 73.50 (*0-8328-1058-4*) Higginson Bk Co.

Setpoint Diet. Gilbert A. Leveille. 1985. mass mkt. 3.95 (*0-345-32196-0*) Ballantine.

Setpoints for Nuclear Safety-Related Instrumentation, Pt. I. 1994. pap. 40.00 (*1-55617-534-5*, S67.04) ISA.

Sets: Naive, Axiomatic & Applied. D. Van Dalen et al. 1978. 155.00 (*0-08-021166-6*, Pub. by Pergamon Repr UK) Franklin.

Sets & Boolean Algebra. Marcel Rueff & Max Jeger. Ed. by A. G. Howson. LC 72-189267. (Mathematical Studies: A Series for Teachers & Students: No. 4). 192p. reprint ed. pap. 54.80 (*0-317-20064-X*, 2023329) Bks Demand.

Sets & Borders. Gwen Marston & Joe Cunningham. (Illus.). 104p. 1987. pap. 14.95 (*0-89145-923-5*, 1821) Collector Bks.

Sets & Groups: A First Course in Algebra. J. A. Green. 256p. 1988. pap. text ed. 16.50 (*0-7102-1227-5*, RKP) Routledge.

Sets, Functions & Logic. 2nd ed. Keith Devlin. 208p. (C). (gr. 13). 1992. text ed. 72.95 (*0-412-45970-1*, A7067); pap. text ed. 27.95 (*0-412-45980-9*, A7071) Chapman & Hall.

Sets, Graphs, & Numbers: A Birthday Salute to Vera T. Sos & Andras Hajnal. Ed. by G. Halasz et al. (Colloquia Mathematica Societatis Janos Bolyai Ser.: Vol. 60). 752p. 1992. 311.25 (*0-444-98681-2*) Elsevier.

Sets in Motion: Art Direction & Film Narrative. Charles Affron & Mirella Affron. LC 94-39443. (Illus.). 300p. (C). 1995. text ed. 55.00 (*0-8135-2160-2*); pap. text ed. 22.50 (*0-8135-2161-0*) Rutgers U Pr.

Sets, Logic, & Axiomatic Theories. 2nd ed. Robert R. Stoll. LC 74-8932. 244p. reprint ed. pap. 69.60 (*0-317-08628-6*, 2055554) Bks Demand.

Sets of Mathematics Teaching Aids. Joan W. Teller et al. LC 90-5516. (Soviet Studies in Mathematics Education). (Illus.). 377p. 1990. pap. 25.00 (*0-87353-290-2*) NCTM.

Sets of Multiples. Richard R. Hall. (Cambridge Tracts in Mathematics Ser.: No. 118). 150p. (C). 1996. text ed. 59.95 (*0-521-40424-X*) Cambridge U Pr.

Setsuko Migishi: A Retrospective. Yasuto Ota et al. LC 91-7707. (Illus.). 136p. 1991. pap. 21.95 (*0-940979-16-0*, NE U Pr) Natl Museum Women.

Setswana-English, English-Setswana Dictionary. Brown. (ENG.). write for info. (*0-7859-7470-9*) Fr & Eur.

Sette Sfere di Cristallo. Herge. (Illus.). 62p. (ITA.). (J). pap. 19.95 (*0-8288-5070-4*) Fr & Eur.

Settecento Musicale in Europa. Antonio Capri. LC 77-5523. (Music Reprint Ser.). 1977. reprint ed. lib. bdg. 49.50 (*0-306-77413-5*) Da Capo.

Settimo Libro de'Madrgali a Cinque Voci (1595) Luca Marenzio. (Secular Works Ser.: No. 14). 1980. pap. 50.00 (*0-8450-7114-9*) Broude.

Setting. Jack M. Bickham. (Elements of Fiction Writing Ser.). 176p. 1994. 14.99 (*0-89879-635-0*, Wrtrs Digest Bks) F & W Pubns Inc.

Setting a Course for Health. D. Catesby. 236p. 1995. pap. 45.00 (*1-85609-077-9*, Pub. by Witherby & Co UK) St Mut.

Setting a Research Agenda. Ed. by Judith T. Sowder. (Research Agenda in Mathematics Education Ser.: Vol. 5). (Illus.). 64p. 1989. pap. 7.50 (*0-87353-269-4*) NCTM.

Setting a Trap for God: The Aramaic Prayer of Jesus. rev. ed. Rocco Errico. LC 96-20661. Orig. Title: The Ancient Aramaic Prayer of Jesus: The Lords Prayer. 136p. 1997. pap. 10.95 (*0-87159-124-3*, 36) Unity Bks.

Setting Agendas & Defining Problems: The Wesley Vale Pulp Mill Proposal, Vol. 2. Ralph J. Chapman. 1992. pap. 53.00 (*0-7300-2018-5*, PTSSSO, Pub. by Deakin Univ AT) St Mut.

Setting Allocation Priorities & Genetic & Reproductive Technologies. Ed. by Robert H. Blank & Andrea L. Bonnicksen. (Emerging Issues in Biomedical Policy Ser.: Vol. 1). 315p. 1993. pap. 19.50 (*0-231-07411-5*) Col U Pr.

Setting an Agenda: Research Priorities for the Gifted & Talented Through the Year 2000. (Illus.). 53p. (Orig.). (C). 1994. pap. text ed. 20.00 (*0-7881-0618-X*) DIANE Pub.

Setting Arteries in the Holy Land. Adina N. Etkes. LC 94-71872. (Illus.). 200p. (Orig.). 1996. pap. 14.95 (*0-9641200-8-9*) Donsun Pubng.

Setting Boundaries: The Anthropology of Spatial & Social Organization. Ed. by Deborah Pellow. LC 95-12840. 248p. 1996. text ed. 59.95 (*0-89789-428-6*, Bergin & Garvey) Greenwood.

Setting Captives Free. Bruce Stevens. 1995. pap. 13.50 (*0-551-02912-9*) Zondervan.

Setting Credit Lines. Credit Research Foundation Staff. 17p. 1982. 40.00 (*0-939050-39-0*) Credit Res NYS.

Setting Domestic Priorities: What Can Government Do? Ed. by Henry J. Aaron & Charles L. Schultze. 318p. (C). 1992. 42.95 (*0-8157-0054-7*); pap. 18.95 (*0-8157-0053-9*) Brookings.

Setting European Community Priorities. Peter Ludlow & Daniel Gros. 154p. 1994. 25.00 (*0-08-041314-5*) Elsevier.

Setting European Community Priorities, 1991-92. Centre for European Policy Studies Staff. 154p. 1991. pap. 39.95 (*0-08-040969-5*, Pub. by Brasseys UK) Brasseys Inc.

***Setting Foot on the Shores of Connemara & Other: Writings.** Tim Robinson. 218p. 9700. 45.00 (*1-874675-79-1*); pap. 19.95 (*1-874675-74-0*) Dufour.

Setting for Guitar. M. Powell. 8p. 1993. pap. 7.95 (*0-7935-2306-0*) H Leonard.

Setting Free the Actor: Overcoming Creative Blocks. Ann Brebner. LC 90-5875. 192p. (Orig.). 1990. pap. 12.95 (*0-916515-80-X*) Mercury Hse Inc.

Setting Free the Bears. John Irving. 352p. 1990. mass mkt. 6.99 (*0-345-36741-3*) Ballantine.

***Setting Free the Bears.** John Irving. 1997. pap. 11.00 (*0-345-41798-4*) Ballantine.

Setting Global Telecommunication Standards. Gerd D. Wallenstein. LC 89-27445. (Artech House Telecommunications Library). (Illus.). 274p. 1990. reprint ed. pap. 78.10 (*0-608-00567-3*, 2061450) Bks Demand.

Setting Global Telecommunications Standards: The Stakes, the Players, & the Process. Gerd D. Wallenstein. (Telecommunications Management Library). 256p. 1990. write for info. (*0-89006-390-7*) Artech Hse.

Setting Goals. Ruth C. Rosen. LC 92-15262. (Life Skills Library). (Illus.). 48p. (YA). (gr. 7-12). 1992. lib. bdg. 14.95 (*0-8239-1451-8*) Rosen Group.

Setting Goals. 3rd ed. John Renesch. 170p. 1983. 15.00 (*0-932654-08-8*) Context Pubns.

Setting Hearts on Fire: A Spirituality for Leaders. Timothy B. Brown & Patricia A. Sullivan. LC 96-50064. 144p. (Orig.). 1997. pap. 12.95 (*0-8189-0771-1*) Alba.

Setting in the American Short Story of Local Color, 1865-1900. Robert D. Rhode. (Studies in English Literature: No. 30). 190p. (Orig.). 1975. pap. text ed. 55.40 (*90-279-3281-6*) Mouton.

Setting It Free: An Exhibition of Modern Alaskan Eskimo Ivory Carving. Dorothy J. Ray. Ed. by Dinah Larsen. (Illus.). 110p. (Orig.). 1982. pap. 10.00 (*0-931163-08-0*) U Alaska Museum.

Setting Limits: How to Raise Responsible, Independent Children by Providing Reasonable Boundaries. Robert Mac Kenzie. (Illus.). 352p. (Orig.). 1992. pap. 12.95 (*1-55958-220-0*) Prima Pub.

Setting Limits: Medical Goals in An Aging Society, with "A Reponse to My Critics" Daniel Callahan. LC 94-34439. 272p. 1995. pap. 15.95 (*0-87840-572-0*) Georgetown U Pr.

Setting Limits: Parents, Kids & Drugs. William LaFountain. 36p. 1982. 3.00 (*0-89486-145-X*, 1418B) Hazelden.

Setting Limits in the Classroom: How to Move Beyond Classroom Dance. Robert J. Mackenzie. 304p. 1996. per., pap. 15.00 (*0-7615-0033-2*) Prima Pub.

Setting Love in Order: Hope & Healing for the Homosexual. Mario Bergner. LC 94-40047. 208p. (YA). (gr. 10). 1995. pap. 11.99 (*0-8010-5186-X*, Hamewith MI) Baker Bks.

Setting Municipal Priorities: American Cities & the New York Experience. Ed. by Charles Brecher & Raymond D. Horton. 560p. (C). 1984. text ed. 48.00 (*0-8147-1066-2*); pap. text ed. 20.00 (*0-8147-1067-0*) NYU Pr.

***Setting Municipal Priorities '83.** Brecher. (C). 1984. text ed. write for info. (*0-8147-1042-5*) NYU Pr.

Setting Municipal Priorities, 1981. Ed. by Charles Brecher & Raymond D. Horton. LC 80-67392. 212p. 1981. text ed. 38.50 (*0-86598-010-1*) Rowman.

Setting Municipal Priorities, 1986. Ed. by Charles Brecher & Raymond D. Horton. 476p. (C). 1985. text ed. 48.00 (*0-8147-1081-6*); pap. text ed. 24.00 (*0-8147-1082-4*) NYU Pr.

Setting Municipal Priorities, 1988. Ed. by Charles Brecher & Raymond D. Horton. 320p. (C). 1988. text ed. 48.00 (*0-8147-1103-0*); pap. text ed. 20.00 (*0-8147-1104-9*) NYU Pr.

Setting Municipal Priorities, 1990. Ed. by Charles Brecher & Raymond D. Horton. 384p. (C). 1989. text ed. 40.00 (*0-8147-1136-7*); pap. text ed. 20.00 (*0-8147-1137-5*) NYU Pr.

***Setting National Priorities: Budget Choices for the Next Century.** Ed. by Robert D. Reischauer. LC 96-45888. 320p. 1996. 42.95 (*0-8157-7398-6*); pap. 18.95 (*0-8157-7397-8*) Brookings.

Setting National Priorities: Policy for the Nineties. Ed. by Henry J. Aaron. 317p. (C). 1990. 34.95 (*0-8157-0048-2*); pap. 14.95 (*0-8157-0047-4*) Brookings.

Setting New Priorities in Health Care. Jack A. Meyer et al. (Illus.). 50p. (Orig.). 1993. pap. text ed. write for info. (*0-9629870-2-6*) Milbank Memorial.

Setting Objectives: For College Reading & Learning Prodiciency. 2nd ed. Clifford Brooks. 214p. 1993. pap. 32.95 (*0-945483-25-2*) E Bowers Pub.

Setting of Silver. Jean Vaughn. LC 94-60945. 87p. (Orig.). 1996. pap. 7.95 (*1-55523-718-5*) Winston-Derek.

***Setting of the Sermon on the Mount.** W. D. Davies. 547p. 1961. 98.95 (*1-55540-403-0*) Scholars Pr GA.

Setting of the Sermon on the Mount. William Davies. LC 64-630. 563p. reprint ed. pap. 160.50 (*0-317-26320-X*, 2024449) Bks Demand.

Setting Out to Begin a New World: Colonial Georgia. Ed. by Edward J. Cashin. (Documentary History Ser.). 248p. 1995. 35.00 (*0-88322-014-8*) Beehive GA.

Setting Priorities & Measuring Results at the National Institute of Standards & Technology. Mark Bello & Michael A. Baum. 38p. (Orig.). (C). 1995. pap. text ed. 25.00 (*0-7881-2326-2*) DIANE Pub.

Setting Priorities for Clinical Practice Guidelines. Marilyn J. Field. 1995. pap. text ed. 33.00 (*0-309-05247-5*) Natl Acad Sci.

Setting Priorities for Land Conservation. National Research Council Staff. 150p. (Orig.). (C). 1993. pap. text ed. 39.95 (*0-309-04836-2*) Natl Acad Pr.

Setting Priorities, Getting Results: A New Direction for EPA. Center for Competitive, Sustainable Economies Staff. 221p. (Orig.). 1995. pap. 20.00 (*0-9646874-5-3*) Nat Acad Public Admin.

Setting Priorities in Health Care. Ed. by Mo Malek. 332p. 1994. text ed. 62.95 (*0-471-94394-0*) Wiley.

Setting Rates for Hospital & Nursing Home Care. Paul L. Grimaldi. LC 84-17838. 360p. 1985. text ed. 27.50 (*0-88331-196-8*) Luce.

***Setting Rules for Your 11-15 Year Old.** Greg Anderson. (Illus.). 8p. (Orig.). 1996. pap. 2.50 (*1-884241-82-4*, AN1029) Energeia Pub.

Setting Safety Standards: Regulation in the Public & Private Sectors. Ross E. Cheit. LC 89-20339. (Illus.). 320p. 1990. 42.00 (*0-520-06733-9*) U CA Pr.

Setting Standards & Educating Teachers: A National Conversation. Mary E. Diez et al. 1994. 18.00 (*0-89333-116-3*) AACTE.

Setting Standards for Financial Reporting: FASB & the Struggle for Control of a Critical Process. Robert Van Riper. LC 94-2987. 216p. 1994. text ed. 55.00 (*0-89930-907-0*, Quorum Bks) Greenwood.

Setting Standards for Professional Nursing: The Marker Model. Carolyn G. Smith-Marker. 1987. 39.00 (*0-932491-84-7*) Res Appl Inc.

Setting Stones with Beads: An Instruction Manual & Source of Inspiration. 2nd ed. Barbara A. Volk. Ed. by Alice Scherer. (Illus.). 88p. (Orig.). 1998. pap. 16.95 (*1-883153-16-6*) B Stone Pr.

Setting Stratigical Goals. 2nd ed. Richard. Date not set. pap. text ed. 39.75 (*0-314-85291-3*) West Pub.

Setting Sun. rev. ed. Osamu Dazai. Tr. by Donald Keene from JPN. LC 56-13350. (Illus.). 1968. reprint ed. pap. 9.95 (*0-8112-0032-9*, NDP258) New Directions.

Setting Sun & the Rolling World: Selected Short Stories. Charles Mungoshi. LC 89-42588. 208p. (Orig.). 1989. pap. 12.00 (*0-8070-8321-6*) Beacon Pr.

Setting the Captives Free. Bob Buess. LC 42-1127. 1975. reprint ed. pap. 4.00 (*0-934244-02-2*) Sweeter Than Honey.

Setting the Captives Free: Victims of the Church Tell Their Stories. Austin Miles. 239p. (C). 1990. 24.95 (*0-87975-617-9*) Prometheus Bks.

Setting the East Ablaze. Peter Hopkirk. 272p. 13.00 (*1-56836-102-5*) FS&G.

Setting the East Ablaze: Lenin's Dream of an Empire in Asia. Peter Hopkirk. Ed. by John Urda. (Kodansha Globe Ser.). (Illus.). 272p. 1995. pap. 14.00 (*1-58636-102-3*, Kodansha Globe) Kodansha.

Setting the Foundations: A Guide to the Study of the Life & Teaching of Jesus Christ As Presented in the First Three Gospels. Rosalyn A. Kendrick. 256p. (C). 1983. pap. 35.00 (*0-7175-1156-1*, Pub. by S Thornes Pubs UK) St Mut.

Setting the Gospel Free: Experiential Faith & Contemplative Practice. Brian C. Taylor. 128p. 1996. 17.95 (*0-8264-0938-5*) Continuum.

Setting the Heart to Understand. Jane Kopp. 1987. pap. 7.00 (*0-941179-03-6*) Latitudes Pr.

Setting the Legal Information Agenda for the Year 2000: Based on a Workshop of the American Association of Law Libraries National Legal Resources Committee Washington, D. C. October 23-26, 1988, 3 vols. Ed. by Mary K. Price & Margaret M. Axtmann. LC 91-21935. (American Association of Law Libraries Publications Ser.: No. 42). 1994. 240.00 (*0-8377-0142-2*) Rothman.

***Setting the Mood with Aromathera.** Carly Wall. Date not set. write for info. (*0-8069-9871-7*) Sterling.

Setting the North-South Agenda United States - Latin American Relations in the 1990s. Ed. by Henry Hamman. 116p. 1991. pap. 14.95 (*0-935501-34-7*) U Miami N-S Ctr.

Setting the Pace. David Halecroft. (Alden All Stars Ser.). (Illus.). 128p. (J). (gr. 3-7). 1991. pap. 2.95 (*0-14-034547-7*, Puffin) Puffin Bks.

Setting the Pace. Lauraine Snelling. (High Hurdles Ser.: Vol. 3). 176p. (Orig.). (J). (gr. 6-9). 1996. pap. 5.99 (*1-55661-507-8*, Hampshire MN) Bethany Hse.

Setting the PACE: Managing Transition to Patient-Centered Care. Ed. by Phyllis B. Risner et al. LC 94-43730. 324p. 1995. pap. 38.00 (*1-56793-024-7*, 0954) Health Admin Pr.

Setting the Pace in Product Development: A Guide to Product & Cycle-Time Excellence. rev. ed. Ed. by Michael E. McGrath. 184p. 1996. pap. 17.95 (*0-7506-9789-X*) Buttrwrth-Heinemann.

***Setting the Record Straight.** Allen. Date not set. write for info. (*0-312-16703-2*) St Martin.

Setting the Record Straight: Give & Take on the National Standards for Arts Education. Consortium of National Arts Education Associations Staff. 12p. (Orig.). (C). 1994. pap. 1.50 (*1-56545-065-5*, 1608) Music Ed Natl.

***Setting the Record Straight: Responses to Misconceptions about Public Education in the United States.** Gerald W. Bracey. LC 96-51260. 1997. pap. 20.95 (*0-87120-279-4*) Assn Supervision.

Setting the Right Price for Your Design & Illustration. Barbara Ganim. (Illus.). 160p. 1994. pap. 24.99 (*0-89134-569-8*, North Lght Bks) F & W Pubns Inc.

Setting the Scene: The Great Hollywood Art Directors. Robert S. Sennett. LC 94-4556. 1994. 39.95 (*0-8109-3846-4*) Abrams.

Setting the Seen: Creative Visualization for Healing. Alan Cohen. (Illus.). 27p. (Orig.). (C). 1982. pap. 2.95 (*0-910367-33-7*) A Cohen.

***Setting the Stage: How to Deliver an Anger Management Program: The Cage Your Rage for Teens Facilitator's Manual.** Murray C. Cullen & Ronald R. Cullen. Ed. by Alice Fins. 95p. (Orig.). 1996. pap. 5.00 (*1-56991-037-5*, 555) Am Correctional.

Setting the Stage & the House That Jack Built. David Lynx & Alvin Martin. LC 92-70719. (Illus.). 16p. (Orig.). (C). 1992. pap. 5.95 (*1-880269-08-2*) D H Sheehan.

Setting the Standard for the New Auditor's Report: An Analysis of Attempts to Influence the Auditing Standards Board. Marshall A. Geiger. LC 93-1462. (Studies in Managerial Aid & Financial Accounting). 1993. write for info. (*1-55938-561-8*) Jai Pr.

Setting the Table: Women in Theological Conversation. Ed. by Rita N. Brock et al. 300p. (Orig.). 1995. pap. 19.99 (*0-8272-3433-3*) Chalice Pr.

Setting the Tempo: Fifty Years of Great Jazz Liner Notes. Ed. & Intro. by Tom Piazza. 256p. 1996. pap. 14.00 (*0-385-48000-8*, Anchor NY) Doubleday.

Setting the Tone for Future Trends. Ed. by Julia Elam & Ann H. Taylor. (NAFEO Conference Ser.). 286p. 1987. pap. text ed. 27.95 (*0-695-60054-0*) Follett Pr.

Setting the Trap. Jeff Nesbit. LC 93-41025. (High Sierra Adventure Ser.). (J). 1994. pap. 5.99 (*0-8407-9256-5*) Nelson.

Setting the Virgin on Fire: Lazaro Cardenas, Michoacan Peasants & the Mexican Revolution. Marjorie Becker. LC 94-40327. (Illus.). 194p. 1996. 45.00 (*0-520-08418-7*); pap. 17.00 (*0-520-08419-5*) U CA Pr.

Setting Them Straight. Betty Berzon. 1999. pap. 21.95 (*0-525-93990-3*) Viking Penguin.

Setting Them Straight: You Can Do Something about Bigotry & Homophobia in Your Life. Betty Berzon. 204p. 1996. pap. 10.95 (*0-452-27421-4*, Plume) NAL-Dutton.

Setting Tile. Michael Byrne. LC 95-947. (Illus.). 260p. 1995. pap. 19.95 (*1-56158-080-5*) Taunton.

Setting up a Bank Records Management Program. Nan H. Morrissette. LC 92-37466. 192p. 1993. text ed. 59.95 (*0-89930-748-5*, MTX/, Quorum Bks) Greenwood.

***Setting Up a Freshwater Aquarium: An Owner's Guide to a Happy, Healthy Pet.** Gregory Skomal. LC 96-49348. 1997. 12.95 (*0-87605-502-1*) Howell Bk.

Setting up a Home Page on the World-Wide Web. Uniforum Staff. 48p. 1995. pap. 25.00 (*0-936593-34-2*) UniForum.

Setting up a Library: How to Begin or Begin Again. rev. ed. Ruth S. Smith. (Guide Ser.: No. 1). 23p. 1994. pap. 5.50 (*0-614-02894-9*) CSLA.

Setting up a Library: How to Begin or Begin Again. 2nd rev. ed. Ruth S. Smith. (Guide Ser.: No. 1). 23p. (Orig.). 1994. pap. 7.00 (*0-915324-37-7*) CSLA.

***Setting up a Saltwater Aquarium: An Owner's Guide to a Happy, Healthy Pet.** Gregory Skomal. 128p. 1997. 12.95 (*0-87605-529-3*) Howell Bk.

Setting up an Effective Marketing Operation. Peter J. Youdale. (Illus.). 168p. 1972. 29.00 (*0-8464-0840-6*) Beekman Pubs.

Setting up an Internet Site for Dummies. James Coombs. 400p. 1996. pap. 19.99 (*1-56884-335-6*) IDG Bks.

***Setting up an Internet Site for Dummies.** 2nd ed. Jason Coombs & Ted Coombs. (Illus.). 400p. (Orig.). 1997. pap. 29.99 (*0-7645-0115-1*) IDG Bks.

Setting up an Office in Japan. American Chamber of Commerce in Japan Staff. (Illus.). 198p. (Orig.). 1994. pap. 28.00 (*0-8048-3009-6*) C E Tuttle.

***Setting up & Troubleshooting Windows PCs.** Michael F. Hordeski. LC 96-51615. 1997. pap. write for info. (*0-7506-9772-5*) Buttrwrth-Heinemann.

Setting up Enterprise in Japan 1995. 635p. 1996. pap. text ed. 133.00 (*4-8224-0710-1*, Pub. by JETRO JA) Taylor & Francis.

Setting up for Infant Care: Guidelines for Centers & Family Day Care Homes. Ed. by Annabelle Godwin & Lorraine Schrag. LC 88-61099. 92p. 1988. pap. text ed. 5.00 (*0-935989-14-5*, NAEYC #228) Natl Assn Child Ed.

***Setting up for Infant/Toddler Care: Guidelines for Centers & Family Child Care Homes.** rev. ed. Ed. by Annabelle Godwin & Lorraine Schrag. LC 96-68452. (Illus.). 126p. 1996. pap. text ed. 5.00 (*0-935989-75-7*, 228) Natl Assn Child Ed.

Setting up Home. Mary Gilliatt. 1986. pap. 16.95 (*0-316-31383-1*) Little.

Setting up in Beijing & Northern China. (Setting up in China Ser.). 184p. 1995. 330.00 (*962-7708-46-1*, Pub. by Euromoney UK) Am Educ Systs.

Setting up in Guangdong & the Sez's. (Setting up in China Ser.). 208p. 1995. 330.00 (*962-7708-45-3*, Pub. by Euromoney UK) Am Educ Systs.

Setting up in Shanghai. (Setting up in China Ser.). 208p. 1995. 330.00 (*962-7708-44-5*, Pub. by Euromoney UK) Am Educ Systs.

Setting up Our Own City: The Black Community in Morristown: An Oral History Project. Cheryl C. Turkington. (Illus.). xii, 104p. 1992. pap. 12.50 (*0-940631-04-0*) JFP Lib Morristown.

Setting Up Radio Control Helicopters. Dave Day. (R-C Handbook Ser.). (Illus.). 61p. 1988. pap. text ed. 12.95 (*0-85242-975-4*, Pub. by Nexus UK) Motorbooks Intl.

Setting up Your Own Pony Stud. Nicholas Arrowsmith-Brown. 132p. 1990. pap. 21.00 (*0-85131-386-8*, Pub. by J A Allen & Co UK) St Mut.

Setting up Your Own Prepaid Plan: A Do-It-Yourself Guide. Dale E. Wagman. 283p. 1989. 10.00 (*0-87814-340-8*, D4272) PennWell Bks.

Setting up Your Own Woodworking Shop. Bill Stankus. LC 92-43351. (Illus.). 192p. 1993. pap. 14.95 (*0-8069-8314-0*) Sterling.

Setting up Your Sewing Space: From Small Areas to Complete Workshops. Myrna Giesbrecht. (Illus.). 164p. 1996. pap. 12.95 (*0-8069-0496-8*) Sterling.

Setting Wonder Free. Maryke Barnes. (Illus.). 24p. (J). 1993. pap. 4.95 (*1-55037-238-6*, Pub. by Annick CN); lib. bdg. 14.95 (*1-55037-241-6*, Pub. by Annick CN) Firefly Bks Ltd.

Setting You Free to Make Right Choices: Leader's Guide. Josh McDowell. 48p. 1995. teacher ed., pap. 5.95 (*0-8054-9829-X*, 7800-10) Broadman.

Setting You Free to Make Right Choices: Workbook for Junior High & High School Students. Josh McDowell. 144p. (YA). (gr. 7-12). 1995. wbk. ed., pap. 9.95 (*0-8054-9828-1*, 7800-08) Broadman.

*__Setting Your Career & Life Direction.__ Patricia Duffy. (Hire Learning, Schooling That Works Ser.). 1997. wbk. ed., pap. text ed. 6.95 (*1-56370-188-X*) JIST Works.

*__Setting Your Church.__ Anderson. 17.75 (*0-8307-1682-3*) Regal.

Setting Your Church Free Conference Workbook. Neil T. Anderson & Charles Mylander. (Illus.). 43p. (Orig.). (C). student ed. 3.99 (*1-884284-30-2*) Freedom in Christ.

Setting Your House in Order. Ray Llarena. 182p. 1993. pap. 6.99 (*1-884369-02-2*) McDougal Pubng.

Setting Your Weight. (Fitness, Health & Nutrition Ser.). (Illus.). 144p. 1988. 17.27 (*0-8094-6191-9*); lib. bdg. 23.27 (*0-8094-6192-7*) Time-Life.

Settings: From Our Past to Your Presentation. 1991. 24.95 (*0-685-41176-1*) JWL Talladega.

Settings & Costumes of the Modern Stage. Ed. by Theodore Komisarjevsky & Lee Simonson. LC 65-19618. (Illus.). 1972. reprint ed. 27.95 (*0-405-08716-0*) Ayer.

Settings of Silver: An Introduction to Judaism. Stephen M. Wylen. 416p. 1989. pap. 15.95 (*0-8091-3071-8*) Paulist Pr.

Settle College Algebra. Date not set. student ed., pap. text ed. 18.50 (*0-314-05480-4*) West Pub.

Settle It out of Court: How to Resolve Business & Personal Disputes Using Mediation, Arbitration, & Negotiation. Thomas E. Crowley. 256p. 1994. pap. text ed. 16.95 (*0-471-30634-7*) Wiley.

Settle It Yourself: Who Needs a Lawyer. 2nd ed. Fred Benjamin & Dorothea Kaplan. 145p. 1992. pap. 12.95 (*0-929387-99-6*) Bonus Books.

Settled Asbestos Dust Sampling & Analysis. Steven M. Hays. 256p. 1994. 59.95 (*0-87371-948-4*, L948) Lewis Pubs.

Settled Out of Court. Henry Cecil. 184p. pap. 8.95 (*1-55882-104-X*) Intl Polygonics.

Settled out of Court: The Social Process of Insurance Claims Adjustment. 2nd ed. H. Laurence Ross. LC 80-68523. 285p. 1980. pap. text ed. 26.95 (*0-202-30296-2*); lib. bdg. 47.95 (*0-202-30286-5*) Aldine de Gruyter.

Settled Out of Court see **Henry Cecil Reprint Series**

Settlement. Henry G. Miller. (Art of Advocacy Ser.). 1983. Looseleaf updates available. write for info. (*0-8205-1041-6*) Bender.

*__Settlement.__ Ross. Date not set. pap. text ed. write for info. (*0-582-02425-0*, Pub. by Longman UK) Longman.

Settlement: The Most Important Productive Medium of Economic Man. Ed. by W. Tietze. 92p. (C). 1975. pap. 23.00 (*0-08-019671-3*, Pergamon Pr) Elsevier.

Settlement Analysis. Ed. by ASCE Staff. LC 94-37791. (Adapted Technical Engineering & Design Guides from the U.S. Corp of Army Engineers Ser.: Vol. 9). 1994. 36.00 (*0-7844-0021-0*) Am Soc Civil Eng.

Settlement & Development in the River Blindness Control Zone. Thayer Scudder et al. LC 92-39287. (Technical Paper Ser.: No. 192). 136p. 1992. 7.95 (*0-8213-2296-6*, 12296) World Bank.

Settlement & Development in the River Blindness Control Zone: Case Study, Burkina Faso. Della E. McMillan et al. LC 93-9380. (Technical Paper, Series on River Blindness Control in West Africa: No. 200). 178p. 1993. 10.95 (*0-8213-2381-4*, 12381) World Bank.

Settlement & Development in the River Blindness Control Zone: Case Study-Burkina Faso. Della E. McMillan et al. (Technical Paper Ser.: No. 200). 178p. (FRE.). 1994. 10.95 (*0-8213-2719-4*, 12719) World Bank.

*__Settlement & Economy in Italy, 1500 BC to AD 1500: Papers of the Fifth Conference of Italian Archaeology.__ Ed. by Neil Christie. (Oxbow Monographs in Archaeology: No. 41). (Illus.). 625p. 1995. 145.00 (*0-946897-89-1*, Pub. by Oxbow Bks UK) David Brown.

Settlement & Famine in Ethiopia: The Villagers' Experience. Alula Pankhurst. LC 91-18748. (Themes in Social Anthropology Ser.). 224p. 1992. text ed. 69.95 (*0-7190-3537-6*, Pub. by Manchester Univ Pr UK) St Martin.

Settlement & Growth of Copper-Tolerant Populations of Ectocarpus Siliculosus (Dillw.) Lyngbye on Different Antifouling Surfaces & Coatings. 66p. 1982. write for info. (*0-318-60083-8*, 306) Intl Copper.

Settlement & Land Use in Micheldever Hundred, 700-1100. Eric Klingelhofer. LC 91-55253. (Transactions Ser.: Vol. 81, Pt. 3). (Illus.). 160p. (Orig.). (C). 1991. pap. 20.00 (*0-87169-813-7*, T813-KLE) Am Philos.

Settlement & Social Change in Asia, Vol. 1. Wolfram Eberhard. 536p. reprint ed. pap. 152.80 (*0-317-11153-1*, 2020775) Bks Demand.

Settlement & Social Organization: The Merovingian Region of Metz. Guy Halsall. 360p. (C). 1995. text ed. 69.95 (*0-521-44256-7*) Cambridge U Pr.

*__Settlement & Story of Oakham, Mass. with Ten Fold-Out Maps.__ H. B. Wright & E. D. Harvey. (Illus.). 361p. 1997. reprint ed. lib. bdg. 45.00 (*0-8328-5960-5*) Higginson Bk Co.

Settlement & Survival: Building Towns in the Chippewa Valley, 1850-1925. Tim Pfaff. Ed. by Susan McLeod. (Illus.). 120p. (Orig.). 1994. pap. 12.95 (*0-9636191-1-X*) Chippewa Val Mus.

Settlement & Survival (Supplement) Building Towns in the Chippewa Valley, 1850-1925, a Case Study. Jim Oberly. Ed. by Susan McLeod. (Illus.). 16p. (Orig.). 1994. pap. 3.00 (*0-9636191-2-8*) Chippewa Val Mus.

Settlement Archaeology of Cerro de las Mesas, Veracruz, Mexico. Ed. by Barbara L. Stark. LC 91-12996. (Monographs: No. 34). (Illus.). 66p. (Orig.). 1991. pap. 10.00 (*0-917956-71-0*) UCLA Arch.

Settlement Conference: A Handbook for Judges & Lawyers. Kenneth E. Conn. Ed. by Carmelita J. Conn. LC 88-2308. 96p. (Orig.). 1988. pap. 19.95 (*0-943663-01-6*) San Joaquin Eagle.

Settlement Cookbook. Ed. by Simon Kander & Schoenfeld. 228p. 1996. reprint ed. pap. 14.95 (*1-55709-436-5*) Applewood.

*__Settlement Development in the North Jazira: A Study of the Archaeological Landscape.__ T. J. Wilkinson & D. J. Tucker. (Iraq Archaeological Reports: Vol. 3). (Illus.). 240p. (Orig.). 1995. pap. 75.00 (*0-85668-658-1*, Pub. by Aris & Phillips UK) David Brown.

Settlement Ecology: The Social & Spatial Organization of Kofyar Agriculture. Glenn D. Stone. LC 96-9997. (Studies in Human Ecology). 310p. (C). 1996. text ed. 47.50 (*0-8165-1567-0*) U of Ariz Pr.

Settlement, Economy, & Cultural Change at the End of the European Iron Age: Excavations at Kelheim in Bavaria, 1987-1991. Peter S. Wells. (Archaeological Ser.: Vol. 6). (Illus.). viii, 181p. 1993. pap. 22.50 (*1-879621-12-6*); lib. bdg. 35.00 (*1-879621-13-4*) Intl Mono Prehstry.

Settlement Excavations at Borgo Le Ferriere - Satricum, Vol. 1. Marianne Maaskant-Kleibrink. (Illus.). viii, 356p. (C). 1987. 93.00 (*90-6980-013-6*, Pub. by Egbert Forsten NE) Benjamins North Am.

Settlement Excavations at Borgo le Ferriere (Satricum), Vol. 2: The Campaigns 1983, 1985, 1987. Marianne Maaskant-Kleibrink. (Illus.). 384p. 1993. 130.00 (*90-6980-048-9*, Pub. by Egbert Forsten NE) Benjamins North Am.

Settlement Folk: Social Thought & the American Settlement Movement, 1885-1930. Mina Carson. LC 89-20319. 294p. 1990. 32.50 (*0-226-09501-0*) U Ch Pr.

Settlement for Cambodia: The Khmer Rouge Dilemma. MacAlister Brown & Joseph J. Zasloff. (Pew Case Studies in International Affairs). 50p. (C). 1993. pap. text ed. 3.50 (*1-56927-356-1*) Geo U Inst Dplmcy.

Settlement Horizon. Robert A. Woods & Albert J. Kennedy. 515p. (C). 1990. 49.95 (*0-88738-323-8*) Transaction Pubs.

Settlement Horizon: A National Estimate. Robert A. Woods & Albert J. Kennedy. LC 79-112562. (Rise of Urban America Ser.). 1970. reprint ed. 30.95 (*0-405-02488-6*) Ayer.

Settlement House Movement in New York City, 1886-1914. Harry P. Kraus. Ed. by Francesco Cordasco. LC 80-872. (American Ethnic Groups Ser.). 1981. lib. bdg. 35.95 (*0-405-13434-7*) Ayer.

Settlement Houses & the Great Depression. Judith A. Trolander. LC 74-20994. 217p. reprint ed. pap. 61.90 (*0-7837-3631-2*, 2043497) Bks Demand.

Settlement Idea: A Vision of Social Justice. Arthur C. Holden. LC 70-112549. (Rise of Urban America Ser.). 1974. reprint ed. 18.95 (*0-405-02455-X*) Ayer.

Settlement in a School of Whales & Other Poems. Roger Nash. (C). 1989. 45.00 (*0-907839-26-6*, Pub. by Brynmill Pr Ltd UK) St Mut.

Settlement in the West. Henry O'Reilly. 468p. 1993. reprint ed. lib. bdg. 99.00 (*0-7812-5193-1*) Rprt Serv.

Settlement of Disputes in Early Medieval Europe. Ed. by Wendy Davies & Paul Fouracre. 327p. (C). 1992. pap. text ed. 19.95 (*0-521-42895-5*) Cambridge U Pr.

Settlement of Disputes on the New Natural Resources: Workshop 1982. Rene-Jean Dupuy. 1983. lib. bdg. 129.00 (*90-247-2901-7*) Kluwer Ac.

Settlement of Estates & Fiduciary Law in Massachusetts, 3 vols. 4th ed. Guy Newhall. 1992. Suppl. 1992. suppl. ed. 50.00 (*0-317-03269-0*) Lawyers Cooperative.

Settlement of Estates & Fiduciary Law in Massachusetts, 3 vols., Set. 5th ed. Guy Newhall. LC 94-79126. 125.00 (*0-318-11944-7*) Lawyers Cooperative.

*__Settlement of Germantown & the Beginning of German Emigration to North America.__ Samuel W. Pennypacker. (Illus.). 310p. 1997. reprint ed. lib. bdg. 38.50 (*0-8328-6414-5*) Higginson Bk Co.

Settlement of Germantown, Pennsylvania, & the Beginning of German Emigration to North America. Samuel W. Pennypacker. LC 69-13248. (Illus.). 1972. reprint ed. 26.95 (*0-405-08847-7*) Ayer.

Settlement of Illinois, 1778-1830. Arthur C. Boggess. LC 71-128873. (Select Bibliographies Reprint Ser.). 1977. 28.95 (*0-8369-5493-9*) Ayer.

Settlement of Labor Disputes on Rights in Australia. Paul F. Brissenden. (Monograph & Research Ser.: No. 13). 131p. 1966. 5.00 (*0-89215-014-9*) U Cal LA Indus Rel.

Settlement of Pendleton District, 1777-1800. Frederick Van Clayton. (Illus.). 112p. 1988. pap. 20.00 (*0-89308-639-8*, SC 87) Southern Hist Pr.

Settlement of Polynesia: A Computer Simulation. Michael Levison et al. LC 72-92337. 145p. reprint ed. pap. 41.40 (*0-317-39704-4*, 2055888) Bks Demand.

Settlement of Shallow Foundations on Cohesionless Soils: Design & Performance. Ed. by William O. Martin. LC 86-70535. (Geotechnical Special Publication Ser.: No. 5). (Illus.). 98p. reprint ed. pap. 28.00 (*0-8357-6879-1*, 2056884) Bks Demand.

Settlement of the Jews in North America. C. P. Daly. 1972. 59.95 (*0-8490-1027-6*) Gordon Pr.

Settlement Planning & Participation under Principles of Pluralism. Ed. by T. Fenster. (Progress in Planning Ser.: Vol. 39). 80p. 1993. pap. 66.25 (*0-08-042332-9*, Pergamon Pr) Elsevier.

*__Settlement Predictions in Sparta.__ Robert H. Lafferty, 3rd et al. (Illus.). 299p. 1981. pap. 6.50 (*1-56349-038-2*, RS14) AR Archaeol.

*__Settlement, Subsistence, & Society in Late Zuni Prehistory.__ Keith W. Kintigh. (Anthropological Papers: No. 44). 142p. 1985. write for info. (*0-8165-1737-1*) U of Ariz Pr.

Settlement, Subsistence & Society in Late Zuni Prehistory. Keith W. Kintigh. LC 84-22769. (Anthropological Papers of the University of Arizona: No. 44). (Illus.). 142p. 1985. reprint ed. pap. 40.50 (*0-608-00927-X*, 2061720) Bks Demand.

Settlement System in India, Set, Vols. 1 & 2. (C). 1991. Set, Vol. 1: Rural, Vol. 2: Urban. 64.00 (*0-8364-2656-8*, Pub. by Chugh Pubns II) S Asia.

Settlement, the Immigrant & the Public School: A Study of the Influence of the Settlement Movement & the New Migration Upon Public Education, 1890-1924. Morris I. Berger. Ed. by Francesco Cordasco. LC 80-841. (American Ethnic Groups Ser.). 1981. lib. bdg. 24.95 (*0-405-13405-3*) Ayer.

Settlements & Israel-Palestinian Negotiations: An Overview. Geoffrey Aronson. 57p. 1996. pap. 4.95 (*0-88728-263-6*) Inst Palestine.

Settlements & the Law: A Juridicial Analysis of the Israeli Settlements in the Occupied Territories. Sally V. Mallison & Thomas W. Mallison. (Illus.). 1982. pap. 1.00 (*0-318-01027-5*) Am Educ Trust.

Settlements in the Americas: Cross-Cultural Perspectives. Ralph Bennett. LC 90-50411. (Illus.). 296p. 1993. 45.00 (*0-87413-411-0*) U Delaware Pr.

Settlements of Hope: An Account of Tibetan Refugees in Nepal. Ann A. Forbes. (Cultural Survival Reports: No. 31). (Orig.). 1989. 10.00 (*0-939521-45-8*); pap. 10.00 (*0-939521-44-X*) Cultural Survival.

Settlements of Western Perthshire. James Stewart. 315p. (C). 1989. text ed. 70.00 (*0-946270-82-1*, Pub. by Pentland Pr UK) St Mut.

Settlements on the Eastern End of Long Island, Vol. 5, No. 2. W. E. Moran. 1993. reprint ed. lib. bdg. 89.00 (*0-7812-5325-X*) Rprt Serv.

Settlements to Society, 1607-1763: A Documentary History of Colonial America. Ed. by Jack P. Greene. 400p. (C). 1975. reprint ed. pap. text ed. 12.95 (*0-393-09232-1*) Norton.

Settlements, Trade & Politics in the Seventeenth-Century Gold Coast. Ray A. Kea. LC 81-23609. (Johns Hopkins Studies in Atlantic History & Culture Ser.). (Illus.). 496p. reprint ed. pap. 141.40 (*0-8357-6617-9*, 2035262) Bks Demand.

Settler. Janice F. Simmons. 96p. 9600. pap. 13.95 (*1-897648-28-6*, Pub. by Salmon Poetry IE) Dufour.

Settler Economies: Studies in the Economic History of Kenya & Southern Rhodesia, 1900-1963. Paul Mosley. LC 82-12896. (African Studies: No. 35). (Illus.). 336p. 1983. text ed. 85.00 (*0-521-24339-4*) Cambridge U Pr.

Settler Regimes in Africa & the Arab World: The Illusion of Endurance. Ed. by Ibrahim Abu-Lughod & Baha Abu-Laban. (Monographs: No. 4). 255p. 1974. 10.95 (*0-914456-06-7*); pap. text ed. 6.95 (*0-914456-07-5*) Assn Arab-Amer U Grads.

Settler Sayings. Bobbie Kalman. (Historic Communities Ser.). (Illus.). 32p. (Orig.). (J). (gr. k-9). 1994. pap. 7.95 (*0-86505-518-1*); lib. bdg. 19.16 (*0-86505-498-3*) Crabtree Pub Co.

Settler Self-Government, 1840-1900: Select Documents on the Constitutional History of the British Empire & Commonwealth. Ed. by Frederick Madden & David Fieldhouse. LC 84-21213. (Documents in Imperial History Ser.: No. 4). 864p. 1990. text ed. 115.00 (*0-313-27326-X*, MGO/) Greenwood.

Settlers. Vilhelm Moberg. 1984. 3.63 (*0-446-38117-9*) Warner Bks.

Settlers. large type ed. Vivian Stuart. 832p. 1983. 27.99 (*0-7089-8106-2*) Ulverscroft.

Settlers. Vilhelm Moberg. LC 95-15948. (Emigrant Novels Ser.: Bk. 3). xxix, 399p. 1995. reprint ed. pap. 15.95 (*0-87351-321-5*, Borealis Book) Minn Hist.

Settlers along the Shores of Virginia's York River: With Banks, Farthing, Knewstep, Philbates, Richardson & Their Neighbors. Compiled by June B. Evans. (Illus.). 320p. 1989. 33.95 (*0-9611114-6-1*) Bryn Ffyliaid.

Settlers & Convicts: Or Recollections of Sixteen Years' Labour in the Australian Backwoods. Alexander Harris. 272p. 1996. reprint ed. pap. 19.95 (*0-522-83944-4*, Pub. by Melbourne Univ Pr AT) Paul & Co Pubs.

Settlers & Residents Series - Southern Columbia County, NY. Arthur C. Kelly. 1989. lib. bdg. write for info. (*1-56012-093-2*) Kinship Rhinebeck.

*__Settlers & Residents Town of Poestenkill, Renssalaer Co., NY, Vol. 4.__ Ed. by Arthur C. Kelly. 105p. (Orig.). 1997. pap. 18.00 (*1-56012-148-3*) Kinship Rhinebeck.

Settlers & Residents, Vol. I, Pt. II: Town of Germantown, 1790-1875. Arthur C. Kelly. LC 74-155407. 229p. 1973. lib. bdg. 33.00 (*1-56012-023-1*, 22B) Kinship Rhinebeck.

Settlers & Residents, Vol. I, Pt. 1: Town of Germantown, 1710-1899. Arthur C. Kelly. LC 74-155407. 238p. 1973. lib. bdg. 35.00 (*1-56012-022-3*, 22A) Kinship Rhinebeck.

Settlers & Residents, Vol. 2, Pt. 1: Town of Clermont, 1756-1899. Arthur C. Kelly. 407p. 1975. lib. bdg. 34.00 (*1-56012-028-2*, 27) Kinship Rhinebeck.

Settlers & Residents, Vol. 2, Pt. 2: Town of Clermont, 1790-1875. Arthur C. Kelly. 212p. 1975. lib. bdg. 19.00 (*1-56012-030-4*, 29) Kinship Rhinebeck.

Settlers & Residents, Vol. 3, Pt. 1: Town of Livingston, 1710-1899. Arthur C. Kelly. 338p. 1978. lib. bdg. 39.00 (*1-56012-039-8*, 38) Kinship Rhinebeck.

Settlers & Residents, Vol. 3, Pt. 2: Town of Livingston, 1790-1875. Arthur C. Kelly. 449p. 1976. lib. bdg. 34.00 (*1-56012-032-0*, 31) Kinship Rhinebeck.

Settlers & Residents, Vol. 3, Pt. 3: Town of Livingston, 1803-1850. Arthur C. Kelly. LC 74-155407. 208p. 1989. lib. bdg. 38.00 (*1-56012-103-3*, 95) Kinship Rhinebeck.

Settlers & Sojourners: A Study of Serbian Adaptation in Milwaukee, Wisconsin. Deborah Padgett. LC 88-46193. (Immigrant Communities & Ethnic Minorities in the U. S. & Canada Ser.: No. 39). 1989. 57.50 (*0-404-19449-4*) AMS Pr.

Settlers' Children: Growing up on the Great Plains. Elizabeth Hampsten. LC 90-50689. (Illus.). 288p. 1991. 24.95 (*0-8061-2342-7*) U of Okla Pr.

Settlers from Delaware River Come to Roanoke & New River. Patricia G. Johnson. LC 95-21802. 1995. 21.00 (*1-878188-05-4*) Walpa Pub.

Settler's Guide: Old-Time Bush Skill for Australians. Keith Smith. (Illus.). 176p. (Orig.). 1995. pap. 19.95 (*0-85091-510-4*, Pub. by Lothian Pub AT) Seven Hills Bk.

*__Settlers in the Ohio & Mississippi River Valleys: 1788-1810.__ Clifford N. Smith. 49p. (Orig.). 1997. pap. 20.00 (*1-890950-07-6*, l FLS 8) Westland Pubns.

*__Settlers in the Ohio & Mississippi River Valleys: 1788-1810.__ Clifford N. Smith. 42p. (Orig.). 1997. pap. 20.00 (*1-890950-08-4*, 1 FLS 9) Westland Pubns.

*__Settlers in the Ohio & Mississippi River Valleys: 1788-1810.__ Clifford N. Smith. 40p. 1997. pap. 20.00 (*1-890950-09-2*, l FLS 10) Westland Pubns.

*__Settlers in the Ohio & Mississippi River Valleys Pt. 1: 1788-1810.__ Clifford N. Smith. 49p. (Orig.). 1997. pap. 20.00 (*1-890950-00-9*, 1 FLS 1) Westland Pubns.

*__Settlers in the Ohio & Mississippi River Valleys Pt. 2: 1788-1810.__ Clifford N. Smith. 48p. (Orig.). 1997. pap. 20.00 (*1-890950-01-7*, 1 FLS 2) Westland Pubns.

*__Settlers in the Ohio & Mississippi River Valleys Pt. 3: 1788-1810.__ Clifford N. Smith. 51p. (Orig.). 1997. pap. 20.00 (*1-890950-02-5*, 1 FLS 3) Westland Pubns.

*__Settlers in the Ohio & Mississippi River Valleys Pt. 4: 1788-1810.__ Clifford N. Smith. 52p. (Orig.). 1997. pap. 20.00 (*1-890950-03-3*, 1 FLS 4) Westland Pubns.

*__Settlers in the Ohio & Mississippi River Valleys Pt. 5: 1788-1810.__ Clifford N. Smith. 48p. (Orig.). 1997. pap. 20.00 (*1-890950-04-1*, 1 FLS 5) Westland Pubns.

*__Settlers in the Ohio & Mississippi River Valleys Pt. 6: 1788-1810.__ Clifford N. Smith. 47p. 1997. pap. 20.00 (*1-890950-05-X*, 1 FLS 6) Westland Pubns.

*__Settlers in the Ohio & Mississippi River Valleys Pt. 7: 1788-1810.__ Clifford N. Smith. 47p. 1997. pap. 20.00 (*1-890950-06-8*, l FLS 7) Westland Pubns.

Settlers of Bajavista: Social & Economic Adaptation in a Mexican Squatter Settlement. James F. Hopgood. LC 79-21191. (Papers in International Studies: Latin America Ser.: No. 7). 157p. reprint ed. pap. 44.80 (*0-7837-1330-4*, 2041478) Bks Demand.

Settlers of Kenya. Elspeth Huxley. LC 74-33894. (Illus.). 126p. 1975. reprint ed. text ed. 45.00 (*0-8371-5457-X*, HUSK, Greenwood Pr) Greenwood.

Settlers of Maryland: 1701-1730. Peter W. Coldham. 216p. 1996. 25.00 (*0-8063-1488-5*) Genealog Pub.

Settlers of Maryland: 1731-1750. Peter W. Coldham. 306p. 1996. 30.00 (*0-8063-1500-8*) Genealog Pub.

Settlers of Maryland: 1751-1765. Peter W. Coldham. 367p. 1996. 32.50 (*0-8063-1514-8*) Genealog Pub.

*__Settlers of Maryland, 1766-1783.__ Peter W. Coldham. 204p. 1996. text ed. 25.00 (*0-8063-1519-9*) Genealog Pub.

*__Settlers of the Marsh.__ Frederick P. Grove. 1996. pap. text ed. 6.95 (*0-7710-9961-4*) McCland & Stewart.

Settlers on the Eastern Shore 1607-1750. John A. Scott. (Library of American History). (Illus.). 144p. (YA). 1990. 17.95 (*0-8160-2327-1*) Facts on File.

*__Settlers' Press.__ A. Gordon-Brown. (Illus.). 160p. 1979. 55.00 (*0-86961-117-8*, Pub. by A A Balkema NE) Ashgate Pub Co.

Settlers, Southerners, Americans: The History of Essex County, Virginia, 1608-1984. James B. Slaughter. LC 84-81011. (Illus.). 400p. 1984. 40.00 (*0-9613549-0-9*) Essex Cty Bd Sup.

Settlin In: The Relocation Magazine for Massachusetts. Ed. by Robert E. Curtin. 1995. pap. 6.95 (*0-916247-15-5*) Suburban MA.

*__Settling: Poems.__ Mary Logue. 72p. 1997. pap. 11.00 (*0-922811-33-4*) Mid-List.

Settling a Dispute: Towards a Legal Anthropology of Late Antique Egypt. Traianos Gagos & Peter. LC 94-31945. (New Texts from Ancient Cultures Ser.). 1994. pap. text ed. 27.95 (*0-472-06590-4*) U of Mich Pr.

Settling a Dispute: Towards a Legal Anthropology of Late Antique Egypt. Traianos Gagos & Peter. LC 94-31945. (New Texts from Ancient Cultures Ser.). 1995. pap. text ed. 47.50 (*0-472-09590-0*) U of Mich Pr.

An Asterisk (*) at the beginning of an entry indicates that the title is appearing in BIP for the first time.

***Settling Accounts: Violence, Justice, & Accountability in Postsocialist Europe.** John Borneman. LC 97-12041. (Studies in Culture/Power/History). 1997. write for info. (*0-691-01682-8*); pap. write for info. (*0-691-01681-X*) Princeton U Pr.

Settling an Estate Without Probate: Illinois Edition. Robert S. Hunter. (Klear-E-Lex Ser.). 258p. (Orig.). 1993. pap. 17.95 (*1-884177-00-X*) Justice IL.

Settling & Safeguarding Estates in California Without an Attorney: With Forms. 10th rev. ed. Clive Hinckley. LC 79-74698. 1988. pap. 20.00 (*0-9602984-1-X*) C Hinckley.

Settling Civil Suits: Litigators' Views About Appropriate Roles & Effective Techniques for Federal Judges. 180p. 1984. pap. 15.00 (*0-685-29684-9*, 410-0002-01) Amer Bar Assn.

Settling Disputes: Conflict Resolution in Business, Families, & the Legal System. 2nd ed. Linda R. Singer. LC 94-17711. (C). 1994. pap. text ed. 21.50 (*0-8133-8656-X*) Westview.

***Settling Down.** Sybil Downing. (Colorado Heritage Ser.). 1979. pap. text ed. 5.95 (*1-878611-08-9*) Silver Rim Pr.

Settling Estates in North Carolina: A Simple Step-by-Step Guide & Checklist for Executors. Jane Young. Ed. by Jerry Bledsoe. LC 92-72658. 128p. (Orig.). 1992. pap. 9.95 (*1-878086-17-0*) Down Home NC.

Settling for More: Mastering Negotiating Strategies & Techniques. Alvin L. Goldman. LC 90-19282. (Illus.). 269p. 1991. reprint ed. pap. 76.70 (*0-608-00706-4*, 2061478) Bks Demand.

Settling in Michigan & Other True Pioneer Stories. Lynne Deur. (Illus.). 80p. (Orig.). (J). (gr. 3-6). 1992. pap. 9.95 (*0-938682-22-9*) River Rd Pubns.

Settling of Copper City, Michigan. (Copper Country Local History Ser.: Vol. 21). (Illus.). 92p. 1983. 2.50 (*0-942363-20-5*) C J Monette.

Settling the Canadian-American West, 1890-1915: Pioneer Adaptation & Community Building. John W. Bennett & Seena B. Kohl. LC 95-1826. (Illus.). xiii, 297p. 1995. text ed. 50.00 (*0-8032-1254-2*) U of Nebr Pr.

Settling the Dust. Robert J. Ege. 1981. pap. 6.95 (*0-933147-03-1*) Werner Pubn.

Settling the Rogue Valley. 100p. 1995. per. 13.95 (*0-9623847-9-8*) B Hegne.

Settling the Score: Music & the Classical Hollywood Film. Kathryn Kalinak. LC 92-6853. (Wisconsin Studies in Film). (Illus.). 266p. (Orig.). (C). 1992. pap. 17.95 (*0-299-13364-8*) U of Wis Pr.

***Settling the Upper Illinois Valley: Patterns of Change in the I & M Canal Corridor, 1830-1900.** Ed. by Michael P. Conzen et al. LC 89-15702. (Studies on the Illinois & Michigan Canal Corridor: Vol. 3). 1989. pap. 15.00 (*0-89065-134-5*) U Ch Pr.

Settling the West see American Story

Settling the West Series, 6 Vol., Set. (Illus.). 96p. (J). (gr. 5-8). 1995. lib. bdg. 101.88 (*0-8050-3967-8*) TFC Bks NY.

Settling Things: Six Case Studies in Environmental Mediation. Allan R. Talbot. LC 82-25255. 115p. reprint ed. pap. 32.80 (*0-7837-1209-X*, 2041741) Bks Demand.

Settlings. Frank L. Fleckenstein. (Illus.). 32p. (Orig.). 1988. pap. 3.00 (*0-945073-03-8*) Nightsun MD.

Setup Phase of Project Open Book. Paul Conway & Shari Weaver. 24p. 1994. pap. 10.00 (*1-887334-34-3*) Comm Preserv & Access.

Setva Svemira: Macedonian Poetry. Jozo T. Boskovski. 234p. 1989. 20.00 (*0-89304-704-X*); pap. 10.00 (*0-89304-705-8*) Cross-Cultrl NY.

Seules les Larmes Seront Comptees. Hector Bianciotti. 441p. (FRE.). 1991. pap. 14.95 (*0-7859-2178-8*, 2070384276) Fr & Eur.

Seumas O'Kelly. George B. Saul. LC 74-126030. (Irish Writers Ser.). 101p. 1975. pap. 1.95 (*0-8387-7661-2*) Bucknell U Pr.

Seumas O'Kelly's the Weaver's Grave. Michael O. Aodha. (New Abbey Theatre Ser.). 1984. pap. 2.95 (*0-912262-81-8*) Proscenium.

Seurat. Catherine Barry. (Pocket Painters Ser.). (Illus.). 1994. 6.50 (*0-517-59969-4*, Clarkson Potter) Crown Bks Yng Read.

***Seurat.** Catherine Barry. Date not set. 1.99 (*0-517-17604-1*) Random Hse Value.

Seurat. Pierre Courthion. 1988. 22.95 (*0-8109-1519-7*) Abrams.

Seurat. John Russell. (World of Art Ser.). (Illus.). 286p. 1985. pap. 14.95 (*0-500-20032-7*) Thames Hudson.

Seurat: A Biography. John Rewald. (Illus.). 240p. 1990. 75.00 (*0-8109-3814-6*) Abrams.

Seurat: A Biography. John Rewald. (Illus.). 240p. 1992. pap. 34.98 (*0-8109-8124-6*, Abradale Pr) Abrams.

Seurat: His Complete Works. M. F. Zimmerman. (Illus.). 492p. 1991. boxed 225.00 (*1-55660-277-4*) A Wofsy Fine Arts.

***Seurat & the Bathers.** Richard Thomson. 1997. 50.00 (*0-300-07328-3*) Yale U Pr.

***Seurat & the Language of the Avant-Garde.** Paul Smith. LC 96-34527. 1997. write for info. (*0-300-07002-0*) Yale U Pr.

Seurat & the Science of Painting. William I. Homer. LC 84-80600. (Illus.). 327p. 1985. reprint ed. lib. bdg. 45.00 (*0-87817-295-5*) Hacker.

Seurat at Gravelines: The Last Landscapes. Ellen W. Lee. LC 90-83128. (Illus.). 80p. 1990. 29.95 (*0-936260-56-4*); pap. 19.95 (*0-936260-55-6*) Ind Mus Art.

Seussisms. Dr. Seuss. (Dr. Seuss Book & Cassette Classics Ser.). (J). 1997. 6.99 (*0-679-88356-8*, Bullseye Bks) Random Bks Yng Read.

Sev. Mark Dunster. 14p. (Orig.). 1993. pap. 4.00 (*0-89642-221-6*) Linden Pubs.

***Sevastopol: On Photographs of War.** William Allen. LC 97-20264. 1997. write for info. (*1-879378-30-2*); pap. write for info. (*1-879378-29-9*) Xenos Riverside.

***Seve.** Lauren St. John. LC 97-9974. (Illus.). 320p. 1997. 19.95 (*1-55853-489-X*) Rutledge Hill Pr.

Seven. Anthony Bruno. 1995. mass mkt. 4.99 (*0-312-95704-1*) St Martin.

Seven-Ability Plan. Arnold B. Skromme. LC 89-91773. (Illus.). 160p. (Orig.). (J). 1989. text ed. 14.95 (*0-9623508-1-8*); pap. text ed. 10.95 (*0-9623508-0-X*) Self Confidence.

Seven African-American Scientists. rev. ed. Robert Hayden. (Achievers: African Americans in Science & Technology Ser.). (Illus.). 173p. (J). (gr. 5-8). 1992. reprint ed. lib. bdg. 15.98 (*0-8050-2134-5*) TFC Bks NY.

***Seven African American Scientists: Achievers: African Americans in Science & Technology.** Robert Hayden. (J). 1992. 18.60 (*0-516-07858-5*) Childrens.

Seven Against Thebes. Aeschylus. Tr. by Anthony Hecht & Helen H. Bacon. 104p. 1991. reprint ed. pap. 7.95 (*0-19-507007-0*) OUP.

Seven Against Thebes. Henry David Thoreau. Ed. by Leo M. Kaiser. LC 80-2522. (Emerson Society Quarterly Fifty-Nine, 1-30). reprint ed. 27.50 (*0-404-19070-7*) AMS Pr.

Seven Against Thebes see Prometheus Bound & Other Plays

Seven Against Thebes-Septem Contra Thebas. Aeschylus. 280p. 1994. reprint ed. pap. 24.95 (*0-19-814999-9*) OUP.

Seven Ages of Childhood. Wells. (J). 14.95 (*0-671-75282-0*, S&S Bks Young Read) S&S Childrens.

Seven Ages of Dan: A Two Act Comedy. Charles Avery. (Illus.). 57p. (Orig.). 1993. pap. 4.00 (*0-88680-387-X*) I E Clark.

***Seven Ages of Frank Lloyd Wright: A New Appraisal.** unabridged ed. Donald W. Hoppen. (Illus.). 192p. 1997. reprint ed. pap. text ed. 12.95 (*0-486-29420-X*) Dover.

Seven Ages of Frank Lloyd Wright: A New Appraisal. Donald W. Hoppen. (Illus.). 160p. (Orig.). (C). 1992. reprint ed. lib. bdg. 49.00 (*0-8095-4112-2*) Borgo Pr.

***Seven Ages of Man.** Ralph W. Bergengren. 108p. Date not set. 13.95 (*0-8369-0203-3*) Ayer.

Seven Ages of the British Army. Field Marshall Lord Carver. (Illus.). 344p. 1985. 22.50 (*0-8253-0241-2*) Beaufort Bks NY.

Seven Ages of Venice. C. M. Smith. 1977. lib. bdg. 59.95 (*0-8490-2594-X*) Gordon Pr.

Seven Ages of Woman. Elizabeth Parker. Ed. by Evelyn Breck. LC 60-8739. 621p. reprint ed. pap. 177.00 (*0-317-07935-2*, 2014853) Bks Demand.

***Seven A.M. Practice: Stories of Family Life.** Roy MacGregor. 1997. 14.95 (*0-7710-5600-1*) McCland & Stewart.

Seven American Poets from MacLeish to Nemerov: An Introduction. Ed. by Denis Donoghue. LC 74-22560. (Minnesota Library on American Writers). 337p. 1975. reprint ed. pap. 96.10 (*0-7837-2966-9*, 2057488) Bks Demand.

Seven American Stylists from Poe to Mailer: An Introduction. Ed. by George T. Wright. LC 72-95441. (Minnesota Library on American Writers). 314p. reprint ed. pap. 89.50 (*0-685-15927-2*, 2056206) Bks Demand.

Seven Ancient Wonders: A Pop-up Book. Celia King. (Illus.). 7p. (J). 1990. 10.95 (*0-87701-707-7*) Chronicle Bks.

***Seven & Three in Mississippi.** Linda Crockem. 12p. (J). 1997. 14.99 (*1-887637-07-9*) First Bk Prodns.

***Seven Animal Stories from the Bible, Vol. 1.** Howard Bogot. (Illus.). 48p. (J). (ps-1). 1997. 15.95 (*0-943706-40-8*) Pitspopany.

***Seven Anti-Aging Secrets.** Bob Goldman & Ronald Klatz. Ed. by Lisa Song et al. (Orig.). 1996. pap. 14.95 (*0-614-19146-7*) Elite Spts Med.

Seven Arias con Tromba Sola. Alessandro Scarlatti. Ed. by Henry Meredith. LC 80-28901. 1980. pap. text ed. 24.00 (*0-914282-51-4*) Brass Pr.

Seven Arrows. Hyemeyohsts Storm. 374p. 1985. pap. 18.00 (*0-345-32901-5*, Ballantine Trade) Ballantine.

Seven Arts, Set, Vols. 1-2. reprint ed. Set. lib. bdg. 157.50 (*0-404-19551-2*) AMS Pr.

Seven at One Blow. (J). Date not set. pap. 3.95 (*0-590-20600-1*) Scholastic Inc.

***Seven Barrel Brewery Brewers' Handbook.** Gregory J. Noonan et al. 307p. (Orig.). 1996. pap. text ed. 9.95 (*1-887167-00-5*) G W Kent.

Seven Basic Macrobiotic Principles. Georges Aihara. 1992. pap. 5.50 (*0-685-57009-6*) Happiness Pr.

***Seven Basic Quarrels of Marria.** Betcher & McCauley. 1997. pap. 11.95 (*0-345-41818-2*) Ballantine.

Seven Basic Quarrels of Marriage: Recognize, Defuse, Negotiate, & Resolve Your Conflicts. Robie Macauley & William Betcher. 1993. mass mkt. 4.99 (*0-345-37649-8*) Ballantine.

7 Basic Steps to Successful Fasting & Prayer. Bill Bright. 24p. 1995. pap. 0.99 (*1-56399-073-3*) NewLife Pubns.

Seven Bells to Bethelehem: The "O" Antiphons. Oliver Treanor. 133p. (Orig.). 1995. pap. 9.95 (*0-85244-329-3*, Pub. by Gracewing UK) Morehouse Pub.

Seven Bible Ways to Properly Relate to Your Pastor. Mark T. Barclay. 32p. 1982. pap. 2.25 (*0-88144-024-8*) Christian Pub.

Seven Black Stones. Jean Hager. 256p. 1996. mass mkt. 5.99 (*0-446-40386-5*, Mysterious Paperbk) Warner Bks.

Seven Blind Mice. Ed Young. LC 90-35396. (Illus.). 40p. (J). (ps-3). 1992. 17.95 (*0-399-22261-8*, Philomel Bks) Putnam Pub Group.

Seven Block. Dixon & Jorge Zaffino. 48p. 1990. 4.50 (*0-87135-698-8*) Marvel Entmnt.

Seven Bodies of Man. E. J. Gold. LC 89-38914. (Illus.). 144p. 1989. 15.95 (*0-89556-060-7*) Gateways Bks & Tapes.

Seven Books of History Against the Pagans. Paulus Orosius. Tr. by Ray J. Deferrari. LC 64-8670. (Fathers of the Church Ser.: Vol. 50). 415p. 1964. 24.95 (*0-8132-0050-4*) Cath U Pr.

Seven Brave Women. Betsy Hearne. LC 96-10414. (Illus.). 24p. (J). (gr. k up). 1997. 15.00 (*0-688-14502-7*); lib. bdg. 14.93 (*0-688-14503-5*) Greenwillow.

***Seven Brides for Seven Brothers: Vocal Selections.** Ed. by Carol Cuellar. 32p. (Orig.). (C). 1992. pap. text ed. 9.95 (*0-7692-0482-1*, TSF0069) Warner Brothers.

Seven Brothers. Aleksis Kivi. Tr. by Richard A. Impola from FIN. 310p. 1991. pap. 12.00 (*1-880474-00-X*) FATA.

Seven Brothers & the Big Dipper/Hungbu, Nolbu & the Magic Gourds. Duance Vorhees & Mark Mueller. (Korean Folk Tales for Children Ser.: Vol. 4). (Illus.). 46p. (J). (gr. 2-5). 1991. lib. bdg. 10.95 (*0-930878-74-4*) Hollym Intl.

Seven by Seven: Interviews with American Science Fiction Writers of the West & Southwest. Neal Wilgus. LC 87-814. (Milford Series: Popular Writers of Today: Vol. 44). 136p. 1996. 29.00 (*0-89370-173-4*, 15164305); pap. 19.00 (*0-89370-273-0*, 15164305) Borgo Pr.

Seven Candles for Kwanzaa. Andrea D. Pinkney. LC 92-3698. (Illus.). 32p. (J). (gr. k up). 1993. pap. 14.99 (*0-8037-1292-8*); pap. 14.89 (*0-8037-1293-6*) Dial Bks Young.

Seven Candles of Unity: The Story of Abdu'l-Baha in Edinburgh. Anjam Khursheed. 270p. 1991. pap. 21.95 (*1-870989-12-0*) Bahai.

***Seven-Card Stud: The Complete Course in Winning.** Roy West. LC 95-72652. 156p. (Orig.). 1996. pap. 24.95 (*1-884466-21-4*) Poker Plus.

Seven Card Stud for Advanced Players. 3rd ed. David Sklansky et al. Ed. by Lynne Loomis. 218p. 1994. pap. text ed. 29.95 (*1-880685-02-7*) Two Plus NV.

Seven Cardinal Virtues. Ed. by Alison Fell. LC 90-60281. (Masks Ser.). (Illus.). 224p. (Orig.). 1990. pap. 13.95 (*1-85242-169-X*) Serpents Tail.

***Seven Cartons of Love: Do Siblings Care?** unabridged ed. Jack Hedger, pseud. (Illus.). 58p. (J). 1996. 19.95 (*1-882416-18-X*) Akela West Pubs.

Seven Cats & the Art of Living. Jo Coudert. LC 96-3144. 208p. 1996. 17.95 (*0-446-51961-8*) Warner Bks.

Seven Centuries in the Kneeland Family. S. F. Kneeland. (Illus.). 583p. reprint ed. pap. 87.50 (*0-8328-0738-9*); reprint ed. lib. bdg. 95.50 (*0-8328-0737-0*) Higginson Bk Co.

Seven Centuries of English Cooking. Maxime De la Falaise. LC 92-2350. 242p. (Orig.). 1992. pap. 15.95 (*0-8021-3296-0*, Grove) Grove-Atltic.

Seven Centuries of Poetry. Ed. by A. Norman Jeffares. (Granger Index Reprint Ser.). 1977. 31.95 (*0-8369-6068-8*) Ayer.

Seven Centuries of Sea Travel. B. W. Bathe. 1990. 24.99 (*0-517-01754-7*) Random Hse Value.

***Seven Challenges: Challenging Ourselves to Make Wise Decisions about Alcohol & Other Drugs.** Robert Schwebel. 112p. (Orig.). (YA). (gr. 7-12). 1995. pap. text ed. 18.95 (*0-9645482-0-8*) Viva Pr.

***Seven Challenges Workbooks, 7 vols.** Robert Schwebel. (YA). (gr. 7-12). 1996. write for info. (*1-890164-00-3*) Viva Pr.

Seven Chant Masses: Accompaniment. Bartholomew Sayles & Cecile Gertken. 88p. spiral bd. 9.95 (*0-8146-2149-X*) Liturgical Pr.

Seven Chant Masses: Melody Edition. Bartholomew Sayles & Cecile Gertken. 56p. pap. 4.95 (*0-8146-2148-1*) Liturgical Pr.

Seven Chinese Brothers. Margaret Mahy. 40p. (J). 1992. pap. 4.99 (*0-590-42057-7*) Scholastic Inc.

Seven Chinese Brothers. Margaret Mahy. (Illus.). 40p. (SPA.). (J). pap. 3.95 (*0-590-25211-9*) Scholastic Inc.

Seven Chocolate Sins: A Devilishly Delicious Collection of Chocolate Recipes. Ruth Moorman & Lalla Williams. (Cookbook Ser.: No. 2). (Illus.). 80p. 1979. pap. 5.95 (*0-937552-01-1*) Quail Ridge.

Seven Choices. Elizabeth H. Neeld. 1990. 19.95 (*0-517-57371-7*, C P Pubs) Crown Pub Group.

***Seven Choices: Taking the Steps to New Life after Losing Someone You Love. 3rd rev. ed. Elizabeth H. Neeld. LC 96-48252. 364p. 1997. pap. 14.95 (*0-937897-90-6*) Centerpoint Pr.**

"This book, SEVEN CHOICES, saved my life."--a doctor & new widower, speaking on "Oprah." "SEVEN CHOICES is one of the best books ever written on grief & mourning."--VALUE & VISIONS, Cultural Information Service. "Readers will welcome SEVEN CHOICES ... sound advice on how to adjust to change & form new life patterns & human bonds."--PUBLISHERS WEEKLY. "I have read thirty-five books since my husband died last September; SEVEN CHOICES is the one that has helped me the most."--C. Lahr, BEREAVEMENT MAGAZINE. "This is the best book I have ever read on grieving; & I have read many. This is the most empowering book I have ever used in working with grieving people; & I have worked with many."--Bill Moore, National Trainer, AARP, Widowed Persons Services. A profoundly moving book, SEVEN CHOICES offers hope to anyone experiencing any type of loss -- e.g., death, divorce, job loss, etc. The poignant story of the death of Dr. Neeld's young husband serves as the author's starting point as she describes the seven phases in this life-transforming process & identifies the growth-engendering choices that culminate in release from the past & discovery of a stronger & balanced self. *Publisher Provided Annotation.*

Seven Churches. 36p. (Orig.). pap. 0.95 (*0-937408-20-4*) GMI Pubns Inc.

Seven Churches. Marshall Neal. (Illus.). 108p. (Orig.). 1977. pap. 4.25 (*0-89084-062-8*, 003624) Bob Jones Univ Pr.

Seven Churches: (Of the Revelation) Kingdom Quotes Staff. pap. write for info. (*0-930179-18-8*) Johns Enter.

Seven Churches of Asia. Robert M. McCheyne. 5.99 (*0-614-11464-0*, Pub. by Christian Focus UK); 5.99 (*0-906731-51-8*, Pub. by Christian Focus UK) Spring Arbor Dist.

Seven Churches of Prophecy, Vol. 1. Gordon Lindsay. (Revelation Ser.: Vol. 2). 1962. 1.95 (*0-89985-977-1*) Christ for the Nations.

Seven Churches of Prophecy, 2, Vol. 2. Gordon Lindsay. (Revelation Ser.: 2). 1962. 1.95 (*0-89985-978-X*) Christ for the Nations.

Seven Clans of the Cherokee Society. Marcelina Reed. (Illus.). 32p. (Orig.). 1993. pap. 3.50 (*0-935741-17-8*) Cherokee Pubns.

***7 Classic Strategies in Selling, 7 vols.** Dartnell Corp. Staff. Incl. Vol. 1. Planning the Sale. 70p. 1998. pap. 7.95 (*0-85013-301-7*); Vol. 2. Getting Better Interviews. 64p. 1998. pap. 7.95 (*0-85013-302-5*); Vol. 3. Making the Presentation. 64p. 1998. pap. 7.95 (*0-85013-303-3*); Vol. 4. Disposing of Objections. 64p. 1998. pap. 7.95 (*0-85013-304-1*); Vol. 5. Closing the Sale. 64p. 1998. pap. 7.95 (*0-85013-305-X*); Vol. 6. Managing Your Time. 64p. 1998. pap. 7.95 (*0-85013-306-8*); Vol. 7. Way to Leadership. 64p. 1998. pap. 7.95 (*0-85013-307-6*); 39.95 (*0-85013-300-9*) Dartnell Corp.

***7 Client/Server Applications in Visual Basic.** Mark McCall. (Toolbox of Templates Ser.). (Illus.). 430p. (Orig.). 1997. pap. 119.00 (*1-883884-42-X*) Midrange Comput.

Seven Clues in Pebble Creek. Kathy Stinson. (Blue Kite Adventure Ser.). (Illus.). (J). (gr. 2 up). 1995. pap. 6.95 (*1-55028-036-8*); bds. 16.95 (*1-55028-038-4*) Formac Dist Ltd.

Seven Clues to the Origin of Life: A Scientific Detective Story. A. G. Cairns-Smith. (Canto Book Ser.). (Illus.). 144p. (C). 1990. pap. text ed. 9.95 (*0-521-39828-2*) Cambridge U Pr.

Seven Colors of the Rainbow: Torah Ethics for Non-Jews. Yirmeyahu Bindman. LC 95-19163. (Or L'amim Ser.). 173p. pap. 14.95 (*0-89390-332-9*) Resource Pubns.

Seven Comedies by Marivaux. Pierre C. De Marivaux. Ed. & Tr. by Oscar Mandel from FRE. Tr. by Adrienne S. Mandel from FRE. LC 68-16386. 366p. 1968. 19.95 (*0-910278-36-9*) Boulevard.

Seven Comedies by Marivaux. Pierre C. De Marivaux. Ed. by Adrienne S. Mandel & Oscar Mandel. LC 68-16386. (Illus.). 380p. 1968. 39.00 (*0-686-60850-X*) Irvington.

Seven Comedies by Marivaux. Pierre C. De Marivaux. Ed. by Oscar Mandel & Adrienne S. Mandel. LC 68-16386. (Illus.). 380p. 1968. pap. text ed. 14.50 (*0-8290-2023-3*) Irvington.

***Seven Comedies of Marivaux.** Pierre C. De Marivaux. Ed. by Oscar Mandel. LC 68-16386. 382p. 1968. reprint ed. pap. 108.90 (*0-608-04422-9*, AU00483) Bks Demand.

Seven Concentric Circles. Jim Goure. 56p. (Orig.). 1983. pap. 5.00 (*0-915235-05-6*) United Res.

Seven Concertos of Beethoven. Anthony Hopkins. 112p. 1996. 51.95 (*1-85928-245-8*, Pub. by Scolar Pr UK) Ashgate Pub Co.

Seven Contemporary Austrian Plays. Ed. by Richard H. Lawson. LC 95-14086. (Studies in Austrian Literature, Culture, & Thought). 284p. 1995. pap. 24.50 (*1-57241-017-5*) Ariadne CA.

Seven Contemporary Chinese Women Writers. 280p. 1995. lib. bdg. 29.00 (*0-8095-4518-7*) Borgo Pr.

***Seven Contemporary Chinese Women Writers.** 282p. 1985. pap. 7.95 (*0-8351-1600-X*) China Bks.

Seven Contemporary Short Novels. 3rd ed. Charles Clerc & Louis H. Leiter. (C). 1982. text ed. 34.50 (*0-673-15569-2*) Addson-Wesley Educ.

***Seven Continents, Vol. 2.** Sayre. 1998. 16.98 (*0-8050-5194-5*) St Martin.

***Seven Continents, Vol. 3.** Sayre. 1998. 16.98 (*0-8050-5195-3*) St Martin.

***Seven Continents, Vol. 4.** Sayre. 1998. 16.98 (*0-8050-5196-1*) St Martin.

***Seven Continents, Vol. 5.** Sayre. Date not set. 16.98 (*0-8050-5197-X*) St Martin.

***Seven Continents, Vol. 6.** Sayre. Date not set. 16.98 (*0-8050-5198-8*) St Martin.

***Seven Continents, Vol. 7.** Sayre. Date not set. 16.98 (*0-8050-5199-6*) St Martin.

Seven Conundrums. E. Phillips Oppenheim. LC 78-134973. (Short Story Index Reprint Ser.). (Illus.). 1977. 20.95 (*0-8369-3704-X*) Ayer.

Seven Conversations with Jorge Luis Borges. Fernando Sorrentino. Tr. by Clark M. Zlotchew from SPA. LC 80-54425. 235p. (C). 1981. 18.50 (*0-87875-214-5*) Whitston Pub.

7 Council Fires. David Seals. (7 Council Fires of Sweet Medicine Ser.: Act 7). 1996. audio 17.00 (*1-887786-33-3*) Sky & Sage Bks.

7 Council Fires. David Seals. (Sweet Medicine Ser.: Act 7). 200p. 1996. 18.95 (*1-887786-16-3*) Sky & Sage Bks.

Seven Council Fires of Sweet Medicine: 7 Acts in 5 Volumes of Indigenous Mythology. David Seals. (C). 1996. audio 129.00 (*1-887786-34-1*) Sky & Sage Bks.

An Asterisk (*) at the beginning of an entry indicates that the title is appearing in BIP for the first time.

Seven Council Fires of Sweet Medicine: 7 Acts in 5 Volumes of Indigenous Mythology, 5 vols., Set. David Seals. (Illus.). 2100p. 1997. 125.00 (*1-887786-21-X*) Sky & Sage Bks.

Seven Countries: A Multivariate Analysis of Death & Coronary Heart Disease. Ancel Keys. LC 79-9163. (Commonwealth Fund Publications). (Illus.). 392p. 1980. 44.50 (*0-674-80237-3*) HUP.

Seven Countries Study: A Scientific Adventure in Cardiovascular Disease Epidemiology. D. Kromhout et al. 218p. 1994. write for info. (*90-6960-048-X*) H Blackburn.

Seven Crowns for the White Lady of the Other World & Blood Poems. Mark Craver. LC 91-27166. 80p. (Orig.). 1992. pap. 10.00 (*0-914061-25-9*) Orchises Pr.

Seven Crucial Moments in Christ's Life & in Ours. John W. Yates, II. LC 91-44982. 104p. (Orig.). 1992. pap. 6.95 (*0-8192-1581-3*) Morehouse Pub.

Seven Crystal Balls. Herge. (Illus.). 62p. (J). (gr. 3-8). 19.95 (*0-8288-5071-2*) Fr & Eur.

Seven Crystal Balls. Herge. (Adventures of Tintin Ser.). (Illus.). (ENG.). 1975. pap. 8.95 (*0-316-35840-1*, Joy St Bks) Little.

Seven Cycles: Public Rituals. Mary B. Edelson. (Illus.). 64p. (Orig.). 1980. pap. 10.00 (*0-9604650-0-6*) Edelson.

Seven Dada Manifestoes. Tristan Tzara. Tr. by Barbara Wright from FRE. (Orig.). 1979. pap. 11.95 (*0-7145-3762-4*) Riverrun NY.

Seven Daughters & Seven Sons. Barbara Cohen & Bahija Lovejoy. 1995. 18.75 (*0-8446-6806-0*) Peter Smith.

Seven Daughters & Seven Sons. Barbara Cohen & Bahija Lovejoy. Ed. by Amy Cohn. LC 94-80. 128p. (YA). (gr. 7 up). 1994. reprint ed. pap. 4.95 (*0-688-13563-3*) Morrow.

Seven Daughters of the Theater. Edward Wagenknecht. (Quality Paperbacks Ser.). (Illus.). 234p. 1981. reprint ed. pap. 7.95 (*0-306-80153-1*) Da Capo.

Seven-Day-a-Week Church. Lyle E. Schaller. 192p. 1992. pap. 12.95 (*0-687-38144-4*) Abingdon.

Seven-Day Afghans. Jean Leinhauser & Rita Weiss. LC 89-22038. (Illus.). 144p. 1990. pap. 14.95 (*0-8069-5709-3*) Sterling.

***7-Day Art Workshop.** Barbara C. Russell. Ed. & Des. by Bonnie A. Bradsaw. (Illus.). 100p. (Orig.). (YA). (gr. 8 up). 1996. pap. 24.95 (*0-9642945-0-8*) J&B Pubng MO.

Seven Day Circle: The History & Meaning of the Week. Eviatar Zerubavel. LC 88-30393. xiv, 220p. 1989. pap. 11.95 (*0-226-98165-7*) U Ch Pr.

***7 Day Cookbook: The Easy Answer to "What's for Dinner?"** unabridged ed. Nadine Nemechek & Sharon N. Gerardi. (Illus.). 240p. 1997. 13.95 (*0-9657500-0-0*) Redbank Ranch.

Seven Day Journey with Thomas Merton. Ester De Waal. LC 93-16820. (Illus.). 116p. 1993. reprint ed. pap. 12.99 (*0-89283-789-6*, Charis) Servant.

Seven-Day Magic. Edward Eager. (Illus.). 208p. (J). (gr. 3-7). 1989. pap. 6.00 (*0-15-272916-X*, Odyssey) HarBrace.

Seven Day Professional Image Update. Meridian Education Corporation Staff. (Illus.). 50p. (Orig.). 1993. student ed., pap. 3.50 (*1-56191-280-8*, 12100); teacher ed., pap. 2.83 (*1-56191-281-6*, 12101) Meridian Educ.

Seven-Day Scriptural Rosary. Larry London. LC 88-63552. (Orig.). 1989. pap. 5.95 (*0-87973-524-4*, 524); audio 12.95 (*0-87973-192-3*) Our Sunday Visitor.

***Seven Days.** Thomas Owens & Derrick Owens. Ed. by Douglas Reed. (Orig.). 1997. pap. write for info. (*1-889732-08-7*) Word-For-Word.

Seven Days: The Emergence of Lee. Clifford Dowdey. LC 92-37791. (Illus.). xx, 380p. (C). 1993. pap. 14.00 (*0-8032-6594-8*, Bison Books) U of Nebr Pr.

Seven Days a Week: Women & Domestic Service in Industrializing America. David M. Katzman. (Illus.). 402p. 1981. reprint ed. pap. text ed. 13.95 (*0-252-00882-0*) U of Ill Pr.

Seven Days Art Columns. Peter Schjeldahl. 1990. pap. 12.50 (*0-935724-41-9*) Figures.

***Seven Days from Midnight.** large type ed. Rona Randall. (Large Print Ser.). 304p. 1997. 27.50 (*0-7089-3673-3*) Ulverscroft.

Seven Days in Dekalb. Margaret O. Kirk. 168p. 1993. 29.95 (*1-883987-00-8*) Riverbend Bks.

Seven Days in June: A Novel of the American Revolution. Howard Fast. LC 94-20163. 1994. 18.95 (*1-55972-256-8*, Birch Ln Pr) Carol Pub Group.

Seven Days in May. Fletcher Knebel. 1995. reprint ed. lib. bdg. 29.95 (*1-56849-610-9*) Buccaneer Bks.

***Seven Days in San Francisco: A Personal Tour.** Mark Jackson. (Illus.). iv, 60p. 1997. 9.95 (*0-9658611-0-4*, 79916001) ASCI.

Seven Days in Tucson. Steve Levin. 192p. 1994. 32.95 (*1-883987-01-6*) Riverbend Bks.

Seven Days in Winston-Salem. Ed. by Rob Levin & Jennifer Eanes. 240p. 1994. 32.95 (*1-883987-02-4*) Riverbend Bks.

Seven Days Makes One Week: I Would Rather Be in L.A. Than the Outskirts of Los Angeles. Craig Gullickson. 200p. 1993. pap. write for info. (*1-883710-00-6*) C Gullickson Pub.

Seven Days Makes One Week: I Would Rather Be in L.A. Than the Outskirts of Los Angeles, 3 vols., Set. Craig Gullickson. 600p. pap. write for info. (*1-883710-03-0*) C Gullickson Pub.

Seven Days Makes One Week Vol. I: I Would Rather Be in L.A. Than the Outskirts of Los Angeles. (Illus.). 225p. (Orig.). 1993. pap. 25.00 (*0-614-13520-6*) C Gullickson Pub.

Seven Days of Creation. Sara Aronow. (Bible Stories in Rhymes Ser.: Vol. 1). (Illus.). 32p. (J). (ps-2). 1985. pap. 5.95 (*0-87203-119-5*) Hermon.

***Seven Days of Creation: A Study Guide to Genesis.** Dana Cottrell. LC 95-61623. 142p. (Orig.). 1995. pap. 8.95 (*0-7880-0634-7*) CSS OH.

Seven Days of Kwanzaa. Angela S. Medearis. 128p. (J). (gr. 4-6). 1994. pap. 3.50 (*0-590-46360-8*) Scholastic Inc.

***7 Days of Kwanzaa: Kwanzaa Step Board Book.** Harriet Ziefert. (J). 1997. pap. 10.99 (*0-670-87327-6*) Viking Penguin.

Seven Days of Man. Abdel-Hakim Kassem. Tr. by Joseph N. Bell. LC 96-3731. 220p. 1996. 24.95 (*0-8101-1415-1*, Hydra Bks) Northwestern U Pr.

Seven Days to a Brand New Life. Conford. (J). 1993. pap. 2.95 (*0-685-66035-4*) Scholastic Inc.

Seven Days to Brand New Me. Ellen Conford. 128p. (J). (gr. 7-9). 1990. pap. 3.50 (*0-590-43824-7*) Scholastic Inc.

***Seven Days to Calvary: The Crucifixion.** Maurice Pearce. 177p. 1996. pap. 12.95 (*1-57502-252-4*) Morris Pubng.

Seven Days to Faster Reading. William S. Schaill. 1976. pap. 7.00 (*0-87980-141-7*) Wilshire.

Seven Days/Seven Rays: A Week of Kundalini Yoga. Ravi Singh. (Illus.). 110p. 1995. pap. text ed. 15.95 (*0-9615707-9-2*) White Lion Pr.

7 Deadly Lawsuits: How Ministers Can Avoid Litigation & Regulations. Thomas F. Taylor. 160p. (Orig.). 1996. pap. 12.95 (*0-687-00822-0*) Abingdon.

Seven Deadly Problems in Education. Carl W. Salser. 71p. 1990. pap. 5.00 (*0-89420-264-2*, 440000) Natl Book.

Seven Deadly Sinnes of London. Thomas Dekker. (BCL1-PR English Literature Ser.). 72p. 1992. reprint ed. lib. bdg. 59.00 (*0-7812-7201-7*) Rprt Serv.

Seven Deadly Sins. Alison Fell. 1989. pap. 10.95 (*1-85242-140-1*) Serpents Tail.

***Seven Deadly Sins.** Steve Schwartz. 1997. 16.00 (*0-02-861496-8*) Macmillan.

Seven Deadly Sins. Sunday Times, London Staff. LC 75-117848. (Essay Index Reprint Ser.). 1977. 17.95 (*0-8369-1722-7*) Ayer.

Seven Deadly Sins: Essays by Angus Wilson, Edith Sitwell, Cyril Connolly, Patrick Leigh-Fermor. Charles G. Waugh et al. 1992. pap. 8.00 (*0-688-11613-2*, Quill) Morrow.

***Seven Deadly Sins: Jewish, Christian, & Classical Reflections on Human Psychology.** Solomon Schimmel. (Illus.). 320p. 1997. pap. 14.95 (*0-19-511945-2*) OUP.

Seven Deadly Sins: Or How I Spent My Summer Vacation. Michael G. Michaud. (Illus.). 8p. (Orig.). 1995. pap. 10.00 (*1-882585-03-8*) MGM Pr.

Seven Deadly Sins: Society & Evil. rev. ed. Stanford M. Lyman. LC 88-82176. 368p. 1989. pap. text ed. 24.95 (*0-930390-81-4*) Gen Hall.

Seven Deadly Sins: Society & Evil. 2nd rev. ed. Stanford M. Lyman. LC 88-82176. 368p. 1989. text ed. 39.95 (*0-930390-82-2*) Gen Hall.

Seven Deadly Sins: Stories on Human Weakness & Virtue. Andrew M. Greeley et al. LC 91-13401. 144p. 1991. reprint ed. pap. 7.95 (*0-89243-506-2*, Triumph Books) Liguori Pubns.

Seven Deadly Sins in the Contemporary Church. Richard W. Bailey. 21p. 1993. pap. 1.49 (*0-87509-541-0*) Chr Pubns.

***Seven Deadly Sins of Data Warehousing.** Douglas Hackney. (C). 1997. pap. text ed. write for info. (*0-201-18379-X*) Addison-Wesley.

Seven Deadly Sins of Love: The Still Unfabulous Social Life of Ethan Green. Eric Orner. 128p. 1994. pap. 8.95 (*0-312-10539-8*) St Martin.

***7 Deadly Sins That Will Kill Your Small Business... And How to Avoid Them.** Bette Price & Charlie Dismore. 224p. (Orig.). 1997. pap. 14.95 (*1-57410-076-9*, 6101-2401, Upstart) Dearborn Finan.

Seven Deadly Sins Today. Henry Fairlie. LC 79-893. (Illus.). 1979. reprint ed. pap. 13.00 (*0-268-01698-4*) U of Notre Dame Pr.

Seven Decades of Rural Social Work: From Country Life Commission to Rural Caucus. Emilia E. Martinez-Brawley. LC 80-24185. 288p. 1981. text ed. 65.00 (*0-275-90678-7*, C0678, Praeger Pubs) Greenwood.

Seven Decades of the Union: The Humanities & Materialism. Henry A. Wise. LC 72-154164. (Select Bibliographies Reprint Ser.). 1977. reprint ed. 27.95 (*0-8369-5780-6*) Ayer.

Seven Decades That Changed America. 440p. 1979. 19.95 (*0-916150-17-8*, HO579) Am Soc Ag Eng.

Seven Decades 1900-1970: Painting & Sculpture by Alumni of Phillips Academy. Bartlett H. Hayes, Jr. (Illus.). 64p. 1969. pap. write for info. (*1-879886-18-9*) Addison Gallery.

Seven Decisive Battles of the Middle Ages. Joseph Dahmus. LC 83-13490. (Illus.). 270p. (Orig.). 1983. lib. bdg. 33.95 (*0-8304-1030-9*) Nelson-Hall.

Seven Defenses of Paracelsus. Paracelsus. (Orig.). 1994. pap. 7.95 (*1-55818-280-2*) Holmes Pub.

Seven Delivery Systems for God's Healing Power. Peter Popoff. Ed. by Don Tanner. LC 81-69730. (Illus.). 70p. 1981. pap. 1.50 (*0-938544-07-1*) Faith Messenger.

Seven Descents of Myrtle *see* **Kingdom of Earth**

Seven Dials. large type ed. Claire Rayner. (General Ser.). 592p. 1993. 25.99 (*0-7089-2812-9*) Ulverscroft.

Seven Dials Mystery. Agatha Christie. 272p. 1991. mass mkt. 4.99 (*0-06-100275-5*, Harp PBks) HarpC.

Seven Dilemmas in World Religions. G. Lynn Stephens & Gregory Pence. LC 94-12102. 126p. (C). 1995. text ed. 16.95 (*1-55778-702-6*) Paragon Hse.

Seven Dips: Level Two. Lavaun Linde & Mary Quishenberry. (Bible Stories for Early Readers Ser.: Bk. 4). (Illus.). 32p. (Orig.). (J). (gr. 1). 1988. pap. text ed. 4.99 (*0-945107-08-0*) Bradshaw Pubs.

Seven Dollar Shoes. Sparrow T. Laughingwand. 20p. (Orig.). 1994. pap. 3.00 (*0-916397-24-6*) Manic D Pr.

***Seven Doors to Islam: Spirituality & the Religious Life of Muslims.** John Renard. 317p. 1996. pap. 16.95 (*0-614-21343-6*, 1452) Kazi Pubns.

Seven Doors to Islam: Spirituality & the Religious Life of Muslims. John Renard. LC 95-45130. 317p. 1996. pap. 16.95 (*0-520-20417-4*) U CA Pr.

Seven Doors to Islam: Spirituality & the Religious Life of Muslims. John Renard. LC 95-45130. (Illus.). 317p. (C). 1996. 45.00 (*0-520-20095-0*) U CA Pr.

Seven Dreamers. Annie T. Slosson. LC 79-98602. (Short Story Index Reprint Ser.). 1977. 20.95 (*0-8369-3168-8*) Ayer.

***Seven Dumbest Relationship Mistakes That Smart People Make.** Carolyn N. Bushong. LC 96-50913. 1997. 19.95 (*0-679-44829-2*, Villard Bks) Random.

***Seven Dynamic Laws of Spirituality & Prosperity.** C. M. Ufkin. 76p. (Orig.). 1997. pap. 8.95 (*0-614-29649-8*) Shiloh Press.

***Seven Dynamic Laws of Spirituality & Prosperity.** C. M. Ufkin. Date not set. write for info. (*1-889868-02-7*) Shiloh Press.

Seven Dynamic Word Studies in the New Testament. Charles D. Goodwin & William D. McBrayer. LC 90-91667. 144p. (Orig.). 1990. pap. 9.95 (*0-9626544-1-8*) Original Word.

Seven Early Accounts of the Pomo Indians & Their Culture. Ed. by Robert F. Heizer. LC 76-621633. (Illus.). 71p. 1975. reprint ed. pap. 25.00 (*0-608-01712-4*, 2062367) Bks Demand.

Seven Early Churches of Nashville. A. L. Crabb et al. (Illus.). 1972. 35.00 (*0-918450-07-1*) C Elder.

Seven Ears of Corn. Ed. by Betty Harman & Nancy Meador. (Illus.). 149p. (J). (gr. 5-9). 1991. pap. 6.00 (*0-9630661-0-2*) Harman & Meador.

Seven Elements of a Successful Safety & Health Program. 125p. 1994. pap. 37.95 (*0-87912-181-5*, 12138-0000) Natl Safety Coun.

Seven-Eleven Diet. Bill Adler. (Critic's Choice Paperbacks Ser.). 1988. pap. 3.50 (*1-55547-280-X*, Univ Books) Carol Pub Group.

Seven English Cities. William Dean Howells. (Notable American Authors Ser.). 1992. reprint ed. lib. bdg. 75.00 (*0-7812-3279-1*) Rprt Serv.

Seven Essays. George Sampson. LC 79-115398. reprint ed. 24.50 (*0-404-05556-7*) AMS Pr.

Seven Ethical Theories. Robert Mellert. 172p. 1995. pap. text ed. 18.31 (*0-7872-0567-2*) Kendall-Hunt.

Seven Exegetical Works. Ambrose. Tr. by Michael P. McHugh. LC 71-157660. (Fathers of the Church Ser.: Vol. 65). 494p. 1972. reprint ed. pap. 140.80 (*0-7837-9201-8*, 2049951) Bks Demand.

***Seven Experiments That Could Change the World: A Do-It-Yourself Guide to Revolutionary Science.** Rupert Sheldrake. 304p. 1996. pap. 14.00 (*1-57322-564-9*, Riverhd Trade) Berkley Pub.

***Seven Faces.** Max Brand. LC 97-22023. 1998. write for info. (*0-8032-1281-X*) U of Nebr Pr.

Seven Faces: Brazilian Poetry since Modernism. Charles A. Perrone. LC 96-78. (Illus.). 280p. 1996. text ed. 49.95 (*0-8223-1807-5*); pap. text ed. 16.95 (*0-8223-1814-8*) Duke.

Seven Faces of Love. Andre Maurois. 1977. reprint ed. 20.95 (*0-518-10169-X*) Ayer.

Seven Faces of Philanthropy: A New Approach to Cultivating Major Donors. Russ A. Prince & Karen F. File. LC 94-8095. (Nonprofit Sector Ser.). 247p. text ed. 27.95 (*0-7879-0008-7*) Jossey-Bass.

Seven Fallen Pillars. Jon Kimche. LC 76-6848. (Middle East in the 20th Century Ser.). 1976. reprint ed. lib. bdg. 49.50 (*0-306-70820-5*) Da Capo.

Seven Famous Greek Plays. Incl. Prometheus Bound. Aeschylus. Ed. by Whitney J. Oates & Eugene O'Neill, Jr. 1955. pap. (*0-318-55460-7*); Agamemnon. Aeschylus. Ed. by Whitney J. Oates & Eugene O'Neill, Jr. 1955. pap. (*0-318-55461-5*); Oedipus the King-Oedipus Rex. Sophocles. Ed. by Whitney J. Oates & Eugene O'Neill, Jr. 1955. pap. (*0-318-55462-3*); Medea. Euripides. Ed. by Whitney J. Oates & Eugene O'Neill, Jr. 1955. pap. (*0-318-55463-1*); Aristophanes: Frogs. Aristophanes. Ed. by Whitney J. Oates & Eugene O'Neill, Jr. 1955. pap. (*0-318-55464-X*); Antigone. Sophocles. Ed. by Whitney J. Oates & Eugene O'Neill, Jr. 1955. pap. (*0-318-55465-8*); Alcestis. Euripides. Ed. by Whitney J. Oates & Eugene O'Neill, Jr. 1955. pap. (*0-318-55466-6*); 446p. 1966. pap. 9.00 (*0-394-70125-9*) Random.

Seven Famous Greek Plays. Ed. by Eugene O'Neill, Jr. 1950. pap. text ed. write for info. (*0-07-553629-3*) McGraw.

Seven Fantasias for Four Viols Vol. 1: Paris Fantasias. John Ward. Ed. by Virginia Brookes. (Viol Consort Ser.: No. 16). 52p. 1993. pap. text ed. 18.00 (*1-56571-070-3*, VC016) PRB Prods.

Seven Fat Years: And How to Do It Again. Robert L. Bartley. 352p. 1992. 22.95 (*0-02-901915-X*, Free Press) Free Pr.

Seven Fat Years: And How to Do It Again. Robert L. Bartley. 256p. 1994. pap. 12.95 (*0-02-901695-9*, Free Press) Free Pr.

Seven Fat Years: And How to Do It Again. Robert L. Bartley. 1995. pap. 12.00 (*0-02-874022-X*) Free Pr.

7 Fatal Management Sins: Understanding & Avoiding Managerial Malpractice. John Collis. (Illus.). 300p. (Orig.). 1997. pap. 29.95 (*1-57444-015-2*) St Lucie Pr.

Seven Festivals of the Messiah. Edward Chumney. 210p. (Orig.). 1994. pap. 9.95 (*1-56043-767-7*) Destiny Image.

Seven Figure Selling: Success Secrets of the Top Salespeople in the Business. Danielle Kennedy. 240p. 1996. pap. text ed. 12.00 (*0-425-15302-9*) Berkley Pub.

Seven Financial Conspiracies Which Enslaved the American People. 1992. lib. bdg. 75.00 (*0-8490-8719-8*) Gordon Pr.

Seven Firefights in Vietnam. John A. Cash et al. (Illus.). 159p. (Orig.). (C). 1993. pap. text ed. 20.00 (*1-56806-563-9*) DIANE Pub.

Seven Fires: An Ojibway Prophecy. Gaikesheyongai & Tobias. 1994. per. 6.95 (*0-920813-92-5*, Pub. by Sister Vision CN) LPC InBook.

Seven for a Secret. Victoria Holt. 1993. mass mkt. 5.99 (*0-449-22177-6*, Crest) Fawcett.

Seven for Banner Pass. large type ed. Marshall Grover. (Linford Western Library). 304p. 1987. pap. 15.99 (*0-7089-6418-4*) Ulverscroft.

Seven for Oregon. rev. ed. Cornelia Shields. 1989. 10.50 (*0-9617393-1-2*) Green Springs Pr.

Seven for Vengeance. large type ed. James Keene. (Linford Western Library). 448p. 1995. pap. 15.99 (*0-7089-7703-0*, Linford) Ulverscroft.

Seven Four, & Three. Thompson L. Casey. 320p. 1995. 45.00 (*1-887189-07-6*); pap. text ed. 29.50 (*1-887189-08-4*) Symi Pub.

Seven French Chroniclers: Witnesses to History. Paul Archambault. LC 73-16652. 224p. 1974. 39.95 (*0-8156-0099-2*) Syracuse U Pr.

Seven Fresh Wineskins. Ed. by William Barclay. (C). 1990. pap. 24.00 (*0-85305-276-X*, Pub. by J Arthur Ltd UK) St Mut.

Seven Friends. Louis Marlow. (Illus.). 176p. 1992. text ed. 45.00 (*1-872736-07-6*, Pub. by Mandrake Pr UK) Holmes Pub.

Seven Friends. Louis Marlow. LC 76-58445. (English Biography Ser.: No. 31). 1977. lib. bdg. 48.95 (*0-8383-2132-1*) M S G Haskell Hse.

***Seven from Heaven: A Biography of a Bantu Slave 1790-1860.** John A. Cullis. LC 96-84881. 150p. (Orig.). 1996. pap. text ed. 9.95 (*1-56226-288-2*) CT Pub.

Seven Ghostly Fancies, for SAT Recorders. Freda Burford. (Contemporary Consort Ser.: No. 23). 8p. 1992. pap. text ed. 3.50 (*1-56571-068-1*, CC023) PRB Prods.

Seven Ghosts: Perils of Mickey. Walt Disney Staff. (J). (ps-3). 1993. pap. 2.25 (*0-307-12793-1*) Western Pub.

***Seven Gifts of Sri Da Avabhasa's Grace: An Introductory Course of Study on the Way of the Heart.** 184p. 15.00 (*0-614-24034-4*) Dawn Horse Pr.

***Seven Gods of Luck.** David Kudler. LC 96-27402. (Illus.). (J). 1997. 15.00 (*0-395-78830-7*) HM.

Seven Golden Chapters of Hermes. Hermes M. Trismegistus. 1984. reprint ed. pap. 4.95 (*0-916411-82-6*) Holmes Pub.

Seven Golden Prophecies for the Year 2000. Michael X. 81p. 1985. reprint ed. spiral bd. 14.00 (*0-7873-0612-6*) Hlth Research.

Seven Gothic Dramas, 1789-1825. Ed. by Jeffrey N. Cox. LC 91-31262. 425p. (C). 1994. pap. text ed. 24.95 (*0-8214-1065-2*) Ohio U Pr.

Seven Gothic Tales. Isak Dinesen. LC 39-27353. 420p. 1980. 9.95 (*0-394-60496-2*, Modern Lib) Random.

Seven Gothic Tales. Isak Dinesen. LC 91-50030. (Vintage International Ser.). 432p. 1991. pap. 14.00 (*0-679-73641-7*, Vin) Random.

Seven Gothic Tales. Isak Dinesen. 546p. 1994. 17.50 (*0-679-60086-8*) Random.

Seven Great Explorations. Celia King. (Illus.). 7p. 1996. 10.95 (*0-8118-1375-4*) Chronicle Bks.

Seven Great Inventions: A Pop-Up Book. Celia King. (Illus.). 7p. 1995. 9.95 (*0-8118-0912-9*) Chronicle Bks.

Seven Great Religions. Annie Besant. 1990. pap. 9.50 (*81-7059-152-X*) Theos Pub Hse.

Seven Great Sacred Cantatas. Johann Sebastian Bach. 1985. pap. 12.95 (*0-486-24950-6*) Dover.

***Seven Greatest Signs Ever Performed: A Contemporary Treatment.** Eric A. Mayes, Jr. Ed. by Robert Brown. 84p. (Orig.). 1994. pap. write for info. (*1-890025-03-8*) B E A M Oklhma City.

Seven Greeks. Tr. by Guy Davenport from GRE. LC 95-4227. 256p. (Orig.). 1995. pap. 16.95 (*0-8112-1288-2*, NDP799) New Directions.

Seven Guides to Effective Prayer. Colin C. Whittaker. LC 87-34106. 224p. (Orig.). 1988. pap. 9.99 (*1-55661-011-4*) Bethany Hse.

Seven Guitars. August Wilson. LC 95-50536. 160p. 1996. pap. 19.95 (*0-525-94196-7*, Dutton) NAL-Dutton.

***Seven Guitars.** August Wilson. 1997. pap. 9.95 (*0-452-27692-6*, Plume) NAL-Dutton.

7 Habits for Highly Happy People. Bix Bender. LC 95-42292. 128p. 1996. pap. 8.95 (*0-87905-731-9*, Peregrine Smith) Gibbs Smith Pub.

***7 Habits of a Healthy Home: Preparing the Ground in Which Your Children Can Grow.** William Carmichael. LC 96-48809. 1997. pap. 11.99 (*0-8423-1293-5*) Tyndale.

7 Habits of Highly Defective People: And Other Bestsellers That Won't Go Away; A Parody. Cathy Crimmins. 96p. 1996. pap. 5.95 (*0-7871-0748-4*, Dove Bks) Dove Audio.

***Seven Habits of Highly Effective Families.** Stephen Covey. LC 97-23152. 1997. write for info. (*0-307-44008-7*, Golden Bks Adult Pub) Western Pub.

Seven Habits of Highly Effective People. Stephen R. Covey. 1996. 25.00 (*0-684-82608-9*) S&S Trade.

Seven Habits of Highly Effective People. Stephen R. Covey. 1989. 24.00 (*0-671-66398-4*) S&S Trade.

Seven Habits of Highly Effective People. Stephen R. Covey. 352p. 1990. pap. 14.00 (*0-671-70863-5*, Fireside) S&S Trade.

***Seven Habits of Highly Effective People.** Stephen R. Covey. LC 97-4210. 585p. 1997. 27.95 (*0-7838-8115-0*, GK Hall) Thorndike Pr.

Seven Habits of Highly Ineffective People: Low-Effort Lessons in Mismanaging for Success. Herman Minor, IV. LC 94-20355. 1994. pap. 8.95 (*0-8065-1582-1*, Citadel Pr) Carol Pub Group.

S

Seven Habits of Highly Successful Web Sites: A Style Guide for Web Masters. David Sachs. 1996. pap. text ed. 26.95 (*0-13-490087-1*) P-H.

Seven Habits of Successful Web Sites. David Sachs & Henry Stair. 1996. 29.95 (*0-614-14498-1*) P-H.

Seven Habits of Winning Relationships. Randal Ross. 150p. (Orig.). 1992. pap. text ed. 11.95 (*1-882745-00-0*) YMTN-Stone.

Seven Habits of Winning Relationships. Randal Ross. 1992. pap. 8.00 (*0-927936-50-X*) Vincom Inc.

Seven Hands, Seven Hearts: Prose & Poems. Elizabeth Wood. LC 94-32230. 192p. (Orig.). 1994. pap. 13.95 (*0-933377-30-4*) Eighth Mount Pr.

Seven Hands, Seven Hearts: Prose & Poems. Elizabeth Woody. LC 94-32230. 192p. (Orig.). 1994. lib. bdg. 22.95 (*0-933377-31-2*) Eighth Mount Pr.

7 Heavens: A Game of Consciousness. DJ'R. LC 95-90018. (Illus.). 360p. 1995. 25.00 (*1-886180-07-5*) For Unltd Nurturing.

Seven Hells. Thaddeus Stabholz. Ed. by Sol Lewis. Tr. by Jacques Grunblatt & Hilda R. Grunblatt from POL. LC 90-19307. (Illus.). 325p. 1991. 21.95 (*0-89604-146-8*, Holocaust Library) US Holocaust.

Seven Herbs: Plants As Teachers. Matthew Wood. (Illus.). 132p. (Orig.). 1986. pap. 8.95 (*0-938190-91-1*) North Atlantic.

S

***Seven Hermetic Letters.** Georg Lomer. Tr. by Gerhard Hanswille from GER. 125p. (Orig.). 1997. pap. text ed. 16.95 (*1-885928-09-2*) Merkur Pubng.

Seven Hindrances to Healing. Kenneth Hagin, Jr. 1980. pap. 0.75 (*0-89276-705-7*) Hagin Ministries.

Seven Hindu Goddesses of Spiritual Transformation: The Iconography of the Saptamatrikas. Katherine A. Harper. LC 89-34814. (Studies in Women & Religion: Vol. 28). (Illus.). 336p. 1990. lib. bdg. 99.95 (*0-88946-061-2*) E Mellen.

Seven Horizons. Stephen Stephanchev. LC 96-23218. 80p. (Orig.). Date not set. pap. 12.95 (*0-914061-63-1*) Orchises Pr.

Seven Hours to Sundown. Ryga. per. 12.95 (*0-88922-124-3*) Genl Dist Srvs.

Seven Human Temperaments. 6th ed. Geoffrey Hodson. 1977. 7.50 (*81-7059-052-3*) Theos Pub Hse.

Seven Hundred & Seventy-Six Even Stupider Things Ever Said. Ross Petras & Kathryn Petras. LC 93-44804. 224p. (Orig.). 1994. pap. 10.00 (*0-06-095059-5*, PL) HarpC.

Seven Hundred Fifty French Verbs & Their Uses. Ed. by Jan R. Zamir et al. LC 92-1048. 400p. 1992. pap. text ed. 16.95 (*0-471-54589-9*) Wiley.

Seven Hundred Fifty German Verbs & Their Uses. Jan R. Zamir & Rolf Neumeier. LC 91-14754. 416p. 1992. pap. text ed. 16.95 (*0-471-54026-9*) Wiley.

750 Italian Verbs & Their Uses. Brunella N. Dutton. Ed. by Jan R. Zamir & Sonia N. Zamir. LC 95-44005. (750 Verbs & Their Uses Ser.). 1996. pap. write for info. (*0-471-01627-6*) Wiley.

Seven Hundred Fifty Over-the-Counter Stocks. Carol Mull. LC 84-71342. 438p. 1986. 31.00 (*0-86690-279-1*, M2614-014) Am Fed Astrologers.

750 Racer: Everything You Need to Know about Designing, Building & Racing a Formula 750 Sports-Racing Car. Peter Herbert. (Illus.). 176p. 1996. 39.95 (*1-85260-447-6*, Pub. by J H Haynes & Co UK) Motorbooks Intl.

Seven Hundred Fifty Russian Verbs & Their Uses. Issa R. Zauber. LC 94-41643. (Seven Hundred Fifty Verbs & Their Uses Ser.). 512p. 1996. pap. text ed. 19.95 (*0-471-01274-2*) Wiley.

Seven Hundred Fifty Spanish Verbs & Their Uses. Jan R. Zamir et al. LC 92-8103. 352p. 1992. pap. text ed. 16.95 (*0-471-53939-2*) Wiley.

Seven Hundred Fifty Years of a Scottish School. John Strawhorn. 112p. 1985. 50.00 (*0-907526-10-1*, Pub. by Alloway Pub UK) St Mut.

700 Great Rail Trails: A National Directory. Greg Smith & Karen-Lee Ryan. (Illus.). 155p. (Orig.). 1996. pap. 9.95 (*0-925794-11-2*) Rails Trails.

700 Illustrations & Ideas for Speakers. Herbert V. Prochnow. (Prochnow Speaker's Library). 168p. (C). 1995. reprint ed. pap. 8.99 (*0-8010-7145-3*) Baker Bks.

***Seven Hundred Kisses: A Yellow Silk Book of Erotic Writing.** LC 96-38100. 1997. 14.00 (*0-06-251484-9*) Harper SF.

***700 North Adams Street.** Dennis Gephardt & Lacy Bullard. Ed. by Rhea Chiles & Kimbel Orr. (Illus.). 144p. 1997. 50.00 (*0-9654772-0-7*) Gov Mansion Fnd.

***700 Old-Time Color Illustrations, 2 vols., Set.** Carol B. Grafton. pap. 12.90 (*0-486-25861-0*) Dover.

701 Things That P-ss Me off about Work. I. M. Peeved & Ed Strand. LC 96-5344. 288p. 1996. pap. 7.95 (*0-399-52231-X*, Perigee Bks) Berkley Pub.

701 Toughest Movie Trivia Questions of All Time. William MacAdams & Paul Nelson. LC 95-19763. 224p. 1995. pap. 9.95 (*0-8065-1700-X*, Citadel Pr) Carol Pub Group.

Seven Hundred Science Experiments for Everyone. rev. ed. UNESCO Staff. LC 64-10638. (Illus.). 252p. (J). (gr. 5-9). 1964. 17.95 (*0-385-05275-8*) Doubleday.

777 & Other Qabalistic Writings. Aleister Crowley. LC 83-160567. 178p. 1986. pap. 12.50 (*0-87728-670-1*) Weiser.

776 Nastiest Things Ever Said. Ross Petras & Kathryn Petras. 224p. 1995. pap. 7.95 (*0-06-095060-9*, PL) HarpC.

Seven Hundred Seventy-Six Stupidest Things. Kathryn Petras & Ross Petras. 240p. 1993. pap. 10.00 (*0-385-41928-7*) Doubleday.

Seven Hundred Sixty-First Tank Battalion. Kathryn B. Pfeifer. (African-American Soldiers Ser.). (Illus.). 80p. (J). (gr. 4-7). 1994. lib. bdg. 14.98 (*0-8050-3057-3*) TFC Bks NY.

Seven Hundred Solved Problems in Vector Mechanics for Engineers, Vol II: Dynamics. Joseph F. Shelley. 1991. pap. text ed. 20.95 (*0-07-056687-9*) McGraw.

***735 Baffling Bible Questions Answered.** Larry Richards. (Bible Difficulties Solved Ser.). 392p. (Orig.). 1997. pap. 12.99 (*0-8007-5632-0*) Revell.

Seven Hundred Three American Sephardim: Diversity Within Cohesiveness. Judith Mizrahi. 100p. 1992. 12.50 (*0-9635425-0-8*) Gemini Books.

722 Miles: The Building of the Subways & How They Transformed New York. Clifton Hood. (Illus.). 336p. 1995. reprint ed. pap. 15.95 (*0-8018-5244-7*) Johns Hopkins.

700 Years of Golf: A History of the Game by Numbers. Al Hand. Date not set. write for info. (*1-888857-07-2*) Links Pub CA.

Seven Ideas That Shook the Universe. Nathan Spielberg & Bryon D. Anderson. 263p. 1987. text ed. 47.95 (*0-471-85974-5*); pap. text ed. 19.95 (*0-471-84816-6*) Wiley.

Seven Ideas that Shook the Universe. 2nd ed. Nathan Spielberg & Bryond D. Anderson. LC 94-32986. 400p. (C). 1995. pap. text ed. 31.95 (*0-471-30606-1*) Wiley.

Seven Ideas That Shook the Universe: Supplementary Notes. 8th ed. Thomas Emmons. 128p. (C). 1996. per., pap. text ed. 15.22 (*0-8403-5765-6*) Kendall-Hunt.

Seven Imperatives for Fair, Legal & Productive Interviewing: A Guide for Anyone Who Makes or Influences Hiring Decision. 2nd ed. Drake Beam Morin, Inc. Staff. (Illus.). 80p. 1993. reprint ed. pap. 10.95 (*1-880030-09-8*) DBM Pub.

Seven Irish Plays, Nineteen Forty-Six to Nineteen Sixty-Four. Ed. by Robert Hogan. LC 67-20594. 478p. reprint ed. pap. 136.30 (*0-317-39702-8*, 2055878) Bks Demand.

Seven Japanese Tales. Junichiro Tanizaki. Tr. by Howard Hibbett. 1996. pap. 13.00 (*0-679-76107-1*) Random Hse Value.

Seven Jewish Cultures: A Reinterpretation of Jewish History & Thought. Efraim Shmueli. Tr. by Gila Shmueli. 350p. (C). 1990. text ed. 75.00 (*0-521-37381-6*) Cambridge U Pr.

Seven Journeys Eastward Eighteen Ninety-Eight to Nineteen Twelve. Gustav J. Ramstedt. Tr. by John R. Krueger from SWE. (Mongolia Society Occasional Papers: No. 9). Orig. Title: Seitseman Retkea Itaan. 1978. pap. 15.00 (*0-910980-19-5*) Mongolia.

Seven Key Scriptures to Lead Someone to the Lord. Jeannie Griffin. 128p. (Orig.). (YA). (gr. 12). 1990. pap. 5.00 (*0-9625016-3-8*) Jeannie Griffin.

Seven Keys to Baldpate. Earl D. Biggers. 1976. reprint ed. lib. bdg. 28.95 (*0-89966-076-2*) Buccaneer Bks.

Seven Keys to Calm. Matthews. 1997. 16.00 (*0-671-00026-8*) PB.

Seven Keys to Family Power. Billy J. Daugherty. 32p. (Orig.). 1993. pap. 0.50 (*1-56267-079-4*) Victory Ctr OK.

Seven Keys to Power. Lewis De Claremont. 9.95 (*0-685-22105-9*) Wehman.

Seven Keys to Successful Study. Peter Edwards. (Illus.). 152p. 1996. pap. 16.95 (*0-86431-176-1*, Pub. by Aust Coun Educ Res AT) Paul & Co Pubs.

Seven Keys to Vibrant Health. Terry Lemerond. LC 95-78606. 144p. (Orig.). 1995. pap. 14.95 (*0-9647489-0-8*) IMPAKT Communs.

Seven Killers East: Larry & Stretch. large type ed. Marshall Grover. (Linford Western Library). 1991. pap. 15.99 (*0-7089-7094-X*) Ulverscroft.

Seven Kinds of Death. Kate Wilhelm. 256p. 1994. reprint ed. mass mkt., pap. text ed. 4.50 (*0-8439-3570-7*) Dorchester Pub Co.

Seven Kinds of Smart: Identifying & Developing Your Many Intelligences. Thomas Armstrong. LC 92-21353. 240p. (Orig.). 1993. pap. 12.95 (*0-452-26819-2*, Plume) NAL-Dutton.

Seven Kisses in a Row. Patricia MacLachlan. LC 82-47718. (Charlotte Zolotow Bk.). (Illus.). 64p. (J). (gr. 2-5). 1983. lib. bdg. 13.89 (*0-06-024084-9*) HarpC Child Bks.

Seven Kisses in a Row. Patricia MacLachlan. LC 82-47718. (Charlotte Zolotow Bk.). (Illus.). 64p. (J). (gr. 2-5). 1988. pap. 3.95 (*0-06-440231-2*, Trophy) HarpC Child Bks.

Seven Kisses in a Row: A Study Guide. Marcia Tretler. (Novel-Ties Ser.). 1989. student ed., teacher ed., pap. text ed. 15.95 (*0-88122-042-6*) Lrn Links.

Seven Lady Godivas. Dr. Seuss. LC 86-31541. (Illus.). 80p. 1987. 9.95 (*0-394-56269-0*) Random.

Seven Lady Godivas. limited ed. Dr. Seuss. LC 86-31541. (Illus.). 80p. 1987. 50.00 (*0-394-56779-X*) Random.

Seven Lamps of Advocacy. Edward A. Parry. LC 68-16965. (Essay Index Reprint Ser.). 1977. reprint ed. 17.95 (*0-8369-0773-6*) Ayer.

Seven Lamps of Architecture. John Ruskin. 1991. 20.75 (*0-8446-6469-3*) Peter Smith.

Seven Lamps of Architecture. John Ruskin. 1989. pap. 8.95 (*0-486-26145-X*) Dover.

Seven Language Dictionary. David Shumaker. 1993. 9.99 (*0-517-05795-6*) Random Hse Value.

Seven Language Dictionary of Analagous Forms: Dictionnaire des Formes Analogues en Sept Langues. Raymond Geysen. 831p. (DUT, ENG, FRE, GER, ITA, LAT & SPA.). 1986. 150.00 (*0-8288-1450-3*, M2315) Fr & Eur.

Seven Last Words. Michael H. Crosby. LC 93-33911. (Illus.). 112p. (Orig.). 1994. pap. 12.50 (*0-88344-938-2*) Orbis Bks.

Seven Last Words. Fulton J. Sheen. LC 95-43410. 63p. 1996. pap. 3.95 (*0-8189-0760-6*) Alba.

Seven Last Words of Christ: For Soli, Chorus, & Orchestra with Harp & Timpani. T. Dubois. 80p. (ENG & LAT.). 1986. pap. 4.95 (*0-7935-5490-X*, 50323850) H Leonard.

Seven Last Words of Christ: The Message of the Cross for Today. Judith Mattison. LC 92-19355. 80p. 1992. pap. 8.99 (*0-8066-2628-3*, 9-2628) Augsburg Fortress.

Seven Last Words of Jesus. Alfred A. McBride & O. Praem. 87p. 1991. pap. 4.95 (*0-86716-149-3*) St Anthony Mess Pr.

***Seven Laws of Money.** Michael Phillips. 128p. 1997. pap. 9.00 (*1-57062-277-9*) Shambhala Pubns.

Seven Laws of Teaching. rev. ed. John M. Gregory. 128p. (Orig.). 1995. pap. 7.99 (*0-8010-5272-6*) Baker Bks.

Seven Laws of the Harvest. John W. Lawrence. 128p. 1995. pap. 7.99 (*0-8254-3151-4*) Kregel.

Seven Laws of the Learner. Bruce Wilkinson. (Illus.). 350p. 1992. student ed., text ed. 19.99 (*0-88070-464-0*, Multnomah Bks) Multnomah Pubs.

7 Lb., 2 Oz. Valentine. Marie Ferrarella. (Yours Truly Ser.). 1996. mass mkt. 3.50 (*0-373-52013-1*, 1-52013-9) Silhouette.

Seven League Boots. Albert Murray. 1997. pap. 13.00 (*0-679-75858-5*) Knopf.

Seven League Boots: A Novel. Albert Murray. 369p. 1996. 25.00 (*0-679-43986-2*) Pantheon.

Seven Lears & Golgo. Howard Barker. 128p. (Orig.). 1990. pap. 11.95 (*0-7145-4183-4*) Riverrun NY.

Seven Lectures on Shakespeare & Milton. Samuel Taylor Coleridge. Ed. by John P. Collier. LC 72-962. reprint ed. 37.50 (*0-404-01617-0*) AMS Pr.

Seven Lectures on the Law & History of Copyright in Books. Augustine Birrell. 228p. 1971. reprint ed. 20.00 (*0-8377-1929-1*) Rothman.

Seven Lectures to Young Men. Henry W. Beecher. (Works of Henry Ward Beecher). 1989. reprint ed. lib. bdg. 79.00 (*0-7812-1918-3*) Rprt Serv.

Seven Lessons for Children of Substance Abusive Families: A Survivor's Manual. Christena Struben. 1993. pap. 8.95 (*1-55691-092-4*, 924) Learning Pubns.

Seven Letters from Heaven. Wim Malgo. 9.95 (*0-937422-26-6*); pap. 6.95 (*0-937422-25-8*) Midnight Call.

Seven Letters Investment Guide. rev. ed. Clarence Wolf, Jr. LC 88-71472. (Illus.). 128p. 1995. pap. 4.95 (*0-916224-87-2*) Seven Letters Pub.

Seven Levels of Change: The Secrets Used by the World's Largest Corporations to Create, Innovate & Motivate. Rolf Smith. LC 96-51302. 1997. pap. 16.95 (*1-56530-207-9*) Summit TX.

Seven Levels of Healing. Lilla Bek & Philippa Pullar. 160p. 1987. pap. 15.95 (*0-7126-9473-0*, Pub. by Century UK) Trafalgar.

Seven Levels of Marriage. Cynthia Smith. 224p. 1986. 16.95 (*0-8184-0413-2*) Carol Pub Group.

Seven Liberal Arts: A Study in Medieval Culture. Paul Abelson. LC 76-176501. (Columbia University. Teachers College. Contributions to Education Ser.: No. 11). reprint ed. 39.50 (*0-404-55011-8*) AMS Pr.

Seven Liberal Arts in the Middle Ages. Ed. by David L. Wagner. LC 83-47660. 296p. (C). 1984. 29.95 (*0-253-35185-5*) Ind U Pr.

Seven Liberal Arts in the Middle Ages. David L. Wagner. LC 83-47660. (Illus.). 295p. 1983. reprint ed. pap. 84.10 (*0-7837-9670-6*, 2059304) Bks Demand.

***Seven Lies about Sex.** Alice Fryling. 32p. 1997. pap. 0.99 (*0-87784-061-X*, 061) InterVarsity.

***Seven Life Lessons of Chaos.** John Briggs & David F. Peat. 192p. 1997. 20.00 (*0-06-018246-6*) HarpC.

Seven Lifetime Sports. 2nd ed. Jerry Clark. 238p. 1991. pap. 28.95 (*0-945483-17-1*) E Bowers Pub.

Seven Little Hippos. Mike Thaler. (J). 1994. pap. 4.95 (*0-671-89907-4*) S&S Trade.

***Seven Little Hippos.** Mike Thaler. (J). 1991. pap. 13.95 (*0-671-72964-0*, S&S Bks Young Read) S&S Childrens.

Seven Little Monsters. Maurice Sendak. LC 76-18400. (Illus.). (J). (gr. 1 up). 1977. lib. bdg. 14.89 (*0-06-025478-5*) HarpC Child Bks.

Seven Little Monsters. Maurice Sendak. (J). (ps-3). 1986. pap. text ed. 4.95 (*0-06-443139-8*) HarpC.

Seven Little Rabbits. John Becker. (Illus.). 32p. (J). 1991. pap. 4.99 (*0-590-44849-8*, Blue Ribbon Bks) Scholastic Inc.

Seven Little Rabbits. 2nd ed. John Becker. Tr. by Barbara Cooney. (Illus.). 32p. (J). (ps-3). 1994. reprint ed. 5.95 (*0-8027-8311-2*) Walker & Co.

Seven Loaves of Bread. Ferida Wolff. LC 92-34313. (Illus.). 32p. (J). (ps up). 1993. 16.00 (*0-688-11101-7*, Tambourine Bks); lib. bdg. 15.93 (*0-688-11112-2*, Tambourine Bks) Morrow.

Seven Long Times. Piri Thomas. LC 94-8661. 1994. pap. 9.95 (*1-55885-105-4*) Arte Publico.

Seven Long Years Until College. Mary J. Auch. LC 91-2094. 176p. (J). (gr. 3-7). 1991. 13.95 (*0-8234-0901-5*) Holiday.

Seven Long Years until College. Mary J. Auch. Ed. by Lisa Clancy. 176p. (YA). (gr. 3-6). 1994. reprint ed. mass mkt. 2.99 (*0-671-78140-5*, Minstrel Bks) PB.

Seven Lost Secrets of Success. Joe Vitale. 128p. (C). 1992. pap. 12.95 (*1-881760-00-6*) Brockton Pubng.

Seven Magic Brothers: Siete Hermanos Magicos. Kuang-ts'ai Hao. Tr. by Beatriz Zeller from CHI. (Illus.). 32p. (ENG & SPA.). (J). (gr. 2-4). 1994. 16.95 (*957-32-2165-9*) Pan Asian Pubns.

Seven Magic Steps to Speed Sight Reading. Duane Shinn. 40p. 1971. pap. 39.95 incl. audio (*0-912732-02-4*) Duane Shinn.

***Seven Majestic Hymn Introductions.** Ed. by Dale Tucker. 16p. (Orig.). (C). 1997. pap. text ed. 6.95 (*0-7692-0084-2*) Warner Brothers.

Seven Making History: A Mayoral Retrospective. League of Women Voters of Cleveland Educational Fund, Inc. Staff. 51p. 1990. pap. 10.00 (*1-880746-01-8*) LOWV Cleve Educ.

Seven Marriages of Marriage. Mel Krantzler. 256p. 1994. mass mkt. 5.50 (*0-06-104303-6*, Harp PBks) HarpC.

Seven Martyrs of Hurmuzak. Muhammad Labib. Tr. & Frwd. by Moojan Momen. (Illus.). 80p. 1981. 11.50 (*0-85398-105-1*); pap. 5.50 (*0-85398-104-3*) G Ronald Pub.

Seven Master Keys to Triumphant Christian Living. Gordon Lindsay. 1967. 2.95 (*0-89985-006-5*) Christ for the Nations.

Seven Master Printmakers: Innovations in the Eighties. Notes by Guy Davenport. (Illus.). 120p. 1991. 37.50 (*0-87070-194-0*); pap. 19.95 (*0-87070-190-8*) Mus of Modern Art.

Seven Masters of Supernatural Fiction. Edward Wagenknecht. LC 91-15989. (Contributions to the Study of Science Fiction & Fantasy Ser.: No. 46). 224p. 1991. text ed. 49.95 (*0-313-27960-8*, WKM, Greenwood Pr) Greenwood.

Seven Matched Hollow Gold Jaguars from Peru's Early Horizon. Heather Lechtman et al. LC 75-21192. (Studies in Pre-Columbian Art & Archaeology: No. 16). (Illus.). 49p. 1975. pap. 6.00 (*0-88402-060-6*) Dumbarton Oaks.

Seven Matrices: The Forest of Fecundity. Alan M. Olson. LC 90-72009. 134p. (Orig.). 1992. pap. 10.00 (*1-56002-090-3*, Univ Edtns) Aegina Pr.

Seven Medieval Historians. Joseph Dahmus. LC 81-11332. 320p. (C). 1981. text ed. 33.95 (*0-88229-712-0*) Nelson-Hall.

Seven Memphite Tomb Chapels, Vol. 65: British School of Egyptian Archaeology. Petrie. 1969. 19.95 (*0-85668-116-4*, Pub. by Aris & Phillips UK) David Brown.

Seven Men at Mimbres Springs. Will Henry. 208p. 1989. reprint ed. pap. 2.95 (*0-380-70605-9*) Avon.

Seven Men at Nimbres Springs. large type ed. Will Henry. LC 94-32524. (Nightingale Ser.). 304p. 1995. pap. 16.95 (*0-7838-1153-5*, GK Hall) Thorndike Pr.

Seven Men Who Rule the World from the Grave. Dave Breese. 1990. pap. 11.99 (*0-8024-8448-4*) Moody.

Seven Men Who Rule the World from the Grave. David Breese. 23p. (Orig.). 1994. pap. 2.50 (*1-879366-63-0*) Hearthstone OK.

***Seven Methods for Transforming Corporate Data into Business Intelligence.** Vasant Dhar & Roger Stein. LC 96-37191. 269p. 1996. pap. 29.95 (*0-13-282006-4*) P-H.

Seven Military Classics of Ancient China. Tr. by Ralph D. Sawyer. (History & Warfare Ser.). 568p. (C). 1993. text ed. 35.00 (*0-8133-1228-0*) Westview.

Seven Minor Epics of the English Renaissance. Ed. by Paul W. Miller. LC 67-10125. 1977. 50.00 (*0-8201-1034-5*) Schol Facsimiles.

Seven-Minute Rotator Cuff Solution. Jerry Robinson & Joseph Horrigan. (Illus.). 64p. (Orig.). 1990. pap. 16.95 (*0-944831-25-7*) Health Life.

Seven Minutes: The Life & Death of the American Animated Cartoon. Norman M. Klein. 296p. 1996. pap. 20.00 (*1-85984-150-3*, Pub. by Vrso UK) Norton.

Seven Miracles at Calvary. Everitt M. Fjordbak. 340p. 1972. pap. 8.95 (*1-882449-09-6*) Messenger Pub.

Seven Modern American Novelists: An Introduction. William V. O'Connor. LC 64-18175. 308p. reprint ed. pap. 87.80 (*0-317-29452-0*, 2055894) Bks Demand.

Seven Modern Wonders of the World: A Pop-up Book. Celia King. (Seven Wonders Ser.). (Illus.). 7p. (J). (gr. 3 up). 1992. 9.95 (*0-8118-0159-4*) Chronicle Bks.

Seven Mohave Myths. fac. ed. A. L. Kroeber. Ed. by Ronald L. Olson et al. (University of California Publications: No. 11:1). 75p. (C). 1948. reprint ed. pap. 6.85 (*1-55567-099-7*) Coyote Press.

Seven Months of Sin. Ned E. Wick. LC 74-78891. 1974. 3.50 (*0-931446-00-7*) Honor Bks.

Seven More Poems by Nicholas Bozon. M. Amelia Klenke. (History Ser.). ix, 162p. 1951. pap. 3.50 (*1-57659-081-X*) Franciscan Inst.

Seven Mountains. Marilyn Mason. LC 96-41986. 160p. 1997. pap. 18.95 (*0-525-93980-6*) NAL-Dutton.

***Seven Mountains: The Inner Climb to Committment & Caring.** Marilyn Mason. 1998. pap. 9.95 (*0-452-27417-6*) NAL-Dutton.

Seven Mountains of Thomas Merton. Michael Mott. 1993. pap. 21.00 (*0-15-680681-9*) HarBrace.

Seven Movements, One Song. Carolyn North. 325p. (Orig.). 1991. pap. 14.95 (*0-916147-17-7*) Regent Pr.

***Seven Moves.** Anshaw. 1997. pap. 11.00 (*0-395-87756-3*) HM.

Seven Moves. Carol Anshaw. LC 96-16134. 220p. 1996. 21.95 (*0-395-69131-1*) HM.

***Seven M's of Missionary Service.** Carlos E. Asay. 1996. 12.95 (*1-57008-287-1*) Bookcraft Inc.

Seven Mysteries In The First Epistle Of John. Witness Lee. 79p. per. 3.00 (*0-87083-089-9*, 10086001) Living Stream Ministry.

Seven Mysteries of Europe. Jules Romains. Tr. by Germaine Bree from FRE. LC 78-152210. (Essay Index Reprint Ser.). 1977. reprint ed. 20.95 (*0-8369-2294-8*) Ayer.

Seven Mysteries of Life: An Exploration in Science & Philosophy. Guy Murchie. 1981. pap. 15.95 (*0-395-30537-3*) HM.

Seven Mysteries...Solved!, Vol. 1. Howard A. Peth. (Illus.). 433p. (Orig.). 1988. pap. 14.95 (*0-9618580-0-1*); write for info. (*0-317-68279-2*) Lessons Heaven.

Seven Mysteries...Solved!, Vol. 2. Howard A. Peth. (Illus.). 545p. (Orig.). 1988. pap. 14.95 (*0-9618580-1-X*) Lessons Heaven.

Seven Mysterious Wonders: A Pop-up Book. Celia King. LC 93-8179. (J). 1993. 9.95 (*0-8118-0361-9*) Chronicle Bks.

An Asterisk (*) at the beginning of an entry indicates that the title is appearing in BIP for the first time.

Seven Mythical Creatures: A Pop-Up Book. Celia King. Ed. by Victoria Rock. (Illus.). 16p. 1994. 9.95 (*0-8118-0673-1*) Chronicle Bks.

Seven Myths about Small Groups. Dan Williams. LC 91-14011. 134p. (Orig.). 1991. pap. 8.99 (*0-8308-1721-2*, 1721) InterVarsity.

Seven Myths of Housing. Nathan Straus. LC 73-11910. (Metropolitan America Ser.). (Illus.). 362p. 1974. reprint ed. 28.95 (*0-405-05426-2*) Ayer.

***7 Myths Promoted by Conservatives, No. 7001.** Gregory N. Austin. 136p. (Orig.). 1996. pap. 10.95 (*0-9653296-0-7*) GLS Publng.

Seven Natural Wonders of the World: A Pop-up Book. Celia King. (Illus.). 7p. (J). (ps up). 1991. 9.95 (*0-8118-0001-6*) Chronicle Bks.

7 Ne Ofanziva - 7 Non Offensives. Ivo Omrcanin. 72p. (Orig.). (CRO.). 1996. pap. 10.00 (*0-614-15880-X*) Ivor Pr.

Seven New Artists: Pittsburgh Today. John R. Caldwell. 24p. (Orig.). 1984. pap. 4.00 (*0-88039-008-5*) Mus Art Carnegie.

Seven New QC Tools: Practical Applications for Managers. Yoshinobu Nayatani et al. Tr. by John H. Loftus from JPN. (Illus.). 180p. 1994. pap. text ed. 34.95 (*4-88319-004-8*, 190048, Pub. by Three A JA) Qual Resc.

Seven Nights. Jorge Luis Borges. Tr. by Eliot Weinberger from SPA. LC 84-1018. Orig. Title: Siete Noches. 128p. 1984. pap. 7.95 (*0-8112-0905-9*, NDP576) New Directions.

Seven Novelettes for Piano. Albert De Vito. 1971. pap. 4.95 (*0-934286-15-9*) Kenyon.

Seven Novelists in the American Naturalist Tradition: An Introduction. Ed. by Charles C. Walcutt. LC 74-14209. (Minnesota Library on American Writers: Vol. 8). 337p. reprint ed. pap. 96.10 (*0-685-15920-5*, 2056204) Bks Demand.

Seven Nuns at Las Vegas. Natalie E. White. 1954. pap. 5.25 (*0-8222-1013-4*) Dramatists Play.

Seven Nuns South of the Border. Natalie E. White. 1962. pap. 5.25 (*0-8222-1014-2*) Dramatists Play.

Seven of Diamonds. large type ed. Max Brand. LC 90-11278. 384p. 1990. reprint ed. lib. bdg. 16.95 (*1-56054-076-1*) Thorndike Pr.

Seven Old English Poems. Ed. by John C. Pope. (Orig.). 1966. pap. 5.55 (*0-672-60976-2*, LL8, Bobbs) Macmillan.

Seven Old English Poems. Ed. by John C. Pope. 240p. (Orig.). (C). 1981. reprint ed. pap. text ed. 9.95 (*0-393-95174-X*) Norton.

Seven on Style. William C. Wantling. 1975. pap. 5.00 (*0-915016-02-8*) Second Coming.

Seven Pagodas on the Coromandal Coast. C. Carr et al. (Illus.). 244p. 1986. reprint ed. 37.50 (*0-8364-1726-7*, Pub. by Usha II) S Asia.

***7 Pamphlets: 1806-11 Editions.** Joseph Lancaster. Ed. & Intro. by Jeffrey Stern. (Classics in Education Ser.). 314p. 1996. reprint ed. write for info. (*1-85506-291-7*) Bks Intl VA.

Seven Papers in Applied Mathematics. Ed. by D. V. Anosov et al. LC 84-21681. (AMS Translations Ser.: Series 2, Vol. 125). 130p. 1985. text ed. 61.00 (*0-8218-3087-2*, TRANS2/125) Am Math.

Seven Papers on Algebra. S. N. Cernikov et al. LC 51-5559. (Translations Ser.: Series 2, Vol. 69). 256p. 1968. 47.00 (*0-8218-1769-8*, TRANS 2-69) Am Math.

Seven Papers on Algebra, Algebraic Geometry & Algebraic Topology. Ju. I. Manin et al. LC 51-5559. (Translations Ser.: Series 2, Vol. 63). 279p. 1967. 50.00 (*0-8218-1763-9*, TRANS2/63) Am Math.

Seven Papers on Analysis. Ja. L. Engel'son et al. LC 51-5559. (Translations Ser.: Series 2, Vol. 60). 283p. 1967. 50.00 (*0-8218-1760-4*, TRANS2/60) Am Math.

Seven Papers on Equations Related to Mechanics & Heat. A. A. Andronov et al. LC 51-5559. (Translations Ser.: Series 2, Vol. 75). 255p. 1968. 47.00 (*0-8218-1775-2*, TRANS2/75) Am Math.

Seven Papers Translated from the Russian. I. Kovalishina & V. Potapov. LC 87-33650. (Translations Ser.: Series 2, Vol. 138). 77p. 1988. 50.00 (*0-8218-3114-3*, TRANS2/138) Am Math.

***Seven Partly Underground Rooms for Water, Ice, & Midgets.** Mary-Ann Ray. LC 97-4042. (Pamphlet Architecture Ser.: Vol. 20). (Illus.). 64p. (Orig.). 1997. pap. 11.95 (*1-56898-103-1*) Princeton Arch.

***7 Paths to Purify: Spiritual Solutions to Everyday Problems.** rev. ed. Phillip H. Porter & W. Terry Whalin. 208p. 1997. 22.00 (*0-06-039205-3*, ReganBooks) HarpC.

Seven Pathways of Learning: Teaching Students & Parents about Multiple Intelligences. David Lazear. LC 93-33054. 256p. 1994. pap. 35.00 (*0-913705-92-6*) Zephyr Pr AZ.

Seven Pauline Letters. Peter F. Ellis. LC 82-15252. 296p. (Orig.). 1983. pap. 14.95 (*0-8146-1245-8*) Liturgical Pr.

Seven-Percent Solution. large type ed. Nicholas Meyer. 1977. 25.99 (*0-7089-0052-6*) Ulverscroft.

Seven-Percent Solution: Being a Reprint from the Reminiscences of John H. Watson, M.D. Ed. by Nicholas Meyer. 256p. 1993. pap. 9.95 (*0-393-31119-8*) Norton.

Seven Persian Treasures. 20.00 (*0-686-23322-0*) Rochester Folk Art.

Seven Phantazias for Five Viols. William Simmes. Ed. by Rita Morey. iii, 64p. 1992. pap. text ed. 20.00 (*1-56571-049-5*, VC5) PRB Prods.

Seven Pieces for SATB Recorders. Ernst Pepping. Ed. by Peter Ballinger. (Contemporary Consort Ser.: No. 4). 34p. 1989. pap. text ed. 10.00 (*1-56571-009-6*) PRB Prods.

Seven Pillars of Faith. Yitzchak Breiter. Tr. by Avraham Greenbaum from HEB. 64p. 1989. pap. text ed. 3.00 (*0-930213-49-1*) Breslov Res Inst.

***Seven Pillars of Health: Nutritional Secrets for Good Health & Long Life.** Jay Solomon. LC 97-1000. 368p. 1997. per., pap. 15.00 (*0-7615-0862-7*) Prima Pub.

Seven Pillars of Popular Culture. Marshall W. Fishwick. LC 84-8994. (Contributions to the Study of Popular Culture Ser.: No. 10). (Illus.). 224p. 1985. text ed. 55.00 (*0-313-23263-6*, FIF/, Greenwood Pr) Greenwood.

Seven Pillars of Sales Success. Jonathan Evetts. 192p. (C). 1990. reprint ed. lib. bdg. 35.00 (*0-8095-7553-1*) Borgo Pr.

Seven Pillars of Wisdom. T. E. Lawrence. 1976. 36.95 (*0-8488-0562-3*) Amereon Ltd.

Seven Pillars of Wisdom. Mark L. McElhaney. (Orig.). 1996. pap. 8.95 (*0-533-11202-8*) Vantage.

Seven Pillars of Wisdom: A Triumph. T. E. Lawrence. 784p. 1991. pap. 15.95 (*0-385-41895-7*) Doubleday.

Seven Pillories of Wisdom. David Hall. LC 91-27412. 144p. (C). 1990. 18.95 (*0-86554-369-0*, MUP-H306) Mercer Univ Pr.

Seven Pines: Its Occupants & Their Letters, 1825-1872. rev. ed. Camilla D. Trammell. LC 86-10209. (Illus.). 304p. 1987. 17.95 (*0-87074-218-3*) SMU Press.

Seven Place Natural Trigonometrical Functions: Together with Many Miscellaneous Tables. rev. ed. LC 39-17191. 230p. reprint ed. pap. 65.60 (*0-317-09161-1*, 2016481) Bks Demand.

Seven Plagues of the Revelation. Kingdom Quotes Staff. pap. write for info. (*0-930179-35-8*) Johns Enter.

Seven Plays. Pierre Corneille. Tr. by Samuel Solomon from FRE. LC 68-14514. 657p. 1969. 35.00 (*0-910278-95-4*) Boulevard.

Seven Plays. Voltaire. Tr. by William F. Fleming from FRE. 507p. 1988. lib. bdg. 49.50 (*0-86527-371-5*) Fertig.

Seven Plays. Ernst Toller. LC 90-34112. xii, 434p. 1991. reprint ed. lib. bdg. 47.50 (*0-86527-399-5*) Fertig.

Seven Plays from American Literature. rev. ed. Adapted by George P. McCallum. 1977. pap. 3.75 (*0-87789-062-5*); audio 39.50 (*0-87789-126-5*) ELS Educ Servs.

Seven Plays of the Sea. Eugene O'Neill. 199p. 1972. pap. 10.00 (*0-394-71856-9*, Vin) Random.

Seven Poems. George Barker. (C). 1990. 75.00 (*0-906887-01-1*, Pub. by Greville Pr UK) St Mut.

Seven Poems. Larry Fagin. (Orig.). 1976. 3.00 (*0-929844-09-2*) Big Sky Bolinas.

Seven Poems. 2nd ed. Boris Pasternak. Tr. by George L. Kline from RUS. LC 76-134742. (Keepsake Ser.). 1970. 15.00 (*0-87775-083-1*); pap. 6.95 (*0-87775-005-X*) Unicorn Pr.

Seven Poems. Resi Nachman. 1971. reprint ed. pap. 1.00 (*0-918230-01-2*) Barnstable.

Seven Poems Suspended in the Temple at Mecca. Mu'Allakat. LC 73-12764. reprint ed. 27.50 (*0-404-11238-2*) AMS Pr.

Seven Portholes in Hell: Poems of the Holocaust. Asher Torren. LC 91-7169. 135p. 1991. 18.95 (*0-89604-150-6*, Holocaust Library); pap. 9.95 (*0-89604-151-4*, Holocaust Library) US Holocaust.

7 Possibilities for Train 713 Departing from Auschwitz. Armand Gatti. Tr. by Teresa L. Jillson from FRE. (Classics Ser.: No. 137). 180p. (Orig.). 1997. pap. 12.95 (*1-55713-303-4*) Sun & Moon CA.

Seven Principal Musical Notes of the Hindus. Sourindro M. Tagore. (C). reprint ed. 8.50 (*0-685-39096-9*, Pub. by Low Price II) S Asia.

Seven Principles in Action: Improving Undergraduate Education. John E. Ross. 168p. (C). 1995. pap. text ed. 23.95 (*1-882982-05-3*) Anker Pub.

Seven Principles of Effective Youth Ministry: A Handbook for Spiritual Growth. Mark Springer & Cheryl Smith. LC 95-33155. 184p. 1995. pap. text ed. 17.95 (*0-89390-341-8*) Resource Pubns.

Seven Principles of Man. Annie Besant. 86p. 1996. pap. 12.95 (*1-56459-628-1*) Kessinger Pub.

Seven Promises of a Promise Keeper. Bill Bright et al. LC 94-4124. 210p. 1994. 17.99 (*1-56179-222-5*) Focus Family.

Seven Promises of a Promise Keeper. Ed. by Al Janssen. LC 94-4124. 1994. audio 19.99 (*1-56179-223-3*) Focus Family.

Seven Psalms: A Commentary on the Penitential Psalms. Ed. by Alexander Barratt. Tr. by Dame Eleanor Hull. (Early English Text Society-Original Ser.: Vol. 307). (Illus.). 370p. (C). 1996. 75.00 (*0-19-722309-5*) OUP.

Seven Queens. Alaka Shankar. (Illus.). 16p. (Orig.). (J). (gr. k-3). 1980. pap. 2.50 (*0-89744-217-2*, Pub. by Childrens Bk Trust II) Auromere.

Seven Ravens. Jacob W. Grimm & Wilhelm K. Grimm. LC 83-61777. (Illus.). 28p. (J). (gr. k up). 1991. pap. 5.95 (*0-685-24951-4*, Picture Book Studio) S&S Childrens.

Seven Ravens. Jacob W. Grimm & Wilhelm K. Grimm. Tr. by Anthea Bell. LC 93-20122. (Pixies Ser.: No. 28). (Illus.). (J). (ps-8). 1993. 4.95 (*0-88708-326-9*, Picture Book Studio) S&S Childrens.

Seven Ravens. adapted ed. Jacob W. Grimm & Wilhelm K. Grimm. LC 93-8161. (Illus.). 32p. (J). (gr. k-4). 1994. lib. bdg. 15.89 (*0-06-023553-5*) HarpC Child Bks.

Seven Ravens: A Fairy Tale. Jacob W. Grimm & Wilhelm K. Grimm. Tr. by Anthea Bell from GER. LC 95-13138. (Illus.). 32p. (J). (gr. k-3). Date not set. lib. bdg. 15.88 (*1-55858-459-5*) North-South Bks NYC.

Seven Ray Energy Cards: An Intuitive Tool for Working with the Seven Rays. John Berges. 50p. 1994. 29.95 (*0-9641549-0-0*) Planetwrk Pr.

Seven Rays. Ernest Wood. LC 76-4909. 191p. 1976. reprint ed. pap. 7.95 (*0-8356-0481-0*, Quest) Theos Pub Hse.

Seven Rays & Nations - France & the United States Compared. Kurt Abraham. LC 87-81909. 96p. (Orig.). 1987. pap. 9.80 (*0-9609002-3-3*) Lampus Pr.

Seven Rays Made Visual: An Illustrated Introduction to the Teaching on the Seven Rays. Helen S. Burmester. LC 85-63216. (Illus.). 142p. (Orig.). 1986. pap. 14.95 (*0-87516-563-X*) DeVorss.

Seven Rays of Development. A. H. Ward. 30p. 1959. reprint ed. spiral bd. 5.50 (*0-7873-0931-1*) Hlth Research.

Seven Rays of Life. Alice A. Bailey. 365p. (Orig.). 1995. pap. 13.00 (*0-85330-142-5*) Lucis.

***Seven Reasons Why.** Neesa Hart. 1997. pap. 3.99 (*0-373-24122-4*, 1-24122-3) Silhouette.

Seven Red Sundays. Ramon J. Sender. 288p. 1990. pap. text ed. 9.95 (*0-929587-29-4*, Elephant Paperbacks) I R Dee.

Seven Renaissance Bicinia. Ed. by E. G. Evans & K. Wollitz. (Renaissance Recorder Ser.: No. 2). 1971. 2.75 (*0-913334-10-3*, CM1012) Consort Music.

***Seven Rivers to Cross: A Mostly British Council Life.** Bruce Nightingale. (Illus.). 225p. 1996. text ed. 39.50 (*1-86064-131-8*, Pub. by I B Tauris UK) St Martin.

Seven Robins. Neile Graham. 80p. 1983. 6.95 (*0-920806-55-4*, Pub. by Penumbra Pr CN) U of Toronto Pr.

Seven Roles of Women: Impact of Education, Migration & Employment on Ghanian Mothers. Christine Oppong & Katharine Abu. (Women, Work & Development Ser.: No. 13). xi, 127p. (Orig.). (C). 1987. pap. 18.00 (*92-2-105858-1*) Intl Labour Office.

Seven Roman Statesmen of the Later Republic. Charles W. Oman. LC 75-156699. (Essay Index Reprint Ser.). 1977. reprint ed. 30.95 (*0-8369-2288-3*) Ayer.

Seven Rs of Volunteer Development: A YMCA Resource Kit. Celeste J. Wroblewski. LC 94-19994. 312p. 1994. ring bd. 50.00 (*0-87322-756-5*, Y5239, YMCA USA) Human Kinetics.

Seven Sacraments. Lawrence G. Lovasik. (Saint Joseph Picture Bks.). (Illus.). (J). (gr. 1-6). 1978. pap. 1.25 (*0-89942-278-0*, 278-00) Catholic Bk Pub.

Seven Sages, in Scotish Metre. John Rolland. Ed. by David Laing. LC 74-144429. (Bannatyne Club, Edinburgh. Publications: No. 57). reprint ed. 57.50 (*0-404-52767-1*) AMS Pr.

Seven Sages of Ancient Greece. Constantine Cavarnos. (Illus.). 64p. 1996. 12.00 (*1-884729-16-9*) Inst Byzantine.

***Seven Sages of Ancient Greece.** Constantine Cavarnos. (Illus.). 64p. 1996. pap. 6.50 (*1-884729-17-7*) Inst Byzantine.

Seven Sages of Rome, (Southern Version) (EETS, OS Ser.: No. 191). 1974. reprint ed. 50.00 (*0-527-00191-0*) Periodicals Srv.

Seven Salient Subjects. Freedom Barry. Date not set. 15.00 (*0-9634250-6-4*) J & L Pubns.

Seven Samurai: And Other Screenplays. Akira Kurosawa. Tr. by Donald Richie from JPN. (Classic Screenplay Ser.). (Illus.). 227p. (Orig.). 1992. pap. 14.95 (*0-571-16224-X*) Faber & Faber.

Seven Sayings of the Saviour on the Cross. A. W. Pink. 8.50 (*1-85792-059-7*, Pub. by Christian Focus UK) Spring Arbor Dist.

Seven Sayings of the Saviour on the Cross. Arthur W. Pink. LC 58-59715. 138p. (gr. 10). 1984. pap. 7.99 (*0-8010-7084-8*) Baker Bks.

***Seven Sayings One Friday.** Kenn Filkens. (Small Group Studies). 64p. (Orig.). Date not set. pap. 4.99 (*0-89900-707-4*, T96-707-4) College Pr Pub.

Seven Schools of Macroeconomic Thought: The Arne Ryde Memorial Lectures. Edmund S. Phelps. 124p. 1990. 32.00 (*0-19-828333-4*) OUP.

Seven Schools of Yoga: An Introduction. Ernest Wood. LC 72-13120. Orig. Title: The Occult Training of the Hindus. 120p. 1973. reprint ed. pap. 5.95 (*0-8356-0435-7*, Quest) Theos Pub Hse.

Seven Science Fiction Novels. H. G. Wells. 1015p. (J). (gr. 9 up). 29.95 (*0-486-20264-X*) Dover.

***Seven Science Fiction Novels: The First Men in the Moon, The Island of Dr. Moreau, The War of the Worlds, The Invisible Man, The Time Machine, The Food of the Gods, In the Days of the Comet.** H. G. Wells. 1995. 29.00 (*0-8446-4842-6*) Peter Smith.

Seven Science Fiction Novels by H. G. Wells. H. G. Wells. 5.00 (*0-89190-452-2*) Amereon Ltd.

Seven Scots Stories. Jane H. Findlater. LC 75-121542. (Short Story Index Reprint Ser.). 1977. 21.95 (*0-8369-3498-9*) Ayer.

Seven Seal Judgements. pap. 0.95 (*0-686-88510-4*) GMI Pubns Inc.

Seven Seals of the Revelation. Kingdom Quotes Staff. pap. write for info. (*0-930179-20-X*) Johns Enter.

Seven Seas of Billy's Bathtub. Ray Nelson, Jr. & Douglas Kelly. Ed. by Michelle Roehm. LC 95-78728. (Flying Rhinoceros Ser.). (Illus.). 48p. (J). (gr. 1-3). 1995. 12.95 (*1-885223-27-7*) Beyond Words Pub.

Seven Seas of Billy's Bathtub. Ray Nelson, Jr. & Douglas Kelly. (Illus.). 48p. (J). (gr. 1-5). 1993. 12.95 (*1-883772-00-1*) Flying Rhino.

Seven Seas of Billy's Bathtub. Ray Nelson & Douglas Kelly. (Illus.). 48p. (J). (gr. k-6). 1994. 14.95 (*1-56977-406-4*) Flying Rhino.

Seven Seas University (SSU) R. Gray Powell. 238p. 1994. pap. text ed. 16.00 (*0-9648373-0-7*) Filac Pubs.

Seven Seasons of a Man's Life. Patrick M. Morley. 288p. 1995. pap. 19.99 (*0-7852-7827-3*) Nelson.

***Seven Seasons of a Man's Life.** Patrick M. Morley. 1995. audio 14.99 (*0-7852-7604-1*) Nelson.

***Seven Seasons of a Man's Life: Examining the Unique Challenges Men Face.** Patrick M. Morley. LC 97-22998. 1997. write for info. (*0-310-22019-X*) Zondervan.

7 Second Marketing: How to Use Memory Hooks to Make You Instantly Stand Out in a Crowd. Ivan R. Misner. 128p. 1996. pap. text ed. 12.95 (*1-885167-15-6*) Bard Press.

***Seven-Second Marketing: How to Use Memory Hooks to Make You Instantly Stand out in a Crowd.** Ivan R. Misner. LC 96-9716. 1996. write for info. (*1-885167-21-0*) Bard Press.

***Seven Secrets for a Happy Family.** Paul D. Meier. 128p. 1997. mass mkt. 4.99 (*0-8007-8642-4*, Spire) Revell.

Seven Secrets for Successful Living: Tapping the Wisdom of Ralph Waldo Emerson to Achieve Love... Marianne Parady. 1995. pap. 12.00 (*0-8217-5091-7*, Zebra Kensgtn) Kensgtn Pub Corp.

7 Secrets of a Healthy Dating Relationship. Les Parrott, III. 112p. (YA). 1995. per., pap. 7.99 (*0-8341-1554-9*) Beacon Hill.

Seven Secrets of a Healthy Dating Relationship Leader Guide. Leslie Parrott. 78p. 1996. pap. text ed. 6.95 (*0-8341-1571-9*) Beacon Hill.

7 Secrets of Effective Fathers. Ken Canfield. 244p. 1993. pap. 9.99 (*0-8423-5918-4*) Tyndale.

Seven Secrets of Effective Fathers. Ken R. Canfield. LC 92-17686. 1992. pap. 9.99 (*0-8423-5915-X*) Tyndale.

Seven Secrets of Financial Success: Applying the Time-Tested Principles of Creating, Managing & Building Personal Wealth. Jack B. Root, Sr. & Douglas L. Mortensen. 275p. 1996. text ed. 25.00 (*0-7863-0459-6*) Irwin Prof Pubng.

Seven Secrets of Influence. Elaina Zuker. 1991. audio 9.95 (*0-07-073084-9*) McGraw.

Seven Secrets of School Success. Jim Grant. 40p. (Orig.). 1992. pap. text ed. 6.00 (*0-935493-92-1*) Programs Educ.

***Seven Secrets of Slim People.** Vikki Hansen & Shawn Goodman. LC 97-20667. 128p. 1997. 12.95 (*1-56170-396-6*, 823) Hay House.

Seven Secrets of Success & Other Talks on Making Good. Madison C. Peters. 108p. 1997. pap. 9.00 (*0-89540-289-0*, SB-289) Sun Pub.

***Seven Secrets of Successful Parents.** Randy Rolfe. LC 96-31883. 1997. write for info. (*0-8092-3156-5*) Contemp Bks.

***7 Secrets of Successful Women.** Donna Brooks & Lynn Brooks. LC 97-5058. 256p. 1997. text ed. 19.95 (*0-07-008229-4*) McGraw.

***7 Secrets of Successful Women.** Donna Brooks & Lynn Brooks. 1997. 19.95 (*0-614-28012-5*) McGraw.

***Seven Secrets to Success: A Story of Hope.** Richard Webster. (Orig.). 1997. pap. 6.95 (*1-56718-797-8*) Llewellyn Pubns.

Seven Secrets to Successful Apartment Leasing. Eric Cumley. LC 95-81075. 253p. 1996. pap. 16.95 (*1-883697-44-1*) Hara Pub.

***7 Secrets to Successful Sales Management: The Sales Manager's Manual.** Jack D. Wilner. 230p. 1997. 39.95 (*1-57444-088-8*) St Lucie Pr.

Seven Sermons. Ed. by Phil Schroeder. LC 86-71906. (Augustana Historical Society Publications: Vol. 34). 32p. 1986. pap. write for info. (*0-910184-34-8*) Augustana.

Seven Sermons & One Eulogy As Preached in the Chapel of Princeton University from 1965 to 1980. Frederic E. Fox. Ed. by Donald H. Fox. LC 82-90693. 88p. (Orig.). 1982. pap. 5.95 (*0-910521-02-6*) D Fox Head.

Seven Sermons before Edward the Sixth: 1549. Hugh Latimer. Ed. by Edward Arber. 208p. 1993. pap. 20.00 (*0-87556-144-6*) Saifer.

Seven Serpents & Seven Moons. Demetrio Aguilera-Malta. Tr. by Gregory Rabassa from SPA. (Texas Pan-American Ser.). 315p. (SPA.). reprint ed. pap. 89.80 (*0-8357-7735-9*, 2036092) Bks Demand.

Seven Seven Seven: A Study of the Kabbalah. Aleister Crowley. 1973. lib. bdg. 250.00 (*0-87968-105-5*) Krishna Pr.

Seven Shaikhdoms: Life in the Trucial State Before the Federation of the United Arab Emirates. Ronald Codrai. 1990. 49.95 (*0-86685-472-X*) Intl Bk Ctr.

Seven Short & Very Short Plays. Jean-Claude Van Itallie. 1973. pap. 5.25 (*0-8222-1203-X*) Dramatists Play.

Seven Short Plays. Isabella A. Gregory. 1988. reprint ed. lib. bdg. 49.00 (*0-7812-0043-1*) Rprt Serv.

Seven Short Plays. Isabella A. Gregory. LC 77-131727. 1970. reprint ed. 29.00 (*0-403-00614-7*) Scholarly.

Seven Short Plays. Isabelle A. Gregory. LC 76-40386. (One-Act Plays in Reprint Ser.). 1976. reprint ed. 25.00 (*0-8486-2002-X*) Roth Pub Inc.

***Seven Significant Positions in Education.** William J. Bailey et al. (Educational Leadership for the 21st Century Ser.). 180p. 1996. 39.95 (*1-56676-236-7*, 762367) Technomic.

Seven Signs of a Born Again Person. Wim Malgo. 1996. reprint ed. 1.45 (*0-937422-14-2*) Midnight Call.

Seven Sillies. Joyce Dunbar. (Illus.). 32p. (J). (ps-3). 1994. 13.95 (*0-307-17504-9*, Golden Books) Western Pub.

Seven Silly Eaters. Mary A. Hoberman. LC 95-18186. (Illus.). (J). 1997. 15.00 (*0-15-200096-8*, Browndeer Pr) HarBrace.

***Seven Silly Stories.** Taylor. Date not set. pap. text ed. write for info. (*0-582-18518-1*, Pub. by Longman UK) Longman.

Seven Simple Tools...Plus. Tennessee Associates International Staff. 20p. 1993. pap. 4.95 (*1-883999-02-2*) Pressmark Intl.

Seven Sinners in Grand Opera: Level 6. Bruce Barkman. Ed. by Jean A. McConochie. (Regents Readers Ser.). 1987. pap. text ed. write for info. (*0-13-807389-9*, 21066) Prentice ESL.

Seven Sins. Sax Rohmer. 1972. 8.50 (*0-685-33437-6*) Bookfinger.

Seven Sins Against the Holy Spirit. Everitt M. Fjordbak. 303p. 1972. pap. 8.95 (*1-882449-07-X*) Messenger Pub.

S

Seven Sisters: Manuscript Edition. Edith Ellis. 1944. pap. 13.00 (0-8222-1015-0) Dramatists Play.

Seven Sisters & Other Nepalese Tales. Kesar Lall. 1988. 20.00 (0-7855-0286-6, Pub. by Ratna Pustak Bhandar) St Mut.

Seven Sisters & Other Nepalese Tales. Kesar Lall. (Illus.). (C). 1988. 35.00 (0-89771-082-7, Pub. by Ratna Pustak Bhandar) St Mut.

Seven Sisters Follow a Star: A P.E.O. Saga As Told Through Paper Dolls. Betty J. Mills. 1987. pap. 8.95 (0-89672-162-0) Tex Tech Univ Pr.

Seven Sisters of Sleep. Mordicai C. Cooke. LC 89-90881. 407p. 1991. 45.00 (0-88000-146-1) Quarterman.

***Seven Sisters of Sleep: The Celebrated Drug Classic.** Mordecai Cooke. LC 97-22404. 304p. 1997. pap. 16.95 (0-89281-748-8) Inner Tradit.

Seven Sixes Are Forty-Three. Kiran Nagarkar. (Asian Writers Ser.). 177p. 1995. pap. 10.95 (0-435-95088-6, 95088) Heinemann.

***Seven Skills for Effective Leaders.** Jeff Arnold. 1997. pap. text ed. 8.00 (1-57683-020-9) NavPress.

Seven Slayers. Paul Cain. 194p. 1987. 14.95 (0-940941-03-1) Blood & Guts Pr.

Seven Slayers. limited ed. Paul Cain. 194p. 1987. 35.00 (0-940941-04-X) Blood & Guts Pr.

Seven Sleepers of Ephesus. James De Voragine. 1991. pap. 0.50 (0-89981-125-6) Eastern Orthodox.

Seven Solitudes of Lorsa Lopez. Sony L. Tansi. Tr. by Clive Wake from FRE. (African Writers Ser.). 129p. 1995. pap. 10.95 (0-435-90594-5, 90594) Heinemann.

Seven Sonatas for Flute & Piano. George F. Handel. 68p. 1986. pap. 7.95 (0-7935-5416-0, 50334450) H Leonard.

Seven Songs - In Memoriam. Frieda Luther-Heyeckhaus. 42p. 1995. spiral bd. 34.95 (0-9615847-2-6) Marwolf Pub.

Seven Songs for the Harpsichord or Forte Piano. Francis Hopkinson. (Illus.). 1954. reprint ed. pap. 10.00 (0-8450-2597-X) Broude.

***Seven Songs of Merlyn.** Thomas A. Barron. LC 97-9619. (Lost Years of Merlin Ser.: Bk. 2). 336p. (YA). (gr. 5 up). 1997. 19.95 (0-399-23019-X, Philomel Bks) Putnam Pub Group.

Seven Soul Types. Max Stibbe. Tr. by Jakob Cornelis. 128p. 1995. 14.95 (1-869890-44-2, Pub. by Hawthorn Press UK) Anthroposophic.

Seven South: The Adventures & Times of a Small Vermont Restaurant, 1972-1982. Roy M. Newton. (Illus.). 250p. 1985. 14.95 (0-930721-00-4) Newton Pub.

Seven Soviet Poets. Ed. by R. C. Porter. 104p. (C). 1988. pap. 15.95 (0-631-15567-8, Pub. by Blckwell Pubs UK) Focus Pub-R Pullins.

Seven Spanish Realists. LC 86-60887. (Illus.). 52p. (Orig.). 1986. pap. 12.00 (0-936827-02-5) C Bernard Gallery Ltd.

Seven Spiders Spinning. Gregory Maguire. (Trophy Bk.). (Illus.). 144p. (J). (gr. 3-7). 1995. pap. 4.50 (0-06-440595-8, Trophy) HarpC Child Bks.

Seven Spiders Spinning. Gregory Maguire. LC 93-30478. (J). (gr. 1 up). 1994. 14.95 (0-395-68965-1, Clarion Bks) HM.

Seven Spirits of God. Ron Auch. LC 93-84462. 192p. (Orig.). 1993. pap. 9.95 (0-89221-238-1) New Leaf.

Seven Spiritual Laws of Success: A Practical Guide to the Fulfillment of Your Dreams. Deepak Chopra. 128p. 1995. 14.00 (1-878424-11-4) Amber-Allen Pub.

***Seven Spiritual Laws of Success for Parents: Daily Lessons for Children to Live By.** Deepak Chopra. LC 97-19609. 1997. 16.95 (0-609-60077-X, Harmony) Crown Pub Group.

***Seven Spiritual Laws/Business.** Deepak Chopra. 1998. write for info. (0-609-60078-8, Harmony) Crown Pub Group.

Seven Splendid Moments. Carmen Benson. 88p. 1992. mass mkt. 1.99 (0-88368-054-8) Whitaker Hse.

Seven Springs Sampler: Herb Recipes from Historic Homes of Powder Springs, Georgia. Sarah F. Miller & Susan K. Smith. (Illus.). 218p. (Orig.). 1991. pap. 17.50 (1-882063-12-0) Cottage Pr MA.

Seven Stairs: An Adventure of the Heart. Stuart Brent. (Illus.). 240p. 1989. pap. 11.00 (0-671-67394-7, Touchstone Bks) S&S Trade.

***Seven Stars.** Anthea Fraser. LC 97-8809. 1997. 20.95 (0-312-15650-2) St Martin.

Seven Stars & Orion: Reflections of the Past. Esther H. Mumford. (Illus.). 112p. (Orig.). 1986. pap. 7.95 (0-9605670-1-1) Ananse Pr.

***Seven States of California: A Human & Natural History.** Philip Fradkin. LC 96-34575. (Illus.). 1997. pap. 14.95 (0-520-20942-7) U CA Pr.

Seven States of California: A Human & Natural History. Philip L. Fradkin. (Illus.). 416p. 1995. 30.00 (0-8050-1947-2) H Holt & Co.

Seven Steps along the Way. F. Dale Simpson. 1981. pap. 7.75 (0-89137-527-9) Quality Pubns.

Seven Steps for Judging Prophecy. Kenneth E. Hagin. 1982. pap. 1.95 (0-89276-024-9) Hagin Ministries.

Seven Steps of the Ladder of Spiritual Love. John Ruysbroeck. 1990. pap. 7.95 (1-55818-130-X) Holmes Pub.

Seven Steps of the Ladder of Spiritual Love. Jan Van Ruysbroeck. 63p. 1992. reprint ed. pap. 6.95 (1-56459-018-6) Kessinger Pub.

Seven Steps to a Better Resume: A Step by Step Guide for Actors. Paul Haber. Ed. by R. Sommers & R. Nicholas. (Orig.). (C). 1988. pap. 4.95 (0-9631332-0-9, TXU 334 722) P Haber Grp.

Seven Steps to a Quality Decision. Buddy Harrison. 80p. (Orig.). 1996. pap. 5.99 (0-89274-736-6, HH-736) Harrison Hse.

***Seven Steps to a Successful Nonprofit Merger, No. 135.** Thomas McLaughlin. 28p. (Orig.). 1996. pap. 16.00 (0-925299-54-5) Natl Ctr Nonprofit.

***Seven Steps to an Effective Leadership Transition: How to Find a New Leader for Your Nonprofit Organization.** Sheila Albert. 32p. (Orig.). 1996. pap. 18.00 (0-925299-51-0) Natl Ctr Nonprofit.

Seven Steps to Better Vision: Easy, Practical & Natural Techniques That Will Improve Your Eyesight. Richard Leviton. (Illus.). 144p. 1992. pap. 8.95 (0-936184-13-2) Boston Common Pr.

7 Steps to Bible Skills: An Easy Step-by-Step Guide for Learning to Use Your Bible. Dorothy Hellstern. (Illus.). 168p. 1991. student ed., pap. text ed. 9.99 (1-56322-029-6); teacher ed., ring bd. 16.99 (1-56322-028-8) V Hensley.

Seven Steps to Effective Prayer. William L. Asher, Jr. 36p. (Orig.). 1978. pap. 2.00 (0-915235-01-3) United Res.

Seven Steps to Freedom. Derin Carmack. 31p. 1986. pap. 3.00 (0-937093-25-4) Jewel Pr.

Seven Steps to Freedom II: How to Escape the American Rat Race. Benjamin D. Suarez. 676p. 1993. 32.00 (1-884889-00-X) Suarez.

Seven Steps to Freedom II: How to Escape the American Rat Race. 2nd ed. Benjamin D. Suarez. 700p. 1994. 32.00 (1-884889-01-8) Suarez.

Seven Steps to Getting Published. Claire Ottenstein. LC 92-73827. 56p. (Orig.). 1992. pap. 6.00 (1-878149-14-8) Counterpoint Pub.

Seven Steps to Home: Coming to Internal Harmony. Ati. Ed. by Bob Murray & Alicia Fortinberry. 32p. 1995. pap. 5.00 (1-885610-05-X) European Amer.

Seven Steps to Improving Your Relationships: How to Set Yourself--& Your Lover--Free for Love. Bonnie Jacobson. 1994. pap. 5.50 (1-56171-321-X, S P I Bks) Sure Seller.

Seven Steps to Inner Power: A Martial Arts Master Reveals Her Secrets for Dynamic Living. Tae Yun Kim. LC 91-178213. 120p. 1991. pap. 9.95 (0-931432-70-7) New Wrld Lib.

***Seven Steps to Inner Power Workbook.** unabridged ed. Tae Y. Kim. 176p. (Orig.). 1997. wbk. ed., pap. 19.95 (0-9656959-1-3) NorthStar CA.

7 Steps to Midnight. Richard Matheson. 320p. 1995. pap. 5.99 (0-8125-5057-9) Tor Bks.

7 Steps to Normal Bladder Control: Simple, Practical Tips & Techniques for Staying Dry. Elizabeth Vierck. (Illus.). 72p. (Orig.). 1998. pap. write for info. (0-936197-29-3) Harbor Pr.

Seven Steps to Peak Performance: The Mental Training Manual for Athletes. Richard M. Suinn. LC 86-10427. 64p. 1987. spiral bd. 12.90 (0-920887-12-0) Hogrefe & Huber Pubs.

Seven Steps to Personal Safety: How to Avoid, Deal with or Survive the Aftermath of a Violent Confrontation. Richard B. Isaacs & Tim Powers. LC 93-90239. 188p. (Orig.). 1993. lib. bdg. 19.95 (1-883633-00-1) Ctr Personal Def.

Seven Steps to Personal Safety: How to Avoid, Deal with or Survive the Aftermath of a Violent Confrontation. large type ed. Richard B. Isaacs & Tim Powers. LC 93-90239. (Illus.). 188p. (Orig.). 1994. pap. 14.95 (1-883633-01-X) Ctr Personal Def.

Seven Steps to Revitalizing the Small-Town Church. Paul Hazelton. 112p. (Orig.). 1993. pap. 7.99 (0-8341-1445-3) Beacon Hill.

Seven Steps to Salvation. Doug Batchelor. (Anchor Ser.). 127p. 1992. pap. 8.99 (0-8163-1071-8) Pacific Pr Pub Assn.

Seven Steps to Successful Home Landscaping. Dennis Ulrey. (Illus.). 94p. (Orig.). 1989. pap. text ed. write for info. (0-318-65961-1) Porter Pubns.

Seven Steps to Treason. Michael Hartland. 1984. 14.95 (0-02-548530-X) Macmillan.

Seven Steps to Treason. large type ed. Michael Hartland. 544p. 1994. 25.99 (0-7089-3134-0) Ulverscroft.

Seven Steps Toward God. Bill Beatty. LC 85-82315. 102p. (Orig.). 1986. pap. 4.50 (0-937779-01-6) Greenlawn Pr.

Seven Storey Mountain. Thomas Merton. 300p. 1991. reprint ed. lib. bdg. 22.95 (0-89966-864-X) Buccaneer Bks.

Seven Storey Mountain. Thomas Merton. LC 78-7109. 429p. 1978. reprint ed. pap. 14.00 (0-15-680679-7, Harvest Bks) HarBrace.

Seven Stories. 1993. pap. 5.25 (0-19-585470-5) OUP.

Seven Stories. James A. Hall. Ed. by Mary Burtschi. LC 75-23549. 114p. 1975. 8.00 (0-9601642-1-9) Little Brick Hse.

Seven Stories. Pancyh. (NFS Canada Ser.). 1993. pap. 10.95 (0-88922-281-9) Genl Dist Srvs.

Seven Stories about Modern Art in Africa. Whitechapel Art Gallery Staff. (Illus.). 320p. 1995. 55.00 (2-08-013599-6, Pub. by Flammarion FR) Abbeville Pr.

***Seven Stories by Maria von Ebner-Eschenbach.** (GERM Ser.). xlii, 118p. 1986. 27.00 (1-879751-47-X) Camden Hse.

Seven Stories by Marie von Ebner-Eschenbach. Tr. & Intro. by Helga Harriman. LC 86-70738. (Studies in German Literature, Linguistics & Culture: Vol. 26). (Illus.). 180p. 1986. 27.00 (0-938100-45-9) Camden Hse.

Seven Stories from Spanish America. Ed. by G. Brotherston & Mario Vargas Llosa. 1968. pap. text ed. 4.60 (0-08-012675-8, Pergamon Pr) Elsevier.

Seven Stories from Spanish America. Ed. by G. Brotherston & Mario Vargas Llosa. (Bristol Spanish Texts Ser.). (SPA.). 1995. pap. 14.95 (1-85399-464-2, Pub. by Brstl Class Pr UK) Focus Pub-R Pullins.

Seven Stories of Christmas Love. Leo F. Buscaglia. (Illus.). 112p. 1992. 12.95 (0-8050-2434-4) H Holt & Co.

Seven Stories of Christmas Love. Leo F. Buscaglia. (Illus.). 110p. (J). 1987. 12.95 (1-55642-019-6) SLACK Inc.

Seven Stories of Modern Japan. Ed. & Tr. by Leith Morton from JPN. Tr. by H. D. Clarke et al. from JPN. (University of Sydney East Asian Ser.: No. 5). 96p. 1991. pap. text ed. 16.00 (0-9590735-9-0, Pub. by Wild Peony Pty AT) UH Pr.

Seven Stories with Basement & Attic. Donald G. Mitchell. 1972. reprint ed. pap. text ed. 8.95 (0-8290-0672-9); reprint ed. lib. bdg. 29.50 (0-8422-8096-0) Irvington.

Seven Story Mountain. Thomas Merton. 528p. 1990. 18.00 (0-15-181354-X) HarBrace.

Seven Story Mountain: The Union Campaign at Vicksburg. Phillip M. Thienel. LC 94-32408. (Illus.). 277p. 1994. lib. bdg. 27.50 (0-7864-0014-5) McFarland & Co.

Seven Stranded Coal Towns: A Study of an American Depressed Area. Malcolm Brown & John N. Webb. LC 76-165680. (Research Monographs: Vol. 23). 1971. reprint ed. lib. bdg. 25.00 (0-306-70355-6) Da Capo.

Seven Strange & Ghostly Tales. Brian Jacques. 144p. (YA). 1993. pap. 3.99 (0-380-71906-1, Camelot) Avon.

Seven Strange & Ghostly Tales. Brian Jacques. LC 91-9889. (Illus.). 160p. (J). (gr. 3 up). 1991. 14.95 (0-399-22103-4, Philomel Bks) Putnam Pub Group.

Seven Strategies for Wealth & Happiness. Jim Rohn. 1988. pap. 9.95 (0-914629-73-5) Prima Pub.

7 Strategies for Wealth & Happiness: Power Ideas from America's Foremost Business Philosopher. Jim Rohn. 176p. 1996. per., pap. 12.00 (0-7615-0616-0) Prima Pub.

Seven Strategies for Wealth & Happiness: Power Ideas from America's Foremost Business Philosopher. John Rohn. 168p. (Orig.). 1987. 13.95 (0-914629-02-6) Prima Pub.

Seven Strong Reasons Why You Should Believe in Jesus Christ. Foster H. Shannon. LC 95-76161. 64p. 1995. pap. 3.99 (0-938462-18-0) Green Leaf CA.

Seven Summers. Mulk-Raj Anand. 242p. 1973. pap. 3.00 (0-88253-124-7) Ind-US Inc.

Seven Summits. Dick Bass & Frank Wells. 352p. 1988. pap. 14.99 (0-446-38516-6) Warner Bks.

***Seven Surahs: For the Classroom.** unabridged ed. Ed. by Hina Akhtar & Huda Quraishi. LC 96-79298. 126p. (YA). (gr. 6-12). 1996. pap. text ed. 8.00 (1-56316-114-1) Iqra Intl Ed Fdtn.

***7 Survival Skills.** William N. Yeomans. 1997. pap. 12.95 (0-452-27490-7, Plume) NAL-Dutton.

***7 Survival Skills for a Reengineered World.** William N. Yeomans. Date not set. pap. write for info. (0-452-27715-9, Plume) NAL-Dutton.

7 Survival Skills for a Reengineered World. William N. Yeomans. LC 96-19398. 320p. 1996. pap. 24.95 (0-525-94233-5) NAL-Dutton.

Seven Sutherland Sisters. rev. ed. Clarence O. Lewis. 56p. 1991. reprint ed. 4.00 (0-614-13513-3) Niagara Cnty Hist Soc.

***Seven Sweet Blessings of Christ: And How to Make Them Yours.** Gerald Vann. LC 97-16979. Orig. Title: The Divine Pity: A Study in the Social Implications of the Beatitudes. 288p. 1997. reprint ed. pap. 14.95 (0-918477-55-7) Sophia Inst Pr.

Seven Synonyms for God. Max Kappeler. Tr. by Kathleen Lee from GER. LC 83-83266. 361p. 1984. 38.00 (0-942958-09-8) Kappeler Inst Pub.

Seven Systems of Indian Philosophy. Pandit R. Tigunait. LC 81-85537. 250p. (Orig.). (C). 1983. pap. 14.95 (0-89389-076-6) Himalayan Inst.

Seven Tablets of Creation, 2 vols., Set. Enuma Elish. LC 73-18850. (Luzac's Semitic Text & Translation Ser.: Nos. 12 & 13). (Illus.). reprint ed. 75.00 (0-404-11344-3) AMS Pr.

***Seven Tales & a Fable.** Gwyneth Jones. 132p. (Orig.). 1995. pap. 8.00 (0-9629066-5-4) Edgewood Pr.

Seven Tales by H. C. Andersen. Hans Christian Andersen. LC 59-16151. (Trophy Picture Bk.). (Illus.). 144p. (J). (gr. k up). 1991. pap. 7.95 (0-06-443172-X, Trophy) HarpC Child Bks.

Seven Taoist Masters: A Folk Novel of China. Tr. by Eva Wong from CHI. LC 89-43307. (Illus.). 208p. (Orig.). 1990. pap. 14.00 (0-87773-544-1) Shambhala Pubns.

***Seven Tattoos.** Peter Trachtenberg. 1998. pap. write for info. (0-609-80189-9, Crown) Crown Pub Group.

Seven Tattoos: A Memoir in the Flesh. Trachtenberg. 1997. 23.00 (0-517-70172-3) Random Hse Value.

Seven Tears for Apollo. Phyllis A. Whitney. 320p. 1992. mass mkt. 4.99 (0-06-100256-9, Harp PBks) HarpC.

Seven Tell Their Story. Robert J. Mueller. Ed. by Michael L. Sherer. (Orig.). 1988. pap. 3.50 (1-55673-019-5, 8803) CSS OH.

***Seven That Were Hanged.** Leonid Andreyev. Date not set. lib. bdg. 20.95 (0-8488-1867-9) Amereon Ltd.

Seven Theories of Human Nature. 2nd ed. Leslie Stevenson. 160p. 1987. 24.95 (0-19-505291-9) OUP.

Seven Theories of Human Nature. 2nd ed. Leslie Stevenson. 160p. 1988. pap. text ed. 13.95 (0-19-505214-5) OUP.

Seven Theories of Human Society. Tom Campbell. 254p. (C). 1981. pap. text ed. 19.95 (0-19-876105-8) OUP.

Seven Theories of Religion. Daniel L. Pals. 304p. 1996. 25.00 (0-19-508724-0) OUP.

Seven Theories of Religion. Daniel L. Pals. 304p. (C). 1996. reprint ed. pap. text ed. 16.95 (0-19-508725-9) OUP.

Seven Things Children Need. 2nd ed. John M. Drescher. LC 88-10173. 144p. 1988. pap. 6.99 (0-8361-3475-3) Herald Pr.

Seven Things States Can Do To Promote Responsible Fatherhood. Wade F. Horn & Eric Brenner. LC 96-19203. 1996. pap. 8.95 (0-934842-15-9) CSPA.

Seven Things You Should Know about Divine Healing. Kenneth E. Hagin. 1979. pap. 3.95 (0-89276-400-7) Hagin Ministries.

7,604 Keisling Kin with Variant Spelling. J. Draper Keisling. 624p. Date not set. 45.00 (0-9627837-0-6) Keisling Bks.

Seven Thunderers Utter Their Voices: History & Verse by Verse Study in the Book of Revelation of the Bible. 2nd ed. E. Warren Anglin. 176p. (Orig.). pap. 7.95 (0-318-04199-5) Total Comm Ministries.

Seven Thunders. Ronald C. Ware. 1996. 19.95 (0-533-11627-9) Vantage.

Seven Thunders of the Millennial Dawn. B. H. Shadduck. 32p. 1988. reprint ed. pap. 1.95 (1-883858-36-4) Witness CA.

Seven Thunders of the Soul: A Unified General Theory of Behavior. Henry M. Jacobs, Jr. 168p. (Orig.). 1995. pap. 20.00 (0-9646021-3-X) Trinity Res Ctr.

Seven Times Eight. David Updike. (Illus.). 40p. (J). (gr. 2-5). 1990. lib. bdg. 14.95 (0-945912-10-2) Pippin Pr.

Seven Times Monday. Ernest Pendrell. 1961. pap. 5.25 (0-8222-1016-9) Dramatists Play.

Seven Times Seven. Maria T. Daviess. Ed. by Annette K. Baxter. LC 79-8786. (Signal Lives Ser.). (Illus.). 1980. reprint ed. lib. bdg. 37.95 (0-405-12834-7) Ayer.

Seven Times the Sun: Guiding Your Child Through the Rhythms of the Day. Shea Darian. LC 93-46003. (Illus.). 224p. (Orig.). 1994. pap. 15.95 (0-931055-96-2) Innisfree Pr.

***Seven Toeic Tests: Practice for Higher Scores.** Steven A. Stupak. LC 97-3862. 1997. pap. write for info. (0-13-619933-X); pap. write for info. (0-13-619941-0) P-H.

Seven Tools of TQC. 4th ed. John S. McConnell. (Illus.). 176p. 1986. pap. 35.00 (0-9588324-0-4, Pub. by Delaware Grp AT) Am Overseas Bk Co.

Seven Trails West. Arthur K. Peters. (Illus.). 252p. 1996. 39.95 (1-55859-782-4) Abbeville Pr.

Seven Treasure Hunts. Betsy C. Byars. LC 90-32043. (Trophy Bk.). (Illus.). 80p. (J). (gr. 2-6). 1992. pap. 3.95 (0-06-440435-8, Trophy) HarpC Child Bks.

Seven Trumpets of the Revelation. Kingdom Quotes Staff. pap. write for info. (0-930179-36-6) Johns Enter.

Seven Tutula Writers. Clara Reid et al. (Illus.). 82p. (Orig.). 1989. 5.00 (0-930773-15-2) Black Heron Pr.

Seven Types of Adventure Tale: An Etiology of a Major Genre. Martin Green. 232p. 1991. 32.50 (0-271-00780-X) Pa St U Pr.

Seven Types of Ambiguity. William Empson. LC 48-78. 1947. pap. 11.95 (0-8112-0037-X, NDP204) New Directions.

Seven Underground Kings, & The Fiery God of the Marrans. Alexander M. Volkov. Tr. & Afterword by Peter L. Blystone. LC 90-83409. (Tales of Magic Land Ser.: No. 2). 384p. (Orig.). (J). (gr. 4 up). 1993. pap. 13.95 (1-878941-18-6) Red Branch Pr.

Seven Underwater Wonders of the World. Rick Sammon. LC 92-6413. 180p. 1992. 29.95 (0-934738-78-5) Lickle Pubng.

Seven Universal Laws of Customer Value: How to Win Customers & Influence Markets. Stephen C. Broydrick. 160p. 1996. per. 24.95 (0-7863-0732-3) Irwin Prof Pubng.

Seven Valleys. Baha'u'llah. 96p. 1994. pap. 8.95 (1-85168-031-4) Onewrld Pubns.

Seven Valleys & Four Valleys. Baha'u'llah. Tr. by Marzieh Gail. (Illus.). 120p. 1992. pap. 13.25 (1-870989-16-3) Bahai.

Seven Valleys & the Four Valleys. 3rd rev. ed. Baha'u'llah. Tr. by Marzieh Gail. LC 77-23326. 1978. 13.95 (0-87743-113-2, 103-015) Bahai.

Seven Valleys & the Four Valleys. 4th ed. Baha'u'llah. Tr. by Marzieh Gail from PER. 65p. 1955. 8.00 (0-87743-226-0); pap. 3.50 (0-87743-227-9) Bahai.

***Seven Veils of Our Lady of Guadalulpe.** Miguel Guadalupe. 420p. (Orig.). 1997. pap. text ed. write for info. (1-882972-79-1) Queenship Pub.

Seven Verdi Librettos. Tr. by William Weaver. (Illus.). 1977. pap. 15.95 (0-393-00852-5) Norton.

Seven Viking Romances. Tiruvalluvar. Tr. by Paul Edwards & Hermann Palsson. (Classics Ser.). 304p. 1986. pap. 11.95 (0-14-044474-2, Penguin Classics) Viking Penguin.

***Seven Visions, Vol. 183.** Sergei Paradjanov. (Sun & Moon Classics Ser.). 1997. pap. text ed. 14.95 (1-55713-311-5) Sun & Moon CA.

Seven Visions & Other Poems. Arthur Johnson. (Illus.). (Orig.). 1987. pap. 4.95 (0-942943-00-7) Silent Hse Pubns.

Seven Visions of Bull Lodge: As Told by His Daughter, Garter Snake. Ed. by George P. Horse Capture. LC 91-41602. (Illus.). 125p. 1992. reprint ed. pap. 10.95 (0-8032-7256-1, Bison Books); reprint ed. text ed. 25.00 (0-8032-2361-7) U of Nebr Pr.

Seven Vital Steps to Publishing Reports & Booklets. 1987. lib. bdg. 175.00 (0-8490-3870-7) Gordon Pr.

Seven Vital Steps to Receiving the Holy Spirit. 2nd ed. Kenneth E. Hagin. 1980. pap. 1.95 (0-89276-003-6) Hagin Ministries.

Seven Voices Speak. Catharose De Petri. Ed. by Lectorium Rosicrucianum Staff. Orig. Title: Zeven Stemmen Spreken. 79p. (DUT.). 1991. pap. 11.00 (90-6732-043-9) Rosycross Pr.

***Seven Voyages of Sinbad the Sailor.** John Yeoman. 1997. 19.95 (0-689-81368-6) S&S Trade.

***Seven Voyages of Sindbad the Snail.** Dennis L. Armstrong. LC 96-86559. (Illus.). 80p. (Orig.). (J). (gr. 4-6). 1996. pap. 7.50 (0-9654326-0-2) Cupcake Pr.

Seven Ways of Knowing: Teaching for Multiple Intelligences. 2nd ed. David Lazear. LC 91-67598. (Illus.). 256p. (Orig.). 1991. pap. text ed. 39.95 (0-932935-39-7) IRI-SkyLght.

Seven Ways of Teaching: The Artistry of Teaching with Multiple Intelligences. David Lazear. LC 91-65666. (Illus.). 192p. (Orig.). 1991. pap. text ed. 33.95 (0-932935-32-X) IRI-SkyLght.

7 Ways to Easy A's in Literature. 119p. 1996. 14.95 (1-889123-02-1) Tutors Pr.

7 Ways to Easy A's in Writing. (Illus.). 143p. 1996. 14.95 (*1-889123-03-X*) Tutors Pr.

Seven Ways to Pray for Spiritual Leaders. Linda Corbin. (Christian Living Ser.). 1996. pap. 1.99 (*0-87509-608-5*) Chr Pubns.

***7 Ways to Teach the Bible to Children: Includes 25 Lessons, Plus Activities That Satisfy Different Learning Styles.** Barbara Bruce. LC 96-42570. 112p. 1996. pap. 14.95 (*0-687-02068-9*) Abingdon.

Seven Wedding Dances. Georg P. Telemann. 1986. 4.00 (*0-685-51180-4*, CM1046) Consort Music.

Seven Weeks to a Settled Stomach. Ronald L. Hoffman. Ed. by Julie Rubenstein. 352p. 1991. reprint ed. mass mkt. 5.99 (*0-671-73425-3*) PB.

Seven Weeks to Better Sex. Domeena Renshaw. 304p. 1997. pap. 12.95 (*0-440-50752-9*, Dell Trade Pbks) Dell.

***Seven Weeks to Better Sex.** Domeena Renshaw. Date not set. 7.99 (*0-517-19289-6*) Random Hse Value.

Seven Weeks to Better Sex. D[illegible]meena Renshaw. 1995. write for info. (*0-615-00*[illegible]) Random.

Seven Weeks to Better Sex. Domeena C. Renshaw. LC 94-18120. 280p. 1995. 22.00 (*0-679-43546-8*) Random.

***Seven Weeks to Better Sex: An American Medical Association Book.** Domeena Renshaw. 22.00 (*0-614-19675-2*, OP830095WE) AMA.

***Seven Weeks to Safe Social Drinking: How to Effectively Moderate Your Alcohol Intake.** D. J. Cornett. 1996. 19.95 (*1-55972-376-9*, Birch Ln Pr) Carol Pub Group.

Seven Weeks to Sobriety. Larsen. Date not set. pap. write for info. (*0-345-40235-9*) Ballantine.

Seven Weeks to Sobriety: The Proven Program to Fight Alcoholism Through Nutrition. Joan M. Larson. (Illus.). 336p. 1993. pap. 11.00 (*0-449-90896-8*, Columbine) Fawcett.

Seven Wild Pigs. Helme Heine. LC 87-3448. (Illus.). 128p. (J). (gr. k up). 1988. lib. bdg. 18.95 (*0-689-50439-X*, McElderry) S&S Childrens.

Seven Windows to a Child's World: 100 Ideas for the Multiple Intelligences Classroom - Grades Pre-K - 3. Anna T. O'Connor & Sheila Callahan-Young. LC 94-78533. 256p. 1994. pap. 25.95 (*0-932935-77-X*, NB1261) IRI-SkyLght.

***Seven Winters in Paris.** Thomas McCarthy. Date not set. pap. 14.95 (*0-85646-224-1*, Pub. by Anvil Press UK) Dufour.

Seven Wise Men of Colonial America. Richard M. Gummere. LC 67-27084. 125p. 1967. 16.95 (*0-674-80250-0*) HUP.

Seven Witches. Marie-Helene Delval. (I Love to Read Collection). (Illus.). 46p. (J). (gr. 2-4). 1992. lib. bdg. 12.79 (*0-89565-897-6*) Childs World.

Seven with One Blow. Maria McLaren. LC 94-32722. 24p. (J). (gr. 1-6). 1994. pap. 6.00 (*0-88734-517-4*) Players Pr.

Seven Wives: A Novel. Jonathan Baumbach. 128p. 1994. 18.95 (*0-932511-86-4*); pap. 8.95 (*0-932511-87-2*) Fiction Coll.

Seven Wives of Bluebeard. Anatole France. LC 73-144154. (Short Story Index Reprint Ser.). 1977. reprint ed. 19.95 (*0-8369-3769-4*) Ayer.

Seven Wonders of the Ancient World. Ed. by Peter Clayton & Martin Price. (Illus.). 192p. 1988. text ed. 29.95 (*0-415-00279-6*) Routledge.

Seven Wonders of the Ancient World. Ed. by Peter Clayton & Martin Price. (Illus.). 192p. (gr. 13). 1990. pap. 13.95 (*0-415-05036-7*, A4490) Routledge.

Seven Wonders of the Ancient World. Reg Cox & Neil Morris. LC 95-30827. (Wonders of the World Ser.). (Illus.). 32p. (J). (gr. 4 up). 1996. lib. bdg. 14.95 (*0-382-39266-3*) Silver Burdett Pr.

Seven Wonders of the Ancient World. Reg Cox & Neil Morris. LC 95-30827. (Wonders of the World Ser.). (Illus.). 32p. (J). (gr. 4 up). 1996. pap. 7.95 (*0-382-39267-1*) Silver Burdett Pr.

Seven Wonders of the Historic World. Reg Cox & Neil Morris. (Wonders of the World Ser.). (Illus.). 32p. (J). (gr. 4 up). 1996. lib. bdg. 14.95 (*0-382-39269-8*, Dillon Silver Burdett) Silver Burdett Pr.

Seven Wonders of the Historic World. Reg Cox & Neil Morris. (Illus.). (J). 1996. pap. 7.95 (*0-382-39270-1*) Silver.

Seven Wonders of the Modern World. Reg Cox & Neil Morris. (Wonders of the World Ser.). (Illus.). 32p. (J). (gr. 4 up). 1996. pap. 7.95 (*0-382-39272-8*, Dillon Silver Burdett); lib. bdg. 14.95 (*0-382-39271-X*, Dillon Silver Burdett) Silver Burdett Pr.

Seven Wonders of the Natural World. Reg Cox & Neil Morris. LC 95-42387. (Wonders of the World Ser.). (Illus.). 32p. (J). (gr. 4 up). 1996. pap. 7.95 (*0-382-39274-4*, Dillon Silver Burdett); lib. bdg. 14.95 (*0-382-39273-6*, Dillon Silver Burdett) Silver Burdett Pr.

Seven Wonders of the World. Kenneth McLeish. 32p. (J). (gr. 4-7). 1986. text ed. 20.95 (*0-521-26538-X*) Cambridge U Pr.

Seven Wonders of the World. Kenneth McLeish. (Illus.). 32p. (J). 1989. pap. text ed. 14.95 (*0-521-37911-3*) Cambridge U Pr.

Seven Wonders of the World: A History of the Modern Imagination. John Romer & Elizabeth Romer. (Illus.). 244p. 1995. 52.50 (*1-85479-933-9*, Pub. by M OMara Books UK) Trans-Atl Phila.

Seven Wonders of the World: Meditations on the Last Words of Christ. George W. Rutler. LC 92-71940. 168p. 1993. pap. 10.95 (*0-89870-417-0*) Ignatius Pr.

***Seven Words for Wind: Personal Essays from Alsaka's Pribilof Islands.** Sumner MacLeish. Ed. by Valerie Griffith. (Illus.). 160p. 1997. 16.95 (*0-945397-35-6*) Epicenter Pr.

Seven Works of Vasubandhu: The Buddhist Psychological Doctor. Stefan Anacker. x, 493p. 1986. 23.00 (*0-317-61124-0*, Pub. by Motilal Banarsidass II) S Asia.

Seven Worlds to Win. Morris G. Watkins. 240p. (Orig.). (YA). (gr. 7 up). 1987. pap. 19.95 (*0-939925-00-1*) R C Law & Co.

Seven Year Atomic Make-Over Guide & Other Stories. Christine Bell. LC 95-36170. 176p. 1996. 21.00 (*0-393-03945-5*) Norton.

Seven Year Balance Sheet of the Sovereign, Military & Hospitaller Order of St. John of Jerusalem, of Rhodes & of Malta: From May 1st, 1778 to End of April 1785. Chevalier Bosredon de Ransijat. Ed. by Marcel V. Dingli-Attard-Inguanez. (Illus.). 79p. (Orig.). 1984. pap. 10.00 (*0-9610740-2-7*) U Intel Data Bank.

Seven Year Itch. Robert A. Arthur. 1956. pap. 5.25 (*0-8222-1017-7*) Dramatists Play.

Seven-Year Itch. Ruth J. Dale. (Love & Laughter Ser.). 1996. mass mkt. 3.50 (*0-373-44006-5*, 1-44006-4) Harlequin Bks.

Seven Year Itch. Peggy Moreland. (Desire Ser.). 1994. mass mkt. 2.99 (*0-373-05837-3*, 5-05837-5) Silhouette.

Seven Year Itch see Best American Plays: Fourth Series, 1952-1957

Seven-Year Stretch: How Families Work Together to Grow through Adolescence. Laura Kastner & Jennifer Wyatt. LC 96-48027. 1997. 23.00 (*0-395-73526-2*) HM.

***Seven-Year Stretch: How Families Work Together to Grow Through Adolescence.** Laura S. Kastner & Jennifer F. Wyatt. 1997. 22.95 (*0-614-28003-6*) HM.

Seven Years among Prisoners of War. Chris Christiansen. Tr. by Ida E. Winther from DAN. (Illus.). 240p. 1994. text ed. 34.95 (*0-8214-1069-5*) Ohio U Pr.

Seven Years among the Freedmen. 2nd enl. rev. ed. M. Waterbury. LC 79-178484. (Black Heritage Library Collection). 1977. reprint ed. 25.95 (*0-8369-8934-1*) Ayer.

Seven Years in Ceylon: Stories of Mission Life. Mary Leitch. 1993. reprint ed. 24.00 (*81-7013-105-7*, Pub. by Navrang) S Asia.

Seven Years in South Africa, Set. Emil Holub. 1881. 49.00 (*0-403-00390-3*) Scholarly.

Seven Years in Tibet. Heinrich Harrer. (Illus.). 320p. 1996. pap. 12.95 (*0-87477-847-6*, Tarcher Putnam) Putnam Pub Group.

***Seven Years in Tibet.** Heinrich Harrer. 320p. 1997. 14.95 (*0-87477-888-3*, Tarcher Putnam) Putnam Pub Group.

Seven Years in Tibet. large type ed. Heinrich Harrer. 528p. 1982. 25.99 (*0-7089-0854-3*) Ulverscroft.

***Seven Years of Highly Defective People: The Origins & Evolutions of Dilbert.** Scott Adams. (Illus.). 256p. (Orig.). 1997. pap. 12.95 (*0-8362-3668-8*) Andrews & McMeel.

Seven Years of Shaking: A Vision. Michael D. Evans. 222p. 1995. pap. 8.00 (*0-935199-04-7*) Bedfrd Books.

Seven Years of the King's Theatre. John Ebers. LC 79-88490. 1972. reprint ed. 26.95 (*0-405-08481-1*, Pub. by Blom Pubns UK) Ayer.

***Seven Years War & the Old Regime in France: The Economic & Financial Toll.** James C. Riley. LC 86-42847. (Illus.). 280p. reprint ed. pap. 79.80 (*0-608-04518-7*, 2065263) Bks Demand.

***Seven Years with the Group of Seven.** Joyce Putnam. (Illus.). 160p. 1991. 39.95 (*1-55082-013-3*, Pub. by Quarry Pr CN) LPC InBook.

Seven You Will Remember. Peter Tarnov. 162p. 1983. pap. 8.00 (*0-911109-00-5*) Oxymora Bk Pr.

Sevenfold Journey: Reclaiming Mind, Body & Spirit Through the Chakras. Anodea Judith & Selene Vega. LC 92-35719. 325p. 1993. pap. 18.95 (*0-89594-574-6*) Crossing Pr.

Sevenfold Path to Peace. Alan Bond. 1986. 4.75 (*0-89536-774-2*, 6801) CSS OH.

Sevenoaks: A Story of To-Day. Josiah G. Holland. (Muckrakers Ser.). 471p. 1986. reprint ed. pap. text ed. 8.95 (*0-8290-2003-9*) Irvington.

Sevenoaks: A Story of Today. Josiah G. Holland. LC 68-57531. (Muckrakers Ser.). 471p. reprint ed. lib. bdg. 29.00 (*0-8398-0785-6*) Irvington.

Sevenoaks Journal: Poetry for the Contemporary Ear. DelVecchio et al. Ed. by Denise A. Collins. (Quarterly Newsletter Ser.). (Illus.). 16p. 1996. pap. 3.00 (*1-887213-05-8*) Blck Oak Pr.

Seventeen. Rachel Hall. 45p. (Orig.). (YA). 1989. pap. 5.00 (*0-9624855-0-0*) R Hall.

Seventeen. Booth Tarkington. 18.95 (*0-8488-1481-9*) Amereon Ltd.

Seventeen. Booth Tarkington. 190p. 1981. lib. bdg. 21.95 (*0-89966-174-2*) Buccaneer Bks.

17 Abstract Artists of East Hampton: The Pollock Years, 1946-56. Intro. by Ronald G. Pisano. LC 80-81980. (Illus.). 32p. (Orig.). 1980. pap. text ed. 4.00 (*0-943526-40-X*) Parrish Art.

Seventeen Against the Dealer. Cynthia Voigt. 224p. 1990. mass mkt. 4.50 (*0-449-70375-4*, Juniper) Fawcett.

Seventeen Against the Dealer. Cynthia Voigt. LC 88-27488. 192p. (YA). (gr. 7 up). 1989. lib. bdg. 18.00 (*0-689-31497-3*, Atheneum Bks Young) S&S Childrens.

Seventeen & in Between. (YA). 1985. pap. 2.95 (*0-590-44770-X*) Scholastic Inc.

Seventeen & In Between. Florence J. Glickman. 3.95 (*0-686-10139-1*) Wagon & Star.

Seventeen & In-Between: A Novel. Barthe DeClements. LC 92-37596. 176p. (J). (gr. 7 up). 1993. pap. 3.99 (*0-14-036475-7*, Puffin) Puffin Bks.

Seventeen & J. Kenzaburo Oe. 1996. pap. 17.95 (*1-56201-091-3*, North Star Line) Blue Moon Bks.

Seventeen Commandments Not from Heaven but Earth. James Carroll. 1985. pap. 3.95 (*0-89826-013-2*) Natl Paperback.

Seventeen Divertimenti for Various Instruments. Wolfgang Amadeus Mozart. 256p. 1979. reprint ed. pap. 10.95 (*0-486-23862-8*) Dover.

1789: The Emblems of Reason. Jean Starobinski. Tr. by Barbara Bray. 304p. 1988. reprint ed. pap. 20.00 (*0-262-69122-1*) MIT Pr.

Seventeen Eighty-Nine Boston Directory. Ed. by Emil R. Salvini. (Illus.). 56p. (Orig.). 1989. pap. 5.00 (*0-933433-00-X*) Wheal Grace.

Seventeen Eighty-Nine Ephemeris. Grant. 40p. 4.50 (*0-86690-226-0*, G1638-044) Am Fed Astrologers.

Seventeen Eighty-Nine, the Emblems of Reason. Jean Starobinski. Tr. by Barbara Bray. LC 81-13135. 304p. 1982. pap. 86.70 (*0-7837-8443-0*, 2049247) Bks Demand.

Seventeen Eighty-One Ephemeris. Grant. 78p. 1945. 4.50 (*0-86690-224-4*, G>1636-044) Am Fed Astrologers.

Seventeen Eighty-Seven: American Housewife. rev. ed. Julianne Belote. (Illus.). 183p. 1987. pap. 5.95 (*0-911954-02-3*, Nitty Gritty Ckbks) Bristol Pub Ent CA.

Seventeen Eighty-Seven: The Grand Convention. Clinton Rossiter. (Illus.). 464p. 1987. reprint ed. pap. 13.95 (*0-393-30404-3*) Norton.

Seventeen Eighty-Seven Ephemeris. Grant. 78p. 1947. 4.50 (*0-86690-225-2*, G1637-044) Am Fed Astrologers.

Seventeen F the Life of Ian Fleming. Donald McCormick. 232p. 9400. 35.00 (*0-7206-0888-0*, Pub. by P Owen Ltd UK) Dufour.

Seventeen Farrington Way. Lawrence H. Bank. LC 87-19344. 1988. 22.95 (*0-87949-267-8*) Ashley Bks.

Seventeen Fifty M, Eighteen Sixty, Nineteen Sixty, Processors & Related Product. 1993. pap. 23.95 (*1-55512-217-5*) Intel Corp.

1745: A Military History of the Last Jacobite Rising. Stuart Reid. (Illus.). 264p. 1996. 24.95 (*1-885119-28-3*) Sarpedon.

Seventeen Grams of Soul. Emilio De Grazia. LC 94-72988. (Illus.). 185p. (Orig.). 1995. pap. 9.95 (*1-883477-07-7*) Lone Oak MN.

Seventeen Guide to Guys & Dating. Barry. (J). 1997. pap. 8.95 (*0-689-81086-5*) S&S Childrens.

Seventeen Guide to Guys & Dating. Barry. (J). 1998. 17.00 (*0-689-81087-3*) S&S Childrens.

Seventeen Guide to Sex & Your Body. Sabrina Solin. LC 96-16230. (YA). (gr. 6 up). 1996. 17.00 (*0-689-80796-1*, S&S Bks Young Read) S&S Childrens.

***Seventeen Guide to Sex & Your Body.** Sabrina Solin. 1996. pap. 8.99 (*0-689-80795-3*, S&S Bks Young Read) S&S Childrens.

Seventeen-Hundred Eighty-Nine: The Long & the Short of It. Ed. by David Williams. (Illus.). 271p. 1991. 40.00 (*1-85075-286-9*, Pub. by Sheffield Acad UK) CUP Services.

***Seventeen Hundred Forty (1740) Description by Daniel Tilas of Stratigraphy & Petroleum Occurrence at Osmundsberg in the Siljan Region of Central Sweden.** Hollis D. Hedberg. LC 88-16683. 105p. 1988. reprint ed. pap. 30.00 (*0-608-03027-9*, 2063478) Bks Demand.

Seventeen Hundred Seven: The Union of Scotland & England. P. H. Scott. 72p. (C). 1989. 39.00 (*0-550-20265-X*, Pub. by Saltire Soc) St Mut.

Seventeen Hundred Twelve Shortcuts to Better Living. Cheryl Winters. 1991. 7.98 (*0-88365-774-0*) Galahad Bks.

Seventeen Kings & Forty-Two Elephants. Margaret Mahy. LC 87-5311. (Illus.). 32p. (J). (ps-3). 1987. pap. 15.99 (*0-8037-0458-5*) Dial Bks Young.

Seventeen Kings & Forty-Two Elephants. Margaret Mahy. Ed. by Phyllis J. Fogelman. LC 87-5311. (Illus.). 32p. (J). (ps-3). 1990. pap. 4.95 (*0-8037-0781-9*) Dial Bks Young.

Seventeen Kings & Forty-Two Elephants. Margaret Mahy. 1993. pap. 5.99 (*0-14-054597-2*) NAL-Dutton.

17 Laws of Successful Investing: Ignore Them at Your Own Risk. Richard S. Rodman. (Illus.). 119p. 1996. 14.95 (*0-9651353-2-2*) Alidan Pr.

Seventeen Lectures on the Study of Medieval & Modern History & Kindred Subjects Delivered at Oxford, under Statutory Obligation in the Years 1867-1884. William Stubbs. vi, 455p. 1992. reprint ed. 45.00 (*0-8377-2652-2*) Rothman.

Seventeen Little Miricals: Fun & Success in a Family with 17 Children! Martin J. Mirical. LC 91-67483. (Illus.). 228p. (Orig.). 1992. pap. 9.95 (*0-9631593-6-4*) Wydaily Pub.

17 Little Piano Studies. Claudette Sorel. 16p. 1995. pap. 4.95 (*0-7935-4721-0*, 00290043) H Leonard.

***17 Love Poems with No Despair.** B. J. Ward. LC 96-39838. 35p. 1997. pap. 6.50 (*1-55643-243-7*) North Atlantic.

Seventeen More Poems. Roshen Alkazi. (Writers Workshop Redbird Ser.). 1975. 8.00 (*0-88253-628-1*); pap. text ed. 4.00 (*0-88253-627-3*) Ind-US Inc.

Seventeen Morton Street. large type ed. Catherine Hiller. LC 90-22237. 425p. 1991. reprint ed. lib. bdg. 18.95 (*1-56054-082-6*) Thorndike Pr.

1790 Census of Maine. annot. ed. (Maine Genealogical Society Special Publication: No. 20). 128p. 1995. pap. 17.50 (*0-89725-127-X*, 1440) Picton Pr.

1795 Census of Kentucky. T.L.C. Genealogy Staff. 195p. 1991. spiral bd., pap. 18.00 (*1-886633-01-0*) TLC Genealogy.

Seventeen Ninety-Four: Janie Miller's Whiskey Rebellion Saga. Anna T. Connor & Laura C. Zajdel. (Illus.). (Orig.). (YA). 1994. pap. 11.95 (*0-9640994-0-3*) L C Zajdel.

Seventeen Ninety to Eighteen Forty Censuses: Provincetown, Barnstable Co., Mass. Edith P. Ferguson. iv, 123p. (Orig.). 1983. pap. 14.00 (*0-917890-26-4*) Heritage Bk.

Seventeen Ninety-Two Ephemeris. Grant. 42p. 1959. 4.50 (*0-86690-227-9*, G1639-044) Am Fed Astrologers.

Seventeen O NMR Spectroscopy in Organic Chemistry. David W. Boykin. (Illus.). 248p. 1990. 217.00 (*0-8493-4867-6*) CRC Pr.

Seventeen Papers on Analysis. M. A. Aizerman et al. LC 51-5559. (Translations Ser.: Series 2, Vol. 26). 351p. 1963. 41.00 (*0-8218-1726-4*, TRANS2/26) Am Math.

Seventeen Papers on Analysis. V. I. Arnol'd et al. LC 51-5559. (Translations Ser.: Series 2, Vol. 28). 344p. 1963. 38.00 (*0-8218-1728-0*, TRANS2/28) Am Math.

Seventeen Papers on Functions of Complex Variables. M. M. Dzrbasjan et al. LC 51-5559. (Translations Ser.: Series 2, Vol. 32). 393p. 1963. 44.00 (*0-8218-1732-9*, TRANS2/32) Am Math.

Seventeen Papers on Topology & Differential Geometry. A. M. Ancikov et al. LC 51-5559. (Translations Ser.: Series 2, Vol. 92). 284p. 1970. 49.00 (*0-8218-1792-2*, TRANS2/92) Am Math.

Seventeen Poems. Roshen Alkazi. 8.00 (*0-89253-549-0*) Ind-US Inc.

***17 RPF Subfile Programs.** Ron Harvey. (Toolbox of Templates Ser.). (Illus.). 300p. (Orig.). 1997. pap. 119.00 (*1-883884-43-8*) Midrange Comput.

Seventeen Sacred Songs: Low Voice Piano for Church or General Use. 96p. 1986. pap. 11.95 (*0-7935-3813-0*, 50328280) H Leonard.

17 Secrets of the Master Prospectors. John Kalench. 268p. 1994. pap. 14.95 (*0-9629447-2-6*) Millionaires.

1771-1772, Vol. 12. Denis Diderot. (Correspondance Complete de Diderot). 1970. pap. 24.95 (*0-8288-9593-7*) Fr & Eur.

1777: The Year of the Hangman. John S. Pancake. LC 76-30797. 280p. 1992. pap. 17.95 (*0-8173-0687-0*) U of Ala Pr.

Seventeen Seventy-Seven Ephemeris. Grant. 78p. 1947. 4.50 (*0-86690-223-6*, G1635-044) Am Fed Astrologers.

Seventeen Seventy-Six: The Adventure of the American Revolution Told with Pictures. Irving Werstein. LC 61-18885. (Illus.). (Orig.). pap. 23.00 (*0-8154-0246-5*); lib. bdg. 44.00 (*0-8154-0247-3*) Cooper Sq.

***1776: Year of Illusion.** T. Fleming. 1996. 12.98 (*0-7858-0724-1*) Bk Sales Inc.

Seventeen Seventy-Six Ephemeris. Grant. 78p. 1944. 4.50 (*0-86690-222-8*, G1634-044) Am Fed Astrologers.

1776 Vocal Selections. S. Edwards. 84p. 1987. pap. 10.95 (*0-7935-2485-7*, 50453960) H Leonard.

Seventeen Simple Lectures on General Relativity Theory. H. A. Buchdahl. LC 81-11376. 190p. 1981. 32.95 (*0-471-09684-9*) Krieger.

Seventeen Sixty-Nine Transit of Venus: The Baja California Observations of Jean-Baptiste Chappe d'Auteroche, Vicente de Doz, & Joaquin Velazquez Cardenas de Leon. Ed. by Doyce B. Nunis, Jr. Tr. by James Donahue et al. from FRE. LC 82-3548. (Baja California Travels Ser.: No. 46). (Illus.). 185p. 1982. 60.00 (*0-938644-18-1*) Nat Hist Mus.

1767, Vol. 7. Denis Diderot. (Correspondance Complete de Diderot). 1970. pap. 24.95 (*0-8288-9588-0*) Fr & Eur.

1767 Chronicle. Armand F. Lucier. 174p. (Orig.). 1995. pap. 17.50 (*0-7884-0356-7*, L813) Heritage Bk.

1766-1770, Vol. II. George Washington. Ed. by Donald Jackson & Dorothy Twohig. 1976. text ed. 37.50 (*0-8139-0688-1*) U Pr of Va.

Seventeen Sports Cars 1919-1930: Landmarks in Automobile Design. Peter Hull & Nigel Arnold-Forster. LC 76-17410. (Illus.). 240p. 1976. 12.50 (*0-8376-0085-5*) Bentley.

Seventeen Steps to 221B: A Sherlockian Collection by English Writers. Intro. by James E. Holroyd. LC 93-42879. (Illus.). 188p. 1994. reprint ed. pap. 8.00 (*1-883402-72-7*) S&S Trade.

17 Super Christmas Hits. 48p. 1984. pap. 7.95 (*0-7935-2735-X*, 00361052) H Leonard.

17 Super Christmas Hits. (Easy Piano Ser.). 48p. 1984. pap. 7.95 (*0-7935-3020-2*, 00361053) H Leonard.

Seventeen Super Christmas Hits. 48p. 1984. pap. 7.95 (*0-7935-3079-2*, 00702071) H Leonard.

17 Super Christmas Hits: Big-Note for Piano. 48p. 1985. pap. 6.95 (*0-7935-1885-7*, 00240867) H Leonard.

17 Super Christmas Hits: Trumpet. 1985. pap. 12.95 incl. audio (*0-7935-3147-0*, 00845064) H Leonard.

17 Super Christmas Hits: Violin. 1985. pap. 12.95 incl. audio (*0-7935-3148-9*, 00845066) H Leonard.

Seventeen Syllables. Ed. by Hosaye Yamamoto & King-Kok Cheung. LC 93-31171. (Woman Writers: Text & Contexts Ser.). 230p. (C). 1994. text ed. 35.00 (*0-8135-2052-5*); pap. text ed. 14.00 (*0-8135-2053-3*) Rutgers U Pr.

Seventeen Syllables & Other Stories. Hisaye Yamamoto. 170p. (Orig.). (C). 1988. 23.95 (*0-913175-15-3*); pap. 11.95 (*0-913175-14-5*) Kitchen Table.

Seventeen Teen Body Book. (YA). Date not set. 14.95 (*0-02-043975-X*) Macmillan.

Seventeen (The Political Being) & J (The Sexual Being) Kenzaburo Oe. (Orig.). 1996. pap. 16.95 (*1-56201-082-4*, North Star Line) Blue Moon Bks.

Seventeen Times As High As the Moon: Stories by Julia Oliver. Julia Oliver. LC 92-37457. 160p. 1993. 18.00 (*1-881320-04-9*, Black Belt) Black Belt Comm.

Seventeen Toutle River Haiku. James Hanlen. LC 84-80654. (Illus.). 60p. (Orig.). 1984. pap. 12.00 (*0-912767-00-6*) Intertxt AK.

Seventeen Toutle River Haiku. deluxe limited ed. James Hanlen. LC 84-80654. (Illus.). 60p. (Orig.). 1984. 25.00 (*0-685-08291-1*) Intertxt AK.

***Seventeen Watts? The First 20 Years of British Rock Guitar, the Musicians, & Their Stories.** Mo Foster. 256p. pap. 29.95 (*1-86074-182-7*, SG 00614, Pub. by Sanctuary Pr UK) Music Sales.

Seventeen Wishes. Robin J. Gunn. LC 93-11278. (Christy Miller Ser.: Vol. 9). (YA). 1993. pap. 5.99 (*1-56179-169-5*) Focus Family.

S

Seventeen Years among the Sea Dyaks of Borneo: A Record of Intimate Association with the Natives of the Bornean Jungles. Edwin H. Gomes. LC 77-86993. (Illus.). 408p. reprint ed. 64.50 (*0-404-16718-7*) AMS Pr.

***Seventeenth- & Eighteenth-Century British Literature, 4 bks.** (Modern Critical Interpretations Ser.). 64.90 (*0-7910-3572-7*) Chelsea Hse.

***Seventeenth- & Eighteenth-Century British Writers, 2 bks.** (Modern Critical Views Ser.). 99.85 (*0-7910-3580-8*) Chelsea Hse.

Seventeenth Airborne Division Association. Seventeenth Airborne Division Staff. LC 87-50352. 128p. 1987. 48.00 (*0-938021-11-7*) Turner Pub KY.

17th & 18th Century American Poetry. Ed. by Dan Woodward. (Illus.). 100p. 1996. 16.95 (*1-882935-24-1*) Westphalia.

Seventeenth & Eighteenth Century Art. Julius Held & Donald Posner. 1976. 60.00 (*0-8109-0032-7*) Abrams.

Seventeenth & Eighteenth Century Art: Baroque Painting, Sculpture & Architecture. Julius Held & Donald Posner. Ed. by H. W. Janson. (Illus.). 492p. (C). 1972. text ed. 71.47 (*0-13-807339-2*) P-H.

Seventeenth & Eighteenth Century British Philosophy, 9 vols., Set. (British Philosophy Ser.). 3172p. (C). (gr. 13). 1992. text ed. 695.00 (*0-415-07973-X*, A9582) Routledge.

Seventeenth & Eighteenth Century European Drawings. Ed. by Richard P. Wunder. (Illus.). 1966. 7.50 (*0-8079-0099-0*); pap. 5.00 (*0-8079-0100-8*) October.

Seventeenth & Eighteenth Century Italian Schools. Michael Levey. (National Gallery Publications). (Illus.). 1989. pap. text ed. 25.00 (*0-300-06142-0*) Yale U Pr.

17th Annual BDA International Design Awards. Ed. by Lynne M. Grasz. (Illus.). x, 224p. 1996. 45.00 (*0-9644038-2-X*) Design Ed.

17th Annual Current Developments in Bankruptcy & Reorganization, 2 vols., Set. (Commercial Law & Practice Course Handbook Ser.). 1704p. 1995. pap. 149.00 (*0-614-17146-6*, A4-4474) PLI.

17th Annual Fall Technical Conference of the ASME Internal Combustion Engine Division Vol. 25-3: Alternate Fuels & Natural Gas. Ed. by J. A. Caton. 132p. 76.00 (*0-614-97060-1*, G0980C) ASME.

17th Annual Fall Technical Conference of the ASME Internal Combustion Engine Division Vol. 25-4: Combustion & Emissions. Ed. by J. A. Caton. 128p. 76.00 (*0-614-97061-X*, G0980D) ASME.

17th Annual Fall Technical Conference of the ASME Internal Combustion Engine Division Vol. 25-2: Simulations, Controls, & Lubrication. Ed. by J. A. Caton. 156p. 84.00 (*0-614-97059-8*, G098B) ASME.

Seventeenth Biennial Conference Proceedings. ICHCA Staff. (C). 1988. 500.00 (*0-685-37351-7*, Pub. by ICHCA UK) St Mut.

17th Bomb Group. Turner Publishing Company Staff. LC 94-61012. 128p. 1994. 48.00 (*1-56311-161-6*) Turner Pub KY.

Seventeenth Century. Ed. by Andrew Lossky. LC 67-10426. (Orig.). 1967. pap. 14.95 (*0-02-919400-8*, Free Press) Free Pr.

Seventeenth Century. Madeleine Mainstone & Rowland Mainstone. LC 80-40039. (Cambridge Introduction to Art Ser.). (Illus.). 100p. 1981. text ed. 29.95 (*0-521-22162-5*); pap. text ed. 13.95 (*0-521-29376-6*) Cambridge U Pr.

Seventeenth Century. Jacques R. Boulenger. LC 70-181913. (National History of France Ser.: No. 4). reprint ed. 45.00 (*0-404-50794-8*) AMS Pr.

Seventeenth Century: Bacon Through Marvell. Arthur E. Barker. LC 76-4657. (Goldentree Bibliographies Series in Language & Literature). (C). 1980. pap. text ed. write for info. (*0-88295-548-9*) Harlan Davidson.

Seventeenth Century: Directions Old & New. E. Moles & N. A. Peacock. 144p. 1993. 49.00 (*0-85261-344-X*, Pub. by Univ of Glasgow UK) St Mut.

Seventeenth Century: Studies in the History of English Thought & Literature from Bacon to Pope. Richard F. Jones et al. vi, 378p. 1951. 49.50 (*0-8047-0408-2*) Stanford U Pr.

Seventeenth Century Albany: A Dutch Profile. rev. ed. Charlotte Wilcoxen. LC 80-70608. (Illus.). 201p. pap. 8.95 (*0-939072-02-5*) Albany Hist & Art.

Seventeenth-Century America: Essays in Colonial History. Ed. by James M. Smith. LC 79-17749. 238p. 1980. reprint ed. text ed. 67.50 (*0-313-22075-1*, SMSC, Greenwood Pr) Greenwood.

Seventeenth Century Background: Studies in the Thought of the Age in Relation to Poetry & Religion. Basil Willey. LC 34-21849. 315p. 1942. text ed. 53.50 (*0-231-01395-7*) Col U Pr.

Seventeenth-Century Barberini Documents & Inventories of Art. Compiled by Marilyn Aronberg Lavin. LC 75-29413. 741p. (C). 1975. text ed. 160.00 (*0-8147-4962-3*) NYU Pr.

Seventeenth Century Britain. Ed. by Boris Ford. (Cultural History of Britain Ser.). (Illus.). 352p. (C). 1992. pap. text ed. 24.95 (*0-521-42884-X*) Cambridge U Pr.

Seventeenth-Century British Nondramatic Poets: First Series, Vol. 121. Ed. by M. Thomas Hester. LC 92-24073. (Dictionary of Literary Biography Ser.: Vol. 121). 1992. 140.00 (*0-8103-7598-2*) Gale.

Seventeenth-Century British Nondramatic Poets: Second Series, Vol. 126. Ed. by M. Thomas Hester. LC 92-42318. (Dictionary of Literary Biography Ser.: Vol. 126). 1993. 140.00 (*0-8103-5385-7*) Gale.

Seventeenth-Century British Philosophers. Ed. by Vere Chappell. (Essays on Early Modern Philosophers Ser.: Vol. 6). 345p. 1992. text ed. 57.00 (*0-8153-0579-6*, B1131) Garland.

Seventeenth Century Colonial Ancestors of Members of the National Society Colonial Dames Seventeenth Century, 3 vols. in 1. Mary L. Hutton. LC 83-80251. 468p. 1991. reprint ed. 30.00 (*0-8063-1025-1*) Genealog Pub.

***Seventeenth-Century Cultural Discourse: France & the Preaching of Bishop Camus.** Thomas Worcester. LC 97-6660. (Religion & Society Ser.: Vol. 28). x, 306p. (C). 1997. lib. bdg. 168.90 (*3-11-015220-7*) Mouton.

Seventeenth Century Dutch & Flemish Painting: The Thyssen Bornemisza Collection. Ivan Gaskell. (Illus.). 552p. 1990. 250.00 (*0-85667-352-8*) Sothebys Pubns.

Seventeenth-Century Dutch Drawings: A Selection from the Maida & George Abrams Collection. William W. Robinson. (Illus.). 234p. 1991. pap. 39.95 (*0-685-63136-2*) Pierpont Morgan.

Seventeenth-Century Dutch Drawings: A Selection from the Maida & George Abrams Collection. William W. Robinson. (Pierpont Morgan Library). (Illus.). 236p. 1994. pap. 39.95 (*0-87598-107-0*) Pierpont Morgan.

Seventeenth Century English Essay. Elbert N. Thompson. LC 67-30818. (English Literature Ser.: No. 33). 1969. reprint ed. lib. bdg. 75.00 (*0-8383-0722-1*) M S G Haskell Hse.

Seventeenth-Century English Hymn: A Mode for Sacred & Secular Concerns. Thelma B. Thompson. (American University Studies: Fine Arts: Ser. XX, Vol. 5). 234p. (C). 1989. text ed. 39.95 (*0-8204-0695-3*) P Lang Pubng.

Seventeenth-Century English Keyboard Music: Benjamin Cosyn. Orhan Memed. LC 92-43441. (Outstanding Dissertations in Music from British Universities Ser.). 480p. 1993. text ed. 147.00 (*0-8153-0949-X*) Garland.

Seventeenth Century English Poetry: The Annotated Anthology. Terence Dawson & Robert Dupree. 608p. 1994. pap. text ed. 38.00 (*0-13-302597-7*) P-H.

***Seventeenth Century Essays, from Bacon to Clarendon.** Ed. by Jacob Zeitlin. 346p. Date not set. 21.95 (*0-8369-2881-4*) Ayer.

Seventeenth Century Europe: State, Conflict & the Social Order in Europe 1598-1700. Thomas Munck. LC 89-10893. 480p. 1990. text ed. 45.00 (*0-312-04011-3*) St Martin.

Seventeenth Century Europe 1598-1700: State, Conflict & the Social Order in Europe. Thomas Munck. 1990. pap. text ed. 14.95 (*0-333-28641-3*) St Martin.

Seventeenth-Century Exposure of Superstition: Select Texts of Claude Pithoys (1587-1676) P. J. Whitmore. (International Archives of the History of Ideas Ser.: No. 49). 307p. 1972. lib. bdg. 104.50 (*90-247-1298-X*) Kluwer Ac.

Seventeenth Century French Drama. Incl. Tartuffe: Acting Edition. Moliere. 1967. (*0-318-54371-0*); Would Be Gentleman. Moliere. LC 67-17879. 1967. (*0-318-54372-9*); Precious Damsels. Moliere. LC 67-17879. 1967. (*0-318-54373-7*); Phaedra. Jean-Baptiste Racine. LC 67-17879. (*0-318-54374-5*); Athaliah. Jean B. Racine. LC 67-17879. 1967. (*0-318-54375-3*); Cid. Pierre Corneille. LC 67-17879. (*0-318-54376-1*); LC 67-17879. (Modern Library College Editions). (C). 1967. pap. text ed. write for info. (*0-07-553656-0*, 30977) McGraw.

Seventeenth Century German Prose. Hans J. Von Grimmelshausen et al. Ed. by Lynne Tatlock. (German Library: Vol. 7). 324p. 1993. 29.50 (*0-8264-0710-2*); pap. text ed. 16.95 (*0-8264-0711-0*) Continuum.

Seventeenth Century Interior Decoration in England, France & Holland. Peter Thornton. LC 77-91067. (Illus.). 439p. 1981. pap. 35.00 (*0-300-02776-1*) Yale U Pr.

Seventeenth-Century Ireland: The War of Religions. Brendan Fitzpatrick. LC 88-23589. (Illus.). 308p. (C). 1988. lib. bdg. 55.50 (*0-389-20814-0*, N8372) B&N Imports.

Seventeenth Century Isle of Wight County, Virginia. John B. Boddie. LC 73-2146. (Illus.). 756p. 1994. reprint ed. 40.00 (*0-8063-0559-2*, 525) Genealog Pub.

Seventeenth Century Isle of Wight County, Virginia. John B. Boddie. (Illus.). 768p. 1993. reprint ed. pap. text ed. 43.00 (*1-55613-887-3*) Heritage Bk.

Seventeenth-Century Italian Prints from the Collection of Mr. & Mrs. Marcus S. Sopher. Claudia Lazzaro-Bruno. LC 78-61801. (Illus.). 1978. pap. 10.00 (*0-937031-11-9*) Stanford Art.

Seventeenth-Century Letter-Book: A Facsimile Editon of Folger MS V.A. 321. Comment by A. R. Braunmuller. LC 81-50652. 464p. 1983. 68.50 (*0-87413-201-0*) U Delaware Pr.

Seventeenth Century Life in the Country Parish. Ed. by E. Trotter. 242p. 1968. reprint ed. 38.50 (*0-7146-1363-0*, Pub. by F Cass Pubs UK) Intl Spec Bk.

Seventeenth-Century New England. Ed. by David G. Allen & David Hall. xx, 340p. 1984. text ed. 40.00 (*0-8139-1048-X*) U Pr of Va.

Seventeenth Century North America: French & Spanish Accounts. Carl O. Sauer. (New World Writing Ser.). (Illus.). 1977. 19.95 (*0-913666-23-8*); pap. 9.95 (*0-913666-22-X*) Turtle Isl Foun.

Seventeenth Century Paintings from the Low Countries. Gilbert Creighton. (Illus.). 1966. 10.50 (*0-8079-0117-2*) October.

Seventeenth Century Prose & Poetry. 2nd enl. ed. Alexander M. Witherspoon & Frank J. Warnke. 1124p. (C). 1983. text ed. 46.75 (*0-15-580237-2*) HB Coll Pubs.

Seventeenth-Century Resolve: A Historical Anthology of a Literary Form. fac. ed. Ed. by John L. Lievsay. LC 79-4004. 221p. 1980. pap. 63.00 (*0-7837-7595-4*, 2047348) Bks Demand.

Seventeenth-Century Roman Palaces: Use & the Art of the Plan. Patricia Waddy. (Illus.). 480p. 1990. 55.00 (*0-262-23156-5*) MIT Pr.

Seventeenth-Century Sheriff: A Comparative Study of the Sheriff in England & the Chesapeake Colonies 1607-1689. Cyrus H. Karraker. 1977. 16.95 (*0-8369-7164-7*, 7996) Ayer.

Seventeenth Century Songs & Lyrics. Ed. by John P. Cutts. LC 70-80373. (Granger Index Reprint Ser.). 1977. 23.95 (*0-8369-6055-6*) Ayer.

Seventeenth-Century Spanish Poetry: The Power of Artifice. Arthur Terry. LC 92-40121. 320p. (C). 1993. text ed. 64.95 (*0-521-44421-7*) Cambridge U Pr.

Seventeenth Century Studies, 2 Vols. Robert Shafer. text ed. 39.95 (*0-8369-9354-3*, 19725) Ayer.

Seventeenth Century Studies. Edmund W. Gosse. LC 70-136381. reprint ed. 37.50 (*0-404-02885-3*) AMS Pr.

Seventeenth Century Studies. Edmund W. Gosse. (BCL1-PR English Literature Ser.). 350p. 1992. reprint ed. lib. bdg. 89.00 (*0-7812-7086-3*) Rprt Serv.

Seventeenth Century Studies. Edmund W. Gosse. 1971. reprint ed. 16.00 (*0-403-00995-2*) Scholarly.

Seventeenth Century Studies. First Series. Ed. by Robert Shafer. LC 68-16976. (Essay Index Reprint Ser.). 1977. 20.95 (*0-8369-0866-X*) Ayer.

Seventeenth Century Studies. Second Series. Ed. by Robert Shafer. LC 68-16976. (Essay Index Reprint Ser.). 1977. 20.95 (*0-8369-0867-8*) Ayer.

Seventeenth Century, the Intellectual & Cultural Context of English Literature, 1603-1700. Graham Parry. (Literature in English Ser.). 336p. (Orig.). (C). 1989. pap. text ed. 27.50 (*0-582-49376-5*, 73590) Longman.

17th Century Wisdom for 21st Century Problems. Theo Brooks. LC 95-80432. 112p. 1995. pap. 5.95 (*0-9645322-4-7*) Akkad Pr.

Seventeenth Conference Proceedings. ICHCA Staff. (C). 1988. 280.00 (*0-685-36611-1*, Pub. by ICHCA UK) St Mut.

***17th Heat Treating Society Conference Proceedings Including the 1st International Induction Heat Treating Symposium.** Ed. by D. Milam et al. (Illus.). 1400p. 1997. 187.00 (*0-87170-610-5*, 6634) ASM.

***17th IEEE Real-Time Systems Symposium.** LC 10-528725. 368p. 1996. pap. text ed. 80.00 (*0-8186-7689-2*) IEEE Comp Soc.

Seventeenth International Byzantine Congress: Major Papers. Compiled by U. S. National Committee for Byzantine Studies. (Illus.). 750p. 1986. lib. bdg. 75.00 (*0-89241-443-X*) Caratzas.

17th National Passive Solar Conference Proceedings. 291p. 1992. pap. 100.00 (*0-89553-207-7*) Am Solar Energy.

***XVII Olympiad, Rome 1960 & Innsbruck 1964.** LC 97-14156. (Olympic Century Ser.). (Illus.). 1996. 21.95 (*1-888383-15-1*, Wrld Spt) Wld Sport Resch.

Seventeenth Space Simulation Conference: Terrestrial Test for Space Success. 1992. 100.00 (*0-685-63214-8*) Inst Environ Sci.

Seventeenth Summer. (YA). Date not set. pap. 2.25 (*0-590-02554-6*) Scholastic Inc.

Seventeenth Summer. Maureen Daley. (YA). (gr. 7-11). 1942. 10.95 (*0-396-02322-3*, Putnam) Putnam Pub Group.

Seventeenth Summer. Maureen Daly. (YA). (gr. 7 up). mass mkt. 3.99 (*0-671-61931-4*, Archway) PB.

Seventeenth Summer. Maureen Daly. 293p. (YA). (gr. 7 up). 1981. reprint ed. lib. bdg. 23.95 (*0-89966-355-9*) Buccaneer Bks.

Seventeenth Summer. Maureen Daly. 288p. (YA). (gr. 7 up). 1981. reprint ed. lib. bdg. 19.95 (*0-89967-029-6*) Harmony Raine.

Seventeenth Texas Symposium on Relativistic Astrophysics & Cosmology, Vol. 759. Ed. by Hans Bohringer et al. LC 95-34165. (Annals of the New York Academy of Sciences Ser.). 1995. write for info. (*0-89766-941-X*); pap. 190.00 (*0-89766-942-8*) NY Acad Sci.

Seventeenth Virginia Cavalry. Nelson Harris. (Virginia Regimental Histories Ser.). (Illus.). 91p. 1994. 19.95 (*1-56190-062-1*) H E Howard.

Seventeenth Virginia Infantry. Lee A. Wallace. (Virginia Regimental Histories Ser.). (Illus.). 154p. 1990. 19.95 (*1-56190-003-6*) H E Howard.

Seventh. Richard Stark. LC 80-39928. 158p. 1981. 25.00 (*0-89366-264-X*) Ultramarine Pub.

Seventh Air Force Story. Kenn Rust. (Illus.). 72p. 1993. pap. text ed. 15.95 (*0-911852-84-0*) Aviation Heritage.

Seventh & Walnut, Life in Colonial Philadelphia. James E. Knight. LC 81-24036. (Illus.). 32p. (J). (gr. 5-9). 1995. pap. 2.95 (*0-89375-741-1*) Troll Communs.

7th Angel: God's Last Trumpet Call. Carroll U. Kendrick, Jr. 342p. (Orig.). 1994. per., pap. text ed. 12.95 (*0-9643347-0-4*) C U Kendrick.

Seventh Annual Digest of Law School Transfer Policies. 1997. 27.50 (*0-938609-14-9*) Graduate Group.

Seventh Annual Directory of Law School Summer Programs in the United States & Abroad. 1995. 27.50 (*0-614-01209-0*) Graduate Group.

Seventh Annual Institute on Proxy Statements, Annual Meeting, & Disclosure Documents. Edward F. Greene. iv, 628p. write for info. (*0-318-61626-2*) HarBrace.

Seventh Annual Internships in Federal Government. 1994. 27.50 (*0-685-71246-X*) Graduate Group.

Seventh Annual Labor & Employment Law Institute: The 1990s: Transitional Years in Labor-Management Relations. Ed. by Marlin M. Volz. LC 95-24087. vi, 311p. 1996. 72.50 (*0-8377-1242-4*) Rothman.

Seventh Annual Report of the Secretaries of State, 1989: American Foreign Policy: The Challenges, the Opportunities, the Dangers. 1990. 5.00 (*0-685-34508-4*) Southern Ctr Intl Stud.

Seventh Annual Report on Carcinogens (1994) Summary. 473p. (Orig.). (C). 1995. pap. text ed. 50.00 (*0-7881-1880-3*) DIANE Pub.

Seventh Annual Services Marketing Conference Proceedings: Designing a Winning Service Strategy. Mary J. Bitner & Lawrence A. Crosby. LC 88-38392. 113p. (Orig.). 1989. pap. text ed. 27.00 (*0-87757-195-3*) Am Mktg.

***Seventh Annual Women Artists & the West: Show & Sale, Invitational, Best of the West.** Tisa R. Sherman & Robert A. Yassin. (Illus.). 20p. (Orig.). 1997. pap. 6.00 (*0-911611-09-6*) Tucson Mus Art.

Seventh Arkansas Confederate Infantry. Desmond W. Allen. (Illus.). 52p. 1988. pap. 14.00 (*0-941765-28-8*) Arkansas Res.

Seventh Army Report of Operations: 1944-1945, 2 vols., Set. (Combat Arms Ser.). (Illus.). 1064p. 1988. reprint ed. 99.95 (*0-89839-124-5*) Battery Pr.

Seventh Assembling. Ed. by Richard Kostelanetz & Henry J. Korn. (Illus.). 376p. 1977. pap. 26.00 (*0-915066-28-9*) Assembling Pr.

Seventh Avenue Murder. Liza Bennett. 1990. mass mkt. 3.50 (*0-373-26041-5*) Harlequin Bks.

Seventh Babe. Jerome Charyn. 352p. (C). 1996. pap. 16.95 (*0-87805-882-6*) U Pr of Miss.

Seventh Bearer. John C. Boland. Ed. by Dana Isaacson. 256p. (Orig.). 1993. mass mkt. 4.99 (*0-671-74100-4*) PB.

Seventh Book of Junior Authors & Illustrators. Ed. by Sally H. Holtze. LC 95-47983. (Illus.). 1996. write for info. (*0-8242-0873-0*) Wilson.

Seventh Carrier. P. Albano. 1987. pap. 4.50 (*0-8217-3612-4*) NAL-Dutton.

Seventh Carrier. Peter Albano. 1987. mass mkt. 3.95 (*0-8217-2056-2*, Zebra Kensgtn) Kensgtn Pub Corp.

Seventh Cavalry's Own Colonel Tommy Tompkins: A Military Heritage & Tradition. John M. Carroll. (Illus.). 31.95 (*0-8488-0013-3*, J M C & Co) Amereon Ltd.

Seventh Census of the United States, Eighteen Fifty. U. S. Census Office Staff. LC 75-22851. (America in Two Centuries Ser.). 1976. reprint ed. 106.95 (*0-405-07718-1*) Ayer.

Seventh Century in the West-Syrian Chronicles. Tr. by Andrew Palmer et al. from LAT. (Translated Texts for Historians Ser.). 272p. (Orig.). 1993. pap. text ed. 18.95 (*0-85323-238-5*, Pub. by Liverpool Univ Pr UK) U of Pa Pr.

Seventh Chords & Arpeggios for Bass. William L. Fowler. LC 84-71709. (Illus.). 64p. 1991. pap. text ed. 8.00 (*0-943894-14-X*) Fowler Music.

Seventh Chords & Arpeggios for Guitar. William L. Fowler. LC 84-71709. (Illus.). 64p. 1991. pap. text ed. 8.00 (*0-943894-15-8*) Fowler Music.

Seventh Circle in Bible Prophecy. Wayne L. Atchison. LC 96-90067. (Illus.). 1996. pap. 10.95 (*0-533-11872-7*) Vantage.

Seventh Commandment. Lawrence Sanders. 368p. (Orig.). 1992. mass mkt. 6.99 (*0-425-13329-X*) Berkley Pub.

Seventh Commandment. large type ed. Lawrence Sanders. (General Ser.). 303p. 1992. pap. 16.95 (*0-8161-5342-6*, GK Hall) Thorndike Pr.

Seventh Commandment. large type ed. Sarah A. Shears. 1979. 25.99 (*0-7089-0388-6*) Ulverscroft.

Seventh Congress of the International Organization for Septuagint & Cognate Studies. Ed. by Claude Cox. (Society of Biblical Literature Septuagint & Cognate Studies Ser.). 496p. (C). 1991. 44.95 (*1-55540-647-5*, 060431); pap. 29.95 (*1-55540-648-3*, 060431) Scholars Pr GA.

Seventh Continent: Antarctica in a Resource Age. Deborah Shapley. LC 85-5581. (Illus.). 405p. reprint ed. pap. 115.50 (*0-7837-5931-2*, 2045730) Bks Demand.

Seventh Cross. Anna Seghers. Tr. by James A. Galston from GER. (Voices of Resistance Ser.). 384p. 1987. reprint ed. pap. 13.00 (*0-85345-712-3*) Monthly Rev.

Seventh Crystal. Gary Paulsen. (World of Adventure Ser.: No. 12). (Illus.). 80p. (J). (gr. 3-7). 1996. pap. 3.99 (*0-440-41051-7*, YB BDD) BDD Bks Young Read.

Seventh-Day Adventist Attitudes Toward Roman Catholicism: 1844 - 1965. Reinder Bruinsma. LC 94-72955. 390p. 1994. pap. 19.99 (*1-883925-04-5*) Andrews Univ Pr.

Seventh-Day Adventist Church in Latin America & the Caribbean, 2 vols. Floyd Greenleaf. LC 92-71515. 1019p. 1993. 45.99 (*0-943872-57-X*) Andrews Univ Pr.

Seventh Day Adventist Encyclopedia, Vol. 1. 2nd rev. ed. 1995. write for info. (*0-8280-0917-1*) Review & Herald.

Seventh Day Adventist Encyclopedia, Vol. 2. 2nd rev. ed. 1995. write for info. (*0-8280-0918-X*) Review & Herald.

Seventh-Day Adventist Reform Movement. Helmut H. Kramer. 89p. (Orig.). 1988. pap. 3.95 (*0-925675-08-3*) BRI DC.

Seventh-Day-Adventists: Cult or Christians? Walter C. Thompson. Ed. by Creation Enterprises International Staff. 92p. 1992. pap. 6.95 (*0-9628512-1-3*) Creation Enter Intl.

***Seventh Day & After.** Don Webb. 78p. 1993. 7.95 (*1-877655-05-8*) Wordcraft Oregon.

Seventh-Day Baptists in Europe & America, Vol. 1. Seventh-Day Baptists General Conference Staff. 1980. 88.95 (*0-405-12478-3*) Ayer.

Seventh-Day Baptists in Europe & America, Vol. 2. Seventh-Day Baptists General Conference Staff. 1980. 88.95 (*0-405-12479-1*) Ayer.

An Asterisk (*) at the beginning of an entry indicates that the title is appearing in BIP for the first time.

Seventh-Day Baptists in Europe & America: A Series of Historical Papers Written in Commemoration of the One Hundred Anniversary of the Organization, 2 Vols., Set. Seventh-Day Baptists General Conference Staff. Ed. by Edwin S. Gaustad. LC 79-52605. (Baptist Tradition Ser.). (Illus.). 1980. reprint ed. lib. bdg. 176.95 (*0-405-12470-8*) Ayer.

Seventh-Day Diet: How the Healthiest People in America Live Better, Longer, Slimmer & Why. Jan Hoffman. 1991. 19.00 (*0-394-58473-2*) Random.

Seventh-Day Men: Sabbatarians & Sabbatarianism in England & Wales, 1600-1800. Bryan W. Ball. LC 92-30811. (Illus.). 416p. 1994. 75.00 (*0-19-826752-5*, Old Oregon Bk Store) OUP.

Seventh Division 1888. 60p. 5.50 (*0-318-18049-9*) Mobile PO.

Seventh Door. Norman Leach. (Illus.). (J). 1995. 13.99 (*0-85953-947-4*) Childs Play.

Seventh Dragon: The Riddle of Equal Temperament. Anita T. Sullivan. LC 84-22627. (Illus.). 100p. (Orig.). (C). 1985. 12.95 (*0-943920-22-1*) Metamorphous Pr.

Seventh E. C. Photovoltaic Solar Energy Conference. Ed. by A. Goetzberger et al. 1987. lib. bdg. 358.00 (*90-277-2449-0*) Kluwer Ac.

Seventh Enemy: A Brady Coyne Mystery. William G. Tapply. LC 94-29386. 1995. 21.00 (*1-883402-99-9*) S&S Trade.

Seventh Five-Year Plan: Performance & Perspectives. Ed. by J. Mahender Reddy et al. xvi, 254p. 1989. text ed. 30.00 (*81-207-1021-5*, Pub. by Sterling Pubs II) Apt Bks.

7th Floor Ain't Too High for Angels to Fly: A Collection of Thoughts on Relationships & Self-Understanding. John M. Eades. 200p. 1995. pap. 10.95 (*1-55874-356-1*, 3561) Health Comm.

Seventh Garfield Treasury. Jim Davis. (Illus.). 120p. 1993. pap. 10.95 (*0-345-38427-X*, Ballantine Trade) Ballantine.

Seventh Garment. Eugenia Fakinoll. Tr. by Ed Emery from GRE. 128p. (Orig.). 1992. pap. 11.99 (*1-85242-186-X*) Serpents Tail.

Seventh Gate. Tracy Hickman & Margaret Weis. 368p. 1995. mass mkt. 6.50 (*0-553-57325-X*, Spectra) Bantam.

Seventh Gate. Margaret Weis & Hickman. 336p. 1994. 14.99 (*0-593-02395-1*) Bantam.

***Seventh General Programme of Work Covering the Period 1984-1989.** 1982. text ed. write for info. (*92-4-180008-9*) World Health.

Seventh Generation of One Hundred & One Aggie Jokes. Illus. by Bob Taylor. (One Hundred & One Aggie Jokes Ser.). 50p. (Orig.). 1977. write for info. (*0-945430-07-8*) Gigem Pr.

Seventh Global Warming International Conference & Expo, April 1-3, 1996, Vienna Austria: Abstracts. Sinyan Shen. (Global Warming International Center Ser.). (Illus.). 120p. (C). 1995. pap. 105.00 (*0-88473-602-4*) Supcon Intl.

Seventh Grade Math TAAS Instructional Packet. Patricia Enselek & Susan Griffin. (TAAS Instructional Packets (TIPs) Ser.). 72p. 1991. 19.95 (*1-883396-13-1*) Educ Etc.

Seventh Grade Reading TAAS Instructional Packet. Patricia Enselek & Susan Griffin. (TAAS Instructional Packets (TIPs) Ser.). 73p. 1991. 19.95 (*1-883396-11-5*) Educ Etc.

Seventh Grade Writing TAAS Instructional Packet. Patricia Enselek & Susan Griffin. (TAAS Instructional Packets (TIPs) Ser.). 71p. 1991. 19.95 (*1-883396-12-3*) Educ Etc.

7th Guest: A Novel. Matthew J. Costello & Graig S. Gardner. 1995. boxed 21.95 (*0-7615-0086-3*) Prima Pub.

Seventh Guilty Man. large type ed. Marshall Grover. (Linford Western Library). 282p. 1989. pap. 15.99 (*0-7089-6676-4*, Linford) Ulverscroft.

***Seventh Heart.** Marian Fitch. 320p. 1997. mass mkt. 5.99 (*0-441-00451-2*) Ace Bks.

Seventh Heaven. Margaret Astridge. (Rainbow Romances Ser.: No. 886). 160p. 1994. 14.95 (*0-7090-4937-4*, Hale-Parkwest) Parkwest Pubns.

Seventh Heaven. Alice Hoffman. 1991. mass mkt. 5.99 (*0-449-22018-4*) Fawcett.

Seventh Heaven. large type ed. Margaret Astridge. (Romance Ser.). 288p. 1995. pap. 15.99 (*0-7089-7666-2*, Linford) Ulverscroft.

Seventh Hero: Thomas Carlyle & the Theory of Radical Activism. Phillip Rosenberg. LC 73-87659. 288p. 1974. 25.95 (*0-674-80260-8*) HUP.

***Seventh hGH Symposium.** Ed. by J. Girard & J. S. Christiansen. (Journal Ser.: Vol. 46, No. 4-5). (Illus.). 104p. 1996. pap. 88.75 (*3-8055-6432-5*) S Karger.

Seventh Hour. Grace L. Hill. 22.95 (*0-8488-0087-7*) Amereon Ltd.

Seventh Hour. Grace L. Hill. (Grace Livingston Hill Ser.: Vol. 26). 267p. 1992. pap. text ed. 4.99 (*0-8423-5884-6*) Tyndale.

Seventh Infantry Division. Turner Publishing Company Staff. LC 90-71732. 112p. 1991. 48.00 (*1-56311-027-X*) Turner Pub KY.

***Seventh Ingot Metallurgy Forum Symposium.** 148p. 1994. 50.00 (*0-614-21923-X*) Iron & Steel.

Seventh International Colloquium on Amphipoda. Ed. by L. Watling. (Developments in Hydrobiology Ser.). (C). 1900. lib. bdg. 222.00 (*0-7923-1459-X*) Kluwer Ac.

Seventh International Conference on Sarcoidosis & Other Granulomatous Disorders, Vol. 278. Ed. by Louis E. Siltzbach. (Annals Ser.). 1976. 55.00 (*0-89072-057-6*) NY Acad Sci.

Seventh International Congress-Cold Forging. FMJ Intl. Publ. Ltd. Staff. 192p. (C). 1985. 495.00 (*0-685-36809-2*, Pub. by Fuel Metallurgical Jrnl UK) St Mut.

7th International Congress International Association of Engineering Geology, Lisbon, Portugal, 5-9 September 1994, 6 vols. Ed. by R. Oliviera et al. (Illus.). 5240p. (C). 1994. text ed. 490.00 (*90-5410-503-8*, Pub. by A A Balkema NE) Ashgate Pub Co.

***Seventh International Congress of Egyptologists: Abstracts of Papers.** 210p. 1995. pap. 22.00 (*0-946897-92-1*, Pub. by Oxbow Bks UK) David Brown.

Seventh International Mineral Processing Congress: Proceedings, 1965. Ed. by Nathaniel Arbiter. 612p. 1965. pap. text ed. 161.00 (*0-677-10695-5*) Gordon & Breach.

7th International Symposium on Corrosion in the Pulp & Paper Industry Proceedings. TAPPI Staff. (Illus.). 361p. 1992. 128.00 (*0-89852-862-3*) NACE Intl.

Seventh International Symposium on Experimental Methods for Microgravity Materials Science. Robert A. Schiffman. (Illus.). 288p. 1995. 20.00 (*0-87339-311-2*, 3112) Minerals Metals.

Seventh International Symposium on Individual & Small Community Sewage Systems: On-Site Wastewater. LC 94-73062. (Illus.). 600p. (Orig.). 1994. pap. 45.00 (*0-929355-58-X*, P1894) Am Soc Ag Eng.

Seventh International Symposium on Very High Energy Cosmic Ray Interactions: Proceedings of the Conference Held in Ann Arbor, MI, June 1992. Ed. by L. Jones. (AIP Conference Proceedings Ser.: No. 276). (Illus.). 748p. 1993. text ed. 145.00 (*1-56396-038-9*, AIP) Am Inst Physics.

Seventh Man. John Berger. 1981. pap. 6.95 (*0-906495-90-3*) Writers & Readers.

***Seventh Mesa.** Mary S. Rain. Date not set. reprint ed. pap. 12.95 (*1-57174-061-9*) Hampton Roads Pub Co.

Seventh Mesa: A Novel. Mary S. Rain. 272p. 1994. text ed. 19.95 (*1-57174-012-0*) Hampton Roads Pub Co.

Seventh Michigan Volunteer Infantry: The Gallant Men & Flag in the Civil War 1861 to 1865. David G. Townshend. 429p. 1994. 39.95 (*0-9639912-0-5*) Southeast Pubns.

Seventh Millennium. Jodie Whitehead. 24p. (Orig.). 1995. pap. write for info. (*1-56167-218-1*) Am Literary Pr.

Seventh Million: Israel Confronts the Holocaust. Tom Segev. Tr. by Haim Watzman. 1993. 27.50 (*0-8090-8563-1*) Hill & Wang.

Seventh Million: The Israelis & the Holocaust. Tom Segev. 594p. 1994. pap. 15.00 (*0-8090-1570-6*) Hill & Wang.

***Seventh Million: The Israelis & the Holocaust.** Tom Segev. 594p. 9.98 (*0-8317-7120-8*) Smithmark.

Seventh National Space Symposium Proceedings Report. Ed. by Diana L. Nitschke et al. (Illus.). 224p. 1991. pap. 50.00 (*0-9616962-5-7*) US Space Found.

Seventh National Wild Turkey Symposium. Ed. by James Dickson. LC 95-53675. 1996. write for info. (*0-8117-1105-6*) Stackpole.

Seventh Night. Amanda Stevens. (Shadows Ser.). 1993. mass mkt. 3.50 (*0-373-27014-3*, 5-27014-5) Silhouette.

Seventh of Joyce. Ed. by Bernard Benstock. LC 81-47775. 281p. (Orig.). reprint ed. pap. 80.10 (*0-7837-1745-8*, 2057279) Bks Demand.

***VII Olympiad, Antwerp 1920 & Chamonix 1924.** (Olympic Century Ser.). (Illus.). 1997. 21.95 (*1-888383-07-0*, Wrld Spt) Wld Sport Resch.

Seventh Omni Book of Science Fiction. Ed. by Ellen Datlow. 384p. 1989. mass mkt. 4.50 (*0-8217-2688-9*, Zebra Kensgtn) Kensgtn Pub Corp.

Seventh Plan Perspectives, India. Malcolm S. Adiseshiah. 1985. 26.00 (*0-8364-1449-7*, Pub. by Lancer II) S Asia.

Seventh Portal. Christine Loren. LC 95-91048. (Orig.). 1996. pap. 8.95 (*0-533-11832-8*) Vantage.

Seventh Ray: Revealer of the New Age. Alice A. Bailey. 1995. pap. 11.00 (*0-85330-141-7*) Lucis.

Seventh Sacrament, Vol 1. James Bradberry. 1995. mass mkt. 4.99 (*0-312-95636-3*) St Martin.

***Seventh Sanctuary.** Daniel Easterman. mass mkt. 6.99 (*0-06-105777-0*, Harp PBks) HarpC.

Seventh Scroll. Wilbur Smith. 1996. mass mkt. 6.99 (*0-312-95757-2*) Tor Bks.

7th Scroll. Wilbur Smith. 1995. pap. 24.95 (*0-7871-0438-8*, Dove Bks) Dove Audio.

Seventh Scroll: A Novel. Wilbur Smith. 496p. 1995. 24.95 (*0-312-11999-2*, Thomas Dunne Bks) St Martin.

Seventh Seal. Melvyn Bragg. (Illus.). 72p. (C). 1993. pap. 9.95 (*0-85170-391-7*, Pub. by British Film Inst UK) Ind U Pr.

Seventh Secret. Irving Wallace. 1986. pap. 4.95 (*0-451-14557-7*, Sig) NAL-Dutton.

Seventh Sense: A Collection of True Unsolved Mysteries from the Animal World. Diane Arrington. LC 96-13167. (Illus.). 224p. 1996. 14.95 (*0-87605-683-4*) Howell Bk.

Seventh Sentinel. Mary Kirchoff. (Defenders of Magic Ser.). 320p. (Orig.). 1995. pap. 5.99 (*0-7869-0117-9*) TSR Inc.

Seventh Sinner. Elizabeth Peters. 256p. 1989. mass mkt. 5.99 (*0-445-40778-6*, Mysterious Paperbk) Warner Bks.

Seventh Sister. Cindy Chang. LC 92-43179. (Legends of the World Ser.). (Illus.). 32p. (J). (gr. 2-5). 1994. lib. bdg. 13.95 (*0-8167-3411-9*) Troll Communs.

Seventh Sister. Cindy Chang. LC 92-43179. (Legends of the World Ser.). (Illus.). 32p. (J). (gr. 2-5). 1996. pap. 4.95 (*0-8167-3412-7*) Troll Communs.

Seventh Sleeper. William R. Dantz. 368p. 1992. mass mkt. 4.99 (*0-380-71032-3*) Avon.

Seventh Solitude: Metaphysical Homelessness in Kierkegaard, Dostoevsky, & Nietzsche. Ralph Harper. LC 65-11662. 163p. 1967. pap. 11.95 (*0-8018-0257-1*) Johns Hopkins.

Seventh Son. David Archambeau. LC 94-90220. 240p. (Orig.). 1995. pap. 8.00 (*1-56002-466-6*, Univ Edtns) Aegina Pr.

Seventh Son. Orson Scott Card. (Alvin Maker Ser.: No. 1). 256p. 1993. mass mkt. 4.99 (*0-8125-3305-4*) Tor Bks.

Seventh Son of a Seventh Son: The Life Story of a Healer. Finbarr Nolan & Martin Duffy. (Illus.). 192p. 1993. 19.95 (*1-85158-414-5*, Pub. by Mnstream UK) Trafalgar.

Seventh Spirit of the Sun: The Seventh Sojourn. Gary Bryant. Ed. by Charles Hilton & Lynn Laffie. 639p. (Orig.). 1994. pap. 13.95 (*0-9640780-9-0*) Futuristic Pub.

Seventh Stone. Nancy Freedman. 448p. 1993. pap. 5.99 (*0-451-17520-4*, Sig) NAL-Dutton.

Seventh Stream: The Emergence of Rocknroll in American Popular Music. Philip H. Ennis. LC 92-53859. (Illus.). 460p. 1992. pap. 24.00 (*0-8195-6257-2*, Wesleyan Univ Pr) U Pr of New Eng.

***Seventh Sunrise.** large type ed. Judy Cornwell. (Large Print Ser.). 560p. 1996. 25.99 (*0-7089-3586-9*) Ulverscroft.

Seventh Sword, 2: The Coming of Wisdom. Dave Duncan. 1988. mass mkt. 5.99 (*0-345-35292-0*, Del Rey) Ballantine.

Seventh Symposium by the 8 Winners of the Grants from Sandoz Foundation for Gerontological Research: Annual Meeting of the Japan Gerontological Society Osaka, October 20, 1995. Ed. by H. Orimo. (Journal: Gerontology Ser.: Vol. 42, Suppl. 11, 1996). (Illus.). iv, 78p. 1996. pap. 25.25 (*3-8055-6334-5*) S Karger.

Seventh Symposium on Salt: Proceedings of the Seventh International Symposium on Salt, Kyoto, Japan, 6-9 April, 1992, 2 vols., Set. Ed. by H. Kakihana et al. LC 93-20216. 1378p. 1993. 387.25 (*0-444-89143-9*) Elsevier.

Seventh Terminal Operations Conference. ICHCA-Cargo Systems Editors. (C). 1992. text ed. 350.00 (*0-907499-80-5*, Pub. by Cargo Systs UK) St Mut.

Seventh Trumpet. Mark Link. LC 78-53943. 1978. 14.50 (*0-89505-014-5*, 21004) Tabor Pub.

Seventh Trumpet: Teacher's Manual. Mark Link. 207p. (YA). (gr. 9-12). 1978. 21.95 (*0-89505-030-7*, 21005) Tabor Pub.

Seventh U. K. Computer & Telecommunications Performance Engineering Workshop, Edinburgh, 22-23 July 1991. Ed. by J. Hillston et al. (Workshops in Computing Ser.). (Illus.). 224p. 1992. 50.95 (*0-387-19733-8*) Spr-Verlag.

Seventh Victim. Susan Kelly. 288p. 1995. pap. 8.95 (*0-340-60995-8*, Pub. by H & S UK) Trafalgar.

Seventh Virginia Cavalry. Richard L. Armstrong. (Virginia Regimental Histories Ser.). (Illus.). 259p. 1993. 19.95 (*1-56190-040-0*) H E Howard.

Seventh Virginia Infantry. David F. Riggs. (Virginia Regimental Histories Ser.). (Illus.). 107p. 1982. 19.95 (*0-930919-02-5*) H E Howard.

Seventh Walnut. Genevieve Petit. LC 92-10588. (J). 1992. 13.95 (*0-922984-10-7*) Wellington IL.

***Seventh West Coast Conference on Formal Linguistics: Proceedings.** 389p. 1988. pap. text ed. 18.95 (*0-937073-40-7*) Cambridge U Pr.

Seventh Wife. Andrei Moscovit, pseud. Tr. by Anthony Olcott from RUS. 468p. 1994. 23.00 (*1-880909-16-2*) Baskerville.

Seventh Workshop on Grand Unification - ICOBAN '86: Proceedings of Workshop, Toyama , Japan, April 16-18, 1986. Ed. by J. Arafune. 527p. 1987. pap. 49.00 (*9971-5-0131-7*); text ed. 131.00 (*9971-5-0130-9*) World Scientific Pub.

Seventh Workshop on Parallel & Distributed Simulation (PADS '93) Ed. by Rajive Bagrodia & David Jefferson. 168p. 1993. pap. 60.00 (*1-56555-055-2*, PADS-93) Soc Computer Sim.

Seventh World Congress on Animal, Plant & Microbial Toxins: Proceedings of the International Symposium, 7th, Brisbane, Australia, July 11-16, 1982. International Symposium on Animal, Plant & Microbial Toxins Staff & R. Endean. (Illus.). 544p. 1983. pap. 145.00 (*0-08-029803-6*, Pergamon Pr) Elsevier.

***70's & 80's Pop Music.** Ed. by Carol Cuellar. (Warner Brothers Presents Ser.). 372p. (Orig.). 1995. pap. text ed. 18.95 (*0-7692-0057-5*, MF9502) Warner Brothers.

70s Pop Hits. (Easy Piano Ser.). 12.95 (*0-7935-4895-0*, 00310075) H Leonard.

Seventies Rock Score. (Illus.). 80p. 1990. pap. 14.95 (*0-8256-1304-3*, AM79567) Music Sales.

Seventieth Week of Daniel 9:27 As a Literary Key for Understanding the Structure of the Apocalypse of John. John A. McLean. LC 95-24323. (Biblical Press Ser.: Vol. 38). 332p. 1996. text ed. 99.95 (*0-7734-2434-2*, Mellen Biblical Pr) E Mellen.

70 Anos de Milagros (70 Years of Miracles) Richard Harvey. (SPA.). mass mkt. 3.99 (*0-88965-072-1*, Pub. by Horizon Books CN) Chr Pubns.

Seventy Birth Control Clinics: A Survey & Analysis Including the General Effects of Control on Size & Quality of Population. Caroline H. Robinson. LC 71-169398. (Family in America Ser.). 380p. 1972. reprint ed. 18.95 (*0-405-03875-5*) Ayer.

Seventy Classic Quilting Patterns: Ready-to-Use Designs & Instructions. Gwen Marston & Joe Cunningham. (Illus.). 96p. (Orig.). 1987. pap. 4.95 (*0-486-25474-7*) Dover.

Seventy Common Cacti of the Southwest. Pierre C. Fisher. Ed. by T. J. Priehs & Carolyn Dodson. LC 89-61677. (Illus.). 84p. (Orig.). 1989. 6.95 (*0-911408-82-7*) SW Pks Mnmts.

78 Great, Fun & Challenging Bible Word Searches. 208p. 1993. pap. 4.99 (*0-8423-1147-5*) Tyndale.

Seventy-Eight Infantry Division History. Seventy-Eight Infantry Division Association Staff. LC 87-71200. 128p. 1987. 48.00 (*0-938021-15-X*) Turner Pub KY.

Seventy-Eight's Refund Table: One to One Hundred-Eighty Months, Forty-Five Days to First Payment. 32p. 1972. pap. 8.00 (*0-87600-838-4*) Finan Pub.

Seventy-Eight's Refund Table: One to One Hundred-Eighty Months, Sixty Days to First Payment. Financial Publishing Company Staff. 32p. 1972. pap. 8.00 (*0-87600-839-2*) Finan Pub.

Seventy-Eight's Refund Table: One to One Hundred-Eighty Months, Thirty Days to First Payment. Financial Publishing Company Staff. 32p. 1972. pap. 8.00 (*0-87600-837-6*) Finan Pub.

70 Essential TCM Formulas for Beginners. Bob Flaws. 265p. (Orig.). 1994. pap. 21.95 (*0-936185-59-7*) Blue Poppy Pr.

Seventy Facets: A Commentary on the Torah from the Pages of the Jerusalem Report. Ed. by Gershom Gorenberg. LC 96-14581. 318p. 1996. 30.00 (*1-56821-904-0*) Aronson.

Seventy-Fifth Anniversary Book - From Spark to Space. 1989. 10.00 (*0-87259-259-6*) Am Radio.

75th Anniversary of the Manassas National Jubilee of Peace. Ed. by Douglas K. Harvey. 21p. 1986. pap. 1.00 (*1-886826-02-1*) Manassas Mus.

75th Art Directors Annual. Rotovision S. A. Staff. 1996. 70.00 (*0-8230-6550-2*) Watsn-Guptill.

Seventy-Fifth Farm Show: A History of Pennsylvania's Annual Agricultural Exposition. Dan Cupper. (Illus.). 89p. (Orig.). 1991. pap. 7.95 (*0-89271-048-9*) Pa Hist & Mus.

Seventy-Fifth Jubilee Conference on the Helium -4: Proceedings of the Jubilee Conference, St. Andrew, Scotland, Aug. 1-5, 1983. J. G. Armitage. 232p. 1984. 41.00 (*9971-966-23-9*) World Scientific Pub.

Seventy-First Came to Gunskirchen Lager. U. S. Army, Seventy First Infantry Division Staff. LC 79-51047. (Witness to the Holocaust Ser.: No. 1). (Illus.). 28p. 1983. reprint ed. pap. 1.50 (*0-89937-036-5*) Witness Holocaust.

Seventy-Five Activities for Celebrating Seventy-Five Years of Votes for Women: A Resource Guide. Jocelyn Riley. 150p. 1995. 20.00 (*1-877933-55-4*) Her Own Words.

Seventy-Five Bible Questions Your Instructors Pray You Won't Ask. 2nd ed. Gary North. LC 96-28357. 238p. (Orig.). (C). 1996. pap. 5.95 (*0-930462-03-3*) Inst Christian.

***75 Cage-Rattling Questions to Change the Way You Work: Shake-Em-Up Questions to Open Meetings, Ignite Discussion & Spark Creativity.** Dick Whitney & Melissa Giovagnoli. LC 97-12468. 300p. 1997. pap. text ed. 14.95 (*0-07-070019-2*) McGraw.

Seventy-Five Creative Ways to Publish Students' Writing. Cherlyn Sunflower. 208p. 1993. pap. 19.95 (*0-590-49270-5*) Scholastic Inc.

Seventy-Five Fun Things to Make & Do by Yourself. Karen G. Ruelle. (Illus.). 80p. (J). (gr. 3-7). 1995. pap. 6.95 (*0-8069-0332-5*) Sterling.

75 Great Hikes. Philip Ferranti et al. 192p. 1995. pap. text ed. 14.95 (*0-7872-1203-2*) Kendall-Hunt.

75 Great Small Town Getaways. Midwest Living Magazine Staff. 1996. spiral bd., pap. 14.95 (*0-696-20043-0*) Meredith Bks.

75 Hikes in California's Lassen Park & Mount Shasta Regions. John R. Soares. 1996. pap. text ed. 14.95 (*0-89886-466-6*) Mountaineers.

75 Hikes in New Mexico. Craig Martin. 1995. pap. 12.95 (*0-89886-441-0*) Mountaineers.

Seventy-Five Life Lines. James Broughton. 48p. 1988. 10.00 (*0-912330-64-3*) Jargon Soc.

Seventy-Five Life Lines. deluxe ed. James Broughton. 48p. 1988. 30.00 (*0-912330-65-1*) Jargon Soc.

Seventy Five Lightbulb Jokes. Jeffrey Armstrong. (Illus.). 152p. (Orig.). 1993. pap. text ed. 4.50 (*1-883532-02-7*) Carmel Bay.

75 Luxury Bath Plans. (Illus.). (Orig.). 1993. pap. 20.00 (*0-922070-02-4*, COLLECTION A1) M Tecton Pub.

Seventy-Five Melodious & Progressive Studies Bk. 1: Violin Opus 36. J. F. Mazas. 44p. 1986. pap. 5.95 (*0-7935-3774-6*) H Leonard.

Seventy-Five Melodious & Progressive Studies Bk. 3: Violin Opus 36. J. F. Mazas. 52p. 1986. pap. 7.95 (*0-7935-3683-9*) H Leonard.

Seventy-Five Picture Prompts for Young Writers. Rick Brown. 88p. 1993. pap. 10.95 (*0-590-49408-2*) Scholastic Inc.

Seventy-Five Readings: An Anthology. 4th ed. LC 92-26977. 1993. pap. text ed. write for info. (*0-07-046734-X*) McGraw.

75 Readings: An Anthology. 6th ed. Santi V. Buscemi & Charlotte Smith. LC 96-26255. 1996. pap. text ed. write for info. (*0-07-052157-3*) McGraw.

Seventy Five Readings Plus. 2nd ed. Santi V. Buscemi & Charlotte Smith. LC 93-29713. 1993. pap. text ed. write for info. (*0-07-009352-0*) McGraw.

Seventy-Five Readings Plus. 3rd ed. Ed. by Santi V. Buscemi et al. LC 95-19930. (C). 1996. pap. text ed. write for info. (*0-07-009482-9*) McGraw.

***75 Readings Plus.** 4th ed. Santi V. Buscemi & Charlotte Smith. LC 97-21489. 1997. write for info. (*0-07-009488-8*) McGraw.

Seventy-Five Receipts for Pastry, Cakes & Sweetmeats. Eliza Leslie. 88p. 1988. reprint ed. pap. 7.95 (*1-55709-116-1*) Applewood.

Seventy-Five Seasons: The Complete Story of the National Football League, 1920-1995. Ed. by Will McDonough et al. LC 94-3580. 1994. 39.95 (*1-57036-056-1*) Turner Pub GA.

Seventy-Five Short Masterpieces. Roger Goodman. 304p. 1985. mass mkt. 5.50 (*0-553-25141-4*) Bantam.

75 Ways to End Reading. Mary Leonhardt. 1996. pap. write for info. (*0-517-88419-4*) Random.

75 Ways to Liven up Your Training. Martin Orridge. LC 96-8092. (Illus.). 250p. 1996. 59.95 (*0-566-07774-4*, Pub. by Gower UK) Ashgate Pub Co.

S

An Asterisk (*) at the beginning of an entry indicates that the title is appearing in BIP for the first time.

Seventy-Five Windows. F. Sims Pounds. LC 78-56418. 120p. 1978. 9.00 (0-86690-143-4, P1377-014) Am Fed Astrologers.

Seventy-Five Works, Seventy-Five Years: Collecting the Art of California. LC 93-810. 1993. 75.00 (0-940872-18-8); pap. 29.95 (0-940872-19-6) Laguna Beach.

Seventy-Five Year History of the Texas Section of the Mathematical Association of America 1920-1995. R. G. Dean. xii, 394p. 1995. 30.00 (0-9645251-0-0) TSMAA.

Seventy-Five Years, an Informal History of Shaker Heights. Ed. by David G. Molyneaux & Sue Sackman. (Illus.). (Orig.). 1987. pap. text ed. 8.50 (0-9619188-0-2) Shaker Hgts Pub Lib.

Seventy-Five Years at Oakland Hills: A Jubilee Celebration. Bryon A. Perry. Ed. by Shelby Cook. (Illus.). 120p. 1991. 55.00 (0-9629299-0-5) B A Perry & Assocs.

Seventy-Five Years, Central Park Baptist Church, Birmingham, Alabama, 1910-1985. Ed. by F. Wilbur Helmbold. (Illus.). (Orig.). 1985. 25.00 (0-87121-447-4) Banner Pr AL.

Seventy-Five Years in California: Recollections & Remarks by One Who Visited These Shores in 1831, & Again in 1833 & Except When Absent on Business Was a Resident from 1838 until 1909. William H. Davis. (American Biography Ser.). 345p. 1991. reprint ed. lib. bdg. 79.00 (0-7812-8104-0) Rprt Serv.

Seventy-Five Years in Old Virginia. John H. Claiborne. (Illus.). 360p. (Orig.). 1994. pap. text ed. 24.00 (0-7884-0010-X) Heritage Bk.

Seventy-Five Years of a Great Idea. Hilda R. Watrous. LC 94-62024. (Illus.). (Orig.). 1995. pap. 24.95 (0-938588-13-3) LWV NYS.

***75 Years of All-Time Favorites.** Better Homes & Gardens Editors. (Illus.). 320p. 1997. 29.95 (0-696-20633-1) Meredith Bks.

75 Years of Chevrolet. George H. Dammann. LC 86-72731. (Crestline Ser.). (Illus.). 350p. 1992. 39.95 (0-87938-692-4, Crestline Pub) Motorbooks Intl.

Seventy-Five Years of Children Book Week Posters. Intro. by Leonard S. Marcus. (Illus.). (J). (ps up). 1994. 30.00 (0-679-85106-2) Knopf Bks Yng Read.

Seventy-Five Years of Concerns for Children: History of the Association for Childhood Education International, 1892-1967. Winifred E. Bain. Ed. by Margaret Rasmussen. LC 67-20740. (Illus.). 96p. reprint ed. pap. 27.40 (0-7837-0548-4, 2040881) Bks Demand.

Seventy-Five Years of Geography at the University of Cincinnati. Bruce Ryan. 36p. (Orig.). 1983. pap. 4.95 (0-9611212-0-3) Univ of Cincinnati.

Seventy-Five Years of Hirayama Asteroid Families No. 63: The Role of Collisions in the Solar System History. Ed. by Yoshihide Kozai et al. 303p. 1994. 28.00 (0-937707-82-1) Astron Soc Pacific.

Seventy-Five Years of I. F. M. A., 1917-1992: The Nondenominational Missions Movement. Edwin L. Frizen, Jr. LC 92-72008. (Illus.). 336p. (Orig.). 1992. pap. text ed. 15.95 (0-87808-235-2, WCL235-2) William Carey Lib.

Seventy-Five Years of Progress: History of the Huntsville Rotary Club. Bill Easterling. Ed. by Michael R. Kaylor. (Illus.). 150p. 1992. 19.95 (0-916039-05-6) Kaylor & Kaylor.

Seventy-Five Years of Progress: Prospects for School Mathematics. Ed. by Iris M. Carl. LC 95-10255. (Illus.). 340p. 1995. 20.00 (0-87353-418-2) NCTM.

Seventy-Five Years of Progress in Oil Field Science & Technology: A Symposium to Mark the 75th Anniversary of the Foundation of the Oil Technology Course at the Royal School of Mines, Imperial College of Science, Technology & Medicine, 12 July 1988. Ed. by M. Ala et al. (Illus.). 215p. (C). 1991. text ed. 105.00 (90-6191-108-7, Pub. by A A Balkema NE) Ashgate Pub Co.

75 Years of Radon Transform. Ed. by Simon Gindikin & Peter Michor. (Series in Mathematical Physics). (C). 1994. text ed. 42.00 (1-57146-008-X) Intl Pr Boston.

Seventy-Five Years of Service: Cooperative Extension in Iowa. Dorothy Schwieder. LC 93-14941. (Illus.). 284p. (C). 1993. text ed. 36.95 (0-8138-0388-8) Iowa St U Pr.

75 Years of the ASME Materials Division. Ed. by Vijay K. Stokes. (1995 ASME International Mechanical Engineering Congress & Exposition Ser.: MD-Vol. 70). 80p. 1995. 20.00 (0-7918-1760-1, H01042) ASME.

Seventy-Five Years of Western Electric Tube Manufacturing: A Log Book History of over 750 W.E. Tubes Including Dates of Manufacture. Bernard Magers. 148p. 1992. pap. 16.95 (0-9632440-1-9) Antique Elect.

74 More Bible Crosswords. 208p. 1991. mass mkt. 4.99 (0-8423-0488-6) Tyndale.

Seventy Generations of Selection for Oil & Protein in Maize. Ed. by J. W. Dudley. 212p. 1974. 10.00 (0-89118-502-X) Crop Sci Soc Am.

70 Great Christians. G. Hanks. 16.99 (1-871676-80-0, Pub. by Christian Focus UK) Spring Arbor Dist.

***Seventy Instructions on How to Make Certain Drawings.** Irene Seigel. 8.50 (0-614-18208-5) Visual Studies.

Seventy Miles from a Lemon. Emma Yates. (American Autobiography Ser.). 234p. 1995. reprint ed. lib. bdg. 79.00 (0-7812-8668-9) Rprt Serv.

Seventy Negro Spirituals, for High Voice. William A. Fisher. LC 72-1637. reprint ed. 42.50 (0-404-09921-1) AMS Pr.

Seventy-Nine Park Avenue. Harold Robbins. sp. 1993. pap. 6.99 (0-671-87496-9) PB.

79 Park Avenue. Harold Robbins. 1995. reprint ed. lib. bdg. 29.95 (1-56849-643-5) Buccaneer Bks.

Seventy Ninety-One: A Tale of San Domingo. E. W. Gilliam. LC 70-37591. (Black Heritage Library Collection). 1977. reprint ed. 26.95 (0-8369-8967-8) Ayer.

Seventy on the Seventies: A Decade's History in Verse. Ed. by Robert McGovern & Richard Snyder. 100p. 1981. pap. 7.00 (0-912592-24-9) Ashland Poetry.

Seventy Percent Factor: Accumulating Savings Through Residential Real Estate Buying. 2nd ed. C. Mark Leaphart & J. Kirk Leaphart. (Forms Library). 62p. (Orig.). 1994. pap. write for info. (0-9644909-1-9) VCI Invest.

Seventy Percent Factor: Accumulating Savings Through Residential Real Estate Buying. 2nd ed. J. Kirk Leaphart, Jr. & C. Mark Leaphart. 233p. (Orig.). 1994. pap. write for info. (0-9644909-0-0) VCI Invest.

Seventy Prophetic Weeks of Daniel. Noah W. Hutchings. 24p. (Orig.). 1994. pap. 2.50 (1-879366-56-8) Hearthstone OK.

Seventy Scenes of Halloween. J. Jones. 1990. pap. 5.95 (0-88145-076-6) Broadway Play.

***Seventy Scottish Songs.** Helen Hopekirk. pap. 11.95 (0-486-27029-7) Dover.

***Seventy-Seven Branches of Faith.** Al-Imam Bayhaqi. 66p. 1996. pap. 7.50 (0-614-21344-4, 1122) Kazi Pubns.

Seventy-Seven Furniture Projects You Can Build. Family Handyman Magazine Editors. 1980. 21.95 (0-8306-9921-X, 1122); pap. 14.95 (0-8306-1122-3) McGraw-Hill Prof.

***77 Habits of Highly Ineffective Christians.** Chris Fabry. LC 96-50475. 96p. 1997. 10.99 (0-8308-1963-0, 1963) InterVarsity.

Seventy-Seven Habits of Highly Ineffective People. Jim Becker et al. LC 93-50210. (Illus.). 96p. 1994. pap. 6.95 (0-8362-1752-7) Andrews & McMeel.

Seventy-Seven Keys to the Civilization of Japan. Intro. by Tadao Umesao. (Illus.). 315p. 1986. reprint ed. pap. 9.95 (0-89346-267-5) Heian Intl.

Seventy-Seven Neo-Latin Letters: An Anthology. Ed. by F. F. Blok. (Illus.). ix, 256p. 1985. 50.00 (90-6088-091-9, Pub. by Boumas Boekhuis NE) Benjamins North Am.

77 No Talent, No Experience, & (Almost) No Cost Businesses You Can Start Today! Kelly Reno. 1995. pap. 12.95 (0-7615-0246-7) Prima Pub.

Seventy-Seven One-Weekend Woodworking Projects. Percy W. Blandford. (Illus.). 304p. (Orig.). 1987. pap. 18.95 (0-8306-2774-X) McGraw-Hill Prof.

Seventy Seven Poems. R. Rabindranath Menon. (Writers Workshop Redbird Ser.). 78p. 1975. 14.00 (0-88253-630-3); pap. text ed. 4.80 (0-88253-629-X) Ind-US Inc.

77th St. Requiem: A Maggie MacGowan Mystery. Wendy Hornsby. 384p. 1996. pap. 5.99 (0-451-40675-3, Sig) NAL-Dutton.

Seventy-Seven Uses for an Ex. Ed. by Garner. (Illus.). 80p. (Orig.). 1993. pap. 4.95 (0-939515-28-8) Newport Hse.

77 Variations on Suzuki Melodies: Technique Builders for Violin. William Starr. 80p. 1994. pap. text ed. 12.95 (0-87487-617-6) Summy-Birchard.

77 Ways to Beat Cold. Charles B. Inlander. 128p. 1996. mass mkt. 4.99 (0-553-57420-5) Bantam.

Seventy-Seven Ways to Energize Your Sunday School Class. Judy G. Smith. 88p. (Orig.). 1992. pap. 11.95 (0-687-38114-2) Abingdon.

77th Street Requiem: A Maggie MacGowen Mystery. Wendy Hornsby. LC 95-11475. 272p. 1995. pap. 21.95 (0-525-93998-9, Dutton) NAL-Dutton.

77th Street Requiem: A Maggie MacGowen Mystery. large type ed. Wendy Hornsby. LC 95-11475. (Large Print Bks.). 1996. pap. 20.95 (1-56895-334-8) Wheeler Pub.

Seventy Six: One World & the Cantos of Ezra Pound. Forrest Read. LC 80-15892. 488p. reprint ed. pap. 139.10 (0-8357-4406-X, 2037226) Bks Demand.

Seventy-Six Disney Songs for the Harp. Sylvia Woods. (Illus.). (Orig.). 1994. pap. 28.95 (0-936661-17-8) Woods Mus Bks.

Seventy-Six Hours: The Invasion of Tarawa. Eric Hammel & John E. Lane. (Illus.). 288p. 1985. 25.00 (0-935553-00-2) Pacifica Pr.

Seventy-Six Most Common Grammar Errors. Communication Briefings Editors. 48p. (Orig.). 1992. pap. 12.50 (1-878604-08-2) Comn Pubns & Resources.

76 Sermons on the Old Testament of the Bible, by Jesus. Daniel G. Samuels. 202p. 1989. pap. 16.00 (1-887621-11-3) Found Ch Divine Truth.

Seventy-Six United Statesiana: Seventy-Six Works of American Scholarship Relating to America as Published During Two Centuries from the Revolutionary Era of the United States Through the Nation's Bicentennial Year, 1776-1976. Ed. by Edward C. Lathem. LC 76-151831. 170p. reprint ed. pap. 48.50 (0-8357-2718-1, 2039832) Bks Demand.

Seventy-Six Ways to Get Organized for Christmas. Bonnie R. McCullough. 1992. mass mkt. 3.99 (0-312-92940-4) St Martin.

76th Infantry Division. Turner Publishing Company Staff. LC 91-67156. 128p. 1992. 48.00 (1-56311-048-2) Turner Pub KY.

Seventy Steps to Vocabulary Power. 2nd rev. ed. Keith D. Holmes. (Illus.). 100p. (Orig.). (C). 1983. reprint ed. boxed 4.95 (0-9608250-1-0) Educ Serv Pub.

Seventy Steps Toward Wisdom. 2nd ed. Sigmund Lowe. 95p. 1981. pap. 3.50 (0-87516-050-6) DeVorss.

Seventy Stories about Boston University, 1923-1993: A Memoir. George K. Makechnie. LC 93-4005. 1993. write for info. (0-87270-104-2, Boston University) U Pr of Amer.

Seventy-Three North. Dudley Pope. LC 88-61812. (Illus.). 320p. 1988. 31.95 (0-87021-660-0) Naval Inst Pr.

73 Poems. Kenneth Goldsmith. 96p. 1994. pap. 50.00 (0-9638489-0-9) Permanent NY.

Seventy Times Seven. John Ilich. (Illus.). 96p. 1983. pap. 7.95 (0-935650-02-4) Bengal Pr.

Seventy Times Seven. Sandi Z. Rebert. 180p. (Orig.). 1982. pap. 4.95 (0-89084-156-X, 018176) Bob Jones Univ Pr.

72 Days at the Baccarat Table. Erick St. Germain. 312p. (Orig.). 1995. pap. 24.95 (0-9640595-1-7) Zumma Pubng.

Seventy-Two Essays: A Selection. Walter L. Murdoch. LC 76-90665. (Essay Index Reprint Ser.). 1977. reprint ed. 23.95 (0-8369-1813-4) Ayer.

Seventy-Two Hour Emergency Preparedness Checklist: Prepare Every Needful Thing. 2nd rev. ed. Barry G. Crockett & Lynette B. Crockett. LC 83-73117. (Illus.). 64p. 1990. pap. 10.95 (0-915131-06-4) Crockett Pub Co.

Seventy Two Hours in Hell. Raymond P. Pope. 176p. (Orig.). 1989. pap. 10.00 (0-944765-01-7) Agape Bks.

Seventy-Two Hours to Success: The Definitive Workbook for Personal Fulfillment. Wolfgang Aulenbacher. 384p. (Orig.). 1992. pap. 24.95 (1-881845-11-7) Blue Phoenix Bks.

***72 Market St. Dishes It Out! A Collection of Recipes & Portraits from a Classic Venice Restaurant.** Roland Gibert & Robert Lia. LC 97-17386. 1998. write for info. (0-9642359-2-7) Wave Pubng.

Seventy-Two Stories of God, Good, & Goods. Yogi Bhajan. Ed. by Tej K. Khalsa. (Illus.). 241p. (Orig.). (YA). (gr. 10). 1989. pap. 9.95 (0-685-29452-8) Harimander Pub.

Seventy-Two Versetl Sammt Twelve Toccaten see Monuments of Music & Music Literature in Facsimile: Series One

Seventy Weeks & the Great Tribulation. Philip Mauro. 285p. 1975. pap. 11.99 (0-87377-058-7) GAM Pubns.

Seventy Weeks, Leviticus, & the Nature of Prophecy, 7 vols., Set. Ed. by Frank B. Holbrook. (Daniel & Revelation Committee Ser.: Vol. 3). 394p. (Orig.). 1986. Vol. 3. pap. 12.95 (0-925675-02-4) BRI DC.

Seventy Weeks of Daniel: An Exposition of Daniel 9: 24-27. Marjorie B. Matheny & James F. Matheny. 133p. (Orig.). 1990. pap. 6.95 (0-939422-03-4) Jay & Assocs.

***70x7 Forgiveness to the Extreme.** 1994. write for info. (1-890553-00-X, CV 600 VSN) Double Vision.

Seventy-Year Ebb & Flow of Chinese Library & Information Services: May 4, 1919 to the Late 1980s. John Barclay. LC 94-27784. 351p. 1995. 42.50 (0-8108-2713-1) Scarecrow.

Seventy Years in Archaeology. William M. Petrie. LC 72-88921. 307p. 1969. reprint ed. text ed. 38.50 (0-8371-2241-4, PESA, Greenwood Pr) Greenwood.

Seventy Years in Organic Chemistry. Tetsuo Nozoe. Ed. by Jeffrey I. Seeman. LC 90-876. (Profiles, Pathways, & Dreams Ser.). (Illus.). 267p. 1990. 34.95 (0-8412-1769-6) Am Chemical.

Seventy Years of It: An Autobiography. Edward A. Ross. Ed. by Walter P. Metzger. LC 76-55183. (Academic Profession Ser.). (Illus.). 1977. reprint ed. lib. bdg. 29.95 (0-405-10010-8) Ayer.

Seventy Years of Life & Labor: An Autobiography by Samuel Gompers. abr. ed. Intro. by Nick Salvatore. LC 84-10765. (Illus.). 280p. 1984. reprint ed. pap. 13.95 (0-87546-109-3, ILR Press) Cornell U Pr.

Seventy Years of Miami Architecture: Commercial & Institutional Architecture in Dade County. Aristides J. Millas. LC 91-70266. (Illus.). 96p. (Orig.). 1991. pap. 14.95 (1-880511-01-0) Bass Museum.

Seventy Years of Miracles. Richard Harvey. 150p. 1993. reprint ed. mass mkt. 4.99 (0-88965-101-9, Pub. by Horizon Books CN) Chr Pubns.

***70 Years of Radio Tubes & Valves: A Guide for Electronic Engineers, Historians & Collectors.** 2nd rev. ed. John W. Stokes. LC 97-13766. (Illus.). 266p. 1997. pap. 29.95 (1-886606-11-0) Sonoran Pub.

Seventy Years on Hope Street: A History of the Church of the Open Door 1915-1985. G. Michael Cocoris. (Illus.). 151p. 1985. 195.95 (0-935729-30-5); text ed. 25.00 (0-935729-09-7) Church Open Door.

***Seventy Years on the Frontier: Alexander Majors' Memoirs of a Lifetime on the Border.** Alexander Majors. Ed. by Prentiss Ingraham. LC 88-31597. (Illus.). 325p. 1989. reprint ed. pap. 92.70 (0-608-02731-6, 2063396) Bks Demand.

Seventy Years on the Frontier: Alexander Majors' Memoirs of a Lifetime on the Border. Alexander Majors. (American Biography Ser.). 325p. 1991. reprint ed. lib. bdg. 79.00 (0-7812-8263-2) Rprt Serv.

***Seventy Years Young: Memories of Elizabeth, Countess of Fingall.** Pamela Hinkson. 454p. 1995. pap. 21.00 (0-946640-74-2, Pub. by Lilliput Pr Ltd IE) Irish Bks Media.

Seventy's Course in Theology. B. H. Roberts. 1000p. (C). 1995. 49.95 (0-910523-16-9) Grandin Bk Co.

Several Complex Variables. Ed. by J. J. Kohn et al. 280p. 1984. 54.00 (0-8176-3189-5) Birkhauser.

Several Complex Variables. Raghavan Narasimhan. LC 75-166949. (Chicago Lectures in Mathematics). 184p. (Orig.). 1974. pap. text ed. 22.00 (0-226-56817-2) U Ch Pr.

Several Complex Variables: Proceedings, 2 pts., Pt. 1. Ed. by R. O. Wells. LC 77-23168. (Proceedings of Symposia in Pure Mathematics Ser.: Vol. 30). 390p. 1977. reprint ed. 58.00 (0-8218-0249-6, PSPUM/30.1) Am Math.

Several Complex Variables: Proceedings, 2 pts., Pt. 2. Ed. by R. O. Wells. LC 77-23168. (Proceedings of Symposia in Pure Mathematics Ser.: Vol. 30). 328p. 1977. reprint ed. 58.00 (0-8218-0250-X, PSPUM/30.2) Am Math.

Several Complex Variables: Proceedings, 2 pts., Set. Ed. by R. O. Wells. LC 77-23168. (Proceedings of Symposia in Pure Mathematics Ser.: Vol. 30). 718p. 1977. reprint ed. 101.00 (0-8218-1430-3, PSPUM/30) Am Math.

Several Complex Variables: Proceedings of the Mittag-Leffler Institute, 1987-1988. Ed. by John E. Fornaess. 452p. (Orig.). 1990. pap. text ed. 49.50 (0-691-08579-X) Princeton U Pr.

***Several Complex Variables & Banach Algebras.** 3rd ed. Herbert Alexander & John Wermer. LC 97-16661. (Graduate Texts in Mathematics Ser.). 1997. write for info. (0-387-98253-1) Spr-Verlag.

Several Complex Variables & Complex Geometry, Pt. I. Steven G. Krantz et al. (Proceedings of Symposia in Pure Mathematics Ser.: Vol. 52.1). 262p. 1991. 60.00 (0-8218-1489-3, PSPUM/52.1) Am Math.

Several Complex Variables & Complex Geometry, Pt. II. Steven G. Krantz et al. (Proceedings of Symposia in Pure Mathematics Ser.: Vol. 52.2). 625p. 1991. 114.00 (0-8218-1490-7, PSPUM/52.2) Am Math.

Several Complex Variables & Complex Geometry, Pt. III. Steven C. Krantz et al. (Proceedings of Symposia in Pure Mathematics Ser.: Vol. 52.3). 368p. 1991. 75.00 (0-8218-1491-5, PSPUM/52.3) Am Math.

Several Complex Variables & Complex Geometry, 3 pts., Set. Steven G. Krantz et al. LC 91-11227. (Proceedings of Symposia in Pure Mathematics Ser.: Vol. 52). 1255p. 1991. 228.00 (0-8218-1488-5, PSPUM/52) Am Math.

Several Complex Variables & Complex Manifolds, Pt. II. Margaret J. Field. LC 81-21590. (London Mathematical Society Lecture Note Ser.: No. 66). 220p. 1982. pap. text ed. 42.95 (0-521-28888-6) Cambridge U Pr.

Several Complex Variables & the Geometry of Real Hypersurfaces. John P. D'Angelo. 288p. 1993. 61.95 (0-8493-8272-6, QA331) CRC Pr.

Several Complex Variables I. Ed. by A. G. Vitushkin. (Encyclopedia of Mathematical Sciences Ser.: Vol. 7). 265p. 1989. 118.95 (0-387-17004-9) Spr-Verlag.

Several Complex Variables III. Ed. by G. M. Khenkin. (Encyclopedia of Mathematical Sciences Ser.: Vol. 9). vii, 261p. 1989. 118.95 (0-387-17005-7) Spr-Verlag.

Several Complex Variables in China. Ed. by Chung-Chun Yang & Sheng Gong. LC 92-44828. (Contemporary Mathematics Ser.: Vol. 142). 173p. 1993. 36.00 (0-8218-5164-0, CONM/142) Am Math.

Several Complex Variables, IV. Ed. by S. G. Gindikin & G. M. Khenkin. (Encyclopedia of Mathematical Sciences Ser.: Vol. 10). 264p. 1989. 118.95 (0-387-18174-1) Spr-Verlag.

Several Complex Variables VI: Complex Manifolds, a Volume in Honour of Reinhold Remmert. Ed. by R. V. Gamkrelidze et al. (Encyclopedia of Mathematical Sciences Ser.: Vol. 69). (Illus.). x, 310p. 1996. 109.50 (0-387-52788-5) Spr-Verlag.

Several Complex Variables VII: Sheaf-Theoretical Methods in Complex Analysis. Ed. by H. Grauert et al. LC 93-32959. (Encyclopedia of Mathematical Sciences Ser.: Vol. 74). (Illus.). 400p. 1994. 118.95 (0-387-56259-1) Spr-Verlag.

Several Complex Variables 2: Function Theory in Classical Domains: Complex Potential Theory. Ed. by G. M. Khenkin & A. G. Vitushkin. LC 92-45735. (Encyclopedia of Mathematical Sciences Ser.: Vol. 8). 1994. 118.95 (0-387-18175-X) Spr-Verlag.

Several Complex Variables 5: Complex Analysis in Partial Differential Equations & Mathematical Physics. Ed. by G. M. Khenkin. LC 93-4830. (Encyclopedia of Mathematical Sciences Ser.: Vol. 54). 1993. 118.95 (0-387-54451-8) Spr-Verlag.

***Several Lives of Chester Himes.** Edward Margolies & Michael Fabre. 1997. 28.00 (0-87805-908-3) U Pr of Miss.

Several More Lives to Live: Thoreau's Political Reputation in America. Michael Meyer. LC 76-56622. (Contributions in American Studies: No. 29). 216p. 1977. text ed. 49.95 (0-8371-9477-6, MES/, Greenwood Pr) Greenwood.

Several Papers Relating to Money, Interest & Trade, Etc. John Locke. LC 87-17243. (Reprints of Economic Classics Ser.). 328p. 1989. reprint ed. 57.50 (0-678-00334-3) Kelley.

Several Worlds of Pearl S. Buck: Essays Presented at a Centennial Symposium, Randolph-Macon Woman's College, March 26-28, 1992. Ed. by Elizabeth J. Lipscomb et al. LC 93-43752. (Contributions in Women's Studies: No. 144). 184p. 1994. text ed. 55.00 (0-313-29152-7, Greenwood Pr) Greenwood.

Severance: A Comprehensive Survey of Canadian Severance Practices. Right Associates Staff. 121p. (Orig.). pap. 250.00 (0-9628438-2-2) Right Assocs.

Severance Benefits & Outplacement Services. (PPF Survey Ser.: No. 143). 46p. 1986. 30.00 (0-87179-974-X) BNA Books.

Severance Genealogy. David C. Dewsnap. (Illus.). 516p. (Orig.). 1995. pap. 36.00 (0-7884-0357-5, D187) Heritage Bk.

Severance Pay. Avery Cloud. 458p. (Orig.). 1996. mass mkt. 6.99 (1-55197-063-5, Pub. by Comnwlth Pub CN) Partners Pubs Grp.

Severans: The Changed Roman Empire. Michael Grant. LC 95-45816. 224p. 1996. 21.00 (0-415-12772-6) Routledge.

Severe. Anthony Lombardy. LC 94-18349. (Illus.). 67p. 1995. 20.00 (0-9624631-7-5) Bennett & Kitchel.

Severe & Unusual Weather. 2nd ed. Joe R. Eagleman. (Illus.). 394p. (C). 1990. pap. text ed. 41.95 (1-877696-03-X) Trimedia Pub.

Severe Asthma. Ed. by Leung & S. J. Szefler. (Lung Biology in Health & Disease Ser.: Vol. 86). 640p. 1995. 195.00 (0-8247-9511-3) Dekker.

Severe Behavior Disorders in the Mentally Retarded: Nondrug Approaches to Treatment. Ed. by Rowland P. Barrett. (Applied Clinical Psychology Ser.). 426p. 1986. 75.00 (0-306-42162-3, Plenum Pr) Plenum.

An Asterisk (*) at the beginning of an entry indicates that the title is appearing in BIP for the first time.

Severe Behavior Problems: A Functional Communication Training Approach. V. Mark Durand. LC 90-44746. (Treatment Manuals for Practitioners Ser.). 183p. 1990. pap. text ed. 19.95 (*0-89862-217-4*) Guilford Pr.

Severe Burns: A Family Guide to Medical & Emotional Recovery. Andrew M. Munster. LC 93-870. (Illus.). 256p. (C). 1994. 24.95 (*0-8018-4653-6*) Phoenix Soc.

Severe Communication Disorders: Intervention Strategies. Ed. by Katharine G. Butler. LC 93-36267. 240p. 1993. 33.00 (*0-8342-0589-0*) Aspen Pub.

Severe Depression: A Practitioner's Guide. Philip J. Barker. LC 92-33173. 1992. 42.50 (*1-56593-051-7*, 0299) Singular Publishing.

Severe Depressive Disorders. Ed. by Leon Grunhaus & John F. Greden. (Progress in Psychiatry Ser.: No. 44). 368p. 1994. text ed. 44.00 (*0-88048-472-1*, 8472) Am Psychiatric.

***Severe Head Injuries: Pathology, Diagnosis & Treatment.** B. L. Bauer & T. J. Kuhn. LC 97-16897. 1997. write for info. (*3-540-62701-4*) Spr-Verlag.

Severe Learning Disabilities & Challenging Behaviors. 2nd ed. John P. Wattis et al. LC 86-5291. 192p. 1993. pap. 49.95 (*1-56593-130-0*, 0442) Singular Publishing.

Severe Local Storm Forecasting Primer. John S. Sturtevant. Ed. by Debi Iacovelli & Richard S. Sturtevant. LC 95-91009. (Illus.). 216p. (Orig.). 1995. per. 40.00 (*0-9650482-0-9*) Weather Scratch.

Severe Local Storms. David Atlas et al. (Meteorological Monograph: Vol. 5, No. 27). (Illus.). 247p. 1963. pap. 20.00 (*0-933876-17-3*) Am Meteorological.

Severe Mercy. Sheldon Vanauken. LC 86-46210. (Illus.). 240p. 1987. pap. 13.00 (*0-06-068824-6*) Harper SF.

Severe Open Tibial Fracture. J. O. Small & R. A. Mollan. (Illus.). 192p. Date not set. 90.00 (*0-7506-1376-9*) Buttrwrth-Heinemann.

Severe Personality Disorders: Psychotherapeutic Strategies. Otto F. Kernberg. 384p. (C). 1993. reprint ed. pap. text ed. 20.00 (*0-300-05349-5*) Yale U Pr.

Severe Queer Review of New York. Betty & Pansy. (Severe Queer Reviews Ser.). 112p. 1994. pap. 9.95 (*0-9633048-3-6*) Bedpan Prods.

Severe Queer Review of San Francisco No. 4. 4th ed. Betty & Pansy. (Severe Queer Review Travel Ser.). (Illus.). 131p. 1995. pap. 10.95 (*0-9633048-4-4*) Bedpan Prods.

Severe Queer Review of Washington, DC. 2nd ed. Betty & Pansy. 96p. 1993. pap. 8.95 (*0-9633048-2-8*) Bedpan Prods.

Severe Storm Engineering for Structural Design. M. Melaragno. 450p. 1995. pap. text ed. 45.00 (*2-88449-126-0*) Gordon & Breach.

Severe Storm Engineering for Structural Design. M. Melaragno. 450p. 1996. text ed. 90.00 (*2-88449-150-3*) Gordon & Breach.

Severe Stress & Mental Disturbance in Children. Ed. by Cynthia R. Pfeffer. 697p. 1996. text ed. 69.95 (*0-88048-657-0*, 8657) Am Psychiatric.

Severe Weather Flying. 2nd ed. Dennis W. Newton. Ed. by ASA Staff. LC 91-71566. (Illus.). 190p. 1991. pap. 16.95 (*1-56027-072-1*, ASA-SWF) Av Suppl & Acad.

Severed Hand & the Upright Corpse: The Declamations of Marcus Antonius Polemo. William W. Reader. LC 96-22492. (SBL Texts & Translations, Graeco-Roman Ser.). 540p. 1996. 49.95 (*0-7885-0282-4*, 060242) Scholars Pr GA.

Severed Head. Iris Murdoch. 208p. 1976. pap. 11.95 (*0-14-002003-9*, Penguin Bks) Viking Penguin.

Severed Wasp. Madeleine L'Engle. 388p. 1983. pap. 13.00 (*0-374-51783-5*) FS&G.

Severed Word: Ovid's "Heriodes" & the Novella Sentimental. Martina S. Brownlee. (Illus.). 273p. (C). 1990. text ed. 45.00 (*0-691-06809-7*) Princeton U Pr.

Severely Disturbed Youngsters & the Parental Alliance. Ed. by Jacquelyn S. Sanders & Barry L. Childress. LC 92-1554. (Residential Treatment for Children & Youth Ser.). 100p. (C). 1996. 39.95 (*1-56024-319-8*) Haworth Pr.

Severely Disturbed Youngsters & the Parental Alliance. Ed. by Jacquelyn S. Sanders & Barry L. Childress. LC 92-1554. 100p. (C). 1996. reprint ed. pap. 14.95 (*0-7890-0093-8*) Haworth Pr.

Severing the Ties That Bind: Government Repression of Indigenous Religious Ceremonies on the Prairies. Katherine Pettipas. (Manitoba Studies in Native History: 7). 304p. 1994. pap. 18.95 (*0-88755-638-8*) U Manitoba Pr.

Severini Futurista: 1912-1917. Anne C. Hanson. LC 95-24939. (Illus.). 192p. 1997. pap. 37.95 (*0-89467-071-9*) Yale Art Gallery.

Severini's Graphic Work. limited ed. Francesco Meloni. (Illus.). 218p. (ITA.). 1982. 275.00 (*1-55660-001-1*) A Wofsy Fine Arts.

Severin's Veterinary Ophthalmology Notes. 3rd ed. Glenn A. Severin. (Illus.). 546p. 1995. pap. text ed. 50.00 (*0-9646143-0-8*) Vet Ophthal Notes.

***Severity in Sandy Shoes.** Doris D. Caruso. (Illus.). 80p. (Orig.). 1997. pap. 8.95 (*1-57502-497-7*, PO1478) Morris Pubng.

Severn Barrage: Conference Proceedings. 246p. 1982. 63.00 (*0-7277-0156-8*, Pub. by T Telford UK) Am Soc Civil Eng.

Severn Enterprise. Christopher Jordan. (Illus.). 112p. (C). 1989. 30.00 (*0-7223-1536-8*, Pub. by A H S Ltd UK) St Mut.

***Severn Estuary: Landscape Evolution & Wetland Reclamation.** Stephen Rippon. LC 96-27923. 1997. write for info. (*0-7185-0069-5*, Pub. by Leicester Univ Pr) Bks Intl VA.

Severn to Solent Walk. Alan Proctor. (C). 1988. pap. 35.00 (*0-904110-91-5*, Pub. by Thornhill Pr UK) St Mut.

Severo Bonini's Discorsi e Regole: A Bilingual Edition. Don Severo Bonini. Ed. & Tr. by MaryAnn Bonino from ITA. LC 77-18514. (Illus.). 1979. text ed. 12.95 (*0-8425-0997-6*) Frnds of the Libry.

Severus of Minorca: Letter on the Conversion of the Jews. Severus of Minorca Staff. Tr. by Scott Bradbury. (Oxford Early Christian Texts Ser.). 160p. 1996. 55.00 (*0-19-826764-9*) OUP.

***Sevice Operations Management: Strategy, Design & Delivery.** Christine Witt. LC 97-10602. 1997. pap. text ed. 34.00 (*0-13-149915-7*) P-H.

Sevier County, Arkansas Census, 1850 & Marriage Records Through 1852. Bobbie J. McLane & Capitola Glazner. 72p. (Orig.). 1964. pap. text ed. 12.00 (*0-929604-00-8*) Arkansas Ancestors.

Sevier County, Arkansas Census, 1860 & Marriage Records, Bk. 2. Bobbie J. McLane & Capitola Glazner. 145p. (Orig.). 1967. pap. 15.00 (*0-929604-06-7*) Arkansas Ancestors.

Sevier County, Tennessee Buyer's Guide for Houses or Land. Virginia Almy. Ed. by Juanitta Baldwin. 230p. (Orig.). 1996. pap. 15.00 (*1-880308-06-1*) Suntop.

***Sevierville, Gatlinburg, & Maryville, TN.** E. Zimmerman. (Images of America Ser.). pap. 16.99 (*0-7524-0520-9*, Arcdia) Chalford.

Sevigne Letters. William Eisner. Ed. by Jeff Putnam. 201p. 1994. 18.00 (*1-880909-27-8*) Baskerville.

Sevilla HGH Symposium: Clinical Aspects of Growth Hormone Replacement Therapy, Proceedings, Seville, Spain, April 1990. Ed. by J. Girard & J. S. Christiansen. (Illus.). iv, 108p. 1990. pap. 48.75 (*3-8055-5290-4*) S Karger.

Sevilla y America. A. Jimenez Nunez. (Gran Enciclopedia de Espana y America Ser.). (Illus.). (SPA.). 1989. 200.00 (*84-87053-16-5*) Elliots Bks.

Sevillana Medicina, Burgos, 1545. Juan De Avinon. Ed. by Eric W. Naylor. (Medieval Spanish Medical Texts Ser.: No. 8). 6p. (SPA.). 1987. 10.00 incl. fiche (*0-940639-03-3*) Hispanic Seminary.

Seville. (New Eyewitness Travel Guides Ser.). 1996. pap. 22.95 (*0-614-97903-X*) DK Pub Inc.

Seville. Tom Burns. (Everything under the Sun Ser.). (Illus.). 176p. 1995. pap. 6.95 (*0-8442-9205-2*, Passport Bks) NTC Pub Grp.

Seville & Andalusia. LC 95-4500. (Eyewitness Travel Guides Ser.). 272p. 1996. pap. 22.95 (*0-7894-0427-3*) DK Pub Inc.

***Seville Architecture & Design Expo '92.** Francesco D. Co et al. (Illus.). 366p. 1996. boxed 85.00 (*1-55859-833-2*) Abbeville Pr.

Seville Architecture & Design Expo '92. Francesco Dal Co et al. (Illus.). 366p. 1995. 80.00 (*1-55859-580-5*) Abbeville Pr.

Seville Pocket Guide. Berlitz Editors. (Pocket Guides Ser.). (Illus.). 128p. 1991. pap. 7.95 (*2-8315-2356-7*) Berlitz.

Seving Minnesota's Mentally Ill: An Introduction. League of Women Voters of Minnesota Education Fund Staff. 1988. write for info. (*0-9613566-6-9*) League Wmn Voters MN.

Sevres Porcelain: Makers & Marks of the Eighteenth Century. Carl C. Dauterman. (Illus.). 264p. 1986. 45.00 (*0-87099-227-9*, 0-8109-6473-2) Metro Mus Art.

Sevso Treasure: Art Historical Description & Inscriptions; Methods of Manufacture & Scientific Analyses. Marlia M. Mango & Anna Bennett. (JRA Supplementary Ser.: No. 12, Pt. 1). (Illus.). 480p. 1994. 198.00 (*1-887829-12-1*) Jour Roman Arch.

Sew a Beautiful Wedding. Karen Dillon & Gail Brown. 128p. (C). 1980. pap. 8.95 (*0-935278-05-2*) Palmer-Pletsch.

***Sew a Circle of Friends: Adorable Cloth Doll Projects.** Anne McKinney. LC 97-7716. 1997. write for info. (*0-8069-8611-5*) Sterling.

***Sew a Work of Art Inside & Out.** Charlotte Bird. Ed. by Barbara Weiland. LC 96-31340. (Illus.). 88p. (Orig.). 1996. pap. 22.95 (*1-56477-172-5*, B287) That Patchwork.

Sew & Go: Easy Convertible Projects for the Active Life-Style. Jasmine Hubble. LC 95-48895. (Creative Machine Arts Ser.). 1996. pap. 16.95 (*0-8019-8658-3*) Chilton.

Sew & Repair Your Outdoor Gear. Louise L. Sumner. LC 88-29293. (Illus.). 144p. (Orig.). 1988. pap. 16.95 (*0-89886-057-1*) Mountaineers.

Sew & Serge Pillows! Pillows! Pillows! Jackie Dodson & Jon Saunders. (Illus.). 100p. 1995. pap. 13.95 (*0-8019-8530-7*) Chilton.

Sew & Serge Terrific Textures. Jackie Dodson & Jan Saunders. (Illus.). 100p. 1995. pap. 13.95 (*0-8019-8526-9*) Chilton.

Sew Any Patch Pocket. Claire B. Shaeffer. (Illus.). 128p. 1992. pap. 9.95 (*0-932086-25-X*) Krause Pubns.

Sew Any Set-In Pocket. Claire B. Shaeffer. LC 92-54915. (Illus.). 128p. 1994. pap. 14.95 (*0-8019-8399-1*) Chilton.

Sew Easy to Kill. Sarah J. Mason. 208p. 1996. mass mkt. 5.99 (*0-425-15310-X*) Berkley Pub.

Sew Far Sew Good: The Comprehensive Sourcebook for Home & Professional Sewers, Quilters, Beaders, Needleworkers, Weavers, Knitters & Other Creative Persons. Heather M. Clans. Ed. by Grant Moser. (Illus.). 416p. (Orig.). 1996. pap. 29.95 (*0-9652103-5-9*) Oracle Publns.

***Sew Find It, Sew Craft It! Product & Service Resource Directory for Sewing & Craft Enthusiasts.** 2nd rev. ed. Joselyn Smith-Greene. 71p. (Orig.). 1996. pap. 11.95 (*0-9655489-0-2*) J Greene Ent.

Sew-Fit Manual. Ruth Oblander & Joan Anderson. LC 77-84538. (Illus.). (C). 1978. 29.95 (*0-933956-03-7*) Sew-Fit.

Sew Hilarious. Mary A. Roehr. (Illus.). 64p. (Orig.). 1995. pap. 9.95 (*0-9619229-4-X*) M Roehr Bks & Vid.

***Sew Inspired: Jeannette's Adventure - Designer Sewing.** Jeannette E. Sellers. (Illus.). 186p. 1996. write for info. (*0-9653581-2-7*) Jeannettes Adven.

Sew It Tonight, Give It Tomorrow: Fifty Fast, Fun & Fabulous Gifts to Make in an Evening. Ed. by Stacy L. Klaman. LC 94-38409. (Illus.). 256p. 1995. 27.95 (*0-87596-645-4*) Rodale Pr Inc.

Sew It Yourself Nursery Ensembles. Robyn A. Massey. Ed. & Illus. by Jack Braunstein. LC 96-11025. 64p. (Orig.). 1996. pap. 14.95 (*1-885588-04-6*) Chitra Pubns.

Sew Many Gifts, Sew Little Time: More Than 50 Special Projects to Be Cherished & Enjoyed. Chris Rankin. LC 93-44538. (Illus.). 128p. 1994. 27.95 (*0-8069-0606-5*) Sterling.

Sew Many Gifts, Sew Little Time: More Than 50 Special Projects to Be Cherished & Enjoyed. Chris Rankin. (Illus.). 128p. 1995. pap. 14.95 (*0-8069-0607-3*) Sterling.

Sew News Time Saving Tips A to Z. Sew News Magazine Editors. 1996. pap. 19.95 (*0-8487-1489-X*) Oxmoor Hse.

Sew-No-More Home Decor. LC 93-85971. 1993. 19.95 (*0-942237-33-1*) Leisure AR.

Sew Romantic. Ruth Seeley-Scheel. (Illus.). 1988. pap. 6.95 (*0-9619815-3-9*) Laugh Goose.

Sew Sensational Gifts. Naomi Baker & Tammy Young. LC 92-56584. 192p. 1993. pap. 16.95 (*0-8019-8237-5*) Chilton.

Sew Simple: A Step-by-Step Guide to Dressmaking. 2nd ed. Tootal Sewing Products Staff. (Illus.). 232p. 1987. pap. 50.00 (*0-7487-0365-9*, Pub. by S Thornes Pubs UK) St Mut.

Sew Simple Step by Step Guide to Dressmaking. Ed. by T. Tootal. (C). 1989. 90.00 (*0-09-172845-2*, Pub. by S Thornes Pubs UK) St Mut.

Sew Smart with Ultra Suede Fabric & Other Luxury Suedes. Clotilde Yurick & Judy M. Lawrence. (Illus.). 106p. (C). 1981. pap. 5.95 (*0-9605860-0-8*) Sewing Knits.

Sew to Speak: The Fabric Art of Mary Milne. Linda Pershing. (Folk Art & Artists Ser.). (Illus.). 72p. 1995. 32.50 (*0-87805-786-2*); pap. 16.95 (*0-87805-787-0*) U Pr of Miss.

Sew to Success! How to Make Money in a Home-Based Sewing Business. Kathleen Spike. 128p. 1995. pap. 10.95 (*0-935278-17-6*) Palmer-Pletsch.

Sew up a Storm: All the Way to the Bank!: How to Succeed in a Sewing-Related Business. Karen L. Maslowski. LC 95-92592. 213p. (Orig.). 1995. pap. 19.95 (*0-9648729-1-9*) SewStorm.

Sew Wonderful Gourmet Garments. Cheryl Arrants. Ed. by Kristi St. Amant. (Illus.). 96p. (Orig.). 1982. pap. text ed. 6.95 (*0-943704-01-4*) Arrants & Assoc.

Sew Wonderful Silk: The Guide to Gourmet Sewing with Silk & Silk-like Fabrics. rev. ed. Cheryl Arrants & Jan Asbjornsen. Ed. by Kristi Amant. (Illus.). 128p. 1981. pap. text ed. 5.95 (*0-943704-02-2*) Arrants & Assoc.

Sew Your Own Riding Clothes. Linnea A. Sheppard. (Illus.). 195p. 1994. 19.95 (*0-914327-56-9*) Breakthrgh NY.

***Sew Yourself a Garden: A Little Book Made Special with Ribbon Embroidery.** Andrews & McMeel Staff. (Little Library to Make It Special). 1997. 4.95 (*0-8362-3613-0*) Andrews & McMeel.

Sewage. Valerie Hannah. Ed. by George H. Herrick. 152p. (Orig.). 1991. pap. 5.95 (*0-941281-81-7*) V H Pub.

Sewage & Industrial Effluent Treatment: A Practical Guide. John Arundel. LC 95-659. 256p. 1995. 75.00 (*0-632-03898-5*) Blackwell Sci.

Sewage District Superintendent. Jack Rudman. (Career Examination Ser.: C-3343). 1994. pap. 39.95 (*0-8373-3343-1*) Nat Learn.

Sewage into 2000: Developments & Upgrading in Sewerage & Wastewater Treatment. Ed. by R. R. Kruize. (Water Science & Technology Ser.: Vol. 27). 496p. 1993. pap. 231.00 (*0-08-042327-2*, Pergamon Pr) Elsevier.

Sewage Organisms: A Color Atlas. J. Carl Fox et al. (Illus.). 116p. 1986. 110.00 (*0-87371-031-2*) Lewis Pubs.

Sewage Plant Operations Supervisor. Jack Rudman. (Career Examination Ser.: C-3017). 1994. pap. 34.95 (*0-8373-3017-3*) Nat Learn.

Sewage Plant Operator. Jack Rudman. (Career Examination Ser.: C-2443). 1994. pap. 27.95 (*0-8373-2443-2*) Nat Learn.

Sewage Plant Operator Trainee. Jack Rudman. (Career Examination Ser.: C-2281). 1994. reprint ed. pap. 23.95 (*0-8373-2281-2*) Nat Learn.

Sewage Pump Operator. Jack Rudman. (Career Examination Ser.: C-3018). 1994. pap. 29.95 (*0-8373-3018-1*) Nat Learn.

Sewage Sludge: Land Utilization & the Environment. Ed. by C. E. Clapp et al. LC 94-29183. (SSSA Miscellaneous Publications). 1994. pap. 30.00 (*0-89118-813-4*) Am Soc Agron.

Sewage, Sludge & Its Contents of Potential Cancer-Causing Substances: Index of New Information & Research Reference Book. Martin C. Wrayer. 150p. 1996. 47.50 (*0-7883-1134-4*); pap. 44.50 (*0-7883-1135-2*) ABBE Pubs Assn.

Sewage Sludge Application in Semiarid Grasslands: Effects on Vegetation & Water Quality. Richard Aguilar et al. (Illus.). 107p. (Orig.). (C). 1995. pap. text ed. 35.00 (*0-7881-1568-5*) DIANE Pub.

Sewage Treatment in Hot Climates. David D. Mara. LC 75-23421. 437p. reprint ed. pap. 124.60 (*0-8357-3399-8*, 2039656) Bks Demand.

Sewage Treatment Operator. Jack Rudman. (Career Examination Ser.: C-1488). 1994. pap. 27.95 (*0-8373-1488-7*) Nat Learn.

Sewage Treatment Operator Trainee. Jack Rudman. (Career Examination Ser.: C-1489). 1994. pap. 23.95 (*0-8373-1489-5*) Nat Learn.

Sewage Treatment Plant Supervisor. Jack Rudman. (Career Examination Ser.: C-1490). 1994. pap. 34.95 (*0-8373-1490-9*) Nat Learn.

Sewage Treatment Using Plants: Crop Protection from Sewage. John E. Butler. 180p. 1994. text ed. 64.95 (*0-13-807041-5*) P-H.

Sewage Treatment Worker. Jack Rudman. (Career Examination Ser.: C-734). 1994. pap. 27.95 (*0-8373-0734-1*) Nat Learn.

Sewage Treatment Worker Trainee. Jack Rudman. (Career Examination Ser.: C-735). 1994. pap. 23.95 (*0-8373-0735-X*) Nat Learn.

Sewall Wright & Evolutionary Biology. William B. Provine. LC 85-24651. (Illus.). xvi, 560p. 1989. pap. text ed. 23.00 (*0-226-68473-3*) U Ch Pr.

Sewall's Point: The History of a Peninsular Community on Florida's Treasure Coast. Sandra H. Thurlow. (Illus.). 196p. 1992. 39.95 (*0-9630788-0-1*) Sewalls Pt.

Sewanee. William A. Percy. LC 82-60214. (Illus.). 40p. 1982. 14.95 (*0-913720-37-2*) Beil.

Sewanee. William A. Percy. 16p. 1941. pap. 7.50 (*0-918769-35-3*) Univ South Pr.

Sewanee: A University Portrait. Illus. by William Strode & Tommy L. Thompson. 22p. (Orig.). 1994. pap. 3.95 (*0-918769-36-1*) Harmony Hse Pub.

Sewanee in Ruins. Richard Tillinghast. 39p. 1983. pap. 15.00 (*0-918769-05-1*) Univ South Pr.

Sewanee Medieval Colloquium, No. 1: Occasional Papers - 1982. Edward B. King. Ed. by Jacqueline T. Schaefer. LC 82-50575. (Illus.). 65p. (Orig.). 1982. pap. 10.00 (*0-918769-28-0*) Univ South Pr.

Sewanee Medieval Colloquium, No. 2: Occasional Papers - 1985. Edward B. King. LC 82-50575. (Illus.). 120p. (Orig.). 1985. pap. 15.00 (*0-918769-29-9*) Univ South Pr.

Sewanee Sampler. Arthur B. Chitty & Elizabeth N. Chitty. 198p. 1978. pap. 15.00 (*0-9627687-7-4*) Univ South Pr.

Sewanee Seasons on the Domain. Illus & Photos by Tommy Thompson. LC 92-75619. 112p. 1993. 39.95 (*1-56469-014-8*) Harmony Hse Pub.

Sewanee-the University of the South. William Strode. (Illus.). 96p. 1984. 30.00 (*0-916509-01-X*) Harmony Hse Pub.

Seward, Alaska - A History of the Gateway City Vol. 1: Prehistory to 1914. Mary J. Barry. LC 86-71202. (Illus.). 182p. (Orig.). 1987. pap. 25.00 (*0-9617009-0-4*) M J P Barry.

Seward, Alaska - A History of the Gateway City Vol. 2: 1914-1923. Mary J. Barry. LC 86-71202. (Illus.). 225p. (YA). (gr. 8 up). 1993. pap. 25.00 (*0-9617009-2-0*) M J P Barry.

Seward, Alaska - A History of the Gateway City Vol. 3: Growth, Tragedy, Recovery, Adaptation, 1924-1993. Mary J. Barry. LC 86-71202. (Illus.). 408p. (YA). (gr. 8 up). 1995. reprint ed. pap. 37.50 (*0-9617009-4-7*) M J P Barry.

Seward & the Declaration of Paris. Charles F. Adams, Jr. (Works of Charles Francis Adams Jr. (1835-1915)). 1989. reprint ed. lib. bdg. 79.00 (*0-685-27453-5*) Rprt Serv.

Seward County, 1992: A Photographic Journey. Jane Graff. LC 92-37197. (Illus.). 1992. write for info. (*0-89865-846-2*) Donning Co.

Seward's Bedside Diagnosis. 13th ed. David M. Mattingly & Charles Seward. (Illus.). 373p. 1989. pap. text ed. 45.00 (*0-443-04077-X*) Churchill.

Sewell: The Sewells of the Isle of Wight, England, with an Account of Some of the Families Connected by Marriage. M. C. Owen. 204p. 1993. reprint ed. pap. 32.00 (*0-8328-3749-0*); reprint ed. lib. bdg. 42.00 (*0-8328-3748-2*) Higginson Bk Co.

Sewell Diary. Sewell. Ed. by Comigan. (Masterworks of Literature Ser.). 1991. write for info. (*0-8084-0445-8*) NCUP.

Sewer As a Physical, Chemical, & Biological Reactor: Selected Proceedings of the International Specialized Conference Held in Aalborg, Denmark, May 16-18, 1994. Ed. by T. Hvitved-Jacobsen et al. (Water Science & Technology Ser.). (Illus.). 380p. 1995. pap. 138.50 (*0-08-042657-3*, Pergamon Pr) Elsevier.

Sewer Charges for Wastewater Collection & Treatment. 46p. (Orig.). (C). 1982. pap. 9.00 (*0-943244-39-0*, MOO35PA) Water Environ.

Sewer City Short Line of the Southern Oregon Live Steamers. Bert Webber & Margie Webber. LC 93-6884. 120p. 1993. pap. 11.95 (*0-936738-70-7*) Webb Research.

Sewer, Gas & Electric: The Public Works Trilogy. Matt Ruff. 384p. 1996. 23.00 (*0-87113-641-4*, Atlntc Mnthly) Grove-Atltic.

Sewer Inspector. Jack Rudman. (Career Examination Ser.: C-2454). 1994. pap. 29.95 (*0-8373-2454-8*) Nat Learn.

Sewer People. David L. Preston. Date not set. pap. 18.00 (*0-670-82023-7*) Viking Penguin.

Sewer People. David L. Preston. 1999. pap. write for info. (*0-14-010611-1*, Viking) Viking Penguin.

Sewer Socialists: A History of the Socialist Party of Wisconsin, 1897-1940, 2 vols. John E. Westburg. (Illus.). 1982. pap. 30.00 (*0-87423-031-4*) Westburg.

Sewer Soup. M. M. Ragz. Ed. by Patricia MacDonald. 128p. (Orig.). pap. 3.50 (*0-671-75881-0*) PB.

Sewerage & Sewage Treatment: International Practice. Ed. by William D. Haworth. LC 83-1300. (Wiley-Interscience Publications). 553p. reprint ed. pap. 157.70 (*0-7837-3276-7*, 2052463) Bks Demand.

Sewering the Cities: An Original Anthology. Ed. by Barbara G. Rosenkrantz. LC 76-40352. (Public Health in America Ser.). (Illus.). 1977. reprint ed. lib. bdg. 23.95 (*0-405-09879-0*) Ayer.

***Sewers: Rehabilitation & New Construction.** write for info. (*0-340-54472-4*, Pub. by E Arnold UK) Routledge Chapman & Hall.

S

S

Sewers - Rehabilitation & New Construction Pt. 1: Repair & Renovation. Ed. by Geoffrey F. Read & Ian G. Vickridge. 448p. 1996. text ed. 175.00 (0-470-23564-0) Halsted Pr.

Sewers of Oblivion. Michael A. Stackpole. (Illus.). 1980. 5.95 (0-940244-13-6) Flying Buffalo.

***Sewing.** Ann Sadler. (Illus.). (FRE.). (J). (gr. k-5). pap. 7.99 (0-590-24055-2) Scholastic Inc.

***Sewing.** unabridged ed. Judy A. Sadler. (Kids Can Easy Crafts Ser.). (Illus.). 32p. (Orig.). (J). (gr. k up). 1997. pap. 4.95 (1-55074-101-2, Pub. by Kids Can Pr CN) Genl Dist Srvs.

***Sewing & Sculpting Dolls: Easy-to-Make Dolls from Fabric, Modeling Paste & Polymer Clay.** Eloise Piper. LC 96-46185. 1997. write for info. (0-8019-8872-1) Chilton.

Sewing As a Home Business. Mary A. Roehr. (Illus.). 135p. (Orig.). (C). 1987. reprint ed. pap. 14.95 (0-9619229-2-3) M Roehr Bks & Vid.

Sewing As a Home or Small Business: Possibilties. rev. ed. Center for Self-Sufficiency Staff. 83p. 1992. ring bd. 25.95 (0-910811-65-2) Ctr Self Suff.

Sewing at Once with a Double Thread: Collections of Poems by Writers in Delaware, Maryland, Virginia, & the District of Columbia. Compiled & Pref. by Joseph D. Adams. (Poet's Domain Ser.: Vol. 9). xiv, 98p. (Orig.). 1994. pap. 7.50 (1-880016-14-1) Road Pubs.

Sewing Book. Ann Ladbury. 1990. 14.99 (0-517-00193-4) Random Hse Value.

Sewing by Hand. Christine Hoffman. LC 92-9516. (Illus.). 32p. (J). (ps-3). 1994. 14.00 (0-06-021146-6); lib. bdg. 13.89 (0-06-021147-4) HarpC Child Bks.

Sewing Church Linens. Elizabeth Joseph. LC 91-19242. (Illus.). 48p. (Orig.). 1991. pap. 9.95 (0-8192-1577-5) Morehouse Pub.

Sewing Circle: Hollywood's Greatest Secret--Female Stars Who Loved Other Women. Axel Madsen. (Illus.). 368p. 1995. 22.50 (1-55972-275-4, Birch Ln Pr) Carol Pub Group.

Sewing Connection, No. 1. rev. ed. Shirley Adams. (Illus.). 64p. 1994. 15.00 incl. vhs (1-884389-23-6) Sewing Connection.

Sewing Connection, Vol. 11. Shirley Adams. Ed. by Rebecca Adams. (Series II). (Illus.). 64p. (Orig.). 1995. wbk. ed. 15.00 (1-884389-24-4) Sewing Connection.

Sewing Connection, Vol. 12. Shirley Adams. Ed. by Rebecca Adams. (Illus.). 64p. (Orig.). 1995. student ed., pap. 15.00 (1-884389-26-0) Sewing Connection.

Sewing Connection, Vol. 13. Shirley Adams. Ed. by Rebecca Adams. (Illus.). 64p. (Orig.). 1996. wbk. ed., pap. 15.00 (1-884389-29-5, SCB013) Sewing Connection.

***Sewing Connection, Vol. 14.** Shirley K. Adams. (Illus.). 64p. (Orig.). 1996. pap. text ed. 15.00 (1-884389-31-7, SCB014) Sewing Connection.

***Sewing Connection, Vol. 15.** Shirley Adams. Ed. by Rebecca Adams. (Illus.). 64p. (Orig.). 1997. pap. 15.00 (1-884389-33-3, SCB015) Sewing Connection.

***Sewing Connection, Vol. 16.** Shirley Adams. (Illus.). 64p. (Orig.). 1997. pap. 15.00 (1-884389-35-X, SCB016) Sewing Connection.

Sewing Connection Series, No. 1. Shirley Adams. (Illus.). 64p. (Orig.). 1990. vhs 58.95 (1-884389-12-0) Sewing Connection.

Sewing Connection Series, No. 2. Shirley Adams. (Illus.). 64p. (Orig.). 1991. student ed. 15.00 (1-884389-01-5); vhs 58.95 (1-884389-13-9) Sewing Connection.

Sewing Connection Series, No. 3. Shirley Adams. (Illus.). 64p. (Orig.). 1991. student ed. 15.00 (1-884389-02-3); vhs 58.95 (1-884389-14-7) Sewing Connection.

Sewing Connection Series, No. 4. Shirley Adams. (Illus.). 64p. (Orig.). 1991. student ed. 15.00 (1-884389-03-1); vhs 58.95 (1-884389-15-5) Sewing Connection.

Sewing Connection Series, No. 5. Shirley Adams. (Illus.). 64p. (Orig.). 1992. student ed. 15.00 (1-884389-04-X); vhs 58.95 (1-884389-16-3) Sewing Connection.

Sewing Connection Series, No. 6. Shirley Adams. (Illus.). 64p. (Orig.). 1992. student ed. 15.00 (1-884389-05-8); vhs 58.95 (1-884389-17-1) Sewing Connection.

Sewing Connection Series, No. 7. Shirley Adams. (Illus.). 64p. (Orig.). 1993. student ed. 15.00 (1-884389-06-6); vhs 58.95 (1-884389-18-X) Sewing Connection.

Sewing Connection Series, No. 8. Shirley Adams. (Illus.). 64p. (Orig.). 1993. student ed. 15.00 (1-884389-07-4); vhs 58.95 (1-884389-19-8) Sewing Connection.

Sewing Connection Series, No. 9. Shirley Adams. Ed. by R. Adams. (Illus.). 64p. (Orig.). 1994. student ed., pap. text ed. 15.00 (1-884389-08-2); vhs 58.95 (1-884389-20-1) Sewing Connection.

Sewing Connection Series No. 10. Shirley Adams. (Illus.). 64p. (Orig.). 1994. vhs 58.95 (1-884389-22-8) Sewing Connection.

Sewing Connection Series No. 10. Shirley Adams. Ed. by Rebecca Adams. (Illus.). 64p. (Orig.). 1994. student ed., pap. text ed. 15.00 (1-884389-21-X, SCB010) Sewing Connection.

Sewing Essentials. LC 84-42637. (Illus.). 1984. pap. 9.95 (0-394-72757-6) Random.

Sewing Essentials. Decosse, Cy, Inc., Staff & Singer Co. Staff. LC 96-18129. 1996. 18.95 (0-86573-307-4); pap. 16.95 (0-86573-308-2) Cowles Creative.

Sewing Etc. Donna L. Salyers. Ed. by Lynda Watcke. LC 84-40063. (Illus.). 120p. (Orig.). 1984. pap. 14.95 (0-916525-00-7) A Scott Pub Co.

Sewing Express. Nancy L. Zieman. 1994. pap. 14.95 (0-8487-1413-X) Oxmoor Hse.

Sewing for Children. Cy DeCosse Incorporated Staff. LC 88-23701. (Singer Sewing Reference Library). (Illus.). 128p. 1988. 18.95 (0-86573-243-4); pap. 16.95 (0-86573-244-2) Cowles Creative.

Sewing for Conservative Men. Teresa Brunk. 1994. spiral bd. 8.95 (0-87813-555-3) Christian Light.

Sewing for Fashion Design. 2nd ed. Nurie Relis & Gail Strauss. LC 96-26800. 1996. 42.00 (0-13-496753-4) P-H.

Sewing for Profits. rev. ed. Judith Smith & Allan Smith. (Illus.). 208p. 1991. reprint ed. pap. text ed. 12.00 (0-931113-01-6) Success Publ.

Sewing for Special Occasions. Cy DeCosse Incorporated Staff. LC 93-17641. (Singer Sewing Reference Library). 128p. 1994. 18.95 (0-86573-286-8); pap. 16.95 (0-86573-287-6) Cowles Creative.

Sewing for Style: Details & Techniques Beyond the Basics. (Singer Reference Library). 1985. pap. 11.95 (0-394-73411-4) Random.

Sewing for the Apparel Industry: Industrial Sewing Techniques. Claire B. Shaeffer. 515p. 1997. 49.00 (1-56367-079-8) Fairchild.

Sewing for the Holidays. DeCosse, Cy, Incorporated Staff. LC 94-679. (Singer Sewing Reference Library). 128p. 1994. 18.95 (0-86573-295-7); pap. 16.95 (0-86573-296-5) Cowles Creative.

Sewing for the Home. rev. ed. Cy DeCosse Inc. Staff. 1994. pap. 16.95 (0-86573-299-X) Cowles Creative.

Sewing for the Home. rev. ed. Cy DeCosse Inc. Staff. 1994. 18.95 (0-86573-305-8) Cowles Creative.

***Sewing for Twentieth Century Dolls.** Johana G. Anderson. (Illus.). 264p. 1996. reprint ed. 24.95 (0-87588-467-9, 5200) Hobby Hse.

Sewing Fun Stuff! Soft Sculpture Shortcuts. Lynne Farris. LC 95-47447. (Great Sewing Projects Ser.). (Illus.). 160p. 1996. 24.95 (0-8069-6164-3) Sterling.

***Sewing Inspirations from Yester Year: Martha's Sewing Room Series 500.** Martha C. Pullen. LC 96-70808. (Illus.). 218p. 1996. text ed. 19.95 (1-878048-09-0) M Pullen.

Sewing Kids' Stuff: Fun Things for Kids to Wear & Share. Ed. by Cindy Kacynski. LC 91-90458. (Illus.). 176p. 1991. pap. 17.95 (0-9621148-3-9, Sew News) PJS Pubns.

Sewing Little Girls & Ladies Nightwear: A New & Easy Way. June H. Fleming. LC 93-70556. (Illus.). 100p. 1993. pap. 24.95 (1-883165-32-6) Fernholm Pub.

Sewing Little Girls Clothing & Ladies Too: Fast & Easy Outfits. June H. Fleming. LC 93-79250. (Illus.). 100p. 1993. pap. 24.95 (1-883165-33-4) Fernholm Pub.

***Sewing Luxurious Pillows: Artistic Designs for Home Decor.** Linda Lee. LC 96-37103. 1997. 27.95 (0-8069-9808-3) Sterling.

Sewing Machine. Beatrice Siegel. LC 83-40397. (Inventions That Changed Our Lives Ser.). 64p. (J). (gr. 5 up). 1984. lib. bdg. 10.85 (0-8027-6532-7) Walker & Co.

Sewing Machine Fun. Nancy Smith & Lynda S. Milligan. Ed. by Sharon Holmes. (Illus.). 72p. (J). (gr. 1-12). 1993. pap. 15.95 (1-880972-04-2, DreamSpinners) Pssblts Denver.

Sewing Machine Fun: Activity Kit. Nancy Smith & Lynda S. Milligan. Ed. by Sharon Holmes. (Illus.). 72p. (J). (gr. 1-12). 1993. pap. 29.95 (1-880972-10-7, DreamSpinners) Pssblts Denver.

***Sewing Machine Guide.** John Giordano. LC 97-13895. (Illus.). 112p. 1996. pap. 15.95 (1-56158-220-4, 070308) Taunton.

Sewing Projects for the Home. Cy DeCosse Incorporated Staff. LC 91-4680. (Singer Sewing Reference Library). 128p. 1991. 18.95 (0-86573-262-0); pap. 16.95 (0-86573-263-9) Cowles Creative.

Sewing Publications, Pattern Companies, Fabric Outlets, Etc. A How to Find or Locate Workbook. Center for Self Sufficiency, Research Division Staff. LC 83-90722. 60p. 1983. ring bd. 24.95 (0-910811-30-X) Ctr Self Suff.

Sewing Room. large type ed. Barbara C. Crafton. LC 93-37650. 1994. lib. bdg. 21.95 (0-8161-5910-6, GK Hall) Thorndike Pr.

***Sewing Room: Uncommon Reflections on Life, Love & Work.** Barbara Crafton. 270p. 1997. pap. 12.95 (0-8192-1723-9) Morehouse Pub.

Sewing Secrets from the Fashion Industry: Proven Methods to Help You Sew Like the Pros. Ed. by Susan Huxley. (Illus.). 256p. 1996. 29.95 (0-87596-719-1) Rodale Pr Inc.

Sewing Specialty Fabrics. Singer Sewing Machine Company Staff. LC 85-13050. (Illus.). 128p. 1986. 10.95 (0-394-74416-0) Random.

Sewing Step-by-Step. (Illus.). 1992. write for info. (1-886614-06-7) Intl Masters Pub.

Sewing Techniques for the Blind Girl. large type rev. ed. S. Jones. 40p. (YA). (gr. 9 up). 1973. 10.50 (0-317-01934-1, J-23520-00) Am Printing Hse.

Sewing the New Classics: Clothes with Easy Style. Carol Parks. LC 95-20037. (Illus.). 160p. 1995. 27.95 (0-8069-3193-0) Lark Books.

Sewing the New Classics: Clothes with Easy Style. Carol Parks. (Illus.). 144p. (Orig.). 1996. pap. 14.95 (0-8069-3194-9) Sterling.

***Sewing the New Fleece: Techniques with Synthetic Fleece & Pile.** Rochelle Harper. LC 97-15277. 144p. (Orig.). 1997. pap. 21.95 (1-56158-172-0, 070301) Taunton.

Sewing Tips & Trade Secrets. Threads Magazine Editors. (Illus.). 128p. Date not set. pap. 14.95 (1-56158-109-7) Field & Wood Inc Medical.

***Sewing Together: A Birthday Quilt.** Jocelyn Riley. 114p. 1996. 45.00 (1-877933-66-X, 19002) Her Own Words.

Sewing Tools & Trinkets. Helen L. Thompson. (Illus.). 192p. (Orig.). 1996. 24.95 (0-89145-736-4, 4729) Collector Bks.

Sewing Victorian Doll Clothes: Authentic Costumes from Museum Collections. Michelle Hamilton. (Illus.). 224p. 1996. 27.95 (1-887374-06-X) Lark Books.

Sewing with an Overlock. Cy DeCosse Incorporated Staff. LC 88-31343. (Singer Sewing Reference Library). 128p. 1989. 18.95 (0-86573-247-7); pap. 16.95 (0-86573-248-5) Cowles Creative.

Sewing with Scraps. Phyllis Guth & Georgeanna Goff. (Illus.). (YA). (gr. 10 up). 1977. pap. 6.95 (0-8306-6878-0, 878) McGraw-Hill Prof.

Sewing with Sergers: The Complete Handbook for Overlock Sewing. rev. ed. Wisner Associates Staff et al. LC 85-60347. (Illus.). 128p. (Orig.). 1985. pap. 8.95 (0-935278-11-7) Palmer-Pletsch.

Sewing Without Pins. Ruth Oblander. LC 76-53269. 1986. 5.95 (0-933956-01-0) Sew-Fit.

***Sex.** Jack Nadel & Beverly Cohn. (Nit-Wits Ser.). 80p. 1997. pap. 4.95 (0-922658-07-2) Nadel Wrldwide.

***Sex: A Man's Guide.** Bechtel. 512p. 1997. pap. 17.95 (0-87596-458-3) Rodale Pr Inc.

Sex: A Man's Guide. Stefan Bechtel et al. 1996. 31.95 (0-87596-299-8) Rodale Pr Inc.

Sex: A User's Manual. Diagram Group Staff. 352p. 1985. reprint ed. mass mkt. 6.99 (0-425-08972-X) Berkley Pub.

Sex: An Encyclopedia for the Bewildered. K. S. Daly. (Illus.). 256p. 1996. 14.95 (1-85410-359-8, Pub. by Aurum Pr UK) London Brdge.

***Sex! Choosing Who, When, Where & How Much.** Douglas Ruben. 200p. (Orig.). Date not set. pap. text ed. 15.95 (1-879899-11-6) Newjoy Pr.

Sex: Desiring the Best. Barry St. Clair & Bill Jones. (Love/Sex/Dating/Series). 140p. (YA). 1993. pap. 7.99 (1-56476-190-8, 6-3190, Victor Bks) Chariot Victor.

***Sex: Even More Fun Without Laughing.** W. Cole. 1997. 5.98 (0-7858-0808-6) Bk Sales Inc.

Sex: Everything You Want to Know & Why! Charmaine Saunders. 160p. (Orig.). 1996. pap. 12.95 (1-86351-153-9, Pub. by Sally Milner AT) Seven Hills Bk.

Sex: Hot, Love; Warm. Jim DeWitt. (Illus.). 64p. (Orig.). 1978. pap. 3.95 (0-915199-97-1) Pen-Dec.

Sex: It's Worth Waiting For. Greg Speck. (Illus.). (Orig.). (J). 1989. pap. 9.99 (0-8024-7692-9) Moody.

***Sex: Most Fun You Can Without Laughing.** W. Cole. 1997. 5.98 (0-7858-0807-8) Bk Sales Inc.

Sex: Real People Talk about What They Really Do. Harry Maurer. 560p. 1995. pap. 13.95 (0-14-017145-2, Penguin Bks) Viking Penguin.

Sex: The Catholic Experience. Andrew M. Greeley. (Illus.). 168p. 1994. 19.95 (0-88347-285-6, 7285) Res Christian Liv.

Sex: The Myth & the Magic. E. Lonnie Melashenko. LC 93-41886. 1993. pap. 1.99 (0-8163-1214-1) Pacific Pr Pub Assn.

Sex: The Relationship Between Sex & Spiritual Development. J. G. Bennett. 80p. 1981. pap. 6.95 (0-87728-533-0) Weiser.

Sex: There's More to It Than You've Been Told. William A. Ross. Ed. by Robert Carlson. 96p. (Orig.). 1988. pap. 4.95 (0-9619246-0-8) Playful Wisdom.

Sex Vol. 3: True Homosexual Experiences from S. T. H. Writers. Ed. by Boyd McDonald. (Illus.). 192p. (Orig.). 1996. reprint ed. pap. 14.95 (0-917342-98-4) Gay Sunshine.

***Sex - God's Way.** Steven Lamb. (Orig.). 1996. pap. write for info. (0-88290-586-4) Horizon Utah.

Sex a Spiritual Guide for the Youth of Today. NanSea. LC 94-93913. (Illus.). 128p. (YA). (gr. 7-12). 1995. pap. text ed. 9.95 (0-9643852-0-1) Spirit Script.

Sex, Abortion, & Unmarried Women. Paul Sachdev. LC 92-33303. (Contributions in Women's Studies: No. 133). 336p. 1993. text ed. 55.00 (0-313-24071-X, SAU, Greenwood Pr) Greenwood.

Sex Abuse Hysteria Salem Witches Trials Revisited: Causes of the Present Child Sex Abuse Hysteria in the United States. Richard A. Gardner. LC 90-20218. 150p. 1991. 18.00 (0-933812-22-1) Creative Therapeutics.

Sex Addiction: Case Studies & Management. Ralph H. Earle et al. LC 95-30129. 288p. 1995. text ed. 33.95 (0-87630-785-3) Brunner-Mazel.

Sex Addiction Workbook: How to Quit the Bible Way. Ray Geide. 105p. (Orig.). 1991. pap. 7.95 (0-9628012-2-4) Dexter KS.

***Sex after Baby.** Phil Goode. 1997. pap. 3.99 (1-57644-051-6) CCC Pubns.

Sex after Blood Pressure Medication: Really! Jessica Flemming & Bill Tyson. LC 93-83996. (Illus.). 160p. (Orig.). 1993. pap. 12.95 (1-883445-01-9) Plain Brown.

Sex after Sixty. Alan Francis. 120p. (Orig.). 1995. pap. 2.95 (0-8362-0823-4) Andrews & McMeel.

Sex After Sixty: A Guide for Men & Women for Their Later Years. large type ed. Robert N. Butler & Myrna I. Lewis. 1977. 18.95 (0-8161-6507-6, GK Hall) Thorndike Pr.

Sex after 40. Alan Francis. 120p. (Orig.). 1996. pap. 2.95 (0-8362-1318-1) Andrews & McMeel.

Sex after 50. Alan Francis. 120p. (Orig.). 1996. pap. 2.95 (0-8362-1320-3) Andrews & McMeel.

Sex, Age & Work: The Changing Composition of the Labor Force. Juanita Kreps & Robert Clark. LC 75-34452. (Policy Studies in Employment & Welfare Ser.: No. 23). (Illus.). 108p. 1976. 16.00 (0-8018-1806-0) Johns Hopkins.

Sex Allocation & Sex Change: Experiments & Models. Ed. by M. Mangel. LC 90-45411. (LLSCI Ser.: Vol. 22). 205p. 1990. pap. text ed. 43.00 (0-8218-1172-X, LLSCI/22) Am Math.

Sex, America, & Other Insights. Colin Wilson. 60p. 1992. reprint ed. pap. 15.00 (0-946650-34-9); reprint ed. lib. bdg. 25.00 (0-8095-6767-9) Borgo Pr.

***Sex, American Style: An Illustrated Romp Through the Golden Age of Heterosexuality.** Jack Boulware. 1997. pap. 14.95 (0-922915-46-6) Feral Hse.

***Sex among Allies: Military Prostitution in U. S.-Korea Relations.** Katharine H. Moon. LC 97-2641. 1997. write for info. (0-231-10642-4); pap. write for info. (0-231-10643-2) Col U Pr.

Sex & Advantage: A Comparative, Macro-Structural Theory of Sex Stratification. Janet S. Chafetz. LC 83-19077. 142p. (C). 1984. 41.00 (0-86598-159-0); pap. 20.00 (0-86598-161-2) Rowman.

Sex & Age Distribution of Population. 1990. 37.00 (92-1-151220-4, E 90.XIII.33) UN.

Sex & Age Distribution of World Population. (Population Studies: No. 144). 858p. 1994. pap. 45.00 (92-1-151274-3, E.95.XIII.2) UN.

Sex & Age Distribution of World Population. rev. ed. (Population Studies: No. 134). 397p. 1992. 45.00 (92-1-151251-4, E.93.XIII.3) UN.

Sex & All You Can Eat. Louise D. Campanelli. 1975. 7.95 (0-8184-0202-4) Carol Pub Group.

Sex & America's Teenagers. 88p. 1994. pap. 30.00 (0-939253-34-8) Guttmacher Inst.

Sex & Back Pain: Advice on Restoring Comfortable Sex Lost to Back Pain. Lauren Andrew Hebert. LC 92-70997. (Illus.). 108p. (Orig.). 1992. pap. 12.95 (1-879864-00-2) IMPACC USA.

Sex & Bisexuality: Index of Modern Information. Rosalie F. Zoltano. LC 88-47995. 150p. 1990. 44.50 (1-55914-200-6); pap. 39.50 (1-55914-201-4) ABBE Pubs Assn.

Sex & Broadcasting: A Handbook on Building a Radio Station for the Community. Lorenzo W. Milam. (Illus.). 375p. 1988. pap. 12.95 (0-917320-01-8) Mho & Mho.

Sex & Celibacy: Establishing Balance in Intimate Relationships Through Temporary Sexual Abstinence. Dwight L. Wolter. 160p. 1992. pap. 9.95 (0-925190-53-5) Fairview Press.

Sex & Character. Otto Weininger. LC 72-11295. reprint ed. 40.00 (0-404-57507-2) AMS Pr.

Sex & Conflict. William Hairston. LC 92-62004. 136p. 1993. pap. 8.95 (1-56002-240-X, Univ Edtns) Aegina Pr.

Sex & Conquest: Gendered Violence, Political Order, & the European Conquest of the Americas. Richard C. Trexler. (Illus.). 300p. 1997. 39.95 (0-8014-3224-3) Cornell U Pr.

***Sex & Conquest: Gendered Violence, Political Order, & the European Conquest of the Americas.** Richard C. Trexler. (Illus.). 300p. 1997. pap. 16.95 (0-8014-8482-0) Cornell U Pr.

Sex & Danger in Buenos Aires: Prostitution, Family, & Nation in Argentina. Donna J. Guy. LC 91-8664. (Engendering Latin America Ser.). (Illus.). ix, 260p. 1991. text ed. 40.00 (0-8032-2139-8); pap. text ed. 14.00 (0-8032-7048-8, Bison Books) U of Nebr Pr.

Sex & Death in Protozoa: History of an Obsession. Graham Bell. (Illus.). 224p. (C). 1989. text ed. 59.95 (0-521-36141-9) Cambridge U Pr.

Sex & Death in Victorian Literature. Ed. by Regina Barreca. LC 89-11020. 272p. 1990. 39.95 (0-253-31015-6) Ind U Pr.

Sex & Death to the Age Fourteen. Spalding Gray. LC 85-40682. 272p. 1986. pap. 13.00 (0-394-74257-5, Vin) Random.

Sex & Drugs: A Journey Beyond Limits. 2nd ed. Robert A. Wilson. LC 88-83351. 208p. 1991. reprint ed. pap. 14.95 (1-56184-001-7) New Falcon Pubns.

Sex & Education: A Reply to Dr. E. H. Clarke's Sex in Education. Ed. by Julia W. Howe. LC 72-2608. (American Women Ser.: Images & Realities). 208p. 1978. reprint ed. 18.95 (0-405-04463-1) Ayer.

Sex & Equality: An Original Anthology. Ed. by Annette K. Baxter. LC 74-3972. (Women in America Ser.). 220p. 1977. reprint ed. 23.95 (0-405-06121-8) Ayer.

Sex & Eroticism in Mesopotamian Literature. Gwendolyn Leick. LC 93-49776. (Illus.). 336p. (C). (gr. 13). 1994. text ed. 62.95 (0-415-06534-8, B4367) Routledge.

Sex & Existence: Simone de Beauvoir's "The Second Sex" rev. ed. Eva Lundgren-Gothlin. Tr. by Linda Schenck from SWE. LC 96-1887. 343p. 1996. pap. 17.95 (0-8195-6303-X, Wesleyan Univ Pr); text ed. 45.00 (0-8195-5295-X, Wesleyan Univ Pr) U Pr of New Eng.

***Sex & Family Planning - How We Teach the Young: Report on a Study.** B. Lewin. (Public Health in Europe Ser.: No. 23). 170p. 1984. pap. text ed. 19.00 (92-890-1159-9) World Health.

Sex & Fly Fishers: A Delightful & Insightful Celebration of Fly Fishing. Keith Russell et al. LC 92-61020. (Illus.). 336p. 1993. 29.95 (0-913276-61-8) Stone Wall Pr.

Sex & Friendship in Baboons. Barbara B. Smuts. (Biological Foundations of Human Behavior Ser.). (Illus.). 319p. (C). 1985. lib. bdg. 52.95 (0-202-02027-4) Aldine de Gruyter.

Sex & Gender. John Archer & Barbara Lloyd. (Illus.). 228p. 1985. pap. text ed. 19.95 (0-521-31921-8) Cambridge U Pr.

Sex & Gender. Phillip R. Shaver. (Review of Personality & Social Psychology Ser.: Vol. 7). (Illus.). 328p. (Orig.). (C). 1987. text ed. 54.00 (0-8039-2929-3); pap. text ed. 24.95 (0-8039-2930-7) Sage.

Sex & Gender. Phillip R. Shaver. LC 90-153948. (Review of Personality & Social Psychology Ser.: Vol. 7). (Illus.). 328p. 1987. pap. 93.50 (0-7837-8967-X, 2049748) Bks Demand.

Sex & Gender. rev. ed. James Park. (Love among Authentic Persons Ser.: No. 4). 1995. pap. 3.75 (0-89231-504-0) Existential Bks.

Sex & Gender: A Theological & Scientific Inquiry. Ed. by Mark F. Schwartz et al. LC 83-27048. 385p. (Orig.). 1983. pap. 19.95 (0-935372-13-X) Pope John Ctr.

Sex & Gender: An Introduction. 2nd rev. ed. Hilary M. Lips. LC 92-20228. 482p. (C). 1993. pap. text ed. 36.95 (1-55934-090-8, 1090) Mayfield Pub.

Sex & Gender: An Introduction. 3rd rev. ed. Hilary M. Lips. LC 96-21490. 513p. (C). 1996. pap. text ed. 36.95 (1-55934-630-2, 1630) Mayfield Pub.

Sex & Gender: On the Development of Masculinity & Femininity. Robert J. Stoller. 400p. 1994. pap. text ed. 36.95 (*0-946439-03-6*, Pub. by Karnac Bks UK) Brunner-Mazel.

Sex & Gender: The Human Experience. 2nd ed. James A. Doyle & Michele A. Paludi. 400p. (C). 1991. pap. write for info. (*0-697-05949-9*) Brown & Benchmark.

Sex & Gender: The Human Experience. 3rd ed. James A. Doyle. 384p. (C). 1994. per. write for info. (*0-697-12735-4*) Brown & Benchmark.

***Sex & Gender Differences in Communication.** Ed. by Daniel J. Canary & Kathryn Dindia. (Communication Ser.). 300p. 1998. text ed. write for info. (*0-8058-2333-6*) L Erlbaum Assocs.

***Sex & Gender Differences in Communication.** Ed. by Daniel J. Canary & Kathryn Dindia. (Communication Ser.). 1998. pap. text ed. write for info. (*0-8058-2334-4*) L Erlbaum Assocs.

Sex & Gender Hierarchies. Ed. by Barbara D. Miller. (Publications of the Society for Psychological Anthropology). (Illus.). 376p. (C). 1993. text ed. 65.00 (*0-521-41297-8*); pap. text ed. 24.95 (*0-521-42368-6*) Cambridge U Pr.

Sex & Gender in Historical Perspective. Ed. by Edward Muir & Guido Ruggiero. Tr. by Margaret A. Gallucci et al. from ITA. LC 90-31730. (Selections from Quaderni Storici Ser.). 264p. 1990. pap. text ed. 14.95 (*0-8018-4072-4*) Johns Hopkins.

Sex & Gender in Medieval & Renaissance Texts: The Latin Tradition. Ed. by Barbara K. Gold et al. LC 96-16249. (SUNY Series in Medieval Studies). 330p. 1997. text ed. 68.50 (*0-7914-3245-9*); pap. text ed. 22.95 (*0-7914-3246-7*) State U NY Pr.

Sex & Gender in Society. 2nd ed. Jean Stockard & Miriam M. Johnson. 352p. (C). 1991. pap. text ed. 42.00 (*0-13-807496-8*) P-H.

Sex & Gender in Society: Perspectives on Stratification. 2nd ed. Joyce M. Nielsen. 293p. (Orig.). (C). 1990. pap. text ed. 15.95 (*0-88133-456-1*) Waveland Pr.

Sex & Gender in the Social Sciences: Reassessing the Introductory Courses. Judith Gappa & Janice Pearce. 176p. 1982. 10.50 (*0-317-36342-5*) Am Sociological.

***Sex & Gender Instructor's Manual.** 3rd rev. ed. Hilary M. Lips. 143p. (C). 1996. pap. text ed. write for info. (*1-55934-631-0*, 1631) Mayfield Pub.

Sex & Gender Issues: A Handbook of Tests & Measures. Carole A. Beere. LC 90-32466. 448p. 1990. text ed. 99.50 (*0-313-27462-2*, BGC, Greenwood Pr) Greenwood.

***Sex & Germs: The Politics of AIDS.** Cindy Patton. 182p. (Orig.). 45.99 (*0-920057-82-9*, Pub. by Black Rose Bks CN); pap. 16.99 (*0-920057-80-2*, Pub. by Black Rose Bks CN) Consort Bk Sales.

Sex & Germs: The Politics of AIDS. Cindy Patton. LC 85-26240. 182p. (Orig.). (C). 1985. 35.00 (*0-89608-260-1*); pap. 12.00 (*0-89608-259-8*) South End Pr.

Sex & God: Some Varieties of Women's Religious Experience. Ed. by Linda Hurcombe. LC 86-29846. 288p. (Orig.). (C). 1987. pap. text ed. 14.95 (*0-7102-0945-2*, RKP) Routledge.

Sex & Human Life. 2nd ed. Eric T. Pengelley. LC 77-77720. (Life Sciences Ser.). (Illus.). 1978. pap. text ed. write for info. (*0-201-05770-0*) Addison-Wesley.

Sex & Insanity. Melvin Anchell. LC 83-81798. 169p. 1983. pap. 9.95 (*0-89420-238-3*, 110020, Halcyon) Natl Book.

Sex & Love. J. C. Willke. 1979. pap. 3.95 (*0-910728-10-0*) Hayes.

Sex & Love: Addiction, Treatment, & Recovery. Eric Griffen-Shelley. LC 90-21283. 224p. 1991. text ed. 49.95 (*0-275-93794-1*, C3794, Praeger Pubs) Greenwood.

***Sex & Love: Addiction, Treatment & Recovery.** Eric Griffin-Shelley. LC 90-21283. 1997. pap. text ed. 22.95 (*0-275-96065-X*, Praeger Pubs) Greenwood.

Sex & Love Addicts Anonymous. Augustine Fellowship Staff. 280p. 1986. text ed. 23.50 (*0-9615701-0-5*); pap. text ed. 13.50 (*0-9615701-1-3*) Augustine Fellow.

Sex & Love in Golden Age Spain. Ed. by Alain Saint-Saens. (Iberian Studies: No. 1). 220p. 1996. pap. 49.95 (*1-889431-01-X*) Univ Pr South.

Sex & Love Quotations: A Worldwide Dictionary of Pronouncements about Gender & Sexuality Throughout the Ages. Michael C. Thomsett & Jean F. Thomsett. LC 94-35595. 234p. 1995. lib. bdg. 35.00 (*0-7864-0048-X*) McFarland & Co.

Sex & Love When You're Single Again. Thomas F. Jones. 1990. pap. 9.99 (*0-8407-9571-8*) Nelson.

Sex & Marriage. Herbert I. Kavet. 96p. 1993. 5.95 (*0-88032-434-1*) Ivory Tower Pub.

Sex & Marriage: Eros in Contemporary Life. Havelock Ellis. LC 77-7264. 219p. 1977. reprint ed. text ed. 55.00 (*0-8371-9667-1*, ELSM, Greenwood Pr) Greenwood.

***Sex & Marriage in Ancient Ireland.** Patrick C. Power. 96p. 1997. pap. 12.95 (*0-8023-1318-3*) Dufour.

Sex & Marriage in the Unification Movement: A Sociological Study. James H. Grace. LC 85-2961. (Studies in Religion & Society: Vol. 13). 284p. 1985. lib. bdg. 89.95 (*0-88946-861-3*) E Mellen.

Sex & Masochism: Index of New Information. Jerry S. Hartford. 150p. 1997. 47.50 (*0-7883-0962-5*); pap. 44.50 (*0-7883-0963-3*) ABBE Pubs Assn.

Sex & Morality: Who Is Teaching Our Sex Standards? Ruth K. Westheimer. 212p. 1991. 3.99 (*0-517-69948-6*) Random Hse Value.

***Sex & One Single Beer Can: Probing the Mass Media & American Culture.** Walt Brasch. 256p. (Orig.). 1997. pap. 19.95 (*0-9624613-6-9*) Mayfly Prodns.

Sex & Orgasm Research: Index of Modern Information. rev. ed. Helen M. Markle. LC 88-48009. 150p. 1991. 47.50 (*1-55914-478-5*); pap. 44.50 (*1-55914-479-3*) ABBE Pubs Assn.

Sex & Other Sacred Games: Love, Desire, Power & Possession. Kim Chernin & Renate Stendhal. 1989. 17.95 (*0-8129-1676-X*, Times Bks) Random.

Sex & Other Touchy Subjects. Shelley L. Stockwell. LC 88-71940. (Illus.). 340p. (Orig.). 1990. pap. 14.95 (*0-912559-12-8*) Creativity Unltd Pr.

Sex & Pay in the Federal Government: Using Job Evaluation Systems to Implement Comparable Worth. Doris M. Werwie. LC 86-33576. (Contributions in Women's Studies: No. 82). (Illus.). 198p. 1987. text ed. 49.95 (*0-313-25499-0*, WUJ/, Greenwood Pr) Greenwood.

Sex & Pedophilia: Index of New Information Including Analysis & Results. Arlene S. Shank. LC 96-12663. 1996. 44.50 (*0-7883-0772-X*); pap. 39.50 (*0-7883-0773-8*) ABBE Pubs Assn.

Sex & Personality. H. J. Eysenck. 262p. 1976. text ed. 17.50 (*0-292-77529-6*) U of Tex Pr.

Sex & Peyronie's Disease (Penile Induration-Strabismus) Index of New Information. Hector H. Blickstein. 150p. 1994. 44.50 (*0-7883-0048-2*); pap. 39.50 (*0-7883-0049-0*) ABBE Pubs Assn.

Sex & Politicians: Affairs of State. Kerry Segrave. 330p. 1990. 19.95 (*0-8283-1938-3*) Branden Pub Co.

Sex & Power: The Rise of Women in America, Russia, Sweden, & Italy. Donald B. Meyer. LC 87-6080. 749p. 1987. reprint ed. pap. 180.00 (*0-608-02312-4*, 2062953) Bks Demand.

Sex & Pregnancy in Adolescence. Melvin Zelnick et al. LC 81-13541. (Sage Library of Social Research: No. 133). (Illus.). 272p. reprint ed. pap. 77.60 (*0-8357-4868-5*, 2037800) Bks Demand.

Sex & Prostitution: Index of Modern Information. Harold P. Drummond. LC 88-47978. 150p. 1990. 44.50 (*1-55914-182-4*); pap. 39.50 (*1-55914-183-2*) ABBE Pubs Assn.

Sex & Psyche: Gender & Self-Viewed Cross-Culturally. John E. Williams & Deborah L. Best. (Cross-Cultural Research & Methodology Ser.: Vol. 13). (Illus.). 240p. (C). 1990. 42.00 (*0-8039-3769-5*); pap. 20.95 (*0-8039-3770-9*) Sage.

Sex & Psychic Energy. Betty Bethards. 127p. 1990. pap. 12.95 (*0-918915-25-2*) Inner Light Found.

Sex & Psychology of Sexual Offenses: Index of New Information with Authors, Subjects & Bibliography. Joanna J. Levitt. 180p. 1993. 49.50 (*1-55914-768-7*); pap. 39.50 (*1-55914-769-5*) ABBE Pubs Assn.

Sex & Psychosexual Development: Index of New Information with Authors, Subjects & Bibliography. Allison C. Ledger. 180p. 1993. 47.50 (*1-55914-824-1*); pap. 44.50 (*1-55914-825-X*) ABBE Pubs Assn.

Sex & Purity. (Cross Training Ser.: Vol. 2). 64p. (YA). (gr. 10-12). 1994. pap. 29.95 (*1-57405-018-4*) CharismaLife Pub.

Sex & Race, 3 vols. J. A. Rogers. (Illus.). 1074p. 44.85 (*0-9602294-3-4*) H M Rogers.

Sex & Race, Vol. I: The Old World. J. A. Rogers. (Illus.). 411p. 1940. reprint ed. 14.95 (*0-9602294-0-X*) H M Rogers.

Sex & Race, Vol. II: The New World. J. A. Rogers. (Illus.). 304p. 1942. reprint ed. 14.95 (*0-9602294-1-8*) H M Rogers.

Sex & Race, Vol. III: Why White & Black Do Mate. J. A. Rogers. (Illus.). 359p. 1944. reprint ed. 14.95 (*0-9602294-2-6*) H M Rogers.

Sex & Racism in America. Calvin C. Hernton. 208p. 1992. pap. 10.95 (*0-385-42433-7*, Anchor NY) Doubleday.

Sex & Racism in America. Intro. by Calvin C. Hernton. LC 87-37254. 192p. 1988. pap. 8.95 (*0-8021-3089-5*, Grove) Grove-Atltic.

Sex & Reality: The Time Has Come! Meha Mondaito. LC 95-74971. (Illus.). 192p. (Orig.). 1996. pap. 14.95 (*1-56184-082-3*) New Falcon Pubns.

Sex & Reason. Richard A. Posner. 458p. (C). 1992. text ed. 29.95 (*0-674-80279-9*) HUP.

Sex & Reason. Richard A. Posner. 458p. (C). 1994. pap. text ed. 15.95 (*0-674-80280-2*) HUP.

Sex & Recovery: A Woman's Guide. rev. ed. Gayle Rosellini. 1994. pap. 0.50 (*0-89230-150-3*) Do It Now.

Sex & Religion. Clifford Howard. LC 72-9654. reprint ed. 36.00 (*0-404-57463-7*) AMS Pr.

Sex & Revolution: Women in Socialist Cuba. Lois M. Smith & Alfred Padula. 256p. (C). 1996. 39.95 (*0-19-509490-5*); pap. text ed. 17.95 (*0-19-509491-3*) OUP.

Sex & Russian Society. Ed. by Igor S. Kon & James Riordan. LC 92-33636. 176p. 1993. 31.50 (*0-253-33200-1*); pap. 11.95 (*0-253-33201-X*) Ind U Pr.

Sex & Salmonella. Kathleen Taylor. 288p. (Orig.). 1996. mass mkt. 5.50 (*0-380-78355-X*) Avon.

Sex & Sanity: The Myths & Realities of Human Sexuality. 2nd rev. ed. Tom-Blaise Shepherd. 60p. (Orig.). 1996. pap. 7.98 (*1-888716-09-6*) Xandex Pr.

Sex & Science. LC 73-20652. (Sex, Marriage & Society Ser.). 202p. 1974. reprint ed. 21.95 (*0-405-05817-9*) Ayer.

Sex & Scientific Inquiry. Ed. by Sandra Harding & Jean F. O'Barr. (Illus.). viii, 326p. (C). 1987. pap. text ed. 15.95 (*0-226-31627-0*) U Ch Pr.

Sex & Secrets: Crimes Involving Australian Women since 1880. Judith A. Allen. 304p. 1990. pap. 32.00 (*0-19-554839-6*) OUP.

Sex & Sense: A Contemporary Guide for Teenagers. Gary F. Kelly. 240p. (YA). 1993. pap. 8.95 (*0-8120-1446-4*) Barron.

Sex & Sensibility: Stories of a Lesbian Generation. Arlene Stein. LC 96-12500. 1997. 45.00 (*0-520-20257-0*); pap. 16.95 (*0-520-20674-6*) U CA Pr.

Sex & Sensibility: The Vanity of Bonfires. Marcia Pally. LC 93-40142. 1994. pap. 13.00 (*0-88001-364-8*) Ecco Pr.

Sex & Sexual Harassment: Index of New Information. Simon H. Bonner. LC 95-14593. 1995. 47.50 (*0-7883-0422-4*); pap. 44.50 (*0-7883-0423-2*) ABBE Pubs Assn.

***Sex & Sexuality.** Feldman. 1987. pap. text ed. write for info. (*0-582-29698-6*, Pub. by Longman UK) Longman.

Sex & Sexuality: From Repression to Expression. Mildred W. Weil. 376p. (Orig.). (C). 1990. pap. text ed. 28.50 (*0-8191-7648-6*); lib. bdg. 47.00 (*0-8191-7647-8*) U Pr of Amer.

***Sex & Sexuality: Risk & Relationships in the Age of AIDS.** Dana Lear. LC 97-4596. 157p. 1997. 42.00 (*0-7619-0477-8*); pap. 19.95 (*0-7619-0478-6*) Sage.

Sex & Sexuality in Ian McEwan's Work. Christina Byrnes. 39p. 1995. lib. bdg. 23.00 (*0-8095-6780-6*) Borgo Pr.

***Sex & Sexuality in Ian McEwan's Work.** Christina Byrnes. 39p. 1995. pap. 13.00 (*0-946650-56-X*) Borgo Pr.

Sex & Sexuality in Latin America. Ed. by Daniel Balderston & Donna J. Guy. LC 96-35697. 320p. (C). 1997. 55.00 (*0-8147-1289-4*); pap. 19.95 (*0-8147-1290-8*) NYU Pr.

***Sex & Sins in the Cemetery: Poems by John Silveira.** John E. Silveira. (Illus.). viii, 104p. (Orig.). 1996. pap. 12.95 (*0-9655203-0-7*) Backwoods Home Mag Inc.

Sex & Society: Studies in the Social Psychology of Sex. William I. Thomas. LC 73-14185. (Perspectives in Social Inquiry Ser.). 338p. 1974. reprint ed. 19.95 (*0-405-05529-3*) Ayer.

Sex & Society in Graeco-Roman Egypt. Dominic Montserrat. (Illus.). 280p. 1996. 76.50 (*0-7103-0530-3*, Pub. by Kegan Paul Intl UK) Col U Pr.

Sex & Society in the World of the Orthodox Slavs, 900-1700. Eve Levin. LC 89-30075. (Illus.). 344p. 1989. 45.00 (*0-8014-2260-4*) Cornell U Pr.

Sex & Society in the World of the Orthodox Slavs, 900-1700. Eve Levin. (Illus.). 344p. 1995. pap. 16.95 (*0-8014-8304-2*) Cornell U Pr.

***Sex & Spirit.** Clifford Bishop. (Living Wisdom Ser.). (Illus.). 184p. (Orig.). 1997. pap. 15.95 (*0-316-09606-7*) Little.

Sex & Spirit: Exploring Gay Men's Spirituality. Ed. by Robert Barzan. LC 95-60287. 144p. (Orig.). 1995. pap. 10.95 (*0-9645384-0-7*) White Crane.

Sex & Spirit: God, Woman, & the Ministry. Victoria B. Demarest. LC 76-42915. (Illus.). 146p. 1977. 6.95 (*0-912760-38-9*); pap. 10.00 (*0-912760-29-X*) Valkyrie Pub Hse.

Sex & Spiritual Emergence: A Study of Pain & Confusion. 1991. lib. bdg. 76.95 (*0-8490-4589-4*) Gordon Pr.

Sex & Status: Hierarchies in the Health Workforce. Ruth J. Simmons. LC 85-72881. 80p. 1985. 12.00 (*0-87553-134-2*) Am Pub Health.

Sex & Subjection: Attitudes to Women in Early-Modern Society. Margaret R. Sommerville. LC 95-14733. 1995. text ed. 49.95 (*0-340-64573-5*, Pub. by E Arnld UK); text ed. 19.95 (*0-340-64574-1*, Pub. by E Arnld UK) St Martin.

Sex & Subterfuge: Women Writers to 1850. Eva Figes. 1988. pap. 10.95 (*0-89255-129-1*) Persea Bks.

Sex & Suffrage in Britain, 1860-1914. Susan K. Kent. 336p. (Orig.). 1987. text ed. 49.50 (*0-691-05497-5*); pap. text ed. 17.95 (*0-691-00852-3*) Princeton U Pr.

Sex & Suits: The Evolution of Modern Dress. Anne Hollander. Ed. by Philip Turner & Deborah Baker. (Kodansha Globe Ser.). (Illus.). 224p. 1995. pap. 13.00 (*1-56836-101-7*, Kodansha Globe) Kodansha.

***Sex & Sunsets.** Tim Sandlin. LC 96-53695. 272p. 1997. reprint ed. pap. 12.00 (*1-57322-628-9*, Riverhd Trade) Berkley Pub.

Sex & Supervision: Guarding Male & Female Inmates. Jocelyn M. Pollock. LC 86-9987. (Contributions in Criminology & Penology Ser.: No. 12). 175p. 1986. text ed. 49.95 (*0-313-25410-9*, PSS/, Greenwood Pr) Greenwood.

Sex & Sweethearts. Vernon Howard. 1981. pap. 1.50 (*0-911203-05-2*) New Life.

Sex & Temperament in Three Primitive Societies. Margaret Mead. 1971. pap. 12.95 (*0-688-06016-1*, Quill) Morrow.

Sex & the Bible. Dale Conaway. 192p. (Orig.). 1996. pap. 14.99 (*1-56043-256-X*) Destiny Image.

Sex & the Bible. Gerald A. Larue. LC 83-60201. 173p. 1983. 28.95 (*0-87975-206-8*); pap. 20.95 (*0-87975-229-7*) Prometheus Bks.

Sex & the Biology of Coitus: Index of Modern Authors & Subjects with Guide for Rapid Research. Helen M. Markle. LC 88-47980. 153p. 1991. 47.50 (*1-55914-220-0*); pap. 44.50 (*1-55914-221-9*) ABBE Pubs Assn.

Sex & the Christian Teen. Jim Auer. LC 94-75179. 64p. (Orig.). 1994. pap. 3.95 (*0-89243-632-8*) Liguori Pubns.

***Sex & the Church: Gender, Homosexuality & the Transformation of Christian Ethics.** Kathy Rudy. LC 96-50190. 1997. 24.00 (*0-8070-1034-0*) Beacon Pr.

Sex & the City. Candace Bushnell. 208p. 1996. 21.00 (*0-87113-642-2*, Atlntc Mnthly) Grove-Atltic.

***Sex & the City.** Candace Bushnell. LC 97-15901. 240p. 1997. pap. 12.99 (*0-446-67354-4*) Warner Bks.

Sex & the City: A Serpent's Tail Compilation. Ed. by Marsha Rowe. 240p. (Orig.). 1990. pap. 9.95 (*1-85242-165-7*) Serpents Tail.

Sex & the Dinosaur. Perry A. Sperber. LC 77-111907. 212p. 1970. 8.00 (*0-87527-075-1*) Green.

Sex & the Empire That Is No More: Gender & the Politics of Metaphor in Oyo Yoruba Religion. J. Lorand Matory. LC 93-37980. (C). 1994. pap. text ed. 19.95 (*0-8166-2227-2*) U of Minn Pr.

Sex & the Human Psyche. John R. Yungblut. LC 75-19951. 32p. (Orig.). 1975. pap. 3.00 (*0-87574-203-3*) Pendle Hill.

Sex & the Italian Male. Andrea Blanche. (Illus.). 160p. 1997. 35.00 (*1-57687-014-6*, pwerHse Bks) pwerHse Cultrl.

Sex & the Italian Male. limited ed. Andrea Blanche & Gore Vidal. (Illus.). 160p. 1997. boxed 125.00 (*1-57687-015-4*, pwerHse Bks) pwerHse Cultrl.

Sex & the Liberated Man. Albert Ellis. 384p. 1976. 12.95 (*0-8184-0222-9*) Carol Pub Group.

Sex & the Marriage Covenant: A Basis for Morality. John F. Kippley. LC 91-72141. 364p. (Orig.). (C). 1991. pap. 14.95 (*0-9601036-9-4*) Couple to Couple.

Sex & the Modern Jewish Woman (1986) Annotated Bibliography & Essays. Compiled by Joan S. Brewer. 128p. (C). 1986. pap. 8.00 (*0-930395-01-8*) Biblio NY.

Sex & the New You. 2nd ed. Illus. by Rich Bimler. (Learning about Sex Ser.: Bk. 4). 64p. (J). (gr. 6-9). 1995. pap. 8.99 (*0-570-03555-4*, 14-2104) Concordia.

Sex & the Office. Helen G. Brown. 1983. pap. 2.95 (*0-380-64048-1*, 64048-1) Avon.

Sex & the Origins of Death. William R. Clark. (Illus.). 208p. 1996. 22.00 (*0-19-510644-X*) OUP.

Sex & the Outer Planets. Barbara Watters. LC 75-159422. 228p. 1971. 4.95 (*0-86690-169-8*, W1512-024) Am Fed Astrologers.

Sex & the Penitentials: The Development of a Sexual Code 550-1150. Pierre J. Payer. 232p. 1984. 35.00 (*0-8020-5649-0*) U of Toronto Pr.

Sex & the Population Crisis. John A. Loraine. LC 85-24774. 213p. 1986. reprint ed. text ed. 55.00 (*0-313-22505-2*, LOSP, Greenwood Pr) Greenwood.

Sex & the Sanctity of Human Life. William E. May. 141p. (Orig.). 1984. pap. 6.95 (*0-931888-17-4*) Christendom Pr.

Sex & the Single Camel. Phil Clendenen. 185p. (Orig.). 1994. pap. 13.95 (*1-879194-18-X*) GLB Pubs.

Sex & the Single Girl. Helen G. Brown. 1983. pap. 2.95 (*0-380-64030-9*, 64030-9) Avon.

Sex & the Single Person: Dealing Honestly with the Need for Intimacy. Robert G. DeMoss, Jr. 192p. 1995. pap. 10.99 (*0-310-20009-1*) Zondervan.

Sex & the Sober Alcoholic. Toby R. Drews. 180p. 1987. 9.95 (*0-9615995-0-2*) Recover Comns.

Sex & the Social Worker. Leonard Davis. 112p. (Orig.). 1994. pap. 14.95 (*1-85756-069-8*, Pub. by Janus Pubng UK) Paul & Co Pubs.

Sex & the Teenager. Mabel Fonseca. 1990. pap. text ed. 4.95 (*0-7069-5305-3*, Pub. by Vikas II) S Asia.

Sex & the Teenager: Choices & Decisions. Kieran Sawyer. LC 89-82512. 112p. (Orig.). (YA). (gr. 9-12). 1990. student ed., pap. text ed. 4.95 (*0-87793-423-1*); teacher ed., spiral bd. 13.95 (*0-87793-424-X*) Ave Maria.

Sex & the Workplace: The Impact of Sexual Behavior & Harassment on Women, Men, & Organizations. Barbara A. Gutek. LC 85-45054. (Management Ser.). 232p. text ed. 32.95 (*0-87589-656-1*) Jossey-Bass.

Sex & the Zodiac. Helen Terrell. LC 74-82754. 1976. 12.95 (*0-87212-058-9*) Libra.

Sex & Transsexualism: Index of Modern Information. Rosalie F. Zoltano. LC 88-47994. 150p. 1989. 44.50 (*1-55914-048-8*); pap. 39.50 (*1-55914-049-6*) ABBE Pubs Assn.

Sex & Violence: Issues in Representation & Experience. Ed. by Peter Gow & Penelope Harvey. LC 94-1689. 240p. (C). 1994. pap. 16.95 (*0-415-05734-5*, B4365) Routledge.

Sex & Violence: Issues in Representation & Experience. Ed. by Peter Gow & Penelope Harvey. LC 94-1689. 240p. (C). (gr. 13). 1994. text ed. 62.95 (*0-415-05733-7*, B4361) Routledge.

Sex & Your Stars: An Astrological Guide to Everybody's Favorite Pastime. Toni Goffe. Ed. by Cliff Carle. 1996. pap. 5.95 (*1-57644-007-9*) CCC Pubns.

Sex & Zen & a Bullet in the Head: The Essential Guide to Hong Kong's Mind-Bending Films. Stefan Hammond & Mike Wilkins. (Illus.). 256p. 1996. pap. 12.00 (*0-684-80341-0*, Fireside) S&S Trade.

Sex Aphrodisiacs. 1991. lib. bdg. 77.95 (*0-8490-4593-2*) Gordon Pr.

Sex Appeal. Kate Botting. 192p. 1996. 24.95 (*0-312-14412-1*) St Martin.

Sex, Art, & American Culture. Camille Paglia. LC 91-50933. 1992. pap. 14.00 (*0-679-74101-1*, Vin) Random.

Sex As a Heap of Malfunctioning Rubble: More of the Best of the Journal of Irreproducible Results. Ed. by Mark Abrahams. LC 92-50286. 208p. 1993. pap. 9.95 (*1-56305-312-8*, 3312) Workman Pub.

Sex As a Political Variable: Women As Candidates & Voters in U. S. Elections. Jody Newman et al. LC 97-9105. 240p. 1997. lib. bdg. 45.00 (*1-55587-636-6*, 876366) Lynne Rienner.

***Sex As a Political Variable: Women As Candidates & Voters in U. S. Elections.** Richard Seltzer et al. LC 97-9105. 1997. pap. write for info. (*1-55587-736-2*) Lynne Rienner.

Sex As a Sublimation for Tennis: From the Secret Writings of Freud. Theodore Saretsky. LC 84-40673. (Illus.). 112p. (Orig.). 1985. pap. 5.95 (*0-89480-912-1*, 912) Workman Pub.

Sex As a Symbol: The Ancient Light in Modern Psychology. Alvin B. Kuhn. 345p. 1992. pap. 27.00 (*1-56459-179-4*) Kessinger Pub.

***Sex at Risk: Lifetime Number of Partners, Frequency of Intercourse, & the Low AIDS Risk of Vaginal Intercourse.** Stuart Brody. LC 97-12110. 1997. 32.95 (*1-56000-309-X*) Transaction Pubs.

Sex at Work. Hearn. 1995. text ed. 55.00 (*0-312-12956-4*) St Martin.

Sex at Work. Jeff Hearn. 1995. text ed. 18.95 (*0-312-12957-2*) St Martin.

S

S

Sex at Work: The Power & Paradox of Organization Sexuality. Jeff Hearn & Wendy Parkin. LC 86-27997. 224p. 1987. text ed. 12.95 (*0-312-00460-5*) St Martin.

Sex Backpack. Tony Raskob. (Illus.). (YA). (gr. 7-12). 1994. pap. 9.95 (*0-9642469-0-2*) Lrning to Lrn.

Sex Barrier in Business. Eleanor B. Schwartz. LC 81-6287. 116p. 1971. pap. 19.95 (*0-88406-184-1*) GA St U Busn Pr.

Sex-Based Discrimination - Text, Cases & Materials on Sex-Based Discrimination. 4th ed. Herma H. Kay & Martha S. West. (American Casebook Ser.). 1260p. 1996. text ed. write for info. (*0-314-09633-7*) West Pub.

Sex-Based Discrimination, 1994 Supplement to Cases & Materials on. Herma H. Kay. (American Casebook Ser.). 425p. 1994. pap. text ed. 18.00 (*0-314-04235-0*) West Pub.

Sex-Based Employment Discrimination. Susan M. Omilian. 1990. 130.00 (*0-685-46258-7*) Clark Boardman Callaghan.

Sex Before Golf. Martin A. Ragaway. (Illus.). 48p. (Orig.). 1982. pap. 2.95 (*0-8431-0313-2*) Putnam Pub Group.

Sex Behavior: Medical Subject Analysis & Research Bibliography. American Health Research Institute Staff. LC 84-45662. 150p. 1985. 39.50 (*0-88164-204-5*); pap. 34.50 (*0-88164-205-3*) ABBE Pubs Assn.

Sex Behavior, HIV & AIDS: Index of New Information with Authors & Subjects. Martine M. Yannock. 180p. 1992. 47.50 (*1-55914-648-6*); pap. 44.50 (*1-55914-649-4*) ABBE Pubs Assn.

Sex Behind Bars: A Novella, Short Stories & True Accounts. Robert N. Boyd. 240p. (Orig.). 1995. reprint ed. pap. 14.95 (*0-917342-34-8*) Gay Sunshine.

Sex Between Men: An Intimate History of the Sex Lives of Gay Men Postwar to Present. Douglas Sadownick. LC 95-25895. 1996. pap. write for info. (*0-06-251269-2*) Harper SF.

Sex Between Men: An Intimate History of the Sex Lives of Gay Men Postwar to Present. Douglas Sadownick. LC 95-25895. 288p. 1996. 25.00 (*0-06-251268-4*) Harper SF.

Sex Bias in School Leadership. Jacqueline P. Clement. LC 75-3712. 1975. 2.70 (*0-912008-10-5*) Equity & Excel.

Sex Bias in the Schools: The Research Evidence. Ed. by Janice Pottker & Andrew Fishel. LC 74-200. 571p. 1976. 50.00 (*0-8386-1464-7*) Fairleigh Dickinson.

Sex Book for Those Who Think They Know It All. Charles L. Pelton. Ed. by Sheryl Klinkel. (Illus.). 227p. 1980. pap. 14.95 (*0-931470-04-8*); lib. bdg. 24.95 (*0-931470-03-X*) Fam Health Media.

Sex Box: Man - Sex - Woman. LC 96-6780. 528p. 1996. boxed 29.95 (*0-8118-1372-X*) Chronicle Bks.

Sex by Prescription: The Startling Truth about Today's Sex Therapy. Thomas Szasz. 224p. 1990. reprint ed. pap. 14.95 (*0-8156-0250-2*) Syracuse U Pr.

Sex, Career & Family: Including an International Review of Women's Roles. Michael P. Fogarty et al. LC 70-158823. 582p. reprint ed. pap. 165.90 (*0-317-29679-5*, 2021900) Bks Demand.

Sex, Cells, & Same-Sex Desire: The Biology of Sexual Preference. Dececco. LC 95-6140. 1994. pap. text ed. 19.95 (*1-56023-060-6*) Harrington Pk.

Sex, Cells, & Same-Sex Desire: The Biology of Sexual Preference. Ed. by David A. Parker & John P. De Cecco. LC 95-6140. 1995. 49.95 (*1-56024-700-2*) Haworth Pr.

***Sex Changes: The Politics of Transgenderism.** Pat Califia. LC 97-19966. 250p. (Orig.). 1997. pap. 16.95 (*1-57344-072-8*) Cleis Pr.

Sex-Charge. Perry Brass. Ed. by John Hammond. LC 90-83699. (Illus.). 76p. (Orig.). 1991. pap. 6.95 (*0-9627123-0-2*) Belhue Pr.

Sex Chromosome Aneuploidy: Prospective Studies on Children. Ed. by Arthur Robinson et al. LC 78-13921. (Alan R. Liss Ser.: Vol. 15, No. 1). 1979. 38.00 (*0-685-03298-1*) March of Dimes.

Sex Chromosomes & Sex Determination in Vertebrates. Alberto J. Solari. LC 93-7964. 352p. 1993. 172.95 (*0-8493-4571-5*, QH600) CRC Pr.

Sex, Church, & the Jungle. Comment by Garry De Young. pap. 15.00 (*0-936128-28-3*) De Young Pr.

Sex, Class & Culture. Lillian Robinson. 388p. 1986. pap. text ed. 13.95 (*0-416-01241-8*, 9874) Routledge Chapman & Hall.

Sex, Class, & Culture. Lillian S. Robinson. LC 77-15762. 373p. reprint ed. pap. 106.40 (*0-317-27848-7*, 2056052) Bks Demand.

Sex, Class & Realism: British Cinema 1956-63. John Hill. 228p. 1986. 37.50 (*0-85170-132-9*, Pub. by British Film Inst UK); pap. 16.95 (*0-85170-133-7*, Pub. by British Film Inst UK) Ind U Pr.

***Sex, Color & Mate Choice in Guppies.** Anne E. Houde. LC 96-49200. (Monographs in Behavior & Ecology). 1997. pap. write for info. (*0-691-02789-7*) Princeton U Pr.

***Sex, Color & Mate Choice in Guppies.** Anne E. Houde. LC 96-49200. (Monographs in Behavior & Ecology). 1997. write for info. (*0-691-02790-0*) Princeton U Pr.

Sex, Contraception, & Motherhood in Jamaica. Eugene B. Brody. LC 81-4133. (Commonwealth Fund Publications). (Illus.). 288p. (C). 1981. 32.00 (*0-674-80277-2*) HUP.

Sex Counseling - Guidelines, Assessment & Treatment: Index of Modern Authors & Subjects with Guide for Rapid Research. Clayton R. Mellows. LC 90-56284. 160p. 1991. 44.50 (*1-55914-350-9*); pap. 39.50 (*1-55914-351-7*) ABBE Pubs Assn.

Sex, Crime & Society. Jogeshwar Mahanta. viii, 112p. (C). 1993. 15.00 (*81-7024-548-6*, Pub. by Ashish Pub Hse II) Nataraj Bks.

Sex Crime Investigation: The Complete Investigator's Handbook. F. D. Jordan. (Illus.). 328p. 1996. pap. 35.00 (*0-87364-874-9*) Paladin Pr.

Sex Crimes. Ronald M. Holmes. (Illus.). 160p. 1991. 45.00 (*0-8039-3952-3*); pap. 19.95 (*0-8039-3953-1*) Sage.

***Sex Crimes.** Shute Jenefer. 240p. 1998. pap. 10.95 (*0-385-31968-1*) Doubleday.

Sex Crimes. Donald J. West. (International Library of Criminology & Criminal Justice). 352p. 1994. 99.95 (*1-85521-358-3*, Pub. by Dartmth Pub UK) Ashgate Pub Co.

Sex Crimes: A Novel. Shute Jenefer. LC 96-7456. 176p. 1996. 18.95 (*0-385-48504-2*) Doubleday.

Sex Crimes: Ten Years on the Front Lines Prosecuting Rapists & Confronting Their Collaborators. Alice Vachss. LC 94-17954. 1994. pap. 12.95 (*0-8050-3502-8*) H Holt & Co.

Sex Crimes Against Children: Tracking the Child Abuse Report from Community Concern Through Criminal Prosecution & Sentencing. 68p. (Orig.). (C). 1993. pap. text ed. 20.00 (*0-7881-0030-0*) DIANE Pub.

Sex Crimes Investigation. Burt Rapp. LC 87-83444. 200p. (Orig.). 1988. pap. 16.95 (*0-915179-72-5*, 55071) Loompanics.

Sex Crimes on Trial: The Use of Sexual Evidence in Scottish Courts. Beverley Brown et al. (Edinburgh Law & Society Ser.). 234p. 1994. text ed. 45.00 (*0-7486-0408-1*, Pub. by Edinburgh U Pr UK) Col U Pr.

Sex, Culture, & Modernity in China. Frank Dikotter. LC 94-46204. (Illus.). 200p. (C). 1995. text ed. 28.00 (*0-8248-1676-5*) UH Pr.

***Sex, Culture & Modernity in China: Medical Science & the Construction of Sexual Identities in the Early Republican Period.** Ed. by Frank Dikotter. 240p. 1995. pap. 42.50 (*962-209-382-5*, Pub. by Hong Kong Univ Pr HK) Coronet Bks.

Sex, Death & Enlightenment: A True Story. Mark Matousek. 288p. 1996. 22.95 (*1-57322-032-9*, Riverhead Books) Putnam Pub Group.

Sex, Death & Fly-Fishing. John Gierach. 208p. 1990. pap. 11.00 (*0-671-68437-X*) S&S Trade.

Sex, Death, & God in L. A. Ed. by David Reid. LC 93-38872. 1994. pap. 13.00 (*0-520-08640-6*) U CA Pr.

Sex, Death, & Hierarchy in a Chinese City: An Anthropological Account. William R. Jankowiak. (Illus.). 376p. 1992. text ed. 49.50 (*0-231-07960-5*); pap. text ed. 18.50 (*0-231-07961-3*) Col U Pr.

Sex, Death & Starshine. Clive Barker. 1992. pap. 7.95 (*1-56060-144-2*) Eclipse Bks.

Sex, Death & the Angry Young Man: Conversations with Riane Eisler & David Loye. Mathew Callahan. (Illus.). 120p. (Orig.). 1993. pap. 8.50 (*0-87810-040-7*) Times Change.

Sex, Death, & the Education of Children: Our Passion for Ignorance in the Age of AIDS. Jonathan Silin. (Politics of Identity Ser.). 264p. (C). 1995. text ed. 39.00 (*0-8077-3406-3*); pap. text ed. 18.95 (*0-8077-3405-5*) Tchrs Coll.

***Sex Death Enlightenment: A True Story.** Mark Matousek. 365p. 1997. reprint ed. pap. 12.00 (*1-57322-581-9*, Riverhd Trade) Berkley Pub.

Sex Determination. G. Bacci & G. A. Kerkut. LC 65-17948. (International Series of Monographs on Pure & Applied Mathematics: Vol. 26). 1965. 138.00 (*0-08-011291-9*, Pub. by Pergamon Repr UK) Franklin.

Sex Determination & Sexual Dimorphism in Mammals. Alfred Glucksmann & M. I. Smith. LC 78-63273. (Wykeham Science Ser.: No. 54). 174p. (C). 1979. pap. 18.00 (*0-8448-1370-2*, Crane Russak) Taylor & Francis.

Sex Determination, Differentiation & Intersexuality in Placental Mammals. R. H. Hunter. (Illus.). 314p. (C). 1995. text ed. 80.00 (*0-521-46218-5*) Cambridge U Pr.

Sex Determination in Immature Cockatiels. David M. Slater. (Illus.). 13p. (C). 1989. pap. text ed. write for info. (*0-318-66533-6*, 1050) Starbird Pubns.

***Sex Determination in Mouse & Man.** 157p. 1989. text ed. 80.00 (*0-521-38003-0*) Cambridge U Pr.

Sex Diary of a Metaphysician. Colin Wilson. 256p. 1994. pap. 12.95 (*0-914171-59-3*) Ronin Pub.

Sex, Diet & Debility in Jacksonian America: Sylvester Graham & Health Reform. Stephen Nissenbaum. LC 79-8280. (Contributions in Medical History Ser.: No. 4). xvii, 198p. 1980. text ed. 49.95 (*0-313-21415-8*, NSY/, Greenwood Pr) Greenwood.

Sex, Diet, & Debility in Jacksonian America: Sylvester Graham & Health Reform. Stephen Nissenbaum. 198p. (C). 1989. reprint ed. pap. 24.95 (*0-534-10915-2*) Wadsworth Pub.

Sex Differences: Modern Biology & the Unisex Fallacy. Yves Christen. Tr. by Nicholas Davidson from FRE. 256p. (C). 1990. 34.95 (*0-88738-869-8*) Transaction Pubs.

Sex Differences & Learning: An Annotated Bibliography of Educational Research, 1979-1989. Jean D. Grambs & John C. Carr. LC 90-19600. (Bibliographies in Contemporary Education Ser.: Vol. 11). 304p. 1991. text ed. 40.00 (*0-8240-6641-3*) Garland.

Sex Differences in Behaviour: Their Relevance for Adult Educators. L. C. Berryman. (C). 1988. text ed. 45.00 (*0-685-22140-7*, Pub. by Univ Nottingham UK) St Mut.

Sex Differences in Britain. 2nd ed. Ed. by Ivan Reid & Drica Stratta. (Illus.). 1989. text ed. 64.95 (*0-566-05595-3*, Pub. by Gower UK); pap. text ed. 21.95 (*0-566-05804-9*, Pub. by Gower UK) Ashgate Pub Co.

Sex Differences in Cognitive Abilities. 2nd ed. Diane F. Halpern. 336p. (C). 1992. pap. 32.50 (*0-8058-0845-0*); text ed. 69.95 (*0-8058-0844-2*) L Erlbaum Assocs.

Sex Differences in Depression. Susan Nolen-Hoeksema. LC 89-27303. 270p. 1990. 42.50 (*0-8047-1640-4*) Stanford U Pr.

Sex Differences in Depression. Susan Nolen-Hoeksema. 270p. (C). 1993. pap. 14.95 (*0-8047-2180-7*) Stanford U Pr.

Sex Differences in Human Performance. fac. ed. Ed. by Mary A. Baker. LC 86-9182. (Wiley Series on Studies in Human Performance). (Illus.). 218p. 1987. reprint ed. pap. 62.20 (*0-608-00969-5*, 2061816) Bks Demand.

Sex Differences in Political Participation: Processes of Change in Fourteen Nations. Carol Christy. LC 87-9336. 208p. 1987. text ed. 55.00 (*0-275-92433-5*, C2433, Praeger Pubs) Greenwood.

Sex Differences in Social Behavior: A Social-Role Interpretation. Alice Eagly. (MacEachran Memorial Lectures). 192p. (C). 1987. text ed. 29.95 (*0-89859-804-4*) L Erlbaum Assocs.

Sex Differences in the Human Life Cycle. 7th ed. Madeleine J. Goodman & Lenn E. Goodman. (Illus.). 430p. 1987. pap. text ed. 30.00 (*0-917232-22-4*) Gee Tee Bee.

Sex Differences in the Professional Life Changes of Chemists. Barbara F. Reskin. Ed. by Harriet Zuckerman & Robert K. Merton. LC 79-9041. (Dissertations on Sociology Ser.). 1980. lib. bdg. 44.95 (*0-405-12987-4*) Ayer.

Sex Differentiation & Chromosomal Abnormalities. Ed. by Robert Summit & Daniel Bergsma. (Alan R. Liss, Inc. Ser.: Vol. 14, No. 6c). 1978. 61.00 (*0-686-23951-2*) March of Dimes.

Sex Differentiation & Ovarian Function: Tokyo Conference of Reproductive Physiology III, Tokyo, August 1995. Ed. by Y. Yoshimura & O. Tsutsumi. (Journal: Hormone Research Ser.: Vol. 46, Suppl. 1, 1996). (Illus.). iv, 52p. 1996. pap. 26.25 (*3-8055-6342-6*) S Karger.

***Sex Discrimination.** Babcock. 1996. 60.00 (*0-316-07488-8*) Little.

Sex Discrimination: Employment Law & Practices. Arjun Aggarwal. 352p. 1994. boxed 75.00 (*0-409-90674-3*, CN) MICHIE.

Sex Discrimination Handbook. Ed. by Barbara S. Gamble. LC 92-24161. 411p. 1992. pap. 40.00 (*0-87179-763-1*, 0763) BNA Books.

Sex Discrimination in a Nutshell. 2nd ed. Thomas C. Sherman. LC 82-2657. (Nutshell Ser.). 395p. (C). 1991. reprint ed. pap. 16.50 (*0-314-89418-7*) West Pub.

Sex Discrimination in European Community Law. Julian Currall. (European Community Law Ser.). (C). 1994. text ed. 85.00 (*0-485-70005-0*, Pub. by Athlone Pr UK) Humanities.

Sex Discrimination in the Labour Market: The Case for Comparable Worth. Ed. by Richard Perlman & Maureen Pike. 240p. 1994. text ed. 59.95 (*0-7190-3336-5*, Pub. by Manchester Univ Pr UK) St Martin.

Sex Discrimination in the Legal Profession. Bernard F. Lentz & David N. Laband. LC 95-3777. 256p. 1995. text ed. 55.00 (*0-89930-928-3*, Quorum Bks) Greenwood.

Sex Discrimination in the Workplace: A Legal Handbook. rev. ed. Women's Legal Defense Fund Staff. 71p. 1989. pap. 7.95 (*0-932689-21-3*) Women's Legal Defense.

Sex Discrimination Law. Evelyn Ellis. 1988. text ed. 59.95 (*0-566-05355-1*, Pub. by Dartmth Pub UK) Ashgate Pub Co.

***Sex, Disease & Society: A Comparative History of Sexually Transmitted Diseases & HIV AIDS in Asia & the Pacific.** Mioton J. Lewis et al. LC 96-28065. (Contributions in Medical Studies). 312p. 1997. text ed. 69.50 (*0-313-29442-9*, Greenwood Pr) Greenwood.

Sex Disorders: Medical Subject Analysis & Research Guidebook with Bibliography. American Health Research Institute Staff. Ed. by John C. Bartone. LC 84-45866. 150p. 1987. 44.50 (*0-88164-288-6*); pap. 34.50 (*0-88164-289-4*) ABBE Pubs Assn.

Sex, Dissidence & Damnation: Minority Groups in the Middle Ages. Jeffrey Richards. 192p. (C). (gr. 13). 1994. pap. 15.95 (*0-415-07147-X*, C0428) Routledge.

Sex, Drink & Fast Cars. Stephen Bayley. LC 86-42976. (Illus.). 192p. 1987. 7.95 (*0-394-75046-2*) Pantheon.

Sex Drugs & Aphrodisiacs. Adam Gottlieb. 90p. (Orig.). 1996. pap. 9.95 (*0-914171-56-9*) Ronin Pub.

***Sex, Drugs, & Madness in Poetry from William Blake to Christina Rossetti: Woman's Pain, Woman's Pleasure.** Eijun Senaha. LC 96-44964. 176p. 1997. text ed. 79.95 (*0-7734-2276-5*, Mellen Univ Pr) E Mellen.

***Sex, Drugs & Rock 'N' Roll.** Chris Charlesworth. (Illus.). 192p. pap. 19.95 (*0-7119-3445-2*, BO 10146) Omnibus NY.

Sex, Drugs, & the Continuing Spread of AIDS. Clyde B. McCoy & James A. Inciardi. LC 94-13908. (Illus.). 181p. (Orig.). (C). 1995. pap. text ed. write for info. (*0-935732-64-0*) Roxbury Pub Co.

Sex, Drugs & Windmills: The Horrible Truth about Holland. Hans Van Der Neut et al. 120p. 1996. 22.00 (*90-802267-3-4*, Pub. by NeXed Edits NE) Intl Spec Bk.

Sex, Drugs, Death & the Law: An Essay on Human Rights & Overcriminalization. David A. Richards. LC 81-23392. (Philosophy & Society Ser.). 328p. 1982. 60.00 (*0-8476-7063-5*); pap. 24.50 (*0-8476-7525-4*) Rowman.

Sex, Drugs, Rock & Roll. Eric Bognasian. LC 96-36475. 136p. (Orig.). 1996. pap. 10.95 (*1-55936-124-7*) Theatre Comm.

Sex, Ecology, Spirituality: The Spirit of Evolution. Ken Wilber. LC 94-3701. 816p. 1995. 40.00 (*1-57062-072-5*) Shambhala Pubns.

Sex, Economy, Freedom & Community. Wendell Berry. 208p. 1994. pap. 11.00 (*0-679-75651-5*) Pantheon.

***Sex Ed.** Miriam Stoppard. 96p. 1997. pap. 9.95 (*0-7894-2077-5*); pap. text ed. write for info. (*0-7894-1751-0*) DK Pub Inc.

***Sex Ed.** Miriam Stoppard. LC 97-14341. (J). 1997. write for info. (*0-7894-2385-5*) DK Pub Inc.

Sex Education. Jenny Davis. 160p. (YA). (gr. 7 up). 1995. reprint ed. mass mkt. 3.99 (*0-440-20483-6*, LLL BDD) BDD Bks Young Read.

Sex Education: An Islamic Perspective. Shahid Athar. 102p. (Orig.). 1995. pap. 12.50 (*0-934905-30-4*) Kazi Pubns.

Sex Education: Political Issues in Britain & Europe. Philip Meredith & Alan Beattie. 250p. (C). 1989. lib. bdg. 49.95 (*0-415-00604-X*) Routledge.

Sex Education: Teacher's Guide & Resource Manual. rev. ed. Steven Bignell. Ed. by Jane Hiatt & Mary Nelson. 277p. 1982. 29.95 (*0-941816-08-7*) ETR Assocs.

Sex Education: The Final Plague. Randy Engel. LC 92-60958. 229p. 1993. reprint ed. pap. 12.00 (*0-89555-471-2*) TAN Bks Pubs.

Sex Education Activities. Patricia R. Toner. LC 93-14860. (Just for the Health of It Ser.: Unit 4). 1993. pap. 18.95 (*0-87628-851-4*) Ctr Appl Res.

Sex Education & Family Life for Visually Handicapped Children & Youth: A Resource Guide. Ed. by Irving R. Dickman. 96p. reprint ed. pap. 27.40 (*0-685-16094-7*, 2027352) Bks Demand.

Sex Education & Successful Parenting. Ann Murphy & John Murphy. LC 94-4980. 100p. 1996. pap. 4.95 (*0-8198-6960-0*) Pauline Bks.

Sex Education & the Law: Issues & Implications. Ed. by Neville Harris. 150p. 1996. pap. 27.50 (*1-874579-66-0*, Pub. by Natl Childrens Bur UK) Paul & Co Pubs.

Sex Education Dictionary for Today's Teens & Preteens. Dean Hoch & Nancy Hoch. LC 89-63577. (Illus.). 128p. (Orig.). (YA). (gr. 5-12). 1990. pap. 12.95 (*0-9624209-0-5*) Landmark ID.

Sex Education for Persons with Disabilities That Hinder Learning: A Teacher's Guide. 1988. 19.95 (*1-56304-010-7*) J Stanfield.

Sex Education for Physically Handicapped Youth. C. Edmund Hopper & William A. Allen. (Illus.). 154p. 1980. text ed. 23.95 (*0-398-03935-6*) C C Thomas.

Sex Education for Physically Handicapped Youth. Edmund Hopper & William A. Allen. (Illus.). 154p. 1980. pap. 16.95 (*0-398-06336-2*) C C Thomas.

Sex Education for Teenagers & Young Adults. Anne E. Jordheimi. 69p. (YA). (gr. 7-12). 1992. pap. 6.95 (*1-57515-021-2*) PPI Pubng.

Sex Education Handbook. Richard N. Diggs. (Illus.). 216p. (YA). (gr. 6-12). 1994. pap. text ed. 17.95 (*0-937157-13-9*) Progressive Pubns.

Sex Education in a Church Setting: The OCTOPUS Training Manual. Fred Isberner et al. LC 86-13014. 128p. (Orig.). 1986. pap. text ed. 12.95 (*0-8093-1315-4*) S Ill U Pr.

Sex Education in the Classroom. J. C. Willke. 1977. 4.95 (*0-910728-11-9*) Hayes.

Sex Education in the Eighties: The Challenge of Healthy Sexual Evolution. Ed. by Lorna Brown. LC 81-15738. (Perspectives in Sexuality Ser.). 278p. (C). 1981. 49.50 (*0-306-40762-0*, Plenum Pr) Plenum.

Sex Education on Film: A Guide to Visual Aids & Programs. Laura J. Singer & Judith Buskin. LC 75-154694. 176p. reprint ed. pap. 50.20 (*0-685-15316-9*, 2026230) Bks Demand.

Sex Education, Rationale & Reaction. Ed. by Rex S. Rogers. LC 73-89764. 295p. reprint ed. pap. 84.10 (*0-317-26377-3*, 2024519) Bks Demand.

Sex Education: Syllabus. Lester A. Kirkendall & Ruth F. Osborne. 1971. pap. text ed. 7.80 (*0-89420-087-9*, 216786); audio 82.60 (*0-89420-184-0*, 180800) Natl Book.

Sex Equality. Jane English. LC 76-53000. (Illus.). 256p. 1977. write for info. (*0-13-807594-8*) P-H.

Sex Equality Law in the European Union. Ed. by Tamara K. Hervey & David O'Keeffe. 1996. text ed. 75.00 (*0-471-96436-0*) Wiley.

***Sex Equality Policy in Western Europe.** Ed. by Frances Gardiner. 224p. (C). 1997. text ed. 65.00 (*0-415-14404-3*) Routledge.

Sex Equity & Sexuality in Education. Ed. by Susan S. Klein. LC 91-4161. 381p. 1992. text ed. 64.50 (*0-7914-1033-1*); pap. text ed. 21.95 (*0-7914-1034-X*) State U NY Pr.

Sex Equity in Education: Readings & Strategies. Anne O. Carelli. (Illus.). 412p. 1988. pap. text ed. 44.95 (*0-398-06628-0*) C C Thomas.

Sex Equity in Education: Readings & Strategies. Anne O. Carelli. (Illus.). 412p. (C). 1988. text ed. 59.95 (*0-398-05415-0*) C C Thomas.

Sex Errors of the Body: Dilemmas, Education, Counseling. John Money. LC 68-15447. (Illus.). 160p. reprint ed. pap. 45.60 (*0-7837-3393-3*, 2043351) Bks Demand.

Sex Errors of the Body & Related Syndromes: A Guide to Counseling Children, Adolescents, & Their Families. 2nd ed. John Money. LC 94-14341. 160p. 1994. 29.95 (*1-55766-150-2*) P H Brookes.

Sex Ethics in the Writings of Moses Maimonides. Fred Rosner. LC 94-19613. 144p. 1994. pap. 20.00 (*1-56821-323-9*) Aronson.

Sex, Ethnics, & Equal Talent: Between Mathematics & Psychology. J. Fang. 1995. pap. 19.95 (*0-318-72910-5*) PAIDEIA & PM.

Sex, Evolution, & Behavior. 2nd ed. Martin Daly & Margo Wilson. 402p. (C). 1983. pap. 33.95 (*0-87150-767-6*) Wadsworth Pub.

Sex Exposed: Sexuality & the Pornography Debate. Ed. by Lynne Segal & Mary McIntosh. LC 92-29843. 344p. (C). 1993. 45.00 (*0-8135-1937-3*); pap. 15.95 (*0-8135-1938-1*) Rutgers U Pr.

Sex Factor & the Management of Schools. Neal Gross & Anne E. Trask. LC 75-34337. 286p. reprint ed. 81.60 (*0-8357-9977-8*, 2055256) Bks Demand.

An Asterisk (*) at the beginning of an entry indicates that the title is appearing in BIP for the first time.

Sex Facts: A Handbook for the Carnally Curious. Leslee Welch. 108p. 1995. pap. 7.95 (0-8065-1678-X, Citadel Pr) Carol Pub Group.
Sex, Family & the Woman in Society. Torkom Saraydarian. LC 86-71759. 1987. 25.00 (0-911794-53-0); pap. 20.00 (0-911794-54-9) Aqua Educ.
Sex-Fiend Monologues. Thaddeus Rutkowski. 33p. 1994. per., pap. 4.00 (1-886206-11-2) Venom Pr.
Sex for Beginners. Errol Selkirk. (Writers & Readers Documentary Comic Bks.). (Illus.). (Orig.). 1987. pap. 7.95 (0-86316-011-5) Writers & Readers.
Sex for Christians. rev. ed. Lewis B. Smedes. 256p. 1994. pap. 12.00 (0-8028-0743-7) Eerdmans.
Sex for Dummies. Ruth K. Westheimer. 1995. pap. 16.99 (1-56884-384-4) IDG Bks.
Sex for One: The Art of Male Masturbation. Gary Griffin. (Illus.). 80p. 1995. pap. 9.95 (1-879967-15-4) Added Dimensns.
Sex for One: The Joy of Selfloving. Betty Dodson. (Illus.). 1992. pap. 12.00 (0-517-58832-3, Harmony) Crown Pub Group.
Sex for One: The Joy of Selfloving. Betty Dodson. 192p. 1996. pap. 14.00 (0-517-88607-3) Crown Pub Group.
Sex for Straights: A Call for Critical Thinking by Teenagers Who Oppose Sexual Perversion. Madonna Knot. (Illus.). 34p. (YA). (gr. 7-12). 1993. lib. bdg. 49.95 (0-9623133-5-1) Oxner Inst.
Sex for the Common Man. LC 73-20654. 222p. 1974. reprint ed. 23.95 (0-405-05819-5) Ayer.
Sex for the Soul. Nancy Simmons. (Illus.). 152p. (Orig.). (C). 1989. pap. 12.95 (0-929680-00-6) Inner Voice.
Sex, Gay Men, & AIDS. Ed. by Peter M. Davies et al. LC 93-16012. (Social Aspects of AIDS Ser.). 1993. 85.00 (0-7507-0095-5, Falmer Pr); pap. 29.00 (0-7507-0096-3, Falmer Pr) Taylor & Francis.
Sex, Gender & Care Work. Ed. by Gordon Horobin. LC 87-9787. (Research Highlights in Social Work Ser.). 112p. 1987. text ed. 29.95 (0-312-01141-5) St Martin.
Sex, Gender & Christian Ethics. Lisa S. Cahill. (New Studies in Christian Ethics: No. 9). 318p. (C). 1996. text ed. 49.95 (0-521-44011-4) Cambridge U Pr.
Sex, Gender & Christian Ethics. Lisa S. Cahill. (New Studies in Christian Ethics: No. 9). 318p. (C). 1996. pap. text ed. 16.95 (0-521-57848-5) Cambridge U Pr.
***Sex, Gender & Desire in the Plays of Christopher Marlowe.** Sara M. Deats. LC 96-40157. 1997. write for info. (0-87413-613-X) U Delaware Pr.
Sex, Gender, & the Politics of ERA: A State & the Nation. Donald G. Mathews & Jane S. De Hart. (Illus.). 304p. 1992. reprint ed. pap. 18.95 (0-19-507852-7) OUP.
Sex, Guilt & Forgiveness. Josh McDowell. 89p. 1990. pap. 2.99 (0-8423-5908-7, 725908-7) Tyndale.
Sex, Health, & Long Life: Manuals of Taoist Practice. Tr. by Thomas Cleary. LC 94-22555. 144p. (Orig.). 1995. pap. 6.00 (1-57062-059-8) Shambhala Pubns.
Sex, Health, & Long Life: Manuals of Taoist Practice. Tr. by Thomas Cleary. (Orig.). 1995. pap. text ed. 48.00 (1-57062-060-1) Shambhala Pubns.
Sex, Honor & Power in the Deuteronomistic History: A Narratological & Anthropological Analysis. Ken Stone. (JSOTS Ser.: No. 234). 200p. 1997. 45.00 (1-85075-640-6, Pub. by Sheffield Acad UK) CUP Services.
Sex Hormones. IARC Working Group on the Evaluation of the Carcinogenic Risk of Chemicals to Man (1976: Lyon, France) Staff. (IARC Monographs on the Evaluation of the Carcinogenic Risk of Chemicals to Humans: No. 6). 245p. reprint ed. pap. 69.90 (0-8357-6458-3, 2035829) Bks Demand.
Sex Hormones & Antihormones in Endocrine Dependent Pathology: Proceedings of an International Symposium, Milano, 10-14 April 1994. Ed. by Marcella Motta & Mario Serio. LC 94-32151. (International Congress Ser.: Vol. 1064). 448p. 1994. 233.50 (0-444-81879-0) Elsevier.
Sex, Hormones & Behaviour. CIBA Foundation Staff. (CIBA Foundation Symposium: New Ser.: No. 62). 390p. reprint ed. pap. 111.20 (0-317-29765-1, 2022185) Bks Demand.
***Sex Hormones II: The Evaluation of Carcinogenic Risks to Humans.** (IARC Monographs: No. 21). 583p. 1979. text ed. 72.00 (92-832-1221-5) World Health.
Sex Imperative: An Evolutionary Tale of Sexual Survival. K. Maxwell. (Illus.). 332p. (C). 1994. 24.95 (0-306-44649-9, Plenum Pr) Plenum.
Sex in America. Robert T. Michael et al. 320p. 1995. pap. 12.99 (0-446-67183-5) Warner Bks.
Sex in America: A Definitive Survey. Robert T. Michael et al. 1994. 22.95 (0-316-07524-8) Little.
Sex in China: Studies in Sexology in Chinese Culture. F. F. Ruan & M. Matsumura. (Perspectives in Sexuality Ser.). (Illus.). 230p. 1991. 39.50 (0-306-43860-7, Plenum Pr) Plenum.
Sex in Civilization. Samuel D. Schmalhausen. LC 72-9630. reprint ed. 75.00 (0-404-57429-7) AMS Pr.
Sex in Education: or A Fair Chance for the Girls. Edward Clarke. LC 74-180566. (Medicine & Society in America Ser.). 190p. 1977. reprint ed. 17.95 (0-405-03943-3) Ayer.
Sex in Films. Parker Tyler. (Illus.). 256p. 1993. pap. 16.95 (0-8065-1465-5, Citadel Pr) Carol Pub Group.
Sex in Georgian England: Attitudes & Prejudices from the 1720s to the 1820s. A. D. Harvey. LC 94-28904. 1994. text ed. 49.95 (0-312-12418-X) St Martin.
Sex in History. Reay Tannahill. LC 79-15053. 480p. 1982. pap. 16.95 (0-8128-8540-6, Scrbrough Hse) Madison Bks UPA.
Sex in Human Relationships. Magnus Hirschfeld. LC 72-9649. reprint ed. 47.50 (0-404-57459-9) AMS Pr.
Sex in Literature, Vol. 1. John Atkins. 1981. pap. 12.95 (0-7145-0523-4) Riverrun NY.
Sex in Literature, Vol. 2. John Atkins. 1980. pap. 12.95 (0-7145-1138-2) Riverrun NY.
Sex in Literature, Vol. 3. John Atkins. 1981. pap. 12.95 (0-7145-3861-2) Riverrun NY.
Sex in Literature, Vol. 4: The Eighteenth Century. John Atkins. 400p. 1982. pap. 12.95 (0-7145-3977-5) Riverrun NY.
***Sex in Long-Term Relationships: Men & Women Talk about Sex.** Ed. by Klay Lamprell. 185p. (Orig.). 1997. pap. 14.95 (1-86448-234-6, Pub. by Allen & Unwin Aust Pty AT) IPG Chicago.
Sex in Middlesex: Popular Mores in a Massachusetts County, 1649-1699. Roger Thompson. LC 85-24630. 272p. 1986. pap. 17.95 (0-87023-656-3); lib. bdg. 32.50 (0-87023-516-8) U of Mass Pr.
Sex in My Confessional. Eric Von Rinkel. pap. 4.95 (0-9628439-0-3) Rusco Pubs.
Sex in Nature. Chris Catton & James Gray. LC 85-236716. 224p. reprint ed. pap. 63.90 (0-8357-3489-7, 2039748) Bks Demand.
Sex in Prison: The Mississippi Experiment with Conjugal Visiting. Columbus B. Hopper. LC 70-86491. 176p. reprint ed. pap. 50.20 (0-317-28745-1, 2051649) Bks Demand.
***Sex in Public: The Incarnation of Early Soviet Ideology.** Eric Naiman. LC 96-43642. 328p. 1997. text ed. 39.50 (0-691-02626-2) Princeton U Pr.
***Sex in Pulbic: Austrialian Sexual Cultures.** Ed. by Jill J. Matthews. (Illus.). 232p. 1997. pap. 24.95 (1-86448-049-1, Pub. by Allen & Unwin Aust Pty AT) Paul & Co Pubs.
Sex in Question: French Feminism. Ed. by Lisa Adkins & Diana Leonard. 208p. 1995. 75.00 (0-7484-0293-4); pap. 23.95 (0-7484-0294-2) Taylor & Francis.
Sex in Society. Alex Comfort. 172p. 1975. pap. 2.95 (0-8065-0064-6, Citadel Pr) Carol Pub Group.
Sex in the Afternoon. Joe Keirland. (Illus.). 250p. (Orig.). 1989. pap. write for info. (0-318-66526-3) Great Jones Pr.
***Sex in the Christian Marriage.** Paul D. Meier et al. 160p. 1997. mass mkt. 5.99 (0-8007-8644-0, Spire) Revell.
Sex in the Family, Bk. 1. King George. Ed. by Marian L. Cunningham. (Illus.). 192p. 1989. 12.95 (0-9622148-0-9) Yassum Pubs.
Sex in the Forbidden Zone. Peter Rutter. 1991. mass mkt. 5.99 (0-449-14727-4, GM) Fawcett.
***Sex in the Forbidden Zone.** Peter Rutter. 1997. pap. 12.00 (0-449-00069-9) Fawcett.
Sex in the Head: Visions of Femininity & Film in D. H. Lawrence. Linda R. Williams. LC 93-60763. (Contemporary Film & Television Ser.). 190p. 1993. text ed. 34.95 (0-8143-2507-6); pap. text ed. 16.95 (0-8143-2508-4) Wayne St U Pr.
***Sex in the Marketplace: American Women at Work.** Juanita M. Kreps. LC 75-155165. (Policy Studies in Employment & Welfare: No. 11). (Illus.). 128p. 1971. reprint ed. pap. 36.50 (0-608-04025-8, 2064761) Bks Demand.
Sex in the Middle Ages: A Book of Essays. Joyce E. Salisbury. LC 91-3959. (Medieval Casebooks Ser.: Vol. 3). 273p. 1991. text ed. 40.00 (0-8240-5766-X, H1360) Garland.
Sex in the Movies. Sam Frank. 1989. pap. 14.95 (0-8065-1115-X, Citadel Pr) Carol Pub Group.
Sex in the Outdoors: A Humerous Approach to Recreation. Robert Rose & Buck Tilton. LC 93-27919. (Illus.). 96p. (Orig.). 1993. pap. 6.99 (0-934802-86-6) ICS Bks.
Sex in the Parish. Karen Lebacqz & Ronald Barton. 256p. (Orig.). 1991. pap. 20.00 (0-664-25087-4) Westminster John Knox.
Sex in the Scriptures. 1991. lib. bdg. 78.00 (0-8490-4597-5) Gordon Pr.
Sex in the Scriptures of All Places: Of Course! Where Else! R. C. Cosbert. 280p. 1990. 14.95 (0-944957-30-7) Rivercross Pub.
Sex in the Therapy Hour: A Case of Professional Incest. Carolyn M. Bates & Annette M. Brodsky. LC 88-19032. 236p. 1988. lib. bdg. 36.95 (0-89862-726-5) Guilford Pr.
Sex in the Therapy Hour: A Case of Professional Incest. Carolyn M. Bates & Annette M. Brodsky. LC 88-19032. 236p. 1993. pap. text ed. 15.95 (0-89862-098-8) Guilford Pr.
Sex in the Western World: The Development of Attitudes & Behaviour. Jean-Louis Flandrin. 368p. 1991. text ed. 106.00 (3-7186-5201-3, Harwood Acad Pubs) Gordon & Breach.
***Sex in Your Garden.** Angela Overy. LC 96-42380. 1997. pap. 19.95 (1-55591-335-0) Fulcrum Pub.
***Sex Industry: An Australian Survey.** Fran Boyle et al. (Illus.). 160p. 1997. text ed. 55.95 (1-85972-625-9, Pub. by Ashgate UK) Ashgate Pub Co.
***Sex Industry & Public Policy.** Ed. by Sally-Anne Gerull & Boronia Halstead. (Australian Institute Conference Proceedings Ser.: Vol. 14). 257p. 1992. pap. 30.00 (0-642-18291-4, Pub. by Aust Inst Criminology) Willow Tree NY.
Sex Inequalities in Urban Employment in the Third World. Richard Anker & Catherine Hein. LC 85-27781. 304p. 1986. text ed. 39.95 (0-312-71341-X) St Martin.
Sex Information, May I Help You? Isadora Alman. LC 92-6939. Orig. Title: Aural Sex & Verbal Intercourse. 176p. (Orig.). (YA). (gr. 11 up). 1992. pap. 9.50 (0-940208-14-8) Down There Pr.
Sex Instructor, Retired. Andrew G. Carrigan. 18p. (Orig.). 1993. pap. 7.50 (1-884763-02-2) Ltd Mailing.
Sex Is a Game. Bob Zahn. Ed. by Cliff Carle. 1996. pap. text ed. 5.95 (1-57644-003-6) CCC Pubns.
Sex Is a Serious Pleasure. Norman Abel. 1995. 13.95 (0-533-11137-4) Vantage.
Sex Is God's Idea. Earl Paulk. 175p. (Orig.). 1985. pap. 7.95 (0-917595-04-1) Kingdom Pubs.
Sex Is Holy. Mary Rousseau & Chuck Gallagher. (Wellspring Bks.). 160p. (Orig.). 1986. pap. 9.95 (0-916349-11-X) Amity Hse Inc.
Sex Is Like a Hot Fudge Sundae. Pauline Falstrom & Gregory A. Cook. LC 93-72014. 256p. 1993. pap. 12.95 (0-939339-12-9) AFCOM Pub.
Sex Is More Than a Plumbing Lesson: A Parent's Guide to Sexuality Education. 2nd ed. Patty Stark. 203p. 1991. pap. text ed. 12.95 (0-9629463-0-3) Preston Hollow.
Sex Is Not a Four-Letter Word! Talking Sex with Children Made Easier. Patricia F. Miller. 176p. (Orig.). 1994. pap. 14.95 (0-8245-1437-8) Crossroad NY.
Sex Is Not a Natural Act & Other Essays. Leonore Tiefer. LC 94-33592. (Psychology, Gender, & Theory Ser.). 232p. (C). 1994. pap. text ed. 21.50 (0-8133-1659-6) Westview.
Sex Jokes & Male Chauvinism. George Fine. (Illus.). 192p. 1981. 9.95 (0-8065-0753-5, Citadel Pr) Carol Pub Group.
***Sex, Kids, & Politics: Health Services in Schools.** Catherine Emihovich & Carolyn Herrington. LC 97-16422. 416p. (Orig.). 1997. pap. 21.95 (0-8077-3635-X) Tchrs Coll.
***Sex, Kids, & Politics: Health Services in Schools.** Catherine Emihovich & Carolyn Herrington. 416p. 1997. 46.00 (0-8077-3636-8) Tchrs Coll.
Sex Law: A Legal Sourcebook on Critical Sexual Issues for the Non-Lawyer. Scott E. Friedman. LC 90-52665. 175p. 1990. pap. 31.50 (0-89950-540-6) McFarland & Co.
Sex, Law & Marriage in the Middle Ages. James A. Brundage. (Collected Studies: Vol. 397). 300p. 1993. 82.95 (0-86078-367-7, Pub. by Variorum UK) Ashgate Pub Co.
***Sex, Laws & Cyberspace: Freedom &Censorship on the Frontiers of the Online Revolution.** Jonathan Wallace. 1997. pap. 14.95 (0-8050-5298-4, Owl) H Holt & Co.
Sex, Laws & Stereotypes. N. Elizabeth Fried. (Leadership Ser.). (Illus.). 238p. (Orig.). Date not set. pap. 19.95 (0-614-10788-1) Natl Pr Pubns.
Sex, Laws & Stereotypes: Authentic Workplace Anecdotes & Practical Tips for Dealing with ADA, Sexual Harassment, Workplace Violence & Beyond... N. Elizabeth Fried. LC 93-91792. 256p. 1994. 25.00 (0-9637481-0-6) Intermed Pr.
Sex, Lies, & Forgiveness: Couples Speaking Out on Healing from Sex Addiction. Bertrand Schneider. 285p. 1991. pap. 11.00 (0-89486-734-2) Hazelden.
Sex, Lies & Leprechauns. Renee Roszel. (Temptation Ser.). 1994. mass mkt. 2.99 (0-373-25583-7, 1-25583-5) Harlequin Bks.
Sex, Lies, & Newsprint: Tales from a North Dallas Police Blotter & Other Texas Publications. Kevin J. Shay. LC 91-67911. (Illus.). 88p. 1993. pap. 4.95 (1-881365-72-7) Shay Pubns.
Sex, Lies & Stereotypes: Perspectives of a Mad Economist. Julianne M. Malveaux. 350p. (Orig.). 1994. pap. 14.95 (0-9636952-5-8) Pines One.
Sex, Lies & the Truth. 95p. 1994. student ed., pap. 24.99 (1-56179-226-8) Focus Family.
Sex, Lies & the Truth. Focus on the Family Staff. 1994. mass mkt. 4.99 (0-8423-1730-9) Tyndale.
Sex, Lies & Video Games: How to Write a Macintosh Arcade Game. Bill Hensler. 496p. 1996. pap. 34.95 incl. disk (0-201-40757-4) Addison-Wesley.
Sex-Life: A Critical Commentary on the History of Sexuality. Don Milligan. LC 92-36245. 169p. (C). 55.50 (0-7453-0611-X, Pub. by Pluto Pr UK); pap. 19.50 (0-7453-0612-8, Pub. by Pluto Pr UK) LPC InBook.
Sex Life in Europe. Max Hodann. LC 72-9652. reprint ed. 45.00 (0-404-57461-0) AMS Pr.
Sex Life in Marriage. Oliver M. Butterfield. (Illus.). 9.95 (0-87523-035-0) Emerson.
Sex Life of Slugs. Lorraine J. Moffett. (All Life Speaks Out Ser.). 10p. 1992. pap. write for info. (0-9633997-0-5) Rolaine Pub.
Sex Life of the Foot & Shoe. William A. Rossi. LC 90-24686. 272p. 1993. reprint ed. 32.50 (0-89464-573-0); reprint ed. pap. 28.50 (0-89464-756-3) Krieger.
***Sex Linkage of Intelligence: The X-Factor.** Robert Lehrke. LC 96-53612. (Human Evolution, Behavior & Intelligence Ser.). 208p. 1997. text ed. 55.00 (0-275-95903-1, Praeger Pubs) Greenwood.
Sex, Literature & Censorship. D. H. Lawrence. 122p. 1953. 19.50 (0-8290-0206-5); pap. text ed. 8.95 (0-8290-2394-1) Irvington.
Sex Lives: A Sexual Self-Portrait of America. Baker. LC 96-42941. 1997. pap. 14.00 (0-671-70254-8) PB.
Sex Lives of Animals Without Backbones. Haig H. Najarian. LC 75-4447. 125p. (Orig.). 1976. lib. bdg. 9.50 (0-684-14613-4) Krieger.
***Sex Lives of Hollywood Idols.** Nigel Cawthorne. 288p. 1997. pap. 11.95 (1-85375-249-5, Pub. by Prion UK) Trafalgar.
Sex Lives of Superheroes. Stephen Gregg. 1990. 3.00 (0-87129-418-4, S92) Dramatic Pub.
***Sex Lives of the Great Dictators.** Nigel Cawthorne. 288p. 1996. pap. 11.95 (1-85375-210-X, Pub. by Prion UK) Trafalgar.
***Sex Lives of the Hollywood Goddesses.** Nigel Cawthorne. 288p. 1997. pap. 11.95 (1-85375-250-9, Pub. by Prion UK) Trafalgar.
***Sex Lives of the Kings & Queens of England.** Nigel Cawthorne. 288p. 1997. pap. 11.95 (1-85375-208-8, Pub. by Prion UK) Trafalgar.
***Sex Lives of the Popes.** Nigel Cawthorne. 280p. 1996. pap. 11.95 (1-85375-207-X, Pub. by Prion UK) Trafalgar.
***Sex Lives of the U. S. Presidents.** Nigel Cawthorne. 288p. 1996. pap. 11.95 (1-85375-209-6, Pub. by Prion UK) Trafalgar.
Sex Love & the Sad Soul. Ron Manfredi. LC 91-67437. 60p. (Orig.). 1992. pap. 7.00 (1-56002-127-6) Aegina Pr.
Sex, Love, & Violence: Strategies for Transformation. Cloe Madanes. (C). 1990. 25.95 (0-393-70096-8) Norton.
Sex, Love & You: Making the Right Decision. Tom Lickona et al. LC 94-71887. (Illus.). 192p. (Orig.). (YA). (gr. 9-12). 1994. pap. 7.95 (0-87793-540-8) Ave Maria.
Sex-Love-Marriage & Divorce: A Male Primer. Joseph H. Hughes, Jr. 1977. pap. 4.95 (0-686-28626-X) Aaron-Jenkins.
Sex, Love, or Infatuation: How Can I Really Know? expanded rev. ed. Ray E. Short. LC 90-31178. 224p. 1990. pap. 5.99 (0-8066-2460-4, 9-2460) Augsburg Fortress.
Sex Macabre. Ed. by Amarantha Knight. (Orig.). 1996. mass mkt. 6.95 (1-56333-392-9, Rhinoceros) Masquerade.
Sex Magazines in the Library Collection: A Scholarly Study of Sex in Serials & Periodicals. Ed. by Peter Gellatly. LC 80-15011. (Serials Librarian Supplement Ser.: No. 1). 138p. 1981. text ed. 32.95 (0-917724-16-X) Haworth Pr.
Sex Magic, Tantra & Tarot: The Way of the Secret Lover. 2nd rev. ed. Christopher S. Hyatt & Lon M. DuQuette. LC 95-90459. (Illus.). 192p. (Orig.). 1991. pap. 14.95 (1-56184-044-0) New Falcon Pubns.
***Sex, Magick, & Spirit: Enlightenment Through Ecstacy.** Bonnie L. Johnston & Peter L. Schuerman. (Illus.). 264p. (Orig.). 1998. pap. 17.95 (1-56718-378-6) Llewellyn Pubns.
Sex, Marriage & Chastity: Reflections of a Catholic Layman, Spouse & Parent. 2nd ed. William E. May. 170p. 1981. reprint ed. pap. 8.95 (0-8199-0821-5, 0821-5, Frncscn Herld) Franciscan Pr.
Sex, Marriage & Society, 35 bks. Ed. by Charles E. Rosenberg & Carroll Smith-Rosenberg. 1974. 832.00 (0-405-05790-3) Ayer.
Sex, Mind & Habit Compatibility. Marc Robertson. 56p. 1975. 8.00 (0-86690-148-5, R1404-014) Am Fed Astrologers.
Sex, Money & Power. Linda Barbanel. LC 96-20129. 304p. 1996. 14.95 (0-02-861120-9) Macmillan.
Sex, Money & Power: An Essay on Christian Social Ethics. Philip Turner. LC 84-72481. 135p. (Orig.). 1985. pap. 9.95 (0-936384-22-0) Cowley Pubns.
***Sex, Morality, & the Law.** Ed. by Lori Gruen & George E. Panichas. 448p. (C). 1996. text ed. 65.00 (0-415-91635-6, Routledge NY) Routledge.
***Sex Morality & the Law.** George E. Panichas. 448p. (C). 1996. pap. 22.95 (0-415-91636-4, Routledge NY) Routledge.
Sex Murder & Sex Aggression: Phenomenology, Psychopathology, Psychodynamics & Prognosis. Eugene Revitch & Louis B. Schlesinger. (Illus.). 152p. 1989. pap. 26.95 (0-398-06346-X) C C Thomas.
Sex Murder & Sex Aggression: Phenomenology, Psychopathology, Psychodynamics & Prognosis. Eugene Revitch & Louis B. Schlesinger. (Illus.). 152p. (C). 1989. text ed. 39.95 (0-398-05556-4) C C Thomas.
Sex, Murder, Art: Films of Jorg Buttgereit. David Kerekes. (Illus.). 180p. (Orig.). 1994. pap. 19.95 (0-9523288-2-8, Pub. by Red Notes UK) AK Pr Dist.
Sex Mythology. Sha Rocco. (Illus.). 55p. (C). 1982. reprint ed. 6.00 (0-911826-34-3, 5440) Am Atheist.
***Sex, Nation & Dissent in Irish Writing.** Ed. by Eibhear Walshe. 210p. 1997. 54.95 (1-85918-013-2, Pub. by Cork Univ IE) Intl Spec Bk.
***Sex, Nation & Dissent in Irish Writing.** Ed. by Eibhear Walshe. 210p. 1997. pap. 26.95 (1-85918-014-0, Pub. by Cork Univ IE) Intl Spec Bk.
***Sex, Nation, & Dissent in Irish Writing.** Eibhear Walshe. LC 97-1637. 1997. text ed. 55.00 (0-312-17446-2); text ed. 19.95 (0-312-17447-0) St Martin.
Sex of Labour Law in Europe. Giota Kravaritou-Manitake & European Culture Research Centre Staff. LC 96-8632. 1996. 145.00 (90-411-0259-0) Kluwer Law Tax Pubs.
Sex of Things: Gender & Consumption in Historical Perspective. Ed. by Victoria De Grazia & Ellen Furlough. (Illus.). 443p. 1996. 50.00 (0-520-20034-9); pap. 19.95 (0-520-20197-3) U CA Pr.
Sex Offender: A Novel. Matthew Stadler. 224p. 1995. pap. 12.00 (0-06-092655-4, PL) HarpC.
Sex Offender Vol. I: Corrections, Treatment, & Legal Practice. Ed. by Barbara K. Schwartz & Henry R. Cellini. 585p. 1995. 95.95 (1-887554-00-9) Civic Res Inst.
***Sex Offender Vol. II: New Insights, Treatment Innovations & Legal Developments.** Ed. by Barbara K. Schwartz & Henry R. Cellini. 432p. 1997. 95.95 (1-887554-02-5) Civic Res Inst.
***Sex Offender Registration Laws: A Federal & State Megan's Laws Sourcebook.** Fred Cohen & Elizabeth Rahmberg-Walsh. 200p. 1997. 95.95 (1-887554-05-X, MEG) Civic Res Inst.
Sex Offender Treatment: A Psychoeducational Model. Geral Blanchard. 154p. (Orig.). 1989. student ed. 15.00 (0-685-30795-6) Golden Val Inst Behav Med.
Sex Offender Treatment: Biological Dysfunction, Intrapsychic Conflict, Interpersonal Violence. Ed. by Eli Coleman et al. LC 96-20107. (Offender Rehabilitation Monographs: Vol. 23, Nos. 3/4). 177p. 1996. 39.95 (1-56024-834-3) Haworth Pr.
Sex Offender Treatment: Psychological & Medical Approaches. Ed. by Eli Coleman et al. LC 92-48795. (Journal of Offender Rehabilitation: Vol. 18, Nos. 3/4). (Illus.). 233p. 1996. 34.95 (1-56024-438-0); pap. 19.95 (0-7890-0069-5) Haworth Pr.
Sex Offenders. E. Schorsch et al. 150p. 1990. pap. 64.00 (0-387-51042-7) Spr-Verlag.

S

An Asterisk (*) at the beginning of an entry indicates that the title is appearing in BIP for the first time.

*Sex Offenders: A Challenge for Community Corrections. Gad J. Bensinger & Arthur J. Lurigio. 65p. (Orig.). 1996. pap. 10.00 (0-942854-21-7) Loyola U Crim.

Sex Offenders: Perspectives & Approaches to Understanding & Management. Adele Mayer. LC 86-45796. 300p. 1988. pap. 19.95 (0-918452-95-3, 953) Learning Pubns.

Sex Offenses: Medical & Psychological Subject Analysis with Research Index & Bibliography. Harold P. Drummond. LC 84-45994. 150p. 1987. 44.50 (0-88164-310-6); pap. 39.50 (0-88164-311-4) ABBE Pubs Assn.

Sex on Architecture. Ed. by Diana Agrest et al. LC 96-5552. (Illus.). 320p. 1996. pap. 19.95 (0-8109-2683-0) Abrams.

*Sex on Campus. 1997. pap. 12.95 (0-375-75011-8, Villard Bks) Random.

*Sex on Campus: The Naked Truth about the Real Sex Lives of College Students. John Katzman & Cynthia Brantley. (Princeton Review Ser.). 1997. pap. 12.00 (0-679-74630-7) Random.

Sex on Dr.'s Orders. 2nd ed. Alizarin Lake. 1996. mass mkt. 5.95 (1-56333-402-X) Masquerade.

*Sex on the Beach! Cosmic Cocktails, Space-Age Shots & Other Rituals for the Jaded & Refined. Beverly West & Kim Doi. 160p. 1997. pap. 10.00 (0-425-15852-7, Berkley Trade) Berkley Pub.

Sex on the Beach & Other Great Stories. Random House Value Publishing Staff. 1997. 5.99 (0-517-18501-6) Random Hse Value.

*Sex on the Brain: The Biological Differences Bewteen Men & Women. Deborah Blum. 1997. 23.95 (0-614-28188-1) Viking Penguin.

Sex on the Net. Charisse Van Der Lyn. (Orig.). 1995. mass mkt. 5.95 (1-56333-399-6) Masquerade.

Sex on the Screen: Eroticism in Film. Gerard Lenne. (Illus.). 352p. 1985. pap. 15.95 (0-312-71335-5) St Martin.

Sex on Your Terms: What to Say to Explain Your Limits, to Repel Sexual Pressure, to Avoid Being Falsely Accused, to Escape Disease. Elizabeth Powell. LC 95-23581. 1995. pap. 15.95 (0-205-17925-8) Allyn.

Sex or Symbol: Erotic Images of Greece & Rome. Catherine Johns. (Illus.). 160p. 1982. reprint ed. pap. 29.95 (0-292-77634-9) U of Tex Pr.

Sex, Orgasm & Depression: Their Inner Relationship in a Changing Society. Samuel O. Okpaku. LC 83-63524. 160p. (Orig.). 1984. 12.95 (0-916085-00-7) Chrisolith Bks.

Sex Oriented, Woman Convected Guy Doing His Own Thing: Bern Porter on Henry Miller, a Manuscript Sampler. Bern Porter. (Illus.). 50p. (Orig.). 1996. pap. 20.00 (0-614-13981-3) R Jackson.

Sex over Coffee. Cherie Vogelstein. 128p. pap. 6.95 (1-55783-270-6) Applause Theatre Bk Pubs.

Sex over Forty. Saul H. Rosenthal. 288p. 1989. pap. 9.95 (0-87477-495-0, Tarcher Putnam) Putnam Pub Group.

Sex Pistols: Never Mind the Bollocks, Here's the Sex Pistols. 19.95 (0-7935-5156-0, 00690076) H Leonard.

*Sex Pistols: Retrospecitve, a Visual History. Music Book Services Staff. 1996. pap. text ed. 26.99 (1-886894-43-4) Mus Bk Servs.

Sex Pistols Chaos: Chaos. Photos by Bob Gruen. (Illus.). 128p. pap. 19.95 (0-7119-2121-0, OP45798) Omnibus NY.

Sex Pistols File. Photos & Compiled by Ray Stevenson. (Illus.). 72p. pap. 15.95 (0-86001-464-9, OP 40302, Pub. by Bobcat Bks UK) Omnibus NY.

Sex, Politics, & Science in the Nineteenth-Century Novel. Ruth B. Yeazell. LC 85-45043. (Selected Papers from the English Institute; 1982-83, New Ser.: No. 10). 209p. reprint ed. pap. 59.60 (0-8357-6742-6, 2035397) Bks Demand.

Sex, Politics, & Science in the Nineteenth-Century Novel. Ed. by Ruth B. Yeazell. LC 85-45043. (Selected Papers from the English Institute; 1982-83, New Ser.). 224p. 1991. reprint ed. pap. 13.95 (0-8018-4211-5) Johns Hopkins.

Sex, Politics & Society: The Regulation of Sexuality since 1800. 2nd ed. Jeffrey Weeks. 336p. (C). 1989. pap. text ed. 29.50 (0-582-02383-1, 78029) Longman.

Sex, Pornography & Justice. Albert B. Gerber. (Illus.). 1965. 10.00 (0-8184-0079-X) Carol Pub Group.

Sex Positives? Cultural Politics of Dissident Sexualities. Ed. by Thomas Foster et al. 320p. (C). 1997. 55.00 (0-8147-2664-X); pap. 17.95 (0-8147-2663-1) NYU Pr.

Sex, Power, and Boundaries: Understanding and Preventing Sexual Harassment. Peter Rutter. 272p. 1996. 23.95 (0-553-09954-X, Bantam Trade Bks) Bantam.

Sex Power & Health for the Middle-Aged & Senior. Irwinn N. Krimm. LC 74-82897. 158p. 1974. pap. 6.95 (0-9606402-2-3) Happy Health.

Sex, Power & Justice: Historical Perspectives on Law in Australia. Ed. by Diane Kirkby. 328p. 1996. pap. 37.50 (0-19-553734-3) OUP.

*Sex, Power & Pleasure. Mariana Valverde. 200p. (Orig.). reprint ed. pap. 11.95 (0-88961-097-5, Pub. by Wmns Pr CN) LPC InBook.

Sex, Power, Conflict: Evolutionary & Feminist Perspectives. Ed. by David M. Buss & Neil M. Malamuth. LC 95-15685. 352p. 1996. pap. 29.95 (0-19-510357-2) OUP.

Sex Preferences. 2nd rev. ed. Mon Roes. 190p. (C). 1990. 14.00 (0-9618960-5-1) M M Fain.

Sex Preferences: Origins & Influences. Mon Roes. 126p. (Orig.). (C). 1988. pap. 8.95 (0-9618960-0-0) M M Fain.

Sex, Preferences & Family: Essays on Law & Nature. Ed. by David M. Estlund & Martha C. Nussbaum. LC 95-49825. (Illus.). 365p. 1997. 35.00 (0-19-509894-3) OUP.

Sex, Priests, & Power: Anatomy of a Crisis. A. W. Sipe. LC 94-45136. 240p. 1995. 24.95 (0-87630-769-1) Brunner-Mazel.

Sex, Race & Science: Eugenics in the Deep South. Edward J. Larson. LC 94-28124. 264p. 1995. text ed. 35.00 (0-8018-4938-1) Johns Hopkins.

Sex, Race, & Science: Eugenics in the Deep South. Edward J. Larson. 264p. 1996. reprint ed. pap. text ed. 14.95 (0-8018-5511-X) Johns Hopkins.

Sex, Race & the Law: Legislating for Equality. Jeanne Gregory. (Contemporary Criminology Ser.: Vol. 1). 208p. (C). 1988. text ed. 69.95 (0-8039-8106-6); pap. text ed. 14.95 (0-8039-8107-4) Sage.

*Sex Rebels. Marcia Seligison. Date not set. write for info. (0-688-05015-8) Morrow.

Sex Redeemed. Michel Pochet. 64p. 1991. pap. 5.95 (0-904287-31-9) New City.

Sex Research-Early Literature from Statistics to Erotica: Guide to the Microfilm Collection. Ed. by Research Publications, Inc. Staff. 130p. 1983. 65.00 (0-89235-075-X) Primary Srce Media.

Sex Researchers. Edward Brecher. 410p. 1979. 9.50 (0-317-34150-2) Specific Pr.

Sex Respect: The Option of True Sexual Freedom: A Public Health Guide for Parents. Coleen K. Mast. (Illus.). 61p. (Orig.). (J). (gr. 7-9). 1986. pap. text ed. 8.95 (0-945745-01-X) Respect Inc.

Sex Respect: The Option of True Sexual Freedom: A Public Health Guide for Parents. rev. ed. Coleen K. Mast. Ed. by Julienne Forrestal. (Illus.). 180p. (Orig.). 1990. pap. text ed. 8.95 (0-945745-04-4) Respect Inc.

Sex Respect: The Option of True Sexual Freedom: A Public Health Manual for Teachers. Coleen K. Mast. (Illus.). 61p. (Orig.). (J). (gr. 7-9). 1986. pap. 12.95 (0-945745-00-1) Respect Inc.

Sex Respect: The Option of True Sexual Freedom: A Public Health Manual for Teachers. rev. ed. Coleen K. Mast. Ed. by Julienne Forrestal. (Illus.). 182p. (Orig.). 1990. pap. text ed. 12.95 (0-945745-03-6) Respect Inc.

Sex Respect: The Option of True Sexual Freedom: A Public Health Workbook for Students. Coleen K. Mast. (Illus.). 61p. (Orig.). (J). (gr. 7-9). 1986. pap. text ed. 7.95 (0-945745-02-8) Respect Inc.

Sex Respect: The Option of True Sexual Freedom: A Public Health Workbook for Students. rev. ed. Coleen K. Mast. Ed. by Julienne Forrestal. (Illus.). 118p. (Orig.). (YA). (gr. 7-9). 1990. pap. text ed. 8.95 (0-945745-05-2) Respect Inc.

Sex Revolts: Gender, Rebellion, & Rock 'n' Roll. Simon Reynolds & Joy Press. LC 94-30683. 428p. 1995. text ed. 24.95 (0-674-80272-1, REYSER) HUP.

Sex Revolts: Gender, Rebellion, & Rock 'n' Roll. Simon Reynolds & Joy Press. 432p. 1996. pap. 15.95 (0-674-80273-X) HUP.

Sex Role Attitudes among High School Seniors: Views about Work & Family Roles. A. Regula Herzog & Jerald G. Bachman. 272p. (Orig.). 1982. pap. 16.00 (0-87944-275-1) Inst Soc Res.

Sex Role Attitudes & Cultural Change. Ira Gross et al. 1982. lib. bdg. 93.00 (90-277-1340-5) Kluwer Ac.

Sex Role Changes: Technology, Politics & Policy. Marcia L. Whicker & Jennie J. Kronenfeld. LC 85-16763. 203p. 1985. text ed. 55.00 (0-275-90041-X, C0041, Praeger Pubs) Greenwood.

Sex Role Identity & Ego Development. Jeanne H. Block. LC 84-7918. (Jossey-Bass Social & Behavioral Science Ser.). 351p. reprint ed. pap. 100.10 (0-7837-2516-7, 2042675) Bks Demand.

Sex Role Research: Measuring Social Change. Ed. by Barbara L. Richardson & Jeana Wirtenberg. LC 83-2426. 286p. 1983. text ed. 36.95 (0-275-91063-6, C1063, Praeger Pubs) Greenwood.

Sex Role Stereotyping & Affirmative Action Policy. Ed. by Barbara A. Gutek. (Monograph & Research Ser.: No. 32). 227p. 1982. 8.50 (0-89215-116-1) U Cal LA Indus Rel.

Sex Role Stereotyping in Occupational Choices: A Career Counseling Manual. Claudia G. Meer et al. 62p. 1982. 6.00 (0-941312-01-1) Inst Mgmt & Labor.

Sex Roles: Rights & Values in Conflict. Ed. by Jeanne Burr. LC 79-3760. 224p. reprint ed. pap. 63.90 (0-685-23991-8, 2031564) Bks Demand.

Sex Roles & Aging: Theory & Research from a Systems Perspective. Jan D. Sinnott. (Contributions to Human Development Ser.: Vol. 15). xiv, 134p. 1986. 35.25 (3-8055-4207-0) S Karger.

Sex Roles & Personal Awareness. Barbara E. Kovach. 432p. (C). 1990. reprint ed. pap. 34.00 (0-8191-7735-0) U Pr of Amer.

Sex Roles & Psychopathology. Ed. by Cathy S. Widom. 390p. 1984. 60.00 (0-306-41406-6, Plenum Pr) Plenum.

Sex Roles & Social Change in Native Lower Central American Societies. Ed. by Christine A. Loveland & Franklin O. Loveland. LC 80-27814. (Illus.). 232p. 1982. text ed. 24.95 (0-252-00858-8) U of Ill Pr.

Sex Roles & Social Patterns. Ed. by Frances A. Boudreau et al. LC 85-12247. 336p. 1985. text ed. 65.00 (0-275-90196-3, C0196, Praeger Pubs) Greenwood.

Sex Roles, Family & Community in Turkey. Ed. by Ilhan Basgoz & Cigdem Kagitcibasi. (Turkish Studies Ser.: Vol. 3). 414p. (C). 1982. 14.95 (0-685-29321-1) IN Univ Turkish.

Sex Roles in Contemporary American Communes. Ed. by Jon Wagner. LC 81-47571. 256p. 1982. 12.95 (0-253-35187-1) Ind U Pr.

Sex Roles, Population & Development in West Africa. Ed. by Christine Oppong. LC 87-27386. 242p. (C). 1988. 40.00 (0-435-08022-9, 08022) Heinemann.

Sex Roles, Sex Inequality, & Sex Role Development. Jean Stockard & Miriam M. Johnson. (Illus.). 1980. pap. text ed. write for info. (0-13-807560-3) P-H.

*Sex Rx. Theresa Crenshaw. 288p. 1998. pap. 12.00 (0-06-272052-X, PL) HarpC.

Sex Satisfaction & Happy Marriage. Alfred H. Tyrer. (Illus.). 1951. 9.95 (0-87523-039-3) Emerson.

Sex, Scams, & Street Life: The Sociology of New York City's Times Square. Ed. by Robert P. McNamara. LC 95-9307. 144p. 1995. text ed. 52.95 (0-275-95002-6, Praeger Pubs); pap. text ed. 14.95 (0-275-95359-9, Praeger Pubs) Greenwood.

Sex Scandal: The Private Parts of Victorian Fiction. William A. Cohen. LC 96-7641. (Series Q). 272p. 1996. text ed. 49.95 (0-8223-1856-3); pap. text ed. 16.95 (0-8223-1848-2) Duke.

Sex Scells: Light Verses Celebrate the Way of All Flesh. Kenneth Leonhardt. 72p. (Orig.). 1994. pap. 8.95 (1-56474-104-4) Fithian Pr.

*Sex Scientists. Ed. by Brannigan. LC 97-15833. (C). 1998. text ed. write for info. (0-321-01139-2) Addson-Wesley Educ.

Sex, Scotch & Scholarship: Selected Writings. Khushwant Singh. Ed. by Rohini Singh. (C). 1992. pap. 9.00 (81-85674-50-7, Pub. by UBS Pubs Dist II) S Asia.

Sex Secrets from China. 64p. 15.00 (0-317-31558-7) Chans Corp.

*Sex Seen: The Emergence of Modern Sexuality in America. Sharon Ullman. 1998. pap. text ed. 16.95 (0-520-20955-9) U CA Pr.

Sex Segregation in Librarianship: Demographic & Career Patterns of Academic Library Administrators. Betty J. Irvine. LC 84-21228. (Contributions in Librarianship & Information Science Ser.: No. 53). (Illus.). xiv, 171p. 1985. text ed. 49.95 (0-313-24260-7, IRA/) Greenwood.

Sex Segregation in the Workplace: Trends, Explanations, Remedies. Ed. by Barbara F. Reskin. LC 84-8342. 323p. reprint ed. pap. 92.10 (0-7837-5357-8, 2045119) Bks Demand.

Sex, Sense & Nonsense: A Workbook for Human Sexuality. 2nd ed. Brenda D. Wilder. (Illus.). 158p. 1990. pap. text ed. 19.95 (0-9609098-6-9) Biomat Pub Co.

Sex, Sensibility & the Gendered Body. Ed. by Janet Holland & Lisa Adkins. 256p. 1996. 17.95 (0-312-16082-8) St Martin.

Sex, Sensibility & the Gendered Body. Ed. by Janet Holland & Lisa Adkins. 256p. 1996. text ed. 45.00 (0-312-16081-X) St Martin.

Sex, Sex, Sex. Ariel Books Staff. (Illus.). 80p. 1995. 4.95 (0-8362-3116-3, Arie Bks) Andrews & McMeel.

Sex Shops & the Law. Colin Manchester. 200p. 1986. text ed. 59.95 (0-566-05232-6, Pub. by Dartmth Pub UK) Ashgate Pub Co.

Sex Show. Robert Bahr. (Orig.). 1994. mass mkt. 4.95 (1-56333-225-6, Badboy) Masquerade.

Sex Side of Life: Mary Ware Dennett's Pioneering Battle for Birth Control & Sex Education. Constance M. Chen. 368p. 1996. 25.00 (1-56584-132-8) New Press NY.

*Sex Side of Life Mary Ware Dennett's Pioneering Battle for Birth Control & Sex Education. Constance M. Chen. 1997. pap. 15.00 (1-56584-133-6) New Press NY.

Sex Signs. Judith Bennett. 413p. 1981. pap. 13.95 (0-312-71339-8) St Martin.

Sex Signs. Judith Bennett. 1990. pap. 6.99 (0-312-91597-7) St Martin.

*Sex Signs. Judith Bennett. LC 96-44813. 1997. 24.95 (0-312-15205-1) Thomas Dunne Bks.

Sex, Sin, & Blasphemy: A Guide to America's Censorship Wars. Marjorie Heins. LC 92-50837. 224p. (Orig.). 1993. 22.95 (1-56584-062-3); pap. 11.95 (1-56584-048-8) New Press NY.

Sex, Sin & Grace: Women's Experience & the Theologies of Reinhold Niebuhr & Paul Tillich. Judith Plaskow. LC 79-5434. 1980. pap. text ed. 21.00 (0-8191-0882-0) U Pr of Amer.

Sex, Sin & Mayhem: Notorious Trials of the 90's. Edward W. Knappman. (Illus.). 216p. 1995. pap. 12.95 (0-7876-0476-3) Visible Ink Pr.

Sex Slave, How to Find One, How to be One. M. Winthrope. 1991. pap. 5.95 (0-88032-404-X) Ivory Tower Pub.

*Sex Slave Murders, Vol. 1. R. Barri Flowers. 1996. mass mkt. 5.99 (0-312-95989-3) St Martin.

Sex Slave Murders: The Terrifying True Story of Gerald & Charlene Gallego, America's First... R. Barri Flowers. LC 94-72114. 1995. pap. 11.95 (0-918751-34-9) Act Direct.

Sex, Society & History. Vern Bullough. 1976. 15.00 (0-88202-154-0) Watson Pub Intl.

Sex Songs of the Ancient Letts. Bud Berzing. LC 69-10779. 320p. 1969. 5.95 (0-8216-0151-2, Univ Bks) Carol Pub Group.

Sex-Specific Mortality & the Economic Value of Children in 19th Century Massachusetts. Caren A. Ginsburg. (Studies in Historical Demography). 225p. 1990. reprint ed. text ed. 15.00 (0-8240-4351-0) Garland.

Sex, Spirit & You. John-Roger. LC 77-81389. 1977. pap. 5.00 (0-914829-18-1) Mandeville LA.

*Sex Spoken Here: Good Vibrations Erotic Reading Circle Selections. Ed. by Carol Queen & Jack Davis. 176p. 1997. pap. 14.50 (0-940208-19-9) Down There Pr.

*Sex Squad. Leddick. Date not set. write for info. (0-312-18174-4) St Martin.

Sex Stereotyping & Bias: Their Origin & Effects. rev. ed. Reeve Love & Alicia S. Sosa. 40p. (Orig.). 1995. pap. text ed. 8.50 (1-878550-57-8) Inter Dev Res Assn.

Sex Stereotyping in Schools: A Report of the Educational Research. vi, 218p. 1982. pap. 27.00 (90-265-0406-3) Swets.

Sex Steroids & Bone. Ed. by R. Ziegler et al. LC 93-43028. (Schering Foundation Workshop Ser.). (Illus.). 205p. 1993. write for info. (0-347-57374-6) Spr-Verlag.

Sex Steroids & Bone. Ed. by R. Ziegler et al. (Schering Foundation Workshop Ser.: Vol. 9). (Illus.). vii, 205p. 1994. 59.00 (0-387-57374-7) Spr-Verlag.

*Sex Steroids & Cardiovascular System: The Proceedings of the 1st Interdisciplinary Workshop, Tubingen, Germany, October 1996. Lippert, T. H., Ary Workshop Staff. Ed. by T. H. Lippert et al. LC 97-7110. (Illus.). 200p. 1997. 55.00 (1-85070-956-4) Prthnon Pub.

Sex Steroids & the Cardiovascular System. Ed. by P. Ramwell et al. LC 92-49749. (Schering Foundation Workshop Ser.: Vol. 5). (Illus.). xii, 201p. 1993. 59.00 (3-540-55728-8); 64.95 (0-387-55728-8) Spr-Verlag.

Sex Stop. Ed. by John W. Dagion. (True Revelations & Strange Happenings Ser.: Vol. 3). 192p. (Orig.). 1987. pap. 10.95 (0-943595-03-7) Leyland Pubns.

Sex Stuff for Boys: Sperm, Squirm & Other Squiggly Stuff. Carole Marsh. (Smart Sex Stuff Ser.). 1994. 29.95 (1-55609-189-3); pap. 19.95 (1-55609-207-5) Gallopade Pub Group.

Sex Stuff for Girls: A Period Is More Than a Punctuation Mark. Carole Marsh. (Smart Sex Stuff Ser.). (Orig.). 1994. 29.95 (1-55609-190-7); pap. 19.95 (1-55609-206-7) Gallopade Pub Group.

Sex Stuff for Kids 7-17: A Book of Practical Information & Ideas for Kids & Their Teachers & Parents, Contains Chapter on 'AIDS' Carole Marsh. (J). (gr. 2-12). 1994. 29.95 (1-55609-200-8); teacher ed. 29.95 (1-55609-204-0); pap. 19.95 (1-55609-201-6) Gallopade Pub Group.

Sex Stuff for Parents: The Painless, Foolproof, "Really Works!" Way to Teach 7-17-Year-Olds about Sex So They Won't Get AIDS, a Disease or a Baby (& You Won't Get Embarrassed!): For Alabama Parents. Carole Marsh. (Carole Marsh Alaska Bks.). (Illus.). 1994. lib. bdg. 29.95 (0-7933-2330-4); lib. bdg. 29.95 (0-7933-2339-8); lib. bdg. 29.95 (0-7933-2357-6); lib. bdg. 29.95 (0-7933-2366-5); lib. bdg. 29.95 (0-7933-2375-4); lib. bdg. 29.95 (0-685-37842-X); lib. bdg. 29.95 (0-7933-2393-2); lib. bdg. 29.95 (0-7933-2402-5); lib. bdg. 29.95 (0-7933-2411-4); lib. bdg. 29.95 (0-7933-2420-3); lib. bdg. 29.95 (0-7933-2429-7); lib. bdg. 29.95 (0-7933-2438-6); lib. bdg. 29.95 (0-7933-2447-5); lib. bdg. 29.95 (0-7933-2456-4); lib. bdg. 29.95 (0-7933-2465-3); lib. bdg. 29.95 (0-7933-2474-2); lib. bdg. 29.95 (0-7933-2483-1); lib. bdg. 29.95 (0-7933-2492-0); lib. bdg. 29.95 (0-7933-2501-3); lib. bdg. 29.95 (0-7933-2510-2); lib. bdg. 29.95 (0-7933-2519-6); lib. bdg. 29.95 (0-7933-2528-5); lib. bdg. 29.95 (0-7933-2537-4); lib. bdg. 29.95 (0-7933-2546-3); lib. bdg. 29.95 (0-7933-2555-2); lib. bdg. 29.95 (0-7933-2564-1); lib. bdg. 29.95 (0-7933-2573-0); lib. bdg. 29.95 (0-7933-2582-X); lib. bdg. 29.95 (0-7933-2591-9); lib. bdg. 29.95 (0-7933-2600-1); lib. bdg. 29.95 (0-7933-2609-5); lib. bdg. 29.95 (0-7933-2618-4); lib. bdg. 29.95 (0-7933-2627-3); lib. bdg. 29.95 (0-7933-2636-2); lib. bdg. 29.95 (0-7933-2645-1); lib. bdg. 29.95 (0-7933-2654-0); lib. bdg. 29.95 (0-7933-2663-X); lib. bdg. 29.95 (0-7933-2672-9); lib. bdg. 29.95 (0-7933-2681-8); lib. bdg. 29.95 (0-7933-2690-7); lib. bdg. 29.95 (0-7933-2699-0); lib. bdg. 29.95 (0-7933-2708-3); lib. bdg. 29.95 (0-7933-2717-2); lib. bdg. 29.95 (0-7933-2726-1); lib. bdg. 29.95 (0-7933-2735-0); lib. bdg. 29.95 (0-7933-2744-X); lib. bdg. 29.95 (0-7933-2753-9); lib. bdg. 29.95 (0-7933-2762-8); lib. bdg. 29.95 (0-7933-2771-7) Gallopade Pub Group.

Sex Stuff for Parents: The Painless, Foolproof, "Really Works!" Way to Teach 7-17-Year-Olds about Sex So They Won't Get AIDS, a Disease or a Baby (& You Won't Get Embarrassed!): For Alabama Parents. Carole Marsh. (Carole Marsh Alabama Bks.). (Illus.). 1997. lib. bdg. 29.95 (0-7933-2321-5) Gallopade Pub Group.

*Sex, Stupidity, & Greed: The Underbelly of the American Movie Industry. Ian Grey. 1997. pap. text ed. 19.95 (0-9651042-7-3) Juno Bks.

Sex Surveyed, 1949-1994: From Mass-Observation's Little Kinsey' to the National Survey & the Hite Reports. Liz Stanley. 272p. 1995. 75.00 (0-7484-0367-1); pap. 25.95 (0-7484-0368-X) Taylor & Francis.

Sex Swappers Library, 5 vols., Set. 1992. lib. bdg. 999.75 (0-8490-5336-6) Gordon Pr.

Sex Symbol Dynasty. Heavy Metal Books Staff. 1996. 24.95 (1-882931-20-3) Heavy Metal Magazine.

Sex Symbolism in Religion, 2 vols. James B. Hannay. 1991. lib. bdg. 188.75 (0-8490-5035-9) Gordon Pr.

Sex Symbolism in Religion, 2 vols., Set. J. B. Hannay. 1184p. 1993. reprint ed. spiral bd. 41.50 (0-7873-0367-4) Hlth Research.

*Sex, Symbols & Dreams. Janice H. Baylis. LC 96-93018. (Illus.). 242p. (Orig.). 1997. pap. 17.00 (0-917738-05-5) Sun Man Moon.

Sex Talk: The Ultimate Collection of Ribald, Raunchy, & Provocative Quotations. Compiled by James Wolfe. LC 94-20519. 1994. 10.95 (0-8065-1564-3, St Ansgars Scan) Carol Pub Group.

Sex Test. Patty Salier. (Desire Ser.). 1996. mass mkt. 3.50 (0-373-76032-9, 1-76032-1) Silhouette.

Sex, the Most Fun You Can Have Without Laughing. William Cole. 1994. pap. 6.95 (0-312-11886-4, Thomas Dunne Bks) St Martin.

Sex Therapy. Mary Melfi. (Drama Ser.: No. 13). 120p. Date not set. pap. 12.00 (1-55071-035-4) Guernica Editions.

Sex Therapy: A Practical Guide. Keith E. Hawton. (Illus.). 280p. 1985. pap. 39.50 (0-19-261413-4) OUP.

*Sex Therapy for Married & Unmarried Couples. Leon Zussman & Shirley Zussman. Date not set. write for info. (0-688-05118-9) Morrow.

Sex Therapy Handbook: A Clinical Manual for the Diagnosis & Treatment of Sexual Disorders. E. C. Krohne. LC 80-26504. (Illus.). 128p. 1982. text ed. 19.50 (0-88331-197-6) Luce.

S

An Asterisk (*) at the beginning of an entry indicates that the title is appearing in BIP for the first time.

Sex Therapy in Britain. Martin Cole & Wendy Dryden. (Psychotherapy in Britain Ser.). 320p. 1988. 95.00 (*0-335-09838-X*, Open Univ Pr); pap. 42.00 (*0-335-09828-2*, Open Univ Pr) Taylor & Francis.

***Sex Therapy Manual.** P. Gillan. (Illus.). 352p. 1987. write for info. (*0-632-01938-7*) Blackwell Sci.

***Sex Therapy Manual.** Patricia Gillan. (Illus.). 352p. 1987. pap. write for info. (*0-632-01866-6*) Blackwell Sci.

***Sex These Days: Essays on Theology, Sexuality & Society.** Ed. by Jon Davies & Gerard Loughlin. (Studies in Theology & Sexuality). 250p. 1997. 55.00 (*1-85075-662-7*, Pub. by Sheffield Acad UK) CUP Services.

***Sex These Days: Essays on Theology, Sexuality & Society.** Ed. by Jon Davies & Gerard Loughlin. (Studies in Theology & Sexuality). 250p. 1997. pap. 19.95 (*1-85075-804-2*, Pub. by Sheffield Acad UK) CUP Services.

Sex Tips for Girls. Cynthia Heimel. 208p. 1983. pap. 10.00 (*0-671-47725-0*) S&S Trade.

Sex Tips for Modern Girls. Edward Astley et al. 99p. 1989. pap. text ed. 5.95 (*0-685-28071-3*) New Mus Theater Lib.

***Sex Tips for Straight Women from a Gay Man.** Dan Anderson. 1997. 16.00 (*0-06-039232-0*, ReganBooks) HarpC.

Sex Token. deluxe ed. James Shreeve. (Treacle Story Ser.: No. 3). (Illus.). 48p. 1976. 12.50 (*0-914232-11-8*) McPherson & Co.

***Sex Toy Tricks: More Than 125 Ways to Accessorize Good Sex.** Jay Wiseman. (Tricks Ser.). 128p. (Orig.). 1996. pap. 11.95 (*0-9639763-4-6*) Greenery Pr.

Sex Toys of the Gods. Christian McLaughlin. LC 97-23041. 1997. pap. 24.95 (*0-525-94058-8*) NAL-Dutton.

Sex Variant Women in Literature. Jeannette H. Foster. 432p. 1985. reprint ed. pap. 8.95 (*0-930044-65-7*) Naiad Pr.

Sex Variants: A Study of Homosexual Patterns, 2 vols., Set. George W. Henry. LC 78-22292. (Gay Experience Ser.). (Illus.). reprint ed. 75.00 (*0-404-61525-2*) AMS Pr.

Sex, Violence, & Power in Sports: Rethinking Masculinity. Michael A. Messner & Donald F. Sabo. LC 94-18562. 216p. 1994. pap. 12.95 (*0-89594-688-2*) Crossing Pr.

Sex, Violence, Drugs & America: The Definition of A Culture. John Oshodi. 114p. (Orig.). 1994. pap. 11.95 (*0-9644455-0-6*) Oshodi Fnd.

Sex War & Others: A Survey of Recent Murders, Principally in France. Rayner Heppenstall. (Illus.). 192p. 1973. 17.95 (*0-8464-1170-9*) Beekman Pubs.

Sex Wars: Free Adaptations of Ibsen & Strinberg. Charles Marowitz. LC 82-1133. 192p. 1983. 16.95 (*0-7145-2721-1*); pap. 9.95 (*0-7145-2722-X*) M Boyars Pubs.

Sex Wars: Sexual Dissent & Political Culture. Lisa Duggan & Nan D. Hunter. 288p. (gr. 13). 1995. pap. 16.95 (*0-415-91037-4*, B4372, Routledge NY) Routledge.

Sex Wars: Sexual Dissent & Political Culture. Lisa Duggan & Nan D. Hunter. 288p. (C). (gr. 13). 1995. text ed. 62.95 (*0-415-91036-6*, B4368, Routledge NY) Routledge.

Sex Werkdays & Agis. Ed. by L. A. Houwen. (Mediaevalia Groningana Ser.: Vol. 10). 132p. (Orig.). 1991. pap. 29.00 (*90-6980-035-7*, Pub. by Egbert Forsten NE) Benjamins North Am.

***Sex What That.** Sam Lansford. 1993. pap. 6.99 (*0-8054-9967-9*) Broadman.

***Sex, What You Don't Know Can Kill You.** Joe S. Mcilhaney & Marion Mcilhaney. LC 96-43362. 1997. 8.99 (*0-8010-5737-X*) Baker Bks.

***Sex Which Prevails: Biology & the Social Construction of Sexuality.** Anne Fausto-Sterl. 1998. 25.00 (*0-465-07713-7*) Basic.

***Sex Which Prevails: The Biology & Social Construction of Sexuality.** Anne Fausto-Sterl. Date not set. pap. 15.00 (*0-465-07714-5*) Basic.

Sex with a Mountain Bike & Other Stories. Gary Wockner. (Orig.). 1993. pap. 12.00 (*0-9631362-1-6*) B-Store Pr.

Sex with God. rev. ed. Thomas O'Neil. LC 93-61845. (Illus.). 156p. (Orig.). 1994. pap. 6.95 (*0-9622398-1-X*) Wexford Pr.

Sex with Strangers. Geoffrey Rees. LC 93-1242. 1993. 20.00 (*0-374-26165-2*) FS&G.

Sex Without Consent Vol. I: A Peer Education Training Manual for Secondary Schools. Toby Simon & Cathy Harris. 1993. pap. 21.95 (*1-55691-097-5*, 975) Learning Pubns.

Sex Without Consent, Vol. II: A Peer Education Training Manual for Colleges & Universities. Toby Simon & Cathy Harris. 1993. pap. 21.95 (*1-55691-098-3*, 983) Learning Pubns.

Sex Without Guilt. Albert Ellis. 1976. pap. 7.00 (*0-87980-145-X*) Wilshire.

Sex Without Guilt. rev. ed. Albert Ellis. 1966. 4.95 (*0-8184-0121-4*) Carol Pub Group.

Sex Without Love: A Philosophical Exploration. Russell Vannoy. LC 79-57534. 226p. (C). 1980. pap. 20.95 (*0-87975-129-0*) Prometheus Bks.

Sex, Woman & Religion. Arthur F. Ide. LC 84-91148. (Woman in History Ser.: 100). (Illus.). xi, 212p. (Orig.). (C). 1984. pap. 15.00 (*0-930383-00-1*) Monument Pr.

Sex Work: Writings by Women in the Sex Industry. Ed. by Frederique Delacoste & Priscilla Alexander. LC 86-72847. 360p. (Orig.). (C). 1991. reprint ed. pap. 16.95 (*0-939416-11-5*) Cleis Pr.

Sex Work & Sex Workers in Australia. Ed. by Roberta Perkins et al. 1995. pap. 27.95 (*0-86840-174-9*, Pub. by New South Wales Univ Pr AT) Intl Spec Bk.

Sex Work on the Streets: Prostitutes & Their Clients. Neil McKeganey & Marina U. Barnard. LC 95-51048. 114p. (C). 1996. 79.00 (*0-335-19401-X*, Open Univ Pr); pap. 24.95 (*0-335-19400-1*, Open Univ Pr) Taylor & Francis.

Sex Workers & Sex Work, Vol. 11, No. 4. Anne McClintock. 1994. pap. 8.00 (*0-8223-6412-3*) Duke.

Sex Worship & Symbolism: An Interpretation. Sanger Brown. LC 72-9624. reprint ed. 36.50 (*0-404-57419-X*) AMS Pr.

Sexaholics & Other Plays. Murray Schisgal. 1995. pap. 5.25 (*0-8222-1438-5*) Dramatists Play.

Sexaholics Anonymous. LC 89-10261. 212p. (Orig.). 1989. pap. 10.00 (*0-9622887-0-5*) SA Literature.

***Sexational Secrets, Vol. 1.** Bakos. 1997. mass mkt. write for info. (*0-312-96341-6*) St Martin.

Sexational Secrets: Exotic Advice Your Mother Never Told You. Susan C. Bakos. 240p. 1996. 22.95 (*0-312-14413-X*) St Martin.

Sex...Bet You Don't Know It All! Noreen Shub & Sue Demore. 43p. 1992. pap. text ed. write for info. (*0-9634453-0-8*) Hawkeye Pr AZ.

Sexbomb: The Life & Death of Jane Mansfield. Guus Luitjters & Gerard Timmer. Tr. by Josh Pachter from DUT. (Illus.). 164p. 1988. pap. 12.95 (*0-8065-1049-8*, Citadel Pr) Carol Pub Group.

***Sexed Work: Gender, Race & Resistance in a Brooklyn Drug Market.** Lisa Maher. LC 97-8002. (Clarendon Studies in Criminology). 300p. 1997. 45.00 (*0-19-826495-X*, Clarendon Pr) OUP.

Sexercise. Herrin. 1982. 14.95 (*0-02-499780-3*, Macmillan Coll) P-H.

Sexes & Genealogies. Luce Irigaray. Tr. by Gillian C. Gill from FRE. LC 92-32495. 192p. (C). 1993. pap. 15.00 (*0-231-07033-0*); text ed. 49.50 (*0-231-07032-2*) Col U Pr.

Sexes at Work. Lois B. Hart & David Dalke. 300p. 1995. teacher ed., ring bd. 79.95 (*0-87425-251-2*) HRD Press.

Sexfacts: The Handbook for Healthy Sexuality. June Morris. (Illus.). 44p. (Orig.). 1995. pap. 10.95 (*0-85572-244-4*) Seven Hills Bk.

Sexing the Benefit: Women, Social Security & Financial Independence in EC Sex Equality Law. Julia Sohrab. (Socio-Legal Studies). 250p. 1996. text ed. 67.95 (*1-85521-705-8*, Pub. by Dartmth Pub UK) Ashgate Pub Co.

Sexing the Cherry. Jeanette Winterson. LC 90-50478. 192p. 1991. pap. 10.00 (*0-679-73316-7*, Vin) Random.

***Sexing the Groove: Popular Music & Gender.** Sheila Whiteley. LC 97-5416. 336p. 1997. pap. write for info. (*0-415-14671-2*) Routledge.

***Sexing the Groove: Popular Music & Gender.** Sheila Whiteley. LC 97-5416. 336p. (C). 1997. text ed. write for info. (*0-415-14670-4*) Routledge.

Sexing the Millennium: Women & the Sexual Revolution. Linda Grant. LC 93-41427. 304p. 1995. pap. 12.00 (*0-8021-3349-5*, Grove) Grove-Atltic.

Sexing the Mind: Nineteenth-Century Fictions of Hysteria. Evelyne Ender. LC 95-11137. 320p. 1995. 42.50 (*0-8014-2826-2*); pap. 17.95 (*0-8014-8083-3*) Cornell U Pr.

Sexing the Self: Gendered Positions in Cultural Studies. Elspeth Probyn. LC 92-22143. 226p. (C). 1993. pap. 15.95 (*0-415-07356-1*, B0135, Routledge NY) Routledge.

Sexing the Self: Gendered Positions in Cultural Studies. Elspeth Probyn. LC 92-22143. 226p. (C). (gr. 13). 1993. text ed. 49.95 (*0-415-07355-3*, B0131, Routledge NY) Routledge.

Sexism. Maurianne Adams. 106p. (C). 1994. 21.00 (*0-7872-0039-5*) Kendall-Hunt.

Sexism. Maurianne Adams. 176p. (C). 1995. 21.00 (*0-7872-1677-1*) Kendall-Hunt.

***Sexism: Going, Going, Gone but Not Forgotten.** Jerry Cooper. 24p. (Orig.). 1996. pap. 3.95 (*1-889419-18-4*) J Cooper.

Sexism & Decency in Advertising: Government Regulation & Industry Self Regulation in 47 Countries. J. J. Boddewyn. 70p. 1989. 70.00 (*0-317-02009-9*) Intl Advertising Assn.

Sexism & God-Talk: Toward a Feminist Theology. Rosemary R. Ruether. LC 92-33119. 320p. 1993. pap. 15.00 (*0-8070-1205-X*) Beacon Pr.

***Sexism & Reentry: Job Realities for Women Librarians.** Katherine M. Dickson. LC 97-7884. 286p. 1997. 32.50 (*0-7618-0747-0*) U Pr of Amer.

Sexism & Science. Evelyn Reed. LC 77-92144. (Illus.). 1978. reprint ed. pap. 15.95 (*0-87348-541-6*); reprint ed. lib. bdg. 45.00 (*0-87348-540-8*) Pathfinder NY.

Sexism & the Female Offender: An Organizational Analysis. Loraine Gelsthorpe. (Cambridge Criminology Ser.). 196p. 1989. text ed. 59.95 (*0-566-05443-4*, Pub. by Avebury Pub UK) Ashgate Pub Co.

Sexism & the War System. Betty A. Reardon. 132p. (C). 1996. pap. 14.95 (*0-8156-0348-7*, RESWP) Syracuse U Pr.

Sexism in Award-Winning Picture Books. Suzanne M. Czaplinski. (Illus.). 1973. pap. 2.50 (*0-912786-21-3*) Know Inc.

Sexism in Indian Education. Narendra N. Kalia. 193p. 1979. 15.95 (*0-7069-0809-0*) Asia Bk Corp.

Sexism in the Computer Industry. Dick Whitson. 1984. ring bd. 99.95 (*0-917194-16-0*) Prog Studies.

Sexism Is a Sin: The Biblical Basis of Female Equality. J. R. Hyland. 150p. (Orig.). 1995. pap. 12.95 (*0-945703-01-5*) Viatoris Ministries.

Sexism of Social & Political Theory: Women & Reproduction from Plato to Nietzsche. Ed. by Lorenne Clark & Lynda Lange. LC 79-17862. 1979. pap. 14.95 (*0-8020-6375-6*) U of Toronto Pr.

***Sexist.** Richard C. Sukin. 1997. mass mkt. 4.99 (*1-55197-302-2*, Pub. by Comnwlth Pub CN) Partners Pubs Grp.

Sexless Oysters & Self-Tipping Hats: 100 Years of Invention in the Pacific Northwest. Adam Woog. (Illus.). 256p. (Orig.). 1991. pap. 14.95 (*0-912365-47-1*) Sasquatch Bks.

SexMagick: Women Conjuring Erotic Fantasy. Ed. by Cecilia Tan. 88p. 1997. reprint ed. pap. 8.95 (*1-885865-14-7*) Circlet Pr.

SexMagick 2: Men Conjuring Erotic Fantasy. Ed. by Cecilia Tan. 152p. (Orig.). 1997. pap. 9.95 (*1-885865-09-0*) Circlet Pr.

***Sexo, las Mentiras y la Verdad - Sex, Lies & the Truth.** (Enfoque a la Familia - Focus on the Family Ser.). 174p. (SPA.). 1995. write for info. (*0-7899-0173-0*) Editorial Unilit.

Sexo Total. Ed. by Frank Calderon. (SPA.). pap. 4.95 (*1-56259-011-1*) Editorial Amer.

Sexo y Comunicacion en el Matrimonio. Kevin Leman. (Serie Enfoque a la Familia - Focus on the Family Ser.). 30p. (SPA.). 1992. pap. 1.79 (*1-56063-260-7*, 497416) Editorial Unilit.

Sexo y el Soltero. Marcos Richards. 40p. (YA). 1995. pap. text ed. 1.15 (*1-885630-34-4*) HLM Producciones.

Sexo y Juventud. Luis Palau. (SPA.). 1987. 3.99 (*0-8423-6522-2*, 498019) Editorial Unilit.

***Sexo y Juventud.** Luis Palau. 136p. (SPA.). 1987. pap. write for info. (*0-614-27140-1*) Editorial Unilit.

Sexo y Mas. M. Lawson & D. Skip. (SPA.). 1988. 3.50 (*0-8423-6521-4*, 490249) Editorial Unilit.

***Sexo y Mas.** M. Lawson & D. Skipp. 112p. (SPA.). 1988. pap. write for info. (*0-614-27139-8*) Editorial Unilit.

Sexo y Mas: Guia Para la Juventud. Michael Lawson & David Skipp. (Illus.). 110p. (Orig.). (SPA.). (YA). (gr. 10-12). 1988. pap. 2.95 (*0-945792-02-6*) Editorial Unilit.

Sexocize: A Female Genitourinary Program. 2nd ed. Janan Clark. (Illus.). 38p. 1989. pap. text ed. 12.95 (*0-929593-01-4*) West Pine Pub.

Sexologisches Woerterbch. Preben Hertoft. 218p. (GER.). 1993. 85.00 (*0-7859-8461-5*, 3769102274) Fr & Eur.

Sexology. William H. Walling. LC 73-20641. (Sex, Marriage & Society Ser.). 238p. 1974. reprint ed. 23.95 (*0-405-05822-5*) Ayer.

Sexology Encyclopedia: Index & Reference Books of New Information Vol. 24: Pedophilia. Arlene S. Shank. Ed. by John C. Bartone. 150p. 1996. 49.95 (*0-7883-0896-3*); pap. 39.95 (*0-7883-0897-1*) ABBE Pubs Assn.

Sexology Encyclopedia: Index & Reference Books of New Information, 25 vols., Set. Ed. by John C. Bartone. (Illus.). 3750p. 1996. 1,200.00 (*0-7883-1050-X*); pap. 950.00 (*0-7883-1051-8*) ABBE Pubs Assn.

Sexology Encyclopedia Vol. 1: Sex & Intercourse Research: Index & Reference Books of New Information. American Health Research Institute Staff. Ed. by John C. Bartone. (Illus.). 175p. 1996. pap. 39.95 (*0-7883-0851-3*) ABBE Pubs Assn.

Sexology Encyclopedia Vol. 1: Sex & Intercourse Research: Index & Reference Books of New Information, 25 vols., Set. American Health Research Institute Staff. Ed. by John C. Bartone. (Illus.). 175p. 1996. 49.95 (*0-7883-0850-5*) ABBE Pubs Assn.

Sexology Encyclopedia Vol. 2: Vaginitis: Index & Reference Books of New Information. Sandy M. Van Wertz. Ed. by John C. Bartone. (Illus.). 125p. 1996. pap. 39.95 (*0-7883-0853-X*) ABBE Pubs Assn.

Sexology Encyclopedia Vol. 2: Vaginitis: Index & Reference Books of New Information, 25 vols., Set. Sandy M. Van Wertz. Ed. by John C. Bartone. (Illus.). 125p. 1996. 49.95 (*0-7883-0852-1*) ABBE Pubs Assn.

Sexology Encyclopedia Vol. 3: Menopause: Index & Reference Books of New Information. Ruby Q. Mordune. Ed. by John C. Bartone. (Illus.). 154p. 1996. pap. 39.95 (*0-7883-0855-6*) ABBE Pubs Assn.

Sexology Encyclopedia Vol. 3: Menopause: Index & Reference Books of New Information, 25 vols., Set. Ruby Q. Mordune. Ed. by John C. Bartone. (Illus.). 154p. 1996. 49.95 (*0-7883-0854-8*) ABBE Pubs Assn.

Sexology Encyclopedia Vol. 4: Sex Offenses: Index & Reference Books of New Information. Harold P. Drummond. Ed. by John C. Bartone. (Illus.). 157p. 1996. pap. 39.95 (*0-7883-0857-2*) ABBE Pubs Assn.

Sexology Encyclopedia Vol. 4: Sex Offenses: Index & Reference Books of New Information, 25 vols., Set. Harold P. Drummond. Ed. by John C. Bartone. (Illus.). 157p. 1996. 49.95 (*0-7883-0856-4*) ABBE Pubs Assn.

Sexology Encyclopedia Vol. 5: Intra-Uterine Devices: Index & Reference Books of New Information. Doris E. Rockford. Ed. by John C. Bartone. (Illus.). 151p. 1996. pap. 39.95 (*0-7883-0859-9*) ABBE Pubs Assn.

Sexology Encyclopedia Vol. 5: Intra-Uterine Devices: Index & Reference Books of New Information, 25 vols., Set. Doris E. Rockford. Ed. by John C. Bartone. (Illus.). 170p. 1996. 49.95 (*0-7883-0858-0*) ABBE Pubs Assn.

Sexology Encyclopedia Vol. 6: Impotence: Index & Reference Books of New Information. Alexander D. Farrell. Ed. by John C. Bartone. (Illus.). 151p. 1996. pap. 39.95 (*0-7883-0861-0*) ABBE Pubs Assn.

Sexology Encyclopedia Vol. 6: Impotence: Index & Reference Books of New Information, 25 vols., Set. Alexander D. Farrell. Ed. by John C. Bartone. (Illus.). 151p. 1996. 49.95 (*0-7883-0860-2*) ABBE Pubs Assn.

Sexology Encyclopedia Vol. 7: Sexually Transmitted Diseases: Index & Reference Books of New Information. Helen M. Markle & John C. Bartone. (Illus.). 159p. 1996. pap. 39.95 (*0-7883-0863-7*) ABBE Pubs Assn.

Sexology Encyclopedia Vol. 7: Sexually Transmitted Diseases: Index & Reference Books of New Information, 25 vols., Set. Helen M. Markle. Ed. by John C. Bartone. (Illus.). 159p. 1996. 49.95 (*0-7883-0862-9*) ABBE Pubs Assn.

Sexology Encyclopedia Vol. 8: Sex & Transsexualism: Index & Reference Books of New Information. Rosalie F. Zoltano. Ed. by John C. Bartone. (Illus.). 129p. 1996. pap. 39.95 (*0-7883-0865-3*) ABBE Pubs Assn.

Sexology Encyclopedia Vol. 8: Sex & Transsexualism: Index & Reference Books of New Information, 25 vols., Set. Rosalie F. Zoltano. Ed. by John C. Bartone. (Illus.). 129p. 1996. 49.95 (*0-7883-0864-5*) ABBE Pubs Assn.

Sexology Encyclopedia Vol. 9: Incest: Index & Reference Books of New Information. Lottie F. Lydeen. Ed. by John C. Bartone. (Illus.). 163p. 1996. pap. 39.95 (*0-7883-0867-X*) ABBE Pubs Assn.

Sexology Encyclopedia Vol. 9: Incest: Index & Reference Books of New Information, 25 vols., Set. Lottie F. Lydeen. Ed. by John C. Bartone. (Illus.). 163p. 1996. 49.95 (*0-7883-0866-1*) ABBE Pubs Assn.

Sexology Encyclopedia Vol. 10: Homosexuality: Index & Reference Books of New Information. Sanivar H. Clygout. Ed. by John C. Bartone. (Illus.). 155p. 1996. pap. 39.95 (*0-7883-0869-6*) ABBE Pubs Assn.

Sexology Encyclopedia Vol. 10: Homosexuality: Index & Reference Books of New Information, 25 vols., Set. Sanivar H. Clygout. Ed. by John C. Bartone. (Illus.). 155p. 1996. 49.95 (*0-7883-0868-8*) ABBE Pubs Assn.

Sexology Encyclopedia Vol. 11: Sex Disorders: Sex Disorders: Index & Reference Books of New Information. American Health Research Institute Staff. Ed. by John C. Bartone. (Illus.). 153p. 1996. pap. 39.95 (*0-7883-0871-8*) ABBE Pubs Assn.

Sexology Encyclopedia Vol. 11: Sex Disorders: Sex Disorders: Index & Reference Books of New Information, 25 vols., Set. American Health Research Institute Staff. Ed. by John C. Bartone. (Illus.). 153p. 1996. 49.95 (*0-7883-0870-X*) ABBE Pubs Assn.

Sexology Encyclopedia Vol. 12: Vagina Research: Index & Reference Books of New Information. Judy J. Hallcrest. Ed. by John C. Bartone. (Illus.). 143p. 1996. pap. 39.95 (*0-7883-0873-4*) ABBE Pubs Assn.

Sexology Encyclopedia Vol. 12: Vagina Research: Index & Reference Books of New Information, 25 vols., Set. Judy J. Hallcrest. Ed. by John C. Bartone. (Illus.). 143p. 1996. 49.95 (*0-7883-0872-6*) ABBE Pubs Assn.

Sexology Encyclopedia Vol. 13: Prostate Research: Index & Reference Books of New Information. Virginia L. Jensen. Ed. by John C. Bartone. (Illus.). 163p. 1996. pap. 39.95 (*0-7883-0875-0*) ABBE Pubs Assn.

Sexology Encyclopedia Vol. 13: Prostate Research: Index & Reference Books of New Information, 25 vols., Set. Virginia L. Jensen. Ed. by John C. Bartone. (Illus.). 163p. 1996. 49.95 (*0-7883-0874-2*) ABBE Pubs Assn.

Sexology Encyclopedia Vol. 14: Menstruation Disorders: Index & Reference Books of New Information. Bette M. Parkenham. Ed. by John C. Bartone. (Illus.). 150p. 1996. 49.95 (*0-7883-0876-9*); pap. 39.95 (*0-7883-0877-7*) ABBE Pubs Assn.

Sexology Encyclopedia Vol. 15: Sex Behavior: Index & Reference Books of New Information. American Health Research Institute Staff. Ed. by John C. Bartone. (Illus.). 153p. 1996. 49.95 (*0-7883-0878-5*); pap. 39.95 (*0-7883-0879-3*) ABBE Pubs Assn.

Sexology Encyclopedia Vol. 16: Herpes Genitalis: Index & Reference Books of New Information. Marian L. Rice. Ed. by John C. Bartone. (Illus.). 145p. 1996. 49.95 (*0-7883-0880-7*); pap. 39.95 (*0-7883-0881-5*) ABBE Pubs Assn.

Sexology Encyclopedia Vol. 17: Sex & Bisexuality: Index & Reference Books of New Information. Rosalie F. Zoltano. Ed. by John C. Bartone. (Illus.). 149p. 1996. 49.95 (*0-7883-0882-3*); pap. 39.95 (*0-7883-0883-1*) ABBE Pubs Assn.

Sexology Encyclopedia Vol. 18: Sex Research: Index & Reference Books of New Information. Rosalie F. Zoltano. Ed. by John C. Bartone. (Illus.). 167p. 1996. 49.95 (*0-7883-0884-X*); pap. 39.95 (*0-7883-0885-8*) ABBE Pubs Assn.

Sexology Encyclopedia Vol. 19: Vasectomy & Medicine: Index & Reference Books of New Information. Benard I. Valahos. (Illus.). 145p. 1996. 49.95 (*0-7883-0886-6*); pap. 39.95 (*0-7883-0887-4*) ABBE Pubs Assn.

Sexology Encyclopedia Vol. 20: Female Genital Diseases: Index & Reference Books of New Information. Patricia S. Hurley. Ed. by John C. Bartone. (Illus.). 155p. 1996. 49.95 (*0-7883-0888-2*); pap. 39.95 (*0-7883-0889-0*) ABBE Pubs Assn.

Sexology Encyclopedia Vol. 21: Sexual Harassment: Index & Reference Book of New Information. Simon H. Bonner. (Illus.). 143p. 1996. 49.50 (*0-7883-0890-4*); pap. 39.95 (*0-7883-0891-2*) ABBE Pubs Assn.

Sexology Encyclopedia Vol. 22: Rape: Index of Modern Information with Bibliography. Marie R. Drake. (Illus.). 129p. 49.50 (*0-7883-0892-0*); pap. 39.95 (*0-7883-0893-9*) ABBE Pubs Assn.

Sexology Encyclopedia Vol. 23: Premenstrual Syndromes: Index & Reference Books of New Information. Jacob L. Liehaus. (Illus.). 123p. 1996. 49.50 (*0-7883-0894-7*); pap. 39.95 (*0-7883-0895-5*) ABBE Pubs Assn.

Sexology Encyclopedia Vol. 25: Orgasm Research: Index & Reference Books of New Information. Helen M. Markle. Ed. by John C. Bartone. 167p. 1996. 49.95 (*0-7883-0898-X*); pap. 39.95 (*0-7883-0899-8*) ABBE Pubs Assn.

***Sexpectations: Women Talk Candidly on Sex & Dating.** R. Louis. (Illus.). 180p. (Orig.). 1997. pap. 10.95 (*0-9613177-4-4*) Bioenergetics Pr.

Sexpert. Ed. by Pat Califia. (Orig.). 1992. mass mkt. 4.95 (*1-56333-034-2*, Badboy) Masquerade.

S'Expliquer (Myself Freud Explained) Stephen N. Stivers. 64p. 1985. pap. 4.95 (*0-9615274-1-2*) Stivers.

***Explorations: Journeys to the Erogenous Frontier.** Anka Radakovich. 1997. 20.00 (*0-517-70195-2*, Crown) Crown Pub Group.

Sexsational Secrets: Things Your Mother Never Told You. Susan C. Bakos. 1996. 22.95 (*0-614-97013-X*) St Martin.

Sextalk. June Morris. 1995. pap. 26.00 (*0-86431-151-6*, Pub. by Aust Council Educ Res AT) St Mut.

S

Sextant Handbook: Adjustment, Repair, Use & History. 2nd ed. Bruce Bauer. 1995. pap. text ed. 15.95 (*0-07-005219-0*) Intl Marine.

Sextant, Sea & Solitude. large type ed. Hugh Schmitt. 1990. 25.99 (*0-7089-2160-4*) Ulverscroft.

Sextet. Henry Miller. LC 77-20795. (Illus.). 1977. pap. 7.95 (*0-88496-111-7*) Capra Pr.

Sextet. Henry Miller. 1994. 14.95 (*0-7145-3828-0*); pap. 9.95 (*0-7145-3844-2*) Riverrun NY.

Sextet: Six Essays. Henry Miller. LC 95-9979. (I.O. Evans Studies in the Philosophy & Criticism of Literature, 0271-9061: Vol. 29). 192p. 1995. pap. 21.00 (*0-8095-1903-8*); lib. bdg. 31.00 (*0-8095-0903-2*) Borgo Pr.

Sextet One: 6 Powerful American Voices. Kim Addonizio et al. Ed. & Intro. by Victor Di Suvero. 1996. 17.50 (*0-938631-27-6*) Pennywhistle Pr.

Sextette: Translations from the French Symbolists. Tr. by Dorothy Martin. LC 80-10539. (Symbolists Ser.). reprint ed. 34.50 (*0-404-16331-9*) AMS Pr.

Sexton: Selected Criticism. Ed. by Diana H. George. 352p. 1988. text ed. 29.95 (*0-252-01552-5*) U of Ill Pr.

***SexTopia: Enlightened Education for Utopian Futures, Computerogenic Realities, & Life in a New & Perfected Paradise on Earth.** M. O. Thoreau & Alexander P. Thoreau. 160p. (Orig.). 1998. pap. 14.95 (*0-927379-84-8*, ZP64) Zorba Pr.

***Sextus Empiricus: Against the Grammarians.** Sextus Empiricus. Tr. & Comment by D. L. Blank. (Clarendon Later Ancient Philosophers Ser.). 336p. 1997. 65.00 (*0-19-824470-3*, Clarendon Pr) OUP.

Sextus Pompey. Moses Hadas. LC 72-181935. reprint ed. 27.50 (*0-404-03020-3*) AMS Pr.

Sexual Aberrations. Wilhelm Stekel. 1971. pap. 5.95 (*0-87140-246-7*) Liveright.

Sexual Aberrations, 2 Vols. Wilhelm Stekel. (C). Date not set. text ed. 14.95 (*0-87140-837-6*) Liveright.

Sexual Abuse: Causes, Consequences & Treatment of Incestuous & Pedophilic Acts. Adele Mayer. LC 84-80657. 176p. 1985. pap. 19.95 (*1-55691-059-2*, 592) Learning Pubns.

***Sexual Abuse: The Overcomer's Manual.** Wendell E. Miller. (Orig.). Date not set. pap. write for info. (*0-9641441-2-3*) ClearBrook.

Sexual Abuse see Child Abuse: A Multidisciplinary Survey

Sexual Abuse - Incest Survivors: A Categorized Bibliography & Reference List. R. Geffner et al. 95p. 1992. 16.95 (*1-882948-05-X*) Family Violence.

Sexual Abuse - Sacred Wound: Transforming Deep Trauma. Stephanie Mines. 1995. pap. text ed. 15.95 (*1-886449-11-2*) Barrytown Ltd.

Sexual Abuse & Consensual Sex: Women's Developmental Patterns & Outcomes. Michael D. Newcomb et al. (Illus.). 192p. (C). 1993. text ed. 28.00 (*0-8039-4733-X*) Sage.

Sexual Abuse & Eating Disorders. Ed. by Mark F. Schwartz & Leigh Cohn. 240p. Date not set. text ed. 27.95 (*0-87630-794-2*) Brunner-Mazel.

***Sexual Abuse & Incest.** Dale Reinert. LC 97-6704. (Teen Issues Ser.). 104p. (YA). (gr. 6 up). 1997. lib. bdg. 18.95 (*0-89490-916-9*) Enslow Pubs.

Sexual Abuse & the Primary Care Doctor. G. Wakely. 96p. 1991. pap. 19.95 (*0-412-41580-1*, A6372) Chapman & Hall.

Sexual Abuse & the Rights of Children: Reforming Canadian Law. Terrence Sullivan. 288p. (Orig.). 1992. 45.00 (*0-8020-5909-0*); pap. 16.95 (*0-8020-6851-0*) U of Toronto Pr.

Sexual Abuse by Clergy: A Crisis for the Church. Marie M. Fortune & James N. Poling. 60p. 1994. pap. 10.00 (*0-929670-09-4*) JPCP.

***Sexual Abuse in America: The Epidemic of the 21st Century.** Robert Freeman-Longo & Geral Blanchard. 150p. (Orig.). 1997. pap. 20.00 (*1-884444-45-8*) Safer Soc.

Sexual Abuse in Christian Homes & Churches. Carolyn H. Heggen. LC 92-32143. 208p. (Orig.). 1993. pap. 11.99 (*0-8361-3624-1*) Herald Pr.

Sexual Abuse in Residential Treatment. Ed. by Raymond Schimmer. LC 93-2422. (Residential Treatment for Children & Youth Ser.: Vol. 11, No. 1). (Illus.). 145p. 1993. lib. bdg. 29.95 (*1-56024-475-5*) Haworth Pr.

***Sexual Abuse in the Lives of Women Diagnosed with Serious Mental Illness.** Ed. by Maxine Harris & Christine Landis. (New Directions in Therapeutic Intervention Ser.). 1997. text ed. 68.00 (*90-5702-504-3*, Harwood Acad Pubs) Gordon & Breach.

***Sexual Abuse in the Lives of Women Diagnosed with Serious Mental Illness.** Ed. by Maxine Harris & Christine Landis. (New Directions in Therapeutic Intervention Ser.). 1997. pap. text ed. 28.50 (*90-5702-505-1*, Harwood Acad Pubs) Gordon & Breach.

Sexual Abuse of Children, 2 vols. Ed. by W. T. O'Donohue & J. H. Geer. 424p. 1992. Vol. I: Theory & Research. pap. 39.95 (*0-8058-0340-8*); Vol. II: Clinical Issues. pap. 45.00 (*0-8058-0955-4*) L Erlbaum Assocs.

Sexual Abuse of Children, 2 vols. Ed. by W. T. O'Donohue & J. H. Geer. 424p. (C). 1992. Vol. I: Theory & Research. 89.95 (*0-8058-0339-4*); Vol. II: Clinical Issues. 89.95 (*0-8058-0954-6*) L Erlbaum Assocs.

Sexual Abuse of Children, 2 vols., Set. Ed. by W. T. O'Donohue & J. H. Geer. 1992. pap. 70.00 (*0-8058-0957-0*); text ed. 150.00 (*0-8058-0956-2*) L Erlbaum Assocs.

Sexual Abuse of Children: A Comprehensive Guide to Current Knowledge & Intervention Strategies. Jeffrey J. Haugaard & N. Dickon Reppucci. LC 87-46345. (Social & Behavioral Science Ser.). 452p. text ed. 39.95 (*1-55542-077-X*) Jossey-Bass.

Sexual Abuse of Children: A Resource Guide & Annotated Bibliography. Benjamin Schlesinger. 212p. 1982. pap. 11.95 (*0-8020-6481-7*) U of Toronto Pr.

Sexual Abuse of Children: Index of Modern Information. Lottie F. Lydeen. LC 88-47967. 150p. 1990. 44.50 (*1-55914-038-0*); pap. 39.50 (*1-55914-039-9*) ABBE Pubs Assn.

***Sexual Abuse of Children & Adolescents.** Margaret O. Hyde & Elizabeth H. Forsyth. LC 96-36366. (Illus.). 96p. (YA). (gr. 7 up). 1997. lib. bdg. 16.90 (*0-7613-0058-9*) Millbrook Pr.

Sexual Abuse of Children & Adolescents: A Preventive Guide for Parents, Teachers & Counselors. William E. Prendergast. 336p. 1996. 29.50 (*0-8264-0892-3*) Continuum.

Sexual Abuse of Children in the 1980s: Issues & Annotated Bibliography, 1980-1984. Benjamin Schlesinger. 208p. 1986. pap. 16.95 (*0-8020-6622-4*) U of Toronto Pr.

Sexual Abuse of Young Children: Evaluation & Treatment. Kee MacFarlane et al. LC 85-30539. 355p. 1988. pap. text ed. 20.95 (*0-89862-703-6*) Guilford Pr.

Sexual Abuse Prevention: A Course of Study for Teenagers. rev. ed. Rebecca Voelkel-Haugen & Marie M. Fortune. LC 96-458. (Illus.). 56p. 1996. student ed., pap. 8.95 (*0-8298-1082-X*) Pilgrim OH.

Sexual Abuse Recalled: Treating Trauma in the Era of the Recovered Memory Debate. Ed. by Judith L. Alpert. 440p. 1995. 40.00 (*1-56821-363-8*) Aronson.

Sexual Abuse! What Is It? An Informational Book for People Who Are Deaf or Hard of Hearing. Alice LaBarre et al. (Illus.). 71p. (Orig.). (J). (ps-12). 1995. reprint ed. pap. text ed. 9.00 (*0-9629302-1-0*) Ramsey Found.

Sexual Accusations & Social Turmoil. Jules H. Masserman & Chris Masserman. 160p. 1994. pap. 17.95 (*0-916147-42-8*) Regent Pr.

Sexual Accusations & Social Turmoil. Jules H. Masserman & Christine M. Masserman. 160p. 1994. 34.95 (*0-916147-43-6*) Regent Pr.

Sexual Addiction see Out of the Shadows: Understanding Sexual Addiction

Sexual Adjustment: A Guide for the Spinal Cord Injured. Martha F. Gregory. Ed. by Raymond C. Cheever. 70p. 1974. pap. 4.95 (*0-915708-00-0*, #1410) Cheever Pub.

Sexual Adventures of Sherlock Holmes. Larry Townsend. (Orig.). 1993. reprint ed. mass mkt. 4.95 (*1-56333-097-0*, Badboy) Masquerade.

Sexual Aggression. Donald Hall et al. (Issues in Etiology of Assessment & Treatment Ser.). 1993. 54.95 (*1-56032-268-3*) Hemisp Pub.

Sexual Aliveness: A Reichian Gestalt Perspective. Edward W. Smith. LC 87-42521. 136p. 1995. pap. 24.95 (*0-7864-0216-4*) McFarland & Co.

Sexual & Gender Harassment in the Academy: A Guide for Faculty, Students, & Administrators. fac. ed. Modern Language Association of America Staff. LC 81-14059. 79p. 1981. reprint ed. pap. 25.00 (*0-7837-8030-3*, 2047786) Bks Demand.

***Sexual & Reproductive Neurorehabilitation.** Ed. by Mindy L. Aisen. LC 97-12460. (Current Clinical Neurology Ser.). (Illus.). 256p. 1997. 99.50 (*0-89603-376-7*) Humana.

Sexual Animosity Between Men & Women. Gerald Schoenewolf. LC 88-19353. 264p. 1989. 30.00 (*0-87668-933-0*) Aronson.

***Sexual Anorexia: Overcoming Sexual Self-Hatred.** Patrick Carnes. LC 97-12610. 250p. 1997. pap. 14.95 (*1-56838-144-1*) Hazelden.

Sexual Art: Photographs That Test the Limits. Michael A. Rosen. (Illus.). 64p. (Orig.). 1994. pap. 30.00 (*0-936705-03-5*) Shaynew Pr.

Sexual Artifice: Persons, Images, Politics. Ed. by Ann Kibbey et al. (Gender Studies: No. 19). (Illus.). 312p. (C). 1994. 55.00 (*0-8147-4650-0*); pap. 17.95 (*0-8147-4651-9*) NYU Pr.

Sexual Aspects of Cardiovascular Disease. Chris Papadopoulos. LC 89-3973. (Sexual Medicine Ser.: No. 10). 136p. 1989. text ed. 55.00 (*0-275-92523-4*, C2523, Praeger Pubs) Greenwood.

Sexual Aspects of Headaches. Ed. by Seymour Diamond & Michael Maliszewski. LC 91-46626. 520p. (C). 1992. 65.00 (*0-8236-6071-0*) Intl Univs Pr.

Sexual Assault: Will I Ever Feel Okay Again; One Woman's Personal Journey to Wholeness. Kay Scott. 208p. 1993. pap. 9.99 (*1-55661-325-3*) Bethany Hse.

Sexual Assault & Abuse: A Handbook for Clergy & Religious Professionals. Mary D. Pellauer et al. Ed. by Barbara Chester & Jane Boyajian. LC 86-45825. 304p. 1991. pap. 17.00 (*0-06-066507-6*) Harper SF.

Sexual Assault & Abuse: Sociocultural Context of Prevention. Carolyn F. Swift. (Prevention in Human Services Ser.: Vol. 12, No. 2). 159p. 1995. 29.95 (*1-56024-762-2*) Haworth Pr.

Sexual Assault in Canada: A Decade of Legal & Social Change. Ed. by Julian V. Roberts & Renate M. Mohr. 384p. (C). 1994. 50.00 (*0-8020-5928-7*); pap. 19.95 (*0-8020-6868-5*) U of Toronto Pr.

Sexual Assault of Children & Adolescents. Ann W. Burgess et al. 245p. 1978. 16.00 (*0-318-17072-8*) Kempe Nat Ctr.

Sexual Assault of Children & Adolescents. Ann W. Burgess et al. LC 77-10217. 250p. 19.95 (*0-669-01892-9*, Lexington) Jossey-Bass.

***Sexual Assault on the College Campus: The Role of Male Peer Support.** Martin D. Schwartz & Walter S. DeKeseredy. LC 96-51225. 230p. 1997. 49.95 (*0-8039-7026-9*); pap. 23.95 (*0-8039-7027-7*) Sage.

Sexual Assault Survivor's Handbook for People with Developmental Disabilities & Their Advocates. Nora J. Baladerian. 1991. spiral bd. 11.95 (*0-88247-883-4*) R & E Pubs.

Sexual Assault Trials. Paul DerOhannesian, II. 1099p. 1994. 105.00 (*0-614-05964-X*) MICHIE.

***Sexual Assault Trials.** Paul DerOhannesian, II. 1099p. 1994. 105.00 (*1-55834-206-0*, 61175) MICHIE.

Sexual Astrology. Martine. 256p. 1977. mass mkt. 5.99 (*0-440-18020-1*) Dell.

Sexual Astrology. Marlene M. Rathgeb. 304p. (Orig.). 1993. pap. 11.00 (*0-380-76888-7*) Avon.

Sexual Attitudes: Myths & Realities. Vern L. Bullough & Bonnie Bullough. LC 94-47645. 281p. 1995. 29.95 (*0-87975-949-6*) Prometheus Bks.

Sexual Attitudes & Lifestyles. Anne M. Johnson et al. LC 93-11896. (Illus.). 512p. 1994. 50.00 (*0-632-03343-6*) Blackwell Sci.

Sexual Attraction & Childhood Association: A Chinese Brief for Edward Westermarck. Arthur P. Wolf. (Illus.). 624p. (C). 1995. 65.00 (*0-8047-2426-1*) Stanford U Pr.

Sexual Aversion, Sexual Phobias, & Panic Disorder. Helen S. Kaplan & Donald F. Klein. LC 86-28331. 168p. 1987. text ed. 41.95 (*0-87630-450-1*) Brunner-Mazel.

Sexual Awareness: 10th Anniversary Edition. enl. rev. ed. Barry W. McCarthy & Emily McCarthy. LC 84-9502. (Illus.). 272p. 1993. pap. 11.95 (*0-7867-0015-7*) Carroll & Graf.

Sexual Bargaining: Power Politics in the American Marriage. 2nd ed. John H. Scanzoni. LC 81-16222. xvi, 196p. 1982. pap. text ed. 7.50 (*0-226-73565-6*) U Ch Pr.

Sexual Barrier: Legal, Medical, Economic & Social Aspects of Sex Discrimination. Marija M. Hughes. LC 77-83214. 1977. 70.00 (*0-912560-04-5*) Hughes Pr.

Sexual Behavior: Management & Problems. N. McConaghy. (Applied Clinical Psychology Ser.). (Illus.). 400p. (C). 1993. 65.00 (*0-306-44177-2*, Plenum Pr) Plenum.

Sexual Behavior & AIDS in Britain. HMSO Staff. 250p. 1993. pap. 35.00 (*0-11-701748-5*, HM17485, Pub. by Stationery Ofc UK) Bernan Associates.

Sexual Behavior & Preventing Pregnancy. Frances S. Sizer & Eleanor N. Whitney. LC 91-39463. 1993. pap. text ed. 12.25 (*0-314-01685-6*) West Pub.

Sexual Behavior & Risks of HIV Infection: Proceedings of an International Workshop Supported by the European Communities. Ed. by Michel Hubert. 140p. (Orig.). (C). 1994. pap. text ed. 30.00 (*0-7881-1127-2*) DIANE Pub.

Sexual Behavior in Modern China: A Report on the Nationwide Survey of 20,000 Chinese Men & Women. Dalin Liu et al. (Illus.). 400p. 1997. 95.00 (*0-8264-0886-9*) Continuum.

***Sexual Behavior Scale.** Vince Huntington. (Perspectives in Psychotherapy Ser.: Vol. 1). 300p. 1997. pap. text ed. 49.95 (*0-938198-03-3*) Weidner & Sons.

Sexual Behaviour & AIDS. Alfred Spira et al. 279p. 1994. 72.95 (*1-85628-931-1*, Pub. by Avebury Pub UK) Ashgate Pub Co.

Sexual Behaviour & Knowledge about AIDS in the Developing World: Findings from a Multisite Study. Ed. by John Cleland & Benoit Ferry. LC 94-47639. (Social Aspects of AIDS Ser.). 240p. 1994. 75.00 (*0-7484-0343-4*); pap. write for info. (*0-7484-0344-2*) Taylor & Francis.

Sexual Behaviour in Canada: Patterns & Problems. Ed. by Benjamin Schlesinger. LC 77-372192. 340p. reprint ed. pap. 96.90 (*0-8357-8318-9*, 2034076) Bks Demand.

Sexual Being vs. Governments That Promote Homosexuality. Karl Bowman. LC 93-83108. 64p. (Orig.). 1993. pap. 6.00 (*0-914752-32-4*) Sovereign Pr.

Sexual Blood. Mark Amerika. 187p. 1995. pap. 9.00 (*1-57366-000-0*) Fiction Coll.

Sexual Blood. Amerkia Mark. 1995. pap. (*0-573-66000-X*) French.

Sexual Body: An Interdisciplinary Perspective. Arthur Efron. LC 82-642121. 314p. 1985. pap. 18.00 (*0-930195-01-9*) Inst Mind Behavior.

Sexual Body Talk. Susan Quilliam. (Illus.). 128p. 1992. pap. 15.95 (*0-88184-757-7*) Carroll & Graf.

Sexual Bond: Rethinking Families & Close Relationships. John H. Scanzoni et al. (Library of Social Research: Vol. 170). 272p. (C). 1989. text ed. 54.00 (*0-8039-2883-1*); pap. text ed. 24.95 (*0-8039-2884-X*) Sage.

Sexual Brain. Simon LeVay. LC 92-44691. (Illus.). 220p. 1993. 25.00 (*0-262-12178-6*, Bradford Bks) MIT Pr.

Sexual Brain. Simon LeVay. (Illus.). 192p. 1994. pap. 10.95 (*0-262-62093-6*, Bradford Bks) MIT Pr.

Sexual Challenge: Growing up Christian. Bishops' Committee for Pastoral Research Staff & National Conference of Catholic Bishops Staff. 16p. (Orig.). (YA). (gr. 9-12). 1990. pap. 0.95 (*1-55586-364-7*) US Catholic.

Sexual Challenges: Navigating Your Course Through Troubled Waters to Loving Relationships. Barbara Childers & Eugenie G. Wheeler. LC 96-7507. 176p. 1996. pap. 11.95 (*0-934793-58-1*) Pathfinder CA.

Sexual Chaos: Charting a Christian Course Through Turbulent Times. rev. ed. Tim Stafford. LC 93-19209. Orig. Title: The Sexual Christian. 172p. 1993. reprint ed. pap. 9.99 (*0-8308-1349-7*, 1349) InterVarsity.

Sexual Character: Beyond Technique to Intimacy. Marva J. Dawn. LC 93-1216. 192p. (Orig.). (C). 1993. pap. 13.00 (*0-8028-0700-3*) Eerdmans.

***Sexual Chemistry.** E. Grant. Date not set. 9.99 (*0-7493-2485-6*, Reed Trade) Buttrwrth-Heinemann.

Sexual Choices: An Introduction to Human Sexuality. Gilbert D. Nass et al. LC 83-25951. 650p. (C). 1984. reprint ed. pap. text ed. 25.00 (*0-86720-392-7*) Jones & Bartlett.

Sexual Christian see Sexual Chaos: Charting a Christian Course Through Turbulent Times

Sexual Citizenship: The Material Construction of Sexualities. David T. Evans. LC 92-28812. 256p. (C). 1993. pap. 17.95 (*0-415-05800-7*, A7742, Routledge NY) Routledge.

Sexual Citizenship: The Material Construction of Sexualities. David T. Evans. LC 92-28812. 256p. (C). (gr. 13). 1993. text ed. 62.95 (*0-415-05799-X*, A7738, Routledge NY) Routledge.

Sexual Coercion & Reproductive Health: A Focus on Research. Lori L. Heise et al. 60p. 1995. pap. text ed. 10.00 (*0-614-16479-6*) Population Coun.

Sexual Coercion in Dating Relationships. Ed. by E. Sandra Byers & Lucia F. O'Sullivan. LC 96-7979. (Journal of Psychology & Human Sexuality: Vol. 8, Nos. 1/2). 179p. 1996. 29.95 (*1-56024-815-7*); pap. 14.95 (*1-56024-844-0*) Haworth Pr.

Sexual Concerns When Illness or Disability Strikes. Carol L. Sandowski. (Illus.). 304p. 1989. pap. 39.95 (*0-398-06413-X*) C C Thomas.

Sexual Concerns When Illness or Disability Strikes. Carol L. Sandowski. (Illus.). 304p. (C). 1989. text ed. 58.95 (*0-398-05612-9*) C C Thomas.

Sexual Conduct: The Social Sources of Human Sexuality. John H. Gagnon & William Simon. 328p. (C). 1973. lib. bdg. 37.95 (*0-202-30261-X*) Aldine de Gruyter.

***Sexual Consent.** David Archard. 1997. text ed. 49.00 (*0-8133-3081-5*) Westview.

***Sexual Consent.** David Archard. (C). 1997. pap. text ed. 18.95 (*0-8133-3082-3*) Westview.

Sexual Contract. Carole Pateman. LC 87-63007. xii, 264p. 1988. 45.00 (*0-8047-1476-2*); pap. 16.95 (*0-8047-1477-0*) Stanford U Pr.

Sexual Contradictions: Psychology, Psychoanalysis, & Feminism. Janet Sayers. 250p. 1986. 29.95 (*0-422-78780-9*, 9791, Pub. by Tavistock UK); pap. 12.95 (*0-422-78790-6*, 9804, Pub. by Tavistock UK) Routledge Chapman & Hall.

Sexual Correctness: The Gender-Feminist Attack on Women. Wendy McElroy. 200p. 1996. lib. bdg. 28.50 (*0-7864-0226-1*) McFarland & Co.

Sexual Counseling Skills Workshop: A Trainers' Handbook. Robert R. Wilson. 1977. pap. 2.00 (*0-89055-120-0*) Carolina Pop Ctr.

***Sexual Crack-Up.** Mary S. Harman. Date not set. write for info. (*0-688-02580-3*) Morrow.

Sexual Creators: An Ethical Proposal for Concerned Christians. Andre Guindon. 256p. (Orig.). (C). 1986. pap. text ed. 25.00 (*0-8191-5240-4*) U Pr of Amer.

Sexual Crimes & American Law. 1991. lib. bdg. 75.00 (*0-8490-4182-1*) Gordon Pr.

Sexual Crimes & Confrontations: A Criminological Perspective. Donald J. West. (Cambridge Studies in Criminology: Vol. 56). 1987. text ed. 63.95 (*0-566-05380-2*, Pub. by Avebury Pub UK) Ashgate Pub Co.

Sexual Cultures: Community, Values, & Intimacy. Ed. by Jeffrey Weeks & Janet Holland. 288p. 1996. text ed. 49.95 (*0-312-16083-6*); text ed. 18.95 (*0-312-16084-4*) St Martin.

***Sexual Cultures & Migration in the Era of AIDS: Anthropological & Demographic Perspectives.** Ed. by Gilbert Herdt. LC 97-2311. (International Studies in Demography). (Illus.). 280p. 1997. 72.00 (*0-19-829230-9*) OUP.

Sexual Cultures & the Construction of Adolescent Identities. Ed. by Janice M. Irvine. (Health, Society, & Policy Ser.). 336p. 1994. 54.95 (*1-56639-135-0*); pap. 19.95 (*1-56639-136-9*) Temple U Pr.

Sexual Customs in Rural Norway: A Nineteenth-Century Study. Eilert Sundt. Ed. & Tr. by Odin W. Anderson. LC 90-28458. (Illus.). 312p. 1993. text ed. 44.95 (*0-8138-0588-0*) Iowa St U Pr.

Sexual Desire: A Moral Philosophy of the Erotic. Roger Scruton. 428p. 1986. 35.00 (*0-02-929280-8*, Free Press) Free Pr.

Sexual Desire & Love. Eric Fuchs. 1983. write for info. (*0-227-67876-1*, Pub. by J Clarke Co Ltd UK) Parkwest Pubns.

Sexual Desire Disorders. Ed. by Sandra R. Leiblum & Raymond C. Rosen. LC 87-21192. 470p. 1992. reprint ed. pap. text ed. 25.95 (*0-89862-153-4*) Guilford Pr.

Sexual Desire Disorders: Dysfunctional Regulation of Sexual Motivation. Helen S. Kaplan. LC 95-15019. 352p. 1995. text ed. 40.95 (*0-87630-784-5*) Brunner-Mazel.

Sexual Development of Young Children. Virginia Lively & Edwin Lively. 1991. pap. 21.50 (*0-8273-4198-9*) Delmar.

Sexual Development of Young Children. Virginia Lively & Edwin Lively. 1991. teacher ed., pap. 8.50 (*0-8273-4199-7*) Delmar.

***Sexual Deviance: Theory, Assessment & Treatment.** LC 97-25929. 1997. lib. bdg. 60.00 (*1-57230-241-0*, 0241) Guilford Pr.

Sexual Deviancy & Social Proscription: The Social Context of Carnal Behavior. Clifton Bryant. LC 81-6216. 432p. 1982. 52.00 (*0-89885-024-X*); pap. 24.95 (*0-89885-094-0*) Human Sci Pr.

Sexual Deviation. 3rd ed. Ed. by Ismond Rosen. (Illus.). 512p. (C). 1996. 145.00 (*0-19-262516-0*) OUP.

Sexual Deviation in American Society: A Social-Psychological Study of Sexual Nonconformity. Bernard J. Oliver, Jr. 1967. pap. 18.95 (*0-8084-0277-3*) NCUP.

Sexual Deviations & Paraphilias: Medical Analysis Index with Research Bibliography. Harold P. Drummond. LC 85-47570. 150p. 1987. 44.50 (*0-88164-314-9*); pap. 39.50 (*0-88164-315-7*) ABBE Pubs Assn.

Sexual Deviations As Seen in Handwriting. Marie Bernard. LC 90-70215. (Illus.). 408p. 1990. 38.50 (*0-87875-360-5*) Whitston Pub.

Sexual Deviations in the Criminal Law: Homosexual, Exhibitionistic, & Pedophilic Offences in Canada. Alex K. Gigeroff. LC 79-364215. (Clarke Institute of Psychiatry, Monograph Ser.: No. 2). 230p. reprint ed. pap. 65.60 (*0-685-16295-8*, 2026432) Bks Demand.

An Asterisk (*) at the beginning of an entry indicates that the title is appearing in BIP for the first time.

Sexual Difference: A Theory of Social-Symbolic Practice. Milan Women's Bookstore Collective Staff. (Theories of Representation & Difference Ser.). 160p. 1990. 27.50 (*0-253-33826-3*); pap. 11.95 (*0-253-20605-7*, MB-605) Ind U Pr.

Sexual Difference: Masculinity & Psychoanalysis. Stephen Frosh. LC 93-5902. 192p. (C). 1994. pap. 16.95 (*0-415-06844-4*, Routledge NY); text ed. 62.95 (*0-415-06843-6*, Routledge NY) Routledge.

Sexual Differentiation. Ed. by A. A. Gerall et al. (Handbook of Behavioral Neurobiology Ser.: Vol. 11). (Illus.). 390p. 1992. 85.00 (*0-306-43983-2*, Plenum Pr) Plenum.

Sexual Differentiation: Basic & Clinical Aspects. Mario Serio. LC 83-42849. (Serono Symposia Publications from Raven Press: No. 11). (Illus.). 384p. 1984. reprint ed. pap. 109.50 (*0-7837-9577-7*, 2060326) Bks Demand.

Sexual Difficulties in Marriage. David R. Mace. LC 72-75652. (Pocket Counsel Bks.). 64p. (Orig.). reprint ed. pap. 25.00 (*0-685-15400-9*, 2027178) Bks Demand.

Sexual Dilemmas for the Helping Professional. rev. ed. Jerry Edelwich & Archie Brodsky. LC 90-15154. 304p. 1991. pap. 20.95 (*0-87630-627-X*); text ed. 37.95 (*0-87630-628-8*) Brunner-Mazel.

Sexual Dimorphism in Homo Sapiens: A Question of Size. Ed. by Robert L. Hall. LC 81-5907. 446p. 1984. text ed. 89.50 (*0-275-91365-1*, C1365, Praeger Pubs) Greenwood.

Sexual Dimorphism in Human & Mammalian Biology & Pathology. Alfred Glucksmann. LC 80-42373. 374p. 1981. text ed. 149.00 (*0-12-286960-5*) Acad Pr.

Sexual Dimorphism, Ontogeny, & Functional Morphology of Rutiderma Hartmanni Poulsen, 1965: Crustacea: Ostracoda. Louis S. Kornicker. LC 84-600218. (Smithsonian Contributions to Zoology Ser.: No. 408). 32p. reprint ed. pap. 25.00 (*0-317-30425-9*, 2024936) Bks Demand.

***Sexual Discourse.** Ed. by Carroll. (C). 1998. text ed. write for info. (*0-321-01255-0*) Addson-Wesley Educ.

Sexual Discrimination & Sexual Harassment in the Workplace. Lawrence Solotoff & Henry S. Kramer. (Labor & Employment Law Ser.). 1994. write for info. (*0-615-00136-X*) Law Journal.

Sexual Disorders: Treatment, Theory & Research. C. David Tollison & Henry E. Adams. LC 79-20853. 1979. text ed. 34.95 (*0-89876-029-1*) Gardner Pr.

Sexual Display & Body Packaging. 1991. lib. bdg. 98.00 (*0-8490-4657-2*) Gordon Pr.

Sexual Dissidence: Augustine to Wilde, Freud to Foucault. Jonathan Dollimore. 400p. 1991. pap. 18.95 (*0-19-811269-6*) OUP.

Sexual Divisions in Law. K. O'Donovan. (Law in Context Ser.). xii, 242p. 1985. 30.00 (*0-297-78664-4*) Rothman.

Sexual Divisions Revisited. Ed. by Diana Leonard & Sheila Allen. LC 90-8802. 208p. 1991. text ed. 45.00 (*0-312-05210-3*) St Martin.

***Sexual Dynamics of Anti-Social Behavior.** 2nd ed. Ed. by Louis B. Schlesinger & Eugene Revitch. LC 96-36861. (Illus.). 324p. 1997. text ed. 64.95 (*0-398-06694-9*); pap. text ed. 49.95 (*0-398-06695-7*) C C Thomas.

Sexual Dysfunction: A Guide for Assessment & Treatment. John P. Wincze & Michael P. Carey. LC 91-16339. (Treatment Manuals for Practitioners Ser.). 212p. 1991. pap. text ed. 19.95 (*0-89862-218-2*); lib. bdg. 49.95 (*0-89862-207-7*) Guilford Pr.

Sexual Dysfunction: A Neuro-Medical Approach. Ed. by Carlos Singer & William J. Weiner. LC 93-46471. (Illus.). 392p. 1994. pap. 55.00 (*0-87993-582-0*) Futura Pub.

Sexual Dysfunction: Neurologic, Urologic & Gynecologic Aspects. Richard Lechtenberg & Dana A. Ohl. LC 94-450. 1994. 69.50 (*0-8121-1496-5*) Williams & Wilkins.

***Sexual Dysfunction in Human Males & Females Including Analysis, Treatments, Methods & Devices: Index of New Information with References.** Jean H. Devlin. 172p. 1997. 47.50 (*0-7883-1562-5*); pap. 44.50 (*0-7883-1563-3*) ABBE Pubs Assn.

Sexual Dysfunction in Neurological Disorders: Diagnosis, Management, & Rehabilitation. Francois Boller & Ellen Frank. LC 81-85165. (Illus.). 108p. 1982. reprint ed. pap. 30.80 (*0-608-00602-5*, 2061189) Bks Demand.

Sexual Ecology: Aids and the Destiny of Gay Men. Gabriel Rotello. LC 96-49706. 1997. pap. 24.95 (*0-525-94164-9*) NAL-Dutton.

***Sexual Economyths.** Beasley. 1994. text ed. 55.00 (*0-312-12234-9*) St Martin.

Sexual Economyths: Conceiving a Feminist Economics, Vol. 1. Chris Beasley. 1994. text ed. 18.95 (*0-312-12235-7*) St Martin.

Sexual Ecstasy from Ancient Wisdom. Amen Ra. LC 93-93602. (Illus.). 60p. (Orig.). 1993. pap. 15.95 (*0-943217-03-2*) Summum.

Sexual Education of Edith Wharton. Gloria C. Erlich. LC 91-16671. 223p. 1992. 27.50 (*0-520-07583-8*) U CA Pr.

Sexual Energy & the Old Religion: Red Dragon Power of Witchcraft. Rhuddlwm Gawr. LC 85-73748. (Illus.). 156p. (Orig.). 1989. pap. 12.95 (*0-931760-11-9*); text ed. 15.95 (*0-931760-03-8*) Camelot GA.

Sexual Energy & Yoga. Elisabeth Haich. 160p. 1983. 8.95 (*0-943358-03-5*) Aurora Press.

Sexual Energy Ecstasy: A Practical Guide to Lovemaking Secrets of the East & West. David A. Ramsdale & Ellen J. Ramsdale. LC 93-10329. (Illus.). 384p. 1993. pap. 16.95 (*0-553-37231-9*) Bantam.

Sexual Energy Ecstasy: A Practical Guide to Lovemaking Secrets of the East & West. 2nd rev. ed. David A. Ramsdale & Ellen J. Ramsdale. (Illus.). 384p. 1991. 24.95 (*0-917879-04-X*) Peak Skill.

Sexual Equality: Workers in an Asian Plantation System. Shobhita Jain. 200p. 1988. text ed. 25.00 (*81-207-0868-7*, Pub. by Sterling Pubs II) Apt Bks.

Sexual Equality: Workers in an Asian Plantation System. Shobhita Jain. (C). 1988. 140.00 (*0-685-27917-0*) St Mut.

Sexual Equality: Writings by John Stuart Mill, Harriet Taylor Mill, & Helen Taylor. Ed. by Ann P. Robson & John M. Robson. 409p. 1994. 60.00 (*0-8020-0513-6*) U of Toronto Pr.

Sexual Equality: Writings by John Stuart Mill, Harriet Taylor Mill, & Helen Taylor. Ed. by Ann P. Robson & John M. Robson. 352p. 1994. pap. 19.95 (*0-8020-6949-5*) U of Toronto Pr.

Sexual Ethics: A Biblical Perspective. Stanley Grenz. 268p. (C). 1995. reprint ed. spiral bd. 23.95 (*1-57383-045-3*) Regent College.

***Sexual Ethics: An Evangelical Perspective.** Stanley J. Grenz. LC 97-1383. 304p. (Orig.). 1997. pap. 22.00 (*0-664-25750-X*) Westminster John Knox.

Sexual Ethics & the Attack on Traditional Morality. Philip Turner. 24p. 1988. pap. 1.15 (*0-88028-085-9*, 958) Forward Movement.

Sexual Excitement: Dynamics of Erotic Life. Robert J. Stoller. LC 86-17316. 301p. reprint ed. pap. 85.80 (*0-8357-7857-6*, 2036234) Bks Demand.

Sexual Exercises for Women. Anthony Harris. 145p. 1988. pap. 8.95 (*0-88184-412-8*) Carroll & Graf.

Sexual Exploitation. Diane E. Russell. LC 84-6950. 319p. 1984. 54.00 (*0-8039-2354-6*); pap. 24.95 (*0-8039-2355-4*) Sage.

Sexual Exploitation in Professional Relationships. Ed. by Glen O. Gabbard. LC 88-3280. 257p. 1989. text ed. 34.00 (*0-88048-290-7*, 8290) Am Psychiatric.

Sexual Exploitation of Children. S. Goldstein. (Practical Aspects of Criminal & Forensic Investigations Ser.). 440p. 1986. 45.00 (*0-444-01117-X*, HQ72) CRC Pr.

***Sexual Exploitation of Children.** Vitit Muntarbhorn. (Human Rights Study Ser.: Vol. 8). 37p. 1997. pap. 25.00 (*92-1-154123-9*, HQ71) UN.

Sexual Exploitation of Children: A Practical Guide to Assessment. Seth L. Goldstein. (Practical Aspects of Criminal & Forensic Investigations Ser.). 456p. 1992. 54.95 (*0-8493-9508-9*) CRC Pr.

Sexual Exploitation of Patients by Health Professionals. Ed. by Ann W. Burgess & Carol R. Hartman. LC 86-9318. (Sexual Medicine Ser.: Vol. 4). 207p. 1986. text ed. 59.95 (*0-275-92171-9*, C2171, Praeger Pubs) Greenwood.

Sexual Expression: A Manual for Trainers. Carl Hartman et al. LC 81-6760. (Illus.). 152p. 1981. pap. 19.95 (*0-89885-053-3*) Human Sci Pr.

Sexual Face of Violence: Rapists on Rape. Lloyd Vogelman. 224p. (Orig.). 1990. pap. text ed. 24.95 (*0-86975-396-7*, Pub. by Ravan Pr ZA) Ohio U Pr.

***Sexual Fantasies.** Lindsay Welsh. 1997. mass mkt. 6.95 (*1-56333-586-7*, Rosebud) Masquerade.

Sexual Feelings in Psychotherapy: Explorations for Therapists & Therapists-in-Training. Kenneth S. Pope et al. 319p. (Orig.). 1993. pap. text ed. 24.95 (*1-55798-201-5*) Am Psychol.

Sexual Fiction. Maurice Charney. 192p. (C). 1990. per. 32.49 (*0-8403-6323-0*) Kendall-Hunt.

Sexual Fitness. (Fitness, Health & Nutrition Ser.). (Illus.). 144p. 1988. 17.27 (*0-8094-6110-2*); lib. bdg. 23.27 (*0-8094-6111-0*) Time-Life.

Sexual Force or the Winged Dragon. rev. ed. Omraam M. Aivanhov. (Izvor Collection: Vol. 205). 138p. (Orig.). 1987. pap. 6.95 (*2-85566-299-0*, Pub. by Prosveta FR) Prosveta USA.

***Sexual Foreplay.** Alex Comfort. 1997. 12.00 (*0-609-60032-X*) Random Hse Value.

Sexual Freedom see IVP Booklets

Sexual Freedom in Restoration Literature. Warren Chernaik. 318p. (C). 1995. text ed. 59.95 (*0-521-46497-8*) Cambridge U Pr.

Sexual Friendship: A New Dynamics in Relationships. Richard Walters. LC 87-91726. 1988. pap. 12.95 (*0-87212-208-5*) Libra.

***Sexual Function in People with Disability & Chronic Illness: A Health Professional's Guide.** Marca Sipski & Craig Alexander. LC 97-14397. 400p. 1997. 55.00 (*0-8342-0886-5*, 20886) Aspen Pub.

Sexual Geometry. Charlie Clark, III. Ed. by Rose E. Sanfilippo. LC 82-91125. (Illus.). 112p. 1983. 8.95 (*0-9609808-0-6*) New Pen Pub Co.

Sexual Gerrymander: Women & the Economics of Power. Jocelynne A. Scutt. 272p. 1994. pap. 19.95 (*1-875559-16-7*, Pub. by SpiniFex Pr AT) LPC InBook.

Sexual Happiness: A Practical Approach. Maurice Yaffe & Elizabeth Fenwick. LC 87-45839. 318p. 1988. 24.95 (*0-8050-0691-5*) H Holt & Co.

Sexual Happiness for Men: A Practical Approach. rev. ed. Maurice Yaffe & Elizabeth Fenwick. 160p. 1989. pap. 16.95 (*0-8050-2215-5*, Owl) H Holt & Co.

Sexual Happiness for Women: A Practical Approach. Maurice Yaffe & Elizabeth Fenwick. LC 87-45840. (Illus.). 160p. 1989. pap. 14.95 (*0-8050-0689-3*, Owl) H Holt & Co.

Sexual Happiness for Women: A Practical Approach. rev. ed. Maurice Yaffe & Elizabeth Fenwick. (Illus.). 160p. 1989. pap. 16.95 (*0-8050-2214-7*, Owl) H Holt & Co.

Sexual Happiness in Marriage. rev. ed. Herbert J. Miles. 208p. 1987. pap. 9.99 (*0-310-29221-2*) Zondervan.

***Sexual Harasment in Higher Education: New Issues & Perspectives.** Billie W. Dziech & Michael W. Hawkins. Ed. by Philip Altbach. (Garland Studies in Higher Education). 1998. text ed. 45.00 (*0-8153-2036-1*) Garland.

Sexual Harassment. Titus Aaron. 70p. (YA). (gr. 7-12). 1992. pap. 6.95 (*1-57515-009-3*) PPI Pubng.

Sexual Harassment. Lynne Eisaguirre. LC 93-8805. (Contemporary World Issues Ser.). 217p. 1993. lib. bdg. 39.50 (*0-87436-723-9*) ABC-CLIO.

***Sexual Harassment.** Martin Eskenazi & David Gallen. 9.95 (*0-7867-0816-6*) Carroll & Graf.

Sexual Harassment. David W. Felder. 1996. pap. text ed. 8.95 (*0-910959-83-8*, B&G 16D) Wellington Pr.

Sexual Harassment. Hazel Houghton-James. 246p. 1995. pap. 34.00 (*1-85941-040-5*, Pub. by Cavendish UK) Gaunt.

Sexual Harassment. Constance Jones. LC 95-18508. (Library in a Book). 256p. 1996. 24.95 (*0-8160-3273-4*) Facts on File.

Sexual Harassment. Elaine Landau. LC 92-43748. 128p. (J). (gr. 5 up). 1993. 14.95 (*0-8027-8265-5*); lib. bdg. 15.85 (*0-8027-8266-3*) Walker & Co.

Sexual Harassment. Ed. by Carol Wekesser et al. LC 92-23593. (Current Controversies Ser.). 208p. (YA). (gr. 10 up). 1992. pap. text ed. 12.96 (*1-56510-020-4*); lib. bdg. 20.96 (*1-56510-021-2*) Greenhaven.

Sexual Harassment, Pt. 1. (Initiatives Ser.: Vol. 52, No. 4). 1990. 13.00 (*0-614-14209-1*) Natl Assn Women.

Sexual Harassment, Pt. 1. (Initiatives Ser.: Vol. 52, No. 3). 1989. 13.00 (*0-614-14210-5*) Natl Assn Women.

Sexual Harassment: A Challenge to Schools of Education. Judith B. Brandenburg. 1995. 15.00 (*0-89333-127-9*) AACTE.

***Sexual Harassment: A Debate.** Linda LeMoncheck & Mane Hajdin. LC 96-43497. (Point/Counterpoint Ser.: No. 94). 192p. 1997. 52.50 (*0-8476-8424-5*); pap. 16.95 (*0-8476-8425-3*) Rowman.

Sexual Harassment: A Guide for Understanding & Prevention. Arjun P. Aggarwal. 144p. 1992. pap. text ed. 21.95 (*0-409-90852-5*) MICHIE.

Sexual Harassment: A Management Issue. Sandra H. Carey. write for info. (*0-8290-1055-6*) Irvington.

Sexual Harassment: A Question of Power. JoAnn B. Guernsey. LC 94-537. (Frontline Ser.). (Illus.). 112p. (YA). (gr. 6 up). 1995. lib. bdg. 18.95 (*0-8225-2608-5*, Lerner Publctns) Lerner Group.

Sexual Harassment: A Selected, Annotated Bibliography. LyndaJ. Hartell & Helena M. VonVille. LC 95-21267. (Bibliographies & Indexes in Women's Studies: Vol. 23). 176p. 1995. text ed. 59.95 (*0-313-29055-5*, Greenwood Pr) Greenwood.

Sexual Harassment: Building a Concensus for Change. Judith I. Avner. (Illus.). 300p. (Orig.). (C). 1995. pap. text ed. 50.00 (*0-7881-2262-2*) DIANE Pub.

Sexual Harassment: Communication Implications. Gary L. Kreps. LC 92-38370. (Speech Communication Association Applied Communication Ser.). 344p. (C). 1993. text ed. 67.50 (*1-881303-44-6*); pap. text ed. 28.50 (*1-881303-45-4*) Hampton Pr NJ.

***Sexual Harassment: Contemporary Feminist Perspectives.** Alison M. Thomas & Celia Kitzinger. LC 97-567. 1997. write for info. (*0-335-19581-4*, Open Univ Pr); pap. write for info. (*0-335-19580-6*, Open Univ Pr) Taylor & Francis.

Sexual Harassment: Discrimination & Other Claims. Jonathan L. Alder. 380p. 1994. spiral bd. 135.00 incl. disk (*0-250-48600-8*) MICHIE.

Sexual Harassment: Employer Policies & Problems. (PPF Survey Ser.: No. 144). 54p. 1987. 30.00 (*0-87179-975-8*) BNA.

Sexual Harassment: High School Girls Speak Out. June Larkin. 1994. pap. 14.95 (*0-929005-65-1*, Pub. by Second Story Pr CN) LPC InBook.

Sexual Harassment: How & Where to Find Facts & Get Help. Robert D. Reed & Danek S. Kaus. Ed. by Diane Parker. LC 92-53761. (Abuse Ser.). 48p. 1993. pap. 4.50 (*0-88247-944-X*) R & E Pubs.

Sexual Harassment: How to Keep Your Company Out of Court. Lloyd. 88p. 1992. 45.00 (*1-878375-47-4*, 75474) Panel Pubs.

Sexual Harassment: Investigator's Manual. rev. ed. Susan L. Webb. 127p. 1991. ring bd. 189.95 (*1-878269-25-9*) Pacific Resource.

Sexual Harassment: Investigator's Manual. rev. ed. Susan L. Webb. 127p. 1996. ring bd. 189.95 (*1-878269-30-5*) Pacific Resource.
SEXUAL HARASSMENT: INVESTIGATOR'S MANUAL will assist you in conducting comprehensive investigations into complaints of sexual harassment. This manual is for those who are responsible for fact-finding, in-depth investigations into serious allegations of harassment. The best way for a company or organization to stop & prevent harassment, as well as limit their liability, is to take prompt, remedial action on complaints. The first step in the process is a thorough investigation. Only then can additional appropriate action be taken. The information in SEXUAL HARASSMENT: INVESTIGATOR'S MANUAL is based on 10 years experience of Susan Webb, a nationally recognized expert on sexual harassment & complaint investigation. She has used the information successfully in investigating & resolving sexual harassment complaints in both public & private organizations. And a special offer is available now...If you order SEXUAL HARASSMENT: INVESTIGATOR'S MANUAL & send your payment within the next thirty days, we'll immediately send you your choice of one of the products listed on the back for free. Then we'll send the INVESTIGATOR'S MANUAL by September 15. If you're not happy with the MANUAL for any reason, you can return it to us & we'll refund your money. 1997 Updated Edition is now available. ***Publisher Provided Annotation.***

Sexual Harassment: It's Hurting People. Lynn Wallich. 68p. (C). teacher ed. 25.00 (*1-56090-094-6*) Natl Middle Schl.

Sexual Harassment: It's Hurting People. Lynn Wallich. (J). (gr. 5-8). 1994. vhs 176.00 (*1-56090-093-8*) Natl Middle Schl.

Sexual Harassment: Know Your Rights. Martin Eskenazi & David Gallen. 240p. 1992. pap. 9.95 (*0-88184-816-6*) Carroll & Graf.

Sexual Harassment: Litigating, Preventing & Resolving Claims. Beville S. May. 1994. 35.00 (*0-614-06019-2*, 4923); audio 135.00 (*0-614-06020-6*) Natl Prac Inst.

Sexual Harassment: Research & Resources, 1992. rev. ed. Deborah Siegel. Ed. by Susan Hallgarth. 68p. 1992. reprint ed. pap. 9.00 (*1-880547-12-0*) Nat Coun Res Wom.

Sexual Harassment: Shades of Gray - Guidelines for Managers, Supervisors & Employees. rev. ed. Susan L. Webb. 58p. 1996. pap. 6.50 (*1-878269-31-3*) Pacific Resource.

Sexual Harassment: Shades of Gray - Guidelines for Managers, Supervisors & Employees. Susan L. Webb. LC 89-189312. 58p. 1988. reprint ed. pap. 6.50 (*1-878269-00-3*) Pacific Resource.

Sexual Harassment: The Training Manuals. rev. ed. Susan L. Webb. 156p. 1996. ring bd. 275.00 (*1-878269-29-1*) Pacific Resource.

Sexual Harassment: The Training Manuals, 2 bks. Susan L. Webb. 62p. 1988. reprint ed. teacher ed., ring bd. write for info. (*1-878269-03-8*) Pacific Resource.

Sexual Harassment: The Training Manuals, 2 bks. Susan L. Webb. 94p. 1991. reprint ed. teacher ed., ring bd. 75.00 (*1-878269-02-X*) Pacific Resource.

Sexual Harassment: The Training Manuals, 2 bks., Set. Susan L. Webb. 156p. 1988. reprint ed. teacher ed., ring bd. 275.00 (*1-878269-01-1*) Pacific Resource.

Sexual Harassment: Theory, Research, & Treatment. Ed. by William O'Donahue. 356p. (C). 1996. 58.95 (*0-205-16412-9*) Allyn.

Sexual Harassment: What Teens Should Know. Carol R. Nash. LC 95-43806. (Issues in Focus Ser.). (Illus.). 112p. (YA). (gr. 6 up). 1996. lib. bdg. 18.95 (*0-89490-735-2*) Enslow Pubs.

Sexual Harassment: What You Need to Know. Susan Benton-Powers & Lee T. Paterson. LC 91-78106. (Fifty-Minute Ser.). (Illus.). 106p. (Orig.). 1992. pap. 15.95 (*1-56052-153-8*) Crisp Pubns.

Sexual Harassment (Am Arbeitsplatz und Haftung des Arbeitgebers) Stefan Werner. 24p. (GER.). 1995. 20.00 (*0-86640-053-2*) German Am Chamber.

Sexual Harassment & Sexual Abuse: A Handbook for Teachers & Administrators. Andrey Cohan et al. 112p. 1996. 37.00 (*0-8039-6440-4*) Corwin Pr.

Sexual Harassment & Social Change in American Society. Stephen Morewitz. LC 93-48393. 498p. 1996. 69.95 (*1-880921-77-4*); pap. 49.95 (*1-880921-76-6*) Austin & Winfield.

Sexual Harassment & Teens: A Program for Positive Change. Susan Strauss & Pamela Espeland. LC 92-18013. 160p. (Orig.). 1992. pap. 17.95 (*0-915793-44-X*) Free Spirit Pub.

***Sexual Harassment & the Federal Employee.** 2nd ed. Dennis K. Reischl & Ralph R. Smith. 39p. (Orig.). 1992. pap. text ed. 6.95 (*0-936295-28-7*) FPMI Comns.

Sexual Harassment & Training Guide. Matthew B. Stuart. (Illus.). (Orig.). 1991. pap. text ed. 39.95 (*1-880409-01-1*) Pacific Servs.

Sexual Harassment at Work. Mary C. Meyer et al. (Illus.). 256p. 1981. text ed. 17.50 (*0-89433-156-6*) Petrocelli.

Sexual Harassment at Work. Ann Sedley & Melissa Benn. (C). 1988. 35.00 (*0-946088-00-4*, Pub. by NCCL UK) St Mut.

Sexual Harassment Awareness Training: 60 Practical Activities for Trainers. Andrea P. Baridon & David R. Eyler. LC 95-23785. 1995. pap. text ed. 21.95 (*0-07-005429-0*) McGraw.

Sexual Harassment, Impact vs. Intent. 84p. 1993. student ed., ring bd. 200.00 incl. vhs (*0-943397-17-0*, 151) Assn Calif Sch Admin.

Sexual Harassment in Academe: The Ethical Issues. Leslie P. Francis. (Issues in Academic Ethics Ser.). 160p. (C). 1996. lib. bdg. 52.50 (*0-8476-8170-X*) Rowman.

Sexual Harassment in Academe: The Ethical Issues. Leslie P. Francis. (Issues in Academic Ethics Ser.). 160p. (C). 1996. pap. text ed. 21.95 (*0-8476-8171-8*) Rowman.

Sexual Harassment in American Secondary Schools: A Legal Guide for Administrators, Teachers, & Students. Nancy S. Layman. LC 93-11323. 207p. 1993. pap. 18.95 (*0-935061-52-5*) Contemp Res.

Sexual Harassment in American Secondary Schools: A Legal Guide for Administrators, Teachers, & Students. Nancy S. Layman. 207p. 1994. 50.00 (*0-935061-57-6*) Contemp Res.

Sexual Harassment in Education. 2nd ed. John F. Lewis & Susan C. Hastings. 57p. (Orig.). 1994. pap. 21.95 (*1-56534-064-7*) Ed Law Assn.

Sexual Harassment in Employment Law. Barbara Lindemann & David D. Kadue. LC 91-41340. 882p. 1992. pap. text ed. 128.00 (*0-87179-704-6*, 0704) BNA Books.

Sexual Harassment in Higher Education: From Conflict to Community. Robert O. Riggs et al. Ed. & Frwd. by Jonathan D. Fife. (ASHE-ERIC Higher Education Reports: No. 2). 89p. (Orig.). 1993. pap. 18.00 (*1-878380-23-0*) GWU Grad Schl E&HD.

S

An Asterisk (*) at the beginning of an entry indicates that the title is appearing in BIP for the first time.

S

***Sexual Harassment in the Federal Workplace: Trends, Progress, Continuing Challenges.** Evangeline W. Swift. 73p. (Orig.). 1996. pap. 25.00 (*0-7881-3068-4*) DIANE Pub.

Sexual Harassment in the Schools: Preventing & Defending Against Claims. rev. ed. Ed. by Naomi E. Gittins. 120p. 1993. pap. 25.00 (*0-88364-147-X*) Natl Sch Boards.

Sexual Harassment in the Workplace. rev. ed. Ralph H. Baxter, Jr. LC 85-81035. 1989. pap. 19.95 (*1-55840-112-1*) Exec Ent Pubns.

Sexual Harassment in the Workplace. 2nd ed. Aggarwal. 384p. 1992. 75.00 (*0-409-90670-0*) MICHIE.

Sexual Harassment in the Workplace: A Guide to Prevention. Juliana Lightle & Elizabeth H. Doucet. LC 94-68537. (Legal Issues in Business Ser.). 116p. (Orig.). 1995. pap. 10.95 (*1-56052-312-3*) Crisp Pubns.

Sexual Harassment in the Workplace: A Guide to the Law & a Research Overview for Employers & Employees. Titus Aaron & Judith A. Isaksen. LC 92-56628. 231p. 1993. pap. 32.50 (*0-89950-763-8*) McFarland & Co.

Sexual Harassment in the Workplace: Can Your Company Afford to Misunderstand It? Linda A. Wheeler. 71p. 1994. student ed. 69.00 (*0-9639713-2-8*) Human Connect.

Sexual Harassment in the Workplace: Conference Report. Patricia Stover & Yvonne Giles. (Program on Women & Work Ser.). 67p. 1980. pap. 5.00 (*0-87736-346-3*) U of Mich Inst Labor.

Sexual Harassment in the Workplace: Designing & Implementing a Successful Policy, Conducting the Investigation, Protecting the Rights of the Parties. (Litigation & Administrative Practice Ser.). 200p. 1992. pap. text ed. 70.00 (*0-685-56921-7*, H4-5126) PLI.

Sexual Harassment in the Workplace: How to Prevent, Investigate, & Resolve Problems in Your Organization. Ellen J. Wagner. 176p. (Orig.). 1992. pap. 17.95 (*0-8144-7787-9*) AMACOM.

Sexual Harassment in the Workplace: Law & Practice, Vol. 1. 2nd ed. Alba Conte. (Employment Law Library). 464p. 1994. text ed. 120.00 (*0-471-01447-8*) Wiley.

Sexual Harassment in the Workplace: Law & Practice, 2 vols., Vol. 2. 2nd ed. Alba Conte. (Employment Law Library). 948p. 1994. text ed. 240.00 (*0-471-01446-X*); text ed. 120.00 (*0-471-01448-6*) Wiley.

***Sexual Harassment in the Workplace: Law & Practice - 1997 Cumulative Supplement, 2 vols., Vol. 2.** 2nd ed. Alba Conte. 1996. pap. text ed. 83.00 (*0-471-17587-0*) Wiley.

Sexual Harassment in the Workplace: Managing Corporate Policy 1996. Julie M. Tamminen. 1996. suppl. ed., pap. text ed. 55.00 (*0-471-12344-7*) Wiley.

Sexual Harassment in the Workplace: Managing Corporated Policy. Julie M. Tamminen. (Employee Benefits - Human Resources Library). 543p. 1994. text ed. 120.00 (*0-471-58640-4*, Pub. by Wiley Law Pubns) Wiley.

Sexual Harassment in the Workplace: Men & Women in Labor. Lawrence Rifkind & Loretta F. Harper. 224p. (C). 1993. per. 31.44 (*0-8403-8650-8*) Kendall-Hunt.

Sexual Harassment in the Workplace: Perspectives, Frontiers, & Response Strategies. Margaret S. Stockdale. (Women & Work Ser.: Vol. 5). 303p. 1996. 55.00 (*0-8039-5793-9*); pap. 24.95 (*0-8039-5794-7*) Sage.

Sexual Harassment in the Workplace: The Management View. Iris McQueen. Ed. by Joan Levers et al. LC 82-99921. (Illus.). 138p. (Orig.). 1983. pap. 14.95 (*0-9609354-0-1*); text ed. 24.95 (*0-9609354-1-X*) McQueen & Son.

Sexual Harassment in the Workplace & Academia: Psychiatric Issues. Ed. by Diane K. Shrier. LC 95-26269. (Clinical Practice Ser.: No. 38). 304p. 1996. text ed. 38.50 (*0-88048-490-X*, 8490) Am Psychiatric.

***Sexual Harassment Investigator's Kit.** Haight Consulting Staff. 195.00 (*0-614-25558-9*, 00HR44658); 270.00 incl. disk (*0-614-25559-7*, 00HR44659) Print Indus Am.

Sexual Harassment Litigation: Plaintiff's & Defendant's Strategies - A Satellite Program. (Litigation & Administrative Practice Course Handbook, 1983-84 Ser.). 584p. 1994. pap. 99.00 (*0-614-17263-2*, H4-5222) PLI.

Sexual Harassment Litigation 1995. (Litigation & Administrative Practice Course Handbook, 1983-84 Ser.). 256p. 1995. pap. 99.00 (*0-685-69735-5*, H4-5213) PLI.

Sexual Harassment Manual for Managers & Supervisors. 48p. 1991. pap. 12.50 (*0-685-67144-5*, 4839) Commerce.

Sexual Harassment No More. Jim Conway & Sally Conway. LC 93-30246. 216p. (Orig.). 1993. pap. 9.99 (*0-8308-1631-3*, 1631) InterVarsity.

Sexual Harassment of Students: A Guide to Prevention, Intervention & Investigation. Sattel & Whaley. 216p. 1996. 99.00 (*0-8342-0445-2*) Aspen Pub.

Sexual Harassment of Women in the Workplace, 1600-1993. Kerry Segrave. LC 94-2803. 279p. 1994. lib. bdg. 32.50 (*0-7864-0007-2*) McFarland & Co.

Sexual Harassment of Working Women: A Case of Sex Discrimination. Catharine A. MacKinnon. LC 78-9645. (Fastback Ser.: No. 19). 1979. pap. 17.00 (*0-300-02299-9*) Yale U Pr.

Sexual Harassment on Campus. (Initiatives Ser.: Vol. 46, No. 2). 1983. 13.00 (*0-614-14216-4*) Natl Assn Women.

Sexual Harassment on Campus: A Guide for Administrators, Faculty, & Students. Ed. by Bernice R. Sandler & Robert J. Shoop. 1996. text ed. 32.95 (*0-205-16712-8*) Allyn.

Sexual Harassment on College Campuses: Abusing the Ivory Power. Ed. by Michele A. Paludi. LC 95-15813. (SUNY Series, the Psychology of Women). 311p. 1996. text ed. 59.50 (*0-7914-2801-X*); pap. text ed. 19.95 (*0-7914-2802-8*) State U NY Pr.

Sexual Harassment on the Job. 2nd ed. William Petrocelli & Barbara K. Repa. LC 94-30168. 336p. 1995. pap. 18.95 (*0-87337-265-4*) Nolo Pr.

***Sexual Harassment on the Job: What It Is & How to Stop It.** 3rd ed. William Petrocelli. 1997. pap. text ed. 18.95 (*0-87337-403-7*) Nolo Pr.

Sexual Harassment Policy Survey of Fifty States & the District of Columbia. 380p. (Orig.). (C). 1993. pap. text ed. 50.00 (*0-7881-0001-7*) DIANE Pub.

Sexual Harmony. Edmond B. Szekely. (Illus.). 60p. 1977. pap. 3.50 (*0-89564-077-5*) IBS Intl.

Sexual Harrasement in the Work Place: Law & Pratice. 2nd ed. A. Conte. 1995. suppl. ed., pap. write for info. (*0-471-11205-4*) Wiley.

Sexual Harrassment: Confrontations & Decisions. Ed. by Edmund Wall. (Contemporary Issues Ser.). 262p. (Orig.). (C). 1992. pap. 16.95 (*0-87975-787-6*) Prometheus Bks.

Sexual Harrassment & Schools of Social Work: Issues, Costs, & Strategic Responses. Ed. by Marie Weil et al. 180p. (Orig.). (C). 1994. pap. text ed. 10.00 (*0-87293-040-8*) Coun Soc Wk Ed.

Sexual Harrassment & Sexual Abuse: A Handbook for Teachers & Administrators. Andrey Cohan et al. 112p. 1996. pap. 17.00 (*0-8039-6441-2*) Corwin Pr.

***Sexual Harrassment in Employment Law: 1996 Supplement.** Barbara Lindemann & David D. Kadue. Ed. by Christine G. Cooper. (Orig.). 1997. pap. 75.00 (*0-87179-896-4*, 0896) BNA Books.

Sexual Healing: A Guide to Freeing Your Sensual Self. Barbara Keesling. 288p. (C). 1990. reprint ed. lib. bdg. 35.00 (*0-8095-6317-7*) Borgo Pr.

Sexual Healing: God's Plan for the Sanctification of Broken Lives. David K. Foster. 400p. 1995. pap. 18.95 (*0-9645000-0-0*) Master Life.

Sexual Healing: How Good Loving Is Good for You - & Your Relationship. 2nd rev. ed. Barbara Keesling. (Illus.). 256p. 1996. pap. 12.95 (*0-89793-204-8*) Hunter Hse.

Sexual Healing in Marriage. Mary Rousseau & Charles Gallagher. 152p. 1994. reprint ed. pap. text ed. 12.95 (*0-8264-0777-3*) Continuum.

Sexual Healing Journey: A Guide for Survivors of Sexual Abuse. Wendy Maltz. LC 90-55934. (Illus.). 368p. 1992. reprint ed. pap. 13.00 (*0-06-092155-2*, PL) HarpC.

Sexual Health: A Nurse's Guide. Carole S. Zawid. LC 93-34696. (Real Nursing Ser.). 257p. 1993. pap. 20.95 (*0-8273-5685-4*) Delmar.

Sexual Health: A Nurse's Guide. Carole S. Zawid. (Illus.). 224p. (C). 1993. pap. 49.95 (*1-878025-55-4*) Western Schls.

Sexual Health Promotion. Fogel & Philip Lauver. (Illus.). 608p. 1989. text ed. 71.00 (*0-7216-3799-X*) Saunders.

Sexual Health Promotion in General Practice. Ed. by Hilary Curtis. 1995. write for info. (*1-85775-131-0*, Radcliffe Med Pr) Scovill Paterson.

Sexual Homicide: Patterns & Motives. Burgess & Robert K. Ressler. 1995. pap. 25.00 (*0-02-874063-7*) Free Pr.

Sexual Homicide: Patterns, Motives & Procedures for Investigation. Ed. by Robert K. Ressler et al. 256p. 1988. 39.95 (*0-669-16559-X*) Free Pr.

Sexual Hormones: Influence on the Electrophysiology of the Brain. Manuel Alcaraz et al. LC 74-4137. 223p. 1974. text ed. 28.00 (*0-8422-7214-3*) Irvington.

Sexual Humor. Ron Smith. 1993. 4.99 (*1-56171-184-5*) Sure Seller.

Sexual Identity: From a Different View. E. Edward Albracht & William E. Lewis. 1995. 13.95 (*0-533-11255-9*) Vantage.

Sexual Identity on the Job: Issues & Services. Ed. by Alan L. Ellis & Ellen D. Riggle. LC 96-20265. (Journal of Gay & Lesbian Social Services Ser.: Vol. 4, No. 4). 108p. 1996. pap. 12.95 (*1-56023-076-2*) Harrington Pk.

Sexual Identity on the Job: Issues & Services. Ed. by Alan L. Ellis & Ellen D. Riggle. LC 96-20265. (Journal of Gay & Lesbian Social Services: Vol. 4, No. 4). 108p. 1996. 24.95 (*1-56024-760-6*, Haworth Pastrl) Haworth Pr.

***Sexual Imagery in the Early Poetry of Aleister Crowley.** Sunny Shah. Ed. by J. D. Holmes. (Orig.). 1997. pap. 9.95 (*1-55818-355-8*, Contra-Thought) Holmes Pub.

Sexual Images of the Self: The Psychology of Erotic Sensations & Illusions. S. Fisher. 360p. 1989. 69.95 (*0-8058-0439-0*) L Erlbaum Assocs.

Sexual Impotence in the Male & Female. William A. Hammond. LC 73-20626. (Sex, Marriage & Society Ser.). 310p. 1974. reprint ed. 26.95 (*0-405-05802-0*) Ayer.

Sexual Indulgence & Denial. Ed. by Charles E. Rosenberg & Carroll-Smith Rosenberg. LC 73-20650. (Sex, Marriage & Society Ser.). 188p. 1974. reprint ed. 19.95 (*0-405-05818-7*) Ayer.

Sexual Interactions. 3rd ed. Elizabeth R. Allgeier & Albert R. Allgeier. LC 90-83168. 720p. (C). 1991. text ed. 59.16 (*0-669-24320-5*); Instr.'s guide with test item file. teacher ed. 2.66 (*0-669-24322-1*); Study guide. student ed. 20.36 (*0-669-24321-3*) HM College Div.

Sexual Interactions. 4th ed. Albert R. Allgeier & Elizabeth R. Allgeier. 800p. (C). 1995. text ed. 59.16 (*0-669-33337-9*) HM College Div.

***Sexual Interactions.** 4th ed. Jan Campbell. (C). 1995. student ed., text ed. 20.36 (*0-669-33338-7*) HM College Div.

***Sexual Interactions.** 4th ed. Deborah M. Winters & Elizabeth R. Allgeier. (C). 1995. teacher ed., text ed. 2.66 (*0-669-33339-5*) HM College Div.

Sexual Interactions & HIV Risk: New Conceptual Perspectives in European Research. Ed. by Mitchell Cohen et al. LC 95-17936. (Social Aspects of AIDS Ser.). 266p. 1995. 79.00 (*0-7484-0345-0*, Pub. by Tay Francis Ltd UK) Taylor & Francis.

Sexual Interactions & HIV Risk: New Conceptual Perspectives in European Research. Ed. by L. Van Campenhoudt. LC 95-17936. (Social Aspects of AIDS Ser.). 1995. pap. 24.95 (*0-7484-0346-9*) Taylor & Francis.

Sexual Interactions in Plants. Herman Van Den Ende. 1976. text ed. 119.00 (*0-12-711250-2*) Acad Pr.

Sexual Intercourse. Rose Boyt. 192p. 1990. 17.95 (*0-394-58693-X*) Random.

Sexual Intimacy & the Alcoholic Relationship. Al-Anon Family Group Headquarters, Inc., Staff. 144p. 1993. Sexual Intimacy & the Alcoholic Relationship. pap. 2.50 (*0-910034-87-7*) Al-Anon.

Sexual Intimacy Between Therapists & Patients. Kenneth S. Pope et al. LC 86-15165. (Sexual Medicine Ser.: No. 5). 197p. 1986. text ed. 49.95 (*0-275-92253-7*, B2953, Praeger Pubs) Greenwood.

Sexual Intimacy Between Therapists & Patients. Kenneth S. Pope et al. LC 86-15165. (Sexual Medicine Ser.: No. 5). 197p. 1988. pap. text ed. 17.95 (*0-275-92953-1*, Praeger Pubs) Greenwood.

Sexual Inversion. Havelock Ellis & John A. Symonds. LC 75-12312. (Homosexuality: Lesbians & Gay Men in Society, History & Literature Ser.). 1975. reprint ed. 32.95 (*0-405-07363-1*) Ayer.

***Sexual Investigations.** Soble. 1998. pap. 18.95 (*0-8147-8085-7*) NYU Pr.

Sexual Investigations. Alan Soble. (Illus.). 320p. (C). 1996. 26.95 (*0-8147-8004-0*) NYU Pr.

Sexual Involvement with Therapists: Patient Assessment, Subsequent Therapy, Forensics. Kenneth S. Pope. LC 94-11534. 1994. pap. 24.95 (*1-55798-248-1*) Am Psychol.

Sexual Issues. Harold Wahking & Gene Zimmerman. LC 94-5939. (Strategic Pastoral Counseling Resources Ser.). 202p. (C). 1994. 17.99 (*0-8010-9728-2*) Baker Bks.

Sexual Joy Through Self-Hypnosis. Daniel L. Araoz & Robert T. Bleck. Orig. Title: Hypnosex. (Illus.). 1991. reprint ed. audio 15.95 (*0-930298-00-4*) Westwood Pub Co.

***Sexual Justice: Democratic Citizenship & the Politics of Desire.** Morris B. Kaplan. LC 96-30436. 256p. 1997. pap. 16.95 (*0-415-90515-X*) Routledge.

***Sexual Justice: Democratic Citizenship & the Politics of Desire.** Morris B. Kaplan. LC 96-30436. 256p. (C). 1997. text ed. 59.95 (*0-415-90514-1*) Routledge.

Sexual Key to the Tarot. Theodor Lawrence. (Illus.). 1971. 5.95 (*0-8065-0242-8*, Citadel Pr) Carol Pub Group.

Sexual Labyrinth of Nikolai Gogol. Simon Karlinsky. (Illus.). 344p. 1992. pap. 17.50 (*0-226-42527-4*) U Ch Pr.

Sexual Language: An Essay in Moral Theology. Andre Guindon. LC 77-371039. 488p. 1977. reprint ed. pap. 139.10 (*0-608-01992-5*, 2062648) Bks Demand.

Sexual Liberals & the Attack on Feminism. Dorchen Leidholdt & Janice G. Raymond. (Athene Ser.). 256p. 1990. text ed. 35.00 (*0-08-037458-1*, Pergamon Pr); pap. text ed. 16.95 (*0-08-037457-3*, Pergamon Pr) Elsevier.

Sexual Liberals & the Attack on Feminism. Ed. by Dorchen Leidholdt & Janice G. Raymond. (Athene Ser.). 256p. (C). 1990. pap. text ed. 17.95 (*0-8077-6238-5*) Tchrs Coll.

Sexual Life: A Clinician's Guide. S. B. Levine. (Critical Issues in Psychiatry Ser.). (Illus.). 265p. (C). 1992. 39.50 (*0-306-44287-6*, Plenum Pr) Plenum.

Sexual Life in Ancient China: A Preliminary Survey of Chinese Sex & Society from c. 1500 B. C. till 1644 A. D. R. H. Van Gulik. LC 95-3035. 1996. reprint ed. pap. 30.00 (*90-04-10293-0*) E J Brill.

Sexual Life in Ancient Egypt. Lise Manniche. LC 96-16781. (Illus.). 130p. (Orig.). 1996. pap. 29.00 (*0-7103-0551-6*, Pub. by Kegan Paul Intl UK) Col U Pr.

Sexual Life in Ancient Egypt. Lise Manniche. (Illus.). 127p. (Orig.). 1987. 35.00 (*0-7103-0202-9*) Routledge Chapman & Hall.

Sexual Life in Ancient Greece. Hans Licht, pseud. Ed. by Lawrence H. Dawson. Tr. by J. H. Freese from GER. LC 72-9622. (Illus.). reprint ed. 67.50 (*0-404-57417-3*) AMS Pr.

Sexual Life in Ancient India. Johann J. Meyer. 1989. reprint ed. 32.00 (*81-208-0638-7*, Pub. by Motilal Banarsidass II) S Asia.

Sexual Life in Ancient Rome. Otto Kiefer. Tr. by Gilbert Highet & Helen Highet. LC 72-9657. (Illus.). reprint ed. 44.50 (*0-404-57466-1*) AMS Pr.

Sexual Life in Ancient Rome. Otto Kiefer. 380p. 1995. reprint ed. pap. 27.50 (*0-09-474480-7*, Pub. by Constable Pubs UK) Trans-Atl Phila.

***Sexual Life in Eighteenth Century London, Vol. 1.** Trumbach. 1993. lib. bdg. 34.95 (*0-226-81290-1*) U Ch Pr.

Sexual Life of Children. Floyd M. Martinson. LC 93-37847. 168p. 1994. text ed. 47.95 (*0-89789-376-X*, Bergin & Garvey) Greenwood.

Sexual Life of Our Time in Its Relation to Modern Civilization. Iwan Bloch. Tr. by M. Eden Paul. LC 72-9619. reprint ed. 90.00 (*0-404-57415-7*) AMS Pr.

Sexual Life of Savages. Bronislaw Malinowski. LC 86-47760. (Illus.). 650p. 1987. reprint ed. pap. 20.00 (*0-8070-4607-8*, BP 740) Beacon Pr.

Sexual Life of Savages: And Other Stories. Stokes Howell. 192p. 1996. 20.95 (*0-312-14414-8*) St Martin.

Sexual Life of Savages in North-Western Melanesia. Bronislaw Malinowski. 700p. 1982. pap. text ed. 22.50 (*0-7100-6659-7*, RKP) Routledge.

Sexual Life of the Child. Albert Moll. Tr. by Eden Paul from GER. LC 72-11290. reprint ed. 39.00 (*0-404-57483-1*) AMS Pr.

Sexual Love - Love & Friendship Valuepack. Verne & Williams. LC 94-49087. (Philosophy Ser.). 320p. 1995. pap. 26.25 (*0-86720-965-8*) Jones & Bartlett.

***Sexual Love & Western Morality.** 2nd ed. Verene. (Philosophy Ser.). (C). 1995. pap. 31.95 (*0-534-54265-4*) Wadsworth Pub.

Sexual Love & Western Morality: A Philosophical Anthology. Ed. & Intro. by D. P. Verene. (Series in Philosophy). 1995. pap. text ed. 28.75 (*0-86720-964-X*) Jones & Bartlett.

Sexual Magic. Paschal B. Randolph. Tr. by Robert North. (Illus.). 180p. 1989. 14.95 (*0-318-42501-7*) Magickal Childe.

Sexual Magic: The S-M Photographs. Michael A. Rosen. (Illus.). 72p. (Orig.). 1986. pap. 25.00 (*0-936705-69-8*) Shaynew Pr.

Sexual Man. Archibald D. Hart. 1995. pap. 12.99 (*0-8499-3684-5*) Word Pub.

Sexual Matrix: Boy Meets Girl on the Evolutionary Scale. Sam K. Kachigan. LC 90-60730. (Illus.). 171p. (C). 1990. 21.95 (*0-942154-77-0*) Radius Pr.

Sexual Matrix: Boy Meets Girl on the Evolutionary Scale. Sam K. Kachigan. 171p. 1996. pap. 10.95 (*0-942154-78-9*) Radius Pr.

Sexual Meanings: The Cultural Construction of Gender & Sexuality. Ed. by Harriet Whitehead & Sherry B. Ortner. LC 80-26655. 448p. 1981. pap. text ed. 24.95 (*0-521-28375-2*) Cambridge U Pr.

***Sexual Medicine in Primary Care.** Maurice. 450p. (C). (gr. 13). 1998. pap. text ed. 39.95 (*0-8151-2797-9*) Mosby Yr Bk.

Sexual Metaphor. Helen Haste. LC 94-50568. 320p. (C). 1994. text ed. 24.95 (*0-674-80282-9*) HUP.

Sexual Ministry: A Modern Sex Manual. John R. Bohlen & Karen Bohlen. (Illus.). 345p. 1987. pap. 9.95 (*0-9607702-2-4*) Kingdom God.

Sexual Misconduct in Counseling. Peter T. Mosgofian & George W. Ohlschlager. LC 94-41599. (Contemporary Christian Counseling Ser.). 1995. 18.99 (*0-8499-1073-0*) Word Pub.

Sexual Misconduct in Counseling & Ministry. Peter T. Mosgofian. 1995. pap. 12.99 (*0-8499-3676-4*) Word Pub.

Sexual Moralities in France: New Ideas on the Family, Divorce & Homosexuality. Antony Copley. LC 91-40114. 296p. (C). 1992. pap. text ed. 18.95 (*0-415-07711-7*, Routledge NY) Routledge.

Sexual Moralities in Modern France, 1780-1980: New Ideas on the Family, Divorce & Homosexuality. Antony Copley. 288p. 1989. 49.95 (*0-415-00360-1*) Routledge.

Sexual Morality in the World's Religions. Geoffrey Parrinder. 290p. 1995. pap. 14.95 (*1-85168-108-6*) Onewrld Pubns.

***Sexual Mutilations - A Human Tragedy: Proceedings of the Fourth International Symposium Held in Lausanne, Switzerland, August 9-11, 1996.** Ed. by George C. Denniston & Marilyn F. Milos. 252p. (C). 1997. 79.50 (*0-306-45589-7*) Plenum.

Sexual Nature, Sexual Culture. Ed. by Paul R. Abramson & Steven D. Pinkerton. LC 94-36662. (Series on Sexuality, History, & Society). 434p. 1995. pap. text ed. 19.95 (*0-226-00182-2*); lib. bdg. 65.00 (*0-226-00181-4*) U Ch Pr.

Sexual Neurasthenia, Its Hygiene, Causes, Symptoms & Treatment with a Chapter on Diet for the Nervous. 5th ed. George M. Beard. Ed. by A. D. Rockwell. LC 76-180553. (Medicine & Society in America Ser.). 312p. 1972. reprint ed. 20.95 (*0-405-03933-6*) Ayer.

Sexual Nutrition. Morton Walker & Joan Walker. 400p. 1984. mass mkt. 3.95 (*0-8217-1390-6*, Zebra Kensgtn) Kensgtn Pub Corp.

***Sexual Nutrition.** rev. ed. Morton Walker. 264p. 1996. 29.98 (*0-941683-34-6*) Instant Improve.

Sexual Nutrition: How to Nutritionally Improve, Enhance, & Stimulate Your Sexual Appetite. 2nd ed. Morton Walker. LC 93-22227. 272p. pap. 9.95 (*0-89529-565-2*) Avery Pub.

Sexual Obsessions of Saints & Mystics. 1991. lib. bdg. 75.00 (*0-8490-4151-1*) Gordon Pr.

Sexual Odyssey: From Forbidden Fruit to Cybersex. Kenneth Maxwell. (Illus.). 310p. (C). 1996. 25.95 (*0-306-45405-X*, Plenum Pr) Plenum.

***Sexual Odyssey: From Forbidden Fruit to Cybersex.** Kenneth Maxwell. (Illus.). 336p. 1998. 15.95 (*0-87477-896-4*, Tarcher Putnam) Putnam Pub Group.

Sexual Offences. C. H. Gane. 200p. 1992. pap. text ed. 40.00 (*0-406-11520-6*, UK) MICHIE.

Sexual Offences. P. F. Rook & R. Ward. (Waterlow Criminal Law Library). 320p. 1990. 72.01 (*0-685-33555-0*, Waterlow) Macmillan.

Sexual Offences Against Children & the Criminal Process. Wendy Harvey & Paulah E. Dauns. 268p. 1993. boxed 75.00 (*0-409-89376-5*, CN) MICHIE.

Sexual Offending Against Children: Assessment & Treatment of Male Abusers. Ed. by Tony Morrison et al. LC 94-1687. 224p. (C). 1994. pap. 18.95 (*0-415-05505-9*, B4373); text ed. 62.95 (*0-415-05504-0*, B4369) Routledge.

Sexual Options for Paraplegics & Quadriplegics. Thomas O. Mooney et al. (Illus.). 150p. 1975. pap. 29.95 (*0-316-57937-8*) Little.

Sexual Organism: Its Healthful Management. James C. Jackson. LC 73-20632. (Sex, Marriage & Society Ser.). 296p. 1974. reprint ed. 25.95 (*0-405-05807-1*) Ayer.

***Sexual Orientation: Toward Biological Understanding.** Ed. by Lee Ellis & Linda Ebertz. LC 97-8864. 1997. text ed. write for info. (*0-275-95651-2*, Praeger Pubs) Greenwood.

Sexual Orientation - A Human Right: An Essay on International Human Rights Law. Eric Heinze. LC 95-2024. 440p. (C). 1995. lib. bdg. 144.00 (*0-7923-3018-8*, Pub. by M Nijhoff NE) Kluwer Ac.

An Asterisk (*) at the beginning of an entry indicates that the title is appearing in BIP for the first time.

Sexual Orientation & Human Rights: The United States Constitution, the European Convention, & the Canadian Charter. Robert Wintemute. 328p. 1997. pap. 19.95 (*0-19-826488-7*) OUP.

Sexual Orientation & Identity: Heterosexual, Lesbian, Gay, & Bisexual Journeys. Heather Wishik & Carol Pierce. LC 94-69743. 285p. (C). 1995. pap. 15.95 (*0-929767-03-9*) New Dynam Pubns.

Sexual Orientation & the Law. Harvard Law Review Editors. 192p. 1990. pap. text ed. 14.50 (*0-674-80293-4*) HUP.

Sexual Orientation & the Law. National Lawyers Guild, San Francisco Bay Area Chapter, Anti-Sexism Committee et al. LC 84-24213. (Civil Rights Ser.). 1985. ring bd. 135.00 (*0-87632-454-5*) Clark Boardman Callaghan.

Sexual Orientation & U. S. Military Personnel Policy: Options & Assessment. National Defense Research Institute Staff. 546p. 1993. pap. text ed. 16.00 (*0-8330-1441-2*, MR-323-OSD) Rand Corp.

Sexual Orientation in the Workplace: Gay Men, Lesbians, Bisexuals, & Heterosexuals Working Together. George F. Simons. LC 95-35747. 96p. 1995. pap. 17.95 (*0-7619-0119-1*) Sage.

Sexual Orientation in the Workplace: Gays, Lesbians, Bisexuals & Heterosexuals Working Together. Amy J. Zuckerman & George F. Simons. (Illus.). (Orig.). 1994. pap. write for info. (*0-932895-06-9*) G Simons Int.

Sexual Outlaw: A Documentary. John Rechy. LC 83-49452. 304p. 1984. pap. 12.00 (*0-8021-3163-8*, Grove) Grove-Atltic.

Sexual Paradises of Earth: A Single Man's Guide to International Travel. Bill Bronson. (Illus.). 240p. (Orig.). 1993. pap. 18.95 (*0-9633966-0-9*) BB Pr.

Sexual Paradises of the World: Where to Find Them. 1995. lib. bdg. 264.75 (*0-8490-7406-1*) Gordon Pr.

Sexual Paradox: Creative Tensions in Our Lives & in Our Congregations. Celia A. Hahn. LC 90-27105. 256p. 1991. pap. 15.95 (*0-8298-0897-3*) Pilgrim OH.

Sexual Personae: Art & Decadence from Nefertiti to Emily Dickinson. Camille Paglia. LC 91-50024. 736p. 1991. pap. 16.00 (*0-679-73579-8*, Vin) Random.

Sexual Personae: Art & Decadence from Nefertiti to Emily Dickinson. Camille Paglia. LC 89-31659. 712p. (C). 1990. 40.00 (*0-300-04396-1*) Yale U Pr.

Sexual Perspective: Homosexuality & Art in the Last 100 Years in the West. 2nd ed. Emmanuel Cooper. LC 93-41921. (Illus.). 388p. (gr. 13). 1994. pap. 18.95 (*0-415-11101-3*, B4374) Routledge.

Sexual Perspective: Homosexuality & Art in the Last 100 Years in the West. 2nd ed. Emmanuel Cooper. LC 93-41921. (Illus.). 380p. (C). (gr. 13). 1994. 40.00 (*0-415-11100-5*, B4370) Routledge.

Sexual Perversion: Integrative Treatment Approaches for the Clinician. S. Travin & B. Protter. (Illus.). 206p. (C). 1993. 39.50 (*0-306-44380-5*, Plenum Pr) Plenum.

Sexual Perversions & Abnormalities: A Study in the Psychology of Paraphilia. Clifford Allen. LC 78-27783. 346p. 1979. reprint ed. text ed. 65.00 (*0-313-20627-9*, ALSP, Greenwood Pr) Greenwood.

Sexual Perversity in Chicago & the Duck Variations. David Mamet. LC 77-91885. 128p. 1978. pap. 8.95 (*0-8021-5011-X*, Grove) Grove-Atltic.

Sexual Pharmacology. Ed. by Alan J. Riley et al. (Illus.). 248p. 1994. 67.50 (*0-19-262283-8*) OUP.

Sexual Pharmacology: Drugs That Affect Sexual Function. Theresa L. Crenshaw & James P. Goldberg. 500p. (C). 1993. 75.00 (*0-393-70144-1*) Norton.

Sexual Pharmacy: The Complete Guide to Drugs with Sexual Side Effects. M. Laurence Lieberman. 320p. 1988. 18.95 (*0-317-66926-5*) NAL-Dutton.

Sexual, Physical, & Emotional Abuse in Out-of-Home Care. Toni C. Johnson. LC 96-36223. (Illus.). 118p. 1997. 39.95 (*0-7890-0088-1*); pap. 17.95 (*0-7890-0193-4*) Haworth Pr.

Sexual Physiology. R. T. Trall. LC 73-20640. (Sex, Marriage & Society Ser.). 310p. 1974. reprint ed. 26.95 (*0-405-05821-7*) Ayer.

Sexual Plant Reproduction. Ed. by Mauro Cresti & Antonio Tiezzi. LC 92-25601. (Illus.). 253p. 1992. 118. 95 (*0-387-55746-6*) Spr-Verlag.

Sexual Pleasure: Reaching New Heights of Sexual Arousal & Intimacy. Barbara Keesling. LC 93-23625. (Illus.). 224p. 1993. 21.95 (*0-89793-149-1*); pap. 12.95 (*0-89793-148-3*) Hunter Hse.

Sexual Pleasure Enhancement Program. G-Jo Institute Staff. 1980. pap. 4.50 (*0-916878-12-0*) Falkyn Inc.

Sexual Pleasures: A Groundbreaking Book That Shows Women How to Claim the Sexual Passion They... Susan C. Bakos. 1992. mass mkt. 4.99 (*0-312-92847-5*) St Martin.

Sexual Pleasures: Enhancement of Sex Life in Finland, 1971-1992. Osmo Kontula & Elina Haavio-Mannila. LC 94-42388. (Illus.). 260p. 1995. text ed. 62.95 (*1-85521-628-0*, Pub. by Dartmth Pub UK) Ashgate Pub Co.

Sexual Politics: Judy Chicago's Dinner Party in Feminist Art History. Ed. by Amelia Jones. LC 95-50772. 1996. pap. write for info. (*0-943739-19-5*); text ed. write for info. (*0-943739-20-9*) F S Wight Art.

Sexual Politics: Judy Chicago's Dinner Party in Feminist Art History. Laura Meyer et al. LC 95-50772. (Illus.). 264p. (C). 1996. 50.00 (*0-520-20565-0*) U CA Pr.

Sexual Politics: Judy Chicago's Dinner Party in Feminist Art History. Laura Meyer et al. (Illus.). 264p. (C). 1996. pap. 29.95 (*0-520-20566-9*) U CA Pr.

Sexual Politics & Popular Culture. Ed. by Diane Raymond. LC 90-82104. 249p. (C). 1990. 37.95 (*0-87972-501-X*); pap. 18.95 (*0-87972-502-8*) Bowling Green Univ Popular Press.

Sexual Politics & the European Union: The New Feminist Challenge. Ed. by R. Amy Elman. 208p. 1996. 39.95 (*1-57181-062-5*); pap. 14.95 (*1-57181-046-3*) Berghahn Bks.

Sexual Politics & the Male Playwright: The Portrayal of Women in 10 Contemporary Plays. Geetha Ramanathan. LC 95-45246. 200p. 1996. lib. bdg. 32.50 (*0-7864-0063-3*) McFarland & Co.

Sexual Politics in America. Ed. by Oliver C. Trager. LC 94-4766. (Editorials on File Bk.). (Illus.). 224p. 1994. 29. 95 (*0-8160-3024-3*) Facts on File.

Sexual Politics in Cuba: Machismo, Homosexuality, & AIDS. Marvin Leiner. (C). 1994. pap. text ed. 20.95 (*0-8133-2122-0*) Westview.

Sexual Politics in the Enlightenment: Women Writers Read Rousseau. Mary S. Trouille. LC 96-44093. (SUNY Series, the Margins of Literature). (Illus.). 448p. (C). 1997. text ed. 65.50 (*0-7914-3489-3*) State U NY Pr.

Sexual Politics in the Enlightenment: Women Writers Read Rousseau. Mary S. Trouille. LC 96-44093. (SUNY Series, the Margins of Literature). (Illus.). 448p. (C). 1997. pap. text ed. 21.95 (*0-7914-3490-7*) State U NY Pr.

Sexual Politics in the Third Reich: The Persecution of Homosexuals During the Holocaust. rev. ed. Jack N. Porter. (Holocaust Studies). (Illus.). 102p. 1995. reprint ed. pap. 16.95 (*0-932270-05-0*) Spencer Pr.

Sexual Politics Issue. (Review Ser.: No. 1). 124p. 1993. pap. 6.00 (*0-9641292-3-X*) Global Cty Pr.

Sexual Politics of Disability. Ed. by Tom Shakespeare et al. (Sexual Politics Ser.). 256p. 1997. 75.00 (*0-304-33328-X*); pap. 18.95 (*0-304-33329-8*) Cassell.

Sexual Politics of Jean-Jacques Rousseau. Joel Schwartz. LC 83-18141. xii, 208p. 1985. pap. text ed. 9.95 (*0-226-74224-5*) U Ch Pr.

Sexual Politics of Meat: A Feminist-Vegetarian Critical Theory. Carol J. Adams. (Illus.). 256p. 1991. pap. text ed. 15.95 (*0-8264-0513-4*) Continuum.

Sexual Politics, Sexual Communities: The Making of a Homosexual Minority in the United States, 1940-1970. John D'Emilio. LC 82-16000. 268p. (C). 1984. reprint ed. pap. 11.95 (*0-226-14266-3*) U Ch Pr.

Sexual Portraits: Photographs of Radical Sexuality. Michael A. Rosen. (Illus.). 64p. (Orig.). 1990. pap. 30.00 (*0-936705-88-4*) Shaynew Pr.

Sexual Positions. Alex Comfort. 1997. 12.00 (*0-609-60033-8*) Random Hse Value.

Sexual Positions. Janet Wright. 1997. pap. text ed. 12.98 (*0-7651-9539-9*) Smithmark.

Sexual Positions for the Knee Patient. Joanne Arczynski. (Illus.). 72p. 1996. pap. text ed. 9.95 (*0-9650561-0-4*) Sex Life.

Sexual Positions for the Knee Patient. Joanne Arczynski. 1997. pap. text ed. 9.95 (*0-9650561-4-7*) Sex Life.

Sexual Power: Feminism & the Family in America. Carolyn Johnston. LC 92-3421. 432p. (C). 1992. text ed. 39.95 (*0-8173-0583-1*) U of Ala Pr.

Sexual Power in British Romantic Poetry. Daniel P. Watkins. Ed. by Maxine L. Margolis & Martin F. Murphy. LC 95-9219. 192p. (C). 1996. lib. bdg. 29.95 (*0-8130-1438-7*) U Press Fla.

Sexual Practice - Textual Theory: Lesbian Cultural Criticism. Ed. by Susan J. Wolfe & Julia Penelope. LC 92-33731. 1993. 61.95 (*1-55786-100-5*); pap. 25.95 (*1-55786-101-3*) Blackwell Pubs.

Sexual Practices & the Medieval Church. Ed. by Vern Bullough & James A. Brundage. LC 80-85227. 289p. 1984. reprint ed. pap. 23.95 (*0-87975-268-8*) Prometheus Bks.

Sexual Problems: New Insight, New Solutions. 3.00 (*0-686-40911-6*, SR17) Transitions.

Sexual Problems of Adolescents in Institutions. David A. Shore et al. (Illus.). 262p. 1981. pap. 29.95 (*0-398-06424-5*); text ed. 41.95 (*0-398-04143-1*) C C Thomas.

Sexual Psychopaths: Narrating the Erotic Imagination. Vernon A. Rosario, II. LC 96-29552. (Ideologies of Desire Ser.). (Illus.). 256p. 1997. 27.50 (*0-19-510483-8*) OUP.

Sexual Purity. Tony Evans. (Tony Evans Speaks Out on... Ser.). 1995. pap. 4.99 (*0-8024-2561-5*) Moody.

Sexual Racism: The Emotional Barrier to an Integrated Society. Charles H. Stember. LC 76-26869. 234p. 1981. text ed. 39.95 (*0-444-99034-8*, SSR/) Greenwood.

Sexual Realm in Long-Term Marriages: A Longitudinal Study Following Marital Partners over Twenty Years. Ben N. Ard, Jr. LC 90-42211. 196p. 1990. lib. bdg. 79. 95 (*0-7734-9982-2*) E Mellen.

Sexual Rehabilitation of the Spinal-Cord-Injured Patient. Ed. by J. F. Leyson. LC 90-4685. (Illus.). 548p. 1991. 125.00 (*0-89603-145-4*) Humana.

Sexual Relationship: An Object Relations View of Sex & the Family. David E. Scharff. (International Library of Group Psychotherapy & Group Process). 284p. (C). 1988. pap. 14.95 (*0-415-00081-5*) Routledge.

Sexual Repression & Victorian Literature. Russell M. Goldfarb. LC 70-101685. 222p. 1975. 32.50 (*0-8387-7619-1*) Bucknell U Pr.

Sexual Reproduction in Higher Plants. Ed. by Mauro Cresti et al. (Illus.). 530p. 1989. 152.95 (*0-387-18673-5*) Spr-Verlag.

Sexual Reproduction in Seed, Plants, Ferns & Mosses. Ed. by M. T. Willemse. (C). 1991. text ed. 400.00 (*0-89771-676-0*, Pub. by Intl Bk Distr II) St Mut.

Sexual Reproduction in the Mucorinaeae. A. F. Blakeslee. (Bibliotheca Mycologica Ser.: No. 48). 1976. reprint ed. text ed. 32.00 (*3-7682-1064-2*) Lubrecht & Cramer.

Sexual Reproduction of Tree Crops. M. Sedgley & A. R. Griffin. (Applied Botany & Crop Science Ser.). 360p. 1989. text ed. 119.00 (*0-12-634470-1*) Acad Pr.

Sexual Revelations of the Bible. Brown Landone. 260p. 1972. reprint ed. spiral bd. 14.00 (*0-7873-0527-8*) Hlth Research.

Sexual Revolution: Challenge & Response. J. Rinzema. Tr. by Lewis B. Smedes. LC 73-14712. 107p. reprint ed. pap. 30.50 (*0-317-09741-5*, 2012849) Bks Demand.

Sexual Revolution in Russia: From the Age of the Czars to Today. Igor S. Kon. 1995. 25.50 (*0-02-917541-0*, Free Press) Free Pr.

Sexual Rights of Adolescents: Competence, Vulnerability, & Parental Control. Hyman Rodman et al. LC 83-14440. 183p. 1984. text ed. 45.00 (*0-231-04916-1*) Col U Pr.

Sexual Rights of Adolescents: Competence, Vulnerability, & Parental Control. Hyman Rodman et al. LC 83-14440. 183p. 1988. pap. text ed. 15.50 (*0-231-04917-X*) Col U Pr.

Sexual Salvation: Affirming Women's Sexual Rights & Pleasures. Naomi B. McCormick. LC 94-6378. 304p. 1994. text ed. 29.95 (*0-275-94359-3*, Praeger Pubs) Greenwood.

Sexual Sameness: Textual Differences in Lesbian & Gay Writing. Ed. by Joseph Bristow. LC 91-28659. (Illus.). 272p. (C). (gr. 13). 1992. text ed. 59.95 (*0-415-06936-X*, A7199) Routledge.

Sexual Sameness: Textural Differences in Lesbian & Gay Writing. Joseph Bristoe. LC 91-28659. 272p. (C). 1992. pap. 17.95 (*0-415-06937-8*, Pub. by Tavistock UK) Routledge Chapman & Hall.

Sexual Satisfaction: Achieving Sexual Ecstasy Through Higher Consciousness. Ann Rosen. 1995. pap. 16.95 (*0-935016-31-7*) Zinn Communs.

Sexual Scene. 2nd rev. ed. Ed. by John H. Gagnon & William Simon. LC 72-87668. 150p. 1973. reprint ed. 32.95 (*0-87855-048-8*); reprint ed. pap. 18.95 (*0-87855-541-2*) Transaction Pubs.

Sexual Science: The Victorian Construction of Womanhood. Cynthia Russett. LC 88-24521. 250p. 1989. text ed. 32. 00 (*0-674-80290-X*) HUP.

Sexual Science: The Victorian Construction of Womanhood. Cynthia Russett. 256p. 1991. pap. text ed. 14.95 (*0-674-80291-8*, RUSSEY) HUP.

Sexual Science & the Law. Richard Green. LC 92-10458. 323p. (C). 1992. 39.95 (*0-674-80268-3*) HUP.

Sexual Science, Sexual Knowledge: The History of Attitudes to Sexuality. Ed. by Roy Porter & Mikulas Teich. LC 93-28940. 290p. (C). 1994. pap. text ed. 19.95 (*0-521-44891-3*) Cambridge U Pr.

Sexual Science, Sexual Knowledge: The History of Attitudes to Sexuality. Ed. by Roy Porter & Mikulas Teich. LC 93-28940. 290p. (C). 1994. text ed. 69.95 (*0-521-44434-9*) Cambridge U Pr.

Sexual Secrets: A Photographic Guide. 1992. lib. bdg. 255. 95 (*0-8490-5342-0*) Gordon Pr.

Sexual Secrets, the Alchemy of Ecstasy. Nik Douglas & Penny Slinger. LC 79-9479. (Illus.). 384p. 1979. 29.95 (*0-89281-010-6*, Destiny Bks); pap. 19.95 (*0-89281-266-4*, Destiny Bks) Inner Tradit.

Sexual Selection. Malte Andersson. LC 93-33276. (Monographs in Behavior & Ecology). 624p. 1994. text ed. 75.00 (*0-691-03344-7*); pap. text ed. 26.50 (*0-691-00057-3*) Princeton U Pr.

Sexual Selection. James L. Gould. (Illus.). 277p. Date not set. pap. text ed. 19.95 (*0-7167-6018-5*) W H Freeman.

Sexual Selection & Animal Genitalia. William G. Eberhard. LC 85-907. 288p. 1988. reprint ed. pap. 18.50 (*0-674-80284-5*) HUP.

Sexual Selection & the Barn Swallow. Anders P. Moller. LC 93-37324. (Series in Ecology & Evolution). (Illus.). 376p. (C). 1994. 65.00 (*0-19-854029-9*); pap. 35.00 (*0-19-854028-0*) OUP.

Sexual Selection, Lek & Arena Behavior, & Sexual Size Dimorphism in Birds. Robert B. Payne. 52p. 1984. 8.00 (*0-943610-40-0*) Am Ornithologists.

Sexual Selections. James Gould & Carol Gould. (Scientific American Library: No. 29). 256p. 1995. text ed. write for info. (*0-7167-5053-8*) W H Freeman.

Sexual Self: How Character Shapes Sexual Experience. Avodah K. Offit. 336p. 1995. pap. 20.00 (*1-56821-548-7*) Aronson.

Sexual Self-Destruct: Conscience of the West. Karl K. Lewin. LC 79-54918. 166p. 1980. 15.00 (*0-87527-197-9*) Green.

Sexual Size Differences in Mainland Anoles. Henry S. Fitch. (Occasional Papers: No. 50). 21p. 1976. pap. 1.00 (*0-686-80357-4*) U KS Nat Hist Mus.

Sexual Size Differences in Reptiles. Henry S. Fitch. (Miscellaneous Publications: No. 70). 72p. 1981. 5.25 (*0-317-04862-7*) U KS Nat Hist Mus.

Sexual Size Dimorphism in Hawks & Owls of North America. Noel F. Snyder & James W. Wiley. 95p. 1976. 7.00 (*0-943610-20-6*) Am Ornithologists.

Sexual Slang: A Compendium of Offbeat Words & Colorful Phrases, from Shakespeare to Today. 3rd ed. Alan Richter. LC 94-34728. 1995. 12.00 (*0-602-72504-6*, PL) HarpC.

Sexual Solutions: A Guide for Men & the Women Who Love Them. rev. ed. Michael Castleman. 304p. 1989. pap. 11.00 (*0-671-66488-3*, Touchstone Bks) S&S Trade.

Sexual Sorcery. John Teal. Ed. by I.G.O.S. Society Staff. LC 93-79456. (Illus.). 239p. (Orig.). (C). 1993. text ed. 35.00 (*1-883147-10-7*) Intern Guild ASRS.

Sexual Strands: Understanding & Treating Sexual Anomalies in Men. R. Langevin. (Illus.). 560p. (C). 1983. text ed. 99.95 (*0-89859-205-4*) L Erlbaum Assocs.

Sexual Strategies: How Females Choose Their Mates. Mary Batten. 1994. pap. 12.95 (*0-685-74802-2*, Tarcher Putnam) Putnam Pub Group.

Sexual Strategies: How Females Choose Their Mates. Mary Batten. 272p. 1994. pap. 13.95 (*0-87477-757-7*, Tarcher Putnam) Putnam Pub Group.

Sexual Subject: Screen Reader in Sexuality. Screen Editorial Collective Staff. Ed. by Mandy Merck. LC 91-40140. 320p. (C). 1992. pap. 17.95 (*0-415-07467-3*, A7174) Routledge.

Sexual Subject: Screen Reader in Sexuality. Screen Editorial Collective Staff. Ed. by Mandy Merck. LC 91-40140. 320p. (C). (gr. 13). 1992. text ed. 69.95 (*0-415-07466-5*, A7170) Routledge.

Sexual Subjects: Lesbians, Gender, Psychoanalysis. Adria E. Schwartz. LC 97-21490. 256p. (C). 1997. pap. write for info. (*0-415-91093-5*); text ed. write for info. (*0-415-91092-7*) Routledge.

Sexual Subordination & State Intervention: Comparing Sweden & the United States. R. Amy Elman. LC 95-31518. 128p. 1996. 35.00 (*1-57181-071-4*); pap. 14.50 (*1-57181-072-2*) Berghahn Bks.

Sexual Subversions: Three French Feminists. Grosz. 288p. pap. 19.95 (*0-04-351072-8*, Pub. by Allen Unwin AT) Paul & Co Pubs.

Sexual Subversions: Three French Feminists. Elizabeth Grosz. 288p. 1989. text ed. 44.95 (*0-04-301292-2*, Pub. by Allen Unwin AT) Paul & Co Pubs.

Sexual Success: How to Satisfy Your Partner Every Time: A New & Practical Approach. Paul Jacobson. Ed. by Martin Matilda. LC 96-84497. 144p. (Orig.). 1997. pap. 14.95 (*1-889078-07-7*, 298-9581) Al-Galaxy.

Sexual Suicide: Our Deadly Lack of Sexual Forethought. Goshawk. 290p. 1994. text ed. 26.95 (*0-9630463-2-2*) S & D.

Sexual Suspects: Eighteenth-Century Players & Sexual Ideology. Kristina Straub. 212p. 1992. text ed. 39.50 (*0-691-06898-4*); pap. text ed. 14.95 (*0-691-01515-5*) Princeton U Pr.

Sexual Symmetry: Love in the Ancient Novel & Related Genres. David Konstan. LC 93-13282. 296p. (C). 1993. text ed. 42.50 (*0-691-03341-2*) Princeton U Pr.

Sexual Tensions of William Sharp: A Study of the Birth of Fiona Macleod, Incorporating Two Lost Works, "Ariadne in Naxos" & "Beatrice", Vol. 2. Terry L. Meyers. LC 94-29463. (Studies in Nineteenth Century British Literature: Vol. 2). 136p. (C). 1996. 37.95 (*0-8204-2637-7*) P Lang Pubng.

Sexual-Textual Politics. Toril Moi. 200p. 1985. pap. 13.95 (*0-415-02974-0*, 9451) Routledge Chapman & Hall.

Sexual Textualities: Essays on Queerling Latin American Writing. David W. Foster. LC 96-51597. (The Texas Pan American Ser.). 200p. 1997. 28.00 (*0-292-72501-9*) U of Tex Pr.

Sexual Textualities: Essays on Queerling Latin American Writing. David W. Foster. LC 96-51597. (The Texas Pan American Ser.). 200p. 1997. pap. 16.95 (*0-292-72502-7*) U of Tex Pr.

Sexual Trafficking in Children: An Investigation of the Child Sex Trade. Daniel S. Campagna & Donald L. Poffenberger. LC 87-1242. 264p. 1987. text ed. 45.00 (*0-86569-154-1*, T154, Auburn Hse); pap. text ed. 17.95 (*0-86569-155-X*, R155, Auburn Hse) Greenwood.

Sexual Transmission of HIV Infection: Risk Reduction, Trauma, & Adaptation. Ed. by Lena N. Schonnesson. LC 92-49781. (Journal of Psychotherapy & the Family: Vol. 5, Nos. 1-2, 1992). (Illus.). 168p. 1993. 39.95 (*1-56024-332-5*); pap. 14.95 (*1-56023-024-X*) Haworth Pr.

Sexual Trauma & Psychopathology: Clinical Intervention with Adult Survivors. Shanti Shapiro & George M. Dominiak. LC 92-25642. 192p. 29.95 (*0-669-27357-0*, Lexington) Jossey-Bass.

Sexual Trauma in Children & Adolescents: Dynamics & Treatment. Diana S. Everstine & Louis Everstine. LC 88-26309. 224p. 1989. text ed. 33.95 (*0-87630-529-X*) Brunner-Mazel.

Sexual Tyranny in Wessex: Hardy's Witches & Demons of Folklore. Gayla R. Steel. LC 92-40987. (American University Studies: English Language & Literature: Ser. IV, Vol. 164). 146p. 1993. 32.95 (*0-8204-2092-1*) P Lang Pubng.

Sexual Underground. John Preston. Date not set. write for info. (*0-87795-910-2*) Morrow.

Sexual Underworlds of the Enlightenment. Ed. by G. S. Rousseau & Roy Porter. (Illus.). vi, 294p. (C). 1988. text ed. 49.95 (*0-8078-1782-1*) U of NC Pr.

Sexual Unfolding: Sexual Development & Sex Therapies in Late Adolescence. Lorna J. Sarrel & Philip M. Sarrel. (Master Works). 378p. 1995. reprint ed. 30.00 (*1-56821-675-0*) Aronson.

Sexual Values: Opposing Viewpoints. Ed. by Charles P. Cozic. LC 94-4978. (Opposing Viewpoints Ser.). (Illus.). 285p. (YA). (gr. 10 up). 1995. pap. text ed. 12.96 (*1-56510-210-X*); lib. bdg. 20.96 (*1-56510-211-8*) Greenhaven.

Sexual Victimisation: Two Recent Researches into Sex Problems & Their Social Effects. Ed. by D. J. West. 194p. 1985. text ed. 68.95 (*0-566-00832-7*, Pub. by Avebury Pub UK) Ashgate Pub Co.

Sexual Violence. Ed. by Mary Williams. LC 96-40122. (Opposing Viewpoints Ser.). (Illus.). (YA). (gr. 5-12). 1997. pap. 12.96 (*1-56510-559-1*); lib. bdg. 20.96 (*1-56510-560-5*) Greenhaven.

Sexual Violence: Our War Against Rape. Linda A. Fairstein. 288p. 1995. pap. 14.00 (*0-425-14780-0*, Berkley Trade) Berkley Pub.

Sexual Violence: The Unmentionable Sin: An Ethical & Pastoral Perspective. Marie M. Fortune. LC 83-3948. 256p. (Orig.). 1983. pap. 15.95 (*0-8298-0652-0*) Pilgrim OH.

Sexual Violence: Twenty Years in New York's Sex Crimes Prosecution Unit. Linda A. Fairstein. LC 93-1175. 1993. 23.00 (*0-688-06715-8*) Morrow.

An Asterisk (*) at the beginning of an entry indicates that the title is appearing in BIP for the first time.

S

Sexual Visions: Images of Gender in Science & Medicine Between the Eighteenth & Twentieth Centuries. Ludmilla Jordanova. (Science & Literature Ser.). (Illus.). 208p. (C). 1989. text ed. 22.50 (*0-299-12290-5*) U of Wis Pr.

Sexual Visions: Images of Gender in Science & Medicine Between the Eighteenth & Twentieth Centuries. Ludmilla Jordanova. (Science & Literature Ser.). (Illus.). 208p. (C). 1993. reprint ed. pap. 12.95 (*0-299-12294-8*) U of Wis Pr.

Sexual Wholeness. Cindy Bunch & Scott Hotaling. (Created Male & Female Bible Studies). 64p. (Orig.). 1993. wbk. ed., pap. 4.99 (*0-8308-1133-8*, 1133) InterVarsity.

***Sexual Woman.** Arch Hart et al. 224p. 1998. 17.99 (*0-8499-1340-3*) Word Pub.

Sexualidad: Sus Conceptos Basicos. Gloria Mock & Wilfred Martinez. 274p. 1995. pap. text ed. write for info. (*1-56758-053-X*) Edit Cultl.

Sexualitat des Menschen: Handbuch und Atlas. E. J. Haeberle. 559p. (GER.). 1983. 41.55 (*3-11-008753-7*) De Gruyter.

***Sexualities.** Ed. by Marny Hall. LC 96-39366. 119p. 1996. 29.95 (*0-7890-0022-9*) Haworth Pr.

***Sexualities.** Ed. by Marny Hall. LC 96-39366. 119p. 1996. pap. 14.95 (*1-56023-095-9*) Harrington Pk.

Sexualities & Homosexualities. Jaime P. Stubrin. 176p. 1994. pap. text ed. 29.50 (*1-85575-065-1*, Pub. by Karnac Bks UK) Brunner-Mazel.

Sexualities in Victorian Britain. Ed. by Andrew H. Miller & James E. Adams. LC 96-5128. (Illus.). 256p. 1996. text ed. 39.95 (*0-253-33066-1*) Ind U Pr.

Sexuality. (YouthTalk Ser.). 32p. (YA). 1994. teacher ed., pap. 4.95 (*0-8066-0256-2*, 15-5211) Augsburg Fortress.

Sexuality. (YouthTalk Ser.). 48p. (YA). 1994. pap. 5.25 (*0-8066-0255-4*, 15-5210) Augsburg Fortress.

***Sexuality.** Joseph Bristow. 152p. (C). 1997. pap. 9.95 (*0-415-08494-6*); text ed. 49.95 (*0-415-12268-6*) Routledge.

Sexuality. Mary Durkin. (Guidelines for Contemporary Catholics Ser.). (Orig.). 1987. pap. 10.95 (*0-88347-211-2*) Res Christian Liv.

Sexuality. Susan Sprecher & Kathleen McKinney. (Series on Close Relationships: Vol. 6). (Illus.). 200p. (C). 1993. text ed. 38.00 (*0-8039-4290-7*); pap. text ed. 16.95 (*0-8039-4291-5*) Sage.

***Sexuality.** Jeffrey Weeks. (Key Ideas Ser.). 128p. (C). 1986. pap. 12.95 (*0-415-03954-1*) Routledge.

Sexuality. Jeffrey Weeks. (Key Ideas Ser.). 128p. 1986. pap. 9.50 (*0-7458-0002-5*, 9876, Pub. by Tavistock-E Horwood UK) Routledge Chapman & Hall.

***Sexuality.** 2nd unabridged ed. Sophia Mason & Vince Ploscik. (Illus.). 158p. (Orig.). 1994. spiral bd., pap. 21.00 (*1-889805-01-7*) A-C Tapes.

Sexuality, Vol. 4. Ed. by Eleanor C. Goldstein. (Resources Ser.). 1995. suppl. ed. 76.00 (*0-89777-184-2*) Sirs Inc.

Sexuality: A Developmental Approach to Problems. Betty N. Gordon & Carolyn S. Schroeder. LC 95-17305. (Clinical Child Psychology Library). 160p. 1995. 35.00 (*0-306-45039-9*, Plenum Pr); pap. 19.50 (*0-306-45040-2*, Plenum Pr) Plenum.

Sexuality: A Health Education Perspective. rev. ed. Mary E. Nicholson & Richard St. Pierre. (Illus.). 75p. (C). 1991. teacher ed. write for info. (*0-910251-28-2*) Venture Pub PA.

***Sexuality: A Reader.** Ed. by Karen Lebacqz. (Pilgrim Library of Ethics: Vol. 2). 480p. (Orig.). 1997. pap. 26.95 (*0-8298-1210-5*) Pilgrim OH.

Sexuality: An Illustrated History. Sander L. Gilman. 376p. 1989. text ed. 75.00 (*0-471-83792-X*) Wiley.

Sexuality: Challenges & Choices. Michael Theisen. Ed. by Thomas Zanzig. (Horizons Ser.: Level 1, Minicourse 2). (Illus.). 68p. (Orig.). (YA). (gr. 9). 1996. student ed., pap. text ed. 9.95 (*0-88489-348-0*) St Marys.

Sexuality: Connecting Mind, Body, & Spirit. Center for Learning Network Staff. (Centering Faith Ser.). 121p. 1992. pap. text ed. 6.95 (*1-56077-220-4*); teacher ed., spiral bd. 8.95 (*1-56077-219-0*) Ctr Learning.

Sexuality: Health Facts. Lucas Stang & Kathleen R. Miner. LC 93-41374. 1996. 12.95 (*1-56071-187-6*, H307) ETR Assocs.

Sexuality: Insights & Issues. 3rd ed. Jerrold S. Greenberg et al. 672p. (C). 1992. per. write for info. (*0-697-10104-5*) Brown & Benchmark.

Sexuality: New Perspectives. Ed. by Zira DeFries et al. LC 84-28991. (Contributions in Psychology Ser.: No. 6). (Illus.). xii, 362p. 1985. text ed. 65.00 (*0-313-24207-0*, DFS/, Greenwood Pr) Greenwood.

Sexuality: The Sacred Journey: An Awakening to Ecstasy. Marina Raye. (Illus.). 224p. (Orig.). 1994. pap. 12.95 (*1-878010-01-8*) A Schlossberg.

Sexuality: Theological Voices. Kevin T. McMahon. LC 87-18201. 266p. (Orig.). 1987. pap. 14.95 (*0-935372-20-2*) Pope John Ctr.

Sexuality Across the Life Course. Ed. by Alice S. Rossi. LC 93-41706. (John D. & Catherine T. MacArthur Foundation Series on Mental Health & Development). 435p. 1994. 34.95 (*0-226-72833-1*) U Ch Pr.

Sexuality after Spinal Cord Injury: Answers to Your Questions. Stanley H. Ducharme & Kathleen M. Gill. 192p. (Orig.). 1996. pap. 22.00 (*1-55766-265-7*, 2657) P H Brookes.

Sexuality after TBI. 2nd ed. William H. Burke. (Professional Series on Traumatic Brain Injury: Vol. 10). 68p. (Orig.). 1995. pap. 9.50 (*1-882855-41-8*) HDI Pubs.

Sexuality & Aging. rev. ed. Robert L. Solnick. LC 78-51932. 1978. pap. 14.00 (*0-88474-023-4*, 05752-5) Free Pr.

Sexuality & Aging: An Annotated Bibliography. George F. Wharton. LC 81-5097. 251p. 1981. 25.00 (*0-8108-1427-7*) Scarecrow.

Sexuality & Authority in the Catholic Church. Monica M. Miller. LC 92-63037. 1994. write for info. (*0-940866-24-2*) U Scranton Pr.

Sexuality & Catholicism. Thomas C. Fox. LC 95-6367. 384p. 1995. 27.50 (*0-8076-1396-7*) Braziller.

Sexuality & Chronic Illness: A Comprehensive Approach. Leslie R. Schover & Soren B. Jensen. LC 87-23640. 357p. 1988. lib. bdg. 49.95 (*0-89862-715-X*) Guilford Pr.

Sexuality & Disabilities: A Guide for Human Service Practitioners. Deborah Valentine. Ed. by Romel W. Mackelprang. LC 93-354. 159p. (C). 1996. pap. 19.95 (*0-7890-0092-X*) Haworth Pr.

Sexuality & Disabilities: A Guide for Human Service Practitioners. Deborah Valentine. Ed. by Romel W. Mackelprang. LC 93-354. (Journal of Social Work & Human Sexuality: Vol. 8, No. 2). (Illus.). 159p. (C). 1996. 29.95 (*1-56024-375-9*) Haworth Pr.

Sexuality & Eroticism among Males in Moslem Societies. Arno Schmitt & Jehoeda Sofer. LC 91-2316. 210p. 1991. pap. 14.95 (*0-918393-91-4*); lib. bdg. 39.95 (*1-56024-047-4*) Harrington Pk.

Sexuality & Family Planning: Report of a Consultation & Research Findings. T. Langfeldt & M. Porter. 62p. 1986. pap. 8.00 (*92-890-1042-8*) World Health.

Sexuality & Feminism in Shelley. Nathaniel Brown. LC 79-4634. 298p. 1979. 32.00 (*0-674-80285-3*) HUP.

Sexuality & Gender in Early Modern Europe: Institutions, Texts, Images. Ed. by James G. Turner. LC 92-26038. (Illus.). 332p. (C). 1993. pap. text ed. 19.95 (*0-521-44605-8*) Cambridge U Pr.

Sexuality & Gender in Society. Jannell L. Carroll & Paul R. Wolpe. (C). 1995. teacher ed. write for info. (*0-06-500874-X*) Addson-Wesley Educ.

Sexuality & Gender in Society. Jannell L. Carroll & Paul R. Wolpe. LC 95-35191. 864p. (C). 1996. text ed. 58.50 (*0-06-500872-3*); student ed., pap. text ed. 19.95 (*0-06-500873-1*) Addson-Wesley Educ.

Sexuality & Human Bonding: Proceedings of the XII World Congress of Sexology, Yokohama, Japan, 12-16 August, 1995. Ed. by Seiichi Matsumoto. LC 96-533. (International Congress Ser.: Vol. 1095). 536p. 1996. 222.25 (*0-444-82195-3*) Elsevier.

Sexuality & Its Discontents: Meaning, Myths & Modern Sexualities. Jeffrey Weeks. 288p. 1985. 35.00 (*0-7102-0564-3*, RKP); pap. 13.95 (*0-7102-0565-1*, RKP) Routledge.

Sexuality & Its Discontents: Meanings, Myths & Modern Sexualities. Jeffrey Weeks. 288p. (C). 1985. pap. 13.95 (*0-415-04503-7*, Pub. by Tavistock UK) Routledge Chapman & Hall.

Sexuality & Marriage in Colonial Latin America. Ed. by Asuncion Lavrin. LC 88-33980. (Latin American Studies). (Illus.). ix, 349p. 1989. reprint ed. text ed. 40.00 (*0-8032-2885-6*) U of Nebr Pr.

Sexuality & Marriage in Colonial Latin America. Ed. by Asuncion Lavrin. LC 88-33980. (Latin American Studies). (Illus.). ix, 349p. 1989. reprint ed. pap. text ed. 18.00 (*0-8032-7940-X*, Bison Books) U of Nebr Pr.

Sexuality & Medicine Vol. I: Conceptual Roots. 5th ed. Ed. by Earl E. Shelp. (Philosophy & Medicine Ser.: No. 22). 304p. 1986. pap. text ed. 54.50 (*90-277-2386-9*) Kluwer Ac.

Sexuality & Medicine Vol. II: Ethical Viewpoints in Transition. 5th ed. Ed. by Earl E. Shelp. (Philosophy & Medicine Ser.: No. 23). 312p. 1987. pap. text ed. 54.50 (*1-55608-016-6*); lib. bdg. 118.50 (*1-55608-013-1*) Kluwer Ac.

Sexuality & Medicine in the Middle Ages. Danielle Jacquart & Claude Thomasset. Tr. by Matthew Adamson from FRE. 232p. 1989. text ed. 45.00 (*0-691-05550-5*) Princeton U Pr.

Sexuality & Medicine, Vol. I: Conceptual Roots. Ed. by Earl E. Shelp. 308p. (C). 1986. lib. bdg. 118.50 (*90-277-2290-0*, D Reidel) Kluwer Ac.

***Sexuality & Mind.** Chasseguet. (C). 1987. text ed. 36.00 (*0-8147-1400-5*) NYU Pr.

Sexuality & Mind: The Role of the Father & the Mother in the Psyche. Janine Chasseguet-Smirgel. LC 86-12635. (Psychoanalytic Crosscurrents Ser.). 167p. (C). 1988. pap. text ed. 13.20 (*0-8147-1414-5*) NYU Pr.

Sexuality & Modern Culture. Dean. 1997. pap. 16.95 (*0-8057-8640-6*, Hall Reference) Macmillan.

Sexuality & Modern Culture. Carolyn J. Dean. 130p. 1996. 28.95 (*0-8057-8615-5*, Twayne) Scribnrs Ref.

Sexuality & Motherhood. Irene Walton. 171p. 1994. pap. 20.00 (*1-898507-07-4*) Buttrwrth-Heinemann.

Sexuality & Narrative. Boone. 306p. (C). 1990. lib. bdg. 58.00 (*0-226-06466-2*) U Ch Pr.

Sexuality & Patient Care: A Guide for Nurses & Teachers. Els Van Ooijen & Andrew Charnock. LC 93-39266. 1994. 42.50 (*1-56593-305-2*, 0629) Singular Publishing.

Sexuality & People with Intellectual Disability. Lydia Fegan & Anne Rauch. LC 93-20084. 1993. 32.00 (*1-55766-140-5*) P H Brookes.

Sexuality & Politics in Renaissance Drama. Ed. by Carole Levin & Karen Robertson. LC 91-25367. (Studies in Renaissance Literature: Vol. 10). 289p. 1991. lib. bdg. 89.95 (*0-88946-078-7*) E Mellen.

Sexuality & Sexual Behavior, Vol. 10 see History of Women in the United States: Topically Arranged Articles on the Evolution of Women's History in the United States

Sexuality & Social Order: The Debate over the Fertility of Women & Workers in France, 1770-1920. Angus McLaren. LC 81-13299. 240p. 1983. 44.50 (*0-8419-0744-7*) Holmes & Meier.

Sexuality & Space. Ed. by Beatriz Colomina. LC 91-40146. (Princeton Papers on Architecture: No. 1). (Illus.). 288p. (Orig.). 1992. pap. 19.95 (*1-878271-08-3*) Princeton Arch.

***Sexuality & Spirituality: Kundaline Yoga Sets & Meditations of Yogi Bhajan.** Rattana, pseud. & Ann M. Maxwell. (Illus.). 200p. 1995. spiral bd. 25.00 (*1-888029-03-X*, Yoga Tech Pr) Heart Quest.

Sexuality & Subordination: Interdisciplinary Studies of Gender in the Nineteenth Century. Susan Mendus & Jane Rendall. 256p. 1989. 49.50 (*0-415-01368-2*) Routledge.

Sexuality & Subordination: Interdisciplinary Studies of Gender in the Nineteenth Century. Susan Mendus & Jane Rendall. 256p. (C). 1989. pap. text ed. 14.95 (*0-415-01369-0*) Routledge.

Sexuality & Textuality in Henry James: Reading Through the Virginal. Lloyd Davis. (Sexuality & Literature Ser.: Vol. 1). 230p. (C). 1989. text ed. 37.50 (*0-8204-0599-X*) P Lang Pubng.

Sexuality & the Body in Russian Culture. Ed. by Jane T. Costlow et al. LC 92-47410. 288p. 1993. 45.00 (*0-8047-2113-0*) Stanford U Pr.

Sexuality & the Counseling Pastor. Herbert W. Stroup & Norma S. Wood. LC 73-88344. 134p. reprint ed. pap. 38.20 (*0-685-15392-4*, 2027176) Bks Demand.

Sexuality & the Curriculum: The Politics & Practices of Sexuality Education. Ed. by James T. Sears. (Critical Issues in Curriculum Ser.: No. 3). 384p. (C). 1992. text ed. 44.00 (*0-8077-3153-6*); pap. text ed. 22.95 (*0-8077-3152-8*) Tchrs Coll.

Sexuality & the Devil: Symbols of Love, Power & Fear in Male Psychology. Edward J. Tejirian. 272p. (C). 1990. text ed. 39.95 (*0-415-90205-3*, Routledge NY) Routledge.

***Sexuality & the Elderly: A Research Guide.** Bonnie L. Walker. LC 96-52496. (Bibliographies & Indexes in Gerontology Ser.: Vol. 35). 320p. 1997. text ed. 75.00 (*0-313-30133-6*, Greenwood Pr) Greenwood.

Sexuality & the Law: An Encyclopedia of Major Legal Cases, Vol. 3. Ed. by Arthur S. Leonard. LC 92-45133. 736p. 1993. text ed. 95.00 (*0-8240-3421-X*, H1272) Garland.

Sexuality & the Person with Traumatic Brain Injury: A Guide for Families. Ernest R. Griffith & Sally Lemberg. LC 92-32994. (Illus.). 170p. 1992. pap. 18.95 (*0-8036-4408-6*) Davis Co.

***Sexuality & the Psychology of Love.** Freud. 1997. pap. 11.00 (*0-684-83824-9*) S&S Trade.

Sexuality & the Psychology of Love. Sigmund Freud. 213p. (C). 1993. pap. 10.00 (*0-02-050986-3*) Macmillan.

Sexuality & the Reading Encounter. Emma Wilson. LC 95-44944. 224p. (C). 1996. 60.00 (*0-19-815885-8*, Clarendon Pr) OUP.

Sexuality & The Sacred: Sources For Theological Reflection. Ed. by James B. Nelson & Sandra P. Longfellow. LC 93-39390. 432p. (Orig.). 1994. pap. 25.00 (*0-664-25529-9*) Westminster John Knox.

Sexuality & the Schools: Handling the Critical Issues. Joan L. Curcio et al. LC 95-37402. (Road Maps to Success Ser.). 72p. 1995. pap. 11.95 (*0-8039-6265-7*) Corwin Pr.

Sexuality & the Social Sciences: A French Survey on Sexual Behaviour. Ed. by Michel Bozon & Henri Leridon. LC 96-19230. 364p. 1996. text ed. 67.95 (*1-85521-820-8*, Pub. by Dartmth Pub UK) Ashgate Pub Co.

Sexuality & the Young Christian. Joanne E. De Jonge. (Illus.). 128p. (YA). 1992. pap. 9.99 (*0-8010-3009-9*) Baker Bks.

Sexuality & Victorian Literature. Ed. by Don R. Cox. LC 83-21655. (Tennessee Studies in Literature: Vol. 27). (Illus.). 280p. 1984. pap. text ed. 18.95 (*0-87049-438-4*) U of Tenn Pr.

Sexuality & War: Literary Masks of the Middle East. Evelyne Accad. (Feminist Crosscurrents Ser.). 224p. (C). 1990. text ed. 40.00 (*0-8147-0595-2*) NYU Pr.

Sexuality & War: Literary Masks of the Middle East. Evelyne Accad. (Feminist Crosscurrents Ser.). 198p. (C). 1992. pap. 18.50 (*0-8147-0615-0*) NYU Pr.

Sexuality, Body Movement & the Rhythms of Development. Judith S. Kestenberg. LC 94-38258. 526p. 1995. reprint ed. pap. text ed. 40.00 (*1-56821-402-2*) Aronson.

Sexuality Counseling: A Training Program. Kay F. Schepp. LC 86-70572. x, 510p. 1986. 31.95 (*0-915202-47-6*) Accel Devel.

Sexuality Debate in North American Churches, 1988-1993: Controversies, Unresolved Issues, Future Prospects. John J. Carey. LC 94-38866. 324p. 1995. text ed. 99.95 (*0-7734-9111-2*) E Mellen.

Sexuality Debates. Sheila Jeffreys. 550p. 1987. 65.00 (*0-7102-0936-3*, 09363, RKP) Routledge.

***Sexuality Education.** 4th ed. Bruess & Greenberg. 1999. pap. text ed. 30.00 (*0-697-29442-0*) McGraw.

Sexuality Education: A Curriculum for Adolescents. Douglas Kirby. 450p. 1984. pap. text ed. 34.95 (*0-941816-28-1*) ETR Assocs.

Sexuality Education: A Curriculum for Parent-Child Programs. Douglas Kirby. 212p. 1988. pap. text ed. 29.95 (*0-941816-29-X*) ETR Assocs.

Sexuality Education: A Guide to Developing & Implementing Programs. Douglas Kirby. 132p. 1988. pap. text ed. 9.95 (*0-941816-27-3*) ETR Assocs.

Sexuality Education: A Handbook for the Evaluation Programs. Douglas Kirby. 192p. 1988. pap. text ed. 14.00 (*0-941816-30-3*) ETR Assocs.

Sexuality Education: A Resource Book. Carol Cassell & Pamela M. Wilson. LC 88-16994. (Source Books on Education: Vol. 19). 470p. 1989. text ed. 74.00 (*0-8240-7899-3*, SS416) Garland.

Sexuality Education: Theory & Practice. 3rd ed. Clint E. Bruess & Jerrold S. Greenberg. 352p. (C). 1993. per. write for info. (*0-697-17124-8*) Brown & Benchmark.

Sexuality Education across Cultures: Working with Diversities. Janice M. Irvine. LC 95-18042. (Psychology Ser.). 206p. 29.95 (*0-7879-0154-7*) Jossey-Bass.

Sexuality Education Challenge: Promoting Healthy Sexuality in Young People. Judy C. Drolet & Kay Clark. LC 93-43183. 1994. 39.95 (*1-56071-130-2*) ETR Assocs.

Sexuality Education for Youths in Care: A State-by-State Survey. Bronwyn Mayden. (Orig.). 1996. pap. text ed. 12.95 (*0-87868-639-8*) Child Welfare.

***Sexuality Education in Postsecondary & Professional Training Settings.** James W. Maddock. LC 97-14977. 1997. write for info. (*0-7890-0027-X*) Haworth Pr.

Sexuality Education Within Comprehensive School Health Education. 1991. 14.60 (*0-89917-838-3*) Am Sch Health.

Sexuality, Evolution, & Humanity. Paul E. Simonds. 300p. (C). 1996. pap. text ed. 28.29 (*0-8403-7218-3*) Kendall-Hunt.

***Sexuality, Gender, & the Law.** William N. Eskridge & Nan D. Hunter. (University Casebook Ser.). 1185p. 1997. text ed. write for info. (*1-56662-461-4*) Foundation Pr.

***Sexuality Gods Gift.** Alice Cannon. Date not set. pap. text ed. 6.99 (*0-8054-9968-7*) Broadman.

Sexuality in America: Contemporary Perspectives on Sexual Identity, Dysfunction & Treatment. Donald A. Brown & Chanda Clary. LC 81-81824. 1981. 24.50 (*0-87650-132-3*) Pierian.

***Sexuality in America: Understanding Our Sexual Values & Behavior.** Ed. by Robert T. Francoeur et al. 300p. 1998. 29.95 (*0-8264-1003-0*) Continuum.

Sexuality in Ancient Art. Ed. by Natalie B. Kampen. (Studies in New Art History & Criticism). (Illus.). 320p. (C). 1996. text ed. 80.00 (*0-521-47099-4*); pap. text ed. 29.95 (*0-521-47683-6*) Cambridge U Pr.

Sexuality in Catullus. Brian Arkins. (Altertumswissenschaftliche Texte und Studien: Vol. 8). 272p. 1982. 37.70 (*3-487-07277-7*) G Olms Pubs.

Sexuality in Close Relationships. Ed. by Kathleen McKinney & S. Spencer. 240p. (C). 1991. text ed. 45.00 (*0-8058-0719-5*) L Erlbaum Assocs.

Sexuality in Islam. Abdelwahab Bouhdiba. 288p. (C). 1985. text ed. 55.00 (*0-7100-9608-9*, RKP) Routledge.

Sexuality in Plants & Its Hormonal Regulation. M. K. Chailakhyan & V. N. Khrianin. (Illus.). 175p. 1987. 144.95 (*0-387-96488-6*) Spr-Verlag.

Sexuality in the Confessional: A Sacrament Profaned. Stephen Haliczer. (Studies in the History of Sexuality). (Illus.). 280p. 1996. 49.95 (*0-19-509656-8*) OUP.

***Sexuality in the Field of Vision.** Jacqueline Rose. (C). 1996. pap. text ed. 15.00 (*1-85984-141-4*, Pub. by Vrso UK) Norton.

Sexuality in the Horoscope. Ed. by Noel Tyl. LC 94-38857. (New World Astrology Ser.). (Illus.). 384p. 1994. pap. 14.95 (*1-56718-865-6*) Llewellyn Pubns.

Sexuality in the Land of Oz: Searching for Safer Sex at the Movies. Wayne Wilson. 432p. (Orig.). (C). 1994. pap. text ed. 35.00 (*0-8191-9623-1*); lib. bdg. 62.50 (*0-8191-9622-3*) U Pr of Amer.

Sexuality in the Second Decade. Raymond R. Willoughby. (SRCD M Ser.: Vol. 2, No. 3). 1937. pap. 25.00 (*0-527-01496-6*) Periodicals Srv.

Sexuality in Victorian Fiction. Dennis W. Allen. LC 93-16225. (Project for Discourse & Theory Ser.: Vol. 15). 182p. 1994. pap. 12.95 (*0-8061-2583-7*) U of Okla Pr.

Sexuality in Western Art. rev. ed. Edward Lucie-Smith. LC 90-71871. (World of Art Ser.). (Illus.). 288p. 1991. pap. 14.95 (*0-500-20252-4*) Thames Hudson.

Sexuality in World Cinema, 2 vols. James L. Limbacher. LC 83-3019. 1535p. 1983. 85.00 (*0-8108-1609-1*) Scarecrow.

Sexuality Is Hereditary. Charles Gallagher. (Celebrate Love Ser.). 66p. (Orig.). 1990. pap. text ed. 3.95 (*0-911905-33-2*) Past & Mat Rene Ctr.

Sexuality, Learning Difficulties & Doing What's Right. Gavin Fairbairn et al. 176p. 1995. pap. 24.95 (*1-85346-292-6*, Pub. by D Fulton UK) Taylor & Francis.

Sexuality, Magic & Perversion. Francis King. (Illus.). 1972. 6.95 (*0-8065-0289-4*, Citadel Pr) Carol Pub Group.

Sexuality, Magic & Perversion. Francis King. 208p. 1974. reprint ed. pap. 3.45 (*0-8065-0454-4*, Citadel Pr) Carol Pub Group.

***Sexuality, Morals & Justice: A Theory of Lesbian & Gay Rights & the Law.** Nicholas Bamforth. (Lesbian & Gay Studies). 320p. 1997. 79.50 (*0-304-33145-7*) Cassell.

***Sexuality, Morals & Justice: A Theory of Lesbian & Gay Rights & the Law.** Nicholas Bamforth. (Lesbian & Gay Studies). 320p. 1997. pap. 27.50 (*0-304-33147-3*) Cassell.

Sexuality of Christ in Renaissance Art & in Modern Oblivion. 2nd rev. ed. Leo Steinberg. (Illus.). 440p. 1996. pap. text ed. 29.95 (*0-226-77187-3*); lib. bdg. 85.00 (*0-226-77186-5*) U Ch Pr.

Sexuality of Jesus. William E. Phipps. LC 96-30147. 264p. (Orig.). 1996. pap. 16.95 (*0-8298-1144-3*) Pilgrim OH.

Sexuality of Latinas. Ed. by Cherrie Moraga & Ana Castillo. (Illus.). 192p. 1991. pap. 10.95 (*0-943219-07-8*) Third Woman.

Sexuality of Men. Andy Metcalf. Ed. by Martin Humphries. (C). pap. 16.95 (*0-86104-638-2*, Pub. by Pluto Pr UK) LPC InBook.

Sexuality of Organization. Ed. by Jeff Hearn et al. 224p. (C). 1989. text ed. 45.00 (*0-8039-8230-5*); pap. text ed. 18.95 (*0-8039-8231-3*) Sage.

An Asterisk (*) at the beginning of an entry indicates that the title is appearing in BIP for the first time.

Sexuality, Politics & AIDS in Brazil: In Another World? Richard Parker & Herbert Daniel. (Social Aspects of AIDS Ser.). 196p. 1993. 75.00 (*0-7507-0135-8*, Falmer Pr); pap. 25.00 (*0-7507-0136-6*, Falmer Pr) Taylor & Francis.

Sexuality-Related Measures: A Compendium. Ed. by Clive M. Davis et al. 270p. (C). 1988. pap. text ed. 39.50 (*0-9620581-0-6*) Graphic Pub.

Sexuality, Relationships & Spiritual Growth. Agnes Ghaznavi. 200p. (Orig.). 1995. pap. 12.95 (*0-85398-382-8*) G Ronald Pub.

Sexuality, Religion & Magic: A Comprehensive Guide to Sources. Michael A. Koszegi. LC 93-41570. (Religious Information Systems Ser.: Vol. 14). 600p. 1994. text ed. 94.00 (*0-8153-0921-X*, SS856) Garland.

Sexuality, State, & Civil Society in Germany, 1700-1815. Isabel V. Hull. 488p. 1997. 45.00 (*0-8014-3126-3*) Cornell U Pr.

***Sexuality, State, & Civil Society in Germany, 1700-1815.** Isabel V. Hull. 488p. 1997. pap. 18.95 (*0-8014-8253-4*) Cornell U Pr.

Sexuality-Textuality: A Study of the Fabric of Montaigne's "Essais" Robert D. Cottrell. LC 81-2085. 197p. 1981. 42.00 (*0-8142-0326-4*) Ohio St U Pr.

Sexuality, the Bible & Science. Stephen Sapp. LC 76-62617. 152p. reprint ed. pap. 43.40 (*0-685-16263-X*, 2026976) Bks Demand.

Sexuality, the Female Gaze, & the Arts: Women, the Arts, & Society. Ed. by Ronald Dotterer & Susan R. Bowers. LC 38-14370. (Susquehanna Studies). 192p. 1993. 32.50 (*0-945636-32-6*) Susquehanna U Pr.

Sexuality Today. Gilbert D. Nass & Mary P. Fisher. 488p. (C). 1988. 41.25 (*0-86720-408-7*); teacher ed., pap. 10.00 (*0-86720-414-1*) Jones & Bartlett.

***Sexuality Today.** 7th ed. Kelly. Date not set. pap. text ed. 22.00 (*0-697-29431-5*) McGraw.

Sexuality Today: The Human Perspective. 5th ed. Gary F. Kelly. 587p. (C). 1995. per. 31.90 (*0-697-26587-0*) Brown & Benchmark.

Sexuality, Vol. 3: Incl. 1988-1992 Supplements. Ed. by Eleanor C. Goldstein. (Social Issues Resources Ser.). 1993. 95.00 (*0-89777-094-3*) Sirs Inc.

Sexuality, War & Schizophrenia: Collected Psychoanalytic Papers. Victor Tausk. Ed. & Intro. by Paul Roazen. 224p. (C). 1990. 44.95 (*0-88738-365-3*) Transaction Pubs.

Sexualized Children: Assessment & Treatment of Sexualized Children & Children Who Molest. Eliana Gil & Toni C. Johnson. LC 92-49422. 384p. (Orig.). 1993. 35.00 (*1-877872-07-5*, 0020); pap. 21.95 (*1-877872-05-9*) Launch Pr.

Sexualizing the Social: Power & Organisation of Sexuality. Ed. by Lisa Adkins & Vicki Merchant. 248p. 1996. text ed. 49.95 (*0-312-16024-0*) St Martin.

Sexualizing the Social: Power & Organisation of Sexuality. Ed. by Lisa Adkins & Vicki Merchant. 248p. 1996. text ed. 18.95 (*0-312-16025-9*) St Martin.

Sexually Abused Child: A Parent's Guide to Coping & Understanding. Kathleen Flynn Mach. LC 93-80905. 83p. 1994. pap. 9.95 (*0-9640778-0-9*) Family Insight.

Sexually Abused Children: Making Their Placement Work. D. Batty. (C). 1989. 39.00 (*0-903534-94-0*, Pub. by Brit Ag for Adopt & Fost UK) St Mut.

Sexually Abused Children in Foster Care: A Sourcebook for Foster Parents. Ed. by BT Press Staff. 103p. 1988. pap. text ed. 19.95 (*0-938510-58-4*, 25-007) Boys Town Pr.

Sexually Abused Children in Foster Care: Instructor's Manual. Ed. by BT Press Staff. 339p. 1988. ring bd. 74.95 (*0-938510-57-6*, 25-006) Boys Town Pr.

Sexually Abused Male: Application of Treatment Strategies, Vol. 2. Mic Hunter. 276p. 44.95 (*0-669-25005-8*, Lexington) Jossey-Bass.

Sexually Abused Male: Prevalence, Impact, & Treatment, Vol. 1. Mic Hunter. 304p. 44.95 (*0-669-21518-X*, Lexington) Jossey-Bass.

Sexually Adequate Female. Caprio. 1979. pap. 3.00 (*0-87980-146-8*) Wilshire.

Sexually Adequate Male. Caprio. 1979. pap. 3.00 (*0-87980-147-6*) Wilshire.

***Sexually Aggressive Children: Coming to Understand Them.** Sharon K. Araji. LC 97-4819. 264p. 1997. text ed. 48.00 (*0-8039-5175-2*); pap. text ed. 22.95 (*0-8039-5176-0*) Sage.

Sexually Balanced Relationships in the Novels of D. H. Lawrence. Leo J. Dorbad. (American University Studies: Ser. IV, Vol. 76). 157p. (C). 1990. text ed. 31.95 (*0-8204-1275-9*) P Lang Pubng.

Sexually Dangerous Poet. Walta Borawski. 1984. pap. 5.00 (*0-915480-16-6*) Good Gay.

Sexually Disturbed: Treating Psychosexual Disorders. Averil M. Doyle. LC 91-45565. 168p. 1992. text ed. 45.00 (*0-275-94294-5*, C4294, Praeger Pubs) Greenwood.

Sexually Dominant Woman: A Workbook for Nervous Beginners. Lady Green. 100p. 1994. pap. 9.95 (*0-9639763-0-3*) Greenery Pr.

Sexually Fulfilled Man. Rachel Copeland. 1983. pap. 5.00 (*0-87980-403-3*) Wilshire.

Sexually Fulfilled Woman. Rachel Copeland. 1983. pap. 5.00 (*0-87980-402-5*) Wilshire.

Sexually Mature Larval Hemiramphidae from the Hawaiian Islands. O. Schindler. (BMB Ser.). 1974. reprint ed. pap. 25.00 (*0-527-02203-9*) Periodicals Srv.

Sexually Satisfied Woman: The 5-Step Program for Getting Everything You Want in Bed. Ron Edell. 1996. pap. 10.95 (*0-452-27468-0*, Plume) NAL-Dutton.

***Sexually Transmitted Debt: Surety Experience & English Law.** Belinda Fehlberg. (Oxford Socio-Legal Studies). 344p. 1997. 75.00 (*0-19-826473-9*) OUP.

Sexually Transmitted Diseases. 2nd ed. Tsieh Sun. Date not set. write for info. (*0-938607-37-5*) Field & Wood Inc Medical.

***Sexually Transmitted Disease Booklet.** Ed. by Wallace. (C). 1993. text ed. write for info. (*0-321-01515-0*) Addson-Wesley Educ.

Sexually Transmitted Disease Control. Business Communications Co., Inc. Staff. 175p. 1984. 1,500.00 (*0-89336-374-X*, C-049) BCC.

Sexually Transmitted Diseases in Obstetrics & Gynecology. Sebastian Faro. (Illus.). 640p. 1998. text ed. 95.00 (*0-397-51303-8*) Lppncott-Raven.

Sexually Transmitted Diseases. D. Goldmeier & S. Barton. 120p. 1986. 25.95 (*0-387-17056-1*) Spr-Verlag.

Sexually Transmitted Diseases. Ed. by Melanie C. Karaffa. 400p. 1992. text ed. 49.95 (*1-878487-35-3*) Practice Mgmt Info.

Sexually Transmitted Diseases. Marjorie Little. (Encyclopedia of Health Ser.). (Illus.). 112p. (YA). (gr. 7 up). 1991. lib. bdg. 19.95 (*0-7910-0080-X*) Chelsea Hse.

Sexually Transmitted Diseases. A. McMillan & G. Scott. (Colour Aids Ser.). (Illus.). 112p. (Orig.). 1991. pap. text ed. 19.95 (*0-443-04052-4*) Churchill.

Sexually Transmitted Diseases. Alan E. Nourse. LC 91-21707. (Illus.). 128p. (YA). (gr. 9-12). 1992. lib. bdg. 22.70 (*0-531-11065-6*) Watts.

Sexually Transmitted Diseases. David Plummer et al. 120p. (Orig.). 1995. pap. 14.95 (*0-85572-249-5*, Pub. by Hill Content Pubng AT) Seven Hills Bk.

Sexually Transmitted Diseases. Charles E. Rinear. LC 85-42732. 224p. 1986. lib. bdg. 32.50 (*0-89950-185-0*) McFarland & Co.

Sexually Transmitted Diseases. 2nd ed. Ed. by King K. Holmes et al. 1232p. 1989. text ed. 135.00 (*0-07-029677-4*) McGraw-Hill HPD.

***Sexually Transmitted Diseases.** 3rd ed. Ed. by King K. Holmes et al. (Illus.). 1440p. 1997. text ed. 129.00 (*0-07-029688-X*) McGraw-Hill HPD.

Sexually Transmitted Diseases: A Clinical Syndrome Approach. Ed. by Vincent A. Spagna & Richard B. Prior. LC 85-1602. (Reproductive Medicine Ser.: No. 7). 487p. 1985. reprint ed. pap. 138.30 (*0-608-01329-3*, 2062072) Bks Demand.

Sexually Transmitted Diseases: A Guide for Clinicians. Ed. by F. Gashnait & Lawrence C. Parish. (Illus.). xiv, 388p. 1988. 121.00 (*0-387-96776-1*) Spr-Verlag.

Sexually Transmitted Diseases: A Textbook of Genito-Urinary Medicine. Csonka. (Illus.). 576p. 1990. text ed. 135.00 (*0-7020-1258-0*) Saunders.

Sexually Transmitted Diseases: Advances in Diagnosis & Treatment. Ed. by P. Elsner & A. Eichmann. (Current Problems in Dermatology Ser.: Vol. 24, 1996). (Illus.). x, 268p. 1996. 249.75 (*3-8055-6220-9*) S Karger.

***Sexually Transmitted Diseases: Epidemiology, Pathology, Diagnosis, & Treatment.** Kenneth A. Borchardt & Michael A. Noble. LC 96-39561. 1997. write for info. (*0-8493-9476-7*) CRC Pr.

Sexually Transmitted Diseases & AIDS. David Daniels et al. LC 92-2331. (Brainscan MCQs Ser.). 1993. 40.95 (*0-387-19762-1*) Spr-Verlag.

Sexually Transmitted Diseases & Appearance of Warts & Papillomas: Index of Modern Authors & Subjects with Guide for Rapid Research. Helen M. Markle. LC 90-56248. 190p. 1991. 44.50 (*1-55914-264-2*); pap. 39.50 (*1-55914-265-0*) ABBE Pubs Assn.

Sexually Transmitted Diseases & Today's Youth. Anne E. Jordheimi. 58p. (YA). (gr. 7-12). 1993. pap. 6.95 (*1-57515-026-3*) PPI Pubng.

Sexually Transmitted Diseases in Homosexual Men: Diagnosis, Treatment, & Research. Ed. by David G. Ostrow et al. LC 83-10957. (Illus.). 292p. 1983. 65.00 (*0-306-41337-X*, Plenum Pr) Plenum.

Sexually Transmitted Diseases Sourcebook. Ed. by Linda M. Ross. LC 97-17036. (Health Reference Ser.). 1997. lib. bdg. 75.00 (*0-7808-0217-9*) Omnigraphics Inc.

Sexually Transmitted Diseases, 2nd Ed. Companion Handbook. Adaora A. Adimora et al. (Companion Handbook Ser.). (Illus.). 448p. 1993. pap. text ed. 29.50 (*0-07-000380-7*) McGraw-Hill HPD.

Sexually Tuned Body: Exercises Every Woman Should Do for a Better Sex Life. Renee Delaplaine. LC 96-90218. (Illus.). 96p. (Orig.). 1997. pap. 19.95 (*0-9651927-3-3*) Winning Tch.

Sexually Unusual: Guide to Understanding & Helping. Dennis M. Dailey. LC 88-24668. (Journal of Social Work & Human Sexuality Ser.: Vol. 7, No. 1). (Illus.). 169p. 1989. pap. text ed. 14.95 (*0-918393-63-9*) Harrington Pk.

Sexually Unusual: Guide to Understanding & Helping. Ed. by Dennis M. Dailey. LC 88-15292. (Journal of Social Work & Human Sexuality: Vol. 7, No. 1). (Illus.). 169p. 1989. text ed. 39.95 (*0-86656-786-0*) Haworth Pr.

Sexually Victimized Children. David Finkelhor. LC 79-7104. 1981. pap. 16.95 (*0-02-910400-9*, Free Press) Free Pr.

***Sexualpadagogik in Gesellschaftlichem Kontext: Studien Zur Konzeptentwicklung Katholischer Sexualerziehung.** Hans-Georg Ziebertz. (Theologie & Empirie Ser.: Vol. 17). 352p. 1993. pap. 46.00 (*90-390-0054-9*, Pub. by KOK Pharos NE) Eisenbrauns.

Sexus: The Rosy Crucifixion I. Henry Miller. LC 86-35723. 506p. 1987. pap. 13.95 (*0-8021-5180-9*, Grove) Grove-Atltic.

Sexy Bodies: The Strange Carnalities of Feminism. Ed. by Elizabeth A. Grosz & Elspeth Probyn. 320p. (gr. 13). 1995. pap. 16.95 (*0-415-09803-3*) Routledge.

Sexy Bodies: The Strange Carnalities of Feminism. Ed. by Elizabeth A. Grosz & Elspeth Probyn. LC 94-36929. 320p. (C). (gr. 13). 1995. text ed. 62.95 (*0-415-09802-5*) Routledge.

***Sexy Crotchword Puzzles.** Don Grant. 72p. (Orig.). 1997. pap. 5.95 (*1-57644-029-X*) CCC Pubns.

Sexy Dressing Etc. Essays on the Power & Politics of Cultural Identity. Duncan Kennedy. 272p. (Orig.). (C). 1995. pap. text ed. 14.95 (*0-674-80297-7*) HUP.

Sexy Dressing Etcetera. Duncan Kennedy. LC 93-1206. 272p. 1993. 24.95 (*0-674-80294-2*) HUP.

Sexy Legs: How to Get Them & How to Keep Them. Susan L. Peterson & James A. Peterson. LC 83-80741. (Orig.). 1984. pap. 6.95 (*0-88011-162-3*) S&S Trade.

Sexy Robots: Genkosha (Airbrush, Erotic Female Robots) (Illus.). 1990. 29.95 (*4-7683-0001-4*) Bks Nippan.

Seya's Song. Ron Hirschi. LC 92-5029. (Illus.). 32p. (J). (ps up). 1992. text ed. 14.95 (*0-912365-62-5*) Sasquatch Bks.

Seya's Song. Ron Hirschi. (Illus.). 32p. (J). (gr. 1 up). 1993. reprint ed. pap. 7.95 (*0-912365-91-9*) Sasquatch Bks.

Seybold Professional Guide to Adobe Photoshop 2.5. Fink. 1993. 29.95 (*1-56276-081-5*, Ziff-Davis Pr) Que.

Seychelles. George Bennett. (World Bibliographical Ser.). 1993. lib. bdg. 64.00 (*1-85109-182-3*) ABC-CLIO.

***Seychelles.** Sarah Carpin. 232p. 1997. pap. 16.95 (*0-8442-4855-X*) NTC Pub Grp.

Seychelles. Kathleen Trayte. LC 95-22475. (Country Guide Series Report from the AACRAO-AID Project). 1996. 20.00 (*0-929851-58-7*) Am Assn Coll Registrars.

Seychelles. Peter Vine. 208p. (C). 1995. 84.00 (*0-907151-83-3*, Pub. by IMMEL Pubng UK) St Mut.

Seychelles. rev. ed. Camerapix & Spectrum Guides Staff. (Spectrum Guides Ser.). (Illus.). 364p. (Orig.). 1993. pap. 19.95 (*0-86190-405-2*) Hunter NJ.

Seychelles Creole-French Dictionary: Dictionnaire Creole (Seychellois)-Francais. Danielle D'Offay & G. Lionnet. 422p. (CRP & FRE.). 1982. 75.00 (*0-8288-1095-8*, F35790) Fr & Eur.

***Seydou Keita: African Photographer.** Pref. by Andre Magnin. (Illus.). 288p. 1997. 49.95 (*3-931141-46-2*, Pub. by Scalo Pubs) Dist Art Pubs.

Seyidu Kamara Ka Donkiliw. Bourama Soumaoro et al. (Occasional Papers in Mande Studies). 101p. (Orig.). 1976. pap. text ed. 7.00 (*0-941934-18-7*) Indiana Africa.

Seymour: A Pictorial History. Elizabeth Rebber. (Indiana Pictorial History Ser.). (Illus.). 1990. write for info. (*0-943963-24-9*) G Bradley.

Seymour: Past & Present. Hollis A. Campbell et al. (Illus.). 613p. 1995. reprint ed. lib. bdg. 64.00 (*0-8328-4990-1*) Higginson Bk Co.

Seymour - An Introduction see Raise High the Roof Beam, Carpenters & Seymour: An Introduction

Seymour & Opal. Nicole Jussek. 1996. lib. bdg. 16.99 (*0-679-96722-2*) Random.

Seymour & Opal. Nicole Jussek. 1996. 15.00 (*0-679-86722-8*) Random.

Seymour Bleu: A Space Odyssey. Deeter. LC 96-8584. (J). 1997. 16.00 (*0-689-80137-8*, S&S Bks Young Read) S&S Childrens.

Seymour Dexter, Union Army: Journal & Letters of Civil War Service in Company K, 23rd New York Volunteer Regiment of Elmira; with Illustrations. Seymour Dexter. Ed. by Carl A. Morrell. LC 96-33265. (Illus.). 112p. 1996. lib. bdg. 24.50 (*0-7864-0197-4*) McFarland & Co.

***Seymour Duncan's Guide to Guitar Electronics.** Seymour W. Duncan. (Illus.). 300p. (Orig.). 1997. pap. 29.95 (*1-884883-07-9*) Vintage Guitar.

Seymour, Jr. Henry H. Sloan. (Illus.). 52p. (Orig.). (J). 1994. pap. 7.95 (*1-888181-04-4*, Bks of Nature) NW Law Pubng.

Seymour/Carraher's Polymer Chemistry. 4th ed. Charles E. Carraher. LC 96-22846. (Undergraduate Chemistry Ser.: No. 13). 720p. 1996. 59.75 (*0-8247-9752-3*) Dekker.

Seymour's Customary Law in Southern Africa. 5th ed. J. C. Bekker. 520p. 1989. pap. 50.00 (*0-7021-2219-X*, Pub. by Juta SA) Gaunt.

Sezz Who? John Lomax. LC 73-83916. 1974. 21.95 (*0-87949-021-7*) Ashley Bks.

SF in Dimension: A Book of Explorations. 2nd ed. Alexei Panshin & Cory Panshin. LC 80-68572. 1980. pap. 12.00 (*0-911682-24-4*) Advent.

SF Published in Nineteen Seventy-Seven. Joanne Burger. (Orig.). 1978. pap. 4.00 (*0-916188-08-6*) J Burger.

SF Restaurants & Gourmet - 96: For Northern California. Andre Gayot. 368p. 1996. 12.00 (*1-881066-21-5*) Gault Millau.

SF: the Other Side of Realism. Ed. by Thomas D. Clareson. 370p. 1971. 15.95 (*0-87972-022-0*); pap. 9.95 (*0-87972-023-9*) Bowling Green Univ Popular Press.

SF 171: The Federal Employment Application Form. 2nd ed. Pauline J. Heaton. LC 94-32838. 1994. 7.95 (*0-671-89156-1*, Arco) Macmillan Gen Ref.

SFBRI: Science Fiction Book Review Index, Vols. 1-10. Incl. Vol. 1. . Ed. by H. W. Hall. LC 72-625320. 1970. lib. bdg. 22.00 (*0-89370-066-5*); Vol. 2. . Ed. by H. W. Hall. LC 72-625320. 1971. lib. bdg. 22.00 (*0-89370-067-3*); Vol. 3. . Ed. by H. W. Hall. LC 72-625320. 1972. lib. bdg. 22.00 (*0-89370-068-1*); Vol. 4. . Ed. by H. W. Hall. LC 72-625320. 1973. lib. bdg. 22.00 (*0-89370-069-X*); Vol. 5. . Ed. by H. W. Hall. LC 72-625320. 1974. lib. bdg. 22.00 (*0-89370-070-3*); Vol. 6. . Ed. by H. W. Hall. LC 72-625320. 1975. lib. bdg. 22.00 (*0-89370-071-1*); Vol. 7. . Ed. by H. W. Hall. LC 72-625320. 1976. lib. bdg. 22.00 (*0-89370-072-X*); Vol. 8. . Ed. by H. W. Hall. LC 72-625320. 1977. lib. bdg. 22.00 (*0-89370-073-8*); Vol. 9. . Ed. by H. W. Hall. LC 72-625320. 1978. lib. bdg. 22.00 (*0-89370-074-6*); Vol. 10. . Ed. by Hal W. Hall. LC 72-625320. 1980. lib. bdg. 22.00 (*0-89370-075-4*); LC 72-625320. 64p. Set lib. bdg. write for info. (*0-318-51157-6*) Borgo Pr.

SFBRI: Science Fiction Book Review Index, 1975, Vol. 6. Hal W. Hall. LC 72-625320. 1976. 5.50 (*0-935064-01-X*) SFBRI.

SFBRI: Science Fiction Book Review Index, 1981, Vol. 12. 46p. 1981. 7.50 (*0-935064-07-9*) SFBRI.

SFBRI: Science Fiction Book Review Index, 1982, Vol. 13. Ed. by Hal W. Hall. LC 72-625320. 50p. 1983. pap. 7.50 (*0-935064-08-7*) SFBRI.

SFBRI: Science Fiction Book Review Index, 1983, Vol. 14. Ed. by Hal W. Hall. LC 72-625320. 61p. (Orig.). 1984. pap. 7.50 (*0-935064-14-1*) SFBRI.

***SFFWA Fantasy Hall of Fame.** Robert Silverberg. mass mkt. write for info. (*0-06-105456-9*, HarperPrism) HarpC.

***SFFWA Fantasy Hall of Fame.** Ed. by Robert Silverberg. Date not set. mass mkt. write for info. (*0-06-105215-9*, HarperPrism) HarpC.

SFI Reduction & Prediction of Natural Disasters-H. John Rundle. 320p. (C). 1996. 55.95 (*0-201-87048-7*) Addison-Wesley.

Sforno: Commentary on the Torah. Raphael Pellcovitz. (ArtScroll Mesorah Ser.). 1993. 31.99 (*0-89906-238-5*) Mesorah Pubns.

Sforza Hours: Manuscripts in the British Library. Mark Evans. 1992. pap. 21.95 (*1-56131-038-7*) New Amsterdam Bks.

Sforzando! Music Medicine for String Players. American String Teachers Association Staff. Ed. by Anne Mischakoff. 1985. pap. text ed. 7.95 (*0-89917-462-0*) Am String Tchrs.

S

SG: Introductory Geology. 2nd ed. Intelecom Staff. 528p. (C). 1996. per., pap. text ed. 32.49 (*0-7872-0125-1*) Kendall-Hunt.

SG Chemistry. Timberlake. (C). 1990. pap. 11.50 (*0-06-046661-8*, PL) HarpC.

SG Economics. Weiler. (C). 1990. pap. 15.50 (*0-06-047004-6*, PL) HarpC.

SG Macroeconomics. Weiler. (C). 1990. pap. 14.00 (*0-06-047002-X*, PL) HarpC.

SG Microeconomics. Weiler. (C). 1990. pap. 13.00 (*0-06-047003-8*, PL) HarpC.

SG Sociology. Stebbins. (C). 1990. pap. 15.00 (*0-06-046420-8*, PL) HarpC.

S'gana: The Black Whale. Sue Stauffacher. LC 92-17573. 224p. (J). (gr. 2-7). 1992. 15.95 (*0-88240-396-6*) Alaska Northwest.

***Sganarelle: A Farce in One Act by Moliere.** Tr. & Adapted by David Frieze. 24p. 1996. pap. 3.25 (*0-87440-028-7*) Bakers Plays.

SGML: The Billion Dollar Secret. Chet Ensign. 213p. (C). 1996. pap. text ed. 29.95 (*0-13-226705-5*) P-H.

***SGML & HTML Explained.** Martin Bryan. 1997. pap. text ed. 34.95 (*0-201-40394-3*) Addison-Wesley.

***SGML & the DSSSL Standard.** Kate Hamilton. (C). 1997. text ed. 33.75 (*0-13-652371-4*) P-H.

***SGML Buyer's Guide.** Goldfarb. 1997. pap. text ed. 55.00 (*0-13-681511-1*) P-H.

SGML Elements of Style. Ziff-Davis Press Development Staff. 1996. pap. text ed. 29.99 (*1-56276-414-4*, Ziff-Davis Pr) Que.

***SGML FAQ Book: Understanding the Foundation of HTML & XML.** Steven J. Derose. LC 97-20857. (Electronic Publishing Ser.). 1997. write for info. (*0-7923-9943-9*) Kluwer Ac.

***SGML for Dummies.** Dummies Tech Press Staff. 1997. pap. 29.99 (*0-7645-0175-5*) IDG Bks.

***SGML for Software.** Sean McGrath. LC 97-20192. 400p. (C). 1997. text ed. 55.00 (*0-13-488967-3*) P-H.

SGML Handbook. AP Professional Staff. 1996. pap. text ed. 29.95 (*0-12-522450-8*, AP Prof) Acad Pr.

SGML Handbook. Charles F. Goldfarb. (Illus.). 550p. 1991. 95.00 (*0-19-853737-9*) OUP.

SGML Implementation Guide: A Blueprint for SGML Migration. Brian E. Travis & Dale C. Waldt. LC 95-21239. 1995. write for info. (*3-540-57730-0*) Spr-Verlag.

SGML Implementation Guide: A Blueprint for SGML Migration. Dale C. Waldt & Brian E. Travis. (Illus.). 522p. 1996. 54.00 (*0-387-57730-0*) Spr-Verlag.

***SGML on the Block.** Pamela L. Gennusa. (C). 1997. pap. text ed. 31.50 (*0-13-190372-1*) P-H.

***SGML on the Web: Small Steps Beyond H. T. M. L.** Yuri Rubinsky. LC 96-52360. 501p. 1997. pap. text ed. 44.95 incl. cd-rom (*0-13-519984-0*) P-H.

SGML Primer. Spivak. (DF - Computer Applications Ser.). 1996. pap. 14.95 (*0-7895-0194-5*) S-W Pub.

Sgt. Pepper's Lonely Hearts Club Band: With Notes & Tablatures. 88p. 1992. otabind 19.95 (*0-7935-2026-6*, 00694863) H Leonard.

***Sgt. York: His Life, Legend & Legacy: The Remarkable Untold Story of Sgt. Alvin C. York.** John Perry. LC 97-15736. (Illus.). 320p. 1997. pap. 16.99 (*0-8054-6074-8*) Broadman.

***SGTE Casebook: Thermodynamics at Work.** Ed. by K. Hack. (Materials Modelling Ser.). 227p. 1996. 70.00 (*0-901716-74-X*, Pub. by Inst Materials UK) Ashgate Pub Co.

Sh! Sexual Harassment. Sivasailam Thiagarajan. (Games by Thiagi Ser.). 39p. (Orig.). 1995. pap. 20.00 (*0-87425-999-1*) HRD Press.

***Sha-Girls '92.** Hana Kaiga No. 1992. pap. text ed. 29.95 (*4-89011-297-9*) Bks Nippan.

***Sha-Girls '93.** Hana Kaiga No. 1993. pap. text ed. 29.95 (*4-89011-311-8*) Bks Nippan.

***Sha-Girls '94.** Hana Kaiga No. 1994. pap. text ed. 29.95 (*4-89011-330-4*) Bks Nippan.

***Sha'Alos Ve'Tshuvos Admur Hazoken.** Levi Bitstrisky. 512p. (HEB.). Date not set. 17.00 (*0-8266-5511-4*) Kehot Pubn Soc.

***Sha'ar Hakolel.** 3rd ed. Abraham D. Lauut. 476p. (HEB.). 1990. reprint ed. 17.00 (*0-8266-5341-3*) Kehot Pubn Soc.

Shaar Hayichud Veha Emunah - Iggeret Hateshuvah. Schneur Zalman Baruchovitch. Ed. by Uri Kaploun. Tr. by Sholom B. Wineberg. (Lessons in Tanya Ser.: Vol. 3). 320p. 1991. 17.00 (*0-8266-0543-5*) Kehot Pubn Soc.

An Asterisk (*) at the beginning of an entry indicates that the title is appearing in BIP for the first time.

Shaare Armon see Palace Gates: Parables for the Days of Awe

Shaare Rahmin: Sermon Material for the High Holidays in Hebrew. P. S. Pollak. 10.50 (0-87559-104-3) Shalom.

Sha'arei Talmon: Studies in the Bible, Qumran, & the Ancient Near East, Presented to Shemaryahu Talmon. Ed. by Michael Fishbane et al. LC 91-3286. xlix, 596p. (ENG & HEB.). 1991. 59.50 (0-931464-61-7) Eisenbrauns.

***Shaarei T'Shuva.** Dov B. Schneersohn. LC 86-2718. 478p. (HEB.). 1995. 25.00 (0-8266-5575-0) Kehot Pubn Soc.

Shabanu: A Study Guide. Barbara Reeves. Ed. by J. Friedland & R. Kessler. (Novel-Ties Ser.). (YA). (gr. 6-9). 1996. pap. text ed. 15.95 (1-56982-672-2) Lrn Links.

Shabanu: Daughter of the Wind. Suzanne F. Staples. LC 89-2714. (Illus.). 256p. (J). (gr. 7 up). 1989. 18.00 (0-394-84815-2); lib. bdg. 18.99 (0-394-94815-7) Knopf Bks Yng Read.

***Shabbat.** David Sokoloff. (Illus.). 12p. (J). (ps-1). 1998. bds. write for info. (0-614-30938-7) Jewish Educ Toys.

Shabbat: A Family Service. Judith Z. Abrams. LC 91-31640. (Illus.). 24p. (Orig.). (J). (gr. k-3). 1992. pap. text ed. 3.95 (0-929371-29-1) Kar-Ben.

Shabbat Can Be. Audrey F. Marcus & Raymond A. Zwerin. (Illus.). (J). (gr. k-3). 1979. 10.95 (0-8074-0023-8, 102560) UAHC.

Shabbat Cantata see Kadima Kesher Series

Shabbat Fun for Little Hands. Illus. by Sally Springer. 32p. (J). (ps-2). 1994. student ed. 3.95 (0-929371-35-6) Kar-Ben.

Shabbat Haggadah for Celebration & Study. Michael Strassfeld. LC 80-83430. 124p. 1980. pap. 5.50 (0-87495-025-2) Am Jewish Comm.

Shabbat Morning Service Bk. 1: The Shema & Its Blessings. Roberta O. Baum. 86p. 1985. teacher ed., pap. 14.95 (0-87441-430-X) Behrman.

Shabbat Morning Service Bk. 1: The Shema & Its Blessings. Comment by Jules Harlow. 96p. 1985. pap. text ed. 7.25 (0-87441-417-2) Behrman.

Shabbat Morning Service Bk. 2: The Shabbat Amidah. Roberta O. Baum. 109p. 1986. By Roberta O. Baum. teacher ed., pap. 14.95 (0-87441-437-7) Behrman.

Shabbat Morning Service Bk. 2: The Shabbat Amidah. Roberta O. Baum. 96p. 1986. pap. text ed. 7.25 (0-87441-432-6) Behrman.

Shabbat Morning Service Bk. 3: Torah Service & Selected Concluding Prayers. Roberta O. Baum. 7.25 (0-87441-449-0); teacher ed., pap. 14.95 (0-87441-468-7) Behrman.

Shabbat Prayers, Vol. 2. Nissan Mindel. (My Prayer Ser.). 208p. 1989. reprint ed. 12.00 (0-8266-0311-4, Merkos LInyonei Chinuch) Kehot Pubn Soc.

***Shabbat Reader: Universe of Cosmic Joy.** D. Peretz Elkins. LC 97-13469. 1997. pap. write for info. (0-8074-0631-7, 386053) UAHC.

Shabbat Seder. Ron Wolfson. LC 96-46454. 272p. 1996. pap. text ed. 16.95 (1-879045-90-7) Jewish Lights.

Shabbat Seder Booklet of Blessings & Songs. Ron Wolfson. 1996. pap. text ed. 5.00 (1-879045-91-5) Jewish Lights.

Shabbat Seder Teacher's Guide. Ron Wolfson. 1996. pap. text ed. 4.95 (1-879045-92-3) Jewish Lights.

***Shabbat Series: Excellence in Education for Jewish Women.** 224p. (Orig.). 1997. pap. 12.95 (1-889454-50-8) Womans Inst-Cont Jewish Ed.

Shabbat Shalom. Roberta O. Baum. (Illus.). (J). 1995. pap. 4.95 (0-87441-520-9) Behrman.

Shabbat Shalom. Judye Groner & Madeline Wikler. LC 88-83568. (Illus.). 12p. (J). (ps). 1989. bds. 4.95 (0-930494-91-1) Kar-Ben.

Shabbat Shalom: A Renewed Encounter with the Sabbath. Pinchas H. Peli. 1989. 17.95 (0-910250-15-4) Sure Seller.

Shabbath, 3 vols. (ENG & HEB.). 45.00 (0-910218-53-6) Bennet Pub.

Shabbatt Seder: The Sabbath Seder. Ron Wolfson. (Art of Jewish Living Ser.). (Illus.). 1985. teacher ed. 4.95 (0-935665-01-3); pap. 14.95 (0-935665-00-5); audio 4.00 (0-935665-02-1) Fed Jewish Mens Clubs.

Shabbes Goy: A Study in Halakhic Flexibility. Jacob Katz. LC 88-13528. 250p. 1992. reprint ed. pap. text ed. 18.95 (0-8276-0413-0) JPS Phila.

Shabbos. Shimon Finkelman. (Holiday Ser.). 1991. 18.99 (0-89906-601-1); pap. 15.99 (0-89906-602-X) Mesorah Pubns.

***Shabbos Home.** Simcha B. Cohen. pap. 15.99 (0-89906-335-7, HO1P) Mesorah Pubns.

***Shabbos Home, Vol. 1.** Simcha B. Cohen. 18.99 (0-89906-334-9, HO1H) Mesorah Pubns.

Shabbos Is Coming. Ruth Lipson. (Sifrei Rimon Ser.). 1985. pap. 2.95 (0-87306-383-X) Feldheim.

Shabbos Kitchen. S. B. Cohen. 1992. 18.99 (0-89906-882-0); pap. 15.99 (0-89906-883-9) Mesorah Pubns.

***Shabbos Stories: Tales with a Message for Every Week of the Year.** Shimon Finkelman. 17.99 (0-89906-526-0, SSTH); pap. 14.99 (0-89906-527-9, SSTP) Mesorah Pubns.

Shabby Chic: Simple Living, the Comfort of Age & the Beauty of Imperfection. Rachel Ashwell & Glynis Costin. LC 96-32371. (Illus.). 288p. 1996. 30.00 (0-06-098204-7) HarpC.

Shabby Genteel Story & Other Writings. William M. Thackery. Ed. by D. J. Taylor. 384p. 1993. pap. text ed. 8.95 (0-460-87289-3, Everyman's Classic Lib) C E Tuttle.

Shabby Tiger. large type ed. Howard Spring. 1993. 39.95 (0-7066-1009-1, Pub. by Remploy Pr CN) St Mut.

Shabbytown Calendar. Thomas W. Shapcott. 104p. 1988. pap. 14.95 (0-7022-0959-7, Pub. by Univ Queensland Pr AT) Intl Spec Bk.

Shabik'eshchee Village: A Late Basket Maker Site in the Chaco Canyon, New Mexico. Frank Roberts, Jr. (Bureau of American Ethnology Bulletins Ser.). 164p. 1995. lib. bdg. 79.00 (0-7812-4092-1) Rprt Serv.

Shabono. large type ed. Florinda Donner. 480p. 1984. 25.99 (0-7089-1126-9) Ulverscroft.

Shabono: A Visit to a Remote & Magical World in the South American Rainforest. Florinda Donner. LC 91-55379. 320p. 1992. pap. 12.00 (0-06-250242-5) Harper SF.

Shack & Back. Michael Crowley. (J). (ps-3). 1993. 14.95 (0-316-16231-0) Little.

Shackelford's Surgery of the Alimentary Tract, 5 Vol. Set. 4th ed. George D. Zuidema. (Illus.). 3200p. 1995. text ed. 459.00 (0-7216-4982-3) Saunders.

***Shackled.** Ray Garton. 576p. Date not set. mass mkt. 5.99 (0-553-29891-7) Bantam.

Shackles: A Novel. Armijn Pane. Tr. by John H. McGlynn. LC 84-18930. (Monographs in International Studies, Southeast Asia Ser.: No. 67). 136p. reprint ed. pap. 38.80 (0-7837-6478-2, 2046483) Bks Demand.

Shackleton's Boat Journey. F. A. Worsley. (Illus.). 224p. 1987. reprint ed. pap. 12.95 (0-393-30376-4) Norton.

Shacksper of Stratford: A Monumental Design. Paul M. Plunkett. 1995. 13.95 (0-533-11068-8) Vantage.

***Shad Treatment: A Novel.** Garrett Epps. LC 97-15062. (Virginia Bookshelf Ser.). 444p. 1997. pap. 17.95 (0-8139-1776-X) U Pr of Va.

Shadd: The Life & Times of Mary Shadd Cary. Jim Bearden & Linda Butler. (Illus.). 256p. text ed. 19.95 (0-919600-76-X, Pub. by NC Press CN) U of Toronto Pr.

***Shade.** Judy Hogan. Ed. by Lucille A. McClelland. (Illus.). 391p. 1997. pap. 16.95 (0-9652673-0-X) Black Oaks.

Shade & Color with Water-Conserving Plants. James Walter & Balbir Backhaus. LC 91-26607. (Illus.). 240p. 1992. 39.95 (0-88192-214-5) Timber.

Shade & Ornamental Trees: Their Origins & History. Li Hui-Lin. LC 96-26742. (Illus.). 288p. (Orig.). 1996. reprint ed. pap. 15.95 (0-8122-1605-9) U of Pa Pr.

Shade Book. rev. ed. Judy Lindahl. (Illus.). 148p. pap. 9.95 (0-9603032-2-7) Lindahl.

Shade Gardening. A. Cort Sinnes. Ed. by Ken Burke. LC 82-82159. (Illus.). 96p. (Orig.). 1982. pap. 9.95 (0-89721-005-0) Ortho Info.

Shade Gardening. Time-Life Books Editors. Ed. by Janet Cave. LC 95-35804. (Time-Life Complete Gardener Ser.). (Illus.). 160p. 1995. write for info. (0-7835-4107-4) Time-Life.

Shade Gardening. rev. ed. A. Cort Sinnes. Ed. by Jennifer Bennett. LC 95-74576. 96p. (Orig.). 1996. pap. 9.95 (0-89721-288-6) Meredith Bks.

***Shade Gardens.** Warren Schultz. LC 96-42370. (For Your Garden Ser.). 1997. write for info. (1-56799-325-7, Friedman-Fairfax) M Friedman Pub Grp Inc.

Shade Gardens: A Harrowsmith Gardener's Guide. Ed. by Brenda Cole. (Illus.). 96p. 1993. pap. 12.95 (0-921820-63-1, Pub. by Camden Hse CN) Firefly Bks Ltd.

Shade of His Hand. Oswald Chambers. 1979. pap. 10.95 (0-87508-295-5) Chr Lit.

Shade of His Hand. Oswald Chambers. 176p. 1991. pap. 10.99 (0-929239-28-8) Discovery Hse Pubs.

Shade of Homer: A Study in Modern Greek Poetry. David Ricks. 208p. (C). 1990. text ed. 54.95 (0-521-36663-1) Cambridge U Pr.

***Shade of Memmnon.** Gregory L. Walker. (Illus.). 500p. 1998. 24.95 (0-614-30566-7) Pebble Bch Pr Ltd.

***Shade of Pale.** Kihn. LC 97-14693. 1997. 21.95 (0-312-86046-3) St Martin.

Shade of the Raintree. Laurence Lockridge. Date not set. pap. 23.00 (0-670-84136-6) Viking Penguin.

Shade of The Raintree: The Life & Death of Ross Lockridge, Author of Raintree County. Laurence Lockridge. Date not set. pap. 23.00 (0-7139-9111-9) Viking Penguin.

Shade of the Raintree: The Life & Death of Ross Lockridge, Jr. Laurence Lockridge. (Illus.). 528p. 1995. pap. 14.95 (0-14-015871-5, Penguin Bks) Viking Penguin.

Shade of the Tree. Piers Anthony. 352p. 1987. pap. 3.95 (0-8125-3103-5) Tor Bks.

Shade Trees for the Central & Northern United States & Canada. Sharon Yiesla & Floyd A. Giles. (Illus.). 1991. pap. 28.80 (0-87563-379-X) Stipes.

Shades. Sharman Macdonald. 96p. (Orig.). 1993. pap. 8.95 (0-571-16884-1) Faber & Faber.

Shades. Heather McHugh. LC 87-21179. (Wesleyan Poetry Ser.). 83p. 1988. pap. 11.95 (0-8195-1137-4, Wesleyan Univ Pr) U Pr of New Eng.

Shades: An Anthology of Fiction by Gay Men of African Descent. Ed. by Bruce Morrow & Charles H. Rowell. LC 95-48795. 400p. (Orig.). 1996. pap. 12.00 (0-380-78305-3) Avon.

Shades & Shadows: An Anthology of Modern Poetry. Ed. by Louisa Persing. (Illus.). 1973. 5.50 (0-686-05276-5) Palomar.

***Shade's Children.** Garth Nix. LC 97-3841. (Illus.). 288p. (J). (gr. 1-4). 1997. 15.95 (0-06-027324-0); lib. bdg. 15.89 (0-06-027325-9) HarpC Child Bks.

Shades of a Desperado. Sharon Sala. 1997. mass mkt. 3.99 (0-373-07757-2, 1-07757-7) Silhouette.

Shades of Aphrodite. large type ed. Jean Marsh. (Linford Romance Library). 272p. 1994. pap. 15.99 (0-7089-7515-1, Linford) Ulverscroft.

Shades of Beauty. A. Cinnamon Brown. LC 95-78543. (Illus.). 25p. (J). (gr. k-4). 1996. 14.95 (1-55523-761-4) Winston-Derek.

***Shades of Black: Conrad Black & the World's Fastest Growing Press Empire.** Richard Siklos. 1997. 24.95 (0-433-39749-7) Buttrwrth-Heinemann.

Shades of Black: Diversity in African-American Identity. William E. Cross. 1991. pap. 19.95 (0-87722-949-X) Temple U Pr.

***Shades of Blue & Gray: An Introductory Military History of the Civil War.** Herman Hattaway. LC 97-4455. (Illus.). 296p. 1997. pap. 29.95 (0-8262-1107-0) U of Mo Pr.

Shades of Brown: New Perspectives on School Desegregation. Ed. by Derrick Bell. LC 80-21877. 160p. 1980. pap. 45.60 (0-7837-7449-4, 2049041) Bks Demand.

***Shades of Buck.** Frances Moschberger. 1997. mass mkt. 4.99 (1-55197-267-0, Pub. by Comnwlth Pub CN) Partners Pubs Grp.

***Shades of Comfort: Decorative Window Treatments for an Energy Efficient Home. Jill Owen. Ed. by Barbara Weiland. (Illus.). 88p. (Orig.). 1996. pap. 9.95 (0-9654466-0-3) Warm Co.**
With increasing national & global emphasis on the environment, people are looking for more ways to preserve the world's resources. The best way to conserve natural resources is to begin with the home & windows are responsible for the greatest amount of energy loss in the home. More people are looking at energy efficiency along with price, appearance & durability when considering window treatments. SHADES OF COMFORT is a guide for making decorative window treatments for an energy efficient home. Complete step-by-step instructions for measuring, making & installing insulated shades are included. Four styles (Roman, Hobbled, Balloon, & Side-draw shades) will fit any window. These insulated shades reduce heat loss through windows during the winter up to 83% & reduce heat gain in the summer by 79%. They also darken rooms for daytime napping & reduce noise pollution. SHADES OF COMFORT includes timesaving no sew tips, handy worksheets & dozens of creative ideas for adding warmth & style to any home. Order from The Warm Company, 954 East Union Street, Seattle, WA 98122. Phone: 1-800-234-WARM, FAX: 206-320-0974. ***Publisher Provided Annotation.***

***Shades of Conscience: Poems.** Doyle Spence. LC 96-45643. 76p. 1997. pap. 12.95 (0-7734-2703-1, Mellen Poetry Pr) E Mellen.

Shades of Darkness: More of the Ghostly Best Stories of Robert Westall. Robert Westall. LC 93-42229. (J). 1994. 17.00 (0-374-36758-2) FS&G.

Shades of Darkness: Poems. Kenrick E. Mose. LC 92-40838. 1993. pap. 12.95 (0-7734-0029-X, Mellen Poetry Pr) E Mellen.

Shades of Death. Kazuo Koike. 1996. pap. 19.95 (1-56931-061-0) Viz Commns Inc.

Shades of Death, Pt. 1: Crying Freeman Graphic Novel. Kazuo Koike. Ed. by Seiji Horibuchi. Tr. by Satoru Fujii from JPN. (Illus.). 212p. (Orig.). (YA). (gr. 12 up). 1991. pap. 14.95 (0-929279-75-1) Viz Commns Inc.

Shades of Death, Pt. 2: Crying Freeman Graphic Novel. Kazuo Koike. Ed. by Seiji Horibuchi. Tr. by Satoru Fujii from JPN. (Illus.). 212p. (Orig.). (YA). (gr. 12 up). 1992. pap. 14.95 (0-929279-76-X) Viz Commns Inc.

Shades of Death, Pt. 3: Crying Freeman Graphic Novel. Kazuo Koike. Ed. by Seiji Horibuchi. Tr. by Satoru Fujii from JPN. (Illus.). 212p. (YA). (gr. 12 up). 1992. pap. 14.95 (0-929279-77-8) Viz Commns Inc.

Shades of Deception. Linda Faye. LC 95-78974. 256p. (Orig.). (C). 1995. pap. 10.95 (0-9647689-3-3) Little Sistr Pubns.

***Shades of Difference.** Padraig O'Malley. 1998. pap. 29.95 (0-670-85233-3) Viking Penguin.

Shades of Familiar. Caroline Burnes. 1994. mass mkt. 2.99 (0-373-22277-7, 1-22277-7) Harlequin Bks.

Shades of Fortune: A Novel. Stephen Birmingham. 400p. 1989. 18.95 (0-316-09655-5) Little.

***Shades of Freedom: Racial Politics & Presumptions of the American Legal Process.** A. Leon Higginbotham, Jr. LC 96-8718. 352p. 1996. 30.00 (0-19-503822-3) OUP.

Shades of Grace. Barbara Delinsky. LC 95-46709. 368p. 1996. 22.00 (0-06-017781-0) HarpC.

***Shades of Grace.** Barbara Delinsky. 1996. pap. 6.99 (0-06-109282-7, Harp PBks) HarpC.

Shades of Grace. large type ed. Barbara Delinsky. 535p. 1996. 25.95 (0-7838-1642-1, GK Hall) Thorndike Pr.

Shades of Gray. Ronald Bernier. 168p. (Orig.). 1993. pap. 7.95 (1-56043-794-4) Destiny Image.

Shades of Gray. Steve Bristol. (Inter Acta Ser.). (Illus.). 4p. (C). 1994. student ed., ring bd. 3.25 (1-885702-14-0, 741-007s, Inter Acta) WSN Pr.

Shades of Gray. Steve Bristol. (Inter Acta Ser.). (Illus.). 6p. (C). 1994. teacher ed., ring bd. 1.25 (1-885702-15-9, 741-007t, Inter Acta) WSN Pr.

Shades of Gray. Carolyn Reeder. 160p. (J). 1991. pap. 4.50 (0-380-71232-6, Camelot) Avon.

Shades of Gray. Carolyn Reeder. LC 89-31976. 160p. (J). (gr. 3-7). 1989. lib. bdg. 15.00 (0-02-775810-9, Mac Bks Young Read) S&S Childrens.

Shades of Gray. Kathleen Ricter. LC 95-91055. 1996. 10.95 (0-533-11842-5) Vantage.

Shades of Gray. Duncan Searl. Ed. by J. Friedland & R. Kessler. (Novel-Ties Ser.). 1995. student ed., pap. text ed. 15.95 (1-56982-299-9) Lrn Links.

***Shades of Gray: A Primer on Intergenerational Equity in the Era of Entitlement Reform.** Lior J. Strahilevitz. LC 97-10360. 1997. write for info. (0-87772-374-5) UCB IGS.

Shades of Gray: Dispatches from the Modern South. John Egerton. LC 91-12391. 261p. 1991. 24.95 (0-8071-1705-6) La State U Pr.

Shades of Green. Shree Devi. (Writers Workshop Redbird Ser.). 1975. 8.00 (0-88253-632-X); pap. text ed. 4.00 (0-88253-631-1) Ind-US Inc.

***Shades of Green.** Contrib. by Anne Harve. (Illus.). (J). 4.98 (0-8317-3263-6) Smithmark.

***Shades of Green: The Clash of Agricultural Science & Environmental Science.** J. S. Kidd & Renee A. Kidd. LC 97-15968. (Science & Society Ser.). 1997. write for info. (0-8160-3583-0) Facts on File.

***Shades of Grey, Vol. 1.** Barrington Watson. Ed. by Joanna Henning. (Illus.). 200p. 1996. 60.00 (1-883545-03-X) Shields Pub.

Shades of Grey: Glasgow 1956-1987. William McIlvanney. (Illus.). 224p. 1993. 34.95 (1-85158-047-6, Pub. by Mnstream UK) Trafalgar.

Shades of Hades: Ladies in Hades, 2 Vols. Frederic A. Kummer. Ed. by R. Reginald & Douglas Melville. LC 77-84242. (Lost Race & Adult Fantasy Ser.). (Illus.). 1978. reprint ed. lib. bdg. 48.95 (0-405-10990-3) Ayer.

Shades of Heaven. Tina Wainscott. 1995. mass mkt. 5.50 (0-312-95671-1) St Martin.

***Shades of Injustice: Uncovering the Collapse of Hennepin County Detox Center.** Thomas Crain. 175p. (Orig.). 1997. pap. 12.99 (0-9627099-7-2) Zephyr Pub Corp.

Shades of Jade. Virginia H. Lillie. (Illus.). (Orig.). 1991. pap. 5.95 (1-878149-04-0) Counterpoint Pub.

Shades of Knight. Rick Hautala. 1995. mass mkt. 4.99 (0-8217-5097-6, Zebra Kensgtn) Kensgtn Pub Corp.

Shades of L A: Creating a Family Album. Carolyn Cole. (Illus.). 112p. (Orig.). Date not set. pap. 20.00 (1-56584-313-4) New Press NY.

Shades of Life. Jamie Z. Frazier. 300p. (C). 1989. 24.00 (0-317-93618-2) Frazier Pubns.

Shades of Life. Jane A. Hogan. Ed. by Jamie Teasley. LC 89-51630. 44p. 1990. 5.95 (1-55523-286-8) Winston-Derek.

Shades of Life. Cheryl S. Walker. 75p. pap. write for info. (0-9634995-0-5) Creat Truths.

Shades of Love: A Collection of Poetry. JoAnne Berkow. (Illus.). 112p. (Orig.). 1993. pap. 14.95 (0-89334-221-1) Humanics Ltd.

Shades of Mao: The Posthumous Cult of the Great Leader. Ed. by Geremie R. Barme. LC 95-25979. (Illus.). 272p. (gr. 13). 1996. text ed. 65.95 (1-56324-678-3, East Gate Bk); pap. text ed. 24.95 (1-56324-679-1, East Gate Bk) M E Sharpe.

Shades of Minos. Joe E. Pierce. 139p. 1973. pap. 6.95 (0-913244-04-X) Hapi Pr.

Shades of Noir. Ed. by Joan Copjec. 320p. (C). (gr. 13). 1993. pap. text ed. 20.00 (0-86091-625-1, B0531, Pub. by Vrso UK) Norton.

Shades of Noir. Ed. by Joan Copjec. 320p. (C). (gr. 13). 1993. text ed. 60.00 (0-86091-460-7, B0527, Pub. by Vrso UK) Norton.

Shades of Pale. Roediger. 1997. 25.00 (0-02-926885-0, Free Press) Free Pr.

Shades of Pale. Roediger. Date not set. 25.00 (0-684-82812-X) Free Pr.

Shades of Pearl. Debra B. Laurens. (Orig.). 1995. pap. text ed. 6.95 (1-56315-040-9) Sterling Hse.

Shades of Resistance. Joseph L. Matthews. 347p. 1996. pap. 15.95 (0-9647760-0-6) Headlands CA.

Shades of Right: Nativist & Fascist Politics in Canada, 1920-1940. Martin Robin. (Illus.). 384p. (Orig.). 1992. 60.00 (0-8020-5962-7); pap. 16.95 (0-8020-6892-8) U of Toronto Pr.

Shades of Rose. Deb Stover. 384p. 1995. mass mkt. 4.99 (0-8217-0143-6, Zebra Kensgtn) Kensgtn Pub Corp.

Shades of Salem. Ruth W. Schuler. (Illus.). 48p. (Orig.). 1987. pap. text ed. 5.00 (0-910083-10-X) Heritage Trails.

Shades of Scotland 1956-1988. Oscar Marzaroli & Grassie. (By Appointment Only Ser.). 224p. 1989. 34.95 (1-85158-213-4, Pub. by Mnstream UK) Trafalgar.

Shades of Sin: Dangerous Liasons. Wood. 1995. pap. 3.25 (0-373-11765-5) Harlequin Bks.

Shades of Singapore Vol. 1: Sister Sarah Balfour's Memoirs of Judicial Caning in South Africa. Angus Balfour. (Orig.). 1994. mass mkt. 5.95 (1-56201-071-9) Blue Moon Bks.

Shades of Summers Past. Joseph W. Scott. 70p. (Orig.). 1996. pap. 6.95 (1-57502-245-1, D0922) Morris Pubng.

***Shades of Sun at Pigeon Creek.** Phil Coleman et al. 52p. (Orig.). 1996. pap. 6.00 (1-889729-00-0) Pigeon Crk Poets.

Shades of the Battlefield. limited ed. Beatrice Bright. (Illus.). 64p. (Orig.). 1996. 11.00 (1-888578-00-9) R E F Typesetting Pub.

Shades of the Past. Loretta Berner et al. (Illus.). 67p. (Orig.). 1995. pap. 11.00 (0-9610250-5-0) Hist Soc of Long Bch.

Shades of the Past. Sandra Heath. 1996. pap. 4.99 (0-451-18752-0) NAL-Dutton.

Shades of the Sunbelt: Essays on Ethnicity, Race, & the Urban South. Ed. by Randall M. Miller & George E. Pozzetta. LC 87-18164. (Contributions in American History Ser.: No. 128). 246p. 1988. text ed. 55.00 (0-313-25690-X, MET/, Greenwood Pr) Greenwood.

Shades of the Sunbelt: Essays on Ethnicity, Race, & the Urban South. Ed. by Randall M. Miller & George E. Pozzetta. 240p. 1989. pap. text ed. 19.95 (0-8130-0956-1) U Press Fla.

Shades of the Wilderness. Joseph Altsheler. 1990. reprint ed. lib. bdg. 21.95 (0-89968-467-X) Buccaneer Bks.

Shades of Twilight. Linda Howard. 1996. mass mkt. 5.99 (*0-671-79937-1*) PB.

***Shades of Twilight.** large type ed. Linda Howard. LC 96-35551. (Large Print Bks.). 1996. 23.95 (*1-56895-378-X*, Compass) Wheeler Pub.

Shades of Womanhood. Cordia Novell. 1991. 6.95 (*0-533-09120-9*) Vantage.

Shades of Yesteryear. Marion Pond. LC 82-71114. (Illus.). 48p. (Orig.). 1982. pap. 7.50 (*0-941284-13-1*) J Shaw Studio.

Shadesmoor. Jason Foss. 320p. 1996. 20.00 (*0-7278-4784-8*) Severn Hse.

Shadier Garden. Random House Value Publishing Staff. 1997. 9.99 (*0-517-14273-2*) Random Hse Value.

Shading Flowers: The Complete Guide for Rug Hookers. Jeanne Field. LC 91-13129. (Illus.). 168p. 1991. pap. 18.95 (*0-8117-3081-6*) Stackpole.

Shading Our Cities: A Resource Guide for Urban & Community Forests. Ed. by American Forestry Association Staff et al. LC 89-15453. 329p. (Orig.). 1989. 34.95 (*0-933280-96-3*); pap. 19.95 (*0-933280-95-5*) Island Pr.

Shading TV Guide Black Side: A Book. George H. Hill & Robert P. Davenport. (Bibliographic Perspective, 1953-1987 Ser.). 75p. 1987. pap. text ed. 8.00 (*0-685-13976-X*) Daystar Co Carson.

Shadow. Blaise Cendrars. Tr. & Illus. by Marcia Brown. LC 81-9424. Orig. Title: La Feticheuse. 40p. (J). (gr. 2 up). 1982. lib. bdg. 17.00 (*0-684-17226-7*, C Scribner Sons Young) S&S Childrens.

Shadow. Enrique J. Levi. Tr. by Samuel A. Zimmerman from SPA. LC 96-17103. (Discoveries Ser.). (Orig.). (C). 1996. pap. 13.95 (*0-935480-78-1*) Lat Am Lit Rev Pr.

Shadow. Joyce Sweeney. 224p. (YA). (gr. 7 up). 1996. mass mkt. 4.99 (*0-440-21986-8*) Dell.

Shadow. 2nd ed. Blaise Cendrars. Tr. by Marcia Brown from FRE. LC 94-792. Orig. Title: La Feticheuse. (Illus.). 40p. (J). (gr. 4 up). 1995. pap. 4.95 (*0-689-71875-6*, Aladdin Paperbacks) S&S Childrens.

Shadow. Mary W. Ovington. LC 72-4736. (Black Heritage Library Collection). 1977. reprint ed. 31.95 (*0-8369-9118-4*) Ayer.

Shadow: A Novel. Joyce Sweeney. LC 93-32215. 224p. (J). (gr. 6 up). 1994. 15.95 (*0-385-32051-5*) Delacorte.

Shadow: Hitler's Astrologer. O'Neil et al. 64p. 1988. 12.95 (*0-87135-341-5*) Marvel Entmnt.

Shadow: Hitler's Astrologer. O'Neil et al. (Illus.). 64p. 1990. reprint ed. pap. 10.95 (*0-87135-664-3*) Marvel Entmnt.

Shadow Bk. 1: In the Coils of Leviathan. Joel Goss & Michael W. Kaluta. (Illus.). 112p. 1995. pap. 13.95 (*1-56971-024-4*) Dark Horse Comics.

Shadow Academy. Kevin J. Anderson & Rebecca Moesta. (Star Wars: Young Jedi Knights Ser.: No. 2). 224p. (Orig.). (YA). 1995. mass mkt. 4.99 (*1-57297-025-1*) Blvd Books.

Shadow Across the Desert. large type ed. Mary Munro. 1989. 25.99 (*0-7089-2094-2*) Ulverscroft.

Shadow Across the Moon. large type ed. Yvonne Whittal. 273p. 1994. 25.99 (*0-7505-0664-4*) Ulverscroft.

Shadow & a Song: The Struggle to Save An Endangered Species. Mark J. Walters. 238p. 1992. 21.95 (*0-930031-58-X*) Chelsea Green Pub.

Shadow & Act. Ralph Ellison. 1972. pap. 11.00 (*0-394-71716-3*, V-716, Vin) Random.

Shadow & Act. Ralph Ellison. 1995. pap. 14.00 (*0-679-76000-8*, Vin) Random.

***Shadow & Bone.** Peter Levi. 118p. 1989. pap. 17.95 (*0-85646-211-X*, Pub. by Anvil Press UK) Dufour.

Shadow & Claw. Gene Wolfe. LC 77-38283. 256p. 1994. pap. 12.95 (*0-312-89020-6*) Orb NYC.

Shadow & Claw: The Shadow of the Torturer - The Claw of the Conciliator. Gene Wolfe. 416p. 1994. pap. 14.95 (*0-312-89017-6*) Orb NYC.

Shadow & Evil in Fairy Tales. rev. ed. Marie-Louise Von Franz. LC 94-26600. (C. G. Jung Foundation Bks.). 344p. 1995. pap. 18.00 (*0-87773-974-9*) Shambhala Pubns.

Shadow & Flowers. W. Scarfe. 8.00 (*0-89253-733-7*) Ind-US Inc.

Shadow & Its Shadow: Surrealist Writing on the Cinema. Ed. by Paul Hammond. 1991. pap. 15.95 (*0-7486-6115-8*, Pub. by Edinburgh U Pr UK) Col U Pr.

Shadow & Light: A Practical Guide to Caregiving. South Carolina Agencies on Aging Staff. (Illus.). 56p. (Orig.). 1994. pap. write for info. (*0-917069-08-0*) Univ SC Inst Pub Affairs.

Shadow & Light: An Autobiography. Mifflin W. Gibbs. LC 95-4568. (Blacks in the American West Ser.). (Illus.). xxxv, 450p. 1995. pap. 15.00 (*0-8032-7050-X*, Bison Books) U of Nebr Pr.

Shadow & Light: An Autobiography. Mifflin W. Gibbs. LC 68-28998. (American Negro: His History & Literature, Ser. 1). 1969. reprint ed. 18.95 (*0-405-01817-7*) Ayer.

Shadow & Light: An Autobiography. Mifflin W. Gibbs. (American Biography Ser.). 372p. 1991. reprint ed. lib. bdg. 79.00 (*0-7812-8143-1*) Rprt Serv.

***Shadow & Light: Literature & the Life of Faith.** Ed. by Darryl L. Tippens et al. LC 96-84069. 384p. (C). 1997. pap. text ed. 35.95 (*0-89112-068-8*) Abilene Christ U.

Shadow, & Other Stories. Jeffery Farnol. LC 75-122696. (Short Story Index Reprint Ser.). 1977. 19.95 (*0-8369-3529-2*) Ayer.

Shadow & Self: Selected Papers in Analytical Psychology. Joseph L. Henderson. LC 89-36875. 352p. (Orig.). 1990. pap. 3.95 (*0-933029-33-0*) Chiron Pubns.

Shadow & Silk. Ann Maxwell. 432p. 1997. mass mkt. 6.50 (*0-8217-5547-1*, Zebra Kensgtn) Kensgtn Pub Corp.

***Shadow & Silk.** large type ed. Ann Maxwell. LC 97-20273. 1997. write for info. (*1-57490-085-4*, Beeler LP Bks) T T Beeler.

Shadow & Sound: The Historical Thought of a Sumatran People. James T. Siegel. LC 78-17963. (Illus.). 296p. 1979. 30.00 (*0-226-75690-4*) U Ch Pr.

Shadow & Substance: Jimmy Carter & the Camp David Accords. Linda B. Miller. (Pew Case Studies in International Affairs). 50p. (C). 1992. pap. text ed. 3.50 (*1-56927-433-9*) Geo U Inst Dplmcy.

Shadow & Substance: Manuscript Edition. Paul V. Carroll. 1948. pap. 13.00 (*0-8222-1018-5*) Dramatists Play.

Shadow & the Ready Time. Patty Sheehan. (J). (ps up). 1994. 14.95 (*0-911655-13-1*) Advocacy Pr.

Shadow & the Star. Laura Kinsale. 464p. (Orig.). 1991. mass mkt. 4.99 (*0-380-76131-9*) Avon.

Shadow & the Star. large type ed. Beatrice Taylor. (Linford Romance Library). 288p. 1993. pap. 15.99 (*0-7089-7340-X*, Linford) Ulverscroft.

Shadow Architecture at the Crossroads Annual. Paul Zelevansky. LC 80-71667. (Illus.). 230p. (C). 40.00 (*0-317-99909-5*) P Zelevansky.

Shadow at Evening. Max Marlow. 1994. lib. bdg. 20.00 (*0-7278-4699-X*) Severn Hse.

Shadow at Sun Lake. Esther Bender. LC 94-33947. 152p. (Orig.). (J). 1995. pap. 6.99 (*0-8361-9007-6*) Herald Pr.

Shadow Bands. Jeanne Schinto. LC 88-19830. (Illus.). 170p. 1988. pap. 9.95 (*0-86538-065-1*) Ontario Rev NJ.

Shadow Bear. Jean Harlow. (Illus.). (Orig.). (J). (gr. k-3). 1995. pap. 4.95 (*1-56801-798-7*) Sundance Pub.

Shadow Before. William Rollins, Jr. LC 74-22808. reprint ed. 45.00 (*0-404-58464-0*) AMS Pr.

Shadow Behind. Johnston. 1987. pap. 3.50 (*0-445-20204-1*) Warner Bks.

Shadow Between. large type ed. Ruth Abbey. (Dales Large Print Ser.). 284p. 1995. pap. 17.99 (*1-85389-535-0*, Dales) Ulverscroft.

Shadow Born of Earth: New Photography in Mexico. Elizabeth Ferrer. (Illus.). 160p. 1993. 40.00 (*0-87663-645-8*) Universe.

Shadow Born of Earth: New Photography in Mexico. Elizabeth Ferrer. 144p. (Orig.). 1993. pap. 25.00 (*0-917418-96-4*) Am Fed Arts.

***Shadow Box.** D. W. Buffa. LC 97-12861. 1997. 23.95 (*0-8050-5307-7*) H Holt & Co.

Shadow Box. John R. Maxim. LC 96-6789. 384p. 1996. 23.00 (*0-380-97300-6*) Avon.

***Shadow Box.** John R. Maxim. 1997. mass mkt. 6.99 (*0-380-78668-0*) Avon.

Shadow Box. George Plimpton. 352p. 1993. pap. 14.95 (*1-55821-276-0*) Lyons & Burford.

Shadow Boxer. Chris Lynch. LC 92-47490. 224p. (J). (gr. 5 up). 1993. 14.95 (*0-06-023027-4*); lib. bdg. 14.89 (*0-06-023028-2*) HarpC Child Bks.

Shadow Boxer. Chris Lynch. (YA). (gr. 9-12). 1996. 17.50 (*0-8446-6886-9*) Peter Smith.

Shadow Boxer. Chris Lynch. LC 92-47490. (Trophy Bk.). 208p. (YA). (gr. 7 up). 1995. pap. 3.95 (*0-06-447112-8*, Trophy) HarpC Child Bks.

Shadow Breed. Patrick McKinnon. 194p. (Orig.). 1996. mass mkt. 4.99 (*1-55197-208-5*, Pub. by Comnwlth Pub CN) Partners Pubs Grp.

Shadow Bride. Roy A. Heath. 428p. 1996. 24.95 (*0-89255-213-1*) Persea Bks.

Shadow Bride. Jane Peart. (Brides of Montclair Ser.: Vol. 7). 224p. 1991. pap. 8.99 (*0-310-67011-X*) Zondervan.

Shadow Brothers. A. E. Cannon. 192p. (YA). 1992. mass mkt. 3.99 (*0-440-21167-0*) Dell.

Shadow by the Door. Gerardo Di Masso. Tr. by Richard Jacques. LC 87-73441. 104p. 1988. pap. 8.95 (*0-915306-76-X*) Curbstone.

Shadow Castle. Michael Gray. 1983. 1.95 (*0-394-72316-3*) Random.

Shadow Castle. Marian Cockrell. (Illus.). 144p. 1992. reprint ed. lib. bdg. 19.95 (*0-89968-315-0*, Lghtyr Pr) Buccaneer Bks.

Shadow Cat. limited ed. Sylvia Hahn. 16p. 1983. 39.00 (*0-920806-49-X*, Pub. by Penumbra Pr CN) U of Toronto Pr.

Shadow Catcher. Charles Fergus. LC 91-20079. 320p. 1993. pap. 12.00 (*0-939149-91-5*) Soho Press.

***Shadow Catcher.** Andrzej Szczypiorski. Tr. by Bill Johnston from POL. LC 96-47370. 192p. 1997. 21.00 (*0-8021-1601-9*, Grove) Grove-Atltic.

Shadow Catcher: The Life & Work of Edward Sherriff Curtis. Laurie Lawlor. LC 93-40272. 132p. (YA). 1994. 19.95 (*0-8027-8288-4*); lib. bdg. 20.85 (*0-8027-8289-2*) Walker & Co.

Shadow Chaser. Stephen E. Cosgrove. LC 88-1533. (Stephen Cosgrove's Value Tales Ser.). (Illus.). 32p. (J). (gr. k-4). 1990. lib. bdg. 21.36 (*0-89565-663-9*) Childs World.

***Shadow Chasers.** Marty Engle & Johnny R. Barnes, Jr. (Strange Matter Ser.: No. 29). 144p. (Orig.). (J). (gr. 4 up). 1997. pap. 3.99 (*1-56714-085-8*) Montage Bks.

***Shadow Chasing.** Debbie Macomber. (Mira Bks.). 1997. 5.50 (*1-55166-263-9*, 1-66263-4, Mira Bks) Harlequin Bks.

Shadow Children. Steven Schnur. LC 94-5098. 192p. (YA). (gr. 3 up). 1994. 15.00 (*0-688-13281-2*, Morrow Junior); lib. bdg. 13.93 (*0-688-13831-4*, Morrow Junior) Morrow.

Shadow Climber. Mickey Z. Reichert. (Bifrost Guardians Ser.: No. 2). 304p. (Orig.). 1988. reprint ed. mass mkt. 4.99 (*0-88677-284-2*) DAW Bks.

Shadow Counter. Tom Kakonis. 400p. 1994. pap. 5.99 (*0-451-18066-6*) NAL-Dutton.

***Shadow Court.** Brian Campbell. (Changeling Ser.). 1996. pap. text ed. 18.00 (*1-56504-710-9*) White Wolf.

Shadow Creek Ranch: Escape to Shadow Creek Ranch. Charles Mills. (Shadow Creek Ranch Ser.). (J). Date not set. pap. text ed. 5.99 (*0-8280-0830-2*) Review & Herald.

Shadow Creek Ranch: Heart of the Warrior. Charles Mills. (J). Date not set. pap. text ed. 5.99 (*0-8280-0861-2*) Review & Herald.

Shadow Creek Ranch: Mystery in the Attic. Charles Mills. (J). Date not set. pap. text ed. 5.99 (*0-8280-0831-0*) Review & Herald.

Shadow Creek Ranch: River of Fear. Charles Mills. (J). Date not set. pap. text ed. 5.99 (*0-8280-0935-X*) Review & Herald.

Shadow Creek Ranch: Treasure of the Merrilee. Charles Mills. (J). Date not set. pap. text ed. 5.99 (*0-8280-0717-9*) Review & Herald.

Shadow Creek Ranch: Whispers in the Wind. Charles Mills. (J). Date not set. pap. text ed. 5.99 (*0-8280-0767-5*) Review & Herald.

***Shadow Crossing.** Philip S. Donlay. Ed. by Heidi Schlumpf. 250p. 1997. 24.95 (*1-889587-87-7*) Pure Play Pub.

Shadow Culture: Visionary Psychology in America. Eugene Taylor. 1996. write for info. (*0-201-60880-4*) Addison-Wesley.

Shadow Dance. Angela Carter. 182p. 1996. pap. 10.95 (*0-14-025524-9*, Penguin Bks) Viking Penguin.

***Shadow Dance.** Tololwa M. Mollel. LC 96-47332. (J). 1998. write for info. (*0-395-82909-7*) HM.

Shadow Dance. Jessica Palmer. Ed. by Rebecca Todd. 304p. (Orig.). 1994. mass mkt. 5.50 (*0-671-78715-2*) PB.

Shadow Dance. Anne Stuart. 384p. (Orig.). 1993. mass mkt. 4.50 (*0-380-76741-4*) Avon.

Shadow Dancers. Jack L. Chalker. 1992. mass mkt. 3.99 (*0-8125-2073-4*) Tor Bks.

Shadow Dancers. Herbert H. Lieberman. 1990. reprint ed. mass mkt. 5.95 (*0-312-92288-4*) St Martin.

Shadow Dancers: A Novel. Herbert H. Lieberman. 416p. 1989. 18.95 (*0-316-52417-4*) Little.

Shadow Dawn. Chris Claremont. LC 96-45148. 464p. 1997. 22.95 (*0-553-09597-8*, Spectra) Bantam.

Shadow Deer. Butler Radcliffe. (J). 1995. pap. 4.99 (*0-14-054380-5*) NAL-Dutton.

Shadow Distance: A Gerald Vizenor Reader. Gerald Vizenor. LC 94-15403. 372p. 1994. pap. 19.95 (*0-8195-6281-5*, Wesleyan Univ Pr) U Pr of New Eng.

Shadow Educational System: Adult Resource Development. Odd Nordhaug. (Scandinavian University Press Publication). 230p. 1991. 39.50 (*82-00-21347-1*) Scandnvan Univ Pr.

Shadow Eighty-One. large type ed. Lucien Nahum. 1981. 25.99 (*0-7089-0556-0*) Ulverscroft.

Shadow Falls. Claire Lorrimer. 224p. 1995. reprint ed. 22.00 (*0-7278-4796-1*) Severn Hse.

Shadow Flies. Rose Macaulay. LC 70-145153. (Literature Ser.). 484p. 1972. reprint ed. 59.00 (*0-403-01082-9*) Scholarly.

Shadow Flight. Joe Weber. 1991. mass mkt. 5.99 (*0-515-10660-7*) Jove Pubns.

Shadow Forms. Manly P. Hall. pap. 8.95 (*0-89314-398-7*) Philos Res.

Shadow from Ladakh. Bhabani Bhattacharya. 359p. 1969. pap. 3.00 (*0-88253-018-6*) Ind-US Inc.

Shadow from the Heat. Margaret E. Kelchner. 128p. 1994. pap. 7.99 (*0-8341-1515-8*) Beacon Hill.

Shadow Game. Dorinda Kamm. (Orig.). 1979. mass mkt. 1.95 (*0-89083-492-X*, Zebra Kensgtn) Kensgtn Pub Corp.

Shadow Games. Glen Cook. 320p. 1989. pap. 3.95 (*0-8125-3382-8*) Tor Bks.

Shadow Games: A Book of Hand & Puppet Shadows. Illus. by Bill Mayer. 40p. (J). (ps-2). 1995. spiral bd. 10.95 (*1-57054-030-6*) Klutz Pr.

Shadow Gate. Margaret Ball. (Fantasy Ser.). 1991. mass mkt. 5.99 (*0-671-72032-5*) Baen Bks.

Shadow Government: The Hidden World of Public Authorities. Donald Axelrod. LC 91-44086. 352p. 1992. text ed. 24.95 (*0-471-52767-X*) Wiley.

Shadow Hill Book of Mix Easy Cakes. Susan Ashby. (Illus.). 64p. (Orig.). 1984. pap. 3.95 (*0-912661-05-4*) Woodsong Graph.

Shadow Hill Book of Squares, Bars & Brownies. Susan Ashby. LC 84-52106. (Illus.). 144p. 1984. pap. 7.95 (*0-912661-03-8*) Woodsong Graph.

Shadow House. Michael Allegretto. 304p. 1994. 19.95 (*0-7867-0070-X*) Carroll & Graf.

Shadow Hunt. Anne Logston. 1992. mass mkt. 4.50 (*0-441-76007-4*) Ace Bks.

Shadow Hunter. Will Baker. Ed. by Claire Zion. 512p. 1994. reprint ed. mass mkt. 5.50 (*0-671-79045-5*, Pocket Star Bks) PB.

Shadow in a Weary Land. Harry Jones. LC 91-41986. 221p. 1992. 22.00 (*1-877946-15-X*) Permanent Pr.

Shadow in America: Reclaiming the Soul of a Nation. Ed. by Jeremiah Abrams. 280p. 1994. pap. 12.95 (*1-882591-17-8*) Nataraj Pub.

Shadow in Pursuit. large type ed. John N. Chance. LC 94-12703. 182p. 1994. lib. bdg. 16.95 (*0-8161-7422-9*, GK Hall) Thorndike Pr.

Shadow in Red: A Norah Mulcahaney Mystery. Lillian O'Donnell. 240p. 1986. 16.95 (*0-399-13208-2*, Putnam) Putnam Pub Group.

Shadow in the Corn. Jason Foss. 320p. 1994. 20.00 (*0-7278-4536-5*) Severn Hse.

Shadow in the Forest: Idaho's Black Bear. John J. Beecham & Jeff Rohlman. LC 94-1537. (Northwest Naturalist Bks.). 224p. 1994. pap. 18.95 (*0-89301-172-X*) U of Idaho Pr.

Shadow in the Land: Homosexuality in America. William Dannemeyer. LC 89-80470. 243p. (Orig.). 1989. pap. text ed. 9.95 (*0-89870-241-0*) Ignatius Pr.

Shadow Justice: The Ideology & Institutionalization of Alternatives to Court. Christine B. Harrington. LC 84-27923. (Contributions in Political Science Ser.: No. 133). (Illus.). x, 224p. 1985. text ed. 49.95 (*0-313-24332-8*, HID/, Greenwood Pr) Greenwood.

Shadow Killers. Franklin W. Dixon. (Hardy Boys Ser.: No. 92). (J). (gr. 3-6). 1988. pap. 3.99 (*0-671-66309-7*, Minstrel Bks) PB.

Shadow Kills. Rodman Philbrick. 288p. 1985. 15.95 (*0-8253-0283-8*) Beaufort Bks NY.

***Shadow King.** Sidra Stone. 1997. pap. text ed. 12.95 (*1-882591-31-3*) Hay House.

Shadow Knew. George Montgomery. Ed. by Joy Walsh. (Esprit Critique Ser.). 30p. (Orig.). 1988. pap. 9.95 (*0-938838-50-4*) Textile Bridge.

Shadow Knows. Diane Johnson. 1999. pap. 10.95 (*0-452-27736-1*) Viking Penguin.

Shadow Land: Light from the Other Side. E. D'Esperance. 414p. 1969. reprint ed. spiral bd. 24.50 (*0-7873-0236-8*) Hlth Research.

Shadow Land: Stories of the South. Florence H. Robertson. LC 72-3188. (Black Heritage Library Collection). 1977. reprint ed. 19.95 (*0-8369-9077-3*) Ayer.

Shadow Lands: Selected Poems. Johannes Bobrowski. Tr. by Ruth Mead & Matthew Mead from GER. LC 94-9979. 208p. (Orig.). 1994. pap. 10.95 (*0-8112-1276-9*, NDP788) New Directions.

Shadow Lands of C. S. Lewis: The Man Behind the Movie. Peter Kreeft. LC 94-75772. 221p. pap. 12.95 (*0-89870-493-6*) Ignatius Pr.

Shadow Lane. Eve Howard. 1993. mass mkt. 5.95 (*1-56201-050-6*) Blue Moon Bks.

Shadow Lane Vol. III: The Romance of Discipline. Eve Howard. 1996. mass mkt. 7.95 (*1-56201-095-6*) Blue Moon Bks.

Shadow Lane II: Return to Random Point. Eve Howard. (Shadow Land Ser.: Vol. 2). (Orig.). 1994. mass mkt. 5.95 (*1-56201-070-0*) Blue Moon Bks.

Shadow Leader. Tara K. Harper. 1991. mass mkt. 5.95 (*0-345-37163-1*, Del Rey) Ballantine.

Shadow Light-The Photography of Robert Guttke. Robert Guttke. 100p. 1995. 45.00 (*1-880777-22-3*) State Man.

Shadow Like a Leopard. Myron Levoy. 1995. 18.00 (*0-8446-6814-1*) Peter Smith.

Shadow Line. Joseph Conrad. Ed. by Jeremy Hawthorn. (WC-P Ser.). 176p. 1985. pap. 6.95 (*0-19-281686-1*) OUP.

Shadow-Line. Joseph Conrad. Ed. & Intro. by Jacques Berthoud. 160p. 1993. pap. 9.95 (*0-14-018097-4*, Penguin Classics) Viking Penguin.

Shadow-Line. Joseph Conrad. 1976. 18.95 (*0-8488-0257-8*) Amereon Ltd.

Shadow Lines. Amitav Ghosh. (C). 1988. 16.50 (*0-02-516001-X*) S Asia.

Shadow Lines: Austrian Literature from Freud to Kafka. Lorna Martens. LC 95-39266. (Illus.). xii, 293p. 1996. text ed. 40.00 (*0-8032-3186-5*) U of Nebr Pr.

Shadow Lords Tribebook. Brian Campbell & Ethan Skemp. (Werewolf Ser.). (Illus.). 72p. (Orig.). (YA). 1996. suppl. ed., pap. 10.00 (*1-56504-329-4*, 3058) White Wolf.

Shadow Lover. Carly Bishop. 1996. mass mkt. 3.75 (*0-373-22394-3*, 1-22394-0) Harlequin Bks.

Shadow Lover. Lori Handeland. 368p. (Orig.). 1995. mass mkt., pap. text ed. 4.99 (*0-505-52010-9*, Love Spell) Dorchester Pub Co.

Shadow Magic. (Illus.). (J). (ps-2). 1991. pap. 5.10 (*0-8136-5692-3*); lib. bdg. 7.95 (*0-8136-5192-1*) Modern Curr.

Shadow Magic! Illus. by Donata Montanari. (J). (ps up). 1994. bds. 6.95 (*1-55550-991-6*) Universe.

Shadow Maker: The Novels & Stories of Peter Carey. Bruce Woodcock. LC 96-2690. 1997. text ed. 49.95 (*0-7190-4360-3*, Pub. by Manchester Univ Pr UK); text ed. 14.95 (*0-7190-4361-1*, Pub. by Manchester Univ Pr UK) St Martin.

***Shadow Man.** Mary Gordon. 1997. pap. 13.00 (*0-679-74931-4*, Vin) Random.

Shadow Man. Cynthia D. Grant. LC 91-36054. 160p. (YA). (gr. 7 up). 1992. lib. bdg. 13.95 (*0-689-31772-7*, Atheneum Bks Young) S&S Childrens.

Shadow Man. John Katzenbach. 1996. mass mkt. 6.99 (*0-345-38630-2*) Ballantine.

Shadow Man. Melissa Scott. 320p. 1995. 22.95 (*0-312-85800-0*) Tor Bks.

Shadow Man. Sofia Shafquat. LC 92-31128. 269p. 1993. 22.00 (*1-877946-25-7*) Permanent Pr.

Shadow Man. large type ed. Claire Hamilton. (Linford Romance Library). 272p. 1989. pap. 15.99 (*0-7089-6692-6*, Linford) Ulverscroft.

Shadow Man, Vol. 1. Melissa Scott. 1996. pap. 13.95 (*0-312-86206-7*) Tor Bks.

Shadow Man: A Daughter's Search for Her Father. Mary Gordon. LC 95-25690. (Illus.). 274p. 1996. 24.00 (*0-679-42885-2*) Random.

***Shadow Matrix.** Marion Z. Bradley. 1997. 21.95 (*0-88677-743-7*) DAW Bks.

Shadow Merchants: Successful Retailing Without a Storefront. Jordan L. Cooper. LC 93-79018. 152p. 1993. pap. 12.95 (*1-55950-105-7*, 64145) Loompanics.

Shadow Moon. 464p. 1995. pap. 12.99 (*0-593-03926-2*) Bantam.

Shadow Moon. Chris Claremont & George Lucas. 544p. 1996. mass mkt. 5.99 (*0-553-57285-7*) Bantam.

Shadow Mountain Lodge, Typing Practice Set. Olive D. Church. (Illus.). (gr. 9-12). 1977. text ed. 13.24 (*0-07-010835-8*) McGraw.

Shadow of a Bird. D. M. Toliver. LC 88-70672. (First Fiction Ser.). 353p. 1995. 16.95 (*0-933031-13-0*) Coun Oak Bks.

Shadow of a Bird in Flight: A Collection of Persian Verses. Tr. by Shamsur R. Faruqi. (C). 1994. 18.00 (*81-7167-195-0*, Pub. by Rupa II) S Asia.

Shadow of a Bull. Michael Golden. Ed. by J. Friedland & R. Kessler. (Novel-Ties Ser.). 1993. student ed., pap. text ed. 15.95 (*0-88122-906-7*) Lrn Links.

S

An Asterisk (*) at the beginning of an entry indicates that the title is appearing in BIP for the first time.

Shadow of a Bull. Maia Wojciechowska. LC 64-12563. (Illus.). 176p. (YA). (gr. 5 up). 1972. lib. bdg. 16.00 (*0-689-30042-5*, Atheneum Bks Young) S&S Childrens.

Shadow of a Bull. Maia Wojciechowska. LC 91-27716. 160p. (J). (gr. 3-7). 1992. reprint ed. pap. 3.95 (*0-689-71567-6*, Aladdin Paperbacks) S&S Childrens.

Shadow of a Bull: A Literature Unit. Michael Shepherd. (Literature Units Ser.). (Illus.). 48p. (Orig.). (gr. 5-8). 1992. student ed. 7.95 (*1-55734-411-6*) Tchr Create Mat.

Shadow of a Dark Queen. Raymond E. Feist. (SerpentWar Saga Ser.: Vol. 1). 512p. 1995. mass mkt. 5.99 (*0-380-72086-8*) Avon.

Shadow of a Doubt. Margaret Chittenden. (Intrigue Ser.). 1993. mass mkt. 2.99 (*0-373-22242-4*, 1-22242-1) Harlequin Bks.

Shadow of a Doubt. William J. Coughlin. 1993. mass mkt. 5.99 (*0-312-92745-2*) St Martin.

Shadow of a Doubt. large type ed. William J. Coughlin. (General Ser.). 562p. 1992. 18.95 (*0-8161-5346-9*, GK Hall); lib. bdg. 21.95 (*0-8161-5345-0*, GK Hall) Thorndike Pr.

Shadow of a Dream. William Dean Howells. Ed. by Edwin H. Cady. Bd. with Imperative Duty. (Masterworks of Literature Ser.). 1962. pap. 14.95 (*0-8084-0340-0*) NCUP.

Shadow of a Dream. William Dean Howells. (Notable American Authors Ser.). 1992. reprint ed. lib. bdg. 75.00 (*0-7812-3243-0*) Rprt Serv.

Shadow of a Dream: Economic Life & Death in the South Carolina Low Country, 1670-1920. Peter A. Coclanis. (Illus.). 384p. 1989. 60.00 (*0-19-504420-7*) OUP.

Shadow of a Dream: Economic Life & Death in the South Carolina Low Country, 1670-1920. Peter A. Coclanis. 384p. 1991. pap. 19.95 (*0-19-507267-7*) OUP.

Shadow of a Flying Bird: A Folktale from Kurdistan. Illus. & Retold by Mordicai Gerstein. LC 94-7034. 32p. (J). (gr. 1 up). 1994. 15.95 (*0-7868-0016-X*) Hyprn Child.

Shadow of a Flying Bird: A Folktale from Kurdistan. Illus. & Retold by Mordicai Gerstein. LC 94-7034. 32p. (J). (gr. 1 up). 1994. lib. bdg. 15.89 (*0-7868-2012-8*) Hyprn Child.

Shadow of a Gunman. large type ed. Gordon D. Shirreffs. 1989. pap. 15.99 (*0-7089-6675-6*, Trailtree Bookshop) Ulverscroft.

Shadow of a Hero. Peter Dickinson & Kees De Kiefte. 295p. (YA). (gr. 7 up). 1994. mass mkt. 3.99 (*0-440-21963-9*, LLL BDD) BDD Bks Young Read.

Shadow of a Man. Doris M. Disney. 1990. mass mkt. 3.50 (*0-8217-3077-0*, Zebra Kensgtn) Kensgtn Pub Corp.

Shadow of a Man. Harold E. Dye. LC 95-72408. 64p. 1995. pap. 8.95 (*1-881576-75-2*) Providence Hse.

Shadow of a Man. May Sarton. 304p. 1982. reprint ed. pap. 4.95 (*0-393-30030-7*) Norton.

Shadow of a Mighty Rock: An Illustrated History of Presbyterianism in Marshall County, Mississippi. Robert M. Winter. (Illus.). 720p. 1997. text ed. write for info. (*1-881576-87-6*) Providence Hse.

Shadow of a Soul: Collected Poems. Bella Dizhur. Tr. by Sarah W. Bliumis from RUS. (Illus.). 234p. 1990. 22.50 (*0-918825-99-7*); pap. 12.95 (*0-918825-63-6*) Moyer Bell.

Shadow of a Star. large type ed. Mary Raymond. (Romance Ser.). 304p. 1987. 25.99 (*0-7089-1591-4*) Ulverscroft.

***Shadow of a Star: The Neutrino Story of Supernova 1987A.** Alfred K. Mann. (Illus.). 192p. 1997. 22.95 (*0-7167-3097-9*) W H Freeman.

Shadow of an Agony - The Highest Good. Oswald Chambers. 240p. 1992. pap. 10.99 (*0-929239-53-9*) Discovery Hse Pubs.

Shadow of an Angel. Marion D. Cohen. LC 86-27723. (Woman in History Ser.: Vol. 73). (Illus.). 136p. (Orig.). 1986. pap. 9.00 (*0-934659-04-4*) Liberal Pr.

Shadow of Arms. Hwang Suk-Young. Tr. by Chun Kyung-Ja from KOR. (Cornell East Asia Ser.: No. 73). 512p. (Orig.). (C). 1994. lib. bdg. 32.00 (*0-939657-80-5*, 73) Cornell East Asia Pgm.

***Shadow of Ashland.** Terence M. Green. 1997. mass mkt. 5.99 (*0-8125-5526-0*) Tor Bks.

***Shadow of Ashland.** Terence M. Green. 17.95 (*0-614-21925-6*) Forge NYC.

***Shadow of Ashland.** Terence M. Green. 224p. 1996. 17.95 (*0-312-85958-9*) Forge NYC.

Shadow of Calvary. Hugh Martin. 1983. pap. 8.99 (*0-85151-373-5*) Banner of Truth.

Shadow of Christ in the Law of Moses. Vern S. Poythress. 435p. (C). 1995. pap. 14.99 (*0-87552-375-7*, Pub. by Evangelical Pr) Presby & Reformed.

Shadow of Cliff College. Joe Brice. pap. 4.99 (*0-88019-172-4*) Schmul Pub Co.

Shadow of Clorinda. large type ed. Katrina Wright. (Linford Romance Library). 208p. 1992. pap. 15.99 (*0-7089-7284-5*, Trailtree Bookshop) Ulverscroft.

Shadow of Creation: Dark Matters & the Structure of the Universe. Michael Riordan & David N. Schramm. LC 90-241997. 1995. pap. text ed. write for info. (*0-7167-2366-2*) W H Freeman.

Shadow of Dark God & the Sin. Indira Goswami. 200p. 1986. text ed. 25.00 (*81-85006-14-8*, Pub. by Gaurav Pub Hse II) Apt Bks.

Shadow of Death. Thomas C. Callahan & Freda Turner. LC 80-50008. (Illus.). 192p. 1980. 9.95 (*0-936354-01-1*) Val-Hse Pub.

Shadow of Death. Anna M. Coalson. LC 91-67101. 251p. 1992. pap. 8.95 (*1-55523-489-5*) Winston-Derek.

Shadow of Death. Noreen Gilpatrick. LC 92-50658. 384p. 1993. 17.95 (*0-89296-514-2*) Mysterious Pr.

Shadow of Death. Noreen Gilpatrick. 400p. 1996. mass mkt. 5.99 (*0-446-40325-3*) Warner Bks.

Shadow of Death. Philip E. Ginsburg. 464p. (Orig.). 1995. mass mkt. 5.99 (*0-515-11547-9*) Jove Pubns.

Shadow of Death. Paul Hughes. LC 93-72058. 248p. (Orig.). 1993. pap. 8.95 (*0-88270-660-8*) Bridge-Logos.

Shadow of Death. William X. Kienzle. 1985. mass mkt. 5.99 (*0-345-33110-9*) Ballantine.

Shadow of Death. Lilli Schultze. 1981. pap. 3.50 (*0-87813-516-2*) Christian Light.

Shadow of Death: An Analytic Bibliography on Political Violence, Terrorism, & Low-Intensity Conflict. Henry W. Prunckun, Jr. LC 93-32400. (Illus.). 432p. 1995. 77.00 (*0-8108-2773-5*) Scarecrow.

Shadow of Death: The Holocaust in Lithuania. Harry Gordon. LC 91-23548. 200p. 1992. text ed. 22.00 (*0-8131-1767-4*) U Pr of Ky.

***Shadow of Desire.** Rebecca Stowe. (Illus.). 240p. 1997. pap. 12.00 (*0-393-31658-0*) Norton.

Shadow of Desire: A Novel. Rebecca Stowe. 240p. 1996. 22.00 (*0-679-42066-5*) Pantheon.

Shadow of Dionysus: A Contribution to the Sociology of the Orgy. Michel Maffesoli. Tr. by M. K. Palmquist & C. Linse. LC 91-41828. 167p. 1992. pap. 21.95 (*0-7914-1240-7*) State U NY Pr.

Shadow of Dionysus: A Contribution to the Sociology of the Orgy. Michel Maffesoli. Tr. by M. K. Palmquist & C. Linse. LC 91-41828. 167p. 1993. text ed. 64.50 (*0-7914-1239-3*) State U NY Pr.

***Shadow of Doubt.** 1997. pap. 5.50 (*1-57566-146-2*, Knsington) Kensgtn Pub Corp.

Shadow of Doubt. Wayne Barton & Stan Williams. Ed. by Doug Grad. 256p. (Orig.). 1994. mass mkt. 4.50 (*0-671-74578-6*) PB.

Shadow of Doubt. Gellis et al. 1996. pap. 5.99 (*1-57566-002-4*, Knsington) Kensgtn Pub Corp.

Shadow of Doubt. Jonnie Jacobs. 1996. pap. 18.95 (*0-8217-5254-5*) NAL-Dutton.

Shadow of Doubt. large type ed. June Thomson. 432p. 1983. 25.99 (*0-7089-0952-3*) Ulverscroft.

Shadow of Dreams. Mike F. Molaire. 50p. 1996. pap. 7.50 (*0-9649390-2-9*) Norex Publns.

Shadow of Eternity: Belief & Structure in Herbert, Vaughan, & Traherne. Sharon C. Seelig. LC 80-51018. 200p. 1981. 22.00 (*0-8131-1444-6*) U Pr of Ky.

Shadow of Evil: Where Is God in a Violent World. Davis. 132p. 1996. per., pap. text ed. 19.95 (*0-7872-1981-9*) Kendall-Hunt.

Shadow of Fear. Jane Peart. LC 96-14568. (Edgecliffe Manor Mysteries Ser.: No. 2). 176p. 1996. pap. 10.99 (*0-8007-5597-9*) Revell.

Shadow of Heaven. Michele Hays. LC 93-60237. 440p. 1993. 12.95 (*1-55523-601-4*) Winston-Derek.

Shadow of Henry Irving. Henry A. Jones. LC 77-91527. 111p. 1972. 18.95 (*0-405-08674-1*, Pub. by Blom Pubns UK) Ayer.

Shadow of Hiroshima & Other Film-Poems. Tony Harrison. 256p. (Orig.). 1995. pap. 13.95 (*0-571-17675-5*) Faber & Faber.

Shadow of His Wings. Bruce Fergusson. 288p. 1988. pap. 2.95 (*0-380-70415-3*) Avon.

Shadow of His Wings. Gilbert Morris. LC 94-28708. (Appomattox Saga Ser.: No. 6). 352p. 1994. pap. 10.99 (*0-8423-5987-7*) Tyndale.

***Shadow of King.** Hollick. LC 97-18589. 1997. 26.95 (*0-312-17000-9*) St Martin.

Shadow of Life. David J. Halton. 154p. (C). 1988. 39.00 (*0-7212-0772-3*, Pub. by Regency Press UK) St Mut.

Shadow of Moloch Mountain. Jane G. Austin. (Works of Jane (Goodin) Austin). 1989. reprint ed. lib. bdg. 79.00 (*0-7812-1825-X*) Rprt Serv.

Shadow of Our Bones. Keith Wilson. (Illus.). 31p. (Orig.). 1971. pap. 4.00 (*0-932264-19-0*) Trask Hse Bks.

Shadow of Paradise. Vincente Aleixandre. Tr. by Hugh A. Harter. 232p. 1993. pap. 16.00 (*0-520-08257-5*) U CA Pr.

Shadow of Paradise: Sombra del Paraiso. Vincente Aleixandre. Tr. by Hugh A. Harter. LC 86-6942. 186p. 1987. 40.00 (*0-520-05599-3*) U CA Pr.

***Shadow of Pengarron.** large type ed. Pauline Bentley. (Dales Large Print Ser.). 388p. 1996. pap. 17.99 (*1-85389-649-7*, Dales) Ulverscroft.

Shadow of Perfection: Eranos Yearbook 1995. Ed. by Jay Livernois. 120p. 1995. pap. 15.00 (*1-882670-08-6*) Spring Pubns.

Shadow of Scotus: The Shadow & Faith in Pre-Reformation Scotland. Alexander Broadie. 128p. 1997. 33.95 (*0-567-09734-X*, Pub. by T & T Clark UK) Bks Intl VA.

***Shadow of Scotus: The Shadow & Faith in Pre-Reformation Scotland.** Alexander Broadie. 128p. 1997. pap. 19.95 (*0-567-29295-9*, Pub. by T & T Clark UK) Bks Intl VA.

Shadow of Sequoyah: Social Documents of the Cherokees, 1862-1964. Ed. by Jack F. Kilpatrick & Anna G. Kilpatrick. LC 65-24205. (Civilization of the American Indian Ser.: No. 81). 144p. reprint ed. pap. 41.10 (*0-317-27894-0*, 2052156) Bks Demand.

Shadow of Silver Tip. large type ed. Max Brand. 425p. 1995. 22.95 (*0-7838-1470-4*, GK Hall) Thorndike Pr.

Shadow of Silver Tip. Max Brand. 320p. 1994. reprint ed. mass mkt., pap. text ed. 3.99 (*0-8439-3645-2*) Dorchester Pub Co.

Shadow of Slavery: Peonage in the South, 1901-69. Pete Daniel. (Illus.). 240p. 1990. pap. text ed. 11.95 (*0-252-06146-2*) U of Ill Pr.

Shadow of Sorcery. Andrew J. Offut. 240p. (Orig.). 1993. mass mkt. 4.99 (*0-441-76026-0*) Ace Bks.

Shadow of Sparta. Ed. by Anton Powell & Stephen Hodkinson. LC 93-43480. 408p. (C). (gr. 13). 1994. 62.95 (*0-415-10413-0*, Routledge NY) Routledge.

Shadow of Spirit: Postmodernism & Religion. Ed. by Philippa Berry & Andrew Wernick. LC 92-12225. 256p. (C). 1993. pap. 16.95 (*0-415-06639-5*, A6343); text ed. 62.95 (*0-415-06638-7*, A6339) Routledge.

Shadow of Suribachi: Raising the Flags on Iwo Jima. Parker B. Albee, Jr. & Keller C. Freeman. LC 94-34304. 232p. 1995. text ed. 27.95 (*0-275-95063-8*, Praeger Pubs) Greenwood.

Shadow of Terror. Rene Noorbergen. Ed. by Gerald Wheeler. 160p. 1991. pap. 8.99 (*0-8280-0576-1*) Review & Herald.

Shadow of That Thought. Dominique Janicaud. Tr. by Michael Gendre. (Studies in Phenomenology & Existential Philosophy). 136p. 1996. pap. text ed. 18.95 (*0-8101-1215-9*) Northwestern U Pr.

Shadow of That Thought. Dominique Janicaud. Tr. by Michael Gendre. (Studies in Phenomenology & Existential Philsophy). 136p. 1996. text ed. 65.00 (*0-8101-1234-5*) Northwestern U Pr.

Shadow of the Almighty. Elisabeth Elliot. 1989. 10.00 (*0-06-062213-X*) Harper SF.

***Shadow of the Atom: 1950-1960.** (This Fabulous Century Ser.). (Illus.). 288p. 24.95 (*0-8094-8216-9*) Time-Life.

Shadow of the Bamboo. Rajneesh Osho Staff. Ed. by Ma P. Maneesha. LC 84-42807. (Initiation Talks Ser.). 240p. (Orig.). 1984. pap. 3.95 (*0-88050-630-X*) Osho America.

***Shadow of the Black Sun.** (Shatterzone Ser.). 12.00 (*0-87431-246-9*, 21024) West End Games.

Shadow of the Child. Maxine O'Callaghan. 336p. 1996. mass mkt. 5.99 (*0-515-11822-2*) Jove Pubns.

Shadow of the Comet: Official Strategy Guide. Steven A. Schwartz. 1994. pap. 19.95 (*1-55958-608-7*) Prima Pub.

Shadow of the Condor. Jeanne Nickson. 400p. (Orig.). 1994. mass mkt., pap. text ed. 4.99 (*0-505-51975-5*) Dorchester Pub Co.

Shadow of the Cross: Studies in Self-Denial. Walter J. Chantry. 79p. (Orig.). 1981. pap. 4.99 (*0-85151-331-X*) Banner of Truth.

Shadow of the Dragon. Sherry Garland. 368p. (YA). (gr. 7-13). 1993. 11.00 (*0-15-273530-5*, HB Juv Bks); pap. 3.95 (*0-15-273532-1*, HB Juv Bks) HarBrace.

Shadow of the Dragon: Chinese Domestic & Trade Ceramics. Columbus Museum of Art Staff. (Illus.). 100p. (Orig.). 1982. pap. 10.00 (*0-918881-10-2*) Columbus Mus Art.

Shadow of the Eagles. Rebel Montgomery Temple Staff. (Illus.). 157p. (Orig.). (J). 1982. pap. 3.75 (*0-89279-045-8*, TXU 90-499) S&S Trade.

Shadow of the Earth. Lee Wichelns. (Illus.). 300p. (Orig.). 1987. 18.95 (*0-941692-07-8*) Elysian Pr.

Shadow of the East. E. M. Hull. 1976. reprint ed. lib. bdg. 24.95 (*0-89190-733-5*, Rivercity Pr) Amereon Ltd.

Shadow of the Flag. B. C. Gray. LC 94-96548. (Illus.). 416p. 1995. 21.95 (*0-9644106-0-5*) Gold Gryffyn.

Shadow of the Fox. Ellen Steiber. LC 94-1295. (Bullseye Chillers Ser.). 108p. (J). (gr. 2-6). 1994. pap. 3.50 (*0-679-86667-1*, Bullseye Bks) Random Bks Yng Read.

Shadow of the Galilean: The Quest of the Historical Jesus in Narrative Form. Gerd Theissen. Tr. by J. Bowden from GER. LC 86-46431. 212p. (Orig.). 1987. pap. 15.00 (*0-8006-2057-7*, 1-2057, Fortress Pr) Augsburg Fortress.

Shadow of the Gallow. Doyle Trent. 1987. pap. 2.95 (*0-8217-2194-1*) NAL-Dutton.

Shadow of the Grizzly. large type ed. Larry J. Martin. LC 93-28535. 1993. lib. bdg. 18.95 (*0-7862-0063-4*) Thorndike Pr.

Shadow of the Gun. Johnny Quarles. 384p. (Orig.). 1995. mass mkt. 5.50 (*0-380-77657-X*) Avon.

Shadow of the Hunt. Novotny. (C). 1995. pap. 20.76 (*0-395-77172-2*) HM.

Shadow of the Hunter. large type ed. Carole Kerr. (Linford Mystery Library). 320p. 1987. pap. 15.99 (*0-7089-6393-5*, Linford) Ulverscroft.

Shadow of the Hunter: Stories of Eskimo Life. Richard K. Nelson. LC 80-11091. (Illus.). xiv, 296p. 1983. pap. 12.95 (*0-226-57180-7*) U Ch Pr.

Shadow of the Hunter: Stories of Eskimo Life. Richard K. Nelson. LC 80-11091. 296p. reprint ed. pap. 84.40 (*0-685-23649-8*, 2026494) Bks Demand.

Shadow of the Lariat: A Treasury of Frontier Tales. Ed. by Jon Tuska. 592p. 1995. 28.00 (*0-7867-0256-7*) Carroll & Graf.

***Shadow of the Lariat: A Treasury of the Frontier.** Jon Tuska. 1997. 12.99 (*0-88394-099-X*) Galahad Bks.

***Shadow of the Legend.** Gini Leggett. 326p. (Orig.). 1997. mass mkt. 4.99 (*1-55197-605-6*, Pub. by Comnwlth Pub CN) Partners Pubs Grp.

Shadow of the Lynx. Victoria Holt. 320p. 1983. mass mkt. 3.50 (*0-449-20231-3*, Crest) Fawcett.

***Shadow Of The Mary Celeste.** large type ed. Richard Rees. (Ulverscroft Large Print Ser.). 672p. 1997. 27.50 (*0-7089-3726-8*) Ulverscroft.

Shadow of the Mills: Working-Class Families in Pittsburgh, 1870-1907. S. J. Kleinberg. LC 88-23627. (Series in Social & Labor History). (Illus.). 439p. (C). 1991. pap. 19.95 (*0-8229-5445-1*) U of Pittsburgh Pr.

***Shadow of the Moon.** Douglas C. Jones. 480p. 1997. mass mkt. 5.99 (*0-06-101033-2*, Harp PBks) HarpC.

Shadow of the Moon. Douglas C. Jones. LC 95-21735. 1996. 25.00 (*0-8050-3654-7*) H Holt & Co.

Shadow of the Moon. large type ed. Douglas C. Jones. LC 96-2044. (Americana Ser.). 1996. 24.95 (*0-7862-0691-8*, Thorndike Lrg Prnt) Thorndike Pr.

Shadow of the Mountain. Gilbert Morris & Lynn Morris. (Cheney Duvall, M. D. Ser.: No. 2). 336p. 1994. pap. 9.99 (*1-55661-423-3*) Bethany Hse.

Shadow of the Mountains. large type ed. Lynn G. Morris & Gilbert Morris. 481p. 1995. 21.95 (*0-7838-1489-5*, GK Hall) Thorndike Pr.

Shadow of the Ninja. Katsumi Toda. pap. 7.95 (*0-86568-361-1*) Unique Pubns.

Shadow of the North. Joseph Altsheler. 1990. reprint ed. lib. bdg. 19.95 (*0-89968-468-8*) Buccaneer Bks.

Shadow of the Object: Psychoanalysis of the Unthought Known. Christopher Bollas. 274p. 1989. pap. text ed. 16.50 (*0-231-06627-9*) Col U Pr.

***Shadow of the Other: Intersubjectivity & Gender in Psychoanalysis.** Jessica Benjamin. 128p. (C). 1997. pap. 15.95 (*0-415-91237-7*, Routledge NY); text ed. 55.00 (*0-415-91236-9*, Routledge NY) Routledge.

Shadow of the Panther: Huey Newton & the Price of Black Power in America. Hugh Pearson. 422p. 1995. pap. 14.00 (*0-201-48341-6*) Addison-Wesley.

Shadow of the Panther: Huey Newton, Oakland, and the Price of Power. Hugh Pearson. (Illus.). 422p. 1994. 24.00 (*0-201-63278-0*) Addison-Wesley.

Shadow of the Parthenon: Studies in Ancient History & Literature. Peter Green. LC 72-87205. 289p. reprint ed. pap. 82.40 (*0-7837-4820-5*, 2044467) Bks Demand.

Shadow of the Past. large type ed. Stella Ross. (Linford Romance Library). 1989. pap. 15.99 (*0-7089-6793-0*) Ulverscroft.

Shadow of the Plantation. Charles S. Johnson. LC 95-46962. 248p. 1996. pap. text ed. 21.95 (*1-56000-878-4*) Transaction Pubs.

Shadow of the Pomegranate. Jean Plaidy. 1997. mass mkt. 5.99 (*0-449-22346-9*) Fawcett.

Shadow of the Red Moon. Walter D. Myers. LC 94-42298. (Illus.). 288p. (J). (gr. 4 up). 1995. 14.95 (*0-590-45895-7*, Scholastic Hardcover) Scholastic Inc.

***Shadow of the Red Moon.** Walter D. Myers. (J). 1997. mass mkt. 4.50 (*0-590-45896-5*) Scholastic Inc.

Shadow of the Sun. A. S. Byatt. 1993. pap. 13.00 (*0-15-681416-1*) HarBrace.

Shadow of the Swastika. Doug Wilhelm. (Choose Your Own Adventure Ser.: No. 163). (Illus.). 128p. (YA). (gr. 5 up). 1995. mass mkt. 3.50 (*0-553-56619-9*, Choose) BDD Bks Young Read.

Shadow of the Third Century. Alvin B. Kuhn. (African Studies). 525p. reprint ed. 40.00 (*0-938818-75-9*) ECA Assoc.

Shadow of the Third Century: A Revaluation of Christianity. Alvin B. Kuhn. 535p. 1992. pap. 36.00 (*1-56459-178-6*) Kessinger Pub.

***Shadow of the Titanic.** Eva Hart. 1997. pap. 9.95 (*1-874529-29-9*, Pub. by Greenwich Univ Pr UK) NYU Pr.

Shadow of the Wall. Christa Laird. LC 89-34469. (YA). (gr. 7 up). 1990. 12.95 (*0-688-09336-1*) Greenwillow.

***Shadow of the Wall.** Christa Laird. 1997. pap. 4.95 (*0-688-15291-0*, Mulberry) Morrow.

Shadow of the Watching Star: The First Americans, Bk. 8. William Sarabande. (First Americans Ser.). 512p. 1995. mass mkt. 5.99 (*0-553-56029-8*) Bantam.

Shadow of the Well of Souls. Jack L. Chalker. 368p. (Orig.). 1994. mass mkt. 5.99 (*0-345-38846-1*, Avery Pub) Ballantine.

Shadow of the Wolf. Rebecca Flanders. 1995. mass mkt. 3.50 (*0-373-27059-3*, 1-27059-4) Silhouette.

Shadow of the Wolf. F. M. Parker. 192p. 1988. pap. 2.75 (*0-317-66101-9*, Sig) NAL-Dutton.

Shadow of the Wolf. Aimee Thurlo. (Intrigue Ser.). 1993. pap. 2.89 (*0-373-22217-3*, 1-22217-3) Harlequin Bks.

Shadow of the Wolf. Gloria Whelan. LC 96-18652. 1997. pap. 3.99 (*0-679-88108-5*) Random.

Shadow of the Wolf. Gloria Whelan. 1997. lib. bdg. 11.99 (*0-679-98108-X*) Random.

***Shadow of the Wolf: An Apache Tale.** Harry J. Plumlee. LC 96-34556. 216p. 1997. 21.95 (*0-8061-2905-0*) U of Okla Pr.

Shadow of the World's Future: Or, the Earth's Population Possibilities & the Consequences of the Present Rate of Increase of the Earth's Inhabitants. George H. Knibbs. LC 75-38133. (Demography Ser.). 1976. reprint ed. 17.95 (*0-405-07986-9*) Ayer.

Shadow of Truth. Ward Hoffman. 1993. pap. 5.95 (*0-9639018-0-X*) Carma Pubng.

***Shadow of Weng-Chiang.** David A. McIntee. (Dr. Who Missing Adventures Ser.). 275p. 1996. mass mkt. 5.95 (*0-426-20479-4*, Pub. by Virgin Pub UK) London Brdge.

***Shadow of Wings.** June Knox-Mawer. 321p. 1997. 26.00 (*0-297-81567-9*, Weidenfeld) Trafalgar.

Shadow of Wings. Judy Kronenfeld. Ed. by Louise A. Wazbinski. 42p. (Orig.). 1991. pap. 9.00 (*0-934958-06-8*) Bellflower.

Shadow of Z: Spirou & Fantasio, Vol. 2. Andre Franquin. (Spirou & Fantasio Ser.). (Illus.). 64p. (Orig.). (ENG & FRE.). (YA). (gr. 6 up). 1996. pap. 8.95 (*1-887911-56-1*) Fantsy Flight.

Shadow on a Star. large type ed. Juliet Gray. (Linford Romance Large Print Ser.). 1994. pap. 15.99 (*0-7089-7524-0*, Linford) Ulverscroft.

Shadow on a Star. large type ed. Juliet Grey. (Linford Romance Library). 304p. 1994. pap. 14.95 (*0-685-71070-X*, Linford) Ulverscroft.

Shadow on a Tightrope: Writings by Women on Fat Oppression. Ed. by Lisa Schoenfielder & Barb Wieser. LC 88-60189. 243p. (Orig.). (C). 1983. pap. 9.95 (*1-879960-24-9*) Aunt Lute Bks.

Shadow on a Wave. Anne Crawford & Baroness Von Rable. Ed. by John C. Moran & Jesse F. Knight. (Worthies Library: No. 5). (Illus.). 75p. 1988. 7.50 (*0-317-01471-4*) F M Crawford.

Shadow on My Soul: Overcoming Addiction to Suicide. Paula M. Quinn. 188p. (Orig.). 1995. pap. 14.95 (*1-879198-13-4*) Knwldg Ideas & Trnds.

Shadow on Summer. Christy Brown. 274p. (C). 1991. pap. 9.95 (*0-685-63036-6*, A0573) Heinemann.

Shadow on Summer. Christy Brown. LC 74-79420. 228p. 1974. pap. 9.95 (*0-8128-8530-9*, Scrbrough Hse) Madison Bks UPA.

Shadow on the Church: Southwestern Evangelical Religion & the Issue of Slavery, 1783-1860. David T. Bailey. LC 84-45795. 264p. (C). 1985. 39.95 (0-8014-1763-5) Cornell U Pr.

Shadow on the Dial. Anne M. Lindbergh. (J). (gr. 3-7). 1988. pap. 2.75 (0-380-70545-1, Camelot) Avon.

Shadow on the Dial & Other Essays. Ambrose G. Bierce. (Principle Works of Ambrose Gwinett Bierce). 1989. reprint ed. lib. bdg. 79.00 (0-7812-1967-1) Rprt Serv.

Shadow on the Moon. Connis Alexander. 1997. pap. 5.99 (0-451-40745-8, Onyx) NAL-Dutton.

Shadow on the Snow. Anne Schraff. Ed. by Carol Newell. (Standing Tall Mystery Ser.). 49p. (Orig.). (J). (gr. 5-9). 1995. pap. 4.95 (1-56254-156-0, SP1560) Saddleback Pubns.

Shadow on the Snow. Bill Wallace. LC 84-48743. 160p. (J). (gr. 4-7). 1985. 15.95 (0-8234-0557-5) Holiday.

Shadow on the Snow see Danger on Panther Peak

Shadow on the Sun. Rosemary Harris. (Children's Paperbacks Ser.). 192p. (J). (gr. 2-6). 1991. pap. 4.95 (0-571-14185-4) Faber & Faber.

Shadow on the Sun. Richard Matheson. LC 94-2937. 180p. 1994. 18.95 (0-87131-765-6) M Evans.

Shadow on the Tetons: David E. Jackson & the Claiming of the American West. John C. Jackson. Ed. by Daniel Greer. (Illus.). 250p. 1993. 24.00 (0-87842-295-1) Mountain Pr.

Shadow on the Trail. Zane Grey. 352p. 1992. mass mkt. 3.99 (0-06-100443-X, Harp PBks) HarpC.

Shadow on the Trail. large type ed. Zane Grey. LC 93-44658. 1994. lib. bdg. 20.95 (0-7862-0074-X) Thorndike Pr.

Shadow on the Valley. Mitchell. Date not set. write for info. (0-312-09382-9) St Martin.

***Shadow on the Wall.** Jonathan Aycliffe. mass mkt. write for info. (0-06-105484-4, HarperPrism) HarpC.

***Shadow on the Wall.** Jonathan Aycliffe. 240p. 1997. 18.00 (0-06-105226-4) HarpC.

Shadow on the White House: Presidents & the Vietnam War, 1945-1975. Ed. by David L. Anderson. LC 92-35898. (Modern War Studies). (Illus.). 248p. 1993. pap. 14.95 (0-7006-0583-5) U Pr of KS.

Shadow over Afghanistan. Fazel R. Fazel. LC 88-50587. (Illus.). 288p. 1988. 21.50 (0-936029-10-2); pap. 12.50 (0-936029-11-0) Western Bk Journ.

Shadow over Babylon. David S. Mason. 1995. pap. 5.99 (0-451-18063-1, Sig) NAL-Dutton.

Shadow over Babylon. David S. Mason. 1995. pap. write for info. (0-451-17671-5, Sig) NAL-Dutton.

***Shadow over Flodden.** Mary Cummins. LC 97-18508. 1997. pap. write for info. (0-7838-8217-3) G K Hall.

Shadow over Heldon Hall. Nan Herbert. 1978. mass mkt. 1.95 (0-89083-407-5, Zebra Kensgtn) Kensgtn Pub Corp.

Shadow over My Life: A Holocaust Story. Lilo & Cohen. (Illus.). 92p. 1994. text ed. 9.95 (965-229-110-2, Pub. by Gefen Pub Hse IS) Gefen Bks.

Shadow over San Mateo. Lauraine Snelling. (Golden Filly Ser.: Vol. 6). 160p. (Orig.). (gr. 7-10). 1993. pap. 5.99 (1-55661-292-3) Bethany Hse.

Shadow Over Second: A Peach Street Mudders Story. Matt Christopher. LC 95-36024. 64p. (J). (gr. 2-4). 1996. 13.95 (0-316-14078-3) Little.

Shadow over Shangri-la: A Woman's quest for Freedom. Durga Pokhrel & Anthony Willett. (Illus.). 376p. 1996. 24.95 (1-57488-061-6) Brasseys Inc.

Shadow over the Rose. Jerri A. Worthen. LC 92-91193. 87p. 1994. pap. 8.00 (1-56002-284-1, Univ Edtns) Aegina Pr.

Shadow Partisan. Nadja Tesich. (Orig.). 1988. pap. 8.95 (0-89823-108-6) New Rivers Pr.

Shadow Play. Charles Baxter. Date not set. 4.98 (0-8317-5034-0) Smithmark.

Shadow Play. Charles Baxter. 400p. 1994. pap. 11.95 (0-14-023510-8, Penguin Bks) Viking Penguin.

Shadow Play. Paul Fleischman. LC 89-26874. (Charlotte Zolotow Bk.). (Illus.). 48p. (J). (gr. 2 up). 1990. lib. bdg. 14.89 (0-06-021865-7) HarpC Child Bks.

Shadow Play. Katherine Sutcliffe. 432p. 1991. mass mkt. 4.95 (0-380-75941-1) Avon.

Shadow Play. Sally Wentworth. (Presents Ser.). 1995. pap. 3.25 (0-373-11738-8, 1-11738-1) Harlequin Bks.

Shadow Play. Bernie Zubrowski. LC 94-27425. (Illus.). 112p. (J). (gr. 3 up). 1995. pap. 7.95 (0-688-13211-1) Morrow.

Shadow Play. large type ed. Sally Wentworth. 1995. lib. bdg. 18.95 (0-263-13970-0) Thorndike Pr.

Shadow Play: Making Pictures with Light & Lenses. Bernie Zubrowski. LC 94-27425. (Illus.). 112p. (YA). (gr. 3 up). 1995. lib. bdg. 15.93 (0-688-13210-3, Morrow Junior) Morrow.

Shadow Play: Poems, 1987-1991. John Brandi. (Light & Dust Bks.). (Illus.). 80p. (Orig.). 1992. pap. 8.00 (0-87924-070-9) Membrane Pr.

***Shadow Play: The Murder of Robert F. Kennedy, the Trial of Sirhan Sirhan & the Failure of American Justice.** Philip H. Melanson & William Klaber. (Illus.). 384p. 1997. 24.95 (0-312-15398-8) St Martin.

Shadow Play, Night Haiku. Penny Harter. LC 93-39887. (J). 1994. 15.00 (0-671-88396-8, S&S Bks Young Read) S&S Childrens.

Shadow Play, The Rats: Two Novellas. Jose Bianco. Ed. by Yvette E. Miller. Tr. by Daniel Balderston from SPA. LC 83-775. (Discoveries Ser.). 88p. 1983. pap. 9.50 (0-935480-11-0) Lat Am Lit Rev Pr.

***Shadow Players Guide.** Richard Dansky & Ed Huang. (Wraith Ser.). (Illus.). 144p. (Orig.). 1997. pap. 18.00 (1-56504-602-1, 6013) White Wolf.

***Shadow Poems.** Thomas Krampf. (Illus.). 67p. (Orig.). 1997. pap. 15.00 (0-9616797-2-7, 3A) Ischua Bks.

***Shadow President: Ted Kennedy in Opposition.** Burton Hersh. LC 97-3109. (Illus.). 219p. 1997. 21.00 (1-883642-30-2) Steerforth Pr.

Shadow Prey. John Sandford. 1991. mass mkt. 6.99 (0-425-12606-4) Berkley Pub.

Shadow Prince. Terri L. Wilhelm. 384p. 1994. mass mkt. 4.99 (0-06-108227-9, Harp PBks) HarpC.

***Shadow Prince.** Terri L. Wilhelm. 1997. mass mkt. 2.99 (0-06-108551-0) HarpC.

Shadow Queen. Tony Gibbs. 336p. 1993. mass mkt. 4.99 (0-446-40108-0, Mysterious Paperbk) Warner Bks.

***Shadow Queen.** Helen Lillie. 276p. (Orig.). 1997. mass mkt. 4.99 (1-55197-876-8, Pub. by Comnwlth Pub CN) Partners Pubs Grp.

Shadow Ranch. Jo-Ann Mapson. 384p. 1996. 24.00 (0-06-017216-9) HarpC.

***Shadow Ranch: A Novel.** Jo-Ann Mapson. 1997. pap. text ed. 13.00 (0-06-092843-3, PL) HarpC.

***Shadow Rider.** William C. MacDonald. 1996. 17.50 (0-7451-4697-X, Gunsmoke) Chivers N Amer.

Shadow Riders. Louis L'Amour. 176p. 1982. mass mkt. 3.99 (0-553-23132-4) Bantam.

Shadow Riders: The Southern Plains Uprising, 1873. Terry C. Johnston. (Plainsmen Ser.: Bk. 6). 416p. (Orig.). 1991. mass mkt. 5.99 (0-312-92597-2) St Martin.

***Shadow Rift.** 1997. 25.00 (0-7869-0737-1) TSR Inc.

Shadow Rising. Robert Jordan. (Wheel of Time Ser.: Bk. 4). 1008p. 1993. pap. 6.99 (0-8125-1373-8) Tor Bks.

Shadow River. Dick Wilson. LC 91-74113. 242p. 1992. pap. 9.95 (1-55523-470-4) Winston-Derek.

***Shadow Seed: A Novel.** Jim Fraiser. LC 97-515. 224p. 1997. 24.00 (1-881320-69-3, Black Belt) Black Belt Comm.

Shadow Self & Other Tales: Selected Stories & Drawings. Helen Daberstein. (Illus.). 125p. 1996. pap. 15.95 (0-939520-09-5) Ghost Dance.

Shadow Shadow. Roger Weingarten. LC 86-4691. 96p. 1986. 13.95 (0-87923-634-5); pap. 8.95 (0-87923-635-3) Godine.

***Shadow Shoguns: The Rise & Fall of Japan's Postwar Political Machine.** Jacob M. Schlesinger. LC 96-51053. 1997. 26.00 (0-684-81158-8) S&S Trade.

Shadow Shop. Kristin Pedersen. Ed. by Nancy R. Thatch. (Books for Students by Students). (Illus.). 29p. (J). (gr. 3-6). 1994. lib. bdg. 14.95 (0-933849-53-2) Landmark Edns.

***Shadow Side of Prayer.** Dossey. LC 97-15085. 22.00 (0-06-251433-4); pap. 15.00 (0-06-251434-2) HarpC.

***Shadow Soldier. T. L. Davis. LC 97-90015. 312p. 1997. 19.95 (0-9656536-4-1) F&S Press. SHADOW SOLDIER is the story of Jefferson Doddridge Wilkes as he makes his way through the turmoil of the Civil War. As a young man, he saw himself at the end of the war standing in the halls of Congress in the new capitol at Richmond, VA. Instead, he found himself with no history, no future & an awful lot of time left to live. Against his wishes, he is forced out into the Frontier West to fend for himself in a world of cutthroats, thieves & gunslingers. But, SHADOW SOLDIER is the story of a young man's struggle with the world & himself. Early on, Jefferson learns that if he is to survive the Frontier, he is going to have to change. He will have to become more savage, less moral, less careful. The question is, will he go far? And what will he become, if he does? $19.95 plus $3.00 S&H--312 pages, hardcover edition. ISBN 0-9656536-4-1. Order from F&S Press through: BookCrafters Order Department, P.O. Box 459, Chelsea, MI 48118 or call 1-800-879-4214 to place an order.**

Publisher Provided Annotation.

Shadow Song. Neal King. LC 94-38869. 160p. 1995. pap. 10.00 (0-06-095058-7) HarpC.

Shadow Song. large type ed. Terry Kay. LC 94-42481. 1994. 24.95 (1-56895-157-4) Wheeler Pub.

Shadow Song: A Novel. Terry Kay. Ed. by Donna Ng. 400p. 1997. reprint ed. pap. 12.00 (0-671-89260-6, WSP) PB.

***Shadow Song: From Despair to Joy: A Pilgrimage with AIDS.** Maurine S. Georgiades. (Orig.). 1997. pap. 11.95 (1-880451-23-9) Rainbows End.

Shadow Songs: A Collection of Poems. Laura Poole. Ed. by M. A. Myers. LC 91-75715. 55p. (Orig.). 1991. pap. text ed. 7.95 (1-879183-11-0) Bristol Banner.

Shadow State: Government & Voluntary Sector in Transition. Jennifer R. Wolch. LC 89-71543. 1990. pap. 24.95 (0-87954-331-0) Foundation Ctr.

Shadow Stealers. Jane B. Mason. (J). 1996. pap. text ed. 2.99 (0-590-50205-0) Scholastic Inc.

Shadow Steed. Richard A. Knaak. 272p. 1990. mass mkt. 4.99 (0-445-20967-4) Warner Bks.

***Shadow Stone.** TSR Inc. Staff. 1997. pap. 5.99 (0-7869-0666-9) TSR Inc.

***Shadow Story.** Barbara Willard. (J). Date not set. write for info. (0-15-201638-4, HB Juv Bks) HarBrace.

Shadow Strategies of an American Ninja Master. Glenn Morris. LC 95-923. 250p. (Orig.). (C). 1995. pap. 12.95 (1-883319-29-3) Frog Ltd CA.

Shadow Sun. Annette Sanford. 1980. pap. 1.50 (0-373-58004-5) Harlequin Bks.

***Shadow Syndromes: Recognizing & Coping with the Hidden Psychological disorders that Can Influence Your Behavior & Silently Determine the Course of Your Life.** C. Johnson & John J. Ratey. 1997. 25.95 (0-679-43968-4) Pantheon.

Shadow Taker. Blaine M. Yorgason & Carl J. Eaton. 125p. 1990. pap. text ed. 6.95 (0-929985-54-0) Jackman Pubng.

***Shadow Tarot.** Linda Falorio. (Illus.). ii, 81p. (Orig.). 1993. pap. 29.95 (1-890399-09-4, 019) Blck Moon.

Shadow the Deer. Theresa Radcliffe. (Illus.). 32p. (J). (ps-1). 1994. pap. 13.99 (0-670-85052-7) Viking Child Bks.

Shadow Train: A Journey Between Relinquishment & Reunion. Patnaa E. Taylor. LC 95-79077. 1995. pap. 18.95 (0-9651217-0-4) P E Taylor.

Shadow Valley - Fort Vengeance. Gordon D. Shirreffs. 320p. 1993. mass mkt., pap. text ed. 4.50 (0-8439-3477-8) Dorchester Pub Co.

Shadow Vengeance. Wendy Haley. 384p. 1993. mass mkt. 4.50 (0-8217-4097-0, Zebra Kensgtn) Kensgtn Pub Corp.

***Shadow Walk.** Jane Waterhouse. LC 97-14765. 320p. 1997. 23.95 (0-399-14305-X) Putnam Pub Group.

***Shadow Walker.** Connie Mason. 400p. (Orig.). 1997. mass mkt. 5.99 (0-8439-4260-6, Leisure Bks) Dorchester Pub Co.

Shadow Walkers. Nina Romberg. 304p. 1993. mass mkt. 4.50 (1-55817-696-9, Pinncle Kensgtn) Kensgtn Pub Corp.

***Shadow War.** Deborah Chester. 400p. 1997. mass mkt. 6.69 (0-441-00400-8) Ace Bks.

Shadow War: German Espionage & United States Counterespionage in Latin America During World War II. Leslie B. Rout & John Bratzel. LC 85-295633. (Foreign Intelligence Book Ser.). 540p. 1986. text ed. 65.00 (0-313-27005-8, U7005, Greenwood Pr) Greenwood.

Shadow War: The CIA's Secret War in Laos. Kenneth Conboy. (Illus.). 464p. 1995. text ed. 49.95 (0-87364-825-0) Paladin Pr.

***Shadow Warrior: The Official Strategy Guide.** Prima Development Staff. 240p. 1997. per., pap. 19.99 (0-7615-0933-X) Prima Pub.

Shadow Warrior Strategies & Secrets. Ronald Wartow. 256p. 1996. pap. text ed. 19.99 incl. cd-rom (0-7821-1795-3, Strategies & Secrets) Sybex.

***Shadow Warrior 1.** Smith. 1997. mass mkt. 6.99 (0-671-01879-5) PB.

***Shadow Warrior 2.** Oltion. 1997. mass mkt. 6.99 (0-671-01880-9) PB.

***Shadow Warriors.** Cameron Judd. 464p. 1997. mass mkt. 5.99 (0-553-57698-4) Bantam.

Shadow Warriors. Dan Matthews. (Slam Ser.). 1993. mass mkt. 3.50 (0-373-63409-9, 1-63409-6) Harlequin Bks.

Shadow Warriors: The Covert War in Korea. William B. Breuer. LC 95-35856. 288p. 1996. text ed. 27.95 (0-471-14438-X) Wiley.

***Shadow Wars.** Clyde Farnsworth. 416p. 1998. pap. 24.95 (1-55611-518-0) D I Fine.

Shadow Wars. D. Nurkse. 1988. pap. 7.00 (0-914610-53-8) Hanging Loose.

Shadow Wars. Dennis Nurkse. 1988. 15.00 (0-914610-54-6) Hanging Loose.

Shadow Wars. Charles D. Taylor. Ed. by Paul McCarthy. 384p. (Orig.). 1992. mass mkt. 5.50 (0-671-73631-0) PB.

Shadow Whispers. Wendy Haley. 1992. mass mkt. 4.50 (0-8217-3750-3, Zebra Kensgtn) Kensgtn Pub Corp.

Shadow Wife. Dorothy Eden. 1980. pap. 1.95 (0-449-23699-4, Crest) Fawcett.

Shadow Wife. large type ed. Dorothy Eden. 1976. 12.00 (0-85456-425-X) Ulverscroft.

***Shadow Within.** Jeanne Cavelos. (Babylon 5 Ser.: No. 7). 1997. mass mkt. 5.50 (0-440-22348-2) Dell.

***Shadow Woman.** Thomas Perry. 1997. 22.00 (0-679-45302-4) Random.

Shadow Women: Homeless Women's Survival Stories. Marjorie Bard. LC 90-60897. 236p. (Orig.). (C). 1990. pap. 9.95 (1-55612-358-2) Sheed & Ward MO.

Shadow Work. Ivan Illich. 160p. 1981. 15.00 (0-7145-2710-6); pap. 5.95 (0-7145-2711-4) M Boyars Pubs.

Shadow World. Patricia Weber. Ed. by N. Smith. (Illus.). 345p. 1994. 19.95 (0-685-71769-0) Pacifica Editions.

Shadow World. Hamlin Garland. (Collected Works of Hamlin Garland). 1988. reprint ed. lib. bdg. 59.00 (0-7812-1238-3) Rprt Serv.

Shadow World: Life Between the News Media & Reality. Jim Willis. LC 90-40802. 272p. 1991. text ed. 59.95 (0-275-93424-1, C3424, Praeger Pubs); pap. text ed. 17.95 (0-275-93425-X, B3425, Praeger Pubs) Greenwood.

Shadow World: Stormriders. Ian Hammell. 1996. mass mkt. 5.50 (0-441-00302-8) Ace Bks.

Shadow World: The Burning Goddess. Ian Hammell. 208p. (Orig.). 1994. mass mkt. 4.50 (0-441-00086-X) Ace Bks.

Shadow World No. 2: Clock Strikes Sword. Ian Hammell. 272p. (Orig.). 1995. mass mkt. 4.99 (0-441-00136-X) Ace Bks.

Shadow World see Collected Works of Hamlin Garland

Shadowbeat: A Shadowrun Sourcebook. FASA Staff. (Shadowrun Ser.). (Illus.). 128p. 1991. pap. 15.00 (1-55560-159-6, 7109) FASA Corp.

Shadowbirds: A Quest for Rails. William Burt. (Illus.). 192p. 1994. 25.00 (1-55821-293-0) Lyons & Burford.

***Shadowborn.** TSR Inc. Staff. 1997. pap. 5.99 (0-7869-0766-5) TSR Inc.

Shadowcaster Clue Book: Illuminations. Melissa Mead. (Illus.). 80p. (Orig.). 1993. pap. 14.95 (0-929373-15-4) Origin Syst.

***Shadowcatcher.** Micah S. Hackler. 304p. 1997. mass mkt. 5.50 (0-440-22339-3) Dell.

Shadowcatchers: A Directory of Women in California Photography, 2 vols., Vol. 1, Before 1901. Peter E. Palmquist. 1991. reprint ed. lib. bdg. 69.00 (0-8095-5950-1) Borgo Pr.

Shadowcatchers: A Directory of Women in California Photography, 2 vols., Vol. 2, 1901-1920. Peter E. Palmquist. 1991. reprint ed. lib. bdg. 79.00 (0-8095-5951-X) Borgo Pr.

Shadowcatchers: A Journey in Search of the Teachings of Native American Healers. Steve Wall. 288p. 1995. lib. bdg. 35.00 (0-8095-9176-6) Borgo Pr.

Shadowcatchers: A Journey in Search of the Teachings of Native American Healers. Steve Wall. 288p. 1995. pap. 16.00 (0-06-092672-4, PL) HarpC.

Shadowdale. Richard Awlinson. LC 88-51723. (Forgotten Realms Avatar Trilogy Ser.: Bk. 1). 352p. 1989. pap. 5.99 (0-88038-730-0) TSR Inc.

Shadowdance. Robin Bailey. (Illus.). (Orig.). 1996. pap. 5.99 (1-56504-946-2, 13403, Borealis) White Wolf.

Shadowed Dreams: Women's Poetry of the Harlem Renaissance. Ed. by Maureen Honey. LC 88-36972. 210p. 1989. pap. 16.95 (0-8135-1420-7) Rutgers U Pr.

***Shadowed Ground: America's Landscapes of Violence & Tragedy.** Kenneth E. Foote. LC 96-41081. (Illus.). 384p. 1997. 45.00 (0-292-72499-3); pap. 19.95 (0-292-72500-0) U of Tex Pr.

***Shadowed Hills.** Audrey Howard. 425p. 1997. 27.00 (0-340-60952-4, Pub. by H & S UK) Trafalgar.

***Shadowed Hills.** Audrey Howard. 425p. 1997. pap. 10.95 (0-340-66078-3, Pub. by H & S UK) Trafalgar.

Shadowed Light. Antonia B. Laird. LC 92-81641. 80p. 1992. 11.00 (0-8233-0480-9) Golden Quill.

***Shadowed Lives.** 2nd ed. Chavez. (C). 1997. pap. text ed. write for info. (0-15-508089-X) HB Coll Pubs.

Shadowed Lives: Undocumented Immigrants in American Society. George D. Spindler. (Case Studies in Cultural Anthropology). (Illus.). 224p. (Orig.). (C). 1992. pap. text ed. 13.50 (0-03-031037-7) HB Coll Pubs.

Shadowed Memories: Battles of Destiny Shiloh. Al Lacy. 320p. 1995. pap. text ed. 6.99 (0-88070-657-0, Multnomah Bks) Multnomah Pubs.

***Shadowed Promises.** Vickie Moore. (Scarlet Ser.). (Orig.). 1997. mass mkt. 3.99 (1-85487-720-8, Pub. by Scarlet Bks UK) London Brdge.

Shadowed Reflections. Leydel J. Willis. 32p. 1984. pap. 5.00 (0-930416-08-2) Clodele.

Shadowed Reunion. large type ed. Lillian Cheatham. 304p. 1984. 25.99 (0-7089-1197-8) Ulverscroft.

Shadowed Vows. Sue Rich. Ed. by Carolyn Tolley. 272p. (Orig.). 1992. mass mkt. 5.50 (0-671-73626-4) PB.

Shadowfall. (Deathlands Ser.). 1995. mass mkt. 4.99 (0-373-62526-X, 1-62526-8) Harlequin Bks.

Shadowfall: Reflections on Nurturing Family Values. A. Gail Smith. LC 96-10504. vii, 232p. 1996. 15.95 (1-57345-145-2) Deseret Bk.

Shadowfane. Janny Wurts. (Cycle of Fire Ser.: Vol. 3). 304p. 1996. mass mkt. 4.99 (0-06-105470-4, HarperPrism) HarpC.

Shadowfires. Leigh Nichols, pseud. 448p. 1987. pap. 3.95 (0-380-75216-6) Avon.

ShadowFlow. Teresa Kao. LC 94-39254. 417p. (Orig.). 1995. pap. 15.00 (0-9631499-1-1) Gangor Pr.

Shadowgraphs: Anyone Can Make. Phila H. Webb & Jose Corby. LC 90-50896. (Illus.). 32p. (J). (gr. 1-4). 1991. reprint ed. 8.95 (1-56138-014-8) Running Pr.

Shadowing & Surveillance: A Complete Guide Book. Burt Rapp. LC 85-82012. 152p. (Orig.). 1985. pap. 16.95 (0-915179-33-4) Loompanics.

Shadowing the Ground. David Ignatow. LC 90-20872. (Wesleyan Poetry Ser.). 80p. 1991. pap. 11.95 (0-8195-1197-8, Wesleyan Univ Pr) U Pr of New Eng.

Shadowings: The Reader's Guide to Horror Fiction. Ed. by Douglas E. Winter. LC 83-21326. (Starmont Studies in Literary Criticism: No. 1). x, 148p. (Orig.). 1983. pap. 19.00 (0-916732-85-1); lib. bdg. 29.00 (0-916732-86-X) Borgo Pr.

Shadowland. Peter Straub. 480p. 1987. mass mkt. 6.99 (0-425-09726-9) Berkley Pub.

Shadowland: Gordon Anthony Photographs, 1926-1952. (Illus.). 64p. 1987. pap. 19.95 (0-904017-96-6, Pub. by Natl Port Gall UK) Antique Collect.

Shadowland Anthology, 2 vols., Set. Ed. by R. Gordon. 1976. lib. bdg. 200.00 (0-8490-2595-8) Gordon Pr.

Shadowlands. Leonore Fleischer. 1993. pap. 4.99 (0-451-18105-0, Sig) NAL-Dutton.

Shadowlands. William Nicholson. 96p. 1991. pap. 8.95 (0-452-26732-3, Plume) NAL-Dutton.

Shadowlands. limited ed. Peter Straub. (Classics Revisited Ser.). 1995. boxed 60.00 (1-887368-00-0) Gauntlet.

Shadowlife. Martin Grzimek. Tr. by Breon Mitchell from GER. LC 90-47795. 224p. 1991. 22.95 (0-8112-1151-7); pap. 11.95 (0-8112-1152-5, NDP705) New Directions.

Shadowlight. Mike Jefferies. 464p. 1990. mass mkt. 5.99 (0-06-100031-0, Harp PBks) HarpC.

***Shadowlight: A Photographer's Life.** Freeman Patterson. 176p. 1997. 45.00 (0-00-255075-X) HarperColl Wrld.

Shadowmaker. Ron Hansen. LC 85-45272. (Trophy Bk.). (Illus.). 80p. (J). (gr. 2-5). 1989. pap. 3.95 (0-06-440287-8, Trophy) HarpC Child Bks.

Shadowmaker. Joan L. Nixon. LC 93-32314. 208p. (J). 1994. 15.95 (0-385-32030-2) Delacorte.

Shadowmaker. Joan L. Nixon. 208p. (YA). (gr. 7 up). 1995. mass mkt. 3.99 (0-440-21942-6) Dell.

Shadowmakers. E. L. Harris. 200p. (C). 1995. 80.00 (1-886800-00-6) Am Soc Radiologic Techns.

Shadowman. Torsten Barring. (Orig.). 1994. mass mkt. 4.95 (1-56333-178-0, Badboy) Masquerade.

Shadowman. George W. Proctor. 256p. 1980. pap. 1.95 (0-449-14350-3, GM) Fawcett.

Shadowman's Way. Paul Pitts. 128p. (Orig.). (J). (gr. 5). 1992. pap. 3.99 (0-380-76210-2, Camelot) Avon.

An Asterisk (*) at the beginning of an entry indicates that the title is appearing in BIP for the first time.

Shadowmasters, No. 2. Potts et al. 48p. 1989. 3.95 (*0-87135-547-7*) Marvel Entmnt.

Shadowmasters, No. 3. Potts et al. 48p. 1989. 3.95 (*0-87135-548-5*) Marvel Entmnt.

Shadowmasters, No. 4. Potts et al. 48p. 1989. 3.95 (*0-87135-549-3*) Marvel Entmnt.

Shadowmasters, No.1. Pitts et al. 48p. 1989. 3.95 (*0-87135-546-9*) Marvel Entmnt.

Shadowmind. (New Doctor Who Adventures Ser.). 1993. pap. 5.95 (*0-426-20394-1*, Dr Who) Carol Pub Group.

***Shadow/Orphan Shadow.** Craig Czury. 36p. (ENG & SPA.). 1997. pap. 6.00 (*0-930502-27-2*) Pine Pr.

Shadowplay. large type ed. Norman Hartley. 528p. 1987. 25.99 (*0-7089-1654-6*) Ulverscroft.

Shadowplay: The Life of Antony Tudor. Donna Perlmutter. LC 94-39957. (Illus.). 432p. 1995. pap. 17.95 (*0-87910-189-X*) Limelight Edns.

***ShadowPrints.** Susan Jared. 66p. (Orig.). 1996. pap. 12.00 (*1-57502-279-6*, PO978) Morris Pubng.

Shadowrun. 2nd ed. FASA Staff. (Shadowrun Ser.). (Illus.). 232p. 1992. pap. 25.00 (*1-55560-180-4*, 7901) FASA Corp.

Shadowrun: Choose Your Enemy Carefully. Robert N. Charrette. (Secrets of Power Ser.: Vol. 2). 256p. (Orig.). 1991. pap. 5.50 (*0-451-45087-6*, ROC) NAL-Dutton.

Shadowrun: Never Deal with a Dragon. Robert N. Charrette. (Secrets of Power Ser.: Vol. 1). 288p. (Orig.). 1990. pap. 4.99 (*0-451-45078-7*, ROC) NAL-Dutton.

Shadowrun: Preying for Keeps. Mel Odom. 1996. mass mkt. 5.50 (*0-451-45374-3*, ROC) NAL-Dutton.

Shadowrun Companion. (Illus.). 152p. 1996. pap. 15.00 (*1-55560-298-3*) FASA Corp.

Shadowrun Twenty-Four see Steel Rain

***Shadowrun 25.** Nick Pollata. (Shadowrun Ser.: No. 25). 1997. pap. 5.99 (*0-451-45600-9*, ROC) NAL-Dutton.

Shadows. Bonnie Faber. 416p. 1995. mass mkt. 4.50 (*0-8217-4869-6*, Zebra Kensgtn) Kensgtn Pub Corp.

Shadows. Dennis Haseley. (Illus.). 80p. (J). (gr. 2-6). 1991. 12.95 (*0-374-36761-2*) FS&G.

Shadows. Dennis Haseley. (J). (gr. 4-7). 1993. pap. 3.95 (*0-374-46611-4*, Sunburst Bks) FS&G.

Shadows. Chenjerai Hove. (African Writers Ser.). 111p. (C). 1992. pap. 9.95 (*0-435-90591-0*, 90591) Heinemann.

Shadows. Robert F. Mainone. (Haiku Series: Vol. 5). (Illus.). 52p. (Orig.). 1971. pap. 7.00 (*1-888693-05-3*) Wnderlnd MI.

Shadows. Jonathan Nasaw. LC 97-8751. 1997. pap. 24.95 (*0-525-94065-0*) NAL-Dutton.

Shadows. Kimberly Rangel. 320p. (Orig.). 1996. mass mkt. 4.99 (*0-8439-4054-9*, Leisure Bks) Dorchester Pub Co.

Shadows. Kenneth Royce. 288p. 1996. 22.00 (*0-7278-4878-X*) Severn Hse.

***Shadows.** Kenneth Royce. LC 96-52557. 1997. pap. 20.95 (*0-7862-1023-0*) Thorndike Pr.

Shadows. John Saul. 400p. 1993. mass mkt. 6.99 (*0-553-56027-1*) Bantam.

Shadows. C. Ray Shubert. (Orig.). 1996. pap. 7.95 (*0-533-11928-6*) Vantage.

Shadows. Aristotle J. Spock. (Chapbook Ser.). 20p. (Orig.). 1996. pap. 2.50 (*0-9636959-5-9*) Coe Review Pr.

Shadows. Jonathan Tweet. (On the Edge Ser.). 1995. 1.95 (*1-887801-25-1*, Atlas Games) Trident MN.

***Shadows.** Dana Warner. 310p. (Orig.). 1997. mass mkt. 4.99 (*1-55237-017-8*, Pub. by Comnwlth Pub CN) Partners Pubs Grp.

Shadows: A Book of Verse. Kel Lane. LC 91-90777. 61p. (Orig.). 1992. pap. 7.00 (*0-9631621-0-1*) K Lane.

Shadows: A Mayan Way of Knowing. Ruben E. Reina. 1984. 13.95 (*0-88282-008-7*) New Horizon NJ.

Shadows: Here, There, & Everywhere. Ron Goor & Nancy Goor. LC 81-43036. (Illus.). 48p. (J). (gr. k-3). 1981. lib. bdg. 14.89 (*0-690-04133-0*, Crowell Jr Bks) HarpC Child Bks.

***Shadows: Secret of the Shadow Road & Other Tales.** Jonathan Schmidt. LC 97-11750. (J). 1997. write for info. (*1-56565-776-4*) Lowell Hse.

Shadows: The Depiction of Cast Shadows in Western Art. Ernest H. Gombrich. 1995. 12.50 (*0-300-06357-1*) Yale U Pr.

***Shadows: The Life & Times of Eliphalet Ball: the Founder of the Town of Ballston.** Katherine Q. Briaddy. 346p. 1991. pap. 25.00 (*0-614-26420-0*) Purple Mnt Pr.

Shadows after Dark. Ouida Crozier. 224p. 1993. pap. 9.95 (*1-883061-50-4*) Rising NY.

Shadows & Enlightenment. Michael Baxandall. LC 94-40132. 1995. 30.00 (*0-300-05979-5*) Yale U Pr.

***Shadows & Enlightenment.** Michael Baxandall. 1997. pap. text ed. 20.00 (*0-300-07272-4*) Yale U Pr.

Shadows & Goatbones. Barbara F. Lefcowitz. LC 92-51111. (SCOP Ser.: No. 18). 64p. 1992. pap. 9.95 (*0-930526-17-1*) SCOP Pubns.

Shadows & Lace. Teresa Medeiros. 352p. 1996. mass mkt. 5.99 (*0-553-57623-2*, Fanfare) Bantam.

Shadows & Light. Lindsay McKenna. (Special Edition Ser.). 1994. mass mkt. 3.50 (*0-373-09878-2*, 5-09878-5) Silhouette.

Shadows & Light. Ed. by Nicole Walstrum. 1996. 69.95 (*1-57553-006-6*) Watermrk Pr.

Shadows & Light: Midwestern Poetry. Florence H. Willette. LC 79-79103. (Illus.). 1969. 5.00 (*0-87839-000-6*) North Star.

Shadows & Moonlight. Mary Fields. (Illus.). 75p. (Orig.). 1990. pap. 8.50 (*0-9628015-0-X*) M Fields.

Shadows & Reflections. Tana Hoban. LC 89-30461. (Illus.). 32p. (J). (ps up). 1990. 12.95 (*0-688-07089-2*); lib. bdg. 12.88 (*0-688-07090-6*) Greenwillow.

Shadows & Substance: The Chemical Weapons Convention. Ed. by Benoit Morel & Kyle Olson. LC 93-8682. (Ridgeway International Security Studies). 345p. (C). 1993. pap. text ed. 75.00 (*0-8133-8735-3*) Westview.

Shadows & Whispers: Power Politics Inside the Kremlin from Brezhnev to Gorbachev. Dusko Doder. (Illus.). 339p. 1986. 19.95 (*0-685-17620-7*) Random.

Shadows & Wolves. William Herrick. LC 79-20726. 1980. 9.95 (*0-8112-0758-7*) New Directions.

Shadows are About. Ann W. Paul. (Illus.). 32p. (J). 1992. pap. 13.95 (*0-590-44842-0*, Scholastic Hardcover) Scholastic Inc.

Shadows Are About. Ann W. Paul. (J). 1996. pap. text ed. 4.95 (*0-590-44843-9*) Scholastic Inc.

Shadows at Noon: A True Story of Love, Terror & Escape. Margot Webb. Ed. by Marcus Webb. (Illus.). 153p. (J). (gr. 6-10). 1992. write for info. (*0-9631096-1-8*) Ascendant.

Shadows Burning. W. S. DiPiero. 80p. 1995. text ed. 29.95 (*0-8101-5019-0*) Northwestern U Pr.

Shadows Burning. W. S. DiPiero. 80p. (C). 1995. pap. 12.95 (*0-8101-5020-4*) Northwestern U Pr.

Shadow's Daughter. Shirley Meier. 1991. mass mkt. 4.99 (*0-671-72096-1*) Baen Bks.

Shadows End. large type ed. Barbara Whitehead. 368p. 1994. 25.99 (*0-7089-3106-5*) Ulverscroft.

Shadow's End. Sheri S. Tepper. 464p. 1995. reprint ed. mass mkt., pap. 6.50 (*0-553-57326-8*, Spectra) Bantam.

Shadows Fall. Simon R. Green. 448p. (Orig.). 1994. pap. 5.99 (*0-451-45363-8*, ROC) NAL-Dutton.

Shadow's Flame. Alicia Scott. (Intimate Moments Ser.). 1994. mass mkt. 3.50 (*0-373-07546-4*, 5-07546-0) Silhouette.

Shadows Free. Connie Burton. LC 94-70628. (Illus.). 32p. (J). (gr. k-5). 1994. 17.95 (*0-9636274-3-0*); pap. 8.95 (*1-885340-05-2*) Coming Age Pr.

***Shadows from Elseetoss: A Love Story Bridging Two Lifetimes.** White Morning Glory, pseud. 242p. (Orig.). 1996. pap. 11.95 (*1-57502-344-X*, PO1139) Morris Pubng.

Shadows from the Past. Venetia Murray. (C). 1988. 75.00 (*1-85219-060-4*, Pub. by Bishopsgate Pr Ltd UK) St Mut.

Shadows from the Sea. large type ed. Jane Donnelly. 329p. 1980. 25.99 (*0-7089-0479-3*) Ulverscroft.

***Shadows Illuminated: Women in a Rural Culture.** Terry Jaakkola & Julia L. Frericks. Ed. by John C. Massmann. (Illus.). 150p. (Orig.). 1996. pap. 19.95 (*1-882049-00-4*) Stearns Cty Hist Soc.

***Shadows in a Chinese Landscape: The Notes of a Confucian Scholar.** Yun Chi. Ed. & Tr. by David Keenan from CHI. (New Studies in Asian Culture). 165p. (C). (gr. 13). 1997. text ed. 52.95 (*0-7656-0173-7*, East Gate Bk); pap. text ed. 19.95 (*0-7656-0174-5*, East Gate Bk) M E Sharpe.

Shadows in Bronze. Lindsey Davis. 1992. mass mkt. 4.99 (*0-345-37426-6*) Ballantine.

Shadows in My Hands: A Southwestern Odyssey. Jane C. Coleman. 125p. 1993. 23.00 (*0-8040-0972-4*) Swallow.

***Shadows in Paradise.** Eric Remarque. 1998. pap. write for info. (*0-449-91248-5*) Fawcett.

Shadows in the Afternoon. large type ed. Robert T. Stevens. 400p. 1985. 25.99 (*0-7089-1302-4*) Ulverscroft.

Shadows in the Cave: A Phenomenological Approach to Literary Criticism Based on Hispanic Texts. Mario J. Valdes. (Romance Ser.: No. 44). 224p. 1982. 30.00 (*0-8020-5568-0*) U of Toronto Pr.

***Shadows in the Dawn: Lemurs of Madagascar.** Kathryn Lasky. LC 97-6055. (Illus.). (J). 1997. write for info. (*0-15-200258-8*); pap. write for info. (*0-15-200281-2*) HarBrace.

Shadows in the Field: New Perspective for Fieldwork in Ethnomusicology. Ed. by Gregory F. Barz & Timothy J. Cooley. (Illus.). 256p. 1996. pap. 17.95 (*0-19-510911-2*); text ed. 35.00 (*0-19-510910-4*) OUP.

Shadows in the Fire. large type ed. Eva Dane. 336p. 1986. 25.99 (*0-7089-1416-0*) Ulverscroft.

***Shadows in the Flame.** Tess Farraday. 368p. 1997. mass mkt. 5.99 (*0-515-12140-1*) Jove Pubns.

***Shadows in the Forest: Japan & the Politics of Timber in Southeast Asia.** Peter Dauvergne. LC 96-50982. (Politics, Science, & the Environment Ser.). (Illus.). 336p. 1997. 45.00 (*0-262-04160-X*); pap. 22.00 (*0-262-54087-8*) MIT Pr.

Shadows in the Mirror. Roslynn Griffith. 304p. 1995. mass mkt. 4.99 (*0-06-108355-0*) HarpC.

Shadows in the Mist: (O'Connor Trilogy) Karen Young. (Superromance Ser.). 1994. mass mkt. 3.50 (*0-373-70606-5*, 1-70606-8) Harlequin Bks.

Shadows in the Night. Zev Spektor. (Illus.). 150p. (J). (gr. 5-6). 1991. 11.95 (*1-56062-100-1*); pap. 8.95 (*0-685-52958-4*) CIS Comm.

Shadows in the Sand. Elizabeth Harris. 384p. (Orig.). 1994. mass mkt. 4.99 (*0-380-77147-0*) Avon.

Shadows in the Sea: The Sharks, Skates & Rays, Fully Updated Edition. Harold W. McCormick et al. LC 96-32190. 1996. pap. text ed. 18.95 (*1-55821-518-2*) Lyons & Burford.

Shadows in the Sun. Maurice Davin-Power. (Irish Play Ser.). 1980. pap. 2.95 (*0-912262-64-8*) Proscenium.

Shadows in the Sun. R. Rabindranath Menon. 1976. 8.00 (*0-89253-813-9*); text ed. 4.80 (*0-89253-814-7*) Ind-US Inc.

Shadows in the Sun. Chad Oliver. 1993. reprint ed. lib. bdg. 18.95 (*0-89968-357-6*, Lghtyr Pr) Buccaneer Bks.

Shadows in the Sun (Poems) Patricia C. Florit. 32p. (Orig.). 1985. pap. 5.00 (*0-89729-362-2*) Ediciones.

Shadows in the Water: A Starbuck Family Adventure. Kathryn Lasky. LC 92-8139. 224p. (J). (gr. 3-7). 1992. 17.00 (*0-15-273533-X*, HB Juv Bks); pap. 8.00 (*0-15-273534-8*, HB Juv Bks) HarBrace.

Shadows in the Wind. Luanshya Greer. 470p. 1993. 24.95 (*1-85797-079-9*) Trafalgar.

Shadows in Their Blood. large type ed. Marian Babson. LC 93-46829. 1994. lib. bdg. 16.95 (*0-8161-5952-1*, GK Hall) Thorndike Pr.

Shadows in Twilight: A 1940-1945 Testimony. Fred Daniels. 66p. 1992. pap. 8.95 (*965-229-076-9*, Pub. by Gefen Pub Hse IS) Gefen Bks.

Shadows in Velvet. Haywood Smith. 1996. mass mkt. 5.99 (*0-312-95873-0*) St Martin.

Shadows Like These: Poems. Marilyn Taylor. LC 94-26827. (Poets Ser.). 94p. 1994. 12.50 (*0-940473-27-5*) Wm Caxton.

Shadows Linger. Glen Cook. 320p. (Orig.). 1990. pap. 3.95 (*0-8125-0842-4*) Tor Bks.

Shadows Made the Forms of People. James Furiano. 1994. 15.95 (*0-533-11119-6*) Vantage.

Shadows of a Lonely Heart: The Jay T. Andell Story. Carlos H. Sparks. 1994. 15.95 (*0-533-10990-6*) Vantage.

Shadows of a Sound. Hwang Sun-Won. Ed. by J. Martin Holman. LC 89-32146. 237p. (KOR.). 1990. 17.95 (*0-916515-65-6*) Mercury Hse Inc.

***Shadows of Aggar.** 2nd rev. ed. Chris A. Wolfe. 400p. 1997. pap. 12.95 (*1-886383-30-8*) Pride OH.

***Shadows of Alamo Plaza.** Donny D. Atkins. 216p. (Orig.). 1995. pap. 14.95 (*0-9653880-1-8*) Bear Paw.

Shadows of Angels. Marilyn Brown. LC 92-75977. 1993. pap. 10.95 (*1-55503-521-3*, 01111205) Covenant Comms.

Shadows of Asheville. Rennie M. Hickman. 60p. pap. 5.00 (*1-878096-24-9*) Best E TX Pubs.

***Shadows of Childhood.** Elizabeth Gille. Date not set. 23.00 (*1-56584-388-6*) New Press NY.

Shadows of Colors. Peter Iden et al. (Illus.). 120p. 1995. 45.00 (*3-905514-85-0*, Pub. by Edit Stemmle SZ) Dist Art Pubs.

Shadows of Crazy Mountain. H. L. Richardson. (Sam Dodd Western Mystery Ser.: No. 2). 320p. 1996. pap. 10.99 (*0-8499-3856-2*) Word Pub.

Shadows of Darkness. large type ed. Lesley Denny. 1991. 25.99 (*0-7089-2498-0*) Ulverscroft.

Shadows of Death. (Library of Curious & Unusual Facts). 1992. 17.95 (*0-8094-7719-X*); lib. bdg. write for info. (*0-8094-7720-3*) Time-Life.

Shadows of Death. Jenna Washington. 1994. pap. 12.95 (*0-533-11020-3*) Vantage.

Shadows of Doom. Ed Greenwood. (Shadow of the Avatar Ser.). 320p. (Orig.). 1995. pap. 5.99 (*0-7869-0300-7*) TSR Inc.

Shadows of Doom. Dennis L. McKiernan. (Iron Tower Trilogy Ser.: Bk. 2). 304p. 1987. pap. 4.50 (*0-451-45103-1*, Sig) NAL-Dutton.

Shadows of Doubt. Palma Harcourt. 192p. 1985. 13.95 (*0-8253-0264-1*) Beaufort Bks NY.

Shadows of Eden Vol. 1. Linda R. DeJong. 1995. mass mkt. 4.99 (*0-312-95114-0*) St Martin.

Shadows of Empire: Colonial Discourse & Javanese Tales. Laurie J. Sears. LC 95-30518. (Illus.). 352p. 1996. text ed. 49.95 (*0-8223-1685-4*); pap. text ed. 16.95 (*0-8223-1697-8*) Duke.

***Shadows of Fame.** Angie C. Thomas. LC 96-90933. 1997. 11.95 (*0-533-12217-1*) Vantage.

Shadows of Fear. Ed. by David G. Hartwell. (Foundations of Fear Ser.: No. 1). 480p. 1994. mass mkt. 4.99 (*0-8125-1896-9*) Tor Bks.

Shadows of Forgotten Ancestors: A Search for Who We Are. Carl Sagan & Ann Druyan. 528p. 1993. pap. 14.00 (*0-345-38472-5*, Ballantine Trade) Ballantine.

Shadows of Good Things, or the Gospel in Type. R. R. Byrum. (Illus.). 144p. pap. 1.50 (*0-686-29141-7*) Faith Pub Hse.

Shadows of Hiroshima. Wilfred Burchett. 123p. 1983. text ed. 22.95 (*0-86091-080-6*, Pub. by Verso UK); pap. text ed. 14.95 (*0-86091-783-5*, Pub. by Verso UK) Routledge Chapman & Hall.

Shadows of His Coming. large type ed. William M. Juring. (Illus.). 189p. (Orig.). 1993. pap. 8.95 (*0-9634885-0-3*) Hse of Waymark.

Shadows of His Sacrifice. Leslie Hardinge. LC 95-61887. 96p. 1996. reprint ed. per. 7.95 (*1-57258-065-8*) Teach Servs.

Shadows of Hope: Clinton & America's Future. Sam Smith. LC 94-2852. 256p. 1994. 22.50 (*0-253-35284-3*) Ind U Pr.

Shadows of Life & Thought: A Retrospective Review in the Form of Memoirs. Arthur E. Waite. 288p. 1992. pap. 24.95 (*1-56459-242-1*) Kessinger Pub.

Shadows of Love. Ed. by Charles Jurrist. 231p. (Orig.). 1988. pap. 8.95 (*1-55583-136-2*) Alyson Pubns.

Shadows of Love. Carolyn B. Pierce. LC 85-90440. (Illus.). 75p. 1985. 6.95 (*0-9615667-0-1*) Starlight Pubns.

Shadows of My Heart. Virginia Glenham. 1993. pap. 9.95 (*1-883103-03-7*) United NC.

Shadows of Night: The Hidden World of the Little Brown Bat. Barbara Bash. LC 92-22713. (Illus.). 32p. (J). (gr. 1-5). 1993. 16.95 (*0-87156-562-5*) Sierra Club Childrens.

***Shadows of Night: The Hidden World of the Little Brown Bat.** Barbara Bash. (Illus.). (J). 1995. pap. 12.95 (*0-87156-384-3*) Sierra Club Childrens.

Shadows of Night: The Hidden World of the Little Brown Bat. Barbara Bash. (Illus.). 32p. (J). (gr. 1-5). 1995. pap. 6.95 (*0-87156-440-8*) Sierra Club Childrens.

Shadows of Old New Orleans. James Register. 1967. 12.50 (*0-87511-097-5*) Claitors.

Shadows of Pain: Intimacy & Sexual Problems in Family Life. Vimala Pillari. LC 96-14384. 248p. 1997. pap. 40.00 (*0-7657-0009-3*) Aronson.

Shadows of Race & Class. Raymond S. Franklin. 180p. (C). 1991. pap. text ed. 15.95 (*0-8166-1957-3*) U of Minn Pr.

Shadows of Realism: Dramaturgy & the Theories & Practices of Modernism. Nancy Kindelan. LC 95-20545. 184p. 1996. pap. text ed. 18.95 (*0-275-95471-4*, Greenwood Pr) Greenwood.

Shadows of Realism: Dramaturgy & the Theories & Practices of Modernism. Nancy Kinderlan. LC 95-20545. (Contributions in Drama & Theatre Studies: No. 68). 184p. 1996. text ed. 57.95 (*0-313-29736-3*, Greenwood Pr) Greenwood.

***Shadows of Selastos.** (Bloodshadows Ser.). 15.00 (*0-87431-383-X*, 33013) West End Games.

***Shadows of Steel.** Dale Brown. 384p. 1997. mass mkt. 6.99 (*0-425-15716-4*) Berkley Pub.

Shadows of Steel. Dale Brown. LC 96-24248. 400p. 1996. 24.95 (*0-399-14139-1*, Thorndike Lrg Prnt) Thorndike Pr.

Shadows of Steel. large type ed. Dale Brown. LC 96-24248. 1996. lib. bdg. 20.00 (*0-7862-0779-5*, Thorndike Lrg Prnt) Thorndike Pr.

***Shadows of Steel.** large type ed. Dale Brown. 1997. pap. 24.95 (*0-7862-0780-9*, Thorndike Lrg Prnt) Thorndike Pr.

Shadows of Tender Fury: The Letters & Communiques of Subcomandante Marcos & the Zapatista Army of National Liberation. Tr. by Frank Bardacke et al. 288p. 1995. pap. 15.00 (*0-85345-918-5*) Monthly Rev.

***Shadows of the City.** Iron Crown Enterprises Staff. 1993. 15.00 (*1-55806-181-9*) Iron Crown Ent Inc.

Shadows of the Cross. Molly D. Roth. LC 94-19568. (Illus.). 57p. 1994. 21.95 (*0-8294-0810-X*) Loyola Pr.

Shadows of the Dictators, (1925-1950 AD) (Time Frame Ser.). (Illus.). 176p. 1989. 19.93 (*0-8094-6483-7*); lib. bdg. 25.93 (*0-8094-6484-5*) Time-Life.

***Shadows of the Empire.** Dark Horse Comics Staff. (Star Wars Ser.). (Illus.). 1997. pap. text ed. 17.95 (*1-56971-183-6*) Dark Horse Comics.

Shadows of the Empire. Christopher Golden. (Star Wars Ser.). (J). 1996. mass mkt. 4.50 (*0-440-41303-6*) Dell.

Shadows of the Empire. Steve Perry. (Star Wars Ser.). 352p. 1996. 22.95 (*0-553-10089-0*, Spectra) Bantam.

***Shadows of the Empire.** Steve Perry. (Star Wars Ser.). 416p. (YA). (gr. 5 up). 1997. mass mkt. 5.99 (*0-553-57413-2*, Spectra) Bantam.

Shadows of the Empire for Ultra 64. Bradygames Staff. 1996. pap. text ed. 9.99 (*1-56686-549-2*) Brady Pub.

***Shadows of the Empire Game Secrets & Solutions.** Bart Farkas. 144p. 1996. per., pap. 12.99 (*0-7615-0937-2*) Prima Pub.

Shadows of the Future: H. G. Wells, Science Fiction, & Prophecy. Patrick Parrinder. LC 95-21827. (Utopianism & Communitarianism Ser.). (C). 1996. pap. 16.95 (*0-8156-0332-0*, PASFP); text ed. 34.95 (*0-8156-2691-6*, PASF) Syracuse U Pr.

Shadows of the Heart. Tracy Grant. 384p. 1996. mass mkt. 5.50 (*0-440-22164-1*) Dell.

Shadows of the Heart. Smart. Date not set. mass mkt. write for info. (*0-614-08382-6*, Pinncle Kensgtn) Kensgtn Pub Corp.

Shadows of the Heart. James Whitehead. 216p. 1996. pap. text ed. 14.95 (*0-8245-1534-X*) Crossroad NY.

Shadows of the Heart: A Spirituality of the Negative Emotions. James D. Whitehead & Evelyn E. Whitehead. LC 94-18087. 1994. 19.95 (*0-8245-1441-6*) Crossroad NY.

Shadows of the Indian: Stereotypes in American Culture. Raymond W. Stedman. LC 82-40330. (Illus.). 300p. (Orig.). 1986. 34.95 (*0-8061-1822-9*); pap. 17.95 (*0-8061-1963-2*) U of Okla Pr.

***Shadows of the King.** Guy Kettelhack. 1998. write for info. (*0-517-70827-2*) Crown Pub Group.

Shadows of the Lamp. large type ed. Clare F. Holmes. 320p. 1995. 25.99 (*0-7089-3274-6*) Ulverscroft.

Shadows of the Mind: A Search for the Missing Science of Consciousness. Roger Penrose. (Illus.). 480p. 1996. reprint ed. pap. 16.95 (*0-19-510646-6*) OUP.

Shadows of the Mind: On Consciousness, Computation, & the New Physics of the Mind. Roger Penrose. (Illus.). 320p. 1994. 25.00 (*0-19-853978-9*) OUP.

Shadows of the Past. Alma Blair. 1993. 17.95 (*0-8034-9027-5*) Bouregy.

Shadows of the Past. Douglas Hulick. 150p. (YA). (gr. 10 up). 1995. pap. 15.00 (*0-9641722-3-2*) Black Gate.

Shadows of the Pomegranate Tree. Tariq Ali. LC 93-37283. 242p. (gr. 13). 1993. pap. 15.00 (*0-86091-676-6*, Pub. by Vrso UK) Norton.

***Shadows of the Puppet.** Mediha F. Saliba. (Illus.). 15p. (Orig.). 1996. pap. 14.95 (*0-9655497-0-4*) SB Review Pubns.

Shadows of the Sacred: Seeing through Spiritual Illusions. Frances E. Vaughan. LC 95-7201. 306p. 1995. 24.95 (*0-8356-0723-2*, Quest) Theos Pub Hse.

Shadows of the Stage. William Winter. 350p. (C). 1996. reprint ed. pap. text ed. 25.00 (*0-87556-828-9*) Saifer.

Shadows of the Voice. E. Robson & Larry Wendt. 1982. pap. 14.00 (*0-934982-09-0*) Primary Pr.

Shadows of the Voice. deluxe limited ed. E. Robson & Larry Wendt. 1982. 35.00 (*0-934982-08-2*) Primary Pr.

Shadows of Time. Mehr N. Masroor. (C). 1988. 31.00 (*81-7001-030-6*, Pub. by Chanakya II) S Asia.

***Shadows of Vietnam: Lyndon Johnson's Wars.** Frank E. Vandiver. LC 96-50121. (Illus.). 432p. (C). 1997. text ed. 29.95 (*0-89096-747-4*) Tex A&M Univ Pr.

Shadows of Yesterday. Sandra Brown. 272p. 1992. mass mkt. 6.50 (*0-446-36071-6*) Warner Bks.

***Shadows of Yesterday.** Sandra Brown. 1997. mass mkt. 3.99 (*0-446-60566-2*) Warner Bks.

Shadows of Yesterday. large type ed. Sandra Brown. LC 93-20593. 1993. lib. bdg. 19.95 (*1-56054-788-X*) Thorndike Pr.

Shadows of Yesterday. large type ed. Mary Mackie. 224p. 1996. pap. 17.95 (*0-7838-1627-8*, GK Hall) Thorndike Pr.

Shadows of Your Mind. Tom Johnson. LC 83-762. (Illus.). 207p. (Orig.). 1983. pap. 8.95 (*0-941992-02-0*) Los Arboles Pub.

An Asterisk (*) at the beginning of an entry indicates that the title is appearing in BIP for the first time.

***Shadows on a Rock: Letters & Drawings.** B. T. Johnson. (Illus.). 16p. 1996. pap. 2.00 (*1-885710-12-7*) Geekspeak Unique.

Shadows on a Sunset Sea. Sabine Kells. 400p. (Orig.). 1994. mass mkt., pap. text ed. 4.99 (*0-505-51984-4*) Dorchester Pub Co.

Shadows on a Wall. Ray Connolly. 541p. 1995. 24.95 (*0-312-11887-2*) St Martin.

Shadows on Glass: The Indian Photographs of Ben Wittick. Patricia J. Broder. 1991. 49.95 (*0-8476-7631-5*) Rowman.

Shadows on Glass: The Indian World of Ben Wittick. Patricia J. Broder. 160p. 1991. pap. 24.95 (*0-8476-7701-X*) Rowman.

Shadows on My Heart: The Civil War Diary of Lucy Rebecca Buck of Virginia. Ed. by Elizabeth R. Baer. LC 96-766. (Southern Voices from the Past Ser.). 1997. 50.00 (*0-8203-1852-3*) U of Ga Pr.

***Shadows on Stoney Creek.** 208p. (J). 1997. write for info. (*0-7814-3005-4*, Chariot Bks) Chariot Victor.

***Shadows on the Flats: The Saltwater Images of Chet Reneson & Ed Gray.** Ed Gray. (Illus.). 128p. 1997. 35.00 (*1-57223-127-0*, 1270) Willow Creek Pr.

Shadows on the Grass. A. W. Cunningham. (C). 1989. 35.00 (*0-7223-2160-0*, Pub. by A H S Ltd UK) St Mut.

Shadows on the Hill: The Immortal Eyes, Bk. II. Jackie Cassada. (Orig.). 1996. pap. 5.99 (*1-56504-861-X*, 11402, Wrld of Darkness) White Wolf.

***Shadows on the Hudson.** Isaac B. Singer. LC 97-18677. 1997. 30.00 (*0-374-26186-5*) FS&G.

Shadows on the Koyukuk: An Alaskan Native's Life along the River. Sidney Huntington & Jim Rearden. LC 92-38360. 236p. 1993. pap. 12.95 (*0-88240-427-X*) Alaska Northwest.

Shadows on the Mirror. large type ed. Frances Fyfield. (Orig.). 1991. reprint ed. lib. bdg. 18.95 (*1-56054-223-3*) Thorndike Pr.

Shadows on the Mirror. Frances Fyfield. Ed. by Jane Chelius. 224p. (Orig.). 1992. reprint ed. mass mkt. 4.50 (*0-671-70162-2*) PB.

Shadows on the Past: Studies in the Historical Fiction Film. Leger Grindon. LC 93-33042. (Culture & the Moving Image Ser.). (Illus.). 256p. 1994. 54.95 (*1-56639-181-4*); pap. 18.95 (*1-56639-182-2*) Temple U Pr.

Shadows on the Rock. Willa Cather. 1976. 23.95 (*0-8488-0455-4*) Amereon Ltd.

Shadows on the Rock. Willa Cather. LC 95-8915. 1995. pap. 12.00 (*0-679-76404-6*, Vin) Random.

Shadows on the Sand: The Memoirs of Sir Gawain Bell. Gawain Bell. LC 83-40286. (Illus.). 253p. 1984. text ed. 29.95 (*0-312-71418-1*) St Martin.

Shadows on the Shore. large type ed. Jessica Stirling. LC 94-17036. 655p. 1994. lib. bdg. 23.95 (*0-7862-0243-2*) Thorndike Pr.

Shadows on the Snow. large type ed. Phyllida Barstow. (Historical Romance Ser.). 752p. 1993. 25.99 (*0-7089-2981-8*) Ulverscroft.

Shadows on the Sun: Star Trek Ser. Michael J. Friedman. Ed. by Kevin Ryan. 352p. 1994. reprint ed. mass mkt. 5.99 (*0-671-86910-8*) PB.

Shadows on the Sundial. Rainer M. Rilke. Ed. by Stanley H. Barkan. Tr. by Norbert Krapf. (Review Chapbook Ser.: No. 21: Swiss (German) Poetry 1). (Illus.). 48p. (ENG & GER.). 1992. 15.00 (*0-89304-895-X*); pap. 5.00 (*0-89304-896-8*) Cross-Cultrl NY.

Shadows on the Sundial: Selected Early Poems of Rainer Maria Rilke. Tr. by Norbert Krapf from GER. 44p. (Orig.). (C). 1990. pap. 6.00 (*1-878173-01-4*) Birnham Wood.

Shadows on the Wall. (Community Anthology Ser.). 139p. (Orig.). 1989. pap. text ed. 5.00 (*0-940696-20-7*) Monroe County Lib.

Shadows on the Wall. Arch Merrill. LC 87-24477. (Arch Merrill's New York Ser.: Vol. 11). (Illus.). 168p. 1987. reprint ed. pap. 12.95 (*1-55787-000-4*, NY36045, Empire State Bks) Hrt of the Lakes.

Shadows on the Wall. Howard Weeden. LC 72-178485. (Black Heritage Library Collection). 1977. reprint ed. 13.95 (*0-8369-8935-X*) Ayer.

Shadows on the Wall: or Glimpses of the Past. John H. Hewitt. LC 76-166200. reprint ed. 37.50 (*0-404-07225-9*) AMS Pr.

Shadows on the Wasteland: Crossing Antarctica with Ranulph Fiennes. Mike Stroud. 192p. 1996. pap. 12.95 (*0-87951-636-4*) Overlook Pr.

Shadows on the Water. large type ed. Elizabeth Cadell. LC 94-26164. 311p. 1995. pap. 18.95 (*0-7862-0289-0*) Thorndike Pr.

Shadows over Anahuac: An Ecological Interpretation of Crisis & Development in Central Mexico, 1730-1800. Arij Ouweneel. LC 95-41814. 384p. (C). 1996. text ed. 60.00 (*0-8263-1731-6*) U of NM Pr.

Shadows over Cypress Swamp. Patricia Werner. 384p. 1993. mass mkt. 3.99 (*0-8217-4332-5*, Zebra Kensgtn) Kensgtn Pub Corp.

Shadows over Innsmouth. Ramsey Campbell et al. Ed. by Stephen Jones. (Illus.). 450p. 1994. 29.00 (*1-878252-18-6*) Fedogan & Bremer.

Shadows over Innsmouth. deluxe limited ed. Ramsey Campbell et al. Ed. by Stephen Jones. (Illus.). 450p. 1994. Ltd., signed & slipcased ed. boxed 95.00 (*1-878252-19-4*) Fedogan & Bremer.

Shadows over My Berlin: One Woman's Story of World War II. Heidi S. Vance & Janet B. Speer. LC 96-41917. (Illus.). 200p. 1996. 25.00 (*0-913337-30-7*) Southfarm Pr.

Shadows over Stonewycke. Michael Phillips & Judith Pella. (Stonewycke Legacy Ser.: Bk. 2). 464p. (Orig.). 1995. mass mkt. 6.99 (*1-55661-632-5*) Bethany Hse.

Shadows over Stonewycke. Michael R. Phillips & Judith Pella. LC 88-10332. (Stonewycke Legacy Fiction Ser.: Vol. 2). 400p. (Orig.). 1988. pap. 9.99 (*0-87123-901-9*) Bethany Hse.

Shadows over Sunnyside: An Arkansas Plantation in Transition, 1830-1945. Ed. by Jeannie M. Whayne. LC 92-39706. (Illus.). 184p. 1995. pap. 12.00 (*1-55728-417-2*) U of Ark Pr.

***Shadows Planet Collection.** (Star Wars Supplements Ser.). 15.00 (*0-87431-284-1*, 40134) West End Games.

Shadow's Realm. Mickey Z. Reichert. (Bifrost Guardians Ser.: No. 4). 304p. 1990. mass mkt. 4.99 (*0-88677-419-5*) DAW Bks.

Shadows Rise: Abraham Lincoln & the Ann Rutledge Legend. John E. Walsh. LC 92-34284. 224p. 1993. 15.95 (*0-252-02011-1*) U of Ill Pr.

Shadows-Secrets, & Other Poems. Doug Dahl. 1990. 7.95 (*0-533-09375-9*) Vantage.

Shadows Short Story Collection. 1993. mass mkt. 4.99 (*0-373-48263-9*, 5-48263-3) Silhouette.

Shadow's Son. Shirley Meier et al. 1991. mass mkt. 4.99 (*0-671-72091-0*) Baen Bks.

***Shadows Sourcebook.** (Star Wars Ser.). 20.00 (*0-87431-281-7*, 40122) West End Games.

***Shadows Walking Downward.** Bruce Jackson. 142p. Date not set. pap. 9.95 (*0-614-19920-4*) Manic D Pr.

Shadow's Weight. Eugenio De Andrade. Tr. by Alexis Levitin from POR. LC 96-75501. 145p. (Orig.). (ENG & POR.). 1996. pap. text ed. 7.50 (*0-943722-23-3*) Gavea-Brown.

Shadowtech Sourcebook: A Shadowrun Sourcebook. FASA Staff & Karl Wu. (Shadowrun Ser.). (Illus.). 128p. 1991. pap. 15.00 (*1-55560-156-1*, 7110) FASA Corp.

Shadowtime: History & Representation in Hardy, Conrad & George Eliot. Jim Reilly. LC 92-16199. 208p. (C). (gr. 13). 1993. text ed. 49.95 (*0-415-08597-7*, B0372, Routledge NY) Routledge.

Shadowtime: History & Representation in Hardy, Conrad & George Eliot. Jim Reilly. LC 92-16199. 192p. (C). 1994. pap. 18.95 (*0-415-11893-X*, B4788) Routledge.

Shadowville. Michael Bartalos. LC 94-43070. 40p. (J). 1995. pap. 13.99 (*0-670-86161-8*, Viking) Viking Penguin.

Shadowwork. Jane Elsdon. 1993. pap. 6.95 (*0-685-70585-4*) Pudding Hse Pubns.

Shadowy Heroes: Irish Literature of the 1890's. Wayne E. Hall. LC 80-21383. (Irish Studies). (Illus.). 1980. 34.95 (*0-8156-2231-7*) Syracuse U Pr.

Shadrach. Meindert DeJong. LC 53-5250. (Illus.). 192p. (J). (gr. 3-6). 1953. lib. bdg. 14.89 (*0-06-021546-1*) HarpC Child Bks.

Shadrach. Meindert DeJong. LC 53-5250. (Trophy Bk.). (Illus.). 192p. (J). (gr. 3-6). 1980. pap. 3.95 (*0-06-440115-4*, Trophy) HarpC Child Bks.

Shadrach, Meshach, & Abednego. Beverly C. Burgess. (Men of God Ser.). (Illus.). 32p. (Orig.). (J). 1996. 4.98 (*1-879470-06-3*) Burgess Pub.

***Shadrach Minkins: From Fugitive Slave to Citizen.** Gary L. Collison. LC 96-35555. 1997. 27.95 (*0-674-80298-5*) HUP.

Shadrach's Crossing see Smuggler's Island

***Shady Borders.** John Sherwood. 192p. 1996. 22.00 (*0-7278-5111-X*) Severn Hse.

Shady Business: Confronting Corporate Corruption. Irwin Ross. LC 92-29437. 1992. 19.95 (*0-87078-340-8*); pap. 9.95 (*0-87078-341-6*) TCFP-PPP.

***Shady Garden: A Practical Guide to Planning & Planting.** Jane Taylor. (Illus.). 128p. 1997. pap. 16.95 (*0-8069-0842-4*) Sterling.

Shady Grove. Janice H. Giles. LC 78-12454. 260p. 1978. reprint ed. 16.95 (*0-87797-211-7*) Cherokee.

Shady Ladies of the West. Ronald D. Miller. LC 64-25860. (Illus.). 18.95 (*0-87026-023-5*) Westernlore.

Shady Lady. Ruth Gordon. 1983. mass mkt. 3.25 (*0-8217-1187-3*, Zebra Kensgtn) Kensgtn Pub Corp.

Shafarevich Maps & Automorphic Forms. Janos Kollar. LC 94-46270. 1995. write for info. (*0-691-04381-7*) Princeton.

Shafer - Huston - Huston Family History. Francis M. Marvin. (Illus.). 470p. 1994. reprint ed. pap. 47.00 (*0-8328-4236-2*); reprint ed. pap. 47.00 (*0-8328-4548-5*); reprint ed. lib. bdg. 57.00 (*0-8328-4235-4*); reprint ed. lib. bdg. 57.00 (*0-8328-4547-7*) Higginson Bk Co.

Shafici Ulama of East Africa, ca. 1830-1970: A Hagiographic Account. Shaikh A. Farsy. Ed. by Randall L. Pouwels. LC 89-22457. (African Primary Texts Ser.: No. 2). 215p. (Orig.). 1989. pap. 25.00 (*0-942615-06-9*) U Wis African Stud.

Shaft Alignment Handbook. 2nd ed. John Piotrowski. (Mechanical Engineering Ser.: Vol. 98). 608p. 1995. 99.75 (*0-8247-9666-7*) Dekker.

Shaft Seals for Dynamic Applications. Horve. (Mechanical Engineering Series of Reference Books & Textbooks: Vol. 107). 504p. 1996. 150.00 (*0-8247-9716-7*) Dekker.

Shaftesbury: The Great Reformer 1801-1885. Georgina Battiscombe. LC 74-32370. 1975. 15.00 (*0-395-19953-0*) HM.

Shaftesbury & the Culture of Politeness: Moral Discourse & Cultural Politics in Early Eighteenth-Century England. Lawrence E. Klein. 224p. (C). 1994. text ed. 54.95 (*0-521-41806-2*) Cambridge U Pr.

Shaftesbury Avenue. large type ed. Claire Rayner. (General Fiction Ser.). 544p. 1992. 25.99 (*0-7089-2735-1*) Ulverscroft.

***Shaftesbury Collection: 1698-1914 Editions, 4 vols., Set.** 1513p. 1996. reprint ed. write for info. (*1-85506-424-3*) Bks Intl VA.

Shaftesbury's Philosophy of Religion & Ethics: A Study in Enthusiasm. Stanley Grean. LC 67-15457. 320p. reprint ed. pap. 91.20 (*0-317-09231-6*, 2006441) Bks Demand.

Shaftsbury, Rousseau & Kant: An Introduction to the Conflict Between Aesthetic & Moral Values in Modern Thought. John A. Bernstein. LC 78-75190. 192p. 1980. 29.50 (*0-8386-2351-4*) Fairleigh Dickinson.

Shag: Last of the Plains Buffalo. Robert M. McClung. LC 91-7508. (Animal Life Cycle Ser.). (Illus.). 96p. (J). (gr. 3-7). 1991. reprint ed. lib. bdg. 16.50 (*0-208-02313-5*, Linnet Bks) Shoe String.

***Shag: The Legendary Dance of the South.** Bo Bryan. 120p. 1996. pap. write for info. (*0-9648084-1-2*) Fnd Books.

Shag & the Bouncing Ball. Donald F. Lippert. (Illus.). 32p. (J). (ps). 1989. write for info. (*0-318-64643-9*) Pastel Pubns.

Shaggy. Marcus Pfister. (Illus.). (J). Date not set. pap. 6.95 (*1-55858-625-3*) North-South Bks NYC.

Shaggy Birthday. Tuppy Owens. (Illus.). 28p. 1993. 5.00 (*1-872819-02-8*, Pub. by Tuppy Owens UK) AK Pr Dist.

Shaggy Dog Murder Trial (Playscript) Joanna H. Kraus. (Orig.). (J). (gr. 4-7). 1988. 5.00 (*0-87602-274-3*) Anchorage.

Shaggy Dog Story. Eric Partridge. LC 72-117910. (Select Bibliographies Reprint Ser.). (Illus.). 1977. reprint ed. 18.95 (*0-8369-5363-0*) Ayer.

Shaggy Dog's Book of Hours. Ann Koehler. (Illus.). 64p. (Orig.). (C). 1991. reprint ed. lib. bdg. 25.00 (*0-8095-4086-X*) Borgo Pr.

Shaggy Dogs Have Punny Tales. V. Gene Child & Gene Youngmann. 192p. 1992. pap. 7.95 (*0-9633899-1-2*) Vaden Bks.

Shaggy Man of Oz. Jack Snow. (Illus.). 256p. (J). (gr. 3 up). 1991. 24.95 (*0-929605-10-1*); pap. 12.95 (*0-929605-11-X*) Books Wonder.

Shaggy Sheep: Big Book. Lada J. Kratky. (Wonders! Ser.). (Illus.). 16p. (Orig.). (J). (gr. 1-3). 1992. pap. text ed. 29.95 (*1-56334-068-2*) Hampton-Brown.

Shaggy Sheep: Small Book. Lada J. Kratky. (Wonders! Ser.). (Illus.). 16p. (Orig.). (J). (gr. 1-3). 1992. pap. text ed. 6.00 (*1-56334-074-7*) Hampton-Brown.

Shaggy Steed of Physics: Mathematical Beauty in the Physical World. David Oliver. LC 93-33015. (Illus.). 320p. 1994. 48.95 (*0-387-94163-0*) Spr-Verlag.

Shah & I: The Confidential Diary of Iran's Royal Court. Asadollah Alam. LC 93-18498. 576p. 1993. pap. 16.95 (*0-312-09384-5*) St Martin.

Shah & I: The Confidential Diary of Iran's Royal Court, 1969-1977. Asadollah Alam. Ed. & Intro. by Alinaghi Alikhani. 576p. 1993. pap. 16.95 (*0-312-09153-2*) St Martin.

Shah Bano Controversy. Ed. by Asghar Ali Engineer. 352p. 1987. text ed. 27.50 (*0-86131-701-7*, Pub. by Orient Longman Ltd II) Apt Bks.

Shah Commission Begins: India Under Emergency. John Dayal & Ajoy Bose. 1978. 13.50 (*0-8364-0179-4*) S Asia.

***Shah-Namah of Fardusi.** Alexander Rogers. (C). 1995. 14.00 (*81-86142-84-3*, Pub. by Low Price II) S Asia.

Shah of Iran: Biography. Andrew Whitley. Date not set. pap. 18.00 (*0-670-82845-9*) Viking Penguin.

Shah of Shahs. Ryszard Kapuscinski. 1985. pap. 9.00 (*0-394-74074-2*, Vin) Random.

Shah of Shahs. Ryszard Kapuscinski. 1992. pap. 11.00 (*0-679-73801-0*, Vin) Random.

Shah, the Ayatollah & the U. S. James A. Bill. LC 88-70867. (Headline Ser.: No. 285). (Illus.). 72p. 1988. pap. 5.95 (*0-87124-120-X*) Foreign Policy.

Shahed va Mashhoud & Seyr-al Saer va Teyr-al Nader. Shah Maghsoud Sadegh Angha. LC 83-60134. 85p. (Orig.). (PER.). 1983. pap. 18.00 (*0-910735-22-0*) MTO Printing & Pubn Ctr.

Shahmah in Pursuit of Freedom. Frances H. McDougall. LC 71-154082. (Black Heritage Library Collection). 1977. 34.95 (*0-8369-8793-4*) Ayer.

Shahnameh: The Book of Kings, Vol. IV. Abolqasem Ferdowsi. Ed. by Djalal Khaleghi-Motlagh. (Persian Text Ser.: No. 1). 416p. (PER.). 1994. lib. bdg. 65.00 (*1-56859-018-0*) Mazda Pubs.

Shahnameh (The Book of Kings), Vol. 1. Abu'l-Qasem Ferdowsi. Ed. by Djalal Khaleghi-Motlagh. 1987. 65.00 (*0-88706-770-0*) Mazda Pubs.

Shahnameh (The Book of Kings), Vol. III. Abulqasem Ferdowsi. Ed. by Djalal Khaleghi-Motlagh. (Persian Text Ser.: Vol. III). 412p. (PER.). 1993. lib. bdg. 65.00 (*0-939214-86-5*) Mazda Pubs.

***Shahnameh (The Book of Kings), Vol. 5.** Ed. by Djalal Khaleghi-Motlagh. (Persian Text Ser.: Vol. 1). 606p. (PER.). 1997. text ed. 65.00 (*1-56859-049-0*) Mazda Pubs.

Shahnameh, Vol. II: The Book of Kings. Abu'l-Qasem Ferdowsi. Ed. by Djalal Khaleghi-Motlagh. (Persian Text Ser.). 512p. 1990. lib. bdg. 65.00 (*0-939214-65-2*) Mazda Pubs.

Shahre Assal: The Honeymoon. Naguib Mahfouz. (ARA.). pap. 8.95 (*0-86685-161-5*, LDL540, Pub. by Librairie du Liban FR) Intl Bk Ctr.

Shaihu Umar: A Historical Novel about Slavery in Africa. Patricia W. Romero. LC 89-5765. (Topics in World History Ser.). (Illus.). 124p. 1989. 18.95 (*1-55876-012-1*); pap. 9.95 (*1-55876-006-7*) Wiener Pubs Inc.

Shaikh Hassan al-Banna & al-Ikhwan al-Muslimun. Maryam Jameelah. 28p. (Orig.). 1985. pap. 4.50 (*1-56744-382-6*) Kazi Pubns.

***Shaikh Muhyidden A. Qaid Gilani (al-Fathu Rabbani)** Tr. by Muhammad Al-Akili. 130p. 1996. pap. 16.50 (*0-614-21345-2*, 1126) Kazi Pubns.

***Shailer Mathews's Lives of Jesus: The Search for a Theological Foundation for the Social Gospel.** William D. Lindsey. LC 96-52290. 280p. 1997. pap. text ed. 19.95 (*0-7914-3508-3*) State U NY Pr.

***Shailer Mathews's Lives of Jesus: The Search for a Theological Foundation for the Social Gospel.** William D. Lindsey. LC 96-52290. 280p. (C). 1997. text ed. 59.50 (*0-7914-3507-5*) State U NY Pr.

Shaina's Garden. Denise L. Patrick. (Gullah Gullah Island Ser.). 1996. pap. 3.25 (*0-689-80397-4*, S&S Bks Young Read) S&S Childrens.

Shaindy Strikes Again. Sarah Tyberg. (Illus.). 167p. (J). (gr. 6-8). 1993. 10.95 (*1-56871-030-5*) Targum Pr.

Shai's Shabbat Walk. Ellie Gellman. LC 85-80780. (Illus.). 12p. (J). (ps). 1985. bds. 4.95 (*0-930494-49-0*) Kar-Ben.

Shaiva Devotional Songs of Kashmir: A Translation & Study of Utpaladeva's Shivastotravali. Constantina R. Bailly. LC 87-6488. (SUNY Series in the Shaiva Traditions of Kashmir). 196p. 1987. text ed. 44.50 (*0-88706-492-2*); pap. text ed. 14.95 (*0-88706-493-0*) State U NY Pr.

Shaka, King of the Zulus. Diane Stanley & Peter Vennema. (J). 1988. 16.00 (*0-688-07342-5*, Morrow Junior) Morrow.

Shaka, King of the Zulus. Diane Stanley & Peter Vennema. (J). 1988. lib. bdg. 15.93 (*0-688-07343-3*, Morrow Junior) Morrow.

Shaka, King of the Zulus. Diane Stanley & Peter Vennema. LC 87-27376. (Illus.). 40p. (J). (gr. 1-4). 1994. reprint ed. pap. 4.95 (*0-688-13114-X*, Morrow Junior) Morrow.

Shaka Zula. E. A. Ritter. (Nonfiction Ser.). 416p. 1985. pap. 12.95 (*0-14-004826-X*, Penguin Bks) Viking Penguin.

Shaka Zulu: The Rise of the Zulu Empire. E. A. Ritter. 412p. 1990. 35.00 (*0-947898-99-9*, 5588) Stackpole.

***Shaka's Children: A History of the Zulu People.** Stephen Taylor. 288p. 1996. 33.00 (*0-8095-9213-4*) Borgo Pr.

Shaka's Children: A History of the Zulu People. Stephen Taylor. 288p. 1996. pap. 12.00 (*0-00-638468-4*) Harper SF.

Shake & Rattle. Illus. by Carol Nicklaus. (Sesame Street Babies Bks.). 5p. (J). (ps). 1994. 6.99 (*0-679-86387-7*) Random Bks Yng Read.

Shake d'em Halloween Bones. W. Nikola-Lisa. LC 94-49738. (Illus.). (J). 1997. 16.00 (*0-395-73095-3*) HM.

Shake down the Thunder: The Creation of Notre Dame Football. Murray Sperber. (Illus.). 384p. 1993. 25.00 (*0-8050-1874-3*) H Holt & Co.

Shake down the Thunder: The Creation of Notre Dame Football. Murray Sperber. (Illus.). 384p. 1995. pap. 15.95 (*0-8050-4243-1*) H Holt & Co.

***Shake Hand Apple Lie.** Hartley & McKneil. Date not set. pap. text ed. write for info. (*0-85896-044-3*) Addison-Wesley.

Shake Hands with the Devil. Reardon Connor. 312p. reprint ed. lib. bdg. 24.95 (*0-89190-449-2*, Rivercity Pr) Amereon Ltd.

Shake Hands with the Dragon. Carl Glick. 1971. reprint ed. 43.00 (*1-55888-223-5*) Omnigraphics Inc.

Shake Heaven & Earth: Peter Bergson & the Rescue of the Jews of Europe. Louis Rapoport. 1988. 21.95 (*0-940461-06-4*) Seth Pr.

Shake It to the One That You Love the Best. JTG of Nashville Staff. (J). (ps-3). 1996. 19.95 (*1-884832-78-4*) JTG Nashville.

Shake It to the One That You Love the Best: Play Songs & Lullabies from Black Musical Traditions. Ed. by Cheryl W. Mattox. (Illus.). (Orig.). (J). (ps-6). 1990. pap. 7.95 (*0-9623381-0-9*) Warren-Mattox.

***Shake It Up! Fun Food, Cocktails, Canapes.** Oona Vandenberg. 1997. 15.98 (*0-7651-9409-9*) Smithmark.

***Shake It up, Kitty!** Laura Driscoll. (Illus.). 12p. (J). (ps). 1997. bds. 8.95 (*0-448-41626-3*, G&D) Putnam Pub Group.

***Shake It up, Pup!** Laura Driscoll. (Illus.). 12p. (J). (ps). 1997. bds. 8.95 (*0-448-41625-5*, G&D) Putnam Pub Group.

Shake My Hand. Louisa M. Burger. 1990. 7.50 (*0-912449-36-5*) Floating Island.

Shake My Sillies Out. Raffi. LC 87-750478. (Raffi Songs to Read Ser.). (Illus.). 32p. (J). (ps-2). 1990. pap. 5.99 (*0-517-56647-8*) Crown Bks Yng Read.

Shake My Sillies Out. Bert Simpson & Bonnie Simpson. (Raffi Songs to Read Ser.). (Illus.). 32p. (J). (ps-2). 1988. lib. bdg. 11.00 (*0-517-56646-X*) Crown Bks Yng Read.

Shake-Out: Iowa Farm Families in the 1980s. Mark Friedberger. LC 89-36474. 192p. 1990. text ed. 24.00 (*0-8131-1682-1*) U Pr of Ky.

Shake, Rattle & Learn: Classroom-Tested Ideas That Use Movement for Active Learning. Janet M. Grant. 112p. (Orig.). (C). 1995. pap. text ed. 15.00 (*1-57110-019-9*) Stenhse Pubs.

***Shake, Rattle & Roll.** 2nd rev. ed. Planet Dexter Editors. 1997. spiral bd. write for info. (*0-201-15436-6*) Addison-Wesley.

Shake, Rattle & Roll: Cool Things to Do with Dice (That Grown-Ups Don't Even Know About) (Planet Dexter's Ser.). (J). 1995. pap. 14.99 (*0-201-40936-4*) Addison-Wesley.

Shake, Rattle, & Roll: The Golden Age of American Rock 'n Roll, 1952-1955, Vol. 1. Lee Cotten. Ed. by Thomas Schultheiss. (Rock & Roll Reference Ser.: No. 31). (Illus.). 390p. 1990. reprint ed. lib. bdg. 45.00 (*1-56075-017-0*) Popular Culture.

***Shake, Rattle & Roll: The World's Most Amazing Natural Forces.** Spencer Christian & Antonia Felix. (Spencer Christian's World of Wonders Ser.). 128p. (J). 1997. pap. 10.95 (*0-471-15291-9*) Wiley.

***Shake, Rattle & Rot: The Zombie Musical.** Leslie J. Caulfield. 29p. (YA). (gr. 7 up). 1997. pap. 5.50 (*0-87129-749-3*, SB7) Dramatic Pub.

Shake, Rattle, & Strum. Sara Corbett. LC 94-36343. (World of Difference Ser.). (Illus.). 32p. (J). (gr. 3-7). 1995. lib. bdg. 19.50 (*0-516-08194-2*) Childrens.

S

Shake, Rattle, & Strum. Sara Corbett. (World of Difference Ser.). (J). 1995. pap. 6.95 (*0-516-48194-0*) Childrens.

*__Shake Shake Shake.__ Pinkney. 1997. pap. write for info. (*0-15-200632-X*) HarBrace.

*__Shake Shake Shake.__ Andrea Pinkney. (Illus.). (J). 1997. bds. write for info. (*0-614-29232-8*, Red Wagon Bks) HarBrace.

Shake, Tap, & Play a Merry Tune. Tania K. Cowling. 1992. pap. 9.99 (*0-86653-949-2*) Fearon Teach Aids.

Shake the Anger Habit! rev. ed. Betty Doty & Pat Rooney. LC 87-71633. (Illus.). 213p. (Orig.). 1990. reprint ed. pap. 11.95 (*0-930822-10-2*) Bookery.

Shake the Parrot Cage. Betty Parry. 112p. 1994. 10.00 (*0-932616-47-X*) Brick Hse Bks.

Shake Them 'Simmons down & Other Adventures in the Lives of Trees. Janet Lembke. LC 96-14375. (Illus.). 224p. 1996. 22.95 (*1-55821-350-3*) Lyons & Burford.

Shakedown. James Bovard. 144p. 1996. pap. 7.95 (*0-14-025819-1*) Viking Penguin.

Shakedown. Terrance Dicks. (Dr. Who New Adventures Ser.). 256p. (Orig.). 1996. mass mkt. 5.95 (*0-426-20459-X*, Pub. by Virgin Pub UK) London Brdge.

Shakedown. Paul Malone. (Agents Bks.: No. 03). 1992. mass mkt. 3.50 (*0-373-63803-5*) Harlequin Bks.

Shakedown: How the Government Screws You from A to Z. James Bovard. LC 95-18515. 144p. 1995. pap. 14.95 (*0-670-86542-7*, Viking) Viking Penguin.

Shakedown Street. Jonathan Nasaw. 208p. (J). 1995. mass mkt. 3.99 (*0-440-21930-2*) Dell.

*__Shakedown Street.__ unabridged ed. Angelo Thorne. Ed. & Illus. by Michael Quinn. (Moonchild Ser.: No. 2). 333p. (Orig.). 1995. spiral bd. 22.00 (*1-889171-00-X*, 1889171) Moonchild Prod.

*__Shaken Not Stirred.__ Anistatia Miller & Jared Brown. 1997. 14.00 (*0-614-28088-5*, Harper Ref) HarpC.

*__Shaken Not Stirred: A Celebration of the Martini.__ Anistatia R. Miller. LC 97-2496. 1997. pap. text ed. 10.00 (*0-06-273488-1*, Harper Ref) HarpC.

*__Shakepeare's Birthday.__ Peter Levi. 38p. 1985. pap. 11.95 (*0-85646-142-3*, Pub. by Anvil Press UK) Dufour.

Shaker: Life, Work, & Art. June Sprigg & David Larkin. (Illus.). 272p. 1991. pap. 30.00 (*0-395-59927-X*) HM.

Shaker: Life, Work, & Art. June Sprigg & David Larkin. LC 87-9957. (Illus.). 272p. 1994. 50.00 (*1-55670-011-3*) Stewart Tabori & Chang.

Shaker: The Art of Craftmanship: the Mount Lebanon Collection. Timothy D. Rieman. LC 94-36405. 1995. pap. 24.95 (*0-88397-109-7*) Art Srvc Intl.

Shaker Adventure. Marguerite F. Melcher. 319p. 1986. pap. 4.95 (*0-937942-08-1*) Shaker Mus.

Shaker Architecture. Herbert F. Schiffer. LC 79-52439. (Illus.). 190p. 1979. pap. 14.95 (*0-88740-153-8*) Schiffer.

Shaker Band Saw Projects. Mark Duginske. LC 94-16846. (Illus.). 144p. 1994. pap. 12.95 (*0-8069-8248-9*) Sterling.

Shaker Baskets. Martha Wetherbee & Nathan Taylor. Ed. by Mary L. Ray. (Illus.). 230p. (Orig.). 1988. 39.95 (*0-9609384-4-3*) M Wetherbee.

Shaker Baskets & Poplarware: A Field Guide. Gerrie Kennedy. (Shaker Field Guides Ser.: Vol. 3). 1993. pap. 12.95 (*0-936399-21-X*) Berkshire Hse.

Shaker Boy. Mary L. Ray. LC 93-1333. (Illus.). 48p. (J). (gr. k-3). 1994. 16.00 (*0-15-276921-8*, Browndeer Pr) HarBrace.

*__Shaker Boy.__ Mary L. Ray. (J). 1997. pap. write for info. (*0-15-201563-9*, HB Juv Bks) HarBrace.

Shaker Built: The Form & Function of Shaker Architecture. Paul Rocheleau & June Sprigg. Ed. by David Larkin. LC 94-76580. (Illus.). 272p. 1994. 60.00 (*1-885254-03-2*) Monacelli Pr.

Shaker Chair. Charles R. Muller & Timothy D. Rieman. LC 91-40646. (Illus.). 268p. (C). 1992. reprint ed. pap. 26.95 (*0-87023-795-0*) U of Mass Pr.

Shaker Children: True Stories & Crafts. Kathleen Thorne-Thomsen. LC 95-52178. 128p. (Orig.). (J). 1996. pap. 15.95 (*1-55652-250-9*) Chicago Review.

Shaker Cities of Peace, Love, & Union: A History of the Hancock Bishopric. Deborah E. Burns. LC 92-59965. (Illus.). 262p. (C). 1993. pap. 19.95 (*0-87451-613-7*); text ed. 45.00 (*0-87451-612-9*) U Pr of New Eng.

Shaker Communism: Or, Tests of Divine Inspiration. Frederick W. Evans. LC 72-2987. reprint ed. 34.50 (*0-404-10749-4*) AMS Pr.

Shaker Communities, Shaker Lives. Priscilla J. Brewer. LC 85-40930. (Illus.). 293p. 1986. pap. 18.95 (*0-87451-400-2*) U Pr of New Eng.

Shaker Cookbook. C. B. Piercy. 1986. 5.98 (*0-517-62243-2*, 014246) Random Hse Value.

Shaker Cookbook: Recipes & Lore from the Valley of God's Pleasure. rev. ed. Caroline B. Piercy & Arthur P. Tolve. (Illus.). 192p. 1984. pap. 14.95 (*0-911861-02-5*) Gabriels Horn.

Shaker Cooking. Intro. by Bobbie Crosby. (Illus.). 80p. 1991. 7.99 (*0-517-05150-8*, Crescent) Random Hse Value.

Shaker Dance Service Reconstucted. J. G. Davies et al. 1984. pap. 3.00 (*0-941500-34-9*) Sharing Co.

Shaker Days Remembered. Martha Hulings. 1983. pap. 6.00 (*0-317-17252-2*) Shaker Her Soc.

Shaker Design. 1988. pap. 39.95 (*0-393-30544-9*) Norton.

Shaker Experience in America: A History of the United Society of Believers. Stephen J. Stein. (Illus.). 576p. (C). 1992. 47.50 (*0-300-05139-5*); pap. 19.00 (*0-300-05933-7*) Yale U Pr.

Shaker Furniture. Time-Life Books Editors. LC 95-1022. (Art of Woodworking Ser.). (Illus.). 144p. 1995. 19.95 (*0-8094-9533-3*) Time-Life.

Shaker Furniture: The Craftsmanship of an American Communal Sect. Edward D. Andrews & Faith Andrews. (Illus.). 192p. 1937. pap. 8.95 (*0-486-20679-3*) Dover.

Shaker Furniture Makers. Jerry V. Grant & Douglas R. Allen. LC 89-5263. (Illus.). 192p. 1989. 34.95 (*0-87451-488-6*) U Pr of New Eng.

Shaker Hearts. Ann Turner. LC 95-45087. (Illus.). 40p. (J). (gr. 1-4). 1997. 14.95 (*0-06-025369-X*); lib. bdg. 14.89 (*0-06-025370-3*) HarpC Child Bks.

Shaker Herb & Garden. Buchanan. 1996. pap. write for info. (*0-395-73324-3*) HM.

Shaker Herb & Garden Book. Rita Buchanan. LC 96-11239. (Illus.). 160p. 1996. 27.95 (*0-395-73325-1*) HM.

Shaker Herbal Teas: Uses, Taxonomy, Growing Cycle. Herb Dept. Staff. 6p. 1988. pap. 0.75 (*0-915836-11-4*) United Soc Shakers.

Shaker Herbs & Their Medicinal Uses. Dee Herbrandson. (Illus.). 28p. 1985. pap. 4.00 (*0-317-56372-6*) Shaker Her Soc.

Shaker Heritage Guidebook: Exploring the Historic Sites, Museums & Collections. Stuart Murray. LC 93-79992. (Illus.). 261p. (Orig.). 1994. pap. 15.95 (*0-9614876-6-6*) Golden Hl Pr NY.

*__Shaker Hollow Collection.__ 100p. (Orig.). 1997. mass mkt. 10.95 (*1-57532-108-4*) Press-Tige Pub.

Shaker Home. Raymond Bial. LC 93-17917. (J). 1994. 15.95 (*0-395-64047-4*) HM.

Shaker Hymnal: A Facsimile Edition of the Hymnal of the Canterbury Shakers. Intro. by Cheryl P. Anderson. 288p. 1990. 21.95 (*0-87951-402-7*) Overlook Pr.

Shaker Hymnal: A Facsimile Edition of the Hymnal of the Canterbury Shakers. Cheryl P. Anderson. 288p. 1996. pap. 15.95 (*0-87951-640-2*) Overlook Pr.

Shaker Inventions. Sallie Randolph & Nancy O. Bolick. (Illus.). (J). (gr. 4-7). 1990. 12.95 (*0-8027-6933-0*); lib. bdg. 13.85 (*0-8027-6934-9*) Walker & Co.

Shaker Kitchen. Jeffrey M. Paige. 1996. 6.99 (*0-517-16818-9*) Random Hse Value.

Shaker Kitchen: Shaker-inspired Cooking from the Canterbury Village. Jeffrey S. Paige. LC 93-2360. 1994. 22.00 (*0-517-58838-2*, C P Pubs) Crown Pub Group.

Shaker Light. Robert Peters. 127p. 1987. 20.00 (*0-87775-200-1*); pap. 10.95 (*0-87775-201-X*) Unicorn Pr.

Shaker Music: A Manifestation of American Folk Culture. Harold E. Cook. LC 71-161507. (Illus.). 312p. 1975. 39.50 (*0-8387-7953-0*) Bucknell U Pr.

Shaker Music: Inspirational Hymns & Melodies Illustrative of the Resurection, Life & Testimony of the Shakers. Frederick W. Evans. LC 72-2988. reprint ed. 49.50 (*0-404-10750-8*) AMS Pr.

Shaker Music: Original Inspirational Hymns & Songs. fac. ed. 250p. 1991. Facsimile ed. 11.95 (*0-915836-20-3*) United Soc Shakers.

Shaker Sampler: Coloring Book. 2nd ed. Kathleen M. Moriarty. (Illus.). 30p. (J). (gr. k-6). 1991. pap. 4.95 (*0-915836-15-7*) United Soc Shakers.

*__Shaker Sisters Drawings.__ Helena S. Cora. LC 96-40516. 1997. 24.95 (*1-885254-52-0*) Monacelli Pr.

Shaker Style. John Bowman. 1995. 14.98 (*0-8317-1033-0*) Smithmark.

Shaker Style. Michael Horsham. (Illus.). 128p. 1996. write for info. (*1-57215-177-3*) World Pubns.

*__Shaker-Style Wood Projects.__ Robert Sonday. LC 96-44348. 1997. 19.95 (*0-8069-1386-X*) Sterling.

Shaker Textile Arts. Beverly Gordon. LC 78-69899. (Illus.). 343p. 1980. pap. 19.95 (*0-87451-242-5*) U Pr of New Eng.

Shaker Village. Edmund V. Gillon, Jr. LC 86-61201. (Illus.). 46p. 1986. pap. 5.95 (*0-88740-077-9*) Schiffer.

Shaker Village Views: Illustrated Maps & Landscape Drawings by Shaker Artists of the Nineteenth Century. Robert P. Emlen. LC 86-40393. (Illus.). 208p. 1987. pap. 24.95 (*0-87451-420-7*) U Pr of New Eng.

Shaker Villages. Nancy O. Bolick & Sallie G. Randolph. LC 92-34587. (Illus.). 96p. (J). (gr. 5 up). 1993. 12.95 (*0-8027-8209-4*); lib. bdg. 13.85 (*0-8027-8210-8*) Walker & Co.

Shaker, Why Don't You Sing? Maya Angelou. (YA). 1983. 16.00 (*0-394-52144-7*) Random.

Shaker Woodenware: A Field Guide to Collecting, Vol. 1. June Sprigg & Jim Johnson. LC 90-81447. (Shaker Field Guides Ser.). (Illus.). 168p. (Orig.). 1991. pap. 12.95 (*0-936399-06-6*) Berkshire Hse.

Shaker Woodenware: A Field Guide to Collecting, Vol. 2. June Sprigg & Jim Johnson. LC 90-81447. (Shaker Field Guides Ser.). (Illus.). 168p. (Orig.). 1992. pap. 12.95 (*0-936399-10-4*) Berkshire Hse.

*__Shaker World: Art, Life, Belief.__ John T. Kirk. LC 96-52014. 1997. write for info. (*0-8109-4472-3*) Abrams.

Shaker Your Plate: Of Shaker Cooks & Cooking. Frances A. Carr. LC 85-51982. (Illus.). 156p. (Orig.). 1985. pap. 12.95 (*0-915836-02-5*) United Soc Shakers.

Shaker Your Plate: Of Shaker Cooks & Cooking. Frances A. Carr. LC 87-8242. (Illus.). 154p. (Orig.). 1985. pap. 14.95 (*0-87451-404-5*) U Pr of New Eng.

*__Shakerag.__ Amy Littlesugar. LC 97-9618. (Illus.). 32p. (J). (ps-3). 1998. 15.95 (*0-399-23005-X*, Philomel Bks) Putnam Pub Group.

Shakerism & Feminism: Reflections on Women's Religion & the Early Shakers. Marjorie Procter-Smith. (Illus.). 24p. 1991. pap. text ed. 4.95 (*0-937942-16-2*) Shaker Mus.

Shakerism, Its Meaning & Message. fac. ed. Anna White & Leila S. Taylor. 417p. 1991. Facsimile ed. 17.95 (*0-915836-19-X*) United Soc Shakers.

Shakerism, Its Meaning & Message. Anna White & Lelia S. Taylor. LC 73-134421. reprint ed. 57.50 (*0-404-08462-1*) AMS Pr.

Shakers. John Godber & Jane Thornton. 1992. pap. 5.25 (*0-8222-1316-8*) Dramatists Play.

Shakers. L. Edward Purcell. 1991. 10.99 (*0-517-64457-6*) Random Hse Value.

*__Shakers.__ Jean K. Williams. LC 96-51498. (American Religious Experience Ser.). (J). 1997. write for info. (*0-531-11342-6*) Watts.

Shakers: Compendium of the Origin, History, Principles, Rules & Regulations, Government & Doctrines of the United Society of Believers in Christ's Second Appearing. 4th ed. Frederick W. Evans. LC 72-2985. (Communal Societies in America Ser.). reprint ed. 37.50 (*0-404-10747-8*) AMS Pr.

Shakers: Hands to Work Hearts to God. Amy S. Burns. 1990. 19.99 (*0-517-03309-7*) Random Hse Value.

Shakers: Two Centuries of Spiritual Reflection. Ed. by Robley E. Whitson. (Classics of Western Spirituality Ser.). 200p. 1983. pap. 11.95 (*0-8091-2373-8*) Paulist Pr.

Shakers & the World's People. Flo Morse. LC 87-8223. (Illus.). 399p. 1987. pap. 19.95 (*0-87451-426-6*) U Pr of New Eng.

Shakescenes: Shakespeare for Two. Intro. by John R. Brown. (Acting Ser.). 384p. 1991. pap. 8.95 (*1-55783-049-5*) Applause Theatre Bk Pubs.

Shakespeare. Bellerophon Staff. (J). (gr. 1-9). 1992. pap. 4.95 (*0-88388-008-3*) Bellerophon Bks.

Shakespeare. David Bevington. LC 76-5220. (Goldentree Bibliographies Series in Language & Literature). (C). 1978. pap. text ed. write for info. (*0-88295-555-1*) Harlan Davidson.

Shakespeare. James C. Bulman. LC 95-12968. 248p. (C). 1995. pap. 17.95 (*0-415-11626-0*) Routledge.

Shakespeare. James C. Bulman. LC 95-12968. 248p. (C). (gr. 13). 1995. text ed. 62.95 (*0-415-11625-2*) Routledge.

Shakespeare. Anthony Burgess. LC 94-5667. 251p. 1994. pap. 13.95 (*1-56663-056-8*, Elephant Paperbacks) I R Dee.

Shakespeare. Germaine Greer. (Past Masters Ser.). 144p. 1986. pap. 8.95 (*0-19-287538-8*) OUP.

Shakespeare. C. Martin. (Life & Works). (Illus.). 112p. (J). (gr. 7 up). 1989. 14.95 (*0-685-58633-2*); lib. bdg. 19.94 (*0-86592-296-9*) Rourke Corp.

Shakespeare. Joseph Rosenblum. (Magill Bibliographies Ser.). 307p. 1992. 40.00 (*0-8108-2802-2*) Scarecrow.

Shakespeare. Jack Rudman. (ACT Proficiency Examination Program Ser.: PEP-7). 1994. pap. 23.95 (*0-8373-5507-9*) Nat Learn.

Shakespeare. Ed. by Raymond M. Alden. LC 73-113539. reprint ed. 39.50 (*0-404-00307-9*) AMS Pr.

Shakespeare. Charles H. Herford. LC 76-51366. (Studies in Shakespeare: No. 24). 1978. reprint ed. lib. bdg. 46.95 (*0-8383-2160-7*) M S G Haskell Hse.

Shakespeare. Walter Raleigh. LC 74-182702. (English Men of Letters Ser.). reprint ed. 32.50 (*0-404-05206-1*) AMS Pr.

Shakespeare. Walter Raleigh. (BCL1-PR English Literature Ser.). 233p. 1992. reprint ed. lib. bdg. 79.00 (*0-7812-7283-1*) Rprt Serv.

Shakespeare. Jack Rudman. (Regents College Proficiency Examination Ser.: Vol. CPEP-33). 1994. reprint ed. pap. 23.95 (*0-8373-5433-1*) Nat Learn.

Shakespeare. Mark Van Doren. LC 82-2933. viii, 344p. 1982. reprint ed. text ed. 55.50 (*0-313-23536-8*, VDSH, Greenwood Pr) Greenwood.

Shakespeare: "Hamlet" Paul A. Cantor. (Landmarks of World Literature Ser.). (Illus.). 128p. (C). 1989. text ed. 29.95 (*0-521-34190-6*); pap. text ed. 11.95 (*0-521-34983-4*) Cambridge U Pr.

Shakespeare: A Bibliographic Guide. Ed. by Stanley Wells. 448p. 1990. 65.00 (*0-19-871036-4*) OUP.

Shakespeare: A Biographical Handbook. Gerald E. Bentley, Jr. LC 85-27246. 266p. 1986. reprint ed. text ed. 52.50 (*0-313-25042-1*, BESH, Greenwood Pr) Greenwood.

Shakespeare: A Critical Study of His Mind. Edward Dowden. 1972. 59.95 (*0-8490-1029-2*) Gordon Pr.

Shakespeare: A Life in Drama. Stanley Wells. 416p. 1995. 28.50 (*0-393-03765-7*) Norton.

Shakespeare: A Life in Drama. Stanley Wells. 416p. 1997. pap. 17.00 (*0-393-31562-2*) Norton.

Shakespeare: A Portrait Restored. Clara Chambrun. LC 77-109642. (Select Bibliographies Reprint Ser.). 1977. 31.95 (*0-8369-5251-0*) Ayer.

Shakespeare: A Selective Bibliography of Modern Criticism. Linda Woodbridge. LC 87-31134. 266p. (C). 1988. lib. bdg. 5.00 (*0-933951-14-0*) Locust Hill Pr.

Shakespeare: A Study & Research Guide. 3rd rev. ed. David M. Bergeron & Geraldo U. De Sousa. LC 94-37236. viii, 208p. (Orig.). 1995. pap. 12.95 (*0-7006-0693-9*) U Pr of KS.

Shakespeare: A Study & Research Guide. 3rd rev. ed. David M. Bergeron & Geraldo U. De Sousa. LC 94-37236. viii, 208p. (Orig.). 1995. 29.95 (*0-7006-0692-0*) U Pr of KS.

Shakespeare: An Illustrated Stage History. Ed. by Jonathan Bate & Russell Jackson. (Illus.). 276p. (C). 1996. 39.95 (*0-19-812372-8*) OUP.

*__Shakespeare: As You Like It, Vol. 2.__ G. K. Hall & Co. Staff. 1997. 99.00 (*0-7838-1812-2*) G K Hall.

Shakespeare: Aspects of Influence. Ed. by G. Blakemore Evans. (English Studies: No. 7). 210p. 1976. 15.00 (*0-674-80330-2*, EVSA); pap. 5.95 (*0-674-80331-0*, EVSX) HUP.

Shakespeare: Bibliographies & Periodicals: A Guide to the Microfiche Collection. (Shakespeariana Ser.). 25p. (Orig.). 1990. pap. 20.00 (*0-8357-2112-4*) Univ Microfilms.

Shakespeare: Contemporary Critical Approaches. Ed. by Harry R. Garvin. LC 79-50103. (Bucknell Review Ser.: Vol. 25, No. 1). 192p. 1970. 22.00 (*0-8387-2376-4*) Bucknell U Pr.

Shakespeare: Contrasts & Controversies. Kenneth Muir. LC 85-994. 208p. 1985. 29.95 (*0-8061-1940-3*) U of Okla Pr.

Shakespeare: From "Richard II" to "Henry V" Derek Traversi. vii, 198p. 1957. 29.50 (*0-8047-0503-8*) Stanford U Pr.

Shakespeare: Handwriting & Spelling. Gerald H. Rendall. LC 76-169107. (Studies in Shakespeare: No. 24). 1971. reprint ed. lib. bdg. 50.95 (*0-8383-1335-3*) M S G Haskell Hse.

Shakespeare: His Life, Art, & Character, 2 Vols, Set. 4th rev. ed. Henry N. Hudson. LC 72-169453. reprint ed. write for info. (*0-404-03378-4*) AMS Pr.

Shakespeare: His Life, Art & Characters, 2 Vols. Henry N. Hudson. LC 79-124395. (Studies in Shakespeare: No. 24). 1970. reprint ed. lib. bdg. 150.00 (*0-8383-1100-8*) M S G Haskell Hse.

Shakespeare: His Life, Work, & Era. Dennis Kay. 1994. pap. 12.00 (*0-688-13225-1*, Quill) Morrow.

Shakespeare: His Music & Song. A. H. Moncure-Sime. LC 70-177518. 196p. 1972. reprint ed. 26.95 (*0-405-08795-0*, Pub. by Blom Pubns UK) Ayer.

Shakespeare: His World & His Art. 3rd rev. ed. K. R. Iyengar. 712p. (C). text ed. 50.00 (*81-207-0635-8*, Pub. by Sterling Pubs II) Apt Bks.

Shakespeare: His World & His Art. K. Srinivasa Iyengar. 736p. (Orig.). reprint ed. pap. text ed. 15.95 (*0-86590-330-1*, Pub. by Sterling Pubs II) Apt Bks.

Shakespeare: Interdisciplinary Thematic Unit. Robbins. (Illus.). 176p. (J). (gr. 5-8). 1995. wbk. ed., pap. text ed. 14.95 (*1-55734-614-3*) Tchr Create Mat.

Shakespeare: Life & Work. Frederick J. Furnivall & John J. Munro. LC 77-168082. reprint ed. 27.50 (*0-404-02664-8*) AMS Pr.

Shakespeare: Man of the Theater. Ed. by Kenneth Muir et al. LC 82-40346. (Illus.). 272p. 1983. 38.50 (*0-87413-217-7*) U Delaware Pr.

*__Shakespeare: Midsummer Night's Dream, Vol. 2.__ G. K. Hall & Co. Staff. 1997. 99.00 (*0-7838-1814-9*) G K Hall.

Shakespeare: Modern Essays in Criticism. 2nd ed. Ed. by Leonard F. Dean. 486p. (Orig.). (YA). (gr. 9 up). 1967. pap. 19.95 (*0-19-500688-7*) OUP.

Shakespeare: Of an Age & for All Time. Ed. by Charles T. Prouty. LC 72-960. reprint ed. 27.50 (*0-404-05146-4*) AMS Pr.

Shakespeare: Out of Court: Dramatizations of Court Society. Graham Holderness et al. LC 89-70305. 280p. 1990. text ed. 45.00 (*0-312-04616-2*) St Martin.

Shakespeare: Poet & Citizen. Victor G. Kiernan. 300p. (C). (gr. 13). 1993. text ed. 35.00 (*0-86091-392-9*, A9735, Pub. by Vrso UK) Norton.

Shakespeare: Selected Sonnets. deluxe limited ed. William Shakespeare. (Illus.). 1974. Ltd. to 500, signed, numbered, hand sewn. pap. 12.50 (*0-937686-15-8*) Turtles Quill.

Shakespeare: Spokesman of the Third Estate. Lorentz J. Eckhoff. LC 71-164750. reprint ed. 34.50 (*0-404-02244-8*) AMS Pr.

*__Shakespeare: Taming of the Shrew, Vol. 2.__ G. K. Hall & Co. Staff. 1997. 99.00 (*0-7838-1815-7*) G K Hall.

Shakespeare: Text, Subtext, & Context. Ed. by Ronald Dotterer. LC 87-42893. (Illus.). 240p. 1989. 28.50 (*0-941664-92-9*) Susquehanna U Pr.

Shakespeare: The Comedies. Ed. by Clarice Swisher. LC 96-19957. (Literary Companion Series: SubSeries British Literature). (YA). (gr. 9-12). 1996. pap. 12.96 (*1-56510-573-7*); lib. bdg. 20.96 (*1-56510-574-5*) Greenhaven.

Shakespeare: The Comedy of Errors. Ed. by Barbara A. Mowat & Paul Werstine. (New Folger Library Ser.). 96p. 1996. mass mkt. 3.99 (*0-671-72257-3*) S&S Trade.

Shakespeare: The Complete Works. George B. Harrison. (Illus.). 1675p. (C). 1952. text ed. 49.25 (*0-15-580530-4*) HB Coll Pubs.

Shakespeare: The Critical Heritage, 6 Vols., Set. Brian Vickers. Incl. Vol. 1. 1623-1692. 1974. 65.00 (*0-7100-7716-5*); Vol. 2. 1693-1733. 1974. 65.00 (*0-7100-7807-2*); Vol. 3. 1733-1752. 1974. 65.00 (*0-7100-7990-7*); Vol. 4. 1753-1765. 1976. 65.00 (*0-7100-8297-5*); (Critical Heritage Ser.). 1974. 335.00 (*0-7100-0828-7*) Routledge Chapman & Hall.

Shakespeare: The Critical Heritage, 1765-1774, Vol. 5. Ed. by Brian Vickers. (Critical Heriatage Ser.). 1979. 65.00 (*0-7100-8788-8*, RKP) Routledge.

Shakespeare: The Critical Heritage, 1774-1801, Vol. 6. Ed. by Brian Vickers. (Critical Heritage Ser.). 664p. 1981. 65.00 (*0-7100-0629-2*, RKP) Routledge.

Shakespeare: The Dark Comedies to the Last Plays: From Satire to Celebration. R. A. Foakes. LC 70-146536. 192p. reprint ed. pap. 54.80 (*0-7837-0122-5*, 2040401) Bks Demand.

Shakespeare: The Deeper Truths Of. 2nd ed. Ed. by Rosicrucian Fellowship Staff. (Illus.). 143p. (C). 1990. reprint ed. pap. text ed. 4.00 (*0-911274-91-X*) Rosicrucian.

Shakespeare: The Elizabethan Plays. Ed. by Susan Bassnett. LC 93-9838. (English Dramatists Ser.). 1993. text ed. 39.95 (*0-312-09663-1*) St Martin.

Shakespeare: The Globe & the World. limited ed. Samuel Schoenbaum. (Illus.). 208p. 1979. boxed 100.00 (*0-19-502731-0*) OUP.

Shakespeare: The Jacobean Plays. Philip C. McGuire. LC 93-42847. (English Dramatists Ser.). 1994. text ed. 39.95 (*0-312-10628-9*) St Martin.

Shakespeare: The Last Phase. Derek Traversi. vii, 272p. 1955. 37.50 (*0-8047-0508-9*) Stanford U Pr.

Shakespeare: The Later Years. Russell A. Fraser. (Illus.). 384p. (C). 1992. text ed. 34.50 (*0-231-06766-6*) Col U Pr.

Shakespeare: The Later Years. Russell A. Fraser. (Illus.). 384p. (C). 1993. pap. 17.50 (*0-231-06767-4*) Col U Pr.

Shakespeare: The Living Record. Irvin L. Matus. LC 90-8113. 192p. 1991. text ed. 45.00 (*0-312-04704-5*) St Martin.

An Asterisk (*) at the beginning of an entry indicates that the title is appearing in BIP for the first time.

Shakespeare: The Man & His Stage. Edmund A. Lamborn & George B. Harrison. LC 73-153336. reprint ed. 29.50 (*0-404-03805-0*) AMS Pr.

Shakespeare: The Merchant of Venice. Graham Holderness. (Critical Studies). 112p. 1994. pap. 7.00 (*0-14-077268-5*, Penguin Bks) Viking Penguin.

***Shakespeare: The Merchant of Venice, Vol. 2.** G. K. Hall & Co. Staff. 1997. 99.00 (*0-7838-1813-0*) G K Hall.

Shakespeare: The Play of History. Graham Holderness et al. LC 87-50124. 250p. 1987. text ed. 32.95 (*0-87745-180-X*) U of Iowa Pr.

Shakespeare: The Poet in His World. Muriel C. Bradbrook. LC 78-7611. 272p. 1980. pap. text ed. 18.50 (*0-231-04649-9*) Col U Pr.

Shakespeare: The Roman Plays. Ed. by Graham Holderness et al. (Critical Readers Ser.). 200p. (C). 1996. pap. text ed. 17.95 (*0-582-23769-6*) Longman.

Shakespeare: The Roman Plays. Ed. by Graham Holderness et al. (Critical Readers Ser.). 200p. (C). 1996. text ed. 50.95 (*0-582-23770-X*) Longman.

Shakespeare: The Roman Plays. Derek Traversi. 280p. 1963. 37.50 (*0-8047-0182-2*) Stanford U Pr.

Shakespeare: The Sonnets. Ed. by Clarice Swisher. LC 96-23046. (Literary Companion Series: SubSeries British Literature). (YA). (gr. 9-12). 1996. pap. 12.96 (*1-56510-571-0*) Greenhaven.

Shakespeare: The Sonnets. Ed. by Clarice Swisher. LC 96-23046. (Literary Companion Series: SubSeries British Literature). (YA). (gr. 9-12). 1996. lib. bdg. 20.96 (*1-56510-572-9*) Greenhaven.

***Shakespeare: The Theater & the Book.** Robert S. Knapp. LC 88-20917. 270p. 1989. reprint ed. pap. 77.00 (*0-608-02595-X*, 2063252) Bks Demand.

Shakespeare: The Theatrical Dimension. Ed. by Philip C. McGuire & David A. Samuelson. LC 77-78320. (Studies in the Renaissance: No. 3). 1979. lib. bdg. 34.50 (*0-404-16002-6*) AMS Pr.

Shakespeare: The Tragedies. Ed. by Clarice Swisher. LC 96-1292. (Literary Companion Series). 1996. pap. 12.96 (*1-56510-466-8*); lib. bdg. 20.96 (*1-56510-467-6*) Greenhaven.

Shakespeare: The True Authorship. Douglas M. Baker. 1976. pap. 25.00 (*0-906006-90-2*, Pub. by Baker Pubns UK) New Leaf Dist.

Shakespeare: The Truth. Patrick Barlow. 224p. 1995. pap. 11.95 (*0-413-69260-4*, A0755) Heinemann.

Shakespeare: To Teach or Not to Teach: Grades Elementary to High School. rev. ed. Cass Foster & Lynn G. Johnson. Ed. by Mary E. Hawkins. 123p. (Orig.). 1994. per., pap. 19.95 (*1-877749-03-6*) Five Star AZ.

***Shakespeare: Varied Perspectives.** Ed. by Vikram Chopra. 1996. 44.00 (*81-7018-822-9*, Pub. by BR Pub II) S Asia.

Shakespeare: World Views. Ed. by Heather Kerr et al. LC 95-22020. (Illus.). 256p. 1996. 39.50 (*0-87413-565-6*) U Delaware Pr.

Shakespeare - Text, Language & Criticism: Essays in Honour of Marvin Spevak. Ed. by B. Fabian & Karl T. Von Rosador. 376p. 1988. lib. bdg. 65.00 (*3-487-07959-3*) G Olms Pubs.

Shakespeare - The Theater & the Book. Robert S. Knapp. 320p. 1989. text ed. 45.00 (*0-691-06766-X*) Princeton U Pr.

Shakespeare - Who Was He? The Oxford Challenge to the Bard of Avon. Richard F. Whalen. LC 94-11303. 208p. 1994. text ed. 19.95 (*0-275-94850-1*, Praeger Pubs) Greenwood.

Shakespeare a Lawyer. William L. Rushton. LC 72-174790. reprint ed. 24.50 (*0-404-05452-8*) AMS Pr.

Shakespeare A to Z: A Complete Guide to the Poems, the Plays, the Characters, the Life, & More. Charles Boyce. (Illus.). 752p. 1990. 45.00 (*0-8160-1805-7*) Facts on File.

Shakespeare A to Z: The Essential Reference to His Plays, His Poems, His Life & Times, & More. Charles Boyce. 752p. 1991. pap. 19.95 (*0-385-31361-6*, Delta) Dell.

Shakespeare Adaptations. Ed. by Montague Summers. LC 65-27919. 1972. reprint ed. 29.95 (*0-405-09017-X*, Pub. by Blom Pubns UK) Ayer.

Shakespeare Adapted for Reading Classes. Thomas Bulfinch. (Works of Thomas Bulfinch). 1989. reprint ed. lib. bdg. 79.00 (*0-7812-2167-6*) Rprt Serv.

Shakespeare Alive! Ed. by Joseph Papp & Elizabeth Kirkland. 224p. 1988. mass mkt. 5.50 (*0-553-27081-8*) Bantam.

Shakespeare Allusion Books: Fifteen Ninety-Two to Fifteen Ninety-Eight, Pt. 1. C. M. Ingleby. Bd. with Shakespeare's Centurie of Prayse: 1591-1693. (New Shakespeare Society, London, Series 6: Nos. 1 & 2). 1974. reprint ed. Set pap. 80.00 (*0-8115-0239-2*) Periodicals Srv.

Shakespeare Allusions & Parallels. Alfred B. Black & Robert M. Smith. LC 78-113559. reprint ed. 32.50 (*0-404-00893-3*) AMS Pr.

Shakespeare Aloud: A Guide to His Verse on Stage. Edward S. Brubaker. LC 76-52176. 1977. pap. 5.25 (*0-9613496-0-3*) Brubaker.

Shakespeare among School Children: Approaches for the Secondary Classroom. Mary A. Rygiel. 135p. 1992. pap. 11.95 (*0-8141-4381-4*) NCTE.

***Shakespeare among the Moderns.** Richard Halpern. (Illus.). 304p. 1996. pap. 18.95 (*0-8014-8418-9*) Cornell U Pr.

***Shakespeare among the Moderns.** Richard Halpern. LC 96-52892. (Illus.). 304p. 1997. 45.00 (*0-8014-3342-8*) Cornell U Pr.

Shakespeare an Archer. WIlliam Rushton. LC 73-7501. (Studies in Shakespeare: No. 24). 1973. reprint ed. lib. bdg. 49.95 (*0-8383-1696-4*) M S G Haskell Hse.

Shakespeare & Astrology, from a Student's Point of View. William Wilson. LC 77-178308. reprint ed. 20.00 (*0-404-06998-3*) AMS Pr.

Shakespeare & Chapman: A Thesis of Chapman's Authorship of a Lover's Complaint, & His Origination of Timon of Athens. John M. Robertson. (BCL1-PR English Literature Ser.). 302p. 1992. reprint ed. lib. bdg. 89.00 (*0-7812-7293-9*) Rprt Serv.

Shakespeare & Company: New Bison Book Edition. Sylvia Beach. LC 91-15230. (Illus.). xxii, 246p. 1991. reprint ed. pap. 9.95 (*0-8032-6097-0*, Bison Books) U of Nebr Pr.

Shakespeare & Cultural Traditions: The Proceedings of the International Shakespeare Association World Congress, Tokyo, 1991. Ed. by Stanley Wells et al. LC 92-50755. (C). 1994. 59.50 (*0-87413-462-5*) U Delaware Pr.

Shakespeare & "Demi-Science" Felix E. Schelling. LC 75-126687. reprint ed. 24.50 (*0-404-05585-0*) AMS Pr.

Shakespeare & Democracy. E. Salmon. LC 73-9600. (Studies in Shakespeare: No. 24). (C). 1973. reprint ed. lib. bdg. 39.95 (*0-8383-1706-5*) M S G Haskell Hse.

Shakespeare & Dickens. Cumberland Clark. LC 73-9794. (Studies in Dickens: No. 52). 1973. reprint ed. lib. bdg. 39.95 (*0-8383-1703-0*) M S G Haskell Hse.

Shakespeare & Dickens: The Dynamics of Influence. Valerie L. Gager. LC 95-6179. (Illus.). 432p. (C). 1996. text ed. 64.95 (*0-521-45526-X*) Cambridge U Pr.

Shakespeare & Dramatic Tradition: Essays in Honor of S. F. Johnson. Ed. by W. R. Elton & William B. Long. LC 87-40242. (Illus.). 312p. 1989. 42.50 (*0-87413-333-5*) U Delaware Pr.

Shakespeare & England. 200p. 1972. 23.00 (*0-317-62777-5*) Bagehot Council.

***Shakespeare & English Renaissance.** Innes. LC 97-1410. 1997. text ed. 55.00 (*0-312-17457-8*) St Martin.

Shakespeare & France. Ed. by Holger Klein & Jean-Marie Maguin. LC 95-7456. 1995. write for info. (*0-7734-8960-6*) E Mellen.

Shakespeare & His Contemporaries: Eastern & Central European Studies. Ed. by Jerzy Limon & Jay L. Halio. LC 92-53788. (International Studies in Shakespeare & His Contemporaries). 272p. (C). 1993. 39.50 (*0-87413-475-7*) U Delaware Pr.

Shakespeare & His Critics. Charles F. Johnson. LC 70-170816. reprint ed. 31.50 (*0-404-03569-8*) AMS Pr.

Shakespeare & His Forerunners, 2 vols. Sidney Lanier. (BCL1-PR English Literature Ser.). 1992. reprint ed. lib. bdg. 99.00 (*0-7812-7289-0*) Rprt Serv.

Shakespeare & His Forerunners see Centennial Edition of the Works of Sidney Lanier

Shakespeare & His Legal Problems. George W. Keeton. 1972. 59.95 (*0-8490-1030-6*) Gordon Pr.

Shakespeare & His Predecessors. Frederick S. Boas. LC 68-59404. 564p. 1968. reprint ed. 75.00 (*0-87752-011-9*) Gordian.

Shakespeare & His Predecessors. Frederick S. Boas. LC 69-13831. 555p. 1969. reprint ed. text ed. 65.00 (*0-8371-0316-9*, BOSH, Greenwood Pr) Greenwood.

Shakespeare & His Predecessors. Frederick S. Boas. LC 68-24898. (Studies in Shakespeare: No. 24). 1969. reprint ed. lib. bdg. 75.00 (*0-8383-0914-3*) M S G Haskell Hse.

Shakespeare & His Predecessors. Frederick S. Boas. (BCL1-PR English Literature Ser.). 555p. 1992. reprint ed. lib. bdg. 99.00 (*0-7812-7278-5*) Rprt Serv.

Shakespeare & His Predecessors. Frederick S. Boas. 1969. reprint ed. 13.00 (*0-403-00109-9*) Scholarly.

Shakespeare & His Social Context: Essays in Osmotic Knowledge & Literary Interpretation. Margaret L. Ranald. LC 83-45279. (Studies in the Renaissance: No. 10). 1987. 42.50 (*0-404-62280-1*) AMS Pr.

Shakespeare & His Theatre. Gerald E. Bentley. LC 64-11350. 136p. reprint ed. pap. 38.80 (*0-685-23968-3*, 2031527) Bks Demand.

Shakespeare & Holy Scripture. Thomas Carter. LC 74-113574. reprint ed. 41.50 (*0-404-01398-8*) AMS Pr.

***Shakespeare & Hungary: Special Theme Section: The Law & Shakespeare.** Ed. by Holger M. Klein & Peter Davidhazi. LC 96-399755. 464p. 1996. text ed. 109.95 (*0-7734-8727-1*) E Mellen.

Shakespeare & Ibsen. H. G. Turnbull. LC 72-117586. (Studies in Comparative Literature: No. 35). (C). 1970. reprint ed. lib. bdg. 75.00 (*0-8383-1019-2*) M S G Haskell Hse.

***Shakespeare & Ireland.** Burnett. LC 97-14277. 1997. text ed. 59.95 (*0-312-17628-7*) St Martin.

Shakespeare & Italy. Ernesto Grillo. LC 73-10197. (Studies in Shakespeare: No. 24). 1973. reprint ed. lib. bdg. 75.00 (*0-8383-1719-7*) M S G Haskell Hse.

Shakespeare & Jonson: The Macmillan Brown Lectures. S. Musgrove. LC 76-38501. reprint ed. 20.00 (*0-404-04545-6*) AMS Pr.

Shakespeare & Jonson, Jonson & Shakespeare. Russ McDonald. LC 87-19158. 249p. 1988. reprint ed. pap. 71.00 (*0-7837-8894-0*, 2049605) Bks Demand.

Shakespeare & Joyce: A Study of Finnegans Wake. Vincent J. Cheng. LC 82-42781. 256p. (C). 1984. 32.50 (*0-271-00342-1*) Pa St U Pr.

Shakespeare & Literature in Nineteenth Century Russia. Iurii D. Levin. 368p. 70.00 (*0-85496-891-1*); pap. 25.00 (*0-85496-863-6*) Berg Pubs.

Shakespeare & Macbeth. Stewart Ross. (Illus.). 48p. (J). (gr. 5 up). 1994. pap. 16.99 (*0-670-85629-0*) Viking Child Bks.

Shakespeare & Montaigne. William Flygare. 150p. 1987. 12.50 (*0-933704-87-9*) Dawn Pr.

Shakespeare & Multiplicity. Brian Gibbons. LC 92-42706. 248p. (C). 1993. text ed. 59.95 (*0-521-44406-3*) Cambridge U Pr.

Shakespeare & Music. 2nd ed. Edward W. Naylor. LC 65-16244. (Illus.). 1972. reprint ed. 17.95 (*0-405-08814-0*) Ayer.

Shakespeare & Music. Edward W. Naylor. LC 06-1277. reprint ed. 20.00 (*0-404-04652-5*) AMS Pr.

Shakespeare & National Character. Cumberland Clark. LC 76-181002. (Studies in Shakespeare: No. 24). 308p. 1972. reprint ed. lib. bdg. 59.95 (*0-8383-1371-X*) M S G Haskell Hse.

***Shakespeare & National Culture.** John J. Joughin. LC 96-3081. 1997. text ed. 69.95 (*0-7190-4888-5*, Pub. by Manchester Univ Pr UK); text ed. 19.95 (*0-7190-5051-0*, Pub. by Manchester Univ Pr UK) St Martin.

Shakespeare & Opera. Gary Schmidgall. 416p. 1990. 35.00 (*0-19-506450-X*) OUP.

Shakespeare & Our World. Alwin Thaler. LC 66-11626. 240p. 1966. 32.50 (*0-87049-063-X*) U of Tenn Pr.

Shakespeare & Our World. Alwin Thaler. LC 66-11626. 246p. reprint ed. pap. 70.20 (*0-317-28038-4*, 2025562) Bks Demand.

Shakespeare & Ovid. Jonathan Bate. 310p. 1994. reprint ed. pap. 22.00 (*0-19-818324-0*) OUP.

Shakespeare & Psychology. Cumberland Clark. (Studies in Shakespeare: No. 24). 1981. lib. bdg. 75.00 (*0-8383-2143-7*) M S G Haskell Hse.

Shakespeare & Science. Cumberland Clark. LC 79-92956. (Studies in Shakespeare: No. 24). 1970. reprint ed. lib. bdg. 75.00 (*0-8383-0965-8*) M S G Haskell Hse.

Shakespeare & Science. Cumberland Clark. (BCL1-PR English Literature Ser.). 262p. 1992. reprint ed. lib. bdg. 79.00 (*0-7812-7304-8*) Rprt Serv.

Shakespeare & Sexuality. Ed. by Stanley Wells. (Shakespeare Survey Ser.: No. 46). (Illus.). 220p. (C). 1994. 69.95 (*0-521-45027-6*) Cambridge U Pr.

Shakespeare & "Sir Thomas More" Essays on the Play & Its Shakespearian Interest. Ed. by Trevor H. Howard-Hill. 222p. (C). 1989. text ed. 69.95 (*0-521-34658-4*) Cambridge U Pr.

Shakespeare & Sir Walter Raleigh. Henry Pemberton. LC 76-174688. (Studies in Shakespeare: No. 24). 1971. reprint ed. lib. bdg. 39.95 (*0-8383-1340-X*) M S G Haskell Hse.

Shakespeare & South Africa. David Johnson. 288p. (C). 1996. 70.00 (*0-19-818315-1*) OUP.

Shakespeare & Spectator Consciousness. Daisy Aldan. 1987. pap. 4.50 (*0-913152-18-8*) Folder Edns.

Shakespeare & Spenser. Walter B. Watkins. LC 50-9325. 352p. reprint ed. pap. 100.40 (*0-8357-9512-8*, 2011405) Bks Demand.

Shakespeare & the Allegory of Evil: The History of a Metaphor in Relation to His Major Villains. Bernard Spivack. LC 57-12758. 521p. reprint ed. pap. 148.50 (*0-317-28960-8*, 2017840) Bks Demand.

Shakespeare & the Ambiguity of Love's Triumph. Charles R. Lyons. (Studies in English Literature: No. 68). 213p. 1971. text ed. 64.65 (*90-279-1751-5*) Mouton.

Shakespeare & the Archpriest Controversy: A Study of Some New Sources. David Kaula. LC 74-78510. (Studies in English Literature: No. 85). 132p. 1975. pap. text ed. 32.35 (*90-279-3466-5*) Mouton.

Shakespeare & the Art of Humankindness: The Essay Toward Androgyny. Robert Kimbrough. LC 89-29698. (Illus.). 288p. (C). 1992. pap. 18.50 (*0-391-03767-6*) Humanities.

Shakespeare & the Arte of English Poesie. William L. Rushton. LC 70-174792. reprint ed. 27.50 (*0-404-05458-7*) AMS Pr.

Shakespeare & the Arts: A Collection of Essays from the Ohio Shakespeare Conference, Wright State University, Dayton, Ohio, 1981. Ed. by Cecile W. Cary & Henry S. Limouze. LC 82-17486. (Illus.). 256p. (Orig.). 1983. lib. bdg. 56.00 (*0-8191-2819-8*) U Pr of Amer.

Shakespeare & the Arts of Design: Architecture, Sculpture & Painting. Arthur H. Fairchild. LC 70-174863. 1972. reprint ed. 19.95 (*0-405-08494-3*, Pub. by Blom Pubns UK) Ayer.

***Shakespeare & the Authority of Performance.** W. B. Worthen. 250p. (C). 1997. text ed. 49.95 (*0-521-55134-X*) Cambridge U Pr.

***Shakespeare & the Authority of Performance.** W. B. Worthen. 250p. (C). 1997. pap. text ed. 17.95 (*0-521-55899-9*) Cambridge U Pr.

Shakespeare & the Bible. James Rees. LC 70-174307. reprint ed. 34.50 (*0-404-05235-5*) AMS Pr.

Shakespeare & the Classical Tradition: A Critical Guide to Commentary, 1660-1960. John W. Velz. LC 67-14377. 479p. reprint ed. pap. 136.60 (*0-317-27789-8*, 2055955) Bks Demand.

Shakespeare & the Classical Tradition: An Annotated Bibliography, 1961-1985. Lewis Walker. 600p. text ed. 78.00 (*0-8240-6697-9*, H1119) Garland.

Shakespeare & the Classics. James A. Thomson. LC 78-6902. 254p. 1978. reprint ed. text ed. 55.00 (*0-313-20388-1*, THSC, Greenwood Pr) Greenwood.

Shakespeare & the Classroom. Ed. by A. K. Hudson. 1960. 29.50 (*0-317-27585-2*) Elliots Bks.

Shakespeare & the Constant Romans. Geoffrey Miles. (Oxford English Monographs). 232p. (C). 1996. 55.00 (*0-19-811771-X*) OUP.

Shakespeare & the Craft of Tragedy. William Rosen. LC 60-8002. 245p. 1960. reprint ed. pap. 69.00 (*0-7837-4127-8*, 2057950) Bks Demand.

Shakespeare & the Denial of Death. James L. Calderwood. LC 87-5922. 248p. (Orig.). (C). 1988. pap. text ed. 17.95 (*0-87023-583-4*) U of Mass Pr.

Shakespeare & the Dialectic of Certainty. Lee A. Jacobus. LC 92-14285. 1992. text ed. 35.00 (*0-312-08063-8*) St Martin.

Shakespeare & the Dramaturgy of Power. John D. Cox. 312p. 1989. text ed. 42.50 (*0-691-06765-1*) Princeton U Pr.

Shakespeare & the Elizabethans, Vol. 42. Ed. by Stanley Wells. (Shakespeare Survey Ser.). (Illus.). 288p. (C). 1990. text ed. 69.95 (*0-521-38034-0*) Cambridge U Pr.

Shakespeare & the Ends of Comedy. Ejner J. Jensen. LC 90-23962. (Drama & Performance Studies). 176p. 1991. 29.95 (*0-253-33094-7*) Ind U Pr.

Shakespeare & the Englishman. Josiah H. Symon. LC 77-155114. (Studies in Shakespeare: No. 24). 1972. reprint ed. lib. bdg. 39.95 (*0-8383-1288-8*) M S G Haskell Hse.

Shakespeare & the Experience of Love. Arthur C. Kirsch. LC 81-635. 204p. reprint ed. pap. 58.20 (*0-685-20554-1*, 2030601) Bks Demand.

Shakespeare & the Geography of Difference. John Gillies. (Cambridge Studies in Renaissance Literature & Culture: No. 4). (Illus.). 300p. (C). 1994. text ed. 59.95 (*0-521-41719-8*); pap. text ed. 19.95 (*0-521-45853-6*) Cambridge U Pr.

Shakespeare & the Greek Romance: A Study of Origins. Carol Gesner. LC 70-111509. 230p. reprint ed. pap. 65. 60 (*0-8357-8594-7*, 2034968) Bks Demand.

Shakespeare & the Hazards of Ambition. Robert N. Watson. 344p. 1984. 36.00 (*0-674-80390-6*) HUP.

Shakespeare & the Idea of the Play. Anne Barton. LC 76-58419. 223p. 1977. reprint ed. text ed. 65.00 (*0-8371-9446-6*, BASI, Greenwood Pr) Greenwood.

Shakespeare & the Indians - Musical. Dale Wasserman. 1992. pap. 5.50 (*0-87129-151-7*, S59) Dramatic Pub.

Shakespeare & the Influence of the Stars. D. Fraser-Harris. 1973. 69.95 (*0-8490-1031-4*) Gordon Pr.

Shakespeare & the Ireland Forgeries. D. Bodde. LC 75-22073. (Studies in Shakespeare: No. 24). 1975. lib. bdg. 40.95 (*0-8383-2084-8*) M S G Haskell Hse.

Shakespeare & the Jew. Gerald Friedlander. 1972. 59.95 (*0-8490-1032-2*) Gordon Pr.

Shakespeare & the Jew. Gerald Friedlander. LC 74-168084. reprint ed. 29.50 (*0-404-02579-X*) AMS Pr.

Shakespeare & the Jews. James Shapiro. LC 95-23260. 317p. 1995. 29.95 (*0-231-10344-1*) Col U Pr.

***Shakespeare & the Jews.** James Shapiro. 1997. pap. text ed. 17.50 (*0-231-10345-X*) Col U Pr.

Shakespeare & the Late Moral Plays. Alan C. Dessen. LC 85-8625. 208p. 1986. reprint ed. pap. 59.30 (*0-7837-9008-2*, 2049571) Bks Demand.

Shakespeare & the Mannerist Tradition: A Reading of Five Problem Plays. Jean P. Maquerlot. (Illus.). 211p. (C). 1996. text ed. 59.95 (*0-521-41083-5*) Cambridge U Pr.

Shakespeare & the Matter of the Crux: Textual, Topical, Onomastic, Authorial, & Other Puzzlements. Robert F. Fleissner. LC 91-37508. 320p. 1992. lib. bdg. 99.95 (*0-7734-9622-X*) E Mellen.

Shakespeare & the Modern Dramatist. Michael Scott. LC 88-11114. 208p. 1989. text ed. 39.95 (*0-312-02352-9*) St Martin.

Shakespeare & the Modern Stage. Sidney Lee. LC 74-172042. reprint ed. 29.50 (*0-404-03929-4*) AMS Pr.

Shakespeare & the Moral Curriculum: Rethinking the Secondary School Shakespeare Syllabus. Peter Roberts. LC 91-66911. 266p. (Orig.). 1992. pap. text ed. 17.95 (*0-9631311-0-9*) Pripet Pr.

Shakespeare & the Moving Image: The Plays on Film & Television. Ed. by Anthony Davies & Stanley Wells. LC 93-42524. (Illus.). 320p. (C). 1994. pap. text ed. 18. 95 (*0-521-43573-0*) Cambridge U Pr.

Shakespeare & the Moving Image: The Plays on Film & Television. Ed. by Anthony Davies & Stanley Wells. LC 93-42524. (Illus.). 320p. (C). 1994. 59.95 (*0-521-43424-6*) Cambridge U Pr.

Shakespeare & the Musical Stage: A Guide to Sources, Studies. Edward R. Hotaling. (Monograph Ser.). 542p. 1990. 55.00 (*0-8161-9070-4*, Hall Reference) Macmillan.

Shakespeare & the Nature of Women. 2nd ed. Juliet Dusinberre. 356p. 1996. text ed. 18.95 (*0-312-15973-0*) St Martin.

Shakespeare & the Nature of Women. 2nd ed. Juliet Dusinberre. 356p. 1996. text ed. 49.95 (*0-312-15972-2*) St Martin.

Shakespeare & the New Disease: The Dramatic Function of Syphilis in "Troilus & Cressida," "Measure for Measure," & "Timon of Athens" Greg W. Bentley. (American University Studies: English Language & Literature: Ser. IV, Vol. 85). 252p. (C). 1989. text ed. 36.95 (*0-8204-0817-4*) P Lang Pubng.

Shakespeare & the Ocular Proof. Alex Aronson. 1995. pap. 14.95 (*0-533-11146-3*) Vantage.

Shakespeare & the Poet's Life. Gary Schmidgall. LC 89-28667. 248p. 1990. 27.00 (*0-8131-1706-2*) U Pr of Ky.

Shakespeare & the Politics of Protestant England. Donna B. Hamilton. LC 91-47204. (Illus.). 272p. (C). 1992. 35. 00 (*0-8131-1790-9*) U Pr of Ky.

Shakespeare & the Popular Tradition in the Theater: Studies in the Social Dimension of Dramatic Form & Function. Robert Weimann. Ed. by Robert Schwartz. LC 77-13673. 352p. 1987. reprint ed. pap. text ed. 15.95 (*0-8018-3506-2*) Johns Hopkins.

Shakespeare & the Post Horses: A New Study of the Merry Wives of Windsor. John E. Crofts. LC 78-153313. reprint ed. 27.50 (*0-404-01856-4*) AMS Pr.

Shakespeare & the Problem of Meaning. Norman Rabkin. LC 80-18538. 176p. 1982. pap. text ed. 9.95 (*0-226-70178-6*) U Ch Pr.

***Shakespeare & the Question of Theory.** Ed. by Patricia Parker & Geoffrey H. Hartman. 352p. (C). 1986. pap. 22.95 (*0-415-05113-4*) Routledge.

Shakespeare & the Question of Theory. Ed. by Patricia Parker & Geoffrey H. Hartman. 300p. 1986. 27.00 (*0-416-36920-0*, 9479); pap. 19.95 (*0-416-36930-8*, 9480) Routledge Chapman & Hall.

Shakespeare & the Rhetoricians. Marion Trousdale. LC 81-40703. 220p. reprint ed. pap. 62.70 (*0-7837-5237-7*, 2044971) Bks Demand.

Shakespeare & the Rival Poet. Arthur Acheson. LC 79-113535. 1903. 29.50 (*0-404-00277-3*) AMS Pr.

S

Shakespeare & the Romance Tradition. E. Pettet. LC 75-30806. (Studies in Shakespeare: No. 24). 1975. lib. bdg. 75.00 (*0-8383-2081-3*) M S G Haskell Hse.

Shakespeare & the Sense of Performance: Essays in the Tradition of Performance Criticism in Honor of Bernard Beckerman. Ed. by Marvin Thompson & Ruth Thompson. LC 87-40327. (Illus.). 264p. 1989. 40.00 (*0-87413-332-7*) U Delaware Pr.

Shakespeare & the Sixteenth Century Study of Language. Jane Donawerth. LC 82-21740. 296p. 1984. text ed. 29.95 (*0-252-01038-8*) U of Ill Pr.

***Shakespeare & the Spectacles of Strangeness: The Tempest & the Transformation of Renaissance Theatrical Forms.** John G. Demaray. (Language & Literature Ser.: Vol. 24). (Illus.). 200p. (C). 1997. text ed. 48.00 (*0-8207-0284-6*) Duquesne.

Shakespeare & the Story: Aspects of Creation. Joan Rees. 239p. (C). 1978. pap. 18.95 (*0-485-12041-0*, Pub. by Athlone Pr UK) Humanities.

Shakespeare & the Supernatural. Cumberland Clark. LC 72-92957. (Studies in Shakespeare: No. 24). 1970. reprint ed. lib. bdg. 75.00 (*0-8383-0966-6*) M S G Haskell Hse.

Shakespeare & the Supernatural. Cumberland Clark. 346p. reprint ed. 29.00 (*0-403-04266-6*) Somerset Pub.

Shakespeare & the Supernatural. Margaret Lucy. LC 70-144653. reprint ed. 24.50 (*0-404-04065-9*) AMS Pr.

Shakespeare & the Tempest. Francis Neilson. LC 74-30004. 181p. 1970. reprint ed. text ed. 65.00 (*0-8371-7385-X*, NEST, Greenwood Pr) Greenwood.

Shakespeare & the Theatre of Wonder. T. G. Bishop. (Studies in Renaissance Literature & Culture: No. 9). 216p. (C). 1996. text ed. 54.95 (*0-521-55086-6*) Cambridge U Pr.

Shakespeare & the Triple Play: From Study to Stage to Classroom. Ed. by Sidney Homan. LC 86-73239. (Illus.). 240p. 1988. 36.50 (*0-8387-5122-9*) Bucknell U Pr.

Shakespeare & the Uses of Antiquity: An Introductory Essay. Charles Martindale. 240p. (C). 1994. pap. 16.95 (*0-415-10426-2*) Routledge.

Shakespeare & the Uses of Antiquity: An Introductoy Essay on Shakespeare & English Renaissance Classicism. Charles Martindale & Michelle Martindale. 240p. (C). (gr. 13). 1990. text ed. 52.95 (*0-415-02388-2*, A4634) Routledge.

Shakespeare & the Uses of Comedy. J. A. Bryant, Jr. LC 86-7770. 280p. 1986. 30.00 (*0-8131-1595-7*) U Pr of Ky.

Shakespeare & the Uses of Ideology. Sidney Shanker. (Studies in English Literature: No. 105). 224p. 1975. pap. text ed. 56.15 (*90-279-3257-3*) Mouton.

Shakespeare & the Victorian Stage. Ed. by Richard Foulkes. (Illus.). 340p. 1986. text ed. 89.95 (*0-521-30110-6*) Cambridge U Pr.

Shakespeare & the Welsh. Frederick J. Harries. LC 72-1333. (Studies in Shakespeare: No. 24). 1972. reprint ed. lib. bdg. 39.95 (*0-8383-1444-9*) M S G Haskell Hse.

***Shakespeare & This "Imperfect" World: Dramatic Form & the Nature of Knowing.** Giulio Marra. (Studies in Shakespeare: No. 5). 296p. (C). 1997. pap. text ed. 29.95 (*0-8204-3388-8*) P Lang Pubng.

Shakespeare & Tolstoy. G. Wilson Knight. LC 77-100769. (Studies in Comparative Literature: No. 35). 1970. reprint ed. pap. 75.00 (*0-8383-0050-2*) M S G Haskell Hse.

Shakespeare & Tragedy. John Bayley. 224p. (C). 1981. pap. text ed. 9.95 (*0-7100-0607-1*) Routledge Chapman & Hall.

Shakespeare & Voltaire. T. R. Lounsbury. 1973. 59.95 (*0-8490-1033-0*) Gordon Pr.

Shakespeare & Voltaire. Thomas R. Lounsbury. LC 72-172753. reprint ed. 37.50 (*0-404-04029-2*) AMS Pr.

Shakespeare & Voltaire. Thomas R. Lounsbury. LC 68-20237. 1972. reprint ed. 24.95 (*0-405-08754-3*, Pub. by Blom Pubns UK) Ayer.

Shakespeare, Aphra Behn, & the Canon. Ed. by W. R. Owen & Lizbeth Goodman. LC 96-16360. (Approaching Literature Ser.: Bk. 3). 352p. (C). 1996. pap. 18.95 (*0-415-13576-1*); text ed. 65.00 (*0-415-13575-3*) Routledge.

Shakespeare Around the Globe: A Guide to Notable Postwar Revivals. Ed. by Samuel L. Leiter. LC 85-27124. 987p. 1986. text ed. 145.00 (*0-313-23756-5*, LES/, Greenwood Pr) Greenwood.

Shakespeare As a Dramatic Artist. Richard G. Moulton. (BCL1-PR English Literature Ser.). 443p. 1992. reprint ed. lib. bdg. 99.00 (*0-7812-7303-X*) Rprt Serv.

Shakespeare As a Dramatist. John C. Squire. LC 79-159971. (Studies in Shakespeare: No. 24). 1971. lib. bdg. 39.95 (*0-8383-1221-7*) M S G Haskell Hse.

Shakespeare As a Lawyer. Franklin F. Heard. LC 76-51206. (Studies in Shakespeare: No. 24). 1977. lib. bdg. 75.00 (*0-8383-2156-9*) M S G Haskell Hse.

Shakespeare As a Lawyer. Franklin F. Heard. 119p. 1987. reprint ed. lib. bdg. 30.00 (*0-89941-571-7*, 305240) W S Hein.

Shakespeare As an Angler. Henry N. Ellacombe. LC 76-166018. reprint ed. 29.50 (*0-404-02278-2*) AMS Pr.

Shakespeare As Poet & Lover. Louis K. Anspacher. LC 73-9528. (Studies in Shakespeare: No. 24). 1973. reprint ed. lib. bdg. 75.00 (*0-8383-1701-4*) M S G Haskell Hse.

Shakespeare As Prompter: The Amending Imagination in Theatre & Therapy. Murray Cox & Alice Theilgaard. 328p. 1994. 60.00 (*1-85302-158-X*); pap. 33.00 (*1-85302-159-8*) Taylor & Francis.

Shakespeare As Traditional Artist. Geoffrey D. Gunther. 363p. (C). 1994. 20.00 (*1-881084-19-1*) Johannesen.

Shakespeare at Stratford upon Avon, Pt. 3, Posters, Programmes, Playbills, Photographs, & Pictures: The Libraries of the Royal Shakespeare Theatre & the Shakespeare Birthplace Trust. Royal Shakespeare Theatre Library Staff & Shakespeare Birthplace Trust Library Staff. (Library Reference Ser.). 32p. (C). 1991. 2,230.00 (*0-8161-1766-7*) G K Hall.

Shakespeare at Stratford upon Avon, Pt. 4, Pamplet Collection: The Libraries of the Royal Shakespeare Theatre & the Shakespeare Birthplace Trust. Royal Shakespeare Theatre Library Staff & Shakespeare Birthplace Trust Library Staff. (Library Reference Ser.). 546p. (C). 1991. 3,615.00 (*0-8161-1767-5*) G K Hall.

Shakespeare at the Maddermarket: Nugent Monck & the Norwich Players. Franklin J. Hildy. LC 86-16155. (Theater & Dramatic Studies: No. 41). (Illus.). 279p. reprint ed. pap. 79.60 (*0-8357-1775-5*, 2070500) Bks Demand.

Shakespeare at Work. John Jones. 304p. 1996. 65.00 (*0-19-811966-6*) OUP.

Shakespeare, Bacon & the Great Unknown. Andrew Lang. LC 75-75982. reprint ed. 40.00 (*0-404-03871-9*) AMS Pr.

Shakespeare-Bacon Controversy. Arthur M. Young. (Broadside Editions Ser.). (Illus.). 24p. (Orig.). (C). 1987. pap. 4.95 (*0-931191-05-X*) Rob Briggs.

Shakespeare Bibliography. Ed. by Levin L. Schucking. LC 68-20246. 1972. reprint ed. 26.95 (*0-405-08482-X*, Pub. by Blom Pubns UK) Ayer.

Shakespeare Bibliography: A Supplement. Walther Ebisch & Levin L. Schhucking. 1972. 26.95 (*0-405-08483-8*, 901) Ayer.

Shakespeare Bibliography: The Catalogue of the Birmingham Shakespeare Library, 7 vols., Set. W. R. Fredrick. 4311p. 1971. text ed. 600.00 (*0-7201-0180-8*, Mansell Pub) Cassell.

Shakespeare Biography & Other Papers, Chiefly Elizabethan. Felix E. Schelling. LC 68-26473. (Essay Index Reprint Ser.). 1977. reprint ed. 18.95 (*0-8369-0853-8*) Ayer.

Shakespeare Book. Shakespeare Birthplace Trust Library Staff. (Illus.). 32p. 1993. pap. 3.95 (*0-7117-0242-X*) Seven Hills Bk.

Shakespeare Cats. Susan Herbert. (J). 1996. 16.95 (*0-8212-2281-3*) Bulfinch Pr.

Shakespeare Cats. Susan Herbert. 1996. 16.95 (*0-614-95675-7*) Little.

Shakespeare, Chapman & Sir Thomas More. Arthur Acheson. LC 72-113536. reprint ed. 42.75 (*0-404-00278-1*) AMS Pr.

Shakespeare-Characters. Charles C. Clarke. LC 72-961. reprint ed. 49.50 (*0-404-01567-0*) AMS Pr.

Shakespeare Circle. C. M. Mitchell. LC 76-30693. (Studies in Shakespeare: No. 24). 1977. lib. bdg. 46.95 (*0-8383-2166-6*) M S G Haskell Hse.

Shakespeare Comedies. 1995. pap. 5.25 (*0-19-586301-1*) OUP.

Shakespeare Comes to Broadmoor: "The Actors Are Come Hither" Ed. by Murray Cox. 200p. 1992. 57.00 (*1-85302-135-0*); pap. 29.95 (*1-85302-121-0*) Taylor & Francis.

Shakespeare Commentaries. Georg G. Gervinus. Tr. by Fanny E. Bunnett. LC 74-168112. reprint ed. 67.50 (*0-404-02716-4*) AMS Pr.

Shakespeare Companies & Festivals: An International Guide. Ron Engle et al. LC 94-32786. 624p. 1995. text ed. 99.50 (*0-313-27434-7*, Greenwood Pr) Greenwood.

Shakespeare Concordance, 4 vols., Set. John R. Bartlett. 1976. 1,500.00 (*0-87968-266-3*) Gordon Pr.

Shakespeare Country. Anthony Bruce. Date not set. pap. 14.95 (*0-7181-3243-2*) Viking Penguin.

Shakespeare Country. Howard Loxton. 1995. 9.98 (*0-8317-1876-5*) Smithmark.

Shakespeare Documents: A Chronological Catalogue. D. Lambert. 1972. 59.95 (*0-8490-1034-9*) Gordon Pr.

Shakespeare Domesticated: The Eighteenth Century Editions. Colin Franklin. 288p. 1991. text ed. 39.95 (*0-85967-834-2*, Pub. by Scolar Pr UK) Ashgate Pub Co.

Shakespeare East & West. Ed. by Minoru Fujita & Leonard Pronko. 256p. 1996. text ed. 45.00 (*0-312-16145-X*) St Martin.

Shakespeare-Expositor. Thomas Keightley. LC 54-171550. reprint ed. 62.50 (*0-404-03642-2*) AMS Pr.

Shakespeare, Fifteen Sixty-Four to Nineteen Sixty-Four: A Collection of Modern Essays by Various Hands. Ed. by Edward A. Bloom. LC 64-17777. (Brown University Bicentennial Publications). 240p. reprint ed. pap. 68.40 (*0-7837-2618-X*, 2042953) Bks Demand.

Shakespeare Films in The Classroom: A Descriptive Guide. Jo McMurtry. LC 93-39431. (Illus.). ix, 249p. (C). 1994. lib. bdg. 39.50 (*0-208-02369-0*, Archon Bks) Shoe String.

Shakespeare, Fletcher, & "The Two Noble Kinsmen" Ed. by Charles H. Frey. LC 88-27634. 232p. 1989. text ed. 34.95 (*0-8262-0705-7*) U of Mo Pr.

Shakespeare Folio Handbook & Census: Bibliographies & Indexes in World Literature, No. 25. Compiled by Harold M. Otness. LC 89-28650. 146p. 1990. text ed. 49.95 (*0-313-27257-3*, OSA/, Greenwood Pr) Greenwood.

***Shakespeare for All in Primary Schools.** Ed. by Maurice Gilmour. (Education Ser.). (Illus.). 128p. 1996. pap. 19.95 (*0-304-33792-7*); text ed. 65.00 (*0-304-33791-9*) Cassell.

***Shakespeare for All in Secondary Schools.** Ed. by Maurice Gilmour. (Education Ser.). (Illus.). 128p. 1996. pap. 19.95 (*0-304-33916-4*); text ed. 65.00 (*0-304-33915-6*) Cassell.

***Shakespeare for Beginners.** Brandon Toropov. (The For Beginners Ser.). (Illus.). 176p. 11.00 (*0-86316-228-2*) Writers & Readers.

Shakespeare for Children: The Story of Romeo & Juliet. Cass Foster. LC 89-80371. (Illus.). 105p. (J). (gr. 2 up). 1989. pap. 9.95 (*0-9619853-3-X*) Five Star AZ.

Shakespeare for Lovers: All of His Romantic Poems. William Shakespeare. LC 94-17111. 1995. 14.95 (*0-8065-1544-9*, Citadel Pr) Carol Pub Group.

Shakespeare for Students. 2nd ed. Michael Magoulias. 1996. 65.00 (*0-7876-0157-8*) Gale.

Shakespeare for Students: Critical Interpretations of As You Like It, Hamlet, Julius Caesar, Macbeth, the Merchant of Venice, a Midsummer Night's Dream, Othello & Romeo & Juliet. Ed. by Mark W. Scott. 529p. (C). 1992. 65.00 (*0-8103-8247-4*, 101152) Gale.

***Shakespeare for the 21st Century. David Vando. 122p. (Orig.). 1996. pap. 13.95 (*0-9653772-0-2*, V62096) Angel Mgmt.**

"Shakespeare made easy" for the computer era with 500+ hilarious quotes "attributed" to the most unlikely cast of characters. Even those "tapping" into the Bard for the first time will be captivated by the "virtual reality" of his wit & wisdom. Chapter One suggests to whom Shakespeare might speak his famous lines if he were living today: "A plague o' both your houses!"--Ross Perot; "Good night, sweet prince, & flights of angels sing thee to thy rest!"--Princess Diana. Other chapters feature "translations" of useful phrases, "Send out for torturers ingenious."--Report him to the IRS; Mottos, "Lay aside life-harming heaviness."--League of Liposuctionists; Parental Quotes, "Get thee to a nunnery!"-- Madonna's mother; & Epitaphs completes "this strange eventful history, what a piece of work is man."--Mae West. The critical acclaim says it all about this unique book: "Best book I've seen in years in years!"--John Milton. "In my day, we shot people for less."--Joseph Stalin. "One of the funniest books ever, but not as funny as mine."--Mark Twain. "If thou didst think my jibes of fleeting use, just read the ones herein for more abuse!"--William Shakespeare. Order from: Angel Management, 42 W. 38th St., 8th Floor, New York, NY 10018. 212-382-1711, FAX: 212-869-3287. ***Publisher Provided Annotation.***

Shakespeare-from Betterton to Irving, 2 Vols., Set. George C. Odell. LC 63-23277. (Illus.). 1972. reprint ed. 60.95 (*0-405-08824-8*) Ayer.

Shakespeare-from Betterton to Irving, 2 Vols., Vol. 1. George C. Odell. LC 63-23277. (Illus.). 1972. reprint ed. 30.95 (*0-405-08825-6*) Ayer.

Shakespeare-from Betterton to Irving, 2 Vols., Vol. 2. George C. Odell. LC 63-23277. (Illus.). 1972. reprint ed. 30.95 (*0-405-08826-4*) Ayer.

Shakespeare from Text to Stage. Mariangela Tempera. (Renaissance Revisited Ser.: No. 1). 204p. 1995. pap. 20.95 (*88-8091-131-7*) Paul & Co Pubs.

Shakespeare from the Margins: Language, Culture, Context. Patricia Parker. LC 95-36472. 352p. 1996. pap. text ed. 19.95 (*0-226-64585-1*); lib. bdg. 52.00 (*0-226-64584-3*) U Ch Pr.

Shakespeare Garden. Esther Singleton. LC 75-176028. (Illus.). reprint ed. 34.50 (*0-404-06096-X*) AMS Pr.

Shakespeare Glossary. enl. rev. ed. Charles T. Onions. Ed. by Robert D. Eagleson. 360p. 1986. pap. 17.95 (*0-19-812521-6*) OUP.

Shakespeare Handbook. Raymond M. Alden. Ed. by Oscar J. Campbell. LC 75-109639. (Select Bibliographies Reprint Ser.). 1977. 26.95 (*0-8369-5248-0*) Ayer.

Shakespeare Handbook. Ed. by Levi Fox. (Illus.). 272p. 1987. 40.00 (*0-8161-8905-6*, Hall Reference) Macmillan.

Shakespeare, Harsnett, & the Devils of Denham. Frank W. Brownlow. LC 90-51010. (Illus.). 440p. 1993. 49.50 (*0-87413-436-6*) U Delaware Pr.

Shakespeare Head Edition of Smollett's Novels, 11 vols. Tobias G. Smollett. (BCL1-PR English Literature Ser.). 1992. reprint ed. lib. bdg. 825.00 (*0-7812-7402-8*) Rprt Serv.

Shakespeare Head Edition of the Novels & Selected Writings of Daniel Defoe, 14 vols., Set. Daniel Defoe. (BCL1-PR English Literature Ser.). 1992. reprint ed. lib. bdg. 1,050.00 (*0-7812-7341-2*) Rprt Serv.

Shakespeare Hermeneutics. Clement M. Ingleby. LC 73-157552. (Studies in Shakespeare: No. 24). 1971. reprint ed. lib. bdg. 33.95 (*0-8383-1294-2*) M S G Haskell Hse.

Shakespeare Illustrated, 3 Vols, Set. C. Lennox. LC 72-172047. reprint ed. 135.00 (*0-404-03970-7*) AMS Pr.

***Shakespeare in Africa (& Other Venues) Import & the Appropriation of Culture.** Lemuel A. Johnson. LC 96-43385. 400p. 1996. 79.95 (*0-86543-536-7*); pap. 21.95 (*0-86543-537-5*) Africa World.

Shakespeare in America. Esther C. Dunn. LC 68-21212. (Illus.). 1972. reprint ed. 20.95 (*0-405-08475-7*, Pub. by Blom Pubns UK) Ayer.

Shakespeare in American Painting: A Catalog from the Late 18th Century to the Present. Richard Studing. LC 90-55008. (Illus.). 192p. 1993. 65.00 (*0-8386-3408-7*) Fairleigh Dickinson.

Shakespeare in Art. S. Hartmann. LC 78-168251. reprint ed. 34.50 (*0-404-03152-8*) AMS Pr.

Shakespeare in China: A Comparative Study of Two Traditions & Cultures. Xiao Yang Zhang. LC 95-30444. (Illus.). 280p. (C). 1996. 39.50 (*0-87413-536-2*) U Delaware Pr.

Shakespeare in Context: A Documentary Companion. Russ McDonald. 320p. 1996. pap. text ed. 8.50 (*0-312-10075-2*) St Martin.

Shakespeare, in Fact. Irvin L. Matus. LC 93-16327. (Illus.). 352p. 1994. 29.50 (*0-8264-0624-6*) Continuum.

Shakespeare, in Fact. Irvin L. Matus. LC 96-23394. 336p. 1997. pap. text ed. 24.95 (*0-8264-0928-8*) Continuum.

Shakespeare in France - Criticism: Voltaire to Victor Hugo. Charles M. Haines. LC 70-168217. reprint ed. 32.50 (*0-404-07883-4*) AMS Pr.

Shakespeare in France Under the Ancient Regime. J. J. Jusserand. 1972. 59.95 (*0-8490-1035-7*) Gordon Pr.

Shakespeare in Germany in the Sixteenth & Seventeenth Centuries. Albert Cohn. LC 75-166208. (Studies in Shakespeare: No. 24). 1971. reprint ed. lib. bdg. 68.95 (*0-8383-1330-2*) M S G Haskell Hse.

Shakespeare in His Context: The Constellated Globe: The Collected Papers of Muriel Bradbrook, IV. Muriel C. Bradbrook. 207p. (C). 1989. lib. bdg. 54.50 (*0-389-20877-9*) B&N Imports.

Shakespeare in His Time & Ours. Paul N. Siegel. LC 68-12294. 270p. 1968. reprint ed. pap. 77.00 (*0-608-00883-4*, 2061677) Bks Demand.

Shakespeare in India. S. Nagarajan & S. Viswanathan. 128p. 1987. 18.95 (*0-685-21573-3*) Asia Bk Corp.

Shakespeare in Italy. Lacy Collison-Morley. LC 67-23862. 1972. reprint ed. 18.95 (*0-405-08373-4*, Pub. by Blom Pubns UK) Ayer.

Shakespeare in Japan. Graham Bradshaw & Tetsuo Kishi. (C). 1997. 90.00 (*0-485-11499-2*, Pub. by Athlone Pr UK) Humanities.

Shakespeare in Music. Louis C. Elson. LC 76-155627. reprint ed. 31.50 (*0-404-02323-1*) AMS Pr.

Shakespeare in Music: A Collation of the Chief Musical Allusions in the Plays of Shakespeare, with an Attempt at Their Explanation & Derivation, Together with Much of the Original Music. Louis C. Elson. LC 78-113646. (Select Bibliographies Reprint Ser.). 1977. 28.95 (*0-8369-5257-X*) Ayer.

Shakespeare in Performance. William Shakespeare. 1995. 19.99 (*0-517-14091-8*) Random Hse Value.

Shakespeare in Pictorial Art. Malcolm C. Salaman. Ed. by Charles Holme. LC 79-175892. (Illus.). 1972. reprint ed. 22.95 (*0-405-08910-4*) Ayer.

Shakespeare in Production: Whose History? H. R. Coursen. LC 95-34091. (Illus.). 350p. (C). 1996. text ed. 39.95 (*0-8214-1140-3*) Ohio U Pr.

Shakespeare in Sable: A History of Black Shakespearean Actors. Errol Hill. LC 83-18106. (Illus.). 248p. 1986. pap. 17.95 (*0-87023-525-7*) U of Mass Pr.

Shakespeare in the Changing Curriculum. Ed. by Lesley Aers & Nigel Wheale. (Illus.). 240p. (C). (gr. 13). 1991. pap. text ed. 18.95 (*0-415-05393-5*, A5746) Routledge.

Shakespeare in the Classroom. Albert Cullum. 272p. (J). (gr. 4-8). 18.99 (*0-86653-903-4*, FE0903) Fearon Teach Aids.

Shakespeare in the Classroom: What's the Matter? Susan Leach & Frank F. Harrison. 160p. 1992. pap. 27.00 (*0-335-09674-3*, Open Univ Pr) Taylor & Francis.

Shakespeare in the New Europe. Boika D. Sokolova. 35.00 (*1-85075-474-8*, Pub. by Sheffield Acad UK) CUP Services.

Shakespeare in the South: Essays on Performance. Ed. by Philip C. Kolin. LC 83-5954. (Illus.). 298p. 1983. 35.00 (*0-87805-185-6*) U Pr of Miss.

Shakespeare in the Stratford Records. Robert Bearman. (Illus.). 96p. 1994. pap. 15.00 (*0-7509-0632-4*, Pub. by Sutton Pubng UK) Bks Intl VA.

Shakespeare in the Theatre. William Poel. LC 70-143343. reprint ed. 31.50 (*0-404-05067-0*) AMS Pr.

Shakespeare in the Theatre. William Poel. LC 67-31456. 1972. reprint ed. 19.95 (*0-405-08859-0*) Ayer.

***Shakespeare in the Theatre: An Anthology of Criticism.** Ed. & Compiled by Stanley Wells. (Illus.). 352p. 1997. 25.00 (*0-19-871177-8*) OUP.

Shakespeare in the Twentieth Century. Ed. by Stanley Wells. LC 49-1639. (Shakespeare Survey Ser.: No. 36). (Illus.). 200p. 1984. text ed. 69.95 (*0-521-25636-4*) Cambridge U Pr.

***Shakespeare in Theory: The Postmodern Academy & the Early Modern Theater.** Stephen Bretzius. (C). 1997. 32.50 (*0-472-10853-0*) U of Mich Pr.

Shakespeare in Time of War. Francis Colmer. LC 76-30691. (Studies in Shakespeare: No. 24). 1977. lib. bdg. 42.95 (*0-8383-2165-8*) M S G Haskell Hse.

Shakespeare in Wall Street. Edward H. Warren. 1978. reprint ed. pap. 7.00 (*0-87034-055-7*) Fraser Pub Co.

Shakespeare in Warwickshire. Mark Eccles. LC 61-5900. 192p. 1961. reprint ed. pap. 54.80 (*0-608-01956-9*, 2062611) Bks Demand.

Shakespeare, Jonson, & the Myth of Venice. David McPherson. LC 89-40722. (Illus.). 160p. 1991. 33.50 (*0-87413-397-1*) U Delaware Pr.

Shakespeare Key. C. Clark. 1972. 59.95 (*0-8490-1036-5*) Gordon Pr.

Shakespeare Left & Right. Ed. by Ivo Kamps. 288p. (C). 1991. pap. 16.95 (*0-415-90376-9*, A5182, Routledge NY) Routledge.

Shakespeare Lexicon: A Complete Dictionary of All the English Words, Phrases & Constructions in the Work of the Poet, 2 Vols., Set. Alexander Schmidt. Ed. by Gregor Sarrazin. LC 67-30463. 1972. reprint ed. 104.95 (*0-405-08935-X*) Ayer.

Shakespeare Lexicon: A Complete Dictionary of All the English Words, Phrases & Constructions in the Work of the Poet, 2 Vols., Vol. 1. Alexander Schmidt. Ed. by Gregor Sarrazin. LC 67-30463. 1972. reprint ed. 52.95 (*0-405-08936-8*) Ayer.

S

An Asterisk (*) at the beginning of an entry indicates that the title is appearing in BIP for the first time.

Shakespeare Lexicon: A Complete Dictionary of All the English Words, Phrases & Constructions in the Work of the Poet, 2 Vols., Vol. 2. Alexander Schmidt. Ed. by Gregor Sarrazin. LC 67-30463. 1972. reprint ed. 52.95 (*0-405-08937-6*) Ayer.

Shakespeare Lexicon: A Complete Dictionary of all the English Words, Phrases & Constructions in the Works of the Poet, 2 vols. 6th enl. rev. ed. Alexander Schmidt. Ed. by Gregor Sarrazin. (C). 1971. 211.55 (*3-11-002203-6*) De Gruyter.

Shakespeare Lexicon & Quotation Dictionary, 2 vols., 1. Alexander Schmidt. 15.95 (*0-486-22726-X*) Dover.

Shakespeare Lexicon & Quotation Dictionary, 2 vols., 2. Alexander Schmidt. 15.95 (*0-486-22727-8*) Dover.

Shakespeare Library, 3 vols. (Cliffs Notes Hardbound Library). 1989. lib. bdg. 201.50 (*0-931013-25-9*) Moonbeam Pubns.

Shakespeare Library, Pt. 1: The Comedies. (Cliffs Notes Hardbound Authors Library: Vol. 8). (C). 1990. lib. bdg. 106.00 (*0-931013-73-9*) Moonbeam Pubns.

Shakespeare Library, Pt. 2: The Tragedies. (Cliffs Notes Hardbound Authors Library: Vol. 9). (C). 1990. lib. bdg. 62.00 (*0-931013-74-7*) Moonbeam Pubns.

Shakespeare Library, the Comedies: Collection of 11 Titles. (Cliffs Notes Softbound Literary Libraries). 1990. pap. text ed. 40.85 (*1-56271-283-7*) Moonbeam Pubns.

Shakespeare Library, the Sonnets: Collection of 6 Titles. (Cliffs Notes Softbound Literary Libraries). 1990. pap. text ed. 21.95 (*1-56271-285-3*) Moonbeam Pubns.

Shakespeare Library, the Tragedies: Collection of 7 Titles. (Cliffs Notes Softbound Literary Libraries). 1990. pap. text ed. 25.90 (*1-56271-284-5*) Moonbeam Pubns.

Shakespeare Library, Vol. 1: The Comedies. (Cliffs Notes Hardbound Library). 1989. lib. bdg. 93.00 (*0-931013-00-3*) Moonbeam Pubns.

Shakespeare Library, Vol. 10, Pt. 3: Histories: Sonnets, Pt. 3. Elizabeth Jones. (Cliffs Notes Hardbound Authors Library: Vol. 10). (C). 1990. lib. bdg. 62.00 (*0-931013-75-5*) Moonbeam Pubns.

Shakespeare Library, Vol. 2: The Tragedies. (Cliffs Notes Hardbound Library). 1989. lib. bdg. 54.25 (*0-931013-01-1*) Moonbeam Pubns.

Shakespeare Library, Vol. 3: The Histories; Sonnets. (Cliffs Notes Hardbound Library). 1989. lib. bdg. 54.25 (*0-931013-02-X*) Moonbeam Pubns.

Shakespeare Manipulated: The Use of the Dramatic Works of Shakespeare in Teatro Di Figura in Italy. Susan Young. LC 95-21989. (Illus.). 232p. 1996. 38.50 (*0-8386-3578-4*) Fairleigh Dickinson.

Shakespeare Manual. Frederick G. Fleay. LC 76-130621. reprint ed. 32.00 (*0-404-02408-4*) AMS Pr.

Shakespeare, Me Thinks: A Collection of Modern Plays for Oral Reading & Comprehension: Trust - Othello. Jerry Chris. 32p. (Orig.). (YA). (gr. 9-12). 1993. pap. text ed. 5.00 (*0-88092-061-0*) Royal Fireworks.

Shakespeare, Me Thinks - A Collection of Modern Plays for Oral Reading & Comprehension: Quicksand - Macbeth. Jerry Chris. 32p. (YA). (gr. 9-12). 1993. pap. text ed. 5.00 (*0-88092-062-9*) Royal Fireworks.

Shakespeare, Me Thinks - A Collection of Modern Plays for Oral Reading & Comprehension: The Choice - Romeo & Juliet. Jerry Chris. 32p. 1993. teacher ed., pap. 12.00 (*0-614-03213-X*) Royal Fireworks.

Shakespeare, Me Thinks - A Collection of Modern Plays for Oral Reading & Comprehension: The Choice - Romeo & Juliet. Jerry Chris. 32p. (YA). (gr. 9-12). 1993. pap. text ed. 5.00 (*0-88092-059-9*) Royal Fireworks.

Shakespeare, Me Thinks - A Collection of Modern Plays for Oral Reading & Comprehension: The Price of Silence - Julius Caesar. Jerry Chris. 32p. (YA). (gr. 9-12). 1993. pap. text ed. 5.00 (*0-88092-060-2*) Royal Fireworks.

Shakespeare, Me Thinks - A Collection of Modern Plays for Oral Reading & Comprehension: Top Priority - Hamlet. Jerry Chris. 32p. (YA). (gr. 9-12). 1993. pap. text ed. 5.00 (*0-88092-063-7*) Royal Fireworks.

Shakespeare, Me Thinks - A Collection of Modern Plays for Oral Reading & Comprehension: Trust - Othello. Jerry Chris. 32p. 1993. teacher ed., pap. 12.00 (*0-88092-058-0*) Royal Fireworks.

Shakespeare, Meaning & Metaphor. Ann Thompson & John O. Thompson. LC 86-51085. 240p. (C). 1987. text ed. 31.95 (*0-87745-166-4*) U of Iowa Pr.

Shakespeare Memorial Theatre, 1919-1945. Susan Brock & Marian J. Pringle. (Theatre in Focus Ser.). (Illus.). 120p. 1984. pap. 105.00 incl. sl. (*0-85964-157-0*) Chadwyck-Healey.

Shakespeare-Middleton Collaborations. Mark Dominik. LC 87-37358. 184p. (C). 1988. 22.50 (*0-945088-01-9*) Alioth Pr.

***Shakespeare, Milton & Eighteenth-Century Literary Editing: The Beginnings of Interpretative Scholarship.** Marcus Walsh. (Studies in Eighteenth-Century English Literature & Thought: Vol. 35). (Illus.). 241p. (C). 1997. text ed. 59.95 (*0-521-55443-8*) Cambridge U Pr.

Shakespeare Music Catalogue, 5 vols., Set. Ed. by Bryan N. Gooch & David Thatcher. 4376p. 1991. 535.00 (*0-19-812359-0*) OUP.

Shakespeare Music Catalogue, Vol. 1: The Catalogue of Music: All's Well That Ends Well - Love's Labours Lost. Ed. by Bryan N. Gooch & David Thatcher. 790p. 1991. 139.00 (*0-19-812941-6*) OUP.

Shakespeare Music Catalogue, Vol. 2: The Catalogue of Music: Macbeth - The Taming of the Shrew. Ed. by Bryan N. Gooch & David Thatcher. 808p. 1991. 139.00 (*0-19-812942-4*) OUP.

Shakespeare Music Catalogue, Vol. 3: A Catalogue of Music: The Tempest - The Two Noble Kinsmen, the Sonnets, the Poems, Commemmorative Pieces, Anthologies. Ed. by Bryan N. Gooch & David Thatcher. 688p. 1991. 125.00 (*0-19-812943-2*) OUP.

Shakespeare Music Catalogue, Vol. 4: Indices. Ed. by Bryan N. Gooch & David Thatcher. 876p. 1991. 89.00 (*0-19-812944-0*) OUP.

Shakespeare Music Catalogue, Vol. 5: Bibliography. Ed. by Bryan N. Gooch & David Thatcher. 320p. 1991. 79.00 (*0-19-812945-9*) OUP.

***Shakespeare Must Have Been Divorced: Practical Alternatives to Hiring a Divorce Lawyer & Why.** Michael Gregory. 174p. 1997. pap. 16.95 (*1-890801-18-6*) Gwydion Pub.

***Shakespeare Name & Place Dictionary.** Ed. by J. Madison Davis & A. Daniel Frankforter. 546p. 1996. lib. bdg. 95.00 (*1-884964-17-6*) Fitzroy Dearborn.

Shakespeare Name Dictionary. Ed. by J. Madison Davis & A. Daniel Frankforter. LC 94-13784. 552p. 1995. text ed. 75.00 (*0-8240-6341-4*, H976) Garland.

Shakespeare Never Did This. Charles Bukowski. (Illus.). 150p. (C). 1996. reprint ed. 25.00 (*0-87685-969-4*); reprint ed. pap. 15.00 (*0-87685-968-6*) Black Sparrow.

Shakespeare No Deerstealer. C. Holte Bracebridge. LC 76-39517. reprint ed. 34.50 (*0-404-00921-2*) AMS Pr.

Shakespeare Observed: Studies in Performance on Stage & Screen. Samuel Crowl. LC 92-9364. (Illus.). 208p. (C). 1993. reprint ed. pap. 16.95 (*0-8214-1064-4*); reprint ed. text ed. 35.00 (*0-8214-1034-2*) Ohio U Pr.

Shakespeare of Stratford. Tucker Brooke. LC 79-128883. (Select Bibliographies Reprint Ser.). 1977. 20.95 (*0-8369-5503-X*) Ayer.

Shakespeare on Film. Jack J. Jorgens. 352p. (C). 1991. reprint ed. pap. text ed. 32.50 (*0-8191-8157-9*) U Pr of Amer.

***Shakespeare on Golf.** John Tullius. 1997. 15.95 (*0-7868-6320-X*); 95.70 (*0-7868-7946-7*) Hyperion.

Shakespeare on Leadership. Federick Talbott. LC 94-11160. 1994. pap. 10.99 (*0-7852-7983-0*) Nelson.

Shakespeare on Love: Passages from the Plays & Poems. William Shakespeare. 1991. 9.95 (*0-312-05514-5*) St Martin.

Shakespeare on Management: Wise Counsel & Warnings from the Bard. Jay M. Shafritz. (Illus.). 160p. 1992. 12.95 (*1-55972-109-X*, Birch Ln Pr) Carol Pub Group.

Shakespeare on Screen: An International Filmography & Videography. Kenneth S. Rothwell & Annabelle H. Meltzer. 400p. (Orig.). 1990. text ed. 59.95 (*1-55570-049-7*) Neal-Schuman.

Shakespeare on Television: An Anthology of Essays & Reviews. Ed. by J. C. Bulman & H. R. Coursen. LC 87-40511. 336p. 1988. 19.95 (*0-87451-435-5*) U Pr of New Eng.

Shakespeare on Temperance. E. Sherlock. LC 72-928. (Studies in Shakespeare: No. 24). 210p. 1972. reprint ed. lib. bdg. 49.95 (*0-8383-1413-9*) M S G Haskell Hse.

Shakespeare on the American Stage: From the Hallams to Edwin Booth. Charles H. Shattuck. (Special Publications Ser.). 1978. pap. 15.95 (*0-918016-59-2*) Folger Bks.

Shakespeare on the American Stage, Vol. 2: From Booth & Barrett to Sothern & Marlowe. Charles H. Shattuck. LC 75-43999. (Illus.). 344p. 1987. 85.00 (*0-918016-77-0*) Folger Bks.

Shakespeare on the German Stage, Vol. 1: 1586-1914. Simon Williams. (Illus.). 268p. (C). 1990. text ed. 69.95 (*0-521-34464-6*) Cambridge U Pr.

Shakespeare on the Stage. William Winter. LC 78-93173. (Illus.). 1972. First Ser. 36.95 (*0-405-09091-9*); Second Ser. 36.95 (*0-405-09093-5*); Third Ser. 36.95 (*0-405-09094-3*) Ayer.

Shakespeare Once a Printer & Bookman. William Jaggard. LC 70-181003. (Studies in Shakespeare: No. 24). 34p. 1972. reprint ed. 75.00 (*0-8383-1372-8*) M S G Haskell Hse.

Shakespeare, Pattern of Excelling Nature: Shakespearean Criticism in Honor of America's Bicentennial. Ed. by David Bevington & Jay L. Halio. LC 77-82878. 304p. 38.50 (*0-87413-129-4*) U Delaware Pr.

Shakespeare, Philosophy, & Literature Vol. 10: Essays by Morris Weitz. Morris Weitz. Ed. by Margaret C. Weitz. LC 93-29764. (New Studies in Aesthetics: Vol. 10). 200p. (C). 1995. text ed. 45.95 (*0-8204-1679-7*) P Lang Pubng.

Shakespeare Phrase Book. John Bartlett. (Works of John Bartlett). 1989. reprint ed. lib. bdg. 79.00 (*0-7812-1904-3*) Rprt Serv.

Shakespeare Phrase Book, 2 vols., Set. John R. Bartlett. 1973. 600.00 (*0-87968-260-4*) Gordon Pr.

Shakespeare, Plautus & the Humanist Tradition. Wolfgang Riehle. (Illus.). 319p. 1991. 90.00 (*0-85991-305-8*) Boydell & Brewer.

Shakespeare Play As Poem. Shiv Viswanathan. LC 79-41618. 250p. 1980. 44.95 (*0-521-22547-7*) Cambridge U Pr.

Shakespeare Primer. G. Sanders. LC 72-175432. reprint ed. 20.00 (*0-404-05560-5*) AMS Pr.

Shakespeare Problem Restated. Granville G. Greenwood. (BCL1-PR English Literature Ser.). 558p. 1992. reprint ed. lib. bdg. 99.00 (*0-7812-7288-2*) Rprt Serv.

Shakespeare Promptbooks: A Descriptive Catalogue. Charles H. Shattuck. LC 65-11737. 563p. reprint ed. pap. 160.50 (*0-685-23650-1*, 2015039) Bks Demand.

Shakespeare Psychognostic. Wolfgang J. Weilgart. LC 75-144701. reprint ed. 18.00 (*0-404-06897-9*) AMS Pr.

Shakespeare Psychognostic: Character Evolution & Transformation. W. John Weilgart. 1976. lib. bdg. 59.95 (*0-8490-2596-6*) Gordon Pr.

Shakespeare Psychognostic: Character Evolution & Transformation. 2nd ed. W. John Weilgart & John C. Bale. 280p. 1952. pap. 6.00 (*0-912038-29-2*) Cosmic Comm.

Shakespeare, Puritan & Recusant. Thomas Carter. LC 70-129386. reprint ed. 32.50 (*0-404-01397-X*) AMS Pr.

***Shakespeare Reader.** William Shakespeare. (Giant Literary Classics Ser.). 1997. 8.98 (*0-7624-0001-3*) Running Pr.

Shakespeare Recycled: The Making of Historical Drama. Graham Holderness. 272p. (C). 1992. text ed. 69.50 (*0-389-20988-0*) B&N Imports.

Shakespeare Remembers. Lawrence H. Waddy. LC 94-42893. 40p. 1994. pap. 6.00 (*0-88734-292-2*) Players Pr.

Shakespeare Repository, 1 vol., Nos. 1-4. reprint ed. 45.00 (*0-404-19552-0*) AMS Pr.

***Shakespeare Reproduced.** Jean E. Howard & Marion O'Connor. 288p. (C). 1987. pap. 17.95 (*0-415-05880-5*) Routledge.

Shakespeare Reproduced: The Text in History & Ideology. Ed. by Jean E. Howard & Marion O'Connor. 288p. 1988. pap. text ed. 15.95 (*0-416-00932-8*) Routledge Chapman & Hall.

Shakespeare Reread: The Texts in New Contexts. Ed. by Russ McDonald. (Illus.). 296p. 1994. 42.50 (*0-8014-2917-X*); pap. 15.95 (*0-8014-8144-9*) Cornell U Pr.

Shakespeare Reshaped, 1606-1623. Gary Taylor & John Jowett. LC 93-16328. (Oxford Shakespeare Studies). 352p. 1993. 60.00 (*0-19-812256-X*, Old Oregon Bk Store) OUP.

Shakespeare Restored. Lewis Theobald. 194p. 1971. reprint ed. 30.00 (*0-7146-2523-X*, Pub. by F Cass Pubs UK) Intl Spec Bk.

Shakespeare Returns. Robert R. Leichtman. (From Heaven to Earth Ser.). (Illus.). 70p. (Orig.). 1978. pap. 3.50 (*0-89804-051-5*) Ariel GA.

Shakespeare Revealed Through Oxford's Letters. William P. Fowler. (Illus.). 900p. 1986. 35.00 (*0-914339-12-5*) P E Randall Pub.

Shakespeare Revue. Chris Luscombe & Malcolm McKee. 128p. 1994. pap. 14.95 (*1-85459-252-1*, Pub. by N Hern Bks UK) Theatre Comm.

Shakespeare Set Free: Teaching Romeo & Juliet, Macbeth, & A Midsummer Night's Dream. Peggy O'Brien. 304p. (Orig.). 1993. pap. 18.00 (*0-671-76046-7*, WSP) PB.

Shakespeare Set Free III: Teaching Twelfth Night & Othello. Folger Library Staff. 1995. pap. 18.00 (*0-671-76047-5*, WSP) PB.

Shakespeare, Seventeen Hundred to Seventeen Forty: 1700-1740, A Collection of the Editions & Separate Plays with Some Account of T. Johnson & R. Walker. Herbert L. Ford. LC 68-56498. 1972. reprint ed. 24.95 (*0-405-08526-5*, Pub. by Blom Pubns UK) Ayer.

Shakespeare, Sex & the Print Revolution. Gordon Williams. LC 95-31871. 220p. (C). 1996. pap. 25.00 (*0-485-12121-2*, Pub. by Athlone Pr UK); text ed. 90.00 (*0-485-11495-X*, Pub. by Athlone Pr UK) Humanities.

Shakespeare, Shylock & Kabbalah. Daniel Banes. LC 78-58912. 1978. 9.99 (*0-686-10284-3*); pap. 3.60 (*0-686-10285-1*) Malcolm Hse.

Shakespeare Society of New York Publications, 33 vols., Nos. 1-12, 14. reprint ed. lib. bdg. write for info. (*0-404-19553-9*) AMS Pr.

Shakespeare, Sophocles: Dramatic Themes & Modes. Martha H. Shackford. 1960. pap. 8.95 (*0-8084-0045-2*) NCUP.

Shakespeare Sounded Soundly. Delbert Spain. 227p. (Orig.). 1989. 20.00 (*0-88496-273-3*); pap. 13.00 (*0-88496-274-1*) Players Pr.

***Shakespeare, Spenser, & the Crisis in Ireland.** Christopher Highley. (Studies in Renaissance Literature & Culture: Vol. 23). (Illus.). 250p. (C). 1997. text ed. 54.95 (*0-521-58199-0*) Cambridge U Pr.

***Shakespeare Stealer.** Gary L. Blackwood. 1998. pap. 15.99 (*0-525-45863-8*) NAL-Dutton.

***Shakespeare Stories.** Garfield. 1997. pap. write for info. (*0-395-86140-3*) HM.

Shakespeare Stories. Leon Garfield. LC 85-1971. (Illus.). 288p. (J). (gr. 5 up). 1991. 26.00 (*0-395-56397-6*) HM.

Shakespeare Stories II. Leon Garfield. LC 94-10515. (Illus.). 288p. (YA). (gr. 5 up). 1995. 24.95 (*0-395-70893-1*) HM.

Shakespeare Studies, Vol. 21. Ed. by J. Leeds Barroll. 320p. 1993. 52.50 (*0-8386-3520-2*) Fairleigh Dickinson.

Shakespeare Studies, Vol. XXII. Ed. by J. Leeds Barroll. (Illus.). 400p. 1994. 52.50 (*0-8386-3580-6*) Fairleigh Dickinson.

Shakespeare Studies, Vol. XXIII. Ed. by J. Leeds Barroll. (Illus.). 296p. 1995. 52.50 (*0-8386-3640-3*) Fairleigh Dickinson.

***Shakespeare Studies, Vol. XXIV.** Ed. by Susan Zimmerman. 360p. 1996. 55.00 (*0-8386-3700-0*) Fairleigh Dickinson.

Shakespeare Studies: Biographical & Literary. Edgar I. Fripp. LC 72-168062. reprint ed. 38.00 (*0-404-07882-6*) AMS Pr.

Shakespeare Studies & an Essay on English Dictionaries. Thomas S. Baynes. reprint ed. 49.50 (*0-404-00697-3*) AMS Pr.

Shakespeare Study Today: The Horace Howard Furness Memorial Lectures. Ed. by Georgiana Ziegler. LC 84-45436. (Studies in the Renaissance: No. 13). 1986. 34.50 (*0-404-62283-6*) AMS Pr.

Shakespeare Survey, 40 vols., Set. Kenneth Muir. 1986. 1,600.00 (*0-317-52152-7*, Pub. by S Chand II) St Mut.

Shakespeare Survey: An Annual Survey of Shakespearian Study & Production, Vol. II. Ed. by Allardyce Nicoll. LC 49-1639. 139p. reprint ed. pap. 39.70 (*0-317-30413-5*, 2024944) Bks Demand.

***Shakespeare Survey Vol. 29: Shakespeare's Last Plays.** 199p. 1976. text ed. 69.95 (*0-521-21227-8*) Cambridge U Pr.

***Shakespeare Survey Vol. 31: Shakespeare & the Classical World.** 248p. 1979. text ed. 69.95 (*0-521-22011-4*) Cambridge U Pr.

***Shakespeare Survey Vol. 33: King Lear.** 227p. 1981. text ed. 69.95 (*0-521-23249-X*) Cambridge U Pr.

***Shakespeare Survey Vol. 41: Shakespearian Stages & Staging (with an Index to Surveys 31-40)** 312p. 1989. text ed. 69.95 (*0-521-36071-4*) Cambridge U Pr.

Shakespeare Survey Vol. 47: Playing Places for Shakespeare, Vol. 47. Ed. by Stanley Wells. (Illus.). 296p. (C). 1995. text ed. 69.95 (*0-521-47084-6*) Cambridge U Pr.

Shakespeare Survey Vol. 48: Shakespeare & Cultural Exchange. Ed. by Stanley Wells. (Illus.). 310p. (C). 1996. text ed. 69.95 (*0-521-55030-0*) Cambridge U Pr.

***Shakespeare Survey Vol. 49: "Romeo & Juliet" & Its Afterlife.** Ed. by Stanley Wells. (Illus.). 360p. (C). 1996. text ed. 64.95 (*0-521-57047-6*) Cambridge U Pr.

Shakespeare the Actor & the Purposes of Playing. Meredith A. Skura. LC 93-17317. 342p. 1993. pap. text ed. 17.95 (*0-226-76180-0*) U Ch Pr.

Shakespeare the Boy. William J. Rolfe. 251p. 1982. reprint ed. 23.95 (*0-87928-111-1*) Corner Hse.

Shakespeare the Boy. William J. Rolfe. LC 78-128411. (Studies in Shakespeare: No. 24). 1970. reprint ed. lib. bdg. 49.95 (*0-8383-1103-2*) M S G Haskell Hse.

***Shakespeare the Four Folios.** 3882p. (C). 1997. text ed. 95.00 (*0-415-15878-8*) Routledge.

Shakespeare the Historian. Paola Pugliatti. LC 95-31651. 224p. 1996. text ed. 39.95 (*0-312-12840-1*) St Martin.

***Shakespeare, the King's Playwright: Theater in the Stuart Court, 1603-1613.** Alvin Kernan. 1997. pap. text ed. 15.00 (*0-300-07258-9*) Yale U Pr.

Shakespeare, the King's Playwright in the Stuart Court, 1603-1613. Alvin B. Kernan. LC 94-43845. 1995. 27.50 (*0-300-06181-1*) Yale U Pr.

***Shakespeare the Magus.** Arthur Versluis. (Studies in Literature & Religion). 150p. (Orig.). 1997. pap. 18.00 (*0-9650488-3-7*) Grail Pubng.

Shakespeare, the Man. Edmund A. Lamborn. LC 76-30695. (Studies in Shakespeare: No. 24). 1977. lib. bdg. 75.00 (*0-8383-2173-9*) M S G Haskell Hse.

Shakespeare the Man. Godwin Smith. LC 76-30768. (Studies in Shakespeare: No. 24). (C). 1977. lib. bdg. 75.00 (*0-8383-2149-6*) M S G Haskell Hse.

Shakespeare the Man. rev. ed. Alfred L. Rowse. (Illus.). 272p. 1989. reprint ed. pap. 15.95 (*0-312-03425-3*) St Martin.

Shakespeare, the Man. Walter Bagehot. LC 71-126678. reprint ed. 31.50 (*0-404-00446-6*) AMS Pr.

***Shakespeare, the Movie: Popularizing the Plays on Film, TV, & Video.** Richard Burt & Lynda E. Boose. LC 97-312. 272p. 1997. pap. write for info. (*0-415-16585-7*) Routledge.

***Shakespeare, the Movie: Popularizing the Plays on Film, TV, & Video.** Richard Burt & Lynda E. Boose. LC 97-312. 272p. (C). 1997. text ed. write for info. (*0-415-16584-9*) Routledge.

Shakespeare the Playwright: A Companion to the Complete Tragedies, Histories, Comedies & Romances. Victor L. Cahn. LC 90-34319. 888p. 1991. text ed. 75.00 (*0-313-27493-2*, CSO, Greenwood Pr) Greenwood.

Shakespeare the Playwright: A Companion to the Complete Tragedies, Histories, Comedies, & Romances. Victor L. Cahn. LC 95-42501. 888p. 1996. pap. text ed. 29.95 (*0-275-95522-2*, Praeger Pubs) Greenwood.

***Shakespeare the Tempest.** Ed. by Blatchford & Head. (Longman Literature Ser.). 1994. pap. text ed. write for info. (*0-582-22583-3*, Pub. by Longman UK) Longman.

Shakespeare the Theatre-Poet. Robert Hapgood. (Illus.). 280p. 1991. reprint ed. pap. 24.95 (*0-19-811270-X*, 5858) OUP.

Shakespeare Thesaurus. Marvin Spevack. xxvi, 541p. 1993. pap. text ed. 24.95 (*3-487-09776-1*); lib. bdg. 65.00 (*3-487-09775-3*) G Olms Pubs.

Shakespeare Through Eastern Eyes. R. Shahani. 1972. 59.95 (*0-8490-1037-3*) Gordon Pr.

***Shakespeare to Dryden, Vol. 11.** John W. Cunliffe. Date not set. write for info. (*0-8369-4802-5*) Ayer.

Shakespeare to Shaw. Cecil F. Armstrong. LC 70-95402. (BCL Ser.: No. 1). reprint ed. 20.00 (*0-404-00383-4*) AMS Pr.

Shakespeare to Shaw: Studies in the Life's Work of Six Dramatists of the English Stage. Cecil F. Armstrong. LC 68-8435. (Essay Index Reprint Ser.). 1977. 23.95 (*0-8369-0157-6*) Ayer.

Shakespeare to Shaw: Studies in the Life's Work of Six Dramatists of the English Stage. Cecil F. Armstrong. (BCL1-PR English Literature Ser.). 330p. 1992. reprint ed. lib. bdg. 89.00 (*0-7812-7076-6*) Rprt Serv.

Shakespeare to U2: How to Know You're in Love. Tim Murhlhoff. (Life Skills Ser.). (Illus.). 6p. (C). 1995. teacher ed., ring bd. 1.25 (*1-885702-61-2*); student ed., ring bd. 3.25 (*1-885702-60-4*, 742-008s) WSN Pr.

Shakespeare Transcripts. Mark P. Friedlander, Jr. & Robert W. Kenny. LC 93-19407. 1993. 24.95 (*0-918024-94-3*) Ox Bow.

Shakespeare Translation: Annual Publication, 13 vols. Ed. by Toshikazu Oyama et al. 1980. write for info. (*0-404-19572-5*) AMS Pr.

Shakespeare Truth & Tradition. John S. Smart. (BCL1-PR English Literature Ser.). 224p. 1992. reprint ed. lib. bdg. 79.00 (*0-7812-7294-7*) Rprt Serv.

Shakespeare Two Thousand: Two Thousand Questions & Answers on All of Shakespeare's Plays. Fannie Gross. LC 92-44022. 224p. (Orig.). 1993. pap. 17.00 (*0-88734-626-X*) Players Pr.

Shakespeare Unbound. Claudia Haas. (Illus.). 24p. (Orig.). 1996. pap. 3.25 (*0-88680-427-2*) I E Clark.

Shakespeare Verbatim: The Reproduction of Authenticity & the 1790 Apparatus. Margreta De Grazia. (Illus.). 264p. 1991. 80.00 (*0-19-811778-7*, 2094) OUP.

Shakespeare Versus Shallow. Leslie Hotson. LC 74-109652. (Select Bibliographies Reprint Ser.). 1977. 26.95 (*0-8369-5261-8*) Ayer.

Shakespeare Versus Shallow. Leslie Hotson. LC 74-95430. (Studies in Shakespeare: No. 24). 1970. reprint ed. lib. bdg. 75.00 (*0-8383-0981-X*) M S G Haskell Hse.

Shakespeare Without Words & Other Essays. Alfred Harbarge. LC 77-188353. 239p. 1972. 20.00 (*0-674-80395-7*) HUP.

Shakespeare Workbook, 2 vols. Bertram Joseph. 1980. pap. write for info. (*0-318-55925-0*, Thtre Arts Bks) Routledge.

Shakespeare Workbook, 2 vols., Vol. 1. Bertram Joseph. 1980. pap. 14.95 (*0-87830-566-1*, Thtre Arts Bks) Routledge.

Shakespeare Workbook, 2 vols., Vol. 2. Bertram Joseph. 1980. pap. 14.95 (*0-87830-571-8*, Thtre Arts Bks) Routledge.

Shakespeare Yesterday - Today, Vol. 1: Romeo & Juliet - Merchant of Venice. Peter A. Belpulsi & Nathalie B. Belpulsi. 240p. (Orig.). (C). 1989. 20.50 (*0-9623663-0-7*); pap. write for info. (*0-9623663-1-5*) Globe Pubs.

Shakespeare Yesterday - Today, Vol. 3: Macbeth & Midsummer Night's Dream. Peter A. Belpulsi & Nathalie B. Belpulsi. 1990. 19.95 (*0-9623663-4-X*) Globe Pubs.

Shakespeare Yesterday - Today, Vol. 4: Hamlet & As You Like It. Peter A. Belpulsi & Nathalie B. Belpulsi. 1990. 23.95 (*0-9623663-6-6*) Globe Pubs.

Shakespeare Yesterday-Today: Student Classic - Julius Caesar. Peter A. Belpulsi & Nathalie B. Belpulsi. 1990. 23.95 (*0-9623663-3-1*) Globe Pubs.

Shakespeare Yesterday-Today: Student Classics - Hamlet. Peter A. Belpulsi & Nathalie B. Belpulsi. 1990. write for info. (*0-9623663-8-2*) Globe Pubs.

Shakespeare Yesterday-Today: Student Classics - Macbeth. Peter A. Belpulsi & Nathalie B. Belpulsi. 1990. write for info. (*0-9623663-5-8*) Globe Pubs.

Shakespeare Yesterday-Today: Student Classics - Romeo & Juliet. Peter A. Belpulsi & Nathalie B. Belpulsi. 1990. write for info. (*0-9623663-7-4*) Globe Pubs.

Shakespeare Yesterday-Today, Vol. 2: Julius Caesar - Antony & Cleopatra. Peter A. Belpulsi & Nathalie B. Belpulsi. 1990. 23.95 (*0-9623663-2-3*) Globe Pubs.

Shakespeare Yesterday...Today, Set. 1989. lib. bdg. write for info. (*1-882614-00-3*) Globe Pubs.

***Shakespeare Yesterday...Today: King Henry the Sixth, Vol. XII, Pts. 1-3.** Nathalie B. Belpulsi & Peter A. Belpulsi. 450p. 1997. lib. bdg. write for info. (*1-882614-07-0*) Globe Pubs.

Shakespeare Yesterday...Today: King Henry VI, Parts 1, 2 & 3, Vol. XII. Nathalie B. Belpulsi & Peter A. Belpulsi. 300p. 1996. text ed. write for info. (*0-614-15865-6*) Globe Pubs.

Shakespeare Yesterday...Today Vol. X, Pt. 1 & 2: Henry IV, Pts. 1-2. 1995. lib. bdg. 23.95 (*1-882614-05-4*) Globe Pubs.

Shakespeare Yesterday...Today Vol. IX: The Tragedy of King Richard II & Twelfth Night. Contrib. by Nathalie B. Belpulsi & Peter A. Belpulsi. LC 94-76313. 223p. 1994. lib. bdg. 21.50 (*1-882614-04-6*) Globe Pubs.

Shakespeare Yesterday...Today Vol. V: Othello, The Moor of Venice & Taming of the Shrew. Nathalie B. Belpulsi & Peter A. Belpulsi. LC 92-83830. 300p. 1992. lib. bdg. 24.95 (*1-882614-01-1*) Globe Pubs.

Shakespeare Yesterday...Today Vol. VI: The Sonnets & Overview. Nathalie B. Belpulsi & Peter A. Belpulsi. LC 92-74881. 155p. 1992. lib. bdg. 19.95 (*0-9623663-9-0*) Globe Pubs.

Shakespeare Yesterday...Today Vol. XI: The Merry Wives of Windsor & the Life of King Henry the Fifth. Contrib. by Nathalie B. Belpulsi & Peter A. Belpulsi. LC 95-80696. 264p. 1995. lib. bdg. 24.95 (*1-882614-06-2*) Globe Pubs.

Shakespeare Yesterday...Today, Vol. VII: King Lear & The Tempest. Nathalie B. Belpulsi & Peter A. Belpulsi. LC 93-80279. 260p. 1993. lib. bdg. 23.95 (*1-882614-02-X*) Globe Pubs.

Shakespeare Yesterday...Today, Vol. VIII: King John & The Comedy of Errors. Nathalie B. Belpulsi & Peter A. Belpulsi. LC 94-76314. 185p. 1994. lib. bdg. 19.95 (*1-882614-03-8*) Globe Pubs.

Shakespearean Actor Prepares. Adrian Brine & Michael York. 320p. 1996. pap. 16.95 (*1-880399-78-4*) Smith & Kraus.

Shakespearean Actor Prepares. Adrian Brine & Michael York. (Career Development Ser.). 320p. 1996. 35.00 (*1-57525-059-4*) Smith & Kraus.

Shakespearean Adaptations. Montague Summers. Incl. Tempest. LC 68-1979. 1969. lib. bdg. (*0-318-53228-X*); LC 68-1979. (Studies in Shakespeare: No. 24). (Illus.). 388p. (C). 1969. reprint ed. lib. bdg. 75.00 (*0-8383-0682-9*) M S G Haskell Hse.

Shakespearean Anomaly: Shakespeare's Hand in Sir John Oldcastle. Mark Dominik. LC 90-42562. 210p. (C). 1991. 22.50 (*0-945088-02-7*) Alioth Pr.

Shakespearean Comedy. Chintamani N. Desai. LC 79-144595. reprint ed. 37.50 (*0-404-02099-2*) AMS Pr.

Shakespearean Concepts. Simon Trussler. 185p. (C). 1989. 29.95 (*0-413-15940-X*, A0376, Pub. by Methuen UK) Heinemann.

Shakespearean Concepts. Simon Trussler. (Methuen Drama Ser.). 185p. (C). 1990. pap. 16.95 (*0-413-61980-X*, A0440, Pub. by Methuen UK) Heinemann.

***Shakespearean Continuities: Essays in Honor of E. A. J. Honigman.** E. A. Honigmann et al. LC 97-5892. 1997. write for info. (*0-312-17504-3*) St Martin.

Shakespearean Criticism, Vol. 1. Ed. by Laurie L. Harris & Mark W. Scott. LC 84-4010. (Literary Criticism Ser.). (Illus.). 680p. 1984. 140.00 (*0-8103-6125-6*) Gale.

Shakespearean Criticism, Vol. 2. Ed. by Mark W. Scott & Laurie L. Harris. 616p. 1985. 140.00 (*0-8103-6126-4*) Gale.

Shakespearean Criticism, Vol. 3. Ed. by Laurie L. Harris & Mark W. Scott. 600p. 1986. 140.00 (*0-8103-6127-2*) Gale.

Shakespearean Criticism, Vol. 4. Ed. by Mark W. Scott. 600p. 1986. 140.00 (*0-8103-6128-0*) Gale.

Shakespearean Criticism, Vol. 5. Ed. by Mark W. Scott. 635p. 1987. 140.00 (*0-8103-6129-9*) Gale.

Shakespearean Criticism, Vol. 6. Ed. by Mark W. Scott. 600p. 1987. 140.00 (*0-8103-6130-2*) Gale.

Shakespearean Criticism, Vol. 8. Ed. by Mark W. Scott. 600p. 1988. 140.00 (*0-8103-6132-9*) Gale.

Shakespearean Criticism, Vol. 9. Ed. by Mark W. Scott. 1989. 140.00 (*0-8103-6133-7*) Gale.

Shakespearean Criticism, Vol. 10. Ed. by James E. Person, Jr. & Sandra L. Williamson. 1989. 140.00 (*0-8103-6134-5*) Gale.

Shakespearean Criticism, Vol. 12. Ed. by Sandra L. Williamson & James E. Person, Jr. 570p. 1990. 140.00 (*0-8103-6136-1*) Gale.

Shakespearean Criticism, Vol. 13. 1990. 140.00 (*0-8103-6137-X*, 001335-M99406) Gale.

Shakespearean Criticism, Vol. 14. Sandra L. Williamson. 1991. 140.00 (*0-8103-6138-8*) Gale.

Shakespearean Criticism, Vol. 15. Sandra L. Williamson. 1991. 140.00 (*0-8103-6139-6*) Gale.

Shakespearean Criticism, Vol. 16. Sandra L. Williamson. 1991. 140.00 (*0-8103-6140-X*) Gale.

Shakespearean Criticism, Vol. 17. Sandra L. Williamson. 1992. 140.00 (*0-8103-7966-X*) Gale.

Shakespearean Criticism, Vol. 18. Sandra L. Williamson. 1992. 140.00 (*0-8103-7967-8*) Gale.

Shakespearean Criticism, Vol. 19. Sandra L. Williamson. 1992. 140.00 (*0-8103-7968-6*) Gale.

Shakespearean Criticism, Vol. 20. Sandra L. Williamson. 1993. 140.00 (*0-8103-7969-4*) Gale.

Shakespearean Criticism, Vol. 21. Sandra L. Williamson. 1993. 140.00 (*0-8103-7970-8*) Gale.

Shakespearean Criticism, Vol. 22. Sandra L. Williamson. 1993. 140.00 (*0-8103-7971-6*) Gale.

Shakespearean Criticism, Vol. 23. Sandra L. Williamson. 1994. 140.00 (*0-8103-8466-3*) Gale.

Shakespearean Criticism, Vol. 24. Sandra L. Williamson. 1994. 140.00 (*0-8103-8467-1*) Gale.

Shakespearean Criticism, Vol. 27. Ed. by Michael Magoulias. 500p. 1995. 140.00 (*0-8103-8947-9*, 001349) Gale.

Shakespearean Criticism, Vol. 28. Michael Magoulias. 1995. 140.00 (*0-8103-8948-7*) Gale.

Shakespearean Criticism, Vol. 29. Michael Magoulias. 1995. 140.00 (*0-8103-9278-X*) Gale.

Shakespearean Criticism, Vol. 30. Michael Magoulias. 1996. 140.00 (*0-8103-9279-8*) Gale.

Shakespearean Criticism, Vol. 31. Michael Magoulias. 1996. 140.00 (*0-8103-9280-1*) Gale.

***Shakespearean Criticism, Vol. 33.** 1996. 140.00 (*0-8103-9979-2*, 00008652, Gale Res Intl) Gale.

***Shakespearean Criticism, Vol. 35.** 1997. 140.00 (*0-7876-1133-6*, 00156237, Gale Res Intl) Gale.

***Shakespearean Criticism, Vol. 36.** 1997. 140.00 (*0-7876-1134-4*, 00156238, Gale Res Intl) Gale.

***Shakespearean Criticism, Vol. 37.** 1997. 140.00 (*0-7876-1135-2*, 00156239, Gale Res Intl) Gale.

***Shakespearean Criticism, Vol. 38.** 1998. 140.00 (*0-7876-1251-0*, 00156428, Gale Res Intl) Gale.

***Shakespearean Criticism, Vol. 39.** 1998. 140.00 (*0-7876-1250-2*, 00156427, Gale Res Intl) Gale.

***Shakespearean Criticism, Vol. 40.** 1998. 140.00 (*0-7876-1985-X*, 00157502) Gale.

Shakespearean Criticism Vol. 25: Yearbook, Vol. 25. Sandra L. Williamson. 1994. 140.00 (*0-8103-8468-X*) Gale.

Shakespearean Criticism Vol. 26. Ed. by Michael Magoulias. 422p. 1995. 140.00 (*0-8103-8946-0*) Gale.

Shakespearean Criticism, Vol. 11: Excerpts from the Criticism of William Shakespeare's Plays & Poetry, from the First Published Appraisals to Current Evaluations, Vol. 11. Ed. by Sandra L. Williamson & James E. Person, Jr. (Illus.). 570p. 1990. 140.00 (*0-8103-6135-3*, 001333) Gale.

Shakespearean Criticism, Vol. 7, Vol. 7. Ed. by Mark W. Scott. 600p. 1988. 140.00 (*0-8103-6131-0*) Gale.

Shakespearean Design. Mark Rose. LC 72-88129. (Illus.). 201p. reprint ed. pap. 57.30 (*0-7837-4185-5*, 2059035) Bks Demand.

Shakespearean Enigma & an Elizabethan Mania. John F. Forbis. LC 75-136375. 1975. reprint ed. 24.50 (*0-404-02458-0*) AMS Pr.

Shakespearean Films - Shakespearean Directors. Peter S. Donaldson. (Media & Popular Culture Ser.: No. 6). (Illus.). 240p. (C). 1990. pap. 19.95 (*0-04-445230-6*) Routledge Chapman & Hall.

Shakespearean Films-Shakespearean Directors. Peter S. Donaldson. (Illus.). 240p. 1990. 44.95 (*0-685-33056-7*); pap. 14.95 (*0-685-33057-5*) Routledge Chapman & Hall.

Shakespearean Ideal: Shakespeare Production & the Modern Theatre in Britain. Lennart Nyberg. 144p. (Orig.). 1988. pap. 40.00 (*91-554-2275-6*, Pub. by Uppsala Univ Acta Univ Uppsaliensis SW) Coronet Bks.

***Shakespearean Marriage: Merry Wives & Heavy Husbands.** Hopkins. LC 97-23091. 1997. text ed. 55.00 (*0-312-17748-8*) St Martin.

Shakespearean Metadrama: The Argument of the Play in Titus Andronicus, Love's Labour's Lost, Romeo & Juliet, a Midsummer Night's Dream & Richard II. James L. Calderwood. LC 71-141839. 202p. 1971. reprint ed. pap. 57.60 (*0-7837-2973-1*, 2057481) Bks Demand.

Shakespearean Miscellany. Francis G. Waldron. LC 73-131497. (Illus.). 1973. reprint ed. 17.50 (*0-404-06805-7*) AMS Pr.

Shakespearean Mob. Frederick Tupper. (Studies in Shakespeare: No. 24). 1970. reprint ed. pap. 39.95 (*0-8383-0077-4*) M S G Haskell Hse.

Shakespearean Music in the Plays & Early Operas. Frederick Bridge. LC 68-358. (Studies in Shakespeare: No. 24). 1969. reprint ed. lib. bdg. 39.95 (*0-8383-0513-X*) M S G Haskell Hse.

Shakespearean Music in the Plays & Early Operas. John F. Bridge. LC 75-153307. reprint ed. 29.50 (*0-404-07808-7*) AMS Pr.

Shakespearean Mythmaking, Unit C. Deakin University Press Staff. 175p. (C). 1991. student ed., pap. 110.00 (*0-7300-0722-7*, HUL306, Pub. by Deakin Univ AT) St Mut.

Shakespearean Narrative. R. Rawdon Wilson. LC 94-22487. (Illus.). 320p. 1995. 46.50 (*0-87413-525-7*) U Delaware Pr.

Shakespearean Negotiations: The Circulation of Social Energy in Renaissance England. Stephen Greenblatt. (New Historicism: Studies in Cultural Poetics: No. 4). (C). 1988. pap. 14.95 (*0-520-06160-8*) U CA Pr.

Shakespearean Performance as Interpretation. Herbert R. Coursen, Jr. LC 90-50933. 280p. 1992. 42.50 (*0-87413-432-3*) U Delaware Pr.

Shakespearean Power & Punishment. LC 96-50028. 1997. write for info. (*0-8386-3679-9*) Fairleigh Dickinson.

Shakespearean Pragmatism: Market of His Time. Lars Engle. LC 93-140. 280p. 1993. 32.50 (*0-226-20942-3*) U Ch Pr.

***Shakespearean Prompt-Books of the 17th Century: King Lear, Henry VIII, The Merry Wives of Windsor, Twelfth Night, Comedy of Errors, & The Winter's Tale, Vol. 8.** Ed. by G. Blakemore Evans. 1997. 75.00 (*1-883631-03-3*) Biblgraph Soc.

Shakespearean Sentences: A Study in Style & Syntax. John P. Houston. LC 87-28584. 232p. 1988. text ed. 35.00 (*0-8071-1399-9*) La State U Pr.

Shakespearean Stage, 1574-1642. 3rd ed. Andrew Gurr. (Illus.). 280p. (C). 1992. text ed. 69.95 (*0-521-41005-3*); pap. text ed. 22.95 (*0-521-42240-X*) Cambridge U Pr.

Shakespearean Staging, 1599-1642. Thomas J. King. LC 77-127880. (Illus.). 185p. reprint ed. pap. 52.80 (*0-7837-4162-6*, 2059010) Bks Demand.

Shakespearean Subversions: Trixter & the Playtext. Richard Hillman. 296p. (C). 1992. text ed. 59.95 (*0-415-07020-1*, Routledge NY) Routledge.

Shakespearean Suspect Texts: The "Bad" Quartos & Their Contexts. Laurie E. Maguire. 355p. (C). 1996. text ed. 59.95 (*0-521-47364-0*) Cambridge U Pr.

Shakespearean Tarot. Dolores Ashcroft-Nowicki. 160p. 1993. pap. 34.00 (*1-85538-054-4*, Pub. by Aquarian Pr UK) Thorsons SF.

Shakespearean Tragedy. J. Leeds Barroll. LC 82-49309. 312p. 1984. 35.00 (*0-918016-18-5*) Folger Bks.

Shakespearean Tragedy. Ed. by Malcolm Bradbury & David Palmer. LC 84-81206. (Stratford-upon-Avon Studies: No. 20). 192p. 1984. pap. text ed. 15.00 (*0-8419-0982-2*) Holmes & Meier.

Shakespearean Tragedy. Ed. by Malcolm Bradbury & David Palmer. LC 84-81206. (Stratford-upon-Avon Studies: No. 20). 192p. 1986. 39.50 (*0-8419-0981-4*) Holmes & Meier.

Shakespearean Tragedy. D. F. Bratchell. LC 89-10506. 176p. (C). 1990. pap. 16.95 (*0-415-03403-5*, A4943) Routledge.

Shakespearean Tragedy. John Drakakis. (Critical Readers Ser.). 448p. (C). 1991. pap. text ed. 31.95 (*0-582-05114-2*, 79009) Longman.

Shakespearean Tragedy: Genre, Tradition, & Change in Antony & Cleopatra. J. Leeds Barroll. 312p. 1984. 45.00 (*0-918016-68-1*) Folger Bks.

Shakespearean Tragedy: Lectures on Hamlet, Othello, King Lear & Macbeth. A. C. Bradley. (New Shakespeare Library). 480p. 1991. pap. 12.95 (*0-14-053019-3*, Penguin Bks) Viking Penguin.

Shakespearean Tragedy: Lectures on Hamlet, Othello, King Lear, Macbeth. 3rd ed. A. C. Bradley. LC 91-43210. 516p. 1992. text ed. 45.00 (*0-312-07923-0*); text ed. 12.95 (*0-312-07922-2*) St Martin.

Shakespearean Tragedy: Lectures on Hamlet, Othello, King Lear, Macbeth. Andrew C. Bradley. (BCL1-PR English Literature Ser.). 498p. 1992. reprint ed. lib. bdg. 99.00 (*0-7812-7298-X*) Rprt Serv.

Shakespearean Tragedy & Gender. Ed. by Shirley N. Garner & Madelon Sprengnether. LC 95-21677. 1996. 39.95 (*0-253-32964-7*); pap. 17.50 (*0-253-21027-5*) Ind U Pr.

Shakespearean Tragedy & Its Double: The Rhythms of Audience Response. Kent Cartwright. 240p. 1991. 32.50 (*0-271-00738-9*) Pa St U Pr.

Shakespearean Tragedy & the Elizabethan Compromise. Paul N. Siegel. LC 78-39208. (Select Bibliographies Reprint Ser.). 1977. reprint ed. 21.95 (*0-8369-6810-7*) Ayer.

***Shakespearean Whodunnits.** Ed. by Mike Ashley. 416p. 1997. pap. 10.95 (*0-7867-0482-9*) Carroll & Graf.

Shakespearean Wild: Geography, Genus & Gender. Jeanne A. Roberts. LC 90-13037. (Illus.). x, 214p. 1991. text ed. 35.00 (*0-8032-3899-1*) U of Nebr Pr.

Shakespearean Wild: Geography, Genus, & Gender. Jeanne A. Roberts. LC 90-13037. (Illus.). x, 214p. 1991. reprint ed. pap. 12.00 (*0-8032-8950-2*, Bison Books) U of Nebr Pr.

Shakespeareana Genealogica. George R. French. LC 74-168139. reprint ed. 91.50 (*0-404-02575-7*) AMS Pr.

Shakespeareana Genealogica: Identification of the Dramatis Personae in Shakespeare's Historical Plays, Pt. I; Shakespeare & Arden Families & Their Connection, Pt. II, Pts. I & II. G. R. French. 546p. 1990. reprint ed. lib. bdg. 51.00 (*0-8328-1690-6*) Higginson Bk Co.

Shakespeare's Agonistic Comedy: Poetics, Analysis, Criticism. G. Beiner. LC 91-58238. 1993. 44.50 (*0-8386-3467-2*) Fairleigh Dickinson.

Shakespeare's Almanac: "A Midsummer Night's Dream", Marriage & The Elizabethan Calendar. David Wiles. (Illus.). 217p. (C). 1993. 63.00 (*0-85991-398-8*) Boydell & Brewer.

Shakespeare's Alternative Tales. Leah Scragg. LC 95-44853. (Medieval & Renaissance Library). 168p. (C). 1996. text ed. 49.95 (*0-582-24485-4*, Pub. by Longman UK); pap. text ed. 16.95 (*0-582-24484-6*, Pub. by Longman UK) Longman.

Shakespeare's Analogical Scene: Parody As Structural Syntax. Joan Hartwig. LC 83-6845. 256p. 1983. reprint ed. pap. 73.00 (*0-7837-8883-5*, 2049594) Bks Demand.

Shakespeare's Anonymous Editors: Scribe & Compositor in the Folio Text of "2 Henry IV" Eleanor Prosser. LC 79-66179. (Illus.). xiv, 219p. 1981. 35.00 (*0-8047-1033-3*) Stanford U Pr.

Shakespeare's Art from a Comparative Perspective. Ed. by Wendell M. Aycock. LC 80-54322. (Proceedings of the Comparative Literature Symposium Ser.: Vol.12). (Illus.). 197p. (Orig.). 1981. pap. 12.00 (*0-89672-081-0*) Tex Tech Univ Pr.

Shakespeare's Art of Orchestration: Stage Technique & Audience Response. Jean E. Howard. LC 84-56. 224p. 1984. text ed. 24.95 (*0-252-01116-3*) U of Ill Pr.

Shakespeare's Autobiographical Poems. Charles A. Brown. 1972. 59.95 (*0-8490-1038-1*) Gordon Pr.

Shakespeare's Autobiographical Poems. Charles A. Brown. LC 76-39541. reprint ed. 47.50 (*0-404-01127-6*) AMS Pr.

Shakespeare's Bad Quartos: Deliberate Abridgements Designed for Performance by Reduced Cast. Robert E. Burkhart. (Studies in English Literature: No. 101). (Illus.). 124p. 1975. pap. text ed. 32.35 (*90-279-3276-X*) Mouton.

Shakespeare's Bawdy. 3rd ed. Eric Partridge. 240p. (gr. 13). 1990. pap. 16.95 (*0-415-05076-6*, A4700) Routledge.

Shakespeare's Biblical Knowledge. Richmond Noble. 1972. 59.95 (*0-8490-1039-X*) Gordon Pr.

Shakespeare's Birth Place. Ed. by Levi Fox. (Shakespeare Travel Ser.). (Illus.). 20p. (Orig.). 1994. pap. 2.50 (*0-7117-0376-0*) Seven Hills Bk.

Shakespeare's Bones. Clement M. Ingleby. 1972. 59.95 (*0-8490-1040-3*) Gordon Pr.

Shakespeare's Book of Insults, Insights & Infinite Jests. William Shakespeare. Ed. by John Seder. 244p. 1984. pap. 12.95 (*0-87243-128-2*) Templegate.

Shakespeare's Books. Henry R. Anders. LC 76-158251. reprint ed. 34.50 (*0-404-00355-9*) AMS Pr.

Shakespeare's Britain. Derek Brewer & Ernest Frank. (C). 1987. text ed. 80.00 (*0-907115-47-0*, Pub. by Pevensey UK) St Mut.

Shakespeare's Caliban: A Cultural History. Alden T. Vaughan & Virginia M. Vaughan. (Illus.). 300p. (C). 1991. text ed. 59.95 (*0-521-40305-7*) Cambridge U Pr.

Shakespeare's Caliban: A Cultural History. Alden T. Vaughan & Virginia M. Vaughan. (Illus.). 320p. (C). 1993. pap. text ed. 17.95 (*0-521-45817-X*) Cambridge U Pr.

Shakespeare's Cardenio. Charles Hamilton et al. (Illus.). 310p. (C). 1994. pap. 15.00 (*1-56924-886-9*) Marlowe & Co.

Shakespeare's Centurie of Prayse: 1591-1693 see Shakespeare Allusion Books: Fifteen Ninety-Two to Fifteen Ninety-Eight

***Shakespeare's Champion.** Charlaine Harris. LC 97-23063. (A Lily Bard Mystery Ser.). 1997. 20.95 (*0-312-17005-X*) St Martin.

Shakespeare's Characters: A Historical Dictionary. W. H. Thomson. 320p. (C). 1966. text ed. 75.00 (*0-8383-0635-7*) M S G Haskell Hse.

Shakespeare's Characters: A Players Press Guide. Kenneth McLeish. 264p. 1992. 40.00 (*0-88734-608-1*) Players Pr.

***Shakespeare's Characters for Students.** LC 97-8515. 500p. 1997. 65.00 (*0-7876-1300-2*, GML00197-110665) Gale.

Shakespeare's Christian Dimension: An Anthology of Commentary. Ed. by Roy Battenhouse. LC 93-31520. 1994. 35.00 (*0-253-31122-5*) Ind U Pr.

Shakespeare's Church. James H. Bloom. LC 73-116790. (Studies in Shakespeare: No. 24). 1971. reprint ed. lib. bdg. 49.95 (*0-8383-1032-X*) M S G Haskell Hse.

Shakespeare's Clowns. Lane Riosley & Rebecca L. Byars. 28p. (Orig.). (J). 1994. pap. 3.00 (*1-57514-122-1*, 1078) Encore Perform Pub.

Shakespeare's Comedies. Ed. by Gary Waller. (Critical Readers Ser.). 224p. (C). 1992. pap. text ed. 31.95 (*0-582-05926-7*, 79010) Longman.

Shakespeare's Comedies. Ed. by Gary Waller. (C). 1991. text ed. 61.50 (*0-582-05927-5*, Pub. by Longman UK) Longman.

Shakespeare's Comedies: From Roman Farce to Romantic Mystery. Robert E. Ornstein. (Illus.). 272p. 1994. pap. 17.95 (*0-87413-541-9*) U Delaware Pr.

Shakespeare's Comedies: The Consummation. Henry B. Charlton. 1972. 59.95 (*0-8490-1041-1*) Gordon Pr.

An Asterisk (*) at the beginning of an entry indicates that the title is appearing in BIP for the first time.

Shakespeare's Comedies: The Consummation. Henry B. Charlton. LC 71-100738. (Studies in Shakespeare: No. 24). 1970. reprint ed. lib. bdg. 49.95 (*0-8383-0339-0*) M S G Haskell Hse.

Shakespeare's Comedies & Poems. H. H. Gowda. LC 86-81400. 160p. 1986. text ed. 15.95 (*0-938719-01-7*, Envoy Pr) Apt Bks.

Shakespeare's Comedies of Play. J. Dennis Huston. LC 80-21366. 179p. reprint ed. pap. 51.10 (*0-8357-6870-8*, 2035568) Bks Demand.

Shakespeare's Comic Commonwealths. Camille Slight. LC 93-93766. 290p. 1993. 45.00 (*0-8020-2924-8*) U of Toronto Pr.

Shakespeare's Comic Theory: A Study of Art & Artifice in the Last Plays. Thomas A. Nelson. (De Proprietatibus Litterarum, Ser. Practica: No. 57). 95p. (Orig.). 1972. text ed. 13.85 (*3-10-800281-3*) Mouton.

Shakespeare's Comic World. Richard Courtney. 224p. (Orig.). 1995. pap. 17.00 (*0-88924-263-1*, Pub. by Simon & Pierre Pub CN) Empire Pub Srvs.

Shakespeare's Complete Works. William Shakespeare. 1230p. 1991. 85.00 (*0-911156-50-X*) Bern Porter.

Shakespeare's Concept of Tragedy: The Bard As Anti-Elizabethan. Rocco Montano. LC 85-4536. 288p. 1986. pap. 12.00 (*0-89526-810-8*) Regnery Pub.

Shakespeare's Confession. Robert Para. LC 96-68187. 530p. 1996. pap. 19.95 (*1-889120-02-2*) StarsEnd Creations.

Shakespeares Coriolanus in deutscher Bearbeitung: Sieben Beispiele zum literaturaesthetischen Problem der Umsetzung und Vermittlung Shakespeares. Martin Brunkhorst. (Komparatistische Studien: Vol. 3). (C). 1973. 95.40 (*3-11-003997-4*) De Gruyter.

Shakespeare's Courtly Mirror: Reflexivity & Prudence in All's Well That Ends Well. David Haley. LC 91-58000. (Illus.). 320p. 1993. 42.50 (*0-87413-443-9*) U Delaware Pr.

Shakespeare's Craft, Eight Lectures. Ed. by Philip H. Highfill, Jr. LC 81-9386. 185p. 1982. 19.95 (*0-8093-1014-7*) S Ill U Pr.

Shakespeare's Darker Purpose: A Question of Incest. Mark Taylor. LC 81-69124. (Studies in the Renaissance: No. 7). 1982. 34.50 (*0-404-62277-1*) AMS Pr.

Shakespeare's Defense of Poetry: A Midsummer Night's Dream & the Tempest. Diana A. Rhoads. 264p. (Orig.). 1986. pap. text ed. 26.00 (*0-8191-4980-2*); lib. bdg. 58.50 (*0-8191-4979-9*) U Pr of Amer.

Shakespeare's Deliberate Art. William B. Bache & Vernon P. Loggins. LC 96-10396. 276p. 1996. pap. text ed. 36.50 (*0-7618-0301-7*) U Pr of Amer.

Shakespeare's Deliberate Art. William B. Bache & Vernon P. Loggins. LC 96-10396. 276p. 1996. lib. bdg. 57.50 (*0-7618-0300-9*) U Pr of Amer.

Shakespeare's Dilemmas. Richard Horwich. (American University Studies: English Language & Literature: Ser. IV, Vol. 61). 221p. 1988. 31.50 (*0-8204-0541-8*) P Lang Pubng.

Shakespeare's Division of Experience. Marilyn French. 416p. 1983. mass mkt. 5.99 (*0-345-30070-X*) Ballantine.

Shakespeare's Dog. Leon Rooke. 176p. 1986. reprint ed. pap. 8.50 (*0-88001-093-2*) Ecco Pr.

Shakespeare's Dramatic Language. Madeleine Doran. LC 75-32072. 264p. 1976. 32.50 (*0-299-07010-7*) U of Wis Pr.

***Shakespeare's Dramatic Speech.** Anthony J. Gilbert. LC 97-11104. (Studies in Renaissance Literature: No. 15). 300p. 1997. text ed. 89.95 (*0-7734-8652-1*) E Mellen.

Shakespeare's Dramatic Structures. Anthony Brennan. 224p. 1988. pap. text ed. 14.95 (*0-415-00269-9*) Routledge.

Shakespeare's Dramatic Transactions. Michael Mooney. LC 90-2770. 243p. (C). 1990. text ed. 36.95 (*0-8223-1039-2*) Duke.

Shakespeare's Early Comedies. Eustace M. Tillyard. 88p. (C). 1965. reprint ed. pap. 19.95 (*0-485-30015-X*, Pub. by Athlone Pr UK) Humanities.

Shakespeare's Early Comedies: Myth, Metamorphosis, Mannerism. Gunnar Sorelius. (Studia Anglistica Upsaliensia Ser.: No. 83). 218p. (Orig.). 1993. pap. 43.50 (*91-554-3133-X*, Pub. by Uppsala Universitet SW) Coronet Bks.

Shakespeare's Early Contemporaries. W. Schrickx. LC 76-144684. reprint ed. 32.50 (*0-404-05622-9*) AMS Pr.

Shakespeare's Early Tragedies: A Collection of Critical Essays. Ed. by Mark Rose. LC 94-11740. (New Century Views Ser.). 264p. 1994. 12.95 (*0-13-035544-5*) P-H.

Shakespeare's Edward III. Ed. by Eric Sams. 256p. 1997. 30.00 (*0-300-06626-0*) Yale U Pr.

Shakespeare's English: Language in the History Plays. W. F. Bolton. (Language Library). 256p. 1992. text ed. 54.95 (*0-631-16147-3*) Blackwell Pubs.

Shakespeare's English & Roman History Plays: A Marxist Approach. Paul N. Siegel. LC 84-46117. 168p. 1986. 33.50 (*0-8386-3251-3*) Fairleigh Dickinson.

***Shakespeare's English Comedy: The Merry Wives of Windsor in Context.** Jeanne A. Roberts. LC 78-24239. 189p. 1979. reprint ed. pap. 53.90 (*0-608-03477-0*, 2064187) Bks Demand.

Shakespeare's English Histories: A Quest for Form & Genre. Ed. by John W. Velz. LC 94-3351. (Medieval & Renaissance Texts & Studies: Vol. 133). 304p. 1996. 25.00 (*0-86698-140-3*, MR133) MRTS.

Shakespeare's English Kings: History, Chronicle & Drama. Peter Saccio. 276p. 1977. pap. 11.95 (*0-19-502156-8*) OUP.

Shakespeare's English Kings, the People & the Law: A Study in the Relationship Between the Tudor Constitution & the English History Plays. Edna Z. Boris. LC 76-19838. 261p. 1978. 35.00 (*0-8386-1990-8*) Fairleigh Dickinson.

Shakespeare's Euphuism. William L. Rushton. LC 77-174794. reprint ed. 29.50 (*0-404-05454-4*) AMS Pr.

Shakespeare's Europe. rev. ed. Fynes Moryson. LC 66-12287. (Illus.). 570p. 1972. 38.95 (*0-405-08799-3*, Pub. by Blom Pubns UK) Ayer.

Shakespeare's Fellows, Being a Brief Chronicle of the Shakespearian Age. George B. Harrison. LC 70-38844. (Studies in Shakespeare: No. 24). 206p. 1972. reprint ed. lib. bdg. 75.00 (*0-8383-1389-2*) M S G Haskell Hse.

Shakespeare's Festive Comedy. C. L. Barber. 266p. 1972. pap. text ed. 17.95 (*0-691-01304-7*, 271) Princeton U Pr.

Shakespeare's Festive Tragedy: The Ritual Foundations of Genre. Naomi C. Liebler. LC 95-9687. 280p. (C). 1995. pap. 17.95 (*0-415-13183-9*) Routledge.

Shakespeare's Festive Tragedy: The Ritual Foundations of Genre. Naomi C. Liebler. LC 95-9687. 280p. (C). (gr. 13). 1995. text ed. 69.95 (*0-415-08657-4*) Routledge.

Shakespeare's Festive World: Elizabethan Seasonal Entertainment & the Professional Stage. Francois Laroque. Tr. by Janet Lloyd. (European Studies in English Literature). (Illus.). 439p. (C). 1993. pap. text ed. 21.95 (*0-521-45786-6*) Cambridge U Pr.

Shakespeare's Fight with the Pirates & the Problems of the Transmission of His Text. Alfred W. Pollard. (BCL1-PR English Literature Ser.). 110p. 1992. reprint ed. lib. bdg. 69.00 (*0-7812-7310-2*) Rprt Serv.

Shakespeare's Fight with the Pirates & the Problems of the Transmission of the Text. Alfred W. Pollard. LC 73-20426. (Studies in Shakespeare: No. 24). 1974. lib. bdg. 75.00 (*0-8383-1754-5*) M S G Haskell Hse.

Shakespeare's Flowers. 72p. 1995. 9.95 (*0-8118-0836-X*) Chronicle Bks.

Shakespeare's Flowers. Ed. by Levi Fox. (Shakespeare Travel Ser.). (Illus.). 32p. (Orig.). 1994. pap. 3.50 (*0-7117-0130-X*) Seven Hills Bk.

Shakespeare's Flowers. James A. Warner & Margaret J. White. (Illus.). 96p. 1987. 35.00 (*0-912608-40-4*) Mid Atlantic.

***Shakespeare's Flowers.** Jessica Kerr. (Illus.). 96p. 1997. reprint ed. pap. 12.50 (*1-55566-202-1*) Johnson Bks.

Shakespeare's Four Giants. Blanche Coles. 1957. 10.95 (*0-87233-809-6*) Bauhan.

Shakespeare's Garter Plays: Edward Third to Merry Wives of Windsor. Giorgio Melchiori. LC 93-48123. (C). 1994. 29.50 (*0-87413-518-4*) U Delaware Pr.

***Shakespeare's Ghost Writers: Literature As Uncanny Causality.** Marjorie Garber. 240p. (C). 1997. pap. 16.95 (*0-415-91869-3*, Routledge NY) Routledge.

Shakespeare's Ghost Writers: Literature As Uncanny Causality. Marjorie Garber. 200p. 1988. 45.00 (*0-416-07342-5*, A0677); pap. text ed. 14.95 (*0-416-09122-9*, A1537) Routledge Chapman & Hall.

***Shakespeare's Globe Rebuilt.** Ed. by Ronnie Mulryne & Margaret Shewring. (Illus.). 192p. (C). 1997. text ed. 59.95 (*0-521-59019-1*); pap. text ed. 19.95 (*0-521-59988-1*) Cambridge U Pr.

Shakespeare's Greenwood: The Customs in the Country, the Language, the Superstitions. George Morley. LC 70-185021. (Studies in Shakespeare: No. 24). 289p. 1972. reprint ed. lib. bdg. 75.00 (*0-8383-1381-7*) M S G Haskell Hse.

Shakespeare's "Hamlet" Authur Clutton-Brock. LC 76-52923. (Studies in Shakespeare: No. 24). 1977. reprint ed. lib. bdg. 75.00 (*0-8383-2133-X*) M S G Haskell Hse.

Shakespeare's Hamlet. P. V. Rubow. LC 79-174974. (DAN.). reprint ed. 34.50 (*0-404-05448-X*) AMS Pr.

Shakespeare's "Hamlet" Edward Strachey. LC 70-176458. reprint ed. 29.50 (*0-404-06294-6*) AMS Pr.

Shakespeare's Hand in the Play of Sir Thomas More: Papers. Alfred W. Pollard. (BCL1-PR English Literature Ser.). 229p. 1992. reprint ed. lib. bdg. 79.00 (*0-7812-7277-7*) Rprt Serv.

Shakespeare's Haunts Near Stratford. Edgar I. Fripp. LC 71-153322. reprint ed. 32.50 (*0-404-02622-2*) AMS Pr.

Shakespeare's Heraldry. W. Scott-Giles. LC 74-137312. (Illus.). reprint ed. 41.50 (*0-404-05663-6*) AMS Pr.

Shakespeare's Heroical Histories: Henry VI & Its Literary Tradition. David Riggs. LC 75-152701. 206p. 1971. reprint ed. pap. 58.80 (*0-7837-4183-9*, 2059033) Bks Demand.

Shakespeare's Hidden World: A Study of His Unconscious. Johannes Fabricius. 280p. 1996. pap. 39.95 (*1-85302-282-9*, Pub. by J Kingsley Pubs UK) Taylor & Francis.

***Shakespeare's Histories: Mirrors of Elizabethan Policy.** Lily B. Campbell. LC 47-2108. (Huntington Library Publications). 356p. 1978. reprint ed. pap. 101.50 (*0-608-03172-0*, 2063625) Bks Demand.

Shakespeare's Histories at Stratford, 1951. John D. Wilson & Thomas C. Worsley. LC 73-128895. (Select Bibliographies Reprint Ser.). 1977. 18.95 (*0-8369-5515-3*) Ayer.

Shakespeare's History. Norwich. 26.00 (*0-684-81434-X*) S&S Trade.

Shakespeare's History Plays: Richard the Second to Henry the Fifth. Ed. by Graham Holderness. LC 92-9126. (New Casebooks Ser.). 1992. text ed. 39.95 (*0-312-08371-8*) St Martin.

Shakespeare's Holinshed. W. G. Boswell-Stone. LC 66-29420. 1972. reprint ed. 33.95 (*0-405-08291-6*, Pub. by Blom Pubns UK) Ayer.

Shakespeare's Home at New Place. John C. Bellew. LC 76-113553. reprint ed. 54.50 (*0-404-00736-8*) AMS Pr.

Shakespeare's Homeland. William S. Brassington. LC 75-39522. reprint ed. 42.50 (*0-404-01068-7*) AMS Pr.

Shakespeare's Hyperontology: Antony & Cleopatra. H. W. Fawkner. LC 89-45922. 200p. 1991. 38.50 (*0-8386-3383-8*) Fairleigh Dickinson.

Shakespeare's Ideals of Womanhood. George H. Gerwig. 229p. 1996. pap. 19.95 (*1-56459-531-5*) Kessinger Pub.

Shakespeare's Ideals of Womanhood. H. George Gerwig. 1972. 59.95 (*0-8490-1042-X*) Gordon Pr.

Shakespeare's Imagery. Caroline F. Spurgeon. 424p. (C). 1935. pap. text ed. 29.95 (*0-521-09258-2*) Cambridge U Pr.

Shakespeare's Imagery: Versuch einer Definition. Maria Rauschenberger. (Bochum Studies in English: No. 11). x, 731p. (Orig.) (GER.). 1981. pap. 50.00 (*90-6032-203-7*) Benjamins North Am.

***Shakespeare's Imagination: A Study of the Psychology of Association & Inspiration.** Edward A. Armstrong. LC 63-8165. 236p. 1982. reprint ed. pap. 67.30 (*0-608-02691-3*, 2063344) Bks Demand.

Shakespeare's Imagined Persons: The Psychology of Role-Playing & Acting. Peter B. Murray. 320p. (C). 1995. pap. text ed. 36.00 (*0-389-21016-1*) B&N Imports.

Shakespeare's Imagined Persons: The Psychology of Role-Playing & Acting. Peter B. Murray. 320p. (C). 1996. lib. bdg. 57.50 (*0-389-21015-3*) B&N Imports.

Shakespeare's Influence on Sir Walter Scott. Wilmon Brewer. reprint ed. 64.50 (*0-404-01075-X*) AMS Pr.

Shakespeare's Insistent Theme: Essays Literary & Various. Charles Harrison. Ed. by Don K. DuPree. LC 84-51974. 192p. 1985. pap. 10.00 (*0-918769-09-4*) Univ South Pr.

Shakespeare's Insults. Wayne Hill. 1995. pap. 12.00 (*0-517-88539-5*, Crown) Crown Pub Group.

Shakespeare's Insults: Educating Your Wit. Wayne F. Hill & Cynthia J. Ottchen. xii, 308p. (Orig.). 1993. pap. 11.95 (*0-9518684-0-3*) MainSail Pr.

Shakespeare's Insults for Doctors. Wayne F. Hill & Cynthia J. Ottchen. 80p. 1996. 12.50 (*0-517-70446-3*, C P Pubs) Crown Pub Group.

Shakespeare's Insults for Lawyers. Wayne F. Hill & Cynthia J. Ottchen. 80p. 1996. 12.50 (*0-517-70447-1*, C P Pubs) Crown Pub Group.

Shakespeare's Insults for Teachers. Wayne F. Hill. 1996. 12.50 (*0-517-70448-X*, Crown) Crown Pub Group.

Shakespeare's Insults for the Office. Wayne F. Hill. LC 96-29659. 80p. 1996. 12.50 (*0-517-70449-8*, Crown) Crown Pub Group.

***Shakespeare's Italy: Functions of Italian Locations in Renaissance Drama.** Michele Marrapodi. LC 97-16566. 1998. pap. write for info. (*0-7190-5220-3*, Pub. by Manchester Univ Pr UK) St Martin.

Shakespeare's "Jest Book", 2 vols. in 1. William Shakespeare. Ed. by Samuel Singer. LC 71-130234. reprint ed. 34.50 (*0-404-06094-3*) AMS Pr.

Shakespeare's Knowledge & Use of the Bible. 3rd ed. Charles Wordsworth. LC 73-144706. reprint ed. write for info. (*0-404-07039-6*) AMS Pr.

Shakespeare's Labored Art: Stir, Work, & the Late Plays, Vol. 3. Maurice Hunt. (Studies in Shakespeare). 328p. (C). 1995. text ed. 58.95 (*0-8204-2737-3*) P Lang Pubng.

Shakespeare's Ladies. Ed. by Dick Dotterer. LC 92-28173. 64p. (Orig.). 1992. pap. 7.95 (*0-940669-19-6*, D-27) Dramaline Pubns.

Shakespeare's Landlord. Charlaine Harris. 224p. 1996. 20.95 (*0-312-14415-6*) St Martin.

***Shakespeare's Landlord: A Lily Bard Mystery.** Charlaine Harris. 1997. mass mkt. 5.50 (*0-440-22418-7*) Dell.

Shakespeare's Language: A Glossary of Unfamiliar Words in Shakespeare's Plays & Poems. Eugene F. Shewmaker. LC 95-12778. 576p. 1996. 50.00 (*0-8160-3276-9*) Facts on File.

Shakespeare's Language: An Introduction. N. F. Blake. LC 82-22005. 154p. 1984. pap. 11.95 (*0-312-71430-0*) St Martin.

Shakespeare's Language: Dictionaries, Rhetoric, Essays & Critical Theory: A Guide to the Microfiche Collection. (Shakespeariana Ser.). 55p. (Orig.). 1991. pap. 20.00 (*0-8357-2149-3*) Univ Microfilms.

Shakespeare's Last Plays. Basavaraj S. Naikar. 1993. text ed. 30.00 (*81-85231-10-9*, Pub. by Creative Pubs II) Advent Bks Div.

Shakespeare's Last Plays. Frances A. Yates. 1975. 22.50 (*0-7100-8100-6*, RKP) Routledge.

Shakespeare's Last Plays. Eustace M. Tillyard. 88p. (C). 1938. reprint ed. pap. 19.95 (*0-485-30017-6*, Pub. by Athlone Pr UK) Humanities.

Shakespeare's Late Tragedies: A Collection of Critical Essays. Ed. by Susanne L. Wofford. LC 95-10942. (New Century Views Ser.). 368p. 1995. pap. 12.95 (*0-13-807819-X*) P-H.

Shakespeare's Legal Acquirements Considered. John C. Campbell. LC 79-39811. reprint ed. 32.50 (*0-404-01369-4*) AMS Pr.

Shakespeare's Legal Maxims. William L. Rushton. LC 70-174795. reprint ed. 24.50 (*0-404-05456-0*) AMS Pr.

Shakespeare's Library, 6 Vols, Set. 2nd ed. Ed. by William C. Hazlitt. LC 17-24753. reprint ed. 475.00 (*0-404-03250-8*) AMS Pr.

Shakespeare's Life - Fact & Fictions: A Guide to the Microfiche Collection. (Shakespeariana Ser.). 49p. (Orig.). 1991. pap. 20.00 (*0-8357-2146-9*) Univ Microfilms.

Shakespeare's Life & Art. Peter Alexander. LC 78-25749. 247p. 1979. reprint ed. text ed. 35.00 (*0-313-20666-X*, ALSA, Greenwood Pr) Greenwood.

Shakespeare's Lives. Samuel Schoenbaum. (Illus.). 656p. 1991. 35.00 (*0-19-818618-5*) OUP.

Shakespeare's Lives. Samuel Schoenbaum. (Illus.). 640p. 1993. reprint ed. pap. 23.50 (*0-19-283155-0*) OUP.

Shakespeare's London. T. P. Ordish. 1972. 59.95 (*0-8490-1043-8*) Gordon Pr.

Shakespeare's London. Henry T. Stephenson. LC 74-176435. reprint ed. 46.50 (*0-404-06258-X*) AMS Pr.

Shakespeare's Lost Play: Edmund Ironside. Ed. by Eric Sams. LC 85-19579. 416p. 1986. text ed. 45.00 (*0-312-71432-7*) St Martin.

Shakespeare's Lost Years in London. Arthur Acheson. LC 79-152552. (Studies in Shakespeare: No. 24). 1971. reprint ed. lib. bdg. 75.00 (*0-8383-1235-7*) M S G Haskell Hse.

Shakespeare's Lovers: A Text for Performance & Analysis. Libby Appel & Michael Flachmann. LC 82-5444. 156p. 1982. pap. 10.95 (*0-8093-1072-4*) S Ill U Pr.

Shakespeare's Lusty Punning in Love's Labour's Lost. Herbert A. Ellis. LC 73-86159. (Studies in English Literature: Vol. 81). 239p. 1974. text ed. 45.40 (*90-279-2616-6*) Mouton.

Shakespeare's Macbeth. 2nd ed. Walter S. Dalgliesh. LC 74-163664. reprint ed. 24.50 (*0-404-01918-8*) AMS Pr.

Shakespeare's Magic Circle. Alfred J. Evans. LC 72-128884. (Select Bibliographies Reprint Ser.). 1977. 18.95 (*0-8369-5504-8*) Ayer.

Shakespeare's Mannerist Canon: Ut Picturas Poemata. Jeffrey R. Myers. (Literature & the Visual Arts: Ser.: Vol. 2). 224p. (C). 1989. text ed. 52.00 (*0-8204-0891-3*) P Lang Pubng.

Shakespeare's Marriage. Joseph W. Gray. 1972. 59.95 (*0-8490-1044-6*) Gordon Pr.

Shakespeare's Marriage. Joseph W. Gray. LC 75-168182. reprint ed. 42.50 (*0-404-02894-2*) AMS Pr.

Shakespeare's Mature Tragedies. Bernard McElroy. LC 72-5389. 266p. reprint ed. pap. 75.90 (*0-7837-4326-2*, 2044030) Bks Demand.

Shakespeare's Mediated World. Richard Fly. LC 75-32486. 192p. 1976. 27.50 (*0-87023-199-5*) U of Mass Pr.

Shakespeare's Medical Knowledge. Charles W. Stearns. LC 72-959. reprint ed. 31.50 (*0-404-06224-5*) AMS Pr.

Shakespeare's Mercutio: His History & Drama. Joseph A. Porter. LC 88-17236. (Illus.). xiv, 282p. (C). 1989. 45.00 (*0-8078-1824-0*) U of NC Pr.

Shakespeare's Metrical Art. George T. Wright. 1988. 52.50 (*0-520-06057-1*) U CA Pr.

Shakespeare's Metrical Art. George T. Wright. 363p. 1991. reprint ed. pap. 14.95 (*0-520-07642-7*) U CA Pr.

Shakespeare's Middle Tragedies: A Collection of Critical Essays. Ed. by David G. Young. LC 92-17043. (New Century Views Ser.). 1992. pap. 12.95 (*0-13-807884-X*) P-H.

Shakespeare's Midwives: Some Neglected Shakespeareans. Arthur Sherbo. LC 91-50932. 208p. 1993. 36.50 (*0-87413-449-8*) U Delaware Pr.

Shakespeare's Minor Plays Notes. Ed. by Gary Carey. (Cliffs Notes Ser.). 1991. pap. 7.95 (*0-8220-0059-8*) Cliffs.

Shakespeare's Miracle Plays: Pericles, Cymbeline, & The Winter's Tale. H. W. Fawkner. LC 90-56175. 192p. 1992. 36.50 (*0-8386-3442-7*) Fairleigh Dickinson.

***Shakespeare's Monarchies: Ruler & Subject in the Romances.** Constance Jordan. LC 97-13665. 224p. 1997. 35.00 (*0-8014-2828-9*) Cornell U Pr.

Shakespeare's Monarchs. J. C. Stobart. 1972. 59.95 (*0-8490-1045-4*) Gordon Pr.

Shakespeare's Monologues for Women. Ed. by Dick Dotterer. LC 90-81269. 64p. (Orig.). 1990. pap. 8.95 (*0-940669-12-9*, D-24) Dramaline Pubns.

Shakespeare's Monologues They Haven't Heard. Ed. by Dick Dotterer. 64p. 1987. pap. 7.95 (*0-940669-01-3*, D-23) Dramaline Pubns.

Shakespeare's "More Than Words Can Witness" Essays on Visual & Nonverbal Enactment in the Plays. Ed. by Sidney Homan. LC 77-81576. 240p. 1978. 36.50 (*0-8387-2153-2*) Bucknell U Pr.

Shakespeare's Mortal Men: Overcoming Death in History, Comedy, & Tragedy. Patricia L. Carlin. LC 92-8722. (Studies in Shakespeare: Vol. 1). 250p. (C). 1993. text ed. 49.95 (*0-8204-1563-4*) P Lang Pubng.

Shakespeare's Motley. Leslie Hotson. LC 75-117592. (Studies in Shakespeare: No. 24). 1970. reprint ed. lib. bdg. 75.00 (*0-8383-1025-7*) M S G Haskell Hse.

Shakespeare's Mouldy Tales. Leah Scragg. (Medieval & Renaissance Library). 192p. (C). 1992. pap. text ed. 33.50 (*0-582-07070-8*, 79376) Longman.

Shakespeare's Mystery Play: A Study of the Tempest. Colin Still. (BCL1-PR English Literature Ser.). 247p. 1992. reprint ed. lib. bdg. 79.00 (*0-7812-7274-2*) Rprt Serv.

Shakespeare's Mystery Play, a Study of the Tempest. Colin Still. LC 71-131842. 247p. 1921. reprint ed. 49.00 (*0-403-00729-1*) Scholarly.

***Shakespeare's Names: A New Pronouncing Dictionary.** Louis Colaianni. 197p. 1997. pap. write for info. (*0-89676-215-7*, Drama Pubs) QSMG Ltd.

Shakespeare's Names: A Pronouncing Dictionary. Helge Kokeritz. LC 59-6798. (Shakespeare Supplements Ser.). 116p. reprint ed. 33.10 (*0-8357-9507-1*, 2011105) Bks Demand.

Shakespeare's "Othello" A Comprehensive Bibliography. John H. Smith. LC 88-26211. (Studies in the Renaissance: No. 26). 1988. 57.50 (*0-404-62296-8*) AMS Pr.

Shakespeare's Other Anne. W. J. Hutcheson. LC 74-1149. (Studies in Shakespeare: No. 24). 1974. lib. bdg. 33.95 (*0-8383-1793-6*) M S G Haskell Hse.

Shakespeare's Other Language. Ruth Nevo. 160p. 1987. text ed. 39.50 (*0-416-06402-7*) Routledge Chapman & Hall.

Shakespeare's Other Lives. Maurice J. O'Sullivan. LC 91-3473. 1995. text ed. 35.00 (*0-89341-680-0*, Longwood Academic) Hollowbrook.

***Shakespeare's Other Lives: An Anthology of Fictional Depictions of the Bard.** Ed. by Maurice J. O'Sullivan, Jr. LC 97-1050. 256p. 1997. lib. bdg. 39.95 (*0-7864-0335-7*) McFarland & Co.

Shakespeare's Pagan World: The Roman Tragedies. Joseph L. Simmons. LC 73-80126. 214p. reprint ed. pap. 61.00 (*0-7837-4370-X*, 2044080) Bks Demand.

S

An Asterisk (*) at the beginning of an entry indicates that the title is appearing in BIP for the first time.

Shakespeare's Parted Eye: Perception, Knowledge & Meaning in the Sonnets & Plays. Robert B. Schwartz. LC 89-29832. (American University Studies: English Language & Literature: Ser. IV, Vol. 114). 174p. (C). 1990. text ed. 36.95 (*0-8204-1202-3*) P Lang Pubng.

Shakespeare's Pastoral Comedy. Thomas McFarland. LC 72-81325. 228p. reprint ed. pap. 65.00 (*0-7837-3752-1*, 2043569) Bks Demand.

Shakespeare's Patterns of Self-Knowledge. Rolf Soellner. LC 72-5804. 476p. 1972. 42.50 (*0-8142-0171-7*) Ohio St U Pr.

Shakespeare's "Pericles" & "Apolonius of Tyre" A Study in Comparative Literature. Albert H. Smyth. LC 79-126696. reprint ed. 29.50 (*0-404-06129-X*) AMS Pr.

Shakespeare's Perjured Eye: The Invention of Poetic Subjectivity in the Sonnets. Joel Fineman. 1986. 48.00 (*0-520-05486-5*); pap. 15.00 (*0-520-06331-7*) U CA Pr.

Shakespeare's Personality. Norman N. Holland. Ed. by Sidney Homan & Bernard J. Paris. 1989. 40.00 (*0-520-06317-1*) U CA Pr.

Shakespeare's Philosophical Patterns. Walter C. Curry. 1990. 14.50 (*0-8446-0567-0*) Peter Smith.

Shakespeare's Play of King Henry IV from a Contemporary Manuscript see Shakespearian Commentary: The Remarks of Karl Simrock on the Plots of Shakespeare's Plays

Shakespeare's Play Within Play: Medieval Imagery & Scenic Form in Hamlet, Othello, & King Lear. Cherrell Guilfoyle. (Early Drama, Art & Music Monograph: No. 12). 1990. pap. 12.95 (*0-918720-35-4*); boxed 22.95 (*0-918720-34-6*) Medieval Inst.

Shakespeare's Playhouse Practice: A Handbook. Warren D. Smith. LC 74-15448. 133p. reprint ed. pap. 38.00 (*0-317-55652-5*, 2029255) Bks Demand.

Shakespeare's Playhouses. Herbert Berry. LC 85-48061. (Studies in the Renaissance: No.19). 1987. 34.50 (*0-404-62289-5*) AMS Pr.

Shakespeare's Plays in Performance. John R. Brown. 256p. (Orig.). 1993. pap. 15.95 (*1-55783-136-X*) Applause Theatre Bk Pubs.

Shakespeare's Plays in Quarto: A Facsimile Edition of Copies Primarily from the Henry E. Huntington Library. William Shakespeare. Ed. by Michael J. Allen & Kenneth Muir. LC 81-40322. 936p. 1982. boxed 185.00 (*0-520-04077-5*) U CA Pr.

Shakespeare's Plots. William H. Fleming. 1972. 59.95 (*0-8490-1046-2*) Gordon Pr.

Shakespeare's Plots. William H. Fleming. LC 75-131512. reprint ed. 47.50 (*0-404-02437-8*) AMS Pr.

Shakespeare's Pluralistic Concepts of Character: A Study in Dramatic Anamorphism. Imtiaz Habib. LC 91-50662. (Illus.). 256p. 1993. 39.50 (*0-945636-37-7*) Susquehanna U Pr.

Shakespeare's Plutarch. Walter W. Skeat. Ed. by Plutarch. 1875. 34.00 (*0-404-06097-8*) AMS Pr.

Shakespeare's Plutarch, 2 vols., Set. Ed. by C. F. Brooke. 441p. (C). 1966. reprint ed. lib. bdg. 150.00 (*0-8383-0516-4*) M S G Haskell Hse.

Shakespeare's Political Animal: Schema & Schemata in the Canon. Alan Hager. LC 88-40585. 168p. 1990. 28.50 (*0-87413-371-8*) U Delaware Pr.

Shakespeare's Political Drama: The History Plays & the Roman Plays. Alexander Leggatt. 288p. (C). 1989. pap. 15.95 (*0-415-03888-X*) Routledge.

Shakespeare's Political Pageant: Essays in Politics & Literature. Ed. by Joseph Alulis & Vickie Sullivan. 304p. 1996. pap. text ed. 24.95 (*0-8476-8290-0*); lib. bdg. 64.50 (*0-8476-8289-7*) Rowman.

Shakespeare's Political Plays. H. M. Richmond. 1990. 14.50 (*0-8446-2804-2*) Peter Smith.

Shakespeare's Politics. Allan Bloom & Harry V. Jaffa. x, 150p. 1981. pap. text ed. 10.95 (*0-226-06041-1*) U Ch Pr.

Shakespeare's Politics. Allen Bloom & Harry V. Jaffa. LC 81-10342. x, 160p. 1987. pap. text ed. 15.95 (*0-226-06040-3*, Midway Reprint) U Ch Pr.

Shakespeare's Portrayal of Moral Life. Frank Sharp. LC 76-121352. (Studies in Shakespeare: No. 24). 1970. reprint ed. lib. bdg. 75.00 (*0-8383-1069-9*) M S G Haskell Hse.

Shakespeare's Predecessors in the English Drama. John A. Symonds. LC 67-28915. 1967. reprint ed. 53.50 (*0-8154-0301-1*) Cooper Sq.

Shakespeare's Predecessors in the English Drama. John A. Symonds. (BCL1-PR English Literature Ser.). 551p. 1992. reprint ed. lib. bdg. 99.00 (*0-7812-7107-X*) Rprt Serv.

Shakespeare's Principal Plays. 3rd ed. Ed. by Tucker Brooke et al. (Illus.). 1935. 59.50 (*0-89197-402-4*) Irvington.

Shakespeare's Problem Plays. Eustace M. Tillyard. LC 83-45901. 1950. 31.50 (*0-404-20258-6*, PR2976) AMS Pr.

Shakespeare's Professional Career. Peter Thomson. (Illus.). 220p. (C). 1992. text ed. 44.95 (*0-521-35128-6*) Cambridge U Pr.

Shakespeare's Professional Career. Peter Thomson. (Canto Book Ser.). (Illus.). 240p. (C). 1994. pap. text ed. 9.95 (*0-521-46655-5*) Cambridge U Pr.

Shakespeare's Professional Skills. Nevill Coghill. 240p. reprint ed. pap. 68.40 (*0-685-16271-0*, 2027277) Bks Demand.

Shakespeare's Pronunciation. Wilhelm Vietor. LC 76-177864. reprint ed. 35.00 (*0-404-06765-4*) AMS Pr.

Shakespeare's Prophetic Mind. A. C. Harwood. 63p. 1977. reprint ed. pap. 9.95 (*0-85440-318-3*, Steinerbks) Anthroposophic.

Shakespeare's Proverbial Themes: A Rhetorical Context for the Sentenia as Res. Marjorie Donker. LC 92-175. (Contributions to the Study of World Literature Ser.: No. 44). 224p. 1992. text ed. 47.95 (*0-313-28410-5*, DSK/, Greenwood Pr) Greenwood.

Shakespeare's Puck & His Folkslore, 3 Vols, Set. William Bell. reprint ed. 155.00 (*0-404-00740-6*) AMS Pr.

Shakespeare's Queer Children: Appropriation in Contemporary Culture. Kate Chedqzoy. 1996. text ed. 69.95 (*0-7190-4657-2*, Pub. by Manchester Univ Pr UK); text ed. 19.95 (*0-7190-4658-0*, Pub. by Manchester Univ Pr UK) St Martin.

Shakespeare's Quotations: A Players Press Guide. William Shakespeare. Ed. by Trevor R. Griffiths. LC 92-53234. 667p. 1992. 40.00 (*0-88734-620-0*) Players Pr.

Shakespeare's Realist Tragedy: Studies in Titus Andronicus. G. Harold Metz. LC 95-52067. (Illus.). 312p. 1996. 46.50 (*0-8386-3653-5*) Fairleigh Dickinson.

Shakespeare's Reflexive Endings. Robert F. Willson, Jr. LC 90-6051. (Studies in Renaissance Literature: Vol. 6). 160p. 1990. lib. bdg. 79.95 (*0-88946-699-8*) E Mellen.

Shakespeare's Religious Background. Ed. by Peter S. Milward. 312p. 1985. reprint ed. 2.50 (*0-8294-0508-9*) Loyola Pr.

Shakespeare's Reparative Comedies: A Psychoanalytic View of the Middle Plays. Joseph Westlund. LC 83-9305. 200p. (C). 1984. 21.00 (*0-226-89413-4*) U Ch Pr.

Shakespeare's Repentance Plays: The Search for an Adequate Form. Alan R. Velie. LC 72-422. 127p. 1972. 24.50 (*0-8386-1126-5*) Fairleigh Dickinson.

Shakespeare's Revision of King Lear. Steven Urkowitz. LC 79-3234. (Princeton Essays in Literature Ser.). 181p. 1980. reprint ed. pap. 51.60 (*0-7837-9465-7*, 2060207) Bks Demand.

Shakespeare's Rhetoric of Comic Character: Dramatic Convention in Classical & Renaissance Comedy. Karen Newman. 128p. 1985. 18.95 (*0-416-37990-7*, 9116) Routledge Chapman & Hall.

Shakespeare's Rival. Robert Gittings. LC 76-3689. (Illus.). 138p. 1976. reprint ed. text ed. 52.50 (*0-8371-8814-8*, GISR, Greenwood Pr) Greenwood.

Shakespeare's Romance of the Word. Maurice Hunt. LC 89-46251. 184p. 1990. 32.50 (*0-8387-5188-1*) Bucknell U Pr.

Shakespeare's Romances. Richard A. Andretta. 152p. (C). 1981. text ed. 15.00 (*0-7069-1420-1*, Pub. by Vikas II) S Asia.

Shakespeare's Romances: A Study of Some Ways of the Imagination. Hallett D. Smith. LC 72-79314. 244p. 1972. 18.00 (*0-87328-052-0*); pap. 6.00 (*0-87328-053-9*) Huntington Lib.

Shakespeare's Romances As Interrogative Texts: Their Alienation Strategies & Ideology. Boika D. Sokolova. LC 92-11453. 168p. 1992. lib. bdg. 79.95 (*0-7734-9475-8*) E Mellen.

Shakespeare's Romances Reconsidered. Ed. by Carol M. Kay & Henry E. Jacobs. LC 77-17389. 236p. reprint ed. pap. 67.30 (*0-7837-0992-7*, 2041298) Bks Demand.

Shakespeare's Romantic Comedies: The Development of Their Form & Meaning. Peter G. Phialas. LC 66-25355. 330p. reprint ed. pap. 94.10 (*0-7837-0316-3*, 2040638) Bks Demand.

Shakespeare's Rome. Robert S. Miola. LC 83-1777. 244p. 1983. 44.95 (*0-521-25307-1*) Cambridge U Pr.

Shakespeare's Romeo & Juliet: Texts, Contexts, & Interpretation. Ed. by Jay L. Halio. LC 95-7462. 1996. write for info. (*0-87413-579-6*) U Delaware Pr.

***Shakespeare's Romeo & Juliet in Performance: Traditions & Departures.** Katherine L. Wright. LC 96-49599. (Illus.). 312p. 1997. text ed. 99.95 (*0-7734-2284-6*, Mellen Univ Pr) E Mellen.

Shakespeare's "Rough Magic" Ed. by Peter Erickson & Coppelia Kahn. LC 83-40112. (Illus.). 320p. 1985. 48.50 (*0-87413-247-9*) U Delaware Pr.

Shakespeare's Satire. Oscar J. Campbell. LC 74-159036. 239p. (C). 1971. reprint ed. 50.00 (*0-87752-150-6*) Gordian.

Shakespeare's Scepticism. Graham Bradshaw. LC 87-9479. 283p. 1987. pap. 12.95 (*0-685-43929-1*) St Martin.

Shakespeare's Self. W. Shore. LC 72-179265. (Studies in Shakespeare: No. 24). 1971. reprint ed. lib. bdg. 59.95 (*0-8383-1366-3*) M S G Haskell Hse.

Shakespeare's Self Portrait: Passages from His Work. Compiled & Notes by A. L. Rowse. 200p. 1985. lib. bdg. 22.00 (*0-8191-4220-4*) U Pr of Amer.

***Shakespeare's Shakespeare: How the Play Were Made.** John C. Meagher. LC 96-45474. 288p. 1997. 34.50 (*0-8264-1007-3*) Continuum.

Shakespeare's Sister. Doris Gwaltney. 256p. 1995. pap. 11.95 (*1-57174-041-4*) Hampton Roads Pub Co.

Shakespeare's Sisters: Feminist Essays on Women Poets. Ed. by Sandra M. Gilbert. LC 78-9510. 368p. 1979. 35.00 (*0-253-11258-3*) Ind U Pr.

Shakespeare's Sisters: Feminist Essays on Women Poets. Ed. by Sandra M. Gilbert. LC 78-9510. 368p. 1981. pap. 15.95 (*0-253-20263-9*, MB-263) Ind U Pr.

Shakespeare's Skepticism. Graham Bradshaw. LC 90-46406. 270p. pap. 16.95 (*0-8014-9910-0*) Cornell U Pr.

Shakespeare's Soliloquies. Wolfgang Clemen. Tr. by Charity S. Stokes. LC 87-1541. 211p. 1987. 45.00 (*0-416-05862-0*); pap. 13.95 (*0-416-30460-5*) Routledge Chapman & Hall.

Shakespeare's Sonnet Story: 1592-1598. Arthur Acheson. LC 72-164658. (Studies in Shakespeare: No. 24). 1971. reprint ed. lib. bdg. 75.00 (*0-8383-1322-1*) M S G Haskell Hse.

Shakespeare's Sonnets. Comment by Stephen Booth. LC 76-56161. 1980. pap. 23.00 (*0-300-02495-9*) Yale U Pr.

Shakespeare's Sonnets. William Shakespeare. pap. 5.99 (*0-671-66926-5*) Folger.

Shakespeare's Sonnets. William Shakespeare. Ed. by Louis B. Wright & Virginia A. LaMar. (Folger Library). 372p. mass mkt. 3.99 (*0-671-67047-6*, WSP) PB.

Shakespeare's Sonnets: A Record of Twentieth Century Criticism. Tetsumaro Hayashi. LC 77-184764. 163p. 1972. 27.50 (*0-8108-0462-X*) Scarecrow.

Shakespeare's Sonnets: Their Relation to His Life. Barbara A. Mackenzie. LC 78-6965. reprint ed. 21.50 (*0-404-04135-3*) AMS Pr.

Shakespeare's Sonnets & A Lover's Complaint. William Shakespeare. Ed. by Stanley Wells. 208p. 1990. pap. 8.95 (*0-19-282026-5*) OUP.

Shakespeare's Sonnets & Problems of Autobiography. Hugh Calvert. (C). 1989. 45.00 (*0-86303-302-4*, Pub. by Merlin Bks UK) St Mut.

Shakespeare's Sonnets Never Before Interpreted. Gerald Massey. LC 78-172855. reprint ed. 74.50 (*0-404-04238-4*) AMS Pr.

Shakespeare's Sonnets Notes. James K. Lowers. (Cliffs Notes Ser.). 1965. pap. 3.75 (*0-8220-0077-6*) Cliffs.

Shakespeare's Sonnets Reconsidered. Ed. by Samuel Butler. LC 76-136416. reprint ed. 39.50 (*0-404-01249-3*) AMS Pr.

Shakespeare's Sonnets Reconsidered. William Shakespeare & Samuel Butler. (BCL1-PR English Literature Ser.). 315p. 1992. reprint ed. lib. bdg. 89.00 (*0-7812-7275-0*) Rprt Serv.

Shakespeare's Speaking Properties. Frances N. Teague. LC 90-55873. 224p. 1990. 38.50 (*0-8387-5208-X*) Bucknell U Pr.

***Shakespeare's Speech-Headings: Speaking the Speech in Shakespeare's Plays.** Ed. by George W. Williams. LC 87-45811. (Illus.). 240p. 1997. 39.50 (*0-87413-637-7*) U Delaware Pr.

Shakespeare's Stagecraft. J. L. Styan. (Illus.). 252p. (C). 1967. pap. text ed. 21.95 (*0-521-09435-6*) Cambridge U Pr.

Shakespeare's Stories: Comedies. Illus. by Carol Tarrant. LC 88-16947. 126p. (J). (gr. 7-12). 1988. 12.95 (*0-87226-191-3*) P Bedrick Bks.

Shakespeare's Stories: Comedies. Illus. by Carol Tarrant. LC 88-16947. 126p. (J). 1990. pap. 6.95 (*0-87226-225-1*) P Bedrick Bks.

Shakespeare's Stories: Histories. Beverley Birch. LC 88-15693. (Illus.). 126p. (YA). (gr. 7-12). 1990. pap. 6.95 (*0-87226-226-X*) P Bedrick Bks.

Shakespeare's Stories: Histories. Illus. by Robina Green. LC 88-15693. 126p. (J). (gr. 7-12). 1988. 12.95 (*0-87226-192-1*) P Bedrick Bks.

Shakespeare's Stories: Tragedies. Beverley Birch. LC 88-18112. (Illus.). 126p. (YA). (gr. 7-12). 1990. pap. 6.95 (*0-87226-227-8*) P Bedrick Bks.

Shakespeare's Stories: Tragedies. Illus. by Tony Kerins. LC 88-18112. 126p. (J). (gr. 7-12). 1988. 12.95 (*0-87226-193-X*) P Bedrick Bks.

***Shakespeare's Storytellers.** Barbara Hardy. 224p. 9600. 34.95 (*0-7206-0963-1*, Pub. by P Owen Ltd UK) Dufour.

Shakespeare's Stratford. Edgar I. Fripp. LC 70-128886. (Select Bibliographies Reprint Ser.). 1977. 20.95 (*0-8369-5506-4*) Ayer.

Shakespeare's Stratford. Edgar I. Fripp. LC 78-153321. reprint ed. 29.50 (*0-404-02623-0*) AMS Pr.

Shakespeare's Stratford. Edgar I. Fripp. (BCL1-PR English Literature Ser.). 86p. 1992. reprint ed. lib. bdg. 59.00 (*0-7812-7285-8*) Rprt Serv.

Shakespeare's Sweet Thunder: Essays on the Early Comedies. Michael J. Collins. (Illus.). 256p. 1997. 40.50 (*0-87413-582-6*, 96-5747) U Delaware Pr.

Shakespeares-'The Old Faith.' John H. De Groot. LC 68-57315. (Essay Index Reprint Ser.). 1977. 20.95 (*0-8369-0368-4*) Ayer.

Shakespeare's Theater. Jacqueline Morley. LC 94-16386. (Inside Story Ser.). (Illus.). 48p. (J). (gr. 5 up). 1994. lib. bdg. 18.95 (*0-87226-309-6*) P Bedrick Bks.

Shakespeare's Theater of Presence: Language, Spectacle, & the Audience. Sidney Homan. LC 85-48170. 256p. 1986. 38.50 (*0-8387-5105-9*) Bucknell U Pr.

Shakespeare's Theatre. 2nd ed. Peter Thomson. LC 91-33770. 216p. (C). (gr. 13). 1992. pap. 17.95 (*0-415-05148-7*, Pub. by Tavistock UK) Routledge Chapman & Hall.

Shakespeare's Theatre & the Dramatic Tradition. Louis B. Wright. LC 79-65978. (Folger Guides to the Age of Shakespeare Ser.). 1979. pap. 4.95 (*0-918016-05-3*) Folger Bks.

Shakespeare's Theory of Drama. Pauline Kiernan. 228p. (C). 1996. text ed. 49.95 (*0-521-55046-7*) Cambridge U Pr.

Shakespeare's Town & Country. Shakespeare Birthplace Trust Library Staff. (Illus.). 64p. 1993. pap. 6.95 (*0-7117-0534-8*, Pub. by Jarrold Pub UK) Seven Hills Bk.

Shakespeare's Tragedies: An Introduction. Dieter Mehl. 281p. 1987. pap. text ed. 19.95 (*0-521-31690-1*) Cambridge U Pr.

***Shakespeare's Tragedies & Modern Critical Theory.** James Cunningham. LC 96-38007. 240p. 1997. 37.50 (*0-8386-3711-6*) Fairleigh Dickinson.

Shakespeare's Tragedies & Other Studies in Seventeenth Century Drama. Clifford Leech. LC 75-16846. 232p. 1975. reprint ed. text ed. 49.75 (*0-8371-8266-2*, LESTO, Greenwood Pr) Greenwood.

Shakespeare's Tragic Cosmos. T. McAlindon. 328p. (C). 1991. text ed. 65.00 (*0-521-39041-9*) Cambridge U Pr.

Shakespeare's Tragic Cosmos. Thomas McAlindon. 324p. 1996. pap. text ed. 18.95 (*0-521-56605-3*) Cambridge U Pr.

Shakespeare's Tragic Heroes: Slaves of Passion. Lily G. Campbell. 1960. 25.75 (*0-8446-1806-3*) Peter Smith.

Shakespeare's Tragic Heroes, Slaves of Passion. Lily B. Campbell. (BCL1-PR English Literature Ser.). 248p. 1992. reprint ed. lib. bdg. 79.00 (*0-7812-7299-8*) Rprt Serv.

Shakespeare's Tragic Imagination. Nicholas Grene. LC 91-8155. 328p. 1991. text ed. 49.95 (*0-312-06218-4*) St Martin.

Shakespeare's Tragic Imagination. Nicholas Grene. 1996. text ed. 18.95 (*0-312-16184-0*) St Martin.

***Shakespeare's Troy: Drama, Politics, & the Translation of Empire.** Heather James. (Studies in Renaissance Literature & Culture: Vol. 22). (Illus.). 269p. (C). 1997. text ed. 54.95 (*0-521-59223-2*) Cambridge U Pr.

Shakespeare's Typological Satire: A Study of the Falstaff-Oldcastle Problem. Alice-Lyle Scoufos. LC 77-92256. (Illus.). xvii, 378p. 1979. 29.95 (*0-8214-0390-7*) Ohio U Pr.

Shakespeare's Understanding of Honor. John E. Alvis. LC 89-61997. 282p. 1990. lib. bdg. 34.95 (*0-89089-382-9*) Carolina Acad Pr.

***Shakespeare's Universal Wolf: Postmodernist Studies in Early Modern Reification.** Hugh Grady. 256p. 1996. 65.00 (*0-19-813004-X*) OUP.

Shakespeare's Universe: Renaissance Ideas & Conventions: Essays for W. R. Elton. John M. Mucciolo. LC 95-8834. 292p. 1996. 74.95 (*1-85928-193-1*, Pub. by Scolar Pr UK) Ashgate Pub Co.

Shakespeare's Universe of Comedy. William J. Martz. 1976. lib. bdg. 250.00 (*0-87700-268-1*) Revisionist Pr.

***Shakespeare's Unruly Women.** Georgianna Ziegler et al. (Illus.). 112p. 1997. pap. 21.95 (*0-295-97629-2*) U of Wash Pr.

Shakespeare's Use of Music: A Study of the Music & Its Performance in the Original Production of Seven Comedies. John H. Long. LC 77-4643. (Music Reprint Ser.). 1977. reprint ed. lib. bdg. 32.50 (*0-306-77423-2*) Da Capo.

Shakespeare's Use of Music: The Final Comedies. John H. Long. LC 77-5644. (Music Reprint Ser.). 1977. reprint ed. lib. bdg. 29.50 (*0-306-77424-0*) Da Capo.

Shakespeare's Use of Music: Vol. 3, The Histories & Tragedies. John H. Long. LC 61-17588. 1971. 39.95 (*0-8130-0311-3*) U Press Fla.

Shakespeare's Use of Off-Stage Sounds. Frances A. Shirley. LC 63-8119. 276p. reprint ed. pap. 78.70 (*0-7837-1827-6*, 2042027) Bks Demand.

Shakespeare's Use of the Pronoun of Address. Geraldine Byrne. LC 72-121150. (Studies in Shakespeare: No. 24). 1970. reprint ed. lib. bdg. 39.95 (*0-8383-1097-4*) M S G Haskell Hse.

Shakespeare's Use of the Supernatural. J. Paul Gibson. LC 79-144615. reprint ed. 32.50 (*0-404-02719-9*) AMS Pr.

Shakespeare's Vast Romance: A Study of the Winter's Tale. Charles Frey. LC 79-3063. 184p. 1980. text ed. 27.50 (*0-8262-0286-1*) U of Mo Pr.

Shakespeare's Verbal Art in Th'Expence of Spirit. Roman Jakobson & L. G. Jones. (De Proprietatibus Litterarum, Ser. Practica: No. 35). (Orig.). 1970. pap. text ed. 25.40 (*90-279-0512-6*) Mouton.

Shakespeare's Verse. Marina Tarlinskaja. (American University Studies: English Language & Literature: Ser. IV, Vol. 41). 383p. (C). 1987. text ed. 49.90 (*0-8204-0344-X*) P Lang Pubng.

Shakespeare's Villains. Charles N. Coe. LC 72-455. reprint ed. 14.50 (*0-404-01585-9*) AMS Pr.

Shakespeare's Vocabulary: Its Etymological Elements. Eilert Ekwall. LC 78-166013. reprint ed. 27.50 (*0-404-02269-3*) AMS Pr.

Shakespeare's Warwickshire Contemporaries. Charlotte Stopes. LC 76-128956. reprint ed. 41.50 (*0-404-06288-1*) AMS Pr.

Shakespeare's Wild Flowers. Eleanor S. Rohde. LC 76-153350. reprint ed. 32.50 (*0-404-05385-8*) AMS Pr.

Shakespeare's Will. William Shakespeare. Ed. by James O. Halliwell-Philipps. LC 79-144631. reprint ed. 29.50 (*0-404-03086-6*) AMS Pr.

Shakespeare's Women: A Playscript for Performance & Analysis. Libby Appel & Michael Flachmann. LC 85-10859. 176p. (C). 1986. pap. text ed. 15.95 (*0-8093-1241-7*) S Ill U Pr.

Shakespeare's Workshop. W. J. Lawrence. 161p. (C). 1966. text ed. 75.00 (*0-8383-0580-6*) M S G Haskell Hse.

Shakespeare's Workshop. William J. Lawrence. (BCL1-PR English Literature Ser.). 161p. 1992. reprint ed. lib. bdg. 69.00 (*0-7812-7296-3*) Rprt Serv.

Shakespeare's World: Background Readings in the English Renaissance. Ed. by Gerald M. Pinciss & Roger Lockyer. 220p. 1989. reprint ed. pap. text ed. 19.95 (*0-8264-0451-0*) F Ungar Bks.

Shakespeare's World of Death. Richard Courtney. 288p. 1995. pap. 17.00 (*0-88924-261-5*, Pub. by Simon & Pierre Pub CN) Empire Pub Srvs.

Shakespeare's World of Love: The Middle Comedies. Richard Courtney. (Director's Shakespeare Ser.). 180p. 1994. pap. text ed. 17.00 (*0-88924-230-5*, Pub. by Simon & Pierre Pub CN) Empire Pub Srvs.

Shakespeare's World of War: The Early Histories. Richard Courtney & Marian M. Wilson. 180p. 1994. pap. text ed. 17.00 (*0-88924-229-1*, Pub. by Simon & Pierre Pub CN) Empire Pub Srvs.

Shakespeare's Young Lovers. Elmer E. Stoll. LC 75-182721. reprint ed. 24.50 (*0-404-06282-2*) AMS Pr.

Shakespearian Gardens. Ed. by Levi Fox. (Shakespeare Travel Ser.). (Illus.). 32p. (Orig.). 1994. pap. 3.50 (*0-7117-0132-6*) Seven Hills Bk.

Shakespearian Grammar. E. A. Abbott. LC 72-3661. (Studies in Shakespeare: No. 24). 1972. reprint ed. lib. bdg. 75.00 (*0-8383-1571-2*) M S G Haskell Hse.

Shakespearian Players & Performances. Arthur C. Sprague. LC 69-14091. (Illus.). 222p. 1969. reprint ed. text ed. 55.00 (*0-8371-0664-8*, SPPP, Greenwood Pr) Greenwood.

Shakespearian Playing Companies. Andrew Gurr. 496p. 1996. 105.00 (*0-19-812977-7*) OUP.

Shakespearian Properties. Ed. by Levi Fox. (Shakespeare Travel Ser.). (Illus.). 32p. (Orig.). 1994. pap. 3.95 (*0-7117-0247-0*) Seven Hills Bk.

S

An Asterisk (*) at the beginning of an entry indicates that the title is appearing in BIP for the first time.

Shakespearian Properties. Ed. by Levi Fox. (Shakespeare Travel Ser.). (Illus.). 20p. (Orig.). 1994. pap. 2.50 (*0-7117-0257-8*) Seven Hills Bk.

Shakespearian Stage. Victor E. Albright. LC 79-158241. reprint ed. 29.50 (*0-404-00304-4*) AMS Pr.

Shakespere: An Address. George L. Kittredge. LC 78-109653. (Select Bibliographies Reprint Ser.). 1977. 12.95 (*0-8369-5262-6*) Ayer.

Shakespere Allusion-Book: A Collection of Allusions to Shakspere from 1591 to 1700, 2 Vols., Set. Ed. by Clement M. Ingleby et al. LC 72-128892. (Select Bibliographies Reprint Ser.). 1977. 60.95 (*0-8369-5512-9*) Ayer.

Shakespere & Montaigne. Jacob Feis. LC 73-130615. reprint ed. 34.00 (*0-404-02375-4*) AMS Pr.

Shakespere & Typography. William Blades. LC 72-113560. reprint ed. 29.50 (*0-404-00894-1*) AMS Pr.

Shakespere as a Playwright. Brander Matthews. LC 13-21467. reprint ed. 45.00 (*0-404-04269-4*) AMS Pr.

Shakespere Flora. Leo H. Grindon. LC 77-168208. reprint ed. 45.00 (*0-404-02929-9*) AMS Pr.

Shakespere to Sheridan. Alwin Thaler. LC 63-23190. (Illus.). 1972. 26.95 (*0-405-09025-0*) Ayer.

Shakesperean Criticism, Vol. 34. 1996. 140.00 (*0-8103-9980-6*) Gale.

Shakespere's Predecessors in the English Drama. John A. Symonds. LC 68-54300. reprint ed. 29.50 (*0-404-06318-7*) AMS Pr.

Shakespere's Silences. Alwin Thaler. LC 70-128894. (Select Bibliographies Reprint Ser.). 1977. 23.95 (*0-8369-5514-5*) Ayer.

Shakesperian Commentary: The Remarks of Karl Simrock on the Plots of Shakespeare's Plays. Ed. by J. D. Halliwell. Bd. with Shakespeare's Play of King Henry IV from a Contemporary Manuscript. (Shakespeare Society of London Publications: Vol. 19). 1974. reprint ed. Set pap. (*0-8115-0181-7*) Periodicals Srv.

Shakhashiri Chemical. 2nd ed. Mary L. Kotz. (C). 1991. teacher ed., pap. text ed. 25.50 (*0-03-074473-3*) HB Coll Pubs.

Shakin' Loose with Mother Goose, Set. Steve Allen & Jayne Meadows. (Illus.). 128p. (J). (ps-2). 1987. audio 19.95 (*0-89411-010-1*) Kids Matter.

Shakin' the Mess Outta Misery. Shay Youngblood. 1994. pap. 5.00 (*0-87129-297-1*, SA6) Dramatic Pub.

Shaking a Fist at God: Struggling with the Mystery of Undeserved Suffering. Katharine J. Dell. LC 96-26517. 128p. (Orig.). 1997. pap. 9.00 (*0-7648-0030-2*, Triumph Books) Liguori Pubns.

Shaking among God's People. Keavin Hayden. LC 94-21417. 1994. 8.99 (*0-8280-0868-X*) Review & Herald.

Shaking Eve's Tree: Short Stories of Jewish Women. Ed. by Sharon Niederman. 290p. 1990. pap. 14.95 (*0-8276-0369-X*); text ed. 27.50 (*0-8276-0356-8*) JPS Phila.

***Shaking off the Dark.** 2nd rev. ed. Tino Villanueva. (Clasicos Chicanos/Chicano Classics Ser.: Vol. 11). 96p. 1997. pap. 9.00 (*0-927534-73-8*) Biling Rev-Pr.

Shaking Out the Spirits: A Psychologists' Entry into the Healing Mysteries of Global Shamanism. Bradford P. Keeney. LC 93-48357. 1994. pap. 14.95 (*0-88268-164-8*) Station Hill Pr.

Shaking the Nickel Bush. Ralph Moody. (J). 1976. 22.95 (*0-8488-1108-9*) Amereon Ltd.

Shaking the Nickel Bush. Ralph Moody. LC 94-14503. (Illus.). 236p. 1994. reprint ed. pap. 9.95 (*0-8032-8218-4*, Bison Books) U of Nebr Pr.

***Shaking the Pillars of Exile: Voice of a Fool, an Early Modern Jewish Critique of Rabbinic Culture.** Talya Fishman. LC 96-43155. (Jewish History & Culture Ser.). 1997. write for info. (*0-8047-2820-8*) Stanford U Pr.

Shaking the Pumpkin: Traditional Poetry of the Indian North Americas. rev. ed. Jerome Rothenberg. LC 90-39916. 448p. 1991. reprint ed. pap. 17.95 (*0-8263-1246-2*) U of NM Pr.

***Shaking the Rattle: Healing the Trauma of Colonization.** Barbara-Helen Hill. 200p. (Orig.). 1996. pap. 12.95 (*0-919441-75-0*, Pub. by Theytus Bks Ltd CN) Orca Bk Pubs.

Shaking the Tree: A Book of Works & Days. Tom O'Grady. (Illus.). 197p. (Orig.). 1993. pap. 10.95 (*0-614-05294-7*) Dolphin-Moon.

Shaking up Shakespeare: Shakespeare: Dreamwork, Personality & Complexity. Patrick A. O'Dougherty. (Illus.). 169p. (C). 1994. lib. bdg. 19.99 (*0-9626665-4-8*) Hellenist Amer Co.

Shaking up the Insides of the Word: Poems. Rudy Thomas. LC 92-26981. 64p. 1992. pap. 12.95 (*0-7734-0045-1*, Mellen Poetry Pr) E Mellen.

Shaking Your Family Tree. Ralph Crandall. (Illus.). 256p. 1988. reprint ed. pap. 10.95 (*0-89909-148-2*, 80-551-6) Yankee Bks.

Shaking Your Family Tree Workbook: A Basic Guide to Tracing Your Family's Genealogy. Maureen E. Mchugh. 64p. (Orig.). 1990. pap. 9.95 (*0-89909-309-4*, 80-551-7) Yankee Bks.

***Shakira's Magic Dollar.** Kerra Davis. (Illus.). 30p. (Orig.). (J). (ps-2). 1998. pap. 8.99 (*1-55237-476-9*, Pub. by Comnwlth Pub CN) Partners Pubs Grp.

Shakkai: Woman of the Sacred Garden. Lynn V. Andrews. LC 91-58368. (Illus.). 310p. 1993. reprint ed. pap. 13.00 (*0-06-092179-X*, PL) HarpC.

Shakspere. George L. Kittredge. LC 76-126663. reprint ed. 22.50 (*0-404-03709-7*) AMS Pr.

Shakspere & His Forerunners, 2 Vols. Sidney Lanier. LC 74-171656. reprint ed. 95.00 (*0-404-03875-1*) AMS Pr.

Shakspere Coat-of-Arms. Samuel A. Tannenbaum. LC 71-176453. reprint ed. 21.50 (*0-404-06336-5*) AMS Pr.

Shakspere Fabrications. Clement M. Ingleby. LC 78-170065. reprint ed. 29.50 (*0-404-03485-3*) AMS Pr.

Shakspere, His Birthplace & Its Neighbourhood. John R. Wise. LC 76-178313. reprint ed. 34.50 (*0-404-07003-5*) AMS Pr.

Shakspere Fly-Leaves & Jottings. 2nd ed. Henry T. Hall. LC 70-135727. 1970. reprint ed. 45.00 (*0-404-03043-2*) AMS Pr.

Shaksperean Statistics. enl. ed. Henry T. Hall. LC 70-135735. reprint ed. 32.50 (*0-404-03044-0*) AMS Pr.

Shakspere's England: Or, Sketches of Our Social History in the Reign of Elizabeth, 2 Vols, Set. George W. Thornbury. LC 72-177453. reprint ed. 125.00 (*0-404-06425-6*) AMS Pr.

Shakspere's Garden. Sidney Beisly. LC 79-113551. reprint ed. 39.50 (*0-404-00727-9*) AMS Pr.

Shakspere's Passionate Pilgrim. August Hoehnen. LC 77-169473. reprint ed. 20.00 (*0-404-03308-3*) AMS Pr.

Shakti: Hidden Treasure of Power. Dhyanyogi M. Shri. (Illus.). 94p. 1979. pap. 9.00 (*1-883879-01-9*) Dhyanyoga Ctr.

Shakti: Power in the Conceptual Structure of Karimpur Religion. Susan S. Wadley. LC 76-37612. (Studies in Anthropology, Series in Social, Cultural, & Linguistic Anthropology: No. 2). 222p. 1975. pap. 6.00 (*0-916256-01-4*) U Chi Dept Anthro.

Shakti Woman: Feeling Our Fire, Healing Our World. Vicki Noble. LC 89-45959. 279p. 1991. pap. 16.00 (*0-06-250667-6*) Harper SF.

Shaktis Tantra: In Search of Soul - Journey on the Path of Bliss. Barbara Janson. (Illus.). 270p. (Orig.). 1995. pap. 14.95 (*1-57502-045-9*) Morris Pubng.

Shakubuku: A Study of the Nichiren Shoshu Buddhist Movement in America, 1960-1975. David A. Snow. LC 92-39646. (Cults & Nonconventional Religious Groups Ser.). 360p. 1993. text ed. 25.00 (*0-8153-1137-0*) Garland.

Shaky Game: Einstein, Realism & the Quantum Theory. 2nd ed. Arthur Fine. xii, 186p. 1996. pap. text ed. 17.95 (*0-226-24949-2*); lib. bdg. 45.00 (*0-226-24948-4*) U Ch Pr.

***Shaky Ground.** Brewer. 1997. 22.95 (*0-312-15652-9*) St Martin.

Shaky Palaces: Home Owernship & Social Mobility in Boston, 1870-1970. Matthew Edel et al. 440p. 1984. text ed. 70.00 (*0-231-05626-5*, King's Crown Paperbacks); pap. text ed. 24.50 (*0-231-05627-3*, King's Crown Paperbacks) Col U Pr.

Shaky Pianist. G. Curtsinger. 1989. pap. 6.00 (*0-941179-34-6*) Latitudes Pr.

Shaky Tale of Dr. Jakey. I. E. Clark. (Illus.). 40p. 1984. pap. 3.50 (*0-88680-228-8*) I E Clark.

Shaky Tale of Dr. Jakey: Director's Production Script. I. E. Clark. (Illus.). 40p. 1984. 10.00 (*0-88680-229-6*) I E Clark.

Shakyamuni Buddha: A Narrative Biography. rev. ed. Nikkyo Niwano. Tr. by Kojiro Miyasaka from JPN. LC 80-154779. Orig. Title: Bukkyo No Inochi Hokekyo. (Illus.). 128p. 1980. pap. 4.95 (*4-333-01001-2*, Pub. by Kosei Pub Co JA) C E Tuttle.

Shal Forest. Gunomoy Manna. (C). 1990. text ed. 18.00 (*81-7017-268-3*, Pub. by Abhinav II) S Asia.

Shalako. Louis L'Amour. 169p. (Orig.). 1985. reprint ed. mass mkt., pap. 3.99 (*0-553-24858-8*) Bantam.

Shalam: Utopia on the Rio Grande. Lee Priestley. (Southwestern Studies: No. 84). (Orig.). 1988. reprint ed. pap. 10.00 (*0-87404-167-8*) Tex Western.

***Shale.** Vona Groarke. 60p. 1994. pap. 12.95 (*1-85235-131-4*) Dufour.

Shale Barrel Politics: Energy & Legislative Leadership. Eric M. Uslaner. LC 88-31973. (Studies in the New Political History: Vol. 2). 264p. 1989. 39.50 (*0-8047-1703-6*) Stanford U Pr.

Shale Oil, Tar Sands, & Related Fuel Sources: A Symposium Co-Sponsored by the Division of Fuel Chemistry & the Division of Petroleum Chemistry of the American Chemical Society. Ed. by Teh Fu Yen. LC 76-16510. (Advances in Chemistry Ser.: No. 151). (Illus.). 191p. reprint ed. pap. 54.50 (*0-317-10922-7*, 2051257) Bks Demand.

Shale Oil Technology: Status of the Industry. David Eaton. (Working Paper Ser.: No. 7). 39p. 1977. pap. 2.50 (*0-89940-552-5*) LBJ Sch Pub Aff.

Shalinar's Song. Daniel J. Porter. LC 95-46808. (Illus.). 32p. (J). (gr. 2-5). 1996. pap. 6.95 (*0-8091-6631-3*, 6631-3) Paulist Pr.

Shall I See You Again? An Anthology of Love & the British. Ed. by Juliet Stevenson & Philip Franks. (Illus.). 112p. 1994. 29.95 (*1-85793-099-1*, Pub. by Pavilion UK) Trafalgar.

Shall I Study Pharmacy? 7th ed. AACP Staff. 32p. 1980. pap. 0.75 (*0-937526-08-8*) AACP Alexandria.

Shall It Be Again. John K. Turner. 1972. 35.00 (*0-8490-1047-0*) Gordon Pr.

Shall Never Perish: Eternal Security Examined. John F. Strombeck. LC 90-20699. 208p. 1991. reprint ed. pap. 9.99 (*0-8254-3779-2*) Kregel.

Shall Suffer Death. A. J. Bannister. LC 95-81160. (Illus.). 200p. (Orig.). 1996. pap. 15.00 (*1-879418-93-2*) Audenreed Pr.

Shall This Nation Long Endure? Taming the Capitalist Beast. Ross Curtis & Farren Webb. LC 92-12410. 224p. (Orig.). 1992. pap. 10.95 (*1-56474-027-7*) Fithian Pr.

Shall We? Stephen Lang & Adelaide Teninga. (Friendship Ser.). (Illus.). 48p. (Orig.). 1993. reprint ed. pap. write for info. (*1-882536-10-X*, A100-0034) Bible League.

Shall We Amend the Fifth Amendment? Lewis Mayers. LC 78-6206. 341p. 1978. reprint ed. text ed. 65.00 (*0-313-20394-6*, MASH, Greenwood Pr) Greenwood.

Shall We Commit Suicide? Winston S. Churchill. (Churchill Ser.: No. 3). 20p. 1994. pap. 10.00 (*0-614-04946-6*) Intl Churchill Soc.

Shall We Dance? Brian H. Edwards. 1991. pap. 4.99 (*0-85234-190-3*, Pub. by Evangelical Pr) Presby & Reformed.

Shall We Dance? Eight Classic Ballroom Dances in Eight Quick Lessons. Manine R. Golden. LC 96-20585. (Illus.). 64p. 1997. pap. 7.95 (*0-7868-8212-3*) Hyperion.

Shall We Dance? The Life of Ginger Rogers. Sheridan Morley. 96p. 1995. 19.95 (*0-312-14149-1*) St Martin.

Shall We Eat Bread? Is Wheat a Healthful Food? Raymond W. Bernard & Enrenfried E. Pfeiffer. 29p. 1994. reprint ed. spiral bd. 5.00 (*0-7873-1057-3*) Hlth Research.

Shall We Know One Another in Heaven? & Other Sermons. Guy N. Woods. 269p. pap. 10.99 (*0-89225-330-4*) Gospel Advocate.

Shall We Know One Another in Heaven? & Other Sermons. 1,988th deluxe ed. Guy N. Woods. 269p. 19.99 (*0-89225-343-6*) Gospel Advocate.

Shall We Send Flowers? large type ed. Philip Lauben. (Mystery Library). 288p. 1995. pap. 15.99 (*0-7089-7654-9*, Linford) Ulverscroft.

Shall We Tell the President? Jeffrey Archer. 288p. 1987. mass mkt. 5.50 (*0-671-63305-8*) PB.

Shallow Crack Fracture Mechanics Toughness Tests & Applications: First International Conference. (Illus.). 304p. 1992. pap. 285.00 (*1-85573-122-3*, Pub. by Woodhead Pubng UK) Am Educ Systs.

Shallow Deformation Along the Crittenden County Fault Zone Near the Southeastern Margin of the Reelfoot Rift, Northeastern Arkansas. Eugene A. Luzietti et al. (Investigations of the New Madrid Seismic Zone & Professional Paper Ser.). 1996. write for info. (*0-615-00333-8*) US Geol Survey.

Shallow-Draft Vessel Owners, Operators & Managers Vol. 2: U. S. A. Companies Only. Compiled by James L. Pelletier. 170p. 1997. 65.00 (*0-9644915-3-2*) Marine Techn.

***Shallow-Draft Vessel Owners, Operators & Managers Vol. 8: Foreign Companies Only.** Compiled by James L. Pelletier. 35p. 1997. 45.00 (*0-9644915-9-1*) Marine Techn.

Shallow End & The Lost Colony. Wendy Macleod. 1992. pap. 5.25 (*0-8222-1346-X*) Dramatists Play.

***Shallow Grave: A Memoir of the Spanish Civil War.** Walter Gregory. 188p. (Orig.). 1996. pap. 14.99 (*0-907123-61-9*, Pub. by Five Leaves UK) AK Pr Dist.

***Shallow Grave at Trinity.** Farrell. LC 97-14780. 1997. 23.95 (*0-312-17009-2*) St Martin.

Shallow Graves. William Jefferies. (Location Scout Mystery Ser.). 272p. (Orig.). 1992. mass mkt. 4.50 (*0-380-76669-8*) Avon.

Shallow Graves. Jeremiah Healy. 288p. 1993. reprint ed. mass mkt. 5.99 (*0-671-70812-0*) PB.

***Shallow Lake Site: Its Place in Regional Prehistory.** Frank F. Schambach. (Illus.). 231p. 1981. pap. 10.00 (*1-56349-036-6*, RS2) AR Archaeol.

Shallow Lakes: Contributions to Their Limnology. Ed. by M. Dokulil et al. (Developments in Hydrobiology Ser.: No. 3). 218p. 1981. lib. bdg. 59.50 (*0-686-28842-4*) Kluwer Ac.

***Shallow-Level Centers in Semiconductors.** 500p. 1997. 89.00 (*981-02-2928-3*) World Scientific Pub.

Shallow-Level Plutonic Complexes in the Eastern Sierra Nevada, California & Their Tectonic Implications. Richard A. Schweickert. LC 76-11570. (Geological Society of America, Special Paper Ser.: No. 176). 64p. reprint ed. pap. 25.00 (*0-317-29102-5*, 2023742) Bks Demand.

Shallow Man. Coerte V. Felske. 243p. 1995. 21.00 (*0-517-70035-2*, Crown) Crown Pub Group.

Shallow Pool of Time: One Woman Grapples with the AIDS Epidemic. Fran Peavey. (Orig.). 1988. pap. 10.00 (*0-317-93395-7*) Crabgrass Pubs.

Shallow Refraction Seismics. Bengt Sjogren. 256p. (gr. 13). 1984. text ed. 123.95 (*0-412-24210-9*, NO. 9171) Chapman & Hall.

Shallow Sea. Neil Ruzic. 544p. 1992. 19.95 (*0-9632357-0-2*) St Clair Pr.

Shallow-Seismic Evidence for Playa Basin Development by Dissolution-Induced Subsidence on the Southern High Plains, Texas. J. G. Paine. (Reports of Investigations: No. 233). (Illus.). 47p. (Orig.). 1995. pap. 7.00 (*0-614-11611-2*) Bur Econ Geology.

Shallow Subduction Zones: Seismicity, Mechanics & Seismic Potential, Pt. 1. Ed. by R. Dmowska & G. Eckstrom. (PAGEOPH Reprint from Pure & Applied Geophysics Ser.: Vol. 140, No. 2). 220p. 1993. 27.50 (*0-8176-2962-9*) Birkhauser.

Shallow Subduction Zones: Seismicity, Mechanics & Seismic Potential, Part II. R. Dmowska & G. Eckstrom. 240p. 1994. 27.50 (*0-8176-2963-7*) Spr-Verlag.

Shallow Tethys Two: Proceedings of the International Symposium on Shallow Tethys 2, Wagga Wagga, 15-17 September 1986. Ed. by K. G. McKenzie. (Illus.). 587p. (C). 1987. text ed. 130.00 (*90-6191-647-X*, Pub. by A A Balkema NE) Ashgate Pub Co.

Shallow-Water Asteroidea & Ophiuroidea of Hawaii. C. A. Ely. (BMB Ser.). 1974. reprint ed. 25.00 (*0-527-02284-5*) Periodicals Srv.

Shallow Water Bass. Larry Larsen. LC 85-82041. (Illus.). 160p. (Orig.). 1986. pap. 9.95 (*0-936513-00-4*) Larsens Outdoor.

Shallow-Water Dictionary: Grounding in Estuary English. John R. Stilgoe. LC 94-22373. (Illus.). 48p. (Orig.). 1994. pap. 9.95 (*1-56898-029-9*) Princeton Arch.

***Shallow Water Hydrodynamics.** W. Y. Tan. (Oceanography Ser.: Vol. 55). 434p. 1992. 194.00 (*0-444-98751-7*) Elsevier.

Shallow-Water Pycnogonida from the Izu Peninsula, Japan. Koichiro Nakamura & C. Allan Child. LC 83-10183. (Smithsonian Contributions to Zoology Ser.: No. 386). 76p. reprint ed. pap. 25.00 (*0-317-29735-X*, 2022202) Bks Demand.

Shallow Water Wave Equations: Formulation, Analysis & Application. I. Kinnmark. (Lecture Notes in Engineering Ser.: Vol. 15). 187p. 1985. 34.95 (*0-387-16031-0*) Spr-Verlag.

***Shallow Waters, Rising Tide: Shipping & Trade in Java Around 1775.** Gerrit J. Knaap. (Verhandelingen Ser.: No. 172). (Illus.). 265p. (Orig.). 1996. pap. 37.00 (*90-6718-102-1*, Pub. by KITLV Pr NE) Cellar.

Shallows. Tim Winton. LC 93-8867. 256p. 1993. reprint ed. pap. 12.50 (*1-55597-193-8*) Graywolf.

***Shaloh, 2 vols.** Incl. Vol. 1. . 192p. (J). (gr. 3 up). 1945. 5.00 (*0-8266-0303-3*, Merkos LInyonei Chinuch); Vol. 2. . 190p. (J). (gr. 3 up). 1945. 5.00 (*0-8266-0304-1*, Merkos LInyonei Chinuch); write for info. (*0-614-20973-0*) Kehot Pubn Soc.

Shalom. Warren M. Marcus. LC 93-2551. 1993. pap. 9.99 (*0-8407-6790-0*) Nelson.

Shalom: Essays in Honor of Dr. Charles H. Shaw. Ed. by Eugene J. Mayhew. 231p. 1983. pap. 11.95 (*0-912407-01-8*) William Tyndale Col Pr.

Shalom: Hope for the World. Steve Clapp. 178p. (Orig.). 1982. pap. 8.00 (*0-914527-35-5*) C-Four Res.

Shalom: The Bible's Word for Salvation, Justice & Peace. Perry B. Yoder. LC 86-82879. 161p. 1987. pap. 14.95 (*0-87303-120-2*) Faith & Life.

Shalom Aleichem. Noah Golinkin. 77p. 1978. pap. 7.95 (*0-88482-696-1*) Hebrew Pub.

Shalom at Last. Peter J. Dyck. LC 92-11199. (Illus.). 128p. (Orig.). (J). 1992. pap. 5.99 (*0-8361-3615-2*) Herald Pr.

Shalom, Friend: The Life & Legacy of Yitzhak Rabin. Jerusalem Report Staff. Ed. by David Horovitz. (Illus.). 314p. 1996. 24.95 (*1-55704-287-X*) Newmarket.

Shalom, Haver - Goodbye, Friend: Goodbye, Friend. Barbara Sofer. Tr. by Shulamith Basok. LC 96-7065. (Illus.). 48p. (ENG & HEB.). (J). (gr. 3-5). 1996. 16.95 (*0-929371-97-6*) Kar-Ben.

***Shalom, Japan.** Shifra Horn. 320p. 1997. pap. 12.00 (*1-57566-223-X*, Knsington) Kensgtn Pub Corp.

Shalom, Japan: A Sabra's Five Years in the Land of the Rising Sun. Shifra Horn. 320p. 1996. 22.00 (*1-57566-111-X*, Knsington) Kensgtn Pub Corp.

***Shalom on the Range: A Roundup of Recipes & Jewish Traditions from Colorado Kitchens.** (Illus.). 312p. 1997. spiral bd. 21.95 (*0-9656849-0-3*) Frnds Shalom Pk.

Shalom, Salaam, Peace... The Long & Winding Road to Peace in the Middle East. Willem-Jan Van der Wolf & Marianne Van de Pas. 392p. 1994. pap. 140.00 (*90-5644-002-0*) Gaunt.

Shalom Seders: Three Passover Haggadahs. Pref. by Grace Paley. LC 83-25857. (Illus.). 104p. 1984. pap. 12.95 (*0-915361-03-5*, 09747-1) Hemed Bks.

Shalom Sesame Players Present: The Story of Passover. Louise Gikow. (Sharing Passover Ser.). (Illus.). 36p. (J). 1994. 12.95 (*1-884857-00-0*); 14.95 incl. audio (*1-884857-01-9*) Comet Intl.

Shalom Sesame Players Present: The Story of Passover. Illus. by Peter Panas. (Sharing Passover Ser.). 32p. (J). 1994. pap. 5.95 (*1-884857-02-7*) Comet Intl.

Shalom Sesame Presents a Chanukah Party for Kippi. Louise Gikow. (Illus.). 32p. (J). 1995. 12.95 (*1-884857-06-X*) Comet Intl.

Shalom Sesame's Sharing Passover Deluxe Family Kit. (Sharing Passover Ser.). 1994. 36.95 (*1-884857-05-1*) Comet Intl.

Shalom Sesame's Sharing Passover Family Kit. (Sharing Passover Ser.). 1994. 23.95 (*1-884857-04-3*) Comet Intl.

Shalom Zachar. Beverly Geller. 47p. (J). (ps-1). 8.95 (*0-935063-69-2*) CIS Comm.

Sham: Social Change Through Contrived Crises. Bernadine Haag. Ed. by Terri Haag. (Illus.). 418p. 1994. write for info. (*0-9635445-0-0*) Sahuarita Pr.

***Sham Flyers.** Edward Kissam. Date not set. 21.00 (*0-900977-09-4*, Pub. by Anvil Press UK); pap. 14.95 (*0-900977-11-6*, Pub. by Anvil Press UK) Dufour.

Shamail Tirmidhi. M. Hussain. 16.50 (*0-933511-53-1*) Kazi Pubns.

Shaman. Hugh Fox. 1993. pap. 10.95 (*1-882633-00-8*) Permeable.

Shaman. Noah Gordon. 576p. 1993. pap. 6.99 (*0-451-17701-0*, Sig) NAL-Dutton.

Shaman. Noah Gordon. 1993. pap. write for info. (*0-451-17929-3*, Sig) NAL-Dutton.

Shaman. Joan Halifax. LC 87-71938. (Art & Imagination Ser.). (Illus.). 96p. 1988. pap. 15.95 (*0-500-81029-X*) Thames Hudson.

Shaman. Piers Vitebsky. 1995. pap. 14.95 (*0-316-90304-3*) Little.

Shaman: His Symbols & His Healing Power. Spencer L. Rogers. (Illus.). 224p. 1982. pap. 23.95 (*0-398-06406-7*) C C Thomas.

Shaman: His Symbols & His Healing Power. Spencer L. Rogers. (Illus.). 224p. (C). 1982. 38.95 (*0-398-04594-1*) C C Thomas.

Shaman: Patterns of Religious Healing among the Ojibway Indians. John A. Grim. LC 83-47834. (Civilization of the American Indian Ser.: No. 165). (Illus.). 272p. 1988. pap. 14.95 (*0-8061-2106-8*) U of Okla Pr.

Shaman: The Paintings of Susan Seddon Boulet. Susan S. Boulet. LC 88-64077. (Illus.). 128p. (Orig.). 1989. pap. 26.95 (*0-87654-433-2*) Pomegranate Calif.

Shaman & the Medicine Wheel. Evelyn Eaton. LC 81-84490. (Illus.). 220p. (Orig.). 1982. pap. 10.95 (*0-8356-0561-2*, Quest) Theos Pub Hse.

Shaman Bulldog: A Love Story. Renaldo Fischer & Michele St. George. 104p. 1996. 12.00 (*0-446-52029-2*) Warner Bks.

S

An Asterisk (*) at the beginning of an entry indicates that the title is appearing in BIP for the first time.

Shaman from Elko. Meier et al. Ed. & Frwd. by Gareth Hill. 272p. (C). 1978. pap. 17.00 (*0-932630-00-6*) C G Jung Frisco.

Shaman from Elko: Festshrift to Joseph L. Henderson, M. D. Ed. by Ed Hill & Gareth Hill. 320p. 1991. reprint ed. 27.50 (*0-938434-80-2*); reprint ed. pap. 14.95 (*0-938434-79-9*) Sigo Pr.

Shaman Laughs. James D. Doss. LC 95-31795. 272p. 1995. 21.95 (*0-312-13601-3*) St Martin.

***Shaman Laughs.** James D. Doss. 1997. pap. text ed. 5.99 (*0-380-72690-4*) Avon.

Shaman of Tibet: Milarepa - From Anger to Enlightenment. rev. ed. Winged Wolf, pseud. Orig. Title: The Golden Dream. (Illus.). 95p. 1994. pap. 14.95 (*0-932927-10-6*) Higher Consciousness.

Shaman Sings. James D. Doss. 256p. 1995. mass mkt. 5.99 (*0-380-72496-0*) Avon.

Shaman Sings. James D. Doss. 272p. 1994. 20.95 (*0-312-10547-9*, Thomas Dunne Bks) St Martin.

Shaman Songs. Michael Holstein. LC 94-84987. 80p. 1996. pap. text ed. 6.95 (*0-943512-26-3*) Linwood Pub.

Shaman Sorceress. Dong-Ni Kim. 275p. 1988. text ed. 19.95 (*0-7103-0280-0*) Routledge Chapman & Hall.

Shamanic Astrology Handbook: The Archetypes & Symbols of the Signs & Planets & Their Role in Shamanic Astrology. 2nd ed. Daniel Giamario & Carolyn Brent. 168p. 1995. spiral bd. 22.00 (*0-614-09459-3*) JC Assocs.

Shamanic Drum: A Guide to Sacred Drumming. Michael Drake. LC 91-90824. 104p. 1991. pap. 9.95 (*0-9629002-0-6*) Talking Drum.

Shamanic Experience: A Practical Guide to Contemporary Shamanism. Kenneth Meadows. (Illus.). 256p. 1993. pap. 14.95 (*1-85230-226-7*) Element MA.

Shamanic Healing & Ritual Drama: Health & Medicine in Native North American Religious Traditions. Ake Hultkrantz. 192p. 1992. 19.95 (*0-8245-1188-3*) Crossroad NY.

***Shamanic Healing & Ritual Drama: Health & Medicine in the Native North American Religious Traditions.** Ake Hultkrantz. 216p. 1997. pap. 15.95 (*0-8245-1664-8*, Crossrd Herd) Crossroad NY.

Shamanic Healing Within the Medicine Wheel. Marie L. Lorler. LC 89-7393. 272p. 1989. pap. 15.95 (*0-914732-23-4*) Bro Life Inc.

Shamanic Journey of Living As Soul. Winged Wolf & Heather Hughes-Calero. (Illus.). 144p. (Orig.). 1994. pap. 10.00 (*0-932927-11-4*) Higher Consciousness.

Shamanic Odyssey: The Lushootseed Salish Journey to the Land of the Dead. Jay Miller. Ed. by Sylvia B. Vane. LC 88-16761. (Anthropological Papers: No. 32). (Illus.). 217p. 1988. pap. 28.95 (*0-87919-112-0*) Ballena Pr.

***Shamanic Songs & Myths of Tuva.** Ed. by Mongush B. Kennin-Lopsan. 180p. 1996. 42.00 (*963-05-7401-2*, Pub. by A K HU) Intl Spec Bk.

Shamanic Voices: A Survey of Visionary Narratives. Joan Halifax. 188p. (C). 1991. pap. 13.95 (*0-14-019348-0*, Arkana) Viking Penguin.

Shamanica. Martine Ashe. (Illus.). (Orig.). 1996. pap. 19.95 (*1-898307-76-8*, Pub. by Capall Bann Pubng UK) Holmes Pub.

Shamanism. Nevill Drury. 1996. pap. 14.95 (*1-85230-794-3*) Element MA.

Shamanism. Compiled by Shirley Nicholson. LC 86-40405. 402p. (Orig.). 1987. pap. 11.95 (*0-8356-0617-1*, Quest) Theos Pub Hse.

***Shamanism: A Beginner's Guide.** Richard Craze. (Beginner's Ser.). (Illus.). 96p. 1997. pap. 11.95 (*0-340-68010-5*, Pub. by Headway UK) Trafalgar.

Shamanism: Archaic Techniques of Ecstasy. Mircea Eliade. 640p. 1989. pap. 10.95 (*0-14-019155-0*, Penguin Bks) Viking Penguin.

Shamanism: Archaic Techniques of Ectasy. Mircea Eliade. Tr. by W. R. Trask. (Bollingen Ser.: Vol. 76). 630p. 1972. pap. text ed. 17.95 (*0-691-01779-4*) Princeton U Pr.

Shamanism: Soviet Studies of Traditional Religion in Siberia & Central Asia. Ed. by Marjorie M. Balzer. LC 89-77158. 216p. (C). (gr. 13). 1990. 67.95 (*0-87332-624-5*) M E Sharpe.

***Shamanism: The Spirit World of Korea.** Ed. by Richard W. Guisso & Chai-shin Yu. LC 87-71271. (Studies in Korean Religions & Culture: No. 1). 190p. pap. 54.20 (*0-608-04959-X*, 2065538) Bks Demand.

Shamanism & Northern Ecology. Ed. by Juha Pentikaeinen. LC 95-46624. (Religion & Society Ser.: Vol. 36). ix, 386p. (C). 1996. lib. bdg. 131.85 (*3-11-014186-8*) Mouton.

Shamanism & Personal Mastery: Using Symbols, Rituals, & Talismans to Activate the Powers Within You. Gini G. Scott. 288p. (Orig.). 1992. pap. 12.95 (*1-55778-381-0*) Paragon Hse.

Shamanism & the Drug Propaganda: The Demonization of the Ecstatic. Dan Russell. 272p. (C). 1995. pap. 29.95 (*0-9650253-0-6*) Dan Russell.

Shamanism & the Eighteenth Century. Gloria Flaherty. (Illus.). 321p. 1992. text ed. 45.00 (*0-691-06923-9*) Princeton U Pr.

***Shamanism & the Eighteenth Century.** Gloria Flaherty. LC 91-21073. (Illus.). 335p. 1992. reprint ed. pap. 95.50 (*0-608-02533-X*, 2063177) Bks Demand.

Shamanism & the Esoteric Tradition. Angelique S. Cook & G. A. Hawk. LC 92-5607. (New Worlds Spirituality Ser.). (Illus.). 240p. 1992. pap. 12.95 (*0-87542-325-6*) Llewellyn Pubns.

Shamanism & the Mystery Lines: Ley Lines, Spirit Paths, Shape-Shifting & Out-of-Body Travel. Paul Devereux. LC 92-35728. (Illus.). 240p. 1993. pap. 12.95 (*0-87542-189-X*) Llewellyn Pubns.

Shamanism As a Spiritual Practice for Daily Life. Tom Cowan. 260p. (Orig.). 1996. pap. 16.95 (*0-89594-838-9*) Crossing Pr.

Shamanism, Colonialism, & the Wild Man: A Study in Terror & Healing. Michael Taussig. LC 86-11410. (Illus.). xx, 538p. (C). 1987. 35.95 (*0-226-79012-6*) U Ch Pr.

Shamanism, Colonialism, & the Wild Man: A Study in Terror & Healing. Michael Taussig. (Illus.). 538p. 1991. pap. text ed. 19.95 (*0-226-79013-4*) U Ch Pr.

Shamanism for Everyone: A Guide to Discovering the Shaman in You. Gini G. Scott. Ed. by Skye Alexander & Camilla Ayers. LC 88-63396. 213p. (Orig.). 1988. pap. 14.95 (*0-914918-86-9*, Whitford Pr) Schiffer.

Shamanism for the New Age: A Guide to Radionics & Radiesthesia. Jane E. Hartman. LC 86-83375. (Illus.). 157p. (Orig.). 1987. pap. 15.95 (*0-9618045-0-5*) Aquarian Sys.

Shamanism, History, & the State. Ed. by Nicholas Thomas & Caroline Humphrey. (C). 1996. pap. 18.95 (*0-472-08401-1*) U of Mich Pr.

Shamanist Folk Paintings: Korea's Eternal Spirits. Alan C. Covell. LC 83-82586. (Illus.). 120p. 1984. 22.50 (*0-930878-39-6*) Hollym Intl.

Shamans: Opposing Viewpoints. Wendy Stein. LC 91-14498. (Great Mysteries Ser.). (Illus.). 112p. (J). (gr. 5-8). 1991. lib. bdg. 17.96 (*0-89908-088-X*) Greenhaven.

Shamans & Cultures. Ed. by Mihaly Hoppal et al. 324p. 1994. 38.00 (*963-05-6590-0*, Pub. by A K HU) Intl Spec Bk.

Shamans & Elders: Experience, Knowledge, & Power among the Daur Mongols. Caroline Humphrey & Urgunge Onon. (Oxford Studies in Social & Cultural Anthropology). (Illus.). 416p. 1996. pap. 24.95 (*0-19-828068-8*) OUP.

Shamans & Elders: Experience, Knowledge, & Power among the Daur Mongols. Caroline Humphrey & Urgunge Onon. (Oxford Studies in Social & Cultural Anthropology). (Illus.). 416p. 1996. text ed. 80.00 (*0-19-827941-8*) OUP.

Shamans & Kushtakas: North Coast Tales of the Supernatural. Mary G. Beck. LC 90-1295. (Illus.). 128p. (Orig.). 1991. pap. 12.95 (*0-88240-406-7*) Alaska Northwest.

***Shaman's Apprentice.** Mark J. Plotkin & Lynne Cherry. LC 97-5978. (YA). 1998. write for info. (*0-15-201281-8*) HarBrace.

Shaman's Body: A New Shamanism for Transforming Health, Relationships, & the Community. Arnold Mindell. LC 92-56408. 176p. 1993. pap. 12.00 (*0-06-250655-2*) Harper SF.

***Shaman's Bones.** LC 96-52148. 1997. write for info. (*0-380-97424-X*) Avon.

Shaman's Circle: Poems. Nancy Wood. (Illus.). 80p. (J). 1996. 22.50 (*0-385-32222-4*) Doubleday.

Shaman's Doorway: Opening Imagination to Power & Myth. Stephen Larsen. (Illus.). 260p. (Orig.). 1988. reprint ed. pap. 10.95 (*0-88268-072-2*) Station Hill Pr.

Shamans, Housewives & Other Restless Spirits: Women in Korean Ritual Life. Laurel Kendall. LC 84-24138. (Illus.). 248p. 1987. pap. text ed. 15.00 (*0-8248-1142-9*) UH Pr.

Shaman's Knife. Scott Young. 288p. 1994. pap. 5.95 (*0-14-014353-X*, Penguin Bks) Viking Penguin.

Shamans, Mystics & Doctors: A Psychological Inquiry into India & Its Healing Traditions. Sudhir Kakar. LC 90-20821. x, 320p. 1990. pap. text ed. 15.95 (*0-226-42279-8*) U Ch Pr.

Shamans of the Twentieth Century. Ruth-Inge Heinze. LC 90-44703. (Shamanism Ser.). (Illus.). 325p. 1990. 29.95 (*0-8290-2456-5*); pap. 14.95 (*0-8290-2459-X*) Irvington.

Shamans, Priests & Witches: A Cross-Cultural Study of Magico-Religious Practitioners. Michael J. Winkelman. (Anthropological Research Papers: No. 44). (Illus.). viii, 191p. 1992. pap. 27.50 (*0-936249-10-2*) AZ Univ ARP.

Shamans, Prophets, & Sages: An Introduction to World Religions. Denise L. Carmody & John T. Carmody. 320p. (C). 1985. pap. 27.95 (*0-534-04263-5*) Wadsworth Pub.

***Shaman's Secret: The Lost Resurrection Teachings of the Ancient Maya.** Douglas Gilette. LC 96-44808. 1997. 24.95 (*0-553-10154-4*) Bantam.

Shamans, Software, & Spleens: Law & the Construction of the Information Society. James Boyle. LC 95-42433. 288p. 1996. 35.00 (*0-674-80522-4*) HUP.

***Shamans, Software & Spleens: Law & the Construction of the Information Society.** James Boyle. 1997. pap. text ed. 15.95 (*0-674-80523-2*) HUP.

Shaman's Story: The West Va. Petroglyphs. Dean Braley. (Orig.). 1993. pap. 15.00 (*0-9638377-0-2*) D Braley.

Shambala Warriors: Non-Violent Fighters for Peace. Teddy Milne. LC 86-64054. (Illus.). 150p. (Orig.). (J). (gr. 4 up). 1987. pap. 7.95 (*0-938875-07-8*) Pittenbruach Pr.

Shambaugh's Surgery of Ear. 4th ed. Glasscock. (Illus.). 656p. 1990. text ed. 169.00 (*0-7216-2063-9*) Saunders.

Shambhala. Nicholas Roerich. 16.00 (*0-685-00147-4*); pap. 12.00 (*0-686-79666-7*) Agni Yoga Soc.

Shambhala: In Search of the New Era. Nicholas Roerich. 334p. 1990. pap. 10.95 (*0-89281-305-9*) Inner Tradit.

Shambhala: The Fascinating Truth Behind the Myth of Shangri-la. Victoria Lepage. LC 96-18045. 1996. pap. 16.00 (*0-8356-0750-X*, Quest) Theos Pub Hse.

Shambhala: The Sacred Path of the Warrior. Chogyam Trungpa. LC 83-20401. (Dragon Editions Ser.). 216p. 1988. pap. 13.00 (*0-87773-264-7*, Sham Dragon Edits) Shambhala Pubns.

Shambhala: The Sacred Path of the Warrior. Chogyam Trungpa. 1995. pap. 7.00 (*1-57062-128-4*) Shambhala Pubns.

Shambhala Dictionary of Buddhism & Zen. LC 91-52515. (Dragon Editions Ser.). (Illus.). 288p. 1991. pap. 20.00 (*0-87773-520-4*) Shambhala Pubns.

***Shambhala Encyclopedia of Yoga.** Georg Feuerstein. LC 96-42066. 304p. 1997. 30.00 (*1-57062-137-3*) Shambhala Pubns.

***Shambhala Guide to Kabbalah & Jewish Mysticism.** Perle Besserman. LC 97-19190. 1997. pap. 12.00 (*1-57062-215-9*) Shambhala Pubns.

***Shambhala Guide to Sufism.** Carl W. Ernst. LC 97-10189. 1997. pap. 15.00 (*1-57062-180-2*) Shambhala Pubns.

Shambhala Guide to Taoism. Eva Wong. LC 96-14960. (Illus.). 240p. (Orig.). 1997. pap. 14.00 (*1-57062-169-1*) Shambhala Pubns.

Shambhala Guide to Traditional Chinese Medicine. Daniel Reid. LC 95-23897. (Illus.). 224p. (Orig.). 1996. pap. 12.00 (*1-57062-141-1*) Shambhala Pubns.

Shambhala Guide to Yoga. Georg Feuerstein. LC 95-23896. (Illus.). 192p. (Orig.). 1996. pap. 12.00 (*1-57062-142-X*) Shambhala Pubns.

***Shame.** Salman Rushdie. LC 97-5633. 1997. pap. 12.00 (*0-8050-5310-7*) H Holt & Co.

***Shame.** Russell. 1998. 22.00 (*0-684-81527-3*) S&S Trade.

Shame: A Faith Perspective. Robert H. Albers. LC 94-29610. 159p. 1995. lib. bdg. 29.95 (*1-56024-935-8*) Haworth Pr.

Shame: A Faith Perspective. Robert H. Albers. 1995. pap. text ed. 12.95 (*1-56024-957-9*) Harrington Pk.

***Shame: A Novel.** Taslima Nasrin. 1997. 25.95 (*1-57392-165-3*) Prometheus Bks.

Shame! An Other Guide for the Perplexed. John W. McGinley. LC 93-18431. 310p. (Orig.). (C). 1993. pap. text ed. 27.50 (*0-8191-9094-2*); lib. bdg. 49.50 (*0-8191-9093-4*) U Pr of Amer.

Shame: The Exposed Self. Michael Lewis. 276p. 1992. 29.95 (*0-02-918881-4*, Free Press) Free Pr.

Shame: The Exposed Self. Michael Lewis. 304p. 1995. pap. 14.95 (*0-684-82311-X*) Free Pr.

Shame: The Power of Caring. rev. ed. Gershen Kaufman. 261p. 1992. pap. 14.95 (*0-87047-053-1*) Schenkman Bks Inc.

Shame: The Power of Caring. 3rd rev. ed. Gershen Kaufman. 261p. 1992. 22.95 (*0-87047-052-3*) Schenkman Bks Inc.

Shame: The Underside of Narcissism. Andrew P. Morrison. 240p. 1989. text ed. 36.00 (*0-88163-082-9*) Analytic Pr.

Shame - Spiritual Suicide: We Have Faced the Shame & in Facing the Shame We Have Set Ourselves Free. Vicki Underland-Rosow. 144p. 1995. pap. 10.95 (*0-9644944-2-6*) Waterfrd Publ.

Shame about the Street. Diane Langford. 1995. pap. 11.99 (*1-85242-269-6*) Serpents Tail.

Shame about the Title: Poems That Mock the Accepted. Matt Fitzgerald. 96p. (Orig.). 1994. pap. 8.00 (*0-7881-0407-1*) DIANE Pub.

Shame & Glory of the Intellectuals: Babbitt Jr. vs. the Rediscovery of Values. Peter R. Viereck. LC 77-28970. 330p. 1978. reprint ed. text ed. 35.00 (*0-313-20281-8*, VISG, Greenwood Pr) Greenwood.

Shame & Guilt: Masters of Disguise. Jane Middelton-Moz. 1990. pap. 8.95 (*1-55874-072-4*) Health Comm.

Shame & Humiliation: Presidential Decision-Making on Vietnam. Blema S. Steinberg. LC 95-52140. (Policy & Institutional Studies). 321p. (C). 1996. pap. text ed. 17.95 (*0-8229-5598-9*) U of Pittsburgh Pr.

Shame & Its Sisters: A Silvan Tomkins Reader. Ed. by Eve K. Sedgwick & Adam Frank. LC 95-16776. (Illus.). 280p. 1995. text ed. 49.95 (*0-8223-1682-X*); pap. text ed. 15.95 (*0-8223-1694-3*) Duke.

Shame & Necessity. Bernard Williams. LC 92-2212. (Sather Classical Lectures: No. 57). (C). 1993. 25.00 (*0-520-08046-7*) U CA Pr.

Shame & Necessity. Bernard Williams. (Sather Classical Lectures: No. 57). 1994. pap. 15.00 (*0-520-08830-1*) U CA Pr.

Shame & Pride: Affect, Sex, & the Birth of the Self. Donald L. Nathanson. (Illus.). 480p. 1992. 24.95 (*0-393-03097-0*) Norton.

Shame & Pride: Affect, Sex & the Birth of the Self. Donald L. Nathanson. 496p. 1994. pap. 15.95 (*0-393-31109-0*) Norton.

Shame & the Corporation. Ed. by Hugh Cortler. 200p. 1986. 65.00 (*0-930586-31-X*) Haven Pubns.

Shame & the Origins of Self-Esteem: A Jungian Approach. Marion Jacoby & Douglas Witcher. LC 93-15067. 220p. (C). 1993. 49.95 (*0-415-07526-2*, B2570) Routledge.

***Shame & the Origins of Self-Esteem: Jungian Approach.** Jacoby. 144p. (C). 1996. pap. 16.95 (*0-415-10580-3*) Routledge.

Shame & the Self. Francis J. Broucek. LC 91-6797. 168p. 1991. lib. bdg. 30.00 (*0-89862-444-4*) Guilford Pr.

Shame Borne in Silence: Spouse Abuse in the Jewish Community. Abraham J. Twerski. 146p. 1996. pap. 16.95 (*0-9648508-1-8*) Mirkov Pubns.

Shame Experience. Susan Miller. 208p. 1993. reprint ed. pap. text ed. 24.95 (*0-88163-165-5*) Analytic Pr.

Shame Faced: The Road to Recovery. Kojiro Miyasaka. 28p. (Orig.). 1986. pap. 3.00 (*0-89486-358-4*, 5452B) Hazelden.

Shame-Free Parenting. Sandra D. Wilson. LC 92-1656. 180p. (Orig.). 1992. pap. 9.99 (*0-8308-1625-9*, 1625) InterVarsity.

Shame, Guilt & Alcoholism: Treatment Issues in Clinical Practice. Ronald T. Potter-Efron. LC 88-32058. (Addictions Treatment Ser.: Vol. 2). 287p. 1988. pap. text ed. 17.95 (*0-86656-856-5*) Harrington Pk.

Shame, Guilt & Alcoholism: Treatment Issues in Clinical Practice. Ronald T. Potter-Efron. LC 87-29724. (Addiction Treatment Ser.: Vol. 2). 287p. 1989. text ed. 49.95 (*0-86656-855-7*) Haworth Pr.

Shame in Context. Susan S. Miller. LC 96-28331. 248p. 1996. 37.50 (*0-88163-209-0*) Analytic Pr.

Shame in the House of Saud: Contempt for Human Rights in the Kingdom of Saudi Arabia. Minnesota Lawyers International Human Rights Committee Staff. 170p. (Orig.). 1992. pap. 15.00 (*0-929293-12-6*) MN Advocates.

Shame of a Nation. Philip Stern & George De Vincent. (Illus.). 1965. 14.95 (*0-8392-1162-7*) Astor-Honor.

Shame of Man. Piers Anthony. 512p. 1995. mass mkt. 6.99 (*0-8125-5091-9*) Tor Bks.

Shame of Savo: Anatomy of a Naval Disaster. Chris Coultard-Clark. LC 94-66596. (Illus.). 346p. 1994. 35.00 (*1-55750-763-5*) Naval Inst Pr.

***Shame of Savo: Anatomy of a Naval Disaster.** Bruce Loxton & Chris Coultard-Clark. (Bluejacket Bks.). (Illus.). 346p. 1997. pap. 19.95 (*1-55750-838-0*) Naval Inst Pr.

Shame of the Cities. rev. ed. Lincoln Steffens. LC 92-11116. (American Century Ser.). 216p. 1993. 9.00 (*0-374-52373-8*) Hill & Wang.

Shame of the States. Albert Deutsch. LC 73-2394. (Mental Illness & Social Policy; the American Experience Ser.). 1980. reprint ed. 19.95 (*0-405-05202-2*) Ayer.

Shame on You! Sara H. Martin. LC 89-17425. 192p. 1990. 13.99 (*0-8054-6010-1*, 4260-10) Broadman.

***Shame or Shameless?** Pete Doudomis. LC 96-90863. (Orig.). 1997. pap. 8.95 (*0-533-12198-1*) Vantage.

Shame the Devil. Michael Grace. (C). 1988. 39.00 (*0-85439-124-X*, Pub. by St Paul Pubns UK) St Mut.

Shame, Thief of Intimacy: Unmasking the Accuser. Marie Powers. Ed. by Karen Anderson. 200p. (Orig.). 1996. pap. 4.95 (*0-614-17634-4*, 521026) Aglow Communs.

Shameful Admissions: The Losing Battle to Serve Everyone in Our Universities. Angela Browne-Miller. LC 95-32120. (Jossey-Bass Higher & Adult Education Ser.). 304p. 1996. 28.00 (*0-7879-0182-2*) Jossey-Bass.

Shamela see Joseph Andrews

Shameless. F. Rosanne Bittner. 512p. 1993. mass mkt. 5.99 (*0-8217-4056-3*, Zebra Kensgtn) Kensgtn Pub Corp.

***Shameless.** Jennifer Blake. 1997. mass mkt. 5.99 (*0-449-15002-X*, GM) Fawcett.

Shameless. Judy Collins. 1996. pap. 6.50 (*0-671-89234-7*) S&S Trade.

Shameless. Suzanne Forster. 352p. (Orig.). 1994. mass mkt. 5.99 (*0-425-14095-4*) Berkley Pub.

Shameless. Sandy Steen. (Crystal Creek Ser.). 1994. mass mkt. 3.99 (*0-373-82529-3*, 1-82529-8) Harlequin Bks.

Shameless. large type ed. Jennifer Blake. LC 94-27172. 511p. 1994. lib. bdg. 22.95 (*0-7862-0269-6*) Thorndike Pr.

Shameless: A Novel. Judy Collins. 320p. 1995. 23.00 (*0-671-89233-9*, PB Hardcover) PB.

Shameless Nude: A Historic Look at Nudism in the Sixties. Ed. by Ed Lange. LC 91-11562. (Illus.). 140p. 1991. 29.95 (*1-55599-037-1*) Elysium.

Shameless Old Lady. Helen Duberstein. 14.95 (*0-939520-00-1*) Ghost Dance.

Shamesless Old Lady. Helen Duberstein. 14.95 (*0-615-00527-6*) Ghost Dance.

***Shamir, the White Elephant: A Rain Forest Adventure.** Beverly F. Croskery. LC 97-93252. (Illus.). 128p. (J). (gr. 3-6). 1997. 14.95 (*0-9657619-4-0*) Bell-Forsythe.

Shammas. Stewart Weiss. 221p. 1992. 14.95 (*0-944070-75-2*) Targum Pr.

Shamor V'Zachor et Yom Hashabbat L'Kadsho see Mitzvah of the Month

Shamp of the City-Solo. Jaimy Gordon. LC 79-2479. 176p. 1993. pap. 12.00 (*0-929701-34-8*) McPherson & Co.

Shampoo King: F. W. Fitch & His Company. Denny Rehder & Lucius W. Fitch. (Illus.). 160p. 1982. pap. 12.95 (*0-942240-05-7*) D Rehder.

Shampoo Planet. Douglas Coupland. Ed. by Judith Regan. 304p. 1997. reprint ed. pap. 14.00 (*0-671-75506-4*) PB.

***Shamrock.** Courage Books Staff. 1997. 6.98 (*0-7624-0225-3*) Courage Bks.

Shamrock & Sword: Saint Patrick's Battalion in the U. S.-Mexican War. Robert R. Miller. LC 89-5252. (Illus.). 248p. 1989. 29.95 (*0-8061-2204-8*) U of Okla Pr.

***Shamrock & Sword: The Saint Patrick's Battalion in the U. S. - Mexican War.** Robert R. Miller. LC 89-5252. (Illus.). 248p. 1997. pap. 14.95 (*0-8061-2964-6*) U of Okla Pr.

Shamrock & the Swastika: German Espionage in Ireland in World War II. Carolle J. Carter. LC 76-14103. (Illus.). 1977. 19.95 (*0-87015-221-1*) Pacific Bks.

***Shamrock Green.** Jean B. Bradley. 1997. mass mkt. 5.99 (*1-55197-382-0*, Pub. by Comnwlth Pub CN) Partners Pubs Grp.

***Shamrock Road: A Musical.** Rae N. Simmonds. (Orig.). (J). 1998. pap. 5.50 (*0-614-30680-9*) Anchorage.

Shamrock Specialties: Trinity High School Family Cookbook. Trinity High School Cookbook Committee. 256p. 1988. pap. 10.00 (*0-318-37121-9*) Trinity HS Cookbook.

Shamrock Trinity: Rafe, the Maverick. large type ed. Kay Hooper. LC 92-28647. (Nightingale Ser.). 256p. (Orig.). 1993. pap. 14.95 (*0-8161-5627-1*, GK Hall) Thorndike Pr.

***Shamrock Way.** unabridged ed. Mervyn Kaufman. (Illus.). 288p. 1996. 29.95 (*0-910152-16-0*) AZ Hist Foun.

Shamrocks & Sea Silver, & Other Illuminations. Leonard Wibberley. Ed. by Christopher Wibberley & Hazel Wibberley. LC 84-345. (I. O. Evans Studies in the Philosophy & Criticism of Literature: No. 8). 128p. (C). 1992. pap. 17.00 (*0-89370-402-4*, 10375577); lib. bdg. 27.00 (*0-89370-302-8*, 10375577) Borgo Pr.

Shamrocks & Shepherds: The Irish of Morrow County. 2nd ed. John F. Kilkenny. (Illus.). 164p. 1981. pap. 3.95 (*0-87595-099-X*) Oregon Hist.

S

An Asterisk (*) at the beginning of an entry indicates that the title is appearing in BIP for the first time.

Shamrocks, Harps, & Shillelaghs: The Story of the St. Patrick's Day Symbols. Edna Barth. LC 77-369. (Illus.). 96p. (J). (gr. 3-6). 1982. pap. 5.95 (*0-89919-038-3*, Clarion Bks) HM.

Shams or Uncle Ben's Experience with Hypocrites. John S. Draper. LC 71-166712. (Illus.). 1971. reprint ed. 29.00 (*0-403-01430-1*) Scholarly.

Shamu & His Friends. Ellen Weiss. (Shamu's Little Library). (Illus.). (J). (ps). 1994. 5.95 (*1-884506-00-3*) Third Story.

Shamu's Best Friend. Langley, William, Studios Staff. (Shamu & His Crew Adventure Ser.). (Illus.). 32p. (J). (gr. k-4). 1994. 5.95 (*1-884506-04-6*) Third Story.

Shamu's Secrets of the Sea. Jane P. Resnick. (Shamu's Little Library). (Illus.). 12p. (J). (ps). 1994. 6.95 (*1-884506-03-8*) Third Story.

Shan. Eric Van Lustbader. 544p. 1988. mass mkt. 5.99 (*0-449-20598-3*, Crest) Fawcett.

Shan-English Dictionary. Sao T. Moeng. LC 94-67927. 458p. 1995. 79.00 (*0-931745-92-6*) Dunwoody Pr.

Shan for English Speakers. Irving Glick & Sao Tern Moeng. LC 90-86130. 723p. 1991. text ed. 59.00 (*0-931745-73-X*) Dunwoody Pr.

Shan Phonological Drills. Eileen M. Scott & Sao T. Moeng. 221p. 1987. text ed. 43.00 (*0-931745-40-3*) Dunwoody Pr.

Shan Phonological Drills with Workbook. Contrib. by Sao T. Moeng. 1987. audio 24.00 (*0-931745-45-4*) Dunwoody Pr.

Shan States & the British Annexation. Sao Saimong Mangrai. LC 65-8564. (Cornell University Dept. of Asian Studies, Southeast Asian Program. Data Paper: No. 57). 427p. reprint ed. pap. 121.70 (*0-8357-5595-9*, 2035234) Bks Demand.

Shandaa: In My Lifetime. Belle Herbert. Ed. by Bill Pfisterer & Jane McGary. Tr. by Sandy Jamieson. (Illus.). 207p. (Orig.). 1988. reprint ed. pap. text ed. 14.95 (*0-912006-30-7*) U of Alaska Pr.

***Shandong, 1996.** (Telecom Market Reports). 1994. 995.00 (*0-614-18358-8*, IGIC-83) Info Gatekeepers.

Shane. Susin Nielsen. (Degrassi Book Ser.). (J). (gr. 6-9). 1995. pap. 4.95 (*1-55028-235-2*) Formac Dist Ltd.

Shane. Susin Nielsen. (Degrassi Book Ser.). (J). (gr. 6-9). 1995. bds. 16.95 (*1-55028-237-9*) Formac Dist Ltd.

Shane. Jack Schaefer. 128p. (YA). 1983. mass mkt. 4.50 (*0-553-27110-5*) Bantam.

Shane. Jack Schaefer. (Illus.). (J). (gr. 7 up). 1954. 17.00 (*0-395-07090-2*) HM.

Shane. Jack Schaefer. 1991. reprint ed. lib. bdg. 21.95 (*1-56849-041-0*) Buccaneer Bks.

Shane: The Critical Edition. Jack Schaefer. Ed. by James C. Work. LC 83-25948. xviii, 432p. 1984. reprint ed. pap. text ed. 14.95 (*0-8032-9142-6*, Bison Books) U of Nebr Pr.

Shane - Study Guide. Crystal Norris. Ed. by Joyce Friedland & Rikki Kessler. (Novel-Ties Ser.). (YA). (gr. 7-10). 1993. pap. text ed. 15.95 (*0-88122-129-5*) Lrn Links.

***Shane - The Ox-Bow Incident by Jack Schaefer & Walter Van Tilburg Clark: Curriculum Unit.** Center for Learning Network Staff. (Novel - Drama Ser.). 79p. 1996. teacher ed. 18.95 (*1-56077-330-8*) Ctr Learning.

***Shane King Mystery Thriller: The Price of Darkness.** Steve Vance. Ed. by Todd Kelly. 300p. (Orig.). 1998. mass mkt. 5.99 (*0-9648592-4-6*) Serenity LA.

***Shane King Political Thriller: Mutiny in the White House.** Stephen Yoham. 302p. 1998. mass mkt. 5.99 (*0-9648592-5-4*) Serenity LA.

Shane Manuscript Collection: A Genealogical Guide to the Kentucky & Ohio Papers. William K. Hall. LC 90-84653. 136p. 1990. pap. 13.50 (*0-932231-08-X*) Frontier Pr.

***Shane Wright or Wrong.** Roberts. (Clipper Fiction Ser.). 1994. pap. text ed. write for info. (*0-582-80269-5*, Pub. by Longman UK) Longman.

Shane's Bride. Karen R. Smith. (Romance Ser.). 1996. mass mkt. 2.99 (*0-373-19128-6*, 1-19128-7) Silhouette.

Shang Han Lun: Wellspring of Chinese Medicine. Chang Chung-Ching. 1994. pap. 14.95 (*0-941942-02-3*) Orient Heal Arts.

Shang Han Lun: Wellspring of Chinese Medicine. Chang Chung-Ching. Ed. by Hong-Yen Hsu & William G. Peacher. LC 95-1873. (Illus.). 304p. 1995. reprint ed. pap. 14.95 (*0-87983-669-5*) Keats.

Shang Han Lun & Other Traditional Formulas: A Clinical Reference. J. Michael Moore. LC 93-35804. 1993. write for info. (*0-941942-42-2*) Orient Heal Arts.

Shang Ritual Bronzes see Ancient Chinese Bronzes: In the Arthur M. Sackler Collections

Shang Yang's Reforms & State Control in China. Ed. by Yu-Ning Li. LC 76-4301. (China Book Project Ser.). 392p. 1977. reprint ed. pap. 111.80 (*0-8357-2621-5*, 2040109) Bks Demand.

***Shanga.** Mark Horton. (Memoir Ser.: Vol. 14). (Illus.). 458p. 1996. 110.00 (*1-872566-09-X*, Pub. by Brit Inst Estrn Africa UK) David Brown.

Shanghai. China Guide Series Editors. (Illus.). 142p. 1994. pap. 8.95 (*0-8442-9816-6*, Passport Bks) NTC Pub Grp.

Shanghai: From Market Town to Treaty Port, 1074-1858. Linda C. Johnson. LC 94-25034. 1995. 49.50 (*0-8047-2294-3*) Stanford U Pr.

Shanghai: Its Mixed Court & Council Material Relating to the History of the Shanghai Municipal Council. Anatol M. Kotenev. xxvi, 588p. 1987. reprint ed. 58.00 (*0-89941-544-X*, 305090) W S Hein.

Shanghai: Revolution & Development in an Asian Metropolis. Christopher Howe. LC 79-41616. (Contemporary China Institute Publications). (Illus.). 456p. 1981. text ed. 89.95 (*0-521-23198-1*) Cambridge U Pr.

Shanghai: The End of an Era, 1949. Photos by Sam Tata. (Illus.). 144p. (C). 1990. 25.00 (*0-941533-92-1*) New Amsterdam Bks.

Shanghai: The Paris of the Orient. 2nd ed. Lynn Pan. 1994. pap. 14.95 (*0-8442-9686-4*) NTC Pub Grp.

Shanghai: The Paris of the Orient. 3rd ed. Lynn Pan et al. (Illus.). 168p. 1995. pap. 16.95 (*0-8442-9704-6*, Passport Bks) NTC Pub Grp.

Shanghai & Manchuria, 1932: Recollections of a War Correspondent. A. T. Steele. 45p. 1977. pap. 6.00 (*0-939252-06-6*) ASU Ctr Asian.

Shanghai Badlands: Wartime Terrorism & Urban Crime, 1937-1941. Frederic Wakeman, Jr. (Studies in Chinese History, Literature & Institutions). (Illus.). 250p. (C). 1996. text ed. 49.95 (*0-521-49744-2*) Cambridge U Pr.

Shanghai Capitalists & the Nationalist Government, 1927-1937. Parks M. Coble. (East Asian Monographs: No. 94). 371p. (C). 1980. 20.00 (*0-674-80535-6*) HUP.

Shanghai Capitalists & the Nationalist Government, 1927-1937. Parks M. Coble. (East Asian Monographs: No. 94). 371p. 1986. pap. text ed. 18.00 (*0-674-80536-4*) HUP.

Shanghai Common Expressions. 1989. audio 39.00 (*0-931745-53-5*) Dunwoody Pr.

Shanghai Common Expressions. Ed. by Jim Mathias. LC 88-51589. 79p. 1989. 39.00 (*0-931745-38-1*) Dunwoody Pr.

Shanghai Creek Fire. Rob H. Miller. Ed. by Ronald H. Bayes. (Illus.). 1979. pap. 5.00 (*0-932662-30-7*) St Andrews NC.

Shanghai Dialect: An Introduction to Speaking the Contemporary Language. (C). 1994. audio 12.00 (*1-881265-15-3*) Dunwoody Pr.

Shanghai Dialect: An Introduction to Speaking the Contemporary Language. Lance Eccles. LC 93-74961. 230p. (C). 1994. 59.00 (*1-881265-11-0*) Dunwoody Pr.

***Shanghai Express: A Thirties Novel.** Zhang Henshui. Tr. by William A. Lyell. LC 96-40374. (Fiction From Modern China Ser.). 232p. 1997. pap. 12.95 (*0-8248-1830-X*); text ed. 28.00 (*0-8248-1825-3*) UH Pr.

Shanghai Green Gang: Politics & Organized Crime, 1919-1937. Brian G. Martin. LC 95-5017. 279p. (C). 1996. 40.00 (*0-520-20114-0*) U CA Pr.

Shanghai, Nineteen Twenty-Seven to Nineteen Thirty-Seven: Municipal Power, Locality, & Modernization. Christian Henriot. Tr. by Noel Castelino from FRE. LC 92-25054. 1993. 45.00 (*0-520-07096-8*) U CA Pr.

Shanghai on Strike: The Politics of Chinese Labor. Elizabeth J. Perry. LC 92-17774. 352p. (C). 1993. 45.00 (*0-8047-2063-0*) Stanford U Pr.

Shanghai on Strike: The Politics of Chinese Labor. Elizabeth J. Perry. (Illus.). 344p. (C). 1995. pap. 16.95 (*0-8047-2491-1*) Stanford U Pr.

Shanghai on the Metro: Spies, Intrigue, & the French Between the Wars. Michael B. Miller. LC 93-34114. (C). 1994. 35.00 (*0-520-08519-1*) U CA Pr.

Shanghai Owner of the Bonsai Shop. Hilary Davies. 84p. (Orig.). 9100. pap. 16.95 (*1-870612-56-6*, Pub. by Enitha Pr UK) Dufour.

Shanghai Postal System: The Stamps & Postal History. Charles W. Dougan. (Illus.). 200p. 1981. 27.00 (*0-933580-06-1*) Am Philatelic Society.

Shanghai Refuge: A Memoir of the World War II Jewish Ghetto. Ernest G. Heppner. LC 93-20038. (Illus.). xix, 217p. 1995. pap. 10.00 (*0-8032-7281-2*, Bison Books) U of Nebr Pr.

Shanghai Sojourners. Ed. by Frederic E. Wakeman, Jr. & Wen-Hsin Yeh. LC 92-70468. (China Research Monographs: No. 40). 1992. pap. 20.00 (*1-55729-035-0*) IEAS.

Shanghai Star. William H. Lovejoy. 496p. 1996. mass mkt. 5.99 (*0-7860-0329-4*, Pinncle Kensgtn) Kensgtn Pub Corp.

Shanghai Symposium on Marine Geotechnology & Nearshore - Offshore Structures. Ed. by Z. X. Hu & J. P. Liu. LC 84-80006. (Shanghai Symposium Proceedings 1983 Ser.). 644p. (C). 1985. pap. 75.00 (*0-932871-10-0*) Envo Pub Co.

Shanghai Taotai: Linkage Man in a Changing Society, 1843-1890. Leung Yuen-Sang. 252p. (Orig.). 1990. pap. 42.50 (*9971-69-143-4*, Pub. by Sgapore Univ SI) Coronet Bks.

Shanghai Year: A Westerner's Life in the New China. Peter Brigg. LC 87-1949. (Illus.). x, 115p. (Orig.). 1987. 27.00 (*0-930261-88-7*); pap. 17.00 (*0-930261-89-5*) Borgo Pr.

***Shanghai, 1996.** (Telecom Market Reports). 1994. 995.00 (*0-614-18356-1*, IGIC-81) Info Gatekeepers.

***Shanghaied in San Francisco: Politics & Personalities.** Bill Pickelhaupt. LC 96-96781. (Illus.). 270p. 1996. 27.95 (*0-9647312-1-5*); pap. 17.95 (*0-9647312-2-3*) Flyblister Pr.

Shanghaied to China. Dave Jackson & Neta Jackson. 144p. (J). (gr. 4-7). 1993. pap. 5.99 (*1-55661-271-0*) Bethany Hse.

Shanghai's Role in the Economic Development of China: Reform of Foreign Trade & Investment. Gang Tian. LC 95-51430. 248p. 1996. text ed. 65.00 (*0-275-95318-1*, Praeger Pubs) Greenwood.

Shango. James R. Curtis. LC 95-37664. 197p. (Orig.). 1996. pap. 11.95 (*1-55885-096-1*) Arte Publico.

Shango: Ifa & the Spirit of Lightning. Fa'lokum Fatunmbi. 26p. 1993. pap. 4.95 (*0-942272-31-5*) Original Pubns.

Shangri-La: The Return to the World of Lost Horizon. Eleanor Cooney & Daniel Altieri. LC 95-23492. 320p. 1996. 25.00 (*0-688-12872-6*) Morrow.

Shangri-La for Wounded Soldiers: The Greenbrier As a World War II Army Hospital. Louis E. Keefer. (Illus.). 330p. (Orig.). 1995. pap. 19.95 (*0-9644740-0-X*) COTU Pub.

Shangrila & Linda. Alesia Kunz. 256p. (Orig.). 1981. pap. 6.95 (*0-9605794-0-0*) Prickly CA.

Shani on the Hill. Nora B. Blakely. (Illus.). (J). (gr. 1). 1988. pap. 3.95 (*0-88378-123-9*) Third World.

Shani Plus Three. Sarah Goodman. (B. Y. High Ser.: No. 7). 176p. (J). (gr. 6-9). 1993. 9.95 (*1-56871-028-3*) Targum Pr.

***Shania Twain: On My Way.** Dallas Williams. 1997. pap. text ed. 16.95 (*1-55022-297-X*, Pub. by ECW Press CN) Genl Dist Srvs.

Shania Twain: The Woman in Me. Ed. by Jeannette DeLisa. 56p. (Orig.). (YA). 1996. pap. text ed. 18.95 (*1-57623-257-3*, PF9544) Warner Brothers.

Shanie Jacob's Crochet Book. Shanie Jacobs. LC 78-11202. (Illus.). 1979. 15.00 (*0-672-52381-7*, Bobbs) Macmillan.

Shaniko: From Wool Capital to Ghost Town. 2nd ed. Helen G. Rees. LC 81-70285. (Illus.). 176p. 1990. reprint ed. pap. 10.00 (*0-8323-0399-2*) Binford Mort.

Shaniko People. Helen G. Rees. LC 82-73596. (Illus.). 256p. 1982. 10.95 (*0-8323-0414-X*); pap. 7.95 (*0-8323-0415-8*) Binford Mort.

Shani's Scoop. Leah Klein. (B. Y. Times Ser.: Vol. 1). 1991. pap. 7.95 (*0-944070-65-5*) Feldheim.

Shank. Roderick Anscombe. 336p. 1996. 22.95 (*0-7868-6239-4*) Hyperion.

***Shank.** Roderick Anscombe. 1997. mass mkt. 6.99 (*0-7868-8919-5*) Hyperion.

Shankara & Indian Philosophy. Natalia Isayeva. LC 91-44466. (SUNY Series in Religious Studies). 285p. 1992. pap. text ed. 16.95 (*0-7914-1282-2*) State U NY Pr.

Shankara & Indian Philosophy. Natalia Isayeva. LC 91-44466. (SUNY Series in Religious Studies). 285p. 1993. text ed. 49.50 (*0-7914-1281-4*) State U NY Pr.

Shankaracharya. Pranab Bandyopadhyay. (C). 1990. text ed. 11.00 (*81-85328-09-9*, Pub. by Firma KLM II) S Asia.

Shankara's Crest-Jewel of Discrimination (Viveka-Chudamani) Shankara. Tr. by Swami Prabhavananda & Christopher Isherwood from SAN. LC 78-51354. 139p. (C). 1947. pap. 6.95 (*0-87481-038-8*) Vedanta Pr.

Shankara's Universal Philosophy of Religion. Y. Masih. viii, 163p. 1986. text ed. 24.00 (*81-215-0007-9*) Coronet Bks.

***Shanken's Cigar Handbook: A Connoisseur's Guide to Smoking Pleasure.** Marvin R. Shanken. (Companion Ser.). (Illus.). 208p. 1997. 24.95 (*0-7624-0059-5*) Running Pr.

Shank's Mare or Hizakurige: Japan's Great Comic Novel. Ikku Jippensha. Tr. by Thomas Satchell from JPN. LC 60-14370. (Unesco Collection of Representative Works, Series of Translations from the Literature of the Union of Soviet Socialist Republics). (Illus.). 416p. 1988. reprint ed. pap. 14.95 (*0-8048-1580-1*) C E Tuttle.

Shankum Naggum. Jonathan Williams. 28p. 1979. pap. 4.00 (*0-933598-00-9*) NC Wesleyan Pr.

Shanna. Kathleen E. Woodiwiss. 1993. 20.00 (*0-688-12497-6*) Morrow.

Shanna. Kathleen E. Woodiwiss. 672p. 1977. reprint ed. mass mkt. 6.99 (*0-380-38588-0*) Avon.

Shannara. Legend. 1995. pap. 33.00 (*1-880520-21-4*) Legend Enter.

Shannara: The Official Strategy Guide. Corey Cole & Lori Cole. 1995. pap. 19.95 (*0-7615-0295-5*) Prima Pub.

Shannara Trilogy: The Sword of Shannara, The Elfstone of Shannara, & Wishsong of Shannara, 3 vols., Set. Terry Brooks. 1988. Boxed set. boxed, pap. 17.97 (*0-345-35833-3*, Del Rey) Ballantine.

***Shannon.** Girlhood Journeys, Inc., Staff. LC 97-11121. (Girlhood Journeys Ser.: No. 3). (J). 1997. mass mkt. 5.99 (*0-689-81561-1*) S&S Childrens.

Shannon. Kudlinski. (Girlhood Journeys Ser.: Bk. 2). (J). 1997. 12.95 (*0-689-81204-3*) S&S Childrens.

Shannon: A Chinatown Adventure, San Francisco, 1880. Kathleen V. Kudlinski. LC 96-2068. (Girlhood Journeys Ser.). (Illus.). (J). 1996. pap. 5.99 (*0-689-80984-0*, Aladdin Paperbacks) S&S Childrens.

Shannon: An Ojibway Dancer. Sandra King. (Illus.). (J). (gr. 3-6). 1993. pap. 6.95 (*0-8225-9643-1*, First Ave Edns); lib. bdg. 19.95 (*0-8225-2652-2*, Lerner Publctns) Lerner Group.

Shannon: What's It all Mean? Wayne Shannon. Ed. by Dick Murdock & Jayne Murdock. LC 86-62501. (Illus.). 128p. 1987. pap. 5.95 (*0-932916-13-9*) May-Murdock.

Shannon No. 2: A Chinatown Adventure. Kathleen V. Kudlinski & Farnsworth. (J). 1996. 13.00 (*0-689-81138-1*) S&S Childrens.

Shannon-Erne Waterway. Patrick Flanagan. 128p. 1994. pap. 18.95 (*0-86327-429-3*) Dufour.

Shannon Genealogy: A Genealogical Record & Memorials of One Branch in America. G. Hodgdon. (Illus.). 609p. 1989. reprint ed. pap. 91.00 (*0-8328-1061-4*); reprint ed. lib. bdg. 99.00 (*0-8328-1060-6*) Higginson Bk Co.

***Shannon Miller: America's Most Decorated Gymnast.** 2nd rev. ed. Krista Quiner. LC 96-36316. (Illus.). 244p. (Orig.). 1997. pap. 1.95 (*0-9643460-5-2*) Bradford Bk.

***Shannon #2: Lost & Found.** Kathleen V. Kudlinski. (Girlhood Journeys Ser.). (Illus.). (J). (gr. 2-6). 1997. pap. 5.99 (*0-614-29078-3*, Aladdin Paperbacks) S&S Childrens.

Shannondene. Bridget Brian. 73p. 1984. 25.00 (*0-7212-0591-7*, Pub. by Regency Press UK) St Mut.

Shannon's Brigade. large type ed. Vivian Stuart. 400p. 1994. 25.99 (*0-7089-3100-6*) Ulverscroft.

Shannon's Mirror. Luisa Perkins. 150p. (YA). 1994. 10.95 (*0-910523-12-6*) Grandin Bk Co.

Shannon's Story. Ann M. Martin. (Baby-Sitters Club Special Edition Ser.). 160p. (J). (gr. 4-6). 1994. pap. 3.50 (*0-590-47756-0*) Scholastic Inc.

Shannon's Way. large type ed. A. J. Cronin. 384p. 1984. 27.99 (*0-7089-8182-8*) Ulverscroft.

Shannon's Way. A. J. Cronin. 1994. reprint ed. lib. bdg. 24.95 (*1-56849-547-1*) Buccaneer Bks.

Shannon's Way. A. J. Cronin. 320p. 1984. reprint ed. 16.45 (*0-316-16191-8*); reprint ed. mass mkt. 6.95 (*0-316-16185-3*) Little.

Shans. Wilbur W. Cochrane. LC 77-87485. (Illus.). 272p. reprint ed. 47.50 (*0-404-16805-1*) AMS Pr.

Shanties from the Seven Seas. Compiled by Stan Hugill. (Illus.). xxiii, 428p. 1994. pap. 19.95 (*0-913372-70-6*) Mystic Seaport.

Shanties from the Seven Seas: Shipboard Work Songs from the Great Days of Sail. rev. ed. Compiled by Stan Hugill. (Illus.). 416p. 1984. pap. 13.95 (*0-7102-0412-4*, RKP) Routledge.

Shantung Compound: The Story of Men & Women under Pressure. Langdon Gilkey. LC 75-9312. 272p. 1975. pap. 13.00 (*0-06-063112-0*, RD101) Harper SF.

Shantung Question: A Study in Diplomacy & World Politics. Ge-Zay Wood. LC 75-32336. (Studies in Chinese History & Civilization). 372p. 1977. text ed. 65.00 (*0-313-26974-2*, U6974, Greenwood Pr) Greenwood.

Shantung Rebellion: The Wang Lun Uprising of 1774. Susan Naquin. LC 81-1268. (Illus.). 256p. (C). 1981. text ed. 30.00 (*0-300-02638-2*) Yale U Pr.

Shanty Boy: Or, Life in a Lumber Camp. John W. Fitzmaurice. LC 70-104451. 246p. reprint ed. lib. bdg. 11.00 (*0-8398-0557-8*) Irvington.

Shanty Boy: Or, Life in a Lumber Camp. John W. Fitzmaurice. 246p. (C). 1986. reprint ed. pap. text ed. 6.95 (*0-8290-2002-0*) Irvington.

Shanty Town City: The Case of Poona. Bapat. (Progress in Planning Ser.: Vol. 15, Pt. 3). 85p. 1981. pap. 16.25 (*0-08-026811-0*, Pergamon Pr) Elsevier.

Shantyboat: A River Way of Life. Harlan Hubbard. LC 77-73701. (Illus.). 368p. 1977. reprint ed. pap. 14.95 (*0-8131-1359-8*) U Pr of Ky.

Shantyboat Journal. Harlan Hubbard. Ed. by Don Wallis. LC 93-42398. 392p. (C). 1994. 29.95 (*0-8131-1868-9*) U Pr of Ky.

Shantyboat on the Bayous. Harlan Hubbard. LC 89-77898. 160p. 1990. 20.00 (*0-8131-1717-8*) U Pr of Ky.

Shantytown Protest in Pinochet's Chile. Cathy L. Schneider. (Illus.). 240p. (Orig.). (C). 1995. pap. text ed. 19.95 (*1-56639-306-X*); lib. bdg. 59.95 (*1-56639-305-1*) Temple U Pr.

Shao-Lin Chuan: The Rhythm & Power of Tan-Tui. Simmone Kuo. (Illus.). 200p. (Orig.). 1996. pap. 16.95 (*1-55643-229-1*) North Atlantic.

Shaohsing: Competition & Cooperation in Nineteenth-Century China. James H. Cole. LC 86-30825. (Monographs: No. 44). xvi, 315p. 1986. 21.00 (*0-8165-0994-8*) Assn Asian Studies.

Shaolin: An Introduction to Lohan Fighting Techniques see Shaolin Lohan Kung-Fu

Shaolin Chin Na. Yang Jwing-Ming. LC 80-53546. (Illus.). 144p. (Orig.). 1980. pap. 9.95 (*0-86568-012-4*, 207) Unique Pubns.

Shaolin-Do. James Halladay. 128p. 1995. pap. text ed. 19.95 (*0-7872-1242-3*) Kendall-Hunt.

Shaolin Fighting: Theories, Concepts. Douglas L. Wong. LC 76-55613. (Illus.). 1975. pap. 6.50 (*0-86568-006-X*, 205) Unique Pubns.

Shaolin Five Animals Kung-Fu. Doc Fai Wong & Jane Hallander. LC 86-50441. (Orig.). 1987. pap. 9.95 (*0-86568-080-9*, 218) Unique Pubns.

Shaolin Lohan Kung-Fu. P'ng Chye Khim & Donn F. Draeger. Orig. Title: Shaolin: An Introduction to Lohan Fighting Techniques. (Illus.). 170p. 1991. pap. 14.95 (*0-8048-1698-0*) C E Tuttle.

Shaolin Long Fist. Yang Jwing-Ming. LC 81-50513. (Illus.). 250p. (Orig.). 1981. pap. 11.50 (*0-86568-020-5*, 208) Unique Pubns.

Shaolin Nei Jin Qi Gong: Ancient Healing in the Modern World. Peter Fenton. LC 96-15198. (Illus.). 224p. (Orig.). 1996. pap. 14.95 (*0-87728-876-3*) Weiser.

Shaolin Secret Formulas for the Treatment of External Injury. 2nd ed. De Qian. Tr. by Zhang Ting-liang & Bob Flaws from CHI. 185p. 1995. 18.95 (*0-936185-08-2*) Blue Poppy Pr.

Shape. Craig Furnas. 212p. 1996. pap. 14.00 (*1-888656-72-7*) CJF.

Shape. Henry Pluckrose. (Math Counts Ser.). 32p. (J). 1995. lib. bdg. 17.80 (*0-516-05456-2*) Childrens.

Shape. Henry Pluckrose. (Math Counts Ser.). (J). 1995. pap. 4.95 (*0-516-45456-0*) Childrens.

Shape-a-Poem. Janice L. Auld. (J). (gr. 1-3). 1986. pap. 6.99 (*0-8224-6393-8*) Fearon Teach Aids.

Shape-a-Sound. Marilyn Burch. (J). (gr. 1-3). 1986. pap. 6.99 (*0-8224-6394-6*) Fearon Teach Aids.

Shape-a-Story. Janice L. Auld. (J). (gr. 1-3). 1986. pap. 6.99 (*0-8224-6392-X*) Fearon Teach Aids.

Shape Alert. Barbara Helwig & Susan Stewart. (Little Books for Kids). (Illus.). 90p. (J). (gr. 2-6). 1992. spiral bd. 4.95 (*1-881285-04-9*) Arbus Pub.

Shape & Color: The Key to Successful Ceramic Restorations. Gerald Ubassy. (Illus.). 216p. 1993. text ed. 100.00 (*0-86715-207-9*) Quint Pub Co.

Shape & Cook Book. Mary Buckman. (One in a Series of Cook & Learn Books). (Illus.). (J). (gr. k-2). 1982. pap. text ed. 9.95 (*1-879414-02-3*) Mary Bee Creat.

Shape & Form in Plants & Fungi. Ed. by David S. Ingram & Andrew Hudson. (Linnean Society Symposium Ser.: No. 16). (Illus.). 380p. 1994. text ed. 89.00 (*0-12-371035-9*) Acad Pr.

Shape & Form of Puget Sound. Robert E. Burns. LC 84-15354. (Puget Sound Bks.). (Illus.). 114p. (Orig.). (C). 1985. pap. 8.95 (*0-295-96184-8*) U of Wash Pr.

***Shape & Forms of Arabic Letters.** 2nd ed. Assad Busool. (J). (ps-4). 1991. reprint ed. pap. 4.00 (*1-56316-001-3*) Iqra Intl Ed Fdtn.

***Shape & Layout Optimization.** 1995. text ed. 99.00 (*3-211-82363-8*) Spr-Verlag.

S

Shape & Layout Optimization of Structural Systems & Optimality Criteria Methods. Ed. by George I. Rozvany. (CISM International Centre for Mechanical Sciences Ser.: Vol. 325). (Illus.). vi, 496p. 1995. 99.00 (*0-387-82363-8*) Spr-Verlag.

Shape & Style of Proust's Novel. John P. Houston. LC 81-16171. 143p. reprint ed. pap. 40.80 (*0-318-39786-2*, 2033188) Bks Demand.

Shape & the Shaping of the Psalter. J. C. McCann. 35.00 (*1-85075-396-2*, Pub. by Sheffield Acad UK) CUP Services.

Shape Bait. Debby Head & Libby Pollett. (Curiosity Bait Ser.). 93p. 1995. pap. 33.95 (*1-885775-07-5*) BBY Pubns.

Shape, Balance, & Composition. (Shorewood Art Programs for Education Ser.). 8p. 1974. teacher ed. 107.00 (*0-88185-020-9*); 143.00 (*0-685-07218-5*) Shorewood Fine Art.

Shape-Changer. Bill Brittain. LC 93-27268. (Trophy Bk.). 112p. (J). (gr. 3-7). 1994. 14.00 (*0-06-024238-8*); lib. bdg. 13.89 (*0-06-024239-6*) HarpC Child Bks.

Shape-Changer's Wife. Sharon Shinn. 208p. (Orig.). 1995. mass mkt. 4.99 (*0-441-00261-7*) Ace Bks.

Shape Cooks. Ed. by Katherine M. Tomlinson. 100p. (Orig.). 1996. pap. 2.95 (*0-945797-25-7*) Weider Health.

Shape Design Sensitivity Analysis & Optimization Using the Boundary Element Method. Z. X. Zhao. (Lecture Notes in Engineering Ser.: Vol. 62). (Illus.). x, 202p. 1991. 45.95 (*0-387-53518-7*) Spr-Verlag.

Shape, Design, Trace Patterns, Vol. 1, Part 2. Ed. by Ann H. Guest. 95p. 1991. pap. text ed. 23.00 (*3-7186-5182-3*, Harwood Acad Pubs) Gordon & Breach.

Shape Detection in Computer Vision Using the Hough Transform. V. F. Leavers. LC 92-23019. xiv, 201p. 1992. 58.95 (*0-387-19723-0*) Spr-Verlag.

Shape from Shading. Ed. by Berthold K. Horn & Michael J. Brooks. (Artificial Intelligence Ser.). 575p. 1989. 70.00 (*0-262-08183-0*) MIT Pr.

Shape in Chemistry: An Introduction to Molecular Shape & Topology. Paul G. Mezey. LC 93-15622. 1993. 75.00 (*0-89573-727-2*, VCH) Wiley.

***Shape in Chemistry: An Introduction to Molecular Shape & Topology.** Paul G. Mezey. 1993. text ed. 79.95 (*0-471-18741-0*) Wiley.

Shape in Picture: Mathematical Description of Shape in Grey-Level Images. Ed. by Ying-Lie O et al. LC 93-48570. (NATO ASI Series F; Computer & Systems Sciences Ser.: Vol. 126). x, 676p. 1994. 172.95 (*0-387-57578-2*) Spr-Verlag.

Shape It Up. Ginger Primus & Barbara Westlake. 112p. (C). 1994. spiral bd. 25.14 (*0-8403-9936-7*) Kendall-Hunt.

***Shape Memory Alloys.** M. Fremond & S. Miyazaki. (CISM International Centre for Mechnical Sciences Ser.: Vol. 351). (Illus.). 147p. 1996. pap. 40.00 (*3-211-82804-4*) Spr-Verlag.

Shape Memory Alloys. Richard K. Miller & Terri C. Walker. LC 88-81888. (Survey on Technology & Markets Ser.: No. 89). 50p. 1989. pap. text ed. 200.00 (*1-55865-100-4*) Future Tech Surveys.

Shape Memory Alloys, Vol. 1. Ed. by Hiroyasu Funakubo. (Precision Machinery & Robotics Ser.). 276p. 1987. text ed. 310.00 (*2-88124-136-0*) Gordon & Breach.

Shape-Memory Materials & Phenomena - Fundamental Aspects & Applications. Ed. by C. T. Liu et al. (Symposium Proceedings Ser.: Vol. 246). 435p. 1992. text ed. 57.00 (*1-55899-140-9*) Materials Res.

***Shape Modeling & Applications, 1997 International Conference.** LC 96-79897. 264p. 1997. pap. 60.00 (*0-8186-7867-4*) IEEE Comp Soc.

***Shape Modeling & Applications, 1997 International Conference on (SMA '97)** 250p. 1997. pap. text ed. write for info. (*0-8186-5880-0*, PR07867) IEEE Comp Soc.

Shape of a Pear: Poems. Estelle G. Novak. 112p. (Orig.). 1996. pap. 9.95 (*1-56474-147-8*) Fithian Pr.

***Shape of Apocalypse in Modern Russian Fiction.** David M. Bethea. LC 88-12639. 326p. 1989. reprint ed. pap. 93.00 (*0-608-02530-5*, 2063174) Bks Demand.

Shape of Athenian Law. S. C. Todd. (Illus.). 448p. 1995. pap. 29.95 (*0-19-815023-7*) OUP.

Shape of Baptism: The Rite of Christian Initiation. Aidan Kavanagh. 240p. 1992. pap. 16.95 (*0-8146-6036-3*, Pueblo Bks) Liturgical Pr.

***Shape of Belief: African Art from the Dr. Michael R. Heide Collection.** Mary N. Roberts & Allen F. Roberts. (Illus.). 96p. 1997. pap. 15.00 (*0-88401-090-2*) Fine Arts Mus.

Shape of Biblical Language: Chiasmus in & Beyond the Scriptures. John Breck. LC 94-30129. 392p. 1994. pap. 16.95 (*0-88141-139-6*) St Vladimirs.

Shape of Books to Come. James D. Adams. LC 72-167302. (Essay Index Reprint Ser.). 1977. reprint ed. 20.95 (*0-8369-2479-7*) Ayer.

Shape of Catholic Theology: An Introduction to Its Sources, Principles, & History. Aidan Nichols. 250p. (Orig.). 1991. pap. 16.95 (*0-8146-1909-6*) Liturgical Pr.

Shape of Content. Ben Shahn. LC 57-12968. (Charles Eliot Norton Lectures: 1956-1957). (Illus.). 131p. 1972. pap. text ed. 7.95 (*0-674-80570-4*) HUP.

Shape of Culture: A Study of Contemporary Cultural Patterns in the United States. Judith R. Blau. (American Sociological Assn. Rose Monograph Ser.). (Illus.). 224p. (C). 1989. 49.95 (*0-521-37098-1*) Cambridge U Pr.

Shape of Culture: A Study of Contemporary Cultural Patterns in the United States. Judith R. Blau. (American Sociological Assn. Rose Monograph Ser.). (Illus.). 219p. (C). 1992. pap. text ed. 18.95 (*0-521-43793-8*) Cambridge U Pr.

***Shape of Data: Statistics.** rev. ed. Susan J. Russell et al. Ed. by Catherine Anderson & Beverly Cory. (Investigations in Number, Data, & Space Ser.). (Illus.). 105p. (YA). (gr. 4 up). 1997. pap. text ed. 22.95 (*1-57232-748-0*, 43895) Seymour Pubns.

Shape of Death: Life, Death, & Immortality in the Early Fathers. Jaroslav J. Pelikan. LC 78-6030. 128p. 1978. reprint ed. text ed. 38.50 (*0-313-20458-6*, PESD, Greenwood Pr) Greenwood.

Shape of Dread. Marcia Muller. 288p. 1990. mass mkt. 5.99 (*0-445-40916-9*, Mysterious Paperbk) Warner Bks.

***Shape of Fear: Horror & the Fin de Siecle Culture of Decadence.** Susan J. Navarette. (Illus.). 272p. 1997. 37.95 (*0-8131-2013-6*) U Pr of Ky.

Shape of Fear & Other Ghostly Tales. Elia W. Peattie. LC 72-98591. (Short Story Index Reprint Ser.). 1977. 18.95 (*0-8369-3165-3*) Ayer.

Shape of Future Technology. 1990. 49.00 (*0-387-19576-9*) Spr-Verlag.

Shape of Good Nutrition. Lynnrae Francis & Steven Francis. (Illus.). 20p. (Orig.). (J). 1993. 2.50 (*0-9638754-0-X*) Providers Pr.

Shape of Houses: Women's Voices from Holland & Flanders. Tr. by Manfred Wolf. 1974. pap. 6.00 (*0-685-48389-4*) Twowindows Pr.

Shape of Ideas. Bauman. (C). 1994. teacher ed., pap. text ed. 32.00 (*0-15-502183-4*) HB Coll Pubs.

Shape of Ideas. 12th ed. Bauman. (C). 1994. pap. text ed. 26.75 (*0-15-501460-9*) HB Coll Pubs.

Shape of Illusion. William E. Barrett. 22.95 (*0-8488-0426-0*) Amereon Ltd.

Shape of Life: Genes, Development, & the Evolution of Animal Form. Rudolf A. Raff. LC 95-49224. 520p. 1996. pap. text ed. 29.95 (*0-226-70266-9*); lib. bdg. 55.00 (*0-226-70265-0*) U Ch Pr.

Shape of Me & Other Shapes. Linda Haywood & Dr. Seuss. (J). 1997. pap. write for info. (*0-679-87083-0*) Random Bks Yng Read.

Shape of Me & Other Stuff. Dr. Seuss. (Bright & Early Bks.: No. 16). (Illus.). (J). (ps-1). 1973. 7.99 (*0-394-82687-6*); lib. bdg. 11.99 (*0-394-92687-0*) Random Bks Yng Read.

***Shape of Me & Other Stuff.** Dr. Seuss. (J). 1997. 4.99 (*0-679-88631-1*) Random Bks Yng Read.

Shape of Meaning in the Poetry of David Jones. Thomas Dilworth. 1988. 50.00 (*0-8020-2613-3*) U of Toronto Pr.

Shape of Medieval Monetary History. Robert S. Lopez. (Collected Studies: No. CS247). (Illus.). 330p. (C). 1986. reprint ed. lib. bdg. 94.95 (*0-86078-195-X*, Pub. by Variorum UK) Ashgate Pub Co.

Shape of Paradox: An Essay on Waiting for Godot. Bert O. States. (Quantum Bks.: No. 13). 1978. pap. 10.95 (*0-520-03572-0*) U CA Pr.

Shape of Pear. Muriel Karr. 84p. (Orig.). 1996. pap. 10.00 (*0-944920-19-5*) Bellowing Ark Pr.

***Shape of Pneumatology: Studies in the Doctrine of the Holy Spirit.** John McIntyre. 304p. 1997. 47.95 (*0-567-08554-6*, Pub. by T & T Clark UK) Bks Intl VA.

Shape of Powder-Particle Outlines. Arthur E. Hawkins. LC 92-44143. (Materials Science & Technology Ser.: Vol. 1). 150p. 1993. text ed. 89.95 (*0-471-93878-5*) Wiley.

Shape of Q: Signal Essays on the Sayings Gospel. Intro. by John S. Kloppenborg. LC 93-28256. 1994. 20.00 (*0-8006-2600-1*, 1-2600) Augsburg Fortress.

Shape of Reason: Argumentative Writing in College. 2nd ed. John T. Gage. 320p. (C). 1991. pap. text ed. 35.00 (*0-02-340041-2*, Macmillan Coll) P-H.

Shape of Red: Insider-Outsider Reflections. Ruth Hubbard & Margaret Randall. (Illus.). 206p. 1988. pap. 9.95 (*0-939416-19-0*) Cleis Pr.

Shape of Religious Instruction: A Social-Science Approach. James M. Lee. LC 74-29823. 330p. (Orig.). 1971. reprint ed. pap. 17.95 (*0-89135-002-0*); reprint ed. lib. bdg. 17.95 (*0-89135-000-4*) Religious Educ.

Shape of Sacred Space: Four Biblical Studies. Robert L. Cohn. LC 80-11086. (Studies in Religion: No. 23). 79p. 1981. pap. 12.95 (*0-89130-384-7*, 01-00-23) Scholars Pr GA.

Shape of Soteriology. John McIntyre. 144p. 1993. text ed. 23.95 (*0-567-09615-7*, Pub. by T & T Clark UK) Bks Intl VA.

Shape of Soteriology. John McIntyre. 144p. 1996. pap. 23.95 (*0-567-29290-8*, Pub. by T & T Clark UK) Bks Intl VA.

Shape of Space. 2nd ed. Graham Nerlich. LC 93-28935. 320p. (C). 1994. pap. text ed. 23.95 (*0-521-45645-2*) Cambridge U Pr.

Shape of Space. 2nd ed. Graham Nerlich. LC 93-28935. 320p. (C). 1994. text ed. 65.00 (*0-521-45014-4*) Cambridge U Pr.

Shape of Space: How to Visualize Surfaces & Three-Dimensional Manifolds. Jeffrey Weeks. (Pure & Applied Mathematics Ser.: Vol. 96). 346p. 1985. 45.00 (*0-8247-7437-X*) Dekker.

Shape of Space, George Sugarman. Holliday D. Day. Ed. by Jane A. Allen. (Illus.). 144p. (Orig.). 1981. pap. 14.95 (*0-936364-06-8*) Joslyn Art.

Shape of Texas: Maps of Metaphors. Richard V. Francaviglia. LC 95-18635. (Illus.). 144p. (C). 1995. 29.50 (*0-89096-664-8*) Tex A&M Univ Pr.

Shape of the City: Toronto Struggles with Modern Planning. John W. Sewell. (Illus.). 240p. 1993. 50.00 (*0-8020-2901-9*); pap. 18.95 (*0-8020-7409-X*) U of Toronto Pr.

Shape of the Data: Statistics. Susan J. Russell et al. Ed. by Priscilla C. Samii et al. (Investigations in Number, Data, & Space Ser.). (Illus.). 97p. (Orig.). 1994. teacher ed., pap. 22.95 (*0-86651-814-2*, DS21252) Seymour Pubns.

Shape of the Fantastic: Selected Essays from the Seventh International Conference on the Fantastic in the Arts. Ed. by Olena H. Saciuk. LC 89-11807. (Contributions to the Study of Science Fiction & Fantasy Ser.: No. 39). 273p. 1990. text ed. 59.95 (*0-313-26198-9*, SKS/) Greenwood.

Shape of the Future: The Post-Cold War. 2nd ed. Donald M. Snow. LC 94-12522. 264p. (gr. 13). 1994. text ed. 65.95 (*1-56324-423-3*); pap. text ed. 25.95 (*1-56324-424-1*) M E Sharpe.

Shape of the Future: The Post-Cold War World. Donald M. Snow. LC 91-8263. 248p. (C). (gr. 13). 1991. text ed. 58.95 (*0-87332-864-7*); pap. text ed. 25.95 (*0-87332-865-5*) M E Sharpe.

Shape of the Good: Christian Reflections on the Foundation of Ethics. C. Stephen Layman. LC 90-50977. (Library of Religious Philosophy: Vol. 7). (C). 1994. reprint ed. pap. text ed. 15.00 (*0-268-01752-2*) U of Notre Dame Pr.

Shape of the Holy: Early Islamic Jerusalem. Oleg Grabar. LC 95-50443. 248p. (C). 1996. text ed. 65.00 (*0-691-03653-5*) Princeton U Pr.

Shape of the New Europe. Ed. by Gregory F. Treverton. LC 91-23295. 240p. 1992. reprint ed. pap. 68.40 (*0-608-02008-7*, 2062664) Bks Demand.

***Shape of the Past: A Philosophical Approach to History.** Gordon Graham. 246p. 1997. pap. 14.95 (*0-19-289255-X*) OUP.

Shape of the Past: Models & Antiquity. T. F. Carney. (Illus.). 1975. 30.00 (*0-685-01230-1*) Coronado Pr.

Shape of the Puritan Mind: The Thought of Samuel Willard. Ernest B. Lowrie. LC 74-76650. 267p. reprint ed. pap. 76.10 (*0-8357-8319-7*, 2033808) Bks Demand.

Shape of the Round Table: Structures of Middle High German Arthurian Romance. James A. Schultz. 264p. 1983. 30.00 (*0-8020-2466-1*) U of Toronto Pr.

Shape of the Table. David Edgar. 112p. 1990. pap. 11.95 (*1-85459-079-0*, Pub. by N Hern Bks UK) Theatre Comm.

Shape of the Tree: Selected Poems. John J. Conger. 48p. (Orig.). 1993. pap. 6.95 (*0-9635839-0-5*) Equinox Mtn.

Shape of the Turtle: Myth, Art, & Cosmos in Early China. Sarah Allan. LC 90-30424. (SUNY Series in Chinese Philosophy & Culture). 230p. (C). 1991. pap. text ed. 21.95 (*0-7914-0460-9*) State U NY Pr.

Shape of the Turtle: Myth, Art, & Cosmos in Early China. Sarah Allan. LC 90-30424. (SUNY Series in Chinese Philosophy & Culture). 230p. (C). 1991. text ed. 64.50 (*0-7914-0459-5*) State U NY Pr.

Shape of Things. Dayle A. Dodds. LC 93-47255. (Illus.). 32p. (J). 1996. pap. 5.99 (*1-56402-698-1*) Candlewick Pr.

Shape of Things: The Art of Francis Lee Jaques. Patricia C. Johnston. (Illus.). 172p. 1994. 60.00 (*0-9639338-0-9*) Afton Hist Soc.

Shape of Things to Come? User-Led Social Services. Jenny Morris. 1994. pap. 35.00 (*0-902789-94-5*, Pub. by Natl Inst Soc Work) St Mut.

Shape of Things to Consume. Alan Cawson et al. 289p. 1995. 63.95 (*1-85972-052-8*, Pub. by Avebury Pub UK) Ashgate Pub Co.

Shape of This Century: Readings from the Disciplines. Diana W. Rigden & Susan S. Waugh. 738p. (C). 1990. pap. text ed. 15.00 (*0-15-585686-2*); pap. text ed. 5.50 (*0-15-580841-9*) HB Coll Pubs.

Shape of Time: Remarks on the History of Things. George A. Kubler. LC 62-8250. (Illus.). 1962. pap. 11.00 (*0-300-00144-4*, Y140) Yale U Pr.

***Shape of Water.** Pat Boran. 1996. 18.95 (*1-873790-86-4*) Dufour.

***Shape of Water.** Pat Boran. 80p. 9700. pap. 11.95 (*1-873790-85-6*) Dufour.

Shape of Waters. David Swanger. LC 78-17237. 49p. 1978. pap. 3.50 (*0-87886-096-7*, Greenfld Rev Pr) Greenfld Rev Lit.

Shape of Wilderness. Shelley Berc. LC 95-31068. 200p. (Orig.). 1995. pap. 12.95 (*1-56689-036-5*) Coffee Hse.

Shape Optimization & Free Boundaries. Ed. by Michel C. Delfour & Gert Sabidussi. LC 92-18173. (NATO Advanced Study Institutes Series C, Mathematical & Physical Sciences: Vol. 380). 480p. 1992. lib. bdg. 200.00 (*0-7923-1944-3*) Kluwer Ac.

Shape Patterns. Marion Smoothey. LC 92-36223. (Let's Investigate Ser.). (J). (gr. 4 up). 1993. 17.95 (*1-85435-465-5*) Marshall Cavendish.

***Shape Power.** Dan A. Davidson. (Illus.). 176p. (Orig.). 1997. pap. 19.95 (*0-9626321-5-5*) Rivas Pub.

Shape Puzzles. (Jigsaw Puzzles Ser.). 12p. 1996. 4.95 (*0-7894-0614-4*) DK Pub Inc.

Shape Selective Catalysis in Industrial Applications. 2nd expanded rev. ed. N. Y. Chen et al. LC 96-15466. (Chemical Industries Ser.: Vol. 65). 304p. 1996. 140.00 (*0-8247-9737-X*) Dekker.

Shape Shifter: Seven Mediums. Mary B. Edelson. (Illus.). 64p. 1990. pap. 20.00 (*0-9604650-3-0*) Edelson.

***Shape Shifters: Continuous Change for Competitive Advantage.** John L. Mariotti. (Business Technology Ser.). 320p. 1997. text ed. 29.95 (*0-442-02559-9*) Van Nos Reinhold.

Shape Shifters: Shaman Women in Contemporary Society. Michele Jamal. 224p. 1988. pap. 11.95 (*0-14-019057-0*, Penguin Bks) Viking Penguin.

***Shape Shifting: Shamanic Techniques for Self-Transformation.** John Perkins. 176p. 1997. pap. 12.95 (*0-89281-663-5*) Inner Tradit.

***Shape Shuffle.** World Book, Inc. Staff. LC 97-6016. (Mind Benders Ser.). (J). 1997. pap. write for info. (*0-7166-4107-0*) World Bk.

Shape Space. Cathryn Falwell. (Illus.). 32p. (J). (ps-2). 1992. 14.95 (*0-395-61305-1*, Clarion Bks) HM.

Shape, Structure & Pattern Recognition. D. Dori & A. Bruckstein. 400p. 1995. text ed. 113.00 (*981-02-2239-4*) World Scientific Pub.

Shape Theory: An Introduction. J. Dydak & J. Segal. (Lecture Notes in Mathematics Ser.: Vol. 688). 1978. 33.95 (*0-387-08955-1*) Spr-Verlag.

Shape Training: The 8-Week Total Body Makeover. Robert Kennedy & Maggie Greenwood-Robinson. (Illus.). 224p. 1996. pap. 14.95 (*0-8092-3251-0*) Contemp Bks.

Shape under the Sheet: The Complete Stephen King Encyclopedia. Stephen J. Spignesi. LC 91-61010. (Illus.). 800p. 1991. lib. bdg. 85.00 (*1-56075-018-9*) Popular Culture.

***Shape Up: Making Shapes, Eating Polygons.** David A. Adler. LC 97-22236. (Illus.). (J). 1998. write for info. (*0-8234-1346-2*) Holiday.

Shape-up & Hiring Hall. Charles P. Larrowe. LC 75-46614. (Illus.). 250p. 1976. reprint ed. text ed. 65.00 (*0-8371-8750-8*, LASU, Greenwood Pr) Greenwood.

Shape up for Soccer. Pete Broccoletti & Rich Hunter. (Illus.). 232p. 1981. 24.95 (*0-89651-750-0*); ring bd. 16.95 (*0-89651-751-9*) Hardwood Pr.

Shape-Up with Splash: Exercises to Be Done in the Water. Judy D. Conley. (Illus.). 112p. 1988. 10.95 (*0-9619828-1-0*) Judys Splash Aerobics.

Shape up Your Business Workbook. Rodale Press Editors. Ed. by Chris Hill. LC 94-31012. 1994. write for info. (*0-87596-246-7*) Rodale Pr Inc.

Shape Your Swing the Modern Way. rev. ed. Byron Nelson & Larry Dennis. (Classics of Golf Ser.). (Illus.). 126p. 1985. 28.00 (*0-940889-06-4*) Classics Golf.

Shapechangers. Jennifer Roberson. (Chronicles of the Cheysuli Ser.: Bk. 1). (Orig.). 1984. mass mkt. 4.99 (*0-88677-140-4*) DAW Bks.

Shaped & Cut-Out Cakes: The Easy Professional Way. John N. McNamara. (Illus.). 40p. (Orig.). (C). 1984. pap. 9.00 (*0-932770-04-5*) McNamara Pubns.

Shaped by Images: One Who Presides. William S. Adams. 120p. 1995. 18.95 (*0-89869-247-4*) Church Pub Inc.

Shaped by the Bible. William H. Willimon. 1991. pap. 2.10 (*0-687-12656-8*) Abingdon.

Shaped by the Word. M. Robert Mulholland. LC 85-51241. (Orig.). 1985. pap. 9.95 (*0-8358-0519-0*) Upper Room Bks.

***Shaped by the Word.** Mullholland. 13.35 (*0-687-61048-6*) Abingdon.

Shaped Crystal Growth. Y. A. Tatarchenko. (Fluid Mechanics & Its Applications Ser.). 310p. (C). 1993. lib. bdg. 181.00 (*0-7923-2419-6*) Kluwer Ac.

***Shaped Pasta: Cooking with Whimsy - Recipes & Far Fetched Food Fables.** Buckeye Beans & Herbs Staff. 1996. pap. text ed. 9.95 (*0-9652278-0-4*) Buckeye Beans.

Shapedown: Weight Management Program for Adolescents. 4th ed. Laurel M. Mellin. LC 86-71125. (Illus.). 124p. (Orig.). 1987. Parent's Guide 124pp. 16.95 (*0-935902-09-0*); Instr's. Guide 288pp. teacher ed. 29.95 (*0-935902-08-2*); Teen wkbk. 215pp. student ed. 16.95 (*0-935902-07-4*) Balboa Pub.

Shapedown: Weight Management Program for Children. Laurel M. Mellin. LC 88-70316. (Illus.). 1995. 18.95 (*0-935902-23-6*) Balboa Pub.

Shapedown: Weight Management Program for Children. 3rd ed. Laurel M. Mellin. LC 88-70316. (Illus.). 216p. 1989. teacher ed. 16.95 (*0-935902-14-7*) Balboa Pub.

Shapedown: Weight Management Program for Children, Level 1, Ages 6-8. 2nd ed. Laurel M. Mellin. LC 88-70316. (Illus.). 138p. 1989. write for info. (*0-935902-15-5*) Balboa Pub.

Shapedown: Weight Management Program for Children, Level 2, Ages 9-12. 3rd ed. Laurel M. Mellin. LC 88-70316. (Illus.). 124p. 1989. write for info. (*0-935902-16-3*) Balboa Pub.

Shapeless God: Essays on Modern Fiction. Ed. by Harry J. Mooney & Thomas F. Staley. LC 68-21630. 232p. reprint ed. pap. 66.20 (*0-685-15962-0*, 2026314) Bks Demand.

Shapely Fire: Black Writers in Canada. Ed. by Cyril Dabydeen. 175p. 1987. 24.95 (*0-88962-345-7*); pap. 12.95 (*0-88962-344-9*) Mosaic.

***Shaper Book.** Lonnie Bird. LC 96-35740. 144p. 1996. pap. 19.95 (*1-56158-120-8*) Taunton.

Shaper Handbook. Roger W. Cliffe & Michael Holtz. LC 90-40300. (Illus.). 256p. (Orig.). 1990. pap. 17.95 (*0-8069-6798-6*) Sterling.

Shaper Handbook. 2nd ed. Eric Stephenson. LC 87-23713. (Illus.). 192p. (Orig.). 1987. reprint ed. pap. 18.95 (*0-941936-09-0*) Linden Pub Fresno.

Shaper Operations. 1996. lib. bdg. 255.95 (*0-8490-8343-5*) Gordon Pr.

Shaper Poems. James Hoggard. (Illus.). 30p. (Orig.). pap. 6.00 (*0-912435-00-3*) Cedarshouse.

***Shaper Project.** Roger Cliffe. 1998. write for info. (*0-8069-9777-X*) Sterling.

Shapers Legacy. Sheila Finch. (Shaper Exile Ser.: No. 2). 1989. pap. 3.95 (*0-553-28167-4*, Spectra) Random Hse Value.

Shapers of America. Ed. by Richard S. Rennert. LC 92-39962. (Profiles of Great Black Americans Ser.). (YA). (gr. 3 up). 1993. pap. 5.95 (*0-7910-2054-1*); lib. bdg. 15.95 (*0-7910-2053-3*) Chelsea Hse.

Shapers of American Fiction, 1789-1947. George Snell. (BCL1-PS American Literature Ser.). 316p. 1993. reprint ed. lib. bdg. 89.00 (*0-7812-6594-0*) Rprt Serv.

Shapers of Baptist Thought. James E. Tull. LC 84-6545. (Reprints of Scholarly Excellence Ser.: No. 8). 255p. 1984. reprint ed. 14.50 (*0-86554-125-6*, MUP-H116) Mercer Univ Pr.

Shapers of Japanese Buddhism. Ed. by Yusen Kashiwahara & Koyu Sonoda. (Illus.). 440p. 1993. pap. 19.95 (*4-333-01630-4*, Pub. by Kosei Pub Co JA) C E Tuttle.

An Asterisk (*) at the beginning of an entry indicates that the title is appearing in BIP for the first time.

Shapers of Religious Traditions in Germany, Switzerland, & Poland, Fifteen Sixty to Sixteen Hundred. Ed. by Jill Raitt. LC 80-23287. 256p. (C). 1981. text ed. 40.00 (*0-300-02457-6*) Yale U Pr.

Shapes. (Honey Bear Shaped Ser.). (Illus.). 12p. (J). (gr. k-2). 1982. bds. 3.95 (*0-87449-179-7*) Modern Pub NYC.

Shapes. (Active Minds Ser.). (Illus.). 24p. (J). 1993. 4.98 (*1-56173-481-0*) Pubns Intl Ltd.

***Shapes.** (Toby & His Dog Ser.). 1997. 6.95 (*0-7894-2108-9*) DK Pub Inc.

Shapes. (Sticker Activity Ser.). (J). (ps-1). 1993. pap. 6.95 (*1-56458-245-0*) DK Pub Inc.

Shapes. (Sticker Puzzle Bks.). (Illus.). 16p. (J). (ps-3). 1995. pap. 4.95 (*0-7894-0005-7*) DK Pub Inc.

Shapes. (Stickers (Concepts) Ser.). (Illus.). 12p. (J). 1996. pap. 3.95 (*0-7894-1139-3*) DK Pub Inc.

Shapes. (Fit-A-Shape Ser.). (Illus.). 10p. (J). 1996. bds. 5.95 (*1-56138-709-6*) Running Pr.

***Shapes.** (Write & Wipe Bks.). (Illus.). 6p. (J). (gr. k-2). 1997. pap. write for info. (*1-56144-989-X*, Honey Bear Bks) Modern Pub NYC.

Shapes. Richard L. Allington. LC 79-19852. (Beginning to Learn about Ser.). (Illus.). 32p. (J). (gr. k-3). 1985. pap. 3.95 (*0-8114-8238-3*) Raintree Steck-V.

Shapes. Rowan Barnes-Murphy. (Blackboard Bks.). (Illus.). 16p. (J). (ps). 1993. bds. 3.95 (*0-8249-8606-7*, Ideals Child) Hambleton-Hill.

Shapes. Roma Bishop. (Nursery Board Mini Pop Bks.). (Illus.). 14p. (J). (ps). 1991. pap. 2.95 (*0-671-74830-0*, Litl Simon S&S) S&S Childrens.

Shapes. K. Bryant-Mole. (First Learning Ser.). (Illus.). 24p. (J). (ps up). 1991. pap. 3.95 (*0-7460-0593-8*, Usborne) EDC.

***Shapes.** Ivan Bulloch & Wendy Clemson. (Action Math Ser.). (J). 1997. pap. write for info. (*0-7166-4905-5*) World Bk.

***Shapes.** Ivan Bulloch et al. LC 96-49558. (Action Math Ser.). (J). 1997. write for info. (*0-7166-4904-7*) World Bk.

Shapes. Donna Burk et al. (Box It or Bag It Mathematics Ser.). (Illus.). 73p. (C). 1988. teacher ed., ring bd. 9.75 (*1-886131-02-3*, BB1) Math Lrning.

Shapes. Christopher Carrie. (Crayola Kinder Art BKs.). (Illus.). 12p. (Orig.). (J). (gr. 3-6). 1987. pap. 4.70 (*0-86696-202-6*) Binney & Smith.

Shapes. Carson & Dellosa. (Home Workbooks Ser.). (Illus.). 64p. (Orig.). (J). (ps-1). 1995. wbk. ed., pap. 2.49 (*0-88724-311-8*, CD6808) Carson-Dellos.

***Shapes.** Patricia T. Cousin et al. (Visions: African-American Experiences: No. 39). (Illus.). 8p. (Orig.). (J). (gr. k-1). 1995. pap. text ed. 3.00 (*1-57518-038-3*) Arborlake.

***Shapes.** Josep M. Fite. LC 96-44008. (Math for Children Ser.). (Illus.). (J). 1997. pap. 5.95 (*0-382-39885-8*, Silver Pr NJ); lib. bdg. 15.95 (*0-382-39884-X*, Silver Pr NJ) Silver Burdett Pr.

Shapes. Frank Schaffer Publications, Inc. Staff. (Back-to-Basics Ser.). 32p. 1996. wbk. ed. 3.95 (*0-86734-967-0*, FS-30003) Schaffer Pubns.

Shapes. Gabriele. (J). 1985. pap. 1.95 (*0-911211-67-5*) Penny Lane Pubns.

Shapes. Barbara Gregorich. Ed. by Joan Hoffman. (Get Ready! Bks.). (Illus.). 32p. (J). (ps). 1983. student ed. 1.99 (*0-938256-63-7*) Sch Zone Pub Co.

Shapes. Sally Hewitt. LC 95-18460. (Take Off With Ser.). (J). 1996. lib. bdg. 21.40 (*0-8172-4114-0*) Raintree Steck-V.

Shapes. David Kirkby. LC 95-20570. (Math Live Ser.). (Illus.). (J). 1996. lib. bdg. write for info. (*1-57572-041-8*) Rigby Interact Libr.

Shapes. David Kirkby. LC 95-38717. (Mini Math Ser.). (Illus.). (J). 1996. lib. bdg. write for info. (*1-57572-002-7*) Rigby Interact Libr.

Shapes. David Moss. (Pull the Tab Bks.). (Illus.). 10p. (J). (ps). 1989. 4.99 (*0-517-69422-0*) Random Hse Value.

***Shapes.** Chuck Murphy. (J). 1997. 4.99 (*0-689-81500-X*, Atheneum S&S) S&S Trade.

Shapes. Jan Pienkowski. (Nursery Board Bks.). (Illus.). (J). (ps). 1989. 2.95 (*0-671-68135-4*, Litl Simon S&S) S&S Childrens.

Shapes. Tony Ross. LC 94-36610. (Little Princess Board Bks.). (Illus.). 14p. (J). (ps). 1995. pap. 6.00 (*0-15-200319-3*, Red Wagon Bks) HarBrace.

Shapes. Shereen G. Rutman. (Toddler Time Ser.). (Illus.). 16p. (J). 1992. student ed., pap. 2.95 (*1-56293-188-1*) McClanahan Bk.

Shapes. Pamela J. Schroeder & Jean M. Donisch. LC 95-52196. (What's the Big Idea? Ser.). (Illus.). (J). 1996. write for info. (*0-86625-577-X*) Rourke Pubns.

Shapes. Marion Smoothey. LC 92-36224. (Let's Investigate Ser.). (J). (gr. 4 up). 1993. 17.95 (*1-85435-464-7*) Marshall Cavendish.

Shapes. Ellen Steiber. (X Files Ser.: No. 6). 112p. (YA). (gr. 5 up). 1996. pap. 3.95 (*0-06-440633-4*, Trophy) HarpC Child Bks.

Shapes: A Turn-the-Wheel Book. Mavis Smith. (Wheelies Ser.). (Illus.). 12p. (J). (ps-3). 1994. 4.50 (*0-307-17377-1*, Golden Books) Western Pub.

Shapes: Active Minds. Photos by George Siede & Donna Preis. (Active Minds-English Ser.). (Illus.). 24p. (J). (ps-3). 1992. lib. bdg. 10.95 (*1-56674-005-3*) Forest Hse.

Shapes: Barney's Shape Picnic. Margie Larsen & Mary A. Dudko. (Barney's Beginnings Ser.). (Illus.). 16p. (J). (ps-3). 1996. wbk. ed., pap. 2.95 (*1-57064-091-2*) Lyrick Pub.

***Shapes: Barney's Shape Picnic.** Margie Larsen & Mary A. Dudko. (Barney's Beginnings Ser.). (Illus.). 32p. (Orig.). (J). (ps-3). 1997. wbk. ed., pap. 2.95 (*1-57064-224-9*) Lyrick Pub.

Shapes: Circle - Square - Triangle, 3 bks., Set. Bernie Karlin. (Illus.). (J). (ps). 1992. pap. 6.95 (*0-671-74625-1*, Litl Simon S&S) S&S Childrens.

***Shapes: With Ten Magnets.** (Cave Kids Ser.). 1997. 7.95 (*1-57719-203-6*) GT Pubng Corp.

Shapes & Colors. (Ready to Learn Ser.: No. S813-4). (J). 1989. pap. 1.95 (*0-7214-5178-0*, Ladybrd) Penguin.

Shapes & Colors. (Step Ahead Plus Ser.). (Illus.). 64p. (J). (ps-3). 1995. wbk. ed., pap. 3.50 (*0-307-03649-9*, Golden Books) Western Pub.

Shapes & Colors. Lynne Bradbury. (Illus.). 28p. (J). (ps). 1992. Series 921. 3.50 (*0-7214-1510-5*, Ladybrd) Penguin.

Shapes & Colors. Denise Lewis-Patrick. (Illus.). (J). (ps-3). 1990. write for info. (*0-307-06134-5*, Golden Books) Western Pub.

Shapes & Colours. Matthew V. Smith. (Illus.). 12p. (J). 1992. pap. 4.95 (*1-895583-03-9*) MAYA Pubns.

Shapes & Designs: Two-Dimensional Geometry. Glenda Lappan et al. Ed. by Catherine Anderson et al. (Connected Mathematics Ser.). (Illus.). (Orig.). 1995. wbk. ed., pap. 5.95 (*1-57232-150-4*, DS21445) Seymour Pubns.

Shapes & Designs: Two-Dimensional Geometry. Glenda Lappan et al. Ed. by Catherine Anderson et al. (Connected Mathematics Ser.). (Illus.). (Orig.). 1995. teacher ed., pap. 16.50 (*1-57232-151-2*, DS21446) Seymour Pubns.

***Shapes & Designs: Two-Dimensional Geometry.** rev. ed. Glenda Lappan et al. Ed. by Catherine Anderson et al. (Connected Mathematics Ser.). (Illus.). 84p. (YA). (gr. 6 up). 1997. student ed., pap. text ed. 5.95 (*1-57232-624-7*, 45819) Seymour Pubns.

***Shapes & Designs: Two-Dimensional Geometry.** rev. ed. Glenda Lappan et al. Ed. by Catherine Anderson et al. (Connected Mathematics Ser.). (Illus.). 149p. (YA). (gr. 6 up). 1997. teacher ed., pap. text ed. 16.50 (*1-57232-625-5*, 45820) Seymour Pubns.

Shapes & Logic: Individual Sets. Marion W. Stuart. text ed. write for info. (*0-943343-14-3*) Lrn Wrap-Ups.

***Shapes & Opposites.** (Richard Scarry's First Little Learners Ser.). (Illus.). 24p. (J). (gr. k-2). 1995. write for info. (*1-56144-724-2*, Honey Bear Bks) Modern Pub NYC.

Shapes & Patterns. Ellen B. Church. 1996. pap. text ed. 3.95 (*0-590-97702-4*) Scholastic Inc.

Shapes & Patterns. National Education Association Staff. 1983. pap. 1.95 (*0-380-82701-8*) Avon.

Shapes & Shells in Nuclear Structure. Ingemar Ragnarsson & Sven G. Nilsson. (Illus.). 432p. (C). 1995. text ed. 95. 00 (*0-521-37377-8*) Cambridge U Pr.

Shapes & Sizes. (Snapshot Concept Board Bks.). (Illus.). 20p. (J). (ps). 1994. 2.95 (*1-56458-536-0*) DK Pub Inc.

Shapes & Sizes. McClanahan Staff. (I Can Learn Ser.). (Illus.). 24p. (J). (ps-2). 1994. 1.95 (*1-56293-510-0*) McClanahan Bk.

Shapes & Things. Illus. by Tana Hoban. LC 70-102965. 32p. (J). (ps-2). 1970. 15.00 (*0-02-744060-5*, Mac Bks Young Read) S&S Childrens.

***Shapes Are Fun.** (Preschool Concepts Ser.). (Illus.). 32p. (J). (ps). 1996. pap. write for info. (*1-56144-827-3*, Honey Bear Bks) Modern Pub NYC.

***Shapes for Lunch.** Melinda Lilly. (Illus.). 34p. (J). (ps up). 1997. bds. 9.95 (*0-8431-7910-4*) Price Stern Sloan.

***Shapes for Woodturners.** David Weldon. (Illus.). 128p. 1997. pap. 29.95 (*0-7134-8139-0*, Pub. by Batsford UK) Trafalgar.

***Shapes Fun.** (Fisher-Price Little People Toddler Workbooks Ser.). (Illus.). 32p. (J). (ps-1). 1997. pap. write for info. (*1-56144-934-2*, Honey Bear Bks) Modern Pub NYC.

Shapes Galore. (Tab Board Bks.). 12p. (J). 1995. 3.95 (*0-7894-0231-9*, 5-70643) DK Pub Inc.

Shape's Guide to a Fit Pregnancy. Ed. by Barbara Harris. (Illus.). 132p. (Orig.). 1994. pap. 2.95 (*0-945797-21-4*) Weider Health.

Shapes, Halves, & Symmetry: Geometry & Fractions. Joan Akers et al. Ed. by Catherine Anderson et al. (Investigations in Number, Data, & Space Ser.). (Illus.). 209p. (Orig.). (J). (gr. 2). 1996. teacher ed., pap. 32.95 incl. mac ld (*1-57232-217-9*, 21648) Seymour Pubns.

***Shapes, Halves, & Symmetry: Geometry & Fractions.** rev. ed. Joan Akers et al. Ed. by Catherine Anderson et al. (Investigations in Number, Data, & Space Ser.). (Illus.). 219p. (J). (gr. 2 up). 1997. pap. text ed. 32.95 (*1-57232-656-5*, 43803) Seymour Pubns.

Shapes in God's World. Beverly Beckman. LC 56-1462. (In God's World Ser.). (J). (ps). 1984. 6.99 (*0-570-04094-9*, 56-1462) Concordia.

***Shapes in My World.** Claudette C. Mitchell et al. (Visions: African-American Experiences: Vol. 37). (Illus.). 8p. (Orig.). (J). (gr. k-1). 1996. pap. text ed. 3.00 (*1-57518-079-0*) Arborlake.

***Shapes in the City.** (Super Sticker Bks.). (Illus.). 16p. (J). (gr. k-2). 1996. pap. write for info. (*1-56144-453-7*, Honey Bear Bks) Modern Pub NYC.

Shapes, Loops & Images. Susan Jagoda et al. Ed. by Lincoln Bergman & Kay Fairwell. (Great Explorations in Math & Science (GEMS) Ser.). (Illus.). 80p. (Orig.). 1987. teacher ed., pap. 21.00 (*0-912511-68-0*) Lawrence Science.

Shapes of Change: Images of American Dance. Marcia B. Siegel. LC 78-23669. 1985. pap. 14.95 (*0-520-04212-3*) U CA Pr.

Shapes of Christmas. (J). (gr. k-2). 1996. pap. 3.95 (*0-8167-2188-2*) Troll Communs.

Shapes of City Life in Rome & Pompeii: Essays in Honor of Lawrence Richardson, Jr. on the Occasion of His Retirement. Ed. by Harry B. Evans & Mary T. Boatwright. LC 96-27325. (Illus.). 139p. (C). 1996. lib. bdg. 50.00 (*0-89241-446-4*) Caratzas.

Shapes of Clay. Ambrose G. Bierce. (Principle Works of Ambrose Gwinett Bierce). 1989. reprint ed. lib. bdg. 79. 00 (*0-7812-1965-5*) Rprt Serv.

Shapes of Culture. Thomas McFarland. LC 86-14670. 201p. 1987. text ed. 27.95 (*0-87745-162-1*) U of Iowa Pr.

Shapes of Flowers: Spring. Nao Shibukawa. (Illus.). 104p. 1995. pap. 24.95 (*4-7661-0883-3*, Pub. by Graphic Sha JA) Bks Nippan.

Shapes of Flowers: Summer. Nao Shibukawa. (Illus.). 104p. 1995. pap. 24.95 (*4-7661-0884-1*, Pub. by Graphic Sha JA) Bks Nippan.

Shapes of Knowledge: From the Renaissance to the Enlightenment. Ed. by Ronald R. Kelley & Richard H. Popkin. 236p. (C). 1991. lib. bdg. 126.00 (*0-7923-1259-7*, Pub. by Klwr Acad Pubs NE) Kluwer Ac.

Shapes of Philosophical History. Frank E. Manuel. (Modern Revivals in Philosophy Ser.). 176p. 1993. 54.95 (*0-7512-0210-X*, Pub. by Gregg Revivals UK) Ashgate Pub Co.

Shapes of Philosophical History. Frank E. Manuel. 166p. 1965. 24.50 (*0-8047-0248-9*) Stanford U Pr.

Shapes of Philosophical History. Frank E. Manuel. LC 65-13111. (Harry Camp Lectures at Stanford University). 111p. reprint ed. pap. 30.00 (*0-7837-4069-7*, 2044025) Bks Demand.

Shapes of Power: The Development of Ezra Pound's Poetic Sequences. Bruce Fogelman. Ed. by A. Walton Litz. LC 88-9647. (Studies in Modern Literature: No. 95). 236p. reprint ed. 72.20 (*0-8357-1883-2*, 2070713) Bks Demand.

Shapes of Power, Belief & Celebration: African Art from New Orleans Collections. William A. Fagaly. (Illus.). 120p. 1991. pap. 19.95 (*0-295-96880-X*) U of Wash Pr.

Shapes of Revenge: Victimization, Vengeance, & Vindictiveness in Shakespeare. Harry Keyishian. LC 93-13228. (C). 1995. text ed. 39.95 (*0-391-03828-1*) Humanities.

Shapes of Sleep. large type ed. J. B. Priestley. 266p. 1990. 19.95 (*1-85089-299-7*, Pub. by ISIS UK) Transaction Pubs.

Shapes of Time: A New Look at the Philosophy of History. Peter Munz. LC 77-2459. 394p. reprint ed. pap. 112.30 (*0-8357-3533-8*, 2034661) Bks Demand.

***Shapes of Time: The Evolution of Growth & Development.** LC 96-29775. 1997. write for info. (*0-8018-5571-3*) Johns Hopkins.

Shapes, Shapes, Shapes. Tana Hoban. LC 85-17569. (Illus.). 32p. (J). (ps-3). 1986. 16.00 (*0-688-05832-9*); lib. bdg. 15.93 (*0-688-05833-7*) Greenwillow.

Shapes, Shapes, Shapes. Tana Hoban. LC 85-17569. (J). 1996. pap. 4.95 (*0-688-14740-2*, Mulberry) Morrow.

Shapes, Sizes & More Surprises! A Little Hands Early Learning Book. Mary Tomczyk. LC 95-10909. (Williamson Little Hands Book Ser.: No. 3). (Illus.). 144p. (J). (ps-1). 1995. pap. 12.95 (*0-913589-95-0*) Williamson Pub Co.

Shapes, Space & Symmetry. Alan Holden. (Illus.). 208p. reprint ed. pap. 8.95 (*0-486-26851-9*) Dover.

Shaping: New Poems in Traditional Prosodies. Intro. by Philip Jason. LC 77-13081. 1978. pap. text ed. 8.95 (*0-931848-11-3*) Dryad Pr.

Shaping a Business in Shanghai. (China Connection Ser.: No. Q170). 1994. 250.00 (*0-85058-788-3*) Economist Intell.

Shaping a Curriculum: For 4's & 5's. 1980. 17.00 (*0-939418-08-8*) Ferguson-Florissant.

Shaping a Healthy Religion: Especially if You Are Catholic. Thomas Aldworth. 132p. 1985. pap. 12.95 (*0-88347-200-7*) Res Christian Liv.

Shaping a House for the Church. Marchita Mauck. 105p. (Orig.). 1990. pap. 9.95 (*0-929650-06-9*) Liturgy Tr Pubns.

***Shaping a Life: Douglass College First Year Course.** Barbara Balliet & Suzan Armstrong-West. 250p. (C). 1996. per., pap. text ed. 29.34 (*0-7872-2793-5*) Kendall-Hunt.

Shaping a Maritime Empire: The Commercial & Diplomatic Role of the American Navy, 1829-1861. John H. Schroeder. LC 85-942. (Contributions in Military Studies: No. 48). (Illus.). ix, 229p. 1985. text ed. 59.95 (*0-313-24883-4*, SSH/, Greenwood Pr) Greenwood.

***Shaping a Nation.** Carter Wiseman. LC 97-9896. 1997. 29. 95 (*0-393-04564-1*) Norton.

Shaping a National Culture: The Philadelphia Experience, 1750-1800. Ed. by Catherine E. Hutchins. LC 94-22570. 376p. 1994. 35.00 (*0-912724-30-7*); pap. 22.50 (*0-912724-27-7*) Winterthur.

Shaping a National Urban Agenda: The Role of the Association of Collegiate Schools of Planning. Ed. by J. Eugene Grigsby, III & David R. Godschalk. (CAAS Urban Policy Ser.: Vol. 1). 122p. (C). 1993. pap. text ed. 9.00 (*0-934934-41-X*) CAAS Pubns.

Shaping a New Economic Relationship: The Republic of Korea & the United States. Ed. by Jongryn Mo & Ramon H. Myers. LC 93-24019. (Publication Ser.: No. 417). 202p. 1993. pap. 19.95 (*0-8179-9252-9*); text ed. 32.95 (*0-8179-9251-0*) Hoover Inst Pr.

Shaping a New Health Care System: The Explosion of Chronic Illness As a Catalyst for Change. Anselm Strauss & Juliet M. Corbin. LC 88-42801. (Health-Management Ser.). 192p. text ed. 50.00 (*1-55542-116-4*) Jossey-Bass.

Shaping a New World: An Orientation to Latin America. Ed. by Edward L. Cleary. LC 78-156969. 333p. reprint ed. pap. 95.00 (*0-8357-7019-2*, 2033538) Bks Demand.

***Shaping a President: Sculpting for the Roosevelt Memorial.** Kelli Peduzzi. LC 97-7331. (Illus.). 48p. (J). (gr. 3-6). 1997. 14.90 (*0-7613-0207-7*) Millbrook Pr.

***Shaping a President: Sculpting the Roosevelt Memorial.** Kelli Peduzzi. 1997. pap. text ed. 9.95 (*0-7613-0325-1*) Millbrook Pr.

Shaping a Woman's Soul: Daily Devotions to Calm Your Spirit & Lead You into God's Presence. Judith Couchman. 160p. 1996. pap. 9.99 (*0-310-20517-4*) Zondervan.

Shaping Agriculture in the 21st Century. Ed. by Ray Coppock & Stephanie W. Smith. 130p. (Orig.). 1995. pap. text ed. 15.00 (*1-885976-02-X*) U CA Agricult Issues.

Shaping America: The Politics of Supreme Court Appointments. George Watson & John A. Stookey. LC 94-18637. (C). 1995. text ed. 22.50 (*0-06-500863-4*) Addson-Wesley Educ.

Shaping American Global Policy: The Growing Impact of Societal Relations. 52p. (Orig.). (C). 1994. pap. text ed. 25.00 (*0-7881-1212-0*) DIANE Pub.

Shaping an American Institution: Robert E. Wood & Sears, Roebuck. James C. Worthy. LC 83-18157. (Illus.). 326p. 1984. text ed. 27.50 (*0-252-01051-5*) U of Ill Pr.

Shaping an American Landscape: The Art & Architecture of Charles A. Platt. Keith N. Morgan. LC 94-31831. 213p. 1995. pap. 29.95 (*0-87451-705-2*) U Pr of New Eng.

Shaping an American Landscape: The Art & Architecture of Charles A. Platt. Keith N. Morgan. LC 94-31831. 213p. 1995. text ed. 55.00 (*0-87451-704-4*) U Pr of New Eng.

Shaping an American Landscape: The Art & Architecture of Charles Platt. Keith Morgan et al. (Illus.). 1995. pap. 29.95 (*0-614-12960-5*) Hood Mus Art.

***Shaping & Integrating the Next Military: Organization Options for Defense Acquisition & Technology.** Paul Bracken et al. 40p. (Orig.). 1996. pap. text ed. 6.00 (*0-8330-2423-X*, DB-177-OSD) Rand Corp.

Shaping & Lofting: 3D Studio Tips & Tricks. Michele Bousquet. (3D Studio Tips & Tricks Ser.). 144p. 1994. pap. 26.50 (*0-8273-7015-6*) Delmar.

Shaping Britain for the Twenty-First Century. RICS Staff. (C). 1991. pap. text ed. 125.00 (*0-85406-501-6*, Pub. by R-I-C-S Bks UK) St Mut.

Shaping Childhood: Themes of Uncertainty in the History of Adult-Child Relationships. Roger Cox. 240p. (C). 1996. text ed. 65.00 (*0-415-11044-0*) Routledge.

Shaping Chinese Foreign Policy. O'Leary. (Australian National University Press Ser.). 1996. write for info. (*0-08-033000-2*, Pergamon Pr) Elsevier.

Shaping Cities: The Environmental & Human Dimensions. Marcia D. Lowe. 70p. (Orig.). 1991. pap. 5.00 (*1-878071-06-8*) Worldwatch Inst.

Shaping College Writing. 5th ed. Gallo. (C). 1991. teacher ed., pap. text ed. 3.00 (*0-15-580866-4*) HB Coll Pubs.

***Shaping College Writing.** 6th ed. Gallo. (C). 1996. pap. text ed. write for info. (*0-15-501551-6*) HB Coll Pubs.

Shaping College Writing: Paragraph & Essay. 5th ed. Joseph D. Gallo & Henry W. Rink. 170p. (Orig.). (C). 1990. pap. text ed. 17.50 (*0-15-580865-6*) HB Coll Pubs.

***Shaping Communities No. VI: Perspectives in Vernacular Architecture.** Ed. by Carter L. Hudgins & Elizabeth C. Cromley. (Illus.). 302p. 1997. pap. text ed. 30.00 (*0-87049-951-3*) U of Tenn Pr.

Shaping Competitive Advantages: Conceptual Framework & the Korean Approach. Wolfgang Hillebrand. LC 95-46990. (German Development Institute Ser.: No. 6). 280p. (Orig.). (C). 1996. pap. 29.50 (*0-7146-4247-9*, Pub. by F Cass Pubs UK) Intl Spec Bk.

Shaping Concensus: The North Commission on the Environment & NAFTA. (Illus.). 60p. (Orig.). (C). 1994. pap. text ed. 40.00 (*0-7881-1222-8*) DIANE Pub.

***Shaping Concepts of Technology: From Philosophical Perspective to Mental Images.** Mard D. Vries & Arley Tamir. LC 97-23318. 1997. write for info. (*0-7923-4647-5*) Kluwer Ac.

Shaping Constitutional Values: Elected Government, the Supreme Court, & the Abortion Debate. Neal Devins. LC 95-39584. (Interpreting American Politics Ser.). 224p. (C). 1996. text ed. 47.50 (*0-8018-5284-6*); pap. text ed. 14.95 (*0-8018-5285-4*) Johns Hopkins.

Shaping Education Policy in the States. Ed. by Susan Fuhrman & Alan Rosenthal. 140p. 1981. lib. bdg. 15.00 (*0-318-03011-X*) Inst Educ Lead.

Shaping Education Policy in the States. Ed. by Susan Fuhrman & Alan Rosenthal. 140p. 1981. pap. 9.50 (*0-318-03625-8*) Inst Educ Lead.

Shaping Educational Change: The First Century of the University of Northern Colorado at Greeley. Robert W. Larson. LC 88-352. (Illus.). 504p. (C). 1989. 39.95 (*0-87081-172-X*) Univ Pr Colo.

Shaping English Liturgy. Ed. by Peter Finn & James M. Schellman. 368p. (Orig.). (C). 1990. pap. 34.95 (*0-912405-72-4*) Pastoral Pr.

Shaping Europe's Military Order: The Origins & Consequences of CFE Treaty. Richard A. Falkenrath. (CSIA Studies in International Security: No. 6). 320p. 1995. 39.95 (*0-262-06177-5*) MIT Pr.

Shaping Europe's Military Order: The Origins & Consequences of the CFE Treaty. Richard A. Falkenrath. (CSIA Studies in International Security: No. 6). 320p. 1995. pap. 17.95 (*0-262-56086-0*) MIT Pr.

Shaping Florida: The Effects of Immigration - 1970-2020. Leon F. Bouvier et al. (Illus.). 16p. (Orig.). 1995. pap. 6.00 (*1-881290-14-X*) Ctr Immigrat.

Shaping Forces in Music. Ernst Toch. 1948. 12.95 (*0-910468-07-9*) Criterion Mus.

Shaping Forces in Music: An Inquiry into the Nature of Harmony, Melody, Counterpoint, Form. Ernst Toch. 1977. reprint ed. pap. text ed. 7.95 (*0-486-23346-4*) Dover.

Shaping Future Florists. Shirley L. Haas. 388p. 1995. per. 39.37 (*0-8403-5549-1*) Kendall-Hunt.

Shaping Georgia: The Effects of Immigration - 1970-2020. John L. Martin & Leon F. Bouvier. (Illus.). 16p. (Orig.). 1995. pap. 6.00 (*1-881290-16-6*) Ctr Immigrat.

Shaping Higher Education's Future: Demographic Realities & Opportunities, 1990-2000. Levine, Arthur, & Associates Staff. LC 89-45576. (Higher Education Ser.). 213p. text ed. 35.00 (*1-55542-191-1*) Jossey-Bass.

Shaping History: The Role of Newspapers in Hawai'i. Helen G. Chapin. LC 95-43101. (Illus.). 400p. (C). 1996. pap. 29.95 (*0-8248-1718-4*) UH Pr.

Shaping History Through Prayer & Fasting. Derek Prince. 1973. pap. 5.95 (*0-686-12766-8*) Derek Prince.

Shaping History Through Prayer & Fasting. Derek Prince. 224p. 1994. mass mkt. 4.99 (*0-88368-339-3*) Whitaker Hse.

Shaping Identity in Canadian Society. John D. Haas et al. 1978. pap. 14.00 (*0-13-808204-9*) P-H.

Shaping Identity in Eastern Europe & Russia: Soviet & Polish Accounts of Ukrainian History, 1914-1991. Stephen Valeychenko. LC 92-17764. 1993. text ed. 35.00 (*0-312-08552-4*) St Martin.

Shaping Illinois: The Effects of Immigration - 1970-2020. Leon F. Bouvier & Rosemary E. Jenks. (Illus.). 16p. (Orig.). 1996. pap. 6.00 (*1-881290-13-1*) Ctr Immigrat.

Shaping Invention. Carolyn C. Cooper. 1991. text ed. 49.50 (*0-231-06868-9*) Col U Pr.

Shaping Melbourne's Future? Town Planning, the State & Civil Society. J. Brian McLoughlin. (Illus.). 320p. (C). 1993. text ed. 69.95 (*0-521-41334-6*) Cambridge U Pr.

Shaping Modern Liberalism: Herbert Croly & Progressive Thought. Edward A. Stettner. LC 92-29943. (American Political Thought Ser.). 240p. 1993. 29.95 (*0-7006-0580-0*) U Pr of KS.

Shaping Modern Times in Rural France: The Transformation & Reproduction of an Aveygronnais Community. Susan C. Rogers. (Illus.). 235p. 1991. text ed. 49.50 (*0-691-09458-6*); pap. text ed. 17.95 (*0-691-02858-3*) Princeton U Pr.

Shaping National Responses to Climate Change: A Post-Rio Policy Guide. Ed. by Henry Lee. 352p. 1995. text ed. 48.00 (*1-55963-343-3*); pap. text ed. 24.95 (*1-55963-344-1*) Island Pr.

Shaping New Vision: Gender & Values in American Culture. Ed. by Clarissa W. Atkinson et al. LC 87-13854. (Studies in Religion: No. 5). 236p. reprint ed. pap. 67.30 (*0-8357-1803-4*, 2070625) Bks Demand.

Shaping of a Christian Family. Elisabeth Elliot. (Illus.). 240p. 1992. 15.99 (*0-8407-9136-4*) Nelson.

***Shaping of a Christian Family.** Elisabeth Elliot. 1997. pap. text ed. 12.99 (*0-7852-7449-9*) Nelson.

Shaping of a Community: The Rise & Reformation of the English Parish, c.1400-1560. Beat A. Kumin. (St. Andrews Studies in Reformation History: Vol. 1). (Illus.). 376p. 1996. 74.95 (*1-85928-164-8*, Pub. by Scolar Pr UK) Ashgate Pub Co.

Shaping of a Jewish Identity in Nineteenth Century France. Jay R. Berkovitz. LC 89-16507. 308p. (C). 1989. 34.95 (*0-8143-2011-2*) Wayne St U Pr.

Shaping of a Jewish Identity in Nineteenth-Century France. Jay R. Berkovitz. 308p. 1995. reprint ed. pap. text ed. 15.95 (*0-8143-2012-0*) Wayne St U Pr.

***Shaping of a Profession: Physicians in Norway, Past & Present.** Ivind Larsen & Bent O. Olsen. LC 96-46645. 1996. write for info. (*0-88135-168-7*) Watson Pub Intl.

Shaping of Adventism: The Case of W. W. Prescott. Gilbert M. Valentine. LC 91-75693. 330307p. 1991. 19.99 (*0-943872-56-1*) Andrews Univ Pr.

Shaping of America: A Geographical Prespective on 500 Years of History, Vol. 2: Continental. Donald W. Meinig. 1995. pap. text ed. 22.00 (*0-300-06290-7*) Yale U Pr.

Shaping of America Vol. 2: A Geological Perspective on 500 Years of American History: Continental America, 1800-1867. Donald W. Meinig. (Illus.). 656p. (C). 1993. 50.00 (*0-300-05658-3*) Yale U Pr.

Shaping of America, Vol. 1: A Geographical Perspective on 500 Years of History. Donald W. Meinig. LC 85-17962. 512p. (C). 1988. reprint ed. 22.00 (*0-300-03882-8*) Yale U Pr.

Shaping of American Congregationalism. John Von Rohr. LC 92-29485. 512p. (Orig.). 1992. pap. 29.95 (*0-8298-0921-X*) Pilgrim OH.

Shaping of Art History: Wilhelm Voge, Adolph Goldschmidt & the Study of Medieval Art. Kathryn Brush. (Illus.). 256p. (C). 1996. text ed. 69.95 (*0-521-47541-4*) Cambridge U Pr.

Shaping of Black America. Lerone Bennett, Jr. LC 74-20659. 365p. 1975. 19.95 (*0-87485-071-1*) Johnson Chi.

Shaping of Black America: The Struggles & Triumphs of African Americans, 1619-1990s. Lerone Bennett, Jr. 368p. 1993. pap. 13.95 (*0-14-017568-7*, Penguin Bks) Viking Penguin.

Shaping of British Policy During the Nationalist Revolution in China. Richard Stremski. LC 80-110682. Orig. Title: Soochow University Political Science Series. 179p. 1980. text ed. 20.00 (*0-931712-02-5*) Alpine Guild.

Shaping of Environmentalism in America. Victor B. Scheffer. LC 90-40577. (Illus.). 260p. 1991. 19.95 (*0-295-97060-X*) U of Wash Pr.

Shaping of Euro-Indian Philosophy: A Challenging Perspective. Anil K. Sarkar. 179p. 1995. reprint ed. pap. 51.10 (*0-608-01605-5*, AU0477) Bks Demand.

Shaping of Foreign Policy. Ed. by Harold K. Jacobson. (Controversy Ser.). 214p. 1969. 12.95 (*0-202-24071-1*); pap. 6.95 (*0-202-24072-X*) Lieber-Atherton.

Shaping of History & Poetry in Late Medieval France. Cynthia J. Brown. LC 85-61597. 215p. 1986. 18.95 (*0-917786-10-6*) Summa Pubns.

Shaping of Israeli Identity: Myth, Memory & Trauma. Ed. by Robert Wistrich & David Ohana. 240p. 1995. pap. 19.50 (*0-7146-4163-4*, Pub. by F Cass Pubs UK) Intl Spec Bk.

Shaping of Israeli Identity: Myth, Memory & Trauma. Ed. by Robert Wistrich & David Ohana. LC 95-15852. (Israel Affairs Ser.: Vol. 1, No. 3). 240p. 1995. 45.00 (*0-7146-4641-5*, Pub. by F Cass Pubs UK) Intl Spec Bk.

Shaping of Liberal Politics in Revolutionary France: A Comparative Perspective. Anne Sa'adah. 278p. 1990. text ed. 39.50 (*0-691-07824-6*) Princeton U Pr.

Shaping of Longfellow's John Endicott: A Textual History, Including Two Early Versions. Edward L. Tucker. LC 84-19652. 1985. text ed. 26.50 (*0-8139-1039-0*) U Pr of Va.

Shaping of Middle-Earth. J. R. R. Tolkien. LC 86-10338. (History of Middle Earth Ser.). (Illus.). 380p. (YA). 1986. 24.95 (*0-395-42501-8*) HM.

Shaping of Middle Earth: The Quenta, the Ambarkanta, & the Annals. J. R. R. Tolkien. 1986. 16.95 (*0-317-47339-5*) HM.

Shaping of Middle-Earth: The Quenta, The Ambarkanta & The Annals. J. R. R. Tolkien. (History of Middle-earth Ser.: No. 4). 1995. mass mkt. 6.99 (*0-345-40043-7*) Ballantine.

Shaping of Modern America, 1877-1920. 2nd ed. Vincent De Santis. (Forum's American History Ser.). 344p. (C). 1989. pap. text ed. 14.95 (*0-88273-136-X*) Forum Pr IL.

Shaping of Modern French Poetry: Reflections on Unrhymed Poetic Form, 1840-1990. Roger Little. 144p. 1996. pap. 18.95 incl. Apple II (*0-614-09904-8*, Pub. by Carcanet Pr UK); pap. 18.95 (*1-85754-189-8*, Pub. by Carcanet Pr UK) Paul & Co Pubs.

Shaping of Modern India. Ed. by Daniel Thorner. 1981. 28.00 (*0-8364-0678-8*, Pub. by Allied II) S Asia.

Shaping of Modern Psychology. Leslie S. Hearnshaw. 1989. pap. 14.95 (*0-415-03903-7*) Routledge.

Shaping of Modern Psychology: An Historical Introduction. Leslie S. Hearnshaw. 408p. 1987. text ed. 49.95 (*0-7102-0576-7*, 05767, RKP) Routledge.

Shaping of Musical Elements, Vol. 1. Armand Russell & Allen R. Trubitt. 410p. (C). 1992. 35.00 (*0-02-872080-6*); teacher ed., pap. write for info. (*0-02-872201-9*) Schirmer Bks.

Shaping of Musical Elements Vol. 2, Vol. 2. Armand Russell & Allen R. Trubitt. 494p. (C). 1992. 35.00 (*0-02-872120-9*) Schirmer Bks.

Shaping of Musical Elements Workbook, Vol. 1. Armand Russell & Allen R. Trubitt. 337p. (C). 1992. student ed. 19.00 (*0-02-872090-3*) Schirmer Bks.

Shaping of Musical Elements Workbook, Vol. 2. Armand Russell & Allen R. Trubitt. 429p. (C). 1992. student ed. 19.00 (*0-02-872200-0*) Schirmer Bks.

Shaping of Nineteenth-Century Law: John Appleton & Responsible Individualism. David M. Gold. LC 89-25706. (Contributions in Legal Studies: No. 57). 256p. 1990. text ed. 59.95 (*0-313-27340-5*, GBL/, Greenwood Pr) Greenwood.

Shaping of Peace: Canada & the Search for World Order, Vol. 1. John W. Holmes. LC 80-462171. 367p. reprint ed. pap. 104.60 (*0-8357-3764-0*, 2036493) Bks Demand.

Shaping of Quebec Politics & Society: Colonialism, Power, & the Transition to Capitalism in the 19th Century. Gerald Bernier & Daniel Salee. 250p. 1992. 49.00 (*0-8448-1697-3*, Crane Russak) Taylor & Francis.

Shaping of Scotland: Eighteenth Century Patterns of Land Use & Settlement. R. J. Brien. (Illus.). 150p. 1989. pap. text ed. 17.90 (*0-08-036572-8*, Pub. by Aberdeen U Pr) Macmillan.

Shaping of Somali Society: Reconstructing the History of a Pastoral People, 1600 to 1900. Lee V. Cassanelli. LC 81-43520. (Ethnohistory Ser.). 328p. reprint ed. pap. 93.50 (*0-7837-3007-1*, 2042934) Bks Demand.

Shaping of Southern Politics: Suffrage Restriction & the Establishment of the One-Party South, 1880-1910. fac. ed. J. Morgan Kousser. LC 73-86905. (Yale Historical Publications: Miscellany: No. 102). 337p. pap. 96.10 (*0-7837-7444-3*, 2082325) Bks Demand.

Shaping of Text: Style, Imagery, & Structure in French Literature, Essays in Honor of John Porter Houston. Ed. by Emanuel J. Mickel, Jr. LC 91-58183. 168p. (C). 1993. 32.50 (*0-8387-5227-6*) Bucknell U Pr.

Shaping of the American High School, Vol. 1, 1880-1920. Edward A. Krug. LC 64-12801. 504p. 1969. reprint ed. pap. text ed. 15.00 (*0-299-05165-X*) U of Wis Pr.

Shaping of the American High School, Vol. 2: Nineteen Twenty to Nineteen Forty-One. Edward A. Krug. LC 64-12801. 392p. 1972. 25.00 (*0-299-05980-4*) U of Wis Pr.

Shaping of the American Past. 5th ed. Robert Kelley. 976p. (C). 1989. Casebound. text ed. 57.80 (*0-13-808387-8*) P-H.

Shaping of the American Past, I. 5th ed. Robert Kelley. 976p. (C). 1989. pap. text ed. 36.00 (*0-13-808361-4*) P-H.

Shaping of the Dynasts: A Study in Thomas Hardy. Walter F. Wright. LC 67-19159. 356p. reprint ed. pap. 101.50 (*0-7837-1831-4*, 2042031) Bks Demand.

Shaping of the Elizabethan Regime. Wallace T. MacCaffrey. 528p. 1994. pap. text ed. 19.95 (*0-691-00767-5*, 250) Princeton U Pr.

Shaping of the Elizabethan Regime. Wallace T. MacCaffrey. LC 68-27409. 517p. reprint ed. 147.40 (*0-8357-9513-6*, 2014636) Bks Demand.

Shaping of the Foundations: Being at Home in the Transcendental Method. Philip McShane. 24.00 (*0-8191-0209-1*) U Pr of Amer.

Shaping of the Modern Middle East. rev. ed. Bernard Lewis. (Illus.). 224p. (C). 1994. 31.95 (*0-19-507281-2*); pap. text ed. 16.95 (*0-19-507282-0*) OUP.

Shaping of the Modern World from the Enlightenment to the Present. Date not set. pap. text ed. 20.50 (*0-314-05755-2*) West Pub.

Shaping of the Socio-Economic Systems. Thomas Baumgartmer et al. (Studies in Cybernetics: Vol. 11). xiv, 360p. 1986. text ed. 87.00 (*2-88124-003-8*) Gordon & Breach.

Shaping of the Socio-Economic Systems. Thomas Baumgartmer et al. (Studies in Cybernetics: Vol. 2). xiv, 360p. 1986. pap. text ed. 48.00 (*2-88124-027-5*) Gordon & Breach.

Shaping of the Welfare State. R. C. Birch. (Seminar Studies in History). 126p. (C). 1974. pap. text ed. 6.95 (*0-582-35200-2*) Longman.

Shaping of Vermont: From the Wilderness to the Centennial 1749-1877. J. Kevin Graffagnino. LC 82-84526. (Illus.). 180p. 1983. 49.50 (*0-911853-01-4*) Vermont Herit Pr.

Shaping of Vermont: From the Wilderness to the Centennial 1749-1877. limited ed. J. Kevin Graffagnino. LC 82-84526. (Illus.). 180p. 1983. 250.00 (*0-911853-00-6*) Vermont Herit Pr.

Shaping Our Environmental Conscience. Gary Cochran. 1995. pap. text ed. 8.95 (*1-882270-29-0*, ORC Pr) Old Rugged Cross.

Shaping Our Future: Challenges for the Church in the Twenty-First Century. Ed. by J. Stephen Freeman. LC 94-12570. 208p. 1994. pap. 14.95 (*1-56101-097-9*) Cowley Pubns.

Shaping Political Attitudes: The Impact of Interpersonal Communication & Mass Media. Silvo Lenart. LC 94-15533. 192p. 1994. 39.95 (*0-8039-5708-4*); pap. 18.50 (*0-8039-5709-2*) Sage.

Shaping Political Consciousness: The Language of Politics in America from McKinley to Reagan. fac. ed. David Green. LC 87-47598. reprint ed. pap. 83.30 (*0-608-01016-2*, 2061874) Bks Demand.

Shaping Postwar Europe: European Unity & Disunity, 1945-1957. Ed. by Peter M. Stirk & David Willis. 232p. 1991. text ed. 49.95 (*0-312-06143-9*) St Martin.

Shaping Psychology: How We Got Where We're Going. Timothy Gannon. (Sources in Semiotics Ser.: Vol. X). 322p. (C). 1991. lib. bdg. 54.50 (*0-8191-7757-1*) U Pr of Amer.

Shaping Revolution. Ed. by Elspeth Attwooll. (Enlightenment Rights & Revolution Ser.). 160p. 1991. pap. 37.90 (*0-08-040925-3*, Pub. by Aberdeen U Pr) Macmillan.

Shaping Romance: Interpretation, Truth, & Closure in Twelfth-Century French Fictions. Matilda T. Bruckner. LC 93-2069. (Middle Ages Ser.). 304p. (C). 1993. text ed. 39.95 (*0-8122-3169-4*) U of Pa Pr.

Shaping School Policy: Guide to Choices, Politics, & Community Relations. Karen S. Gallagher. LC 92-4571. 112p. 1992. pap. 18.00 (*0-8039-6022-0*) Corwin Pr.

Shaping Seattle Architecture: A Historical Guide to the Architects. Ed. by Jeffrey K. Ochsner. LC 94-17618. (Illus.). 446p. 1994. 40.00 (*0-295-97365-X*); pap. 19.95 (*0-295-97366-8*) U of Wash Pr.

Shaping South Asia's Future Role of Regional Cooperation. Kant K. Bhargava. Ed. by Heinz Bongartz & Farooq Sobhan. (C). 1995. 28.00 (*0-7069-9225-3*, Pub. by Vikas II) S Asia.

Shaping Space. Paul Zelanski. 304p. (C). 1987. pap. text ed. 37.25 (*0-03-001078-0*) HB Coll Pubs.

***Shaping Space.** 2nd ed. Zelansk. (C). 1995. pap. write for info. (*0-03-076546-3*) HB Coll Pubs.

Shaping Space: The Dynamics of Three-Dimensional Design. Paul Zelanski & Mary P. Fisher. 286p. (C). 1987. pap. text ed. write for info. (*0-318-69120-5*) HB Coll Pubs.

Shaping Spokane: Jay P. Graves & His Times. John Fahey. LC 94-3347. (Illus.). 168p. 1994. text ed. 25.00 (*0-295-97395-1*) U of Wash Pr.

Shaping Standardization: A Study of Standards Processes & Standards Policies in the Field of Telematic Services. Tineke Egyedi. 329p. (Orig.). 1996. pap. 87.50 (*90-407-1201-8*, Pub. by Delft U Pr NE) Coronet Bks.

Shaping Strategic Change. Andrew Pettigrew et al. (Illus.). 336p. (C). 1992. 75.00 (*0-8039-8778-1*); pap. 27.95 (*0-8039-8779-X*) Sage.

***Shaping Structures: Statics.** Waclaw Zalewski & Edward Allen. text ed. write for info. (*0-471-16968-4*) Wiley.

Shaping Suburbia: How Political Institutions Organize Urban Development. Paul G. Lewis. LC 95-52088. (Pitt Series in Policy & Institutional). 208p. (C). 1996. pap. 19.95 (*0-8229-5595-4*); text ed. 44.95 (*0-8229-3938-X*) U of Pittsburgh Pr.

Shaping Technology - Building Society: Studies in Sociotechnical Change. Ed. by Wiebe E. Bijker & John Law. (Inside Technology Ser.). (Illus.). 400p. 1992. 35.00 (*0-262-02338-5*) MIT Pr.

Shaping Technology, Building Society: Studies in SocioTechnical Change. Ed. by Wiebe E. Bijker & John Law. (Inside Technology Ser.). (Illus.). 352p. 1994. pap. 17.50 (*0-262-52194-6*) MIT Pr.

Shaping Texas: The Effects of Immigration - 1970-2020. John L. Martin & Leon F. Bouvier. (Illus.). 16p. (Orig.). 1995. pap. 6.00 (*1-881290-18-2*) Ctr Immigrat.

Shaping the Accountancy Profession: The Story of Three Scottish Pioneers. Ed. by Thomas A. Lee. LC 95-49826. (New Works in Accounting History). (Illus.). 264p. 1996. reprint ed. text ed. 52.00 (*0-8153-2269-0*) Garland.

Shaping the City. Gregory F. Gilmartin. 1996. pap. 20.00 (*0-517-88610-3*) Random Hse Value.

***Shaping the City.** Gregory F. Gilmartin. 1996. 9.99 (*0-517-17193-7*) Random Hse Value.

Shaping the College Curriculum: Academic Plans in Action. Joan S. Stark & Lisa R. Lattuca. 496p. 1996. 41.95 (*0-205-16706-3*) Allyn.

Shaping the College Experience Outside the Classroom. James Scannell & Kathleen Simpson. (Illus.). 168p. (C). 1996. 45.00 (*1-878822-68-3*) Univ Rochester Pr.

Shaping the Community College Image. Ed. by Steven W. Jones. LC 92-83906. 154p. (Orig.). 1993. pap. 25.00 (*0-9635800-1-9*) Nat Coun Mkt.

Shaping the Corporate Image: An Analytical Guide for Executive Decision Makers. Marion G. Sobol et al. LC 91-38239. 184p. 1992. text ed. 45.00 (*0-89930-564-4*, SOF, Quorum Bks) Greenwood.

Shaping the Culture of Schooling: The Rise of Outcome-Based Education. Cheryl T. Desmond. LC 95-44256. (SUNY Series, Education & Culture). 181p. (C). 1996. text ed. 49.50 (*0-7914-2955-5*); pap. text ed. 17.95 (*0-7914-2956-3*) State U NY Pr.

Shaping the Defense Civilian Work Force: Economics, Politics, & National Security. Martin Binkin & Rolf H. Clark. LC 78-14897. (Studies in Defense Policy). 113p. 1978. pap. 7.95 (*0-8157-0967-6*) Brookings.

Shaping the Earth: Tectonics of Continents & Oceans. Eldridge M. Moores. (C). 1995. text ed. write for info. (*0-7167-2141-4*) W H Freeman.

Shaping the Easter Feast. Anscar J. Chupungco. (NPM Studies in Church Music & Liturgy). (Orig.). 1992. pap. text ed. 9.95 (*0-912405-95-3*) Pastoral Pr.

Shaping the Eighteen Amendment: Temperance Reform, Legal Culture, & the Polity, 1880-1920. Richard F. Hamm. LC 94-17948. (Studies in Legal History). 380p. 1995. pap. text ed. 18.95 (*0-8078-4493-4*); lib. bdg. 49.95 (*0-8078-2181-0*) U of NC Pr.

Shaping the First Amendment: The Development of Free Expression. John D. Stevens. LC 82-10556. (Sage Commtext Ser.: No. 11). 157p. reprint ed. pap. 44.80 (*0-8357-8512-2*, 2034809) Bks Demand.

Shaping the Future: Biology & Human Values. National Research Council Staff. 132p. 1989. 17.95 (*0-309-03947-9*) Natl Acad Pr.

Shaping the Future: Business Design Through Information Technology. Peter G. Keen. 1991. text ed. 29.95 (*0-07-103289-4*) McGraw.

Shaping the Future: Business Design Through Information Technology. Peter G.W. Keen. 288p. 1991. 29.95 (*0-87584-237-2*) Harvard Busn.

Shaping the Future: Challenges & Opportunities. Ed. by Helen S. Lepke. (Reports of the Northeast Conference on the Teaching of Foreign Languages). 164p. 1989. pap. 10.95 (*0-915432-89-7*) NE Conf Teach Foreign.

***Shaping the Future: Higher Education Finance in the 1990s.** Patrick M. Callan & Joni E. Finney. (Ace/Oryx Series on Higher Education). 256p. (C). 1997. text ed. 39.95 (*1-57356-116-9*) Oryx Pr.

***Shaping the Future of Feminist Psychology: Education, Research, & Practice.** Ed. by Judith Worell & Norine G. Johnson. LC 97-17947. 280p. 1997. text ed. 39.95 (*1-55798-448-4*, 431-6940) Am Psychol.

***Shaping the Landscape Image, 1865-1910: John Douglas Woodward.** Sue Rainey et al. LC 97-6008. (Illus.). 1997. pap. 24.95 (*0-8139-1768-9*) U Pr of Va.

Shaping the Local Economy: Current Perspectives on Economic Development. Ed. by Cheryl A. Farr. LC 84-6693. (Practical Management Ser.). (Illus.). 182p. (Orig.). 1984. pap. text ed. 23.95 (*0-87326-034-1*) Intl City-Cnty Mgt.

***Shaping the Nature of Future Literacy: A Synopsis.** unabridged ed. Martin L. Ernst. 20p. (Orig.). 1996. pap. text ed. write for info. (*1-879716-37-2*, I-96-3) Ctr Info Policy.

Shaping the Netherlandish Canon: Karel Van Mander's Schilder-Boeck. Walter S. Melion. LC 91-2806. (Illus.). 385p. 1992. 52.00 (*0-226-51959-7*) U Ch Pr.

Shaping the New Social Work. Alfred J. Kahn. LC 73-4189. (Social Work & Social Issues Ser.). 221p. 1977. pap. text ed. 21.00 (*0-231-08356-4*) Col U Pr.

Shaping the Novel: Textual Interplay in the Fiction of Malraux, Hebert & Modiano. Constantina T. Mitchell & Paul R. Cote. LC 95-36839. 240p. 1996. 49.95 (*1-57181-036-6*) Berghahn Bks.

Shaping the Political Arena: Critical Junctures, the Labor Movement, & Regime Dynamics in Latin America. Ruth B. Collier & David Collier. (Illus.). 845p. 1991. text ed. 95.00 (*0-691-07830-0*); pap. text ed. 26.95 (*0-691-02313-1*) Princeton U Pr.

Shaping the Preschool Agenda: Early Literacy, Public Policy, & Professional Beliefs. Anne McGill-Franzen. LC 91-34722. (SUNY Series, Literacy, Culture, & Learning: Theory & Practice). (Illus.). 227p. (C). 1992. text ed. 64.50 (*0-7914-1195-8*); pap. text ed. 21.95 (*0-7914-1196-6*) State U NY Pr.

Shaping the Schools of the Canadian West. Ed. by David C. Jones et al. 256p. (Orig.). (C). 1979. pap. text ed. 13.95 (*0-920490-01-8*) Temeron Bks.

Shaping the Shorter Essay. Patricia S. Taylor. (C). 1991. pap. text ed. 33.50 (*0-673-39678-9*) Addson-Wesley Educ.

Shaping the Superintendency: A Reexamination of Callahan & the Cult of Efficiency. Ed. by William E. Eaton. 224p. (C). 1989. text ed. 27.00 (*0-8077-2985-X*) Tchrs Coll.

***Shaping the Superintendency: A Reexamination of Callahan & the Cult of Efficiency.** Ed. by William E. Eaton. LC 89-38171. 224p. pap. 63.90 (*0-608-05095-4*, 2065651) Bks Demand.

Shaping Things to Come. Griscom Morgan et al. 1980. pap. 1.00 (*0-910420-27-0*) Comm Serv OH.

Shaping Time: Music, the Brain & Performance. David Epstein. 598p. 1995. 48.00 (*0-02-873320-7*) Schirmer Bks.

Shaping Tomorrow, Starting Today. Ed. by G. Grogan. 10.99 (*1-85792-007-4*, Pub. by Christian Focus UK) Spring Arbor Dist.

An Asterisk (*) at the beginning of an entry indicates that the title is appearing in BIP for the first time.

Shaping Tradition: Art & Diversity in the Essay. Sandra F. Tropp. 800p. (C). 1992. pap. text ed. 21.50 (*0-03-049518-0*); pap. text ed. 4.00 (*0-03-049519-9*) HB Coll Pubs.

Shaping U. S. Foreign Policy: Profiles of Twelve Secretaries of State. Edward F. Dolan & Margaret M. Scariano. (Democracy in Action Ser.). (Illus.). 128p. (YA). (gr. 7-12). 1996. lib. bdg. 22.70 (*0-531-11264-0*) Watts.

Shaping Up. Shirley Lowe & Angela Ince. 256p. 1992. 24.95 (*0-340-52830-3*, Pub. by H & S UK) Trafalgar.

Shaping Up for a Healthy Pregnancy. Barbara B. Holstein. LC 87-38757. (Illus.). 240p. (Orig.). 1988. pap. text ed. 26.00 (*0-87322-926-6*, BHOL0926) Human Kinetics.

***Shaping up for Sight Word Success.** Valerie F. Harris & Eula V. Jones. 30p. (J). (gr. k-6). Date not set. wbk. ed. write for info. (*1-889654-03-5*) Enricharamics.

Shaping up to Womanhood: Gender & Girls' Physical Education. Sheila Scraton. (Gender & Education Ser.). 160p. 1992. pap. 27.00 (*0-335-09693-X*, Open Univ Pr) Taylor & Francis.

Shaping up Your English. Pat Wellington. LC 94-8812. 1994. pap. text ed. 28.00 (*0-205-13785-7*) Allyn.

Shaping Welfare Consensus: U. S. Catholic Bishops Contribution. Philip Land. 217p. (Orig.). (C). 1988. pap. text ed. 7.95 (*0-934255-07-5*) Center Concern.

Shaping Women's Work: Gender, Employment, & Information Technology. Juliet Webster. LC 96-459. (Sociology Ser.). (C). 1996. pap. text ed. 14.95 (*0-582-21810-1*, Pub. by Longman UK) Longman.

Shaping Women's Work: Gender, Employment, & Information Technology. Juliet Webster. LC 96-459. (Sociology Ser.). 1996. write for info. (*0-582-21811-X*, Pub. by Longman UK) Longman.

Shaping Wood: A New Woodworking Approach. Douglas Hackett. 1992. pap. text ed. 14.95 (*0-07-157867-6*) McGraw.

Shaping Wood: A New Woodworking Approach. Douglas Hackett. 176p. 1992. pap. 14.95 (*0-8306-3936-5*) McGraw-Hill Prof.

***Shaping World History: Breakthroughs in Ecology, Technology, Science, & Politics.** Mary K. Matossian. LC 96-29807. (Sources & Studies in World History). 264p. (C). (gr. 13). 1997. pap. 22.95 (*0-7656-0062-5*) M E Sharpe.

***Shaping World History: Breakthroughs in Ecology, Technology, Science, & Politics.** Mary K. Matossian. LC 96-29807. (Sources & Studies in World History). 256p. (C). (gr. 13). 1997. 62.95 (*0-7656-0061-7*) M E Sharpe.

Shaping Written Knowledge: The Genre & Activity of the Experimental Article in Science. Charles Bazerman. LC 88-40187. (Rhetoric of the Human Sciences Ser.). 400p. (C). 1988. text ed. 40.00 (*0-299-11690-5*); pap. text ed. 17.50 (*0-299-11694-8*) U of Wis Pr.

Shaping Written Knowledge: The Genre & Activity of the Experimental Article in Science. Charles Bazerman. LC 88-40187. (Rhetoric of the Human Sciences Ser.). 368p. 1988. reprint ed. pap. 104.90 (*0-7837-9775-3*, 2060504) Bks Demand.

Shaping Your Life: The Power of Creative Imagery. Laurel J. Fuller. 224p. 1994. pap. 9.95 (*0-944386-14-8*) SOM Pub.

Shaping Your Puppy's Future: A Commonsense Guide to Positive Training. Shirley G. Sullivan. 80p. (Orig.). 1996. pap. 15.00 (*0-938872-23-0*) Black Buzzard.

***Shapinsky's Karma, Boggs Balls.** Lawrence Weschler. 1998. pap. write for info. (*0-679-77751-2*, Vin) Random.

Shapiro Diamond. large type ed. Michael Legat. 448p. 1984. 27.99 (*0-7089-8213-1*) Ulverscroft.

Shapiro's C. P. L. Explanatory Quizzer. Irving Shapiro. 260p. 1997. ring bd. 10.95 (*0-930137-46-9*) Looseleaf Law.

Shapiro's C. P. L. R. Explanatory Quizzer for New York State. Irving Shapiro & Peter J. McGuinness. 280p. 1997. ring bd. 15.95 (*0-930137-61-2*) Looseleaf Law.

Shapiro's Penal Law Explanatory Quizzer N.Y.S. Irving Shapiro. 260p. 1997. ring bd. 10.95 (*0-930137-03-5*) Looseleaf Law.

Shapley. The Shapleigh, Shapley & Shappley Families: A Comprehensive Genealogy, 1635-1993. Brian J. Berry. (Illus.). 534p. 1995. reprint ed. pap. 79.50 (*0-8328-4890-5*); reprint ed. lib. bdg. 89.50 (*0-8328-4889-1*) Higginson Bk Co.

Shapley Value: Essays in Honor of Lloyd S. Shapley. Ed. by Alvin E. Roth. (Illus.). 320p. 1988. text ed. 85.00 (*0-521-36177-X*) Cambridge U Pr.

Shapley. Westward, the American Shapleys: The Family & Descendants of David Shapley, a 17th-Century Marblehead (MA.), with Pedigrees of Spouses...& English Ancestry & American Descent of Five Additional Shapley Immigrants. Brian J. Berry. (Illus.). 466p. 1995. reprint ed. pap. 69.50 (*0-8328-4888-3*); reprint ed. lib. bdg. 79.50 (*0-8328-4887-5*) Higginson Bk Co.

Shaq. Peter C. Bjarkman. 64p. 1994. 9.98 (*0-8317-7983-7*) Smithmark.

Shaq. Dennis Eichhorn. (Illus.). 79p. (Orig.). (YA). (gr. 7-12). 1995. pap. 4.25 (*0-89872-221-7*) Turman Pub.

Shaquille O'Neal. Ed. by James Beckett. 1995. pap. 15.00 (*0-614-15518-5*, Harvest Bks) HarBrace.

Shaquille O'Neal. Michael E. Goodman. LC 93-49103. (Ovations Ser.). (Illus.). 32p. (YA). (gr. 4 up). 1998. lib. bdg. 14.95 (*0-88682-633-0*) Creative Ed.

***Shaquille O'Neal.** Gutman. (J). 1998. mass mkt. 3.99 (*0-671-01541-9*) PB.

***Shaquille O'Neal.** Paul Joseph. LC 96-25155. (Awesome Athletes Ser.). (J). 1997. lib. bdg. 13.95 (*1-56239-642-0*) Abdo & Dghtrs.

Shaquille O'Neal. Richard Rambeck. LC 95-6462. (Sports Superstars Ser.). (Illus.). 24p. (J). (gr. 2-6). 1995. lib. bdg. 21.36 (*1-56766-199-8*) Childs World.

Shaquille O'Neal. Ken Rappoport. LC 93-38561. 128p. (YA). 1994. 15.95 (*0-8027-8294-9*); lib. bdg. 16.85 (*0-8027-8295-7*) Walker & Co.

Shaquille O'Neal. Edward Tallman. LC 94-18182. (Taking Part Ser.). (J). 1994. text ed. 13.95 (*0-87518-637-8*, Dillon Silver Burdett) Silver Burdett Pr.

Shaquille O'Neal. Edward Tallman. (Taking Part Ser.). 72p. (J). 1994. pap. 7.95 (*0-382-24727-2*, Dillon Silver Burdett) Silver Burdett Pr.

Shaquille O'Neal. Tim Ungs. LC 95-9263. (Basketball Legends Ser.). (Illus.). 64p. (J). (gr. 3 up). 1996. lib. bdg. 15.95 (*0-7910-2437-7*) Chelsea Hse.

Shaquille O'Neal. Bob Woods. LC 94-22752. (Illus.). 32p. (J). (gr. 3-6). 1995. pap. 2.25 (*0-8167-3568-9*, Whistlstop) Troll Communs.

Shaquille O'Neal: A Biography. Bill Gutman. (YA). (gr. 5 up). 1993. pap. 3.99 (*0-671-88088-8*) PB.

Shaquille O'Neal: Basketball Sensation. Bill Gutman. (Sports World Ser.). (Illus.). 48p. (J). (gr. 3-6). 1994. pap. 6.95 (*1-56294-869-5*); lib. bdg. 14.90 (*1-56294-460-6*) Millbrook Pr.

Shaquille O'Neal: Center of Attention. Brad Townsend. LC 93-35558. (Sports Achievers Biographies Ser.). (Illus.). (J). (gr. 4-9). 1994. lib. bdg. 19.95 (*0-8225-2879-7*, Lerner Publctns) Lerner Group.

Shaquille O'Neal: Center of Attention. Brad Townsend. (Sports Achievers Biographies Ser.). (Illus.). (J). (gr. 4-9). 1994. pap. 5.95 (*0-8225-9655-5*, First Ave Edns) Lerner Group.

***Shaquille O'Neal: Center of Attention.** Brad Townsend. (Lerner Sports Achievers Ser.). (J). 1997. pap. text ed. 5.95 (*0-8225-9780-2*) Lerner Group.

Shaquille O'Neal: Shaq Attack. Ted Cox. LC 93-19781. (Sports Stars Ser.). (Illus.). 48p. (J). (gr. 2-8). 1993. pap. 4.50 (*0-516-44379-8*); lib. bdg. 17.50 (*0-516-04379-X*) Childrens.

Shaquille O'Neal: Star Center. Glen Macnow. LC 96-3425. (Sports Reports). (Illus.). (J). (gr. 4-10). 1996. lib. bdg. 18.95 (*0-89490-656-9*) Enslow Pubs.

Shar Dea, Empress of Peace. Robert V. Gerard. LC 87-71722. 192p. (Orig.). 1988. pap. 8.95 (*0-916383-40-7*) Aegina Pr.

Shar-Pei. Ellen W. Debo. (Illus.). 256p. 1986. 24.95 (*0-86622-154-9*, PS-818) TFH Pubns.

Shar-Pei. Tanya B. Ditto. (Complete Pet Owner's Manual Ser.). (Illus.). 64p. 1992. pap. 6.95 (*0-8120-4834-2*) Barron.

Shar Pei, AKC Rank No. 25. Anna K. Nicholas. (KW Dog Ser.). (Illus.). 224p. 1996. pap. 9.95 (*0-7938-2359-5*, KW156S) TFH Pubns.

Sharad Pawar: The Making of a Modern Maratha. P. K. Ravindranath. (C). 1992. 14.00 (*81-85674-46-9*, Pub. by UBS Pubs Dist II) S Asia.

Sharafuddin Maneri: The Hundred Letters. Ed. by Paul Jackson. LC 79-56754. (Classics of Western Spirituality Ser.). 480p. 1980. pap. 9.95 (*0-8091-2229-4*) Paulist Pr.

Sharaku: Masterworks of Ukiyo-E. Muneshige Narazaki. Tr. by Bonnie F. Abiko. (Illus.). 96p. 1995. 40.00 (*4-7700-1910-6*) Kodansha.

Shard at Lynchburg. large type ed. John Blaze. LC 96-10451. (Nightingale Ser.). 184p. 1996. pap. 17.95 (*0-7838-1735-5*, GK Hall) Thorndike Pr.

***Shard Brand.** large type ed. B. J. Holmes. (Linford Western Large Print Ser.). 272p. 1997. pap. 16.99 (*0-7089-5053-1*) Ulverscroft.

Shard Calls the Tune. large type ed. Philip McCutchan. 320p. 1994. 25.99 (*0-7505-0537-0*, Pub. by Magna Print Bks UK) Ulverscroft.

***Shards.** David A. Bolduc. 70p. (Orig.). 1994. pap. 7.95 (*0-9646610-1-2*) Toth Pr.

Shards. Tom Piccirilli. 214p. 1996. 20.95 (*1-885173-23-7*) Write Way.

***Shards.** Tom Piccirilli. 1997. pap. text ed. 5.95 (*1-885173-41-5*) Write Way.

Shards. Frank Stella. LC 82-22304. (Illus.). (Orig.). 1983. pap. 6.95 (*0-902825-19-4*) Petersburg Pr.

Shards from the Heart: A Spiritual Odyssey in Twentieth Century America. Bernard J. Garber. LC 64-13358. (Freedeeds Library). 160p. 1965. pap. 6.95 (*0-8334-1015-6*, Freedeeds Libr) Garber Comm.

***Shards of Alderaan.** Kevin J. Anderson. (Star Wars Young Jedi Knights Ser.). 1997. mass mkt. 5.99 (*1-57297-207-6*) Blvd Books.

Shards of Empire. Susan Shwartz. 384p. 1996. 23.95 (*0-312-85716-0*) Tor Bks.

***Shards of Empire.** Susan Shwartz. 1996. mass mkt. 5.99 (*0-8125-4817-5*) Tor Bks.

Shards of Glass: Children Reading & Writing Beyond Gendered Identity. Bronwyn Davies & Judith L. Green. LC 93-11086. (Language & Social Processes Ser.). 228p. 1993. pap. text ed. 19.50 (*1-881303-18-7*) Hampton Pr NJ.

Shards of Honor. Lois M. Bujold. 1991. mass mkt. 5.99 (*0-671-72087-2*) Baen Bks.

Shards of Love: Exile & the Origins of the Lyric. Maria R. Menocal. LC 93-26530. 312p. 1993. text ed. 49.95 (*0-8223-1405-3*); pap. text ed. 18.95 (*0-8223-1419-3*) Duke.

Shards of Memory. Ruth P. Jhabvala. 224p. 1996. pap. 11.00 (*0-385-47723-6*, Anchor NY) Doubleday.

Share & Grow Rich. Jim Sims. 100p. (Orig.). (C). 1989. pap. text ed. 19.95 (*0-9622643-0-X*) Altaverde Pub.

***Share Bear.** Paul Stickland. 1997. pap. 4.99 (*0-525-45681-3*) NAL-Dutton.

Share Bears. (Illus.). 14p. (J). (ps). 1995. bds. 4.95 (*0-87406-759-6*) Willowisp Pr.

Share Economy: Conquering Stagflation. Martin L. Weitzman. 176p. (C). 1984. 23.50 (*0-674-80582-8*) HUP.

Share Economy: Conquering Stagflation. Martin L. Weitzman. (Illus.). 176p. 1986. pap. text ed. 8.95 (*0-674-80583-6*) HUP.

Share in Death. large type ed. Deborah Crombie. LC 93-21675. 316p. 1993. reprint ed. lib. bdg. 20.95 (*0-7862-0012-X*) Thorndike Pr.

Share in Death. Deborah Crombie. 208p. 1994. reprint ed. pap. 5.50 (*0-425-14197-7*, Prime Crime) Berkley Pub.

Share in the Kingdom: A Commentary on the Rule of St. Benedict for Oblates. Benet Tvedten. 80p. 1989. pap. 4.95 (*0-8146-1808-1*) Liturgical Pr.

Share It. (J). 1993. pap. 8.98 (*1-879496-57-7*) Lightyear Entrtnmnt.

***Share Life's Defining Moments: Relating to Your Grown Children.** Eldon Weisheit. LC 97-8383. 1997. write for info. (*0-570-04990-3*) Concordia.

Share of Financial Intermediaries in National Wealth & National Assets, 1900-1949. Raymond W. Goldsmith. (Occasional Papers: No. 42). 135p. 1954. reprint ed. 35.10 (*0-87014-356-5*); reprint ed. mic. film 20.00 (*0-685-61293-7*) Natl Bur Econ Res.

Share of Freedom. June R. Wood. LC 95-45022. 256p. (J). (gr. 4-8). 1996. pap. 4.95 (*0-7868-1085-8*) Hyprn Child.

Share of Freedom. June R. Wood. LC 94-6578. 256p. (YA). 1994. 15.95 (*0-399-22767-9*, Putnam) Putnam Pub Group.

Share of the Harvest: Kinship, Property, & Social History among the Malays of Rembau. Michael G. Peletz. 448p. 1988. 50.00 (*0-520-06153-5*) U CA Pr.

Share of the Harvest: Kinship, Property & Social History among the Malays of Rembau. Michael G. Peletz. 1992. pap. 17.00 (*0-520-08086-6*) U CA Pr.

Share of Thomas Aquinas in the Growth of the Witchcraft Delusion. Charles E. Hopkin. LC 79-8103. 208p. reprint ed. 39.50 (*0-404-18415-4*) AMS Pr.

Share of Top Wealth-Holders in National Wealth, 1922-56. Robert J. Lampman. (General Ser.: No. 74). 316p. 1962. reprint ed. 82.20 (*0-87014-073-6*) Ayer.

Share of Top Wealth-Holders in National Wealth, 1922-56. Robert J. Lampman. LC 84-19118. xxvii, 286p. 1984. reprint ed. text ed. 79.50 (*0-313-24425-1*, LAST, Greenwood Pr) Greenwood.

Share Rental Survival Guide: Open Your Door to Fun & Profit. Barbara W. Nelson. (Orig.). 1989. write for info. (*0-318-63724-3*) Mediawrite.

Share Systems & Unemployment: A Theoretical Analysis. Franco Cugno & Mario Ferraro. LC 90-43871. 144p. 1991. text ed. 65.00 (*0-312-05015-1*) St Martin.

Share the Care: An Evaluation of a Family-Based Respite Care Service. Kirsten Stalker. 160p. 1990. 42.50 (*1-85302-038-9*) Taylor & Francis.

Share the Care: How to Organize a Group to Care For Someone Who is Seriously Ill. Cappy Capossela & Sheila Warnock. 320p. 1995. pap. 13.00 (*0-684-81136-7*, Fireside) S&S Trade.

Share the Experience Vol. 9. Ed. by Virginia Thomas. (Brewery Operations Ser.). (Illus.). 330p. (Orig.). 1992. pap. 25.95 (*0-937381-32-2*) Brewers Pubns.

***Share the Fire.** Guy Chevreau. 1997. pap. 8.99 (*1-56043-688-3*) Falcon Pr MT.

Share the Fire: Cycle A. Francis P. Sullivan. LC 89-61222. 256p. (Orig.). 1989. pap. 14.95 (*1-55612-305-1*) Sheed & Ward MO.

***Share the Journey: Navigating the Currents of Incurable Illness.** Catherine M. Ray. LC 96-41070. 1997. pap. 10.95 (*0-553-37801-5*) Bantam.

***Share the Olympic Dream.** Date not set. 12.95 (*1-55734-064-1*) Tchr Create Mat.

***Share the Olympic Dream Vol. 1.** (U. S. Olympic Committee's Curriculum Guide Ser.: Vol. 1). 32p. 1996. teacher ed., pap. 5.98 (*1-882180-56-9*) Griffin CA.

***Share the Olympic Dream Vol. 2.** (U. S. Olympic Committee's Curriculum Guide Ser.: Vol. 2). 144p. 1996. teacher ed., pap. 12.95 (*1-882180-52-6*) Griffin CA.

Share the Vision: Ideas for Mission Involvement. Judy Edwards. Ed. by Becky Nelson. 44p. (Orig.). 1992. pap. text ed. 4.95 (*1-56309-051-1*) Womans Mission Union.

Share Valuation Cases. 2nd ed. Nigel A. Eastaway et al. 110p. 1994. pap. text ed. 240.00 (*0-406-02659-9*, UK) MICHIE.

Share Valuation Handbook: Techniques for the Valuation of Shares in Private Companies. Leslie Livens. 207p. (C). 1986. 104.00 (*0-906840-98-8*, Pub. by Fourmat Pub UK) St Mut.

Share Valuation Handbook: Techniques for the Valuation of Shares in Private Companies. 2nd ed. Leslie Livens. 250p. 1993. 96.00 (*0-85459-811-1*, Pub. by Tolley Pubng UK) St Mut.

Share with a Friend Love Above All. Frances R. Johnson. LC 92-61594. (Illus.). 44p. (J). (gr. k-3). 1993. pap. 5.95 (*1-55523-564-6*) Winston-Derek.

Share Your Blessings. Chris Thornton. 100p. 1990. pap. text ed. 9.50 (*1-56770-226-0*) S Scheewe Pubns.

Sharecroppers: The Way We Really Were. Roy G. Taylor. LC 84-90379. (Illus.). 242p. 1984. 16.95 (*0-9613485-0-X*) J Mark.

Sharecroppers of the Sertao: Economics & Dependence on a Brazilian Plantation. Allen W. Johnson. LC 74-130827. (Illus.). x, 156p. 1971. 24.50 (*0-8047-0758-8*) Stanford U Pr.

Sharecropping & Sharecroppers. Ed. by T. J. Byres. (Illus.). 284p. 1983. 35.00 (*0-7146-3223-6*, Pub. by F Cass Pubs UK) Intl Spec Bk.

***Shared Affections.** David A. Bolduc & Mark I. Hallman. 62p. (Orig.). 1993. pap. 4.95 (*0-9646610-0-4*) Toth Pr.

Shared Agenda for General & Special Educators Module 1. York et al. (Staff Development Series for General & Special Educators). 48p. 1995. student ed. 14.00 (*1-55766-206-1*); teacher ed., spiral bd. 30.00 (*1-55766-205-3*) P H Brookes.

Shared Anxiety: Selected Plays. George F. Walker. 527p. 1994. 26.95 (*0-88910-472-7*, Pub. by Talonbooks CN) Genl Dist Srvs.

Shared Authority: Essays on the Craft & Meaning of Oral & Public History. Michael Frisch. LC 88-37030. (SUNY Series in Oral & Public History). (Illus.). 273p. 1990. text ed. 59.50 (*0-7914-0132-4*); pap. text ed. 19.95 (*0-7914-0133-2*) State U NY Pr.

Shared Burdens: Stories of Caring Practices among Mennonites. Sue V. Schlabach & Glen A. Roth. LC 93-38443. 180p. (Orig.). 1993. pap. 6.95 (*1-56148-100-9*) Good Bks PA.

Shared Care: A Model for Clinical Management. Peter Edwards et al. LC 95-47038. 1996. write for info. (*1-85775-165-5*, Radcliffe Med Pr) Scovill Paterson.

***Shared Creation: Words & Music in the Hofmannsthal-Strauss Operas.** Joanna Bottenberg. LC 95-52949. (German Studies in Canada: Bd. 6). 368p. 1996. pap. 61.95 (*0-8204-2974-0*, ML410) P Lang Pubng.

Shared Decision Making. Frank F. Maple. LC 77-12109. (Sage Human Services Guides Ser.: No. 4). 135p. 1977. reprint ed. pap. 38.50 (*0-608-01472-9*, 2059516) Bks Demand.

Shared Destiny: Initiatives for the Near East. Ed. by Joyce R. Starr. 208p. 1983. text ed. 45.00 (*0-275-91083-0*, C1083, Praeger Pubs) Greenwood.

Shared Differences: Multicultural Media & Practical Pedagogy. Ed. by Diane Carson & Lester D. Friedman. LC 94-29251. 296p. 1995. text ed. 49.95 (*0-252-02150-9*); pap. text ed. 17.95 (*0-252-06450-X*) U of Ill Pr.

Shared Expectations. Joseph Petruzzini. Ed. by Mari-Lynn Hankinson. (AT&T Quality Library). (Illus.). 102p. (Orig.). 1994. pap. 24.95 (*0-932764-42-8*) AT&T Customer Info.

Shared Expectations: Sustaining Customer Relationships. Wayne A. Little. LC 95-12450. (Management Master Ser.). (Illus.). 64p. 1995. 15.95 (*1-56327-149-4*) Prod Press.

Shared Expectations: Sustaining Customer Relationships. Wayne A. Little. LC 95-12450. (Management Master Ser.). (Illus.). 88p. 1996. pap. 12.95 (*1-56327-096-X*) Prod Press.

Shared Experience: The History, Architecture & Historical Designations of the Lower Rio Grande Heritage Corridor. Ed. by Mario L. Sanchez. 336p. 1994. pap. 25.00 (*1-886811-00-8*) TX Hist Comm.

Shared Experience: The History, Architecture & Historical Designations of the Lower Rio Grande Heritage Corridor. Ed. by Mario L. Sanchez. 336p. 1994. 40.00 (*1-886811-01-6*) TX Hist Comm.

Shared Experience: The Psychoanalytic Dialogue. Luciana Nissim-Momigliano & Andreina Robutti. 278p. 1992. pap. text ed. 35.95 (*1-85575-034-1*, Pub. by Karnac Bks UK) Brunner-Mazel.

***Shared Experience of Illness: Stories of Patients, Families, & Their Therapists.** Susan H. McDaniel et al. LC 97-2010. 1997. write for info. (*0-465-09737-5*) Basic.

Shared Experiences in Human Communication. Ed. by Stewart L. Tubbs & Robert M. Carter. 299p. 1978. pap. text ed. 34.95 (*0-8104-6089-0*) Transaction Pubs.

Shared Fate: A Theory & Method of Adoptive Relationships. rev. ed. H. David Kirk. LC 63-16589. 215p. 1984. reprint ed. pap. 13.50 (*0-914539-00-0*) Ben-Simon.

Shared Governance for Nursing: A Creative Approach to Professional Accountability. Tim Porter-O'Grady & Sharon Finnigan. LC 84-16814. 256p. (C). 1984. text ed. 66.00 (*0-89443-874-3*, 43874) Aspen Pub.

Shared Governance Implementation Manual. Tim Porter-O'Grady. 208p. (C). (gr. 13). 1992. pap. text ed. 36.95 (*0-8016-6317-2*) Mosby Yr Bk.

***Shared Happiness: A Collection of Poems.** Barbara D. Johnson. LC 97-72234. (Illus.). 64p. 1997. 12.95 (*0-9658206-0-2*) B J Burton.

***Shared Heart: Portraits & Stories Celebrating Lesbian, Gay, & Bisexual Young People.** Adam Mastoon. LC 97-3276. 96p. 1997. 22.00 (*0-688-14931-6*) Morrow.

Shared Heart: Relationship Initiations & Celebrations. Barry Vissell & Joyce Vissell. LC 83-62976. (Illus.). 186p. (Orig.). 1984. pap. 9.95 (*0-9612720-0-7*) Ramira Pub.

Shared Heart: Relationship Initiations & Celebrations. Barry Vissell & Joyce Vissell. LC 85-10981. 186p. (Orig.). 1985. reprint ed. lib. bdg. 29.00 (*0-89370-883-6*) Borgo Pr.

Shared Heritage: Art by Four African Americans. William E. Taylor & Harriet G. Warkel. (Illus.). 192p. (Orig.). 1996. 49.95 (*0-253-33079-3*) Ind U Pr.

Shared Heritage: Art by Four African Americans. William E. Taylor & Harriet G. Warkel. (Illus.). 192p. (Orig.). (C). 1996. pap. 29.95 (*0-936260-62-9*) Ind Mus Art.

Shared Heritage: The Historical Legacy of Sackets Harbor & Madison Barracks. Ed. by Jan M. Saltzgaber. (Illus.). 128p. 1993. pap. write for info. (*0-9610556-3-4*) Ithaca Coll.

***Shared Hope: Environment & Development Agendas for the 21st Century.** Mary MacDonald. 208p. (C). 1997. text ed. 65.00 (*0-415-15491-X*) Routledge.

Shared Hopes, Separate Fears: Fifty Years of U. S.-Indonesian Relations. Paul F. Gardner. 310p. 1997. text ed. 75.00 (*0-8133-3190-0*) Westview.

Shared Hopes, Separate Fears: Fifty Years of U. S.-Indonesian Relations. Paul F. Gardner. (C). 1997. pap. text ed. 24.00 (*0-8133-3191-9*) Westview.

S

Shared Horizon. Ed. by Tom O'Neill. 216p. 1989. 39.50 (*0-7165-2414-7*, Pub. by Irish Acad Pr IE) Intl Spec Bk.

Shared Housing for the Elderly. Ed. by Dale J. Jaffe. LC 89-11938. (Contributions to the Study of Aging Ser.: No. 15). 214p. 1989. text ed. 55.00 (*0-313-26284-5*, JSH/, Greenwood Pr) Greenwood.

Shared in an Evil Time. Jeanne Phillips. LC 90-72004. 119p. 1992. pap. 10.00 (*1-56002-085-7*, Univ Edtns) Aegina Pr.

Shared Journey...Leaders Growing Leaders: A Teacher's Handbook for Taking Quality One Step Further into the Classroom. Carolyn R. Wicks. 275p. 1995. pap. text ed. 24.95 (*0-9646935-1-8*) Pact Pubng.

Shared Legacy. Alfred P. Ingegno. 291p. 1992. 22.00 (*0-9636017-7-6*); pap. 14.00 (*0-9636017-6-8*) API-BBI.

Shared Life. D. Macleod. 5.99 (*1-85792-128-3*, Pub. by Christian Focus UK) Spring Arbor Dist.

Shared Life. Katherine Soniat. LC 93-13695. (Edwin Ford Piper Poetry Award Cowinner, 1992 Ser.). 112p. (Orig.). 1993. pap. 10.95 (*0-87745-429-9*) U of Iowa Pr.

Shared Lives: A Memoir. Lyndall Gordon. (Illus.). 352p. 1992. 24.95 (*0-393-03164-0*) Norton.

Shared Manufacturing: A Global Perspective. David I. Cleland et al. 300p. 1993. text ed. 46.00i (*0-07-157812-9*) McGraw.

Shared Meaning: An Introduction to Speech Communication. 4th ed. Margot Olson & Mary Forrest. 350p. (C). 1996. per., pap. text ed. 37.74 (*0-7872-2367-0*) Kendall-Hunt.

Shared Memory Multiprocessing. Ed. by Norihisa Suzuki. (Illus.). 518p. 1992. 50.00 (*0-262-19322-1*) MIT Pr.

Shared Minds: The New Technologies of Collaboration. Michael Schrage. 256p. 1990. 21.00 (*0-394-56587-8*) Random.

Shared Moments. Lenore Turkeltaub. LC 87-83182. (Illus.). 72p. (Orig.). 1988. pap. 7.95 (*0-9614768-4-2*); pap. 7.95 (*0-9614768-3-4*) Lenjalin Pubns.

Shared Moments: Learning Games for Disabled Children. Sally M. Rogow & Julia L. Hass. 64p. 1993. pap. 8.95 (*0-936389-33-8*) Tudor Pubs.

Shared Motherhood. Chieko N. Okazaki. 1994. pap. 1.95 (*0-88494-932-X*) Bookcraft Inc.

Shared Pain & Sorrow: The Reflections of a Secondary Sufferer. James I. Cook. (Looking up Ser.). 24p. (Orig.). 1991. pap. 1.95 (*0-8298-0903-1*) Pilgrim OH.

Shared Parking. Barton-Aschman Associates Inc. Staff. LC 83-51648. 86p. (Orig.). 1983. pap. 57.95 (*0-87420-652-9*, S-22) Urban Land.

Shared Past: Texas & the United States since Reconstruction. William C. Hardt. 140p. pap. text ed. 10.00 (*0-87611-118-5*) Tex St Hist Assn.

Shared Perspectives: The Printmaker & Photographer in New York, 1900-1950. Berenise Abbott. (Illus.). 1994. pap. 15.00 (*0-910961-04-2*) Mus City NY.

Shared Pleasures: A History of Movie Presentation in the United States. Douglas Gomery. LC 91-30618. (Wisconsin Studies in Film). (Illus.). 404p. (Orig.). (C). 1992. pap. 15.95 (*0-299-13214-5*) U of Wis Pr.

Shared Power: What Is It? How Does It Work? How Can We Make It Work Better? John M. Bryson & Robert C. Einsweiler. (Readings for Leaders Ser.: Vol. IV). 420p. (Orig.). (C). 1992. pap. text ed. 43.50 (*0-8191-8458-6*); lib. bdg. 71.00 (*0-8191-8457-8*) U Pr of Amer.

Shared Praise. Contrib. by Teresa Wilhelmi. 1991. 8.99 (*0-685-68272-2*, MB-633) Lillenas.

***Shared Purpose: Business Strategies to Create Strong Families & High-Performance Organizations.** Maria G. Mackavey & Richard J. Levin. 224p. 1997. 24.95 (*0-8144-0388-3*) AMACOM.

Shared Reading: Safe. (J). 1993. pap. 7.95 (*0-590-71698-0*) Scholastic Inc.

Shared Reading in Practice. Chris Davis & Rosemary Stubbs. 128p. 1989. 80.00 (*0-335-09510-0*, Open Univ Pr); pap. 27.00 (*0-335-09509-7*, Open Univ Pr) Taylor & Francis.

Shared Reading in the Middle & High School Years: In the Middle & High School Years. Frank McTeague. LC 92-39116. 93p. 1992. pap. text ed. 16.50 (*0-435-08735-5*, 08735) Heinemann.

Shared Responsibility: Families & Social Policy. Robert M. Moroney. Ed. by James K. Whittaker. LC 85-20950. (Modern Applications of Social Work Ser.). (Illus.). 229p. (Orig.). 1986. pap. text ed. 24.95 (*0-202-36042-3*); lib. bdg. 46.95 (*0-202-36041-5*) Aldine de Gruyter.

Shared Search: Doing Theology in Conversation with One's Friends. Maurice F. Wiles. 288p. (Orig.). 1994. pap. 19.75 (*0-334-02559-1*, SCM Pr) TPI PA.

Shared Sightings: An Anthology of Bird Poems. Ed. by Sheila G. Johnson. (Illus.). 144p. (Orig.). 1995. pap. 12.00 (*1-880284-12-X*) J Daniel.

Shared Solitude. D. A. Blyler. (Illus.). 68p. (Orig.). 1995. pap. 7.95 (*0-9645655-1-X*) BurnhillWolf.

Shared Space: Folklife in the Arizona-Sonora Borderlands. James S. Griffith. (Illus.). 1995. 34.95 incl. disk (*0-87421-198-0*); pap. 19.95 incl. disk (*0-87421-187-5*) Utah St U Pr.

Shared Space, Divided Space: Essays on Conflict & Territorial Organization. Ed. by Michael Chisholm & David M. Smith. (Illus.). 288p. (C). (gr. 13). 1990. text ed. 65.00 (*0-04-445153-9*) Routledge Chapman & Hall.

Shared Space, Divided Space: Essays on Conflict & Territorial Organization. Ed. by Michael Chisholm & David M. Smith. (Illus.). 288p. (C). 1990. pap. 29.95 (*0-04-445714-6*) Routledge Chapman & Hall.

Shared Spaces: Contexts of Interaction in Chicago's Ethnic Communities. Carucci et al. LC 89-31161. (Immigrant Communities & Ethnic Minorities in the U. S. & Canada Ser.: No. 63). 1989. 49.50 (*0-404-19473-7*) AMS Pr.

Shared Spaces: Solutions for Child Care Providers. Georgia B. Houle. (Illus.). 80p. (Orig.). (C). 1991. pap. text ed. 10.95 (*0-940139-24-3*) Consortium RI.

Shared Spirits: Wildlife & Native Americans. Dennis L. Olson. LC 95-15129. (Illus.). 144p. 1995. 29.95 (*1-55971-474-3*) NorthWord.

Shared Surprise. Vivian Hamburg. (Illus.). 30p. (J). (gr. 2-4). 1995. 7.95 (*0-533-11298-2*) Vantage.

Shared Symbols, Contested Meanings: Gros Ventre Culture & History, 1778-1984. Loretta Fowler. LC 86-47977. (Illus.). 336p. (C). 1987. pap. 16.95 (*0-8014-9450-8*) Cornell U Pr.

Shared Taste. John Thorne. Date not set. pap. 16.95 (*0-670-81809-7*) Viking Penguin.

Shared Threads: Quilting Together - Past & Present. Jacqueline M. Atkins. (Illus.). 144p. 1994. pap. 39.95 (*0-525-93441-3*) Studio Bks.

Shared Values: Our Common Bond. Susan Annitto. (AT&T Quality Library). (Illus.). 124p. (Orig.). 1992. pap. 24.95 (*0-932764-37-1*, 500-479A) AT&T Customer Info.

Shared Values for a Troubled World: Conversations with Men & Women of Conscience. Rushworth M. Kidder. LC 93-33139. (Public Administration Ser.). 356p. 1994. pap. 26.00 (*1-55542-603-4*) Jossey-Bass.

Shared Views in the Family During Adolescence. Ed. by Roberta L. Paikoff. LC 85-644581. (New Directions for Child Development Ser.: No. CD 51). 1991. 19.00 (*1-55542-787-1*) Jossey-Bass.

Shared Vision: Transformational Leadership in America Community Colleges. John E. Roueche et al. 1989. 34.00 (*0-87117-190-2*, 1100) Am Assn Comm Coll.

Shared Visions: Native American Painters & Sculptors in the Twentieth Century. Ed. by Margaret Archuleta & Rennard Strickland. LC 92-50853. (Illus.). 112p. 1993. pap. 20.00 (*1-56584-069-0*) New Press NY.

Shared Visions: Native American Painters & Sculptors in the Twentieth Century, Conference, May 8-11, 1991, Phoenix, Arizona, Proceedings. rev. ed. LC 92-43942. 1992. write for info. (*0-934351-41-4*) Heard Mus.

Shared Visions of Statewide Higher Education Structures: Leadership Styles & Organizations That Work. Edgar B. Schick et al. LC 92-26124. 1992. write for info. (*0-88044-132-1*) AASCU Press.

***Shared Visions, Shared Lives: Communal Living Around the Globe.** Bill Metcalf. (Illus.). 192p. (Orig.). 1996. pap. 13.95 (*1-899171-01-0*, Pub. by Findhorn Pr UK) Words Distrib.

Shared Vulnerability: The Media & American Perceptions of the Bhopal Disaster. Lee Wilkins. LC 86-25838. (Contributions to the Study of Mass Media & Communications Ser.: No. 8). (Illus.). 184p. 1987. text ed. 45.00 (*0-313-25265-3*, WIV/) Greenwood.

Shared Wisdom: A Guide to Case Study Reflection in Ministry. Jeffrey H. Mahan et al. LC 93-4458. 144p. (Orig.). 1993. pap. 12.95 (*0-687-38335-8*) Abingdon.

Shared Wisdom: Development & Succession Planning. Ed. by Robert A. Levit & Christina Gikakis. (Best Practices Ser.: No. 2). 300p. 1994. pap. text ed. 25.00 (*1-881115-05-4*) Human Res Plan.

Shareholder Derivative Actions: Law & Practice. Deborah A. DeMott. LC 86-31029. 1990. 140.00 (*0-685-17693-2*) Clark Boardman Callaghan.

Shareholder Derivative Actions: Law & Practice. annuals Deborah A. DeMott. 1990. suppl. ed. write for info. (*0-318-61654-8*) Clark Boardman Callaghan.

Shareholder Litigation, 1984-1990, 3 vols. Roger Magnuson. LC 81-6078. 350.00 (*0-685-09306-9*) Clark Boardman Callaghan.

Shareholder Proposal Rule: SEC Interpretations & Lawsuits. Helen E. Booth. Ed. by Carolyn Mathiasen. 114p. (Orig.). 1987. pap. 25.00 (*0-931035-14-7*) IRRC Inc DC.

Shareholder Rebellion: How Investors Are Changing the Way America's Companies Are Run. George P. Schwartz. 250p. 1995. text ed. 24.95 (*1-55738-883-0*) Irwin Prof Pubng.

Shareholder Use & Understanding Financial Information. T. A. Lee & D. P. Tweedie. (Accounting History & Thought Ser.). 400p. 1990. reprint ed. text ed. 10.00 (*0-8240-3321-3*) Garland.

Shareholder Value: Key to Corporate Development. Ed. by Christopher J. Clarke. LC 92-46885. 132p. 1993. text ed. 95.75 (*0-08-040668-8*, Pergamon Pr) Elsevier.

Shareholder Voting Almanac, 1991. Bill Sander. 250p. 1991. 50.00 (*0-931035-77-5*) IRRC Inc DC.

Shareholders' Liability: The Comparative Law Yearbook of International Business Special Issue, 1993. Ed. by Dennis Campbell & Jennifer Powers. LC 93-46209. (Comparative Law Yearbook Ser.). 528p. (C). 1994. lib. bdg. 179.50 (*1-85966-048-7*, Pub. by Graham & Trotman UK) Kluwer Ac.

Shareholders Rights & Remedies. Peter Willcocks. 150p. 1991. pap. 48.00 (*1-86287-050-0*, Pub. by Federation Pr AU) Gaunt.

Shareholder's Use of Corporate Annual Reports. Marc J. Epstein & Moses L. Pava. LC 93-41149. (Studies in Managerial Aid & Financial Accounting: Vol. 2). 1993. write for info. (*1-55938-562-6*) Jai Pr.

ShareHouse Blues. Joan Morrison. 160p. (C). 1990. pap. 30.00 (*0-86439-002-5*, Pub. by Boolarong Pubns AT) St Mut.

Sharelle. John Neufeld. 240p. 1984. pap. 2.50 (*0-451-12783-8*, Sig Vista) NAL-Dutton.

Sharendel. large type ed. Margaret A. Carr. (Linford Mystery Library). 368p. 1987. pap. 15.99 (*0-7089-6390-0*, Linford) Ulverscroft.

Shares. William Gray. 320p. 1996. 22.00 (*0-684-81096-4*) S&S Trade.

***Shares.** large type ed. William Gray. LC 96-27672. (Cloak & Dagger Ser.). 503p. 1996. 21.95 (*0-7862-0856-2*, Thorndike Lrg Prnt) Thorndike Pr.

Shares & Other Fiction. Richard Stern. 202p. 1992. 20.00 (*1-883285-06-2*) Delphinium.

Shares of Upper Income Groups in Income & Savings. Simon Kuznets. (Occasional Papers: No. 35). 72p. 1950. reprint ed. 20.00 (*0-87014-350-6*) Natl Bur Econ Res.

Shares of Upper Income Groups in Income & Savings. Simon Kuznets & Elizabeth Jenks. (General Ser.: No. 55). 768p. 1953. reprint ed. 160.00 (*0-87014-054-X*) Natl Bur Econ Res.

Shareware Compendium: The ASP Shareware Catalog, 1993. Rob Rosenberg. 1993. pap. 25.00 (*1-55623-914-9*) Irwin Prof Pubng.

Shareware for Kids: With Ready-to-Run Programs for the IBM for Ages 2 Through 5. Debra Schepp & Brad Schepp. LC 92-35447. (J). (ps). 1993. write for info. (*0-8306-4248-X*) McGraw-Hill Prof.

Shareware Plus: Featuring 4 DOS. 2nd ed. David D. Busch. Ed. by Susan Glinert. 325p. 1992. DOS 5 compatible. per., pap. 40.00 incl. disk (*1-55623-575-5*) Irwin Prof Pubng.

Shareware Plus: Featuring 4DOS. David D. Busch. 1990. pap. 40.00 (*1-55623-411-2*) Irwin Prof Pubng.

Sharh al-Aqidah al-Tahawiyah al-Mussamat "Bayan al-Sunnah wa-al-Jamaah" Abd-al-Ghani Al-Ghunaymi al-Maydani. 160p. (Orig.). (ARA.). 1995. pap. 3.95 (*1-57547-228-7*) Dar Al-Fikr.

Sharh Qawaid al-Irab. Ibn-Hisham. 304p. 1995. 9.95 (*1-57547-212-0*) Dar Al-Fikr.

Shari 'a in Songhay: The Replies of al-Maghili to the Questions of Askia al-Hajj Muhammad. J. O. Hunwick. (Fontes Historiae Africanae, Series Arabica: Vol. V). (Illus.). 1985. 19.98 (*0-19-726032-2*) David Brown.

Shari Lewis' Lamb Chop & Friends Blue Ribbon Kitten. Jean Lewis. (Illus.). 24p. (J). (ps). 1995. pap. 1.49 (*0-307-10564-4*, Golden Books) Western Pub.

Shari Lewis Presents One Hundred-One Magic Tricks for Kids to Do. Shari Lewis & Dick Zimmerman. LC 89-10360. (Illus.). 96p. (Orig.). (J). 1990. pap. 6.95 (*0-394-82059-2*); lib. bdg. 9.99 (*0-394-92059-7*) Random Bks Yng Read.

Shari Urquhart Fiber: December 3, 1993 Thru January 28, 1994. Ed. by Judy Collischan. LC 94-16141. 1994. 10.00 (*0-933699-31-X*) Hillwood Art.

Shar'ia: An Introduction to the Law of the Islam. Rodolphe J. De Seife. LC 93-31399. 103p. 1994. 49.95 (*1-880921-39-1*); pap. 34.95 (*1-880921-38-3*) Austin & Winfield.

Shari'at & Ambiguity in South Asian Islam. Katherine P. Ewing. (Comparative Studies on Muslim Societies: No. 4). 1988. 50.00 (*0-520-05575-6*) U CA Pr.

Shariati on Shariati: An Autobiographical Biography & English Guide to the Collected Works. Laleh Bakhtiar. 144p. (Orig.). (C). 1989. pap. text ed. 14.00 (*1-871031-05-2*) Abjad Bk.

***Shariati on Shariati & the Muslim Woman.** Laleh Bakhtiar. 1996. pap. 19.95 (*1-871031-50-8*) Abjad Bk.

Sharing. Dan Carr. (God I Need to Talk to You About... Ser.). (Illus.). 24p. (J). (gr. k-4). 1984. pap. 0.99 (*0-570-08728-7*, 56-1472) Concordia.

Sharing. Stephen Cosgrove. LC 91-71221. (Illus.). 72p. 1991. 24.95 (*1-55868-066-7*) Gr Arts Ctr Pub.

Sharing. Gill Davies & Stephanie Longfoot. (Now I Am Big Ser.). (Illus.). 24p. (J). (ps-1). 1996. 3.49 (*1-85854-369-X*) Brimax Bks.

Sharing. Shelly Nielsen. Ed. by Rosemary Wallner. LC 91-73045. (Values Matter Ser.). (J). 1992. lib. bdg. 14.98 (*1-56239-063-5*) Abdo & Dghtrs.

Sharing. Debbie Pincus. (Illus.). 80p. (J). (gr. 4-8). 1983. student ed. 10.99 (*0-86653-117-3*, GA 468) Good Apple.

Sharing. Janet Riehecky. LC 87-26811. (Values to Live By Ser.). (Illus.). 32p. (J). (ps-2). 1988. lib. bdg. 21.36 (*0-89565-416-4*) Childs World.

Sharing. O. B. Rozell. (Illus.). 19p. (Orig.). 1980. pap. 3.00 (*0-88680-172-9*) I E Clark.

Sharing, Reading Level 2. Elaine Goley. (Learn the Value Ser.: Set II). (Illus.). 32p. (J). (gr. 1-4). 1989. 11.95 (*0-685-58791-6*); lib. bdg. 15.94 (*0-86592-388-4*) Rourke Corp.

Sharing: A Manual for Program Directors. Thomas Zanzig. (Sharing Program Ser.). 219p. 1985. ring bd. 54.00 (*0-88489-167-4*) St Marys.

Sharing: A Manual for Volunteer Teachers, No. I. Thomas Zanzig. (Sharing Program Ser.). (Illus.). 196p. 1985. spiral bd. 18.95 (*0-88489-163-1*) St Marys.

Sharing: A Manual for Volunteer Teachers, No. II. Thomas Zanzig. (Sharing Program Ser.). 239p. 1985. spiral bd. 18.95 (*0-88489-164-X*) St Marys.

Sharing: A Manual for Volunteer Teachers, No. III. Thomas Zanzig. (Sharing Program Ser.). 237p. 1985. spiral bd. 18.95 (*0-88489-165-8*) St Marys.

Sharing: A Manual for Volunteer Teachers, No. IV. Thomas Zanzig. (Sharing Program Ser.). 237p. 1988. spiral bd. 18.95 (*0-88489-166-6*) St Marys.

Sharing: Self Discovery in Relationships. Kathy Oddenino. 354p. (Orig.). 1990. pap. 14.95 (*0-923081-02-X*) Joy Pubns MD.

Sharing: What Does It Mean? Sue Riley. LC 77-16293. (What Does It Mean? Ser.). (Illus.). (J). (ps-2). 1978. lib. bdg. 18.50 (*0-89565-015-0*) Childs World.

***Sharing - A Challenge for All: Conference Proceedings of the 11th Annual Conference of the International Association of School Librarianship, Red Deer, Alberta, Canada, August 1-6, 1982.** Ed. by John Wright. 420p. 25.00 (*1-890861-01-4*) IASL.

Sharing a Heritage: American Indian Arts. 2nd ed. Charlotte Heth. (Contemporary American Indian Issues Ser.). 214p. 1984. pap. 15.00 (*0-935626-00-X*) U Cal AISC.

Sharing a Robin's Life. Linda Johns. (Illus.). 164p. 1993. pap. 12.95 (*1-55109-055-4*, Pub. by Nimbus Publishing Ltd CN) Chelsea Green Pub.

Sharing a Song Activity Book. B. Schneider. 1987. pap. text ed. 8.41 (*0-201-16510-4*) Addison-Wesley.

Sharing a Sunshine Umbrella: A Mimmy & Simmy Story. Yaffa Ganz. (Illus.). (J). 1989. 10.95 (*0-87306-496-8*) Feldheim.

Sharing a Vision. Phoebe Willetts. 116p. 1978. pap. 7.50 (*0-227-67842-7*) Attic Pr.

Sharing & Responding Guide. 2nd ed. Peter Elbow & Patricia Belanoff. 1994. pap. text ed. write for info. (*0-07-019695-8*) McGraw.

Sharing Authority Effectively. Kenneth P. Mortimer & T. R. McConnell. LC 76-50721. (Jossey-Bass Series in Higher Education). 344p. reprint ed. pap. 98.10 (*0-8357-4913-4*, 2037843) Bks Demand.

Sharing Birth: A Father's Guide to Giving Support During Labor. Carl Jones. LC 89-6658. (Illus.). 192p. (Orig.). 1989. reprint ed. text ed. 29.95 (*0-89789-209-7*, Bergin & Garvey); reprint ed. pap. text ed. 12.95 (*0-89789-208-9*, Bergin & Garvey) Greenwood.

***Sharing Blessings: Children's Stories for Exploring the Spirit of the Jewish Holidays.** Rachel Musleah & Michael Klayman. LC 96-30047. (Illus.). 64p. (J). (gr. 1-5). 1997. 18.95 (*1-879045-71-0*) Jewish Lights.

Sharing Child Care in Early Parenthood. Malcolm Hill. 336p. 1987. lib. bdg. 67.00 (*0-7102-0497-3*, RKP) Routledge.

***Sharing Christ When You Feel You Can't: Making It Easier to Tell Your Friends & Family about Your Faith in Christ.** Daniel Owens. LC 96-52236. (Orig.). 1997. pap. 10.99 (*0-89107-935-1*) Crossway Bks.

Sharing Christ with Black Muslims: An Introduction to the Orientation of Black Muslims. Gary Banks & Eddie Kinley. Ed. by Teri Thomas. 64p. (Orig.). 1996. pap. 7.95 (*0-9651234-0-5*) BKin Lght Minist.

Sharing Christ with Your Mormon Friends. Cary Trivanovich. Ed. by Margaret Wallace. 112p. (Orig.). 1991. pap. 6.95 (*0-939497-22-0*) Promise Pub.

Sharing CIM Solutions: The Link Between Innovation & Growth. J. K. Knudsen et al. LC 94-7881. (Advances in Design & Manufacturing Ser.: Vol. 5). 416p. (gr. 12). 1994. 99.00 (*90-5199-194-0*) IOS Press.

Sharing Circle: Themes for Home & School Involvement. Carol Spangler. 240p. (J). (ps-k). 1996. 16.99 (*0-86653-868-2*, FE3868) Fearon Teach Aids.

Sharing Circle Handbook: Topics for Teaching Self-Awareness, Communication, & Social Skills. Susanna Palomares et al. Ed. by Dianne Schilling. 181p. (Orig.). 1992. pap. text ed. 12.95 (*1-56499-007-9*) Innerchoice Pub.

Sharing Danny's Dad. 2nd ed. Angela Shelf. (Let Me Read Ser.). (Illus.). (J). (ps-2). 1995. bds. 2.95 (*0-673-36275-2*, GoodYrBooks) Addson-Wesley Educ.

Sharing Faith: A Comprehensive Approach to Religious Education. Thomas H. Groome. 1991. pap. 29.95 (*0-06-063497-9*) Harper SF.

***Sharing Faith Across the Hemisphere.** Mary M. McGlone. 260p. (Orig.). 1997. pap. 20.00 (*1-57075-132-3*) Orbis Bks.

***Sharing Faith Across the Hemisphere.** Mary M. McGlone. (Illus.). 302p. (Orig.). (C). 1997. pap. 19.95 (*1-57455-015-2*) US Catholic.

Sharing Faith with Children: Rethinking the Children's Sermon. Sara C. Juengst. LC 93-31960. 128p. (Orig.). 1994. pap. 12.00 (*0-664-25439-X*) Westminster John Knox.

***Sharing Four Cultures: A Journey of Love.** Barbara H. Burrus. (Illus.). 224p. 1997. 24.95 (*1-57736-045-1*) Providence Hse.

Sharing Geographic Information. Ed. by Harlan J. Onsrud & Gerard Rushton. LC 94-19192. (Illus.). 528p. (C). 1995. 44.95 (*0-88285-152-7*) Ctr Urban Pol Res.

Sharing Gifts: A Spirituality of Time, Talent, & Treasure. Joseph M. Champlin. 40p. (Orig.). 1991. pap. 2.95 (*0-8146-2054-X*) Liturgical Pr.

Sharing God's Feelings. B. J. Whitley, Jr. LC 84-51661. 201p. (Orig.). 1985. pap. 9.95 (*0-9615536-0-X*) Spirit Christ.

Sharing God's Greatest Gift: A Guide to Building Witnessing Relationships. Tammy F. Davis. Ed. by Judy Edwards. 50p. (Orig.). 1993. pap. text ed. 4.95 (*1-56309-059-7*, New Hope) Womans Mission Union.

Sharing God's Life. St. Paul Publications Staff. (C). 1988. 39.00 (*0-85439-148-7*, Pub. by St Paul Pubns UK) St Mut.

***Sharing God's Work Through the Year: A Small Group Guide for Young Adults.** Ed. by Ron Bagley. 200p. 1997. pap. 19.95 (*1-890516-03-1*) Ctr Minist Dev.

Sharing Groups in Youth Ministry. Walt Marcum. 1991. pap. 13.95 (*0-687-38344-7*) Abingdon.

Sharing Hanukkah. Janet McDonnell. LC 93-13250. (Circle the Year with Holidays Ser.). (Illus.). 32p. (J). (ps-2). 1993. pap. 3.95 (*0-516-40685-X*); lib. bdg. 17.50 (*0-516-00685-1*) Childrens.

Sharing Heaven's Music: The Heart of Christian Preaching. Ed. by Barry L. Callen. 272p. 1995. 18.95 (*0-687-01108-6*) Abingdon.

Sharing His Love. Eddie Roush. (Orig.). 1995. pap. 7.95 (*0-533-11520-5*) Vantage.

Sharing in Development: A Programme of Employment, Equity & Growth for the Philippines. A WEP Study. xxvii, 687p. 1974. 37.80 (*92-2-101111-9*) Intl Labour Office.

***Sharing Information: A Guide to Federal Laws on Confidentiality & Disclosure of Information for Child Welfare Agencies.** Alice Bussiere et al. LC 97-25093. 1997. write for info. (*1-57073-464-X*) Amer Bar Assn.

An Asterisk (*) at the beginning of an entry indicates that the title is appearing in BIP for the first time.

Sharing Innovation: Global Perspectives on Food, Agriculture & Rural Development. Ed. by Neil G. Kotler. LC 90-53151. 286p. 1990. pap. text ed. 14.95 (*0-87474-874-7*) Smithsonian.

Sharing Innovations: The Program Exchange Compendium. Kim P. Helfgott. 1992. 9.95 (*0-87868-504-9*) Child Welfare.

Sharing International Responsibilities among the Trilateral Countries. Nobuhiko Ushiba et al. (Triangle Papers: No. 25). (Illus.). 102p. (Orig.). 1982. pap. 6.00 (*0-930503-20-1*) Trilateral Comm.

Sharing Is Caring. Carol Cummings. (Learn with Me Ser.). (Illus.). 24p. (Orig.). (J). (ps-3). 1992. pap. 4.99 (*0-9614574-9-X*) Teaching WA.

Sharing Is Fun. Beverly Amstutz. (Illus.). 24p. (J). (gr. k-7). 1979. pap. 2.50 (*0-937836-00-1*) Precious Res.

Sharing It All: The Rewards & Struggles of Two-Career Families. Lucia A. Gilbert. LC 88-19478. (Illus.). 250p. 1988. 18.95 (*0-306-42961-6*, Plenum Pr) Plenum.

Sharing Jesus Effectively. Jerry Savelle. 144p. (Orig.). 1994. pap. 7.99 (*0-89274-251-8*, HH-251) Harrison Hse.

Sharing Land with Wildlife: A Practical Guidebook for Those Living in the Urban Districts, Suburbs, or Rural Areas That May Encounter Wildlife. John Trout, Jr. (Illus.). 250p. 1996. write for info. (*0-614-12973-7*) Midwest Pubng.

Sharing Literature with Children: A Thematic Anthology. Francelia Butler. (Illus.). 492p. (C). 1989. reprint ed. pap. text ed. 29.95 (*0-88133-463-4*) Waveland Pr.

***Sharing Love.** P. Lewis. (30 Days Smart Family Ser.). 1997. pap. 4.99 (*0-310-21587-0*) Zondervan.

Sharing Makes Me Happy. Dot Cachiaras. Ed. by Shirley Beegle. (Happy Day Bks.). (Illus.). 24p. (Orig.). (J). (ps-3). 1994. reprint ed. pap. 1.99 (*0-7847-0264-0*, 04214) Standard Pub.

Sharing Maths Learning with Children. Pat Costello et al. (C). 1990. 65.00 (*0-86431-101-X*, Pub. by Aust Council Educ Res AT) St Mut.

Sharing More Than a Pastor. Joan C. McKeown. (Illus.). 128p. (Orig.). 1993. pap. 9.95 (*0-9636183-0-X*) Arc Res.

Sharing Music: An Introductory Guide to Music Education. J. G. Martin. (Academic Ser.). 260p. (C). 1987. pap. 16.95 (*0-910075-06-9*) Hardin-Simmons.

Sharing My Faith: A Teen's Guide to Evangelism. Ed. by Mark Gilroy. (Illus.). 104p. (YA). 1991. pap. 6.99 (*0-8341-1384-8*) Beacon Hill.

Sharing Nature with Children. Joseph Cornell. LC 78-74650. (Illus.). 143p. (J). 1979. pap. 7.95 (*0-916124-14-2*, ES2) Dawn CA.

Sharing of Expertise & Experience, Vol. 7. 672p. (Orig.). 1989. pap. 63.00 (*0-88034-040-1*) Am Soc Assn Execs.

Sharing of Love. Illus. by Flavia. 32p. 1993. 6.95 (*0-8362-4701-9*) Andrews & McMeel.

Sharing Our Best: Recipes from Nebraska 4-H. (Illus.). 176p. 1996. pap. 11.95 (*0-9652002-0-5*) NE Four-H Dev.

Sharing Our Biblical Story: A Guide to Using Liturgical Readings As the Core of Church & Family Education. rev. ed. Joseph P. Russell. LC 88-8399. 325p. 1988. reprint ed. pap. 19.95 (*0-8192-1425-6*) Morehouse Pub.

Sharing Ownership: The Business Manager's Guide to ESOP's & Other Ownership Incentive Plans. Darien A. McWhirter. LC 92-46584. 288p. 1993. text ed. 34.95 (*0-471-57733-2*) Wiley.

Sharing Passover: A Guide to Celebration with Your Kids. Melanie Berman. 38p. 1994. pap. 3.95 (*1-884857-03-5*) Comet Intl.

Sharing Peace: Sharing Peace. Mouse Works Staff. (J). 1995. 7.98 (*1-57082-281-6*) Mouse Works.

Sharing Pedagogies: Students & Teachers Write about Dialogic Practices. Ed. by Gail Tayko & John Tassoni. 1996. pap. text ed. 26.00 (*0-86709-412-5*, 0412) Boynton Cook Pubs.

Sharing Power: Public Governance & Private Markets. Donald F. Kettl. LC 92-41705. 219p. (C). 1993. 38.95 (*0-8157-4906-6*); pap. 16.95 (*0-8157-4907-4*) Brookings.

Sharing Research Data. Ed. by Stephen E. Fienberg et al. LC 84-27275. 235p. reprint ed. pap. 67.00 (*0-8357-6595-4*, 2035991) Bks Demand.

Sharing Responsibility. Larry May. LC 92-12658. 216p. 1992. 34.95 (*0-226-51168-5*) U Ch Pr.

Sharing Responsibility. Larry May. 204p. 1996. reprint ed. pap. text ed. 15.95 (*0-226-51169-3*) U Ch Pr.

Sharing Sam. Katherine Applegate. (Love Stories Ser.: No. 2). 192p. (J). (gr. 4-8). 1995. mass mkt. 3.99 (*0-553-56660-1*) Bantam.

Sharing Secrets. Mary R. Palmer. LC 91-65294. (Illus.). 60p. (J). (ps-4). 1991. pap. 4.00 (*0-932433-82-0*) Windswept Hse.

Sharing Secrets with Stalin: How the Allies Traded Intelligence, 1941-1945. Bradley F. Smith. LC 96-2395. (Modern War Studies). 336p. 1996. 35.00 (*0-7006-0800-1*) U Pr of KS.

Sharing Silence: Meditation Practices & Mindful Living. Gunilla Norris. LC 92-44971. 1993. 13.00 (*0-517-59506-0*, Bell Tower) Crown Pub Group.

Sharing Sisters. 224p. 1993. pap. 4.95 (*0-88184-984-7*) Carroll & Graf.

Sharing Social Science Data: Advantages & Challenges. Joan E. Sieber. (Focus Editions Ser.: Vol. 128). (Illus.). 208p. 1991. 54.00 (*0-8039-4082-3*); pap. 24.95 (*0-8039-4083-1*) Sage.

Sharing Susan. Eve Bunting. LC 90-27097. (Trophy Bk.). 128p. (J). (gr. 4-7). 1994. pap. 3.95 (*0-06-440430-7*, Trophy) HarpC Child Bks.

Sharing the American Dream: A Second Look. 2nd rev. ed. Patsy Van Ouwerkerk et al. 219p. 1995. pap. 49.00 (*1-889394-08-4*) Credit Union Execs.

Sharing the Articles of Faith: Child-Centered Learning Activities. Christena C. Nelson. (Illus.). (Orig.). 1994. pap. 6.95 (*0-87579-943-4*) Deseret Bk.

***Sharing the Asset Message Speaker's Kit.** 1996. ring bd. 175.00 (*1-57482-368-X*) Search Inst.

Sharing the Burden: Strategies for Public & Private Long-Term Care Insurance. Joshua M. Wiener et al. 290p. (C). 1994. 42.95 (*0-8157-9378-2*); pap. 18.95 (*0-8157-9377-4*) Brookings.

Sharing the Challenge: Floodplain Management into the 21st Century. 1996. lib. bdg. 253.99 (*0-8490-5981-X*) Gordon Pr.

Sharing the City: Community Participation in Urban Management. John Abbott. (Illus.). 256p. 1996. 56.00 (*1-85383-323-1*, Pub. by Erthscan Pubns UK); pap. 24.95 (*1-85383-328-2*, Pub. by Erthscan Pubns UK) Island Pr.

Sharing the Course: A Guide to Group Study & Individual Application of Spiritual Principles. Nancy H. Glende. LC 93-83759. 416p. 1993. pap. 25.00 (*0-9636216-9-6*) Noelani Pub.

Sharing the Dance: Contact Improvisation & American Culture. Cynthia J. Novack. LC 89-40534. (New Directions in Anthropological Writing Ser.). (Illus.). 272p. (Orig.). 1990. pap. text ed. 16.95 (*0-299-12444-4*) U of Wis Pr.

Sharing the Darkness: The Spirituality of Caring. Sheila Cassidy. LC 91-28462. 1992. pap. 12.50 (*0-88344-779-7*) Orbis Bks.

Sharing the Delirium: Second Generation AIDS Plays & Performances. Ed. by Therese Jones. LC 93-44972. 342p. (C). 1994. pap. 16.95 (*0-435-08633-2*, 08633) Heinemann.

Sharing the Desert: The Tohono O'odham in History. Winston P. Erickson. LC 94-12391. (Illus.). 182p. 1994. text ed. 36.00 (*0-8165-1490-9*) U of Ariz Pr.

Sharing the Difference: Feminist Debates in Holland. Ed. by Alkeline Van Lenning & Joke Hermsen. 240p. (C). 1991. pap. text ed. 17.95 (*0-415-06139-3*, A6177) Routledge.

Sharing the Earth: Cross-Cultural Experiences in Population, Wildlife & the Environment. Ed. by Patricia Waak & Kennth Strom. (Illus.). 152p. 1992. 34.95 (*0-930698-34-7*); pap. 24.95 (*0-930698-35-5*) Natl Audubon.

***Sharing the Earth: The Rhetoric of Sustainable Development.** Tarla R. Peterson. LC 97-4737. (Studies in Rhetoric/Communication). 240p. 1997. 29.95 (*1-57003-173-8*) U of SC Pr.

***Sharing the Effort: Options for Differentiating Commitments on Climate Change.** Ed. by Matthew Paterson & Michael Grubb. 80p. 1996. pap. 14.95 (*1-899658-75-0*, Pub. by Royal Inst Intl Affairs UK) Brookings.

Sharing the Faith: The Beliefs & Values of Catholic High School Teachers. Peter L. Benson & Michael J. Guerra. 85p. 1985. 11.40 (*0-318-18578-4*) Natl Cath Educ.

Sharing the Faith with Your Child: From Age Seven to Fourteen. Mary J. Pedersen & Joan Burney. LC 92-81360. 160p. (Orig.). 1992. pap. 5.95 (*0-89243-444-9*) Liguori Pubns.

Sharing the Faith with Your Child: From Birth to Age Six. Phyllis Chandler & Joan Burney. LC 84-80854. 96p. 1984. pap. 3.95 (*0-89243-205-5*) Liguori Pubns.

***Sharing the Final Journey.** Norma Wylie. Date not set. pap. 9.95 (*0-88999-608-3*, Pub. by Lancelot Pr CN) BookWorld Dist.

Sharing the Gains of Productivity. Brian F. Moore. (Studies in Productivity: No. 24). 57p. 1982. pap. 55.00 (*0-08-029505-3*) Work in Amer.

Sharing the Ganges: The Politics & Technology of River Development. Ben Crow et al. LC 94-32113. 230p. 1995. text ed. 26.00 (*0-8039-9203-3*) Sage.

Sharing the Good News with Children: Stories for the Common Lectionary. Thomas W. Goodhue. 322p. 1992. spiral bd. 19.95 (*0-86716-136-1*) St Anthony Mess Pr.

***Sharing the Good News with the Poor.** Ed. by Bruce J. Nicholls & Beulah Woods. (World Evangelical Fellowship Ser.). 288p. (C). 1996. pap. 22.99 (*0-8010-2099-9*) Baker Bks.

Sharing the Harvest the Road to Self-Reliance: Report of the National Round Table on Aboriginal Economic Development & Resources. 361p. (Orig.). 1993. pap. 38.95 (*0-660-15367-X*, Pub. by Canada Commun Grp CN) Accents Pubns.

Sharing the House. Jan Seale. Ed. by Dorey Schmidt. (Poetry Ser.: No. 3). (Illus.). 50p. (Orig.). 1982. pap. 6.95 (*0-938884-05-0*) Riversedge Pr.

Sharing the Journey. Robert Wuthnow. 304p. 1996. pap. 15.00 (*0-684-82623-2*) Free Pr.

***Sharing the Journey: Personal Stories of MS Caregiving.** David H. Oberlander. (Illus.). 200p. (Orig.). pap. 15.95 (*0-9654493-2-7*) D H Oberlander.

Sharing the Journey: Support Groups & America's New Quest for Community. Robert Wuthnow. 300p. 1994. 24.95 (*0-02-935625-3*, Free Press) Free Pr.

Sharing the Joy of Nature: Nature Activities for All Ages. Joseph Cornell. (Illus.). 176p. (Orig.). 1989. pap. 9.95 (*0-916124-52-5*, ES4) Dawn CA.

***Sharing the Lectionary for Lent: A Small-Group Faith-Sharing Process.** Jeff Keyes & St. Barnabas Catholic Community. 96p. (Orig.). 1997. pap. 7.95 (*0-89390-415-5*) Resource Pubns.

Sharing the Light of Faith: National Catechetical Directory for Catholics of the United States. United States Catholic Conference of Bishops Staff. (Illus.). 182p. (Orig.). 1979. pap. 9.95 (*1-55586-001-X*) US Catholic.

***Sharing the Lite!** Glynna M. Gunnell & Linda L. Church. LC 96-78076. 224p. 1996. 15.95 (*0-9654484-0-1*) Lite-Side Pubns.

Sharing the Maths Cultures: IMPACT LEA Maths for Parents, Children & Teachers. Ruth Merttens & Jeff Vass. 200p. 1990. 55.00 (*1-85000-875-2*, Falmer Pr); pap. 28.00 (*1-85000-876-0*, Falmer Pr) Taylor & Francis.

Sharing the Ministry: A Practical Guide for Transforming Volunteers into Ministry. Jean M. Trumbauer. 1995. ring bd. 49.95 (*0-8066-0280-5*, 23-2326) Augsburg Fortress.

***Sharing the Pie.** Brouwer. Date not set. write for info. (*0-8050-5206-2*) St Martin.

Sharing the Pie: A Disturbing Picture of the U. S. Economy. Steve Brouwer. (Illus.). 88p. (Orig.). (C). 1992. pap. 8.00 (*0-9622152-2-8*) Big Picture Bks.

Sharing the Pie: A Disturbing Picture of the U. S. Economy in the 1980s. Steve Brouwer. (Illus.). 240p. (C). 1988. 7.95 (*0-317-93354-X*) Big Picture Bks.

Sharing the Quest. Muz Murray. (Illus.). 272p. 1990. pap. 13.95 (*1-85230-087-6*) Element MA.

***Sharing the Reformed Tradition: The Dutch - North American Exchange, 1846-1996.** (Illus.). 188p. 1997. pap. 34.50 (*90-5383-519-9*, Pub. by VUB Univ Pr BE) Paul & Co Pubs.

***Sharing the Resources of the South China Sea.** 1997. lib. bdg. 121.00 (*90-411-0411-9*) Kluwer Ac.

Sharing the Risk: How the Nation's Businesses, Homes, & Autos Are Insured. 2nd rev. ed. James R. Marks & John D. Craigie. LC 81-65769. 191p. reprint ed. pap. 54.50 (*0-685-23719-2*, 2032707) Bks Demand.

Sharing the Road with Idiots: A Hilarious Guide to a Wild Ride. Bob Glickman. Ed. by Cliff Carle. 1993. pap. 4.95 (*0-918259-55-X*) CCC Pubns.

Sharing the Same Bowl: A Socioeconomic History of Women & Class in Accra, Ghana. Claire C. Robertson. LC 89-20660. (Illus.). 320p. 1990. pap. 15.95 (*0-472-06444-4*); lib. bdg. 39.50 (*0-472-09444-0*) U of Mich Pr.

Sharing the Season: A Collection of Christmas Warmth. Debbie Hansen. Ed. by Patrick Caton. LC 96-76125. 68p. 1996. 6.50 (*1-56245-274-6*) Great Quotations.

Sharing the Secrets: Open Source Intelligence & the War on Drugs. J. F. Holden-Rhodes. LC 95-40090. 224p. 1997. text ed. 55.00 (*0-275-95454-4*, Praeger Pubs) Greenwood.

***Sharing the Sky.** D. Levy & L. Lebofsky. 346p. (C). 1997. write for info. (*0-306-45638-9*, Plenum Pr) Plenum.

***Sharing the Sky: A Parent's & Teacher's Guide to Astronomy.** David H. Levy et al. (Illus.). 52p. 1997. pap. 18.95 (*0-306-45639-7*) Plenum.

Sharing the Sun. Lee Klein. LC 94-27638. (Illus.). (J). (gr. 1-4). 1995. pap. 4.95 (*0-8091-6621-6*) Paulist Pr.

Sharing the Sun: A Kid's Guide to South Florida. Debbie Fox & Marie-Helene Paquette Suarez. (Illus.). (Orig.). (J). (gr. k-7). 1996. pap. text ed. 14.95 (*0-9633461-7-2*) Valiant Pr.

Sharing the Sunday Scriptures with Youth: Cycle B. Robert P. Stamschror. 136p. (Orig.). 1996. teacher ed., pap. 24.95 (*0-88489-410-X*) St Marys.

***Sharing the Universe.** Seth Shostak. 1998. pap. text ed. 15.95 (*0-9653774-3-1*) Berkeley Hills.

Sharing the Wealth: Privatization Through Broad-Based Ownership Strategies. Stuart Bell. LC 95-13317. (World Bank Discussion Papers: Vol. 285). 40p. 1995. 6.95 (*0-8213-3230-9*, 13230) World Bank.

Sharing the Wonder of Birds with Kids. Laura Erickson. Ed. by Susan Gustafson. (Illus.). 192p. (Orig.). 1996. pap. 14.95 (*1-57025-129-0*) Pfeifer-Hamilton.

***Sharing the Word: Preaching in the Roundtable Church.** Lucy A. Rose. 176p. (Orig.). 1997. pap. 17.00 (*0-664-25658-9*) Westminster John Knox.

***Sharing the Word Through the Liturgical Year.** Gustavo Gutierrez. Tr. by Collettee J. Dees. LC 97-19495. 272p. 1997. reprint ed. pap. 18.00 (*1-57075-138-2*) Orbis Bks.

Sharing the Work: An Analysis of the Issues in Worksharing & Jobsharing. Noah M. Meltz et al. LC 81-188245. 98p. reprint ed. pap. 28.00 (*0-317-39707-9*, 2055826) Bks Demand.

Sharing the World with Animals. Marjorie B. Shaw & Ann Elwood. LC 95-49375. (Zoobooks Ser.). (Illus.). 24p. (J). (gr. 3 up). 1996. lib. bdg. 14.95 (*0-88682-778-7*) Creative Ed.

Sharing the World with Animals. Marjorie B. Shaw & Ann Elwood. (Zoobooks Ser.). 24p. (J). (gr. 1-7). 1995. 13.95 (*1-888153-02-4*) Wildlife Educ.

Sharing the World with Animals: Saving Our Animal Friends. Wildlife Education, Ltd. Staff. (Zoobooks Ser.). (Illus.). (J). 1990. pap. 2.75 (*0-937934-68-2*) Wildlife Educ.

Sharing the World's Resources. Oscar Schachter. LC 76-28422. 1977. text ed. 37.50 (*0-231-04110-1*) Col U Pr.

Sharing Thinking Strategies. John Langrehr. Ed. by Barbara Z. Presseisen. 121p. (Orig.). 1990. teacher ed. 22.95 (*1-879639-09-2*) Natl Educ Serv.

Sharing Thoughts & Feelings. Al Bouwense, Jr. (Orig.). 1996. pap. write for info. (*1-57553-174-7*) Watermrk Pr.

Sharing Time: A Guide to Quality Kindergarten Enrichment. Carol A. Larson. 64p. 1990. 9.00 (*0-911943-22-6*) Leadership Pub.

Sharing Time, Family Time, Anytime. Beth Lefgren & Jennifer Jackson. 1992. pap. 7.95 (*0-88494-846-3*) Bookcraft Inc.

Sharing Time, Family Time, Anytime Bk. 2. Beth Lefgren & Jennifer Jackson. 1994. pap. 7.95 (*0-88494-941-9*) Bookcraft Inc.

Sharing Time for Special Occassions. Christena C. Nelson. (Illus.). 51p. 1993. pap. 6.95 (*0-87579-815-2*) Deseret Bk.

Sharing Time Troubles. Grace Maccarone. LC 95-36015. (Hello Reader! Ser.: Level 1). (Illus.). (J). 1997. 3.50 (*0-590-73879-8*) Scholastic Inc.

Sharing Treasure, Time, & Talent: A Parish Manual for Sacrificial Giving or Tithing. Joseph M. Champlin. LC 82-16178. 88p. (Orig.). 1982. pap. 6.95 (*0-8146-1277-6*) Liturgical Pr.

Sharing Treasures: Book Reviews by John Holt. Ed. by Jane P. Holcomb. 86p. (Orig.). 1990. pap. text ed. 5.95 (*0-913677-08-6*) Holt Assocs.

Sharing Wisdom. Mary B. McKinney. 192p. 1987. pap. 9.95 (*0-89505-449-3*, 21101) Tabor Pub.

Sharing with Children: New Ideas on the Evolution of Life. Lynn Margulis. (Illus.). 23p. (Orig.). (C). 1985. pap. 3.00 (*0-918374-21-9*) City Coll Wk.

Sharing Without Reckoning: Imperfect Right & the Norms of Reciprocity. Millard Schumaker. (Editions SR Ser.: Vol. 14). 128p. (C). 1992. pap. 17.95 (*0-88920-208-7*) Wilfrid Laurier.

Sharing Writing: Peer Response Groups in English Classes. Karen I. Spear. LC 87-23067. 172p. (Orig.). (C). 1987. pap. text ed. 21.50 (*0-86709-189-4*, 0189) Boynton Cook Pubs.

Sharing Your Faith. Carolyn Nystrom. (Discipleship Ser.). 64p. 1992. pap. 4.99 (*0-310-54741-5*) Zondervan.

Sharing Your Faith. Harold Odor & Ruth S. Odor. (Illus.). 16p. (J). (gr. 3-7). 1985. 0.75 (*0-87239-902-8*, 03302) Standard Pub.

Sharing Your Faith: Ministry Training Program for Facilitators: Leader's Guide. Gemma Fisher et al. (Illus.). 32p. 1987. 3.95 (*1-55612-082-6*) Sheed & Ward MO.

Sharing Your Faith: Ministry Training Program for Facilitators: Participant. Gemma Fisher et al. (Illus.). 36p. 1987. pap. text ed. 2.95 (*1-55612-085-0*) Sheed & Ward MO.

S

Sharing Your Faith with a Muslim. Adiyah Akbar Abdul-Haqq. LC 80-16020. 192p. (Orig.). 1980. pap. 8.99 (*0-87123-553-6*) Bethany Hse.

Sharing Your Good Ideas: A Workshop Facilitator's Handbook. Peggy A. Sharp. LC 93-17871. 178p. (C). 1993. pap. 16.95 (*0-435-08783-5*, 08783) Heinemann.

Sharing Your Home. Christine Orton. (C). 1989. 30.00 (*0-86242-060-1*, Pub. by Age Concern Eng UK) St Mut.

***Shari's Passover Surprise.** Ed. by Debbie Cavalier. (Illus.). (Orig.). (J). 1997. pap. text ed. 19.95 (*1-57623-982-9*, PF9713) Warner Brothers.

Shariyat-Ki-Sugmad, Bk. 1. Paul Twitchell. 258p. 1998. pap. 14.00 (*1-57043-048-9*) ECKANKAR.

Shariyat-Ki-Sugmad, Bk. 2. Paul Twitchell. 270p. Date not set. pap. 14.00 (*1-57043-049-7*) ECKANKAR.

Shark. Michael Chinery. LC 90-33361. (Life Story Ser.). (Illus.). 32p. (J). (gr. 4-6). 1991. lib. bdg. 12.95 (*0-8167-2104-1*) Troll Communs.

Shark. Michael Chinery. LC 90-33361. (Life Story Ser.). (Illus.). 32p. (J). (gr. 4-6). 1997. pap. 4.95 (*0-8167-2105-X*) Troll Communs.

Shark. Miranda MacQuitty. LC 92-4712. (Eyewitness Bks.). (Illus.). 64p. (J). 1992. 19.00 (*0-679-81683-6*); lib. bdg. 20.99 (*0-679-91683-0*) Knopf Bks Yng Read.

***Shark.** Joyce Pope. LC 97-16490. (Pockets Ser.). 1997. write for info. (*0-7894-2045-7*) DK Pub Inc.

***Shark.** Adam Woog. LC 97-21348. (Overview Series). (Illus.). (J). (gr. 4-12). 1997. lib. bdg. 17.96 (*1-56006-462-5*) Lucent Bks.

Shark: A Photographer's Story. Jeremy Stafford-Deitsch. LC 87-4798. (Illus.). 200p. 1988. reprint ed. pap. 25.00 (*0-87156-733-4*) Sierra.

***Shark: Endangered Predator of the Sea.** Marty Snyderman. LC 97-9751. 1997. pap. write for info. (*1-57145-604-X*) Thunder Bay CA.

Shark: Lord of the Sea. 6th ed. Sandra D. Romashko. LC 76-150452. (Illus.). 64p. 1991. pap. 4.95 (*0-89317-001-1*) Windward Pub.

Shark! Nature's Masterpiece. R. D. Lawrence. (Curious Naturalist Ser.). (Illus.). 180p. 1994. reprint ed. pap. 12.95 (*1-881527-57-3*) Chapters Pub.

***Shark among Dolphins.** Steve Hubbard. LC 97-23129. 1997. 25.00 (*0-345-41204-4*) Ballantine.

Shark & Dolphin. Rod Theodorou & Carole Telford. LC 96-5554. (Discover the Difference Ser.). (Illus.). (J). 1996. lib. bdg. write for info. (*1-57572-101-5*) Rigby Interact Libr.

Shark & Ray. Vincent Serventy. LC 84-15097. (Animals in the Wild Ser.). (Illus.). 24p. (J). (gr. k-5). 1984. pap. 3.95 (*0-8114-6888-7*) Raintree Steck-V.

Shark & Whale. (Ultimate Sticker Bks.). (Illus.). 20p. (J). 1994. pap. 6.95 (*1-56458-717-7*) DK Pub Inc.

Shark Attack! Richie Cheval. (Super Eye Adventure Ser.: No. 4). (J). 1996. mass mkt. 3.99 (*0-553-48324-2*, Skylark BDD) BDD Bks Young Read.

***Shark Attack.** Longman Publishing Staff. Date not set. pap. text ed. write for info. (*0-17-556693-3*) Addison-Wesley.

***Shark Attack.** Mac Mcdiarmid. 1996. 9.98 (*0-7651-9698-0*) Smithmark.

Shark Attack Almanac. Beth Pickett. LC 96-42324. (J). 1997. pap. 5.99 (*0-679-87769-X*) Random Bks Yng Read.

Shark Attack!, Rescue at Nordic Valley, Emergency at Chitek Lake. Deborah Morris. (Real Kids, Real Adventures Ser.: Vol. 4). 104p. (J). (gr. 3-10). 1995. pap. 4.99 (*0-8054-4054-2*, 4240-54) Broadman.

***Shark Bait.** Graham Salisbury. LC 96-54708. (J). 1997. write for info. (*0-385-32237-2*) Delacorte.

Shark Beneath the Reef. Jean Craighead George. LC 88-25194. 192p. (YA). (gr. 7 up). 1989. 13.95 (*0-06-021992-0*); lib. bdg. 13.89 (*0-06-021993-9*) HarpC Child Bks.

Shark Beneath the Reef. Jean Craighead George. LC 88-25194. (Trophy Bk.). 192p. (YA). (gr. 7 up). 1991. pap. 3.95 (*0-06-440308-4*, Trophy) HarpC Child Bks.

***Shark Bites: True Stories of Survival.** Greg Ambrose. (Illus.). 144p. (Orig.). 1996. pap. 9.95 (*1-57306-054-2*) Bess Pr.

Shark Callers. Eric Campbell. LC 93-44881. 224p. (YA). (gr. 5 up). 1994. 11.00 (*0-15-200007-0*); pap. 5.00 (*0-15-200010-0*) HarBrace.

An Asterisk (*) at the beginning of an entry indicates that the title is appearing in BIP for the first time.

*Shark Cartilage. Rita Elkins. (The Woodland Health Ser.). 1997. pap. text ed. 3.95 (1-885670-38-9) Woodland UT.

Shark Dialogues. Kiana Davenport. Ed. by Lee Goerner. 512p. 1994. 22.00 (0-689-12191-1, Pub. by Ctrl Bur voor Schimmel NE) Macmillan.

Shark Dialogues. Kiana Davenport. LC 95-737. 1995. pap. 13.95 (0-452-27458-3, Plume) NAL-Dutton.

Shark Facts. Lynn M. Stone. LC 96-7965. (Read All about Sharks Ser.). (J). 1996. write for info. (0-86593-445-2) Rourke Corp.

Shark in School. Patricia R. Giff. (Illus.). 103p. (J). (gr. 3-7). 1995. pap. 3.50 (0-440-41127-0, YB BDD) BDD Bks Young Read.

Shark in the Dining Room. Mier Ponte. Ed. by Rose Merkle & Junah Burnstein. LC 95-81155. (Illus.). 96p. (Orig.). 1995. pap. text ed. 14.95 (0-9649763-0-7) Heavenly Wind.

Shark in the Sea. Joanne Ryder. LC 96-16963. (Just for a Day Bks.). (Illus.). (J). 1997. 16.00 (0-688-14909-X, Morrow Junior); lab manual ed., lib. bdg. 15.93 (0-688-14910-3, Morrow Junior) Morrow.

Shark Infested Custard. Charles Willeford. 320p. 1996. mass mkt. 4.99 (0-440-21881-0) Dell.

Shark-Infested Waters: Young British Artists in the Saatchi Collection. Sarah Kent. (Illus.). 272p. 1994. 39.95 (0-302-00648-6, Pub. by P Wilson Pubs) Sothebys Pubns.

Shark Lady. Ann McGovern. (Illus.). 96p. (J). (gr. k-3). 1991. pap. 2.95 (0-590-44771-8) Scholastic Inc.

*Shark Liver Oil. 1997. mass mkt. 5.99 (1-57566-202-7) Kensgtn Pub Corp.

Shark Mazes: Educational Activity-Coloring Book. Peter M. Spizzirri. Ed. by Linda Spizzirri. (Illus.). 32p. (J). (gr. k-5). 1984. pap. 1.25 (0-86545-056-0) Spizzirri.

*Shark Never Sleeps. Rosenhaus. 1997. 24.00 (0-671-01525-7, PB Hardcover) PB.

Shark of the Confederacy: The Story of the CSS Alabama. Charles M. Robinson, III. LC 94-13816. (Illus.). 230p. 1994. 26.95 (1-55750-728-7) Naval Inst Pr.

Shark of the Confederacy: The Story of the CSS Alabama. Charles M. Robinson, III. (Illus.). 212p. 1995. 39.50 (0-85052-435-0, Pub. by L Cooper Bks UK) Trans-Atl Phila.

Shark Shock. Donna J. Napoli. LC 93-43975. (Illus.). 192p. (J). (gr. 3-7). 1994. pap. 13.99 (0-525-45267-2) Dutton Child Bks.

Shark Shock. Donna J. Napoli. 176p. (J). 1996. pap. 3.99 (0-14-037742-5) Viking Penguin.

Shark Stickers. Nina Barbaresi. (Illus.). (J). (gr. k-3). 1993. pap. 1.00 (0-486-27664-3) Dover.

*Shark Stories Vol. 1: Amazing But True. Fred Barnett. (Illus.). 128p. (Orig.). 1996. pap. 9.95 (1-887394-00-1, 1) F Barnett Studios.

*Shark Tank. Fine. LC 97-23036. 1997. 23.95 (0-312-17019-X) St Martin.

Shark Watcher's Guide. Guido Dingerkus. (Illus.). 144p. (YA). (gr. 7 up). 1989. pap. 5.95 (0-671-68815-4, Julian Messner) Silver Burdett Pr.

Shark Who Learned a Lesson. Gill McBarnet. (Illus.). 32p. (J). (gr. k-2). 1990. 8.95 (0-9615102-5-0) Ruwanga Trad.

Sharkbait. large type ed. Butler. (Dales Large Print Ser.). 1995. pap. 17.99 (1-85389-570-9, Dales) Ulverscroft.

Sharkproof. H. Mackay. pap. 5.98 (0-8317-0044-0) Smithmark.

Sharks. (Explorers Ser.). (Illus.). 40p. (J). (gr. 2-6). 1996. pap. 4.99 (0-7214-5606-5, Ladybrd) Penguin.

*Sharks. (Eyes on Nature Ser.). (Illus.). 32p. (J). (gr. 1 up). write for info. (1-56156-422-2) Kidsbks.

Sharks. Donna Bailey. LC 90-22114. (Animal World Ser.). (Illus.). 32p. (J). (gr. 1-4). 1992. pap. 4.95 (0-8114-4618-2); lib. bdg. 21.40 (0-8114-2649-1) Raintree Steck-V.

Sharks! June Behrens. LC 89-25375. (Sea Life Ser.). (Illus.). 48p. (J). (gr. 1-4). 1990. lib. bdg. 17.50 (0-516-00571-5) Childrens.

Sharks. Ruth Berman. LC 94-21468. (J). Date not set. pap. 7.95 (0-87614-897-6, Carolrhoda) Lerner Group.

Sharks. Ruth Berman. LC 94-21468. (Nature Watch Bks.). 47p. (J). (gr. 3-5). 1995. lib. bdg. 14.96 (0-87614-870-4, Carolrhoda) Lerner Group.

*Sharks. Chelsea House Publishing Staff. (Concise Collection). 1997. 15.95 (1-85627-782-8) Chelsea Hse.

Sharks. Sheena Coupe. (Great Creatures of the World Ser.). 72p. (J). (gr. 5-12). 1990. 17.95 (0-8160-2270-4) Facts on File.

*Sharks. DK Publishing, Inc. Staff. LC 97-20872. (Really Horrible Guides Ser.). 1997. 9.95 (0-7894-2050-3) DK Pub Inc.

Sharks. Russell Freedman. LC 85-42881. (Illus.). 40p. (J). (gr. 1-4). 1985. lib. bdg. 14.95 (0-8234-0582-6) Holiday.

Sharks. Gail Gibbons. LC 91-31524. (Illus.). 32p. (J). (ps-3). 1992. lib. bdg. 15.95 (0-8234-0960-0) Holiday.

Sharks. Gail Gibbons. (Illus.). (J). 1993. pap. 6.95 (0-8234-1068-4) Holiday.

Sharks. Gail Gibbons. (Illus.). (J). (gr. k-4). 1992. pap. 15.95 incl. audio (0-87499-275-3) Live Oak Media.

Sharks. Gail Gibbons. (Illus.). (J). (gr. k-4). 1992. 22.95 incl. audio (0-87499-276-1) Live Oak Media.

Sharks. John Green. (Little Activity Bks.). (J). 1994. pap. 1.00 (0-486-28096-9) Dover.

*Sharks. Judith Hodge. LC 97-19632. (Animals of the Oceans Ser.). 1997. pap. text ed. 5.95 (0-7641-0260-5) Barron.

*Sharks. Kevin J. Holmes. LC 97-12203. (Animals Ser.). (J). 1998. write for info. (1-56065-600-X) Capstone Pr.

Sharks. Casey Horton. (Endangered! Ser.). 32p. (J). (gr. 3-5). 1996. lib. bdg. 14.95 (0-7614-0220-9, Benchmark NY) Marshall Cavendish.

Sharks. Houghton Mifflin Company Staff. (Literature Experience 1991 Ser.). (J). (gr. 8). 1990. pap. 9.84 (0-395-55188-9) HM.

*Sharks. Bobbie Kalman & Niki Walker. LC 97-4089. (Crabapple Ser.). (Illus.). 32p. (J). (gr. k-7). 1997. lib. bdg. 16.95 (0-86505-637-4) Crabtree Pub Co.

*Sharks. Bobbie Kalman & Niki Walker. LC 97-4089. (Crabapple Ser.). (Illus.). 32p. (J). (gr. k-7). 1997. pap. 5.95 (0-86505-737-0) Crabtree Pub Co.

*Sharks. Gerald Legg. LC 97-5964. (Worldwise Ser.). (J). 1998. write for info. (0-531-14461-5) Watts.

Sharks. Gary Lopez. (Nature Bks.). 32p. (J). (gr. 2-6). 1991. lib. bdg. 22.79 (0-89565-705-8) Childs World.

*Sharks. Christopher Maynard. LC 97-16537. (Infomania Ser.). (Illus.). 90p. (J). 1997. 14.99 (0-7636-0328-7) Candlewick Pr.

Sharks. Ann McGovern. 64p. (J). (gr. k-3). 1995. pap. 4.95 (0-590-41360-0) Scholastic Inc.

Sharks. Jo E. Moore. (Illus.). 48p. (J). (gr. 3-6). 1992. pap. 5.95 (1-55799-215-0, EMC 255) Evan-Moor Corp.

Sharks. Peter Murray. (Baby Zoobks.). (Illus.). 32p. (YA). (gr. 3 up). 1998. lib. bdg. write for info. (0-88682-838-4) Creative Ed.

Sharks. Steve Parker. (What If...Ser.). (Illus.). 32p. (J). (gr. 4-6). 1996. lib. bdg. 14.90 (0-7613-0456-8, Copper Beech Bks) Millbrook Pr.

Sharks. Steve Parker. (What If...Ser.). (Illus.). 32p. (J). (gr. 4-6). 1996. pap. 5.95 (0-7613-0471-1, Copper Beech Bks) Millbrook Pr.

Sharks. Doug Perrine. LC 94-42427. (WorldLife Library). (Illus.). 72p. 1995. pap. 14.95 (0-89658-270-1) Voyageur Pr.

Sharks. Lee Server. (Illus.). 128p. (J). 1989. 14.99 (0-517-69091-8) Random Hse Value.

Sharks. Seymour Simon. LC 95-1593. (Illus.). 32p. (J). (gr. 2-5). 1995. 15.95 (0-06-023029-0); lib. bdg. 15.89 (0-06-023032-0) HarpC Child Bks.

Sharks. Seymour Simon. LC 95-1593. (Trophy Nonfiction Bk.). (Illus.). 32p. (J). (gr. k-3). 1996. pap. 5.95 (0-06-446187-4, Trophy) HarpC Child Bks.

Sharks. Eileen Spinelli. (Childrens' Nature Library). (Illus.). 64p. (J). (gr. k-4). 1992. lib. bdg. 14.95 (1-878363-89-1, HTS Bks) Forest Hse.

Sharks. Ed. by John Stevens. (Illus.). 240p. (J). 1987. 35.00 (0-8160-1800-6) Facts on File.

Sharks. Jane Walker. (Fascinating Facts Ser.). (Illus.). 32p. (J). (gr. 2-4). 1995. pap. 5.95 (1-56294-896-2) Millbrook Pr.

Sharks. Jane Walker. (Fascinating Facts Ser.). (Illus.). 32p. (J). (gr. 2-4). 1995. lib. bdg. 14.90 (1-56294-606-4) Millbrook Pr.

*Sharks. Waters. 1996. pap. 8.95 (0-8050-4783-2) St Martin.

*Sharks. Waters. LC 97-8729. 1997. pap. 18.98 (0-8050-4782-4) St Martin.

Sharks. John B. Wexo. (Zoobooks Ser.). 24p. (J). (gr. 3). 1988. lib. bdg. 14.95 (0-88682-229-7) Creative Ed.

*Sharks. John B. Wexo. (Zoobooks). (Illus.). 24p. (J). (gr. 1-7). 1997. 13.95 (1-888153-31-8, 229-7) Wildlife Educ.

Sharks. Wildlife Education, Ltd. Staff. (Zoobooks Ser.). (Illus.). 20p. (YA). (gr. 5 up). 1983. pap. 2.75 (0-937934-15-1) Wildlife Educ.

Sharks! Lynn Wilson. (All Aboard Bks.). (Illus.). 32p. (J). (ps-3). 1992. pap. 2.95 (0-448-40300-5, G&D) Putnam Pub Group.

Sharks, 4 bks., Set. Gail Gibbons. (Illus.). (J). (gr. k-4). 1992. pap. 36.95 incl. audio (0-87499-277-X) Live Oak Media.

Sharks: A Portrait of the Animal World. Andrew Cleave. 1995. 10.98 (0-8317-0963-4) Smithmark.

Sharks: A Source Guide. 1991. lib. bdg. 69.00 (0-8490-4878-8) Gordon Pr.

Sharks: An Educational Coloring Book. Spizzirri Publishing Co. Staff. Ed. by Linda Spizzirri. (Illus.). 32p. (J). (gr. 1-8). 1981. pap. 1.99 (0-86545-029-3) Spizzirri.

Sharks: Challengers of the Deep. Mary M. Cerullo. LC 92-14206. 64p. (J). (gr. 4 up). 1993. pap. 16.99 (0-525-65100-4, Cobblehill Bks) Dutton Child Bks.

*Sharks: Challengers of the Deep. Photos by Jeffrey L. Rotman. (Illus.). (J). (gr. 6). 1995. 8.20 (0-395-73271-9) HM.

*Sharks: Challengers of the Deep. large type ed. Text by Mary M. Cerullo. 78p. (J). (gr. 6). 19.50 (0-614-20618-9, L-38205-00 APHB) Am Printing Hse.

*Sharks: Pop-Up Book. Intervisual Books Staff. (Illus.). (J). 1997. 14.95 (1-888443-03-0) Intervisual Bks.

Sharks: Shark Magic for Kids. Patricia Corrigan. LC 96-16947. (Animal Magic for Kids Ser.). (Illus.). (J). 1996. lib. bdg. 18.60 (0-8368-1633-1) Gareth Stevens Inc.

Sharks: The History of a Crew & a Shipwreck. Jens Bjorneboe. Tr. by Esther G. Murer from NOR. 241p. 9300. pap. 24.00 (1-870041-20-8, Pub. by Norvik Pr UK) Dufour.

Sharks: The Perfect Predators. rev. ed. Howard Hall. Ed. by Vicki Leon. (Marine Life Ser.). (Illus.). 48p. (Orig.). (J). (gr. 5 up). 1993. pap. 9.95 (0-685-69340-6) Blake Pub.

Sharks: The Perfect Predators. rev. ed. Howard Hall. Ed. by Vicki Leon. LC 94-31828. (Close up: A Focus on Nature Ser.). (Illus.). 48p. (YA). (gr. 5 up). 1994. pap. 7.95 (0-382-24892-9); lib. bdg. 14.95 (0-382-24891-0) Silver Burdett Pr.

*Sharks: The Supper Fish. Helen R. Sattler. (J). Date not set. lib. bdg. write for info. (0-688-03994-4) Lothrop.

Sharks! True Stories & Legends. Catherine Gourley. LC 95-45005. (Illus.). 96p. (J). (gr. 4-6). 1996. lib. bdg. 20.90 (0-7613-0001-5) Millbrook Pr.

Sharks: Voracious Hunters of the Sea. Isidro Sanchez et al. (Secrets of the Animal World Ser.). (Illus.). 32p. (J). (gr. 3 up). 1996. lib. bdg. 18.60 (0-8368-1396-0) Gareth Stevens Inc.

Sharks - Shorelines of America: The Story Behind the Scenery. Peter C. Howorth. LC 91-60038. (Shorelines of America Ser.). (Illus.). 48p. (Orig.). 1991. pap. 7.95 (0-88714-063-7) KC Pubns.

Sharks, a Fisherman's Point of View. Mitchell Waite. LC 91-68227. (Illus.). 115p. (Orig.). 1992. pap. text ed. 7.95 (1-881260-01-1) Southwest Pubns.

Sharks Activity & Game Book. Elvira Gamiello. (Illus.). (Orig.). (J). (gr. 4-6). 1988. pap. 1.95 (0-942025-46-6) Kidsbks.

Sharks & Other Creatures of the Deep. Philip Steele. LC 91-72484. (See & Explore Library). (Illus.). 64p. (J). (gr. 3 up). 1991. 12.95 (1-879431-16-5) DK Pub Inc.

Sharks & Other Dangerous Sea Creatures. Idaz Greenberg & Jerry Greenberg. (Illus.). 64p. 1981. pap. 7.95 (0-913008-09-5) Seahawk Pr.

Sharks & Other Fish. (Information Ser.). 32p. (J). 3.50 (0-7214-1746-9, Ladybrd) Penguin.

Sharks & People. Lynn M. Stone. LC 96-7969. (Read All about Sharks Ser.). (J). 1996. write for info. (0-86593-446-0) Rourke Corp.

Sharks & Rays. Keith Banister. (Look Inside Ser.). (Illus.). 16p. (J). (gr. 2-5). 1995. bds. 10.99 (0-89577-690-1) Rdrs Dgst Yng Fam.

*Sharks & Rays. Leighton R. Taylor, Jr. et al. LC 97-10718. (Nature Company Guides Ser.). (Illus.). 288p. 1997. write for info. (0-7835-4940-7) Time-Life.

Sharks & Rays of Australia. P. Last & J. Stevens. (Illus.). 600p. 1993. 95.00 (0-643-05143-0, Pub. by CSIRO AT) Aubrey Bks.

*Sharks & Rays of New Zealand. Geoffrey Cox. (Illus.). 32p. (Orig.). (YA). 1996. pap. 19.95 (0-908812-60-4, Pub. by Canterbury Univ NZ) Aubrey Bks.

Sharks & Rays of the Pacific Coast. Ava Ferguson & Gregor Caillet. (Natural History Ser.). (Illus.). 64p. (Orig.). 1990. pap. 9.95 (1-878244-02-7) Monterey Bay Aquarium.

Sharks & Shark Products in Prehistoric South Florida. Laura Kozuch. (Institute of Archaeology & Paleoenvironmental Studies, Monograph: No. 2). 50p. 1993. pap. 5.00 (1-881448-01-0) IAPS Bks.

Sharks & Shipwrecks. Hugh Edwards. LC 74-33219. (Illus.). 128p. 1975. write for info. (0-8129-0559-8, Times Bks) Random.

Sharks Are People Too! Leigh Rubin. LC 82-99813. (Illus.). 80p. 1982. pap. 4.95 (0-943384-02-8) Rubes Pubns.

Shark's Cove. Alicia Baldwin. 176p. (YA). (gr. 5 up). 1996. pap. 3.99 (0-679-88133-6, Bullseye Bks) Random Bks Yng Read.

Sharks Don't Get Cancer: How Shark Cartilage Could Save Your Life. I. William Lane & Linda Comac. LC 92-782. 216p. pap. 11.95 (0-89529-520-2) Avery Pub.

Sharks for Kids. Patricia Corrigan. LC 95-6206. (Wildlife for Kids Ser.). (Illus.). 48p. (Orig.). (J). (gr. 3-7). 1995. pap. 6.95 (1-55971-476-X) NorthWord.

Sharks Have No Bones: 1001 Things Everyone Should Know About Science. James S. Trefil. (Illus.). 320p. 1993. pap. 12.00 (0-671-79627-5, Fireside) S&S Trade.

Sharks Hawai'i. Arnold Suzumoto. (Illus.). 44p. 1991. 4.95 (0-930897-67-6) Bishop Mus.

Sharks in Question: The Smithsonian Answer Book. Victor G. Springer & Joy P. Gold. LC 88-18185. (Illus.). 192p. (C). 1989. pap. 16.95 (0-87474-877-1) Smithsonian.

Sharks of Arabia. John E. Randall. 148p. (C). 1990. 125.00 (0-907151-09-4, Pub. by IMMEL Pubng UK) St Mut.

Sharks of Arabia. John E. Randall. (Illus.). 148p. 1995. 81.00 (0-614-07670-6, Pub. by IMMEL Pubng UK) St Mut.

Sharks of Hawai'i: Their Biology & Cultural Significance. Leighton Taylor. LC 93-10424. (Illus.). 126p. (C). 1993. 19.00 (0-8248-1562-9) UH Pr.

Sharks of North American Waters. Jose I. Castro. LC 82-16720. (W. L. Moody Jr. Natural History Ser.: Vol. 5). (Illus.). 192p. (Orig.). (C). 1996. reprint ed. pap. 17.95 (0-89096-143-3) Tex A&M Univ Pr.

Sharks of Steel. Paul Stillwell & Robert Y. Kaufman. LC 92-35231. (Illus.). 176p. 1993. 45.00 (1-55750-451-2) Naval Inst Pr.

Sharks of the Seas. Lynn M. Stone. LC 96-19187. (Read All about Sharks Ser.). (J). 1996. write for info. (0-86593-441-X) Rourke Corp.

Sharks of the World. Rodney Steel. (Of the World Ser.). (Illus.). 192p. 1985. 25.95 (0-8160-1086-2) Facts on File.

Sharks of the World Coloring Book. Llyn Hunter. (Illus.). (J). 1989. pap. 2.95 (0-486-26137-9) Dover.

Sharks of Tropical & Temperate Seas. R. H. Johnson. (Illus.). 170p. 1995. pap. 16.95 (1-55992-085-8, 2085) Gulf Pub.

Sharks over China: The 23rd Fighter Group in World War II. Carl Molesworth. (World War II Commemorative Ser.). (Illus.). 256p. 1995. 23.95 (0-02-881094-5) Brasseys Inc.

Sharks, Rays, & Eels: Golden Junior Guide. Christopher Lampton. (Illus.). 36p. (J). (ps-3). 1995. 5.50 (0-307-11437-6, Golden Books) Western Pub.

Sharks, Sharks, Sharks. Tina Anton. (Real Readers Ser.). (Illus.). 32p. (J). (gr. 1-4). 1989. pap. 4.95 (0-8114-6731-7); lib. bdg. 21.40 (0-8172-3531-0) Raintree Steck-V.

Sharks, Ships & Potato Chips: Curriculum Integrated Library Instruction. Ruth Toor & Hilda K. Weisburg. (Illus.). 260p. 1986. 33.95 (0-931315-02-6) Lib Learn Res.

Sharks Still Don't Get Cancer: The Continuing Story of Shark Cartilage Therapy. I. William Lane & Linda Comac. LC 96-4749. 272p. 1996. pap. 12.95 (0-89529-722-1) Avery Pub.

Shark's Teeth Nose Art. Jeffrey L. Ethell. (Illus.). 128p. 1992. pap. 9.98 (0-87938-584-7) Motorbooks Intl.

Shark's World. Lynn M. Stone. LC 96-7967. (Read All about Sharks Ser.). (J). 1996. write for info. (0-86593-444-4) Rourke Corp.

Sharky's Machine. William Diehl. 1995. mass mkt. 6.99 (0-345-40239-1) Ballantine.

*Sharlot Hall on the Arizona Strip: A Diary of a Journey Through Northern Arizona in 1911. rev. ed. Sharlot M. Hall. Ed. by C. Gregory Crampton. (Illus.). 96p. (YA). (gr. 8-12). 1997. reprint ed. pap. 11.95 (0-927579-08-1) Sharlot Hall Mus Pr.

Sharlot Herself: Selected Writings of Sharlot Hall. Ed. by Nancy K. Wright. 126p. 1992. pap. 11.95 (0-614-14695-X) Sharlot Hall Mus Pr.

Sharman Macdonald Plays, No. 1. Sharman Macdonald. 384p. (Orig.). 1995. pap. 13.95 (0-571-17621-6) Faber & Faber.

Sharon: An Israeli Caesar. Uzi Benziman. LC 85-13461. 276p. 1985. 17.95 (0-915361-23-X) Hemed Bks.

Sharon: Memoirs of a Coed Call Girl. 1991. pap. 4.50 (0-8216-5088-2, Univ Books) Carol Pub Group.

Sharon, Connecticut, Probate Records 1757-83. 1984. pap. 12.00 (0-914385-03-8) Catoctin Pr.

Sharon Lee's Original Animal-Free Salad Dressings! Sharon L. Davies-Tight. 48p. 1993. pap. 8.95 (1-885099-02-9) Rainbow Sunshine.

Sharon, Lois & Bram's Mother Goose Songs, Finger Rhymes, Tickling Verses, Games & More. Sharon et al. (Illus.). 92p. (J). (ps-2). 1986. 16.95 (0-316-78281-5, 782815) Little.

Sharon Oehler: Pediatrician. Jennifer Bryant. (Working Moms: A Portrait of Their Lives Ser.). (Illus.). 40p. (J). (gr. 2-4). 1991. lib. bdg. 15.98 (0-941477-53-3) TFC Bks NY.

Sharon, PA. Historical Briefs, Inc. Staff. Ed. by Thomas Antonucci & Michael Antonucci. 176p. 1992. pap. 14.95 (0-89677-045-1) Hist Briefs.

Sharon Shares from Where Eagles Soar. Sharon Reed. 95p. (Orig.). 1993. pap. text ed. 12.95 (0-9629735-1-3) Sharon Reed.

Sharon Shares Her Heart. 55p. 1991. 10.00 (0-9629735-0-5) Sharon Reed.

*Sharon Stone. David Sandison. (Superstars of Film Ser.). (Illus.). 48p. (YA). (gr. 7 up). 1997. lib. bdg. 15.95 (0-7910-4650-8) Chelsea Hse.

Sharon's Hope. Neva Coyle. 288p. (J). 1996. pap. 10.99 (0-7852-7660-2) Nelson.

Sharp & Sticky Stuff. Lynn M. Stone. LC 96-8997. (Animal Weapons Ser.). 1996. write for info. (1-57103-167-7) Rourke Pr.

Sharp End. David Drake. LC 93-10739. 384p. 1993. 20.00 (0-671-72192-5) Baen Bks.

Sharp End. David Drake. 384p. 1994. mass mkt. 5.99 (0-671-87632-5) Baen Bks.

Sharp Quillets of the Law. Charles S. Desmond. xix, 245p. 1949. lib. bdg. 34.00 (0-89941-595-4, 500310) W S Hein.

Sharp Rocks. Edgar Heap of Birds. (Illus.). 14p. 1986. pap. 12.00 (0-939784-14-9) CEPA Gall.

Sharp Teeth of Love. Doris Betts. LC 96-38583. 1997. 24.00 (0-679-45072-6) McKay.

*Sharp the Bugle Calls. large type ed. Steve Frazee. 1996. lib. bdg. 17.95 (1-57490-050-1, Sagebrush LP West) T T Beeler.

*Sharp. The Sharps of Chester Co., Pa. & Abstracts of Records in Gt. Britain. W. C. Sharpe. 36p. 1996. lib. bdg. 17.00 (0-8328-6578-8) Higginson Bk Co.

Sharpe Genealogy & Miscellany. W. C. Sharpe. 178p. 1995. reprint ed. pap. 29.00 (0-8328-4836-0); reprint ed. lib. bdg. 39.00 (0-8328-4835-2) Higginson Bk Co.

Sharpe, Vol. I, Nos. 1-32: The Sharpe Family Magazine. (Illus.). 212p. 1991. reprint ed. pap. 34.50 (0-8328-2200-0); reprint ed. lib. bdg. 44.50 (0-8328-2199-3) Higginson Bk Co.

Sharpen the Sickle. Reginald Groves. LC 74-22744. (Labor Movement in Fiction & Non-Fiction Ser.). 1976. reprint ed. 37.50 (0-404-58496-9) AMS Pr.

*Sharpen Your Bridge Technique: How to Think Like an Expert. Hugh Kelsey. 160p. 1997. pap. 17.95 (0-575-06437-4, Pub. by V Gollancz UK) Trafalgar.

Sharpen Your School Law Focus. Jennifer Jacobs et al. 500p. 1996. ring bd. 200.00 (0-88364-199-2) Natl Sch Boards.

*Sharpen Your Skills in Motivating People to Perform. Trevor J. Bentley. LC 96-9742. 1996. write for info. (0-07-709072-1) McGraw.

*Sharpen Your Tactics! 1125 Brilliant Sacrifices, Combinations, & Studies. Anatoly Lein & Boris Archangelsky. Ed. by Lou Hays. 270p. 1996. pap. 19.95 (1-880673-13-4) Hays Pub.

*Sharpen Your Team's Skills in Coaching. Tony Voss & Dennis C. Kinlaw. LC 96-36299. 1996. pap. write for info. (0-07-709278-3) McGraw.

*Sharpen Your Team's Skills in Creativity. Trevor J. Bentley. LC 96-46524. 1996. pap. write for info. (0-07-709282-1) McGraw.

*Sharpen Your Team's Skills in Effective Selling. Trevor J. Bentley & Herbert R. Miller. LC 96-9743. 1996. write for info. (0-07-709279-1) McGraw.

*Sharpen Your Team's Skills in People Skills. Dianne Kamp. LC 96-34473. 1997. pap. text ed. 24.95 (0-07-709276-7) McGraw.

*Sharpen Your Team's Skills in Project Management. Jean Harris. LC 96-41876. (Sharpen Your Team's Skills Ser.). 1996. pap. write for info. (0-07-709140-X) McGraw.

*Sharpen Your Team's Skills in Supervision. Susan Clayton. LC 96-34950. 1996. pap. write for info. (0-07-709280-5) McGraw.

*Sharpen Your Team's Skills in Time Management. Jane Allan. LC 96-46035. (Sharpen Your Team's Skills Ser.). 1997. pap. write for info. (0-07-709275-9) McGraw.

An Asterisk (*) at the beginning of an entry indicates that the title is appearing in BIP for the first time.

Sharpened Axe of Reason: Approaches to Walter Benjamin. Ed. by Gerhard Fischer. (Illus.). 256p. 1996. 45.95 (*1-85973-044-2*); pap. 16.95 (*1-85973-054-X*) Berg Pubs.

Sharpening. Nick Engler. LC 93-37564. (Workshop Companion Ser.). 1994. 19.95 (*0-87596-584-9*) Rodale Pr Inc.

Sharpening: A Complete Guide. Jim Kingshott. (Illus.). 160p. 1994. pap. 17.95 (*0-946819-48-3*, Pub. by Guild Mstr Craftsman UK) Sterling.

Sharpening & Knife Making. Jim Watson. LC 87-62895. (Illus.). 176p. 1987. 12.95 (*0-88740-118-X*) Schiffer.

Sharpening & Tool Care. Ed. by Time-Life Books Editors. LC 94-26232. (Art of Woodworking Ser.). (Illus.). 144p. 1994. 19.95 (*0-8094-9933-9*) Time-Life.

Sharpening Basics. Patrick Spielman. LC 91-19984. (Basics Ser.). (Illus.). 128p. 1991. pap. 10.95 (*0-8069-7226-2*) Sterling.

Sharpening Pocket Reference Book: Techniques & Equipment. Jim Kingshott. (Illus.). 160p. 1996. pap. 12.95 (*1-86108-007-7*, Pub. by Guild Mstr Craftsman UK) Sterling.

Sharpening Small Tools. Ian Bradley. pap. 7.00 (*0-85242-459-0*) Apple Blossom.

Sharpening the Combat Edge: The Use of Analysis to Reinforce Military Judgment. 1995. lib. bdg. 255.95 (*0-8490-6579-8*) Gordon Pr.

Sharpening the Focus of the Church. Gene A. Getz. 360p. 1984. pap. 12.99 (*0-89693-393-8*, 6-2393, Victor Bks) Chariot Victor.

Sharpening the Marketing Edge. Harvard Business Review Staff. (Marketing in Action Ser.). 111p. 1991. pap. 19.95 (*0-87584-282-8*) Harvard Busn.

Sharpening the Marketing Edge. Harvard Business School Press Staff. 1991. pap. text ed. 19.95 (*0-07-103342-4*) McGraw.

Sharpening the Sword: A Call to Strong & Courageous Leadership. Stephen D. Hower. LC 96-14011. 368p. 1996. 19.87 (*0-570-04872-9*, 12-3295) Concordia.

***Sharpening the Warrior's Edge: The Psychology & Science of Training.** Bruce K. Siddle. 1996. 19.95 (*0-614-19156-4*) PPCT Res Publns.

***Sharpening with Waterstones: A Perfect Edge in 60 Seconds.** Ian J. Kirby. (Illus.). 96p. (Orig.). 1997. pap. 14.95 (*0-9643999-3-8*) Cambium Pr.

Sharpening Your Image: How to Get, Keep & Expand a Healthcare Business. Lisa Mosing. 238p. 1992. pap. 29.95 (*0-9633990-0-4*) Nutrition Wks.

Sharpening Your People Skills: Twelve Tools for Success in Any Relationship. William J. Diehm. LC 96-11432. 176p. 1996. pap. 10.99 (*0-8054-6288-0*, 4262-88) Broadman.

Sharper Edge. T. T. Riffig. 154p. (Orig.). 1989. pap. text ed. 5.95 (*0-9621755-0-1*) Metahomin Pub.

Sharper Edge: Your Very Best Effort Game, and-or Performance Can Be Made Routine: Then, Duely Improved Upon. A. S. Igwe. Ed. by David Wilde. 52p. (Orig.). 1993. pap. text ed. 15.00 (*1-882204-06-9*) Wilde Pub.

Sharpe's Battle. Bernard Cornwell. LC 95-10347. 320p. 1995. 20.00 (*0-06-017677-6*, HarpT) HarpC.

Sharpe's Battle. Bernard Cornwell. 432p. 1996. mass mkt. 5.99 (*0-06-109537-0*, Harp PBks) HarpC.

Sharpe's Battle: Richard Sharpe & the Battle of Fuentes de Onoro, May 1811. large type ed. Bernard Cornwell. 534p. 1996. 23.95 (*0-7862-0572-5*, Thorndike Lrg Prnt) Thorndike Pr.

Sharpe's Company, No. 4. Bernard Cornwell. 288p. 1987. pap. 9.95 (*0-14-014443-9*, Penguin Bks) Viking Penguin.

Sharpe's Company: The Siege of Badajoz. Bernard Cornwell. 288p. 1984. pap. 10.95 (*0-14-007023-0*, Penguin Bks) Viking Penguin.

Sharpe's Devil. Bernard Cornwell. 368p. 1993. mass mkt. 5.99 (*0-06-109028-X*, Harp PBks) HarpC.

Sharpe's Eagle. large type ed. Bernard Cornwell. 480p. 1983. 25.99 (*0-7089-0945-0*) Ulverscroft.

Sharpe's Eagle. Bernard Cornwell. 1991. reprint ed. lib. bdg. 29.95 (*1-56849-076-3*) Buccaneer Bks.

Sharpe's Eagle, No. 2. Bernard Cornwell. 270p. 1987. pap. 10.95 (*0-14-009921-2*, Penguin Bks) Viking Penguin.

Sharpe's Enemy, No. 6. Bernard Cornwell. 368p. 1987. pap. 10.95 (*0-14-010430-5*, Penguin Bks) Viking Penguin.

Sharpe's Enemy: The Defense of Portugal, Christmas 1812. Bernard Cornwell. 1985. mass mkt. 5.95 (*0-14-007655-7*, Penguin Bks) Viking Penguin.

Sharpe's Gold, No. 3. Barnard Cornwell. 1987. pap. 10.95 (*0-14-024305-4*, Penguin Bks) Viking Penguin.

Sharpe's Honor, No. 7. Barnard Cornwell. 1990. pap. 9.95 (*0-14-014597-4*, Penguin Bks) Viking Penguin.

Sharpe's Honor: The Vitoria Campaign, February to June, 1813. Bernard Cornwell. 360p. 1986. pap. 3.50 (*0-14-008013-9*, Penguin Bks) Viking Penguin.

Sharpe's Regiment, No. 8. Barnard Cornwell. 1987. pap. 10.95 (*0-14-024306-2*, Penguin Bks) Viking Penguin.

Sharpe's Revenge, No. 10. Bernard Cornwell. 320p. 1990. pap. 10.95 (*0-14-008472-X*, Penguin Bks) Viking Penguin.

Sharpe's Rifles, No. 1. Bernard Cornwell. 304p. 1989. pap. 9.95 (*0-14-011014-3*, Penguin Bks) Viking Penguin.

Sharpe's Siege, No. 9. Bernard Cornwell. 320p. 1990. pap. 9.95 (*0-14-014442-0*, Penguin Bks) Viking Penguin.

Sharpe's Sword, No. 5. Barnard Cornwell. 1987. pap. 10.95 (*0-14-024304-6*, Penguin Bks) Viking Penguin.

***Sharpe's Tiger.** Bernard Cornwell. 1997. mass mkt. 5.99 (*0-06-101269-6*, Harp PBks) HarpC.

Sharpest Sight: A Novel. Louis Owens. LC 91-33072. (American Indian Literature & Critical Studies Ser.: Vol. 1). 272p. 1995. pap. 11.95 (*0-8061-2574-8*) U of Okla Pr.

***Sharpeville Commemoration.** write for info. (*0-929917-04-9*) Magnolia PA.

Sharpeville Commemoration...the Legacy. Ed. by Rob Penny & Valerie Lawrence. LC 88-61292. 60p. (Orig.). 1988. pap. 8.95 (*0-685-22522-4*) Magnolia PA.

Sharpham Miscellany: Essays in Spirituality & Ecology. Maurice Ash et al. 192p. 1995. pap. 14.95 (*0-9518298-0-7*, Pub. by Buddhist Pub UK) Assoc Pubs Grp.

***Sharpie: The Life Story of Evelyn Sharp Nebraska's Aviatrix.** Diane R. Bartels. Ed. by Linda J. Dageforde. LC 96-85189. 344p. (Orig.). 1996. pap. 21.95 (*1-886225-16-8*, 2000) Dageforde Pub.

Sharpie Book. Reuel B. Parker. 1993. pap. text ed. 19.95 (*0-87742-304-0*) Intl Marine.

Sharpie Book. Reuel B. Parker. 1994. pap. text ed. 19.95 (*0-07-158013-1*) McGraw.

Sharples. Katherine M. Knox. LC 70-87456. (Library of American Art). 133p. 1972. reprint ed. lib. bdg. 42.50 (*0-306-71529-5*) Da Capo.

Sharpness on the Neck. Fred Saberhagen. 352p. 1996. 23.95 (*0-312-85799-3*) St Martin.

Sharps & Flats. Jack A. Westrup. LC 79-134156. (Essay Index Reprint Ser.). 1977. 20.95 (*0-8369-1937-8*) Ayer.

Sharps & Flats Forever. Dan Carlson. LC 90-71982. 96p. (Orig.). 1994. pap. 6.95 (*1-56002-042-3*, Univ Edtns) Aegina Pr.

Sharps & Flats in Five Decades. William Finn. (American Autobiography Ser.). 342p. 1995. lib. bdg. 89.00 (*0-7812-8518-6*) Rprt Serv.

Sharps Firearms. Frank M. Sellers. (Illus.). 1995. 50.00 (*0-9608122-0-2*) F Sellers.

Sharps Rifle: The Gun That Shaped American Destiny. Martin Rywell. 160p. 1956. 6.00 (*0-913150-21-5*) Pioneer Pr.

Sharps Rifles & Spanish Mules: The San Antonio-El Paso Mail, 1851-1881. Wayne R. Austerman. LC 84-40557. (Illus.). 336p. 1985. 34.95 (*0-89096-220-0*) Tex A&M Univ Pr.

Sharpshooter: A Novel of the Civil War. David Madden. LC 96-9994. (Illus.). 176p. 1996. 19.95 (*0-87049-948-3*) U of Tenn Pr.

Sharpshooter: Hiram Berdan, His Famous Sharpshooters & Their Sharps Rifles. Wiley Sword. LC 88-62056. (Illus.). 125p. 1988. 18.00 (*0-917218-37-X*) A Mowbray.

***Sharpshooter Blues.** Lewis Nordan. 1997. pap. text ed. 11.95 (*1-56512-182-1*) Algonquin Bks.

Sharpshooter Blues: A Novel. Lewis Nordan. LC 95-15306. 300p. 1995. 17.95 (*1-56512-083-3*, 72083) Algonquin Bks.

***Sharpshooters.** Christopher Piliero. 1997. mass mkt. 4.99 (*1-55197-297-2*, Pub. by Comnwlth Pub CN) Partners Pubs Grp.

Sharpshooters. Bruce H. Thorstad. 256p. (Orig.). 1993. mass mkt. 3.99 (*0-671-75906-X*) PB.

Sharpshooting at Kinkajous. Jim DeWitt. (Illus.). 136p. (J). (gr. 4-12). 1987. pap. 6.00 (*0-915199-06-8*) Pen-Dec.

Sharra's Exile. Marion Zimmer Bradley. (Darkover Ser.). 368p. 1981. mass mkt. 5.99 (*0-88677-309-1*) DAW Bks.

Sharra's Exile. Marion Z. Bradley. (Darkover Ser.). 368p. 1996. reprint ed. 24.00 (*0-7278-4799-6*) Severn Hse.

Shasta & the Shebang Machine. Katy D. Oana. LC 77-18350. (Sound Ser.). (Illus.). 32p. (J). (gr. 2-4). 1978. lib. bdg. 9.95 (*0-87783-152-1*) Oddo.

Shasta & the Shebang Machine. Katy D. Oana. LC 77-18350. (Illus.). (J). (gr. k-2). 1978. lib. bdg. 5.95 (*0-89508-066-4*) Rainbow Bks.

Shasta Dam Boomtowns: Community Building in the New Deal Era. Al M. Rocca. LC 93-84961. (Illus.). 180p. (Orig.). 1993. pap. 12.95 (*1-884055-00-1*) Redding Mus.

Shasta Ethnography. fac. ed. catherine Holt. Ed. by Robert H. Lowie et al. (University of California Publications: No. 3:4). 56p. (C). 1946. reprint ed. pap. 5.30 (*1-55567-078-4*) Coyote Press.

Shasta Indian Tales. Rosemary Holsinger. LC 82-22364. (Illus.). 48p. 1982. pap. 5.95 (*0-87961-129-4*) Naturegraph.

Shasta Indians of California & Their Neighbors. Elizabeth Renfro. Ed. by Keven Brown. (Illus.). 126p. (Orig.). 1992. pap. 8.95 (*0-87961-221-5*) Naturegraph.

Shasta Route, 1863 to 1887: The Railroad Link Between the Sacramento & the Columbia. William H. Boyd. Ed. by Stuart Bruchey. LC 80-1276. (Railroads Ser.). 1981. lib. bdg. 18.95 (*0-405-13751-6*) Ayer.

Shastra evam Vidhi ke Sidhant (Jurisprudence & Legal Theory in Hindi) Subba Rao. 377p. 1981. 52.50 (*0-317-54630-9*) St Mut.

Shastra on the Door to Understanding the Hundred Dharmas. Bodhisattva Vasubhandu. Tr. by Buddhist Text Translation Society from CHI. 130p. (Orig.). 1983. pap. 6.50 (*0-88139-003-8*) Buddhist Text.

Shatted Lantern: Rediscovering the Felt Presence of God. Ronald Rohleiser. 172p. (Orig.). 1995. pap. 11.95 (*0-8245-1497-1*) Crossroad NY.

Shatter. John Farris. 1993. mass mkt. 4.99 (*0-8125-3522-7*) Tor Bks.

Shatter. Brian Harper. 1995. pap. 4.99 (*0-451-17338-4*, Sig) NAL-Dutton.

Shattered. Dean R. Koontz. 304p. 1986. mass mkt. 7.50 (*0-425-09933-4*) Berkley Pub.

Shattered. John Peel. 224p. (Orig.). (J). (gr. 6 up). 1993. pap. 3.50 (*0-671-79406-X*, Archway) PB.

Shattered: In the Eye of the Storm. Faye D. Resnick. 1996. pap. 17.95 (*0-7871-0730-1*, Dove Bks) Dove Audio.

Shattered: In the Eye of the Storm. Faye D. Resnick. 1996. pap. 17.95 (*0-7871-0727-1*, Dove Bks) Dove Audio.

***Shattered & Other Stories.** (Shatterzone Ser.). 6.95 (*0-87431-237-X*, 21104) West End Games.

Shattered Applause! The Eva Le Gallienne Story. Robert A. Schanke. LC 94-13104. 320p. 1992. pap. 18.00 (*1-56980-023-5*) Barricade Bks.

Shattered Applause: The Lives of Eva Le Gallienne. Robert A. Schanke. LC 92-4414. (Illus.). 328p. (C). 1992. 39.95 (*0-8093-1820-2*) S Ill U Pr.

Shattered Assumptions: Towards a New Psychology of Trauma. Ronnie Janoff-Bulman. 250p. 1992. 29.95 (*0-02-916015-4*, Free Press) Free Pr.

***Shattered Bone.** Chris Stewart. LC 97-20580. 1997. write for info. (*0-87131-831-8*) M Evans.

Shattered Chain. Marion Zimmer Bradley. (Darkover Ser.). 1976. pap. 5.99 (*0-88677-308-3*) DAW Bks.

Shattered Chains. Clayton Emery. (Magic: The Gathering Ser.). 288p. 1995. mass mkt. 4.99 (*0-06-105419-4*, Harp PBks) HarpC.

Shattered Crystal Ball. James G. Blight. 224p. (C). 1990. lib. bdg. 47.50 (*0-8476-7609-9*, R 7609) Rowman.

Shattered Crystal Ball: Fear & Learning in the Cuban Missile Crisis. James G. Blight. 224p. (C). 1990. pap. text ed. 14.95 (*0-8226-3015-X*, R 7609) Littlefield.

***Shattered Crystals.** Mia A. Kanner. LC 97-66098. (Illus.). 406p. (YA). (gr. 9-12). Date not set. 24.95 (*1-56062-317-9*) CIS Comm.

Shattered Dream. Aleksander Szurek. (East European Monographs: No. 263). 384p. 1989. text ed. 75.50 (*0-88033-160-7*) East Eur Monographs.

Shattered Dream: A Southern Bride at the Turn of the Century. Margaret Sloan. Ed. by Harold Woodell. (Women's Diaries & Letters of the Nineteenth-Century South Ser.). 247p. 1990. text ed. 24.95 (*0-87249-712-7*) U of SC Pr.

Shattered Dream: America's Search for Its Soul. Walter T. Davis, Jr. LC 94-10248. 208p. (Orig.). (C). 1994. pap. 16.00 (*1-56338-095-1*) TPI PA.

Shattered Dreams: A Nightmare in a Nursing Home. Nellie Collar Anson. LC 87-80849. 240p. (Orig.). Date not set. 19.95 (*0-89896-328-1*); pap. 11.95 (*0-89896-324-9*) Larksdale.

Shattered Dreams: How to Avoid Costly Mistakes in Multi-Level Marketing. Gary Tartaglia. (In Plain English Ser.: No. 2). (Illus.). 119p. (Orig.). 1985. pap. 14.95 (*0-9614404-0-6*) Calaciura Pr.

Shattered Dreams - Lonely Choices: Birthparents of Babies with Disabilities Talk about Adoption. Joanne Finnegan. LC 92-38706. 208p. 1993. text ed. 29.95 (*0-89789-286-0*, H286, Bergin & Garvey) Greenwood.

Shattered Dreams & Broken Hearts: An Inspiring Story of Triumph Through Continual Adversity. Michael Shaw & Victoria Lee. Ed. by Edward A. Clark. (Illus.). 210p. (Orig.). 1995. pap. 12.95 (*1-888225-00-9*) A Touch of Heart.

Shattered Dreams on Pike's Peak: (Jones Park, Lake Moraine & Seven Lakes) Ivan Brunk. (Illus.). 64p. (Orig.). 1989. pap. 3.95 (*0-9624008-1-5*) Pulpit Rock.

Shattered Eagles: Balkan Fragments. T. Winifrith. 39.95 (*0-7156-2635-3*, Pub. by Duckworth UK) Focus Pub-R Pullins.

Shattered Echoes. Barbara Shapiro. 352p. (Orig.). 1993. mass mkt. 4.99 (*0-380-76747-3*) Avon.

***Shattered Faith.** Sheila R. Kennedy. 256p. 1997. 23.00 (*0-679-43995-1*) Pantheon.

Shattered Faith: A Holocaust Legacy. Leon Wells. LC 95-8408. 192p. 1995. 19.95 (*0-8131-1931-6*) U Pr of Ky.

Shattered Forms: Art Brut, Phantasms, Modernism. Allen S. Weiss. LC 91-36290. (SUNY Series in Aesthetics & the Philosophy of Art). 158p. (C). 1992. text ed. 24.50 (*0-7914-1117-6*) State U NY Pr.

Shattered Glass. Elaine Bergstrom. 384p. 1994. reprint ed. mass mkt. 4.99 (*0-441-00067-3*) Ace Bks.

Shattered Glass: A Dramatic Pattern in Shakespeare's Early Plays. John P. Cutts. LC 68-22253. 154p. reprint ed. 43.90 (*0-685-16235-4*, 2027603) Bks Demand.

Shattered Helmet. Franklin W. Dixon. LC 72-90825. (Hardy Boys Ser.: Vol. 52). (Illus.). 196p. (J). (gr. 5-9). 1973. 5.95 (*0-448-08952-1*, G&D) Putnam Pub Group.

Shattered Hope: The Guatemalan Revolution & the United States, 1944-54. Piero Gleijeses. (Illus.). 450p. 1991. pap. text ed. 18.95 (*0-691-02556-8*) Princeton U Pr.

Shattered Hopes. Barbara C. Schaaf. LC 93-15904. 1993. 18.99 (*0-9623032-9-1*) Barricade Bks.

Shattered Hopes. Barbara C. Schaaf. 432p. 1996. mass mkt. 5.99 (*0-06-100848-6*) HarpC.

Shattered Illusion: The History of Ukrainian Pro-Communist Organizations in Canada. John Kolasky. (Illus.). 255p. 1979. pap. 7.95 (*0-88778-190-X*) Genl Dist Srvs.

***Shattered Illusions.** Anne Mather. 1997. mass mkt. 3.50 (*0-373-11911-9*, 1-11911-4) Harlequin Bks.

Shattered Images: The Phenomenological Language of Sexual Trauma. Dee Spring. LC 92-50849. (Illus.). 305p. (Orig.). 1993. pap. 36.00 (*0-9613309-2-9*) Magnolia St Pub.

Shattered Innocence: A Practical Guide for Counseling Women Survivors of Childhood Sexual Abuse. Neil Weiner & Sharon E. Robinson-Kurpius. 240p. 1995. 49.95 (*1-56032-347-7*); pap. 24.95 (*1-56032-348-5*) Taylor & Francis.

Shattered Innocence, Shattered Dreams. Susan Hightower. 1995. mass mkt. 4.99 (*0-7860-0219-0*, Pinncle Kensgtn) Kensgtn Pub Corp.

Shattered Mind. Howard Gardner. 1976. pap. 10.36 (*0-394-71946-8*, Vin) Random.

***Shattered Mirror: Representations of Women in Mexican Literature.** Marla E. Valdes. LC 97-16813. (Texas Pan American Ser.). 1998. write for info. (*0-292-71591-9*); pap. write for info. (*0-292-71590-0*) U of Tex Pr.

Shattered Mirrors: Our Search for Identity & Community in the AIDS Era. Monroe E. Price. LC 89-33265. 160p. 1989. text ed. 27.00 (*0-674-80590-9*) HUP.

Shattered Nerves: Doctors, Patients, & Depression in Victorian England. Janet Oppenheim. 400p. 1991. 35.00 (*0-19-505781-3*) OUP.

Shattered Oath: Prince of Sidhe, Vol. 1. Josepha Sherman. 416p. 1995. mass mkt. 5.99 (*0-671-87672-4*) Baen Bks.

Shattered Rainbows. Mary J. Putney. 384p. 1996. mass mkt., pap. 5.99 (*0-451-40614-1*, Topaz) NAL-Dutton.

Shattered Reflections. Deborah Nicholas. 416p. 1995. mass mkt. 4.99 (*0-8217-5076-3*) Kensgtn Pub Corp.

Shattered Rhythms. Phyllis Knight. 1995. 8.95 (*0-312-11888-0*, Stonewall Inn) St Martin.

Shattered Romance. Janet Stein. (Illus.). 24p. (Orig.). 1982. pap. 3.00 (*0-917061-12-8*) Top Stories.

Shattered Rose. Jo Beverley. 1996. pap. text ed. 5.99 (*0-8217-5310-X*, Zebra Kensgtn) Kensgtn Pub Corp.

Shattered Secrets. Mary Millard. 408p. (Orig.). 1992. pap. 16.95 (*0-9624022-5-7*) Venture Bk Pubns.

Shattered Self: A Psychoanalytic Study of Trauma. Richard B. Ulman & Doris Brothers. 344p. 1993. reprint ed. pap. text ed. 26.50 (*0-88163-174-4*) Analytic Pr.

Shattered Self: E. T. A. Hoffman's Tragic Vision. Horst S. Daemmrich. LC 73-1490. 143p. reprint ed. pap. 40.80 (*0-685-23356-1*, 2032285) Bks Demand.

Shattered Selves: Multiple Personality in a Postmodern World. James M. Glass. LC 92-33928. 200p. 1993. 32.50 (*0-8014-2809-2*) Cornell U Pr.

Shattered Selves: Multiple Personality in a Postmodern World. James M. Glass. 200p. 1995. pap. 12.95 (*0-8014-8256-9*) Cornell U Pr.

Shattered Silence. Judith Marshall. 352p. 1993. mass mkt. 4.50 (*1-55817-704-3*, Pinncle Kensgtn) Kensgtn Pub Corp.

Shattered Silence: Letters from Former Soviets Struggling with Freedom at Home. Barbara DeKovner-Mayer. (Illus.). 160p. 1993. pap. 14.95 (*0-935047-13-1*) Americas Group.

Shattered Silk. Barbara Michaels. 320p. 1996. mass mkt. 5.99 (*0-06-101008-1*, Harp PBks) HarpC.

Shattered Sphere. Roger M. Allen. 416p. 1995. mass mkt. 5.99 (*0-8125-3016-0*) Tor Bks.

Shattered Synthesis: New England Puritanism Before the Great Awakening. James W. Jones. LC 73-77154. 219p. reprint ed. pap. 62.50 (*0-8357-8320-0*, 2033773) Bks Demand.

Shattered Thoughts: A Collection of Poems. Scott Shaw. (Illus.). 56p. (Orig.). Date not set. pap. 5.99 (*0-9642793-0-4*) S Shaw.

Shattered Visage. Richard E. Baker. 103p. (Orig.). 1982. pap. 3.50 (*0-942648-01-3*) Vardaman Pr.

Shattered Visage: The Real Face of Atheism. Ravi Zacharias. LC 90-41933. 206p. (Orig.). (C). 1993. pap. 12.99 (*0-8010-9938-2*) Baker Bks.

Shattered Vision. Rabah Belamri. Tr. by Hugh A. Harter from FRE. (French Expressions Ser.). 180p. 1994. 19.95 (*0-8419-1258-0*) Holmes & Meier.

Shattered Vows. Jasmine Cresswell. (Weddings by DeWilde Ser.). 1996. mass mkt. 4.50 (*0-373-82537-4*, 1-82537-1, Wrldwide Lib) Harlequin Bks.

Shattered Vows. Pat Warren. 352p. 1995. mass mkt. 4.99 (*0-8217-4943-9*, Pinncle Kensgtn) Kensgtn Pub Corp.

Shattered Vows: Priests Who Leave. David Rice. LC 91-29569. 288p. 1992. pap. 9.95 (*0-89243-507-0*, Triumph Books) Liguori Pubns.

Shattered World: Adaptation & Survival among Vietnam's Highland Peoples During the Vietnam War. Gerald C. Hickey. LC 92-45143. (Illus.). 336p. (Orig.). (C). 1993. text ed. 36.95 (*0-8122-3172-4*); pap. text ed. 15.95 (*0-8122-1417-X*) U of Pa Pr.

***Shattered World: Adaptation & Survival among Vietnam's Highland Peoples During the Vietnam War.** Gerald C. Hickey. LC 92-45143. 333p. pap. 95.00 (*0-608-04818-6*, 2065475) Bks Demand.

Shatterhouse. Leo Connellan. (Hollow Spring Poetry Ser.). (Illus.). 50p. (Orig.). 1983. pap. 6.95 (*0-936198-04-4*) Hollow Spring Pr.

Shattering: Food, Politics, & the Loss of Genetic Diversity. Cary Fowler & Pat Mooney. LC 89-49378. 278p. (Orig.). 1990. pap. 17.95 (*0-8165-1181-0*); lib. bdg. 34.95 (*0-8165-1154-3*) U of Ariz Pr.

Shattering Air. David Biespiel. (New Poets of America Ser.: Vol. 17). 71p. 1996. 20.00 (*1-880238-34-9*); pap. 12.50 (*1-880238-35-7*) BOA Edns.

Shattering an American Myth. Moeller. 1976. 29.95 (*0-8488-1551-3*) Amereon Ltd.

***Shattering an American Myth: Unfurling the History of the Stars & Stripes.** Henry W. Moeller. Date not set. lib. bdg. 14.95 (*0-8488-1531-9*) Amereon Ltd.

Shattering Glass. Nancy-Gay Rotstein. 352p. 21.00 (*0-374-26223-3*) FS&G.

***Shattering Hero's Checkered Past.** Janet Christensen-O'Brien. 154p. (Orig.). 1996. pap. 9.95 (*0-9658633-0-1*) Skykomish.

Shattering Illusions: West Indians in British Politics. Carter. (C). 1986. pap. 17.50 (*0-85315-674-3*, Pub. by Lawrence & Wishart UK) NYU Pr.

Shattering of Silence. Farida Karodia. (African Writers Ser.). 288p. 1993. pap. 9.95 (*0-435-90593-7*, 90593) Heinemann.

Shattering Our Assumptions: Breaking Free of Expectations - Others & Our Own. Miriam Neff & Debra Klingsporn. LC 96-45769. 256p. 1996. pap. 10.99 (*1-55661-686-4*) Bethany Hse.

***Shattering Rules of Graphic Design.** Lycette Nelson. 1997. 55.00 (*1-56830-417-X*) Hayden.

***Shattering Silence: Women, Nationalism, & Political Subjectivity in Northern Ireland.** Begona Aretxaga. LC 97-4176. 1997. write for info. (*0-691-03755-8*); pap. write for info. (*0-691-03754-X*) Princeton U Pr.

Shattering Stereotypes: A Demographic Look at the Facts about Children in the United States. Janice H. Outtz. 52p. 1994. 12.00 (*0-937846-45-7*) Inst Educ Lead.

Shattering the Darkness: The Crisis of the Cross in the Church Today. Joseph L. Foreman. LC 92-52941. 186p. (Orig.). 1992. pap. 9.95 (*0-935883-03-7*) Cooling Spring.

S

Shattering the Glass Ceiling: The Woman Manager. Marilyn J. Davidson & Cary L. Cooper. 192p. 1992. pap. 29.95 (*1-85396-132-9*, Pub. by Paul Chapman UK) Taylor & Francis.

Shattering the Icon of Abraham Lincoln: A New Look at the Lincoln Myth. S. Dickson. 1987. lib. bdg. 79.00 (*0-8490-3956-8*) Gordon Pr.

Shattering the Myth: Plays by Hispanic Women. Ed. by Linda Feyder. LC 91-40997. 1992. pap. 13.00 (*1-55885-041-4*) Arte Publico.

Shattering the Myth: Signposts on Custer's Road to Disaster. Kevin M. Sullivan. 136p. (Orig.). 1995. pap. 8.95 (*1-57087-195-7*) Prof Pr NC.

***Shattering the Myths of Darwinism.** Richard Milton. LC 97-9962. 272p. 1997. 24.95 (*0-89281-732-1*) Inner Tradit.

***Shattering the Two-Income Income Myth: Daily Secrets for Living Well on One Income.** Andy Dappen. LC 97-93080. 410p. (Orig.). 1997. pap. 14.95 (*0-9632577-1-4*) Brier Bks.

***Shattering Your Strongholds.** 1997. wbk. ed. 5.50 (*0-88270-736-1*) Bridge-Logos.

Shattering Your Strongholds. Liberty S. Savard. LC 92-74981. 205p. (Orig.). 1992. pap. 8.95 (*0-88270-713-2*) Bridge-Logos.

***Shatterzone.** 30.00 (*0-87431-227-2*, 21001) West End Games.

***Shatterzone Players' Guide.** 15.00 (*0-87431-229-9*, 21002) West End Games.

***Shatterzone Rule Book.** 15.00 (*0-87431-230-2*, 21004) West End Games.

***Shatterzone Universe Guide.** 15.00 (*0-87431-228-0*, 21003) West End Games.

Shaughnessy: Humanization of Freddie Mouse. Nathan Zimelman & Richard Blake. Ed. by May Davenport. 64p. (J). (gr. 3-5). 1984. pap. 3.50 (*0-943864-38-0*) Davenport.

Shave Ice. Tom Stevens. (Illus.). 208p. (Orig.). 1989. pap. 10.00 (*0-9622212-0-1*) Maui Pub Co.

Shave Ten Strokes in Twelve Days: A Woman Golfer's Guide to a More Successful Game. Sandy LaBauve & George Kehoe. (Illus.). 128p. (Orig.). 1994. pap. 9.95 (*0-399-51860-6*, Perigee Bks) Berkley Pub.

Shave the Whales. Scott Adams. (Illus.). 128p. 1994. pap. 9.95 (*0-8362-1740-3*) Andrews & McMeel.

Shaver Mystery & the Inner Earth. Timothy G. Beckley. 95p. 1985. reprint ed. spiral bd. 14.00 (*0-7873-0084-5*) Hlth Research.

***Shavetails & Bell Sharps: The History of the U. S. Army Mule.** Emmett M. Essin. LC 96-45626. 256p. 1997. text ed. 37.50 (*0-8032-1819-2*) U of Nebr Pr.

***Shaving.** Stephen Berg. LC 96-61434. 1997. 21.95 (*1-884800-17-3*) Four Way Bks.

***Shaving Effects on Eccentrically Cut Gears.** A. O. Andrisano. (1987 Fall Technical Meeting). 1987. pap. text ed. 30.00 (*1-55589-491-7*) AGMA.

Shaving Mug & Barber Bottle Book, with Value Guide. Keith Estep. LC 94-44836. (Illus.). 240p. 1995. 69.95 (*0-88740-761-7*) Schiffer.

Shaving the Inside of Your Skull: Crazy Wisdom for Discovering Who You Really Are. Mel Ash. (Illus.). 256p. (Orig.). 1997. pap. 15.95 (*0-87477-841-7*, Tarcher Putnam) Putnam Pub Group.

Shaving with Occam's Razor. Peter Schorer. (Illus.). 216p. (Orig.). 1985. pap. 8.95 (*0-9614238-0-3*) Occam Pr.

***Shavuos.** (Holiday Ser.). 17.99 (*0-89906-625-9*, SHVH) Mesorah Pubns.

***Shavuos.** (Holiday Ser.). pap. 14.99 (*0-89906-626-7*, SHVP) Mesorah Pubns.

Shavuos. Y. Ganz. (ArtScroll Youth Holiday Ser.). (YA). 1992. 8.99 (*0-89906-982-7*) Mesorah Pubns.

Shavuot Anthology. Ed. by Philip Goodman. LC 74-25802. (Holiday Anthologies Ser.). (Illus.). 370p. 1992. reprint ed. pap. 15.95 (*0-8276-0391-6*) JPS Phila.

Shaw. Stanley Weintraub. (Annual of Bernard Shaw Studies: Vol. 2). (Illus.). 224p. 1982. 35.00 (*0-271-00305-7*) Pa St U Pr.

Shaw. Ed. by Stanley Weintraub. (Annual of Bernard Shaw Studies: Vol. 4). 232p. (C). 1985. 35.00 (*0-271-00366-9*) Pa St U Pr.

Shaw. Ed. by Stanley Weintraub. (Annual of Bernard Shaw Studies: Vol. 6). 180p. (C). 1986. 35.00 (*0-271-00426-6*) Pa St U Pr.

***Shaw, No. 16.** Ed. by Dan H. Laurence & Margot Peters. (Annual of Bernard Shaw Studies). 252p. 1996. 35.00 (*0-271-01577-2*) Pa St U Pr.

Shaw: An Exhibit. Compiled by Dan H. Laurence. LC 76-620047. (Illus.). 1977. 20.00 (*0-87959-081-5*); pap. 15.00 (*0-87959-082-3*) U of Tex H Ransom Ctr.

Shaw: Interviews & Recollections. Ed. by A. M. Gibbs. LC 88-51147. (Illus.). 584p. 1990. text ed. 44.95 (*0-87745-232-6*) U of Iowa Pr.

***Shaw: Shaw & Speculative Fiction.** Ed. by Milton Wolf. (Annual of Bernard Shaw Studies: No. 16). 288p. 1997. 35.00 (*0-271-01681-7*) Pa St U Pr.

Shaw: The Neglected Plays. Ed. by Alfred Turco, Jr. LC 86-63274. (Annual of Bernard Shaw Studies: Vol. 7). 376p. 1987. 35.00 (*0-271-00492-4*) Pa St U Pr.

Shaw Abroad. Ed. by Rodelle Weintraub. LC 84-43058. (Annual of Bernard Shaw Studies: Vol. 5). 326p. 1985. 35.00 (*0-271-00384-7*) Pa St U Pr.

Shaw & Ibsen: Bernard Shaw's the Quintessence of Ibsenism & Related Writings. George Bernard Shaw. LC 79-14858. 278p. reprint ed. pap. 79.30 (*0-8357-6393-5*, 2035749) Bks Demand.

Shaw & Joyce: The Last Word in Stolentelling. Martha F. Black. LC 94-27516. (Florida James Joyce Ser.). 456p. (C). 1995. lib. bdg. 49.95 (*0-8130-1328-3*) U Press Fla.

Shaw & Politics. Ed. by T. F. Evans. (Annual of Bernard Shaw Studies: Vol. 11). 304p. 1991. 35.00 (*0-271-00733-8*) Pa St U Pr.

Shaw & Religion. Ed. by Charles A. Berst. LC 81-956. (Annual of Bernard Shaw Studies: Vol 1). 264p. 1981. 35.00 (*0-271-00280-8*) Pa St U Pr.

Shaw & Society: An Anthology & Symposium. Ed. by Cyril E. Joad. 1976. lib. bdg. 59.95 (*0-8490-2597-4*) Gordon Pr.

Shaw & the Nineteenth Century Theater. Martin Meisel. LC 75-25495. (Illus.). 477p. 1976. reprint ed. text ed. 87.50 (*0-8371-8416-9*, MESN, Greenwood Pr) Greenwood.

Shaw, Books & Libraries. Dan H. Laurence. LC 76-620048. (Bibliographical Monograph: No. 9). (Illus.). 1976. 8.00 (*0-87959-022-X*) U of Tex H Ransom Ctr.

Shaw en el Mundo Hispanico. Asela Rodriguez-Seda de Laguna. LC 79-22415. (Coleccion Mente y Palabra). 142p. (SPA.). 1981. 9.60 (*0-8477-0564-1*); pap. 8.00 (*0-8477-0565-X*) U of PR Pr.

***Shaw Festival's "Sherlock Holmes"** William Gillette et al. Ed. by Christopher Newton. (Illus.). 208p. 1994. spiral bd., pap. 16.00 (*1-896032-10-9*) Battered Silicon.

Shaw in His Time. Ivor J. Brown. LC 79-17319. (Illus.). 212p. 1979. reprint ed. text ed. 55.00 (*0-313-21999-0*, BRSW, Greenwood Pr) Greenwood.

Shaw, Lady Gregory & the Abbey: A Correspondence & a Record. Ed. by Dan H. Laurence & Nicholas Grene. (Illus.). 272p. 1996. 45.00 (*0-86140-278-2*) OUP.

Shaw, Lady Gregory & the Abbey: A Correspondence & a Record, Vol. 2. F. M. Kamm. (Oxford Ethics Ser.). 400p. 1996. 55.00 (*0-19-508459-4*) OUP.

Shaw Offstage: The Nondramatic Writings. Ed. by Fred D. Crawford. LC 88-19770. (Annual of Bernard Shaw Studies: Vol. 9). (Illus.). 243p. 1989. lib. bdg. 35.00 (*0-271-00652-8*) Pa St U Pr.

Shaw on Music. Ed. by Eric Bentley. 320p. (Orig.). 1995. pap. 12.95 (*1-55783-149-1*) Applause Theatre Bk Pubs.

Shaw on Shakespeare. George Bernard Shaw. Ed. by Edwin Wilson. LC 77-134134. (Essay Index Reprint Ser.). 1980. 29.95 (*0-8369-2175-5*) Ayer.

Shaw on Women. limited ed. George Bernard Shaw. Ed. by Mary C. Stratton. (Bucknell University, Limited Editions, Ellen Clarke Bertrand Library). (Illus.). 72p. 1992. 175.00 (*0-916375-16-1*) Press Alley.

Shaw Records: A Memorial of Roger Shaw, 1594-1661. H. F. Farwell. (Illus.). 435p. 1989. reprint ed. pap. 65.00 (*0-8328-1067-3*); reprint ed. lib. bdg. 73.00 (*0-8328-1066-5*) Higginson Bk Co.

Shaw Saville Line. R. P. De Kerbrech. 1990. 69.00 (*0-9516038-3-3*, Pub. by Ship Pictorial Pubng UK) St Mut.

Shaw the Dramatist. Louis Crompton. LC 69-11202. 273p. reprint ed. pap. 77.90 (*0-685-15994-9*, 2056172) Bks Demand.

Shaw 12. Ed. by Fred D. Crawford. (Annual of Bernard Shaw Studies). (Illus.). 368p. 1992. text ed. 55.00 (*0-271-00811-3*) Pa St U Pr.

Shaw 15. Ed. by Fred D. Crawford. (The Annual of Bernard Shaw Studies). 256p. 1995. 35.00 (*0-271-01422-9*) Pa St U Pr.

Shawangunk Ridge Conservation & Design Guidebook. David Church & John Myers. (Illus.). 66p. (Orig.). 1993. pap. 10.00 (*0-9616712-1-1*) Catskill Ctr.

Shawangunk Rock Climbs: Near Trapps & Millbrook, 3 vols., Set. 3rd ed. Dick Williams. (Illus.). 224p. 1993. pap. 18.00 (*0-930410-37-8*) Amer Alpine Club.

Shawangunk Rock Climbs: Skytop, 3 vols., Set. 3rd ed. Dick Williams. (Illus.). 200p. 1993. pap. 18.00 (*0-930410-38-6*) Amer Alpine Club.

Shawangunk Rock Climbs: The Trapps, 3 vols., Set. 3rd ed. Dick Williams. (Illus.). 348p. 1993. pap. 22.50 (*0-930410-36-X*) Amer Alpine Club.

Shawano Paper Mill Centennial 1894-1994. George Putz, Jr. (Illus.). 112p. 1994. write for info. (*0-942495-41-1*); pap. write for info. (*0-942495-42-X*) Amherst Pr.

Shawcross & Beaumont: Air Law, 3 vols. Ed. by Peter Martin et al. U.K. ring bd. 990.00 (*0-406-37319-1*) MICHIE.

Shawl. Susan Daitch. 1990. pap. 6.95 (*0-679-72942-9*) Random.

Shawl. Cynthia Ozick. 1989. 12.95 (*0-394-57976-3*) Knopf.

Shawl. Cynthia Ozick. LC 89-40638. 74p. 1990. pap. 7.95 (*0-679-72926-7*, Vin) Random.

Shawl & Prairie du Chien. David Mamet. LC 85-14884. 120p. 1985. pap. 6.95 (*0-8021-5172-8*, Grove) Grove-Atltic.

Shawl from Kashmir & Other Stories. Manuel A. Viray. 109p. (Orig.). 1992. pap. 9.50 (*971-10-0451-8*, Pub. by New Day Pub PH) Cellar.

Shawl Straps. Louisa May Alcott. (Works of Louisa May Alcott). 1989. reprint ed. lib. bdg. 79.00 (*0-7812-1631-1*) Rprt Serv.

Shawls. Pamela Clabburn. 1989. pap. 25.00 (*0-85263-579-6*, Pub. by Shire UK) St Mut.

***Shawn & Uncle John.** John L. Steptoe. (J). Date not set. write for info. (*0-688-05600-8*); lib. bdg. write for info. (*0-688-05601-6*) Lothrop.

***Shawn Colvin: A Few Small Repairs.** Ed. by Jennette DeLisa & Aaron Stang. (Illus.). 100p. (Orig.). (YA). 1997. pap. text ed. 19.95 (*1-57623-956-X*, PG9702) Warner Brothers.

Shawn Colvin - Cover Girl. Ed. by Milton Okun. 32p. (Orig.). (YA). pap. 12.95 (*0-89524-867-0*, 02506918) Cherry Lane.

Shawn Colvin - Fat City: Guitar Arrangements. pap. 14.95 (*0-685-75223-2*) Cherry Lane.

Shawn Colvin - Steady On: Piano - Vocal. Ed. by Milton Okun. (Illus.). 55p. (Orig.). 1990. pap. text ed. 14.95 (*0-89524-516-7*) Cherry Lane.

Shawn Goes to School. Petronella Breinburg. LC 73-8003. (Illus.). 32p. (J). (ps-2). 1974. lib. bdg. 14.89 (*0-690-00277-7*, Crowell Jr Bks) HarpC Child Bks.

***Shawn Kemp.** Mike Bonner. (Basketball Legends Ser.). (Illus.). 64p. (YA). (gr. 7 up). 1997. lib. bdg. 15.95 (*0-7910-4576-5*) Chelsea Hse.

Shawn Robbins' Prophecies for the End of Time. Shawn Robbins. 240p. (Orig.). 1995. mass mkt. 4.99 (*0-380-77694-4*) Avon.

Shawnee. Jerry E. Clark. LC 93-14114. 120p. 1993. 15.00 (*0-8131-1839-5*) U Pr of Ky.

***Shawnee.** Elaine Landau. (First Bks.). 64p. (J). 1997. pap. 6.95 (*0-531-15818-7*) Watts.

Shawnee. Elaine Landau. LC 96-5375. (First Books-Indians of the Americas). 64p. (J). (gr. 4-6). 1997. lib. bdg. 21.00 (*0-531-20247-X*) Watts.

Shawnee: Kohkumthena's Grandchildren. Dark Rain Thom. 300p. 1994. 22.95 (*1-878208-53-5*); pap. 16.95 (*1-878208-29-2*) Guild Pr IN.

Shawnee: The Ceremonialism of a Native Indian Tribe & Its Cultural Background. James H. Howard. LC 80-23752. (Illus.). xvi, 454p. 1981. pap. 19.95 (*0-8214-0614-0*) Ohio U Pr.

Shawnee see Indians of North America

Shawnee Bill's Enchanted Five-Ride Carousel. Cooper Edens. (J). 1994. 15.00 (*0-671-75952-3*, Green Tiger S&S) S&S Childrens.

Shawnee County Cemeteries, Vol. II. Topeka Genealogical Society Staff. LC 80-133984. 187p. 1977. pap. 17.25 (*0-943259-07-X*) Topeka Geneal Soc.

Shawnee County Cemeteries, Vol. III. Topeka Genealogical Society Staff. LC 80-133984. 189p. 1987. pap. 17.25 (*0-943259-06-1*) Topeka Geneal Soc.

Shawnee County Kansas Cemeteries, Vol. IV. Ed. by Margaret Smith. (Illus.). 78p. (Orig.). 1993. pap. 11.25 (*0-943259-14-2*) Topeka Geneal Soc.

Shawnee County, Kansas Probate Court Records: Index Books III-V (1877-1908) Topeka Genealogical Society Staff. LC 82-184706. 142p. 1977. pap. 9.50 (*0-943259-04-5*) Topeka Geneal Soc.

***Shawnee High School Aviation Magnet Case Study Report.** Ivan Charner & Susan Hubbard. (Cross Case Report & Case Studies). 50p. 1995. teacher ed., text ed. 20.00 (*0-614-24538-9*); teacher ed., pap. text ed. 10.00 (*0-614-24539-7*) Natl Inst Work.

Shawnee Indians see Junior Library of American Indians

Shawnee Moon. Judith E. French. (Indian Moon Ser.). 400p. (Orig.). 1995. mass mkt. 5.50 (*0-380-77705-3*) Avon.

Shawnee-Northeast see Indians of North America

Shawnee Pottery: An Identification & Value Guide. Jim Mangus. 1996. 24.95 (*0-89145-574-4*) Collector Bks.

Shawnee Pottery: The Full Encyclopedia. Pam Curran. LC 95-20256. (Illus.). 304p. 1995. 59.95 (*0-88740-845-1*) Schiffer.

Shawnee Prophet. R. David Edmunds. LC 82-23830. (Illus.). xii, 272p. 1983. pap. 12.95 (*0-8032-6711-8*, Bison Books) U of Nebr Pr.

Shawnee Trail. Ralph Compton. 1994. mass mkt. 5.99 (*0-312-95241-4*, Thomas Dunne Bks) St Martin.

***Shawnee Trail.** large type ed. Ralph Compton. (Niagara Large Print Ser.). 438p. 1997. 29.50 (*0-7089-5861-3*, Linford) Ulverscroft.

Shawnees: People of the Eastern Woodlands. Laurie A. O'Neill. LC 94-42234. (Native Americans Ser.). (Illus.). 64p. (J). (gr. 4-6). 1995. lib. bdg. 16.40 (*1-56294-533-5*) Millbrook Pr.

Shawnese Traditions. Charles C. Trowbridge. Ed. by Vernon Kinietz & Erminie W. Voegelin. LC 76-43871. (Michigan Univ. Museum of Anthrolpology. Occasional Contributions Ser.: No. 9). reprint ed. 41.50 (*0-404-15729-7*) AMS Pr.

Shawn's Fundamentals of Dance, Vol. 2. T. Shawn. Ed. by Ann H. Guest. 108p. 1988. pap. text ed. 47.00 (*2-88124-219-7*) Gordon & Breach.

Shaw's Daughters: Dramatic & Narrative Constructions of Gender. J. Ellen Gainor. (Theater: Theory - Text - Performance Ser.). (Illus.). 240p. (C). 1991. text ed. 39.50 (*0-472-10219-2*) U of Mich Pr.

Shaw's Directory of Courts. Ed. by Gordon Morris. (C). 1988. pap. 110.00 (*0-7219-0983-3*, Pub. by Scientific UK) St Mut.

Shaw's Directory of Courts in the United Kingdom. Ed. by Gordon Morris. (C). 1987. pap. 85.00 (*0-7219-0980-9*, Pub. by Scientific UK) St Mut.

Shaw's Guide to the Rent (Agriculture) Act, 1976. Hugh Rossi. (C). 1977. 75.00 (*0-7219-0750-4*, Pub. by Scientific UK) St Mut.

Shaw's People: Victoria to Churchill. Stanley Weintraub. LC 95-15481. (Illus.). 264p. 1996. 29.50 (*0-271-01500-4*) Pa St U Pr.

Shaw's Plays in Performance. Daniel J. Leary. LC 83-2188. (Annual of Bernard Shaw Studies: Vol. 3). 268p. 1983. 35.00 (*0-271-00346-4*) Pa St U Pr.

Shaw's Pygmalion & Arms & the Man Notes. James K. Lowers. (Orig.). 1981. pap. 3.95 (*0-8220-1103-4*) Cliffs.

Shaw's Ready Reckoner for the Calculation of (Metric) Areas. William H. Cutmore. (C). 1982. 30.00 (*0-7219-0390-8*, Pub. by Scientific UK) St Mut.

Shaw's Sense of History. J. L. Wisenthal. 208p. 1988. 75.00 (*0-19-812892-4*) OUP.

Shawshank Redemption. Stephen King. 1994. pap. 6.99 (*0-451-18394-0*, Sig) NAL-Dutton.

Shawshank Redemption: The Shooting Script. Frank Darabont. 1996. pap. 15.95 (*1-55704-246-2*) Newmarket.

Shay Pendray's Needlecraft Projects. Embroidery Studio Staff. LC 96-15464. (Illus.). 128p. 1996. 24.95 (*0-8069-4864-7*, Chapelle) Sterling.

Shaykh Ahmad Sirhindi: An Outline of His Thought & a Study of His Image in the Eyes of Posterity. Yohanan Friedmann. LC 76-165593. (McGill Islamic Studies: No. 2). 144p. 1971. reprint ed. pap. 41.10 (*0-7837-1017-8*, 2041328) Bks Demand.

Shaykh & Effendi: Changing Patterns of Authority among the El Shabana of Southern Iraq. Robert A. Fernea. LC 70-88804. (Harvard Middle Eastern Studies: No. 14). (Illus.). 243p. reprint ed. pap. 69.30 (*0-7837-4104-9*, 2011602) Bks Demand.

Shayna Maidel. Barbara Lebow. 1988. pap. 5.25 (*0-8222-1019-3*) Dramatists Play.

***Shayndl & Salomea.** Salomea Genin. LC 97-2492. 1997. write for info. (*0-8101-1183-7*); pap. write for info. (*0-8101-1168-3*) Northwestern U Pr.

***Shayne: The Pretender.** Joann Ross. 1997. pap. 3.50 (*0-373-25746-5*, 1-25746-8) Harlequin Bks.

Shays' Rebellion: Selected Essays. Ed. by Martin Kaufman. (Illus.). 104p. (Orig.). (C). 1987. pap. 6.00 (*0-685-26790-3*) WSC Inst MA Studies.

Shays' Rebellion: The Making of an Agrarian Insurrection. David P. Szatmary. LC 79-22522. 208p. 1980. pap. 15.95 (*0-87023-419-6*) U of Mass Pr.

Shazaam! The Fractured Phrases of Basketball. Bill Levy. (Illus.). 96p. 1996. pap. 6.95 (*1-885590-18-0*) Golden West Pub.

Shazam! Simple Science Magic. Laurence B. White, Jr. & Ray Broekel. Ed. by Judith Mathews. LC 90-42441. (Illus.). 48p. (J). (gr. 3-7). 1991. lib. bdg. 12.95 (*0-8075-7332-9*) A Whitman.

Shazam! Simple Science Magic. Laurence B. White. (Albert Whitman Prairie Book Ser.). (J). (ps-3). 1994. pap. 4.95 (*0-8075-7333-7*) A Whitman.

Shazam! User's Reference Manual, Version 7.0. Kenneth J. White. 1993. pap. text ed. write for info. (*0-07-069862-7*) McGraw.

She. H. Rider Haggard. (Airmont Classics Ser.). (J). (gr. 8 up). 1967. mass mkt. 1.95 (*0-8049-0146-5*, CL-146) Airmont.

She. H. Rider Haggard. 352p. 1994. pap. 5.95 (*0-451-52584-1*, Sig Classics) NAL-Dutton.

She. H. Rider Haggard. (World's Classics Ser.). (Illus.). 384p. 1991. pap. 7.95 (*0-19-282767-7*, 6021) OUP.

S/HE. Minnie B. Pratt. LC 95-3894. 192p. 1995. pap. 11.95 (*1-56341-059-1*); lib. bdg. 24.95 (*1-56341-060-5*) Firebrand Bks.

She. M. L. Rosenthal. (American Poets Continuum Ser.: No. 2). 40p. 1977. pap. 7.00 (*0-918526-06-X*) BOA Edns.

She. H. Rider Haggard. 1976. reprint ed. lib. bdg. 23.95 (*0-89190-705-X*, Rivercity Pr) Amereon Ltd.

She. H. Rider Haggard. 1990. reprint ed. lib. bdg. 20.95 (*0-89968-514-5*) Buccaneer Bks.

She: Anthology of Big Bitch. Spain Rodriguez. 1993. pap. 14.95 (*0-86719-398-0*) Last Gasp.

She: Understanding Feminine Psychology. rev. ed. Robert A. Johnson. LC 89-45098. 94p. 1989. reprint ed. pap. 9.50 (*0-06-096397-2*, PL) HarpC.

She & Allan. H. Rider Haggard. reprint ed. lib. bdg. 25.95 (*0-89190-706-8*, Rivercity Pr) Amereon Ltd.

She Bop: The Definitive History of Women in Rock, Pop, & Soul. Lucy O'Brien. LC 95-40456. (Illus.). 480p. (Orig.). 1996. pap. 14.95 (*0-14-025155-3*, Penguin Bks) Viking Penguin.

S/He Brain: Science, Sexual Politics, & the Myths of Feminism. Robert L. Nadeau. LC 96-3211. 184p. 1996. text ed. 19.95 (*0-275-95593-1*, Praeger Pubs) Greenwood.

She Calls Me Daddy: Seven Things Every Man Needs to Know about Building a Complete Daughter. Robert D. Wolgemuth. LC 96-2303. 219p. 1996. 16.99 (*1-56179-461-9*) Focus Family.

She Came Back. Patricia Wentworth. 256p. 1996. mass mkt. 4.99 (*0-06-104399-0*) HarpC.

She Came by the Book. Mary Wings. LC 95-21205. 256p. 1996. 21.95 (*0-425-15147-6*, Prime Crime); pap. 10.00 (*0-425-15144-1*) Berkley Pub.

***She Came by the Book.** Mary Wings. 272p. 1997. reprint ed. mass mkt. 5.99 (*0-425-15697-4*, Prime Crime) Berkley Pub.

She Came Preaching. Barry L. Callen. 1992. pap. 3.99 (*0-87162-601-2*, D1390) Warner Pr.

She Came to Stay. Simone De Beauvoir. 1990. pap. 12.95 (*0-393-30646-1*) Norton.

***She Came to the Castro.** Mary Wings. LC 96-31690. 272p. 1997. 21.95 (*0-425-15629-X*, Prime Crime) Berkley Pub.

***She Came to the Castro.** Mary Wings. 1998. mass mkt. write for info. (*0-425-16222-2*, Prime Crime) Berkley Pub.

She Can Laugh at the Days to Come: Strengthening the Soul for the Journey Ahead. Valerie Bell. 208p. 1996. 14.99 (*0-310-20569-7*) Zondervan.

She Can Read: Feminist Reading Strategies for Biblical Narrative. Emily Cheney. LC 96-24734. 192p. (Orig.). 1996. pap. 18.00 (*1-56338-167-2*) TPI PA.

She Carried Me All the Way, the Fastest Buggy Horse in Alpine. Polly Block. LC 96-68805. (Nurturing the Spirit Ser.: Vol. II). (Illus.). 266p. 1996. reprint ed. pap. 10.95 (*1-57636-017-2*) SunRise Pbl.

She Caught the Sheriff. Anne M. Duquette. (Harlequin Superromance Ser.: No. 700). 1996. mass mkt. 3.99 (*0-373-70700-2*, 1-70700-9) Harlequin Bks.

She Changes: A Goddess Myth for Modern Women. Teresa Mark. 234p. (Orig.). 1991. pap. 12.95 (*1-878980-03-3*) Delphi IL.

She Child. Mardiningsih Arquette. (Illus.). 32p. (Orig.). 1982. pap. 4.00 (*0-9605594-1-8*) Monkey Man.

She Come Bringing Me That Little Baby Girl. Eloise Greenfield. LC 74-8104. (Illus.). 32p. (J). (gr. k-3). 1990. lib. bdg. 15.89 (*0-397-32478-2*, Lipp Jr Bks) HarpC Child Bks.

She Come Bringing Me That Little Baby Girl. Eloise Greenfield. LC 74-8104. (Trophy Picture Bk.). (Illus.). 32p. (J). (ps-3). 1993. pap. 5.95 (*0-06-443296-3*, Trophy) HarpC Child Bks.

An Asterisk (*) at the beginning of an entry indicates that the title is appearing in BIP for the first time.

She Comes When You're Leaving. Bruce Boston. 64p. (Orig.). 1982. pap. 5.95 (0-917658-14-0) BPW & P.
She Comes When You're Leaving & Other Stories. Bruce Boston. 62p. 1991. reprint ed. lib. bdg. 25.00 (0-8095-6007-0) Borgo Pr.
***She Cookbook: Over 200 Quick, Easy & Delicious.** Ed. by Richard Ehrlich. (Illus.). 192p. 1997. pap. 29.95 (1-85793-940-9, Pub. by Pavilion UK) Trafalgar.
She Cookbook: Over 200 Quick, Easy & Delicious Recipes. Richard Ehrlich. (Illus.). 192p. 1996. 40.00 (1-85793-758-9, Pub. by Pavilion UK) Trafalgar.
She-Crab Soup. Dawn L. Simmons. LC 93-72370. 260p. 1993. 16.95 (0-9629880-2-2) ACME Pr.
She Dared to Fly, Bessie Coleman. Dolores Johnson. LC 96-2404. (Benchmark Biographies Ser.: Group 1). (Illus.). 48p. (J). (gr. 3 up). 1996. lib. bdg. 14.95 (0-7614-0487-2, Benchmark NY) Marshall Cavendish.
She-Devils. Pierre Louys. (Velvet Ser.: Vol. 2). 192p. (Orig.). 1996. pap. 12.95 (1-871592-51-8) Creation Bks.
She Didn't Float. Mary Kane. 1994. pap. 5.00 (1-885141-03-3) Harlequin Ink.
She Died Like Good Old Jacob, Deathbed Scenes & Inversions of Power in New England, 1675-1775. Erik R. Seeman. 29p. 1995. pap. 6.00 (0-944026-63-X) Am Antiquarian.
She Died Too Young. Lurlene McDaniel. (One Last Wish Ser.: No. 9). 160p. (YA). 1994. mass mkt. 3.99 (0-553-56263-0) Bantam.
She Died Twice. Jessica Lauren. LC 91-10551. 192p. (Orig.). 1991. pap. 8.95 (0-934678-34-0) New Victoria Pubs.
***She Died Young.** Charles Livingston. LC 96-70174. 250p. (Orig.). 1996. pap. 8.95 (1-889120-04-9) StarsEnd Creations.
She Does Math! Real-Life Problems from Women on the Job. Ed. by Marla Parker. LC 95-76294. (Classroom Resource Material Ser.). 272p. 1995. pap. text ed. 27.50 (0-88385-702-2) Math Assn.
She Drove Without Stopping. Jaimy Gordon. 408p. 1990. 18.95 (0-945575-24-6, 71524) Algonquin Bks.
She Drove Without Stopping. Jaimy Gordon. LC 89-77062. 390p. 1993. reprint ed. pap. 14.00 (0-929701-36-4) McPherson & Co.
She Flew No Flags. Joan B. Manley. LC 94-27623. 272p. (J). (gr. 5-9). 1995. 15.95 (0-395-71130-4) HM.
She Flew the Coop. Michael L. West. 400p. 1995. pap. 13.50 (0-06-092620-1, PL) HarpC.
She Fulfilled the Impossible Dream. DeWitt S. Williams. Ed. by Gerald Wheeler. (Banner Ser.). 126p. (Orig.). 1985. pap. 7.99 (0-8280-0274-6) Review & Herald.
She Goes to War. Edith Pargeter. 313p. 1991. pap. 9.95 (0-7472-3277-6, Pub. by Headline UK) Trafalgar.
She Got Her Man. Marie Ferrarella. (Special Edition Ser.). 1993. mass mkt. 3.50 (0-373-09843-X, 5-09843-9) Silhouette.
She (Graphic Album) Haggard. (Illus.). 1990. pap. 5.95 (0-913035-47-5) Eclipse Bks.
She Had Some Horses. Joy Harjo. 80p. 1983. pap. 8.95 (0-938410-06-7) Thunders Mouth.
***She Had Some Horses.** 2nd ed. Joy Harjo. 96p. 1997. pap. 10.95 (1-56025-119-0) Thunders Mouth.
She Has Reddish Hair & Her Name Is Sabina: A Novel by Julieta Campos. Julieta Campos. Tr. by Leland H. Chambers from SPA. LC 92-39710. 152p. 1993. 19.95 (0-8203-1467-6) U of Ga Pr.
She Hath Done What She Could. Jane McWhorter. 1973. 6.50 (0-89137-405-1) Quality Pubns.
She Hath Done What She Could: A History of Women's Participation in the Church of the Brethren. Frwd. by Pamela K. Brubaker & Ruby Rhoades. LC 85-6622. (Illus.). 240p. reprint ed. pap. 68.40 (0-8357-5590-8, 2035222) Bks Demand.
She-Hulk. Bryne et al. 176p. 1992. pap. 12.95 (0-685-59753-9) Marvel Entmnt.
She-Hulk. John Bryne. (Illus.). 1992. pap. 12.95 (0-87135-892-1) Marvel Entmnt.
She Hulk Ceremony, Pt. I. McDuffie et al. 48p. 1990. 3.95 (0-87135-632-5) Marvel Entmnt.
She Hulk Ceremony, Pt. II. McDuffie et al. 48p. 1990. 3.95 (0-87135-633-3) Marvel Entmnt.
***She Incomparable Siddons.** Florence M. Parson. Date not set. write for info. (0-8369-5193-X) Ayer.
She Is a Cat. Mocco Wollert. (C). 1990. 60.00 (0-86439-038-6, Pub. by Boolarong Pubns AT) St Mut.
She Is Beautiful. Claudia Hazard. (Orig.). 1996. pap. write for info. (1-57553-298-0) Watermrk Pr.
***She Is Darkness.** Cook. LC 97-13701. 1997. 23.95 (0-312-85907-4) St Martin.
She Is Me. Bensalem Association of Women Writers Staff. Ed. by Susan S. Stets. (Illus.). 68p. (Orig.). 1986. pap. 5.95 (0-930069-08-0) Jasmine Pr.
She Is Worthy: Encounters with Biblical Women. Marjorie L. Kimbrough. LC 94-37754. 144p. (Orig.). 1994. pap. 9.95 (0-687-00790-9) Abingdon.
She Just Wants the Hot Wax! A Herman Collection. Jim Unger. (Illus.). 104p. (Orig.). 1991. pap. 6.95 (0-8362-1875-2) Andrews & McMeel.
She King, or the Book of Poetry, Vol. III. Tr. by James Legge. (CHI & ENG.). 1991. 35.00 (957-638-041-3, Pub. by SMC Pub CC) Oriental Bk Store.
She, King Solomon's Mines & Allan Quartermain. H. Rider Haggard. 636p. pap. 10.95 (0-486-20643-2) Dover.
She Laughs & the World Laughs with Her. Ann E. Weeks. LC 95-70771. (Illus.). 49p. (Orig.). 1995. pap. 10.95 (1-886036-07-1) Passages Pbg.
She Loved Gravity & Would Fall Down Exquisitely Anywhere. Ian MacCallum. (Illus.). 32p. 1987. pap. 4.00 (0-907791-17-4) Synerg AZ.
***She Loved Me Once & Other Stories.** Lester Goran. LC 97-10220. 1997. write for info. (0-87338-576-4) Kent St U Pr.
She Loved People: The Story of Joyce Warnke. Mabel Warnke. 1989. 13.95 (0-533-08254-4) Vantage.
She Loves Me. 24p. 1994. pap. 9.95 (1-57007-036-9, XW1651) Astor Bks.
She Loves Me. Joe Masteroff. (Illus.). 96p. 1995. 11.99 (1-56865-142-2, GuildAmerica) Dbldy Direct.
She Loves Me, She Loves Me Knot. Joseph Matzner. (Illus.). 32p. (Orig.). 1993. pap. 8.95 (0-317-05730-8) J Matzner.
She Loves Me-Vocal Selections: Broadway Revival Edition. 52p. (Orig.). 1994. pap. 12.95 (0-89724-157-6, VF2108) Warner Brothers.
***She Loves You.** Segal. LC 97-12321. 1997. 16.95 (0-684-83895-8, S&S Editions) S&S Trade.
She Made Friends & Kept Them: An Anecdotal Memoir. Fleur Cowles. (Illus.). 416p. 1996. 32.50 (0-06-018713-1) HarpC.
She Made Many Rich: Sister Emma Francis of the Virgin Islands. Catherine B. Herzel. (Illus.). 24p. (J). (gr. 6 up). 1990. reprint ed. pap. 4.50 (0-935357-06-8) CRIC Prod.
***She Magazine Names for Baby Book.** Catriona Luke. 176p. 1995. pap. write for info. (1-85479-752-2, Pub. by M OMara UK) Assoc Pubs Grp.
She Must Have Been a Giant. Marilyn Recht. 41p. (Orig.). 1994. pap. write for info. (1-877649-22-8) Tesseract SD.
She Needed Me. (0-8317-5846-5) Smithmark.
She Needed Me. Walter Kirn. Ed. by Judith Regan. 240p. 1993. reprint ed. pap. 10.00 (0-671-78093-X, WSP) PB.
She Offered Them Christ: The Legacy of Women Preachers in Early Methodism. Paul W. Chilcote. LC 92-31400. 176p. (Orig.). 1993. pap. 11.95 (0-687-38345-5) Abingdon.
She Poems. Carol L. Sanchez. LC 95-2806. 41p. (Orig.). 1995. 7.95 (0-9619111-9-0) Chicory Blue.
She Pushes with Her Hands. limited ed. Dale Going. 25p. 1992. pap. 55.00 (0-9632085-1-9) Em Pr.
She-rab Dong-bu, or Prajnya Danda: A Metrical Translation in Tibetan of a Sanskirt Ethical Work. Nagarjuna. Ed. by W. L. Campbell. LC 78-70103. reprint ed. 27.50 (0-404-17354-3) AMS Pr.
She Said - He Said. Nancy Henley & Barrie Thorne. 1976. per. 3.50 (0-912786-36-1) Know Inc.
She Said, He Said: What Women & Men Really Think about Sex, Money, Politics & Other Issues of Essence... Floris Wood. 1991. pap. 11.95 (0-8103-9411-1) Visible Ink Pr.
She Said No: But He Crossed the Line Between Passion & Violence. Kay D. Rizzo. LC 93-28923. 1994. pap. 10.99 (0-8163-1179-X) Pacific Pr Pub Assn.
She Said, She Said: Strong Words from Strong-Minded Women. Ed. & Selected by Gloria Alder. 256p. (Orig.). 1995. pap. 8.00 (0-380-77728-2) Avon.
She Said What? Interviews with Women Columnists. Maria Braden. LC 92-36460. (Illus.). 216p. 1993. 24.00 (0-8131-1819-0) U Pr of Ky.
***She Say, He Say: Urban Girls Write Their Lives.** Brett E. Blake. LC 96-45352. 160p. (C). 1997. pap. text ed. 14.95 (0-7914-3480-X) State U NY Pr.
***She Say, He Say: Urban Girls Write Their Lives.** Brett E. Blake. LC 96-45352. 160p. (C). 1997. text ed. 44.50 (0-7914-3479-6) State U NY Pr.
She Sells Seashells by the Seashore: A Tongue Twister Story. Grace Kim. LC 94-39721. (Hello Reader! Ser.). (Illus.). 32-48p. (J). 1996. pap. 2.95 (0-590-26584-9, Cartwheel) Scholastic Inc.
She Shall Be Called Woman. Marsha Newman & Gene Newman. 1981. pap. write for info. (0-318-56398-3) Wellspring Utah.
She Shall Be Called Woman Vol. 2: New Testament Women. Ed. by Sheila Jones & Linda Brumley. 154p. 1995. pap. 7.99 (1-884553-41-9) Discipleshp.
She Shall Be Called Woman Vol. I: Old Testament Women. Ed. by Sheila Jones & Linda Brumley. 160p. 1994. pap. 7.99 (1-884553-24-9) Discipleshp.
She Shoots She Scores. Barbara Stewart. 208p. 1993. pap. 18.95 (0-385-25426-1) Doubleday.
She Speaks, He Listens: Women on the French Analysts' Couch. Ed. by Elaine H. Baruch & Lucienne J. Serrano. 208p. (C). 1995. pap. 16.95 (0-415-91127-3, Routledge NY) Routledge.
She Speaks, He Listens: Women on the French Analysts' Couch. Ed. by Elaine H. Baruch & Lucienne J. Serrano. 208p. (C). 1995. text ed. 62.95 (0-415-91126-5, Routledge NY) Routledge.
She Started It! A Baby Blues Cartoon Collection. Rick Kirkman & Jerry Scott. LC 95-30787. 128p. 1995. pap. 8.95 (0-8092-3266-9) Contemp Bks.
She Stays. Bettye Shelton & Andy Landis. (Illus.). 256p. 1995. 16.99 (0-7852-7742-0, J Thoma Bks) Nelson.
***She Stoops to Conquer.** Goldsmith. 1994. pap. text ed. write for info. (0-582-25397-7, Pub. by Longman UK) Longman.
She Stoops to Conquer. Oliver Goldsmith. 1994. 3.00 (0-87129-477-X, S31) Dramatic Pub.
She Stoops to Conquer. Oliver Goldsmith. Ed. by Katherine G. Balderston. LC 51-6755. (Crofts Classics Ser.). 96p. (C). 1951. pap. text ed. write for info. (0-88295-039-8) Harlan Davidson.
She Stoops to Conquer. Oliver Goldsmith. (Illus.). 34p. 1965. pap. 3.25 (0-88680-173-7) I E Clark.
She Stoops to Conquer. Oliver Goldsmith. LC 93-16949. 1993. pap. 7.00 (0-88734-268-X) Players Pr.
She Stoops to Conquer. Oliver Goldsmith. Ed. by Harry Shefter. (Enriched Classics Edition Ser.). 176p. mass mkt. 4.99 (0-671-50998-5, WSP) PB.
She Stoops to Conquer. Oliver Goldsmith. Ed. by J. A. Lavin. (New Mermaid Ser.). (C). 1980. pap. text ed. 6.95 (0-393-90046-0) Norton.
She Stoops to Conquer. Oliver Goldsmith. (Thrift Editions Ser.). 80p. reprint ed. pap. 1.00 (0-486-26867-5) Dover.
She Stoops to Conquer: Director's Script. Oliver Goldsmith. (Illus.). 34p. 1965. pap. 10.00 (0-88680-174-5) I E Clark.
She Talks to Herself in the Language of an Educated Woman. Frances Jaffer. (Illus.). 48p. 1981. 4.25 (0-932716-13-X) Kelsey St Pr.
She Taught Me to Eat Artichokes: The Discovery Of The Heart Of Friendship. Mary K. Shanley. (Illus.). 1993. 13.95 (1-882835-10-7) STA-Kris.
She, the Tale of a Sail. D. Smith Nath. 30p. (J). (gr. k-2). pap. 5.95 (1-886134-03-0) Miraculous Fngerprnt.
***She Took My Arm As If She Love.** Herbert Gold. LC 96-53663. 1997. 21.95 (0-312-15653-7) St Martin.
She Tries Her Tongue: Her Silence Softly Breaks. M. Nourbese Philip. 100p. 1995. pap. 12.95 (0-921556-03-9, Pub. by Gynergy-Ragweed CN) LPC InBook.
She Walks in Beauty. Sarah Shankman. Ed. by Jane Chelius. 352p. 1992. reprint ed. mass mkt. 4.99 (0-671-73658-2) PB.
She Walks in Beauty: Jennifer, a Celebration of Life. Barbara Mellen. (Illus.). 80p. (Orig.). 1993. pap. 10.00 (0-9636524-0-0) B Mellen.
She Walks These Hills. Sharyn McCrumb. 448p. 1995. pap. 6.99 (0-451-18472-6, Sig) NAL-Dutton.
***She Walks These Hills.** large type ed. Sharyn McCrumb. LC 96-31684. (Large Print Bks.). 1996. 24.95 (1-56895-357-7, Compass) Wheeler Pub.
She Walks These Hills: A Novel of Suspense. Sharyn Mccrumb. 320p. 1994. 21.00 (0-684-19556-9) S&S Trade.
She Wants a Share of His Law Practice: Divorce Simulation. David W. Felder. 44p. 1996. pap. text ed. 8.95 (0-910959-94-3, B&G 18E) Wellington Pr.
She Was a Queen. Maurice Collis. LC 90-21153. (New Directions Classics Ser.). (Illus.). 304p. 1991. reprint ed. pap. 12.95 (0-8112-1169-X, NDP716) New Directions.
She Was a Sister Sailor: The Whaling Journals of Mary Brewster, 1845-1851. Ed. by Joan Druett. (Illus.). xx, 449p. 1992. 39.95 (0-913372-60-9) Mystic Seaport.
She Was Born, She Died. rev. ed. Marion Cohen. (Illus.). 24p. (Orig.). 1996. pap. 3.25 (1-56123-044-8) Centering Corp.
She Was Only a Garbageman's Daughter: But She Was Nothing to Be Sniffed At. Earl Reimer. 63p. (Orig.). 1995. pap. 4.50 (1-57514-229-5, 0091) Encore Perform Pub.
She Was Only Twenty-Two. James A. Stewart. 1966. pap. 0.99 (1-56632-074-7) Revival Lit.
She Was There All the Time: A Woman's Journey of Self-Discovery. Ralene Friend. 40p. 1995. pap. text ed. 8.95 (0-9649590-0-3) Creating Futures.
She Went to War: The Rhonda Cornum Story. Rhonda Cornum. LC 92-7288. 240p. 1993. pap. 9.95 (0-89141-507-6) Presidio Pr.
She Who Dwells Within: A Feminist Vision of a Renewed Judaism. Lynn Gottlieb. LC 94-36296. 240p. 1995. pap. 16.00 (0-06-063292-5) Harper SF.
She Who Is: The Mystery of God in Feminist Theological Discourse. Elizabeth A. Johnson. 300p. 1992. 24.95 (0-8245-1162-X) Crossroad NY.
She Who Is: The Mystery of God in Feminist Theological Discourse. Elizabeth A. Johnson. 316p. 1993. reprint ed. pap. 16.95 (0-8245-1376-2) Crossroad NY.
She Who Loves a Garden. Mary Engelbreit. (Illus.). 48p. 1993. 6.95 (0-8362-4612-8); pap. 4.95 (0-8362-4618-7) Andrews & McMeel.
She Who Remembers. Linda L. Shuler. 1989. pap. 6.99 (0-451-16053-3, Sig) NAL-Dutton.
She Who Walks the Sunrise, Vol. 1. Sandy Corcoran. LC 95-623. (Illus.). 32p. (J). 1996. 16.95 (0-9629978-4-6) Sights Prods.
She Who Was Lost Is Remembered: Healing from Incest Through Creativity. Ed. by Louise M. Wisechild. LC 91-21464. (Illus.). 304p. (Orig.). 1991. pap. 18.95 (1-878067-09-5) Seal Pr WA.
She Wields a Pen: American Women Poets of the Nineteenth Century. Ed. by Janet Gray. (Everyman Paperback Classics Ser.). 384p. (Orig.). (C). 1996. pap. 8.95 (0-460-87652-X, Everyman's Classic Lib) C E Tuttle.
***She Wields a Pen: American Women Poets of the Nineteenth Century.** Ed. by Janet Gray. LC 96-61104. 420p. (Orig.). 1997. 29.95 (0-87745-574-0); pap. 15.95 (0-87745-575-9) U of Iowa Pr.
She Works, He Works: How Two-Income Families Are Happier, Heathier & Better-Off. Rosalind Barnett & Caryl Rivers. 272p. 1996. 24.00 (0-06-251080-0, HarpT) HarpC.
She Works/He Works: How Two-Income Families Are Happier, Healthier, & Better-Off. Rosalind Barnett & Caryl Rivers. LC 96-10442. 1996. pap. write for info. (0-06-251189-0) Harper SF.
She Would If She Could. George Etherege. Ed. by Charlene M. Taylor. LC 76-128913. (Regents Restoration Drama Ser.). 162p. reprint ed. pap. 46.20 (0-8357-7770-7, 2036130) Bks Demand.
Sheaf of Cinquain. Irene Stanley. 15.00 (0-686-00950-9) Wagon & Star.
Sheaf of Studies. Edmund K. Chambers. LC 74-99622. (Essay Index Reprint Ser.). 1977. 20.95 (0-8369-1398-1) Ayer.
***Sheaf Theory.** 2nd ed. Glen E. Bredon. LC 96-44232. (Graduate Texts in Mathematics Ser.: Vol. 170). 512p. 1997. 59.95 (0-387-94905-4) Spr-Verlag.
Shear. Tim Parks. LC 94-7058. 224p. 1994. 21.00 (0-8021-1552-7, Grove) Grove-Atltic.
Shear. Tim Parks. LC 94-7058. 216p. 1995. pap. 11.00 (0-8021-3360-6, Grove) Grove-Atltic.
Shear in Reinforced Concrete, 1. American Concrete Institute Staff. LC 73-94112. (American Concrete Institute Publication Ser.: SP-42). (Illus.). reprint ed. pap. 108.30 (0-317-10241-9) Bks Demand.
Shear in Reinforced Concrete, 2. American Concrete Institute Staff. LC 73-94112. (American Concrete Institute Publication Ser.: SP-42). (Illus.). reprint ed. pap. 131.00 (0-317-10242-7) Bks Demand.
Shear Reinforcement for Slabs. 12p. 1992. 12.75 (0-685-72321-6, 421.1R-92BOW6) ACI.
Shear Stability of Multigrade Crankcase Oil-DS49. 1973. pap. 7.75 (0-8031-0090-6, 05-049000-12) ASTM.
Shear Stability of Multigrade Oils-IP Fleet Test-DS49-S1. 36p. 1974. pap. 4.00 (0-8031-0566-5, 05-049001-12) ASTM.
Shear Strength of Reinforced & Prestressed Concrete Beams: CEB Approach. Bruno Thurlimann. (IBA Ser.: No. 93). 23p. 1980. 18.50 (0-8176-1131-2) Birkhauser.
Shear Structures in Layered Geological Bodies. L. M. Plotnikov. Ed. by S. P. Sychanthavong. (Russian Translation Ser.: No. 104). (Illus.). 171p. (C). 1994. text ed. 55.00 (90-5410-220-9, Pub. by A A Balkema NE) Ashgate Pub Co.
Shear-Wave Exploration. Ed. by S. Danbom & S. N. Domenico. LC 87-60488. (Geophysical Developments Ser.: No. 1). 282p. 1987. text ed. 61.00 (0-931830-45-1, 451) Soc Expl Geophys.
Shear Waves in Marine Sediments. Ed. by Jens M. Hovem et al. (C). 1991. lib. bdg. 238.00 (0-7923-1357-7) Kluwer Ac.
Shear Zones in Rocks: Papers Presented at the International Conference Held at the University of Barcelona, May 1979. J. Carreras et al. 200p. 1980. pap. 48.00 (0-08-026244-9, Pergamon Pr) Elsevier.
Shearer Furniture Designs. R. Fastnedge. 1966. 18.00 (0-685-52092-7) Transatl Arts.
Shearer's Manual of Human Dissection. 7th ed. John J. Jacobs. 320p. 1989. pap. text ed. 32.00 (0-07-032177-9) McGraw-Hill HPD.
Shearers' War: The Story of the 1891 Shearer's Strike. Stuart Svensen. 250p. (Orig.). 1989. pap. text ed. 34.95 (0-7022-2165-1, Pub. by Univ Queensland Pr AT) Intl Spec Bk.
Shearwall-Frame Interaction: A Design Aid. rev. ed. 18p. 1970. pap. 6.00 (0-89312-111-8, EB066D) Portland Cement.
Sheathing the Sword: The U. N. Secretary-General & the Prevention of Internation Conflict. Thomas E. Boudreau. LC 90-47520. (Contributions in Political Science Ser.: No. 273). 208p. 1991. text ed. 55.00 (0-313-26109-1, BDK/, Greenwood Pr) Greenwood.
Sheaves: Poems & Songs. 2nd ed. Rabindranath Tagore. Tr. by Nagendranath Gupta. LC 78-98878. 152p. 1971. reprint ed. text ed. 59.75 (0-8371-3149-9, TASH, Greenwood Pr) Greenwood.
Sheaves in Geometry & Logic: A First Introduction to Topos Theory. S. Mac Lane & Izak Moerdijk. (Universitext Ser.). (Illus.). 616p. 1994. 60.95 (0-387-97710-4) Spr-Verlag.
Sheaves of Friendship. Ruth Adams Bevell. xxii, 247p. 1982. text ed. 7.50 (0-88053-325-0, S-100) Macoy Pub.
Sheaves on Manifolds. Masaki Kashiwara & P. Schapira. Ed. by M. Berger et al. (Grundlehren der Mathematischen Wissenschaften Ser.: Bd. 292). 528p. 1994. 142.95 (0-387-51861-4) Spr-Verlag.
Sheba. Jack Higgins. 272p. (Orig.). 1995. mass mkt. 5.99 (0-425-14670-7) Berkley Pub.
Sheba. Jack Higgins. (Orig.). 1995. pap. 17.95 (0-7871-0230-X, Dove Bks) Dove Audio.
Sheba. large type ed. Jack Higgins. LC 95-5409. (Large Print Bks.). 1995. pap. 22.95 (1-56895-126-4, Compass) Wheeler Pub.
Sheba Consumes Whatever She Can. D. H. James. 98p. (J). 1990. 19.95 (1-878950-01-0) Sheba Bks Intl.
Sheba Learns the Great Outdoors. J. Hamlyn. (Sheba Does Ser.). 65p. (J). (gr. 1-4). 1990. pap. 5.25 (1-878950-00-2) Sheba Bks Intl.
Sheba's Daughters. Harris S. Philby. LC 83-45836. reprint ed. 55.00 (0-404-20201-2) AMS Pr.
Sheba's Daughters. Harry S. Philby. (Illus.). xix, 485p. reprint ed. write for info. (0-318-71552-X) G Olms Pubs.
***Shebeen Tales: Messages from Harare.** Chenjerai Hove. 1997. pap. 12.95 (1-897959-32-X, Pub. by Serif UK) LPC InBook.
Shebeen Tales Messages From... Messages from Harare. Chenjerai Hove. 121p. 1996. 10.95 (1-897959-16-8, Pub. by Serif UK) LPC InBook.
Sheboygan County: 150 Years of Progress. Janice Hildebrand. 140p. 1995. pap. 16.95 (0-89781-479-7) Am Historical Pr.
Shebu'oth. (ENG & HEB.). 18.00 (0-910218-75-7) Bennet Pub.
Shechem I: The Middle Bronze IIB Pottery. Dan P. Cole. LC 84-3004. (Excavation Reports of the American Schools of Oriental Research). (Illus.). xiv, 203p. 1984. text ed. 50.00 (0-89757-206-8) Am Sch Orient Res.
Shechita: Religious & Historical Research on the Method of Slaughter. Ed. by Elie Munk et al. (Illus.). 1976. 12.95 (0-87306-992-7) Feldheim.
Shed a Soft Mongolian Tear: The Komplete Kat Komics. George Herriman. 1991. pap. 9.95 (0-913666-51-3) Turtle Isl Foun.
Shed Antler Records of North American Big Game: A Record Book for the Recognition of North America's Big Game Shed Antlers. Jeff LeBaron. Ed. by Sandi Falck. 210p. 1994. text ed. 29.95 (0-9644514-4-1) NAm Shed Hunt.
***Shed for Your Salvation.** Nicholas A. Mazzei. 48p. (Orig.). (J). (gr. 7). 1996. pap. 3.50 (0-9655903-0-5) N A Mazzei.

S

S

***Shed Side on Merseyside: The Locomotive Depots of Liverpool & Birkenhead.** Kenn Pearce. (Illus.). 1997. 33.95 (*0-7509-1369-X*, Pub. by Sutton Pubng UK) Bks Intl VA.

Shedding a Little Light on Your Skin. Richard G. Mora. LC 91-67754. 126p. (Orig.). 1992. pap. 17.95 (*1-56002-162-4*) Aegina Pr.

Shedding & Literally Dreaming. Verena Stefan. Tr. by Johanna Moore et al. from GER. 200p. 1994. 32.50 (*1-55861-081-2*); pap. 14.95 (*1-55861-084-7*) Feminist Pr.

***Shedding Life: Disease, Politics, & Other Human Conditions.** Miroslav Holub. Tr. by David Young from CZE. LC 97-10712. 280p. 1997. 22.95 (*1-57131-217-X*) Milkweed Ed.

Shedding Light. Peter Lauria. 135p. 1992. pap. write for info. (*0-9635713-1-1*) Longshot Prod.

Shedding Light on Our Dark Side. Charles R. Swindoll. (Swindoll Bible Study Guide Ser.). 1993. pap. 5.99 (*0-8499-8477-7*) Word Pub.

Shedding Light on the New Age. Judy Hamlin. (Searching for Answers Ser.). 64p. (Orig.). 1993. pap. 1.00 (*1-56476-075-8*, 6-3075, Victor Bks) Chariot Victor.

Shedding Silence. Janice Mirikitani. 176p. 1995. pap. 9.95 (*0-89087-493-X*) Celestial Arts.

Shedding Skin. Robert Ward. Ed. by Donna Ng. LC 95-30615. 256p. 1995. reprint ed. pap. 10.00 (*0-671-53613-3*, WSP) PB.

Shedding the Veil: Mapping the European Discovery of America & the World. T. Suarez. 200p. 1994. text ed. 75.00 (*981-02-0869-3*) World Scientific Pub.

Shedding the Years. James C. Bennett. 383p. 1971. reprint ed. spiral bd. 22.50 (*0-7873-0091-8*) Hlth Research.

Sheds: The Do-It-Yourself Guide for Backyard Builders. David Stiles. (Illus.). 142p. 1993. 29.95 (*0-944475-38-8*, Pub. by Camden Hse CN); pap. 17.95 (*0-944475-37-X*, Pub. by Camden Hse CN) Firefly Bks Ltd.

Sheehan. Terry Trueman. (Illus.). 43p. (Orig.). 1992. pap. 6.95 (*0-9629744-0-4*) Siobhan Pr.

Sheep. Peter Brady. (Beginning Reader Science Bks.). 24p. (J). (ps-4). 1996. lib. bdg. 13.35 (*1-56065-346-9*) Capstone Pr.

***Sheep.** Peter Brady. (Early Reader Science Bks.). (Illus.). 24p. (J). (gr. k-3). 1996. 13.25 (*0-516-20118-2*) Childrens.

Sheep. Ruth Gatenby. 154p. 1991. 9.95 (*0-333-52310-5*) Macmillan.

Sheep. Ann L. Hansen. LC 96-709. (J). 1997. lib. bdg. 12.95 (*1-56239-606-4*) Abdo & Dghtrs.

Sheep. Hans A. Muller. (Complete Pet Owner's Manuals Ser.). (Illus.). 1989. pap. 6.95 (*0-8120-4091-0*) Barron.

***Sheep.** Peter Murray. LC 97-5953. (J). 1997. lib. bdg. write for info. (*1-56766-379-6*) Childs World.

Sheep. Tessa Potter. LC 89-22022. (Animal World Ser.). (Illus.). 32p. (J). (gr. 1-4). 1990. lib. bdg. 21.40 (*0-8114-2630-0*) Raintree Steck-V.

Sheep. Lynn M. Stone. (Farm Animals Discovery Library). (Illus.). 24p. (J). (gr. k-5). 1990. lib. bdg. 11.94 (*0-86593-038-4*); lib. bdg. 8.95 (*0-685-36313-9*) Rourke Corp.

Sheep: A Guide to Management. Edward Hart. (Illus.). 128p. 1994. pap. 22.95 (*1-85223-828-3*, Pub. by Crowood Pr UK) Trafalgar.

Sheep: Life on the South Dakota Range. Archer B. Gilfillan. LC 92-42162. xlv, 272p. 1993. reprint ed. pap. 10.95 (*0-87351-285-5*, Borealis Book) Minn Hist.

Sheep Ailments: T. V. Vet Sheep Book. 6th ed. (T. V. Vet Ser.). (Illus.). 192p. 1992. 36.95 (*0-85236-212-9*, Pub. by Farming Pr UK) Diamond Farm Bk.

Sheep & Goat Breeding. (Better Farming Ser.: No. 12). 51p. 1977. pap. 5.00 (*92-5-100152-9*, F70, Pub. by FAO IT) Bernan Associates.

Sheep & Goat Practice. Boden. 1991. pap. text ed. 46.00 (*0-7020-1555-5*) HarBrace.

***Sheep & Goat Practice 2.** 2nd ed. Boden. 1997. text ed. write for info. (*0-7020-2330-2*) Saunders.

***Sheep & Goat Science.** Ensminger & Parker. (Illus.). 1998. text ed. 73.25 (*0-8134-3116-6*) Interstate.

Sheep & Goat Science. 5th ed. Ensminger & Parker. (Illus.). 1986. text ed. 66.95 (*0-8134-2464-X*) Interstate.

Sheep & Man. M. Ryder. 1983. 103.95 (*0-7156-1655-2*, Pub. by Duckworth UK) Focus Pub-R Pullins.

Sheep & Sheep Hunting. J. O'Connor. (Illus.). 398p. 1992. 35.00 (*0-940143-73-9*) Safari Pr.

Sheep & Wool: Science, Production & Management. M. P. Botkin et al. (Illus.). 512p. 1988. text ed. 50.80 (*0-13-808494-7*) P-H.

***Sheep & Wool Production.** David Crean & Geoff Bastian. (Illus.). 144p. 1996. pap. write for info. (*0-7506-8915-3*) Buttrwrth-Heinemann.

Sheep As an Experimental Animal. J. F. Hecker. 1983. text ed. 99.00 (*0-12-336050-1*) Acad Pr.

Sheep, Goats & Soap. large type ed. John Malcolm. 275p. 1992. pap. 14.95 (*0-8161-5475-9*, GK Hall) Thorndike Pr.

Sheep, Goats & Wolves. Mark T. Barclay. 54p. (Orig.). 1985. pap. 5.00 (*0-944802-06-0*) M Barclay Pubns.

Sheep, Goats, Pigs: And Other People Who Attend Your Church. Jeffrey B. Krall. 40p. (Orig.). 1996. pap. 3.50 (*1-57688-000-1*, 000-1) Branch & Vine.

Sheep Grass. large type ed. Padder Nash. (Linford Mystery Library). 1996. pap. 15.99 (*0-7089-7863-0*, Linford) Ulverscroft.

Sheep Herder. Alex Velasquez. Ed. by Paulie Grissom. (Illus.). 108p. (Orig.). 1995. pap. text ed. 10.00 (*1-887294-01-5*) Black Ball Pr.

Sheep Housing & Equipment Handbook. 4th ed. Harvey J. Hirning et al. Ed. by C. J. Huffman. LC 93-26802. (Illus.). 90p. 1994. pap. 10.00 (*0-89373-090-4*, MWPS-3) MidWest Plan Serv.

Sheep Hunting in Alaska: The Dall Sheep Hunters' Guide. Tony Russ. LC 93-86886. 160p. (Orig.). 1994. pap. text ed. 19.95 (*0-9639869-0-2*) Northern Pubng.

Sheep in a Jeep. Nancy Shaw. LC 86-3101. (Illus.). 32p. (J). (ps). 1986. 13.95 (*0-395-41105-X*) HM.

Sheep in a Jeep. Nancy Shaw. (Illus.). 32p. (J). (ps). 1988. pap. 3.95 (*0-395-47030-7*, Sandpiper) HM.

Sheep in a Jeep. Nancy Shaw. (Illus.). 32p. (J). (ps). 1991. audio 8.95 (*0-395-60167-3*, Sandpiper) HM.

***Sheep In A Jeep.** Nancy Shaw. 1997. 4.95 (*0-395-86786-X*) HM.

Sheep in a Shop. Nancy Shaw. LC 90-4139. (Illus.). 32p. (J). (ps). 1991. 13.95 (*0-395-53681-2*) HM.

***Sheep in a Shop.** Nancy Shaw. 1997. 4.95 (*0-395-87276-6*) HM.

Sheep in a Shop. Nancy Shaw. (Illus.). (J). 1994. pap. 4.95 (*0-395-70672-6*) HM.

Sheep in a Shop. Nancy Shaw. (Illus.). 32p. (J). (ps-k). 1996. pap. 8.95 incl. audio (*0-395-77940-5*) HM.

Sheep in Wolves' Clothing. Satoshi Kitamura. 40p. (J). (gr. k-4). 1996. 15.00 (*0-374-36780-9*) FS&G.

Sheep Is Life: An Assessment of Livestock Reduction in the Former Navajo-Hopi Joint Use Area. rev. ed. John J. Wood et al. (Northern Arizona University Anthropological Papers: No. 1). (Illus.). xxiii, 182p. 1982. pap. 13.50 (*0-910953-00-7*) N Arizona U Bkstore.

Sheep Management & Production. Stanley, Thornes, Publishers Ltd. Staff. (C). 1989. 90.00 (*0-09-138091-X*, Pub. by S Thornes Pubs UK) St Mut.

Sheep Management & Wool Technology. 3rd ed. J. B. D'Arcy. 352p. 1990. reprint ed. pap. 34.95 (*0-86840-036-X*, Pub. by New South Wales Univ Pr AT) Intl Spec Bk.

Sheep May Safely Graze: A Personal Essay on Tradition & a Contemporary Sheep Ranch. Louie W. Attebery. (Northwest Folklife Ser.). 192p. (Orig.). (C). 1993. pap. text ed. 15.95 (*0-89301-158-4*) U of Idaho Pr.

Sheep of His Pasture: A Study of the Hebrew Noun 'AM(M) & its Semitic Cognates. Robert M. Good. LC 83-90934. (Harvard Semitic Monographs). 214p. (C). 1984. 17.00 (*0-89130-628-5*, 04 00 29) Scholars Pr GA.

Sheep on a Ship. Nancy Shaw. (Illus.). (J). (ps). 1989. 13.95 (*0-395-48160-0*) HM.

Sheep on a Ship. Nancy Shaw. (J). (ps-3). 1992. pap. 4.95 (*0-395-64376-7*) HM.

Sheep Out to Eat. Nancy Shaw. LC 91-38425. (Illus.). 32p. (J). (ps-1). 1992. 14.00 (*0-395-61128-8*) HM.

Sheep Out to Eat. Nancy Shaw. LC 91-38425. (Illus.). 32p. (J). (ps-2). 1995. pap. 3.95 (*0-395-72027-3*, Sandpiper) HM.

Sheep Production & Management. C. V. Ross. 512p. 1989. boxed 50.80 (*0-13-808510-2*) P-H.

Sheep Production-Health Records & Binder. 1995. 12.95 (*0-944079-15-6*) Lessiter Pubns.

Sheep Production in the Tropics. A. B. Carles. (Oxford Tropical Handbooks Ser.). (Illus.). 200p. 1984. 55.00 (*0-19-859449-6*) OUP.

Sheep Production in Tropics & Subtropics. Ed. by Scientific Publishers Staff. 1994. pap. 300.00 (*81-7233-072-3*, Pub. by Scientific Pubs II) St Mut.

Sheep Raiser's Manual. William K. Kruesi. LC 84-25765. (Illus.). 288p. (Orig.). 1985. Incl. index, appendix & bibliography. pap. 13.95 (*0-913589-10-1*) Williamson Pub Co.

Sheep, Sheep, Sheep, Help Me Fall Asleep. Arlene Alda. (Illus.). 32p. (J). (ps-3). 1995. pap. 4.99 (*0-440-40957-8*) Dell.

Sheep, Stars, & Solitude: Adventure Saga of a Wilderness Trail. Francis R. Line. LC 86-11154. (Illus.). 166p. (Orig.). 1986. pap. 8.95 (*0-938109-02-2*) Wide Horiz Pr.

Sheep Stell: The Autobiography of a Shepherd. Jane White. (Illus.). 218p. 1993. 34.95 (*0-7126-4624-8*, Pub. by Sumach UK) Trafalgar.

Sheep Take a Hike. Nancy Shaw. LC 93-30725. (Illus.). 32p. (J). (ps-1). 1994. 13.95 (*0-395-68394-7*) HM.

Sheep Take a Hike. Nancy Shaw. (Illus.). 32p. (J). (ps-1). 1996. pap. 4.95 (*0-395-81658-0*) HM.

Sheep Thief: The Second Shepherds' Play. Ford Ainsworth. (Illus.). 24p. (Orig.). 1979. pap. 3.25 (*0-88680-175-3*) I E Clark.

***Sheep Trick or Treat.** Nancy Shaw. LC 96-43140. (Illus.). (J). 1997. 15.00 (*0-395-84168-2*) HM.

Sheep Who Was Allergic to Wool. Mother Goof. LC 92-60096. (Illus.). 32p. (J). (gr. 3 up). 1992. 8.95 (*0-9623184-1-8*) Sunflower Hill.

Sheep Will Be Scattered. Don Wiltfong. 1994. pap. 3.95 (*1-55673-515-4*) CSS OH.

Sheepdog in the Snow. Lucy Daniels. LC 96-1843. (Animal Ark Ser.). (Illus.). (J). 1996. 3.95 (*0-8120-9782-3*) Barron.

Sheepdog Training: An All-Breed Approach. rev. ed. Mari Taggart. LC 90-19715. (Illus.). 200p. 1991. 19.95 (*0-931866-50-2*) Alpine Pubns.

Sheepeaters. W. A. Allen. 1989. boxed 14.95 (*0-87770-464-3*) Ye Galleon.

Sheepfarmer's Daughter. Elizabeth Moon. (Deed of Paksenarrion Ser.: Bk. 1). 512p. (Orig.). 1988. pap. 5.99 (*0-671-65416-0*) Baen Bks.

Sheepish Beauty, Civilian Love. Erin Moure. 136p. (Orig.). 1992. pap. 9.95 (*1-55065-028-9*, Pub. by Vehicule Pr CN) Genl Dist Srvs.

Sheepish Riddles. Katy Hall & Lisa Eisenberg. LC 93-32212. (Easy-to-Read Bks.). (Illus.). 48p. (J). (ps-3). 1996. pap. 12.89 (*0-8037-1536-6*) Dial Bks Young.

Sheepish Riddles. Katy Hall & Lisa Eisenberg. LC 93-32212. (Illus.). 48p. (J). (ps-8). 1996. pap. 12.99 (*0-8037-1535-8*) Dial Bks Young.

Sheepskin & Morning Star. Joan Kalbacken. LC 94-90737. (Illus.). 64p. (Orig.). (J). (gr. 3-6). 1996. pap. 7.00 (*1-56002-527-1*, Univ Edtns) Aegina Pr.

Sheer Anecdotages Leaves from a Reporter's Diary. D. R. Mankekar. 1984. 12.50 (*0-8364-1167-6*, Pub. by Allied II) S Asia.

***Sheer Chance.** Goodwin. LC 97-8210. 1997. 22.95 (*0-312-15654-5*) St Martin.

***Sheer Chance.** large type ed. Suzanne Goodwin. (Ulverscroft Large Print Ser.). 448p. 1997. 27.50 (*0-7089-3808-6*) Ulverscroft.

Sheer Delight: Handwoven Transparencies. Doramay Keasbey. Ed. by Seymour Bress. (Illus.). 136p. 1990. 34.95 (*0-9623468-3-7*) Stellar Pub Hse.

Sheer Fiction. Paul West. LC 86-33252. 224p. 1988. reprint ed. 17.95 (*0-914232-82-7*); reprint ed. pap. 10.00 (*0-914232-98-3*) McPherson & Co.

Sheer Fiction, Vol. 2. Paul West. LC 86-33252. 198p. 1991. 20.00 (*0-929701-08-9*) McPherson & Co.

Sheer Fiction, Vol. 3. Paul West. 216p. 1994. 22.00 (*0-929701-38-0*) McPherson & Co.

Sheer Gall. Michael A. Kahn. 320p. 1996. pap. 23.95 (*0-525-94188-6*) NAL-Dutton.

***Sheer Gall.** Michael A. Kahn. 1998. mass mkt. 5.99 (*0-451-40733-4*, Onyx) NAL-Dutton.

Sheer Guts: A Journalist's Recovery from Head Injury. Sharon Sopher. 1992. write for info. (*0-201-57771-2*) Addison-Wesley.

Sheer Joy of Celestial Mechanics. Nathaniel Grossman. LC 95-34467. 1995. write for info. (*3-7643-3832-6*) Birkhauser.

Sheer Joy of Celestial Mechanics. Nathaniel Grossman. LC 95-34467. 181p. 1995. 38.00 (*0-8176-3832-6*) Birkhauser.

Sheer Pleasures. Stella Cameron. 1995. mass mkt. 5.99 (*0-8217-5093-3*, Zebra Kensgtn) Kensgtn Pub Corp.

Sheer Shame. E. L. Rogers. LC 96-60637. 200p. 1997. pap. 9.95 (*1-55523-800-9*) Winston-Derek.

She'erit Yoseph (Hebrew) Yoseph Katz. Ed. by Asher Siev. LC 83-50567. 350p. 1984. 18.50 (*0-87203-116-0*) Hermon.

Sheesh: A Gil Thorp Collection. Jack Berrill. 256p. 1991. pap. 19.95 (*0-930099-07-9*) Take Five Pubs.

Sheet Flutter & Windage Problems Seminar, 1990: Westin Seattle, Seattle, WA, September 28-29. Technical Association of the Pulp & Paper Industry Staff. (TAPPI Notes Ser.). 81p. reprint ed. pap. 25.00 (*0-8357-2960-5*, 2039222) Bks Demand.

Sheet Flutter & Windage Problems Seminar, 1991: Opryland Hotel, Nashville, TN, October 4-5. Technical Association of the Pulp & Paper Industry Staff. (TAPPI Proceedings Ser.). (Illus.). 128p. reprint ed. pap. 36.50 (*0-7837-1143-3*, 2041671) Bks Demand.

Sheet Formability of Alpha-Brass: Effect of Material Properties, Anisotrophy, & Processing Parameters. Drexel Institute of Technology Staff. 127p. 1973. 19.05 (*0-317-34545-1*, 129) Intl Copper.

Sheet Forming. Ed. by D. Bhattacharyya. 1996. write for info. (*0-614-17894-0*) Elsevier.

Sheet-Forming Process. Ed. by J. D. Parker. LC 72-75337. 104p. 1972. pap. 33.00 (*0-685-45540-8*, 0102BS09) TAPPI.

Sheet Metal. L. A. Meyer. (Illus.). 316p. 1995. 26.96 (*0-8269-1907-3*); student ed. 10.96 (*0-8269-1908-1*); teacher ed. 8.96 (*0-8269-1909-X*) Am Technical.

Sheet Metal, Level 1. National Center for Construction Education & Research Staff. (Wheels of Learning Ser.). 1996. teacher ed., pap. text ed. 50.00 (*0-13-462755-5*) P-H.

Sheet Metal, Level 2. National Center for Construction Education & Research Staff. (Wheels of Learning Ser.). 1996. teacher ed., ring bd. 80.00 (*0-13-265604-3*) P-H.

Sheet Metal, Level 3. Ed. by National Center for Construction Staff. 1996. teacher ed., pap. text ed. 80.00 (*0-13-462797-0*) P-H.

Sheet Metal, Level 4. National Center for Construction Education & Research Staff. (Wheels of Learning Ser.). 1996. teacher ed., ring bd. 80.00 (*0-13-265620-5*) P-H.

Sheet Metal: Level 1. Ed. by National Center for Construction Staff. 1996. pap. text ed. 50.00 (*0-13-462748-2*) P-H.

Sheet Metal: Level 2. Ed. by National Center for Construction Staff. 1996. pap. text ed. 80.00 (*0-13-462763-6*) P-H.

Sheet Metal: Level 2. Ed. by National Center for Construction Staff. 1996. teacher ed., pap. text ed. 80.00 (*0-13-462771-7*) P-H.

Sheet Metal: Level 3. Ed. by National Center for Construction Staff. 1996. pap. text ed. 80.00 (*0-13-462789-X*) P-H.

Sheet Metal: Level 4. Ed. by National Center for Construction Staff. 1996. pap. text ed. 80.00 (*0-13-462805-5*) P-H.

Sheet Metal: Level 4. Ed. by National Center for Construction Staff. 1996. teacher ed., pap. text ed. 80.00 (*0-13-462813-6*) P-H.

Sheet Metal: Trainee, Level 1. National Center for Construction Education & Research Staff. (Wheels of Learning Ser.). 1996. student ed., pap. text ed. 50.00 (*0-13-266479-8*) P-H.

Sheet Metal: Trainee, Level 2. National Center for Construction Education & Research Staff. (Wheels of Learning Ser.). 1996. student ed., pap. text ed. 80.00 (*0-13-265976-X*) P-H.

Sheet Metal: Trainee, Level 3. National Center for Construction Education & Research Staff. (Wheels of Learning Ser.). 1996. pap. text ed. 80.00 (*0-13-265984-0*) P-H.

Sheet Metal: Trainee, Level 4. National Center for Construction Education & Research Staff. (Wheels of Learning Ser.). 1996. student ed., pap. text ed. 80.00 (*0-13-265992-1*) P-H.

Sheet Metal & Stamping Symposium: Thirty-three Papers. 318p. 1993. 29.00 (*1-56091-329-0*, SP-944) Soc Auto Engineers.

Sheet Metal Blueprint Reading: For the Building Trades. 2nd ed. Claude J. Zinngrabe. LC 79-2748. 138p. (C). 1980. pap. 26.50 (*0-8273-1352-7*); teacher ed., pap. 12.50 (*0-8273-1353-5*) Delmar.

Sheet Metal Cutting: Collected Articles & Technical Papers. Ed. by Amy J. Nickel. (Illus.). 144p. (Orig.). (C). 1994. pap. 29.95 (*1-881113-05-1*) Croydon Grp.

***Sheet Metal Drawing.** Dickason. 1990. pap. text ed. write for info. (*0-582-99482-9*, Pub. by Longman UK) Longman.

Sheet Metal Fabrication. Jack Rudman. (Occupational Competency Examination Ser.: OCE-31). 1994. pap. 27.95 (*0-8373-5731-4*) Nat Learn.

Sheet Metal Forming & Energy Conservation: Proceedings of the Biennial Congress of the International Deep Drawing Research Group, 9th, Ann Arbor, Michigan, U. S. A., October 13-14, 1976. International Deep Drawing Research Group Staff. LC 76-27547. (Illus.). 292p. reprint ed. pap. 83.30 (*0-317-10787-9*, 2050982) Bks Demand.

Sheet Metal Hand Processes. Claude J. Zinngrabe & F. W. Schumacher. LC 73-2159. 1974. pap. 19.95 (*0-8273-0220-7*) Delmar.

Sheet Metal Layout. 2nd ed. Leo A. Meyer. (Illus.). 1979. text ed. 35.95 (*0-07-041731-8*) McGraw.

Sheet Metal Layout Simplified, 3 vols., Vol. 1. Hugh B. Reid. 1981. 19.50 (*0-685-77694-8*) H B Reid.

Sheet Metal Layout Simplified, 3 vols., Vol. 2. Hugh B. Reid. 1981. 19.50 (*0-685-41577-5*) H B Reid.

Sheet Metal Layout Simplified, 3 vols., Vol. 3. Hugh B. Reid. 1981. 19.50 (*0-685-41578-3*) H B Reid.

Sheet Metal Layout Tables for the Heating, Ventilation & Air Conditioning Industry. Richard S. Budzik. 1996. 29.95 (*0-912914-31-9*) Practical Pubns.

Sheet Metal Machine Processes. Claude J. Zinngrabe & F. W. Schumacher. LC 73-2160. (C). 1975. pap. 28.50 (*0-8273-0222-3*) Delmar.

Sheet Metal Machinery. Leo Rizzo. LC 82-730275. 1982. student ed. 7.00 (*0-8064-0253-9*, 518); audio, vhs 419.00 (*0-8064-0254-7*) Bergwall.

Sheet-Metal Pattern Drafting & Shop Problems. rev. ed. J. S. Daugherty & R. E. Powell. 196p. (C). 1975. pap. text ed. 18.20 (*0-02-665680-9*) Glencoe.

Sheet Metal Punching: Collected Articles & Technical Papers. Ed. by Amy Boeselager. (Illus.). 216p. (Orig.). (C). 1993. pap. 24.95 (*1-881113-03-5*) Croydon Grp.

Sheet Metal Shop Fabrication Projects Including Over Three Hundred Fifty Graded Parts. Richard S. Budzik. LC 80-84009. (Illus.). (gr. 7-12). 1980. 29.95 (*0-912914-07-6*) Practical Pubns.

***Sheet Metal Stamping: Development Application.** 29p. 1997. 94.00 (*1-56091-933-7*) Soc Auto Engineers.

Sheet Metal Stamping for Automotive Applications: 1996 International Congress & Exposition. (Special Publications). 163p. 1996. pap. 55.00 (*1-56091-764-4*, SP-1134) Soc Auto Engineers.

Sheet Metal Technology. 2nd ed. Richard S. Budzik. 1981. 19.96 (*0-672-97360-X*, Bobbs); teacher ed. 3.67 (*0-672-97361-8*, Bobbs); student ed. 10.28 (*0-672-97362-6*, Bobbs) Macmillan.

***Sheet Metal Technology.** 4th ed. Richard S. Budzik. 44.95 (*0-912914-64-5*) Practical Pubns.

Sheet Metal Technology Student's Workbook, Vol. 1. 4th ed. Budzik. 1995. 11.95 (*0-912914-66-1*) Practical Pubns.

Sheet Metal Toolbox Manual. David Tenenbaum. (On-the-Job Reference Ser.). 320p. 1991. pap. 14.00 (*0-13-808650-8*, Arco) Macmillan Gen Ref.

Sheet Metal Welding Code (D9.1-90) (Illus.). 51p. 1990. pap. 27.00 (*0-87171-329-2*) Am Welding.

***Sheet Metal Work.** Date not set. 24.95 (*0-8464-4417-8*) Beekman Pubs.

Sheet Metal Work. John D. Bies. 472p. 1985. 19.95 (*0-8161-1706-3*) Macmillan.

Sheet Metal Work. R. E. Wakeford. (Workshop Practice Ser.: No. 8). (Illus.). 152p. (Orig.). 1985. pap. 18.50 (*0-85242-849-9*, Pub. by Nexus Special Interests UK) Trans-Atl Phila.

Sheet Metal Worker. Jack Rudman. (Career Examination Ser.: C-736). 1994. pap. 23.95 (*0-8373-0736-8*) Nat Learn.

Sheet Metals, Level 3. National Center for Construction Education & Research Staff. (Wheels of Learning Ser.). 1996. teacher ed., ring bd. 80.00 (*0-13-265612-4*) P-H.

Sheet Metalwork. John Nagle. LC 79-730773. 1977. student ed. 9.00 (*0-8064-0231-8*, 507); audio, vhs 359.00 (*0-8064-0232-6*) Bergwall.

Sheet Molding Compound Materials: Science & Technology. Hamid G. Kia. 266p. (C). 1993. text ed. write for info. (*1-56990-154-6*) Hanser-Gardner.

Sheet Music Price Guide. Debbie Dillon. 160p. pap. 9.95 (*0-89145-284-2*) L-W Inc.

Sheet Music Reference & Price Guide. 2nd ed. Anna M. Guiheen & Marie-Reine A. Pafik. 320p. 1995. pap. 19.95 (*0-89145-648-1*, 3973) Collector Bks.

Sheet of Glass. Stefanie Marlis. 40p. (Orig.). 1994. pap. 8.00 (*0-912449-47-0*) Floating Island.

Sheeted Paper Identifiers Specification. Ed. by Alan Kotok & Norman W. Scharpf. 30p. 1990. 29.95 (*0-933505-19-1*) Graph Comm Assn.

Sheetfed Offset Press Operating. 2nd ed. Lloyd P. DeJidas & Thomas M. Destree. Ed. by Deborah L. Stevenson. LC 94-76299. (Illus.). 400p. (Orig.). (C). 1994. text ed. 60.00 (*0-88362-171-1*) Graphic Arts Tech Found.

Sheetfed Pressroom Manager's Guide Book. 1989. 25.00 (*0-318-35509-4*) F Drazan.

Sheetfed Printers by Size & Geographic Area see 1996 PIA Ratios

An Asterisk (*) at the beginning of an entry indicates that the title is appearing in BIP for the first time.

Sheeting & Packaging Seminar, 1986: Notes of TAPPI, Mead Inn, Wisconsin Rapids, WI, May 18-21, 1986. Technical Association of the Pulp & Paper Industry. 138p. pap. 39.40 (0-685-17840-4, 2029190) Bks Demand.

Sheeting & Packaging Short Course, 1990: Holiday Inn, Chillicothe, OH, May 6-9. Technical Association of the Pulp & Paper Industry Staff. (Illus.). 92p. reprint ed. pap. 26.30 (0-8357-4229-6, 2037016) Bks Demand.

Sheeuwwitje - Snow White. Adapted by Sarah Harris. (Comes to Life Bks.). 16p. (DUT & ENG.). (J). (ps-2). 1995. write for info. (1-57234-031-2) YES Ent.

Sheffield: History & Guide. David Fine. LC 92-21234. (History & Guide Ser.). 128p. 1992. pap. 16.00 (0-7509-0819-X, Pub. by Sutton Pubng UK) Bks Intl VA.

Sheffield Gang Wars. J. P. Bean. 135p. (C). 1992. pap. text ed. 55.00 (0-9507645-0-7, Pub. by D&D Pubns UK) St Mut.

Sheffield Outrages Inquiry: Report Presented to the Trades Unions Commissioners. Great Britain Sheffield Outrages Staff. LC 72-108850. xix, 452p. 1971. reprint ed. lib. bdg. 65.00 (0-678-07766-5) Kelley.

Sheffield Steel & America: A Century of Commercial & Technological Interdependence 1830-1930. Geoffrey Tweedale. (Illus.). 320p. 1987. 69.95 (0-521-33458-6) Cambridge U Pr.

Sheffielder. George Shaw. LC 93-28808. 1993. 18.00 (0-7509-0433-X, Pub. by Sutton Pubng UK) Bks Intl VA.

Shehu Shegari: My Vision of Nigeria. Ed. by Aminu Tijjani & David Williams. (Illus.). 446p. 1981. 39.50 (0-7146-3181-7, Pub. by F Cass Pubs UK) Intl Spec Bk.

***Sheik.** Connie Mason. 400p. (Orig.). 1997. mass mkt. 5.99 (0-8439-4328-9, Leisure Bks) Dorchester Pub Co.

Sheik. E. M. Hull. 1976. reprint ed. lib. bdg. 23.95 (0-89190-734-3, Rivercity Pr) Amereon Ltd.

Sheik. E. M. Hull. 1990. reprint ed. lib. bdg. 27.95 (0-89968-529-3) Buccaneer Bks.

Sheik & the Vixen. Elizabeth Mayne. 1996. pap. 3.99 (0-373-07755-6, 1-07755-1) Silhouette.

Sheik Daddy. Barbara McMahon. (Romance Ser.). 1996. mass mkt. 3.25 (0-373-19132-4, 1-19132-9) Silhouette.

Sheikh & Disciple. M. R. Muhaiyaddeen. LC 83-1565. (Illus.). 120p. 1983. 12.00 (0-914390-26-0) Fellowship Pr PA.

***Sheikh & the Dustbin.** George M. Frasher. 190p. (Orig.). 1997. pap. 8.00 (0-00-617681-X) HarperColl Wrld.

Sheikh's Revenge. Emma Darcy. (Presents Ser.). 1993. mass mkt. 2.99 (0-373-11604-7, 1-11604-5) Harlequin Bks.

Sheik's Glory. Carole Howey. 400p. (Orig.). 1996. mass mkt., pap. text ed. 5.50 (0-8439-3903-6) Dorchester Pub Co.

Sheik's Promise. Carole Howey. 400p. (Orig.). 1994. mass mkt., pap. text ed. 4.99 (0-505-51938-0, Love Spell) Dorchester Pub Co.

Sheik's Spell. Eboni Snoe. 1992. pap. 4.95 (1-878634-06-2) Odyssey Bks.

Sheila. John Benton. 192p. (J). (gr. 7-12). 1982. pap. 3.50 (0-8007-8419-7) J Benton Bks.

Sheila - a Healing Through Dying. Ed. by Saxon Walker. (C). 1990. pap. text ed. 30.00 (0-85305-290-5, Pub. by J Arthur Ltd UK) St Mut.

***Sheila Elias: Secret Gardens.** Sheila Elias et al. LC 97-16534. 1997. pap. write for info. (0-9648614-1-0) Lowe Art Mus.

Sheila la Magnifica - Sheila the Great. Judy Blume. Tr. by Olvido Salazar-Alonso. 151p. (SPA.). (J). (gr. 5-8). 1991. pap. 8.50 (84-204-4577-0) Santillana.

Sheila Lake & the Universal Explorers: The People of Glass. Victor E. Swanson. LC 91-77269. 416p. 1992. 24.95 (0-9627771-6-1) Hologlobe Pr.

Sheila Lukins All Around the World Cookbook. Sheila Lukins. LC 94-2421. 512p. 1994. 27.95 (1-56305-636-4, 3636); pap. 18.95 (1-56305-237-7, 3237) Workman Pub.

Sheila Rae, the Brave. Kevin Henkes. LC 86-25761. (Illus.). 32p. (J). (gr. k-3). 1987. 16.00 (0-688-07155-4); lib. bdg. 15.93 (0-688-07156-2) Greenwillow.

Sheila Rae, the Brave. Kevin Henkes. (J). (ps-3). 1990. pap. 3.95 (0-14-050835-X, Puffin) Puffin Bks.

Sheila Rae, the Brave. Kevin Henkes. LC 86-25761. 32p. (J). (ps up). 1996. pap. 4.95 (0-688-14738-0, Mulberry) Morrow.

Sheila's Show Biz Days. Adrianne T. Allen. (Illus.). 64p. (Orig.). (J). (gr. k-6). 1993. pap. 5.95 (1-56883-044-0) Colonial Pr AL.

Shekhina: Forty Poems. Norma Farber. LC 83-73424. 96p. 1984. 15.95 (0-9610662-1-0); pap. 9.95 (0-9610662-2-9) Capstone Edns.

Shekhinah - Spirit: Divine Presence in Jewish & Christian Religion. Michael E. Lodahl. LC 92-5525. (Stimulus Bks.). 272p. 1992. pap. 11.95 (0-8091-3311-3) Paulist Pr.

***Shel Silverstein.** Ruth K. MacDonald. LC 97-15204. (Twayne's United States Authors Ser.). 1997. write for info. (0-8057-1606-8) Irvington.

Shelborne Manufacturing Inc. Manual Practice Set. Leland Mansuetti & Keith Weidkamp. 184p. (C). 1994. student ed., text ed. 28.50 (0-256-17337-0) Irwin.

Shelburne Essays, 11 vols., Set. Ed. by Paul E. More. Incl. Vol. 1. 1904. LC 67-17764. 253p. 1967. 25.00 (0-685-22556-9); Vol. 2. 1905. LC 67-17764. 253p. 1967. 25.00 (0-685-22557-7); Vol. 3. 1906. LC 67-17764. 265p. 1967. 25.00 (0-685-22558-5); Vol. 4. 1906. LC 67-17764. 286p. 1967. 25.00 (0-685-22559-3); Vol. 5. 1908. LC 67-17764. 216p. 1967. 25.00 (0-685-22560-7); Vol. 6. Studies in Religious Dualism, 1909. LC 67-17764. 355p. 1967. 25.00 (0-685-22561-5); Vol. 7. 1910. LC 67-17764. 272p. 1967. 25.00 (0-685-22562-3); Vol. 8. Drift of Romanticism, 1913. LC 67-17764. 316p. 1967. 25.00 (0-685-22563-1); Vol. 9. Aristocracy & Justice, 1915. LC 67-17764. 253p. 1967. 25.00 (0-685-22564-X); Vol. 10. With the Wits, 1919. LC 67-17764. 323p. 1967. 25.00 (0-685-22565-8); Vol. 11. New England Group & Others, 1921. LC 67-17764. 300p. 1967. 25.00 (0-685-22566-6); LC 67-17764. 1967. reprint ed. 250.00 (0-87753-028-9) Phaeton.

Shelby. Cynthia Cooksey. 48p. 1995. 4.50 (1-887945-01-6) CTTC.

Shelby. Pete McCormack. LC 93-27527. 267p. 1994. 22.00 (1-877946-47-8) Permanent Pr.

Shelby Avenue Gang. Auguste R. Black. (Illus.). 66p. (Orig.). (J). (gr. 2-5). 1990. pap. 3.95 (0-9628010-0-3) A R Black.

Shelby Cobra: The Shelby American Original Color Archives 1963-1965. Dave Friedman. (Color Archives Ser.). (Illus.). 168p. 1994. 29.95 (0-87938-757-2) Motorbooks Intl.

Shelby Cobra G.P. 1962-1969. R. M. Clarke. (Gold Portfolio Ser.). (Illus.). 180p. 1990. pap. 24.95 (1-85520-023-6, Pub. by Brooklands Bks UK) Motorbooks Intl.

Shelby Cobra, Mustang & Dodge. Steve Statham. (Enthusiast Color Ser.). (Illus.). 96p. 1996. pap. 12.95 (0-7603-0124-7) Motorbooks Intl.

Shelby County, Ohio, Index for the 1910 Census. Gwyne L. Jensen. LC 89-84493. 88p. 1989. 8.00 (0-9624164-0-1) G L Jensen.

Shelby County, Texas in the Civil War. Kathryn H. Davis & Carolyn R. Ericson. 333p. 1993. pap. 35.00 (0-911317-56-2) Ericson Bks.

Shelby Foote: Novelist & Historian. Robert L. Phillips, Jr. LC 91-26636. 1992. 35.00 (0-87805-531-2) U Pr of Miss.

Shelby GT 40: The Shelby American Original Color Archives. Dave Friedman. (Illus.). 160p. 1995. 39.95 (0-7603-0013-5) Motorbooks Intl.

Shelby Mustang. Tom Corcoran. (Muscle Car Color History Ser.). (Illus.). 128p. 1992. pap. 19.95 (0-87938-620-7) Motorbooks Intl.

Shelby Oakland & Most Pure Heart of Mary Cemeteries. 350p. 1994. lib. bdg. 30.00 (0-9644381-0-0) Richland Shelby.

***Shelby Racing History.** Dave Friedman. LC 97-21674. (Racing History Ser.). (Illus.). 192p. 1997. pap. 24.95 (0-7603-0309-6) Motorbooks Intl.

Shelby's Plan. Michelle R. Anderson. LC 96-96141. 192p. 1996. 17.95 (0-8034-9200-6) Bouregy.

***Shelbyville: A Pictorial History.** Beverly Oliver. (Indiana Pictorial History Ser.). (Illus.). 1996. write for info. (0-943963-53-2) G Bradley.

Sheldon Collection, 2 vols. Garrett W. Sheldon. Incl. What Would Jesus Do?. 192p. 1993. 14.99 (0-8054-6067-5, 4260-67); 240p. 1995. 27.99 (0-8054-6281-3, 4262-81) Broadman.

***Sheldon Harnick Songbook.** Ed. by Carol Cuellar. 136p. (Orig.). (C). 1996. pap. text ed. 19.95 (1-57623-347-2, PF9539) Warner Brothers.

Sheldon Jacobs' Guide to Successful No-Load Fund Investing. Sheldon Jacobs. 300p. 1995. text ed. 17.50 (0-7863-0436-7) Irwin Prof Pubng.

Sheldon Memorial Art Gallery Cookbook. Ed. by Jean L. Martin et al. LC 78-10588. (Illus.). 212p. 1978. pap. 13. 95 (0-9602018-1-5) Nebraska Art.

Sheldon's Lunch. Bruce Lemerise. LC 94-11355. (Parents Magazine Press Read-Aloud Library). 1994. lib. bdg. 17. 27 (0-8368-0991-2) Gareth Stevens Inc.

Sheldon's Lunch. Bruce Lemerise. LC 80-10449. (Illus.). (J). (ps-3). 1980. 5.95 (0-8193-1025-5) Parents.

Sheldon's Major Stores & Chains. 111th ed. 1996. pap. 25. 00 (0-942239-13-9) P S & M Inc.

Sheldon's Major Stores & Chains. 112th ed. 1996. pap. 175.00 (0-942239-15-6) P S & M Inc.

Sheldon's Retail. 106th ed. 650p. 1996. 175.00 (0-685-55414-7) B Klein Pubns.

Shelee & Me: Journeys of Intimate Discovery. Paul D. Cohn. 392p. 1996. pap. 11.95 (0-9645876-3-7) Burns-Cole Pub.

Shelf Access in Libraries. Richard J. Hyman. LC 81-22764. (ALA Studies in Librarianship: No. 9). 190p. 1982. reprint ed. pap. 54.20 (0-7837-9680-3, 2060409) Bks Demand.

Shelf in Woop's Clothing. Mac Wellman. LC 88-43065. (New American Poetry Ser.: No. 4). 88p. 1990. pap. 8.95 (1-55713-035-3) Sun & Moon CA.

Shelf Life: A Key to Sharpening Your Competitive Edge: Proceedings. Food Processors Institute Staff. 64p. (Orig.). 1981. pap. 10.00 (0-937774-05-7) Food Processors.

Shelf Life: Essays, Memoirs, & an Interview. Thomas Gunn. LC 93-27163. (Poets on Poetry Ser.). 240p. 1993. 39.50 (0-472-09541-2); pap. 13.95 (0-472-06541-6) U of Mich Pr.

Shelf Life: Modern Packaging Design 1920-1945. Jerry Jankowski. (Illus.). 120p. 1992. pap. 16.95 (0-8118-0075-X) Chronicle Bks.

Shelf-Life Dating of Foods. Theodore P. Labuza. 500p. 1982. 77.00 (0-917678-14-1) Food & Nut Pr.

Shelf Life Studies of Foods & Beverages: Chemical, Biological, & Physical Aspects. Ed. by George Charalambous. LC 93-34767. (Developments in Food Science Ser.: No. 33). 1224p. 1993. 405.00 (0-444-89459-4) Elsevier.

Shelf Life Technology for Processed Foods. Dorothy Kroll. 160p. 1995. 2,750.00 (0-614-10908-6, GA-088) BCC.

Shelf List see Catalogs of the Scripps Institution of Oceanography Library

Shelf List of Documents, Reports & Translations Collection see Catalogs of the Scripps Institution of Oceanography Library

Shelf List of the Union Theological Seminary Library. Union Theological Seminary Library Staff. 1980. 1,075. 00 (0-8161-1306-8, Hall Library) G K Hall.

Shelf of Lincoln Books: A Critical, Selective Bibliography of Lincolniana. Paul M. Angle. LC 46-25256. 162p. reprint ed. pap. 46.20 (0-317-10291-5, 2050456) Bks Demand.

Shelf of Old Books. Annie Fields. (Notable American Authors Ser.). 1992. reprint ed. lib. bdg. 75.00 (0-7812-2825-5) Rprt Serv.

Shelf Sand & Sandstone Bodies: Geometry, Facies & Sequence Stratigraphy. D. P. Swift et al. (International Association of Sedimentologists Special Publication Ser.: No. 14). (Illus.). 544p. 1992. pap. 125.00 (0-632-03237-5) Blackwell Sci.

Shelf Sands & Sandstone Reservoirs. Roderick W. Tillman et al. (Short Course Notes Ser.: No. 13). 708p. 1985. pap. 49.00 (0-918985-57-9) SEPM.

Shelf-Stable & Refrigerated Microwaveable Meals. Ed. by Peter Allen. 149p. 1988. pap. 795.00 (0-941285-37-5) FIND-SVP.

***Shelf Talker.** Kilpatrick. 1997. pap. write for info. (0-684-00546-8, Touchstone Bks) S&S Trade.

Shelfbreak: Critical Interface on Continental Margins. Ed. by Daniel J. Stanley & George T. Moore. (Special Publications: No. 33). 467p. 1983. 33.50 (0-918985-13-7) SEPM.

Shelflife Evaluation of Foods. Ed. by Adrian Jones. Date not set. text ed. 129.00 (0-7514-0033-5, Blackie & Son-Chapman NY) Routledge Chapman & Hall.

Shell. Alex Arthur. LC 88-13449. (Eyewitness Bks.). (Illus.). 64p. (J). (gr. 5 up). 1989. 19.00 (0-394-82256-0) Knopf Bks Yng Read.

Shell. Alex Arthur. LC 88-13449. (Eyewitness Bks.). (Illus.). 64p. (J). (gr. 5 up). 1989. lib. bdg. 18.99 (0-394-92256-5) Knopf Bks Yng Read.

Shell Alps. (Baedeker-Shell Roadmaps Ser.). 6.95 (0-317-51998-0) P-H.

Shell & the Kernel: Renewals of Psychoanalysis. Nicolas Abraham & Maria Torok. Tr. by Nicholas T. Rand. LC 93-47621. (Illus.). 240p. 1994. pap. text ed. 15.95 (0-226-00088-5); lib. bdg. 40.00 (0-226-00087-7) U Ch Pr.

Shell & the Pearl. Roger White. 32p. 1985. pap. 3.00 (0-85398-205-8) G Ronald Pub.

Shell & Tube Heat Exchangers: Second Symposium: Proceedings of a Conference, 14-16 September 1981, Houston, TX. Symposium on Shell & Tube Heat Exchangers Staff. Ed. by William R. Apblett, Jr. LC 82-72486. (Materials-Metalworking Technology Ser.). (Illus.). 430p. reprint ed. pap. 122.60 (0-8357-3534-6, 2034324) Bks Demand.

Shell Art: A Handbook for Making Shell Flowers, Mosaics, Jewelry. rev. ed. Helen K. Krauss. LC 75-21356. (Illus.). 136p. 1976. reprint ed. pap. 4.95 (0-486-23255-7) Dover.

She'll Be Comin' Round the Mountain. Tom Birdseye & Debbie Birdseye. LC 92-37641. (Illus.). 32p. (J). (ps-3). 1994. lib. bdg. 15.95 (0-8234-1032-3) Holiday.

She'll Be Comin' Round the Mountain. Kathleen Bullock. LC 92-17340. (J). 1993. pap. 14.00 (0-671-79153-2, S&S Bks Young Read) S&S Childrens.

***She'll Be Coming Around the Mountain.** Emily Coplon et al. LC 96-30711. (Bank Street Ready-to-Read Bks.). (Illus.). 48p. (J). (ps-2). 1997. lib. bdg. 17.27 (0-8368-1689-7) Gareth Stevens Inc.

She'll Be Coming Round the Mountain. Emily Coplon et al. LC 93-20627. (Bank Street Ready-to-Read Ser.). (Illus.). 32p. (J). (gr. 4 up). 1994. pap. 3.99 (0-553-37340-4) Bantam.

Shell-Bearing Land Snails of Ohio. Celeste Taft. (Bulletin New Ser.: Vol. 1, No. 3). 1961. 4.00 (0-86727-045-4) Ohio Bio Survey.

Shell Book. Barbara H. Lember. LC 96-22172. (J). 1997. 14.95 (0-395-72030-3) HM.

Shell Book: A Complete Guide to Collecting & Identifying. 6th ed. Sandra D. Romashko. LC 76-360976. (Illus.). 64p. 1992. pap. 5.95 (0-89317-000-3) Windward Pub.

Shell Burst Pond. Richard E. Baker. (Illus.). 1982. pap. 3.00 (0-942648-02-1) Vardaman Pr.

Shell-Corner Method. Li Kung Shaw. LC 83-60572. 332p. 1984. Standard words ed. 30.00 (0-9607806-5-3); Xin hua words ed. write for info. (0-9607806-6-1) Li Kung Shaw.

Shell Craft. Virginie F. Elbert. LC 93-28187. (Illus.). 288p. 1993. reprint ed. pap. text ed. 8.95 (0-486-27730-5) Dover.

Shell Design: Circular Cylindrical Shells Engineered by the Beam Method. Richard Weingardt. LC 89-85337. 125p. (C). 1964. text ed. 50.00 (0-932446-49-3) Jacqueline Enter.

Shell Dredging & Its Influence on Gulf Coast Environments. Ed. by Arnold H. Bouma. LC 75-39416. (Illus.). 464p. reprint ed. pap. 132.30 (0-685-44465-1, 2032861) Bks Demand.

Shell Europe. write for info. (0-318-59695-4) S&S Trade.

Shell for Angela. Ofelia D. Lachtman. LC 94-36140. 208p. (Orig.). 1995. pap. 9.95 (1-55885-123-2) Arte Publico.

Shell from Cape Cod to Cape May: With Special Reference to the New York City Area. Morris K. Jacobson & W. K. Emerson. (Illus.). 1988. 15.25 (0-8446-6329-8) Peter Smith.

Shell Game. Melissa Crandall. Ed. by Dave Stern. (Star Trek Ser.: No. 63). 288p. 1993. mass mkt. 5.50 (0-671-79572-4) PB.

Shell Game: A True Account of Beads & Money in North America. Jerry Martien. 256p. (Orig.). 1996. pap. 14.95 (1-56279-080-3) Mercury Hse Inc.

Shell Game: A True Story of Banking, Spies, Lies, Politics - & the Arming of Saddam Hussein. Peter Mantius. LC 95-8564. 304p. 1995. 23.95 (0-312-13169-0) St Martin.

Shell Game: Reflections on Rowing & the Pursuit of Excellence. Stephen Kiesling. LC 82-22128. 200p. reprint ed. pap. 11.95 (0-9638461-9-1) Nordic Knight.

***Shell Gorgets: Styles of Late Prehistoric & Protohistoric Southeast.** Jeffrey P. Brain & Philip Phillips. (Illus.). 544p. 1996. pap. 79.95 (0-87365-812-4) Peabody Harvard.

Shell Guide to English Parish Churches. Robert Harbison. (Illus.). 306p. 1993. 34.95 (0-233-98793-2, Pub. by A Deutsch UK) Trafalgar.

Shell Guide to Ireland. rev. ed. Lord Killanin & Michael Duignan. (Illus.). 340p. 1995. pap. 20.00 (0-7171-2310-3, Pub. by Gill & MacMill IE) Irish Bks Media.

Shell Guide to the Gardens of England & Wales. Sarah Hollis. (Illus.). 367p. 1989. 39.95 (0-233-98391-0, Pub. by A Deutsch UK) Trafalgar.

Shell Guide to Yacht Navigation. Ed. by John Cotte. 128p. (C). 1987. 115.00 (0-571-14691-0, Pub. by Imray Laurie Norie & Wilson UK) St Mut.

Shell Hacker's Guide to X & Motif: Custom Power Tools & Window Manager Tricks. Alan Southerton. 382p. 1994. Book. pap. text ed. 34.95 (0-471-59722-8) Wiley.

Shell Hacker's Guide to X & Motif: Custom Power Tools & Window Manager Tricks. Alan Southerton. 382p. 1994. Incl. diskette. pap. text ed. 49.95 (0-471-59723-6); Diskette. disk 15.00 (0-471-30431-X) Wiley.

Shell-Heaps of the Lower Fraser River, British Columbia. Harlan I. Smith. LC 73-3519. (Jesup North Pacific Expedition. Publications: Vol. 2, Pt. 4). reprint ed. 37.50 (0-404-58120-X) AMS Pr.

Shell Mazes: An Educational-Activity Coloring Book. Spizzirri Publishing Co. Staff. (Illus.). 32p. (J). (gr. 1-8). 1989. pap. 1.25 (0-86545-145-1) Spizzirri.

Shell Model & Nuclear Structure: Where Do We Stand? Ed. by Aldo Covello. 668p. (C). 1989. text ed. 131.00 (9971-5-0757-9) World Scientific Pub.

Shell Money of the Slave Trade. Jan S. Hogendorn & Marion Johnson. (African Studies: No. 49). (Illus.). 230p. 1986. text ed. 80.00 (0-521-32086-0) Cambridge U Pr.

Shell Oil Co. A Report on the Company's Environmental Policies & Practices. (Illus.). 50p. (C). 1994. reprint ed. pap. text ed. 250.00 (0-7881-0983-9, Coun on Econ) DIANE Pub.

Shell Pilot to the English Channel. Tom Cunliffe. (Illus.). 350p. (C). 1995. text ed. 57.95 (0-85288-278-5, Pub. by Imray Laurie Norie & Wilson UK) Bluewater Bks.

Shell Process Foundry Practice. 164p. pap. 50.00 (0-87433-082-3, GM9204) Am Foundrymen.

Shell Process Foundry Practice. 2nd ed. 158p. 1973. 50.00 (0-317-32670-8, GM7311) Am Foundrymen.

Shell Scandinavia. (Baedeker-Shell Roadmaps Ser.). 6.95 (0-317-52003-2) P-H.

Shell Seekers. Rosamunde Pilcher. 560p. 1987. 23.95 (0-312-01058-3, Thomas Dunne Bks) St Martin.

***Shell Seekers.** Rosamunde Pilcher. 1997. 25.00 (0-312-17023-8) Thomas Dunne Bks.

Shell Seekers. Rosamunde Pilcher. 592p. 1989. reprint ed. mass mkt. 7.50 (0-440-20204-3) Dell.

***Shell Seekers, Vol. 1.** Pilcher. 1997. mass mkt. 7.99 (0-312-96132-4) St Martin.

Shell-Shock & Other Neuropsychiatric Problems Presented in Five Hundred & Eighty-Nine Case Histories from the War Literature, 1914-1918. Elmer E. Southard. LC 73-2416. (Mental Illness & Social Policy; the American Experience Ser.). 1973. reprint ed. 68.95 (0-405-05226-X) Ayer.

Shell Theory. F. I. Niordson. (Applied Mathematics & Mechanics Ser.: Vol. 29). 408p. 1985. 77.25 (0-444-87640-5, North Holland) Elsevier.

***Shell Theory.** Vekue. Date not set. pap. text ed. write for info. (0-273-08692-8) Addison-Wesley.

Shell Theory of the Nucleus. Eugene Feenberg. LC 54-9017. (Investigations in Physics Ser.: No. 3). 223p. reprint ed. pap. 63.60 (0-317-09267-7, 2000630) Bks Demand.

Shell Woman & the King: A Chinese Folktale. Illus. by Yang Ming-Yi. LC 92-9583. 32p. (J). (gr. k-3). 1993. pap. 13.89 (0-8037-1395-9) Dial Bks Young.

Shella. Andrew Vachss. 1994. pap. 12.00 (0-679-75681-7, Vin) Random.

***Shellcase.** Andrew Lansdale. 299p. (Orig.). 1997. mass mkt. 4.99 (1-55237-192-1, Pub. by Comnwlth Pub CN) Partners Pubs Grp.

Shellcraft Animals. Patricia Pope. LC 75-15906. (Short-Time Projects for Beginners Ser.). (Illus.). 32p. (Orig.). 1975. pap. 1.00 (0-8200-0507-X) Great Outdoors.

Shellcraft Critters. Kellum. (Short Time Projects for Beginners Ser.). (Illus.). 32p. 1977. pap. 1.00 (0-8200-0509-6) Great Outdoors.

Shellcraft Instruction. Marjorie Pelosi & Frank Pelosi. 80p. (Orig.). 1959. pap. 4.95 (0-8200-0501-0) Great Outdoors.

Shelley. David Pirie. (Open Guides to Literature Ser.). 128p. 1988. 75.00 (0-335-15091-8, Open Univ Pr); pap. 22.00 (0-335-15082-9, Open Univ Pr) Taylor & Francis.

***Shelley.** Tomalin. 1992. pap. text ed. write for info. (0-17-555984-8) Addison-Wesley.

S

Shelley. John A. Symonds. LC 68-58400. (English Men of Letters Ser.). reprint ed. 27.50 (*0-404-51732-3*) AMS Pr.

Shelley: A Critical Biography. George B. Smith. LC 73-16290. (Studies in Shelley: No. 25). 1974. lib. bdg. 75.00 (*0-8383-1727-8*) M S G Haskell Hse.

Shelley: A Critical Reading. Earl R. Wasserman. LC 70-138036. (Illus.). 512p. 1977. reprint ed. pap. 15.95 (*0-8018-2017-0*) Johns Hopkins.

Shelley: An Essay. Adolphus A. Jack. 1972. 35.00 (*0-8490-1048-9*) Gordon Pr.

Shelley: His Theory of Poetry. Melvin T. Solve. LC 75-30014. reprint ed. 34.50 (*0-404-14020-3*) AMS Pr.

Shelley: His Theory of Poetry. Melvin T. Solve. (BCL1-PR English Literature Ser.). 207p. 1992. reprint ed. lib. bdg. 79.00 (*0-7812-7657-8*) Rprt Serv.

Shelley: His Thought & Work. 3rd ed. Desmond G. King-Hele. LC 83-14242. 416p. 1984. 35.00 (*0-8386-3199-1*) Fairleigh Dickinson.

Shelley: Poems. Percy Bysshe Shelley. (Poetry Library). 320p. 1985. pap. 11.95 (*0-14-058504-4*, Penguin Bks) Viking Penguin.

Shelley: Poet & Legislator of the World. Ed. by Betty T. Bennett & Stuart Curran. 304p. 1996. text ed. 45.00 (*0-8018-5175-0*); pap. text ed. 15.95 (*0-8018-5176-9*) Johns Hopkins.

S

Shelley: Selected Poetry & Prose. Ed. by Alasdair MacRae. (English Texts Ser.). 256p. (C). 1991. pap. text ed. 14.95 (*0-415-01607-X*, A5370) Routledge.

Shelley: The Critical Heritage. Ed. by James E. Barcus. (Critical Heritage Ser.). 1975. 69.50 (*0-7100-8148-0*, RKP) Routledge.

Shelley: The Golden Years. Kenneth N. Cameron. LC 73-80566. 681p. reprint ed. pap. 180.00 (*0-7837-3865-X*, 2043687) Bks Demand.

Shelley: The Last Phase. Ivan Roe. LC 72-97078. (Illus.). 256p. 1973. reprint ed. lib. bdg. 53.50 (*0-8154-0464-6*) Cooper Sq.

Shelley: The Pursuit. Richard Holmes. 11.95 (*0-7043-3111-X*, Pub. by Quartet UK) Charles River Bks.

Shelley: The Pursuit. Richard Holmes. (Elizabeth Sifton Bks.). (Illus.). 848p. 1987. pap. 12.95 (*0-14-058037-9*, Penguin Bks) Viking Penguin.

Shelley--Alastor & Other Poems, Prometheus Unbound with Other Poems, Adonais. Ed. by P. H. Butter. (Illus.). 368p. 1980. reprint ed. pap. 13.95 (*0-7121-0145-4*) Trans-Atl Phila.

Shelley & Byron. Isabel Clarke. LC 74-118006. (English Literature Ser.: No. 33). 1970. reprint ed. lib. bdg. 75.00 (*0-8383-1062-1*) M S G Haskell Hse.

***Shelley & Greece: Rethinking Romantic Hellenism.** Jennifer Wallace. LC 96-49850. 1997. text ed. 49.95 (*0-312-16548-X*) St Martin.

***Shelley & His Audiences.** Stephen C. Behrendt. LC 88-31621. 309p. 1989. reprint ed. pap. 88.10 (*0-608-02689-1*, 2063342) Bks Demand.

Shelley & His Circle: Seventeen Seventy-Three to Eighteen Twenty-Two, 6 Vols. Incl. Vol. 1. . Percy Bysshe Shelley. LC 60-5393. (Illus.). l, 474p. 1961. (*0-318-53186-0*); Vols. 1 & 2. . Ed. by Kenneth N. Cameron. LC 60-5393. (Illus.). xvi, 545p. 1990. boxed 100.00 (*0-674-80610-7*); Vol. 3. . Ed. by Donald H. Reiman. LC 60-5393. (Illus.). xxxvi, 485p. 1970. (*0-318-53187-9*); Vols. 3 & 4. . Percy Bysshe Shelley. LC 60-5393. (Illus.). xviii, 529p. 1990. boxed 100.00 (*0-674-80611-5*); Vol. 3. . Percy Bysshe Shelley. LC 60-5393. (Illus.). 1990. boxed 100.00 (*0-674-80612-3*); Vols. 7 & 8. . Ed. by Donald J. Reiman. LC 60-5393. 1308p. 1990. boxed 122.00 (*0-674-80613-1*); LC 60-5393. (Carl H. Pforzheimer Library). write for info. (*0-318-53185-2*) HUP.

Shelley & His Friends in Italy. Helen R. Angeli. LC 72-3197. (Studies in Shelley: No. 25). 1972. reprint ed. lib. bdg. 75.00 (*0-8383-1539-9*) M S G Haskell Hse.

Shelley & His Poetry. Edward W. Edmunds. LC 76-52970. (Studies in Shelley: No. 25). 1977. lib. bdg. 39.95 (*0-8383-2124-0*) M S G Haskell Hse.

Shelley & Keats as They Struck Their Contemporaries. E. Blunden. LC 70-174689. (English Literature Ser.: No. 33). 1971. reprint ed. lib. bdg. 75.00 (*0-8383-1341-8*) M S G Haskell Hse.

Shelley, & Other Essays. George H. Cowling. LC 67-23198. (Essay Index Reprint Ser.). 1977. 19.95 (*0-8369-0344-7*) Ayer.

Shelley & the Chaos of History: A New Politics of Poetry. Hugh Roberts. LC 96-20029. (Literature & Philosophy Ser.). 1997. 75.00 (*0-271-01640-X*); pap. 25.00 (*0-271-01641-8*) Pa St U Pr.

Shelley & the Revolution in Taste: The Body & the Natural World. Timothy Morton. (Studies in Romanticism: No. 10). (Illus.). 320p. (C). 1995. text ed. 59.95 (*0-521-47135-4*) Cambridge U Pr.

Shelley & the Revolutionary Idea. Gerald McNiece. LC 75-88808. 317p. reprint ed. pap. 90.40 (*0-8357-9178-5*, 2011601) Bks Demand.

Shelley & the Romantic Revolution. F. Lea. LC 71-164028. (Studies in Shelley: No. 25). 1971. reprint ed. lib. bdg. 52.95 (*0-8383-1328-0*) M S G Haskell Hse.

Shelley & the Romantics. limited ed. Alan Catlin. 20p. (Orig.). 1994. 7.00 (*0-938566-64-4*) Adastra Pr.

Shelley & the Unromantics. Olwen W. Campbell. LC 68-1189. (Studies in Shelley: No. 25). 1969. reprint ed. lib. bdg. 75.00 (*0-8383-0652-7*) M S G Haskell Hse.

Shelley-Byron Conversation. William D. Brewer. LC 94-11299. 216p. 1994. lib. bdg. 39.95 (*0-8130-1300-3*) U Press Fla.

Shelley Correspondence in the Bodleian Library. Ed. by R. E. Hill. LC 75-30870. (Studies in Shelley: No. 25). 1975. lib. bdg. 75.00 (*0-8383-2101-1*) M S G Haskell Hse.

Shelley, Godwin, & Their Circle. Henry N. Brailsford. (BCL1-PR English Literature Ser.). 256p. 1992. reprint ed. lib. bdg. 79.00 (*0-7812-7093-6*) Rprt Serv.

Shelley II: Middle of My Century. Shelley Winters. Ed. by William Grose. (Illus.). 576p. 1990. reprint ed. mass mkt. 5.95 (*0-671-70142-8*) PB.

Shelley II: The Middle of My Century. Shelley Winters. 1989. 14.95 (*0-671-69320-4*) S&S Trade.

Shelley in America in the Nineteenth Century. Julia Power. LC 70-90370. 233p. (C). 1969. reprint ed. 50.00 (*0-87752-088-7*) Gordian.

Shelley in America in the Nineteenth Century. Julia Power. LC 65-15892. (Studies in Shelley: No. 25). 1969. reprint ed. lib. bdg. 75.00 (*0-8383-0611-X*) M S G Haskell Hse.

Shelley-Leigh Hunt: How Friendship Made History. Reginald Johnson. LC 72-3431. (Studies in Shelley: No. 25). 1972. reprint ed. lib. bdg. 56.95 (*0-8383-1536-4*) M S G Haskell Hse.

Shelley Library. Maurice B. Forman. LC 78-116794. (Studies in Shelley: No. 25). 1970. reprint ed. lib. bdg. 49.95 (*0-8383-1036-2*) M S G Haskell Hse.

Shelley Library. Thomas J. Wise. LC 78-122990. (Studies in Shelley: No. 25). 1970. reprint ed. lib. bdg. 75.00 (*0-8383-1123-7*) M S G Haskell Hse.

Shelley Library, an Essay in Bibliography. H. Buxton Forman. LC 74-30296. (Shelley Society, Fourth Ser.: No. 1). reprint ed. 29.50 (*0-404-11513-6*) AMS Pr.

Shelley Memorials. Jane G. Shelley. 1859. reprint ed. 24.00 (*0-403-00299-0*) Scholarly.

Shelley Memorials: From Authentic Sources. Jane G. Shelley. (BCL1-PR English Literature Ser.). 308p. 1992. reprint ed. lib. bdg. 89.00 (*0-7812-7656-X*) Rprt Serv.

***Shelley on Love.** Richard Holmes. Date not set. 36.00 (*0-85646-063-X*, Pub. by Anvil Press UK) Dufour.

***Shelley on Love.** Richard Holmes. 248p. 1980. pap. 21.95 (*0-85646-101-6*, Pub. by Anvil Press UK) Dufour.

Shelley Poetry Pros. Cameron. (C). 1951. pap. text ed. 25.00 (*0-03-008100-9*) HB Coll Pubs.

Shelley Primer. Henry S. Salt. LC 74-30299. (Shelley Society, Fourth Ser.: No. 4). reprint ed. 29.50 (*0-404-11516-0*) AMS Pr.

Shelley Society's Papers: Papers Read Before the Society & Abstracts of Any Not Fully Reported. Shelley Society, London Staff. (First Ser.: No. 1). reprint ed. 60.00 (*0-404-11501-2*) AMS Pr.

Shelley, the Hyperactive Turtle. Deborah Moss. LC 88-40248. (Illus.). 24p. (J). (gr. k up). 1989. lib. bdg. 12.95 (*0-933149-31-X*) Woodbine House.

Shelley the Man & the Poet. Arthur Clutton-Brock. 1977. 18.95 (*0-8369-7106-X*, 7940) Ayer.

Shelleyan Eros: The Rhetoric of Romantic Love. William A. Ulmer. (Illus.). 201p. (C). 1990. text ed. 29.50 (*0-691-06829-1*) Princeton U Pr.

Shelley's Adonais: A Critical Edition. Anthony D. Knerr. LC 83-7451. 360p. 1984. text ed. 40.00 (*0-231-05466-1*) Col U Pr.

Shelley's Ambivalence. Christine Gallant. LC 88-26379. 224p. 1989. text ed. 45.00 (*0-312-02471-1*) St Martin.

***Shelley's Annus Mirabilis: The Maturing of an Epic Vision.** Stuart Curran. LC 75-318514. (Illus.). 277p. 1975. reprint ed. pap. 79.00 (*0-608-03173-9*, 2063626) Bks Demand.

Shelley's "Charles the First" Notebook, Vol. XII, No. E.17. Contrib. by Nora Crook. LC 90-21087. (Bodleian Shelley Manuscripts). 910313p. 1991. text ed. 185.00 (*0-8240-5871-2*) Garland.

Shelley's Critical Prose. Percy Bysshe Shelley. Ed. by Bruce R. McElderry, Jr. LC 66-19856. (Regents Critics Ser.). 207p. reprint ed. pap. 59.00 (*0-318-34733-4*, 2031990) Bks Demand.

Shelley's "Devils" Notebook, Vol. XIV, No. E.9. Ed. by Timothy Webb. (Bodleian Shelley Manuscripts). 930722p. 1992. text ed. 210.00 (*0-8240-5898-4*) Garland.

Shelley's Eccentricities. Carl H. Grabo. LC 50-63247. 84p. 1982. reprint ed. lib. bdg. 27.00 (*0-89370-732-5*) Borgo Pr.

Shelley's First Love: The Love Story of Percy Bysshe Shelley & Harriet Grove. Desmond Hawkins. (Illus.). xviii, 162p. (C). 1992. lib. bdg. 29.50 (*0-208-02363-1*, Archon Bks) Shoe String.

Shelley's Goddess. Barbara C. Gelpi. (Illus.). 336p. 1992. 55.00 (*0-19-507383-5*) OUP.

Shelley's Goddess: Maternity, Language, Subjectivity. Barbara C. Gelpi. (Illus.). 336p. 1992. pap. 24.00 (*0-19-507384-3*) OUP.

Shelley's Heart. Charles McCarry. 1996. pap. 6.99 (*0-449-22168-7*) Fawcett.

Shelley's Heart. Charles McCarry. 1997. mass mkt. 6.99 (*0-8041-1474-9*) Ivy Books.

Shelley's Heart: A Novel. Charles McCarry. 1995. 23.00 (*0-679-41533-5*) Random.

Shelley's Hymn of Pan: Music Composed March 1864. P. Florence Shelley. LC 74-30280. (Shelley Society, Extra Ser.: No. 3). reprint ed. 22.50 (*0-404-11521-7*) AMS Pr.

Shelley's Idols of the Cave. Peter Butter. LC 68-24118. (Studies in Shelley: No. 25). 1969. reprint ed. lib. bdg. 75.00 (*0-8383-0781-7*) M S G Haskell Hse.

Shelley's Italian Experience. Alan M. Weinberg. LC 91-12029. 280p. 1991. text ed. 55.00 (*0-312-06584-1*) St Martin.

Shelley's Last Notebook: Bodleian MSS Shelley Adds, Nos. e.15 & e.20. 9,003th ed. Contrib. by Donald H. Reiman. (Bodleian Shelley Manuscripts: Vol. VII). 665p. 1990. text ed. 195.00 (*0-8240-6983-8*) Garland.

Shelley's Lost Letters to Harriet. Percy Bysshe Shelley. LC 74-7113. (Studies in Shelley: No. 25). 1974. lib. bdg. 46.95 (*0-8383-1925-4*) M S G Haskell Hse.

Shelley's Major Verse: The Narrative & Dramatic Poetry. Stuart M. Sperry. LC 87-35923. (Illus.). 272p. 1988. 37.50 (*0-674-80625-5*) HUP.

Shelley's Pisan Winter Notebook, 1820-1821: A Facsimile of Bodleian MS Shelley Adds. E. 8, No. e.8. Contrib. by Carlene A. Adamson. LC 91-43949. (Bodleian Shelley Manuscripts: Vol. VI). 568p. 1992. text ed. 95.00 (*0-8240-6982-X*) Garland.

Shelley's Platonic Answer to a Platonic Attack on Poetry. Joseph E. Baker. 72p. 1965. pap. 10.00 (*0-87745-006-4*) U of Iowa Pr.

***Shelley's Poetry.** Ed. by Haines. LC 96-27679. 1997. text ed. 59.95 (*0-312-16551-X*) St Martin.

Shelley's Poetry & Prose. Percy Bysshe Shelley. Ed. by Donald H. Reiman. LC 76-26929. (Critical Editions Ser.). (C). 1977. pap. text ed. 15.95 (*0-393-09164-3*) Norton.

Shelley's Principles. Henry S. Salt. LC 76-57707. (Studies in Shelley: No. 25). 1977. lib. bdg. 33.95 (*0-8383-2161-5*) M S G Haskell Hse.

Shelley's Principles: Has Time Refuted or Confirmed Them? Henry S. Salt. 1972. 59.95 (*0-8490-1049-7*) Gordon Pr.

Shelley's Prose. Ed. by David L. Clark. LC 54-6517. 1954. 20.00 (*0-8263-0015-4*) Lib Soc Sci.

***Shelley's Quest.** Evelyn Malloy & Dean Addison. LC 95-90899. (Illus.). 64p. (Orig.). (J). 1997. pap. 9.00 (*1-56002-627-8*, Univ Edtns) Aegina Pr.

Shelley's Satire: Violence, Exhortation, & Authority. Steven E. Jones. LC 93-45747. 250p. (C). 1994. lib. bdg. 30.00 (*0-87580-186-2*) N Ill U Pr.

Shelley's Style. William Keach. 269p. (C). 1985. text ed. 32.50 (*0-416-30320-X*, NO. 4149) Routledge Chapman & Hall.

Shelley's Vegetarianism. William E. Axon. LC 79-116789. (Studies in Shelley: No. 25). 1971. reprint ed. lib. bdg. 39.95 (*0-8383-1031-1*) M S G Haskell Hse.

Shelley's Venomed Melody. Nora Crook & Derek Guiton. (Illus.). 288p. 1986. text ed. 75.00 (*0-521-32084-4*) Cambridge U Pr.

Shelley's 1819-1821 Huntington Notebook, Vol. VI, No. HM 2176. Contrib. by Mary A. Quinn. LC 83-49271. (Manuscripts of the Younger Romantics & the Bodleian Shelley Manuscripts). 484p. 1994. 195.00 (*0-8240-5870-4*, SSSHELL) Garland.

Shellfish. Joanne Van Roden. 36p. (Orig.). 1981. pap. 3.25 (*0-940844-01-X*) Wellspring.

Shellfish. Ed. by Chuck Williams. (Williams-Sonoma Kitchen Library). (Illus.). 108p. 17.95 (*0-7835-0305-9*) Time-Life.

Shellfish: A Guide to Oysters, Mussels, Scallops, Clams & Similar Products for the Commercial User. Ian Dore. LC 90-48601. (Illus.). 272p. (gr. 13). 1991. text ed. 87.95 (*0-442-00203-3*) Chapman & Hall.

Shellfish: A Particular Palate Cookbook. Michele Scicolone. 1989. pap. 6.95 (*0-517-57337-7*, Harmony) Crown Pub Group.

Shellfish & Public Health: Lead, Cadmium, Chromium, Arsenic, & Nickel in Shellfish. Michael A. Adams et al. (Illus.). 212p. (Orig.). (C). 1994. pap. text ed. 50.00 (*0-7881-0588-4*) DIANE Pub.

Shellfish & Seaweed Harvests on Puget Sound. Daniel P. Cheney & Thomas F. Mumford, Jr. (Illus.). 180p. 1984. pap. 8.95 (*0-295-95990-8*) U of Wash Pr.

Shelling Peanuts: And Other Odd Odes. Howard Nelson. 118p. (Orig.). 1996. pap. 5.00 (*1-57502-240-0*, P0913) Morris Pubng.

Shelling San Sal. Betty Lawson. (Illus.). 63p. (Orig.). 1993. pap. text ed. 12.00 (*0-935909-44-3*) Bahamian.

Shellmounds of the San Francisco Bay Region. fac. ed. N. C. Nelson. (University of California Publications in American Archaeology & Ethnology: Vol. 7: 4). 51p. (C). 1909. reprint ed. pap. text ed. 4.70 (*1-55567-178-0*) Coyote Press.

Shells. LC 91-60532. (What's Inside? Ser.). (Illus.). 24p. (J). (ps-3). 1991. 8.95 (*1-879431-10-6*) DK Pub Inc.

Shells. R. Tucker Abbott. (Illus.). 160p. 1989. 19.99 (*0-517-68850-6*) Random Hse Value.

Shells. Catherine Chambers. (Would You Believe It! Ser.). 1996. lib. bdg. 19.97 (*0-8172-4101-9*) Raintree Steck-V.

Shells. Jennifer Coldrey. LC 92-54311. (Eyewitness Explorers Ser.). (Illus.). 64p. (J). (gr. 3 up). 1993. 9.95 (*1-56458-229-9*) DK Pub Inc.

Shells. Dance. 1995. 12.98 (*0-8317-1886-2*) Smithmark.

Shells. S. Peter Dance. LC 91-58223. (Eyewitness Handbks.). (Illus.). 300p. 1992. 29.95 (*1-56458-032-6*); pap. 17.95 (*1-56458-060-1*) DK Pub Inc.

***Shells.** Mary Maguire. (New Crafts Ser.). (Illus.). 96p. 1997. 14.95 (*1-85967-376-7*, Lorenz Bks) Anness Pub.

Shells. Clare Nicholson. (Design Motifs Ser.). (Illus.). 64p. 1996. 9.95 (*1-85967-149-7*, Lorenz Bks) Anness Pub.

Shells. Graham Saunders. (Spotter's Guides Ser.). (Illus.). 64p. (YA). (gr. 8 up). 1993. pap. 4.95 (*0-86020-454-5*, Usborne) EDC.

Shells. Fred Woodward. 1993. 6.98 (*1-55521-841-5*) Bk Sales Inc.

Shells: Jewels from the Sea. M. G. Harasewych. (Illus.). 224p. 1996. 19.98 (*1-56138-766-5*) Courage Bks.

Shells: Jewels of the Sea. Leonard Hill. 1996. 75.00 (*0-88363-595-X*) H L Levin.

Shells - Classic Natural History Prints. S. Peter Dance & David Heppell. (Illus.). 128p. 1991. 35.00 (*1-85170-392-6*) Am Malacologists.

Shells & Insects: Alaska Sea Week Curriculum Series Grade 2. C. Kelsey et al. (Report Ser.: No. 84-04). (Illus.). 169p. 1984. teacher ed., pap. 12.50 (*1-56612-016-0*) AK Sea Grant CP.

Shells for Pathfinders: A Basic Youth Enrichment Skill Honor Packet. L. S. Gattis, III. (Illus.). 26p. (Orig.). (J). (gr. 5 up). 1989. teacher ed., pap. 5.00 (*0-936241-47-0*) Cheetah Pub.

***Shells from the Sands of Time: 1876 Edition.** Rosina B. Lytton. Ed. & Intro. by Marie M. Roberts. (Her Write His Name Ser.). 272p. 1996. reprint ed. pap. write for info. (*1-85506-386-7*) Bks Intl VA.

Shell's Golf Guide to Greater Houston. 2nd ed. Kevin Newberry. (Illus.). 484p. 1993. pap. 14.95 (*1-883369-02-9*) Twnty-Frst Media.

Shells of Hawai'i. E. Alison Kay & Olive Schoenberg-Dole. LC 91-2710. (Illus.). 96p. 1991. pap. 12.95 (*0-8248-1316-2*) UH Pr.

Shells of North American Shores. Katherine S. Orr. (NaturEncyclopedia Library). (Illus.). 48p. (Orig.). 1989. pap. 5.95 (*0-88045-097-5*) Stemmer Hse.

Shells of Revolution: Developments in Civil Engineering, No. 30. Z. E. Mazurkiewicz & R. T. Nagorski. 640p. 1991. 272.50 (*0-444-98779-7*) Elsevier.

Shells of the Florida Coast. rev. ed. Frances W. Hall. 32p. 1979. pap. 2.95 (*0-8200-0207-0*) Great Outdoors.

Shells Stained Glass Coloring Book. John Green. (Illus.). (J). (gr. k-3). 1993. pap. 1.00 (*0-486-27530-2*) Dover.

Shells, Whales, & Fish Tales: Science in Art, Song, & Play. Rhonda Vansant & Barbara L. Dondiego. (Illus.). 1995. pap. text ed. 12.95 (*0-07-017915-8*) McGraw.

Shellshock. Richard S. Prather. 352p. 1988. pap. 3.95 (*0-8125-0783-5*) Tor Bks.

***Shellsong.** large type ed. Rowan Edwards. (Linford Romance Library). 304p. 1996. pap. 15.99 (*0-7089-7903-3*) Ulverscroft.

Shelly & Nonviolence. Art Young. (Studies in English Literature: No. 103). 174p. (Orig.). 1975. pap. text ed. 38.50 (*90-279-3031-7*) Mouton.

Shelly His Thought & Work. 27.50 (*0-8386-1022-6*) Fairleigh Dickinson.

Shel's Sister. Terrence Ortwein. 1994. 3.00 (*0-87129-476-1*, S32) Dramatic Pub.

Shelta - Bearlagair Na Saer Vocabularies. Intro. by Jean Hunt. 46p. 1991. pap. 15.00 (*0-9626812-3-7*) Hunt Asso LA.

***Shelter.** Cecil Fernando. (Illus.). 48p. 1997. pap. 9.95 (*1-56163-190-6*, Comics Lit) NBM.

Shelter. Laura Jensen. LC 85-12861. 120p. 1985. pap. 7.00 (*0-937872-29-6*) Dragon Gate.

Shelter. Jayne Anne Phillips. 336p. 1995. pap. 11.95 (*0-385-31389-6*, Delta) Dell.

Shelter. Jayne Anne Phillips. LC 94-8391. 1994. 21.95 (*0-395-48890-7*) HM.

Shelter. Shelter Publications Staff. Ed. by Lloyd Kahn. LC 90-60125. (Illus.). 176p. 1995. pap. 20.00 (*0-679-76948-X*) Shelter Pubns.

Shelter: Hanging Moon, No. 2. Paul Ledd. 256p. (Orig.). 1980. mass mkt. 1.95 (*0-89083-637-X*, Zebra Kensgtn) Kensgtn Pub Corp.

Shelter: Human Habitats from Around the World. Charles Knevitt. LC 95-71975. 168p. 1996. pap. 29.95 (*0-87654-600-9*) Pomegranate Calif.

Shelter: Need & Response - Housing, Land, & Settlement Policies in Seventeen Third World Nations. Jorge E. Hardoy & David Satterthwaite. LC 80-41417. (Illus.). 302p. reprint ed. pap. 86.10 (*0-685-44485-6*, 2031495) Bks Demand.

Shelter: Savage Night, No. 15. Paul Ledd. 1983. mass mkt. 2.25 (*0-685-07875-2*, Zebra Kensgtn) Kensgtn Pub Corp.

Shelter: Wichita Gunman, No. 16. Paul Ledd. 1983. pap. 2.25 (*0-8217-1299-3*, Zebra Kensgtn) Kensgtn Pub Corp.

Shelter Affordability for Blacks: Crisis or Clamor? Wilhelmina A. Leigh. 90p. (Orig.). 1982. pap. 18.95 (*0-87855-901-9*) Transaction Pubs.

***Shelter & Service Issues for Aging Populations: International Perspectives.** Leon A. Pastalan. LC 97-16059. 207p. 1997. 49.95 (*0-7890-0314-7*) Haworth Pr.

Shelter & Shade: Creating a Healthy & Profitable Environment for Your Livestock with Trees. John Mortimer & Bunny Mortimer. LC 96-18694. (Illus.). 160p. 1996. pap. 20.00 (*0-9632460-4-6*) Green Park.

Shelter & Subsidies: Who Benefits from Federal Housing Policies? Henry J. Aaron. LC 72-306. (Brookings Institution Studies in Social Experimentation). 254p. reprint ed. pap. 72.40 (*0-317-30177-2*, 2025359) Bks Demand.

Shelter & the Family. Bearl Brooks. (Social Studies Ser.). 24p. (gr. 4-6). 1976. student ed. 5.00 (*0-8209-0249-7*, SS-16) ESP.

***Shelter Blues: Sanity & Selfhood among the Homeless.** Robert R. Desjarlais. LC 97-8656. (Contemporary Ethnography Ser.). 1997. write for info. (*0-8122-3407-3*); pap. write for info. (*0-8122-1622-9*) U of Pa Pr.

***Shelter Cats.** Karen Commings. 1998. 12.95 (*0-87605-676-1*) Howell Bk.

Shelter Folks. Virginia L. Kroll. (Illus.). 40p. 1995. pap. 7.00 (*0-8028-5131-2*) Eerdmans.

Shelter Folks. Virginia L. Kroll. LC 95-13431. (Illus.). 40p. (J). (gr. 1-3). 1995. 15.00 (*0-8028-5106-1*) Eerdmans.

Shelter for the Rural Poor. J. P. John & N. Sridharan. (C). 1992. 19.50 (*81-7024-458-7*, Pub. by Ashish II) S Asia.

***Shelter for the Spirit: How to Make Your Home a Haven in a Hectic World.** Victoria Moran. 240p. 1997. 20.00 (*0-06-017415-3*) HarpC.

Shelter for the Spiritually Homeless. Donna E. Schaper. 96p. (Orig.). 1995. pap. 8.99 (*0-8272-3434-1*) Chalice Pr.

Shelter from Compassion. Ruth E. Durr. LC 56-6375. (Orig.). 1956. pap. 3.00 (*0-87574-087-1*) Pendle Hill.

Shelter from the Storm. Betty Dellacorte. 306p. 1985. pap. 9.95 (*0-933843-00-3*) Villa Pr AZ.

***Shelter from the Storm.** Anthony P. Dunbar. LC 97-10844. 1997. write for info. (*0-399-14301-7*) Putnam Pub Group.

Shelter from the Storm. Patricia Rice. 384p. (Orig.). 1993. pap. 4.99 (*0-451-40358-4*, Onyx) NAL-Dutton.

***Shelter from the Storm.** Maris Soule. (Loveswept Ser.: Vol. 859). 1997. mass mkt. 3.50 (*0-553-44595-2*, Loveswept) Bantam.

An Asterisk (*) at the beginning of an entry indicates that the title is appearing in BIP for the first time.

Shelter Hill: An Analysis of Faunal Remains & Artifacts from a Marin County Shellmound (04-MRN-14) Lynn M. Riley. xiv, 206p. (C). 1985. reprint ed. pap. text ed. 20.15 (*1-55567-014-8*) Coyote Press.

Shelter, Home & Housing Self-Sufficiency References in American Literature. Center for Self-Sufficiency, Research Division Staff. 60p. 1985. pap. text ed. 9.95 (*0-910811-41-5*) Ctr Self Suff.

Shelter, Housing, & Homes: A Social Right. Arnold Bennett. LC 95-79357. 193p. 1996. 48.99 (*1-55164-043-0*, Pub. by Black Rose Bks CN); pap. 19.99 (*1-55164-042-2*, Pub. by Black Rose Bks CN) Consort Bk Sales.

Shelter in His Arms. Elane Osborn. (Intimate Moments Ser.). 1995. mass mkt. 3.75 (*0-373-07642-8*, 1-07642-1) Silhouette.

Shelter in India. Aromar Revi. 1990. text ed. 27.95 (*0-7069-4937-4*, Pub. by Vikas II) S Asia.

Shelter in Saudi Arabia. Kaizer Talib. 144p. 1984. pap. 19.50 (*0-312-71693-1*) St Martin.

***Shelter in the Forest.** Karen R. Schultz. Ed. by Kjellberg Printers. (Illus.). 44p. (J). (gr. 4-6). 1997. 13.95 (*0-912868-00-7*) Inner Space.

Shelter in the Light: Poetry of the Islamic Awakening. Ed. by Nura Kly. 108p. (Orig.). 1996. pap. 9.95 (*0-932863-11-6*) Clarity Pr.

Shelter Inspector (Civil Defense) Jack Rudman. (Career Examination Ser.: C-737). 1994. pap. 34.95 (*0-8373-0737-6*) Nat Learn.

Shelter Investment: A Step-by-Step Approach to Make Buying a Home Easy. 15.95 (*0-318-20249-2*) UWIM CCA.

Shelter Island & Presbyterian Church. Jacob E. Mallmann. 1976. 25.95 (*0-8488-0874-6*) Amereon Ltd.

***Shelter Island, NY.** L. Green. (Images of America Ser.). 1997. pap. 16.99 (*0-7524-0491-1*, Arcdia) Chalford.

***Shelter of Each Other.** Mary Pipher. 1997. pap. 12.95 (*0-345-40603-6*) Ballantine.

Shelter of Each Other: Rebuilding Our Families. Mary Pipher. 288p. 1996. 24.95 (*0-399-14144-8*, Grosset-Putnam) Putnam Pub Group.

Shelter of Her Arms. Jean Barrett. (Intrigue Ser.). 1995. pap. 2.99 (*0-373-22308-0*, 1-22308-0) Harlequin Bks.

Shelter of His Wings. Joan W. Brown. (Illus.). 64p. 1994. 8.95 (*0-8378-7688-5*) Gibson.

Shelter of One's Own. Spencer. LC 90-72118. 50p. 1992. pap. 5.95 (*1-55523-421-6*) Winston-Derek.

Shelter Poverty: New Ideas on Housing Affordability. Michael E. Stone. LC 92-32768. 352p. (C). 1993. 59.95 (*1-56639-050-8*); pap. 19.95 (*1-56639-092-3*) Temple U Pr.

***Shelter Provision & Employment Generation.** xxii, 249p. 1995. pap. 27.00 (*92-2-108523-6*) Intl Labour Office.

Shelter, Settlement & Development. Ed. by Lloyd Rodwin. LC 87-1038. 448p. (C). 1987. text ed. 39.95 (*0-04-711023-6*) Routledge Chapman & Hall.

Shelter, Sign & Symbol. Ed. by Paul Oliver. LC 77-77089. (Illus.). 1977. 40.00 (*0-87951-068-4*) Overlook Pr.

Shelter, Sign & Symbol. Ed. by Paul Oliver. LC 77-77089. (Illus.). 1980. pap. 16.95 (*0-87951-112-5*) Overlook Pr.

Shelter the Pilgrim. Fred Licht. (Classic Short Stories Ser.). 48p. (J). (gr. 6). 1990. lib. bdg. 13.95 (*0-88682-307-2*) Creative Ed.

Shelter What You Make Minimize the Take. Beverly Tanner et al. 1983. 36.95 (*0-8359-6999-1*, Reston) P-H.

Shelter, Woman, & Development: First & Third World Perspectives. Hemalata C. Dandekar. 1993. pap. 37.50 (*0-911586-96-2*) Wahr.

Sheltered Accommodations for Elderly People in an International Perspective. Ed. by G. Dooghe. (NIDI-CBGS Publications, Population & Family Study Center Ser.: Vol. 29). xii, 152p. 1993. pap. 26.75 (*90-265-1352-6*) Swets.

***Sheltered by God's Love: 52 Bible Lessons for Senior Adults.** Morton B. King. LC 96-37714. 176p. 1997. pap. 9.95 (*0-687-04795-1*) Abingdon.

Sheltered by Islands: New & Selected Poems 1985-1995. Daniel T. Moran. LC 95-95187. (Orig.). 1995. pap. text ed. 15.00 (*0-9629221-2-9*) D T Moran.

***Sheltered Content Instruction.** Echevarria & Graves. 1997. pap. text ed. 26.00 (*0-205-16874-4*) P-H.

Sheltered English: Teaching Handbook. Linda Gonzales & Dan Watson. (Illus.). 69p. (Orig.). (C). 1992. pap. text ed. 11.00 (*0-942787-05-6*) Binet Intl.

Sheltered English Training Manual. L. Gonzales & D. Watson. (Illus.). 200p. (C). 1992. write for info. (*0-942787-34-X*) Binet Intl.

Sheltered Housing for the Elderly. Alan Butler et al. 1983. 80.00 (*0-317-54602-3*, Pub. by Natl Inst Soc Work) St Mut.

Sheltered Housing for the Elderly: Policy, Practice & the Consumer. Alan Butler et al. (National Institute Social Services Library: No. 44). 1983. text ed. 34.95 (*0-04-362055-8*) Routledge Chapman & Hall.

Sheltered Land. Xavier Pons. 368p. 1995. pap. 29.95 (*1-86373-639-5*, Pub. by Allen Unwin AT) Paul & Co Pubs.

Sheltered Life. Harry Dean. LC 91-4431. v, 37p. (Orig.). 1991. pap. 5.00 (*0-926487-09-4*) Rowan Mtn Pr.

Sheltered Life. Ellen Glasgow. LC 93-41095. 352p. (C). 1994. pap. 12.95 (*0-8139-1514-7*) U Pr of Va.

***Sheltered Nest.** Sean Dunne. 58p. 1992. pap. 12.95 (*1-85235-084-9*) Dufour.

***Sheltered Quarter.** Hamza Bogary. Ed. by Salma K. Jayyusi. Tr. by Olive Kenny. 141p. 1996. pap. 9.95 (*0-614-21653-2*, 1129) Kazi Pubns.

Sheltered Quarter: A Tale of a Boyhood in Mecca. Hamza Bogary. Ed. by Salma Jayyusi. Tr. by Kenny Reed et al. from ARA. (Modern Middle Eastern Literature in Translation Ser.). 141p. (Orig.). 1992. pap. 8.95 (*0-292-72752-6*) U of Tex Pr.

Sheltering Arms Hospital: One Hundred Years of Caring. Anne R. Lower. (Illus.). 100p. (Orig.). 1989. pap. (*0-318-65239-0*); lib. bdg. 20.00 (*0-685-26159-X*) Sheltering Arms.

Sheltering Rebecca. Mary Baylis-White. 112p. (J). (gr. 5-9). 1993. pap. 3.99 (*0-14-036448-X*, Puffin) Puffin Bks.

Sheltering Sky. Paul Bowles. 1991. pap. 9.95 (*0-685-48186-7*, Vin) Random.

Sheltering Sky. Paul Bowles. (Vintage International Ser.). 1990. pap. 13.00 (*0-679-72979-8*, Vin) Random.

Sheltering the Jews: Stories of Holocaust Rescuers. Mordecai Paldiel. 1995. pap. 16.00 (*0-8006-2897-7*) Augsburg Fortress.

Sheltering Tree. Mary A. Whitley. LC 84-27100. 90p. 1985. 11.95 (*0-8027-6587-4*) Walker & Co.

Shelters, Shacks & Shanties. D. C. Beard. LC 87-82272. 272p. 1987. reprint ed. pap. text ed. 9.95 (*0-915179-69-5*) Loompanics.

Sheltie Talk. 2nd ed. Betty J. McKinney. LC 75-45831. (Illus.). 320p. 1985. 34.95 (*0-931866-17-0*) Alpine Pubns.

Shelton: A History of the Shelton Family of England & America. M. C. Whitaker. (Illus.). 275p. 1995. reprint ed. pap. 43.00 (*0-8328-4838-7*); reprint ed. lib. bdg. 53.00 (*0-8328-4837-9*) Higginson Bk Co.

Shelton: The First Century Plus Ten. abr. rev. ed. Fredi Perry & Berwyn B. Thomas. (Illus.). 112p. 1996. lib. bdg. 20.00 (*0-935693-17-3*) Mason Cty Hist.

Shelton Conspiracy. large type ed. Rae Foley. LC 93-26720. 1993. lib. bdg. 18.95 (*0-7862-0026-X*) Thorndike Pr.

Shelton, Washington: The First Century, 1885-1985. 2nd ed. Berwyn B. Thomas. LC 85-21653. (Illus.). 88p. 1987. 11.95 (*0-935693-06-8*) Mason Cty Hist.

Shelton Wininger & Pace Families. Alvin Casey & Robert B. Casey. LC 87-71662. (Illus.). 600p. 1987. 40.00 (*0-9619051-0-7*) Brooks TX.

Shelton's Barefoot Airlines. Phillip Schleit. Ed. by Anthony Drummond. LC 82-70498. (Illus.). 148p. 1982. pap. 8.95 (*0-942720-01-6*) Fishergate.

Shelves & Cabinets. Time-Life Books Editors. LC 95-983. (Home Repair & Improvement Ser.). (Illus.). 128p. 1995. 14.95 (*0-7835-3883-9*) Time-Life.

Shelves, Closets & Cabinets. Peter Jones. LC 77-83698. (Illus.). 304p. (Orig.). 1987. pap. 17.95 (*0-943822-96-3*) Sterling.

***Shelving & Storage.** Creative Homeowner Press Staff. (Quick Guide Ser.). 1997. pap. text ed. 7.95 (*1-880029-91-X*) Creative Homeowner.

Shem, Ham & Japheth: The Papers of W. O. Tuggle, Comprising His Indian Diary, Sketches & Observations, Myths & Washington Journal in the Territory & at the Capital, 1879-1882. William O. Tuggle. Ed. by Eugene Current-Garcia. LC 68-55755. 372p. reprint ed. pap. 106.10 (*0-318-34883-7*, 2031194) Bks Demand.

Shema & Company. rev. ed. Joel L. Grishaver. (Shema Is for Real Ser.). (Illus.). (J). (gr. 5-8). 1991. student ed. 6.95 (*0-933873-62-X*) Torah Aura.

Shema Is For Real. Joel L. Grishaver. (Illus.). 128p. (Orig.). (YA). 1994. pap. text ed. 7.50 (*0-933873-35-2*) Torah Aura.

Shema Is for Real Lab Book. Joel L. Grishaver. (Illus.). 163p. 1988. pap. 6.50 (*0-933873-34-4*) Torah Aura.

Shema Yisroel: The Three Portions of the Shema Including the Bedtime Shema. Meir Zlotowitz. (ArtScroll Mesorah Ser.). 64p. 1982. 9.99 (*0-89906-187-7*); pap. 5.99 (*0-89906-188-5*) Mesorah Pubns.

Shemirath Shabbath, Vol 1. Rabbi Yehoshja Y. Neuwirth. Tr. by W. Grangewood from HEB. 360p. 1984. 19.95 (*0-87306-298-1*); pap. 16.95 (*0-87306-375-9*) Feldheim.

Shemirath Shabbath, Vol. 2. 1989. 19.95 (*0-87306-477-1*); pap. 16.95 (*0-87306-478-X*) Feldheim.

Shemittah & Yobel. I. Grunfeld. 151p. 1986. pap. 7.95 (*0-900689-91-9*) Soncino Pr.

Shemois, Vol 6. Menachem M. Schneerson. (Likkutei Sichos Ser.). 420p. (HEB & YID.). reprint ed. 15.00 (*0-8266-5724-9*) Kehot Pubn Soc.

Shemoneh Esrei. A. C. Feuer. 1990. 19.99 (*0-89906-603-8*); pap. 16.99 (*0-89906-604-6*) Mesorah Pubns.

Shemoneh Essre: Las Dieciocho Bendiciones. R. Amram Amselem. 350p. (SPA.). 1993. write for info. (*1-883932-27-0*) A Amselem.

Shemoneh Essre: Las Dieciocho Bendiciones. deluxe ed. R. Amram Amselem. 350p. (SPA.). 1993. write for info. (*1-883932-26-2*) A Amselem.

Shemos, Vol. 21. Menachem M. Schneerson. (Likkutei Sichos Ser.). 521p. (HEB & YID.). Date not set. reprint ed. 15.00 (*0-8266-5739-7*) Kehot Pubn Soc.

Shemos, Vol. 26. Menachem M. Schneerson. (Likkutei Sichos Ser.). 462p. (HEB & YID.). Date not set. reprint ed. 15.00 (*0-8266-5749-4*) Kehot Pubn Soc.

Shemos, Vol. 31. Menachem M. Schneerson. (Likkutei Sichos Ser.). 366p. (HEB & YID.). 1992. 15.00 (*0-8266-5776-1*) Kehot Pubn Soc.

Shemot Vol. 16. Menachem M. Schneerson. (Likkutei Sichos Ser.). 664p. (HEB & YID.). reprint ed. 15.00 (*0-8266-5735-4*) Kehot Pubn Soc.

Shemuel Hanagid. 1982. 9.95 (*0-87306-220-5*); pap. 7.95 (*0-87306-362-7*) Feldheim.

Shen of the Sea. Arthur B. Chrisman. (Illus.). (J). (gr. 4-7). 1968. pap. 15.99 (*0-525-39244-0*) Dutton Child Bks.

Shen Pao-chen & China's Modernization in the Nineteenth Century. David Pong. (Studies in Chinese History, Literature & Institutions). (Illus.). 325p. (C). 1994. text ed. 54.95 (*0-521-44163-3*) Cambridge U Pr.

Shenandoah. (Vocal Score Ser.). 148p. 1982. pap. 40.00 (*0-88188-049-3*, 00384715) H Leonard.

Shenandoah. large type ed. Fred Harrison. (Linford Western Library). 272p. 1995. pap. 15.99 (*0-7089-7705-7*, Linford) Ulverscroft.

Shenandoah: An Anthology. Ed. by James Boatwright. LC 85-60719. 1985. 28.00 (*0-916366-33-2*) Pushcart Pr.

Shenandoah: Daughter of the Stars. Photos by Lucian Niemeyer. LC 94-18981. (Illus.). 224p. 1994. 39.95 (*0-8071-1966-0*) La State U Pr.

Shenandoah: The Story Behind the Scenery. rev. ed. Hugh Crandall. LC 88-82821. (Illus.). 48p. (Orig.). 1990. pap. 7.95 (*0-88714-027-0*) KC Pubns.

Shenandoah: Vocal Selections. (Illus.). 104p. 1982. 10.95 (*0-88188-109-0*, 00384716) H Leonard.

Shenandoah & Other Verse Plays. Delmore Schwartz. 168p. 1992. 25.00 (*0-918526-90-6*); pap. 12.50 (*0-918526-91-4*) BOA Edns.

Shenandoah Autumn. Ronald Amos. 42p. (Orig.). 1994. pap. 4.00 (*1-57514-123-X*, 1167) Encore Perform Pub.

Shenandoah Campaign of Eighteen Sixty-Two & Eighteen Sixty-Four, & the Appomattox Campaign. (Papers of the Military Historical Society of Massachusetts: Vol. 6). (Illus.). 518p. 1989. reprint ed. 40.00 (*1-56837-010-5*) Broadfoot.

Shenandoah Co. VA: The 1870 Census. Marvin J. Vann. 609p. 1995. pap. text ed. 39.50 (*0-7884-0143-2*) Heritage Bk.

Shenandoah County: Virginia Publick Claims. Janice L. Abercrombie & Richard Slatten. (Virginia Publick Claims Ser.). ix, 26p. 1991. pap. 5.00 (*0-8095-8692-4*) Borgo Pr.

Shenandoah County: Virginia Publick Claims. Janice L. Abercrombie & Richard Slatten. (Virginia Publick Claims Ser.). ix, 26p. (C). 1991. reprint ed. lib. bdg. 25.00 (*0-8095-8360-7*) Borgo Pr.

Shenandoah County in the Civil War: The Turbulent Years. Richard B. Kleese. (Virginia Civil War Battles & Leaders Ser.). (Illus.). 177p. 1992. 19.95 (*1-56190-034-6*) H E Howard.

Shenandoah County Marriage Bonds, 1772-1850. John Vogt & T. William Kethley, Jr. (Virginia Historic Marriage Register Ser.). (Illus.). ix, 417p. (Orig.). 1984. pap. 15.00 (*0-935931-18-X*) Borgo Pr.

***Shenandoah County Marriage Bonds, 1772-1850.** Bernice M. Ashby. 518p. 1996. reprint ed. pap. 36.50 (*0-614-23517-0*, 9040) Clearfield Co.

Shenandoah County Marriage Bonds, 1772-1850. John Vogt & T. William Kethley, Jr. (Virginia Historic Marriage Register Ser.). ix, 417p. (Orig.). (C). 1984. reprint ed. lib. bdg. 39.00 (*0-8095-8232-5*) Borgo Pr.

Shenandoah County Pioneer & Descendants: Matthias Sheetz (Schutz) Thomas M. Spratt. v, 166p. 1993. 49.00 (*0-8095-8298-8*); pap. 20.00 (*0-8095-8690-8*) Borgo Pr.

Shenandoah County, Virginia: A Study of the 1860 Census. Marvin J. Vann. (Illus.). 422p. (Orig.). 1996. pap. 32.00 (*0-7884-0394-X*) Heritage Bk.

Shenandoah County Virginia: A Study of the 1860 Census with Supplemental Data. Marvin J. Vann. (Illus.). 433p. (Orig.). 1993. pap. text ed. 30.00 (*1-55613-852-0*) Heritage Bk.

Shenandoah County, Virginia Men in Gray, 2 vols., Set. Thomas M. Spratt. xix, 902p. 1992. pap. 36.00 (*0-8095-8691-6*); lib. bdg. 66.00 (*0-8095-8189-2*) Borgo Pr.

Shenandoah Heritage: The Story of the People Before the Park. Carolyn Reeder & Jack Reeder. LC 78-61240. 88p. 1995. 7.00 (*0-915746-10-7*) Potomac Appalach.

Shenandoah in Flames. (Civil War Ser.). (Illus.). 176p. 1987. 18.95 (*0-8094-4784-3*); lib. bdg. 25.93 (*0-8094-4785-1*) Time-Life.

Shenandoah National Park: An Interpretive Guide. John A. Conners. LC 88-23118. (Illus.). ix, 214p. (Orig.). 1988. pap. 15.95 (*0-939923-02-5*) M & W Pub Co.

Shenandoah National Park, VA. rev. ed. Ed. by Trails Illustrated Staff. (Illus.). 1995. 8.99 (*0-925873-86-1*) Trails Illustrated.

Shenandoah Noah. Jim Aylesworth. LC 84-22554. (Illus.). 32p. (J). (gr. k-2). 1985. 11.95 (*0-03-003749-2*, Bks Young Read) H Holt & Co.

***Shenandoah River Atlas.** William E. Trout, III. (Illus.). 109p. (Orig.). 1997. spiral bd., pap. 15.00 (*1-888838-06-X*) VA Canals & Navigat.

Shenandoah Saga: A Narrative History of the U. S. Navy's First Pioneering Large Helium-Filled Rigid Airship. 4th rev. ed. Thomas S. Hook. Ed. by T. G. Settle. LC 73-84973. (Famous Airships Ser.). (Illus.). xiv, 208p. (C). 1989. pap. 12.95 (*0-9601506-1-7*) Airsho Pubs.

Shenandoah Secrets. Carolyn Reeder & Jack Reeder. 184p. 1991. pap. 12.95 (*0-915746-41-7*) Potomac Appalach.

Shenandoah Spector. William Opie. 120p. (Orig.). (YA). 1989. pap. write for info. (*0-318-65487-3*) Opie Pub.

Shenandoah Valley Family Data 1799-1813. Johannes Braun. Ed. & Tr. by Klaus Wust from GER. 1978. pap. 10.00 (*0-917968-05-0*) Shenandoah Hist.

Shenandoah Valley Pioneer Settlers: A Few of Them & Some Notes of Interest. 2nd ed. G. P. Hammond. Ed. by Rachael W. Hammond. LC 93-79852. (Illus.). 88p. (C). 1994. pap. 14.75 (*1-878014-04-8*) G P Hammond Pub.

Shenandoah Valley Pioneer Settlers: A Few of Them & Some Notes of Interest. Gene P. Hammond. Ed. by Jason Hammond. 88p. 1991. reprint ed. 23.75 (*1-878014-01-3*) G P Hammond Pub.

Shenandoah Valley Pioneers & Their Descendants: A History of Frederick County, Virginia from Its Formation in 1733 to 1908 Compiled Mainly from Original Records of Old Frederick County, Now Hampshire, Berkeley, Shenandoah, Jefferson, Hardy, Clarke, Warren, Morgan & Frederick. T. K. Cartmell. vii, 572p. 1995. reprint ed. pap. 57.50 (*0-685-65674-8*, 9075) Clearfield Co.

Shenandoah Valley Pioneers & Their Descendants: A History of Frederick County, Virginia from Its Formation in 1733 to 1908 Compiled Mainly from Original Records of Old Frederick County, Now Hampshire, Berkeley, Shenandoah, Jefferson, Hardy, Clarke, Warren, Morgan & Frederick. T. K. Cartmell. (Illus.). 598p. 1989. reprint ed. pap. 60.00 (*1-55613-243-3*) Heritage Bk.

Shenandoah Vestiges: What the Mountain People Left Behind. Carolyn Reeder & Jack Reeder. LC 80-81761. 72p. 1993. pap. 5.00 (*0-915746-14-X*) Potomac Appalach.

Shenandoah Voices: Folklore, Legends & Traditions of the Valley. 2nd ed. John L. Heatwole. LC 95-8763. (Illus.). 147p. 1995. 25.00 (*1-883522-07-2*) Rockbridge Pub.

***Shenandoah 1862.** Ed. by Time-Life Books Editors. LC 97-3198. (Voices of the Civil War Ser.). 168p. (YA). (gr. 6-12). 1997. 24.95 (*0-7835-4711-0*) Time-Life.

Shenanigans. Casey Roberts. (Superromance Ser.). 1993. mass mkt. 3.39 (*0-373-70547-6*, 1-70547-4) Harlequin Bks.

Shenson on Consulting. Howard L. Shenson. LC 90-30240. 200p. 1990. text ed. 37.95 (*0-471-50661-3*) Wiley.

Shenson on Consulting: Success Strategies from the "Consultant's Consultant" Howard L. Shenson. 200p. 1994. pap. text ed. 14.95 (*0-471-00925-3*) Wiley.

Sheolah's Easy Ways to Elegant Cooking. Sheilah Kaufman. 288p. 1983. pap. 7.95 (*0-671-50383-9*) S&S Trade.

Sheople Incidents. Gail Blanton. 1995. pap. 8.99 (*0-8341-9438-4*, MP-767) Nazarene.

Shepard: Ralph Shepard, Puritan. R. H. Shepard. 50p. 1991. reprint ed. pap. 10.00 (*0-8328-1764-3*) Higginson Bk Co.

Shepard Alonzo Mount: His Life & Art. Deborah J. Johnson. LC 87-36561. (Illus.). 64p. (Orig.). 1988. pap. 7.50 (*0-943924-12-X*) Mus Stony Brook.

Shepard Looks at Psalm 23. anniversary ed. W. Phillip Keller. (Zondervan Classics Ser.). 144p. 1996. 15.99 (*0-310-20994-3*) Zondervan.

Shepard's Acts & Cases by Popular Names: Federal & State. 3rd ed. write for info. (*0-318-60411-6*, Shepards) McGraw.

Shepard's Arizona Case Names Citator: A Compilation of Case Names & Citations of Arizoan Cases Decided from 1866 to the Present. 2nd ed. Shepard's McGraw-Hill Staff. 1994. write for info. (*0-318-72810-9*) Shepards.

Shepard's Arkansas Citations. 5th ed. 1993. write for info. (*0-318-71664-X*) Shepards.

Shepard's Atlantic Reporter Citations. 3rd ed. Shepard's McGraw-Hill Staff. write for info. (*0-318-60757-3*, Shepards) McGraw.

Shepard's Atlantic Reporter Citations, Cases. 4th ed. Shepard's Magraw-Hill Staff. 1994. write for info. (*0-615-00155-6*) Shepards.

***Shepard's Christmas.** Arch Books Staff. 1997. 1.99 (*0-570-07540-8*) Concordia.

Shepard's Citations for ALR, 2 vols., Set. LC 89-10695. 1993. 225.00 (*0-318-68085-8*) Lawyers Cooperative.

Shepard's Code of Federal Regulations Citations: A Compilation of Citations to the Code of Federal Regulations, Presidential Proclamations, Executive Orders & Reorganization Plans. 2nd ed. write for info. (*0-318-60412-4*, Shepards) McGraw.

Shepard's Colorado Citations. 6th ed. 1994. write for info. (*0-318-72494-4*) Shepards.

Shepard's Contemporary Health Care Issues. Ed. by James H. Cooper & Vera D. Cooper. LC 94-19056. 1994. write for info. (*0-07-172577-6*) Shepards.

Shepard's Horizons. Gene A. Kelly. 296p. 1995. text ed. 16.95 (*0-8059-3657-2*) Dorrance.

Shepard's Illinois Case Names Citator. Shepard's Citation, Inc. Staff. write for info. (*0-318-59779-9*) McGraw.

Shepard's Iowa Case Names Citator: A Compilation of Case Names & Citations of Iowa Cases Decided from 1855 to the Present. 2nd ed. 1994. write for info. (*0-615-00127-0*) Shepards.

Shepard's Iowa Case Names Citator: A Compilation of Case Names & Citations of Iowa Cases Decided from 1925 to the Present: the Case Names & Citations Appear in Iowa Reports, Northwestern Reporter (Iowa Cases), Northwestern Reporter, Second Series (Iowa Cases) Shepard's McGraw-Hill Staff. write for info. (*0-318-59324-6*) McGraw.

Shepard's Iowa Citations. 7th ed. 1993. write for info. (*0-318-72257-7*) Shepards.

Shepard's Kansas Citations. Shepard's Citation, Inc. Staff. write for info. (*0-318-59780-2*) McGraw.

Shepard's Kansas Citations. 5th ed. Shepard's McGraw-Hill Staff. 1994. write for info. (*0-318-72809-5*) Shepards.

Shepard's Kentucky Case Names Citator: A Compilation of Case Names & Citations of Kentucky Cases Decided from 1940 to the Present. Shepard's McGraw-Hill Staff. write for info. (*0-318-60759-X*, Shepards) McGraw.

Shepard's Law Review Citations: A Compilation of Citations to Law Reviews & Legal Periodicals. 4th ed. Shepard's McGraw-Hill Staff. write for info. (*0-318-60760-3*, Shepards) McGraw.

Shepard's Maryland Case Names Citator. write for info. (*0-318-59778-0*) McGraw.

Shepard's Massachusetts Case Names Citator: A Compilation of Case Names & Citations of Massachusetts Cases Decided from 1873 to the Present. 2nd ed. Shepard's Magraw-Hill Staff. 1994. lib. bdg. write for info. (*0-615-00073-8*) Shepards.

Shepard's Massachusetts Citations: A compilation of Citations to the United States Constitution & Statues, Massachusetts Constitution, General Laws, Acts & Resolves, Court Rules, Charters & Ordinances. 7th ed. Shepard's McGraw-Hill Staff. 1993. write for info. (*0-318-71652-6*) Shepards.

S

Shepard's Michigan Citations. 9th ed. 1994. write for info. (*0-318-72732-3*) Shepards.

Shepard's Missouri Citations. 7th ed. Shepard's McGraw-Hill Staff. 1994. write for info. (*0-318-72887-7*) Shepards.

Shepard's Nebraska Citations. 7th ed. 1994. write for info. (*0-318-72574-6*) Shepards.

Shepard's New Jersey Citations. 8th ed. 1994. write for info. (*0-318-72611-4*) Shepards.

Shepard's New York Court of Appeals Citations: A Compilation of Citations to New York Court of Appeals, Common Law & Chancery Cases. 6th ed. 1993. write for info. (*0-318-72256-9*) Shepards.

Shepard's New York Miscellaneous Citations. 6th ed. Shepard's Magraw-Hill Staff. 1994. write for info. (*0-615-00284-6*) Shepards.

Shepard's North Carolina Case Names Citator: A Compilation of Case Names & Citations of North Carolina Cases Decided from 1887 to the Present. 2nd ed. 1994. write for info. (*0-318-72733-1*) Shepards.

Shepard's Northwestern Reporter Citations: A Compilation of Citations to All Cases in the Northwestern Reporter, Including Affirmances, 5 vols. Shepard's Citation, Inc. Staff. LC 52-2849. 1985. Supplements available. 640.00 (*0-686-90097-9*) Shepards.

S

Shepard's Ohio Case Names Citator see Shepard's Ohio Citations: Case Name Table: A Compilation of Case Names & Citations of Ohio Cases Decided from 1940 to the Present

Shepard's Ohio Citations. 1994. write for info. (*0-318-72765-X*) Shepards.

Shepard's Ohio Citations: Case Name Table: A Compilation of Case Names & Citations of Ohio Cases Decided from 1940 to the Present. 2nd ed. Orig. Title: Shepard's Ohio Case Names Citator. 1994. reprint ed. write for info. (*0-318-72956-3*) Shepards.

Shepard's Oklahoma Case Names Citator: A Compilation of Case Names & Citations of Oklahoma Cases Decided from 1940 to the Present. write for info. (*0-318-60413-2*) McGraw.

Shepard's Pacific Reporter Citations: A Compilation of Citations to All Cases Reported in the Pacific Reporter. 5th ed. 1994. write for info. (*0-615-00235-8*) Shepards.

Shepard's Pennsylvania Case Names Citator: A Compilation of Case Names & Citations of Pensylvania Cases Decided from 1910 to the Present. 2nd ed. 1993. write for info. (*0-318-72297-6*) Shepards.

Shepard's Products Liability Citations, 2 vols. 2nd ed. Shepard's Magraw-Hill Staff. LC 93-18537. 1993. 270.00 (*0-685-64753-6*) Shepards.

Shepard's Southern Reporter Citations: A Compilation of Citations to All Cases Reported in the Southern Reporter. Shepard's Magraw-Hill Staff. 1994. write for info. (*0-318-72584-3*) Shepards.

Shepard's Southern Reporter Citations: A Compilation of Citations to All Cases Reported in the Southern Reporter, 7 vols. 3rd ed. McGraw-Hill Staff Shepard's. LC 86-15597. 1986. 798.00 (*0-685-67639-0*) Shepards.

Shepard's Southwestern Reporter Citations, 7 vols. 5th ed. Shepard's Magraw-Hill Staff. LC 93-18536. 1993. 868.00 (*0-685-64754-4*) Shepards.

Shepard's Tennessee Citations: A Compilation of Citations to Tennessee Cases Reported in the Various Series of Tennessee Reports & in the Southwestern Reporter, 2 vols. 5th ed. LC 93-12613. 1993. 320.00 (*0-685-64928-8*) Shepards.

Shepard's United States Citation: A Compilation of Citations to United States Supreme Court Decisions. 7th ed. 1994. write for info. (*0-318-72918-0*) McGraw.

Shepard's United States Citations: Statutes - Court Rules..., 32 vols. 7th ed. LC 86-17769. 1986. 2,976.00 (*0-685-67640-4*) Shepards.

Shephard Technologies & Neoclassical Production Functions. T. Junius. (Tilburg Studies in Econometrics: No. 2). 1977. lib. bdg. 55.00 (*90-207-0727-2*) Kluwer Ac.

Shepheardes Calender. Edmund Spenser. LC 79-691. 1979. reprint ed. 50.00 (*0-8201-1328-X*) Schol Facsimiles.

Shepheardes Calender: An Introduction. Lynn S. Johnson. (Illus.). 240p. 1991. lib. bdg. 32.50 (*0-271-00699-4*) Pa St U Pr.

Shepheards Devises: Edmund Spenser's Shepheardes Calender & the Institutions of Elizabethan Society. Robert Lane. LC 92-27594. (Illus.). 256p. 1993. 40.00 (*0-8203-1514-1*) U of Ga Pr.

Shepherd. Julian F. Thompson. 176p. (YA). (gr. 7 up). 1996. pap. 4.99 (*0-14-037502-3*, Puffin) Puffin Bks.

Shepherd. large type ed. Joseph F. Girzone. LC 93-36171. 1994. lib. bdg. 23.95 (*0-8161-5740-5*, GK Hall) Thorndike Pr.

Shepherd. large type ed. Joseph F. Girzone. LC 93-36171. 1994. pap. 17.95 (*0-8161-5741-3*, GK Hall) Thorndike Pr.

Shepherd: A Biography of Dr. Arthur A. Peters. Flossie E. Thompson-Peters. (African-American Heritage Ser.). 251p. 1979. 10.00 (*1-880784-00-9*) Atlas Pr.

Shepherd: A Novel. Joseph F. Girzone. 256p. (Orig.). 1992. pap. 9.95 (*0-02-019908-2*) Macmillan.

Shepherd & His Love: Instrument Parts-Piccolo, Viola, Piano. K. Mechem. 8p. 1993. pap. 5.95 (*0-7935-2695-7*) H Leonard.

Shepherd & His Sheep. William A. Rogers. 1983. pap. 6.99 (*1-56632-011-9*) Revival Lit.

Shepherd & His Shepherdess Are Leading Their Sheep to the Ark Vol. I. Danille Roshelle. Ed. by Ariel Roshelle. 340p. (Orig.). 1995. pap. 21.00 (*0-9644530-0-2*) AR-L Pubns.

Shepherd Boy. Marvin Good. 1978. pap. 2.00 (*0-686-24054-5*) Rod & Staff.

Shepherd Boy. Kim Lewis. LC 89-23679. (Illus.). 32p. (J). (ps-1). 1990. lib. bdg. 13.95 (*0-02-758581-6*, Four Winds Pr) S&S Childrens.

Shepherd Boy (El Nino Pastor) Kristine L. Franklin. Tr. by Alma F. Ada. LC 93-34823. (Illus.). 40p. (J). (ps-1). 1994. lib. bdg. 14.95 (*0-689-31809-X*, Atheneum Bks Young); lib. bdg. 14.95 (*0-689-31918-5*, Atheneum Bks Young) S&S Childrens.

***Shepherd Boy Who Loved God: A Baal Shem Tov Story.** Sterna Citron. LC 96-78002. (Children's Ser.). (Illus.). 24p. (J). (gr. k-2). 1996. 12.95 (*1-889727-15-6*) Kerem Pubng.

***Shepherd Boy's Christmas.** Mary Calhoun. (J). Date not set. write for info. (*0-688-15176-0*, Morrow Junior); lib. bdg. write for info. (*0-688-15177-9*, Morrow Junior) Morrow.

Shepherd Discourse of John Ten & Its Context. Ed. by Johannes Beutler & Robert T. Fortna. (Society for New Testament Studies Monographs: No. 67). (Illus.). 200p. (C). 1991. text ed. 59.95 (*0-521-39211-X*) Cambridge U Pr.

Shepherd God: The 23rd Psalm for Today. Paul Nagano. Ed. by Rennie Mau. 30p. (Orig.). 1989. pap. write for info. (*0-318-66304-X*); audio write for info. (*0-318-66305-8*) Media Bridge.

***Shepherd in Combat Boots: Chaplain Emil Kapaun of the 1st Cavalry Division.** William L. Maher. LC 97-19800. 1997. 24.95 (*1-57249-069-1*) Brewster & Vine Pub.

***Shepherd King: Activity Center Leader's Guide.** 1997. teacher ed., pap. 5.49 (*1-885428-35-9*) CPA.

***Shepherd King: Age-Level Leader's Guide.** 1997. teacher ed., pap. 5.49 (*1-885428-34-0*) CPA.

***Shepherd King: All-in-One Planning Book.** (Illus.). 216p. 1997. teacher ed. 24.99 (*1-885428-54-5*) CPA.

***Shepherd King: Songbook.** 1997. teacher ed., pap. 1.99 (*1-885428-36-7*) CPA.

***Shepherd King: Storyteller's Guide.** (Storyteller Ser.). 1997. teacher ed., pap. 4.99 (*1-885428-33-2*) CPA.

Shepherd Looks at Psalm 23. large type ed. W. Phillip Keller. (Illus.). 142p. 1974. 10.99 (*0-310-26797-8*) Zondervan.

Shepherd Looks at Psalm 23. W. Phillip Keller. (Illus.). 142p. 1970. reprint ed. 12.99 (*0-310-26790-0*) Zondervan.

Shepherd of an Immigrant People: The Story of Erland Carlsson. Emory K. Lindquist. LC 78-108120. (Augustana Historical Society Publications: No. 26). 236p. 1978. 7.50 (*0-910184-26-7*) Augustana.

Shepherd of Democracy? America & Germany in the Twentieth Century. Ed. by Carl C. Hodge & Cathal J. Nolan. LC 92-5421. (Contributions in Political Science Ser.: No. 305). 248p. 1992. text ed. 55.00 (*0-313-27945-4*, NSH, Greenwood Pr) Greenwood.

Shepherd of Guadaloupe. Zane Grey. 320p. 1992. mass mkt. 3.99 (*0-06-100500-2*, Harp PBks) HarpC.

Shepherd of Hermas, Martyrdom of Polycarp, Epistle to Diognetus see Works of Apostolic Fathers

Shepherd of Hermas the Gentle Apocalypse. Adapted & Intro. by William Jardine. 170p. (Orig.). 1992. pap. 10.00 (*0-9630606-2-7*) Proteus CA.

Shepherd of Jerusalem. Dov P. Elkins. LC 75-39436. (Illus.). (J). (gr. 8-12). 1976. 11.95 (*0-88400-045-1*) Shengold.

Shepherd of Jerusalem: A Biography of Rabbi Abraham Isaac Kook. Dov P. Elkins. LC 95-8311. 138p. (J). 1995. pap. 20.00 (*1-56821-597-5*) Aronson.

Shepherd of Men: An Official Commentary on the Sermon of Hermes Trismegistos. A. S. Raleigh. 145p. 1995. reprint ed. pap. 16.95 (*1-56459-493-9*) Kessinger Pub.

Shepherd of the Hills. Harold B. Wright. 1975. lib. bdg. 27.95 (*0-89966-206-4*) Buccaneer Bks.

Shepherd of the Hills. Harold B. Wright. LC 91-18605. 352p. 1992. pap. 4.95 (*0-88289-884-1*) Pelican.

Shepherd of the Hills. rev. ed. Harold B. Wright. Ed. by Michael R. Phillips. LC 88-10311. 256p. 1988. pap. 7.99 (*0-87123-916-7*) Bethany Hse.

Shepherd of the Hills. Harold B. Wright. LC 87-61206. 269p. 1987. reprint ed. write for info. (*0-911978-04-6*) McCormick-Armstrong.

Shepherd of the Sun. Benjamin Appel. (Illus.). (J). (gr. 5 up). 1961. 10.95 (*0-8392-3033-8*) Astor-Honor.

Shepherd of the Wolves. William S. Slusher. 1995. mass mkt. 5.99 (*0-671-89546-X*, PB Trade Paper) PB.

Shepherd Psalm. Frederick B. Meyer. LC 91-9805. 128p. 1991. reprint ed. pap. 8.99 (*0-8254-3276-6*, Kregel Class) Kregel.

Shepherd under Christ. Armin W. Schuetze & Irwin J. Habezk. LC 74-81794. 395p. 1974. text ed. 23.99 (*0-8100-0046-6*, 15N0351) Northwest Pub.

Shepherd Who Planted a Forest. Diana Noonan. LC 93-11828. (J). 1994. write for info. (*0-383-03774-3*) SRA McGraw.

Shepherdess: Notes from the Field. Joan J. Ellison. LC 95-4199. (Illus.). 182p. (Orig.). (C). 1995. pap. 14.95 (*1-55753-070-X*) Purdue U Pr.

Shepherdess of Elk River Valley. 2nd ed. Margaret D. Brown. (Illus.). 1967. 5.50 (*0-87315-037-6*) Golden Bell.

Shepherding: Workbook 3. Robert D. Noble. (Welcome in Ser.). 68p. (Orig.). 1987. 10.00 (*0-944687-03-2*) Gather Family Inst.

***Shepherding a Child's Heart.** Tedd Tripp. 237p. (Orig.). 1995. pap. 11.95 (*1-879737-19-1*) Calvary Press.

Shepherding God's Flock: A Handbook on Pastoral Ministry, Counseling, & Leadership. Jay E. Adams. (Jay Adams Library). 544p. 1986. pap. 24.99 (*0-310-51071-6*, 12119P) Zondervan.

***Shepherding the Church: Effective Spiritual Leadership in a Changing Culture.** Joseph M. Stowell. 336p. 1997. pap. 14.99 (*0-8024-7821-2*) Moody.

Shepherding the Flock of God: The Pastoral Theology of John Chrysostom. Robert A. Krupp. LC 90-17583. (American University Studies: Theology & Religion: Ser. VII, Vol. 101). 294p. (C). 1991. text ed. 49.95 (*0-8204-1515-4*) P Lang Pubng.

***Shepherds Abiding in the Fields: The Challenge of Pastoral Leadership.** Leonard M. Young & Reorganized Church of Jesus Christ of Latter Day Saints, Board of Publication Staff. LC 97-7399. 1997. write for info. (*0-8309-0765-3*) Herald Hse.

Shepherds & Shoppers. Wendy Lord et al. Ed. by Helen Johns. LC 92-72129. (Illus.). 56p. (Orig.). 1992. pap. 6.95 (*0-916035-49-2*) Evangel Indiana.

Shepherd's Calendar. James Hogg. Ed. by Douglas S. Mack. (Collected Works of James Hogg). 287p. 1994. 45.00 (*0-7486-0474-X*, Pub. by Edinburgh U Pr UK) Col U Pr.

Shepherd's Calendar. 2nd ed. John Clare. Ed. by Eric Robinson et al. LC 92-44091. 1993. 10.00 (*0-19-283154-2*) OUP.

Shepherd's Calendar. John Clare. LC 91-30167. 258p. 1991. reprint ed. 48.00 (*1-85477-062-4*, Pub. by Woodstock Bks UK) Cassell.

Shepherd's Calendar. Edmund Spenser. (BCL1-PR English Literature Ser.). 242p. 1992. reprint ed. lib. bdg. 79.00 (*0-7812-7225-4*) Rprt Serv.

Shepherd's Care. William Goulooze. 1959. pap. 0.70 (*0-686-23475-8*) Rose Pub MI.

Shepherd's Care: Reflections on the Changing Role of Pastor. NCCB Committee on Priestly Life & Ministry. 84p. (Orig.). 1987. pap. 4.95 (*1-55586-166-0*) US Catholic.

Shepherd's Castle. George MacDonald & Mike Phillips. 288p. (Orig.). 1983. pap. 8.99 (*0-87123-579-X*) Bethany Hse.

Shepherd's Castle. George MacDonald & Michael Phillips. 298p. (Orig.). 1995. mass mkt. 5.99 (*1-55661-633-3*) Bethany Hse.

Shepherd's Crowns: A Volume of Essays. Pamela G. Grey. LC 67-30216. (Essay Index Reprint Ser.). 1977. 18.95 (*0-8369-0498-2*) Ayer.

Shepherd's Life. William H. Hudson. reprint ed. 64.50 (*0-404-03406-3*) AMS Pr.

Shepherd's Man. David F. Gray. LC 93-87253. 384p. (Orig.). 1994. pap. 9.95 (*0-89221-258-6*) New Leaf.

Shepherds of Bethlehem. James H. Schackel. 1989. pap. 2.25 (*1-55673-144-2*, 9869) CSS OH.

Shepherds of Britain: Scenes from Shepherd Life Past & Present. Compiled by Adelaide L. Gosset. LC 78-174415. (Illus.). 356p. 1972. reprint ed. 26.95 (*0-405-08565-6*, Pub. by Blom Pubns UK) Ayer.

Shepherds of Saint Francis. Lowell Swortzell. 1995. 3.00 (*0-87129-584-9*, SA9) Dramatic Pub.

Shepherds of the Night. Jorge Amado. 384p. 1988. pap. 7.95 (*0-380-75471-1*) Avon.

***Shepherds' Paradise.** Walter Montagu. Ed. by Sarah Poynting. 175p. 1997. 49.95 (*0-19-729035-3*) OUP.

Shepherd's Path. David F. Gray. LC 92-60940. 336p. (Orig.). 1992. pap. 9.95 (*0-89221-227-6*) New Leaf.

Shepherd's Pie. Kenneth J. Roberts & Anna M. Waters. 217p. (Orig.). Date not set. pap. 9.95 (*0-9610984-4-9*) PAX Tapes.

Shepherd's Pipe, & Other Stories. Arthur Schnitzler. Tr. by O. F. Theis. LC 74-140340. (Short Story Index Reprint Ser.). 1977. 13.95 (*0-8369-3732-5*) Ayer.

Shepherd's Pipe Songs from the Holy Night: A Christmas Cantata for Children's Voices or Youth Choir. Georg J. Gick & Marlys Swinger. LC 71-85805. (Illus.). 64p. (J). (gr. k up). 1969. pap. 4.00 (*0-87486-011-3*) Plough.

Shepherd's Purse: Organic Pest Control Handbook. rev. ed. Pest Publications Staff. LC 92-25525. (Illus.). 80p. 1993. pap. 9.95 (*0-913990-98-1*) Book Pub Co.

Shepherd's Son. Robert Van DeWeyer & Annabel Spenceley. LC 92-40284. 24p. (J). (gr. k-3). 1993. 10.00 (*0-8170-1188-9*) Judson.

Shepherds Song. Julie Miner. Date not set. pap. 13.89 (*0-8037-1197-2*) Dial Bks Young.

Shepherd's Song: Finding the Heart to Go On. Lynn Anderson. LC 96-14377. 240p. 1996. 14.99 (*1-878990-62-4*) Howard Pub LA.

***Shepherd's Story: A Musical Story Based on Luke 2:1-20 for Unison & Two-Part Children's Voices: IntroPak.** Hal H. Hopson. 1992. spiral bd. 19.95 incl. audio (*0-687-38376-5*) Abingdon.

***Shepherd's Story: A Musical Story Based on Luke 2:1-20 for Unison & Two-Part Children's Voices: Leader/Accompanist Edition.** Hal H. Hopson. 72p. 1992. spiral bd. 14.95 (*0-687-38374-9*) Abingdon.

***Shepherd's Story: A Musical Story Based on Luke 2:1-20 for Unison & Two-Part Children's Voices: PreviewPak.** Hal H. Hopson. 1995. pap. 6.00 incl. audio (*0-687-08294-3*) Abingdon.

***Shepherd's Story: A Musical Story Based on Luke 2:1-20 for Unison & Two-Part Children's Voices: Singer's Edition.** Hal H. Hopson. 16p. 1992. pap. 3.50 (*0-687-38375-7*) Abingdon.

Shepherd's System for Medical Device Incident Investigation & Reporting. Marvin D. Shepherd. (Illus.). 220p. 1992. ring bd. 195.00 (*0-930844-35-1*) Quest Pub.

***Shepherd's Tools: Administrative Guides for Pastors.** Mark A. Tabb. (Christian Life Focus System Ser.). 1997. ring bd. 8.99 (*0-8024-2681-6*) Moody.

Shepherd's Trade. deluxe limited ed. R. J. Berman. 1984. lib. bdg. 100.00 (*0-8239-0617-5*, Pelion Pr) Rosen Group.

Shepherdstown: An American Treasure. Martin R. Conway. LC 90-83219. (Illus.). 72p. 1991. text ed. 14.95 (*0-938634-10-0*) Carabelle.

Sheppard Lee. Robert M. Bird. (Works of Robert Montgomery Bird). 1989. reprint ed. lib. bdg. 79.00 (*0-7812-1991-4*) Rprt Serv.

Shepperton Studios: An Independent View. Derek Threadgall. 1994. pap. 21.95 (*0-85170-422-0*, Pub. by British Film Inst UK) Ind U Pr.

Sheppey: A Play in Three Acts. W. Somerset Maugham. LC 75-30396. (Works of W. Somerset Maugham). 1977. reprint ed. 23.95 (*0-405-07848-X*) Ayer.

Shepton Mallet Prison: Three Hundred Eighty Years of Prison Regimes. Francis Disney. 312p. (C). 1992. text ed. 110.00 (*0-9511470-2-1*, Pub. by F J Disney UK) St Mut.

Sherard Families of South Carolina & Beyond. Anita W. Roof. (Illus.). 100p. 1993. 35.00 (*0-9623070-1-7*) A W Roof.

Sheraton World Cookbook. Ed. by Vera Krijn. 304p. (Orig.). 1983. pap. write for info. (*0-672-52761-8*) Macmillan.

Sheraton World Cookbook: Great Recipes from Great Chefs. 1981. write for info. (*0-672-52672-7*) Macmillan.

Sherazade. Leila Sebbar. Tr. by Dorothy S. Blair from ARA. 264p. 1991. 19.95 (*0-7043-2778-3*, Pub. by Quartet UK) Interlink Pub.

Sherazade & Her Two Lovers. A. K. Belkaoui. 200p. (Orig.). 1995. pap. 10.95 (*1-57532-011-8*) Press-Tige Pub.

***Sherbet.** Adams Media Staff. (Just Desserts Ser.). 1997. pap. text ed. 4.95 (*1-55850-734-5*) Adams Media.

Sherborne: A Cotswold Village. W. Tuftnell et al. (Illus.). 192p. 1992. 28.00 (*0-7509-0081-4*, Pub. by Sutton Pubng UK) Bks Intl VA.

Sherbro of Sierra Leone. H. U. Hall. (Illus.). 15p. 1938. pap. 10.00 (*0-686-17762-2*) U PA Mus Pubns.

Sherbrooke Bride. Catherine Coulter. 1992. mass mkt. 6.99 (*0-515-10766-2*) Jove Pubns.

Sherbrooke Bride. large type ed. Catherine Coulter. LC 95-9761. 465p. 1995. 23.95 (*0-7838-1293-0*, GK Hall) Thorndike Pr.

***Sherburne Illustrated: History of the Village of Sherburne, Its Scenery, Development & Business Enterprises.** John P. Gomph. 110p. 1997. reprint ed. pap. 15.00 (*0-8328-6239-8*) Higginson Bk Co.

Sherds. limited ed. Ray Ragosta. (Burning Deck Poetry Chapbooks Ser.). 32p. (Orig.). 1982. pap. 15.00 (*0-930901-08-8*) Burning Deck.

Sheridan. W. A. Darlington. LC 74-7188. (Studies in Drama: No. 39). 1974. lib. bdg. 75.00 (*0-8383-1926-2*) M S G Haskell Hse.

Sheridan. Roy Morris. 1994. 23.50 (*0-8446-6753-6*) Peter Smith.

Sheridan: Interviews & Recollections. Ed. by E. H. Mikhail. LC 88-35562. (Illus.). 200p. 1990. text ed. 39.95 (*0-312-03013-4*) St Martin.

Sheridan: The Life & Wars of General Phil Sheridan. Roy Morris, Jr. LC 92-50621. (Civil War Library). 1993. pap. 16.00 (*0-679-74398-7*, Vin) Random.

Sheridan & Goldsmith. Katharine Worth. LC 92-8838. (English Dramatists Ser.). 176p. 1992. text ed. 39.95 (*0-312-08392-0*) St Martin.

Sheridan & the Drama of Georgian England. John C. Loftis. 186p. 1976. 23.50 (*0-674-80632-8*) HUP.

Sheridan in the Shenandoah. 2nd ed. Edward J. Stackpole. LC 61-14913. (Illus.). 448p. 1992. reprint ed. pap. 14.95 (*0-8117-3061-1*) Stackpole.

***Sheridan Le Fanu.** W. J. McCormack. (Illus.). 336p. 1997. pap. 22.95 (*0-7509-1489-0*, Pub. by Sutton Pubng UK) Bks Intl VA.

***Sheridan Road.** Date not set. write for info. (*0-688-09449-X*) Morrow.

Sheridan Studies. Ed. by James Morwood & David Crane. (Illus.). 275p. (C). 1996. text ed. 54.95 (*0-521-46466-8*) Cambridge U Pr.

Sheridan to Robertson: A Study of the Nineteenth-Century London Stage. Ernest B. Watson. LC 63-23191. (Illus.). 1972. 33.95 (*0-405-09055-2*) Ayer.

Sheridan's Comedies: Their Contexts & Achievements. Mark S. Auburn. LC 77-7205. 231p. reprint ed. pap. 65.90 (*0-7837-6459-6*, 2046463) Bks Demand.

Sheridan's Troopers on the Borders. Debenneville R. Keim. 308p. 1973. reprint ed. 26.95 (*0-87928-043-3*) Corner Hse.

Sheridan's Troopers on the Borders: A Winter Campaign on the Plains. Debenneville R. Keim. LC 78-133523. (Select Bibliographies Reprint Ser.). (Illus.). 1977. reprint ed. 23.95 (*0-8369-5555-2*) Ayer.

Sheridan's Troopers on the Borders: A Winter Campaign on the Plains. Debenneville R. Keim. LC 84-25754. 338p. 1985. reprint ed. pap. 96.40 (*0-608-00486-3*, 2061305) Bks Demand.

Sheriff. Jack Rudman. (Career Examination Ser.: C-794). 1994. pap. 27.95 (*0-8373-0794-5*) Nat Learn.

***Sheriff & the Branding Iron Murders.** D. R. Meredith. LC 96-48192. (Nightingale Ser.). 1997. pap. 18.95 (*0-7838-2044-5*) G K Hall.

Sheriff & the Branding Iron Murders. Doris R. Meredith. 160p. 1986. pap. 2.95 (*0-380-70050-6*) Avon.

Sheriff & the Branding Iron Murders. Doris R. Meredith. 159p. 1985. 14.95 (*0-8027-4050-2*) Walker & Co.

Sheriff & the Folsom Man Murders. Doris R. Meredith. 208p. 1987. pap. 2.95 (*0-380-70364-5*) Avon.

Sheriff & the Folsom Man Murders. Doris R. Meredith. 192p. 1987. 16.95 (*0-8027-5663-8*) Walker & Co.

Sheriff & the Panhandle Murders. Doris R. Meredith. 1991. mass mkt. 4.99 (*0-345-36951-3*) Ballantine.

Sheriff & the Pheasant Hunt Murders. Doris R. Meredith. 1993. mass mkt. 4.50 (*0-345-36948-3*) Ballantine.

Sheriff at Waterstop. Andy Thompson. Ed. by Olivia Tschappler. (Light Line Ser.). (Illus.). 133p. (Orig.). (J). (gr. 4-6). 1987. pap. 6.49 (*0-89084-371-6*, 031443) Bob Jones Univ Pr.

***Sheriff Brady, Vol. 5.** J. A. Jance. Date not set. write for info. (*0-688-13822-5*) Morrow.

An Asterisk (*) at the beginning of an entry indicates that the title is appearing in BIP for the first time.

Sheriff of Devil's Fork. Regan Forest. (Temptation Ser.). 1993. mass mkt. 2.99 (*0-373-25564-0*, 1-25564-5) Harlequin Bks.

Sheriff of Nottingham. Richard Kluger. 496p. 1993. pap. 12.00 (*0-14-017703-5*, Penguin Bks) Viking Penguin.

Sheriff of Rottenshot. Jack Prelutsky. LC 81-6420. (Illus.). 32p. (J). (gr. k-3). 1982. lib. bdg. 14.93 (*0-688-00198-X*) Greenwillow.

Sheriff of Rottenshot. Jack Prelutsky. Ed. by Amy Cohn. LC 81-6420. (Illus.). 48p. (J). (gr. k up). 1994. reprint ed. pap. 4.95 (*0-688-13635-4*, Mulberry) Morrow.

Sheriff of Whiskey City. Robin Gibson. 1995. 17.95 (*0-8034-9100-X*, 094642) Bouregy.

Sheriff Pat Garrett's Last Days. Colin Richards. LC 85-25020. (Illus.). 96p. (Orig.). 1986. pap. 8.95 (*0-86534-079-X*) Sunstone Pr.

Sheriff Rod of Whistling Meadows. Edwin W. Holden. 1994. 14.95 (*0-533-10856-X*) Vantage.

***Sheriff Sixsmith.** large type ed. John Blaze. (Dales Large Print Ser.). 224p. 1997. pap. 18.99 (*1-85389-737-X*, Dales) Ulverscroft.

***Sheriff Star's "Round up the Sin Gang" Drama Skit Book.** (J). teacher ed., pap. 9.95 (*0-614-18229-8*) Let Us Tch Kids.

***Sheriff Star's "Round up the Sin Gang" Drama/Puppet Tape.** (J). teacher ed., pap. 9.95 incl. audio (*0-614-18228-X*) Let Us Tch Kids.

***Sheriff Star's Skits & Tape.** (J). pap. 17.90 incl. audio (*0-614-18216-6*) Let Us Tch Kids.

***Sheriff Star's Skits & Tape.** (J). pap. 9.95 (*0-614-18217-4*) Let Us Tch Kids.

***Sheriff Star's Skits & Tape.** (J). audio 9.95 (*0-614-18218-2*) Let Us Tch Kids.

Sheriff Takes the Stand. Herman Pierce & Thel Spencer. LC 92-19120. (Illus.). 192p. 1992. 14.95 (*0-87714-173-8*) Denlingers.

***Sheriff Was a Lady.** Frank Kunkel. 156p. (Orig.). 1998. mass mkt. 4.99 (*1-55237-414-9*, Pub. by Comnwlth Pub CN) Partners Pubs Grp.

Sheriff William Brady: Tragic Hero of the Lincoln County War. Donald R. LaVash. LC 85-8025. (Illus.). 128p. (Orig.). 1986. pap. 10.95 (*0-86534-064-1*) Sunstone Pr.

Sheriffs: 1911-1989: A History of Murders in the Wilderness of Washington's Last County. 2nd ed. Tony Bamonte. LC 91-70632. (Illus.). 251p. 1996. 26.00 (*0-87062-206-4*) A H Clark.

Sheriff's Blood. John Legg. 288p. 1994. mass mkt. 3.50 (*0-8217-4440-2*, Zebra Kensgtn) Kensgtn Pub Corp.

***Sheriffs' Insignia of the United States: A Guide to the Uniform Emblems Worn by the Nation's Sheriffs.** James V. Claflin. LC 96-75680. (Illus.). 144p. 1997. 49.95 (*1-882824-17-2*); pap. 29.95 (*1-882824-16-4*) Graphic Pubs.

Sheriff's Ordinary Court: Practice & Procedure. 2nd ed. D. B. White. 272p. 1994. 81.00 (*0-85459-864-2*, Pub. by Tolley Pubng UK) St Mut.

Sheriff's Proposal. Karen R. Smith. 1996. pap. 3.99 (*0-373-24074-0*, 1-24074-6) Silhouette.

***Sheriff's Son.** Stella Bagwell. (Twins on the Doorstep Ser.). 1997. mass mkt. 3.25 (*0-373-19218-5*, 1-19218-6) Silhouette.

Sherlock Chick & the Case of the Night Noises. Robert Quackenbush. LC 89-70984. (Illus.). 48p. (J). (ps-3). 1990. 5.95 (*0-8193-1194-4*) Parents.

Sherlock Chick & the Giant Egg Mystery. Robert Quackenbush. LC 88-4093. (Illus.). (J). (ps-3). 1989. 5.95 (*0-8193-1178-2*) Parents.

Sherlock Chick & the Giant Egg Mystery. Robert Quackenbush. (Parents Magazine Whole Language Library). (Illus.). 42p. (J). (gr. 1 up). lib. bdg. 17.27 (*0-8368-0897-5*) Gareth Stevens Inc.

Sherlock Chick & the Peekaboo Mystery. Robert Quackenbush. LC 87-3591. (Illus.). 48p. (J). (ps-3). 1987. 5.95 (*0-8193-1149-9*) Parents.

Sherlock Chick's First Case. (Parents Magazine Press Read-Aloud Library). (Illus.). 42p. (J). (ps-3). 1993. lib. bdg. 17.27 (*0-8368-0892-4*) Gareth Stevens Inc.

Sherlock Chick's First Case. Robert Quackenbush. LC 86-9398. (Illus.). 48p. (J). (ps-3). 1986. 5.95 (*0-8193-1148-0*) Parents.

Sherlock Holmes. Arthur Conan Doyle. (Airmont Classics Ser.). (YA). (gr. 5 up). 1966. mass mkt. 2.50 (*0-8049-0097-3*, CL-97) Airmont.

Sherlock Holmes. Arthur Conan Doyle. LC 79-24106. (Short Classics Ser.). (Illus.). 48p. (J). (gr. 4 up). 1983. lib. bdg. 24.26 (*0-8172-1657-X*) Raintree Steck-V.

Sherlock Holmes. Arthur Conan Doyle. LC 79-24106. 1991. pap. 4.95 (*0-8114-6839-9*) Raintree Steck-V.

Sherlock Holmes. Arthur Conan Doyle. 1996. pap. 17.95 (*0-312-13824-5*) St Martin.

Sherlock Holmes. Arthur Conan Doyle. (Little Brown Notebook Ser.). (Illus.). 256p. 6.95 (*1-897954-25-5*) Sterling.

Sherlock Holmes. Arthur Conan Doyle. 1996. 15.95 (*0-679-45104-8*) McKay.

Sherlock Holmes. Ed. by Milton Okun. pap. 19.95 (*0-89524-745-3*) Cherry Lane.

Sherlock Holmes: A Case of Blind Fear. Martin Powell. (Illus.). 113p. 1990. pap. 9.95 (*0-944735-50-9*) Malibu Comics Ent.

***Sherlock Holmes: Four Great Novels.** (Works). 358p. 1996. pap. 6.99 (*1-57215-205-2*, JG1204) World Pubns.

Sherlock Holmes: From Victorian Sleuth to Modern Hero. Ed. by Joseph A. King et al. 356p. 1996. 34.50 (*0-8108-3180-5*) Scarecrow.

***Sherlock Holmes: In the Dreaming Detective.** Ralph Vaughan. 1997. reprint ed. pap. 9.95 (*0-936071-65-6*) Gryphon Pubns.

Sherlock Holmes: My Life & Crimes. Michael Hardwick. LC 85-17594. (Illus.). 208p. 1986. pap. 7.95 (*0-03-007193-3*, Owl) H Holt & Co.

Sherlock Holmes: Scarlet in Gaslight, An Adventure in Terror. 2nd ed. Martin Powell & Wayne R. Smith. (Illus.). 120p. 1988. pap. 7.95 (*0-944735-09-6*) Malibu Comics Ent.

Sherlock Holmes: Screen & Sound Guide. Gordon E. Kelley. LC 94-4386. (Illus.). 343p. 1994. 37.50 (*0-8108-2859-6*) Scarecrow.

Sherlock Holmes: Selected Stories. Arthur Conan Doyle. (World's Classics Paperback Ser.). 435p. 1982. pap. 7.95 (*0-19-281530-X*) OUP.

***Sherlock Holmes: Short Stories.** (Works). 764p. 1996. pap. 6.99 (*1-57215-204-4*, JG1203) World Pubns.

***Sherlock Holmes: The Adventure at Sir Arthur Sullivan's.** unabridged ed. Timothy Heath. Ed. by William-Alan Landes. LC 97-25397. 55p. 1997. pap. 12.00 (*0-88734-926-9*) Players Pr.

Sherlock Holmes: The Adventure of the Ancient Gods. 2nd ed. Ralph E. Vaughan. Ed. by Gary Lovisi. (Illus.). 40p. 1992. 5.95 (*0-936071-19-2*) Gryphon Pubns.

Sherlock Holmes: The Complete Novels & Stories, Vol. I. Arthur Conan Doyle. 944p. 1986. mass mkt. 5.95 (*0-553-21241-9*, Bantam Classics) Bantam.

Sherlock Holmes: The Complete Novels & Stories, Vol. II. Arthur Conan Doyle. 688p. 1986. mass mkt. 5.95 (*0-553-21242-7*, Bantam Classics) Bantam.

Sherlock Holmes: The Detective & the Collector: Essays on the John Bennett Shaw Collection. Ed. by Lucy M. Brusic. (Illus.). 204p. 1995. 35.00 (*0-9632976-1-9*) A Givens Sr Collect.

Sherlock Holmes: The Major Stories with Contemporary Critical Essays. Arthur Conan Doyle. Ed. by John A. Hodgson. 464p. 1993. pap. text ed. 12.50 (*0-312-08945-7*) St Martin.

Sherlock Holmes: The Major Stories with Contemporary Critical Essays. Ed. by John A. Hodgson. 448p. 1993. text ed. 39.95 (*0-312-10304-2*) St Martin.

Sherlock Holmes: The Red Headed League & Other Stories. Edith Meiser & Frank Giacoia. Ed. by Tom Mason. (Illus.). 132p. 1991. pap. 17.95 (*0-944735-68-1*) Malibu Comics Ent.

***Sherlock Holmes: The Truth about Ludwig II: Zeua Weinstein.** Peter Neugebauer. Tr. by Richard R. Rutter from GER. 232p. 1995. 24.00 (*1-896032-42-7*) Battered Silicon.

Sherlock Holmes: Travels in the Canadian West. Ronald C. Weyman. 160p. 1994. pap. text ed. 17.00 (*0-88924-245-3*, Pub. by Simon & Pierre Pub CN) Empire Pub Srvs.

***Sherlock Holmes - Selected Stories.** Arthur Conan Doyle. Date not set. lib. bdg. 29.95 (*0-8488-1672-2*) Amereon Ltd.

Sherlock Holmes - The Four Long Stories: A Study on Scarlet; The Sign of Four; The Hounds of the Baskervilles; The Valley of Fear. large type ed. Arthur Conan Doyle. 650p. 1995. lib. bdg. 25.00 (*0-939495-89-9*) North Bks.

Sherlock Holmes, a Graphic Novel: 100 Year Anniversary Edition. Arthur Conan Doyle & William Barry. Ed. by Joan Harryman. (Illus.). 80p. (Orig.). 1987. pap. 8.95 (*0-944099-00-9*) Comic Art.

Sherlock Holmes among the Pirates: Copywright & Conan Doyle in America 1890-1930. Donald A. Redmond. LC 89-27280. (Contributions to the Study of World Literature Ser.: No. 36). 304p. 1990. text ed. 59.95 (*0-313-27230-1*, RSH/, Greenwood Pr) Greenwood.

Sherlock Holmes & Much More. Doris E. Cook. (Illus.). 112p. 1970. pap. 3.50 (*0-940748-42-8*) Conn Hist Soc.

Sherlock Holmes & the Arabian Princess. John North. 124p. 1991. 25.00 (*0-86025-270-1*, Pub. by Ian Henry Pubns UK) Empire Pub Srvs.

Sherlock Holmes & the Brighton Pavilion Mystery. Val Andrews. 124p. 1991. 25.00 (*0-86025-269-8*, Pub. by Ian Henry Pubns UK) Empire Pub Srvs.

Sherlock Holmes & the Curse of the Sign of Four. Arthur Conan Doyle. 1975. pap. 5.25 (*0-8222-1020-7*) Dramatists Play.

Sherlock Holmes & the Earthquake Machine. Austin Mitchelson & Nicholas Utechin. 1994. 25.00 (*0-86025-283-3*, Pub. by Ian Henry Pubns UK) Empire Pub Srvs.

Sherlock Holmes & the Egyptian Hall Adventure. Val Andrews. 112p. 1995. pap. 9.00 (*0-947533-43-5*) LPC InBook.

Sherlock Holmes & the Eminent Thespian. Val Andrews. 124p. 1991. 25.00 (*0-86025-268-X*, Pub. by Ian Henry Pubns UK) Empire Pub Srvs.

Sherlock Holmes & the German Nanny. John North. 144p. 1991. 25.00 (*0-86025-273-6*, Pub. by Ian Henry Pubns UK) Empire Pub Srvs.

***Sherlock Holmes & the Hellbirds.** Austin Mitchelson & Nicholas Utechin. LC 95-13261. 1995. 35.00 (*0-86025-284-1*) Players Pr.

Sherlock Holmes & the Hentzau Affair. David S. Davies. 160p. 1991. 25.00 (*0-86025-274-4*, Pub. by Ian Henry Pubns UK) Empire Pub Srvs.

Sherlock Holmes & the Houdini Birthright. Val Andrews. 160p. 1995. pap. 10.00 (*0-947533-91-5*) LPC InBook.

Sherlock Holmes & the Jewel & Other Short Plays. M. Chokai. (Sangam English Supplementary Readers Ser.). (Illus.). 169p. (J). (gr. 6). 1983. pap. 3.95 (*0-86131-330-5*) Apt Bks.

Sherlock Holmes & the Mark of the Beast. Ronald C. Weyman. (Illus.). 132p. (Orig.). 1993. pap. 16.00 (*0-88924-219-4*, Pub. by Simon & Pierre Pub CN) Empire Pub Srvs.

Sherlock Holmes & the Mysterious Friend of Oscar Wilde. Russell A. Brown. (Stonewall Inn Mysteries Ser.). 192p. 1990. 8.95 (*0-312-03932-8*) St Martin.

Sherlock Holmes & the Red Demon. John Watson. Ed. & Intro. by Larry Millett. LC 96-6723. 320p. 1996. pap. 22.95 (*0-670-87039-0*, Viking) Viking Penguin.

***Sherlock Holmes & the Shakespeare Solution.** Peter C. Donat & Barney Gould. 90p. 1997. 25.00 (*1-55246-016-9*) Battered Silicon.

***Sherlock Holmes & the Shakespeare Solution.** Peter C. Donat & Barney Gould. 90p. 1997. pap. 10.00 (*1-55246-017-7*) Battered Silicon.

Sherlock Holmes & the Somerset Hunt. Rosemary Michaud. 200p. 1993. 25.00 (*0-86025-276-0*, Pub. by Ian Henry Pubns UK) Empire Pub Srvs.

***Sherlock Holmes & the Strange Events at the Bank of England.** unabridged ed. Graham Avery. Ed. by William-Alan Landes. (Illus.). 160p. 1997. pap. 20.00 (*0-88734-927-7*) Players Pr.

Sherlock Holmes & the Ultimate Disguise. Ronald C. Weyman. (Illus.). 160p. (Orig.). 1993. pap. 16.00 (*0-88924-232-1*, Pub. by Simon & Pierre Pub CN) Empire Pub Srvs.

Sherlock Holmes by Gas-Lamp: Highlights from the First Four Decades of the Baker Street Journal. Ed. by Philip A. Shreffler. LC 88-81014. viii, 423p. 1989. 22.50 (*0-8232-1221-1*) Fordham.

Sherlock Holmes, Consulting Detective: Official Strategy Guide. Bruce Shelley. 1994. pap. 19.95 (*1-55958-603-6*) Prima Pub.

Sherlock Holmes Crossword Puzzle Book II. Ruth L. Tepper. (Illus.). 1979. pap. 8.95 (*0-393-00947-5*) Norton.

***Sherlock Holmes Demo.** Lawrence Millett. 1997. pap. 9.95 (*0-14-025882-5*) Penguin.

Sherlock Holmes Handbook. Christopher Redmond. 254p. 1994. 30.00 (*0-88924-246-1*, Pub. by Simon & Pierre Pub CN) Empire Pub Srvs.

Sherlock Holmes in Gibraltar. Sam Benady. (C). 1989. text ed. 25.00 (*0-948466-15-4*, Pub. by Gibraltar Bks UK) St Mut.

Sherlock Holmes in London: A Photographic Record of Conan Doyle's Stories. Charles Viney. 1995. 12.98 (*0-8317-1889-7*) Smithmark.

***Sherlock Holmes in Orbit.** Ed. by Martin H. Greenberg & Mike Resnick. (Orig.). 1997. 8.98 (*1-56731-182-2*, MJF Bks) Fine Comms.

Sherlock Holmes in Orbit. Ed. by Mike Resnick & Martin H. Greenberg. 320p. (Orig.). 1995. pap. 5.50 (*0-88677-636-8*) DAW Bks.

Sherlock Holmes in The Deerstalker: Chameleons' Dramascripts. Terence Mustoo. 50p. (Orig.). 1991. pap. 10.00 (*0-86025-886-6*) Players Pr.

Sherlock Holmes IQ Book. Eamonn Butler & Madsen Pirie. LC 96-20656. 208p. 1996. pap. 9.95 (*0-7867-0330-X*) Carroll & Graf.

Sherlock Holmes Is Missing. Alexander Simmons. (J). 1998. pap. 5.99 (*0-679-88204-9*, Bullseye Bks) Random Bks Yng Read.

Sherlock Holmes Letters. Ed. by R. L. Green. LC 86-50620. 272p. 1987. 32.95 (*0-87745-161-3*) U of Iowa Pr.

Sherlock Holmes Murder File. Kelvin I. Jones. 104p. 1985. 16.95 (*0-685-35563-2*) Samson Pubs.

Sherlock Holmes Mysteries: New Expanded Edition. Arthur Conan Doyle. (YA). 1985. pap. 5.95 (*0-451-52431-4*, Sig Classics) NAL-Dutton.

Sherlock Holmes of Baker Street: A Life of the World's First Consulting Detective. William S. Baring-Gould. LC 95-12302. 1995. write for info. (*0-614-05426-5*) Random.

Sherlock Holmes on the Roof of the World. Thomas K. Miller. LC 88-34116. 75p. (C). 1988. reprint ed. lib. bdg. 27.00 (*0-89370-526-8*) Borgo Pr.

***Sherlock Holmes' Puzzles of Deduction.** Tom Bullimore. LC 96-49893. 1997. write for info. (*0-8069-9675-7*) Sterling Pubng.

Sherlock Holmes Reader. Arthur Conan Doyle. (Literary Classics Ser.). 224p. (YA). 1994. 5.98 (*1-56138-429-1*) Courage Bks.

Sherlock Holmes Scrapbook. Ed. by P. Haining. (Illus.). 1991. 5.99 (*0-517-17248-8*) Random Hse Value.

Sherlock Holmes Short Stories. (Fiction Ser.). (YA). 1993. pap. text ed. 6.50 (*0-582-09676-6*, 79827) Longman.

Sherlock Holmes Solves the Science Scandals. Colin Jack. LC 97-6866. (C). 1997. 23.00 (*0-201-46139-0*) Addison-Wesley.

Sherlock Holmes Two Complete Adventures: Miniature Edition. Arthur Conan Doyle. (Illus.). 192p. 1995. 4.95 (*1-56138-521-2*) Running Pr.

Sherlock Holmes, Vol. 1: The Classic Comic Strips. Edith Meiser & Frank Giacoia. (Illus.). 140p. 1989. pap. 17.95 (*0-944735-15-0*) Malibu Comics Ent.

Sherlock Holmes's London: Following the Footsteps of London's Master Detective. Tsukasa Kobayashi & William LeBlond. LC 85-30895. (Illus.). 132p. (Orig.). 1989. reprint ed. pap. 18.95 (*0-87701-380-2*) Chronicle Bks.

***Sherlock in Black.** Philip R. Brogdon. 29p. (Orig.). 1995. pap. 8.00 (*1-896032-45-1*) Battered Silicon.

Sherlock in Love. Sena J. Naslund. 232p. 1993. 21.95 (*0-87923-977-8*) Godine.

Sherlock Street Detectives Package, 4 bks., Set. Mary B. Christian. Ed. by Janet L. Bolinske. (Sherlock Street Detectives Ser.). (Illus.). (Orig.). (J). (gr. 1-3). 1989. pap. text ed. 18.00 (*0-88335-592-2*) Milliken Pub Co.

Sherlock Takes a Wife & Other Modern Tales. Ira B. Dworkin. LC 93-90974. (Illus.). 100p. (Orig.). 1994. pap. 10.00 (*0-9639979-0-4*) Creative Writers.

***Sherlockian Star Chamber.** Steve Clarkson. (Illus.). 108p. 1996. 30.00 (*1-896648-71-1*) Battered Silicon.

***Sherlockian Star Chamber.** Steve Clarkson. (Illus.). 184p. 1996. pap. 12.00 (*1-896648-88-6*) Battered Silicon.

***Sherlockian Star Chamber.** Steve Clarkson. (Illus.). 292p. 1996. lib. bdg. 14.00 (*1-896648-89-4*) Battered Silicon.

Sherlock's Last Case. Charles Marowitz. 1984. pap. 5.25 (*0-8222-1021-5*) Dramatists Play.

Sherlock's London Today: A Walking Tour of the London of Sherlock Holmes. Gunnar E. Sundin. (Illus.). 1985. pap. 17.00 (*0-934935-00-9*) Sherlocks Book.

***Sherlock's Men: Masculinity, Conan Doyle & Cultural History.** Joseph A. Kestner. LC 97-18794. (Nineteenth Century Studies). (Illus.). 304p. 1997. text ed. 68.95 (*1-85928-394-2*, Pub. by Scolar Pr UK) Ashgate Pub Co.

Sherlock's Veiled Secret: Based on a Story by K. C. Brown & Arne Zaslove. K. C. Brown. 1996. pap. 5.25 (*0-8222-1492-X*) Dramatists Play.

Sherm Morgan's Classic Aviation Humor Bk. III. Sherman F. Morgan. 1992. pap. 6.95 (*1-881001-06-7*) Pendragon TX.

Sherman: A Soldier's Passion for Order. John F. Marszalek. LC 92-24533. 635p. 1992. 35.00 (*0-02-920135-7*, Free Press) Free Pr.

Sherman: A Soldier's Passion for Order. John F. Marszalek. 1994. pap. 17.00 (*0-679-74989-6*) Random.

Sherman: Fighting Prophet. Lloyd Lewis. LC 93-11132. (Illus.). xxi, 720p. 1993. reprint ed. pap. 20.00 (*0-8032-7945-0*, Bison Books) U of Nebr Pr.

Sherman: Merchant of Terror, Advocate of Peace. Charles E. Vetter. LC 91-31713. (Illus.). 400p. 1992. 25.00 (*0-88289-860-4*) Pelican.

Sherman: Soldier, Realist, American. Basil H. Liddell-Hart. (Illus.). 480p. 1993. reprint ed. pap. 15.95 (*0-306-80507-3*) Da Capo.

Sherman: Soldier, Realist, American. Basil H. Liddell-Hart. LC 78-536. 456p. 1978. reprint ed. text ed. 52.50 (*0-313-20288-5*, LHSH, Greenwood Pr) Greenwood.

Sherman Antitrust Act & Foreign Trade. Andre Simmons. LC 63-63263. (University of Florida Monographs: Social Sciences: No. 16). 78p. reprint ed. pap. 25.00 (*0-7837-5002-1*, 2044669) Bks Demand.

Sherman Be Nimble. Le Rap. (Nursery Rhymes Ser.). 15p. (J). (gr. k-2). 1991. pap. text ed. 4.50 (*1-56843-091-4*) BGR Pub.

Sherman Be Nimble: Big Book. Le Rap. (Nursery Rhymes Ser.). 15p. (J). (gr. k-2). 1991. pap. text ed. 23.00 (*1-56843-044-2*) BGR Pub.

Sherman Brothers Songbook. Ed. by Ronny S. Schiff et al. (Piano-Vocal-Guitar Ser.). (Illus.). 120p. (Orig.). 1991. pap. 14.95 (*0-7935-0425-2*, 00490548) H Leonard.

Sherman Day: Artist, Engineer & Forty Niner. Murphy D. Smith. LC 80-81543. 127p. 1980. 30.00 (*0-89453-152-2*) Scholarly Res Inc.

Sherman Fighting Prophet. Lloyd Lewis. 1994. 12.98 (*0-8317-3287-3*) Smithmark.

Sherman in Action. (Armor in Action Ser.). (Illus.). 1984. pap. 7.95 (*0-89747-049-4*, 2016) Squad Sig Pubns.

Sherman Letter. Leonard Palmer. 200p. 1995. 18.95 (*1-885173-08-3*) Write Way.

Sherman Letters. 2nd ed. Ed. by Rachel S. Thorndike. LC 68-8693. (American Scene Ser.). 1969. reprint ed. lib. bdg. 45.00 (*0-306-71175-3*) Da Capo.

Sherman Letters. William T. Sherman. Ed. by Rachel S. Thorndike. LC 70-168056. (Illus.). 414p. 1972. reprint ed. 55.00 (*0-404-04626-6*) AMS Pr.

Sherman Medium Tank. Steven J. Zaloga. (New Vanguard Ser.: No. 3). (Illus.). 48p. pap. 12.95 (*1-85532-296-X*, 9338, Pub. by Osprey UK) Stackpole.

Sherman Minton: Hoosier Justice. William Radcliff. LC 96-75160. 300p. 1996. 29.95 (*1-878208-81-0*) Guild Pr IN.

***Sherman Minton: New Deal Senator, Cold War Justice.** Linda C. Gugin & James E. St. Clair. LC 97-3899. 1997. 29.95 (*0-87195-116-9*) Ind Hist Soc.

Sherman Tank in U. S. & Allied Service. Steven J. Zaloga. (Vanguard Ser.: No. 26). (Illus.). 48p. pap. 10.95 (*0-85045-427-1*, 9315, Pub. by Osprey UK) Stackpole.

Sherman the Sheep. Kevin Kiser. LC 92-22745. (Illus.). 32p. (J). (gr. k-3). 1994. lib. bdg. 14.95 (*0-02-750825-0*, Mac Bks Young Read) S&S Childrens.

Sherman's Battle for Atlanta. Jacob D. Cox. LC 94-11264. Orig. Title: Atlanta. (Illus.). 294p. 1994. reprint ed. pap. 12.95 (*0-306-80588-X*) Da Capo.

Sherman's Guide to Hugh Moore Park. Lance E. Metz. LC 87-25622. 1988. pap. 3.00 (*0-930973-07-0*) Canal Hist Tech.

Sherman's Horseman: Union Cavalry Operations in the Atlanta Campaign. David Evans. LC 95-47981. (Illus.). 688p. 1996. 39.95 (*0-253-32963-9*) Ind U Pr.

***Sherman's Lagoon: Ate That, What's Next.** Jim Toomey. (Illus.). 128p. (Orig.). 1997. pap. 9.95 (*0-8362-3660-2*) Andrews & McMeel.

Sherman's March. (Civil War Ser.). (Illus.). 176p. 1986. 18.95 (*0-8094-4812-2*); lib. bdg. 25.93 (*0-8094-4813-0*) Time-Life.

Sherman's March. Cynthia Bass. 1994. 21.00 (*0-679-43033-4*, Publishers Consult) Random.

Sherman's March. Burke Davis. LC 79-5550. (Illus.). 1988. 21.95 (*0-394-50739-8*) Random.

Sherman's March. Cynthia Bass. LC 95-15143. 288p. 1995. reprint ed. pap. 12.95 (*0-553-37547-4*) Bantam.

Sherman's March. Burke Davis. Ed. by Jeff Stone & Carolyn Reidy. LC 87-45927. (Vintage Civil War Library). 356p. 1988. reprint ed. pap. 13.00 (*0-394-75763-7*, Publishers Media) Random.

Shermans March & Vietnam. James Reston. 1985. 14.95 (*0-02-602300-8*) Macmillan.

Sherman's March Through North Carolina: A Chronology. Wilson Angley et al. 129p. (Orig.). 1996. pap. 10.00 (*0-86526-266-7*) NC Archives.

Sherman's March Through the Carolinas. John G. Barrett. LC 56-14242. x, 325p. 1956. 27.50 (*0-8078-0701-X*) U of NC Pr.

Sherman's March Through the Carolinas. John G. Barrett. LC 56-14242. 335p. (C). 1996. pap. 15.95 (*0-8078-4566-3*) U of NC Pr.

S

An Asterisk (*) at the beginning of an entry indicates that the title is appearing in BIP for the first time.

S

Sherman's March to the Sea: Hood's Tennessee Campaign & the Carolina Campaigns of 1865. Jacob D. Cox. LC 94-11263. Orig. Title: The March to the Sea: Franklin & Nashville. (Illus.). 289p. 1994. reprint ed. pap. 12.95 (0-306-80587-1) Da Capo.

***Sheroes, Suga' Mommas, Sistah Girlfriends & Me.** Nichelle Holliday. (Illus.). iv, 23p. 1996. pap. 7.95 (0-9605288-1-4) Gwethine Pub Co.

Sherpa of Khumbu: People, Livestock & Landscape. B. Brower. (C). 1991. text ed. 75.00 (0-7855-0160-6, Pub. by Ratna Pustak Bhandar) St Mut.

Sherpa of Khumbu: People, Livestock, & Landscape. Barbara Brower. (Illus.). 230p. 1993. reprint ed. pap. 10. 95 (0-19-563137-4) OUP.

Sherpas: Reflections on Change in Himalayan Nepal. James F. Fisher. (Illus.). 1990. 55.00 (0-520-06770-3); pap. 16.00 (0-520-06941-2) U CA Pr.

Sherpas Through their Rituals. Sherry B. Ortner. LC 76-62582. (Cambridge Studies in Cultural Systems). (Illus.). 196p. 1978. pap. text ed. 18.95 (0-521-29216-6) Cambridge U Pr.

***Sherraby Brides.** Kay Gregory. 400p. (Orig.). 1997. mass mkt. 3.99 (1-85487-713-5, Pub. by Scarlet Bks UK) London Brdge.

***Sherrard Family of Steubenville, (Together with Letters, Records & Genealogies of Related Families, Edited by Thomas J. Sherrard)** Robert A. Sherrard. 409p. 1996. reprint ed. pap. 63.00 (0-8328-5286-4); reprint ed. lib. bdg. 73.00 (0-8328-5285-6) Higginson Bk Co.

Sherri. Leila P. Golding. LC 85-71472. (Springsong Books Ser.). 176p. (Orig.). (YA). (gr. 7-10). 1995. mass mkt. 4.99 (1-55661-586-8) Bethany Hse.

Sherrick Chronicle 1732-1992. Catharine L. Sherrick. (Illus.). 200p. 1994. lib. bdg. 25.00 (0-9641870-0-0) H Hse Pubns.

Sherrie Levine: Newborn. Ann Temkin. LC 93-33117. 1993. pap. 14.95 (0-87633-090-1) Phila Mus Art.

Sherrington: His Life & Thought. John C. Eccles & W. C. Gibson. LC 78-11359. (Illus.). 1979. 37.95 (0-387-09063-0) Spr-Verlag.

Sherris Medical Microbiology. 3rd ed. Kenneth J. Ryan. (Illus.). 1008p. 1994. text ed. 57.95 (0-8385-8541-8, A8541-3) Appleton & Lange.

Sherry. 4th ed. Julian Jeffs. (Illus.). 320p. 1993. 29.95 (0-571-16445-5) Faber & Faber.

***Sherwood.** Jane Yolen. (J). Date not set. 19.95 (0-399-23182-X) Putnam Pub Group.

Sherwood. Parke Godwin. 608p. 1992. reprint ed. mass mkt. 5.99 (0-380-70995-3, AvoNova) Avon.

Sherwood: Daniel L. Sherwood & His Paternal Ancestors, Including Sherwood Evidences Both in England & America from the First Mention of the Name in History Down to Thomas Sherwood, the American Pioneer & Francis Sherwood, the Md. Pioneer, & Some Descendants. A. Sherwood. (Illus.). 390p. 1992. reprint ed. pap. 59.50 (0-8328-2721-5); reprint ed. lib. bdg. 69. 50 (0-8328-2720-7) Higginson Bk Co.

Sherwood Anderson. Irving Howe. xvi, 272p. 1951. 42.50 (0-8047-0236-5); pap. 14.95 (0-8047-0237-3) Stanford U Pr.

Sherwood Anderson. C. B. Chase. LC 72-3565. (Studies in Fiction: No. 34). 1972. reprint ed. lib. bdg. 75.00 (0-8383-1543-7) M S G Haskell Hse.

Sherwood Anderson. Brom Weber. LC 64-64450. (University of Minnesota Pamphlets on American Writers Ser.: No. 43). 48p. (Orig.). reprint ed. pap. 25.00 (0-7837-2856-5, 2057599) Bks Demand.

Sherwood Anderson: A Collection of Critical Essays. Ed. by Walter B. Rideout. (Twentieth Century Views Ser.). 192p. 1974. 12.95 (0-13-036558-0, Spectrum IN); pap. 2.45 (0-13-036533-5, Spectrum IN) Macmillan Gen Ref.

***Sherwood Anderson: Great American Short Stories I.** Illus. by James Balkovek. LC 94-75020. (Classic Short Stories Ser.). 80p. 1994. pap. 5.95 (0-7854-0619-0, 40009) Am Guidance.

Sherwood Anderson: Selected Letters. Sherwood Anderson. Ed. by Charles E. Modlin. LC 83-6530. (Illus.). 280p. 1983. text ed. 34.00 (0-87049-404-X) U of Tenn Pr.

Sherwood Anderson & the American Short Story. P. A. Abraham. (C). 1995. 15.00 (81-85231-24-9, Pub. by Sterling Plns Pvt II) S Asia.

Sherwood Anderson Diaries, 1936-1941. Ed. by Hilbert H. Campbell. LC 86-19311. (Illus.). 1987. 24.95 (0-8203-0908-7) U of Ga Pr.

Sherwood Anderson's Love Letters to Eleanor Copenhaver Anderson. Ed. by Charles E. Modlin. LC 89-4895. (Illus.). 352p. 1990. 24.95 (0-8203-1150-2) U of Ga Pr.

Sherwood Anderson's Secret Love Letters: For Eleanor, a Letter a Day. Sherwood Anderson. Ed. by Ray L. White. LC 90-13331. (Illus.). 292p. 1991. text ed. 35.00 (0-8071-1610-6) La State U Pr.

***Sherwood Anderson's Winesburg, Ohio: With Variant Readings & Annotations.** Sherwood Anderson. Ed. by Ray L. White. LC 97-711. (Illus.). 285p. 1997. text ed. 44.95 (0-8214-1180-2) Ohio U Pr.

***Sherwood Forest & the East Midlands Walks.** Jarrold Publishing Staff. (Pathfinder Guides Ser.). 80p. 1997. pap. 16.95 (0-7117-0878-9, Pub. by Jarrold Pub UK) Seven Hills Bk.

Sherwood Game. Esther Friesner. 384p. (Orig.). 1995. mass mkt. 5.99 (0-671-87641-4) Baen Bks.

Sherwood Ring. Elizabeth M. Pope. (J). (gr. 6 up). 1990. 19.50 (0-8446-6416-2) Peter Smith.

***Sheryl Crow: Guitar.** Ed. by Jeannette DeLisa. (Illus.). 124p. (Orig.). 1997. pap. text ed. 22.95 (1-57623-882-2, 4847A) Warner Brothers.

***Sheryl Crow: Piano/Vocal/Chords.** Ed. by Jeannette DeLisa. (Illus.). 72p. (Orig.). 1997. pap. text ed. 19.95 (1-57623-924-1, 4846A) Warner Brothers.

***Sheryl Crow/Tuesday Night Music Club.** Ed. by Carol Cuellar. 60p. (Orig.). (C). 1995. pap. text ed. 16.95 (0-89724-459-1, VF2174) Warner Brothers.

***Sheryl Swoopes.** Chris W. Sehnert. LC 97-25522. (Awesome Athletes Ser.). 1998. write for info. (1-56239-845-8) Abdo & Dghtrs.

***Sheryl Swoopes, All-Star Basketball Player.** Liza N. Burby. (Making Their Mark Ser.). (J). 1997. write for info. (0-8239-5069-7) Rosen Group.

Sheryl Visits Cyril: An Ecological Tale. Valerie Hannah. Ed. by George Herrick. (Illus.). (J). 1992. pap. 6.95 (0-941281-87-6) V H Pub.

She's a Momma, Not a Movie Star: A Rose Is Rose Collection. Pat Brady. (Illus.). 128p. (Orig.). 1996. pap. 8.95 (0-8362-1087-5) Andrews & McMeel.

She's a Moving Weapon. Ayn Imperato. 32p. 1993. 3.00 (1-887151-03-6) Andromeda CA.

She's a Rebel: The History of Women in Rock & Roll. Gillian G. Gaar. LC 92-16977. (Illus.). 472p. (Orig.). 1992. pap. 16.95 (1-878067-08-7) Seal Pr WA.

She's Always Liked the Girls Best: Lesbian Plays. Claudia Allen. LC 92-44359. 228p. (Orig.). 1993. pap. 12.95 (1-879427-11-7) Third Side Pr.

She's Back. Linda Lerner. Ed. by Victoria Rivas. (Illus.). 64p. (Orig.). 1996. per. 9.50 (1-889289-04-3) Ye Olde Font Shoppe.

She's Been Away & Hidden City. Stephen Poliakoff. (Methuen Screenplay Ser.). 189p. (Orig.). (C). 1989. pap. 13.95 (0-413-62210-X, A0399, Pub. by Methuen UK) Heinemann.

***She's Been Blessed.** Dorothy M. Hazzard. 365p. (Orig.). Date not set. pap. 20.00 (0-9655177-0-5) Flamingo Pub Co.

***She's Been Working on the Railroad.** Nancy S. Levinson. LC 97-1058. 1997. pap. 16.99 (0-525-67545-0) NAL-Dutton.

She's Come Undone. Wally Lamb. 1996. pap. 14.00 (0-671-00375-5, WSP) PB.

***She's Come Undone.** Wally Lamb. 1997. 23.00 (0-671-01473-0, Pocket Books) PB.

***She's Come Undone.** Wally Lamb. LC 97-15909. 1997. lib. bdg. write for info. (1-56895-460-3, Compass) Wheeler Pub.

She's Not Fat...She's My Mom: The Journal of Amy Spellos. Amy Spellos. 128p. 1991. pap. 8.95 (0-9631004-0-8) Olive Tree.

She's Not What She Seems. Francine Pascal. (Sweet Valley High Ser.: No. 92). 160p. (YA). 1993. 3.99 (0-553-29849-6) Bantam.

She's That Universal Lady! More Information to Those Who Would Remove to America. Richard Poor. 1994. 17.95 (0-533-10910-8) Vantage.

***She's the One & the Brothers Mcmullen.** Edward Burns. 1997. pap. text ed. 14.95 (0-571-19072-3) Faber & Faber.

***She's Tricky Like Coyote: Annie Miner Peterson, an Oregon Coast Indian Woman.** Lionel Youst. LC 97-12529. (Civilization of the American Indian Ser.: Vol. 224). (Illus.). 320p. 1997. 24.95 (0-8061-2972-7) U of Okla Pr.

She's Wearing a Dead Bird on Her Head. Kathryn Lasky. LC 94-18204. (Illus.). 40p. (J). (gr. k-4). 1995. 14.95 (0-7868-0065-8); lib. bdg. 14.89 (0-7868-2052-7) Hyprn Child.

She's Wearing a Dead Bird on Her Head. Kathryn Lasky. LC 94-18204. (Illus.). 40p. (J). (ps-4). 1997. pap. 4.95 (0-7868-1164-1) Hyprn Child.

Sheshunoff Banksearch Book: Sold by State, Set. 1993. 295.00 (0-685-66714-6) Sheshunoff.

Shete Ha'Qesawot: The Two Extremes Novel. 2nd ed. R A Braudes. (Literaria Judaica Section 2 Ser.: No. 5). reprint ed. 47.50 (0-404-13861-6) AMS Pr.

***Shetland.** Anna Ritchie. (Exploring Scotland's Heritage Ser.). (Illus.). 176p. 1997. pap. 18.95 (0-11-495289-2, Pub. by Statnry Ofc UK) Seven Hills Bk.

Shetland: An Illustrated Architectural Guide. Mike Finnie. (Illus.). 104p. (C). 1990. pap. 40.00 (1-85158-390-4, Pub. by Rutland Pr UK) St Mut.

Shetland: Land of the Ocean. Jim Crumley. (Illus.). 120p. 1996. pap. 19.95 (0-948661-65-8, Pub. by Colin Baxter Ltd UK) Voyageur Pr.

Shetland Horses. Janet L. Gammie. LC 95-2237. (Horses Ser.). (J). (gr. k-3). 1995. lib. bdg. 13.98 (1-56239-438-X) Abdo & Dghtrs.

Shetland Ponies. (Illus.). 192p. 1996. 34.95 (1-873580-26-6, Pub. by Whittet Bks UK) Diamond Farm Bk.

Shetland Pony. Gail B. Stewart. (Learning about Horses Ser.). (Illus.). 48p. (J). (gr. 3-9). 1995. lib. bdg. 17.80 (1-56065-300-0) Capstone Pr.

Shetland Pony. Gail B. Stewart. (Illus.). 48p. (J). (gr. 3-7). 1995. 13.35 (0-516-35300-4) Childrens.

Shetland Sheepdog. Cathy Merrithew. (Owner's Guide to a Happy, Healthy Pet Ser.). (Illus.). 160p. 1995. 12.95 (0-87605-385-1) Howell Bk.

Shetland Sheepdog at Work. Joanne Carriera. (Illus.). 200p. Date not set. write for info. (0-931866-90-1) Alpine Pubns.

Shetland Sheepdogs. Jaime J. Sucher. (Complete Pet Owner's Manuals Ser.). (Illus.). 79p. (Orig.). 1990. pap. text ed. 6.95 (0-8120-4264-6) Barron.

Shetland Sheepdogs, AKC Rank No. 13. Beverly Pisano. (KW Dog Ser.). (Illus.). 224p. 1996. pap. 9.95 (0-7938-2357-9, KW079S) TFH Pubns.

Shetland Sheepdogs Today. Maurice Baker. (Illus.). 160p. 1993. 24.95 (0-948955-40-6, Pub. by Ringpr Bks UK) Seven Hills Bk.

Shetland Summer. Billie T. Signer. LC 88-18480. (Illus.). 125p. (Orig.). (J). (gr. 5-8). 1990. pap. 3.95 (0-8198-6884-1) Pauline Bks.

Shevchenko & the Critics, Eighteen Sixty-One to Nineteen Eighty. Ed. by George S. Luckyj. 1981. pap. 11.95 (0-8020-6377-2) U of Toronto Pr.

Shevchenko & the Critics, 1861-1980. Ed. by George S. Luckyj. Tr. by Dolly Ferguson & Sophia Yurkevich. LC 81-192007. 536p. reprint ed. pap. 152.80 (0-8357-4731-X, 2037647) Bks Demand.

Shevilei Hahagadah. 1980. 5.00 (0-686-46793-0) T Black.

Shewa, Menilek, & the Ethiopian Empire. R. H. Darkwah. (Illus.). 233p. (C). Date not set. 37.95 (0-8419-5310-4, Africana) Holmes & Meier.

Shewhart-Type Charts in Statistical Process Control. C. B. Roes. 119p. 1995. pap. 23.50 (90-5170-365-1, Pub. by Thesis Pubs NE) IBD Ltd.

Shewings of Julian of Norwich. Ed. by Georgia R. Crampton. (Teams Middle English Text Ser.). 1996. pap. 10.00 (1-879288-45-1) Medieval Inst.

***Shh! Listen.** (J). 1942. write for info. (1-56476-356-0, Chariot Bks) Chariot Victor.

Shh! The Whale Is Smiling. Josephine Nobisso. LC 91-21521. (Illus.). 40p. (J). (ps-1). 1992. 14.00 (0-671-74908-0, Green Tiger S&S) S&S Childrens.

Shh! We're Writing the Constitution. Jean Fritz. (Illus.). 64p. (J). (gr. 3-7). 1987. pap. 8.95 (0-399-21404-6, Putnam) Putnam Pub Group.

***Shhh!** Julie Sykes. LC 96-30794. (Illus.). (J). 1996. 14.95 (1-888444-07-X) Little Tiger.

Shhh! A Lift the Flap Book. Sally Grindley. 32p. (J). (ps-3). 1992. 13.95 (0-316-32899-5, Joy St Bks) Little.

Shhh: How to Keep Trade Secrets...Secret. Philip L. Williams. LC 92-97388. 235p. (Orig.). 1993. pap. 39.95 (0-9631484-5-1) Voyager Rec.

Shhh, I'm Thinking: Poems. Gretna Wilkinson. 30p. 1996. pap. 7.00 (1-886841-02-0, Hummingbird Folios) Ladybug Publ.

Shhh Is a Four Letter Word! Laughs for Library Lovers. Andy Gibbons & Jeanne D. Nelson. LC 83-62296. 120p. (Orig.). (C). 1984. pap. 10.95 (0-88247-702-1) R & E Pubs.

Shhh! It's the Principal. Lamar Dodson. LC 91-70634. 160p. 1991. pap. 9.95 (1-879384-05-1); boxed 17.95 (1-879384-06-X) Cypress Hse.

***Shhhh.** (J). 1985. pap. write for info. (0-88207-072-X, Chariot Bks) Chariot Victor.

Shhhh. Kevin Henkes. LC 88-18771. (Illus.). 24p. (J). (ps up). 1989. 11.95 (0-688-07985-7); lib. bdg. 11.88 (0-688-07986-5) Greenwillow.

Shi, Its Religion: A History of Islam in Persia & Iraq. Dwight M. Donaldson. 1976. lib. bdg. 59.95 (0-8490-2598-2) Gordon Pr.

Shi'a Islam: From Religion to Revolution. Heinz Halm. Ed. by Bernard Lewis & Heath W. Lowry. Tr. by Allison Brown from GER. (Princeton Series on the Middle East). Orig. Title: Der Schiitische Islam: Von der Religion zur Revolution. 260p. 1997. pap. text ed. 16.95 (1-55876-135-7) Wiener Pubs Inc.

***Shi'a Islam: From Religion to Revolution.** Heinz Halm. Ed. by Bernard Lewis & Heath W. Lowry. Tr. by Allison Brown from GER. (Princeton Series on the Middle East). Orig. Title: Der Schiitische Islam: Von der Religion zur Revolution. 260p. 1997. 39.95 (1-55876-134-9) Wiener Pubs Inc.

Shia Origin & Faith. Ed. by Kashif Al-Gita. Tr. by M. Fazal Haq from ARA. 284p. 1984. pap. 3.00 (0-941724-23-9) Islamic Seminary.

***Shias Are the Ahl Al-Sunnah.** Muhammad A. Al-Samawi. Ed. by Nasir Shamsi. Tr. by Yasin T. Al-Jibouri. LC 96-90442. 350p. 1997. 18.95 (0-533-12055-1) Vantage.

Shiatsu. Ray Ridolfi. (Tuttle Alternative Health Ser.). (Illus.). 128p. (Orig.). 1993. pap. 12.95 (0-8048-1834-7) C E Tuttle.

Shiatsu. Ray Ridolfi. (Alternative Health Ser.). (Illus.). 114p. (Orig.). 1996. pap. 11.95 (0-356-20994-6, Pub. by Optima UK) Trafalgar.

***Shiatsu: A Fully Illustrated Guide to Safe Effective Home Treatment.** Susanne Franzen. (New Life Library). (Illus.). 64p. 1997. 9.95 (1-85967-400-3, Lorenz Bks) Anness Pub.

Shiatsu: Japanese Finger-Pressure Therapy. Tokujiro Namikoshi. LC 68-19983. (Illus.). 84p. 1994. pap. 12.00 (0-87040-169-6) Japan Pubns USA.

Shiatsu: Japanese Finger Pressure Therapy. William Shultz. (Illus.). 1991. 5.99 (0-517-22525-5) Random Hse Value.

Shiatsu: The Complete Guide. Chris Jarmey & Gabriel Mojay. (Illus.). 1992. pap. 28.00 (0-7225-2243-6) Thorsons SF.

Shiatsu for Beginners: A Step-by-Step Guide: Achieve Overall Health & Well-Being with Finger-Pressure Massage. Nigel Dawes. 1995. pap. 16.95 (0-7615-0132-0) Prima Pub.

Shiatsu for Women: The Complete Guide to Restoring Health, Vitality & Well-Being. Ray Ridolfi & Suzanne Franzen. (Illus.). 176p. (Orig.). 1996. pap. 17.00 (1-85538-482-5, Pub. by Aquarian Pr UK) Thorsons SF.

Shiatsu Handbook: A Guide to the Traditional Art of Shiatsu Acupressure. Shizuko Yamamoto & Patrick McCarty. LC 95-2396. (Illus.). 276p. Date not set. pap. 14.95 (0-89529-714-0) Avery Pub.

Shiatsu Manual: Step-by-Step Techniques for a Full Body Treatment. Gerry Thompson. LC 94-12944. (Illus.). 144p. 1994. pap. 14.95 (0-8069-0738-X) Sterling.

Shiatsu Therapy: Theory & Practice. Ti Namikoshi. pap. 18.95 (0-685-70705-9) Wehman.

Shiatsu Way to Health: Relaxation & Relief at a Touch. Toru Namikoshi. Tr. by Susan K. McCandless. LC 87-81676. (Illus.). 160p. 1988. pap. 22.00 (0-87011-796-3) Kodansha.

***Shiatsu/Shin Tai Vol. 1: The Evolution & Synthesis of Traditional Bodywork.** Saul Goodman. (Illus.). 200p. (Orig.). 1996. pap. 19.95 (0-940843-01-3) Infi-Tech Pubns.

Shibas. Richard K. Tomita. (KW Ser.). (Illus.). 192p. 1992. 9.95 (0-86622-220-0, KW-226) TFH Pubns.

***Shibboleth: My Revolting Life.** Penny Rimbaud. 1997. pap. text ed. 9.95 (1-873176-40-6) AK Pr Dist.

***Shibboreth or Every Man a Freemason.** 1996. pap. 12.95 (1-56459-996-5) Kessinger Pub.

Shibori: Japanese Shaped Resist Dyeing. Yoshiko Wada et al. LC 82-48789. (Illus.). 304p. 1983. 120.00 (0-87011-559-6) Kodansha.

Shibumi. Trevanian. 448p. 1983. mass mkt. 6.99 (0-345-31180-9) Ballantine.

Shibumi. large type ed. Trevanian. 619p. 1981. 27.99 (0-7089-8004-X) Ulverscroft.

Shidduchim & Zivugim: The Torah's Perspective on Choosing Your Mate. Yehudah Lebovits. 176p. (Orig.). 1988. 14.95 (0-944070-01-9) Targum Pr.

Shiel in Diverse Hands: A Collection of Essays. Moskowitz et al. LC 82-61695. 501p. 1983. pap. 32.50 (0-685-04346-0) Reynolds Morse.

Shiel in Diverse Hands: A Collection of Essays in M. P. Shiel see Works of M. P. Shiel

Shield, 5 vols. in 1. Incl. Vol. 1. Russia & the Jews. Maxim Gorky. (ENG & RUS.). 1975. 35.00 (0-318-52735-9, Greenwood Pr); Vol. 2. First Step. Leonid Andreyev. (ENG & RUS.). 1975. 35.00 (0-318-52736-7, Greenwood Pr); Vol. 3. Jewish Question in Russia. Paul Milyukov. (ENG & RUS.). 1975. 35.00 (0-318-52737-5, Greenwood Pr); Vol. 4. Jewish Question As a Russian Question. Dmitri S. Merezhkovsky. (ENG & RUS.). 1975. 35.00 (0-318-52738-3, Greenwood Pr); LC 74-97305. 209p. (ENG.). 1975. reprint ed. Set text ed. 35. 00 (0-8371-2633-9, GOSH, Greenwood Pr) Greenwood.

Shield & Storm: Personal Recollections of the Air War in the Gulf. John Godden. (Illus.). 156p. 1994. 27.00 (1-85753-002-0, Pub. by Brasseys UK) Brasseys Inc.

Shield & Sword: Jewish Polemics Against Christianity in France & Spain 1100-1500. Hanne Trautner-Kromann. (Texts & Studies in Medieval & Early Modern Judaism: No. 8). 216p. 1993. 110.00 (3-16-145995-4, Pub. by J C B Mohr GW) Coronet Bks.

Shield & Sword: Neutrality & Engagement in American Foreign Policy. Elliott Abrams. 1994. text ed. 22.95 (0-02-900165-X, Free Press) Free Pr.

Shield Between the Worlds. Adrienne Martine-Barnes & Diana L. Paxson. 336p. 1995. mass mkt. 4.99 (0-380-75802-4, AvoNova) Avon.

Shield Continuity Testing. Norman H. Haskell, Jr. (ABC Pocket Guide for the Field Ser.). (Illus.). 19p. 1980. pap. 6.95 (1-56016-030-6) ABC TeleTraining.

Shield Devices of the Greeks in Art & Literature. G. H. Chase. (Illus.). 90p. 1979. reprint ed. pap. 12.50 (0-89005-260-3) Ares.

Shield Five Cent Series: A Comprehensive Listing of Known Varieties. Edward L. Fletcher, Jr. (Illus.). 229p. (C). 1994. pap. 37.00 (0-9642451-1-6); lib. bdg. 95.00 (0-9642451-0-8); spiral bd. 40.00 (0-9642451-2-4) Dead End Pubng.

Shield in Space? Technology, Politics, & the Strategic Defense Initiative. Sanford Lakoff & Herbert F. York. (California Studies in Global Conflict & Cooperation: Vol. 1). 1989. 45.00 (0-520-06650-2) U CA Pr.

Shield of Achilles & the Poetics of Ekphrasis: Theory, Philology, & the Shield of Achilles. Andrew S. Becker. 200p. (C). 1995. pap. text ed. 22.95 (0-8476-7998-5); lib. bdg. 56.00 (0-8476-7997-7) Rowman.

Shield of Faith. deluxe ed. Martyria Madauss. 1974. 0.95 (3-87209-659-1) Evang Sisterhood Mary.

Shield of Fear. Franklin W. Dixon. Ed. by Ann Greenberg. (Hardy Boys Ser.: No. 91). 160p. (J). (gr. 3-6). reprint ed. pap. 3.99 (0-671-66308-9, Minstrel Bks) PB.

Shield of Homer: Narrative Structure in the Iliad. Keith Stanley. LC 92-2410. 492p. (C). 1993. text ed. 49.50 (0-691-06938-7) Princeton U Pr.

Shield of Honor. Gilbert Morris. LC 94-45604. (Wakefield Dynasty Ser.: Vol. 3). 400p. 1995. pap. 11.99 (0-8423-5930-3) Tyndale.

Shield of Perseus: The Vision & Imagination of Howard Nemerov. Julia A. Bartholomay. LC 70-137851. 176p. reprint ed. pap. 50.20 (0-8357-6714-0, 2035346) Bks Demand.

Shield of Republic - Sword of Empire: A Bibliography of United States Military Affairs, 1783-1846. Compiled by John C. Fredriksen. LC 89-25620. (Bibliographies & Indexes in American History Ser.: No. 15). 446p. 1990. text ed. 89.50 (0-313-25384-6, FUM/, Greenwood Pr) Greenwood.

Shield of the Young Methodist. Hilary T. Hudson. 88p. 1990. write for info. (0-8187-0126-9) Harlo Press.

Shield of Time. Poul Anderson. 1991. mass mkt. 4.99 (0-8125-1000-3) Tor Bks.

Shield of Zion: The Israel Defense Forces. Netanel Lorch. (Illus.). 144p. 1992. 34.95 (0-943231-47-7) Howell Pr VA.

Shield the Source: San Antonio Reporter Endures Jail to Uncover Corruption & Murder. Brian Karem. LC 92-80433. 1992. 21.95 (0-88282-104-0) New Horizon NJ.

Shieldbreaker's Story: The Last Book of Swords. Fred Saberhagen. (Swords Ser.). 256p. 1995. 4.99 (0-8125-0577-8) Tor Bks.

Shielded Metal Arc Welding. Gellerman. (Welding Ser.). 1998. 18.95 (0-8273-7611-1) Delmar.

Shielded Metal Arc Welding. Gellerman. (Welding Ser.). 1998. 12.95 (0-8273-7612-X) Delmar.

Shielded Metal Arc Welding. Gellerman. (Welding Ser.). 1997. 26.96 (0-8273-7613-8) Delmar.

An Asterisk (*) at the beginning of an entry indicates that the title is appearing in BIP for the first time.

Shielding Aspects of Accelerators, Targets & Irradiation Facilities. 392p. (Orig.). 1995. pap. 63.00 (*92-64-14327-0*) OECD.

Shielding Design Methodology & Procedures. Donald R. White. LC 85-80685. (Illus.). 128p. 1986. 98.00 (*0-932263-26-7*) emf-emi Control.

Shielding Fundamentals & Methods see Engineering Compendium on Radiation Shielding

***Shielding Our Innocents: A Prevention Plan on Child Sexual Abuse.** LC 97-93262. 208p. 1997. write for info. (*0-9657496-0-6*) Metallo Hse.

***Shield's Lady.** Jayne Ann Krentz, pseud. 1996. mass mkt. 5.99 (*0-446-60267-1*) Warner Bks.

Shield's Lady. large type ed. Jayne Ann Krentz. LC 96-10394. 1996. 25.95 (*0-7862-0687-X*) Thorndike Pr.

Shields of Pride. Elizabeth Chadwick. 1994. mass mkt. 4.99 (*0-345-38839-9*) Ballantine.

Shields of Pride. large type ed. Elizabeth Chadwick. LC 94-33627. 471p. 1995. 22.95 (*0-7838-1154-3*, GK Hall) Thorndike Pr.

Shieling, 1600-1840: The Case of the Central Scottish Highlands. Albert Bil. 400p. (C). 1996. 90.00 (*0-85976-158-4*, Pub. by J Donald UK) St Mut.

Shielography Updated see Works of M. P. Shiel

***Shiflet. The Shiflets of Georgia.** Marteal Wells. 283p. 1996. reprint ed. pap. 43.00 (*0-8328-5352-6*); reprint ed. lib. bdg. 53.00 (*0-8328-5351-8*) Higginson Bk Co.

Shifra Stein's Day Trips from Baltimore: Getaways Less Than Two Hours Away. 3rd ed. Bob Willis & Gwyn Willis. Ed. by Shifra Stein. LC 95-52617. (Shifra Stein's Day Trips Ser.). (Illus.). 176p. (Orig.). 1996. pap. 10.95 (*1-56440-878-7*) Globe Pequot.

***Shifra Stein's Day Trips from Cincinnati: Getways Less Than 2 Hours Away.** 4th rev. ed. Amy Weirick. LC 97-22544. (Shifra Stein's Day Trips Ser.). (Illus.). 224p. (Orig.). 1997. pap. 12.95 (*0-7627-0053-X*) Globe Pequot.

***Shifra Stein's Day Trips from Houston: Getaways Less Than Two Hours Away.** 7th rev. ed. Carol Barrington. (Illus.). 240p. 1998. pap. 12.95 (*0-7627-0110-2*) Globe Pequot.

Shifra Steins Day Trips from Phoenix, Tucson & Flagstaff: Getaways Less Than Two Hours Away. 4th ed. Pam Hait. LC 96-9611. (Shifra Stein's Day Trips Ser.). (Illus.). 192p. 1995. pap. 12.95 (*1-56440-759-4*) Globe Pequot.

***Shifra Stein's Day Trips from Phoenix, Tucson, & Flagstaff: Getaways Less Than Two Hours Away.** 5th rev. ed. Pam Hait. (Shifra Stein's Day Trips Ser.). (Illus.). 192p. 1997. pap. 12.95 (*0-7627-0111-0*) Globe Pequot.

Shifra Stein's Kansas City. Ed. by Shifra Stein. (Illus.). 64p. (Orig.). 1986. pap. 9.95 (*0-9609752-5-X*) S Stein Prods.

Shift. George Foy. LC 95-48837. (Bantam Spectra Bk.). 480p. 1996. pap. 12.95 (*0-553-37544-X*) Bantam.

***Shift.** George Foy. 528p. 1997. mass mkt. 5.99 (*0-553-57471-X*) Bantam.

Shift. Jeredith Merrin. LC 95-39347. (Phoenix Poets Ser.). (Illus.). 96p. 1996. lib. bdg. 20.00 (*0-226-52063-3*) U Ch Pr.

Shift. Jeredith Merrin. 96p. 1996. pap. 9.95 (*0-226-52064-1*) U Ch Pr.

Shift & Shape of Spectral Lines. R. Breene & R. Belcher. LC 60-14951. (International Series of Monographs on Analytical Chemistry: Vol. 61). 1961. 155.00 (*0-08-009549-6*, Pub. by Pergamon Repr UK) Franklin.

Shift in Value Added Minus Payroll & the Forecasting of Growth for Industries in Maine. Benjamin H. Stevens & J. R. Rower. (Discussion Paper Ser.: No. 125). 20p. (Orig.). 1981. pap. 10.00 (*1-55869-002-6*) Regional Sci Res Inst.

Shift of the Wind. Clodine Ross. 1996. 12.95 (*0-533-11027-0*) Vantage.

Shift Register Sequences. rev. ed. Solomon W. Golomb. 1981. pap. 34.80 (*0-89412-048-4*) Aegean Park Pr.

Shift Work Swindle. Jean Coussins. 1979. 25.00 (*0-317-54920-0*, Pub. by NCCL UK) St Mut.

Shifting. Paul Krapfel. (Illus.). 180p. (Orig.). 1989. pap. 11.75 (*0-933421-48-6*) Redwood Seed.

Shifting Agriculture & Sustainable Development. P. S. Ramakrishnan. (Man & the Biosphere Ser.: Vol. 10). (Illus.). 550p. (C). 1992. 85.00 (*1-85070-383-3*) Prthnon Pub.

***Shifting Alliances: Church & State in English Schools.** Priscilla Chadwick. 128p. 1997. pap. 31.95 (*0-304-70124-6*) Cassell.

Shifting & Incidence of Taxation. 5th rev. ed. Edwin R. Seligman. LC 68-30543. (Reprints of Economic Classics Ser.). (Illus.). xiii, 431p. 1969. reprint ed. 49.50 (*0-678-00478-1*) Kelley.

Shifting Borders: East European Poetry of the Eighties. Ed. by Walter Cummins. LC 91-58885. 488p. 1993. 59.50 (*0-8386-3497-4*) Fairleigh Dickinson.

Shifting Boundaries: Contextual Approaches to the Structure of Theological Education. Ed. by Edward Farley & Barbara G. Wheeler. 288p. (Orig.). 1991. pap. 24.00 (*0-664-25172-2*) Westminster John Knox.

Shifting Circles of Support: Contextualising Kinship & Gender in South Asia & Sub-Saharan Africa. Ed. by Rajni Palriwala & Carla Risseeuw. LC 95-30053. (Illus.). 343p. 1996. 35.00 (*0-8039-9275-0*) AltaMira Pr.

Shifting Contexts: The Generation of Effective Psychotherapy. Bill O'Hanlon & James Wilk. LC 86-26986. 289p. 1987. lib. bdg. 34.95 (*0-89862-677-3*) Guilford Pr.

Shifting Contexts: Transformations in Anthropological Knowledge. Ed. by Marilyn Strathern. LC 94-46811. (Uses of Knowledge Ser.). 208p. (C). 1995. pap. 17.95 (*0-415-10795-4*) Routledge.

Shifting Contexts: Transformations in Anthropological Knowledge. Ed. by Marilyn Strathern. LC 94-46811. (Uses of Knowledge Ser.). 208p. (C). (gr. 13). 1995. text ed. 59.95 (*0-415-10794-6*) Routledge.

Shifting Cultivation in India. Sachchidananda. (C). 1989. 17.50 (*81-7022-040-8*, Pub. by Concept II) S Asia.

Shifting Cultivation in Southeastern Asia. Joseph E. Spencer. 1978. 45.00 (*0-520-03517-8*) U CA Pr.

Shifting Cultivation in Southeastern Asia. Joseph E. Spencer. LC 67-63051. (University of California Publications in Social Welfare: Vol. 19). 256p. reprint ed. pap. 73.00 (*0-317-29507-1*, 2021275) Bks Demand.

Shifting for Himself. Horatio Alger, Jr. (Works of Horatio Alger Jr.). 1989. reprint ed. lib. bdg. 79.00 (*0-685-27562-0*) Rprt Serv.

***Shifting Fortunes: The Rise & Decline of American Labor, from the 1820s to the Present.** Daniel Nelson. LC 97-22108. (American Ways Ser.). 192p. 1997. 22.50 (*1-56663-179-3*) I R Dee.

***Shifting Fortunes: The Rise & Decline of American Labor, from the 1820's to the Present.** Daniel Nelson. LC 97-22108. (American Ways Ser.). 1997. pap. write for info. (*1-56663-180-7*) I R Dee.

Shifting Fortunes of Wilhelm Raabe: A History of Criticism as a Cautionary Tale. Jeffrey L. Sammons. (LCGERM Ser.: Vol. 69). xiv, 164p. 1991. pap. 36.00 (*1-879751-08-9*) Camden Hse.

Shifting Frames: English - Literature - Writing. Kevin Hart. 95p. (C). 1988. 60.00 (*0-7300-0257-8*, Pub. by Deakin Univ AT) St Mut.

Shifting Frontiers in Late Antiquity. Ed. by Ralph W. Mathisen & Hagith Sivan. 400p. 1996. 89.95 (*0-86078-588-2*, Pub. by Variorum UK) Ashgate Pub Co.

Shifting Gears. Nuala Beck. 208p. 1995. 20.00 (*0-00-215785-3*, HarpT) HarpC.

Shifting Gears. Gary Bishop. Ed. by Cindy McClain. 190p. (Orig.). 1992. pap. text ed. 7.95 (*1-56309-017-1*, New Hope) Womans Mission Union.

Shifting Gears: A Bicycling Guide to West Virginia. Kurt B. Detwiler. LC 95-39712. (Illus.). 160p. (Orig.). 1995. spiral bd. 14.95 (*0-939009-93-5*) EPM Pubns.

Shifting Gears: Changing Labor Relations in the U. S. Automobile Industry. Harry C. Katz. 248p. 1987. reprint ed. pap. 9.95 (*0-262-61050-7*) MIT Pr.

Shifting Gears: Technology, Literature, Culture in Modernist America. Cecelia Tichi. LC 86-16161. (Illus.). xviii, 310p. (C). 1987. pap. 19.95 (*0-8078-4167-6*) U of NC Pr.

Shifting Genres, Changing Realities: Reading the Late Eighteenth-Century Novel. Laurie Fitzgerald. LC 93-37794. (Age of Revolution & Romanticism Ser.: Vol. 8). 140p. (C). 1995. text ed. 46.95 (*0-8204-2305-X*) P Lang Pubng.

Shifting Ground: Exile Literature from the Spanish Civil War. Michael Ugarte. LC 88-16957. 256p. (C). 1988. text ed. 41.95 (*0-8223-0857-6*) Duke.

Shifting Histories: Transforming Education for Social Change. Ed. by Gladys Capella-Noya et al. (Harvard Educational Review Reprint Ser.: No. 26). 420p. (Orig.). (C). 1995. pap. 19.95 (*0-916690-28-8*) Harvard Educ Rev.

Shifting Identities, Shifting Racisms: A Feminism & Psychology Reader. Ed. by Kum-Kum Bhavnani & Ann Phoenix. 224p. 1994. 69.95 (*0-8039-7786-7*); pap. 22.95 (*0-8039-7787-5*) Sage.

Shifting into Miracle Thinking. David Hiller & Margaret F. Hiller. 42p. (Orig.). (C). 1994. pap. 5.95 (*1-878555-07-3*) Oakbridge Univ Pr.

Shifting Involvements: Private Interest & Public Action. Albert O. Hirschman. LC 81-47922. (Eliot Janeway Lectures on Historical Economics: No. 1979). (Illus.). 149p. reprint ed. pap. 42.50 (*0-8357-3974-0*, 2036427) Bks Demand.

Shifting Landscape. Henry Roth. 320p. 1994. pap. 13.95 (*0-312-11139-8*) St Martin.

Shifting Lines in the Sand: Kuwait's Elusive Frontier with Iraq. David H. Finnie. 221p. 1992. 34.50 (*0-674-80639-5*) HUP.

Shifting Loyalties. Daniel Cano. LC 95-13564. 1995. pap. 9.95 (*1-55885-144-5*) Arte Publico.

Shifting Paradigms: New Approaches to Horace's "Ars Poetica" Bernard Frischer. (American Classical Studies). 160p. 1991. 24.95 (*1-55540-619-X*, 40 04 27); pap. 16.95 (*1-55540-620-3*, 40 04 27) Scholars Pr GA.

Shifting Paradigms in Software Engineering: Proceedings of the 7th Joint Conference of the Austrian Computer Society (OCG) & the John Von Neumann Society for Computing Sciences (NJSZT) in Klagenfurt, Austria, 1992. Ed. by R. Mittermeir. (Illus.). x, 252p. 1992. 41.95 (*0-387-82408-1*) Spr-Verlag.

Shifting Paradigms in Student Affairs: Culture, Context, Teaching & Learning. Fried, Jan, & Associates Staff. 242p. (Orig.). (C). 1995. lib. bdg. 49.00 (*1-883485-07-X*) Am Coll Personnel.

Shifting Paradigms in Student Affairs: Culture, Context, Teaching & Learning. Fried, Jan, & Associates Staff. 242p. (Orig.). (C). 1995. pap. text ed. 24.95 (*1-883485-08-8*) Am Coll Personnel.

Shifting Perspectives & the Stylish Style: Mannerism in Shakespeare & His Jacobean Contemporaries. John Greenwood. 228p. 1988. 45.00 (*0-8020-2617-6*) U of Toronto Pr.

Shifting Point: Theatre, Film, Opera, 1946-1987. Peter Brook. LC 94-2600. (Illus.). 1994. pap. 10.95 (*1-55936-081-X*) Theatre Comm.

Shifting Realities of Philip K. Dick. Ed. & Intro. by Lawrence Sutin. 384p. 1996. pap. 13.00 (*0-679-74787-7*, Vin) Random.

Shifting Relations: Science, Technology & Technoscience. Ed. by Peter Medway. 110p. 1995. pap. 40.00 (*0-7300-1606-4*, ESC810, Pub. by Deakin Univ AT) St Mut.

Shifting Safety & Health Paradigms. F. David Pierce. 250p. 1996. text ed. 59.00 (*0-86587-527-8*) Gov Insts.

Shifting Sands. Suzanne Ellison. (Superromance Ser.: No. 488). 1992. mass mkt. 3.29 (*0-373-70488-7*, 1-70488-1) Harlequin Bks.

Shifting Sands. N. N. Bray. LC 70-180321. reprint ed. 39.50 (*0-404-56216-7*) AMS Pr.

Shifting Sands: Government-Group Relationships in the Health Care Sector. Joan P. Boase. LC 93-90659. (Canadian Public Administration Ser.). 240p. 1994. 39.95 (*0-7735-1158-X*, Pub. by McGill CN) U of Toronto Pr.

Shifting Sands: The British in South Arabia. David Ledger. 232p. (C). 1995. 51.00 (*0-907151-08-6*, Pub. by IMMEL Pubng UK) St Mut.

Shifting Sands Beneath the State: Unemployment, the Labor Market, & the Local Community, 1893-1922. Peter C. Seixas. LC 92-38642. (Non-profit Institutions in America Ser.). 320p. 1993. text ed. 25.00 (*0-8153-0943-0*) Garland.

Shifting Scenes: Interviews on Women, Writing, & Politics in Post-68 France. Ed. by Alice A. Jardine et al. (Gender & Culture Ser.). 222p. (C). 1993. pap. 15.00 (*0-231-06773-9*); text ed. 35.00 (*0-231-06772-0*) Col U Pr.

Shifting Scenes of the Modern European Theatre. Hallie Flanagan. LC 79-187832. (Illus.). 1980. reprint ed. 34.95 (*0-405-08522-2*, Pub. by Blom Pubns UK) Ayer.

***Shifting Song.** Peter J. Davis. (Altertumswissenschaftliche Texte und Studien: Bd. 26). iv, 274p. (GER.). 1993. write for info. (*3-487-09748-6*) G Olms Pubs.

Shifting Sources of Power & Influence. Charles E. Dwyer. LC 92-74648. 80p. (Orig.). (C). 1993. pap. text ed. 25.95 (*0-924674-12-1*) Am Coll Phys Execs.

***Shifting Stars.** Page Lambert. LC 96-53930. 1997. 23.95 (*0-312-86324-1*) St Martin.

Shifting Target. (Executioner Ser.). 1994. mass mkt. 3.50 (*0-373-61181-1*, 1-61181-3) Harlequin Bks.

Shifting the Boundaries: Transformation of the Languages of Public & Private in the 18th Century. Ed. by Castiglione & Sharpe. 272p. 1995. text ed. 59.95 (*0-85989-444-4*, Pub. by Univ Exeter Pr UK) Northwestern U Pr.

Shifting the Burden: The Struggle over Growth & Corporate Taxation. Cathie J. Martin. (American Politics & Political Economy Ser.). (Illus.). 260p. 1991. pap. text ed. 19.50 (*0-226-50833-1*) U Ch Pr.

Shifting the Burden: The Struggle over Growth & Corporate Taxation. Cathie J. Martin. (American Politics & Political Economy Ser.). (Illus.). 260p. 1991. lib. bdg. 52.00 (*0-226-50832-3*) U Ch Pr.

***Shifting the Ground: American Women Writers' Revisions of Nature, Gender, & Race.** Rachel Stein. LC 97-9841. 240p. 1997. text ed. 32.50 (*0-8139-1741-7*) U Pr of Va.

Shifting the Instructional Focus to the Learner. Ed. by Sally S. Magnan. LC 55-34379. (Reports of the Northeast Conference on the Teaching of Foreign Languages). 177p. 1990. pap. 10.95 (*0-915432-90-0*) NE Conf Teach Foreign.

Shifting Time & Space: The Story of Videotape. Eugene Marlow & Eugene Secunda. LC 90-7808. 192p. 1991. text ed. 49.95 (*0-275-93408-X*, C3408, Praeger Pubs) Greenwood.

Shifting Town: Glass Plate Images of Clermont & Its People. G. C. Pullar. LC 86-16070. (Illus.). 232p. 1987. text ed. 49.95 (*0-7022-2012-4*, Pub. by Univ Queensland Pr AT) Intl Spec Bk.

Shifting Web: New & Selected Poems. Lewis Turco. LC 85-1056. 199p. 1989. pap. 16.00 (*1-55728-091-6*) U of Ark Pr.

Shifting Winds & Strong Currents: George Bush Charts a Trade-Policy Approach to Japan. Michael J. Fratantuono. (Pew Case Studies in Internationl Affairs). 50p. (C). 1993. pap. text ed. 3.50 (*1-56927-153-4*) Geo U Inst Dplmcy.

Shifting World: Social Change & Nostalgia in the American Novel. David C. Stineback. LC 74-31510. 192p. 1976. 29.50 (*0-8387-1686-5*) Bucknell U Pr.

Shifts & Transpositions in Medieval Narrative: A Festschrift for Dr. Elspeth Kennedy. Ed. by Karen Pratt. (Illus.). 224p. (C). 1994. 53.00 (*0-85991-421-6*, DS Brewer) Boydell & Brewer.

Shifts in the Functions of Cities & Towns of India, Nineteen Sixty-One to Nineteen Seventy-One. Asok Mitra et al. 1981. 47.50 (*0-8364-0719-9*, Pub. by Abhinav II) S Asia.

Shifts in the Social Contract: Understanding Change in American Society. Beth A. Rubin. LC 95-13200. (Illus.). 224p. (Orig.). (C). 1995. pap. 17.95 (*0-8039-9040-5*) Pine Forge.

***Shiftwork: Problems & Solutions.** Ed. by W. Peter Colquhoun et al. (Arbeitswissenschaft in der Betrieblichen Praxis Ser.: Bd. 7). 224p. (GER.). 1996. pap. 42.95 (*0-8204-3151-6*) P Lang Pubng.

***Shiftwork: Problems & Solutions.** Ed. by W. Peter Colquhoun et al. (Arbeitswissenschaft in der Betrieblichen Praxis Ser.: Bd. 7). 224p. (GER.). 1996. pap. 42.95 (*3-631-49133-6*) P Lang Pubng.

***Shiftwork, Capital Hours & Productivity Change.** Murray F. Foss. LC 97-20551. 1997. text ed. write for info. (*0-7923-9955-2*) Kluwer Ac.

Shiftwork Safety & Performance: A Manual for Managers & Trainers. Glenn McBride & Peggy Westfall. 270p. 1992. 99.50 (*0-9638482-0-8*) McBride Pubns.

Shiftwork Swindle. Jean Cousins. (C). 1988. 21.00 (*0-901108-81-2*, Pub. by NCCL UK) St Mut.

Shiga Hero. William F. Sibley. LC 79-14120. 230p. 1979. lib. bdg. 25.50 (*0-226-75620-3*) U Ch Pr.

Shih-Ching: The Classic Anthology Defined by Confucius. Tr. by Ezra Pound. 335p. 1976. pap. text ed. 7.95 (*0-674-13397-8*) HUP.

Shih Fa Chieh Pu li i Nian Hsin see Ten Dharma Realms Are Not Beyond a Single Thought

***Shih Tzu.** Parker & Collins. (Illus.). 157p. 1997. pap. 9.95 (*0-7938-2326-9*, KW-084S) TFH Pubns.

Shih-Tzu. JoAnn White. (Owner's Guides to a Happy Healthy Pet Ser.). (Illus.). 160p. 1996. 12.95 (*0-87605-388-6*) Howell Bk.

Shih-Tzus. Jaime J. Sucher. (Complete Pet Owner's Manuals Ser.). 64p. 1991. pap. 6.95 (*0-8120-4524-6*) Barron.

Shihaja World Bank in Changing. 1995. lib. bdg. 274.00 (*90-411-0115-2*) Kluwer Ac.

Shihouette du Scandale. Marcel Ayme. 208p. (FRE.). 1973. pap. 14.95 (*0-7859-0385-2*, M3019) Fr & Eur.

Shi'is of Iraq. Yitzhak Hakash. 340p. (C). 1994. pap. text ed. 17.95 (*0-691-00643-1*) Princeton U Pr.

Shiis of Iraq. Yitzhak Nakash. LC 93-31786. 340p. 1994. text ed. 45.00 (*0-691-03431-1*) Princeton U Pr.

Shiism. Heinz Halm. (Islamic Surveys Ser.). 220p. 1995. pap. 25.00 (*0-7486-0509-6*, Pub. by Edinburgh U Pr UK) Col U Pr.

Shiism. Janet C. Watson. 288p. 1992. text ed. 65.00 (*0-7486-0268-2*, Pub. by Edinburgh U Pr UK) Col U Pr.

Shi'ism: Doctrines, Thought, & Spirituality. Ed. by Hamid Dabashi et al. LC 87-10258. 401p. 1988. pap. text ed. 24.95 (*0-88706-690-9*) State U NY Pr.

Shi'ism: Doctrines, Thought, & Spirituality. Ed. by Hamid Dabashi et al. LC 87-10258. 401p. 1988. text ed. 74.50 (*0-88706-689-5*) State U NY Pr.

Shiitake: The Healing Mushroom. Kenneth Jones. (Illus.). 126p. 1994. pap. 8.95 (*0-89281-499-3*, Heal Arts VT) Inner Tradit.

Shiitake Way. Jennifer Snyder. LC 93-30032. 112p. 1993. pap. 7.95 (*0-913990-41-8*) Book Pub Co.

Shi'ite Anthology. Ed. & Tr. by William C. Chittick from ARA. 160p. 1981. text ed. 59.50 (*0-87395-510-2*); pap. text ed. 19.95 (*0-87395-511-0*) State U NY Pr.

Shi'ite Islam. Muhammad H. Al-Tabataba'i. Tr. by Seyyed H. Nasr. LC 74-8289. 253p. 1979. text ed. 59.50 (*0-87395-272-3*); pap. text ed. 19.95 (*0-87395-390-8*) State U NY Pr.

Shi'ite Islam. Muhammad Tabatabai. Tr. by Sayyed H. Nasr from PER. 253p. 1979. pap. 12.95 (*0-941722-19-8*) Book Dist Ctr.

Shiite Islam: Polity, Ideology & Creed. Yann Richard. Tr. by Antonia Nevill from FRE. LC 94-15820. (Studies in Social Discontinuity). 256p. (C). 1995. text ed. 63.95 (*1-55786-469-1*); pap. text ed. 24.95 (*1-55786-470-5*) Blackwell Pubs.

Shi'ite Pilgrimage to Mecca, 1885-1886: The Safarnameh of Mirza Mohammad Hosayn Farahani. Mirza M. Farahani. Tr. by Hafez Farmayan & Elton L. Daniel from ARA. (Illus.). 432p. 1990. pap. 19.95 (*0-292-77622-5*); text ed. 40.00 (*0-292-77620-9*) U of Tex Pr.

Shi'ite Religion: A History of Islam in Persia & Irak. Dwight M. Donaldson. LC 80-1933. 64.50 (*0-404-18959-8*) AMS Pr.

Shiites: Ritual & Popular Piety in a Muslim Community. David Pinault. 224p. 1993. text ed. 17.95 (*0-312-10024-8*) St Martin.

Shikar. Jamshed Butt. 1967. pap. 2.35 (*0-88253-128-X*) Ind-US Inc.

Shikchashtak. Swami P. Saraswati. (Illus.). 138p. 1986. pap. 10.00 (*1-881921-02-6*) Intl Soc Divine Love.

Shiki: Four Seasons in the Eden. Riri Nakasone. (Illus.). 20p. (ENG & JPN.). 1988. pap. 25.00 (*0-944290-02-7*) Light Speed.

***Shikijyo: Sexual Desire.** Nobuyoshi Araki. 1997. 55.00 (*3-908162-44-0*) Dist Art Pubs.

Shikimic Acid: Metabolism & Metabolites. Edwin Haslam. LC 93-7365. 387p. 1993. text ed. 175.00 (*0-471-93999-4*) Wiley.

Shikimic Acid Pathway. Ed. by Eric E. Conn. LC 86-8885. (Recent Advances in Phytochemistry Ser.: Vol. 20). 356p. 1986. 75.00 (*0-306-42283-2*, Plenum Pr) Plenum.

Shikitei Sanba & the Comic Tradition in Edo Fiction. Robert W. Leutner. (Harvard-Yenching Institute Monographs: No. 25). 300p. 1986. 28.00 (*0-674-80646-8*) HUP.

Shilappadikaram: The Ankle Bracelet. Ilango Adigal. Tr. by Alain Danielou. LC 64-16823. (Orig.). 1965. pap. 12.95 (*0-8112-0001-9*, NDP162) New Directions.

Shilling for Candles. Josephine Tey. (Josephine Tey Mysteries Ser.). 240p. 1988. pap. 6.00 (*0-02-054530-4*, Collier S&S) S&S Trade.

Shilling for Candles. Josephine Tey. 22.95 (*0-8488-1203-4*) Amereon Ltd.

Shilling for Carmarthen...the Town They Nearly Tamed. Pat Molloy. 201p. (C). 1993. pap. 22.00 (*0-86383-182-6*, Pub. by Gomer Pr UK) St Mut.

Shilling for the Gate. Mary John. 68p. (YA). 1991. pap. 23.00 (*0-86383-763-8*, Pub. by Gomer Pr UK) St Mut.

Shilling for Your Scowl. James S. Grant. (C). 1992. text ed. 50.00 (*0-86152-898-0*, Pub. by Acair Ltd UK) St Mut.

Shiloh. Gabriel Arquilevic. (Literature Units Ser.). 48p. 1996. wbk. ed., pap. 7.95 (*1-55734-566-X*) Tchr Create Mat.

***Shiloh.** Blackbirch. LC 97-17229. 1998. 16.98 (*0-8050-5229-1*) H Holt & Co.

Shiloh. Shelby Foote. 1985. 23.95 (*0-8488-0158-X*, J M C & Co) Amereon Ltd.

Shiloh. Shelby Foote. 1976. 21.00 (*0-394-40873-X*) Random.

Shiloh. Shelby Foote. LC 90-50941. 240p. 1991. pap. 12.00 (*0-679-73542-9*, Vin) Random.

S

An Asterisk (*) at the beginning of an entry indicates that the title is appearing in BIP for the first time.

S

Shiloh. Phyllis R. Naylor. 144p. (J). (gr. 3-7). 1992. pap. 4.99 (*0-440-40752-4*, YB BDD) BDD Bks Young Read.

Shiloh. Phyllis Reynolds Naylor. LC 90-603. 144p. (J). (gr. 3-7). 1991. lib. bdg. 14.00 (*0-689-31614-3*, Atheneum Bks Young) S&S Childrens.

***Shiloh.** Scholastic Staff. (Literature Guide Ser.). (J). 1997. pap. text ed. 3.95 (*0-590-37356-0*) Scholastic Inc.

Shiloh. Anne Spencer. Ed. by J. Friedland & R. Kessler. (Novel-Ties Ser.). 1993. pap. text ed. 15.95 (*0-88122-911-3*) Lrn Links.

***Shiloh.** Ed. by Time-Life Books Editors. LC 96-33040. (Voices of the Civil War Ser.). 167p. 1996. 24.95 (*0-7835-4707-2*) Time-Life.

Shiloh. large type ed. Phyllis R. Naylor. 1993. 38.50 (*0-614-09869-6*, L-15921-00) Am Printing Hse.

Shiloh. large type ed. Phyllis R. Naylor. 160p. (J). (gr. 4-8). 1995. lib. bdg. 16.95 (*1-885885-10-5*, Cornerstone FL) Pages Inc FL.

Shiloh: A Biblical City in Tradition & History. Donald G. Schley. (Journal for the Study of the Old Testament Supplement Ser.: Vol. 63). 256p. 52.00 (*1-85075-161-7*, Pub. by Sheffield Acad UK) CUP Services.

Shiloh: Bloody April. Wiley Sword. (Illus.). 519p. 1983. reprint ed. pap. 17.50 (*0-89029-770-3*) Morningside Bkshop.

***Shiloh: The Battle that Changed the Civil War.** Larry J. Daniel. LC 96-51539. 1997. 26.00 (*0-684-80375-5*) S&S Trade.

Shiloh & Other Stories. Bobbie Ann Mason. LC 95-16581. 264p. 1995. 18.00 (*0-8131-1948-0*) U Pr of Ky.

Shiloh & Other Stories. Bobbie Ann Mason. LC 82-47541. 256p. 1993. reprint ed. pap. 12.00 (*0-06-091330-4*, PL1330, PL) HarpC.

Shiloh Autumn. Bodie Thoene & Brock Thoene. 480p. 1996. 21.99 (*0-7852-8066-9*) Nelson.

***Shiloh Autumn.** Bodie Thoene & Brock Thoene. 1996. audio 24.99 (*0-7852-7273-9*) Nelson.

***Shiloh Autumn: A Novel.** Bodie Thoene & Brock Thoene. 480p. 1997. pap. 12.99 (*0-7852-7134-1*) Nelson.

Shiloh Campaign: March-April 1862. rev. ed. David G. Martin. (Great Campaigns Ser.). (Illus.). 256p. 1995. 24.95 (*0-938289-69-1*) Combined Pub.

Shiloh-in Hell Before Night. James L. McDonough. LC 76-18864. (Illus.). 272p. 1977. 31.95 (*0-87049-199-7*); pap. 16.95 (*0-87049-232-2*) U of Tenn Pr.

Shiloh Season. Phyllis R. Naylor. LC 95-32558. (J). (gr. 3-7). 1996. 15.00 (*0-689-80647-7*, Atheneum Bks Young) S&S Childrens.

Shiloh Season. Phyllis R. Naylor. (J). 1998. mass mkt. 4.50 (*0-689-80646-9*) S&S Childrens.

Shiloh. The Pre-Hellenistic Remains: The Danish Excavations at Tall Sailun, Palestine in 1926, 1929, 1932, & 1963. Marie-Louise Buhl & Svend Holm-Nielsen. (Publications of the National Museum, Archaeological-Historical Ser.: No. 1, 12). (Illus.). 120p. (C). 1963. pap. 25.00 (*0-614-11378-4*, Pub. by Aarhus Univ Pr DK) David Brown.

Shiloh. The Remains from the Hellenistic to the Mamluk Periods: The Dansih Excavations at Tall Sailun, Palestine in 1926, 1929, 1932, & 1963. Flemming G. Andersen. (Publications of the National Museum, Archaeological-Historical Ser.: No. 23). (Illus.). 126p. (C). 1985. pap. 37.00 (*87-480-0567-3*, Pub. by Aarhus Univ Pr DK) David Brown.

Shiloh's Choice. Lee Roddy. (Giants of the Hill Ser.: No. 3). 288p. 1996. pap. 10.99 (*0-8499-3833-3*) Word Pub.

Shilpa: Folk Dances, Music, Crafts & Puppetry of India. rev. ed. Carol Hansen et al. LC 90-12985. (Illus.). 205p. (J). 1990. teacher ed., ring bd. 54.95 (*0-930141-38-5*) World Eagle.

Shim Eighty-Nine: Proceedings of the First International Symposium on Swift Heavy Ions in Matter, Caen, France, May 18-19, 1989: A Special Issue of the Journal Radiation Effects & Defects in Solids. Ed. by J. Remillieux et al. x, 228p. 1989. pap. text ed. 375.00 (*0-677-25960-3*) Gordon & Breach.

Shimanto Belt, Southwest Japan: Studies on the Evolution of an Accretionary System. Ed. by Asahiko Taira & Yujiro Ogawa. (Modern Geology Ser.: Vol. 12, Nos. 1-4). 536p. 1988. pap. text ed. 757.00 (*0-677-25680-9*) Gordon & Breach.

Shimer: History & Genealogy of the Shimer Family in America. A. R. Shimer. (Illus.). 147p. 1992. reprint ed. pap. 22.00 (*0-8328-2723-1*); reprint ed. lib. bdg. 32.00 (*0-8328-2722-3*) Higginson Bk Co.

Shimmee & the Taste-Me Tree. Shaindel Weinbach. (Illus.). (J). (ps-2). 2.95 (*0-87306-991-9*) Feldheim.

Shimmer & Other Texts. John O'Keefe. LC 89-20312. 72p. (Orig.). 1989. pap. 6.95 (*1-55936-002-X*) Theatre Comm.

Shimmering Door: Tales of Sorcery. Ed. by Katharine Kerr. 464p. 1996. pap. 12.00 (*0-06-105342-2*, HarperPrism) HarpC.

Shimmering Ghost of Riversend. Norma Lehr. (Lerner Mysteries Ser.). 168p. (J). (gr. 4-7). 1991. 18.95 (*0-8225-0732-3*, Lerner Publctns) Lerner Group.

Shimmering Ghost of Riversend. Norma Lehr. 168p. (J). (gr. 4-7). 1991. pap. 3.95 (*0-8225-9589-3*, First Ave Edns) Lerner Group.

***Shimmering Light.** Faquir M. Hunzai. 1997. text ed. 19.95 (*1-86064-151-2*, Pub. by I B Tauris UK) St Martin.

Shimmering Light: An Anthology of Isma'ili Poetry. Tr. & Compiled by Faquir M. Hunzai. 192p. 1996. text ed. 39.50 (*1-85043-907-9*, Pub. by I B Tauris UK) St Martin.

Shimmering Maya & Other Essays. Catherine S. Brosman. LC 94-6065. 168p. 1994. 24.95 (*0-8071-1874-5*) La State U Pr.

Shimmering Splendor. Roberta Gellis. 416p. 1995. mass mkt. 5.99 (*0-8217-0132-0*, Zebra Kensgtn) Kensgtn Pub Corp.

Shimmering Splendor. Roberta Gellis. 1995. mass mkt. 5.99 (*0-7860-0132-1*, Pinncle Kensgtn) Kensgtn Pub Corp.

Shimmering Stone. Carol Reinsma. (Really Reading! Bks.). (Illus.). 48p. (Orig.). (J). (gr. k-3). 1994. pap. 4.49 (*0-7847-0007-9*, 03957) Standard Pub.

Shimmershine Queens. Camille Yarbrough. 128p. (J). (gr. 5-8). 1989. 14.95 (*0-399-21465-8*, Putnam) Putnam Pub Group.

Shimmershine Queens. Camille Yarbrough. 114p. (J). (gr. 5-9). 1996. pap. 4.95 (*0-698-11369-1*, Paperstar) Putnam Pub Group.

Shimmy Shimmy Shimmy Like My Sister Kate: Looking at the Harlem Renaissance Through Poems. Nikki Giovanni. LC 95-38617. 177p. (YA). (gr. 9 up). 1996. 16.95 (*0-8050-3494-3*) H Holt & Co.

Shimmy the Youngest. Miriam Elias. LC 94-77433. (Illus.). 32p. (J). 1994. 8.95 (*0-922613-71-0*); pap. text ed. 6.95 (*0-922613-72-9*) Hachai Pubns.

Shin-hanga: New Prints in Modern Japan. Kendall H. Brown & Hollis Goodall-Cristante. (Illus.). 120p. 1996. pap. 35.00 (*0-295-97517-2*) U of Wash Pr.

Shin-Ju. Laura J. Rowland. LC 94-10181. 1994. 21.00 (*0-679-43422-4*) Random.

Shin Sutras to Live By. Ed. by Ruth M. Tabrah. Tr. by Shoji Matsumoto et al. from SAN. (New Century Publication Ser.). (Orig.). (C). 1990. pap. 5.95 (*0-938474-12-X*) Buddhist Study.

***Shin Takamastu & Gabriel E. Lahyahi: Architects Associates.** Noriko Ueshina. 120p. 1996. pap. text ed. 48.00 (*3-7643-5539-5*) Birkhauser.

Shin Takamatsu. Ed. by Paolo Polledri. LC 92-37714. 1993. write for info. (*0-918471-28-1*) San Fran MOMA.

***Shin Takamatsu: Architecture & Nothingness.** Maurizio Vitta. 1997. pap. text ed. 49.99 (*88-7838-016-4*, Pub. by Yeol-rin Munhwa KO) Consort Bk Sales.

Shin Takamatsu: The Architecture & Nothingness. Maurizio Vitta. (Illus.). 198p. 1996. pap. write for info. (*1-56496-342-X*) Rockport Pubs.

Shinano!, Vol. 1. Joseph F. Enright & James W. Ryan. 1988. pap. 3.95 (*0-312-90967-5*) St Martin.

Shindano-Swahili Essays & Other Stories. Alice Grant et al. (Foreign & Comparative Studies Program, African Ser.: No.6). 55p. (C). 1971. pap. 6.00 (*0-686-70992-6*) Syracuse U Foreign Comp.

Shine: Life & Times of Franklin County. large type ed. A. Rodger Doss et al. (Illus.). 200p. 1996. pap. 12.95 (*0-9641867-1-3*) Docar Pubng.

***Shine: The Screenplay.** Jan Sardi. 192p. (Orig.). 1997. pap. 12.00 (*0-8021-3508-0*, Grove) Grove-Atltic.

Shine, All-Stars Shine! Gregory Spalding. (Illus.). 180p. (Orig.). 1995. pap. 20.00 (*1-886094-18-7*) Chicago Spectrum.

Shine Boys. Vincent Younis. 120p. (Orig.). 1994. pap. text ed. 10.00 (*1-883968-06-2*) Blinking Yellow.

Shine Hawk. Charlie Smith. 368p. 1988. 17.95 (*0-945167-01-6*) British Amer Pub.

***Shine, Jesus, Shine.** 1989. pap. 1.20 (*0-8341-9074-5*) Lillenas.

Shine On. Fred Pfeil. 1987. pap. 8.00 (*0-89924-047-X*) SPD-Small Pr Dist.

Shine on, Bright & Dangerous Object. Laurie Colwin. LC 94-24622. 192p. 1995. pap. 11.00 (*0-06-097632-2*, HarpT) HarpC.

***Shine on Us.** 1995. pap. 1.20 (*0-8341-9451-1*) Lillenas.

Shine Perishing Republic. Rudolph Gilbert. LC 65-15883. (Studies in Poetry: No. 38). 1969. reprint ed. lib. bdg. 75.00 (*0-8383-0556-3*) M S G Haskell Hse.

Shine, Sun! Carol Greene. LC 82-19853. (Rookie Reader Ser.). (Illus.). 32p. (J). (ps-2). 1983. pap. 3.50 (*0-516-42038-0*); lib. bdg. 15.00 (*0-516-02038-2*) Childrens.

Shiner Fishing Techniques. Glen Hunter. 1991. pap. 9.95 (*0-937866-21-0*) Atlantic Pub Co.

Shiner's Return. Nolan Carlson. LC 95-78134. (Illus.). 146p. (YA). (gr. 4-8). 1995. pap. 6.95 (*1-882420-25-X*) Hearth KS.

***Shingebiss.** Van Laan. 1997. 16.00 (*0-395-82745-0*) HM.

Shingebiss: An Ojibwe Legend. Retold by Nancy Van Laan. LC 95-40274. (Illus.). (J). 1997. write for info. (*0-316-89627-6*) Little.

Shingle Style & the Stick Style: Architectural Theory & Design from Richardson to the Origins of Wright. rev. ed. Vincent Scully. (Publications in the History of Art: No. 20). (Illus.). 1971. pap. 22.00 (*0-300-01519-4*) Yale U Pr.

***Shingler: Genealogy of the Shingler Family of So. Carolina.** Edward M. Shingler. 110p. 1996. reprint ed. pap. 18.00 (*0-8328-5611-8*); reprint ed. lib. bdg. 28.00 (*0-8328-5610-X*) Higginson Bk Co.

Shingles & PHN. rev. ed. Thomas C. Thomsen & Eleanor Mann. 168p. 1994. pap. 10.95 (*0-945288-03-4*) Cross River Pr.

Shingling the Fog & Other Plains Lies. Roger L. Welsch. LC 79-18730. viii, 160p. 1980. text ed. 25.00 (*0-8032-4709-5*) U of Nebr Pr.

Shingling the Fog & Other Plains Lies. Roger L. Welsch. LC 79-18730. viii, 160p. 1980. pap. 6.95 (*0-8032-9700-9*, Bison Books) U of Nebr Pr.

Shingo Production Management System: Improving Process Functions. Shigeo Shingo. Tr. by Andrew P. Dillon from JPN. (Illus.). 238p. 1992. 50.00 (*0-915299-52-6*) Prod Press.

***Shingu: Message from Nature.** Susumu Shingu et al. LC 97-3460. (Illus.). 288p. 1997. 125.00 (*0-7892-0380-4*) Abbeville Pr.

Shingwauk's Vision: A History of Native Residential Schools. J. R. Miller. (Illus.). 700p. 1996. 70.00 (*0-8020-0833-X*); pap. 29.95 (*0-8020-7858-3*) U of Toronto Pr.

Shinichi Suzuki: His Speeches & Essays. Shinichi Suzuki. 51p. 1989. pap. text ed. 8.95 (*0-87487-588-9*) Summy-Birchard.

Shinichi Suzuki: Man of Love. Kyoko I. Selden. 72p. (Orig.). (J). (gr. 7-12). 1984. pap. text ed. 7.95 (*0-87487-199-9*, Suzuki Method) Summy-Birchard.

Shinichi Suzuki: The Man & His Philosophy. Evelyn Hermann. 220p. 1995. pap. text ed. 22.95 (*0-87487-589-7*) Summy-Birchard.

Shiniest Rock of All. Nancy R. Patterson. (Illus.). 80p. (J). (gr. 3 up). 1991. 13.00 (*0-374-36805-8*) FS&G.

Shiniest Rock of All. Nancy R. Patterson. (J). (ps-3). 1994. pap. 3.95 (*0-374-46615-7*) FS&G.

Shinin' Trails: A Possibles Bag of Fur Trade Trivia. John P. Legg. Ed. by Monte Smith. (Illus.). 112p. 1988. per. 7.95 (*0-943604-20-6*, BOO/13) Eagles View.

Shining. Mark Dunster. 14p. (Orig.). 1993. pap. 4.00 (*0-89642-219-4*) Linden Pubs.

Shining. Stephen King. LC 76-24212. 464p. 1990. 25.00 (*0-385-12167-9*) Doubleday.

***Shining.** Stephen King. 1997. mass mkt. 7.50 (*0-451-19388-1*, Sig) NAL-Dutton.

Shining. Terea D. Shaffer. LC 95-48904. (Illus.). (J). 1997. write for info. (*0-15-200773-3*) HarBrace.

Shining. Stephen King. 464p. 1978. reprint ed. pap. 6.99 (*0-451-16091-6*, Sig) NAL-Dutton.

Shining Affliction: A Story of Harm & Healing in Psychotherapy. Annie G. Rogers. LC 94-45171. 322p. 1995. pap. 23.95 (*0-670-85727-0*, Viking) Viking Penguin.

Shining Affliction: A Story of Harm & Healing in Psychotherapy. Annie G. Rogers. 336p. 1996. pap. 12.95 (*0-14-024012-8*, Penguin Bks) Viking Penguin.

Shining Brow. Paul Muldoon. 80p. (Orig.). 1993. pap. 8.95 (*0-571-16789-6*) Faber & Faber.

Shining City on a Hill: Ronald Reagan's Economic Rhetoric, 1951-1989. Amos Kiewe & Davis W. Houck. LC 91-9595. 264p. 1991. text ed. 55.00 (*0-275-93634-1*, C3634, Praeger Pubs) Greenwood.

Shining Company. Rosemary Sutcliff. 1990. 14.95 (*0-374-36807-4*) FS&G.

Shining Company. Rosemary Sutcliff. (YA). 1992. pap. 4.95 (*0-374-46616-5*) FS&G.

***Shining down upon Us.** Daniel R. Voboril. 196p. (Orig.). 1997. mass mkt. 4.99 (*1-55237-165-4*, Pub. by Comnwlth Pub CN) Partners Pubs Grp.

Shining Eyes of Dawn. Marilyn K. Smith. LC 88-17171. 176p. 1988. 13.75 (*0-930950-25-9*); pap. 8.75 (*0-930950-26-7*) Nopoly Pr.

Shining Falcon. Josepha Sherman. 352p. (Orig.). 1989. pap. 3.95 (*0-380-75436-3*) Avon.

Shining Gateway. James Allen. 58p. 1997. pap. 6.00 (*0-89540-328-5*, SB-328) Sun Pub.

Shining Light. Ruth Glover. 216p. 1993. pap. 9.99 (*0-8341-1514-X*) Beacon Hill.

***Shining Light on Constipation: Rectal Descent & Other Colon, Rectal & Anal Problems.** Christopher J. Lahr. Ed. by Brian J. Lindgren. (Illus.). 112p. (Orig.). 1997. pap. 12.95 (*0-9648176-4-0*) TRIAD Svcs.

***Shining Lights: Illuminating Stories of Faith & Inspiration.** Ruchoma Shain. LC 97-10971. 1997. write for info. (*0-87306-791-6*) Feldheim.

Shining Moment: (Musical) Kathryn S. Miller. (J). 1989. Playscript. 5.00 (*0-87602-286-7*) Anchorage.

Shining Moments: Tanka Poems in English. Edward G. Seidensticker. (Illus.). 140p. 1993. 12.00 (*0-944676-39-1*) AHA Bks.

Shining Moments of a Mystic. Earlyne C. Chaney. LC 76-24187. 78p. 1976. pap. 3.95 (*0-918936-19-5*) Astara.

Shining Mountain Shadows. Dixie Connor. (Illus.). 1977. pap. 5.00 (*0-918292-02-6*) Griggs Print.

Shining of Love. Emma Darcy. (Presents Ser.). 1994. mass mkt. 2.99 (*0-373-11632-2*, 1-11632-6) Harlequin Bks.

Shining Ones. David Eddings. (Tamuli Ser.: Bk. 2). 480p. 1994. mass mkt. 6.99 (*0-345-38866-6*, Avery Pub) Ballantine.

Shining Path of Peru. 2nd ed. David S. Palmer. 1994. text ed. 19.95 (*0-312-10619-X*) St Martin.

Shining Place of an Image. Barbara S. Marshall. LC 88-37853. 168p. (C). 1989. lib. bdg. 36.00 (*0-8191-7300-2*) U Pr of Amer.

Shining Princess of the Slender Bamboo. Sylvia Ashby. (Illus.). 44p. (Orig.). (J). (gr. 6 up). 1987. pap. 4.00 (*0-88680-266-0*) I E Clark.

Shining Pyramid. Sam Adams & Roland Mathias. 163p. (C). 1970. pap. 22.00 (*0-85044-484-5*, Pub. by Gomer Pr UK) St Mut.

Shining Pyramid. Ed. by Sam Adams & Roland Mathias. 163p. 1970. pap. 20.00 (*0-85088-484-5*, Pub. by Gomer Pr UK) St Mut.

Shining Reader. Ed. by Anthony S. Magistrale. LC 89-29631. (Starmont Studies in Literary Criticism: No. 30). xii, 220p. 1990. lib. bdg. 35.00 (*1-55742-107-2*) Borgo Pr.

***Shining Sands: Artist in Newlyn & St. Ives 1880-1930.** Tom Cross. 1997. pap. text ed. 29.95 (*0-7188-2926-3*) Parkwest Pubns.

Shining Sands: Artists in Newlyn & St. Ives 1880-1930. Tom Cross. LC 95-82207. (Illus.). 1996. 48.95 (*0-7188-2925-5*, Lutterworth-Parkwest) Parkwest Pubns.

Shining Seas. G. Weir et al. 500p. 1995. write for info. (*0-471-59645-0*) Wiley.

Shining Season: The True Story of John Baker as Told by William J. Buchanan. William J. Buchanan. LC 87-19072. (Illus.). 248p. 1987. reprint ed. pap. 14.95 (*0-8263-1016-8*) U of NM Pr.

Shining Shining Path. Carroll D. Short. 400p. 1995. 24.00 (*1-881320-59-6*, Black Belt) Black Belt Comm.

***Shining Souls.** Chris Hannan. 96p. (Orig.). 1996. pap. 14.95 (*1-85459-361-7*, Pub. by N Hern Bks UK) Theatre Comm.

Shining Star. Joyce Esely. (Illus.). 124p. (Orig.). (J). (gr. 3-6). 1995. pap. 5.00 (*0-88092-145-5*) Royal Fireworks.

Shining Star. Joyce Esely. (Illus.). 124p. (Orig.). (J). (gr. 3-6). 1995. lib. bdg. 15.00 (*0-88092-146-3*) Royal Fireworks.

Shining Star Quilts: Lone Star Variations. Judy Martin. 144p. 1987. pap. 19.95 (*0-943721-00-8*) Leman Pubns.

Shining Stars. Ghislaine Vautier. (Illus.). 32p. (J). 1989. pap. text ed. 9.95 (*0-521-37914-8*) Cambridge U Pr.

Shining Steel. Lawrence Watt-Evans. 224p. 1986. pap. 2.95 (*0-380-89671-0*) Avon.

Shining Still. Richard Hawley. (Illus.). 192p. (YA). 1989. 12.95 (*0-374-36811-2*) FS&G.

***Shining Sword.** Charles G. Coleman. LC 96-33537. (Illus.). 1996. write for info. (*0-87213-084-3*) Loizeaux.

Shining the Light Vol. 1, Vol. 1. Technology Research Staff. 193p. (Orig.). 1994. pap. 12.95 (*0-929385-66-7*) Light Tech Comns Servs.

***Shining the Light Book III.** Arthur Fanning. 1996. pap. text ed. 14.95 (*0-929385-71-3*) Light Tech Comns Servs.

***Shining the Light Book IV.** Arthur Fanning. 1996. pap. text ed. 14.95 (*0-929385-93-4*) Light Tech Comns Servs.

Shining the Light II Vol. II. Technology Research Staff. 418p. (Orig.). 1995. pap. 14.95 (*0-929385-70-5*) Light Tech Comns Servs.

Shining Through. Susan Isaacs. 1989. mass mkt. 5.99 (*0-345-35803-1*) Ballantine.

Shining Through. large type ed. Susan Isaacs. (General Ser.). 595p. 1990. lib. bdg. 21.95 (*0-8161-4755-8*, GK Hall) Thorndike Pr.

***Shining Through: Pulling All Together after Sexual Abuse.** 2nd rev. ed. Mindy B. Loiselle & Leslie B. Wright. 128p. (J). (gr. 5-11). 1996. pap. 14.00 (*1-884444-39-3*) Safer Soc.

Shining Through: Pulling It Together after Sexual Abuse. Mindy B. Loiselle & Leslie B. Wright. 100p. (Orig.). (J). (gr. 4-10). 1994. student ed., pap. 14.00 (*1-884444-13-X*) Safer Soc.

Shining Tide. Karen Rhodes. 320p. 1992. mass mkt. 3.99 (*0-8217-3839-9*, Zebra Kensgtn) Kensgtn Pub Corp.

Shining Time Station: Station House. Quality Family Entertainment, Inc. Staff. (Pop-Up Sound-Up Bks.). 2p. (J). (ps-2). 1993. write for info. (*1-883366-10-0*) YES Ent.

***Shining Tree Self-Work-Book: A Technical Support Manual for the Tantric-Alchemical Kaballah.** Jerry C. Welch. (Illus.). 256p. (Orig.). 1997. spiral bd. 22.95 (*0-9657371-0-1*) As You Like MA.

Shining Trumpets: A History of Jazz. 2nd rev. ed. Rudi Blesh. LC 74-28309. (Roots of Jazz Ser.). (Illus.). xxxii, 412p. 1975. reprint ed. lib. bdg. 39.50 (*0-306-70658-X*) Da Capo.

Shining Woman Tarot Cards. Rachel Pollack. 1993. pap. 34.00 (*1-85538-098-6*) Thorsons SF.

Shining Your Armour: The Lost Art of Romance. Gabriel H. Vaughn. 1992. pap. 8.95 (*0-9628733-0-6*) KQ Pub.

Shinju. Laura J. Rowland. 384p. 1996. mass mkt. 5.99 (*0-06-100950-4*) HarpC.

***Shinju.** Laura J. Rowland. 384p. mass mkt. write for info. (*0-06-101035-9*, Harp PBks) HarpC.

***Shinjuku Nights.** Sachi Mizuno. (Orig.). 1997. mass mkt. 6.50 (*1-56333-493-3*) Masquerade.

Shinkage-Ryu Sword Technique, Vol. 2. Tadashige Watanabe. (Illus.). 150p. (Orig.). 1993. pap. 32.00 (*0-87040-926-3*) Japan Pubns USA.

Shinkage-Ryu Sword Techniques, Vol. 1: Traditional Japanese Martial Arts. Shihan Tadashige Watanabe. (Illus.). 150p. (Orig.). 1993. pap. 32.00 (*0-87040-887-9*) Japan Pubns USA.

Shinnecock Bay & Boston Poems. Lawrence Homer. 32p. 1985. reprint ed. per. 6.95 (*0-9615306-1-8*); reprint ed. Lawrence Homer-Selected Poems Harvard Poetry Archives Edition. audio 9.95 (*0-9615306-2-6*) Poets Playwrights.

Shining's Orphan. Joanna Campbell. (Thoroughbred Ser.: No. 12). 192p. (J). (gr. 4-7). 1994. mass mkt. 3.99 (*0-06-106281-2*) HarpC Child Bks.

Shinohara. 1982. pap. 7.00 (*0-614-02678-4*) Japan Soc.

Shinohata, a Portrait of a Japanese Village. Ronald P. Dore. LC 93-41319. (C). 1994. 14.95 (*0-520-08628-7*) U CA Pr.

Shinran: His Life & Thought. Norihiko Kikumura. LC 70-172538. 192p. (C). 1972. 12.95 (*0-685-65548-2*) Nembutsu Pr.

Shinran's Gospel of Pure Grace. 8th ed. Alfred Bloom. LC 64-8757. (Monographs: No. 20). xiv, 97p. 1991. reprint ed. pap. 10.00 (*0-8165-0405-9*) Assn Asian Studies.

Shin's Tricycle. Tatsuharu Kodama. Tr. by Kazuko Hokumen-Jones from JPN. LC 95-7326. (Illus.). 32p. (J). (gr. 2-5). 1995. 15.95 (*0-8027-8375-9*); lib. bdg. 16.85 (*0-8027-8376-7*) Walker & Co.

Shintaido: An Art of Movement & Life Expression. Hiroyuki Aoki. Tr. by Michael Thompson & Haruyoshi Ito from JPN. LC 82-80496. (Illus.). 120p. 1982. pap. 8.95 (*0-942634-00-4*) Shintaido.

Shintani Zeta Functions. Akihiko Yukie. LC 92-45913. (London Mathematical Society Lecture Note Ser.: No. 183). 200p. (C). 1994. pap. text ed. 44.95 (*0-521-44804-2*) Cambridge U Pr.

Shintaro's Umbrellas. Marjorie Jackson. (Books for Young Learners). (Illus.). 16p. (Orig.). (J). (gr. k-2). 1996. pap. 5.00 (*1-57274-025-6*) R Owen Pubs.

Shinto, 2 vols. J. W. Mason. 1973. 500.00 (*0-8490-1050-0*) Gordon Pr.

Shinto: The Kami Way. Sokyo Ono. (Illus.). 144p. 1994. pap. 8.95 (*0-8048-1960-2*) C E Tuttle.

Shinto & the State, 1868-1988. Helen Hardacre. 219p. 1989. pap. text ed. 16.95 (*0-691-02052-3*) Princeton U Pr.

An Asterisk (*) at the beginning of an entry indicates that the title is appearing in BIP for the first time.

Shinto Animism: A Special Custom-Order Catalogue of Japanese Designs. Ed. by Michael P. Jones. (Illus.). 22p. (Orig.). 1983. pap. text ed. 3.00 (*0-89904-053-5*) Crumb Elbow Pub.

Shinto Bengi Oshigata. Hawley. 1986. reprint ed. 42.50 (*0-910704-63-5*) Hawley.

Shinto-Bibliography in Western Languages: Bibliography on Shinto & Religious Sects, Intellectual Schools & Movements Influenced by Shintoism. Arcadio Schwade. xiv, 126p. 1986. pap. 41.50 (*90-04-08173-9*) E J Brill.

Shinto Bijutsu see Arts of Shinto

Shinto, the Way of Japan. Floyd H. Ross. LC 83-12970. (Illus.). xvii, 187p. 1983. reprint ed. text ed. 52.50 (*0-313-24240-2*, RSHI, Greenwood Pr) Greenwood.

Shinto, the Way of the Gods. W. G. Aston. 1973. lib. bdg. 300.00 (*0-87968-076-8*) Krishna Pr.

***Shintoism.** Paula Hartz. LC 96-47016. (World Religions Ser.). 1997. write for info. (*0-8160-3577-6*) Facts on File.

Shiny Objects. Dianne Benedict. LC 82-10853. (Iowa Short Fiction Award Ser.). 170p. 1982. 19.95 (*0-87745-116-8*); pap. 12.95 (*0-87745-117-6*) U of Iowa Pr.

Shiny Red Sled. Barbara Davoll. (Christopher Churchmouse Classics Ser.). (Illus.). 24p. (J). 1989. 8.99 (*0-89693-498-5*, 6-1498, Victor Bks) Chariot Victor.

Shiny Red Sled. Barbara Davoll. (Illus.). 24p. (J). 1989. audio 11.99 (*0-89693-031-9*, 3-1203, Victor Bks) Chariot Victor.

***Shiny Science.** 1997. pap. 19.95 (*0-8069-9885-7*) Sterling.

Shiny Shoes & Sparkling Brass. Hershell F. Winship. 202p. 1993. pap. 8.95 (*0-9636868-0-1*) H F Winship.

Shiny Shoes on Dusty Paths, Vol. 1. Joanne Kroeker. 294p. 1995. pap. 9.99 (*1-56043-845-2*) Destiny Image.

***Shiny Shoes on Dusty Paths Vol. 2: The Polishing of Grace.** 2nd ed. Joanne Kroeker. LC 96-132577. (Illus.). 286p. (Orig.). 1996. pap. text ed. 11.95 (*1-56226-317-X*) CT Pub.

Shiny Skates. Elizabeth Koda-Callan. LC 92-50293. (J). (ps-3). 1992. 12.95 (*1-56305-309-8*, 3309) Workman Pub.

***Shiny Water.** Anna Salter. 288p. 1997. 23.00 (*0-671-00310-0*) PB.

Shinzo: Hachiman Imagery & Its Development. Christine G. Kanda. (East Asian Monographs: No. 119). 1985. 35.00 (*0-674-80650-6*) HUP.

Shion: Blade of the Minstrel. Yu Kinutani. Ed. by Seiji Horibuchi. Tr. by Gerard Jones from JPN. (Illus.). 80p. (Orig.). 1990. pap. 9.95 (*0-929279-38-7*) Viz Commns Inc.

Ship. Chris L. Demarest. LC 94-74412. (Illus.). 16p. (J). (ps). 1995. pap. 4.95 (*0-15-200267-7*, Red Wagon Bks) HarBrace.

Ship. David Macaulay. (J). (gr. 4-7). 1993. 19.95 (*0-395-52439-3*) HM.

Ship. David Macaulay. (Illus.). 96p. (YA). (gr. 5 up). 1995. pap. 8.95 (*0-395-74518-7*, Sandpiper) HM.

Ship Ahoy. Judy Delton. LC 95-3285. (Lottery Luck Ser.: Bk. 5). (Illus.). 96p. (Orig.). (J). (gr. 2-5). 1995. pap. 3.95 (*0-7868-1022-X*) Hyprn Ppbks.

Ship & Aircraft Fairing & Development: For Draftsman & Loftsmen & Sheet Metal Workers. S. S. Rabl. LC 41-51932. (Illus.). 109p. 1941. spiral bd., pap. 19.95 (*0-87033-096-9*) Cornell Maritime.

Ship & Aircraft Mortgages. Nigel Meeson. 217p. 1988. 110.00 (*1-85044-104-9*) LLP.

Ship Ashore! The U. S. Lifesavers of Coastal North Carolina. Joe A. Mobley. (Illus.). 197p. (Orig.). (YA). (gr. 8-12). 1996. pap. 10.00 (*0-86526-260-8*) NC Archives.

***Ship Avenged.** S. M. Stirling. LC 96-36977. 352p. 1997. 21.00 (*0-671-87766-6*) Baen Bks.

Ship Building: Architectura Navalis. Josef Furttenbach. (Printed Sources of Western Art Ser.). (Illus.). 150p. (GER.). 1981. reprint ed. boxed 65.00 (*0-915346-62-1*) A Wofsy Fine Arts.

***Ship-Building & Navigation in the Indian Ocean Region, AD 1400-1800.** Ed. & Intro. by K. S. Mathew. 1996. 29.50 (*81-215-0739-1*, Pub. by M Manoharial II) Coronet Bks.

Ship Carver's Handbook. Jay S. Hanna. 1987. text ed. 17.95 (*0-07-155438-6*) McGraw.

Ship Choice in the Container Age. Ed. by Cargo Systems Staff. 1980. 200.00 (*0-905394-07-0*, Pub. by Cargo Systs UK) St Mut.

Ship Construction. 4th ed. D. J. Eyres. LC 94-15957. 1994. pap. text ed. 42.95 (*0-7506-1842-6*) Buttrwrth-Heinemann.

Ship Construction Sletches & Notes. 3rd ed. Kemp. 1971. pap. 36.95 (*0-7506-0381-X*) Buttrwrth-Heinemann.

Ship Design & Construction. Ed. by Robert Taggart. 748p. 1980. 70.00 (*0-614-06719-7*) Soc Naval Arch.

Ship Design & Construction. 3rd ed. Ed. by Robert Taggart. LC 80-52966. (Illus.). 748p. 1980. 70.00 (*0-9603048-0-0*) Soc Naval Arch.

Ship Errant. Jody L. Nye. 416p. 1996. 21.00 (*0-671-87754-2*) Baen Bks.

***Ship Errant.** Jody L. Nye. (Brain/Brawn Ser.). 1997. mass mkt. 5.99 (*0-671-87854-9*) Baen Bks.

Ship Fever: Stories. Andrea Barrett. LC 95-14562. 224p. 1996. 21.00 (*0-393-03853-X*) Norton.

***Ship Fever Stories: Stories.** Andrea Barrett. 256p. 1997. pap. 12.00 (*0-393-31600-9*) Norton.

Ship Finance: Credit Expansion & the Boom-Bust Cycle. Peter Stokes. 263p. 1992. 130.00 (*1-85044-437-4*) LLP.

Ship Financing in Singapore. Hairani Saaban. xxi, 305p. 1983. 69.00 (*9971-70-030-1*) MICHIE.

Ship Fires & the Law: Through the Eyes of a Firefighter. Frank Rushbrook. 450p. 1995. 125.00 (*1-85044-838-8*) LLP.

Ship Forms. Marc Miller & Larry Bond. (Harpoon Ser.). (Illus.). (Orig.). 1988. pap. 8.00 (*0-943580-61-7*) Game Designers.

Ship Handling in Narrow Channels. 3rd enl. ed. Carlyle J. Plummer. LC 78-15384. 165p. reprint ed. pap. 47.10 (*0-317-55498-0*, 2029228) Bks Demand.

Ship Hyrodynamics, Water Waves & Asymptotics. F. Ursell. (Advanced Fluid Mechanics Ser.). 800p. 1994. text ed. 187.00 (*981-02-1455-3*) World Scientific Pub.

Ship in the Field. Henny Buschini & Luciano Buschini. LC 77-174719. (Illus.). 32p. (J). (gr. k-3). 1973. 6.95 (*0-87592-045-4*) Scroll Pr.

Ship in the Harbor. Mary H. Dyer. LC 93-84468. 160p. (Orig.). 1993. pap. 8.95 (*1-882587-00-6*) Paradigm San Diego.

Ship Information Questionnaire for Bulk Oil Carriers. OCIMF Staff. (C). 1989. 85.00 (*0-948691-91-3*, Pub. by Witherby & Co UK) St Mut.

Ship Information Questionnaire for Liquefied Gas Carriers. OCIMF Staff & SIGTTO Staff. (C). 1990. 125.00 (*0-948691-99-9*, Pub. by Witherby & Co UK) St Mut.

Ship Lovers Guide to California. Martin P. Riegel. LC 88-60110. (California Heritage Ser.: Vol. II). (Illus.). 168p. (Orig.). 1988. 16.00 (*0-944871-03-8*); pap. 9.95 (*0-944871-02-X*) Riegel Pub.

Ship Lovers Guide to the Pacific Northwest. Martin P. Riegel. (Illus.). 110p. (Orig.). 1990. 15.95 (*0-944871-30-5*); pap. 9.95 (*0-944871-31-3*) Riegel Pub.

Ship Lovers Guide to the Pacific Northwest, Vol. 1: Oregon. Martin P. Riegel. (Illus.). 52p. (Orig.). 1989. 11.00 (*0-944871-24-0*); pap. 4.95 (*0-944871-25-9*) Riegel Pub.

Ship Lovers Guide to the Pacific Northwest, Vol. 2: Washington. Martin P. Riegel. (Illus.). 52p. (Orig.). 1989. 11.00 (*0-944871-26-7*); pap. 4.95 (*0-944871-27-5*) Riegel Pub.

Ship Management. 2nd ed. John Spruyt. 250p. 1994. 105.00 (*1-85044-532-X*) LLP.

Ship Management, Arrest, Collision, Berth, Detention, Lien, Negligence: 1919-1991. (Lloyd's Law Reports Consolidated Index, 1919-1994 Ser.: Vol. 4). 1992. 125.00 (*1-85044-430-7*) LLP.

Ship Model Basin: Tool of the Naval Architect. Jack Brandau. 64p. (Orig.). (C). 1986. pap. 10.00 (*0-934114-82-X*, BK-550) Marine Educ.

Ship Model Builder's Assistant. Charles G. Davis. (Illus.). 288p. 1988. reprint ed. pap. 7.95 (*0-486-25584-0*) Dover.

Ship Model Building. 3rd ed. Gene Johnson. LC 61-17424. (Illus.). 1961. pap. 12.95 (*0-87033-369-0*) Cornell Maritime.

Ship Modeler's Shop Notes. Ed. by Merritt Edson et al. (Illus.). viii, 216p. 1979. pap. 19.95 (*0-9603456-0-4*) Nautical Res.

Ship Modeling from Scratch: Tips & Techniques for Building Without Kits. Edwin B. Leaf. (Illus.). 176p. 1993. pap. 17.95 (*0-87742-389-X*) Intl Marine.

Ship Modeling from Scratch: Tips & Techniques for Building Without Kits. Edwin B. Leaf. (Illus.). 176p. 1994. pap. text ed. 18.95 (*0-07-036817-1*) McGraw.

Ship Modeling from Stem to Stern. Milton Roth. 1988. pap. text ed. 18.95 (*0-07-155060-7*) McGraw.

Ship Modeling from Stem to Stern. Milton Roth. (Illus.). 288p. 1988. pap. 17.95 (*0-8306-2844-4*) McGraw-Hill Prof.

Ship Modeling Simplified: Tips & Techniques for Model Construction from Kits. Frank Mastini. 1990. pap. text ed. 18.95 (*0-87742-272-9*) Intl Marine.

Ship Modeling Simplified: Tips & Techniques for Model Construction from Kits. Frank Mastini. 1990. pap. text ed. 18.95 (*0-07-155867-5*) McGraw.

Ship Modeling Techniques. Portia Takakjian. Ed. by Jeff Phillips. (Illus.). (C). 1990. 18.95 (*0-9615021-4-2*) Phoen Pubns.

Ship Models. 2nd ed. Richard B. McLanathan. (Illus.). 48p. (Orig.). 1957. reprint ed. pap. 3.95 (*0-87846-220-1*) Mus Fine Arts Boston.

Ship Models: How to Build Them. Charles G. Davis. 1990. 19.25 (*0-8446-6280-1*) Peter Smith.

Ship Models: How to Build Them. Charles G. Davis. 192p. 1986. reprint ed. pap. 6.95 (*0-486-25170-5*) Dover.

Ship Models: Their Purposes & Development from 1650 to the Present. Brian Lavery & Simon Stephens. (Illus.). 256p. 1995. 80.00 (*0-302-00654-0*, Pub. by Zwemmer Bks UK) Sothebys Pubns.

Ship Names: Origins & Usages During 45 Centuries. Don H. Kennedy. LC 73-94274. 325p. 1974. text ed. 25.00 (*0-8139-0531-1*) U Pr of Va.

Ship of Courage. Brendan Whiting. (Illus.). 224p. 1995. pap. 34.95 (*1-86373-653-0*, Pub. by Allen Unwin AT) Paul & Co Pubs.

Ship of Dreams. 1994. 179.50 (*0-8109-5092-8*) Abrams.

Ship of Dreams. Brian Lumley. LC 86-81017. (Illus.). 192p. 1986. 21.00 (*0-932445-25-X*); pap. 7.50 (*0-932445-24-1*) Ganley Pub.

Ship of Dreams. Brian Lumley. 256p. 1994. mass mkt. 4.99 (*0-8125-2420-9*) Tor Bks.

Ship of Dreams. Dean Morrissey. (Illus.). 37p. (J). 1994. 17.95 (*0-8109-3848-0*) Abrams.

Ship of Fools. Sebastian Brant. 1991. pap. 9.95 (*0-486-25791-6*) Dover.

Ship of Fools. Sebastian Brant. 1990. 21.50 (*0-8446-6403-0*) Peter Smith.

Ship of Fools. Katherine Anne Porter. 31.95 (*0-8488-1129-1*) Amereon Ltd.

Ship of Fools. Cristina P. Rossi. Tr. by Psiche Hughes from SPA. LC 88-61390. (Readers International Ser.). 225p. (Orig.). 1989. pap. 11.95 (*0-930523-54-7*) Readers Intl.

***Ship of Fools.** Dave Stone. (Orig.). 1997. mass mkt. 5.95 (*0-426-20510-3*, Pub. by Virgin Pub UK) London Brdge.

Ship of Fools, 2 Vols. Sebastian Brant. Ed. by T. H. Jamieson. Tr. by Alexander Barclay. LC 14-11937. reprint ed. 95.00 (*0-404-01065-2*) AMS Pr.

Ship of Fools. Katherine Anne Porter. 516p. 1984. reprint ed. pap. 14.95 (*0-316-71390-2*) Little.

Ship of Force. Alan Evans. 256p. 1986. 15.95 (*0-8027-0894-3*) Walker & Co.

Ship of Force. large type ed. Alan Evans. 453p. 1980. 25.99 (*0-7089-0555-2*) Ulverscroft.

Ship of Gold in the Deep Blue Sea: The History & Discovery of America's Richest Shipwreck. Gary Kinder. 352p. 1997. 24.00 (*0-87113-464-0*, Atlntc Mnthly) Grove-Atltic.

Ship of Ishtar. limited ed. Abraham Merritt. 1990. 35.00 (*0-87505-355-6*) Borden.

Ship of Terror. Jason Steele. 96p. (J). (gr. 5-8). 1994. pap. 2.99 (*0-87406-694-8*) Willowisp Pr.

***Ship of the Hunted.** Yehuda Elberg. LC 96-47894. (Library of Modern Jewish Literature). 400p. 1997. reprint ed. 26.95 (*0-8156-0449-1*) Syracuse U Pr.

Ship of the Line. C. S. Forester. 1985. pap. 14.95 (*0-316-28936-1*) Little.

Ship of Widows. I. Grekova. Tr. by Cathy Porter from RUS. (European Classics Ser.). 192p. 1994. reprint ed. pap. 14.95 (*0-8101-1144-6*) Northwestern U Pr.

Ship or Sheep. Ann Baker. (Cambridge English Language Learning Ser.). (Illus.). 1981. pap. 11.95 (*0-521-28354-X*) Cambridge U Pr.

Ship Performance. C. N. Hughes. 112p. 1987. 75.00 (*1-85044-149-9*) LLP.

Ship Production. 2nd ed. Richard L. Storch et al. 512p. 1995. 80.00 (*0-614-06715-4*) Soc Naval Arch.

Ship Production. 2nd ed. Richard L. Storch et al. (Illus.). 456p. (C). 1995. text ed. 80.00 (*0-87033-461-1*) Cornell Maritime.

Ship Registration. 2nd ed. N. P. Ready. 216p. 1994. 105.00 (*1-85044-824-8*) LLP.

Ship Repair & Alteration. George V. Haliday & W. E. Swanson. LC 42-17459. (Illus.). 383p. reprint ed. pap. 109.20 (*0-317-08204-3*, 2022553) Bks Demand.

Ship Ride Down the Spring Branch. Jess Carr. LC 78-60480. 200p. 1978. 12.95 (*0-89227-048-9*) Commonwealth Pr.

Ship Safety Handbook. 3rd ed. Bureau Veritas Staff. 346p. 1995. pap. 90.00 (*1-85044-814-0*) LLP.

Ship Sale & Purchase: First Supplement to the Second Edition. 1995. pap. 70.00 (*1-85044-973-2*) LLP.

Ship Sale & Purchase: Law & Technique. 2nd ed. I. S. Goldrein. LC 86-101708. 458p. 1993. 230.00 (*1-85044-455-2*) LLP.

Ship, Sea & Sky: The Marine Art of James Edward Buttersworth. Richard B. Grassby. LC 93-42623. 128p. 1994. 35.00 (*0-8478-1805-5*) Rizzoli Intl.

***Ship Shapes.** Mouse Works. (J). 1997. 5.98 (*1-57082-710-9*) Mouse Works.

Ship-Shore Safety Check List Guidelines. Ed. by ICS Staff et al. (C). 1982. 50.00 (*0-685-26149-2*, Pub. by Witherby & Co UK) St Mut.

Ship Squat Manual. (C). 1989. 195.00 (*0-89771-717-1*, Pub. by Lorne & MacLean Marine) St Mut.

Ship Squat Manual. Lorne & MacLean Marine & Offshore Publications Staff. (C). 1987. 300.00 (*0-685-33851-7*, Pub. by Lorne & MacLean Marine) St Mut.

Ship Squat Manual. OCS Marine Staff. (C). 1989. text ed. 290.00 (*0-906314-07-0*, Pub. by Lorne & MacLean Marine) St Mut.

***Ship St. Andrew, Galley: A Hypothesis.** Alfred T. Meschter. 1992. pap. 3.00 (*0-935980-08-3*) Schwenkfelder Lib.

Ship Stability for Masters & Mates. 4th ed. Demott. 1990. 56.95 (*0-7506-0380-1*) Buttrwrth-Heinemann.

Ship Stability Notes & Examples. 2nd ed. Kemp. 1971. pap. 38.95 (*0-7506-0099-3*) Buttrwrth-Heinemann.

Ship Structural Design. Owen F. Hughes. LC 88-62642. 566p. 1988. 100.00 (*0-939773-04-X*) Soc Naval Arch.

Ship Structural Design: A Rationally-Based, Computer-Aided Optimization Approach (Plate Bending) 43p. 1991. 32.00 (*0-614-06729-4*) Soc Naval Arch.

Ship Structural Design: A Rationally-Based, Computer-Aided Optimization Approach (Ship Structural Design) 566p. 1988. 100.00 (*0-614-06728-6*) Soc Naval Arch.

Ship Structural Design: A Rationally-Based, Computer-Aided Optimization Approach (Ship Structural Design with Plate Bending Supplement) Owen F. Hughes. 120.00 (*0-614-06727-8*) Soc Naval Arch.

Ship Structural Design Concepts. rev. ed. Ed. by J. Harvey Evans. LC 89-156923. (Illus.). 841p. reprint ed. pap. 180.00 (*0-8357-6424-9*, 2035792) Bks Demand.

Ship That Died of Shame, & Other Stories. Nicholas Monsarrat. LC 70-163044. (Short Story Index Reprint Ser.). 1977. reprint ed. 18.95 (*0-8369-3958-1*) Ayer.

Ship That Flew. Hilda Lewis. LC 58-5903. (Illus.). (J). (gr. 3-7). 1958. 29.95 (*0-87599-067-3*) S G Phillips.

Ship That Held the Line: The U. S. S. Hornet & the First Year of the Pacific War. Lisle A. Rose. LC 95-8683. (Illus.). 328p. 1995. 34.95 (*1-55750-729-5*) Naval Inst Pr.

Ship That Sailed to Mars. William M. Timlin. (Illus.). 104p. (J). (gr. 4-5). 1992. reprint ed. 25.00 (*0-9633212-6-9*) V Wagner Pubns.

Ship That Torpedoed Herself. Ed. by Maritime Books Staff. (C). 1986. text ed. 60.00 (*0-685-38770-4*, Pub. by Maritime Bks UK) St Mut.

Ship That Would Not Die. F. Julian Becton & Joseph Morschauser, III. LC 80-16263. (Illus.). 316p. 1987. pap. 8.95 (*0-933126-87-5*) Pictorial Hist.

Ship to Ship Transfer Guide. ICS Staff & OCIMF Staff. (C). 1988. 95.00 (*0-948691-49-2*, Pub. by Witherby & Co UK) St Mut.

***Ship to Ship Transfer Guide (Liquefied Gases)** ICS Staff et al. 1995. pap. 60.00 (*1-85609-082-5*, Pub. by Witherby & Co UK) St Mut.

Ship to Ship Transfer Guide (Liquefield Gases) ICS Staff & OCIMF Staff. 1980. 75.00 (*0-900886-51-X*, Pub. by Witherby & Co UK) St Mut.

Ship to Ship Transfer Guide (Petroleum) ICS-OCIMF Staff. (C). 1988. 80.00 (*0-948691-36-0*, Pub. by Witherby & Co UK) St Mut.

Ship to Shore. Peter D. Jeans. 425p. 1993. lib. bdg. 55.00 (*0-87436-717-4*) ABC-CLIO.

Ship to Shore, Vol. I. Ed. by Jan Robinson & Cheryl A. Fowler. (Illus.). 336p. 1983. pap. 14.95 (*0-9612686-0-3*) Ship-Shore.

Ship to Shore, Vol. II. Jan Robinson. (Illus.). 288p. 1986. pap. 14.95 (*0-9612686-1-1*) Ship-Shore.

Ship to Shore: Caribbean Charter Yacht Recipes. Compiled by Jan Robinson. (Illus.). 448p. (Orig.). 1987. reprint ed. pap. 15.95 (*0-13-808932-9*) P-H.

Ship Too Far: The Truth about the Loss of the Derbyshire. Dave Ramwell & Tim Madge. 256p. 1992. 34.95 (*0-340-56997-2*, Pub. by H & S UK) Trafalgar.

Ship Translator. H. E. Eklund. 360p. (ENG, FIN, RUS, SPA & SWE.). 1984. 49.95 (*0-8288-0427-3*, M7322) Fr & Eur.

Ship Versus Shore: Civil War Engagements Between Land & Sea. Dave Page. LC 94-15005. (Illus.). 320p. (J). 1994. 22.95 (*1-55853-267-6*) Rutledge Hill Pr.

Ship Who Sang. Anne McCaffrey. 1985. mass mkt. 5.99 (*0-345-33431-0*) Ballantine.

Ship Who Searched. Anne McCaffrey & Mercedes Lackey. 320p. 1992. mass mkt. 5.99 (*0-671-72129-1*) Baen Bks.

Ship Who Searched. large type ed. Anne McCaffrey & Mercedes Lackey. LC 95-52488. 440p. 1996. pap. 20.95 (*0-7862-0645-4*, Thorndike Lrg Prnt) Thorndike Pr.

Ship Who Won. Anne McCaffrey & Jody L. Nye. (Brain-Brawn Ser.). 336p. 1994. 21.00 (*0-671-87595-7*) Baen Bks.

Ship Who Won. Anne McCaffrey & Jody L. Nye. 336p. 1995. mass mkt. 5.99 (*0-671-87657-0*) Baen Bks.

Ship Who Won. Anne McCaffrey. 1993. pap. 17.95 (*0-7871-0237-7*, Dove Bks) Dove Audio.

***Ship Who Won.** large type ed. Anne McCaffrey & Jody L. Nye. LC 97-12887. 1997. write for info. (*0-7862-1113-X*, Thorndike Lrg Prnt) Thorndike Pr.

Ship Without an Udder. Robert L. Steed. (Illus.). 160p. 1995. 17.95 (*1-56352-252-7*) Longstreet Pr Inc.

Shipboard Acoustics. Ed. by J. Buiten. (C). 1987. lib. bdg. 323.50 (*90-247-3420-7*) Kluwer Ac.

Shipboard Antennas. 2nd ed. Preston E. Law. LC 86-70448. (Artech House Antenna Library). (Illus.). 566p. reprint ed. pap. 161.40 (*0-7837-4725-X*, 2044290) Bks Demand.

Shipboard Antennas. Preston E. Law. LC 82-72892. (Illus.). 561p. reprint ed. pap. 159.90 (*0-318-39756-0*, 2033130) Bks Demand.

Shipboard Electromagnetics. Preston E. Law. LC 87-19293. (Artech House Antenna Library). (Illus.). 278p. reprint ed. pap. 79.30 (*0-8357-7926-2*, 2036352) Bks Demand.

Shipboard Fish Scouting & Electronavigational Equipment. V. P. Averkiev. Tr. by S. K. Kane from RUS. 485p. (C). 1985. text ed. 140.00 (*90-6191-436-1*, Pub. by A A Balkema NE) Ashgate Pub Co.

Shipboard Handling of Unitised Cargo. Ed. by Mike Curtis & Keith Mowat. (C). 1979. 45.00 (*0-906297-02-8*, Pub. by ICHCA UK) St Mut.

Shipboard Handling of Unitised Cargo, No. 2. ICHCA Staff. (C). 1988. 90.00 (*0-685-46501-2*, Pub. by ICHCA UK) St Mut.

Shipboard Operational Problems. C. Hughes. 1989. 85.00 (*1-85044-237-1*) LLP.

Shipboard Operations. 2nd ed. R. V. Lavery. 1990. pap. 47.95 (*0-7506-1857-4*) Buttrwrth-Heinemann.

Shipboard Refrigeration & Fish Processing Equipment. Ed. by N. G. Kondrashova. Tr. by B. Karekar from RUS. 266p. (C). 1986. text ed. 130.00 (*90-6191-432-9*, Pub. by A A Balkema NE) Ashgate Pub Co.

Shipboard Wedding. Francine Pascal. (Sweet Valley University Ser.: No. 14). 240p. (YA). (gr. 9-12). 1995. mass mkt. 3.99 (*0-553-56693-8*) Bantam.

Shipbrokering & Chartering Practice. 4th ed. L. Gorton et al. 1995. 140.00 (*1-85044-971-6*) LLP.

***Shipbuilders.** Leonard E. Fisher. LC 96-34136. (Colonial Craftsmen Ser.: Group 2). (Illus.). 48p. (J). (gr. 4 up). 1997. lib. bdg. 14.95 (*0-7614-0508-9*, Benchmark NY) Marshall Cavendish.

***Shipbuilders of Esses: A Chronicle of Yankee Endeavor.** Dana A. Story. 1996. text ed. 39.95 (*0-07-061784-8*) McGraw.

Shipbuilders of Essex: A Chronicle of Yankee Ingenuity. Dana A. Story. (Illus.). 0408p. 1995. 39.95 (*0-938459-09-0*) Ten Pound Isl Bk.

Shipbuilders of the Venetian Arsenal: Workers & Workplace in the Preindustrial City. Robert C. Davis. LC 90-43807. (Studies in Historical & Political Science: 109th Series, No. 1 (1991)). (Illus.). 256p. 1991. text ed. 39.95 (*0-8018-4095-3*) Johns Hopkins.

Shipbuilding Contracts. 2nd ed. Ed. by M. Clarke. 265p. 1992. 110.00 (*1-85044-482-X*) LLP.

Shipbuilding in Colonial America. Joseph A. Goldenberg. LC 74-32136. xiii, 306p. 1976. text ed. 35.00 (*0-8139-0588-5*) U Pr of Va.

Shipbuilding Industry: A Guide to Historical Records. Ed. by Lewis A. Ritchie. LC 92-9472. (Studies in British Business Archives). 1992. text ed. 59.95 (*0-7190-3805-7*, Pub. by Manchester Univ Pr UK) St Martin.

***Shipbuilding on Prince Edward Island: Enterprise in a Maritime Setting, 1787-1920.** Nicolas J. De Jong & Marven E. Moore. (Mercury Ser.: No. 46). (Illus.). 418p. 1994. pap. 34.95 (*0-660-14021-7*, Pub. by Can Mus Civil CN) U of Wash Pr.

Shipbuilding Technology & Education. National Research Council Staff. 160p. (Orig.). 1996. pap. text ed. 29.00 (*0-309-05382-X*) Natl Acad Pr.

S

An Asterisk (*) at the beginning of an entry indicates that the title is appearing in BIP for the first time.

Shipbuilding Timber for the British Navy: Parliamentary Papers, 1729-1792. Intro. by R. J. Knight. LC 93-2507. (Scholars' Facsimiles & Reprints, Maritime History Ser.: Vol. 482). 1993. 75.00 (*0-8201-1482-0*) Schol Facsimiles.

Shipcarver's Handbook. Jay S. Hanna. (Illus.). 140p. 1988. 17.95 (*0-937822-14-0*) WoodenBoat Pubns.

Shipfitter. Jack Rudman. (Career Examination Ser.: C-1031). 1994. pap. 27.95 (*0-8373-1031-8*) Nat Learn.

Shiphandling for the Mariner. 3rd ed. Daniel H. MacElrevey. LC 95-5938. (Illus.). 344p. 1995. text ed. 35.00 (*0-87033-464-6*) Cornell Maritime.

Shiphandling Simulation: Application to Waterway Design. National Research Council Staff. Ed. by William C. Webster. 172p. 1992. pap. text ed. 19.00 (*0-309-04338-7*) Natl Acad Pr.

Shiphandling with Tugs. George H. Reid. LC 86-47712. (Illus.). 279p. 1986. text ed. 18.00 (*0-87033-354-2*) Cornell Maritime.

Shipley: The Shipleys of Maryland: a Genealogical Study. Shipley Clan Of Maryland Staff. (Illus.). 281p. 1993. reprint ed. pap. 44.00 (*0-8328-2979-X*); reprint ed. lib. bdg. 54.00 (*0-8328-2978-1*) Higginson Bk Co.

Shipley Associates Style Guide for Oil & Gas Professionals. rev. ed. Terry R. Bacon & Lawrence H. Freeman. 1990. 38.95 (*0-933427-01-8*) Shipley.

Shipmans of East Hawai'i. Emmett Cahill. LC 95-47621. (Illus.). 296p. 1996. pap. 24.95 (*0-8248-1680-3*) UH Pr.

Shipmaster's Handbook on Ship's Business. 2nd ed. James R. Aragon. LC 87-47998. 283p. 1988. text ed. 24.00 (*0-87033-378-X*) Cornell Maritime.

Shipment Clerk. Jack Rudman. (Career Examination Ser.: C-738). 1994. pap. 23.95 (*0-8373-0738-4*) Nat Learn.

Shipment of Edible Oils. Keith Farrer. 176p. (C). 1990. 475.00 (*1-85271-120-5*, Pub. by IBC Tech Srvs UK) St Mut.

Shipowners Guide to Yard Repairs. (C). 1989. 225.00 (*0-685-54758-2*, Pub. by Lorne & MacLean Marine) St Mut.

Shipowners Guide to Yard Repairs. Lorne & MacLean Marine & Offshore Publications Staff. (C). 1987. 195.00 (*0-685-33859-2*, Pub. by Lorne & MacLean Marine) St Mut.

Shipowners Guide to Yard Repairs. OCS Marine Staff. (C). 1989. text ed. 310.00 (*0-906314-29-1*, Pub. by Lorne & MacLean Marine) St Mut.

Shipowners' Liability for Loss of or Damage to Cargo under the Hague Rules: Gold Clause Agreement. 1987. 30.00 (*0-317-61474-6*, Pub. by Witherby & Co UK) St Mut.

***Shippen. Genealogy of the Descendants of Dr. William Shippen, the Elder, of Philadelphia, Member of the Continental Congress.** Roberdeau Buchanan. 16p. 1996. lib. bdg. 15.00 (*0-8328-6579-6*) Higginson Bk Co.

Shipping: A Techno-Economic Approach. C. Hughes. 1989. 80.00 (*1-85044-238-X*) LLP.

***Shipping: An Overview of the Worldwide Shipping Industry.** Niko Wijnolst & Tor Wergeland. (Marine Technology Ser.). (Illus.). 591p. (Orig.). 1996. pap. 87.50 (*90-407-1380-4*, Pub. by Delft U Pr NE) Coronet Bks.

***Shipping & Culture Vol. 1: The Norwegian Fish Club of San Francisco 1914-1996.** unabridged ed. Olaf T. Envig. Ed. by David Hull. LC 96-71767. (Illus.). 192p. 1996. 40.00 (*0-9655451-0-5*) Craft Pr CA.

Shipping & Development Policy: An Integrated Assessment. Alexander J. Yeats. LC 81-4989. 190p. 1981. text ed. 55.00 (*0-275-90745-7*, C0745, Praeger Pubs) Greenwood.

Shipping & the Environment. Lloyd's Shipping Economist Staff. (Orig.). 1991. pap. 30.00 (*0-685-66240-3*) LLP.

Shipping & Trade Between the Baltic Area & Western Europe 1784-95. Hans Johansen. (Odense Studies in History & Social Sciences: No. 82). 139p. (Orig.). 1983. Incl. 4 microfiche. pap. 43.50 (*87-7492-433-8*, Pub. by Odense Universitets Forlag DK) Coronet Bks.

Shipping & Trade (1750-1950) Proceedings of the Tenth International Economic History Congress, Leuven, Belgium, August 1990. Ed. by L. Fischer & H. Nordvik. (Studies in Social & Economic History: No. 10). 120p. (Orig.). 1990. pap. 32.50 (*90-6186-382-1*, Pub. by Leuven Univ BE) Coronet Bks.

Shipping Board's "Other Agency Ships" SubBoats & Merchants. Mark H. Goldberg. (Illus.). 350p. (Orig.). 1994. pap. write for info. (*1-879180-10-3*) AMM Mus Found.

Shipping Business & Maritime Economics: An Annotated International Bibliography. annot. ed. James McConville & Glenys Rickaby. LC 94-23314. 512p. 1995. 140.00 (*0-7201-2180-9*, Mansell Pub) Cassell.

Shipping Container Code & Symbol Guidelines for the U. S. Book Industry. rev. ed. Distribution Committee of Book Industry Study Group, Inc. (Illus.). 22p. 1996. pap. 8.00 (*0-940016-58-3*) Bk Indus Study.

Shipping Days of Old Boothbay (Maine) George W. Rice. LC 84-61955. (Illus.). 463p. 1984. reprint ed. 45.00 (*0-89725-054-0*, 1203) Picton Pr.

***Shipping Developments in Far Eastern: The Korean Experience.** Tae-Woo Lee. (Plymouth Studies in Contemporary Shipping). 272p. 1996. text ed. 67.95 (*1-85972-493-0*, Pub. by Avebury Pub UK) Ashgate Pub Co.

Shipping Finance. (C). 1990. 325.00 (*1-85564-039-2*) St Mut.

Shipping Finance. 2nd ed. Euromoney Staff. Ed. by Graham Burns. 300p. 1995. pap. 170.00 (*1-85564-380-4*, Pub. by Euromoney UK) Am Educ Systs.

Shipping Finance Annual 1995/96. Ed. by Adrian Hornbrook. 220p. 1995. 170.00 (*0-614-17076-1*, Pub. by Euromoney UK) Am Educ Systs.

Shipping Futures. James Gray. 180p. 1990. 105.00 (*1-85044-322-X*) LLP.

Shipping in International Trade Relations. Ademuni-Odeke. 600p. 1988. text ed. 110.00 (*0-566-05371-3*, Pub. by Dartmth Pub UK) Ashgate Pub Co.

***Shipping in the Baltic Region.** Ed. by Michael Roe. (Plymouth Studies in Contemporary Shipping). 96p. 1997. text ed. 49.95 (*1-85972-501-5*, Pub. by Avebury Pub UK) Ashgate Pub Co.

Shipping Industry: The Technology & Economics of Specialization, Vol. 5. Edmund J. Gubbins. (Transportation Studies: Vol. 5). 126p. 1986. text ed. 101.00 (*2-88124-063-1*) Gordon & Breach.

Shipping Law. M. Davies & A. Dickey. 1995. 120.00 (*0-455-21355-0*, Pub. by Law Bk Co AT) Gaunt.

Shipping Law. M. Davies & A. Dickey. 1995. pap. 75.00 (*0-455-21356-9*, Pub. by Law Bk Co AT) Gaunt.

Shipping Law. Martin Davies & Anthony Dickey. lxxii, 431p. 1990. 89.50 (*0-455-20936-7*, Pub. by Law Bk Co AT) Gaunt.

Shipping Law Faces Europe: European Policy, Competition & Environment. P. Aspden et al. (International Colloquium Ser.). 255p. 1996. pap. 58.00 (*90-6215-476-X*, Pub. by Maklu Uitgevers BE) Gaunt.

Shipping Law Handbook. Michael Bundock. ring bd. 125.00 (*1-85044-889-2*) LLP.

Shipping Literature of the Great Lakes: A Catalog of Company Publications, 1852-1990. Compiled by LeRoy Barnett. LC 92-53725. 1992. 27.95 (*0-87013-317-9*) Mich St U Pr.

Shipping, Maritime Trade, & the Economic Development of Colonial North America. James F. Shepherd. LC 76-176256. 265p. reprint ed. pap. 75.60 (*0-317-20814-4*, 2024536) Bks Demand.

Shipping News. E. Annie Proulx. 352p. 1994. pap. 10.00 (*0-02-036078-9*) Macmillan.

Shipping News. E. Annie Proulx. 352p. 1994. pap. 12.00 (*0-671-51005-3*, Scribners PB Fict) S&S Trade.

Shipping News: A Novel. E. Annie Proulx. Ed. by B. Grossman. 352p. 1993. 20.00 (*0-684-19337-X*) S&S Trade.

Shipping Out. 1997. pap. 12.95 (*0-939837-06-4*) Paradise Cay Pubns.

***Shipping Out.** Alan E. Spears. 1996. pap. text ed. 12.95 (*0-07-066052-2*) McGraw.

Shipping Policy in the European Community. Paul Hart et al. LC 92-38911. 107p. 1992. 63.95 (*1-85628-348-8*, Pub. by Avebury Pub UK) Ashgate Pub Co.

Shipping Pools. 2nd ed. William Packard. 200p. 1995. 85.00 (*1-85044-512-5*) LLP.

Shipping Regulation: Cases, Vols. 1-26, 1961-1995. Pike & Fischer, Inc. Staff. LC 61-31808. 1978. reprint ed. 1,925.00 (*0-89941-206-8*, 200950) W S Hein.

Shipping Revolution: The Modern Merchant Ship. Ed. by Robert Gardiner & Alastair Couper. (Conway's History of the Ship Ser.). (Illus.). 208p. 1993. 46.95 (*1-55750-765-1*) Naval Inst Pr.

Shipping, Technology & Imperialism: Papers Presented to the Third British-Dutch Maritime History Conference. Ed. by Gordon Jackson & David M. Williams. (Illus.). 304p. 1996. 76.95 (*1-85928-344-6*, Pub. by Scolar Pr UK) Ashgate Pub Co.

Shippo: The Art of Enameling in Japan. George Kuwayama. LC 86-31839. (Illus.). 56p. (Orig.). 1987. pap. 9.95 (*0-87587-136-4*) LA Co Art Mus.

Ships. LC 93-46382. (Look Inside Cross-Sections Ser.). (Illus.). 32p. (J). (gr. 1-4). 1994. pap. 5.95 (*1-56458-521-2*) DK Pub Inc.

***Ships.** (Illus.). (J). pap. 8.99 (*0-590-24342-X*) Scholastic Inc.

Ships. Donna Bailey. LC 89-21727. (Facts About Ser.). (Illus.). 48p. (J). (gr. 2-6). 1990. pap. 4.95 (*0-8114-6631-0*); lib. bdg. 24.26 (*0-8114-2502-9*) Raintree Steck-V.

Ships. Bellerophon Staff. (J). (gr. 1-9). 1992. pap. 3.95 (*0-88388-016-4*) Bellerophon Bks.

Ships. Richard Humble. LC 93-19705. (Pointers Ser.). (Illus.). 32p. (J). (gr. 4-6). 1993. lib. bdg. 22.83 (*0-8114-6158-0*) Raintree Steck-V.

Ships. Richard Humble. (Illus.). (J). 1995. pap. text ed. 4.95 (*0-8114-6337-0*) Raintree Steck-V.

Ships. Daisy Kerr. (Worldwise Ser.). (Illus.). 48p. (J). (gr. 4-6). 1995. lib. bdg. 22.70 (*0-531-14379-1*) Watts.

Ships. Daisy Kerr. (Worldwise Ser.). (Illus.). 48p. (J). (gr. 4-6). 1996. pap. 7.00 (*0-531-15284-7*) Watts.

***Ships.** Neil Morris. LC 97-12533. (J). 1997. write for info. (*0-382-39789-4*); pap. write for info. (*0-382-39790-8*) Silver Burdett Pr.

Ships. Roberto Quesada. Tr. by Hardie St. Martin. LC 92-7988. 214p. 1992. 17.95 (*0-941423-65-4*) FWEW.

Ships. Roy Richards. LC 95-23172. (Through Time Ser.). (J). 1996. lib. bdg. 24.26 (*0-8172-4138-8*) Raintree Steck-V.

Ships. Joy Richardson. LC 93-49730. (Picture Science Ser.). (Illus.). 32p. (J). 1994. lib. bdg. 20.00 (*0-531-14326-0*) Watts.

***Ships.** Snapshot Staff. (Shape Board Books Ser.). 1997. 3.95 (*0-7894-2210-7*) DK Pub Inc.

Ships: An Educational Coloring Book. Spizzirri Publishing Co. Staff. Ed. by Linda Spizzirri. (Illus.). 32p. (J). (gr. 1-8). 1981. pap. 1.99 (*0-86545-035-8*) Spizzirri.

Ships! Come Aboard. Siegfried Aust. LC 92-12761. (Fun with Technology Ser.). (Illus.). 32p. (J). (gr. 2-5). 1993. lib. bdg. 9.50 (*0-8225-2156-3*, Lerner Publctns) Lerner Group.

Ships: Crossing the World's Oceans. Sean M. Grady. LC 92-9162. (Encyclopedia of Discovery & Invention Ser.). (Illus.). 96p. (J). (gr. 5-8). 1992. lib. bdg. 18.96 (*1-56006-220-7*) Lucent Bks.

Ships: Sailors & the Sea. Richard Humble. LC 91-6805. (Timelines Ser.). (Illus.). 48p. (J). (gr. 5-8). 1991. 13.95 (*0-531-15234-0*) Watts.

Ships: Sailors & the Sea. Richard Humble. (Timelines Ser.). (Illus.). 48p. (J). (gr. 5-8). 1996. reprint ed. pap. 7.95 (*0-531-15286-3*) Watts.

Ships Afire. J. J. Marcelo. Tr. by Sarah Arvio. 336p. (Orig.). 1988. pap. 7.95 (*0-380-89741-5*) Avon.

Ship's Agent, Docks & Ports, Towage, Lighterage, Pilotage: 1919-1991. (Lloyd's Law Reports Consolidated Index, 1919-1994 Ser.: Vol. 5). 1992. 125.00 (*1-85044-433-1*) LLP.

Ships, Aircraft & Weapons of the U. S. Navy. (Illus.). 67p. (Orig.). (C). 1994. pap. text ed. 25.00 (*0-7881-0739-9*) DIANE Pub.

Ships & Aircraft of the Royal Navy. 1989. pap. 15.00 (*0-907771-54-8*, Pub. by Maritime Bks UK) St Mut.

Ships & Aircraft of the Royal Navy. Maritime Books Staff. (C). 1986. pap. text ed. 55.00 (*0-907771-23-8*, Pub. by Maritime Bks UK) St Mut.

Ships & Aircraft of the U. S. Fleet: 1939, '41, '42 & '45 Editions, 4 Vols., Set. Ed. by James C. Fahey. (Illus.). 208p. 1976. boxed 27.95 (*0-87021-171-4*) Naval Inst Pr.

Ships & Aircraft of the U. S. Fleet: 1950, '58, & '65 Editions, 3 Vols., Set. James C. Fahey. LC 76-15840. (Illus.). 192p. 1980. 26.95 (*0-87021-647-3*) Naval Inst Pr.

Ships & Boats Punch Out Stencils. Theodore Menten. (J). 1986. pap. 3.50 (*0-486-25049-0*) Dover.

Ships & Marine Technology see 1997 Annual Book of ASTM Standards: Iron & Steel Products, Section 1

Ships & Memories: Merchant Seafarers in Canada's Age of Steam. Eric W. Sager. (Illus.). 176p. 1993. 29.95 (*0-7748-0443-2*) U of Wash Pr.

Ships & Men of the Great Lakes. Dwight Boyer. 208p. 1960. pap. 12.75 (*0-912514-51-5*) Freshwater.

Ships & Sailing: Poetry, Folklore, Sayings, Comics. Michael J. Cushman. 40p. 1995. pap. 3.00 (*0-9648667-0-6*) Cushmn Pubng.

Ships & Sailors: Ancient & Modern. C. C. Cotterill & E. Little. 1977. lib. bdg. 69.95 (*0-8490-2599-0*) Gordon Pr.

Ships & Sailors: The Story of Our Merchant Marine. William H. Clark. LC 74-22736. (Illus.). reprint ed. 37.50 (*0-404-58488-8*) AMS Pr.

Ships & Sea-Power Before the Great Persian War: The Ancestry of the Ancient Trireme. H. T. Wallinga. LC 92-16496. (Mnemosyne Ser.: Supplement 121). 1992. 100.00 (*90-04-09650-7*) E J Brill.

Ships & Seafaring in Ancient Times. Lionel Casson. (Illus.). 160p. (Orig.). 1994. pap. 24.95 (*0-292-71162-X*) U of Tex Pr.

Ships & Seamanship in the Ancient World. Lionel Casson. (Illus.). 469p. 1995. pap. text ed. 19.95 (*0-8018-5130-0*) Johns Hopkins.

Ships & Seamanship in the Ancient World. Lionel Casson. LC 78-112996. (Illus.). 577p. reprint ed. pap. 164.50 (*0-7837-0564-6*, 2040908) Bks Demand.

Ships & Shipwrecks. Steven Blackman. (Technology Craft Topics Ser.). (Illus.). 32p. (J). (gr. 5-7). 1993. lib. bdg. 20.00 (*0-531-14278-7*) Watts.

Ships & Shipwrecks of the Americas: A History Based on Underwater Archaeology. Ed. by George F. Bass. LC 88-50246. (Illus.). 272p. 1996. pap. 24.95 (*0-500-27892-X*) Thames Hudson.

Ships & Submarines. Richard Humble. 1997. pap. 17.99 (*0-670-86778-0*) Viking Penguin.

Ships & the River. David Canright. Ed. by Janet Cambell. (Illus.). 32p. (J). (gr. 2-6). 1975. pap. 2.00 (*0-913344-22-2*) South St Sea Mus.

Ships & Their Cargoes. Brown, Son & Ferguson Ltd. Staff. 60p. (C). 1987. 75.00 (*0-85174-073-1*, Pub. by Brwn Son Ferg) St Mut.

Ships & Voyages. Jon Nichol. (Resource Units, Middle Ages, 1066-1485, Ser.). (Illus.). 24p. 1974. reprint ed. teacher ed., pap. text ed. 12.95 (*0-582-39388-4*) Longman.

Ship's Bell. Karl Wede. (Illus.). 60p. 1972. 1.00 (*0-913344-10-9*) South St Sea Mus.

Ships' Bilge Pumps: A History of Their Development, 1500-1900. Thomas J. Oertling. LC 96-21939. (Studies in Nautical Archaeology: No. 2). (Illus.). 123p. (Orig.). 1996. pap. 17.95 (*0-89096-722-9*) Tex A&M Univ Pr.

Ships Chronometer. Marvin E. Whitney. (Illus.). 490p. 1984. 75.00 (*0-918845-08-4*) Am Watchmakers.

Ship's Clock: A Family Chronicle. large type ed. Catherine M. Rae. LC 93-22972. 1993. lib. bdg. 21.95 (*0-7862-0000-6*) Thorndike Pr.

Ships Data 1. Ed. by Arnold S. Lott & Robert F. Sumrall. (Illus.). 32p. 1982. 3.00 (*0-915268-07-8*) USS North Car.

Ship's Doctor. Terrence Riley. LC 95-8186. (Illus.). 312p. 1995. 31.95 (*1-55750-721-X*) Naval Inst Pr.

Ships' Figureheads. Hans J. Hansen & Clas B. Hansen. LC 90-63800. (Illus.). 128p. 1991. 24.95 (*0-88740-299-2*) Schiffer.

Ship's Figureheads. Michael K. Stammers. 1990. 4.50 (*0-913714-63-1*) Legacy Books.

Ships Figureheads. Michael K. Stammers. 1989. pap. 25.00 (*0-85263-650-4*, Pub. by Shire UK) St Mut.

Ships Fire-Fighting Manual. (C). 1989. 150.00 (*0-89771-704-X*, Pub. by Lorne & MacLean Marine) St Mut.

Ships Fire-Fighting Manual. Ed. by Lorne & MacLean Marine & Offshore Publications Staff. 1987. 235.00 (*0-317-43641-4*, Pub. by Lorne & MacLean Marine) St Mut.

Ships Fire-Fighting Manual. OCS Marine Staff. (C). 1989. text ed. 195.00 (*0-906314-03-8*, Pub. by Lorne & MacLean Marine) St Mut.

Ships for the Seven Seas: Philadelphia Shipbuilding in the Age of Industrial Capitalism. Thomas R. Heinrich. LC 96-27104. (Johns Hopkins Studies in Industry & Society). (Illus.). 288p. 1997. text ed. 39.95 (*0-8018-5387-7*) Johns Hopkins.

Ships Going into the Blue: Essays & Notes on Poetry. Louis Simpson. LC 94-16874. (Poets on Poetry Ser.). 176p. 1994. pap. 13.95 (*0-472-06559-9*) U of Mich Pr.

Ships Going into the Blue: Essays & Notes on Poetry. Louis Simpson. LC 94-16874. (Poets on Poetry Ser.). 176p. 1994. 39.50 (*0-472-09559-5*) U of Mich Pr.

Ships Gone Missing: The Great Lakes Storm of 1913. Robert J. Hemming. 208p. 1993. pap. 16.95 (*0-8092-3715-6*) Contemp Bks.

Ships in Bottles. Guy De Marco. LC 84-52714. (Illus.). 64p. 1985. pap. 6.95 (*0-88740-033-7*) Schiffer.

Ships in Bottles. Neil Curry. 96p. 8800. reprint ed. pap. 12.95 (*1-870612-30-2*, Pub. by Enitha Pr UK) Dufour.

Ships in Bottles: A Step-by-Step Guide to a Venerable Nautical Craft. 2nd ed. Donald Hubbard. LC 88-90507. (Illus.). 133p. 1988. reprint ed. pap. 19.95 (*0-943665-00-0*) Sea Eagle Pubns.

Ships in the Making: A History of Ship Model Testing at Teddington & Feltham, 1910. David Bailey. 400p. 1995. 85.00 (*1-85044-943-0*) LLP.

Ships in the Sky: the Story of the Great Dirigibles see Great Dirigibles: Their Triumph & Disasters

Ship's Log. Henry Beard & Roy McKie. (Illus.). 96p. 1983. pap. 7.95 (*0-89480-574-6*, 574) Workman Pub.

***Ship's Log.** Weems & Plath Staff. (Illus.). 98p. 1990. reprint ed. pap. 15.95 (*1-878797-08-5*) C Plath North Amer.

Ship's Log Book II. Frank F. Farrar. 448p. 1993. pap. 19.95 (*0-9637291-3-6*) Sextant Pr.

Ships' Medicine Chest & Medical Aid at Sea, 2 vols., Set. 1994. lib. bdg. 595.00 (*0-8490-5746-9*) Gordon Pr.

Ships, Money & Politics: Seafaring & Naval Enterprise in the Reign of Charles I. Kenneth R. Andrews. (Illus.). 248p. (C). 1991. text ed. 59.95 (*0-521-40116-X*) Cambridge U Pr.

Ships, Oceans & Empire: Studies in European Maritime & Colonial History, 1400-1750. Geoffrey V. Scammell. (Collected Studies: Vol. CS478). 300p. 1995. 81.95 (*0-86078-475-4*, Pub. by Variorum UK) Ashgate Pub Co.

Ships of Catalina Island. Martin P. Riegel. LC 88-61279. (California Heritage Ser.: Vol. IV). (Illus.). 88p. (Orig.). 1988. 14.00 (*0-944871-07-0*); pap. 8.95 (*0-944871-06-2*) Riegel Pub.

Ships of Children. Richard A. Taylor. LC 91-71745. (Illus.). 192p. 1992. pap. 14.95 (*0-942963-01-6*) Distinctive Pub.

Ships of China. Valentin A. Sokoloff. LC 82-90290. (Illus.). 54p. 1982. 29.75 (*0-9607438-0-4*) Sokoloff.

Ships of Christopher Columbus. Xavier Pastor. (Anatomy of the Ship Ser.). (Illus.). 128p. 1992. 39.95 (*1-55750-755-4*) Naval Inst Pr.

***Ships of Collingwood.** Skip Gillham. (Great Lakes Marine History Ser.). (Illus.). 200p. 1992. pap. 19.95 (*0-9697606-2-0*, Pub. by Riverbank Trade CN) Partners Pubs Grp.

Ships of Earth. Orson Scott Card. (Homecoming Saga Ser.: No. 2). 384p. 1994. 22.95 (*0-312-85659-8*) Tor Bks.

Ships of Earth. Orson Scott Card. (Homecoming Saga Ser.: No. 3). 384p. 1995. mass mkt. 5.99 (*0-8125-3263-5*) Tor Bks.

Ships of Earth. deluxe limited ed. Orson Scott Card. (Homecoming Saga Ser.: No. 3). 384p. 1994. 200.00 (*0-312-85660-1*) Tor Bks.

Ships of Our Ancestors. Michael J. Anuta. LC 93-70622. (Illus.). viii, 380p. 1996. reprint ed. pap. 34.95 (*0-8063-1381-1*, 125) Genealog Pub.

***Ships of Port Weller.** Skip Gillham. (Great Lakes Marine History Ser.). (Illus.). 96p. 1992. pap. 15.95 (*0-9697606-3-9*, Pub. by Riverbank Trade CN) Partners Pubs Grp.

Ships of the Air. Lynn Curlee. LC 94-10746. (Illus.). 32p. (J). (gr. 3-7). 1996. 14.95 (*0-395-69338-1*) HM.

Ships of the American Revolution. John F. Millar. Ed. by Harry Knill. (Illus.). 48p. (Orig.). 1976. pap. 3.95 (*0-88388-036-9*) Bellerophon Bks.

Ships of the California Gold Rush. Martin P. Riegel. LC 88-92421. (Illus.). 48p. (Orig.). (YA). 1988. 11.00 (*0-944871-11-9*); pap. 4.95 (*0-685-24979-4*) Riegel Pub.

Ships of the French Arm. Timothy B. Brown. (Traveller Ser.: No. 2300). 96p. (Orig.). 1987. pap. 10.00 (*0-943580-34-X*) Game Designers.

Ships of the German Fleet, 1848-1945. rev. ed. Hans J. Hansen. (Illus.). 192p. 1988. reprint ed. 41.95 (*0-87021-654-6*) Naval Inst Pr.

Ships of the Great Lakes: 300 Years of Navigation. 3rd rev. ed. James P. Barry. (Illus.). 274p. 1996. reprint ed. 40.00 (*1-882376-27-7*); reprint ed. pap. 24.95 (*1-882376-26-9*) Thunder Bay Pr.

***Ships of the Great Lakes Books.** rev. ed. 1996. pap. 5.00 (*0-942618-63-7*) Penrod-Hiawatha.

Ships of the Great Lakes in Miniature. John Heinz. Ed. by Jeffrey A. Phillips. (Illus.). 98p. (C). 1987. 14.95 (*0-9615021-2-6*) Phoen Pubns.

Ships of the Inland Sea: The Story of the Puget Sound Steamboats. 2nd ed. Gordon R. Newell. (Illus.). 257p. 1960. 14.95 (*0-8323-0039-X*) Binford Mort.

Ships of the Orange Coast. Martin P. Riegel. LC 88-92522. (Illus.). 40p. (Orig.). (YA). (gr. 9 up). 1988. pap. 4.75 (*0-944871-09-7*); lib. bdg. 11.00 (*0-944871-08-9*) Riegel Pub.

***Ships of the Paterson Fleet.** Gene Onchulenko & Skip Gillham. (Great Lakes Marine History Ser.). (Illus.). 144p. 1996. pap. 19.95 (*0-9697606-4-7*, Pub. by Riverbank Trade CN) Partners Pubs Grp.

Ships of the Redwood Coast. Jack McNairn & Jerry MacMullen. 111p. reprint ed. pap. 30.00 (*0-7837-2354-7*, 2042570) Bks Demand.

***Ships of the Star Fleet, Vol. 1.** rev. ed. Todd Guenther. LC 92-114105. (Illus.). 120p. (Orig.). 1991. pap. 29.95 (*0-9656016-0-9*) Mstrcom Data.

***Ships of the Star Fleet Vol. 2, No. 1: Akyazi-Class Perimeter Action Ships.** Todd Guenther. LC 92-114105. (Illus.). 67p. (Orig.). 1993. pap. 17.95 (0-9656016-1-7) Mstrcom Data.

***Ships of the United States Navy & Their Sponsors, 1958-1990.** Marylin Jackson & John D. Beecher. (Illus.). 216p. 1991. 21.95 (1-55750-751-1) Naval Inst Pr.

***Ships of the World: An Historical Encyclopedia.** Lincoln P. Paine. LC 97-12872. 1997. 45.00 (0-395-71556-3) HM.

***Ships of Upper Lakes Shipping.** Skip Gillham & Garnet Wilcox. (Great Lakes Marine History Ser.). (Illus.). 150p. 1994. pap. 17.95 (0-9697606-1-2, Pub. by Riverbank Trade CN) Partners Pubs Grp.

Ships Passenger Lists, Port of Galveston, Texas: 1846-1871. Galveston County Genealogical Society Staff. 1984. 28.00 (0-89308-343-7) Southern Hist Pr.

Ship's Pasture: Poems. Jon Silkin. 96p. 1986. pap. 11.95 (0-7102-0841-3, 08413, RKP) Routledge.

Ships Routing. IMO Staff. (ENG, FRE & SPA.). (C). 1991. English ed. ring bd. 800.00 (0-7855-0012-X, IMO 927E, Pub. by Intl Maritime Org UK); French ed. ring bd. 800.00 (0-685-74515-5, IMO 928F, Pub. by Intl Maritime Org UK); Spanish ed. ring bd. 800.00 (0-685-74516-3, IMO 929S, Pub. by Intl Maritime Org UK) St Mut.

Ships, Sailors & the Sea. J. Miles. 1989. lib. bdg. 15.95 (0-88110-365-9, Usborne) EDC.

Ships, Sailors & the Sea. J. Miles. 1989. pap. 7.95 (0-7460-0285-8, Usborne) EDC.

Ships, Seafaring & Society: Essays in Maritime History. Ed. by Timothy J. Runyan. LC 87-17769. 382p. 1987. 29.95 (0-8143-1990-4); pap. 17.95 (0-8143-1991-2) Wayne St U Pr.

Ships, Submarines & the Sea. P. J. Gates & N. M. Lynn. Ed. by Geoffrey Till. (Sea Power Ser.: Vol. 2). 176p. 1990. 40.00 (0-08-034735-5, Pub. by Brasseys UK); 25.00 (0-08-033626-4, Pub. by Brasseys UK) Brasseys Inc.

Ship's Surgeon's Yarn, & Other Stories. Francis B. Young. LC 72-134985. (Short Story Index Reprint Ser.). 1977. 20.95 (0-8369-3715-5) Ayer.

Ships That Brought Us So Far. Peter Stanford. (Illus.). pap. 5.95 (0-686-15903-9) Sea Hist Pr.

Ships That Changed History. Adolph A. Hoehling. 1994. pap. 13.95 (1-56833-019-7) Madison Bks UPA.

Ships That Changed History. Adolph A. Hoehling. 1992. 19.95 (0-8191-8072-6) U Pr of Amer.

Ship's Value. 2nd ed. Kaj Pineus. 1986. 85.00 (1-85044-062-X) LLP.

***Shipshape.** Ferenc Mate. Date not set. pap. 29.95 (0-920256-33-3) Norton.

Shipton Quebec Canada 1825 Census. Jay M. Hobrook. LC 76-364055. 15p. 1976. pap. 5.00 (0-931248-07-8) Holbrook Res.

Shipur Halashon. rev. ed. Shifra Babad. 109p. (Orig.). (HEB.). wbk. ed. write for info. (0-9645822-1-X) S Babad.

Shipwreck. BBN Staff. (MS - Middle School Science Ser.). 1998. teacher ed. 70.00 (0-538-66304-9) S-W Pub.

Shipwreck. BBN Staff. (MS - Middle School Science Ser.). 1998. student ed., pap. 13.95 (0-538-66305-7) S-W Pub.

Shipwreck! A Comprehensive Directory of Over 3700 Shipwrecks on the Great Lakes. David D. Swayze. (Illus.). 260p. 1992. pap. 19.95 (0-937360-12-0) Harbor Hse MI.

***Shipwreck! Stories of the Graveyard of the Atlantic.** Mary Maden. Ed. by Eric Schroeder. LC 97-65801. (Illus.). 20p. (Orig.). (J). (gr. 1-6). 1997. pap. 5.95 (1-890479-50-0) Dog & Pony Enter.

Shipwreck & Adventure of Monsieur Pierre Viaud. Tr. by Robin F. Fabel. 128p. 1990. lib. bdg. 24.95 (0-8130-1000-4) U Press Fla.

Shipwreck & Adventures among the South Sea Islanders: Wreck of the Minerva. John P. Twyning & Peter Bays. 238p. 1996. pap. 14.95 (0-87770-575-5) Ye Galleon.

Shipwreck & Adventures among the South Sea Islanders & Wreck of the Minerva. 2nd ed. John P. Twyning & Peter Bays. LC 96-2261. 238p. 1996. 24.95 (0-87770-574-7) Ye Galleon.

Shipwreck Diving: A Complete Diver's Handbook to Mastering the Skills of Wreck Diving. Daniel Berg. (Illus.). 88p. (Orig.). 1991. pap. 12.95 (0-9616167-5-X) Aqua Explorers.

***Shipwreck Eyewitness Books.** LC 97-9278. 1997. 19.00 (0-679-88562-5) Knopf.

***Shipwreck Eyewitness Books.** Eyewitness Books Staff. LC 97-9278. (J). 1997. lib. bdg. 20.99 (0-679-98562-X) Knopf Bks Yng Read.

Shipwreck Guide to the Bahamas, Turks, & Caicos. Tony Jaggers. (Illus.). 280p. 1994. 29.95 (0-9647791-0-2) T Jaggers.

Shipwreck in Haven. Keith Waldrop. 1989. pap. 10.00 (0-942433-15-7) Awede Pr.

Shipwreck of the Mesquite: Death of a Coast Guard Cutter. Frederick Stonehouse. Ed. by Paul L. Hayden. LC 91-62082. (Illus.). 112p. (Orig.). 1991. pap. 14.95 (0-942235-10-X) LSPC Inc.

Shipwreck of Their Hopes: The Battles for Chattanooga. Peter Cozzens. LC 94-6269. (Illus.). 536p. 1994. 34.95 (0-252-01922-9) U of Ill Pr.

Shipwreck on the Lights. Joan R. Biggar. (Adventure Quest Ser.). 160p. (Orig.). (J). (gr. 5-8). 1992. pap. 4.99 (0-570-04710-2, 56-1669) Concordia.

Shipwreck, Pirates, & Privateers: Sunken Treasures of the Upper South Carolina Coast, 1521-1865. Edward L. Spence. LC 95-69597. (Illus.). 160p. (Orig.). 1995. 19.95 (1-886391-06-8); pap. text ed. 12.95 (1-886391-07-6) Narwhal Pr.

Shipwreck with Spectator: Paradigm of a Metaphor for Existence. Hans Blumenberg. (Studies in Contemporary German Social Thought). (Illus.). 112p. 1996. 19.00 (0-262-02411-X) MIT Pr.

Shipwrecked. Katherine Applegate. (Ocean City Ser.: No. 9). 224p. 1995. mass mkt. 3.99 (0-06-106304-5, Harp PBks) HarpC.

Shipwrecked. Ditz. 1993. 34.95 (0-226-15381-9) U Ch Pr.

Shipwrecked at Samoa, California: The Loss of the Navy Cruiser U. S. S. Milwaukee Launched 1906 Lost 1917. 2nd ed. Raymond W. Hillman. LC 93-93681. (Illus.). 53p. 1994. pap. 15.95 (0-9644191-0-6) Pride Riv.

Shipwrecked in the Tunnel of Love. Martha Smith & Maureen Croteau. (Illus.). 96p. (Orig.). 1984. pap. text ed. 4.95 (0-932413-00-5) Recreat Pub.

***Shipwrecked on Padre Island.** Isabel R. Marvin. LC 92-43073. (Illus.). 160p. (J). (gr. 4 up). 1993. pap. 9.95 (1-885777-17-5) Hendrick-Long.

***Shipwrecks.** Cathie Cush. LC 97-141. 1997. write for info. (1-56799-475-X, Friedman-Fairfax) M Friedman Pub Grp Inc.

Shipwrecks. Akira Yoshimura. Tr. by Mark Ealey from JPN. LC 95-40514. 174p. 1996. 22.00 (0-15-100194-4) HarBrace.

Shipwrecks: A Novel. Akira Yoshimura. Tr. by Mark Ealey from JPN. 1996. 21.00 (0-15-100211-8, Harvest Bks) HarBrace.

Shipwrecks: An Encyclopedia of the World's Worst Disasters at Sea. David Ritchie. LC 95-15664. 320p. 1996. 40.00 (0-8160-3163-0) Facts on File.

Shipwrecks: Diving the Graveyard of the Atlantic. rev. ed. Roderick Farb. LC 85-7233. (Illus.). 380p. (Orig.). 1990. pap. 14.95 (0-89732-064-6) Menasha Ridge.

Shipwrecks: Terror & Treasure. Kathryn L. Humphrey. LC 91-16962. (Full-Color First Bks.). (Illus.). 64p. (J). (gr. 5-8). 1991. lib. bdg. 21.00 (0-531-20031-0) Watts.

Shipwrecks along the Atlantic Coast. William P. Quinn. 240p. 1988. 34.95 (0-940160-40-4) Parnassus Imprints.

***Shipwrecks & Maritime Disasters of the Maine Coast.** Peter D. Bachelder. LC 97-13640. 1997. write for info. (0-931675-03-0) Prov Pr Maine.

Shipwrecks & Rescues on the Northwest Coast - Documentary. Bert Webber & Margie Webber. LC 95-50880. (Illus.). 264p. (Orig.). 1996. pap. 14.95 (0-936738-90-1) Webb Research.

Shipwrecks & Sea Monsters of California's Central Coast. Randall A. Reinstedt. LC 76-350548. (Illus.). 168p. 1975. pap. 8.95 (0-933818-02-5) Ghost Town.

Shipwrecks & Sunken Treasures Coloring Book. Peter F. Copeland. (Illus.). (J). (gr. k-3). 1992. pap. 2.95 (0-486-27286-9) Dover.

Shipwrecks Around Boston. William P. Quinn. LC 96-70036. (Illus.). 240p. 1997. 45.00 (0-940160-67-6) Parnassus Imprints.

Shipwrecks Around Cape Cod. William P. Quinn. LC 73-92326. (Illus.). 240p. 1973. pap. 25.00 (0-936972-01-7) Lower Cape.

Shipwrecks Around Land's End. Richard Larn. (C). 1989. pap. 35.00 (0-85025-307-1, Pub. by Tor Mark Pr UK) St Mut.

Shipwrecks Around Maine. William P. Quinn. 1983. pap. 25.00 (0-936972-11-4) Lower Cape.

Shipwrecks Around New England. William P. Quinn. LC 79-88076. (Illus.). 240p. 1979. pap. 25.00 (0-936972-05-X) Lower Cape.

Shipwrecks Around the Lizard. Richard Larn. (C). 1990. pap. 24.95 (0-85025-306-3, Pub. by Tor Mark Pr UK) St Mut.

Shipwrecks at the Golden Gate. James Delgado & Stephen Haller. (Illus.). 192p. (Orig.). 1989. 25.95 (0-938530-50-X); pap. 15.95 (0-938530-49-6) Lexikos.

Shipwrecks in Florida Waters: A Billion Dollar Graveyard. Robert F. Marx. LC 78-65775. (Illus.). ix, 147p. 1986. 12.50 (0-913122-55-6); pap. 7.95 (0-913122-51-3) Mickler Hse.

Shipwrecks in New York Waters. Paul C. Morris & William P. Quinn. (Illus.). 240p. 1989. 34.95 (0-940160-44-7) Parnassus Imprints.

Shipwrecks in the Americas. Robert F. Marx. (Illus.). 544p. 1987. reprint ed. pap. 10.95 (0-486-25514-X) Dover.

Shipwrecks in the Vicinity of Jupiter Inlet. Bessie W. DuBois. (Illus.). 31p. 1981. pap. 2.95 (0-317-19706-1) Florida Classics.

Shipwrecks, Legends & Ghost Stories of Cape May. Charles J. Adams, III & David J. Seibold. (Illus.). 115p. 1987. pap. 6.95 (0-9610008-5-6) Exeter Hse.

Shipwrecks Near Barnegat Inlet. 2nd ed. David J. Seibold & Charles J. Adams, III. (Illus.). 78p. reprint ed. pap. 6.95 (1-880683-04-0) Exeter Hse.

Shipwrecks Near Wabasso Beach. Ernie S. Richards & Robert F. Weller. (Illus.). 96p. (Orig.). 1995. pap. 9.95 (0-9628359-4-3) R Weller.

Shipwrecks North Coast: St. Ives to Bude. Richard Larn. (C). 1990. pap. 35.00 (0-85025-324-1, Pub. by Tor Mark Pr UK) St Mut.

Shipwrecks of Delaware & Maryland. Gary Gentile. (Illus.). 200p. 1990. pap. 20.00 (0-9621453-2-7) GGP.

Shipwrecks of Florida: A Comprehensive Listing. Steven D. Singer. LC 91-45895. (Illus.). 368p. 1992. 24.95 (1-56164-006-9) Pineapple Pr.

Shipwrecks of Isle Royale National Park. Daniel F. Lenihan. LC 94-77712. (Illus.). 212p. 1994. pap. 34.95 (0-942235-18-5) LSPC Inc.

Shipwrecks of Lake Huron: The Great Sweet Water Sea. 4th ed. Jack Parker. LC 86-70155. (Illus.). 175p. (Orig.). 1986. pap. 11.95 (0-932212-45-X) Avery Color.

Shipwrecks of Lake Superior. James R. Marshall. LC 87-80682. (Illus.). 100p. (Orig.). 1987. pap. 19.95 (0-942235-00-2) LSPC Inc.

Shipwrecks of New Jersey. Gary Gentile. (Illus.). 172p. (Orig.). 1988. pap. 14.95 (0-9616399-2-X) Sea Sports Pubns.

Shipwrecks of New York. Gary Gentile. (Illus.). 240p. 1996. pap. 20.00 (1-883056-04-7) GGP.

Shipwrecks of North Carolina: From Hatteras Inlet South. Gary Gentile. (Illus.). 232p. 1992. pap. 20.00 (0-9621453-5-1) GGP.

Shipwrecks of North Carolina: From the Diamond Shoals North. Gary Gentile. (Illus.). 240p. 1993. pap. 20.00 (0-9621453-7-8) GGP.

Shipwrecks of North East Scotland 1444-1990. David M. Ferguson. (Aberdeen University Press Bks.). (Illus.). 150p. 1991. pap. 13.90 (0-08-041217-3, Pub. by Aberdeen U Pr) Macmillan.

***Shipwrecks of Sanilac.** 2nd ed. Pat Stayer & Jim Stayer. Ed. by Tim Juhl & Dave Fritz. (Illus.). 103p. (Orig.). 1995. pap. 11.95 (0-9627084-1-0) Lakeshore Charters.

Shipwrecks of Southern California. Bonnie J. Cardone & Patrick Smith. LC 89-37758. (Illus.). 201p. 1989. pap. 14.95 (0-89732-094-8) Menasha Ridge.

Shipwrecks of the Atlantic: Montauk to Cape May, New Jersey. Bill Davis. Ed. by Linda Barrett. (Fisherman Library). (Illus.). 248p. (Orig.). (C). 1991. pap. text ed. 18.95 (0-923155-12-0) Fisherman Lib.

Shipwrecks of the Era of Revolution: Sunken History of South Carolina & Georgia, 1763-1783. Edward L. Spence. LC 95-69599. (Illus.). 128p. (Orig.). 1996. 19.95 (1-886391-10-6); pap. text ed. 12.95 (1-886391-11-4) Narwhal Pr.

Shipwrecks of the Lakes. Dana T. Bowen. 1952. pap. 12.75 (0-912514-21-3) Freshwater.

Shipwrecks of the Pacific Coast. 2nd ed. James A. Gibbs. LC 57-13208. (Illus.). 352p. 1989. reprint ed. pap. 14.95 (0-8323-0391-7) Binford Mort.

Shipwrecks of the Straits of Mackinac. Charles E. Feltner & Jeri Baron Feltner. LC 91-62285. (Illus.). 354p. (Orig.). 1991. pap. 17.95 (0-9609014-1-8) Seajay.

Shipwrecks of Virginia. Gary Gentile. (Illus.). 216p. 1992. pap. 20.00 (0-9621453-3-5) GGP.

Shipwrecks off Central New Jersey Coast. William O. Davis. 1987. write for info. (0-318-62717-5) Wm O Davis.

Shipwrecks off Juan De Fuca. James A. Gibbs. LC 68-28924. (Illus.). 288p. 1968. 14.95 (0-8323-0012-8); 3.50 (0-8323-0051-9) Binford Mort.

Shipwrecks off Ocean City (N. J.) David J. Seibold & Charles J. Adams, III. (Illus.). 112p. 1986. pap. 6.95 (0-9610008-4-8) Exeter Hse.

Shipwrecks on the Chesapeake: Maritime Disasters on Chesapeake Bay & Its Tributaries, 1608-1978. Donald G. Shomette. LC 81-85606. (Illus.). 336p. 1982. 19.95 (0-87033-283-X, Tidewtr Pubs) Cornell Maritime.

Shipwrecks on the Virginia Coast & the Men of the United States Life-Saving Service. Richard A. Pouliot & Julie Pouliot. LC 85-41004. (Illus.). 240p. 1986. 18.95 (0-87033-352-6, Tidewtr Pubs) Cornell Maritime.

Shipwrecks, Sea Stories & Legends of the Delaware Coast. David J. Seibold & Charles J. Adams, III. (Illus.). 171p. 1989. pap. 10.95 (0-9610008-8-0) Exeter Hse.

Shipwrecks, Smugglers, & Maritime Mysteries. 3rd ed. Eugene D. Wheeler & Robert Kalmann. 176p. 1991. reprint ed. lib. bdg. 29.00 (0-8095-5909-9) Borgo Pr.

Shipwrecks, Smugglers & Maritime Mysteries. 3rd rev. ed. Eugene D. Wheeler & Robert E. Kallman. LC 84-25106. (Illus.). 176p. (Orig.). 1994. pap. 9.95 (0-934793-03-4) Pathfinder CA.

Shipwrecks, Smugglers, & Spanish Silver: Sunken Treasures of the Lower South Carolina Coast, 1521-1865. Edward L. Spence. LC 95-69598. (Illus.). 160p. (Orig.). 1996. 19.95 (1-886391-08-4); pap. text ed. 12.95 (1-886391-09-2) Narwhal Pr.

Shipwrecks Through War, Weather, & Error, 1812-1816: Sunken Treasures of the Gulf, Caribbean, & Atlantic. Edward L. Spence. LC 95-69600. (Illus.). 240p. (Orig.). 1996. 19.95 (1-886391-12-2); pap. 14.95 (1-886391-13-0) Narwhal Pr.

Shipyard. Juan C. Onetti. (Extraordinary Classics Ser.). 1993. pap. 14.99 (1-85242-191-6) Serpents Tail.

***Shipyard in Maine: Percy & Small & the Great Schooners.** Ralph L. Snow & Douglas K. Lee. (Illus.). 348p. 1997. 49.95 (0-88448-193-X) Tilbury Hse.

Shir Hashirim-Song of Songs. Meir Zlotowitz. (Art Scroll Tanach Ser.). 224p. 1977. 17.99 (0-89906-008-0); pap. 14.99 (0-89906-009-9) Mesorah Pubns.

Shira: A Novel. S. Y. Agnon. Tr. by Zeva Shapiro. LC 96-9552. (Library of Modern Jewish Literature). 585p. 1996. reprint ed. pap. 16.95 (0-8156-0425-4, AGSHP) Syracuse U Pr.

Shiralee. D'Arcy Niland. 250p. 1992. reprint ed. lib. bdg. 25.95 (0-89966-941-7) Buccaneer Bks.

Shira's New Start. Libby Lazewnik. (J). (gr. 6-9). 1988. 12.95 (0-87306-471-2); pap. 9.95 (0-87306-472-0) Feldheim.

Shira's Summer. Libby Lazewnik. (YA). (gr. 6-9). 1988. 12.95 (0-87306-467-4); pap. 9.95 (0-87306-468-2) Feldheim.

Shiraz, Persian City of Saints & Poets. Arthur J. Arberry. LC 60-8752. (Centers of Civilization Ser.: No.2). (Illus.). 191p. reprint ed. pap. 54.50 (0-317-11173-6, 2016192) Bks Demand.

***Shirazeh Houshiary: Turning around the Centre.** Anne B. Morgan. LC 93-61863. (Illus.). 24p. 1994. pap. 15.00 (0-929597-03-6) UMass Univ Gallery.

Shire Horse. Keith Chivers. 872p. 1990. 100.00 (0-85131-245-4, Pub. by J A Allen & Co UK) St Mut.

Shirim: Songs of My Jewishness. Meir Zlotowitz. LC 85-62081. 64p. 1986. 4.95 (0-9615631-0-9) Almin.

Shirim al Galgalim: Songs on Wheels. Debbie Friedman. Ed. & Tr. by Randee Friedman. 1994. audio 10.95 (1-890161-19-5) Sounds Write.

Shirim al Galgalim: Songs on Wheels. Debbie Friedman. Ed. & Tr. by Randee Friedman from HEB. (Illus.). 31p. (J). (ps up). 1994. pap. 12.95 (0-9626286-4-6) Sounds Write.

***Shirim al Galgalim: Songs on Wheels.** Debbie Friedman. Ed. & Tr. by Randee Friedman. 1995. audio compact disk 17.95 (1-890161-20-9) Sounds Write.

Shirkutu of Babylonian Deities. Raymond P. Dougherty. LC 78-63548. (Yale Oriental Series: Researches: No. 5, Pt. 2). reprint ed. 25.00 (0-404-60295-9) AMS Pr.

Shirley. Charlotte Bronte. Ed. by Margaret Smith & Herbert Rosengarten. (World's Classics Paperback Ser.). 768p. 1983. pap. 6.95 (0-19-281562-8) OUP.

***Shirley.** Charlotte Bronte. LC 97-9954. 1997. 19.50 (0-679-60275-5, Modern Lib) Random.

Shirley. Charlotte Bronte. Ed. by Andrew Hook & Judith Hook. (English Library). 624p. 1974. pap. 6.95 (0-14-043095-4, Penguin Classics) Viking Penguin.

Shirley Adams'Belt Bazaar. Shirley Adams. LC 94-33446. (Starwear Ser.). 96p. 1995. 17.95 (0-8019-8528-5) Chilton.

Shirley Baker & the King of Tonga. Noel Rutherford. (Pasifika Library). 1996. pap. 19.95 (0-8248-1856-3) UH Pr.

Shirley Boohers Makes Me Sick. Garbo. 58p. (Orig.). 1992. pap. 7.95 (1-881152-05-7) Big Breakfast.

Shirley Chisholm. Jill S. Pollack. LC 93-31175. (First Bks.). (Illus.). 64p. (J). (gr. 5-8). 1994. lib. bdg. 21.00 (0-531-20168-6) Watts.

Shirley Chisholm: A Bibliography of Writings by & about Her. Compiled by Susan Duffy. LC 88-2073. 143p. 1988. 22.50 (0-8108-2105-2) Scarecrow.

Shirley Chisholm, Congresswoman. Garnet N. Jackson. (Illus.). (J). (gr. 1-4). 1994. pap. 4.95 (0-8136-5247-2); lib. bdg. 9.95 (0-8136-5241-3) Modern Curr.

Shirley Holmquist & Aunt Wilma, Who Dunit? Janet L. Martin. Ed. by Eunice W. Pearson. (Illus.). 120p. (Orig.). 1988. pap. 7.95 (0-9613437-2-9, Martin Hse Pubns) Redbird Prods.

Shirley Hughes Nursery Collection. Shirley Hughes. LC 93-47395. (Illus.). (J). 1994. 17.00 (0-688-13583-8) Lothrop.

Shirley Jackson. Ed. by Lenemaja Friedman. LC 74-31244. (Twayne's United States Authors Ser.). 182p. (C). 1975. pap. text ed. write for info. (0-672-61507-X, Bobbs) Macmillan.

Shirley Jones & Marty Ingels: Hollywood's Whacky & Wonderful Love Story. Shirley Jones & Marty Ingles. 336p. 1993. reprint ed. pap. 5.50 (1-56171-236-1, S P I Bks) Sure Seller.

Shirley Letters. Louise Clappe. LC 77-141468. (Illus.). 224p. 1970. pap. 14.95 (0-87905-004-7, Peregrine Smith) Gibbs Smith Pub.

Shirley MacLaine & the New Age Movement. James W. Sire. LC 88-12792. (Viewpoint Pamphlet Ser.). 32p. (Orig.). 1988. pap. 3.99 (0-8308-1106-0, 1106) InterVarsity.

Shirley, Massachusetts, Uplands & Intervale. Ethel S. Bolton. (Illus.). 394p. 1993. reprint ed. lib. bdg. 42.00 (0-8328-2906-4) Higginson Bk Co.

Shirley Temple Dolls & Fashions: A Collector's Guide to the World's Darling. Edward R. Pardella. LC 92-60624. (Illus.). 176p. 1992. pap. 29.95 (0-88740-420-0) Schiffer.

Shirley Valentine & One for the Road. Willy Russell. 106p. (C). 1988. pap. 9.95 (0-413-18950-3, A0335, Pub. by Methuen UK) Heinemann.

***Shirley's Book: Poems for Practicing Vertical Print.** Shirley A. Christopher. 80p. (Orig.). 1994. teacher ed., pap. 10.70 (1-890666-14-9, SB1) Peterson Direct.

***Shirley's Book Vol. 2: Poems for Practicing Slanted Print.** Shirley A. Christopher. 80p. (Orig.). 1994. teacher ed., pap. 10.70 (1-890666-15-7, SB2) Peterson Direct.

***Shirley's Book Vol. 3: Poems for Printing Practice.** Shirley A. Christopher. 80p. (Orig.). 1994. teacher ed., pap. 10.70 (1-890666-16-5, SB3) Peterson Direct.

***Shirley's Book Vol. 4: Poems for Practicing Beginning Cursive.** Shirley A. Christopher. (Illus.). 48p. (Orig.). 1994. teacher ed., pap. 10.70 (1-890666-17-3, SB4) Peterson Direct.

Shiro in Love. Wendy Tokuda & Richard Hall. (Illus.). 32p. (J). (gr. 1-3). 1989. 12.95 (0-89346-306-X) Heian Intl.

Shiro to Shoin see Feudal Architecture of Spain

Shirobamba. Yasushi Inoue. 200p. 9100. 30.00 (0-7206-0837-6) Dufour.

***Shirobamba.** Yasushi Inoue. 341p. 1997. pap. 25.99 (2-84011-189-6) Ulverscroft.

Shirobamba: A Childhood in Old Japan. Yasushi Inoue. Tr. & Intro. by Jean O. Moy. (Illus.). 200p. 1993. pap. 12.95 (0-8348-0269-4) Weatherhill.

Shirt Book. Carol Konop. (Illus.). 108p. 1995. 19.00 (0-9648720-0-5) Cappiello & Chabrowe.

Shirt Drafting & Grading Book, No. 1. rev. ed. L. H. Warmkessel. (Illus.). 1977. spiral bd. 12.00 (0-686-21214-2) Master Design.

Shirt Sleeve Approach to Long Range Planning for the Smaller Growing Corporation. R. Linneman. 1980. text ed. 53.33 (0-13-808972-8) P-H.

Shirt-Sleeve Diplomacy. Jonathan B. Bingham. LC 77-133512. (Select Bibliographies Reprint Ser.). 1977. 21.95 (0-8369-5544-7) Ayer.

Shirt-Sleeve Diplomat. Josephus Daniels. LC 73-11621. (Illus.). 547p. 1973. reprint ed. text ed. 75.00 (0-8371-7082-6, DASD, Greenwood Pr) Greenwood.

Shirt-Sleeves Bookkeeping: Manual Systems. J. H. White. 55p. 1996. pap. 19.95 (1-889206-03-2) J H White.

Shirt-Sleeves Management. James F. Evered. LC 80-67962. 188p. reprint ed. pap. 53.60 (0-317-10215-X, 2022625) Bks Demand.

Shirtmaking: Developing Skills for Fine Sewing. David Coffin. LC 92-27291. (Illus.). 192p. 1993. 29.95 (1-56158-015-5, 070156) Taunton.

***Shirts & Skin.** Tim Miller. LC 97-26917. 214p. (Orig.). 1997. pap. 11.95 (1-55583-425-6) Alyson Pubns.

S

Shirts of Steel: An Anatomy of the Turkish Officer Corps. Mehmet A. Birand. 1991. text ed. 59.95 (*1-85043-326-7*, Pub. by I B Tauris UK) St Martin.

Shirtsleeve Philosophy. Mike Dante. 1992. 10.95 (*0-533-10019-4*) Vantage.

Shisendo: Hall of the Poetry Immortals. J. Thomas Rimer et al. (Illus.). 224p. (Orig.). 1991. pap. 29.95 (*0-8348-0241-4*) Weatherhill.

Shish Mahal Cook Book. Ali Aslam. (C). 1988. pap. 50.00 (*0-907526-08-X*, Pub. by Alloway Pub UK) St Mut.

Shisler - A Portrait of Our Ancestors Jury, Troxell, Shisler & Parrish Vol. III: Shisler. Irene P. Baker. (Illus.). ix, 238p. 1995. pap. 37.50 (*0-8328-4590-6*); lib. bdg. 47.50 (*0-8328-4589-2*) Higginson Bk Co.

Shit Happens: A Gift Book of Unlikely Quotes. Buck Tilton. LC 96-22018. (Orig.). 1996. 10.95 (*1-57034-051-X*) ICS Bks.

Shit of God: The Texts of Diamanda Galas. Diamanda Galas. (High Risk Ser.). (Illus.). 200p. (Orig.). 1996. 16.99 (*1-85242-432-X*) Serpents Tail.

Shiur Qomah: Texts & Recensions. Martin S. Cohen. 250p. 1985. lib. bdg. 74.50 (*3-16-144907-X*, Pub. by J C B Mohr GW) Coronet Bks.

Shiurei HaRav (Shiure Ha-Rav) A Conspectus of the Public Lectures of Rabbi Joseph B. Soloveitchik. Ed. by Joseph Epstein. LC 94-10838. 1994. 25.00 (*0-88125-499-1*) Ktav.

Shiurim Basefer Hatnya: Shaar Haylchud Vehaemunah, Igeret Hatshuva. 510p. (YID.). 1984. 17.00 (*0-8266-5527-0*) Kehot Pubn Soc.

Shiurim Besefer Hatanya. 780p. (YID.). 1982. 17.00 (*0-8266-5526-2*) Kehot Pubn Soc.

Shiurim Besefer Hatenya: Kuntress Acharon. 671p. (YID.). 1986. 17.00 (*0-8266-5528-9*) Kehot Pubn Soc.

Shiva. Shakti M. Gupta. (Illus.). xv, 151p. (C). 1993. 16.00 (*81-7039-203-9*, Pub. by Somaiya Publns II) Nataraj Bks.

***Shiva Dancing.** Bharti Kirchner. 1998. pap. 23.95 (*0-525-94367-6*) NAL-Dutton.

Shiva Descending. Gregory Benford & William Rotsler. 400p. mass mkt. 5.99 (*0-8125-1690-7*) Tor Bks.

Shiva-Sutra Vimarsini of Ksemaraja. Tr. by P. T. Iyengar. (C). 1994. text ed. 12.00 (*81-7030-390-7*, Pub. by Sri Satguru Pubns II) S Asia.

Shivaji & His Diplomats. T. T. Mahajan. (C). 1991. 16.00 (*81-7169-110-2*, Pub. by Commonwealth II) S Asia.

Shivaji & His Times. 5th ed. Jonathan Sarkar. 1993. 35.00 (*0-685-66308-6*, Pub. by Disha Bks II) Apt Bks.

Shiva's Dancing Ground. Harvey. LC 96-20111. 1997. 21.00 (*0-06-250905-5*) Harper SF.

Shiva's Other Children: Religion & Social Identity Amongst Overseas Indians. David J. Mearns. 296p. 1995. 29.95 (*0-8039-9249-1*) AltaMira Pr.

Shiver. Brian Harper. 432p. (Orig.). 1992. pap. 5.99 (*0-451-17424-0*, Sig) NAL-Dutton.

Shivering Babe, Victorious Lord: The Nativity in Poetry & Art. Linda C. Sledge. LC 81-9728. 199p. reprint ed. pap. 56.80 (*0-317-30162-4*, 2025344) Bks Demand.

Shivering in the Sun. William Fadiman. 296p. 1988. 17.95 (*1-55713-043-4*) Sun & Moon CA.

Shivering Sands. Victoria Holt. 288p. 1986. mass mkt. 5.99 (*0-449-21361-7*, Crest) Fawcett.

Shivers & Shakes. Larry Weinberg. LC 93-24445. (J). 1993. pap. 2.95 (*0-8167-3281-7*) Troll Communs.

***Shivers for Christmas.** large type ed. (Large Print Ser.). 512p. 1996. 25.99 (*0-7089-3656-3*) Ulverscroft.

Shivers for Christmas, Vol. 1. Richard Dalby. LC 96-20056. 1996. 22.95 (*0-312-14731-7*) Thomas Dunne Bks.

***Shivers II: Harvest of Souls: The Official Strategy Guide.** Jeff Campbell. 288p. 1997. per. 19.99 (*0-7615-1072-9*) Prima Pub.

Shivers, Shakes & Screams. Denver M. Hensley. Ed. by Judy Hilovsky. LC 89-369. (Illus.). 1991. pap. 13.95 (*0-87949-292-9*) Ashley Bks.

Shivr Koma. R. Moshe Cordovero. (HEB.). 1983. write for info. (*0-943688-38-8*) Res Ctr Kabbalah.

Shiwan Ceramics: Beauty, Color, & Passion. Manni Liu et al. Tr. by Li He from ENG. LC 94-71002. (Illus.). 110p. (Orig.). (CHI.). 1995. pap. 28.00 (*0-9609784-0-2*); text ed. 38.00 (*0-9609784-6-1*) CCF San Francisco.

Shizuko's Daughter. Kyoko Mori. 240p. 1994. mass mkt. 4.50 (*0-449-70433-5*, Juniper) Fawcett.

Shizuko's Daughter. Kyoko Mori. LC 92-26956. 240p. (YA). (gr. 7 up). 1993. 15.95 (*0-8050-2557-X*, Bks Young Read) H Holt & Co.

Shizuo Kakutani: Selected Mathematical Papers, 2 Vols., 1. Robert R. Kallman. (Contemporary Mathematicians Ser.). 1987. 176.00 (*0-8176-3277-8*) Birkhauser.

Shizuo Kakutani: Selected Mathematical Papers, 2 Vols., 2. Robert R. Kallman. (Contemporary Mathematicians Ser.). 1987. 176.00 (*0-8176-3278-6*) Birkhauser.

Shizuo Kakutani: Selected Mathematical Papers, 2 Vols., Set. Robert R. Kallman. (Contemporary Mathematicians Ser.). 1987. 291.50 (*0-8176-3279-4*) Birkhauser.

Shlamo Homelich & the Ashmedai. Illus. by Rochel Denkels & Miriam Silberman. write for info. (*0-9614920-0-7*) Shain F.

Shlemiel & Fools. Houghton Mifflin Company Staff. (Literature Experience 1993 Ser.). (J). 1992. pap. 9.84 (*0-395-61842-8*) HM.

Shlepping the Exile. Michael Wex. 144p. 1995. lib. bdg. 39.00 (*0-8095-4817-8*) Borgo Pr.

***Shlichus - Outreach Insights: A Panorama of Programs & Projects.** Ed. by Chana T. Piekarski. (Illus.). 480p. 1996. 25.00 (*0-8266-0397-1*, Neshei Chabad) Kehot Pubn Soc.

Shlomo's Stories: Selected Tales. Shlomo Carlebach & Susan Y. Mesinai. LC 94-7560. 296p. 1995. 30.00 (*1-56821-215-1*) Aronson.

Shlomo's Stories: Selected Tales. Shlomo Carlebach & Susan Y. Mesinai. LC 94-7560. 296p. 1997. pap. 24.95 (*1-56821-960-1*) Aronson.

Shlosha Yamin, No. 5, Three New Holidays see Kadima Hagim Series

Sh'ma B'ni. M. Lavry. (BJE Choral Ser.). 6p. (HEB.). 0.65 (*0-318-13634-1*, 44-604) Board Jewish Educ.

Sh'ma Kolaynu: Hear Our Voice. Ed. by Laura Utterbach. 64p. (Orig.). 1994. pap. 8.95 (*0-89716-551-9*) P B Pubng.

Shmerkii & the Booger Picker. Rhyk Gilbar. LC 95-92814. (Illus.). 32p. (J). 1996. pap. 6.95 (*1-888588-05-5*, Star Bear); lib. bdg. 14.95 (*1-888588-04-7*, Star Bear) Positive Press.

Shmuel Aleph. David Benvenisty. (Illus.). 84p. pap. 3.25 (*965-17-0058-0*, 14-523) Board Jewish Educ.

Shmuel Bet. David Benvenisty. (Illus.). 63p. pap. 3.25 (*965-17-0059-9*, 14-524) Board Jewish Educ.

Shmuel Yosef Agnon: A Revolutionary Traditionalist. Gershon Shaked. (Modern Jewish Masters Ser.). 304p. (C). 1989. 40.00 (*0-8147-7894-1*) NYU Pr.

***Shmueli Family Bk. 2: More Cartoon Adventures.** Adaia Shumsky & Abraham Shumsky. 1975. pap. 6.00 (*0-8074-0227-3*, 405311) UAHC.

Sho: Japanese Calligraphy. C. J. Earnshaw. LC 88-51194. (Illus.). 180p. 1988. pap. 24.95 (*0-8048-1568-2*) C E Tuttle.

Sho & the Demons of the Deep. Annouchka G. Galouchko. (Illus.). 32p. (J). (gr. 1-3). 1995. lib. bdg. 17.95 (*1-55037-398-6*, Pub. by Annick CN) Firefly Bks Ltd.

Sho et les Dragons d'Eau. Annouchka G. Galouchko. 32p. (FRE.). (J). (gr. 2-3). 1995. lib. bdg. 17.95 (*1-55037-399-4*, Pub. by Annick CN) Firefly Bks Ltd.

Shoah. Harry Smart. 96p. (Orig.). 1993. pap. 9.95 (*0-571-16793-4*) Faber & Faber.

***Shoah: A Jewish Perspective on Tragedy in the Context of the Holocaust.** Yoel Schwartz & Yitzchak Goldstein. 19.99 (*0-89906-402-7*, SHOH); pap. 16.99 (*0-89906-403-5*, SHOP) Mesorah Pubns.

Shoah: The Complete Text of the Acclaimed Holocaust Film. rev. ed. Claude Lanzmann. (Illus.). 208p. 1995. reprint ed. pap. 12.95 (*0-306-80665-7*) Da Capo.

SHOAH The Paradigmatic Genocide: Essays in Exegesis & Eisegesis. Zev Garber. (Studies in the Shoah: VIII). 232p. (Orig.). (C). 1994. pap. text ed. 29.50 (*0-8191-9659-2*) U Pr of Amer.

SHOAH The Paradigmatic Genocide: Essays in Exegesis & Eisegesis, Vol. VIII. Zev Garber. (Studies in the Shoah: VIII). 232p. (Orig.). (C). 1994. lib. bdg. 52.00 (*0-8191-9658-4*) U Pr of Amer.

Shoal & Sheaf: Orkneys Pictorial Heritage. David M. Tinch. (Illus.). 184p. 8900. 30.00 (*0-85640-411-X*, Pub. by Blackstaff Pr IE) Dufour.

Shoal of Time: A History of the Hawaiian Islands. Gavan Daws. LC 73-92053. 510p. 1974. reprint ed. pap. 10.95 (*0-8248-0324-8*) UH Pr.

Shoals of Capricorn. Francis D. Ommanney. LC 74-15555. (Illus.). 322p. 1975. reprint ed. text ed. 59.75 (*0-8371-7823-1*, OMSC, Greenwood Pr) Greenwood.

Shoals to Sand Dunes - Your Alabama Travel Guide. Lynn Edge. (Illus.). 240p. (Orig.). 1991. pap. 9.95 (*1-878561-03-0*) Seacoast AL.

Shoalwater's Finest Dinners: Cooking for Wine. Ann Kischner et al. 200p. 1991. write for info. (*1-880166-01-1*) Harris & Friedrich.

***Shoayb: The Prophet of Madyan.** Amina I. Ali. Ed. by J. C. Cinquino. (Prophets' Stories for Children from the Holy Qur'an Ser.: No. 11). (Illus.). 28p. (Orig.). (J). (gr. 4-6). 1996. write for info. (*1-881963-24-1*); pap. 2.50 (*1-881963-25-X*) Al-Saadawi Pubns.

Shobe: A Genealogy of the Shobe, Kirkpatrick & Dilling Families. rev. ed. F. D. Shobe. (Illus.). 182p. 1991. reprint ed. pap. 31.00 (*0-8328-2166-7*); reprint ed. lib. bdg. 41.00 (*0-8328-2165-9*) Higginson Bk Co.

Shobkan Paul Site (CA-LAN-958) Archaeological Investigations of a Coastal Millingstone Horizon Occupation. Roy A. Salls. (Archives of California Prehistory Ser.: Vol. 43). (Illus.). (Orig.). (C). 1995. pap. 10.65 (*1-55567-581-6*) Coyote Press.

***Shobogenzo: Or the Treasure House of the Eye of the True Teachings.** Great Master Dogen. Ed. by Daizui MacPhillamy. Tr. by Hubert Nearman from CHI. LC 96-68739. 193p. (Orig.). 1996. pap. 15.00 (*0-930066-17-0*, B112) Shasta Abbey.

Shobogenzo: Zen Essays by Dogen. Dogen. Tr. by Thomas Cleary from JPN. LC 85-20979. 132p. (C). 1991. pap. text ed. 14.00 (*0-8248-1401-0*) UH Pr.

Shobun: A Forgotton War Crime in the Pacific. Michael J. Goodwin. LC 95-22759. (Illus.). 176p. 1995. 19.95 (*0-8117-1518-3*) Stackpole.

Shocco Tales: Southern Fried Sagas. Jim Ritchie. 1991. 17.95 (*1-879034-07-7*) MS River Pub.

***Shocco Tales: Southern Fried Sagas.** 2nd ed. Jim Ritchie. (Illus.). 204p. 1991. reprint ed. 17.95 (*0-9656002-0-3*) Shocco Stories.

Shock. Eddie Strachan & Betty Strachan. LC 93-92780. 176p. (Orig.). 1994. pap. 8.95 (*1-56002-377-5*, Univ Edtns) Aegina Pr.

Shock: Metabolism, Physiology & Therapeutics. Ed. by James B. Heneghan. 1990. 49.95 (*0-915340-17-8*) PJD Pubns.

***Shock Absorber Design Manual.** John Dixon. 1997. write for info. (*0-7680-0050-5*) Soc Auto Engineers.

***Shock & Awe: Achieving Rapid Dominance.** James P. Wade et al. LC 96-29748. 1996. write for info. (*1-57906-030-7*) Natl Defense.

Shock & Detonation Waves. John G. Kirkwood. Ed. by W. W. Wood. LC 68-7145. (Documents on Modern Physics Ser.). (Illus.). xvi, 124p. 1967. text ed. 178.00 (*0-677-00380-3*) Gordon & Breach.

Shock & Impact on Structures. C. A. Brebbia. Ed. by V. Sanchez-Galvez. LC 94-68173. (Computational Mechanics). 278p. 1994. 100.00 (*1-56252-221-3*, 2971) Computational Mech MA.

Shock & Resuscitation. Ed. by Evan R. Geller. (Illus.). 592p. 1993. text ed. 75.00 (*0-07-023500-7*) McGraw-Hill HPD.

Shock & the Adult Respiratory Distress Syndrome. Ed. by W. J. Kox & D. J. Bihari. (Current Concepts in Critical Care Ser.). (Illus.). 255p. 1990. 46.95 (*0-387-17484-2*) Spr-Verlag.

Shock & Upheaval. Motohisa Honda. (Illus.). 120p. 1993. pap. 11.95 (*0-8059-3404-9*) Dorrance.

Shock & Vibration Engineering. Charles T. Morrow. LC 63-7556. 404p. reprint ed. pap. 115.20 (*0-317-08532-8*, 2011956) Bks Demand.

Shock & Vibration Handbook. 4th ed. Cyril M. Harris. LC 95-38224. 1995. text ed. 125.00 (*0-07-026920-3*) McGraw.

***Shock Army of the British Empire: The Canadian Corps in the Last 100 Days of the Great War.** Shane B. Schreiber. LC 96-31916. (War Studies Ser.). 192p. 1997. text ed. 55.00 (*0-275-95513-3*, Praeger Pubs) Greenwood.

***Shock Around the Clock.** David H. Dorian. (KidBacks Ser.). (Illus.). (J). (gr. 3-7). 1997. pap. 5.99 (*0-614-28941-6*) Random Bks Yng Read.

Shock Around the Clock: Timely Tales of Terror. LC 96-53147. (J). 1997. pap. 5.99 (*0-679-88186-7*) McKay.

***Shock Compression of Condensed Materials.** R. F. Trunin. (Illus.). 174p. (C). 1997. text ed. 49.95 (*0-521-58290-3*) Cambridge U Pr.

Shock Compression of Condensed Matter - 95: Proceedings of the Conference of the American Physical Society Topical Group on Shock Compression of Condensed Matter Held at Seattle, Washington, August 13-18, 1995, Pt. 1. Steven C. Schmidt & William C. Tao. (AIP Press Conference Proceedings Ser.: No. 370). (Illus.). 1996. write for info. (*1-56396-615-8*, AIP) Am Inst Physics.

Shock Compression of Condensed Matter - 95: Proceedings of the Conference of the American Physical Society Topical Group on Shock Compression of Condensed Matter Held at Seattle, Washington, August 13-18, 1995, Pt. 2. Steven C. Schmidt & William C. Tao. (AIP Press Conference Proceedings Ser.: No. 370). (Illus.). 1996. write for info. (*1-56396-616-6*, AIP) Am Inst Physics.

Shock Compression of Condensed Matter - 95: Proceedings of the Conference of the American Physical Society Topical Group on Shock Compression of Condensed Matter Held at Seattle, Washington, August 13-18, 1995, 2 vols., Set. Steven C. Schmidt & William C. Tao. (AIP Press Conference Proceedings Ser.: No. 370). (Illus.). 1427p. 1996. 265.00 (*1-56396-566-6*, CP 370, AIP) Am Inst Physics.

Shock Compression of Condensed Matter, 1991: Proceedings of the American Physical Society Topical Conference Held in Williamsburg, Virginia, June 17-20, 1991. Ed. by S. C. Schmidt et al. LC 92-20810. 1992. 295.75 (*0-444-89732-1*, North Holland) Elsevier.

Shock Dynamics. Z. Han & X. Yin. LC 92-10614. (Fluid Mechanics & Its Applications Ser.: Vol. 11). 320p. (C). 1993. lib. bdg. 166.50 (*0-7923-1746-7*) Kluwer Ac.

Shock, from Molecular & Cellular Level to Whole Body: Proceedings of the Third International Shock Congress, Shock '95, Hamamatsu, Japan, 21-23 October 1995. Ed. by Kazuo Okada & Hiromaru Ogata. LC 96-5881. (International Congress Ser.: No. 1102). 410p. 1996. 194.50 (*0-444-82285-2*) Elsevier.

Shock Induced Transitions & Phase Structures in General Media. Ed. by J. E. Dunn et al. LC 93-4682. (IMA Volumes in Mathematics & Its Applications: Vol. 52). (Illus.). 250p. 1993. write for info. (*3-540-94084-7*) Spr-Verlag.

Shock Induced Transitions & Phase Structures in General Media. Ed. by J. E. Dunn et al. LC 93-4682. (IMA Volumes in Mathematics & Its Applications Ser.: Vol. 52). 1993. 63.95 (*0-387-94084-7*) Spr-Verlag.

Shock Jock. Franklin W. Dixon. (Hardy Boys Casefiles Ser.: No. 106). (J). (gr. 6 up). 1995. mass mkt. 3.99 (*0-671-50429-0*, Archway) PB.

Shock Lines. Warren N. Beath. 384p. 1993. mass mkt. 4.50 (*0-8217-4036-9*, Zebra Kensgtn) Kensgtn Pub Corp.

***Shock Marketing: Advertising, Influence, & Family Values.** Joe Marconi. LC 97-12070. 250p. 1997. 29.95 (*1-56625-081-1*) Bonus Books.

Shock Masters of the Cinema. Lois Curci. Ed. by Margot Winick. (Illus.). 151p. (Orig.). 1996. pap. 19.95 (*1-888214-00-7*) Fantasma Bks.

***Shock of Arrival: Reflections on Postcolonial Experience.** Meena Alexander. 224p. 1996. 40.00 (*0-89608-546-5*) South End Pr.

Shock of Arrival: Reflections on Postcolonial Experience. Meena Alexander. LC 96-15058. 224p. 1996. pap. 15.00 (*0-89608-545-7*) South End Pr.

Shock of Men: Homosexual Hermeneutics in French Writing. Lawrence R. Schehr. 252p. 1995. 32.50 (*0-8047-2417-2*) Stanford U Pr.

Shock of the New. Robert Hughes. 1991. pap. 45.00 (*0-679-72876-7*) Knopf.

Shock of the New. 2nd ed. Robert Hughes. 1991. pap. text ed. write for info. (*0-07-031127-7*) McGraw.

Shock of War: Unknown Battles That Ruined Hitler's Plan for a Second Blitzkrieg in the West, December-January 1944-45, Vol. 1. Joseph C. Doherty. LC 95-60258. (Illus.). 381p. (Orig.). 1994. pap. 13.95 (*0-9613980-4-3*) Vert Milon Pr.

***Shock of War Vol. II: Unknown Battles That Ruined Hitler's Plan for a Second Blitzkrieg in the West, December-January, 1944-45.** J. C. Doherty. Ed. by Lionel Adda. (Illus.). 442p. (Orig.). 1996. pap. 13.95 (*0-9613980-5-1*) Vert Milon Pr.

***Shock of War, Picture Annex, Unknown Battles That Ruined Hitler's Plan for a Second Blitzkrieg in the West, December-January 1944-45.** J. C. Doherty. LC 95-60258. (Illus.). 52p. (Orig.). 1997. pap. 6.50 (*0-9613980-6-X*) Vert Milon Pr.

Shock Radio. Leigh Clark. 1996. 24.95 (*0-312-85724-1*) St Martin.

Shock Rock. Ed. by Jeff Gelb & Claire Zion. 288p. (Orig.). 1992. mass mkt. 4.99 (*0-671-70150-9*) PB.

Shock Rock II. Ed. by Jeff Gelb & Claire Zion. 368p. (Orig.). 1994. mass mkt. 5.50 (*0-671-87088-2*) PB.

***Shock, Sepsis & Organ Failure: I-Brain Damage Secondary to Hemorrhagic-Traumatic Shock: II-Brain Damage Secondary to Sepsis: III-Brain Damage Secondary to Traumatic Brain Injury.** Gunther O. Schlag et al. LC 96-40408. 1997. write for info. (*0-387-62419-8*) Spr-Verlag.

***Shock, Sepsis & Organ Failure: I-Brain Damage Secondary to Hemorrhagic-Traumatic Shock: II-Brain Damage Secondary to Sepsis: III-Brain Damage Secondary to Traumatic Brain Injury.** Daniel L. Traber. LC 96-40408. 1997. write for info. (*3-540-62419-8*) Spr-Verlag.

Shock, Sepsis, & Organ Failure: Proceedings of the Third Wiggers Bernard Conference on Cytokine Networks, 1992, Styria, Austria. Gunther O. Schlag & Daniel L. Traber. LC 93-12635. 1993. write for info. (*0-387-55339-8*) Spr-Verlag.

Shock, Sepsis & Organ Failure-Nitric Oxide. Gunther O. Schlag. 488p. 1995. 140.00 (*3-540-58549-4*) Spr-Verlag.

Shock Shots: Ghosts. Dona Smith. 48p. (J). (gr. 4-6). 1993. pap. 1.25 (*0-590-47568-1*) Scholastic Inc.

Shock Shots: Monsters. Dona Smith. 48p. (J). (gr. 4-7). 1993. pap. 1.25 (*0-590-47566-5*) Scholastic Inc.

Shock Shots: Mummies. Dona Smith. 48p. (J). (gr. 4-6). 1993. pap. 1.25 (*0-590-47571-1*) Scholastic Inc.

Shock Shots: Werewolves. Dona Smith. 48p. (J). (gr. 4-6). 1993. pap. 1.25 (*0-590-47570-3*) Scholastic Inc.

Shock Shots: Zombies. Dona Smith. 48p. (J). (gr. 4-6). 1993. pap. 1.25 (*0-590-47567-3*) Scholastic Inc.

Shock Tactic. 1995. mass mkt. 4.99 (*0-373-61444-6*, 1-61444-5) Harlequin Bks.

Shock Therapy for a Brain Dead World. Gyeorgos C. Hatonn. (Phoenix Journals). 211p. 1994. pap. 6.00 (*1-56935-032-9*) Phoenix Source.

Shock Therapy in Poland: The Response of State-Owned Enterprises. Jan Kulig & Adam Lipowski. LC 93-32160. 1993. pap. 6.95 (*1-55815-286-5*) ICS Pr.

Shock Therapy of Gradualism? A Comparative Approach to Anti Inflation Policies. William Fellner et al. (Occasional Papers: No. 8). 87p. 1981. pap. write for info. (*1-56708-007-3*) Grp of Thirty.

Shock to the System: A Donald Strachey Mystery. Richard Stevenson. LC 95-34505. 192p. 1995. 19.95 (*0-312-13610-2*) St Martin.

Shock to the System: A Donald Strachey Mystery. Richard Stevenson. 192p. 1996. pap. 9.95 (*0-312-14732-5*) St Martin.

Shock to the System: Restructuring America's Electricity Industry. Timothy J. Brennan et al. LC 96-20204. (Illus.). 160p. 1996. pap. text ed. 18.95 (*0-915707-80-2*) Resources Future.

Shock Treatment. Karen Finley. (Illus.). 128p. (Orig.). 1990. pap. 8.95 (*0-87286-252-6*) City Lights.

Shock Value: A Tasteful Book about Bad Taste. 2nd ed. John Waters. (Illus.). 256p. (Orig.). 1995. pap. 12.95 (*1-56025-092-5*) Thunders Mouth.

***Shock Wave.** Robert T. Abbott. (Time Surfers Ser.: No. 7). (YA). 1997. mass mkt. 3.50 (*0-553-48464-8*, Skylark BDD) BDD Bks Young Read.

Shock Wave. Clive Cussler. 1996. mass mkt. 7.99 (*0-671-00030-6*) PB.

***Shock Wave.** Clive Cussler. 1996. mass mkt. 7.99 (*0-614-20518-2*, Pocket Star Bks) PB.

Shock Wave. Clive Cussler. 448p. 1996. 25.00 (*0-684-80297-X*) S&S Trade.

***Shock Wave.** Burton Seavey. 1997. pap. 13.99 (*1-56043-283-7*) Destiny Image.

Shock-Wave. large type ed. Basil Copper. (Linford Mystery Library). 1994. pap. 15.99 (*0-7089-7629-8*, Linford) Ulverscroft.

Shock Wave. large type ed. Clive Cussler. 860p. 1996. lib. bdg. 27.95 (*0-7838-1579-4*) S&S Trade.

***Shock Wave.** large type ed. Clive Cussler. 1997. pap. 25.95 (*0-614-25129-X*, GK Hall) Thorndike Pr.

Shock Wave. large type ed. Clive Cussler. 1997. pap. 25.95 (*0-7838-1578-6*) G K Hall.

Shock-Wave & High-Strain-Rate Phenomena in Materials. Meyers et al. (Mechanical Engineering Ser.: Vol. 77). 1184p. 1992. 275.00 (*0-8247-8579-7*) Dekker.

Shock Wave Engine Design. Helmut E. Weber. 175p. 1994. text ed. 69.95 (*0-471-59724-4*) Wiley.

Shock Wave Lithotripsy, Vol. 1: State of the Art. Ed. by James E. Lingeman & D. M. Newman. (Illus.). 432p. 1988. 110.00 (*0-306-43112-2*, Plenum Pr) Plenum.

Shock Wave Lithotripsy, Vol. 2: Urinary & Biliary Lithotripsy. Ed. by James E. Lingeman & D. M. Newman. LC 89-70948. (Illus.). 476p. 1989. 110.00 (*0-306-43416-4*, Plenum Pr) Plenum.

Shock Wave Reflection Phenomena. G. Ben-Dor. (Illus.). 328p. 1991. 99.95 (*0-387-97707-4*) Spr-Verlag.

Shock Wave Two-Thousand. Robert Sungenis et al. LC 94-67493. 160p. (Orig.). 1994. pap. 7.95 (*0-89221-269-1*) New Leaf.

An Asterisk (*) at the beginning of an entry indicates that the title is appearing in BIP for the first time.

Shock Waves. Carolyn Keene. (Nancy Drew & Hardy Boys Supermystery Ser.). (YA). (gr. 7 up). 1991. mass mkt. 3.99 (*0-671-74393-7*, Archway) PB.

***Shock Waves: Eastern Europe after the Revolutions.** John Feffer. (Orig.). 48.99 (*1-895431-47-6*, Pub. by Black Rose Bks CN); pap. 19.99 (*1-895431-46-8*, Pub. by Black Rose Bks CN) Consort Bk Sales.

Shock Waves: Eastern Europe after the Revolutions. John Feffer. LC 92-3916. 350p. (Orig.). 1992. 40.00 (*0-89608-440-X*); pap. 16.00 (*0-89608-439-6*) South End Pr.

Shock Waves: Proceedings of the 18th International Symposium on Shock Waves, Held at Sendai, Japan, 21-26 July 1991. Ed. by K. Takayama. LC 92-29581. 1993. 258.95 (*0-387-55686-9*) Spr-Verlag.

***Shock Waves: Proceedings of the 20th International Symposium, 2 vols.** 2000p. 1997. 293.00 (*981-02-2593-8*) World Scientific Pub.

Shock Waves & Reaction-Diffusion Equations. Joel A. Smoller. (Grundlehren der Mathematischen Wissenschaften Ser.: Vol. 258). (Illus.). 581p. 1983. 73.00 (*0-387-90752-1*) Spr-Verlag.

Shock Waves & Reaction-Diffusion Equations. 2nd ed. Joel A. Smoller. LC 93-50712. (Grundlehren der Mathematischen Wissenschaften Ser.: Vol. 258). (Illus.). 664p. 1994. 86.95 (*0-387-94259-9*) Spr-Verlag.

Shock Waves & Shock Tubes: Proceedings of the Fifteenth International Symposium on Shock Waves & Shock Tubes. Ed. by Daniel Bershader & Ronald Hanson. (Illus.). xvi, 922p. 1986. 69.50 (*0-8047-1310-3*) Stanford U Pr.

Shock Waves & Shock Tubes: Proceedings of the Fifteenth International Symposium on Shock Waves & Shock Tubes, Berkeley, California, July 28-August 2, 1985. fac. ed. International Symposium on Shock Waves & Shock Tubes Staff. Ed. by Daniel Bershader & Ronald Hanson. LC 86-5871. (Illus.). 111p. 1986. reprint ed. pap. 30.00 (*0-7837-7906-2*, 2047662) Bks Demand.

Shock Waves at Marseille. International Symposium on Shock Waves Staff. Ed. by R. Brun & L. Z. Dumitrescu. LC 95-132636. 1995. write for info. (*0-615-00736-8*) Spr-Verlag.

Shock Waves at Marseille: Proceedings of the 19th International Symposium on Shock Waves Held at Marseille, France, 26-30 July 1993, 4 vols., Set. Ed. by R. Brun & L. Dumitrescu. 1995. 412.95 (*0-387-57713-0*) Spr-Verlag.

Shock Waves at Marseille Vol. 1: Proceedings of the 19th International Symposium on Shock Waves Held at Marseille, France, 26-30 July 1993: Hypersonics, Shock Tube & Shock Tunnel Flow. Ed. by R. Brun & L. Dumitrescu. (Illus.). 504p. 1995. 132.95 (*0-387-57710-6*) Spr-Verlag.

Shock Waves at Marseille Vol. 2: Proceedings of the 19th International Symposium on Shock Waves Held at Marseille, France, 26-30 July 1993: Physico-Chemical Processes & Nonequilibrium Flow. Ed. by R. Brun & L. Dumitrescu. (Illus.). 464p. 1995. 132.95 (*0-387-57711-4*) Spr-Verlag.

Shock Waves at Marseille Vol. 3: Proceedings of the 19th International Symposium on Shock Waves Held at Marseille, France, 26-30 July 1993: Shock Waves in Condensed Matter & Heterogenous Media. Ed. by R. Brun & L. Dumitrescu. (Illus.). 504p. 1995. 132.95 (*0-387-57712-2*) Spr-Verlag.

Shock Waves at Marseille Vol. 4: Proceedings of the 19th International Symposium on Shock Waves Held at Marseille, France, 26-30 July 1993: Shock Structure & Kinematics, Blast Waves & Detonation. Ed. by R. Brun & L. Dumitrescu. LC 95-13595. (Shock Waves at Marseilles Ser.: Vol. 4). 544p. 1995. 132.95 (*3-540-58862-0*) Spr-Verlag.

Shock Waves for Industrial Applications. Ed. by Lawrence E. Murr. LC 88-27516. (Illus.). 533p. 1989. 78.00 (*0-8155-1170-1*) Noyes.

Shock Waves in Chemistry. Ed. by Assa Lifshitz. LC 81-5375. (Illus.). 400p. reprint ed. pap. 114.00 (*0-7837-0744-4*, 2041064) Bks Demand.

Shock Waves in Condensed Matter. Ed. by Y. M. Gupta. 940p. 1986. 155.00 (*0-306-42276-X*, Plenum Pr) Plenum.

Shock Waves in Condensed Matter: 1981 (Menlo Park) Ed. by W. J. Nellis et al. LC 82-70014. (AIP Conference Proceedings Ser.: No. 78). 715p. 1982. lib. bdg. 43.00 (*0-88318-177-0*) Am Inst Physics.

Shock Waves in Condensed Matter & Heterogeneous Media: Proceedings of the 19th International Symposium on Shock Waves, Held at Marseille, France, July 1993. Ed. by R. Brun & L. Z. Dumitrescu. LC 95-13594. (Shock Waves at Marseilles Ser.: Vol. 3). 1995. write for info. (*3-540-57712-2*) Spr-Verlag.

Shock Waves in Materials Science. Akira B. Sawaoka. LC 93-13476. 1993. 103.95 (*0-387-70119-2*) Spr-Verlag.

Shock Waves Through Los Angeles: The Northridge Earthquake. Carole G. Vogel. LC 95-52104. (Illus.). 32p. (J). (gr. 3-7). 1996. 15.95 (*0-316-90240-3*) Little.

Shocker Handbook: Stories, Stats, & Stuff about Wichita State Sports. Kirk Seminoff. (Illus.). 160p. (Orig.). 1995. pap. 9.95 (*1-880652-47-1*) Wichita Eagle.

Shocker on Shock Street. R. L. Stine. (Goosebumps Ser.: Vol. 35). 160p. (J). (gr. 4-6). 1995. pap. text ed. 3.99 (*0-590-48340-4*) Scholastic Inc.

Shocking Ballad Picture Show: German Popular Literature & Cultural History. Tom Cheesman. LC 94-10059. 256p. 1994. 45.95 (*0-85496-893-8*) Berg Pubs.

Shocking Crimes of Japan. Mark Schreiber. 1995. pap. text ed. 9.95 (*4-900737-34-8*, Pub. by Yen Bks JA) C E Tuttle.

Shocking Discovery. Connie Griffith. LC 93-8422. (Tootie McCarthy Ser.: Bk. 5). 112p. (J). (gr. 5-8). 1994. pap. 6.99 (*0-8010-3866-9*) Baker Bks.

***Shocking Pink.** Spindler. 1998. mass mkt. 5.99 (*1-55166-415-1*) Harlequin Bks.

***Shocking Science.** 1997. pap. 19.95 (*0-8069-9886-5*) Sterling.

Shocking Science: 500 Years of Mishaps & Misunderstandings. Steve Parker. LC 95-18380. (Illus.). 64p. (YA). (gr. 8-12). 1996. 16.95 (*1-57036-269-6*) Turner Pub GA.

Shocking the Web, Macintosh Edition. Cathy Clarke et al. 464p. 1996. 44.95 (*0-201-88663-4*) Peachpit Pr.

Shocking the Web, Windows Edition. Carhy Clarke et al. 464p. 1997. 44.95 (*0-201-88662-6*) Peachpit Pr.

Shocking Truth about Cholesterol: And How to Lower Yours Quickly & Still Eat Eggs. William F. Welles. Ed. by Bethany Gilmore. LC 90-90197. (Truth Ser.). (Illus.). 95p. (Orig.). 1990. pap. 5.95 (*1-878043-00-5*) Welles Enterprises.

Shocking Truth about Water: Learn How & Why You Need Pure Safe Water! 27th rev. ed. Patricia Bragg. (Illus.). 128p. Date not set. pap. 7.95 (*0-87790-063-9*) Hlth Sci.

Shockley on Eugenics & Race: The Application of Science to the Solution of Human Problems. William B. Shockley. Ed. by Roger Pearson. (Illus.). 304p. (Orig.). (C). 1992. pap. text ed. 28.00 (*1-878465-03-1*) Scott-Townsend Pubs.

Shocks. Burton Goodman. 151p. (J). (gr. 5). 1994. pap. 12.30 (*0-89061-750-3*) Jamestown Pubs.

Shocks & Rocks: Seismology in the Plate Tectonics Revolution: The Story of Earthquakes & the Great Earth Science Revolution of the 1960s. J. E. Oliver. LC 96-2723. 1996. write for info. (*0-87590-280-4*) Am Geophysical.

Shocks in Astrophysics: Proceedings of the International Conference on Shocks in Astrophysics. Ed. by T. J. Millar & A. C. Raga. 336p. (C). 1996. lib. bdg. 195.00 (*0-7923-3899-5*) Kluwer Ac.

Shockware for MacIntosh. Yeaman. 208p. 1996. 30.00 (*1-56830-275-4*) Hayden.

Shockwave. Colin Forbes. 558p. (Orig.). 1990. pap. 16.95 (*0-330-31279-0*, Pub. by Pan Books UK) Trans-Atl Phila.

Shockwave! Breathe New Life into Web Pages. Darryl Plant & Dan Gray. 350p. 1996. pap. 49.95 incl. cd-rom (*1-56604-441-3*) Ventana Communs.

Shockwave for Director for Dummies. Harvey. 1996. pap. 19.99 (*0-7645-0029-5*) IDG Bks.

***Shockwave for Dummies.** 2nd ed. Greg Harvey. 1997. pap. 24.99 (*0-7645-0255-7*) IDG Bks.

***Shockwave for Web Innovators: Designing Multimedia for the Web.** Bob Schmitt. 1997. pap. text ed. 39.95 incl. cd-rom (*1-56592-231-X*) OReilly & Assocs.

Shockwave Power Techniques. Noel Rabinowitz. LC 96-23739. 528p. 1996. pap. text ed. 44.99 (*1-56205-646-8*) New Riders Pub.

Shockwave Rider. John Brunner. 288p. 1984. mass mkt. 5.99 (*0-345-32431-5*, Del Rey) Ballantine.

Shockwaves: The Global Impact of Sexual Harassment. Susan L. Webb. 1993. 19.95 (*0-942361-91-1*); pap. 9.95 (*0-942361-90-3*) MasterMedia Pub.

Shodo: The Art of Coordinating Mind, Body, & Brush. William Reed. LC 88-81760. (Illus.). 212p. (Orig.). 1990. pap. 22.00 (*0-87040-784-8*) Japan Pubns USA.

***Shodo Suzuki Pt. 2: Landscapes & Natural Harmony.** Process Architecture Editorial Staff. (Process Architecture Ser.: No. 131). (Illus.). 168p. 1997. pap. 44.95 (*4-89331-131-X*, Pub. by Process Archit JA) Bks Nippan.

***Shoe.** Gordon Legge. 1989. 16.00 (*0-7486-6080-1*, Pub. by Polygon UK) Subterranean Co.

Shoe & Canoe or Pictures of Travel in the Canadas, 2 Vols, Set. John J. Bigsby. LC 69-19549. 1969. reprint ed. 115.00 (*0-404-00880-1*) AMS Pr.

Shoe Bird. Eudora Welty. LC 93-30729. (Illus.). 88p. (J). (gr. 4-6). 1993. 14.95 (*0-87805-668-8*) U Pr of Miss.

Shoe Book: Learn to Tie Your Shoes! Kate Mason. (Illus.). 16p. (Orig.). (J). (ps-2). 1996. pap. 6.95 (*0-8167-3871-8*, Watermill Pr) Troll Communs.

Shoe Box Centers Writing Activities: Shoe Box Centers. Jo E. Moore. (Illus.). 64p. (J). (gr. 1-3). 1992. pap. 7.95 (*1-55799-224-X*, EMC 261) Evan-Moor Corp.

Shoe Business, Inc: Practice Set for Understanding Annual Reports. Timothy J. Louwers. 76p. (C). 1995. 28.35 (*0-256-19077-1*) Irwin.

***Shoe Chew.** Pat Pollari. (Barf-O-Rama Ser.: No. 13). 128p. (J). 1997. mass mkt. 3.50 (*0-553-48469-9*, Skylark BDD) BDD Bks Young Read.

Shoe City: Growing up in Brockton, Mass. During the Roaring Twenties. Arthur F. Joy. (Illus.). 1978. pap. 5.50 (*0-317-28503-3*) Saturscent Pubns.

Shoe for You, Vol. 7. Shirley A. Barone. (Illus.). 44p. (Orig.). (J). (ps-2). 1989. pap. write for info. (*0-318-66617-0*) Toad Hse Bks.

Shoe Goes to Wrigley Field: How Many Next Years Do You Get in Baseball? Jeff MacNelly. (Illus.). 59p. (Orig.). 1988. pap. 5.95 (*0-933893-51-5*) Bonus Books.

Shoe Monster. North Shuswap Elementary School Students. 32p. (J). (gr. k-3). 1994. pap. 3.50 (*0-87406-687-5*) Willowisp Pr.

Shoe Shine Parlor Poems Et Al. W. R. Rodriguez. 48p. 1984. pap. 6.50 (*0-941160-08-4*) Ghost Pony Pr.

Shoe Stats 1996. 250p. 1995. spiral bd. 325.00 (*0-318-17504-5*) Footwear Indus.

Shoebag. James. 144p. (J). 1992. pap. 3.50 (*0-590-43030-0*, Apple Paperbacks) Scholastic Inc.

Shoebag. Mary James. 144p. (J). (gr. 5-7). 1990. 13.95 (*0-590-43029-7*) Scholastic Inc.

Shoebag Returns. Mary James. LC 95-26123. (J). (gr. 3-7). 1996. 15.95 (*0-590-48711-6*) Scholastic Inc.

Shoebox Center: Math Activities. Jo E. Moore. (Illus.). 64p. (J). (gr. 1-3). 1993. pap. text ed. 7.95 (*1-55799-252-5*, EMC 108) Evan-Moor Corp.

Shoebox of Desire. Allen Woodman. LC 86-63358. (Illus.). 70p. (Orig.). 1987. 16.75 (*0-930501-10-1*); pap. 8.95 (*0-930501-11-X*) Livingston U Pr.

Shoebox of Violets. Martha Byrd. LC 95-41108. 1995. pap. write for info. (*0-9623388-5-0*) Laney-Smith.

Shoebox Syndrome (Record-Keeping) Selma H. Lamkin. (Orig.). (C). 15.00 (*0-686-32948-1*) Nikmal Pub.

Shoefull of Shamrock. Mary F. Shura. 96p. (J). 1991. pap. 2.95 (*0-380-76169-6*, Camelot Young) Avon.

***Shoei Yoh: In Response to Natural Phenomena.** Maurizio Vitta. 1997. pap. text ed. 39.99 (*88-7838-022-9*, Pub. by Yeol-rin Munhwa KO) Consort Bk Sales.

Shoeing for Performance: In the Sound & Lame Horse. Haydn Price & Rod Fisher. (Illus.). 144p. 1995. pap. 16.95 (*1-57076-033-0*, Trafalgar Sq Pub) Trafalgar.

Shoeing Right: Advice to Horse Owners from a Working Farrier. David Krolick. (Illus.). 208p. 1992. pap. 14.95 (*0-914327-39-9*) Breakthrgh NY.

Shoelaces & Brussel Sprouts. Nancy Levene. LC 87-5267. 120p. (J). (gr. 3-6). 1994. pap. 4.99 (*1-55513-301-0*, Chariot Bks) Chariot Victor.

Shoeless Joe. W. P. Kinsella. 256p. 1987. mass mkt. 5.99 (*0-345-34256-9*, Del Rey) Ballantine.

***Shoeless Joe.** W. P. Kinsella. 1996. pap. 11.00 (*0-345-41007-6*) Ballantine.

Shoeless Joe Jackson. Jack Kavanagh. LC 94-21264. (Illus.). 64p. (J). (gr. 3 up). 1995. lib. bdg. 15.95 (*0-7910-2170-X*) Chelsea Hse.

Shoeless Joe Jackson & Ragtime Baseball. Harvey Frommer. LC 91-43040. 256p. 1993. reprint ed. pap. 10.95 (*0-87833-820-9*) Taylor Pub.

Shoeless Joe Jackson Comes to Iowa. W. P. Kinsella. LC 93-3935. 168p. (Orig.). 1993. 19.95 (*0-87074-355-4*); pap. 9.95 (*0-87074-356-2*) SMU Press.

Shoemaker & the Elves. Naomi Fox. (Illus.). 24p. (J). (ps-1). 1993. Incl. cassette. pap. 9.95 (*1-882179-15-3*) Confetti Ent.

Shoemaker & the Elves. Jacob W. Grimm & Wilhelm K. Grimm. (Illus.). 32p. (J). (ps-3). 1992. 6.95 (*0-8362-4923-2*) Andrews & McMeel.

Shoemaker & the Elves. Jacob W. Grimm & Wilhelm K. Grimm. (Illus.). 16p. 1975. 60.00 (*0-945303-04-1*) Evanescent Pr.

Shoemaker & the Elves. Ilse Plume. (Illus.). 32p. (J). (ps-3). 1991. 15.00 (*0-15-274050-3*, HB Juv Bks) HarBrace.

Shoemaker Fooze. Illus. by Lola E. Frank. LC 68-56827. (Sound Ser.). 48p. (J). (gr. 2-5). 1969. lib. bdg. 10.95 (*0-87783-036-3*) Oddo.

Shoemaker Martin. Leo Tolstoy. LC 86-60489. (Illus.). 32p. (J). (gr. k-3). 1986. 14.95 (*1-55858-044-1*) North-South Bks NYC.

***Shoemaker Martin.** Leo Tolstoy. 1997. pap. text ed. 6.95 (*1-55858-772-1*) North-South Bks NYC.

***Shoemakers.** Leonard E. Fisher. LC 96-40975. (Colonial Craftsmen Ser.). (Illus.). 48p. (YA). (gr. 4 up). 1997. lib. bdg. 14.95 (*0-7614-0510-0*, Benchmark NY) Marshall Cavendish.

Shoemaker's Battery. J. J. Shoemaker. 108p. 1984. reprint ed. 22.50 (*0-942211-23-5*) Olde Soldier Bks.

Shoemaker's Battery, Stuarthouse Artillery. J. J. Shoemaker. 28.00 (*0-8488-1165-8*) Amereon Ltd.

Shoemaker's Best Selections, No. 1. Ed. by J. W. Shoemaker. LC 79-116415. (Granger Index Reprint Ser.). 1977. 18.95 (*0-8369-6156-0*) Ayer.

Shoemaker's Best Selections, Vol. 2. Ed. by J. W. Shoemaker. LC 79-116415. (Granger Index Reprint Ser.). 1977. 18.95 (*0-8369-6185-4*) Ayer.

Shoemaker's Best Selections, Vol. 3. Ed. by J. W. Shoemaker. LC 79-116415. (Granger Index Reprint Ser.). 1977. 18.95 (*0-8369-6157-9*) Ayer.

Shoemaker's Best Selections, Vol. 4. Ed. by J. W. Shoemaker. LC 79-116415. (Granger Index Reprint Ser.). 1977. 18.95 (*0-8369-6158-7*) Ayer.

Shoemaker's Best Selections, Vol. 5. Ed. by J. W. Shoemaker. LC 79-116415. (Granger Index Reprint Ser.). 1977. 17.95 (*0-8369-6175-7*) Ayer.

Shoemaker's Best Selections, Vol. 6. Ed. by J. W. Shoemaker. LC 79-116415. (Granger Index Reprint Ser.). 1977. 18.95 (*0-8369-6186-2*) Ayer.

Shoemaker's Best Selections, Vol. 7. Ed. by J. W. Shoemaker. LC 79-116415. (Granger Index Reprint Ser.). 1977. 17.95 (*0-8369-6176-5*) Ayer.

Shoemaker's Best Selections, Vol. 9. Compiled by J. W. Shoemaker. LC 79-116415. (Granger Index Reprint Ser.). 1977. No. 9, 1881. 20.95 (*0-8369-6378-4*) Ayer.

Shoemaker's Best Selections, Vol. 10. Compiled by J. W. Shoemaker. LC 79-116415. (Granger Index Reprint Ser.). 1977. No. 10, 1882. 18.95 (*0-8369-6379-2*) Ayer.

Shoemaker's Best Selections, Vol. 11. Compiled by J. W. Shoemaker. LC 79-116415. (Granger Index Reprint Ser.). 1977. No. 11, 1883. 20.95 (*0-8369-6380-6*) Ayer.

Shoemaker's Best Selections: For Reading & Recitations, Vol. 14. Ed. by J. W. Shoemaker. LC 79-116415. (Granger Index Reprint Ser.). 1977. reprint ed. 17.95 (*0-8369-6273-7*) Ayer.

Shoemaker's Best Selections: For Readings & Recitations. Compiled by J. W. Shoemaker. Incl. No. 25. 1977. reprint ed. 20.95 (*0-8369-6414-4*); (Granger Index Reprint Ser.). 1973. write for info. (*0-8369-9375-6*); write for info. (*0-318-50889-3*) Ayer.

Shoemaker's Boy. Joan Aiken. LC 93-6613. (Illus.). (J). (ps-6). 1994. pap. 14.00 (*0-671-86647-8*, S&S Bks Young Read) S&S Childrens.

Shoemaker's Dream. Mildred Schell. (J). (ps-3). 1982. 10.00 (*0-8170-0945-0*) Judson.

Shoemaker's Gift. Lyndell Ludwig. LC 82-73196. (Illus.). 36p. (J). (ps-1). 1983. pap. 4.95 (*0-916870-53-7*) Star Dust Bks.

Shoemaker's Holiday. Thomas Dekker. 1979. pap. 4.95 (*0-8120-0314-4*) Barron.

Shoemaker's Holiday. 2nd ed. Thomas Dekker. Ed. by Anthony Parr. (New Mermaid Ser.). 102p. (C). 1990. pap. text ed. 6.95 (*0-393-90062-2*) Norton.

Shoemaker's Holiday. Thomas Dekker. Ed. by R. L. Smallwood & Stanley Wells. LC 79-87579. (Revels Plays Ser.). 241p. reprint ed. pap. 68.70 (*0-7837-4270-3*, 2043962) Bks Demand.

Shoemaker's Holiday see Six Elizabethan Plays

Shoemaker's Tale. Mark Ari. 240p. 1993. 19.00 (*0-939010-38-0*); pap. 10.00 (*0-939010-39-9*) Zephyr Pr.

Shoemaking. June Swanno. 1989. pap. 25.00 (*0-85263-778-0*, Pub. by Shire UK) St Mut.

Shoes. Robert Novak. 1975. 4.00 (*0-685-67937-3*) Windless Orchard.

Shoes. Elizabeth Winthrop. LC 85-45841. (Illus.). 32p. (J). (ps-2). 1986. 14.00 (*0-06-026591-4*); lib. bdg. 14.89 (*0-06-026592-2*) HarpC Child Bks.

Shoes. Elizabeth Winthrop. LC 85-45841. (Trophy Picture Bk.). (Illus.). 32p. (J). (ps-3). 1988. pap. 4.95 (*0-06-443171-1*, Trophy) HarpC Child Bks.

Shoes. Elizabeth Winthrop. (J). (ps-1). 1988. 22.95 incl. audio (*0-87499-113-7*); pap. 15.95 incl. audio (*0-87499-112-9*) Live Oak Media.

Shoes. Elizabeth Winthrop. LC 85-45841. (Tell Me a Story Book Ser.). (Illus.). 24p. (J). (ps-3). 1996. pap. 7.95 incl. audio (*0-694-70037-1*) HarpC.

Shoes. Charlotte Yue & David Yue. LC 96-17220. 1997. 14.95 (*0-395-72667-0*) HM.

Shoes, 4 bks., Set. Elizabeth Winthrop. (J). (ps-1). 1988. student ed., pap. 31.95 incl. audio (*0-87499-114-5*) Live Oak Media.

Shoes: A Celebration of Footwear Through the Ages. Linda O'Keefe. LC 96-20755. 512p. 1996. pap. 10.95 (*0-7611-0114-4*, 10114) Workman Pub.

Shoes: Fashion & Fantasy. Colin McDowell. LC 93-61542. (Illus.). 224p. 1994. pap. 24.95 (*0-500-27755-9*) Thames Hudson.

***Shoes & Pattens: Medieval Finds from Excavations in London.** Francis Grew. 1996. pap. text ed. 24.95 (*0-11-290443-2*) Her Majesty s Stationery Office.

Shoes Big Book. Elizabeth Winthrop. LC 85-45841. (Trophy Picture Bk.). (Illus.). 24p. (J). (ps-3). 1993. pap. 19.95 (*0-06-443320-X*, Trophy) HarpC Child Bks.

Shoes Board Book. Elizabeth Winthrop. LC 85-45841. (Illus.). 24p. (J). (ps-1). 1996. bds. 6.95 (*0-694-00844-3*, Festival) HarpC Child Bks.

Shoes for Everyone: A Story about Jan Matzeliger. Barbara Mitchell. (Creative Minds Ser.). (Illus.). 64p. (J). (gr. 3-6). 1986. lib. bdg. 14.21 (*0-87614-290-0*, Carolrhoda) Lerner Group.

Shoes for Everyone: A Story about Jan Matzeliger. Barbara Mitchell. (Creative Minds Bks.). (Illus.). (J). (gr. 3-6). 1987. reprint ed. pap. 5.95 (*0-87614-473-3*, First Ave Edns) Lerner Group.

Shoes from Grandpa. Mem Fox. LC 89-35401. (Illus.). 32p. (J). (ps-1). 1992. pap. 6.95 (*0-531-07031-X*) Orchard Bks Watts.

***Shoes in the Freezer, Beer in the Flowerbed.** Wilen. 1997. pap. 10.00 (*0-684-80456-5*, Fireside) S&S Trade.

Shoes like Miss Alice's. Angela Johnson. LC 93-4872. (Illus.). 32p. (J). (ps-2). 1995. 15.95 (*0-531-06814-5*); lib. bdg. 16.99 (*0-531-08664-X*) Orchard Bks Watts.

Shoes of Glass. Libby Yalom. (Illus.). 164p. 1989. pap. 15.95 (*0-915410-56-7*, 3035) Antique Pubns.

Shoes of Maidanek. Arthur P. Goldstein. (Studies in the Shoah). (Orig.). (C). 1992. pap. text ed. 14.50 (*0-8191-8664-3*); lib. bdg. 33.50 (*0-8191-8663-5*) U Pr of Amer.

Shoes of Satin, Ribbons of Silk: Tales from the Ballet. Ed. by Antonia Barber et al. LC 95-1352. (Illus.). 79p. (J). (gr. 3-6). 1995. 16.95 (*1-85697-593-2*, Kingfisher LKC) LKC.

Shoes of Tanboury. Shimon Ballas. 40p. 1970. 4.95 (*0-88482-767-4*) Hebrew Pub.

Shoes of the Fisherman. Morris West. 1991. mass mkt. 6.99 (*0-312-92466-6*) St Martin.

Shoes of the Fisherman. large type ed. Morris West. (General Ser.). 434p. 1991. lib. bdg. 22.95 (*0-8161-5140-7*, GK Hall) Thorndike Pr.

Shoes of the Fisherman. Morris L. West. 1993. reprint ed. lib. bdg. 21.95 (*1-56849-146-8*) Buccaneer Bks.

Shoes on, Shoes Off. Catherine Compher. Ed. by Karen Gross. 24p. (Orig.). (J). (ps). 1993. pap. text ed. 6.95 (*1-56309-076-7*, New Hope) Womans Mission Union.

Shoes or Zapatos: A Bilingual Story. Valerie Hannah. Ed. by George H. Herrick. Tr. by Lissa Lee. (Illus.). (ENG & SPA.). 1993. pap. 4.95 (*0-941281-57-4*) V H Pub.

Shoes, Shoes, Shoes. Ann Morris. LC 94-46649. (Illus.). 32p. (J). (gr. k-2). 1995. 15.00 (*0-688-13666-4*); lib. bdg. 14.93 (*0-688-13667-2*) Lothrop.

Shoes, Shoes, Shoes. John Speirs. (Head to Toe Ser.). (Illus.). 16p. (J). (ps-3). 1995. bds. 2.95 (*0-307-17650-9*, Golden Books) Western Pub.

Shoes, Shoes, Shoes. Andy Warhol. 1997. 10.95 (*0-8212-2319-4*) Bulfinch Pr.

Shoes That Danced & Other Poems. Anna H. Branch. LC 77-89722. (One-Act Plays in Reprint Ser.). 1988. reprint ed. 25.00 (*0-8486-2027-5*) Roth Pub Inc.

Shoes That Fit Our Feet: Sources for a Constructive Black Theology. Dwight N. Hopkins. LC 92-38713. 230p. (Orig.). 1993. pap. 15.00 (*0-88344-848-3*) Orbis Bks.

Shoeshine Girl. Clyde R. Bulla. LC 75-8516. (Illus.). 80p. (J). (gr. 3-5). 1989. lib. bdg. 14.89 (*0-690-04830-0*, Crowell Jr Bks) HarpC Child Bks.

Shoeshine Girl. Clyde R. Bulla. LC 75-8516. (Trophy Bk.). (Illus.). 64p. (J). (gr. 2-5). 1989. reprint ed. pap. 3.95 (*0-06-440228-2*, Trophy) HarpC Child Bks.

Shoeshine Girl: A Study Guide. Dina Claydon. Ed. by Joyce Friedland & Rikki Kessler. (Novel-Ties Ser.). 20p. (YA). (gr. 9-12). 1990. pap. text ed. 15.95 (*0-88122-396-4*) Lrn Links.

S

Shoeshine Girl Literature Mini-Unit. Janet Lovelady. (Illus.). 32p. (J). (gr. 3-5). 1990. student ed. 4.95 (*1-56096-017-5*) Mari.

Shoestring Marketing: Marketing 101 for Small Business, Indispensable Marketing Tools... Larry Mersereau. 1996. pap. text ed. 14.95 (*1-882180-57-7*) Griffin CA.

Shoestring Memories: Through the Depression on a Hill Ranch. Stacy Adams. 208p. 1994. pap. 10.00 (*0-9640521-0-5*) Wild Rose Pr.

Shoestrings: Spiritual Learning Stories. Peter Saint James. (Illus.). 128p. 1997. pap. 12.95 (*1-887936-25-4*) Khabir Pr.

Shoetown: Poems by Gerald McCarthy. Gerald McCarthy. LC 92-71673. (Annual Prize for Poetry (1992) Ser.). 64p. (Orig.). (C). 1992. pap. text ed. 24.95 (*1-55605-207-3*) Wyndham Hall.

Shofar Calls to Us. Illus. by Katherine J. Kahn. LC 91-60592. 12p. (J). (ps). 1991. bds. 4.95 (*0-929371-61-5*) Kar-Ben.

Shofar Sounders' Reference Manual. Arthur L. Finkle. LC 93-15670. 1993. 2.50 (*0-933873-82-4*) Torah Aura.

Shofar That Lost Its Voice. David E. Fass. (Illus.). 48p. 1982. 6.95 (*0-8074-0168-4*, 103500) UAHC.

Shogakukan-Robert: Grand Dictionnaire Francais-Japonais. Robert. 2597p. (FRE & JPN.). 1990. 895.00 (*0-7859-9214-6*) Fr & Eur.

Shoghi Effendi: Recollections. Ugo Giachery. (Illus.). 248p. 1973. 22.25 (*0-85398-050-0*) G Ronald Pub.

Shogi: Japan's Game of Strategy. Trevor P. Leggett. 100p. 1993. pap. 14.95 (*0-8048-1903-3*) C E Tuttle.

Shogi for Beginners. John Fairbairn. 1984. pap. 11.95 (*4-87187-201-7*, S1) Ishi Pr Intl.

***Shogi Set.** Charles E. Tuttle. 1996. pap. 64.00 (*0-8048-1773-1*) C E Tuttle.

Shogun. James Clavell. 816p. 1983. 25.00 (*0-385-29224-4*) Delacorte.

Shogun. James Clavell. 1152p. (YA). 1976. mass mkt. 6.99 (*0-440-17800-2*) Dell.

Shogun! The Shogun Age Exhibition. Shogun Age Exhibition Executive Committee. (Illus.). 280p. 1984. pap. 29.95 (*0-295-96197-X*) U of Wash Pr.

Shogun see James Clavell Library

Shogunal Politics: Arai Hakuseki & the Premises of Tokugawa Rule. Kate W. Nakai. LC 87-30517. (East Asian Monographs: No. 134). 400p. 1988. 28.00 (*0-674-80653-0*) HUP.

Shogun's Agents. Akahige Namban. 213p. 1996. mass mkt. 7.95 (*0-929654-07-2*, 49) Blue Moon Bks.

Shogun's City: A History of Tokyo. Noel Nouet. Tr. by John Mills & Michele Mills. 160p. (C). 1989. text ed. 35.00 (*0-904404-61-7*, Pub. by Curzon Press UK) UH Pr.

***Shogun's City: A History of Tokyo.** Noel Nouet. Tr. by John Mills & Michele Mills. 160p. (C). 1989. text ed. 35.00 (*0-904404-62-5*, Pub. by Curzon Press UK) UH Pr.

Shogun's Ghost: The Dark Side of Japanese Education. Ken Schoolland. LC 90-32124. 224p. 1990. text ed. 29.95 (*0-89789-218-6*, H218, Bergin & Garvey) Greenwood.

Shogun's Reluctant Ambassadors: Japanese Sea Drifters in the North Pacific. Katherine Plummer. (Illus.). 320p. 1991. pap. 19.95 (*0-87595-235-6*) Oregon Hist.

***Shogun's Scrolls: On Controlling All Aspects of the Realm.** LC 96-40265. 1997. write for info. (*0-8048-3122-X*) C E Tuttle.

Shogun's Shrine, No. 1: Plant & Bird Carvings. Sieg Inc. Staff. (Illus.). 114p. 1994. pap. 49.95 (*4-7661-0778-0*, Pub. by Graphic Sha JA) Bks Nippan.

Shogun's Shrine, No. 2: Human & Animal Carvings. Sieg Inc. Staff. (Illus.). 114p. 1994. pap. 49.95 (*4-7661-0779-9*, Pub. by Graphic Sha JA) Bks Nippan.

Shoji: How to Design, Build & Install Japanese Screens. Jay Van Arsdale. LC 87-82860. (Illus.). 96p. (Orig.). 1988. pap. 17.00 (*0-87011-864-1*) Kodansha.

Shoji Hamada: A Potter's Way & Work. Susan Peterson. LC 95-21872. (Illus.). 240p. 1995. pap. 22.95 (*0-8348-0345-3*) Weatherhill.

***Shoke Cards - The Black Angels Vol. 1: A Healing Tool for African American Women.** Earthlyn M. Manuel. (Illus.). i, 90p. (Orig.). (J). 1996. pap. 29.95 (*0-9654420-0-4*) LeaderSpirit.

Shokuhin No Nenchosei see Consistency of Foodstuffs

Sholari Pack. Joseph S. Coleman. Ed. by Janice Sellers. (Skyrealms of Jorune Ser.). (Illus.). 112p. (Orig.). 1994. pap. text ed. 18.00 (*1-883240-02-6*) Chessex.

Sholem Aleichem in the Theater. Jacob Weitzner. 190p. 1995. 35.00 (*0-8386-3636-5*) Fairleigh Dickinson.

Sholem Aleichem's Wandering Star & Other Plays of Jewish Life. David S. Lifson. LC 86-73240. 216p. 1988. 19.95 (*0-8453-4810-8*, Cornwall Bks) Assoc Univ Prs.

Sholom Aleichem: A Non-Critical Introduction. Sol Gittleman. (De Proprietatibus Litterarum Ser. Didactica: No. 3). 1974. pap. text ed. 32.35 (*90-279-2606-9*) Mouton.

Sholom Chefs! Family Favorites from Temple Beth Sholom. Ed. by Mary E. Hawkins. 52p. (Orig.). 1995. spiral bd. 9.95 (*1-877749-17-6*) Five Star AZ.

***Shomei Tomatsu.** Toshihara Ito. (Illus.). 96p. 1997. 29.95 (*4-7713-2831-5*) Dist Art Pubs.

Shompen. S. N. Rizvi. (Andaman & Nicobar Island Tribes Ser.). (C). 1990. 7.50 (*81-7046-075-1*, Pub. by Seagull Bks II) S Asia.

Shona. Robert Johnson, Jr. & Gary Van Wyk. LC 96-47359. (Heritage Library of African Peoples: set 4). (Illus.). 64p. (YA). (gr. 7-12). 1997. lib. bdg. 15.95 (*0-8239-2011-9*, D2011-9) Rosen Group.

Shona & Their Neighbors. David Beach. LC 92-36819. (Peoples of Africa Ser.). 1994. 42.95 (*0-631-17678-0*) Blackwell Pubs.

Shona & Zimbabwe Nine Hundred to Eighteen Fifty: An Outline of Shona History. D. N. Beach. LC 80-14116. 424p. 1980. 54.50 (*0-8419-0624-6*, Africana) Holmes & Meier.

Shona Basic Course, Set 10. 519p. pap. text ed. 185.00 incl. audio (*0-88432-290-4*, AFSH10) Audio-Forum.

Shondan Language. David C. Morrow. 20p. (Orig.). 1995. pap. 5.00 (*0-9641836-2-5*) Textar Media.

***Shonnji Ryu Jujitsu Training Manual.** George Alexander & Ken Penland. (Illus.). 150p. (Orig.). 1997. pap. 34.95 (*0-9631775-6-7*) Yamazato Pubns.

Shonto: A Study of the Role of the Trader in a Modern Navaho Community. Ed. by William Y. Adams. 1988. reprint ed. lib. bdg. 75.00 (*0-7812-0219-1*) Rprt Serv.

Shonto: Study of the Role of the Trader in a Modern Navaho Community. William Y. Adams. (Bureau of American Ethnology Bulletins Ser.). 329p. 1995. lib. bdg. 99.00 (*0-7812-4188-X*) Rprt Serv.

Shonto Begay Biography. (J). 1995. pap. write for info. (*0-590-39348-0*) Scholastic Inc.

Shoo King, or the Book of Historical Documents, Vol. II. Tr. by James Legge. (CHI & ENG.). 1991. 35.00 (*957-638-040-5*, Pub. by SMC Pub CC) Oriental Bk Store.

Shoo-Shoo Baby: A Lucky Lady of the Sky. George E. Merva. (Illus.). 1988. pap. 10.00 (*0-9622271-0-2*) Patterson Productions.

***Shook over Hell: Post-Traumatic Stress, Vietnam & the Civil War.** Eric T. Dean. LC 97-9737. 1997. write for info. (*0-674-80651-4*) HUP.

Shoot! George Bowering. 304p. 1995. 22.95 (*0-312-14045-2*) St Martin.

***Shoot.** Jay Cronley. LC 96-6558. 1997. 19.95 (*0-312-15655-3*) St Martin.

Shoot! Everything You Ever Wanted to Know about 35mm Photography. Ed. by Liz Harvey. LC 92-39858. (Illus.). 256p. 1993. pap. 29.95 (*0-8174-5869-7*, Amphoto) Watsn-Guptill.

Shoot Better II: Ballistics Tables. Charles W. Matthews. (Illus.). 521p. (Orig.). 1989. pap. 18.95 (*0-9613734-1-5*) B Matthews Inc.

Shoot Better Three-Ballistics Tables. Charles W. Matthews. (Illus.). (Orig.). (YA). 1994. pap. 19.45 (*0-9613734-3-1*) B Matthews Inc.

Shoot Down. (Executioner Ser.). 1995. mass mkt. 3.50 (*0-373-61198-6*, 1-61198-7) Harlequin Bks.

Shoot-Em-Ups Ride Again: A Supplement to Shoot-Em-Ups. Buck Rainey. LC 90-34151. (Illus.). 319p. 1990. 62.50 (*0-8108-2132-X*) Scarecrow.

Shoot-Em-Ups Ride Again: A Supplement to Shoot-Em-Ups. Buck Rainey. LC 90-34151. (Illus.). 309p. 1990. pap. 19.95 (*0-936505-12-5*) World Yesterday.

Shoot for the Hoop. Matt Christopher. (J). (gr. 3-7). 1995. pap. 3.95 (*0-316-14125-9*) Little.

***Shoot for the Moon.** 2nd ed. Allen A. Johnson. Ed. by Carol Panaccione & Frederick M. Sawyer. (Illus.). 37p. 1996. pap. 12.95 (*0-9656023-1-1*) Saunderstown Pr.

Shoot for the Moon: Even If You Miss You Will Land among the Stars. Meiji Stewart. (Illus.). 160p. 1996. pap. 6.95 (*0-9647349-3-1*) Keep Coming Back.

Shoot for the Star. Bill Bates & Bill Butterworth. LC 94-30584. 1994. 19.99 (*0-8499-1170-2*) Word Pub.

Shoot for the Star. Bill Bates. 272p. 1996. mass mkt. 5.99 (*0-8499-3986-0*) Word Pub.

Shoot for the Stars Basketball Handbook, Vol. 1. Lynette Woodard & Kevin Cook. Ed. by Lewis Bunch. (Illus.). 60p. (YA). (gr. 9-12). 1989. text ed. write for info. (*0-318-65726-0*) Worldwide Sports.

Shoot Low, Boys - They're Ridin' Shetland Ponies. Lewis Grizzard. 1987. mass mkt. 5.99 (*0-345-34097-3*) Ballantine.

Shoot, Luke! The Air Is Full of Pigeons. James D. Blakely. (Illus.). 249p. 1989. 20.00 (*0-9607256-7-9*) Rich Pub Co.

Shoot, Luke, the Air Is Full of Pigeons. James D. Blakely. 1989. 20.00 (*0-317-01817-5*) Doc Blakely.

Shoot Organization in Vascular Plants. Kenneth J. Dormer. LC 70-39412. (Illus.). 256p. (C). 1972. text ed. 39.95 (*0-8156-5032-9*) Syracuse U Pr.

Shoot Out. James L. Berkman. 32p. (Orig.). 1983. pap. 10.00 (*0-943662-02-8*, 1-166-723) Runaway Pubns.

Shoot Pool. Ian Pannel. 1996. 6.98 (*0-7858-0546-X*) Bk Sales Inc.

Shoot Pool. Ian Pannell. 1989. 12.98 (*1-55521-413-4*) Bk Sales Inc.

Shoot Straight & Stay Alive: A Lifetime of Hunting Experiences. Fred Bartlett. LC 94-60939. (Illus.). 262p. 1994. 85.00 (*1-882458-04-4*) Trophy Rm Bks.

***Shoot the Moon.** Klempner. Date not set. 24.95 (*0-312-15424-0*) St Martin.

Shoot the Piano Player. David Goodis. LC 90-50255. (Vintage Crime - Black Lizard Ser.). 176p. 1990. pap. 10.00 (*0-679-73254-3*, Vin) Random.

Shoot the Piano Player. Francois Truffaut. Ed. by Peter Brunette. LC 92-32702. (Films in Print Ser.: Vol. 18). (Illus.). 275p. (C). 1993. text ed. 40.00 (*0-8135-1941-1*); pap. text ed. 17.00 (*0-8135-1942-X*) Rutgers U Pr.

Shoot the Stars: How to Become a Celebrity Photographer. Brad Elterman. LC 85-71055. (Illus.). (YA). (gr. 10 up). 1985. pap. 12.95 (*0-933781-00-8*) Cal Features.

Shoot the Teacher. large type ed. David Belbin. (Illus.). (J). 1996. 16.95 (*0-7451-4727-5*, Galaxy Child Lrg Print) Chivers N Amer.

Shoot the Works. William McCay. LC 89-37749. (Three Investigators Crimebusters Ser.: No. 8). 144p. (J). (gr. 5 up). 1990. pap. 2.95 (*0-679-80157-X*) Random Bks Yng Read.

Shoot to Kill. large type ed. Brett Halliday. (Linford Mystery Library). 288p. 1994. pap. 15.99 (*0-7089-7232-2*, Linford) Ulverscroft.

Shoot to Kill: Cops Who Have Used Deadly Force. Charles W. Sasser. Ed. by Eric Tobias. 288p. (Orig.). 1994. mass mkt. 4.99 (*0-671-78929-5*) PB.

Shoot Wrestling: Shooto Training Guide. Yorinaga Nakamura. (Shoot Wrestling Training Ser.: Vol. I). 52p. 1993. pap. 14.99 (*0-9633592-2-3*) Third Eye Pub.

Shoot/Don't Shoot. J. A. Jance. 384p. 1996. mass mkt. 6.50 (*0-380-76548-9*) Avon.

Shooter. Paul A. Hawkins. 352p. (Orig.). 1994. pap. 5.99 (*0-451-17879-3*, Sig) NAL-Dutton.

Shooter. Eric Kinkopf. 320p. 1994. mass mkt. 4.99 (*0-380-72215-1*) Avon.

Shooter. Dennis L. Stull. 176p. 1993. pap. 12.95 (*1-880365-45-6*) Prof Pr NC.

Shooter. Gregory G. Vanhee. 256p. 1989. pap. 3.95 (*0-380-70822-1*) Avon.

***Shooters.** Terrill Lankford. LC 96-29344. 1996. 20.95 (*0-312-86272-5*) Forge NYC.

Shooters. Leon C. Metz. LC 76-21578. (Illus.). 300p. 1976. 19.95 (*0-930208-04-8*) Mangan Books TX.

Shooters. Jay Shaffer. (Orig.). 1995. mass mkt. 4.95 (*1-56333-284-1*, Badboy) Masquerade.

Shooters: A Gallery of Notorious Gunmen from the American West. Leon C. Metz. 304p. 1996. pap. text ed. 13.00 (*0-425-15450-5*) Berkley Pub.

Shooters: TV News Photographers & Their Work. D. M. Lindekugel. LC 93-23672. 192p. 1994. text ed. 49.95 (*0-275-94603-7*, Praeger Pubs) Greenwood.

Shooter's Bible No. 88: 1997. rev. ed. William Jarrett. (Illus.). 576p. 1996. pap. 22.95 (*0-88317-192-9*) Stoeger Pub Co.

Shooter's Bible, 1940. (Illus.). 512p. 1989. pap. 16.95 (*0-88317-154-6*) Stoeger Pub Co.

***Shooter's Bible, 1998, No. 89.** William Jarrett. (Illus.). 576p. 1997. pap. 22.95 (*0-88317-198-8*) Stoeger Pub Co.

Shootin' Sheriff & The Bandit of Bloody Run. Nelson Nye. (Two-in One Western Ser.). 1979. mass mkt. 1.95 (*0-89083-444-X*, Zebra Kensgtn) Kensgtn Pub Corp.

Shooting. J. Henry FitzGerald. (World's Great Gun Books Ser.). 1993. 29.00 (*1-879356-21-X*) Wolfe Pub Co.

Shooting & Fishing (1888-1906), 40 vols., Set. (Illus.). Date not set. reprint ed. 2,400.00 (*0-916107-93-0*) Broadfoot.

***Shooting at Brook City.** large type ed. Steven Gray. (Dales Large Print Ser.). 240p. 1996. pap. 17.99 (*1-85389-640-3*, Dales) Ulverscroft.

Shooting at Loons. Margaret Maron. 256p. 1995. mass mkt. 5.50 (*0-446-40424-1*, Mysterious Paperbk) Warner Bks.

Shooting at Loons. large type ed. Margaret Maron. 1994. pap. 19.95 (*1-56895-083-7*) Wheeler Pub.

Shooting at the Moon: The Story of America's Clandestine War in Laos. Roger Warner. LC 96-45758. (Illus.). 436p. 1997. pap. 18.00 (*1-883642-36-1*) Steerforth Pr.

Shooting Back from the Reservation: A Photographic View of Life by Native American Youth. Jim Hubbard. LC 94-19844. 112p. 1994. 17.00 (*1-56584-206-5*) New Press NY.

Shooting Blanks: War Making That Doesn't Work. James F. Dunnigan & Albert A. Nofi. 516p. 1995. pap. 15.00 (*0-688-14066-1*, Quill) Morrow.

Shooting Dope: Career Patterns of Hard-Core Heroin Users. Charles E. Faupel. (American Social Problems Ser.). 256p. (C). 1991. lib. bdg. 39.95 (*0-8130-1070-5*) U Press Fla.

Shooting Elvis. Robert Eversz. 224p. 1996. pap. 21.00 (*0-8021-1582-9*, Grove) Grove-Atltic.

***Shooting Elvis.** Robert M. Eversz. 224p. 1997. reprint ed. pap. 12.00 (*0-8021-3501-3*, Grove) Grove-Atltic.

Shooting Field: One Hundred Fifty Years with Holland & Holland. Peter King. (Illus.). 176p. 1985. 40.00 (*0-940143-36-4*) Safari Pr.

Shooting for Glory. Paul Henderson & Mike Leonetti. (Illus.). 208p. 1992. 24.95 (*0-7737-2646-2*) Genl Dist Srvs.

Shooting for Stock. George Schaub. (Illus.). 144p. 1987. pap. 22.50 (*0-8174-5871-9*, Amphoto) Watsn-Guptill.

Shooting Forever: The Complete What to Shoot & How Manual for Handguns. Don Paul & David B. Smith. LC 96-67855. (Illus.). 172p. (Orig.). 1995. pap. 14.95 (*0-938263-19-6*) Path Finder.

Shooting from the Hip: Selected Writings. Shobha De. (C). 1995. 12.50 (*81-86112-30-8*, Pub. by UBS Pubs Dist II) S Asia.

***Shooting from the Outside.** Tara Vanderveer & Joan Ryan. LC 97-3231. 1997. write for info. (*0-380-97588-2*) Avon.

***Shooting Gallery.** Yuko Tsushima. Tr. by Geraldine Harcourt. LC 96-54025. (Classic Ser.). 144p. 1997. pap. 11.95 (*0-8112-1356-0*, NDP846) New Directions.

Shooting Gallery & Play for Germs: Two Short Plays. Israel Horovitz. 1972. pap. 3.25 (*0-8222-1022-3*) Dramatists Play.

Shooting It Straight. Diana Noonan. LC 93-21248. (J). 1994. 4.25 (*0-383-03731-X*) SRA McGraw.

Shooting Man's Dog: A Complete Guide to Gun Dogs. David Hudson. (Illus.). 160p. 1996. 34.95 (*1-85310-560-0*, Pub. by Swan Hill UK) Voyageur Pr.

Shooting of Dan McGrew. Robert W. Service. (Illus.). 64p. 1989. pap. 5.95 (*0-88839-224-9*) Hancock House.

Shooting of Dan McGrew. Robert W. Service. (Illus.). 32p. (J). (gr. k-3). 1995. pap. 10.95 (*1-56792-065-9*) Godine.

Shooting of Dan McGrew & Other Poems. Robert W. Service. LC 92-44604. (Thrift Editions Ser.). 96p. 1993. reprint ed. pap. 1.00 (*0-486-27556-6*) Dover.

***Shooting of Rabbit Wells: An American Tragedy.** William Lorzeaux. 272p. 1998. 24.95 (*1-55970-380-6*) Arcade Pub Inc.

Shooting Outdoor Videos. Don Steffans. (Illus.). 160p. 1992. 24.95 (*0-87742-350-4*, 60312); pap. 12.95 (*0-87742-325-3*, 60312) Intl Marine.

Shooting Outdoor Videos. Don Steffens. 1993. pap. text ed. 12.95 (*0-07-060944-6*) McGraw.

Shooting Rats, Other Plays & Poems. Peter Turrini. Tr. by Richard Dixon from GER. (Studies in Austrian Literature, Culture, & Thought). (Orig.). 1996. pap. 21.50 (*0-929497-98-8*) Ariadne CA.

Shooting Scripts. Adam Cornford. (Illus.). 1979. pap. 10.00 (*0-686-28251-5*) Black Stone.

Shooting Simone. Lynne Kaufman. 1994. 5.25 (*0-87129-470-2*, S22) Dramatic Pub.

Shooting Sports for Women. Morrow. LC 96-22850. 240p. 1996. 24.95 (*0-312-14733-3*) St Martin.

Shooting Star. Barbara Bretton. 1995. mass mkt. 4.99 (*1-55166-074-1*, 1-66074-5, Mira Bks) Harlequin Bks.

***Shooting Star.** Roberta Burditt. 1998. 23.00 (*0-345-40139-5*) Ballantine.

Shooting Star. Herge. (Illus.). (J). (gr. 3-8). ring bd. 19.95 (*0-8288-5073-9*) Fr & Eur.

Shooting Star. Herge. 1978. pap. 8.95 (*0-316-35851-7*, Joy St Bks) Little.

Shooting Star. Wallace Stegner. 448p. 1996. pap. 12.95 (*0-14-025241-X*, Viking) Viking Penguin.

***Shooting Star.** Wallace Stegner. Date not set. 22.75 (*0-8446-6919-9*) Peter Smith.

Shooting Star. Brock Thoene & Bodie Thoene. LC 93-16175. (Saga of the Sierras Ser.: Vol. 7). 208p. (Orig.). 1993. pap. 7.99 (*1-55661-320-2*) Bethany Hse.

Shooting Star. large type ed. Brock Thoene & Bodie Thoene. LC 93-33578. (Orig.). 1994. lib. bdg. 21.95 (*0-8161-5908-4*, GK Hall) Thorndike Pr.

Shooting Star: A Novel about Annie Oakley. Sheila S. Klass. LC 96-16121. 192p. (J). (gr. 4-6). 1996. 15.95 (*0-8234-1279-2*) Holiday.

Shooting Star: Annie Oakley, the Legend. Debbie Dadey. LC 96-24821. (Illus.). 32p. (J). (gr. k-3). 1997. 15.95 (*0-8027-8484-4*); lib. bdg. 16.85 (*0-8027-8485-2*) Walker & Co.

Shooting Star & Other Poems. Martha LaBare. 64p. (Orig.). 1982. pap. 4.50 (*0-9609090-2-8*) Swollen Magpie.

Shooting Star Summer. Candice F. Ransom. LC 91-77621. (Illus.). 32p. (J). (ps-3). 1992. lib. bdg. 14.95 (*1-56397-005-8*) Boyds Mills Pr.

Shooting Stars. Franklyn M. Branley. LC 88-14190. (Let's-Read-&-Find-Out Science Bk.). (Illus.). 32p. (J). (ps-1). 1989. lib. bdg. 14.89 (*0-690-04703-7*, Crowell Jr Bks) HarpC Child Bks.

Shooting Stars. Rod Kierkegaard, Jr. (Illus.). 48p. 1987. 12.95 (*0-87416-028-6*) Catalan Communs.

Shooting Stars. Molly Newman. 1988. pap. 5.25 (*0-8222-1023-1*) Dramatists Play.

Shooting Stars. Wendell Trogdon. 1990. pap. 7.95 (*0-913617-13-X*) Highlander Pr.

***Shooting Stars: Champion Archery Techniques.** Date not set. 35.95 (*0-8464-4418-6*) Beekman Pubs.

Shooting Stars: Heroes & Heroines of Western Film. Ed. by Archie P. McDonald. LC 85-45988. (Illus.). 287p. reprint ed. pap. 81.80 (*0-8357-3957-0*, 2057053) Bks Demand.

Shooting Superstars: Me, My Camera, & the Show-Biz Legends. Zinn Arthur & Pat Hornsey. (Illus.). 240p. (C). 1989. 24.95 (*0-685-27244-3*) Artique Pr.

Shooting the Black Powder Cartridge Rifle. Paul A. Matthews. 129p. 1994. 22.50 (*1-879356-38-4*) Wolfe Pub Co.

Shooting the Boh: A Woman's Voyage down the Wildest River in Borneo. Tracy Johnston. LC 92-53825. 1992. pap. 12.00 (*0-679-74010-4*, Publishers Media) Random.

***Shooting the Bull.** Kenny Dadismun. 117p. 1996. pap. 9.50 (*0-87012-563-X*) McClain.

Shooting the Pianist: The Role of Government in the Arts. Phillip Parsons. (C). 1990. 45.00 (*0-86819-176-0*) Aubrey Bks.

***Shooting the Stars.** John Metcalf. 256p. 1993. pap. 14.95 (*0-88984-166-7*, Pub. by Porcupines Quill CN) Genl Dist Srvs.

Shooting the Sun: Ritual & Meaning in West Sepik. Ed. by Bernard Juillerat. LC 92-4511. (Series in Ethnographic Inquiry). (Illus.). 320p. (C). 1992. text ed. 37.50 (*1-56098-168-7*) Smithsonian.

Shooting the War: Memoirs of a World War II U-Boat Officer. Otto Giese & James E. Wise, Jr. LC 93-21242. 289p. 1994. 31.95 (*1-55750-307-9*) Naval Inst Pr.

Shooting the Works: On Poetry & Pictures. W. S. Di Piero. 230p. 1996. 29.95 (*0-8101-5051-4*); pap. 14.95 (*0-8101-5052-2*) TriQuarterly.

Shooting to Live. W. E. Fairbairn & E. A. Sykes. (Illus.). 112p. 1987. pap. 10.00 (*0-87364-027-6*) Paladin Pr.

Shootout at the Ol' Pancake Corral. Dave Fisher. (Illus.). 1994. pap. 3.95 (*1-885766-15-7*) Brand Cross.

Shootout in Sendero. Jim Miller. Ed. by Doug Grad. (Ex-Rangers Ser.: No. 8). 224p. (Orig.). 1992. pap. 3.50 (*0-671-74826-2*) PB.

Shootout on Wall Street: The Four Thousand to 1,000,000 Dollar Formula in Less Than A Year. Gerald A. Cannon. 1993. 13.95 (*0-533-10483-1*) Vantage.

***Shootout with Father, Vol. 156.** Marianne Hauser. (Sun & Moon Classics Ser.). 1997. pap. text ed. 11.95 (*1-55713-312-3*) Sun & Moon CA.

Shoowa Design: African Textiles from the Kingdom of Kuba. Georges Meurant. (Illus.). 200p. 1986. 60.00 (*0-500-59733-2*) Thames Hudson.

Shop Accessories You Can Build. Fine Woodworking Magazine Editors. (Best of Fine Woodworking Ser.). 128p. 1996. pap. 14.95 (*1-56158-118-6*, 070249) Taunton.

Shop-by-Mail: The Mail Order Bible. Elysa Lazar. 1992. pap. 9.95 (*1-881642-00-3*) Lazar Comms.

Shop Carpenter. Jack Rudman. (Career Examination Ser.: C-739). 1994. pap. 23.95 (*0-8373-0739-2*) Nat Learn.

Shop Clerk. Jack Rudman. (Career Examination Ser.: C-740). 1994. pap. 23.95 (*0-8373-0740-6*) Nat Learn.

An Asterisk (*) at the beginning of an entry indicates that the title is appearing in BIP for the first time.

Shop Committee in the United States. Carroll E. French. LC 78-641100. (Johns Hopkins University. Studies in the Social Sciences. Thirtieth Ser. 1912: 2). 112p. 1982. reprint ed. 37.50 (*0-404-61225-3*) AMS Pr.

***Shop Coupon Queen.** Michele Easter. 1991. pap. 3.99 (*0-425-13260-9*) Berkley Pub.

Shop Drawings of Shaker Furniture & Woodenware, Vol. 1. 2nd ed. Ejner Handberg. 1991. pap. 8.95 (*0-936399-17-1*) Berkshire Hse.

Shop Drawings of Shaker Furniture & Woodenware, Vol. 2. 2nd ed. Ejner Handberg. 1991. pap. 8.95 (*0-936399-18-X*) Berkshire Hse.

Shop Drawings of Shaker Furniture & Woodenware, Vol. 3. 2nd ed. Ejner Handberg. 1991. pap. 8.95 (*0-936399-19-8*) Berkshire Hse.

Shop Drawings of Shaker Iron & Tinware. Ejner Handberg. 1993. pap. 8.95 (*0-936399-45-7*) Berkshire Hse.

Shop Expense: Analysis & Control. Nicholas T. Ficker. Ed. by Richard P. Brief. LC 80-1492. (Dimensions of Accounting Theory & Practice Ser.). 1980. reprint ed. lib. bdg. 28.95 (*0-405-13522-X*) Ayer.

Shop Floor Bargaining & the State: Historical & Comparative Perspectives. Ed. by Steven Tolliday & Jonathan Zeitlin. 268p. 1985. text ed. 59.95 (*0-521-26711-0*) Cambridge U Pr.

Shop Floor Citizens: Engineering Democracy in 1940s Britain. James Hinton. 232p. 1994. 70.00 (*1-85898-081-X*) E Elgar.

Shop Floor Control. Steven A. Melnyk et al. LC 85-70568. 1985. text ed. 47.50 (*0-87094-628-5*) Irwin Prof Pubng.

Shop Floor Control Principles & Practices & Case Studies. Steven A. Melnyk & Phillip L. Carter. LC 87-72180. 535p. 1987. pap. text ed. 60.00 (*0-935406-95-6*) Am Prod & Inventory.

***Shop Floor Control Systems.** Bauer et al. (Illus.). 368p. 1994. pap. text ed. 45.95 (*0-412-58150-7*, Chap & Hall NY) Chapman & Hall.

Shop Floor Control Systems: From Design to Implementation. A. Bauer et al. (Illus.). 364p. 1991. 67.95 (*0-442-31329-2*) Chapman & Hall.

Shop Floor Controls Training Aid. APICS Milwaukee Chapter Staff. 30p. 1979. 35.00 (*0-935406-08-5*) Am Prod & Inventory.

Shop Like a Coupon Queen. Michelle Easter. 1991. pap. 3.99 (*0-425-13259-5*) Berkley Pub.

Shop Math. National Machine Tool Builders Association Staff. LC 82-13534. (NMTBA Shop Practices Ser.). 140p. (C). 1982. pap. 13.95 (*0-471-07841-7*) P-H.

Shop Math. Henry Ortiz. LC 84-730297. (Series 950). (Orig.). 1984. student ed., pap. 7.00 (*0-8064-0435-3*); audio, vhs 219.00 (*0-8064-0436-1*) Bergwall.

Shop Mathematics. Jack Rudman. (General Aptitude & Abilities Ser.: No. CS-36). 1994. pap. 23.95 (*0-8373-6736-0*) Nat Learn.

Shop Mathematics. 6th ed. Charles A. Felker. 1984. 20.64 (*0-02-816310-9*); teacher ed. 9.28 (*0-02-816330-3*) Glencoe.

Shop NY Downtownstyle. Meg Castaldo. (Illus.). 240p. (Orig.). 1996. pap. 15.95 (*1-885492-32-4*) City & Co.

Shop NY Jewelry. Andrea DiNoto. (Illus.). 240p. (Orig.). 1996. pap. 15.95 (*1-885492-34-0*) City & Co.

Shop Rules see Human Relations & Industrial Relations Books & Management Tools

Shop Savvy. Roy Moungovan. (Illus.). 342p. (Orig.). (C). 1990. reprint ed. lib. bdg. 43.00 (*0-8095-7560-4*) Borgo Pr.

Shop Subjects. Jack Rudman. (Teachers License Examination Ser.: T-53). 1994. pap. 27.95 (*0-8373-8053-7*) Nat Learn.

Shop Talk: A Prevocational Language Program for Students with Developmental Disabilities. Louise Kent-Udolf & Eileen R. Sherman. LC 83-61810. 236p. 1983. pap. 25.95 (*0-87822-229-4*, 2294) Res Press.

Shop Talk: Papers on Historical Business & Commercial Records of New England. Ed. by James Lawton. 1975. 3.00 (*0-89073-002-2*) Boston Public Lib.

Shop Talk: Studies in Honor of Seymour Slire. Cynthia P. Schneider et al. (Illus.). 426p. 1996. 65.00 (*0-917624-85-8*, 85-9, Woodstocker Bks) A Schwartz & Co.

Shop Talk: Studies in Honor of Seymour Slive: Presented on His Seventy-Fifth Birthday. Alice I. Davies & William W. Robinson. Ed. & Pref. by Cynthia P. Schneider. LC 95-40406. (Illus.). (Orig.). 1995. 65.00 (*0-916724-85-9*) Harvard Art Mus.

Shop Techniques from the Henry Ford Trade School. Ford Trade School Staff. (Illus.). 267p. 1991. reprint ed. pap. 19.00 (*1-877767-43-3*) Univ Publng Hse.

***Shop-Tested Large Furniture You Can Make: From the Editors of Wood Magazine.** Ben Allen. (Illus.). 96p. 1997. pap. 9.95 (*0-696-20742-7*) Meredith Bks.

***Shop-Tested Outdoor Furniture You Can Make: From the Editors of Wood Magazine.** Ben Allen. (Illus.). 96p. 1997. pap. 9.95 (*0-696-20746-X*) Meredith Bks.

***Shop-Tested Router Techniques & Projects You Can Make: From the Editors of Wood Magazine.** Ben Allen. (Illus.). 96p. 1997. pap. 9.95 (*0-696-20743-5*) Meredith Bks.

***Shop-Tested Scrollsaw Techniques & Projects You Can Make: From the Editors of Wood Magazine.** Ben Allen. (Illus.). 96p. 1997. pap. 9.95 (*0-696-20741-9*) Meredith Bks.

***Shop-Tested Small Furniture You Can Make: From the Editors of Wood Magazine.** Ben Allen. (Illus.). 96p. 1997. pap. 9.95 (*0-696-20744-3*) Meredith Bks.

***Shop-Tested Wookworking Tools You Can Make: From the Editors of Wood Magazine.** Ben Allen. (Illus.). 96p. 1997. pap. 9.95 (*0-696-20745-1*) Meredith Bks.

Shop Testing of Automatic Liquid-Level Gages. 49p. 1961. 18.00 (*0-317-33099-3*, 85225092) Am Petroleum.

Shop Theory from the Henry Ford Trade School. 1996. lib. bdg. 259.99 (*0-8490-8307-9*) Gordon Pr.

Shop 'Til You Drop. (YA). (gr. 7 up). 1995. 20.00 (*0-922242-94-1*) Bepuzzled.

Shop till You Drop, Then Sit down & Buy Shoes. Cathy Guisewite. (Main Street Gift Bks.). (Illus.). 1996. 6.95 (*0-8362-1068-9*) Andrews & McMeel.

Shop Tips: Expert Advice on Making the Most of Your Shop Time & Tools. Rodale Press Woodworking Editors. LC 93-6356. (Illus.). 312p. 1994. 27.95 (*0-87596-591-1*) Rodale Pr Inc.

***Shop Tips: Expert Advice on Making the Most of Your Time & Tools.** Rodale Press Incorporated Staff. 320p. 1997. pap. 14.95 (*0-87596-961-5*) Rodale Pr Inc.

Shop Tools. 5th rev. ed. Ed. by Deere & Company Staff. (Fundamentals of Service Ser.). (Illus.). 56p. 1992. pap. text ed. 7.95 (*0-86691-140-5*, FOS5105NC) Deere & Co.

***Shop Tools.** 5th rev. ed. Ed. by Deere & Company Staff. (Fundamentals of Service Ser.). 47p. 1992. sl. 47.95 (*0-614-24205-3*, FOS5105S) Deere & Co.

Shop Windows. Rotovision S. A. Staff. (Commercial Spaces Ser.). (Illus.). 160p. 1995. pap. 35.00 (*0-8230-6472-7*, Whitney Lib) Watsn-Guptill.

Shop Windows: Cosmetics. Rotovision S. A. Staff. 1996. pap. text ed. 35.00 (*0-8230-6558-8*) Watsn-Guptill.

***Shopfloor Matters: Labor-Management Relations in 20th Century American Manufacturing.** David Fairris. LC 97-4318. 256p. (C). 1997. text ed. write for info. (*0-415-12123-X*) Routledge.

ShopFloor Politics of New Technology. Barry Wilkinson. viii, 120p. 1983. text ed. 44.00 (*0-435-82950-5*, Pub. by Avebury Pub UK); pap. text ed. 16.50 (*0-566-05261-X*, Pub. by Avebury Pub UK) Ashgate Pub Co.

Shopkeeper's Handbook. Peter Levene. (C). 1989. pap. text ed. 18.50 (*1-85333-171-6*, Pub. by Graham & Trotman UK); lib. bdg. 39.00 (*1-85333-170-8*, Pub. by Graham & Trotman UK) Kluwer Ac.

Shopkeeper's Millennium: Society & Revivals in Rochester, New York, 1815-1837. Paul E. Johnson. (American Century Ser.). 224p. 1979. pap. 11.00 (*0-8090-0136-5*) Hill & Wang.

Shoplifting. Charles A. Sennewald & John H. Christman. 180p. 1992. 32.95 (*0-7506-9036-4*) Buttrwrth-Heinemann.

Shoplifting: The Antishoplifting Guidebook. Kathleen L. Farrell & John A. Ferrara. LC 85-3613. 176p. 1985. text ed. 55.00 (*0-275-90096-7*, C0096, Praeger Pubs) Greenwood.

Shoplifting & Employee Theft Investigation. Burt Rapp. LC 88-46126. 178p. 1989. pap. text ed. 14.95 (*0-915179-87-3*) Loompanics.

Shoplifting Control: Theft Prevention for Business. Read Hayes. (Illus.). 75p. (Orig.). (C). 1993. pap. 14.99 (*0-9632762-0-4*) Prevent Pr.

Shopmade Jigs & Fixtures. LC 93-34103. (Art of Woodworking Ser.). 144p. 1993. 19.95 (*0-8094-9508-2*) Time-Life.

Shoppell's Modern Houses 1887. Ed. by Donald J. Berg. (Yesterday's Home Ser.). (Illus.). 48p. (Orig.). 1983. pap. 6.00 (*0-937214-06-X*) Antiquity Re.

***Shoppers' Guide to Better Food Choices: By Betsy Lydon & Mothers & Others for a Livable Planet.** Betsy Lydon. Ed. by Mindy Pennybacker. (Illus.). x, 100p. (Orig.). 1996. pap. 15.00 (*0-9653607-0-9*, 8883264636) Mothers & Others.

Shopper's Guide to Fat in Your Food: A Carry-Along Guide to the Fat, Calories, & Fat Percentages in Brand Name Foods. Karen J. Bellerson. 96p. mass mkt. 2.50 (*0-89529-610-1*) Avery Pub.

Shopper's Guide to Japan: Getting the Most for Your Yen. Boye L. De Mente. 128p. 1991. pap. 5.95 (*0-8048-1642-5*) C E Tuttle.

Shopper's Guide to Long-Term Care Insurance. rev. ed. 54p. (C). 1995. pap. text ed. 15.00 (*0-7881-1945-1*) DIANE Pub.

Shopper's Guide to Natural Foods: A Consumer's Guide to Buying & preparing Foods for Good Health. Ed. by East West Journal Staff. LC 87-1098. 224p. pap. 12.95 (*0-89529-233-5*) Avery Pub.

Shopping. (Sticker Activity Ser.). (Illus.). 16p. (J). (ps-1). 1993. pap. 6.95 (*1-56458-396-1*) DK Pub Inc.

Shopping. (Talkabouts Ser.: No. 735-4). (Illus.). (J). (ps). 3.50 (*0-7214-1120-7*, Ladybrd) Penguin.

Shopping. (Butterfly Bks.). (Illus.). (ARA.). 12.95 (*0-86685-619-6*, LDL360, Pub. by Librairie du Liban FR) Intl Bk Ctr.

Shopping & Traveling in Exotic Asia: Your Passport to Exciting Hong Kong, Thailand, Indonesia, Singapore, & Malaysia. Ronald L. Krannich et al. (Impact Guides Ser.). 584p. 1991. pap. 16.95 (*0-942710-38-X*) Impact VA.

Shopping & Traveling in Exotic Hong Kong. rev. ed. Caryl R. Krannich et al. (Impact Guides Ser.). 247p. 1991. pap. 12.95 (*0-942710-43-6*) Impact VA.

Shopping & Traveling in Exotic Singapore & Malaysia. 2nd rev. ed. Ronald L. Krannich & Caryl R. Krannich. 284p. 1993. pap. 13.95 (*0-942710-54-1*) Impact VA.

Shopping & Traveling in Exotic Thailand. rev. ed. Ronald L. Krannich & Caryl R. Krannich. 297p. 1991. pap. 13.95 (*0-942710-55-X*) Impact VA.

Shopping & Traveling the Exotic Caribbean. John W. Edmiston et al. (Impact Guides Ser.). 304p. (Orig.). 1991. pap. 13.95 (*0-942710-03-7*) Impact VA.

Shopping Around: Feminine Culture & the Pursuit of Pleasure. Hilary Radner. 224p. (C). 1994. pap. 17.95 (*0-415-90540-0*, A6797, Routledge NY) Routledge.

Shopping Around: Feminine Culture & the Pursuit of Pleasure. Hilary Radner. 224p. (C). (gr. 13). 1994. text ed. 62.95 (*0-415-90539-7*, A6793) Routledge.

Shopping at the Ani-Mall. Gloria S. Bullock & Jane B. Crocitto. Ed. by Jane Weinberger. LC 90-70908. (Illus.). 44p. (J). (ps-3). 1991. pap. 3.95 (*0-932433-72-3*) Windswept Hse.

Shopping at the Mall see Set 2

Shopping Bag Design. (Illus.). 160p. 1994. 34.95 (*1-56496-077-3*) Rockport Pubs.

***Shopping Bag Design.** Photo Book Company Staff. 1988. 52.50 (*0-688-07925-3*) Morrow.

***Shopping Bag Design.** 2nd ed. PBC International Staff. 1992. 55.00 (*0-688-10921-7*) Morrow.

***Shopping Bag Design, No. 2.** Ed. by Rockport Publishers Editorial Staff. (Illus.). 160p. 1997. 34.99 (*1-56496-299-7*) Rockport Pubs.

Shopping Bag Design: People, Process, Products. Lori Gilbertson et al. (Illus.). 33p. 1992. pap. 4.00 (*0-939719-05-3*) UMN Goldstein Gall.

Shopping Bag Graphics. P.I.E. Books Editorial Staff. (Illus.). 224p. 1996. 79.95 (*4-89444-021-0*, Pub. by PIE Bks JA) Bks Nippan.

Shopping Bag Ladies of New York. Joan Roth. Ed. by Robert Walter. LC 81-85387. (Illus.). 122p. (Orig.). 1982. pap. 10.95 (*0-942160-00-2*) Jolen Pr.

Shopping Basket. 2nd ed. John Burningham. (Illus.). 32p. (J). 1996. 15.99 (*1-56402-688-4*) Candlewick Pr.

Shopping Basket. John Burningham. LC 95-25945. (Illus.). 32p. (J). (ps up). 1997. reprint ed. pap. 5.99 (*0-7636-0098-9*) Candlewick Pr.

***Shopping Cart Soldiers.** John Mulligan. LC 96-37883. 1997. 22.95 (*1-880684-48-9*) Curbstone.

Shopping Center & Store Leases, 2 vols. Emanuel B. Halper. 1500p. 1979. ring bd. 140.00 (*0-318-12031-3*, 00548) NY Law Pub.

Shopping Center Appraisal & Analysis. James D. Vernor & Joseph S. Rabianski. LC 92-46567. 340p. 1993. 35.00 (*0-922154-10-4*) Appraisal Inst.

Shopping Center DealMaker's Handbook: Practical Transaction Guide with Ready-to-Use Forms on Computer Diskettes. Bruce G. Zimmerman. LC 93-90557. (Illus.). 630p. 1993. 140.00 (*1-881250-88-1*); disk 140.00 (*1-881250-94-6*); disk 140.00 (*1-881250-90-3*); disk 140.00 (*1-881250-91-1*); disk 140.00 (*1-881250-93-8*) Busn Source Pub.

Shopping Center Development Handbook. 2nd ed. Urban Land Institute, Commercial & Office Development Council Staff. LC 85-50127. (Community Builders Handbook Ser.). 338p. 1985. 64.95 (*0-87420-634-0*) Urban Land.

Shopping Center Management. Alan A. Alexander & Richard F. Muhlebach. LC 91-40796. (Illus.). 424p. 1992. text ed. 44.95 (*0-944298-68-0*, 752) Inst Real Estate.

Shopping Center Management: The Guide for the 1990s. Alan A. Alexander. 403p. 1992. 45.95 (*0-685-71712-7*, 752) Inst Real Estate.

Shopping Centers: Planning, Development, & Administration. Edgar Lion. LC 75-33374. 208p. reprint ed. pap. 59.30 (*0-685-16180-3*, 2056295) Bks Demand.

Shopping Centers & Malls, No. 4. Ed. by Robert D. Rathbun. (Illus.). 224p. 1992. 49.95 (*0-934590-45-1*) Retail Report.

Shopping Centers & Malls, Vol. II. Ed. by Robert D. Rathbun. (Illus.). 192p. 1988. 44.95 (*0-934590-25-7*) Retail Report.

Shopping Centers & Malls, Vol. III. Intro. by Robert D. Rathbun. (Illus.). 224p. 1990. 49.95 (*0-934590-34-6*) Retail Report.

Shopping Centers & Other Retail Properties: Their Investment, Development, Financing & Management. John R. White. 624p. 1996. text ed. 80.00 (*0-471-04002-9*) Wiley.

***Shopping Centre Design.** Scott. (Illus.). 250p. text ed. 92.50 (*0-419-14880-9*, E & FN Spon) Routledge Chapman & Hall.

Shopping Centre Design. N. Keith Scott. (Illus.). 216p. 1989. 83.95 (*0-7476-0045-7*) Chapman & Hall.

Shopping Centres. 1986. pap. 40.00 (*0-86022-168-7*, Pub. by Build Servs Info Assn UK) St Mut.

Shopping Centres: Retail Development Design & Management. 2nd ed. Nadine Beddington. (Library of Planning & Design). 268p. 1991. 115.00 (*0-7506-1213-4*) Buttrwrth-Heinemann.

Shopping Centres Canada, 1993-1994: Basic Facts & Economic Impacts. 64p. 1996. pap. 109.95 (*0-927547-70-8*) Intl Coun Shop.

Shopping for a Better World: A Quick & Easy Guide to Socially Responsible Supermarket Shopping. Rosalyn Will et al. LC 94-8231. 432p. 1994. 14.00 (*0-87156-471-8*) CEP.

Shopping for a Home. Kevin McQueen. Ed. by Gary Askerooth & Kathryn Fisher. (Realizing the American Dream Ser.). (Illus.). 39p. (Orig.). 1995. wbk. ed., pap. 3.00 (*1-884356-06-0*); teacher ed., pap. 5.00 (*1-884356-11-7*) Neighborhd Reinvest.

Shopping for Buddhas. Jeff Greenwald. (Illus.). 220p. 1996. pap. 10.95 (*0-86442-471-X*) Lonely Planet.

Shopping for Enlightenment. Laura Eisen. LC 88-62976. 1989. pap. 5.95 (*0-89087-555-3*) Celestial Arts.

Shopping for Food & Drink in Northern France & Belgium. Marc Millon & Kim Millon. (Illus.). 192p. 1995. pap. 17.95 (*1-85793-147-5*, Pub. by Pavilion UK) Trafalgar.

***Shopping for Food & Making Meals in Minutes Using the Dietary Guidelines.** 1997. lib. bdg. 250.95 (*0-8490-6122-9*) Gordon Pr.

***Shopping for God: A Guide to Your Spiritual Evolution.** Richard K. Livett. 250p. (Orig.). 1996. pap. write for info. (*0-9654201-0-8*) Soul Star.

Shopping for Health: A Nutritionist's Aisle-by-Aisle Guide to Smart Low-Fat Choices at the Supermarket. Suzanne Havala. LC 95-38389. 224p. 1996. pap. 6.99 (*0-06-095077-3*, PL) HarpC.

***Shopping for Miracles: A Practical Guide to Psychics & Psychic Powers.** Joanne D. McMahon & Anna Lascurain. LC 97-20452. 1997. write for info. (*1-56565-782-9*) Lowell Hse.

Shopping For Safer Boat Care: 101 Health & Environmental Ratings. Neil Smith & Phil Troy. LC 96-30476. (Illus.). 144p. 1996. pap. text ed. 13.95 (*0-07-059271-3*) Intl Marine.

Shopping for Safety: Providing Consumer Automative Safety Information. National Research Council Committee for the Future of Irrigation in the Face of Competing Demands. LC 96-11131. (Special Report Transportation Research Board, National Research Council Ser.: No. 248). 160p. 1996. pap. 20.00 (*0-309-06209-8*) Transport Res Bd.

***Shopping for School.** Claudette C. Mitchell et al. (Visions: African-American Experiences: Vol. 24). (Illus.). 8p. (Orig.). (J). (gr. k-1). 1996. pap. text ed. 3.00 (*1-57518-066-9*) Arborlake.

Shopping for Women. Philip Oakes. 256p. 1994. 24.95 (*0-233-98861-0*, Pub. by A Deutsch UK) Trafalgar.

***Shopping Guide for Caring Consumers, 1997.** Peta People for the Ethical Treatment of Animals Staff. 1996. pap. 7.95 (*1-57067-034-X*) Book Pub Co.

***Shopping Guide for Caring Consumers 1997: A Guide to Products That Are Not Tested on Animals.** Peta People for the Ethical Treatment of Animals Staff. LC 81-12p. 1996. pap. text ed. 7.95 (*1-57067-342-X*) Book Pub Co.

S

Shopping in Exciting Australia & Papua New Guinea: Your Passport to the Unique & Exotic. Ronald L. Krannich et al. 347p. (Orig.). 1989. pap. 13.95 (*0-942710-22-3*) Impact VA.

Shopping in Exotic Indonesia: Your Passport to the World's Most Exciting Islands & Cultures. Ronald L. Krannich & Caryl R. Krannich. (Impact Guides Ser.). 270p. (Orig.). 1991. pap. 12.95 (*0-942710-27-4*) Impact VA.

Shopping in Exotic Places: Your Passport to Exciting Hong Kong, Korea, Thailand, Indonesia, & Singapore. 2nd rev. ed. Ronald L. Krannich et al. 478p. 1989. pap. 14.95 (*0-942710-18-5*) Impact VA.

Shopping in Regency York: Butcher, Baker, Candlestick-Maker. Prudence Bebb. 1995. pap. 45.00 (*1-85072-148-3*, Pub. by W Sessions UK) St Mut.

Shopping in Space: Essays in American Blank Generation Fiction. Elizabeth Young & Graham Caveney. 256p. (Orig.). (C). pap. 15.99 (*1-85242-255-6*) Serpents Tail.

Shopping in Space: Essays on America's Blank Generation Fiction. Elizabeth Young & Graham Caveney. LC 94-7071. 288p. 1994. pap. 12.00 (*0-8021-3394-0*, Grove) Grove-Atltic.

Shopping in Thousand Oaks: An Illustrated Guide to the Malls & Shopping Centers in Thousand Oaks, Newbury Park, Oak Park & Westlake Village. Debbie Trice. (Illus.). 128p. (Orig.). 1995. pap. 10.95 (*0-9643018-3-0*) Rabbit Hollow Pr.

Shopping LA: The Insiders' Sourcebook for Film & Fashion. Marcy Froehlich et al. 560p. (Orig.). 1995. pap. 40.00 (*0-9647815-0-6*) Shopping LA.

***Shopping LA: The Insiders' Sourcebook for Film & Fashion.** 2nd rev. ed. Marcy Froehlich et al. 560p. (Orig.). 1997. pap. 40.00 (*0-9647815-1-4*) Shopping LA.

***Shopping List.** Peach. 7.40 (*1-877719-54-4*) Brownlow Pub Co.

***Shopping List.** Williamsburg. 7.40 (*1-877719-55-2*) Brownlow Pub Co.

Shopping List of Mystery Classics. Karen T. McCallum & Pamela Granovetter. (Copperfield Collections: Vol. 1). 96p. (Orig.). 1986. pap. 6.95 (*0-9617037-0-9*) Copperfld NY.

Shopping Mall High School: Winners & Losers in the Educational Marketplace. Arthur G. Powell et al. 1986. pap. 12.95 (*0-395-42638-3*) HM.

Shopping Manhattan: The Discriminating Buyer's Guide to Finding Almost Anything. Corky Pollan. 512p. (Orig.). 1989. pap. 12.95 (*0-14-012401-2*, Penguin Bks) Viking Penguin.

Shopping on the Internet & Beyond. Jaclyn Easton. 1995. pap. 19.99 (*1-883577-33-0*) Coriolis Grp.

Shopping Savvy. Ruth C. Rosen. (Life Skills Library). (Illus.). 48p. (YA). (gr. 7-12). 1992. lib. bdg. 14.95 (*0-8239-1455-0*) Rosen Group.

Shopping Secrets of Southern California: The Bargain Hunter's Guide. Mindy Glazer. 288p. (Orig.). 1995. pap. 14.95 (*0-9633263-1-7*) Helpful Pubns.

Shopping Smart Booklet. 1989. 0.95 (*1-56066-239-5*) Great Performance.

Shopping Spree: Identifying Shapes. Monica Weiss. LC 91-3986. (Frimble Family First Learning Adventures Ser.). (Illus.). 24p. (J). (gr. k-2). 1992. lib. bdg. 10.95 (*0-8167-2490-3*) Troll Communs.

Shopping Spree: Identifying Shapes. Monica Weiss. LC 91-3986. (Frimble Family First Learning Adventures Ser.). (Illus.). 24p. (J). (gr. k-2). 1997. pap. 3.50 (*0-8167-2491-1*) Troll Communs.

Shopping Surprises! Little Peek-in Book. Tr. by Joanne Barkan from ITA. (Peek-in Books Ser.). (Illus.). (J). 1995. bds., spiral bd. 3.99 (*0-88705-785-3*, Wshng Well Bks) Joshua Morris.

Shopping the Exotic South Pacific: Your Passport to Exciting Australia, New Zealand, Papua New Guinea, Fiji, & Tahiti. Ronald L. Krannich & Caryl R. Krannich. 479p. (Orig.). 1990. pap. 16.95 (*0-942710-21-5*) Impact VA.

Shopping the Insider's Way. Leil Lowndes. 192p. 1985. pap. 5.95 (*0-8065-0939-2*, Citadel Pr) Carol Pub Group.

S

Shopping Trip. Helen Oxenbury. LC 81-69274. (Very First Bks.). 14p. (J). (ps). 1982. bds. 3.50 (*0-8037-7939-9*) Dial Bks Young.

Shopping Trip. Helen Oxenbury. LC 81-69274. (Illus.). 14p. (J). (ps). 1991. pap. 3.95 (*0-8037-0997-8*) Dial Bks Young.

Shopping Trip. Arnold Shapiro. (J). (ps-3). 1992. pap. 12.95 (*0-8167-2747-3*) Troll Communs.

Shopping Trip. R. W. Thompson, Jr. (Illus.). 16p. (J). (ps-3). 1995. 8.95 (*0-9636442-2-X*) N Pole Chron.

*__Shopping with Benjamin.__ Sterling Publishing Company, Inc. Staff. (Balloon Bks.). 1997. 4.95 (*0-8069-0395-3*) Sterling.

Shopping with Fancy Pig. Pam Howard. (HRL Little Bks.). (Illus.). 8p. (Orig.). (J). (ps-k). 1995. pap. text ed. 10.95 (*1-57332-060-9*) HighReach Lrning.

Shopping with Fancy Pig. Pam Howard. (HRL Big Bks.). (Illus.). 8p. (Orig.). (J). (ps-k). 1995. pap. text ed. 10.95 (*1-57332-061-7*) HighReach Lrning.

Shopping with Freud. Rachel Bowlby. LC 92-37663. 192p. (C). 1993. pap. 16.95 (*0-415-06007-9*, A7958, Routledge NY) Routledge.

Shopping with Freud. Rachel Bowlby. LC 92-37663. 192p. (C). (gr. 13). 1993. text ed. 49.95 (*0-415-06006-0*, A7954, Routledge NY) Routledge.

Shops & Boutiques. Grant Kirkpatrick. 192p. 1995. 42.50 (*0-86636-291-6*) Rizzoli Intl.

Shops & Boutiques. Grant Kirkpatrick. 184p. 1996. pap. 34.95 (*0-86636-381-5*) St Martin.

*__Shops & Boutiques.__ PBC International Staff. 1995. 42.50 (*0-688-13827-6*) Morrow.

*__Shops & Boutiques.__ PBC International Staff. 1996. pap. 29.95 (*0-688-15048-9*) Morrow.

Shops & Shopkeeping in Eighteenth-Century England. Hoh-cheung Mui & Lorna H. Mui. 400p. 1989. 55.00 (*0-7735-0620-9*, Pub. by McGill CN) U of Toronto Pr.

*__Shops & Shopping.__ (Sense of History Ser.). Date not set. pap. text ed. write for info. (*0-582-04022-1*, Pub. by Longman UK) Longman.

Shoptalk: Conversations about Theater & Film with Twelve Writers, One Producer - & Tennessee Williams' Mother. Dennis Brown. (Illus.). 224p. 1992. pap. 19.95 (*1-55704-128-8*) Newmarket.

Shoptalk: Conversations about Theater & Film with Twelve Writers, One Producer - & Tennessee Williams' Mother. Dennis Brown. 1993. pap. 10.95 (*1-55704-170-9*) Newmarket.

Shoptalk: Learning to Write with Writers. Donald M. Murray. LC 89-77216. 208p. (Orig.). 1990. pap. 12.95 (*0-86709-258-0*, 0258) Boynton Cook Pubs.

Shoptalk Ideas for Elementary School Librarians. Ed. by Linworth Publishing, Inc. Staff. LC 93-50677. (Professional Growth Ser.). (Illus.). 75p. 1994. pap. text ed. 17.95 (*0-938865-30-7*) Linworth Pub.

Shopwalks Paris: Shopping Maps & Guide. Jane Magidson & Susan Harney. (Illus.). 1994. pap. 5.95 (*0-9638326-0-3*) Shopwalks.

Shore. limited ed. William Heyen. (Chapbook Ser.: No. 7). (Illus.). 29p. 1991. 45.00 (*0-937035-20-3*); pap. 30.00 (*0-937035-17-3*) Stone Hse NY.

Shore Bird Decoys. Henry A. Fleckenstein, Jr. LC 80-52024. (Illus.). 144p. 35.00 (*0-916838-32-3*) Schiffer.

Shore Bird Patterns. William Veasey. LC 83-61646. (Blue Ribbon Pattern Ser.: Bk. V). (Illus.). 64p. 1983. pap. 14.95 (*0-916838-88-9*) Schiffer.

*__Shore Birds.__ Delma Morton. (Illus.). (J). (gr. k-3). 1991. write for info. (*1-57842-078-4*) Delmas Creat.

Shore Dimly Seen. Ellis G. Arnall. (History - United States Ser.). 312p. 1993. reprint ed. lib. bdg. 89.00 (*0-7812-4917-1*) Rprt Serv.

Shore Diver: A Diver's Guide to Long Island Beach Sites. Daniel Berg. (Illus.). 96p. (Orig.). 1987. pap. 12.95 (*0-9616167-1-7*) Aqua Explorers.

Shore Ecology of the Gulf of Mexico. Joseph C. Britton & Brian Morton. (Illus.). 403p. 1989. 52.95 (*0-292-77610-1*); pap. 29.95 (*0-292-77626-8*) U of Tex Pr.

Shore Environment, Vol. 1: Methods. Ed. by J. R. Price et al. (Systematics Association Special Ser.: No.17). 1981. text ed. 189.00 (*0-12-564701-8*) Acad Pr.

Shore Environment, Vol. 2: Ecosystems. Ed. by J. H. Price et al. (Systematics Association Special Ser.: No. 17). 1981. text ed. 189.00 (*0-12-564702-6*) Acad Pr.

Shore Establishments of the Royal Navy. 1989. 120.00 (*0-907771-52-1*, Pub. by Maritime Bks UK) St Mut.

*__Shore Fishes of Hawaii.__ John E. Randall. (Illus.). 216p. (Orig.). 1996. pap. 14.95 (*0-939560-21-6*) Natural World.

Shore Ghosts & Other Stories of New Jersey. Larona Homer. (Illus.). 154p. (J). (gr. 4-8). 8.95 (*0-912608-82-X*) Mid Atlantic.

Shore Ghosts & Other Stories of New Jersey. Larona Homer. (Illus.). 154p. (J). (gr. 4-8). 1986. 8.95 (*0-912608-14-5*) Mid Atlantic.

Shore Party & Other Tales of War. Michael Harac. (Illus.). 104p. 1995. pap. text ed. 9.00 (*0-8059-3766-8*) Dorrance.

Shore Road Mystery. Franklin W. Dixon. (Hardy Boys Ser.: Vol. 6). (Illus.). 180p. (J). (gr. 5-9). 1928. 5.95 (*0-448-08906-8*, G&D) Putnam Pub Group.

*__Shore Road Mystery.__ fac. ed. Franklin W. Dixon. LC 97-14799. (Hardy Boys Mystery Stories Ser.: No. 6). (Illus.). 210p. (J). (gr. 4-8). 1997. 12.95 (*1-55709-149-8*) Applewood.

*__Shore Stories: Tales of the Jersey Shore.__ Ed. by Rich Youmans. (Illus.). 280p. 1997. 22.95 (*0-945582-50-1*) Down the Shore Pub.

Shore to Die. Valerie Wolzien. 1996. mass mkt. 5.50 (*0-449-14958-7*) Fawcett.

*__Shore Unknown.__ Coral S. Saxe. 368p. (Orig.). 1997. mass mkt. 5.50 (*0-8439-4273-8*, Leisure Bks) Dorchester Pub Co.

*__Shore Walker.__ Jim Arnosky. 1997. 7.99 (*0-679-86718-X*) Random.

Shore Wildflowers of California, Oregon, & Washington. Philip A. Munz. (Illus.). (Orig.). 1965. pap. 10.95 (*0-520-00903-7*) U CA Pr.

Shore Writers' Sampler: Best Stories by Eastern Shore Writers. Ed. by George H. Gillelan et al. LC 87-81639. (Illus.). 248p. (Orig.). 1987. pap. 9.50 (*0-9618993-0-1*) Friendly Harbor.

Shore Writer's Sampler II: Stories & Poems by Eastern Shore Writers Selected with the Help of Cynthia Voigt & David Bergman. Ed. by Sue Megargee & Frank Megargee. (Illus.). xii, 222p. (Orig.). 1988. pap. 9.50 (*0-9618993-1-X*) Friendly Harbor.

Shorebird Carving. Rosalyn L. Daisey. LC 89-63675. (Illus.). 256p. 1990. text ed. 49.95 (*0-88740-219-4*) Schiffer.

Shorebird Management Manual. Douglas L. Helmers. 58p. 1992. pap. text ed. 10.00 (*1-883861-05-5*) Wetlnds Amer.

Shorebirds. Peter Hayman et al. 1986. write for info. (*0-318-60127-3*) HM.

Shorebirds: An Identification Guide. John Marchant & Tony Prater. (Illus.). 416p. 1991. pap. 29.95 (*0-395-60237-8*) HM.

Shorebirds: Beautiful Beachcombers. Arthur Morris. (Wildlife Ser.). (Illus.). 160p. (Orig.). 1996. pap. write for info. (*1-55971-567-7*) NorthWord.

Shorebirds: The Birds, the Hunters, the Decoys. John M. Levinson & Somers G. Headley. LC 91-50581. (Illus.). 158p. 1991. 49.95 (*0-87033-424-7*, Tidewtr Pubs) Cornell Maritime.

Shorebirds of the Pacific Northwest. Dennis Paulson. LC 92-19050. (Illus.). 448p. 1993. 40.00 (*0-295-97233-5*) U of Wash Pr.

Shoreham & the Rise & Fall of the Nuclear Power Industry. Kenneth F. McCallion. LC 94-32930. 240p. 1995. text ed. 59.95 (*0-275-94299-6*, Praeger Pubs) Greenwood.

Shorehaven. Gayl Teller. LC 95-50789. (Illus.). 120p. 1996. pap. 19.95 (*0-7734-2678-7*, Mellen Poetry Pr) E Mellen.

*__Shoreline.__ Graphis Staff. 1995. 85.00 (*0-688-14788-7*) Morrow.

Shoreline. Barbara Taylor. LC 92-53491. (Look Closer Ser.). (Illus.). 32p. (J). (gr. 1-4). 1993. 9.95 (*1-56458-213-2*) DK Pub Inc.

Shoreline & Vegetation-Line Movement, Texas Gulf Coast, 1974 to 1982. J. G. Paine & R. A. Morton. (Geological Circular Ser.: GC 89-1). (Illus.). 50p. 1989. pap. 3.00 (*0-317-03108-2*) Bur Econ Geology.

Shoreline Nurse. large type ed. Jeanne Bowman. (Romance Ser.). 1994. pap. 15.99 (*0-7089-7614-X*, Linford) Ulverscroft.

Shoreline or Steamers, Stumps & Strawberries. LouAnn Bivins. (Illus.). 132p. 1987. pap. write for info. (*0-939116-18-9*) Frontier OR.

Shoreline Suite, for Four Recorders (SAAT) rev. ed. Leonie Jenkins. (Contemporary Consort Ser.: No. 3). i, 13p. 1994. pap. text ed. 9.00 (*1-56571-118-1*) PRB Prods.

Shorelines. Suzanne Rosenblatt. (Open Meeting Bks.). (Illus.). 64p. 1991. pap. 15.00 (*0-87924-072-5*) Membrane Pr.

Shorelines: Poetic Thoughts & Stories. Photos by Alexander West. (Illus.). 88p. (Orig.). 1986. pap. 6.00 (*0-9603414-2-0*) DeLong & Assocs.

Shorelines: The Camera at Water's Edge. Ed. by B. Martin Pedersen. (Illus.). 104p. 1995. 85.95 (*0-8230-6462-X*, Amphoto) Watsn-Guptill.

Shorelines & Beaches in Coastal Management: A Bibliography, No. 876. Ed. by Joseph M. Heikoff. 1975. 6.50 (*0-686-20368-2*, Sage Prdcls Pr) Sage.

Shorelines of the Great Lakes. F. Erick Carne. (Illus.). 127p. 1996. pap. 24.95 (*1-882376-25-0*) Thunder Bay Pr.

Shorelines Past & Present, 3 vols. Ed. by William F. Tanner. 745p. 1980. pap. 50.00 (*0-686-83996-X*) FSU Geology.

Shores & Headlands. Emily Grosholz. (Contemporary Poets Ser.). 80p. 1988. pap. 9.95 (*0-691-01448-5*); text ed. 21.95 (*0-691-06749-X*) Princeton U Pr.

*__Shores of a Dream: Yasuo Kuniyoshi's Early Work in America.__ Jane E. Myers & Tom Wolf. LC 96-31120. (Illus.). 80p. 1997. pap. 24.95 (*0-88360-086-2*) Amon Carter.

Shores of America: Thoreau's Inward Exploration. Sherman Paul. LC 58-6998. 447p. reprint ed. pap. 127.40 (*0-685-23651-X*, 2014928) Bks Demand.

Shores of Darkness. Demetrios Capetanakis. LC 73-76897. (Essay Index Reprint Ser.). 1977. 19.95 (*0-8369-0010-3*) Ayer.

Shores of Darkness. Edward B. Hungerford. 1990. 14.50 (*0-8446-2285-0*) Peter Smith.

*__Shores of Desire.__ Tracy Grant. 1997. mass mkt. 5.50 (*0-440-22168-4*, Dell Trade Pbks) Dell.

Shores of Discovery: How Expeditionaries Have Constructed the World. Eric J. Leed. 336p. 1996. pap. text ed. 14.00 (*0-465-02160-3*) HarpC.

*__Shores of Dusk.__ TSR Inc. Staff. 1997. 19.99 (*0-7869-0741-X*) TSR Inc.

Shores of Home. Jeanne-Marie Alexander. (Orig.). 1992. pap. 9.95 (*0-9631080-9-3*) Moonspun Bks.

Shores of Light: A Literary Chronicle of the 1920s & 1930s. Edmund Wilson. 832p. (C). 1985. reprint ed. pap. text ed. 16.95 (*0-930350-68-5*) NE U Pr.

Shores of Love. large type ed. Doris Howe. 448p. 1989. 25.99 (*0-7089-1944-8*) Ulverscroft.

*__Shores of Saco Bay: Historical Guide to Biddeford Pool, Old Orchard Beach, Pine Point, Prout's Neck.__ J. S. Locke. (Illus.). 107p. 1997. reprint ed. pap. 15.00 (*0-8328-5882-X*) Higginson Bk Co.

Shoresaver's Handbook: A Citizen's Guide. Tucker Coombe. 128p. (Orig.). 1996. pap. 12.95 (*1-55821-401-1*, 14011) Lyons & Burford.

Shorewood Collection. Shorewood Staff. (Illus.). 216p. 1983. ring bd. 21.00 (*0-88185-000-4*) Shorewood Fine Art.

Shorewood Collection Art Reference Guide. Shorewood Staff. 84p. (Orig.). 1985. 18.50 (*0-88185-026-8*) Shorewood Fine Art.

Shorin-Ryu: Okinawan Karate Question & Answer Book. William Cummins & Robert Scaglione. 86p. 1985. pap. 11.95 (*0-8048-1426-0*) C E Tuttle.

Shorin Ryu Karate Training Manual. George W. Alexander. (Illus.). 187p. 1995. pap. 34.95 (*0-614-13756-X*) Yamazato Pubns.

Short. Charles Doria. 50p. (Orig.). pap. 10.00 (*0-915066-98-X*) Assembling Pr.

Short. deluxe limited ed. Charles Doria. 50p. (Orig.). 15.00 (*0-915066-97-1*) Assembling Pr.

Short "a" & Long "a" Play a Game. Jane B. Moncure. LC 79-10300. (Sound Box Library). (Illus.). 32p. (J). (ps-2). 1979. lib. bdg. 21.36 (*0-89565-089-4*) Childs World.

Short Account of Early Muslim Architecture. K. A. Creswell. 1968. 22.00 (*0-86685-010-4*) Intl Bk Ctr.

Short Account of the Destruction of the Indies. Bartolome De Las Casas. Tr. by Nigel Griffin. (Illus.). 192p. 1992. pap. 10.95 (*0-14-044562-5*, Penguin Classics) Viking Penguin.

Short Account of the History of Mathematics. 4th ed. W. W. Ball. 544p. (C). 1908. pap. 11.95 (*0-486-20630-0*) Dover.

Short Account of the Life & Writings of the Late Rev. William Law, A. M. Richard Tighe. 48p. 1977. reprint ed. spiral bd. 12.00 (*0-7873-0871-4*) Hlth Research.

Short Account of the Malignant Fever, Lately Prevalent in Philadelphia. Mathew Carey. LC 73-112531. (Rise of Urban America Ser.). 1970. reprint ed. 15.95 (*0-405-02441-X*) Ayer.

Short Account of the Writings of the Late Rev. William Law. Richard Tighe. 126p. 1996. pap. 15.95 (*1-56459-689-3*) Kessinger Pub.

Short & Long. Elizabeth Gregory. (Illus.). (J). 1981. 6.95 (*0-933184-09-3*); pap. 4.95 (*0-933184-10-7*) Flame Intl.

Short & Long Term Changes in Climate, Vol. I. Felix G. Sulman. 192p. 1982. 103.00 (*0-8493-6420-5*, QC981, CRC Reprint) Franklin.

Short & Long Term Changes in Climate, Vol. II. Felix G. Sulman. 184p. 1982. 105.00 (*0-8493-6421-3*, QC981, CRC Reprint) Franklin.

Short & Long Term Effects see Child Abuse: A Multidisciplinary Survey

*__Short & Long Vowels.__ Scholastic, Inc. Staff. (Fun with Phonics Ser.). (J). 1997. pap. text ed. 6.95 (*0-590-76494-2*) Scholastic Inc.

Short & Profitable Treatise Touching the Cure of the Morbus Gallicus by Unctions. William Clowes. LC 75-38166. (English Experience Ser.: No. 443). 118p. 1972. reprint ed. 20.00 (*90-221-0443-5*) Walter J Johnson.

Short & Shivery. Robert D. San Souci. (Illus.). 192p. (J). 1989. lib. bdg. 7.95 (*0-385-26426-7*) Doubleday.

Short & Simple Account of the Country Guinea & Its Nature. Erik Tilleman. Ed. & Tr. by Selena A. Winsnes from DAN. LC 94-25765. Orig. Title: Liden Enfoldig Beretning om det Landskab Guinea og dets Beskaffenhed. (ENG.). 1994. write for info. (*0-942615-23-9*) U Wis African Stud.

Short & Sweet: Quick Creative Writing Activities That Encourage Imagination, Humor & Enthusiasm about Writing. Randy Larson. 36p. 1993. 10.95 (*1-877673-19-6*, SS) Cottonwood Pr.

Short & Tall. Rod Theodorou & Carole Telford. (Animal Opposites Ser.). (Illus.). (J). 1996. lib. bdg. write for info. (*1-57572-065-5*) Rigby Interact Libr.

*__Short Answer Questions in Anaesthesia.__ G. B. Rushman. (Greenwich Medical Media Ser.). 140p. 1997. pap. 32.50 (*1-900151-23-5*) OUP.

Short Apprehensive History of the World. Illus. by Anthony Beal. 189p. 20.99 (*0-9635524-1-4*); pap. 10.99 (*0-9635524-0-6*) Brainerd Bks.

Short Arm of the Law & Other Anomalies. W. R. Torpid. LC 96-90605. vii, 120p. 1996. per. write for info. (*0-9651357-0-5*) Bakala Pubns.

Short Arms see Rudolph J. Nunnemacher Collection of Projectile Arms

Short Attention Span User's Guide to IBMCAD: CAD Edition. 3rd ed. Howard A. Goodman. 42p. 1995. pap. text ed. 9.95 (*0-914465-01-5*) H A Goodman & Assocs.

Short Audit Case: The Valley Publishing Company. 6th ed. Ben Barr et al. 284p. (C). 1990. per. 24.95 (*0-256-07725-8*) Irwin.

Short Audit Case: Valley Publishing Company. 7th ed. Ben Barr & William Morris. 350p. (C). 1995. 25.95 (*0-256-12807-3*) Irwin.

*__Short Bible Catechism.__ John C. Kersten. 96p. 1989. pap. 4.00 (*0-89942-455-4*, 455/04) Catholic Bk Pub.

Short Bible Reference System. Ed. by R. G. Bratcher. viii, 148p. 1961. pap. 6.99 (*0-8267-0030-6*, 102669) Untd Bible Soc.

Short Bike Rides in & Around Los Angeles. Robert M. Winning. LC 92-44919. (Short Bike Rides Ser.). (Illus.). 224p. (Orig.). 1993. pap. 11.95 (*1-56440-168-5*) Globe Pequot.

Short Bike Rides in & Around New York City. 2nd ed. Phil Harrington & Wendy Harrington. LC 95-50822. (Short Bike Rides Ser.). 192p. (Orig.). 1996. pap. 9.95 (*1-56440-892-2*) Globe Pequot.

Short Bike Rides in & Around Philadelphia. Anne Lembo & Joe Surkiewicz. LC 93-48965. (Short Bike Rides Ser.). (Illus.). 128p. 1994. pap. 9.95 (*1-56440-073-5*) Globe Pequot.

*__Short Bike Rides in & Around Philadelphia.__ 2nd rev. ed. Joe Surkiewicz & Ann Lembo. LC 97-18714. (Short Bike Rides Ser.). (Illus.). 160p. 1997. pap. 9.95 (*0-7627-0078-5*) Globe Pequot.

Short Bike Rides in & Around San Francisco. Henry Kingman. (Short Bike Rides Ser.). (Illus.). 192p. (Orig.). 1996. pap. text ed. 10.95 (*1-56440-653-9*) Globe Pequot.

Short Bike Rides in & Around Washington, D. C. 3rd ed. Michael Leccese. LC 95-53719. (Short Bike Rides Ser.). 176p. (Orig.). 1993. pap. 10.95 (*1-56440-893-0*) Globe Pequot.

Short Bike Rides in Colorado. Michael Leccesse. LC 95-13956. (Short Bike Rides Ser.). (Illus.). 224p. (Orig.). 1995. pap. 10.95 (*1-56440-640-7*) Globe Pequot.

Short Bike Rides in Connecticut. 5th ed. Edwin Mullen. LC 94-24080. (Short Bike Rides Ser.). (Illus.). 144p. 1995. pap. 9.95 (*1-56440-641-5*) Globe Pequot.

Short Bike Rides in Eastern Massachusetts. Howard Stone. LC 93-39144. (Short Bike Rides Ser.). (Illus.). 360p. 1994. pap. 14.95 (*1-56440-393-9*) Globe Pequot.

*__Short Bike Rides in Eastern Massachusetts.__ 2nd rev. ed. Howard Stone. LC 96-50083. (Short Bike Rides Ser.). (Illus.). 400p. 1997. pap. 14.95 (*0-7627-0077-7*) Globe Pequot.

Short Bike Rides in Eastern Pennsylvania. 3rd ed. William Simpson. LC 96-16420. (Short Bike Rides Ser.). (Illus.). 176p. (Orig.). 1996. pap. 9.95 (*1-56440-891-4*) Globe Pequot.

*__Short Bike Rides in Hawaii.__ William L. Walters. (Short Bike Rides Ser.). (Illus.). 224p. 1997. pap. 10.95 (*0-7627-0116-1*) Globe Pequot.

Short Bike Rides in Michigan. Pamela Stovall. LC 94-46754. (Short Bike Rides Ser.). 224p. (Orig.). 1995. pap. 10.95 (*1-56440-642-3*) Globe Pequot.

Short Bike Rides in New Jersey. 3rd ed. Robert Santelli. LC 95-3427. (Short Bike Rides Ser.). (Illus.). 192p. (Orig.). 1995. pap. 9.95 (*1-56440-529-X*) Globe Pequot.

Short Bike Rides in Rhode Island. 5th ed. Howard Stone. LC 95-3427. (Short Bike Rides Ser.). (Illus.). 240p. 1995. pap. 10.95 (*1-56440-633-4*) Globe Pequot.

*__Short Bike Rides in Vermont.__ Sandy Duling. LC 96-54274. (Short Bike Rides Ser.). (Illus.). 224p. (Orig.). 1997. pap. 10.95 (*0-7627-0045-9*) Globe Pequot.

*__Short Bike Rides in Western Massachusetts.__ 2nd rev. ed. Howard Stone. LC 96-39641. (Short Bike Rides Ser.). (Illus.). 240p. 1997. pap. 12.95 (*0-7627-0076-9*) Globe Pequot.

Short Bike Rides in Western Washington. Judy Wagonfeld. LC 93-19378. (Short Bike Rides Ser.). (Illus.). 288p. (Orig.). 1993. pap. 12.95 (*1-56440-236-3*) Globe Pequot.

Short Bike Rides in Western Washington. 2nd rev. ed. Judy Wagonfeld. LC 96-24054. (Short Bike Rides Ser.). (Illus.). 288p. (Orig.). 1997. pap. 13.95 (*1-56440-988-0*) Globe Pequot.

*__Short Bike Rides in Wisconsin.__ Greg Marr. LC 97-13800. (Short Bike Rides Ser.). (Illus.). 224p. (Orig.). 1997. pap. 10.95 (*0-7627-0046-7*) Globe Pequot.

Short Bike Rides on Cape Cod, Nantucket, & the Vineyard. 5th ed. Edwin Mullen & Jane Griffith. LC 93-40253. (Short Bike Rides Ser.). (Illus.). 160p. 1994. pap. 9.95 (*1-56440-392-0*) Globe Pequot.

*__Short Bike Rides on Cape Cod, Nantucket & the Vineyard.__ 6th ed. Edwin Mullen & Jane Griffith. LC 96-41635. (Short Bike Rides Ser.). (Illus.). 160p. 1997. pap. 10.95 (*0-7627-0075-0*, East Woods) Globe Pequot.

Short Bike Rides on Long Island. 4th ed. Phil Angelillo. LC 95-43031. (Short Bike Rides Ser.). (Illus.). 176p. (Orig.). 1996. pap. 9.95 (*1-56440-901-5*) Globe Pequot.

Short Biography of John Leeth: With an Account of His Life among the Indians. John Leeth. (American Biography Ser.). 90p. 1991. reprint ed. lib. bdg. 59.00 (*0-7812-8240-3*) Rprt Serv.

Short Biography of John Leeth, with an Account of His Life Among the Indians. Ewel Jeffries. Ed. by Reuben G. Thwaites. LC 74-180034. 1977. 20.95 (*0-405-08669-5*, Pub. by Blom Pubns UK) Ayer.

Short-Bus Kid. Willard Helmuth. (Orig.). (J). (gr. 6-9). 1995. pap. 5.00 (*0-88092-112-9*); lib. bdg. 15.00 (*0-88092-113-7*) Royal Fireworks.

Short Business Letters for Dictation & Transcription. Charles E. Zoubek. (Diamond Jubilee Ser.). 1970. text ed. 28.50 (*0-07-073075-X*) McGraw.

Short but Foamy History of Beer: The Drink That Invented Itself. William Haiber & Robert Haiber. LC 93-78823. (Illus.). 200p. (Orig.). 1993. per. 19.99 (*0-944089-09-7*) Info Devels.

Short Calculus for Business, Economics, & the Social Sciences. Joseph N. Fadyn. Ed. by Marshall. 662p. (C). 1991. text ed. 64.25 (*0-314-77292-8*) West Pub.

Short Calculus Workbook. Turner. (C). 1990. 24.00 (*0-673-46318-4*) Addson-Wesley Educ.

*__Short Cases for Paediatric Exams.__ Adam Glasser et al. (Illus.). 225p. 1997. pap. write for info. (*0-7020-2162-8*, Pub. by W B Saunders UK) Saunders.

Short Cases for the MRCP. Charles R. Hind. 172p. 1990. pap. text ed. 22.00 (*0-443-04190-3*) Churchill.

Short Cases in Surgery. Charnley. 1996. text ed. write for info. (*0-7020-2061-3*) HarBrace.

Short Catechism of Mary. Charles Journet. (Illus.). 80p. 1991. pap. 1.95 (*0-89942-050-8*, 50/04) Catholic Bk Pub.

Short Chain Fatty Acids. Konrad H. Soergel. LC 93-48419. 304p. (C). 1994. lib. bdg. 102.00 (*0-7923-8849-6*) Kluwer Ac.

An Asterisk (*) at the beginning of an entry indicates that the title is appearing in BIP for the first time.

Short Change Game: How to Stop the School from Depriving Your Retarded or Handicapped Child. Maryn Baker. LC 81-3653. 1983. 13.95 (0-87949-211-2) Ashley Bks.

Short-Changed. Rhonda Sharp & Ray Broomhill. 216p. 1991. pap. text ed. 18.95 (0-04-320219-5, Pub. by Allen Unwin AT) Paul & Co Pubs.

Short-Changed: Africa in World Trade. Michael Barratt-Brown & Pauline M. Tiffen. LC 92-34001. (Transnational Institute Ser.). 220p. (C). 63.00 (0-7453-0694-2, Pub. by Pluto Pr UK); pap. 18.95 (0-7453-0699-3, Pub. by Pluto Pr UK) LPC InBook.

Short Chinese TV Plays: An Intermediate Course. Teng Shou-Hsin & Liu Yuehua. LC 86-71550. (C & T Asian Language Ser.). 484p. (Orig.). (C). 1992. pap. text ed. 29.95 (0-88727-168-5) Cheng & Tsui.

Short Chronology of American History, Fourteen Ninety-Two to Nineteen Fifty. Irving S. Kull & Nell M. Kull. LC 79-24781. 388p. 1980. reprint ed. text ed. 65.00 (0-313-22259-2, KUSC, Greenwood Pr) Greenwood.

***Short Circuit.** Olga Litowinsky. 1996. pap. text ed. 3.95 (0-8114-9323-7) Raintree Steck-V.

***Short Circuit: Strengthening Local Economies for Security in an Unstable World.** Richard Douthwaite. 386p. 9700. pap. 29.95 (1-874675-60-0) Dufour.

***Short-Circuit Characteristics of Insulated Cable.** 15.00 (0-614-18677-3, P-32-382-1994) Insulated Cable.

***Short-Circuit Performance of Metallic Shielding & Sheaths.** 15.00 (0-614-18684-6, P-45-482-1994) Insulated Cable.

Short Circuits. Bruce Boston. (Illus.). 88p. 1990. 25.00 (0-938075-15-2); pap. 10.95 (0-938075-16-0) Ocean View Bks.

Short Circuits. Donald R. Gallo. 224p. (J). 1993. mass mkt. 5.50 (0-440-21889-6) Dell.

Short Circular Walks Around Nottinghamshire. 64p. 1987. 29.00 (0-907496-58-X, Pub. by JNM Pubns UK) St Mut.

Short Circular Walks on the Northern Moors. 64p. 1987. 29.00 (0-907496-59-8, Pub. by JNM Pubns UK) St Mut.

Short Commentary on Aristotle's Prior Analytics. Al-Farabi. Tr. by Nicholas Rescher. LC 63-10581. 132p. reprint ed. pap. 37.70 (0-317-09047-X, 2010487) Bks Demand.

Short Commentary on Kant's Critique of Pure Reason. 2nd ed. A. C. Ewing. LC 39-13499. 1967. reprint ed. pap. text ed. 16.95 (0-226-22778-2, P265) U Ch Pr.

Short Communications see European Nutrition Conference: Proceedings, 2nd, Munich, 1976

Short Constitutional History of England. 3rd ed. H. St. Clair Feilden & W. Gray Etheridge. xx, 358p. 1986. reprint ed. lib. bdg. 42.50 (0-8377-2130-X) Rothman.

Short Course: A Basic Guide for Planning Boards & Zoning Boards of Appeals in New York State. Harry J. Willis et al. (Illus.). 90p. (Orig.). 1996. pap. 16.00 (0-8113-0002-1) NY Plan Fed.

Short Course in Adolescent Psychiatry. Ed. by Joseph R. Novello. LC 93-74373. 288p. 1994. pap. 30.00 (1-56821-195-3) Aronson.

Short Course in Algebra & Trigonometry. A. W. Goodman. (Illus.). 139p. 1985. pap. text ed. 16.95 (0-912675-11-X) Ardsley.

Short Course in Bacterial Genetics: A Laboratory Manual & Handbook for Escherichia Coli & Related Bacteria, 2 vols., Set. Jeffrey H. Miller. (Illus.). 876p. 1992. student ed. 110.00 (0-87969-349-5) Cold Spring Harbor.

Short Course in Bacterial Genetics: Handbook for Escherichia Coli & Related Bacteria. Jeffrey H. Miller. (Illus.). 1992. pap. 75.00 (0-614-06575-5) Cold Spring Harbor.

Short Course in Basic. Stewart M. Venit. Date not set. pap. text ed. 35.50 (0-314-62283-7) West Pub.

Short Course in Biochemistry. Albert L. Lehninger. LC 72-93199. (Illus.). 452p. (C). 1973. text ed. 65.95 (0-87901-024-X) Worth.

Short Course in Calculus with Applications to Management, Life & Social Sciences. Bodh Gulati. 512p. (C). 1994. per., pap. text ed. 41.94 (0-8403-9871-9) Kendall-Hunt.

Short Course in Clinical Pharmacokinetics. Dennis A. Noe. LC 93-74962. 154p. (Orig.). (C). 1994. pap. text ed. 27.00 (0-915486-19-9) Applied Therapeutics.

Short Course in Cloud Physics. 3rd ed. R. R. Rogers & M. K. Yau. (International Series in Natural Philosophy). (Illus.). 307p. 1989. pap. 39.95 (0-08-034863-7, Pergamon Press) Buttrwrth-Heinemann.

Short Course in Epidemiology. Staffan E. Norell. 208p. 1991. pap. text ed. 39.50 (0-88167-842-2, 2325) Lppncott-Raven.

Short Course in General Relativity. James Foster. LC 94-21438. 1994. 29.95 (0-387-94295-5) Spr-Verlag.

Short Course in Geometry. Patricia Juelg. 320p. (C). 1990. text ed. 24.40 (0-02-361471-4, Macmillan Coll) P-H.

***Short Course in International Business Culture.** (Short Course in International Trade Ser.). (Illus.). 192p. (Orig.). 1997. pap. 19.95 (1-885073-54-2) Wrld Trade Pr.

***Short Course in International Contracts.** (Short Course in International Trade Ser.). (Illus.). 192p. (Orig.). 1997. pap. 19.95 (1-885073-55-0) Wrld Trade Pr.

***Short Course in International Economics.** (Short Course in International Trade Ser.). (Illus.). 192p. (Orig.). 1997. pap. 19.95 (1-885073-53-4) Wrld Trade Pr.

***Short Course in International Entrepreneurial Trade.** (Short Course in International Trade Ser.). 192p. (Orig.). 1997. pap. 19.95 (1-885073-58-5) Wrld Trade Pr.

***Short Course in International Marketing.** (Short Course in International Trade Ser.). (Illus.). 192p. (Orig.). 1997. pap. 19.95 (1-885073-52-6) Wrld Trade Pr.

***Short Course in International Negotiating.** Jeffrey E. Curry. (Short Course in International Trade Ser.). (Illus.). 182p. (Orig.). 1997. pap. 19.95 (1-885073-51-8) Wrld Trade Pr.

***Short Course in International Payments.** Edward G. Hinkleman & Molly Thurmond. (Short Course in International Trade Ser.). (Illus.). 176p. (Orig.). 1997. pap. 19.95 (1-885073-50-X) Wrld Trade Pr.

***Short Course in Matrix Theory.** Erwin Kleinfeld & Margaret Kleinfeld. 155p. (C). 1997. lib. bdg. 27.50 (1-56072-422-6) Nova Sci Pubs.

Short Course in Pathology. Nancy Standler. LC 94-3037. 1994. pap. text ed. 29.95 (0-443-08955-8) Churchill.

Short Course in Permanent Magnet Materials. William A. Cassady. (Illus.). 192p. 1993. pap. text ed. 39.95 (1-882637-34-8) SJL Pub.

Short Course in Photography. 2nd ed. Barbara London. 1994. pap. text ed. 24.50 (0-8230-4976-0) Watsn-Guptill.

Short Course in Photography. 3rd ed. Barbara London & Jim Stone. (Illus.). 264p. 1995. pap. 27.00 (0-8230-4977-9, Amphoto) Watsn-Guptill.

Short Course in Photography: An Introduction to Black-&-White Photographic Technique. 3rd ed. Barbara London & Jim Stone. (Illus.). (C). 1995. teacher ed. write for info. (0-673-54294-7) Addson-Wesley Educ.

Short Course in Photography: An Introduction to Black-&-White Photographic Technique. 3rd ed. Barbara London & Jim Stone. LC 95-31003. (Illus.). 192p. (C). 1996. text ed. 28.95 (0-673-52439-6) Addson-Wesley Educ.

Short Course in PL-I PL-C. Ann L. Clark & Steven L. Mandell. (Data Processing & Information Systems Ser.). 190p. 1978. pap. text ed. 38.25 (0-8299-0219-8); write for info. (0-8299-0465-4) West Pub.

Short Course in QBASIC. Stewart M. Venit. LC 95-37484. 300p. (C). 1996. pap. text ed. 39.75 (0-314-06526-1) West Pub.

Short Course in Spoken English. Ronald Mackin. 1975. pap. 5.95 (0-87789-137-0); audio 55.00 (0-87789-140-0) ELS Educ Servs.

Short Course in the Secret War. Christopher Felix. 280p. reprint ed. pap. 14.95 (0-8191-8470-5) U Pr of Amer.

Short Course in Windows 95. Stewart M. Venit. (Illus.). 240p. (Orig.). (C). 1996. pap. text ed. 16.00 (1-881991-44-X) Scott Jones Pubng.

Short Course in Writing: Composition, Collaborative Learning & Constructive Reading. 4th ed. Kenneth A. Bruffee. (C). 1993. text ed. 31.95 (0-673-52190-7) Addson-Wesley Educ.

Short Course of Economics. David H. Blake. LC 93-12209. 1993. 15.95 (0-07-707726-1) McGraw.

Short Course on Computer Viruses. F. Cohen. (Orig.). (C). 1990. 48.00 (1-878109-01-4) ASP PA.

Short Course on Computer Viruses. 2nd ed. Frederick B. Cohen. 288p. (Orig.). 1994. pap. text ed., pap. 44.95 (0-471-00769-2); disk 10.00 (0-471-00770-6) Wiley.

Short Course on Computer Viruses. 2nd ed. Frederick B. Cohen. 288p. (Orig.). 1994. pap. text ed. 34.95 (0-471-00768-4) Wiley.

Short Course on Functional Equations: Based upon Recent Applications to the Social & Behavioural Sciences. J. Aczel. 1986. pap. text ed. 45.50 (90-277-2377-X); lib. bdg. 100.00 (90-277-2376-1) Kluwer Ac.

Short Cut. June M. Milam. Ed. by Chris Gilmer. (Drugless Douglass Tales Ser.). (Illus.). 20p. (J). (ps). 1994. pap. text ed. 42.95 (1-884307-05-1); student ed. 4.95 (1-884307-06-X) Dev Res Educ.

***Short Cut.** June M. Milam. Ed. by Charlotte C. Daley. Tr. by Carmen Miranda. (Drugless Douglass Tales Ser.). (Illus.). 24p. (SPA.). (J). (ps). 1997. pap. 32.95 (1-884307-24-8) Dev Res Educ.

***Short Cut.** June M. Milam. Ed. by Charlotte C. Daley. Tr. by Carmen Miranda. (Drugless Douglass Tales Ser.). (Illus.). 24p. (SPA.). (J). (ps). 1997. student ed., pap. 6.95 (1-884307-25-6) Dev Res Educ.

Short Cut. Ennio Flaiano. Tr. by Stuart Hood from ITA. LC 93-80761. 270p. 1994. reprint ed. pap. 12.95 (1-56897-019-6) Marlboro Pr.

Short-Cut Cook. Jacques Pepin. LC 90-6306. 320p. 1990. 19.95 (0-688-09448-1) Morrow.

Short-Cut Math. Gerard W. Kelly. (Popular Science Ser.). 112p. 1984. reprint ed. pap. 2.95 (0-486-24611-6) Dover.

Short-Cut Quilts: Sixty Patterns for Creating Quilts from 5" Squares. Doreen C. Burbank. Ed. by Lauri Linch-Zadel. (Illus.). 144p. (Orig.). 1994. pap. 19.95 (0-943721-13-X) Leman Pubns.

Short Cut to Easy Street: How to Get Money in Your Mailbox Every Day Plus Automatic Income for the Rest of Your Life. Stephen W. Kenyon. 256p. 1993. pap. text ed. 19.95 (1-883256-75-5) Life Unltd.

***Short Cut to Good Fortune: The Meng.** Lily Chung. LC 97-2437. 288p. (Orig.). 1997. pap. 14.95 (1-56718-133-3) Llewellyn Pubns.

Short Cut to the Stars. large type ed. Jan Tempest. 384p. 1986. 25.99 (0-7089-1410-1) Ulverscroft.

Short Cuts. Sigmund Brouwer. LC 93-26411. (Accidental Detective Ser.: Vol. 11). 132p. (Orig.). (J). (gr. 3-7). 1993. pap. 4.99 (1-56476-158-4, Victor Bks) Chariot Victor.

Short Cuts. Sigmund Brouwer. LC 93-26411. (Accidental Detective Ser.: No. 11). 132p. (Orig.). (J). (gr. 3-7). 1995. pap. 5.99 (1-56476-380-3, 6-3380, Victor Bks) Chariot Victor.

Short Cuts: A Screenplay. Robert Altman & Frank Barhydt. (Illus.). 224p. (Orig.). 1993. lib. bdg. 43.00 (0-8095-4118-1) Borgo Pr.

Short Cuts: An Interactive English Course, Vol. 1. James R. Mentel. 1996. pap. text ed. write for info. (0-07-041886-1) McGraw.

***Short Cuts: An Interactive English Course, Vol. 2.** James R. Mentel. 1996. pap. text ed. write for info. (0-07-041887-X) McGraw.

Short Cuts: An Interactive English Course, Vol. 2. James R. Mentel. 1996. pap. text ed. write for info. (0-07-041891-8) McGraw.

Short Cuts: Selected Stories. Raymond Carver. LC 93-19747. (Contemporaries Ser.). 1993. pap. 10.00 (0-679-74864-4, Vin) Random.

Short Cuts: The Dictionary of Useful Abbreviations. Ed. by Steven R. Kleinedler & Richard A. Spears. 320p. 1996. pap. 12.95 (0-8442-0905-8) NTC Pub Grp.

Short-Cuts for Round Layouts. 4th ed. Joseph J. Kaberlein. 1985. 23.36 (0-02-819450-0) Glencoe.

***Short Cuts to Designer Style: Decorative Effects.** Jo Avison. 1997. 24.95 (0-7063-7516-5, Pub. by Ward Lock UK) Sterling.

***Short Cuts to Designer Style: Soft Furnishings.** Jo Avison. (Illus.). 128p. 1997. 19.95 (0-7063-7515-7, Pub. by Ward Lock UK) Sterling.

Short Dance in the Sun. George Benet. 160p. 1988. pap. 9.95 (0-932499-58-9) Lapis Pr.

Short Days Long Nights: New & Selected Poems. Helen Dunmore. 192p. (Orig.). 9100. pap. 18.95 (1-85224-150-0, Pub. by Bloodaxe Bks UK) Dufour.

Short Dialysis. Ed. by Vincenzo Cambi. (Topics in Renal Medicine Ser.). (C). 1987. lib. bdg. 152.00 (0-89838-858-9) Kluwer Ac.

Short Diary of a School Girl Louisa Salome Cutler: Florence Village - 1881 Northampton, Massachusetts. limited ed. Louisa S. Cutler. Ed. by Florence Civic & Business Association, Book Committee Staff. 76p. 1993. pap. 46.50 (0-685-71474-8) Florence Civic Busn Assn.

***Short Dictionary of Alaska Peninsula Sugtestun & Alaska Peninsula Alutiiq: Orthography 1996.** 2nd rev. ed. Matrona Christiansen et al. Orig. Title: A Short Dictionary of Alaska Peninsula Sugcestun & Alaska Peninsula Alutiiq. x, 66p. 1996. wbk. ed., pap. 6.00 (1-55500-060-6) Alaska Native.

Short Dictionary of Anglo-Saxon Poetry: In a Normalized Early West-Saxon Orthography. Jess B. Bessinger. LC 61-2144. 105p. reprint ed. pap. 30.00 (0-317-09527-7, 2020454) Bks Demand.

Short Dictionary of Eighteenth Century Russian. Charles E. Gribble. 103p. (RUS.). 1977. pap. 12.95 (0-89357-172-5) Slavica.

Short Dictionary of the Psalms. Jean-Pierre Prevost. Tr. by Mary M. Misrahi. LC 96-36930. 104p. (Orig.). 1997. pap. text ed. 9.95 (0-8146-2370-0, Litrg Pr Bks) Liturgical Pr.

Short Discourse of the Three Kinds of Peppers in Common Use. Walter Bailey. LC 77-38145. (English Experience Ser.: No. 425). 48p. 1972. reprint ed. 20.00 (90-221-0425-7) Walter J Johnson.

Short Discourse on Tyrannical Government. William Ockham. Ed. by John Kilcullen & Arthur S. McGrade. (Cambridge Texts in the History of Political Thought Ser.). (Illus.). 400p. (C). 1995. pap. text ed. 24.95 (0-521-35804-3) Cambridge U Pr.

Short Discourse on Tyrannical Government. William of Ockham. Ed. by A. S. McGrade. (Cambridge Texts in the History of Political Thought Ser.). 280p. (C). 1992. text ed. 59.95 (0-521-35242-8) Cambridge U Pr.

Short Discoverie of the Dangers of Ignorant Practisers of Physicke. John Cotta. LC 72-38168. (English Experience Ser.: No. 445). 144p. 1972. reprint ed. 21.00 (90-221-0445-1) Walter J Johnson.

Short "e" & Long "e" Play a Game. Jane B. Moncure. LC 79-10305. (Sound Box Library). (Illus.). 32p. (J). (ps-2). 1979. lib. bdg. 21.36 (0-89565-090-8) Childs World.

Short Economic & Social History of Twentieth Century England. Walford Johnson et al. LC 67-21370. ix, 208p. 1967. 29.50 (0-678-06002-9) Kelley.

Short Energy History of the United States & Some Thoughts about the Future. Joseph M. Dukert. (Decisionmakers Bookshelf Ser.: Vol. 7). (Illus.). 88p. (Orig.). 1980. pap. 2.50 (0-931032-07-5) Edison Electric.

Short Engagement. large type ed. Marjorie Lewty. 352p. 1984. 25.99 (0-7089-1213-3) Ulverscroft.

Short Essays. 5th ed. Gerald Levin. 512p. (C). 1989. pap. text ed. 18.75 (0-15-580920-2) HB Coll Pubs.

Short Essays. 6th ed. Gerald Levin. 544p. (C). 1992. pap. text ed. 20.00 (0-15-580922-9) HB Coll Pubs.

Short Essays. 7th ed. Levin. (C). 1994. pap. text ed. 26.75 (0-15-501188-X) HB Coll Pubs.

Short Essays. 7th ed. Levin. (C). 1994. teacher ed., pap. text ed. 33.75 (0-15-502145-1) HB Coll Pubs.

Short Essays. 8th ed. Levin. (C). 1997. pap. text ed. write for info. (0-15-503969-5) HarBrace.

Short Eyes. Miguel Pinero. 128p. 1975. pap. 10.00 (0-374-52147-6) FS&G.

Short Fiber Reinforced Composite Materials - STP 772. Ed. by B. Sanders. 258p. 1982. 27.50 (0-8031-0697-1, 04-772000-30) ASTM.

Short Fibre-Polymer Composites. Ed. by S. K. De & J. R. White. 256p. 1995. boxed 165.00 (1-85573-220-3, Pub. by Woodhead Pubng UK) Am Educ Systs.

***Short Fiction.** W. B. Yeats. lib. bdg. 22.95 (0-8488-1880-6) Amereon Ltd.

***Short Fiction: A Critical Companion.** Ed. by Robert C. Evans et al. LC 96-52058. 400p. (C). 1997. lib. bdg. 50.00 (0-933951-73-6) Locust Hill Pr.

Short Fiction: Classic & Contemporary. 3rd ed. Ed. by Charles H. Bohner. LC 93-2730. 1183p. (C). 1993. pap. text ed. 39.33 (0-13-146051-X) P-H.

Short Fiction & the Press in France 1829 - 1841: Followed by a Selection of Short Fiction from the Periodical & Daily Press. David Bryant. LC 95-3920. (Studies in French Literature: Vol. 24). 396p. 1995. text ed. 99.95 (0-7734-8956-8) E Mellen.

Short Fiction by Black Women, 1900-1920. Compiled by Elizabeth Ammons. (Schomburg Library of Nineteenth-Century Black Women Writers). 640p. 1991. 39.95 (0-19-506195-0) OUP.

Short Fiction by Hispanic Writers of the United States. Ed. by Nicolas Kanellos. LC 92-20826. 256p. (Orig.). 1993. pap. 15.00 (1-55885-044-9) Arte Publico.

Short Fiction of Charles W. Chesnutt. Ed. by Sylvia L. Render. LC 81-6314. 428p. (C). 1981. pap. 12.95 (0-88258-092-2) Howard U Pr.

Short Fiction of D. H. Lawrence. Janice H. Harris. 284p. 1984. text ed. 40.00 (0-8135-1046-5) Rutgers U Pr.

Short Fiction of Edgar Allan Poe: An Annotated Edition. Ed. by Stuart Levine & Susan Levine. 672p. 1990. pap. text ed. 16.95 (0-252-06125-X) U of Ill Pr.

Short Fiction of Ernest Hemingway: A Study in Major Themes. Syed A. Hamod. ix, 167p. 1985. 16.50 (81-7024-008-5, Pub. by Ashish Pub Hse II) Nataraj Bks.

***Short Fiction of Kurt Vonnegut.** Peter J. Reed. LC 97-2236. (Contributions to the Study of American Literature: Vol. 1). 184p. 1997. text ed. 55.00 (0-313-30235-9, Greenwood Pr) Greenwood.

Short Fiction of Mary Wilkins Freeman & Sarah Orne Jewett. Ed. by Barbara H. Solomon. (Orig.). 1979. pap. 4.95 (0-451-51192-1, CE1192, Sig Classics) NAL-Dutton.

Short Fiction of Rudolph Fisher. Ed. by Margaret Perry. LC 86-29580. (Contributions in Afro-American & African Studies: No. 107). 242p. 1987. text ed. 49.95 (0-313-21348-8, FPF, Greenwood Pr) Greenwood.

Short Fictions. Mark Sonnenfeld. 32p. Date not set. pap. 3.00 (1-887379-05-3) M Sonnenfeld.

Short Flights. Patrick P. Garrett. 138p. 1994. pap. 12.95 (0-9649194-1-9) P P Garrett.

Short Friday & Other Stories. large type ed. Isaac B. Singer. (YA). (gr. 10-12). reprint ed. 10.00 (0-89064-057-2) NAVH.

Short Game. Derek Lawrenceson. (Golf Basic Ser.). (Illus.). 112p. (Orig.). 1996. pap. 14.95 (1-57243-120-2) Triumph Bks.

Short Grammar of Biblical Aramaic. rev. ed. Alger F. Johns. LC 93-72717. (Monograph Ser.). 120p. (C). 1982. reprint ed. pap. text ed. 14.99 (0-943872-74-X) Andrews Univ Pr.

***Short Grammar of Latvian.** Terje Mathiassen. 236p. 1997. pap. 22.95 (0-89357-270-5) Slavica.

***Short Grammar of Lithuanian.** Terje Mathiassen. 256p. (Orig.). 1996. pap. 22.95 (0-89357-267-5) Slavica.

Short Guide to Business Writing. Harry Bruce et al. LC 94-11834. 208p. 1994. pap. text ed. 32.60 (0-13-124728-X) P-H.

Short Guide to Business Writing. Morton. (C). 1996. pap. text ed. 21.00 (0-15-501635-0) HB Coll Pubs.

Short Guide to Classical Mythology. Kirkwood. 109p. (C). 1960. pap. text ed. 14.75 (0-03-008865-8) HB Coll Pubs.

Short Guide to Classical Mythology. G. M. Kirkwood. LC 95-43579. viii, 110p. 1995. reprint ed. pap. 8.00 (0-86516-309-X) Bolchazy-Carducci.

Short Guide to Life. J. Thomas, pseud. 76p. 1993. pap. 4.95 (0-9637794-0-0) Machia.

Short Guide to Reading & Writing about Chemistry. Beall & John Trimbur. 208p. (C). 1994. text ed. 15.95 (0-673-46882-8) Addson-Wesley Educ.

***Short Guide to Writing.** Steven Lynn. LC 96-30523. 154p. 1996. pap. 18.00 (0-205-18934-2) Allyn.

Short Guide to Writing a Research Proposal. Andrew H. Ziegler, Jr. 28p. 1995. pap. text ed. 4.95 (1-884778-11-9) Old Mountain.

Short Guide to Writing about Art. 4th ed. Sylvan Barnet. LC 92-26229. (Short Guide Ser.). (C). 1992. 11.00 (0-673-52293-8) Addson-Wesley Educ.

Short Guide to Writing about Art. 4th ed. Sylvan Barnet. (Illus.). 208p. 1995. pap. text ed. 16.95 (0-8230-4960-4) Watsn-Guptill.

Short Guide to Writing about Art. 5th ed. Sylvan Barnet. LC 95-51667. (Short Guide Ser.). (C). 1997. text ed. 15.95 (0-673-52487-6) Addson-Wesley Educ.

Short Guide to Writing about Art. 5th ed. Sylvan Barnet. 1996. pap. text ed. 15.00 (0-8230-4980-9) Watsn-Guptill.

Short Guide to Writing about Biology. 2nd ed. Jan A. Pechenik. LC 92-10923. (Short Guide Ser.). (C). 1993. text ed. 15.95 (0-673-52128-1) Addson-Wesley Educ.

Short Guide to Writing about Biology. 2nd ed. Jan A. Pechenik. 240p. 1996. reprint ed. pap. 15.95 (1-886746-70-2) Talman.

***Short Guide to Writing about Biology.** 3rd ed. Jan A. Pechenik. LC 96-35994. (C). 1997. pap. text ed. 15.95 (0-673-52503-1) Longman.

Short Guide to Writing about Chemistry. Herbert Beall & John Tribur. 160p. 1996. pap. 15.95 (1-886746-71-0) Talman.

Short Guide to Writing about Film. Timothy Corrigan. LC 93-21631. (Short Guide Ser.). (C). 1994. text ed. 16.95 (0-673-52299-7) Addson-Wesley Educ.

Short Guide to Writing about Film. 2nd ed. Timothy Corrigan. 190p. 1995. pap. text ed. 16.95 (0-8230-4955-8) Watsn-Guptill.

***Short Guide to Writing about Film.** 3rd ed. Ed. by Corrigan. LC 97-13118. (C). 1998. text ed. write for info. (0-321-01110-4) Addson-Wesley Educ.

Short Guide to Writing about History. Richard C. Marius. (C). 1987. pap. text ed. 7.50 (0-316-54621-6) Little.

Short Guide to Writing about History. 2nd ed. Richard Marius. LC 94-8774. (C). 1995. text ed. 16.95 (0-673-52348-9) Addson-Wesley Educ.

Short Guide to Writing about History. 2nd ed. Richard Marius. 192p. reprint ed. pap. 13.95 (1-886746-07-9, 93369) Talman.

Short Guide to Writing about Literature. 6th ed. Sylvan Barnet. 304p. 1995. reprint ed. pap. 16.95 (1-886746-53-2) Talman Pub.

Short Guide to Writing about Literature. 7th ed. Sylvan Barnet. 400p. 1995. pap. 18.95 (0-8230-5009-2) Watsn-Guptill.

Short Guide to Writing about Literature. 7th ed. Sylvan Barnet. LC 95-9732. 416p. (C). 1996. text ed. 17.95 (0-673-52395-0) Addson-Wesley Educ.

S

An Asterisk (*) at the beginning of an entry indicates that the title is appearing in BIP for the first time.

Short Guide to Writing about Science. David Porush. LC 94-3119. (Short Guide Ser.). (C). 1994. text ed. 16.95 (*0-06-500754-9*) Addson-Wesley Educ.

Short Guide to Writing about Science. David Porush. 275p. 1996. reprint ed. pap. 15.95 (*1-886746-69-9*) Talman.

Short Guide to Writing about Social Science. 2nd ed. Lee Cuba. 182p. 1996. reprint ed. pap. 15.95 (*1-886746-68-0*) Talman.

***Short Guide to Writing about Social Science.** 3rd ed. Lee J. Cuba. LC 96-34858. (C). 1997. text ed. 15.95 (*0-673-52494-9*) Longman.

Short Guide to Writing about Social Sciences. 2nd ed. Lee J. Cuba. LC 92-20281. (C). 1992. 16.00 (*0-673-52194-X*) Addson-Wesley Educ.

***Short Guide to Writing Mathematics.** Ed. by Maurer. (C). 1998. text ed. write for info. (*0-321-01578-9*) Addson-Wesley Educ.

Short Handbook & Style Sheet. Thomas Pinney. 58p. (Orig.). (C). 1977. pap. text ed. 8.00 (*0-15-580925-3*) HB Coll Pubs.

Short Handbook for Writers. Johnathon F. Schell. LC 90-44129. 1991. pap. text ed. write for info. (*0-07-055288-6*) McGraw.

Short Handbook for Writers. Gerald J. Schiffhorst. 1991. teacher ed., text ed. write for info. (*0-07-055345-9*) McGraw.

Short Handbook for Writers. Gerald J. Schiffhorst. 1991. spiral bd. write for info. (*0-07-055409-9*) McGraw.

***Short Handbook for Writers.** 2nd ed. Gerald J. Schiffhorst. 1996. pap. text ed. write for info. (*0-07-057761-7*); wbk. ed., pap. text ed. write for info. (*0-07-057765-X*) McGraw.

***Short Handbook for Writers: The Mcgraw-Hill Brief Guide to Persuasion & Critical Thinking in Writing.** 2nd ed. Gerald J. Schiffhorst. 1996. pap. text ed. write for info. (*0-07-057763-3*) McGraw.

***Short Handbook for Writers: The Mcgraw-Hill Brief to Avoiding Bias in Writing.** 2nd ed. Gerald J. Schiffhorst. 1996. pap. text ed. write for info. (*0-07-057764-1*) McGraw.

***Short Handbook for Writers Exercise Book.** 2nd ed. Gerald J. Schiffhorst. 1996. pap. text ed. write for info. (*0-07-057766-8*) McGraw.

Short Handbook of Communist Ideology: Synopsis of the Osnovy Marksizma-Leninizma. H. Fleischer. Tr. by Thomas J. Blakeley from GER. (Sovietica Ser.: No. 20). 98p. 1965. lib. bdg. 49.00 (*90-277-0053-2*) Kluwer Ac.

Short Handbook of Fiqh. T. B. Badayum. pap. 3.50 (*0-933511-54-X*) Kazi Pubns.

Short Happy Life of the Brown Oxford. Philip K. Dick. 1990. pap. 12.95 (*0-8065-1153-2*, Citadel Pr) Carol Pub Group.

Short Hikes & Easy Walks: In Grand Teton National Park. Bill Hayden & Jerry Freillich. Ed. by NPS Staff. (Illus.). 15p. 1988. pap. 1.00 (*0-931895-13-8*) Grand Teton NHA.

Short Hikes in God's Country. Carl F. Dillon, Jr. LC 95-92730. (Explore Pennsylvania's North Central Highlands Ser.). (Illus.). 256p. (Orig.). 1995. pap. 10.95 (*0-9639328-3-7*) Pine Creek Pr.

Short Hikes in Rocky Mountain National Park. Kent Dannen & Donna Dannen. Orig. Title: Walks With Nature in Rocky Mountain National Park. (Illus.). 64p. (Orig.). 1986. reprint ed. pap. 4.95 (*0-9606768-1-3*) Tundra Pubns.

Short Hikes in Shenandoah National Park. Shenandoah National Park Staff. Ed. by Ann Grogg. (Illus.). 16p. (YA). 1994. pap. 1.00 (*0-931606-15-2*) Shenandoah Nat Assn.

Short Historical English Grammar. Henry Sweet. 1892. 49.00 (*0-685-20268-2*) Scholarly.

Short Historical English Grammar. Henry Sweet. 1988. reprint ed. lib. bdg. 49.00 (*0-7812-0008-3*) Rprt Serv.

***Short History of a Prince.** Jane Hamilton. 1998. write for info. (*0-679-45755-0*) Random.

Short History of a Small Place. T. R. Pearson. 408p. 1986. mass mkt. 5.95 (*0-345-33263-6*) Ballantine.

Short History of A Small Place. T. R. Pearson. 1994. pap. 12.00 (*0-8050-3320-3*) H Holt & Co.

Short History of Africa. Roland A. Oliver & J. D. Fage. 304p. 1988. mass mkt. 6.95 (*0-14-022759-8*, Penguin Bks) Viking Penguin.

Short History of Africa. 6th ed. Roland A. Oliver. 1990. pap. 13.95 (*0-14-013601-0*) Viking Penguin.

Short History of African Art. Werner Gillon. (Illus.). 416p. 1987. pap. 12.95 (*0-14-022508-0*, Penguin Bks) Viking Penguin.

Short History of African Art. Werner Gillon. 1991. pap. 18.95 (*0-14-013611-8*) Viking Penguin.

Short History of Agriculture in the British Colonies. Geoffrey B. Masefield. LC 77-26015. 179p. 1978. reprint ed. text ed. 49.75 (*0-313-20094-7*, MAAG, Greenwood Pr) Greenwood.

Short History of American Catholicism. Martin E. Marty. 240p. (Orig.). 1995. pap. 10.95 (*0-88347-320-8*) Res Christian Liv.

Short History of American Railways. Slason Thompson. LC 70-150203. (Select Bibliographies Reprint Ser.). 1977. reprint ed. 66.95 (*0-8369-5716-4*) Ayer.

***Short History of Anaesthesia: The First 150 Years.** G. B. Rusham et al. LC 96-31494. 1996. write for info. (*0-7506-3066-3*) Buttrwrth-Heinemann.

Short History of Ancient Egypt. T. G. James. 196p. 1996. 24.95 (*0-304-34711-6*, Pub. by Cassell UK) Sterling.

Short History of Ancient Egypt. David O'Connor. LC 89-85826. (Illus.). 48p. (Orig.). (C). 1990. pap. text ed. 7.95 (*0-911239-16-2*) Carnegie Mus.

Short History of Anglo-Saxon Freedom. James K. Hosmer. (Notable American Authors Ser.). 1992. reprint ed. lib. bdg. 75.00 (*0-7812-3178-7*) Rprt Serv.

Short History of Aryan Medical Science. Bhagavat Simhaji. LC 75-23683. reprint ed. 45.00 (*0-404-13236-7*) AMS Pr.

Short History of Astronomy: From Earliest Times Through the 19th Century. Arthur Berry. (Illus.). (C). 1961. reprint ed. pap. 10.95 (*0-486-20210-0*) Dover.

Short History of Biology. Isaac Asimov. LC 80-15464. (American Museum Science Bks.). (Illus.). ix, 189p. 1980. reprint ed. text ed. 45.00 (*0-313-22583-4*, ASSB, Greenwood Pr) Greenwood.

Short History of Botany in the United States. Ed. by Joseph Ewan. 174p. 1969. lib. bdg. 12.50 (*0-02-844360-8*) Lubrecht & Cramer.

Short History of Breast Cancer. Daniel De Moulin. 1983. lib. bdg. 32.50 (*90-247-2814-2*) Kluwer Ac.

Short History of Breast Cancer. Daniel De Moulin. (C). 1989. pap. text ed. 80.00 (*0-7923-0524-8*) Kluwer Ac.

Short History of British Psychology, 1840-1940. Leslie S. Hearnshaw. LC 86-22840. (Methuen's Manuals of Modern Psychology Ser.). 342p. 1986. reprint ed. text ed. 89.50 (*0-313-25278-5*, HEAS, Greenwood Pr) Greenwood.

Short History of Buddhism. Edward Conze. 160p. 1994. pap. 8.95 (*1-85168-066-7*) Onewrld Pubns.

Short History of Byzantium: Based on the Great Three-Volume Work. abr. ed. John J. Norwich. LC 96-44458. 1997. 35.00 (*0-679-45088-2*) McKay.

Short History of California. Rockwell D. Hunt. 1992. reprint ed. lib. bdg. 75.00 (*0-7812-5052-8*) Rprt Serv.

Short History of Cambridge University Press. Michael H. Black. 123p. 1992. pap. text ed. 15.95 (*0-521-42921-8*) Cambridge U Pr.

Short History of Canada. Desmond Morton. 351p. (Orig.). 1995. pap. 14.95 (*0-7710-6516-7*) McCland & Stewart.

Short History of Canada. Donald C. Masters. LC 80-12913. (Anvil Ser.). 192p. 1980. reprint ed. pap. text ed. 11.50 (*0-89874-201-3*) Krieger.

Short History of Cardiology. James B. Herrick. LC 75-23720. reprint ed. 49.50 (*0-404-13278-2*) AMS Pr.

Short History of Ceylon. H. W. Codrington. (C). 1994. text ed. 18.50 (*81-206-0946-8*, Pub. by Asian Educ Servs II) S Asia.

Short History of Ceylon. Humphrey W. Codrington. LC 72-140353. (Select Bibliographies Reprint Ser.). 1977. 28.95 (*0-8369-5596-X*) Ayer.

***Short History of Charleston.** Robert N. Rosen. LC 97-7228. (Orig.). 1997. pap. 14.95 (*1-57003-197-5*) U of SC Pr.

Short History of Charleston. rev. ed. Robert N. Rosen. Ed. by M. Rita Howe & Tom Cole. (Illus.). 176p. (Orig.). 1992. 19.95 (*0-9635154-1-1*); pap. 13.95 (*0-9635154-0-3*) Peninsula SC.

***Short History of Charleston.** Robert N. Rosen. 176p. (Orig.). 1997. reprint ed. 21.95 (*1-57003-196-7*) U of SC Pr.

Short History of Chemistry. James R. Partington. 1989. pap. 10.95 (*0-486-65977-1*) Dover.

Short History of Chemistry. Isaac Asimov. LC 78-25789. (Illus.). 263p. 1979. reprint ed. text ed. 55.00 (*0-313-20769-0*, ASSH, Greenwood Pr) Greenwood.

Short History of Chicago. Robert Cromie. (Short History Ser.). (Illus.). 160p. (Orig.). 1984. pap. 12.95 (*0-938530-28-3*) Lexikos.

Short History of Chinese Art. Ludwig Bachhofer. LC 83-45695. reprint ed. 47.50 (*0-404-20014-1*) AMS Pr.

Short History of Chinese Art. Hugo Munsterberg. LC 70-88990. (Illus.). 227p. 1969. reprint ed. text ed. 55.00 (*0-8371-2117-5*, MUCA, Greenwood Pr) Greenwood.

***Short History of Chinese Philosophy.** Fung Yu-Lan. Ed. by Derk Bedde. Orig. Title: History of Chinese Philosophy. 1997. pap. 17.95 (*0-684-83634-3*, Free Press) Free Pr.

Short History of Chinese Philosophy. abr. ed. Fung Yu-Lan. Ed. by Derk Bedde. Orig. Title: History of Chinese Philosophy. 1966. pap. 18.95 (*0-02-910980-9*, Free Press) Free Pr.

Short History of Christian Doctrine: From the First Century to the Present. rev. ed. Bernhard Lohse. Tr. by F. Ernest Stoeffer from GER. LC 66-21732. 320p. 1978. pap. 16.00 (*0-8006-1341-4*, 1-1341, Fortress Pr) Augsburg Fortress.

Short History of Christian Missions. Frank W. Patterson. 176p. 1985. pap. 12.50 (*0-311-72663-1*) Casa Bautista.

Short History of Christian Thought. exp. rev. ed. Linwood P. Urban. 384p. (C). 1995. pap. text ed. 21.95 (*0-19-509348-8*) OUP.

Short History of Christianity. 2nd exp. rev. ed. Martin E. Marty. LC 80-8042. 336p. (Orig.). 1987. pap. 20.00 (*0-8006-1944-7*, 1-1944) Augsburg Fortress.

Short History of Classical Arabic Literature. 2nd enl. rev. ed. Ignaz Goldziher. Tr. & Rev. by J. DeSomogyi. (Olms Paperbacks Ser.: Vol. 23). x, 172p. 1966. pap. 24.57 (*0-685-66471-6*, 05101243) G Olms Pubs.

Short History of Clinical Midwifery: The Development of Ideas in the Professional Management of Childbirth. Philip Rhodes. 200p. 1995. pap. 24.95 (*1-898507-22-8*) Buttrwrth-Heinemann.

Short History of Dumbartonshire. I. M. MacPhail. 136p. (C). 1986. 40.00 (*0-907590-01-2*) St Mut.

Short History of Economic Progress: A Course in Economic History. Y. S. Brenner. LC 68-21447. (Illus.). viii, 304p. 1969. 37.50 (*0-678-05014-7*) Kelley.

Short History of Egypt. M. V. Seton-Williams. (Illus.). 96p. (C). 1989. pap. 17.95 (*0-948695-12-9*, Pub. by Rubicon Pr UK) David Brown.

***Short History of English Church Music.** Erik Routley. 160p. (C). 1997. pap. text ed. 19.95 (*0-916642-63-1*, 1995) Hope Pub.

Short History of English Drama. Benjamin I. Evans. LC 77-27446. 146p. 1978. reprint ed. text ed. 45.00 (*0-8371-9072-X*, EVED, Greenwood Pr) Greenwood.

Short History of English Liberalism. W. Lyon Bease. 1976. lib. bdg. 59.95 (*0-8490-2600-8*) Gordon Pr.

Short History of English Literature. 2nd ed. Robert Barnard. 282p. 1994. pap. 17.95 (*0-631-19088-0*) Blackwell Pubs.

Short History of English Literature. 2nd ed. Robert Barnard. 238p. 1995. write for info. (*82-00-03993-5*) Scandnvan Univ Pr.

***Short History of English Literature.** 2nd ed. Harry Blamires. 448p. (C). 1984. pap. text ed. 18.95 (*0-415-05078-2*) Routledge.

Short History of Ethics. Alasdair MacIntyre. 280p. 1966. pap. 11.00 (*0-02-087260-7*) Macmillan.

***Short History of Ethics.** Alasdair MacIntyre. LC 97-22280. (C). 1997. reprint ed. pap. write for info. (*0-268-01759-X*) U of Notre Dame Pr.

***Short History of Ethics: A History of Moral Philosophy from the Homeric Age to the Twentieth Century.** Alasdair Macintyre. 1996. pap. text ed. 13.00 (*0-684-82677-1*, Scrbnr) Scribnrs Ref.

***Short History of Europe.** Alcock. Date not set. pap. 18.95 (*0-312-21036-1*); text ed. 59.95 (*0-312-21003-5*) St Martin.

Short History of Existentialism. Jean A. Wahl. pap. 0.95 (*0-685-19412-4*, 100, Citadel Pr) Carol Pub Group.

Short History of Financial Euphoria. John Kenneth Galbraith. 128p. 1994. 7.95 (*0-685-70794-6*, Penguin Bks) Viking Penguin.

Short History of Financial Euphoria. John Kenneth Galbraith. 1994. pap. 9.95 (*0-14-023856-5*, Penguin Bks) Viking Penguin.

Short History of Finland. Fred Singleton. (Illus.). 224p. (C). 1990. text ed. 59.95 (*0-521-32275-8*); pap. text ed. 18.95 (*0-521-31136-5*) Cambridge U Pr.

Short History of France from Early Times to 1972. 2nd ed. J. H. Jackson. (Illus.). 260p. 1974. pap. 10.95 (*0-521-09864-5*) Cambridge U Pr.

Short History of Freethought, Ancient & Modern. John M. Robertson. LC 74-169215. (Atheist Viewpoint Ser.). 464p. 1972. reprint ed. 29.95 (*0-405-03804-6*) Ayer.

Short History of Genetics: The Development of Some of the Main Lines of Thought, 1864-1939. Leslie C. Dunn. LC 91-18890. (History of Science & Technology Reprint Ser.). (Illus.). 286p. (C). 1991. reprint ed. pap. text ed. 19.95 (*0-8138-0447-7*) Iowa St U Pr.

Short History of Geomorphology. Keith J. Tinkler. LC 84-24364. (Illus.). 336p. 1985. 64.50 (*0-389-20544-3*, BNB-08108) B&N Imports.

Short History of German Literature. James K. Hosmer. (Notable American Authors Ser.). 1992. reprint ed. lib. bdg. 75.00 (*0-7812-3176-0*) Rprt Serv.

Short History of Glass. Chloe Zerwick. LC 89-17779. (Illus.). 112p. 1990. pap. 9.95 (*0-87290-146-7*) Corning.

Short History of God, Me & the Universe. Russell Stannard. (J). (gr. 1-5). 1995. 8.95 (*0-345-39741-X*) Ballantine.

Short History of Greek Literature. Jacqueline DeRomilly. Tr. by Lillian Doherty from FRE. LC 84-16457. (Illus.). 304p. 1985. lib. bdg. 32.50 (*0-226-14311-2*) U Ch Pr.

Short History of Greek Mathematics. James Gow. LC 68-21639. 24.95 (*0-8284-0218-3*) Chelsea Pub.

Short History of Ilunl Usul. rev. ed. Muhammad B. Sadr. Tr. by Islamic Seminary Staff from ARA. 130p. (C). 1985. reprint ed. pap. 7.00 (*0-941724-37-9*) Islamic Seminary.

Short History of Ireland. Richard Killeen. (Illus.). 72p. 1994. pap. 7.95 (*0-7171-2156-9*, Pub. by Gill & MacMill IE) Irish Bks Media.

***Short History of Ireland.** Sean McMahon. 224p. 1997. pap. 16.95 (*0-8023-1319-1*) Dufour.

Short History of Ireland. John O. Ranelagh. 320p. (C). 1995. pap. text ed. 18.95 (*0-521-46944-9*) Cambridge U Pr.

Short History of Ireland. John O. Ranelagh. 320p. (C). 1995. text ed. 65.00 (*0-521-47548-1*) Cambridge U Pr.

Short History of Ireland. 2nd ed. Martin Wallace. (Appletree Pocket Guides Ser.). 94p. (Orig.). 1986. pap. 7.95 (*0-86281-171-6*, Pub. by Appletree Pr IE) Irish Bks Media.

Short History of Irish Literature. Seamus Deane. LC 85-52218. (C). 1994. reprint ed. pap. text ed. 17.50 (*0-268-01751-4*) U of Notre Dame Pr.

Short History of Islam. William M. Watt. 160p. 1995. pap. 8.95 (*1-85168-109-4*) Onewrld Pubns.

Short History of Islam. rev. ed. Sayyid F. Mahmud. (Illus.) 442p. 1989. pap. 19.95 (*0-19-577384-5*) OUP.

Short History of Islamic Spain. William M. Watt & Pierre A. Cachia. 1979. pap. 13.50 (*0-85224-332-4*, Pub. by Edinburgh U Pr UK) Col U Pr.

Short History of Jazz. Bob Yurochko. 300p. 1992. pap. text ed. 23.95 (*0-8304-1331-6*) Nelson-Hall.

Short History of Judaism. Dan Cohn-Sherbok. 160p. 1995. pap. 10.95 (*1-85168-069-1*) Onewrld Pubns.

Short History of Judaism: Three Meals, Three Epochs. Jacob Neusner. LC 92-7929. 244p. (Orig.). 1992. pap. 18.00 (*0-8006-2552-8*, 1-2552, Fortress Pr) Augsburg Fortress.

Short History of Linguistics. 3rd ed. R. H. Robins. (Linguistics Library). 288p. (C). 1990. pap. text ed. 24.85 (*0-582-29145-3*, 78586) Longman.

Short History of Logic. Robert Adamson. Ed. by W. R. Sorley. (Reprints in Philosophy Ser.). reprint ed. lib. bdg. 39.50 (*0-697-00001-X*) Irvington.

Short History of Los Angeles. Gordon DeMarco. (Illus.). 156p. (Orig.). 1987. pap. 12.95 (*0-938530-37-2*) Lexikos.

Short History of Lyme Regis. John Fowles. (Illus.). 56p. 1983. 13.50 (*0-316-28987-6*) Little.

Short History of Marriage: Marriage Rites, Customs, & Folklore in Many Countries & All Ages. Ethel L. Urlin. LC 89-43338. 276p. 1990. reprint ed. lib. bdg. 42.00 (*1-55888-879-9*) Omnigraphics Inc.

Short History of Medicine. rev. ed. Erwin H. Ackerknecht. LC 81-48194. 304p. (C). 1982. reprint ed. pap. 14.95 (*0-8018-2726-4*) Johns Hopkins.

Short History of Medieval Philosophy. Julius R. Weinberg. 320p. 1964. pap. text ed. 15.95 (*0-691-01956-8*) Princeton U Pr.

Short History of Modern Arabic Literature. M. M. Badawi. LC 92-23257. 320p. (C). 1993. 58.00 (*0-19-826542-5*) OUP.

Short History of Modern Bulgaria. R. J. Crampton. (Illus.). 224p. 1987. 59.95 (*0-521-25340-3*); pap. text ed. 22.95 (*0-521-27323-4*) Cambridge U Pr.

Short History of Modern Egypt. Afaf L. Marsot. 168p. 1985. pap. text ed. 17.95 (*0-521-27234-3*) Cambridge U Pr.

Short History of Modern Philosophy: From Descartes to Wittgenstein. 2nd rev. ed. Roger Scruton. LC 95-16864. Orig. Title: From Descartes to Wittgenstein. 320p. (C). 1995. pap. 10.95 (*0-415-13035-2*) Routledge.

Short History of Modern Philosophy: From Descartes to Wittgenstein. 2nd rev. ed. Roger Scruton. LC 95-13864. Orig. Title: From Descartes to Wittgenstein. 320p. (C). (gr. 13). 1995. text ed. 45.00 (*0-415-13327-0*) Routledge.

Short History of Music. Donald N. Ferguson. LC 73-5266. (Illus.). 500p. 1974. reprint ed. text ed. 35.00 (*0-8371-6881-3*, FEHM, Greenwood Pr) Greenwood.

Short History of Nautical Medicine. Louis H, Roddis. LC 75-23757. reprint ed. 39.50 (*0-404-13363-0*) AMS Pr.

Short History of Nepal. Netra B. Thapa. 1992. 38.00 (*0-7855-0265-3*, Pub. by Ratna Pustak Bhandar) St Mut.

Short History of Nepal. enl. rev. ed. Netra B. Thapa. 188p. (C). 1990. 75.50 (*0-89771-070-3*, Pub. by Ratna Pustak Bhandar) St Mut.

Short History of North Africa. Jane S. Nickerson. LC 68-54233. 1961. 35.00 (*0-8196-0219-1*) Biblo.

Short History of Norway. Thomas K. Derry. LC 79-10688. (Illus.). 281p. 1979. reprint ed. text ed. 79.50 (*0-313-21467-0*, DESH, Greenwood Pr) Greenwood.

Short History of Opera. 3rd ed. Donald J. Grout & Hermine W. Williams. (Illus.). 933p. 1988. text ed. 49.50 (*0-231-06192-7*) Col U Pr.

Short History of Oriental Trade. Joseph Desomogyi. 281p. 1968. lib. bdg. 37.70 (*0-317-93808-8*, 05101831) G Olms Pubs.

Short History of Oriental Trade. Joseph Desomogyi, pseud. 281p. 1968. write for info. (*0-318-71499-X*) G Olms Pubs.

Short History of Parliament, Twelve Ninety-Five - Sixteen Forty-Two. Faith Thompson. LC 53-10471. 294p. reprint ed. pap. 83.80 (*0-317-28170-4*, 2055965) Bks Demand.

Short History of Philosophy. Robert C. Solomon & Kathleen M. Higgins. 336p. 1996. 30.00 (*0-19-508647-3*) OUP.

Short History of Philosophy. Robert C. Solomon & Kathleen M. Higgins. 336p. (C). 1996. pap. 17.95 (*0-19-510196-0*) OUP.

Short History of Planet Earth: Mountains, Mammals, Fire, & Ice. J. D. MacDougall. LC 95-46399. (Illus.). 256p. 1996. text ed. 24.95 (*0-471-14805-9*) Wiley.

Short History of Political Thinking. Paul W. Ward. LC 70-134151. (Essay Index Reprint Ser.). 1977. 17.95 (*0-8369-2080-5*) Ayer.

Short History of Portland. Lexikos Publishing Staff. 1990. pap. 12.95 (*0-938530-46-1*) Lexikos.

***Short History of Presidential Elections.** Robert T. Masella. (Orig.). 1997. mass mkt. 4.99 (*1-55197-593-9*, Pub. by Comnwlth Pub CN) Partners Pubs Grp.

Short History of Quebec. John A. Dickinson. (C). 1993. pap. text ed. 25.95 (*0-7730-5283-6*) Addison-Wesley.

Short History of Reconstruction. Eric Foner. LC 89-45653. 1990. pap. 13.50 (*0-06-096431-6*, PL) HarpC.

Short History of Reconstruction, 1863-1877. abr. ed. Eric Foner. (Illus.). 288p. 1990. pap. 8.95 (*0-685-48926-4*, PL) HarpC.

Short History of Religion in America. Lester B. Scherer. (Illus.). 145p. (Orig.). 1980. pap. 8.95 (*0-89894-011-7*) Advocate Pub Group.

Short History of Religions. Ernest E. Kellett. LC 71-156671. (Essay Index Reprint Ser.). 1977. reprint ed. 33.95 (*0-8369-2281-6*) Ayer.

Short History of Renaissance & Reformation Europe: Dances over Fire & Water. Jonathan W. Zophy. LC 95-30635. 1995. pap. text ed. 29.00 (*0-13-320433-2*) P-H.

Short History of Renaissance Europe: Dances over Fire & Water. Jonathan W. Zophy. 1996. pap. text ed. 26.40 (*0-13-181579-2*) P-H.

Short History of Reno. Myrick E. Land & Barbara N. Land. LC 94-32428. (Illus.). 136p. 1995. pap. 14.95 (*0-87417-262-4*) U of Nev Pr.

Short History of Revivalist Movement in Islam. S. Abul Ala Maududi. 165p. (Orig.). 1985. pap. 5.50 (*1-56744-383-4*) Kazi Pubns.

Short History of Roman Law. Olga Tellegen-Couperus. LC 92-21949. (Illus.). 192p. (C). 1993. pap. 17.95 (*0-415-07251-4*, B0364, Routledge NY); text ed. 49.95 (*0-415-07250-6*, B0360, Routledge NY) Routledge.

Short History of Roman Law. Paul F. Girard. Tr. by Augustus H. Lefroy & John H. Cameron. LC 93-79695. 228p. 1994. reprint ed. 48.00 (*1-56169-053-8*, Pub. by Longman Far East HK) Gaunt.

Short History of Rosalia, Washington. Alice Campbell. 10p. 1970. reprint ed. pap. 1.50 (*0-87770-037-0*) Ye Galleon.

Short History of San Diego. Michael McKeever. (Short History Ser.). (Illus.). 144p. (Orig.). 1985. pap. 12.95 (*0-938530-32-1*) Lexikos.

Short History of San Francisco. Tom Cole. LC 81-2588. (Illus.). 144p. (Orig.). 1981. pap. 12.95 (*0-938530-00-3*, 00-3) Lexikos.

An Asterisk (*) at the beginning of an entry indicates that the title is appearing in BIP for the first time.

Short History of Saracens. Syed A. Ali. 1990. 19.95 (*0-933511-55-8*) Kazi Pubns.

Short History of Sierra Leone. Christopher Fyfe. (Illus.). 1979. pap. text ed. 5.50 (*0-582-60358-7*) Longman.

Short History of Socialist Money. Gavin Peebles. 192p. 1992. text ed. 34.95 (*1-86373-113-X*, Pub. by Allen Unwin AT); pap. text ed. 19.95 (*1-86373-071-0*, Pub. by Allen Unwin AT) Paul & Co Pubs.

Short History of Sociological Thought. Alan Swingewood. LC 84-40119. 350p. 1984. text ed. 12.95 (*0-312-72151-X*) St Martin.

Short History of Sociological Thought. 2nd ed. Alan Swingewood. 1991. text ed. 18.95 (*0-312-06736-4*); text ed. 45.00 (*0-312-06735-6*) St Martin.

Short History of Solicitors. Edmund B. Christian. xiv, 255p. 1983. reprint ed. lib. bdg. 25.00 (*0-8377-0448-0*) Rothman.

Short History of Spanish Literature: Revised & Updated Edition. James R. Stamm. LC 78-53803. (Gotham Library). (C). 1979. pap. text ed. 18.00 (*0-8147-7792-9*) NYU Pr.

Short History of Spanish Music. Ann Livermore. LC 72-196469. 272p. reprint ed. pap. 77.60 (*0-317-42003-8*, 2026116) Bks Demand.

***Short History of St. George's Hospital & the Origins of Its Ward Names.** Terry Gould & David Uttley. LC 96-39214. (Illus.). 200p. 1997. 39.95 (*0-485-11504-2*, Pub. by Athlone Pr UK); pap. 19.95 (*0-485-12126-3*, Pub. by Athlone Pr UK) Humanities.

Short History of Surgery. D'Arcy Power. LC 75-23751. reprint ed. 32.50 (*0-404-13357-6*) AMS Pr.

Short History of Switzerland. Edgar Bonjour et al. LC 84-25253. viii, 388p. 1985. reprint ed. 52.50 (*0-313-24675-0*, BOSZ, Greenwood Pr) Greenwood.

Short History of Technology: From Ancient Times to A. D. 1900. T. K. Derry & Trevor I. Williams. LC 92-46454. (Illus.). 782p. 1993. reprint ed. pap. 16.95 (*0-486-27472-1*) Dover.

Short History of the American Bison. rev. ed. Martin S. Garretson. LC 79-169759. (Select Bibliographies Reprint Ser.). 1977. reprint ed. 15.95 (*0-8369-5979-5*) Ayer.

Short History of the American Nation. 6th ed. John A. Garraty. (C). 1992. 34.00 (*0-06-500741-7*) Addson-Wesley Educ.

Short History of the American Nation. 6th ed. John A. Garraty. 556p. reprint ed. pap. 36.00 (*1-886746-41-9*, 93489) Talman.

***Short History of the American Nation.** 7th ed. Ed. by Garraty. (C). 1997. student ed., pap. text ed. 21.95 (*0-673-98028-6*) Addison-Wesley.

Short History of the American Nation. 7th ed. John Garraty. 556p. 1996. reprint ed. pap. 34.00 (*1-886746-84-2*) Talman.

Short History of the American Nation. 7th ed. John A. Garraty. (C). 1997. text ed. 34.50 (*0-673-98027-8*) Addson-Wesley Educ.

Short History of the American Nation, 1. John A. Garraty. (C). 1993. 18.50 (*0-06-500848-0*) Addson-Wesley Educ.

Short History of the American Nation, 2 vols., 1. 6th ed. John A. Garraty. (C). 1992. 22.50 (*0-06-500742-5*) Addson-Wesley Educ.

Short History of the American Nation, 2. John A. Garraty. (C). 1993. 19.00 (*0-06-501329-8*) Addson-Wesley Educ.

Short History of the American Nation, 2 vols., 2. 6th ed. John A. Garraty. (C). 1992. 22.50 (*0-06-500743-3*) Addson-Wesley Educ.

***Short History of the American Nation Chapters 1-16.** 7th ed. Garraty. (C). 1997. pap. text ed. 25.00 (*0-201-32640-X*) Addison-Wesley.

***Short History of the American Nation Chapters 17-32.** 7th ed. Garraty. (C). 1997. pap. text ed. 25.00 (*0-201-32641-8*) Addison-Wesley.

Short History of the American Negro. Benjamin G. Brawley. (History - United States Ser.). 288p. 1993. reprint ed. lib. bdg. 79.00 (*0-7812-4870-1*) Rprt Serv.

Short History of the American Revolution. James L. Stokesbury. LC 92-26180. 1993. pap. 10.00 (*0-688-12304-X*, Quill) Morrow.

Short History of the American Teilhard Association. Winifred McCulloch. 1979. pap. 3.00 (*0-89012-013-7*) Am Teilhard.

Short History of the Ancient Near East (Custom Pub) John Takanikos-Quinones & Barbara Takanikos. 1994. pap. text ed. write for info. (*0-07-052022-4*) McGraw.

Short History of the Arab Peoples. John Glubb. LC 69-16907. 1970. pap. 12.95 (*0-8128-1351-0*, Scrbrough Hse) Madison Bks UPA.

Short History of the Art of Distillation from the Beginnings up to the Death of Cellier Blumenthal. Robert J. Forbes. LC 79-8608. reprint ed. 41.00 (*0-404-18470-7*) AMS Pr.

Short History of the Baha'i Faith. Peter Smith. 160p. 1995. pap. 8.95 (*1-85168-070-5*) Onewrld Pubns.

Short History of the Bible. Bronson C. Keeler. 133p. 1965. reprint ed. spiral bd. 8.50 (*0-7873-0488-3*) Hlth Research.

Short History of the Bible Being a Popular Account of the Formation & Development of the Canon (1881) Bronson C. Keeler. 133p. 1996. pap. 16.95 (*1-56459-696-6*) Kessinger Pub.

***Short History of the British School at Rome.** T. P. Wiseman. (Illus.). 43p. 1990. pap. 11.50 (*0-904152-13-8*, Pub. by British Schl Rome UK) David Brown.

Short History of the Browntail Moth. William Curtis. 1969. 45.00 (*0-317-07175-0*) St Mut.

Short History of the Cartography of Africa. Jeffrey C. Stone. LC 95-14845. (African Studies: Vol. 39). (Illus.). 288p. 1995. text ed. 89.95 (*0-7734-8898-7*) E Mellen.

Short History of the Catholic Church. Denis Meadows. 246p. 1959. 14.95 (*0-8159-6813-2*) Devin.

Short History of the Catholic Church. Jose Orlandis. Tr. by Michael Adams from SPA. 163p. 1992. pap. 9.95 (*0-906127-86-6*, Pub. by Four Courts Pr IE) Scepter Pubs.

Short History of the Catholic Church. rev. ed. Ed. by J. Derek Holmes & B. W. Bickers. 320p. 1994. pap. 27.00 (*0-86012-211-5*, Pub. by Srch Pr UK) St Mut.

Short History of the Civil War. James L. Stokesbury. LC 95-7093. 320p. 1995. 25.00 (*0-688-11523-3*) Morrow.

***Short History of the Civil War.** James L. Stokesbury. 368p. 1997. pap. 14.00 (*0-688-15129-9*, Quill) Morrow.

***Short History of the Civil War: Ordeal by Fire.** Fletcher Pratt. LC 97-4264. (Illus.). 448p. 1997. reprint ed. pap. text ed. 11.95 (*0-486-29702-0*) Dover.

***Short History of the Coast.** Tony Gibbs. Date not set. write for info. (*0-688-10323-5*) Morrow.

Short History of the Early American Microscopes, Vol. 12. Donald L. Padgitt. LC 74-30750. (Illus.). 1975. 30.00 (*0-904962-04-0*) Microscope Pubns.

Short History of the Early Church. Harry R. Boer. LC 75-25742. 1976. pap. 12.00 (*0-8028-1339-9*) Eerdmans.

Short History of the English Colonies in America. Henry C. Lodge. 560p. (Orig.). 1995. pap. text ed. 35.00 (*0-7884-0189-0*) Heritage Bk.

Short History of the English Drama. Benjamin G. Brawley. LC 71-102227. (Select Bibliographies Reprint Ser.). 1977. 26.95 (*0-8369-5112-3*) Ayer.

Short History of the English Language. Torben Kisbye. Ed. by Knud Sorensen. 180p. (C). 1992. pap. 27.00 (*87-7288-406-1*, Pub. by Aarhus Univ Pr DK) David Brown.

Short History of the English Microscope, Vol. 11. Harold Malies. LC 80-83457. (Illus.). 1981. 20.00 (*0-904962-09-1*) Microscope Pubns.

Short History of the European Working Class. Wolfgang Abendroth. Tr. by Nicholas Jacobs & Brian Trench. LC 72-81766. 204p. 1972. reprint ed. pap. 58.20 (*0-7837-9614-5*, 2060371) Bks Demand.

Short History of the Franciscan Family. Damien Vorreux & Aaron Pembleton. 108p. 1989. pap. 4.95 (*0-8199-0955-6*, Frncscn Herld) Franciscan Pr.

Short History of the French Revolution. Jeremy D. Popkin. LC 94-35480. 240p. 1995. pap. text ed. 22.00 (*0-13-288424-0*) P-H Gen Ref & Trav.

***Short History of the French Revolution.** 2nd ed. Popkin. LC 97-11955. 1997. pap. text ed. 21.33 (*0-13-647421-7*) P-H.

Short History of the French Revolution, 1789-1799. Albert Soboul. Tr. by Geoffrey Symcox. 1977. pap. 11.00 (*0-520-03419-8*) U CA Pr.

Short History of the French Revolution 1789-1799. Albert Soboul. Tr. by Geoffrey Symcox. LC 77-152588. 198p. reprint ed. pap. 56.50 (*0-7837-4690-3*, 2044437) Bks Demand.

Short History of the Future. W. Warren Wagar. LC 89-32019. (Illus.). 338p. 1989. 29.95 (*0-226-86901-6*) U Ch Pr.

Short History of the Future. W. Warren Wagar. xiv, 340p. 1992. pap. 16.95 (*0-226-86902-4*) U Ch Pr.

Short History of the Georgian Church. Platon Ioseliani. 208p. 1983. reprint ed. pap. 6.00 (*0-317-30451-8*) Holy Trinity.

Short History of the German Language. W. Walker Chambers & John R. Wilkie. 1970. pap. 12.95 (*0-416-18220-8*, NO. 2130) Routledge Chapman & Hall.

Short History of the Glenview Art League. Robert T. Sherman. (Illus.). 31p. (Orig.). 1994. pap. 4.00 (*0-9613031-1-5*) R T Sherman.

Short History of the Gravel Springs Distillery & Bottling Works. Kenneth B. Farnsworth. LC 96-13950. (Kampsville Studies in Archeology & History: No. 2). 1996. pap. 10.00 (*0-942118-36-7*) Ctr Amer Arche.

Short History of the Indians of the United States. Edward H. Spicer. LC 83-11320. 320p. (C). 1984. reprint ed. pap. text ed. 16.50 (*0-89874-657-4*) Krieger.

Short History of the Interpretation of the Bible. 2nd enl. rev. ed. Robert M. Grant & David Tracy. LC 83-18485. 224p. 1984. pap. 16.00 (*0-8006-1762-2*, 1-1762, Fortress Pr) Augsburg Fortress.

Short History of the Jewish People. rev. ed. Cecil Roth. 1969. 14.95 (*0-685-05778-X*); pap. 6.95 (*0-87677-183-5*) Hartmore.

Short History of the Korean War. James L. Stokesbury. LC 89-39419. 276p. 1990. pap. 8.95 (*0-688-09513-5*, Quill) Morrow.

Short History of the Labour Party. 9th ed. Henry Pelling. 215p. 1991. text ed. 49.95 (*0-312-05272-3*) St Martin.

Short History of the Labour Party. 10th ed. Henry Pelling. LC 93-16705. (Illus.). 225p. 1993. text ed. 45.00 (*0-312-09676-3*) St Martin.

Short History of the Labour Party. 11th ed. Henry Pelling & Alistair J. Reid. 224p. 1996. text ed. 59.95 (*0-312-15934-X*, Pub. by E Arnold UK) St Martin.

Short History of the Liberal Party, 1900-1984. 2nd ed. Chris Cook. write for info. (*0-318-59186-3*) Macmillan.

Short History of the Long Ball. Justin Cronin. LC 90-80294. (National Novella Winner Ser.). 91p. 1995. 12.95 (*0-933031-23-8*) Coun Oak Bks.

Short History of the Mississippi Valley. James K. Hosmer. (Notable American Authors Ser.). 1992. reprint ed. lib. bdg. 75.00 (*0-7812-3179-5*) Rprt Serv.

Short History of the Movies. 5th ed. Gerald Mast. 562p. 1992. 35.00 (*0-02-580510-X*) Macmillan.

Short History of the Movies. 6th ed. Gerald Mast. LC 95-35138. (Illus.). 1996. pap. text ed. 48.00 (*0-02-377075-9*, Macmillan Coll) P-H.

Short History of the Printed Word. Warren Chappell. 1981. 19.95 (*0-405-13093-7*) Ayer.

***Short History of the Roman Mass.** Michael Davies. 50p. 1996. pap. 2.00 (*0-89555-546-8*) TAN Bks Pubs.

Short History of the Romantic Movement in Spain. Edgar A. Peers. LC 76-28478. reprint ed. 32.50 (*0-404-15034-9*) AMS Pr.

Short History of the Saracens. A. A. Syed. 702p. 1984. 360.00 (*1-85077-034-4*, Pub. by Darf Pubs Ltd UK) St Mut.

***Short History of the Shadow.** Victor I. Stoichita. (Essays in Art & Culture Ser.). (Illus.). 264p. 1997. pap. 24.95 (*1-86189-000-1*, Pub. by Reaktion Bks UK) Consort Bk Sales.

Short History of the Slocums, Slocumbs, & Slocombs of America, Genealogy & Biography from 1637 to 1881, Vol. I. Charles E. Slocum. (Illus.). 644p. 1989. reprint ed. pap. 96.50 (*0-8328-1079-7*); reprint ed. lib. bdg. 104.50 (*0-8328-1078-9*) Higginson Bk Co.

Short History of the Slocums, Slocumbs & Slocombs of America, Vol. II: Supplement. (Illus.). 549p. 1989. reprint ed. pap. 86.00 (*0-8328-6581-8*); reprint ed. lib. bdg. 96.00 (*0-8328-6580-X*) Higginson Bk Co.

Short History of the Twelve Buddhist Sects. Tr. by Bunyiu Nanjio from JPN. LC 79-52924. (Studies in Japanese History & Civilization). 172p. 1979. reprint ed. text ed. 59.95 (*0-313-26989-0*, U6989, Greenwood Pr) Greenwood.

Short History of the Twelve Japanese Buddhist Sects. Compiled by Bunyiu Nanjio. LC 78-70104. reprint ed. 37.50 (*0-404-17355-1*) AMS Pr.

Short History of the Universe. Joseph Silk. LC 94-21771. 1995. text ed. write for info. (*0-7167-5048-1*) W H Freeman.

***Short History of the Universe.** Joseph Silk. (Illus.). 246p. 1997. pap. 19.95 (*0-7167-6020-7*) W H Freeman.

Short History of the University of Michigan. Wilfred B. Shaw. 1934. 19.50 (*0-911586-31-8*) Wahr.

Short History of the Vietnam War. Ed. by Allan R. Millett. LC 77-23623. 189p. reprint ed. pap. 54.50 (*0-7837-1758-X*, 2057294) Bks Demand.

Short History of the Western Liturgy. 2nd ed. Theodor Klauser. Tr. by John Halliburton from GER. 250p. 1979. pap. text ed. 16.95 (*0-19-213223-7*) OUP.

Short History of the Westminster Assembly. William Beveridge. 160p. (C). 1993. pap. text ed. 10.95 (*1-884416-00-4*) A Press.

***Short History of the World.** J. M. Roberts. LC 96-49811. 544p. 1997. reprint ed. pap. text ed. 14.95 (*0-19-511504-X*) OUP.

Short History of Tompkins County. Jane M. Dieckmann. LC 85-25440. (Illus.). 229p. (Orig.). 1986. 16.95 (*0-942690-34-6*); pap. 9.95 (*0-942690-33-8*) DeWitt Hist.

Short History of Tuberculosis. George N. Meachen. LC 75-23738. reprint ed. 31.50 (*0-404-13295-2*) AMS Pr.

Short History of Vertebrate Palaeontology. Eric Buffetaut. (Illus.). 256p. 1987. 65.00 (*0-7099-3962-0*, Pub. by Croom Helm UK) Routledge Chapman & Hall.

Short History of Western Civilization. 8th ed. Richard E. Sullivan et al. LC 93-14409. 1994. text ed. write for info. (*0-07-026897-5*) McGraw.

Short History of Western Civilization, 1. 8th ed. Richard E. Sullivan et al. LC 93-42015. 1994. pap. text ed. write for info. (*0-07-026899-1*) McGraw.

Short History of Western Civilization, Set. 7th ed. John B. Harrison et al. (Illus.). 832p. 1990. text ed. write for info. (*0-07-557080-7*) McGraw.

Short History of Western Civilization, Vol. 2. 8th ed. Richard E. Sullivan et al. LC 93-42015. 1994. pap. text ed. write for info. (*0-07-026900-9*) McGraw.

Short History of Western Civilization: Renaissance to the Present, Vol. 3. 8th ed. Richard E. Sullivan et al. LC 93-42399. 1994. pap. text ed. write for info. (*0-07-026901-7*) McGraw.

Short History of Western Civilization Vol. I: To 1776. 8th ed. Joyce E. Salisbury. 1994. student ed., pap. text ed. write for info. (*0-07-026902-5*) McGraw.

Short History of Western Legal Theory. John M. Kelly. 388p. 1992. 75.00 (*0-19-876244-5*); pap. 35.00 (*0-19-876243-7*) OUP.

***Short History of Women.** Linda G. Depauw. Date not set. write for info. (*0-688-10641-2*) Morrow.

Short History of Women's Rights. 2nd rev. ed. Eugene A. Hecker. LC 72-98839. 313p. 1971. reprint ed. text ed. 59.75 (*0-8371-3106-5*, HEWR, Greenwood Pr) Greenwood.

Short History of World War I. James L. Stokesbury. LC 80-22207. (Illus.). 352p. 1981. pap. 11.00 (*0-688-00129-7*, Quill) Morrow.

Short History of World War Two. James L. Stokesbury. LC 79-20896. (Illus.). 1980. pap. 11.50 (*0-688-08587-3*, Quill) Morrow.

Short History of Writing Instruction: From Ancient Greece to Twentieth-Century America. Ed. by James J. Murphy. (Illus.). 241p. (Orig.). (C). 1990. 19.50 (*0-9611800-7-2*, Hermagoras); pap. 12.95 (*0-9611800-6-4*, Hermagoras) L Erlbaum Assocs.

Short Hours, Short Shrift: Causes & Consequences of Part-Time Work. Chris Tilly. (Studies). 44p. 1990. 10.00 (*0-944826-29-6*) Economic Policy Inst.

Short "i" & Long "i" Play a Game. Jane B. Moncure. LC 79-10303. (Sound Box Library). (Illus.). 32p. (J). (ps-2). 1979. lib. bdg. 21.36 (*0-89565-091-6*) Childs World.

Short Introduction to English Grammar. Robert Lowth. LC 79-4675. (American Linguistics Ser.). 1979. reprint ed. lib. bdg. 50.00 (*0-8201-1332-8*) Schol Facsimiles.

***Short Introduction to Islamic Philosophy, Theology & Mysticism.** Majid Fakhry. 1997. pap. 13.95 (*1-85168-134-5*) Onewrld Pubns.

***Short Introduction to Judaism.** Lavinia Cohn-Sherbok & Dan Cohn-Sherbok. 1997. pap. 13.95 (*1-85168-145-0*) Onewrld Pubns.

Short Introduction to Modal Logic. Grigori Mints. LC 92-2924. (Center for the Study of Language & Information-Lecture Notes Ser.: No. 30). 112p. (Orig.). (C). 1992. text ed. 44.95 (*0-937073-76-8*); pap. text ed. 15.95 (*0-937073-75-X*) CSLI.

Short Introduction to Moral Philosophy. Francis Hutcheson. LC 78-67529. (Scottish Enlightenment Ser.). reprint ed. 34.50 (*0-404-17194-X*) AMS Pr.

Short Introduction to Moral Philosophy, in Three Books: Containing the Elements of Ethicks & the Law of Nature. Francis Hutcheson. Ed. by Bernhard Fabian. (Collected Works: Vol. IV). 347p. 1990. reprint ed. 63.70 (*3-487-02255-9*) G Olms Pubs.

Short Introduction to the Ancient Greek Theater. Graham Ley. (Illus.). 118p. 1991. pap. 6.95 (*0-226-47760-6*) U Ch Pr.

Short Introduction to the Apostles Creed. Bruno Forte. 123p. 1994. pap. 11.50 (*0-85439-464-8*, Pub. by St Paul Pubns UK) St Mut.

***Short Introduction to the Bahai Faith.** Moojan Momen. 180p. 1997. pap. 11.95 (*1-85168-120-5*) Onewrld Pubns.

Short Introduction to the Catholic Church. Severino Dianich. 110p. 1994. pap. 11.50 (*0-85439-490-7*, Pub. by St Paul Pubns UK) St Mut.

Short Introduction to the Old Testament Prophets. E. W. Heaton. 200p. 1996. pap. 13.99 (*1-85168-114-0*) Onewrld Pubns.

Short Introduction to X-Bar Syntax & Transformations. Thomas Walsh. 67p. (C). 1995. pap. text ed. 10.95 (*0-9644636-2-8*) Parlay Enter.

Short Latin Stories. Philip Dunlop. 72p. 1987. pap. text ed. 10.95 (*0-521-31592-1*) Cambridge U Pr.

Short Learn Clarisworks. Date not set. pap. text ed. 21.95 (*0-314-04041-2*) West Pub.

Short Legs Tall. TV Associates Self Esteem Staff. (Simply Grand Quigley's Band Ser.: Vol. 7). 1995. pap. 12.99 (*0-310-24469-2*) Zondervan.

Short Lexicon of Alchemy: Explaining the Chief Terms Used by Paracelsus & Other Hermetic Philosophers. A. E. Waite. 1990. pap. 6.95 (*1-55818-164-4*) Holmes Pub.

Short Life of Christ. Everett F. Harrison. (Highlights in the Life of Christ Ser.). 1968. pap. 16.00 (*0-8028-1824-2*) Eerdmans.

Short Life of Kierkegaard. Walter Lowrie. 284p. 1942. pap. text ed. 15.95 (*0-691-01957-6*) Princeton U Pr.

Short Life of Sri Ramakrishna. Tejasananda Swami. 114p. 1988. pap. 1.50 (*0-87481-081-7*, Pub. by Advaita Ashrama II) Vedanta Pr.

Short Life of Swami Vivekananda. Swami Tejasananda. pap. 1.50 (*0-87481-091-4*, Pub. by Advaita Ashrama II) Vedanta Pr.

***Short Life of the ASTP.** Francis N. Iglehart. LC 97-72032. 112p. (Orig.). 1997. pap. 10.50 (*1-56167-377-3*) Am Literary Pr.

Short Life of the Five Minute Dancer. Barry Wallenstein. (Illus.). 64p. (Orig.). (C). 1993. pap. 7.95 (*1-56439-028-4*) Ridgeway.

Short Life of the Holy Mother. Swami Pavitrananananda. pap. 1.50 (*0-87481-122-8*, Pub. by Advaita Ashrama II) Vedanta Pr.

Short Line to Cripple Creek. Tivis E. Wilkins. LC 70-102682. (Colorado Rail Annual Ser.: No. 16). (Illus.). 180p. 1983. 29.95 (*0-918654-16-5*) CO RR Mus.

Short-Line War. Samuel Merwin & Henry K. Webster. LC 67-29273. (Americans in Fiction Ser.). 340p. reprint ed. pap. text ed. 5.95 (*0-89197-935-2*); reprint ed. lib. bdg. 29.50 (*0-8398-1256-6*) Irvington.

Short Lines: Classic American Railroad Stories. Illus. by Ron Hazlitt. 256p. 1996. 23.95 (*0-312-14046-0*) St Martin.

Short-Lived Exploration of Isadore Meyerowitz. Rosaline Levenson. LC 94-77679. (Illus.). 80p. (Orig.). 1994. pap. 9.95 (*0-936029-35-8*) Western Bk Journ.

Short-Lived Radionuclides in Chemistry & Biology. Ed. by John W. Root & Kenneth A. Krohn. LC 81-19148. (Advances in Chemistry Ser.: No. 197). 1982. 80.95 (*0-8412-0603-1*) Am Chemical.

***Short-Lived Radionuclides in Chemistry & Biology.** Ed. by John W. Root & Kenneth A. Krohn. LC 81-19148. (Advances in Chemistry Ser.: Vol. 197). 562p. 1981. reprint ed. pap. 160.20 (*0-608-03502-5*, 2064221) Bks Demand.

Short Log & Timber Book see Log & Timber Home Building: Using the Post & Beam Modular Method

Short Lyric Poems of Jean Froissart: Fixed Forms of the Expression of the Courtly Ideal. Kristen M. Figg. LC 93-38223. (Studies in Medieval Literature: Vol. 10). 304p. 1994. text ed. 20.00 (*0-8153-1351-9*, H1749) Garland.

Short Meditations, 3 vols., Set. J. G. Bellett. pap. 12.95 (*0-88172-003-8*) Believers Bkshelf.

Short Meditations on the Bible & Peanuts. Robert L. Short. (Illus.). 128p. (Orig.). 1990. pap. 10.00 (*0-664-25152-8*) Westminster John Knox.

Short Meditations on the Bible & Peanuts, 12 bks., Set. Robert L. Short. (Illus.). 128p. (Orig.). 1990. pap. 110.00 (*0-664-25240-0*) Westminster John Knox.

Short Modern Dances in Labanotation. Nadia Chilkovsky. (Illus.). 35p. 1957. pap. text ed. 10.00 (*0-932582-67-2*, Pub. by Dance Bks UK) Princeton Bk Co.

***Short Money.** Pete Hautman. 1997. mass mkt. 5.99 (*0-671-00303-8*) PB.

Short Money: A Novel. Pete Hautman. LC 94-47963. 1995. 21.00 (*0-684-80211-2*) S&S Trade.

Short Narrative of the Horrid Massacre in Boston: Perpetrated in the Evening of the Fifth Day of March, Seventeen Seventy, by Soldiers of the Twenty Ninth Regiment. Boston Staff. LC 71-150170. (Select Bibliographies Reprint Ser.). 1977. reprint ed. 23.95 (*0-8369-5683-4*) Ayer.

S

An Asterisk (*) at the beginning of an entry indicates that the title is appearing in BIP for the first time.

Short Narrative of the Life & Actions of His Grace John, D. of Marlborough. Daniel Defoe. LC 92-23651. (Augustan Reprints Ser.: No. 168). 1974. reprint ed. 14. 50 (*0-404-70168-X*, DA462) AMS Pr.

***Short Nature Walks in Connecticut.** 5th ed. Eugene Keyarts. Ed. by Carolyn Battista. LC 96-50082. (Short Nature Walks Ser.). (Illus.). 176p. 1997. pap. 9.95 (*0-7627-0079-3*) Globe Pequot.

Short Nature Walks on Cape Cod, Nantucket, & the Vineyard. 5th ed. Hugh Sadlier & Heather Sadlier. Ed. by Karl Luntta. LC 95-38794. (Short Nature Walks Ser.). 128p. 1996. pap. 9.95 (*1-56440-894-9*) Globe Pequot.

Short Nature Walks on Long Island. 5th ed. Rodney Albright & Priscilla Albright. LC 95-43039. (Short Nature Walks Ser.). 176p. 1996. pap. 9.95 (*1-56440-895-7*) Globe Pequot.

Short Novels. Leo Tolstoy. Ed. & Intro. by Ernest J. Simmons. LC 65-12448. 1979. 8.95 (*0-394-60482-2*, Modern Lib) Random.

Short Novels & Other Writings. Theodor Fontane. Ed. by Peter Demetz. LC 81-17505. (German Library: Vol. 46). 326p. 1982. 29.50 (*0-8264-0250-X*); pap. text ed. 16.95 (*0-8264-0260-7*) Continuum.

Short Novels of John Steinbeck: Critical Essays. Ed. by Jackson J. Benson. LC 89-27255. 360p. (Orig.). (C). 1990. pap. text ed. 22.95 (*0-8223-0994-7*) Duke.

Short Novels of the Masters. Intro. by Charles Neider. 642p. (C). 1989. pap. 12.95 (*0-88184-487-X*) Carroll & Graf.

Short Novels of the Masters. Ed. & Intro. by Charles Neider. 656p. 1996. pap. 15.95 (*0-7867-0324-5*) Carroll & Graf.

Short Novels of Thomas Wolfe. Thomas Wolfe. LC 75-35061. (Hudson River Editions Ser.). 324p. 1976. reprint ed. 40.00 (*0-684-14554-5*) S&S Trade.

Short "o" & Long "o" Play a Game. Jane B. Moncure. LC 79-10304. (Sound Box Library). (Illus.). 32p. (J). (ps-2). 1979. lib. bdg. 21.36 (*0-89565-092-4*) Childs World.

***Short Orders: Writings on Film.** Jonathan Romney. 1998. pap. text ed. 16.00 (*1-85242-512-1*) Serpents Tail.

Short Oxford History of English Literature. Andrew Sanders. LC 93-32330. 688p. 1994. 39.95 (*0-19-811202-5*, Old Oregon Bk Store) OUP.

Short Oxford History of English Literature. rev. ed. Andrew Sanders. 680p. 1996. pap. 17.95 (*0-19-871156-5*) OUP.

Short Papers of the U. S. Geological Survey Uranium Workshop. Ed. by Kendell A. Dickinson. (Illus.). 56p. (Orig.). (C). 1993. pap. text ed. 30.00 (*1-56806-325-3*) DIANE Pub.

Short Papers on American Liberal Education. Andrew F. West. LC 73-165745. (American Education Series 2). 1978. reprint ed. 18.95 (*0-405-03616-7*) Ayer.

***Short Parliamentary Diary of Sir Thomas Aston 1640.** J. D. Maltby. (Camden Fourth Ser.). 27.00 (*0-86193-116-5*) David Brown.

Short Path. C. H. Harvey. LC 96-90081. 1996. 12.95 (*0-533-11883-2*) Vantage.

Short Pathwaye to the Ryghte & True Understanding of the Holye & Sacred Scriptures. Ulrich Zwingli. Tr. by J. Veron. LC 77-7443. (English Experience Ser.: No. 901). 1977. reprint ed. lib. bdg. 35.00 (*90-221-0901-1*) Walter J Johnson.

***Short People Who Made it Big: A Short History.** Joan K. Slomanson. LC 97-9911. 1998. write for info. (*0-7892-0333-2*) Abbeville Pr.

Short Pieces from the New Dramatists. Ed. by Stan Chervin. 92p. (Orig.). 1985. pap. 5.95 (*0-88145-029-4*) Broadway Play.

Short Plays see Oxford Chekhov

Short Plays & Monologues. David Mamet. 1981. pap. 5.25 (*0-8222-0720-6*) Dramatists Play.

Short Plays & Sketches. David Mamet. Date not set. pap. write for info. (*0-679-76940-4*) Random.

***Short Plays for Teen Audiences Vol. 2: Basic Drama Sketches.** Judy Miller. 1992. pap. 8.95 (*1-57514-019-5*) Encore Perform Pub.

Short Plays for Young Actors. Ed. by Craig Slaight & Jack Sharrar. (Young Actors Ser.). 256p. (YA). (gr. 9 up). 1996. pap. 16.95 (*1-880399-74-1*) Smith & Kraus.

Short Plays of Theatre Classics. Selected by Aurand Harris. (YA). 1991. 30.00 (*0-87602-032-5*) Anchorage.

Short Poems by a Short Person (In Ascending Order) Leanne Grabel. 42p. (Orig.). 1996. pap. 4.00 (*1-882550-18-8*) Quiet Lion Pr.

Short Practical Russian Grammar. I. G. Miloslavskii. 244p. (ENG & RUS.). (C). 1988. 45.00 (*0-685-39367-4*) Collets.

***Short Practice of Anaesthesia.** G. Hall & M. Morgan. 784p. 1997. 119.95 (*0-412-71890-1*) Chapman & Hall.

***Short Practice of Spinal Surgery.** 2nd ed. Henry V. Crock. (Illus.). 319p. 1993. 154.00 (*3-211-82351-4*) Spr-Verlag.

Short Practice of Spinal Surgery. 2nd rev. ed. Henry V. Crock. LC 92-48889. (Illus.). 344p. 1993. 169.00 (*0-387-82351-4*) Spr-Verlag.

Short Prayers for the Long Day. Compiled by Giles Harcourt & Melville Harcourt. LC 96-12966. 256p. 1996. pap. 11.00 (*0-89243-929-7*, Triumph Books) Liguori Pubns.

Short Preludes & Fugues for Piano. Johann Sebastian Bach. (Carl Fischer Music Library: No. 516). 1914. pap. 6.95 (*0-8258-0132-X*, L516) Fischer Inc NY.

Short Primer for Unsettled Laymen. Hans U. Von Balthasar. Tr. by Michael Waldstein from GER. LC 84-81790. 134p. (Orig.). 1985. pap. 9.95 (*0-89870-037-X*) Ignatius Pr.

Short Prose: An Illustrated Essay. M. Kasper. Ed. by Gloria V. Hickok. 6p. (Orig.). 1994. pap. 2.50 (*1-884235-05-0*) Helicon Nine Eds.

Short Prose Reader. Funk & Day. LC 96-2772. 448p. (C). 1996. pap. text ed. 28.00 (*0-13-205584-8*) P-H.

Short Prose Reader. 6th ed. Harvey S. Wiener & Gilbert H. Muller. 1991. pap. text ed. write for info. (*0-07-044135-9*) McGraw.

Short Prose Reader. 7th ed. Ed. by Harvey S. Wiener. LC 93-29710. 1993. pap. text ed. write for info. (*0-07-044249-5*) McGraw.

Short Prose Reader. 8th ed. Gilbert H. Muller & Harvey S. Wiener. LC 96-24813. 1996. pap. text ed. write for info. (*0-07-044016-6*) McGraw.

Short Protocols in Molecular Biology. 2nd ed. Ed. by Frederick M. Ausubel et al. 740p. 1992. pap. text ed. 79. 95 (*0-471-57735-9*) Wiley.

Short Protocols in Molecular Biology: A Compendium of Methods from Current Protocols in Molecular Biology. 3rd ed. Roger Brent et al. Ed. by Frederick M. Ausubel. 900p. 1995. pap. text ed. 79.95 (*0-471-13781-2*) Wiley.

Short Race: Late Intermediate. J. Tiner. 4p. 1994. pap. 3.95 (*0-7935-3639-1*, 00290466) H Leonard.

Short Range Radio Telemetry for Rotating Instrumentation. Joseph H. Valentich. LC 77-78670. (Illus.). 156p. reprint ed. pap. 44.50 (*0-7837-5146-X*, 2044874) Bks Demand.

Short Reader in Judaism. Lavinia Cohn-Sherbok & Dan Cohn-Sherbok. 191p. 1996. pap. 14.99 (*1-85168-112-4*, 573) Onewrld Pubns.

Short Reference Grammar of Moroccan Arabic. Richard S. Harrell. (Richard Slade Harrell Arabic Ser.). 263p. 1962. pap. 11.95 (*0-87840-006-0*); audio 5.00 (*0-87840-016-8*) Georgetown U Pr.

Short Reign of Pippin IV. John Steinbeck. 176p. 1977. mass mkt. 4.95 (*0-14-004290-3*, Penguin Bks) Viking Penguin.

Short Reign of Pippin IV. John Steinbeck. 176p. 1994. pap. 10.95 (*0-14-018749-9*, Penguin Classics) Viking Penguin.

Short Residence in Sweden & Memoirs. Mary Wollstonecraft Shelley & William Godwin. 320p. 1987. pap. 11.95 (*0-14-043269-8*, Penguin Classics) Viking Penguin.

***Short Route to Chaos: Conscience, Community, & the Re-Constitution of American Schooling.** Stephen Arons. LC 96-51512. 232p. 1997. pap. 14.95 (*1-55849-078-7*); lib. bdg. 40.00 (*1-55849-077-9*) U of Mass Pr.

Short Run SPC. Donald J. Wheeler. 72p. (Orig.). (C). 1991. pap. text ed. 15.00 (*0-945320-12-4*) SPC Pr.

Short Russian-English Business Dictionary. I. F. Zhdanova. 175p. (C). pap. text ed. 8.95 (*0-8285-4994-X*) Firebird NY.

Short Russian Grammar. I. M. Pulkina. 352p. 1984. 65.00 (*0-317-42778-4*) St Mut.

Short Russian Reference Grammar. 2nd ed. I. M. Pulkina. Ed. by P. S. Kuznetsov. ii, 354p. 1969. text ed. 72.00 (*0-677-20820-0*) Gordon & Breach.

Short Scenes from Shakespeare: Nineteen Cuttings for the Classroom. William Shakespeare. Ed. by Samuel Selden. LC 93-4582. 144p. 1993. pap. 10.00 (*0-88734-632-4*) Players Pr.

Short Sea Shipping. OECD Staff. 128p. (Orig.). 1993. pap. 21.00 (*92-821-1181-4*) OECD.

Short Sea Shipping. David Tinsley. 225p. 1991. pap. 225.00 (*1-85044-355-6*) LLP.

Short Season & Other Stories. Jerry Klinkowitz. LC 87-46311. (Poetry & Fiction Ser.). 208p. 1988. 16.95 (*0-8018-3614-X*) Johns Hopkins.

Short Season Between Two Silences. Madeline Moore. (Illus.). 240p. (C). 1984. text ed. 39.95 (*0-04-800022-1*) Routledge Chapman & Hall.

Short Season Between Two Silences: The Mystical & the Political in the Novels of Virginia Woolf. Madeline Moore. 216p. 1986. pap. text ed. 12.95 (*0-04-800098-1*) Routledge Chapman & Hall.

Short Season Flowering Plants. S. P. Singh. 254p. (C). 1987. 100.00 (*0-317-92319-6*, Pub. by Scientific UK) St Mut.

Short Selling. James E. Meeker. LC 75-2648. (Wall Street & the Security Market Ser.). 1975. reprint ed. 25.95 (*0-405-06973-1*) Ayer.

Short Sermons for Worship: One Hundred Fifty Bible-Based Themes, Vol. 2. Richard A. Brown. 160p. (Orig.). 1990. pap. text ed. 12.00 (*0-8309-0632-0*) Herald Hse.

Short, Sharp Knock. Kim S. Robinson. 176p. 1996. reprint ed. mass mkt. 5.99 (*0-553-57461-2*, Spectra) Bantam.

Short Sharp Shock. Kim S. Robinson. 160p. 1990. 18.00 (*0-929480-18-X*) Mark Ziesing.

Short Sharp Shock. limited ed. Kim S. Robinson. 160p. 1990. 45.00 (*0-929480-19-8*) Mark Ziesing.

Short, Sharp Shock & The Dragon Masters. Jack Vance & Kim S. Robinson. 1990. pap. 3.50 (*0-8125-0895-5*) Tor Bks.

Short Short Short Stories. Accorsi. 1995. 3.98 (*0-8317-1111-6*) Smithmark.

Short, Short Stories. Ed. by Jack David & Jon Redfern. 202p. (C). 1986. pap. 12.00 (*0-920763-98-7*, Pub. by ECW Press CN) Genl Dist Srvs.

Short Shorts. Ed. by Ilana W. Howe. 288p. 1983. mass mkt. 4.99 (*0-553-27440-6*, Bantam Classics) Bantam.

Short-Shorts: A Couple of Dozen Stories. Elizabeth B. Hill. LC 92-93280. (Illus.). 121p. (Orig.). 1992. pap. 5.95 (*0-9632163-0-9*) D Scouten.

Short Shots..A Drill a Day: The Easy Way to Language Literacy. 2nd ed. James A. Kleman. 44p. (J). (gr. 4-8). 1982. student ed. 5.00 (*0-938464-09-4*) JML Enter MD.

Short Shrift. Bill Yake. (Wind Room Ser.: No. 7). 16p. (Orig.). 1996. pap. 4.00 (*1-887853-10-3*) Radiolarian.

***Short Sicilian Novels.** Giovanni Verga. 171p. pap. 11.95 (*1-873982-40-2*, Pub. by Dedalus Bks UK) Hippocrene Bks.

Short Sixes: Stories to Be Read While the Candle Burns. Henry C. Bunner. 1972. reprint ed. lib. bdg. 27.00 (*0-8422-8014-6*) Irvington.

Short Sketch of Tajik Grammar. Ed. & Tr. by Herbert H. Paper. LC 64-63907. (General Publications). 1993. reprint ed. 19.90 (*0-933070-28-4*) Res Inst Inner Asian Studies.

Short Sketch of the Evolution of the Bungalow see California Bungalows of the Twenties

***Short Stature: From Folklore to Fact.** Elaine Landau. LC 96-42347. (First Bks.). 1997. lib. bdg. 21.00 (*0-531-20265-8*) Watts.

Short Stop. Zane Grey. 298p. reprint ed. lib. bdg. 22.95 (*0-89190-760-2*, Rivercity Pr) Amereon Ltd.

***Short Stories.** Agnes Adachi. LC 95-94393. (Orig.). (YA). (gr. 9-12). 1995. pap. 10.00 (*0-9621930-2-X*) A Adachi.

Short Stories. Ed. by Joseph Blotner. (William Faulkner Manuscripts). 552p. 1987. text ed. 70.00 (*0-8240-6836-X*) Garland.

Short Stories. Harold Brodkey. 1996. write for info. (*0-8050-4832-4*) H Holt & Co.

Short Stories. Ed. by Constance C. Harrison. LC 71-94731. (Short Story Index Reprint Ser.). 1977. 19.95 (*0-8369-3111-4*) Ayer.

***Short Stories.** Ernest Hemingway. LC 96-53349. 1997. 27. 50 (*0-684-83786-2*, Scribners PB Fict) S&S Trade.

Short Stories. Aramais Hovsepian. 144p. 1984. pap. 5.95 (*0-933706-24-3*) Ararat Pr.

Short Stories. Langston Hughes. Ed. by Akiba S. Harper. 299p. 1996. 25.00 (*0-8090-8658-1*) Hill & Wang.

***Short Stories.** Langston Hughes. 1997. pap. text ed. 14.00 (*0-8090-1603-6*) Hill & Wang.

Short Stories. A. M. Klein. Ed. by M. W. Steinberg. (Collected Works of A. M. Klein). 344p. 1983. 40.00 (*0-8020-5598-2*); pap. 18.95 (*0-8020-6469-8*) U of Toronto Pr.

Short Stories. Roxana Robinson. Date not set. pap. 17.95 (*0-670-82792-4*) Viking Penguin.

Short Stories. Roxana Robinson. Date not set. pap. write for info. (*0-14-012147-1*) Viking Penguin.

Short Stories. Anita B. Rothgeb. LC 95-67130. 1995. 8.95 (*0-8158-0512-8*) Chris Mass.

Short Stories. Hjalmar Soderberg. Tr. by Carl Lofmark from SWE. LC 88-60363. 150p. 8800. pap. 18.95 (*1-870041-03-8*, Pub. by Norvik Pr UK) Dufour.

Short Stories. Linda Stewart & Paul Champanier. Ed. by J. Friedland & R. Kessler. (Novel-Ties Ser.). 1989. student ed., pap. text ed. 15.95 (*0-88122-865-6*) Lrn Links.

Short Stories. Warriner. 1981. text ed. 28.25 (*0-15-348340-7*); teacher ed., pap. text ed. 9.00 (*0-15-348341-5*) HR&W Schl Div.

Short Stories. rev. ed. George Meredith. LC 73-144162. (Short Story Index Reprint Ser.). 1977. reprint ed. 20.95 (*0-8369-3777-5*) Ayer.

Short Stories. unabridged ed. Louisa May Alcott. (Thrift Editions Ser.). 64p. 1996. pap. text ed. 1.00 (*0-486-29063-8*) Dover.

Short Stories. unabridged ed. Andreev. (World Classic Literature Ser.). (RUS.). pap. 8.95 (*2-87714-276-0*, Pub. by Bookking Intl FR) Distribks Inc.

Short Stories. unabridged ed. Anton P. Chekhov. (World Classic Literature Ser.). (RUS.). pap. 8.95 (*2-87714-277-9*, Pub. by Bookking Intl FR) Distribks Inc.

Short Stories. unabridged ed. Theodore Dreiser. (Thrift Editions Ser.). 96p. (Orig.). 1994. reprint ed. pap. text ed. 1.00 (*0-486-28215-5*) Dover.

Short Stories. unabridged ed. Leskov. (World Classic Literature Ser.). (RUS.). pap. 8.95 (*2-87714-273-6*, Pub. by Bookking Intl FR) Distribks Inc.

Short Stories. unabridged ed. Tolstoi. (World Classic Literature Ser.). (RUS.). pap. 8.95 (*2-87714-274-4*, Pub. by Bookking Intl FR) Distribks Inc.

Short Stories. unabridged ed. Edith Wharton. LC 94-32905. (Thrift Editions Ser.). 112p. 1994. pap. text ed. 1.00 (*0-486-28235-X*) Dover.

Short Stories. Conrad P. Aiken. LC 72-178434. (Short Story Index Reprint Ser.). 1977. reprint ed. 29.95 (*0-8369-4034-2*) Ayer.

Short Stories, 10 Vols. Alexandre Dumas. LC 72-5898. (Short Story Index Reprint Ser.). 1977. reprint ed. 55.95 (*0-8369-4212-4*) Ayer.

Short Stories. Louis C. Schroeter. 169p. reprint ed. pap. 48. 20 (*0-7837-6500-2*, AU00441) Bks Demand.

Short Stories, Pt. 1, Texts. Ed. by James A. Bellamy et al. xiii, 93p. 1963. write for info. (*0-318-51708-6*) UM Dept NES.

Short Stories, Pt. 2, Notes & Glossaries. Ed. by James A. Bellamy et al. 1963. write for info. (*0-318-51709-4*) UM Dept NES.

Short Stories, 2 pts., Set. Ed. by James A. Bellamy et al. (Contemporary Arabic Readers Ser.: Vol. IV). (ARA.). 1963. 19.95 (*0-916798-14-3*) Intl Bk Ctr.

Short Stories: Reading, Thinking, Writing. 2nd rev. ed. Richard Panman & Sandra Panman. Ed. by Linda Gluck. (Illus.). 192p. 1995. pap. text ed. 10.95 (*0-912813-23-7*) Active Lrn.

Short Stories: The First Forty-Nine Stories with a Brief Introduction by the Author. Ernest Hemingway. 1995. pap. 14.00 (*0-684-80334-8*) S&S Trade.

Short Stories: The Pedlar's Revenge. Liam O'Flaherty. 1991. pap. 10.95 (*0-86327-225-8*) Dufour.

Short Stories see Houghton Books in Literature

Short Stories about States & Capitals. Edward T. Garrison, Jr. (Illus.). (J). (gr. 5 up). write for info. (*0-9634033-0-3*) E G Photoprint.

Short Stories & Other. Lyndon Teeples. 89p. 1988. 12.95 (*1-888129-03-4*) Story Pubng.

Short Stories & The Unbearable Bassington. Saki. Ed. by John Carey. LC 93-45276. (World's Classics WC Ser.). 336p. 1994. pap. 9.95 (*0-19-283169-0*) OUP.

Short Stories Are Not Real Life. David R. Slavitt. LC 91-18913. 184p. 1991. 18.95 (*0-8071-1665-3*) La State U Pr.

***Short Stories by Charles Dickens.** Ed. by Mike Royston. (Thornes Classic Short Stories Ser.). (Orig.). 1997. pap. 10.95 (*0-7487-3095-8*, Pub. by Stanley Thornes UK) Trans-Atl Phila.

Short Stories by Cubena. Ian I. Smart. LC 86-71821. 103p. (Orig.). 1987. pap. 7.50 (*0-939423-00-6*) Afro Hispanic Inst.

***Short Stories by Edgar Allen Poe.** Ed. by Mike Royston. (Thornes Classic Short Stories Ser.). (Orig.). 1997. pap. 10.95 (*0-7487-3096-6*, Pub. by Stanley Thornes UK) Trans-Atl Phila.

***Short Stories by H. G. Wells.** Ed. by Mike Royston. (Thornes Classic Short Stories Ser.). (Orig.). 1997. pap. 10.95 (*0-7487-3132-6*, Pub. by Stanley Thornes UK) Trans-Atl Phila.

Short Stories by Latin American Women: The Magic & the Real. 2nd ed. Ed. by Celia C. De Zapata. LC 89-36298. 224p. 1990. pap. 13.50 (*1-55885-002-3*) Arte Publico.

Short Stories by Marjorie Kinnan Rawlings. Marjorie K. Rawlings. Ed. by Rodger L. Tarr. LC 93-30649. (Illus.). 392p. (C). 1994. pap. 24.95 (*0-8130-1253-8*); lib. bdg. 44.95 (*0-8130-1252-X*) U Press Fla.

Short Stories by Sir Walter Scott. Walter Scott. 1988. reprint ed. lib. bdg. 65.00 (*0-7812-0135-7*) Rprt Serv.

Short Stories by Sir Walter Scott. Walter Scott. LC 71-145286. 1971. reprint ed. 49.00 (*0-403-01200-7*) Scholarly.

***Short Stories by Turkish Women Writers.** 2nd ed. Tr. by Nilufer M. Reddy from TUR. LC 94-76980. (Turkish Studies: Vol. 8). 172p. 1994. pap. text ed. 16.95 (*1-878318-07-1*) IN Univ Turkish.

***Short Stories for Students.** 3rd ed. 1998. 55.00 (*0-7876-2218-4*, 00157826) Gale.

***Short Stories for Students: Presenting Analysis, Context & Criticism on Commonly Studied Short Stories, Vol. 1.** Ed. by Kathleen Wilson. 400p. 1997. 55.00 (*0-7876-1690-7*) Gale.

***Short Stories for Students: Presenting Analysis, Context & Criticism on Commonly Studied Short Stories, Vol. 2.** Ed. by Kathleen Wilson. 400p. 1997. 55.00 (*0-7876-1691-5*) Gale.

Short Stories for Young & Old. G. Polizoides. (GRE.). 1977. pap. text ed. 3.00 (*0-685-81640-0*) Divry.

Short Stories from Abruzzo. G. Talbot. Ed. by Dante Marianacci. 172p. (Orig.). 1993. pap. 10.95 (*0-7165-2514-3*, Pub. by Irish Acad Pr IE) Intl Spec Bk.

Short Stories from Another Day: Eighteenth-Century Periodical Fiction. Keith J. Fennimore. LC 88-43155. 334p. (C). 1989. 27.00 (*0-87013-268-7*) Mich St U Pr.

Short Stories from the Balkans. Tr. by Edna W. Underwood. LC 75-122590. reprint ed. 47.50 (*0-404-06703-4*) AMS Pr.

Short Stories from the Bible. (Value Bks). 128p. 1996. mass mkt. 0.99 (*1-55748-818-5*) Barbour & Co.

Short Stories from the History of Mathematics. Robert E. Knauff. (Illus.). (Orig.). 1996. pap. 10.50 (*0-89278-435-0*) Carolina Biological.

Short Stories from the Irish Renaissance: An Anthology. Ed. by Alexander Gonzalez. LC 91-75023. 593p. 1993. 25.00 (*0-87875-421-0*) Whitston Pub.

Short Stories of Chen Ruoxi, Translated from the Original Chinese: A Writer at the Crossroads. Chen Ruoxi. Ed. by Hsin-sheng C. Kao. LC 92-29960. 420p. 1992. 109.95 (*0-7734-9190-2*) E Mellen.

Short Stories of Ernest Hemingway. Ernest Hemingway. (Hudson River Editions Ver.). 512p. 1977. 50.00 (*0-684-15155-3*) S&S Trade.

Short Stories of Ernest Hemingway: Critical Essays. Jackson L. Benson. LC 74-75815. xv, 375p. 1975. reprint ed. pap. text ed. 20.95 (*0-8223-0386-8*) Duke.

Short Stories of F. Scott Fitzgerald. F. Scott Fitzgerald. Ed. by Matthew J. Bruccoli. 656p. 1989. 29.95 (*0-684-19160-1*) S&S Trade.

Short Stories of F. Scott Fitzgerald. F. Scott Fitzgerald. Ed. by Matthew S. Bruccoli. 775p. (YA). 1995. pap. 17. 00 (*0-684-80445-X*) S&S Trade.

Short Stories of F. Scott Fitzgerald: New Approaches in Criticism. Ed. by Jackson R. Bryer. 416p. 1982. pap. 12.95 (*0-299-09084-1*) U of Wis Pr.

Short Stories of F. Scott Fitzgerald Read. Sub. Matthew J. Bruccoli. 1990. write for info. (*0-02-992032-9*, Free Press) Free Pr.

Short Stories of God's Blessings. Anna F. Gahr. 36p. (J). (gr. 2-8). 1992. pap. text ed. 12.00 (*1-883702-08-9*) Aiello Grp.

Short Stories of Grace Livingston Hill. Grace L. Hill. Ed. by J. E. Clauss. 1976. lib. bdg. 17.95 (*0-89190-101-9*, Rivercity Pr) Amereon Ltd.

Short Stories of H. G. Wells. H. G. Wells. (BCL1-PR English Literature Ser.). 1015p. 1992. reprint ed. lib. bdg. 119.00 (*0-7812-7552-0*) Rprt Serv.

Short Stories of Jack London. Jack London. Ed. by Robert C. Leitz, III et al. 784p. 1992. pap. 16.00 (*0-02-022371-4*) Macmillan.

Short Stories of John Galsworthy. J. Henry Smit. LC 68-877. (Studies in Fiction: No. 34). 1969. reprint ed. lib. bdg. 75.00 (*0-8383-0681-0*) M S G Haskell Hse.

Short Stories of Sean O'Faolain. Jo S. Rippier. 162p. 7600. 26.00 (*0-901072-30-3*, Pub. by Colin Smythe Ltd UK) Dufour.

Short Stories of the Far East. Graham Brash Editorial Staff. (Illus.). 184p. 1983. pap. 8.95 (*9971-947-62-5*) Heian Intl.

Short Stories of the Traditional People of Nigeria: African Folks, Back Home. John E. Njoku. LC 91-38739. (Studies in African Literature: Vol. 7). 172p. 1992. lib. bdg. 79.95 (*0-7734-9631-9*) E Mellen.

Short Stories of the Twentieth Century. Lorraine Massey. LC 94-90219. 128p. (Orig.). 1995. pap. 9.00 (*1-56002-469-0*, Univ Edtns) Aegina Pr.

An Asterisk (*) at the beginning of an entry indicates that the title is appearing in BIP for the first time.

Short Stories of the World, 5 vols. 1996. 135.00 (*0-19-521229-0*) OUP.

Short Stories, Vol. 1: A Sahib's War & Other Stories. Rudyard Kipling. Ed. by Andrew Rutherford. 1977. pap. 5.95 (*0-685-13408-3*, Penguin Bks) Viking Penguin.

Short Stories, Vol. 2: Friendly Brook & Other Stories. Rudyard Kipling. Ed. by Andrew Rutherford. (Modern Classics Ser.). 1977. pap. 5.95 (*0-685-13410-5*, Penguin Bks) Viking Penguin.

Short Story. Charles May. (Studies in Genre). 1995. 23.95 (*0-8057-0953-3*, Twayne) Scribnrs Ref.

Short Story. Sean O'Faolain. pap. 9.95 (*0-8159-6814-0*) Devin.

Short Story. Sean O'Faolain. 1989. pap. 19.95 (*0-85342-860-3*) Dufour.

***Short Story.** Miles T. Shatto. 40p. 1996. pap. 7.00 (*0-8059-3909-1*) Dorrance.

***Short Story, Vol. 2.** Naylor. 1997. pap. 14.95 (*0-316-59923-9*) Little.

Short Story: An Introduction. 2nd ed. Wilfred Stone & Nancy H. Packer. 640p. 1983. text ed. write for info. (*0-07-061693-0*) McGraw.

Short Story: An Introduction. 2nd ed. Wilfred Stone et al. 1983. teacher ed., pap. text ed. write for info. (*0-07-061695-7*) McGraw.

Short Story: Fifty Masterpieces. Ed. by Ellen C. Wynn. LC 82-60462. 650p. (C). 1983. pap. text ed. 16.50 (*0-312-72216-8*) St Martin.

Short Story: The Reality of Artifice. May. 1995. pap. 14.95 (*0-8057-9238-4*, Hall Reference) Macmillan.

Short Story: The Story of Zacchaeus. Kevin Foreman et al. (Bible Sing & Tell Ser.). (Illus.). 24p. (Orig.). (J). (ps-2). 1996. pap. 7.95 incl. audio (*0-88347-303-8*) Res Christian Liv.

Short Story: Thirty Masterpieces. 2nd ed. Beverly Lawn. LC 90-71633. 512p. (C). 1992. pap. text ed. 9.50 (*0-312-04835-1*) St Martin.

***Short Story Collection.** Jerry Spinelli. 1997. write for info. (*0-679-88638-9*) Knopf.

***Short Story Compilaton.** Rebecca Y. Winslow. 245p. (Orig.). 1997. mass mkt. 4.99 (*1-55237-242-1*, Pub. by Comnwlth Pub CN) Partners Pubs Grp.

Short Story Criticism, Vol. 1. Ed. by Laurie L. Harris & Sheila Fitzgerald. 450p. 1987. 99.00 (*0-8103-2550-0*) Gale.

Short Story Criticism, Vol. 2. Ed. by Sheila Fitzgerald. 550p. 1988. 99.00 (*0-8103-2551-9*) Gale.

Short Story Criticism, Vol. 2. Kalesky. 1996. 99.00 (*0-7876-0754-1*) Gale.

Short Story Criticism, Vol. 3. Ed. by Sheila Fitzgerald. 435p. 1989. 99.00 (*0-8103-2552-7*) Gale.

Short Story Criticism, Vol. 4. Ed. by Thomas Votteler. 1989. 99.00 (*0-8103-2553-5*) Gale.

Short Story Criticism, Vol. 7. Thomas Votteler. 1991. 99.00 (*0-8103-2556-X*) Gale.

Short Story Criticism, Vol. 8. Thomas Votteler. 1991. 99.00 (*0-8103-2557-8*) Gale.

Short Story Criticism, Vol. 9. Thomas Votteler. 1992. 99.00 (*0-8103-2558-6*) Gale.

Short Story Criticism, Vol. 10. Thomas Votteler. 1992. 99.00 (*0-8103-2559-4*) Gale.

Short Story Criticism, Vol. 11. Thomas Votteler. 1993. 99.00 (*0-8103-7953-8*) Gale.

Short Story Criticism, Vol. 12. Thomas Votteler. 1993. 99.00 (*0-8103-7955-4*) Gale.

Short Story Criticism, Vol. 13. Thomas Votteler. 1993. 99.00 (*0-8103-8469-8*) Gale.

Short Story Criticism, Vol. 14. Thomas Votteler. 1994. 99.00 (*0-8103-8470-1*) Gale.

Short Story Criticism, Vol. 19. Kalasky. 1995. 99.00 (*0-8103-9283-6*) Gale.

Short Story Criticism, Vol. 20. Kalasky. 1995. 99.00 (*0-8103-9284-4*) Gale.

Short Story Criticism, Vol. 21. Kalasky. 1996. 99.00 (*0-7876-0753-3*) Gale.

Short Story Criticism, Vol. 23. Kalasky. 1996. 99.00 (*0-7876-0755-X*) Gale.

***Short Story Criticism, Vol. 24.** 1997. 99.00 (*0-7876-0756-8*, 00153389, Gale Res Intl) Gale.

***Short Story Criticism, Vol. 25.** 1997. 99.00 (*0-7876-0757-6*, 00153390, Gale Res Intl) Gale.

***Short Story Criticism, Vol. 26.** 1997. 99.00 (*0-7876-1486-6*, 00156747, Gale Res Intl) Gale.

***Short Story Criticism, Vol. 27.** 1998. 99.00 (*0-7876-1663-X*, 00157019) Gale.

***Short Story Criticism, Vol. 128.** 1998. 99.00 (*0-7876-2051-3*, 00157605) Gale.

Short Story Criticism Vol. 15: Excerpts from Criticism of the Work of Short Fiction Writers. Ed. by David Segal. 1994. 99.00 (*0-8103-8930-4*) Gale.

Short Story Criticism Vol. 16: Excerpts from Criticism of the Works of Short Fiction Writers. Ed. by David Segal. 560p. 1994. 99.00 (*0-8103-8931-2*) Gale.

Short Story Criticism Vol. 17: Excerpts from Criticism of the Works of Short Fiction Writers, Vol. 17. Ed. by David Segal. 555p. 1995. 99.00 (*0-8103-9281-X*) Gale.

Short Story Criticism Vol. 18: Excerpts from Criticism of the Works of Short Fiction Writers, Vol. 18. Ed. by David Segal. 550p. 1995. 99.00 (*0-8103-9282-8*, 004723) Gale.

Short Story Criticism, Vol. 5: Excerpts from Criticism of the Works of Short Fiction Writers, Vol. 5. Ed. by Thomas Votteler. LC 88-641014. (Illus.). 501p. 1990. 99.00 (*0-8103-2554-3*, 004710) Gale.

Short Story Criticism, Vol. 6: Excerpts from Criticism of the Works of Short Fiction Writers, Vol. 6. Ed. by Thomas Votteler. LC 88-641014. (Illus.). 520p. 1990. 99.00 (*0-8103-2555-1*) Gale.

Short Story Cycle: A Genre Companion & Reference Guide. Susan G. Mann. 243p. 1988. lib. bdg. 49.95 (*0-318-39872-9*, MSS/, Greenwood Pr) Greenwood.

Short Story in America, 1900-1950. Ray B. West. LC 68-55863. (Essay Index Reprint Ser.). 1979. 23.95 (*0-8369-0982-8*) Ayer.

Short Story in English: An Annotated Biography. Dean Baldwin & Gregory Morris. LC 94-15580. (Magill Bibliographies). 45.00 (*0-8108-2834-0*) Scarecrow.

Short Story Index: Basic Volume, 1900-1949. Incl. Supplement 1950-1954. Ed. by Dorothy E. Cook & Estelle A. Fidell. 394p. 1956. 65.00 (*0-8242-0385-2*); Supplement 1955-1958. Ed. by Estelle A. Fidell & Esther V. Flory. LC 53-8991. 341p. 1960. 65.00 (*0-8242-0386-0*); Supplement 1959-1963. Ed. by Estelle A. Fidell. LC 53-8991. 487p. 1965. 65.00 (*0-8242-0387-9*); Supplement 1964-1968. Ed. by Estelle A. Fidell. LC 53-8991. 599p. 1969. 65.00 (*0-8242-0399-2*); Supplement 1969-1973. Ed. by Estelle A. Fidell. LC 53-8991. 639p. 1974. 65.00 (*0-8242-0497-2*); Supplement, 1974-1978. Ed. by Gary L. Bogart. LC 75-649762. 802p. 1953. 95.00 (*0-686-66656-9*); Short Story Index: Supplement 1979-83. LC 75-649762. 918p. 1984. 115.00 (*0-685-05424-1*); Supplement 1953. Ed. by Dorothy E. Cook & Isabel S. Monro. LC 75-649762. 1533p. 1953. 55.00 (*0-8242-0384-4*); LC 53-8991. 1553p. 1953. 65.00 (*0-318-56461-0*) Wilson.

Short Story Index: Collections Indexed 1900-1978. LC 79-24887. 349p. 1979. 45.00 (*0-8242-0643-6*) Wilson.

Short Story Index: Supplement 1979-83. LC 75-649762. (Short Story Index). 918p. 1984. 115.00 (*0-685-05424-1*) Wilson.

Short Story Index: Supplement 1979-83 see Short Story Index: Basic Volume, 1900-1949

Short Story Index. 1984-1988. LC 75-649762. 1200p. (C). 1989. 135.00 (*0-685-45834-2*) Wilson.

***Short Story Longs, 8 bks.** Ann B. Herrick. Incl. Have You Ever Been on a Flower Ride?. (Illus.). 12p. (J). (ps-2). 1997. pap. 2.50 (*1-890656-01-1*); Little Squirrel Went Passing By. (Illus.). 12p. (J). (ps-2). 1997. pap. 2.50 (*1-890656-02-X*); Have You Ever Been on a Turtle Ride?. (Illus.). 12p. (J). (ps-2). 1997. pap. 2.50 (*1-890656-03-8*); Elephant Is Tall & Wide. (Illus.). 12p. (J). (ps-2). 1997. pap. 2.50 (*1-890656-04-6*); Once upon a Cricket Jump. (Illus.). 12p. (J). (ps-2). 1997. pap. 2.50 (*1-890656-05-4*); Have You Ever Been on a Butterflight?. (Illus.). 12p. (J). (ps-2). 1997. pap. 2.50 (*1-890656-06-2*); Pollywog Is So Unique. (Illus.). 12p. (J). (ps-2). 1997. pap. 2.50 (*1-890656-07-0*); Walk Down to the Sea with Me. (Illus.). 12p. (J). (ps-2). 1997. pap. 2.50 (*1-890656-08-9*); 17.95 (*1-890656-00-3*) Seascape Pubs.

Short Story Masterpieces. Ed. by Robert Penn Warren & Albert Erskine. 528p. 1954. mass mkt. 7.50 (*0-440-37864-8*, LE) Dell.

Short-Story Masterpieces: Vol. 3, Russian. Tr. by John Cournos from RUS. LC 79-179299. (Short Story Index Reprint Ser.). 1977. reprint ed. 18.95 (*0-8369-4038-5*) Ayer.

Short Story Sequencing. Joy Evans & Jo E. Moore. (Illus.). 48p. (J). (gr. 1-2). 1983. teacher ed., pap. text ed. 4.95 (*1-55799-029-8*, EMC 140) Evan-Moor Corp.

Short Story Theories. Ed. by Charles E. May. LC 75-36982. xiv, 251p. 1977. pap. 9.95 (*0-8214-0221-8*) Ohio U Pr.

Short Story Theory at a Crossroads. Ed. by Susan Lohafer & JoEllen Clarey. LC 89-30723. (Illus.). 280p. 1989. pap. 16.95 (*0-8071-1586-X*); text ed. 35.00 (*0-8071-1546-0*) La State U Pr.

Short Story Writers, 3 vols. Ed. by Salem Press Editors. LC 97-23079. (Illus.). 1100p. (YA). (gr. 9-12). 1997. lib. bdg. 175.00 (*0-89356-950-X*) Salem Pr. This 3 volume reference compiles essays on more than 100 frequently read & studied short story writers from around the world, including such early masters of short fiction as Chaucer, European masters such as Rudyard Kipling, & American Masters such as Ray Bradbury, John Cheever, Ernest Hemingway & Eudora Welty. Other authors in this reference work are: Boccaccio, Mavis Gallant, Bret Harte, Zora Neale Hurston, Shirley Jackson, Guy de Maupassant & Alice Walker. For more information call Salem Press at 800-221-1592 or FAX: 201- 871-8668.** ***Publisher Provided Annotation.

Short Story Writers & Their Work: A Guide to the Best. 2nd ed. Brad Hooper. LC 92-11944. 100p. (C). 1992. pap. text ed. 16.00 (*0-8389-0587-0*) ALA.

Short Story Writers & Their Work: A Guide to the Best. Brad Hooper. LC 88-10393. 69p. reprint ed. pap. 25.00 (*0-7837-5912-6*, 2045710) Bks Demand.

Short Story Writing. 1966. pap. 1.50 (*0-686-32332-7*) Rod & Staff.

Short Straw: Memoirs of Korea, by a Fighter Pilot/ Forward Air Controller. Bernard W. Peterson. LC 95-83262. (Illus.). 560p. 1996. 29.95 (*0-9631875-3-8*) Chuckwalla Pub.

Short Straw Bride. Dallas Schulze. 1996. mass mkt. 4.99 (*0-373-28939-1*, 1-28939-6) Harlequin Bks.

Short Studies in Shakespeare. G. Bradby. LC 76-30728. (Studies in Shakespeare: No. 24). 1977. lib. bdg. 75.00 (*0-8383-2169-0*) M S G Haskell Hse.

Short Studies of American Authors. enl. ed. Thomas W. Higginson. 78p. 1967. reprint ed. pap. 6.50 (*0-910120-01-3*) Americanist.

Short Studies of American Authors. Thomas W. Higginson. (BCL1-PS American Literature Ser.). 78p. 1992. reprint ed. lib. bdg. 59.00 (*0-7812-6611-4*) Rprt Serv.

Short Studies of Great Lawyers. Irving Browne. iv, 382p. 1982. reprint ed. lib. bdg. 30.00 (*0-8377-0330-1*) Rothman.

***Short Surahs Vol. 1: Islam, the Qur'an, 'Iman, Arkan.** unabridged ed. Abdullah Ghazi & Tasneema Ghazi. Ed. by Noura Dourke & Fadel Abdullah. LC 95-76090. (Illus.). 85p. (Orig.). (J). (gr. 1-6). 1993. pap. text ed. 5.00 (*1-56316-101-X*) Iqra Intl Ed Fdtn.

Short Surahs Workbook. Noura Dourkee. Ed. by Abidullah Ghazi & Tasneema Ghazi. (Illus.). 42p. 1994. student ed. 4.00 (*1-56316-103-6*) Iqra Intl Ed Fdtn.

Short Suras for Prayer. M. A. Qazi. 16p. (Orig.). 1985. pap. 4.50 (*1-56744-384-2*) Kazi Pubns.

Short Survey of Surrealism. David Gascoyne. (Illus.). 162p. 1971. reprint ed. 32.50 (*0-7146-2262-1*, BHA-02262, Pub. by F Cass Pubs UK) Intl Spec Bk.

Short, Sweet & All That: Something to Think About. Juanita Bratcher. (Illus.). 94p. (Orig.). 1997. pap. 10.00 (*0-9635616-2-6*) Bratcher-McMillan.

Short, Swift Time of Gods on Earth: The Hohokam Chronicles. Donald Bahr et al. LC 93-41131. 1994. 45.00 (*0-520-08467-5*); pap. 16.95 (*0-520-08468-3*) U CA Pr.

Short Tail. Barbara Davoll. (Christopher Churchmouse Classics Ser.). (Illus.). 24p. (J). 1989. 8.99 (*0-89693-499-3*, 6-1499, Victor Bks) Chariot Victor.

Short Tail. Barbara Davoll & Dennis Hockerman. 24p. (J). 1989. audio 11.99 (*0-89693-032-7*, 3-1204) SP Pubns.

Short-Tailed Fruit Bat: A Study in Plant-Animal Interactions. Theodore H. Fleming. (Wildlife Behavior & Ecology Ser.). (Illus.). 384p. 1988. lib. bdg. 60.00 (*0-226-25328-7*) U Ch Pr.

Short Tails & Treats from Three Dog Bakery. Dan Dye & Mark Beckloff. (Illus.). 128p. (Orig.). 1996. pap. 14.95 (*0-8362-2155-9*) Andrews & McMeel.

Short Takes: A Look at the South's Newest Books. Ed. by Bob Hall & Bonnie Campbell. (Southern Exposure Ser.). (Illus.). 64p. (Orig.). (C). 1987. pap. 5.00 (*0-943810-24-8*) Inst Southern Studies.

Short Takes: Brief Personal Narratives & Other Works by American Teen Writers. Ed. by R. James Stahl & Kathryn Kulpa. LC 94-39802. (American Teen Writer Ser.). (Illus.). 128p. (Orig.). (YA). (gr. 7-12). 1996. pap. 9.75 (*1-886427-00-3*) Merlyns Pen.

Short Takes: Model Essays for Basic Composition. 5th ed. 448p. (C). 1995. teacher ed., pap. 18.75 (*0-673-99464-3*) Addson-Wesley Educ.

Short Takes: Model Essays for Basic Composition. 5th ed. Elizabeth Penfield & Theodore Hill. LC 94-20373. 320p. (C). 1996. pap. text ed. 25.50 (*0-673-99463-5*) Addson-Wesley Educ.

Short Takes: Model Essays for Composition. 4th ed. Elizabeth Penfield. LC 92-22100. (C). 1992. 18.50 (*0-673-46598-5*, HarpT); 10.00 (*0-673-46599-3*, HarpT) HarpC.

Short Tales in Fiction: Critical Thinking, Reading & Writing. R. Saitz & F. Sterglitz. 1993. pap. text ed. 14.67 (*0-201-51677-2*) Longman.

Short Talks Around the Lord's Table. Harry L. Thomson. 1985. pap. 5.95 (*0-89137-559-7*) Quality Pubns.

Short Talks on Huna. 2nd rev. ed. Max F. Long. 1978. pap. 5.00 (*0-910764-02-6*) Huna Res Inc.

Short Talks on Many Subjects. Manly P. Hall. 6.95 (*0-89314-828-8*) Philos Res.

Short Talks on Masonry. Joseph F. Newton. x, 243p. 1994. reprint ed. pap. 10.00 (*0-88053-036-7*, M-85) Macoy Pub.

Short Talks with the Dead, & Others. Hilaire Belloc. LC 67-23175. (Essay Index Reprint Ser.). 1977. 20.95 (*0-8369-0192-4*) Ayer.

Short, Tall, Big or Small? Kari J. Gold. Ed. by Janet Reed. (Early Learning Program Ser.). (Illus.). 16p. (J). (ps-1). 1996. pap. 14.95 (*1-56784-308-5*) Newbridge Comms.

Short, Tall, Big or Small? Mini-Book. Kari J. Gold. Ed. by Janet Reed. (Illus.). 16p. (J). (ps-1). 1996. pap. 2.95 (*1-56784-333-6*) Newbridge Comms.

Short Tall Bridge Tales: Funny Stories about Tricky Hands. Stanley T. Burkoff et al. 192p. (Orig.). 1996. pap. 13.95 (*1-888745-00-2*, 4-1996-1) Zookeeper Pubng.

Short Term: Testbank. Terry S. Maness. Date not set. suppl. ed., teacher ed., pap. text ed. write for info. (*0-314-02002-0*) West Pub.

Short-Term America. Michael T. Jacobs. 1992. text ed. 24.95 (*0-07-103310-6*) McGraw.

Short-Term America: The Causes & Cures of Our Business Myopia. Michael T. Jacobs. 288p. 1993. pap. 14.95 (*0-87584-409-X*) Harvard Busn.

Short-Term America: The Causes & Cures of Our Business Myopia. Michael T. Jacobs. 288p. 1993. 24.95 (*0-87584-300-X*) Harvard Busn.

Short-Term America: The Causes & Cures of Our Business Myopia. Michael T. Jacobs. 1993. pap. text ed. 16.95 (*0-07-103397-1*) McGraw.

Short-Term Approaches to Psychotherapy. Ed. by Henry Grayson & Paul T. Olsen. LC 78-27605. (New Directions in Psychotherapy Ser.: Vol. III). 285p. 1979. 35.95 (*0-87705-345-6*) Human Sci Pr.

Short-Term Bioassays in the Analysis of Complex Environmental Mixtures, Pt. 5. Ed. by Shahbeg S. Sandhu et al. LC 87-27388. (Environmental Science Research Ser.: Vol. 36). (Illus.). 422p. 1987. 105.00 (*0-306-42772-9*, Plenum Pr) Plenum.

Short Term Consumption Behavior, Seasonality, & Labor Market Uncertainty in Rural India. CFNPP Staff et al. (Working Papers). (C). 1993. pap. 7.00 (*1-56401-136-4*) Cornell Food.

Short-Term Counseling. David Dillon. (Contemporary Christian Counseling Ser.: Vol. 3). 1992. 18.99 (*0-8499-0775-6*) Word Pub.

Short-Term Counseling: A Psychoanalytic Approach. Barbara W. Tilley. LC 84-9008. xii, 358p. (C). 1985. 47.50 (*0-8236-6072-9*, BN#06072) Intl Univs Pr.

Short-Term Counseling: Guidelines Based on Recent Research. Irving L. Janis. LC 83-3488. 240p. 1983. pap. 15.00 (*0-300-03125-4*, Y-480) Yale U Pr.

Short-Term Counseling: Theory & Practice. Kathleen Black. 1982. pap. write for info. (*0-201-00073-3*, 00073, Health Sci) Addison-Wesley.

Short-Term Couples Therapy Bk. 8027: The Imago Model in Action. Wade Luquet. LC 96-1961. 224p. 1996. pap. text ed. 38.95 (*0-87630-802-7*) Brunner-Mazel.

Short-Term Dynamic Hypnotherapy & Hypnoanalysis: Clinical Research & Treatment Strategies. Milton V. Kline. (Illus.). 334p. 1992. pap. 39.95 (*0-398-06206-4*) C C Thomas.

Short-Term Dynamic Hypnotherapy & Hypnoanalysis: Clinical Research & Treatment Strategies. Milton V. Kline. (Illus.). 334p. (C). 1992. text ed. 59.95 (*0-398-05796-6*) C C Thomas.

Short-Term Dynamic Psychotherapy. Ed. by Habib Davanloo. LC 80-67986. 416p. 1992. pap. 40.00 (*0-87668-301-4*) Aronson.

Short-Term Dynamic Psychotherapy: Evaluation & Technique. 2nd ed. Peter E. Sifneos. LC 87-2346. (Topics in General Psychiatry Ser.). 316p. 1987. 49.50 (*0-306-42341-3*, Plenum Pr) Plenum.

S

Short-Term Economic Forecasting. (Studies in Income & Wealth: No. 17). 516p. 1955. reprint ed. 134.20 (*0-87014-172-4*) Ayer.

Short-Term Economic Forecasting. (Studies in Income & Wealth: No. 17). 516p. 1955. reprint ed. mic. film 67.10 (*0-685-61301-1*) Natl Bur Econ Res.

Short-Term Economic Indicators Central & Eastern Europe: Sources & Definitions. OECD Staff. 127p. (Orig.). 1993. pap. 9.00 (*92-64-03864-7*) OECD.

***Short-Term Economic Indicators Central & Eastern Europe: Sources & Definitions.** OECD Staff. 127p. (Orig.). 1993. pap. 9.00 (*92-64-03863-9*) OECD.

Short-Term Economic Indicators Transition Economies: Sources & Definitions. OECD Staff. 400p. (Orig.). 1996. pap. 46.00 (*92-64-04838-3*, Pub. by Org for Econ FR) OECD.

Short-Term Economic Statistics: Central & Eastern Europe. Organization for Economic Cooperation & Development Staff. 390p. (Orig.). 1992. pap. 32.00 (*92-64-03523-0*) OECD.

Short-Term Energy Outlook. 1995. lib. bdg. 250.00 (*0-8490-6502-X*) Gordon Pr.

Short-Term Energy Outlook Annual Supplement. 1994. lib. bdg. 250.00 (*0-8490-5753-1*) Gordon Pr.

Short Term Financial Management. 3rd ed. Ned C. Hill & William L. Sartoris. (Illus.). 608p. (C). 1994. text ed. 80.00 (*0-02-354832-0*, Macmillan Coll) P-H.

Short-Term Financial Management: Text, Cases, & Readings. Terry S. Maness & John T. Zietlow. Ed. by Burvikovs. LC 92-32830. 550p. (C). 1993. text ed. 69.25 (*0-314-01268-0*) West Pub.

Short-Term Futures Trading: Systems, Strategies & Techniques for the Day- Trader. Jake Bernstein. 300p. 1992. pap. 32.50 (*1-55738-474-6*, 474) Irwin Prof Pubng.

Short-Term Group Counseling. 3rd ed. Ellis S. Grayson. (Illus.). 150p. 1993. pap. text ed. 20.50 (*0-929310-91-8*, 189) Am Correctional.

Short-Term Losses. Mark Lindensmith. LC 96-15669. 200p. 1996. 22.50 (*0-87074-406-2*); pap. 12.95 (*0-87074-407-0*) SMU Press.

Short Term Macro-Economic Policy in Latin America. Conference on Planning & Short Term Macroeconomic Policy in Latin America Staff. Ed. by Jere R. Behrman & James Hanson. LC 78-24053. 392p. reprint ed. pap. 111.80 (*0-8357-3238-X*, 2057132) Bks Demand.

Short Term Markets. (How to Borrow Workbooks Ser.). Date not set. 83.00 (*0-614-17081-8*, Pub. by IFR Pub UK) Am Educ Systs.

Short-Term Missions Boom: A Guide to International & Domestic Involvement. Ed. by Michael J. Anthony. LC 94-26120. 240p. (Orig.). 1994. pap. 14.99 (*0-8010-0233-8*) Baker Bks.

Short-Term Pastoral Counseling. Brian H. Childs. 1990. pap. 12.95 (*0-687-38432-X*) Abingdon.

***Short-Term Play Therapy for Disruptive Children.** Cheryl B. McNeel et al. 129p. 1996. write for info. (*1-882732-51-0*) Ctr Applied Psy.

Short-Term Psychotherapy & Brief Treatment Techniques: An Annotated Bibliography, 1920-1980. Harvey P. Mandel. LC 81-221. 704p. 1981. 95.00 (*0-306-40658-6*, Plenum Pr) Plenum.

Short Term Psychotherapy & Emotional Crisis. Peter E. Sifneos. LC 78-172323. (Illus.). 219p. 1972. 29.50 (*0-674-80720-0*) HUP.

Short-Term Surplus Funds Management for the State of Texas. Contrib. by Richard L. Schott. (Policy Research Project Report: No. 17). 68p. 1977. pap. 2.00 (*0-89940-610-6*) LBJ Sch Pub Aff.

Short Term Survival Techniques. John Tomikel. LC 84-70534. (Illus.). 144p. 1984. pap. 4.95 (*0-910042-45-4*) Allegheny.

Short-Term Tests for Chemical Carcinogens. Ed. by H. F. Stich & R. H. San. (Topics in Environmental Physiology & Medicine Ser.). (Illus.). 518p. 1981. 227.00 (*0-387-90496-4*) Spr-Verlag.

Short-Term Therapy Techniques. Christ L. Zois & Margaret Scarpa. 352p. 1997. 40.00 (*0-7657-0026-3*) Aronson.

Short-Term Therapy with Children: A Multi-Modal Approach to Helping Children with Their Problems. rev. ed. Lawrence E. Shapiro. (Illus.). 206p. (Orig.). (C). 1994. text ed. 34.95 (*1-882732-13-8*) Ctr Applied Psy.

Short-Term Toxicity Tests for Non-Genotoxic Effects. Ed. by Philippe Bourdeau et al. LC 89-22693. (Scientific Committee on Problems of the Environment Ser.: No. 41). 353p. 1990. text ed. 385.00 (*0-471-92506-3*) Wiley.

Short-Term Treatment in Occupational Therapy. Diane Gibson & Kathy Kaplan. LC 84-9115. (Occupational Therapy in Mental Health Ser.: Vol. 4, No. 3). 114p. 1984. 29.95 (*0-86656-342-3*) Haworth Pr.

Short Text Book of Surgery, Vol. II. B. P. Chatterjee. (C). 1989. 170.00 (*0-89771-365-6*, Pub. by Current Dist II); 170.00 (*0-89771-364-8*, Pub. by Current Dist II) St Mut.

Short Text Book of Zoology. G. K. Ghosh & M. Manna. (C). 1989. 55.00 (*0-89771-422-9*, Pub. by Current Dist II) St Mut.

Short Textbook of Clinical Imaging. Ed. by D. Sutton & J. W. Young. 868p. 1990. 155.00 (*0-387-19592-0*) Spr-Verlag.

***Short Textbook of Clinical Imaging.** David Sutton & Jeremy W. Young. 856p. 1990. 145.00 (*3-540-19592-0*) Spr-Verlag.

Short Textbook of Medical Jurisprudence. C. C. Mallik. 1985. 100.00 (*0-317-38795-2*, Pub. by Current Dist II) St Mut.

Short Textbook of Otolaryngology. A. L. Mukherjee. 1985. 59.00 (*0-317-39560-2*, Pub. by Current Dist II) St Mut.

Short Textbook of Radiotherapy. 4th ed. J. Walter. (Illus.). 299p. 1979. 52.00 (*0-443-01389-6*) Churchill.

Short Textbook of Surgery, 2 vols. C. Chatterjee. (C). 1981. 340.00 (*0-685-46427-X*, Pub. by Current Dist II) St Mut.

Short Time. Fred Misurella. LC 96-46780. (VIA Folios Ser.: Vol. 8). (Illus.). 49p. (C). 1996. pap. 7.00 (*1-884419-07-0*) Bordighera.

Short-Time Compensation: A Formula for Work Sharing. Ed. by Ramelle McCoy & Martin J. Morand. LC 83-13265. 223p. 1984. 31.00 (*0-08-030148-7*, 29/59/4) Work in Amer.

Short Time to Live. large type ed. Gwen Moffat. 368p. 1995. 25.99 (*0-7089-3336-X*) Ulverscroft.

Short Time to Stay: Comments on Time, Literature & Oral Performance. Ruth Finnegan. LC 81-70548. (Hans Wolff Memorial Lecture Ser.). 55p. 1982. pap. text ed. 5.00 (*0-941934-35-7*) Indiana Africa.

***Short Timers Guidebook. Edward A. Temple, Jr. (Illus.). 134p. (Orig.). 1995. pap. 7.95 (*0-9655781-1-9*) P Temple.**
This is the perfect going away gift for any active duty military member. All the armed services know what a SHORT TIMER is. That's the person who is counting down the days until military life ends & civilian life begins. This hilarious, fully illustrated cartoon book can ease that stressful transition with a good laugh. It took a Marine to capture the SHORT TIMER concept in a book. Advertised in LEATHERNECK magazine to include a book review, Nov. 1995. Everyone who joins the military will someday get 'SHORT'; Lord willing. Edward A. Temple, Jr., c/o P.TEMPLE, P.O. Box 15586, Alexandria, VA 22060. 703-799-3688; FAX: 703-658-3930. ***Publisher Provided Annotation.***

Short-Title Catalogue of Books Printed in England, Scotland, & Ireland & of English Books Printed Abroad, 3 vols., Set. 2nd rev. ed. Ed. by A. W. Pollard et al. 1992. 750.00 (*0-19-721797-4*) OUP.

Short-Title Catalogue of Books Printed in England, Scotland, & Ireland & of English Books Printed Abroad, 1475-1640, 2 vols., Vol. 1. 2nd ed. Ed. by Alfred W. Pollard & G. R. Redgrave. (Bibliographical Society Ser.). 612p. 1987. 350.00 (*0-19-721789-3*) OUP.

Short-Title Catalogue of Books Printed in England, Scotland, & Ireland & of English Books Printed Abroad, 1475-1640, 2 vols., Vol. 2. 2nd ed. Ed. by Alfred W. Pollard & G. R. Redgrave. (Bibliographical Society Ser.). 506p. 1976. 250.00 (*0-19-721790-7*) OUP.

Short-Title Catalogue of Books Printed in England, Scotland, & Ireland, & of English Books Printed Abroad, 1475-1640: Vol. III: Addenda, Corrigenda, & Indexes. 2nd ed. Ed. by Alfred W. Polland et al. (Illus.). 430p. 1991. 350.00 (*0-19-721791-5*) OUP.

Short-Title Catalogue of Books Printed in England, Scotland, Ireland, Wales & North America & of English Books Printed in Other Countries, 1641-1700, 3 vols., Vol. 1. 2nd enl. rev. ed. Compiled by Donald Wing. LC 70-185211. xxxi, 954p. 1994. lib. bdg. 400.00 (*0-87352-044-0*, Z2100) Modern Lang.

Short-Title Catalogue of Books Printed in England, Scotland, Ireland, Wales & North America & of English Books Printed in Other Countries, 1641-1700, 3 vols., Vol. 2. 2nd enl. rev. ed. Compiled by Donald Wing. LC 70-185211. xvii, 690p. 1982. lib. bdg. 400.00 (*0-87352-045-9*, Z2200) Modern Lang.

Short-Title Catalogue of Books Printed in England, Scotland, Ireland, Wales & North America & of English Books Printed in Other Countries, 1641-1700, 3 vols., Vol. 3. 2nd enl. rev. ed. Compiled by Donald Wing. LC 70-185211. xxvii, 766p. 1988. lib. bdg. 400.00 (*0-87352-046-7*, Z2300) Modern Lang.

Short-Title Catalogue of Books Printed in Hungary Before 1850. Geoffrey Arnold. (Catalogues of the British Library Collections). 329p. 1994. 120.00 (*0-7123-0313-8*, Pub. by Brit Library UK) U of Toronto Pr.

Short Title Catalogue of Eighteenth-Century Spanish Books, 3 vols., Set. Harold Whitehead. (Catalogues of the British Library Collections). 820p. 1994. 300.00 (*0-7123-0342-1*, Pub. by Brit Library UK) U of Toronto Pr.

Short-Title Catalogue of Music Printed Before 1825 in the Fitzwilliam Museum, Cambridge. Ed. by Valerie Rumbold & Iain Fenlon. (Illus.). 179p. (C). 1992. text ed. 95.00 (*0-521-41535-7*) Cambridge U Pr.

Short Title Catalogue of the Emblem Books & Related Works in the Stirling Maxwell Collection of Glasgow University Library (1499-1917) Hester M. Black. Ed. by David Weston. 150p. 1988. text ed. 34.95 (*0-85967-751-6*, Pub. by Scolar Pr UK) Ashgate Pub Co.

Short Title Catalogue of the Frank Kacmarcik Rare Book Collection. Maureen M. Watry & Paul B. Watry. LC 95-67221. 1995. write for info. (*0-9644805-0-6*) Order St Benedict.

Short Title Catalogue of Works on Psychical Research. Harry Price. (Hypnosis & Altered States of Consciousness Ser.). 468p. 1982. lib. bdg. 49.50 (*0-306-76166-1*) Da Capo.

Short Track Driving Techniques. Butch Miller & Steve Smith. (Illus.). 80p. (Orig.). 1989. pap. text ed. 12.95 (*0-936834-65-X*) S S Autosports.

Short Treatise Declaringe the Detestable Wickednesse of Magicall Sciences. Francis Coxe. LC 72-5971. (English Experience Ser.: No. 501). 32p. 1972. reprint ed. 20.00 (*90-221-0501-6*) Walter J Johnson.

Short Treatise of Geometrie. John Babington. LC 76-25837. (English Experience Ser.: No. 296). 200p. 1971. reprint ed. 50.00 (*90-221-0296-3*) Walter J Johnson.

Short Treatise of Lawfull & Unlawfull Recreations. Dudley Fenner. LC 77-6740. (English Experience Ser.: No. 870). 1977. reprint ed. lib. bdg. 15.00 (*90-221-0870-8*) Walter J Johnson.

Short Treatise on the Virgin Mary. Rene Laurentin. 1991. 14.95 (*1-56036-015-1*, 38347) AMI Pr.

Short Trips in & Around Dallas. Laura Trim. (Illus.). 298p. (Orig.). 1984. pap. 11.95 (*0-317-18943-3*) LDT Pr.

Short Trips in the Pacific Northwest: Fifty-Two Weekend Destinations from Seattle & Portland. Barry Anderson. 1992. pap. 14.00 (*0-517-57542-6*, C P Pubs) Crown Pub Group.

Short "u" & Long "u" Play a Game. Jane B. Moncure. LC 79-10306. (Sound Box Library). (Illus.). 32p. (J). (ps-2). 1979. lib. bdg. 21.36 (*0-89565-093-2*) Childs World.

Short Victorious War. David Weber. (Honor Harrington Ser.: Vol. 3). 416p. (Orig.). 1994. mass mkt. 5.99 (*0-671-87596-5*) Baen Bks.

Short View of Legal Bibliography: Bridgman's Legal Bibliography. Richard W. Bridgman. xviii, 430p. 1958. reprint ed. 55.00 (*0-89941-353-6*, 502140) W S Hein.

Short View of the English Stage, 1900-1926. James Agate. LC 70-94263. (Select Bibliographies Reprint Ser.). 1977. 19.95 (*0-8369-5037-2*) Ayer.

Short View of the English Stage 1900-1926. James Agate. LC 75-91887. 1972. reprint ed. 21.95 (*0-405-08194-4*, Pub. by Blom Pubns UK) Ayer.

Short View of the Immorality, & Profaneness of the English Stage. 3rd ed. Jeremy Collier. LC 74-3401. reprint ed. 21.50 (*0-404-01619-7*) AMS Pr.

Short View of the Profaneness & Immorality of the English Stage, Etc. Jeremy Collier. (Anglistica & Americana Ser.: No. 46). x, 437p. 1969. reprint ed. 110.00 (*0-685-66453-8*, 05102589) G Olms Pubs.

Short View of Tragedy. Thomas Rymer. LC 79-118069. 1968. reprint ed. 29.50 (*0-404-05478-1*) AMS Pr.

Short View of Tragedy. Thomas Rymer. 184p. 1971. reprint ed. 26.00 (*0-7146-2519-1*, Pub. by F Cass Pubs UK) Intl Spec Bk.

Short Vowel, Long Vowel, Digraph Readers & Workbooks, 450 vols., Set. E. Reid et al. (Start Reading Ser.: Sets A,B,C). 6600p. (J). (ps-3). 1986. pap. text ed. 949.95 (*1-56422-049-4*) Start Reading.

Short Vowel Readers, 5 vols., Set. E. Reid et al. (Start Reading Ser.: Set A). 40p. (J). (ps-3). 1986. pap. text ed. 14.95 (*1-56422-036-2*) Start Reading.

Short Vowel Readers & Workbooks, 10 vols., Set. E. Reid et al. (Start Reading Ser.: Set A). 132p. (J). (ps-3). 1986. pap. text ed. 28.95 (*1-56422-042-7*); pap. text ed. 369.95 (*1-56422-046-X*) Start Reading.

Short Vowel Workbooks, 5 vols., Set. E. Reid et al. (Start Reading Ser.: Set A). 92p. (J). (ps-3). 1986. pap. text ed. 14.95 (*1-56422-039-7*) Start Reading.

Short Vowels. Barbara Gregorich. Ed. by Joan Hoffman. (I Know It! Bks.). (Illus.). 32p. (J). (gr. 1-3). 1981. student ed. 1.99 (*0-938256-40-8*) Sch Zone Pub Co.

***Short Vowels.** Scholastic, Inc. Staff. (Fun with Consonants Ser.). (J). 1997. pap. text ed. 6.95 (*0-590-76491-8*) Scholastic Inc.

Short Vowels. Rozanne L. Williams. (Fun Phonics Ser.: Vol. 2). (Illus.). 24p. (Orig.). (J). (gr. k-2). 1993. wbk. ed., pap. 10.98 (*1-57471-092-3*) Creat Teach Pr.

***Short Vowels (Language)** Jo E. Moore. (Reading & Writing Ser.). (Illus.). 32p. (J). (gr. 1-2). 1996. teacher ed., pap. 2.95 (*1-55799-405-6*, 4007) Evan-Moor Corp.

Short Wait Between Trains. Robert McLaughlin. 1976. 21.95 (*0-8488-0829-0*) Amereon Ltd.

Short Walk Around the Pyramids & Through the World of Art. Philip M. Isaacson. LC 91-8854. (Illus.). 112p. (J). (gr. 3-7). 1993. lib. bdg. 20.99 (*0-679-91523-0*) Knopf Bks Yng Read.

Short Walk Around the Pyramids & Through the World of Art. Phillip M. Isaacson. LC 91-8854. (Illus.). 112p. (J). (gr. 3-7). 1993. 25.00 (*0-679-81523-6*) Knopf Bks Yng Read.

***Short Walk in the Rain.** Hugh Hood. 176p. 1989. pap. 10.95 (*0-88984-134-9*, Pub. by Porcupines Quill CN) Genl Dist Srvs.

Short Walk to Death. large type ed. R. A. Bennett. 250p. 1996. pap. 17.99 (*1-85389-588-1*, Dales) Ulverscroft.

Short Wave Length Microscopy, Vol. 306. Parson. 1978. 45.00 (*0-89072-062-2*) NY Acad Sci.

***Short Wave Listening Guide.** Ian Poole. 1997. pap. text ed. 29.95 (*0-7506-2631-3*) Buttrwrth-Heinemann.

Short-Wave Mystery. rev. ed. Franklin W. Dixon. (Hardy Boys Ser.: Vol. 24). 180p. (J). (gr. 5-9). 1945. 5.95 (*0-448-08924-6*, G&D) Putnam Pub Group.

Short Wavelength Coherent Radiation: Generation & Applications. LC 88-60866. (Proceedings Ser.: Vol. 2). 180p. (Orig.). 1988. lib. bdg. 82.00 (*1-55752-044-5*) Optical Soc.

Short Wavelength Coherent Radiation: Generation & Applications. Ed. by D. T. Attwood & J. Bokor. LC 86-71674. (AIP Conference Proceedings Ser.: No. 147). 480p. 1986. lib. bdg. 70.00 (*0-88318-346-3*) Am Inst Physics.

Short Wavelength Coherent Radiation: Generation & Applications. Ed. by Phillip H. Bucksbaum & Natale M. Ceglio. LC 90-63178. (Proceedings Ser.: Vol. 11). 350p. 1991. lib. bdg. 75.00 (*1-55752-185-9*) Optical Soc.

Short-Wavelength Lasers. Ed. by C. Yamanaka. (Proceedings in Physics Ser.: Vol. 30). (Illus.). xiv, 410p. 1988. 74.00 (*0-387-50311-0*) Spr-Verlag.

Short Wavelength Lasers & Their Applications. Ed. by V. V. Korobkin & M. Y. Romanovsky. 405p. 1992. 145.00 (*1-56072-020-4*) Nova Sci Pubs.

Short-Wavelength Magnetic Recording: New Methods & Analysis. J. J. Ruigrok. 566p. 1990. 190.25 (*0-946395-56-X*) Elsevier.

Short Wavelength V: Physics with Intense Laser Pulses. Ed. by Michael D. Perry & Paul B. Corkum. LC 92-62909. (Proceedings Ser.: Vol. 17). 350p. (Orig.). 1993. lib. bdg. 75.00 (*1-55752-298-7*) Optical Soc.

Short Weeks of Summer. large type ed. Elisabeth Hargreaves. 416p. 1982. 25.99 (*0-7089-0804-7*) Ulverscroft.

***Shortbread: Thirty Sweet & Savory Recipes.** Jann Johnson. LC 97-6174. 1997. 9.95 (*0-8118-1359-2*) Chronicle Bks.

Shortchanged: Minorities & Women in Banking. Rodney Alexander & Elisabeth Sapary. 182p. 1972. 9.95 (*0-614-16163-0*) CEP.

Shortchanged Review. Michael D. Moody. 1976. pap. 5.25 (*0-8222-1024-X*) Dramatists Play.

***Shortchangers.** Arnold Silver. LC 96-44056. 192p. (Orig.). 1997. pap. 12.95 (*0-89407-119-X*, 119X) Strawberry Hill.

Shortchanging Girls, Shortchanging America-Executive Summary: A Nationwide Poll That Assesses Self-Esteem, Educational Experiences, Interest in Math & Science & Career Aspirations of Girls & Boys, Ages 9-15. 2nd ed. Greenberg-Lake Staff & Analysis Group Staff. LC 94-27744. 20p. 1994. pap. 11.95 (*1-879922-02-9*) Am Assoc U Women.

Shortchanging the Workforce: The Job Training Partnership Act & the Overselling of Privatized Training. John D. Donahue. (Illus.). 40p. 1990. 12.00 (*0-944826-18-0*) Economic Policy Inst.

Shortcut. Donald Crews. LC 91-36312. (Illus.). 32p. (J). (ps-6). 1992. 16.00 (*0-688-06436-1*); lib. bdg. 15.93 (*0-688-06437-X*) Greenwillow.

Shortcut. Donald Crews. (J). 1996. pap. 4.95 (*0-688-13576-5*, Mulberry) Morrow.

Shortcut. David Macaulay. (J). 1995. 15.95 (*0-395-52445-8*) HM.

Shortcut. David Macaulay. LC 95-2542. (Illus.). 64p. (J). 1995. 15.95 (*0-395-52436-9*) HM.

***Shortcut Cook Book No. 1: Breaking the Cooking Mold.** Terrie MacFarlane & Lisa Rubino. (Illus.). 160p. (Orig.). 1996. pap. write for info. (*0-9654204-7-7*) TeriLee Prods.

Shortcut Through Adventureland, Vol. I. Jack Cassidy et al. write for info. (*0-318-58217-1*) P-H.

Shortcut Through Adventureland, Vol. II: Infocom. Richard Lynn et al. write for info. (*0-318-58218-X*) P-H.

Shortcut Through Therapy: Ten Principles of Growth-Oriented, Contented Living. Richard Carlson. 224p. (Orig.). 1995. pap. 10.95 (*0-452-27383-8*, Plume) NAL-Dutton.

Shortcut to French. Colette Dulac. (J). (gr. 9 up). 1977. pap. text ed. 5.45 (*0-88345-300-2*, 18441); audio 25.00 (*0-685-79306-0*, 58442) Prentice ESL.

Shortcut to French. Colette Dulac. 1987. pap. text ed. 30.20 (*0-13-809195-1*) Prentice ESL.

Shortcut to Reading. Richard P. Archer. 29p. 1983. 10.00 (*0-317-02255-5*) Concept Spelling.

Shortcut to Santa Fe. Medora Sale. 256p. 1994. 20.00 (*0-684-19680-8*) S&S Trade.

Shortcut User's Guide. David Schargel. (Illus.). 75p. (Orig.). 79.95 (*1-878777-00-9*) Aladdin Systs.

Shortcuts: A Concise Guide to Metric Rotary Cutting. Donna L. Thomas. Ed. by Liz McGehee. LC 91-34298. (Illus.). 52p. (Orig.). 1991. pap. 12.95 (*0-943574-96-X*, B124M) That Patchwork.

Shortcuts: A Concise Guide to Rotary Cutting. Donna L. Thomas. Ed. by Liz McGehee. LC 91-4275. (Illus.). 52p. (Orig.). 1991. pap. 12.95 (*0-943574-87-0*, B124) That Patchwork.

Shortcuts for Accenting Your Garden: Over Five Hundred Easy & Inexpensive Tips. Marianne Binetti. Ed. by Sandra Webb. LC 92-54654. (Illus.). 144p. (Orig.). 1993. 18.95 (*0-88266-830-7*, Garden Way Pub); pap. 9.95 (*0-88266-829-3*, Garden Way Pub) Storey Comm Inc.

Shortcuts for Fall. Marilynn G. Barr. (Illus.). 80p. (J). (ps-4). 1992. pap. 8.95 (*1-878279-43-2*) Monday Morning Bks.

Shortcuts for Librarians & Teachers. Susan Pagnucci. (Illus.). 64p. (Orig.). 1993. pap. 8.95 (*0-929326-05-9*) Bur Oak Pr Inc.

Shortcuts for Spring. Marilynn G. Barr. (Illus.). 80p. (J). (gr. k-4). 1992. pap. 8.95 (*1-878279-45-9*) Monday Morning Bks.

Shortcuts for Teachers: Strategies for Reducing Classroom Workload. Jean Enk & Meg Hendricks. LC 81-81392. (J). (gr. k-6). 1981. pap. 8.99 (*0-8224-6373-3*) Fearon Teach Aids.

Shortcuts for Teaching Language Usage. Flora Joy. (Illus.). 144p. (J). (gr. 2-8). 1994. 13.99 (*0-86653-805-4*, GA1497) Good Apple.

Shortcuts for Teaching Phonics. Flora Joy. (Illus.). 144p. 1990. 13.99 (*0-86653-514-4*, GA1143) Good Apple.

Shortcuts for Teaching Reading Comprehension. Flora Joy. (Illus.). 144p. 1990. 13.99 (*0-86653-515-2*, GA1144) Good Apple.

Shortcuts for Teaching Vocabulary. Flora Joy. 144p. (gr. 3-6). 1991. 13.99 (*0-86653-591-8*, GA1304) Good Apple.

Shortcuts for Teaching Writing. Flora Joy. 144p. (J). (gr. 3-6). 1991. 13.99 (*0-86653-590-X*, GA1303) Good Apple.

Shortcuts for the Older Child Beginner. Ruth Schoening. 38p. 1987. 5.75 (*0-913191-33-7*) AGEI Pub.

Shortcuts for Winter. Marilynn G. Barr. (Illus.). 80p. (J). (gr. k-4). 1992. pap. 8.95 (*1-878279-44-0*) Monday Morning Bks.

Shortcuts in Gun Dog Training. Ronald D. Mohn. (Illus.). 112p. (Orig.). 1991. pap. 11.95 (*0-9629840-9-4*) RDM Enter.

Shortcuts on Wine: Everything the Wine Lover Needs to Know. Edmond Masciana. 160p. (Orig.). 1996. pap. 10.95 (*0-88496-404-3*) Capra Pr.

Shortcuts Sampler. Roxanne Carter. Ed. by Barbara Weiland. LC 92-40607. (Illus.). 20p. (Orig.). 1992. pap. 5.95 (*1-56477-023-0*, LSC8) That Patchwork.

***Shortcuts to a Great Yard.** Marinelli. 1996. 25.00 (*0-8050-4415-9*) St Martin.

Shortcuts to a Perfect Sewing Pattern. Rusty Bensussen. LC 88-30833. (Illus.). 160p. (Orig.). 1993. pap. 12.95 (*0-8069-6822-2*) Sterling.

Shortcuts to Basic Writing Skills: An Innovative Approach to Composition. 2nd ed. Gary Steele. 336p. (C). 1985. pap. text ed. 22.00 (*0-03-069731-X*) HB Coll Pubs.

Shortcuts to Becoming Rich. Robert E. Shindler. 1979. 12.00 (*0-915451-01-8*) New Start Pubns.

Shortcuts to Beginning Reading: A How-To Manual. Marie L. Myers. LC 96-9173. 184p. 1996. pap. 16.50 (*0-8108-3213-5*) Scarecrow.

Shortcuts to Better Living. Cherly W. Tetreau. 1996. 11.98 (*0-88365-949-2*) Galahad Bks.

Shortcuts to Business Success. Dianne J. Moore. 27p. 1992. pap. 4.00 (*1-880670-01-1*) Write On Servs.

Shortcuts to Great Gardens. Nigel Colborn. 1993. pap. 24.95 (*0-316-15052-5*) Little.

Shortcuts to Increase Your Typing Speed. Elza Dinwiddie-Boyd. 1988. pap. 8.95 (*0-399-51489-9*, Perigee Bks) Berkley Pub.

Shorte & Briefe Narration of the Two Navigations to Newe Fraunce. Jacques Cartier. Tr. by J. Florio. LC 73-6110. (English Experience Ser.: No. 718). 1975. reprint ed. 25.00 (*90-221-0718-3*) Walter J Johnson.

Shorte Introduction of Grammar. William Lily. LC 45-4059. 1977. reprint ed. 50.00 (*0-8201-1208-9*) Schol Facsimiles.

Shorte Treatise of Politike Power. Compiled by John Poynet. LC 72-38220. (English Experience Ser.: No. 484). 184p. 1972. reprint ed. 35.00 (*90-221-0484-2*) Walter J Johnson.

Shortened History of England. George M. Trevelyan. 1976. pap. 7.95 (*0-14-020443-1*, Penguin Bks) Viking Penguin.

Shortened History of England. George M. Trevelyan. 1988. pap. 12.00 (*0-14-010241-8*, Penguin Bks) Viking Penguin.

Shortened History of England. George M. Trevelyan. 1988. pap. 14.95 (*0-14-023323-7*) Viking Penguin.

Shortened Path: Autobiography of a Western Yogi. abr. ed. Sri Kriyananda. 209p. 1980. pap. 6.95 (*0-916124-19-3*, DJ1) Crystal Clarity.

ShortEnglish Grammar: An Accidence to the English Tongue. Hugh Jones. (Notable American Authors Ser.). 1992. reprint ed. lib. bdg. 75.00 (*0-7812-3509-X*) Rprt Serv.

Shortening in Foods. Ahmad Sakr. Ed. by Al I. Obaba. 49p. (Orig.). 1974. pap. text ed. 1.50 (*0-916157-65-2*) African Islam Miss Pubns.

Shortening Manufacturing Cycle Time. 19p. 1970. 15.00 (*0-318-19678-6*) Clothing Mfrs.

Shortening Structures in Eastern & Northwestern Himalayan Rocks. W. Schwan. (Current Trends in Geology Ser.: Vol. III). 70p. 1980. 12.00 (*0-88065-189-X*, Messers Today & Tomorrow) Scholarly Pubns.

Shortening Time to the Doctoral Degree. 234p. (Orig.). (C). 1993. pap. text ed. 50.00 (*0-7881-0016-5*) DIANE Pub.

Shorter Book of Blessings. 576p. 15.95 (*1-55586-373-6*) US Catholic.

***Shorter Book of Blessings.** 576p. 1990. 16.95 (*0-89942-565-8*, 565/10) Catholic Bk Pub.

***Shorter Book of Blessings.** 576p. 1990. lthr. 21.95 (*0-89942-566-6*, 565/13) Catholic Bk Pub.

Shorter Cambridge Medieval History: The Twelfth Century to the Renaissance, Vol. 2. Charles W. Previte-Orton. LC 75-31398. 579p. reprint ed. pap. 165.10 (*0-318-34767-9*, 2031627) Bks Demand.

Shorter Catechism: A Baptist Version. 50p. (Orig.). (YA). (gr. 5 up). 1991. pap. 7.95 (*0-9622508-4-8*) Simpson NJ.

An Asterisk (*) at the beginning of an entry indicates that the title is appearing in BIP for the first time.

***Shorter Catechism: A Modest Revision for Baptists Today.** rev. ed. Ed. by James A. Hufstetler & Samuel E. Waldron. Orig. Title: The Westminster Shorter Catechism. 38p. (YA). (gr. 4 up). 1991. pap. 2.50 (*1-889520-08-X*) Truth for Eternity.

Shorter Catechism: A Study Manual, 2 vols., 1. G. I. Williamson. LC 77-139855. 1970. pap. 7.99 (*0-87552-539-3*, Pub. by Evangelical Pr) Presby & Reformed.

Shorter Catechism: A Study Manual, 2 vols., 2. G. I. Williamson. LC 77-139855. 1970. pap. 7.99 (*0-87552-540-7*, Pub. by Evangelical Pr) Presby & Reformed.

Shorter Catechism Explained from Scripture. Thomas Vincent. (Puritan Paperbacks Ser.). 282p. (Orig.). 1980. reprint ed. pap. 7.50 (*0-85151-314-X*) Banner of Truth.

Shorter Catechism of the Orthodox Church. pap. 0.50 (*0-89981-094-2*) Eastern Orthodox.

Shorter Catechism with Scripture Proofs. Westminster Assembly Staff. 1975. 1.00 (*0-85151-265-8*) Banner of Truth.

Shorter Christian Prayer. National Conference of Catholic Bishops. 670p. 1988. vinyl bd. 9.95 (*0-89942-408-2*, 408/10) Catholic Bk Pub.

Shorter Classics. Eugen Von Bohm-Bawerk. 370p. 1962. pap. 12.95 (*0-910884-12-9*) Libertarian Press.

Shorter College German. 3rd ed. M. Blakemore Evans et al. LC 56-5843. (Illus.). 1956. text ed. 15.95 (*0-89197-403-2*); pap. text ed. 8.95 (*0-89197-404-0*) Irvington.

Shorter Compositions for Piano: Most from the Weimar Years. Ed. by Joel Sachs. LC 89-754020. (J. N. Hummel: The Complete Works for Piano Ser.: Vol. 4). 512p. 1990. text ed. 45.00 (*0-8240-3789-8*) Garland.

Shorter Compositions for Piano: Most from the Weimar Years. Ed. by Joel Sachs. (J. N. Hummel: The Complete Works for Piano Ser.: Vol. 3). 424p. 1990. reprint ed. text ed. 45.00 (*0-8240-3788-X*) Garland.

Shorter Connection: A. J. Wilkinson, Clarice Cliff, Crown Devon, a Family Pottery 1874-1974. Irene Hopwood. (Illus.). 132p. 1992. pap. 50.00 (*0-903685-31-0*, Pub. by R Dennis UK) Antique Collect.

Shorter Contributions to The Stratigraphy & Geochronology of Upper Cretaceous Rocks in Southwestern Montana. LC 94-34009. (U.S. Geological Survey Bulletin Ser.: 2113). 1995. write for info. (*0-615-00152-1*) US Geol Survey.

Shorter Course of Theoretical Physics, Set. L. D. Landau & E. M. Lifshitz. Incl. Vol. 1. Mechanics & Electrodynamics. LC 74-167927. 1972. text ed. 135.00 (*0-08-016739-X*, CRC Reprint); LC 74-167927. 1992. Set text ed. write for info. (*0-08-025049-1*, Pub. by Pergamon Repr UK) Franklin.

Shorter Dictionary of Catch Phrases: Based on the Work of Eric Partridge & Paul Beale. Rosalind Fergusson. LC 93-43539. 176p. (gr. 13). 1994. pap. 16.95 (*0-415-10051-8*) Routledge.

Shorter Dictionary of Spoken Russian: Abkuerzungswoertereuch der Russischen Sprache. 3rd ed. D. I. Alekseev. (GER & RUS.). 1983. 29.95 (*0-8288-1162-8*, M15324) Fr & Eur.

Shorter Encyclopedia of Islam. Hamilton A. Gibb & J. H. Kramers. (Illus.). viii, 671p. 1995. reprint ed. 78.00 (*90-04-00681-8*) E J Brill.

Shorter English Nepali Dictionary. T. Warren. 1988. reprint ed. 11.50 (*81-206-0304-4*, Pub. by Asian Educ Servs II) S Asia.

Shorter English-Persian Dictionary. Soleyman Haim. 890p. 1984. 18.00 (*0-939214-50-4*) Mazda Pubs.

Shorter English-Persian Dictionary. Soleyman Haim. 700p. (ENG & PER.). 1985. 35.00 (*0-8288-0544-X*, F 46380) Fr & Eur.

Shorter Essay Writing Text. Smilkstein. (C). pap. text ed. 18.75 (*0-15-501168-5*) HB Coll Pubs.

Shorter Etymological Dictionary of the Spanish Language: Breve Diccionario Etimologico de la Lengua Espanola. 3rd ed. Joan Corominas i Vigneaux & J. A. Pascual. 628p. (SPA.). 1990. write for info. (*0-7859-4949-6*) Fr & Eur.

Shorter Forms of Building Contract. 3rd ed. H. Clamp. 208p. 1993. 64.95 (*0-632-03384-3*) Blackwell Sci.

Shorter Homeric Hymns. Lee T. Pearcy. 53p. (Orig.). (C). 1989. pap. text ed. 6.00 (*0-929524-62-4*) Bryn Mawr Commentaries.

Shorter Hours: A Study of the Movement since the Civil War. Marion C. Cahill. LC 68-54258. (Columbia University. Studies in the Social Sciences: No. 380). 1971. reprint ed. 34.50 (*0-404-51380-8*) AMS Pr.

Shorter Hours, Shorter Weeks: Spreading the Work to Reduce Unemployment. Sar A. Levitan & Richard Belous. LC 77-4787. (Johns Hopkins University Policy Studies in Employment & Welfare: No. 30). (Illus.). 107p. reprint ed. 30.50 (*0-8357-9286-2*, 2016573) Bks Demand.

Shorter Illustrated History of the World. J. M. Roberts. 616p. Date not set. pap. write for info. (*1-85986-053-2*) OUP.

***Shorter Illustrated History of Ulster.** Jonathan Bardon. 326p. 9700. pap. 29.95 (*0-85640-586-8*, Pub. by Blackstaff Pr IE) Dufour.

Shorter Latin Poems of Master Henry of Avranches Relating to England. Henry Of Avranches. Ed. by Josiah C. Russell & John P. Heironimus. (Mediaeval Academy of America Publications: Vol. 21). 1935. 30.00 (*0-527-01693-4*) Periodicals Srv.

Shorter Lexicon of the Greek New Testament. 2nd rev. ed. Frederick W. Danker. LC 82-10933. 240p. 1983. lib. bdg. 29.95 (*0-226-13613-2*) U Ch Pr.

Shorter Life of Christ. Donald Guthrie. LC 71-120039. (Contemporary Evangelical Perspective Ser.). 186p. 1970. 14.99 (*0-310-25441-8*, 6500P) Zondervan.

***Shorter Model Theory.** Wilfred Hodges. LC 96-36603. 250p. (C). 1997. pap. text ed. 34.95 (*0-521-58713-1*) Cambridge U Pr.

Shorter Modern Poems: 1900-1931. Ed. by David Morton. LC 74-116411. (Granger Index Reprint Ser.). 1977. 15.95 (*0-8369-6152-8*) Ayer.

Shorter Morning & Evening Prayer: The Psalter of the Liturgy of the Hours. 562p. (C). 1989. pap. 17.95 (*0-8146-1939-8*) Liturgical Pr.

Shorter New Oxford Book of Carols. Ed. by Hugh Keyte et al. 360p. 1993. 16.95 (*0-19-353324-3*) OUP.

Shorter Novels: Elizabethan & Jacobean, Jacobean & Restorations & Eighteenth Century, 3 vols., Set. (BCL1-PR English Literature Ser.). 1992. reprint ed. lib. bdg. 225.00 (*0-7812-7156-8*) Rprt Serv.

Shorter Novels of Herman Melville. Herman Melville. (Black & Gold Library). 1978. pap. 12.95 (*0-87140-122-3*) Liveright.

Shorter Pepys. Samuel Pepys. Ed. & Selected by Robert Latham. LC 85-40210. 1152p. 1985. 50.00 (*0-520-03426-0*) U CA Pr.

Shorter Persian-English Dictionary. Soleyman Haim. 850p. 1984. 18.00 (*0-939214-49-0*) Mazda Pubs.

Shorter Persian-English Dictionary. Soleyman Haim. 814p. (ENG & PER.). 1984. 35.00 (*0-8288-0545-8*, F 46510) Fr & Eur.

Shorter Plays & Scenarios of Norm Moser. Ed. by Norman Moser. 48p. (Orig.). 1981. pap. 3.00 (*0-941442-00-4*) Illuminations Pr.

Shorter Poems. Gerald Burns. LC 92-29476. 128p. 1993. pap. 9.95 (*1-56478-026-0*) Dalkey Arch.

Shorter Poems. Alastair J. Minnis. (Oxford Guides to Chaucer Ser.: Vol. 3). 580p. 1995. 79.00 (*0-19-811193-2*) OUP.

Shorter Poems of Matthew Prior. Matthew Prior. 1977. 16.95 (*0-8369-7120-5*, 7954) Ayer.

Shorter Poems of the Eighteenth Century: An Anthology. Iolo A. Williams. (BCL1-PR English Literature Ser.). 478p. 1992. reprint ed. lib. bdg. 99.00 (*0-7812-7140-1*) Rprt Serv.

Shorter Poems, 1807-1820. William Wordsworth. Ed. by Carl H. Ketcham. LC 88-15969. (Cornell Wordsworth Ser.). (Illus.). 704p. 1990. 90.00 (*0-8014-2175-6*) Cornell U Pr.

Shorter Prose Writings of Samuel Johnson, 2 vols., Set. Samuel Johnson. Ed. by O M Brack, Jr. (Studies in the Eighteenth Century: No. 24). 1992. 125.00 (*0-404-63524-5*) AMS Pr.

***Shorter Road to Success.** Linda J. Nash. LC 96-92278. 192p. (Orig.). 1996. pap. 10.00 (*0-9636702-1-2*) PRISM MO.

Shorter Science & Civilisation in China, Vol. 1. Colin A. Ronan. LC 77-82513. (Illus.). 337p. 1980. pap. text ed. 30.95 (*0-521-29286-7*) Cambridge U Pr.

Shorter Science & Civilisation in China, Vol. 2. Colin A. Ronan. LC 77-82513. (Illus.). 250p. 1985. pap. text ed. 32.95 (*0-521-31536-0*) Cambridge U Pr.

Shorter Science & Civilisation in China, Vol. 3. Colin A. Ronan. 280p. 1986. text ed. 69.95 (*0-521-25272-5*); pap. text ed. 26.95 (*0-521-31560-3*) Cambridge U Pr.

Shorter Science & Civilisation in China Vol. 4: An Abridgement of Joseph Needham's Original Text of Volume IV. Colin A. Ronan. 350p. 1994. text ed. 80.00 (*0-521-32995-7*); pap. text ed. 35.95 (*0-521-33873-5*) Cambridge U Pr.

Shorter Science & Civilisation in China Vol. 5. Colin A. Ronan. (Illus.). 360p. (C). 1995. text ed. 80.00 (*0-521-46214-2*); pap. text ed. 35.95 (*0-521-46773-X*) Cambridge U Pr.

***Shorter Shakespeare.** William Shakespeare. 1996. 9.95 (*0-614-20640-5*) Macmillan.

Shorter Slang Dictionary. Eric Partridge & Paul Beale. Ed. by Rosalind Fergusson. 240p. (gr. 13). 1993. pap. 15.95 (*0-415-08866-6*, B0566) Routledge.

Shorter Socratic Writings: "Apology of Socrates to the Jury," "Oeconomicus," & "Symposium" Xenophon. Ed. by Robert C. Bartlett. LC 95-37619. 216p. 1996. 29.95 (*0-8014-3214-6*) Cornell U Pr.

Shorter Summa: The Most Essential Philosophical Passages of St. Thomas Aquinas' Summa Theologica. Peter J. Kreeft. LC 92-75065. 162p. (C). 1993. pap. 10.95 (*0-89870-438-3*) Ignatius Pr.

Shorter Tales. Joseph Conrad. LC 71-128727. (Short Story Index Reprint Ser.). 1977. 24.95 (*0-8369-3618-3*) Ayer.

***Shorter Term Treatments for Borderline Personality Disorders.** John D. Preston. 160p. 1997. text ed. 39.95 (*1-57224-092-X*) New Harbinger.

Shorter Testament of Secrets: The Heart of the Dawn Horse Testament. Adi D. Samraj. 1996. pap. text ed. 24.95 (*1-57097-029-7*) Dawn Horse Pr.

Shorter Works & Fragments Vol. 11: The Collected Works of Samuel Taylor Coleridge. Samuel Taylor Coleridge. 1760p. (C). 1995. text ed. 150.00 (*0-691-09878-6*) Princeton U Pr.

Shorter Works for Pianoforte Solo. Franz Schubert. 199p. 1970. pap. 10.95 (*0-486-22648-4*) Dover.

Shorter Works of Stephen King. Michael R. Collings & David Engebretson. LC 85-2822. (Starmont Studies in Literary Criticism: No. 9). vi, 202p. 1985. pap. 23.00 (*0-930261-02-X*); lib. bdg. 33.00 (*0-930261-03-8*) Borgo Pr.

Shorter Workweek in the 1980's. William McGaughey, Jr. LC 80-54666. 320p. (Orig.). 1981. pap. 6.95 (*0-9605630-0-8*) Thistlerose.

Shorter Writings of J. I. Packer, Vol. 1. J. I. Packer. Ed. by Jim Lyster. 369p. (C). 1996. ring bd. write for info. (*1-57383-061-5*) Regent College.

Shorter Writings of J. I. Packer, Vol. 2. J. I. Packer. Ed. by Jim Lyster. 323p. (C). 1996. ring bd. write for info. (*1-57383-062-3*) Regent College.

Shorter Writings of J. I. Packer, Vol. 3. J. I. Packer. Ed. by Jim Lyster. 353p. (C). 1996. ring bd. write for info. (*1-57383-063-1*) Regent College.

Shorter Writings of J. I. Packer, Vol. 4. J. I. Packer. Ed. by Jim Lyster. (C). 1996. ring bd. write for info. (*1-57383-064-X*) Regent College.

Shortest Day: Murder at the Revels. Jane Langton. LC 95-14266. (Homer Kelly Mystery Ser.). (Illus.). 288p. 1995. pap. 19.95 (*0-670-84710-0*, Viking) Viking Penguin.

Shortest Day: Murder at the Revels. Jane Langton. (Illus.). 272p. 1996. pap. 5.95 (*0-14-017377-3*, Viking) Viking Penguin.

Shortest Disciple. Steve Jensen. LC 93-3902. (Devotions for Today Ser.). (J). 1993. 8.75 (*1-56212-036-0*) CRC Pubns.

Shortest Distance: The Pursuit of Independence for Persons with Acquired Brain Injury. Ed. by Brian T. McMahon & Randall W. Evans. LC 93-87363. 156p. 1994. pap. text ed. 32.50 (*1-878205-68-4*) GR Press.

***Shortest Distance Between You & Published Book: Everything You Need to Know in the Order You Need to Know It.** Susan Page. 256p. 1997. pap. 13.00 (*0-553-06177-1*) Broadway BDD.

***Shortest Distance to Danger.** Patrick O. Kendley. 588p. (Orig.). 1997. mass mkt. 5.99 (*1-55237-101-8*, Pub. by Comnwlth Pub CN) Partners Pubs Grp.

Shortest Journey. large type ed. Hazel Holt. LC 94-37507. 232p. 1995. pap. 17.95 (*0-7838-1138-1*, GK Hall) Thorndike Pr.

Shortest Kid in the World. Corinne D. Bliss. LC 93-45421. (Illus.). (J). (gr. 1-3). 1995. pap. 3.99 (*0-679-85809-1*); lib. bdg. 11.99 (*0-679-95809-6*) Random Bks Yng Read.

Shortest Paths. N. Crisper & G. Froelich. (Illus.). 54p. pap. text ed. 11.99 (*0-614-05327-7*, GM 6653) COMAP Inc.

Shortest Paths for Sub-Riemannian Metrics on Rank-Two Distributions. Wensheng Liu & Hector J. Sussmann. LC 95-34455. (Memoirs of the American Mathematical Society Ser.: No. 564). 124p. 1995. pap. 35.00 (*0-8218-0404-9*, MEMO/118/564) Am Math.

Shortest Paths Variational Problems: Survey of Recent East European Mathematical Literature. L. Lyusternik & P. Collins. LC 64-14145. (Popular Lectures in Mathematics: Vol. 13). 1964. 49.00 (*0-08-010647-1*, Pub. by Pergamon Repr UK) Franklin.

Shortest Way to Hades. Sara Caudwell. 320p. 1995. mass mkt. 4.99 (*0-440-21233-2*) Dell.

Shortest Way to Style: Rhetorical Strategies. May F. McMillan. LC 84-20567. xxii, 274p. (C). 1984. 19.45 (*0-86554-132-9*, H123) Mercer Univ Pr.

Shortgrass Song. Mike Blakely. 608p. 1995. 4.99 (*0-8125-3029-2*) Forge NYC.

Shorthand Collection in the New York Public Library: A Catalogue of Books, Periodicals & Manuscripts. Ed. by Karl Brown & Daniel C. Haskell. LC 77-137704. (New York Public Library Publications in Reprint). 1971. reprint ed. 51.95 (*0-405-01746-4*) Ayer.

Shorthand Fashion Sketching. 3rd ed. Patricia L. Rowe. LC 60-6848. (Illus.). 145p. reprint ed. pap. 41.40 (*0-685-44413-9*, 2032487) Bks Demand.

***Shorthand for Today.** Longman Publishing Staff. Date not set. pap. text ed. write for info. (*0-85896-830-4*) Addison-Wesley.

Shorthand in Four Days. rev. ed. Benjamin Friedlander. LC 52-3478. 24p. 1980. pap. 9.95 (*0-917520-02-5*) Fineline.

Shorthand Reporter. Jack Rudman. (Career Examination Ser.: C-741). 1994. pap. 23.95 (*0-8373-0741-4*) Nat Learn.

Shortline to Paradise. Hank Johnston. 1962. 5.95 (*0-685-28945-1*) Flying Spur Pr.

Shortness of Breath: A Guide to Better Living & Breathing. 5th ed. Andrew Ries. 128p. (C). (gr. 13). 1995. pap. text ed. 9.95 (*0-8151-7339-3*) Mosby Yr Bk.

Shorts. Caryl Churchill. 304p. 1990. pap. 19.95 (*1-85459-085-5*, Pub. by N Hern Bks UK) Theatre Comm.

Shorts. David Edgar. 160p. 1989. pap. 16.95 (*1-85459-051-0*, Pub. by N Hern Bks UK) Theatre Comm.

Shorts. Milo Manara. Tr. by Tom Leighton from FRE. (Illus.). 49p. (Orig.). 1989. pap. 9.95 (*0-87416-060-X*) Catalan Communs.

Shorts. Milo Manara. 48p. (Orig.). 1995. pap. 9.95 (*1-56163-128-0*, Eurotica) NBM.

***Shorts: A Gateway into New Markets.** Colleen F. Bollen. 80p. (Orig.). 1996. pap. 8.95 (*0-9654384-0-6*) Turtle Isl WA.

Shorts: For Fun, Not for Instruction. J. Chester Johnson. LC 85-81660. (Orig.). 1985. pap. 6.50 (*0-914426-02-8*) Juliet Pr.

Shorts: On Reaching Forty. J. Chester Johnson. LC 85-82179. (Orig.). 1986. pap. 6.50 (*0-914426-03-6*) Juliet Pr.

S.H.O.R.T.S. Some Humorous Opinions Regarding Today's Society. Jack Lacy. Ed. by Mary E. Gilliland. (Illus.). 120p. (Orig.). 1995. pap. 9.95 (*0-9643918-0-5*) Triple J Pr.

Shorts Aircraft since 1900. 2nd ed. C. H. Barnes. (Putnam Aviation Ser.). (Illus.). 766p. 1989. 45.00 (*0-87021-662-7*) Naval Inst Pr.

***Shortsight: (Blind Ambition)** Douglas Greer. iii, 508p. (Orig.). 1996. 24.95 (*0-9655625-0-6*) G P Gibralter.

Shortstop from Tokyo. 1995. pap. 8.75 (*0-15-305219-8*) HB Schl Dept.

Shortstop from Tokyo. Matt Christopher. (Illus.). (J). (gr. 3-6). 1988. mass mkt. 3.95 (*0-316-13992-0*) Little.

***Shortstop from Tokyo.** HarBrace Staff. (J). 1995. pap. 11.00 (*0-15-305595-2*) HarBrace.

***Shortstop Who Knew Too Much, Vol. 1.** Dan Gutman. (Sandlot Ser.). 1997. pap. 3.99 (*0-590-13760-3*, Apple Paperbacks) Scholastic Inc.

***Shortstop's Son: Essays & Journalism.** Philip Martin. LC 97-14766. 1997. write for info. (*1-55728-483-0*); pap. write for info. (*1-55728-484-9*) U of Ark Pr.

Shortwave Clandestine Confidential. Gerry L. Dexter. (Illus.). 86p. (Orig.). 1984. pap. 8.95 (*0-916661-02-4*, 203) Universal Elect.

Shortwave Directory. 8th ed. Robert B. Grove. Ed. by Larry Van Horn. LC 87-51078. (Illus.). 256p. 1993. 9.95 (*0-944543-00-6*, BOK14) Grove Enterp.

Shortwave Listening Guidebook: The Complete Guide to Hearing the World. 2nd ed. Harry L. Helms. LC 93-1030. 352p. 1993. pap. 19.95 (*1-878707-11-6*) HighText.

Shortwave Listening Handbook. Harry L. Helms. (Illus.). 224p. 1987. 18.50 (*0-13-809591-4*) P-H.

Shortwave Listening on the Road: The World Traveler's Guide. A. Yoder. 1995. pap. text ed. 17.95 (*0-07-076509-X*) McGraw.

Shortwave Radio Listening for Beginners. Anita L. McCormick. 1993. text ed. 12.95 (*0-07-044991-0*); pap. text ed. 19.95 (*0-07-044990-2*) McGraw.

Shortwave Radio Listening for Beginners. Anita L. McCormick. LC 92-41603. 1993. 18.95 (*0-8306-4136-X*); pap. 10.60 (*0-8306-4135-1*) McGraw-Hill Prof.

***Shortwave Receivers Past & Present: Communications Receivers 1945-1996.** 2nd ed. Fred Osterman. (Illus.). 351p. (Orig.). 1997. per., pap. 19.95 (*1-882123-06-9*, 0002) Universal Radio Rsch.

Shortwinged Hawks: A Review of Ancient & Modern Hawking. E. W. Jameson, Jr. (Illus.). 175p. 1993. 135.00 (*0-9606576-3-0*) E W Jameson Jr.

Shorty Gordy. D. W. Hayes. LC 91-65922. (Illus.). (J). (gr. k-3). 1992. 7.95 (*1-55523-449-6*) Winston-Derek.

Shorty McCabe Gets the Hail. Sewell Ford. LC 79-125211. (Short Story Index Reprint Ser.). 1977. 20.95 (*0-8369-3578-0*) Ayer.

Shorty McCabe Looks 'em Over. Sewell Ford. LC 73-122702. (Short Story Index Reprint Ser.). (Illus.). 1977. 21.95 (*0-8369-3535-7*) Ayer.

Shorty Society. Sheri C. Sinykin. 144p. (J). (gr. 5 up). 1994. pap. 14.99 (*0-670-85248-1*) Viking Child Bks.

Shorty Society. Sheri C. Sinykin. 144p. (J). 1996. pap. 3.99 (*0-14-036724-1*) Puffin Bks.

Shosankenshu: Japanese Sword Mounts. Henri Joly. 1970. 45.00 (*0-87556-133-0*) Saifer.

Shosha. Isaac B. Singer. 278p. 1996. pap. text ed. 12.00 (*0-374-52480-7*, Noonday) FS&G.

Shoshaman: A Tale of Corporate Japan. Shinya Arai. Tr. by Chieko Mulhern from JPN. (Voices from Asia Ser.: No. 3). 232p. 1991. pap. 15.95 (*0-520-07142-5*) U CA Pr.

Shoshin Issho & Niwano Nikkyo Jiden see Lifetime Beginner: An Autobiography

Shoshinge: The Heart of Shin Buddhism. Alred Bloom. Tr. by T. Nagatani & Ruth Tabrah. LC 86-26379. 108p. (Orig.). 1986. pap. 8.95 (*0-938474-06-5*) Buddhist Study.

***Shoshone.** LC 96-49702. (The Junior Library of the Indians of North America). (J). 1997. pap. 7.95 (*0-7910-4601-X*, Am Art Analog) Chelsea Hse.

***Shoshone: Indians of North America.** Chelsea House Publishers Staff. LC 96-49702. 1996. pap. 9.95 (*0-7910-4452-1*) Chelsea Hse.

Shoshone - Southwest see Indians of North America

Shoshone-Bannock Subsistence & Society. fac. ed. Robert Fand & Yolanda Murphy. Ed. by J. H. Rowe et al. (University of California Publications: No. 16:7). 51p. (C). 1960. reprint ed. pap. 4.70 (*1-55567-148-9*) Coyote Press.

Shoshone Ghost Dance Religion: Poetry Songs & Great Basin Context. Judith Vander. (Music in American Life Ser.). 656p. 1996. text ed. 65.00 (*0-252-02214-9*) U of Ill Pr.

Shoshone Indians see Junior Library of American Indians

Shoshone Mike. Frank Bergon. (Western Literature Ser.). 304p. 1994. pap. 13.00 (*0-87417-244-6*) U of Nev Pr.

Shoshone Tales. Compiled by Anne M. Smith. (American West Ser.: Vol. 31). (Illus.). 248p. (C). 1993. 24.95 (*0-87480-405-1*) U of Utah Pr.

Shoshonean Dialects of California. fac. ed. A. L. Kroeber. (University of California Publications in American Archaeology & Ethnology: Vol. 4: 3). 101p. (C). 1907. reprint ed. pap. text ed. 9.05 (*1-55567-164-0*) Coyote Press.

Shoshoni. Alden R. Carter. LC 89-31102. (First Bks.). (Illus.). 64p. (J). (gr. 3-5). 1989. lib. bdg. 21.00 (*0-531-10753-1*) Watts.

Shoshoni. Alden R. Carter. (First Bks.). (Illus.). 64p. (J). (gr. 3 up). 1991. pap. 6.95 (*0-531-15605-2*) Watts.

Shoshoni. rev. ed. Dennis B. Fradin. LC 88-11821. (New True Bks.). (Illus.). 48p. (J). (gr. k-4). 1993. pap. 5.50 (*0-516-41156-X*); lib. bdg. 19.00 (*0-516-01156-1*) Childrens.

Shoshoni Cookbook: Vegetarian Recipes from the Shoshoni Yoga Spa. Ann Saks & Faith Stone. LC 93-8782. 208p. 1993. pap. 12.95 (*0-913990-49-3*) Book Pub Co.

Shoshoni-Crow Sun Dance. Fred W. Voget. LC 83-40332. (Civilization of the American Indian Ser.: Vol. 170). (Illus.). 368p. 1984. 28.95 (*0-8061-1886-5*) U of Okla Pr.

Shoshoni Frontier & the Bear River Massacre. Ed. by Brigham D. Madsen. (Illus.). 304p. 1995. reprint ed. pap. 17.95 (*0-87480-494-9*) U of Utah Pr.

Shoshoni Man: A Tale of Self-Discovery & Love. Rose Sparrow. LC 94-29889. 1994. 13.95 (*1-885275-10-2*) C J Howie.

Shoshoni River Witching Hour. 2nd ed. Dean Phelps. 44p. 1975. pap. 3.00 (*0-914974-04-1*) Holmgangers.

Shoshoni Vengeance. John Legg. 304p. 1993. mass mkt. 3.50 (*0-8217-4334-1*, Zebra Kensgtn) Kensgtn Pub Corp.

Shoshonis: Sentinels of the Rockies. Virginia C. Trenholm & Maurine Carley. (Civilization of the American Indian Ser.: No. 74). (Illus.). 1964. pap. 18.95 (*0-8061-1055-4*) U of Okla Pr.

S

S

Shostakovich. Eric Roseberry. (Illustrated Lives of the Great Composers Ser.). (Illus.). 192p. 1996. 14.95 (0-7119-0258-5, OP 42449) Omnibus NY.

Shostakovich: A Life Remembered. Elizabeth Wilson. 574p. (C). 1994. pap. text ed. 18.95 (0-691-04465-1) Princeton U Pr.

Shostakovich: The Man & His Music. Christopher Norris. LC 82-4172. 235p. 1983. 25.00 (0-7145-2778-5) M Boyars Pubs.

Shostakovich Studies. Ed. by David Fanning. 320p. (C). 1995. text ed. 59.95 (0-521-45239-2) Cambridge U Pr.

Shot! (Illus.). 120p. 1995. pap. 29.95 (0-85493-237-2, Pub. by Withrby UK) Trafalgar.

***Shot.** Jamie Murphy. Ed. by Carol White. 1996. pap. 17.95 incl. audio (0-9630373-2-3) Earth Healing.

Shot: La Detonacion. Antonio B. Vallejo. (Hispanic Classics Ser.). 1990. 49.95 (0-85668-455-4, Pub. by Aris & Phillips UK); pap. 22.00 (0-85668-456-2, Pub. by Aris & Phillips UK) David Brown.

Shot at a Rose, to the Bite of a Gator: The '75-'78 Ohio State Football Saga. Todd W. Skipton. LC 93-72628. (Illus.). 330p. (Orig.). pap. 22.95 (0-9638057-1-1) Brawny Pug.

Shot by Shot: A Practical Guide to Filmmaking. 2nd ed. John Cantine et al. (Illus.). 156p. (Orig.). (C). 1995. pap. text ed. 12.50 (0-9637433-1-7) Pittsbrgh Film.

Shot-Countershot: Film Tradition & Women's Cinema. Lucy Fischer. 320p. 1989. text ed. 55.00 (0-691-04756-1); pap. text ed. 17.95 (0-691-00605-9) Princeton U Pr.

Shot Glasses: An American Tradition. Mark Pickvet. (Illus.). 167p. 1990. pap. 6.48 (0-915410-62-1, 3070) Antique Pubns.

Shot Heard 'Round the World: The Beginnings of the American Revolution. Ed. by Jeanne M. Bracken. LC 94-71898. (Perspectives on History Ser.). (Illus.). 64p. (Orig.). (YA). 1995. pap. 5.95 (1-878668-32-3) Disc Enter Ltd.

Shot in the Cathedral. Mario Bencastro. LC 96-16942. 220p. 1996. 18.95 (1-55885-164-X) Arte Publico.

Shot in the Dark. Tony Gibbs. 320p. 1997. mass mkt. 5.99 (0-446-40519-1, Mysterious Paperbk) Warner Bks.

Shot in the Dark: Why the P In DPT Vaccination May Be Hazardous to Your Child's Health. Harris L. Coulter & Barbara L. Fisher. LC 91-21991. 256p. (Orig.). pap. 10.95 (0-89529-463-X) Avery Pub.

Shot in the Heart. Mikal Gilmore. 416p. 1994. 25.00 (0-385-42293-8) Doubleday.

Shot in the Heart. Mikal Gilmore. 416p. 1995. reprint ed. pap. 14.95 (0-385-47800-3, Anchor NY) Doubleday.

Shot on Location. Stan Cutler. 336p. 1994. pap. 4.99 (0-451-40391-6, Sig) NAL-Dutton.

Shot on Location. large type ed. Hazel W. Jones. 1993. 21.95 (0-7089-2788-2, Charnwood) Ulverscroft.

Shot on This Site: A Traveler's Guide to the Places & Locations Used to Film Famous Movies & Television Shows. William A. Gordon. (Illus.). 304p. 1995. pap. 14.95 (0-8065-1647-X, Citadel Pr) Carol Pub Group.

Shot Peening. A. Niku-Lari. 1981. pap. 26.00 (0-08-027600-8, Pergamon Pr) Elsevier.

***Shot Peening & the Fatigue of Metals.** H. F. Moore. (Technical Papers). 1944. pap. text ed. 30.00 (1-55589-221-3) AGMA.

***Shot Peening in Gear Design.** J. C. Straub. (Technical Papers). 1964. pap. text ed. 30.00 (1-55589-225-6) AGMA.

***Shot Peening in the Design of Gears.** J. C. Straub. (Technical Papers). 8p. 1953. pap. text ed. 30.00 (1-55589-224-8) AGMA.

Shot Shell Boxes. 2nd ed. Bob Strauss & Beverly Strauss. (Illus.). 148p. (Orig.). 1991. pap. text ed. 12.00 (1-879170-00-0) Circus Promotions.

Shotblasting Equipment & Abrasives U. S. Markets, Technologies & Opportunities: 1992-1997 Analysis. Dennis M. Zogbi. 127p. (Orig.). 1993. pap. 995.00 (0-929717-20-1) Paumanok Pubns.

Shotcrete. 76p. 1992. 53.75 (0-685-62962-7, C-18BOW6) ACI.

Shotcrete for Underground Support, No. IV. Ed. by Elwyn H. King. LC 85-81285. 194p. 1985. pap. 30.00 (0-939204-27-4, 82-18) Eng Found.

Shotcrete for Underground Support, Vol. III. Ed. by Robin Mason. 346p. (Orig.). 1980. pap. 30.00 (0-939204-04-5, 78-14) Eng Found.

Shotcrete for Underground Support, Vol. 7. 328p. (Orig.). 1995. pap. 40.00 (0-7844-0087-3) Am Soc Civil Eng.

Shotcrete for Underground Support 5: Proceedings of the Engineering Foundation Conference, Uppsala, Sweden, June 3-7, 1990. Ed. by John C. Sharp & Tomas Franzen. LC 93-204. 576p. 1993. 48.00 (0-87262-944-9) Am Soc Civil Eng.

Shotcrete for Underground Support 6: Proceedings of the Engineering Foundation Conference, Niagara-on-the-Lake, Canada, May 2-6, 1993. LC 93-3587. 208p. 1993. 24.00 (0-87262-949-X) Am Soc Civil Eng.

Shotcreting: Equipment & Procedures. (Illus.). (Orig.). 1996. pap. 11.95 (0-924659-77-7, 1280) Aberdeen Group.

Shotgun. Geoffrey Boothroyd. (Illus.). 240p. 1993. 35.00 (0-940143-92-5) Safari Pr.

Shotgun! Kit Dalton. (Buckskin Giant Special Edition Ser.). 368p. (Orig.). 1995. mass mkt., pap. text ed. 4.99 (0-8439-3730-0) Dorchester Pub Co.

***Shotgun.** Kevin W. Dwyer. 280p. (Orig.). 1997. 18.95 (1-889501-12-3, Sherlock Pr); mass mkt. 7.99 (1-889501-11-5, Sherlock Pr) Sovereign.

Shotgun. Ed McBain. 1982. pap. 2.50 (0-451-11971-1, Sig) NAL-Dutton.

Shotgun. Robert Olmsted. 16p. 1991. pap. 1.50 (0-89754-077-8) Dan River Pr.

***Shotgun Baby.** Tara T. Quinn. 1997. pap. 3.99 (0-373-70750-9, 1-70750-4) Harlequin Bks.

Shotgun Canyon. Doyle Trent. 1990. mass mkt. 3.50 (0-8217-3229-3, Zebra Kensgtn) Kensgtn Pub Corp.

Shotgun Digest. 4th ed. Ed. by Jack Lewis. LC 74-80333. (Illus.). 256p. (Orig.). 1993. pap. 17.95 (0-87349-137-8, SD4) DBI.

Shotgun in Combat. Tony Lesce. (Illus.). 152p. 1984. pap. 12.00 (0-87364-314-3) Paladin Pr.

Shotgun Marriage. Day Leclaire. 1997. mass mkt. 3.25 (0-373-03440-7, 1-03440-4) Silhouette.

***Shotgun Marriage.** large type ed. Day Leclaire. (Fairytale Weddings Trilogy Ser.). 1997. mass mkt. 3.25 (0-373-15686-3) Harlequin Bks.

Shotgun Saturday Night. Bill Crider. 1987. 16.95 (0-8027-5684-0) Walker & Co.

Shotgun Shooting. Boy Scouts of America Staff. (Illus.). 64p. (Orig.). 1989. pap. 2.40 (0-8395-3331-4, 33331) BSA.

Shotgun Stuff. Don Zutz. 176p. (Orig.). 1991. pap. 19.95 (0-925012-01-7) Shotgun Sports.

Shotgun Wedding. Barbara Catlin. (Special Edition Ser.: No. 724). 1992. mass mkt. 3.29 (0-373-09724-7, 5-09724-1) Harlequin Bks.

Shotgun Wedding. Charlotte Lamb. (Presents Ser.: No. 480). 1992. pap. 2.89 (0-373-11480-X) Harlequin Bks.

***Shotgun Wedding.** Alexandra Sellers. 1997. mass mkt. 3.50 (0-373-52055-7, 1-52055-0) Silhouette.

Shotgun Wedding. Cathy G. Thacker. (American Romance Ser.). 1995. mass mkt. 3.50 (0-373-16587-0, 1-16587-7) Harlequin Bks.

Shotgunner's Notebook: The Advice & Reflections of a Wingshooter. rev. ed. Gene Hill. LC 89-60724. (Illus.). 199p. 1989. 25.00 (0-924357-00-2, 21301-A) Countrysport Pr.

Shotgunning: The Art & the Science. Bob Brister. LC 82-62603. 1976. 18.95 (0-8329-1840-7, Winchester Pr) New Win Pub.

Shotgunning: Trends in Transition. Don Zutz. (Illus.). 288p. 1990. 29.50 (0-935632-86-7) Wolfe Pub Co.

Shotguns & Gunsmiths. Geoffrey Boothroyd. (Illus.). 240p. 1993. 35.00 (0-940143-91-7) Safari Pr.

Shotguns & Shooting. Michael McIntosh. (Illus.). 280p. 1995. 30.00 (0-924357-48-7, 21150-A) Countrysport Pr.

Shotguns & Shooting. deluxe limited ed. Michael McIntosh. (Illus.). 274p. 1995. lthr. 95.00 (0-924357-49-5, 21150-B) Countrysport Pr.

Shotguns by Keith. Elmer Keith. (Library Classics Ser.). 1988. 39.00 (0-935632-58-1) Wolfe Pub Co.

Shoto Clay: Clay Artifacts from the Lower Columbia River. Robert Slocum & Kenneth Matsen. 32p. 1968. pap. 5.95 (0-8323-0133-7) Binford Mort.

Shoto Kan Karate: The Ultimate in Self-Defense. Peter Ventresca. 158p. 1990. pap. 11.95 (0-8048-1658-1) C E Tuttle.

Shotokan Karate. K. Enoeda & Mack. pap. 13.95 (0-901764-24-8, 93219) Talman.

Shotokan Karate: Its History & Evolution. rev. ed. Randall G. Hassell. (Illus.). 200p. 1995. pap. 15.95 (0-911921-20-6) Focus Pubns MO.

***Shotokan Karate Handbook: Beginner to Black Belt.** Gursharan Sahota. 1996. pap. text ed. 24.95 (0-9524638-0-6) Seven Hills Bk.

Shots at Big Game. C. Boddington. (Illus.). 198p. 1993. pap. 15.95 (0-940143-89-5) Safari Pr.

Shots for Lower Scoring: How to Play the Trickier Shots. Beverly Lewis. 1994. 4.98 (0-8317-4036-1) Smithmark.

***Shots in the Dark: An Auvo Biography.** David Zawalski. (Illus.). 20p. (Orig.). 1997. pap. 8.00 (0-9657670-0-0) D Johnsson Pub.

Shots in the Dark: Films of 1949-1951. Edgar Anstel. 1976. lib. bdg. 59.95 (0-8490-2601-6) Gordon Pr.

Shots, Moves & Strategies: As Taught by the Game's Greatest Players. Eddie Robin et al. Ed. & Intro. by Lloyd F. Welcome. (Pocket Billiards Ser.). (Illus.). 328p. 1996. 42.00 (0-936362-04-9) Billiard Wld.

***Shots, Moves & Strategies: As Taught by the Game's Greatest Players.** deluxe ed. Eddie Robin et al. Ed. & Intro. by Lloyd F. Welcome. (Illus.). 328p. 1996. bond lthr. 59.00 (0-936362-17-0) Billiard Wld.

***Shots on Goal.** Rich Wallace. LC 97-11310. 1997. 17.00 (0-679-88670-2); pap. write for info. (0-679-88671-0); lib. bdg. 18.99 (0-679-98670-7) Knopf Bks Yng Read.

Shotwell: Annals of Our Colonial Ancestors & Their Descendants. A. M. Shotwell. (Illus.). 291p. 1990. reprint ed. pap. 44.00 (0-8328-1625-6); reprint ed. lib. bdg. 52.00 (0-8328-1624-8) Higginson Bk Co.

Should a Christian be a Mason? 1991. lib. bdg. 54.95 (0-8490-4463-4) Gordon Pr.

Should a Christian Be a Mason? E. M. Storms. LC 80-83598. (Orig.). 1994. pap. text ed. 4.00 (0-932050-08-5) New Puritan.

Should a Christian Wear Purple Sweat Socks? How to Decide What's Right or Wrong for "You" James Watkins. 144p. (Orig.). 1987. pap. 7.95 (0-89827-039-1, BKE55) Wesleyan Pub Hse.

Should a Master's Degree Be Required of All Virginia Teachers? An Examination of the Issue. 1988. 4.00 (0-318-40064-2) U VA Ctr Pub Serv.

Should America Go to War? The Debate over Foreign Policy in Chicago, 1939-1941. James C. Schneider. LC 88-10644. 313p. 1989. reprint ed. pap. 89.30 (0-608-02073-7, 2062726) Bks Demand.

Should Auld Acquaintance Be Forgot...? Institutions of Communism, the Transition to Capitalism & Personal Networks - The Case of East Germany. Beate Volker. 300p. 1995. pap. 26.50 (90-5170-346-5, Pub. by Thesis Pubs NE) IBD Ltd.

Should Business & Non-Business Accounting Be Different? Robert N. Anthony. 1989. pap. text ed. 14.95 (0-07-103202-9) McGraw.

Should Christians Attend Movies? Gordon Lindsay. 1964. 1.95 (0-89985-007-3) Christ for the Nations.

Should Christians Fear God Today. John A. Korsgaard. 61p. (Orig.). 1991. pap. write for info. (0-925703-37-0) Crown MA.

Should Christians Support Israel? John C. Hagee. Ed. by Rick Randall. 169p. (Orig.). 1987. per. 10.00 (1-56908-000-3) Global Evang.

Should Drugs Be Legalized? Susan N. Terkel. (Illus.). 160p. (YA). (gr. 9-12). 1990. lib. bdg. 22.70 (0-531-10944-5) Watts.

Should Eighty-Five Percent of Social Security Benefits Be Taxed? John C. Goodman. 1990. pap. 5.00 (0-943802-80-6, BG101) Natl Ctr Pol.

Should Federal Law Provide Monetary Damages for Harassment? Ann E. Reesman. 30p. 1991. pap. 10.00 (0-614-06157-1, 2028-PP-4040) EPF.

***Should God Get Tenure? Essays on Religion & Higher Education.** Ed. by David W. Gill. LC 97-14229. 261p. (Orig.). 1997. pap. 24.00 (0-8028-4307-7) Eerdmans.

Should Healthy People Pay More for Health Insurance? John C. Goodman. (Illus.). 17p. 1992. pap. 5.00 (0-943802-94-6, BG115) Natl Ctr Pol.

Should I Become a Board Member? A Guide for People Thinking of Joining a Nonprofit Board. Dorian Dodson. LC 93-71371. (Illus.). 70p. (Orig.). 1993. pap. text ed. 10.95 (0-9632445-2-3) Adolfo St.

Should I Get Married? M. Blaine Smith. LC 90-32638. 213p. (Orig.). 1990. pap. 9.99 (0-8308-1730-1, 1730, Saltshaker Bk) InterVarsity.

Should I Go to the Teacher? Developing a Cooperative Relationship with Your Child's School Community. Susan M. Benjamin & Susan Sanchez. LC 95-31723. 151p. 1995. pap. 12.00 (0-435-08126-8, 08126) Heinemann.

Should I Have This Baby? What to Do When Your Pregnancy Is Unwanted or Unexpected. Carl Jones. 18.95 (0-8065-1752-2, Citadel Pr) Carol Pub Group.

Should I Have This Baby? What to Do When Your Pregnancy Is Unwanted or Unexpected. Carl Jones. LC 95-47106. 256p. 1996. 19.95 (1-55972-359-9, Birch Ln Pr) Carol Pub Group.

***Should I Home School? How to Decide What's Right for You & Your Child.** Elizabeth Hamilton & Dan Hamilton. LC 97-19046. 150p. 1997. pap. 9.99 (0-8308-1976-2, 1976) InterVarsity.

Should I Keep My Baby? Martha Zimmerman. LC 83-6068. 96p. (Orig.). 1983. pap. 5.99 (0-87123-578-1) Bethany Hse.

***Should I Keep My Baby? Caring, Practical Help for Teenage Girls Facing Pregnancy Alone.** Martha Zimmerman. LC 97-21019. 96p. Date not set. pap. 7.99 (1-55661-983-9) Bethany Hse.

Should I Laugh or Cry? Betty Brandt. Ed. by Laura Brandt. (Illus.). 128p. (YA). (gr. 6-12). 1990. 8.95 (0-9622014-1-3) Beaver Valley.

Should I Leave? Kramer. LC 97-19060. 1997. 25.00 (0-684-81343-2) S&S Trade.

Should Income Tax Rates for Wealthy Taxpayers Be Increased? John C. Goodman. 1990. pap. 5.00 (0-943802-81-4, BG102) Natl Ctr Pol.

Should Intercity Bus Drivers Be Allowed to Use CB Radios? (Special Reports: No. 205). 93p. 1984. 12.00 (0-309-03721-2) Transport Res Bd.

Should Medical Care Be Rationed by Age? Ed. by Timothy M. Smeeding et al. 192p. 1987. 57.00 (0-8476-7521-1) Rowman.

Should Pension Assets Be Managed for Social-Political Purposes? Employee Benefit Research Institute Staff. Ed. by Dallas L. Salisbury. LC 80-65232. 381p. (Orig.). 1980. pap. 15.00 (0-86643-001-6) Empl Benefit Res Inst.

***Should Psychology Be a Science? Pros & Cons.** Jock Abra. LC 97-21853. 1998. text ed. write for info. (0-275-95476-5, Praeger Pubs) Greenwood.

Should Textbooks Challenge Students? The Case for Easier or Harder Books. Jeanne S. Chall & Sue S. Conard. 176p. (C). 1991. text ed. 41.00 (0-8077-3065-3); pap. text ed. 18.95 (0-8077-3064-5) Tchrs Coll.

Should the Baby Live? The Problem of Handicapped Infants. Helga Kuhse & Peter Singer. (Modern Revivals in Philosophy Ser.). 240p. 1994. 55.95 (0-7512-0313-0, Pub. by Gregg Revivals UK) Ashgate Pub Co.

Should the Children Pray? A Historical, Judicial, & Political Examination of Public School Prayer. Lynda B. Fenwick. LC 89-62659. 249p. (Orig.). 1989. 29.95 (0-918954-51-7) Baylor Univ Pr.

***Should the Federal Minimum Wage Be Increased?** Richard Vedder & Lowell Gallaway. 21p. 1995. pap. 10.00 (1-56808-054-9, 190) Natl Ctr Pol.

Should the Maastricht Treaty Be Saved? Barry Eichengreen. LC 92-46576. (Studies in International Finance: No. 74). 74p. (C). 1992. pap. 11.00 (0-88165-246-6) Princeton U Int Finan Econ.

Should the Reagan Administration Have Signed the U. N. Convention on the Law of the Sea? Alberto R. Coll. (Pew Case Studies in International Affairs). 50p. (C). 1994. pap. text ed. 3.50 (1-56927-403-7) Geo U Inst Dplmcy.

***Should Trees Have Standing? And Other Essays on Law, Morals & the Environment.** 3rd ed. Christopher D. Stone. LC 96-35448. 181p. 1996. pap. text ed. 30.00 (0-379-21381-8) Oceana.

Should War Be Eliminated? Philosophical & Theological Investigations. Stanley Hauerwas. LC 84-60236. (Pere Marquette Lectures). 75p. (C). 1984. 15.00 (0-87462-539-4) Marquette.

Should We Burn Babar? Essays on Children's Literature & the Power of Stories. Herbert R. Kohl. 192p. Date not set. pap. 11.00 (1-56584-259-6) New Press NY.

Should We Burn Babar? Essays on Children's Literature & the Power of Stories. Herbert R. Kohl. 192p. 1995. 18.95 (1-56584-258-8) New Press NY.

Should We Consent to Be Governed? A Short Introduction to Political Philosophy. Stephen Nathanson. 134p. (C). 1992. pap. 20.95 (0-534-16746-2) Wadsworth Pub.

Should We Disown Milton Friedman? Thomas B. Silver. (Occasional Paper of the Study of Statesmanship & Political Philosophy: No. 6). 14p. (Orig.). (C). 1983. pap. text ed. 2.00 (0-930783-12-3) Claremont Inst.

Should We Have Capital Punishment? JoAnn B. Guernsey. (Pro-Con Ser.). (Illus.). 96p. (J). (gr. 6 up). 1992. lib. bdg. 19.95 (0-8225-2602-6, Lerner Publctns) Lerner Group.

Should We Limit Science & Technology. Ed. by Leo Steg. 70p. 1976. pap. 19.75 (0-08-019981-X, Pergamon Pr) Elsevier.

***Should We Worry about Ozone?** Jane S. Shaw & Richard L. Stroup. 22p. 1995. pap. 10.00 (1-56808-056-5, 191) Natl Ctr Pol.

Should You Go into Business for Yourself? Travis Young. (Orig.). 1997. pap. 12.95 (0-9650566-4-3, F-004) Active Edit.

Should You Incorporate? Council of New York Law Associates Staff. 24p. (ENG & SPA.). 1977. 3.00 (0-685-08021-8) Coun NY Law.

Should You Shut Your Eyes When You Kiss? Or, How to Survive "The Best Years of Your Life" Carol M. Wallace. LC 83-5458. (Illus.). 112p. (J). (gr. 7 up). 1983. 13.45i (0-316-91998-5) Little.

Shoulder. 1986. pap. 9.00 (0-912452-66-8, P-54) Am Phys Therapy Assn.

Shoulder. E. A. Codman. (Illus.). 550p. 95.00 (0-930405-67-6) Norman SF.

Shoulder, 2 vol. Charles A. Rockwood, Jr. (Illus.). 1184p. 1990. text ed. 259.00 (0-7216-2828-1) Saunders.

Shoulder. Ed. by Carter R. Rowe. (Illus.). 1988p. 1987. 175.00 (0-443-08457-2) Churchill.

Shoulder, 2. 2nd ed. Charles A. Rockwood. 1998. text ed. write for info. (0-7216-8134-4) Saunders.

Shoulder: A Balance of Mobility & Stability. Ed. by Frederick A. Matsen, III et al. LC 93-30015. 653p. 1993. 105.00 (0-89203-091-7) Amer Acad Ortho Surg.

Shoulder: A Method of Evaluation & Assessment. David W. Altchek. 1995. text ed. 55.00 (0-07-001284-9) McGraw.

Shoulder: Periarticular Degenerative Pathology. Ed. by L. Celli. Tr. by S. Notini. (Current Concepts in Orthopedic Surgery Ser.: Vol. 1). (Illus.). 144p. 1991. 135.00 (0-387-82219-4) Spr-Verlag.

Shoulder: Rupture of the Supraspinatus Tension & Other Lesions in or about the Subacronial Bursa. E. A. Codman. LC 83-25154. 495p. 1984. reprint ed. 84.50 (0-89874-731-7) Krieger.

Shoulder & Elbow, Vols. 5 & 5a. Jules R. Kalisch & Harold Williams. (Courtroom Medicine Ser.). 1970. write for info. (0-8205-1246-X, 246); ring bd. write for info. (0-318-67989-2); ring bd. write for info. (0-318-67990-6) Bender.

Shoulder Arthrography. Ed. by Amy B. Goldman et al. (Radiology Library). 1982. 52.50 (0-316-31931-7) Little.

Shoulder Arthroscopy. Stephen J. Snyder. (Illus.). 288p. 1993. text ed. 155.00 (0-07-059526-7) McGraw-Hill HPD.

Shoulder Arthroscopy. Stephen J. Snyder. 1994. vhs 95.00 (0-07-059528-3); vhs 95.00 (0-07-059529-1) McGraw-Hill HPD.

***Shoulder Bags.** rev. ed. Val Love. (Illus.). 8p. 1997. pap. 7.00 (1-886828-07-5) Dovetail Desgn.

Shoulder Dystocia & Birth Injury: Prevention & Treatment. James A. O'Leary. (Illus.). 200p. 1992. pap. text ed. 42.00 (0-07-105393-X) McGraw-Hill HPD.

Shoulder in Hemiplegia. Rene Cailliet. LC 79-18598. (Illus.). 130p. 1980. text ed. 15.95 (0-8036-1602-3) Davis Co.

Shoulder Injuries in Sport: Evaluation, Treatment, & Rehabilitation. Jerome V. Ciullo. LC 95-41120. (Illus.). 304p. 1996. text ed. 55.00 (0-87322-651-8, BCIU0651) Human Kinetics.

Shoulder Injuries in Sports. Phillip J. Marone. LC 91-44364. 188p. 1992. text ed. 93.50 (0-8342-0338-3) Lppncott-Raven.

Shoulder Injuries in the Athlete: Surgical Repair & Rehabilitation. Ed. by Richard J. Hawkins & Gary W. Misamore. LC 95-36792. (Illus.). 470p. 1995. 125.00 (0-443-08947-7) Churchill.

Shoulder (Master Techniques in Orthopaedic Surgery) Master Techniques in Orthopaedic Surgery. Ed. by Edward V. Craig. (Master Techniques in Orthopaedic Surgery Ser.). (Illus.). 496p. 1995. text ed. 189.00 (0-7817-0035-3) Lppncott-Raven.

Shoulder Pain. 3rd ed. Rene Cailliet. (Pain Ser.). (Illus.). 277p. 1991. pap. 19.95 (0-8036-1614-7) Davis Co.

Shoulder Pathophysiology: Rehabilitation & Treatment. Scott V. Haig. 360p. 1995. 54.00 (0-8342-0622-6) Aspen Pub.

Shoulder Reconstruction. Neer. 624p. 1990. text ed. 179.00 (0-7216-2832-X) Saunders.

Shoulder Replacement. Ed. by R. Kolbel et al. Tr. by Terry C. Telger from GER. (Illus.). 240p. 1987. 96.95 (0-387-17129-0) Spr-Verlag.

Shoulder Sleeve Insignia of the U. S. Armed Forces, 1941-1945. 2nd ed. Richard W. Smith. (Illus.). 256p. 1991. reprint ed. 30.00 (0-9618883-2-6); reprint ed. pap. 25.00 (0-9618883-3-4) R W Smith.

Shoulder Sleeve Insignia of the U. S. Army, 1946- 1989. rev. ed. Richard W. Smith. (Illus.). 108p. 1990. 22.00 (0-9618883-0-X); pap. 18.00 (0-9618883-1-8) R W Smith.

Shoulder Surgery. Copeland. 1996. text ed. 97.00 (0-7020-2063-X) Saunders.

An Asterisk (*) at the beginning of an entry indicates that the title is appearing in BIP for the first time.

Shoulder the Sky. D. E. Stevenson. 23.95 (*0-8488-1472-X*) Amereon Ltd.
Shoulder the Sky. D. E. Stevenson. 275p. 1976. lib. bdg. 23.95 (*0-89966-166-1*) Buccaneer Bks.
***Shoulder to Shoulder: Strengthening Your Church by Supporting Your Pastor.** Dan Reiland. LC 96-39916. 192p. 1997. pap. 10.99 (*0-7852-7248-8*) Nelson.
Shoulder to Shoulder? The American Federation of Labor, the United States, & the Mexican Revolution, 1910-1924. Gregg Andrews. LC 91-11343. 295p. 1991. 20.00 (*0-520-07230-8*) U CA Pr.
***Shoulder to Shoulder: The Journey from Isolation to Brotherhood.** Rodney L. Cooper. LC 97-1611. 192p. 1997. 16.99 (*0-310-21187-5*) Zondervan.
Shoulder to Shoulder: Unlocking the Power of Unity. Steven D. Grandy. 160p. (Orig.). 1993. pap. 6.95 (*0-9635014-0-2*) Jubilee Ridge.
Shoulders. Georgia Cotrell. LC 87-7413. 258p. (Orig.). 1987. pap. 9.95 (*0-932379-25-7*); lib. bdg. 20.95 (*0-932379-26-5*) Firebrand Bks.
Shoulders of Atlas. Mary E. Wilkins Freeman. LC 76-51665. (Rediscovered Fiction by American Women Ser.). 1977. reprint ed. lib. bdg. 33.95 (*0-405-10044-2*) Ayer.
Shoulders of Giants. E. Gaylon McCollough. (Illus.). 224p. 1986. 15.95 (*0-932919-04-9*) Albright & Co.
Shoulders of Giants: A History of Human Flight to 1919. Phil Scott. 304p. (C). 1995. 23.08 (*0-201-62722-1*) Addison-Wesley.
Shoulders, Upper Back & Neck: Free Yourself from Pain! Rosemarie Atencio. LC 94-79485. (Illus.). 128p. (Orig.). 1995. pap. 17.95 (*0-9637360-9-4*) HWD Pub.
Shouldn't I Be Happy? Emotional Problems of Pregnant & Post Partum Women. Shaila Misri. 1995. 23.00 (*0-02-921405-X*, Free Press) Free Pr.
Shout. Philip Norman. 1996. pap. 13.00 (*0-684-83067-1*) S&S Trade.
Shout! The Beatles in Their Generation. Philip Norman. (Illus.). 1995. 8.98 (*1-56731-087-7*, MJF Bks) Fine Comms.
Shout at the Devil. Wilbur Smith. 1996. mass mkt. 6.99 (*0-7493-2431-7*, Reed Trade) Buttrwrth-Heinemann.
Shout at the Devil. Wilbur Smith. 336p. 1989. mass mkt. 6.99 (*0-449-21554-7*, Crest) Fawcett.
***Shout Because You're Free: The African-American Ring Shout Tradition in Coastal Georgia.** Art Rosenbaum. (Illus.). 216p. 1998. 24.95 (*0-8203-1934-1*) U of Ga Pr.
Shout for Joy. 1990. 29.95 (*1-55568-120-4*) Gospel Films.
Shout in Silence: Visual Arts & the Deaf. 2nd abr. ed. Rawley A. Silver. (Illus.). 36p. (C). 1993. reprint ed. pap. text ed. 9.00 (*0-9621429-5-6*) Ablin Pr.
Shout in the Street: An Excursion into the Modern City. Peter Jukes. (Illus.). 276p. 1991. reprint ed. pap. 14.95 (*0-520-07553-6*) U CA Pr.
Shout in the Street: The Story of Church House in Bridgeton. Sally Magnusson. (C). 1992. pap. 35.00 (*0-86153-150-7*, Pub. by St Andrew UK) St Mut.
Shoutin Sextet. C. Fuller. 1995. pap. text ed. 20.00 (*0-7935-4836-5*) H Leonard.
Shouting at Midnight. Dale Jacobson. 55p. (Orig.). 1992. pap. 4.95 (*1-882191-00-5*) Spirit Horse Pr.
Shouting at No One. Lawrence Joseph. LC 82-20052. (Poetry Ser.). 72p. 1983. pap. 10.95 (*0-8229-5350-1*) U of Pittsburgh Pr.
Shouting at the Wolf: A Guide to Identifying & Warding off Evil in Everyday Life. Anderson Reed. 1990. pap. 11.95 (*0-8065-1170-2*, Citadel Pr) Carol Pub Group.
***Shouting in the Evening: British Theater, 1956-1996.** Ed. by Cathy Henderson & Dave Oliphant. (Illus.). 1996. pap. 20.00 (*0-87959-137-4*) U of Tex H Ransom Ctr.
Shouting Sharon: A Riotous Counting Rhyme. David Pace. LC 94-76897. (Illus.). 32p. (J). (ps-3). 1995. 12.95 (*0-307-17518-9*, Golden Books) Western Pub.
Shouting Signpainters: A Literary & Political Account of Quebec Revolutionary Nationalism. Malcolm Reid. LC 75-158922. 320p. 1972. pap. 10.00 (*0-85345-283-0*) Monthly Rev.
Shouting to the Wind. Mario Edlosi. Ed. by Janet Leih. 224p. (Orig.). 1996. pap. text ed. 12.95 (*1-877649-25-2*) Tesseract SD.
***Shouts & Whispers: Stories from the Southern Chesapeake Bay.** James A. Charbeneau. LC 96-43891. (Illus.). 175p. (Orig.). 1996. pap. 12.95 (*1-883911-11-7*) Brandylane.
***Shouts from the Wall: Posters & Photographs Brought Home from the Spanish Civil War by American Volunteers.** 19.95 (*0-252-06606-5*) U of Ill Pr.
Shove: An English Ancestry: an Account of the Ancestry of Edward Melvin Shove & His Siblings. James K. Raywalt. (Illus.). 149p. 1992. reprint ed. pap. 21.00 (*0-8328-2413-5*); reprint ed. lib. bdg. 31.00 (*0-8328-2412-7*) Higginson Bk Co.
Shovel & the Loom. Carl Friedman. Tr. by Jeannette K. Ringold from DUT. 176p. 1996. 20.00 (*0-89255-216-6*) Persea Bks.
Shovel of Stars: The Making of the American West 1800 to Present, Pt. 2. Ted Morgan. (Illus.). 560p. 1996. pap. 16.00 (*0-684-81492-7*, Touchstone Bks) S&S Trade.
Shovel of Stars: The Settling of the North American Continent 1850-1994. Ted Morgan. (Illus.). 544p. 1995. 30.00 (*0-671-79439-6*) S&S Trade.
Shoveful of Earth. Lorus J. Milne & Margery Milne. LC 86-4735. (Illus.). 112p. (J). (gr. 4-6). 1987. 12.95 (*0-8050-0028-3*, Bks Young Read) H Holt & Co.
***Shoveling Smoke: Selected Mystery Stories.** Margaret Maron. 240p. 1997. pap. 16.00 (*1-885941-15-3*) Crippen & Landru.
***Shoveling Smoke: Selected Mystery Stories.** limited ed. Margaret Maron. 240p. 1997. 40.00 (*1-885941-14-5*) Crippen & Landru.
Shovelling Out Paupers: Female Emigration from Irish Workhouses, 1840-70. Dympna McLoughlin. 192p. 1997. 39.95 (*0-7165-2563-1*, Pub. by Irish Acad Pr IE) Intl Spec Bk.
Shovels & Speculation - Archeologists Hunt Custer. Sandy Barnard. (Illus.). 64p. (Orig.). 1990. pap. 10.00 (*0-9618087-1-3*) AST Pr.
Show! Robert Montgomery. LC 90-20586. (Gary Carter's Iron Mask Ser.). (Illus.). 176p. (J). (gr. 5-8). 1997. pap. 2.95 (*0-8167-1985-3*) Troll Communs.
Show a Little Love. Janeen Brady. (Illus.). 48p. (J). (gr. k-6). 1981. audio 8.95 (*0-944803-28-8*) Brite Music.
Show a Little Love: Songbook. Janeen Brady. (Illus.). 48p. (J). (gr. k-6). 1981. 7.95 (*0-944803-26-1*) Brite Music.
Show & Sell: 133 Business Building Ways to Promote Your Trade Show Exhibit. Margit B. Weisgal. Ed. by Adrienne Hickey. LC 96-9494. 320p. 1996. 55.00 (*0-8144-0330-1*) AMACOM.
Show & Tell. Margaret Bard. Ed. by Jane Chelius. 400p. (Orig.). 1995. mass mkt. 5.99 (*0-671-86592-7*) PB.
Show & Tell. Tony Bennett. LC 94-12936. (Culture). (Illus.). 320p. (C). (gr. 13). 1995. pap. 19.95 (*0-415-05388-9*, C0144); text ed. 69.95 (*0-415-05387-0*, C0143) Routledge.
Show & Tell. Sharon Gordon. LC 86-30855. (Illus.). 32p. (J). (gr. k-2). 1997. pap. 2.50 (*0-8167-0995-5*) Troll Communs.
Show & Tell. Robert Munsch & Michael Martchenko. (J). (ps-2). 1991. pap. 5.95 (*1-55037-197-5*, Pub. by Annick CN); lib. bdg. 15.95 (*1-55037-195-9*, Pub. by Annick CN) Firefly Bks Ltd.
Show & Tell. Barney Saltzburg. LC 93-47365. (Illus.). 32p. (J). (gr. k-3). 1994. 14.95 (*0-7868-0020-8*); lib. bdg. 14.89 (*0-7868-2016-0*) Hyprn Child.
Show & Tell. Joanne Smith. (Rookie Readers Ser.). (Illus.). 32p. (J). (ps-3). 1994. pap. 3.50 (*0-516-42026-7*); lib. bdg. 15.00 (*0-516-02026-9*) Childrens.
Show & Tell: Education. Vivian A. Phillips. (Illus.). 10p. (Orig.). (J). Date not set. pap. write for info. (*1-888413-00-X*) Seasoning Quilting.
Show & Tell No. 2: A Husband's View of the Patchwork Passion. 2nd ed. Don Tyler. LC 95-36065. (Illus.). 72p. (Orig.). 1989. pap. 6.95 (*0-939009-92-7*) EPM Pubns.
Show & Tell Day. Anne Rockwell. LC 95-26349. (Illus.). 32p. (J). (ps-k). 1997. 14.95 (*0-06-027300-3*); lib. bdg. 14.89 (*0-06-027301-1*) HarpC Child Bks.
Show-&-Tell Frog. (LVL Ser.: No. 2). 32p. (J). 1992. pap. 3.99 (*0-553-35147-8*) Bantam.
Show-&-Tell War. Janice L. Smith. (Trophy Chapter Bk.: No. 4). (Illus.). 96p. (J). (gr. 1-4). 1995. pap. 3.95 (*0-06-442006-X*, Trophy) HarpC Child Bks.
Show-&-Tell War: And Other Stories about Adam Joshua. Janice L. Smith. LC 85-45842. (Trophy Bk.). (Illus.). 176p. (J). (gr. 1-4). 1990. pap. 3.95 (*0-06-440312-2*, J312, Trophy) HarpC Child Bks.
***Show & the Gaze of Theatre: A European Perspective.** Erika Fischer-Lichte. (Studies in Theatre History & Culture). (Illus.). 448p. 1997. text ed. 49.95 (*0-87745-607-0*) U of Iowa Pr.
***Show & the Gaze of Theatre: A European Perspective.** Erika Fischer-Lichte. (Studies in Theatre History & Culture). (Illus.). 448p. 1997. pap. text ed. 22.95 (*0-87745-608-9*) U of Iowa Pr.
Show Biz, from Vaude to Video. Abel Green & Joe Laurie, Jr. LC 82-49223. (Cinema Classics Ser.). 613p. 1985. lib. bdg. 23.00 (*0-8240-5761-9*) Garland.
Show Biz Kids: How to Make Your Kid a Film, Television & Recording Star. Ruthie O. Grant. (Illus.). 350p. (Orig.). 1995. pap. 16.95 (*0-935016-36-8*) Zinn Communs.
Show Biz Tricks for Cats: Thirty Fun & Easy Tricks You Can Teach Your Cat. Anne Gordon & Steve Duno. (Illus.). 144p. 1996. pap. 7.95 (*1-55850-613-6*) Adams Media.
Show Boat. Edna Ferber. 1994. pap. 5.95 (*0-451-52600-7*, Sig Classics) NAL-Dutton.
Show Boat. Edna Ferber. 1992. reprint ed. lib. bdg. 35.95 (*0-89968-281-2*, Lghtyr Pr) Buccaneer Bks.
Show Boat: The Story of a Classic American Musical. Miles Kreuger. (Quality Paperbacks Ser.). (Illus.). 256p. 1990. reprint ed. pap. 16.95 (*0-306-80401-8*) Da Capo.
Show Boat: Vocal Selections. (Illus.). 32p. 1987. pap. 8.95 (*0-88188-637-8*, 01121012) H Leonard.
Show Border Collie. Joyce Collis. (Illus.). 144p. 1993. 24.95 (*0-948955-35-X*, Pub. by Ringpr Bks UK) Seven Hills Bk.
Show Business. Kevin Coyne. (Masks Ser.). 1993. pap. 14.99 (*1-85242-251-3*) Serpents Tail.
Show Business. Shashi Tharoor. 352p. 1992. 19.95 (*1-55970-181-1*) Arcade Pub Inc.
Show Business. Shashi Tharoor. 312p. 1993. pap. 11.95 (*1-55970-227-3*) Arcade Pub Inc.
Show Business Is No Business. Al Hirschfeld. (Theatre, Film & Literature Ser.). 142p. 1983. reprint ed. lib. bdg. 25.00 (*0-306-76221-8*) Da Capo.
Show Business Is Two Words or What to Do While Waiting for Your Options to Be Dropped. Bob Vincent. (Illus.). 1979. 12.50 (*0-933866-00-3*, TXU10-020) Main Track.
Show Business Kills. Iris Rainer Dart. LC 94-22947. 1995. 21.95 (*0-316-17334-7*) Little.
Show Business Kills. Iris Rainer Dart. 400p. 1996. mass mkt. 6.50 (*0-446-36511-4*) Warner Bks.
Show Business Kills. large type ed. Iris Rainer Dart. 543p. 1995. reprint ed. 23.95 (*0-7862-0487-7*, GK Hall) Thorndike Pr.
Show Business Law: Motion Pictures, Television, Videos. Peter Muller. LC 90-40699. 280p. 1990. text ed. 59.95 (*0-89930-493-1*, MBC, Quorum Bks) Greenwood.
Show Business Personalities Available on Tape: A Catalogue of Recorded Sound, 2 vols. 1991. lib. bdg. 179.75 (*0-8490-5175-4*) Gordon Pr.
Show Control. Keith Snyder. 267p. 1996. 20.95 (*1-885173-11-3*) Write Way.
Show Dogs: Their Points & Characteristics. Theodore Marples. 1991. lib. bdg. 88.95 (*0-8490-5238-6*) Gordon Pr.
Show, Don't Tell: A Writer's Guide. William Noble. 208p. 1991. 19.95 (*0-8397-7766-3*) Eriksson.
Show, Don't Tell: A Writer's Guide. William Noble. LC 91-16580. 224p. 1993. reprint ed. pap. 12.95 (*0-8397-7767-1*) Eriksson.
Show! Don't Tell! How to Personalize College Applications. Shannon Barth. Ed. by Susan Berescik. (Illus.). 175p. (Orig.). 1993. spiral bd. 19.95 (*0-9638297-0-X*) Intl Editing.
Show Grooming. 2nd ed. Charlene Strickland. (Illus.). 1995. 29.95 (*0-914327-57-7*) Breakthrgh NY.
Show Grooming: The Look of a Winner. 2nd ed. Charlene Strickland. LC 86-70656. (Illus.). 224p. 1995. 29.95 (*0-914327-12-7*) Breakthrgh NY.
Show Him Your Love: 101 Gift Ideas for the Man in Your Life. Haya Gil-Lubin. (Illus.). 160p. (Orig.). 1996. pap. 12.95 (*1-886094-30-6*) Chicago Spectrum.
Show Horse. Bonnie Bryant. (Saddle Club Ser.: No. 25). 144p. (J). (gr. 4-7). 1992. pap. 3.99 (*0-553-48072-3*) Bantam.
Show Houses: Twin Cities Style. Kirk J. Besse. LC 93-60772. (Illus.). 160p. (Orig.). 1997. pap. text ed. 24.95 (*1-883141-02-8*) Victoria Pubns.
***Show in Destitute Times.** Joe DiMattio. Ed. by Noel Brooks. (Illus.). 74p. (Orig.). Date not set. pap. text ed. 12.00 (*0-9641891-1-9*) Chelsea Lit.
Show Jumper Wanted. Patricia Leitch. LC 96-2764. (Horseshoes Ser.: Vol. 5). 112p. (J). (gr. 3-7). 1997. pap. 3.95 (*0-06-440638-5*, Trophy) HarpC Child Bks.
Show Jumping. Jane Wallace. (Threshold Picture Guides Ser.: No. 24). (Illus.). 24p. 1992. pap. 12.00 (*1-872082-36-X*, Pub. by Kenilworth Pr UK) Half Halt Pr.
Show-Man. Andree Chedid. Tr. by Felicia H. Londre from FRE. (Publications: No. 8). 120p. (Orig.). 1984. pap. text ed. 8.95 (*0-913745-07-3*) Ubu Repertory.
***Show Me!** D. Caroline Coile. LC 96-3193. 1997. pap. 9.95 (*0-8120-9710-6*) Barron.
Show Me. Janet Dailey. (Janet Dailey Americana Ser.: No. 875). 1992. mass mkt. 3.59 (*0-373-89875-4*, 1-89875-8) Harlequin Bks.
Show Me: Storyboard Workbook & Template. Harry I. Forsha. 62p. 1994. pap. 20.00 (*0-87389-320-4*, H0816A) ASQC Qual Pr.
Show Me: The Complete Guide to Storyboarding & Problem Solving. Harry I. Forsha. LC 94-24724. (Illus.). 300p. 1994. 42.00 (*0-87389-255-0*, H0816) ASQC Qual Pr.
Show Me a Face. A. Child. (Cityscapes Ser.). 14p. (J). (ps). 1992. pap. text ed. 23.00 (*1-56843-006-X*); pap. text ed. 4.50 (*1-56843-056-6*) BGR Pub.
Show Me a Hero: Great Contemporary Stories about Sports. Ed. & Intro. by Jeanne Schinto. LC 94-47955. 265p. (Orig.). (YA). 1995. pap. 13.95 (*0-89255-209-3*) Persea Bks.
Show Me, Branson, MO. George Sheldon. (Archer Bks.). 208p. 1992. pap. 9.95 (*1-881204-49-9*) Archer Pubns.
Show Me God: What the Message from Space Is Telling Us about God. Fred Heeren. (Wonders Ser.: No. 1). (Illus.). 336p. 1996. 19.99 (*1-885849-51-6*) Searchlight.
***Show Me God: What the Message from Space Is Telling Us about God.** rev. ed. Fred Heeren. LC 97-6547. (Wonders Ser.). (Illus.). 405p. 1997. 22.99 (*1-885849-52-4*) Day Star Prods.
Show Me Helen: How to Use Quilting Designs. Helen Squire. LC 92-40648. 1993. 15.95 (*0-89145-990-1*) Collector Bks.
Show Me How: A Manual for Parents of Preschool Visually Impaired & Blind Children. Mary Brennan. 56p. 1982. pap. 10.95 (*0-89128-113-4*) Am Foun Blind.
Show Me How I Can Cook. Sarah Maxwell. (Illus.). 48p. (J). (gr. 1-4). 1995. 7.98 (*0-8317-7684-6*) Smithmark.
Show Me How I Can Experiment. Steve Parker. 48p. (J). (gr. 5). 1996. 7.98 (*0-8317-7263-8*) Smithmark.
Show Me How I Can Grow Things. Sally Walton. 48p. 1995. 7.98 (*0-8317-0719-4*) Smithmark.
Show Me How I Can Make Music. Michael Purton. (J). (ps-3). 1996. 7.98 (*0-8317-7264-6*) Smithmark.
Show Me How I Can Make Things. Sally Walton. (Illus.). 48p. (J). (gr. 1-4). 1995. 7.98 (*0-8317-8083-5*) Smithmark.
Show Me How I Can Paint. Petra Boase. (Illus.). 48p. (J). (gr. 1-4). 1995. 7.98 (*0-8317-7698-6*) Smithmark.
***Show Me How to Paper Piece.** Carol Doak. 1997. pap. text ed. 5.95 (*1-56477-204-7*) That Patchwork.
***Show Me How to Paper Piece.** Carol Doak. Ed. by Ursula Reikes. (Illus.). 24p. 1997. pap. 5.95 (*1-56477-205-5*, B316) That Patchwork.
Show Me How to Write an Experimental Science Fair Paper: A Fill-in-the-Blank Handbook. Judy F. Shubkagel. 44p. (J). (gr. 4-8). 1993. student ed., pap. 9.95 (*1-883484-00-6*) Show Me How.
Show Me Missouri Women, Vol. 2. Ed. by Mary Dains & Sue Sadler. (Illus.). 262p. 1993. lib. bdg. 25.00 (*0-943549-22-1*) TJU Pr.
Show Me Missouri Women: Selected Biographies. Ed. by Mary K. Dains. LC 89-19882. (Missouri Women's History Project Ser.). (Illus.). 272p. (C). 1990. lib. bdg. 42.50 (*0-943549-05-1*) TJU Pr.
Show Me No Mercy: A Compelling Story of Remarkable Courage. Robert Perske. LC 83-21384. 144p. (Orig.). (YA). (gr. 12 up). 1984. pap. 2.99 (*0-687-38435-4*) Abingdon.
***Show Me One Soul: A True Haunting.** Nancy L. Stallings. LC 96-69088. 376p. 1996. 27.95 (*1-56167-316-1*) Noble Hse MD.
Show Me PCs. Joe Kraynak. (Show Me Ser.). (Illus.). 121p. (Orig.). 1993. 12.95 (*1-56761-260-1*, Alpha Ref) Macmillan Gen Ref.
Show-Me State. Lloyd Rees. 176p. 1995. pap. 16.95 (*1-85411-145-0*, Pub. by Seren Bks UK) Dufour.
***Show Me Tell Me Bk. 1.** Sheldon. Date not set. pap. text ed. write for info. (*0-05-004149-5*); pap. text ed. write for info. (*0-05-004150-9*) Addison-Wesley.
Show Me the Evidence. Alane Ferguson. 176p. 1990. mass mkt. 3.99 (*0-380-70962-7*, Flare) Avon.
Show Me the Good Parts: The Reader's Guide to Sex in Literature. Robert G. Reisner. 1964. pap. 2.45 (*0-8065-0049-2*, C262, Citadel Pr) Carol Pub Group.
Show Me the MAC. R. Lewis. (Show Me Ser.). (Illus.). 125p. 1993. 12.95 (*1-56761-265-2*, Alpha Ref) Macmillan Gen Ref.
***Show Me the Money: Business Opportunity Networks.** Michael Collins et al. Ed. by Daniel Broun. 59p. (Orig.). (C). 1997. pap. 20.00 (*0-9636927-5-5*) Reg Tech Strat.
Show Me the Way: Readings for Each Day of Lent. Henri J. Nouwen. 144p. 1994. reprint ed. pap. 9.95 (*0-8245-1353-3*) Crossroad NY.
Show Me the Way to Go Home. Simmons Jones. 336p. 1991. 19.95 (*0-945575-41-6*) Algonquin Bks.
Show Me the Way to Go Home. Simmons Jones. (Stonewall Inn Editions Ser.). 336p. 1993. pap. 9.95 (*0-312-09387-X*) St Martin.
Show Me the Way to Go Home. Larry Rose. LC 94-61038. 150p. (Orig.). 1995. pap. 10.95 (*0-943873-08-8*) Elder Bks.
***Show Me the Way to Home.** Nan Shelby. (J). Date not set. write for info. (*0-688-05126-X*); lib. bdg. write for info. (*0-688-05127-8*) Greenwillow.
Show Me Where It Hurts! Chiropractic Care. Alan Rosenthal & Illana Katz. (J). (gr. k-6). 1993. pap. 9.95 (*1-882388-10-0*) Real Life Strybks.
Show Me Where It Hurts, Chiropractic Care. Illana Katz & Alan D. Rosenthal. (Illus.). 40p. (J). (gr. k-6). 1993. 16.95 (*1-882388-01-1*) Real Life Strybks.
Show Me Word for Windows 6.0. Peter Aitken. 1993. 12.95 (*1-56761-347-0*, Alpha Ref) Macmillan Gen Ref.
Show Music on Record: The First One Hundred Years. rev. ed. Jack Raymond. LC 91-23483. 440p. 1992. text ed. 45.00 (*1-56098-151-2*) Smithsonian.
Show Must Go On. (Babar Story Bks.). (Illus.). 48p. (J). 1990. 6.99 (*0-517-05206-7*) Random Hse Value.
Show Must Go On: The Life of Freddie Mercury. Rick Sky. LC 93-46587. 1994. 10.95 (*0-8065-1506-6*, Citadel Pr) Carol Pub Group.
Show Must Go On - Seeing Someone - If Walls Could Talk. Laurence Klavan. 1990. pap. 5.25 (*0-8222-1025-8*) Dramatists Play.
Show of Evil. William Diehl. 1995. mass mkt. 6.99 (*0-345-40133-6*) Ballantine.
Show of Evil. William Diehl. 1996. mass mkt. 6.99 (*0-345-37536-X*) Ballantine.
***Show of Hands.** D. A. Crossman. LC 96-45604. 288p. 1997. 22.95 (*0-89272-412-9*) Down East.
Show of Hands: Say It in Sign Language. Mary B. Sullivan et al. LC 84-48782. (Trophy Nonfiction Bk.). (Illus.). 96p. (J). (gr. 2-6). 1985. reprint ed. pap. 4.95 (*0-06-446007-X*, Trophy) HarpC Child Bks.
Show of Justice: Racial 'Amalgamation' in Nineteenth Century New Zealand. Alan Ward. 382p. 1995. pap. 29.95 (*1-86940-121-2*, Pub. by Auckland Univ NZ) Paul & Co Pubs.
Show Planner. Jennifer Gilbert & Christopher Long. (Illus.). 20p. (Orig.). 1994. pap. 8.95 (*1-887724-02-8*) Fremantle Pr.
Show Pomeranians. Lilla Ives. (Pomeranian Dog Ser.). 1991. lib. bdg. 88.95 (*0-8490-5234-3*) Gordon Pr.
Show Red for Danger: A Captain Heimrich Mystery. large type ed. Richard Lockridge & Frances Lockridge. LC 93-31000. (Popular Ser.). 1994. lib. bdg. 17.95 (*1-56054-303-5*) Thorndike Pr.
Show Ring Success: A Rider's Guide to Winning Strategies. Kathleen Oberland. LC 93-15115. (Illus.). 192p. 1993. pap. 24.00 (*0-87605-965-5*) Howell Bk.
Show Starts on the Sidewalk: An Architectural History of the Movie Theatre, Starring S. Charles Lee. Maggie Valentine. LC 93-24977. (Illus.). 288p. 1994. 40.00 (*0-300-05527-7*) Yale U Pr.
Show Starts on the Sidewalk: An Architectural History of the Movie Theatre, Starring S. Charles Lee. Maggie Valentine. (Illus.). 1996. pap. 25.00 (*0-300-06647-3*); pap. 22.50 (*0-614-97683-9*) Yale U Pr.
Show Stopper. Mary M. Pulver. (Orig.). 1993. mass mkt. 4.50 (*0-425-15828-4*, Prime Crime) Carol Pub Group.
Show Stopper. Zachary. 1996. pap. 13.00 (*0-02-874121-8*) Free Pr.
Show Stopper: A Kori & Peter Brichter Mystery. Mary M. Pulver. 204p. 1992. 19.95 (*0-8027-3210-0*) Walker & Co.
Show Stoppers! Seventy Easy-to-Present Classroom Art Lessons for Elementary Teachers. Gene Baer. 224p. 1989. pap. text ed. 24.95 (*0-13-809237-0*) P-H.
Show Time. 48p. 1990. pap. 5.95 (*0-7935-0120-2*, 00001276) H Leonard.
Show Time. 1990. pap. 4.95 (*0-7935-0177-6*, 00001393) H Leonard.
***Show Time.** Gene Brown. LC 97-16529. 1997. write for info. (*0-02-862072-0*) Macmillan.
Show Time! Hank Herman. (Super Hoops Ser.: No. 6). 96p. (J). (gr. 2-5). 1996. mass mkt. 3.50 (*0-553-48278-5*, Skylark BDD) BDD Bks Young Read.
Show Time! Barbie. Patricia Jensen. (Golden Look-Look Bks.). (Illus.). 24p. (J). (ps-3). 1992. pap. 2.25 (*0-307-12691-9*, 12691, Golden Pr) Western Pub.
Show Time at the Polk Street School: Plays You Can Do Yourself. Patricia R. Giff. LC 91-46163. (Illus.). 112p. (J). (gr. 1-4). 1992. 14.00 (*0-385-30794-2*) Delacorte.

S

Show Time at the Polk Street School: Plays You Can Do Yourself or In. Patricia R. Giff. (Polk Street Special Ser.: No. 5). 80p. (J). (gr. 4-7). 1995. pap. 3.99 (*0-440-40962-4*) Dell.

Show Time for Young Scientists: Entertaining with Science see Fun with Science: Forty Six Entertaining Demonstrations

Show Trial under Lenin. Marc C. Jansen. 1982. lib. bdg. 88.00 (*90-247-2698-0*) Kluwer Ac.

Show Trials: Stalinist Purges in Eastern Europe, 1948-1954. George H. Hodos. LC 87-13769. 208p. 1987. text ed. 55.00 (*0-275-92783-0*, C2783, Praeger Pubs) Greenwood.

Show Tunes 1905-1991: The Songs, Shows & Careers of Broadway's Major Composers. rev. ed. Steven Suskin. LC 91-23643. 768p. 1992. reprint ed. pap. 27.50 (*0-87910-146-6*) Limelight Edns.

Show Us Life: Toward a History & Aesthetics of the Committed Documentary. Ed. by Thomas Waugh. LC 84-5603. 536p. 1984. 45.00 (*0-8108-1706-3*); pap. 19.50 (*0-8108-2217-2*) Scarecrow.

Show Us Your Face Lord, & We Shall Work Wonders. Valentino Del Mazza. LC 93-10461. 136p. 1993. reprint ed. pap. 4.95 (*0-8198-6959-7*) Pauline Bks.

***Show What You Know on Ohio's Fourth Grade Proficiency Test.** Marilyn Axtmann et al. 288p. 1996. teacher ed., pap. 14.95 (*1-884183-08-5*) Englfld & Arnold.

Show What You Know on Ohio's Fourth Grade Proficiency Test. Deborah Tong et al. (Illus.). 96p. (J). (gr. 3-4). 1996. student ed., wbk. ed., pap. 9.95 (*1-884183-03-4*) Englfld & Arnold.

Show What You Know on Ohio's Sixth Grade Proficiency Test. Patricia Nay et al. (J). (gr. 5-6). 1996. student ed., wbk. ed., pap. 9.95 (*1-884183-05-0*) Englfld & Arnold.

Show What You Know on Ohio's Sixth Grade Proficiency Test. Patricia Nay et al. 1996. teacher ed., pap. write for info. (*1-884183-04-2*) Englfld & Arnold.

***Show Your Mini! A Complete How-to Workbook for the First Time Exhibitor.** Toni M. Leland. LC 95-74741. (Illus.). 86p. 1996. ring bd. 11.95 (*1-887932-06-2*, SYM, Small Horse Pr) Equine Graph Pubng.

Show Your Tongue. Gunter Grass. 237p. 1989. 34.95 (*0-15-182090-2*); pap. 19.95 (*0-15-682330-6*) HarBrace.

Showa: The Age of Hirohito. Dorothy Hoobler & Thomas Hoobler. 228p. (YA). (gr. 7 up). 1990. 15.95 (*0-8027-6966-7*); lib. bdg. 16.85 (*0-8027-6967-5*) Walker & Co.

Showa: The Japan of Hirohito. Ed. by Carol Gluck & Stephen R. Graubard. 384p. 1993. pap. 10.95 (*0-393-31064-7*) Norton.

Showa Anthology: Modern Japanese Short Stories. Ed. by Van C. Gessel et al. 464p. 1993. pap. 13.00 (*4-7700-1708-1*) Kodansha.

Showbiz Bookkeeper: The Tax Record-Keeping System for Professionals Working in the Arts. rev. ed. Annie Chadwick & Wallace Norman. 120p. (Orig.). 1992. spiral bd., pap. 16.95 (*0-933919-22-0*) Theatre Directories.

Showbiz Goes to War. large type ed. Eric Taylor. (Charnwood Ser.). (Illus.). 352p. 1994. 27.99 (*0-7089-8745-1*, Charnwood) Ulverscroft.

Showboat. Sage. (J). 1998. write for info. (*0-15-201398-9*) HarBrace.

Showboat Cookbook. 1996. 14.99 (*0-517-15049-2*) Random Hse Value.

Showcard Alphabets: 100 Complete Fonts. Contrib. & Selected by Dan X. Solo. (Pictorial Archive Ser.). 1996. pap. write for info. (*0-486-28976-1*) Dover.

Showcase of Interior Design: Commercial Edition. LC 92-13464. 123p. 1992. 35.00 (*0-9624596-4-X*) Rockport Vitae Pub.

Showcase of Interior Design: Eastern II. Ed. by John C. Aves. LC 94-2454. 232p. 1994. 39.00 (*1-883065-01-1*) Rockport Pubs.

Showcase of Interior Design: Eastern II. Ed. by John C. Aves. LC 94-2454. 230p. 1994. pap. 18.95 (*1-883065-02-X*) Rockport Vitae Pub.

Showcase of Interior Design: Forty-Three Designers & Their Work. Ed. by John C. Aves. (Illus.). 128p. 1989. 36.00 (*0-9624596-0-7*); pap. 15.00 (*0-9624596-1-5*) Rockport Vitae Pub.

***Showcase of Interior Design: Midwest.** LC 96-36119. 1996. write for info. (*1-883065-11-9*) Rockport Vitae Pub.

Showcase of Interior Design: Midwest Edition. 2nd ed. Elaine Markoutsas. 200p. 1993. 35.00 (*0-9624596-7-4*) Rockport Vitae Pub.

Showcase of Interior Design: Pacific Edition. Ed. by John C. Aves. 235p. 1992. 37.50 (*0-9624596-3-1*) Rockport Vitae Pub.

Showcase of Interior Design: Pacific Edition 2. Joyce MacRae. LC 95-44671. 235p. 1996. 39.00 (*1-883065-08-9*) Rockport Vitae Pub.

Showcase of Interior Design: Pacific Edition 2. Joyce MacRae. LC 95-44671. 200p. 1996. pap. 18.95 (*1-883065-09-7*) Rockport Vitae Pub.

Showcase of Interior Design: Southern. 2nd ed. Lisa Newsom. LC 95-41521. 207p. 1996. 39.00 (*1-883065-06-2*) Rockport Vitae Pub.

Showcase of Interior Design: Southern Edition. Ed. by John C. Aves. 236p. 1993. 35.00 (*0-9624596-5-8*); pap. 20.00 (*0-9624596-9-0*) Rockport Vitae Pub.

Showcase of Interior Design: Southern Edition 2. Lisa Newsom. 214p. 1996. pap. 19.95 (*1-883065-07-0*) Rockport Vitae Pub.

Showcasing Your Stamp Collection. C. E. Foster. LC 78-62408. (Illus.). 1978. reprint ed. pap. 10.00 (*0-917922-08-5*) Hobby Pub Serv.

Showdown. 1995. mass mkt. 4.99 (*0-373-61445-4*, 1-61445-2, Wrldwide Lib) Harlequin Bks.

***Showdown.** Elizabeth Drew. 1997. pap. 14.00 (*0-684-82551-1*, Touchstone Bks) S&S Trade.

Showdown. Erdman. Date not set. text ed. 12.95 (*0-312-15900-5*) St Martin.

Showdown. Errol Flynn. 1976. 22.95 (*0-8488-1317-0*) Amereon Ltd.

***Showdown.** Errol Flynn. Date not set. lib. bdg. 24.95 (*0-8488-1976-4*) Amereon Ltd.

Showdown. Shannon Gilligan. (Choose Your Own Adventure Ser.: No. 127). 128p. (J). 1992. pap. 3.50 (*0-553-29297-8*) Bantam.

Showdown. Errol Flynn. 1976. reprint ed. lib. bdg. 25.95 (*0-89966-094-0*) Buccaneer Bks.

Showdown: Confronting Modern America in the Western Film. John H. Lenihan. LC 79-25271. (Illus.). 224p. 1985. pap. text ed. 11.95 (*0-252-01254-2*) U of Ill Pr.

Showdown: The Lithuanian Rebellion & the Breakup of the Soviet Empire. Richard J. Krikus. LC 96-26870. 272p. 1996. 24.95 (*1-57488-058-6*) Brasseys Inc.

Showdown: The Struggle Between the Gingrich Congress & the Clinton White House. Elizabeth Drew. 448p. 1996. 25.00 (*0-684-81518-4*, S&S) S&S Trade.

***Showdown: U. S. A. vs. Militia.** Ian Slater. 1997. mass mkt. 5.99 (*0-449-14933-1*, GM) Fawcett.

Showdown at Armageddon. George E. Vandeman. 94p. 1987. pap. 0.97 (*0-8163-0735-0*) Pacific Pr Pub Assn.

Showdown at Centerpoint. Roger M. Allen. (Star Wars: The Corellian Trilogy Ser.: Bk. 3). 320p. (YA). 1995. mass mkt. 5.99 (*0-553-29806-2*) Bantam.

Showdown at Crazy Man Creek. large type ed. Elliot Long. (Linford Western Library). 208p. 1996. pap. 15.99 (*0-7089-7879-7*, Linford) Ulverscroft.

Showdown at Drowning Creek No. 203: Showdown at Drounding Creek. Jake Logan. (Jack Logan Ser.: No. 203). 192p. (Orig.). 1996. mass mkt. 4.50 (*0-515-11782-X*) Jove Pubns.

Showdown at Fire Hill. Roe Richmond. (Orig.). 1979. mass mkt. 1.95 (*0-89083-560-8*, Zebra Kensgtn) Kensgtn Pub Corp.

Showdown at Gucci Gulch. Jeffrey H. Birnbaum & Alan S. Murray. 1987. 18.95 (*0-394-56024-8*) Random.

Showdown at Gucci Gulch: Lawmakers, Lobbyists, & the Unlikely Triumph of Tax Reform. Jeffrey H. Birnbaum & Alan S. Murray. Ed. by Peter Osnos. LC 87-45971. 336p. 1988. reprint ed. pap. 15.00 (*0-394-75811-0*, Vin) Random.

Showdown at Lonesome Pellet. Paul Ratz de Tagyos. LC 93-25733. (J). 1994. 14.95 (*0-395-67645-2*, Clarion Bks) HM.

Showdown at Medicine Creek. large type ed. J. D. Kincaid. (Linford Western Library). 240p. 1992. pap. 15.99 (*0-7089-7175-X*, Trailtree Bookshop) Ulverscroft.

Showdown at Mesa Verde. large type ed. Amy Sadler. (Dales Western Ser.). 208p. 1993. pap. 17.99 (*1-85389-358-7*) Ulverscroft.

Showdown at Seven Springs. Jason Manning. 224p. 1992. mass mkt. 3.50 (*0-8217-3999-9*, Zebra Kensgtn) Kensgtn Pub Corp.

Showdown at Six-Gun Mine. John P. Legg. (gr. k). 1989. mass mkt. 2.95 (*0-8217-2660-9*, Zebra Kensgtn) Kensgtn Pub Corp.

Showdown at Slickrock. Pat Bagley. (Illus.). 32p. (J). (gr. k-5). 1996. 16.95 (*1-885628-02-1*) Buckaroo Bks.

Showdown at the Aracade. Mercer Mayer. (School Time Readers Ser.). (Illus.). 48p. (J). (ps-3). 1994. 3.50 (*0-307-15958-2*, Golden Books) Western Pub.

***Showdown at the Mall, Vol. 2.** Gallagher. (Teenage Witch: No. 2). (J). 1997. pap. 3.99 (*0-671-01434-X*) S&S Trade.

***Showdown at the OP Corral: A Satire on Ecological Madness & Political Foolery.** Richard Hale. 537p. 1996. 24.95 (*0-9651888-8-4*); pap. 19.95 (*0-9651888-7-6*); pap. 19.95 (*0-9651888-9-2*) Ecol Pr.

Showdown at Viking Cave. Clifford Blair. LC 93-37908. 198p. 1994. 19.95 (*0-8027-4136-3*) Walker & Co.

Showdown at Viking Cave. large type ed. Clifford Blair. LC 94-27154. 255p. 1994. pap. 18.95 (*0-8161-7473-3*, GK Hall) Thorndike Pr.

Showdown at Yellow Butte. Louis L'Amour. 192p. 1983. 3.99 (*0-553-27993-9*) Bantam.

***Showdown at Yellow Butte.** Louis L'Amour. 1997. 9.95 (*0-553-06278-6*) Bantam.

Showdown in High Valley. large type ed. Wallace Ford. (Linford Western Library). 1991. pap. 15.99 (*0-7089-7125-3*) Ulverscroft.

***Showdown in Memphis: An Epic Tale of the Forties.** unabridged ed. Thomas C. Hammond. (Illus.). 450p. 1997. 30.00 (*0-9643846-4-7*) Retrospect Prods.

Showdown in Salt Fork. large type ed. Jim Bowden. (Linford Western Library). 1991. pap. 15.99 (*0-7089-7034-6*) Ulverscroft.

Showdown in Sonora. large type ed. Gordon D. Shirreffs. (Linford Western Library). 336p. 1986. pap. 15.99 (*0-7089-6200-9*, Linford) Ulverscroft.

Showdown in Washington: State, Treasury, & Congress. Intro. by David S. Wyman. (America & the Holocaust Ser.: Vol. 6). 460p. 1990. text ed. 95.00 (*0-8240-4538-6*) Garland.

Showdown with the Devil. Kenneth Hagin, Jr. 1983. pap. 0.75 (*0-89276-715-4*) Hagin Ministries.

Shower of Games for Brides & Babies. Novella Isom. (Game & Party Bks.). 48p. (gr. 10). 1975. pap. 4.99 (*0-8010-5029-4*) Baker Bks.

***Shower of Jewels: Feng Shui: An Amusing Yet Practical Guide to Ancient Principles of Placement & Geoenergy Manipulation.** Richard Tan & Cheryl Warnke. Ed. by Keith Robbins & Harvey Berger. (Illus.). 229p. (Orig.). 1996. pap. 26.00 (*0-9654512-0-8*) T&W Bks.

***Shower of Stars: The Medal of Honor & the 27th Maine.** John J. Pullen. LC 96-43138. 288p. 1997. 24.95 (*0-8117-0075-5*) Stackpole.

Shower of Summer Days. May Sarton. 256p. 1995. pap. 10.00 (*0-393-31250-X*) Norton.

Showers: The Complete Guide to Hosting a Perfect Bridal or Baby Shower. Beverly Clark. Ed. by Celine Burk. (Illus.). 168p. (Orig.). 1989. pap. 8.95 (*0-934081-03-4*) Wlshre Pubns.

Showers of Blessings. Helen Steiner Rice. 96p. (gr. 10). 1987. 13.99 (*0-8007-1567-5*) Revell.

Showers of Blessings: A Journal of Ohio Valley Life. Alma D. Hall & Patricia M. Mote. (Illus.). 112p. (Orig.). 1993. pap. 7.95 (*0-9633083-2-7*) Quixote Pubns.

Showers of Flowers. Marilyn Kleinhardt. 6p. 1993. pap. 6.00 (*1-884694-04-7*) Wood n Needle.

Showgirls: Portrait of a Film. Paul Verhoeven. (Newmarket Pictorial Moviebook Ser.). 1995. 39.95 (*1-55704-253-5*) Newmarket.

Showgirls: Portrait of a Film. Paul Verhoeven. (Newmarket Pictorial Moviebook Ser.). 1995. pap. 24.95 (*1-55704-267-5*) Newmarket.

Showhouse Recipes. 2nd ed. (Illus.). 238p. (Orig.). 1980. 7.50 (*0-686-32905-8*) Jr League Binghamton.

***Showing.** Lucy Smith. (Riding School Ser.). (Illus.). 32p. (J). (gr. 2-6). 1997. pap. 5.95 (*0-7460-2440-1*, Usborne); lib. bdg. 13.95 (*0-88110-906-1*, Usborne) EDC.

Showing America a New Way Home: Expanding Opportunities for Home Ownership. James A. Johnson. LC 96-14977. (Public Administration Ser.). 1996. write for info. (*0-7879-0272-1*) Jossey-Bass.

Showing Dairy Cattle. Bill Telfer. (Illus.). 80p. 1994. text ed. 29.95 (*0-85236-272-2*, Pub. by Farming Pr UK) Diamond Farm Bk.

***Showing for Beginners.** Hallie I. McEvoy. LC 96-30498. (Illus.). 176p. 1996. pap. 16.95 (*1-55821-500-X*) Lyons & Burford.

***Showing How: The Act of Teaching.** Gabriel Moran. LC 96-50492. 256p. (Orig.). 1997. pap. 20.00 (*1-56338-187-7*) TPI PA.

Showing Masterclass: With Allister Hood & Wendy King. Vanessa Britton. (Illus.). 160p. 1996. 27.95 (*0-7153-0310-4*, Pub. by D & C Pub UK) Sterling.

Showing Mercy: Getting What You Give. David Lambert. (Beatitudes Ser.). 64p. 1993. 4.99 (*0-310-59663-7*) Zondervan.

Showing My Age. Edmund Skellings. LC 78-2459. 1978. 14.95 (*0-8130-0548-5*) U Press Fla.

***Showing My Color: Impolite Essays on Race & Identity.** Clarence Page. 320p. 1997. pap. 13.00 (*0-06-092801-8*, PL) HarpC.

Showing My Color: Impolite Essays on Race in America. Clarence Page. 224p. 1996. 23.00 (*0-06-017256-8*) HarpC.

Showing Off: The Geltung Hypothesis. Philip Wagner. LC 95-50184. 176p. 1996. text ed. 30.00 (*0-292-79102-X*) U of Tex Pr.

Showing Off: The Geltung Hypothesis. Philip L. Wagner. LC 95-50184. 176p. 1996. pap. 12.95 (*0-292-79103-8*) U of Tex Pr.

Showing Our Colors: Afro-German Women Speak Out. Ed. by May Opitz et al. Tr. by Anne V. Adams from GER. LC 91-17061. (Illus.). 272p. (C). 1991. pap. 17.95 (*0-87023-760-8*); lib. bdg. 40.00 (*0-87023-759-4*) U of Mass Pr.

Showing Our Mussel: The Great Lakes Sea Grant Network Report on Zebra Mussel Research & Outreach. Kelly Kershner & Jeffrey M. Reutter. Ed. by Maran B. Hilgendorf. (OHSU Ser.: No. TB-026). (Illus.). 1993. 5.00 (*1-883756-01-4*) Ohio St U Res.

Showing Sheep: Select, Feed, Fit & Show. Laura Lawson. LC 94-78838. (Illus.). 224p. (Orig.). 1994. pap. 12.95 (*0-9633923-2-8*) LDF Pubns.

Showing Signs of Violence: The Cultural Politics of a Twentieth-Century Headhunting Ritual. Kenneth M. George. LC 95-36929. (Illus.). 356p. 1996. 48.00 (*0-520-20041-1*); pap. 18.00 (*0-520-20361-5*) U CA Pr.

Showing the Ridden Pony. Caroline Akrill. 174p. (C). 1990. 52.00 (*0-85131-513-5*, Pub. by J A Allen & Co UK) St Mut.

***Showing the Ridden Pony.** 3rd rev. ed. Caroline Akrill. (Illus.). 1996. 46.00 (*0-85131-649-2*, Pub. by J A Allen & Co UK) St Mut.

Showing the Spirit: A Theological Exposition of I Corinthians 12-14. D. A. Carson. LC 87-21457. 229p. (C). 1996. pap. 12.99 (*0-8010-2521-4*) Baker Bks.

Showing to Win. Carolyn Henderson & Lynn Russell. (Illus.). 128p. 1994. 29.95 (*1-85310-389-6*, Pub. by Swan Hill UK) Voyageur Pr.

***Showing You Know: A Sourcebook for Learning Through Speaking.** Robert Wolsch & Lois A. Wolsch. 144p. 1996. pap. text ed. write for info. (*0-07-071764-8*) McGraw.

Showing Your Colors: A Designer's Guide to Coordinating Your Wardrobe. Jeanne Allen. LC 86-2656. (Designers Guide Ser.). (Illus.). 134p. (Orig.). 1986. pap. 10.95 (*0-87701-381-0*) Chronicle Bks.

Showman Shepherd. David Turner. (Illus.). 120p. 1990. 32.95 (*0-85236-204-8*, Pub. by Farming Pr UK) Diamond Farm Bk.

Showmanship in the Dining Room. Bruce H. Axler. 1974. pap. 5.01 (*0-672-96117-2*, Bobbs) Macmillan.

Showmen of Wiltshire. John Girvan. 1990. 48.00 (*0-614-08408-3*, Pub. by Picton UK) St Mut.

Shown to Be Holy: An Introduction to Eastern Christian Moral Thought. 89p. (Orig.). 1990. pap. text ed. 7.00 (*1-887158-05-7*) God With Us.

Showplace of America: Cleveland's Euclid Avenue, 1850-1910 c. Jan Cigliano. LC 91-9019. (Illus.). 416p. 1991. 45.00 (*0-87338-445-8*) Kent St U Pr.

Showroom Stock Race Car Preparation. Nigel MacKnight. (Illus.). 160p. 1992. pap. 6.98 (*0-87938-652-5*) Motorbooks Intl.

***Showrooms.** PBC International Staff. 1993. 42.50 (*0-688-12231-0*) Morrow.

***Shows & Tells: A Book about Archaeology.** Scholastic Inc. Staff. (Magic School Bus Ser.). 1997. pap. text ed. 2.99 (*0-590-92242-4*) Scholastic Inc.

Shows of Force: Power, Politics, & Ideology in Art Exhibitions. Timothy W. Luke. LC 91-20018. 264p. 1992. pap. text ed. 17.95 (*0-8223-1123-2*); lib. bdg. 39.95 (*0-8223-1188-7*) Duke.

Shows of London. Richard D. Altick. LC 77-2755. 576p. 1978. 50.00 (*0-674-80731-6*) Belknap Pr.

Shows on a Shoestring. Nellie McCaslin. 106p. 1979. 9.95 (*0-679-20952-2*) New Plays Inc.

Showshoe Country. Florence P. Jaques. LC 89-2787. (Illus.). ii, 110p. 1989. reprint ed. pap. 8.50 (*0-87351-236-7*, Borealis Book) Minn Hist.

Showstopper! The Breakneck Race to Create Windows NT & the Next Generation at Microsoft. G. Pascal Zachary. 1994. 22.95 (*0-02-935671-7*, Free Press) Free Pr.

Showstoppers: Busby Berkeley & the Tradition of Spectacle. Martin Rubin. Ed. by John Belton. LC 92-37956. (Film & Culture Ser.). 352p. (C). 1993. 34.50 (*0-231-08054-9*) Col U Pr.

Showstoppers Ragtime. CPP Belwin Staff. 1987. pap. 17.95 (*0-89898-674-5*, F2867SMX) Warner Brothers.

Showstoppers 90's. CPP Belwin Staff. 1995. pap. text ed. 18.95 (*0-89724-979-8*, F3223SMA) Warner Brothers.

Showtime. Gene Brown. LC 97-16529. 1998. 22.95 (*0-02-860830-5*) Macmillan.

Showtime: How to Make THrousands Vacationing in Hawaii. Art Fettig. 96p. 1994. pap. 9.95 (*0-916927-19-9*) Growth Unltd.

Showtime at the Apollo. Ted Fox. LC 83-4299. (Illus.). 336p. 1985. pap. 9.95 (*0-03-060534-2*, Owl) H Holt & Co.

Showtime at the Apollo. Ted Fox. (Illus.). 336p. 1993. reprint ed. pap. 13.95 (*0-306-80503-0*) Da Capo.

Showtime's Act One Festival '94: One-Act Plays. Ed. by Marisa Smith. (Contemporary Playwrights Ser.). 240p. 1995. pap. 16.95 (*1-880399-96-2*) Smith & Kraus.

***Showtune.** Jerry Herman & Stasi. 1997. pap. 12.95 (*1-55611-537-7*) D I Fine.

Showtune: A Memoir. Jerry Herman & Marilyn Stasio. (Illus.). 320p. 1996. pap. 24.95 (*1-55611-502-4*) D I Fine.

Showy Science: Exciting Hands-on Activities That Explore the World Around Us. Hy Kim. (Illus.). 320p. (Orig.). (J). (gr. 3-6). 1994. pap. 19.95 (*0-673-36091-1*, GoodYrBooks) Addson-Wesley Educ.

Shpalera. Aleksandr Radashkevich. LC 84-60082. (Russica Poetry Ser.: No. 5). 90p. (Orig.). (RUS.). 1986. pap. 8.95 (*0-89830-073-8*) Russica Pubs.

Shpeter: A Latecomer in Early History. Meir U. Gottesman. (Judaica Youth Ser.). (Illus.). (J). (gr. 1-3). 1981. 5.95 (*0-910818-35-5*); pap. 4.95 (*0-910818-36-3*) Judaica Pr.

Shpeter: From the Depths to the Heights. Meir U. Gottesman. (Judaica Youth Ser.). (Illus.). (J). (gr. 1-3). 1981. 5.95 (*0-910818-39-8*); pap. 4.95 (*0-910818-40-1*) Judaica Pr.

Shraddhenjali. Kalyan K. De. 2870p. pap. 9.95 (*1-57087-030-6*) Prof Pr NC.

Shraga Mendlowitz. Hillel Seidman. LC 76-502. (HEB.). 1976. 10.00 (*0-88400-042-7*) Shengold.

Shraman Mahavir: His Life & Teachings. Yuvacharya Shri Mahaprajna. 334p. 1980. 12.00 (*0-88065-213-6*, Messers Today & Tomorrow) Scholarly Pubns.

Shrapnel in the Heart: Letters & Remembrances from the Vietnam Veterans Memorial. Laura Palmer. 1988. pap. 12.00 (*0-394-75988-5*, Vin) Random.

Shrapnel in the Heart: Letters & Remembrances from the Vietnam Memorial. Laura Palmer. LC 87-42652. (Illus.). 272p. 1987. 17.95 (*0-394-56027-2*) Random.

Shrapnel of the Heart. Ronald W. Wynkoop, Jr. LC 90-91429. (Orig.). 1990. pap. write for info. (*0-9626848-0-5*) Wynkoop Pr.

Shred Jam Trax for Guitar. Ralph Agresta. 1994. 9.95 (*0-8256-1414-7*, AM91475) Omnibus NY.

Shred of Evidence. Jill McGown. 1997. mass mkt. 5.99 (*0-449-22499-6*) Ballantine.

Shred of Evidence. Jill McGown. 304p. 1996. 21.00 (*0-449-91066-0*) Fawcett.

***Shred of God.** Steven Schwartz. LC 97-23601. 1998. write for info. (*0-688-15401-8*) Morrow.

Shredding of Families. Lillian D. Dunsmore & Richard A. Dunsmore. 100p. (Orig.). 1994. pap. 13.95 (*0-9640590-0-2*) Fallowfield.

Shree Rajneesh: A Man of Many Climates, Seasons & Rainbows: Through the Eye of the Camera. Photos by Divyananda et al. (Photobiography Ser.). 112p. 1989. 49.95 (*3-89338-051-5*, Pub. by Rebel Hse GW) Osho America.

Shreek of Wagons. Richard M. May. 154p. 1993. 29.95 (*1-883543-00-2*); pap. 19.95 (*1-883543-01-0*) Rigel Pubns.

Shrek! William Steig. 32p. 1990. 10.95 (*0-374-36877-5*) FS&G.

Shrek! William Steig. (J). (gr. 4-7). 1993. pap. 4.95 (*0-374-46623-8*) FS&G.

Shreveport & Bossier City. Photos & Text by Neil Johnson. LC 94-18981. (Illus.). (C). 1995. 39.95 (*0-8071-1995-4*) La State U Pr.

Shreveport & Vicinity, LA. (Streetfinder Ser.). (Illus.). 1995. pap. 17.95 (*0-528-91337-9*) Rand McNally.

Shreveport Plan: An Experiment in the Delivery of Legal Services. Raymond F. Marks et al. LC 74-77636. xi, 95p. Date not set. pap. 15.00 (*0-910058-61-X*, 305020) W S Hein.

Shrew! - Musical. Richard Barbie. 110p. 1977. pap. 5.50 (*0-87129-108-8*, S03) Dramatic Pub.

An Asterisk (*) at the beginning of an entry indicates that the title is appearing in BIP for the first time.

Shrews Can't Hoop!? Ray Nelson & Douglas Kelly. (Illus.). 48p. (J). (gr. k-6). 1994. 14.95 (*1-56977-418-8*) Flying Rhino.

Shrewsbury Edition of the Works of Samuel Butler, 20 vols., Set. Samuel Butler. (BCL1-PR English Literature Ser.). 1992. reprint ed. lib. bdg. 1,500.00 (*0-7812-7469-9*) Rprt Serv.

Shrewsbury, NJ. Randall Gabrielan. (Images of America Ser.). 1996. pap. 16.99 (*0-7524-0433-4*, Arcdia) Chalford.

Shrewsbury School Library Bindings, Vol. 17. James B. Oldham. (History of Bookbinding & Design Ser.). (Illus.). 296p. 1990. reprint ed. text ed. 70.00 (*0-8240-4046-5*) Garland.

Shreya of Sonargh. Uma Vasudev. (C). 1993. pap. 14.00 (*81-85944-23-7*, Pub. by UBS Pubs Dist II) S Asia.

Shri Bhagavad Gita. Winthrop Sargeant. 293p. 1993. pap. 9.95 (*0-7914-1888-X*) State U NY Pr.

Shri Lanka: Serendipity. Gillian Wright. (India Guides Ser.). (Illus.). 288p. 1996. pap. 16.95 (*0-8442-9695-3*, Passport Bks) NTC Pub Grp.

Shri Sayajirao Gaikwad, Maharaja of Baroda: The Prime Promoter of Public Libraries. Murari L. Nagar. Ed. by Sarla D. Nagar. LC 92-2528. (Spectrum of Alpha: America's Library Promotional Heritage in Asia: No. 5). 72p. (Orig.). 1992. pap. 18.00 (*0-943913-24-1*) Intl Lib Ctr.

Shri Varadrajswamy Temple-Kanchi. N. S. Raman. (Illus.). 206p. 1975. 29.95 (*0-318-36252-X*) Asia Bk Corp.

Shrichakrasambhara Tantra: A Buddhist Tantra. Tr. by Kazi Dawa-Samdup from TIB. 255p. 1984. reprint ed. lib. bdg. 29.50 (*0-88181-000-2*) Canon Pubns.

***Shriek in the Forest Night.** R. D. Lawrence. 224p. 1997. pap. 13.95 (*0-7737-5917-4*, Pub. by Stoddart Pubng CN) Genl Dist Srvs.

Shriek in the Forest Night: Wilderness Encounters. R. D. Lawrence. 224p. 1996. 19.95 (*0-7737-2941-0*, Pub. by Stoddart Pubng CN) Genl Dist Srvs.

Shriek of Silence: A Phenomenology of the Holocaust Novel. David Patterson. LC 91-17269. 192p. 1991. text ed. 24.00 (*0-8131-1768-2*) U Pr of Ky.

Shriek One. Ed. by Steve Bissette & Thomas Skulan. (Illus.). 1989. pap. 4.95 (*0-938782-14-2*) Fantaco.

Shriek Two. Ed. by Steve Bissette & Thomas Skulan. (Illus.). (Orig.). 1989. pap. 4.95 (*0-938782-15-0*) Fantaco.

Shrieking Silence: A Library Landscape. David Gerard. LC 87-32248. (Illus.). 297p. 1988. 29.50 (*0-8108-2069-2*) Scarecrow.

Shrikant. Saratchandra Chattopadhyaya. 168p. 1969. pap. 2.50 (*0-88253-028-3*) Ind-US Inc.

Shrikant Verma's Magadha. Tr. by Ajit Khullar. (C). 1990. 11.00 (*81-7023-285-6*, Pub. by Allied II) S Asia.

Shrike. Joseph Kramm. 1953. pap. 5.25 (*0-8222-1026-6*) Dramatists Play.

***Shrikes: A Guide to the Shrikes of the World.** Norbert Lefranc. 1997. 35.00 (*0-300-07336-4*) Yale U Pr.

Shrimp: Supply, Products & Marketing in the Aquaculture Age. Ian Dore. 368p. 1993. 79.00 (*1-881693-01-5*) Urner Barry Pubns.

Shrimp Captive & Culture Fisheries of the United States. Edwin S. Iversen et al. LC 93-7535. 247p. 1993. text ed. 79.95 (*0-470-22090-2*) Halsted Pr.

Shrimp Culture in North America & the Caribbean. Ed. by Paul A. Sandifer. (Advances in World Aquaculture Ser.: Vol. 4). (Illus.). (C). 1991. text ed. 45.00 (*0-9624529-3-9*) World Aquaculture.

***Shrimp Diet for Giants: 365 Shrimp Recipes to Bust Yer Gut!** Robert L. Albee. (Illus.). 160p. (Orig.). 1996. otabind, pap. text ed. 11.95 (*0-9624441-2-X*) Writers Express.

***Shrimper.** Bang. 1998. 15.95 (*0-8050-5396-4*) H Holt & Co.

Shrimper's Maui: A Guide to Coral Reef Biology. Charles J. Flora. (Illus.). 365p. (Orig.). 1996. pap. 22.95 (*0-9631036-3-6*) Jero Enter.

Shrimps, Lobsters & Crabs: Their Fascinating Life Story. Dorothy E. Bliss. (Morningside Bk.). (Illus.). 256p. 1990. pap. text ed. 22.00 (*0-231-07203-1*) Col U Pr.

Shrine. James Herbert. 464p. 1990. pap. 5.95 (*0-451-16669-8*, Sig) NAL-Dutton.

Shrine. John Iorio. (Juniper Bk. Ser.: No. 51). 68p. (Orig.). 1987. pap. 8.00 (*1-55780-080-4*) Juniper Pr WI.

Shrine. Christina Odone. 224p. 1996. 26.00 (*0-297-81661-6*, Weidenfeld) Trafalgar.

Shrine & Choma's Drum: Two Short Novels. Shivram K. Karanth. Tr. by U. R. Kalkur from KAN. 137p. 1984. 14.95 (*0-86578-246-6*) Ind-US Inc.

Shrine of Party: Congressional Voting Behavior, 1841 to 1852. Joel H. Silbey. LC 81-6341. (Illus.). x, 292p. 1981. reprint ed. text ed. 35.00 (*0-313-22661-X*, SISP, Greenwood Pr) Greenwood.

Shrine, Shelter, Cave. David McAleavey. LC 80-19572. 72p. 1980. 4.00 (*0-87886-110-6*, Greenfld Rev Pr) Greenfld Rev Lit.

Shrines of Ireland. John Dunne. 126p. 1989. pap. 22.00 (*1-85390-028-1*, Pub. by Veritas IE) St Mut.

Shringar: The Golden Book of Indian Hair Styles. Earl Cumine. (Illus.). (TAM & URD.). 1975. pap. 2.50 (*0-88253-454-8*) Ind-US Inc.

Shrink Rap: Sixty Psychotherapists Discuss Their Work, Their Lives, & the State of Their Field. Lee D. Kassan. LC 96-18541. 600p. 1996. 40.00 (*0-7657-0017-4*) Aronson.

Shrink Wrap. P. S. Mueller. (Illus.). 126p. 1992. pap. 6.95 (*0-930753-12-7*) Spect Ln Pr.

Shrinking Circle: Memories of Nazi Berlin, 1933-39. Zena Sulkes. 128p. (YA). (gr. 7-9). 1990. teacher ed., pap. 5.00 (*0-8074-0447-0*, 201500) UAHC.

Shrinking Circle: Memories of Nazi Berlin, 1933-39. Marion F. Wolff. 128p. (YA). (gr. 7-9). 1989. pap. 7.95 (*0-8074-0419-5*, 147501) UAHC.

Shrinking Circle: The Commonwealth in British Foreign Policy, 1945-1974. B. Vivekanandan. 1984. 37.50 (*0-8364-1039-4*, Pub. by Somaiya II) S Asia.

Shrinking Corporate Waistline. Brian P. Woolf. 1993. pap. 14.95 (*0-9632025-1-0*) Teal Bks.

***Shrinking Fields: Crop Land Loss in a World of Eight Billion.** Gary Gardner. 70p. (Orig.). 1996. pap. 5.00 (*1-878071-33-5*) Worldwatch Inst.

Shrinking Forests. Jenny E. Tesar. (Our Fragile Planet Ser.). (Illus.). 128p. (YA). (gr. 7-12). 1991. 18.95 (*0-8160-2492-8*) Facts on File.

Shrinking Lessons: Adventure Mystery for Kids Ages 8-12. Ann Gerfin. (Spider Tales Ser.). (Orig.). (J). (gr. 3-7). 1995. 14.00 (*0-922242-79-8*) Bepuzzled.

Shrinking Library Dollar. Dantia Quirk & Patricia Whitestone. 170p. 1982. 27.95 (*0-685-47122-5*) G K Hall.

Shrinking Library Dollar. Dantia Quirk & Patricia Whitestone. LC 81-12319. (Communications Library). 170p. 1982. 27.95 (*0-685-02844-5*) G K Hall.

Shrinking Man. Richard Matheson. 1993. reprint ed. lib. bdg. 27.95 (*0-89968-352-5*, Lghtyr Pr) Buccaneer Bks.

Shrinking Mouse. Pat Hutchins. LC 96-5393. (Illus.). 32p. (J). (ps up). 1997. 15.00 (*0-688-13961-2*); lib. bdg. 14.93 (*0-688-13962-0*) Greenwillow.

Shrinking of Treehorn. Florence P. Heide. LC 78-151753. (Illus.). 64p. (J). (gr. 3-6). 1971. pap. 4.95 (*0-8234-0975-9*); lib. bdg. 15.95 (*0-8234-0189-8*) Holiday.

Shrinking Pains. E. Maureen Goldman. LC 96-12343. 224p. (J). (gr. 4-8). 1996. pap. 14.99 (*0-670-86321-1*) Viking Penguin.

Shrinking Planet: U. S. Information Technology & Sustainable Development. John Elkington. LC 88-50613. 88p. (Orig.). 1988. pap. 10.00 (*0-915825-20-1*) World Resources Inst.

Shrinking the Corporate Waistline. 240p. (Orig.). 1992. pap. 20.00 (*0-9632025-0-2*) Teal Bks.

***Shrinking the Globe into Your Company's Hands: The Step-by-Step International Trade Guide for Small Businesses.** Sidney R. Lawrence. 192p. (Orig.). 1997. pap. 24.95 (*1-877810-46-0*) Rayve Prodns.

***Shrinking the Truth.** Marc Darrow. (Mystery in the Monterey Bay Area Ser.). 220p. (Orig.). 1997. pap. 9.95 (*0-9617681-9-3*) Otter B Bks.

Shrinking World? Ed. by John Allen & Chris Hamnett. (Shape of the World Ser.: Vol. 2). (Illus.). 272p. (C). 1996. text ed. 48.00 (*0-19-874186-3*); pap. text ed. 21.25 (*0-19-874187-1*) OUP.

Shrinklits. Maurice Sagoff. LC 79-56532. (Illus.). 112p. 1980. pap. 6.95 (*0-89480-079-5*, 413) Workman Pub.

SHRM Legislative Fact Sheets. Society for Human Resource Management Staff. Ed. by Deanna R. Gelak. 54p. (Orig.). 1996. pap. 10.00 (*0-939900-70-X*) Soc Human Resc Mgmt.

***Shrodinger's Machines: The Quantum Technology Reshaping Everyday Life.** Gerard J. Milburn. LC 96-51024. 188p. 1997. 21.95 (*0-7167-3106-1*, Sci Am Yng Rdrs) W H Freeman.

Shropshire. Ellis Peters & Roy Morgan. LC 92-13684. 168p. 1993. 35.00 (*0-89296-516-9*) Mysterious Pr.

Shropshire: The Records; Editorial Apparatus, 2 vols., Set. J. Alan Somerset. 834p. 1994. 175.00 (*0-8020-0648-5*) U of Toronto Pr.

Shropshire Christmas. Compiled by Lyn Briggs. LC 93-33701. 1993. 15.00 (*0-7509-0098-9*, Pub. by Sutton Pubng UK) Bks Intl VA.

***Shropshire Lad.** 34.95 (*1-85253-071-5*, XC7138, Pub. by Ashland Buchan & Enright UK) Cimino Pub Grp.

Shropshire Lad. Alfred E. Housman. (Illus.). 1997. pap. 3.95 (*0-8283-1455-1*, 7, Intl Pocket Lib) Branden Pub Co.

Shropshire Lad. Alfred E. Housman. LC 93-41351. (Decadents, Symbolists, Anti-Decadents Ser.). 96p. 1995. 43.00 (*1-85477-147-7*, Pub. by Woodstock Bks UK) Cassell.

Shropshire Lad. Alfred E. Housman. 64p. 1990. pap. 1.00 (*0-486-26468-8*) Dover.

Shropshire Lad. Intro. by Ian Rogerson. (Illus.). 109p. 1996. 11.95 (*1-57076-058-6*, Trafalgar Sq Pub) Trafalgar.

Shropshire Lad. Alfred E. Housman. 100p. 1981. reprint ed. lib. bdg. 21.95 (*0-89966-285-4*) Buccaneer Bks.

Shropshire Lad. Alfred E. Housman. 300p. 1990. reprint ed. lib. bdg. 16.95 (*0-89966-284-6*) Buccaneer Bks.

Shroud for a Nightingale. P. D. James. 288p. 1988. mass mkt. 5.99 (*0-446-31303-3*) Warner Bks.

Shroud for a Scholar. Audrey Peterson. 1995. mass mkt. 5.50 (*0-671-79510-4*) PB.

Shroud for an Archbishop. Peter Tremayne. LC 96-8481. 352p. 1996. 23.95 (*0-312-14734-1*) St Martin.

***Shroud for the Archbishop.** large type ed. Peter Tremayne. (Magna Large Print Ser.). (Illus.). 436p. 1996. 25.99 (*0-7505-0930-9*) Ulverscroft.

Shroud for Waldo. Kim Deitch. 64p. 1992. pap. 7.95 (*1-56097-081-2*) Fantagraph Bks.

Shroud in the Family. Lionel G. Garcia. LC 93-48366. (Orig.). 1994. 9.95 (*1-55885-113-5*) Arte Publico.

Shroud of Madness: An Earthdawn Novel. Carl Sargent. (Earthdawn Ser.). 320p. 1995. pap. 5.99 (*1-55560-275-4*, 6501) FASA Corp.

Shroud of Shadow. Gael Baudino. 352p. 1993. pap. 4.99 (*0-451-45294-1*, ROC) NAL-Dutton.

Shroud of Sophia: The Secret of Wisdom. Aurora Terrenus. 145p. (Orig.). 1988. pap. 8.95 (*0-945717-88-1*) Celestial Comns.

***Shroud of the Gnome: Poems.** James Tate. 96p. 1997. 23.00 (*0-88001-561-6*); pap. write for info. (*0-88001-562-4*) Ecco Pr.

Shroud of Turin & the C-14 Dating Fiasco: A Scientific Detective Story. Thomas W. Case. LC 96-60013. (Illus.). 104p. (Orig.). 1996. pap. 10.50 (*0-9648310-1-5*) Whte Hrse Pr.

Shroud Society. Robert Crawford. 192p. 1993. 18.50 (*0-7451-8620-3*, Black Dagger) Chivers N Amer.

***Shrouded.** Carol A. Davis. (Bloodlines Ser.). 212p. 1997. pap. 14.95 (*1-899344-17-9*, Pub. by Do-Not Pr UK) Dufour.

Shrouded Secrets: Japan's War on Mainland Australia 1942-1944. Richard Connaughton. (Illus.). 150p. 1994. 30.00 (*1-85753-160-4*, Pub. by Brasseys UK) Brasseys Inc.

Shrouds of Glory: From Atlanta to Nashville: The Last Great Campaign of the Civil War. Winston Groom. LC 94-37242. (Illus.). 256p. 1994. 23.00 (*0-87113-591-4*, Atlntc Mnthly) Grove-Atltic.

Shrouds of Glory: From Atlanta to Nashville: The Last Great Campaign of the Civil War. Winston Groom. 320p. 1996. pap. 14.00 (*0-671-56250-9*) PB.

SHRP-LTPP General Pavement Studies: Five-Year Report. William O. Hadley. 79p. (Orig.). (C). 1994. pap. text ed. 10.00 (*0-309-05766-3*, SHRP-P-387) SHRP.

SHRP-LTPP International Participation: Five-Year Report. Compiled by SHRP Staff. 140p. (Orig.). (C). 1994. pap. text ed. 15.00 (*0-309-05769-8*, SHRP-P-389) SHRP.

SHRP-LTPP Overview: Five-Year Report. William O. Hadley. (SHRP Ser.: P-416). (Illus.). 315p. (Orig.). (C). 1994. pap. text ed. 20.00 (*0-309-05815-5*) Natl Res Coun.

SHRP-LTPP Specific Pavement Studies: Five-Year Report. Amir N. Hanna et al. 164p. (Orig.). (C). 1994. pap. text ed. 15.00 (*0-309-05772-8*, SHRP-P-395) SHRP.

SHRP-LTPP Traffic Data Collection & Analysis: Five-Year Report. John L. German & Charlie Copeland, Jr. Ed. by William O. Hadley. 39p. (Orig.). (C). 1993. pap. text ed. 10.00 (*0-309-05765-5*, SHRP-P-386) SHRP.

Shrub Identification Book. George W. Symonds. LC 63-7388. 1973. pap. 19.50 (*0-688-05040-9*, Quill) Morrow.

Shrub It Up: A Guide for Pacific Northwest Landscaping. George R. McNair. Ed. by Chris McNair. (Illus.). 66p. 1986. pap. 7.96 (*0-9619034-0-6*) CGM Pub Co.

Shrub Roses & Climbing Roses: With Hybrid Tea & Floribunda Roses. David Austin. (Illus.). 225p. (Orig.). 1993. pap. 25.00 (*1-85149-166-X*) Antique Collect.

Shrub-Steppe: Balance & Change in a Semi-Arid Terrestrial Ecosystems. Ed. by W. H. Rickard et al. (Developments in Agricultural & Managed-Forest Ecology Ser.: No. 20). 284p. 1988. 220.75 (*0-444-42990-5*) Elsevier.

Shrubs. Roger Phillips. (Illus.). 288p. 1989. pap. 27.50 (*0-679-72345-5*, Vin) Random.

Shrubs: Over 1900 Shrubs in Full-Colour Photographs. Roger Phillips & Martyn E. Rix. (Garden Plant Ser.). (Illus.). 288p. (Orig.). 1989. pap. 44.50 (*0-330-30258-2*, Pub. by Pan Books UK) Trans-Atl Phila.

Shrubs: The New Glamour Plants. Ed. by Bob Hyland & Brooklyn Botanic Garden Staff. (21st-Century Gardening Ser.). (Illus.). 112p. 1994. per., pap. 9.95 (*0-945352-86-7*) Bklyn Botanic.

Shrubs & Climbers. LC 95-43914. (Eyewitness Handbks.). 336p. 1996. pap. 19.95 (*0-7894-0429-X*) DK Pub Inc.

Shrubs & Hedges. A. Cort Sinnes & Michael Mckinley. Ed. by Cedric Crocker. LC 90-80074. (Illus.). 112p. 1990. reprint ed. pap. 9.95 (*0-89721-223-1*) Meredith Bks.

Shrubs & Trees of the Southwest Deserts. Janice E. Bowers. Ed. by Ronald J. Foreman & T. J. Priehs. LC 93-84560. (Illus.). 120p. (Orig.). (C). 1993. pap. 9.95 (*1-877856-34-7*) SW Pks Mnmts.

Shrubs & Trees of the Southwest Uplands. 2nd ed. Francis H. Elmore. Ed. by Earl Jackson. LC 76-14115. (Popular Ser.: No. 19). (Illus.). 216p. (Orig.). 1976. pap. 9.95 (*0-911408-41-X*) SW Pks Mnmts.

Shrubs & Vines for Southern Landscapes. fac. ed. William D. Adams. LC 76-15455. (Illus.). 80p. pap. 25.00 (*0-7837-7408-7*, 2047202) Bks Demand.

Shrubs & Woody Vines of Florida. Gil Nelson. (Illus.). 464p. 1996. 30.95 (*1-56164-106-5*); pap. 21.95 (*1-56164-110-3*) Pineapple Pr.

***Shrubs for Everyone.** Peter Seabrook. Ed. by Jane Robinson. (Illus.). 128p. (Orig.). 1997. 25.95 (*0-903001-70-5*, Pub. by Burall Floraprint UK) J Markham & Assocs.

***Shrubs for Everyone.** Peter Seabrook. Ed. by Jane Robinson. (Illus.). 128p. (Orig.). 1997. pap. 21.95 (*0-903001-71-3*, Pub. by Burall Floraprint UK) J Markham & Assocs.

Shrubs for Pathfinders: A Basic Youth Enrichment Skill Honor Packet. L. S. Gattis, III. (Illus.). 20p. (Orig.). (J). (gr. 5 up). 1989. teacher ed., pap. 5.00 (*0-936241-41-1*) Cheetah Pub.

Shrubs for the Rocky Mountain & Plains States. Gayle Weinstein. (Illus.). 300p. 1996. pap. text ed. 30.00 (*0-9629743-3-1*) Shereth Grp.

Shrubs, Gardener's Collection. Better Homes & Gardens Editors. (Better Homes & Gardens Ser.). (Illus.). 64p. 1995. pap. 4.95 (*0-696-02578-7*) Meredith Bks.

Shrubs in the Wild and in Gardens. Bruno P. Kremer. LC 94-46431. (Illus.). 240p. 1995. pap. 13.95 (*0-8120-9203-1*) Barron.

Shrubs of Michigan. 2nd ed. Cecil Billington. LC 44-1024. (Bulletin Ser.: No. 20). (Illus.). 339p. 1949. text ed. 12.00 (*0-87737-005-2*) Cranbrook.

Shrubs of Ontario. James H. Soper & Margaret L. Heimburger. 1994. pap. 35.00 (*0-88854-283-6*, Pub. by Royal Ont Mus CN) U of Toronto Pr.

Shrubs of the Great Basin: A Natural History. Hugh N. Mozingo. LC 86-7070. (Great Basin Ser.: No. 4). 364p. (Orig.). 1987. pap. 34.95 (*0-87417-112-1*) U of Nev Pr.

***Shrunken Dream.** Jane T. Creider. (International Connections Ser.). 360p. pap. 15.95 (*0-88961-175-0*, Pub. by Wmns Pr CN) LPC InBook.

Shrunken Planets. Robert Louthan. LC 79-54883. 64p. 1980. pap. 3.95 (*0-914086-28-6*) Alicejamesbooks.

Shtetl: A Creative Anthology of Jewish Life in Eastern Europe. Ed. & Tr. by Joachim Neugroschel. 584p. 1989. 25.00 (*0-87951-356-X*) Overlook Pr.

Shtetl: A Creative Anthology of Jewish Life in Eastern Europe. Ed. & Tr. by Joachim Neugroschel. 584p. 1990. pap. 15.95 (*0-87951-380-2*) Overlook Pr.

***Shtetl: The Life & Death of a Small Town & the World of Polish Jews.** Eva Hoffman. LC 97-2615. 1997. 25.00 (*0-395-82295-5*) HM.

Shtetl & Other Yiddish Novellas. Ed. by Ruth R. Wisse. LC 86-15794. 344p. 1986. reprint ed. 34.95 (*0-8143-1848-7*); reprint ed. pap. 17.95 (*0-8143-1849-5*) Wayne St U Pr.

Shtetl Book. rev. ed. David G. Roskies. pap. 16.95 (*0-87068-455-8*) Ktav.

Shtetl Finder Gazetteer: Jewish Communities in the 19th & Early 20th Centuries in the Pale of Settlement of Russia & Poland, & in Lithuania, Latvia, Galicia, & Bukovina, with Names of Residents. Chester G. Cohen. 154p. (Orig.). 1989. pap. 18.50 (*1-55613-248-4*) Heritage Bk.

Shtetl in the Adirondacks: The Story of Gloversville & Its Jews. Herbert M. Engel. LC 91-36221. (Illus.). 220p. (Orig.). 1996. reprint ed. pap. 18.00 (*0-935796-22-3*) Purple Mnt Pr.

Shtetl Life. Florence B. Helzel. (Illus.). 160p. (Orig.). 1993. pap. 19.95 (*0-943376-59-9*) Magnes Mus.

Shu Ting: Selected Poems. Shu Ting. Tr. & Pref. by Eva Hung. 134p. (Orig.). 1994. pap. 14.95 (*0-614-05343-9*, Pub. by Renditions Papbk HK) SPD-Small Pr Dist.

Shua. William Burke. LC 90-8566. (Illus.). 110p. (Orig.). 1990. pap. 8.95 (*0-87946-050-4*, 119) ACTA Pubns.

Shub-Niggurath Cycle: 15 Horror Tales Involving Shub-Niggurath & Her Thousand Young. Ramesy Campbell et al. (Chaosium Fiction Ser.). (Illus.). 256p. (Orig.). 1994. pap. 10.95 (*1-56882-017-8*, 6004) Chaosium.

Shuberts of Broadway: A History Drawn from the Collection of the Shubert Archive. Brooks McNamara. (Illus.). 258p. 1990. 35.00 (*0-19-506542-5*) OUP.

Shuck Beans, Stack Cakes, & Honest Fried Chicken: The Heart & Soul of Southern Country Kitchens. Ronni Lundy. LC 91-18142. (Illus.). 400p. 1994. pap. 15.00 (*0-87113-600-7*, Atlntc Mnthly) Grove-Atltic.

Shuckin' & Jivin': Folklore from Contemporary Black Americans. Daryl C. Dance. LC 77-23635. 416p. 1978. 35.00 (*0-253-35220-7*) Ind U Pr.

Shuckin' & Jivin': Folklore from Contemporary Black Americans. Daryl C. Dance. LC 77-23635. 416p. 1981. pap. 15.95 (*0-253-20265-5*, MB-265) Ind U Pr.

Shudda, Cudda, Wudda: Affirmations to Cope with Self-Doubt. A. J. Chevalier. 380p. 1996. pap. 8.95 (*1-55874-387-1*) Health Comm.

Shudder. Brian Harper. 416p. 1994. 4.99 (*0-451-17693-6*, Sig) NAL-Dutton.

Shudder Again. Ed. by Michele B. Slung. 384p. 1995. 5.99 (*0-451-45346-8*, ROC) NAL-Dutton.

Shudder Pulps: A History of the Weird Menace Magazines of the 1930s. Robert K. Jones. LC 74-82614. xv, 238p. 1974. lib. bdg. 35.00 (*0-913960-04-7*) Borgo Pr.

Shuddering Dawn: Religious Studies & the Nuclear Age. Ed. by Ira Chernus & Edward T. Linenthal. LC 88-38013. 210p. 1989. text ed. 64.50 (*0-7914-0084-0*); pap. text ed. 21.95 (*0-7914-0085-9*) State U NY Pr.

Shuddhi Movement in India: A Study of Its Socio-Political Dimensions. R. K. Ghai. (C). 1990. 28.50 (*81-7169-042-4*, Commonwealth) S Asia.

Shuey: History of the Shuey Family in America, 1732 to 1919. 2nd ed. D. B. Shuey. 381p. 1993. reprint ed. pap. 58.00 (*0-8328-3403-3*); reprint ed. lib. bdg. 68.00 (*0-8328-3402-5*) Higginson Bk Co.

Shuffleboard: Those Capricious Discs. Floyd Swem. (Illus.). 84p. (Orig.). 1975. pap. 3.95 (*0-8200-0611-4*) Great Outdoors.

Shuffleboard Pilots: The History of the Women's Air Raid Defense in Hawaii, 1941-1945. Candace A. Chenoweth & A. Kam Napier. (Illus.). 88p. (Orig.). 1991. pap. 8.95 (*0-9631388-0-4*) AZ Mem Mus.

Shufflebrain. Paul Pietsch. LC 80-21726. 287p. reprint ed. pap. 81.80 (*0-7837-6490-1*, AU00447) Bks Demand.

Shug: The Life & Times of Auburn's Ralph 'Shug' Jordan. Rich Donnell. 1994. 22.95 (*0-9638568-0-4*) Owl Bay Pubs.

***Shugah & Doops.** Will D. Campbell. (Father Thyme Bks.). 32p. 1997. 14.95 (*1-57736-019-2*) Providence Hse.

Shugborough. John M. Robinson. (Illus.). 96p. 1989. pap. 9.95 (*0-7078-0101-X*, Pub. by Natl Trust UK) Trafalgar.

Shukar Balan: The White Lamb. Mela M. Lindsay. 1976. 16.50 (*0-914222-02-3*) Am Hist Soc Ger.

Shukis Upsidedown Dream. Yaffa Ganz. (J). (gr. k-3). 1986. 7.95 (*0-87306-384-8*) Feldheim.

Shukshin: Snowball Berry Red (Kalina Krasnaya) Ed. by D. Holohan. (Russian Texts Ser.). (RUS.). pap. 16.95 (*1-85399-419-7*, Pub. by Brstl Class Pr UK) Focus Pub-R Pullins.

Shulamite's Song: A Feminist Approach to the Bible. Ilana Pardes. (Illus.). 240p. (C). 1992. text ed. 29.95 (*0-674-80733-2*) HUP.

Shulamith. Meera Mahadevan. 208p. 1980. pap. 3.25 (*0-86578-061-7*) Ind-US Inc.

Shulchan Aruch Choshan Mishpot: With Commentaries, 2 Vols. (HEB.). 35.00 (*0-87559-081-0*) Shalom.

Shulchon Oruch, Vol. 1. Schneur Z. Baruchovitch. (HEB.). reprint ed. 11.25 (*0-8266-5502-5*) Kehot Pubn Soc.

Shulchon Oruch, Vol. 2. Schneur Z. Baruchovitch. (HEB.). reprint ed. 11.25 (*0-8266-5503-3*) Kehot Pubn Soc.

S

An Asterisk (*) at the beginning of an entry indicates that the title is appearing in BIP for the first time.

Shulchon Oruch, Vol. 3. Schneur Z. Baruchovitch. (HEB.). reprint ed. 11.25 (0-8266-5504-1) Kehot Pubn Soc.

Shulchon Oruch, Vol. 4. Schneur Z. Baruchovitch. (HEB.). reprint ed. 11.25 (0-8266-5505-X) Kehot Pubn Soc.

***Shultz. Genealogy of the Schultz, Cupp, Weyand & Pisel Families Which Have Descended from Michael Shultz, a Pioneer Settler in SOmerset Co., Pa., Many of Whose Descendants Have Also been Pioneers Throughout the U. S. & Canada.** Charles R. Schultz. (Illus.). 205p. 1996. reprint ed. pap. 32.00 (0-8328-5284-8) Higginson Bk Co.

***Shultz. Genealogy of the Schultz, Cupp, Weyand & Pisel Families Which Have Descended from Michael Shultz, a Pioneer Settler in Somerset Co., Pa., Many of Whose Descendants Have Also Been Pioneers Throughout the U. S. & Canada.** Charles R. Schultz. (Illus.). 205p. 1996. reprint ed. lib. bdg. 42.00 (0-8328-5283-X) Higginson Bk Co.

Shum Zemli: Stikhi. Vladimir Gandelsman. LC 91-40906. 100p. (RUS.). 1991. pap. 8.00 (1-55779-046-9) Hermitage.

Shunka: Life with an Arctic Wolf. Marika L. Morgan. (Illus.). 192p. 1996. reprint ed. pap. 15.00 (1-880158-09-4) J N Townsend.

Shunned. Willis Brubacher. (Orig.). 1996. pap. 12.95 (0-533-11734-8) Vantage.

***Shunning, Vol. 1.** Beverly Lewis. LC 97-4648. (The Heritage of Lancaster County Ser.). 288p. 1997. pap. 9.99 (1-55661-866-2) Bethany Hse.

Shunpiker's Guide to the Northeast: Washington to Boston Without Turnpikes or Interstates. Peter Exton. LC 88-11054. (Illus.). 160p. (Orig.). 1988. pap. 9.95 (0-939009-10-2) EPM Pubns.

Shunt Book. J. M. Drake & C. Sainte-Rose. (Illus.). 160p. 1994. pap. 26.95 (0-86542-220-6) Blackwell Sci.

Shunts. rev. ed. 1989. write for info. (0-944093-05-1) Am Brain Tumor.

Shunts & Problems in Shunts. Ed. by M. Choux. (Monographs in Neural Sciences: Vol. 8). (Illus.). x, 230p. 1982. pap. 92.00 (3-8055-2465-X) S Karger.

Shupton's Fancy: A Tale of the Fly-Fishing Obsession. Paul Schullery. LC 96-769. (Illus.). 64p. 1996. 15.00 (0-8117-1534-5) Stackpole.

Shurangama Sutra, 7 vols. Incl. Vol. 6. . Tr. by Buddhist Text Translation Society from CHI. (Illus.). 200p. (Orig.). (C). 1981. pap. Not sold separately (0-917512-97-9); Vol. 1. . Tr. by Buddhist Text Translation Society from CHI. (Illus.). 289p. (Orig.). 1977. pap. Not sold separately (0-917512-17-0); Vol. 2. . Tr. by Buddhist Text Translation Society from CHI. (Illus.). 212p. (Orig.). 1979. pap. Not sold separately (0-917512-25-1); Vol. 3. . Tr. by Buddhist Text Translation Society from CHI. (Illus.). 240p. (Orig.). (C). 1980. pap. Not sold separately (0-917512-94-4); Vol. 4. . Tr. by Buddhist Text Translation Society from CHI. (Illus.). 285p. (Orig.). (C). 1980. pap. Not sold separately (0-917512-95-2); Vol. 5. . Tr. by Buddhist Text Translation Society from CHI. (Illus.). 250p. (Orig.). (C). 1980. pap. Not sold separately (0-917512-91-X); Vol. 7. . Tr. by Buddhist Text Translation Society from CHI. (Illus.). 270p. (Orig.). (C). 1982. pap. Not sold separately (0-917512-93-6); 59.50 (0-685-57675-2) Buddhist Text.

Shurangama Sutra: The Fifty Skandha-Demon States. Ed. & Tr. by Buddhist Text Translation Society Staff. Orig. Title: Leng Yen Ching Wu Shih Yin Mo Chien Shih. (CHI & ENG.). 1996. write for info. (0-88139-400-9) Buddhist Text.

***Shurangama Sutra, Great Strength Bodhisattva's Perfect Penetration Through Mindfulness of the Buddha: Ba Simple Explanation.** Hs Uan Hua. LC 96-52639. 1997. write for info. (0-88139-307-X) Buddhist Text.

Shurik. Kyra P. Wayne. 224p. 1992. pap. 9.95 (1-55821-144-6) Lyons & Burford.

Shurikendo. Ikku-Ken. pap. 13.95 (0-901764-94-9, 93210) Talman.

Shurtleff: Descendants of William Shurtleff of Plymouth & Marshfield, Massachusetts. B. Shurtleff. (Illus.). 738p. 1992. reprint ed. pap. 165.00 (0-8328-2276-0); reprint ed. lib. bdg. 175.00 (0-8328-2275-2) Higginson Bk Co.

Shurtleff & Lawton Families: Genealogy & History. William R. Shurtleff. 220p. 1994. pap. 39.00 (0-942515-07-2) Pine Hill CA.

Shuruk, No. 1. Harvey Jackins et al. (ARA.). 1993. 2.00 (0-913937-83-5) Rational Isl.

Shurut al-Nahdah. Malik Bin-Nabi. (Mushkilat al-Hadarah Ser.). 176p. 1987. pap. 4.95 (1-57547-027-6) Dar Al-Fikr.

Shushan Chronicle: The Story of Purim. Yaffa L. Gottlieb. (Illus.). 56p. (J). (gr. 2-6). 1991. 11.95 (0-922613-39-7); pap. 9.95 (0-922613-40-0) Hachai Pubns.

Shuster Mission & the Persian Constitutional Revolution. Robert A. McDaniel. LC 72-96966. (Studies in Middle Eastern History: No. 1). 1974. 30.00 (0-88297-004-6) Bibliotheca.

Shuswap. James A. Teit. LC 73-3522. (Jesup North Pacific Expedition. Publications: No. 2, Pt. 7). reprint ed. 79.50 (0-404-58123-4) AMS Pr.

Shuswap Language. Aert H. Kuipers. LC 73-85775. (Janua Linguarum, Ser. Practica: No. 225). 297p. 1974. pap. text ed. 81.55 (90-279-2672-7) Mouton.

***Shut the Door.** Claudette C. Mitchell et al. (Visions: African-American Experiences: Vol. 15). (Illus.). 8p. (Orig.). (J). (gr. k-1). 1996. pap. text ed. 3.00 (1-57518-057-X) Arborlake.

Shut Those Thick Lips! A Study of Slum School Failure. Gerry Rosenfeld. 120p. (C). 1983. reprint ed. pap. text ed. 9.50 (0-88133-022-1) Waveland Pr.

Shut up & Make More Money: The Recruiter's Guide to Talking Less & Billing More. William G. Radin. Ed. by Betsy Smith. (Illus.). 224p. 1995. pap. 49.95 (0-9626147-3-4) Innovative Consulting.

Shut up & Paint. Alfred S. Cosentino. 1989. write for info. (0-929991-17-6) A S Cosentino Bks.

Shut up & Sell! Tested Techniques for Closing the Sale. Don Sheehan. LC 81-66235. 165p. 1984. pap. 16.95 (0-8144-7615-5) AMACOM.

Shut up, Fag! Quotations from the Files of Congressman Bob Dornan. Ed. by Nathan Callahan & William Payton. 120p. (Orig.). 1994. pap. 8.95 (0-9641241-0-6) Mainstreet Media.

Shutdown at Youngstown: Public Policy for Mass Unemployment. Terry F. Buss & F. Stevens Redburn. LC 82-5686. (SUNY Series in Urban Public Policy). 219p. 1983. text ed. 59.50 (0-87395-646-X); pap. text ed. 19.95 (0-87395-647-8) State U NY Pr.

Shuteyes. Mary James. 376p. (J). (gr. 4-7). 1994. pap. 3.25 (0-590-45070-0) Scholastic Inc.

***Shutter of Snow.** Emily H. Coleman. (American Literature Ser.). 245p. 1997. reprint ed. pap. 12.95 (1-56478-147-X) Dalkey Arch.

Shutterbug. Stan Hayward. (Henry's Cat Ser.). (Illus.). (J). (ps-5). 1987. pap. 2.25 (0-671-63776-2) S&S Trade.

Shutterbug's Guide to Better Photography. Compiled by Edward S. Balian. 96p. 1992. pap. 9.95 (0-9634576-0-8) Patch Pub.

Shuttered Eye. Julia Copus. 64p. 1996. pap. 16.95 (1-85224-338-4, Pub. by Bloodaxe Bks UK) Dufour.

Shuttered Heart. Meg Buchanan. (Rainbow Romances Ser.). 160p. 1994. 14.95 (0-7090-5005-4, 910, Hale-Parkwest) Parkwest Pubns.

Shuttered Heart. large type ed. Meg Buchanan. (Linford Romance Library). 288p. 1995. pap. 15.99 (0-7089-7778-2, Linford) Ulverscroft.

Shuttle. Frances Hodgson Burnett. 22.95 (0-8488-0253-5) Amereon Ltd.

Shuttle, 2 cassettes, Set. (Read-Along Ser.). (YA). 1986. student ed., pap. 34.95 incl. audio (0-88432-969-0, S23914) Audio-Forum.

Shuttle Craft: An Educational Coloring Book. Spizzirri Publishing Co. Staff. Ed. by Linda Spizzirri. (Illus.). 32p. (J). (gr. 1-8). 1986. pap. 1.99 (0-86545-077-3) Spizzirri.

Shuttle Diplomacy in the 1980s: U. S. Mediations in the Falkland - Malvinas Crisis. Chaim D. Kaufmann. (Pew Case Studies in International Affairs). 50p. (C). 1994. pap. text ed. 3.50 (1-56927-431-2) Geo U Inst Dplmcy.

Shuttle Mission. Desjarlais. (New Readers Ser.). 1993. pap. text ed. write for info. (0-15-599354-2) HB Schl Dept.

Shuttle Plus One - A New View of Space: Proceedings of the 12th Conference on Space Simulation, May 1982, Pasadena, California. 363p. 1982. 55.00 (0-686-92542-4) Inst Environ Sci.

Shuttle Propulsion Systems: Presented at the Winter Annual Meeting of the American Society of Mechanical Engineers, Phoenix, Arizona, November 14-19, 1982. American Society of Mechanical Engineers Staff. Ed. by John W. Robinson. LC 82-73179. (AD Ser.: No. 05). (Illus.). 93p. reprint ed. pap. 26.60 (0-8357-2906-0, 2039143) Bks Demand.

Shuttle-Spacelab: The New Transportation System & Its Utilization. Ed. by Dietrich E. Koelle & George V. Butler. LC 57-43769. (Advances in the Astronautical Sciences Ser.: Vol. 43). (Illus.). 342p. 1981. pap. text ed. 35.00 (0-87703-146-0); lib. bdg. 45.00 (0-87703-144-4) Univelt Inc.

Shuttlecock. Graham Swift. 1992. pap. 10.00 (0-679-73933-5, Vin) Random.

Shuttlecock. Phil Andros. 174p. 1992. reprint ed. pap. 7.95 (1-55583-226-1) Alyson Pubns.

Shu'ubiyya in Al-Andalus: The Risala of Ibn Garcia & Five Refutations. James T. Monroe. LC 77-627464. (University of California Publications, Near Eastern Studies: No. 13). (Illus.). 113p. reprint ed. pap. 32.30 (0-685-20581-9, 2030679) Bks Demand.

Shuzo Kuki & Jean Paul Sartre: Influence & Counter-Influence in the Early History of Existential Phenomenology. Stephen Light. LC 86-11861. (Journal of the History of Philosophy Monograph Ser.). 168p. (Orig.). 1987. pap. text ed. 13.95 (0-8093-1271-9) S Ill U Pr.

Shy Ann. Nancy Ball. LC 88-51305. (Illus.). 55p. (Orig.). (J). (gr. k-4). 1989. pap. 3.95 (0-931563-03-8) Wishing Rm.

Shy Charles. Rosemary Wells. LC 87-27247. (Illus.). 32p. (J). (ps-3). 1988. lib. bdg. 11.89 (0-8037-0564-6) Dial Bks Young.

Shy Charles. Rosemary Wells. LC 87-27247. (Illus.). 32p. (J). (ps-3). 1992. pap. 4.99 (0-14-054537-9, Puff Pied Piper) Puffin Bks.

Shy Charles: Giant Book. Rosemary Wells. LC 87-27247. (Illus.). 32p. (J). (ps-3). 1992. pap. 17.99 (0-14-054570-0, Puff Pied Piper) Puffin Bks.

***Shy Life: Understanding, Hope & Healing.** Bernardo Carducci. 256p. Date not set. 24.00 (0-06-018247-4) HarpC.

Shy Little Kitten. Cathleen Schurr. (Little Golden Bks.). (Illus.). 24p. (J). (ps-2). 1992. bds. write for info. (0-307-00145-8, 312-10, Golden Books) Western Pub.

***Shy Little Turtle.** Howard Goldsmith. 1997. text ed. 14.95 (0-07-024541-X, Lrning Triangle) McGraw.

Shy Man Syndrome: Why Men Become Love Shy & How They Can Overcome It. Brian G. Gilmartin. LC 88-37066. 228p. 1989. 18.95 (0-8191-7009-7) Madison Bks UPA.

Shy Man's Guide to Success with Women. Terry A. Heggy. 1994. pap. 12.95 (0-9640544-0-X) Perf Press CO.

Shy Man's Guide to the Secrets of Attracting Women. Dale J. Kroll. 56p. (Orig.). 1986. pap. 5.95 (0-9616728-0-3) Summerdale Ent.

Shy Man's Guide to the Secrets of Attracting Women in the '90s. Dale J. Kroll. (Illus.). 123p. (Orig.). 1993. pap. 12.95 (0-9616728-1-1) Summerdale Ent.

Shy Nude. J. T. Elias. 227p. 1990. 19.95 (1-878648-00-4) Flying Eightball Prodns.

***Shy Persons Guide to a Happier Love Life.** Eric Weber & Judi Miller. 1979. reprint ed. pap. 19.95 (0-914094-52-1) Symphony.

Shy Roland. Marilyn Talbot. (Illus.). 32p. (J). (ps). 1994. 14.95 (0-86264-405-4, Pub. by Andersen Pr UK) Trafalgar.

Shy Salamanders. D. M. Souza. LC 94-9108. (Creatures All Around Us Ser.). (Illus.). 40p. (J). (gr. 1-4). 1994. lib. bdg. 14.96 (0-87614-826-7, Carolrhoda) Lerner Group.

***Shy Sophie.** (Little Monsters Ser.). (J). 1997. write for info. (0-614-21786-5, Pub. by Splash UK) Assoc Pubs Grp.

Shy Tulip Murders. Rebecca Rothenberg. 336p. 1996. 21.95 (0-89296-607-6) Mysterious Pr.

Shy Tulip Murders. Rebecca Rothenberg. 304p. 1997. mass mkt. 5.99 (0-446-40462-4, Mysterious Paperbk) Warner Bks.

Shy Vi. Wendy C. Lewison. LC 91-39658. (Illus.). 40p. (J). (ps-2). 1993. pap. 14.00 (0-671-76968-5, S&S Bks Young Read) S&S Childrens.

Shy Young Denbury. large type ed. Audrey Blanshard. (General Ser.). 304p. 1993. 25.99 (0-7089-2835-8) Ulverscroft.

Shyann Am! Tuvan Folk Tales. Kira Van Deusen. LC 95-92426. (Illus.). 64p. (Orig.). 1995. pap. 9.95 (0-9647716-0-8) Udagan Bks.

Shylock: A Legend & Its Legacy. John Gross. 384p. 1994. 13.00 (0-671-88386-0, Touchstone Bks) S&S Trade.

Shylock: The History of a Character. Hermann Sinsheimer. LC 63-23188. (Illus.). 1972. reprint ed. 18.95 (0-405-08977-5, Pub. by Blom Pubns UK) Ayer.

Shylock & Others: Eight Studies. G. H. Radford. LC 72-13311. (Essay Index Reprint Ser.). 1977. reprint ed. 18.95 (0-8369-8172-3) Ayer.

Shylock & Shakespeare. Abraham Morevski. LC 67-19382. 112p. 1967. 3.35 (0-87527-056-5) Green.

***Shylock & the Jewish Question.** Martin D. Jaffe. LC 97-3012. (Jewish Studies). 1998. write for info. (0-8018-5648-5) Johns Hopkins.

Shylock & the King of England. Edna Krane. 1995. 17.95 (0-533-11519-1) Vantage.

Shylock's Daughter. Erica Jong. 272p. 1995. mass mkt. 6.50 (0-06-100830-3) HarpC.

Shylock's Rights: A History of Lockian Doctrine. Edward Andrew. 192p. 1987. 35.00 (0-8020-2611-7); pap. 15.95 (0-8020-6660-7) U of Toronto Pr.

Shyness. Philip G. Zimbardo. 1990. pap. 12.00 (0-201-55018-0) Addison-Wesley.

Shyness: Perspectives on Research & Treatment. Ed. by Warren H. Jones et al. (Emotions, Personality, & Psychotherapy Ser.). 410p. 1986. 52.50 (0-306-42033-3, Plenum Pr) Plenum.

Shyness: What It Is, What to Do About It. Philip G. Zimbardo. LC 77-73069. 1977. pap. write for info. (0-201-08794-4) Addison-Wesley.

Shyness & Embarrassment: Perspectives from Social Psychology. Ed. by W. Ray Crozier. (Illus.). 368p. (C). 1990. text ed. 64.95 (0-521-35529-X) Cambridge U Pr.

Shyp of Folys of the Worlde. Sebastian Brant. Tr. by Alexander Barcley. LC 74-25743. (English Experience Ser.: No. 229). 1970. reprint ed. 85.00 (90-221-0229-7) Walter J Johnson.

Shy's, Wise, Y's: The Griot's Tale. Amiri Baraka. 86p. 1994. 14.95 (0-88378-150-6) Third World.

SI: The International System of Units. 2nd ed. Robert A. Nelson. (Illus.). 132p. 1983. 14.00 (0-917853-84-9, OP45) Am Assn Physics.

Si Amas a Tu Adolescente. Ross Campbell. Tr. by Juan S. Araujo from ENG. 144p. (SPA.). 1986. pap. 3.95 (0-88113-030-3) Edit Betania.

Si Amas a Tu Hijo. Ross Campbell. Tr. by Juan S. Araujo from ENG. 144p. (SPA.). 1986. pap. 3.95 (0-88113-031-1) Edit Betania.

Si Belles et Fraiches Etaient les Roses. Nella Bielski. 224p. (FRE.). 1984. pap. 10.95 (0-7859-2226-1, 207037551X) Fr & Eur.

Si de Las Ninas. Moratin. 130p. (SPA.). 1980. 4.95 (0-8288-7104-3) Fr & Eur.

Si de las Ninas. unabridged ed. Moratin. (SPA.). pap. 5.95 (84-410-0055-7, Pub. by Bookking Intl FR) Distribks Inc.

Si Dios Me Ama, Por Que Me Sale Todo Mal? Lorraine Peterson. Tr. by Rhode F. Ward from ENG. 160p. (SPA.). 1988. reprint ed. pap. 4.95 (0-88113-269-1) Edit Betania.

SI Drilling Manual. Canadian Association of Oilwell Drilling Contractors Staff. LC 82-15466. 820p. 1982. ring bd. 195.00 (0-87201-211-5) Gulf Pub.

***Si Estoy Perdonado, Por que Me Siento Culpable? - If I'm Forgiven Why Do I...?** Bangley. 101p. (SPA.). 1995. write for info. (1-56063-523-1) Editorial Unilit.

Si Haulte Architecture: The Design of Sceve's Delie. Doranne Fenoaltea. LC 81-71432. (French Forum Monographs: No. 35). 246p. (Orig.). 1982. pap. 16.95 (0-917058-34-8) French Forum.

Si J'Etais Vous... Julien Green. (FRE.). 1983. pap. 16.95 (0-7859-2695-X, 2020006181) Fr & Eur.

Si le Das un Panecillo a un Alce. Laura J. Numeroff. Tr. by Teresa Mlawer. LC 94-37255. (Illus.). 32p. (SPA.). (J). (ps-2). 1995. 14.95 (0-06-025440-8, HpArco Iris) HarpC Child Bks.

Si le Das una Galletita a un Raton. Laura J. Numeroff. Tr. by Teresa Mlawer. LC 94-37254. (Illus.). 32p. (SPA.). (J). (ps-2). 1995. 12.95 (0-06-025438-6, HpArco Iris) HarpC Child Bks.

Si le Grain Ne Meurt. Andre Gide. (FRE.). 1976. pap. 11.95 (0-8288-3687-6, F102381) Fr & Eur.

Si le Grain ne Meurt: Memoires. Andre Gide. (Folio Ser.: No. 875). (FRE.). 1966. pap. 10.50 (2-07-036875-0) Schoenhof.

SI Metric System of Units & SEG Tentative Metric Standard. 158p. 1981. pap. 15.00 (0-931830-21-4, 492) Soc Expl Geophys.

Si, No, Pequeno Hipopotamo. Jane B. Moncure. (Castillo Magico Ser.). (Illus.). 32p. (SPA.). (J). (ps-2). 1989. lib. bdg. 21.36 (0-89565-933-6) Childs World.

***Si Si Knows You Need to Feel Safe! A Guide for Parents - Caregiver - Professionals.** Nancy Parks. Ed. by Ann Corfman & Ken Davis. (Illus.). 8p. (Orig.). 1996. wbk. ed., pap. 1.50 (1-888282-02-9) Little Otter.

***Si Si Knows You Need to Feel Safe: A Guide for Young People.** Nancy Parks. Ed. by Ann Corfman & Ken Davis. (Illus.). 19p. (Orig.). (J). (gr. 2-4). 1996. student ed., pap. 3.25 (1-888282-01-0) Little Otter.

Si Silicon. 8th ed. (Gmelin Handbook of Inorganic & Organometallic Chemistry Ser.: Vol. B). 386p. 1994. 1,725.00 (0-387-93693-9) Spr-Verlag.

Si-Silicon: History. 1984. 460.00 (0-387-93508-8) Spr-Verlag.

Si Silicon Vol. B 5d2: Silicon Nitride: Chemical Reactions. R. C. Sangster. Ed. by F. Schroder. xiii, 303p. 1995. 1,346.00 (3-540-93716-1) Spr-Verlag.

Si-SiO2 System. Ed. by P. Balk. (Materials Science Monographs: No. 32). 366p. 1988. 175.00 (0-444-42603-5) Elsevier.

***Si Solo le Hubiera Decho.** A. Campolo. (SPA.). 1.50 (0-8297-0327-6) Life Pubs Intl.

Si Su Hijo Tartamudea: Una Guia para los Padres. (Publications on Stuttering: No. 15). 48p. (SPA.). pap. 1.00 (0-933388-12-8) Stuttering Fnd Am.

Si Te Quieres por el Pico Divertir: Historia del Pregon Musical Latinoamericano. Cristobal D. Ayala. LC 88-92157. (Illus.). 371p. (Orig.). (SPA.). 1988. pap. 25.00 (0-89729-525-0) Ediciones.

SI-Ten Asme Steam Charts, SI Metric & U. S. Customary Units. J. H. Potter. 128p. 1976. pap. text ed. 25.00 (0-685-62575-3, E00090) ASME.

Si Tu Quieres Predicar. Don DeWelt. Tr. by Victor S. Fernandois. 176p. 1988. pap. 4.99 (0-89900-322-2) College Pr Pub.

SI Unit Conversion Guide. Michael Laposata. (Illus.). 110p. (Orig.). 1992. spiral bd. 14.95 (0-910133-38-7) Mass Med Pub Div.

***SI Units for Clinical Measurement.** Ed. by Donald S. Young & Edward J. Huth. LC 96-30174. (Medical Writing & Communication Ser.). 100p. (Orig.). (C). 1997. pap. text ed. 25.00 (0-943126-51-7) Amer Coll Phys.

SI Units for the HVAC - R Professional. Wilbert F. Stoecker. LC 92-18208. 80p. 1992. 10.95 (0-912524-73-1) Busn News.

SI Units in Radiation Protection & Measurements. LC 85-3052. (Report Ser.: No. 82). 68p. (Orig.). 1985. pap. text ed. 25.00 (0-913392-74-X) NCRP Pubns.

Si Youssef. Anouar Majid. 160p. 1993. 19.95 (1-7043-7032-8, Pub. by Quartet UK) Interlink Pub.

Si-Yu-Ki: Buddhist Records of the Western World. Samuel Beal. (C). 1994. text ed. 38.00 (81-208-1107-0, Pub. by Motilal Banarsidass II) S Asia.

SIA, Japanese Electronics Giants, & Global Competition in Semiconductors. Michael Ryan et al. (Pew Case Studies in International Affairs). 50p. (C). 1995. pap. text ed. 3.50 (1-56927-707-9, GU Schl Foreign) Geo U Inst Dplmcy.

Siah Armajani - Hannes Brunner: Common Houses. Carin Kuoni & Marjorie Welish. LC 93-87754. (Illus.). 32p. (Orig.). 1994. write for info. (1-884692-00-1) Swiss Inst.

Sialadenosis & Sialadenitis. Ed. by R. Chilla. (Advances in Oto-Rhino-Laryngology Ser.: Vol. 26). (Illus.). viii, 252p. 1981. 126.50 (3-8055-1669-X) S Karger.

Sialic Acids: Chemistry, Metabolism, & Function. Ed. by R. Schauer. (Cell Biology Monographs: Vol. 10). (Illus.). 344p. 1983. 144.95 (0-387-81707-7) Spr-Verlag.

Siam: The Crossroads. Josiah Crosby. LC 72-179186. reprint ed. 32.50 (0-404-54817-2) AMS Pr.

Siam: The Land of the White Elephant, As It Was & Is. George B. Bacon. LC 77-87064. reprint ed. 35.00 (0-404-16792-6) AMS Pr.

Siam Becomes Thailand. Judith A. Stowe. LC 90-23778. 400p. (C). 1991. text ed. 42.00 (0-8248-1393-6); pap. text ed. 18.95 (0-8248-1394-4) UH Pr.

Siam in Transition: A Brief Survey of Cultural Trends in the Five Years Since the Revolution of 1932. Kenneth P. Landon. LC 68-57615. (Illus.). 328p. 1969. reprint ed. text ed. 38.50 (0-8371-0521-8, LASI, Greenwood Pr) Greenwood.

Siam Mapped: A History of the Geo-Body of a Nation. Winichakul Thongchai. LC 93-34494. (Illus.). 280p. 1994. text ed. 34.00 (0-8248-1337-5) UH Pr.

***Siam Mapped: A History of the Geo-Body of a Nation.** Thongchai Winichakul. (Illus.). 280p. 1997. reprint ed. pap. text ed. 18.95 (0-8248-1974-8) UH Pr.

Siam Then: The Foreign Colony in Bangkok Before & After Anna. William L. Bradley. LC 81-12196. (Illus.). 207p. (Orig.). 1981. pap. 9.95 (0-87808-185-2) William Carey Lib.

Siamang in Malaya: A Field Study of a Primate in Tropical Rain Forest. D. J. Chivers et al. Ed. by H. Hofer & A. H. Schultz. (Contributions to Primatology Ser.: Vol. 4). (Illus.). 250p. 1974. 137.75 (3-8055-1668-1) S Karger.

Siamese Cat. Stuart A. Kallen. LC 95-7579. (Cats Ser.). (J). (gr. k-3). 1995. lib. bdg. 13.98 (1-56239-444-4) Abdo & Dghtrs.

Siamese Cats. Marjorie Collier. (Complete Pet Owner's Manuals Ser.). (Illus.). 64p. 1992. pap. 6.95 (0-8120-4764-8) Barron.

Siamese Cats. Ron Reagan. (Illus.). 96p. 1988. 12.95 (0-87666-860-0, KW-062) TFH Pubns.

An Asterisk (*) at the beginning of an entry indicates that the title is appearing in BIP for the first time.

S

Siamese Cats. Dimare Spiotta. (Illus.). 80p. 1985. pap. 6.95 (*0-86622-430-0*, PB-135) TFH Pubns.

Siamese-English Dictionary. Edward B. Michell. (ENG & THA.). 1977. reprint ed. 43.95 (*0-518-19004-8*) Ayer.

***Siamese Fighting Fish.** Gene A. Lucas. (Illus.). 64p. 1997. 12.95 (*0-7938-0120-6*, WW-017) TFH Pubns.

Siamese Fighting Fish. Gene Wolfsheimer. 64p. 1996. pap. 6.95 (*0-7938-0352-7*, RE603) TFH Pubns.

Siamese Mauser. Francis C. Allan & Roger L. Wakelam. Ed. by Joseph P. Koss, Jr. (Illus.). 50p. 1987. pap. 7.95 (*0-9614814-2-0*) AK Enterprises.

Siamese State Ceremonies: With Supplementary Notes. H. Quaritch Wales. (Illus.). 340p. (C). 1992. text ed. 49.00 (*0-7007-0269-5*, Pub. by Curzon Press UK) UH Pr.

Siamese Turtle Mystery. Bob Wright. Tr. by Phyllis Bourne & Eugenia Tusquets. (Tom & Ricky Spanish-English Readers Ser.). (Illus.). 96p. (ENG & SPA.). (J). (gr. 1-5). 1988. pap. 4.95 (*0-87879-658-4*) High Noon Bks.

Siamese Twin Mystery. Ellery Queen. LC 93-8120. 1993. pap. 6.95 (*1-883402-11-5*) S&S Trade.

***Siamese Twins.** Solberg. 1996. 15.95 (*0-8050-5051-5*) H Holt & Co.

Sian Incident: A Pivotal Point in Modern Chinese History. Tien-wei Wu. (Michigan Monographs in Chinese Studies: No. 26). 1976. pap. text ed. 20.00 (*0-89264-026-X*) Ctr Chinese Studies.

Siaya: The Historical Anthropology of an African Landscape. David W. Cohen & E. S. Odhiambo. LC 88-15182. 192p. (Orig.). 1988. pap. 14.95 (*0-8214-0902-6*) Ohio U Pr.

Sibawaihi the Phonologist. A. A. Al-Nassir. (Library of Arabic Linguistics). 240p. 1992. 115.00 (*0-7103-0356-4*, A3926) Routledge Chapman & Hall.

Sibawaihi's Buch Uber die Grammatik, 4 pts.in 2, Set. Sibawaihi. xxvii, 2168p. 1969. reprint ed. write for info. (*0-318-71566-X*) G Olms Pubs.

SIBD, 92-93: The Business Directory for the Soviet Region, Vol. 2. FYI Information Resources Staff & IIA Sistema-Reserve Staff. 1200p. (Orig.). 1992. pap. write for info. (*0-9632263-0-4*) FYI Info Res.

Sibelius. (Dent Master Musicians Ser.). (Illus.). (C). pap. write for info. (*0-19-816482-3*) OUP.

Sibelius. David Burnett-James. (Illustrated Lives of the Great Composers Ser.). (Illus.). 128p. 1989. pap. 14.95 (*0-7119-1683-7*, OP45004) Omnibus NY.

Sibelius. Robert Layton. (Master Musicians Ser.). (Illus.). 247p. 1993. 30.00 (*0-02-871322-2*) Schirmer Bks.

Sibelius: A Symposium. G. Abraham. 1972. 250.00 (*0-8490-1051-9*) Gordon Pr.

Sibelius: The Symphonies. Cecil Gray. LC 78-114879. (Select Bibliographies Reprint Ser.). 1977. 13.95 (*0-8369-5283-9*) Ayer.

Sibelius: The Symphonies. Cecil Gray. (Music Book Index Ser.). 77p. 1992. reprint ed. lib. bdg. 59.00 (*0-7812-9480-0*) Rprt Serv.

***Sibelius: 20th Century Composers.** Guy Richards. 1997. pap. text ed. 19.95 (*0-7148-3581-1*, Pub. by Phaidon Press UK) Chronicle Bks.

Sibelius Companion. Ed. by Glenda D. Goss. LC 96-5833. 456p. 1996. text ed. 85.00 (*0-313-28393-1*, Greenwood Pr) Greenwood.

Sibelius, Symphony No. 5. Ed. by James A. Hepokoski. LC 92-21614. (Cambridge Music Handbooks Ser.). (Illus.). 128p. (C). 1993. text ed. 34.95 (*0-521-40143-7*); pap. text ed. 11.95 (*0-521-40958-6*) Cambridge U Pr.

***Siberia.** Date not set. write for info. (*0-688-09121-0*) Morrow.

Siberia. David N. Collins. (World Bibliographical Ser.). 1991. lib. bdg. 75.00 (*1-85109-157-2*) ABC-CLIO.

Siberia: Problems & Prospects for Regional Development. Ed. by Alan Wood. 240p. 1987. lib. bdg. 49.95 (*0-7099-3655-9*, Pub. by Croom Helm UK) Routledge Chapman & Hall.

***Siberia: Worlds Apart.** Victor L. Mote. (Post-Soviet Republics Ser.). 1997. 49.95 (*0-8133-1298-1*); pap. text ed. 17.95 (*0-8133-1837-8*) Westview.

Siberia & Other Plays. Felix Mitterer. (Studies in Austrian Literature, Culture, & Thought). 1994. pap. 33.50 (*0-929497-68-6*) Ariadne CA.

Siberia & the Soviet Far East: Strategic Dimensions in Multinational Perspective. Ed. by Roger Swearingen. 298p. (C). 1987. text ed. 16.95 (*0-8179-8361-9*) Hoover Inst Pr.

Siberia on Fire: Stories & Essays by Valentin Rasputin. Valentin Rasputin. Tr. by Gerald Mikkelson & Margaret Winchell from RUS. 252p. 1989. 30.00 (*0-87580-152-8*); pap. 14.00 (*0-87580-547-7*) N Ill U Pr.

Siberia, Outer Mongolia, Central Asia: Crosslands of Civilization. Christine De Weck. 1992. 17.95 (*0-533-10229-4*) Vantage.

Siberia, Siberia. Valentin Rasputin. Tr. by Margaret Winchell & Gerald Mikkelson. 380p. 1996. 40.00 (*0-8101-1287-6*) Northwestern U Pr.

Siberian & Other Folk-Tales: Primitive Literature from the Empire of the Tsars. Charles F. Coxwell. LC 78-67702. (Folktale Ser.). 1056p. reprint ed. 87.50 (*0-404-16076-X*) AMS Pr.

Siberian Bam Railway Guide. Athol Yates. 1996. pap. text ed. 21.95 (*1-873756-06-2*, Pub. by Trlblazer Pubn UK) Seven Hills Bk.

Siberian Development & East Asia: Threat or Promise? Allen S. Whiting. LC 81-50057. 296p. 1981. 42.50 (*0-8047-1109-7*) Stanford U Pr.

Siberian Forest Adventure. E. Boronina. Ed. by G. A. Birkett. LC 66-25018. (RUS.). (C). 1966. pap. text ed. 2.75 (*0-89197-485-7*) Irvington.

Siberian Ginseng. Betty Kamen. (Good Health Guide Ser.). 32p. (Orig.). 1988. pap. 3.95 (*0-87983-485-4*) Keats.

Siberian Huskies. Kerry Kern. (Complete Pet Owner's Manuals Ser.). 80p. 1990. pap. 6.95 (*0-8120-4265-4*) Barron.

***Siberian Huskies: AKC Rank #17.** Beverly Pisano. (Illus.). 224p. 1997. 9.95 (*0-7938-2327-7*, KW-068S) TFH Pubns.

Siberian Husky. Joan M. Brearley. (TS Ser.). (Illus.). 512p. 1992. text ed. 59.95 (*0-86622-631-1*, TS148) TFH Pubns.

Siberian Husky. Betsy S. Siino. (Owner's Guides to a Happy Healthy Pet Ser.). (Illus.). 160p. 1996. 12.95 (*0-87605-395-9*) Howell Bk.

Siberian Husky Champions, 1952-1980. Jan L. Pata. (Illus.). 151p. 1982. pap. 36.95 (*0-940808-11-0*) Camino E E & Bk.

Siberian Husky Champions, 1981-1986. Camino E. E. & Bk. Co. Staff. (Illus.). 114p. 1988. pap. 28.95 (*0-940808-66-8*) Camino E E & Bk.

Siberian Iris. Currier McEwen. LC 95-14643. (Illus.). 242p. 1996. 39.95 (*0-88192-329-X*) Timber.

Siberian Journey: The Journal of Hans Fries, 1774-1776. Ed. by Walter Kirchner. (Illus.). 183p. 1974. 32.50 (*0-7146-2964-2*, Pub. by F Cass Pubs UK) Intl Spec Bk.

***Siberian Light.** Robin White. 384p. 1997. 23.95 (*0-385-31688-7*) Doubleday.

***Siberian Tiger.** Jason Cooper. LC 96-52095. (Giants among Us Ser.). (J). 1997. write for info. (*1-55916-186-8*) Rourke Bk Co.

Siberian Tiger Sponsorship Kit. Merryl Lambert. 1995. 19.95 (*0-9641742-7-8*) Pequot Pubng.

Siberian Yupik Eskimo: The Language & Its Contacts with Chukchi. Willem J. De Reuse. 424p. (C). 1994. 50.00 (*0-87480-397-7*) U of Utah Pr.

Sibirskaia Sovetskaia Entsiklopediia Vol. IV, Vol. IV. Ed. by B. Shumiatskii et al. LC 92-60511. (Illus.). xviii, 566p. (RUS.). 1992. lib. bdg. 195.00 (*0-88354-358-3*) N Ross.

Sibley Music Library Catalog of Sound Recordings. 1977. 1,630.00 (*0-8161-0063-2*, Hall Library) G K Hall.

***Sibley's Harvard Graduates, Vol. 1.** John L. Sibley. xx, 618p. 1996. 50.00 (*0-934909-72-5*) Mass Hist Soc.

***Sibley's Harvard Graduates, Vol. 2.** John L. Sibley. viii, 557p. 1996. 50.00 (*0-934909-73-3*) Mass Hist Soc.

***Sibley's Harvard Graduates, Vol. 3.** John L. Sibley. viii, 457p. 1996. 50.00 (*0-934909-74-1*) Mass Hist Soc.

Sibling Abuse: Hidden Physical & Sexual Abuse. Vernon R. Wiehe. 186p. 32.95 (*0-669-24362-0*, Lexington) Jossey-Bass.

***Sibling Abuse: Hidden Physical, Emotional & Sexual Trauma.** 2nd ed. Vernon R. Wiehe. LC 97-4600. 224p. 1997. 48.00 (*0-7619-1008-5*); pap. 21.95 (*0-7619-1009-3*) Sage.

***Sibling Bond: 15th Anniversary Edition: The First Major Account of the Powerful Emotional Connections Among Brothers & Sisters Throughout Life.** rev. ed. Stephen P. Bank & Michael D. Kahn. LC 97-9634. 384p. 1997. 35.00 (*0-465-07817-6*) Basic.

Sibling Connection: Seeds of Life & Death. Roy Fanti. 279p. 1995. 21.95 (*0-9648883-3-5*) R Fanti.

Sibling Groups & Social Work. Peter Wedge & Greg Mantle. 107p. 1991. text ed. 55.95 (*1-85628-195-7*, Pub. by Avebury Pub UK) Ashgate Pub Co.

Sibling Interaction Across Cultures. Ed. by P. G. Zukow. 230p. 1988. 71.95 (*0-387-96784-2*) Spr-Verlag.

Sibling Loss. Joanna H. Fanos. 192p. 1996. pap. 18.50 (*0-8058-1778-6*); text ed. 39.95 (*0-8058-1777-8*) L Erlbaum Assocs.

Sibling Love & Incest in Jane Austen's Fiction. Glenda A. Hudson. 1992. text ed. 49.95 (*0-312-06796-8*) St Martin.

Sibling Relationships: Their Causes & Consequences. Judy Dunn et al. Ed. by Gene H. Brody. (Advances in Applied Developmental Psychology Ser.: Vol. 10). (Illus.). 263p. 1996. pap. 39.50 (*1-56750-181-8*); text ed. 73.25 (*1-56750-180-X*) Ablex Pub.

Sibling Relationships: Their Nature & Significance Across the Lifespan. Ed. by Michael E. Lamb & Brian Sutton-Smith. 416p. 1982. 79.95 (*0-89859-189-9*) L Erlbaum Assocs.

Sibling Relationships Across the Life Span. Victor G. Cicirelli. 250p. 1995. 39.50 (*0-306-45025-9*) Plenum.

Sibling Rivalry. Seymour V. Reit. 224p. 1988. mass mkt. 5.99 (*0-345-35553-9*) Ballantine.

Sibling Rivalry: Brothers & Sisters at Odds. Elaine Landau. (Illus.). 48p. (J). (gr. 4-6). 1994. lib. bdg. 14.90 (*1-56294-328-6*) Millbrook Pr.

Sibling Rivalry in God's Family. Elmer Morgan. 147p. (Orig.). 1993. pap. 5.95 (*1-56794-033-1*, C2292) Star Bible.

Sibling Scrapbook: An Activity Book for the New Big Brother & Big Sister. Betsy Monroe. (Medical Ser.: No. 5). (Illus.). 24p. (Orig.). (J). (gr. k-4). 1989. pap. write for info. (*1-878083-00-7*) Color Me Well.

Sibling Society. Robert Bly. 272p. 1996. 25.00 (*0-201-40646-2*) Addison-Wesley.

***Sibling Society.** Robert Bly. LC 96-36867. 1997. pap. 13.00 (*0-679-78128-5*, Vin) Random.

Sibling Society. limited ed. Robert Bly. 288p. 1996. 100.00 (*0-201-46133-1*) Addison-Wesley.

Sibling Species of Titmice in the Parus Inorntus Complex: Aves: Paridae. Carla Cicero. LC 95-46527. (Publications in Zoology: Vol. 128). (Illus.). 232p. (C). 1996. pap. 27.00 (*0-520-09808-0*) U CA Pr.

Siblinghood of Humanity: An Introduction to Philosophy. 2nd ed. Joseph Agassi. LC 91-16766. 1991. pap. 20.00 (*0-88206-511-4*) Caravan Bks.

Siblings: Love, Envy, & Understanding. Judy Dunn & Carol Kendrick. LC 81-7251. (Developing Child Ser.). (Illus.). 304p. 1982. 32.00 (*0-674-80735-9*) HUP.

Siblings: Rabbinic Judaism & Early Christianity. Hayim Perelmuter. 1989. pap. 11.95 (*0-8091-3104-8*) Paulist Pr.

Siblings & the Children's Story. Klaus Mann. Tr. by Tanya Alexander & Peter Eyre from GER. 160p. 1991. 19.95 (*0-7145-2939-7*) M Boyars Pubs.

Siblings in South Asia: Brothers & Sisters in Cultural Context. Ed. by Charles W. Nuckolls. LC 92-30076. (Culture & Human Development Ser.). 200p. 1993. lib. bdg. 26.00 (*0-89862-146-1*) Guilford Pr.

***Siblings in the Unconscious & Psychopathology: Womb Fantasies, Claustrophobias, Fear of Pregnancy, Murderous Rage, Animal Symbolism, Christmas & Easter Neuroses, & Twinnings or Identifications with Sisters & Brothers.** Vamik D. Volkan & Gabriele Ast. LC 96-30832. 1997. 27.50 (*0-8236-6067-2*) Intl Univs Pr.

Siblings in Therapy: Life Span & Clinical Issues. Ed. by Michael D. Kahn & Karen G. Lewis. (Professional Bks.). (Illus.). 1988. 34.95 (*0-393-70058-5*) Norton.

Siblings of Children with Autism: A Guide for Families. Sandra L. Harris. Ed. by Michael D. Powers. LC 94-18177. (Topics in Autism Ser.). 132p. (Orig.). 1994. pap. 12.95 (*0-933149-71-9*) Woodbine House.

Siblings of the Mentally Ill. Wendy Carlisle. 160p. (Orig.). (C). 1984. pap. 12.95 (*0-88247-705-6*) R & E Pubs.

***Siblings Should Never Be in the Same Family.** Charles M. Schulz. (Peanuts Program Ser.). (Illus.). 144p. (J). 10.95 (*0-06-757449-1*) HarpC.

Siblings Without Rivalry: How to Help Your Children Live Together So You Can Live Too. Adele Faber & Elaine Mazlish. 1988. pap. 12.00 (*0-380-70527-3*) Avon.

Siblingship in Oceania: Studies in the Meaning of Kin Relations. Ed. by Mac Marshall. LC 83-14516. (ASAO Monographs: No. 8). (Illus.). 434p. (C). 1983. reprint ed. pap. text ed. 31.00 (*0-8191-3430-9*) U Pr of Amer.

Sibs. F. Paul Wilson. 384p. 1995. 5.99 (*0-8125-3124-8*) Tor Bks.

Sibshops: Implementing Workshops for Brothers & Sisters of Children with Special Health & Developmental Needs. Donald J. Meyer & Patricia F. Vadasy. LC 94-8827. (Illus.). 256p. 1994. pap. 32.00 (*1-55766-169-3*) P H Brookes.

Sibton Abbey Cartularies & Charters Pt. III. Ed. by Philippa Brown. (Suffolk Records Society-Suffolk Charters Ser.: No. 9). 1987. 39.00 (*0-85115-474-3*) Boydell & Brewer.

Sibton Abbey Cartularies & Charters Pt. IV. Ed. by Philippa Brown. (Suffolk Records Society-Suffolk Charters Ser.: No. 10). 180p. 1988. 39.00 (*0-85115-499-9*) Boydell & Brewer.

Sibton Abbey Cartularies & Charters Pt. II: II. Ed. by Philippa Brown. (Suffolk Charters Ser.: No. VIII). 330p. 1987. 39.00 (*0-85115-443-3*) Boydell & Brewer.

Sibton Abbey Estates: Selected Documents, 1325-1509. Ed. by A. H. Denney. (Suffolk Records Society Ser.: No. II). 166p. 1970. 20.00 (*0-900716-12-6*) Boydell & Brewer.

Sibyl. Par Lagerkvist. Tr. by Naomi Walford. 1963. pap. 9.00 (*0-394-70240-9*, Vin) Random.

Sibyl see Angelos Sikelianos & the Delphic Idea

Sibyll Seebill & Sybil. Agoston Zarand. LC 90-55252. 439p. (Orig.). 1991. pap. 15.00 (*1-56002-061-X*) Aegina Pr.

Sibylline Books. Cyril Toker. LC 89-90986. 352p. (Orig.). 1989. pap. 13.95 (*0-9622200-0-0*) Cumaean Pr.

Sibylline Guide to Craps. Alfred Di Mauro. (Sibylline Game Library). (Illus.). 110p. (Orig.). 1993. pap. 9.95 (*0-9631961-1-1*) Sibylline Bks.

Sibylline Guide to Single Deck Blackjack. Ken Schmidt. (Sibylline Game Library). (Illus.). (Orig.). 1993. pap. write for info. (*0-9631961-2-X*) Sibylline Bks.

Sibylline Leaves. Samuel Taylor Coleridge. LC 90-31895. 328p. 1990. reprint ed. 55.00 (*1-85477-042-X*, Pub. by Woodstock Bks UK) Cassell.

Sibylline Oracles. Ed. by Robert Navon. Tr. by Milton Terry. (Great Works of Philosophy Ser.: Vol. 7). 267p. 1995. reprint ed. pap. 22.50 (*0-933601-08-5*) Selene Bks.

Sibylline Oracles. Tr. by Milton S. Terry from GRE. LC 72-176141. reprint ed. 32.50 (*0-404-06362-4*) AMS Pr.

Sibyls & Sibylline Prophecy in Classical Antiquity. H. W. Parke. Ed. by Brian C. McGing. 256p. 1988. lib. bdg. 42.50 (*0-415-00343-1*) Routledge.

Sibyls & Sibylline Prophecy in Classical Antiquity. H. W. Parke. LC 91-43625. 256p. (C). 1992. pap. 18.95 (*0-415-07638-2*, Pub. by Tavistock UK) Routledge Chapman & Hall.

Sibyl's Dreams. deluxe ed. Mary Helen. 1980. 14.95 (*0-912492-18-X*) Pyquag.

Sibyl's Legend of Mammy Jane. Sibyl J. Pischke. 1981. 14.95 (*0-9608532-0-0*) S J Pischke.

***Sibyls, Seers & Sages in Hellenistic-Roman Judaism.** John J. Collins. 248p. 1997. text ed. 93.75 (*90-04-10752-5*) E J Brill.

Sibyl's Stories. Carolyn Van Langenberg. 141p. (C). 1990. 45.00 (*0-947087-03-6*, Pub. by Pascoe Pub AT) St Mut.

SIC: Sean Landers. Sean Landers. LC 95-1046. (Illus.). 464p. (Orig.). 1995. pap. 15.00 (*1-57322-507-X*, Riverhd Trade) Berkley Pub.

(Sic) Humor. Ed. by Diane S. Heath. (Illus.). 212p. (Orig.). (C). 1995. pap. 30.00 (*0-935229-23-X*) Am Assoc Med.

SiC, Natural & Synthetic Diamond & Related Materials: Proceedings of Symposium C on Properties & Application of SiC, Natural & Synthetic Diamond & Related Materials of the 1990 E-MRS Fall Conference, Strasbourg, France, 27-30 November 1990. J. P. Sellschop. (European Materials Research Society Symposia Proceedings Ser.: Vol. 20). xii, 380p. 1992. 236.25 (*0-444-89416-0*) Elsevier.

Sicarii. William Moore. LC 89-63164. 192p. (Orig.). 1990. pap. 8.95 (*0-945563-01-9*) Penumbra Pub.

Sicconis Polentoni Scriptorum Illustrium Latinaelinguae Libri XVIII. Sicco Polenton. Ed. by Berthold L. Ullman. LC 29-7429. (American Academy in Rome. Papers & Monographs: Vol. 6). 540p. 1928. reprint ed. pap. 170.20 (*0-685-15597-8*, 2026721) Bks Demand.

SICE Nineteen Ninety-Four Proceedings of the 33rd SICE Annual Conference. Industrial Electronics Society & Tokyo Section Staff. Ed. by Institute of Electrical & Electronics Engineers, Inc. Staff. 275p. 1994. pap. write for info. (*0-7803-2024-7*, 94TH0683-3); fiche write for info. (*0-7803-2025-5*) Inst Electrical.

***Sichem: Eine Archaologische und Religionseschichtliche Studie Mit Besanderer Berucksichtigung Von Jos 24.** Karl Jaros. (Orbis Biblicus et Orientalis Ser.: Vol. 11). 1976. 55.50 (*3-7278-0153-0*) Eisenbrauns.

Sicherheitsadressbuch Deutschland, Osterreich, Schweiz 1996/97. 400p. 1996. 125.00 (*3-598-23076-1*) K G Saur.

***Sicherung von Altlasten.** H. L. Jessberger. 272p. 1993. 70.00 (*90-5410-312-4*, Pub. by A A Balkema NE) Ashgate Pub Co.

***Sicherung von Altlasten.** H. L. Jessberger. 268p. 1994. 70.00 (*90-5410-385-X*, Pub. by A A Balkema NE) Ashgate Pub Co.

***Sicherungs-, Stutz- und Gebirgsverbesserungmassnahmen Im Untertagebau-** 177p. 1988. pap. 90.00 (*90-6191-863-4*, Pub. by A A Balkema NE) Ashgate Pub Co.

S

***Sichos in English: Exerpts of Rabbi Menachem M. Schneerson's Public Addresses.** Menachem M. Schneerson. 334p. Date not set. 10.00 (*0-8266-0560-5*) Kehot Pubn Soc.

***Sichos in English: Exerpts of Rabbi Menachem M. Schneerson's Public Addresses, Vol. 20.** Menachem M. Schneerson. 306p. 1986. 10.00 (*0-8266-0580-X*) Kehot Pubn Soc.

***Sichos in English: Exerpts of Rabbi Menachem M. Schneerson's Public Addresses, Vol. 22.** Menachem M. Schneerson. 298p. 1986. 10.00 (*0-8266-0582-6*) Kehot Pubn Soc.

***Sichos in English: Exerpts of Rabbi Menachem M. Schneerson's Public Addresses, Vol. 23.** Menachem M. Schneerson. 284p. 1987. 10.00 (*0-8266-0583-4*) Kehot Pubn Soc.

***Sichos in English: Exerpts of Rabbi Menachem M. Schneerson's Public Addresses, Vol. 24.** Menachem M. Schneerson. 318p. 1986. 10.00 (*0-8266-0584-2*) Kehot Pubn Soc.

***Sichos in English: Exerpts of Rabbi Menachem M. Schneerson's Public Addresses, Vol. 26.** Menachem M. Schneerson. 320p. 1987. 10.00 (*0-8266-0586-9*) Kehot Pubn Soc.

***Sichos in English: Exerpts of Rabbi Menachem M. Schneerson's Public Addresses, Vol. 27.** Menachem M. Schneerson. 360p. 1987. 10.00 (*0-8266-0587-7*) Kehot Pubn Soc.

***Sichos in English: Exerpts of Rabbi Menachem M. Schneerson's Public Addresses, Vol. 28.** Menachem M. Schneerson. 320p. 1988. 10.00 (*0-8266-0588-5*) Kehot Pubn Soc.

***Sichos in English: Exerpts of Rabbi Menachem M. Schneerson's Public Addresses, Vol. 29.** Menachem M. Schneerson. 318p. 1988. 10.00 (*0-8266-0589-3*) Kehot Pubn Soc.

***Sichos in English: Exerpts of Rabbi Menachem M. Schneerson's Public Addresses, Vol. 30.** Menachem M. Schneerson. 304p. 1988. 10.00 (*0-8266-0590-7*) Kehot Pubn Soc.

***Sichos in English: Exerpts of Rabbi Menachem M. Schneerson's Public Addresses, Vol. 31.** Menachem M. Schneerson. 288p. 1988. 10.00 (*0-8266-0591-5*) Kehot Pubn Soc.

***Sichos in English: Exerpts of Rabbi Menachem M. Schneerson's Public Addresses, Vol. 32.** Menachem M. Schneerson. 232p. 1989. 10.00 (*0-8266-0592-3*) Kehot Pubn Soc.

***Sichos in English: Exerpts of Rabbi Menachem M. Schneerson's Public Addresses, Vol. 33.** Menachem M. Schneerson. 320p. 1989. 10.00 (*0-8266-0593-1*) Kehot Pubn Soc.

***Sichos in English: Exerpts of Rabbi Menachem M. Schneerson's Public Addresses, Vol. 34.** Menachem M. Schneerson. 276p. 1990. 10.00 (*0-8266-0594-X*) Kehot Pubn Soc.

***Sichos in English: Exerpts of Rabbi Menachem M. Schneerson's Public Addresses, Vol. 35.** Menachem M. Schneerson. 320p. 1990. 10.00 (*0-8266-0595-8*) Kehot Pubn Soc.

***Sichos in English: Exerpts of Rabbi Menachem M. Schneerson's Public Addresses, Vol. 36.** Menachem M. Schneerson. 276p. 1991. 10.00 (*0-614-20958-7*) Kehot Pubn Soc.

***Sichos in English: Exerpts of Rabbi Menachem M. Schneerson's Public Addresses, Vol. 41.** Menachem M. Schneerson. 320p. 1992. 10.00 (*0-8266-0601-6*) Kehot Pubn Soc.

***Sichos in English: Exerpts of Rabbi Menachem M. Schneerson's Public Addresses, Vol. 42.** Menachem M. Schneerson. 328p. 1993. 10.00 (*0-8266-0602-4*) Kehot Pubn Soc.

***Sichos in English: Exerpts of Rabbi Menachem M. Schneerson's Public Addresses, Vol. 43.** Menachem M. Schneerson. 352p. 1991. 10.00 (*0-614-20957-9*) Kehot Pubn Soc.

***Sichos in English: Exerpts of Rabbi Menachem M. Schneerson's Public Addresses, Vol. 44.** Menachem M. Schneerson. 318p. 1991. 10.00 (*0-8266-0604-0*) Kehot Pubn Soc.

***Sichos in English: Exerpts of Rabbi M Schneerson's Public Addresses, Vol. 45.** M Schneerson. 300p. 1991. 10.00 (*0-8266-0*

***Sichos in English: Exerpts of Rabbi Schneerson's Public Addresse Schneerson. 246p. 1991. 10 Pubn Soc.

An Asterisk (*) at the beginning of an entry indicates that the title is appearing in BIP for the first time.

***Sichos in English: Exerpts of Rabbi Menachem M. Schneerson's Public Addresses, Vol. 47.** Menachem M. Schneerson. 246p. 1991. 10.00 (*0-8266-0607-5*) Kehot Pubn Soc.

***Sichos in English: Exerpts of Rabbi Menachem M. Schneerson's Public Addresses, Vol. 48.** Menachem M. Schneerson. 260p. 1992. 10.00 (*0-8266-0608-3*) Kehot Pubn Soc.

***Sichos in English Vol. 17: Exerpts of Rabbi Menachem M. Schneerson's Public Addresses, 51 vols.** Menachem M. Schneerson. 314p. 1989. 10.00 (*0-8266-0577-X*) Kehot Pubn Soc.

***Sichos in English Vol. 49: Exerpts of Rabbi Menachem M. Schneerson's Public Addresses, 51 vols.** Menachem M. Schneerson. 280p. 1992. 10.00 (*0-8266-0609-1*) Kehot Pubn Soc.

***Sichos in English Vol. 50: Exerpts of Rabbi Menachem M. Schneerson's Public Addresses, 51 vols.** Menachem M. Schneerson. 288p. 1992. 10.00 (*0-8266-0610-5*) Kehot Pubn Soc.

***Sichos in English Vol. 51: Exerpts of Rabbi Menachem M. Schneerson's Public Addresses, 51 vols.** Menachem M. Schneerson. 1992. 10.00 (*0-8266-0611-3*) Kehot Pubn Soc.

Sichtwechsel: Developing Language Sensitivity. Martin Hog et al. (Illus.). 104p. (C). 1989. pap. text ed. 15.95 (*0-521-31190-X*) Cambridge U Pr.

Sichtwechsel: Developing Language Sensitivity. Martin Hog et al. (Illus.). (C). 1989. digital audio 27.95 (*0-521-33140-4*) Cambridge U Pr.

Sichtwechsel NEU: Allgemeine Einfuehrung 1, 2, 3. Gerd Wessling et al. 48p. (Orig.). (GER.). (C). 1995. pap. text ed. 9.75 (*3-12-675022-2*, Pub. by Klett Edition GW) Intl Bk Import.

Sichtwechsel NEU Level 1: Text- und Arbeitsbuch. Gerd Wessling et al. 176p. (Orig.). (GER.). (C). 1995. pap. text ed. 27.00 (*3-12-675020-6*, Pub. by Klett Edition GW); audio 34.25 (*3-12-675023-0*, Pub. by Klett Edition GW) Intl Bk Import.

Sichtwechsel NEU Level 1: Unterrichtsbegleiter. 48p. (GER.). (C). 1995. pap. text ed. 9.75 (*3-12-675015-X*, Pub. by Klett Edition GW) Intl Bk Import.

Sichuan: Four Rivers. May Holdsworth. (Illus.). 248p. 1994. pap. 15.95 (*0-8442-9793-3*, Passport Bks) NTC Pub Grp.

Sichuan Panda Forests. Terri Willis. LC 94-41786. (Wonders of the World Ser.). (J). 1995. lib. bdg. 25.68 (*0-8114-6367-2*) Raintree Steck-V.

***Sichuan Rhododendrom of China.** (CHI & LAT.). 1986. 179.00 (*0-7855-0534-2*, Pub. by Wanhai Books CH) St Mut.

***Sichuan Rhododendrom of China.** (ENG & LAT.). 1986. 198.00 (*0-7855-0535-0*, Pub. by Wanhai Books CH) St Mut.

***Sichuan, 1996.** 995.00 (*0-614-26463-4*) Info Gatekeepers.

Sicilian! Jon Edwards & Ron Henley. (ChessBase University Power Play! Ser.). (Illus.). 64p. (Orig.). 1993. pap. 10.95 (*1-883358-05-1*) R&D Pub NJ.

Sicilian. Georgette Hall. 1974. 15.95 (*0-88289-060-3*) Pelican.

Sicilian. large type ed. Mario Puzo. (Charnwood Large Print Ser.). 1986. 27.99 (*0-7089-8317-0*, Charnwood) Ulverscroft.

Sicilian: Poisoned Pawn Variation. L. M. Kovaca. 220p. 1986. 27.90 (*0-08-029755-2*, Pergamon Pr) Elsevier.

Sicilian: Sveshnikov Variation. A. Adorjan & T. Horvath. (Chess Openings Ser.). 150p. 1987. 27.90 (*0-08-029735-8*, P115, Pergamon Pr) Elsevier.

Sicilian see Misanthrope & Other Plays

***Sicilian Accelerated Dragon.** Peter Heine & Carsten Hansen. (New American Batsford Chess Library). 192p. (Orig.). 1997. pap. 22.50 (*1-879479-53-2*) ICE WA.

Sicilian Accelerated Dragon: ICON: 1.e4c52.Nf3Nc63. d4ed44.Nd4g6. John Donaldson. Ed. by Philip Peterson. (Inside Chess Opening Novelties Ser.). 156p. (Orig.). 1995. pap. 14.95 (*1-879479-24-9*) ICE WA.

Sicilian Alapin: ICON: 1.e4c52.c3. John Donaldson. Ed. by Eric Woro. (Inside Chess Opening Novelties Ser.). 104p. (Orig.). 1994. pap. 14.95 (*1-879479-22-2*) ICE WA.

Sicilian Antigruppo. Ed. by Stanley H. Barkan & Saverio A. Scammacca. (Illus.). 30p. 1976. 25.00 (*0-89304-099-1*, CCC106); boxed 30.00 (*0-89304-008-8*); 15.00 (*0-89304-096-7*) Cross-Cultrl NY.

Sicilian Campaign: The Navy, 1943. 1994. lib. bdg. 250.95 (*0-8490-5804-X*) Gordon Pr.

***Sicilian Carousel.** Lawrence Durrell. 1997. pap. text ed. 12.95 (*1-56924-783-8*) Marlowe & Co.

Sicilian Defence, Bk. 1. Svetozar Gligoric & V. Sokolov. 1972. pap. 140.00 (*0-08-017276-8*, Pergamon Pr) Elsevier.

***Sicilian Defence Closed Variation Vol. 1: (B23)** Adolf Neumann. Ed. by S. L. Edritrice. (Illus.). 176p. 1996. pap. 17.95 (*88-86127-48-0*) Thinkers Pr.

***Sicilian Defence Closed Variation Vol. 2: (B24-B25)** Adolf Neumann. Ed. by S. L. Edritrice. (Illus.). 234p. 1996. pap. 19.95 (*88-86127-49-9*) Thinkers Pr.

***Sicilian Defence Closed Variation Vol. 3: (B26)** Adolf Neumann. Ed. by S. L. Edritrice. (Illus.). 160p. 1996. pap. 17.50 (*88-86127-50-2*) Thinkers Pr.

Sicilian Defence Najdorf Poisoned Pawn: (B97) S. Edritrice. (Illus.). (Orig.). 1995. pap. 21.50 (*88-86127-44-8*) Thinkers Pr.

***Sicilian Defence 4.Qd4 (B53)** Ed. by S. L. Edritrice. (Illus.). 120p. 1996. pap. 15.95 (*88-86127-52-9*) Thinkers Pr.

***Sicilian Defence 5.f3.** Adolf Neumann. Ed. by S. L. Edritrice. (Illus.). 60p. 1996. pap. 15.50 (*88-86127-55-3*) Thinkers Pr.

Sicilian Defense: Taimanov System. Mark Taimanov. 208p. 1989. pap. 14.95 (*0-02-029863-3*) Macmillan.

Sicilian Defense in the Last Decade (1986-95) 250 Good & Bad Ideas. Nikolay Minev. Ed. by Michael J. Franett. (Illus.). (Orig.). 1995. pap. 14.95 (*1-879479-28-1*) ICE WA.

Sicilian Defense O'Kelly Variation. W. John Lutes. (Orig.). 1993. pap. 14.95 (*0-945470-26-6*) Chess Ent.

Sicilian Defense, Velimirovic Attack. Bruce Leverett. (Illus.). 70p. (Orig.). 1983. pap. 6.00 (*0-931462-23-1*) Chess Ent.

Sicilian Defense, Wing Gambits. Tomasz Kapitaniak. 71p. (Orig.). 1985. pap. 6.00 (*0-931462-41-X*) Chess Ent.

Sicilian Dragon. Laszlo Sapi. 1989. pap. 14.95 (*0-02-029803-X*) Macmillan.

Sicilian Dragon: Classical & Levenfish Variations. Laszlo Sapi & Attila Schneider. 240p. 1990. pap. 14.95 (*0-02-029804-8*) Macmillan.

Sicilian Dragon Jugoslav Attack. Eric Schiller & Jonathan Goldman. 136p. (Orig.). 1987. pap. 6.50 (*0-931462-68-1*) Chess Ent.

Sicilian Dragon, Yugoslav Attack II. Eric Schiller. 125p. (Orig.). 1989. pap. 7.95 (*0-931462-88-6*) Chess Ent.

Sicilian-English, English-Sicilian Concise Dictionary. Marco Guarneri. LC 96-42097. 210p. 1996. pap. 11.95 (*0-7818-0457-4*) Hippocrene Bks.

Sicilian Erotica. Tr. by Onat Claypole. LC 96-53354. (Pueti d'Arba Sicula/Poets of Arba Sicula Ser.: Vol. V). (Illus.). 200p. 1997. pap. 20.00 (*1-881901-10-6*) LEGAS.

Sicilian Folk Medicine. Giuseppe Pitre. (Illus.). 320p. 1971. 48.50 (*0-87291-013-X*) Coronado Pr.

Sicilian Gentleman's Cookbook. 2nd rev. ed. Don Baratta. (Illus.). 272p. (Orig.). 1992. pap. 15.95 (*1-55958-230-8*) Prima Pub.

Sicilian Hoard: A Novel. David Weimer. LC 95-74724. 330p. 1996. 19.95 (*0-9648186-5-5*); pap. 9.95 (*0-9648186-6-3*) Colossus Pr.

Sicilian in America. John Brucato. 448p. 1992. 18.95 (*0-9635292-0-X*) Green Hills.

Sicilian Labyrinth, 2 vols., Set. Lyev Polugayevsky. (Russian Chess Ser.). 370p. 1991. pap. 45.00 (*0-08-037798-X*, P115) Macmillan.

Sicilian Labyrinth, Vol. 1. Lyev Polugayevsky. (Russian Chess Ser.). 185p. 1991. pap. 25.00 (*0-08-032047-3*, Pub. by CHES UK) Macmillan.

Sicilian Labyrinth, Vol. 2. Lyev Polugayevsky. (Russian Chess Ser.). 185p. 1991. pap. 25.00 (*0-08-037796-3*) Macmillan.

Sicilian Love: The Book of the Sicilian Defence Theme Tournament, Buenos Aires 1994. Lev Polugaevsky et al. 256p. 1996. 35.00 (*0-917237-13-7*) Chess Combi.

Sicilian Mafia: The Business of Private Protection. Diego Gambetta. LC 93-9612. 345p. 1993. 42.50 (*0-674-80741-3*) HUP.

Sicilian Mafia: The Business of Private Protection. Diego Gambetta. 352p. 1996. pap. 18.95 (*0-674-80742-1*) HUP.

***Sicilian Matchmaker.** (Orig.). 1997. pap. write for info. (*0-9651561-1-7*) J Sparacino.

Sicilian Origin of the Odyssey. L. G. Pocock. Tr. by Nina Scammacca & Nat Scammacca. 206p. 1986. 36.00 (*0-89304-593-4*); pap. 15.00 (*0-89304-568-3*) Cross-Cultrl NY.

Sicilian Richter-Rauzer with...a6. Eric Schiller. 120p. (Orig.). 1987. pap. 5.00 (*0-931462-66-5*) Chess Ent.

Sicilian Romance. Ann Radcliffe. Ed. by Alison Milbank. LC 92-25480. (World's Classics Ser.). 256p. (C). 1993. 8.95 (*0-19-282212-8*) OUP.

Sicilian Romance. Ann Radcliffe. LC 75-131338. (Gothic Novels Ser.). 1972. reprint ed. 46.95 (*0-405-00809-0*) Ayer.

***Sicilian Romance 1792, 2 vols. in 1.** Ann Radcliffe. 498p. 1995. 65.00 (*1-85477-190-6*, Pub. by Woodstock Bks UK) Cassell.

***Sicilian Sun.** Andrew J. Montalbano. LC 97-91452. (Illus.). 600p. 1997. write for info. (*0-9656710-0-3*) New Writers Ink.

***Sicilian Tamanov.** Plaskett. 1997. pap. 19.95 (*1-901259-01-3*) Macmillan.

Sicilian Vegetarian Cooking: 99 More Recipes You Can't Refuse. John Penza. LC 96-8210. (Illus.). 160p. (Orig.). 1997. pap. 16.95 (*0-89815-868-0*) Ten Speed Pr.

Sicilian Vengeance. Sara Wood. (Presents Ser.: No. 470). 1992. pap. 2.89 (*0-373-11470-2*, 1-11470-1) Harlequin Bks.

Sicilian Vengeance. large type ed. Sara Wood. 1991. reprint ed. lib. bdg. 18.95 (*0-263-12600-5*) Thorndike Pr.

Sicilian Vespers: A History of the Mediterranean World in the Later Thirteenth Century. Steven Runciman. (Canto Book Ser.). (Illus.). 370p. (C). 1992. pap. text ed. 11.95 (*0-521-43774-1*) Cambridge U Pr.

Sicilian Writers. Stanley H. Barkan & Nat Scammacca. 1991. boxed 75.00 (*0-89304-917-4*); boxed 50.00 (*0-89304-916-6*) Cross-Cultrl NY.

Sicilianische Marchen, 2 vols. in 1. Laura Gonzenbach. (Volkskundliche Quellen Ser.: No. III). lvii, 632p. 1976. reprint ed. write for info. (*3-487-06032-9*) G Olms Pubs.

Sicilians Wanted the Inquisition. Calogero Messina. LC 92-43674. 1993. pap. 12.00 (*1-881901-01-7*) LEGAS.

Sicily. (Panorama Bks.). (Illus.). (FRE.). 3.95 (*0-685-11562-3*) Fr & Eur.

Sicily. Berlitz Editors. (Pocket Guides Ser.). (Illus.). 1993. pap. 7.95 (*2-8315-2315-X*) Berlitz.

Sicily. Dana Facaros & Michael Pauls. LC 93-48979. (Cadogan Country Guides Ser.). 224p. 1994. pap. 12.95 (*1-56440-176-6*) Globe Pequot.

Sicily. Roland Flint. LC 87-62888. 32p. (Orig.). 1987. pap. 5.00 (*0-933598-03-3*); 10.00 (*0-317-65523-X*) NC Wesleyan Pr.

***Sicily.** Insight Guides Staff. (Insight Guides Ser.). 1996. pap. 22.95 (*0-395-82689-6*) HM.

***Sicily.** Enzo Sellerio. 1996. 50.00 (*1-86046-055-0*) Harvill Pr UK.

Sicily: An Informal History. Peter Sammartino & William C. Roberts. LC 92-1374. (Illus.). 144p. 1993. 16.95 (*0-8453-4843-4*, Cornwall Bks) Assoc Univ Prs.

Sicily: The Insecure Base: A History of British Occupation of Sicily, 1806-1815. Desmond Gregory. LC 86-46244. (Illus.). 184p. 1988. 32.50 (*0-8386-3306-4*) Fairleigh Dickinson.

Sicily: The U. S. Army Campaigns of World War II. 1994. lib. bdg. 250.95 (*0-8490-5805-8*) Gordon Pr.

Sicily As Metaphor: Conversations Presented by Marcelle Padovani. Leonardo Sciascia. Tr. by James Marcus from ITA. LC 93-79805. 196p. 1994. 19.95 (*0-910395-98-5*) Marlboro Pr.

Sicily Enough & More. Claire Rabe. 128p. (C). 1989. reprint ed. lib. bdg. 29.00 (*0-8095-4048-7*) Borgo Pr.

***Sicily Map.** 1997. 8.95 (*2-06-700432-8*, 432) Michelin.

Sicily-Salerno-Anzio, January 1943-June 1944 see History of the United States Naval Operations in World War Two

Sicily Under the Roman Empire. R. J. Wilson. (Archaeologists' Guides to the Roman World Ser.). (Illus.). 464p. 1990. 249.00 (*0-85668-552-6*, Pub. by Aris & Phillips UK); pap. 135.00 (*0-85668-160-1*, Pub. by Aris & Phillips UK) David Brown.

Sick. Jay R. Bonansinga. 336p. (Orig.). 1995. mass mkt. 5.99 (*0-446-36516-5*) Warner Bks.

Sick a Geranium in Your Hat & Be Happy: Mini Book. Barbara Johnson. 1993. 4.99 (*0-8499-5026-0*) Word Pub.

Sick & Tired of Being a Minister's Wife. Shirley D. Wise. 173p. (Orig.). 1988. pap. 8.00 (*0-685-22589-5*) Wise Works Inc.

Sick & Tired of Being Sick & Tired: Black Women's Health Activism in America, 1890-1950. Susan L. Smith. (Studies in Health, Illness, & Caregiving). (Illus.). 288p. 1995. text ed. 34.95 (*0-8122-3237-2*); pap. text ed. 16.95 (*0-8122-1449-8*) U of Pa Pr.

Sick & Tired of Feeling Sick & Tired: Living with Invisible Chronic Illness. Paul J. Donoghue & Mary E. Siegel. 288p. 1992. 22.95 (*0-393-03408-9*) Norton.

Sick & Tired of Feeling Sick & Tired: Living with Invisible Chronic Illness. Paul J. Donoghue. 1994. pap. 12.95 (*0-393-31154-6*) Norton.

Sick Building Syndrome. I. N. Potter. (C). 1988. 220.00 (*0-86022-212-8*, Pub. by Build Servs Info Assn UK) St Mut.

***Sick Building Syndrome.** Ed. by J. Rostron. (Illus.). 360p. 1997. text ed. 110.00 (*0-419-21530-1*, E & FN Spon) Routledge Chapman & Hall.

***Sick Building Syndrome: A Special Industry Report.** Ed. by Larry Siegelman. 26p. 1996. spiral bd. 40.00 (*0-9633003-0-X*) IAQ Pubns.

Sick Building Syndrome: How Indoor Air Pollution Is Poisoning Your Life & What You Can Do. Nicholas Tate. 1993. 23.95 (*0-88282-085-0*); pap. 13.95 (*0-88282-082-6*) New Horizon NJ.

Sick Building Syndrome: Sources, Health Effects, Mitigation. M. C. Baechler et al. LC 91-20423. (Pollution Technology Review Ser.: No. 205). (Illus.). 328p. 1992. 64.00 (*0-8155-1289-9*) Noyes.

Sick Buildings: Definition, Diagnosis and Mitigation. Thaddeus Godish. 416p. 1994. 69.95 (*0-87371-346-X*, L346) Lewis Pubs.

Sick Burn Cut. Deran Ludd. 1992. pap. 7.00 (*0-936756-85-3*) Autonomedia.

***Sick Child.** Rosenberry. 1998. 15.95 (*0-8050-5405-7*) H Holt & Co.

Sick Child Care: Employers' Prescriptions for the 1990s. (BNA Special Report Series on Work & Family: No. 14). 32p. 1989. 35.00 (*1-55871-046-9*) BNA Plus.

Sick for Justice. Ed. by Joseph Hughes. (Southern Exposure Ser.). (Illus.). 128p. (Orig.). (C). 1978. pap. 3.00 (*0-943810-06-X*) Inst Southern Studies.

Sick Friends. Ivan Gold. Ed. by Jane Rosenman. 384p. (Orig.). 1992. pap. 10.00 (*0-671-75604-4*, WSP) PB.

Sick Heart of Modern Europe: The Problem of the Danubian Lands. Hugh Seton-Watson. LC 74-30170. 89p. 1975. 20.00 (*0-295-95360-8*) U of Wash Pr.

Sick Heart River. John Buchan. Ed. & Intro. by David Daniell. 256p. (C). Date not set. pap. write for info. (*0-19-282937-8*) OUP.

Sick Humor: Outrageous but True Medical Stories from the ER to the OR. Allan Zullo & Martha Moffett. LC 95-26021. (Illus.). 112p. (Orig.). 1996. 7.95 (*0-8362-1050-6*) Andrews & McMeel.

***Sick Little Sagas.** (Tales from the Crypt Ser.). 15.00 (*0-87431-493-3*, 28009) West End Games.

Sick Nations of the Modern Age. S. Abul Ala Maududi. 16p. (Orig.). 1985. pap. 3.00 (*1-56744-385-0*) Kazi Pubns.

Sick Newborn Baby. 3rd ed. Christopher J. Kelnar. 1995. pap. text ed. 29.00 (*0-7020-1647-0*) Saunders.

Sick, Not Dead: The Health of British Workingmen During the Mortality Decline. James C. Riley. LC 96-26961. 384p. 1997. text ed. 58.00 (*0-8018-5411-3*) Johns Hopkins.

Sick of Shadows. Sharyn McCrumb. 240p. 1989. mass mkt. 5.99 (*0-345-35653-5*) Ballantine.

***Sick or Healthy Building?** O'Reilly. (Occupational Health & Safety Ser.). 1997. text ed. 69.95 (*0-442-02507-6*) Van Nos Reinhold.

Sick Rose: A Pastoral Elegy. Haruo Sato. Tr. by Francis Tenny from JPN. LC 93-27266. 240p. 1993. pap. text ed. 12.95 (*0-8248-1539-4*) UH Pr.

Sick Rose: A Pastoral Elegy. Haruo Sato. Tr. by Francis Tenny from JPN. LC 93-27266. 240p. 1993. text ed. 28.00 (*0-8248-1534-3*) UH Pr.

Sick Societies: Challenging the Myth of Primitive Harmony. Robert B. Edgerton. LC 92-13948. 350p. 1992. 24.95 (*0-02-908925-5*, Free Press) Free Pr.

Sick Surfers Ask the Surf Docs & Dr. Geoff. Mark Renneker. 1993. pap. 12.95 (*0-923521-26-7*) Bull Pub.

Sicke Womans Private Looking Glasse Wherein Methodically Are Handled All Uterine Affects, or Diseases Arising from Ye Wombe. John Sadler. LC 77-7430. (English Experience Ser.: No. 891). 1977. reprint ed. lib. bdg. 25.00 (*90-221-0891-0*) Walter J Johnson.

***Sicken & So Die.** Brett. 1998. mass mkt. 5.50 (*0-373-26262-0*) Harlequin Bks.

Sicken & So Die. Simon Brett. 1997. 21.00 (*0-684-82459-0*) S&S Trade.

Sickle & Crescent No. 61: The Communist Revolt of 1926 in Banten. Michael C. Williams. 81p. 1982. pap. 6.00 (*0-87763-027-5*) Cornell Mod Indo.

Sickle Cell Anemia. Ed. by George Beshore. LC 94-15513. (Venture Bks.). (Illus.). 112p. (YA). (gr. 7-12). 1994. lib. bdg. 22.00 (*0-531-12510-6*) Watts.

Sickle Cell Anemia. Cerami & Washington. LC 72-93681. 1973. 25.95 (*0-89388-068-X*) Okpaku Communications.

Sickle Cell Anemia. R. L. Nagle & Samuel Charache. (Illus.). 600p. 1995. write for info. (*0-86542-060-2*) Blackwell Sci.

Sickle Cell Anemia. Laura Silverstein-Nunn et al. LC 96-22643. (Diseases & People Ser.). (Illus.). 112p. (YA). (gr. 6 up). 1997. lib. bdg. 18.95 (*0-89490-711-5*) Enslow Pubs.

Sickle Cell Anemia: A Preliminary Survey, Nos. 1042-1043. 2nd ed. Lenwood G. Davis. 1976. 9.50 (*0-686-20397-6*, Sage Prdcls Pr) Sage.

Sickle Cell Anemia: A Source Guide. 1991. lib. bdg. 250.00 (*0-8490-4868-0*) Gordon Pr.

Sickle Cell Disease. 2nd ed. Graham R. Serjeant. (Illus.). 656p. 1992. pap. 65.00 (*0-19-262231-5*) OUP.

Sickle Cell Disease: A Psychosocial Approach. Kenny Midence & James Elander. 1994. 39.95 (*1-870905-14-8*, Radcliffe Med Pr) Scovill Paterson.

Sickle Cell Disease: Basic Principles & Clinical Practice. Ed. by Stephen H. Embury et al. LC 93-50787. 928p. 1994. text ed. 148.00 (*0-7817-0142-2*) Lppncott-Raven.

Sickle Cell Disease: Pathophysiology, Diagnosis, & Management. Ed. by Vipul N. Mankad & Blaine R. Moore. LC 91-32168. 432p. 1992. text ed. 85.00 (*0-275-92503-X*, C2503, Praeger Pubs) Greenwood.

Sickle Cell Disease: Psychological & Psychosocial Issues. Ed. by Anita L. Hurtig & Carol T. Viera. LC 85-5400. 168p. 1986. text ed. 24.95 (*0-252-01186-4*) U of Ill Pr.

Sickle Cell Disease: Screening, Diagnosis, Management & Counseling in Newborns & Infants. 1994. lib. bdg. 250.00 (*0-8490-8401-6*) Gordon Pr.

Sickle Cell Disease: Screening, Diagnosis, Management, & Counseling in Newborns & Infants. 1995. lib. bdg. 253.99 (*0-8490-6805-3*) Gordon Pr.

Sickle Cell Hemoglobinopathies: A Comprehensive Bibliography 1973-75. Charles W. Triche, 3rd & Diane S. Triche. LC 73-85959. 1976. 9.50 (*0-87875-104-1*) Whitston Pub.

Sickle Cell, Thalassaemia & Other Haemoglobinopathies - Report of Working Committee. HMSO Staff. 126p. 1994. pap. 19.00 (*0-11-321699-8*, HM16998, Pub. by Stationery Ofc UK) Bernan Associates.

Sickled Cell. Stuart J. Edelstein. LC 86-2003. (Illus.). 224p. 1986. 37.00 (*0-674-80737-5*) HUP.

Sickles the Incredible: A Biography of Daniel Edgar Sickles. W. A. Swanberg. (Illus.). 433p. 1991. reprint ed. 25.00 (*1-879664-02-X*); reprint ed. pap. 14.95 (*1-879664-03-8*) Stan Clark Military.

***Sickly Simon.** (Little Monsters Ser.). (J). 1997. write for info. (*0-614-21787-3*, Pub. by Splash UK) Assoc Pubs Grp.

Sickness: Physical, Mental or Demons? David Mendez. 16p. (Orig.). 1989. pap. 4.00 (*1-56428-013-6*) Logos Intl Pub.

Sickness & Death in the Christian Family. Peter Jeffrey. 1993. pap. 4.99 (*0-85234-308-6*, Pub. by Evangelical Pr) Presby & Reformed.

Sickness & Healing: An Anthropological Perspective. Robert A. Hahn. LC 94-3382. 327p. 1995. 35.00 (*0-300-06088-2*) Yale U Pr.

Sickness & Health: An Anthropological Perspsective. Robert A. Hahn. 1996. pap. 17.00 (*0-300-06871-9*) Yale U Pr.

Sickness & Health in America: Readings in the History of Medicine & Public Health. 2nd rev. ed. Ed. by Judith W. Leavitt & Ronald L. Numbers. LC 85-40370. (Illus.). 560p. 1985. pap. text ed. 16.95 (*0-299-10274-2*) U of Wis Pr.

***Sickness & Health in America: Readings in the History of Medicine & Public Health.** 3rd rev. ed. Ed. by Judith W. Leavitt & Ronald L. Numbers. LC 96-44916. (Illus.). 600p. 1997. 65.00 (*0-299-15320-7*); pap. 27.95 (*0-299-15324-X*) U of Wis Pr.

Sickness & Senility Are Unnecessary. Leon De Seblo. 111p. 1959. reprint ed. spiral bd. 10.00 (*0-7873-0270-8*) Hlth Research.

Sickness & the State: Health & Illness in Colonial Malaya, 1870-1940. Lenore Manderson. (Illus.). 360p. (C). 1996. text ed. 69.95 (*0-521-56008-X*) Cambridge U Pr.

Sickness & Wellness Publications Vol. 3. Gerald R. Shields. 1997. pap. 39.50 (*0-934272-38-7*) J G Burke Pub.

***Sickness Behavior & the Sick Role.** Andrew C. Twaddle. LC 81-5269. (Illus.). 257p. reprint ed. pap. 73.30 (*0-608-05329-5*, 2065034) Bks Demand.

Sickness Called Man. Ferdinando Camon. Tr. by John Shepley from ITA. LC 92-60850. 180p. 1992. 18.95 (*0-910395-90-X*) Marlboro Pr.

Sickness Called Man. Ferdinando Camon. Tr. by John Shepley. 177p. 1996. pap. 14.95 (*0-8101-6015-3*) Marlboro Pr.

Sickness in Small Scale Industries. K. C. Reddy. (C). 1988. 32.00 (*81-7024-212-6*, Pub. by Ashish II) S Asia.

Sickness, Recovery, & Death: A History & Forecast of Ill Health. James C. Riley. LC 88-51148. (Illus.). 288p. 1989. text ed. 36.95 (*0-87745-233-4*) U of Iowa Pr.

An Asterisk (*) at the beginning of an entry indicates that the title is appearing in BIP for the first time.

Sickness unto Death. Soren Kierkegaard. Tr. & Intro. by Alastair Hannay. 320p. 1989. pap. 11.95 (0-14-044533-1, Penguin Classics) Viking Penguin.

Sickness unto Death. Ed. by Robert L. Perkins. LC 87-5614. (International Kierkegaard Commentary Ser.: No. 19). 272p. 1987. 18.95 (0-86554-271-6, H234) Mercer Univ Pr.

Sickness Unto Death: A Christian Psychological Exposition for Upbuilding & Awakening. Soren Kierkegaard. Tr. by Howard V. Hong & Edna H. Hong. LC 79-3218. (Kierkegaard's Writings: Vol. XIX). 216p. 1980. text ed. 45.00 (0-691-07247-7); pap. text ed. 14.95 (0-691-02028-0) Princeton U Pr.

Sickroom in Victorian Fiction: The Art of Being Ill. Miriam Bailin. (Cambridge Studies in Nineteenth-Century Literature & Culture: No. 1). 200p. (C). 1994. text ed. 54.95 (0-521-44526-4) Cambridge U Pr.

SICSA Cookbook. Society for the Improvement of Stray Animals Staff. LC 85-61448. (Illus.). 181p. 1985. 9.95 (0-9615105-0-1) SICSA.

Sicuanga Runa: The Other Side of Development in Amazonian Ecuador. Norman E. Whitten, Jr. LC 84-155. (Illus.). 328p. 1985. text ed. 29.95 (0-252-01117-1) U of Ill Pr.

Siculo Arabic. Dionisius A. Agius. LC 95-15881. (Library of Arabic Linguistics: No. 12). 1995. 93.50 (0-7103-0497-8) Routledge Chapman & Hall.

***Sid.** Dalton. Date not set. 21.95 (0-312-15520-4) St Martin.

***Sid: Sid Vicious, Rock 'n' Roll Star.** Malcolm Butt. 160p. 1996. pap. 15.95 (0-85965-234-3, Pub. by Plexus UK) Publishers Group.

***Sid! The Sports Legends, the Inside Scoops, & the Close Personal Friends.** Sid Hartman & Patrick Reusse. LC 97-14451. (Illus.). 300p. (YA). (gr. 8 up). 1997. 24.95 (0-89658-352-X) Voyageur Pr.

Sid & Sal's Famous Channel Marker Diner. Priscilla Cummings. LC 91-65255. (Illus.). 30p. (J). (gr. k-5). 1991. bds. 8.95 (0-87033-423-9, Tidewtr Pubs) Cornell Maritime.

Sid & Sam. Nola Buck. LC 94-36711. (My First I Can Read Bks.). (Illus.). 32p. (J). (ps). 1996. 14.95 (0-06-025371-1); lib. bdg. 14.89 (0-06-025372-X) HarpC Child Bks.

***Sid & Sam.** Nola Buck. LC 94-36711. (My First I Can Read Book Ser.). (Illus.). 32p. (J). (ps). 1997. pap. 3.75 (0-06-444211-X, Trophy) HarpC Child Bks.

Sid & Sol. Arthur Yorinks. (J). (gr. 4-8). 1991. pap. 3.95 (0-374-46634-3, Sunburst Bks) FS&G.

***Sid, Chinuch Yitz, Yair.** 12.50 (0-89906-646-1) Mesorah Pubns.

SID Internaitonal Symposium Digest of Technical Papers, May 1986. 70.00 (0-318-20633-1) SID.

SID International Symposium Digest of Technical Papers, Baltimore, May 1989. 1989. 70.00 (0-317-02012-9) SID.

SID International Symposium Digest of Technical Papers, May 1987. 465p. 1989. 70.00 (0-317-01767-5) SID.

SID International Symposium Digest of Technical Papers, May, 1988. 494p. 1989. 70.00 (0-317-01768-3) SID.

SID International Symposium Digest of Technical Papers, Orlando, April-May 1985. 70.00 (0-318-20632-3) SID.

Sid Meier's Civilization. Johnny L. Wilson & Alan Emrich. (Illus.). 376p. (Orig.). 1992. pap. 19.95 (1-55958-191-3) Prima Pub.

***Sid Meier's Civilization: Advanced Strategies, No. II.** Michael Rymeszewski. 144p. 1996. per., pap. 16.99 (0-7615-0917-8) Prima Pub.

Sid Meier's Civilization II: The Official Strategy Guide. Dave Ellis. 1996. pap. text ed. 19.99 (0-7615-0106-1) Prima Pub.

Sid Meier's Civnet Official Secrets & Solutions. Jonatha Caspian-Kaufman. 1996. pap. text ed. 12.95 (0-7615-0140-1) Prima Pub.

Sid Meier's Colonization Vol. 1: The Official Strategy Guide. Bruce Shelley. (Illus.). 272p. 1994. pap. 19.95 (1-55958-622-2) Prima Pub.

***Sida: Lo Que los Jouenes Deben Saber: Guia para el Estudiante.** 41p. 1991. pap. 3.25 (0-88314-496-4, A4964) AAHPERD.

***Sida: Lo Que los Jouenes Deben Saber: Guia para el Instructor.** William L. Yarber. 66p. 1991. pap. 10.00 (0-88314-495-6, A4956) AAHPERD.

SIDA, Adiccion, Bienestar. (Mart Ser.). 5.00 (1-885565-05-4) Mart.

***SIDA Comprendiendo Biologia Molecular: Jorge & Eddy, Libro Para Adolescences.** Pedro Z. Taussig. (Illus.). 80p. (SPA.). 1997. text ed. 45.00 (1-889167-04-5) Doctors Pr.

***Sida Comprendiendo Biologia Molecular: La Invasion Del Rey Jorge, Libro Para Nonios.** Pedro Z. Taussig. (Illus.). 64p. (SPA.). (YA). (gr. 9-12). 1997. 35.00 (1-889167-03-7) Doctors Pr.

Siddartha, the Pilgrim. Edmond B. Szekely. (Illus.). 32p. (Orig.). 1993. pap. 2.95 (0-89564-082-1) IBS Intl.

Siddhanta Darsanam of Vyasa. Vyasa. Tr. by Mohan L. Sandal. LC 73-3822. (Sacred Books of the Hindus: No. 29). reprint ed. 17.00 (0-404-57829-2) AMS Pr.

Siddhartha. Hermann Hesse. 160p. (YA). (gr. 10-12). 1982. mass mkt. 4.99 (0-553-20884-5) Bantam.

Siddhartha. Hermann Hesse. 1994. 5.98 (1-56731-007-9, MJF Bks) Fine Comms.

Siddhartha. Hermann Hesse. Tr. by Hilda Rosner. LC 51-13669. 1951. pap. 5.95 (0-8112-0068-X, NDP65) New Directions.

Siddhartha. deluxe ed. Hermann Hesse. Tr. by Hilda Rosner. LC 51-13669. 1964. 16.95 (0-8112-0292-5) New Directions.

Siddhartha. Hermann Hesse. 191p. 1983. reprint ed. lib. bdg. 21.95 (0-89966-447-4) Buccaneer Bks.

***Siddhartha Becomes the Buddha.** Sri Chinmoy. 1974. pap. 6.95 (0-88497-116-3) Aum Pubns.

Siddhartha, Demian, & Other Writings. Hermann Hesse. Tr. by Denver Lindley et al. from GER. LC 92-562. (German Library: Vol. 71). 324p. 1992. 29.50 (0-8264-0714-5); pap. text ed. 16.95 (0-8264-0715-3) Continuum.

Siddhartha Gautam, Buddha, + Teacher's Guide. pap. text ed. 4.95 (1-878099-10-8) Vidya Bks.

Siddhi Kur: Tales of the Bewitched Vampire, the Vetalapan-cavimsatika. (Mongolia Society Special Papers: Issue III). 7.50 (0-910980-23-3) Mongolia.

Siddie Sidey: Descendants of John Siddie. Barbara J. Thompson. (Illus.). 455p. 1993. text ed. 95.00 (0-9631097-1-5) Barriclyn.

***Siddur: Ashkenaz.** (HEB.). 12.50 (0-89906-097-8, SHAD) Mesorah Pubns.

***Siddur: Ashkenaz.** deluxe ed. (HEB.). 11.99 (0-614-18312-X, SRCH) Mesorah Pubns.

Siddur: The Complete ArtScroll Siddur - Ashkenaz. Meir Zlotowitz. (ArtScroll Siddur Ser.). 992p. 25.99 (0-89906-650-X); Rabbinical Council ed. 26.99 (0-89906-662-3); Pocket sized. 15.99 (0-89906-655-0); Pocket sized paper. 29.99 (0-89906-661-5) Mesorah Pubns.

Siddur: The Complete ArtScroll Siddur - Ashkenaz. deluxe ed. Meir Zlotowitz. (ArtScroll Siddur Ser.). 992p. 44.99 (0-89906-653-4); Pocket sized leather gift bd. 24.95 (0-318-32593-4) Mesorah Pubns.

Siddur: The Complete ArtScroll Siddur - Ashkenaz. large type ed. Meir Zlotowitz. (ArtScroll Siddur Ser.). 992p. 49.99 (0-89906-656-9) Mesorah Pubns.

Siddur: The Prayer Book. Comment by Ben Z. Bokser. 15.00 (0-317-70173-8); pap. 15.00 (0-317-70174-6) Behrman.

Siddur Vol. 1: For Messianic Jews. 3rd ed. Tr. by John Fischer. 208p. (ENG & HEB.). 1995. reprint ed. 20.00 (0-944414-00-1) R E F Typesetting Pub.

***Siddur - Pocket Size: Ashkenaz.** 18.99 (0-89906-654-2) Mesorah Pubns.

***Siddur - Weekday Pocket Size: Ashkenaz.** 13.99 (0-89906-693-3, SAWH) Mesorah Pubns.

***Siddur - Weekday Pocket Size: Ashkenaz.** pap. 9.99 (0-89906-694-1, SAWP) Mesorah Pubns.

Siddur Aravit L'Hol: Traditional. large type ed. 32p. (J). (gr. 3 up). 1991. student ed. 1.40 (0-933873-56-5) Torah Aura.

Siddur Aravit L'Hol Reform. large type ed. 32p. (J). 1991. student ed. 1.40 (0-933873-57-3) Torah Aura.

Siddur Avodat Yisrael. 79.50 (0-88482-013-0) Hebrew Pub.

Siddur Hadash: A New Prayer Book for Sabbath & Festival Mornings. Ed. by Sidney Greenberg & Jonathan D. Levine. LC 92-60062. 590p. 1992. 18.95 (0-87677-081-2) Prayer Bk.

***Siddur House of Mourning: Ashkenaz.** Jacob J. Schacter & David Weinberger. 19.99 (0-89906-774-3, SMOH) Mesorah Pubns.

Siddur Leshabbat Veyom Tov: Prayer Book for Sabbath & Festivals. large type ed. Philip Birnbaum. 384p. 1978. 26.00 (0-88482-126-9) Hebrew Pub.

Siddur Leshabbat Veyom Tov: Prayer Book for Sabbath & Festivals with Torah Readings. Philip Birnbaum. 724p. 1978. 23.00 (0-88482-062-9) Hebrew Pub.

Siddur Tefilas Mikal Hashana. 832p. (HEB.). 1981. 20.00 (0-8266-5574-2) Kehot Pubn Soc.

***Siddur Tefilas Shlomo: Sefard.** 7.25 (0-89906-651-8) Mesorah Pubns.

Siddur Tefillot: A Woman's Ladino Prayer Book (Paris B. N., Esp. 668; 15th C.) Ed. by Moshe Lazar & Robert Dilligan. LC 95-81321. (Sephardic Classical Library: Vol. 10). (Illus.). 302p. (HEB & LAD.). (C). 1995. 55.00 (0-911437-67-3) Labyrinthos.

***Siddur Tehillat Hashem: Shabat & Weekdays.** Schneur Zalman of Liadi. 256p. (HEB.). Date not set. reprint ed. 7.00 (0-8266-0255-X, Merkos LInyonei Chinuch) Kehot Pubn Soc.

***Siddur Tehillat Hashem with English Translation.** Schneur Z. M'Liadi. Tr. by Nissan Mangel from HEB. LC 86-81508. 854p. 1995. reprint ed. 14.00 (0-8266-0260-6) Kehot Pubn Soc.

***Siddur Tehillat Hashom with Tehillim.** 2nd ed. Schneur Zalman of Liadi. LC 86-1587. 746p. (HEB.). 1995. reprint ed. 12.00 (0-8266-0257-6, Merkos LInyonei Chinuch) Kehot Pubn Soc.

Siddur Torah Ohr Im Perush Shaar Hakollel. Schneur Z. M'Liadi & Avraham D. Lavut. LC 86-149. 778p. (HEB.). 1987. reprint ed. 20.00 (0-8266-5340-5) Kehot Pubn Soc.

Siddurenu. Sidney Greenberg & Morris Silverman. (J). (gr. 3-7). 8.95 (0-87677-099-5) Prayer Bk.

Side by Side. Ted Cooper & Amy Glennon. 24p. 1994. pap. text ed. 4.95 (0-913277-32-0) Summy-Birchard.

Side by Side. Martha Humphreys. (First Love Ser.). 186p. 1998. pap. 6.50 (0-671-53402-5) Silhouette.

Side by Side. Isabel Miller. 256p. 1990. pap. 9.95 (0-941483-77-0) Naiad Pr.

Side by Side, 2 Vols. Wiener. (C). 1995. pap. 28.76 (0-395-71925-9) HM.

Side by Side, 2 Vols. Wiener. (C). 1995. suppl. ed., teacher ed., pap. 11.96 (0-395-75052-0) HM.

Side by Side, Bk. 1. 2nd ed. Bliss & Steven J. Molinsky. 1989. teacher ed., pap. text ed. 16.95 (0-13-811167-7) P-H.

Side by Side, Bk. 1. 2nd ed. Steven J. Molinsky & Bill Bliss. 1988. pap. text ed. 12.50 (0-13-811076-X) P-H.

Side by Side, Bk. 2. Steven J. Molinsky & Bill Bliss. 1995. text ed. 12.95 (0-13-456195-3) P-H.

Side by Side, Bk. 2. 2nd ed. Bill Bliss & Steven J. Molinsky. (Illus.). 130p. 1988. pap. text ed. 9.00 (0-13-811241-X) P-H.

Side by Side, Bk. 3. 2nd ed. Bliss & Steven J. Molinsky. 1989. teacher ed., pap. text ed. 15.50 (0-13-811779-9) P-H.

Side by Side, Bk. 3. 2nd ed. Steven J. Molinsky. 1989. pap. text ed. 9.00 (0-13-811761-6) P-H.

Side by Side, Bk. 4. 2nd ed. Bliss & Steven J. Molinsky. 1989. teacher ed., pap. text ed. 16.95 (0-13-811829-9) P-H.

Side by Side, Bk. 4. 2nd ed. Steven J. Molinsky. 1989. pap. text ed. 9.00 (0-13-811811-6) P-H.

Side by Side: A History of Denver's Witter-Cofield Historic District. Witter-Cofield Historic District Committee Staff. (Illus.). 247p. (Orig.). 1995. pap. 19.95 (0-9645824-0-6) BenchMark CO.

Side by Side: An Autobiography. H. Joseph. (C). 1986. pap. 15.00 (0-86232-565-X, Pub. by Zed Bks Ltd UK); text ed. 45.00 (0-86232-564-1, Pub. by Zed Bks Ltd UK) Humanities.

***Side by Side: Animals Who Help Each Other, Vol. 4.** Marilyn Baillie. (Amazing Things Animals Do Ser.). (Illus.). 32p. (J). (gr. k up). 1997. 17.95 (1-895688-56-6, Pub. by Owl Bks CN); pap. 6.95 (1-895688-57-4, Pub. by Owl Bks CN) Firefly Bks Ltd.

Side by Side: English Grammar Through Guided Conversation 1A. Steven J. Molinsky & Bill Bliss. 128p. (C). 1982. pap. text ed. 8.50 (0-13-809715-1); pap. text ed. 6.50 (0-13-809525-6) P-H.

Side by Side: English Grammar through Guided Conversation 1B. Steven J. Molinsky & Bill Bliss. 128p. (C). 1982. pap. text ed. 8.50 (0-13-809723-2) P-H.

Side by Side: English Grammar through Guided Conversation 1B. Steven J. Molinsky & Bill Bliss. 128p. (C). 1983. Study guide. student ed., pap. text ed. 6.50 (0-13-809582-5) P-H.

Side by Side: English Grammar Through Guided Conversation 2A. Steven J. Molinsky & Bill Bliss. 128p. (C). 1982. pap. text ed. 8.50 (0-13-809772-0) P-H.

Side by Side: English Grammar Through Guided Conversation 2A. Steven J. Molinsky & Bill Bliss. 128p. (C). 1983. pap. text ed. 6.50 (0-13-809640-6) P-H.

Side by Side: English Grammar Through Guided Conversation 2B. Steven J. Molinsky & Bill Bliss. 128p. (C). 1982. pap. text ed. 8.50 (0-13-809798-4) P-H.

Side by Side: English Grammar Through Guided Conversation 2B. Steven J. Molinsky & Bill Bliss. 128p. (C). 1983. Wkbk. student ed., pap. text ed. 6.50 (0-13-809699-6) P-H.

Side by Side: English Grammar Through Guided Conversations, Bk. I. Steven J. Molinsky & Bill Bliss. 1980. pap. text ed. 15.95 (0-13-809848-4) P-H.

Side by Side: English Grammar Through Guided Conversations Bk. II. Steven J. Molinsky & Bill Blass. 1980. pap. text ed. 15.95 (0-13-809855-7) P-H.

Side by Side: Essays on Teaching to Learn. Nancie Atwell. LC 91-6670. 164p. 1991. pap. 16.95 (0-435-08586-7, 08586) Heinemann.

Side by Side: Exploring Your Neighborhood Through Intergenerational Activities: A Curriculum Guide. Matt S. Kaplan. LC 94-8908. 1994. pap. 15.95 (0-944661-21-1) MIG Comns.

Side by Side: Mentoring Guide for Congregational Youth Ministry. Lavon J. Welty. LC 89-84089. 108p. 1989. pap. 9.95 (0-87303-996-3) Faith & Life.

Side by Side: Poems to Read Together. Ed. by Lee B. Hopkins. LC 87-33025. (Illus.). 96p. (J). (gr. 1 up). 1988. pap. 16.00 (0-671-63579-4, S&S Bks Young Read) S&S Childrens.

Side by Side: Poems to Read Together. Ed. by Lee B. Hopkins. (J). (gr. 1 up). 1991. pap. 9.95 (0-671-73622-1, S&S Bks Young Read) S&S Childrens.

***Side by Side: Twelve Multicultural Puppet Plays.** Jean M. Pollock. LC 97-20542. (School Library Media). 1997. pap. write for info. (0-8108-3362-X) Scarecrow.

Side by Side Bk. 1. Steven J. Molinsky & Bill Bliss. LC 95-23474. 176p. 1995. pap. 9.95 (0-13-440124-7) P-H.

Side by Side Bk. 1. Steven J. Molinsky & Bill Bliss. LC 95-23474. 1995. boxed, text ed. 12.95 (0-13-456187-2) P-H.

Side by Side Bk. 2: Global Village Edition. Steven J. Molinsky. 1995. pap. text ed. 9.00 (0-13-467334-4) P-H.

Side by Side Bk. 3: Global Village Edition. Steven J. Molinsky. 1995. pap. text ed. 9.00 (0-13-467812-5) P-H.

Side by Side Bk. 4: Global Village Edition. Steven J. Molinsky. 1995. pap. text ed. 9.00 (0-13-467821-4) P-H.

Side by Side Bilingual Books - Latin America. (BBC Phrase Books for Teenagers). 1995. pap. 11.95 (0-8442-0812-4, Passport Bks) NTC Pub Grp.

Side by Side Core Conversation, Intermediate Text. 2nd ed. Steven J. Molinsky & Bill Bliss. (C). 1991. pap. text ed. 15.95 (0-13-811878-7) P-H.

Side by Side Grammar: French & English. (BBC Phrase Bks.). 128p. 1994. pap. 7.95 (0-8442-1224-5, Passport Bks) NTC Pub Grp.

Side by Side Grammar: Spanish & English. (BBC Phrase Bks.). 128p. 1995. pap. 7.95 (0-8442-7140-3, Passport Bks) NTC Pub Grp.

Side-by-Side Strategies: How Two-Career Couples Can Thrive in the Nineties. Jane H. Cuozzo & S. Diane Graham. LC 90-35139. 240p. 1991. pap. 10.95 (0-942361-39-3) MasterMedia Pub.

Side by Side Student Text 1: Global Village Edition. Steven J. Molinsky. 1995. pap. text ed. 9.00 (0-13-467292-5) P-H.

Side Chain Liquid Crystal Polymers. Ed. by Ciaran B. McCardle. (Illus.). 416p. 1989. 150.00 (0-412-01761-X, Chap & Hall NY) Chapman & Hall.

***Side-Chain Liquid Crystalline Polycarbonates: Synthesis, Mesomorphic Properties & Dielectric & Mechanical Analysis.** Johannes C. Jansen. (Illus.). 210p. (Orig.). 1996. pap. 77.50 (90-407-1348-0, Pub. by Delft U Pr NE) Coronet Bks.

***Side Dishes Creative & Simple: Vegetable & Fruit Accompaniments for All Occasions.** Deirdre Davis. Ed. by Rux Martin. LC 96-37468. (Illus.). 208p. 1997. pap. 14.95 (1-57630-027-7) Chapters Pub.

Side Effects. Allen. 1988. 21.95 (0-8488-0365-5) Amereon Ltd.

Side Effects. Woody Allen. 160p. 1986. mass mkt. 5.99 (0-345-34335-2) Ballantine.

Side Effects. Nancy Fisher. 384p. (Orig.). 1994. mass mkt. 4.99 (0-451-18130-1, Sig) NAL-Dutton.

Side Effects. Bobby Hutchinson. 1997. mass mkt. 3.99 (0-373-70723-1, 1-70723-1) Silhouette.

Side Effects. Michael Palmer. 368p. 1991. mass mkt. 6.50 (0-553-27618-2) Bantam.

Side-Effects of Anti-Inflamatory Drugs 3. Ed. by Kim D. Rainsford & G. P. Velo. (Inflammation & Drug Therapy Ser.). (C). 1992. lib. bdg. 185.00 (0-7923-8966-2) Kluwer Ac.

***Side Effects of Anti-Inflammatory Drugs IV.** Ed. by K.D. Rainsford. 384p. 1997. lib. bdg. 215.00 (0-7923-8713-9) Kluwer Ac.

Side-Effects of Antiinflammatory Analgesic Drugs. Ed. by Kim D. Rainsford & G. P. Velo. LC 83-13940. (Advances in Inflammation Research Ser.: Vol. 6). 320p. 1984. reprint ed. pap. 91.20 (0-608-00436-7, 2061151) Bks Demand.

Side Effects of Drugs Annual 16: A Yearly Critical Survey of the World's Literature on Adverse Reactions to Drugs. Ed. by M. N. Dukes & J. K. Aronson. 646p. 1993. 221.00 (0-444-89657-0) Elsevier.

Side Effects of Drugs Annual, 18. Ed. by J. K. Aronson & C. J. Van Boxtel. 558p. 1995. 233.50 (0-444-81939-8) Elsevier.

Side Effects of Drugs Annual, No. 13. M. N. Dukes & L. Beeley. 1990. 208.75 (0-444-81091-9, SED 1989) Elsevier.

Side Effects of Drugs, Annual 12. Ed. by M. N. Dukes. 500p. 1988. 201.25 (0-444-90491-3) Elsevier.

***Side Effects of Drugs Annual 15/1991, Vol. 15.** M. N. Dukes & J. K. Aronson. 586p. 1991. 221.75 (0-444-89171-4) Elsevier.

Side Effects of Drugs Annual 17: A Worldwide Yearly Critical Survey of New Data & Trends. Ed. by J. K. Aronson & C. J. Van Boxtel. 648p. 1994. 227.25 (0-444-82005-1) Elsevier.

***Side Effects of Drugs Annual 19.** Ed. by J. K. Aronson & C. J. Van Boxtel. 532p. 1996. 228.25 (0-444-82531-2) Elsevier.

Side Effects of Drugs Annual 1990, No. 14. Ed. by M. N. Dukes & L. Beeley. 500p. 1991. 203.75 (0-444-81346-2) Elsevier.

Side Effects of Drugs Essays. Ed. by M. N. Dukes. 200p. 1991. 110.00 (0-444-81435-3) Elsevier.

Side Effects of Estrogen Drug Therapy. Harold E. Simmons. 1979. pap. 8.00 (0-87312-007-8) Psychogenic Disease.

Side Glimpses from the Colonial Meeting House. William R. Bliss. 1970. reprint ed. 40.00 (1-55888-224-3) Omnigraphics Inc.

Side-Impact Occupant Protection Technologies. 152p. 1991. pap. 55.00 (1-56091-115-8, SP-851) Soc Auto Engineers.

Side-Lights on Maryland History, 2 Vols., Set. Hester D. Richardson. (Illus.). 990p. 1995. 85.00 (0-8063-0296-8) Genealog Pub.

Side of the Angels. Alexander Federoff. 1960. 12.95 (0-8392-1103-1) Astor-Honor.

Side Orders: Small Helping of Southern Cookery & Culture. John Egerton. LC 90-41766. 224p. 1990. 14.95 (1-56145-005-7) Peachtree Pubs.

Side Orders: Small Helpings of Southern Cookery & Culture. John Egerton. 1993. pap. 9.95 (1-56145-016-2) Peachtree Pubs.

Side Saddle Riding: Four-H Manual. Linda A. Bowlby & Mary L. Thomas. (Illus.). 23p. (Orig.). (YA). (gr. 9-12). 1984. pap. 5.00 (1-884011-01-2) Wrld Sidesaddle.

Side Saddle Riding: Four-H Manual. 2nd rev. ed. Linda A. Bowlby & Mary L. Thomas. (Illus.). 24p. (Orig.). (YA). (gr. 9-12). 1993. pap. 5.00 (1-884011-06-3) Wrld Sidesaddle.

Side Saddle Riding: Notes for Teachers & Pupils. Betty Skelton. (Illus.). 64p. 1989. 22.95 (0-948253-24-X, Pub. by Sportmans Pr UK) Trafalgar.

Side Saddles. Linda A. Bowlby. (Illus.). 12p. 1985. pap. 2.00 (1-884011-00-4) Wrld Sidesaddle.

Side Scan Sonar Record Interpretation. Charles Mazel. 146p. 1985. 48.95 (0-932146-50-3) Peninsula CA.

Side Show: 1991 Short Story Annual. Ed. by Shelley Anderson et al. 276p. 1991. 12.50 (0-9630563-0-1) Somersault.

Side Show: 1994 Annual Anthology of Contemporary Fiction. Ed. by Shelley Anderson et al. 257p. 1994. 12.00 (0-9630563-2-8) Somersault.

Side Show: 1995 Annual Anthology of Contemporary Fiction. Ed. by Shelley Anderson et al. 308p. 1995. 12.50 (0-9630563-3-6) Somersault.

Side Show: 1996 Annual Anthology of Contemporary Fiction. Ed. by Shelley Anderson et al. 320p. (Orig.). 1996. pap. 13.00 (0-9630563-4-4) Somersault.

Side Show 1992-93: An Annual of Contemporary Fiction. Ed. by Shelley Anderson et al. (Annual Ser.). 448p. (Orig.). 1992. 15.00 (0-9630563-1-X) Somersault.

Side Stepping with Shorty. Sewell Ford. 1977. 20.95 (0-8369-4242-6, 6053) Ayer.

***Side Steps: A Communicative Course for Learners of English.** LC 96-51583. (YA). 1997. pap. write for info. (0-13-619891-0) P-H.

Side Street: San Francisco. Proctor Jones. LC 89-91212. 324p. (Orig.). 1990. pap. 4.95 (0-9608860-6-0) Proctor Jones.

S

Side Tracks. Teresa Stores. 256p. 1996. pap. 10.95 (*1-56280-122-8*) Naiad Pr.
Side Trips: The Photography of Sumner W. Matteson. Louis B. Casagrande & Phillips Bourns. LC 83-61682. (Illus.). 249p. 1983. 12.50 (*0-89326-095-9*) Milwaukee Pub Mus.
Sidecar Motorcycles. Jesse Young. (Motorcycles Ser.). 48p. (J). (gr. 3-4). 1994. lib. bdg. 17.80 (*1-56065-225-X*) Capstone Pr.
***Sidecar Motorcycles.** Jesse Young. (Motorcycles Ser.). (Illus.). 48p. (J). (gr. 3-6). 1995. 18.40 (*0-516-35225-3*) Childrens.
Sidelight on Anglo-American Relations 1839-1858: Furnished by the Correspondence of Lewis Tappan & Others with the British & Foreign Anti-Slavery Society. Lewis Tappan. Ed. by Annie H. Abel. LC 73-117503. 407p. 1970. reprint ed. 49.50 (*0-678-00650-4*) Kelley.
Sidelight on History. James McHenry. LC 75-140875. (Eyewitness Accounts of the American Revolution Ser., No. 1). 1971. reprint ed. 15.95 (*0-405-01225-X*) Ayer.
Sidelights. Charlotte J. Blennerhassett. Tr. by E. Gulcher. LC 68-54329. (Essay Index Reprint Ser.). 1977. 19.95 (*0-8369-0216-5*) Ayer.
Sidelights: Incidents in the Life of Eugene V. Debs. Theodore Debs. (Illus.). 32p. 1980. pap. 4.00 (*0-88286-091-7*) C H Kerr.
Sidelights, Fanlights & Transoms Stained Glass Pattern Book. Ed Sibbett, Jr. 64p. (Orig.). 1987. pap. 4.95 (*0-486-25328-7*) Dover.
Sidelights of New London & Newer New York. Gilbert K. Chesterton. 1988. reprint ed. lib. bdg. 49.00 (*0-7812-0466-6*) Rprt Serv.
Sidelights of New London & Newer York, & Other Essays. Gilbert K. Chesterton. LC 68-8447. (Essay Index Reprint Ser.). 261p. 1977. reprint ed. 18.95 (*0-8369-0298-X*) Ayer.
Sidelights of Robert Browning's the Ring & the Book. Louis Snitslaar. LC 68-1061. (Studies in Browning: No. 4). 1969. reprint ed. lib. bdg. 75.00 (*0-8383-0626-8*) M S G Haskell Hse.
Sidelights on Greek History. Marcus N. Tod. 96p. 1974. 20.00 (*0-89005-039-2*) Ares.
Sidelights on Negro Soldiers see Negro Soldiers in World War One: The Human Side
Sidelights on New London & Newer New York. Gilbert K. Chesterton. 1981. reprint ed. lib. bdg. 29.00 (*0-403-00551-5*) Scholarly.
Sidelights on Relativity. Albert Einstein. (Popular Science Ser.). 56p. 1983. reprint ed. pap. 3.95 (*0-486-24511-X*) Dover.
Sidelights on the Catholic Revival. Francis J. Sheed. LC 74-99649. (Essay Index Reprint Ser.). 1977. 20.95 (*0-8369-2176-3*) Ayer.
Sideline Help. Marshall K. Steele. LC 95-38863. (Illus.). 152p. (Orig.). 1996. pap. 14.95 (*0-87322-786-7*, PSTE0786) Human Kinetics.
Sidelines - Behind the Scenes of America's Favorite Sport. Ben Higgs. 1992. 40.00 (*0-9629648-2-4*) Cadmus Publ.
Sidelines Activist: Charles S. Johnson & the Struggle for Civil Rights. Richard Robbins. 224p. 1996. text ed. 45.00 (*0-87805-904-0*); pap. text ed. 17.00 (*0-87805-932-6*) U Pr of Miss.
***Sideman.** Debra Davis. Date not set. write for info. (*0-688-03909-X*) Morrow.
***Sideman: The Autobiography of Billy Bauer.** William Bauer. Ed. by Thea Luba. (Illus.). xxxvii, 215p. Date not set. pap. 19.95 (*0-9657237-0-4*) W H Bauer.
Sidereal Astrological Almanac, 1987. P. Krishna Warriar et al. 100p. (Orig.). 1986. pap. text ed. 11.00 (*0-9618070-0-8*) Personal Insight.
Sidereal Astrological Almanac, 1988. P. Krishna Warriar et al. 105p. (Orig.). 1987. pap. text ed. 11.00 (*0-9618070-1-6*) Personal Insight.
Sidereal Astrological Almanac, 1989. Molly F. Seeligson & Sally W. Gorreu. Ed. by David A. Zimmerman. 118p. (Orig.). 1988. pap. 12.00 (*0-9618070-2-4*) Personal Insight.
Sidereal Astrological Almanac, 1990. Molly F. Seeligson & Sally W. Gorsell. Ed. by David A. Zimmermann. 118p. (Orig.). 1989. pap. text ed. 12.00 (*0-9618070-3-2*) Personal Insight.
Sidereal Astrological Almanac, 1991. Molly F. Selligson & Sally W. Gorsell. Ed. by David A. Zimmermann. 118p. (Orig.). 1990. pap. text ed. 12.00 (*0-9618070-4-0*) Personal Insight.
Sidereal Astrological Almanac, 1992. Molly F. Seeligson & Sally W. Gorsell. Ed. by David A. Zimmermann. 118p. (Orig.). 1991. pap. text ed. 14.00 (*0-9618070-5-9*) Personal Insight.
Sidereal Astrological Almanac, 1993. Molly F. Suligson & Sally W. Garrell. 118p. (Orig.). 1992. pap. text ed. 14.00 (*0-9618070-6-7*) Personal Insight.
Sidereal Zodiac. Powell & Treadgold. 52p. 1979. 10.00 (*0-904693-07-4*, P2533-014) Am Fed Astrologers.
Sidereus Nuncius. Galileo Galilei. (Mapping of the Stars Ser.). (Illus.). 64p. (LAT.). (C). 1989. reprint ed. 75.00 (*1-85297-019-7*, Pub. by Archival Facs UK) St Mut.
***Sidereus Nuncius & Stella Polaris: The Scientific Relations Between Italy & Sweden in Early Modern History.** Marco Beretta & Tore Angsmyr. LC 96-38088. (Uppsala Studies in the History of Science). 1997. write for info. (*0-88135-188-1*) Watson Pub Intl.
Sidereus Nuncius, Or the Sidereal Messenger. Galileo Galilei. Tr. by Albert Van Helden. LC 88-25179. (Illus.). 144p. 1989. pap. text ed. 8.95 (*0-226-27903-0*) U Ch Pr.
Siderophores from Microorganisms & Plants. (Structure & Bonding Ser.: Vol. 58). (Illus.). 160p. 1985. 69.95 (*0-387-13649-5*) Spr-Verlag.
Sidesaddle Legacy: How to Ride Aside the American Way. Linda A. Bowlby & Martha C. Friddle. (Illus.). 105p. 1994. 21.95 (*1-884011-08-X*) Wrld Sidesaddle.
Sideshow. Anne LeClaire. 352p. 1995. pap. 5.99 (*0-451-40610-9*, Onyx) NAL-Dutton.
***Sideshow.** Anne D. LeClaire. 308p. 1995. 3.98 (*0-8317-4551-7*) Smithmark.
Sideshow. Sheri S. Tepper. 496p. 1993. mass mkt. 6.50 (*0-553-56098-0*, Spectra) Bantam.
Sideshow War: The Italian Campaign, 1943-1945. George F. Botjer. LC 96-14400. (Texas A&M University Military History Ser.: No. 49). (Illus.). 232p. 1996. 29.95 (*0-89096-718-0*) Tex A&M Univ Pr.
Sideshows. B. K. Smith. LC 94-75777. (Illus.). 136p. 1994. 23.95 (*0-942979-15-X*); pap. text ed. 12.95 (*0-942979-16-8*) Livingston U Pr.
Sidestepping the Barbarians. Merle Bagley. (American Autobiography Ser.). 45p. 1995. reprint ed. lib. bdg. 69.00 (*0-7812-8445-7*) Rprt Serv.
Sidesteps: A Collection of Compositions. Chad Sychtysz. LC 93-94981. 120p. (Orig.). pap. 8.00 (*1-56002-397-X*) Aegina Pr.
Sideswipe. Charles Willeford. 288p. 1996. mass mkt. 4.99 (*0-440-21882-9*) Dell.
***Sidetrack City.** Kaz. 64p. 1995. pap. 9.95 (*1-56097-198-3*) Fantagraph Bks.
Sidetracked Home Executives. Pam Young & Peggy Jones. (Orig.). 1983. pap. 10.99 (*0-446-37765-1*) Warner Bks.
Sidetracked in the Wilderness: Learn the Way Back to a Victorious, Abundant Life. Michael Wells. LC 90-49987. 192p. (gr. 10). 1991. pap. 9.99 (*0-8007-5386-0*) Revell.
Sidetracked to Danger. Carolyn Keene. Ed. by Ruth Ashby. (Hardy Boys Ser.: No. 130). 160p. (Orig.). (J). (gr. 3-6). 1995. pap. 3.99 (*0-671-87214-1*, Minstrel Bks) PB.
Sidewalk: Reflections & Images. William M. Barbieri. LC 79-99433. (Illus.). 95p. reprint ed. pap. 27.10 (*0-8357-7020-6*, 2033539) Bks Demand.
Sidewalk Art see Homeplay: Joyful Learning for Children & Adults, Series I
Sidewalk Chalk Games. Golden Staff. (Illus.). (J). (ps-3). 1994. pap. 4.95 (*0-307-16600-7*, Golden Books) Western Pub.
Sidewalk Games Around the World. Arlene Erlbach. LC 96-8715. (Illus.). 64p. (J). (gr. 2-5). 1997. lib. bdg. 17.90 (*0-7613-0008-2*) Millbrook Pr.
Sidewalk Squares & Triangle Birds: God's Wonderful World of Shapes. Glenda Palmer. LC 92-34717. (Almost on My Own Ser.). (Illus.). 32p. (J). 1993. pap. 4.99 (*0-7814-0711-7*, Chariot Bks) Chariot Victor.
Sidewalk Story. Sharon B. Mathis. (Novels Ser.). 64p. (J). (gr. 2-6). 1986. pap. 3.99 (*0-14-032165-9*, Puffin) Puffin Bks.
Sidewalk Story: A Study Guide. Duncan Searl. Ed. by J. Friedland & R. Kessler. (Novel-Ties Ser.). (J). (gr. 3). 1996. pap. text ed. 15.95 (*1-56982-614-5*) Lrn Links.
Sidewalk Talk: A Naturalistic Study of Street Kids. rev. ed. Katherine C. Lundy. LC 94-42201. (Children of Poverty Ser.). 248p. 1995. text ed. 58.00 (*0-8153-2014-0*) Garland.
Sidewalks Are Free see Melov's Legacy
Sidewalks of America: Folklore, Legends, Sagas, Traditions, Customs, Songs, Stories, & Sayings of City Folk. Benjamin A. Botkin. LC 76-44361. (Illus.). 605p. 1977. reprint ed. text ed. 85.00 (*0-8371-9312-5*, BOSA, Greenwood Pr) Greenwood.
Sidewalks of St. Louis: Places, People & Politics in an American City. George Lipsitz. (Illus.). 152p. (C). 1991. 19.95 (*0-8262-0814-2*) U of Mo Pr.
***Sidewalks on the Moon: The Journey of a Mystic Architect Through Tradition, Technology & Transformation.** 2nd ed. Nader Khalili. 325p. 1994. reprint ed. pap. 14.95 (*1-889625-02-7*) Cal-Earth.
Sideways Arithmetic from Wayside School. Louis Sachar. 96p. (J). (gr. 4-6). 1992. pap. 2.99 (*0-590-45726-8*, Apple Paperbacks) Scholastic Inc.
Sideways Stories from Wayside School. Louis Sachar. 144p. 1985. pap. 4.50 (*0-380-69871-4*, Camelot) Avon.
Sideways Stories from Wayside School. Louis Sachar. (Louis Sachar GLB Reprints Ser.). 128p. (J). (gr. 2-6). 1990. reprint ed. lib. bdg. 12.99 (*0-679-90413-1*) Random Bks Yng Read.
Sidewinder. Mike Dunn. 1991. mass mkt. 4.95 (*0-380-76371-0*) Avon.
Sidewinders & Accolades: Poems. Michael E. Waldecki. (Ohio Writers Ser.). 60p. (Orig.). 1994. pap. 6.95 (*0-933087-34-9*) Bottom Dog Pr.
Sidgwick's Greek Prose Composition. A. Sidgwick. 1986. pap. 19.95 (*0-7156-1675-7*, Pub. by Duckworth UK) Focus Pub-R Pullins.
Sidgwick's Greek Prose Composition. A. Sidgwick. 287p. 1990. reprint ed. pap. text ed. 14.95 (*0-89341-625-8*, Longwood Academic) Hollowbrook.
Sidhartha. Hermann Hesse. 1976. 19.95 (*0-8488-1361-8*) Amereon Ltd.
Sidney: The Story of a Kingfisher. Jane H. Stroschin. (Illus.). 32p. (J). (gr. k-6). 1991. text ed. 15.00 (*1-883960-08-8*) Henry Quill.
Sidney: The Story of a Kingfisher. Jane H. Stroschin. (Illus.). 32p. (J). (gr. k-6). 1991. pap. 7.00 (*1-883960-09-6*) Henry Quill.
Sidney & Sally: The Danger of Strangers. Roberta A. Wofford. (Illus.). 38p. (J). (gr. k-4). 1987. pap. text ed. 1.85 (*0-9616198-0-5*) Pt Orchard Spec.
Sidney & Spenser: The Poet As Maker. S. K. Heninger, Jr. LC 88-39036. 880p. 1990. lib. bdg. 67.50 (*0-271-00666-8*) Pa St U Pr.
Sidney Bechet: The Wizard of Jazz. John Chilton. LC 95-43924. (Illus.). 380p. 1996. reprint ed. pap. 14.95 (*0-306-80678-9*) Da Capo.
Sidney Centennial Jubilee, Sidney Plains, Delaware County, New York. Compiled by Ira Sherman. 87p. 1994. 38.00 (*0-9614858-6-8*) RSG Pub.
Sidney Drell on Arms Control. Ed. by Kenneth W. Thompson. LC 88-14287. (W. Alton Jones Foundation Series on Arms Control: Vol. VII). 228p. (Orig.). (C). 1988. pap. text ed. 21.00 (*0-8191-6814-9*, Pub. by White Miller Center); lib. bdg. 45.00 (*0-8191-6813-0*, Pub. by White Miller Center) U Pr of Amer.
Sidney Family Romance: Mary Wroth, William Herbert & the Early Modern Construction of Gender. Gary Waller. LC 92-42532. (Illus.). 324p. 1993. text ed. 39.95 (*0-8143-2436-3*) Wayne St U Pr.
Sidney Godolphin: Servant of the State. Roy A. Sundstrom. LC 90-51012. 328p. 1992. 47.50 (*0-87413-438-2*) U Delaware Pr.
Sidney Godolphin, Lord Treasurer, 1702-1710. William C. Dickinson. LC 89-12979. (Studies in British History: Vol. 18). 300p. 1990. lib. bdg. 89.95 (*0-88946-469-3*) E Mellen.
Sidney Goodman: Paintings & Drawings, 1959-95. John B. Ravenal. (Illus.). 1995. write for info. (*0-87633-099-5*) Phila Mus Art.
Sidney Goodman: Recent Paintings. Howard D. Spencer. LC 84-52236. (Illus.). 28p. 1984. pap. 5.00 (*0-939324-16-4*) Wichita Art Mus.
Sidney Hook: A Checklist of Writings. Compiled by Barbara Levine. LC 88-15043. 120p. 1989. 19.95 (*0-8093-1510-6*) S Ill U Pr.
Sidney Hook: Philosopher of Democracy & Humanism. Ed. by Paul Kurtz. LC 82-62459. 360p. 1982. 33.95 (*0-87975-191-6*) Prometheus Bks.
Sidney Howard. Sydney H. White. Ed. by Sylvia E. Bowman. LC 77-24471. (Twayne's United States Authors Ser.). 175p. (C). 1977. lib. bdg. 17.95 (*0-8057-7191-3*) Irvington.
Sidney in Retrospect: Selections from "English Literary Renaissance" Ed. by Arthur F. Kinney & English Literary Renaissance Staff. LC 87-15639. 240p. (Orig.). (C). 1988. pap. text ed. 17.95 (*0-87023-599-0*) U of Mass Pr.
Sidney Ironworks Accounts 1541-73. D. W. Crossley. (Camden Fourth Ser.: No. 15). 27.00 (*0-901050-25-3*) David Brown.
Sidney Kingsley: Five Prizewinning Plays. Sidney Kingsley. Ed. by Nena Couch. LC 95-10843. (Theatre Studies Series of Occasional Publications). (Illus.). 408p. (C). 1995. 42.50 (*0-8142-0665-4*) Ohio St U Pr.
Sidney Lanier. Edwin Mims. 1972. 59.95 (*0-8490-1052-7*) Gordon Pr.
Sidney Lanier: Poems & Letters. Sidney Lanier. LC 76-83323. 239p. reprint ed. pap. 68.20 (*0-317-39701-X*, 2025824) Bks Demand.
Sidney Lanier: Poet of the Marshes. Jack DeBellis. (Georgia Humanities Council Publications). 56p. 1991. pap. 9.95 (*0-8203-1319-X*) U of Ga Pr.
Sidney Lanier at Rockingham Springs. John W. Wayland. LC 70-148905. (Select Bibliographies Reprint Ser.). 1977. reprint ed. 17.95 (*0-8369-5668-0*) Ayer.
Sidney Lanier, Poet & Prosodist. Richard Webb. (BCL1-PS American Literature Ser.). 108p. 1993. reprint ed. lib. bdg. 69.00 (*0-7812-6983-0*) Rprt Serv.
Sidney Lumet: Film & Literary Vision. Frank R. Cunningham. LC 91-10230. (Illus.). 304p. 1992. text ed. 35.00 (*0-8131-1745-3*) U Pr of Ky.
Sidney M. Jourard: Selected Writings. Ed. by Michael Lowman et al. (Illus.). 371p. (Orig.). (C). 1994. pap. text ed. 23.95 (*0-917982-49-5*) Capitol Enquiry.
Sidney Nolan: Landscapes & Legends. Jane Clark. (Illus.). 176p. 1988. 69.95 (*0-521-35301-7*) Cambridge U Pr.
Sidney Nolan: The Ned Kelly Story. Andrew Sayers. LC 94-1494. (Illus.). 64p. 1994. 9.95 (*0-87099-703-3*) Metro Mus Art.
Sidney Poet Heroical. Amiri Baraka. LC 78-66005. 1979. pap. 5.95 (*0-918408-12-1*) Reed & Cannon.
Sidney Poitier: Actor. Carol Bergman. Ed. by Nathan I. Huggins. (Black Americans of Achievement Ser.). (Illus.). 112p. (Orig.). (YA). (gr. 5 up). 1988. pap. 8.95 (*0-7910-0209-8*) Chelsea Hse.
***Sidney Rella & the Glass Sneaker.** Bernice Myers. (J). (gr. 3). 1995. 7.56 (*0-395-73226-3*) HM.
Sidney Rella & the Glass Sneaker. Bernice Myers. LC 85-3044. (Illus.). 32p. (J). (gr. k-3). 1985. lib. bdg. 14.95 (*0-02-767790-7*, Mac Bks Young Read) S&S Childrens.
***Sidney Rella & the Glass Sneaker.** large type ed. Bernice Myers. 54p. (J). (gr. 3). 13.50 (*0-614-20619-7*, L-38214-00 APHB) Am Printing Hse.
Sidney Ridgon: A Portrait of Religious Excess. Richard S. Van Wagoner. LC 92-17137. (Illus.). x, 493p. 1994. 28.95 (*1-56085-030-2*) Signature Bks.
Sidney Sime: Master of the Mysterious. Simon Heneage & Henry Ford. 1980. pap. 8.95 (*0-500-27154-2*) Thames Hudson.
Sidney Sussex College, Cambridge: Historical Essays in Commemoration of the Quatercentenary. Ed. by D. E. Beales & H. B. Nisbet. (Illus.). 310p. (C). 1996. 63.00 (*0-85115-629-0*) Boydell & Brewer.
Sidney's Appearance: A Study in Elizabethan Portraiture. Alexander C. Judson. LC 73-179730. (Biography Index Reprint Ser.). 1977. reprint ed. 21.95 (*0-8369-8098-0*) Ayer.
Sidney's Arcadia, a Comparison Between the Two Versions. Reinard W. Zandvoort. (BCL1-PR English Literature Ser.). 215p. 1992. reprint ed. lib. bdg. 79.00 (*0-7812-7220-3*) Rprt Serv.
Sidney's Poetic Justice: The Old Arcadia, Its Eclogues, & Renaissance Pastoral Traditions. Robert E. Stillman. LC 84-46096. 280p. 1986. 40.00 (*0-8387-5085-0*) Bucknell U Pr.
Sido. Sidonie-Gabrielle Colette. Bd. with Vrilles De la Vigne. (FRE.). 1958. Set pap. 10.95 (*0-8288-9163-X*, F97320) Fr & Eur.
Sidon: A Study in Oriental History. Frederick C. Eiselen. LC 70-166011. (Columbia University. Oriental Studies: No. 4). reprint ed. 32.50 (*0-404-50494-9*) AMS Pr.
Sidon Sets. Jorge M. Lopez & Kenneth A. Ross. (Lecture Notes in Pure & Applied Mathematics Ser.: Vol. 13). 208p. 1975. 110.00 (*0-8247-6289-4*) Dekker.
Sidon, the Canal That Faith Built. Melvin M. Fillerup. (Illus.). 155p. 1988. write for info. (*0-318-63720-0*) Ptarmigan Co.
Sidonius Apollinaris & His Age. Courtenay E. Stevens. LC 78-21112. 224p. 1979. reprint ed. text ed. 55.00 (*0-313-20850-6*, STSA, Greenwood Pr) Greenwood.
Sidonius Apollinaris & the Fall of Rome 407-485 A.D. Jill Harries. 304p. 1995. text ed. 49.95 (*0-19-814472-5*) OUP.
Sidrah Stories: A Torah Companion. Steven M. Rosman. 120p. (J). (gr. 4-6). 1989. pap. 7.95 (*0-8074-0429-2*, 121723) UAHC.
Sidrot. Abraham Chill. 102p. 1992. 12.95 (*965-229-012-2*, Pub. by Gefen Pub Hse IS) Gefen Bks.
SIDS: A Parent's Guide to Understanding & Preventing Sudden Infant Death Syndrome. William M. Sears. 1995. 19.95 (*0-316-77912-1*) Little.
SIDS: A Parent's Guide to Understanding & Preventing Sudden Infant Death Syndrome. William M. Sears. (Illus.). 256p. 1996. 12.95 (*0-316-77953-9*) Little.
SIDS Survival Guide: Information & Comfort for Grieving Family & Friends & Professionals Who Seek to Help Them. Joani N. Horchler & Robin D. Morris. 290p. (Orig.). 1994. pap. 14.95 (*0-9641218-7-5*) SIDS Educ Srvs.
***SIDS Survival Guide: Information & Comfort for Grieving Family & Friends & Professionals Who Seek to Help Them.** 2nd rev. ed. Joani N. Horchler & Robin R. Morris. (Illus.). 316p. (Orig.). 1997. pap. 16.95 (*0-9641218-8-3*) SIDS Educ Srvs.
Siduri's Net. P. K. McAllister. (Cloudships of Orion Ser.: No. 1). 336p. (Orig.). 1994. pap. 4.99 (*0-451-45319-0*, ROC) NAL-Dutton.
Sieben Hauptlaster see Saemtliche Werke
Sieben Kristallkugeln. Herge. (Illus.). 62p. (GER.). (J). pap. 19.95 (*0-8288-5072-0*) Fr & Eur.
Sieben S-Immunglobulin zur intravenoesen Anwendung. Ed. by F. R. Seiler & R. G. Geursen. (Beitraege zur Infusionstherapie und Klinische Ernaehrung Ser.: Vol. 9). (Illus.). viii, 176p. 1982. pap. 40.00 (*3-8055-3632-1*) S Karger.
Siebenbuergisch-Saechsisches Woerterbuch, 3 vols. Incl. Vol 3 (g). . 355p. 1971. 55.40 (*3-11-003707-6*); Vol. 4 (h-j). . 416p. 1972. 118.50 (*3-11-004097-2*); Vol. 5 (k). . 420p. 1976. 146.15 (*3-11-006645-9*); (GER.). (C). write for info. (*0-318-51648-9*) De Gruyter.
Siecle de Louis XIV, 2 vols. Voltaire, pseud. Ed. by Antoine Adam. 200p. 1984. pap. 11.95 (*0-7859-1660-1*, 2904144048) Fr & Eur.
Siecle de Louis XIV see Histoire de l'Architecture Classique en France
Siecle De Picasso, Vol. 1: La Naissance Du Cubisme 1881-1912. Pierre Cabanne. 416p. (FRE.). 1992. pap. 18.95 (*0-7859-1681-4*, 2070326500) Fr & Eur.
Siecle Des Lumieres. Alejo Carpentier. 461p. (FRE.). 1977. pap. 11.95 (*0-7859-1862-0*, 2070369811) Fr & Eur.
Siecle Litteraire de Louis XV: ou Lettres sur les Hommes Celebres, 2 vols. in 1. Pierre-Louis D' Aquin de Chateau-Lyon. LC 76-43913. (Music & Theatre in France in the 17th & 18th Centuries Ser.). reprint ed. 57.50 (*0-404-60156-1*) AMS Pr.
Sieg Heil! The Nineteen Forty Book Catalogue of the Central Publishing House of the Nazi Party. LC 85-421. (Studies in Judaica & the Holocaust: No. 4). 80p. pap. write for info. (*0-89370-930-1*); lib. bdg. write for info. (*0-89370-830-5*) Borgo Pr.
Sieg Heil! An Illustrated History of Germany from Bismarck to Hitler. (Illus.). 1981. 24.95 (*0-918058-03-1*) Authors Edn MA.
Sieg Heil! War Letters of Tank Gunner Karl Fuchs, 1937-1941. Tr. & Compiled by Horst F. Richardson. LC 87-1327. (Illus.). viii, 171p. (C). 1987. lib. bdg. 29.50 (*0-208-02141-8*, Archon Bks) Shoe String.
Siegal-Margolis Dog Library: The Golden Years. Mardecai Siegal & Matthew Margolis. 1996. 18.95 (*0-316-79017-6*) Little.
Siegal-Margolis Dog Library: The Good Shepherd: A Pet Owner's Guide to the German Shepherd. Mordecai Siegal & Matthew Margolis. 1996. 18.95 (*0-316-79019-2*) Little.
Siege. Bill Baldwin. 320p. (Orig.). 1994. mass mkt. 5.50 (*0-446-36503-3*, Aspect) Warner Bks.
Siege. Peter David. (Star Trek: Deep Space Nine Ser.: No. 2). 288p. (Orig.). 1993. mass mkt. 5.50 (*0-671-87083-1*) PB.
***Siege.** Simon Hawke. (Birthright Ser.). 1997. pap. 5.99 (*0-7869-0759-2*) TSR Inc.
Siege. Paul Mayersberg. Date not set. pap. write for info. (*0-670-81367-2*) Viking Penguin.
Siege: A Novel. Graham Petrie. LC 95-9076. 195p. 1996. 21.00 (*1-56947-076-6*) Soho Press.
Siege: A Story of Bosnia. Michael Kelly. 224p. 1998. 23.00 (*0-679-41121-6*) Fodors Travel.
***Siege - 1759: The Campaign Against Niagara.** 2nd rev. ed. Brian L. Dunnigan. (Illus.). 168p. (Orig.). 1996. pap. 14.95 (*0-941967-15-8*) Old Fort Niagara Assn.
Siege & Reduction of Fort Pulaski. Quincy A. Gillmore. (Illus.). 112p. (C). 1988. reprint ed. pap. 7.95 (*0-939631-07-5*) Thomas Publications.
Siege & Survival: The Odussey of a Leningrader. Elena Skrjabina. (Soviet Union at War Ser.: Vol. 1). 186p. 1971. 32.95 (*0-88738-511-7*) Transaction Pubs.

An Asterisk (*) at the beginning of an entry indicates that the title is appearing in BIP for the first time.

*__Siege & Survival: The Odyssey of a Leningrader.__ Elena Skriabina. LC 97-12341. 1997. write for info. (*1-56000-538-6*) Transaction Pubs.

Siege Artillery in the Campaigns Against Richmond with Notes on the 15-Inch Gun. Henry L. Abbot. (Illus.). 192p. (C). 1986. reprint ed. 24.95 (*0-939631-04-0*) Thomas Publications.

Siege at Forlorn River. Romer Z. Grey. (Zane Grey's Yaqui Ser.). 288p. 1985. mass mkt., pap. text ed. 2.75 (*0-8439-2192-7*) Dorchester Pub Co.

Siege City: The Story of Derry & Londonderry. Brian Lacy. (Town History Ser.). 288p. (Orig.). 9000. pap. 26.00 (*0-85640-443-8*, Pub. by Blackstaff Pr IE) Dufour.

Siege in Peking: China Against the World. William A. Martin. LC 72-79832. (China Library). 1972. reprint ed. lib. bdg. 23.00 (*0-8420-1376-8*) Scholarly Res Inc.

Siege of Boston. Allen French. LC 68-58326. (Illus.). 1969. reprint ed. 20.00 (*0-87152-052-4*) Reprint.

Siege of Burgos, the Retreat from Burgos the Campaign of Vittoria, the Battles of the Pyrennes, Sept. 1, 1812-Aug. 5, 1813 see History of the Peninsular War

Siege of Charleston. Ed. by Bernard A. Uhlendorf. LC 67-29028. (Eyewitness Accounts of the American Revolution Ser., No. 1). 1976. reprint ed. 25.95 (*0-405-01125-3*) Ayer.

Siege of Charleston, 1861-1865. E. Milby Burton. LC 70-120584. xxii, 390p. 1976. pap. 14.95 (*0-87249-345-8*) U of SC Pr.

Siege of Darkness. R. A. Salvatore. (Forgotten Realms Ser.). 352p. (Orig.). 1995. pap. 5.99 (*0-7869-0164-0*) TSR Inc.

Siege of Dome. Stephen R. Lawhead. (Empyrion Saga Ser.: Vol. 2). 464p. 1996. pap. 13.00 (*0-310-20508-5*) Zondervan.

*__Siege of Eternity.__ Pohl. LC 97-15567. 1997. 22.95 (*0-312-86375-6*) St Martin.

Siege of Fort Cumberland, 1776. Ernest Clarke. 1995. 39.95 (*0-7735-1323-X*, Pub. by McGill CN) U of Toronto Pr.

Siege of Fort Macon. Ed. by Paul R. Branch, Jr. (Illus.). 105p. (Orig.). 1982. pap. 5.00 (*0-9614000-0-5*) P Branch.

Siege of Gibraltar, Seventeen Seventy-Nine to Seventeen Eighty-Three. T. H. McGuffie. LC 64-25508. (Illus.). 1965. 15.95 (*0-8023-1074-5*) Dufour.

Siege of Jerusalem. (EETS, OS Ser.: No. 188). 1974. reprint ed. 40.00 (*0-527-00188-0*) Periodicals Srv.

Siege of Krishnapur. J. G. Farrell. 344p. 1985. pap. 4.95 (*0-88184-195-1*) Carroll & Graf.

*__Siege of Krishnapur.__ J. G. Farrell. 368p. 1997. pap. 12.95 (*0-7867-0484-5*) Carroll & Graf.

Siege of Leningrad. Leon Goure. LC 62-8662. (Illus.). xiv, 367p. 1962. 47.50 (*0-8047-0115-6*) Stanford U Pr.

Siege of Leningrad. Leon Goure. LC 62-8662. 111p. reprint ed. pap. 30.00 (*0-7837-1225-1*, 2041756) Bks Demand.

Siege of London. Henry James. 1972. 59.95 (*0-8490-1053-5*) Gordon Pr.

Siege of Mazagao: A Perilous Moment in the Defence of Christendom Against Islam. John R. Martyn. LC 93-15019. (American University Studies). 264p. (C). 1994. text ed. 43.95 (*0-8204-2210-X*) P Lang Pubng.

Siege of Ocean Valkyrie. John-Allen Price. 1992. mass mkt. 4.50 (*0-8217-3662-0*, Zebra Kensgtn) Kensgtn Pub Corp.

Siege of Penobscot by the Rebels & the Proceedings of the General Assembly & of the Council of the State of Massachusetts Bay Relating to the Penobscot Expedition. Ed. by John Calef. LC 78-140857. (Eyewitness Accounts of the American Revolution Ser., No. 1). (Illus.). 1971. reprint ed. 14.95 (*0-405-01226-8*) Ayer.

Siege of Petersburg. Noah A. Trudeau. (Civil War Ser.). (Illus.). 52p. (Orig.). 1995. pap. 4.95 (*0-915992-82-5*) Eastern Acorn.

Siege of Rabaul. Henry Sakaida. LC 95-72892. (Illus.). 96p. (Orig.). 1996. pap. 16.95 (*1-883809-09-6*) Phalanx Pub.

Siege of Savannah. Franklin B. Hough. LC 77-165683. (Era of the American Revolution Ser.). 187p. 1974. reprint ed. lib. bdg. 27.50 (*0-306-70619-9*) Da Capo.

Siege of Savannah. Charles C. Jones, Jr. 184p. 1996. reprint ed. 20.00 (*1-881454-05-3*) Amer Hist Bks.

Siege of Savannah, in 1779 As Described in Two Contemporaneous Journals of French Officers in the Fleet of Count D'estaing. Ed. by Charles C. Jones, Jr. LC 67-29027. (Eyewitness Accounts of the American Revolution Ser., No. 1). 1976. reprint ed. 16.95 (*0-405-01115-6*) Ayer.

Siege of Shadows. Lynn Abbey. 1996. mass mkt. 6.50 (*0-441-00306-0*) Ace Bks.

Siege of South Africa: What the Press Doesn't Tell You. Ivor Benson. 1986. lib. bdg. 79.50 (*0-8490-3820-0*) Gordon Pr.

Siege of Suffolk: The Forgotten Campaign April 11-May 4, 1863. Steven A. Cormier. (Virginia Civil War Battles & Leaders Ser.). (Illus.). 445p. 1989. 19.95 (*0-930919-82-3*) H E Howard.

Siege of the Castle of Edinburgh. Ed. by Robert Bell. LC 78-39425. (Bannatyne Club, Edinburgh. Publications: No. 23). reprint ed. 22.00 (*0-404-52729-9*) AMS Pr.

Siege of Three Eighteen: Thirteen Mystical Stories. Davis Grubb. LC 78-61067. 180p. 1978. 12.00 (*0-686-37046-5*) Back Fork Bks.

Siege of Wonder. Mark S. Geston. LC 75-36624. 180p. 1976. 25.00 (*0-385-11359-5*) Ultramarine Pub.

Siege Perilous: Essays in Biblical Anthropology & Kindred Subjects. Samuel H. Hooke. LC 73-130552. (Select Bibliographies Reprint Ser.). 1977. reprint ed. 20.95 (*0-8369-5525-0*) Ayer.

Siege Perilous, & Other Stories. Maud Diver. LC 78-122694. (Short Story Index Reprint Ser.). 1977. 19.95 (*0-8369-3527-6*) Ayer.

Siege Train: The Journal of a Confederate Artilleryman in the Defense of Charleston. Ed. by Warren Ripley. 386p. 1986. 24.95 (*0-87249-491-8*) U of SC Pr.

Siege Train: The Journal of a Confederate Artilleryman in the Defense of Charleston. Ed. by Warren Ripley. (Illus.). 386p. 1996. pap. 16.95 (*1-57003-127-4*) U of SC Pr.

*__Siege Warfare: Fortress in the Early Modern World 1494-1660.__ Christopher Duffy. 304p. (C). 1997. pap. 19.95 (*0-415-14649-6*) Routledge.

Siegel Criminal Justice 94. rev. ed. Date not set. pap. text ed. write for info. (*0-314-05383-2*) West Pub.

Siegel Criminology. 5th ed. Date not set. student ed., pap. text ed. 19.00 (*0-314-05814-1*) West Pub.

Siegel Film: An Autobiography. Don Siegel. (Illus.). 600p. 1993. 24.95 (*0-571-16270-3*) Faber & Faber.

Siegel Film: An Autobiography. Don Siegal. (Illus.). 300p. 1996. reprint ed. pap. 17.95 (*0-571-17831-6*) Faber & Faber.

Siegel's Q's & A's on Civil Procedure. 3rd rev. ed. Brian Siegel. 165p. 1996. pap. text ed. 15.95 (*1-56542-341-0*) E Pub Corp.

*__Siegel's Q's & A's on Constitutional Law.__ Brian Siegel. 205p. 1997. pap. text ed. 15.95 (*1-56542-345-3*) E Pub Corp.

Siegel's Q's & A's on Contracts 1993. 160p. 1993. pap. text ed. 15.95 (*1-56542-333-X*) E Pub Corp.

Siegel's Q's & A's on Criminal Law 1993. 160p. 1993. pap. text ed. 15.95 (*1-56542-334-8*) E Pub Corp.

Siegel's Q's & A's on Criminal Procedure 1993. 160p. 1996. pap. text ed. 15.95 (*1-56542-335-6*) E Pub Corp.

Siegel's Q's & A's on Evidence. 3rd rev. ed. Brian Siegel. 180p. 1996. pap. text ed. 15.95 (*1-56542-342-9*) E Pub Corp.

Siegel's Q's & A's on Evidence 1993. 160p. pap. text ed. 14.95 (*1-56542-336-4*) E Pub Corp.

*__Siegel's Q's & A's on Professional Responsibility.__ (Siegel's Ser.). (Orig.). (C). 1997. pap. text ed. 15.95 (*1-56542-343-7*) E Pub Corp.

Siegel's Q's & A's on Real Property 1993. 160p. 1996. pap. text ed. 15.95 (*1-56542-337-2*) E Pub Corp.

Siegel's Q's & A's on Torts 1993. 160p. 1994. pap. text ed. 15.95 (*1-56542-338-0*) E Pub Corp.

Siegel's Q's & A's on Wills & Trusts 1993. 160p. 1995. pap. text ed. 15.95 (*1-56542-339-9*) E Pub Corp.

Sieges: A Comparative Study. Bruce W. Watson. LC 92-46422. 192p. 1993. text ed. 52.95 (*0-275-94034-9*, C4034, Praeger Pubs) Greenwood.

*__Siegfreid Sassoon.__ Moeyes. LC 96-46418. 1997. text ed. 35.00 (*0-312-17277-X*) St Martin.

Siegfried. Jean Giraudoux. pap. 9.50 (*0-685-33926-2*) Fr & Eur.

Siegfried. Richard Wagner. Ed. by Nicholas John. Tr. by Andrew Porter from GER. (English National Opera Guide Series: Bilingual Libretto, Articles: No. 28). (Illus.). 1984. pap. 9.95 (*0-7145-4040-4*) Riverrun NY.

Siegfried: Libretto. Richard Wagner. 84p. (GER.). 1989. pap. 4.95 (*0-7935-4715-6*, 50340500) H Leonard.

*__Siegfried: Translation & Commentary.__ Richard Wagner. (Illus.). 1997. pap. 14.95 (*0-7148-3653-2*, Pub. by Phaidon Press UK) Chronicle Bks.

Siegfried see Theatre

Siegfried et le Limousin. Jean Giraudoux. (FRE.). 1956. pap. 26.95 (*0-8288-9806-5*, F104230) Fr & Eur.

Siegfried Sassoon: A Memorial Exhibition. Illus. by David Price. LC 77-628295. 1969. pap. 8.00 (*0-87959-007-6*) U of Tex H Ransom Ctr.

Siegfried Sassoon Diaries: 1915-1918. Siegfried Sassoon. Ed. by Rupert Hart-Davis. 296p. 1983. 22.95 (*0-571-11997-2*) Faber & Faber.

Siegfried Sassoon Diaries: 1920-1922. Siegfried Sassoon. Ed. by Rupert Hart-Davis. 304p. 1983. 23.95 (*0-571-11685-X*) Faber & Faber.

Siegfried Sassoon Diaries: 1923-1925. Ed. by Rupert Hart-Davis. 300p. 1984. 27.95 (*0-571-13322-3*) Faber & Faber.

Siegfried's Journey: 1916-1920. Siegfried Sassoon. 224p. (C). 1982. reprint ed. pap. 5.95 (*0-571-11917-4*) Faber & Faber.

*__Siembra y Cosecha, Vol. 1.__ L. Walker. (SPA.). 5.95 (*0-8297-0297-0*) Life Pubs Intl.

*__Siembra y Cosecha, Vol. 2.__ L. Walker. (SPA.). 5.95 (*0-8297-0298-9*) Life Pubs Intl.

*__Siembra y Cosecha, Vol. 3.__ L. Walker. 5.95 (*0-8297-0299-7*) Life Pubs Intl.

*__Siembra y Cultiva.__ Marilyn Lashbrook. (SPA.). 1997. pap. 3.50 (*0-8254-1419-9*, Edit Portavoz) Kregel.

*__Siemens: 1918-1945.__ Wilfried Feldenkirchen. 1997. 69.50 (*0-614-27830-9*) Ohio St U Pr.

*__Siemens, 1918-1945.__ Wilfried Feldenkirchen. LC 97-23348. (Historical Perspectives on Business Enterprise Ser.). 1998. 96.75 (*0-8142-0723-5*) Ohio St U Pr.

Siempre Junto a Ti. Rafael Crespo. (Romance Real Ser.). 192p. (SPA.). 1981. pap. 1.50 (*0-88025-004-6*) Roca Pub.

Siempre la Lluvia. Jose A. Felippe. LC 94-71766. (Coleccion Caniqui). 277p. (Orig.). (SPA.). 1994. pap. 19.00 (*0-89729-741-5*) Ediciones.

Siempre Puede Ser Peor: It Could Always Be Worse. Margot Zemach. Tr. by Aida E. Marcuse. (Illus.). 32p. (SPA.). (J). (ps-3). 1992. 17.00 (*0-374-36907-0*, Mirasol) FS&G.

Siempre Sere tu Nina Pequena. H. Norman Wright. Orig. Title: Always Daddy's Girl. 240p. (SPA.). 1991. pap. 8.99 (*0-8254-1890-9*, Edit Portavoz) Kregel.

Siempre Te Amare. N. Norman Wright. 231p. (SPA.). 1994. pap. 7.99 (*1-56063-580-0*, 498438) Editorial Unilit.

Siempre Te Querre (Love You Forever) Robert Munsch. (Illus.). 32p. (J). 1992. pap. 4.95 (*1-895565-01-4*) Firefly Bks Ltd.

*__Siempre Unidos.__ Rita Rainville. (SPA.). 1997. mass mkt. 3.50 (*0-373-35184-4*, 1-35184-0) Harlequin Bks.

Siena & the Sienese in the Thirteenth Century. Daniel Waley. (Illus.). 300p. (C). 1991. 59.95 (*0-521-40312-X*) Cambridge U Pr.

Siena, Biblioteca Comunale Degli Intronati, MS K. I. 2. Ed. by Brown et al. (Renaissance Music in Facsimile Ser.: Vol. 17). 464p. 1986. text ed. 35.00 (*0-8240-1466-9*) Garland.

Siena, Florence, & Padua: Art, Society, & Religion, 1280-1400, Vol. 2. Diana Norman. (Case Studies). 1995. pap. 27.50 (*0-300-06127-7*) Yale U Pr.

*__Siena, Florence, & Padua Vol. II: Art, Society, & Religion, 1280-1400.__ Ed. by Diana Norman. 1996. 55.00 (*0-300-06126-9*) Yale U Pr.

Sienese Altarpieces, 1215-1460: Form, Content, Function, Volume Two: 1344-1460. Henk Van Os. (Mediaevalia Groningana Ser.: Vol. 9). 261p. 1990. 63.00 (*90-6980-027-6*, Pub. by Egbert Forsten NE); pap. 49.95 (*90-6980-028-4*, Pub. by Egbert Forsten NE) Benjamins North Am.

Sienese Altarpieces, 1215-1460, Vol. 1: 1215-1344. 2nd ed. Henk Van Os. (Illus.). 163p. (Orig.). (C). 1988. pap. 29.95 (*90-6980-022-5*, Pub. by Egbert Forsten NE) Benjamins North Am.

Sienese Painting in the Age of the Renaissance. Bruce Cole. LC 84-48246. (Illus.). 216p. 1985. 39.95 (*0-253-18130-5*) Ind U Pr.

Sienese Renaissance Tomb Monuments. Robert Munman. LC 92-85343. (Memoirs Ser.: Vol. 205). (Illus.). 295p. (C). 1993. 25.00 (*0-87169-205-8*, M205-MUR) Am Philos.

Sienese Trecento Painter Bartolo di Fredi. Patricia Harpring. LC 90-55831. (Illus.). 192p. (C). 1993. 65.00 (*0-8386-3401-X*) Fairleigh Dickinson.

Sieneser Domkanzel des Nicola Pisano. Joachim Poeschke. LC 72-81565. (Beitraege zur Kunstgeschichte Ser.: Vol. 9). (C). 1973. 62.35 (*3-11-003961-3*) De Gruyter.

Sienitieteelinen Sanasto Suomi-Venaja-Latina. A. Novitsky. 190p. (FIN, LAT & RUS.). 1984. 29.95 (*0-8288-1250-0*, F22445) Fr & Eur.

Sienna, Florence & Padua: Art, Society & Religion 1280-1400, Vol. 1. LC 94-25653. 1995. pap. 27.50 (*0-300-06125-0*) Yale U Pr.

Sienna, Florence & Padua: Art, Society & Religion 1280-1400, Vol. 1. Ed. by Diana Norman. LC 94-25653. 1995. 55.00 (*0-300-06124-2*) Yale U Pr.

Sienna Red. Stephen Poliakoff. (Methuen Modern Plays Ser.). 106p. (C). 1992. pap. 9.95 (*0-413-66430-9*, A0633, Pub. by Methuen UK) Heinemann.

Sierra. Shari MacDonald. 257p. 1995. pap. 8.99 (*0-88070-726-7*, Multnomah Bks) Multnomah Pubs.

Sierra. Connie Mason. 448p. (Orig.). 1995. mass mkt., pap. text ed. 5.99 (*0-8439-3815-3*) Dorchester Pub Co.

Sierra. Diane Siebert. LC 90-30522. (Illus.). 32p. (J). (ps-3). 1991. 16.00 (*0-06-021639-5*); lib. bdg. 15.89 (*0-06-021640-9*) HarpC Child Bks.

Sierra. Diane Siebert. LC 90-30522. (Trophy Picture Bk.). (Illus.). 32p. (J). (ps-3). 1996. pap. 4.95 (*0-06-443441-9*, Trophy) HarpC Child Bks.

Sierra: A Novel of the California Gold Rush. Richard S. Wheeler. LC 96-8305. 384p. 1996. 24.95 (*0-312-86185-0*) Forge NYC.

*__Sierra: A Novel of the California Gold Rush.__ large type ed. Richard S. Wheeler. LC 96-43643. 696p. 1997. 24.95 (*0-7862-0916-X*, Thorndike Lrg Prnt) Thorndike Pr.

Sierra: Sierra Mountain Flowers. Millie Miller. (Pocket Nature Guides Ser.). (Illus.). 40p. (Orig.). 1981. pap. 5.95 (*0-933472-57-9*) Johnson Bks.

Sierra Adventures. Fraser Bridges. (Driver's Guide Ser.). (Illus.). 352p. pap. 14.95 (*0-9694136-7-X*) Amer Traveler.

*__Sierra Baron.__ Tom W. Blackburn. 304p. 1997. reprint ed. mass mkt. 4.99 (*0-8439-4304-1*, Leisure Bks) Dorchester Pub Co.

Sierra Big Trees. abr. ed. John Muir. Ed. by William R. Jones. (Illus.). 80p. 1981. reprint ed. pap. 4.95 (*0-89646-069-X*) Vistabooks.

Sierra Classics: 100 Best Climbs in the High Sierra. John Moynier & Claude Fiddler. (Illus.). 318p. (Orig.). 1993. pap. 25.00 (*0-934641-60-9*) Chockstone Pr.

Sierra Club: One Hundred Years of Protecting Nature. Tom Turner. (Illus.). 288p. 1991. 49.50 (*0-8109-3820-0*) Abrams.

Sierra Club Alaska Postcard Collection: A Portfolio. Art Wolfe. 1989. pap. 8.95 (*0-87156-606-0*) Sierra.

Sierra Club Book of Great Mammals. Linsay Knight. LC 92-11373. (Illus.). 72p. (YA). (gr. 5 up). 1992. 16.95 (*0-87156-507-2*) Sierra Club Childrens.

Sierra Club Book of Small Mammals. Linsay Knight. LC 92-28859. (Illus.). 72p. (YA). (gr. 5 up). 1993. 16.95 (*0-87156-525-0*) Sierra Club Childrens.

Sierra Club Desert Reader: A Literary Companion. Ed. by Gregory McNamee. LC 95-5603. 384p. (Orig.). 1995. pap. 16.00 (*0-87156-426-2*) Sierra.

Sierra Club Family Outdoors Guide. rev. ed. Marlyn Doan. LC 94-35087. 1995. pap. 12.00 (*0-87156-442-4*) Sierra.

Sierra Club Green Guide: Everybody's Desk Reference to Environmental Information. Andrew J. Feldman. LC 95-2438. 304p. (Orig.). 1996. pap. 25.00 (*0-87156-402-5*) Sierra.

*__Sierra Club Guide to Natural Areas of California.__ John Perry. 352p. 1997. pap. 15.00 (*0-87156-850-0*) Sierra.

Sierra Club Guide to Safe Drinking Water. Scott A. Lewis. LC 95-38942. 120p. (Orig.). 1996. pap. 10.00 (*0-87156-355-X*) Sierra.

Sierra Club Guide to Sketching in Nature. Cathy Johnson. LC 90-45266. (Illus.). 224p. 1991. 30.00 (*0-87156-691-5*); pap. 18.00 (*0-87156-554-4*) Sierra.

*__Sierra Club Guide to Sketching in Nature.__ Cathy Johnson. 240p. 1997. pap. 20.00 (*0-87156-932-9*) Sierra.

Sierra Club Guide to the National Parks of the Rocky Mountains & the Great Plains: The Rocky Mountains & the Great Plains. rev. ed. Text by Conger Beasley, Jr. et al. LC 95-11447. (Sierra Club Guides to the National Parks Ser.). (Illus.). 280p. 1995. pap. 24.95 (*0-679-76496-8*) Stewart Tabori & Chang.

Sierra Club Guide to the Natural Areas of California. John Perry & Jane G. Perry. LC 82-16939. (Sierra Club Guides to the Natural Areas of the United States Ser.). (Illus.). 352p. (Orig.). 1983. pap. 12.00 (*0-87156-333-9*) Sierra.

Sierra Club Guide to the Natural Areas of Colorado & Utah. John Perry & Jane G. Perry. LC 84-22215. (Guides to the Natural Areas of the United States Ser.). (Illus.). 416p. (Orig.). 1985. pap. 10.00 (*0-87156-832-2*) Sierra.

Sierra Club Guide to the Natural Areas of Florida. John Perry & Jane G. Perry. LC 92-905. (Guides to the Natural Areas of the United States Ser.). 416p. (Orig.). 1992. pap. 12.00 (*0-87156-551-X*) Sierra.

Sierra Club Guide to the Natural Areas of Idaho, Montana & Wyoming. John Perry & Jane G. Perry. LC 87-26312. (Guides to the Natural Areas of the United States Ser.). 416p. (Orig.). 1988. pap. 14.00 (*0-87156-781-4*) Sierra.

*__Sierra Club Guide to the Natural Areas of New England.__ John Perry. 1997. pap. 15.00 (*0-87156-940-X*) Sierra.

Sierra Club Guide to the Natural Areas of New England: Maine, Vermont, New Hampshire, Massachusetts, Rhode Island, & Connecticut. John Perry & Jane G. Perry. LC 89-37536. (Guides to the Natural Areas of the United States Ser.). (Illus.). 400p. 1990. pap. 14.00 (*0-87156-744-X*) Sierra.

S

Sierra Club Guide to the Natural Areas of New Mexico, Arizona, & Nevada. John Perry & Jane G. Perry. LC 85-18481. (Guides to the Natuareal Areas of the United States Ser.). (Illus.). 448p. 1986. pap. 12.00 (*0-87156-753-9*) Sierra.

*__Sierra Club Guide to the Natural Areas of Oregon & Washington.__ John Perry. 352p. 1997. pap. 15.00 (*0-87156-939-6*) Sierra.

Sierra Club Guide to 35MM Landscape Photography. Tim Fitzharris. 112p. 1996. pap. 20.00 (*0-87156-902-7*) Sierra.

Sierra Club Guides to the National Parks of California, Hawaii, & American Samoa: California, Hawaii, & American Samoa. rev. ed. Text by Joseph E. Brown et al. LC 95-11450. (Sierra Club Guides to the National Parks Ser.). (Illus.). 352p. 1995. pap. 24.95 (*0-679-76497-6*) Stewart Tabori & Chang.

Sierra Club Guides to the National Parks of the Desert Southwest: The Desert Southwest. rev. ed. Ed. by James V. Murfin & Irene Pavitt. LC 95-11448. (Sierra Club Guides to the National Parks Ser.). (Illus.). 400p. 1995. pap. 24.95 (*0-679-76493-3*) Random.

Sierra Club Guides to the National Parks of the East & Middle West: The East & the Middle West. rev. ed. Text by William A. Bake et al. LC 95-11446. (Sierra Club Guides to the National Parks Ser.). (Illus.). 412p. 1995. pap. 24.95 (*0-679-76494-1*) Random.

Sierra Club Guides to the National Parks of the Pacific Northwest & Alaska: The Pacific Northwest & Alaska. rev. ed. Text by Robert Belous et al. LC 95-11449. (Sierra Club Guides to the National Parks Ser.). (Illus.). 400p. 1995. pap. 24.95 (*0-679-76495-X*) Random.

Sierra Club Handbook of Seals & Sirenians. Randall R. Reeves et al. LC 92-946. (Illus.). 350p. (Orig.). 1992. pap. 18.00 (*0-87156-656-7*) Sierra.

Sierra Club Handbook of Whales & Dolphins. Stephen Leatherwood & Randall R. Reeves. LC 83-388. (Illus.). 320p. 1983. pap. 18.00 (*0-87156-340-1*) Sierra.

Sierra Club Home Planet Postcard Collection: Images from the Home Planet. Kevin W. Kelley. 1989. pap. 8.95 (*0-87156-605-2*) Sierra.

Sierra Club Mother Earth Postcard Collection: Through the Eyes of Women Photographers. Ed. by Judith Boice. LC 92-2681. (Illus.). 46p. 1993. pap. 9.00 (*0-87156-456-4*) Sierra.

Sierra Club Mountain Light Postcard Collection: A Portfolio. Galen A. Rowell. LC 87-13201. (Illus.). 64p. (Orig.). 1987. pap. 9.00 (*0-87156-779-2*) Sierra.

Sierra Club Naturalist's Guide to Southern New England. Neil Jorgensen. LC 77-28543. (Naturalist's Guides Ser.). (Illus.). 448p. 1982. pap. 18.00 (*0-87156-183-2*) Sierra.

Sierra Club Naturalist's Guide to the Deserts of the Southwest. Peggy Larson & Lane Larson. LC 76-24835. (Naturalist's Guides Ser.). (Illus.). 288p. 1982. pap. 12.00 (*0-87156-186-7*) Sierra.

Sierra Club Naturalist's Guide to the Middle Atlantic Coast: Cape Hatteras to Cape Cod. Bill Perry. LC 83-18691. (Naturalist's Guides Ser.). (Illus.). 448p. (Orig.). 1985. pap. 14.00 (*0-87156-816-0*) Sierra.

Sierra Club Naturalist's Guide to the North Atlantic Coast: Cape Cod to Newfoundland. Michael Berrill & Deborah Berrill. LC 80-23086. (Naturalist's Guides Ser.). (Illus.). 512p. 1982. pap. 16.00 (*0-87156-243-X*) Sierra.

Sierra Club Naturalist's Guide to the North Woods of Michigan, Wisconsin, Minnesota & Southern Ontario. Glenda Daniel & Jerry Sullivan. LC 80-28742. (Naturalist's Guides Ser.). (Illus.). 384p. 1982. pap. 16.00 (*0-87156-277-4*) Sierra.

Sierra Club Naturalist's Guide to the Pacific Northwest. Stephen Whitney. LC 88-23937. (Naturalist's Guides Ser.). (Illus.). 352p. 1989. pap. 16.00 (*0-87156-696-6*) Sierra.

Sierra Club Naturalist's Guide to the Sierra Nevada. Stephen Whitney. LC 79-766. (Naturalist's Guides Ser.). (Illus.). 544p. 1982. pap. 18.00 (*0-87156-216-2*) Sierra.

Sierra Club Naturalist's Guide to the Southern Rockies: The Rocky Mountain Regions of Southern Wyoming, Colorado, & Northern New Mexico. Audrey D. Benedict. LC 89-10569. (Naturalist's Guides Ser.). (Illus.). 512p. 1991. 30.00 (*0-87156-741-5*); pap. 18.00 (*0-87156-647-8*) Sierra.

Sierra Club Nature Writing Handbook: A Creative Guide. John A. Murray. LC 95-5601. 208p. (Orig.). 1995. pap. 14.00 (*0-87156-436-X*) Sierra.

Sierra Club Summer Book. Linda Allison. (Illus.). 160p. (J). (gr. 3-7). 1989. pap. 7.95 (*0-316-03433-9*) Little.

Sierra Club Summer Book. Linda Allison. LC 93-41481. (Illus.). 160p. (J). 1994. 8.99 (*0-517-10082-7*) Random Hse Value.

Sierra Club Wetlands Reader: A Literary Companion. Ed. by Sam Wilson & Tom Moritz. LC 95-5602. 288p. (Orig.). 1996. pap. 15.00 (*0-87156-425-4*) Sierra.

Sierra Club Yosemite Postcard Collection: A Portofolio. Galen A. Rowell. 1989. pap. 8.95 (*0-87156-604-4*) Sierra.

Sierra Cycle. Lani Steele. (Illus.). 31p. (Orig.). 1989. write for info. (*0-9616635-3-7*) Oblong Pr.

Sierra Flower Finder: A Guide to Sierra Nevada Wildflowers. Glenn Keator. (Illus.). 128p. 1980. pap. 3.75 (*0-912550-09-0*) Nature Study.

Sierra High Route. Paul K. Edwards, Jr. LC 95-69763. (Illus.). 60p. (Orig.). 1995. pap. 8.00 (*0-9649604-0-0*) Surfrider.

***Sierra High Route: Traversing Timberline Country.** 2nd rev. ed. Steve Roper. LC 96-49269. (Illus.). 224p. (Orig.). 1997. pap. 16.95 (*0-89886-506-9*) Mountaineers.

Sierra Leone. M. Binns. (World Bibliographical Ser.). 1992. lib. bdg. 81.50 (*1-85109-101-7*) ABC-CLIO.

***Sierra Leone: A Final Report.** 102p. (Orig.). 1996. pap. text ed. 10.50 (*1-885205-05-8*) African-Amer.

Sierra Leone after a Hundred Years. E. G. Ingham. (Illus.). 368p. 1968. reprint ed. 42.00 (*0-7146-1819-5*, Pub. by F Cass Pubs UK) Intl Spec Bk.

Sierra Leone As It Was & Is: Its Progress, People, Native Customs, & Undeveloped Wealth. Thomas J. Alldridge. 1976. lib. bdg. 59.95 (*0-8490-2602-4*) Gordon Pr.

Sierra Leone's Settler Women Traders: Women on the Afro-European Frontier. E. Frances White. (Women & Culture Ser.). (Illus.). 200p. 1987. text ed. 42.50 (*0-472-10080-7*) U of Mich Pr.

Sierra Mountaineering. Leonard Daughenbaugh. (Illus.). 1990. 32.50 (*0-939919-11-7*) Bear Flag Bks.

Sierra Nevada: A Mountain Journey. Tim Palmer. LC 88-13019. (Illus.). 334p. 1988. 31.95 (*0-933280-54-8*); pap. 15.95 (*0-933280-53-X*) Island Pr.

Sierra Nevada Big Trees: History of the Exhibitions 1850-1903. Dennis G. Kruska. 1985. 30.00 (*0-87093-188-1*) Dawsons.

Sierra Nevada Byways: Backcountry Drives for the Whole Family. Tony Huegel. 1994. pap. 10.95 (*0-9636560-4-X*) Post ID.

***Sierra Nevada Flora.** 4th ed. Norman F. Weedon. (Illus.). 1996. pap. 15.95 (*0-89997-204-7*) Wilderness Pr.

Sierra-Nevada Lakes. George Hinkle & Bliss Hinkle. LC 87-13795. (Vintage West Ser.). (Illus.). 286p. 1987. reprint ed. pap. 14.95 (*0-87417-123-7*) U of Nev Pr.

Sierra Nevada Natural History: An Illustrated Handbook. Tracy I. Storer & Robert L. Usinger. (Illus.). 1963. pap. 14.95 (*0-520-01227-5*) U CA Pr.

***Sierra Nevada Tree Identifier.** Jim Paruk. (Illus.). 96p. 1996. pap. 9.95 (*0-939666-83-9*) Yosemite Assn.

Sierra Nevadan Wildlife Region. 4th rev. ed. Vinson Brown. LC 95-42041. (Illus.). 144p. 1996. pap. 8.95 (*0-87961-227-4*) Naturegraph.

***Sierra North.** 7th ed. Thomas Winnett et al. LC 97-18964. (Illus.). 312p. (Orig.). 1997. pap. 14.95 (*0-89997-212-8*) Wilderness Pr.

Sierra Pacific: A Family History: A Forester's Perspective. J. Bud Tomascheski. LC 91-66688. 400p. 1991. text ed. 30.00 (*0-9630947-1-8*) B Tomascheski.

Sierra Railroad: A Portfolio. Lowell Amrine. LC 86-2307. 32p. 1986. reprint ed. lib. bdg. 25.00 (*0-89370-554-3*) Borgo Pr.

Sierra South. 6th ed. Thomas Winnett et al. (Illus.). 296p. 1993. pap. 14.95 (*0-89997-162-8*) Wilderness Pr.

***Sierra Stories: True Tales of Tahoe.** Mark McLaughlin. LC 97-93297. (Illus.). 120p. (Orig.). 1997. pap. 11.95 (*0-9657202-1-7*) Mic Mac Pub.

Sierra Sue II: The Story of a P-51 Mustang. John Christgau. (Illus.). 188p. (Orig.). 1994. pap. 15.00 (*0-9640256-0-4*) Great Planes.

Sierra Summer. Mary J. Kelso. (Lynne Garrett Adventure Ser.: No. 3). (Illus.). 120p. (Orig.). (YA). (gr. 6 up). 1992. pap. 4.95 (*0-9621406-3-5*) MarKel Pr.

Sierra Trout Guide. rev. ed. Ralph Cutter. (Illus.). 112p. (Orig.). 1991. reprint ed. pap. 19.95 (*1-878175-02-5*) F Amato Pubns.

Sierra Tucson Cookbook: Recipes for a New Healthstyle. Sierra Tucson Staff. 192p. 1993. pap. 14.95 (*0-922641-81-1*) Stem Pubns.

Sierra Valley Memories: With Artie Strang, Frank Dotta & Rita Bradley. Ed. by Helen M. Blue. (Illus.). 122p. 1990. lib. bdg. 35.50 (*1-56475-348-4*); fiche write for info. (*1-56475-349-2*) U NV Oral Hist.

Sierra Wildlife Coloring Book. Illus. by W. Berry et al. 16p. 1971. pap. 1.25 (*0-939666-15-4*) Yosemite Assn.

Sierra's Steeplechase. Joanna Campbell. (Thoroughbred Ser.: No. 8). 192p. (J). (gr. 4-7). 1993. mass mkt. 3.99 (*0-06-106164-6*, Harp PBks) HarpC.

Sierraville Experience: An Intriguing Anthology. Thomas. 272p. (Orig.). 1996. pap. 21.95 (*1-57087-212-0*) Prof Pr NC.

Siervos entre los Pobres. Viv Grigg. (Nueva Creacion Ser.). 246p. (SPA.). 1994. pap. text ed. 13.00 (*0-8028-0925-1*) Eerdmans.

***Sies Horas de un Viernes.** M. Lucado. (SPA.). 9.95 (*0-8297-0324-1*) Life Pubs Intl.

Siesta. Berry Fleming. LC 87-60785. 352p. 1987. 22.00 (*0-933256-66-3*) Second Chance.

Siesta de Tres Anos - Boy of the Three Year Nap. Dianne Snyder. (J). 1995. pap. text ed. 12.95 (*1-56014-182-4*) Santillana.

Siete Bolas de Cristal. Herge. (Illus.). 62p. (SPA.). (J). 19.95 (*0-8288-5074-7*) Fr & Eur.

Siete Cosas Que James Aceptare: El Secreto Para Vivir En Perdon, Paz, Confianza, Fuerza, Victoria Abundancia y Salud. Victor Ricardo. 30p. 1992. pap. 1.15 (*1-885630-00-X*) HLM Producciones.

Siete del Valle: A Collection of Rio Grande Valley Stories. Esperanza Ochoa. Ed. by Patricia De La Fuente. (Illus.). 209p. 1995. pap. text ed. 15.95 (*0-938738-14-3*) U TX Pan Am Pr.

***Siete Etapas en la Vida de un Hombe.** Patrick M. Morley. 1997. 10.99 (*0-88113-422-8*) Edit Betania.

Siete Hermanos Chinos - The Seven Chinese Brothers. Margaret Mahy. 40p. (J). (ps-3). 1994. pap. 5.95 (*0-590-48131-2*) Scholastic Inc.

Siete Impedimentos Para Recibir Sanidad. Kenneth Hagin, Jr. (SPA.). 1983. pap. 0.75 (*0-89276-175-X*) Hagin Ministries.

Siete Leyes de la Cosecha. John W. Lawrence. 128p. (SPA.). 1996. pap. 5.99 (*0-8254-1444-X*, Edit Portavoz) Kregel.

Siete Leyes Espirituales Del Exito: Una Guia Practica para la Realizacion de Tus Suenos. Deepak Chopra. 128p. 1995. pap. 10.95 (*1-878424-19-X*) Amber-Allen Pub.

Siete Libros de Diana. Jorge De Montemayor. Ed. by Enrique Moreno Baez. 239p. (SPA.). 1968. 100.00 (*0-614-00109-9*) Elliots Bks.

Siete Libros de Diana. Jorge De Montemayor. Ed. by Enrique Moreno Baez. 239p. (SPA.). 1968. pap. 100.00 (*0-614-00214-1*) Elliots Bks.

Siete Libros de la Diana. Jorge De Montemayor. Ed. by Julian Arribas. (Illus.). 384p. (C). 1996. 53.00 (*1-85566-044-X*, Pub. by Tamesis Bks Ltd UK) Boydell & Brewer.

Siete Necesidades Basicas Del Nino. John M. Drescher. 128p. (SPA.). 1986. reprint ed. pap. 7.99 (*0-311-46085-2*) Casa Bautista.

Siete Noches see Seven Nights

Siete Pasos a las Oracion Efectiva. William L. Asher, Jr. 44p. (Orig.). (SPA.). 1982. pap. 2.00 (*0-915235-07-2*) United Res.

Siete Pasos Para Recibir El Espiritu Santo. 2nd ed. Kenneth E. Hagin. (SPA.). 1983. pap. 1.95 (*0-89276-103-2*) Hagin Ministries.

***Siete Pecados Capitales de un Padre.** Daniel De Leon. Date not set. write for info. (*0-88113-410-4*) Edit Betania.

***Siete Promesas de un Cumplidor de Promesas.** (Serie Enfoque a la Familia - Focus on the Family Ser.). 230p. (SPA.). 1995. write for info. (*1-56063-878-8*) Editorial Unilit.

***Sietet Pasos Basicos para Ayunar y Orar con Exito - Seven Basic Steps to Successful Fasting & Prayer.** Bright. 24p. (SPA.). 1995. write for info. (*0-7899-0190-0*) Editorial Unilit.

Sieve & Other Scenes. Heather Stephens. 48p. (Orig.). (J). (gr. 3-9). 1996. pap. 12.00 (*0-9522224-0-X*) Empire Pub Srvs.

Sieve & Other Scenes. Heather Stephens. LC 96-26468. 48p. (Orig.). (J). (gr. 3-9). 1996. pap. 12.00 (*0-88734-683-9*) Players Pr.

Sieve Elements. Ed. by H. D. Behnke & R. D. Sjolund. (Illus.). 240p. 1990. 163.95 (*0-387-50783-3*) Spr-Verlag.

Sieve Methods & Prime Numbers Theory. Y. Motohashi. (Tata Institute Lectures on Mathematics). xi, 205p. 1984. 26.95 (*0-387-12281-8*) Spr-Verlag.

***Sieve Methods, Exponential Sums, & Their Applications in Number Theory.** G. R. Greaves et al. (London Mathematical Society Lecture Note Ser.: Vol. 237). (Illus.). 354p. (C). 1997. pap. text ed. 39.95 (*0-521-58957-6*) Cambridge U Pr.

Sieyes: His Life & His Nationalism. Glyndon G. Van Deusen. LC 68-58632. (Columbia University. Studies in the Social Sciences: No. 362). reprint ed. 29.50 (*0-404-51362-X*) AMS Pr.

***SIF Sociological Theory.** Maynard. 1989. pap. text ed. write for info. (*0-582-00427-6*) Addison-Wesley.

Sifra: An Analytical Translation: Introduction, Vayyiqra Dibura Denedabah & Vayyiqra Dibura Dehobah. Jacob Neuser. (Brown Judaic Studies). 377p. 1988. 39.95 (*1-55540-205-4*, 14 01 38) Scholars Pr GA.

Sifra: The Rabbinic Commentary on Leviticus. Tr. by Jacob Neusner & Roger Brooks. (Brown Judaic Studies). 162p. (C). 1985. pap. 19.25 (*0-89130-914-4*, 14 01 02) Scholars Pr GA.

Sifra Vol. III: An Analytical Translation: Ahare Mot Qedoshim, Emor, Behar & Behuqotai. Jacob Neusner. 437p. 1988. 51.95 (*1-55540-207-0*, 140140) Scholars Pr GA.

Sifra in Perspective: The Documentary Comparison of the Midrashim of Ancient Judaism. Jacob Neusner. LC 88-10073. (Brown Judaic Studies). 277p. 1988. 41.95 (*1-55540-232-1*, 14-01-46) Scholars Pr GA.

Sifra on Leviticus: Vayiqra Dibura DeHobah, Vol. 3. Medieval Hebrew Masters Staff. 550p. (HEB.). (C). 1992. 24.00 (*1-881255-10-7*) OFEQ Inst.

Sifra on Leviticus, Vol. I: Baraita de-R. Ishmael (The 13 Hermeneutic Rules of R. Ishmael) Medieval Hebrew Masters Staff. LC 91-60934. 142p. (HEB.). (C). 1991. 14.00 (*1-881255-09-3*) OFEQ Inst.

Sifre: A Tannaitic Commentary on the Book of Deuteronomy. Tr. by Reuven Hammer from HEB. LC 85-29556. (Yale Judaica Ser.: No. 24). 560p. 1987. text ed. 60.00 (*0-300-03345-1*) Yale U Pr.

Sifre to Deuteronomy: An Analytical Transtation, Vol. I: Pisqaot One Through One Hundred Forty-Three. Jacob Neusner. LC 87-9779. (Brown Judaic Studies: Vol. 1). 366p. 1987. 31.95 (*1-55540-145-7*, 14-00-98) Scholars Pr GA.

Sifre to Deuteronomy: An Introduction to the Rhetorical, Lofical, & Topical Program. Jacob Neusner. LC 87-16687. (Brown Judaic Studies). 210p. 1987. 25.95 (*1-55540-168-6*, 14-01-24) Scholars Pr GA.

Sifre to Numbers: An American Translation & Explanation: Sifre to Numbers 59-115, Vol. II. Jacob Neuser. (Brown Judaic Studies). 186p. (C). 1986. pap. 20.95 (*1-55540-011-6*, 140119) Scholars Pr GA.

Sifre to Numbers Vol. I: An American Translation & Explanation: Sifre to Numbers 1-58. Jacob Neuser. (Brown Judaic Studies). (C). 1986. pap. 23.95 (*1-55540-009-4*) Scholars Pr GA.

***Sifreinu.** H. V. Vasserman & A. Thorov. 194p. (HEB.). 1976. reprint ed. pap. 4.00 (*0-8266-0203-7*, Merkos LInyonei Chinuch) Kehot Pubn Soc.

***Sifreinu, 2 vols.** H. V. Vasserman & A. Thorov. Incl. Vol. 2. . (HEB.). 96p. 1976. reprint ed. pap. text ed. 3.00 (*0-8266-0202-9*, Merkos LInyonei Chinuch); Vol. 1. . 12th ed. (HEB.). 96p. 1976. reprint ed. pap. text ed. 2.00 (*0-8266-0201-0*, Merkos LInyonei Chinuch); write for info. (*0-8266-0200-2*) Kehot Pubn Soc.

Sifriyas Lubavitch. 237p. (HEB.). 15.00 (*0-8266-5337-5*) Kehot Pubn Soc.

Sifron Hanukkah. (Illus.). 54p. 3.50 (*0-318-13637-6*, 15-300) Board Jewish Educ.

Sifrut Al Ketzeh HaLashon, or Literature on the Tip of the Tongue: Intermediate Hebrew. Edna G. Grad. (Illus.). 317p. (C). 1988. student ed. 19.95 (*0-8101-0769-4*); pap. text ed. 23.95 (*0-8101-0768-6*) Northwestern U Pr.

Sift & Shout. Randy Granovetter & Jeanne James. (Illus.). 1987. pap. text ed. 8.95 (*0-88076-122-9*, 16821) Kaplan Pr.

***Sifting Through Science.** Laura Lowell & Carolyn Willard. Ed. by Lincoln Bergman et al. (Great Explorations in Math & Science GEMS Ser.). (Illus.). 104p. (Orig.). 1997. teacher ed., pap. 13.50 (*0-912511-35-4*) Lawrence Science.

***Sifting Through the Years: A History of Bay State Milling Company.** Tara Blanc. 110p. 1997. 18.99 (*0-929690-31-1*) Herit Pubs AZ.

Siftings. Jens Jensen. 1990. pap. 13.95 (*0-8018-4021-X*) Johns Hopkins.

***Siftings from the Morrilton Democrat Newspaper, 1929: Published in Morrilton, Arkansas.** Cathy Barnes. 185p. (Orig.). 1997. pap. 25.00 (*1-56546-106-1*) Arkansas Res.

***Sigamos: Grammar.** Lydia Velez & Jacqueline Kiraithe-Cordova. 1997. pap. text ed. write for info. (*0-07-053783-6*) McGraw.

***Sigamos: Reader.** Lydia Velez & Jacqueline Kiraithe-Cordova. 1997. pap. text ed. write for info. (*0-07-053814-X*) McGraw.

Sigari del Faraone. Herge. (Illus.). 62p. (ITA.). (J). pap. 19.95 (*0-8288-5075-5*) Fr & Eur.

SiGe Based Technologies: Proceedings of Symposium A, 1992 E-MRS Spring Conference, Strasbourg, France 2-4 June 1992. Ed. by Erich Kasper et al. (European Materials Research Society Symposia Proceedings Ser.: 31). 280p. 1993. 228.50 (*0-444-89905-7*) Elsevier.

***Sigel Regiment: The 26th Wisonsin Volunteer Infantry, 1862-1865.** James S. Pula. 1997. 29.95 (*1-882810-20-1*) Stackpole.

Sigfluence: Enduring Positive Influence. John F. Loase. (American University Studies: Psychology: Ser. VIII, Vol. 10). 269p. 1988. 46.50 (*0-8204-0534-5*) P Lang Pubng.

Sigfluence: Long-Term Positive Influence. John F. Loase. LC 93-48962. 168p. (Orig.). lib. bdg. 48.00 (*0-8191-9449-2*) U Pr of Amer.

Sigfluence: Long-Term Positive Influence. John F. Loase. LC 93-48962. 168p. (Orig.). 1994. pap. text ed. 27.50 (*0-8191-9450-6*) U Pr of Amer.

Sigfluence III: The Key to: "It's a Wonderful Life" John F. Loase. LC 95-43442. 114p. (C). 1996. lib. bdg. 26.50 (*0-7618-0207-X*) U Pr of Amer.

Siggraph Conference Proceedings, August 1988. ACM Press Staff. 1988. pap. text ed. 53.75 (*0-201-09196-8*) Addison-Wesley.

Siggraph '89 Conference Proceedings Vol. 23, No. 3: Computer Graphics. Richard J. Beach. (C). 1989. pap. text ed. 46.95 (*0-201-50434-0*) Addison-Wesley.

Siggraph '90 Conference Proceedings Vol. 24, No. 4: Computer Graphics. Richard J. Beach. 1990. pap. 50.50 (*0-201-50933-4*) Addison-Wesley.

***Siggy Lindo.** A. A. Attanasio. Date not set. write for info. (*0-688-04381-X*) Morrow.

Siggy's Baseball Bat Factory. Peggy Thomson. LC 95-24172. (Illus.). (J). Date not set. write for info. (*0-688-13890-X*, Tambourine Bks); lib. bdg. write for info. (*0-688-13891-8*, Tambourine Bks) Morrow.

Siggy's Spaghetti Works. Peggy Thomson. LC 92-13186. (Illus.). 32p. (J). (gr. 1 up). 1993. lib. bdg. 13.93 (*0-688-11374-5*, Tambourine Bks) Morrow.

Sigh, a Tear. Clarence L. Freed. (Illus.). 36p. 1983. 14.95 (*0-914715-00-3*) Spectracolor-Reynolds.

Sigh of Relief: The First-Aid Handbook for Childhood Emergencies. 2nd rev. ed. Martin I. Green. LC 92-36406. 384p. 1994. pap. 16.95 (*0-553-35180-X*) Bantam.

Sigh on the Breeze. large type ed. Miriam MacGregor. 336p. 1986. 25.99 (*0-7089-1423-3*) Ulverscroft.

Sighing for Eden: Sin, Evil & the Christian Faith. William H. Willimon. LC 84-14555. 208p. 1985. pap. 8.95 (*0-687-38447-8*) Abingdon.

***Sight.** Sue Hurwitz. LC 96-29958. (Library of the Five Senses (Plus the Sixth Sense)). (J). 1997. write for info. (*0-8239-5055-7*) Rosen Group.

Sight. Andreu Llamas. (Five Senses of the Animal World Ser.). (Illus.). (J). 1996. lib. bdg. 15.95 (*0-7910-3491-7*) Chelsea Hse.

Sight. J. M. Parramon & J. J. Puig. (Five Senses Ser.). (Illus.). 32p. (Orig.). (J). (ps). 1985. pap. 6.95 (*0-8120-3564-X*); pap. 6.95 (*0-8120-3605-0*) Barron.

***Sight.** Maria Rius et al. (Five Senses Ser.). (J). 1985. 6.95 (*0-8120-5737-6*) Barron.

Sight. Mandy Suhr. LC 93-44193. (I'm Alive Ser.). (Illus.). (J). (ps-1). 1993. lib. bdg. 14.21 (*0-87614-834-8*, Carolrhoda) Lerner Group.

Sight & Insight: Essays on Art & Culture in Honor of E. H. Gombrich at 85. John Onians. (Illus.). 420p. (C). 1994. 59.95 (*0-7148-2971-4*, Pub. by Phaidon Press UK) Chronicle Bks.

***Sight & Song 1892; Underneath the Bough 1893, 2 vols. in 1.** Michael Field. 292p. 1993. 49.50 (*1-85477-143-4*, Pub. by Woodstock Bks UK) Cassell.

Sight & Sound: Film Review Volume, January-December 1993. Sight & Sound Staff. (Illus.). 260p. 1994. 55.00 (*0-85170-482-4*) Ind U Pr.

Sight & Sound: Film Review Volume May 1991-April 1992. (Illus.). 300p. (C). 1992. 50.00 (*0-85170-335-6*, Pub. by British Film Inst UK) Ind U Pr.

Sight & Sound: Film Review Volume May 1992-December 1992. (Illus.). 168p. (C). 1993. 45.00 (*0-85170-417-4*, Pub. by British Film Inst UK) Ind U Pr.

Sight & Sound: Students' Manual. Arpad Darazs & Stephen Jay. LC 64-25360. (J). (gr. 3-6). 1965. pap. text ed. 5.00 (*0-913932-03-5*) Boosey & Hawkes.

Sight & Sound: Teachers' Manual. Arpad Darazs & Stephen Jay. LC 64-25360. 1965. 7.50 (*0-913932-02-7*) Boosey & Hawkes.

Sight & Sound: The Sensible & Sensitive Use of Audio-Visual Aids. Ed. by Mills F. Edgerton, Jr. 1969. pap. 10.95 (*0-915432-69-2*) NE Conf Teach Foreign.

Sight & Sound Anthology 1936-1955, 6 vols. Ed. by R. Gordon. 1976. lib. bdg. 950.95 (*0-8490-2603-2*) Gordon Pr.

Sight & Sound Film Review Volume, January-December 1994. Sight & Sound Staff. 1996. pap. text ed. 60.00 (*0-85170-529-4*, Pub. by British Film Inst UK) Ind U Pr.

Sight for a Lifetime. 1989. write for info. (*0-929199-07-3*) Plantain Pub.

***Sight for Sound.** Baird. Date not set. 42.50 (*0-688-15687-8*) Morrow.

Sight Lines. Al Beck. (Illus.). 87p. (Orig.). 1996. pap. 6.00 (*0-934852-63-4*) Lorien Hse.

Sight Lines. Arlene Croce. 1988. 19.95 (*0-317-68135-4*) Knopf.

Sight of a Marsh Hawk. Gilbert Byron. (Illus.). 58p. (Orig.). 1985. pap. 5.95 (*0-9615275-4-4*) Unicorn Bkshop.

Sight of Sound: Music, Representation, & the History of the Body. Richard Leppert. LC 92-39075. 345p. 1995. pap. 17.95 (*0-520-20342-9*) U CA Pr.

Sight of Sound: Music, Representation, & the History of the Body. Richard D. Leppert. LC 92-39075. 1993. 45.00 (*0-520-08174-9*) U CA Pr.

Sight out of Mind: Essays & Criticism on Art. Dennis Adrian. LC 85-8434. (Contemporary American Art Critics Ser.: No. 5). 243p. reprint ed. pap. 69.30 (*0-8357-1676-7*, 2070490) Bks Demand.

Sight Read Successfully, Bk. 1. Louise Guhl. 40p. 1991. 4.95 (*0-8497-9433-1*, WP320) Kjos.

Sight Read Successfully, Bk. 2. Louise Guhl. 40p. 1991. 4.95 (*0-8497-9434-X*, WP321) Kjos.

Sight Read Successfully, Bk. 3. Louise Guhl. 40p. 1991. 4.95 (*0-8497-9435-8*, WP322) Kjos.

***Sight-Reading - Class Guitar 1-3.** Ed. by Aaron Stang. 52p. (Orig.). (C). 1985. pap. text ed. 9.95 (*0-7692-0974-2*, EL02942) Warner Brothers.

***Sight Reading for the Classical Guitar: Levels IV-V.** Robert Benedict. Ed. by Aaron Stang. 64p. 1985. pap. text ed. 12.95 (*0-7692-1285-9*) Warner Bros.

Sight Singing. 2nd ed. Alfred Adler. LC 96-28217. (C). 1997. pap. text ed. 25.95 (*0-393-97072-8*) Norton.

Sight Singing: Pitch, Interval, Rhythm. Samuel Adler. (Illus.). (C). 1979. pap. text ed. 22.95 (*0-393-95052-2*) Norton.

Sight Singing Through Melodic Analysis. Leland D. Bland. LC 83-8184. 512p. (C). 1983. text ed. 43.95 (*0-8304-1003-1*); pap. text ed. 30.95 (*0-88229-820-8*) Nelson-Hall.

Sight So Nobly Grand: Josel Palmen on Mt. Hood in 1845. Joel Palmer & John P. Spencer. (Illus.). 67p. (Orig.). 1994. pap. 6.95 (*0-87595-252-6*) Oregon Hist.

Sight, Sound, & Sense. Ed. by Thomas A. Sebeok. LC 77-21520. (Advances in Semiotics Ser.). 298p. reprint ed. pap. 85.00 (*0-685-44455-4*, 2056718) Bks Demand.

Sight-Sound-Motion: Applied Media Aesthetics. 2nd ed. Herbert Zettl. 408p. (C). 1990. text ed. 54.95 (*0-534-07952-0*) Wadsworth Pub.

Sight Through Sound. Goldberg. 1984. text ed. 635.00 (*0-7216-1103-6*) HarBrace.

***Sight to Sound: Guitar.** Leon White. Ed. by Aaron Stang. 100p. 1985. pap. text ed. 12.95 (*0-7692-1283-2*) Warner Bros.

Sight Unseen. Dan Gilroy. 1992. mass mkt. 4.50 (*1-55817-520-2*, Pinncle Kensgtn) Kensgtn Pub Corp.

***Sight Unseen.** Gloria Kroeze. (Acts 2 Ser.). 59p. (Orig.). 1996. pap. 4.10 (*1-56212-227-4*, 1360-0560) CRC Pubns.

Sight Unseen. Donald Margulies. 1992. pap. 5.25 (*0-8222-1317-6*) Dramatists Play.

Sight Unseen: A Field Guide to the Invisible. Wayne Biddle. 1997. 24.00 (*0-8050-5069-8*) H Holt & Co.

Sight Unseen: And Other Plays. Donald Margulies. 304p. (Orig.). 1995. pap. 15.95 (*1-55936-103-4*) Theatre Comm.

An Asterisk (*) at the beginning of an entry indicates that the title is appearing in BIP for the first time.

Sight Unseen: Beckett, Pinter, Stoppard, & Other Contemporary Dramatists on Radio. Elissa S. Guralnick. 256p. (C). 1995. text ed. 29.95 (*0-8214-1128-4*) Ohio U Pr.
Sight Unseen: The Art of Active Seeing, Grades 4-8. John Schaefer. (Illus.). 192p. (Orig.). 1994. pap. 11.95 (*0-673-36123-3*, GoodYrBooks) Addson-Wesley Educ.
Sighted Singer: Two Works on Poetry for Readers & Writers. Allen Grossman & Mark Halliday. LC 91-2944. 256p. 1991. pap. 15.95 (*0-8018-4243-3*); text ed. 55.00 (*0-8018-4242-5*) Johns Hopkins.
***Sighted Sub Sank Same.** Donald F. Mason. 246p. (Orig.). 1997. mass mkt. 4.99 (*1-55237-208-1*, Pub. by Comnwlth Pub CN) Partners Pubs Grp.
Sighting. Luci Shaw. LC 81-9342. (Wheaton Literary Ser.). (Illus.). 95p. 1981. pap. 5.95 (*0-87788-768-3*) Shaw Pubs.
Sighting the Slave Ship. Pauline Stainer. 80p. (Orig.). 9200. pap. 14.95 (*1-85224-176-4*, Pub. by Bloodaxe Bks UK) Dufour.
Sightings. Susan Michaels. (Illus.). 256p. 1996. pap. 11.00 (*0-684-82369-1*, Fireside) S&S Trade.
Sightings. Charles D. Taylor. Ed. by Paul McCarthy. 416p. (Orig.). 1993. mass mkt. 5.50 (*0-671-73632-9*, Pocket Star Bks) PB.
***Sightings: A Maine Coast Odyssey.** Peter Ralston. LC 97-7742. (Illus.). 160p. 1997. 50.00 (*0-89272-408-0*) Down East.
Sightings: Essays in Humanistic Psychology. Ed. by Fred Richards & I. David Welch. LC 72-96552. 228p. (C). 1973. pap. 6.95 (*0-88310-002-9*) Publishers Consult.
***Sightings UFO.** Michaels. LC 97-19475. 1997. pap. 11.00 (*0-684-83630-0*, Fireside) S&S Trade.
Sightreading. Howard Roberts & Bob Grebb. (Howard Roberts Guitar Manuals Ser.). (Illus.). 63p. 1972. pap. text ed. 9.95 (*0-89915-003-9*) Playback Mus Pub.
Sightreading at the Keyboard. Robert Spillman. 267p. (C). 1990. 32.00 (*0-02-872381-3*) Schirmer Bks.
***Sightreading on Guitar.** Leigh Powers. Ed. by Aaron Stang. 100p. 1985. pap. text ed. 12.95 (*0-7692-1286-7*) Warner Bros.
Sights - Three Novellas. Anna Holmes. LC 63-22335. (Orig.). 1963. pap. 1.85 (*0-87376-001-8*) Red Dust.
***Sights & Insights: A Guide to the Findhorn Foundation Community.** Cathy Miller. 1995. pap. text ed. 4.00 (*1-899171-50-9*, Pub. by Findhorn Pr UK) Words Distrib.
Sights & Sounds: The Very Special Senses. Charles E. Kupchella. LC 75-1446. 1975. pap. text ed. 6.95 (*0-672-63695-6*, Bobbs) Macmillan.
Sights & Sounds of Cinema & Television: How the Aesthetic Experience Influences Our Feelings. Robert Edmonds. (C). 1982. pap. text ed. 17.95 (*0-8077-2679-6*) Tchrs Coll.
Sights & Sounds of Steamboatin' The Life & Times of Captain William H. Laughton. Virginia W. French. (Illus.). 136p. (Orig.). 1992. pap. 11.95 (*0-9622783-1-9*) Cottonwood Hill Pub.
Sights of Hawaii Color/Sticker Book. Bernard O. Atkins. (Illus.). 20p. (Orig.). (J). (ps-6). 1995. pap. 4.95 (*0-9642050-4-1*) Great Creations.
Sights on the Sixties. Ed. by Barbara L. Tischler. LC 91-29234. (Perspectives on the Sixties Ser.). 300p. (C). 1992. text ed. 45.00 (*0-8135-1792-3*); pap. text ed. 16.00 (*0-8135-1793-1*) Rutgers U Pr.
Sights Unseen. Kaye Gibbons. 240p. 1996. mass mkt. 6.99 (*0-380-72681-5*) Avon.
Sights Unseen. Kaye Gibbons. 256p. 1995. 19.95 (*0-399-13986-9*, Putnam) Putnam Pub Group.
Sightseeing: A Space Panorama. Peter Riva & Barbara Hitchcock. LC 85-40347. (Illus.). 120p. 1985. 24.95 (*0-394-54243-6*) Knopf.
Sightseeing...Huntsville, Alabama. Elfrida Hassen-Richter. 70p. (Orig.). 1985. pap. text ed. 6.95 (*0-916039-03-X*) Kaylor & Kaylor.
Sightsinging. Henry. LC 96-33609. 352p. (C). 1997. pap. text ed. 38.67 (*0-13-121336-9*) P-H.
Sightsinging - Complete. 5th ed. Bruce Benward & Maureen A. Carr. 336p. (C). 1991. spiral bd. write for info. (*0-697-05845-X*) Brown & Benchmark.
***Sightsinging Complete.** 6th ed. Benward & Carr. 1997. pap. text ed. 26.00 (*0-697-34395-2*) McGraw.
Sigillate Pottery of the Roman Empire. (Illus.). 1937. 3.00 (*0-87535-041-0*) Hispanic Soc.
SIGIR '94: Proceedings of the Seventeenth Annual International Information Retrieval. Held in Dublin, Ireland, July 3-6, 1994. Ed. by W. B. Croft & C. J. Van Rijsbergen. 363p. 1994. 126.95 (*0-387-19889-X*) Spr-Verlag.
Sigismond Thalberg (1812-1871) Ed. by Jeffrey Kallberg. LC 92-776265. (Piano Music of the Parisian Virtuosos, 1810-1860 Ser.: Vol. 2). 344p. 1993. text ed. 110.00 (*0-8153-0848-5*) Garland.
Sigismond Thalberg (1812-1871) Selected Works. Ed. by Jeffrey Kallberg. LC 92-776265. (Piano Music of the Parisian Virtuosos, 1810-1860 Ser.). (Illus.). 376p. 1993. text ed. 120.00 (*0-8153-0847-7*) Garland.
Sigismund. Lars Gustafsson. Tr. by John Weinstock from SWE. LC 84-1021. 224p. 1985. 16.50 (*0-8112-0923-7*); pap. 7.95 (*0-8112-0924-5*, NDP584) New Directions.
Sigismund, Prince of Poland: A Baroque Entertainment. Oscar Mandel. LC 88-204. (Illus.). 72p. (Orig.). (C). 1988. pap. text ed. 13.50 (*0-8191-6931-5*); lib. bdg. 25.50 (*0-8191-6930-7*) U Pr of Amer.
Siglas y Abreviaturas Latinas con Su Significado por Orden Alfabetico de un Catalogo de las Abreviaturas Que Se Usan en los Documentos Pontificios. Ramon A. De la Brana. 216p. 1978. reprint ed. write for info. (*3-487-06454-5*) G Olms Pubs.
Sigler & Flanders' Nonprescription Drug Cards. Jeffrey D. Sigler. 106p. (C). 1993. ring bd. 29.95 (*1-880579-06-5*) Sigler & Flanders.
Siglo de las Luces. 2nd ed. Alejo Carpentier. 420p. 1989. pap. 15.95 (*0-7859-5172-5*) Fr & Eur.
Siglo de Literatura Infantil Puertorriquena: A Century of Puerto Rican Children's Literature. Flor Pineiro De Rivera. LC 85-8705. (Illus.). 139p. (SPA.). 1985. 25.00 (*0-8477-3531-1*); pap. 20.00 (*0-8477-3532-X*) U of PR Pr.
Siglo de Oro Tradition & Modern Adolescent Psychology in Pepita Jimenez. Robert E. Lott. LC 75-172751. (Catholic University of America. Studies in Romance Languages & Literatures: No. 58). reprint ed. 42.50 (*0-404-50358-6*) AMS Pr.
SIGMA: A Knowledge-Based Aerial Image Understanding System. Takashi Matsuyama & S. S. Hwang. LC 89-29221. (Advances in Computer Vision & Machine Intelligence Ser.). (Illus.). 296p. 1990. 75.00 (*0-306-43301-X*, Plenum Pr) Plenum.
Sigma & Phencyclidine Like Compounds as Molecular Probes in Biology. Ed. by E. F. Domino & J. M. Kamenka. LC 87-62521. (Illus.). 819p. 1988. 90.00 (*0-916182-05-3*) NPP Bks.
Sigma Molecular Orbital Theory. Oktay Sinanoglu & Kenneth Wiberg. LC 77-89906. (Yale Series in the Sciences. A Chemistry-Physics Interface). (Illus.). 465p. reprint ed. pap. 120.90 (*0-8357-8321-9*, 2033891) Bks Demand.
Sigma Plot for Scientists. M. Brent Charland. 392p. (C). 1995. per. write for info. (*0-697-28800-5*) Wm C Brown Pubs.
Sigma Receptors. Ed. by Yossef Itzhak. (Neuroscience Perspectives Ser.). (Illus.). 360p. 1994. text ed. 74.00 (*0-12-376350-9*) Acad Pr.
Sigma Text + 5" Software: Graphical Simulation V2.1. 2nd ed. Lee W. Schruben. (QM - Quantitative Methods Ser.). 1993. text ed. 65.95 (*0-89426-216-5*) S-W Pub.
Sigmar Polke. (Illus.). 152p. 1992. 50.00 (*0-918471-18-4*) San Fran MOMA.
Sigmar Polke: Drawings, 1963-1969. (Illus.). 216p. 1991. 175.00 (*3-906127-02-8*, Pub. by Gachnang & Springer SZ) Dist Art Pubs.
Sigmar Polke: Join the Dots. Thomas McEvilley et al. (Illus.). 112p. (C). 1996. pap. 30.00 (*1-85437-153-3*, Pub. by Tate Gallery UK) U of Wash Pr.
Sigmar Polke: Photoworks. (Illus.). 1995. 60.00 (*0-614-96882-8*) DAP Assocs.
Sigmar Polke: The Early Drawings, 1963-1969. (Illus.). 106p. 1991. pap. 65.00 (*3-906127-27-3*, Pub. by Gachnang & Springer SZ) Dist Art Pubs.
***Sigmar Polke: The Three Lies of Painting.** Hans Belting et al. (Illus.). 360p. 1997. 75.00 (*3-89322-925-6*) Dist Art Pubs.
Sigmar Polke - Photoworks: When Pictures Vanish. Paul Schimmel & Maria M. Hambourg. (Illus.). 250p. 1995. 85.00 (*0-914357-44-1*) Los Angeles Mus Contemp.
Sigmatic Aorist in Indo-European: Evidence for the Space-Time Hypothesis. Bridget Drinka. (Journal of Indo-European Studies Monograph: No. 13). 210p. (C). 1995. pap. text ed. 40.00 (*0-941694-46-1*) Inst Study Man.
Sigmatropic Additions & Cyclosubstitutions in Five-Membered Heterocyclic Compounds Containing Exocyclic Double Bonds, Vol. 1. V. N. Drozd & N. S. Zefirov. (Sulfur Reports). 45p. 1981. pap. text ed. 62.00 (*3-7186-0081-1*) Gordon & Breach.
Sigmet Active: A Novel. Thomas Page. LC 78-53307. 1978. write for info. (*0-8129-0774-4*, Times Bks) Random.
Sigmons of Virginia. Juanita S. Halstead. (Family History Ser.). (Illus.). 301p. 1986. 35.00 (*0-9617449-0-1*) J S Halstead.
Sigmund & Freud: Critical Assessments. Ed. by Laurence Spurling. 500p. 1989. 295.00 (*0-415-02088-3*, A3445) Routledge.
Sigmund Freud. Ed. by Robert Bocock. (Key Sociologists Ser.). 128p. 1983. pap. 6.95 (*0-85312-580-5*, NO. 3754, Pub. by Tavistock-E Horwood UK) Routledge Chapman & Hall.
Sigmund Freud. Michael Jacobs. (Key Figures in Counselling & Psychotherapy Ser.). 160p. (C). 1992. text ed. 44.00 (*0-8039-8464-2*); pap. text ed. 18.95 (*0-8039-8465-0*) Sage.
Sigmund Freud. Barry Mann. LC 92-42548. (Biographies Ser.). (J). 1993. 19.93 (*0-86625-491-9*); 14.95 (*0-685-66534-8*) Rourke Pubns.
***Sigmund Freud.** Ralph Steadman. 1997. pap. text ed. 19.95 (*1-55209-174-0*) Firefly Bks Ltd.
***Sigmund Freud.** Stephen Wilson. (Get a Life...Pocket Biographies Ser.). (Illus.). 128p. Date not set. pap. 10.95 (*0-7509-1530-7*, Pub. by Sutton Pubng UK) Bks Intl VA.
Sigmund Freud. Richard Wollheim. 316p. 1990. pap. text ed. 22.95 (*0-521-28385-X*) Cambridge U Pr.
Sigmund Freud. Ed. by Paul Roazen. (Series in Science). vi, 186p. 1987. reprint ed. pap. 9.95 (*0-306-80292-9*) Da Capo.
Sigmund Freud: An Introduction. Walter Hollitscher. LC 72-119931. (Select Bibliographies Reprint Ser.). 1977. reprint ed. 16.95 (*0-8369-5374-6*) Ayer.
***Sigmund Freud: Exploring the Unconscious.** Margaret Muckenhoupt. (Oxford Portraits in Science Ser.). (Illus.). 144p. (J). 1997. lib. bdg. 20.00 (*0-19-509933-8*) OUP.
Sigmund Freud: Father of Psychoanalysis. Alan L. Paley. Ed. by D. Steve Rahmas. LC 74-14694. (Outstanding Personalities Ser.: No. 73). 32p. 1974. lib. bdg. 7.25 (*0-87157-573-6*) SamHar Pr.
Sigmund Freud: His Life & Mind. Helen W. Puner. 295p. (C). 1992. pap. 24.95 (*1-56000-611-0*) Transaction Pubs.
Sigmund Freud: His Life in Pictures & Words. Ed. by Ernst Freud et al. (Illus.). 352p. 1985. reprint ed. pap. 17.95 (*0-393-30285-7*) Norton.
Sigmund Freud: His Personality, His Teaching & His School. Fritz Wittels. Tr. by Eden Paul & Cedar Paul from GER. LC 79-161001. (Select Bibliographies Reprint Ser.). 1977. reprint ed. 23.95 (*0-8369-5869-1*) Ayer.
Sigmund Freud: Man & Father. Martin Freud. 224p. 1983. 30.00 (*0-87668-722-2*) Aronson.
Sigmund Freud see Modern Critical Views Series
Sigmund Freud - The Standard Edition: Jokes & Their Relation to the Unconscious. Sigmund Freud. Tr. by James Strachey. 1990. pap. 9.95 (*0-393-00145-8*) Norton.
Sigmund Freud - The Standard Edition: The Ego & the Id. Sigmund Freud. Ed. by James Strachey. Tr. by Joan Riviere. 1990. pap. 7.95 (*0-393-00142-3*) Norton.
Sigmund Freud - The Standard Edition: The Psychopathology of Everyday Life. Sigmund Freud. Ed. by James Strachey. Tr. by Alan Tyson. 1990. pap. 7.95 (*0-393-00611-5*) Norton.
Sigmund Freud & Art: His Personal Collection of Antiquities. Peter Gay. 1993. pap. 24.95 (*0-8109-2551-6*) Abrams.
Sigmund Freud & Lou Andreas-Salome: Letters. Sigmund Freud & Lou Andreas-Salome. Ed. by Ernst Pfeiffer. 256p. 1985. pap. 6.95 (*0-393-30261-X*) Norton.
Sigmund Freud As a Consultant. Edoardo Weiss. 81p. (C). 1991. 32.95 (*0-88738-423-4*) Transaction Pubs.
Sigmund Freud Presente par Lui-Meme. Sigmund Freud. (FRE.). 1987. pap. 10.95 (*0-7859-2804-9*) Fr & Eur.
Sigmund Freud: The Standard Edition: Group Psychology & the Analysis of the Ego. Sigmund Freud. Ed. & Tr. by James Strachey. 1990. reprint ed. pap. 7.95 (*0-393-00770-7*) Norton.
Sigmund Freud: The Standard Edition: Inhibitions, Symptoms, & Anxiety. Sigmund Freud. Ed. by James Strachey. Tr. by Alix Strachey. 1990. pap. 6.95 (*0-393-00874-6*) Norton.
Sigmund Freud: The Standard Edition: New Introductory Lectures on Psychoanalysis. Sigmund Freud. Ed. & Tr. by James Strachey. 1990. pap. 9.95 (*0-393-00743-X*) Norton.
Sigmund Freud: The Standard Edition: On the History of the Psycho-Analytic Movement. Sigmund Freud. Ed. by James Strachey. Tr. by Joan Riviere. 1990. pap. 4.95 (*0-393-00150-4*) Norton.
Sigmund Freud: The Standard Edition: Totem & Taboo. Sigmund Freud. Tr. by James Strachey. 1990. pap. 7.95 (*0-393-00143-1*) Norton.
Sigmund Freud's Dreams. Alexander Grinstein. LC 79-2485. 486p. 1980. 65.00 (*0-8236-6074-5*) Intl Univs Pr.
Sigmund Freud's Mission: An Analysis of His Personality & Influence. Erich Fromm. 1990. 19.75 (*0-8446-4544-3*) Peter Smith.
Sigmund Freud's Writings: A Comprehensive Bibliography. Ed. by Alexander Grinstein. LC 76-46812. 181p. 1977. 30.00 (*0-8236-6076-1*) Intl Univs Pr.
Sigmund Says: A Lighter Look at Freud Through His Id, Ego, & Super Ego. Monte Elchoness. LC 88-4229. (Illus.). 96p. (Orig.). 1988. pap. 6.95 (*0-936781-04-1*) Monroe Pr.
***Sigmund Spaeth - Song Session.** Ed. by Carol Cuellar. 200p. (Orig.). (C). 1995. pap. text ed. 9.95 (*0-7692-0536-4*, VF0247) Warner Brothers.
Sign. rev. ed. Robert Van Kampen. LC 92-18465. 512p. 1993. pap. 19.99 (*0-89107-756-1*) Crossway Bks.
Sign. rev. ed. Robert Van Kampen. LC 92-18465. 512p. 1994. student ed., pap. 12.99 (*0-89107-757-X*) Crossway Bks.
Sign & Culture: A Reader for Students of American Sign Language. Ed. by William C. Stokoe. LC 80-82122. 1980. reprint ed. pap. text ed. 18.95 (*0-932130-07-0*) Linstok Pr.
Sign & Its Masters. Thomas A. Sebeok. LC 88-20906. (Sources in Semiotics Ser.: Vol. VIII). 372p. (C). 1989. reprint ed. pap. text ed. 29.00 (*0-8191-7195-6*); reprint ed. lib. bdg. 44.00 (*0-8191-7194-8*) U Pr of Amer.
Sign & School: Using Signs in Deaf Children's Development. Jim Kyle. 230p. 1987. 79.00 (*0-905028-89-9*, Pub. by Multilingual Matters UK); pap. 29.95 (*0-905028-88-0*, Pub. by Multilingual Matters UK) Taylor & Francis.
Sign & Subject: Semiotic & Psychoanalytic Investigations into Poetry. Daniel Laferriere. (Studies in Semiotics: No. 14). 103p. (Orig.). 1978. pap. 17.00 (*90-316-0138-1*, Pub. by Gruner NE) Benjamins North Am.
***Sign & Symbol in the Church of the Brethren.** Patricia K. Helman. (Illus.). 112p. 1991. reprint ed. pap. 32.00 (*0-608-04176-9*, 2064910) Bks Demand.
Sign & the Seal. Graham Hancock. 608p. 1993. pap. 19.95 (*0-385-25414-8*) Doubleday.
Sign & the Seal: The Quest for the Lost Ark of the Covenant. Graham Hancock. 512p. 1992. 22.00 (*0-517-57813-1*, Crown) Crown Pub Group.
Sign & the Seal: The Quest for the Lost Ark of the Covenant. Graham Hancock. LC 93-16159. (Illus.). 608p. 1993. pap. 15.00 (*0-671-86541-2*, Touchstone Bks) S&S Trade.
***Sign-Based Methods in Linear Statistical Models.** M. V. Boldin et al. LC 97-3452. (Translations of Mathematical Monographs: Vol. 162). 1997. 99.00 (*0-8218-0371-9*, MMONO/162) Am Math.
Sign Change Tutorial: Speaker Identification Course. David Kennedy. (Advanced Court Reporting Technology Ser.). 82p. 1991. pap. text ed. 7.56 (*1-881086-02-X*) Middle Wasley.
Sign Design: Easy Type Guide. Don Dewsnap. 160p. 1993. pap. 16.95 (*1-56496-035-8*, 30502) Rockport Pubs.
Sign Design & Layout. Kenneth Woodward. 72p. 1983. pap. 18.95 (*0-911380-60-4*) ST Pubns.
Sign Design Gallery. (Illus.). 192p. 1994. 39.99 (*1-56496-070-6*, 30601) Rockport Pubs.
Sign Design Gallery 2. 39.99 (*1-56496-196-6*) Rockport Pubs.
Sign Designer's Sketchbook. Keigo Helotie. LC 88-29859. (Illus.). (Orig.). 1988. pap. 16.95 (*0-911380-81-7*) ST Pubns.
Sign Electrician's Workbook. James G. Stallcup. (Illus.). 90p. 1992. 22.96 (*0-8269-1731-3*) Am Technical.
***Sign Gallery.** Date not set. 35.00 (*0-688-15359-3*); pap. 29.95 (*0-688-15780-7*) Morrow.
***Sign Gallery.** Sign Of The Times Staff. 1997. pap. text ed. 35.00 (*0-8230-4823-3*) Watsn-Guptill.
***Sign Here.** Jane H. Paterson. (Illus.). 96p. (Orig.). 1997. pap. 10.95 (*1-85398-106-0*, Pub. by Ashgrove UK) Words Distrib.
***Sign Here: How to Understand Any Contract Before You Sign.** 2nd rev. ed. Mari P. Ulmer. Ed. by Lee Ellison. 1997. pap. write for info. (*0-9643161-8-8*) Columb Pub.
Sign Here! Your Complete Autograph Kit. Illus. by Carrie Abel. (J). (gr. 3-7). 1995. 8.95 (*0-448-40961-5*, G&D) Putnam Pub Group.
Sign in Music & Literature. Ed. by Wendy Steiner. LC 80-27915. 243p. (C). 1981. text ed. 25.00 (*0-292-77563-6*) U of Tex Pr.
Sign in Sidney Brustein's Window see Raisin in the Sun
Sign in the Subway. Caraveth Mitchell. (Orig.). 1988. pap. 5.95 (*1-55673-056-X*, 8853) CSS OH.
Sign is Just a Sign. Thomas A. Sebeok. LC 90-42289. (Advances in Semiotics Ser.). (Illus.). 190p. 1991. 31.50 (*0-253-35131-6*); pap. 13.95 (*0-253-20625-1*, MB-625) Ind U Pr.
Sign is Mendel's Window. Mildred Phillips & Zemach. (J). 1996. pap. 5.99 (*0-689-80979-4*) S&S Childrens.
Sign Language: A Photograph Album of Visual Puns & Peculiarities. Ann Sanfedele. (Illus.). 1992. pap. 7.95 (*0-8065-1356-X*, Citadel Pr) Carol Pub Group.
Sign Language: Athletes & Autographs. Phil Schaaf. (Illus.). 192p. 1994. pap. 12.95 (*1-57028-010-X*) Masters Pr IN.
Sign Language: Contemporary Southwest Native America. Skeet McAuley. (Illus.). 80p. 1989. 29.95 (*0-89381-333-8*) Aperture.
Sign Language: Fourth Most Used Language in the U. S. A. Louie J. Fant, Jr. LC 77-93544. (Illus.). 1977. pap. 19.95 (*0-917002-13-X*, 159) Joyce Media.
Sign Language: Street Signs As Folk Art. Photos & Text by John Baeder. LC 95-34057. (Illus.). 144p. 1996. pap. 19.95 (*0-8109-2642-3*) Abrams.
Sign Language: The Study of Deaf People & Their Language. Jim Kyle et al. (Illus.). 300p. 1985. text ed. 85.00 (*0-521-26075-2*) Cambridge U Pr.
Sign Language: The Study of Deaf People & Their Language. Jim Kyle et al. (Illus.). 300p. 1988. pap. text ed. 29.95 (*0-521-35717-9*) Cambridge U Pr.
Sign Language & Deaf Culture. rev. ed. Janet L. Duvall. (Illus.). 166p. (C). 1994. pap. text ed. 29.50 (*1-882457-02-1*) Sharp Image.
Sign Language & the Deaf Community: Essays in Honor of William Stokoe. Charlotte Baker & Robbin M. Battison. (Illus.). 267p. 1981. text ed. 15.00 (*0-913072-37-0*); pap. text ed. 8.95 (*0-913072-36-2*) Natl Assn Deaf.
Sign Language & the Health Care Professional. Debbie L. Cole. LC 89-20083. 92p. (C). 1990. pap. 12.50 (*0-89464-417-3*) Krieger.
Sign Language Animals. Frank A. Paul et al. 16p. 1985. pap. 4.50 (*0-915035-01-4*) Dawn Sign.
Sign Language Clowns. Ben Bahan et al. 16p. (J). 1983. pap. 4.50 (*0-915035-00-6*, 4160) Dawn Sign.
Sign Language Dot-to-Dot. Ed. by J. A. Belcher. 32p. (J). (ps-3). 1979. 2.95 (*0-917002-40-7*) Joyce Media.
Sign Language Feelings. Ralph Miller et al. 16p. (J). 1985. pap. 4.50 (*0-915035-05-7*, 4165) Dawn Sign.
Sign Language Flash Cards, Vol. I. rev. ed. Harry W. Hoemann & Shirley A. Hoemann. (Illus.). 120p. 1988. reprint ed. pap. text ed. 19.95 (*0-9614621-5-9*) Bowling Gr Pr.
Sign Language Flash Cards, Vol. II. Harry W. Hoemann et al. (Illus.). 120p. 1988. reprint ed. pap. text ed. 19.95 (*0-9614621-4-0*) Bowling Gr Pr.
Sign Language for Everyone. California State Department of Health Staff et al. LC 75-70066. (Illus.). 11.95 (*0-917002-02-4*) Joyce Media.
Sign Language for Everyone: A Basic Course in Communication with the Deaf. Cathy Rice. LC 77-14592. 1978. 19.99 (*0-8407-9002-3*) Nelson.
Sign Language Fun. Ralph Miller et al. 16p. (J). 1984. pap. 4.50 (*0-915035-02-2*, 4163) Dawn Sign.
Sign Language House. Frank A. Paul et al. 16p. (J). 1984. pap. 4.50 (*0-915035-03-0*, 4162) Dawn Sign.
Sign Language Interpreting: A Basic Resource Book. Sharon Newmann-Solow. (Illus.). 107p. (C). 1981. pap. text ed. 9.95 (*0-913072-44-3*) Natl Assn Deaf.
Sign Language Lecture Notes on Stories from the Attic, Vol. 2: The Magic Pot. Harry W. Hoemann. 40p. (Orig.). (C). 1991. pap. text ed. 3.95 (*0-9614621-6-7*) Bowling Gr Pr.
Sign Language Lecture Notes on Stories from the Attic, Vol. 3: The Father, the Son & the Donkey. Harry W. Hoemann. 56p. (Orig.). (C). 1991. pap. text ed. 3.95 (*1-880064-00-6*) Bowling Gr Pr.
Sign Language Lecture Notes on Stories from the Attic, Vol. 4: The Village Stew. Harry W. Hoemann. 56p. (Orig.). (C). 1991. pap. text ed. 3.95 (*1-880064-01-4*) Bowling Gr Pr.
***Sign Language Made Simple.** Karen Lewis. LC 97-9233. 1997. pap. 12.95 (*0-385-48857-2*) Doubleday.
***Sign Language Made Simple.** 2nd ed. Edgar D. Lawrence. LC 96-6501. 1997. write for info. (*0-88243-500-0*) Gospel Pub.

S

An Asterisk (*) at the beginning of an entry indicates that the title is appearing in BIP for the first time.

Sign Language Made Simple: A Complete Manual for Learning Sign Language in Sentence Form. Edgar D. Lawrence. LC 79-10417. (Illus.). 240p. (J). (gr. k up). 1975. text ed. 16.95 (*0-88243-604-X*, 02-0604) Gospel Pub.

Sign Language of the Mysteries, Vols. 1-2. J. S. Ward. 270p. 1993. pap. 17.95 (*1-56459-391-6*) Kessinger Pub.

Sign Language Opposites. Ralph Miller et al. 16p. (J). 1985. pap. 4.50 (*0-915035-04-9*, 4164) Dawn Sign.

Sign Language Research: Theoretical Issues. Ed. by Ceil Lucas. LC 89-28131. (Illus.). 398p. 1990. text ed. 49.95 (*0-930323-58-0*) Gallaudet Univ Pr.

Sign Language Research & Application. Ed. by Siegmund Prillwitz & Tomas Vollhaber. (International Studies on Sign Language & the Communication of the Deaf: Vol. 13). 304p. 1990. text ed. 39.95 (*3-927731-12-9*, Pub. by Signum-Verlag GW) Gallaudet Univ Pr.

***Sign Language Research 1994.** Ed. by Heleen Bos & Trude Schermer. (International Studies on Sign Language & the Communication of the Deaf: Vol. 29). 360p. 1995. text ed. 45.00 (*3-927731-57-9*, Pub. by Signum-Verlag GW) Gallaudet Univ Pr.

Sign Language Study. 2nd rev. ed. Kelley Higgens-Nelson. (Exambusters Ser.). (Illus.). 250p. (YA). (gr. 7 up). 1996. pap. 9.95 (*1-881374-95-5*, Exambusters) Ace Acad.

Sign Languages: Stories. James Hannah. LC 93-12820. 168p. (C). 1993. 22.50 (*0-8262-0900-9*) U of Mo Pr.

Sign Languages of Aboriginal Australia: Cultural, Semiotic, & Communicative Perspectives. Adam Kendon. 450p. 1989. 79.95 (*0-521-36008-0*) Cambridge U Pr.

Sign Languages of Deaf People & Psycholinguistics. A. Van Uden. viii, 120p. 1986. 33.75 (*90-265-0701-1*) Swets.

Sign Maze: Approaches the Development of Signs, Labels, Markings, & Instruction Manuals. Thomas F. Bresnahan et al. LC 93-30075. (Illus.). 70p. (Orig.). 1993. pap. 21.00 (*0-939874-94-6*, 4346) ASSE.

Sign-Me-Fine: Experiencing American Sign Language. Laura Greene & Eva B. Dicker. LC 90-5148. (Illus.). 120p. (YA). (gr. 7-12). 1990. reprint ed. pap. 6.95 (*0-930323-76-9*, Pub. by K Green Pubns) Gallaudet Univ Pr.

Sign Numbers. Nancy Bartusch. (Illus.). 54p. (Orig.). (J). (ps-3). 1988. pap. 5.00 (*0-916708-17-9*) Modern Signs.

Sign of a Promise & Other Stories. James C. Schaap. 263p. (Orig.). 1979. pap. 6.95 (*0-932914-02-0*) Dordt Coll Pr.

Sign of Angellica. Janet M. Todd. 1992. pap. text ed. 17.50 (*0-231-07135-3*) Col U Pr.

Sign of Angellica: Women, Writing, & Fiction, 1660-1800. Janet M. Todd. 326p. 1989. text ed. 49.50 (*0-231-07134-5*) Col U Pr.

Sign of Chaos. Roger Zelazny. (Amber Ser.: Vol. 8). 224p. 1988. mass mkt. 4.99 (*0-380-89637-0*, AvoNova) Avon.

Sign of Contradiction. Pope John Paul, II. (C). 1988. 39.00 (*0-85439-158-4*, Pub. by St Paul Pubns UK) St Mut.

Sign of Death. Barbara Merrell. (YA). (gr. 7 up). 1981. mass mkt. 2.50 (*0-89083-781-3*, Zebra Kensgtn) Kensgtn Pub Corp.

Sign of Fear. R. L. Stine. (Fear Street Ser.: No. 4). (J). 1996. mass mkt. 3.99 (*0-671-00291-0*) PB.

Sign of Four. Arthur Conan Doyle. Ed. by Christopher Roden. (Oxford Sherlock Holmes Ser.). 200p. (C). 1993. 11.00 (*0-19-212316-5*, 14614) OUP.

Sign of Four. Arthur Conan Doyle. (J). 1997. pap. 2.95 (*0-8167-0851-7*) Troll Communs.

Sign of Four. large type ed. Arthur Conan Doyle. Bd. with Study in Scarlet. 1969. 12.00 (*0-7089-0190-5*) Ulverscroft.

Sign of Her Heart. John M. Haffert. 270p. 1971. pap. 4.50 (*0-911988-03-3*, 42955) AMI Pr.

Sign of Jonah. Boeli Van Leeuwen. Tr. by Andre Lefevere. LC 94-31750. 203p. 1995. 22.00 (*1-877946-62-1*) Permanent Pr.

Sign of Jonas. Thomas Merton. LC 79-10283. 362p. 1979. pap. 10.95 (*0-15-682529-5*, Harvest Bks) HarBrace.

Sign of Misfortune. Vasil Bykov. Tr. by Alan Myers from RUS. (Stebbins Ser.). 256p. 1990. 19.95 (*0-89864-049-0*) Allerton Pr.

Sign of Reconciliation & Conversion: The Sacrament of Penance for Our Times. Monika K. Hellwig. LC 82-80404. (Message of the Sacraments Ser.: Vol. 4). 157p. 1982. pap. 12.95 (*0-8146-5272-7*) Liturgical Pr.

***Sign of the Beaver.** Elizabeth G. Speare. 1997. mass mkt. 2.69 (*0-440-22730-5*) Dell.

Sign of the Beaver. Elizabeth G. Speare. 144p. (YA). (gr. 5 up). 1983. 14.95 (*0-395-33890-5*) HM.

Sign of the Beaver. Elizabeth G. Speare. 144p. (J). (gr. 5-9). 1905. mass mkt. 4.50 (*0-440-47900-2*, YB BDD) BDD Bks Young Read.

Sign of the Beaver. braille ed. Elizabeth G. Speare. 172p. (J). 1994. vinyl bd. 13.76 (*1-56956-563-5*, BR9513, YB BDD) BDD Bks Young Read.

Sign of the Beaver: A Literature Unit. John Carratello & Patty Carratello. (Literature Units Ser.). (Illus.). 48p. (Orig.). (gr. 3-5). 1991. student ed. 7.95 (*1-55734-402-7*) Tchr Create Mat.

Sign of the Beaver: A Study Guide. Rosemary Villanella. (Novel-Ties Ser.). 1989. student ed., teacher ed., pap. text ed. 15.95 (*0-88122-052-3*) Lrn Links.

Sign of the Carousel. Jane Peart. (International Romance Ser.). 216p. (Orig.). 1993. pap. 7.99 (*0-8007-5461-1*) Revell.

Sign of the Chrysanthemum. Katherine Paterson. LC 72-7553. (Trophy Bk.). (Illus.). 128p. (J). (gr. 6 up). 1988. reprint ed. pap. 3.95 (*0-06-440232-0*, Trophy) HarpC Child Bks.

Sign of the Crooked Arrow. rev. ed. Franklin W. Dixon. LC 71-100119. (Hardy Boys Ser.: Vol. 28). (Illus.). 180p. (J). (gr. 5-9). 1949. 5.95 (*0-448-08928-9*, G&D) Putnam Pub Group.

Sign of the Cross. John Bligh. (C). 1988. 39.00 (*0-85439-109-6*, Pub. by St Paul Pubns UK) St Mut.

Sign of the Cross. John Damascus et al. 1987. pap. 1.00 (*0-89981-200-7*) Eastern Orthodox.

***Sign of the Cross.** David Horton. 1997. pap. text ed. 9.99 (*1-56476-611-X*, Victor Bks) Chariot Victor.

Sign of the Cross: Travels in Catholic Europe. Colm Toibin. 304p. 1996. pap. 13.00 (*0-679-75855-0*) McKay.

Sign of the Cross: Travels in Catholic Europe. Colm Toibin. LC 95-7299. 304p. 1995. 24.00 (*0-679-44203-0*) Pantheon.

Sign of the Dove: The Exciting Sequel to Dragon's Milk. Susan Fletcher. LC 95-584. 224p. (J). (gr. 4-8). 1996. 17.00 (*0-689-80460-1*, Atheneum Bks Young) S&S Childrens.

Sign of the Falcon. Carolyn Keene. (Nancy Drew Ser.: No. 130). (J). (gr. 3-6). 1996. pap. 3.99 (*0-671-50508-4*, Minstrel Bks) PB.

Sign of the Four. Arthur Conan Doyle. LC 93-50112. 297p. 1994. 14.95 (*1-55709-301-6*) Applewood.

Sign of the Four. Arthur Conan Doyle. 1989. lib. bdg. 15.95 (*0-89966-230-7*) Buccaneer Bks.

Sign of the Four. Arthur Conan Doyle. Ed. & Intro. by Christopher Roden. (World's Classics Ser.). 200p. 1995. reprint ed. pap. 5.95 (*0-19-282379-5*) OUP.

Sign of the Fox. Sara Stambaugh. LC 91-70665. 182p. 1991. 16.95 (*1-56148-011-8*) Good Bks PA.

Sign of the Golden Grasshopper: A Life of Sir Thomas Gresham. Perry Gresham & Carol Jose. LC 95-9972. 1995. 24.95 (*0-915463-71-7*) Jameson Bks.

"Sign" of the Last Days--When? Carl O. Jonsson & Wolfgang Herbst. LC 86-72140. (Illus.). 288p. (C). 1987. pap. 7.95 (*0-914675-09-5*) Comment Pr.

Sign of the Raven. Poul Anderson. (Last Viking Ser.: No. 3). (Orig.). 1981. mass mkt. 2.50 (*0-8217-0625-X*, Zebra Kensgtn) Kensgtn Pub Corp.

***Sign of the Scales.** Marianne Brandis. 224p. 1990. pap. 9.95 (*0-88984-103-9*, Pub. by Porcupines Quill CN) Genl Dist Srvs.

Sign of the Scorpion. J. Gonzo Smith. 1996. mass mkt. 7.95 (*1-56201-094-8*) Blue Moon Bks.

Sign of the Seahorse: A Tale of Greed & High Adventure in Two Acts. Graeme Base. (Illus.). 44p. 1992. 19.95 (*0-8109-3825-1*) Abrams.

Sign of the Serpent. large type ed. Sara Hely. 400p. 1985. 25.99 (*0-7089-1387-3*) Ulverscroft.

***Sign of the Stag.** Joseph McKenna. Ed. by Edward D. Ives & Pauleena M. MacDougall. (Northeast Folklore Ser.). (Illus.). 97p. (C). 1997. pap. text ed. write for info. (*0-943197-24-4*) ME Folklife Ctr.

Sign of the Twisted Candle. Carolyn Keene. (Nancy Drew Ser.: Vol. 9). (Illus.). 196p. (J). (gr. 3-9). 1959. 5.95 (*0-448-09509-2*, G&D) Putnam Pub Group.

Sign of the Twisted Candles. Carolyn Keene. LC 96-28382. (Nancy Drew Mystery Stories Ser.: No. 9). (Illus.). 210p. (J). (gr. 3-10). 1997. reprint ed. 12.95 (*1-55709-163-3*) Applewood.

Sign of the Unicorn. Roger Zelazny. 192p. (YA). (gr. 9 up). 1986. reprint ed. mass mkt. 5.99 (*0-380-00831-9*, AvoNova) Avon.

Sign of Three: Dupin, Holmes, Peirce. Ed. by Umberto Eco & Thomas A. Sebeok. LC 82-49207. (Advances in Semiotics Ser.). (Illus.). 250p. 1984. 31.50 (*0-253-35235-5*) Ind U Pr.

Sign of Three: Dupin, Holmes, Peirce. Ed. by Umberto Eco & Thomas A. Sebeok. LC 82-49207. (Advances in Semiotics Ser.). (Illus.). 250p. 1988. pap. 13.95 (*0-253-20487-9*, MB-487) Ind U Pr.

Sign Off. Jon Katz. 368p. 1996. mass mkt. 5.99 (*0-553-57569-4*) Bantam.

***Sign-Off for the Old Met: The Metropolitan Opera Broadcasts 1950-1966, 2 vols.** Paul Jackson. LC 97-19864. (Saturday Afternoons at the Old Met Ser.). (Illus.). 1200p. 1997. 89.95 (*1-57467-031-X*, Amadeus Pr) Timber.

***Sign-Off for the Old Met: The Metropolitan Opera Broadcasts 1950-1966.** Paul Jackson. LC 97-19864. (Saturday Afternoons at the Old Met Ser.: Vol. 2). (Illus.). 600p. 1997. 49.95 (*1-57467-030-1*, Amadeus Pr) Timber.

Sign on Rosie's Door. Maurice Sendak. LC 60-9451. (Illus.). 48p. (J). (gr. k-3). 1960. 14.95 (*0-06-025505-6*) HarpC Child Bks.

Sign on the Dotted Line: Two Hundred Years of U. S. Constitution Silly Trivia. Carole Marsh. (Quantum Leap Ser.). (Illus.). (Orig.). (gr. 3-9). 1994. 29.95 (*1-55609-191-5*); pap. 19.95 (*0-935326-76-6*) Gallopade Pub Group.

Sign Painter. Jack Rudman. (Career Examination Ser.: C-2090). 1994. reprint ed. pap. 27.95 (*0-8373-2090-9*) Nat Learn.

Sign Painter's Dream. Roger Roth. 32p. (J). 1995. pap. 6.99 (*0-517-88541-7*) Crown Pub Group.

Sign Painter's Secret: The Story of a Revolutionary Girl. Dorothy Hoobler & Thomas Hoobler. (Her Story Ser.). (Illus.). 64p. (J). (gr. 4-6). 1991. pap. 3.95 (*0-382-24345-5*); lib. bdg. 9.95 (*0-382-24143-6*) Silver Burdett Pr.

Sign Painting & Graphics Course. Lonnie Tettaton. LC 80-12135. (Illus.). 240p. 1981. pap. 30.95 (*0-88229-768-6*) Nelson-Hall.

Sign Painting Techniques: Beginner to Professional. Ralph Gregory. (Illus.). 1973. 21.95 (*0-911380-29-9*) ST Pubns.

Sign, Semiotics Around the World. Ed. by Bailey & Ladislav Matejka. (Michigan Slavic Contributions Ser.: No. 9). 1980. 10.00 (*0-930042-28-X*) Mich Slavic Pubns.

Sign, Sentence, Discourse: Language in Medieval Thought & Literature. Ed. by Julian N. Wasserman & Lois Roney. 344p. 1988. 45.00 (*0-8156-2445-X*); pap. 18.95 (*0-8156-2451-4*) Syracuse U Pr.

Sign Structures & Foundations: A Guide for Designers & Estimators. Peter Horsley. (Illus.). 1984. pap. 24.95 (*0-911380-65-5*) ST Pubns.

Sign, Symbol, Script: An Exhibition on the Origins of Writing & the Alphabet. Ed. by Martha L. Carter & Keith N. Schoville. viii, 88p. 1984. pap. 5.95 (*0-614-11210-9*) Eisenbrauns.

Sign, System & Function: Papers of the First & Second Polish-American Semiotics Colloquia. Ed. by Jerzy Pelc et al. LC 84-3288. (Approaches to Semiotics Ser.: No. 67). xiii, 503p. 1984. 180.80 (*90-279-3270-0*) Mouton.

Sign, Textuality, World. Floyd Merrell. LC 91-26984. (Advances in Semiotics Ser.). (Illus.). 288p. 1992. text ed. 19.95 (*0-253-33748-8*) Ind U Pr.

***Sign, Textuality, World.** Floyd Merrell. LC 91-26984. (Advances in Semiotics Ser.). (Illus.). 282p. pap. 80.40 (*0-608-05034-2*, 2059695) Bks Demand.

Sign the Speech: An Introduction to Theatrical Interpreting. Julie Gebron. 96p. (Orig.). 1996. pap. 14.95 (*1-884362-04-4*) Butte Pubns.

Sign User's Guide: A Marketing Aid. rev. ed. James R. Claus & Karen Claus. Ed. by William Dorsey. LC 88-201992. (Illus.). 165p. 1988. 15.00 (*0-911380-83-3*, 92) ST Pubns.

Sign Wars: The Cluttered Landscape of Advertising. Goldman & Papson. LC 95-9396. (Critical Perspectives Ser.). 323p. 1996. lib. bdg. 44.50 (*1-57230-014-0*, 0014) Guilford Pr.

Sign Wars: The Cluttered Landscape of Advertising. Robert L. Goldman & Papson. LC 95-9396. (Critical Perspectives Ser.). (Illus.). 323p. 1996. pap. text ed. 19.95 (*1-57230-034-5*, 0034) Guilford Pr.

Sign with Me: Building Concepts Workbook-ASL. Mary P. Moeller & Brenda Schick. 1994. pap. text ed. 8.95 (*0-938510-63-0*, 76-003) Boys Town Pr.

***Sign with Me Vol. 3: Positive Parenting (ASL)** Mary P. Moeller & Brenda Schick. (Orig.). 1997. wbk. ed., pap. 8.95 (*1-889322-03-2*, 76-005(ASL)) Boys Town Pr.

***Sign with Me Vol. 3: Positive Parenting (MCE)** Mary P. Moeller & Brenda Schick. (Orig.). 1996. wbk. ed., pap. 8.95 (*0-938510-84-3*, 76-006(MCE)) Boys Town Pr.

Sign with Me Vol. I: Building Conversations Workbook-ASL. Mary P. Moeller & Brenda Schink. 1994. pap. text ed. 8.95 (*0-938510-62-2*, 76-001) Boys Town Pr.

Sign with Me Colors. (Illus.). 24p. (J). 1987. pap. 3.95 (*0-939849-02-X*, 105P) Sugar Sign Pr.

Sign with Me Weather. 24p. (J). 1987. pap. 3.95 (*0-939849-03-8*, 106P) Sugar Sign Pr.

Signage. Alan Davies. LC 87-60108. (Roof Bks.). 150p. (Orig.). 1987. pap. 10.95 (*0-937804-24-X*) Segue NYC.

Signal: Blackbird. Robert Tralins. 1992. mass mkt. 4.50 (*1-55817-595-4*, Pinncle Kensgtn) Kensgtn Pub Corp.

Signal Analysis. Athanasios Papoulis. (C). 1977. text ed. write for info. (*0-07-048460-0*) McGraw.

Signal Analysis & Estimation. Ronald Fante. LC 87-21707. 448p. 1988. text ed. 112.00 (*0-471-62425-X*) Wiley.

Signal Analysis in Linear Systems. Ronald C. Houts. (Oxford Series in Electrical & Computer Engineering). (Illus.). 432p. (C). 1995. text ed. 69.00 (*0-03-028744-8*); Solutions manual. teacher ed., text ed. write for info. (*0-03-028747-2*) OUP.

***Signal & Data Processing of Small Targets.** Ed. by Oliver E. Drummond. 68p. 1997. pap. 107.00 (*0-8194-2585-0*) SPIE.

Signal & Image Processing Sourcebook. Robert Libbey. 512p. 1994. text ed. 69.95 (*0-442-30861-2*) Van Nos Reinhold.

Signal & Image Processing with Neural Networks: C Sourcebook. Timothy Masters. 417p. 1994. pap. text ed. 44.95 (*0-471-04963-8*) Wiley.

Signal & Linear System Analysis. Gordon E. Carlson. 768p. 1994. text ed. write for info. (*0-471-12499-0*) Wiley.

Signal, & Other Stories. Wsewolod M. Garshin. Tr. by Rowland Smith from RUS. LC 77-163027. (Short Story Index Reprint Ser.). 1977. reprint ed. 23.95 (*0-8369-3941-7*) Ayer.

Signal & Power Integrity in Digital Systems: TTL, CMOS, & BiCMOS. James E. Buchanan. LC 95-38799. 1995. text ed. 60.00 (*0-07-008734-2*) McGraw.

Signal Approach to Children's Books. Ed. by Nancy Chambers. LC 81-8824. 352p. 1981. 27.50 (*0-8108-1447-1*) Scarecrow.

Signal Averaged Electrocardiography: Concepts, Methods, & Applications. J. Anthony Gomes. LC 93-5136. 608p. (C). 1993. lib. bdg. 222.00 (*0-7923-2390-4*) Kluwer Ac.

Signal-Boxes & Semaphores of the Leicester Gap. Mike Spencer. LC 94-26297. 1994. 30.00 (*0-7509-0587-5*, Pub. by Sutton Pubng UK) Bks Intl VA.

Signal Coding & Processing. 2nd ed. Graham Wade. LC 93-37133. (Illus.). 450p. (C). 1994. text ed. 90.00 (*0-521-41230-7*); pap. text ed. 44.95 (*0-521-42336-8*) Cambridge U Pr.

***Signal Compression, Coding of Speech, Audio, Image & Video.** 200p. 1997. lib. bdg. 29.00 (*981-02-2694-2*) World Scientific Pub.

***Signal Conditioning & PC-Based Data Acquisition Handbook: A Reference on Analog & Digital Signal Conditioning for PC-Based Data Acquisition.** Steve Lekas et al. (Illus.). 128p. 1997. pap. 25.95 (*0-9656789-0-3*) IOtech.

Signal Corps in the War of the Rebellion. Joseph W. Brown. (Illus.). 916p. (C). 1996. reprint ed. 60.00 (*0-935523-54-5*) Butternut & Blue.

Signal Corps, U. S. A. in the War of the Rebellion. Willard J. Brown. LC 74-4670. (Telecommunications Ser.). (Illus.). 916p. 1974. reprint ed. 63.95 (*0-405-06036-X*) Ayer.

Signal Detection: Mechanisms, Models, & Applications. Michael L. Commons et al. 304p. (C). 1991. text ed. 59.95 (*0-8058-0823-X*) L Erlbaum Assocs.

Signal Detection & Estimation. Mourad Barkat. LC 91-13451. 449p. reprint ed. pap. 128.00 (*0-7837-5847-2*, 2045566) Bks Demand.

Signal Detection & Recognition by Human Observers. John A. Swets. LC 87-63305. 734p. 1989. reprint ed. 54.95 (*0-932146-21-X*) Peninsula CA.

Signal Detection Theory & Psychophysics. David M. Green & John A. Swets. LC 88-62297. 521p. 1989. reprint ed. 54.95 (*0-932146-23-6*) Peninsula CA.

Signal Detection Theory & ROC Analysis in Psychology & Diagnostics: Collected Papers. John A. Swets. (Scientific Psychology Ser.). 328p. 1996. text ed. 69.95 (*0-8058-1834-0*) L Erlbaum Assocs.

Signal Electrician. Jack Rudman. (Career Examination Ser.: C-2440). 1994. pap. 27.95 (*0-8373-2440-8*) Nat Learn.

Signal Lives Series, 51 bks., Set. Ed. by Annette K. Baxter. 1980. lib. bdg. 1,889.50 (*0-405-12815-0*) Ayer.

Signal Maintainer. Jack Rudman. (Career Examination Ser.: C-742). 1994. pap. 23.95 (*0-8373-0742-2*) Nat Learn.

Signal Molecules in Plants & Plant-Microbe Interactions. Ed. by B. J. Lugtenberg. (NATO ASI Series H: Vol. 36). (Illus.). 448p. 1990. 189.95 (*0-387-50381-1*) Spr-Verlag.

Signal Noise. Miriam Goodman. LC 82-71819. 64p. 1982. pap. 3.95 (*0-914086-39-1*) Alicejamesbooks.

Signal Peptidases. Gunnar Von Heijne. (Molecular Biology Intelligence Unit Ser.). 120p. 1994. 89.95 (*1-57059-184-9*) R G Landes.

Signal Perception & Transduction in Higher Plants. Ed. by R. Ranjeva & A. M. Boudet. (NATO ASI Series H: Cell Biology: Vol. 47). (Illus.). ix, 344p. 1990. 142.95 (*0-387-51772-3*) Spr-Verlag.

Signal Processing: A Vector Space Approach. Gregory H. Wakefield. 1995. text ed. write for info. (*0-07-067808-1*) McGraw.

Signal Processing: Model Based Approach. J. V. Candy. 256p. 1986. text ed. write for info. (*0-07-009725-9*) McGraw.

Signal Processing: Principles & Applications. D. Brook & R. J. Wynne. (Illus.). 288p. (C). 1988. pap. text ed. 19.95 (*0-7131-3564-6*, Pub. by E Arnold UK) Routledge Chapman & Hall.

Signal Processing - A First Introduction. Ed. by J. F. Martin. 272p. (C). 1990. pap. text ed. 145.00 (*0-273-03256-9*, Pub. by Pitman Pubng UK) St Mut.

Signal Processing - Theories & Applications: Proceedings of the European Conference, 5th, Barcelona, Spain, 18-21 Sept., 1990, 3 vols., Set. Ed. by L. Torres et al. 2100p. 1990. 558.25 (*0-444-88636-2*) Elsevier.

Signal Processing - Theories, Implementation & Applications: ISSPA 87: Proceedings IASTED Symposium, Brisbane, Australia, August 24-28, 1987 (Co-Sponsored by IEEE, IREE, IE Australia), 2 vols., 1. Ed. by Boualem Boashash. 907p. 1988. write for info. (*0-85814-141-8*) Acta Pr.

Signal Processing - Theories, Implementation & Applications: ISSPA 87: Proceedings IASTED Symposium, Brisbane, Australia, August 24-28, 1987 (Co-Sponsored by IEEE, IREE, IE Australia), 2 vols., 2. Ed. by Boualem Boashash. 907p. 1988. write for info. (*0-85814-142-6*) Acta Pr.

Signal Processing - Theories, Implementation & Applications: ISSPA 87: Proceedings IASTED Symposium, Brisbane, Australia, August 24-28, 1987 (Co-Sponsored by IEEE, IREE, IE Australia), 2 vols., Set. Ed. by Boualem Boashash. 907p. 1988. 98.00 (*0-85814-143-4*, 120) Acta Pr.

Signal Processing Algorithms in FORTRAN & C. Samuel D. Stearns & Ruth A. David. LC 92-20876. 1993. write for info. (*0-13-816307-3*) P-H Gen Ref & Trav.

Signal Processing Algorithms in MATLAB. Samuel D. Stearns & Ruth A. David. LC 95-49046. (Prentice-Hall Signal Processing Ser.). 3720p. (C). 1996. text ed. 66.00 (*0-13-045154-1*) P-H.

Signal Processing Algorithms Using Fortran & C. Samuel D. Stearns et al. 384p. 1992. text ed. 62.00 (*0-13-812694-1*) P-H.

Signal Processing & Digital Filtering: Proceedings of the International Symposium Held in Lugano, Switzerland, June 18-21, 1990. M. H. Hamza. 319p. 1990. 90.00 (*0-88986-158-7*, 166) Acta Pr.

Signal Processing & Its Applications. Ed. by N. K. Bose. LC 93-18104. (Handbook of Statistics Ser.: Vol. 10). 1010p. 1993. 190.00 (*0-444-89205-2*, North Holland) Elsevier.

Signal Processing & Linear Systems. B. P. Lathi. (Illus.). 750p. (C). 1997. text ed. 74.95 (*0-944413-35-8*) Berkeley-Cambridge.

***Signal Processing & Pattern Recognition for Non-Destructive Evaluation.** (Engineering NDE Ser.). (Illus.). 352p. (C). (gr. 13 up). 1997. text ed. 49.95 (*0-412-43130-0*, Chap & Hall NY) Chapman & Hall.

Signal Processing & Pattern Recognition in Nondestructive Evaluation of Materials. Ed. by C. H. Chen. (NATO Asi Series F: Vol. 44). viii, 344p. 1988. 100.95 (*0-387-19100-3*) Spr-Verlag.

Signal Processing & Systems Theory: Selected Topics. Charles K. Chui & Guanrong Chen. Ed. by T. S. Huang et al. LC 92-14512. (Information Sciences Ser.: Vol. 26). (Illus.). xi, 267p. 1992. 54.50 (*0-387-55442-4*) Spr-Verlag.

Signal Processing Design Techniques. Britt Rorabaugh. (Illus.). 304p. 1986. 32.50 (*0-8306-0457-X*, NO. 2657) McGraw-Hill Prof.

Signal Processing for Computer Vision. Ed. by Gosta H. Granlund. 437p. (C). 1994. lib. bdg. 146.00 (*0-7923-9530-1*) Kluwer Ac.

Signal Processing for Industrial Diagnostics. T. M. Romberg et al. LC 96-5957. (Series in Measurement Science & Technology). 1996. text ed. 74.95 (*0-471-96166-3*) Wiley.

Signal Processing Handbook. Chen. (Electrical Engineering & Electronics Ser.: Vol. 51). 840p. 1988. 215.00 (*0-8247-7956-8*) Dekker.

Signal Processing in C. Christopher E. Reid et al. 352p. 1991. pap. text ed. 49.95 (*0-471-52713-0*) Wiley.

Signal Processing in C. Christopher E. Reid & Thomas B. Passin. 352p. 1992. 77.95 incl. disk (*0-471-56955-0*) Wiley.

***Signal Processing in Electronic Communications: For Engineers & Mathematicians.** Michael J. Chapman et al. 300p. 1997. pap. 35.00 (*1-898563-30-6*, Pub. by Albion Pubng UK) Paul & Co Pubs.

Signal Processing in Measurement. Ed. by K. Havrilla & I. Kollar. (Illus.). 276p. (C). 1988. text ed. 125.00 (*0-941743-42-X*) Nova Sci Pubs.

Signal Processing in Telecommunications: Proceedings of the 7th International Thyrrhenian Workshop on Digital Communications, Viagreggio, Italy, September 10-14, 1995. Ed. by Ezio Biglieri & Marco Luise. 400p. 1996. pap. 69.95 (*3-540-76019-9*) Spr-Verlag.

Signal Processing IV: Theories & Applications, 3 vols., Set. Ed. by J. L. Lacoume et al. 1770p. 1988. 543.25 (*0-444-70516-3*, North Holland) Elsevier.

Signal Processing Methods for Audio, Images & Telecommunications. Ed. by Peter Clarkson & Henry Stark. (Signal Processing & Its Applications Ser.). (Illus.). 452p. 1995. boxed 49.95 (*0-12-175790-0*) Acad Pr.

Signal Processing of HDTV, No. III. Ed. by H. Yasuda & L. Chiariglione. LC 92-13878. 1992. 269.50 (*0-444-89491-8*) Elsevier.

Signal Processing of HDTV: Proc. of the 2nd Internat. Workshop at L'Aquila, Italy, 29 Feb. to March 2, 1988. Ed. by L. Chiariglione. 698p. 1989. 253.75 (*0-444-70518-X*, North Holland) Elsevier.

Signal Processing of HDTV: Proceedings of the International Workshop on HDTV, 3rd, Turin, Italy, 30 Aug.-1 Sept., 1989, No. 2. Ed. by L. Chiariglione. 920p. 1990. 249.50 (*0-444-88833-0*) Elsevier.

Signal Processing of HDTV: Proceedings of the International Workshop on HDTV '94, Turin, Italy, October 26-28, 1994. Ed. by Y. Niomiya & L. Chiariglione. 592p. 1995. text ed. 321.00 (*0-444-82283-6*) Elsevier.

Signal Processing of HDTV, IV. Ed. by E. Dubois & L. Chiariglione. 846p. 1993. 337.25 (*0-444-81551-1*) Elsevier.

Signal Processing of HDTV, V: Proceedings of the International Workshop on HDTV '93, Ottawa, Canada, October 26-28, 1993. Ed. by L. Chiarliiglione et al. LC 94-29287. 868p. 1994. 292.00 (*0-444-81844-8*) Elsevier.

Signal Processing, Part I: Signal Processing Theory. Ed. by L. Auslander et al. (IMA Volumes in Mathematics & Its Applications Ser.: Vol. 22). (Illus.). xiii, 251p. 1990. 42.95 (*0-387-97215-3*) Spr-Verlag.

Signal Processing, Part II: Control Theory & Applications. Ed. by L. Auslander et al. (IMA Volumes in Mathematics & Its Applications Ser.: Vol. 23). (Illus.). xiii, 411p. 1990. 56.95 (*0-387-97230-7*) Spr-Verlag.

Signal Processing, Scattering & Operator Theory, & Numerical Methods. M. A. Kaashoek et al. (Progress in Systems & Control Theory Ser.: Vol. 5). 555p. 1990. 137.50 (*0-8176-3471-1*) Birkhauser.

***Signal Processing, Sensor Fusion, & Target Recognition VI.** Ed. by Ivan Kadar. 80p. 1997. pap. 116.00 (*0-8194-2483-8*) SPIE.

***Signal Processing, Speech & Music.** Ed. by Stan Tempelaars. LC 96-46383. (Studies on New Music Research: Vol. 1). 360p. 1996. 91.00 (*90-265-1481-6*) Swets.

Signal Processing Systems: Theory & Design. Nicholas Kalouptsidis. LC 96-12447. (Series in Telecommunications & Signal Processing). 1996. text ed. write for info. (*0-471-11220-8*) Wiley.

Signal Processing Technology & Applications. Ed. by John G. Ackenhusen. LC 94-46444. (Technology Update Ser.). 1995. write for info. (*0-7803-2469-2*) Inst Electrical.

***Signal Processing Using Optics: Fundamentals, Devices, Architecture, & Applications.** Bradley G. Boone. (Johns Hopkins University Applied Physics Laboratory Series in Science & Engineering). (Illus.). 480p. (C). 1997. text ed. 75.00 (*0-19-508424-1*) OUP.

Signal Processing VI: Theories & Applications: Proceedings of EUSIPCO-92, Sixth European Signal Processing Conference, Brussels, Belgium, August 24-27, 1992, 3 vols., Set. Ed. by J. Vandewalle et al. LC 92-24842. 1992. 602.50 (*0-444-89587-6*) Elsevier.

Signal Processing with Alpha-Stable Distribution & Applications. Chrysostomos L. Nikias & Min Shao. LC 95-1482. (Adaptive & Learning Systems for Signal Processing, Communications & Control Ser.). 184p. 1995. text ed. 69.95 (*0-471-10647-X*, Wiley-Interscience) Wiley.

Signal Processing with Fractals: A Wavelet-Based Approach. Gregory Wornell. LC 95-25228. 177p. 1995. text ed. 56.00 (*0-13-120999-X*) P-H.

Signal Processing with Lapped Transforms. Henrique S. Malvar. (Telecommunications Library). 375p. 1992. text ed. write for info. (*0-89006-467-9*) Artech Hse.

***Signal Processing with Lapped Transforms.** Henrique S. Malvar. LC 91-35984. (Artech House Telecommunications Library). (Illus.). 379p. 1992. reprint ed. pap. 108.10 (*0-608-02497-X*, 2063141) Bks Demand.

***Signal Processing Workshop on High-Order Statistics, 1997.** 550p. 1997. pap. 120.00 (*0-8186-8005-9*) IEEE Comp Soc.

Signal Processing Workshop on Statistical Signal & Array Processing: SSAP 96. LC 96-75525. 608p. 1996. pap. 130.00 (*0-8186-7576-4*) IEEE Comp Soc.

Signal Recovery & Synthesis. (Technical Digest Series, 1989: Vol. 15). 250p. (Orig.). 1989. Postconference ed. lib. bdg. 66.00 (*1-55752-096-8*) Optical Soc.

Signal Recovery & Synthesis. LC 95-67806. (1995 Technical Digest Ser.: Vol. 11). 128p. (Orig.). 1995. pap. 66.00 (*1-55752-392-4*) Optical Soc.

Signal Recovery & Synthesis IV. LC 92-80620. (Technical Digest Series, 1992: Vol. 11). 300p. (Orig.). 1992. pap. 66.00 (*1-55752-236-7*) Optical Soc.

Signal Recovery from Noise in Electronic Instrumentation. 2nd ed. T. H. Wilmshurst. (Illus.). 248p. 1990. 107.00 (*0-7503-0059-0*); pap. 36.00 (*0-7503-0058-2*) IOP Pub.

Signal Routing in Integrated Circuit Layout. Chi-Ping Hsu. Ed. by Harold Stone. LC 86-1382. (Computer Science: Very Large Systems Integration Ser.: No. 1). 126p. reprint ed. 35.70 (*0-8357-1744-5*, 2070393) Bks Demand.

Signal Success in Bridge. Danny Roth. (Illus.). 142p. 1993. pap. 15.95 (*0-575-05539-1*, Pub. by V Gollancz UK) Trafalgar.

Signal Theory & Processing. Frederic De Coulon. LC 85-73435. (Artech House Communications & Electronic Defense Library). (Illus.). 630p. reprint ed. pap. 179.60 (*0-8357-5586-X*, 2035217) Bks Demand.

Signal to Depart. M. H. Salmon. LC 95-95042. (Illus.). 214p. 1995. 21.95 (*0-944383-33-5*); pap. 12.95 (*0-944383-32-7*) High-Lonesome.

***Signal to Noise.** Carla Sinclair. 1997. 22.50 (*0-06-251533-0*) Harper SF.

Signal To Syntax: Bootstrapping from Speech to Grammar in Early Acquisition. Ed. by James L. Morgan & Katherine Demuth. 500p. 1995. pap. 36.00 (*0-8058-1266-0*); text ed. 69.95 (*0-8058-1265-2*) L Erlbaum Assocs.

Signal Transduction: A Practical Approach. Ed. by G. Milligan. (Practical Approach Ser.). (Illus.). 192p. 1992. 95.00 (*0-19-963296-0*, IRL Pr); pap. 55.00 (*0-19-963295-2*, IRL Pr) OUP.

Signal Transduction: Prokaryotic & Simple Eukaryotic Systems. Ed. by Janet Kurjan & Barry L. Taylor. (Illus.). 463p. 1993. text ed. 99.95 (*0-12-429350-6*) Acad Pr.

***Signal Transduction: Single Cell Techniques.** Bert V. Duijn & Anneke Wiltink. LC 97-21326. (Springer Lab Manual Ser.). 1997. write for info. (*3-540-62563-1*) Spr-Verlag.

Signal Transduction & Bacterial Virulence. Rino Rappuoli. LC 95-6581. (Medical Intelligence Unit Ser.). 157p. 1995. 69.00 (*1-57059-231-4*) R G Landes.

Signal Transduction & Protein Phosphorylation. Ed. by Ludwig M. Heilmeyer, Jr. LC 87-15398. (NATO ASI Series A, Life Sciences: Vol. 135). (Illus.). 410p. 1987. 105.00 (*0-306-42615-3*, Plenum Pr) Plenum.

***Signal Transduction by G Protein-Coupled Receptors.** Paul Nederkoorn & Henk Timmerman. (Molecular Biology Intelligence Unit Ser.). 97p. 1997. 89.95 (*1-57059-415-5*, 0-412-137119) R G Landes.

***Signal Transduction in Health & Disease.** Ed. by Jackie D. Corbin & Sharron H. Francis. (Advances in Second Messenger & Phosphoprotein Research Ser.: Ser. 31). 500p. 1997. text ed. 129.00 (*0-397-51685-1*) Lppncott-Raven.

Signal Transduction in Human Endothelial Cells & Endothelial Cell & Platelet Activation In Vivo in Man. V. Van Geet. No. 34. 112p. (Orig.). 1990. pap. 32.50 (*90-6186-426-7*, Pub. by Leuven Univ BE) Coronet Bks.

Signal Transduction in Leukocytes: G Protein-Related & Other Pathways. Ed. by Pramod M. Lad et al. 384p. 1995. 139.95 (*0-8493-6694-1*, 6694, CRC Reprint) CRC Pr.

Signal Transduction in Lung Cells. Brody et al. (Lung Biology in Health & Disease Ser.: Vol. 65). 680p. 1993. 240.00 (*0-8247-8813-3*) Dekker.

Signal Transduction in Photoreceptor Cells: Proceedings of an International Workshop Held at the Research Centre Julich, FRG 8-11 August 1990. Ed. by Paul A. Hargrave et al. (Research Reports in Physics). (Illus.). 328p. 1992. 79.95 (*0-387-53765-1*) Spr-Verlag.

Signal Transduction in Plant Growth & Development. Ed. by Desh P. Verma. (Plant Gene Research Ser.). (Illus.). 330p. 1996. 149.00 (*3-211-82745-5*) Spr-Verlag.

***Signal Transduction in Plants.** Ed. by P. Aducci. LC 96-48484. (Molecular & Cell Biology Update Ser.). 1997. 88.00 (*0-8176-5307-4*) Birkhauser.

***Signal Transduction in Plants.** Ed. by P. Aducci. LC 96-48484. (Molecular & Cell Biology Update Ser.). 192p. 1997. 88.00 (*3-7643-5307-4*) Birkhauser.

Signal Transduction in Testicular Cells. Ed. by V. Hansson et al. (Ernst Schering Research Foundation Workshop Ser.: Suppl. 2). 351p. 1996. 62.00 (*3-540-60910-5*) Spr-Verlag.

Signal Transduction in Testicular Cells: Basic & Clinical Aspects. Ed. by V. Hansson et al. LC 96-10610. (Ernst Schering Research Foundation Workshop Ser.: Supplement No. 2). 1996. write for info. (*0-387-60910-5*) Spr-Verlag.

Signal Transduction Mechanisms, Vol. 15. Ed. by Junor A. Barnes et al. LC 95-35226. (Developments in Molecular & Cellular Biochemistry Ser.). 928p. (C). 1995. lib. bdg. 275.00 (*0-7923-3663-1*) Kluwer Ac.

Signal Transduction Mechanisms in Cancer. Hans Grunicke. LC 95-23489. (Medical Intelligence Unit Ser.). 233p. 1995. 79.00 (*1-57059-245-4*) R G Landes.

Signal Transduction Protocols. Ed. by David A. Kendall & Stephen J. Hill. LC 95-2769. (Methods in Molecular Biology Ser.: Vol. 41). (Illus.). 320p. 1995. 64.50 (*0-89603-298-1*) Humana.

Signal Treatment & Signal Analysis in NMR. Ed. by D. N. Rutledge. (Data Handling in Science & Technology Ser.: Vol. 18). 566p. 1996. text ed. 324.25 (*0-444-81986-X*) Elsevier.

***Signal Victory: The Lake Erie Campaign, 1812-1813.** David C. Skaggs & Gerard T. Altoff. LC 97-12236. (Illus.). 304p. 1997. 34.95 (*1-55750-030-4*) Naval Inst Pr.

Signaling & Communicating at Sea: An Original Anthology. Ed. by David L. Woods & Christopher H. Sterling. LC 80-484. (Historical Studies in Telecommunications). (Illus.). 1980. lib. bdg. 80.95 (*0-405-13195-X*) Ayer.

Signaling & Communicating at Sea, Vol. 1. David L. Woods. 1980. 40.95 (*0-405-13196-8*) Ayer.

***Signaling & the Cytoskeleton.** Kermit Carraway. 220p. 1997. 89.95 (*0-412-13941-3*) R G Landes.

Signaling Games in Political Science, Vol. 46. Jeffrey Banks. (Fundamentals of Pure & Applied Economics Ser.). 90, viiip. 1991. pap. text ed. 45.00 (*3-7186-5087-8*, Harwood Acad Pubs) Gordon & Breach.

***Signaling in Broadband Networks, Vol. 2.** Uyless D. Black. (ATM Ser.). (C). 1997. text ed. 65.00 (*0-13-571837-6*) P-H.

***Signaling in Telecommunication Networks.** John G. Van Bosse. LC 96-43761. 1997. text ed. write for info. (*0-471-57377-9*) Wiley.

Signaling Mechanisms & Gene Expression in the Ovary. Ed. by G. Gibori. (Serono Symposia Ser.). (Illus.). xxix, 487p. 1991. 157.00 (*0-387-97653-1*) Spr-Verlag.

Signaling Mechanisms in Secretory & Immune Cells. Ed. by J. R. Martinez et al. (Illus.). 1990. 10.00 (*0-614-11704-6*) San Francisco Pr.

***Signaling Student Success: Thematic Learning Stations & Integrated Units for Middle Level Classrooms.** Sandra Schurr. LC 96-35190. 1996. pap. write for info. (*1-56090-112-8*) Natl Middle Schl.

Signaling System No. 7. Travis Russell. LC 94-49007. (Series on Computer Communications). 1995. text ed. 65.00 (*0-07-054991-5*) McGraw.

***Signalled Love.** D. W. Hartnett. 62p. 1985. pap. 14.95 (*0-85646-144-X*, Pub. by Anvil Press UK) Dufour.

***Signalling by Inositides: A Practical Approach.** Ed. by Stephen Shears. (The Practical Approach Ser.: No. 176). (Illus.). 272p. 1997. pap. 55.00 (*0-19-963638-9*, IRL Pr) OUP.

***Signalling by Inositides: A Practical Approach.** Ed. by Stephen Shears. (Practical Approach Ser.: No. 176). (Illus.). 272p. 1997. 110.00 (*0-19-963639-7*, IRL Pr) OUP.

Signalling Mechanisms: From Transcription Factors to Oxidative Stress. Ed. by Lester Packer & Karel W. Wirtz. LC 95-10171. (NATO ASI Series H: Vol. 92). (Illus.). 472p. 1995. 217.95 (*3-540-59127-3*) Spr-Verlag.

Signalling Through Space Without Wires: Being a Description of the Work of Hertz & His Successors. 3rd ed. Oliver J. Lodge. LC 74-9688. (Telecommunications Ser.). (Illus.). 138p. 1974. 17.95 (*0-405-06051-3*) Ayer.

Signalman & Other Ghost Stories. Charles Dickens. 152p. 1985. pap. 6.00 (*0-89733-307-1*) Academy Chi Pubs.

Signalman & Other Ghost Stories. Charles Dickens. (Pocket Classics Ser.). 272p. 1996. pap. 8.95 (*0-86299-858-1*, Pub. by Sutton Pubng UK) Bks Intl VA.

Signalman's Nightmare. Adrian Vaughan. (Illus.). 164p. 1989. 34.95 (*0-7195-4285-5*, Pub. by John Murray UK) Trafalgar.

Signals. Allan Pease. 240p. (Orig.). 1984. pap. 11.95 (*0-553-34366-1*) Bantam.

Signals: The Science of Telecommunications. John R. Pierce & Michael A. Noll. LC 89-70207. (Illus.). (C). 1995. text ed. write for info. (*0-7167-5026-0*) W H Freeman.

Signals & Cells - Three Views: Recent Work by Paul Harryn. Paul Harryn. (Illus.). (Orig.). 1991. 10.00 (*0-9624021-3-3*) Ursinus College.

Signals & Discards for You. Andrew Kambites. 96p. 1995. pap. 13.95 (*0-575-05813-7*, Pub. by V Gollancz UK) Trafalgar.

Signals & Filters. Goldblatt. (Electrical Engineering Ser.). 1994. teacher ed., pap. write for info. (*0-442-01851-7*) Van Nos Reinhold.

***Signals & Images.** Ed. by Madeleine Bastide. LC 97-868. 1997. lib. bdg. 160.00 (*0-7923-4466-9*) Kluwer Ac.

Signals & Instructions, Seventeen Seventy-Six to Seventeen Ninety-Four. Julian S. Corbett. (C). 1987. 115.00 (*0-685-45016-3*) St Mut.

Signals & Linear Systems. 3rd ed. Robert A. Gabel & Richard A. Roberts. LC 86-7748. 496p. 1986. text ed. 81.95 (*0-471-82513-1*) Wiley.

Signals & Linear Systems. 3rd ed. Robert A. Gabel & Richard A. Roberts. 470p. 1987. teacher ed. 17.50 (*0-471-62806-9*) Wiley.

***Signals & Noise in Physics: Concepts & Methods.** 250p. 1998. lib. bdg. 38.00 (*981-02-2691-8*) World Scientific Pub.

Signals & Systems. B. P. Lathi. LC 86-72954. 531p. 1987. text ed. 59.95 (*0-941413-33-0*) Berkeley-Cambridge.

***Signals & Systems.** Tervo. (Electrical Engineering Ser.). Date not set. pap. 49.95 (*0-534-95205-4*) PWS Pubs.

***Signals & Systems.** 2nd ed. Balmer. LC 97-11053. 1997. pap. text ed. 66.00 (*0-13-495672-9*) P-H.

Signals & Systems. 2nd ed. M. L. Meade & C. R. Dillon. (Tutorial Guides in Electronic Engineering Ser.: No. 8). 160p. 1991. pap. 27.95 (*0-412-40110-X*) Chapman & Hall.

Signals & Systems. 2nd ed. Alan V. Oppenheim & Willsky. 760p. (C). 1996. text ed. 84.00 (*0-13-814757-4*) P-H.

Signals & Systems. 2nd ed. Alexander D. Poularikas & Samuel Seely. LC 93-48738. 1038p. 1994. reprint ed. 120.00 (*0-89464-875-6*) Krieger.

Signals & Systems: Continuous & Discrete. 3rd ed. Rodger E. Ziemer et al. (Illus.). 640p. (C). 1992. text ed. 84.00 (*0-02-431641-5*, Macmillan Coll) P-H.

Signals & Systems for Speech & Hearing. Stuart Rosen & Peter Howell. 332p. (C). 1991. pap. text ed. 53.00 (*0-12-597231-8*) Acad Pr.

Signals & Systems Made Ridiculously Simple. Zoher Z. Karu. LC 94-90623. (Illus.). 140p. (Orig.). (C). 1995. pap. text ed. 32.00 (*0-9643752-1-4*) ZiZi Pr.

Signals from the Corner. Tom Frye. 125p. (Orig.). 1995. pap. 6.95 (*1-881663-49-3*) Poudre Canyon Pr.

Signals from the Falklands: The British Navy in the Falklands Conflict: An Anthology of Personal Experience. Ed. by John Winton. 238p. 1995. 47.50 (*0-85052-429-6*, Pub. by L Cooper Bks UK) Trans-Atl Phila.

Signals from the Heartland. Tony Fitzpatrick. LC 92-15732. 230p. 1993. 22.95 (*0-8027-1260-6*) Walker & Co.

Signals from the Hill: Congressional Oversight & the Challenge of Social Regulation. Christopher H. Foreman, Jr. 246p. (C). 1989. reprint ed. text ed. 37.50 (*0-300-04410-0*) Yale U Pr.

Signals from the Hill: Congressional Oversight & the Challenge of Social Regulation. Christopher H. Foreman, Jr. 224p. (C). 1990. reprint ed. pap. 15.00 (*0-300-04900-5*) Yale U Pr.

***Signals in Plant Development.** J. Krekule et al. 181p. 1989. pap. 39.00 (*90-5103-028-2*, Pub. by SPB Acad Pub NE) Balogh.

Signals in the Air: Native Broadcasting in America. Michael C. Keith. LC 94-32919. (Media & Society Ser.). 200p. 1995. text ed. 52.95 (*0-275-94876-5*, Praeger Pubs) Greenwood.

Signals Intelligence in World War II: A Research Guide. Compiled by Donal J. Sexton. LC 96-6348. (Bibliographies of Battles & Leaders Ser.). 208p. 1996. text ed. 69.50 (*0-313-28304-4*, Greenwood Pr) Greenwood.

Signals, Noise & Active Sensors: Radar, Sonar & Laser Radar. John R. Minkoff. LC 91-16515. 264p. 1992. text ed. 79.95 (*0-471-54572-4*) Wiley.

Signals of Distress. Jim Crace. LC 95-10100. 277p. 1995. 22.00 (*0-374-26379-5*) FS&G.

Signals of Distress. 2nd ed. Jim Crace. LC 96-47426. 288p. 1997. reprint ed. pap. 15.00 (*0-88001-486-5*) Ecco Pr.

Signals of Recession & Recovery: An Experiment with Monthly Reporting. Julius Shiskin. (Occasional Papers: No. 77). 208p. 1961. reprint ed. 54.10 (*0-685-61329-1*) Natl Bur Econ Res.

Signals of the Sea & Heroes of the Surf. Arthur Hewitt & John R. Spears. Ed. & Intro. by William R. Jones. (Illus.). 24p. 1996. reprint ed. pap. 3.95 (*0-89646-088-6*) Vistabooks.

Signals of War: The Falklands Conflict of 1982. Lawrence Freedman & Virginia Gamba-Stonehouse. 476p. 1991. text ed. 65.00 (*0-691-07890-4*); pap. text ed. 18.95 (*0-691-02344-1*) Princeton U Pr.

Signals, Sound, & Sensation. William M. Hartmann. LC 96-43808. (Modern Acoustics & Signal Processing Ser.). (Illus.). 580p. 1996. 80.00 (*1-56396-283-7*, AIP) Am Inst Physics.

Signals, Systems, & Filters. Paul M. Chirlian. LC 93-12670. 1993. text ed. 59.95 (*0-442-01324-8*) Van Nos Reinhold.

Signals, Systems, & the Computer. Paul Chirlian. 615p. (C). 1986. text ed. 64.95 (*0-938862-81-2*) Weber Systems.

Signals, Systems & Transforms. Leland B. Jackson. (Illus.). 500p. (C). 1991. text ed. 66.75 (*0-201-09589-0*) Addison-Wesley.

Signals, Systems, & Transforms. Charles L. Phillips & John M. Parr. LC 94-6083. 800p. 1994. text ed. 84.00 (*0-13-795253-8*) P-H.

Signals to the Blind. Danny L. Rendleman. LC 72-19183. 50p. 1972. 2.95 (*0-87886-015-0*, Greenfld Rev Pr) Greenfld Rev Lit.

Signaturas Libristicas: Normas para Su Aplicacion en Bibliotecas de Habla. Donald J. Lehnus. (Serie Bibliotecologica). 35p. 1975. pap. text ed. 1.50 (*0-8477-0903-5*) U of PR Pr.

Signature. Mark Sonnenfeld. 44p. pap. 3.00 (*0-9632820-2-6*) M Sonnenfeld.

Signature: Wiley Command Reference. Christine Rivera. 352p. 1992. pap. text ed. 12.95 (*0-471-55818-4*) Wiley.

***Signature Bets: A Guide to Recognizing Roulette Advantage Play.** Marcia A. McDowell. (Illus.). 60p. (C). Date not set. pap. text ed. 8.95 (*0-9648090-1-X*) Cndlelight Bks.

***Signature by Mail: Broker Success Kit.** 9th ed. Tyler G. Hicks. 176p. 1998. pap. 100.00 (*1-56150-223-5*) Intl Wealth.

Signature Collection Country Music Cookbook. IFCO, International Fan Club Organization Staff. (Orig.). Date not set. pap. text ed. write for info. (*1-56944-109-X*) Terrell Missouri.

Signature in Blood. William E. Pettit. 256p. 1995. 24.95 (*0-925591-39-4*) Covenant Hse Bks.

Signature in Time: Contemporary Samplers in Stitch. Vanessa-Ann Collection Staff. LC 86-63721. (Illus.). 168p. 1987. write for info. (*0-02-496790-4*, Macmillan Coll) P-H.

***Signature Killers.** Keppel. 1997. mass mkt. 6.50 (*0-671-00130-2*) PB.

Signature Loans by Mail Broker Success Kit, 2 bks., Set. 8th ed. Tyler G. Hicks. 176p. 1996. pap. 100.00 (*1-56150-173-5*) Intl Wealth.

Signature Macros. Art Campbell & Bonnie Allen. LC 92-5326. (Illus.). 304p. 1993. pap. 32.95 (*0-8306-4047-9*, 4185, Windcrest) TAB Bks.

Signature Man: Tales of a Detached Rear. Harvet W. Olsen. 1993. pap. 11.95 (*0-533-10126-3*) Vantage.

Signature of All Things; of the Supersensual Life; of Heaven & Hell; Discourse Between Two Souls. Jacob Boehme. 300p. 1992. pap. 27.00 (*1-56459-215-4*) Kessinger Pub.

S

***Signature of God.** Grant R. Jeffrey. 19.95 (0-921714-32-7, Pub. by Frontier Res CN); pap. 13.95 (0-921714-28-9, Pub. by Frontier Res CN) Spring Arbor Dist.
Signature of God. Velma Ruch. 1986. pap. 30.00 (0-8309-0428-X) Herald Hse.
Signature of God: A Positive Identification of Christ & His Prophets by Computer Wordprints. Robert L. Hamson. LC 81-51809. (Illus.). 111p. (C). 1982. 8.95 (0-940356-01-5) Sandpiper CA.
Signature of Jesus. Brennan Manning. 210p. 1996. pap. 9.99 (0-88070-859-X, Multnomah Bks) Multnomah Pubs.
Signature of Power: Buildings, Communication, & Policy. Harold D. Lasswell. 224p. (C). 1978. text ed. 44.95 (0-87855-289-8) Transaction Pubs.
Signature of Power & Patronage: The Medici Coat of Arms, 1299-1492. Roy Brogan. LC 93-25229. (Currents in Comparative Romance Languages & Literatures Ser.: Vol. 20). 349p. (C). 1994. text ed. 49.95 (0-8204-2213-4) P Lang Pubng.
Signature of Silence. Sheila Gujral. (Illus.). 56p. 1993. 18. 95 (81-207-1361-3) Apt Bks.
Signature of the Spiral. Daniel W. Schreck. LC 87-16469. 64p. (Orig.). 1989. pap. 6.95 (0-86534-114-1) Sunstone Pr.
Signature Pieces: On the Institution of Authorship. Peggy Kamuf. LC 88-47731. 256p. 1988. 39.95 (0-8014-2209-4) Cornell U Pr.
Signature Quilt: Traditions, Techniques & Signature Block Collection. Pepper Cory & Susan McKelvey. Ed. by Mary Penders. (Illus.). 144p. 1995. pap. 29.95 (1-881588-14-9) EZ Quilting.
Signatures in Steel. Greg McDonnell. Ed. by Noel Hudson. (Illus.). 208p. 50.00 (0-7737-2554-7, Pub. by Boston Mills Pr CN) Genl Dist Srvs.
Signatures of Hiroshige. Hawley & Metzgar. 1993. pap. 6.95 (0-910704-76-7) Hawley.
Signatures of Naganobu. Hawley. 1992. pap. 4.95 (0-910704-33-3) Hawley.
Signatures of Steel. Greg McDonnell. 1995. 50.00 (1-55046-162-1, Pub. by Boston Mills Pr CN) Genl Dist Srvs.
Signatures of the Visible. Fredric Jameson. LC 92-16583. 256p. (C). (gr. 13). 1992. pap. 15.95 (0-415-90012-3, A1194, Routledge NY) Routledge.
Signatures on Water. Osho. Ed. by Ma D. Sarito. (Zen Ser.). 352p. 1992. 36.00 (81-7261-005-X, Pub. by Rebel Hse GW) Osho America.
Signboards of Old London Shops. Ambrose Heal. LC 76-174401. (Illus.). 220p. 1972. reprint ed. lib. bdg. 20.95 (0-405-08608-3, Pub. by Blom Pubns UK) Ayer.
Signe Ascendant. Andre Breton. Bd. with Fata Morgana. Andre Breton. ; Etats-generaux. Andre Breton. ; Des epingles tremblantes. Andre Breton. ; Xenophile. Andre Breton. ; Ode a Charles Fourier. Andre Breton. ; Constellation. Andre Breton. ; Le la. Ed. by Andre Breton. (Poesie Ser.). (FRE.). Set pap. 9.95 (2-07-030046-3) Schoenhof.
Signe Ascendant, Fata Morgana, les Etats Generaux des Epingles Tremblantes, Xenophiles, Ode a Charles Fourier, Constellations. Andre Breton. (FRE.). 1968. pap. 10.95 (0-8288-3816-X, F89600) Fr & Eur.
Signe et le Texte: Etudes sur L'ecriture au XVIe Siecle en France. Ed. by Lawrence D. Kritzman. LC 89-81170. (French Forum Monographs: No. 72). 190p. (Orig.). 1990. pap. 17.95 (0-917058-74-7) French Forum.
***Signe Toksvig's Irish Diaries 1926-1937.** Lisa Pihl. 450p. 9400. 39.95 (1-874675-26-0) Dufour.
Signed English for the Classroom. Harry Bornstein. LC 75-2974. (Signed English Ser.). 80p. (J). (ps-6). 1979. pap. 6.50 (0-913580-37-6, Pub. by K Green Pubns) Gallaudet Univ Pr.
Signed English Starter, Pt. I. Harry Bornstein & Karen L. Saulnier. LC 84-4042. (Signed English Ser.). (Illus.). 230p. (J). (ps-6). 1984. teacher ed., pap. 13.95 (0-913580-82-1, Clerc Bks) Gallaudet Univ Pr.
Signed English Starter, Pt. I. Harry Bornstein & Karen L. Saulnier. LC 84-4042. 1995. teacher ed. 34.95 incl. vhs (1-56368-038-6, Clerc Bks) Gallaudet Univ Pr.
Signed English Starter, Pt. II. Harry Bornstein & Karen L. Saulnier. LC 84-4042. 1995. teacher ed. 34.95 incl. vhs (1-56368-040-8, Clerc Bks) Gallaudet Univ Pr.
Signed English Starter Book & Videotape Set. Harry Bornstein & Karen L. Saulnier. LC 84-4042. 388p. 1995. teacher ed. 75.00 incl. vhs (1-56368-041-6, Clerc Bks) Gallaudet Univ Pr.
Signed, Sealed, & Delivered: True Life Stories of Women in Pop Music. Sue Steward & Sheryl Garratt. LC 84-40384. 160p. (Orig.). 1984. 25.00 (0-89608-241-5); pap. 8.00 (0-89608-240-7) South End Pr.
Signers Declaration of Independence. R. G. Ferris. 1976. 26.95 (0-8488-0214-4, J M C & Co) Amereon Ltd.
Signers of the Constitution. C. Edward Quinn. (Bicentennial of U. S. Constitution Ser.). (Illus.). 112p. 1986. 20.00 (0-941980-18-9) Bronx County.
Signers of the Constitution. Robert G. Ferris & James H. Charleton. LC 86-81140. (Illus.). 280p. 1986. reprint ed. pap. 14.95 (0-936478-10-1) Interpretive Pubns.
Signers of the Declaration of Independence. Robert G. Ferris & Richard E. Morris. LC 82-82219. (Illus.). 180p. 1982. reprint ed. pap. 10.95 (0-936478-07-1) Interpretive Pubns.
Signers of the Declaration of Independence. C. Edward Quinn. Ed. by Gary D. Hermalyn & LLoyd Ultan. (Bicentennial of U. S. Constitution Ser.). (Illus.). 132p. 1988. reprint ed. 20.00 (0-685-25265-5) Bronx County.
***Signers of the Declaration of Independence: A Biographical & Genealogical Reference.** Della G. Barthelmas. LC 97-11663. 1997. 55.00 (0-7864-0318-7) McFarland & Co.
Signes & Sothe: Language in the Piers Plowman Tradition. Helen Barr. LC 94-19105. (Piers Plowman Studies: No. X). 202p. (C). 1994. 63.00 (0-85991-419-4, DS Brewer) Boydell & Brewer.
Signes et les Prodiges. Francoise Mallet-Joris. 416p. (FRE.). 1966. pap. 10.95 (0-8288-9843-X, F110821); pap. 3.95 (0-686-56316-6) Fr & Eur.
Signes et Paraboles see Signs & Parables: Semiotics & Gospel Texts
Signet Classic Book of American Short Stories. Ed. & Intro. by Burton Raffel. 1985. pap. 6.95 (0-451-52279-6, Sig Classics) NAL-Dutton.
Signet Classic Book of Mark Twain's Short Stories. Mark Twain. 688p. (J). (gr. 5 up). 1989. pap. 4.50 (0-451-52220-6, Sig Classics) NAL-Dutton.
Signet Classic Book of Mark Twain's Stories. Intro. by Justin E. Kaplan. 1985. pap. 3.95 (0-451-51960-4, Sig Classics) NAL-Dutton.
Signet Classic Book of Southern Short Stories. Ed. by Susan Koppelman. 496p. 1991. mass mkt. 6.95 (0-451-52395-4, Sig) NAL-Dutton.
Signet Classic Mark Twain. Mark Twain. 1985. pap. 6.95 (0-451-52440-3) NAL-Dutton.
Signet Handbook of Parapsychology. Ed. by Martin Ebon. 528p. (Orig.). 1980. pap. 4.95 (0-451-15478-9, Sig) NAL-Dutton.
Signet-Mosby Medical Encyclopedia. C. V. Mosby Company Staff. 704p. 1987. pap. 5.95 (0-451-15059-7, Sig) NAL-Dutton.
Signet-Mosby Medical Encyclopedia. rev. ed. 912p. 1996. mass mkt. 7.99 (0-451-18409-2, Sig) NAL-Dutton.
Signet of Atlantis: War in Heaven Bypass. Barbara H. Clow. LC 92-12392. (Mind Chronicles Ser.). (Illus.). 208p. 1992. pap. 12.95 (1-879181-02-9) Bear & Co.
Signet Ultimate Basketball Quiz Book. Patrick Mullooly. 176p. (Orig.). 1993. pap. 3.99 (0-451-17764-9, Sig) NAL-Dutton.
Signet World Atlas. Ed. by B. M. Willet. (Illus.). 136p. (Orig.). 1991. pap. 5.99 (0-451-17203-5, Sig) NAL-Dutton.
Signets: Reading H. D. Ed. by Susan S. Friedman & Rachel B. DuPlessis. LC 90-50088. 368p. (Orig.). (C). 1991. text ed. 40.00 (0-299-12680-3); pap. text ed. 17.50 (0-299-12684-6) U of Wis Pr.
Significacion Del Genero: Estudio Semiotico De las Novelas y Ensayos De Ernesto Sabato. Nicasio Urbina. LC 91-76701. (Coleccion Polymita). 202p. (Orig.). (SPA.). 1992. pap. 20.00 (0-89729-627-3) Ediciones.
Significado del Velo de la Mujer Cristiana. Merle Ruth. 1980. 0.65 (0-317-02032-3) Rod & Staff.
Significados de la Muerte. John Bowker. 360p. (SPA.). (C). 1996. pap. text ed. 17.95 (0-521-47832-4) Cambridge U Pr.
Significance & Basic Postulates of Economic Theory. Terence W. Hutchison. LC 65-16994. (Reprints of Economic Classics Ser.). xxi, 192p. 1965. reprint ed. 35. 00 (0-678-00091-3) Kelley.
Significance & Impact of Gregorio Maranon. Gary D. Keller. LC 76-45295. 1977. pap. 20.00 (0-916950-18-2); lib. bdg. 30.00 (0-916950-04-2) Biling Rev-Pr.
Significance & Regulation of Soil Biodiversity. Ed. by Harold P. Collins et al. LC 95-14925. (Developments in Plant & Soil Sciences Ser.: Vol. 63). 1995. lib. bdg. 170. 00 (0-7923-3138-9) Kluwer Ac.
Significance & Treatment of VOCs in Water Supplies. Ed. by Neil M. Ram et al. (Illus.). 576p. 1990. 95.00 (0-87371-123-8, L123) Lewis Pubs.
Significance of Anthony Trollope. Spencer V. Nichols. 1977. lib. bdg. 59.95 (0-8490-2604-0) Gordon Pr.
Significance of Art: A Phenomenological Approach to Aesthetics. Moritz Geiger. Ed. by Klaus Berger. LC 86-13250. (Current Continental Research Ser.: No. 402). 238p. (Orig.). (C). 1987. pap. text ed. 22.50 (0-8191-5485-7, Ctr Adv Res); lib. bdg. 48.00 (0-8191-5484-9, Ctr Adv Res) U Pr of Amer.
Significance of Birthdays. W. J. Colville. 161p. 1967. reprint ed. spiral bd. 5.50 (0-7873-1230-4) Hlth Research.
Significance of Birthdays (1911) W. J. Colville. 161p. 1996. pap. 17.95 (1-56459-706-7) Kessinger Pub.
Significance of Cytokines in the Treatment of Infectious Diseases, Vol. 4. Ed. by Uwe Ullmann & Axel Dalhoff. x, 175p. 1993. pap. 50.00 (3-437-11487-5, Pub. by G Fischer Verlag GW) Lubrecht & Cramer.
Significance of Defects in Welded Structures: Proceedings of the Japan-U. S. Seminar, 1973, Tokyo, Japan. Ed. by Takeshi Kanazawa & Albert S. Kobayashi. LC 78-321441. 431p. 1974. reprint ed. pap. 122.90 (0-608-01224-6, 2061912) Bks Demand.
Significance of Fatima: A Seventy-Five Year Perspective. Frederick L. Miller. 1993. 2.00 (1-56036-078-X, 38003) AMI Pr.
Significance of Flesh. Joseph P. Clancy. 159p. (C). 1984. pap. 20.00 (0-86383-061-7, Pub. by Gomer Pr UK) St Mut.
Significance of Free Will. Robert L. Kane. 280p. 1996. 45. 00 (0-19-510550-8) OUP.
Significance of Infant Observational Research for Clinical Work with Children, Adolescents, & Adults. Ed. by Scott Dowling & Arnold Rothstein. (Workshop Series of the American Psychoanalytic Association: Monograph 5). 300p. 1989. 40.00 (0-8236-6073-7) Intl Univs Pr.
Significance of Lourdes, Fatima, & Medjugorje As Explained in Scripture. Wilmott G. Brown. LC 95-94530. (Illus.). 72p. (Orig.). 1995. pap. 1.50 (0-9647294-0-7) W G Brown.
Significance of Mary for Women. Joyce A. Little. (Queen of Apostles Ser.: Vol. III). 1995. 0.75 (0-911988-86-6, 49716) AMI Pr.
Significance of N-Nitrosation of Drugs. Ed. by G. Eisenbrand et al. (Drug Development & Evaluation Ser.: Vol. 16). 290p. 1990. pap. text ed. 70.00 (0-89574-319-1, Pub. by G Fischer Verlag GW) Lubrecht & Cramer.
Significance of Neoplatonism. Ed. by R. Baine Harris. LC 76-21254. 370p. 1976. text ed. 24.50 (0-87395-800-4) State U NY Pr.
Significance of Organizational Conflict on the Legislative Evolution of the Accounting Profession in the United States. Myron S. Lubell. Ed. by Richard P. Brief. LC 80-1515. (Dimensions of Accounting Theory & Practice Ser.). 1980. lib. bdg. 49.95 (0-405-13494-0) Ayer.
Significance of Philosophical Scepticism. Barry Stroud. 294p. 1984. pap. 23.00 (0-19-824761-3) OUP.
Significance of Satan: New Testament Demonology & Its Contemporary Relevance. Trevor Ling. LC 79-8110. (Satanism Ser.). 120p. 1985. reprint ed. 21.50 (0-404-18424-3) AMS Pr.
Significance of Schooling: Life-Journeys in an African Society. Robert Serpell. (Illus.). 416p. (C). 1993. text ed. 69.95 (0-521-39478-3) Cambridge U Pr.
***Significance of Shri Sukta: Laxmi's Invocation for National Prosperity.** Yadunath. 100p. (Orig.). 1996. pap. 10.00 (1-890041-00-9); text ed. 25.00 (1-890041-01-7) S V Y M Ent.
Significance of Sibling Relationships in Literature. Ed. by Joanna S. Mink & Janet D. Ward. LC 92-75707. 174p. (C). 1993. 38.95 (0-87972-612-1); pap. 14.95 (0-87972-613-X) Bowling Green Univ Popular Press.
Significance of Silence. Arnold T. Olson. LC 80-70698. (Heritage Ser.: Vol. 2). 208p. 1981. 8.95 (7-100-07628-5) Free Church Pubns.
***Significance of Sinclair Lewis.** Stuart P. Sherman. 20p. 1971. 11.95 (0-8369-5660-5) Ayer.
Significance of Spiritual Research for Moral Action. Rudolf Steiner. Tr. by Alan P. Cottrell from GER. 17p. 1981. pap. 3.95 (0-88010-101-6) Anthroposophic.
***Significance of Strain Limits for Elevated Temperature Design, EUR 16812.** H. Kasti. 234p. 1996. pap. 40.00 (92-827-7459-7, CRNA-16812-ENC, Pub. by Europ Com UK) Bernan Associates.
Significance of Testing & Properties of Concrete & Concrete-Making Materials. 4th ed. Ed. by Joseph F. Lamond & Paul Klieger. LC 94-16746. (Special Technical Publications: Vol. 169C). (Illus.). 630p. 1994. 110.00 (0-8031-2053-2, 0416903007) ASTM.
Significance of Tests & Properties of Concrete & Concrete-Making Materials- STP 169B. 882p. 1985. 65.00 (0-8031-0612-2, 04-169020-07) ASTM.
Significance of the Christian Woman's Veiling. Merle Ruth. 1980. 1.25 (0-686-30769-0) Rod & Staff.
Significance of the Father: Four Papers from the FSAA Biennial Meeting, Washington, D.C., April, 1959. Family Service Association of America Staff. 78p. reprint ed. pap. 25.00 (0-317-10308-3, 2007668) Bks Demand.
Significance of the Frontier in American History. Frederick J. Turner. (Irvington Reprint Series in American History). (Illus.). (C). 1991. reprint ed. pap. text ed. 2.90 (0-8290-2610-X, H-214) Irvington.
Significance of the Human Factor in African Economic Development. Ed. by Senyo Adjibolosoo. LC 94-8545. 280p. 1995. text ed. 62.95 (0-275-94895-1, Praeger Pubs) Greenwood.
Significance of the Media in American History. W. David Sloan & James D. Startt. 400p. 1993. pap. 24.95 (0-9630700-4-5) Vision AL.
Significance of the One. Don Bradley. (Illus.). (Orig.). 1996. pap. 14.95 (1-888298-01-4) Native Planet.
Significance of the Physical Constitution in Mental Disease: Medicine Monographs, Vol. X. F. I. Wertheimer & Florence E. Hesketh. Ed. by Gerald N. Grob. LC 78-22594. (Historical Issues in Mental Health Ser.). (Illus.). 1980. reprint ed. lib. bdg. 15.95 (0-405-11944-5) Ayer.
Significance of the Slave Plantation for Southern Economic Development. Eugene Genovese. (Irvington Reprint Series in American History). (C). 1991. reprint ed. pap. text ed. 1.00 (0-8290-2612-6, H-394) Irvington.
Significance of the Women's Movement to Marketing. Alladi Venkatesh. LC 85-19106. 224p. 1985. text ed. 49. 95 (0-275-90232-3, C0232, Praeger Pubs) Greenwood.
Significance of the Young Child's Motor Development. Ed. by Georgianna Engstrom. LC 70-177238. 55p. (Orig.). 1971. pap. text ed. 3.50 (0-912674-32-6, NAEYC #128) Natl Assn Child Ed.
Significance of Theory. Terry Eagleton. 1992. pap. 17.95 (0-631-17271-8) Blackwell Pubs.
Significance of Various Kinds of Preparation for the City-Elementary School Principalship in Pennsylvania with Implications for a Program for Preparing for the Elementary-School Principalship in. Marion E. Macdonald. LC 77-177020. (Columbia University. Teachers College. Contributions to Education Ser.: No. 416). reprint ed. 37.50 (0-404-55416-4) AMS Pr.
Significance Test for Time Series & Other Ordered Observations. W. Allen Wallis & Geoffrey H. Moore. (Technical Papers: No. 1). 71p. 1941. reprint ed. 20.00 (0-87014-446-4); reprint ed. mic. film 20.00 (0-685-61223-6) Natl Bur Econ Res.
Significant Acts of Kindness: Works of the Heart. 128p. (Orig.). 1996. pap. 5.95 (1-889116-01-7) Penbrooke Pub.
Significant & the Insignificant: Five Studies in Herodotus' View of History. J. E. Van Der Veen. (Amsterdam Studies in Classical Philology: No. 6). viii, 146p. 1996. lib. bdg. 57.00 (90-5063-296-3, Pub. by Gieben NE) Benjamins North Am.
Significant Aspects of Ground Water Aquifers Related to Well Head Protection Considerations. A. G. Everett. LC 91-65689. 1991. spiral bd. 18.00 (0-918334-70-5) WRP.
Significant Benefits: The High/Scope Perry Preschool Study Through Age 27. Lawrence J. Schweinhart et al. 275p. 1993. 25.95 (0-929816-57-9) High-Scope.
Significant Decisions of the Supreme Court, 1975-1976 Term. Bruce E. Fein. LC 77-26165. (AEI Studies: No. 183). 204p. reprint ed. pap. 58.20 (0-8357-4529-5, 2037409) Bks Demand.
Significant Decisions of the Supreme Court, 1976-1977 Term. Bruce E. Fein. LC 78-5056. (AEI Studies: No. 187). 172p. reprint ed. pap. 49.10 (0-8357-4530-9, 2037410) Bks Demand.
Significant Decisions of the Supreme Court, 1977-1978 Term. Bruce E. Fein. (AEI Studies: No. 257). 168p. reprint ed. pap. 47.90 (0-8357-4531-7, 2037411) Bks Demand.
Significant Decisions of the Supreme Court, 1978-1979 Term. Bruce E. Fein. (AEI Studies: No. 282). 205p. reprint ed. pap. 58.50 (0-8357-4532-5, 2037412) Bks Demand.
Significant Decisions of the Supreme Court, 1979-1980 Term. Bruce E. Fein. (AEI Studies: No. 413). 254p. (Orig.). reprint ed. pap. 72.40 (0-8357-4533-3, 2037413) Bks Demand.
Significant Decisions of the Supreme Court, 1979-1980 Term, No. 11. Bruce E. Fein. vi, 248p. (Orig.). 1985. pap. 22.50 (0-8377-1135-5) Rothman.
Significant Decisions of the Supreme Court, 1980-1981 Term. Paul B. Stephan, III. 108p. (Orig.). 1985. pap. 15. 00 (0-8377-1136-3) Rothman.
Significant Decisions of the Supreme Court, 1980-1981 Term. Paul B. Stephan. (AEI Studies: No. 418). 114p. (Orig.). reprint ed. pap. 32.50 (0-8357-4534-1, 2037414) Bks Demand.
Significant Developments in Continuing Higher Education. A. A. Liverwright & Freda H. Goldmann. 1965. 2.50 (0-87060-016-8, OCP 12) Syracuse U Cont Ed.
Significant Developments in Engineering Practice & Research: A Tribute to Chester P. Siess. Ed. by Mete A. Sozen. LC 81-69911. (American Concrete Institute Publication Ser.: No. SP-72). 425p. 1981. reprint ed. pap. 121.20 (0-608-01430-3, 2062192) Bks Demand.
Significant Developments in the Taxation of Insurance Companies & Their Products. Ed. by Stephen C. Eldridge. 250p. 1992. ring bd. 95.00 (1-56423-016-3) Ntl Ctr Tax Ed.
Significant Developments in the Taxation of Insurance Companies & Their Products, 1990-1991. Ed. by Stephen C. Eldridge. 240p. 1991. ring bd. 95.00 (1-56423-000-7) Ntl Ctr Tax Ed.
Significant Differences: Feminism in Psychology. Corinne Squire. 176p. 1989. 45.00 (0-415-01224-4, A2447); pap. 12.95 (0-415-01225-2, A3580) Routledge.
Significant Harm: Unravelling Child Protection Decisions & Substitute Care Careers of Children. Elizabeth Fernandez. 322p. 1996. 63.95 (1-85972-210-5, Pub. by Avebury Pub UK) Ashgate Pub Co.
***Significant Incident: Canada's Army, the Airborne, & the Murder in Somalia.** David Bercuson. 1997. 26.95 (0-7710-1113-X) McCland & Stewart.
Significant Incidents of Political Violence Against Americans. (Illus.). 51p. (Orig.). (C). 1992. pap. text ed. 20.00 (1-56806-022-X) DIANE Pub.
Significant Losses: Artists Who Have Died from AIDS. Terry Gips & Bradley Spence. LC 94-78476. 50p. (Orig.). 1994. pap. 15.00 (0-937123-32-3) Art Gal U MD.
Significant Others. Sandra Kitt. 1996. mass mkt. 5.99 (0-451-18824-1, Sig) NAL-Dutton.
Significant Others. Armistead Maupin. 336p. 1994. pap. 13. 00 (0-06-092481-0, PL) HarpC.
***Significant Others.** large type ed. Sandra Kitt. LC 96-41772. (Romance Ser.). 597p. 1996. lib. bdg. 23.95 (0-7862-0920-8) Thorndike Pr.
Significant Others: Creativity & Intimate Partnership. Ed. by Whitney Chadwick & Isabelle De Courtivron. LC 92-62321. (Interplay Ser.). (Illus.). 256p. 1996. pap. 17.95 (0-500-27874-1) Thames Hudson.
***Significant Others: Exploring the Potential of Manufacturing Networks.** Brian Bosworth & Stuart Rosenfeld. 52p. (Orig.). 1993. pap. 7.00 (0-9636927-0-4) Reg Tech Strat.
Significant Others: Gender & Culture in Film & Literature East & West. Ed. by William Burgwiukle et al. LC 93-7608. (Literary Studies: Vol. 6). 136p. 1993. pap. text ed. 15.00 (0-8248-1564-5) UH Pr.
Significant Phased Array Papers. Robert C. Hansen. LC 73-81240. (Modern Frontiers in Applied Science Ser.). (Illus.). 287p. reprint ed. pap. 81.80 (0-8357-4179-6, 2036957) Bks Demand.
Significant Social Revolution: Cross-Cultural Aspects of the Evolution of Compulsory Education. Ed. by James A. Mangan. 232p. 1994. 37.50 (0-7130-0189-5, Pub. by Woburn Pr UK) Intl Spec Bk.
Significant State Anti-Crime Legislation. Donna Hunzeker. (State Legislative Reports: Vol. 19, No. 6). 10p. 1994. 5.00 (1-55516-377-7, 7302-1906) Natl Conf State Legis.
Significant Tornadoes, 1680-1991. Thomas P. Grazulis. (Illus.). 1340p. 1993. 95.00 (1-879362-03-1) Environ Films.
Significant Violence: Oppression & Resistance in the Later Narrative of Juan Goytisolo, 1970-1990. Brad Epps. (Oxford Hispanic Ser.). 288p. 1996. 82.00 (0-19-815890-4) OUP.
Signification & Significance: A Study of the Relations of Signs & Values. Charles G. Morris. 1968. pap. 9.95 (0-262-63014-1) MIT Pr.
Significs & Language. Victoria L. Welby. LC 84-28456. (Foundations of Semiotics Ser.: No. 5). cclxvii, 220p. 1985. 94.00 (90-272-3275-X) Benjamins North Am.
Signifier & the Signified. Frits Noske. 1977. lib. bdg. 135. 00 (90-247-1995-X) Kluwer Ac.

Signifying Acts: Structure & Meaning in Everyday Life. R. S. Perinbanayagam. LC 84-5474. 205p. 1985. 29.95 (*0-8093-1181-X*) S Ill U Pr.

Signifying Animal: The Grammar of Language & Experience. Ed. by Irmengard Rauch & Gerald F. Carr. LC 79-3624. (Advances in Semiotics Ser.). (Illus.). 304p. reprint ed. pap. 86.70 (*0-8357-6696-9*, 2056876) Bks Demand.

Signifying Animals: Human Meaning in the Natural World. Ed. by R. G. Willis. (One World Archaeology Ser.). 288p. (C). 1994. pap. 18.95 (*0-415-09555-7*, B3903) Routledge.

Signifying Animals: Human Meaning in the Natural World. Ed. by Roy Willis. (One World Archaeology Ser.). 320p. 1990. text ed. 65.00 (*0-04-445014-1*) Routledge Chapman & Hall.

Signifying Monkey: A Theory of Afro-American Literary Criticism. Henry Louis Gates, Jr. (Illus.). 320p. 1989. pap. 15.95 (*0-19-506075-X*) OUP.

Signifying Nothing. A. W. Felton. 280p. (C). 1989. text ed. 69.00 (*1-872795-45-5*, Pub. by Pentland Pr UK) St Mut.

Signifying Nothing: The Semiotics of Zero. Brian Rotman. LC 87-15632. 210p. 1988. pap. 12.95 (*0-318-32465-2*) St Martin.

Signifying Nothing: The Semiotics of Zero. Brian Rotman. (Illus.). 111p. (C). 1993. reprint ed. pap. 12.95 (*0-8047-2129-7*) Stanford U Pr.

***Signifying Rappers: Rap & Race in the Urban Present.** Mark Costello & David F. Wallace. 1997. pap. text ed. 11.00 (*0-88001-535-7*) Ecco Pr.

Signifying Woman: Culture & Chaos in Rousseau, Burke, & Mill. Linda M. Zerilli. LC 93-31618. (Contestations Ser.). 232p. 1994. 35.00 (*0-8014-2958-7*); pap. 14.95 (*0-8014-8177-5*) Cornell U Pr.

Signing. Bornstein. 1996. pap. write for info. (*0-517-88487-9*) Random Hse Value.

Signing: How to Speak with Your Hands. rev. ed. Elaine Costello. LC 94-46156. (Illus.). 288p. 1995. pap. 17.95 (*0-553-37539-3*) Bantam.

Signing: Signed English - A Basic Guide. Harry Bornstein & Karen L. Saulnier. (Illus.). 240p. 1988. pap. 10.00 (*0-517-56132-8*, Crown) Crown Pub Group.

Signing at School. S. Harold Collins. (Beginning Sign Language Ser.). (Illus.). 32p. (Orig.). (J). (gr. 1-6). 1992. pap. 2.95 (*0-931993-47-4*, GP-047) Garlic Pr OR.

Signing English: Exact or Not - A Collection of Articles. Ed. by G. Gustason. 1988. pap. 13.25 (*0-916708-18-7*) Modern Signs.

Signing Everyday Phrases. Mickey Flodin. LC 96-23260. 256p. 1996. pap. 13.00 (*0-399-52236-0*, Perigee Bks) Berkley Pub.

Signing Exact English. Gerilee Gustason & Esther Zawolkow. LC 93-86649. (Illus.). 472p. (J). (gr. k-12). 1993. text ed. 39.95 (*0-916708-22-5*, SL025); pap. text ed. 29.95 (*0-916708-23-3*) Modern Signs.

Signing Exact English. Gerilee Gustason & Esther Zawolkow. LC 93-86649. (Illus.). 472p. (J). (gr. k-12). 1994. pap. 21.95 (*0-916708-26-8*) Modern Signs.

Signing for Kids: The Fun Way for Anyone to Learn American Sign Language. Mickey Flodin. (Perigee's Signing Library). (Illus.). 144p. (J). (gr. 3-9). 1991. pap. 11.00 (*0-399-51672-7*, Perigee Bks) Berkley Pub.

Signing Illustrated: The Complete Learning Guide. Mickey Flodin. 288p. (Orig.). 1994. pap. 15.00 (*0-399-52134-8*, Perigee Bks) Berkley Pub.

Signing Is Fun. Mickey Flodin. LC 95-22018. 1995. pap. 9.00 (*0-399-52173-9*, Perigee Bks) Berkley Pub.

Signing Made Easy. Rod R. Butterworth & Mickey Flodin. 224p. 1989. pap. 12.00 (*0-399-51490-2*, Perigee Bks) Berkley Pub.

Signing Naturally: Student Videotext & Workbook - Level One. expanded ed. Cheri Smith et al. (Vista Curriculum Ser.). 200p. 1993. per., pap. text ed. 39.95 incl. vhs (*0-915035-20-0*, 1315) Dawn Sign.

Signing Naturally: Student Videotexts & Workbook - Level Two. expanded ed. Cheri Smith et al. 192p. 1995. per., pap. text ed. 49.95 incl. vhs (*0-915035-16-2*, 1325) Dawn Sign.

Signing Naturally: Teacher's Curriculum Guide - Level One. Cheri Smith et al. (Vista Curriculum Ser.). 336p. 1990. pap. text ed., spiral bd. 84.95 incl. vhs (*0-915035-07-3*, 1300) Dawn Sign.

Signing Naturally: Teacher's Curriculum Guide - Level Two. Cheri Smith et al. (Vista Curriculum Ser.). 228p. 1988. pap. text ed., spiral bd. 84.95 incl. vhs (*0-915035-08-1*, 1301) Dawn Sign.

Signing Off: How to Have Fun with Names. Homer. 140p. 1980. pap. 3.95 (*0-936944-00-5*) Comm Creat.

Signing with Your Clients: A Practical Manual for Audiologists & Speech - Language Pathologists. Florence C. Vold et al. LC 90-13968. (Illus.). 334p. 1990. spiral bd. 29.95 (*0-930323-53-X*, Clerc Bks) Gallaudet Univ Pr.

Signmaker's Assistant. Tedd Arnold. LC 90-19537. (Illus.). 32p. (J). (ps-3). 1992. pap. 15.99 (*0-8037-1010-0*); pap. 14.89 (*0-8037-1011-9*) Dial Bks Young.

***Signmaker's Assistant.** Tedd Arnold. 1997. pap. 5.99 (*0-14-056097-1*) Viking Penguin.

Signmaking, Carving & Lettering: A Complete Illustrated Manual. Roger Schroeder & Greg Krockta. (Illus.). 150p. (Orig.). 1997. pap. 24.95 (*1-56523-078-7*) Fox Chapel Pub.

Signo Del Caballito De Mar: Un Intenso Episidio, En Dos Actos, De Codicia Y Aventuras. Graeme Base. 1994. 19.95 (*0-8109-4458-8*) Abrams.

Signo del Castor - The Sign of the Beaver. Elizabeth G. Speare. 1996. pap. text ed. 9.75 (*84-279-3188-3*) Lectorum Pubns.

Signor Bruschino. Gioachino Rossini. Ed. by Arrigo Fazzanigo. Tr. by Bruno Cagli et al. from ITA. (Works of Gioachino Rossini Ser.). xxxv, 504p. 1987. XXXV, 426 p. plus one vol. pap., 78 p. lib. bdg. 216.00 (*0-226-72836-6*, 728366) U Ch Pr.

Signor Faranta's Iron Theatre. Boyd Cruise & Merle Harton. LC 82-83592. (Illus.). xii, 148p. 1982. 14.95 (*0-917860-13-6*) Historic New Orleans.

Signore: Shogun of the Warring States. Kunio Tsuji. Tr. & Intro. by Stephen Snyder. 210p. 1990. 17.95 (*0-87011-939-7*) Kodansha.

Signore: Shogun of the Warring States. Kunio Tsuji. Tr. & Intro. by Stephen Snyder. 210p. 1996. pap. 12.00 (*4-7700-2066-X*) Kodansha.

Signors of the Night. Max Pemberton. LC 74-132123. (Short Story Index Reprint Ser.). 1977. 20.95 (*0-8369-3680-9*) Ayer.

Signos Para el Ingles Exacto: A Book for Spanish-Speaking Families of Deaf Children in Schools Using Signing Exact English. Esther Zawolkow et al. LC 82-61647. (Illus.). 160p. 1983. pap. 14.95 (*0-916708-06-3*) Modern Signs.

Signos Que Apareceran. Berceo. 308p. (SPA.). 1980. 16.75 (*0-8288-7010-1*, S37437) Fr & Eur.

Signpost to Romance. large type ed. Mandy Brown. 288p. 1988. 25.99 (*0-7089-1861-1*) Ulverscroft.

Signposts. Patricia Loomis. Ed. by Kathleen Muller. (Illus.). 97p. 1982. 22.95 (*0-914139-06-1*) Hist Mus San Jose.

Signposts: A Collection of Articles on the Russian Intelligentsia. Ed. by Michael Gershenzon. Tr. by Marshall S. Shatz & Judith E. Zimmerman. LC 86-22038. xxviii, 179p. (C). 1986. pap. 19.50 (*1-884445-15-2*) C Schlacks Pub.

Signposts: Reading African American Culture. Norman Harris. 210p. pap. write for info. (*1-878531-05-0*) Black Res Ctr.

Signposts: Spanish. Edith Baer & Margaret Wightman. (Illus.). 104p. (C). 1990. pap. text ed. 11.95 (*0-521-28193-8*) Cambridge U Pr.

Signposts Aloft - Chinese Edition. Moody Institute of Science Staff. Tr. by CRM Staff. 15p. (CHI.). 1985. 0.40 (*1-56582-068-1*) Christ Renew Min.

Signposts for Pilgrims: An Inspirational Collection of Papal Quotes. Margaret R. Bunson. LC 91-60012. 112p. 1991. lib. bdg. 9.95 (*0-87973-452-3*) Our Sunday Visitor.

Signposts French. Edith Baer. 104p. 1983. pap. text ed. 11. 95 (*0-521-28192-X*) Cambridge U Pr.

Signposts from Proverbs: An Introduction to Proverbs. Rhiannon Weber. (Illus.). 128p. (Orig.). (J). 1988. spiral bd. 10.99 (*0-85151-517-7*) Banner of Truth.

Signposts German. Edith Baer. 104p. 1982. pap. text ed. 11. 95 (*0-521-28186-5*) Cambridge U Pr.

Signposts II. Patricia Loomis. (Illus.). 104p. 1985. 22.95 (*0-914139-02-9*) Hist Mus San Jose.

Signposts in a Strange Land. Walker Percy. 1991. 25.00 (*0-374-26391-4*) FS&G.

Signposts in a Strange Land. Walker Percy. 432p. 1992. pap. 16.00 (*0-374-52345-2*) FS&G.

Signposts on the Road to Success. E. W. Kenyon. 72p. (Orig.). (C). 1938. pap. 3.75 (*1-57770-014-7*) Kenyons Gospel.

Signposts to Peace: An Independent Survey of the Violence in Natal, South Africa. International Commission of Jurists. 36p. reprint ed. pap. 25.00 (*0-7837-5224-5*, 2044956) Bks Demand.

Signs. Maurice Merleau-Ponty. Tr. by Richard C. McCleary. (Studies in Phenomenology & Existential Philosophy). 355p. 1964. pap. 24.95 (*0-8101-0253-6*) Northwestern U Pr.

Signs: An Introduction to Semiotics. Thomas A. Sebeok. (Toronto Studies in Semiotics). (Illus.). 144p. 1994. 40. 00 (*0-8020-2958-2*); pap. 14.95 (*0-8020-7780-3*) U of Toronto Pr.

Signs Across America. Edgar H. Shroyer & Susan P. Shroyer. LC 84-21219. (Illus.). 304p. 1984. pap. 17.95 (*0-913580-96-1*) Gallaudet Univ Pr.

Signs along the River: Learning to Read the Natural Landscape. Kayo Robertson. 64p. 1986. pap. 6.95 (*0-911797-22-X*) R Rinehart.

Signs & Guiding for Libraries. Linda Reynolds & Stephen Barrett. LC 80-140234. 158p. 1981. reprint ed. pap. 45. 10 (*0-608-02471-6*, 2063115) Bks Demand.

***Signs & Instruments of Liberation: The Confederation of Latin American Religious (CLAR) & a Contextural Theology of Religious Life from 1966 until 1991.** John Kiesler. 338p. 1996. pap. 39.00 (*90-390-0524-9*, Pub. by KOK Pharos NE) Eisenbrauns.

Signs & Meaning in the Cinema. enl. ed. Peter Wollen. LC 72-82722. (Cinema One Ser.: No. 9). (Illus.). 176p. 1973. pap. 11.95 (*0-253-18141-0*) Ind U Pr.

Signs & Parables: Semiotics & Gospel Texts. Entrevernes Group Staff. Tr. by Gary Phillips from FRE. LC 78-12840. (Pittsburgh Theological Monographs: No. 23). Orig. Title: Signes et Paraboles. 1978. pap. 12.00 (*0-915138-35-2*) Pickwick.

Signs & Portents. Chelsea Q. Yarbro. 232p. 1984. lib. bdg. 15.00 (*0-910489-02-5*) Scream Pr.

Signs & Portents: Monstrous Births from the Middle Ages to the Enlightenment. Dudley B. Wilson. LC 92-18149. (Illus.). 240p. (C). (gr. 13). 1993. text ed. 85.00 (*0-415-03236-9*, A7813) Routledge.

Signs & Printed Words, General Vocabulary see **Sport Signs**

Signs & Seasons. John Burroughs. (Works of John Burroughs). 1989. reprint ed. lib. bdg. 79.00 (*0-7812-2184-6*) Rprt Serv.

Signs & Seats of Power. (Illus.). 28p. (C). 1986. pap. 2.00 (*0-912303-36-0*) Michigan Mus.

Signs & Shadows: Reading John 5-12. Francis J. Moloney. LC 96-11618. 224p. 1996. 22.00 (*0-8006-2936-1*, Fortress Pr) Augsburg Fortress.

Signs & Spaces: International Survey of the Leading Environmental Design Firms. Rockport - Allworth Editions Staff. (Illus.). 200p. 1993. 49.99 (*1-56496-031-5*, 30509) Rockport Pubs.

Signs & Strategies for Educating Children with Brain Injuries: A Practical Guide for Teachers & Schools. Sue Pearson et al. LC 95-34228. 112p. (Orig.). 1995. teacher ed., pap. 24.95 (*1-882855-33-7*) HDI Pubs.

Signs & Symbols Illustrated & Explained in a Course of Twelve Lectures on Freemasonry. George R. Oliver. 210p. 1993. pap. 17.00 (*1-56459-302-9*) Kessinger Pub.

Signs & Symbols in Chauer's Poetry. Alabama Symposium on English & American Literature Staff. Ed. by John P. Hermann & John J. Burke, Jr. LC 80-11064. (Illus.). 267p. 1981. pap. 76.10 (*0-7837-8379-5*, 2059189) Bks Demand.

Signs & Symbols in Christian Art. George Ferguson. (Illus.). 192p. 1966. reprint ed. pap. 12.95 (*0-19-501432-4*) OUP.

Signs & Symbols of Primordial Man. Albert Churchward. 1991. lib. bdg. 499.99 (*0-87700-998-8*) Revisionist Pr.

Signs & Symbols of Primordial Man. Albert Churchward. 501p. 1986. reprint ed. spiral bd. 62.00 (*0-7873-0173-6*) Hlth Research.

Signs & Symbols of Primordial Man. Albert Churchward. (African Heritage Classical Research Studies). 449p. reprint ed. 60.00 (*0-938818-60-0*) ECA Assoc.

Signs & Symbols of Primordial Man, Vol. I. Albert Churchward. 232p. 1990. pap. text ed. 22.00 (*0-916157-44-X*) African Islam Miss Pubns.

Signs & Symbols of Primordial Man, Vol. II. Albert Churchward. 200p. 1990. pap. text ed. 22.00 (*0-916157-45-8*) African Islam Miss Pubns.

Signs & Symbols of Primordial Man, Vol. III. Albert Churchward. 186p. 1990. pap. text ed. 22.00 (*0-916157-46-6*) African Islam Miss Pubns.

Signs & Symbols of Primordial Man: The Evolution of Religious Doctrines from the Eschatology of the Ancient Egyptians. Albert Churchward. 500p. (Orig.). 1992. pap. 39.95 (*1-56459-105-0*) Kessinger Pub.

Signs & Symbols of Primordial Man: The Evolution of Religious Doctrines from the Eschatology of the Ancient Egyptians. Albert Churchward. 501p. 1994. pap. text ed. 16.95 (*1-881316-73-4*) A&B Bks.

Signs & Symptoms. Klippel & Liang. (C). (gr. 13). 1994. 184.00 (*0-8151-5214-0*) Mosby Yr Bk.

Signs & Symptoms: Adolescent Drug & Alcohol Use: What to Look for, What to Do. Community Intervention, Inc. Staff. 22p. (Orig.). 1986. pap. 3.95 (*0-9613416-3-7*) Comm Intervention.

Signs & Symptoms (Nurse's Ready Reference) Springhouse Publishing Co. Editors. LC 91-4608. 297p. 1991. spiral bd. 26.95 (*0-87434-366-6*) Springhouse Pub.

Signs & Wonders. Carl Dennis. LC 79-3210. (Contemporary Poets Ser.). 69p. 1979. pap. 9.95 (*0-691-01363-2*) Princeton U Pr.

***Signs & Wonders.** Maria B. Woodworth-Etter. LC 97-3118. 569p. (Orig.). 1997. pap. 13.99 (*0-88368-299-0*) Whitaker Hse.

Signs & Wonders: Amazing Evidence As the Boston Revival Gains Momentum. Ed. by Lloyd Hildebrand. 176p. (Orig.). 1995. pap. 8.95 (*0-929685-53-9*) Superior Bks.

Signs & Wonders: Biblical Texts in Literary Focus. Cheryl J. Exum. LC 88-19169. (Society of Biblical Literature Semeia Studies). 246p. 1989. 34.95 (*1-55540-249-6*, 06-06-18); pap. 22.95 (*1-55540-250-X*, 06 06 18) Scholars Pr GA.

Signs & Wonders: Outsider Art Inside North Carolina. Roger Manley. LC 89-60598. (Illus.). 152p. 1989. pap. 19.95 (*0-88259-957-7*) NCMA.

***Signs & Wonders: Poems.** Carl Dennis. LC 79-83985. (Princeton Series of Contemporary Poets). reprint ed. pap. 25.00 (*0-608-04587-X*, 2065357) Bks Demand.

Signs & Wonders: Saints, Miracles & Prayer from the 4th Century to the 14th. Benedicta Ward. (Collected Studies: No. CS361). 320p. 1992. text ed. 89.95 (*0-86078-316-2*, Pub. by Variorum UK) Ashgate Pub Co.

***Signs & Wonders: The Secrets of Mystical Marketing.** Tama Starr & Ed Hayman. (Illus.). 240p. 1996. 27.50 (*0-385-48602-2*, Currency) Doubleday.

Signs & Wonders in Ministry Today. Ed. by Benny C. Aker & Gary B. McGee. 128p. (Orig.). 1996. pap. 7.99 (*0-88243-346-6*) Gospel Pub.

Signs & Wonders Today. Christian Life Magazine Staff & C. Peter Wagner. 120p. 1986. pap. 2.95 (*0-8297-0709-3*) Life Pubs Intl.

Signs Becoming Signs: Our Perfusive, Pervasive Universe. Floyd Merrell. LC 90-49160. (Advances in Semiotics Ser.). (Illus.). 264p. 1991. 16.50 (*0-253-33746-1*) Ind U Pr.

***Signs Becoming Signs: Our Perfusive, Pervasive Universe.** Floyd Merrell. LC 90-49160. (Illus.). 261p. pap. 74.40 (*0-608-05049-0*, 2059710) Bks Demand.

***Signs by Gayle.** 2nd ed. Gayle C. Brown. 50p. 1997. pap. text ed. write for info. (*1-57377-016-7*) Easl Pubns.

Signs, Dialogue & Ideology: Interdisciplinary Approaches to Language, Discourse & Ideology. Augusto Ponzio. LC 93-33214. (Critical Theory Ser.: No. 11). ix, 183p. 1992. 65.00 (*1-55619-179-0*) Benjamins North Am.

Signs Everywhere: A Collection of Signs for Towns, Cities, States, & Provinces in the United States, Canada, & Mexico. Nancy Kelly-Jones & Harley Hamilton. LC 81-80388. (Illus.). 280p. (Orig.). (J). 1981. pap. 14.95 (*0-916708-05-5*) Modern Signs.

Signs for All Seasons. Suzie L. Kirchner. Ed. by John Joyce. LC 77-93546. (Illus.). 1981. pap. 10.95 (*0-917002-19-9*, 149) Joyce Media.

Signs for Catholic Liturgy & Education. 61p. 1990. reprint ed. pap. 7.00 (*0-318-16887-1*) Natl Cath Off Deaf.

Signs for Me: Basic Sign Vocabulary for Children, Parents & Teachers. Benjamin Bahan et al. (Illus.). 112p. 1987. pap. 12.95 (*0-915035-27-8*) Dawn Sign.

Signs from the Heart: California Chicano Murals. Ed. by Holly Barnet-Sanchez. LC 93-17526. (Illus.). 119p. 1993. pap. 25.95 (*0-8263-1448-1*) U of NM Pr.

Signs from the Heart: California Chicano Murals. Shifra M. Goldman et al. Ed. by Holly Barnet-Sanchez. (Illus.). 112p. (Orig.). 1990. pap. 24.95 (*0-9626419-0-1*) SPARC.

Signs, Genres, & Communities in Technical Communication. M. Jimmie Killingsworth & Michael K. Gilbertson. (Technical Communications Ser.). 257p. 1992. text ed. 37.95 (*0-89503-064-0*); pap. text ed. 28.46 (*0-89503-065-9*) Baywood Pub.

Signs Getting Along. Edward Wilson. LC 83-71741. 144p. 1983. 15.00 (*0-86690-246-5*, W2346-014) Am Fed Astrologers.

Signs Grow: Semiosis & Life Processes. Floyd Merrell. (Toronto Studies in Semiotics). 356p. 1996. 65.00 (*0-8020-0778-3*); pap. 24.95 (*0-8020-7142-2*) U of Toronto Pr.

Signs in Action. Pound & Michaux. LC 87-42539. 48p. 1987. pap. 4.00 (*0-87376-057-3*) Red Dust.

Signs in Contemporary Culture: An Introduction to Semiotics. Arthur A. Berger. (Illus.). 196p. (Orig.). (C). 1988. pap. text ed. 17.95 (*0-88133-396-4*) Sheffield WI.

Signs in Culture: Roland Barthes Today. Ed. by Steven Ungar & Betty R. McGraw. LC 89-32171. (Illus.). 190p. 1989. text ed. 26.95 (*0-87745-245-8*) U of Iowa Pr.

Signs in Judaism: A Resource Book for the Jewish Deaf Community. Adele K. Shuart. 196p. 1986. pap. 16.95 (*0-8197-0505-5*) Bloch.

Signs in Society: Psychological & Socio-Cultural Studies in Semiotic Mediation. Ed. by Elizabeth Mertz & Richard A. Parmentier. (Language, Thought & Culture Ser.). 1985. text ed. 80.00 (*0-12-491280-X*) Acad Pr.

Signs in Society: Studies in Semiotic Anthropology. Richard J. Parmentier. LC 93-27758. 252p. 1994. 35.00 (*0-253-32757-1*) Ind U Pr.

Signs in Success: Profiles of Deaf Americans. Ron Podmore. (Illus.). 48p. (Orig.). (J). 1995. pap. text ed. 7.95 (*1-884362-02-8*) Butte Pubns.

Signs in the Heavens. 7.95 (*1-56441-016-1*) M Hickey Min.

Signs in the Heavens. John A. Abent. 392p. (Orig.). 1995. pap. 14.99 (*1-56043-828-2*) Destiny Image.

***Signs in the Heavens.** Imad A. Ahmad. 174p. 1996. pap. 12.00 (*0-614-21610-9*, 1137) Kazi Pubns.

Signs in the Heavens: A Muslin Astronomer's Perspective of Religion & Science. Imad-ad-Dean Ahmad. LC 92-90710. (Illus.). 174p. (Orig.). 1992. pap. 12.00 (*0-9627854-2-3*) Writers Inc.

Signs, Language, & Communication. Roy Harris. LC 96-10472. 304p. (C). 1997. 59.95 (*0-415-10089-5*) Routledge.

Signs, Letters, Words: Archaeology Discovers Writing. W. John Hackwell. LC 86-26237. (Illus.). 72p. (YA). (gr. 7 up). 1987. lib. bdg. 14.95 (*0-684-18807-4*, C Scribner Sons Young) S&S Childrens.

Signs of a Christian. Ray Reeves. 36p. 1995. pap. 3.95 (*0-9647459-0-9*) Kuppinger Pubng.

***Signs of a Prophet: The Prophetic Actions of Jesus.** Morna D. Hooker. 144p. (Orig.). 1997. pap. 14.00 (*1-56338-210-5*) TPI PA.

Signs of Addictive Love. Brenda Schaeffer. 32p. 1986. pap. 3.25 (*0-89486-382-7*, 5207B) Hazelden.

Signs of All Time: The Warning, the Miracle, the Chastisement, the Era of Peace see **Thunder of Justice: The Warning, the Miracle, the Chastisement, the Era of Peace**

Signs of Arrival: Poems. Jeffrey Harrison. LC 96-21673. 71p. (Orig.). 1996. pap. 10.00 (*0-914278-71-1*) Copper Beech.

Signs of Borges. Sylvia Molloy. Tr. by Oscar Montero. LC 93-11260. (Post-Contemporary Interventions Ser.). 160p. 1994. text ed. 35.95 (*0-8223-1406-1*); pap. text ed. 16.95 (*0-8223-1420-7*) Duke.

Signs of Certainty: The Linguistic Imperative in French Classical Literature. Barbara Woshinsky. (Stanford French & Italian Studies: No. 71). 160p. 1991. pap. 46. 50 (*0-915838-87-7*) Anma Libri.

Signs of Change: Premodern--Modern--Postmodern. Ed. by Stephen Barker. LC 94-25974. (SUNY Series in Contemporary Studies in Philosophy & Literature: No. 4). 440p. (C). 1996. pap. text ed. 24.95 (*0-7914-2434-0*) State U NY Pr.

Signs of Change: Premodern--Modern--Postmodern. Ed. by Stephen Barker. LC 94-25974. (SUNY Series in Contemporary Studies in Philosophy & Literature: No. 4). 440p. (C). 1996. text ed. 74.50 (*0-7914-2433-2*) State U NY Pr.

Signs of Change: Urban Iconographies in San Francisco, 1880-1915. Ron Robin. LC 90-3506. (European Immigrants & American Society Ser.). 184p. 1990. reprint ed. text ed. 15.00 (*0-8240-0317-9*) Garland.

Signs of Christ. Harold Balyoz. LC 79-64608. 1979. 18.00 (*0-9609710-0-9*) Altai Pub.

Signs of Christ: A Book of Clip Art. Charles Lehman. (Illus.). 128p. (Orig.). 1995. pap. 24.95 (*1-55612-822-3*) Sheed & Ward MO.

Signs of Christianity in the Work of Walker Percy. Ann M. Futrell. 219p. 1995. 64.95 (*1-883255-11-2*, Cath Scholar Pr); pap. 44.95 (*1-883255-04-X*, Cath Scholar Pr) Intl Scholars.

Signs of Cleopatra: History, Politics, Representation. Mary Hamer. LC 92-10396. (Gender, Culture, & Difference Ser.). 224p. (C). 1993. pap. 16.95 (*0-415-04872-9*, Routledge NY) Routledge.

Signs of Cleopatra: History, Politics, Representation. Mary Hamer. LC 92-10396. (Gender, Culture, & Difference Ser.). 224p. (C). (gr. 13). 1993. text ed. 62.95 (*0-415-04871-0*, A9580, Routledge NY) Routledge.

S

Signs of Crime: A Field of Manual for Police. David Powis. LC 77-30173. (Illus.). 1978. pap. text ed. 5.95 (*0-89444-007-1*) John Jay Pr.
Signs of Design: An Introduction. Design Council Staff. (C). 1990. pap. text ed. 39.00 (*0-85072-268-3*) St Mut.
Signs of Design: English. Design Council Staff. (C). 1991. pap. text ed. 39.00 (*0-85072-271-3*) St Mut.
Signs of Design: Mathematics. Design Council Staff. (C). 1990. pap. text ed. 39.00 (*0-85072-269-1*) St Mut.
Signs of Design: Science. Design Council Staff. (C). 1990. pap. text ed. 39.00 (*0-85072-270-5*) St Mut.
Signs of Design: The Early Years. Design Council Staff. (C). 1991. pap. text ed. 39.00 (*0-85072-290-X*) St Mut.
Signs of Devotion: Stories. Maxine Chernoff. 192p. 1993. 19.00 (*0-671-79812-X*) S&S Trade.
***Signs of Diaspora/Diaspora of Signs: Literacies, Creolization, & Vernacular Practice in African America.** Grey Gundaker. (Commonwealth Center Studies in American Culture). (Illus.). 320p. 1998. 55.00 (*0-19-510769-1*) OUP.
Signs of Drug Use. James Woodward. 1980. pap. text ed. 7.95 (*0-932666-04-3*) T J Pubs.
***Signs of Effectiveness Vol. II: Preventing Alcohol, Tobacco, & Other Drug Use: A Risk Factor/Resiliency-Based Approach.** Ed. by Stephen E. Gardner et al. 93p. (C). 1996. reprint ed. pap. text ed. 25.00 (*0-7881-3619-4*) DIANE Pub.
Signs of Fertility: The Personal Science of Natural Birth Control. Margaret Nofziger. LC 86-90578. (Illus.). 100p. (Orig.). 1988. pap. 6.95 (*0-940847-07-8*) MND Publish.
Signs of God's Love: Baptism & Communion. Jeanne S. Fogle. Ed. by Mary J. Duckert & W. Ben Lane. (Illus.). 32p. (Orig.). (J). (gr. 3-8). 1984. pap. 10.00 (*0-664-24636-2*, Geneva Pr) Westminster John Knox.
Signs of Grace: Sacraments in Poetry & Prose. Ed. by David Brown & David Fuller. LC 96-1298. 224p. 1996. 19.95 (*0-8192-1654-2*) Morehouse Pub.
Signs of Healthy Love. Brenda Schaeffer. 24p. (Orig.). 1986. pap. 3.25 (*0-89486-374-6*, 5206B) Hazelden.
Signs of His Coming. Arthur E. Bloomfield. LC 57-8724. 160p. 1962. pap. 6.99 (*0-87123-513-7*) Bethany Hse.
***Signs of His Coming.** David A. Lewis. LC 97-65169. 272p. (Orig.). 1997. pap. 12.95 (*0-89221-347-7*) New Leaf.
Signs of His Coming. Linda M. McLaughlin. Ed. by Kathryn Hall. (Illus.). 64p. 1994. pap. text ed. 9.95 (*1-56664-068-7*) WorldComm.
Signs of Hope: Developing Small Christian Communities. James O'Halloran. LC 90-46180. 1991. pap. 11.50 (*0-88344-730-4*) Orbis Bks.
Signs of Hope: Working Towards Our Common Future. Linda Starke. 208p. 1990. 45.00 (*0-19-212993-7*) OUP.
Signs of Hope see Small Christian Communities: A Pastoral Companion
***Signs of Hope in the City.** Robert C. Linthicum. 95p. 1996. pap. 7.95 (*0-912552-95-6*) MARC.
***Signs of Human Action.** Ed. by David Williams. 1996. pap. text ed. 72.00 (*90-5702-513-2*, Harwood Acad Pubs) Gordon & Breach.
Signs of Humanity - L'Homme et ses Signes: Proceedings of the IVth IASS Congress. Ed. by Michel Balat et al. LC 92-31588. (Approaches to Semiotics Ser.: Vol. 107). (Illus.). 1804p. (FRE.). 1992. lib. bdg. 536.95 (*3-11-011675-8*) Mouton.
Signs of Jesus' Return. Richard Madison. Ed. by A. Eldredge. 70p. (Orig.). 1994. pap. 8.95 (*1-885857-00-4*) Four Wnds Pubng.
Signs of Judgement, Onomastica Sacra & the Generations from Adam. Michael E. Stone. LC 80-28371. (University of Pennsylvania Armenian Texts & Studies). 277p. (C). 1981. pap. 13.00 (*0-89130-461-4*); text ed. 17.50 (*0-89130-460-6*, 21-02-03) Scholars Pr GA.
Signs of Language. Edward S. Klima & Ursula Bellugi. 432p. 1988. reprint ed. pap. 17.95 (*0-674-80796-0*) HUP.
Signs of Life. Jean Ferris. LC 94-28709. 160p. (J). 1995. 14.00 (*0-374-36909-7*) FS&G.
***Signs of Life.** Harrison. LC 97-8803. 1997. 21.95 (*0-312-15656-1*) St Martin.
Signs of Life. Cherry Wilder. LC 96-41. 352p. 1996. 23.95 (*0-312-86171-0*) St Martin.
***Signs of Life.** 2nd ed. Maasik. 1997. pap. text ed. 2.40 (*0-312-14913-1*); pap. text ed. 5.00 (*0-312-14915-8*) St Martin.
***Signs of Life.** 2nd ed. Sonia Maasik. 1996. pap. text ed. 27.00 (*0-312-16718-0*) St Martin.
Signs of Life: A Memoir of Hospice, Home & Hope. Tim Brookes. 1997. 23.00 (*0-8129-2468-1*, Times Bks) Random.
Signs of Life: Channel-Surfing Through '90s Culture. Ed. by Jennifer Joseph & Lisa Taplin. (Illus.). 240p. (Orig.). 1994. pap. 12.95 (*0-916397-21-1*) Manic D Pr.
Signs of Life: Jews from Wuerttemberg-Reports for the Period after 1933 in Letters & Descriptions. Ed. by Walter Strauss. 35.00 (*0-87068-201-6*) Ktav.
Signs of Life: Observations of Death. Craig E. Betson. Ed. by Susan Farese. LC 94-60686. (Illus.). 92p. (Orig.). 1994. pap. 9.95 (*1-880254-18-2*) Vista.
Signs of Life: Process & Materials. Melissa Feldman. (Illus.). 63p. 1990. pap. 16.00 (*0-88454-049-9*) U of Pa Contemp Art.
Signs of Life: Rebecca Howland, Cara Perlman, Christy Rupp, Kiki Smith. Barry Blinderman. (Illus.). 72p. (Orig.). 1992. pap. 25.00 (*0-945558-19-8*) ISU Univ Galls.
Signs of Life: The Language & Meanings of DNA. Robert Pollack. 1995. pap. 10.95 (*0-395-73530-0*) HM.
Signs of Life: The Letters of Hilde Verdoner-Sluizer from Nazi Transit Camp, Westerbork, 1942 to 1944. Yoka Verdoner & Francisca Kan. 223p. 1990. 18.95 (*0-87491-955-X*) Acrpls Bks CO.
***Signs of Life: 6 Comedies of Menace.** Joan Schenkar. Ed. & Intro. by Vivian Patraka. LC 97-17910. (Illus.). 320p. 1997. text ed. 45.00 (*0-8195-6322-6*, Wesleyan Univ Pr) U Pr of New Eng.
***Signs of Life: 6 Comedies of Menace.** Joan Schenkar. Ed. & Intro. by Vivian Patraka. LC 97-17910. (Illus.). 320p. 1997. pap. 17.95 (*0-8195-6323-4*, Wesleyan Univ Pr) U Pr of New Eng.
Signs of Life in the U. S. Readings on Popular Culture for Writers. Sonia Maasik & James F. Solomon. 768p. 1994. pap. text ed. 22.00 (*0-312-09020-X*) St Martin.
Signs of Life in USA. 2nd ed. Sonia Maasik. 1997. pap. text ed. 22.00 (*0-312-13631-5*) St Martin.
Signs of Life with Rules. 3rd ed. Sonia Maasik. 1996. pap. text ed. 30.15 (*0-312-14959-X*) St Martin.
Signs of Literature: Language, Ideology, & the Literary Text. Hughes. (NFS Canada Ser.). pap. 16.95 (*0-88922-236-3*) Genl Dist Srvs.
Signs of Love: Your Personal Guide to Romantic & Sexual Compatibility. rev. ed. Jeraldine Saunders. (Illus.). 320p. 1995. reprint ed. mass mkt. 6.99 (*1-56718-602-5*) Llewellyn Pubns.
Signs of Meaning in the Universe. Jesper Hoffmeyer. LC 96-14287. (Illus.). 208p. 1997. 24.95 (*0-253-33233-8*) Ind U Pr.
Signs of My Friends. Ed. by Patricia T. Harsch & Leslie K. Harsch. (Illus.). 420p. 1984. boxed 15.95 (*0-931977-00-2*) About Faces Pub.
Signs of My Friends. deluxe ed. Ed. by Patricia T. Harsch & Leslie K. Harsch. (Illus.). 420p. 1984. Gift box ed. 17.95 (*0-931977-01-0*); 23.95 (*0-931977-02-9*) About Faces Pub.
Signs of Nations: A Political Semiotics of Self & Others in Contemporary European Nationalism. Ed. by Ulf Hedetoft. (Illus.). 720p. 1995. text ed. 69.95 (*1-85521-669-8*, Pub. by Dartmth Pub UK) Ashgate Pub Co.
Signs of Our Time: The Secret Meanings of Everyday Life. Jack Solomon. LC 89-45719. 256p. 1990. reprint ed. pap. 12.00 (*0-06-097266-1*, PL) HarpC.
Signs of Our Times. John Margolies & Emily Gwathmey. LC 92-37283. 96p. 1993. 27.50 (*1-55859-209-1*) Abbeville Pr.
Signs of Our Times: Theological Essays on Art in the Twentieth Century. George S. Heyer. LC 79-26805. (Illus.). 108p. reprint ed. pap. 30.80 (*0-317-10532-9*, 2019327) Bks Demand.
Signs of Paradox: Irony, Resentment, & Other Mimetic Structures. Eric L. Gans. LC 96-26518. 1997. write for info. (*0-8047-2769-4*) Stanford U Pr.
Signs of Performance: A Student's Guide. Colin Counsell. LC 95-37692. 232p. (C). 1996. pap. 17.95 (*0-415-10643-5*) Routledge.
Signs of Performance: A Student's Guide. Colin Counsell. LC 95-37692. 232p. (C). 1996. text ed. 59.95 (*0-415-10642-7*) Routledge.
Signs of Protest. Patricia Lakin. LC 94-19717. (My Community Ser.). (Illus.). (J). 1995. lib. bdg. 21.40 (*0-8114-8263-4*) Raintree Steck-V.
Signs of Psyche in Modern & Postmodern Art. Donald Kuspit. LC 93-18347. (Contemporary Artists & Their Critics Ser.). (Illus.). 397p. (C). 1993. pap. text ed. 27.95 (*0-521-44611-2*) Cambridge U Pr.
Signs of Recognition: Powers & Hazards of Representation in an Indonesian Society. Webb Keane. (Illus.). 322p. 1997. 50.00 (*0-520-20474-3*) U CA Pr.
Signs of Recognition: Powers & Hazards of Representation in an Indonesian Society. Webb Keane. (Illus.). 322p. 1997. pap. 20.00 (*0-520-20475-1*) U CA Pr.
Signs of Sexual Behavior. James Woodward. 1980. pap. text ed. 7.95 (*0-932666-02-7*) T J Pubs.
Signs of Sharing: An Elementary Sign Language & Deaf Awareness Curriculum. Sue F. Rakow & Carol B. Carpenter. LC 92-46219. (Illus.). 380p. (Orig.). 1993. spiral bd., pap. 49.95 (*0-398-05851-2*) C C Thomas.
Signs of Taste. Steven M. Weiss. LC 88-11730. 185p. 1988. pap. 9.95 (*0-932576-59-1*) Breitenbush Bks.
Signs of the Apostles. Walter J. Chantry. 1979. pap. 6.99 (*0-85151-175-9*) Banner of Truth.
Signs of the Coming of the Antichrist. Gordon Lindsay. (End of the Age Ser.: Vol. 1). 1.95 (*0-89985-067-7*) Christ for the Nations.
Signs of the Early Modern: I, Vol. 2. unabridged ed. Ed. by David L. Rubin. (EMF Studies in Early Modern France: No. 3). 257p. (C). 1996. lib. bdg. 39.95 (*1-886365-02-4*) Rookwood Pr.
Signs of the Flesh: An Essay on the Evolution of Hominid Sexuality. Daniel Rancour-Laferriere. LC 91-6785. (Illus.). 488p. 1992. pap. text ed. 18.95 (*0-253-20673-1*) Ind U Pr.
Signs of the Flesh: An Essay on the Evolution of Homonid Sexuality. Daniel Rancour-Laferriere. (Approaches to Semiotics Ser.: No. 71). x, 473p. 1986. 161.55 (*0-89925-121-8*) Mouton.
Signs of the Kingdom in the Secular City: Resources for the Urban Church. Ed. by Helen Ujvarosy. 1984. pap. 3.95 (*0-910452-56-3*) Covenant.
Signs of the Last Days: A Scriptural Guide to the Future. Vicki Alder. (Illus.). 248p. 1990. 12.95 (*0-9626559-0-2*) V Alder.
Signs of the Literary Times: Essays, Reviews, Profiles 1970-1992. William O'Rourke. LC 92-43027. (SUNY Series, The Margins of Literature). 250p. (C). 1993. pap. 19.95 (*0-7914-1682-8*) State U NY Pr.
Signs of the Literary Times: Essays, Reviews, Profiles 1970-1992. William O'Rourke. LC 92-43027. (SUNY Series, The Margins of Literature). 250p. (C). 1993. text ed. 59.50 (*0-7914-1681-X*) State U NY Pr.
Signs of the Nineties: The Poet. Don E. Miles. (Illus.). 108p. (Orig.). 1992. pap. 12.50 (*0-9635478-0-1*) Marked Tree.
Signs of the Soon Coming Christ (Senates De la Pronla Venida De Cristo) Gordon Lindsay. (Literature Crusade Ser.). (SPA.). 1960. pap. 0.95 (*0-89985-368-4*) Christ for the Nations.
Signs of the Soon Coming of Christ. Gordon Lindsay. (Literature Crusade Ser.). 1965. pap. 0.95 (*0-89985-355-2*) Christ for the Nations.
***Signs of the Times.** M. R. De Haan. LC 96-32045. (M. R. De Haan Classic Library). 1997. pap. 9.99 (*0-8254-2484-4*) Kregel.
Signs of the Times. Kenneth E. Hagin. 1986. pap. 0.75 (*0-89276-269-1*) Hagin Ministries.
Signs of the Times. John-Roger. 1981. pap. 5.00 (*0-914829-19-X*) Mandeville LA.
Signs of the Times. Klaus Schmidt. Ed. by B. Martin Pedersen. (Illus.). 224p. 1996. 49.95 (*1-888001-11-9*) Graphis US.
Signs of the Times. Edgar H. Shroyer. LC 82-81441. (Illus.). 448p. 1982. pap. text ed. 21.95 (*0-913580-76-7*, Clerc Bks) Gallaudet Univ Pr.
Signs of the Times. Shelley Von Strunckel. 1996. 23.00 (*0-517-70344-0*) Random Hse Value.
Signs of the Times: A Decade of Video, Film & Slide-Tape Installation in Britain 1980-1990. Ed. by Museum of Modern Art Oxford Staff. 87p. 1990. pap. 48.00 (*0-905836-72-3*, Pub. by Museum Modern Art UK) St Mut.
***Signs of the Times: Finding Omens in Everyday Life.** Sarvananda Bluestone. LC 97-1328. 256p. 1997. pap. 12.00 (*0-399-52349-9*, Perigee Bks) Berkley Pub.
***Signs of the Times: Leslie Stephen's Letters to "The Nation" from 1866-1873.** Brian Stenfors. (American University Studies: Series IV: Vol. 147). 288p. (C). 1996. text ed. 46.95 (*0-8204-1885-4*) P Lang Pubng.
Signs of the Times: Some Recurring Motifs in Twentieth-Century Photography. Deborah Irmas. LC 85-2280. (Illus.). 56p. 1985. pap. 9.95 (*0-918471-01-X*) San Fran MOMA.
Signs of the Times: Theological Reflections. Juan L. Segundo. Ed. by Alfred Hennelly. LC 93-941. 225p. (Orig.). 1993. pap. 21.00 (*0-88344-791-6*) Orbis Bks.
Signs of the Times: Trends & Indicators That Influence Our Lives. Roger E. Herman. LC 96-18518. (Illus.). 132p. (Orig.). 1996. pap. 14.95 (*1-886939-05-5*) Oak Hill Pr OH.
Signs of the Times in Cotton Mather's "Paterna" A Study of Puritan Autobiography. Constance J. Post. LC 91-58798. (Studies in Religious Tradition: No. 2). 1992. 39.50 (*0-404-62532-0*) AMS Pr.
Signs of the Times in the Heavens. Gordon Lindsay. 1967. 1.95 (*0-89985-062-6*) Christ for the Nations.
Signs of the Times: The Late Eighteenth Century see Millennium in America: From the Puritan Migration to the Civil War
Signs of the Times, Vols. 18 & 19, The Late Eighteenth Century see Millennium in America: From the Puritan Migration to the Civil War
Signs of the True Church of Christ. Michael T. Griffith. LC 89-83435. 144p. 1989. pap. 9.98 (*0-88290-337-3*, 1034, Pergamon Pr) Elsevier.
Signs of the Unseen: Discourses of Rumi. Wheeler M. Thackston. 132p. 1993. pap. 14.00 (*0-939660-34-2*) Threshold VT.
***Signs of the Unseen: The Discourses of Jalaluddin Rumi.** Tr. by W. M. Thackston, Jr. 284p. 1996. pap. 15.95 (*0-614-21346-0*, 1138) Kazi Pubns.
Signs of the Zodiac. Chancey King. 112p. 1968. 5.50 (*0-86690-121-3*, K1261-014) Am Fed Astrologers.
***Signs of the Zodiac: A Reference Guide to Historical, Mythological & Cultural Associations.** Mary E. Snodgrass. LC 97-5598. 1997. text ed. write for info. (*0-313-30276-6*, Greenwood Pr) Greenwood.
Signs of the Zodiac: Esoteric Bible Study; Astrological Characteristics & Consciousness of the 12 Signs of the Zodiac. Ed. by Health Research Staff. 84p. 1993. reprint ed. spiral bd. 10.00 (*0-7873-0399-2*) Hlth Research.
Signs of These Times: The Ayer Lectures of the Colgate Rochester Divinity School for 1929. Willard L. Sperry. LC 68-29247. (Essay Index Reprint Ser.). 1977. reprint ed. 18.95 (*0-8369-0897-X*) Ayer.
Signs of Time: An Introduction to MesoAmerican Astrology. Bruce Scofield. (Illus.). 216p. (Orig.). 1994. pap. 11.95 (*0-9628031-1-1*) One Reed Pubns.
Signs of Writing. Roy Harris. LC 94-30278. 185p. (C). (gr. 13). 1996. 55.00 (*0-415-10088-7*, C0165) Routledge.
Signs, Omens & Superstitions. Astra Cielo. 1991. lib. bdg. 75.00 (*0-8490-5003-0*) Gordon Pr.
Signs, Omens & Superstitions. Astra Cielo. 159p. 1969. reprint ed. spiral bd. 8.50 (*0-7873-0175-2*) Hlth Research.
Signs, Omens & Superstitions (1918) Astra Cielo. 163p. 1996. pap. 16.95 (*1-56459-899-3*) Kessinger Pub.
Signs. Poems. Margaret Gibson. LC 78-11961. (Illus.). viii, 64p. 1979. 13.95 (*0-8071-0493-0*); pap. 6.95 (*0-8071-0494-9*) La State U Pr.
Signs Preceding the Second Coming of Christ. Kingdom Quotes Staff. pap. write for info. (*0-930179-16-1*) Johns Enter.
Signs Reader: Women, Gender & Scholarship. Ed. by Elizabeth Abel & Emily K. Abel. LC 83-5781. 304p. 1983. pap. 14.95 (*0-226-00075-3*) U Ch Pr.
Signs Reader - 2: Feminist Scholarship, 1983-1996. Ed. by Ruth-Ellen B. Joeres & Barbara Laslett. LC 96-31516. 350p. 1996. pap. 18.95 (*0-226-40061-1*); lib. bdg. 35.00 (*0-226-40060-3*) U Ch Pr.
Signs, Science & Politics: Philosophies of Language in Europe 1700-1830. Lia Formigari. LC 93-32116. (Studies in the History of the Language Sciences: No. 70). x, 261p. 1993. 74.00 (*1-55619-365-3*) Benjamins North Am.
Signs, Search & Communication: Semiotic Aspects of Artificial Intelligence. Ed. by Rene J. Jorna et al. LC 92-35865. (Foundations of Communication & Cognition Ser.). viii, 378p. (C). 1992. lib. bdg. 130.80 (*3-11-013658-9*) De Gruyter.
Signs, Songs, & Memory in the Andes: Translating Quechua Language & Culture. Regina Harrison. LC 89-30889. (Illus.). 253p. 1989. 25.00 (*0-292-77627-6*); pap. 14.95 (*0-292-77628-4*) U of Tex Pr.
***Signs Taken.** Franco Moretti. (C). Date not set. pap. text ed. 18.00 (*1-85984-171-6*) Norton.
Signs Taken for Wonders: Essays in the Sociology of Literary Forms. Franco Moretti. Tr. by Susan Fischer et al. 336p. 1988. text ed. 50.00 (*0-86091-210-8*, A2102, Pub. by Verso UK) Routledge Chapman & Hall.
Signs That Make You Wonder. C. Paul Willis. 32p. (Orig.). 1994. pap. 4.00 (*1-885857-06-3*) Four Wnds Pubng.
Signs that Sell: The Handbook of Successful Merchandise Signing. Sonja Larsen & G. L. Hoffman. (Illus.). 200p. (C). 1991. 29.95 (*0-9629666-0-6*); pap. text ed. write for info. (*0-9629666-1-4*) Insignia Systs.
Signs Unseen, Sounds Unheard. 3rd ed. Carolyn B. Norris. 173p. 1991. 5.00 (*0-933076-02-9*) Alinda Pr.
Signs, Words, & Gestures. Balthasar Fischer. 79p. 1992. pap. 7.95 (*0-8146-6048-7*, Pueblo Bks) Liturgical Pr.
Signs Your Sex Life Is Dead. Jerry King. Ed. by Cliff Carle. 1995. pap. text ed. 5.95 (*0-918259-82-7*) CCC Pubns.
SignWriter Computer Program Package, Version 4.3, Set. Valerie J. Sutton. (Illus.). 1995. student ed., ring bd., pap. 150.00 incl. audio compact disk (*0-914336-63-0*) Ctr Sutton Movement.
Sigodlin: Poems. Robert Morgan. LC 89-30431. (Wesleyan Poetry Ser.). 72p. 1990. pap. 11.95 (*0-8195-1180-3*, Wesleyan Univ Pr); text ed. 25.00 (*0-8195-2178-7*, Wesleyan Univ Pr) U Pr of New Eng.
Sigrid Undset: A Study in Christian Realism. Andreas H. Winsnes. Tr. by P. G. Foote. LC 74-110276. (Illus.). ix, 258p. 1970. reprint ed. text ed. 55.00 (*0-8371-4502-3*, WISU, Greenwood Pr) Greenwood.
***Sigue Hasta la Meta.** 240p. (SPA.). 1996. pap. write for info. (*0-614-27141-X*) Editorial Unilit.
***Sigue Hasta la Meta - Go the Distance.** 240p. (SPA.). 1996. write for info. (*0-7899-0258-3*) Editorial Unilit.
Sigue Tus Pies see Homeplay: La Alegria de Aprender Entre Ninos y Adultos, Series I
Sigueme. Ralph W. Neighbour, Jr. 128p. 1986. reprint ed. student ed. 7.50 (*0-311-13836-5*); reprint ed. 5.50 (*0-311-13837-3*) Casa Bautista.
Sigueme, Edicion para Ninos. Ralph W. Neighbour, Jr. Tr. by Mary J. Geiger & Shirley Ditmore from ENG. (Illus.). 64p. (Orig.). (SPA.). (J). 1989. pap. 5.50 (*0-311-13848-9*) Casa Bautista.
Sigueme 2. Ralph W. Neighbour, Jr. Tr. by Mario Martinez from ENG. (Illus.). 128p. (Orig.). (SPA.). (J). 1989. pap. 8.99 (*0-311-13843-8*) Casa Bautista.
Sigueme 3. Thomas D. Lea & Bill Latham. Tr. by Mario Martinez from ENG. 128p. (Orig.). (SPA.). (J). (gr. 5 up). 1989. pap. 6.50 (*0-311-13847-0*) Casa Bautista.
Siguiendo Instrucciones A. Joy Evans & Jo E. Moore. Tr. by Jan Mayer et al. from ENG. (Illus.). 32p. (SPA.). (J). (ps-1). 1990. pap. text ed. 4.95 (*1-55799-179-0*, EMC 021) Evan-Moor Corp.
Siguiendo Instrucciones B. Joy Evans & Jo E. Moore. Tr. by Jan Mayer et al. from ENG. (Illus.). 32p. (SPA.). (J). (gr. 1-3). 1990. pap. text ed. 4.95 (*1-55799-178-2*, EMC 020) Evan-Moor Corp.
***Siguiendo la Estrella Actividades - Follow the Star Activity Book.** Parry. (SPA.). (J). write for info. (*1-56063-834-6*) Editorial Unilit.
Siguiendo las Pisadas de Jesus. 2nd ed. C. Wayne Zunkel. Ed. by Marcos R. Inhauser. Tr. by Marian Barriga et al. (Illus.). 124p. (SPA.). 1995. pap. 5.00 (*0-614-98000-3*, 0763) Brethren.
***Siguiriya: A Novel.** Sylvia Lopez-Medina. LC 97-249. 320p. Date not set. 23.00 (*0-06-017271-1*) HarpC.
***Sigundo Mapa.** Elspeth C. Murphy. (Ten Commandments Series for Kids). (SPA.). 1.50 (*0-8297-1898-2*) Life Pubs Intl.
Sigurd Hoel's Fiction: Cultural Criticism & Tragic Vision. Sverre Lyngstad. LC 83-26470. (Contributions to the Study of World Literature Ser.: No. 6). xvi, 198p. 1984. text ed. 49.95 (*0-313-24343-3*, LSH/, Greenwood Pr) Greenwood.
***Sigurd the Volsung: 1911 Edition.** Ed. by Peter Faulkner. (William Morris Library). 346p. 1996. reprint ed. pap. write for info. (*1-85506-253-4*) Bks Intl VA.
Sihanouk: Prince of Light, Prince of Darkness. Milton E. Osborne. LC 93-48520. (C). 1994. 27.95 (*0-8248-1638-2*); pap. 17.95 (*0-8248-1639-0*) UH Pr.
Sijobang: Sung Narrative Poetry of West Sumatra. Nigel Phillips. LC 80-42227. (Cambridge Studies in Oral & Literate Culture: No. 1). (Illus.). 248p. 1981. text ed. 74.95 (*0-521-23737-8*) Cambridge U Pr.
***Sik Asian Yearbook International Law 96.** 1996. lib. bdg. 262.00 (*90-411-0872-6*) Kluwer Law Tax Pubs.
Sik-Ki-Mi. Peter Roop. (Indian Culture Ser.). 32p. (J). (gr. 3-6). 1984. pap. 3.95 (*0-89992-091-8*) Coun India Ed.
Sikandar Nama: E Bara, or Book of Alexander the Great Written AD 1200. Nizam Nizami. Tr. by H. Wilberforce Clarke. 857p. reprint ed. text ed. 67.50 (*0-685-13397-4*) Coronet Bks.
Sikano l'Amerikano! Italian Stories. Nat Scammacca. 214p. 1989. 30.00 (*0-89304-509-8*); pap. 15.00 (*0-89304-508-X*) Cross-Cultrl NY.
Sikh. Catherine Chambers. LC 94-47348. (Beliefs & Cultures Ser.). (Illus.). 32p. (J). (gr. 4-6). 1996. lib. bdg. 19.50 (*0-516-08079-2*) Childrens.
Sikh Architecture in the Punjab. P. S. Arshi. 1986. 70.00 (*0-8364-1945-6*, Pub. by Intellectual Pub Hse II) S Asia.

An Asterisk (*) at the beginning of an entry indicates that the title is appearing in BIP for the first time.

Sikh Diaspora. Ed. by N. G. Barrier. (C). 1989. 44.00 (*0-685-35370-2*) S Asia Pubs II.

Sikh Festivals, Reading Level 4. Kapoor. (Holidays & Festivals Ser.: Set II). (Illus.). 48p. (J). (gr. 3-8). 1989. 11.95 (*0-685-58774-6*); lib. bdg. 15.94 (*0-86592-984-X*) Rourke Corp.

Sikh Gurus: Their Lives & Teachings. K. S. Duggal. LC 87-27712. 240p. 1987. pap. 14.95 (*0-317-65457-8*) Himalayan Inst.

Sikh Gurus: Their Lives & Teachings. K. S. Duggal. (C). 1993. pap. 6.00 (*81-85674-99-X*, Pub. by UBS Pubs Dist II) S Asia.

Sikh Gurus - Their Lives & Teachings. K. S. Duggal. 240p. 1996. 19.95 (*0-318-36784-X*) Asia Bk Corp.

Sikh Gurus & the Sikh Society. Niharranjan Ray. 1975. 14. 50 (*0-8364-2615-0*, Pub. by Munshiram Manoharial II) S Asia.

Sikh History & Religion in the Twentieth Century. Joseph T. O'Connell et al. (C). 1988. reprint ed. 34.00 (*0-9692907-4-8*, Pub. by Ctre South Asian CN) S Asia.

Sikh Identity & National Integration. Rajinder Kaur. xii, 158p. 1992. 10.00 (*81-7076-401-7*) Nataraj Bks.

Sikh Identity & National Integration. Rajinder Kaur. (C). 1992. 17.50 (*0-685-66245-4*, Pub. by Intellectual II) S Asia.

Sikh Moral Tradition. Nripender Singh. (C). 1990. 32.50 (*0-945921-12-8*, Pub. by S Asia Pubs II) S Asia.

Sikh People: Yesterday & Today. K. S. Duggal. (C). 1994. text ed. 7.50 (*81-85944-36-9*, Pub. by UBS Pubs Dist II) S Asia.

Sikh Psyche: A Study of the Fictional Writings of Bhai Vir Singh. Harcharan S. Sobti. x, 170p. (C). 1990. 15.00 (*81-85133-42-5*, Pub. by Estrn Bk Linkers II) Nataraj Bks.

Sikh Religion, 6 vols. in 3. Max A. MacAuliffe. 1963. text ed. 125.00 (*0-685-13749-X*) Coronet Bks.

Sikh Religion, 6 vols., Set. Max A. Macauliffe. 1270p. 1986. 400.00 (*0-317-52153-5*, Pub. by S Chand II) St Mut.

Sikh Religion: Its Gurus Sacred Writings & Authors, 3 vols., Set. Max A. MacAuliffe. 1990. reprint ed. 62.50 (*81-85395-94-2*, Pub. by Low Price II) S Asia.

Sikh Religion & Economic Development. Upinder J. Kaur. 1990. 52.00 (*81-85135-48-7*, Pub. by Natl Bk Org II) S Asia.

Sikh Separatism: The Politics of Faith. Rajiv A. Kapur. 240p. 1986. text ed. 34.95 (*0-04-320179-2*) Routledge Chapman & Hall.

Sikh Struggle: Origin, Evolution & Present Phase. Ram N. Kumar. (C). 1991. 47.50 (*81-7001-083-7*, Pub. by Chanakya II) S Asia.

Sikh Theology of Liberation. Dharam Singh. 1991. text ed. 25.00 (*81-85151-49-0*) Advent Bks Div.

***Sikhism.** Babraa. 1990. pap. text ed. write for info. (*0-582-31787-8*, Drumbeat) Longman.

Sikhism. Owen Cole. 160p. (Orig.). 1995. pap. 11.95 (*0-8442-3747-7*, Teach Yourslf) NTC Pub Grp.

Sikhism. Ed. by W. H. McLeod. LC 84-410. (Textual Sources for the Study of Religion Ser.). 208p. 1984. 50. 00 (*0-389-20479-X*, 08041) B&N Imports.

Sikhism. Sue Penney. (J). 1996. lib. bdg. 24.26 (*0-8172-4398-4*) Raintree Steck-V.

Sikhism. Piara S. Sambhi. 108p. 1989. pap. 21.00 (*1-871402-12-3*) Dufour.

Sikhism. Nikkyh-Guninder Singh. (World Religions Ser.). (Illus.). 128p. (YA). (gr. 7-12). 1992. bds. 17.95 (*0-8160-2446-4*) Facts on File.

Sikhism: A Short Expose. Ujagar S. Bawa. (Books on Sikhism Ser.). 30p. (J). 1988. pap. 2.00 (*0-942245-02-4*) Wash Sikh Ctr.

Sikhism & Christianity: A Comparative Study. W. Owen Cole & Piara S. Sambhi. LC 93-24508. 1993. text ed. 39. 95 (*0-312-10365-4*) St Martin.

Sikhism & the Sikhs: An Annotated Bibliography. Compiled by Priya M. Rai. LC 88-38308. (Bibliographies & Indexes in Religious Studies: No. 13). 272p. 1989. text ed. 75.00 (*0-313-26130-X*, RSI/, Greenwood Pr) Greenwood.

***Sikhism & Women.** Raj Pruthi & Bela R. Sharma. (C). 1995. 32.00 (*81-7488-087-9*, Pub. by Anmol II) S Asia.

***Sikhism Festivals.** John Coutts. LC 96-52641. (Celebrate Ser.). (J). 1997. write for info. (*0-431-06963-8*) Heinemann.

Sikhism in Pictures. Satinder S. Singh. 1982. 4.50 (*0-318-36779-3*) Asia Bk Corp.

Sikhs. W. Owen Cole & Piara S. Sambhi. (Library of Religious Beliefs & Practices). 210p. (C). 1986. pap. text ed. 13.95 (*0-415-04028-0*, 8843-4) Routledge.

Sikhs. Gene R. Thursby. LC 91-30520. (Iconography of Religions Ser.: Vol. 13-16). (Illus.). ix, 42p. 1992. 57.00 (*90-04-09554-3*) E J Brill.

Sikhs: An Ethnology. A. E. Barstow. (C). 1994. reprint ed. 10.00 (*0-614-04745-5*, Pub. by Low Price II) S Asia.

Sikhs: History, Religion, & Society. W. H. McLeod. 188p. 1989. text ed. 49.50 (*0-231-06814-X*) Col U Pr.

Sikhs: History, Religion, & Society. W. H. McLeod. 1991. pap. text ed. 14.50 (*0-231-06815-8*) Col U Pr.

Sikhs: Their Literature on Culture, History, Philosophy, Politics, Religion & Traditions. Rajwat Singh. 1989. 58. 50 (*81-85004-19-6*, Indian Biblio Bureau) S Asia.

Sikhs: Their Religion, Gurus, Sacred Writings & Authors, 6 vols., Set. Max A. Macauliffe. (C). 1988. 500.00 (*0-7855-0054-5*, Pub. by Print Hse II) St Mut.

Sikhs: Their Religious Beliefs. W. Owen Cole. 1985. pap. 9.00 (*0-7100-8843-4*, RKP) Routledge.

***Sikhs: Their Religious Beliefs & Practices.** W. Owen Cole & Piara S. Sambhi. 220p. pap. 24.95 (*0-614-21935-3*, Pub. by Sussex Acad Pr UK) Intl Spec Bk.

Sikhs: Their Religious Beliefs & Practices. W. Owen & Piara S. Sambhi. 1995. pap. 24.95 (*1-898723-13-3*, Pub. by Sussex Acad Pr UK) Intl Spec Bk.

Sikhs & Sikhism: A View with a Bias. I. J. Singh. (C). 1995. 17.50 (*0-945921-41-1*) South Asia Pubns.

Sikhs in Britain. Allan De Souza. (Communities in Britain Ser.). (Illus.). 72p. 1986. 19.95 (*0-7134-5100-9*, Pub. by Batsford UK) Trafalgar.

Sikhs in Indian Politics: Study of a Minority. Devinder P. Sandhu. (C). 1992. 18.00 (*81-7050-149-0*, Pub. by Patriot II) S Asia.

Sikhs in Kashmir. Jasbir S. Sarna. (Illus.). 98p. 1993. 10.00 (*81-7116-139-1*, Pub. by National Bk Shop II) Nataraj Bks.

Sikhs in North America: An Annotated Bibliography. Darshan S. Tatla. LC 90-13998. (Bibliographies & Indexes in Sociology Ser.: No. 19). 208p. 1991. text ed. 49.95 (*0-313-27336-7*, TSN/, Greenwood Pr) Greenwood.

Sikhs of Northern California, 1904-1975. Ed. by Bruce La Brack. LC 87-45787. (Immigrant Communities & Ethnic Minorities in the U. S. & Canada Ser.: No. 22). 1988. 67.50 (*0-404-19432-X*) AMS Pr.

Sikhs of the Punjab. J. S. Grewal. (New Cambridge History of India Ser.: II: 3). (Illus.). 272p. (C). 1991. text ed. 49. 95 (*0-521-26884-2*) Cambridge U Pr.

Sikhs of the Punjab: Unheard Voices of the State & Guerrilla Violence. Joyce M. Pettigrew. LC 95-13677. (Politics in Contemporary Asia Ser.). (Illus.). 256p. (C). 1995. pap. 25.00 (*1-85649-356-3*, Pub. by Zed Bks Ltd UK); text ed. 59.95 (*1-85649-355-5*, Pub. by Zed Bks Ltd UK) Humanities.

Sikhs of Vancouver. James G. Chadney. LC 83-45350. (Immigrant Communities & Ethnic Minorities in the U. S. & Canada Ser.: No. 1). (Illus.). 1984. 71.50 (*0-404-19403-6*) AMS Pr.

Sikhs Today: Their Religion, History, Culture, Customs. K. Singh. 94p. 1989. 8.95 (*0-318-36780-7*) Asia Bk Corp.

Sikkim. P. N. Chopra. 114p. 1979. 11.95 (*0-940500-65-5*) Asia Bk Corp.

Sikkim: A Himalayan Tragedy. Nari Rustomji. 173p. 1987. 21.00 (*0-8364-2056-X*, Pub. by Allied II) S Asia.

Sikkim: Customs & Folklore. C. D. Stocks. (Illus.). 189p. 1975. 12.95 (*0-318-36323-2*) Asia Bk Corp.

Sikkim: Democracy & Social Change. Madhumit Bhadra. (C). 1992. 16.00 (*81-85195-45-5*, Pub. by Abhinav II) S Asia.

Sikkim: Problems & Prospects. Manas D. Gupta. (C). 1992. 19.50 (*81-85182-73-6*, Pub. by Indus Pub II) S Asia.

Sikkim: Report of a Mission to Sikkim & the Tibetan Frontier, with a Memoir on Our Relation with Tibet. Ed. by Colman Mascaulay. (Illus.). 105p. (C). 1977. reprint ed. 55.00 (*0-89771-100-9*, Pub. by Ratna Pustak Bhandar) St Mut.

Sikkim: Society, Polity, Economy, Environment. Ed. by Mahendra P. Lama. (C). 1994. text ed. 30.00 (*81-7387-013-6*, Pub. by Indus Pub II) S Asia.

Sikkim since Independence. Amal Datta. (C). 1991. 21.50 (*81-7099-267-2*, Pub. by Mittal II) S Asia.

Siksha Samuccaya: A Compendium of Buddhist Doctrine. Ed. by Cecil Bendall & W. H. Rouse. 1981. 18:50 (*0-8364-0793-8*, Pub. by Motilal Banarsidass II) S Asia.

Siksha-Samuccaya, a Compendium of Buddhist Doctrine. Tr. by Cecil Bendall & W. D. Rouse. LC 78-70114. reprint ed. 33.50 (*0-404-17368-3*) AMS Pr.

SIL - a Simulation Language: User's Guide. N. Houbak. Ed. by G. Goos & J. Hartmanis. (Lecture Notes in Computer Science Ser.: Vol. 426). vii, 192p. 1990. 29.95 (*0-387-52497-5*) Spr-Verlag.

S'il Braille, Lache-Le. Chester Himes. 320p. (FRE.). 1984. pap. 12.95 (*0-7859-2500-7*, 2070376184) Fr & Eur.

Silage Fermentation. Woolford. (Microbiology Ser.: Vol. 14). 368p. 1984. 180.00 (*0-8247-7039-0*) Dekker.

Silage UK. 6th ed. Intro. by Mike Wilkinson. (Illus.). 191p. 1990. pap. text ed. 27.50 (*0-948617-01-2*, Pub. by Chalcombe Pubns UK) Scholium Intl.

Silane Coupling Agents. 2nd ed. Edwin P. Plueddemann. LC 90-21011. (Illus.). 245p. 1990. 65.00 (*0-306-43473-3*, Plenum Pr) Plenum.

Silanes & Other Coupling Agents. Ed. by K. L. Mittal. 588p. 1992. 147.50 (*90-6764-142-1*) Coronet Bks.

Silanes, Surfaces & Interfaces Vol. 1: Proceedings of the Silanes, Surfaces & Interfaces Symposium, Snowmass, Colorado, June 19-21, 1985: Chemically Modified Surfaces, Vol. 1. Ed. by Donald E. Leyden. 600p. 1986. text ed. 226.00 (*2-88124-085-2*) Gordon & Breach.

Silas. Nora DeLoach. 160p. (Orig.). 1993. mass mkt. 3.95 (*0-87067-383-1*) Holloway.

Silas: The Antarctic Diaries & Memoir of Charles S. Wright. Charles S. Wright. Ed. by Colin Bull & Pat F. Wright. LC 92-9407. (Illus.). 419p. (C). 1993. 62.50 (*0-8142-0548-8*) Ohio St U Pr.

Silas & the Mad-Sad People. Amber Jayant. LC 80-83882. (Illus.). (J). (gr. 1-5). 1981. pap. 6.95 (*0-938678-08-6*) New Seed.

Silas Downer - Forgotten Patriot: His Life & Writings. Carl Bridenbaugh. LC 74-83462. (Rhode Island Revolutionary Heritage Ser.: Vol. 1). (Illus.). 1974. 8.95 (*0-917012-01-1*) RI Pubns Soc.

Silas E. Ross: Recollections of Life at Glendale, Nevada, Work at the University of Nevada, & Western Funeral Practice, Set. Ed. by Mary E. Glass. 633p. 1971. lib. bdg. 81.50 (*1-56475-094-9*); Microfiche set. fiche write for info. (*1-56475-097-3*) U NV Oral Hist.

Silas Marner. 1995. pap. 5.25 (*0-19-422708-1*) OUP.

Silas Marner. 1995. pap. 5.25 (*0-19-586311-9*) OUP.

***Silas Marner.** (Classics Illustrated Study Guides Ser.). (Illus.). (Orig.). 1997. mass mkt. write for info. (*1-57840-050-3*) Acclaim Bks.

***Silas Marner.** Eliot. 1994. pap. text ed. write for info. (*0-582-23662-2*, Pub. by Longman UK) Longman.

Silas Marner. George Eliot. (Airmont Classics Ser.). (YA). (gr. 9 up). 1963. mass mkt. 2.50 (*0-8049-0014-0*, CL-14) Airmont.

Silas Marner. George Eliot. LC 92-54293. 1993. 15.00 (*0-679-42030-4*, Everymans Lib) Knopf.

Silas Marner. George Eliot. 192p. 1981. 2.95 (*0-553-21229-X*, Bantam Classics) Bantam.

Silas Marner. George Eliot. Ed. by Mary Bousted. (Literature Ser.). 256p. (C). 1996. pap. text ed. 7.95 (*0-521-48572-X*) Cambridge U Pr.

Silas Marner. George Eliot. Ed. by Anne Smith. 256p. 1993. pap. 4.95 (*0-460-87263-X*, Everyman's Classic Lib) C E Tuttle.

Silas Marner. George Eliot. (FRE.). 1980. pap. 11.95 (*0-7859-2434-5*, 2070371913) Fr & Eur.

Silas Marner. George Eliot. 192p. (YA). (gr. 7 up). 1960. pap. 3.95 (*0-451-52427-6*, Sig Classics) NAL-Dutton.

Silas Marner. George Eliot. Ed. by Q. D. Leavis. (English Library). 272p. 1968. pap. 6.95 (*0-14-043030-X*, Penguin Classics) Viking Penguin.

Silas Marner. George Eliot & Carro. 1997. pap. 6.95 (*0-14-043480-1*) Viking Penguin.

Silas Marner. George Eliot. 1997. pap. 2.95 (*0-89375-996-1*) NAL-Dutton.

Silas Marner. Hughes. (Book Notes Ser.). (C). 1985. pap. 2.95 (*0-8120-3538-0*) Barron.

Silas Marner. unabridged ed. George Eliot. 160p. reprint ed. pap. text ed. 1.50 (*0-486-29246-0*) Dover.

Silas Marner. George Eliot. 188p. 1987. reprint ed. lib. bdg. 19.95 (*0-89966-621-3*) Buccaneer Bks.

***Silas Marner: The Reaver of Raveloe.** George Eliot. Ed. & Intro. by Terence Cave. (The World's Classics Ser.). 232p. 1996. pap. 4.95 (*0-19-283210-7*) OUP.

Silas Marner: The Weaver of Naveloe. large type ed. George Eliot. (Isis Clear Type Classic Ser.). 196p. 1992. 24.95 (*1-85089-538-4*, Pub. by ISIS UK) Transaction Pubs.

Silas Marner, Brother Jacob, the Lifted Veil. rev. ed. George Eliot. Ed. by Peter Mudford. (Everyman Paperback Classics Ser.). 348p. (C). 1996. pap. 6.95 (*0-460-87568-X*, Everyman's Classic Lib) C E Tuttle.

Silas Marner Notes. William Holland. 1966. pap. 3.95 (*0-8220-1192-1*) Cliffs.

***Silas Rat.** Dermot O'Donovan. Date not set. pap. 8.95 (*0-947962-02-6*) Dufour.

Silas Rat & the Nuclear Tail. Dermot O'Donovan. (Illus.). 125p. (J). 1988. reprint ed. pap. 7.95 (*0-947962-22-0*, Pub. by Childrens Pr IE) Irish Bks Media.

Silas Talbot - Captain of Old Ironsides. William M. Fowler, Jr. (Illus.). 233p. 1995. 29.95 (*0-913372-73-0*) Mystic Seaport.

Silas, the Bookstore Cat. Karen T. Mather. LC 94-72357. (Illus.). 32p. (J). (gr. 1-4). 1994. 14.95 (*0-89272-352-1*) Down East.

Silba por Willie: (Whistle for Willie) Ezra J. Keats. (Illus.). 40p. (SPA.). (J). (ps-1). 1992. pap. 14.00 (*0-670-84395-4*) Viking Child Bks.

Silbale a Willie: A Study Guide. Marina Petralia. Ed. by J. Friedland & R. Kessler. (Novel-Ties Ser.). (SPA.). (J). (gr. k-2). 1996. pap. text ed. 14.95 (*1-56982-727-3*) Lrn Links.

Silbale a Willie: Whistle for Willie. Ezra J. Keats. Tr. by Ernesto L. Grosman. (Illus.). 32p. (SPA.). (J). 1996. pap. 4.99 (*0-14-055766-0*) Viking Penguin.

Silberstang's Encyclopedia of Games & Gambling. 7th ed. Edwin Silberstang. LC 94-69490. (Illus.). 552p. 1995. pap. 17.95 (*0-940685-55-8*) Cardoza Pub.

Silchester Ampitheatre: Excavations of 1979-85. Michael Fulford. (Illus.). 264p. 1993. text ed. 55.00 (*0-86299-627-9*, Pub. by Sutton Pubng UK) Bks Intl VA.

***Silciclastic Shelf Sediments: Based on a Symposium Sponsored by the Society of Economic Paleontologists & Mineralogists.** Ed. by Roderick W. Tillman & Charles T. Siemers. LC 84-225177. (Society of Economic Paleontologists & Mineralogists Ser.: No. 34). (Illus.). 276p. 1984. reprint ed. pap. 78.70 (*0-608-02972-6*, 2063440) Bks Demand.

Silence. 1972. 15.00 (*0-686-23327-1*) Rochester Folk Art.

Silence. Shusaku Endo. Tr. by William Johnston from JPN. LC 78-27168. 1980. pap. 9.95 (*0-8008-7186-3*) Taplinger.

***Silence.** Shusaku Endo. Tr. by William Johnston from JPN. 312p. 1996. pap. write for info. (*0-7206-1007-9*, Pub. by P Owen Ltd UK) Dufour.

Silence. Peter Ganick. 16p. (Orig.). 1996. pap. 5.00 (*1-57141-019-8*) Runaway Spoon.

Silence. Lily Lerner & S. L. Stuart. 1980. 10.95 (*0-8184-0306-3*) Carol Pub Group.

***Silence.** Charles Maclean. 1997. mass mkt. 5.99 (*0-06-101233-5*) HarpC.

Silence: A Thirteenth-Century French Romance. Ed. & Tr. by Sarah Roche-Mahdi. (Medieval Texts & Studies: No. 10). 343p. 1992. 15.95 (*0-937191-31-0*); pap. text ed. 16. 95 (*0-937191-32-9*) Colleagues Pr Inc.

***Silence: Interdisciplinary Perspectives.** Adam Jaworski. LC 97-11161. (Studies in Anthropological Linguistics). 1997. write for info. (*3-11-015459-5*) De Gruyter.

Silence: Lectures & Writings. John Cage. LC 61-14238. 288p. 1973. pap. 18.95 (*0-8195-6028-6*, Wesleyan Univ Pr) U Pr of New Eng.

Silence: Lectures & Writings. John Cage. 276p. reprint ed. lib. bdg. 39.00 (*0-685-14865-3*) Rprt Serv.

***Silence: Making the Journey to Inner Quiet.** Barbara Erakko Taylor. LC 97-11593. (Illus.). 160p. (Orig.). 1997. pap. 13.95 (*1-880913-21-6*) Innisfree Pr.

Silence: Our Eye on Eternity. David A. Seeger. LC 94-7414. 32p. pap. 3.00 (*0-87574-318-8*) Pendle Hill.

Silence: The Phenomenon & Its Ontological Significance. Bernard P. Dauenhauer. LC 80-7683. 222p. 1980. reprint ed. pap. 63.60 (*0-7837-6099-X*, 2059145) Bks Demand.

Silence: The Ultimate Protector of Individual Rights. 3rd rev. ed. Carl Watner. 1984. pap. 9.95 (*0-911752-39-0*) Neo-Tech Pub.

Silence Afterwards: Selected Poems of Rolf Jacobsen. Rolf Jacobsen. Ed. & Tr. by Roger Greenwald. LC 85-42671. (Lockert Library of Poetry in Translation). 290p. 1985. text ed. 49.50 (*0-691-06647-7*) Princeton U Pr.

Silence All Round Marked: An Historical Play in Hysteria Writ. Douglas Messerli. (Blue Corner Drama Ser.). 40p. (Orig.). 1991. pap. 5.95 (*1-55713-125-2*) Sun & Moon CA.

Silence & Invisibility: A Study of the Literatures of the Pacific, Australia, & New Zealand. Norman Simms. LC 82-40407. (Illus.). 227p. (Orig.). 1986. 26.00 (*0-89410-362-8*, Three Contnts); pap. 16.00 (*0-89410-363-6*, Three Contnts) Lynne Rienner.

Silence & License. William L. Fox. 1994. pap. 10.00 (*0-87924-086-5*) Membrane Pr.

Silence & Metaphor. William Bronk. 1975. 16.00 (*0-685-56226-3*); pap. 8.00 (*0-685-56227-1*) Elizabeth Pr.

Silence & Narrative: The Early Novels of Gertrude Stein. Janice L. Doane. LC 85-9854. (Contributions in Women's Studies: No. 62). 189p. 1986. text ed. 45.00 (*0-313-24936-9*, DSN/, Greenwood Pr) Greenwood.

Silence & Other Stories. Krishna B. Vaid. (Writers Workshop Greenbird Ser.). 94p. 1975. 14.00 (*0-88253-634-6*); pap. text ed. 4.80 (*0-88253-633-8*) Ind-US Inc.

Silence & Other Stories by Mary E. Wilkins Freeman. Mary E. Wilkins Freeman. LC 74-101812. (Short Story Index Reprint Ser.). 1977. 20.95 (*0-8369-3200-5*) Ayer.

Silence & Power: A Reevaluation of Djuna Barnes. Ed. by Mary L. Broe. LC 89-56358. (Illus.). 384p. (C). 1991. 34.95 (*0-8093-1250-6*); pap. 15.95 (*0-8093-1255-7*) S Ill U Pr.

Silence & Solitude: Inspirations for Meditation & Spiritual Growth. Ed. by Eileen Campbell. LC 95-4229. 176p. 1995. 15.00 (*0-06-251271-4*) Harper SF.

Silence & Sound: Theories of Poetics from the Eighteenth Century. Richard Bradford. LC 90-56225. 232p. 1992. 35.00 (*0-8386-3435-4*) Fairleigh Dickinson.

Silence and the Blue Night. Angela Greene. 83p. 9300. pap. 11.95 (*1-897648-06-5*, Pub. by Salmon Poetry IE) Dufour.

Silence & the Gift: Prayers & Drawings. Richard Beale. LC 94-11027. (Illus.). 1994. pap. 7.50 (*0-939485-08-7*) St Andrew Pr.

Silence As Yoga. 4th ed. Swami Paramananda. 1974. pap. 3.95 (*0-911564-11-X*) Vedanta Ctr.

Silence Bell: Poeme Haiku. Florentin Smarandache. Ed. by R. Muller. Tr. by Rodica Stefanescu. 180p. (Orig.). 1993. pap. text ed. 8.99 (*1-879585-35-9*) Erhus Univ Pr.

***Silence Calling: Australians in Antarctica 1947-97.** Tim Bowden. (Illus.). 624p. 1997. 59.95 (*1-86448-311-3*, Pub. by Allen Unwin AT) Paul & Co Pubs.

Silence de la Mer et Autres Recits. Jean Vercors, pseud. pap. 7.50 (*0-685-36630-8*) Fr & Eur.

Silence de la Mer et Autres Recits. Jean Vercors. 1953. pap. 3.95 (*0-685-11564-X*) Fr & Eur.

Silence de la Mer, Vercors: Critical Monographs in English. William Kidd. 72p. 1993. pap. 32.00 (*0-85261-316-4*, Pub. by Univ of Glasgow UK) St Mut.

***Silence Descends: The Decline & Fall of the Information Age, 2000-2500.** George Case. 1997. pap. text ed. 10.95 (*1-55152-041-9*, Pub. by Arsenal Pulp CN) LPC InBook.

Silence et le Mensonge see Isma

Silence, Exile & Cunning: The Fiction of Ruth Prawer Jhabvala. 2nd ed. Yasmine Gooneratne. 1993. 30.00 (*0-86311-144-0*, Pub. by Sangam Bks II) Apt Bks.

Silence in Hanover Close. Anne Perry. 1989. mass mkt. 6.99 (*0-449-21686-1*, Crest) Fawcett.

Silence in Hanover Close. large type ed. Anne Perry. (Mystery Ser.). 1990. 25.99 (*0-7089-2324-0*) Ulverscroft.

Silence in Heaven. Gilbert Morris. (Price of Liberty Ser.: Vol. 5). 1994. pap. 9.99 (*0-8499-3511-3*) Word Pub.

Silence in Heaven: A Book of Women's Preaching. Ed. by Susan Durber & Heather Walton. 160p. (Orig.). 1994. pap. 16.00 (*0-334-01543-X*, SCM Pr) TPI PA.

Silence in Henry James: The Heritage of Symbolism & Decadence. John Auchard. LC 85-21750. 192p. 1986. 28.50 (*0-271-00420-7*) Pa St U Pr.

Silence in the Garden. William Treavor. 208p. 1989. pap. 10.95 (*0-14-012065-3*, Penguin Bks) Viking Penguin.

Silence in the Garden. William Trevor. 204p. 1989. pap. 7.95 (*0-14-012712-7*, Penguin Bks) Viking Penguin.

Silence in the Novels of Elie Wiesel. Simon P. Sibelman. LC 94-27525. 1995. text ed. 39.95 (*0-312-12214-4*) St Martin.

Silence in the Snowy Fields: Poems. Robert Bly. LC 62-18340. (Wesleyan Poetry Program Ser.: Vol. 15). 60p. 1962. pap. 11.95 (*0-8195-1015-7*, Wesleyan Univ Pr) U Pr of New Eng.

Silence Is Not Golden: A Critical Anthology of Ethiopian Literature. Ed. by Tadesse Adera & Ali J. Ahmed. 222p. (Orig.). (C). 1994. 49.95 (*0-932415-46-6*); pap. 16. 95 (*0-932415-47-4*) Red Sea Pr.

***Silence Is Thy Praise.** Esther Austern. 15.99 (*0-89906-568-6*, SILH); pap. 12.99 (*0-89906-569-4*, SILP) Mesorah Pubns.

Silence, Le Mensonge. Nathalie Sarraute. pap. 4.95 (*0-685-36549-2*) Fr & Eur.

Silence Made Visible: Howard O'Hagan & Tay John. Ed. by Margery Fee. 160p. (C). 1992. pap. text ed. 25.00 (*1-55022-167-1*, Pub. by ECW Press CN) Genl Dist Srvs.

Silence Now. May Sarton. 1990. pap. 9.95 (*0-393-30635-6*) Norton.

Silence of Adam: Becoming Men of Courage in a World of Chaos. Larry Crabb et al. 224p. 1995. 18.99 (*0-310-48530-4*) Zondervan.

S

Silence of Angels. Dale C. Allison, Jr. LC 95-35121. 144p. (Orig.). (C). 1995. pap. 15.00 (*1-56338-131-1*) TPI PA.

Silence of Bartleby. Dan McCall. LC 89-627. 240p. 1989. pap. 13.95 (*0-8014-9593-8*) Cornell U Pr.

Silence of Constitutions: An Essay in Constitutional History. Michael Foley. 192p. (C). 1990. text ed. 59.95 (*0-415-03068-4*, A3949) Routledge.

Silence of Dreams. Barbara Faith. (Shadows Ser.). 1993. mass mkt. 3.50 (*0-373-27013-5*, 5-27013-7) Silhouette.

Silence of Entropy or Universal Discourse: The Postmodernist Poetics of Heiner Muller. Arlene A. Teraoka. LC 84-15431. (New York University Ottendorfer Ser.: Vol. 21). 240p. (C). 1984. text ed. 26.50 (*0-8204-0190-0*) P Lang Pubng.

Silence of Eternity. Lloyd H. Efflandt. (Illus.). 150p. (Orig.). 1990. pap. 8.95 (*0-9617938-1-3*) Rock Isl Arsenal Hist Soc.

Silence of God. John Foster. 125p. (C). 1993. text ed. 50.00 (*0-85439-424-9*, Pub. by St Paul Pubns UK) St Mut.

Silence of God. Robert Anderson. LC 78-9528. (Sir Robert Anderson Library). 232p. 1978. reprint ed. pap. 7.99 (*0-8254-2128-4*, Kregel Class) Kregel.

Silence of God: Creative Response to the Films of Ingmar Bergman. Arthur Gibson. LC 76-85048. 171p. 1978. pap. 79.95 (*0-88946-951-2*) E Mellen.

Silence of God: Meditations on Prayer. James P. Carse. LC 95-10094. 128p. 1995. pap. 11.00 (*0-06-061410-2*) Harper SF.

Silence of God: The Answer of the Buddha. Raimundo Panikkar. Tr. by Robert R. Barr from ITA. LC 89-2950. (Faith Meets Faith Series in Interreligious Dialogue). 400p. 1989. pap. 19.50 (*0-88344-446-1*) Orbis Bks.

Silence of God see Silencio de Dios

Silence of History. Eva Ancsel. 110p. (C). pap. 30.00 (*963-05-4907-7*, Pub. by Akad Kiado HU) St Mut.

Silence of Isaac Babel. Brent. 1994. pap. text ed. 14.95 (*0-226-07396-3*) U Ch Pr.

***Silence of Jesus.** James Breech. 1983. pap. 14.95 (*0-8006-0691-4*, Fortress Pr) Augsburg Fortress.

Silence of Light. Judith R. Platz. (Salt River Poetry Ser.). 32p. (Orig.). 1990. pap. 6.95 (*1-882021-15-0*) Salt River Pr.

Silence of Mary. Ignacio Larranaga. Tr. by V. Gaudet. LC 91-34526. 215p. (Orig.). 1991. pap. 12.95 (*0-8198-6911-2*) Pauline Bks.

Silence of Memory: Armistice Day, 1919-1946. Adrian Gregory. Ed. by Jay Winter. (Legacy of the Great War Ser.). (Illus.). 288p. 1994. 45.95 (*0-85496-955-1*); pap. 19.95 (*1-85973-001-9*) Berg Pubs.

Silence of Midnight. Karen Stone. (Superromance Ser.: No. 500). 1992. mass mkt. 3.39 (*0-373-70500-X*, 1-70500-3) Harlequin Bks.

Silence of My Love. Kay D. Rizzo. LC 92-43132. 1993. pap. 10.99 (*0-8163-1135-8*) Pacific Pr Pub Assn.

Silence of Strangers. Audrey Howard. 487p. 1995. 27.00 (*0-340-60949-4*, Pub. by H & S UK) Trafalgar.

Silence of the Body: Materials for the Study of Medicine. Guido Ceronetti. Tr. by Michael Moore from ITA. 1993. 22.00 (*0-374-26405-8*) FS&G.

Silence of the "Good" People. Garry De Young. pap. 17.95 (*0-936128-11-9*) De Young Pr.

Silence of the Hams. Jill Churchill. 1996. mass mkt. 5.99 (*0-380-77716-9*) Avon.

Silence of the Heart Pt. 2: Reflection of the Christ Mind. Paul Ferrini. (Reflections of the Christ Mind Ser.: Pt. 2). (Illus.). 218p. (Orig.). 1996. 14.95 (*1-879159-16-3*) Heartways Pr.

***Silence of the Lamberts: A Close to Home Collection.** John McPherson. LC 96-79242. (Illus.). 128p. (Orig.). 1997. pap. 7.95 (*0-8362-2698-4*) Andrews & McMeel.

Silence of the Lambs. Thomas Harris. 1991. mass mkt. 6.99 (*0-312-92458-5*) St Martin.

***Silence of the Langford: Essays (& Some Stories)** David Langford. Ed. by Ben Yalow. LC 96-69346. (Illus.). 286p. 1996. pap. 15.00 (*0-915368-62-5*) New Eng SF Assoc.

Silence of the Maharajah. Marie Corelli. 74p. 1972. reprint ed. spiral bd. 5.50 (*0-7873-0206-6*) Hlth Research.

Silence of the Maharajah (1895) Marie Corelli. 74p. 1996. pap. 12.95 (*1-56459-916-7*) Kessinger Pub.

Silence of the North. large type ed. Olive A. Fredrickson & Ben East. 1978. 25.99 (*0-7089-0183-2*) Ulverscroft.

Silence of the Sea. Hilaire Belloc. LC 74-107682. (Essay Index Reprint Ser.). 1977. 18.95 (*0-8369-2038-4*) Ayer.

Silence of the Sea - Le Silence de la Mer: A Novel of French Resistance During the Second World War by "Vercors" Ed. by Lawrence D. Stokes & James W. Brown. 112p. (C). 1992. pap. text ed. 15.95 (*0-85496-378-2*) Berg Pubs.

Silence of the Spheres: The Deaf Experience in the History of Science. Harry G. Lang. LC 93-20838. 224p. 1994. text ed. 49.95 (*0-89789-368-9*, Bergin & Garvey) Greenwood.

Silence of Unknowing: The Key to the Spiritual Life. Terence Grant. LC 95-10762. 208p. (Orig.). 1995. pap. 10.95 (*0-89243-828-2*, Triumph Books) Liguori Pubns.

***Silence of Yesterday.** Ed. by Nicole Walstrum. 1997. 69.95 (*1-57553-350-2*) Nat Lib Poetry.

Silence on Fire: The Prayer of Awareness. William H. Shannon. 160p. 1993. reprint ed. pap. 10.95 (*0-8245-1211-1*) Crossroad NY.

Silence Opens. Amy Clampitt. 112p. 1996. pap. 13.00 (*0-679-75022-3*) McKay.

Silence Opens: Poems. Amy Clampitt. LC 93-26889. 1994. 20.00 (*0-679-42997-2*) Knopf.

Silence, Please: Stories after the Works of Juan Munoz. John Berger. 144p. 1996. 27.50 (*3-931141-21-7*, Pub. by Scalo Pubs) Dist Art Pubs.

Silence, Simplicity & Solitude: A Guide for Spiritual Retreat. David A. Cooper. 320p. 1992. 18.00 (*0-517-58620-7*, Bell Tower) Crown Pub Group.

Silence, Simplicity & Solitude: A Guide for Spiritual Retreat. David A. Cooper. 1994. pap. 12.00 (*0-517-88186-1*, Bell Tower) Crown Pub Group.

***Silence Speaks: From the Chalkboard of Baba Hari Dass.** 2nd rev. ed. Baba H. Dass. Ed. by Karuna K. Ault. LC 96-92500. (Illus.). 272p. 1996. pap. 16.95 (*0-918100-19-4*) Sri Rama.

Silence Speaks for Love. Emma Goldrick. (Presents Ser.: No. 465). 1992. pap. 2.89 (*0-373-11465-6*, 1-11465-1) Harlequin Bks.

Silence Spoken Here. Samuel Hazo. LC 88-60731. 128p. 1988. 18.95 (*0-910395-38-1*) Marlboro Pr.

Silence That Is Not Golden. Tibbie S. Kposowa. LC 95-94743. 333p. (Orig.). 1995. pap. text ed. 18.99 (*1-887935-00-2*) Tabay Pubns.

***Silence the Ultimate Protector of Individual Rights.** Carl Watner. 36p. 1984. pap. 9.95 (*0-911752-81-1*) Neo-Tech Pub.

Silence, the Word & the Sacred. Ed. by E. D. Blodgett & Harold G. Coward. 224p. (C). 1989. text ed. 35.00 (*0-88920-981-2*) Wilfrid Laurier.

Silence to the Drums. Margaret Perry. LC 74-19806. (Contributions in Afro-American & African Studies: No. 18). 194p. 1976. text ed. 27.50 (*0-8371-7847-9*, PSD/, Greenwood Pr) Greenwood.

Silence Was a Weapon see Stalking the Vietcong: Inside Operation Phoenix, a Personal Account

***Silenced: Caribbean Domestic Workers Talk with Makeda Silvera.** Makeda Silvera. 115p. Date not set. pap. 12.95 (*0-920813-73-9*, Pub. by Sister Vision CN) LPC InBook.

Silenced Rivers: The Ecology & Politics of Large Dams. Patrick McCully. 320p. 1996. 60.00 (*1-85649-435-7*, Pub. by Zed Bks Ltd UK); pap. 25.00 (*1-85649-436-5*, Pub. by Zed Bks Ltd UK) Humanities.

Silenced Sextet: Six Nineteenth-Century Canadian Women Novelists. Carrie MacMillan et al. (Illus.). 240p. 1993. 44.95 (*0-7735-0945-3*, Pub. by McGill CN) U of Toronto Pr.

Silenced Theatre: Czech Playwrights Without a Stage. Marketa Goetz-Stankiewicz. LC 79-13423. 343p. reprint ed. pap. 97.80 (*0-318-34721-0*, 2031931) Bks Demand.

Silencehotels: Relais du Silence. Pierre Monthule. 192p. (ENG, FRE & GER.). 1994. pap. 9.95 (*0-7859-7426-1*) Fr & Eur.

Silencer. Simon Louvish. LC 92-24536. (Emerging Voices: New International Fiction Ser.). 264p. (Orig.). 1993. 29.95 (*1-56656-116-7*); pap. 10.95 (*1-56656-108-6*) Interlink Pub.

Silencer Theory. Henry C. Landa. (Illus.). 1979. pap. 11.00 (*0-931974-09-7*) FICOA.

***Silencers.** Daniel McCarthy. 280p. (Orig.). 1996. pap. text ed. 11.95 (*0-9653465-0-1*) Paine Pr.

Silencers for Hand Firearms. 1991. lib. bdg. 76.95 (*0-8490-4742-0*) Gordon Pr.

Silencers for Hand Firearms. Siegfried F. Huebner. LC 76-13260. (Illus.). 100p. 1976. pap. 18.00 (*0-87364-055-1*) Paladin Pr.

Silencers Graphic Novel. R. G. Taylor & Mark Askwith. (Illus.). 96p. 1994. 18.95 (*0-941613-46-1*) Stabur Pr.

Silences. J. P. Das. 100p. 1989. text ed. 10.95 (*0-317-93100-8*, Pub. by Vikas II) S Asia.

Silences. Vijay Munshi. (Redbird Ser.). 24p. 1975. 8.00 (*0-88253-846-2*); pap. text ed. 4.80 (*0-88253-715-6*) Ind-US Inc.

Silences. Tillie Olsen. 320p. 1979. pap. 12.95 (*0-385-28893-X*, Delta) Dell.

Silences. Tillie Olsen. 1984. 22.50 (*0-8446-6091-4*) Peter Smith.

***Silences: Poems.** Augustine Towey. LC 96-38777. 72p. 1996. pap. 12.95 (*0-7734-2693-0*, Mellen Poetry Pr) E Mellen.

Silences de Colonel Bramble. Dicours. Nouveau Discours du Dr. O'Grady. Andre Maurois. (FRE.). 1992. pap. 12.95 (*0-7859-3085-X*, 2253012769) Fr & Eur.

Silences de Paris see Voix et Silences: Les Meilleures Pieces Radiophoniques Francaises

Silences du Colonel Bramble. Andre Maurois. Bd. with Discours et Nouveaux discours ou Docteur O'Grady. Set pap. 6.50 (*0-685-23886-5*, 90) Fr & Eur.

Silences du Colonel Bramble: Avec: Discours, Nouveaux Discours du Dr. O'Grady. Andre Maurois. 14.50 (*0-686-55498-1*) Fr & Eur.

Silence's Roar: The Life & Drama of Nikolai Erdman. John Freedman. (Illus.). 220p. 1992. pap. 16.95 (*0-88962-489-5*) Mosaic.

Silence's Roar: The Life & Times of Nikolai Erdman. John Freedman. (Illus.). 220p. 1995. lib. bdg. 43.00 (*0-8095-4905-0*) Borgo Pr.

Silencing a People: The Destruction of Civil Society in Haiti. Ed. by Human Rights Watch Staff. 152p. (Orig.). 1993. pap. 15.00 (*1-56432-094-4*) Hum Rts Watch.

***Silencing Guns in Haiti.** Stotzky. LC 97-19494. 1997. 24.95 (*0-226-77626-3*) U Ch Pr.

Silencing Ivan Illich: A Foucauldian Analysis of an Intellectual Exclusion. David A. Gabbard. LC 93-3747. 115p. 1993. 54.95 (*1-880921-33-2*); pap. 34.95 (*1-880921-17-0*) Austin & Winfield.

Silencing Jeremiah. Peter Schmiesser. Date not set. pap. 8.95 (*0-14-013402-6*) Viking Penguin.

Silencing Jeremiah. Peter Schmiesser. Date not set. pap. 22.00 (*0-670-83373-8*) Viking Penguin.

Silencing of Leonardo Boff: The Vatican & the Future of World Christianity. Harvey Cox. LC 87-43277. 224p. (Orig.). 1988. pap. 9.95 (*0-940989-35-2*) Meyer Stone Bks.

Silencing of the Lambs: How Long Shall They Kill Our Prophets. Ricardo A. Scott. (Reggae Book of Light Ser.). (Illus.). 70p. (Orig.). pap. write for info. (*1-883427-28-2*) Crnerstone GA.

Silencing Science: National Security Controls & Scientific Communication. Harold C. Relyea. LC 93-50697. (Information Management, Policies & Services Ser.). 272p. 1994. pap. 39.50 (*1-56750-097-8*); text ed. 73.25 (*1-56750-096-X*) Ablex Pub.

Silencing Sentries. Oscar Diaz-Cobo. LC 88-45738. 104p. 1988. pap. text ed. 14.95 (*0-915179-84-9*) Loompanics.

Silencing the Enemy. Robert Gay. LC 93-79313. 108p. (Orig.). 1993. pap. 7.99 (*0-88419-349-7*) Creation House.

Silencing the Opposition: Government Strategies of Suppression of Freedom of Expression. Ed. by Craig R. Smith. (SUNY Series in Speech Communication). 285p. (C). 1996. text ed. 65.50 (*0-7914-3085-5*); pap. text ed. 21.95 (*0-7914-3086-3*) State U NY Pr.

Silencing the Past: Power & the Production of History. Michel-Rolph Trouillot. LC 95-17665. 192p. (C). 1995. 22.00 (*0-8070-4310-9*) Beacon Pr.

***Silencing the Past: Power & the Production of History.** Michel-Rolph Trouillot. 1997. pap. text ed. 12.50 (*0-8070-4311-7*) Beacon Pr.

Silencing the Self: Women & Depression. Dana C. Jack. 256p. (C). 1991. text ed. 24.00 (*0-674-80815-0*) HUP.

***Silencing the Voices: One Woman's Triumph over Multiple Personality Disorder.** Jean D. Cline. 416p. 1997. mass mkt. 6.99 (*0-425-15693-1*) Berkley Pub.

Silencio de Dies. Jose Escoto. 160p. (SPA.). 1994. pap. text ed. 9.00 (*1-57139-025-1*) Hernandez Translat.

Silencio de Dios. Robert Anderson. Orig. Title: The Silence of God. 192p. (SPA.). 1983. mass mkt. 5.25 (*0-8254-1022-3*, Edit Portavoz) Kregel.

Silens in Attic Black-Figure Vase-Painting: Myth & Performance. Guy M. Hedreen. (Illus.). 300p. (C). 1992. text ed. 42.50 (*0-472-10295-8*) U of Mich Pr.

Silent. A. Attanasio & Robert S. Henderson. 312p. 1996. 30.00 (*0-939767-24-4*) D McMillan.

Silent Abduction: Journeys of the Stranger, Bk. 2. Al Lacy. 320p. 1994. pap. 9.99 (*0-88070-877-8*, Multnomah Bks) Multnomah Pubs.

Silent After. Linda Stuart. LC 91-68086. 55p. 1992. 7.95 (*1-55523-499-2*) Winston-Derek.

Silent Alarm: On the Edge with a Deaf EMT. Steven L. Schrader. LC 95-34074. 144p. 1995. pap. text ed. 17.95 (*1-56368-044-0*) Gallaudet Univ Pr.

***Silent & Deadly.** Gary A. Linderer. 1997. mass mkt. 5.99 (*0-8041-1567-2*) Ivy Books.

Silent & Violent: Artists' Editions for Parkett. Text by Susan Tallman. (Illus.). 183p. 1996. pap. 55.00 (*3-89322-796-2*, Pub. by Parkett Pubs SZ) Dist Art Pubs.

Silent Angel. Heinrich Boll. Tr. by Breon Mitchell. 176p. 1994. 19.95 (*0-312-11064-2*) St Martin.

Silent Angel: A Novel. Heinrich Boll. Tr. by Breon Mitchell from GER. 192p. 1995. pap. 12.00 (*0-312-13171-2*) St Martin.

Silent Arrows. 3rd ed. Earl F. Moore. LC 23-939860. 1977. 12.95 (*0-939860-03-1*) Tremaine Graph & Pub.

Silent Boundaries: Cultural Constraints on Sickness & Diagnosis of Iranians in Israel. Karen L. Pliskin. LC 86-32492. 293p. reprint ed. pap. 83.60 (*0-7837-4551-6*, 2080342) Bks Demand.

Silent Brotherhood: Inside America's Racist Underground. Kevin Flynn & Gary Gerhardt. 496p. 1990. pap. 6.99 (*0-451-16786-4*, Sig) NAL-Dutton.

Silent Bullet: The Adventures of Craig Kennedy, Scientific Detective. Arthur B. Reeve. LC 75-32795. (Literature of Mystery & Detection Ser.). (Illus.). 1976. reprint ed. 34.95 (*0-405-07896-X*) Ayer.

Silent But for the Word: Tudor Women as Patrons, Translators, & Writers of Religious Works. Ed. by Margaret P. Hannay. LC 84-27802. 314p. reprint ed. pap. 89.50 (*0-7837-5125-7*, 2044853) Bks Demand.

***Silent Chain, Its Application to the Drive Problems of Industry.** J. M. Bryant. (Technical Papers). 1938. pap. text ed. 30.00 (*1-55589-445-3*) AGMA.

Silent Christmas. Illus. by Josse Goffin. LC 90-83430. 24p. (J). (ps). 1991. 14.95 (*1-878093-08-8*) Boyds Mills Pr.

Silent Cinema: An Annotated Critical Bibliography. Leona R. Phillips. 1977. lib. bdg. 250.00 (*0-8490-1368-2*) Gordon Pr.

Silent Cinema Music in the Nederlands. Theodore Van Houten. (Illus.). 328p. (Orig.). 1992. 78.00 (*0-913746-39-8*); pap. 53.00 (*0-913746-40-1*) Organ Lit.

Silent Cities: A Tombstone Registry of Old Lexington District South Carolina. June A. Seay. LC 86-114293. (Registry of Tombstone Epitaphs Ser.: Vol. I). (Illus.). 428p. (Orig.). 1984. pap. write for info. (*0-9617786-5-2*) June A Seay.

Silent Cities: A Tombstone Registry of Old Lexington District South Carolina, Set. June A. Seay. LC 86-114293. (Registry of Tombstone Epitaphs Ser.: Vol. I). (Illus.). 428p. (Orig.). 1984. pap. 32.50 (*0-9617786-4-4*) June A Seay.

Silent Cities: The Evolution of the American Cemetery. Kenneth Jackson & Camilo J. Vergara. LC 89-33672. (Illus.). 136p. (Orig.). 1990. pap. 14.95 (*0-910413-22-3*) Princeton Arch.

Silent Cities of Mexico & the Maya. 2nd ed. Norman F. Carver, Jr. (Illus.). 216p. 1986. 34.95 (*0-932076-06-8*); pap. 27.95 (*0-932076-07-6*) Documan.

Silent City. 2nd rev. ed. Erez Yakin. LC 95-39748. (Illus.). 104p. 1996. pap. 24.95 (*0-87816-385-9*) Kitchen Sink.

***Silent City.** 2nd rev. ed. Erez Yakin. (Illus.). 104p. 1996. 40.00 (*0-87816-447-2*) Kitchen Sink.

Silent City of Rocks: And the Almo Creek Massacre of 1861. Lovina C. Tuttle. Ed. & Illus. by Tedi T. Wixom. 24p. (Orig.). 1994. pap. 3.50 (*1-885227-11-6*) TNT Bks.

Silent City on a Hill: Landscapes of Memory & Boston's Mount Auburn Cemetery. Blanche Linden-Ward. (Urban Life & Urban Landsapes Ser.). (Illus.). 400p. 1989. 62.00 (*0-8142-0469-4*) Ohio St U Pr.

Silent Close No. 6. Monika Maron. Tr. by David N. Marinelli from GER. 192p. (Orig.). (C). 1993. 19.95 (*0-930523-93-8*); pap. 11.95 (*0-930523-94-6*) Readers Intl.

***Silent Clots, Life's Biggest Killers: Lockstep Medicine's Conspiracy to Suppress the Test That Should Be Done in Emergency Rooms Throughout the World.** large type unabridged ed. James R. Privitera & Alan Stang. LC 96-72237. (Illus.). 290p. (Orig.). 1997. pap. 19.95 (*0-9656313-0-3*) Catacombs Pr.

Silent Clowns. Walter Kerr. 1975. 20.00 (*0-394-46907-0*) Knopf.

Silent Clowns. Walter Kerr. (Quality Paperbacks Ser.). (Illus.). 384p. 1990. pap. 19.95 (*0-306-80387-9*) Da Capo.

Silent Comedians. Richard D. MacCann. LC 93-11399. (American Movies: The First Thirty Years Ser.). (Illus.). 257p. 1993. 29.50 (*0-8108-2725-5*); pap. 16.50 (*0-8108-2730-1*) Scarecrow.

Silent Command. deluxe limited ed. Robert Dante. (Illus.). 24p. 1992. 12.00 (*0-930324-24-2*) Wings Pr.

Silent Community: Public Homosexual Encounters. Edward W. Delph. LC 78-629. (Sociological Observations Ser.: No. 3). 186p. reprint ed. pap. 53.10 (*0-317-08749-5*, 2021886) Bks Demand.

***Silent Conscience.** Craig L. Andrews. 243p. (Orig.). 1997. mass mkt. 5.99 (*1-55197-446-0*, Pub. by Comnwlth Pub CN) Partners Pubs Grp.

***Silent Conspiracy: A Lincoln Keller Mystery.** Lee E. Meadows. LC 96-72290. 270p. 1997. 24.95 (*1-882792-38-6*) Proctor Pubns.

***Silent Coup: Confronting the Big Business Takeover of Canada.** Tony Clarke. 160p. 1997. pap. 19.95 (*1-55028-556-4*, Pub. by J Lorimer CN) Formac Dist Ltd.

***Silent Coup: Confronting the Big Business Takeover of Canada.** Tony Clarke. 160p. 1997. bds. 34.95 (*1-55028-557-2*, Pub. by J Lorimer CN) Formac Dist Ltd.

Silent Coup: The Removal of a President. Len Colodny. 1992. mass mkt. 5.99 (*0-312-92763-0*) St Martin.

Silent Cry. Kenzaburo Oe. Ed. by S. Shaw. 288p. 1994. pap. 11.00 (*4-7700-1965-3*) Kodansha.

Silent Cry. Kenzaburo Oe. Ed. by S. Shaw. Tr. by John Bester. 284p. 1994. 25.00 (*4-7700-0450-8*) Kodansha.

***Silent Cry.** Anne Perry. LC 97-16848. 1997. 24.95 (*0-449-90848-8*) Fawcett.

Silent Cry (Ray, Deke & Me) The Key to Stopping the Violence. E. J. Bassette. Ed. by Derrick K. Baker. 272p. 1994. 21.95 (*0-9642800-0-0*) ThreeB Pubng.

Silent Dancing: A Partial Remembrance of a Puerto Rican Childhood. 2nd ed. Judith Ortiz Cofer. LC 89-77428. 120p. (YA). (gr. 9 up). 1990. pap. 9.50 (*1-55885-015-5*) Arte Publico.

Silent Day in Tangiers. Tahar B. Jelloun. 1991. 17.95 (*0-15-182631-5*) HarBrace.

***Silent Death.** Iron Crown Enterprises Staff. 1991. 40.00 (*1-55806-088-X*) Iron Crown Ent Inc.

***Silent Death Unleaded.** Iron Crown Enterprises Staff. 1991. 20.00 (*1-55806-122-3*) Iron Crown Ent Inc.

Silent Decent. Couch. Date not set. 4.98 (*0-8317-6726-X*) Smithmark.

Silent Depression: The Fate of the American Dream. Wallace C. Peterson. LC 93-1295. 1994. 25.00 (*0-393-03586-7*) Norton.

Silent Depression: Twenty-Five Years of Wage Squeeze & Middle Class Decline. Wallace C. Peterson & Anthony Burgess. 320p. 1995. pap. 13.95 (*0-393-31282-8*, Norton Paperbks) Norton.

Silent Descent. Dick Couch. 400p. 1994. pap. text ed. 5.99 (*0-425-14335-X*) Berkley Pub.

Silent Dialogue: A Study in the Social Psychology of Professional Socialization. Virginia L. Olesen & Elvi W. Whittaker. LC 68-21320. (Jossey-Bass Behavioral Science Ser.). 328p. reprint ed. pap. 93.50 (*0-317-41981-1*, 2025678) Bks Demand.

Silent Dialogue: Zen Letters to a Trappist Abbot. David G. Hackett. 176p. 1996. 17.95 (*0-8264-0780-3*) Continuum.

Silent Disease: Hypertension. Lawrence Galton. 1974. pap. 3.95 (*0-451-13702-7*, AE2098, Sig) NAL-Dutton.

Silent Drums: The First Frontier Series, Bk. 2. Mike Roarke. 1994. mass mkt. 4.99 (*0-312-95224-4*) St Martin.

Silent Duchess. Dacia Maraini. 1993. 23.95 (*1-55082-053-2*, Pub. by Quarry Pr CN) LPC InBook.

Silent Duchess. Elspeth Spottiswood. 235p. 9200. 30.00 (*0-7206-0859-7*, Pub. by P Owen Ltd UK) Dufour.

Silent Enemies. Justina H. Hill. LC 79-134093. (Essay Index Reprint Ser.). 1977. 23.95 (*0-8369-1954-8*) Ayer.

Silent Enemies: The Story of the Diseases of War & Their Control. Justina H. Hill. (Essay Index Reprint Ser.). 275p. 1982. reprint ed. lib. bdg. 17.00 (*0-8290-0789-X*) Irvington.

Silent Energy: New Art from China. Intro. by David Elliott & Lydie Mepham. 1993. pap. 24.00 (*0-905836-86-3*, Pub. by Museum Modern Art UK) St Mut.

Silent Escape: Three Thousand Days in Romanian Prisons. Lena Constante. Tr. by Franklin Philip from FRE. LC 94-10627. (Society & Culture in East Central Europe Ser.: No. 9). 257p. 1995. 22.00 (*0-520-08209-5*) U CA Pr.

Silent Feminists: America's First Women Directors. rev. ed. Anthony Slide. LC 96-1178. Orig. Title: Early Women Directors. 160p. 1996. pap. 29.50 (*0-8108-3053-1*) Scarecrow.

Silent Fifties. Roger Bowen. (Orig.). 1994. pap. write for info. (*0-9602986-2-2*) Normandie.

Silent Film. Ed. & Intro. by Richard Abel. LC 95-12437. (Depth of Field Ser.). (Illus.). 300p. (C). 1995. text ed. 52.00 (*0-8135-2225-0*); pap. text ed. 20.00 (*0-8135-2226-9*) Rutgers U Pr.

An Asterisk (*) at the beginning of an entry indicates that the title is appearing in BIP for the first time.

Silent Film Necrology: Births & Deaths of over 9,000 Performers, Directors, Producers & Other Filmmakers of the Silent Era, Through 1993. Eugene M. Vazzana. LC 95-14462. 381p. 1995. lib. bdg. 55.00 (*0-7864-0132-X*) McFarland & Co.

Silent Film Performers: An Annotated Bibliography of Published, Unpublished & Archival Sources for over 350 Actors & Actresses. Roy Liebman. LC 95-20915. 391p. 1995. lib. bdg. 75.00 (*0-7864-0100-1*) McFarland & Co.

Silent Films on Video: A Filmography of over 700 Silent Features Available on Videocassette, with a Directory of Sources. Robert K. Klepper. LC 96-11757. 198p. 1996. lib. bdg. 45.00 (*0-7864-0157-5*) McFarland & Co.

***Silent Fox.** 125p. (Orig.). 1997. pap. 10.00 (*0-9657054-0-4*) Whspering Winds.

Silent Friends: A Quaker Quilt. Margaret Lacey. LC 91-66321. 108p. 1992. 14.95 (*0-935153-15-2*) Stormline Pr.

Silent Game: The Real World of Imaginary Spies. rev. ed. David Stafford. LC 90-28594. 280p. 1991. reprint ed. pap. 18.00 (*0-8203-1343-2*) U of Ga Pr.

Silent Garden: Raising Your Deaf Child. Paul W. Ogden. LC 96-34322. 328p. 1996. pap. 29.95 (*1-56368-058-0*, 2902) Gallaudet Univ Pr.

Silent Gasp. Lyn Lifshin. Ed. by Joyce Carbone. (Illus.). 40p. (Orig.). 1995. pap. 4.95 (*1-878116-52-5*) JVC Bks.

***Silent Grief: Living in the Wake of Suicide.** Christopher Lukas & Henry M. Seiden. LC 96-37735. (Master Works). 1997. pap. 24.95 (*0-7657-0056-5*) Aronson.

***Silent Groom: The Rose Tattoo.** Kelsey Roberts. (Intrigue Ser.). 1997. mass mkt. 3.75 (*0-373-22412-5*, 1-22412-0) Harlequin Bks.

Silent Hattie Speaks: The Personal Journal of Senator Hattie Caraway. Hattie W. Caraway. Ed. by Diane D. Kincaid. LC 78-22136. (Contributions in Women's Studies: No. 9). (Illus.). 151p. 1979. text ed. 47.95 (*0-313-20820-4*, KSI/, Greenwood Pr) Greenwood.

Silent Health: Women, Health & Representation. Camerawork Ltd. Staff. 96p. (C). 1990. 59.00 (*1-871103-03-7*, Pub. by Camerawork UK) St Mut.

Silent Heart. Claire McNab. 192p. 1993. pap. 10.95 (*1-56280-036-1*) Naiad Pr.

Silent Heart: Flynn of the Inland. Max Griffiths. 176p. (Orig.). 1995. pap. 16.95 (*0-86417-617-1*, Pub. by Kangaroo Pr AT) Seven Hills Bk.

Silent Herald of Unity: The Life of Bl. Gabrielle Sagheddu. Martha Driscoll. (Cistercian Studies: No. 119). 142p. 1990. 19.95 (*0-87907-619-4*); pap. 10.95 (*0-87907-919-3*) Cistercian Pubns.

Silent Heroes. Jack Campbell. 276p. (Orig.). 1987. pap. text ed. 9.95 (*0-942761-42-1*) JONopher Pub.

***Silent Heroes among Us: Final Flights of the Mighty 8th.** Ed. by James Clements. (Illus.). (Orig.). Date not set. pap. 24.95 (*1-884687-07-5*) N Horzns Pub.

Silent Holocaust: Romania & Its Jews. I. C. Butnaru. LC 91-21181. (Contributions to the Study of World History Ser.: No. 31). 304p. 1992. text ed. 59.95 (*0-313-27985-3*, BFK, Greenwood Pr) Greenwood.

Silent Honor. Danielle Steel. LC 96-8248. 360p. 1996. 24.95 (*0-385-31301-2*) Delacorte.

***Silent Honor.** Danielle Steel. 432p. 1997. mass mkt. 7.50 (*0-440-22405-5*) Dell.

Silent Honor. large type ed. Danielle Steel. 360p. 1996. 29.95 (*0-385-31712-3*) Doubleday.

Silent Hunger: A Biblical Approach to Overcoming Compulsive Eating & Overweight. Judy Halliday & Arthur Halliday. LC 93-33904. (Illus.). 208p. (Orig.). (gr. 10). 1994. pap. 8.99 (*0-8007-5524-3*) Revell.

Silent Hunter Official Secrets & Solutions. Prima Publishing Staff. 1996. pap. text ed. 14.99 (*0-7615-0144-4*) Prima Pub.

***Silent Hunters: German U-Boat Commanders of WW II.** Ed. by Theodore P. Savas. (Illus.). 238p. 1997. write for info. (*1-882810-17-1*) Savas Woodbury.

Silent in the Land. Photos by Chip Cooper. (Illus.). 192p. 1993. 45.00 (*0-9636713-0-8*) CKM Pr.

Silent in the Saddle. large type ed. Norman A. Fox. LC 92-37236. (Popular Ser.). 262p. 1993. reprint ed. lib. bdg. 15.95 (*1-56054-548-8*) Thorndike Pr.

***Silent Instrument: A Spiritual Experience.** Nina I. Alenti. (Orig.). 1996. pap. 10.95 (*0-533-12033-0*) Vantage.

Silent Interviews: On Language, Race, Sex, Science Fiction, & Some Comics. Samuel R. Delany. LC 93-35913. (Illus.). 334p. (C). 1994. pap. 17.95 (*0-8195-6280-7*, Wesleyan Univ Pr) U Pr of New Eng.

Silent Intruder: Surviving the Radiation Age. Charles Panati & Michael Hudson. 224p. 1981. 9.95 (*0-685-02309-5*) HM.

Silent Invasion. Ellen Crystall. 1996. mass mkt. 6.50 (*0-312-95935-4*) St Martin.

Silent Journey. Betty L. Jasmin. (Orig.). 1996. pap. write for info. (*1-57553-240-9*) Watermrk Pr.

***Silent Justice: Court Experiences of People Who Are Deaf or Hard of Hearing.** Wynne Harrison. (Illus.). 20p. 1997. pap. write for info. (*0-938870-79-3*, 793) Am Judicature.

Silent Knife: Cesarean Prevention & Vaginal Birth after Cesarean. Nancy W. Cohen & Lois J. Estner. LC 82-24276. (Illus.). 456p. 1983. pap. text ed. 19.95 (*0-89789-027-2*, Bergin & Garvey) Greenwood.

Silent Knife: Vaginal Birth After Cesarean (VBAC) & Cesarean Prevention. Nancy W. Cohen & Lois J. Estner. 464p. 1983. 13.46 (*0-318-17499-5*) C Sec.

Silent Knight. Jim Buckley. LC 76-28107. (Illus.). 79p. (J). 1976. 4.95 (*0-9649167-0-3*) P Plough.

Silent Knight. Tori Phillips. 1996. pap. 4.99 (*0-373-28943-X*, 1-28943-8) Harlequin Bks.

Silent Lamp: The Thomas Merton Story. William H. Shannon. 320p. 1994. reprint ed. pap. 14.95 (*0-8245-1281-2*) Crossroad NY.

Silent Language. Edward T Hall. LC 72-97265. 224p. reprint ed. 9.95 (*0-385-05549-8*, Anchor NY) Doubleday.

Silent Language. Edward T. Hall. LC 79-25399. xviii, 217p. 1980. reprint ed. text ed. 59.75 (*0-313-22277-0*, HASN, Greenwood Pr) Greenwood.

Silent Language of Psychotherapy: Social Reinforcement of Unconscious Processes. 2nd ed. Ernst G. Beier & David M. Young. LC 84-6287. 307p. (C). 1984. pap. text ed. 26.95 (*0-202-26098-4*); lib. bdg. 49.95 (*0-202-26097-6*) Aldine de Gruyter.

Silent Life. Thomas Merton. 178p. 1975. pap. 12.00 (*0-374-51281-7*) FS&G.

Silent Lotus. Jeanne Lee. (Illus.). 32p. (J). (gr. k-3). 1991. 14.95 (*0-374-36911-9*) FS&G.

Silent Lotus. Jeanne M. Lee. (J). (ps-3). 1994. pap. 4.95 (*0-374-46646-7*, Sunburst Bks) FS&G.

Silent Majority: Families of Emotionally Healthy College Students. William A. Westley & Nathan B. Epstein. LC 77-75937. (Jossey-Bass Behavioral Science Ser.). 208p. reprint ed. pap. 59.30 (*0-8357-9347-8*, 2013780) Bks Demand.

Silent Man. Said Salah. (Dual Language Ser.). 46p. 1995. pap. 12.00 (*1-887584-29-3*) Intl Prom Art.

Silent Masquerade. Molly Rice. (Intrigue Ser.). 1995. pap. 3.50 (*0-373-22315-3*, 1-22315-5) Harlequin Bks.

Silent Master: Awakening the Power Within. Tae Yun Kim. LC 93-46044. 192p. (Orig.). 1994. pap. 10.95 (*1-880032-41-4*) New Wrld Lib.

***Silent Memory.** Mary Balogh. 368p. 1997. mass mkt. 5.99 (*0-425-15862-4*) Berkley Pub.

Silent Meow: A Manual for Kittens, Strays, & Homeless Cats. Paul Gallico & Suzanne Szasz. (Illus.). 160p. 1985. pap. 12.00 (*0-517-55683-9*, Crown) Crown Pub Group.

Silent Minority: Children with Disabilities in Asian Families. 2nd ed. Robina Shah. 128p. 1995. pap. 25.00 (*1-874579-44-X*) Paul & Co Pubs.

Silent Minority: Deaf Education. Susan J. Plann. LC 96-10171. (Illus.). 1997. 40.00 (*0-520-20471-9*) U CA Pr.

Silent Mobius, Vol. 1. Kia Asamiya. Ed. by Seiji Horibuchi. Tr. by Satoru Fujii from JPN. (Illus.). 120p. 1992. pap. 14.95 (*0-929279-87-5*) Viz Commns Inc.

Silent Mobius, Vol. 2. Kia Asamiya. Ed. by Seiji Horibuchi. Tr. by Satoru Fujii from JPN. (Illus.). 120p. 1992. pap. 14.95 (*0-929279-88-3*) Viz Commns Inc.

Silent Movies. Neil Sinyard. 192p. 1994. 15.98 (*0-8317-7800-8*) Smithmark.

Silent Movies: A Picture Quiz Book. Stanley Appelbaum. 128p. 1974. pap. 4.95 (*0-486-23054-6*) Dover.

***Silent Music.** 2nd rev. ed. William Johnston. LC 97-3400. 200p. 1997. 30.00 (*0-8232-1774-4*) Fordham.

***Silent Music.** 2nd rev. ed. William Johnston. LC 97-3400. 200p. 1997. pap. 17.00 (*0-8232-1775-2*) Fordham.

Silent Music, 3 vols., Set. Nicholas. (Illus.). 144p. 1998. pap. 25.00 (*0-9649124-1-4*) Cygnet Pubng.

Silent Myocardial Ischemia: A Critical Appraisal. Ed. by J. J. Kellermann & E. Braunwald. (Advances in Cardiology Ser.: Vol. 37). (Illus.). viii, 358p. 1990. 207.00 (*3-8055-5196-7*) S Karger.

Silent Myocardial Ischemia & Angina. Bramah N. Singh. 1988. text ed. 45.00 (*0-07-105311-5*) McGraw.

Silent Myocardial Ischemia & Infarction. 3rd ed. Pete F. Cohn. LC 92-48488. (Fundamental & Clinical Cardiology Ser.: Vol. 13). 288p. 1993. 95.00 (*0-8247-9054-5*) Dekker.

Silent New World: Ford Madox Ford's Parade's End. M. A. Calderaro. 136p. 1995. pap. 12.95 (*88-8091-132-5*) Paul & Co Pubs.

Silent Night. (Lights & Music of Christmas Ser.). (Illus.). 16p. (J). 1993. 12.98 (*1-56173-706-2*) Pubns Intl Ltd.

Silent Night. Gary Amo. 1991. mass mkt. 4.50 (*1-55817-510-5*, Pinncle Kensgtn) Kensgtn Pub Corp.

Silent Night. Mary Higgins Clark. 1996. mass mkt. 5.99 (*0-671-00042-X*) PB.

Silent Night. Mary Higgins Clark. LC 95-36717. 154p. 1995. 16.00 (*0-684-81545-1*) S&S Trade.

***Silent Night.** Linda Granfield. (Illus.). (J). 1997. write for info. (*0-614-29318-9*) Tundra Pubns.

Silent Night. Andy Holmes. (J). (ps-3). 1992. 5.99 (*0-929216-50-4*) KindrVision.

Silent Night. Illus. by Susan Jeffers. LC 84-8113. (Unicorn Paperbacks Ser.). 32p. (J). (ps up). 1984. pap. 4.95 (*0-8037-4443-9*) Dutton Child Bks.

Silent Night. Susan Jeffers. (Illus.). (J). 1992. pap. 4.99 (*0-525-44431-9*) Dutton Child Bks.

Silent Night. Joseph Mohr. LC 84-8113. (J). 1988. pap. 4.95 (*0-685-57131-9*) Dutton Child Bks.

Silent Night. Joseph Mohr. 1992. pap. 4.99 (*0-14-054877-7*) NAL-Dutton.

Silent Night. Will Moses. LC 96-18585. (J). 1997. 16.95 (*0-399-23100-5*, Philomel Bks) Putnam Pub Group.

***Silent Night.** Illus. by Laura Rader. (Little Angels Ser.). 4p. (J). (ps up). 1997. bds. 2.99 (*1-57584-163-0*) Rdrs Dgst Yng Fam.

***Silent Night.** Illus. by Laura Rader. (Little Angels Ser.). 6p. (J). (ps). 1997. bds. 2.99 (*0-7847-0633-6*, 24-03743) Standard Pub.

Silent Night. R. L. Stine. Ed. by Patricia MacDonald. (Fear Street Super Chiller Ser.). 224p. (Orig.). (J). (gr. 7 up). mass mkt. 3.99 (*0-671-73822-4*, Archway) PB.

Silent Night. large type ed. Mary Higgins Clark. 1995. 18.00 (*0-684-81546-X*) S&S Trade.

Silent Night, No. 2. R. L. Stine. Ed. by Pat MacDonald. (Fear Street Super Chiller Ser.). 224p. (Orig.). (YA). (gr. 7 up). 1993. mass mkt. 3.99 (*0-671-78619-9*, Archway) PB.

Silent Night: A Christmas Book with Lights & Music. Kathy Mitchell. (Illus.). 12p. (J). (ps-3). 1989. bds. 11.95 (*0-689-71330-4*, Aladdin Paperbacks) S&S Childrens.

Silent Night: A Christmas Carol Sample. Illus. by Belinda Downes. 32p. 1995. 18.00 (*0-679-86959-X*) Random.

Silent Night: A Mouse Tale. Betsy Hernandez & Donny Monk. (Illus.). 48p. (J). (ps-5). 1992. write for info. (*0-917143-17-5*) Sparrow TN.

Silent Night: A Mouse Tale. Betsy Hernandez & Donny Monk. (Illus.). 48p. (J). (ps-5). 1992. 12.95 (*0-917143-10-8*) Sparrow TN.

Silent Night: A Pop-up Book. Mary Engelbreit. (Illus.). 8p. (J). 1995. 4.95 (*0-8362-0026-8*) Andrews & McMeel.

Silent Night: Christmas. Mary M. Simon. (Hear Me Read Bible Stories Ser.). (Illus.). 24p. (J). (ps-1). 1991. pap. 2.49 (*0-570-04700-5*, 56-1659) Concordia.

Silent Night: Glitter Glow. Brooke House Staff. 12p. (J). 1996. pap. 4.99 (*0-689-80932-8*) S&S Childrens.

***Silent Night: Its Story & Song.** Margaret Hodges. LC 97-16408. (Illus.). (J). 1997. 16.00 (*0-8028-5138-X*) Eerdmans.

***Silent Night: The Song from Heaven.** Linda Granfield. (Illus.). 24p. (J). (gr. 1 up). 1997. 15.95 (*0-88776-395-2*) Tundra Bks.

Silent Night: Tree Ornament Book. Lion Publishing Staff. 8p. (J). (gr. 1 up). 1992. 1.99 (*0-7814-0759-1*, Lion) Chariot Victor.

***Silent Night (Collectors Edition)** R. L. Stine. (Fear Street Ser.). (J). 1997. mass mkt. 7.99 (*0-671-00886-2*) PB.

Silent Night 3. R. L. Stine. (Fear Street Super Chiller Ser.: No. 11). (J). 1996. mass mkt. 3.99 (*0-671-52970-6*) PB.

Silent Observer. Christy MacKinnon. (Awareness & Caring Ser.). (Illus.). 48p. (J). (gr. k-6). 1995. lib. bdg. 17.95 (*1-56674-075-4*) Forest Hse.

Silent Observer. Christy MacKinnon. LC 93-4510. (Illus.). 48p. (J). 1993. 15.95 (*1-56368-022-X*, Pub. by K Green Pubns) Gallaudet Univ Pr.

Silent One & Other Poems. Emma L. Moffatt. 16p. (Orig.). 1995. pap. write for info. (*1-885206-10-0*, Iliad Pr) Cader Pubng.

Silent Operas. Li Yu. Ed. & Intro. by Patrick Hanan. (Illus.). xiii, 201p. (Orig.). 1990. pap. 14.95 (*962-7255-07-6*, Pub. by Renditions Papbk HK) SPD-Small Pr Dist.

***Silent Option.** Larry Simmmons. 1997. mass mkt. 6.50 (*0-671-55281-3*, Pocket Books) PB.

Silent Pain - Is It Arthritis? Reflections of a Clinical Rheumatologist. William E. Byrd. LC 95-25169. (Illus.). 240p. 1995. 22.50 (*1-55618-155-8*) Brunswick Pub.

Silent Partner. Jonathan Kellerman. 512p. 1990. mass mkt. 6.99 (*0-553-28592-0*) Bantam.

Silent Partner. Greg Williamson. LC 95-15725. (Ruerich Poetry Prize Winner Ser.). 88p. 1995. pap. 11.95 (*1-885266-11-1*) Story Line.

***Silent Partner.** large type ed. Jonathan Kellerman. LC 96-31678. 1996. pap. 23.95 (*1-56895-362-3*, Compass) Wheeler Pub.

***Silent Partner.** Elizabeth S. Phelps. LC 82-25306. 1983. reprint ed. pap. 12.95 (*0-935312-08-0*) Feminist Pr.

Silent Partner. Elizabeth S. Ward. (Americans in Fiction Ser.). 310p. reprint ed. pap. text ed. 10.95 (*0-89197-936-0*); reprint ed. lib. bdg. 29.00 (*0-8398-2151-4*) Irvington.

Silent Partner: The History of the American Film Manufacturing Company 1910-1921, Vol. 7. Timothy J. Lyons. LC 73-21590. 266p. 1974. 18.95 (*0-405-04872-6*) Ayer.

***Silent Passage.** Sheehy. 1998. pap. 12.00 (*0-671-01774-8*, PB Trade Paper) PB.

Silent Passage. Gail Sheehy. Ed. by Julie Rubenstein. 336p. 1995. pap. 12.00 (*0-671-51951-4*) PB.

Silent Passage: Menopause. Gail Sheehy. 1992. 16.00 (*0-679-41388-X*) Random.

Silent Passage: Menopause. Gail Sheehy. Ed. by Julie Rubenstein. 256p. 1997. reprint ed. mass mkt. 6.50 (*0-671-79931-2*) PB.

Silent Path to God. James E. Griffiss. LC 79-8903. 110p. reprint ed. pap. 31.40 (*0-317-55552-9*, 2029620) Bks Demand.

Silent People Dwelling in a World Without Sound: All About Deaf Mutes. J. N. Williams. 1972. 250.00 (*0-8490-1054-3*) Gordon Pr.

Silent Piano, Vol. 10. Hilda Stahl. (Elizabeth Gail Ser.: Vol. 10). 128p. (J). (gr. 3-9). 1989. pap. 5.99 (*0-8423-0810-5*) Tyndale.

Silent Picture: Numbers One-Nineteen. 1977. 52.95 (*0-405-09898-7*, 11492) Ayer.

Silent Pictures. Katie Maratta. 128p. 1992. pap. 9.95 (*0-943728-49-5*) Lone Eagle Pub.

Silent Pilgrimage to God: The Spirituality of Charles de Foucauld. Jeremy Moiser. LC 74-32516. 100p. reprint ed. pap. 28.50 (*0-8357-4072-2*, 2036762) Bks Demand.

Silent Pilots: Figureheads in Mystic Seaport Museum. Georgia W. Hamilton. (Illus.). 116p. 1984. pap. 19.95 (*0-913372-30-7*) Mystic Seaport.

Silent Places. Stewart E. White. 1976. lib. bdg. 14.25 (*0-89968-123-9*, Lghtyr Pr) Buccaneer Bks.

Silent Places. Stewart E. White. 15.95 (*0-8488-1511-4*) Amereon Ltd.

Silent Poetry: Deafness, Sign, & Visual Culture in Modern France. Nicholas Morzoeff. LC 94-42545. 320p. 1995. text ed. 29.95 (*0-691-03789-2*) Princeton U Pr.

Silent Portraits: Stars of the Silent Screen in Historic Photographs. Anthony Slide. LC 89-22589. (Illus.). 280p. (Orig.). 1989. pap. 24.95 (*0-911572-78-3*) Madison Bks UPA.

Silent Power. Stuart Wilde. 64p. (Orig.). 1996. pap. 3.95 (*1-56170-323-0*, 187) Hay House.

Silent Presence. Ernest E. Larkin. 1984. pap. 8.95 (*0-87193-172-9*) Dimension Bks.

Silent Prey. John Sandford. 384p. 1993. mass mkt. 6.99 (*0-425-13756-2*) Berkley Pub.

Silent Printers: Anonymous Printing at Venice in the Sixteenth Century. Dennis E. Rhodes. (British Library Studies in the History of the Book). (Illus.). 306p. 1995. 120.00 (*0-7123-0385-5*) U of Toronto Pr.

Silent Prophet. Joseph Roth. Tr. by David Le Vay from GER. LC 79-67676. 216p. 1980. 22.50 (*0-87951-110-9*) Overlook Pr.

Silent Prophet. Joseph Roth. Tr. by David Le Vay. 224p. 1990. pap. 11.95 (*0-87951-384-5*) Overlook Pr.

Silent Rage: The Thirty-Year Odyssey of a Serial Killer. Michael Newton. 384p. 1994. mass mkt. 5.99 (*0-440-21313-4*) Dell.

Silent Rain: A Search for the Child Within. Nancy V. Rawlins. 232p. 1993. 14.95 (*1-879908-04-2*) Milton Pub.

***Silent Rescue.** William M. Jones. (Illus.). 220p. (Orig.). 1997. pap. 14.95 (*0-9639984-9-8*) Eastern Dakota.

Silent Retreats. Philip F. Deaver. LC 87-14313. (Flannery O'Connor Award for Short Fiction Ser.). 240p. 1988. 19.95 (*0-8203-0981-8*) U of Ga Pr.

Silent Revolution. Miriam S. Zakon. 1992. 16.99 (*0-89906-105-2*); pap. 13.99 (*0-89906-106-0*) Mesorah Pubns.

Silent Revolution: Development of Conventional Weapons, 1945-1985. Guy Hartcup. (Illus.). 276p. 1993. 35.00 (*0-08-036702-X*, Pub. by Brasseys UK) Brasseys Inc.

Silent Revolution: Media, Democracy, & the Free Trade Debate. Ed. by James P. Winter. 196p. 1990. pap. 22.00 (*0-7766-0296-9*, Pub. by Univ Ottawa Pr CN) Paul & Co Pubs.

Silent Revolution: The Informal Sector in Five Asian & Near Eastern Countries. Ed. by A. Lawrence Chickering & Mohamed Salahdine. 245p. 1991. 29.95 (*1-55815-163-X*); pap. 12.95 (*1-55815-162-1*); 5.00 (*1-55815-177-X*) ICS Pr.

S

***Silent Revolution: The Rebirth of American Civil Life & What It Means for All of Us.** Everett C. Ladd. 1998. 25.00 (*0-684-83735-8*) Free Pr.

Silent Revolution: The Rise of Market Economics in Latin America. Duncan Green. (Global Issues Ser.). (Illus.). 256p. 1996. 60.00 (*0-304-33455-3*) Cassell.

Silent Revolution: The Rise of Market Economies in Latin America. Duncan Green. (Illus.). 180p. (Orig.). (C). 1995. pap. text ed. 16.00 (*0-85345-969-X*, Pub. by Lat Am Bur UK) Monthly Rev.

Silent Revolution: The Transformation of Divorce Law in the United States. Herbert Jacob. 220p. 1988. 27.00 (*0-226-38951-0*) U Ch Pr.

Silent Revolution in Africa: Debt, Development & Democracy. Fantu Cheru. LC 89-22579. 160p. (C). 1989. pap. 17.50 (*0-86232-891-8*, Pub. by Zed Bks Ltd UK); text ed. 49.95 (*0-86232-890-X*, Pub. by Zed Bks Ltd UK) Humanities.

Silent Revolution in Europe: Integrational Change in Post-Industrial Societies. Ronald Inglehart. (Reprint Series in Political Science). (C). 1993. reprint ed. pap. text ed. 2.30 (*0-8290-2736-X*, PS-486) Irvington.

Silent Rights: The Ninth Amendments & the Constitution's Unemurated Rights. Calvin R. Massey. 280p. (Orig.). (C). 1995. 54.95 (*1-56639-311-6*); pap. text ed. 22.95 (*1-56639-312-4*) Temple U Pr.

Silent River: A Pastoral Elegy in the Form of a Recollection of Arctic Adventure. Charles R. Metzger. (Illus.). xi, 161p. (Orig.). 1984. pap. 7.95 (*0-9613094-0-7*) Omega LA.

Silent Road. Pole. 157p. 1960. pap. 11.95 (*0-85435-443-3*, Pub. by C W Daniel UK) Natl Bk Netwk.

Silent Road. Wellesley T. Pole. 240p. (Orig.). 17.95 (*0-8464-4290-6*) Beekman Pubs.

Silent Rose. Kasey Mars. 512p. 1994. mass mkt. 4.99 (*0-7860-0081-3*, Pinncle Kensgtn) Kensgtn Pub Corp.

Silent Running: My Years on a World War II Attack Submarine. James F. Calvert. LC 95-15447. 320p. 1995. text ed. 27.95 (*0-471-12778-7*) Wiley.

Silent Sabotage: Rescuing Our Careers, Our Companies & Our Lives from the Creeping Paralysis of Anger & Bitterness. William J. Morin. 192p. 1995. 19.95 (*0-8144-0300-X*) AMACOM.

Silent Sam, & Other Stories of Our Day. Harvey J. O'Higgins. 1977. 23.95 (*0-8369-4251-5*, 6061) Ayer.

Silent Sam's Salvation. Myrna Temte. (Special Edition Ser.: No. 745). 1992. mass mkt. 3.39 (*0-373-09745-X*, 5-09745-6) Harlequin Bks.

Silent Scream. Diane Hoh. (Nightmare Hall Ser.: No. 1). 176p. (YA). (gr. 7-9). 1993. pap. 3.50 (*0-590-46014-5*) Scholastic Inc.

Silent Scream: Alfred Hitchcock's Sound Track. Elisabeth Weis. LC 80-71093. (Illus.). 192p. 1982. 29.50 (*0-8386-3079-0*) Fairleigh Dickinson.

Silent Screams. Peter A. Wysocki. LC 93-93894. (Illus.). 66p. 1993. pap. 16.95 (*1-883565-00-6*) Photo Concepts.

***Silent Screams from the Russian Underground.** Gail Gelburd & Alexander Borovsky. (Illus.). 1980p. (Orig.). Date not set. pap. write for info. (*1-890789-04-6*) Coun for Creat Proj.

Silent Screen & My Talking Heart: The Autobiography of Nell Shipman. 2nd rev. ed. Nell Shipman. Ed. by Tom Trusky. LC 86-71541. (Hemingway Western Studies). (Illus.). 300p. (Orig.). 1988. pap. 15.95 (*0-932129-04-8*) Heming W Studies.

Silent Sea. Catherine Martin. Ed. by Rosemary Foxton. 569p. 1996. pap. 34.95 (*0-86840-373-3*, Pub. by New South Wales Univ Pr AT) Intl Spec Bk.

Silent Sea. Tom McCaughren. (Illus.). 111p. (Orig.). (YA). 1988. reprint ed. pap. 7.95 (*0-947962-20-4*, Pub. by Childrens Pr IE) Irish Bks Media.

***Silent Seasons.** 4th ed. Russell Chatham et al. LC 88-72163. (Illus.). 240p. 1996. reprint ed. 24.95 (*0-944439-76-4*) Clark City Pr.

Silent Seasons: Fishing Adventures by Seven American Experts. Russell Chatham et al. LC 88-72163. (Illus.). 240p. (Orig.). 1988. pap. 14.95 (*0-944439-05-5*) Clark City Pr.

***Silent Seduction.** Tanya Bishop. (Orig.). 1997. mass mkt. 5.95 (*0-352-33193-3*, Pub. by Black Lace UK) London Brdge.

***Silent Seeds.** Nicholas Rogowsky. LC 96-90987. (Orig.). 1997. pap. 8.95 (*0-533-12243-0*) Vantage.

Silent Self: A Journal of Spiritual Discovery. George Benson. 86p. (Orig.). 1992. pap. 3.95 (*0-88028-133-2*, 1175) Forward Movement.

Silent Sellout. Arthur Fletcher. LC 73-83161. 121p. 1973. 29.95 (*0-89388-100-7*) Okpaku Communications.

Silent Sentinel on the Potomac, Fort McNair 1791-1991. Phyllis I. McClellan. (Illus.). 280p. (Orig.). 1993. pap. text ed. 24.00 (*1-55613-848-2*) Heritage Bk.

Silent September. rev. ed. Joyce L. Heatherley. 64p. 1988. reprint ed. pap. 5.95 (*0-929488-01-6*) Balcony Pub Inc.

Silent Service: U. S. Submarines in World War II. Hughston E. Lowder. LC 87-90657. 504p. (C). 1987. 24.95 (*0-9619189-0-X*) Silent Serv Bks.

Silent Shepherd. John MacArthur. LC 96-18173. 168p. 1996. 9.99 (*1-56476-579-2*, 6-3579) SP Pubns.

Silent Shofar. Carol K. Hubner. (Judaica Youth Ser. Devorah Doresh Mysteries Ser.). (Illus.). (J). (gr. 3 up). 1983. pap. 6.95 (*0-910818-54-1*) Judaica Pr.

Silent Siege Three; Japanese Attacks on North America in World War Two - Ships Sunk, Air Raids, Bombs Dropped, Civilians Killed: Documentary. Bert Webber. LC 92-38606. (Illus.). 304p. (Orig.). 1992. 48.95 (*0-936738-74-X*); pap. 28.95 (*0-936738-73-1*) Webb Research.

Silent Silos: A Counterbomb Haiku Sequence. Johnny Baranski. (Sunburst Matchbooks Ser.: No. 1). (Illus.). 16p. (Orig.). 1985. pap. 3.00 (*0-934648-10-7*) Sunburst Pr.

Silent Sisters: An Ethnography of Homeless Women. Betty G. Russell. (Health Care for Women International Publication). 160p. 1991. 33.95 (*1-56032-098-2*) Hemisp Pub.

Silent Sky: Aviation's War on the American Public. Dick Amann. 200p. 1991. 99.95 (*0-917194-19-5*) Prog Studies.

***Silent Soldier: Fox Conner - Eisenhower's Mentor.** unabridged ed. Hal Willard. (Illus.). 1998. write for info. (*0-614-28419-8*) Avondale Press.

Silent Son. Gallatin Warfield. 416p. 1995. mass mkt. 5.99 (*0-446-60199-3*) Warner Bks.

Silent Songs. A. C. Crispin & Kathleen O'Malley. (Starbridge Ser.: No. 05). 304p. (Orig.). 1994. mass mkt. 4.99 (*0-441-00061-4*) Ace Bks.

Silent Sons: A Book for and About Men. Robert Ackerman. 240p. 1994. pap. 11.00 (*0-671-89286-X*, Fireside) S&S Trade.

Silent Sorrow: Pregnancy Loss: Guidance & Support for You & Your Family. Ingrid Kohn & Moffitt. 464p. 1993. pap. 12.95 (*0-440-50713-8*) Dell.

Silent South. George W. Cable. (Works of George Cable). 1988. reprint ed. 59.00 (*0-685-48940-X*) Rprt Serv.

Silent South: Including the Freedman's Case in Equity, the Convict Lease System & to Which Has Been Added Eight Hitherto Uncollected Essays by Cable on Prison & Asylum Reform & an Essay on Cable by Arlin Turner. George W. Cable. LC 69-14915. (Criminology, Law Enforcement, & Social Problems Ser.: No. 57). 1969. 22.00 (*0-87585-057-X*) Patterson Smith.

Silent South see Collected Works of George W. Cable

Silent Spaces: The Last of the Great Aisled Barns. Malcolm Kirk. LC 94-3863. (Illus.). 176p. 1994. 50.00 (*0-8212-2093-4*) Bulfinch Pr.

Silent Speaker. Rex Stout. (Crime Line Ser.). 288p. 1994. mass mkt. 4.99 (*0-553-23497-8*) Bantam.

Silent Speech of Politicians: Body Language in Government. Miriam D. Blum. Ed. by Lee Rathbone. (Illus.). 128p. (Orig.). 1988. pap. 7.95 (*0-929535-00-6*) Brenner Info Group.

Silent Spokesman: Bishop Robert Clarence Lawson. Alexander C. Stewart & Sherry S. DuPree. (Illus.). 80p. 1995. pap. 9.95 (*0-614-07533-5*) Displays Sch.

Silent Spring. Rachel L. Carson. 1994. pap. 13.00 (*0-395-68329-7*) HM.

***Silent Spring.** large type ed. Rachel Carson. LC 96-49681. 398p. 1997. 23.95 (*0-7838-8053-7*, GK Hall) Thorndike Pr.

Silent Spring. Rachel Carson. 1994. reprint ed. lib. bdg. 27.95 (*1-56849-552-8*) Buccaneer Bks.

Silent Spring Revisited. Ed. by Gino J. Marco et al. 1987. 44.95 (*0-8412-0980-4*); pap. 34.95 (*0-8412-0981-2*) Am Chemical.

Silent Stalker. Richie T. Cusick. Ed. by Patricia MacDonald. 224p. (Orig.). (YA). (gr. 7 up). 1993. pap. 3.99 (*0-671-79402-7*, Archway) PB.

Silent Stones, Empty Passageways: Poetry & Photography from the Anasazi Homeland. Jean Dubois & Lee Dubois. (Illus.). 59p. (Orig.). 1992. pap. 7.95 (*0-9622932-8-8*) San Miguel Pr.

Silent Stones Sacred Light: Sacred Light. Kathleen L. Mendel. LC 94-60584. (Illus.). 40p. (Orig.). (C). 1994. pap. 6.10 (*1-878142-37-2*) Telstar FL.

Silent Storm. Sherry Garland. LC 92-33690. 288p. (J). (gr. 3-7). 1993. 15.00 (*0-15-274170-4*) HarBrace.

Silent Storm. Sherry Garland. 288p. (J). (gr. 3-7). 1995. pap. 5.00 (*0-15-200016-X*) HarBrace.

***Silent Stranger.** Amy Midgley. LC 97-439. (J). 1997. write for info. (*0-380-97486-X*) Avon.

***Silent Stream.** large type ed. Rowan Edwards. (Ulverscroft Large Print Ser.). 320p. 1997. 27.50 (*0-7089-3790-X*) Ulverscroft.

Silent Strength. Linda J. Montgomery. Ed. by Nick Alicino & Jane Zopf. LC 89-81213. (Illus.). 48p. (Orig.). 1989. pap. 16.95 (*0-9624768-0-3*) Divine Designs.

Silent Strength: God's Wisdom for Daily Living. Lloyd J. Ogilvie. LC 90-3582. Orig. Title: Silent Strength for My Life. 400p. (Orig.). 1995. reprint ed. pap. 11.99 (*1-56507-398-3*) Harvest Hse.

Silent Strength for My Life see Silent Strength: God's Wisdom for Daily Living

Silent Strength of Stones. Nina K. Hoffman. 256p. (Orig.). 1995. mass mkt. 4.99 (*0-380-77760-6*, AvoNova) Avon.

Silent Striders: Tribebook. Teeuwynn & Ethan Skemp. (Werewolf Ser.). (Illus.). 72p. (Orig.). 1996. pap. 10.00 (*1-56504-330-8*, 3059) White Wolf.

Silent Subject: Reflections on the Unborn in American Culture. Brad Stetson. LC 95-31397. 288p. 1996. text ed. 59.95 (*0-275-95032-8*, Praeger Pubs); pap. text ed. 22.95 (*0-275-95392-0*, Praeger Pubs) Greenwood.

Silent Success: Master's Education in the United States. Clifton F. Conrad et al. LC 92-1612. 384p. 1993. text ed. 35.95 (*0-8018-4508-4*) Johns Hopkins.

Silent Sufferers. Phyllis Carter. 154p. (Orig.). 1996. pap. 7.99 (*1-56043-581-X*) Destiny Image.

Silent Suitor. Elisabeth Fairchild. (Signet Regency Romance Ser.). 224p. (Orig.). 1994. pap. 3.99 (*0-451-18070-4*, Sig) NAL-Dutton.

Silent Summer. Sukey S. Gross. (Girls of Riukah Gross Academy Ser.). (Illus.). 139p. (J). (gr. 7-9). 1989. 10.95 (*1-56062-004-8*); pap. 7.95 (*1-56062-005-6*) CIS Comm.

Silent Sun. Solomon Gross. LC 91-58258. (Illus.). 120p. 1992. 19.95 (*0-8453-4840-X*, Cornwall Bks) Assoc Univ Prs.

Silent Superstitions. Catherine Marshall. LC 95-13126. (Christy Ser.: Vol. 2). 128p. (J). (gr. 5-9). 1995. pap. 4.99 (*0-8499-3687-X*) Word Pub.

***Silent Syndicate.** Hank Messick. Date not set. lib. bdg. 24.95 (*0-8488-1809-1*) Amereon Ltd.

Silent Tears. Sima Fei. 1995. pap. 15.95 (*0-533-11388-1*) Vantage.

Silent Tears, Joyous Joys. Jane Blair & Ruth J. Oleksowicz. 18p. (Orig.). 1986. 15.00 (*0-910147-29-9*); pap. 12.00 (*0-317-60033-8*) World Poetry Pr.

Silent Tears No More. Judy Baer. LC 89-82689. (Cedar River Daydreams Ser.: Bk. 7). 144p. (Orig.). (J). (gr. 7-10). 1990. mass mkt. 4.99 (*1-55661-119-6*) Bethany Hse.

Silent Temples, Songful Hearts: Traditional Music of Cambodia. Sam-Ang Sam & Patricia S. Campbell. Ed. by Judith C. Tucker. (Illus.). 144p. (Orig.). 1991. pap. 24.95 incl. audio (*0-937203-36-X*) World Music Pr.

Silent Temples, Songful Hearts: Traditional Music of Cambodia. Sam-Ang Sam & Patricia S. Campbell. Ed. by Judith C. Tucker. (Illus.). 144p. (Orig.). 1996. pap. 24.95 incl. audio compact disk (*0-937203-74-2*) World Music Pr.

Silent Testimony: A True Story. Roger W. Walker. LC 88-91220. 297p. 1989. 19.95 (*0-939713-05-5*) Carriage House.

Silent Testimony: A True Story. Roger W. Walker. 1990. mass mkt. 4.95 (*0-312-92141-1*) St Martin.

Silent Thief. Judy Baer. (Cedar River Daydreams Ser.: Bk. 23). 160p. (YA). (gr. 7-10). 1995. pap. 4.99 (*1-55661-588-4*) Bethany Hse.

Silent Thunder. Eduardo Lopez. 1995. pap. 5.95 (*0-88145-116-9*) Broadway Play.

Silent Thunder: A Novel. Peter Tasker. Ed. by Pockell. LC 92-9997. 288p. 1992. 20.00 (*4-7700-1685-9*) Kodansha.

Silent Times, No. 17. pap. 0.15 (*0-87377-144-3*) GAM Pubns.

Silent Tower. Barbara Hambly. 384p. 1986. mass mkt. 5.99 (*0-345-33764-6*, Del Rey) Ballantine.

Silent Travelers: Germs, Genes, & the "Immigrant Menace" Alan M. Kraut. (Illus.). 382p. 1995. pap. text ed. 15.95 (*0-8018-5096-7*) Johns Hopkins.

Silent Traveller in San Francisco. Chiang Yee. (Illus.). 1964. 12.50 (*0-393-08422-1*) Norton.

Silent Treatment. large type ed. Michael Palmer. LC 95-19989. 632p. 1995. 26.95 (*0-7838-1406-2*, GK Hall) Thorndike Pr.

Silent Treatment. large type ed. Michael Palmer. LC 95-19989. (Core Collection). 632p. 1996. 23.95 (*0-7838-1405-4*, GK Hall) Thorndike Pr.

Silent Treatment. Michael Palmer. 480p. 1996. reprint ed. mass mkt. 6.50 (*0-553-57221-0*) Bantam.

Silent Trumpets of Justice: Integration's Failure in Prince Edward County. Vonita White & Gerald A. Foster. (Illus.). 107p. (Orig.). 1993. 14.95 (*1-56411-062-1*) Untd Bros & Sis.

Silent Twins. Marjorie Wallace. 320p. 1987. mass mkt. 5.99 (*0-345-34802-8*) Ballantine.

Silent Twins. Marjorie Wallace. (Illus.). 230p. 1991. 3.99 (*0-517-69503-0*) Random Hse Value.

***Silent Valley.** Carey Cleaver. 576p. 31.50 (*0-7089-3699-7*) Ulverscroft.

Silent Veterans: The Rage, Despair & Healing of a Vietnam Veteran. Thomas J. Evansew. LC 93-61128. 63p. (Orig.). 1993. pap. 12.95 (*0-9638359-0-4*) Zena Bk PA.

Silent Voice. Trevor Romain. 32p. (J). (gr. k-5). 1994. 13.95 (*1-880092-23-9*) Bright Bks TX.

Silent Voices. Ms. Celia. (Orig.). 1996. pap. 7.95 (*0-533-11726-7*) Vantage.

Silent Voices. Ed. by Doug A. Newsom & Bob J. Carrell. (Illus.). 256p. (Orig.). (C). 1995. lib. bdg. 52.00 (*0-8191-9854-4*) U Pr of Amer.

Silent Voices. Ed. by Doug A. Newsom & Bob J. Carrell. 256p. (Orig.). (C). 1995. pap. text ed. 29.50 (*0-8191-9855-2*) U Pr of Amer.

Silent Voices: An Anthology of Contemporary Romanian Women Poets. Tr. by A. Deletant & B. Walker. LC 85-80386. 161p. 8900. reprint ed. pap. 21.00 (*0-948259-03-5*, Pub. by Forest Bks UK) Dufour.

Silent Voices: Recent American Poems on Nature. Ed. by Paul Feroe. LC 78-54317. 1978. pap. 6.95 (*0-915408-17-1*) Ally Pr.

Silent Voices, Sacred Lives: Women's Readings for the Liturgical Year. Ed. by Carolyn A. Osiek et al. LC 92-26234. 448p. 1992. pap. 17.95 (*0-8091-3336-9*) Paulist Pr.

Silent Voices Speak: Women & Prohibition in Truk. Mac Marshall & Leslie B. Marshall. 190p. (C). 1990. pap. 22.95 (*0-534-12384-8*) Wadsworth Pub.

Silent Voyage. James Pattinson. 1959. 10.95 (*0-8392-1105-8*) Astor-Honor.

Silent War. Mark Patinkin & Ira C. Magaziner. LC 89-40489. 1990. pap. 15.00 (*0-679-72827-9*, Vin) Random.

Silent War. John A. Mitchell. LC 68-57541. (Muckrakers Ser.). 222p. 1979. reprint ed. lib. bdg. 24.00 (*0-8398-1263-9*) Irvington.

Silent War. John A. Mitchell. (Muckrakers Ser.). (Illus.). 222p. (C). 1986. reprint ed. pap. text ed. 6.95 (*0-8290-2004-7*) Irvington.

Silent War: Infection Control for Emergency Responders. OnGuard Inc. Staff. 410p. 1992. teacher ed., ring bd. 34.95 (*1-56916-402-9*) OnGuard.

Silent War: Infection Control for Emergency Responders. OnGuard Inc. Staff. (Student Textbook Ser.). 232p. 1992. student ed., pap. text ed. 12.95 (*1-56916-403-7*) OnGuard.

Silent War: Infection Control for Law Enforcement. OnGuard Inc. Staff. Ed. by Susan Peterson. (Illus.). 144p. 1996. pap. text ed. 9.95 (*1-56916-710-9*, 40SWP) OnGuard.

Silent War: Infection Control for Law Enforcement: Post-Incident Procedures. OnGuard Inc. Staff. (Illus.). 116p. (Orig.). 1993. teacher ed., ring bd. 19.95 (*1-56916-709-5*) OnGuard.

Silent War: Infection Control for Law Enforcement: Reducing Your Risk. OnGuard Inc. Staff. (Illus.). 59p. (Orig.). 1993. teacher ed., ring bd. 19.95 (*1-56916-706-0*) OnGuard.

Silent War: Infection Control for Law Enforcement: Understanding Contagious Diseases. OnGuard Inc. Staff. (Illus.). 53p. (Orig.). 1993. teacher ed., ring bd. 19.95 (*1-56916-703-6*) OnGuard.

Silent Warfare: Understanding the World of Intelligence. 2nd rev. ed. Abram N. Shulsky. (Intelligence & National Security Library). 304p. 1993. 22.95 (*0-02-881025-2*) Brasseys Inc.

***Silent Warrior.** Donna Kauffman. 240p. 1997. mass mkt. 3.50 (*0-553-44539-1*, Loveswept) Bantam.

Silent Warriors. Richard P. Henrick. 1989. mass mkt. 4.50 (*0-8217-3026-6*, Zebra Kensgtn) Kensgtn Pub Corp.

Silent Warriors: A Memoir of America's 442nd Regimental Combat Team. Jack K. Wakamatsu. 1995. 17.95 (*0-533-11430-6*) Vantage.

Silent Warriors of World War II: The Alamo Scouts Behind the Japanese Lines. Lance Q. Zedric. LC 94-46996. 288p. 1995. 22.95 (*0-934793-56-5*) Pathfinder CA.

Silent Way, English - A Thousand Sentences. rev. ed. Caleb Gattegno. 1995. reprint ed. pap. 4.50 (*0-87825-007-7*) Ed Solutions.

Silent Way, English - Eight Tales. Caleb Gattegno. (Illus.). 109p. 1968. pap. 4.00 (*0-87825-026-3*) Ed Solutions.

Silent Way, English - Short Passages. Caleb Gattegno. 1968. pap. 4.00 (*0-87825-027-1*) Ed Solutions.

Silent Way, French - Huit Contes. Caleb Gattegno. (FRE.). 1967. pap. 4.00 (*0-87825-199-5*) Ed Solutions.

Silent Winds: Poetry of One Hopi. 3rd ed. Ramson Lomatewama. LC 83-61654. 64p. 1983. reprint ed. pap. 5.00 (*0-935825-00-2*) Badger Claw Pr.

Silent Winds: Poetry of One Hopi. 4th ed. Ramson Lomatewama. 1987. pap. 5.00 (*0-934351-32-5*) Heard Mus.

Silent Wings. Gordon A. Alcorn. (Illus.). 83p. 1982. pap. 5.95 (*0-87770-277-2*) Ye Galleon.

Silent Witness. Mary Germano. 320p. 1993. mass mkt. 4.50 (*1-55817-677-2*, Pinncle Kensgtn) Kensgtn Pub Corp.

Silent Witness. Gorman. 1997. 17.95 (*0-7862-0749-3*) Thorndike Pr.

***Silent Witness.** David Kaufmann. LC 97-65401. (C). 1997. 24.95 (*1-56062-316-0*) CIS Comm.

Silent Witness. Lionel A. Luckloo & John R. Thompson. LC 94-24278. 1995. pap. text ed. 12.99 (*0-7852-8007-3*) Nelson.

Silent Witness. Nancy Myer. 1995. mass mkt. 4.99 (*0-312-95481-6*) St Martin.

***Silent Witness.** Richard N. Patterson. 1997. mass mkt. 7.99 (*0-345-40476-9*) Ballantine.

Silent Witness. Patricia H. Rushford. (Jennie McGrady Mystery Ser.: No. 2). 176p. (YA). (gr. 7 up). 1993. pap. 4.99 (*1-55661-332-6*) Bethany Hse.

Silent Witness. Collin Wilcox. 1992. mass mkt. 3.99 (*0-8125-1149-2*) Tor Bks.

***Silent Witness.** Margaret Yorke. 1975. 5.95 (*0-8027-5318-3*) Walker & Co.

Silent Witness. Edward Yourdon. LC 82-90213. 184p. 1982. 7.95 (*0-917072-28-6*, Yourdon) P-H.

Silent Witness. large type ed. Gorman. Date not set. 20.00 (*0-7862-0772-8*, Thorndike Lrg Prnt) Thorndike Pr.

***Silent Witness.** large type ed. Richard N. Patterson. 494p. 1997. pap. 25.95 (*0-679-77416-5*) Random.

***Silent Witness.** large type ed. Richard N. Patterson. 1997. pap. 25.95 (*0-7838-8059-6*) Thorndike Pr.

***Silent Witness: A Novel.** Richard N. Patterson. 512p. 1997. 25.95 (*0-679-45040-8*) Knopf.

Silent Witness: The Karla Brown Murder Case. Don W. Weber & Charles Bosworth, Jr. (Illus.). 448p. (Orig.). 1993. pap. 6.99 (*0-451-40423-8*, Sig) NAL-Dutton.

Silent Witness: The True Story of a Psychic Detective. Nancy Czetli & Steve N. Czetli. 224p. 1993. 17.95 (*1-55972-200-2*, Birch Ln Pr) Carol Pub Group.

***Silent Witnesses: Representations of Working-Class Women in America, 1933-1945.** Jacqueline Ellis. LC 97-3115. (Illus.). 200p. 1997. write for info. (*0-87972-743-8*); pap. write for info. (*0-87972-744-6*) Bowling Green Univ Popular Press.

Silent Witnesses: Russian Films 1908-1919. Ed. by Paolo C. Usai et al. (Illus.). 622p. 1990. 75.00 (*0-85170-265-1*, Pub. by British Film Inst UK) Ind U Pr.

Silent Woman. Edmund Marston. 1995. mass mkt. 5.99 (*0-449-22375-2*) Fawcett.

Silent Woman: Sylvia Plath & Ted Hughes. Janet Malcolm. LC 93-33848. 1994. 23.00 (*0-685-70236-7*) Knopf.

Silent Woman: Sylvia Plath & Ted Hughes. Janet Malcolm. 1994. 23.00 (*0-679-43158-6*) Knopf.

Silent Woman: Sylvia Plath & Ted Hughes. Janet Malcolm. 1995. pap. 12.00 (*0-679-75140-8*, Vin) Random.

Silent Woman (or Epicoene) Ben Jonson. (Swan Theatre Plays Ser.). (Illus.). 62p. (Orig.). (C). 1989. pap. 9.95 (*0-413-62060-3*, A0397, Pub. by Methuen UK) Heinemann.

Silent Woods. Bob. 1992. pap. 3.95 (*1-55850-202-5*) Adams Media.

Silent Words. Joan M. Drury. 224p. 1996. pap. 10.95 (*1-883523-13-3*) Spinsters Ink.

***Silent World of Doctor & Patient.** Jay Katz. 1997. pap. text ed. 15.95 (*0-8018-5780-5*) Johns Hopkins.

***Silent World of Nicholas Q.** Colin Dexter. 1997. mass mkt. 5.99 (*0-8041-1487-0*) Ivy Books.

Silent World of Nicholas Quinn. Colin Dexter. 224p. 1988. mass mkt. 5.99 (*0-553-27238-1*) Bantam.

Silently Seduced: When Parents Make Their Children Partners. Kenneth M. Adams. 1991. pap. 7.95 (*1-55874-131-3*) Health Comm.

Silents. Charlotte Abrams. LC 96-19638. (Illus.). 272p. 1996. 24.95 (*1-56368-055-6*, 2899) Gallaudet Univ Pr.

Silenus. Thomas Woolner. LC 76-148336. reprint ed. 32.50 (*0-404-07033-7*) AMS Pr.

Siletz: Survival for an Artifact. 2nd ed. Leone L. Kasner. (Illus.). 82p. 1980. reprint ed. pap. text ed. 9.95 (*0-911443-04-5*) Lincoln Coun Hist.

***Silhouette Alex & the Angel.** Dixie Browning. (Silhouette Ser.). 1997. 20.95 (*0-373-59818-1*) Harlequin Bks.

Silhouette Christmas Stories. 1987. mass mkt. 3.95 (*0-373-48212-4*) Harlequin Bks.

Silhouette Christmas Stories 1988. 1988. pap. 4.99 (*0-373-48253-1*) Silhouette.

Silhouette Christmas Stories, 1989. 1989. mass mkt. 4.25 (*0-373-48218-3*) Harlequin Bks.

Silhouette Christmas Stories, 1990. 1990. mass mkt. 4.50 (*0-373-48230-2*) Harlequin Bks.

Silhouette Christmas Stories, 1993, Set. Lisa Jackson et al. 1993. mass mkt. 4.99 (*0-373-48264-7*, 5-48264-1) Silhouette.

Silhouette Collectibles: On Glass. Shirley Mace. (Illus.). 160p. 1992. 24.95 (*0-9633674-5-5*) Shadow Enter.

Silhouette Cutting for Fun & Money. Ann Woodward & Deidre Woodward. LC 87-90602. (Illus.). 102p. (Orig.). 1987. pap. 12.50 (*0-944095-00-3*) Profile VA.

Silhouette Designs for Artists & Craftspeople. Rico Prosperoso. LC 94-37319. (Illus.). 1995. pap. write for info. (*0-486-28452-2*) Dover.

Silhouette in Diamonds: The Life of Mrs. Potter Palmer. Isabel Ross. LC 75-1868. (Leisure Class in America Ser.). (Illus.). 1975. reprint ed. 25.95 (*0-405-06934-0*) Ayer.

Silhouette in Scarlet. Elizabeth Peters. 224p. 1994. mass mkt. 5.50 (*0-446-36482-7*) Warner Bks.

Silhouette of a Saint: Albert Pepper. Danny R. Morrow. 1985. 5.95 (*0-86544-027-1*) Salv Army Suppl South.

***Silhouette of the Bridge.** Keith Waldrop. (Orig.). 1997. pap. 8.95 (*0-614-29377-4*) AVEC Bks.

***Silhouette of the Bridge: (Memory Stand-Ins)** Keith Waldrop. 80p. (Orig.). 1997. pap. 8.95 (*1-880713-08-X*) AVEC Bks.

Silhouette on a Wide Land. Alan S. Kesselheim. LC 92-53049. 240p. 1992. 8.99 (*1-55591-092-0*) Fulcrum Pub.

Silhouette Shadow. Anne Stuart. 1992. mass mkt. 4.99 (*0-373-48246-9*) Silhouette.

Silhouette Spring Fancy Collection, 1994. 1994. pap. 4.99 (*0-685-68119-X*, 5-48266-6) Silhouette.

Silhouette Summer Sizzlers, 1994. 1994. mass mkt. 4.99 (*0-373-48321-X*) Harlequin Bks.

Silhouette Summer Sizzlers-89. 1989. mass mkt. 3.95 (*0-373-48217-5*) Harlequin Bks.

Silhouettes. Paul Patti. 256p. 1991. mass mkt. 3.99 (*0-312-92672-3*) St Martin.

Silhouettes. Edmund W. Gosse. LC 78-156654. (Essay Index Reprint Ser.). 1977. reprint ed. 26.95 (*0-8369-2399-5*) Ayer.

Silhouettes: A Pictorial Archive of Varied Illustrations. Ed. by Carol B. Grafton. (Illus.). 1979. pap. 5.95 (*0-486-23781-8*) Dover.

Silhouettes: With London Nights. Arthur Symons. LC 93-31598. (Decadents, Symbolists, Anti-Decadents Ser.). 1994. 55.00 (*1-85477-155-8*, Pub. by Woodstock Bks UK) Cassell.

Silhouettes & Shadows: Poetry of Another Persuasion. Robert T. Kostello. LC 91-91332. 208p. 1992. 29.95 (*0-9631351-5-5*) Thundersong.

Silhouettes at Eventide. John C. Pine. 32p. (Orig.). 1989. pap. 4.50 (*0-943430-04-6*) Moveable Feast Pr.

Silhouettes in Cross Stitch. Julie Hasler. (Illus.). 76p. 1996. 18.95 (*1-870586-11-5*, D Porteous) Parkwest Pubns.

Silhouettes of American Life. Rebecca H. Davis. (C). 1972. reprint ed. lib. bdg. 26.50 (*0-8422-8033-2*) Irvington.

Silhouettes of American Life. Rebecca H. Davis. (C). 1986. reprint ed. pap. text ed. 6.95 (*0-8290-1965-0*) Irvington.

Silhouettes of American Lives. Rebecca H. Davis. Ed. by Jane Rose. (Masterworks of Literature Ser.). pap. 12.95 (*0-8084-0478-4*) NCUP.

S

An Asterisk (*) at the beginning of an entry indicates that the title is appearing in BIP for the first time.

Silhouettes of Woman. Phyliss Shanken. (Illus.). 1976. pap. 7.95 (*0-918836-01-8*) Philmer.

Silica: Physical Behavior, Geochemistry & Materials Applications. Ed. by P. J. Heaney et al. (Reviews in Mineralogy Ser.: Vol. 29). 606p. 1994. per. 28.00 (*0-939950-35-9*) Mineralogical Soc.

Silica & Me: The Career of an Industrial Chemist. Guy Alexander. LC 73-75723. (Chemistry in Action Ser.). 111p. 1973. pap. 8.95 (*0-8412-0162-5*) Am Chemical.

Silica & Silica-Induced Lung Diseases: Current Concepts. William E. Wallace. 432p. 1995. 199.95 (*0-8493-4709-2*, 4709) CRC Pr.

***Silica & Some Silicates: The Evaluation of Carcinogenic Risk of Chemicals to Humans.** (IARC Monographs). 289p. 1987. text ed. 72.00 (*92-832-1242-8*) World Health.

***Silica-Based Buried Channel Waveguides & Devices.** Ladouceur & Love. (Optical & Quantum Electronics Ser.). (Illus.). 216p. (Orig.). 1995. text ed. 84.00 (*0-412-57930-8*, Chap & Hall NY) Chapman & Hall.

Silica, Calcium, & Clay: Processes in Mineral, Plant, Animal, & Man. Friedrich Benesch & Klaus Wilde. Ed. by Charlene Breedlove. Tr. by Eva Lauterbach. LC 95-46337. (Illus.). 1995. pap. 14.95 (*0-935690-05-0*) Schaumburg Pubns.

Silica Gel & Bonded Phases: Their Production, Properties, & Use in LC. Raymond P. Scott. (Separation Science Ser.). 261p. 1993. text ed. 79.95 (*0-471-93985-4*) Wiley.

Silica Glass & Its Application: Glass Science & Technology, No. 11. Ed. by I. Fanderlik. 304p. 1991. 158.25 (*0-444-98755-X*) Elsevier.

Silica in Sediments: Nodular & Bedded Chert. Ed. by Earle F. McBride. (Reprint Ser.: No. 8). 184p. 1979. pap. 14.00 (*0-918985-34-X*) SEPM.

Silica in Sediments: Proceedings of the Symposium, Los Angeles, 1958. Silica in Sediments Symposium Staff. Ed. by H. Andrew Ireland. LC 60-50. (Society of Economic Paleontologists & Mineralogists, Special Publication Ser.: No. 7). 197p. reprint ed. pap. 56.20 (*0-317-27166-0*, 2024734) Bks Demand.

Silica, Silicosis & Cancer: Controversy in Occupational Medicine. Ed. by David F. Goldsmith et al. LC 85-640225. (Cancer Research Monographs: Vol. 2). 592p. 1985. text ed. 65.00 (*0-275-91305-8*, C1305, Praeger Pubs) Greenwood.

***Silica, Some Silicates, Coal Dust & Para-Aramid Fibrils: The Evaluation of Carcinogenic Risks to Humans.** (IARC Monographs: No. 68). 506p. 1997. text ed. 80.00 (*92-832-1268-1*) World Health.

Silica, the Amazing Gel: An Essential Mineral for Radiant Health, Recovery & Rejuvenation. Klaus Kaufmann. LC 93-910249. (Illus.). 159p. (Orig.). 1993. pap. 9.95 (*0-920470-30-0*) Alive Bks.

Silica The Forgotten Nutrient: Healthy Skin, Shiny Hair, Strong Bones, Beautiful Nails. Klaus Kaufmann. LC 89-903875. (Illus.). 106p. 1993. pap. 9.95 (*0-920470-25-4*) Alive Bks.

Silica the Forgotten Nutrient: Healthy Skin, Shiny Hair, Strong Bones, Beautiful Nails. Klaus Kaufmann. LC 89-903875. (Illus.). 128p. 1993. pap. 9.95 (*0-920470-24-6*) Alive Bks.

Silica The Forgotten Nutrient: Healthy Skin, Shiny Hair, Strong Bones, Beautiful Nails. 2nd ed. Klaus Kaufmann. LC 89-903875. (Illus.). 128p. 1993. 19.95 (*0-920470-26-2*) Alive Bks.

Silicate Glass Technology Methods. Clarence L. Babcock. LC 76-30716. (Wiley Series in Pure & Applied Optics). 336p. reprint ed. pap. 95.80 (*0-317-28068-6*, 2055768) Bks Demand.

Silicate Melt Equilibria. Wilhelm Eitel. Tr. by J. G. Philips et al. from GER. LC 51-62230. 169p. reprint ed. pap. 48.20 (*0-317-11176-0*, 2050514) Bks Demand.

***Silicate Melts.** Sharon L. Webb. LC 97-23668. (Lecture Notes in Earth Sciences). 1997. lib. bdg. write for info. (*3-540-63129-1*) Spr-Verlag.

Silicate Melts & Mantle Petrogenesis: Collection of Papers in Memory of Christopher M. Scarfe. 296p. 1990. reprint ed. 25.00 (*0-87590-766-0*, CR0317660) Am Geophysical.

Siliceous Deposits of the Tethys & Pacific Regions. Ed. by James R. Hein & J. Obradovic. (Illus.). 350p. 1988. 137.95 (*0-387-96704-4*) Spr-Verlag.

Siliceous Microfossil & Microplankton Studies of the Monterey Formation & Modern Analogs. Ed. by Richard E. Casey. (Illus.). 154p. (Orig.). 1986. pap. 8.00 (*1-878861-27-1*) Pac Section SEPM.

Siliciclastic Sequence Stratigraphy: Recent Developments & Applications. Ed. by Paul Weimer & Henry W. Posamentier. (AAPG Memoir Ser.: No. 58). (Illus.). vii, 492p. 1994. 59.00 (*0-89181-337-3*, 586) AAPG.

Siliciclastic Sequence Stratigraphy in Well Logs, Cores, & Outcrops: Concepts for High-Resolution Correlation of Time & Facies. J. C. Van Wagoner et al. (Methods in Exploration Ser.: No. 7). (Illus.). 55p. 1996. 53.00 (*0-89181-657-7*, 549) AAPG.

Siliciclastic Shelf Sediments. Ed. by Roderick W. Tillman & Charles T. Siemers. (Special Publications: No. 34). 268p. 1984. 36.50 (*0-918985-14-5*) SEPM.

Silicide Thin Films - Fabrication, Properties & Applications: Materials Research Society Symposium Proceedings, Vol. 402. Ed. by Ray Tung et al. (MRS Symposium Proceedings Ser.: Vol. 402). 648p. 1996. 73.00 (*1-55899-305-3*) Materials Res.

Silicides for VLSI Applications. Ed. by Shyam P. Murarka. 1983. text ed. 61.00 (*0-12-511220-3*) Acad Pr.

Silicides, Germanides, & Their Interfaces Vol. 320: Materials Research Society Symposium Proceedings. L. J. Schowalter & King N. Tu. 495p. 1994. text ed. 71.00 (*1-55899-219-7*) Materials Res.

Silicoflagellates & Actiniscus: Vertical Fluxes at Pacific & Atlantic Sediment Trap Stations. Kozo Takahashi. Ed. by Susumu Honjo. (Ocean Biocoenosis Ser.: No. 2). (Illus.). 35p. 1991. pap. 10.00 (*1-880224-01-1*) Woods Hole Ocean.

Silicoflagellates from Central North Pacific Core Sediments. H.-Yi Ling. 48p. 1970. write for info. (*0-614-17836-3*) Paleo Res.

Silicon. (Metals & Minerals Ser.). 1993. lib. bdg. 250.95 (*0-8490-8938-7*) Gordon Pr.

Silicon. Ed. by J. Grabmaier. (Crystals - Growth, Properties & Applications Ser.: Vol. 5). (Illus.). 215p. 1981. 118.95 (*0-387-10932-3*) Spr-Verlag.

Silicon & Siliceous Structures in Biological Systems. Ed. by T. L. Simpson & B. E. Yolcani. (Illus.). 587p. 1981. 267.00 (*0-387-90592-8*) Spr-Verlag.

Silicon & Silicones. Eugene G. Rochow. (Illus.). 190p. 1987. 20.95 (*0-387-17565-2*) Spr-Verlag.

Silicon-Based Millimeter-Wave Devices: Series in Electronics & Photonics. J. F. Luy & P. Russer. LC 94-12946. 1994. 75.95 (*0-387-58047-6*) Spr-Verlag.

Silicon-Based Optoelectronic Materials. Ed. by R. T. Collins et al. (Symposium Proceedings Ser.: Vol. 298). 461p. 1993. text ed. 65.00 (*1-55899-194-8*) Materials Res.

Silicon-Based Polymer Science: A Comprehensive Resource. Ed. by John M. Zeigler & F. W. Fearon. LC 89-17843. (Advances in Chemistry Ser.: No. 224). (Illus.). 828p. 1989. 129.95 (*0-8412-1546-4*) Am Chemical.

Silicon-Based Structural Ceramics. Ed. by Brian W. Sheldon & Stephen C. Danforth. LC 94-26453. (Ceramic Transactions Ser.: Vol. 42). 345p. 1994. 83.00 (*0-944904-76-9*, 1CBI00D) Am Ceramic.

Silicon Carbide & Related Materials 1995: Proceedings of the Sixth International Conference, Kyoto, Japan, 18-21 September 1995. H. Matsunami. Ed. by S. Nakashima et al. LC 96-11373. (Institute of Physics Conference Ser.: Vol. 142). (Illus.). 1200p. 1996. 450.00 (*0-7503-0335-2*) IOP Pub.

Silicon-Chemical Etching. Ed. by H. C. Freyhardt. (Crystals - Growth, Properties & Applications Ser.: Vol. 8). (Illus.). 255p. 1982. 150.95 (*0-387-11862-4*) Spr-Verlag.

Silicon Chips: The Magical Mineral in Your Telephone, Calculator, Toys, Automobile, Hospital, Air Conditioning, Factory, Furnace, Sewing Machine, & Countless Other Future Inventions. C. D. Renmore. LC 80-24153. (Illus.). 160p. 1980. 8.95 (*0-8253-0022-3*) Beaufort Bks NY.

Silicon Compilation. Daniel D. Gajski. LC 87-1365. (Illus.). 608p. (C). 1988. text ed. 36.76 (*0-201-09915-2*) Addison-Wesley.

Silicon-Containing Polymers. Ed. by Richard G. Jones. 197p. 1995. 88.00 (*0-85404-745-X*) CRC Pr.

***Silicon-Crystal Growth & Wafer Manufacturing.** Abe. (Illus.). 352p. 1997. text ed. write for info. (*0-412-71820-0*, Chap & Hall NY) Chapman & Hall.

Silicon Destiny: The History of Application Specific Integrated Circuits & LSI Logic Corporation. Rob Walker. 256p. 1992. 24.95 (*0-9632654-0-7*) CMC.

SiO2 & Its Interfaces. Ed. by G. Lucovsky & Sokrates T. Pantelides. (Symposium Proceedings Ser.: Vol. 105). 1988. text ed. 30.00 (*0-931837-73-1*) Materials Res.

Silicon Dioxide in Solid State Electronics. O. Engstrom. 300p. 1997. text ed. 86.00 (*981-02-2017-0*) World Scientific Pub.

Silicon Dreams: Information, Man, & Machine. Robert Lucky. LC 90-19224. 1991. pap. 13.95 (*0-312-05517-X*) St Martin.

***Silicon Embrace.** John Shirley. 1996. 29.95 (*0-929480-44-9*) Mark Ziesing.

Silicon Forest: High Tech in the Portland Area, 1945-1986. Gordon Dodds & Craig Wollner. LC 90-41708. 210p. 1990. 19.95 (*0-87595-230-5*) Oregon Hist.

Silicon Geochemistry & Biogeochemistry. S. R. Aston. 1983. text ed. 115.00 (*0-12-065620-5*) Acad Pr.

Silicon-Heteroatom Bond: Updates from the Chemistry of Functional Groups. Robert J. P. Corriu et al. LC 90-43887. (Chemistry of Functional Groups Ser.: No. 1078). 529p. 1991. text ed. 369.00 (*0-471-92904-2*) Wiley.

Silicon Implementation of Pulse Coded Neural Networks. Ed. by Mona E. Zaghloul et al. LC 93-48181. (International Series in Engineering & Computer Science, VLSI, Computer Architecture, & Digital Screen Processing). 304p. (C). 1994. lib. bdg. 93.50 (*0-7923-9449-6*) Kluwer Ac.

Silicon in Polymer Synthesis. Ed. by H. R. Kricheldorf. LC 95-52299. 1996. write for info. (*3-540-58294-0*) Spr-Verlag.

Silicon in Polymer Synthesis. Ed. by H. R. Kricheldorf. (Illus.). 500p. 1996. 157.00 (*0-387-58294-0*) Spr-Verlag.

***Silicon Karma.** Tom Eastonn. (Orig.). 1997. pap. 11.99 (*1-56504-818-0*, 11818) White Wolf.

Silicon Landscapes. Peter Hall & Ann R. Markusen. (Illus.). 160p. (C). 1985. text ed. 29.95 (*0-04-338122-7*) Routledge Chapman & Hall.

Silicon Mage. Barbara Hambly. LC 87-91378. 352p. 1988. mass mkt. 5.99 (*0-345-33763-8*, Del Rey) Ballantine.

***Silicon Man.** Charles Platt. LC 97-19832. (Cortext: Science Fiction That Changed the World Ser.). 1997. write for info. (*1-888869-14-3*) HardWired.

Silicon Man. Charles Platt. LC 93-60317. 232p. 1993. reprint ed. 19.95 (*0-9623712-7-0*) Tafford Pub.

Silicon Material Preparation & Economical Wafering Methods. Ed. by Ralph Lutwack & Andrew Morrison. LC 84-5968. (Illus.). 586p. 1984. 54.00 (*0-8155-0990-1*) Noyes.

***Silicon Materials: Science & Technology for Microelectronics.** Fumio Shimura. LC 96-27170. 1997. write for info. (*0-471-96773-4*) Wiley.

***Silicon Microengineering.** Young. 448p. (C). (gr. 13 up). 1997. text ed. 121.00 (*0-412-36270-8*, Chap & Hall NY) Chapman & Hall.

Silicon Micromachining & Microstructures. Richard K. Miller & Terri C. Walker. LC 88-80901. (Survey on Technology & Markets Ser.: No. 17). 50p. 1989. pap. text ed. 200.00 (*1-55865-016-4*) Future Tech Surveys.

Silicon-Molecular Beam Epitaxy, Vol. I. Ed. by Erich Kasper & John C. Bean. 272p. 1988. 147.00 (*0-8493-6830-8*, QC611, CRC Reprint) Franklin.

Silicon-Molecular Beam Epitaxy, Vol. II. Ed. by Erich Kasper & John C. Bean. 256p. 1988. 174.00 (*0-8493-6831-6*, QC611, CRC Reprint) Franklin.

Silicon Molecular Beam Epitaxy Vol. 220: Materials Research Society Symposium Proceedings. Ed. by J. C. Bean et al. 649p. 1991. text ed. 70.00 (*1-55899-114-X*) Materials Res.

***Silicon Nitride & Silicon Dioxide Thin Insulating Films: 3rd International Symposium.** Ed. by V. J. Kapoor & W. D. Brown. (Illus.). 617p. 1994. 80.00 (*1-56677-048-3*, PV94-16) Electrochem Soc.

***Silicon Nitride & Silicon Dioxide Thin Insulating Films: 4th International Symposium.** Ed. by M. J. Deen et al. Date not set. 78.00 (*1-56677-137-4*, PV97-10) Electrochem Soc.

Silicon Nitride in Electronics. V. I. Belyi et al. (Materials Science Monographs: No. 34). 340p. 1989. 152.50 (*0-444-42689-2*, North Holland) Elsevier.

Silicon Nitride Report. 3rd ed. A. J. Fletcher. 350p. 1993. 1,176.00 (*1-85617-186-8*, Pub. by Elsevier Applied Sci UK) Elsevier.

Silicon on Insulator. Furukawa. 1985. lib. bdg. 182.50 (*90-277-1940-3*) Kluwer Ac.

Silicon-on-Insulator & Buried Metals in Semiconductors. Ed. by C. K. Chen et al. (Symposium Proceedings Ser.: Vol. 107). 1988. text ed. 30.00 (*0-931837-75-8*) Materials Res.

Silicon-on-Insulator Technology: Materials to VLSI. Jean-Pierre Colinge. (C). 1991. lib. bdg. 81.00 (*0-7923-9150-0*) Kluwer Ac.

***Silicon-on-Insulator Technology & Devices: 7th International Symposium.** Ed. by P. L. Hemment et al. 440p. 1996. 71.00 (*1-56677-153-6*, PV96-3) Electrochem Soc.

***Silicon-on-Insulator Technology & Devices VIII.** Ed. by S. Cristoloveanu et al. Date not set. 73.00 (*1-56677-176-5*, PV97-23) Electrochem Soc.

Silicon Processing for the VLSI Era: Process Technology, Vol. 1. Stanley Wolf & Richard N. Tauber. (Illus.). 660p. 1986. 59.95 (*0-9616721-3-7*) Lattice Pr.

Silicon Processing for the VLSI Era Vol. 3: The Submicron MOSFET. Stanley Wolf. (Illus.). 722p. (C). 1995. 94.95 (*0-9616721-5-3*) Lattice Pr.

Silicon Processing for the VLSI Era, Vol. 2: Process Integration. Stanley Wolf. (Illus.). 752p. (C). 1990. text ed. 89.95 (*0-9616721-4-5*) Lattice Pr.

Silicon Processing-STP 804. Ed. by D. C. Gupta. LC 82-83529. 559p. 1983. text ed. 60.00 (*0-8031-0243-7*, 04-804000-46) ASTM.

Silicon Reagents. E. W. Colvim. 147p. 1988. text ed. 88.00 (*0-12-182560-4*) Acad Pr.

Silicon Samurai: How Japan Conquered the World's IT Industry. Tom Forester. 244p. 1993. 27.95 (*1-55786-292-3*) Blackwell Pubs.

Silicon Semiconductor Data. Helmut F. Wolf. 1969. 306.00 (*0-08-013019-4*, Pub. by Pergamon Repr UK) Franklin.

Silicon Semiconductor Technology. W. R. Runyan. LC 64-24607. (Texas Instruments Electronics Ser.). (Illus.). 284p. reprint ed. pap. 81.00 (*0-317-09126-3*, 2055600) Bks Demand.

***Silicon Sensors & Circuits: On-Chip Compatibility.** Ed. by Wolffenbuttel. (Sensor Physics & Technology Ser.). (Illus.). 336p. 1995. text ed. 65.00 (*0-412-70970-8*, Chap & Hall NY) Chapman & Hall.

Silicon Snake Oil: Second Thoughts on the Information Highway. Clifford Stoll. 256p. 1996. pap. 14.00 (*0-385-41994-5*, Anchor NY) Doubleday.

Silicon Society. David Lyon. LC 86-194046. (London Lectures in Contemporary Christianity: 1979). 127p. (Orig.). reprint ed. pap. 36.20 (*0-685-23726-5*, 2032740) Bks Demand.

Silicon Sumo: U. S. - Japan Competition & Industrial Policy in the Semiconductor Equipment Industry. Ross Young. Ed. by Nancy Richey. (Illus.). 384p. (Orig.). (C). 1994. pap. text ed. 79.50 (*0-9613880-9-9*) Semiconductor.

***Silicon Valley Business Traveler's Guide: Easy Access to Sites Virtual & Tangible.** Dana Abbott. (Illus.). 112p. (Orig.). 1997. pap. 12.95 (*0-9638781-8-2*) Silicon CA.

Silicon Valley C.A.R.D. Cycle America Resource Directory. Martin Krieg. (Illus.). 64p. 1990. pap. 2.95 (*0-9611490-1-9*) Cycle Amer.

Silicon Valley Job Guide. Madeline Bailey. 250p. 1996. pap. 19.95 (*0-9639688-3-1*) Q C C.

Silicone Oil in the Treatment of Complicated Retinal Detachments: Techniques, Results, & Complications. K. Lucke & H. Laqua. (Illus.). xix, 161p. 1990. 64.00 (*0-387-53035-5*) Spr-Verlag.

Silicone Oil in Vitreoretinal Surgery. R. Zivojnovic. (Monographs in Ophthalmology). (C). 1987. lib. bdg. 175.00 (*0-89838-879-1*) Kluwer Ac.

Silicone Rubbers. Trego & Winnan. (Rapra Review Reports: Vol. 3). 1991. pap. 115.00 (*0-08-041725-6*, Pergamon Pr) Elsevier.

Silicone Toxicity. Ed. by Nachman Brautbar et al. (International Journal of Occupational Medicine, Immunology, & Toxicology Ser.: Vol. 4, No. 1). (Illus.). 252p. 1995. pap. text ed. 70.00 (*0-911131-99-X*) Princeton Sci Pubs.

Silicones & Industry. Andreas Tomanek. 172p. (C). 1991. text ed. 24.00 (*1-56990-099-X*) Hanser-Gardner.

Silicones & Industry: A Compendium for Practical Use, Instruction & Reference. Andreas Tomanek. LC 92-16110. (C). 1993. write for info. (*0-19-520960-5*) OUP.

Silicones Chemistry & Technology. Koerner. 1992. 76.00 (*0-8493-7740-4*) CRC Pr.

Silicones for Biomedical & Pharmaceutical Applications: Seminar Notes - Oct. 1995. 1995. 89.95 (*1-56676-392-4*) Technomic.

Silicosis: Records of International Conference, Johannesburg, August, 1930, (I. L. O. Studies & Reports) (Series F: No. 13, Vol. 31). 1974. reprint ed. 65.00 (*0-8115-3263-1*) Periodicals Srv.

Silius Italicus - Concordantia in Silii Italici Punica, 2 vols., Set. Silius Italicus. Ed. by Manfred Wacht. (Alpha-Omega, Reihe A Ser.: Bd. CII). 1297p. (GER.). 1990. write for info. (*3-487-09175-5*) G Olms Pubs.

Silius Italicus & His View of the Past. Carlos Santini. (London Studies in Classical Philology: No. 25). 129p. 1991. 44.00 (*90-5063-029-4*, Pub. by Gieben NE) Benjamins North Am.

Silk. Jacques Anquetil. (Illus.). 200p. 1996. 60.00 (*2-08-013616-X*, Pub. by Flammarion FR) Abbeville Pr.

Silk. Chris Deshpande. Ed. by Rebecca Stefoff. (Threads Ser.). (Illus.). 25p. (J). (gr. 2-4). 1995. lib. bdg. 15.93 (*1-56074-061-2*) Garrett Ed Corp.

***Silk.** Caitlin Kiernan. 1998. mass mkt. 12.95 (*0-451-45668-8*, ROC) NAL-Dutton.

Silk. Robert Mackintosh. 1992. pap. 4.99 (*0-685-53101-5*) Pinnacle MO.

Silk. Grace D. Mazur. 238p. 1996. pap. 15.95 (*1-57129-028-1*) Brookline Bks.

Silk: An Expose of Commercial Fishing. Soren Roegdke & Kay Busse. LC 94-61842. 364p. (Orig.). (C). 1995. pap. 20.00 (*0-9629242-3-7*) WKB Enterp.

Silk: The Luxurious Fabric, Vol. 1, No. 1. S. Jill Miller-Lewis. (Illus.). 34p. (Orig.). 1987. pap. text ed. 8.00 (*0-934155-04-6*) Miller Des.

Silk & Bamboo Music in Shanghai: The Jiangnan Sizhu Instrumental Ensemble Tradition. J. Lawrence Witzleben. LC 94-9092. (World Music Ser.). (Illus.). 224p. 1995. text ed. 35.00 (*0-87338-499-7*) Kent St U Pr.

***Silk & Metal Threads on Canvas.** expanded ed. Sandy Rodgers. LC 96-61312. 94p. 1996. pap. text ed. 27.95 (*0-9649081-7-4*) Yarn Cellar.

Silk & Religion: An Exploration of Material Life & Thought of People, AD 600-1200. Xinru Liu. (Illus.). 248p. (C). 1996. 22.95 (*0-19-563655-4*) OUP.

Silk & Secrets. Mary J. Putney. 400p. (Orig.). 1992. pap. 4.99 (*0-451-40301-0*, Onyx) NAL-Dutton.

Silk & Shadows. Mary J. Putney. 432p. 1991. pap. 4.99 (*0-451-40277-4*, Onyx) NAL-Dutton.

Silk & Splendor. Ellen T. Marsh. 432p. 1986. pap. 3.95 (*0-380-89677-X*) Avon.

Silk & Stone. Deborah Smith. 528p. 1994. mass mkt. 5.99 (*0-553-29689-2*) Bantam.

Silk & Stone: The Art of Asia: The Third Hali Annual. Ed. by Jill Tilden. 1996. 75.00 (*1-898113-20-3*, Pub. by L King Pubng UK) Antique Collect.

Silk Designs of the Eighteenth Century: From the Victoria & Albert Museum, London. Ed. & Intro. by Clare Browne. LC 95-62053. (Illus.). 112p. 1996. pap. 19.95 (*0-500-27880-6*) Thames Hudson.

Silk Domino. Jean Musson. (Rainbow Romances Ser.). 160p. 1993. 14.95 (*0-7090-4924-2*, Hale-Parkwest) Parkwest Pubns.

Silk Domino. large type ed. Jean Musson. (Romance Ser.). 1994. pap. 15.99 (*0-7089-7609-3*, Linford) Ulverscroft.

Silk Exports & Development Information: Procedures & Guidelines. T. D. Koshy. 1990. 32.50 (*81-7024-320-3*, Pub. by Ashish II) S Asia.

Silk Expressions. Deonne B. Wright. 31p. (Orig.). 1986. pap. 10.00 (*4-15-109253-6*) D B Wright.

Silk Flags & Cold Steel: The Civil War in North Carolina: The Piedmont. William Trotter. LC 90-28706. (Civil War in North Carolina Ser.). (Illus.). 385p. 1991. reprint ed. pap. 12.95 (*0-89587-086-X*) Blair.

Silk Flowers. Anne Hamilton & Kathleen White. LC 88-45280. 144p. 1988. 22.50 (*0-87923-765-1*) Godine.

Silk Flowers: Complete Color & Style Guide for the Creative Crafter. Judith Blacklock. 128p. 1995. pap. 19.95 (*0-8019-8649-4*) Chilton.

Silk Glove Hegemony: Finnish-Soviet Relations, 1944-1974: A Case Study of the Theory of the Soft Sphere of Influence. John P. Vloyantes. LC 74-27387. 222p. reprint ed. pap. 63.30 (*0-317-55823-4*, 2029409) Bks Demand.

Silk Hope, N. C. Lawrence Naumoff. 1995. pap. 12.00 (*0-15-600207-8*) HarBrace.

Silk Hope, N. C. A Novel. Lawrence Naumoff. 1994. 21.95 (*0-15-188900-7*) HarBrace.

Silk Industry. Sarah Bush. 1989. pap. 25.00 (*0-85263-706-3*, Pub. by Shire UK) St Mut.

Silk Industry: Problems & Prospects. Abdul Aziz & H. G. Hanumappa. 1985. 18.50 (*0-8364-1511-6*, Pub. by Ashish II) S Asia.

Silk Industry in Ch'ing China. Shih Min-hsiung. Tr. by E-tu Zen Sun from CHI. (Michigan Abstracts of Chinese & Japanese Works on Chinese History: No. 5). (Illus.). 98p. 1976. pap. text ed. 15.00 (*0-89264-905-4*) Ctr Chinese Studies.

Silk King. large type ed. Mary Wells. 416p. 1989. 25.99 (*0-7089-2018-7*) Ulverscroft.

Silk Painting. Born Vibeke. 1996. 18.95 (*1-870586-25-5*, Pub. by D Porteous UK) Parkwest Pubns.

Silk Painting: New Ideas & Textures. Jill Kennedy & Jane Varrall. LC 93-6115. 1994. reprint ed. write for info. (*0-486-27909-X*) Dover.

Silk Painting: The Artist's Guide to Gutta & Wax Resist Techniques. Susan L. Moyer. (Illus.). 144p. 1991. pap. 24.95 (*0-8230-4828-4*, Watsn-Guptill) Watsn-Guptill.

S

Silk Painting For Fashion & Fine Art: Techniques for Making Ties, Scarves, Dresses, Decorative Pillows & Fine Art Paintings. Susan L. Moyer. (Illus.). 144p. 1995. pap. 24.95 (*0-8230-4831-4*) Watsn-Guptill.

Silk Painting Workshop: Painting, Marbling & Batik for Beginners. Jane Venables. 128p. 1994. 29.95 (*0-7153-0000-8*, Pub. by D & C Pub UK) Sterling.

***Silk Peony, Parade Dragon.** Elizabeth Steckman. LC 94-70684. (Illus.). 32p. (J). (ps-1). 1997. 14.95 (*1-56397-233-6*) Boyds Mills Pr.

Silk Polymers: Materials Science & Biotechnology. Ed. by David Kaplan et al. LC 93-37155. (ACS Symposium Ser.: No. 544). (Illus.). 370p. 1994. 94.95 (*0-8412-2743-8*) Am Chemical.

Silk Production, Processing & Marketing. Mahesh Nanavaty. (C). 1990. 52.00 (*81-224-0282-8*) S Asia.

***Silk Ribbon: Applique Embellishments.** Cathy Grafton. 1997. pap. 16.95 (*0-89145-885-9*) Collector Bks.

***Silk Ribbon Embroidery: Beautiful Projects & Elegant Design Ideas.** Sheena Cable. LC 96-38705. 1997. write for info. (*0-89577-934-X*) RD Assn.

Silk Ribbon Embroidery: For Gifts & Garments. Jenny Bradford. (Illus.). 72p. 1991. pap. 12.95 (*1-86351-009-5*, Pub. by S Milner AT) Sterling.

Silk Ribbon Embroidery: Step by Step. Di VanNiekerk. 70p. 1995. 19.95 (*0-9629056-3-1*) Quilters Res.

***Silk Ribbon Machine Embroidery.** Nancy Bednar. LC 96-52099. (Great Sewing Projects Ser.). (Illus.). 128p. 1997. 27.95 (*0-8069-9493-2*) Sterling.

Silk Ribbon Treasures: Smocking & Embroidery. Martha C. Pullen. LC 96-92281. (Illus.). 240p. (Orig.). 1996. pap. text ed. 24.95 (*1-878048-07-4*) M Pullen.

Silk Ribbons by Machine. Jeanie Sexton. LC 96-9202. 72p. 1996. 15.95 (*0-89145-880-8*, 4783, Am Quilters Soc) Collector Bks.

Silk Road. China Guides Editors. (China Guides Ser.). 224p. 1994. pap. 12.95 (*0-8442-9823-9*, Passport Bks) NTC Pub Grp.

Silk Road. Sven A. Hedin. (C). 1994. text ed. 52.00 (*81-7303-025-1*, Pub. by Book Faith II) S Asia.

Silk Road. Sven Heiden. 1994. pap. 144.00 (*0-7855-0485-0*, Pub. by Ratna Pustak Bhandar) St Mut.

Silk Road: From Xian to Kashgar. 2nd ed. Judy Boravia. 320p. 1994. pap. 16.95 (*0-8442-9951-0*, Passport Bks) NTC Pub Grp.

Silk Road & the Shoso-In. Ryoichi Hayashi. Tr. by Robert Ricketts from JPN. LC 75-23081. (Heibonsha Survey of Japanese Art Ser.: Vol. 6). (Illus.). 184p. 1975. 20.00 (*0-8348-1022-0*) Weatherhill.

Silk Road Today. Christine De Weck. 1989. 12.95 (*0-533-08031-2*) Vantage.

Silk Route. John S. Major. LC 92-38169. (Illus.). 32p. (J). 1995. 14.95 (*0-06-022924-1*) HarpC.

Silk Route. John S. Major. LC 92-38169. (Illus.). 32p. (J). (gr. 4-9). 1995. lib. bdg. 14.89 (*0-06-022926-8*) HarpC.

Silk Route: 7,000 Miles of History. John S. Major. LC 92-38169. (Trophy Picture Bk.). (Illus.). 32p. (J). (gr. 3-5). 1996. pap. 5.95 (*0-06-443468-0*, Trophy) HarpC Child Bks.

***Silk Route by Rail.** 2nd rev. ed. Dominic Streatfeild-James. (World Rail Guides Ser.). (Illus.). 320p. 1997. pap. 17.95 (*1-873756-14-3*, Pub. by Trlblazer Pubn UK) Seven Hills Bk.

Silk-Screen Printing for Artists & Craftsmen. Mathilda V. Schwalbach & James A. Schwalbach. (Illus.). 150p. 1981. reprint ed. pap. 8.95 (*0-486-24046-0*) Dover.

Silk Screen Techniques. J. I. Biegeleisen & J. A. Cohn. (Illus.). 1958. pap. 4.95 (*0-486-20433-2*) Dover.

Silk Screen Techniques. J. I. Biegeleisen & M. A. Cohn. (Illus.). 1990. 20.00 (*0-8446-0491-7*) Peter Smith.

***Silk Stalkings: More Women Write of Murder.** Victoria Nichols & Susan Thompson. LC 97-24372. 1997. write for info. (*0-8108-3393-X*) Scarecrow.

Silk Stockings & Ballot Boxes: Women & Politics in New Orleans, 1920-1963. Pamela Tyler. LC 95-11197. 1996. 40.00 (*0-8203-1790-X*) U of Ga Pr.

Silk Tree, Guanacaste, Monkey's Earring: A Generic System for the Synandrous Mimosacene of the Americas, Pt. I: Aberima, Albizia, & Allies. Rupert C. Barneby & Jim Grimes. (Memoirs of the New York Botanical Garden Ser.: No. 74). (Illus.). 288p. 1996. 45.00 (*0-89327-395-3*, MEM 74(1)) NY Botanical.

Silk Vendetta. Victoria Holt. 1989. mass mkt. 3.50 (*0-449-21548-2*, Crest) Fawcett.

Silk Worker's Notebook. rev. ed. Cheryl Kolander. LC 85-80616. (Illus.). 168p. 1986. reprint ed. pap. 12.00 (*0-934026-18-1*) Interweave.

Silke on South African Income Tax: Eleventh Memorial Edition, 2 vols., Set. C. Divaris & M. L. Stein. 1991. ring bd. 274.00 (*0-7021-2268-8*, Pub. by Juta SA) Gaunt.

***Silken Betrayal.** Francis Ray. 256p. 1997. mass mkt. 4.99 (*0-7860-0426-6*, Pinncle Kensgtn) Kensgtn Pub Corp.

***Silken Bonds.** Marion Chesney. LC 97-17828. 1997. 25.95 (*0-7838-8269-6*) G K Hall.

Silken Cage. Sophie Danson. (Black Lace Ser.). 1995. mass mkt. 5.95 (*0-352-32928-9*, Pub. by Virgin Pub UK) London Brdge.

***Silken Chains.** Jodi Nicol. 256p. (Orig.). 1997. mass mkt. 5.95 (*0-352-33143-7*, Pub. by Black Lace UK) London Brdge.

Silken Dreams. Sharon Green. 384p. (Orig.). 1994. mass mkt. 4.50 (*0-380-77393-7*) Avon.

Silken Inspirations: Shadow Work Embroidery Designs. Allison Seils. (Illus.). 90p. 1994. 22.95 (*0-9640616-0-0*) Contessa Patterns.

***Silken Love.** Carmen Green. 240p. 1997. mass mkt. 4.99 (*0-7860-0434-7*, Pinncle Kensgtn) Kensgtn Pub Corp.

***Silken Net.** large type ed. Rachelle Edwards. (Linford Romance Large Print Ser.). 336p. 1997. pap. 16.99 (*0-7089-5119-8*, Linford) Ulverscroft.

Silken Sorcery see Handkerchief Magic

***Silken Thread: Stories & Sketches.** Cora Sandel. 175p. 8600. 28.00 (*0-7206-0658-6*, Pub. by P Owen Ltd UK) Dufour.

Silken Twine: A Study of the Works of Michael McLaverty. Sophia H. King. 269p. 1993. pap. 17.95 (*1-85371-173-X*) Dufour.

Silken Web. Sandra Brown. 336p. 1993. mass mkt. 6.50 (*0-446-36479-7*) Warner Bks.

Silken Web. large type ed. Sandra Brown. LC 92-43519. 522p. 1993. reprint ed. lib. bdg. 21.95 (*1-56054-638-7*) Thorndike Pr.

Silken Web. large type ed. Sandra Brown. LC 92-43519. 522p. 1993. reprint ed. pap. 14.95 (*1-56054-886-X*) Thorndike Pr.

Silkroads & Shadows. Susan Shawartz. 352p. 1988. pap. 3.95 (*0-8125-5411-6*) Tor Bks.

Silkscreen: Arnold Hoffmann Jr. & the Art of the Print. Helen A. Harrison. LC 95-6493. (Illus.). 12p. 1995. pap. 5.00 (*0-943924-19-7*) Mus Stony Brook.

***Silkworm Egg Production.** R. Otsuki. (Illus.). 204p. 1997. 38.00 (*1-57808-009-6*) Science Pubs.

***Silkworm Rearing.** K. Veda. (Illus.). 440p. 1997. 59.00 (*1-57808-008-8*) Science Pubs.

Silkworms. Sylvia A. Johnson. LC 82-250. (Natural Science Bks.). (Illus.). 48p. (J). (gr. 4 up). 1982. pap. 5.95 (*0-8225-9557-5*, First Ave Edns) Lerner Group.

***Silkworms.** L. Patricia Kite. (Illus.). 120p. (Orig.). (J). 1997. pap. write for info. (*1-57502-542-6*, P01591) Morris Pubng.

***Silkworms.** Arthur Morton. (Illus.). (J). (gr. k-3). 1995. write for info. (*1-57842-080-6*) Delmas Creat.

Silky Terriers. Martin Weil. (Illus.). 192p. 1981. 9.95 (*0-86622-822-5*, KW-115) TFH Pubns.

***Silky Terriers Today.** Nancy Wren. LC 96-36644. 1997. 25.95 (*0-87605-325-8*) Howell Bk.

Silky, the Woods Cat. Helen Moss. (Illus.). 80p. (J). (gr. 2-4). 1993. 10.95 (*0-89015-867-3*) Sunbelt Media.

Sill Family: Old Silltown: Something of Its History & People, Being Principally a Brief Account of the Early Generations of the Sill Family. S. S. Burt. (Illus.). 148p. 1991. reprint ed. pap. 22.00 (*0-8328-1940-9*); reprint ed. lib. bdg. 32.00 (*0-8328-1939-5*) Higginson Bk Co.

Silla de Pedro. Ezra Jack Keats. Tr. by Maria A. Fiol from SPA. LC 95-9962. Orig. Title: Peter's Chair. (Illus.). 40p. (SPA.). (J). (ps-3). 1996. pap. 5.95 (*0-06-443433-8*, HpArco Iris) HarpC Child Bks.

Silla de Pedro. Ezra Jack Keats. Tr. by Maria Fiol from SPA. LC 95-9962. Orig. Title: Peter's Chair. (Illus.). 40p. (J). (ps-3). 1996. 15.95 (*0-06-026655-4*, HpArco Iris) HarpC Child Bks.

Sillas Especiales. Jean A. Zollars. Ed. by Macrina C. Montano. Tr. by Alejandra Millar. (Illus.). 95p. (Orig.). (SPA.). 1993. pap. 20.00 (*1-882632-02-8*); pap. 19.95 (*1-882632-04-4*) PAX Pr.

Silliest Joke Book Ever. Victoria G. Hartman. LC 92-22161. (Illus.). (J). 1993. 14.00 (*0-688-10109-7*); lib. bdg. 13.93 (*0-688-10110-0*) Lothrop.

***Sillitoe Selection.** Marland. Date not set. pap. text ed. write for info. (*0-582-23373-9*, Pub. by Longman UK) Longman.

Sillon para Mama (A Chair for My Mother) Vera B. Williams. (Illus.). (J). 1994. lib. bdg. 15.93 (*0-688-13616-8*) Morrow.

Sillon Para Mama (A Chair For My Mother) Spanish Edition. Vera B. Williams. Tr. by Aida E. Marcuse from ENG. LC 81-7010. (Books in Spanish). (Illus.). 32p. (SPA.). (J). (ps up). 1994. reprint ed. pap. 4.95 (*0-688-13200-6*, Mulberry) Morrow.

Sillon para Mi Mama. Vera B. Williams. (Illus.). (SPA.). (J). (gr. k-4). 1994. pap. 15.95 incl. audio (*0-87499-335-0*) Live Oak Media.

Sillon Para Mi Mama, 4 bks., Set. Vera B. Williams. (Illus.). (J). (gr. k-4). 1994. pap. 31.95 incl. audio (*0-87499-337-7*) Live Oak Media.

Sills Family & Related Lines. Louise J. Sills. 1969. pap. 8.00 (*0-686-05558-6*) L C Bryant.

Sills for the Office. S. Seah & F. Foster. (C). 1985. 80.00 (*0-85950-396-8*, Pub. by S Thornes Pubs UK) St Mut.

***Silly AB Seas.** Kathleen Estes. (Illus.). 48p. (J). (gr. 1). 1997. 17.95 (*1-880851-27-X*) Greene Bark Pr.

Silly Animal Jokes. Gary Perkins. LC 92-20776. (J). 1992. pap. 2.50 (*0-8167-2966-2*) Troll Communs.

Silly Animal Stickers. Nina Barbaresi. (Illus.). (J). (gr. k-3). 1993. pap. 1.00 (*0-486-27196-X*) Dover.

Silly Animals Punch-Out Masks. Carolyn Bracken. (Illus.). (J). (gr. k-3). 1993. pap. 2.95 (*0-486-27702-X*) Dover.

Silly Billy! Pat Hutchins. LC 91-32561. (Illus.). 32p. (J). (ps-6). 1992. 14.00 (*0-688-10817-2*); lib. bdg. 13.93 (*0-688-10818-0*) Greenwillow.

***Silly Chester.** Betty Jo Stanovich. (J). Date not set. write for info. (*0-688-04053-5*); lib. bdg. write for info. (*0-688-04054-3*) Lothrop.

Silly Christmas Scenes. Illus. by Bill Ross. 14p. (J). (ps-2). 1991. pap. 3.50 (*0-8249-8523-0*, Ideals Child) Hambleton-Hill.

Silly Circus! Puzzles, Jokes, & Things to Make & Do. Martin Chatterton. (Illus.). 32p. (J). (ps up). 1994. pap. 2.99 (*1-56402-405-9*) Candlewick Pr.

Silly Daddy: The Long Goodbye. Joe Chiappetta. (Silly Daddy Ser.). (Illus.). 98p. (Orig.). (YA). 1994. pap. text ed. 7.95 (*0-9644323-0-7*) J Chiappetta.

***Silly Dog.** Eddie Bowman. (J). 1997. write for info. (*1-56763-324-2*); pap. write for info. (*1-56763-325-0*) Ozark Pub.

Silly Egg. Nancy Reese. Ed. by Alton Jordan. (I Can Read Ser.). (Illus.). (J). (gr. k-3). 1984. 7.95 (*0-89868-004-2*, Read Res); pap. 3.95 (*0-89868-037-9*, Read Res) ARO Pub.

Silly Flyers. Ed. by Meg Bowman. (Illus.). 112p. 1995. spiral bd. 8.95 (*0-940483-11-4*) Hot Flash Pr.

Silly Ghost Riddles. Roger Salinas. (Illus.). 32p. (Orig.). (J). (gr. 3-5). 1987. pap. 2.95 (*0-942673-00-X*) Salinas Salinas & Matthews.

Silly Goofy Jokes. Gary Perkins. LC 92-20779. (Illus.). 64p. (J). (gr. 2-6). 1994. pap. 1.95 (*0-8167-2965-4*) Troll Communs.

Silly Goose. Jack Kent. LC 82-21441. (Illus.). 32p. (J). (gr. k-4). 1982. pap. 5.95 (*0-671-66677-0*, S&S Bks Young Read); lib. bdg. 10.95 (*0-671-66676-2*, S&S Bks Young Read) S&S Childrens.

***Silly Gooses.** Sue Denim. LC 96-52916. (J). 1997. write for info. (*0-590-94733-8*, Blue Sky Press) Scholastic Inc.

***Silly Gooses Build a House.** Sue Denim. LC 96-52435. (J). 1997. write for info. (*0-590-94741-9*, Blue Sky Press) Scholastic Inc.

Silly Haunted Jokes. Gary Perkins. LC 92-20760. (Illus.). 64p. (J). (gr. 2-6). 1994. pap. 1.95 (*0-8167-2963-8*) Troll Communs.

Silly Heads. 16p. (J). 1996. 15.95 (*0-7894-0219-X*) DK Pub Inc.

***Silly Holes.** Sophie Fatus. (Silly Shapes Ser.). (Illus.). 12p. (J). 1997. bds. 5.95 (*0-7892-0317-0*, Abbeville Kids) Abbeville Pr.

Silly Jokes. (Sound Mixers Ser.). 8p. (J). (ps-2). 1994. write for info. (*1-883366-45-3*) YES Ent.

Silly Jokes & Riddles. Elvira Gamiello. (Illus.). 96p. (Orig.). (J). 1988. pap. 1.95 (*0-942025-32-6*) Kidsbks.

Silly Me. Michael G. Michaud. LC 89-92010. 123p. (Orig.). 1989. pap. 8.95 (*0-9620574-1-X*) MGM Pr.

Silly People Mix-Ups. Christopher Carrie. (Crayola Color & Activity Ser.). (Illus.). 32p. (J). (gr. k up). 1991. 1.49 (*0-86696-304-9*) Binney & Smith.

Silly Sally. Audrey Wood. (J). 1992. 15.00 (*0-15-274428-2*, HB Juv Bks) HarBrace.

Silly Sally. Audrey Wood. LC 91-15839. (Illus.). 32p. (J). (ps-2). 1994. pap. 20.00 (*0-15-200072-0*, HB Juv Bks) HarBrace.

Silly Sam. Russell Hoban. (J). Date not set. pap. 3.95 (*0-590-20744-X*) Scholastic Inc.

Silly School Jokes. Gary Perkins. LC 92-20437. (Illus.). 64p. (J). (gr. 2-6). 1992. pap. text ed. 2.50 (*0-8167-2964-6*) Troll Communs.

Silly Science: Strange & Startling Projects to Amaze Your Family & Friends. Shar Levine & Leslie Johnstone. LC 94-24698. 95p. (J). 1995. pap. text ed. 9.95 (*0-471-11013-2*) Wiley.

Silly Science Tricks. Peter Murray. LC 92-18903. (Umbrella Bks.). 32p. (J). (gr. 2-6). 1992. lib. bdg. 21.36 (*0-89565-976-X*) Childs World.

Silly Sentences. (Sound Mixers Ser.). 8p. (J). (ps-2). 1994. write for info. (*1-883366-46-1*) YES Ent.

***Silly Sheep.** Mouse Works Staff. (J). 1997. 4.98 (*1-57082-574-2*) Mouse Works.

Silly Sheepdog. H. Amery. (Farmyard Tales Ser.). (Illus.). 16p. (J). (ps-3). 1992. pap. 3.95 (*0-7460-1412-0*) EDC.

***Silly Sheepdog Sticker Book.** Heather Amery. (Farmyard Tales Sticker Storybook Ser.). (Illus.). 18p. (Orig.). (J). (ps up). 1997. pap. 5.95 (*0-7460-2995-0*, Usborne) EDC.

***Silly Sidney.** (Little Monsters Ser.). (J). 1997. write for info. (*0-614-21788-1*, Pub. by Splash UK) Assoc Pubs Grp.

Silly Sidney. Morgan Matthews. LC 85-14063. (Illus.). 48p. (Orig.). (J). (gr. 1-3). 1997. pap. 3.50 (*0-8167-0611-5*) Troll Communs.

***Silly Sights New York City.** Jacki L. Drucker. LC 96-70492. (Illus.). 32p. (J). (ps-4). 1997. 16.95 (*0-9647857-1-4*); pap. 9.95 (*0-9647857-2-2*) Peeking Duck Bks.

Silly Sights Washington, DC. Jacki L. Drucker. LC 95-74712. (Illus.). 32p. (Orig.). (J). (ps-4). 1996. pap. 8.95 (*0-9647857-0-6*) Peeking Duck Bks.

***Silly Signs 'n Stuff.** Jerry Cooper. 24p. (Orig.). 1996. pap. 3.95 (*1-889419-14-1*) J Cooper.

Silly Songs. (Play - a - Sound Ser.). (Illus.). 24p. (J). 1993. 12.98 (*0-7853-0054-6*) Pubns Intl Ltd.

Silly Songs for Kids in Five Finger Patterns with Crayons. 1992. pap. 6.95 (*0-7935-1595-5*, 00290379) H Leonard.

***Silly Soup.** Carol Korty. Ed. by William-Alan Landes. LC 96-50267. (Illus.). 113p. (Orig.). (J). (gr. k-6). 1997. pap. 17.00 (*0-88734-679-0*) Players Pr.

***Silly Spots.** Sophie Fatus. (Silly Shapes Ser.). (Illus.). 12p. (J). 1997. bds. 5.95 (*0-7892-0315-4*, Abbeville Kids) Abbeville Pr.

***Silly Squares.** Sophie Fatus. (Silly Shapes Ser.). (Illus.). 12p. (J). 1997. bds. 5.95 (*0-7892-0318-9*, Abbeville Kids) Abbeville Pr.

Silly Stories. Stuart A. Kallen. LC 92-14773. (J). 1992. lib. bdg. 13.98 (*1-56239-132-1*) Abdo & Dghtrs.

Silly Story: Nothing Less Nothing More. Mercer Mayer. (Illus.). 48p. (J). 1992. reprint ed. pap. 5.95 (*1-879920-02-6*) Rain Bird Prods.

Silly Story of Goldilocks & the Three Squares. Grace Maccarone. LC 95-13226. (Hello Math Reader Ser.: Level 2). (Illus.). 32-40p. (J). 1996. pap. 3.50 (*0-590-54344-X*, Cartwheel) Scholastic Inc.

***Silly Stripes.** Sophie Fatus. (Silly Shapes Ser.). (Illus.). 12p. (J). 1997. bds. 5.95 (*0-7892-0316-2*, Abbeville Kids) Abbeville Pr.

***Silly Stunts & Terrific Tricks for Kids.** Bob Phillips. 154p. (Orig.). (J). (gr. 5-12). 1997. pap. 6.99 (*1-56507-573-0*) Harvest Hse.

Silly Tail Book. (Parents Magazine Press Read-Aloud Library). (J). 1994. lib. bdg. 17.27 (*0-8368-0986-6*) Gareth Stevens Inc.

Silly Tail Book. Marc Brown. LC 83-2250. (Illus.). 48p. (J). (ps-3). 1983. 5.95 (*0-8193-1109-X*); pap. 2.95 (*0-8193-1158-8*) Parents.

***Silly Tails.** Jan Mark. 32p. (J). 3.98 (*0-7651-0098-3*) Smithmark.

***Silly the Seed.** Scott Sussman. LC 96-92618. (Illus.). 48p. (J). (gr. k-8). 1997. 11.95 (*1-889691-00-3*); pap. 7.95 (*1-889691-01-1*) SenSation.

Silly Tillie. Jeanine Wine. LC 87-38311. 32p. (J). (gr. k-3). 1990. 12.95 (*0-934672-62-8*) Good Bks PA.

Silly Tilly & the Easter Bunny. Lillian Hoban. LC 86-7682. (Harper Early I Can Read Bk.). (Illus.). 32p. (J). (ps-3). 1987. lib. bdg. 14.89 (*0-06-022393-6*) HarpC Child Bks.

Silly Tilly & the Easter Bunny. Lillian Hoban. LC 86-7682. (Trophy Early I Can Read Bk.). (Illus.). 32p. (J). (ps-2). 1989. pap. 3.50 (*0-06-444127-X*, Trophy) HarpC Child Bks.

Silly Tilly's Thanksgiving Dinner. Lillian Hoban. LC 89-29287. (I Can Read Bk.). (Illus.). 64p. (J). (gr. k-3). 1990. 14.95 (*0-06-022422-3*); lib. bdg. 14.89 (*0-06-022423-1*) HarpC Child Bks.

Silly Tilly's Thanksgiving Dinner. Lillian Hoban. LC 89-29287. (Trophy I Can Read Bk.). (Illus.). 64p. (J). (gr. k-3). 1991. pap. 3.75 (*0-06-444154-7*, Trophy) HarpC Child Bks.

***Silly Tilly's Valentine.** Lillian Hoban. LC 96-38239. (I Can Read Bks.). (J). Date not set. write for info. (*0-06-027400-X*); lib. bdg. write for info. (*0-06-027401-8*) HarpC.

Silly Times with Two Silly Trolls. Nancy Jewell. LC 95-4319. (I Can Read Bk.). (Illus.). 48p. (J). (gr. k-3). 1996. 14.95 (*0-06-024292-2*); lib. bdg. 14.89 (*0-06-024293-0*) HarpC Child Bks.

***Silly Times with Two Silly Trolls.** Nancy Jewell. LC 95-4319. (I Can Read Bk.). (Illus.). 48p. (J). (ps-3). 1997. pap. 3.75 (*0-06-444228-4*, Trophy) HarpC Child Bks.

Silly Willy. Maryann Cocca-Leffler. (All Aboard Reading Picture Readers Ser.). (Illus.). 32p. (J). (ps-1). 1995. pap. 3.95 (*0-448-40969-0*, G&D) Putnam Pub Group.

Silly Wish Jellyfish. Illus. by John Blackman. 14p. (J). (gr. k-2). 1996. 7.99 (*0-88705-925-2*, Wshng Well Bks) Joshua Morris.

Silly Zoo Animals. (Sound Mixers Ser.). 8p. (J). (ps-2). 1994. write for info. (*1-883366-44-5*) YES Ent.

Sillycomb. Hunce Voelcker. 136p. 1973. 6.95 (*0-915572-10-9*) Panjandrum.

SillyOZbul of OZ & the Magic Merry-Go-Round. Roger S. Baum. 32p. (J). 1992. 15.95 (*0-9630101-2-3*) Yellow Brick Rd.

SillyOZbul of OZ & Toto. Roger S. Baum. (Illus.). (J). 1992. 15.95 (*0-9630101-1-5*) Yellow Brick Rd.

SillyOZbul Trilogy, 3 vols. Roger S. Baum. (J). boxed 47.85 (*0-9630101-3-1*) Yellow Brick Rd.

SillyOZbuls of OZ. Roger S. Baum. LC 91-66003. (Illus.). (J). 1991. 15.95 (*0-9630101-0-7*) Yellow Brick Rd.

Sillysaurs: Dinosaurs That Could Have Been. R. Gary Raham. (Illus.). 16p. (Orig.). (J). (gr. k-4). 1990. 2.95 (*0-9626301-0-1*) Biostration.

Silmarillion. J. R. R. Tolkien. 480p. 1985. mass mkt. 5.95 (*0-345-32581-8*) Ballantine.

Silmarillion. J. R. R. Tolkien. 1983. pap. 15.95 (*0-395-34646-0*) HM.

Silo: Obras Completas, Vol. I. unabridged ed. Silo. 502p. (Orig.). (SPA.). 1994. pap. 16.95 (*1-878977-24-5*) Latitude Pr.

Silo Sajes: Prensip Filozofi Lavi. Serge Madhere. 103p. 1992. pap. text ed. write for info. (*1-881686-02-7*) Madhere.

Silozane Polymers. J. Anthony Semlyen. 560p. 1993. text ed. 115.00 (*0-13-816315-4*) P-H.

Silpa-Sri: Studies in Indian Art & Culture. A. L. Srivastava. 1990. 80.00 (*81-85067-29-5*, Pub. by Sundeep II) S Asia.

Silparatnakosa: Glossary of Orissan Temple Architecture. Sthapaka N. Mahapatra. (C). 1994. 38.00 (*0-614-96185-8*, Pub. by Motilal Banarsidass II) S Asia.

Silurian & Lower Devonian Basin & Basin-Slope Limestones, Copenhagen Canyon, Nevada. Jonathan C. Matti et al. LC 74-19734. (Geological Society of America, Special Paper Ser.: No. 159). 56p. reprint ed. pap. 25.00 (*0-317-28377-4*, 2025458) Bks Demand.

Silurian Conodonts from Wills Mountain Anticline, Virginia. Charles T. Helfrich. LC 74-28984. (Geological Society of America, Special Paper Ser.: No. 161). 198p. reprint ed. pap. 56.50 (*0-317-28375-8*, 2025456) Bks Demand.

Silurian Nuculoid Modio-Morphid Bivalves from Sweden. Louis Liljedahl. (Fossils & Strata: No.33). 89p. 1994. pap. 30.00 (*82-00-37648-6*) Scandnvan Univ Pr.

Silurian Oncocerid Cephalopods from Gotland. Sven Stridsberg. (Fossils & Strata: No. 18). 65p. 1985. pap. 26.00 (*82-00-07575-3*) Scandnvan Univ Pr.

Silurian Paulinitid Polychaetes from Gotland. Claes F. Bergman. (Fossils & Strata: No. 25). 128p. 1989. pap. 44.00 (*82-00-37424-6*) Scandnvan Univ Pr.

Siluro-Devonian Microfaunal Biostratigraphy in Nevada, No. 274 see Bulletins of American Paleontology: Vol. 62

Silva de Romances Viejos. Jacob W. Grimm. xxviii, 318p. reprint ed. write for info. (*0-318-71622-4*) G Olms Pubs.

Silva Method: Thank & Grow Fit. Jose Silva. 216p. (Orig.). 1996. pap. 14.99 (*1-56414-221-3*) Career Pr Inc.

Silva Mind Control: An Anthropological Inquiry. Analine M. Powers. LC 91-39376. (Cults & Nonconventional Religious Groups Ser.). 336p. 1992. text ed. 25.00 (*0-8153-0770-5*) Garland.

Silva Mind Control Method. Jose Silva. 1991. mass mkt. 6.99 (*0-671-73989-1*) PB.

Silva Mind Control Method for Business Managers. Jose Silva & Robert B. Stone. 1991. mass mkt. 6.99 (*0-671-73968-9*) PB.

Silva Mind Control Method for Business Managers. Jose Silva & Robert B. Stone. LC 83-13888. 241p. 1986. 16.95 (*0-13-811018-2*, Busn) P-H.

An Asterisk (*) at the beginning of an entry indicates that the title is appearing in BIP for the first time.

Silva Mind Control Method for Getting Help from Your Other Side. Jose Silva & Robert B. Stone. 288p. 1989. pap. 6.99 (*0-671-67944-9*) PB.

Silva Mind Control Through Psychorientology. Harry F. McKnight. 5.95 (*0-913343-40-4*) Inst Psych Inc.

Silva Mind Mastery for the Nineties. Judith L. Powell & Tag Powell. Ed. by Yvonne Fawcett & Carol Van Horn. LC 91-10758. (Illus.). 256p. 1996. reprint ed. pap. 17.95 (*1-56087-116-4*) Top Mtn Pub.

Silvae. Statius. Ed. by E. Courtney. (Oxford Classical Texts Ser.). 198p. 1990. 55.00 (*0-19-814683-3*) OUP.

Silvae IV. Statius. Ed. & Tr. by K. M. Coleman. (Illus.). 280p. 1988. 80.00 (*0-19-814031-2*) OUP.

Silvae Mycologicae Berolinensis. C. G. Ehrenberg. 1972. reprint ed. 27.00 (*90-6123-253-8*) Lubrecht & Cramer.

Silvae, Thebaid, Achilleid, 2 vols. Statius. No. 206-207. 1928. write for info. (*0-318-53188-7*) HUP.

Silvae, Thebaid, Achilleid, 2 vols., 1. Statius. (Loeb Classical Library: No. 206-207). 604p. 1928. 18.95 (*0-674-99226-1*) HUP.

Silvae, Thebaid, Achilleid, 2 vols., 2. Statius. (Loeb Classical Library: No. 206-207). 602p. 1928. 18.95 (*0-674-99228-8*) HUP.

Silvana. Meg Berenson. 368p. 1996. pap. 5.99 (*0-451-18148-4*, Sig) NAL-Dutton.

Silvarum Libri. Statius. Ed. by Friedrich Vollmer. xvi, 598p. 1971. reprint ed. write for info. (*0-318-71227-X*) G Olms Pubs.

Silvarum Libri. Publius P. Statius. xvi, 598p. (GER.). 1971. reprint ed. write for info. (*0-318-70485-4*) G Olms Pubs.

Silver. (Metals & Minerals Ser.). 1993. lib. bdg. 255.95 (*0-8490-8955-7*) Gordon Pr.

Silver. Penny Jordan. 1990. mass mkt. 5.95 (*0-373-97120-6*) Harlequin Bks.

Silver. Ira Levin. 1992. 5.99 (*0-685-53447-2*) Bantam.

Silver. Norma F. Mazer. 208p. (J). 1989. mass mkt. 4.50 (*0-380-75026-0*, Flare) Avon.

Silver. Norma F. Mazer. LC 88-18652. 272p. (YA). (gr. 7 up). 1988. 16.00 (*0-688-06865-0*, Morrow Junior) Morrow.

Silver. G. Rickard. (Spotlight on Resources Ser.). (Illus.). 48p. (J). (gr. 5 up). 1985. 12.95 (*0-685-58323-6*); lib. bdg. 17.27 (*0-86592-273-X*) Rourke Corp.

Silver. Gloria Whelan. LC 87-26612. (Stepping Stone Bks.). (Illus.). 64p. (Orig.). (J). (gr. 2-4). 1988. lib. bdg. 5.99 (*0-394-99611-9*) Random Bks Yng Read.

Silver. Gloria Whelan. LC 87-26612. (Stepping Stone Bks.). (Illus.). 64p. (Orig.). (J). (gr. 2-4). 1988. pap. 3.99 (*0-394-89611-4*) Random Bks Yng Read.

Silver. large type ed. Hilma Wolitzer. (General Ser.). 384p. (J). 1989. lib. bdg. 20.95 (*0-8161-4743-4*, GK Hall) Thorndike Pr.

Silver. large type ed. Hilma Wolitzer. (General Ser.). 384p. (J). 1989. pap. 13.95 (*0-8161-4933-X*, GK Hall) Thorndike Pr.

Silver: A Study Guide. Mary E. Snodgrass. Ed. by Joyce Friedland & Rikki Kessler. (Novel-Ties Ser.). (J). (gr. 2-5). 1991. pap. text ed. 15.95 (*0-88122-571-1*) Lrn Links.

Silver: An Analysis of Factors Affecting Its Price. 2nd ed. Y. S. Leong. (Brookings Institution Reprint Ser.). reprint ed. lib. bdg. 39.50 (*0-697-00162-8*) Irvington.

Silver: Economics, Metallurgy, & Use. Ed. by Allison Butts. LC 74-34002. 498p. 1975. reprint ed. 54.50 (*0-88275-278-2*) Krieger.

Silver: History & Design. Ed. by Philippa Glanville. LC 96-22288. (Illus.). 144p. 1997. 35.00 (*0-8109-4471-5*) Abrams.

Silver: Practical Guide to Collecting Silverware. Joel Langford. 1991. 12.98 (*1-55521-710-9*) Bk Sales Inc.

Silver Age: Russian Art in the Early Twentieth Century & the World Art Group. 2nd ed. John Bowlt. (Illus.). 456p. 1982. 38.00 (*0-89250-063-8*) Orient Res Partners.

Silver Age: The Commonwealth of Both Nations, No. I. Pawel Jasienica. Tr. by Alexander Jordan. LC 92-81177. 1987. 25.00 (*0-87052-394-5*) Am Inst Polish.

Silver Age in Russian Literature. Ed. by John D. Elsworth. LC 92-1018. (Selected Papers from the Fourth World Congress for Soviet & East European Studies, Harrogate, 1990). 200p. 1992. text ed. 45.00 (*0-312-08044-1*) St Martin.

Silver Age of Superman: The Greatest Covers of Action Comics from the '50s to the '70s. Intro. by Mark Waid. LC 95-3952. (Illus.). 144p. 1995. 19.98 (*0-89660-055-6*, Artabras) Abbeville Pr.

Silver Amalgam in Clinical Practice. 3rd ed. I. D. Gainsford & Stephen M. Dunne. (Illus.). 176p. 1992. pap. text ed. 45.00 (*0-7236-2315-5*) Buttrwrth-Heinemann.

Silver & Entrepreneurship in Seventeenth-Century Potosi: The Life & Times of Antonio Lopez de Quiroga. Peter Bakewell. LC 94-41720. (Illus.). 272p. 1995. pap. 14.95 (*0-87074-386-4*) SMU Press.

Silver & Entrepreneurship in Seventeenth-Century Potosi: The Life & Times of Antonio Lopez de Quiroga. Peter J. Bakewell. LC 88-14227. 268p. reprint ed. pap. 76.40 (*0-7837-5862-6*, 2045581) Bks Demand.

Silver & Gold. Bull. 1997. write for info. (*0-15-200094-1*) HarBrace.

Silver & Gold: Courtly Splendour from Augsburg. Lorenz Seelig et al. (Illus.). 128p. 1995. 39.95 (*3-7913-1456-4*, Pub. by Prestel GW) te Neues.

Silver & Politics in Nevada: 1892-1902. Mary E. Glass. LC 72-92547. (Lancehead Ser.). (Illus.). xi, 256p. 1970. 16. 95 (*0-87417-026-5*) U of Nev Pr.

Silver & Sapphires. Shelly Thacker. 384p. (Orig.). 1993. mass mkt. 4.50 (*0-380-77034-2*) Avon.

Silver & Silver Alloys-Sulfonic Acids see Encyclopedia of Chemical Technology

Silver & Steel. Susan Amarillas. (Historical Ser.). 1994. mass mkt. 3.99 (*0-373-28833-6*, 1-28833-6) Harlequin Bks.

Silver & Stone. Lyle McIntyre. (Illus.). 96p. 32.00 (*1-55046-114-1*, Pub. by Boston Mills Pr CN) Genl Dist Srvs.

Silver Angel. Johanna Lindsey. 432p. (Orig.). 1988. mass mkt. 6.50 (*0-380-75294-8*) Avon.

Silver Anniversary Directory. 1983. pap. write for info. (*0-916984-13-3*) SSAR.

Silver Answer. large type ed. Margaret Maddocks. 1990. 25.99 (*0-7089-2126-4*) Ulverscroft.

***Silver Anthology of Canadian Fiction.** Ed. by Geoff Hancock. 1997. pap. 14.95 (*1-55082-178-4*, Pub. by Quarry Pr CN) LPC InBook.

Silver Apples, Golden Apples. Ed. by Frank Delaney. LC 87-24296. 157p. 1987. pap. 14.95 (*0-85640-391-1*) Dufour.

Silver Apples, Golden Apples: Best Loved Irish Verse. Ed. by Frank Delaney. LC 87-24296. 157p. 1987. pap. 14.95 (*0-685-25871-8*, Pub. by Blackstaff Pr IE) Dufour.

Silver Arm. Jim Fitzpatrick. (Illus.). 112p. pap. 19.95 (*0-905895-54-1*) Avery BookStores Inc.

Silver Arrow & Other Indian Romances of the Dune Country. E. H. Reed. 1977. lib. bdg. 59.95 (*0-8490-2605-9*) Gordon Pr.

Silver at the Essex Institute. Martha G. Fales. LC 83-80762. (E.I. Museum Booklet Ser.). (Illus.). 64p. (Orig.). 1983. pap. 5.95 (*0-88389-086-0*, Essx Institute) Peabody Essex Mus.

Silver at Williamsburg: Drinking Vessels. John A. Hyman. LC 93-46616. (Wallace Gallery Decorative Arts Publications). (Illus.). 134p. 1994. pap. 19.95 (*0-87935-125-X*) Colonial Williamsburg.

Silver at Your Service: A Collectors Guide to Railroad Dining Car Flatware Patterns. Arthur L. Dominy & Rudolph A. Morgenfrug. LC 87-70565. (Illus.). 191p. 1995. 32.50 (*0-9626759-0-3*) D&M Pub CA.

Silver Azide Cyanide. Salomon. (Solubility Data Ser.). 1979. 130.00 (*0-08-023950-1*, Pergamon Pr) Elsevier.

***Silver Balloon.** Susan Bonners. 1997. 14.00 (*0-374-36913-5*) FS&G.

Silver Bay Association: A Pictorial History. Mark C. Johnson et al. LC 93-144870. (Illus.). 50.00 (*0-9634001-0-X*) Silver Bay Assn YMCA.

Silver Bells. 1990. pap. 5.95 (*0-7935-0160-1*, 00001312) H Leonard.

Silver Bells. 30.00 (*0-7935-5082-3*, 00861320) H Leonard.

***Silver Bells.** Lisa T. Bergren et al. 256p. 1997. pap. 8.99 (*1-57673-119-7*, Palisades OR) Multnomah Pubs.

Silver Bells. Lynn Emery et al. 448p. 1996. mass mkt. 4.99 (*0-7860-0333-2*, Pinncle Kensgtn) Kensgtn Pub Corp.

Silver Bells. White Heat Ltd. Staff. (J). 1995. 14.95 (*0-689-80180-7*, Litl Simon S&S) S&S Childrens.

Silver Berries & Christmas Magic. Urslan J. Gaffington. LC 96-67682. (Illus.). 32p. (J). (ps-3). 1996. 18.95 (*0-9647811-0-7*) RiverMoon Bks.

Silver Bindings. Miriam D. Irwin. (Illus.). 48p. 1984. 24.00 (*0-88014-076-3*) Mosaic Pr OH.

***Silver Bird.** Spenser. 29.95 (*1-85532-668-X*, Pub. by Osprey UK) Stackpole.

Silver Bird of Prey. large type ed. Lewis. 1996. 20.00 (*0-7838-1889-0*, GK Hall) Thorndike Pr.

Silver Blades, 4 vols., Set. Melissa Lowell. 1994. pap. 14.00 (*0-553-63494-1*) Bantam.

***Silver Blades: Now or Never.** Melissa Lowell. (Gold Medal Dreams Ser.: No. 2). 128p. (Orig.). (J). (gr. 4-7). 1998. pap. 3.50 (*0-553-48519-9*) BDD Bks Young Read.

***Silver Blades: On the Edge.** Melissa Lowell. (Gold Medal Dreams Ser.: No. 1). 128p. (Orig.). (J). (gr. 4-7). 1997. pap. 3.50 (*0-553-48515-6*) BDD Bks Young Read.

Silver Blaze. Arthur Conan Doyle. (Classic Short Stories Ser.). 64p. (J). (gr. 6). 1990. lib. bdg. 13.95 (*0-88682-302-1*) Creative Ed.

Silver Boat. Ann Adams. (Illus.). 1990. pap. 11.50 (*0-938837-02-8*) Behav Sci Ctr Pubs.

Silver Boat II: The Journey. Ann Adams. (Illus.). 40p. (Orig.). 1994. pap. 11.50 (*0-938837-17-6*) Behav Sci Ctr Pubs.

Silver Bonanza: How to Profit from the Coming Bull Market in Silver. James Blanchard. 272p. 1995. 25.00 (*0-671-50297-2*) S&S Trade.

Silver Bough. Neil M. Gunn. 328p. 1989. 22.95 (*0-8027-1089-1*) Walker & Co.

Silver Bough, 4 vols., Set. F. Marian Mcneill. 1982. 160.00 (*0-686-45783-8*, Pub. by Stuart Titles Ltd UK) St Mut.

Silver Bough, Vol. II: A Calendar of Scottish National Festivals, Candlemas to Harvest Home. F. Marian McNeill. 163p. (C). 1988. 40.00 (*0-317-93231-4*, Pub. by Stuart Titles Ltd UK) St Mut.

Silver Bough, Vol. III: A Calendar of Scottish National Festivals Hallowe'en to Yule. F. Marian McNeill. 180p. (C). 1988. 40.00 (*0-85335-162-7*, Pub. by Stuart Titles Ltd UK) St Mut.

Silver Bough, Vol. IV: The Local Festivals of Scotland. F. Marian McNeill. 272p. (C). 1988. 40.00 (*0-85335-002-7*, Pub. by Stuart Titles Ltd UK) St Mut.

Silver Bough, Vol. 1: Scottish Folklore & Folk Belief. F. Marian McNeill. 220p. (C). 1988. 40.00 (*0-85335-161-9*, Pub. by Stuart Titles Ltd UK) St Mut.

Silver Boxes. Florence Littauer. 154p. 1989. 14.99 (*0-8499-0720-9*) Word Pub.

Silver Boxes. large type ed. Florence Littauer. 272p. pap. 14.99 (*0-8499-3940-2*, 2434) Word Dist.

Silver Boxes: The Gift of Encouragement. Florence Littauer. 1994. 4.99 (*0-8499-5073-2*) Word Pub.

Silver Branch. Patricia Kennealy. (Tale of Aeron Ser.: Bk. 2). 464p. 1991. pap. 5.99 (*0-451-45114-7*, ROC) NAL-Dutton.

Silver Branch. Compiled by Sean O'Faolain. LC 68-58822. (Granger Index Reprint Ser.). 1977. 15.95 (*0-8369-6035-1*) Ayer.

Silver Branch. Rosemary Sutcliff. LC 93-7950. (J). 1993. 4.95 (*0-374-46648-3*) FS&G.

Silver Branch. Rosemary Sutcliff. (J). 1994. 18.25 (*0-8446-6780-3*) Peter Smith.

Silver Buckle Mystery. Bob Wright. Tr. by Phyllis Bourne & Eugenia Tusquets. (Illus.). 96p. (ENG & SPA.). (J). (gr. 1-5). pap. 6.95 (*0-87879-664-9*) High Noon Bks.

Silver Bullet. Defelice. 1995. mass mkt. 4.99 (*0-312-95570-7*) St Martin.

Silver Burdett Countries, 10 bks., Set. (Illus.). 576p. (YA). (gr. 5 up). 1992. lib. bdg. 149.50 (*0-382-09648-7*) Silver Burdett Pr.

Silver Burdett Countries: China. Merton. 1989. 15.96 (*0-382-09253-8*) Silver Burdett Pr.

Silver Burdett Mathematical Dictionary. R. E. Abdelnoor. LC 86-45568. (Illus.). 126p. (J). (gr. 5-12). 1986. 8.95 (*0-382-09485-9*); pap. 5.95 (*0-382-09309-7*) Silver Burdett Pr.

***Silver Burdett Mathematics Dictionary for Young People.** Eula E. Monroe. LC 97-1069. (J). 1998. write for info. (*0-382-39630-8*); pap. write for info. (*0-382-39631-6*) Silver Burdett Pr.

Silver by Paul de Lamerie at the Clark Art Institute. Beth S. Carver & Eleen M. Casey. (Illus.). 74p. 1978. 25.00 (*1-55660-185-9*) A Wofsy Fine Arts.

***Silver Candelabra & Other Stories: A Century of Argentine Jewish Literature.** Rita Gardiol. LC 97-15868. 1997. pap. text ed. 16.95 (*0-935480-88-9*) Lat Am Lit Rev Pr.

Silver Canyon. Louis L'Amour. 176p. 1957. mass mkt. 3.99 (*0-553-24743-3*) Bantam.

***Silver Canyon.** large type ed. Louis L'Amour. LC 96-35016. 225p. 1997. 23.95 (*0-7838-1949-8*, GK Hall) Thorndike Pr.

Silver Caress. Charlotte Simms. 400p. 1990. pap. 3.95 (*0-380-76179-3*) Avon.

***Silver Castle.** Clive James. 1998. write for info. (*0-375-50093-6*) Random.

Silver Chair. C. S. Lewis. LC 93-14299. (Chronicles of Narnia Ser.). (Illus.). 208p. (J). (gr. 3 up). 1994. pap. 5.95 (*0-06-440504-4*, Trophy) HarpC Child Bks.

Silver Chair. C. S. Lewis. LC 93-14299. (Chronicles of Narnia Ser.: Bk. 4). (Illus.). 208p. (J). (gr. 3 up). 1994. 15.00 (*0-06-023495-4*); lib. bdg. 14.89 (*0-06-023496-2*) HarpC Child Bks.

Silver Chair. C. S. Lewis. LC 93-14299. (Chronicles of Narnia Ser.: No. 6). (Illus.). 208p. (J). (gr. 3 up). 1994. pap. 3.95 (*0-06-447109-8*) HarpC Child Bks.

Silver Chariot Killer. Richard A. Lupoff. LC 96-20058. 1996. 21.95 (*0-312-14736-8*) St Martin.

Silver Chief: Dog of the North. Jack O'Brien. 250p. 1991. reprint ed. lib. bdg. 20.95 (*0-89966-823-2*) Buccaneer Bks.

***Silver Christmas Ornaments: A Collector's Identification & Price Guide.** Clara J. Scroggins. (Illus.). 240p. 1997. 29.95 (*0-87341-516-7*, XORN) Krause Pubns.

Silver City. Li Rui. LC 97-23508. 1997. write for info. (*0-8050-4895-2*) H Holt & Co.

Silver City. David Norman. (Frontier Rakers Ser.: No. 4). (Orig.). 1982. mass mkt. 2.95 (*0-89083-921-2*, Zebra Kensgtn) Kensgtn Pub Corp.

Silver City Scandal. large type ed. Gerald Hammond. 272p. 1987. 25.99 (*0-7089-1639-2*) Ulverscroft.

***Silver Cloud Cafe.** Alfredo Vea, Jr. 352p. 1996. 23.95 (*0-614-19894-1*) NAL-Dutton.

***Silver Cloud Cafe.** Alfredo Vea, Jr. 1997. pap. 13.95 (*0-452-27664-0*, Plume) NAL-Dutton.

Silver Coach. C. S. Adler. 112p. (J). (gr. 3-7). 1988. pap. 2.50 (*0-380-75498-3*, Camelot) Avon.

Silver Coach: A Study Guide. Elyse Fischer. Ed. by Joyce Friedland & Rikki Kessler. (Novel-Ties Ser.). (J). (gr. 3-5). 1991. pap. text ed. 15.95 (*0-88122-577-0*) Lrn Links.

Silver Cobweb. Carolyn Keene. (Nancy Drew Ser.: No. 71). (Illus.). 192p. (Orig.). (J). 1983. 8.95 (*0-671-46464-7*); pap. 3.50 (*0-685-42563-0*) S&S Trade.

Silver Cobweb. Carolyn Keene. Ed. by Meg F. Schneider. (Nancy Drew Ser.). (Illus.). 192p. (Orig.). (J). (gr. 3-7). 1983. 9.95 (*0-671-46463-9*) S&S Trade.

Silver Coinage of Crete: A Metrological Note. G. Macdonald. (Illus.). 29p. 1974. pap. 5.00 (*0-916710-13-0*) Obol Intl.

Silver Coins of England. Edward Hawkins. LC 76-12920. (Illus.). 1977. reprint ed. lib. bdg. 65.00 (*0-915262-05-3*) S J Durst.

Silver, Copper & Gold Halates. A. S. Miyamoto. 266p. 1990. 111.25 (*0-08-029208-9*, Pergamon Pr) Elsevier.

Silver Cord. Marti Barham & Tom Greene. LC 85-63215. 197p. (Orig.). 1986. pap. 12.00 (*0-87516-562-1*) DeVorss.

***Silver Cord: Photographs.** David Armstrong. 1997. 45.00 (*3-931141-48-9*) Dist Art Pubs.

Silver Cow: A Welsh Tale. Susan Cooper. LC 91-234. (Illus.). 32p. (J). (gr. k-3). 1991. reprint ed. pap. 5.99 (*0-689-71512-9*, Aladdin Paperbacks) S&S Childrens.

Silver Cowboy. large type ed. Gene Tuttle. (Linford Western Library). 320p. 1996. pap. 15.99 (*0-7089-7823-1*, Linford) Ulverscroft.

Silver Creek City. James L. Jensen. LC 93-94365. 384p. (Orig.). 1995. pap. 10.00 (*1-56002-434-8*, Univ Edtns) Aegina Pr.

Silver Creek, ID. W. David Joye. Ed. by Jeff Findley. (River Journal Ser.: Vol. 1, No. 2). (Illus.). 48p. (Orig.). 1993. pap. 14.95 (*1-878175-33-5*) F Amato Pubns.

Silver Creek Riders: Back in the Saddle, No. 1. Beth Kincaid. 192p. (Orig.). (J). (gr. 4-7). 1994. mass mkt. 3.99 (*0-515-11480-4*) Jove Pubns.

Silver Creek Riders: True Romance, No. 2. Beth Kincaid. 192p. (Orig.). (J). (gr. 4-7). 1994. mass mkt. 3.50 (*0-515-11489-8*) Jove Pubns.

Silver Creek Riders No. 3: Winning. Beth Kincaid. 192p. (Orig.). 1995. mass mkt. 3.99 (*0-515-11499-5*) Jove Pubns.

Silver Crown. William Bridges. 1995. pap. 5.99 (*1-56504-882-2*, 11301) White Wolf.

Silver Crown. Joel Rosenburg. (Book of Guardians of the Flame Ser.: No. 3). 304p. 1985. pap. 4.99 (*0-451-15983-7*, ROC) NAL-Dutton.

Silver Dagger. David French. 136p. (Orig.). 1993. pap. 11. 95 (*0-88922-325-4*) Genl Dist Srvs.

Silver Dandelion see Bunny's Nutshell Library

Silver Dandelion Pop-Up Surprise Book. Gill Speirs. (Illus.). 14p. (J). (ps-3). 1995. pap. 3.50 (*0-307-14408-9*, Golden Books) Western Pub.

Silver Darlings. Sarah Litsey. LC 93-80690. 64p. 1994. 10. 00 (*0-8233-0490-6*) Golden Quill.

Silver Days. Sonia Levitin. LC 91-22581. 192p. (J). (gr. 3-7). 1992. reprint ed. pap. 3.95 (*0-689-71570-6*, Aladdin Paperbacks) S&S Childrens.

Silver Deceptions. Deborah Martin. 384p. 1994. 4.99 (*0-451-40434-3*, Topaz) NAL-Dutton.

Silver Dental Fillings: The Toxic Timebomb. Sam Ziff. 220p. 1984. pap. 14.95 (*0-943358-24-8*) Aurora Press.

***Silver Desires.** Stef A. Holm. 400p. 1997. mass mkt. 5.99 (*0-8439-4155-3*) Dorchester Pub Co.

Silver Dollar. Carol A. Russell. 57p. (Orig.). 1995. pap. 8.95 (*0-931122-81-3*) West End.

Silver Dollar City's ABC Words & Rhymes. Darrell Wiskur. Ed. by Silver Dollar City, Inc. Staff. (City Stories Ser.). (Illus.). (J). (ps-1). 1977. 1.99 (*0-686-19127-7*) Silver Dollar.

Silver Dollar Series No. 1. Robert Suttmeir. 200p. (Orig.). 1997. pap. 10.95 (*1-57532-053-3*) Press-Tige Pub.

Silver Dollars & Trade Dollars of the United States, Vols. 1-2: A Complete Encyclopedia. Q. David Bowers. (Illus.). 2192p. 1993. 195.00 (*0-943161-50-9*) Bowers & Merena.

Silver Dollars & Trade Dollars of the United States, Vols. 1-2: A Complete Encyclopedia, Set. Q. David Bowers. (Illus.). 2192p. 1993. text ed. 149.00 (*0-943161-48-7*); pap. text ed. 99.00 (*0-943161-49-5*) Bowers & Merena.

Silver Dolphin. Diana Lord. 448p. 1995. mass mkt. 4.99 (*0-8217-5040-2*, Zebra Kensgtn) Kensgtn Pub Corp.

Silver Dolphin. large type ed. Anne Weale. 1975. 25.99 (*0-85456-315-6*) Ulverscroft.

Silver Drawing Test of Cognition & Emotion. 2nd ed. Rawley A. Silver. LC 88-83150. (Illus.). 140p. (C). 1996. pap. text ed. 32.00 (*0-9621429-6-4*) Ablin Pr.

Silver Dreams: A Myth of the Sixth Sense. Joyce Petschek. LC 90-82143. (Illus.). 208p. (YA). (gr. 8-12). 1990. 29. 95 (*0-89087-619-3*); pap. 19.95 (*0-89087-620-7*) Celestial Arts.

Silver Drum: A Japanese Imperial Memoir. Princess Chichibu. 160p. 1996. 24.95 (*1-86034-004-0*, Pub. by Global Bks UK) Talman.

Silver Elephant, No. 2. Els. (J). 1987. 4.95 (*0-02-970370-0*, Free Press) Free Pr.

***Silver Fangs Tribebook.** Chris Howard. 1997. pap. text ed. 10.00 (*1-56504-331-6*) White Wolf.

Silver Flame. Hannah Howell. 384p. (Orig.). 1992. mass mkt. 4.50 (*0-380-76504-7*) Avon.

Silver Flame. Susan Johnson. (Orig.). 1993. 5.50 (*0-553-29959-X*) Bantam.

Silver Flatware: An Illustrated Guide to Pieces, Manufacturers & Care. Helen Cox. Ed. by Tracy Cox. (Illus.). 133p. (Orig.). 1994. pap. 12.95 (*0-9643982-0-6*) As You Like It.

Silver Flatware - English, Irish & Scottish: 1660-1980. Ian Pickford. (Illus.). 232p. 1983. 59.50 (*0-907462-35-9*) Antique Collect.

Silver Flower Coo. Charles H. Ford. pap. 3.50 (*0-686-73475-0*) Kulchur Foun.

Silver Folding Fruit Knives. Bill Karsten. (Illus.). 34p. 1986. pap. 5.00 (*0-940362-11-2*) Knife World.

Silver Fountain. large type ed. Michael Legat. 608p. 1984. 27.99 (*0-7089-8189-5*) Ulverscroft.

Silver Frenzy: A Guide to Huge Profits in Silver. James Digeorgia. Ed. by Martin D. Weiss. 69p. (Orig.). pap. text ed. 72.00 (*0-941739-04-X*) M D Weiss Pub.

Silver Fury. Jon Sharpe. (Trailsman Ser.: No. 138). 176p. (Orig.). 1993. pap. 3.50 (*0-451-17615-4*, Sig) NAL-Dutton.

Silver Gelatin: A User's Guide to Liquid Photographic Emulsions. Sarah Jones. 1996. pap. text ed. 29.95 (*0-8174-5848-4*, Amphoto) Watsn-Guptill.

***Silver Gelatin: A User's Guide to Liquid Photographic Emulsions.** Sarah Jones. 1996. pap. text ed. 29.95 (*0-8174-5885-9*) Watsn-Guptill.

Silver Ghost. Charlotte MacLeod. 1992. 4.50 (*0-446-77519-3*) Warner Bks.

Silver Gryphon. Mercedes Lackey & Larry Dixon. 352p. 1996. 21.95 (*0-88677-684-8*) DAW Bks.

Silver Gryphon. Mercedes Lackey & Larry Dixon. 1997. mass mkt. 5.99 (*0-88677-685-6*) DAW Bks.

Silver Guilt. large type ed. Laurence Meynell. 1989. 25.99 (*0-7089-2060-8*) Ulverscroft.

Silver-Halide Recording Materials: For Holography & Their Processing. 2nd ed. Arthur L. Schawlow & Hans I. Bjelkhagen. (Springer Series in Optical Sciences: Vol. 66). (Illus.). 440p. 1995. 74.95 (*3-540-58619-9*) Spr-Verlag.

Silver Halide Recording Materials for Holography & Their Processing. Hans I. Bjelkhagen. LC 93-3705. (Optical Sciences Ser.: Vol. 66). (Illus.). 450p. 1993. 89.00 (*0-387-56576-0*); write for info. (*3-540-56576-0*) Spr-Verlag.

Silver Hammer. Edward Ross. LC 92-46184. 192p. (Orig.). 1993. pap. 7.95 (*0-9635448-0-2*) Thornhse Pr.

S

An Asterisk (*) at the beginning of an entry indicates that the title is appearing in BIP for the first time.

Silver Hand. Stephen R. Lawhead. (Song of Albion Ser.: Bk. 2). 400p. 1993. mass mkt. 5.99 (*0-380-71647-X*, AvoNova) Avon.

Silver Highway. Marian Wells. (Treasure Quest Ser.: Vol. 3). 368p. (Orig.). 1989. pap. 8.99 (*1-55661-060-2*) Bethany Hse.

Silver Hills. Sandra Cox. LC 90-71999. 214p. (Orig.). 1992. pap. 8.95 (*1-56002-080-6*, Univ Edtns) Aegina Pr.

Silver Hillside: The Life & Times of Virginia City. Barbara Richnak. (Illus.). 200p. 1985. 29.95 (*0-915933-01-2*) Comstock NV Pub Co.

Silver Hollowware for Dining Elegance. Richard Osterberg. (Illus.). 256p. 1996. 39.95 (*0-88740-955-5*) Schiffer.

Silver Horde. Rex E. Beach. 1975. lib. bdg. 17.25 (*0-89966-013-4*) Buccaneer Bks.

Silver in England. Philippa Glanville. (Illus.). 366p. 1988. 85.00 (*0-04-748004-1*) Routledge Chapman & Hall.

***Silver in the Fur Trade, 1680-1820.** Martha W. Hamilton. 236p. 1997. pap. 45.00 (*0-9646087-0-7*, F1060) M Hamilton Pub.

Silver in the Golden State: Images & Essays Celebrating the History & Art of Silver in California. Ed. by Edgar Morse & Thomas Curran. (Artisans & the Arts Ser.). (Illus.). 130p. 1986. lib. bdg. 43.00 (*0-8026-0021-2*) Univ Pub Assocs.

Silver in the Unaka. Buddy Johnson. (Illus.). 147p. 1989. pap. 8.95 (*0-932807-36-4*) Overmountain Pr.

Silver in the Viking Age: A Regional-Economic Study. Birgittta Hardh & Lars-Gunnar Larsson. (Acta Archaeologica Lundensia Series 8: No. 25). (Illus.). 221p. (Orig.). 1996. pap. 46.50 (*91-22-01702-X*) Coronet Bks.

Silver Insights. Scott D. Dial. (Illus.). 105p. (Orig.). 1982. reprint ed. pap. 25.00 (*0-912497-00-9*) Silver D Invest Inc.

Silver Investments Volatility & Boredon for the Enduring. Michael E. Odell. Ed. by Joe Palmquist. (Illus.). 176p. (C). 1989. pap. text ed. 14.95 (*0-924380-01-2*) Veritas Rsch Pub.

Silver Jackass. large type ed. Frank Gruber. (Linford Mystery Library). 368p. 1994. pap. 15.99 (*0-7089-7479-1*, Linford) Ulverscroft.

***Silver Jewellery of Oman.** Rajab. Date not set. pap. write for info. (*1-86064-310-8*, Pub. by I B Tauris UK) St Martin.

Silver Jewelry Designs: Good, Better, Best. Nancy N. Schiffer. LC 96-15206. (Illus.). 304p. 1996. 59.95 (*0-7643-0052-0*) Schiffer.

Silver Jewelry Treasures. Nancy N. Schiffer. LC 92-63101. (Illus.). 144p. (Orig.). 1993. pap. 16.95 (*0-88740-458-8*) Schiffer.

Silver Key. TSR Hobbies Staff. 1996. 7.95 (*0-7869-0366-X*) TSR Inc.

Silver Key. A. Sepharial. 94p. 1963. reprint ed. spiral bd. 5.50 (*0-7873-0767-X*) Hlth Research.

Silver Key: A Guide to Speculators. 1991. lib. bdg. 79.95 (*0-8490-4539-8*) Gordon Pr.

Silver Key: A Guide to Speculators. A. Sepharial. 96p. 1996. pap. 14.95 (*1-56459-818-7*) Kessinger Pub.

Silver Key: A Scientific Guide to Speculation. A. Sepahrial. 136p. 1995. pap. 12.00 (*0-89540-240-8*, SB-240, Sun Bks) Sun Pub.

Silver Kingdom: Iran in History & Prophecy. Mark Hitchcock. 100p. (Orig.). 1993. pap. 5.95 (*1-879366-41-X*) Hearthstone OK.

Silver Kiss. Annette C. Klause. 208p. (J). (gr. 7 up). 1992. mass mkt. 3.99 (*0-440-21346-0*, LLL BDD) BDD Bks Young Read.

Silver Lady. Mary Lyons. 1993. mass mkt. 2.99 (*0-373-11610-1*, 1-11610-2) Harlequin Bks.

Silver Lady. large type ed. Jean Innes. (Linford Romance Library). 1991. pap. 15.99 (*0-7089-6978-X*) Ulverscroft.

Silver Lake Community Center: Clerk Type Job Sim. 3rd ed. Shinn. (KM - Office Procedures Ser.). 1989. pap. 24. 95 (*0-538-25890-X*) S-W Pub.

Silver Lake Community Center: Clerk-Typist Objectives. 3rd ed. Shinn. (KM - Office Procedures Ser.). 1989. 84. 95 (*0-538-25892-6*); 84.95 (*0-538-25895-0*) S-W Pub.

Silver Lake Community Center: Clerk-Typist Objectives. 3rd ed. Shinn. (KM - Office Procedures Ser.). 1989. 84. 95 (*0-538-25893-4*); 84.95 (*0-538-25894-2*) S-W Pub.

Silver Lake Community Center: Clerk Typist S. 3rd ed. Shinn. (KM - Office Procedures Ser.). 1989. 84.95 (*0-538-25891-8*) S-W Pub.

Silver Lake Twp. (Susquehanna Co. Pa.) Tax Rolls, 1878-1879. Compiled by D. P. Hawley. 64p. 1995. reprint ed. write for info. (*0-8328-6549-4*) Higginson Bk Co.

Silver Latin Epic. H. M. Currie. (Orig.). 1985. pap. 13.00 (*0-86516-129-1*) Bolchazy-Carducci.

Silver Leopard. large type ed. Zoe Cass. 379p. 1980. 25.99 (*0-7089-0554-4*) Ulverscroft.

Silver Lining. Christiane Heggan. 400p. (Orig.). 1995. mass mkt. 4.99 (*0-451-40594-3*, Onyx) NAL-Dutton.

Silver Lining: Personalized Scriptural Wake Services. Josephine M. Ford. LC 87-50614. 116p. 1987. 19.95 (*0-89622-331-0*) Twenty-Third.

Silver Lining: The Unexpected Advantage of Divorced Women. Nancy Summers. 273p. (Orig.). 1992. pap. 10. 00 (*0-9632318-0-4*) Vinyard Pubns.

Silver Linings: Thoughts on Finding the Bright Side. Andrews & McMeel Staff. (Illus.). 80p. 1994. 4.95 (*0-8362-3094-9*) Andrews & McMeel.

Silver Linings. Jayne Ann Krentz. 352p. (Orig.). 1991. mass mkt. 6.50 (*0-671-67624-5*); mass mkt. 4.95 (*0-671-31268-5*) PB.

***Silver Linings.** Kate Samperi. 1994. pap. text ed. 6.95 (*1-875169-29-6*, Pub. by S Milner AT) Sterling.

Silver Linings. Ted Tally. 1983. pap. 5.25 (*0-8222-1027-4*) Dramatists Play.

Silver Linings: Living with Cancer. Margaret C. Gilseth. 1995. 15.95 (*0-533-11253-2*) Vantage.

***Silver Linings: On a Cloudy Day Look For.** Dayle A. Shockley. LC 96-36052. 1997. pap. write for info. (*0-8163-1371-7*) Pacific Pr Pub Assn.

Silver Linings: Selling to the Expanding Mature Market. Herschell G. Lewis. LC 96-21808. 250p. 1996. 40.00 (*1-56625-058-7*) Bonus Books.

***Silver Linings: The Other Side of Cancer.** Ed. by Shirley Gollo & Elaine Glass. (Illus.). 260p. (Orig.). 1997. pap. 19.50 (*1-890504-01-7*) Oncology Nursing.

Silver Linings: Triumph of the Challenger 7. June S. Rogers. LC 95-36078. (Illus.). 128p. 1995. 14.95 (*1-57312-034-0*) Smyth & Helwys.

***Silver Linings: Triumphs of the Chronically Ill & Physical Challenged.** Shaena Engle. 1997. 24.95 (*1-57392-171-8*) Prometheus Bks.

Silver Linings - 2 Collection. Albert E. Gardner. (Illus.). 32p. (Orig.). 1994. pap. 19.95 (*0-9651248-0-0*) Gardner Graphics.

Silver Link. large type ed. Juliet Gray. (Linford Romance Library). 272p. 1992. 25.99 (*0-7089-2677-0*) Ulverscroft.

Silver Link. large type ed. Claire Lorrimer. (Charnwood Large Print Ser.). 736p. 1995. 27.99 (*0-7089-8815-6*, Charnwood) Ulverscroft.

Silver Link, the Silken Tie. large type ed. Lynn Granger. 1990. 25.99 (*0-7089-2327-5*) Ulverscroft.

Silver Locket. JoAnn Sands. 1994. 17.95 (*0-8034-9077-1*, 094431) Bouregy.

Silver Locket: A Charleston Christmas Storybook. Bruce Smith. LC 94-78135. (Illus.). 110p. (Orig.). (J). (ps up). 1994. pap. 11.95 (*0-9642620-0-2*) Marsh Wind Pr.

Silver Mania: A Study into the Causes of High Price Volatility of Silver. W. J. Streeter. 1984. lib. bdg. 73.00 (*90-277-1795-8*) Kluwer Ac.

Silver Masters of Mexico: Hector Aguilar & the Taller Borda. Penny C. Morrill. LC 96-1894. 224p. (gr. 10-13). 1996. 49.95 (*0-88740-961-X*) Schiffer.

***Silver Moon Song.** Genell Dellin. 336p. (Orig.). 1996. mass mkt. 5.99 (*0-380-78602-8*) Avon.

***Silver Morning.** Pearson. (J). 1998. write for info. (*0-15-274786-9*) HarBrace.

Silver Mountain. Dan Cushman. 448p. 1995. mass mkt., pap. text ed. 4.99 (*0-8439-3846-3*) Dorchester Pub Co.

Silver Nemesis. 1993. pap. 5.95 (*0-426-20340-2*, Dr Who) Carol Pub Group.

Silver Nights. Jane Feather. 352p. (Orig.). 1989. mass mkt. 4.99 (*0-380-75569-6*) Avon.

***Silver Noose.** Patricia G. Evans. 1998. mass mkt. 4.50 (*0-373-81047-4*, 1-81047-2) Harlequin Bks.

Silver Nutmeg. Norah Lofts. reprint ed. lib. bdg. 26.95 (*0-89190-229-5*, Rivercity Pr) Amereon Ltd.

Silver of Tiffany & Co., 1850-1987. Charles H. Carpenter, Jr. & Jane Zapata. Ed. by Katharine O. Parker & Editorial Associates Staff. LC 87-62188. (Illus.). 64p. 1987. pap. 8.00 (*0-87846-292-9*) Mus Fine Arts Boston.

Silver on the Tree. Susan Cooper. LC 77-5361. 256p. (J). (gr. 4-8). 1977. lib. bdg. 17.00 (*0-689-50088-2*, McElderry) S&S Childrens.

Silver on the Tree. Susan Cooper. LC 86-3341. (Dark Is Rising Sequence Ser.). 288p. (YA). (gr. 6 up). 1987. reprint ed. pap. 3.95 (*0-689-71152-2*, Collier Bks Young) S&S Childrens.

***Silver Packages: An Appalachian Christmas Story.** Cynthia Rylant. LC 96-53876. (Illus.). 32p. (J). (gr. k-3). 1997. 15.95 (*0-531-30051-X*); lib. bdg. 16.99 (*0-531-33051-6*) Orchard Bks Watts.

Silver Palate Cookbook. Julee Rosso et al. LC 81-43782. (Illus.). 416p. 1982. 22.95 (*0-89480-203-8*, 316); pap. 13. 95 (*0-89480-204-6*, 402) Workman Pub.

Silver Palate Cookbook in Large Print. large type ed. Julee Rosso & Sheila Lukins. LC 93-9108. (Illus.). 650p. 1993. reprint ed. pap. 18.95 (*0-8161-5765-0*, GK Hall) Thorndike Pr.

Silver Palate Cookbook in Large Print. large type ed. Julee Rosso & Sheila Lukins. LC 93-9108. (Illus.). 650p. 1993. reprint ed. 24.95 (*0-8161-5764-2*, GK Hall) Thorndike Pr.

Silver Palate Desserts: Recipes from the Classic American Cookbooks. Julee Rosso & Sheila Lukens. (Miniature Editions Ser.). (Illus.). 128p. 1995. 4.95 (*1-56138-498-4*, Running Pr Mini Edtns) Running Pr.

Silver Palate Good Times Cookbook. Julee Rosso et al. LC 85-5368. (Illus.). 416p. (Orig.). 1985. 22.95 (*0-89480-832-X*, 832) Workman Pub.

Silver Palate Good Times Cookbook. Julee Rosso et al. LC 85-5368. (Illus.). 416p. (Orig.). 1985. pap. 14.95 (*0-89480-831-1*, 831) Workman Pub.

Silver Path. Harris. (CHI & ENG.). (J). 16.95 (*1-85430-323-6*, 93425) Talman.

Silver Path. Christine Harris. LC 93-72342. (Illus.). 32p. (J). (gr. 2-5). 1994. 14.95 (*1-56397-338-3*) Boyds Mills Pr.

Silver Path. Christine Harris. (ENG & VIE.). (J). 16.95 (*1-85430-327-9*, 93381) Talman.

Silver Pen: Starting a Profitable Writing Business from a Lifetime of Experience. Alan N. Canton. LC 95-79412. 380p. (Orig.). 1996. pap. 22.95 (*1-883422-11-6*) Adams-Blake.

Silver Pencil. Alice Dalgliesh. 1995. 18.25 (*0-8446-6794-3*) Peter Smith.

Silver Pencil. Alice Dalgliesh. (Illus.). 248p. (YA). (gr. 7 up). 1991. pap. 4.99 (*0-14-034792-5*, Puffin) Puffin Bks.

Silver Pennies. Blanche J. Thompson. 16.95 (*0-8488-1487-8*) Amereon Ltd.

Silver Pennies. Blanche J. Thompson. (Illus.). 140p. 1991. reprint ed. lib. bdg. 25.95 (*0-89966-836-4*) Buccaneer Bks.

***Silver Petals.** Albert E. Gardner. (Illus.). 68p. (Orig.). 1996. pap. 19.95 (*0-9651248-1-9*) Gardner Graphics.

Silver Pigs. Lindsey Davis. 256p. 1991. mass mkt. 4.99 (*0-345-36907-6*) Ballantine.

Silver Pilgrimage. M. Anantanarayanan. (Indian Novels Ser.). 160p. 1976. pap. 2.75 (*0-89253-022-7*) Ind-US Inc.

Silver Pillow: A Tale of Witchcraft. Thomas M. Disch. 1988. pap. 10.00 (*0-9612970-7-7*) Mark Ziesing.

Silver Pitchers & Other Stories. Louisa May Alcott. (Works of Louisa May Alcott). 1989. reprint ed. lib. bdg. 79.00 (*0-7812-1635-4*) Rprt Serv.

Silver-Plated Age. Tom B. Jones. 185p. 1971. pap. 8.50 (*0-87291-018-0*) Coronado Pr.

Silver Poets of the Sixteenth Century. Ed. & Intro. by Douglas Brooks-Davies. 512p. 1994. 9.50 (*0-460-87440-3*, Everyman's Classic Lib) C E Tuttle.

Silver Point: The Ancient Art of Drawing in Solid Silver & How to Add Colour to It. Patricia Carter. (Illus.). 32p. (Orig.). 1996. pap. 10.95 (*0-85532-800-2*, 28002, Pub. by Search Pr UK) A Schwartz & Co.

Silver Pony. Lynd Ward. (J). (ps-3). 1992. pap. 6.95 (*0-395-64377-5*) HM.

Silver Pony: A Story in Pictures. Lynd Ward. LC 72-5402. (Illus.). 192p. (J). (gr. k-3). 1973. 17.95 (*0-395-14753-0*) HM.

Silver Princess, Golden Knight. Sharon Green. 352p. (Orig.). 1993. mass mkt. 4.99 (*0-380-76625-6*, AvoNova) Avon.

***Silver Princess in Oz.** Ruth P. Thompson. (Illus.). 304p. (J). (gr. 3 up). 1996. reprint ed. pap. 12.95 (*0-929605-56-X*) Books Wonder.

Silver Queen: The Fabulous Story of Baby Doe Tabor. Caroline Bancroft. (Illus.). 80p. 1955. pap. 4.95 (*0-933472-21-8*) Johnson Bks.

***Silver Rain Brown.** Mary-Claire Helldorfer. LC 97-17738. (Illus.). (J). 1998. write for info. (*0-395-73093-7*) HM.

Silver Recovery Techniques: AIIM TR4-1989 (A1993) Association for Information & Image Management Staff. (Technical Reports). 16p. (Orig.). 1989. pap. 33.00 (*0-89258-191-3*, TR04) Assn Inform & Image Mgmt.

Silver Ribbon Skinny. Marilyn W. Seguin. (Illus.). 96p. (J). (gr. 4-10). 1996. pap. 12.95 (*0-8283-2020-9*) Branden Pub Co.

Silver Rights. Constance Curry. LC 95-21731. 288p. 1995. 21.95 (*1-56512-095-7*, 72095) Algonquin Bks.

Silver Rights. Constance Curry. 288p. 1996. pap. 13.00 (*0-15-600479-8*); pap. 21.95 (*0-15-600485-2*) HarBrace.

Silver Rings & Other Stories. Gershon Kranzler. (Illus.). 162p. (YA). reprint ed. 10.00 (*0-8266-0329-7*, Merkos Llnyonei Chinuch) Kehot Pubn Soc.

Silver Rose. Ellen Cooney. LC 79-52862. 104p. (Orig.). 1979. pap. 5.95 (*0-9602912-8-8*) Duir Press.

***Silver Rose.** Jane Feather. 1997. mass mkt. 5.99 (*0-553-57524-4*, Fanfare) Bantam.

Silver Saddles. Cap Iversen. (Dakota Ser.: No. 2). 222p. (Orig.). 1993. pap. 7.95 (*1-55583-213-X*) Alyson Pubns.

Silver San Juan. Ernest Ingersoll. Ed. by William R. Jones. (Illus.). 24p. 1977. reprint ed. pap. 2.95 (*0-89646-025-8*) Vistabooks.

Silver Scream. David J. Schow. 512p. 1988. pap. 3.95 (*0-8125-2555-8*) Tor Bks.

Silver Screen in the Silver City: A History of Cinemas in Aberdeen, 1896-1987. M. Thomson. (Illus.). 350p. 1988. pap. 20.00 (*0-08-036402-0*, Pub. by Aberdeen U Pr) Macmillan.

Silver Season: Twenty-Five Years of Braves Baseball in Atlanta. Ed. by Jackie Blackburn-Tyson. LC 90-70280. (Illus.). 64p. (Orig.). 1990. pap. 6.95 (*0-9626248-0-2*) SportsPrint.

Silver Seasons: The Story of the Rochester Red Wings. Jim Mandelaro & Scott Pitoniak. LC 95-50078. (Illus.). (C). 1996. pap. 17.95 (*0-8156-0379-7*, MASSP); text ed. 39. 95 (*0-8156-2703-3*, MASS) Syracuse U Pr.

***Silver Seekers.** Remi Nadeau. (Illus.). 300p. (Orig.). 1997. pap. 16.95 (*0-9627104-7-4*) Crest Pubs.

Silver Shadows. Elaine Cunningham. (Forgotten Realms Ser.). 1996. pap. 5.99 (*0-7869-0498-4*) TSR Inc.

***Silver Shadows.** Sylvie Kurtz. 320p. (Orig.). 1997. mass mkt. 4.99 (*0-505-52202-0*, Love Spell) Dorchester Pub Co.

Silver Shadows: A Directory & History of Early Photography in Chico & the Twelve Counties of Northern California. Peter Palmquist et al. LC 92-73662. 84p. 1993. pap. 24.95 (*0-9634512-0-0*) Chico Mus Assn.

Silver Ships-Green Fields. Sara C. Juengst. (Illus.). 52p. (Orig.). (J). (gr. 1-6). 1986. pap. 5.95 (*0-377-00161-9*) Friendship Pr.

***Silver Shoes for a Princess.** James P. Hogan. 288p. 1997. mass mkt. 5.99 (*0-671-87792-5*) Baen Bks.

Silver Shot: A Derby Man Adventure. Gary McCarthy. LC 96-68189. (Derby Man Ser.: Vol. 7). (Illus.). 224p. 1997. 20.00 (*0-938313-16-9*) E B Houchin.

Silver Shroud. large type ed. Donna Creekmore. (Linford Mystery Library). 448p. 1992. pap. 15.99 (*0-7089-7224-1*) Ulverscroft.

Silver Simply Elegant: 25th Anniversary of Simply Elegant. Pearl S. Gordon. (Illus.). 136p. 1995. lib. bdg. 21.95 (*0-9600492-5-8*) Simply Elegant.

Silver Sinners & Saints: A History of Old Silver Reef, Utah. Paul D. Proctor & Morris A. Shirts. (Illus.). 225p. (Orig.). 1991. text ed. 19.95 (*0-9625042-1-1*); pap. text ed. 17.95 (*0-9625042-2-X*) Paulmar.

Silver Situation in the United States. Frank W. Taussig. LC 73-95079. (Select Bibliographies Reprint Ser.). 1977. 21.95 (*0-8369-5079-8*) Ayer.

Silver Skates. William A. Kottmeyer. 1972. text ed. 7.96 (*0-07-034019-6*) McGraw.

Silver Slaughter. Jon Sharpe. 1989. pap. 2.95 (*0-318-42960-8*, Sig) NAL-Dutton.

Silver Slippers. Elizabeth Koda-Callan. LC 89-40370. (Illus.). 40p. (J). (ps-3). 1989. 12.95 (*0-89480-618-1*, 1618) Workman Pub.

Silver Spitfire. large type ed. Roger Harvey. 1991. 25.99 (*0-7089-2391-7*) Ulverscroft.

Silver Splendor. Barbara D. Smith. 384p. 1989. pap. 3.95 (*0-380-75731-1*) Avon.

Silver Spoon & the Passers by. John Galsworthy. 23.95 (*0-8488-0064-8*) Amereon Ltd.

Silver Spoon Murders. D. W. Smith. 272p. 1988. 15.95 (*0-8184-0460-4*) Carol Pub Group.

Silver Spoon Restaurant Cookbook: Bakery Recipes from Duvall. Donna D. Beeson. (Illus.). 1995. pap. 8.95 (*0-9641540-1-3*) L D Pubng.

Silver Spoons & Tarnished Times: Events & Occasions, 1921-1940. Louis Hill. LC 89-38509. 192p. (Orig.). 1990. pap. 9.95 (*0-931832-41-1*) Fithian Pr.

Silver Sports Series, 4 vols., Set. Carol Nicklaus. (Illus.). (J). (ps-1). 1991. pap. 11.80 (*0-671-31272-3*, Silver Pr NJ) Silver Burdett Pr.

Silver Springs. Carolyn Lampman. 384p. 1996. mass mkt. 3.99 (*0-06-108432-8*, Harp PBks) HarpC.

Silver Stallion: A Novel of Korea. Ahn Junghyo. LC 89-39219. 269p. 1993. pap. 13.00 (*1-56947-003-0*) Soho Press.

Silver Stampede. Neill C. Wilson. LC 74-165650. (Select Bibliographies Reprint Ser.). 1977. reprint ed. 26.95 (*0-8369-5969-8*) Ayer.

Silver Stampede: The Career of Death Valley's Hell-Camp, Old Panamint. Neill C. Wilson. (Illus.). 360p. 1986. reprint ed. pap. 12.00 (*0-87380-156-3*) Rio Grande.

***Silver Star, Vol. 20.** Gilbert Morris. LC 97-4647. (House of Winslow Ser.). 336p. 1997. pap. text ed. 9.99 (*1-55661-688-0*) Bethany Hse.

Silver State: Nevada's Heritage Reinterpreted. James W. Hulse. LC 90-19349. (Wilbur S. Shepperson Series in History & Humanities). (Illus.). 392p. 1991. 31.95 (*0-87417-165-2*); pap. 14.95 (*0-87417-166-0*) U of Nev Pr.

***Silver Stirrups.** Bonnie Bryant. (The Saddle Club Ser.: No. 65). 144p. (J). 1997. pap. 3.99 (*0-553-48420-6*, Skylark BDD) BDD Bks Young Read.

Silver Stone: Keeper of the Hidden Ways, Bk. 2. Joel Rosenberg. 1996. 23.00 (*0-688-13715-6*) Morrow.

Silver Strand. large type ed. Gimone Hall. (Romance Ser.). 448p. 1992. 25.99 (*0-7089-2747-5*) Ulverscroft.

Silver Street Woman. Les Savage, Jr. 352p. (Orig.). 1995. mass mkt., pap. text ed. 4.99 (*0-8439-3854-4*) Dorchester Pub Co.

Silver Strike: The True Story of Silver Mining in the Coeur d'Alenes. William T. Stoll. LC 91-402. (Idaho Yesterdays Ser.). (Illus.). 287p. (C). 1991. reprint ed. pap. 15.95 (*0-89301-147-9*) U of Idaho Pr.

Silver Sunbeam: A Practical & Theoretical Text-Book on Sun-Drawing & Photographic Printing, Comprehending All the Wet & Dry Processes at Present Known As Collodion, Albumen, Gelatine, Wax, Resin & Silver... 4th ed. J. Towler. 378p. 1995. reprint ed. lib. bdg. 45.00 (*0-8328-4493-4*) Higginson Bk Co.

Silver Sunset for the Lazy T. Ronald B. Parsley. 1994. pap. 10.95 (*0-533-11003-3*) Vantage.

Silver Surfer. Stan Lee & John Buscema. (Marvel Masterworks Ser.: Vol. 15). 206p. 1990. 34.95 (*0-87135-631-7*) Marvel Entmnt.

Silver Surfer: Homecoming. Jim Starlin & Bill Reinhold. 64p. 1991. 12.95 (*0-87135-855-7*) Marvel Entmnt.

Silver Surfer: Judgement Day. Stan Lee & John Buscema. 64p. 1988. 14.95 (*0-87135-427-6*) Marvel Entmnt.

Silver Surfer: Judgment Day. Stan Lee & John Buscema. 64p. 1990. reprint ed. pap. 10.95 (*0-87135-663-5*) Marvel Entmnt.

Silver Surfer: Parable. Stan Lee & Moebius. (Illus.). 72p. 1988. 19.95 (*0-87135-491-8*) Marvel Entmnt.

Silver Surfer: Rebirth of Thanos. Jim Starlin. (Illus.). 1993. pap. 12.95 (*0-87135-968-5*) Marvel Entmnt.

Silver Surfer: The Enslavers. Stan Lee et al. 80p. 1990. 16. 95 (*0-87135-617-1*) Marvel Entmnt.

Silver Surrender. 1996. pap. 2.99 (*0-8217-5482-3*) Kensgtn Pub Corp.

Silver Swimmer: Poems. Rosalie Boyle. LC 74-33990. 1975. pap. 5.00 (*0-914562-01-0*) Merriam-Eddy.

Silver Swimmer: The Struggle for Survival of the Wild Atlantic Salmon. Richard Buck. 320p. 1993. 35.00 (*1-55821-251-5*) Lyons & Burford.

Silver Sword. Ian Serraillier. LC 59-6556. (Illus.). (J). (gr. 7-9). 1959. 30.95 (*0-87599-104-1*) S G Phillips.

Silver Thorns. Amanda Harte & Christine Tayntor. 384p. 1996. mass mkt. 4.99 (*0-7860-0302-2*, Pinncle Kensgtn) Kensgtn Pub Corp.

Silver Thread: The Ups & Downs of a Mennonite Family in Mission (1895-1995) Joseph C. Shenk. LC 96-23958. (Illus.). 224p. 1996. pap. 9.95 (*1-56148-207-2*) Good Bks PA.

Silver Threads. Arthur Bradley. (Illus.). 1994. 19.95 (*0-9636777-1-3*) Aplomb Pub.

Silver Threads: A Life Alone. John Williams. 1996. 23.95 (*0-563-36941-8*, BBC-Parkwest) Parkwest Pubns.

Silver Threads: A Personal Look at the First Twenty-Five Years of the Registry of Interpreters for the Deaf. Lou Fant. 152p. (Orig.). (C). 1990. pap. text ed. 12.95 (*0-916883-08-6*) RID Pubns.

Silver Threads: Twenty-Five Years of Parapsychology Research. Ed. by Beverly Kane et al. LC 92-28551. 384p. 1993. text ed. 75.00 (*0-275-94161-2*, C4161, Praeger Pubs) Greenwood.

Silver Tombstone. large type ed. Frank Gruber. (Linford Mystery Large Print Ser.). 336p. 1995. pap. 15.99 (*0-7089-7730-8*, Linford) Ulverscroft.

Silver Tombstone of Edward Schieffelin. Lonnie E. Underhill. LC 78-66100. (Illus.). 64p. 1979. 19.95 (*0-933234-01-5*); pap. 10.95 (*0-933234-00-7*) Roan Horse.

***Silver Tomorrows.** Susan Plunkett. 352p. 1997. mass mkt. 5.99 (*0-515-12047-2*) Jove Pubns.

Silver-Tongued Devil. Jennifer Blake. 336p. 1996. mass mkt. 4.99 (*0-449-14938-2*) Fawcett.

An Asterisk (*) at the beginning of an entry indicates that the title is appearing in BIP for the first time.

*Silver-Tongued Devil. Jennifer Blake. 384p. 1996. 24.00 (0-7278-5114-4) Severn Hse.
Silver-Tongued Devil. large type ed. Jennifer Blake. 541p. 1996. 23.95 (0-7862-0669-1, Thorndike Lrg Prnt) Thorndike Pr.
Silver Tower. Dale Brown. 1989. mass mkt. 6.99 (0-425-11529-1) Berkley Pub.
Silver Treasure: Myths & Legends of the World. Geraldine McCaughrean. (Illus.). 130p. (J). 1997. 19.95 (0-689-81322-8) S&S Childrens.
Silver Treasure from Early Byzantium: The Kaper Karaon & Related Treasures. Marlia Mundell Mango. LC 86-50138. (Illus.). 125p. (Orig.). 1986. pap. 35.00 (0-911886-32-X) Walters Art.
Silver Unicorn: A Telecommunications Simulation. Olsen. (KM - Office Procedures Ser.). 1994. pap. 19.95 (0-538-61066-2) S-W Pub.
Silver Wands. Marion M. Boyd. LC 70-144724. (Yale Series of Younger Poets: No. 17). reprint ed. 18.00 (0-404-53817-7) AMS Pr.
Silver Waves. Vella Munn. (American Romance Ser.: No. 444). 1992. mass mkt. 3.39 (0-373-16444-0, 1-16444-1) Harlequin Bks.
Silver Wedding. Maeve Binchy. 432p. 1990. reprint ed. mass mkt. 6.99 (0-440-20777-0) Dell.
Silver Wheel: Women's Myths & Mysteries in the Celtic Tradition. Marguerite Elsbeth & Kenneth Johnson. LC 96-43652. (Celtic Wisdom Ser.). (Illus.). 224p. (Orig.). 1996. pap. 14.95 (1-56718-371-9) Llewellyn Pubns.
Silver Whistle. Patrick B. Mace. (Orig.). (J). (gr. k up). 1986. pap. 5.00 (0-87602-250-6) Anchorage.
Silver Whistle. Robert E. McEnroe. 1950. pap. 5.25 (0-8222-1028-2) Dramatists Play.
Silver Wings. Grace L. Hill. (Grace Livingston Hill Ser.: No. 37). 288p. 1996. pap. 4.99 (0-8423-5914-1) Tyndale.
Silver Wings. large type ed. Grace L. Hill. (General Ser.). 315p. 1992. lib. bdg. 19.95 (0-8161-4722-1, GK Hall) Thorndike Pr.
Silver Wings. Grace L. Hill. reprint ed. lib. bdg. 23.95 (0-89190-030-6, Rivercity Pr) Amereon Ltd.
Silver Wings: A History of the United States Air Force. Walter J. Boyne. LC 92-42939. (Illus.). 336p. 1993. 50.00 (0-671-78537-0) S&S Trade.
Silver Wings: RAF Biplane Fighters Between the Wars. Owen Thetford & Alec Lumsden. (Illus.). 228p. 1994. 39.95 (1-85532-374-5, Pub. by Osprey Pubng Ltd UK) Motorbooks Intl.
Silver Wings in Pacific Skies Australia's First Trans-Pacific Airline: British Commonwealth Pacific Airlines. Harry N. Moore. 166p. 1995. 59.00 (0-614-11878-6, Pub. by Boolarong Pubns AT) St Mut.
Silver Wings, Pinks & Greens: Uniforms, Wings & Insignia of USAAF Airmen in WWII. Jon A. Maguire. (Illus.). 224p. 1994. 45.00 (0-88740-578-9) Schiffer.
Silver Wings Santiago Blue. Janet Dailey. 1994. pap. 6.50 (0-671-87515-9) PB.
Silver Witch. Sue Rich. Ed. by Carolyn Tolley. 320p. (Orig.). 1995. mass mkt. 5.99 (0-671-79409-4) PB.
Silver Wood. James Facos. 1977. pap. 1.75 (0-686-38383-4) Eldridge Pub.
Silver Years of the Alaska Canned Salmon Industry: An Album of Historical Photos. Alaska Geographic Staff & Laurence Freeburn. (Alaska Geographic Ser.: Vol. 3, No. 4). (Illus.). 168p. 1991. reprint ed. pap. 19.95 (0-88240-082-7) Alaska Geog Soc.
Silver-Zinc Battery: Best Practices, Facts & Reflections. Albert Himy. 1995. 24.50 (0-533-11413-6) Vantage.
Silverado Squatters. limited ed. Robert Louis Stevenson. (Illus.). 160p. 1996. 425.00 (0-614-16023-5) Arion Pr.
Silverado Squatters. Robert Louis Stevenson. 115p. 1989. reprint ed. lib. bdg. 14.95 (0-89966-587-X) Buccaneer Bks.
Silverado Squatters. Robert Louis Stevenson. 112p. 1996. reprint ed. pap. 10.95 (1-56279-097-8) Mercury Hse Inc.
Silvergirls Surgery: The Breast. Shumacker. 1991. write for info. (0-941432-30-0) Mosby Yr Bk.
Silverhand: The Arcana, Bk. I. Morgan Llywelyn & Michael Scott. (Arcana Ser.: Bk. I). 432p. (Orig.). 1995. 22.00 (0-671-87652-X) Baen Bks.
Silverhand No. 1: The Arcana, Bk. I. Morgan Llywelyn & Michael Scott. 432p. 1996. mass mkt. 5.99 (0-671-87714-3) Baen Bks.
Silverhawks: The Planet-Eater. Illus. by Fernando Fernandez. (J). (gr. k-5). 1987. pap. 1.95 (0-448-48631-8, G&D) Putnam Pub Group.
Silverhawks: The Sun Bandits. Illus. by Fernando Fernandez. (J). (gr. k-5). 1987. pap. 1.95 (0-448-48632-6, G&D) Putnam Pub Group.
Silverhawks: The Terror of the Time-Stopper. Illus. by Fernando Fernandez. (J). (gr. k-5). 1987. pap. 1.95 (0-448-48633-4, G&D) Putnam Pub Group.
Silverheels (Graphic Album) Jones et al. (Illus.). 1990. pap. 7.95 (0-913035-22-X) Eclipse Bks.
Silverhill. Phyllis A. Whitney. 192p. 1981. mass mkt. 5.99 (0-449-24094-0) Fawcett.
Silvering the Flute. Sandra Soli. 24p. 1995. reprint ed. 5.00 (0-936908-06-8) Broncho Pr.
Silverlake Heat. Carol Schmidt. 224p. 1993. pap. 9.95 (1-56280-031-0) Naiad Pr.
Silverlake Stranger, Vol. 11. Sally Marcey. LC 92-36889. (Choice Adventures Ser.: Vol. 11). (J). 1993. pap. 4.99 (0-8423-5048-9) Tyndale.
Silverless Mirrors: Book, Self, & Postmodern American Fiction. Charles Caramello. LC 83-14841. 1983. pap. 27.95 (0-8130-0722-4) U Press Fla.
*Silverlight. Morgan Llywelyn & Michael Scott. (Arcana Ser.: Vol. 2). 432p. 1997. mass mkt. 5.99 (0-671-87790-9) Baen Bks.
Silverlight Bk. 2: The Arcana. Morgan Llywelyn & Michael Scott. 416p. 1996. 21.00 (0-671-87728-3) Baen Bks.
Silverlock. John M. Myers. (Orig.). 1993. reprint ed. lib. bdg. 18.95 (0-89968-409-2, Lghtyr Pr) Buccaneer Bks.
Silverlock, Bk. 5. John Myer. LC 83-1039. 544p. (Orig.). (J). (gr. 3-5). 1984. mass mkt. 6.99 (0-441-76674-9) Ace Bks.
Silverlock Companion: The Life & Works of John Myers Myers. Ed. by Fred Lerner. (Illus.). 52p. (Orig.). 1988. pap. 7.95 (0-910619-02-6) Niekas Pubns.
Silverlock Companion: The Life & Works of John Myers Myers. Fred Lerner. LC 89-861. 52p. (Orig.). (C). 1989. reprint ed. lib. bdg. 25.00 (0-8095-6850-0) Borgo Pr.
Silvermane & Other Stories. large type ed. Zane Grey. (General Ser.). 218p. 1991. lib. bdg. 17.95 (0-8161-5076-1, GK Hall) Thorndike Pr.
Silverman's Game: A Special Class of Two-Person Zero-Sum Games. Gerald A. Heuer & U. Leopold-Wildburger. (Lecture Notes in Economics & Mathematical Systems Ser.: No. 424). (Illus.). 283p. 1995. 65.00 (3-540-59232-6) Spr-Verlag.
Silverplated Flatware. 4th rev. ed. Tere Hagan. (Illus.). 368p. 1995. pap. 14.95 (0-89145-428-4, 2096) Collector Bks.
Silverpoints: With Spirtual Poems. John Gray. LC 93-41357. (Decadents, Symbolists, Anti-Decadents Ser.). 1994. 48.00 (1-85477-144-2, Pub. by Woodstock Bks UK) Cassell.
Silversmith in Eighteenth-Century Williamsburg. rev. ed. Colonial Williamsburg Foundation Staff. (Historic Trades Ser.). (Illus.). 37p. (Orig.). 1972. pap. 2.95 (0-910412-21-9) Colonial Williamsburg.
Silversmithing & Art Metal for Schools, Tradesmen, Craftsmen. rev. ed. Murray Bovin. LC 64-2766. (Illus.). 176p. (C). 1977. 22.95 (0-910280-04-5); pap. 17.95 (0-910280-03-7) Bovin.
Silversmithing (FET) William Seitz & Finegold. LC 82-70657. 480p. 1983. 39.95 (0-8019-7232-9) Chilton.
Silversmiths. 2nd ed. Leonard E. Fisher. LC 96-16607. (Colonial Craftsmen Ser.). (Illus.). 48p. (J). (gr. 4 up). 1996. reprint ed. lib. bdg. 14.95 (0-7614-0478-3, Benchmark NY) Marshall Cavendish.
Silversmith's Manual. Bernard Cuzner. (Illus.). 209p. 1979. 35.00 (0-7198-0062-5, Pub. by NAG Press UK) Antique Collect.
Silversmiths of Birmingham & Their Marks: 1750-1980. Kenneth Jones. (Illus.). 410p. 1981. 95.00 (0-7198-0002-1, Pub. by NAG Press UK) Antique Collect.
Silversmiths of Lancaster, Pennsylvania 1730-1850. Vivian S. Gerstell. LC 72-86855. (Illus.). 160p. 1972. 9.50 (0-915010-17-8) Sutter House.
Silversmiths of North Carolina,1696-1860. rev. ed. Mary R. Peacock. (Illus.). xxix, 301p. 1984. pap. 12.00 (0-86526-215-2) NC Archives.
Silversmiths of North Carolina,1696-1860. rev. ed. Mary R. Peacock. (Illus.). xxix, 301p. 1984. 20.00 (0-86526-201-2) NC Archives.
Silversmiths of Virginia. George B. Cutten. (Illus.). 1976. reprint ed. 17.50 (0-87517-040-4) Dietz.
Silverswept. Linda Ladd. (Avon Romance Ser.). 368p. 1987. pap. 3.95 (0-380-75204-2) Avon.
Silversword. Phyllis A. Whitney. 1988. mass mkt. 5.99 (0-449-21278-5) Fawcett.
Silverthorn. Raymond E. Feist. 352p. 1986. mass mkt. 6.50 (0-553-27054-0, Spectra) Bantam.
*Silverthrone. Wayne Davis. 256p. 1997. mass mkt. 4.99 (0-425-15764-4) Berkley Pub.
Silvertip's Roundup. large type ed. Max Brand. (General Ser.). 246p. 1990. lib. bdg. 17.95 (0-8161-4979-8, GK Hall) Thorndike Pr.
Silverton. rev. ed. Jack L. Benham. (Illus.). 64p. (Orig.). 1981. reprint ed. pap. 3.95 (0-941026-02-7) Bear Creek Pub.
Silverton - Ouray - Telluride - Lake City, CO. rev. ed. Ed. by Trails Illustrated Staff. (Illus.). 1995. Folded topographical map. 8.99 (0-925873-92-6) Trails Illustrated.
Silverton - Then & Now: A Pictorial Journey Through Silverton, Colorado 1874-1922. Allan G. Bird. (Illus.). 90p. (Orig.). 1990. pap. text ed. 4.95 (0-9619382-3-4) A G Bird.
Silverton Gold: The Story of Colorado's Largest Gold Mine. rev. ed. Allan G. Bird. (Illus.). 1986. pap. text ed. 9.95 (0-9619382-4-2) A G Bird.
Silverton Gold: The Story of Colorado's Largest Underground Gold Mine - 1873 to 1986. Allan G. Bird. (Illus.). 1986. pap. 9.95 (0-9619382-2-6) A G Bird.
Silvertown 1917. Michael Paris. 1993. pap. 8.00 (0-86025-401-1, Pub. by Ian Henry Pubns UK) Empire Pub Srvs.
*Silverware of the 20th Century: The Top 250 Patterns. 1997. pap. 24.95 (0-676-60086-7) Random.
*Silverwing. Kenneth Oppel. LC 97-10977. (J). 1997. 16.00 (0-689-81529-8) S&S Childrens.
Silverwork & Jewelry Handbook of 1903. William R. Lethaby. (Illus.). 343p. 1988. reprint ed. pap. 25.00 (0-87556-362-7) Saifer.
Silvester & the Oogaloo Boogalo. Teddi Doleski. (J). 1990. pap. 2.95 (0-8091-6596-1) Paulist Pr.
Silvestre y la Piedrecita Magica. William Steig. Tr. by Teresa Mlawer from ENG. (Illus.). 40p. (J). (gr. 3). 1990. pap. 5.95 (0-9625162-7-9); lib. bdg. 12.95 (0-9625162-0-1) Lectorum Pubns.
Silvestre y La Piedrecita Magica. William Steig. (Illus.). (SPA.). (J). (gr. 2-5). 1992. 22.95 incl. audio (0-87499-272-9); pap. 15.95 incl. audio (0-87499-271-0) Live Oak Media.
Silvestre y La Piedrecita Magica, 4 bks., Set. William Steig. (Illus.). (J). (gr. 2-5). 1992. pap. 33.95 incl. audio (0-87499-273-7) Live Oak Media.
Silvestre y la Piedrecita Magica: A Study Guide. Marina Petralia. Ed. by J. Friedland & R. Kesslere. (Novel-Ties Ser.). (SPA.). (J). (gr. k-2). 1996. pap. text ed. 14.95 (1-56982-728-1) Lrn Links.
Silvia Dubois: A Biografy of the Slav Who Whipt Her Mistres & Gand Her Fredom. Cornelius W. Larison. Tr. & Intro. by Jared C. Lobdell. (Schomburg Library of Nineteenth-Century Black Women Writers). 288p. 1988. 29.95 (0-19-505239-0) OUP.
Silvia Dubois: A Biografy of the Slav Who Whipt Her Mistres & Gand Her Fredom. C. W. Larison. Tr. & Intro. by Jared C. Lobdell. (Schomburg Library of Nineteenth-Century Black Women Writers). (Illus.). 168p. 1990. reprint ed. pap. 9.95 (0-19-506671-5) OUP.
Silvia Kolbowski: Eleven Projects. Silvia Kolbowski et al. Tr. by Donald McGrath & Joachim Neugroschel from FRE. (Critical Convergence Ser.). (Illus.). 112p. (Orig.). (ENG, FRE & GER.). (C). 1992. pap. 20.00 (0-9633328-0-5) Border Edits.
Silvicultural Manual for the Solomon Islands. G. Chaplin. 305p. 1993. pap. 90.00 (0-902500-44-9, Pub. by Nat Res Inst UK) St Mut.
Silvicultural of Indian Trees, 3 vols., Set. R. S. Troup. 1280p. (C). 1986. reprint ed. pap. 2,250.00 (81-7089-045-4, Pub. by Intl Bk Distr II) St Mut.
Silvicultural Systems. John D. Matthews. (Illus.). 304p. 1991. reprint ed. pap. 45.00 (0-19-854670-X) OUP.
Silviculture. W. Kostler. 436p. 1990. 245.00 (81-7089-128-0, Pub. by Intl Bk Distr II) St Mut.
Silviculture & Propagation of Indian Forest Trees. Ram Parkash. 400p. 1990. 210.00 (81-7089-113-2, Pub. by Intl Bk Distr II) St Mut.
Silviculture Research Code. A. L. Griffith. (C). 1991. 275.00 (81-7136-022-X, Pub. by Periodical Expert II) St Mut.
Silvie's Life. Marianne Rogoff. Ed. by Wendy Logsdon. LC 95-60133. 135p. (Orig.). 1995. pap. 9.95 (1-57143-045-8, Zenobia Pr) RDR Bks.
Silvija: A Riga Nocturne. Karlis Freivalds. Ed. by Bradley R. Strahan. (Black Buzzard Illustrated Poetry Chapbook Ser.). (Illus.). 20p. (Orig.). 1989. pap. 4.50 (0-938872-11-7) Black Buzzard.
Silvio: Congressman for Everyone, a Biography of Silvio Conti. Peter E. Lynch. (Illus.). 192p. 1997. 24.95 (0-86534-256-3) Sunstone Pr.
Silvio E. Petricciani: the Evolution of Gaming in Nevada: The Twenties to the Eighties. Intro. by Kathryn M. Totton. 440p. 1982. lib. bdg. 62.50 (1-56475-224-0); fiche write for info. (1-56475-225-9) U NV Oral Hist.
Silvio Gesell: Money Reformer. L. Wise. 1982. lib. bdg. 59.95 (0-87700-393-9) Revisionist Pr.
Silvio Scionti: Remembering a Master Pianist & Teacher. Jack Guerry. LC 91-10498. (Illus.). 220p. 1991. 25.00 (0-929398-27-0) UNTX Pr.
Silvo. large type ed. Vic J. Hanson. (Linford Western Library). 240p. 1996. pap. 15.99 (0-7089-7881-9, Linford) Ulverscroft.
Silyated Surfaces, Vol. 2. D. Leyden & W. Collins. (Midland Macromolecular Monographs). 380p. 1980. text ed. 318.00 (0-677-13370-7) Gordon & Breach.
Sim & Cain: Practice & Procedure of the High Court & Court of Appeal of New Zealand. 12th ed. ring bd. write for info. (0-409-66761-7, NZ) MICHIE.
Sim & Scott's "A" Level English Law. 7th ed. R. S. Sim & P. J. Pace. 1991. pap. 26.00 (0-406-51760-6, U.K.) MICHIE.
*Sim Chung & the River Dragon: A Folktale from Korea. Ellen Schecter. LC 96-30692. (Bank Street Ready-to-Read Bks.). (Illus.). 48p. (J). (gr. 2-4). 1997. lib. bdg. 17.27 (0-8368-1695-1) Gareth Stevens Inc.
Sim Chung & the River Dragon, Level Three: A Folktale from Korea. Ellen Schecter. LC 92-7652. 48p. (J). (ps-3). 1993. pap. 3.99 (0-553-37109-6) Bantam.
SimCity 2000: Authorized Strategy Guide. Bradygames Staff. (Illus.). 304p. (Orig.). 1995. 19.99 (1-56686-205-1) Brady Pub.
Sim Gadgetronics -- a Retail Decision Making Simulation. Simon & Schuster Staff. (SB - Marketing Education Ser.). 1985. pap. 19.95 (0-538-19010-8) S-W Pub.
SIM-Simplified. 3rd ed. Goodman & Fosegan. (KG - Filing/Records Management Ser.). 1987. 21.95 (0-538-11146-1) S-W Pub.
Sim Strategy -- a Computer-Assisted Simulation. Patton & Tangedahl. (DF - Computer Applications Ser.). 1986. pap. 13.95 (0-538-10070-2) S-W Pub.
Sim Webb, Casey Jone's Fireman. Nancy Farmer. (Illus.). 1997. pap. write for info. (0-8037-1929-9); lib. bdg. write for info. (0-8037-1930-2) Dial Bks Young.
*Sima Milka. Thomas Kammerer. write for info. (3-927120-47-2, Pub. by Ugarit-Verlag GW) Eisenbrauns.
Simas. Jurgis Gliauda. 1971. 5.00 (0-87141-042-7) Manyland.
Sima7 Come Join Me. Lorna Williams & Mary Longman. (Illus.). 96p. (Orig.). (J). 1991. pap. 8.95 (0-88865-077-9, Pub. by Pacific Educ Pr CN) Orca Bk Pubs.
*Simba & Nala: Best Friends. Golden Books Staff. (Lion King Ser.). (Illus.). (J). 1997. pap. text ed. 2.29 (0-307-03442-9, Golden Books) Western Pub.
Simba & the Lost Waterfall. (Creative Classic Ser.). 16p. (J). (ps-1). 1995. 7.98 (1-57082-221-2) Mouse Works.
*Simba Book on Media. 1997. 545.00 (0-614-25708-5) Simba Info.
Simba Plays: The Lion King. Golden Press Staff. (Magic Corner Bks. Ser.). (Illus.). 14p. (J). (ps-3). 1994. 8.95 (0-307-76028-6, 66028, Golden Books) Western Pub.
Simba Roars. (Squeeze Me Ser.). (J). 1996. 6.98 (1-57082-388-X) Mouse Works.
Simbambene: The Voices of Women at Mboza. Hanlie Griesel et al. 49p. 1988. pap. text ed. 8.95 (0-86975-319-3, Pub. by Ravan Pr ZA) Ohio U Pr.
Simba's Adventure. (Slide-n-Show Ser.). 20p. (J). 1994. 9.98 (1-57082-152-6) Mouse Works.
Simba's Counting Wheel. (Wheel & Window Ser.). 6p. (J). 1995. 7.98 (1-57082-193-3) Mouse Works.
Simba's Journey. (Giant Carousel Book). 12p. (J). (ps-1). 1995. 6.98 (1-57082-244-1) Mouse Works.
Simbi & the Satyr of the Dark Jungle. Amos Tutuola. 144p. (Orig.). 1988. pap. 6.95 (0-87286-214-3) City Lights.
*Simbul's Gift. TSR Inc. Staff. 1997. pap. 5.99 (0-7869-0763-0) TSR Inc.
Simchas Yaavetz Haggadah. D. Cohen. 1993. 18.99 (0-89906-073-0); pap. 14.99 (0-89906-074-9) Mesorah Pubns.
Simchat Torah: A Family Celebration. Judith Abrams. (Illus.). 24p. (Orig.). (J). (ps up). 1995. pap. 3.95 (0-929371-87-9) Kar-Ben.
SimCity Classic Strategies & Secrets. Nick Dargahi. LC 91-75246. 253p. 1991. 12.95 (0-89588-890-4, Strategies & Secrets) Sybex.
SimCity 2000: Power, Politics, & Planning. Nick Dargahi. 1994. pap. 19.95 (1-55958-192-1) Prima Pub.
SimCity 2000: Power, Politics, & Planning. Nick Dargahi. 1995. pap. 19.95 (0-7615-0075-8) Prima Pub.
Simcity 2000 Strategies & Secrets. Daniel A. Tauber & Brenda Kienan. LC 94-66143. 292p. 1994. pap. 14.99 (0-7821-1518-7, Strategies & Secrets) Sybex.
SimCity 2000 Strategies & Secrets Special Edition: Special Edition. 2nd ed. Daniel A. Tauber & Brenda Kienan. LC 94-74148. 323p. 1995. 16.99 (0-7821-1664-7, Strategies & Secrets) Sybex.
SIMD Model of Parallel Computation. Robert Cypher & Jorge L. Sanz. LC 93-27497. 1994. 44.95 (0-387-94139-8) Spr-Verlag.
SimEarth: The Official Strategy Guide. Rusel DeMaria. 336p. (Orig.). 1991. pap. 18.95 (1-55958-103-4) Prima Pub.
Simenon. De Fallois. pap. 8.95 (0-685-36579-4, F126930) Fr & Eur.
Simenon: A Critical Biography. Stanley G. Eskin. LC 86-43084. (Illus.). 318p. 1987. lib. bdg. 45.00 (0-89950-281-4) McFarland & Co.
Simeon Chamber. Steve Martini. 320p. 1994. reprint ed. mass mkt. 6.99 (0-515-11371-9) Jove Pubns.
Simeon North: First Official Pistol Maker of the United States. North. reprint ed. 15.95 (0-88227-001-X) Gun Room.
Simeon Pearce's Randwick: Dream & Reality. Brendan O'Keefe. (Illus.). 75p. pap. 9.95 (0-86840-305-9, Pub. by New South Wales Univ Pr AT) Intl Spec Bk.
Simeon Solution: One Woman's Spiritual Odyssey. Anne O. Poelman. LC 94-46883. vii, 151p. 1995. 13.95 (0-87579-967-1) Deseret Bk.
Simeon's Bride. Alison G. Taylor. 339p. 1996. mass mkt. 5.50 (0-553-57579-1, Loveswept) Bantam.
Simeon's Sandbox. Suranna. (J). 1997. 4.99 (0-689-81312-0) S&S Childrens.
SimFarm Almanac: The Official Guide to Maxis' Simfarm. Paula Spiese. (Illus.). 176p. (Orig.). 1994. pap. 19.95 (1-55958-326-6) Prima Pub.
Simha: Visages Limunieux. I. Besancon. Ed. by A. Dimermanas. 169p. (FRE.). 1989. pap. 9.00 (0-930213-25-4) Breslov Res Inst.
Simhat Torah. Norma Simon. (Festival Series of Picture Storybooks). (Illus.). (J). (ps). 1960. bds. 4.50 (0-8381-0704-4) USCJE.
Simian Immuno-Deficiency Virus. Ed. by N. L. Letvin & R. C. Desrosiers. (Currents Topics in Microbiology & Immunology Ser.: Vol. 188). (Illus.). 250p. 1994. 158.95 (0-387-57274-0) Spr-Verlag.
Simians, Cyborgs, & Women: The Reinvention of Nature. Donna J. Haraway. (Illus.). 288p. (gr. 13). 1990. pap. 17.95 (0-415-90387-4, A4811, Routledge NY) Routledge.
Similar Facts. J. R. Forbes. xxvi, 242p. 1987. 55.50 (0-455-20764-X, Pub. by Law Bk Co AT) Gaunt.
Similarities & Differences Between Children & Adults: Implications for Risk Assessment. Ed. by P. S. Guzelian et al. LC 92-81193. 300p. 1992. pap. text ed. 35.00 (0-944398-07-3) ILSI.
*Similarity & Analogical Reasoning. 608p. 1989. pap. text ed. 36.95 (0-521-38935-6) Cambridge U Pr.
Similarity & Clustering in Chemical Information Systems. John Willett. LC 86-31433. (Chemometrics Research Studies). 254p. 1987. text ed. 169.00 (0-471-91463-0) Wiley.
Similarity & Dimensional Methods in Mechanics. 10th ed. L. I. Sedov. 496p. 1993. 163.00 (0-8493-9308-6, TA347) CRC Pr.
Similarity & Equivalent Fractions: Middle Grades Mathematics Project. Glenda Lappan. 1986. text ed. 18.95 (0-201-21476-8) Addison-Wesley.
Similarity in Visually Perceived Forms. Erich Goldmeier. LC 72-83230. (Psychological Issues Monograph: No. 29, Vol. 8, No. 1). 135p. 1972. 27.50 (0-8236-6077-X) Intl Univs Pr.
Similarity Laws & Modeling. Jhurgen Zierep. LC 74-157835. (Gasdynamics Ser.: Vol. 2). 171p. reprint ed. pap. 48.80 (0-317-28555-6, 2055016) Bks Demand.
Similarity Methods in Engineering Dynamics: Theory & Practice of Scale Modeling. 2nd ed. W. E. Baker et al. (Fundamental Studies in Engineering: No. 12). 384p. 1991. 188.50 (0-444-88156-5) Elsevier.
Similarity Models in Organic Chemistry, Biochemistry & Related Fields. Ed. by R. I. Zalewski et al. (Studies in Organic Chemistry: No. 42). 688p. 1991. 292.00 (0-444-88161-1) Elsevier.
Similarity of Automorphisms of the Torus. R. L. Adler & B. Weiss. LC 52-42839. (Memoirs Ser.: No. 1/98). 43p. 1970. pap. 16.00 (0-8218-1298-X, MEMO/1/98) Am Math.

An Asterisk (*) at the beginning of an entry indicates that the title is appearing in BIP for the first time.

S

***Similarity of Automorphisms of the Torus.** Roy L. Adler & Benjamin Weiss. LC 52-42839. (American Mathematical Society Ser.: No. 98). (Illus.). 47p. pap. 25.00 (*0-608-05169-1*, 2052590) Bks Demand.

Similarity Problems & Completely Bounded Maps. Gilles Pisier. LC 95-44959. (Lecture Notes in Mathematics Ser.: No. 1618). 156p. 1995. 38.95 (*3-540-60322-0*) Spr-Verlag.

Simile & Prophetic Language in the Old Testament. Terry L. Brensinger. LC 96-7048. (Biblical Press Ser.: No. 43). 216p. 1996. 89.95 (*0-7734-2413-X*, Mellen Biblical Pr) E Mellen.

Similes Dictionary. Lawrence Urdang. LC 87-36109. 1993. 75.00 (*0-8103-4361-4*) Gale.

Similes Dictionary. 2nd ed. Sommer. 1900. 75.00 (*0-8103-5467-5*) Gale.

Similiar to Fire: Poems. Bob Stuart. 59p. (Orig.). 1992. pap. 10.95 (*0-9630164-2-3*) Canios Edit.

Similitude & Approximation Theory. S. J. Kline. (Illus.). 250p. 1986. reprint ed. 69.00 (*0-387-16518-5*) Spr-Verlag.

Similkameen Treasure. N. L. Barlee. 96p. 1989. reprint ed. pap. 9.95 (*0-88839-990-1*) Hancock House.

Siminare des Probabilites XXI. Ed. by J. Azema et al. (Lecture Notes in Mathematics Ser.: Vol. 1247). iv, 579p. 1987. 79.95 (*0-387-17768-X*) Spr-Verlag.

SimIsle: The Official Strategy Guide. Selby Bateman. 1995. pap. text ed. 19.95 (*0-7615-0085-5*) Prima Pub.

Simisola. Ruth Rendell. 336p. 1996. mass mkt. 6.50 (*0-7704-2714-6*) Bantam.

***Simisola.** Ruth Rendell. 1996. 5.99 (*0-517-17252-6*) Random Hse Value.

Simisola. Ruth Rendell. 327p. 1995. 23.00 (*0-517-70073-5*, Crown) Crown Pub Group.

Simisola. Ruth Rendell. 336p. 1995. 27.95 (*0-385-25498-9*) Doubleday.

Simisola. Ruth Rendell. 432p. 1996. mass mkt. 5.99 (*0-440-22202-8*) Dell.

Simisola. large type ed. Ruth Rendell. 512p. 1995. pap. 22.00 (*0-7838-1588-3*, GK Hall) Thorndike Pr.

Simisola: Autographed Edition. Ruth Rendell. 1995. 23.00 (*0-517-70480-3*) Crown Pub Group.

Simkin Handbook of Therapeutic Monitoring. 2nd ed. Ed. by William J. Taylor & Daniel J. Robinson. LC 93-83709. v, 174p. 1993. pap. 14.00 (*0-929375-10-6*) H W Bks.

Simkin's Soldiers, Vol. 1. Picton Publishing (Chippenham) Ltd. Staff. (C). 1987. 60.00 (*0-685-39341-0*, Pub. by Picton UK) St Mut.

Simkin's Soldiers Vol. 1: The British Army in 1890: The Cavalry & the Royal Artillery with a Special Section on the Royal Marines. P. S. Walton. (Illus.). 112p. (C). 1990. pap. 27.00 (*0-9506885-1-7*, Pub. by Picton UK) St Mut.

Simkin's Soldiers, the British Army in 1890 Vol. 2: The Infantry. Ed. by P. S. Walton. (Illus.). 205p. (C). 1990. pap. 39.00 (*0-948251-02-6*, Pub. by Picton UK) St Mut.

Simla Village Tales, or, Folk Tales from the Himalayas. Alice E. Dracott. 1976. lib. bdg. 59.95 (*0-8490-2606-7*) Gordon Pr.

SimLife: The Official Strategy Guide. Michael Bremmer & Ken Karakotsios. (Illus.). 368p. (Orig.). 1993. pap. 18.95 (*1-55958-190-5*) Prima Pub.

Simmel & Parsons: Two Approaches to the Study of Society. Donald N. Levine. Ed. by Harriet Zuckerman & Robert K. Merton. LC 79-9011. (Dissertations on Sociology Ser.). 1980. lib. bdg. 30.95 (*0-405-12979-3*) Ayer.

Simmel & Since. David Frisby. 224p. (C). (gr. 13 up). 1992. text ed. 52.95 (*0-415-00975-8*, Routledge NY) Routledge.

Simmel & Since. David Frisby. 224p. (C). 1992. pap. 16.95 (*0-415-07275-1*) Routledge.

***Simmel on Culture: Selected Writings.** Georg Simmel. Ed. by David Frisby & Mike Featherstone. (Theory, Culture & Society Ser.). 340p. 1997. 85.00 (*0-8039-8651-3*) Sage.

***Simmel on Culture: Selected Writings.** Georg Simmel. Ed. by David Frisby & Mike Featherstone. (Theory, Culture & Society Ser.). 340p. 1997. pap. 28.95 (*0-8039-8652-1*) Sage.

Simmering Suppers: Classic & Creative One-Pot Meals. Ed. by JoAnne B. Cats-Baril & Rux Martin. (Illus.). 240p. (Orig.). 1988. pap. 16.95 (*0-920656-69-2*, Pub. by Camden Hse CN) Firefly Bks Ltd.

***Simmering Suppers: Classic & Creative One-Pot Meals.** Harrowsmith Magazine Editors. 1997. pap. text ed. 19.95 (*1-55209-182-1*) Firefly Bks Ltd.

Simmons: History of Our Simmons Family Through Ten Generations, & Brief Sketches of Allied Families of Bartlett, Moore & Mann. M. E. Simmons. (Illus.). 244p. 1993. reprint ed. pap. 38.50 (*0-8328-3405-X*); reprint ed. lib. bdg. 48.50 (*0-8328-3404-1*) Higginson Bk Co.

Simmons E. C. Hardware Co. 1930 Keen Kutter & Winchester Pocket Knives. 1974. pap. 3.50 (*0-915706-07-5*) Am Reprints.

Simms: A Literary Life. John C. Guilds. LC 91-35919. (Illus.). 456p. 1992. pap. 24.00 (*1-55728-378-8*) U of Ark Pr.

Simms Family of Stafford County, Virginia: A Record of the Descendents of Three Brothers...Richard Simms (1752-1850) of Clay County, MO; Presley Simms (ca. 1754-1852) of Montgomery County, IN; Rhodam Simms (1756-1853) of Ralls County MO. Wilma Chappell & William K. Hall. LC 71-11244. 250p. 1969. reprint ed. pap. 71.30 (*0-7837-9009-0*, AU00461) Bks Demand.

SimoLink Version 1 for Windows. Mathworks, Inc. Staff. 1995. student ed., pap. text ed. 73.33 (*0-13-452427-6*) P-H.

Simon. Arthur Blessitt. LC 87-7213. 128p. 1987. pap. 5.00 (*0-934461-04-X*) Blessitt Pub.

Simon. Arthur Fanning. 56p. (Orig.). 1992. pap. 9.95 (*0-929385-32-2*) Light Tech Comns Servs.

Simon. Ivar T. Mattson. Ed. by Ella M. King. 188p. (Orig.). 1992. pap. 6.99 (*0-9625584-5-1*) Super G Pub Co.

Simon. George Sand, pseud. 184p. (FRE.). 1991. pap. 19.95 (*0-7859-1582-6*, 2903950490) Fr & Eur.

Simon. Fred E. Hanson. (Illus.). 54p. (J). (gr. 3-5). 1990. reprint ed. pap. 6.00 (*0-9624292-1-X*) Black Willow Pr.

Simon & Garfunkel: Bridge over Troubled Water (All Organ Edition) (Illus.). 40p. 1989. pap. 12.95 (*0-86001-305-7*, PS10362) Music Sales.

Simon & Garfunkel: Bridge over Troubled Water (Piano Edition) (Illus.). 48p. 1989. pap. 14.95 (*0-7119-0205-4*, PS10172) Music Sales.

Simon & Garfunkel: Old Friends a Dual Biography. Joe Morella & Patricia Barey. (Illus.). 256p. 1991. 19.95 (*1-55972-089-1*, Birch Ln Pr) Carol Pub Group.

Simon & Garfunkel: The Concert in Central Park. (Illus.). 112p. 1996. pap. 19.95 (*0-8256-3308-7*, PS 11170) Music Sales.

Simon & Garfunkel: The Definitive Biography. Victoria Kingston. (Illus.). 254p. 1996. 33.50 (*0-283-06267-3*, Pub. by Sidgwick & Jackson UK) Trans-Atl Phila.

***Simon & Garfunkel: The Definitive Biography.** Victoria Kingston. (Illus.). 320p. (Orig.). 1997. pap. 17.95 (*0-330-34970-8*, Pub. by Pan Books UK) Trans-Atl Phila.

Simon & Garfunkel Collection. (Illus.). 80p. 1988. pap. 14.95 (*0-7119-0064-7*, PS10776) Music Sales.

Simon & Garfunkel's Greatest Hits: Easy Guitar. (Illus.). 48p. pap. 14.95 (*0-86001-323-5*, PS10206) Music Sales.

Simon & Garfunkel's Greatest Hits: Organ Edition. (Illus.). 64p. 1993. pap. 12.95 (*0-86001-304-9*, PS10008) Music Sales.

Simon & Garfunkel's Greatest Hits: Piano-Vocal Edition. (Illus.). 64p. 1993. pap. 14.95 (*0-86001-277-8*, PS10008) Music Sales.

Simon & Halbig Dolls: The Artful Aspect. Jan Foulke. (Illus.). 236p. 1984. 25.00 (*0-87588-219-6*) Hobby Hse.

Simon & His Boxes. Gilles Tibo. (Illus.). 24p. (ENG & SPA.). (J). (ps-1). 1996. 12.95 (*1-57227-033-0*); 12.95 (*1-57227-034-9*); 12.95 (*1-57227-035-7*) Pan Asian Pubns.

Simon & His Boxes. Gilles Tibo. LC 92-80416. (Illus.). 24p. (J). (gr. k-4). 1992. lib. bdg. 10.95 (*0-88776-287-5*) Tundra Bks.

Simon & His Boxes. Gilles Tibo. (Illus.). 24p. (J). (ps up). 1995. pap. 4.95 (*0-88776-345-6*) Tundra Bks.

***Simon & His Boxes.** Gilles Tibo. (Illus.). 1996. pap. 4.95 (*0-88776-346-4*) Tundra Bks.

Simon & His Boxes: English - Hmong. Gilles Tibo. (Illus.). 24p. (J). (ps-1). 1996. 12.95 (*1-57227-036-5*) Pan Asian Pubns.

Simon & His Shrinking Socks. Michael Steinbaum & Diana Cohen. (Ms. Stories Tell Tales Ser.). (Illus.). 64p. (J). (ps-4). 1993. pap. 9.95 (*0-8449-4253-7*) Good Morn Tchr.

***Simon & Janner's Color Atlas of Pediatric Diseases with Differential Diagnosis.** 4th ed. Ed. by R. Soll. LC 97-3047. 384p. (C). (gr. 13 up). 1996. text ed. 169.00 (*0-412-08131-8*) Chapman & Hall.

Simon & Schuster Beginner's Guide to Understanding Wine. Michael Schuster. (Illus.). 140p. (Orig.). 1991. pap. 14.00 (*0-671-72893-8*, Fireside) S&S Trade.

Simon & Schuster Children's Guide to Insects & Spiders. Johnson. LC 96-27600. (J). 1997. 19.95 (*0-689-81163-2*) S&S Childrens.

***Simon & Schuster Children's Guide to Marine Animals.** Jinny Johnson. LC 97-8227. (J). 1998. 19.95 (*0-689-81534-4*) S&S Childrens.

Simon & Schuster Childrens's Guide to Birds. Jinny Johnson. 96p. (J). (gr. 2 up). 1996. 19.95 (*0-689-80199-8*, S&S Bks Young Read) S&S Childrens.

Simon & Schuster Concise Handbook. rev. ed. Lynn Q. Troyka. 576p. (C). 1992. pap. text ed. 26.60 (*0-13-175571-4*) P-H.

Simon & Schuster concise Workbook. Emily Gordon & Lynn Q. Troyka. 1992. pap. text ed. 21.40 (*0-13-174285-X*) P-H.

Simon & Schuster Crossward Book, Vol 186. John M. Samson. 1995. pap. 8.00 (*0-684-80257-0*, Fireside) S&S Trade.

Simon & Schuster Crossword, No. 175. Ed. by Eugene T. Maleska. 1993. pap. 7.50 (*0-671-87194-3*, Fireside) S&S Trade.

***Simon & Schuster Crossword Puzzle Book, 197.** Samson. 1997. pap. 8.00 (*0-684-81475-7*, Fireside) S&S Trade.

***Simon & Schuster Crossword Puzzle Book, 198.** Samson. 1997. pap. 8.00 (*0-684-81476-5*, Fireside) S&S Trade.

***Simon & Schuster Crossword Puzzle Book, 199.** Samson. 1997. pap. 8.00 (*0-684-84274-2*) S&S Trade.

Simon & Schuster Crossword Puzzle Book, No. 152. Eugene T. Maleska & John M. Samson. 1989. pap. 6.95 (*0-671-67988-0*, Fireside) S&S Trade.

Simon & Schuster Crossword Puzzle Book, No. 185. John M. Samson. 1995. pap. 8.00 (*0-684-80256-2*, Fireside) S&S Trade.

Simon & Schuster Crossword Puzzle Book, No. 193. John M. Samson. 64p. 1996. pap. 8.00 (*0-684-81471-4*) S&S Trade.

Simon & Schuster Crossword Puzzle Book, No. 194. John M. Samson. 1996. pap. 8.00 (*0-684-81472-2*) S&S Trade.

***Simon & Schuster Crossword Puzzle Book, Vol. 200.** John M. Samson. 1997. pap. 8.00 (*0-684-84275-0*, Fireside) S&S Trade.

***Simon & Schuster Crostics, 118.** Middleton. 1997. pap. 8.00 (*0-684-83502-9*) S&S Trade.

Simon & Schuster Crostics, No. 83. Thomas H. Middleton. 1980. 3.95 (*0-686-61340-6*, 25464) S&S Trade.

Simon & Schuster Crostics, No. 110. Thomas H. Middleton. 1993. pap. 7.00 (*0-671-87192-7*, Fireside) S&S Trade.

Simon & Schuster Crostics, No. 112. Ed. by Thomas H. Middleton. 1994. pap. 7.00 (*0-671-89711-X*, Fireside) S&S Trade.

Simon & Schuster Crostics, No. 113. Thomas H. Middleton. 1995. pap. 7.00 (*0-684-80261-9*) S&S Trade.

Simon & Schuster Crostics, No. 115. Thomas H. Middleton. 64p. 1996. pap. 7.00 (*0-684-82431-0*, Fireside) S&S Trade.

Simon & Schuster Crostics 116. Thomas H. Middleton. 1996. pap. 7.00 (*0-684-82963-0*) S&S Trade.

Simon & Schuster Fun With Crostics, No. 7. Charles A. Duerr. 1993. pap. 8.00 (*0-671-86735-0*, Fireside) S&S Trade.

Simon & Schuster Fun with Crostics, No. 10. Ed. by Charles A. Duerr. 1994. pap. 8.00 (*0-671-89712-8*, Fireside) S&S Trade.

Simon & Schuster Guide to Briefcase Computers. Ashley D. Grayson. 1985. pap. 12.95 (*0-685-08680-1*) S&S Trade.

Simon & Schuster Guide to Shells. Harold Feinberg. (Illus.). 1980. pap. 15.00 (*0-671-25320-4*) S&S Trade.

Simon & Schuster Guide to Writing. 2nd abr. ed. Donald H. Cunningham & Jeanette Harris. LC 96-31246. 1996. pap. 33.33 (*0-13-456583-5*) P-H.

Simon & Schuster Guide to Writing: Full Edition. 2nd ed. Jeanette Harris & Donald Cunningham. LC 96-30357. 736p. (C). 1996. text ed. 36.67 (*0-13-456575-4*) P-H.

Simon & Schuster Handbook for Writers. 3rd ed. Lynn Q. Troyka. 864p. 1992. text ed. 27.40 (*0-13-813767-6*) P-H.

Simon & Schuster Handbook for Writers. 4th ed. Lynn Q. Troyka. LC 95-35914. 1995. text ed. 30.00 (*0-13-204215-0*) P-H.

Simon & Schuster International Dictionary: English-Spanish, Spanish-English. 1632p. (SPA.). 1973. 55.00 (*0-671-21267-2*) S&S Trade.

***Simon & Schuster International Dictionary Spanish - English.** Ed. by Tana De Gamez. 1997. 49.95 (*0-02-862013-5*) Macmillan.

Simon & Schuster Pocket Book of Chess. Raymond Keene. LC 88-30555. (J). (gr. 4 up). 1989. pap. 8.95 (*0-671-67924-4*, S&S Bks Young Read) S&S Childrens.

***Simon & Schuster Pocket Guide to Beer.** 6th ed. Michael Jackson. 1997. pap. 12.00 (*0-684-84381-1*, Fireside) S&S Trade.

Simon & Schuster Pocket Guide to the Wines of Burgundy. Serena Sutcliffe. write for info. (*0-671-61163-1*) S&S Trade.

Simon & Schuster Pocket Guide to the Wines of Germany. Ian Jamieson & Hugh Johnson. LC 92-19088. 328p. 1993. pap. 13.00 (*0-671-79709-3*, Fireside) S&S Trade.

Simon & Schuster Quick Access Reference for Writers. Lynn Q. Troyka. LC 94-26630. 304p. 1994. pap. text ed. 26.00 (*0-13-101882-5*) P-H.

***Simon & Schuster Quick Access Reference for Writers.** 2nd ed. Lynn Q. Troyka & Simon & Schuster, Inc. Staff. LC 97-14280. 1997. 28.00 (*0-13-621541-6*) P-H.

Simon & Schuster Super Crossword, Bk. 9. Eugene T. Maleska. 1996. pap. 9.00 (*0-684-82964-9*) S&S Trade.

Simon & Schuster Super Crossword, No. 8. Ed. by Eugene T. Maleska. 1994. pap. 9.00 (*0-671-89709-8*, Fireside) S&S Trade.

Simon & Schuster Super Crossword Series, No. 6. William Shakespeare. 1990. pap. 3.50 (*0-671-73355-9*, Folger Lib) PB.

Simon & Schuster Two Minute Crosswords No. 3, No. 3. Albert. 1995. pap. 5.95 (*0-684-80263-5*, Fireside) S&S Trade.

Simon & Schuster Workbook for Writers. 4th ed. Lynn Q. Troyka. (C). 1996. wbk. ed., pap. text ed. 19.87 (*0-13-455396-9*) P-H.

Simon & Schuster World Coin Catalogue 1979-1980. Gunter Schon. (Illus.). 1979. pap. 13.25 (*0-671-24639-9*) S&S Trade.

Simon & Schuster Young Reader's Atlas. Jill Wright. (YA). 1993. pap. 8.95 (*0-671-88089-6*, S&S Bks Young Read) S&S Childrens.

Simon & Schuster Young Readers' Book of Planet Earth. Martyn Bramwell. LC 91-38216. (Illus.). 192p. (J). (gr. 4 up). 1992. pap. 13.00 (*0-671-77830-7*, S&S Bks Young Read) S&S Childrens.

Simon & Schuster Young Readers' Illustrated Dictionary. (Illus.). (J). (gr. 3 up). 1985. pap. 9.99 (*0-671-50821-0*) S&S Trade.

Simon & Schuster Young Readers' Thesaurus. George Beal. Ed. by Wendy Barish. (Illus.). 192p. (J). (gr. 3-7). 1984. pap. 6.95 (*0-685-09127-9*, Litl Simon S&S) S&S Childrens.

Simon & Schuster Young Readers' Thesaurus. George Beal. (Illus.). 192p. (YA). 1984. pap. 8.99 (*0-671-50816-4*, S&S Bks Young Read) S&S Childrens.

Simon & Schuster's Complete Guide to Plants & Flowers. Ed. by Frances Perry. (Illus.). 1976. pap. 15.00 (*0-671-22247-3*) S&S Trade.

Simon & Schuster's Computer Study Guide for the SAT: Apple. 1988. 34.95 (*0-671-66439-5*) S&S Trade.

Simon & Schuster's Crossword Book Of Quotations, No. 13. Ed. by Eugene T. Maleska. 1981. pap. 4.95 (*0-686-73805-5*, Fireside) S&S Trade.

Simon & Schuster's Crossword Puzzle Book, No. 173. Eugene T. Maleska. 1993. pap. 7.50 (*0-671-86408-4*, Fireside) S&S Trade.

Simon & Schuster's Crossword Puzzle Book No. 183. Ed. by Eugene T. Maleska & John M. Samson. 64p. 1995. pap. 8.00 (*0-671-51056-8*, Fireside) S&S Trade.

Simon & Schuster's Crossword Puzzle Book No. 184. Ed. by Eugene T. Maleska & John M. Samson. 64p. 1995. pap. 8.00 (*0-671-51131-9*, Fireside) S&S Trade.

Simon & Schuster's Crossword Puzzle Book Series, No. 168. Eugene T. Maleska. 1992. pap. 6.99 (*0-671-77850-1*) S&S Trade.

Simon & Schuster's Crossword Puzzle Book Series, No. 171. Ed. by Eugene T. Maleska & John M. Samson. 64p. 1993. pap. 7.00 (*0-671-79787-5*, Fireside) S&S Trade.

Simon & Schuster's Crostics Treasury Series, No. 3. Thomas H. Middleton. 1994. pap. 7.00 (*0-671-87221-4*, Fireside) S&S Trade.

Simon & Schuster's Fun with Crostics, No. 16. Charles A. Duerr. 1996. pap. 8.00 (*0-684-82959-2*, Fireside) S&S Trade.

Simon & Schuster's Fun with Crostics No. 11. Charles A. Duerr. 64p. 1995. pap. 8.00 (*0-671-51130-0*, Fireside) S&S Trade.

Simon & Schuster's Fun with Crostics Series, No. 8. Charles A. Duerr. 1994. pap. 8.00 (*0-671-87220-6*, Fireside) S&S Trade.

Simon & Schuster's Guide to Birds. John Bull. 1981. pap. 15.00 (*0-671-42235-9*, Fireside) S&S Trade.

Simon & Schuster's Guide to Bonsai. Gianfranco Giorgi. 256p. 1991. pap. 14.00 (*0-671-73488-1*, Fireside) S&S Trade.

Simon & Schuster's Guide to Cats. Pugnetti. Ed. by Mordecai Siegal. (Illus.). 256p. 1983. pap. 13.00 (*0-671-49170-9*) S&S Trade.

Simon & Schuster's Guide to Dogs. Elizabeth M. Schuler. 1980. pap. 14.00 (*0-671-25527-4*) S&S Trade.

Simon & Schuster's Guide to Fossils. Paolo Arduini & Giorgio Teruzzi. (Nature Guide Ser.). (Illus.). 320p. 1987. pap. 14.00 (*0-671-63132-2*, Fireside) S&S Trade.

Simon & Schuster's Guide to Freshwater & Marine Aquarium Fishes. LC 76-56863. 1977. pap. 14.00 (*0-671-22809-9*) S&S Trade.

Simon & Schuster's Guide to Garden Flowers. Guido Moggi et al. Ed. by Stanley Schuler. (Illus.). 512p. 1983. pap. 15.00 (*0-671-46678-X*) S&S Trade.

Simon & Schuster's Guide to Gems & Precious Stones. Curzio Cipriani & Alessando Borelli. Ed. by Kennie Lyman. 384p. 1986. pap. 14.00 (*0-671-60430-9*) S&S Trade.

Simon & Schuster's Guide to Herbs & Spices. Walter Simonetti. 256p. 1991. pap. 14.00 (*0-671-73489-X*, Fireside) S&S Trade.

Simon & Schuster's Guide to Horses & Ponies. Murizio Bongianni. 256p. 1988. pap. 14.00 (*0-671-66068-3*, Fireside) S&S Trade.

Simon & Schuster's Guide to House Plants. Alessandro Chiusoli & Maria L. Boriani. (Nature Guide Ser.). (Illus.). 320p. 1987. pap. 14.00 (*0-671-63131-4*, Fireside) S&S Trade.

Simon & Schuster's Guide to Insects. Ross Arnett & Richard Jacques, Jr. (Illus.). 1981. pap. 15.00 (*0-671-25014-0*) S&S Trade.

***Simon & Schuster's Guide to Insects & Spiders.** Jinny Johnson. (Simon & Schuster Children's Guide Ser.). (Illus.). (YA). (gr. 3 up). 1997. 19.95 (*0-614-29072-4*) S&S Childrens.

Simon & Schuster's Guide to Mammals. Ed. by Sydney Anderson. (Illus.). 512p. 1984. pap. 15.00 (*0-671-42805-5*) S&S Trade.

Simon & Schuster's Guide to Mushrooms. Gary H. Lincoff. (Illus.). 512p. 1982. pap. 15.00 (*0-671-42849-7*) S&S Trade.

Simon & Schuster's Guide to Orchids. Alberto Fanfani. 256p. 1989. pap. 14.00 (*0-671-67798-5*, Fireside) S&S Trade.

Simon & Schuster's Guide to Pet Birds. Matthew M. Vriends. 320p. 1985. pap. 15.00 (*0-671-50696-X*) S&S Trade.

Simon & Schuster's Guide to Reptiles & Amphibians of the World. Massimo Capula. 256p. 1990. pap. 13.00 (*0-671-69098-1*, Fireside) S&S Trade.

Simon & Schuster's Guide to Rocks & Minerals. Martin Prinz et al. (Illus.). 1978. pap. 15.00 (*0-671-24417-5*) S&S Trade.

Simon & Schuster's Guide to Saltwater Fish & Fishing. Angelo Mojetta. (Illus.). 256p. (Orig.). 1992. pap. 14.00 (*0-671-77947-8*, Fireside) S&S Trade.

Simon & Schuster's Guide to Trees. Ed. by Stanley Schuler. (Illus.). 216p. 1978. pap. 14.00 (*0-671-24125-7*) S&S Trade.

Simon & Schuster's Hooked on Cryptics Series, No. 4. Henry Hook. 1994. pap. 8.00 (*0-671-78743-8*, Fireside) S&S Trade.

Simon & Schuster's International Spanish-English Dictionary. 3rd ed. Degamez. (ENG & SPA.). 1996. 55.00 (*0-671-51060-6*) S&S Trade.

Simon & Schuster's Large Type Crosswords No. 18. Ed. by Eugene T. Maleska & John M. Samson. 96p. 1995. pap. 8.00 (*0-671-51134-3*, Fireside) S&S Trade.

Simon & Schuster's Super Crossword Book, No. 7. Eugene T. Maleska. 1992. pap. 9.00 (*0-671-79232-6*, Fireside) S&S Trade.

Simon & Schuster's Super Crostics Book No. 3. Thomas H. Middleton. 256p. 1995. pap. 9.00 (*0-671-51132-7*, Fireside) S&S Trade.

Simon & Schuster's Two-Minute Crossword No. 2. David King. 224p. 1995. pap. 5.95 (*0-671-88575-8*, Fireside) S&S Trade.

Simon & Shuster's Guide to Cacti & Succulents. Ed. by Stanley Schuler. 1985. pap. 14.00 (*0-671-60231-4*) S&S Trade.

***Simon & Spy.** Laird. 1990. pap. text ed. write for info. (*0-582-04611-4*, Pub. by Longman UK) Longman.

Simon & the Holy Night. Eve Tharlet. Tr. by Andrew Clements. (Illus.). 28p. (J). (gr. k up). 1991. pap. 14.95 (*0-88708-185-1*, Picture Book Studio) S&S Childrens.

An Asterisk (*) at the beginning of an entry indicates that the title is appearing in BIP for the first time.

Simon & the Holy Night. Eve Tharlet. LC 93-306. (Pixies Ser.: Vol. 26). (Illus.). (J). 1993. 4.95 (*0-88708-324-2*, Picture Book Studio) S&S Childrens.
Simon & the Snowflakes. Gilles Tibo. LC 88-50259. (Illus.). 24p. (J). (ps-4). 1991. pap. 4.95 (*0-88776-274-3*) Tundra Bks.
***Simon & the Snowflakes.** Gilles Tibo. (Illus.). 1996. pap. 4.95 (*0-88776-275-1*) Tundra Bks.
Simon & the Wind. Gilles Tibo. LC 89-50777. (Illus.). 24p. (J). (gr. k-4). 1989. 10.95 (*0-88776-234-4*) Tundra Bks.
Simon & the Wind. Gilles Tibo. LC 89-50776. (Illus.). 24p. (J). (ps-4). 1991. pap. 4.95 (*0-88776-276-X*) Tundra Bks.
***Simon at the Circus.** Gilles Tibo. (J). 1997. write for info. (*0-614-29317-0*) Tundra Pubns.
***Simon at the Circus.** Gilles Tibo. (Illus.). 24p. (J). (ps-1). 1997. 10.95 (*0-88776-414-2*) Tundra Bks.
***Simon at the Circus.** Gilles Tibo. (Illus.). 24p. (J). (ps-1). 1997. pap. 4.95 (*0-88776-416-9*) Tundra Bks.
Simon Au Clair De Lune. Gilles Tibo. LC 93-60333. (Simon Ser.). (Illus.). 24p. (J). (gr. k up). 1993. 10.95 (*0-88776-317-0*) Tundra Bks.
Simon Baruch: Rebel in the Ranks of Medicine, 1840-1921. Patricia S. Ward. Ed. by Lester D. Stephens. LC 93-31300. (History of American Science & Technology Ser.). (Illus.). 416p. 1994. text ed. 49.95 (*0-8173-0589-0*) U of Ala Pr.
Simon Boccanegra. Giuseppe Verdi. Ed. by Nicholas John. Tr. by Sylvia Mulcahy from ITA. LC 85-1831. (English National Opera Guide Series: Bilingual Libretto, Articles: No. 32). (Illus.). 96p. (Orig.). 1985. pap. 9.95 (*0-7145-4064-1*) Riverrun NY.
Simon Boccanegra: Libretto. Giuseppe Verdi. 48p. (ENG & ITA.). 1986. pap. 4.95 (*0-7935-5210-9*, 50340380) H Leonard.
Simon Bolivar. (Hispanic Stories Ser.). (Illus.). 32p. (J). (gr. 3-5). 1988. lib. bdg. 21.40 (*0-8172-2902-7*) Raintree Steck-V.
Simon Bolivar. Dennis Wepman. (World Leaders - Past & Present Ser.). (Illus.). 112p. (YA). (gr. 5 up). 1985. lib. bdg. 19.95 (*0-87754-569-3*) Chelsea Hse.
Simon Bolivar: A Bibliography. Ed. by Raoul Gordon. 1976. lib. bdg. 59.95 (*0-8490-2607-5*) Gordon Pr.
Simon Bolivar: Latin American Liberator. Frank De Varona. LC 92-19459. (Hispanic Heritage Ser.). (Illus.). 32p. (J). (gr. 2-4). 1993. pap. 4.95 (*1-56294-812-1*); lib. bdg. 14.90 (*1-56294-278-6*) Millbrook Pr.
Simon Bolivar & Spanish American Independence, 1783-1830. John J. Johnson. (Anvil Ser.). 224p. (C). 1992. reprint ed. pap. 15.50 (*0-89464-687-7*) Krieger.
Simon Bouquet's Imitations et Traduction de Cent Dix-Huit Emblemes d'Alciat. Simon Bouquet. LC 89-45848. (Studies in the Emblem: No. 5). 1993. 63.00 (*0-404-63705-1*) AMS Pr.
Simon Cameron: Ante Bellum Years. Lee F. Crippen. LC 76-168674. (American Scene Ser.). 1972. reprint ed. lib. bdg. 39.50 (*0-306-70362-9*) Da Capo.
Simon Celebra la Primavera (Simon Welcomes Spring) Gilles Tibo. Tr. by Arturo Salazar from ENG. LC 92-85471. (Illus.). 24p. (Orig.). (SPA.). (J). (gr. k-3). 1993. pap. 4.95 (*0-88776-297-2*) Tundra Bks.
Simon Commission: Report on India, 3 vols., Set. 1987. 2, 500.00 (*0-318-37214-2*) Asia Bk Corp.
Simon Crosby the Emigrant: His English Ancestry & Some of His American Descendents. Eleanor D. Crosby. (Illus.). 195p. 1995. reprint ed. pap. 15.00 (*0-7884-0326-5*) Heritage Bk.
***Simon de Colines.** Fred Schreiber. 330p. 1995. 150.00 (*0-614-24479-X*, 42579) Oak Knoll.
Simon De Cramaud, De Substraccione Obediencie. Ed. by Howard Kaminsky. (Medieval Academy Bks.: No. 92). 1984. 40.00 (*0-910956-84-7*) Medieval Acad.
Simon de Montfort. J. R. Maddicott. LC 93-33224. (Illus.). 424p. (C). 1994. text ed. 69.95 (*0-521-37493-6*) Cambridge U Pr.
Simon de Montfort. J. R. Maddicott. (Illus.). 430p. 1996. pap. text ed. 24.95 (*0-521-37636-X*) Cambridge U Pr.
Simon De Montfort. Margaret W. Labarge. LC 75-22643. (Illus.). 312p. 1975. reprint ed. text ed. 35.00 (*0-8371-8359-6*, LASM, Greenwood Pr) Greenwood.
Simon de Montfort & Baronial Reform. R. F. Treharne. 368p. 1986. text ed. 55.00 (*0-907628-70-2*) Hambledon Press.
Simon De Montfort, Earl of Leicester, 1208-1265. Charles Bemont. Tr. by Ernest F. Jacob. LC 74-9223. (Illus.). 303p. 1974. reprint ed. text ed. 35.00 (*0-8371-7625-5*, BESM, Greenwood Pr) Greenwood.
Simon Drew's Beastly Birthday Book. Simon Drew. 1995. 12.95 (*1-85149-220-8*) Antique Collect.
Simon et la Musique. Gilles Tibo. (Illus.). (J). 1995. 10.95 (*0-88776-360-X*) Tundra Bks.
***Simon et la Musique.** Gilles Tibo. (Illus.). (FRE.). (J). (ps up). 1997. reprint ed. pap. 4.95 (*0-614-29134-8*) Tundra Bks.
***Simon et la Plume Perdu.** Gilles Tibo. (Illus.). (FRE.). (J). (ps up). 1997. reprint ed. pap. 4.95 (*0-614-29136-4*) Tundra Bks.
Simon et la Plume Perdue. Gilles Tibo. LC 94-60138. (Illus.). 24p. (FRE.). (J). (gr. k-4). 1994. 10.95 (*0-88776-341-3*) Tundra Bks.
***Simon et le Petit Cirque.** Gilles Tibo. (Illus.). 24p. (J). (ps-1). 1997. 10.95 (*0-88776-417-7*) Tundra Bks.
***Simon et le Petit Cirque.** Gilles Tibo. (Illus.). 24p. (J). (ps-1). 1997. pap. 4.95 (*0-88776-423-1*) Tundra Bks.
Simon et le Soleil D'Ete. Gilles Tibo. LC 90-72049. (Illus.). 24p. (FRE.). (J). (ps). 1991. 10.95 (*0-88776-262-X*) Tundra Bks.
Simon et le Vent d'Automne. Gilles Tibo. LC 89-50776. (Illus.). 24p. (FRE.). (J). (gr. k-4). 1989. 10.95 (*0-88776-235-2*) Tundra Bks.
Simon Evans: An Anthology. M. Baldwin. 269p. (C). 1989. 45.00 (*0-907083-03-X*, Pub. by S A Baldwin UK) St Mut.
Simon Fete le Printemps. Gilles Tibo. LC 90-70132. (Illus.). 24p. (J). (ps-4). 1990. 10.95 (*0-88776-247-6*) Tundra Bks.
Simon Fete le Printemps. Gilles Tibo. (Illus.). 24p. (J). (gr. k-3). 1993. pap. 4.95 (*0-88776-279-4*) Tundra Bks.
Simon Fete le Printemps. Gilles Tibo. (Illus.). (J). (gr. k-3). 1994. pap. 4.95 (*0-88776-278-6*) Tundra Bks.
Simon Finds a Feather. Gilles Tibo. LC 94-60134. (Illus.). 24p. (J). (gr. k-4). 1994. 10.95 (*0-88776-340-5*) Tundra Bks.
***Simon Finds a Feather.** Gilles Tibo. (Simon Ser.). (Illus.). (J). 1997. pap. text ed. 4.95 (*0-88776-402-9*) Tundra Bks.
***Simon Finds a Feather.** Gilles Tibo. (Illus.). (J). (ps up). 1997. reprint ed. pap. 4.95 (*0-614-29135-6*) Tundra Bks.
***Simon Finds a Treasure.** Gilles Tibo. (Illus.). 1996. 10.95 (*0-88776-375-8*) Tundra Bks.
***Simon Finds a Treasure.** Gilles Tibo. (Illus.). (J). (ps-1). 1996. 10.95 (*0-88776-376-6*); pap. 4.95 (*0-88776-388-X*) Tundra Bks.
Simon Girty the Outlaw. Uriah James Jones. 1931. 30.00 (*0-686-17407-0*) R S Barnes.
Simon Gray: A Casebook. Katherine Burkman. LC 92-319493. (Casebooks on Modern Dramatists Ser.: Vol. 13). 228p. 1992. text ed. 37.00 (*0-8240-5758-9*, H1362) Garland.
Simon Greenleaf Review of Law & Religion, 4 bks., Set, Vols. 1-8. 1989. 300.00 (*0-685-70757-1*) Gaunt.
Simon Gross' U. S. Revenue Cutter Active 1791-1798. Florence Kern. 1977. 3.95 (*0-913377-05-8*) Alised.
Simon in Summer. Gilles Tibo. (Illus.). (J). (ps). pap. 4.95 (*0-88776-358-8*) Tundra Bks.
Simon in Summer. Gilles Tibo. LC 90-72048. (Illus.). 24p. (J). (ps). 1991. 10.95 (*0-88776-261-1*) Tundra Bks.
Simon in Summer. Gilles Tibo. (Illus.). (J). 1995. pap. 4.95 (*0-88776-280-8*) Tundra Bks.
***Simon in Summer.** Gilles Tibo. (Illus.). 1996. pap. 4.95 (*0-88776-281-6*) Tundra Bks.
Simon in the Moonlight. Gilles Tibo. LC 93-60334. (Simon Ser.). (Illus.). 24p. (J). (gr. k up). 1993. 10.95 (*0-88776-316-2*) Tundra Bks.
Simon in the Moonlight. Gilles Tibo. (Simon Ser.). (Illus.). 24p. (J). (ps up). 1995. pap. 4.95 (*0-88776-347-2*) Tundra Bks.
***Simon in the Moonlight.** Gilles Tibo. (Illus.). 1996. pap. 4.95 (*0-88776-348-0*) Tundra Bks.
Simon J. Ortiz. Andrew Wiget. LC 86-70653. (Western Writers Ser.: No. 74). (Illus.). 53p. (Orig.). 1986. pap. 4.95 (*0-88430-048-X*) Boise St U W Writ Ser.
Simon Kenton: The Great Frontiersman. Ray Crain. (Illus.). 52p. (Orig.). 1992. 18.00 (*0-9641149-4-1*); pap. 12.00 (*0-9641149-5-X*) Main Graphics.
Simon Kenton, His Life & Period, 1755-1836. Edna Kenton. LC 70-146406. (First American Frontier Ser.). (Illus.). 1976. reprint ed. 35.95 (*0-405-02865-2*) Ayer.
Simon Kenton, Kentucky Scout. 2nd ed. Thomas D. Clark. LC 93-20718. (Illus.). 256p. (YA). (gr. 6-12). 1993. reprint ed. 17.95 (*0-945084-38-2*) J Stuart Found.
Simon Kuznets. Fogel. 1992. lib. bdg. 34.95 (*0-226-25661-8*) U Ch Pr.
Simon Lash. large type ed. Frank Gruber. 336p. 1995. 25. 99 (*0-7089-3429-3*) Ulverscroft.
Simon le Pathetique. Jean Giraudoux. pap. 9.95 (*0-685-33927-0*) Fr & Eur.
Simon Lobdell, 1646 of Milford, Connecticut, & His Descendants, Also of Nicholas Lobden (Lobdell), 1635 of Hingham, Mass., & Some Descendants. J. H. Lobdell. (Illus.). 425p. 1989. reprint ed. pap. 63.50 (*0-8328-0780-X*); reprint ed. lib. bdg. 71.50 (*0-8328-0779-6*) Higginson Bk Co.
Simon Magus. G. R. Mead. 1978. reprint ed. pap. 12.50 (*0-89005-258-1*) Ares.
Simon Magus: An Essay on the Founder of Simonianism Based on the Ancient Sources with a Re-Evaluation of His Philosophy & Teachings. G. R. Mead. Ed. by J. D. Holmes. 1991. pap. 8.95 (*1-55818-177-6*) Holmes Pub.
Simon Magus: An Essay on the Founder of Simonianism Based on the Ancient Sources with a Re-Evaluation of His Philosophy & Teachings. G. R. Mead. 91p. 1994. pap. 7.95 (*1-56459-439-4*) Kessinger Pub.
Simon Magus & the Gnostics. Milton Ward. (Orig.). 1990. pap. 15.00 (*0-939835-05-3*) Optimus Bks.
Simon Makes Music. Gilles Tibo. LC 95-60977. (Illus.). 24p. (J). (gr. k-2). 1995. 10.95 (*0-88776-359-6*) Tundra Bks.
***Simon Makes Music.** Gilles Tibo. (Simon Ser.). (Illus.). 1997. pap. text ed. 4.95 (*0-88776-398-7*); pap. text ed. 4.95 (*0-88776-381-2*) Tundra Bks.
***Simon Makes Music.** Gilles Tibo. (Illus.). (J). (ps up). 1997. reprint ed. pap. 4.95 (*0-614-29133-X*) Tundra Bks.
***Simon Michael: The Man, the Artist, the Teacher.** Dorothy C. Kucera. LC 88-61736. (Illus.). 80p. 1988. 29. 95 (*0-9658121-0-3*) Waters Edge TX.
Simon of Cyrene. Martin De Porres. 1996. write for info. (*0-9648448-3-4*) CMJ Assocs.
Simon Perkins of the Western Reserve. Mary L. Conlin. 215p. 1968. 15.95 (*0-911704-05-1*) Western Res.
Simon Peter. Hugh Martin. 1984. pap. 9.50 (*0-85151-427-8*) Banner of Truth.
Simon Peter. Eleanor Snyder. LC 94-61288. (Living Stones Ser.). (Illus.). 196p. (J). (ps-8). 1994. pap. 32.95 (*0-87303-234-9*) Faith & Life.
***Simon Peter: The Fisherman from Galilee.** Ivor C. Powell. LC 96-30471. 240p. 1996. pap. 11.99 (*0-8254-3548-X*) Kregel.
Simon Peter - the Disciple. C. Mackenzie. (BibleTime Bks.). (J). 1995. 2.99 (*0-906731-09-7*, Pub. by Christian Focus UK) Spring Arbor Dist.
Simon Pure. Julian F. Thompson. 336p. (YA). (gr. 7-9). 1988. pap. 3.50 (*0-590-41823-8*, Point) Scholastic Inc.
***Simon Said.** Sarah R. Shaber. 1997. 20.95 (*0-312-15207-8*) St Martin.
Simon Says. Sheryl Lynn. (Intrigue Ser.). 1994. mass mkt. 2.99 (*0-373-22258-0*, 1-22258-7) Harlequin Bks.
Simon Says. Gloria Murphy. 416p. (Orig.). 1994. pap. 4.99 (*0-451-18140-9*) NAL-Dutton.
Simon Says, "Croak!" M. T. Coffin. (Spinetinglers Ser.: No. 6). 144p. (Orig.). (J). 1995. pap. 3.50 (*0-380-78232-4*, Camelot) Avon.
Simon Says Is Not the Only Game. large type ed. Ed. by Margaret Von Schneden. LC 82-3943. 150p. 1982. pap. 24.95 (*0-89128-109-6*) Am Foun Blind.
Simon Schuster Pocket Guide to Beer. 5th ed. Michael Jackson. 1996. pap. 12.00 (*0-684-83062-0*) S&S Trade.
Simon Syndrome: A Wholistic Metaphoric Approach to 20th Century Problems of Leaders, Leading & Leadership. E. Gene Rooney. 507p. (Orig.). 1995. 45.00 (*1-881596-06-0*) L E A D Cnslts.
Simon the Coldheart. Georgette Heyer. 1978. 12.00 (*0-685-90568-3*) Bookfinger.
Simon the Coldheart. Georgette Heyer. 1976. reprint ed. lib. bdg. 26.95 (*0-89966-118-1*) Buccaneer Bks.
Simon the Pointer. Joan W. Brown. LC 95-34148. (Illus.). 96p. 1996. pap. 14.95 (*0-670-86662-8*, Viking) Viking Penguin.
Simon the Shepherd at Bethlehem: A Christmas Activity Story Book. Mark Water. (Illus.). 32p. (J). (gr. 1). 1996. pap. 4.99 (*0-8010-4152-X*) Baker Bks.
Simon Wheeler, Detective. Mark Twain. Ed. by Franklin R. Rogers. LC 63-18140. (Levy Pub. Ser.: No. 2). 204p. 1963. 25.00 (*0-87104-161-8*) NY Pub Lib.
Simon Wiesenthal: A Life in Search of Justice. Hella Pick. LC 96-11808. (Illus.). 384p. 1996. 29.95 (*1-55553-273-X*) NE U Pr.
***Simon Wiesenthal: Tracking Down Nazi Criminals.** Laura S. Jeffrey. LC 97-8220. (People to Know Ser.). (Illus.). 128p. (YA). (gr. 6 up). 1997. lib. bdg. 18.95 (*0-89490-830-8*) Enslow Pubs.
Simon Wiesenthal Center Annual, Vol. 1. Ed. by Alex Grobman. (Illus.). 256p. 1984. text ed. 17.95 (*0-940646-30-7*) Rossel Bks.
Simon Willard & His Clocks. John W. Willard. Orig. Title: History of Simon Willard, Inventor & Clockmaker. (Illus.). 1968. reprint ed. pap. 5.95 (*0-486-21943-7*) Dover.
Simon Wolf: Private Conscience & Public Image. Esther L. Panitz. LC 86-45378. (Illus.). 224p. 1987. 35.00 (*0-8386-3293-9*) Lubrecht & Cramer.
Simona Morini's Encyclopedia of Beauty & Health for Women. Simona Morini. LC 75-6403. (Illus.). 512p. 1976. 17.50 (*0-672-51913-5*, Bobbs) Macmillan.
Simone de Beauvoir. Mary Evans. (Women of Ideas Ser.). 128p. (C). 1996. 55.00 (*0-8039-8866-4*); pap. 19.95 (*0-8039-8867-2*) Sage.
Simone de Beauvoir: A Bibliography. Ed. by Joan Nordquist. (Social Theory: A Bibliographic Ser.: No. 23). 60p. (Orig.). (C). 1991. pap. 15.00 (*0-937855-45-6*) Ref Rsch Serv.
Simone de Beauvoir: A Biography. Deirdre Bair. (Illus.). 720p. 1991. pap. 17.00 (*0-671-74180-2*, Touchstone Bks) S&S Trade.
Simone de Beauvoir: A Life, a Love Story. Claude Francis & Fernande Gontier. (Vermilion Bks.). (Illus.). 452p. 1988. pap. 12.95 (*0-312-02324-3*) St Martin.
Simone de Beauvoir: The Making of an Intellectual Woman. Toril Moi. 352p. 1994. pap. 24.95 (*0-631-19181-X*) Blackwell Pubs.
Simone de Beauvoir Aujourd'hui, Six Entretiens. Simone de Beauvoir. 128p. (FRE.). 1984. 24.95 (*0-8288-9683-6*, 271520180X) Fr & Eur.
Simone de Beauvoir et le Cours du Monde. Simone de Beauvoir. 170p. (FRE.). 1978. 95.00 (*0-8288-9684-4*, 225202058X) Fr & Eur.
Simone de Beauvoir on Women. Jean Leighton. LC 74-3615. 230p. 1975. 35.00 (*0-8386-1504-X*) Fairleigh Dickinson.
Simone de Beauvoir ou le Refus de l'Indifference. Gagnebin. (Collection Celebrites). 9.95 (*0-685-37194-8*, F85860) Fr & Eur.
***Simone De Beauvoir's the Second Sex: New Interdisciplinary Essays.** LC 97-21594. (Texts in Culture Ser.). 1998. write for info. (*0-7190-4302-6*, Pub. by Manchester Univ Pr UK); pap. write for info. (*0-7190-4303-4*, Pub. by Manchester Univ Pr UK) St Martin.
Simone Martini. Cecilia Jannella. Tr. by Lisa C. Pelletti. (Library of Great Masters). (Illus.). 80p. (Orig.). 1990. pap. 12.99 (*1-878351-05-2*) Riverside NY.
Simone Martini: Complete Edition. Andrew Martindale. (Illus.). 240p. (C). 1988. text ed. 168.00 (*0-8147-5444-9*) NYU Pr.
Simone Signoret. Catherine David. Tr. by Sally Sampson. LC 92-35037. (Illus.). 225p. 1993. 22.95 (*0-87951-491-4*) Overlook Pr.
Simone Signoret. Catherine David. (Illus.). 225p. 1995. pap. 12.95 (*0-87951-581-3*) Overlook Pr.
Simone Weil. John Dunaway. (World Authors Ser.: No. 723). 152p. 1984. 24.95 (*0-8057-6570-0*, Twayne) Scribnrs Ref.
***Simone Weil.** Stephen Plant. Ed. by Peter Vardy. LC 96-52490. (Great Christian Thinkers Ser.). 112p. 1997. reprint ed. pap. 9.00 (*0-7648-0116-3*, Triumph Books) Liguori Pubns.
Simone Weil: "The Just Balance" Peter Winch. (Modern European Philosophy Ser.). 250p. (C). 1989. pap. 22.95 (*0-521-31743-6*) Cambridge U Pr.
Simone Weil: A Bibliography. Joan Nordquist. (Social Theory: No. 38). 72p. (Orig.). (C). 1995. pap. 15.00 (*0-937855-75-8*) Ref Rsch Serv.
Simone Weil: A Sketch for a Protrait. Richard Rees. LC 77-24990. (Arcturus Books Paperbacks). 215p. 1978. reprint ed. pap. 6.95 (*0-8093-0852-5*) S Ill U Pr.
Simone Weil: An Anthology. Ed. & Tr. by Sian Miles from FRE. LC 86-9242. 304p. 1986. pap. 12.95 (*1-55584-021-3*, Grove) Grove-Atltic.
Simone Weil: An Intellectual Biography. Gabriella Fiori. Tr. by Joseph R. Berrigan. LC 88-20536. (Illus.). 408p. 1989. 40.00 (*0-8203-1102-2*) U of Ga Pr.
Simone Weil: An Introduction. Heinz Abosch. Tr. by Kimberly A. Kenny from GER. 125p. 1994. pap. 9.95 (*1-880055-03-1*) Pennbdg Comm.
Simone Weil: Portrait of a Self-Exiled Jew. Thomas R. Nevin. LC 91-9784. xvi, 488p. (C). 1991. 37.50 (*0-8078-1999-9*) U of NC Pr.
Simone Weil a New York et a Londres. Cabaud. 15.95 (*0-685-36635-9*) Fr & Eur.
Simone Weil & the Socialist Tradition. Louis Patsouras. LC 91-42735. 120p. 1992. pap. text ed. 39.95 (*0-7734-9913-X*) E Mellen.
Simone Weil Reader. Ed. by George A. Panichas. 529p. 1985. pap. 14.95 (*0-918825-01-6*) Moyer Bell.
Simone Weil's Philosophy of Culture: Readings Toward a Divine Humanity. Intro. by Richard H. Bell. LC 92-11490. 353p. (C). 1993. text ed. 69.95 (*0-521-43263-4*) Cambridge U Pr.
Simoniacal Entry into Religious Life from 1000 to 1260: A Social, Economic, & Legal Study. Joseph H. Lynch. LC 76-22670. (Illus.). 286p. 1976. 45.00 (*0-8142-0222-5*) Ohio St U Pr.
Simonides: A Historical Study. J. H. Molyneux. 374p. (Orig.). 1991. 39.00 (*0-86516-222-0*); pap. 24.00 (*0-86516-223-9*) Bolchazy-Carducci.
Simonides in Vietnam & Other Epigrams. R. L. Barth. 16p. (Orig.). 1990. pap. 5.00 (*0-936784-91-1*) J Daniel.
Simon's Book. Henrik Drescher. LC 82-24931. (Illus.). 32p. (J). (gr. k-3). 1983. 16.00 (*0-688-02085-2*); lib. bdg. 15. 93 (*0-688-02086-0*) Lothrop.
Simon's Book. Henrik Drescher. LC 82-24931. (Illus.). 32p. (J). (ps up). 1991. reprint ed. pap. 3.95 (*0-688-10484-3*, Mulberry) Morrow.
Simon's Lady. Julie Tetel. (Historical Ser.). 1994. mass mkt. 3.99 (*0-373-28829-8*, 1-28829-9) Harlequin Bks.
Simon's Masterpiece. James LaVilla-Havelin. 1983. pap. 6.00 (*0-934834-40-7*) White Pine.
Simon's Night. Jon Hassler. 320p. 1986. mass mkt. 5.95 (*0-345-33374-8*) Ballantine.
***Simon's Night.** Jon Hassler. 1997. pap. 12.00 (*0-345-41825-5*) Ballantine.
Simons Says: Faith, Fun, Foible. Leonard N. Simons. LC 89-17074. (Illus.). 368p. 1989. pap. text ed. 14.95 (*0-8143-1780-4*) Wayne St U Pr.
Simon's Sunflowers. Maggie S. Terris & Donna Ruff. (Illus.). Date not set. lib. bdg. write for info. (*0-688-14874-3*) Greenwillow.
Simon's Taxes, 10 vols. 3rd ed. Ed. by B. J. Sims et al. U.K. ring bd. 1,290.00 (*0-406-06860-7*) MICHIE.
Simon's Waif. Mira Stables. 224p. 1981. pap. 1.50 (*0-449-50207-4*, Coventry) Fawcett.
Simonton: Family History, Genealogical, Historical & Biographical, of the Simonton & Related Families. W. Simonton. 199p. 1992. reprint ed. pap. 31.00 (*0-8328-2725-8*); reprint ed. lib. bdg. 41.00 (*0-8328-2724-X*) Higginson Bk Co.
Simpatico. Sam Shepard. 1995. pap. 5.25 (*0-8222-0726-5*) Dramatists Play.
Simpatico. Sam Shepard. Date not set. pap. write for info. (*0-679-44342-8*) Random.
Simpatico: A Play in Three Acts. Sam Shepard. LC 95-43451. 135p. 1996. pap. 10.00 (*0-679-76317-1*) Random.
Simpco Land Use Planning Information System Design: What to Do When the Data Arrives. Kenneth Meyer et al. (Technical Reports: No. 1). 1978. 5.00 (*1-55614-113-0*) U of SD Gov Res Bur.
Simpkin. Quentin Blake. Date not set. pap. write for info. (*0-14-050608-X*) Viking Penguin.
SIMPLAN: A Computer Based Planning System for Government. Thomas H. Naylor et al. LC 74-75956. 189p. reprint ed. pap. 53.90 (*0-317-20449-1*, 2023426) Bks Demand.
Simple Abundance: A Daybook of Comfort & Joy, Vol. 1. Sarah B. Breathnach. 512p. 1995. 20.00 (*0-446-51913-8*) Warner Bks.
Simple Abundance Journal of Gratitude. Sarah B. Breathnach. 160p. 1996. pap. 12.95 (*0-446-52106-X*) Warner Bks.
Simple Acts of Kindness: Volunteering in the Age of AIDS. Ed. by John Griggs. LC 89-5131. 127p. 1989. pap. 5.95 (*0-934459-56-8*) United Hosp Fund.
Simple Algebras, Base Change, & the Advanced Theory of the Trace Formula. James Arthur & Laurent Clozel. 225p. 1989. text ed. 67.50 (*0-691-08517-X*); pap. text ed. 27.50 (*0-691-08518-8*) Princeton U Pr.
Simple American Cooking. Chuck Williams. Ed. by Laurie Wertz. LC 94-7742. (Chuck Williams Collection). 1994. 17.95 (*1-875137-22-X*) Weldon Owen.
Simple & Classic: Greek Elegance for the Everyday Cook. Billie V. Andersson. (Illus.). 88p. (Orig.). 1991. pap. 10. 00 (*0-9615556-0-2*) Andesign.
Simple & Direct: A Rhetoric for Writers. rev. ed. Jacques Barzun. LC 93-47049. 314p. (C). 1994. pap. 14.95 (*0-226-03868-8*) U Ch Pr.
Simple & Direct Guide to Jazz Improvisation. 14.95 (*0-7935-5596-5*, 00841046) H Leonard.
Simple & Easy Taste of Japan. Shufunotomo Staff. (Illus.). 48p. (Orig.). 1996. pap. 12.00 (*0-87040-973-5*) Kodansha.
Simple & Easy Way to Study the Bible. Don Gray & Marjorie Gray. (Outreach Ser.). 31p. 1985. pap. 1.49 (*0-8163-0613-3*) Pacific Pr Pub Assn.

S

An Asterisk (*) at the beginning of an entry indicates that the title is appearing in BIP for the first time.

*Simple & Inexpensive Robot That You Can Build. James M. Conrad. 250p. 1997. write for info. (0-8186-7514-4, BP07514) IEEE Comp Soc.

Simple & Tasty Side Dishes: Great-Tasting Recipes in Minutes. Frank R. Blenn. (Healthy Selects Cookbook Ser.). (Illus.). 72p. 1996. pap. 8.95 (0-945448-45-7) Am Diabetes.

Simple & Vital Design: The Story of the Indiana Post Office Murals. John C. Carlisle. (Illus.). 105p. 1995. pap. 24.95 (0-87195-110-X) Ind Hist Soc.

Simple Animals. Linda Losito et al. (Encyclopedia of the Animal World Ser.). (Illus.). 96p. (YA). 1989. 17.95 (0-8160-1968-1) Facts on File.

Simple Annals. Eugene Lockhart. 132p. (Orig.). 1987. pap. 7.65 (0-9618581-3-3) E Lockhart.

*Simple Annals: Two Centuries of an American Family. Robert H. Allen. LC 96-45312. 220p. 1997. 22.00 (1-56858-090-8) FWEW.

Simple Approach to Digital Signal Processing. Craig Marven. LC 96-2518. 1996. text ed. 39.95 (0-471-15243-9) Wiley.

Simple Art of Greatness. James X. Mullen. Date not set. pap. 9.95 (0-14-023437-3) Viking Penguin.

Simple Art of Murder. Raymond Chandler. LC 87-45923. (Crime Ser.). 288p. 1988. pap. 12.00 (0-394-75765-3, Vin) Random.

Simple Art of Napkin Folding. Linda Hertzer. (Illus.). 128p. 1991. reprint ed. 15.00 (0-688-10280-8) Hearst Bks.

Simple Art of Perfect Baking. rev. ed. Flo Braker. LC 92-11095. (Illus.). 400p. 1992. reprint ed. 24.95 (0-9631591-3-5); reprint ed. pap. 19.95 (0-9631591-2-7) Chapters Pub.

*Simple Art of Silk Flower Arrangement. Emilio Robba. Date not set. write for info. (0-688-14840-9) Hearst Bks.

Simple Attractions. Steve Tomecek. LC 95-18864. (Illus.). 48p. (J). (gr. 4-7). 1995. pap. 9.95 (0-7167-6632-9, Sci Am Yng Rdrs) W H Freeman.

Simple Attractions. Steve Tomecek. LC 95-18864. (Phantastic Physical Phenomena Ser.). (Illus.). 48p. (J). (gr. 4-7). 1995. 14.95 (0-7167-6601-9, Sci Am Yng Rdrs) W H Freeman.

Simple Beauty: The Shakers of America. William Ketchum. 1996. 15.98 (0-8317-8171-8) Smithmark.

Simple Beauty Hints. 1991. lib. bdg. 75.00 (0-8490-4150-3) Gordon Pr.

Simple Biflagellate Holocarpic Phycomycetes. 2nd ed. J. S. Karling. (Illus.). 1981. lib. bdg. 90.00 (0-685-03123-3) Lubrecht & Cramer.

Simple Boat Building. G. Prout. (C). 1987. 40.00 (0-85174-143-6, Pub. by Brwn Son Ferg) St Mut.

Simple Book: An Introduction to Networking Management. 2nd ed. Marshall T. Rose. LC 96-7192. (Series in Innovative Technology). 294p. (C). 1996. text ed. 59.00 (0-13-451659-1) P-H.

*Simple C. Jim McGregor. (C). 1997. pap. text ed. write for info. (0-201-40385-4) Addison-Wesley.

Simple Candle Magick. Keith Morgan. (Orig.). 1995. pap. 7.95 (1-872189-61-X, Pub. by Mandrake Pr UK) Holmes Pub.

Simple Case Books for Small Businesses. Paul D. Ordidge. 96p. (Orig.). 1990. 14.95 (0-8464-1379-5) Beekman Pubs.

*Simple Celebration. David Simon. 1998. pap. write for info. (0-609-80181-3, Crown) Crown Pub Group.

Simple Celebration: A Vegetarian Cookbook for Body, Mind & Spirit. LC 96-47910. 1997. 23.00 (0-517-70732-2) Crown Pub Group.

Simple Ceramics. Dawan Richardson-Hyde. 1996. pap. text ed. 15.95 (0-85091-625-9, Pub. by Lothian Pub AT) Seven Hills Bk.

*Simple, Cheap & Easy: How to Build a Cell Tech Business off Your Kitchen Table. Venus Andrecht. Ed. by Summer Andrecht. (Illus.). 112p. (Orig.). 1996. mass mkt. write for info. (0-941903-17-6) Ransom Hill.

Simple Checkmates. A. J. Gillam. 128p. (Orig.). 1996. pap. 9.00 (0-345-40307-X) Ballantine.

Simple Chemistry Experiments with Everyday Materials. Frances W. Zweifel. LC 94-16757. (Illus.). 128p. (Orig.). 1994. 14.95 (0-8069-0688-X) Sterling.

Simple Chemistry Experiments with Everyday Materials. Frances W. Zweifel. (Illus.). 128p. (Orig.). (J). 1995. pap. 4.95 (0-8069-0689-8) Sterling.

Simple Chess. Michael Stean. 128p. 1987. pap. 7.95 (0-571-11257-9) Faber & Faber.

Simple Chinese Phrase Book. rev. ed. Terry C. Shen. (Illus.). 75p. 1986. pap. 2.50 (0-935655-01-8) Language Intl.

Simple Christian Crafts. Elsa M. Sorensen. (Illus.). 70p. (Orig.). 1993. pap. text ed. 27.85 (1-883894-00-X) Environ Life Sci.

*Simple Christmas: Celebrating the Old-Fashioned Way in a Post-Modern World. Lori Salkin & Rob Sperry. LC 97-14356. (Illus.). 112p. 1997. 14.95 (0-8362-3593-2) Andrews & McMeel.

Simple Circuits. Katina Boulais. (Illus.). 74p. 1994. ring bd. write for info. (0-614-00951-0) E&L Instru.

Simple Cobler of Aggawam in America. Nathaniel Ward. (BCL1-PS American Literature Ser.). 80p. 1993. reprint ed. lib. bdg. 59.00 (0-7812-6942-3) Rprt Serv.

Simple Computing: What Computers Can Do for You. Chauncey Ching. LC 84-33. (Orig.). 1984. pap. 9.95 (0-915805-00-6) Total Concepts.

Simple Conjunctions: An Installation by Phillip Galgiani. James Welling. (Illus.). 16p. 1986. pap. 6.50 (0-918471-09-5) San Fran MOMA.

Simple Contracts for Personal Use. Stephen Elias & Marcia Stewart. LC 86-61365. Orig. Title: Make Your Own Contract. 208p. 1995. pap. 16.95 (0-87337-155-0) Nolo Pr.

Simple Cooking. John Thorne. (Illus.). 290p. 1996. pap. 12.00 (0-86547-504-0, North Pt Pr) FS&G.

Simple Cooperation in the Classroom. Jacqueline Rhoades et al. (Illus.). 165p. (Orig.). (J). (ps up). 1985. pap. 15.95 (0-933935-07-2) ITA Pubns.

Simple Creole Cajun. Floyd Babineaux. 165p. 1986. 12.00 (0-317-69245-3) F Babineaux.

Simple Cuisine. Jean-Georges Vongerichten. 224p. 1996. 16.00 (0-02-860991-3) Macmillan.

*Simple Curtains. Katrin Cargill. 1998. write for info. (0-609-60125-3, C P Pubs) Crown Pub Group.

Simple Daylight: Vocal with Piano. 7.95 (0-7935-4047-X, 50482306) H Leonard.

Simple Decency & Common Sense: The Southern Conference Movement, 1938-1963. Linda Reed. LC 91-7803. (Blacks in the Diaspora Ser.). (Illus.). 288p. 1991. text ed. 31.50 (0-253-34895-1) Ind U Pr.

Simple Decency & Common Sense: The Southern Conference Movement, 1938-1963. Linda Reed. LC 91-7803. (Blacks in the Diaspora Ser.). (Illus.). 288p. 1994. pap. 11.95 (0-253-20912-9) Ind U Pr.

Simple, Decent Place to Live. Millard Fuller. 1995. 19.99 (0-8499-1196-6) Word Pub.

Simple Decorative Paper Techniques. Stephanie Ipert. 48p. 1992. pap. 11.95 (0-85532-728-6, 728-6, Pub. by Search Pr UK) A Schwartz & Co.

Simple Definition of the Feynman Integral, with Applications. R. H. Cameron & A. Storvick. LC 83-15605. (Memoirs Ser.: No. 46/288). 48p. 1983. pap. 16.00 (0-8218-2288-8, MEMO/46/288) Am Math.

Simple Dielectric Liquids: Mobility, Conduction, & Breakdown. T. J. Gallagher. (Oxford Science Research Papers Ser.). (Illus.). 160p. 1975. pap. 89.00 (0-19-851933-8) OUP.

*Simple Earth Science Experiments with Everyday Materials. Louis V. Loeschnig. (Illus.). 128p. (J). 1997. pap. 5.95 (0-8069-0365-1) Sterling.

Simple Earth Science Experiments with Everyday Materials. Frances W. Zweifel. LC 95-53977. (Illus.). 128p. (J). (gr. 3). 1996. 14.95 (0-8069-0898-X) Sterling.

Simple Earth Solutions: Powerful Paths to Health & Healing Through Natural Healing. Ronald J. Vaillancourt. LC 95-90285. 351p. (Orig.). 1995. pap. 29.95 (0-9645645-1-3) Abundant Hlth Pub.

Simple, Easy Candy. (Favorite All Time Recipes Ser.). (Illus.). 96p. 1993. 7.98 (1-56173-281-8, 2012300) Pubns Intl Ltd.

Simple Economic Model of Cocaine Production. Michael Kennedy et al. LC 93-17674. 1994. pap. 13.00 (0-8330-1384-X, MR-201-USDP) Rand Corp.

*Simple Economics & Bookkeeping for Fish Farmers. (Training Ser.: No. 19). 100p. 1992. 30.00 (92-5-103002-2, Pub. by FAO IT) Bernan Associates.

*Simple, Effective Number Sense. Barbara J. Reys et al. Ed. by Joan Gideon. (Number Sense Ser.). (Illus.). 213p. (Orig.). (J). (gr. 6-8). 1996. pap. text ed. 18.95 (1-57232-264-0, 21803) Seymour Pubns.

Simple Electronic Navigation. 2nd ed. Mik Chinery. 64p. (C). 1990. text ed. 59.00 (0-906754-67-4, Pub. by Fernhurst Bks UK) St Mut.

Simple Elegance: A Culinary Collection of Simple to Elegant Recipes. Our Lady of Perpetual Help Church Women's Guild Staff & Rita Leonard. 288p. 1997. reprint ed. 16.95 (0-9633165-0-8) Our Lady Perpet HCWG.

*Simple Elegance Petite Photo Album. Illus. & Des. by Jenny Faw. (Petite Photo Albums Ser.). 15p. 1997. 4.95 (0-88088-650-1) Peter Pauper.

Simple Embroidery Designs. Ondori Publishing Company Staff. (Illus.). 103p. (Orig.). 1985. pap. 10.95 (0-87040-647-7) Japan Pubns USA.

Simple Estate Planning & Will Writing: A Home Study Course. James E. De Martino. (Home Study Ser.). 41p. 1982. 30.00 (0-939926-15-6); audio (0-939926-14-8) Fruition Pubns.

Simple Etiquette in France. Marie T. Byram. (Illus.). 48p. pap. 6.95 (0-904404-81-1) Talman.

Simple Etiquette in Italy. Hugh Shankland. pap. 6.95 (0-904404-82-X, 91987) Talman.

Simple Etiquette in Japan. Helmut Morsbach. 1988. pap. 20.00 (0-904404-46-3, Pub. by P Norbury Pubns Ltd UK) St Mut.

Simple Etiquette in Korea. Lee & Kim. pap. 6.95 (0-904404-65-X, 90811) Talman.

Simple Etiquette in Russia. Irene Slatter. 1990. pap. 20.00 (0-904404-72-2, Pub. by P Norbury Pubns Ltd UK) St Mut.

Simple Etiquette in Spain. McGuiness. pap. 6.95 (1-873411-45-6, 92775) Talman.

Simple Etiquette in Turkey. David Shankland. (Illus.). 48p. 1991. pap. 6.95 (1-873411-00-6, Pub. by A&C Black UK) Talman.

Simple Experiments. Time-Life Books Editors. Ed. by Karin Kinney. (Child's First Library of Learning). (Illus.). 88p. (J). (gr. k-3). 1994. lib. bdg. write for info. (0-8094-9471-X) Time-Life.

Simple Experiments. Time-Life Books Editors. Ed. by Karin Kinney. (Child's First Library of Learning). (Illus.). 88p. (J). (gr. 1-4). 1994. 16.95 (0-8094-9470-1) Time-Life.

*Simple Experiments in Time with Everyday Materials. Frances W. Zweifel. LC 97-992. (Illus.). 96p. (J). 1997. 14.95 (0-8069-3803-X) Sterling.

Simple Eye Care for Health Care Workers. 2nd ed. Helen Keller International Staff. LC 93-1669. 1993. pap. 5.00 (0-915173-23-9) Helen Keller Intl.

Simple Eyes & Other Poems. Michael McClure. LC 93-46673. 144p. (Orig.). 1994. pap. 10.95 (0-8112-1265-3, NDP780) New Directions.

Simple Fact. Cathy Cockrell. LC 87-8677. 1987. 15.00 (0-914610-45-7); pap. 8.00 (0-914610-48-1) Hanging Loose.

Simple Faith. Charles R. Swindoll. 1993. pap. 12.99 (0-8499-3524-5) Word Pub.

Simple Faith. Charles R. Swindoll. 400p. 1996. mass mkt. 5.99 (0-8499-3969-0) Word Pub.

*Simple Faith: Insights for Living in a Complex World. Fletcher C. Spruce. LC 96-39977. 152p. (Orig.). 1997. pap. 9.99 (0-8341-1626-X) Beacon Hill.

Simple Filing Practice Set: Business Records Control. 4th ed. Fosegan & Ginn. (KG - FIling/Records Management Ser.). 1995. 21.95 (0-538-62368-3) S-W Pub.

Simple Filing Practice Set: Replacement Set. 4th ed. Fosegan & Ginn. (KG - FIling/Records Management Ser.). 1995. pap. 15.95 (0-538-62369-1) S-W Pub.

*Simple Flight & Space Experiments. Louis Loeschnig. (J). Date not set. write for info. (0-8069-4246-0) Sterling.

*Simple Flowers. Paula Pryke. 1998. write for info. (0-609-60139-3, C P Pubs) Crown Pub Group.

Simple Food for the Good Life. Helen Nearing. 309p. (Orig.). 1980. reprint ed. pap. 10.00 (0-913299-24-3) Stillpoint.

Simple Foods for a Simple & Healthy Life: A Self-Help Guide to Nutrition. Madeline Goulard. (Illus.). 118p. 1993. pap. 9.00 (0-9642335-1-7) Simple Life Bks.

Simple Foods for the Pack: The Sierra Club Guide to Delicious Natural Foods for the Trail. rev. ed. Claudia Axcell et al. LC 85-22076. (Outdoor Activities Guides Ser.). (Illus.). 224p. 1986. pap. 9.00 (0-87156-757-1) Sierra.

Simple Foods Recipes for a Simple & Healthy Life. Madeline Goulard. 50p. 1992. pap. 5.00 (0-9642335-0-9) Simple Life Bks.

*Simple Football Handbook for Women: A Mom's Answers to Tuff Turf Questions. Cheri Gowen. LC 96-70344. (Illus.). iii, 56p. (Orig.). 1997. pap. 12.95 (0-9653680-5-X) Skeeter Pub.

Simple French Cooking. Chuck Williams. Ed. by Laurie Wertz. (Chuck Williams Collection). 1996. 17.95 (1-875137-10-6) Weldon Owen.

Simple French Cuisine: From Provence & Languedoc. Jenny Baker. (Illus.). 272p. 1992. pap. 12.95 (0-571-14454-3) Faber & Faber.

Simple French Food. Richard Olney. (Illus.). 448p. 1992. reprint ed. pap. 13.00 (0-02-010060-4) Macmillan.

Simple French Phrase Book. Terry C. Shen. Tr. by Sara Mills. (Popular Phrase Bk.). (Illus.). 40p. 1986. pap. 2.50 (0-935655-06-9) Language Intl.

Simple Games for Practicing Basic Skills. Kathleen Morgan. (Illus.). 48p. (J). (ps-1). 1989. pap. text ed. 5.95 (1-55799-147-2, EMC 176) Evan-Moor Corp.

Simple Garden Projects: More Than 75 Projects & Design Ideas for Furnishing the Room Outside. Terence Conran. 1996. 16.99 (0-517-14231-7) Random Hse Value.

*Simple Gift of Islam. Robinson. pap. 9.95 (1-86034-013-X, Pub. by Global Bks UK) Talman.

Simple Gifts. Joanne Greenberg. LC 86-323. 208p. 1987. pap. 7.95 (0-8050-0540-4, Owl) H Holt & Co.

Simple Gifts. Kathleen Korbel. 1994. mass mkt. 3.50 (0-373-07571-5, 5-07571-8) Harlequin Bks.

*Simple Gifts: A Shaker Hymn. Christopher Raschka. LC 97-16734. 1997. write for info. (0-8050-5143-0) H Holt & Co.

Simple Gifts: The Shaker Song. Photos by Solomon Skolnick. LC 92-13543. 48p. 1992. 9.95 (1-56282-915-7) Hyperion.

*Simple Gifts, Abundant Treasures: A Woman's Companion. Beth M. Conny. (Gift Editions Ser.). (Illus.). 56p. 1997. 8.99 (0-88088-499-1) Peter Pauper.

Simple Goals for Nigerian Administrators & Politicians: Options for Social, Political & Economic Development. Sylvester Enaifoghe. (Illus.). (Orig.). 1994. pap. write for info. (0-318-71691-7) Harmattan.

Simple Gospel: Reflections on Christian Faith. Hugh T. Kerr. 80p. (Orig.). 1991. pap. 9.00 (0-664-25171-4) Westminster John Knox.

Simple Graph Art. Erling Freeberg & Dolores Freeberg. (Illus.). 48p. (J). (gr. k-1). 1987. student ed. 7.95 (1-55734-095-1) Tchr Create Mat.

Simple Graphical Procedure to Estimate the Minimum Time to Evacuate a Building. R. L. Francis. 1979. 3.50 (0-686-25955-6, TR 79-5) Society Fire Protect.

Simple Groups of Lie Type. Roger W. Carter. 335p. 1989. pap. text ed. 63.95 (0-471-50683-4) Wiley.

Simple Groups of Lie Type. Roger Carter. LC 72-39228. (Pure & Applied Mathematics Ser.: Vol. 28). 343p. reprint ed. pap. 97.80 (0-317-26151-7, 2024274) Bks Demand.

Simple Guide to Applying & Preparing for the College of Your Choice. Catherine A. Gullo. 19p. (YA). (gr. 11-12). 1992. spiral bd. 10.00 (1-883374-01-4) Scholar Cnslt.

Simple Guide to Arabia & the Gulf States. Bruce Ingham. pap. 8.95 (1-86034-005-9, 92911) Talman.

Simple Guide to Chinese Ingredients & Other Asian Specialties. Martin Yan. 98p. 1994. pap. 4.95 (1-884657-00-1) Yan Can Cook.

Simple Guide to Courier Travel: How to Fly Free Or at Discounted Prices to Cities Around the World. Jesse L. Riddle. 50p. (Orig.). 1989. pap. text ed. 9.95 (0-9626583-0-8) Carriage Group.

Simple Guide to Courier Travel: How to Fly Free or at Discounted Prices to Cities Around the World. 2nd ed. Jesse L. Riddle. 72p. 1991. pap. 14.95 (0-9626583-1-6) Carriage Group.

Simple Guide to Customs & Etiquette in China. 2nd ed. Caroline Mason. pap. 8.95 (1-86034-030-X, 93395, Pub. by Global Bks UK) Talman.

Simple Guide to Customs & Etiquette in England. Peter Hobday. pap. 8.95 (1-86034-015-6, 93356, Pub. by Global Bks UK) Talman.

Simple Guide to Customs & Etiquette in Germany. 2nd ed. Waltraud Coles & Uwe Koreik. pap. 8.95 (1-86034-025-3, 93396, Pub. by Global Bks UK) Talman.

Simple Guide to Customs & Etiquette in Hungary. Laszlo Jotischky. pap. 8.95 (1-86034-035-0, 92912, Pub. by Global Bks UK) Talman.

Simple Guide to Customs & Etiquette in India. Venika Kingsland. (Illus.). 64p. 1996. pap. text ed. 8.95 (1-86034-050-4, Pub. by Global Bks UK) Talman.

Simple Guide to Customs & Etiquette in Ireland. Aidan McNamara. (Illus.). 80p. 1996. pap. text ed. 8.95 (1-86034-060-1, Pub. by Global Bks UK) Talman.

Simple Guide to Customs & Etiquette in Israel. David Starr-Glass. (Illus.). 64p. 1996. pap. text ed. 8.95 (1-86034-055-5, Pub. by Global Bks UK) Talman.

*Simple Guide to Customs & Etiquette in Italy. 2nd ed. Hugh Shankland. 1996. pap. 8.95 (1-86034-080-6, Pub. by Global Bks UK) Talman.

*Simple Guide to Customs & Etiquette in Korea. 2nd ed. J. E. Hoare. 1996. pap. 8.95 (1-86034-065-2, Pub. by Global Bks UK) Talman.

Simple Guide to Customs & Etiquette in Russia. 2nd ed. Irene Slatter. pap. 8.95 (1-86034-020-2, 93357, Pub. by Global Bks UK) Talman.

Simple Guide to Customs & Etiquette in Singapore. Audrey Perera. 64p. 1996. pap. text ed. 8.95 (1-86034-040-7, Pub. by Global Bks UK) Talman.

Simple Guide to Customs & Etiquette in Thailand. 2nd ed. Derek Tonkin & Visnu Kongsiri. (Illus.). 64p. 1996. pap. text ed. 8.95 (1-86034-045-8, Pub. by Global Bks UK) Talman.

Simple Guide to Etiquette in Greece. Alex Martin. pap. 8.95 (1-86034-010-5, 92989, Pub. by Global Bks UK) Talman.

*Simple Guide to Hinduism. Venika Kingsland. (Illus.). 128p. 1997. pap. 9.95 (1-86034-018-0, Pub. by Global Bks UK) Talman.

*Simple Guide to Holland: Customs & Etiquette. Mark T. Hooker. (Illus.). 64p. 1997. pap. 8.95 (1-86034-085-7, Pub. by Global Bks UK) Talman.

*Simple Guide to Islam. Neal Robinson. (Illus.). 128p. 1997. pap. 9.95 (0-614-26975-X, Pub. by Global Bks UK) Talman.

Simple Guide to Japan. 2nd ed. Morsback. pap. 8.95 (1-86034-000-8, 92988) Talman.

*Simple Guide to Judaism. David Starr-Glass. (Illus.). 128p. 1997. pap. 9.95 (1-86034-008-3, Pub. by Global Bks UK) Talman.

Simple Guide to Orthopaedics. R. L. Kuckstep. 450p. (Orig.). 1993. pap. text ed. 24.95 (0-443-04385-X) Churchill.

Simple Guide to Self-Publishing: A Time & Money Saving Handbook to Printing, Distributing & Promoting Your Own Book. 2nd ed. Mark Ortman. LC 95-62025. 64p. (Orig.). 1996. pap. 7.95 (0-9634699-5-9) Wise Owl Bks & Mus.

*Simple Guide to Shinto. Ian Reader. (Illus.). 128p. 1997. pap. 9.95 (1-86034-003-2, Pub. by Global Bks UK) Talman.

*Simple Guide to SPSS for Window Version 6.0. Kirkpatrick. LC 97-8678. (Psychology Ser.). (C). 1998. pap. 19.95 (0-534-34853-X) Wadsworth Pub.

Simple Guide to SPSS/PC+ for Versions 4.0 & 5.0. Lee A. Kirkpatrick & Brooke C. Feeney. LC 95-35565. (Psychology Ser.). 98p. 1996. 14.95 (0-534-34050-4) Brooks-Cole.

*Simple Guide to the Czech Republic: Customs & Etiquette. David Short. (Illus.). 64p. 1997. pap. 8.95 (1-86034-075-X, Pub. by Global Bks UK) Talman.

*Simple Guide to the Roman Catholic Church. Edmund Hartley. (Illus.). 128p. 1997. pap. 9.95 (1-86034-023-7, Pub. by Global Bks UK) Talman.

Simple Guide to Trade Finance. W. White. (C). 1989. 95.00 (0-85297-215-6, Pub. by Inst Bankers UK) St Mut.

Simple Guide to Trauma. 4th ed. Ronald L. Huckstep. (Illus.). 397p. 1986. pap. text ed. 24.95 (0-443-03350-1) Churchill.

Simple Guide to Trauma. 5th ed. Ronald L. Huckstep. LC 95-6577. 1995. write for info. (0-443-04679-4) Churchill.

Simple Guide to Understanding & Applying the Hazard Analysis Critical Control Point Concept. ILSI Europe Scientific Committee on Microbiology Staff. 12p. 1993. pap. text ed. 12.50 (0-944398-18-9) ILSI.

*Simple Guide to Understanding Children by Galen. Galen Southard. Ed. by Margie Southard. (Illus.). 120p. (Orig.). Date not set. pap. 10.95 (1-890090-61-1) Closet Pubng.

*Simple Guide to Vietnam: Customs & Etiquette. Geoffrey Murray. (Illus.). 64p. 1997. pap. 8.95 (1-86034-090-3, Pub. by Global Bks UK) Talman.

*Simple Guidebook for Mortgage Loans. Neil Moser. 135p. 1997. mass mkt. 12.95 (1-57532-101-7) Press-Tige Pub.

Simple Guides to Daily Growth, Problem Solving, or Purposeful Relaxation for Comfort or Effectiveness, Set-SG, Set-SG. Russell E. Mason. 1975. Incl. Tape-1A, T-2, T-5A; Notes; Clinical Applications, Differential Criteria & Implications for Bio. pap. 25.00 incl. audio (0-89533-001-6) F I Comm.

Simple Handmade Jewellery: Over Two Hundred Easy-to-Make Designs. C. De la Bedoyere. (Illus.). 80p. (Orig.). 1993. pap. 17.50 (0-85532-749-9, 749-9, Pub. by Search Pr UK) A Schwartz & Co.

Simple Hands-on Activities Reinforce Education: SHARE. Mickey Sarquis et al. (Illus.). (Orig.). 1989. pap. text ed. 12.95 (1-877991-01-5, AP1833) Flinn Scientific.

An Asterisk (*) at the beginning of an entry indicates that the title is appearing in BIP for the first time.

Simple Heart. Gustave Flaubert. Tr. by Arthur McDowall from FRE. LC 95-47601. (New Directions Classics Ser.). 64p. 1996. pap. 6.00 (*0-8112-1318-8*, 819) New Directions.

Simple Heart see Three Tales

Simple Inorganic Substances: A New Approach. R. T. Sanderson. LC 87-35345. 526p. (Orig.). 1989. pap. 41.50 (*0-89464-232-4*) Krieger.

Simple Inorganic Substances: A New Approach. R. T. Sanderson. LC 87-35345. 526p. (Orig.). 1989. 51.50 (*0-89464-372-X*) Krieger.

Simple Interest Monthly Payment Tables. Financial Publishing Company Staff. 288p. 1983. pap. 9.00 (*0-87600-683-7*) Finan Pub.

Simple Interest Monthly Payment Tables. Financial Publishing Company Staff. 288p. 1984. pap. 9.00 (*0-87600-689-6*); pap. 9.00 (*0-87600-686-1*) Finan Pub.

Simple Interior Design: A Space Planning Program. 2nd ed. Wallach. (OX - Home Economics Ser.). 1988. 40.95 (*0-538-60109-4*) S-W Pub.

Simple Introduction to Numerical Analysis, Vol. 1. R. D. Harding & Douglas A. Quinney. (Illus.). 135p. (C). 1989. pap. 39.00 (*0-85274-821-3*); disk 270.00 (*0-7503-0085-X*) IOP Pub.

Simple Introduction to Numerical Analysis Vol. 2: Interpolation & Approximation. R. D. Harding & Douglas A. Quinney. (Illus.). 184p. 1989. pap. 39.00 (*0-85274-154-5*); disk 270.00 (*0-7503-0089-2*) IOP Pub.

Simple Is Powerful: Anecdotes for a Complex World. Michael J. Roads. Ed. by Doris Ober. LC 91-52848. 216p. 1992. pap. 10.95 (*0-915811-35-9*) H J Kramer Inc.

Simple Isn't Easy. Olivia Goldsmith & Amy F. Collins. 224p. 1995. mass mkt. 5.50 (*0-06-109394-7*, Harp PBks) HarpC.

Simple Italian Cooking. Chuck Williams. Ed. by Laurie Wertz. LC 94-32475. (Chuck Williams Collection). (Illus.). 128p. 1995. 17.95 (*1-875137-13-0*) Weldon Owen.

Simple Japanese Phrase Book. rev. ed. Terry C. Shen. (Illus.). 79p. 1986. pap. 2.50 (*0-685-11951-3*); text ed. 21.95 (*0-935655-02-6*) Language Intl.

Simple Jess. Pamela Morsi. 336p. (Orig.). 1996. mass mkt. 6.50 (*0-515-11837-0*) Jove Pubns.

Simple Jitterbug. (Ballroom Dance Ser.). 1986. lib. bdg. 59. 95 (*0-8490-3296-2*) Gordon Pr.

Simple Jitterbug. (Ballroom Dance Ser.). 1985. lib. bdg. 60. 00 (*0-87700-787-X*) Revisionist Pr.

***Simple Justice.** John M. Wilson. 1997. mass mkt. 5.99 (*0-553-57532-5*) Bantam.

Simple Justice: A Benjamin Justice Mystery. John M. Wilson. 256p. 1996. 21.00 (*0-385-48234-5*) Doubleday.

Simple Justice: How Litigants Fare in the Pittsburgh Court Arbitration Program. Jane W. Adler et al. LC 83-16016. 152p. 1983. pap. 15.00 (*0-8330-0518-9*, R-3071-1CJ) Rand Corp.

Simple Justice: The History of Brown V. Board of Education & Black America's Struggle for Equality. Richard Kluger. 1977. pap. 25.00 (*0-394-72255-8*, Vin) Random.

Simple Kaleidoscopes: 16 Spectacular Scopes to Make. Gary Newlin. (Illus.). 112p. (Orig.). (J). 1996. pap. 14.95 (*0-8069-3155-8*) Sterling.

Simple Kitchen Experiments: Learning Science with Everyday Foods. Frances W. Zweifel. (Illus.). 128p. (J). 1994. pap. 4.95 (*0-8069-8415-5*) Sterling.

***Simple Lace & Other Beaded Jewelry Patterns: For Ages 7 to 70.** Mary E. Harte. Ed. by Monte Smith. LC 96-85695. (Illus.). 32p. (Orig.). 1997. pap. 6.95 (*0-943604-55-9*, BOO/41) Eagles View.

Simple Latin for Family Historians. (C). 1987. 40.00 (*0-317-89820-5*, Pub. by Birmingham Midland Soc UK) St Mut.

Simple Life: Plain Living & High Thinking in American Culture. David E. Shi. 352p. 1986. pap. 14.95 (*0-19-504013-9*) OUP.

Simple Life Coloring Book. Craig Sandberg. 1983. 2.50 (*0-87813-519-7*) Christian Light.

Simple Life Cookbook. Marcine Silver. 102p. (YA). (gr. 7-12). 1992. pap. 6.95 (*1-57515-016-6*) PPI Pubng.

***Simple Life of Rene Guenon.** P. Chacornac. 1996. pap. 16. 00 (*0-614-21611-7*, 1139) Kazi Pubns.

Simple Living. Edward K. Ziegler. LC 74-8716. reprint ed. pap. 37.10 (*0-608-02172-5*, 2062841) Bks Demand.

Simple Living: One Couple's Search for a Better Life. Frank Levering & Wanda Urbanska. 288p. 1993. pap. 11.95 (*0-14-012339-3*, Penguin Bks) Viking Penguin.

***Simple Living & High Thinking: My High Road to a Good Life.** Lawrence C. Gibbs. LC 95-95333. (Illus.). 725p. 1996. write for info. (*0-9654703-0-X*) Gibbs Publng.

***Simple Living Guide.** Janet Luhrs. LC 97-13486. 1997. pap. 18.00 (*0-553-06796-6*) Bantam.

Simple Living Investments: For True Security & Adventure in Old Age. rev. ed. Michael Phillips & Catherine Campbell. LC 84-71943. 72p. 1988. pap. 6.00 (*0-931425-00-X*) Clear Glass.

Simple Logic. Bonevac. (C). 1996. text ed. write for info. (*0-15-503171-6*) HB Coll Pubs.

Simple Logic. Bonevac. (C). 1997. student ed., pap. text ed. 17.75 (*0-15-503173-2*) HB Coll Pubs.

Simple, Low-Cost Wire Antennas for Radio Amateurs. William I. Orr & Stuart D. Cowan. (Illus.). 192p. 1990. pap. 13.95 (*0-8230-8707-7*, RAC Bks) Watsn-Guptill.

Simple Low-Cost Wire Antennas for Radio Amateurs. 2nd ed. William I. Orr & S. D. Cowan. LC 76-190590. (Illus.). 192p. 1972. 11.95 (*0-933616-02-3*) Radio Pubns.

Simple Lust: Collected Poems of South African Jail & Exile. Dennis Brutus. (African Writers Ser.). 176p. (C). 1973. pap. 11.95 (*0-435-90115-X*, 90115) Heinemann.

Simple Machines. Melvin Berger. Ed. by Susan Evento. (Early Science Big Bks.). (Illus.). 16p. (Orig.). (J). (ps-2). 1995. pap. 14.95 (*1-56784-103-1*) Newbridge Comms.

***Simple Machines.** Fran Whittle & Sarah Lawrence. LC 97-20319. (Design & Create Ser.). (J). 1998. write for info. (*0-8172-4890-0*) Raintree Steck-V.

Simple Machines: Hands on Science. John Carratello & Patty Carratello. (Illus.). 32p. (J). (gr. 2-5). 1988. student ed. 5.95 (*1-55734-227-X*) Tchr Create Mat.

Simple Machines: Mini Book. Melvin Berger. Ed. by Susan Evento. (Early Science Big Bks.). (Illus.). 16p. (Orig.). (J). (ps-2). 1995. pap. 2.95 (*1-56784-128-7*) Newbridge Comms.

Simple Machines Made Simple. Ralph E. St. Andre. (Illus.). xix, 150p. 1993. pap. text ed. 20.00 (*1-56308-104-0*) Teacher Ideas Pr.

Simple Machines Theme Pack. Melvin Berger. Ed. by Susan Evento. (Macmillan Early Science Big Bks.). (Illus.). (J). (ps-2). 1995. pap. write for info. (*1-56784-185-6*) Newbridge Comms.

Simple Makeup for Young Actors. Richard Cummings. LC 89-23118. 1990. pap. 14.95 (*0-8238-0290-6*) Plays.

***Simple Map Reading.** Roger Smith. (Illus.). 96p. 1997. pap. 10.00 (*0-11-495775-4*, HM57754, Pub. by Stationery Ofc UK) Seven Hills Bk.

***Simple Math.** (First Learning Adventure Ser.). (Illus.). (J). (ps-2). 1997. 19.95 incl. cd-rom (*0-7894-1710-3*) DK Pub Inc.

Simple Matter of Justice? Ed. by Angelia Wilson. 1995. pap. 14.95 (*0-304-32955-X*) LPC InBook.

Simple Matter of Justice? Ed. by Angelia Wilson. 1995. 55.00 (*0-304-32957-6*) LPC InBook.

Simple Matter of Salt: An Ethnography of Nutritional Deficiency in Spain. Renate L. Fernandez. LC 90-33972. (Comparative Studies of Health Systems & Medical Care: Vol. 25). (Illus.). 225p. 1990. 45.00 (*0-520-06910-2*) U CA Pr.

Simple Men & Trust. Hal Hartley. (Illus.). 256p. (Orig.). 1993. pap. 15.95 (*0-571-16798-5*) Faber & Faber.

***Simple Mental Secrets of Golf: How to Make Them Work for You.** Stan Luker. LC 96-85471. (Illus.). 125p. (Orig.). 1996. pap. 10.95 (*0-9653253-0-X*) Chubasco Pr.

***Simple Method for Calculation of the Ratings of Industrial Gear Units.** Georges Henriot. (1984 Fall Technical Meeting Ser.: Vol. 9). 26p. 1984. pap. text ed. 30.00 (*1-55589-091-1*) AGMA.

***Simple Methods for Aquaculture: Management for Freshwater Fish Culture Ponds.** A. G. Coche et al. (FAO Training Ser.: No. 21/1). 233p. 1997. pap. 45.00 (*92-5-102873-7*, F28737, Pub. by FAO IT) Bernan Associates.

Simple Methods for Aquaculture: Pond Construction for Freshwater Fish Culture. A. G. Coche et al. (Training Ser.: No. 20-2). 224p. 1993. pap. 65.00 (*92-5-102872-9*, F28729, Pub. by FAO IT) Bernan Associates.

***Simple Methods for Aquaculture: Topography for Freshwater Fish Culture: Topographical Surveys.** (Training Ser.: No. 16-2). 266p. 1989. 95.00 (*92-5-102591-6*, Pub. by FAO IT) Bernan Associates.

Simple Methods for Detecting Buying & Selling Points in Securities. James Liveright. LC 68-21699. 1968. reprint ed. pap. 12.00 (*0-87034-028-X*) Fraser Pub Co.

Simple Methods for Identification of Plastic. 2nd ed. Dietrich Braun. 110p. (C). 1986. text ed. 24.00 (*1-56990-006-X*) Hanser-Gardner.

Simple Methods for Identification of Plastics. 3rd rev. ed. Dietrich Braun. Tr. by Edmund Immergut. LC 95-47136. 110p. (C). 1996. text ed. 24.00 (*1-56990-204-6*) Hanser-Gardner.

Simple Methods for the Treatment of Drinking Water. Gabriele Heber. (GATE Ser.). (Illus.). 78p. 1986. pap. 14.00 (*3-528-02021-0*, Pub. by Vieweg & Sohn GW) Informatica.

Simple Methods of Mining Gold. 2nd ed. Terry R. Faulk. (Wild & Woolly West Ser.: No. 10). (Illus.). 1980. pap. 4.00 (*0-910584-98-2*) Filter.

Simple Middle East Cuisine. Lily Sayegh. 1997. pap. 12.95 (*0-86685-372-3*) Intl Bk Ctr.

Simple Midtown Bank: A Bank Teller Simulation. 2nd ed. Sargent. (GB-Basic Business Ser.). 1997. pap. 15.95 (*0-538-60267-8*) S-W Pub.

***Simple Mindedness: In Defense of Naive Naturalism in the Philosophy of Mind.** Jennifer Hornsby. LC 96-40847. 1997. write for info. (*0-674-80818-5*) HUP.

Simple Minds. Dan Lloyd. 330p. 1989. 32.50 (*0-262-12140-9*, Bradford Bks) MIT Pr.

***Simple Model of the Housing Market.** M. J. Dicks. (Bank of England - Discussion Papers: No. 49). 60p. 1990. reprint ed. pap. 25.00 (*0-608-03151-8*, 2063604) Bks Demand.

Simple Models of Complex Nuclei: The Shell Model & Interacting Boson Model. Igal Talmi. LC 92-12901. (Contemporary Concepts in Physics Ser.: Vol. 7). 1993. text ed. 132.00 (*3-7186-0551-1*); pap. text ed. 57.00 (*3-7186-0550-3*) Gordon & Breach.

Simple Models of Equilibrium & Nonequilibrium Phenomena. Ed. by Joel L. Lebowitz. (Studies in Statistical Mechanics: Vol. 13). 272p. 1987. 140.75 (*0-444-87039-3*, North Holland) Elsevier.

Simple Models of Group Behavior. Otomar J. Bartos. 1967. text ed. 70.00 (*0-231-02894-6*) Col U Pr.

Simple Molecular Systems at Very High Density. Ed. by A. Polian et al. (NATO ASI, Series B: Physics: Vol. 186). (Illus.). 449p. 1988. 135.00 (*0-306-43028-2*, Plenum Pr) Plenum.

Simple Nature Experiments with Everyday Materials. Frances W. Zweifel. LC 95-24302. (Illus.). 128p. (J). 1995. 14.95 (*0-8069-1354-1*) Sterling.

***Simple Nature Experiments with Everyday Materials.** Frances W. Zweifel. (Illus.). 128p. (J). 1997. pap. 4.95 (*0-8069-1355-X*) Sterling.

Simple Noise Calculations. P. Dewell. (Handbook Ser.: No. 6). (C). 1991. 51.00 (*0-948237-05-8*, Pub. by H&H Sci Cnslts UK) St Mut.

Simple Noneuclidean Geometry & Its Physical Basis. I. M. Yaglom. (Heidelberg Science Library). (Illus.). 1979. pap. 51.00 (*0-387-90332-1*) Spr-Verlag.

Simple Object Lessons for Children. Tom A. Biller & Martie Biller. (Object Lessons Ser.). 226p. (Orig.). (YA). (gr. 10). 1988. pap. 7.99 (*0-8010-0793-3*) Baker Bks.

Simple Office Filing Procedures: Business Record Control. 6th ed. Goodman & Fosegan. (KG - Filing/Records Management Ser.). 1987. pap. 25.95 (*0-538-11145-3*) S-W Pub.

Simple Office Filing Procedures: Business Records C. 7th ed. Fosegan & Ginn. (KG - Filing/Records Management Ser.). 1995. 25.95 (*0-538-62367-5*) S-W Pub.

Simple Painted Furniture. Annie Sloan. LC 88-33780. 128p. 1989. 19.95 (*0-8021-1428-8*, Grove) Grove-Atltic.

Simple Pascal. James J. McGregor & Alan H. Watt. 190p. (C). 1981. pap. text ed. 80.00 (*0-273-01704-7*, Pub. by Pitman Pubng UK) St Mut.

Simple Passion. Annie Ernaux. Tr. by Tanya Leslie from FRE. LC 93-8702. 72p. 1993. 14.95 (*1-888363-26-6*) Seven Stories.

Simple Passion. Annie Ernaux. 80p. 1994. reprint ed. pap. 8.50 (*0-345-38254-4*) Ballantine.

Simple Past. Driss Chraibi. Tr. by Hugh A. Harter. LC 90-33513. 163p. 1990. 22.00 (*0-89410-399-7*, Three Contnts) Lynne Rienner.

Simple Patchwork. Ondori Publishing Company Staff. (Illus.). 64p. (Orig.). 1993. pap. 15.95 (*0-87040-928-X*) Japan Pubns USA.

Simple Path. Mother Teresa. 288p. 1995. 20.00 (*0-345-39745-2*) Ballantine.

Simple Path. Mother Teresa. 1995. pap. 4.00 (*0-345-40571-4*) Ballantine.

Simple Path. Mother Theresa. 1997. pap. 10.00 (*0-345-40626-5*) Ballantine Trade.

Simple Path. large type ed. Mother Teresa. 464p. 1995. 22. 00 (*0-7838-1582-4*, GK Hall) Thorndike Pr.

Simple Path. large type ed. Mother Teresa. 464p. 1995. 22. 00 (*0-679-44231-6*) Random Hse Lrg Prnt.

Simple Path to Health: A Guide to Oriental Nutrition & Healing. Kim Le. (Illus.). 256p. (Orig.). 1996. pap. 12. 95 (*0-915801-62-0*) Rudra Pr.

Simple Pests & Disease Control. Colin Campbell. Ed. by John Patrick. (Lothian Australian Garden Ser.). (Illus.). 64p. (Orig.). 1995. pap. 10.95 (*0-85091-652-6*, Pub. by Lothian Pub AT) Seven Hills Bk.

Simple Pictures Are Best. Nancy Willard. LC 78-6424. (Illus.). 32p. (J). (ps-3). 1978. pap. 5.00 (*0-15-682625-9*, Voyager Bks) HarBrace.

Simple Pineapple Crochet. Nihon Vogue Staff. (Illus.). 74p. 1995. pap. text ed. 17.00 (*0-87040-951-4*) Japan Pubns USA.

Simple Pink Bubble That Ended the Trouble with Jonathan Hubble. Utz. LC 78-190273. (Illus.). 32p. (J). (gr. 2-3). 1972. lib. bdg. 9.95 (*0-87783-062-2*) Oddo.

Simple Pink Bubble That Ended the Trouble with Jonathan Hubble. deluxe ed. Utz. LC 78-190273. (Illus.). 32p. (J). (gr. 2-3). 1972. pap. 3.94 (*0-87783-108-4*) Oddo.

Simple Plan. Scott Smith. 1994. mass mkt. 5.99 (*0-312-95271-6*) St Martin.

Simple Plants: Traditional Medicinal Herbs of Northern Illinois. Valerie Morris. 84p. 1994. pap. 9.95 (*1-888342-01-3*) Flying Pig.

Simple Plants: Traditional Medicinal Herbs of Northern Illinois. rev. ed. Valerie Morris. 100p. 1996. pap. text ed. 12.95 (*1-888342-02-1*) Flying Pig.

***Simple Pleasures.** John Hadamuscin. Date not set. 4.99 (*0-517-17641-6*) Random Hse Value.

Simple Pleasures: A Bulletin Board Collection. St. Paul Pioneer Press Staff. Ed. by Daniel Kelly. LC 94-19755. 160p. 1994. pap. 6.95 (*0-8362-8083-0*) Andrews & McMeel.

Simple Pleasures: A Journal of Life's Joys. Running Press Staff. 1996. 14.95 (*1-56138-755-X*) Running Pr.

***Simple Pleasures: Soothing Suggestions & Small Comforts for Living Well Year Round.** Robert Taylor et al. (Illus.). 250p. 1997. 14.95 (*1-57324-075-3*) Conari Press.

***Simple Pleasures for Busy Couples.** Dimensions for Living Staff. (Illus.). 64p. 1997. pap. text ed. 5.00 (*0-687-11109-9*) Abingdon.

Simple Pleasures for Busy Families. (Illus.). 64p. (Orig.). 1996. pap. 5.00 (*0-687-05570-9*) Dimen for Liv.

Simple Pleasures for Busy Men. (Illus.). 64p. (Orig.). 1996. pap. 5.00 (*0-687-05540-7*) Dimen for Liv.

Simple Pleasures for Busy Women. (Illus.). 64p. (Orig.). 1996. pap. 5.00 (*0-687-05550-4*) Dimen for Liv.

Simple Pleasures for Christmas. (Illus.). 64p. (Orig.). 1996. pap. 5.00 (*0-687-05590-3*) Dimen for Liv.

***Simple Pleasures for Friends.** Dimensions for Living Staff. (Illus.). 64p. 1997. pap. text ed. 5.00 (*0-687-11119-6*) Abingdon.

***Simple Pleasures for Teachers.** Dimesions for Living Staff. (Illus.). 64p. 1997. pap. text ed. 5.00 (*0-687-11129-3*) Abingdon.

***Simple Pleasures for Teens.** Demensions for Living Staff. (Illus.). 64p. 1997. pap. text ed. 5.00 (*0-687-11139-0*) Abingdon.

***Simple Pleasures of Japan.** J. Condon & C. Condon. 1996. pap. 15.95 (*4-07-973843-9*) Shufu no Tomo-Sha.

Simple Poems: Life Experiences. Alejo Rodriguez. LC 87-51040. 65p. 1988. 6.95 (*1-55523-121-7*) Winston-Derek.

Simple Poems Looking at Life Through a Broken Glass. Alejo Rodriguez. LC 89-50713. 82p. 1990. pap. 5.95 (*1-55523-239-6*) Winston-Derek.

***Simple Prayers.** Ken Boa. 1997. 17.99 (*1-56292-367-6*) Honor Bks OK.

Simple Prayers. Michael Golding. LC 93-8876. 320p. 1994. 17.95 (*0-446-51790-9*) Warner Bks.

Simple Prayers. Michael Golding. 320p. 1996. pap. 11.99 (*0-446-67086-3*) Warner Bks.

Simple Process of Getting Healthy: The Total Book for Good Health & Well-Being. Ted Landau. 66p. (Orig.). 1994. pap. 10.95 (*0-9640599-0-8*) Apollo Pub OR.

Simple Processes at the Gas-Solid Interface. C. H. Bamford & C. F. Tipper. (Comprehensive Chemical Kinetics Ser.: Vol. 19). 436p. 1984. 370.50 (*0-444-42287-0*, I-147-84) Elsevier.

Simple Program: A Contemporary Translation of the Original Big Book of Alcoholics Anonymous. LC 95-40453. 192p. (Orig.). 1996. pap. 9.95 (*0-7868-8136-4*) Hyperion.

Simple Program Design. Robertson. 188p. 1991. pap. 20.95 (*0-87835-709-2*) Course Tech.

Simple Program Design. 2nd ed. Lesley A. Robertson. (C). 1994. pap. 17.95 (*0-87709-283-4*, BF2834) S-W Pub.

Simple Projects in Patchwork. Catherine Grosshans. (Crafty Hands Collection). 48p. 1995. pap. 9.95 (*1-85410-327-X*, Pub. by Aurum Pr UK) London Brdge.

***Simple Psychology: Simple Living in a Complicated World.** Thomas P. Reilly. LC 96-94359. 171p. 1996. 19. 95 (*0-944448-11-9*) Motivation Pr.

Simple Puppets from Everyday Materials. Barbara M. Buetter. LC 96-15475. (Illus.). 80p. (J). 1996. 19.95 (*1-895569-05-2*, Pub. by Tamos Bks CN) Sterling.

***Simple Quantum Physics.** 2nd ed. Peter Landshoff et al. LC 97-25151. (Illus.). 210p. (C). 1997. write for info. (*0-521-62011-2*) Cambridge U Pr.

Simple Quarrels: Negotiations & Adjudication in Divorce. Gwynn Davis et al. 288p. 1994. 65.00 (*0-19-825777-5*) OUP.

Simple Relaxation: The Mitchell Method for Easing Tension. Laura Mitchell. (Illus.). 144p. 1989. pap. 15.95 (*0-7195-4388-6*, Pub. by John Murray UK) Trafalgar.

Simple Remedies for the Home. C. W. Dail & C. S. Thomas. LC 91-61468. (Illus.). 158p. (Orig.). 1991. per. 11.95 (*0-945383-30-4*, 945-5820) Teach Servs.

Simple Repair & Preservation Techniques for Collection Curators, Librarians & Archivists. 3rd ed. J. Gunner. (Illus.). 24p. 1984. pap. 3.00 (*0-913196-44-4*) Hunt Inst Botanical.

Simple Research Techniques for the High School Student. Norman C. Tognazzini. (Illus.). 8p. (YA). 1994. pap. 2.50 (*1-884241-25-5*) Energeia Pub.

Simple Rules: Poems. R. A. Shoaf. LC 91-45813. 64p. 1991. pap. 12.95 (*0-7734-0010-9*, Mellen Poetry Pr) E Mellen.

Simple Rules for a Complex World. Richard A. Epstein. LC 94-40364. 361p. 1995. text ed. 35.00 (*0-674-80820-7*, EPSSIM) HUP.

***Simple Rules for a Complex World.** Richard A. Epstein. 1997. pap. text ed. 17.95 (*0-674-80821-5*) HUP.

Simple Science. Walt Disney Productions Staff. (Walt Disney's Fun-to-Learn Library Ser.: Vol. 10). (Illus.). 44p. (J). (gr. 1-6). 1983. reprint ed. 3.49 (*1-885222-01-7*) Advance Pubs.

Simple Science Experiments. Andrea McLoughlin. (J). 1996. pap. text ed. 2.99 (*0-590-48589-X*) Scholastic Inc.

Simple Science Experiments with Everyday Materials. Muriel Mandell. LC 88-31201. (Illus.). 128p. (YA). (gr. 4-10). 1990. pap. 4.95 (*0-8069-5764-6*) Sterling.

Simple Science Fun: Creative Kids. Fo-Ha-Chr. (Illus.). 160p. (J). (gr. 2 up). 1996. wbk. ed., pap. 12.95 (*1-55734-675-5*) Tchr Create Mat.

Simple Science of Flight: From Insects to Jumbo Jets. Henk Tennekes. LC 95-35554. (Illus.). 152p. 1996. 20.00 (*0-262-20105-4*) MIT Pr.

***Simple Science of Flight: From Insects to Jumbo Jets.** Henk Tennekes. (Illus.). 152p. 1997. reprint ed. pap. 12. 50 (*0-262-70065-4*) MIT Pr.

Simple Science Projects, 8 vols. (Illus.). 256p. (J). (gr. 2-4). 1992. Set. lib. bdg. 148.80 (*0-8368-0773-1*) Gareth Stevens Inc.

Simple Science Projects with Air. John Williams. LC 91-50543. (Simple Science Projects Ser.). (Illus.). 32p. (J). (gr. 2-4). 1992. lib. bdg. 18.60 (*0-8368-0765-0*) Gareth Stevens Inc.

Simple Science Projects with Color & Light. John Williams. LC 91-50544. (Simple Science Projects Ser.). (Illus.). 32p. (J). (gr. 2-4). 1992. lib. bdg. 18.60 (*0-8368-0766-9*) Gareth Stevens Inc.

Simple Science Projects with Electricity. John Williams. LC 91-50545. (Simple Science Projects Ser.). (Illus.). 32p. (J). (gr. 2-4). 1992. lib. bdg. 18.60 (*0-8368-0767-7*) Gareth Stevens Inc.

Simple Science Projects with Flight. John Williams. LC 91-50546. (Simple Science Projects Ser.). (Illus.). 32p. (J). (gr. 2-4). 1992. lib. bdg. 18.60 (*0-8368-0768-5*) Gareth Stevens Inc.

Simple Science Projects with Machines. John Williams. LC 91-50547. (Simple Science Projects Ser.). (Illus.). 32p. (J). (gr. 2-4). 1992. lib. bdg. 18.60 (*0-8368-0769-3*) Gareth Stevens Inc.

Simple Science Projects with Time. John Williams. LC 91-50548. (Simple Science Projects Ser.). (Illus.). 32p. (J). (gr. 2-4). 1992. lib. bdg. 18.60 (*0-8368-0770-7*) Gareth Stevens Inc.

Simple Science Projects with Water. John Williams. LC 91-50549. (Simple Science Projects Ser.). (Illus.). 32p. (J). (gr. 2-4). 1992. lib. bdg. 18.60 (*0-8368-0771-5*) Gareth Stevens Inc.

Simple Science Projects with Wheels. John Williams. LC 91-50550. (Simple Science Projects Ser.). (Illus.). 32p. (J). (gr. 2-4). 1992. lib. bdg. 18.60 (*0-8368-0772-3*) Gareth Stevens Inc.

Simple Screamer: A Guide to the Art of Papier & Cloth Mache. Dan Reeder. (Illus.). 96p. 1984. pap. 17.95 (*0-87905-163-9*, Peregrine Smith) Gibbs Smith Pub.

Simple Screening Instruments for Outreach for Alcohol & Other Drug Abuse & Infectious Diseases. 1995. lib. bdg. 251.95 (*0-8490-6821-5*) Gordon Pr.

S

S

***Simple Secrets of Home Mortgages: What 90,000,000 Homeowners Need to Know about Refinancing.** Richard E. McDowell. (Illus.). 144p. (Orig.). 1997. pap. 16.95 (0-9656885-1-8) Smple Secrets Hme Mrtgages.

Simple Secrets of Parenting: Easy As ABC. John Q. Baucom. LC 97-2301. (Illus.). 64p. (Orig.). 1997. pap. 9.95 (0-87868-638-X) Child Welfare.

Simple Seismics. Nigel A. Anstey. LC 82-80267. (Short Course Handbks.). (Illus.). 168p. 1982. text ed. 29.00 (0-934634-37-8) Intl Human Res.

***Simple Selling: Common Sense That Guarantees Your Success.** Thomas R. Crowel. (Illus.). 200p. (Orig.). 1997. pap. 14.95 (1-884962-09-2) Bkwrld Press.

Simple Sermons That Demand a Decision. Edward Fudge. 2.50 (0-686-12689-0) E Fudge.

Simple Sermons That Say Something. Edward Fudge. pap. 2.50 (0-686-12684-X) E Fudge.

Simple Settings of American Folk Songs & Rhymes for Orff Ensemble, Bk. 1: CDEGA Pentatonic. Isabel M. Carley. 1974. pap. 2.00 (0-918812-06-2, SE 0122) MMB Music.

Simple Settings of American Folk Songs & Rhymes for Orff Ensemble, Bk. 2: CDEGA Pentatonic. 2nd rev. ed. Isabel M. Carley. 1974. reprint ed. pap. 2.00 (0-918812-07-0, SE 0123) MMB Music.

Simple Shrine. Jim Vetter. (New Shoes Ser.). (Illus.). 75p. (Orig.). 1995. pap. 7.00 (0-9641196-4-1) Champion Bks.

Simple Signs. Cindy Wheeler. LC 95-11141. (Illus.). 32p. (J). (gr. k-1). 1995. pap. 12.99 (0-670-86282-7) Viking Child Bks.

***Simple Signs.** Cindy Wheeler. 1997. pap. 4.99 (0-14-055673-7) Viking Penguin.

***Simple Simon.** Ryne D. Pearson. 336p. 1997. mass mkt. 5.99 (0-380-72574-6) Avon.

Simple Simon: A Thriller. Ryne D. Pearson. LC 95-50106. 288p. 1996. 24.00 (0-688-14296-6) Morrow.

***Simple Simon Says.** Evan Skolnick. (Fox-Saban Powerhouse Ser.). 1997. pap. text ed. 4.50 (1-57840-068-6) Acclaim Bks.

Simple Simon Strategist. (Orig.). 1997. mass mkt., pap. 12.50 (0-930305-04-3) Enter Achieve.

Simple Simulations Two: A Collection of Simulation-Games for Political Scientists. Ed. by Charles Walcott. (Instructional Resource Monographs: No. 3). 165p. (Orig.). (C). 1980. pap. text ed. 3.00 (0-915654-42-3) Am Political.

***Simple Skin Surgery.** S. Burge & R. Rayment. (Illus.). 104p. 1986. pap. write for info. (0-632-01368-0) Blackwell Sci.

Simple Skin Surgery. 2nd ed. Susan Burge et al. LC 95-50692. (Illus.). 104p. 1996. pap. 29.95 (0-86542-690-2) Blackwell Sci.

***Simple Social Graces: Recapturing the Joys of Victorian Life.** Linda S. Lichter. (Illus.). 256p. 1997. 23.00 (0-06-039170-7, ReganBooks) HarpC.

Simple Solutions. Elizabeth Gaynor. 1996. write for info. (0-517-70452-8, C P Pubs) Crown Pub Group.

Simple Solutions to Energy Calculations. Richard R. Vaillencourt. LC 94-8311. 1994. 58.00 (0-88173-181-1) Fairmont Pr.

Simple Solutions to Energy Calculations. Richard R. Vaillencourt & Fairmount. (Illus.). 158p. (C). 1994. text ed. 58.00 (0-13-148388-9) P-H.

***Simple Solutions to Energy Calculations.** 2nd ed. Richard Vaillencourt. LC 97-10859. 1997. write for info. (0-88173-263-X) Fairmont Pr.

***Simple Solutions to Energy Calculations.** 2nd ed. Richard R. Vaillencourt & Fairmont Press Staff. (C). 1997. text ed. 69.00 (0-13-675067-2) P-H.

Simple Solutions to Getting Organized: Ten Mistakes That Lead to Disorganization & How to Avoid Them. Jain Gunsauls. LC 94-90880. (Orig.). 5.95 incl. 5.25 hd (0-9644510-0-X) Working Solut.

***Simple Solutions to the Most Common Dog Problems.** Bash Dibra & Elizabeth Randolph. Orig. Title: Teach Your Dog to Behave. (Orig.). Date not set. reprint ed. pap. write for info. (0-9655908-1-X) Petlab.

Simple Songs. Vickie Sears. LC 90-3175. 168p. (Orig.). 1990. pap. 8.95 (0-932379-81-8); lib. bdg. 18.95 (0-932379-82-6) Firebrand Bks.

Simple Soups: Sixty Shortcut Recipes for Every Occasion. Teresa Kennedy. LC 94-21969. 1994. pap. 12.00 (0-517-88225-6) Crown Pub Group.

Simple Southwestern Cooking: Quick Recipes for Today's Busy Lifestyle. Judy Walker. LC 95-9176. (Illus.). 144p. (Orig.). 1995. spiral bd. 12.95 (0-87358-606-9) Northland AZ.

Simple Soybean & Your Health: How Soyfoods Can Lower Your Cholesterol & Reduce Your Risk of Disease & Cancer. Mark Messina et al. LC 93-43374. 272p. pap. 12.95 (0-89529-611-X) Avery Pub.

Simple Spanish Phrase Book. abr. ed. Terry C. Shen. Ed. by Farres. (Popular Phrase Bk.). (Illus.). (Orig.). (J). 1986. pap. 2.50 (0-317-43437-3) Language Intl.

Simple Spectrophotometric Method for the Determination of Thms in Drinking Water. (Illus.). 80p. 1992. pap. 48.00 (0-89867-640-1, 90608) Am Water Wks Assn.

Simple Spells for Love. Barrie Dolricle. 1997. pap. write for info. (0-609-80006-X, Chatham River Pr) Random Hse Value.

Simple Spells for Love: Ancient Practices for Emotional Fulfillment. Barrie Dolnick. LC 94-31885. 1995. 15.00 (0-517-79995-2, Harmony) Crown Pub Group.

Simple Spells for Success. Barrie Dolnick. 1996. 18.00 (0-517-70338-6) Random.

Simple Spells from a Witches' Spellbook. Keith Morgan. (Orig.). 1995. pap. 7.95 (1-872189-75-X, Pub. by Mandrake Pr UK) Holmes Pub.

Simple Squeezes. Hugh Kelsey. (Master Bridge Ser.). 1995. pap. 9.95 (0-395-72858-4) HM.

Simple Squeezes: How to Make Impossible Contracts. Hugh Kelsey. (Illus.). 128p. 1993. pap. 15.95 (0-575-05354-2, Pub. by V Gollancz UK) Trafalgar.

Simple Stage: Its Origins in the Modern American Theater. Arthur Feinsod. LC 90-25222. (Contributions in Drama & Theatre Studies: No. 38). 264p. 1992. text ed. 49.95 (0-313-25715-9, FGE/, Greenwood Pr) Greenwood.

***Simple Stenciling.** Book Sales Incorporated Staff. 1997. pap. text ed. 9.98 (0-7858-0806-X) Bk Sales Inc.

***Simple Steps to Health: A Self-Help Guide.** Madeline Goulard. (Illus.). 250p. (Orig.). 1996. pap. 13.00 (0-9642335-2-5) Simple Life Bks.

Simple Steps to Spiritual Living. Jack McArdle. 128p. (Orig.). 1993. pap. 7.95 (1-85607-080-8, Pub. by Columba Pr IE) Twenty-Third.

Simple Steps to U. S. Citizenship: Bilingual Spanish & English. Marge M. Quinby. Ed. by Marjorie Sowers. Tr. by Olga Contreras from ENG. LC 93-87459. (Illus.). 112p. 1994. pap. text ed. 16.95 (0-9627478-2-3) Oceanside Pr.

Simple Steps to U. S. Citizenship: Complete Information Needed to Obtain U. S. Citizenship. Marge M. Quinby. Ed. by Lee Gallery. LC 90-62900. (Illus.). 102p. (Orig.). 1990. pap. text ed. 12.95 (0-9627478-0-7) Oceanside Pr.

Simple Steps to U.S. Citizenship: Complete Information Needed to Obtain U. S. Citizenship. rev. ed. Marge M. Quinby. Ed. by Lee Gallery. LC 92-83769. (Illus.). 100p. (Orig.). 1993. pap. 14.95 (0-9627478-1-5) Oceanside Pr.

Simple Steps...Costly Choices: A Guide to Inner Peace. Bob Lively. 194p. (Orig.). 1995. wbk. ed., pap. 10.00 (0-9647272-5-0); teacher ed., pap. 5.00 (0-9647272-6-9) Riverbend Pr.

Simple Steps...Costly Choices: A Guide to Inner Peace. Robert D. Lively. 194p. (Orig.). 1995. pap. 14.95 (0-9647272-4-2) Riverbend Pr.

Simple Story. Elizabeth S. Inchbald. Ed. by J. M. Tompkins & Jane Spencer. (World's Classics Ser.). 384p. 1988. pap. 7.95 (0-19-281849-X) OUP.

***Simple Story.** Elizabeth S. Inchbald. 1997. pap. 9.95 (0-14-043473-9) Viking Penguin.

Simple Subs Book. 2nd ed. L. Sellers. 187p. 1985. text ed. 88.00 (0-08-031839-8, CRC Reprint) Franklin.

Simple Suburban Murder. Mark R. Zubro. 224p. 1990. 8.95 (0-312-03933-6) St Martin.

Simple, Successful Prioritizing (SSP) Dora B. Johnson. (TTnT Ser.). 18p. (C). 1990. pap. text ed. 4.75 (0-923285-02-4) Baldwin Ctr.

Simple Sums. Keith Faulkner. (J). (ps-3). 1994. 11.00 (0-671-88555-3, S&S Bks Young Read) S&S Childrens.

***Simple Suppers: The after Work Cookbook.** Hugo Arnold. (Illus.). 224p. 1997. pap. 24.95 (0-7472-7809-1, Pub. by Headline UK) Trafalgar.

Simple Surprises! Use Everyday Objects Like Pencils & Strings to Complete the Pages. (J). (ps up). 1994. bds. 6.95 (1-55550-990-8) Universe.

Simple Surveying. Keith Miller. (C). 1977. 21.00 (0-907649-58-0, Pub. by Expedit Advisory Centre UK) St Mut.

Simple Systems, Complex Environments: Hospital Financial Information Systems. Mari Malvey. LC 80-29597. (Managing Information Ser.: No. 2). 188p. 1981. reprint ed. pap. 53.60 (0-608-01473-7, 2059517) Bks Demand.

Simple Takes a Wife. Langston Hughes. 1994. lib. bdg. 24.95 (1-56849-398-3) Buccaneer Bks.

Simple Talks on the Tabernacle. D. H. Dolman. LC 92-39335. 224p. 1993. pap. 9.99 (0-8254-2457-7) Kregel.

Simple Task-Centered Exercises as an Aid to Social Work Training. Kay McDougall. 1977. 25.00 (0-317-42899-3, Pub. by Natl Inst Soc Work) St Mut.

Simple Tent Camping: The Basics of Camping from Car or Canoe. Zora Aiken & David Aiken. (Illus.). 224p. 1996. pap. text ed. 15.95 (0-07-073021-0, Ragged Mntn) Intl Marine.

Simple Texas Wedding. Ruth J. Dale. (Romance Ser.). 1996. mass mkt. 3.25 (0-373-03424-5, 1-03424-8) Harlequin Bks.

Simple Theory, Hard Reality: The Impact of Sentencing Reforms on Courts, Prisons & Crime. Tamasak Wicharaya. LC 94-31688. (SUNY Series in New Directions in Crime & Justice Studies). 235p. (C). 1995. text ed. 49.50 (0-7914-2507-X); pap. text ed. 16.95 (0-7914-2508-8) State U NY Pr.

Simple Theory of the Self. David W. Mann. 160p. (C). 1994. 25.00 (0-393-70172-7) Norton.

Simple Things. Teri Probasco. 36p. (J). (ps-6). 1994. pap. 5.90 (0-932970-98-2) Prinit Pr.

Simple Things: A Collection of Forty-Six Still Life Photographs. Robert Golden. (Illus.). 64p. 1989. 40.00 (0-685-21903-8); pap. 24.99 (0-685-21904-6) Wits End Pub.

Simple Things & Simple Thoughts. Eldon Taylor. Ed. by Norma Anderson. Tr. by Gary L. Pedrosa. 116p. 1988. pap. 8.95 (0-916095-18-5) R K Bks.

Simple Things of the Christian Life. G. Campbell Morgan. 1984. pap. 3.25 (0-915374-40-4) Rapids Christian.

Simple Things to Make & Do. A. Wilkes & C. Rosen. (Simple Activities Ser.). (Illus.). 72p. (J). (gr. 2-6). 1986. pap. 8.95 (0-7460-0549-0, Usborne) EDC.

Simple Things to the Believer: A Collection of Photos & Verse. Christine M. Moyer. (Illus.). 53p. (Orig.). 1994. pap. 9.95 (1-886453-00-4) Candleberry Pr.

***Simple Things Won't Save the Earth.** J. Robert Hunter. LC 96-35689. 216p. 1997. 35.00 (0-292-73112-4); pap. 15.95 (0-292-73113-2) U of Tex Pr.

Simple Thoughts. Mike Hamill. Ed. by Judy L. Wofter. (Illus.). 78p. (Orig.). 1983. pap. 7.95 (0-912477-00-8, TX 1-086-794) Ogab Pubs.

***Simple Thoughts on Finding Love & Marriage.** Anne Meridien. LC 97-26203. 96p. 1997. pap. 7.00 (1-56170-428-8) Hay House.

Simple Times. Clara Leppert. (Folk Literature Ser.). 48p. 1993. pap. 5.95 (1-87781-07-3) Free River Pr.

Simple Tiny Cross-Stitch. Ondori Publishing Company Staff. (Illus.). 72p. (Orig.). 1990. pap. 12.95 (0-87040-864-X) Japan Pubns USA.

Simple to Sew: Appliques. Helen Milsavijevich. 1996. 7.98 (0-7858-0361-0) Bk Sales Inc.

Simple to Sew: Cross-Stitch. Dorthea Hall. 1996. 7.98 (0-7858-0360-2) Bk Sales Inc.

Simple to Sew: Needlepoint. Hilary More. 1996. 7.98 (0-7858-0362-9) Bk Sales Inc.

Simple to Sew: Patchwork & Quilting. Katherine Guerrici. 1996. 7.98 (0-7858-0363-7) Bk Sales Inc.

Simple Treasures. Lighten Up Enterprises Staff. (Places of the Heart Ser.). 366p. 1994. spiral bd. 8.50 (1-879127-36-9) Lighten Up Enter.

Simple Treasures for a Complex World: A Collection of Inspirational, Practical & Insightful Principles. Linda B. James. 116p. 1994. text ed. 12.95 (0-9639315-4-7) Five-Star NJ.

Simple Truth. Carl Allensworth. 1963. pap. 3.25 (0-8222-1029-0) Dramatists Play.

Simple Truth. Mary-Alice Jafolla. LC 81-69084. 109p. (J). 1993. pap. 9.95 (0-87159-199-5) Unity Bks.

Simple Truth. Elizabeth Hardwick. LC 81-43389. (Neglected Books of the 20th Century Ser.). 278p. 1982. reprint ed. 12.95 (0-912946-98-9) Ecco Pr.

Simple Truth: Ideas & Experiences for Humans from Less-Than-Perfect Families. Thom Rutledge. 105p. 1994. pap. 8.95 (0-9627963-0-1) T W Rutledge.

Simple Truth: Poems. Philip Levine. LC 94-14508. 1994. 20.00 (0-679-43580-8) Knopf.

Simple Truth: Poems. Philip Levine. 1996. pap. 13.00 (0-679-76584-0) Knopf.

Simple Truths. Jack Byrd, Jr. et al. LC 91-65108. (Illus.). 160p. 1991. pap. 14.95 (1-879727-00-5) Think About Pr.

Simple Truths. Jan Dargatz. LC 94-43145. 1995. pap. text ed. 10.99 (0-8407-9139-9) Nelson.

Simple Truths: Clear & Gentle Guidance on the Big Issues in Life. Kent Nerburn. LC 96-5130. 112p. (Orig.). 1996. 14.00 (1-880032-92-9) New Wrld Lib.

***Simple Truths: Thinking Life Through.** Fulton J. Sheen. LC 97-24513. 1998. write for info. (0-7648-0169-4, Triumph Books) Liguori Pubns.

***Simple Truths Signed.** Philip Levine. 1996. 20.00 (0-676-51725-0) Random.

Simple Twist of Fate. Marianne Evans. 1994. pap. 4.99 (0-451-18375-4, Sig) NAL-Dutton.

Simple Twist of Fate. Mary Anne Evans. 1994. pap. write for info. (0-451-18326-6, Sig) NAL-Dutton.

***Simple Upholstery & Slipcovers: Great New Looks for Every Room.** Carol Parks. 1996. 24.95 (0-8069-8158-X, 96-24162) Lark Books.

***Simple Upholstery & Slipcovers: Great New Looks for Every Room.** Carol Parks. 1997. pap. text ed. 14.95 (0-8069-8159-8) Sterling.

Simple Vegetarian Cookery. Paul Cartan. 1974. lib. bdg. 69.95 (0-685-51356-4) Revisionist Pr.

Simple Versions of Disaster. Jerry Bradley. LC 91-8955. (Texas Poets Ser.: Vol. 3). 134p. 1991. pap. 9.95 (0-929398-25-4) UNTX Pr.

Simple Vietnamese for Americans. Nguyen Cuong. 22.50 (0-87559-169-8) Shalom.

Simple Views on Condensed Matter. Pierre-Gilles De Gennes. (Series in Modern Condensed Matter Physics: No. 4). 428p. 1992. text ed. 86.00 (981-02-0909-6); pap. text ed. 48.00 (981-02-0910-X) World Scientific Pub.

Simple Way to Pray. Tr. by C. J. Trapp. 32p. (Orig.). 1983. pap. 1.50 (0-8100-0166-7, 06N0564) Northwest Pub.

Simple Way to Solve the Health Care Crisis: Both the Health Care & the Cost of Health Care. Maynard C. Meierhofer. 1995. 12.95 (0-533-11353-9) Vantage.

Simple Ways to Help Your Kids Become Dollar-Smart. Elizabeth Lewin & Bernard Ryan, Jr. LC 93-36832. 128p. (Orig.). 1994. pap. 8.95 (0-8027-7429-6) Walker & Co.

Simple Ways to Make Teaching Math More Fun: Elementary School Edition. Bob Algozzine & James E. Ysseldyke. (Simple Ways Ser.). (Illus.). 88p. 1994. teacher ed., pap. text ed. 14.95 (1-57035-028-0, 50MATH) Sopris.

***Simple Ways to Pray for Healing.** Matthew Linn et al. (Illus.). 128p. 1998. 9.95 (0-8091-3762-3) Paulist Pr.

Simple Ways to Protect Your Inventions (Ideas) James M. DeVone. LC 90-91834. (Illus.). 50p. (Orig.). (C). 1990. pap. text ed. 49.95 (0-9625092-7-2) Schl Univ Studies.

Simple Ways to Protect Yourself from Lawsuits: A Complete Guide to Asset Protection. Mark Warda. LC 95-74590. 216p. (Orig.). 1995. pap. 24.95 (1-57248-020-3, Leg Surv Guides) Sourcebks.

Simple Ways to Save Money on Insurance, Vol. 1. J. C. Erickson. 120p. (Orig.). 1988. pap. 8.95 (0-9621175-0-1) Finan Mktg Inc.

Simple Ways to Say I Love You. Debbie Hansen. 366p. (Orig.). 1993. pap. 8.95 (1-56245-048-4) Great Quotations.

Simple Ways to Wellness: A Workbook for Self-Healing. Louise Taylor. 1995. pap. 19.95 (0-8048-3048-7) C E Tuttle.

Simple Weather Experiments with Everyday Materials. Frances W. Zweifel. LC 90-37915. (Illus.). 128p. (J). (gr. 4 up). 1991. pap. 4.95 (0-8069-7295-5) Sterling.

Simple Welcome Speeches. Amy Bolding. 112p. (gr. 10). 1973. reprint ed. pap. 6.99 (0-8010-0612-0) Baker Bks.

Simple Will in Ohio. Marilyn J. Maag. (Anderson's Ohio Practice Manual Ser.). 1991. pap. 25.50 (0-87084-550-0) Anderson Pub Co.

***Simple Will in Ohio.** 2nd ed. Marilyn J. Maag. (Ohio Practice Manual Ser.). 131p. 1996. pap. 35.00 (0-87084-547-0) Anderson Pub Co.

Simple Wisdom: Shaker Sayings, Poems, & Songs. Kathleen Mahoney. LC 92-50729. 1993. pap. 13.95 (0-670-84808-5, Viking Studio) Studio Bks.

***Simple Wish: Make a Simple Wish of Your Very Own.** Catherine Daly-Weir. (Simple Wish Ser.). 24p. (Orig.). (J). (gr. 2-5). 1997. pap. 4.95 (0-448-41635-2, G&D) Putnam Pub Group.

***Simple Wish: The Junior Novelization.** Francine Hughes. (Simple Wish Ser.). 24p. (Orig.). (J). (gr. 2-5). 1997. pap. 4.95 (0-448-41636-0, G&D) Putnam Pub Group.

Simple Wonders: The Disarming Pleasure of Looking Beyond the Seen. Christopher De Vinck. 144p. 1995. 12.99 (0-310-49891-0) Zondervan.

Simple WordPerfect for Busy People. Maria Reidelbach. 1992. pap. 27.00 (1-56243-080-7, 4QZ) DDC Pub.

Simple, Yet Elegant: A Cookbook for Busy Schedules. Betsy Starr. 140p. 1992. pap. text ed. 14.00 (0-9635000-0-7) EES Pub FL.

Simple Yet Stunning Quilts. Rita Davis. (Illus.). 80p. 1981. pap. 8.95 (0-942152-07-7) R C Pubns OR.

Simple Yoga & Therapy. Yogeswar. (Illus.). 340p. 1987. 16.95 (0-318-36399-2) Asia Bk Corp.

SimPleat. Lee J. McFarland. 41p. 1988. pap. 6.00 (1-883763-03-7) Kideko Hse.

Simplemente Religioso o Cristiano de Verdad? Henry Bryant. 80p. (SPA.). 1990. pap. 2.99 (0-8254-1080-0, Edit Portavoz) Kregel.

Simplemente Versos y Poesias. Paulino S. Rodriguez. 144p. 1995. lib. bdg. write for info. (1-888598-00-X) P S Rodriguez.

Simplemento Yo. Trini M. Campbell. 62p. (Orig.). 1993. pap. 5.00 (0-913983-06-3) M & A Edns.

***Simpler German Course.** Russon. Date not set. pap. text ed. write for info. (0-582-36168-0, Pub. by Longman UK) Longman.

Simpler Life: Memories of Childhood at Sea, 1902-1910. Burgess Cogill. (Illus.). 1990. 17.95 (0-393-02716-3) Norton.

Simpler Place: A Simpler Time. Odis G. Stephenson. 68p. 1995. pap. 9.95 (0-9646039-0-X) O G Stephenson.

Simpler Times. Anne C. Buchanan. 96p. (Orig.). 1996. 24.99 (1-56507-416-5) Harvest Hse.

Simpler Times. Ray Cunningham. 215p. 1991. pap. 9.95 (0-9631251-1-7) R Cunningham.

Simpler Times: Stories of Early Twentieth Century City Life. J. George Butler. 208p. 1994. 19.95 (0-918339-25-1) Vandamere.

***Simpler Times Guest Book.** Thomas Kinkade. (Illus.). 96p. 1997. 12.99 (1-56507-614-1) Harvest Hse.

***Simpler Times Sketchbook.** Thomas Kinkade. (Illus.). 128p. 1997. spiral bd. 14.99 (1-56507-606-0) Harvest Hse.

Simpler Way. Margaret J. Wheatley & Myron Kellner-Rogers. LC 96-15999. (Illus.). 168p. 1996. 27.95 (1-881052-95-8) Berrett-Koehler.

Simpler Way: Silverton, Colorado. (Illus.). 64p. 1990. pap. 8.95 (0-685-71529-9) Simpler Way.

Simples, Superstitions & Solace see Herbs & Herb Lore of Colonial America

Simplest Game: Intelligent Fan's Guide to the World of Soccer. 3rd ed. Paul Gardner. 384p. 1996. 14.95 (0-02-860401-6) Macmillan.

Simplest Mathematics see Collected Papers of Charles Sanders Peirce

Simplest of Gifts, the Greatest of Powers: A Fable. H. Bradley Stucki. 170p. (Orig.). 1996. pap. 9.95 (1-888106-11-5) Custom Fmly.

Simplex Method. K. H. Borgwardt. (Algorithms & Combinatorics Ser.: Vol. 1). (Illus.). xi, 268p. 1986. 71.95 (0-387-17096-0) Spr-Verlag.

Simplication of American Life: Hollywood's Films of the 1930's. Jeffery M. Paine. 1977. 29.95 (0-405-09893-6, 11489) Ayer.

Simpliciad. Richard Mant. LC 91-3947. 62p. 1991. reprint ed. 35.00 (1-85477-076-4, Pub. by Woodstock Bks UK) Cassell.

Simplicial Algorithms on the Simplotope. T. M. Doup. (Lecture Notes in Economics & Mathematical Systems Ser.: Vol. 318). viii, 262p. 1988. 38.70 (0-387-50233-5) Spr-Verlag.

Simplicial Methods & the Interpretation of "Triple" Cohomolgy. J. Duskin. LC 75-20008. (Memoirs Ser.: No. 3/163). 135p. 1975. pap. 21.00 (0-8218-1863-5, MEMO/3/163) Am Math.

Simplicial Objects in Algebraic Topology. J. Peter May. LC 82-51078. (Chicago Lectures in Mathematics). viii, 170p. (C). 1992. pap. text ed. 26.50 (0-226-51181-2) U Ch Pr.

Simplicissimus. unabridged ed. Grimmelshausen. (World Classic Literature Ser.). (GER.). pap. 7.95 (3-89507-006-8, Pub. by Bookking Intl FR) Distribks Inc.

Simplicissimus: One-Hundred Eighty Satirical Drawings from the Famous German Weekly. Ed. & Tr. by Stanley Appelbaum from GER. LC 74-79171. (Illus.). 172p. 1975. 14.95 (0-486-23099-6) Dover.

Simplicities: Poems. Oscar Mandel. LC 74-79131. 64p. 1974. pap. 4.00 (0-914502-01-8) Spectrum Prods.

Simplicity. Edward G. Dobson. 192p. 1995. pap. 9.99 (0-310-48701-3) Zondervan.

Simplicity. Ruth Stone. LC 94-40667. 136p. (Orig.). 1995. pap. 12.95 (0-9638183-1-7) Paris Pr MA.

Simplicity. John M. Talbot & Dan O'Neill. 179p. (Orig.). (C). 1989. pap. 9.99 (0-89283-635-0) Servant.

Simplicity: A Distinctive Quality of Japanese Spirituality. John T. Brinkman. (Berkeley Insights in Linguistics & Semiotics Ser.: Vol. 23). 275p. (C). 1996. pap. 33.95 (0-8204-2726-8) P Lang Pubng.

Simplicity: A Rich Quaker's View. George Peck. LC 72-97851. (Orig.). 1973. pap. 3.00 (0-87574-189-4) Pendle Hill.

An Asterisk (*) at the beginning of an entry indicates that the title is appearing in BIP for the first time.

***Simplicity: Bed & Bath.** Date not set. pap. 9.95 (*0-87596-965-8*) Rodale Pr Inc.

Simplicity: Kingdom Living Through the Eyes of a Child. Betty Malz. LC 95-43028. 208p. (gr. 10). 1996. 12.99 (*0-8007-9240-8*) Chosen Bks.

Simplicity: Notes, Stories & Exercises for Developing Unimaginable Wealth. Mark A. Burch. 144p. 1995. pap. 12.95 (*0-86571-323-5*); lib. bdg. 34.95 (*0-86571-322-7*) New Soc Pubs.

Simplicity: The Art of Living. Richard Rohr. 180p. 1992. pap. 11.95 (*0-8245-1251-0*) Crossroad NY.

***Simplicity & Complexity: Pondering Literature, Science, & Painting.** Floyd Merrell. (C). 1997. 44.50 (*0-472-10860-3*) U of Mich Pr.

Simplicity & Complexity in Games of the Intellect. Lawrence B. Slobodkin. (Illus.). 266p. (C). 1992. text ed. 27.50 (*0-674-80825-8*) HUP.

Simplicity & Complexity in Games of the Intellect. Lawrence B. Slobodkin. 266p. 1993. pap. text ed. 12.95 (*0-674-80826-6*) HUP.

Simplicity & Joy of Meditation. Stephen R. Daisy. 180p. 1995. pap. 11.95 (*0-87193-285-7*) Dimension Bks.

Simplicity & Ordinariness: Studies in Medieval Cistercian History, Vol. IV. Ed. by John R. Sommerfeldt. (Cistercian Studies: No. 61). (Orig.). 1980. pap. text ed. 2.00 (*0-87907-861-8*) Cistercian Pubns.

Simplicity & Reality of the Bible: A Revolutionary Bible Handbook. Eric Demaree. LC 87-91608. 97p. (Orig.). 1988. pap. 6.00 (*0-9619367-0-3*) Fellowship Bks.

***Simplicity As Evidence of Truth, Vol. 1997 or No. 61.** Richard Swinburne. LC 96-51315. (Aquinas Lectures). 1997. 15.00 (*0-87462-164-X*) Marquette.

Simplicity Fitting Book. rev. ed. Ed. by Jo Kirshon. (Illus.). (Orig.). 1978. pap. 3.50 (*0-685-08975-4*) Simplicity.

Simplicity in Generative Morphology. Harry Bochner. LC 92-28365. (Publications in Language Sciences: Vol. 37). vi, 247p. 1992. pap. 98.50 (*3-11-013594-9*) Mouton.

Simplicity of Life As Lived in the Everyday. Kathleen Storms. LC 83-16812. 322p. (Orig.). (C). 1984. lib. bdg. 52.50 (*0-8191-3601-8*) U Pr of Amer.

Simplicity Wins: How Germany's Mid-Sized Industrial Companies Succeed. Gunter Rommel et al. LC 94-34599. 240p. 1995. 27.95 (*0-87584-504-5*) Harvard Busn.

Simplicity Wins: How Germany's Mid-Sized Industrial Companies Succeed. Gunter Rommel et al. 1995. text ed. 27.95 (*0-07-103617-2*) McGraw.

Simplicity's Quick & Easy Sewing for the Home: Bed & Bath. Simplicity Pattern Co. Staff. (Illus.). 128p. 1995. 19.95 (*0-87596-660-8*) Rodale Pr Inc.

***Simplicity's Quick & Easy Sewing for the Home: Windows.** 128p. 1997. pap. 9.95 (*0-87596-966-6*) Rodale Pr Inc.

Simplicity's Quick & Easy Sewing for the Home: Windows, Vol. 1. Simplicity Pattern Co. Staff. LC 94-44847. (Illus.). 128p. 1995. 19.95 (*0-87596-676-4*) Rodale Pr Inc.

Simplicity's Simply the Best Book of Home Decorating. Simplicity Pattern Co. Staff. (Illus.). 224p. 1993. pap. 20.00 (*0-671-76712-7*, Fireside) S&S Trade.

Simplicius, Commentaire sur les Categories, Traduction Commentee, Fascicule I: Introduction, Premiere Partie. Ed. by Ilsetraut Hadot. LC 89-7342. (Philosophia Antiqua Ser.: Vol. 50). x, 239p. (FRE.). 1990. pap. 62.75 (*90-04-09015-0*) E J Brill.

Simplicius, Commentaire sur les Categories, Traduction Commentee, Fascicule III: Commentaire au Premier Chapitre de Categories. Ed. by Ilsetraut Hadot. LC 89-7342. (Philosophia Antiqua Ser.: Vol. 51). ix, 179p. (FRE.). 1990. pap. 50.00 (*90-04-09016-9*) E J Brill.

***Simplification of Operating Regulations for Public Limited Companies in the in the European Union: Final Report Dec. 1995.** 455p. 1996. pap. 105.00 (*92-827-7243-8*, CM96-96-142-ENC, Pub. by Europ Com UK) Bernan Associates.

Simplifications Staliniennes et Complications Sovietiques. Gabor T. Rittersporn. 384p. 1988. pap. text ed. 86.00 (*2-88124-223-5*) Gordon & Breach.

Simplified Accompaniments: 97 Hymns from The Hymnal 1992. Ed. by John E. Williams. 160p. 1994. pap. 18.95 (*0-89869-197-4*) Church Pub Inc.

Simplified Approach to Electrocardiography. Richard A. Johnson & Mark Schwartz. (Illus.). 331p. 1986. pap. text ed. 32.50 (*0-7216-1738-7*) Saunders.

Simplified Approach to S-370 Assembly Language Programming. Barbara J. Burian. (Illus.). 1977. text ed. write for info. (*0-13-810119-1*) P-H.

Simplified Astronomy for Astrologers. David Williams. 108p. 1969. 6.00 (*0-86690-172-8*, W1525-014) Am Fed Astrologers.

Simplified Baldrige Award Organization Assessment. Donald C. Fisher. LC 92-20055. 240p. 1993. student ed., pap. 32.95 (*1-879111-51-9*) Lincoln-Bradley.

Simplified Basic Programming for IBM PCs, Ps-2s, Compatible & Clones. 2nd ed. Gerald A. Silver & Myrna L. Silver. Orig. Title: Simplified Basic Programming for Microcomputers. (Illus.). 350p. (C). 1988. teacher ed. write for info. (*0-912675-27-6*); pap. text ed. 24.95 (*0-912675-26-8*) Ardsley.

Simplified Basic Programming for Microcomputers see Simplified Basic Programming for IBM PCs, Ps-2s, Compatible & Clones

Simplified Behavior & "Feeling" State Change & Goal Accomplishment, Set-SB. Russell E. Mason. 1975. Incl. Tape 1A, T-2, T-5A, T-3, T-16, T-17; Notes; Cinical Applications (rev. 1979); Outlines 3, Subs. pap. 60.00 incl. audio (*0-89533-002-4*) F I Comm.

Simplified Building Design for Wind & Earthquake Forces. 3rd ed. James E. Ambrose & Dimitry Vergun. (Parker/Ambrose Series of Simplified Design Guides). 336p. 1995. text ed. 59.95 (*0-471-30958-3*) Wiley.

Simplified Buying Guide. 1988. 2.00 (*0-318-33255-8*, 102) Am Bartenders.

Simplified Buying Guide: Child & Adult Care Food Program. California Department of Education Staff. 144p. 1992. pap. 9.00 (*0-8011-0980-9*) Calif Education.

Simplified Catechism. Sandra Greenfield & Ardis Koeller. 85p. (Orig.). (J). 1988. pap. 5.95 (*0-8100-0270-1*, 07N0753) Northwest Pub.

Simplified Catechism-Bible Stories. Sandra Greenfield & Ardis Koeller. 71p. (Orig.). (J). 1988. pap. 5.95 (*0-8100-0285-X*, 07N0755) Northwest Pub.

Simplified Cellular. Dennis Bishop. 160p. 1991. pap. 29.00 (*1-880008-00-9*) Bishop & Assoc.

Simplified Chart Calculations: Step by Step Instructions. Bobbye Bratcher-Nelson & Carol A. Wiggers. (Illus.). 52p. (C). 1991. student ed. 12.00 (*1-878935-13-5*) JustUs & Assocs.

Simplified Chinese Characters. Tan Huay Peng. (Peng's Chinese Treasury Ser.). (Illus.). 128p. 1987. pap. 5.95 (*0-89346-293-4*) Heian Intl.

Simplified Christmas Carols for Piano. Donna R. Wangsgard. 1992. 9.98 (*0-88290-455-8*) Horizon Utah.

Simplified Circuit Analysis: Digital-Analog Logic. Richard D. Sacks et al. LC 79-179386. (Illus.). 174p. reprint ed. pap. 49.60 (*0-317-08020-2*, 2017857) Bks Demand.

Simplified Classics for Piano. Ed. by Marcel Frank. (Carl Fischer's "All Time Favorites" Music Ser.). 160p. (Orig.). 1984. pap. 10.95 (*0-8258-0347-0*, ATF105) Fischer Inc NY.

Simplified Classifieds: 1001 Real Estate Ads That Sell. Bradley Pivar & William H. Plvar. 286p. 1990. pap. 29.95 (*0-7931-0086-0*, 1926-0201) Dearborn Finan.

Simplified Computer Programming: Including the Easy RPG Way. Kelton Carson. LC 73-90739. (Illus.). 240p. 1974. pap. 8.95 (*0-8306-3676-5*, 676) McGraw-Hill Prof.

Simplified Design: Reinforced Concrete Buildings of Moderate Size & Height. 2nd ed. Portland Cement Association Staff. (Illus.). 256p. (C). 1993. 30.00 (*0-89312-129-0*, EB104D) Portland Cement.

Simplified Design for Building Fire Safety. James Patterson. LC 93-1037. (Parker Series of Simplified Design Guides). 344p. 1993. text ed. 54.95 (*0-471-57236-5*) Wiley.

Simplified Design for Building Sound Control. James E. Ambrose & Jeffrey E. Ollswang. LC 94-23802. 350p. 1995. text ed. 59.95 (*0-471-56908-9*) Wiley.

Simplified Design of Building Foundations. 2nd ed. James E. Ambrose. LC 88-17221. (Parker Series of Simplified Design Handbooks). 237p. 1988. text ed. 59.95 (*0-471-85898-6*) Wiley.

Simplified Design of Building Lighting. Mark Schiler. LC 92-771. (Parker Series of Simplified Design Guides: No. 1879). 168p. 1992. text ed. 59.95 (*0-471-53213-4*) Wiley.

Simplified Design of Building Structures. 2nd ed. James E. Ambrose. LC 90-27415. 280p. (C). 1993. reprint ed. lib. bdg. 42.50 (*0-89464-574-9*) Krieger.

Simplified Design of Building Structures. 3rd ed. James E. Ambrose. LC 95-16411. (Parker Ambrose Series of Simplified Design Guides). 288p. 1995. text ed. 59.95 (*0-471-03744-3*) Wiley.

Simplified Design of Concrete Buildings of Moderate Size & Height. 160p. 1984. 15.75 (*0-317-37041-3*) ACI.

Simplified Design of Concrete Structures. 6th ed. James E. Ambrose & Harry Parker. LC 90-37690. (Parker Series of Simplified Design Handbooks). 390p. 1991. text ed. 59.95 (*0-471-52204-X*) Wiley.

Simplified Design of Concrete Stuctures. 7th ed. James E. Ambrose & Harry Parker. LC 96-23740. (Parker-Ambrose Series of Simplified Design). 1996. text ed. 54.95 (*0-471-13918-1*) Wiley.

***Simplified Design of Data Converters.** LC 96-48397. (EDN Series for Design Engineers). 1997. pap. write for info. (*0-7506-9509-0*) Buttrwrth-Heinemann.

Simplified Design of HVAC Systems. William Bobenhausen. (Parker Simplified Design Guides Ser.). 448p. 1994. text ed. 59.95 (*0-471-53280-0*) Wiley.

Simplified Design of IC Amplifiers. John Lenk. (EDN Series for Design Engineers). (Illus.). 240p. 1996. pap. 29.95 (*0-7506-9508-0*) Buttrwrth-Heinemann.

Simplified Design of Linear Power Supplies. John D. Lenk. LC 94-16077. (EDN Ser.). 240p. 1994. 39.95 (*0-7506-9506-4*) Buttrwrth-Heinemann.

Simplified Design of Linear Power Supplies. John D. Lenk. (Illus.). 246p. 1996. pap. 29.95 (*0-7506-9820-9*) Buttrwrth-Heinemann.

***Simplified Design of Masonry Structures.** James E. Ambrose. pap. text ed. 45.00 (*0-471-17988-4*) Wiley.

Simplified Design of Masonry Structures. James E. Ambrose. LC 90-46401. (Parker Series of Simplified Design Handbooks). 201p. 1991. text ed. 69.95 (*0-471-52439-5*) Wiley.

Simplified Design of Micropower & Battery Circuits. John Lenk. LC 95-4867. (EDN Series for Design Engineers). (Illus.). 240p. 1995. pap. 29.95 (*0-7506-9510-2*, Focal) Buttrwrth-Heinemann.

Simplified Design of Steel Structures. 6th ed. Harry Parker & James E. Ambrose. LC 89-22631. 437p. 1990. text ed. 59.95 (*0-471-50539-0*) Wiley.

***Simplified Design of Steel Structures.** 7th ed. James E. Ambrose & Harry Parker. LC 97-51. (Parker-Ambrose Simplified Design Guides Ser.). 1997. 59.95 (*0-471-16574-3*) Wiley.

Simplified Design of Switching Power Supplies. John D. Lenk. LC 94-32727. (EDN Ser.). 248p. 1994. 39.95 (*0-7506-9507-2*) Buttrwrth-Heinemann.

Simplified Design of Switching Power Supplies. John D. Lenk. (Illus.). 246p. 1996. pap. 29.95 (*0-7506-9821-7*) Buttrwrth-Heinemann.

Simplified Design of Wood Structures. 5th ed. Harry Parker & James Ambrose. 368p. 1994. text ed. 59.95 (*0-471-30366-6*) Wiley.

***Simplified Design of Wood Structures.** 5th ed. Harry Parker & James E. Ambrose. pap. text ed. 45.00 (*0-471-17989-2*) Wiley.

Simplified Dictionary of Modern Samoan. R. W. Allardice. 228p. 1986. pap. text ed. 29.00 (*0-908597-02-9*) UH Pr.

Simplified Dictionary of Modern Tongan. Edgar Tu'inukuafe. 240p. 1992. pap. text ed. 27.00 (*0-908597-09-6*) UH Pr.

Simplified Diet Manual: Iowa Dietetic Association. 7th ed. Ed. by Judy Fitzgibbons. (Illus.). 142p. 1995. 26.95 (*0-8138-1426-X*) Iowa St U Pr.

Simplified Diet Manual: Iowa Dietetic Association. 7th ed. Iowa Dietetic Association Staff. Ed. by Judy Fitzgibbons. LC 94-44098. (Illus.). 90p. 1995. student ed., pap. text ed. 19.95 (*0-8138-1427-8*) Iowa St U Pr.

Simplified Drugs & Solutions for Health Care Professionals. 11th ed. Dison. 320p. (C). (gr. 13). 1996. pap. text ed. 19.95 (*0-8151-2505-4*) Mosby Yr Bk.

Simplified EKG Analysis: A Sequential Guide to Interpretation. Ed. by Charles B. Seelig. (Illus.). 600p. (Orig.). 1992. pap. text ed. 20.95 (*1-56053-010-3*) Hanley & Belfus.

Simplified Electrical Wiring Design Handbook. John D. Lenk. LC 92-11463. 336p. 1992. text ed. 52.00 (*0-13-814047-2*) P-H.

Simplified Employee Pensions: What Small Businesses Need to Know. 1991. lib. bdg. 69.00 (*0-8490-5088-X*) Gordon Pr.

Simplified Energy Analysis Using the Modified Bin Method. (Illus.). 240p. 1984. 49.00 (*0-910110-39-5*) Am Heat Ref & Air Eng.

Simplified Engineering for Architects & Builders. 8th ed. James E. Ambrose & Harry Parker. (Parker Series of Simplified Design Guides). 704p. 1993. text ed. 59.95 (*0-471-58703-6*) Wiley.

Simplified Engineering for Architects & Builders. 8th ed. James E. Ambrose. (Parker-Ambrose Series of Simplified Design). 112p. 1993. student ed., pap. text ed. 27.50 (*0-471-58860-1*) Wiley.

Simplified Estimating for Builders & Engineers. 2nd ed. Joseph E. Helton. 224p. 1991. text ed. 66.00 (*0-13-812967-3*) P-H.

Simplified Existence. Lothario. Ed. by Teresa A. Pitts. 17p. (Orig.). 1992. 7.95 (*0-9636309-0-3*, TXU514949) Lothario.

Simplified Extended, Deep, & or Meditative Relaxation, Set-R. Russell E. Mason. 1975. Incl. Tape 1A, T-1, T-6; Clinical Applications (rev. 1979); Brief Outlines 1, Relaxation Trng. pap. 35.00 incl. audio (*0-89533-004-0*) F I Comm.

Simplified Fly Fishing. S. R. Slaymaker, II. LC 87-7088. (Illus.). 160p. 1988. pap. 12.95 (*0-8117-2279-1*) Stackpole.

Simplified Framework Evaluation of Water Resource Project Impacts. Brian W. Clowes. LC 90-43713. (Environment: Problems & Solutions Ser.: Vol. 3). 486p. 1990. text ed. 30.00 (*0-8240-0411-6*) Garland.

Simplified Governmental Budgeting. Edward A. Lehan. LC 81-82463. (Illus.). 86p. 1981. 30.00 (*0-686-84272-3*); student ed. 15.00 (*0-686-84273-1*) Municipal.

Simplified Grammar of the Gujarati Language. W. M. Clair Tisdall. (ENG & GUJ.). 1986. 29.95 (*0-8288-8429-3*) Fr & Eur.

***Simplified Grammar of the Pali Language.** E. Muller. (C). 1995. reprint ed. 18.00 (*81-206-1103-9*, Pub. by Asian Educ Servs II) S Asia.

Simplified Guide to BHS: Critical Apparatus, Masora, Accents, Unusual Letters & Other Markings. 3rd ed. William R. Scott. 96p. 1995. pap. 7.95 (*0-941037-35-5*) BIBAL Pr.

Simplified Guide to Bishops' Transcripts & Marriage Licenses, Their Location & Indexes in England, Wales, & Ireland. J. S. W. Gibson. LC 82-82482. 40p. 1991. reprint ed. pap. 6.00 (*0-8063-0995-4*) Genealog Pub.

Simplified Guide to Common Colorado Grasses. 2nd rev. ed. Janet L. Wingate. (Illus.). 1995. pap. 4.00 (*0-9647543-2-0*) Wingate Cnslt.

***Simplified Guide to Construction Law.** James Acret. 1997. 29.95 (*1-55701-176-1*) BNI Pubns.

Simplified Guide to Custom Stairbuilding & Handrailing. George Di Cristina. LC 94-7753. (Illus.). 278p. 1994. 34.95 (*0-941936-27-9*) Linden Pub Fresno.

Simplified Guide to Microcomputers with Practical Programs & Applications. William A. Bocchino. LC 82-3671. 256p. 1982. 19.95 (*0-13-810085-3*, Busn) P-H.

Simplified Guide to Nutritional Supplements. Sam Ziff & Michael F. Ziff. 160p. (Orig.). 1994. pap. 12.00 (*0-941011-10-0*) Bio-Probe.

Simplified Guide to Probate Jurisdictions: Where to Look for Wills in Great Britain & Ireland. J. S. W. Gibson. LC 82-82481. (Illus.). 72p. 1989. pap. 7.50 (*0-8063-0994-6*) Genealog Pub.

Simplified Guide to Structured COBOL Programming. 2nd ed. Daniel D. McCracken & Donald G. Golden. LC 87-34608. 630p. 1988. Net. pap. text ed. 37.50 (*0-471-88658-0*) Wiley.

Simplified Guide to Using Statistical Techniques with Computer Applications. Margaret N. Morrison. LC 86-3242. 206p. 1986. text ed. 29.95 (*0-13-810185-X*, Busn) P-H.

Simplified Guidelines for Evaluating Transit Service in Small Urban Areas. (National Cooperative Transit Research Program Synthesis Ser.: No. 8). 119p. 1984. 10.40 (*0-309-03852-9*) Transport Res Bd.

Simplified Hairdressing Science. David Salinger & Jon Williams. (Illus.). 180p. 1986. pap. text ed. 15.95 (*0-9614548-4-9*) Intl Assn Trichologists.

Simplified Hazardous Materials Chemistry. Pollution Engineering Staff. 239p. 1994. 39.95 (*0-934165-39-4*) Gulf Pub.

Simplified Indian Cookery. Rebecca Joseph. 1970. pap. 3.00 (*0-88253-144-1*) Ind-US Inc.

Simplified Instrument Flying - Instructing Techniques. William M. Jones. Ed. by Ronald G. Gallagher. (Illus.). 54p. (C). 1995. pap. text ed. 9.95 (*0-9639984-3-9*) Eastern Dakota.

Simplified Introduction to the Wisdom of St. Thomas. Peter A. Redpath. LC 80-5230. 180p. 1980. pap. text ed. 21.00 (*0-8191-1059-0*) U Pr of Amer.

Simplified Inventory System: For Collectors, Investors & Dealers. E. R. Jones. (Illus.). 68p. 1982. 6.75 (*0-9600934-3-5*) E R Jones.

Simplified Irrigation Design. 2nd ed. Pete Melby. 1995. pap. 35.95 (*0-442-01822-3*) Van Nos Reinhold.

Simplified Job-Resume Preparation. 5th ed. Ray G. Hadley. LC 56-1958. (C). 1981. per. 2.97 (*0-9600988-1-X*) R G Hadley.

Simplified Laboratory Procedures for Wastewater Examination. 3rd ed. Water Pollution Control Federation Staff. LC 85-51664. (Special Series Publications). 105p. 1985. pap. 13.00 (*0-943244-62-5*, MOO18) Water Environ.

Simplified Low-cost Maintenance Control. Wilmer Cooling. LC 82-18380. 122p. reprint ed. pap. 34.80 (*0-317-20412-2*, 2023501) Bks Demand.

Simplified Magic: A Beginner's Guide to the New Age Qabala. Ted Andrews. LC 88-45192. (New Age Ser.). (Illus.). 108p. (Orig.). 1989. mass mkt. 4.99 (*0-87542-015-X*) Llewellyn Pubns.

Simplified Mail Order Bookkeeping System. 1987. lib. bdg. 79.95 (*0-8490-3863-4*) Gordon Pr.

Simplified Mechanics & Strength of Materials. 5th ed. Harry Parker. LC 91-42711. (Parker Series of Simplified Design Guides: No. 1879). 408p. 1992. text ed. 59.95 (*0-471-54170-2*) Wiley.

Simplified Methodology for Community Energy Management Planning. (Technical Report). 116p. 1981. 20.00 (*0-318-17715-3*, DG 81-310) Pub Tech Inc.

Simplified Methods for Estimating Vapor Concentration & Dispersion Distances for Continuous LNG Spills into Dikes with Flat or Sloping Floors. 103p. 1978. pap. 6.00 (*0-318-12699-0*, X50978) Am Gas Assn.

Simplified Methods in Pressure Vessel Analysis: Presented at 1978 ASME-CSME Montreal Pressure Vessel & Piping Conference, Montreal , Quebec, Canada, June 25-29, 1978. Ed. by R. S. Barsoum. LC 78-51570. (PVP Ser.: Vol. 29). (Illus.). 133p. reprint ed. pap. 38.00 (*0-685-23447-9*, 2032701) Bks Demand.

Simplified Piano Arrangements of LDS Hymns. Donna R. Wangsgard. 48p. 1990. pap. 9.98 (*0-88290-410-8*) Horizon Utah.

Simplified Practical Filter Design. Irving M. Gottlieb. 1990. text ed. 26.95 (*0-07-155909-4*) McGraw.

Simplified Practical Filter Design. Irving M. Gottlieb. 1990. pap. 16.95 (*0-07-155919-1*) McGraw.

Simplified Practical Filter Design. Irving M. Gottlieb. (Illus.). 220p. 1990. 26.95 (*0-8306-8355-0*, 3355); pap. 16.95 (*0-8306-3355-3*) McGraw-Hill Prof.

Simplified Precision Bridge. C. C. Wei. Ed. by Robert B. Ewen. (Illus.). 64p. 1972. pap. 4.95 (*0-87643-006-X*) Barclay Bridge.

Simplified Procedures for Evaluating Low-Cost TSM Projects - User's Manual. (National Cooperative Highway Research Program Report Ser.: No. 263). 209p. 1983. 12.80 (*0-309-03604-6*) Transport Res Bd.

***Simplified Procedures for Water Examination.** 4th ed. American Water Works Association Staff. LC 97-25864. (AWWA Manual Ser.). 1997. write for info. (*0-89867-914-1*) Am Water Wks Assn.

Simplified Procedures for Water Examination, No. M12. 194p. 1978. pap. 60.00 (*0-89867-070-5*, 30012) Am Water Wks Assn.

Simplified Purposeful Relaxation for Comfort or Effectiveness, Set-PR. Russell E. Mason. 1975. Incl. Tape 1A, T-2, T-6; Notes; Clinical Applications, rev. ed., 1979. pap. 35.00 incl. audio (*0-89533-003-2*) F I Comm.

Simplified Quantity Recipes: Nursing-Convalescent Homes & Hospitals. Mabel Caviani & Muriel Urbashich. 310p. 1986. pap. 37.70 (*0-317-57875-8*, FP783) Natl Restaurant Assn.

Simplified Radiation Heat Transfer Calculations from Large Open Hydrocarbon Fires. Philip J. DiNenno. 1982. 5.35 (*0-686-37674-9*, TR 82-9) Society Fire Protect.

Simplified Reef Keeping. Robert M. Metelsky. Ed. by Steve Morris. (Illus.). 275p. (Orig.). 1996. pap. text ed. 39.95 (*0-9652843-0-1*) Shoreline Res.

Simplified Reinforced Concrete. Edward G. Nawy. (Illus.). 320p. (C). 1986. text ed. 29.95 (*0-317-29670-1*) P-H.

Simplified Relaxation, Problem Solutions & Substitutions, & Value Considerations, Set-S. Russell E. Mason. 1975. pap. 85.00 incl. audio (*0-89533-020-2*) F I Comm.

***Simplified Sentence Skills.** Barbara Hansen & Rebecca McDaniel. 304p. 1997. pap. 18.95 (*0-8442-5970-5*) NTC Pub Grp.

Simplified Site Design. James E. Ambrose & Peter Brandow. LC 91-26269. (Parker Series of Simplified Design Guides). 216p. 1992. text ed. 54.95 (*0-471-53029-8*) Wiley.

Simplified Site Engineering. 2nd ed. James E. Ambrose et al. LC 91-30112. (Parker Series of Simplified Design Handbooks: No. 1879). 192p. 1991. text ed. 59.95 (*0-471-52809-9*) Wiley.

***Simplified Site Engineering.** 2nd ed. Harry Parker & John W. MacGuire. pap. text ed. 45.00 (*0-471-17987-6*) Wiley.

Simplified Small Business Accounting. Daniel Sitarz. (Small Business Library). 256p. (Orig.). 1995. pap. 19.95 (*0-935755-15-2*) Nova Pub IL.

S

An Asterisk (*) at the beginning of an entry indicates that the title is appearing in BIP for the first time.

S

***Simplified Solutions for Weight Management.** Gay Cline. (Illus.). vi, 202p. (Orig.). 1996. pap. 18.00 (*0-9654762-0-0*) Simplified Solns.

Simplified Staking Manual for Overhead Distribution Lines. Southern Engineering Company Staff. LC 92-34057. 1992. write for info. (*0-917599-08-X*) Natl Rural.

Simplified Structured COBOL with Microsoft-Microfocus COBOL. Daniel D. McCracken & Donald G. Golden. LC 89-27937. 696p. 1990. pap. text ed. 50.00 (*0-471-51407-1*) Wiley.

Simplified Systematic Handling Analysis. 3rd ed. Richard Muther et al. (Illus.). 24p. (C). 1994. pap. 12.00 (*0-933684-11-8*) Mgmt & Indus Res Pubns.

Simplified Systematic Layout Planning. Richard Muther & J. D. Wheeler. 1962. 8.00 (*0-933684-04-5*) Mgmt & Indus Res Pubns.

Simplified Systematic Layout Planning. 3rd ed. Richard Muther & J. D. Wheeler. (Illus.). 36p. (C). 1994. pap. 12.00 (*0-933684-09-6*) Mgmt & Indus Res Pubns.

Simplified Systematic Planning of Manufacturing Cells. Richard Muther et al. (Illus.). 24p. 1996. pap. 12.00 (*0-933684-13-4*) Mgmt & Indus Res Pubns.

Simplified Tai Chi Chuan: 24 & 48 Postures with Martial Applications. rev. ed. Shou-Yu Liang et al. LC 95-61982. (Illus.). 168p. (Orig.). 1996. pap. 14.95 (*1-886969-33-7*, B019R) YMAA Pubn.

Simplified Tax System: The Option for Mexico. Alvin Rabushka. LC 92-46379. (Essays in Public Policy Ser.: No. 38). 1993. pap. 5.00 (*0-8179-5432-5*) Hoover Inst Pr.

Simplified Thermal Design of Building Envelopes for Use with ASHRAE Standard 90-75. 544p. 9.00 (*0-937040-15-0*, JR-179) P-PCI.

Simplified V-Springs: A Guncraftsmanship Manual. Kit Ravenshear. 1991. 3.00 (*0-913150-71-1*) Pioneer Pr.

Simplified Wastewater Treatment Plant Operations. Edward Haller. LC 95-60002. 195p. 1995. pap. text ed. 29.95 (*1-56676-216-2*) Technomic.

Simplified Woodworking I: A Business Guide for Woodworkers. A. William Benitez. Ed. by Mary B. Goens. 82p. (Orig.). 1989. pap. 10.00 (*0-9636035-1-5*) A W Benitez.

***Simplifier.** Dr. Seuss. 1998. 14.00 (*0-679-88612-5*) Random Bks Yng Read.

Simplify, Simplify: and Other Quotations from Henry David Thoreau. Ed. by Kevin P. Van Anglen. LC 95-47962. 224p. 1996. 19.95 (*0-231-10388-3*) Col U Pr.

***Simplify Your Life.** St. James. 1997. 16.99 (*0-553-47708-0*) Bantam.

***Simplify Your Life: 100 Ways to Slow Down & Enjoy the Things That Really Matter.** Elaine S. James. 1997. 19.95 (*0-7868-6345-5*) Hyperion.

Simplify Your Life: 100 Ways to Slow Down & Enjoy the Things That Really Matter. Elaine St. James. LC 93-27749. 256p. (Orig.). 1994. pap. 8.95 (*0-7868-8000-7*) Hyperion.

***Simplify Your Life with Kids: 100 Ways to Make Family Life Easier & More Fun.** James St. Elaine. LC 97-15340. 1997. 14.95 (*0-8362-3595-9*) Andrews & McMeel.

Simplifying Contract Terminations. 2nd ed. Margaret G. Rumbaugh. Ed. by Anne M. Rankin. 170p. 1991. pap. 37.45 (*0-940343-29-0*, SCT2) Natl Contract Mgmt.

***Simplifying Phacoemulsification: Safe & Efficient Methods for Cataract Surgery.** 5th ed. Paul S. Koch. LC 97-9765. 1997. write for info. (*1-55642-352-7*) SLACK Inc.

Simplifying Power Supply Technology. Rajesh J. Shah. (Illus.). 160p. 1995. pap. 16.95 (*0-7906-1062-0*) H W Sams.

Simplifying the Complicated in Real Estate & Appraising. Robert V. Anderson. LC 84-70613. (Illus.). 95p. 1984. 14.95 (*0-910436-27-4*) Conway Data.

Simplifying the FAR AIMS: An Essential Guide for the Private Pilot. James E. Guilkey & Christopher Snyder. 378p. (C). 1993. pap. 17.95 (*0-534-17730-1*) Wadsworth Pub.

Simplistic Poet. Ralph P. Prescott. Ed. by Fern Hagar. LC 87-71726. (Illus.). 77p. (Orig.). 1988. pap. 10.80 (*0-9618378-0-2*) Parishs Poetry.

***Simplistic Sailboat: A Family Cruise in a $600.00 Boat.** Dan Hookham. (Illus.). 224p. (Orig.). 1997. pap. 11.95 (*0-9655954-4-7*) Still Water Bks.

Simply - How to Register, Vote & Make It Count. M. R. Ward. Ed. by Diane Parker. LC 92-50869. 60p. 1993. pap. 4.95 (*0-88247-984-9*) R & E Pubs.

Simply a Man of Letters: Panel Discussions & Papers from the Proceedings of a Symposium on Jorge Luis Borges Held at the University of Maine at Orono. Ed. by Carlos Cortinez. 353p. 1982. 27.50 (*0-89101-052-1*); pap. 13.95 (*0-89101-051-3*) U Maine Pr.

Simply Accounting: Practical Accounting. 3rd ed. Insinga. 1995. pap. text ed. 35.20 (*0-13-348764-4*) P-H.

Simply AIX. Casey Cannon & Jones. 310p. (C). 1996. pap. text ed. 42.00 incl. cd-rom (*0-13-568882-5*) P-H.

Simply Amazing Internet. Adam Engst. (Illus.). 250p. (Orig.). 1995. pap. 39.95 incl. cd-rom (*1-56830-230-4*) Hayden.

Simply American. Andrea Gross. 1993. 6.99 (*0-517-10846-1*) Random Hse Value.

Simply American: Painted Furniture Patterns to Pull Out & Trace. Jocasta Innes & Stewart Walton. 28p. 1992. pap. 15.00 (*0-517-58710-6*, Harmony) Crown Pub Group.

Simply Barbara Bush: A Portrait of America's Candid First Lady. Donnie Radcliffe. 256p. 1990. mass mkt. 4.95 (*0-446-36024-4*) Warner Bks.

Simply Benjamin. Beryl E. Newman. LC 94-60119. (Illus.). 320p. 1994. pap. 11.95 (*1-55523-684-7*) Winston-Derek.

Simply Black: Poems. Beverley W. Wells. 46p. (Orig.). 1993. pap. 10.00 (*0-9630164-4-X*) Canios Edit.

***Simply Bradley Christmas Joy.** Ed. by Tony Esposito. 32p. (Orig.). 1997. pap. 8.95 (*0-7692-0139-3*, BP3380A) Warner Brothers.

***Simply Bradley Country Songs.** Ed. by Tony Esposito. 48p. (Orig.). (YA). 1997. pap. 8.96 (*0-7692-0058-3*, BP3376A) Warner Brothers.

***Simply Bradley Favorite Christmas Songs.** Ed. by Tony Esposito. 32p. (Orig.). 1997. pap. 8.95 (*0-7692-0106-7*, BP3379A) Warner Brothers.

***Simply Bradley TV Themes.** Ed. by Tony Esposito. 32p. (Orig.). (J). 1997. pap. 8.95 (*0-7692-0082-6*, BP3377A) Warner Brothers.

Simply Breads. Terri L. Johnson. (Illus.). 105p. (C). 1995. pap. text ed. 6.95 (*0-9644536-1-4*) MTJ Pubs.

***Simply Build Green: A Technical Guide to the Ecological Houses at the Findhorn Foundation.** 2nd rev. ed. John Talbott. (Illus.). 224p. 1995. pap. 17.95 (*1-899171-90-8*, Pub. by Findhorn Pr UK) Words Distrib.

Simply by Design: A Desktop Publishing Guide. 1991. lib. bdg. 79.95 (*0-8490-4949-0*) Gordon Pr.

***Simply C. S. Lewis: A Beginner's Guide to His Life & Works.** Thomas C. Peters. LC 97-8203. 272p. (Orig.). 1997. pap. 11.99 (*0-89107-948-3*) Crossway Bks.

Simply Cakes: Angel, Pound, & Chiffon. Elizabeth Alston. LC 93-26351. (Illus.). 128p. 1994. 12.50 (*0-06-016988-5*, HarpT) HarpC.

***Simply Casseroles: Over 100 Quick & Delicious One-Dish Dinners.** Kim Lila. 150p. (Orig.). 1997. pap. 14.95 (*1-57284-013-7*) Surrey Bks.

Simply Celebrating Children: Parties As Unique & Special As a Child. Dale W. Reinhard. 132p. (J). 1991. 12.95 (*0-9628888-0-X*) Pressed Duck.

***Simply Chilis, Chowders & Stews.** Carol Munson. (Simply Ser.). 160p. (Orig.). 1998. pap. 14.95 (*1-57284-015-3*) Surrey Bks.

***Simply Christmas.** Miriam Gourley. LC 97-2532. (Illus.). 1997. 24.95 (*0-8442-2627-0*) NTC Pub Grp.

***Simply Christmas.** Sheila Pickles. (Illus.). 128p. 1997. pap. 17.95 (*1-85793-935-2*, Pub. by Pavilion UK) Trafalgar.

Simply Classic: A Collection of Recipes to Celebrate the Northwest. Junior League of Seattle Staff. (Illus.). 264p. 1993. 24.95 (*0-9636088-9-4*) Jr Leag Seattle.

Simply Colorado: Nutritious Recipes for Busy People. Colorado Dietetic Association, Staff. Ed. by Kay P. Massey. 200p. (Orig.). 1990. 9.95 (*0-9626337-0-4*) CO Dietetic Assn.

Simply Colorado: Nutritious Recipes for Busy People. rev. ed. Colorado Dietetic Association Staff. Ed. by Kay P. Massey. 260p. 1992. 14.95 (*0-9626337-1-2*) CO Dietetic Assn.

***Simply Containers: Bright Ideas for Your Patio, Balcony, Windows & Walls over 40 Step-by-Step.** Ward Lock U. K. Staff. 1997. pap. text ed. 14.95 (*0-7063-7646-3*, Pub. by Ward Lock UK) Sterling.

***Simply Cosmic.** Mayfair Games Staff. 1996. 20.00 (*1-56905-072-4*) Mayfair Games.

Simply Country Watercolors. Susan Scheewe. (Illus.). 96p. 1992. pap. 9.50 (*1-56770-257-0*) S Scheewe Pubns.

Simply Criminal. 2nd ed. Susan C. Hayes & Gerard Craddock. 1992. pap. 48.00 (*1-86287-077-2*, Pub. by Federation Pr AU) Gaunt.

Simply Delicious. 398p. 1983. 12.00 (*0-317-69863-X*) Ark Assn Ext Home Econ.

Simply Delicious. (Illus.). 1991. write for info. (*1-886614-04-0*) Intl Masters Pub.

Simply Delicious. Darina Allen. (Illus.). 78p. (Orig.). 1989. pap. 13.95 (*0-7171-1687-5*, Pub. by Gill & MacMill IE) Irish Bks Media.

***Simply Delicious.** Arkansas Association of Home Staff. 1983. pap. 14.95 (*0-911184-00-7*) Wimmer Bks.

Simply Delicious. 3rd ed. Ed. by Marilyn Danger. (Illus.). 314p. (Orig.). 1983. reprint ed. pap. 9.95 (*0-9608666-0-4*) Miriam Hosp.

Simply Delicious, No. 2. Darina Allen. (Illus.). 91p. (Orig.). 1990. pap. 15.95 (*0-7171-1770-7*, Pub. by Gill & MacMill IE) Irish Bks Media.

Simply Delicious Christmas. Darina Allen. (Illus.). 122p. 1989. pap. 15.95 (*0-7171-1738-3*, Pub. by Gill & MacMill IE) Irish Bks Media.

Simply Delicious Family Food. Darina Allen. (Simply Delicious Ser.). (Illus.). 108p. (Orig.). 1993. pap. 15.95 (*0-7171-2060-0*, Pub. by Gill & MacMill IE) Irish Bks Media.

Simply Delicious Fish. Darina Allen. (Illus.). 100p. (Orig.). 1991. pap. 15.95 (*0-7171-1822-3*, Pub. by Gill & MacMill IE) Irish Bks Media.

Simply Delicious Meals. Family Circle Editors. 1947. 12.95 (*0-405-11956-9*) Ayer.

Simply Delicious Meals in Minutes. Darina Allen. (Simply Delicious Ser.). (Illus.). 90p. (Orig.). 1996. pap. 15.95 (*0-7171-2375-8*, Pub. by Gill & MacMill IE) Irish Bks Media.

Simply Delicious Recipes for Diabetics: 150 Easy to Make Dishes from Appetizers to Desserts. Christine Roberts et al. (Illus.). 206p. 1996. pap. 13.95 (*0-89529-688-8*) Avery Pub.

Simply Delicious Versatile Vegetables. Darina Allen. (Simply Delicious Ser.). (Illus.). 144p. (Orig.). 1994. pap. 15.95 (*0-7171-2152-6*, Pub. by Gill & MacMill IE) Irish Bks Media.

Simply Disconnected. Simon Gray. (Orig.). 1996. pap. text ed. 10.95 (*0-571-17972-X*) Faber & Faber.

***Simply Disconnected.** Simon Gray. 95p. (Orig.). 1996. pap. 10.95 (*0-614-18274-3*) Faber & Faber.

***Simply Divine.** Second-Ponce de Leon Baptist Church Cookbook Committee. LC 97-91775. (Illus.). 288p. 1997. 17.95 (*0-9658102-0-8*) Sec-Ponce de Leon.

Simply Divine: 200 Inspired (& Effortless) Desserts. Rita M. Harris. LC 95-33229. 1996. pap. 14.95 (*0-7615-0300-5*) Prima Pub.

Simply Elegant: A Guide for Elegant but Simple Entertaining. 10th rev. ed. Pearl S. Gordon. LC 77-13166. (Illus.). 208p. 1984. Incl. recipes & menues. lib. bdg. 21.95 (*0-9600492-4-X*) Simply Elegant.

Simply Elegant: Quick Recipes for Stylish Entertaining. 1995. 25.95 (*0-916103-26-9*) Am Express Food.

Simply Entertaining. Mary Anne Bauer. 180p. 1985. pap. 8.95 (*0-9613619-1-3*); spiral bd. 10.95 (*0-9613619-2-1*) M A Bauer.

***Simply Fat-Loss: The Knight System - A Comprehensive Fat-Loss Workbook.** John Knight. 160p. (Orig.). 1997. wbk. ed., pap. 16.95 (*1-890898-00-7*) Schuyler Instruct.

Simply Fish: A Guide to Identifying, Buying & Eating Fish. Jenny Baker. (Illus.). 288p. 1994. pap. 13.95 (*0-571-14966-9*) Faber & Faber.

Simply Flowers: Beautiful Ideas & Practical Advice for Creating Flower Filled Rooms. Barbara M. Orbach. LC 92-29768. (Illus.). 1993. 22.50 (*0-517-58183-3*, C P Pubs) Crown Pub Group.

***Simply French: Light, Fresh & Healthy Dishes from a Classic Cuisine.** Carole Clements. 1996. 12.98 (*0-7651-9732-4*) Smithmark.

Simply French: Painted Furniture Patterns to Pull Out & Trace. Jocasta Innes & Stewart Walton. 28p. 1992. pap. 15.00 (*0-517-58708-4*, Harmony) Crown Pub Group.

Simply French: Patricia Wells Presents the Cuisine of Joel Robouchon. Patricia Wells & Joel Robouchon. (Illus.). 367p. 1991. 35.00 (*0-688-06642-9*) Morrow.

Simply French: Patricia Wells Presents the Cuisine of Joel Robouchon. Patricia Wells. 1995. pap. 20.00 (*0-688-14356-3*) Hearst Bks.

Simply Fun! A Book of Hand-Me-Down Games. Patricia Zatopa. LC 90-86026. (Frisky Kid Ser.). (Orig.). 1991. pap. 4.95 (*0-9623430-7-2*) Explorers Guide Pub.

Simply Funtastic! Creative Play Ideas from Current (R) Ed. by Donna Cliff. (Illus.). 32p. (J). (gr. 1 up). 1993. pap. 6.10 (*0-944943-31-4*, CODE 21165-7) Current Inc.

***Simply God: Everyday Theology for Everyday People.** rev. ed. James D. Cantelon. LC 96-43230. 324p. (Orig.). 1997. pap. 14.99 (*0-7852-7799-4*) Nelson.

Simply Golf-Golfer's "Tote Book" Swing Analysis of the "Transfer of Power" John T. Johnson. 59p. 1993. pap. text ed. 7.50 (*0-9638212-1-0*) Jon Tees Pub.

Simply Golf-Jon Tee's Handbook: Swing Analysis of the "Transfer of Power" rev. ed. John T. Johnson. 67p. 1995. pap. text ed. 8.50 (*0-9638212-2-9*) Jon Tees Pub.

Simply Good Low Fat-Low Cal Cookbook. Helen M. Bowles. 115p. (Orig.). 1995. pap. 11.95 (*0-9647254-0-1*) H Bowles.

Simply Grammar: An Illustrated Primer. Karen Andreola. 1993. pap. text ed. 24.95 (*1-889209-01-5*) C Mason Res.

Simply Great Cookbook, Vol. II. C. A. Muer Corporation Staff. (Illus.). 165p. (Orig.). 1995. ring bd. 19.95 (*1-879094-38-X*) Momentum Bks.

Simply Great Cookbook: Recipes & the Experience of Fine Dining from the Kitchens of Chuck Muer. Chuck Muer. LC 92-15339. (Illus.). 166p. (Orig.). 1992. pap. 19.95 (*1-879094-13-4*) Momentum Bks.

Simply Halston. Steven Gaines. 320p. 1993. mass mkt. 5.99 (*0-515-11015-9*) Jove Pubns.

Simply Happy: How to Simplify Your Life & Find Happiness. Rebecca K. Merriman. LC 95-26617. 92p. (Orig.). 1996. pap. 5.95 (*1-56825-053-3*, 053-3) Rainbow Books.

Simply Healthful Cakes: Delicious New Low-Fat Recipes. Donna Deane & Minnie Bernardino. LC 92-40573. (Simply Healthful Ser.). (Illus.). 96p. (Orig.). 1993. pap. 9.95 (*1-881527-07-7*) Chapters Pub.

Simply Healthful Fish: Delicious New Low-Fat Recipes. David Ricketts & Susan McQuillan. LC 92-39978. (Simply Healthful Ser.). (Illus.). 96p. (Orig.). 1993. pap. 9.95 (*1-881527-05-0*) Chapters Pub.

Simply Healthful Pasta Salads: Delicious New Low-Fat Recipes. Andrea Chesman. LC 92-39973. (Simply Healthful Ser.). (Illus.). 96p. (Orig.). 1993. pap. 9.95 (*1-881527-06-9*) Chapters Pub.

Simply Healthful Pizzas & Calzones: Delicious New Low-Fat Recipes. David Ricketts & Susan McQuillan. LC 93-45013. (Simply Healthful Ser.). (Illus.). 96p. (Orig.). 1994. pap. 9.95 (*1-881527-34-4*) Chapters Pub.

Simply Healthful Skillet Suppers: Delicious New Low-Fat Recipes. Andrea Chesman. LC 93-45014. (Simply Healthful Ser.). (Illus.). 96p. (Orig.). 1994. pap. 9.95 (*1-881527-33-6*) Chapters Pub.

Simply Healthy: Over Two Hundred Fifty Lowfat Recipes Rich in the Antioxidant Vitamins That Keep You Healthy. Photos by Lisa Koenig. (Illus.). 256p. 1995. 24.95 (*0-929661-28-1*) Rebus.

Simply Heart Smart. Bonnie Stern. 1996. write for info. (*0-8129-2699-4*, Times Bks) Random.

Simply Heaven. Patricia Hagan. 352p. 1995. mass mkt. 5.99 (*0-06-108221-X*, Harp PBks) HarpC.

***Simply Heaven! The Monastery Vegetarian Cookbook.** George Burke. 1996. pap. 19.95 (*0-614-19373-7*) Macmillan.

Simply Heavenly. Langston Hughes. 1958. pap. 5.25 (*0-8222-1030-4*) Dramatists Play.

Simply Heavenly: Monastery Vegetarian Cookbook. (Illus.). 1997. 19.95 (*0-02-861267-1*) P-H Gen Ref & Trav.

Simply Heavenly! The Monastery Vegetarian Cookbook. Abbot G. Burke. (Illus.). 349p. (Orig.). pap. 19.95 (*0-932104-00-2*) St George Pr.

Simply Heavenly! The Monastery Vegetarian Cookbook. rev. ed. Abbot G. Burke. (Illus.). 326p. (Orig.). 1995. pap. 19.95 (*0-932104-07-X*) St George Pr.

Simply His: A Missionary Story of Love, Commitment, & a Willing Heart. Eunice Perryman & Pam Waddell. Ed. by Becky Nelson. 144p. (Orig.). 1996. pap. 9.95 (*1-56309-172-0*) Womans Mission Union.

Simply Homeschooling: A Unique Guide for the Homeschooling Parent. rev. ed. Karen L. Fogle. 108p. (C). 1994. pap. text ed. 20.00 (*0-9643531-0-5*) T E A C H.

***Simply Irresistible.** Geri Guillaume. 256p. 1998. mass mkt. 4.99 (*0-7860-0476-2*, Pinncle Kensgtn) Kensgtn Pub Corp.

Simply Irresistible. Peg Sutherland. (Superromance Ser.). 1994. mass mkt. 3.50 (*0-373-70580-8*, 1-70580-5) Harlequin Bks.

Simply Irresistible. large type ed. Miranda Lee. (Harlequin Ser.). 1994. lib. bdg. 19.95 (*0-263-13651-5*) Thorndike Pr.

Simply Irresistible: A Special Collection of Recipes from Junior Auxiliary of Conway. Gary A. Strain. (Illus.). 222p. 1993. 15.00 (*0-9643867-0-4*) Jr Auxil Conway.

***Simply Italian.** Harris. LC 96-36602. 1997. pap. write for info. (*0-8092-3040-2*) Contemp Bks.

Simply Kosher: Exotic Food from Around the World. Ramona Bachmann. (Illus.). 218p. 1994. 19.95 (*965-229-104-8*, Pub. by Gefen Pub Hse IS) Gefen Bks.

Simply Landscapes. Judy Sisneros. 44p. (Orig.). 1993. pap. text ed. 14.00 (*1-885156-07-3*) Animas Quilts.

Simply Light Cooking: From the Kitchens of Weight Watchers. Weight Watchers International, Inc. Staff. LC 93-13628. (Illus.). 320p. 1993. reprint ed. pap. 16.95 (*0-452-26875-3*, Plume) NAL-Dutton.

***Simply Live It Up: Brief Solutions.** 2nd rev. ed. Teri-E Belf & Charlotte Ward. LC 96-72247. (Illus.). 224p. 1997. mass mkt. 16.95 (*0-9646842-1-7*) Purposeful Pr.

Simply Logical: Intelligent Reasoning by Example. Peter A. Flach. LC 93-48745. 240p. 1994. pap. text ed. 69.95 incl. disk (*0-471-94215-4*) Wiley.

Simply Logical Intelligent Reasoning by Example. Peter A. Flach. LC 93-48745. 240p. 1994. pap. text ed. 60.00 (*0-471-94152-2*) Wiley.

***Simply Love.** Catherine Anderson. 1997. mass mkt. 5.99 (*0-380-79102-1*) Avon.

***Simply Maria, or The American Dream.** Josefina Lopez. 51p. 1996. pap. 3.00 (*0-87129-723-X*, SB4) Dramatic Pub.

Simply Marvelous. Ted Trujillo. (Orig.). 1989. pap. write for info. (*0-318-65905-0*) Santa Fe Pr.

Simply Me, Alexis Satchell. Ed. & Illus. by Alexis Satchell. 65p. (Orig.). 1987. 6.95 (*0-931841-09-7*) Satchells Pub.

Simply Me! An Autobiography: An Autobiography of Beatrice I. Hazley. Beatrice Hazley. Ed. by Marvin L. Smith. LC 96-83528. (Illus.). 104p. 1996. pap. 10.00 (*1-882581-14-8*) Campbell Rd Pr.

Simply Mexican: Painted Furniture Patterns to Pull Out & Trace. Jocasta Innes & Stewart Walton. 28p. 1992. pap. 15.00 (*0-517-58707-6*, Harmony) Crown Pub Group.

Simply Mick: Mick Hucknall of Simply Red - The Inside Story. Robin McGibbon & Rob McGibbon. (Illus.). 224p. 1994. pap. 15.95 (*1-85797-211-2*) Trafalgar.

***Simply Monsters.** Louis Phillips. LC 96-47722. 1998. pap. 11.99 (*0-670-87459-4*) Viking Penguin.

Simply Monstrous Time: And Other Halloween Stories from Highlights. Ed. by Beth Troop. LC 92-75837. (Illus.). 32p. (Orig.). (J). (gr. 2-7). 1993. pap. 4.95 (*1-56397-085-6*) Boyds Mills Pr.

Simply Nutritious. Am Cancer Society Staff & Volunteers. 180p. 1988. 5.00 (*0-317-01470-6*) Am Cancer Syracuse.

Simply Nutritious: Recipes & Recommendations to Reduce Your Risk of Cancer. Sabine M. Artaud-Wild. LC 86-71576. 182p. 1987. lib. bdg. 6.00 (*0-9617128-0-5*); spiral bd. 8.00 (*0-9617128-1-3*) Amer Cancer Soc OR.

Simply Organized! How to Simplify Your Complicated Life. Connie Cox & Cris Evatt. 128p. (Orig.). 1988. pap. 8.95 (*0-399-51451-1*, Perigee Bks) Berkley Pub.

Simply Organized: How to Simplify Your Complicated Life. Connie Cox. 1991. pap. 4.50 (*0-425-13088-6*) Berkley Pub.

***Simply Organized: The Life You Always Searched for...but Were Too Cluttered to Find.** Emilie Barnes. LC 96-35336. 96p. (Orig.). 1997. 12.99 (*1-56507-592-7*) Harvest Hse.

Simply Painting Acrylics: Pictures Anyone Can Paint. Frank Clarke. (Simply Painting Ser.: Bk. 2). (Illus.). 130p. 1996. 24.95 (*0-9512510-7-4*) Oisin Pubns.

Simply Painting Acrylics: Teaches Anyone to Paint Acrylics. Frank Clarke. (Simply Painting Ser.: Bk. 1). (Illus.). 1996. 19.95 (*0-9512510-5-8*) Oisin Pubns.

Simply Painting Watercolours: Pictures Anyone Can Paint. Frank Clarke. (Simply Painting Ser.: Bk. 2). (Illus.). 1996. 24.95 (*0-9512510-6-6*) Oisin Pubns.

Simply Painting Watercolours: Teaches Anyone to Paint. Frank Clarke. (Simply Painting Ser.: Bk. 1). (Illus.). 1996. 19.95 (*0-9512510-4-X*) Oisin Pubns.

Simply Precious: Moments in Time with a Remarkable Cat. Muriel L. Hine. 120p. (Orig.). 1996. pap. 12.95 (*0-9651188-0-0*) M L Hine.

Simply Public Relations: Public Relations Made Challenging, Complete & Concise! Thomas W. Dwyer. 210p. (C). 1992. pap. text ed. 19.95 (*0-913507-25-3*) New Forums.

Simply Ready. Terri L. Johnson. (Illus.). 227p. 1994. pap. text ed. 17.95 (*0-9644536-0-6*) MTJ Pubs.

***Simply Ridiculous.** unabridged ed. Virginia Davis. (Illus.). 32p. (J). (gr. k-2). 1995. 12.95 (*1-55074-107-1*, Pub. by Kids Can Pr CN) Genl Dist Srvs.

Simply Salmon: Fresh, Frozen & Canned. Linda Martinson. 138p. 1986. pap. 9.95 (*0-934363-02-1*) Lance Pubns.

Simply Salmon: Fresh, Frozen & Canned. 2nd rev. ed. Linda Martinson. (Illus.). 134p. 1986. reprint ed. pap. 5.95 (*0-934363-03-X*) Simply Books.

Simply Sam. Greg Mitchell. LC 92-21452. (Voyages Ser.). (Illus.). (J). 1993. 3.75 (*0-383-03652-6*) SRA McGraw.

Simply Sane: The Spirituality of Mental Health. enl. ed. Gerald G. May. LC 93-2581. 176p. 1993. pap. 11.95 (*0-8245-1366-5*) Crossroad NY.

An Asterisk (*) at the beginning of an entry indicates that the title is appearing in BIP for the first time.

Simply Scheme: Introducing Computer Science. Brian Harvey & Matthew Wright. LC 93-34469. (Illus.). 590p. 1993. 52.50 (0-262-08226-8) MIT Pr.

Simply Science: Discovering the Fascinations of Our World. Dean R. Brown. (Illus.). 206p. (YA). (gr. 7-12). 1993. pap. text ed. 24.95 (1-880293-02-1) Alaken.

Simply Scones. Leslie Weiner & Barbara Albright. LC 87-27328. (Illus.). 112p. 1988. pap. 6.95 (0-312-01511-9) St Martin.

Simply Scrappy. Nancy J. Martin. 1995. pap. 24.95 (1-56477-127-X, B245) That Patchwork.

Simply Scrumptious Microwaving. Rosemary D. Stancil & Lorela N. Wilkins. (Illus.). 1982. pap. 10.95 (0-9610160-0-0) Simply Scrumptious.

Simply Scrumptious Southern Sweets. rev. ed. Patricia B. Mitchell. 1991. pap. 4.00 (0-925117-39-0) Mitchells.

Simply Seafood. Vicki Emmons. (Illus.). 224p. (Orig.). 1983. pap. 6.95 (0-89933-043-6) DeLorme Map.

Simply Seafood Cookbook of East Coast Shellfish. R. Marilyn Schmidt. 160p. (Orig.). 1987. pap. 8.95 (0-937996-11-4) Barnegat.

Simply Seders. Date not set. 27.50 (0-02-861259-0) Macmillan.

Simply Seminole: Techniques & Designs in Quiltmaking. Dorothy Hanisko. LC 40-35648. (Illus.). 120p. 1997. pap. 24.95 (0-8442-2647-5) Quilt Digest Pr.

Simply Sensational: Great Christmas Ornament & Stocking Ideas. Carol E. Sterbenz. (Illus.). 70p. 1993. 10.95 (1-56865-023-X, GuildAmerica) Dblday Direct.

Simply Sensational: Great Ideas for Buttons, Beads, Ribbons & Lace. Carol E. Sterbenz. (Illus.). 72p. 1993. 8.95 (1-56865-022-1, GuildAmerica) Dblday Direct.

Simply Sensational: Great Napkin Folds. Carol E. Sterbenz. (Illus.). 70p. 1993. 8.95 (1-56865-021-3, GuildAmerica) Dblday Direct.

Simply Sensational: Great Scarf Ideas. Carol E. Sterbenz. (Illus.). 72p. 1993. 12.95 (1-56865-020-5, GuildAmerica) Dblday Direct.

Simply Serged Fabrics: A Handbook for Overlocking Today's Varied Textiles. Naomi Baker & Tammy Young. LC 89-83400. (Illus.). 200p. 1990. pap. text ed. 14.95 (0-8019-8104-2) Chilton.

Simply Shaker: Groveland & the New York Communities. Fran Kramer. Ed. by H. J. Swinney. 88p. 1991. pap. 14.95 (0-938551-01-9) Rochester Mus & Sci Ctr.

***Simply Shooters: A. K. A. Coast to Coast Shooter Collection.** 2nd rev. ed. Eugene Coolik. 144p. 1997. pap. 12.95 (0-944057-02-0) Just Bev Pubns.

Simply Shooters: Coast to Coast Shooter Collection. Gene Coolik. 144p. (Orig.). 1995. reprint ed. pap. 12.95 (0-944057-01-2) Just Bev Pubns.

Simply Shrimp! R. Marilyn Schmidt. 130p. (Orig.). 1988. pap. 8.95 (0-937996-14-9) Barnegat.

Simply Shrimp: Fresh, Frozen & Canned. Linda Martinson. (Illus.). 130p. (Orig.). 1988. pap. 5.95 (0-934363-04-8) Simply Books.

Simply Silly about Sentences. Suzanna M. Watt. (Illus.). 286p. 1990. spiral bd. 29.00 (0-9609160-6-7) Mayer-Johnson.

Simply Simpatico. Junior League Staff. 1981. 14.95 (0-9609278-0-8) Junior League of Albuquerque Inc.

***Simply Slipcovers.** Sunset Editors. 1997. pap. 18.95 (0-614-27403-6) Sunset Bks Inc.

Simply Sophisticated: What Every Wordly Person Needs to Know. Suzanne Munshower. Ed. by Mike Towle. (Illus.). 178p. 1994. pap. 12.95 (1-56530-148-X) Summit TX.

***Simply SoulStirring: Writing As Meditative Process.** Francis Dorff & O. Praem. 128p. 1998. 9.95 (0-8091-3769-0) Paulist Pr.

***Simply Speaking! The No-Sweat Way to Prepare & Deliver Presentations.** David Greenberg. (Illus.). 180p. (Orig.). 1997. pap. 14.95 (1-890480-00-2) Goldleaf Pubns.

Simply Spiritual: A Sharing. Bill Stelling. (Illus.). 64p. (Orig.). (YA). (gr. 9-12). 1992. pap. 9.95 (0-940829-07-X) Eagle Wing Bks.

Simply Spiritual Exercise Workbook. Bill Stelling. 38p. (Orig.). (YA). (gr. 10 up). 1992. pap. 6.00 (0-940829-08-8) Eagle Wing Bks.

Simply Stars: Quilts That Sparkle. Alex Anderson. Ed. by Lee Jonsson. LC 96-15854. (Illus.). 96p. (Orig.). 1996. pap. 21.95 (1-57120-019-3, 10143) C & T Pub.

Simply State It, Vol. 1: Verses for You to Share. Lynda Claus. LC 92-91189. 64p. (Orig.). 1993. pap. 8.95 (0-9635598-1-8) Simply Stated.

Simply Stews: More Than 100 Savory One-Pot Meals. Susan Wyler. LC 95-25214. 256p. 1995. pap. 14.00 (0-06-095144-3, PL) HarpC.

***Simply Super Bulletin Boards.** Amy Vangsgard. LC 97-10561. 1997. pap. write for info. (0-917846-89-3) Highsmith Pr.

Simply Surrender: Based on the Little Way of Therese of Lisieux. John Kirvan. LC 96-19550. (30 Days with a Great Spiritual Teacher Ser.). 216p. (Orig.). 1996. pap. 6.95 (0-87793-590-4) Ave Maria.

Simply Tennessee. Betty J. McClanahan. LC 95-78262. 128p. 1995. pap. 12.95 (0-913383-40-6) McClanahan Pub.

Simply Thai Cooking. Wandee Young & Byron Ayanoglu. (Illus.). 192p. (Orig.). 1996. pap. text ed. 17.95 (1-896503-18-7, Pub. by R Rose CN) Firefly Bks Ltd.

Simply the Best. Catherine Spencer. (Romance Ser.). 1995. mass mkt. 2.99 (0-373-03365-6, 1-03365-3) Harlequin Bks.

Simply the Best: A Celebration of the First 50 Years in the Life & Times of Best Western International. William H. Boyer. 120p. 1996. write for info. (0-929690-28-1) Herit Pubs AZ.

Simply the Best: Over One Hundred Easy-to-Make, Tasty Cheese Recipes. (Illus.). 96p. 1992. spiral bd. 7.95 (0-9637893-0-9) Sargento.

***Simply the Best! The Inside Story of the 1996 Atlanta Braves.** I. J. Rosenberg. 1996. 29.95 (1-56352-411-2) Longstreet Pr Inc.

Simply the Best Dad. Sharon Steffensen. 366p. (Orig.). 1993. pap. 8.95 (1-56245-077-8) Great Quotations.

Simply the Best Mom. Julie Otlewis. 366p. 1993. spiral bd., pap. 8.95 (1-56245-076-X) Great Quotations.

***Simply the Best Mysteries.** Ed. by Janet Hutchings. 384p. 1997. pap. 12.95 (0-7867-0483-7) Carroll & Graf.

***Simply the Easiest Possible Solution to Pro/ENGINEER, Vol. 1: Getting Started; Vol. 2: Getting Serious.** Teddy D. Bradshaw. (Steps Ser.). (Illus.). 922p. (Orig.). 1996. pap. 79.95 (1-889961-00-0) Green Leaf Graphics.

Simply Trusting. Aletha Hinthorn. (Satisfied Heart Ser.). 104p. (Orig.). 1996. per., pap. 6.99 (0-8341-1604-9) Beacon Hill.

Simply Unforgettable. Pat Warren. 1993. mass mkt. 3.39 (0-373-09797-2, 5-09797-7) Silhouette.

Simply Vegan. 2nd ed. Debra Waserman & Reed Mangels. LC 95-60716. 224p. 1995. pap. 12.95 (0-931411-15-7) Vegetarian Resc.

***Simply Vegetarian.** Lee H. Lin. Tr. by Connie Wolhardt from CHI. (Illus.). 96p. 1997. pap. 19.95 (0-941676-71-4) Wei-Chuan Pub.

***Simply Vegetarian!** Nancy Mair. 1993. pap. 4.99 (0-425-13993-X) Berkley Pub.

Simply Vegetarian! Easy-to-Prepare Recipes for the Vegetarian Gourmet. rev. ed. Nancy Mair & Susan Rinzler. LC 90-131641. 256p. 1989. pap. 11.95 (0-916124-53-3, DES1) Dawn CA.

Simply Watercolor. Susan Scheewe. 106p. 1992. pap. text ed. 11.95 (1-56770-260-0) S Scheewe Pubns.

Simply Whidbey: A Collection of Regional Recipes from Whidbey Island, Washington. Laura Moore & Deborah Skinner. LC 90-81675. (Illus.). 224p. (Orig.). 1991. pap. 16.95 (0-9628766-0-7) Saratoga Pubs.

Simply Windows: Microsoft Windows 3.1. Stacey C. Sawyer et al. (Advantage Series for Computer Education). 200p. 1995. per. 17.00 (0-7863-0445-6) Irwin Prof Pubng.

Simply Windows: Microsoft Windows 3.1. Stacey C. Sawyer et al. (C). 1994. pap. 12.50 (0-256-18310-4) Irwin.

Simply Windows: Microsoft Windows 3.1. 2nd ed. Sarah E. Hutchinson & Glen J. Coulthard. LC 95-37741. (Irwin Advantage Series for Computer Education). 160p. (C). 1995. per. 12.50 (0-256-20246-X) Irwin.

Simply Windows: Microsoft Windows 3.1. 2nd ed. Sarah E. Hutchinson & Glen Coulthard. 136p. (C). 1995. per. 25.00 (0-256-20234-6) Irwin.

Simply Windows: Microsoft Windows 3.1. 2nd ed. Sarah E. Hutchinson & Glen Coulthard. (C). 1996. 10.00 (0-256-24187-2) Irwin.

Simply Windows 95. Sarah E. Hutchinson & Glen Coulthard. 176p. (C). 1996. per. 25.00 (0-256-21998-2) Irwin.

Simply 1-2-3. Lynn Swinson. 208p. (C). 1992. pap. 28.95 (0-87835-771-8) Course Tech.

Simply 1-2-3, Release 2.4. Swinson. (C). 1994. pap. 25.95 (0-87709-300-8, BF3008) S-W Pub.

Simposio Sobre Energia Nuclear y el Desarrollo de Latinoamerica. Centro Nuclear de Puerto Rico Staff. 167p. 1969. pap. 3.00 (0-8477-2304-6) U of PR Pr.

Simposium Sobre Arqueologia en el Estado de Hidalgo: Trabajos Recientes, 1989. Ed. by Enrique Fernandez. 156p. 1994. pap. 7.00 (968-29-5131-3, IN054) UPLAAP.

Simpson County, Kentucky Families Past & Present. Turner Publishing Company Staff. LC 89-50076. 544p. 1989. 49.95 (0-938021-40-0) Turner Pub KY.

Simpson Desert-Natural History & Human Endeavour: RGSA (SA) Adelaide 1991. Mark Shephard. 184p. (C). 1992. 85.00 (0-7855-0330-7, Pub. by Royal Geograp Soc AT) St Mut.

Simpson Fever. Jeff Rovin. 1990. pap. 2.95 (0-312-92502-6) St Martin.

***Simpson the Snail Sings.** John Himmleman. (J). 1997. pap. 3.50 (0-14-038434-0) Viking Penguin.

Simpsons. Bob Italia. Ed. by Rosemary Wallner. LC 91-73050. (Behind the Creation of Ser.). (J). 1991. lib. bdg. 13.95 (1-56239-051-1) Abdo & Dghtrs.

***Simpsons: A Complete Guide to Your Favorite Family.** Matt Groening. 1997. pap. text ed. 14.95 (0-06-095252-0, PL) HarpC.

Simpson's Comics Extravaganza. Matt Groening. 128p. 1994. pap. 11.95 (0-06-095086-2, HarpT) HarpC.

Simpsons Comics Simp-So-Rama. Matt Groening. 128p. 1996. pap. 11.95 (0-06-095199-0) HarpC.

Simpsons Comics Spectacular. Matt Groening. 128p. 1995. pap. 11.95 (0-06-095148-6, PL) HarpC.

Simpson's Comics Strike Back. Matt Groening. (Illus.). 128p. 1996. pap. text ed. 11.95 (0-06-095212-1) HarpC.

***Simpsons Comics Strike Back.** Matt Groening. (Illus.). 1996. pap. 11.95 (0-614-20784-3, PL) HarpC.

***Simpsons Comics Wing Ding.** Matt Groening. 1997. pap. text ed. 11.95 (0-06-095245-8, PL) HarpC.

Simpson's Contemporary Quotations: The Most Notable Quotes from 1950 to the Present. 2nd ed. James B. Simpson. LC 96-51910. 656p. 1996. 30.00 (0-06-270137-1) HarpC.

***Simpson's Forensic Medicine.** 11th ed. Bernard Knight. (Illus.). 336p. 45.00 (0-340-61370-X, Pub. by E Arnold UK) Routledge Chapman & Hall.

Simpsons of Shore Acres. Stephen D. Beckham. (Illus.). 54p. 1992. pap. text ed. 6.95 (0-685-53206-2) Arago Bks.

Simpsons of Shore Acres. 2nd ed. Stephen D. Beckham. (Illus.). 64p. reprint ed. pap. 6.95 (0-930998-05-7) Arago Bks.

Simpsons Uncensored Family Album. Matt Groening. 64p. (Orig.). 1991. pap. 12.95 (0-06-096582-7, PL) HarpC.

Sim's Gold. Noellene Moore. LC 95-60769. 307p. 1996. 11.95 (1-55523-746-0) Winston-Derek.

Sims Reeves, Fifty Years of Music in England. Charles E. Pearce. LC 79-25066. (Music Reprint Ser.). 1980. reprint ed. lib. bdg. 35.00 (0-306-76007-X) Da Capo.

***Simsbury, Being a Brief Historical Sketch of Ancient & Modern Simsbury, 1642-1935.** John E. Ellsworth. (Illus.). 190p. 1997. reprint ed. lib. bdg. 26.50 (0-8328-5686-X) Higginson Bk Co.

SIMSOC: Simulated Society. 4th ed. William A. Gamson. 200p. 1991. student ed., pap. 16.95 (0-02-911201-X, Free Press) Free Pr.

SIMSOC: Simulated Society. 4th ed. William A. Gamson. 1990. teacher ed., pap. 4.95 (0-02-911202-8, Free Press) Free Pr.

Simson see Saemtliche Werke: Ausgaben Deutscher Literatur des 15 bis 18 Jahrhunderts

SimTower: The Vertical Empire: The Official Strategy Guide. Rick Barba. 1995. pap. 19.95 (0-7615-0042-1) Prima Pub.

Simulachres & Historiees Faces Des La Mort see Dance of Death

***Simulacion de Empresa en Direccion Estrategica.** 2nd ed. Arthur A. Thompson. (SPA.). (C). 1996. pap. text ed. 18.00 (84-8086-256-4) Irwin.

Simulacra. Rena Rosenwasser & Kate Delos. LC 86-18836. (Illus.). 48p. (Orig.). 1986. pap. text ed. 23.00 (0-932716-21-0) Kelsey St Pr.

Simulacra & Simulation. Jean Baudrillard. Tr. by Sheila Glaser. (Body in Theory: Histories of Cultural Materialism Ser.). 128p. 1994. pap. text ed. 14.95 (0-472-06521-1) U of Mich Pr.

Simulacra & Simulation. Jean Baudrillard. Tr. by Sheila Glaser. (Body in Theory: Histories of Cultural Materialism Ser.). 128p. 1995. text ed. 37.50 (0-472-09521-8) U of Mich Pr.

Simulated & Virtual Realities: Elements of Perception. Ed. by Karen Carr & Rupert England. 250p. 1995. 85.00 (0-7484-0128-8); pap. 34.95 (0-7484-0129-6, Pub. by Tay Francis Ltd UK) Taylor & Francis.

Simulated Annealing: Parallelization Techniques. Robert Azencott. LC 91-4198. (Interscience Series in Discrete Mathematics). 256p. 1992. text ed. 84.95 (0-471-53231-2) Wiley.

Simulated Annealing & Boltzmann Machines: A Stochastic Approach to Combinatorial Optimization & Neural Computing. Emile H. Aarts & Jan Korst. LC 88-20871. 272p. 1989. text ed. 130.00 (0-471-92146-7) Wiley.

Simulated Annealing for VLSI Design. D. F. Wong et al. (C). 1988. lib. bdg. 75.00 (0-89838-256-4) Kluwer Ac.

Simulated Annealing (SA) & Optimization: Modern Algorithms with VLSI, Optimal Design, & Missile Defense Applications. Ed. by Mark E. Johnson. LC 89-84348. (American Sciences Press Series in Mathematical & Management Sciences: Vol. 17). 1989. 125.00 (0-935950-18-4) Am Sciences Pr.

Simulated Client: A Method for Studying Professionals Working with Clients. R. Emerson Dobash & Fran Wasoff. (Cariff Papers). 112p. (C). 1996. 51.95 (1-85628-920-6, Pub. by Avebury Pub UK) Ashgate Pub Co.

Simulated International Processes: Theories & Research in Global Modeling. Ed. by Harold Guetzkow & Joseph J. Valadez. LC 80-29047. (Illus.). 400p. reprint ed. pap. 114.00 (0-8357-4802-2, 2037739) Bks Demand.

Simulated Real Life Experiences Using Classified Ads in the Classroom. Ellen Hechler. (Illus.). 54p. (Orig.). (J). (gr. 6-10). 1991. pap. 10.00 (0-9638483-3-X) Midmath.

Simulated Test Marketing: Technology for Launching Successful New Products. Kevin J. Clancy et al. LC 94-17718. 306p. 39.95 (0-02-905505-9, Free Press) Free Pr.

Simulated Voyages: Using Simulation Technology to Train & License Mariners. National Research Council Staff. 304p. (Orig.). 1996. pap. text ed. 38.00 (0-309-05383-8) Natl Acad Pr.

Simulated Worlds: A Computer Model of National Decision-Making. Stuart A. Bremer. LC 76-49547. 267p. reprint ed. pap. 76.10 (0-8357-7021-4, 2033405) Bks Demand.

Simulating Clastic Sedimentary Basins: Physical Fundamentals & Computer Programs for Creating Dynamic Systems. Rudy Slingerland et al. LC 93-24602. 240p. (C). 1993. text ed. 85.00 (0-13-814054-5) P-H Gen Ref & Trav.

Simulating Clastic Sedimentation. Tetzlaff & John W. Harbaugh. 224p. (gr. 13). 1988. text ed. 67.95 (0-442-23293-4) Chapman & Hall.

Simulating Computer Systems: Techniques & Tools. Myron H. MacDougall. (Computer Systems Ser.). 290p. (C). 1987. 44.00 (0-262-13229-X) MIT Pr.

Simulating K-3 Christaller Central Place Structures: An Algorithm Using a Constant Elasticity of Substitution Consumption Function. Daniel A. Griffith. (Monograph Ser.: No. 10). (Illus.). 103p. (Orig.). (C). 1989. pap. 15.95 (1-877751-20-0); pap. text ed. 15.95 (1-877751-21-9) Inst Math Geo.

Simulating Nearshore Environments. Paul A. Martinez & John W. Harbaugh. LC 93-29269. (Computer Methods in the Geosciences Ser.: Vol. 12). 280p. 1993. 137.25 (0-08-037937-0, Pergamon Pr) Elsevier.

Simulating Neural Networks. Norbert Hoffman. 244p. 1994. 56.00 (3-528-05376-3) Informatica.

Simulating Neural Networks with Mathematica. James A. Freeman. (Illus.). 352p. (C). 1994. text ed. 39.75 (0-201-56629-X) Addison-Wesley.

Simulating Oil Migration & Stratigraphic Traps. Wendebourg. LC 97-20560. 1997. write for info. (0-08-042431-7, Pergamon Pr) Elsevier.

Simulating Process Control Loops Using BASIC. F. Greg Shinskey. LC 89-24478. 226p. 1990. reprint ed. pap. 64.50 (0-608-01354-4, 2062094) Bks Demand.

Simulating Science: Heuristics, Mental Models, & Technoscientific Thinking. Michael E. Gorman. LC 91-26630. (Science, Technology, & Society Ser.). (Illus.). 292p. 1992. text ed. 45.00 (0-253-32608-7) Ind U Pr.

Simulating Societies: The Computer Simulation of Social Phenomena. Ed. by Nigel Gilbert & Jim Doran. 320p. 1994. 59.95 (1-85728-082-2, Pub. by UCL Pr UK) Taylor & Francis.

Simulating Sovereignty: Intervention, the State & Symbolic Exchange. Cynthia Weber. LC 94-9269. (Studies in International Relations: No. 37). 200p. (C). 1994. pap. text ed. 17.95 (0-521-45559-6) Cambridge U Pr.

Simulating Sovereignty: Intervention, the State & Symbolic Exchange. Cynthia Weber. LC 94-9269. (Studies in International Relations: No. 37). 200p. (C). 1995. text ed. 54.95 (0-521-45523-5) Cambridge U Pr.

Simulating Terrorism. Stephen Sloan. LC 80-5937. (Illus.). 200p. 1981. 27.95 (0-8061-1746-X) U of Okla Pr.

Simulating the Earth: Experimental Geochemistry. J. R. Holloway & B. J. Wood. (Illus.). 192p. 1988. text ed. 49.95 (0-04-552023-2); pap. text ed. 24.95 (0-04-445255-1) Routledge Chapman & Hall.

Simulating the Medical Office. Jerry Belch. Ed. by Valerie Harris. Incl. Getting Started. 86p. 1993. Getting Started, 86p. 8.98 (0-89262-337-3); Record Management. 76p. 1993. Record Management, 76p. 7.98 (0-89262-313-6); Correspondence. 92p. 1993. Correspondence, 92p. 7.98 (0-89262-314-4); Appointments. 60p. 1993. Appointments, 60p. 7.98 (0-89262-315-2); Business Checking Account. 76p. 1993. Business Checking Account, 76p. 7.98 (0-89262-316-0); Office Purchase Orders. 60p. 1993. Office Purchase Orders, 60p. 6.98 (0-89262-317-9); Patient Billing. 108p. 1993. Patient Billing, 108p. 9.98 (0-89262-318-7); Insurance Claims. 60p. 1993. Insurance Claims, 60p. 7.98 (0-89262-319-5); 1993. Set student ed. 249.95 (0-89262-210-5); 695.00 (0-89262-417-5) Career Pub.

Simulating Violators. Chanoch Jacobsen & Richard Bronson. (Topics in Operations Research Ser.). viii, 246p. 1985. pap. 15.00 (1-877640-07-7) INFORMS.

Simulating with Spice. L. G. Meares & C. E. Hymowitz. Ed. by S. N. Marks & J. T. Robson. (Spice Ser.). (Illus.). 283p. (Orig.). 1988. pap. 65.00 (0-923345-00-0) INTUSOFT.

Simulating Workplace Safety Policy. Ed. by Thomas J. Kniesner & John D. Leeth. (Studies in Risk & Uncertainty). 240p. (C). 1994. lib. bdg. 99.00 (0-7923-9519-0) Kluwer Ac.

Simulation. R. D. Hurrion. (International Trends in Manufacturing Technology Ser.). (Illus.). 380p. 1987. 107.95 (0-387-16357-3) Spr-Verlag.

***Simulation.** 2nd ed. Sheldon M. Ross. LC 96-30669. (Statistical Modeling & Decision Science Ser.). (Illus.). 282p. 1996. boxed 59.95 (0-12-598410-3, AP Prof) Acad Pr.

Simulation, 2 Vols. 2nd ed. Jerald R. Smith. (C). 1987. pap. 19.56 (0-395-47037-4) HM.

Simulation: A Problem Solving Approach. Ronald F. Perry & Stewart V. Hoover. (Illus.). 550p. (C). 1989. text ed. 65.75 (0-201-16880-4) Addison-Wesley.

***Simulation: A Problem Solving Approach.** 2nd ed. Stuart Hoover. (C). 1998. text ed. write for info. (0-201-58063-2) Addison-Wesley.

Simulation: A Statistical Perspective. Jack P. Kleijnen & Willem Van-Groenendaal. LC 92-7364. 241p. 1992. pap. text ed. 65.00 (0-471-93055-5) Wiley.

Simulation: Principles & Methods. 2nd ed. Poch. 1992. write for info. (0-318-69402-6, CRC Reprint) Franklin.

Simulation Activities in Library, Communication & Information Science. James G. Williams. Ed. by Patrick R. Penland. LC 75-32390. (Communication Science & Technology Ser.: No. 6). (Illus.). 264p. reprint ed. pap. 75.30 (0-7837-3339-9, 2043297) Bks Demand.

Simulation Analysis of Capital Structure in a Property Insurance Firm. Russell Nye. (C). 1975. 10.50 (0-256-04607-7) Irwin.

Simulation & Ada Software. Unger et al. 274p. 1984. pap. 40.00 (0-911801-03-0, ESC84-1) Soc Computer Sim.

Simulation & AI (Multi '87) (Simulation Ser.: Vol. 18, No. 3). 100p. 1987. 40.00 (0-911801-18-9, SS18-3) Soc Computer Sim.

Simulation & AI, 1989. Ed. by Wade Webster. (Simulation Ser.: Vol. 20, No. 3). (Illus.). 140p. 1989. text ed. 48.00 (0-911801-44-8, SS20-3) Soc Computer Sim.

Simulation & Analysis of Soil-Water Conditions in the Great Plains & Adjacent Areas, Central United States, 1951-80. Jack T. Dugan & Ronald B. Zelt. LC 94-31133. (United States Geological Survey Water-Supply Bulletin Ser.: 2427). 1995. write for info. (0-615-00178-5) US Geol Survey.

Simulation & Artificial Intelligence in Manufacturing: Conference Proceedings: October 14-16, 1987, Long Beach, CA, Vol. 2. Society of Manufacturing Engineers Staff. LC 87-62401. (Illus.). 343p. reprint ed. pap. 97.80 (0-8357-6499-0, 2035870) Bks Demand.

Simulation & Chaotic Behavior of a Stable Stochastic Processes. Janicki & Weron. LC 93-21359. (Pure & Applied Mathematics Ser.: Vol. 178). 376p. 1993. 140.00 (0-8247-8882-6) Dekker.

Simulation & Control of Electrical Power Stations. J. B. Knowles. LC 90-38478. (Engineering Systems Modelling & Control Ser.). 350p. 1991. text ed. 198.00 (0-471-92870-4) Wiley.

S

Simulation & Design of Applied Electromagnetic Systems: Proceedings of the International ISEM Symposium on Simulation & Design of Applied Electromagnetic Systems, Sapporo, Japan, 26-30 January, 1993. Ed. by Toshihisa Honma. LC 93-49566. (Studies in Applied Electromagnetics in Materials: No. 5). 778p. 1993. 256.25 (*0-444-81747-6*) Elsevier.

Simulation & Design of Microsystems & Microstructures: Proceedings of Microsim 95. Ed. by R. A. Adey et al. LC 95-68883. (MICROSIM Ser.: Vol. 1). 352p. 1995. 183.00 (*1-56252-314-7*, 3900) Computational Mech MA.

Simulation & Design of Microsystems & Microstructures II: Proceedings of the Second International Conference. (MICROSIM Ser.: Vol. 2). 400p. Date not set. text ed. 265.00 (*1-85312-408-7*, 4087) Computational Mech MA.

Simulation & Gaming in Social Science. Michael Inbar & Clarice S. Stoll. LC 74-143527. 1972. 27.95 (*0-02-915750-1*, Free Press) Free Pr.

Simulation & Imaging of the Cardiac System. Ed. by Samuel Sideman & Rafael Beyar. (Developments in Cardiovascular Medicine Ser.). 1985. lib. bdg. 212.50 (*0-89838-687-X*) Kluwer Ac.

Simulation & Model-Based Methodologies: An Integrative View. Bernard P. Zeigler. (NATO ASI Series F: Computer & Systems Sciences, Special Programme AET: No. 10). xiv, 651p. 1984. 143.95 (*0-387-12884-0*) Spr-Verlag.

Simulation & Modeling of Turbulent Flows. Ed. by Thomas B. Gatski et al. (ICASE/LaRC Series in Computational Science & Engineering). (Illus.). 336p. 1996. 45.00 (*0-19-510643-1*) OUP.

Simulation & Modelling: Proceedings, IASTED Symposium, Orlando, Florida, U. S. A., November 9-11, 1983. Ed. by M. H. Hamza. 176p. 1983. 65.00 (*0-88986-053-X*, 060) Acta Pr.

Simulation & Modelling '89: Proceedings of IASTED Symposium, Lugano, Switzerland, June 19-22, 1989. Ed. by M. H. Hamza. 404p. 1989. 90.00 (*0-88986-125-0*, 144) Acta Pr.

Simulation & Optimization: Proceedings of the International Workshop on Computationally Intensive Methods in Simulation & Optimization Held at the International Institute for Applied Systems Analysis (IIASA) Laxenburg, Austria, August 23-25, 1990. Ed. by Martin J. Beckmann et al. (Lecture Notes in Economics & Mathematical Systems Ser.: Vol. 374). (Illus.). x, 162p. 1992. 45.95 (*0-387-54980-3*) Spr-Verlag.

Simulation & Optimization of Large Systems. Ed. by Andrzej J. Osiadacz. (Institute of Mathematics & Its Applications Conference Series, New Ser.: New Series 13). (Illus.). 352p. 1988. 79.00 (*0-19-853617-8*) OUP.

Simulation & Systems Analysis in Agriculture. C. Csaki. (Developments in Agricultural Engineering Ser.: Vol. 2). 262p. 1985. 145.25 (*0-444-99622-2*) Elsevier.

Simulation & Systems Management in Crop Protection. R. Rabbinge. 434p. (C). 1976. pap. 335.00 (*81-7089-135-3*, Pub. by Intl Bk Distr II) St Mut.

Simulation & the Monte Carlo Method. Reuven Y. Rubinstein. LC 81-1873. (Probability & Mathematical Statistics Ser.). 278p. 1981. text ed. 106.00 (*0-471-08917-6*) Wiley.

Simulation & the User Interface. Ed. by Ian Hamilton et al. 290p. 1990. 85.00 (*0-85066-803-4*, Pub. by Tay Francis Ltd UK) Taylor & Francis.

Simulation & Theory of Evolving Microstructures: Proceedings of a Symposium Sponsored by Computer Simulation Committee, Held at the Fall Meeting of the Minerals, Metals & Materials Society in Indianapolis, 2-5th October 1989. Minerals, Metals & Materials Society Staff. Ed. by M. P. Anderson & A. D. Rollett. LC 90-61686. (Illus.). 299p. reprint ed. pap. 85.30 (*0-7837-6063-9*, 2052509) Bks Demand.

Simulation & Training Technology for Nuclear Power Plant Safety. Ed. by Albert E. Hickey. 156p. (Orig.). 1981. pap. text ed. 40.00 (*0-89785-975-8*) Am Inst Res.

Simulation Applications in Business Management & MIS. Ed. by Roberts & Monroe. 124p. 1993. pap. 50.00 (*1-56555-023-4*, MC93-3) Soc Computer Sim.

Simulation Applied to Manufacturing Energy & Environmental Studies & Electronics & Computer Engineering. Ed. by S. Tucci et al. 448p. 1989. pap. 80.00 (*0-911801-55-3*, ESM89-2) Soc Computer Sim.

Simulation Approach to Solids: Molecular-Dynamics of Equilibrium Crystals & More. Ed. by Gianni Jacucci. (C). 1991. lib. bdg. 157.50 (*0-7923-0383-0*) Kluwer Ac.

Simulation Approach to the Study of Human Fertility. Gigi Santow. (Publications of the Netherlands Inter-University Demographic Institute & the Population & Family Study Centre Ser.: Vol. 5). 1978. pap. text ed. 64.00 (*90-207-0765-5*) Kluwer Ac.

***Simulation-Based Econometric Methods.** Christian Gourieroux & Alain Monfort. (OUP/CORE Lecture Ser.). (Illus.). 192p. 1997. 35.00 (*0-19-877475-3*) OUP.

Simulation-Based Experiential Learning. Ed. by T. Jonng et al. (NATO ASI Series F: Computer & Systems Sciences, Special Programme AET: Vol. 122). (Illus.). xiv, 274p. 1994. 79.00 (*0-387-57276-7*) Spr-Verlag.

Simulation-Based Reliability Assessment for Structural Engineers. Pavel Marek et al. Ed. by Wai-Fah Chen. (New Directions in Civil Engineering Ser.). 372p. 1995. 89.95 incl. disk (*0-8493-8286-6*, 8286) CRC Pr.

Simulation by Bondgraphs: Introduction to a Graphical Method. J. U. Thoma. (Illus.). 224p. 1990. 87.95 (*0-387-51640-9*) Spr-Verlag.

Simulation Environments & Symbol & Number Processing on Multi & Array Processors. Karplus. (Illus.). 430p. 1988. pap. text ed. 40.00 (*0-911801-39-1*, MC-88-1) Soc Computer Sim.

Simulation Fidelity in Training System Design: Bridging the Gap Between Reality & Training. R. T. Hays & M. J. Singer. (Recent Research in Psychology Ser.). (Illus.). 440p. 1990. 58.95 (*0-387-96846-6*) Spr-Verlag.

Simulation for Decision Making. Arne Thesen. (West - Engineering Ser.). 1992. text ed. 77.95 (*0-534-95466-9*) PWS Pubs.

***Simulation for Emergency Management.** Ed. by David H. Kanecki. 92p. 1994. pap. 60.00 (*1-56555-025-0*, SMC-94-1) Soc Computer Sim.

Simulation Fundamentals. B. S. Bennett. (International Series in Systems & Control Engineering). (C). 1995. text ed. 65.00 (*0-13-813262-3*) P-H.

Simulation Games for Religious Education. Richard J. Reichert. LC 75-142. 106p. 1975. pap. 5.95 (*0-88489-060-0*) St Marys.

Simulation Games in Learning. Ed. by Sarane S. Boocock & E. O. Schild. LC 68-21913. 279p. 1968. reprint ed. pap. 79.60 (*0-608-01474-5*, 2059518) Bks Demand.

Simulation Games 1. Pat Baker & Mary-Ruth Marshall. 1992. pap. 8.50 (*0-85819-582-8*, Pub. by JBCE AT) Morehouse Pub.

Simulation Games 2. Pat Baker & Mary-Ruth Marshall. 1992. pap. 8.50 (*0-85819-583-6*, Pub. by JBCE AT) Morehouse Pub.

Simulation Games 3. Pat Baker & Mary-Ruth Marshall. 1992. pap. 8.50 (*0-85819-586-0*, Pub. by JBCE AT) Morehouse Pub.

Simulation Games 4. Pat Baker & Mary-Ruth Marshall. 1992. pap. 8.50 (*0-85819-802-9*, Pub. by JBCE AT) Morehouse Pub.

Simulation Gaming - On the Improvement of Competence in Dealing with Complexity, Uncertainty & Value Conflicts: Proceedings of the International Simulation & Gaming Association's 19th International Conference, Department of Gamma-Informatics, Utrecht University, the Netherlands, August 16-19, 1988. Ed. by Jan H. Klabbers et al. (Illus.). 382p. 1989. 100.75 (*0-08-037115-9*, Pergamon Pr) Elsevier.

Simulation, Gaming & Language Learning. David Crookall & Oxford. 1990. pap. 27.95 (*0-8384-2673-5*) Heinle & Heinle.

Simulation-Gaming in Education & Training: Proceedings of the International Simulation & Gaming Association's 18th International Conference. David Crookall et al. LC 88-11740. (Illus.). 298p. 1988. 115.00 (*0-08-036465-9*, Prgamon Press) Buttrwrth-Heinemann.

Simulation in Ada. Ed. by Unger et al. 40p. 1985. pap. 10.00 (*0-911801-06-5*, ESC85-1) Soc Computer Sim.

Simulation in Emergency Management & Engineering: Simulation in Health Care. Ed. by Jim D. Sullivan et al. 269p. 1991. Joint vol. pap. 48.00 (*0-911801-86-3*, MC91-2) Soc Computer Sim.

Simulation in Emergency Planning. Carroll. 116p. 1983. 36.00 (*0-685-66784-7*, SS11-2) Soc Computer Sim.

Simulation in Energy Systems, 1991. Ed. by W. Frisch et al. (Simulation Ser.: Vol. 22, No. 4). 174p. 1990. 48.00 (*0-911801-82-0*, SS22-4) Soc Computer Sim.

Simulation in Engineering Education, 1990. Ed. by Michael Ward. 108p. 1990. pap. 36.00 (*0-911801-65-0*, SEE90-1) Soc Computer Sim.

Simulation in Engineering Education, 1991. Ed. by Alfred W. Jones et al. 124p. 1991. pap. 40.00 (*0-911801-85-5*, SEE91-1) Soc Computer Sim.

Simulation in Health Care Delivery Systems, 1984. Stanridge. 120p. 1984. pap. 20.00 (*0-911801-02-2*, MC84-1) Soc Computer Sim.

Simulation in Health Sciences & Services: 1993 Conference. Anderson & Meyer Katzper. 116p. 1993. pap. 48.00 (*1-56555-021-8*, MC93-2) Soc Computer Sim.

Simulation in Inventory & Production Control. Bekiroglu. 64p. 1983. pap. 20.00 (*0-685-67787-7*, MC83-1) Soc Computer Sim.

Simulation in Manufacturing. Ed. by J. E. Lenz. 260p. 1986. 158.95 (*0-387-16329-8*) Spr-Verlag.

Simulation in Manufacturing. N. D. Thomson. (Industrial Control, Computers, & Communications Ser.: No. 12). 1995. write for info. (*0-86380-172-2*) Wiley.

Simulation in Manufacturing. Norman Thomson. (Industrial Control, Computers, & Communications Ser.: No. 12). 200p. 1996. text ed. 74.95 (*0-471-95738-0*) Wiley.

Simulation in Research & Development. Robert Vichnevetsky. LC 72-2231. (American Management Association's Management Bulletins Ser.: No. 125). 19p. reprint ed. pap. 25.00 (*0-317-09918-3*, 2000640) Bks Demand.

Simulation in Strongly Typed Languages: Ada, Pascal, Simula. Bryant & Unger. 172p. 1984. 36.00 (*0-685-67788-5*, SS13-2) Soc Computer Sim.

***Simulation in Synthetic Environments '96: 1996 Simulation for Emergency Management.** Ed. by Ben Delany et al. 74p. 1996. pap. 60.00 (*1-56555-094-3*, SS-28-4) Soc Computer Sim.

Simulation in the Design of Digital Electronic Systems. John B. Gosling. LC 93-14882. (Electronics Texts for Engineers & Scientists Ser.). (Illus.). 284p. (C). 1993. text ed. 95.00 (*0-521-41656-6*); pap. text ed. 42.95 (*0-521-42672-3*) Cambridge U Pr.

Simulation in the Factory of the Future: Simulation in Traffic Control. Ed. by S. Takaba. (Illus.). 234p. 1988. pap. text ed. 32.00 (*0-911801-40-5*, EMC88-2) Soc Computer Sim.

***Simulation in the Health Sciences; 1994.** Ed. by Anderson & Katzper. 151p. 1994. pap. 60.00 (*1-56555-068-4*, MC-94-3) Soc Computer Sim.

***Simulation in the Medical Sciences.** Ed. by James G. Anderson & Meyer Katzper. 226p. 1996. pap. 80.00 (*1-56555-091-9*, HSS-96) Soc Computer Sim.

Simulation Made Easy: A Manager's Guide. Kerim Tumay & Charles Harrell. (Illus.). 311p. 1995. text ed. 50.00 (*0-89806-136-9*) Eng Mgmt Pr.

Simulation Metamodel. Linda W. Friedman. 224p. (C). 1995. lib. bdg. 89.95 (*0-7923-9648-0*) Kluwer Ac.

Simulation Methodology for Statisticians, Operations Analysts, & Engineers, Vol. I. Peter A. Lewis & Endel J. Orav. LC 88-5536. 416p. (C). (gr. 13). 1988. text ed. 73.00 (*0-534-09450-3*) Chapman & Hall.

Simulation Model Design & Execution: Building Digital Worlds. Paul A. Fishwick. LC 94-36756. 432p. 1995. text ed. 83.00 (*0-13-098609-7*) P-H.

***Simulation Model for the Future Analysis of Cardiovascular Disease.** O. J. Frieze et al. 408p. (Orig.). 1996. pap. 69.00 incl. disk (*90-6224-878-0*, Pub. by Uitgeverij Arkel NE) LPC InBook.

Simulation Modeling & Analysis. 2nd ed. Averill M. Law & W. David Kelton. (Industrial Engineering & Management Science Ser.). 784p. 1991. pap. text ed. write for info. (*0-07-036698-5*) McGraw.

Simulation Modeling Using @Risk. Wayne L. Winston. 1996. pap. text ed. 37.95 incl. 3.5 hd (*0-534-26490-5*); pap. text ed. 69.95 incl. 3.5 hd (*0-534-26491-3*) Wadsworth Pub.

Simulation Modeling Using @Risk: With Demonstration Software. Wayne L. Winston. 230p. (C). 1996. pap. text ed. 29.95 incl. 3.5 ld (*0-534-26492-1*) Wadsworth Pub.

Simulation, Modelling & Development - SMD '87: Proceedings IASTED Symposium, Cairo, Egypt, March 3-5, 1987. Ed. by M. H. Hamza. 177p. 1987. 77.00 (*0-88986-110-2*, 121) Acta Pr.

Simulation Modelling in Bioengineering: Proceedings of the BIOSIM '96 Conference. Ed. by M. Cerrolaza & C. A. Brebbia. 350p. 1996. 239.00 (*1-85312-455-9*, 4559) Computational Mech MA.

***Simulation Models, GIS & Nonpoint-Source Pollution: Bibliography, January 1988-June 1992.** David Holloway & Joe Makuch. 34p. (C). 1996. reprint ed. pap. 20.00 (*0-7881-3693-3*) DIANE Pub.

Simulation Models in Corporate Planning. Thomas H. Naylor. LC 78-31258. (Praeger Special Studies). 312p. 1979. text ed. 55.00 (*0-275-90398-2*, C0398, Praeger Pubs) Greenwood.

***Simulation of American History I.** Semonch. (C). 1987. lab manual ed. write for info. incl. 5.25 hd (*0-15-581050-2*) HB Coll Pubs.

***Simulation of American History II.** Semonch. (C). 1987. write for info. incl. 5.25 hd (*0-15-581051-0*) HB Coll Pubs.

***Simulation of American History II.** Semonch. (C). 1989. 29.95 incl. 3.5 hd (*0-15-581053-7*) HB Coll Pubs.

Simulation of Communication Systems. Michael C. Jeruchim et al. (Applications of Communications Theory Ser.). (Illus.). 730p. 1992. 125.00 (*0-306-43989-1*, Plenum Pr) Plenum.

Simulation of Ground-Water Flow & the Movement of Saline Water in the Hueco Bolson Aquifer, El Paso, Texas, & Adjacent Areas. George E. Groschen. LC 95-37536. (U. S. Geological Survey Bulletin Ser.: Vol. 2444). 1996. write for info. (*0-614-08569-1*) US Geol Survey.

Simulation of Ground-Water Flow in Alluvial Basins in South-Central Arizona & Parts of Adjacent States. T. W. Anderson & Geoffrey W. Freethey. (Regional Aquifer-System Analysis--Southwest Alluvial Basins, Arizona & Adjacent States; Professional Paper: Vol. 1406-D). 1995. write for info. (*0-615-00173-4*) US Geol Survey.

Simulation of Human Intelligence. Ed. by Donald Broadbent. LC 92-17187. 232p. 1993. pap. 24.95 (*0-631-18733-2*) Blackwell Pubs.

Simulation of Liquids & Solids: Molecular Dynamics & Monte Carlo Methods in Statistical Mechanics. Ed. by G. Ciccotti et al. 482p. 1987. pap. 75.50 (*0-444-87061-X*, North Holland) Elsevier.

Simulation of Local Area Networks. Matthew N. Sadiku & Mohammad Ilyas. LC 94-23413. 240p. 1994. 69.95 (*0-8493-2473-4*, 2473) CRC Pr.

Simulation of Materials Processing: Theory, Methods, & Applications: Proceedings: International Conference on Numerical Methods in Industrial Forming Processes - NUMIFORM '95 (5th: 1995: Ithaca, NY) Ed. by Shen Shan-Fu & Paul R. Dawson. (Illus.). 1248p. (C). 1995. 170.00 (*90-5410-553-4*, Pub. by A A Balkema NE) Ashgate Pub Co.

***Simulation of Meshing, Transmission Errors & Bearing Contact for Single-Enveloping Worm-Gear Drives.** Faydor L. Litvin & Vadim Kin. (1990 Fall Technical Meeting). 1990. pap. text ed. 30.00 (*1-55589-555-7*) AGMA.

Simulation of Nonlinear Systems in Physics: ENEA Workshop on Nonlinear Dynamics, Vol. 3. Giuseppe Maino et al. 250p. 1991. text ed. 84.00 (*981-02-0402-7*) World Scientific Pub.

Simulation of Recreational Use for Park & Wilderness Management. Mordechai Shechter & Robert C. Lucas. LC 78-17920. (Resources for the Future Ser.). 1979. 25.00 (*0-8018-2160-6*) Johns Hopkins.

Simulation of Recreational Use for Park & Wilderness Management. Mordechai Shechter & Robert C. Lucas. LC 78-17920. (Illus.). 240p. reprint ed. pap. 68.40 (*0-685-23709-5*, 2032165) Bks Demand.

Simulation of Semiconductor Devices & Processes, Vol. 5. Ed. by S. Selberherr et al. (Computational Microelectronics Ser.). 505p. 1993. 158.95 (*0-387-82504-5*) Spr-Verlag.

Simulation of Semiconductor Devices & Processes, Vol. 6. Ed. by H. Ryssel & P. Pichler. 516p. 1995. 174.95 (*3-211-82736-6*) Spr-Verlag.

Simulation of Surveillance: Hyper-Control in Telematic Societies. William Bogard. (Cultural Social Studies). 224p. (C). 1996. text ed. 59.95 (*0-521-55081-5*); pap. text ed. 18.95 (*0-521-55561-2*) Cambridge U Pr.

Simulation of the Maneuverability of Inland Waterway Tows. George L. Petrie. (University of Michigan, Dept. of Naval Architecture & Marine Engineering, Report Ser.: No. 186). 93p. reprint ed. pap. 26.60 (*0-317-27207-1*, 2023871) Bks Demand.

Simulation of Thermal Systems: A Modular Program with an Interactive Preprocessor (EMGP3) Willy L. Dutre. (C). 1991. lib. bdg. 259.00 (*0-7923-1235-X*) Kluwer Ac.

Simulation of Thin Slot Spirals & Dual Circular Patch Antennas Using the Finite Element Method with Mixed Elements. J. Gong et al. LC 95-19796. (University of Michigan Reports: No. 030601-4-T). 94p. 1995. reprint ed. pap. 26.80 (*0-608-02397-3*, 2063038) Bks Demand.

Simulation of Water Based Thermal Solar Systems: Eursol - an Interactive Program. Willy L. Dutre. (C). 1991. lib. bdg. 121.50 (*0-7923-1236-8*) Kluwer Ac.

Simulation of Wave Processes in Excitable Media. V. S. Zykov & A. T. Winfree. (Nonlinear Science: Theory & Applications Ser.). 233p. 1992. text ed. 209.00 (*0-471-93513-1*) Wiley.

Simulation, Optimization & Expert Systems: How Technology Is Revolutionizing the Way Securities Are Underwritten, Analyzed & Traded. Dimitris N. Chorafas. (Institutional Investor Publication Ser.). 450p. 1991. text ed. 70.00 (*1-55738-231-X*) Irwin Prof Pubng.

Simulation, Planning, & Society. Melville C. Branch. LC 96-26291. 224p. 1997. text ed. 59.95 (*0-275-95403-X*) Greenwood.

Simulation Security First Bank: A Banking Custom. 2nd ed. Sargent. (GB - Basic Business Ser.). 1986. 17.95 (*0-538-07175-3*) S-W Pub.

Simulation Software for Robotics. Ed. by J. D. Lee. (Robotics & Computer Integrated Manufacturing Ser.). 116p. 1989. 36.50 (*0-08-037196-5*, Pergamon Pr) Elsevier.

Simulation, Spectacle & the Ironies of Education Reform. Guy Senese & Ralph Page. LC 94-38514. (Critical Studies in Education & Culture). 160p. 1995. text ed. 52.95 (*0-89789-402-2*, Bergin & Garvey); pap. text ed. 16.95 (*0-89789-444-8*, Bergin & Garvey) Greenwood.

Simulation Surgery. Ed. by Toyomi Fujino. LC 93-15923. 261p. 1994. text ed. 160.00 (*0-471-94122-0*) Wiley.

Simulation Symposium, 28th Annual. LC 10-80241. 368p. 1995. pap. 60.00 (*0-8186-7091-6*, PR07091) IEEE Comp Soc.

***Simulation Symposium, 30th Annual.** LC 10-80241. 288p. 1997. pap. 70.00 (*0-8186-7934-4*) IEEE Comp Soc.

Simulation Syndrome. Derderain. Date not set. 21.95 (*0-02-907275-1*, Free Press) Free Pr.

Simulation Teaching of Library Administration. Martha J. Zachert. LC 74-32041. 315p. reprint ed. pap. 89.80 (*0-317-10402-0*, 2004384) Bks Demand.

Simulation Techniques: Models of Communication Signals & Processes. Floyd M. Gardner & John D. Baker. LC 96-31193. 1996. pap. text ed. 0.01 (*0-471-51965-0*, Wiley-Interscience) Wiley.

Simulation Techniques: Models of Communication Signals & Processes & the Staedt..., 2 vols., Set. Floyd M. Gardner. 1996. 245.00 (*0-471-51966-9*) Wiley.

Simulation Techniques Vol. 1: Models of Communication Signals & Processes. Floyd M. Gardner & John D. Baker. LC 95-38580. 300p. 1996. text ed. 95.00 (*0-471-51964-2*) Wiley.

Simulation Techniques & Solutions for Mixed-Signal Coupling in Integrated Circuits. Nishath K. Verghese et al. (International Series in Engineering & Computer Science). 304p. (C). 1994. lib. bdg. 114.00 (*0-7923-9544-1*) Kluwer Ac.

***Simulation Technology, Proceedings of International Conference on (SIMTEC '93)** Ed. by Dost & Lambert. 400p. 1993. pap. 60.00 (*1-56555-060-9*, SIMTEC-93) Soc Computer Sim.

***Simulation Training: Management Framework Improved, but Challenges Remain.** Barry W. Holman et al. (Illus.). 61p. (C). 1997. reprint ed. pap. text ed. 30.00 (*0-7881-4133-3*) DIANE Pub.

Simulation Validation - A Confidence Assessment Methodology. Peter Knepell & Deborah Arangno. LC 92-36123. 168p. 1996. 40.00 (*0-8186-3512-6*, 3512) IEEE Comp Soc.

Simulation with GASP-PL-I: A PL-I Based Continuous-Discrete Simulation Language. Alan B. Pritsker & Robert E. Young. LC 75-23182. 351p. reprint ed. pap. 100.10 (*0-317-11035-7*, 2022490) Bks Demand.

***Simulation with Visual SLAM & AweSim.** A. Alan Pritsker et al. (Illus.). 1997. 69.95 (*0-614-29828-8*) Systems Pub.

Simulations. Jean Baudrillard. 159p. Date not set. 7.00 (*0-936756-02-0*, Semiotexte) Autonomedia.

Simulations: Sixteen Tales of Virtual Reality. Karie Jacobson. LC 92-39509. 1993. 9.95 (*0-8065-1406-X*, Citadel Pr) Carol Pub Group.

Simulations & Gaming Across Disciplines & Cultures: ISAGA at a Watershed. Ed. by David A. Crookall & Kiyoshi Arai. LC 95-12230. 288p. (C). 1995. 46.00 (*0-8039-7102-8*); pap. 22.95 (*0-8039-7103-6*) Sage.

Simulations for Careers & Life Skills. P. Smith. (C). 1986. 115.00 (*0-7487-0273-3*, Pub. by S Thornes Pubs UK) St Mut.

Simulations for Careers & Life Skills. Peter Smith. 176p. (C). 1993. 75.00 (*0-7478-0273-4*, Pub. by Stanley Thornes UK) Trans-Atl Phila.

***Simulations for Op Amps Using EWB.** Antonakos. (C). 1997. pap. text ed. 27.00 (*0-13-632464-9*) P-H.

***Simulations for Op Amps Using PSpice.** Antonakos. (C). 1997. pap. text ed. 27.00 (*0-13-632449-5*) P-H.

An Asterisk (*) at the beginning of an entry indicates that the title is appearing in BIP for the first time.

*Simulations for Solid State Physics: An Interactive Resource for Students & Teachers. Robert H. Silsbee & Jorg Drager. (Illus.). (C). 1997. cd-rom write for info. (0-521-59910-5) Cambridge U Pr.

*Simulations for Solid State Physics: An Interactive Resource for Students & Teachers. Robert H. Silsbee & Jorg Drager. LC 96-48930. (Illus.). 335p. (C). 1997. text ed. 80.00 incl. cd-rom (0-521-59094-9); pap. text ed. 24.95 (0-521-59911-3) Cambridge U Pr.

Simulations in Biomedicine IV. (BIOMED Ser.: Vol. 4). 400p. 1997. 180.00 (1-85312-462-1, 4621) Computational Mech MA.

Simulations in Business. James VanOosting. (C). 1991. pap. 17.96 (0-395-56496-4) HM.

Simulations in English Teaching. Paul J. Bambrough. LC 94-12227. (English, Language & Education Ser.). 128p. 1994. pap. 23.00 (0-335-19151-7, Open Univ Pr) Taylor & Francis.

Simulations in Language Teaching. Ken Jones. LC 82-4557. (New Directions in Language Teaching Ser.). 122p. (Orig.). 1983. pap. 14.95 (0-521-27045-6) Cambridge U Pr.

Simulations of Biological & Polymeric Macromolecular Systems: A Discretized Monte Carlo Approach. J. Skolnick & A. Kolinsky. 200p. (C). 1993. text ed. 49.00 (9971-5-0855-9) World Scientific Pub.

Simulations, Selected Translations. Richard O'Connell. 1993. pap. 25.00 (3-7052-0625-7) Atlantis Edns.

Simulator GPSS-FORTRAN: Version 3. B. Schmidt. 350p. 1987. 60.95 (0-387-96504-1) Spr-Verlag.

*Simulators, Vol. 11. Ed. by Jaime Olmos & Ariel Sharon. 559p. 1994. 120.00 (1-56555-071-4, SS-26-3) Soc Computer Sim.

Simulators International, Vol. 12. Ed. by Maurice Ades & Ariel Sharon. 382p. 1995. 120.00 (1-56555-049-8, SS-27-3) Soc Computer Sim.

*Simulators International, Vol. 12. Ed. by Maurice Ades & Ron Griebenow. 290p. 1996. 120.00 (1-56555-092-7, SS-28-2) Soc Computer Sim.

Simulators IX. Ed. by Ariel Sharon. 343p. 1992. 80.00 (1-56555-004-8, SS-24-4) Soc Computer Sim.

Simulators VI, 1989. Ed. by Ariel Sharon & Mohammad R. Fakory. (Simulation Ser.: Vol. 21, No. 3). 264p. 1989. 48.00 (0-911801-51-0, SS21-3) Soc Computer Sim.

Simulators VII, 1990. Ed. by Ariel Sharon & Mohammad R. Fakory. (Simulation Ser.: Vol. 22, No. 2). 330p. 1990. 48.00 (0-911801-67-7, SS22-2) Soc Computer Sim.

Simulators VIII, 1991. Ed. by Ariel Sharon. (Simulation Ser.: Vol. 24, No. 1). 446p. 1991. 88.00 (0-911801-89-8, SS24-1) Soc Computer Sim.

Simulators X. Ed. by Ariel Sharon. 698p. 1993. 100.00 (1-56555-050-1, SS-25-4) Soc Computer Sim.

SIMULINK: User's Guide. Mathworks, Inc. Staff. 320p. 1995. student ed., pap. text ed. 51.00 (0-13-452435-7) P-H.

Simultan see Three Paths to the Lake

*Simultane Conjointanalyse, Benefitsegmentierung, Produktlinien- & Preisgestaltung. Eberhard Aust. (Illus.). 264p. (GER.). 1996. 51.95 (3-631-49057-7) P Lang Pubng.

Simultaneous Engineering. 1994. 42.95 (0-387-57882-X) Spr-Verlag.

Simultaneous Equations Estimation. Ed. by Carl F. Christ. (International Library of Critical Writings in Economics Ser.: Vol. 3). 560p. 1994. 175.00 (1-85278-661-2) E Elgar.

Simultaneous Horizontal & Cyclovertical Strabismus Surgery. Marc H. Govin & Jos J. Bierlaagh. LC 93-18643. (Monographs in Ophthalmology: Vol. 15). 216p. (C). 1994. lib. bdg. 243.00 (0-7923-2246-0) Kluwer Ac.

Simultaneous Management: Managing Projects in a Dynamic Environment. Alexander Laufer. 300p. 1996. 59.95 (0-8144-0312-3) AMACOM.

Simultaneous Model of Intra-Urban Household Mobility. Daniel H. Weinberg. (Explorations in Economic Research Four Ser.: No. 4). 17p. 1977. reprint ed. 35.00 (0-685-61417-4) Natl Bur Econ Res.

*Simultaneous Orgasm: And Other Joys of Sexual Intimacy. Michael Riskin & Anita Banker-Riskin. LC 97-19824. 1997. pap. 14.95 (0-89793-221-8) Hunter Hse.

*Simultaneous Orgasm: And Other Joys of Sexual Intimacy. Michael Riskin & Anita Banker-Riskin. (Illus.). 224p. 1997. 24.95 (0-89793-222-6) Hunter Hse.

Simultaneous Stabilation of Linear Systems. V. Blondel. (Lecture Notes in Control & Information Sciences Ser.: Vol. 191). (Illus.). 216p. 1993. 45.95 (0-387-19862-8) Spr-Verlag.

Simultaneous Statistical Inference. Rupert G. Miller, Jr. (Series in Statistics). (Illus.). 299p. 1991. 74.95 (0-387-90548-0) Spr-Verlag.

Simultaneous Switching Noise in Printed Circuit Boards. Linda P. Katehi & Karem A. Sakallah. (University of Michigan Reports: No. RL898). 38p. reprint ed. pap. 25.00 (0-7837-6783-8, 2046615) Bks Demand.

Simultaneous Switching Noise of CMOS Devices & Systems. Ramesh Senthinathan & John L. Prince. LC 93-32572. (International Series in Engineering & Computer Science, VLSI, Computer Architecture, & Digital Screen Processing). 232p. (C). 1993. lib. bdg. 105.00 (0-7923-9400-3) Kluwer Ac.

Simultaneous Time: Twin Souls, Soul Mates, & Parallel Lives. Thea Alexander. 48p. (Orig.). 1982. pap. 10.00 (0-913080-09-8) Macro Bks.

Sin. Josephine Hart. 1993. mass mkt. 5.99 (0-8041-1097-2) Ivy Books.

Sin. Wendy MacLeod. 1997. pap. 5.25 (0-8222-1561-6) Dramatists Play.

Sin: A Novel. F. S. Jose. LC 95-39828. 1996. write for info. (0-614-08383-4) Random.

Sin: Radical Evil in Soul & Society. Ted Peters. 312p. (Orig.). (C). 1994. pap. 15.00 (0-8028-0113-7) Eerdmans.

Sin & Censorship: The Catholic Church & the Motion Picture Industry. Frank Walsh. (Illus.). 1996. 35.00 (0-300-06373-3) Yale U Pr.

Sin & Hoodoo Memory. W. Gellis. 44p. 1987. pap. 10.00 (0-917455-04-5) Big Foot NY.

Sin & Its Consequences. 104p. 1990. pap. 20.00 (1-57277-428-2) Script Rsch.

Sin & Its Consequences. rev. ed. Cardinal Henry E. Manning. LC 86-50420. 200p. 1991. reprint ed. pap. 6.00 (0-89555-299-X) TAN Bks Pubs.

Sin & Reconciliation see Torah Anthology: Meam Lo'ez

Sin & Repentance. Ignatius Brianchianinov. 1991. pap. 1.00 (0-89981-119-1) Eastern Orthodox.

Sin & Scientism. Jacob Needleman. (Broadside Editions Ser.). 26p. (Orig.). (C). 1986. pap. 4.95 (0-9609850-7-7) Rob Briggs.

Sin & Self-Consciousness in the Thought of Friedrich Schleiermacher. Robert L. Vance. 1995. write for info. (0-7734-2862-3) E Mellen.

Sin & Sex. R. Briffault. LC 72-6300. (Studies in Philosophy: No. 40). 228p. 1972. reprint ed. lib. bdg. 75.00 (0-8383-1631-X) M S G Haskell Hse.

Sin & Sex. Robert Briffault. LC 72-9623. (Human Sexual Behavior Ser.). reprint ed. 37.50 (0-404-57418-1) AMS Pr.

Sin & Society. John Addy. (Illus.). 240p. (C). 1989. text ed. 39.95 (0-415-01874-9) Routledge.

Sin & Temptation: The Challenge of Personal Godliness. John Ownen. (Classics Faith & Devotion Ser.: Bk. 2). 208p. 1996. pap. text ed. 9.99 (1-55661-830-1) Bethany Hse.

Sin & the Calvinists: Morals Control & the Consistory in the Reformed Tradition. Ed. by Raymond A. Mentzer. LC 94-25541. (Sixteenth Century Essays & Studies: Vol. 32). 1995. 40.00 (0-940474-34-4) Sixteenth Cent.

Sin Anillos-Shadow Play. Sally Wentworth. 1996. mass mkt. 3.50 (0-373-33357-9) Harlequin Bks.

Sin As Addiction. Patrick T. McCormick. 1989. pap. 7.95 (0-8091-3064-5) Paulist Pr.

Sin at Easter. Tumas J. Vaizgantas. 1971. 5.95 (0-87141-038-9) Manyland.

Sin Boldly! Dr. Dave's Irreverent Guide to Acing the College Paper. David R. Williams. 96p. (Orig.). (C). 1995. pap. text ed. 6.66 (0-9644419-0-X) Dr Dave Pub.

Sin City. rev. ed. Frank Miller. (Illus.). 208p. 1992. pap. 15.00 (1-878574-59-0) Dark Horse Comics.

*Sin City: That Yellow Bastard. Frank Miller. 1997. 25.00 (1-56971-187-9); pap. text ed. 15.00 (1-56971-225-5) Dark Horse Comics.

Sin City: The Big Fat Kill. Frank Miller. (Illus.). 184p. 1995. 25.00 (1-56971-076-7) Dark Horse Comics.

Sin City Bk. 1: A Dame to Kill For. rev. ed. Frank Miller. Ed. by Jerry Prosser. (Illus.). 208p. 1994. 25.00 (1-56971-036-8) Dark Horse Comics.

Sin City Bk. 1: A Dame to Kill For. 2nd ed. Fraank Miller. (Illus.). 208p. 1994. pap. 15.00 (1-56971-068-6) Dark Horse Comics.

Sin Compromiso: Beyond All Reason. Cathy Williams. (Bianca Ser.: No. 384). 1996. mass mkt. 3.50 (0-373-33384-6, 1-33384-8) Harlequin Bks.

*Sin Diego: The Underground Guide to Sex, Drugs & Rock & Roll. 2nd rev. ed. Phil Fredricks. Ed. by Roger Warren. (Lecher McRich's Adult Guides Ser.). (Illus.). 400p. 1997. pap. 22.95 (0-945949-07-3) Warren Comns.

Sin Duda. Frank Medley. 1992. pap. 16.95 (0-8384-2378-7) Heinle & Heinle.

Sin Eater. B. Thomas Ellis. 28.95 (0-7156-0940-8, Pub. by Duckworth UK) Focus Pub-R Pullins.

Sin-Eater. Deborah Randall. 8900. pap. 11.95 (1-85224-041-5, Pub. by Bloodaxe Bks UK) Dufour.

Sin Eater. Gary D. Schmidt. LC 96-14372. 192p. (J). (gr. 5-9). 1996. pap. 15.99 (0-525-67541-8) Dutton Child Bks.

Sin-Eater, & Other Tales & Episodes. William Sharp. LC 74-167470. (Short Story Index Reprint Ser.). 1977. reprint ed. 21.95 (0-8369-3996-4) Ayer.

*Sin in the Camp. Ian A. Montgomery. pap. write for info. (1-890538-16-7) Rhiannon Pubns.

*Sin in Valentinianism. Michel Desjardins. 167p. 1990. 19.95 (1-55540-224-0, 062108); pap. 12.95 (1-55540-225-9) Scholars Pr GA.

Sin Loi. Arthur B. Greathead. (Illus.). 50p. (Orig.). 1988. pap. 5.95 (0-945670-00-1) Greathead Pub.

Sin of Familiarity: Those Practicing Excessive Familiarity - a Devastating Sin. Mark T. Barclay. 64p. (Orig.). 1989. pap. 5.00 (0-944802-04-4) M Barclay Pubns.

*Sin of Father Mouret. Emile Zola. Tr. by Sandy Petrey. LC 83-10436. 318p. pap. 90.70 (0-608-04828-3, 2065485) Bks Demand.

Sin of Lawlessness: A Lethal Practice. Mark T. Barclay. 57p. (Orig.). 1989. pap. 5.00 (0-944802-01-X) M Barclay Pubns.

Sin of Monsieur Pettipon & Other Humorous Stories. Richard E. Connell. LC 77-106273. (Short Story Index Reprint Ser.). 1977. 20.95 (0-8369-3310-9) Ayer.

Sin of Obedience. Willard Beecher & Marguerite Beecher. 88p. (Orig.). 1982. pap. 7.75 (0-942350-00-6) Beecher Found.

Sin of Pat Muldoon. John McLiam. 1957. pap. 5.25 (0-8222-1031-2) Dramatists Play.

Sin of the Book: Edmond Jab Es. Ed. by Eric Gould. LC 84-5270. 278p. 1985. reprint ed. pap. 79.30 (0-7837-8888-6, 2049599) Bks Demand.

Sin of Unbelief. Charles H. Spurgeon. 1977. mass mkt. 0.75 (1-56186-333-5) Pilgrim Pubns.

***Sin of Wages: Where the Conventional Pay System Has Led Us & How to Find a Way Out. William B. Abernathy. LC 96-92835. 181p. (Orig.). 1996. pap. 12.00 (0-9655276-0-3) Abernathy & Assocs. Informative & thought-provoking examination of today's conventional pay system & the problems it creates within organizations. Discusses in detail the seven Sins of Wages: Fixed-expense pay, paying for time, corporate socialism, performance-based promotions, management by exception, management by perception, & entitlement thinking. Provides alternatives to these problems that will allow an organization to reward high contribution employees for their performance, link organizational objectives to specific job positions & use these measures as a management tool for feedback, develop an alternative to the annual (an usually subjective) review process, & convert part of our compensation from a fixed to a profit-indexed expense that would have a direct relationship with the way the business cycle goes. Written by William Abernathy, Ph.D., a leading authority on performance management & incentive pay systems. Order from: PerfSys Press, Abernathy & Assoc., 665 Oakleaf Office Lane, Memphis, TN 38117. 901-763-2122.** *Publisher Provided Annotation.*

Sin, Organized Charity, & the Poor Law in Victorian England. Robert Humphreys. 1995. text ed. 65.00 (0-312-12755-3) St Martin.

Sin, Redemption & Sacrifice: A Biblical & Patristic Study. Stanislas Lyonnet & Leopold Sabarin. (Analecta Biblica Ser.: Vol. 48). 1971. pap. 27.00 (88-7653-048-7, Pub. by Biblical Inst Pr IT) Loyola Pr.

Sin Revisited. Solange S. Hertz. 158p. (Orig.). 1996. pap. 10.50 (1-883511-08-9) Veritas Pr CA.

*Sin Santidad Nadie le Vera - Without Holiness He Will Not Be Seen. Avila. 42p. (SPA.). 1995. write for info. (1-56063-742-0) Editorial Unilit.

Sin Tactics. David Gansz. 54p. 1988. 12.00 (0-916258-19-X); pap. 7.50 (0-916258-20-3) Woodbine Pr.

*Sin-Tau. (Complete Biblical Library: Vol. 7). 539p. (ENG & HEB.). Date not set. 39.95 (1-884642-47-0) World Library.

*Sin Tener a Quien Clamar. Doris Van Stone. (SPA.). 4.95 (0-8297-1838-9) Life Pubs Intl.

Sin, the Savior, & Salvation: The Theology of Everlasting Life. Robert P. Lightner. 320p. 1996. pap. 13.99 (0-8254-3153-0) Kregel.

Sin Tiempo ni Distancia. Isabel Rodriguez. LC 90-81212. (Coleccion Cuba y Sus Jueces). (Illus.). 94p. (Orig.). (SPA.). 1990. pap. 9.95 (0-89729-566-8) Ediciones.

Sin Within Her Smile. Jonathan Gash. 240p. 1995. pap. 5.95 (0-14-023839-5, Penguin Bks) Viking Penguin.

Sin Within Her Smile. large type ed. Jonathan Gash. LC 94-30215. 1994. lib. bdg. 21.95 (0-7838-1115-2, GK Hall) Thorndike Pr.

Sin Within Her Smile. large type ed. Jonathan Gash. LC 94-30215. 385p. 1994. 20.95 (0-8161-1115-4, GK Hall) Thorndike Pr.

*Sin 7. Tony Luke. (Illus.). 64p. 1997. pap. 9.95 (1-56163-194-9, Eurotica) NBM.

Sinagua. Christian Downum. 32p. 1992. 5.95 (0-89734-108-2, PL63-1) Mus Northern Ariz.

Sinai: A Photographic Portfolio. Neil Folberg. (Illus.). 1986. 60.00 (0-915361-05-1) Hemed Bks.

*Sinai: A Physical Geography. Ned H. Greenwood. LC 96-27618. (Illus.). 160p. 1997. 35.00 (0-292-72798-4); pap. 16.95 (0-292-72799-2) U of Tex Pr.

*Sinai: Farben Einer Landschaft - Landschaft der Farbe. Werner Lichtner-Aix. (Illus.). 88p. (GER.). (C). 1986. 48.00 (3-8170-2007-4, Pub. by Knstvrlag Weingrtn GW) Intl Bk Import.

Sinai Accord As a Phase of the U. S. Containment Policy. Naseer H. Aruri. (Occasional Papers: No. 2). 7p. (C). 1976. pap. 1.00 (0-937694-41-X) Assn Arab-Amer U Grads.

Sinai & Olympus: A Comparative Study. Joseph P. Schultz & Lois Spatz. 818p. (C). 1995. lib. bdg. 75.50 (0-7618-0032-8) U Pr of Amer.

Sinai & Palestine. A. P. Stanley. 646p. 1986. 350.00 (1-85077-088-3, Pub. by Darf Pubs Ltd UK) St Mut.

Sinai & Zion: An Entry into the Jewish Bible. Jon D. Levenson. 1987. pap. 12.00 (0-06-254828-X) Harper SF.

Sinai Blunder. Indar J. Rikhje. 200p. 1978. 25.50 (0-937722-19-7) Intl Peace.

Sinai Blunder: Withdrawal of the United Nations Emergency Force Leading to the Six-Day War of June, 1967. Indar J. Rikhye. 240p. 1980. 37.50 (0-7146-3136-1, Pub. by F Cass Pubs UK) Intl Spec Bk.

Sinai II: The Politics of International Mediation. Cecilia Albin & Harold H. Saunders. (Pew Case Studies in International Affairs). 114p. 1991. pap. text ed. 3.50 (1-56927-421-5) Geo U Inst Dplmcy.

Sinai Peace Front: U. N. Peacekeeping Operations in the Middle East, 1973-1980. Bertil Stjernfelt. LC 91-39028. 360p. 1992. text ed. 49.95 (0-312-07150-7) St Martin.

Sinai Strategy: Economics & the Ten Commandments. Gary North. 368p. (Orig.). 1986. pap. 12.50 (0-930464-07-9) Inst Christian.

*Sinai Summit: Meeting God with Our Character Crisis. Rick Atchley. (Faith Focus Adult Studies). 1993. 9.95 (0-8344-0228-9) Sweet Pub.

Sinai Summit Study Guide: 13 Studies for Individuals or Groups. Chris Seidman. Ed. by Patty Crowley. LC 95-69738. 84p. (Orig.). 1996. pap. 5.95 (0-8344-0247-5, JACBC) Sweet Pub.

Sinai Two: The Politics of International Mediation. Cecilia Albin & Harold H. Saunders. LC 93-18253. (FPI Case Studies: No. 17). 1993. write for info. (0-941700-78-X) JH FPI SAIS.

Sinai Victory: Command Decisions in History's Shortest War, Israel's Hundred Hour Conquest of Egypt East of Suez, Autumn 1956. Samuel L. Marshall. (Combat Arms Ser.: 11th). (Illus.). 280p. 1958. reprint ed. 29.95 (0-89839-085-0) Battery Pr.

Sinai's Moscow Seminar on Dynamical Systems. Ed. by L. A. Bunimovich et al. (American Mathematical Society Translations Ser.: Series 2, Vol. 171). 247p. 1995. 57.00 (0-8218-0456-1, TRANS2/171) Am Math.

Sinan: Ottoman Architecture & Its Values Today. Godfrey Goodwin. (Illus.). 190p. 1993. 49.95 (0-86356-172-1, Pub. by Saqi Bks UK) Interlink Pub.

Sinatra: A Celebration. Stan Britt. 160p. (Orig.). 1995. 19.95 (0-02-864577-4) Macmillan.

*Sinatra: The Man Behind the Myth. J. Randy Taraborrelli. 1997. 24.95 (1-55972-434-X, Birch Ln Pr) Carol Pub Group.

Sinatra: The Pictorial Biography. Lew Irwin. (Illus.). 128p. 1995. 19.98 (1-56138-453-4) Courage Bks.

*Sinatra: All Or Nothing at All: A Biography. Donald Clarke. LC 97-21885. (Illus.). 320p. reprint ed. 25.95 (0-88064-181-9) Fromm Intl Pub.

*Sinatra Celebrity Cookbook: Barbara, Frank & Friends. Barbara Sinatra Children's Center Staff. 300p. 1996. 24.95 (0-9646756-0-9) B Sinatra Chldrns.

Sinatra Scrapbook. Gary L. Doctor. (Illus.). 256p. (Orig.). 1991. pap. 15.95 (0-8065-1250-4, Citadel Pr) Carol Pub Group.

Sinatra, Sinatra. Paul Fericano. 16p. (Orig.). 1982. pap. 200.00 (0-916296-06-7) Poor Souls Pr.

Sinatra! The Song Is You: A Singer's Art. Will Friedwald. (Illus.). 557p. 1995. 30.00 (0-684-19368-X) S&S Trade.

*Sinatra! The Song Is You: A Singer's Art. Will Friedwald. LC 96-43855. (Illus.). 568p. 1997. reprint ed. pap. 17.95 (0-306-80742-4) Da Capo.

Sinatra 101: The 101 Best Recordings & the Stories Behind Them. Ed O'Brien & Robert Wilson. 192p. 1996. pap. 12.00 (1-57297-165-7) Blvd Books.

Sinbad & the Evil Genii. Jack Melanos. (Orig.). (J). (gr. k up). 1986. pap. 5.00 (0-87602-251-4) Anchorage.

Sinbad the Sailor. Illus. & Retold by Marcia Williams. LC 93-3531. 40p. (J). (gr. 2 up). 1994. 17.95 (1-56402-310-9) Candlewick Pr.

Sinbad the Sailor. Illus. & Retold by Marcia Williams. LC 93-3531. 40p. (J). (gr. 2-6). 1996. reprint ed. pap. 7.99 (1-56402-814-3) Candlewick Pr.

*Sinbad the Sailor & Other Stories. N. J. Dawood. 1997. pap. 3.99 (0-14-036769-1) Viking Penguin.

Sinbad, the Thirteenth Voyage. R. A. Lafferty. 176p. (Orig.). 1989. pap. 9.95 (0-9623824-1-8) Broken Mirrors Pr.

*Sinbad's Guide to Life. Sinbad & David Ritz. 256p. 1997. 22.95 (0-553-10373-3) Bantam.

Sinc Methods for Quadrature & Differential Equations. John Lund & Kenneth Bowers. LC 92-12139. (Miscellaneous Bks.: No. 32). x, 304p. 1992. 49.50 (0-89871-298-X) Soc Indus-Appl Math.

Since Aquino: The Philippine Tangle & the United States. Justus M. Van der Kroef. (Occasional Papers-Reprints Series in Contemporary Asian Studies: No. 6-1987). (C). 1987. pap. text ed. 3.00 (0-942182-80-4) Occasional Papers.

*"Since at Least Plato" & Other Postmodern Myths. M. J. Devaney. LC 97-7781. 1997. write for info. (0-312-17511-6) St Martin.

Since Before the Yellow Fever: A History of Union Planters Bank. John C. Longwith. LC 94-60749. (Illus.). 224p. 1994. 19.95 (0-944897-02-9) Magic Chef.

Since Cezanne. Clive Bell. (Essay Index Reprint Ser.). 1977. 18.95 (0-8369-0034-0) Ayer.

Since Cumorah: The Book of Mormon. Hugh Nibley. LC 88-3862. (Collected Works of Hugh Nibley: Vol. 7). xv, 512p. 1988. 25.95 (0-87579-139-5) Deseret Bk.

Since Daisy Creek. W. O. Mitchell. LC 85-9088. 288p. 1985. 16.95 (0-8253-0303-6) Beaufort Bks NY.

Since Debussy: A View of Contemporary Music. Andre Hodeir. Tr. by Noel Burch. LC 74-28310. (Music Ser.). (Illus.). 256p. 1975. reprint ed. lib. bdg. 29.50 (0-306-70662-8) Da Capo.

Since Eve Ate Apples: Quotations on Feasting, Fasting & Food - From the Beginning. Ed. by March Egerton. 365p. 1994. pap. 17.95 (0-9637709-1-8) Tsunami Pr.

Since Flannery O'Connor: Essays on the Contemporary American Short Story. Ed. by Loren Logsdon & Charles W. Mayer. LC 87-61274. (Essays in Literature Bks.: No. 7). (Illus.). 152p. (Orig.). (C). 1987. pap. 8.00 (0-934312-06-0) WIU Essays Lit.

Since Gandhi: India's Sarvodaya Movement. Mark Shepard. 40p. 1984. pap. 3.50 (0-934676-63-1) Greenlf Bks.

Since Jesus Passed By. Charles Hunter & Frances Hunter. 199p. (SPA.). 1986. pap. 4.00 (0-917726-76-6) Hunter Bks.

Since Jesus Passed By. Frances Hunter & Charles Hunter. 1973. pap. 5.95 (0-917726-38-3) Hunter Bks.

Since Man Began to Eat Himself. Lawrence Ferlinghetti et al. (Illus.). 58p. 1987. write for info. (0-318-64541-6) Perishable Pr.

Since "Megalopolis" The Urban Writings of Jean Gottmann. Ed. by Jean Gottmann & Robert A. Harper. LC 89-45484. 304p. 1990. text ed. 48.50 (0-8018-3812-6); pap. text ed. 16.95 (0-8018-3927-0) Johns Hopkins.

S

An Asterisk (*) at the beginning of an entry indicates that the title is appearing in BIP for the first time.

Since O'Casey & Other Essays on Irish Drama. Robert Hogan. (Irish Literary Studies: Vol. # 15). 178p. 8300. 35.00 (*0-86140-115-8*, Pub. by Colin Smythe Ltd UK) Dufour.

Since Owen: A Parent-to-Parent Guide for Care of the Disabled Child. Charles R. Callanan. LC 84-24678. 448p. 1990. pap. 16.95 (*0-8018-3964-5*); text ed. 45.00 (*0-8018-3963-7*) Johns Hopkins.

Since Predator Came: Notes from the Struggle for American Indian Liberation. Ward Churchill. (Illus.). 448p. (Orig.). 1995. pap. 18.00 (*1-883930-03-0*); lib. bdg. 30.00 (*1-883930-04-9*) AIGIS Pubns.

***Since Records Began: EMI: the First Hundred Years.** Peter Martland. LC 97-2709. (Illus.). 384p. 1997. 39.95 (*1-57467-033-6*, Amadeus Pr) Timber.

Since Seventeen Eighty-Seven: The Franklin & Marshall College Story. Frederic S. Klein. 1968. 2.00 (*0-685-10974-7*); pap. 1.00 (*0-685-10975-5*) Franklin & Marshall.

Since Stanislavski & Vakhtangov: The Method As a System for Today's Actor. Lawrence Parke. 272p. (Orig.). 1986. pap. 12.95 (*0-9615288-8-5*) Acting World Bks.

Since Statehood: Twelve Oklahoma Artists. Contrib. & Intro. by David Rust. 1996. pap. 10.00 (*0-614-13529-X*) Okla City Art.

***Since the Noon Mail Stopped: Poetry.** Wyatt Prunty. LC 97-4993. (Poetry & Fiction Ser.). 88p. 1997. 16.95 (*0-8018-5646-9*) Johns Hopkins.

Since the Revolution: Human Rights in Romania. Helsinki Watch Staff. LC 91-71163. 68p. 1991. pap. 7.00 (*0-929692-88-8*, Helsinki Watch) Hum Rts Watch.

Since the World Began: Walt Disney World: The First 25 Years. Jeff Kurtti. (Illus.). 192p. 1996. pap. 14.95 (*0-7868-8219-0*) Hyperion.

Since the World Began: Walt Disney World, the First 25 Years. Jeff Kurtti. LC 96-23099. 1996. 24.95 (*0-7868-6248-3*) Hyprn Child.

Since Vietnam: The United States in World Affairs, 1973-1994. H. W. Brands. LC 95-2756. 1996. pap. text ed. write for info. (*0-07-007196-9*) McGraw.

Since Yesterday: The 1930s in America. Frederick L. Allen. 376p. 1994. lib. bdg. 35.00 (*0-8095-9160-X*) Borgo Pr.

Since Yesterday - The Nineteen Thirties in America: September 3, 1929 to September 3, 1939. Frederick L. Allen. LC 86-45060. 304p. 1986. reprint ed. pap. 14.00 (*0-06-091322-3*, PL1322, PL) HarpC.

Since You Asked. Bill Flatt. 1983. pap. 6.95 (*0-89137-544-9*) Quality Pubns.

Since You Want Away: World War II Letters from American Women on the Home Front. Ed. by Judy B. Litoff & David C. Smith. (Illus.). 310p. 1995. pap. 15.95 (*0-7006-0714-5*) U Pr of KS.

Since You Went Away: World War II Letters from American Women on the Home Front. Ed. by Judy B. Litoff & David C. Smith. (Illus.). 312p. 1991. 27.50 (*0-19-506795-9*) OUP.

Since You've Been Gone. Michael P. Jones. (Illus.). 155p. 1984. text ed. 20.00 (*0-89904-016-0*) Crumb Elbow Pub.

Since 1600 see Western Experience

Since 1794 the History of the Onondaga County Sheriff Department. Jon Anderson. 110p. 1994. 18.95 (*0-9648622-4-7*) Pine Grve Pr.

Since 1865 see Key Issues in the Afro-American Experience

Since 1945: Politics & Diplomacy in Recent American History. 3rd ed. Robert A. Divine. 1985. pap. text ed. write for info. (*0-07-554644-2*) McGraw.

Sincere & Constant Love. T. S. Wallace. LC 91-24187. 142p. 1992. pap. 10.95 (*0-944350-19-4*) Friends United.

Sincere Cafe: Stories by Leslee Becker. Leslee Becker. (First Ser.). 184p. (Orig.). 1996. pap. 14.00 (*0-922811-28-8*) Mid-List.

Sincere Faith. C. M. Wagner. 75p. 1988. pap. 4.00 (*0-685-19992-4*) Tru-Faith.

Sincere Milk...That You May Grow. Linda Berry. 102p. (Orig.). (YA). (gr. 6-12). 1993. pap. 7.95 (*0-9636797-0-8*) Christ Covenant.

Sincerely. Sandra Kitt. 288p. 1995. mass mkt. 4.99 (*0-8217-0115-0*, Zebra Kensgtn); mass mkt. 4.99 (*0-7860-0115-1*, Pinncle Kensgtn) Kensgtn Pub Corp.

Sincerely, Mom: Letters of Love & Guidance to the Family. Catherine Knobloch. (Illus.). 48p. 1994. pap. 7.00 (*0-8059-3554-1*) Dorrance.

Sincerely Peg. Peggy R. Dobler. (Illus.). 1976. pap. 4.95 (*0-686-17611-1*) New Expressions.

Sincerely Yours: How to Write Great Letters. Elizabeth James & Carol Barkin. 192p. (J). (gr. 4-8). 1993. 14.95 (*0-395-58831-6*, Clarion Bks); pap. 6.95 (*0-395-58832-4*, Clarion Bks) HM.

Sincerely Yours: Letters from the Heart. Patricia G. Opatz. LC 96-19518. 176p. (Orig.). 1996. pap. 11.95 (*0-8146-2422-7*, Litrug Pr Bks) Liturgical Pr.

Sincerity & Authenticity: Six Lectures. Lionel Trilling. LC 72-83468. (Charles Eliot Norton Lectures: 1969-1970). 188p. 1972. pap. 10.50 (*0-674-80861-4*) HUP.

Sincerity & Other Works: The Collected Papters of Donald Meltzer. Ed. by Alberto Hahn. 604p. 1994. pap. text ed. 63.50 (*1-85575-084-8*, Pub. by Karnac Bks UK) Brunner-Mazel.

Sinclair: The Sinclairs of England. 414p. 1991. reprint ed. pap. 61.00 (*0-8328-2168-3*); reprint ed. lib. bdg. 71.00 (*0-8328-2167-5*) Higginson Bk Co.

Sinclair Beiles: Selected Poems. Sinclair Beiles. (Illus.). 112p. (Orig.). (C). 1990. pap. 12.95 (*0-932499-42-2*) Lapis Pr.

***Sinclair Collectibles.** Wayne Henderson & Scott Benjamin. (Illus.). 144p. 1997. pap. 29.95 (*0-7643-0193-4*) Schiffer.

Sinclair Lewis. Sheldon N. Grebstein. (Twayne's United States Authors Ser.). 1962. pap. 13.95 (*0-8084-0278-1*, T14) NCUP.

Sinclair Lewis. Mark Schorer. LC 63-62713. (University of Minnesota Pamphlets on American Writers Ser.: No. 27). 47p. (Orig.). reprint ed. pap. 25.00 (*0-7837-2867-0*, 2057588) Bks Demand.

***Sinclair Lewis: A Descriptive Bibliography.** Stephen R. Pastore & James M. Hutchisson. (Illus.). 397p. 1997. 59.95 (*0-9656275-0-0*) S R Pastore.

***Sinclair Lewis: New Essays in Criticism.** Ed. by James H. Hutchisson. LC 96-61675. viii, 257p. 1997. 29.50 (*0-87875-492-X*) Whitston Pub.

Sinclair Lewis: Our Own Diogenes. Vernon L. Parrington. LC 73-11205. (American Literature Ser.: No. 49). 1974. lib. bdg. 75.00 (*0-8383-1720-0*) M S G Haskell Hse.

Sinclair Lewis: Twentieth Century American Author & Nobel Prize Winner. Alan L. Paley. Ed. by D. Steve Rahmas. LC 73-87626. (Outstanding Personalities Ser.: No. 67). 32p. (Orig.). (YA). (gr. 7-12). 1974. lib. bdg. 7.25 (*0-87157-567-1*) SamHar Pr.

Sinclair Lewis see Modern Critical Views Series

Sinclair Lewis at Thorvale Farm: A Personal Memoir. Ida L. Compton. LC 88-92777. (Illus.). 62p. (Orig.). 1988. pap. 5.00 (*0-915909-01-4*) Ruggles Pub.

Sinclair on Federal Civil Practice. 3rd ed. Kent Sinclair. 200p. 1992. ring bd. 115.00 (*0-685-69495-X*, H6-1538) PLI.

Sinclair Ross: An Annotated Bibliography. David Latham. 395p. (C). 1981. pap. text ed. 9.00 (*0-920763-63-4*, Pub. by ECW Press CN) Genl Dist Srvs.

Sinclair Ross & His Works. Morton Ross. (Canadian Author Studies). 42p. (C). 1991. pap. text ed. 9.95 (*1-55022-056-X*, Pub. by ECW Press CN) Genl Dist Srvs.

Sinclair Ross's As for Me & My House: Five Decades of Criticism. Ed. by David Stouck. 288p. 1991. 45.00 (*0-8020-5897-3*); pap. 16.95 (*0-8020-6835-9*) U of Toronto Pr.

Sincoast Civic Center, Simulation: Office Assistant. 3rd ed. Taylor & Sanchez. (KM - Office Procedures Ser.). 1992. pap. 12.95 (*0-538-60898-6*) S-W Pub.

Sind a Re-Interpretation of the Unhappy Valley. J. Abbott. (C). 1992. 14.00 (*81-206-0759-7*, Pub. by Asian Educ Servs II) S Asia.

***Sind Revisited.** Richard F. Burton. 1996. 42.50 (*81-215-0771-5*, Pub. by M Manoharial II) Coronet Bks.

Sindell Negligence Folio. rev. ed. Joseph M. Sindell & I. David. 24p. 1985. pap. 5.40 (*0-88450-101-9*, 6105) Lawyers & Judges.

Sindh & the Races That Inhabit the Valley of the Indus. Richard Burton. (C). 1992. reprint ed. 28.00 (*81-206-0758-9*, Pub. by Asian Educ Servs II) S Asia.

Sindicalizacion de Trabajadores Agricolas en Mexico: La Experiencia de la Confederacion Nacional Campesina (CNC) Heladio Ramirez-Lopez. (Research Reports: No. 26). 16p. (Orig.). (C). 1981. pap. 5.00 (*0-935391-25-8*, RR-26) UCSD Ctr US-Mex.

Sindon: A Layman's Guide to the Shroud of Turin. Frank O. Adams. Ed. by John A. DeSalvo. LC 82-90138. (Illus.). 1982. 12.50 (*0-86700-008-2*, Synergy Bks) P Walsh Pr.

Sindrome De Down: Hacia un Futuro Mejor Guia Para los Padres. Siegfried M. Pueschel. 286p. (SPA.). 1993. pap. 25.00 (*84-345-2429-5*, Pub. by Ediciones Cientificas SP) P H Brookes.

Sindrome De Down: Problematica Biomedica. Jeanette K. Pueschel & Siegfried M. Pueschel. 352p. (SPA.). 1994. pap. 55.00 (*84-458-0202-X*, Pub. by Ediciones Cientificas SP) P H Brookes.

Sindrome De Down y Educacion. Jesus Florez & Troncoso. 318p. (SPA.). (C). 1991. pap. 29.00 (*84-458-0118-X*, Pub. by Ediciones Cientificas SP) P H Brookes.

Sindrome de la Borrachera Seca. R. J. Solberg. 12p. (Orig.). (SPA.). 1983. pap. 1.50 (*0-89486-219-7*) Hazelden.

***Sindrome Premenstrual - Premenstrual Syndrome.** Marvin Eastlund. (Serie Enfoque a la Familia - Focus on the Family Ser.). 55p. (SPA.). 1995. write for info. (*1-56063-709-9*) Editorial Unilit.

Sine Die: A Guide to the Washington State Legislative Process, 1997 Edition. Edward D. Seeberger. LC 96-36855. 318p. 1996. pap. 19.95 (*0-295-97572-5*) U of Wash Pr.

Sine'ad: Her Life & Music. Jimmy Guterman. 1991. pap. 8.95 (*0-446-39254-5*) Warner Bks.

Sinead Morrissey: There Was Fire in Vancouver. 64p. 1996. pap. 12.95 (*1-85754-230-4*, Pub. by Carcanet Pr UK) Paul & Co Pubs.

SinEater. Elizabeth Massie. 352p. 1994. 21.00 (*0-7867-0061-0*) Carroll & Graf.

Sinergy Graphic Novel. Kyle Garrett et al. (Illus.). 176p. 1994. 14.95 (*0-941613-57-7*) Stabur Pr.

Sinews of Fleece. Clifford E. Bajema. LC 93-60418. 151p. 1994. pap. 7.95 (*1-55523-628-6*) Winston-Derek.

Sinews of Peace, Post-War Speeches. Winston L. Churchill. Ed. by Randolph S. Churchill. LC 83-45733. reprint ed. 30.00 (*0-404-20059-1*) AMS Pr.

Sinews of Power: War, Money & the English State, 1688-1783. John Brewer. 290p. 1990. pap. 15.95 (*0-674-80930-0*) HUP.

***Sinews of Survival: The Living Legacy of Inuit Clothing.** Betty K. Issenman. (Illus.). 225p. 1997. 45.00 (*0-7748-0596-X*, Pub. by U BC Pr) U of Wash Pr.

Sinews of the Heart: A Book of Men's Writings. Ed. by James Ryan. 164p. (Orig.). (YA). (gr. 12). 1995. pap. 14.98 (*0-907123-41-4*, Pub. by Five Leaves UK) AK Pr Dist.

Sinews of the Spirit: The Ideal of Christian Manlines in Victorian Literature & Religious Thought. Norman Vance. 256p. 1985. 75.00 (*0-521-30387-7*) Cambridge U Pr.

Sinews of Ulysses: Form & Convention in Milton's Works. Michael Lieb. LC 88-25651. (Duquesne Studies: Language & Literature Ser.: Vol. 9). 190p. 1989. text ed. 28.95 (*0-8207-0205-6*) Duquesne.

Sinews of War. Arnold Bennett. LC 74-17139. (Collected Works of Arnold Bennett: Vol. 74). 1977. reprint ed. 26.95 (*0-518-19155-9*) Ayer.

Sinews of War: Essays on the Economic History of World War II. Hugh Rockoff. Ed. by Geoffrey T. Mills. LC 92-26832. (Illus.). 284p. 1993. text ed. 44.95 (*0-8138-1312-3*) Iowa St U Pr.

Sinews of War: Hard Cash & the 1890 Maritime Strike. Stuart Svensen. 286p. 1995. pap. 29.95 (*0-86840-398-9*, Pub. by New South Wales Univ Pr AT) Intl Spec Bk.

***Sinews of War: How Technology, Industry, & Transportation Won the Civil War.** Benjamin Bacon. LC 97-531. 1997. 24.95 (*0-89141-626-9*) Presidio Pr.

Sinfonias de Otono (Symphonies of Autumn) Enrique Aguilar. xii, 135p. 1962. pap. 3.50 (*1-57659-113-1*) Franciscan Inst.

Sinful. Susan Johnson. 432p. 1993. mass mkt. 5.99 (*0-553-29312-5*) Bantam.

Sinful Knights: A Study of Middle English Penitential Romance. Andrea Hopkins. 264p. 1990. 85.00 (*0-19-811762-0*) OUP.

Sinful Self, Saintly Self: The Puritan Experience of Poetry. Jeffrey A. Hammond. LC 92-18709. 320p. 1993. 45.00 (*0-8203-1500-1*) U of Ga Pr.

Sinful Tunes & Spirituals: Black Folk Music to the Civil War. Dena J Epstein. LC 77-6315. (Music in American Life Ser.). (Illus.). 460p. 1981. pap. text ed. 16.95 (*0-252-00875-8*) U of Ill Pr.

Sinful Woman. large type ed. James M. Cain. LC 92-27528. (Nightingale Ser.). 160p. 1993. pap. 15.95 (*0-8161-5462-7*, GK Hall) Thorndike Pr.

Sinfulness of Sin. Ralph Venning. 284p. 1993. reprint ed. pap. 7.50 (*0-85151-647-5*) Banner of Truth.

Sing. Ed. by American Camping Association Staff. 95p. 1985. pap. 3.95 (*0-318-41769-3*) Am Camping.

Sing! Ed. by Charles Fowler. 392p. 1988. pap. 27.95 (*0-937276-08-1*) Hinshaw Mus.

Sing. Joe Raposo. (Sing-a-Song Storybooks Ser.). (Illus.). 24p. (J). 1993. 9.95 (*0-7935-1860-1*, 00183012) H Leonard.

Sing. A. L. Singer. 144p. (J). (gr. 7 up). 1989. pap. 2.75 (*0-590-42151-4*) Scholastic Inc.

***Sing - Bein' Green & Other Joe Raposo Classics.** Ed. by Carol Cuellar. 52p. (Orig.). (C). 1996. pap. text ed. 11.95 (*1-57623-293-X*, AF9559) Warner Brothers.

Sing a Happy Song: Beloved Children's Favorites. Clara W. McMaster. (J). 1992. 9.98 (*0-88290-451-5*, 2929) Horizon Utah.

Sing-a-Long. (Illus.). 16p. (J). 1991. audio write for info. (*1-880459-01-9*); audio write for info. (*1-880459-05-1*) Arrow Trad.

Sing-A-Long Christmas Carols, Vol. 289. Date not set. pap. 6.95 (*0-7935-4886-1*, 00100023) H Leonard.

Sing-A-Long Christmas Favorites, Vol. 288. Date not set. pap. 6.95 (*0-7935-4885-3*, 00100022) H Leonard.

Sing-a-Long Christmas Joy. 10.95 (*0-7935-4805-5*, 00310064) H Leonard.

Sing-a-Long for All Occasions. Joseph M. Russo. 62p. (Orig.). 1988. pap. 6.95 (*0-685-29095-6*) Mid-West Music.

Sing-a-Longs for All Occasions. Joseph M. Russo. 62p. (Orig.). 1988. pap. 6.95 (*0-9624214-0-5*, PA-394-638) Mid-West Music.

Sing a Lullaby Big Book, Unit 3. (Networks Ser.). (J). (gr. 1-7). 1991. 19.50 (*0-88106-717-2*, N130) Charlesbridge Pub.

Sing a Message to Freedom: The Freedom Man. Anthony E. McAden. Ed. by Alexis Satchell. (Illus.). 50p. (Orig.). 1986. pap. 6.25 (*0-931841-07-0*) Satchells Pub.

Sing a New Song. Charles Allums. Ed. by Betty Allums. (Illus.). 135p. (Orig.). 1984. pap. 8.75 (*0-932211-00-3*) BA Cross Ctrl.

***Sing a New Song: A Book of Psalms.** Bijou LeTord. LC 96-33231. (Illus.). 32p. (J). (ps-2). 1997. 15.00 (*0-8028-5139-8*, Eerdmans Bks) Eerdmans.

Sing a New Song: Liberating Black Hymnody. Jon M. Spencer. 224p. 1995. pap. 24.00 (*0-8006-2722-9*, Fortress Pr) Augsburg Fortress.

Sing a New Song: The Psalms in the Sunday Lectionary. Irene Nowell. 320p. (Orig.). 1993. pap. 17.95 (*0-8146-2043-4*) Liturgical Pr.

Sing a New Song: Well Loved Hymns & Choruses. 32p. 1995. 11.99 (*0-87788-580-X*) Shaw Pubs.

Sing a New Song! Worship Renewal for Adventists Today. C. Raymond Holmes. LC 84-70077. 208p. (C). 1984. pap. 13.99 (*0-943872-88-X*) Andrews Univ Pr.

Sing a New Song unto the Lord: Poems of Joyful Praise. John C. Biardo. LC 86-83240. 80p. (Orig.). 1987. pap. 3.95 (*0-933181-03-5*) Elmwood Park Pub.

Sing a Rainbow Big Book. Arthur Hamilton. (Illus.). (J). (ps-2). 1988. pap. text ed. 14.00 (*0-922053-21-9*) N Edge Res.

Sing a Sad Song: The Life of Hank Williams. 2nd ed. Roger M. Williams. LC 80-15520. (Music in American Life Ser.). 328p. 1981. 12.95 (*0-252-00861-8*) U of Ill Pr.

Sing a Song: Activity & Idea Book. Karen Finch. (Illus.). 96p. (Orig.). (J). (ps-7). 1994. 7.95 (*1-885476-09-4*) Finch Fmly Games.

Sing a Song of Christmas Twelve Favorites: High Voice. 1994. pap. 19.95 incl. audio compact disk (*0-7935-3418-6*, 00747072) H Leonard.

Sing a Song of Christmas Twelve Favorites: Low Voice. 1994. pap. 19.95 incl. audio compact disk (*0-7935-3417-8*, 00747073) H Leonard.

Sing a Song of Circus. Ward Schumaker. LC 95-47124. (J). 1997. 13.00 (*0-15-201363-6*) HarBrace.

Sing a Song of Concepts. Dina Zeese. LC 87-83701. 112p. (Orig.). (J). (ps-2). 1988. pap. 16.95 (*0-936485-01-9*) Lkng Glass Pubns.

Sing a Song of Death. Catherine Dain. 176p. (Orig.). 1993. mass mkt. 3.99 (*0-515-11057-4*) Jove Pubns.

Sing a Song of Mother Goose. Francis Reid. 40p. (J). 1993. 19.95 (*0-590-71380-9*) Scholastic Inc.

Sing a Song of People. Lois Lenski. (Illus.). 32p. (J). (ps-3). 1996. pap. 4.95 (*0-316-52070-5*) Little.

***Sing a Song of Popcorn: Every Child's Book of Poems.** Illus. by Marcia Brown. (J). (gr. 3-7). 1988. 16.89 (*0-590-40645-0*, 266909) Scholastic Inc.

Sing a Song of Popcorn: Every Child's Book of Poems. Ed. by Eva Moore et al. (Illus.). 160p. (J). (gr. k up). 1988. 18.95 (*0-590-43974-X*, Scholastic Hardcover) Scholastic Inc.

Sing a Song of Scripture. Compiled by Ken Bible. (J). (gr. 3-7). 1985. 6.99 (*0-8341-9050-8*, BCMB-558) Lillenas.

Sing a Song of Scripture, 1. Compiled by Ken Bible. (J). (gr. 3-7). 1986. audio 12.99 (*0-685-68218-8*, TA-9074C) Lillenas.

Sing a Song of Scripture, 2. Compiled by Ken Bible. (J). (gr. 3-7). 1986. audio 12.99 (*0-685-68219-6*, TA-9075C) Lillenas.

Sing a Song of Scripture, Vols. 1 & 2. Compiled by Ken Bible. (J). (gr. 3-7). 1987. audio 19.99 (*0-685-68217-X*, TA-9075B) Lillenas.

***Sing a Song of SETI: The Official Songbook of the SETI League, Inc.** H. Paul Shuch. 32p. (Orig.). 1996. pap. 10.00 (*0-9650707-1-9*) SETI League.

***Sing a Song of Six-Packs.** Jerry Kent. 11.95 incl. audio (*0-9620314-4-5*) Meyer Enter.

Sing a Song of Social Significance. 2nd rev. ed. R. Serge Denisoff. LC 78-186631. 1983. 20.95 (*0-87972-036-0*) Bowling Green Univ Popular Press.

Sing a Song of Sound. Vicki Silvers. LC 72-90695. (Illus.). 32p. (J). (ps-2). 1973. 7.95 (*0-87592-046-2*) Scroll Pr.

Sing Alleluia. 135p. 1985. Pgs. 135, 08/1985. ring bd. 8.50 (*0-919797-41-5*) Kindred Prods.

Sing Alleluia. 32p. 1987. Pgs. 32, 08/1987. suppl. ed. 1.95 (*0-919797-70-9*) Kindred Prods.

Sing Alleluia, Supplement 2. 35p. 1992. ring bd. 2.95 (*0-921788-13-4*) Kindred Prods.

***Sing along Birthday Songs.** Vicki Lansky. (J). Date not set. 9.95 incl. audio (*0-916773-57-4*); 12.95 incl. audio (*0-916773-55-8*); 8.95 incl. audio (*0-916773-56-6*) Book Peddlers.

Sing-Along Book. Lynn E. Robbins. 68p. 1993. pap. 8.00 (*1-888143-07-X*) Robbins Mgmt.

Sing-Along Christmas Carols. William Bay. 3.95 (*0-87166-071-7*, 94117); audio 9.98 (*0-87166-072-5*, 94117C) Mel Bay.

***Sing-Along Christmas Carols.** William Bay. 12.95 incl. audio (*0-87166-073-3*, 94117P) Mel Bay.

Sing Along Favorites. (Easy Play Ser.: Vol. 32). 1990. pap. 5.95 (*0-7935-1490-8*, 1289) H Leonard.

Sing-Along Favorites. (Golden Lyric Book n Tape). (Illus.). (J). (ps-1). 1995. bds. 9.95 (*0-307-05338-5*, Golden Pr) Western Pub.

Sing Along Favorites. (Illus.). 16p. (J). (ps-1). 1996. pap. 6.99 (*1-57234-064-9*) YES Ent.

Sing-Along Fun: Cowboy Classics, Fun-to-Sing, Campfire Favorites & Good 'n Gross, 4 vols., Set. Mark Johnson. (Illus.). 24p. (Orig.). (J). (gr. k-12). 1993. pap. 31.99 (*1-883988-05-5*) RSV Prods.

Sing along Piano Fun. Random House Staff. (J). (gr. k-2). 1994. 7.99 (*0-517-10246-3*) Random Hse Value.

Sing Along-Senior Citizens. Ed. by R. E. Grant. 108p. 1973. spiral bd., pap. 21.95 (*0-398-02772-2*) C C Thomas.

Sing-Along Songbook: A Songbook for Younger Girl Scouts. (Illus.). 80p. (YA). 1990. 9.50 (*0-88441-367-5*, 23-102) Girl Scouts USA.

Sing Along with Elmo. (Super Sing Along Bks.). (Illus.). 20p. (YA). 1995. bds. 19.95 (*0-307-74307-1*, Golden Pr) Western Pub.

Sing Along with Me. Frank DiSilvestro. (Illus.). 52p. (YA). (gr. 8-10). 1985. pap. 7.95 (*0-934591-00-8*) Songs & Stories.

Sing along with Saints & Angels. Mark J. Lenz. 64p. (Orig.). 1985. student ed., pap. 3.50 (*0-8100-0206-X*, 22N0795); teacher ed., pap. 5.50 (*0-8100-0207-8*, 22N0796) Northwest Pub.

***Sing & Cook Italian.** 2nd rev. ed. Andy LoRusso. 160p. 1993. reprint ed. otabind, pap. 19.95 incl. audio (*0-614-29353-7*) Happy Heart.

Sing & Learn. Carolyn Meyer & Kel Pickens. (Illus.). 144p. (J). (ps-3). 1989. student ed. 13.99 (*0-86653-476-8*, GA1078) Good Apple.

Sing & Other Joe Raposo Songs from Sesame Street. (J). 1993. pap. 6.95 incl. audio (*0-7935-2382-6*, 00823027) H Leonard.

Sing & Other Kids' Favorites. Joe Raposo. (Sing 'n' Color Fun! Ser.). (Illus.). (J). 1993. spiral bd. 6.95 (*0-7935-1955-1*, 00823020) H Leonard.

Sing & Play--Preschool Piano Book One. Ann Collins & Linda Clary. (Illus.). 60p. (J). (ps). 1987. spiral bd. 5.00 (*0-87563-307-2*) Stipes.

Sing & Play the Junior Fun-Way. Yoder. 1990. 4.95 (*0-685-32164-9*, H782) Hansen Ed Mus.

Sing & Play with Super Mario Brothers. 48p. 1992. pap. 7.95 (*0-7935-1618-8*, 00222552) H Leonard.

***Sing & Rejoice: Favorite Hymns in Large Print.** Ed. by William D. Auld. 264p. (Orig.). 1997. pap. 15.00 (*0-664-25712-7*) Westminster John Knox.

Sing & Shine On! The Classroom Teacher's Guide to Multicultural Song Leading. Nick Page. LC 95-12279. (Illus.). 177p. 1995. pap. text ed. 20.00 (*0-435-08673-1*, 08673) Heinemann.

Sing & Strum Seven Hawaiian Favorites. 50p. 1986. pap. 9.95 (*0-917822-13-7*) Heedays.

S

An Asterisk (*) at the beginning of an entry indicates that the title is appearing in BIP for the first time.

Sing Carols with the Angels. Mary Leask. LC 95-94890. 192p. 1995. 17.95 (*0-8034-9148-4*) Bouregy.

***Sing Chinese! Popular Children's Songs & Lullabies.** Cindy Mao & Ma Baolin. 64p. 1996. spiral bd. 14.95 (*0-8351-2587-4*); spiral bd. 19.95 incl. audio (*0-8351-2588-2*); audio 7.95 (*0-8351-2589-0*) China Bks.

Sing Choral Music at Sight. Tom Anderson. Ed. by Michael Blakeslee. (Illus.). 128p. (Orig.). (J). (gr. 1-12). 1992. teacher ed., pap. 49.50 (*1-56545-007-8*, 1046) Music Ed Natl.

Sing, Clap, & Play the Recorder, Vol. 1. Heather Cox & Garth Rickard. (Illus.). 1983. Book 1, A Soprano Recorder Book for Beginners. pap. 6.50 (*0-918812-29-1*, SE 0883) MMB Music.

Sing, Clap, & Play the Recorder, Vol. 2. Heather Cox & Garth Rickard. (Illus.). 1983. Book 2, A Soprano Recorder Book for Intermediate Players. pap. 6.50 (*0-918812-30-5*, SE 0884) MMB Music.

Sing, Dance, Laugh & Eat Cheeseburgers. Barbara MacArthur. (Illus.). 35p. (Orig.). (J). (ps-12). 1992. pap. 17.95 incl. audio (*1-881120-06-6*) Frog Pr WI.

Sing, Dance, Laugh & Eat Quiche. rev. ed. Barbara MacArthur. (Illus.). 35p. (FRE.). (J). (ps-12). 1990. reprint ed. pap. 15.88 incl. audio (*1-881120-00-7*) Frog Pr WI.

Sing, Dance, Laugh & Eat Quiche 2. Barbara MacArthur. (Illus.). 35p. (Orig.). (ENG & FRE.). (J). (ps-12). 1989. pap. text ed. 15.88 incl. audio (*1-881120-01-5*) Frog Pr WI.

Sing, Dance, Laugh, & Eat Quiche 3. Barbara MacArthur. (Illus.). 35p. (Orig.). (ENG & FRE.). (J). (ps-12). 1992. pap. 15.88 incl. audio (*1-881120-07-4*) Frog Pr WI.

Sing, Dance, Laugh & Eat Tacos. Barbara MacArthur. (Illus.). 35p. (Orig.). (ENG & SPA.). (J). (ps-12). 1990. pap. text ed. 15.88 incl. audio (*1-881120-04-X*) Frog Pr WI.

Sing, Dance, Laugh & Eat Tacos 2. Barbara MacArthur. (Illus.). 36p. (Orig.). (ENG & SPA.). (J). (ps-12). 1991. pap. text ed. 15.88 incl. audio (*1-881120-05-8*) Frog Pr WI.

Sing, Dance, Laugh & Eat Tacos 3. Barbara MacArthur. (Illus.). 35p. (ENG & SPA.). (J). (ps-12). 1993. pap. 15.88 incl. audio (*1-881120-13-9*) Frog Pr WI.

Sing, Dance, Laugh & Learn German. Barbara MacArthur. (Illus.). 18p. (Orig.). (ENG & GER.). (J). (ps-12). 1993. pap. 12.95 incl. audio (*1-881120-11-2*) Frog Pr WI.

Sing, Dance, Laugh & Learn Spanish. Barbara MacArthur. (Illus.). 18p. (Orig.). (ENG & SPA.). (J). (ps-12). 1993. pap. 12.95 incl. audio (*1-881120-08-2*) Frog Pr WI.

Sing down the Moon. Scott O'Dell. 138p. (J). (gr. 5 up). 1976. mass mkt. 3.99 (*0-440-97975-7*, LLL BDD) BDD Bks Young Read.

Sing Down the Moon. Scott O'Dell. 144p. (J). (gr. 5 up). 1992. mass mkt. 3.99 (*0-440-40673-0*, YB BDD) BDD Bks Young Read.

Sing Down the Moon. Scott O'Dell. LC 71-98513. (J). (gr. 5 up). 1970. 16.00 (*0-395-10919-1*) HM.

***Sing Down the Moon.** Scott O'Dell. 1997. mass mkt. 2.69 (*0-440-22736-4*) Dell.

Sing Down the Moon: A Study Guide. Judith Warshall. (Novel-Ties Ser.). 1987. student ed., teacher ed., pap. text ed. 15.95 (*0-88122-091-4*) Lrn Links.

***Sing Down the Rain.** Judi Moreillon. LC 97-70357. (Illus.). 32p. (J). (gr. k-5). 1997. 14.95 (*1-885772-07-6*) Kiva Pubng.

Sing, Elvis, Sing. Stephanie Spinner & Ellen Weiss. LC 95-51257. (Weebie Zone Ser.: Vol.2). (Illus.). 80p. (J). (gr. 2-4). 1996. pap. 3.95 (*0-06-442032-9*, Trophy) HarpC Child Bks.

Sing, Elvis, Sing! Stephanie Spinner & Ellen Weiss. LC 95-51257. (Weebie Zone Ser.: Vol. 2). (Illus.). 80p. (J). (gr. 2-4). 1996. lib. bdg. 13.89 (*0-06-027337-2*) HarpC Child Bks.

Sing for Freedom: The Story of the Civil Rights Movement Through Its Songs. Ed. by Guy Carawan & Candie Carawan. (Illus.). 312p. 1990. reprint ed. pap. 14.95 (*0-9626704-4-8*); reprint ed. lib. bdg. 39.95 (*0-9626704-5-6*) Sing Out.

Sing for Joy. Review & Herald Publishing Editors. Date not set. pap. 9.99 (*0-8280-0465-X*) Review & Herald.

Sing for the Taxman. Sheenagh Pugh. 63p. 1993. pap. 14.95 (*1-85411-085-3*, Pub. by Seren Bks UK) Dufour.

***Sing for Your Father, Su Phan.** Stella Pevsner & Fay Tran. LC 97-4290. (J). 1997. 14.00 (*0-395-82267-X*, Clarion Bks) HM.

Sing for Your Life. Illus. by Samapatti. 80p. (J). (gr. 3 up). 12.95 (*0-7136-5546-1*, Pub. by A&C Black UK) Talman.

Sing Freedom! Children's Poetry. Ed. by Judith Nicholls. (Illus.). 132p. (J). (gr. 3 up). 1992. pap. 9.95 (*0-571-16514-1*) Faber & Faber.

Sing Glory & Hallelujah! Historical & Biographical Guide to Gospel Hymns Nos. 1 to 6 Complete. Samuel J. Rogal. LC 95-32893. (Music Reference Collection: Vol. 49). 256p. 1996. text ed. 79.50 (*0-313-29690-1*, Greenwood Pr) Greenwood.

***Sing Hallelujah.** 8p. 1994. pap. 1.20 (*0-8341-9168-7*) Lillenas.

***Sing, Henrietta! Sing!** Lynn Downey. LC 96-38638. (Illus.). 32p. (J). (ps-3). 1997. 14.95 (*1-57102-103-5*, Ideals Child) Hambleton-Hill.

Sing Hey Diddle Diddle. Illus. by Frank Harris & Bernard Cheese. 96p. (J). (ps-3). 1991. pap. 14.95 (*0-7136-2334-9*, Pub. by A&C Black UK) Talman.

Sing High! Sing Low! A Book of Essays. Osbert Sitwell. (Essay Index Reprint Ser.). 1977. reprint ed. 18.95 (*0-518-10171-1*) Ayer.

Sing Ho for a Prince - Musical. Joe Grenzeback. 81p. 1949. pap. 4.25 (*0-87129-047-2*, S89) Dramatic Pub.

Sing It! Amy Sit. 1979. pap. 3.50 (*0-917726-39-1*) Hunter Bks.

Sing It! Learn English Through Song, Vol. 1. Millie Grenough. 1993. pap. text ed. 12.94 (*0-07-024705-6*) McGraw.

Sing It! Learn English Through Song, Vol. 2. Millie Grenough. 1994. pap. text ed. 12.94 (*0-07-024708-0*) McGraw.

Sing It! Learn English through Song, Vol. 3. Millie Grenough. 1994. pap. text ed. 16.84 (*0-07-024711-0*) McGraw.

Sing It! Learn English through Song, Vol. 3. Millie Grenough. 1994. pap. text ed. 12.94 (*0-07-024709-9*) McGraw.

Sing It! Learn English Through Song, Vol. 4. Millie Grenough. 1995. pap. text ed. 12.94 (*0-07-024710-2*) McGraw.

Sing It! Learn English Through Song, Vol. 5. Millie Grenough. 1995. pap. text ed. 12.94 (*0-07-024713-7*) McGraw.

Sing It! Learn English Through Song, Vol. 6. Millie Grenough. 1995. pap. text ed. 12.94 (*0-07-024750-1*) McGraw.

Sing It! Learn English Through Song, Vol. 2. Millie Grenough. 1993. wbk. ed., pap. text ed., pap. 26.34 incl. audio (*0-07-911681-7*) McGraw.

Sing It! Learn English Through Song, Levels 1-6, Vol. 7. Millie Grenough. 1993. pap. text ed. 148.94 (*0-07-911680-9*) McGraw.

Sing It! Learn English Through Song Vol. 3: Level 3, Vol. 3. Millie Grenough. 1995. wbk. ed., pap. text ed. 26.34 incl. audio (*0-07-911682-5*) McGraw.

Sing It! Learn English Through Song Vol. 4: Level 4, Vol. 4. Millie Grenough. 1995. wbk. ed., pap. text ed. 26.34 incl. audio (*0-07-911683-3*) McGraw.

Sing It! Learn English Through Song Vol. 5: Level 5, Vol. 5. Millie Grenough. 1995. wbk. ed., pap. text ed. 26.34 incl. audio (*0-07-911693-0*) McGraw.

Sing It! Learn English Through Song Vol. 6: Level 6, Vol. 6. Millie Grenough. 1995. wbk. ed., pap. text ed. 26.34 incl. audio (*0-07-911694-9*) McGraw.

Sing Japanese: The Fun Approach to Studying Japanese. Peter Tse. Ed. by John Ashburne & Hilary Sagar. 144p. 1995. pap. 25.00 incl. audio (*4-7700-1866-5*) Kodansha.

Sing Joyfully. Ed. by Jack Schrader. 683p. 1989. 9.95 (*0-916642-39-9*) Hope Pub.

Sing, Like a Hermit Thrush. Richard G. Green. Ed. by Dianne Longboat. 132p. (Orig.). (J). (gr. 4-8). 1995. pap. 7.95 (*0-911737-01-4*) Ricara Features.

Sing Like the Whippoorwill. Stafford Betty. LC 86-51539. (Illus.). 96p. (Orig.). 1987. pap. 6.95 (*0-89622-324-8*) Twenty-Third.

Sing, Little Sack! Canta, Saquito!, a Folktale from Puerto Rico. Illus. by Ray Cruz. LC 92-10743. 48p. (J). 1993. pap. 3.50 (*0-553-37144-4*) Bantam.

Sing Me a Death Song. Jay Bennett. 144p. (YA). (gr. 7 up). 1991. mass mkt. 4.50 (*0-449-70369-X*, Juniper) Fawcett.

Sing Me a Loveaby? Bill Keane. (Family Circus Ser.). 1995. mass mkt. 3.99 (*0-449-14815-7*, GM) Fawcett.

Sing Me a Mountain. Howard L. Norskog. 35p. (Orig.). 1994. pap. 6.00 (*0-9625171-1-9*) H L Norskog.

Sing Me a Sky. John Sherman. 1978. pap. 4.25 (*0-915358-02-6*) Bridgeberg.

Sing Me a Story. (J). 1993. pap. 9.95 incl. audio (*0-7935-1737-0*, 00330601) H Leonard.

Sing Me a Story. (J). 1993. pap. 12.95 incl. audio compact disk (*0-7935-2273-0*, 00330603) H Leonard.

Sing Me a Story: The Metropolitan Opera's Book of Opera Stories for Children. Jane Rosenberg. LC 88-51929. (Illus.). 160p. (J). 1996. pap. 15.95 (*0-500-27873-3*) Thames Hudson.

***Sing Me Creation.** Desmond O'Grady. 66p. 7700. pap. 11.95 (*0-902996-56-8*) Dufour.

Sing Me in Simple Song. Sheilah G. Shook. Ed. by Rand Hall. (Pocket Poetry Ser.). 60p. (Orig.). 1989. pap. 4.50 (*0-937025-02-X*) Shadowood Pubns.

Sing Me No Lullaby. Robert Ardrey. 1955. pap. 5.25 (*0-8222-1032-0*) Dramatists Play.

Sing Me No More. Lynette Dueck. 1992. pap. 12.95 (*0-88974-046-1*, Pub. by Press Gang CN) LPC InBook.

Sing Me the Creation. Paul Matthews. 226p. 1995. pap. 16.95 (*1-869890-60-4*, Pub. by Hawthorn Press UK) Anthroposophic.

Sing Me the Song of My World. Drutmar Cremer. (C). 1988. 39.00 (*0-85439-191-6*, Pub. by St Paul Pubns UK) St Mut.

Sing Me to Sleep. Mary-Ben Louis. 288p. 1993. mass mkt. 4.50 (*0-8217-4405-4*, Zebra Kensgtn) Kensgtn Pub Corp.

Sing Me to Sleep & Wake Me with a Song. Helen Haidle. 100p. (J). (ps-k). 1996. 9.99 (*0-88070-922-7*, Gold & Honey) Multnomah Pubs.

***Sing 'n Learn Chinese: Introduce Chinese with Favorite Children's Songs.** Trio Jan Jeng & Selina Yoon. LC 97-70085. (Sing 'n Learn Ser.). (Illus.). 32p. (Orig.). (CHI & ENG.). (J). (ps-6). 1997. pap. 14.95 incl. digital audio (*1-888194-06-5*) Master Commn.

***Sing 'n Learn Korean: Introduce Korean with Favorite Children's Songs.** Bo-Kyung Kim & Selina Yoon. LC 97-70086. (Sing 'n Learn Ser.). (Illus.). 32p. (Orig.). (ENG & KOR.). (J). (ps-6). 1997. pap. 14.95 incl. digital audio (*1-888194-08-1*) Master Commn.

Sing 'n' Learn Music Activities Kit: A Complete Sequential Program in Basic Music Theory for Grades 1-6. Malcolm Hines. 352p. 1990. pap. text ed. 42.95 (*0-13-809401-2*) P-H.

Sing 'n' Play with Super Mario Bros. (Xylotone Fun! Ser.). 16p. (J). (gr. 3 up). 1992. Incl. xylotone. 14.95 (*0-7935-1551-3*, 00824010) H Leonard.

Sing No Sad Songs. large type ed. Lys Holland. (Romance Ser.). 1994. pap. 15.99 (*0-7089-7619-0*, Linford) Ulverscroft.

Sing Noel. Jane Yolen & Adam Stemple. LC 95-80779. (Illus.). 96p. (J). (ps up). 1996. 17.95 (*1-56397-420-7*) Boyds Mills Pr.

Sing, O Barren One: A Study in Comparative Midrash. Mary Callaway. LC 86-15554. (Society of Biblical Literature Dissertation Ser.). 150p. 1986. pap. 12.95 (*0-89130-995-0*, 06-01-91) Scholars Pr GA.

Sing On! Sing On! A Guide to the Life-Long Enjoyment of the Voice for Singers & Teachers of the Vocal Art. Herbert Burtis. 96p. (Orig.). (C). 1992. pap. 8.95 (*0-911318-17-8*) E C Schirmer.

***Sing Out!** Boze Hadleigh. 240p. 1997. 21.95 (*1-56980-116-9*) Barricade Bks.

Sing Out Louise! Winer. 288p. 1996. 18.00 (*0-02-864618-5*, Free Press) Free Pr.

Sing Out Louise! 150 Stars of the Musical Theatre Remember 50 Years on Broadway. Dennis McGovern & Deborah G. Winer. (Illus.). 288p. 1993. 28.00 (*0-02-871394-X*) Schirmer Bks.

Sing Out Your Praise, Vol. 1. Ed. by Jim Rolland. 128p. 1989. ring bd., pap. 6.95 (*0-937779-21-0*) Greenlawn Pr.

Sing Out Your Praise, Vol. 2. Ed. by Jim Rolland. 160p. 1993. ring bd., pap. 8.95 (*0-937779-26-1*) Greenlawn Pr.

Sing, Pick & Strum Nineteen Christmas Carols with Your Ukulele. Hideo M. Kimura. (Illus.). 74p. (Orig.). (YA). 1992. pap. 12.95 (*0-917822-27-7*) Heedays.

Sing, Pierrot, Sing: A Picture Book in Mime. Tomie De Paola. LC 83-8403. (Illus.). 32p. (J). (ps-3). 1983. 13.00 (*0-15-274988-8*, HB Juv Bks) HarBrace.

***Sing, Pierrot, Sing: A Picture Book in Mime.** Tomie De Paola. (Voyager Picture Bks.). (Illus.). 32p. (J). (ps-3). 1987. pap. 5.00 (*0-15-274989-6*, Voyager Bks) HarBrace.

Sing Praises to His Name. Louis Pratt. Ed. by Michael L. Sherer. (Orig.). 1986. pap. 7.25 (*0-89536-831-5*, 6845) CSS OH.

Sing Sing Sing. Bruce Murphy. 112p. (C). 1990. 30.00 (*0-8147-5460-0*); pap. 13.50 (*0-8147-5461-9*) NYU Pr.

Sing Soft, Sing Loud. Patricia McConnel. 272p. 1995. pap. 12.00 (*0-9643253-0-6*) Logoria.

Sing Song: A Nursery Rhyme Book. Christina Rossetti. LC 68-55822. (Illus.). x, 130p. (J). (gr. 3-7). 1969. reprint ed. pap. 4.50 (*0-486-22107-5*) Dover.

Sing-Song of Old Man Kangaroo. Rudyard Kipling. LC 90-7382. (Illus.). 32p. (J). (gr. k up). 1991. pap. 14.95 (*0-88708-152-5*, Picture Book Studio) S&S Childrens.

Sing Songs & Some That Don't. Joseph A. Labadie. (Men & Movements in the History & Philosophy of Anarchism Ser.). 1979. lib. bdg. 59.95 (*0-87700-310-6*) Revisionist Pr.

Sing, Sophie! Dayle A. Dodds. LC 96-22411. (Illus.). 32p. (J). (gr. k-3). 1997. 15.99 (*0-7636-0131-4*) Candlewick Pr.

***Sing the Beloved Country: The Struggle for the New South Africa.** Peter Hain. LC 96-26350. 1996. write for info. (*0-7453-0996-8*, Pub. by Pluto Pr UK) LPC InBook.

***Sing the Beloved Country: The Struggle for the New South Africa.** Peter Hain. 1997. pap. 16.95 (*0-7453-0997-6*, Pub. by Pluto Pr UK) LPC InBook.

Sing the Cows Home. 2nd abr. rev. ed. Kerstin Brorson. Ed. by Florence Ekstrand. (Illus.). 176p. 1985. reprint ed. pap. 9.95 (*0-916871-07-X*) Welcome Pr.

Sing the Four Quarters. Tanya Huff. 416p. (Orig.). 1994. mass mkt. 4.99 (*0-88677-628-7*) DAW Bks.

Sing the Joys of Mary. Costante Berselli & Georges Gharib. (Orig.). (C). 1988. 45.00 (*0-85439-188-6*, Pub. by St Paul Pubns UK) St Mut.

Sing the Joys of Mary. Ed. by Costante Berselli & Georges Gharib. Tr. by Phil Jenkins from ITA. 136p. (Orig.). 1983. reprint ed. pap. 7.95 (*0-8192-1329-2*) Morehouse Pub.

Sing the Light. Louise Marley. 304p. (Orig.). 1995. mass mkt. 5.50 (*0-441-00272-2*) Ace Bks.

Sing the Lord's Song in a Strange Land: The Life of Justin Morgan. Betty Bandel. LC 78-73309. 264p. 1981. 35.00 (*0-8386-2411-1*) Fairleigh Dickinson.

***Sing the Warmth.** Louise Marley. 1996. mass mkt. 5.99 (*0-441-00386-9*) Ace Bks.

Sing Them in English!, 2 vols., Set. Frederic Kirchberger. 1993. pap. 87.50 (*0-8108-2746-8*) Scarecrow.

Sing Them in English!, Vol. One: Nine Great German Song Cycles from Beethoven to Mahler in New Singable English Translations. Frederic Kirchberger. (Illus.). 396p. 1993. pap. 49.50 (*0-8108-2715-8*) Scarecrow.

Sing Them in English!, Vol. Two: One Hundred Songs by Franz Schubert, Johannes Brahms & Hugo Wolf in New Singable English Translations. Frederic Kirchberger. (Illus.). 396p. 1993. pap. 49.50 (*0-8108-2745-X*) Scarecrow.

Sing Through the Seasons: Ninety-Nine Songs for Children. Ed. by Bruderhof Staff. LC 70-164916. (Illus.). 144p. (J). (gr. k-6). 1972. 18.00 (*0-87486-006-7*) Plough.

Sing Time. Bruce H. Siegel. LC 95-37195. (J). (gr. 3-6). 1997. 5.95 (*1-881283-14-3*) Alef Design.

Sing to God: Songs & Hymns for Christian Education. (Orig.). 1984. teacher ed., pap. 9.95 (*0-8298-0688-1*); student ed. 6.45 (*0-8298-0689-X*) Pilgrim OH.

Sing to Me of Dreams. Kathryn L. Davis. Ed. by Linda Marrow. 608p. 1992. reprint ed. mass mkt. 5.99 (*0-671-68314-4*) PB.

Sing to Me, Saigon. Kathryn Jensen. Ed. by Linda Marrow. 352p. (Orig.). 1994. mass mkt. 5.50 (*0-671-73197-1*) PB.

Sing to the Earth. Jane L. Reynolds. 16p. (J). (gr. k-4). 1978. The Orange Book for First Chorus. 16p. write for info. (*0-932320-01-5*); The Yellow Book for Second Chorus. 20p. write for info. (*0-932320-02-3*); The Green Book for Third Chorus. 20p. write for info. (*0-932320-03-1*); The Blue Book for Fourth Chorus & Soloists. 24p. write for info. (*0-932320-04-X*); pap. write for info. (*0-932320-00-7*) Solar Studio.

***Sing to the Lord.** 1993. pap. 9.99 (*0-8341-9397-3*); pap. 9.99 (*0-8341-9398-1*); pap. 9.99 (*0-8341-9399-X*); pap. 19.99 (*0-8341-9403-1*) Lillenas.

***Sing to the Lord.** Mary A. Vidakovich. 13.35 (*0-687-61016-8*) Abingdon.

Sing to the Lord: A Survey of Christian Hymnody. Stephen W. Nance. LC 95-32679. 201p. (Orig.). 1996. pap. 16.95 (*0-942597-89-3*, Ragged Edge) White Mane Pub.

Sing to the Lord: Devotions for Advent. Mary A. Vidakovich. 112p. 1994. pap. 9.95 (*0-8358-0706-1*) Upper Room Bks.

Sing to the Lord: Hymnal. 1993. 9.99 (*0-685-01106-2*, MB-665); 19.99 (*0-685-74894-4*, MB-670) Lillenas.

Sing to the Lord: Hymnal. large type ed. 1993. 19.99 (*0-8341-9402-3*, MB-669) Lillenas.

Sing to the Lord: Hymnal, Accompanist - Pulpit Edition. 1993. spiral bd. 39.99 (*0-685-74892-8*, MB-668) Lillenas.

Sing to the Lord: Hymnal, Pew Edition. 1993. 9.99 (*0-685-74891-X*, MB-664) Lillenas.

Sing to the Lord an "Old" Song: Activities, Games & Puzzles for Teaching Hymns. Dolores Hruby & Susan R. Tindall. 1989. pap. 7.50 (*0-912405-47-3*) Pastoral Pr.

Sing to the Sun. Ashley Bryan. LC 91-38359. (Trophy Picture Bk.). (Illus.). 32p. (J). (gr. 1 up). 1996. pap. 4.95 (*0-06-443437-0*, Trophy) HarpC Child Bks.

Sing Together: A Girl Scout Songbook. Girl Scouts of the U. S. A. Staff. (Illus.). 192p. (J). (gr. 1-12). 1973. spiral bd. 8.25 (*0-88441-309-8*, 20-206) Girl Scouts USA.

Sing Unto God a New Song: A Contemporary Reading of the Psalms. Herbert J. Levine. LC 94-21826. 308p. 1995. 39.95 (*0-253-33341-5*) Ind U Pr.

***Sing Unto the Lord Medley.** 1980. 1.35 (*0-8341-9045-1*) Lillenas.

Sing Us a Story: Using Music in Preschool & Family Story Times. Jane Marino. LC 93-6389. 215p. 1994. 40.00 (*0-8242-0847-1*) Wilson.

Sing We Noel. Mary Goetze. 16p. 1984. 4.50 (*0-918812-42-9*, SE 0892) MMB Music.

Sing with Me Christmas Carols. Illus. by Helen Davie. (Sing with Me Songbooks & Cassettes Ser.). 24p. (J). (ps up). 1987. pap. 5.95 incl. audio (*0-394-89060-4*) Random Bks Yng Read.

Sing with Me in English: A Teach Me Tapes Songbook. Compiled by Judy Mahoney. (Illus.). 20p. (Orig.). (J). (ps-6). 1994. pap. 7.95 (*0-934633-90-8*) Teach Me.

Sing with Me in French: A Teach Me Tapes Songbook. Compiled by Judy Mahoney. (Illus.). 20p. (Orig.). (FRE.). (J). (ps-6). 1994. pap. 7.95 (*0-934633-91-6*) Teach Me.

Sing with Me in Spanish: A Teach Me Tapes Songbook. Compiled by Judy Mahoney. (Illus.). 20p. (Orig.). (SPA.). (J). (ps-6). 1994. pap. 7.95 (*0-934633-92-4*) Teach Me.

Sing with Me Mother Goose. Illus. by Lulu Delacre. (Sing with Me Songbooks Ser.). (J). (ps-1). 1987. 5.95 incl. audio (*0-394-88812-X*) Random Bks Yng Read.

Sing with Old MacDonald. (J). 1993. write for info. (*0-7853-0760-5*) Pubns Intl Ltd.

***Sing with the Wind.** Alvin R. Tresselt. Date not set. lib. bdg. write for info. (*0-688-05605-9*) Lothrop.

***Sing with the Wind.** Alvin R. Tresselt. (J). Date not set. write for info. (*0-688-05604-0*) Lothrop.

Sing with the Wind. deluxe ed. Winston O. Abbott. LC 68-56014. 1968. 9.95 (*0-918114-01-2*) Inspiration Conn.

***Sing with Understanding: An Introduction to Christian Hymnology.** rev. ed. Harry Eskew & Hugh T. McElrath. 400p. 29.95 (*0-8054-9825-7*) Broadman.

Sing Without Shame: Oral Traditions in Indo-Portugese Creole Verse. K. David Jackson. LC 89-18358. (Creole Language Library: Vol. 5). xxiv, 257p. 1990. 65.00 (*1-55619-081-6*) Benjamins North Am.

Sing Your Heart Out, Country Boy: Classic Country Songs & Their Inside Stories by the Men & Women Who Wrote Them. expanded rev. ed. Dorothy Horstman. LC 75-12889. 443p. (C). 1996. reprint ed. 24.95 (*0-915608-19-7*) Country Music Found.

Sing Your Joys: The Complete New York Poems, 1968-1980. James R. Hurst. LC 80-54736. viii, 120p. 1980. pap. 15.00 (*0-87423-028-4*) Westburg.

Sing Your Song for All You're Worth: A Book on Living Abundantly for the Young at Heart. Leo J. Fishbeck. Ed. by Raylene Fishbeck. 64p. (Orig.). 1988. 5.50 (*0-9619866-0-3*) L J Fishbeck.

Singalong! (Ultimate Ser.). 292p. 1983. pap. 17.95 (*0-88188-134-1*, 00361418) H Leonard.

Singalong Favorites. (Piano-Vocal-Guitar Ser.). 104p. (Orig.). 1991. pap. 9.95 (*0-7935-0068-0*, HL00490346) H Leonard.

Singalong Fun. 104p. 1993. otabind 12.95 (*0-7935-2195-5*, 00222564) H Leonard.

Singalong Fun, No. 78. 48p. 1986. pap. 5.95 (*0-7935-4841-1*, 00243687) H Leonard.

Singalong Funfest. (Mixed Folios - Piano-Vocal-Guitar Ser.). 96p. (Orig.). 1990. pap. 9.95 (*0-7935-0069-9*, HL00490330) H Leonard.

Singalong Requests, Vol. 43. 48p. Date not set. pap. 5.95 (*0-7935-3486-0*, 00100576) H Leonard.

***Singalong with Sherlock Holmes.** Jim Ballanger. 282p. 1995. pap. 24.00 (*0-9695673-7-5*) Battered Silicon.

Singapore. (Essential Guides Ser.). 1994. 7.95 (*0-8442-8933-7*, Passport Bks) NTC Pub Grp.

Singapore. Karl Baedeker. (Baedeker's City Guides Ser.). 1986. pap. 12.95 (*0-13-058090-2*) P-H.

Singapore. Berlitz Editors. (Pocket Guides Ser.). (Illus.). 144p. 1993. pap. 7.95 (*2-8315-0625-5*) Berlitz.

***Singapore.** Lily Kong et al. text ed. 65.95 (*0-471-97190-1*) Wiley.

***Singapore.** Helen Oon. (Globetrotter Travel Guide Ser.). 1995. pap. 9.95 (*1-85368-359-0*) St Mut.

Singapore. Jon S. Quah. (World Bibliographical Ser.). 1989. lib. bdg. 52.50 (*1-85109-071-1*) ABC-CLIO.

Singapore. 3rd ed. Peter Turner. (Illus.). 288p. 1996. pap. 11.95 (0-86442-400-0) Lonely Planet.

Singapore: A Case Study in Rapid Development. Kenneth Bercuson et al. (Occasional Paper Ser.: No. 119). 75p. 1995. pap. 15.00 (1-55775-463-2) Intl Monetary.

Singapore: A Complete Guide. Passport Books Staff. 1992. pap. 10.95 (0-8442-9720-8, Passport Bks) NTC Pub Grp.

Singapore: City State in South-East Asia. Philippe Regnier. 258p. (C). 1992. text ed. 39.00 (0-8248-1406-1); pap. text ed. 17.95 (0-8248-1407-X) UH Pr.

Singapore: Ideology, Society, Culture. John Clammer. 178p. (C). 1986. text ed. 32.50 (0-317-43158-7, Pub. by Chopmen Singapore SI) Advent Bks Div.

Singapore: Island Nation. 2nd ed. Irene Hoe. (Asian Guides Ser.). 222p. 1992. pap. 12.95 (0-8442-9689-9, Passport Bks) NTC Pub Grp.

Singapore: The Chain of Disaster. Stanley W. Kirby. LC 76-853426. 286p. reprint ed. pap. 81.60 (0-317-26204-1, 2052127) Bks Demand.

Singapore: The Complete Guide with Dining, Shopping & Excursions to Newighboring Malaysia. 9th ed. Fodor's Travel Staff. 1997. pap. 15.00 (0-679-03283-5) Fodors Travel.

*Singapore: The Year in Review 1994. Ed. by Yap M. Teng. 88p. 1995. pap. write for info. (981-210-074-1, Pub. by Times Academic SI) Intl Spec Bk.

*Singapore: The Year in Review 1995. Ed. by Yeo L. Hwee. 96p. 1996. pap. write for info. (981-210-090-3, Pub. by Times Academic SI) Intl Spec Bk.

Singapore see Cultures of the World - Group 1

Singapore see Exploring Cultures of the World

Singapore see Children of the World: Set II

*Singapore Affair. large type ed. Kathleen Farrell. (Dales Large Print Ser.). 309p. 1997. pap. 18.99 (1-85389-729-9) Ulverscroft.

Singapore & Malaysia. Nick Hanna. (Illustrated Travel Guides from Thomas Cook Ser.). (Illus.). 192p. 1994. pap. 12.95 (0-8442-9056-4, Passport Bks) NTC Pub Grp.

Singapore & Malaysia. John Platt et al. (Varieties of English Around the World General Ser.: T4). iv, 138p. (Orig.). 1983. pap. 32.00 (90-272-4712-9) Benjamins North Am.

Singapore & Malaysia. Milton E. Osborne. LC 64-55818. (Cornell University, Southeast Asia Program, Data Paper Ser.: No. 53). 136p. reprint ed. pap. 38.80 (0-8357-3535-4, 2034586) Bks Demand.

*Singapore & Malaysia: Knopf Guide. Knopf Travel Guides Staff. 1996. pap. 25.00 (0-679-75567-5) Knopf.

*Singapore & Malaysia Electronics Industry. Donald Beane et al. LC 97-146. (Electronics Industry Research Ser.). 1997. write for info. (0-8493-3171-4) CRC Pr.

Singapore Books in Print, 1986. 392p. 1987. pap. text ed. 50.00 (0-317-54337-7, Pub. by Chopmen Singapore SI) Advent Bks Div.

Singapore Business: The Portable Encyclopedia for Doing Business with Singapore. Christine Genzberger et al. (Country Business Guide Ser.). 310p. 1994. pap. 24.95 (0-9631864-6-9) Wrld Trade Pr.

Singapore Chance. Russell J. Smith. LC 91-25577. 256p. (Orig.). 1991. pap. 9.95 (0-910155-16-X) Bartleby Pr.

*Singapore Changes Guard. Rodan. Date not set. text ed. write for info. (0-582-87610-9, Pub. by Longman UK) Longman.

Singapore Changes Guard. Ed. by Garry Rodan. LC 93-16580. 272p. 1993. text ed. 49.95 (0-312-09687-9) St Martin.

Singapore Conveyancing Practice: Forms, Precedents & Materials. Hairani Saban. 1992. 236.00 (0-409-99608-4) MICHIE.

Singapore Conveyancing Practice: Forms, Precedents & Materials-Issue 2. Hairani Saban. 944p. 1994. write for info. (0-409-99702-1, ASIA) MICHIE.

Singapore Economy. Gavin Peebles & Peter Wilson. LC 95-36676. (Illus.). 304p. 1996. 95.00 (1-85898-286-3) E Elgar.

Singapore Express. Steve Wilson. 1994. pap. 12.50 (0-941749-31-2) Black Tie Pr.

Singapore Fling. Lynn Leslie. (Superromance Ser.). 1994. mass mkt. 3.50 (0-373-70604-9, 1-70604-3) Harlequin Bks.

Singapore Grip. J. G. Farrell. 455p. 1986. pap. 4.95 (0-88184-124-2) Carroll & Graf.

*Singapore Handbook. Carl Parkes. 1997. pap. text ed. 15.95 (1-56691-078-1) Moon Trvl Hdbks.

Singapore-India Relations: A Primer. Yong Mun Cheong & V. V. Bhanoji Rao. (Southeast Asian Studies). 318p. 1996. pap. 49.95 (9971-69-195-7, Pub. by Singapore Univ Pr SI) Intl Spec Bk.

Singapore, Indonesia, Malaysia, the Philippines & Thailand see Political Economy of East Asia

Singapore Law Review, 15 vols., Set. Date not set. 750.00 (0-614-13284-3) Gaunt.

Singapore Master Tax Guide, 1992. 11th ed. Soin. 950p. 1992. pap. 73.00 (0-685-67181-X, 1521) Commerce.

Singapore, Nineteen Forty-One to Nineteen Forty-Two. Louis Allen. Ed. by Noble Frankland & Christopher Dowling. LC 79-52236. (Politics & Strategy of the Second World War Ser.). 343p. 1979. 27.50 (0-87413-160-X) U Delaware Pr.

Singapore Property Tax Cases (1959-1986) Ed. by Leila B. Rahman. xxii, 413p. 1987. 99.00 (9971-70-057-3) MICHIE.

Singapore Super Computing Conference, '90. Ed. by K. K. Phuq et al. 500p. (C). 1991. text ed. 104.00 (981-02-0700-X) World Scientific Pub.

Singapore Taxation. 2nd ed. Pok S. Yoong & Damian C. Hong. 1990. pap. 108.00 (0-409-99565-7) MICHIE.

Singapore to 2003: Aspiring to the First World. (Research Reports: No. M202). 1994. 445.00 (0-614-12663-0) Economist Intell.

*Singapore Women: Three Decades of Change. Ed. by Aline Wong & Leong W. Kum. 336p. 1993. pap. write for info. (981-210-031-8, Pub. by Times Academic SI) Intl Spec Bk.

Singapore, 1941-1942. Louis Allen. LC 92-20935. 351p. 1993. text ed. 42.50 (0-7146-3473-5, Pub. by F Cass Pubs UK) Intl Spec Bk.

*Singapore's Urban Coastal Area: Strategies for Management. L. S. Chia. (ICLARM Technical Reports: No. 31). 99p. 1992. per. write for info. (971-8709-17-7, Pub. by ICLARM PH) Intl Spec Bk.

Singe en Hiver. Antoine Blondin. 224p. (FRE.). 1987. pap. 10.95 (0-7859-1739-X, 2070363597) Fr & Eur.

Singen Weihnachten. Barbara MacArthur. (Illus.). 14p. (Orig.). (ENG & GER.). (J). (ps-12). 1993. pap. 12.95 incl. audio (1-881120-12-0) Frog Pr WI.

Singer. Peter Flannery. 98p. 1989. pap. 13.95 (1-85459-066-9, Pub. by N Hern Bks UK) Theatre Comm.

Singer. Calvin Miller. LC 74-20097. (Illus.). 152p. (Orig.). 1975. pap. 9.99 (0-87784-639-1, 639) InterVarsity.

Singer: Perspective in Music for Christian Schools. Nancy Tipton. (Illus.). 113p. (Orig.). (gr. 7-12). 1991. pap. text ed. 13.27 (0-89084-564-6, 055160) Bob Jones Univ Pr.

Singer & Accompanist: The Performance of Fifty Songs. Gerald Moore. LC 73-11859. (Illus.). xi, 232p. 1974. reprint ed. lib. bdg. 49.75 (0-8371-7090-7, MOSC, Greenwood Pr) Greenwood.

Singer & Songs of the Church. Joseph Miller. reprint ed. lib. bdg. 75.00 (0-7812-0770-3) Rprt Serv.

Singer & the Sewing Machine: A Capitalist Romance. Ruth Brandon. Ed. by Maya Rao. (Illus.). 256p. 1996. pap. 13.00 (1-56836-146-7, Kodansha Globe) Kodansha.

Singer Children's Clothes, Toys & Gifts Step-by-Step. Cy DeCosse Incorporated Staff. LC 95-30810. 320p. 1995. 29.95 (0-86573-304-X) Cowles Creative.

Singer Creative Gifts & Projects Step-by-Step. Cy DeCosse Incorporated Staff. LC 93-17642. 320p. 1993. 29.95 (0-86573-290-6) Cowles Creative.

Singer Home Decorating Projects Step-by-Step. Cy DeCosse Incorporated Staff. LC 92-16877. 320p. 1992. 29.95 (0-86573-270-1) Cowles Creative.

Singer in the White Pajamas. Louis Phillips. 29p. 1991. pap. 3.00 (0-87129-090-1, S97) Dramatic Pub.

Singer Instructions for Art Embroidery & Lace Work. Ed. by Jules Kliot & Kaethe Kliot. (Illus.). 224p. 1987. pap. 22.00 (0-916896-24-2) Lacis Pubns.

Singer Instructions for Art Embroidery & Lace Work. Singer Sewing Machine Company Staff. (Illus.). 225p. 1989. reprint ed. pap. 26.95 (0-932086-19-5) Krause Pubns.

Singer of Seasons: The Prayers of Beverly Sawyer. Beverly Sawyer. LC 82-70161. 104p. 1991. reprint ed. pap. 8.95 (0-935304-42-8) August Hse.

Singer of Tales. Albert B. Lord. (Studies in Comparative Literature: No. 24). 319p. (C). 1981. pap. 15.95 (0-674-80881-9) HUP.

Singer of Tales in Performance. John M. Foley. LC 94-17638. (Voices in Performance & Text Ser.). 256p. 1995. 31.50 (0-253-32225-1); pap. 15.95 (0-253-20931-5) Ind U Pr.

Singer of the Eclogues: A Study of Virgilian Pastoral. Paul J. Alpers. LC 77-93465. 1979. 42.00 (0-520-03651-4) U CA Pr.

Singer Resumes the Tale. Albert B. Lord. Ed. by Mary L. Lord. (Myth & Poetics Ser.). 336p. 1995. 39.95 (0-8014-3103-4) Cornell U Pr.

Singer Sewing Step-by-Step. Cy DeCosse Incorporated Staff. LC 90-39717. (Illus.). 320p. 1990. 29.95 (0-86573-257-4) Cowles Creative.

Singer to the Sea God. Vivien Alcock. 208p. (J). (gr. 4-7). 1995. pap. 3.99 (0-440-41003-7) Dell.

Singer to the Sea God. Vivien Alcock. (YA). (gr. 9-12). 1996. 17.50 (0-8446-6887-7) Peter Smith.

Singer Trilogy. Calvin Miller. (Illus.). 496p. 1992. reprint ed. pap. 18.99 (0-8308-1321-7, 1321) InterVarsity.

Singer with Love. Shuo-Lun Wu. 270p. 1995. pap. text ed. 12.00 (1-888065-01-X) New Wrld Poetry.

Singermann. Myron Brinig. LC 74-27968. (Modern Jewish Experience Ser.). 1975. reprint ed. 40.95 (0-405-06698-8) Ayer.

Singers & Songwriters. (Illus.). 144p. 1991. pap. 19.95 (0-8256-1318-3, AM85580) Music Sales.

Singers & Storytellers. Ed. by Mody C. Boatright et al. LC 60-15894. (Texas Folklore Society Publications: No. 30). 304p. 1961. 14.95 (0-87074-019-9) UNTX Pr.

Singers & the Song. Gene Lees. 272p. 1987. 24.95 (0-19-504293-X) OUP.

Singers & the Song. Gene Lees. 272p. 1989. pap. 11.95 (0-19-506087-3) OUP.

Singer's Companion to the Church Year: Cycle A. Lawrence J. Johnson. 117p. (Orig.). 1995. pap. text ed. 7.95 (1-56929-059-8) Pastoral Pr.

Singer's Companion to the Church Year Cycle C. Lawrence J. Johnson. 104p. (Orig.). 1994. pap. text ed. 7.95 (1-56929-022-9) Pastoral Pr.

*Singer's Companion to the Church Year, Cycle B. Lawrence J. Johnson. 110p. (Orig.). 1996. pap. 7.95 (1-56929-065-2) Pastoral Pr.

Singer's Fake Book - High Key. spiral bd. 19.95 (0-7935-4411-4, 00240036) H Leonard.

Singer's Fake Book - Low Voice. spiral bd. 19.95 (0-7935-4412-2, 00240038) H Leonard.

Singer's Guide to Languages. rev. ed. Marcie Stapp. LC 95-91010. (Illus.). 220p. 1996. pap. text ed. 25.00 (0-9650473-0-X, 001-96) Teddys Music.

Singer's Guide to the American Art Song, 1870-1980. Victoria E. Villamil. LC 93-34664. 477p. 1993. 49.50 (0-8108-2774-3) Scarecrow.

Singers, Heroes, & Gods in the "Odyssey" Charles Segal. (Myth & Poetics Ser.). 264p. 1994. 37.50 (0-8014-3041-0) Cornell U Pr.

Singers in Late Byzantine & Slavonic Painting. N. K. Moran. (Byzantina Neerlandica Ser.: No. 9). (Illus.). xiv, 173p. 1986. 61.50 (90-04-07809-6) E J Brill.

Singers in the Marketplace: The Economics of the Singing Profession. Ruth Towse. (Illus.). 240p. 1993. 55.00 (0-19-816347-9) OUP.

Singer's Italian: A Manual of Diction & Phonetics. Evelina Colorni. LC 71-113927. 192p. 1970. 13.50 (0-02-870620-X) Schirmer Bks.

Singer's Lock: The Revolution in the Understanding of Weather, Pt. 1. Oscar Singer. LC 83-90086. (Illus.). 351p. 1983. 40.00 (0-9610922-0-3); trans. 10.00 (0-9610922-1-1) Singer Pr.

Singer's Manual of English Diction. Madeleine F. Marshall. 208p. 1953. 15.00 (0-02-871100-9) Schirmer Bks.

Singer's Manual of German & French Diction. Richard D. Cox. 80p. 1970. 13.50 (0-02-870650-1) Schirmer Bks.

Singer's Manual of Spanish Lyric Diction. Nico Castel. LC 94-6333. (Illus.). 164p. (Orig.). (ENG & SPA.). (C). 1994. 15.95 (0-9627226-9-3) Excalibur Pub.

Singer's Movie Anthology: The Men's Edition. 248p. 1994. per. 19.95 (0-7935-3404-6, 00747069) H Leonard.

Singer's Movie Anthology: Women's Edition. 232p. 1995. per. 19.95 (0-7935-3425-9, 00747076) H Leonard.

Singer's Musical Theatre Anthology Vol. 2: Soprano. 224p. 1993. per. 19.95 (0-7935-3050-4, 00747066) H Leonard.

Singers Musical Theatre Anthology, Vol. 1: Soprano. 248p. 1987. 19.95 (0-88188-546-0) H Leonard.

Singer's Musical Theatre Anthology, Vol. 1: Tenor. 232p. 1987. 19.95 (0-88188-549-5, 00361073) H Leonard.

Singer's Musical Theatre Anthology, Vol. 2: Baritone - Bass. (Piano-Vocal Ser.). 224p. (Orig.). 1993. pap. 19.95 (0-7935-2332-X, 00747033) H Leonard.

Singer's Musical Theatre Anthology, Vol. 2: Mezzo-Soprano - Belter. (Piano-Vocal Ser.). 224p. (Orig.). 1993. pap. 19.95 (0-7935-2330-3, 00747031) H Leonard.

Singer's Musical Theatre Anthology, Vol. 2: Soprano. (Piano-Vocal Ser.). 224p. (Orig.). 1993. pap. 18.95 (0-7935-2329-X, 00747030) H Leonard.

Singer's Musical Theatre Anthology, Vol. 2: Tenor. (Piano-Vocal Ser.). 224p. (Orig.). 1993. pap. 19.95 (0-7935-2331-1, 00747032) H Leonard.

Singers of Daybreak: Studies in Black American Literature. Houston A. Baker. LC 82-23280. 107p. 1975. 19.95 (0-88258-017-5); pap. 12.95 (0-88258-025-6) Howard U Pr.

Singers of Italian Opera. John Rosselli. 288p. 1995. pap. text ed. 18.95 (0-521-42697-9) Cambridge U Pr.

Singers of Italian Opera: The History of a Profession. John Rosselli. (Illus.). 275p. (C). 1992. text ed. 59.95 (0-521-41683-3) Cambridge U Pr.

Singers of the Century. J. B. Steane. (Illus.). 288p. 1996. 34.95 (1-57467-009-3, Amadeus Pr) Timber.

Singers of Today. Donald Brook. LC 70-160917. (Biography Index Reprint Ser.). 1977. reprint ed. 22.95 (0-8369-8080-8) Ayer.

Singer's Pilgrimage. Blanche Marchesi. Ed. by Andrew Farkas. LC 76-29951. (Opera Biographies Ser.). (Illus.). 1977. reprint ed. lib. bdg. 29.95 (0-405-09692-5) Ayer.

Singer's Pilgrimage. Blanche Marchesi. LC 77-1941. (Music Reprint Ser.: 1978). (Illus.). 1978. reprint ed. lib. bdg. 37.50 (0-306-70878-7) Da Capo.

Singer's Repertoire, 4 vols., Set. 2nd ed. Berton Coffin. Incl. Vol. 1. Coloratura, Lyric & Dramatic Soprano. LC 60-7265. 1960. text ed. 39.50 (0-8108-0188-4); Vol. 2. Mezzo Soprano & Contralto. LC 60-7265. 1960. text ed. 39.50 (0-8108-0189-2); Vol. 3. Lyric & Dramatic Tenor. LC 60-7265. 1960. text ed. 39.50 (0-8108-0190-6); Vol. 4. Baritone & Bass. LC 60-7265. 1960. text ed. 39.50 (0-8108-0191-4); LC 60-7265. 1960. 135.00 (0-8108-2023-4) Scarecrow.

Singers Wedding Anthology: Duets. 144p. 1995. otabind 14.95 (0-7935-4099-2, 00740005) H Leonard.

Singers Wedding Anthology: High Voice. 208p. 1995. otabind 19.95 (0-7935-4095-X, 00740006) H Leonard.

Singers Wedding Anthology: Low Voice. 208p. 1995. otabind 19.95 (0-7935-4096-8, 00740008) H Leonard.

*Singin & Swingin & Gettin Merry. Maya Angelou. 1997. 20.00 (0-679-45777-1) Random.

Singin' & Swingin' & Gettin' Merry Like Christmas. Maya Angelou. 256p. (gr. 8-12). 1985. mass mkt. 5.50 (0-553-25199-6) Bantam.

Singin' & Swingin' & Gettin' Merry Like Christmas. Maya Angelou. 1976. 22.00 (0-394-40545-5) Random.

*Singin & Swingin & Gettin Merry Like Christmas. Maya Angelou. 256p. 1985. mass mkt. 5.50 (0-553-85179-9) Bantam.

Singin' in the Rain. Peter Wollen. (BFI Film Classics Ser.). (Illus.). 1993. pap. 9.95 (0-85170-351-8, Pub. by British Film Inst UK) Ind U Pr.

Singin' Texas. Francis E. Abernethy. LC 93-39616. (Texas Folklore Society Publications). (Illus.). 183p. (Orig.). 1994. reprint ed. pap. 19.95 (0-929398-71-8) UNTX Pr.

Singin' the Sun Up. Ocala Wings. LC 90-63947. 240p. 1991. 8.95 (0-941300-20-X) Mother Courage.

Singing. Dennis Schmitz. (American Poetry Ser.: Vol. 31). 60p. (Orig.). 1985. pap. 7.50 (0-88001-068-1) Ecco Pr.

Singing. Alyn Shipton. LC 93-20006. (Exploring Music Ser.). (Illus.). 32p. (J). (gr. 1-8). 1993. lib. bdg. 22.83 (0-8114-2315-8) Raintree Steck-V.

Singing. Susan Sutherland. 160p. 1995. pap. 7.95 (0-8442-3900-3, Teach Yourslf) NTC Pub Grp.

Singing. Herbert Witherspoon. LC 80-12944. (Music Reprint Ser.). (Illus.). 126p. 1980. reprint ed. lib. bdg. 25.00 (0-306-76001-0) Da Capo.

Singing, Set. Sue Sutherland. (Teach Yourself Ser.). 160p. (Orig.). 1996. pap. 17.95 incl. audio (0-8442-3902-X, Teach Yourslf) NTC Pub Grp.

Singing: The Mechanism & the Technique. rev. ed. William Vennard. (Music Instruction Bks.). 275p. 1967. pap. 29.95 (0-8258-0055-2, 04685) Fischer Inc NY.

Singing--An Extension of Speech. Russell A. Hammar. LC 78-11756. 216p. 1978. lib. bdg. 27.50 (0-8108-1182-0) Scarecrow.

Singing a Mass for the Dead. Darc Cummings. 24p. (Orig.). 1995. 5.00 (0-936908-07-6) Broncho Pr.

*Singing a New Song: A Study of the Life & Works of Maria Celeste Crostarosa. Hamish F. Swanston. LC 97-7825. 256p. (Orig.). 1997. 24.95 (0-7648-0105-8) Liguori Pubns.

Singing about It: Folk Song in Southern Indiana. George List. (Illus.). 450p. 1991. pap. 32.00 (0-87195-086-3) Ind Hist Soc.

***Singing above the Hi Knowtes. Gene L. Williams, III. LC 97-93048. (Illus.). v, 295p. (Orig.). 1997. pap. 8.95 (1-890440-02-7) Honey Clouds. SINGING ABOVE THE HI KNOWTES, (general) 1996. Fiction sprinkled with humorous over tones. So many knowtes to be sang! An esoteric establishment simplified -- ejecting fictional prose with a bridge to the real world intellect & emotions. Tampering with human nature issues, while squeezing out creative understanding from them to enhance general relationships. SINGING ABOVE THE HI KNOWTES, available in English. A small time nomad lad called Peffamy, yapped & shouted his peace here, there & no telling where, all the way to paradise. He did this through various avenues, including via chu chu train & an unexpected terrible, but terrific fall. Prancing by several bizarre situations, such as the pleasure to talk to a stick figure & meeting actual tear wipers; still he remains nonchalant even when coming in contact with some most extraordinary experiences, generally expresses by plenty of wow-wee's. Of course, Peffamy was not going to be found having escaped his journey without wallowing in remnants of elements connected to a beloved, adoring, cuddly mademoiselle -- re-occurs in his life threatening punitive damages to his heart. All said & done, Peffamy experienced a fantastic presentation in an awkward, prolific, bursting way. SINGING ABOVE THE HI KNOWTES, illus., 5 1/2 x 8 1/2, 300p (ISBN 1-890440-02-7), Card Catalog 97-93048, $8.95. To Order: call 213-860-9907, 213-461-7810 or write Honey Clouds, P.O. Box 1416, Los Angeles, CA 90078-1416.** *Publisher Provided Annotation.*

Singing along with Life: Grace Notes. Mae Mary. 108p. 1996. pap. 9.95 (1-887679-04-9) Foxglove Found.

Singing America: Poems That Define a Nation. Ed. & Intro. by Neil Phillip. (Illus.). 160p. (YA). (gr. 5 up). 1995. pap. 19.99 (0-670-86150-2) Viking Child Bks.

Singing an Indian Song: A Biography of D'Arcy McNickle. Dorothy R. Parker. LC 92-7616. (American Indian Lives Ser.). (Illus.). x, 317p. 1992. pap. 13.00 (0-8032-8730-5, Bison Books) U of Nebr Pr.

Singing & Making Melody. Kay Gowen. 1975. pap. 3.25 (0-685-47448-8) Quality Pubns.

Singing & New Testament Worship. Dave Miller. 1994. pap. 4.95 (0-89137-144-3) Quality Pubns.

Singing & the Etheric Tone: Gracia Ricardo's Approach to Singing Based on Her Work with Rudolf Steiner. Hilda Deighton et al. (Illus.). 96p. (Orig.). 1991. pap. 10.95 (0-88010-356-6) Anthroposophic.

Singing Assembly. Ed. by Virgil C. Funk. (Pastoral Music in Practice Ser.). 148p. (Orig.). 1991. pap. 9.95 (0-912405-80-5) Pastoral Pr.

Singing at the Top of Our Lungs: Women, Love, & Creativity. Claudia Bepko & Jo-Ann Krestan. LC 92-54738. 352p. 1994. reprint ed. pap. 13.00 (0-06-092499-3, PL) HarpC.

*Singing Away the Hunger: Stories from a Life in Lesotho. Mpho M'atsepo Nthunya. Ed. by Limakatso Kendall. 186p. 1997. pap. 22.00 (0-86980-932-6, Pub. by Univ Natal Pr SA) Intl Spec Bk.

*Singing Away the Hunger: The Autobiography of an African Woman. Mpho M. Nthunya & K. Limakatso Kendall. LC 97-18778. 1997. write for info. (0-253-33352-0); pap. write for info. (0-253-21162-X) Ind U Pr.

*Singing Baptists: Studies in Baptist Hymnody in America. Harry Eskew et al. 224p. pap. 19.95 (0-8054-9824-9) Broadman.

Singing Bee! A Collection of Favorite Children's Songs. Ed. by Jane Hart. LC 82-15296. (Illus.). 160p. (J). 1982. reprint ed. 22.95 (0-688-41975-5) Lothrop.

Singing Bee! A Collection of Favorite Children's Songs. Ed. by Jane Hart. LC 82-15296. (Illus.). 160p. (J). 1989. reprint ed. pap. 12.00 (0-688-09113-X) Morrow.

*Singing Bird Will Come: An AIDS Journal. John R. Noonan. Ed. by Mary R. Noonan. LC 96-54910. (Illus.). 150p. (Orig.). 1997. pap. write for info. (0-9641725-4-2) Canticle Press.

Singing Black. Homer A. Rodeheaver. LC 72-1681. reprint ed. 31.50 (0-404-08330-7) AMS Pr.

Singing Bone. R. Austin Freeman. 1976. lib. bdg. 12.95 (0-89968-168-9, Lghtyr Pr) Buccaneer Bks.

Singing Bourgeois: Songs of the Victorian Drawing-Room & Parlour. Derek W. Scott. 176p. 1989. 95.00 (*0-335-15291-0*, Open Univ Pr); pap. 39.00 (*0-335-15296-1*, Open Univ Pr) Taylor & Francis.

Singing Bowls: A Practical Handbook of Instruction & Use. Eva R. Jansen. (Illus.). 95p. (Orig.). 1990. pap. 10.95 (*90-74597-01-7*, Pub. by Binkey Kok NE) Weiser.

***Singing Bowls: A Practical Handbook of Instruction & Use.** Eva R. Jansen. (Orig.). 1993. pap. 9.95 (*90-800594-7-1*, Pub. by Binkey Kok NE) Weiser.

Singing Campaign for Ten Thousand Pounds. rev. ed. Gustavus D. Pike. LC 75-164392. (Black Heritage Library Collection). 1977. reprint ed. 29.95 (*0-8369-8851-5*) Ayer.

Singing Cave. Eilis Dillon. 259p. (YA). (gr. 6 up). 1992. reprint ed. pap. 8.95 (*1-85371-153-5*, Pub. by Poolbeg Pr IE) Dufour.

Singing, Chanting, Telling Tales. Caroline Graham. 96p. (C). 1992. pap. text ed. write for info. (*0-13-808056-9*) P-H.

***Singing Chick.** Stenmarc. 1998. 14.95 (*0-8050-5255-0*) H Holt & Co.

Singing Church. 623p. 1985. 9.95 (*0-916642-25-9*) Hope Pub.

Singing Cowboy Stars. Robert Phillips. (Illus.). 96p. 1994. 19.95 incl. audio compact disk (*0-87905-593-6*, Peregrine Smith) Gibbs Smith Pub.

Singing Cowboys & All That Jazz: A Short History of Popular Music in Oklahoma. William W. Savage, Jr. LC 82-17560. (Illus.). 200p. 1988. 19.95 (*0-8061-1648-X*); pap. 11.95 (*0-8061-2085-1*) U of Okla Pr.

Singing Cowboys & Musical Mountaineers: Southern Culture & the Roots of Country Music. Bill C. Malone. LC 92-12430. (Mercer University Lamar Memorial Lectures: No. 34). 160p. 1993. 24.95 (*0-8203-1483-8*) U of Ga Pr.

Singing Cowboys, Musical Mountaineers: Southern Culture & the Roots of Country Music. Bill C. Malone. LC 92-12430. (Brown Thrasher Bks.). 168p. 1994. pap. 12.95 (*0-8203-1679-2*) U of Ga Pr.

Singing Creek Where the Willows Grow: The Mystical Nature Diary of Opal Whiteley. Opal Whitely. Ed. by Benjamin Hoff. (Illus.). 400p. 1995. reprint ed. pap. 12.95 (*0-14-023720-8*, Penguin Bks) Viking Penguin.

Singing Detective. Dennis Potter. 256p. 1994. 8.99 (*1-56865-113-9*, GuildAmerica) Dblday Direct.

***Singing down the Bones: An Invitation to Poetry.** Ed. by Jeni Couzyn. (Livewire Ser.). (YA). (gr. 6-9). pap. 6.95 (*0-7043-4913-2*, Pub. by Womens Press UK) Trafalgar.

***Singing down the Rain.** Joy Cowley. LC 96-43055. (Illus.). 32p. (J). (gr. 1-4). 1997. 14.95 (*0-06-027602-9*); lib. bdg. 14.89 (*0-06-027603-7*) HarpC Child Bks.

Singing down the Rain. Joy Cowley. LC 96-10179. (Illus.). (J). 1997. write for info. (*0-590-52701-0*) Scholastic Inc.

Singing Early Music: The Pronunciation of European Languages in the Late Middle Ages & Renaissance. Ed. by A. G. Rigg et al. LC 95-22575. (Music--Scholarship & Performance Ser.). 1996. 49.95 (*0-253-32961-2*) Ind U Pr.

Singing Energy in the Gan-Tone Method of Voice Production. Robert Gansert. LC 81-80960. (Illus.). 324p. 38.50 incl. audio (*0-939458-00-4*) Gan-Tone Pub.

Singing Entertainer: A Contemporary Study of the Art & Business of Being a Professional. John Davidson & Cort Casady. 244p. 1979. pap. 14.95 (*0-88284-194-7*, 1488) Alfred Pub.

Singing Faith. Jane P. Huber. LC 86-753277. 142p. (Orig.). 1987. pap. 11.00 (*0-664-24055-0*, Westminster); spiral bd. 13.00 (*0-664-24056-9*, Westminster) Westminster John Knox.

Singing Family of the Cumberlands. Jean Ritchie. LC 88-17337. 264p. 1988. 25.00 (*0-8131-1679-1*); pap. 15.00 (*0-8131-0186-7*) U Pr of Ky.

Singing Farm: Singing Farm, Big Bear, Sing to Me, Muse! Family & Friends. Rosita B. Filipek. LC 90-92142. (Illus.). 88p. (Orig.). 1990. pap. 7.75 (*0-9628245-0-X*) Monte Solare.

Singing Fish & Flying Rhinos: Amazing Animal Habits. Owl Magazine Editors. (Illus.). 48p. (J). (gr. 2 up). 1992. pap. 6.95 (*0-920775-45-4*, Pub. by Greey dePencier CN) Firefly Bks Ltd.

Singing Flame. 2nd ed. Ernie O'Malley. 312p. 1992. reprint ed. pap. 15.95 (*0-947962-32-8*, Pub. by Anvil Bks Ltd IE) Irish Bks Media.

***Singing Fluent American Vowels.** Yale Marshall. Ed. by Edward V. Foreman. 1993. pap. 37.50 (*1-887117-02-4*) Pro musica pr.

Singing for Our Lives - Songbook. Holly Near. 1982. pap. 10.00 (*0-9608774-2-8*) Hereford Pub.

Singing for Power: The Song Magic of the Papago Indians of Southern Arizona. Ruth M. Underhill. LC 93-2396. (Sun Tracks Ser.: Vol. 25). (Illus.). 158p. 1993. reprint ed. pap. 12.95 (*0-8165-1401-1*) U of Ariz Pr.

Singing for Survival: Songs of the Lodz Ghetto, 1940-45. Gila Flam. (Illus.). 224p. 1992. text ed. 27.50 (*0-252-01817-6*) U of Ill Pr.

Singing for the Stars: A Complete Program for Training Your Voice. rev. ed. Seth Riggs. Ed. by John Carratello. (Illus.). (Orig.). 1985. audio 45.00 (*0-88284-472-5*, 2535) Alfred Pub.

Singing for the Stars: A Complete Program for Training Your Voice. rev. ed. Seth Riggs. Ed. by John Carratello. (Illus.). 160p. (Orig.). 1987. pap. 35.00 incl. audio (*0-88284-340-0*, 2200) Alfred Pub.

Singing for the Stars: A Complete Program for Training Your Voice. 5th rev. ed. Seth Riggs. Ed. by John Carratello. (Illus.). (Orig.). 1992. 40.00 incl. cd-rom (*0-88284-528-4*, 3379) Alfred Pub.

Singing for Your Supper: Entertaining Ways to Be a Perfect Guest. Edith Hazard. (Illus.). 224p. 1996. 15.95 (*1-56512-090-6*, 72151) Algonquin Bks.

Singing from the Heart: Discovering Worship That Rejoices & Restores: A Study of the Psalms. Jack W. Hayford & Joseph Snider. LC 93-1416. (Spirit-Filled Life Bible Discovery Guide Ser.). 1993. pap. 6.99 (*0-8407-8347-7*) Nelson.

***Singing from the Heart/Cuando Se Canta de Corazon.** Jack Hayford. 1996. pap. 5.99 (*0-89922-521-7*) Edit Betania.

Singing from the Soul: An Autobiography. Jose Carreras. Ed. by Walter Price. Tr. by Thomas et al. from GER. LC 90-71130. (Library of Courage). (Illus.). 285p. 1991. 30.95 (*1-878756-89-3*) YCP Pubns.

Singing from the Well. Reinaldo Arenas. 224p. 1988. pap. 7.95 (*0-14-009444-X*, Penguin Bks) Viking Penguin.

Singing Games & Playparty Games. Richard Chase. (Illus.). 63p. (J). (gr. 1-4). 1949. pap. 2.95 (*0-486-21785-X*) Dover.

Singing Games & Playparty Games. Richard Chase. (Illus.). (J). (gr. 4-8). 1990. 17.50 (*0-8446-4721-7*) Peter Smith.

***Singing Geese: A Black Tall Tale from Maryland.** Jan Wahl. LC 96-30796. (Illus.). (J). 1998. pap. 15.99 (*0-525-67499-3*, Lodestar Bks) Dutton Child Bks.

Singing Green: New & Selected Poems for All Seasons. Eve Merriam. LC 91-31205. (Illus.). 112p. (J). (gr. 3 up). 1992. 14.00 (*0-688-11025-8*, Morrow Junior) Morrow.

Singing Guns. Max Brand. 1991. pap. 2.95 (*0-671-73542-X*) S&S Trade.

Singing Heart. Margaret Clarkson. LC 87-82067. 203p. (Orig.). 1987. pap. 11.95 (*0-916642-31-3*, 390) Hope Pub.

Singing House. large type ed. Mary Munro. 336p. 1985. 25.99 (*0-7089-1340-7*) Ulverscroft.

Singing in a Dark Language. Terri Drake. 1968. 3.00 (*0-936814-08-X*) New Collage.

Singing in a Strange Land: Praying & Acting with the Poor. William D. Lindsey. LC 90-63488. 120p. (Orig.). (C). 1991. pap. 8.95 (*1-55612-415-5*, LL1415) Sheed & Ward MO.

Singing in Celebration: Hymns for Special Occasions. Jane P. Huber. 96p. (Orig.). 1996. spiral bd. 13.00 (*0-664-25649-X*) Westminster John Knox.

Singing in Celebration: Hymns for Special Occasions. Jane P. Huber. 1996. pap. text ed. 11.00 (*0-664-25648-1*) Westminster John Knox.

Singing in English: A Manual of English Diction for Singers & Choral Directors. Richard Cox. (Monograph Ser.: No. 5). 109p. 1988. 10.00 (*0-614-05592-X*) Am Choral Dirs.

Singing in English: A Manual of English Diction for Singers & Choral Directors. Richard Cox. (Monographs: No. 5). 109p. (C). 1990. pap. 10.00 (*1-882648-04-8*) Am Choral Dirs.

Singing in French: A Manual of French Diction & French Vocal Repertoire. Thomas Grubb. LC 77-18473. 221p. 1979. 19.00 (*0-02-870790-7*) Schirmer Bks.

Singing in Latin. Harold Copeman. (C). 1988. 65.00 (*0-9515798-2-7*, Pub. by H Copeman UK) St Mut.

Singing in My Chains: Violet Formalist Verse. Carol J. Rose. 148p. 1996. 29.00 (*1-878490-66-4*); lib. bdg. 39.00 (*1-878490-67-2*) Rosehips Ink.

Singing in the African American Tradition, 6 cassettes, Set. 35p. 1989. pap. 59.95 incl. audio (*0-614-01595-2*, S11150) Audio-Forum.

***Singing in the Comeback Choir.** Bebe M. Campbell. 320p. 1998. 24.95 (*0-399-14298-3*) Putnam Pub Group.

Singing in the Fire. Faith Cook. 193p. (Orig.). 1995. pap. 9.99 (*0-85151-684-X*) Banner of Truth.

Singing in the Season. Jane Frazee. 20p. 1983. pap. 4.00 (*0-918812-24-0*, SE 0882) MMB Music.

Singing in the Spirit: African-American Sacred Quartets in New York City. Ray Allen. LC 91-16943. (Publications of the American Folklore Society, Bibliographical & Special Ser.). (Illus.). 296p. (Orig.). (C). 1991. text ed. 38.95 (*0-8122-3050-7*); pap. text ed. 16.95 (*0-8122-1331-9*) U of Pa Pr.

Singing Keys Omnibus. 64p. (Orig.). (J). (gr. 6-12). 1946. pap. text ed. 9.95 (*0-87487-651-6*) Summy-Birchard.

Singing Knives. Frank Stanford. LC 78-17914. (Lost Roads Poetry Ser.: No. 18). 1979. pap. 25.00 (*0-918786-19-3*) Lost Roads.

Singing Lead. large type ed. Norman A. Lazenby. (Linford Western Library). 240p. 1989. pap. 15.99 (*0-7089-6678-0*, Linford) Ulverscroft.

Singing Like a Cricket, Hooting Like an Owl: Selected Poems by Yi Kyu-bo. Ch'on Sang Pyong. (Cornell East Asia Ser.: No. 77). 106p. (Orig.). (C). 1995. 18.00 (*1-885445-68-7*, 77) Cornell East Asia Pgm.

Singing Like a Cricket, Hooting Like an Owl: Selected Poems by Yi Kyu-bo. Kry-bo Yi & Kevin D. O'Rourke. (Cornell East Asia Ser.: No. 78). 106p. (Orig.). (C). 1995. pap. 12.00 (*1-885445-78-4*, 78) Cornell East Asia Pgm.

Singing Man: Adapted from a West African Folktale. Terea D. Shaffer. LC 93-4219. (Illus.). 32p. (J). (ps-3). 1994. lib. bdg. 15.95 (*0-8234-1103-6*) Holiday.

Singing Man: Adapted from a West African Folktale. Terea D. Shaffer. (Illus.). 32p. (J). (ps-3). 1995. pap. 6.95 (*0-8234-1208-3*) Holiday.

***Singing-Masters.** John O'Meara. 1996. 24.95 (*0-946640-68-8*, Pub. by Lilliput Pr Ltd IE) Irish Bks Media.

Singing Mountain. Levitin. (J). 1998. 16.00 (*0-689-80809-7*) S&S Childrens.

Singing Mouse Stories. Emerson Hough. 1976. lib. bdg. 12.50 (*0-89968-047-X*, Lghtyr Pr) Buccaneer Bks.

Singing Nightingale. large type ed. Marjorie Warby. 1977. 25.99 (*0-7089-0078-X*) Ulverscroft.

***Singing of Birth & Death: Texts in Performance.** Stuart H. Blackburn. LC 87-30137. 299p. 1988. reprint ed. pap. 85.30 (*0-608-03631-5*, 2064458) Bks Demand.

Singing of Mount Abora: Coleridge's Use of Biblical Imagery & Natural Symbolism in Poetry & Philosophy. H. W. Piper. LC 86-45480. 128p. 1987. 28.50 (*0-8386-3295-5*) Fairleigh Dickinson.

Singing of the Real World: The Philosophy of Virginia Woolf's Fiction. Mark Hussey. LC 86-12763. 185p. 1986. 47.50 (*0-8142-0414-7*) Ohio St U Pr.

Singing of the Source: Nature & God in the Poetry of the Chinese Painter Wu Li. Jonathan Chaves. LC 93-3878. (SHAPS Library of Translations). (Illus.). 288p. (C). 1992. text ed. 42.00 (*0-8248-1485-1*) UH Pr.

Singing on the Throne: And Other Tales of a Country Vet in the South. 2nd ed. Clifton C. McLean. Ed. by MaryBelle Campbell. (Illus.). 160p. 1994. per., pap. 16.95 (*1-879009-16-1*) S P-Persephone Pr.

Singing Performer. James Kenney. 256p. (C). 1987. spiral bd. write for info. (*0-697-00826-6*) Brown & Benchmark.

Singing Professionally: Studying Singing for Actors & Singers. Arabella H. Young. LC 95-17856. 129p. 1995. pap. 17.95 (*0-435-08677-4*, 08677) Heinemann.

Singing Psalms of Joy & Praise. Fred R. Anderson. LC 86-1550. 78p. (Orig.). 1986. pap. 30.00 (*0-664-24696-6*, Westminster) Westminster John Knox.

***Singing Rails: Railroadin' Songs, Jokes & Stories.** Wayne Erbsen. (Illus.). 64p. (Orig.). 1997. pap. 4.95 (*1-883206-26-X*, NGB-900) Native Ground.

***Singing River Traditions.** 256p. 1996. 14.95 (*0-9653139-0-5*) Jr Aux Pascagoula-Moss.

Singing Road: Medium-High Voice, 3 vols., Vol. 1. Arthur E. Ward. 95p. 1939. pap. 12.95 (*0-8258-0218-0*, 02794) Fischer Inc NY.

Singing Sack. Illus. by Mary Currie. 80p. (J). (gr. 2 up). 16.95 (*0-7136-3115-5*, Pub. by A&C Black UK) Talman.

Singing Sam. Clyde R. Bulla. LC 88-19758. (Step into Reading Bks.). (Illus.). 48p. (Orig.). (J). (gr. 1-3). 1989. pap. 3.99 (*0-394-81977-2*); lib. bdg. 11.99 (*0-394-91977-7*) Random Bks Yng Read.

Singing Sands. Josephine Tey. 222p. 1988. pap. 6.00 (*0-02-008825-6*, Collier S&S) S&S Trade.

Singing Sands. Josephine Tey. LC 96-43937. 1996. pap. 9.00 (*0-684-81892-2*) S&S Trade.

Singing Shark. Rane Arroyo. 88p. (Orig.). 1996. pap. 9.00 (*0-927534-61-4*) Biling Rev-Pr.

Singing Shepherd & Other Poems. Annie Fields. (Notable American Authors Ser.). 1992. reprint ed. lib. bdg. 75.00 (*0-7812-2821-2*) Rprt Serv.

***Singing Sky.** large type ed. Margaret Creal. pap. 18.95 (*1-55050-091-0*, Pub. by Coteau CN) Genl Dist Srvs.

Singing Snails: Na Pupu-Kani-Oe. Harvey Hess. 20p. 1992. pap. 3.00 (*0-931909-08-2*) Malama Arts.

Singing Snake. Stefan Czernecki & Timothy Rhodes. LC 92-85515. (Illus.). 40p. (J). (ps-2). 1993. 14.95 (*1-56282-399-X*); lib. bdg. 14.89 (*1-56282-400-7*) Hyprn Child.

Singing Snake. Stefan Czernecki & Timothy Rhodes. LC 92-85515. (Illus.). 40p. (J). (ps-2). 1995. pap. 4.95 (*0-7868-1036-X*) Hyprn Child.

***Singing Snake.** large type ed. Stefan Czernecki & Timothy Rhodes. (Illus.). 40p. (J). (ps-2). 1993. 14.95 (*0-920534-97-X*, Pub. by Hyperion Pr Ltd CN) Sterling.

Singing Softly - Cantando Bajito. Carmen De Monteflores. LC 89-4125. 197p. (Orig.). (ENG & SPA.). 1989. pap. 8.95 (*0-933216-62-9*); lib. bdg. 18.95 (*0-933216-65-3*) Aunt Lute Bks.

Singing Soldiers: A History of the Civil War in Song. Paul Glass & Louis Singer. LC 75-14127. (Quality Paperbacks Ser.). Orig. Title: The Spirit of the Sixties. (Illus.). xx, 300p. 1975. reprint ed. pap. 14.95 (*0-306-80021-7*) Da Capo.

Singing Something: Anna J. Cooper & the Foundations of Womanist Theology. Karen Baker-Fletcher. 160p. 1994. 19.95 (*0-8245-1399-1*) Crossroad NY.

Singing Songs. Meg Tilly. 1995. pap. 9.95 (*0-452-27165-7*, Plume) NAL-Dutton.

Singing Spirit: Early Short Stories by North American Indians. Ed. by Bernd C. Peyer. LC 89-32419. (Sun Tracks Ser.). 175p. 1991. reprint ed. pap. 11.95 (*0-8165-1220-5*) U of Ariz Pr.

Singing Stones. Phyllis A. Whitney. 1991. mass mkt. 5.95 (*0-449-21897-X*, Crest) Fawcett.

Singing Stones. large type ed. Phyllis A. Whitney. LC 93-13154. 338p. 1993. pap. 19.95 (*0-8161-5772-3*) Thorndike Pr.

Singing Swan: An Account of Anna Seward & Her Acquaintance with Doctor Johnson, Boswell & Others of Their Time. Margaret E. Ashmun. LC 68-57589. (Illus.). 1969. reprint ed. text ed. 65.00 (*0-8371-0287-1*, ASSS, Greenwood Pr) Greenwood.

Singing Sword. Jack Whyte. LC 96-19966. 352p. 1996. 23.95 (*0-312-85292-4*) St Martin.

***Singing Sword.** Jack Whyte. (Camulod Chronicles Ser.: No. 2). 1997. mass mkt. 6.99 (*0-8125-5139-7*) Tor Bks.

Singing Teacher. Susan Skramstad. 272p. 1992. 17.95 (*0-945575-69-6*) Algonquin Bks.

Singing Teachers Wear Many Hats. Gordon Myers. (Illus.). 86p. (Orig.). (C). 1992. pap. 8.00 (*1-878617-02-8*) Leyerle Pubns.

Singing the Chaos: Madness & Wisdom in Modern Poetry. William Pratt. 360p. (C). 1996. text ed. 44.95 (*0-8262-1048-1*) U of Mo Pr.

Singing the French Revolution: Popular Culture & Politics, 1787-1799. Laura Mason. LC 96-17694. 280p. 1996. 37.50 (*0-8014-3233-2*) Cornell U Pr.

Singing the Glory Down: Amateur Gospel Music in South Central Kentucky, 1900-1991. William L. Montell. LC 91-8688. (Illus.). 264p. 1991. text ed. 27.00 (*0-8131-1757-7*) U Pr of Ky.

Singing the Land, Signing the Land. Helen Watson & David W. Chambers. 72p. 1989. 75.00 (*0-614-04022-1*, HUS204, Pub. by Deakin Univ AT) St Mut.

Singing the Land, Signing the Land. Helen Watson et al. 72p. (C). 1995. pap. 50.00 (*0-7300-0696-4*, Pub. by Deakin Univ AT) St Mut.

Singing the Lord's Song in a Strange Land: The African-American Churches & Ecumenism. William D. Watley. 54p. 1993. 29.95 (*0-86543-391-7*); pap. 9.95 (*0-86543-392-5*) Africa World.

Singing the Master: The Emergence of African-American Culture in the Plantation South. Roger D. Abrahams. (Illus.). 344p. 1994. reprint ed. pap. 12.95 (*0-14-017919-4*, Penguin Bks) Viking Penguin.

***Singing the Meaning.** Harold Copeman. 200p. 1996. pap. 39.95 (*0-9515798-6-X*, Pub. by H Copeman UK) St Mut.

Singing the Mozart Requiem. Ingrid Wendt. LC 87-5133. 1987. 14.95 (*0-932576-51-6*); pap. 7.95 (*0-932576-52-4*) Breitenbush Bks.

Singing the Psalms: How & Why. Michael Gilligan. 1990. 9.95 (*0-915866-15-3*) Am Cath Pr.

Singing the Sacrament. 1987. 25.00 (*0-947988-16-5*, Pub. by Wild Goose Pubns UK) St Mut.

Singing the Soul Back Home: Shamanism in Daily Life. Caitlin Matthews. 268p. 1995. pap. 14.95 (*1-85230-616-5*) Element MA.

Singing the Stories of the West: Western Songs. Ernie Sites. (Illus.). 40p. (Orig.). (J). (gr. 1-12). 1996. pap. 14.95 incl. audio (*1-57424-027-7*) Centerstream Pub.

Singing the Vietnam Blues: Songs of the Air Force in Southeast Asia. Joseph F. Tuso. LC 89-20529. (Military History Ser.: No. 19). (Illus.). 288p. 1990. 29.50 (*0-89096-383-5*); pap. 15.95 (*0-89096-455-6*) Tex A&M Univ Pr.

Singing Through the Clouds, Pt. 3. Samuel Lewin. Tr. by Joseph Leftwich. LC 85-22377. (Trilogy Ser.). 160p. 1988. 12.95 (*0-8453-4805-1*, Cornwall Bks) Assoc Univ Prs.

Singing to Cuba. Margarita M. Engle. LC 93-13446. 192p. (Orig.). (C). 1993. pap. 9.50 (*1-55885-070-8*) Arte Publico.

Singing to God. Michael Perry. 312p. (Orig.). 1995. pap. 16.95 (*0-916642-59-3*, 1207) Hope Pub.

Singing Tradition of Child's Popular Ballads. Ed. by Bertrand H. Bronson. LC 75-2980. 576p. reprint ed. pap. 164.20 (*0-7837-4324-6*, 2044028) Bks Demand.

***Singing Tradition of Lapp Shamans.** Gyorgy Szomjas-Schiffert. 248p. 1995. 29.00 (*963-05-6940-X*, Pub. by A K HU) Intl Spec Bk.

Singing Tree. Kate Seredy. (J). (gr. 4 up). 1990. pap. 5.99 (*0-14-034543-4*, Puffin) Puffin Bks.

Singing Tree. Kate Seredy. (J). (gr. 4 up). 1992. 18.75 (*0-8446-6588-6*) Peter Smith.

Singing Tree. Anne Weale. 1993. pap. 2.89 (*0-373-03257-9*, 1-03257-2) Harlequin Bks.

Singing Tree. large type ed. Anne Weale. 1992. reprint ed. lib. bdg. 18.95 (*0-263-13136-X*, Pub. by Mills & Boon UK) Thorndike Pr.

Singing Triangle. 55p. 1988. write for info. (*0-318-62776-0*) BMC Pubns.

Singing U. S. A. Hyman. 1992. audio 40.95 (*0-8384-2981-5*) Heinle & Heinle.

Singing U. S. A. Hyman. 1992. teacher ed., pap. 10.95 (*0-8384-2980-7*) Heinle & Heinle.

Singing Underwater. Susan Wicks. 96p. (Orig.). 1992. pap. 8.95 (*0-571-16724-1*) Faber & Faber.

Singing Water. large type ed. Catherine Hay. 320p. 1987. 25.99 (*0-7089-1710-0*) Ulverscroft.

Singing Wheels & Circus Wagons. Gene Plowden. LC 75-21135. (Illus.). 1978. pap. 4.95 (*0-87004-256-4*) Caxton.

***Singing Wilderness.** Sigurd F. Olson. LC 97-13328. (Fesler-Lampert Minnesota Heritage Book Series). 1997. write for info. (*0-8166-2992-7*) U of Minn Pr.

Singing Wilderness. Sigurd F. Olson. (Illus.). 1956. 24.95 (*0-394-44560-0*) Knopf.

Singing Wind: Songs & Melodies from Ecuador. rev. ed. Elizabeth V. Brennan. (Illus.). 48p. (ENG & SPA.). 1996. pap. 11.50 incl. audio (*0-937203-60-2*); pap. 6.95 (*0-937203-61-0*) World Music Pr.

***Singing Winds.** large type ed. Elizabeth Gill. (Magna Large Print Ser.). 557p. 1997. 27.50 (*0-7505-1030-7*) Ulverscroft.

Singing with Coyote. Bruce Aufhammer. 96p. 1990. pap. 7.50 (*1-879025-02-7*) Christopher-Burghardt.

Singing with Sai Baba: The Politics of Revitalization in Trinidad. Morton Klass. 187p. (C). 1996. pap. text ed. 10.95 (*0-88133-901-6*) Waveland Pr.

Singing with the Owls. Michael McPherson. 58p. 1983. pap. 5.95 (*0-932136-05-2*) Petronium HI.

Singing with Whitman's Thrush: Itineraries of the Aesthetic. Frederic Will. LC 93-29913. 212p. 1993. text ed. 89.95 (*0-7734-3046-6*) E Mellen.

Singing with Young Children: Book & Cassette. Bonnie Phipps. (Illus.). 64p. (Orig.). 1991. pap. 17.95 incl. audio (*0-88284-492-X*, 3558) Alfred Pub.

Singing Words. Illus. by Masha. LC 79-38605. (Granger Index Reprint Ser.). 1977. reprint ed. 18.95 (*0-8369-6337-7*) Ayer.

Singing Yet: New & Selected Poems. Stan Rice. 1993. pap. 14.00 (*0-679-74733-8*) Knopf.

Singing Your Own Song: Using the Mind-Body Connection to Enhance Your Health. Susan D. Multer. LC 94-23113. (Illus.). 96p. (Orig.). 1995. pap. 7.95 (*0-942963-51-2*) Distinctive Pub.

Single . . . With Children. Connie Bennett. (Superromance Ser.). 1994. mass mkt. 3.50 (*0-373-70586-7*, 1-70586-2) Harlequin Bks.

Single Adult Journey. Bobbie Read. 1992. pap. 4.99 (*0-87162-616-0*, D7001) Warner Pr.

S

Single Adult Passages: Uncharted Territories. Carolyn A. Koons & Michael J. Anthony. LC 91-2162. (Illus.). 232p. (C). 1995. pap. 12.99 (0-8010-5219-X) Baker Bks.

Single African-American-Christian Vol. 2: Keeping a Clean Life in a Dirty World. Eddie B. Lane. 112p. 1995. text ed. 12.95 (0-9647767-0-7, Blck Fam Pr) Inst Black Fam.

Single Again: Dating & Meeting New Friends the Second Time Around. George Blake. 1995. pap. 11.95 (1-56875-098-6) R & E Pubs.

Single Again: Enjoy Life with or Without a Partner. Mildred H. Witkin. 1994. pap. 12.95 (1-57101-001-7) MasterMedia Pub.

Single-Again Handbook. Thomas F. Jones. LC 93-2516. 1993. pap. 12.99 (0-8407-9190-9) Nelson.

Single & Feeling Good. Harold I. Smith. LC 87-1799. 160p. 1987. pap. 11.95 (0-687-38552-0) Abingdon.

Single Audit: Refinements Can Improve Usefulness. (Illus.). 72p. (Orig.). (C). 1995. pap. text ed. 20.00 (0-7881-2213-4) DIANE Pub.

Single Audits. 96th ed. Broadus. 1995. pap. text ed. write for info. (0-15-602179-X) HB Coll Pubs.

Single Audits of State & Local Governments. 1995. lib. bdg. 251.75 (0-8490-6745-6) Gordon Pr.

Single Bed Blues. Ellen Leroe. Ed. by Elisa B. Fitzgerald. LC 81-23307. 72p. 1981. pap. 5.95 (0-913024-12-0) Tandem Pr.

*__Single Black Female.__ Yvette Richards. 192p. 1996. pap. 9.95 (1-874509-10-7) LPC InBook.

Single Black Mother. Thelma Williams. (Illus.). 24p. (Orig.). 1988. pap. 4.00 (0-945768-00-1) A-Town Pub Co.

Single, but Not Alone. Glen S. Martin. 144p. (Orig.). 1993. pap. 8.95 (0-941005-94-1) Chrch Grwth VA.

Single, but Not Alone. Ellen Weber. LC 89-29552. 144p. (Orig.). 1990. pap. 6.99 (0-8054-5347-4, 4253-47) Broadman.

Single but Not Alone: Meditations for Christian Women. Jane Graver. LC 12-2815. 64p. 1983. pap. 3.99 (0-570-03880-4, 12-2815) Concordia.

Single, but Not Sorry. 2nd rev. ed. Joyce Parks. 235p. 1986. pap. 8.25 (0-89084-307-4, 003632) Bob Jones Univ Pr.

Single Camera Stereo Sound. J. Ratcliff & N. Papworth. (Illus.). 144p. 1992. 44.95 (0-240-51307-X, Focal) Buttrwrth-Heinemann.

Single-Camera Video: The Creative Challenge. Michael H. Adams. 384p. (C). 1992. boxed write for info. (0-697-09760-9) Brown & Benchmark.

Single-Camera Video: The Creative Challenge. Michael H. Adams. 384p. (C). 1994. per. write for info. (0-697-27934-0) Brown & Benchmark.

Single Camera Video Production. Robert B. Musburger. LC 92-13909. (Illus.). 208p. 1992. pap. 22.95 (0-240-80034-6, Focal) Buttrwrth-Heinemann.

Single Card Strategies. Philip Kramer et al. 200p. 1996. pap. 14.95 (1-55622-489-3) Wordware Pub.

Single Case Experimental Designs. 2nd ed. Barlow. (C). 1992. pap. text ed. 55.00 (0-205-14271-0, H4271) Allyn.

Single-Case Research Design & Analysis: New Directions for Psychology & Education. Ed. by Thomas R. Kratochwill & Joel Levin. 240p. 1992. text ed. 59.95 (0-8058-0515-X) L Erlbaum Assocs.

Single-Case Research Designs: Methods for Clinical & Applied Settings. Alan E. Kazdin. (Illus.). 384p. (C). 1982. pap. text ed. 29.95 (0-19-503021-4) OUP.

Single-Cell Mutation Monitoring Systems: Methodologies & Applications. Aftab A. Ansari. Ed. by Frederick J. De Serres. LC 84-3368. (Topics in Chemical Mutagenesis Ser.: Vol. 2). 308p. 79.50 (0-306-41537-2, Plenum Pr) Plenum.

Single Cell Protein. Irving D. Goldberg. (Biotechnology Monographs: Vol. 1). (Illus.). 260p. 1985. 125.95 (0-387-15308-X) Spr-Verlag.

Single Cell Protein--Safety for Animal & Human Feeding: Proceedings of the Protein-Calorie Advisory Group of the United Nations System Symposium, Milan, Italy, March-April 1977. Silvio Garattini et al. LC 78-40993. (Illus.). 220p. 1979. pap. 105.00 (0-08-023764-9, Pub. by Pergamon Repr UK) Franklin.

*__Single-Chain Silicates.__ Ed. by W. A. Deer et al. (Rock-Forming Minerals Ser.: No. 2A). (Illus.). 680p. 1997. 125.00 (1-897799-85-3, Pub. by Geol Soc Pub Hse UK) AAPG.

Single Chamber Processing: Proceedings of the Joint Session on Single Chamber Processing of the 1992 E-MRS Spring Meeting Conference, Strasbourg, France, June 2-5, 1992. Ed. by Yves I. Nissim & Avishay Katz. LC 92-42556. (European Materials Research Society Symposia Proceedings Ser.: Vol. 37). 1993. 162.50 (0-444-89915-4, North Holland) Elsevier.

Single-Channel Recording. 2nd ed. Ed. by Bert Sakmann & Erwin Neher. 660p. (C). 1995. 89.50 (0-306-44870-X, Plenum Pr) Plenum.

Single Charge Tunneling: Goulomb Blockade Phenomena in Nanostructures. Ed. by H. Grabert & M. H. Devoret. (NATO ASI, Series B: Physics: Vol. 294). (Illus.). 350p. (C). 1992. 95.00 (0-306-44229-9, Plenum Pr) Plenum.

Single-Child Family. Ed. by Toni Falbo. LC 83-1612. 304p. 1984. lib. bdg. 35.00 (0-89862-630-7) Guilford Pr.

Single-Chip Computer Cookbook, with 25 One-Evening. Edward V. Hiskes. (Illus.). 224p. 1989. 24.95 (0-8306-9135-9, 3135); pap. 16.95 (0-8306-3135-6, 3135) McGraw-Hill Prof.

Single Circles. Martha McKee. 132p. 1982. 8.95 (0-913428-42-6); pap. 5.95 (0-913428-43-4) Landfall Pr.

Single Combat. Dean Ing. 384p. (Orig.). 1993. mass mkt. 4.99 (0-8125-1164-6) Tor Bks.

Single-Component, Binary, & Ternary Oxide Glasses. Oleg V. Mazurin et al. LC 93-27810. (Handbook of Glass Data Ser., Pt. E, Physical Sciences Data Ser.: Vol. 15). 894p. 1993. 552.00 (0-444-81635-6) Elsevier.

Single Cook's Book: One Hundred & Six Unusual Recipes for One-Person Servings. Larry Luce. (Illus.). 1976. pap. 4.00 (0-686-16919-0) Other Bks.

Single Crystal Diffractometry. Ulrich W. Arndt & B. T. Willis. LC 66-13637. (Cambridge Monographs on Physics). 355p. reprint ed. pap. 101.20 (0-317-26117-7, 2024404) Bks Demand.

Single Cylinder Engine Tests: Caterpillar L38A Test Method - STP 509-A, Pt. 4. 46p. 1980. pap. 7.25 (0-8031-0575-4, 04-509040-12); ring bd. 7.25 (0-8031-0576-2, 04-509041-12) ASTM.

Single Cylinder Engine Tests, Pt. II: Caterpillar 1H2 Test Method, Vol. STP 509A. 94p. 1979. pap. 9.75 (0-8031-0571-1, 04-509020-12); ring bd. 12.75 (0-8031-0572-X, 04-509021-12) ASTM.

Single Dad. Jennifer Greene. (Desire Ser.). 1995. mass mkt. 3.25 (0-373-05931-0, 1-05931-0) Silhouette.

*__Single Dad.__ Jennifer Greene. 1997. 20.95 (0-373-59768-1) Thorndike Pr.

Single Dad see Magia Peligrosa

Single Door: Social Work with Families of Disabled Children. Caroline Glendinning. 240p. 1986. text ed. 49.95 (0-04-361060-9); pap. text ed. 17.95 (0-04-361061-7) Routledge Chapman & Hall.

Single-Dose Therapy of Urinary Tract Infections: Modern Trend in the Treatment of Lower Urinary Tract Infections. Ed. by A. Jardin & J. D. Williams. (Journal: European Urology: Vol. 13, Suppl. 1, 1987). (Illus.). iv, 136p. 1987. pap. 40.00 (3-8055-4559-2) S Karger.

Single Drop of Rain. Richard C. Sather. (Illus.). 20p. (Orig.). (C). 1988. pap. 8.00 (0-9621585-0-X) RCS Prodns.

Single-Electron Tunneling & Mesoscopic Devices. Ed. by H. Koch et al. (Electronics & Photonics Ser.: Vol. 31). (Illus.). 307p. 1992. 86.95 (0-387-55132-8) Spr-Verlag.

Single-Engine Sea, for Private & Commercial Pilots, Practical Test Standards: FAA-S-8081-SEA. Federal Aviation Administration, D. O. T. Staff. (Practical Test Standards Ser.). 102p. 1995. reprint ed. pap. 4.95 (1-56027-223-6, ASA-8081-SEA) Av Suppl & Acad.

*__Single-Entity Asset Real Estate.__ Robert M. Zinman et al. LC 96-51818. 1997. pap. write for info. (1-57073-390-2) Amer Bar Assn.

*__Single European Currency.__ Ed. by Jeffrey Gedmon. 50p. (Orig.). 1997. pap. 9.95 (0-8447-7097-3) Am Enterprise.

Single European Market. Jules Lonbay. 1995. pap. text ed. write for info. (0-406-60940-3, UK) MICHIE.

Single European Market: Prospects for Economic Integration. R. W. Vickerman. LC 92-28598. 1992. text ed. 55.00 (0-312-08771-3) St Martin.

Single European Market & Beyond: A Study of the Wider Implications of the Single European Act. Ed. by Dennis Swann. LC 91-33934. 272p. (C). 1992. pap. 24.95 (0-415-06161-X, A7139) Routledge.

Single European Market & Beyond: A Study of the Wider Implications of the Single European Act. Ed. by Dennis Swann. LC 91-33934. 336p. (C). (gr. 13). 1992. text ed. 79.95 (0-415-06160-1, A7108) Routledge.

Single European Market & Insurance Law & Practice. T. Henry Ellis. 500p. (C). 1994. 555.00 (1-85609-075-2, Pub. by Witherby & Co UK) St Mut.

Single European Market & the Third World, 1992. Ed. by S. Sideri & J. Sengupta. (EADI Book Ser.: No. 13). 224p. 1992. text ed. 35.00 (0-7146-3474-3, Pub. by F Cass Pubs UK) Intl Spec Bk.

*__Single Event Phenomena.__ G. Messenger & M. Ash. LC 96-34533. 250p. (C). (gr. 13 up). 1997. text ed. 59.95 (0-412-09731-1) Chapman & Hall.

Single Eye. Naomi Clark. (QRL Poetry Bks.: Vol. XXXI). 1992. 20.00 (0-614-06450-3) Quarterly Rev.

*__Single Eye of Light: Sacred Visions (Poems & Letters)__ Ronne R. Gleason. LC 97-92974. (Illus.). 180p. (Orig.). 1997. pap. 9.95 (1-57502-420-9, PO1287) Morris Pubng.

Single-Family Selective Rehabilitation. Enterprise Foundation Staff & Rehab Work Group Staff. (Housing Production Manual Ser.). 256p. 1991. text ed. 65.00 (0-442-00815-5) Chapman & Hall.

Single Family Selective Rehabilitation. Robert M. Santucci. Ed. by Jude Cashman & Peter Werwath. (Housing Production Manuals Ser.). 1990. student ed. 45.00 (0-942901-02-9) Enterprise Foundation.

Single Father. Celeste Hamilton. (Special Edition Ser.: No. 738). 1992. mass mkt. 3.39 (0-373-09738-7, 5-09738-1) Harlequin Bks.

Single Fatherhood: The Complete Guide. Chuck Gregg. 212p. (Orig.). 1995. pap. 11.99 (0-945819-57-9) Sulzburger & Graham Pub.

Single Female (Reluctantly) Seeks... Dixie Browning. 1995. mass mkt. 3.50 (0-373-52007-7, 1-52007-1) Silhouette.

Single Fiber Electromyography: Studies in Healthy & Diseased Muscle. 2nd ed. Erik Stalberg & Joze V. Trontelj. LC 94-5646. 304p. 1994. text ed. 79.00 (0-7817-0212-7) Lppncott-Raven.

Single Figure Golfer: How to Get Your Handicap Really Low - & Keep It There. Peter Smith. (Illus.). 128p. 1996. pap. 22.95 (1-85223-913-1, Pub. by Crowood Pr UK) Trafalgar.

Single File. Susan Deitz. 1990. mass mkt. 4.95 (0-312-92425-9) St Martin.

*__Single Flank Testing & Structure-Born Noise Analysis.__ H. J. Stadtfeld. (1993 Fall Technical Meeting). 1993. pap. text ed. 30.00 (1-55589-620-0) AGMA.

Single Frequency Semiconductor Lasers. Jens Buus. 112p. 1991. pap. 20.00 (0-8194-0535-3, TT05) SPIE.

Single Girls! Nice Guys Do Answer Personal Ads: How to Find Excitement, New Friends Maybe Even Love & Marriage - Through the Personal Ads. Sara David. LC 88-70572. 128p. (Orig.). 1989. pap. 8.95 (0-929034-00-7) Palmtree Pr.

Single Gospel. A. Theodore Farabee, Jr. 258p. (Orig.). 1992. pap. text ed. 7.00 (0-9620426-1-7) A T Farabee Pub Co.

Single Grandmother. Tracy E. Hyde. LC 73-88510. 250p. 1974. 27.95 (0-88229-128-9) Nelson-Hall.

Single Handed: Devices & Aids for One Handers & Sources of These Devices. Ed. by Betty Garee. 30p. pap. 3.50 (0-915708-06-X, 1480) Cheever Pub.

Single-Handed Sailing. Frank Mulville. (Illus.). 192p. (Orig.). 1990. pap. 17.50 (0-85036-410-8) Sheridan.

Single Hound. Emily Dickinson. (Notable American Authors Ser.). 1992. reprint ed. lib. bdg. 75.00 (0-7812-2632-5) Rprt Serv.

Single Hound: A Novel. May Sarton. 1991. pap. 8.95 (0-393-30785-9) Norton.

Single Image, Vol. 21. 1996. 19.00 (1-887528-12-1) Scott & Daughters.

*__Single Image, Vol. 22.__ 1997. 19.00 (1-887528-23-7) Scott & Daughters.

*__Single Image, Vol. 23.__ 1997. 19.00 (1-887528-24-5) Scott & Daughters.

*__Single Image, Vol. 24.__ 1997. 19.00 (1-887528-25-3) Scott & Daughters.

Single in a Married World: A Life Cycle Framework for Working with the Unmarried Adult. Natalie Schwartzberg et al. 304p. 1995. 34.00 (0-393-70205-7) Norton.

*__Single in a Relationship World... The Search for Clean Clothes.__ C. Lynn Warren. 156p. (Orig.). 1997. pap. 9.95 (0-9658013-5-7) Window View.

Single in New York. Michael Bergman & Victoria Sandvik. 240p. (Orig.). 1992. pap. 10.95 (1-55850-172-X) Adams Media.

Single in Seattle. Carolyn Zane. (Yours Truly Ser.). 1996. mass mkt. 3.50 (0-373-52021-2, 1-52021-2) Silhouette.

Single in the Church: New Ways to Minister with 52 Percent of God's People. Kay Collier-Slone. LC 92-72459. (Orig.). 1992. pap. 15.95 (1-56699-058-0, AL137) Alban Inst.

Single Ingredient Formulas for Profit. 1992. lib. bdg. 85.95 (0-8490-5501-6) Gordon Pr.

Single Issues. J. A. Fishman. (International Journal of the Sociology of Language Ser.: No. 22). 1979. 60.00 (90-279-7938-3) Mouton.

Single Lady's Guide to Bar Games. Judith A. Ray. 65p. (Orig.). 1989. pap. 4.00 (0-9622689-0-9) J A Ray.

Single-Layer Wire Routing & Compaction: Foundations of Computing. F. Miller Maley. 424p. 1989. 45.00 (0-262-13250-8) MIT Pr.

Single Level Home Plans. 5th ed. LC 95-81707. (Illus.). 256p. 1996. pap. 6.95 (0-938708-66-X) L F Garlinghouse Co.

Single Living. Jack Daly. 100p. 1991. write for info. (0-9631420-0-3) Seacoast.

Single Loop Control Methods: Art Books of Horses/ Illustrated for Children, No. 1. Kevin D. Starr & Jeanie Innis. (Illus.). 109p. (Orig.). (J). (gr. k-12). 1996. pap. text ed. 49.00 (1-882811-08-9) Skyline Pubns.

*__Single Malt Scotch.__ Roderick Martine. LC 97-7238. 1997. write for info. (1-56799-440-7, Friedman-Fairfax) M Friedman Pub Grp Inc.

*__Single Malt Whiskey Companion: A Connoisseur's Guide.__ Helen Arthur. LC 97-3201. 1997. write for info. (0-02-861780-0) Macmillan.

Single-Malt Whiskies of Scotland: For the Discriminating Imbiber. James F. Harris & Mark H. Waymack. LC 92-21777. 212p. 1992. pap. 16.95 (0-8126-9213-6) Open Court.

Single Man. Christopher Isherwood. (Michael di Capua Bks.). 186p. 1987. pap. 11.00 (0-374-52038-0) FS&G.

Single Market & the Law of Banking. 2nd ed. Ross Cranston. 350p. 1995. 110.00 (1-85044-552-4) LLP.

*__Single Market & Tomorrow's Europe.__ European Commission. 162p. 1996. pap. 19.00 (92-827-8701-X, C101-96-010-ENC, Pub. by Europ Com UK) Bernan Associates.

*__Single Market & Tomorrow's Europe: The Monti Report.__ Mario Monti. 1996. pap. text ed. 19.95 (0-7494-2266-1) Kogan Page Ltd.

Single Market Europe: Opportunities & Challenges for Business. Makridakis, Spyros G., & Associates. LC 90-24419. (Management Ser.). 215p. 38.95 (1-55542-343-4) Jossey-Bass.

Single Market Handbook, 1993. 1991. 450.00 (0-8103-9999-7, 100667, Pub. by Euromonitor Pubns UK) Gale.

Single Market Programme As Stimulus to Change: Britain & Germany. David G. Mayes & Peter Hart. (National Institute of Economic & Social Research Occasional Papers: No. 47). (Illus.). 250p. (C). 1994. text ed. 59.95 (0-521-47156-7) Cambridge U Pr.

Single Market to Social Europe. Mark Wise. 1993. pap. 43.95 (0-582-06088-5, Pub. by Longman UK) Longman.

Single Married Separated & Life after Divorce. Myles E. Munroe. 128p. (Orig.). 1992. pap. 7.99 (1-56043-094-X) Destiny Image.

Single Married Separated Workbook. Myles E. Munroe. 48p. (Orig.). 1993. student ed., wbk. ed., pap. 5.95 (1-56043-115-6) Destiny Image.

Single Military Parent: Military Edition. Carol B. Richardson. (Family Forum Library). 16p. 1994. 1.95 (1-56688-166-8) Bur For At-Risk.

Single-Mode Fiber Optics: Principles & Applications. 2nd exp. rev. ed. Luc B. Jeunhomme. (Optical Engineering Ser.: Vol. 23). 360p. 1989. 140.00 (0-8247-8170-8) Dekker.

Single-Mode Fibers. E. G. Neumann. (Optical Sciences Ser.: Vol. 57). (Illus.). 560p. 1988. 123.95 (0-387-18745-6) Spr-Verlag.

Single-Mode Optical Fiber Measurement: Characterization & Sensing. Giovanni Cancellieri. LC 92-32247. (Optoelectronics Library). 350p. (C). 1993. text ed. write for info. (0-89006-602-7) Artech Hse.

Single-Mode Optical Fiber Measurement: Characterization & Sensing. Ed. by Giovanni Cancellieri. LC 92-32247. (Artech House Optoelectronics Library). (Illus.). 348p. 1993. reprint ed. pap. 99.20 (0-608-00568-1, 2061451) Bks Demand.

Single Mother. Jean A. Donathan. (Special Edition Ser.). 1993. mass mkt. 3.50 (0-373-09858-8, 5-09858-7) Silhouette.

Single Mothers. Dee Gregory. 1993. pap. 8.95 (0-8306-2130-X, TAB-Human Servs Inst) TAB Bks.

Single Mothers & Their Children: A New American Dilemma. Irwin Garfinkel & Sara S. McLanahan. (Illus.). 218p. (Orig.). 1986. pap. text ed. 14.95 (0-87766-404-8); lib. bdg. 27.50 (0-87766-405-6) Urban Inst.

Single Mothers & Their Children: Disposal, Punishment & Survival in Australia. Shurlee Swain & Renate Howe. (Studies in Australian History: No. 20). (Illus.). 288p. (C). 1996. text ed. 59.95 (0-521-47443-4) Cambridge U Pr.

Single Mother's Book: A Practical Guide to Managing Your Children, Career, Home, Finances & Everything Else. Joan Anderson. 352p. 1990. pap. 13.95 (0-934601-84-4) Peachtree Pubs.

Single Mothers by Choice: A Guidebook for Single Women Who Are Considering or Have Chosen. Jane Mattes. 1994. pap. 15.00 (0-8129-2246-8, Times Bks) Random.

Single Mother's Companion: Essays & Stories by Women. Ed. by Marsha R. Leslie. LC 94-10613. 288p. (Orig.). 1994. pap. 12.95 (1-878067-56-5) Seal Pr WA.

*__Single Mothers in International Context: Mothers or Workers?__ Ed. by Simon Duncan & Rosalind Edwards. LC 97-3476. (Gender & Society Ser.). 176p. 1997. 69.95 (0-7484-0363-9, Pub. by Tay Francis Ltd UK); pap. 22.95 (0-7484-0364-7, Pub. by Tay Francis Ltd UK) Taylor & Francis.

Single Mother's Survival Manual. Barbara Duncan. LC 83-62294. 180p. (C). 1984. spiral bd. 15.95 (0-88247-707-2) R & E Pubs.

*__Single Mystique.__ Melissa Roth. Date not set. write for info. (0-688-15801-3) Morrow.

Single Neuron Computation. Ed. by Thomas McKenna et al. (Neural Networks: Foundations to Applications Ser.). (Illus.). 644p. 1992. text ed. 67.00 (0-12-484815-X) Acad Pr.

*__Single Older Women in the Workforce: By Necessity, or Choice?__ rev. ed. Jennifer K. Coplon. LC 97-9289. (Studies in the History of American Labor). (Illus.). 178p. 1997. text ed. 50.00 (0-8153-2837-0) Garland.

Single Operatic Arias & Overtures. Ed. by Ernest Warburton. LC 83-48727. (Johann Christian Bach, 1735-1782 The Collected Works: Vol. 12). 520p. 1993. text ed. 195.00 (0-8240-6061-X) Garland.

Single or Joint Venturing? A Comprehensive Approach to Foreign Entry Mode Choice. John Bell. 191p. 1996. 55.95 (1-85972-383-7, Pub. by Avebury Pub UK) Ashgate Pub Co.

Single Out. Ruth Weiss. LC 78-73007. (Illus.). 1978. pap. 7.00 (0-933022-01-8) DAurora Pr.

Single Out. deluxe limited ed. Ruth Weiss. LC 78-73007. (Illus.). 1978. 25.00 (0-685-90846-1) DAurora Pr.

Single Parent. Ruth Bowdoin. (Bowdoin Method II Ser.). (Illus.). 24p. (Orig.). 1991. pap. write for info. (1-55997-107-X) Websters Intl.

Single Parent. Coleen Hume. 32p. 1987. pap. 50.00 (0-85937-145-X, Pub. by K Mason Pubns Ltd UK) St Mut.

Single-Parent Families. LC 96-33555. (At Issue Ser.). (J). (gr. 5-12). 1996. pap. 8.96 (1-56510-543-5) Greenhaven.

Single-Parent Families. LC 96-33555. (At Issue Ser.). (J). (gr. 5-12). 1996. lib. bdg. 14.96 (1-56510-544-3) Greenhaven.

Single Parent Families. Kris Kissman & Jo A. Allen. (Sourcebooks for the Human Services Ser.: Vol. 24). (Illus.). 144p. (C). 1993. text ed. 52.00 (0-8039-4322-9); pap. text ed. 24.95 (0-8039-4323-7) Sage.

Single-Parent Families. Richard Worth. LC 92-14230. (Illus.). 128p. (YA). (gr. 9-12). 1992. lib. bdg. 22.70 (0-531-11131-8) Watts.

Single-Parent Families: A Challenge to the Jewish Community. Chaim I. Waxman. 24p. 1980. pap. 1.00 (0-87495-020-1) Am Jewish Comm.

Single Parent Families: Diversity, Myths & Realities. Ed. by Shirley M. Hanson et al. LC 94-14154. (Illus.). 527p. 1994. 79.95 (1-56024-688-X) Haworth Pr.

Single-Parent Families at Camp: The Essence of an Experience. Bernard Reisman & Gladys Rosen. LC 84-70480. 54p. 1984. pap. 2.50 (0-87495-061-9) Am Jewish Comm.

Single Parent Family. Thomas D. Yawkey & Georgianna M. Cornelius. LC 89-51911. 200p. 1990. pap. 24.95 (0-87762-542-5) Technomic.

*__Single Parent Family Book.__ 200p. 1997. write for info. (0-7814-0269-7, Victor Bks) Chariot Victor.

Single Parent Journey. Bobbie Read. 1992. pap. 4.99 (0-87162-614-4, D7000) Warner Pr.

Single Parenting. Robert G. Barnes. 294p. 1992. mass mkt. 5.99 (0-8423-5920-6) Tyndale.

Single Parenting. Waln K. Brown. 20p. 1989. 2.95 (1-56456-015-5, 209) W Gladden Found.

Single Parenting. Tony Evans. (Tony Evans Speaks Out on. ..Ser.). 1995. pap. 4.99 (0-8024-2563-1) Moody.

Single Parenting: How & Where to Find Facts & Get Help. Robert D. Reed & Danek S. Kaus. Ed. by Diane Parker. LC 92-53756. (Abuse Ser.). 48p. 1993. pap. 4.50 (0-88247-945-8) R & E Pubs.

An Asterisk (*) at the beginning of an entry indicates that the title is appearing in BIP for the first time.

Single Parenting: The Golden Rules for Raising Children Alone. Ed. by Sarah Pirch. (Life's Golden Rules Ser.). 160p. 1994. 5.99 (*1-881649-18-0*) Genl Pub Grp.

Single Parent's Almanac: Real World Answers to Your Everyday Questions. Linda Foust. 314p. 1996. pap. 16.95 (*0-7615-0329-3*) Prima Pub.

Single Parents by Choice: A Growing Trend in Family Life. N. Miller. (Illus.). 238p. (C). 1992. 24.95 (*0-306-44321-X*, Plenum Insight) Plenum.

Single Parents in Black America: A Study in Culture & Legitimacy. Annie S. Barnes. LC 87-51006. 175p. (C). 1987. text ed. 39.95 (*1-55605-023-2*); pap. text ed. 19.95 (*1-55605-024-0*) Wyndham Hall.

Single Parent's Money Guide: Thriving On. Emily W. Card. 208p. 1996. 14.95 (*0-02-861119-5*) Macmillan.

Single Particle Detection & Measurement. R. S. Gilmore. 266p. 1992. 79.00 (*0-85066-755-0*, Pub. by Tay Francis Ltd UK) Taylor & Francis.

Single Pebble. John R. Hersey. 1956. 19.95 (*0-394-44562-7*) Knopf.

Single Pebble. John R. Hersey. 1989. pap. 12.00 (*0-394-75697-5*, Vin) Random.

Single-Period Stationarity in Open Systems of Regions. Gene E. Smith. (Discussion Paper Ser.: No. 71). 1974. pap. 10.00 (*1-55869-112-X*) Regional Sci Res Inst.

Single-Phase to Three-Phase Electric Power Converters: A Concise Application Guide. William A. Moncreif & National Rural Electric Cooperative Association Staff. LC 96-8666. 1996. write for info. (*0-917599-18-7*) Natl Rural.

SPECT Imaging in Clinical Medicine. Hircsh Handmaker & Stephen R. Bunker. (Illus.). 350p. 1996. 195.00 (*0-7506-9533-1*) Buttrwrth-Heinemann.

Single-Photon Ultrashort-Lived Radionuclides: Proceedings. DOE Technical Information Center Staff. Ed. by Peter Paras & J. W. Thiessen. LC 84-26051. (Symposium Ser.). 362p. 1985. pap. 17.00 (*0-87079-520-1*, CONF-830504, DE83017017); fiche 9.00 (*0-87079-521-X*, CONF-830504, DE83017017) DOE.

Single Ply Roofing - Advantages & Concerns RICS Occasional Paper. C. R. Davies. (C). 1989. text ed. 45.00 (*0-685-40839-6*, Pub. by Surveyors Pubns) St Mut.

Single-Point Access to Full Life Cycle Information - The Station Basis Navigator. William C. Cleff & John S. Brtis. (ICONE 4 - Technical Papers). 1996. write for info. (*0-614-16703-5*, 96-NE-2) ASME.

Single Point Mooring Maintenance & Operations Guide. OCIMF Staff. (C). 1985. 200.00 (*0-900886-95-1*, Pub. by Witherby & Co UK) St Mut.

Single Point Mooring Maintenance & Operations Guide. OCIMF Staff. 1993. 80.00 (*1-85609-072-8*, Pub. by Witherby & Co UK) St Mut.

Single Point Moorings of the World. Oilfield Publications Limited Staff. (Illus.). 300p. 1994. pap. 285.00 (*1-870945-48-4*, Pub. by Oilfld Pubns Ltd UK) Am Educ Systs.

Single Point Moorings of the World. 4th ed. Oilfield Publications Limited Staff. (Illus.). 300p. 1994. pap. 285.00 (*1-870945-83-2*, Pub. by Oilfld Pubns Ltd UK) Am Educ Systs.

Single Point Moorings of the World: The World's Only Complete Reference to Every SPM, CALM, SALM, SAL, ALP & Turret Type Installation. Oilfield Publications Limited Staff. 300p. (C). 1993. 580.00 (*1-870945-30-1*, Pub. by Oilfield Pubns UK) St Mut.

Single Point Morning: Maintenance & Operations Guide. OCIMF Staff. 1985. 162.00 (*0-317-61479-7*, Pub. by Witherby & Co UK) St Mut.

Single Pregnancy - Single Parenting: Creating a Positive, Fulfilling Experience. Keri Bowers. (Illus.). 310p. (Orig.). 1996. pap. 12.95 (*0-9652441-0-5*) Park Alxndr.

Single Principles: The Single Woman's 10 Step Guide to Power. Sheron C. Patterson. 111p. (Orig.). 1993. pap. 12.95 (*0-9638853-0-8*) Persever Pr.

***Single Purpose.** Norman H. Wright. LC 97-14143. 1997. 15.99 (*0-8307-1924-5*); pap. write for info. (*0-8307-1932-6*) Regal.

Single-Reed Player's Memo Pad: A Gathering Place for Reed Tips. Harvey R. Snitkin. Orig. Title: The Clarinetist's Scrapbook. (Illus.). 100p. 1987. reprint ed. wbk. ed., spiral bd. 7.95 (*1-888732-06-7*) HMS Pubns CT.

Single-Reed Player's Pocket Memo. Harvey R. Snitkin. (Illus.). 100p. 1987. reprint ed. wbk. ed., spiral bd. 4.25 (*1-888732-09-1*) HMS Pubns CT.

Single Replacement Reactions & Relative Reactivity. H. Anthony Neidig & J. N. Spencer. (Modular Laboratory Program in Chemistry Ser.). 12p. (C). 1990. pap. text ed. 1.35 (*0-87540-389-1*, REAC 389-1) Chem Educ Res.

***Single Room Maternity Care.** Margaret Burns. 160p. 1996. spiral bd. 85.00 (*1-879575-75-2*) Acad Med Sys.

Single Rooms: Stories of an Urban Subculture. Ellie Winberg & Tom Wilson. 100p. 1981. pap. text ed. 11.95 (*0-87073-496-2*) Schenkman Bks Inc.

Single Rose. Barbara Delinsky. 1994. mass mkt. 4.50 (*0-373-83293-1*, 1-83293-0) Harlequin Bks.

***Single Rose - A Collection of Gentle Love Poems.** Faith B. Godbey. (Orig.). 1997. pap. write for info. (*1-57553-492-4*) Watermrk Pr.

Single Salary Schedule: An Analysis & Evaluation. Lyle L. Morris. LC 72-177086. (Columbia University. Teachers College. Contributions to Education Ser.: No. 413). reprint ed. 37.50 (*0-404-55413-X*) AMS Pr.

***Single Season.** Dorothea Donley. 224p. 1997. mass mkt. 4.99 (*0-8217-5672-9*, Zebra Kensgtn) Kensgtn Pub Corp.

Single Secret. Teo Savory. 310p. 1986. 20.00 (*0-87775-197-8*); pap. 10.00 (*0-87775-198-6*) Unicorn Pr.

Single Serve Packaging. BCGS Committee Staff. 177p. 1987. pap. 1,950.00 (*0-89336-541-6*, P-097) BCC.

Single Server Queue. 2nd ed. J. W. Cohen. (Applied Mathematics & Mechanics Ser.: Vol. 8). 694p. 1991. 208.75 (*0-444-85452-5*, North Holland) Elsevier.

***Single Server Queue.** 2nd rev. ed. J. W. Cohen. (North-Holland Series in Applied Mathematics & Mechanics: Vol. 8). 694p. 1982. pap. 92.00 (*0-444-89482-9*, North Holland) Elsevier.

***Single Serving Recipes.** Joyce Herzog. (Illus.). 64p. (Orig.). (J). (gr. k-4). 1997. pap. 8.95 (*1-882514-53-X*) Greenleaf TN.

Single-Session Solutions: A Guide to Practical, Effective, & Affordable Therapy. Moshe Talmon. LC 93-11394. (Illus.). 256p. 1993. 19.95 (*0-201-63239-X*) Addison-Wesley.

Single-Session Therapy: Maximizing the Effect of the First (& Often Only) Therapeutic Encounter. Moshe Talmon. LC 90-36407. (Social & Behavioral Science Ser.). 170p. 28.95 (*1-55542-260-8*) Jossey-Bass.

***Single Shot.** Matthew F. Jones. 256p. 1997. pap. 11.95 (*0-385-31833-2*, Delta) Dell.

Single Shot. Matthew F. Jones. LC 95-43304. 256p. 1996. 22.00 (*0-374-26465-1*) FS&G.

Single-Shot Rifles. James J. Grant. 35.00 (*0-88227-017-6*) Gun Room.

Single-Shot Rifles Finale. James J. Grant. 1992. 36.00 (*1-879356-07-4*) Wolfe Pub Co.

Single-Sideband Systems & Circuits. 2nd ed. Ed. by William E. Sabin & Edgar O. Schoenike. LC 95-6081. 1995. text ed. 75.00 (*0-07-912038-5*) McGraw.

Single Smart. C. Kelly Howard. 160p. (Orig.). 1990. pap. 9.95 (*0-9626232-0-2*) Calico Pub.

Single Solution: A Taxpayer's Guide to Sheltering More of the 20,000, 50,000, or 100,000 Dollars You Make As a Single Person. Mary J. Parson. LC 86-13561. (Illus.). 192p. reprint ed. pap. 54.80 (*0-8357-4253-9*, 2037042) Bks Demand.

Single Solution: The Sexual Survival Guide for Today's Single Christian Woman, Vol. 1. Donna M. Cowan. 176p. 1996. pap. text ed. 9.95 (*0-89221-319-1*) New Leaf.

Single Solutions - An Essential Guide for the Single Career Woman. Charlotte E. Thompson. (Orig.). 1990. pap. 11.95 (*0-8283-1933-2*) Branden Pub Co.

Single Source: A Workbook Reference for Singles. Ed. by Bibliotheca Press Research Division Staff. 75p. 1982. student ed., ring bd. 35.95 (*0-939476-71-1*, Bibliotheca Pr) Prosperity & Profits.

Single Space. Jim Towns. 190p. (Orig.). 1990. pap. 6.99 (*1-56292-719-1*, HB719) Honor Bks OK.

Single Sparks: China's Rural Revolutions. Ed. by Kathleen J. Hartford & Steven M. Goldstein. LC 87-4823. 232p. (gr. 13). 1990. pap. text ed. 30.95 (*0-87332-753-5*, East Gate Bk) M E Sharpe.

Single-Stranded DNA Phages. Ed. by David T. Denhardt et al. LC 78-60445. (Cold Spring Harbor Monograph Ser.). 730p. reprint ed. pap. 180.00 (*0-7837-5840-5*, 2045559) Bks Demand.

Single-Subject Experimental Research: Applications for Literacy. Ed. by Susan B. Neuman & Sandra McCormick. 256p. 1995. pap. 20.95 (*0-87207-128-6*) Intl Reading.

Single-System Designs in the Social Services: Issues & Options for the 1990s. Intro. by Martin Bloom. LC 93-40395. (Journal of Social Service Research). (Illus.). 190p. 1994. lib. bdg. 32.95 (*1-56024-574-3*) Haworth Pr.

Single-System Research Designs. Ed. by Martin Bloom. (Journal of Social Service Research: Vol. 3, No. 1). 134p. 1979. pap. text ed. 14.95 (*0-917724-70-4*) Haworth Pr.

Single Tear: A Family's Persecution, Love & Endurance in Communist China. Ningkun Wu. LC 94-615. 1994. reprint ed. pap. 11.95 (*0-316-95639-2*) Little.

Single-Tier Steel Bracket Library Shelving, Z39.73-1994. National Information Standards Organization Staff. LC 94-45135. (National Information Standards Ser.). 10p. 1995. pap. 40.00 (*1-880124-09-2*) NISO.

***Single Titles Series, 16 vols.** Incl. Medicines from Nature. Peggy Thomas. LC 96-47686. (Illus.). 128p. (YA). (gr. 7 up). 1997. lib. bdg. 17.98 (*0-8050-4168-0*); Alternative Medicine: Cures or Myths?. Howard Facklam. 128p. (YA). (gr. 7 up). 1996. lib. bdg. 17.98 (*0-8050-4169-9*); Bioethics & High-Tech Medicine. Victoria Sherrow. LC 95-34222. 144p. (YA). (gr. 7 up). 1996. lib. bdg. 17.98 (*0-8050-3832-9*); The Information Superhighway. Kathlyn Gay & Martin Gay. LC 95-46281. (Illus.). 112p. (YA). (gr. 7 up). 1996. lib. bdg. 17.98 (*0-8050-3804-3*); Threads of Evidence: Using Forensic Science to Solve Crimes. Herma Silverstein. 128p. (YA). (gr. 7 up). 1996. lib. bdg. 17.98 (*0-8050-4370-5*); Virtual Reality: A Door to Cyberspace. Ann E. Weiss. (Illus.). 128p. (YA). (gr. 7 up). 1996. lib. bdg. 17.98 (*0-8050-3722-5*); Children of Welfare. Joan J. Johnson. LC 96-45193. 128p. (YA). (gr. 7 up). 1997. lib. bdg. 17.98 (*0-8050-3961-9*); Communes & Cults. Kathlyn Gay. 128p. (YA). (gr. 7 up). 1997. lib. bdg. 17.98 (*0-8050-3803-5*); Hardship & Hope: America & the Great Depression. Victoria Sherrow. 128p. (YA). (gr. 7 up). 1997. lib. bdg. 17.98 (*0-8050-4178-8*); Panama & the United States: Divided by the Canal. Edmund Lindop. LC 96-40948. (Illus.). 128p. (YA). (gr. 7 up). 1997. lib. bdg. 17.98 (*0-8050-4768-9*); In Sports, Money Talks. Edward F. Dolan. (Illus.). 144p. (YA). (gr. 7 up). 1996. lib. bdg. 17.98 (*0-8050-4569-4*); Protest!. Michael Kronenwetter. (Illus.). 128p. (YA). (gr. 7 up). 1996. lib. bdg. 17.98 (*0-8050-4103-6*); Living in Two Worlds: The Immigrant Children's Experience. Anna Kosof. LC 96-13004. (Illus.). 112p. (YA). (gr. 7 up). 1996. lib. bdg. 17.98 (*0-8050-4083-8*); Teens & Tobacco: A Fatal Attraction. Susan S. Lang & Beth H. Marks. LC 95-40738. 144p. (YA). (gr. 7 up). 1996. lib. bdg. 17.98 (*0-8050-3768-3*); Mexico & the United States: Cooperation & Conflict. Elaine Pascoe. LC 96-11430. (Illus.). 128p. (YA). (gr. 7 up). 1996. lib. bdg. 17.98 (*0-8050-4180-X*); Puerto Rico: Deciding Its Future. Judith Harlan. LC 96-14714. (Illus.). 128p. (YA). (gr. 7 up). 1996. lib. bdg. 17.98 (*0-8050-4372-1*); 230.14 (*0-8050-5385-9*) TFC Bks NY.

Single to God: Personal Prayers by Single Adults Through Everyday Life. Ed. by Douglas Fagerstrom. LC 93-29535. 128p. (gr. 10). 1994. 14.99 (*0-8010-3565-1*) Baker Bks.

Single-Track Mind: An Illustrated Guide to Mountain-Bike Racing, Technique & Training. Paul Skilbeck. (Illus.). 256p. 1996. pap. 16.95 (*1-884737-10-2*) VeloPress.

Single-Track to Jacksonville; the Rogue River Valley Railway & the Southern Oregon Traction Company: An Oregon Documentary. Bert Webber & Margie Webber. LC 90-47551. (Illus.). 128p. (Orig.). 1991. 24.95 (*0-936738-67-7*); pap. 12.95 (*0-936738-55-3*) Webb Research.

Single Tree. Gary D. Svee. 192p. 1994. 19.95 (*0-8027-4142-8*) Walker & Co.

Single Tree. large type ed. Gary D. Svee. LC 94-45387. 248p. 1995. lib. bdg. 19.95 (*0-7838-1220-5*, GK Hall) Thorndike Pr.

Single Variable Calculus. Bradley & Smith. 1995. pap. text ed. 70.00 (*0-13-207218-1*) P-H.

Single Variable Calculus. John Feroe. (C). 1991. teacher ed., pap. text ed. 20.75 (*0-15-581063-4*) HB Coll Pubs.

Single Variable Calculus. John Feroe. (C). 1991. student ed., pap. text ed. 24.00 (*0-15-581066-9*) HB Coll Pubs.

Single Variable Calculus. Joseph Repka. 880p. (C). 1993. text ed. write for info. (*0-697-15375-4*) Wm C Brown Pubs.

Single Variable Calculus. 2nd ed. James Stewart. 762p. (C). 1991. text ed. 52.00 (*0-534-14532-9*) Brooks-Cole.

Single Variable Calculus. 3rd ed. James Stewart. LC 94-29765. 768p. (C). 1995. text ed. 75.95 (*0-534-21828-8*) Brooks-Cole.

***Single Variable Calculus.** 4th ed. Stewart. (Mathematics Ser.). Date not set. text ed. 71.95 (*0-534-35562-5*) Brooks-Cole.

Single Variable Calculus: Early Transcendentals. 2nd ed. James Stewart. 630p. (C). 1991. pap. 59.95 (*0-534-16410-2*) Brooks-Cole.

Single Variable Calculus: Early Transcendentals. 2nd ed. James Stewart. 752p. (C). 1991. text ed. 69.95 (*0-534-16414-5*) Brooks-Cole.

***Single Variable Calculus: Early Transcendentals.** 5th ed. Edwards & David E. Penney. (C). 1997. pap. text ed. 60.00 (*0-13-617978-9*) P-H.

Single Variable Calculus: Early Transcendentals Version. 3rd ed. James Stewart. LC 94-29766. 768p. (C). 1995. text ed. 71.95 (*0-534-25170-6*) Brooks-Cole.

Single-Variable Calculus with Discrete Mathematics. John Feroe & Charles Steinhorn. 992p. (C). 1991. text ed. 59.00 (*0-15-581062-6*) SCP.

Single Vegan: Simple, Convenient & Appetizing Meals for One. Leah Leneman. (Illus.). 128p. 1989. pap. 10.00 (*0-7225-1454-9*) Thorsons SF.

Single Voices. Ed. by Bruce Yoder & Imo J. Yoder. LC 82-3002. 128p. 1982. pap. 6.99 (*0-8361-1998-3*) Herald Pr.

Single vs. Multiple Languages in Secondary Schools see Language Teacher

Single White Female. John Lutz. Ed. by Julie Rubenstein. 288p. 1992. reprint ed. mass mkt. 4.99 (*0-671-74500-X*) PB.

Single, Whole & Holy: Christian Women & Sexuality. Joy Jacobs & Deborah Strubel. 214p. 1996. pap. 11.99 (*0-88965-125-6*, Pub. by Horizon Books CN) Chr Pubns.

Single, Wild, Sexy...& Safe. Graham Masterton. 256p. (Orig.). 1994. pap. 5.99 (*0-451-17364-3*, Sig) NAL-Dutton.

Single Wing Offense with the Spinning Fullback. John F. Aldrich. LC 83-7060. (Illus.). 183p. 1983. reprint ed. pap. 52.20 (*0-608-00104-X*, 2060869) Bks Demand.

Single with Children. Arlene James. (Fortune's Children Ser.). 1996. pap. 4.50 (*0-373-50182-X*, 1-50182-4) Harlequin Bks.

Single with Children. Caryl W. Krueger. Ed. by Mary C. Dean. LC 93-18280. 176p. (Orig.). 1993. Alk. paper. pap. 9.95 (*0-687-38555-5*) Abingdon.

Single Woman Homesteader. rev. ed. Leona D. Cox. LC 90-89552. (Illus.). 214p. 1991. 21.95 (*0-9627680-7-3*) Inkwell CA.

Single Woman's Guide to the Available Men of Washington. Mary J. Shomon. (Illus.). 52p. (Orig.). 1993. pap. text ed. write for info. (*0-9635604-0-9*) Flies On The Wall.

Single Women. Marcelle Clements. Date not set. write for info. (*0-393-04025-9*) Norton.

Single Women. Urmila Jothani. (C). 1995. 22.00 (*81-7033-240-0*, Pub. by Rawat II) S Asia.

Single Women: Affirming Our Spiritual Journey. Clare Christie. Ed. by Mary O'Brien. 232p. 1993. pap. write for info. (*0-318-70155-3*, Bergin & Garvey) Greenwood.

Single Women: Affirming Our Spiritual Journey. Ed. by Mary O'Brien & Clare Christie. LC 92-39121. 232p. 1993. text ed. 49.95 (*0-89789-321-2*, H321, Bergin & Garvey) Greenwood.

Single Women: On the Margins? Tuula Gordon. LC 93-36034. (C). 1994. pap. 15.00 (*0-8147-3064-7*); text ed. 36.00 (*0-8147-3063-9*) NYU Pr.

Single Women - Family Ties: Life Histories of Older Women. Katherine R. Allen. (New Perspectives on Family Ser.). 152p. (C). 1989. text ed. 48.00 (*0-8039-2804-1*); pap. text ed. 22.95 (*0-8039-2805-X*) Sage.

Single Women in Assamese Hindu Society. Jeuti Barooah. (C). 1993. 22.00 (*81-212-0416-X*, Pub. by Gian Publng Hse II) S Asia.

***Single Women vs. Married Women: A Politically Incorrect Comparison.** Bruce T. Smith & Laura G. Burns. Ed. by Cliff Carle. 1997. pap. 5.95 (*1-57644-058-3*) CCC Pubns.

***Single Women/Family Ties: Life Histories of Older Women.** Katherine R. Allen. LC 89-6383. (New Perspectives on Family Ser.). 152p. 1989. reprint ed. pap. 43.40 (*0-608-02765-0*, 2063831) Bks Demand.

Single-Word Usage, Cognitive Development, & the Beginnings of Combinatorial Speech: A Study of Ten English-Speaking Children. Maris M. Rodgon. LC 75-7211. 173p. reprint ed. pap. 49.40 (*0-317-26378-1*, 2024520) Bks Demand.

Single World, Divided Nations? International Trade & the OECD Labor Markets. Robert Z. Lawrence. LC 96-25252. 100p. 1996. pap. 12.95 (*0-8157-5185-0*) Brookings.

Single World, Divided Nations? International Trade & the OECD Labor Markets. OECD Development Centre Staff. LC 96-25252. 100p. 1996. 32.95 (*0-8157-5186-9*) Brookings.

Single Worry. Martin LaJoyce. LC 93-18944. 200p. (Orig.). 1993. pap. 7.99 (*1-56722-011-8*) Word Aflame.

Singled Out. Simon Brett. LC 94-39141. 1995. 20.00 (*0-684-80248-1*) S&S Trade.

Singled Out. large type ed. Simon Brett. LC 95-17661. 282p. 1995. 24.95 (*0-7838-1377-5*, GK Hall) Thorndike Pr.

***Singled Out for God's Assignment: A Widow's Valley of Learning.** Leona Choy. 234p. 1996. pap. 14.95 (*1-889283-03-7*) Golden Morning.

Singlehanded Sailing: The Experiences & Techniques of the Lone Voyagers. 2nd ed. Richard Henderson. (Illus.). 352p. 1992. pap. 18.95 (*0-87742-359-8*, 60919) Intl Marine.

Singlehanded Sailing: The Experiences & Techniques of the Long Voyagers. 2nd ed. Richard Henderson. 1992. pap. text ed. 18.95 (*0-07-028164-5*) McGraw.

Singlehanded, Vol. 4: True Homosexual Encounters from First Hand. Ed. by Winston Leyland. 192p. (Orig.). 1987. pap. 10.95 (*0-943595-05-3*) Leyland Pubns.

Singlehood That Glorifies God: Living with Eternal Purpose. John Coblentz. 1992. pap. 2.95 (*0-87813-546-4*) Christian Light.

Singleland: Living It, Loving It or Leaving It. Sharon Silver. LC 92-9765. 160p. 1992. pap. 14.95 (*0-942963-24-5*) Distinctive Pub.

Singleness. Charles R. Swindoll. (Swindoll Booklets Ser.). 32p. 1995. pap. 3.99 (*0-310-20090-3*) Zondervan.

Singleness: A Guide to Understanding & Satisfaction. Nadine Peterson & Barbara N. Sofie. LC 87-50532. 184p. (Orig.). 1987. pap. 9.95 (*0-934955-09-3*) Watercress Pr.

Singleness: An Opportunity for Growth & Fulfillment. Edward F. Weising & Gwen E. Weising. LC 82-80197. (Radiant Life Ser.). 128p. (Orig.). 1982. pap. 3.95 (*0-88243-901-4*, 02-0901); teacher ed., pap. 5.50 (*0-88243-196-X*, 32-0196) Gospel Pub.

Singles: Myths & Realities. Leonard Cargan & Matthew Melko. LC 81-23343. (New Perspectives on Family Ser.). (Illus.). 287p. reprint ed. pap. 81.80 (*0-8357-8482-7*, 2034749) Bks Demand.

Singles: Shorter Works, 1981-1986. John A. Scott. (Poetry Ser.). 70p. (Orig.). 1989. pap. text ed. 12.95 (*0-7022-2142-2*, Pub. by Univ Queensland Pr AT) Intl Spec Bk.

Singles Alive! Jim Towns. LC 83-23777. 128p. 1984. 11.95 (*0-88289-421-8*) Pelican.

Singles Ask: Answers to Questions about Relationships & Sexual Issues. Harold I. Smith. LC 88-6368. 160p. 1988. pap. 11.99 (*0-8066-2379-9*, 10-5803, Augsburg) Augsburg Fortress.

***Singles at the Crossroads: A Fresh Perspective on Christian Singleness.** Albert Y. Hsu. LC 97-26147. 180p. 1997. pap. 10.99 (*0-8308-1353-5*, 1353) InterVarsity.

S

S

Singles Cookbooks: How to Find or Locate Cookbooks for Singles Cooking. Ed. by Cookbook Consortium Information Division Staff. 70p. 1992. ring bd. 24.95 (*0-318-00120-9*) Prosperity & Profits.

Single's Guide to Chicagoland. Madeline Binder. (Illus.). 152p. (Orig.). 1994. pap. 11.95 (*0-9642934-0-4*) Two M IL.

Single's Guide to Cruise Vacations. Margaret Russell. 256p. 1997. per., pap. 15.00 (*0-7615-0324-2*) Prima Pub.

Singles Guide to Southern California. Richard Gosse. 208p. 1992. pap. 9.95 (*0-934377-13-8*) Marin Pubns.

***Singles Guide to the San Francisco Bay Area: Where & How to Meet New Friends & a Romantic Partner.** 6th ed. Richard Gosse. 208p. 1997. pap. 9.95 (*0-934377-15-4*) Marin Pubns.

Singles Guide to Writing Personal Ads. Thomas P. Roemer. (Illus.). 96p. (Orig.). 1996. pap. 9.95 (*0-9652893-0-3*) Double Ink Pr.

Singles' Ministry for Today. Bobbie Reed. LC 95-23858. 1996. 12.99 (*0-570-04840-0*, 12-3277) Concordia.

Singles' Philosopher. William Carroll. (New Age Philosophy Ser.). 160p. (Orig.). 1990. pap. 10.00 (*0-910390-26-6*) Auto Bk.

Singles Plus. Ray Mossholder. LC 91-55230. (Orig.). 1991. pap. 10.99 (*0-88419-290-3*) Creation House.

Singles Scene: A Psychoanalytic Study of the Breakdown of Intimacy. Gerald Alper. LC 93-6446. 128p. 1995. 37.95 (*1-883255-15-5*) Intl Scholars.

Singles Scene: A Psychoanalytical Study of the Breakdown of Intimacy. Gerald Alper. LC 93-6446. 1995. pap. 14.95 (*1-883255-14-7*) Intl Scholars.

Singles Sorting It Out. Wilberta L. Chinn. (Illus.). 335p. (Orig.). 1991. pap. 11.95 (*0-937673-08-0*) Peacock Ent LA.

Singlet Oxygen: Reactions with Organic Compounds & Polymers. Ed. by Bengt G. Ranby & J. F. Rabek. LC 77-2793. 341p. reprint ed. pap. 97.20 (*0-685-20685-8*, 2030475) Bks Demand.

Singlet 02 Series, 4 vols. Incl. Vol. I. Physical-Chemical Aspects. Ed. by Aryeh A. Frimer. 248p. 1985. (*0-318-60782-4*); Vol. II, Part I. Reaction Modes & Products. Aryeh A. Frimer. 296p. 1985. (*0-318-60783-2*); Vol.III, Reaction Modes & Products-Part II. Ed. by Aryeh A. Frimer. 288p. 1985. (*0-318-60784-0*); Vol. IV. Polymers & Biomolecules. Ed. by Aryeh A. Frimer. 224p. 1985. (*0-318-60785-9*); 1985. 593.00 (*0-8493-6439-6*, QD281, CRC Reprint) Franklin.

Singlet 02, Vol. 1: Physical Chemical Aspects. A. Frimer. LC 84-4225. 248p. 1985. 141.00 (*0-8493-6442-6*, CRC Reprint) Franklin.

Singlet 02, Vol. 2, Pt. 1: Reaction Modes & Products. A. Frimer. LC 84-4225. 296p. 1985. 167.00 (*0-8493-6443-4*, CRC Reprint) Franklin.

Singlet 02, Vol. 3, Pt. 2: Reaction Modes & Products. A. Frimer. LC 84-4225. 288p. 1985. 159.00 (*0-8493-6444-2*, CRC Reprint) Franklin.

Singlet 02, Vol. 4: Polymers & Biomolecules. A. Frimer. LC 84-4225. 224p. 1985. 127.00 (*0-8493-6445-0*, CRC Reprint) Franklin.

Singletary: Genealogy of the Singletary-Curtis Family. L. Singletary-Bedford. (Illus.). 115p. 1991. reprint ed. pap. 19.50 (*0-8328-2062-8*) Higginson Bk Co.

Singleton. Thomas Haluszczak. 150p. (Orig.). 1996. mass mkt. 4.99 (*1-55197-272-7*, Pub. by Comnwlth Pub CN) Partners Pubs Grp.

Singleton Abbey & the Vivians of Swansea. Ralph A. Griffiths. 67p. (C). 1988. pap. 21.00 (*0-86383-441-8*, Pub. by Gomer Pr UK) St Mut.

***Singleton's Law.** Reginald Hill. LC 97-18507. 1997. 24.95 (*0-7838-8106-1*) G K Hall.

Singletree. William Crow. (Orig.). 1996. mass mkt. 5.99 (*1-55197-069-4*, Pub. by Comnwlth Pub CN) Partners Pubs Grp.

Single...Understanding & Accepting the Reality of It All. William A. White. 1991. teacher ed. 3.95 (*0-87162-515-6*, D7211); pap. text ed. 4.95 (*0-87162-513-X*, D7210) Warner Pr.

Singualarities des Systemes Differentiels de Gauss-Manin. F. Pham. (Progress in Mathematics Ser.: No. 2). 340p. (FRE.). 1980. 56.50 (*0-8176-3002-3*) Birkhauser.

***Singular Beast: Jews, Christians, & the Pig.** Claudine Fabre-Vassas. LC 96-50482. (Illus.). 448p. (C). 1997. 29.50 (*0-231-10366-2*) Col U Pr.

Singular Behavior & Non-Linear Dynamics, 2 vols., Set. S. N. Pnevmatikos et al. 742p. 1989. text ed. 113.00 (*9971-5-0896-6*) World Scientific Pub.

Singular Behaviour & Nonlinear Dynamics, 2 vols., I. S. N. Pnevmatikos et al. 742p. (C). 1989. text ed. 143.00 (*9971-5-0895-8*) World Scientific Pub.

Singular Case of the Duplicate Holmes. Jan Walker. 1994. text ed. 30.00 (*0-86025-278-7*, Pub. by Ian Henry Pubns UK) Empire Pub Srvs.

Singular Control Systems. L. Dai. (Lecture Notes in Control & Information Sciences Ser.: Vol. 118). (Illus.). ix, 332p. 1989. 61.95 (*0-387-50724-8*) Spr-Verlag.

Singular Electromagnetic Fields & Sources. J. Van Bladel. (Oxford Engineering Science Ser.: No. 28). (Illus.). 256p. 1991. 79.00 (*0-19-856200-4*) OUP.

Singular Electromagnetic Fields & Sources. J. Van Bladel. 252p. 1996. 69.95 (*0-7803-1153-1*, PC5624) Inst Electrical.

Singular Elopement. large type ed. Audrey Blanshard. (Romance Ser.). 1994. pap. 15.99 (*0-7089-7613-1*, Linford) Ulverscroft.

Singular Homology Theory. W. S. Massey. LC 79-23309. (Graduate Texts in Mathematics Ser.: Vol. 70). (Illus.). 280p. 1980. 40.00 (*3-540-90456-5*) Spr-Verlag.

Singular Honeymoon. Michaels. 1994. pap. 2.99 (*0-373-15546-8*) Harlequin Bks.

Singular Honeymoon. Leigh Michaels. (Romance Ser.). 1994. mass mkt. 2.99 (*0-373-03300-1*, 1-03300-0) Harlequin Bks.

***Singular Impressions: The Monotype in America.** Joann Moser. LC 96-39416. (Illus.). 224p. 1997. 60.00 (*1-56098-737-5*) Smithsonian.

Singular Integral Equations: Boundary Problems of Function Theory & Their Application to Mathematical Physics. 2nd ed. N. I. Muskhelishvili. 447p. 1992. reprint ed. pap. 12.95 (*0-486-66893-2*) Dover.

***Singular Integral Equations & Discrete Vortices.** Ivan K. Lifanov. (Illus.). 486p. 1996. 267.50 (*90-6764-207-X*, Pub. by VSP NE) Coronet Bks.

Singular Integral Operators. S. G. Michlin & S. Prossdorf. Tr. by A. Bottcher & R. Lehmann from GER. (Illus.). 540p. 1987. 118.95 (*0-387-15967-3*) Spr-Verlag.

***Singular Integral Operators & Related Topics: Joint German-Israeli Workshop, Tel Aviv, March 1-10, 1995.** Albrecht Bottcher & I. Gohberg. LC 96-36429. (Operator Theory, Advances & Applications Ser.). 1996. 122.95 (*0-8176-5466-6*) Birkhauser.

***Singular Integral Operators & Related Topics: Joint German-Israeli Workshop, Tel Aviv, March 1-10, 1995, Vol. 90.** Ed. by A. Bottcher & I. Gohberg. LC 96-36429. (Operator Theory & Its Application Ser.). 324p. 1996. 122.95 (*3-7643-5466-6*) Birkhauser.

Singular Integrals: Proceedings. Pure Mathematics Symposium Staff. Ed. by A. P. Calderon. LC 67-16553. (Proceedings of Symposia in Pure Mathematics Ser.: Vol. 10). 375p. 1968. reprint ed. pap. 51.00 (*0-8218-1410-9*, PSPUM/10) Am Math.

Singular Integrals & Differentiability Properties of Functions. E. M. Stein. (Mathematical Ser.: No. 30). 304p. 1971. text ed. 55.00 (*0-691-08079-8*) Princeton U Pr.

Singular Limits of Dispersive Waves. Ed. by N. M. Ercolani et al. (NATO ASI Series B, Physics: Vol. 320). (Illus.). 364p. 1994. 105.00 (*0-306-44628-6*, Plenum Pr) Plenum.

Singular Man. Emmanuel Bove. Tr. by Dominic Di Bernardi from FRE. LC 92-62875. 200p. 1993. 29.95 (*0-910395-94-2*) Marlboro Pr.

Singular Man. Emmanuel Bove. Tr. by Dominic Di Bernardi. LC 95-37381. 200p. (C). 1995. pap. 12.95 (*0-8101-6002-1*) Northwestern U Pr.

Singular Man. J. P. Donleavy. LC 88-33780. 408p. 1989. pap. 7.95 (*0-87113-265-6*, Atlntc Mnthly) Grove-Atltic.

Singular Manual of Textbook Preparation. M. N. Hegde. (Illus.). 96p. (Orig.). (C). 1991. pap. text ed. 20.00 (*1-879105-49-7*, 0236) Singular Publishing.

Singular Manual of Textbook Preparation. 2nd ed. M. N. Hegoe. 96p. (Orig.). 1996. pap. 24.95 (*1-56593-640-X*, 1326) Singular Publishing.

Singular-Meaning Lexicon of the New Testament. Richard C. Averitt. 205p. 1996. pap. write for info. (*1-887612-00-9*) Script Semantics.

Singular Modular Forms & Theta Relations. E. Freitag. Ed. by A. Dold et al. (Lecture Notes in Mathematics Ser.: Vol. 1487). vi, 172p. 1991. pap. 27.00 (*0-387-54704-5*) Spr-Verlag.

***Singular Nonlinear Partial Differential Equations.** Raymond Gerard & Hidetoshi Tahara. (Aspects of Mathematics Ser.: Vol. 28). 280p. 1996. 70.00 (*3-528-06659-8*) Informatica.

Singular Ordinary Differential Operators & Pseudodifferential Equations. J. Elschner. (Lecture Notes in Mathematics Ser.: Vol. 1128). 200p. 1985. 37.95 (*0-387-15194-X*) Spr-Verlag.

Singular Passion. Geoffrey Wagner. 303p. 1994. 20.00 (*1-880909-22-7*) Baskerville.

Singular Paths: Old Men Living Alone. Robert L. Rubinstein. LC 85-19063. 1986. text ed. 49.50 (*0-231-06206-0*) Col U Pr.

Singular Paths: Old Men Living Alone. Robert L. Rubinstein. LC 85-19063. 1988. pap. text ed. 17.50 (*0-231-06207-9*) Col U Pr.

Singular Perturbation Analysis of Discrete Control Systems. D. S. Naidu & A. K. Rao. (Lecture Notes in Mathematics Ser.: Vol. 1154). 195p. 1985. 37.95 (*0-387-15981-9*) Spr-Verlag.

Singular Perturbation Methods for Ordinary Differential Equations. R. E. O'Malley, Jr. Ed. by F. John et al. (Applied Mathematical Sciences Ser.: Vol. 89). (Illus.). 248p. 1991. 54.95 (*0-387-97556-X*) Spr-Verlag.

Singular Perturbation Methods in Control: Analysis & Design. Peter V. Kokotovic et al. (Mathematics in Science & Engineering Ser.). 1986. text ed. 92.00 (*0-12-417635-6*) Acad Pr.

Singular Perturbation Problems in Chemical Physics: Analytic & Computational Methods, Vol. 97. Ed. by John H. Miller. (Advances in Chemical Physics Ser.). 373p. Date not set. text ed. 125.00 (*0-471-11531-2*) Wiley.

Singular Perturbation Theory: An Introduction with Applications. Donald R. Smith. 576p. 1985. text ed. 90.00 (*0-521-30042-8*) Cambridge U Pr.

Singular Perturbations: Order Reduction in Control System Design. American Society of Mechanical Engineers Staff. LC 72-87029. 68p. reprint ed. pap. 25.00 (*0-317-08441-0*, 2012304) Bks Demand.

Singular Perturbations & Asymptotic Analysis in Control Systems. Ed. by Peter V. Kokotovic et al. (Lecture Notes in Control & Information Sciences Ser.: Vol. 90). vi, 419p. 1987. 75.95 (*0-387-17362-5*) Spr-Verlag.

Singular Perturbations & Differential Inequalities. F. A. Howes. LC 75-44235. (Memoirs Ser.: No. 5/168). 75p. 1976. pap. 21.00 (*0-8218-1868-6*, MEMO 5/168) Am Math.

***Singular Perturbations in Elasticity Theory.** Ed. by L. S. Frank. LC 96-78409. (Analysis & Its Applications Ser.: Vol. 1). 300p. (YA). (gr. 12 up). Date not set. 82.00 (*90-5199-307-2*, 307-2) IOS Press.

Singular Perturbations in Systems & Control. Ed. by M. D. Ardema. (CISM Courses & Lectures: Vol. 280). (Illus.). 337p. 1983. 51.95 (*0-387-81751-4*) Spr-Verlag.

Singular Perturbations, One: Spaces & Singular Perturbations on Manifolds Without Boundary. L. S. Frank. (Studies in Mathematics & Its Applications: No. 23). 556p. 1990. 141.50 (*0-444-88134-4*, North Holland) Elsevier.

Singular Pleasures. Harry Mathews. LC 92-29478. (Illus.). 144p. 1993. 19.95 (*1-56478-024-4*) Dalkey Arch.

Singular Points of Complex Hypersurfaces. John W. Milnor. (Annals of Mathematics Studies: No. 61). 130p. 1969. pap. text ed. 26.50 (*0-691-08065-8*) Princeton U Pr.

Singular Power: An Essay on American Television News. Robert Hershman. 32p. (Orig.). 1982. pap. text ed. 11.50 (*0-8191-5850-X*, Aspen Inst for Humanistic Studies) U Pr of Amer.

Singular Problems of the Single Jewish Parent. Shlomo D. Levine. 39p. (Orig.). 1981. pap. text ed. 1.25 (*0-8381-2115-2*) United Synagogue.

Singular Rebellion. Saiichi Maryua. Tr. by Dennis Keene from JPN. 420p. 1990. pap. 6.95 (*0-87011-989-3*) Kodansha.

Singular Semi-Riemannian Geometry. Demir N. Kupeli. LC 96-10934. (Mathematics & Its Applications Ser.: Vol. 366). 1996. lib. bdg. 99.00 (*0-7923-3996-7*) Kluwer Ac.

***Singular Spectrum Analysis: A New Tool in Time Series Analysis.** Ed. by James B. Elsner & Anastasios A. Tsonis. LC 96-47009. 160p. 1996. 49.50 (*0-306-45472-6*) Plenum.

Singular Spy. Amanda K. Williams. 192p. 1992. pap. 8.95 (*1-56280-008-6*) Naiad Pr.

Singular Stories, Vol. One: Tales from Singapore. Ed. by Robert Yeo. LC 92-34216. 1993. pap. 12.00 (*0-89410-758-5*, Three Contnts) Lynne Rienner.

Singular Texts - Plural Authors: Perspectives on Collaborative Writing. Lisa Ede & Andrea A. Lunsford. LC 89-19712. 300p. (C). 1989. text ed. 34.95 (*0-8093-1447-9*) S Ill U Pr.

Singular Texts - Plural Authors: Perspectives on Collaborative Writing. Lisa Ede & Andrea A. Lunsford. LC 91-17964. 304p. (C). 1992. pap. 19.95 (*0-8093-1793-1*) S Ill U Pr.

Singular Torsion & the Splitting Properties. K. R. Goodearl. LC 72-4344. (Memoirs Ser.: No. 1/124). 89p. 1972. pap. 17.00 (*0-8218-1824-4*, MEMO/1/124) Am Math.

Singular Unitary Representations & Discrete Series for Indefinite Stiefel Manifolds U. T. Kobayashi. LC 91-36299. 106p. 1992. pap. 26.00 (*0-8218-2524-0*, MEMO/95/462) Am Math.

Singular Value Decomposition & Signal Processing: Algorithms, Applications & Architectures. Ed. by E. F. Deprettere. 478p. 1988. 194.50 (*0-444-70439-6*, North Holland) Elsevier.

***Singular Value Decompositions.** Golub. (C). (gr. 13 up). 1997. text ed. 46.00 (*0-412-45010-0*, Chap & Hall NY) Chapman & Hall.

Singular View: The Art of Seeing with One Eye. 5th ed. Frank B. Brady. (Illus.). 144p. 1994. reprint ed. pap. 15.00 (*0-9614639-2-9*) Frank B Brady.

Singular Visions: Long Island Folk Art from the Late 18th Century to the Present. Alyce Assael. LC 85-70640. (Illus.). 48p. (Orig.). 1985. pap. 6.00 (*0-933793-00-6*) Guild Hall.

***Singular Voices.** Playwrights Canada Press Staff. LC 95-213365. 1997. pap. text ed. 14.95 (*0-88754-510-6*, Pub. by Playwrights CN Pr CN) Theatre Comm.

***Singular Voices: Conversations with Americans Who Make a Difference.** Barbaralee Diamonstein. LC 96-35204. 224p. 1997. 19.95 (*0-8109-2698-9*, Abradale Pr) Abrams.

***Singularidad de Jesus - The Uniqueness of Jesus: Introduccion - Introduction.** Bright. (Diez Grados Basicos - Ten Basic Steps Ser.). (SPA.). 1995. write for info. (*1-56063-472-3*) Editorial Unilit.

Singularities. Susan Howe. LC 89-16445. (Wesleyan Poetry Ser.). 80p. 1990. pap. 11.95 (*0-8195-1194-3*, Wesleyan Univ Pr); text ed. 25.00 (*0-8195-2192-2*, Wesleyan Univ Pr) U Pr of New Eng.

Singularities. R. Randell. LC 89-6662. (Contemporary Mathematics Ser.: Vol. 90). 359p. 1989. pap. text ed. 50.00 (*0-8218-5096-2*, CONM/90) Am Math.

***Singularities: Extremes of Theory in the Twentieth Century.** Thomas Pepper. (Literature, Culture, Theory Ser.: No. 22). 285p. (C). 1997. text ed. 54.95 (*0-521-57382-3*); pap. text ed. 17.95 (*0-521-57478-1*) Cambridge U Pr.

Singularities: Lille 1991. Ed. by Jean-Paul Brasselet. (London Mathematical Society Lecture Note Ser.: No. 201). 432p. (C). 1994. pap. text ed. 42.95 (*0-521-46631-8*) Cambridge U Pr.

Singularities: Proceedings of Symposia in Pure Mathematics, Pt. 1. Ed. by Peter Orlik. LC 83-2529. (Proceedings of Symposia in Pure Mathematics Ser.: Vol. 40). 676p. 1983. text ed. 80.00 (*0-8218-1450-8*, PSPUM/40.1) Am Math.

Singularities: Proceedings of Symposia in Pure Mathematics, Pt. 2. Ed. by Peter Orlik. LC 83-2529. (Proceedings of Symposia in Pure Mathematics Ser.: Vol. 40). 680p. 1983. text ed. 80.00 (*0-8218-1466-4*, PSPUM/40.2) Am Math.

Singularities: Proceedings of Symposia in Pure Mathematics, Set. Ed. by Peter Orlik. LC 83-2529. (Proceedings of Symposia in Pure Mathematics Ser.: Vol. 40). 1356p. 1983. text ed. 138.00 (*0-8218-1443-5*, PSPUM/40) Am Math.

Singularities & Bifurcations. Ed. by V. I. Arnold. (Advances in Soviet Mathematics Ser.: Vol. 21). 262p. 1994. 100.00 (*0-8218-0237-2*, ADVSOV/21) Am Math.

***Singularities & Complex Geometry: Seminar on Singularities & Complex Geometry, June 15-20, 1994, Beijing, People's Republic of China.** C. K. Lu et al. LC 96-47630. (AMS/IP Studies in Advanced Mathematics: Vol. 5). 1997. 49.00 (*0-8218-0662-9*, AMSIP/5) Am Math.

Singularities & Constructive Methods for Their Treatment. Ed. by P. Grisvard et al. (Lecture Notes in Mathematics Ser.: Vol. 1121). ix, 346p. 1985. 49.95 (*0-387-15219-9*) Spr-Verlag.

Singularities & Groups in Bifurcation Theory I. Martin Golubitsky & D. Schaeffer. (Applied Mathematical Sciences Ser.: Vol. 51). (Illus.). 320p. 1984. 64.95 (*0-387-90999-0*) Spr-Verlag.

Singularities & Groups in Bifurcation Theory Two. Martin Golubitsky et al. (Applied Mathematical Sciences Ser.: Vol. 69). (Illus.). 550p. 1988. 76.95 (*0-387-96652-8*) Spr-Verlag.

***Singularities & Oscillations.** Ed. by Jeffrey Rauch & Michael E. Taylor. LC 97-2460. (IMA Volumes in Mathematics & Its Applications Ser.: Vol. 91). (Illus.). 164p. 1997. 49.95 (*0-387-98200-0*) Spr-Verlag.

Singularities & Topology of Hypersurfaces. A. Dimca. (Universitext Ser.). xvi, 263p. 1992. 59.95 (*0-387-97709-0*) Spr-Verlag.

Singularities in Boundary Value Problems. Ed. by H. G. Garnir. 370p. 1981. lib. bdg. 112.00 (*90-277-1240-9*) Kluwer Ac.

Singularities in Boundary Value Problems. P. Grisvard. Ed. by P. G. Ciarlet & J. L. Lions. (Recherches en Mathematiques Appliquees Ser.: Vol. 22). (Illus.). 212p. 1992. 61.95 (*0-387-55450-5*) Spr-Verlag.

Singularities in Fluids, Plasmas, & Optics: Proceedings of a NATO Advanced Research Workshop July 6-10, 1992, Herkalion, Greece. Ed. by Russel E. Caflisch & George C. Papanicolaou. LC 93-1726. (NATO Advanced Study Institutes Series C, Mathematical & Physical Sciences: Vol. 403). 356p. (C). 1993. lib. bdg. 196.00 (*0-7923-2333-5*) Kluwer Ac.

Singularities in Linear Wave Propagation. L. Garding. (Lecture Notes in Mathematics Ser.: Vol. 1241). iii, 125p. 1987. 29.95 (*0-387-18001-X*) Spr-Verlag.

Singularities of Caustics & Wave Fronts. V. I. Arnold. (Mathematics & Its Applications, Soviet Ser.). 280p. 1990. lib. bdg. 137.50 (*0-7923-1038-1*) Kluwer Ac.

Singularities of Differentiable Maps. Ed. by Arnold et al. (Monographs in Mathematics: No. 83, Vol. II). 400p. 1988. 120.50 (*0-8176-3185-2*) Birkhauser.

***Singularities of Differentiable Maps.** V. I. Arnold et al. (Monographs in Mathematics: Vol. 83). 492p. 1988. 39.00 (*3-7643-3185-2*) Birkhauser.

Singularities of Differentiable Maps, Vol. 1. Arnold et al. (Monographs in Mathematics). 1985. 86.50 (*0-8176-3187-9*) Birkhauser.

Singularities of Smooth Maps. James J. Eells. (Notes on Mathematics & Its Applications Ser.). x, 104p. (Orig.). 1967. text ed. 120.00 (*0-677-01330-2*) Gordon & Breach.

Singularities of Solutions of Second Order Quasilinear Equations. L. Veron. LC 94-33324. (Pitman Research Notes in Mathematics Ser.). 1995. write for info. (*0-615-00144-0*) Longman.

***Singularities of Solutions of Second Order Quasilinear Equations RN 353.** Laurent Veron. (Pitman Research Notes in Mathematics Ser.). 1996. pap. 67.46 (*0-582-03539-2*) Addison-Wesley.

Singularities, Representation of Algebras, & Vector Bundles. Ed. by G. Greuel & G. Trautmann. (Lecture Notes in Mathematics Ser.: Vol. 1273). xiv, 383p. 1987. pap. 47.90 (*0-387-18263-2*) Spr-Verlag.

Singularity. William Sleator. 170p. (YA). (gr. 7 up). 1995. pap. 3.99 (*0-14-037598-8*) Puffin Bks.

Singularity: Poems. Greg Glazner. 96p. 1996. 19.00 (*0-393-03992-7*) Norton.

Singularity of Thomas Nashe. Stephen S. Hilliard. LC 85-16538. 270p. 1986. reprint ed. pap. 77.00 (*0-608-02134-2*, 2062803) Bks Demand.

Singularity Theory. B. Teisser et al. 996p. 1995. text ed. 162.00 (*981-02-2000-6*) World Scientific Pub.

Singularity Theory & Equivariant Symplectic Maps. Thomas J. Bridges & Jacques E. Furter. LC 93-37171. (Lecture Notes in Mathematics Ser.: Vol. 1558). 1993. 45.95 (*0-387-57296-1*) Spr-Verlag.

***Singularity Theory & Gravitational Lensing: Mathematical Foundations-Physical Applications.** A. O. Petters et al. (Illus.). 350p. 1997. 69.50 (*0-8176-3668-4*) Spr-Verlag.

Singularity Theory & Its Applications Vol. I: Warwick 1989: Symposium Held at the University of Warwick 1988-1989. Ed. by J. A. Montaldi & D. Mond. (Lecture Notes in Mathematics Ser.: Vol. 1462). viii, 428p. 1991. 62.95 (*0-387-53737-6*) Spr-Verlag.

Singularity Theory & Its Applications Vol. II: Warwick 1989: Symposium Held at the University of Warwick 1988-1989. Ed. by I. A. Stewart & R. M. Roberts. (Lecture Notes in Mathematics Ser.: Vol. 1463). x, 352p. 1991. 50.95 (*0-387-53736-8*) Spr-Verlag.

Singularity Theory & Some Problems of Functional Analysis. Ed. by S. G. Gindikin. LC 92-32240. (American Mathematical Society Translations Ser. 2: Vol. 153). 199p. 1992. 101.00 (*0-8218-7502-7*, TRANS2/153) Am Math.

An Asterisk (*) at the beginning of an entry indicates that the title is appearing in BIP for the first time.

Singularity Theory, Rod Theory & Symmetry-Breaking Loads. J. F. Pierce. (Lecture Notes in Mathematics Ser.: Vol. 1377). iv, 177p. 1989. 32.95 (*0-387-51304-3*) Spr-Verlag.

Singularly Perturbed & Weakly Coupled Linear Control Systems: A Recursive Approach. Zoran Gajic et al. (Lecture Notes in Control & Information Sciences Ser.: Vol. 140). (Illus.). 300p. 1990. 45.95 (*0-387-52333-2*) Spr-Verlag.

Singularly Perturbed Evolution Equations with Applications to Kinetic Theory. J. R. Mika & J. Banasiak. (Series on Advances in Mathematics for Applied Sciences). 250p. 1995. text ed. 61.00 (*981-02-2125-8*) World Scientific Pub.

Singweisen Bernarts Von Ventadorn nach den Handschriften mitgeteilt. Carl L. Appel. LC 80-2171. reprint ed. 32.50 (*0-404-19002-2*) AMS Pr.

Sinhala-English. 2nd ed. B. Clough. 838p. 1982. 34.00 (*0-88431-104-X*) IBD Ltd.

Sinhala Village in a Time of Trouble: Politics & Change in Rural Sri Lanka. Jonathan Spencer. (Oxford University South Asian Studies Ser.). 304p. 1991. 32.00 (*0-19-562495-5*) OUP.

Sinhalese: Colloquial Language Course, Set 13. 251p. (SNH.). 1984. pap. text ed. 195.00 incl. audio (*0-88432-394-3*, AFSN20) Audio-Forum.

Sinhalese: Colloquial Language Course, Set 21. 390p. (SNH.). 1981. pap. text ed. 225.00 incl. audio (*0-88432-393-5*, AFSN10) Audio-Forum.

Sinhalese-English - English-Sinhalese Dictionary. T. Moscrop & Vijairantne. 335p. (ENG & SNH.). 1992. 32.75 (*81-85243-66-2*) IBD Ltd.

Sinhalese-English--English Sinhalese Dictionary. T. Moscrop. 335p. (ENG & SNH.). 1992. 31.00 (*0-7859-8920-X*) Fr & Eur.

Sinhalese-English, Dictionary. 276p. 1993. 24.95 (*0-7818-0219-9*) Hippocrene Bks.

Sinhalese-English, English-Sinhalese Dictionary. rev. ed. Moscrop. 336p. (ENG & SNH.). 1992. 49.95 (*0-8288-6986-3*) Fr & Eur.

*__Sinister Gambits.__ Ed. by Richard Peyton. 320p. 1993. pap. 18.95 (*1-55082-068-0*, Pub. by Quarry Pr CN) LPC InBook.

*__Sinister Haunts.__ Date not set. 20.00 (*1-55878-117-X*) Game Designers.

Sinister House. Leland Hall. 1975. 6.50 (*0-685-72184-1*) Bookfinger.

Sinister Ladies of Mystery: The Dark Asteroids of Earth. Ted George & Barbara Parker. LC 87-81809. 145p. (C). 1988. 17.00 (*0-932782-04-3*, G2713-034) Am Fed Astrologers.

Sinister Madonna. Sax Rohmer. (Sumuru Ser.). 1977. reprint ed. 8.50 (*0-685-88226-8*) Bookfinger.

Sinister Paradise. Becky Bohan. LC 93-2011. 1993. pap. 9.95 (*0-9630822-2-1*) Madwoman Pr.

Sinister Ray. Lester Dent. 175p. (Orig.). 1987. pap. 9.95 (*0-936071-04-4*) Gryphon Pubns.

Sinister Romance. Mary H. Vorse. 1989. lib. bdg. 25.00 (*0-910489-20-3*) Scream Pr.

Sinister Secret Salt Marsh. TSR Hobbies Staff. 1981. 5.50 (*0-394-52187-0*) Random.

*__Sinister Side.__ large type ed. Lucilla Andrews. (Ulverscroft Large Print Ser.). 336p. 1997. 27.50 (*0-7089-3768-3*) Ulverscroft.

Sinister Sign Post. Franklin W. Dixon. (Hardy Boys Ser.: Vol. 15). 180p. (J). (gr. 5-9). 1936. 5.95 (*0-448-08915-7*, G&D) Putnam Pub Group.

*__Sinister Smoke Ring.__ Stan Berenstain & Jan Berenstain. (Berenstain Bear Scouts Ser.). (Illus.). (J). (gr. 2-5). 1997. pap. 2.99 (*0-614-29028-7*, Little Apple) Scholastic Inc.

Sinister Spies Dingbats Book. Carole Marsh. (Carole Marsh Dingbats Bks.). (Illus.). (J). (gr. 3-12). 1994. pap. 19.95 (*0-7933-5390-4*); lib. bdg. 29.95 (*0-7933-5389-0*); disk 29.95 (*0-7933-5391-2*) Gallopade Pub Group.

Sinister Stones. Arthur Upfield. 19.95 (*0-8488-1211-5*) Amereon Ltd.

SINIX: UNIX for Commercial Use. John J. Abbott. (Illus.). 240p. (C). 1994. pap. text ed. 32.00 (*0-13-148909-7*) P-H.

Sink down to the Seed. Charlotte Fardelmann. LC 88-64133. (Orig.). 1989. pap. 3.00 (*0-87574-283-1*) Pendle Hill.

Sink or Capture! large type ed. Alan Evans. 1994. 25.99 (*0-7089-3201-0*) Ulverscroft.

*__Sink or Float? Big Book.__ Lisa Trumbauer. Ed. by Jennifer Mooney. (Early Science Ser.). 16p. (J). (ps-2). 1997. pap. 14.95 (*1-56784-322-0*) Newbridge Comms.

*__Sink or Float? Mini Book.__ Lisa Trumbauer. Ed. by Jennifer Mooney. (Early Science Ser.). 16p. (J). (ps-2). 1997. pap. 16.95 (*1-56784-347-6*) Newbridge Comms.

*__Sink or Swim.__ Adapted by Brian Brown & Andrew Melrose. (Storykeepers Juvenile Ser.: Bk. 5). (Illus.). 64p. (J). (gr. 2-5). 1997. mass mkt. 3.99 (*0-310-20341-4*) Zondervan.

*__Sink or Swim.__ Adapted by Brian Brown & Andrew Melrose. (Storykeepers Easy Reader Ser.: Bk. 5). (J). (ps-3). 1997. mass mkt. 3.99 (*0-310-20343-0*) Zondervan.

*__Sink or Swim.__ Gerald Hammond. LC 97-798. 176p. 1997. 19.95 (*0-312-15657-X*) St Martin.

Sink or Swim. Laurie Lawrence. 64p. (C). 1990. pap. 40.00 (*0-86439-092-0*, Pub. by Boolarong Pubns AT) St Mut.

Sink or Swim. John Marshall. LC 95-18945. (Energy & Action Ser.). (J). 1995. write for info. (*1-55916-157-4*) Rourke Bk Co.

Sink or Swim. Betty Miles. 208p. (YA). (gr. 3-7). 1987. pap. 2.95 (*0-380-69913-3*, Camelot) Avon.

Sink or Swim. William Pasnak. (J). (gr. 3-8). 1995. pap. 8.95 (*1-55028-480-0*) Formac Dist Ltd.

Sink or Swim. William Pasnak. (J). (gr. 3-8). 1995. bds. 16.95 (*1-55028-481-9*) Formac Dist Ltd.

*__Sink or Swim.__ large type ed. Gerald Hammond. LC 97-12885. 1997. write for info. (*0-7862-1071-0*, Thorndike Lrg Prnt) Thorndike Pr.

Sink or Swim: College Lifesavers to Help You Stay Afloat. Priscilla Tanner. 167p. (Orig.). 1986. pap. 6.95 (*0-9616673-0-3*) Wilson Crewe.

Sink or Swim: The Politics of Bilingual Education. Colman B. Stein, Jr. LC 86-8196. 249p. 1986. text ed. 49.95 (*0-275-92161-1*, C2161, Praeger Pubs) Greenwood.

Sinking Ark: A New Look at the Problem of Disappearing Species. Norman Myers. LC 79-40232. 1979. 145.00 (*0-08-024501-3*, Pub. by Pergamon Repr UK) Franklin.

*__Sinking Creek.__ John Engels. 208p. 1998. pap. 16.95 (*1-55821-638-3*) Lyons & Burford.

*__Sinking Creek.__ John Engels. 208p. 1998. 25.00 (*1-55821-646-4*) Lyons & Burford.

Sinking Island: The Modern English Writers. Hugh Kenner. LC 88-46121. 304p. 1989. reprint ed. pap. 12.95 (*0-8018-3837-1*) Johns Hopkins.

Sinking of the Merrimac. Richmond P. Hobson. Ed. by Jack Sweetman. (Classics of Naval Literature Ser.). (Illus.). 320p. 1988. reprint ed. 32.95 (*0-87021-632-5*) Naval Inst Pr.

Sinking of the Princess Sophia: Taking the North Down with Her. Ken Coates & Bill Morrison. LC 90-26927. (Illus.). xviii, 220p. 1991. pap. 12.95 (*0-912006-50-1*) U of Alaska Pr.

*__Sinking of the Titanic.__ Ed. by Bruce M. Caplan. LC 96-78295. 215p. 1997. pap. 12.95 (*1-883697-34-4*) Hara Pub.

Sinking of the USS Cairo. John C. Wideman. LC 92-39651. (Civil War Ser.). 248p. 1993. text ed. 22.00 (*0-87805-617-3*) U Pr of Miss.

Sinking Spell. Edward Gorey. (Illus.). 1965. pap. 5.95 (*0-8392-1150-3*) Astor-Honor.

Sinking Your Roots in Christ. Stephen D. Eyre. (Spiritual Encounter Guides Ser.). 96p. (Orig.). 1992. wbk. ed., pap. 4.99 (*0-8308-1177-X*, 1177) InterVarsity.

Sinko & Adams for Justice & Freedom: A Documentary Story. C. E. Ita. 1994. 10.95 (*0-533-10474-2*) Vantage.

Sinn Als Bedeutung: Bedeutungstheoretische Untersuchungen zur Psychoanalyse Sigmund Freuds. Stephan Achim. (Quellen und Studien zur Philosophie Ser.: Vol. 24). xvi, 174p. (GER.). (C). 1989. lib. bdg. 78.25 (*3-11-011949-8*) De Gruyter.

Sinn Fein: The First Election 1908. Ciaran O. Duibhir. Ed. by Prionnsias O'Duignean. (North Leitrim History Ser.). (Illus.). 52p. (Orig.). 1994. pap. 9.95 (*1-873437-02-1*, Pub. by Drumlin Pubns Ltd IE) Irish Bks Media.

Sinn-und Sachverwandten Worter. (Duden Ser.: Vol. 8). 801p. 1986. 33.50 (*3-411-20908-9*, Pub. by Bibliogr Inst Brockhaus GW) Langenscheidt.

Sinne: Beitrage Zur Geschichte der Physiologie und Psychologie Im Ittelalter Aus Hebraischen und Arabisch En Quellen. David Kaufmann. Ed. by Steven Katz. LC 79-7141. (Jewish Philosophy, Mysticism & History of Ideas Ser.). 1980. reprint ed. lib. bdg. 19.95 (*0-405-12267-5*) Ayer.

Sinner. Stewart MacGregor. LC 72-95425. 256p. 1973. 7.95 (*0-87955-903-9*) O'Hara.

Sinner from Toledo & Other Stories. Anton P. Chekhov. Tr. by Arnold Hinchliffe. LC 70-147269. 168p. 1975. 24.50 (*0-8386-7890-4*) Fairleigh Dickinson.

*__Sinners.__ Jackie Collins. 304p. mass mkt. 5.99 (*0-06-101253-X*, Harp PBks) HarpC.

Sinners. Jackie Collins. 1991. mass mkt. 5.99 (*0-671-73787-2*) PB.

Sinners & Saints: Tales of Old Laramie City. Gladys B. Beery. LC 93-38315. 288p. (Orig.). 1993. pap. 12.95 (*0-931271-23-1*) Hi Plains Pr.

Sinners & Shrouds. Jonathan Latimer. LC 82-21449. 1983. pap. 4.95 (*0-685-57776-7*) S&S Trade.

Sinner's Guide. Venerable Louis of Granada. LC 84-51820. 395p. 1994. reprint ed. pap. 12.00 (*0-89555-254-X*) TAN Bks Pubs.

*__Sinners in the Hands of an Angry Church: Finding a Better Way to Influence Our Culture.__ Dean Merrill. LC 97-23181. 1997. pap. write for info. (*0-310-21308-8*) Zondervan.

Sinners in the Hands of an Angry God. Jonathan Edwards. (Orig.). pap. 0.99 (*0-87377-004-8*) GAM Pubns.

Sinners in the Hands of an Angry God. Jonathan Edwards. (Orig.). 1992. pap. 1.99 (*0-87552-233-5*, Pub. by Evangelical Pr) Presby & Reformed.

*__Sinners in the Hands of an Angry God.__ Jonathan Edwards. 64p. (Orig.). 1997. mass mkt. 1.99 (*0-88368-415-2*) Whitaker Hse.

Sinners in the Hands of an Angry God. large type ed. Jonathan Edwards. 28p. (Orig.). 1995. pap. 9.00 (*0-9627423-4-1*) Candlestick.

Sinners in the Hands of an Angry God. rev. ed. Duncan Campbell. 19p. (C). 1992. pap. text ed. 0.95 (*0-942889-06-1*) Christ Life Pubns.

Sinners in the Hands of an Angry God. Jonathan Edwards. (Notable American Authors Ser.). (Orig.). 1992. reprint ed. lib. bdg. 75.00 (*0-7812-2765-8*) Rprt Serv.

Sinners in the Hands of an Angry God, Made Easier to Read. Jonathon Edwards. Ed. by John J. Fanella. 32p. (Orig.). 1996. pap. 1.99 (*0-87552-213-0*) Presby & Reformed.

Sinners' League: A Gun Pedersen Mystery. L. L. Enger. 288p. 1994. 21.00 (*1-883402-64-6*) S&S Trade.

*__Sinners, Lovers, & Heroes: An Essay on Memorializing in Three American Cultures.__ Richard Morris. LC 97-13019. 224p. (C). 1997. pap. text ed. 18.95 (*0-7914-3494-X*) State U NY Pr.

*__Sinners, Lovers, & Heroes: An Essay on Memorializing in Three American Cultures.__ Richard Morris. LC 97-13019. 224p. (C). 1997. text ed. 56.50 (*0-7914-3493-1*) State U NY Pr.

Sinner's Return to God: Or, the Prodigal Son. Michael Mueller. LC 82-74244. 224p. 1993. reprint ed. pap. 11.00 (*0-89555-205-1*) TAN Bks Pubs.

Sinnett Genealogy: Michael Sinnett of Harpswell, Me., His Ancestry & Descendants. Charles N. Sinnett. (Illus.). 137p. 1995. reprint ed. pap. 19.50 (*0-8328-4840-9*); reprint ed. lib. bdg. 29.50 (*0-8328-4839-5*) Higginson Bk Co.

Sinning Saints? Howard Sweeten. 1979. pap. 6.99 (*0-88019-109-0*) Schmul Pub Co.

Sinning with Annie & Other Stories. Paul Theroux. 176p. 1990. mass mkt. 3.95 (*0-8041-0517-0*) Ivy Books.

Sinnliche Gehalt der Wahrnehmung. Richard Schantz. (Introductiones Ser.). 284p. (GER.). (C). 1990. 46.00 (*3-88405-065-6*) Philosophia Pr.

*__Sino-American Alliance: Nationalist China & American Cold War Strategy in Asia.__ John W. Garver. LC 97-5056. 1997. pap. write for info. (*0-7656-0053-6*) M E Sharpe.

*__Sino-American Alliance: Nationalist China & American Cold War Strategy in Asia.__ John W. Garver. LC 97-5056. 450p. (C). (gr. 13). 1997. 76.95 (*0-7656-0025-0*, East Gate Bk) M E Sharpe.

Sino-American Economic Exchanges: The Legal Contributions. Guiguo Wang. LC 84-18108. 236p. 1985. text ed. 49.95 (*0-275-90179-3*, C0179, Praeger Pubs) Greenwood.

Sino-American Foreign Policy & Relations since World War II. Joseph D. Lowe. LC 88-91014. (Illus.). xii, 125p. 1994. pap. 30.00 (*0-930325-07-9*) Lowe Pub.

Sino-American Relations after Normalization. Steven M. Goldstein & Jay Mathews. LC 86-81093. (Headline Ser.: No. 276). (Illus.). 64p. (Orig.). 1985. pap. 5.95 (*0-87124-105-6*) Foreign Policy.

Sino-American Relations, 1945-1955: A Joint Reassessment of a Critical Decade. Harry Harding & Yuan Ming. LC 89-10196. (America in the Modern World: Studies in International History). 343p. 1989. 45.00 (*0-8420-2333-X*) Scholarly Res Inc.

Sino Chinese-English Dictionary. Commercial Press Staff. 564p. (CHI & ENG.). 1980. pap. 14.95 (*0-8288-1601-8*, M14526) Fr & Eur.

Sino-Conflict: A Historical Bibliography. Jessica Brown. (ABC-CLIO Research Guides). 1984. lib. bdg. 49.50 (*0-87436-382-9*) ABC-CLIO.

Sino-Indian Border Dispute: A Legal Study. Chih Lu. LC 85-12713. (Contributions in Political Science Ser.: No. 139). 153p. 1986. text ed. 45.00 (*0-313-25024-3*, LSI/, Greenwood Pr) Greenwood.

Sino-Indian Border Dispute & Sino-Indian Relations. Xuecheng Liu. 236p. (C). 1994. lib. bdg. 46.50 (*0-8191-9699-1*) U Pr of Amer.

Sino Indian Relations. Ed. by Chopra Surendra. 1985. 17.95 (*0-318-37269-X*) Asia Bk Corp.

Sino-Indian Relations, 1948-52: Role of K. M. Panikar. Karunakar Gupta. (C). 1987. 16.00 (*0-8364-2199-X*, Pub. by Minerva II) S Asia.

Sino-Iranica: Chinese Contributions to the History of Civilization in Ancient Iran, with Special Reference to the History of Cultivated Plants & Products. Berthold Laufer. LC 20-5115. (Field Museum of Natural History, Publication 184, Anthropological Ser.: Vol. 15, No. 3). 436p. 1919. reprint ed. pap. 124.30 (*0-608-02108-3*, 2062757) Bks Demand.

Sino Iranica: Chinese Contributions to the History of Civilization in Iran. Berthold Laufer. 1976. lib. bdg. 59.95 (*0-8490-2608-3*) Gordon Pr.

Sino-Iranica see Beginnings of Porcelain in China: Field Museum of Natural History

Sino-Japanese Negotiations of 1915: Japanese & Chinese Documents & Chinese Official Statement. Carnegie Endowment for International Peace Staff. LC 75-36222. reprint ed. 27.50 (*0-404-14473-X*) AMS Pr.

Sino-Japanese Relations since 1894. Joseph D. Lowe. LC 89-91187. (Illus.). xxxii, 375p. 1994. 80.00 (*0-930325-14-1*) Lowe Pub.

Sino-Judaic Bibliographies of Rudolf Loewenthal. Rudolf Loewenthal. Ed. by Michael Pollak. (Bibliographica Judaica Ser.: No. 12). 208p. 1988. pap. 20.00 (*0-87820-910-7*) Hebrew Union Coll Pr.

Sino-Jurchen Vocabulary of the Bureau of Interpreters. Daniel Kane. LC 89-60480. (Uralic & Altaic Ser.: Vol. 153). 461p. 1989. 32.50 (*0-933070-23-3*) Res Inst Inner Asian Studies.

Sino-Latin American Economic Relations. He Li. LC 91-19434. 192p. 1991. text ed. 55.00 (*0-275-93759-3*, C3759, Praeger Pubs) Greenwood.

Sino-Russian St. Petersburg Treaty of 1881: Diplomatic History. Alexei D. Voskressenski. LC 94-41596. 239p. (C). 1995. lib. bdg. 69.00 (*1-56072-208-8*) Nova Sci Pubs.

Sino-Soviet Border Dispute in the 1970's. Tsien-hua Tsui. 220p. 25.00 (*0-88962-215-9*); pap. 14.95 (*0-88962-214-0*) Mosaic.

Sino-Soviet Conflict. Ed. by Leopold Labedz & George Urban. LC 65-18351. 6500. 18.95 (*0-8023-1070-2*) Dufour.

Sino-Soviet Conflict over India. Hemen Ray. (C). 1988. 16.00 (*81-7017-206-3*, Pub. by Abhinav II) S Asia.

Sino-Soviet Confrontation since Mao Zedong: Dispute, Detente, or Conflict. Alfred D. Low. (Social Science Monographs). 322p. 1987. text ed. 68.50 (*0-88033-958-6*) East Eur Monographs.

Sino-Soviet Crisis Politics: A Study of Political Change & Communication. Richard Wich. (East Asian Monographs: No. 96). 321p. 1980. 26.00 (*0-674-80935-1*) HUP.

Sino-Soviet Cultural Frontier: The Ili Kazakh Autonomous Chou. George Moseley. LC 67-827. (East Asian Monographs: No. 22). 171p. 1966. pap. 11.00 (*0-674-80925-4*) HUP.

Sino-Soviet Dispute: An Analysis of the Polemics. Alfred D. Low. LC 74-2949. 364p. 1976. 39.50 (*0-8386-1479-5*) Fairleigh Dickinson.

SINO-Soviet Documents Annual, 1989. Ed. by Stephen Uhalby, Jr. 1993. 95.00 (*0-87569-164-1*) Academic Intl.

Sino-Soviet Normalization & Its International Implications. Lowell Dittmer. LC 91-15770. (Jackson School Publications in International Studies). 352p. 1992. text ed. 35.00 (*0-295-97118-5*) U of Wash Pr.

Sino-Soviet Relations: Nineteen Seventeen to Nineteen Forty-Nine; with Emphasis on the Early Period. Joseph D. Lowe. LC 88-91013. (Illus.). xiv, 55p. 1994. pap. 22.00 (*0-930325-06-0*) Lowe Pub.

Sino-Soviet Relations: Re-examining the Prospects for Normalization. T. G. Hart. (Swedish Institute of International Affairs Ser.). 150p. 1987. text ed. 45.95 (*0-566-05449-3*, Pub. by Dartmth Pub UK) Ashgate Pub Co.

Sino-Soviet Relations since Mao: The Chairman's Legacy. Carl G. Jacobsen. LC 80-27319. 176p. 1981. text ed. 45.00 (*0-275-90652-3*, C0652, Praeger Pubs) Greenwood.

Sino-Vatican Relations: Problems in Conflicting Authority, 1976-1986. Beatrice Leung. (London School of Economics Monographs in International Studies). (Illus.). 384p. (C). 1992. text ed. 85.00 (*0-521-38173-8*) Cambridge U Pr.

Sino-Vietnamese Conflict. Eugene K. Lawson. LC 84-8329. 336p. 1984. text ed. 55.00 (*0-275-91212-4*, C1212, Praeger Pubs) Greenwood.

Sino-Vietnamese Territorial Dispute. Pao-min Chang. LC 85-19445. (Washington Papers: No. 118). 128p. 1985. text ed. 45.00 (*0-275-90022-3*, C0022, Praeger Pubs); pap. text ed. 11.95 (*0-275-91456-9*, B1456, Praeger Pubs) Greenwood.

Sino-Western Calendar for Two Thousand Years. Chung-san Hsueh. 1973. lib. bdg. 300.00 (*0-87968-096-2*) Krishna Pr.

Sinonimos, Lexikon der Spanischen Synonyme. Felipa Moreno Torres. 504p. (GER & SPA.). 1992. 29.95 (*0-7859-8512-3*, 3860470191) Fr & Eur.

Sinonimus Castellanos. 17th ed. Roque Barcia. 590p. (SPA.). 1978. 15.95 (*0-8288-5271-5*, S11889) Fr & Eur.

Sinonoma Bartholomei. John Mirfeld. Ed. by J. L. Mowat. (Anecdota Oxoniensia Ser.: No. 1). 1988. reprint ed. 37.50 (*0-404-63951-8*) AMS Pr.

Sinopah, the Indian Boy. James W. Schultz. LC 83-73494. (J. W. Schultz Reprint Ser.: Bk.3). (Illus.). 103p. (J). (gr. 4-7). 1984. reprint ed. pap. 7.95 (*0-8253-0320-6*) Confluence Pr.

*__Sinopsis de Datos Biologicos y Pesqueros de la Sardina, Sardinops Sagax, Jenyns, 1842, en el Pacifico Suroriental.__ rev. ed. 65p. (SPA.). 1988. 12.00 (*92-5-302702-9*, Pub. by FAO IT) Bernan Associates.

Sinousities: Lesbian Poetic Politics. Jeffner Allen. LC 95-22357. (Illus.). 200p. 1996. 35.00 (*0-253-33022-X*); pap. 15.95 (*0-253-21046-1*) Ind U Pr.

Sins. Judith Gould. 1982. pap. 5.99 (*0-451-15803-2*, Sig) NAL-Dutton.

Sins. F. Sinoil Jose. 207p. 1996. 22.00 (*0-679-42018-5*) Random.

*__Sins & Needles.__ Materson. 1996. write for info. (*0-15-200786-5*) HarBrace.

Sins & Secrets. Ed. by Dorothy M. Ogrizovich. 115p. (Orig.). (C). 1994. pap. 6.95 (*0-9639229-0-4*) Plautz Enter.

Sin's Explosion - Revival or Ruin. Jack Van Impe. 444p. 1988. pap. 9.00 (*0-934803-65-X*) J Van Impe.

Sins for Father Knox. Josef Skvorecky. 1991. pap. 8.95 (*0-393-30787-5*) Norton.

Sins of Appu's Mother. T. Janakiraman. Tr. by Tamil M. Krishnan from TAM. 168p. 1972. pap. 2.75 (*0-88253-042-9*) Ind-US Inc.

*__Sins of Childhood & Other Stories.__ Boleslaw Prus. Tr. by Bill Johnston from POL. 250p. 1997. 42.95 (*0-8101-1274-4*); pap. 14.95 (*0-8101-1462-3*) Northwestern U Pr.

Sins of Commission. Susan Wright. Ed. by Kevin Ryan. (Star Trek: The Next Generation Ser.). 288p. (Orig.). 1994. mass mkt. 5.50 (*0-671-79704-2*) PB.

Sins of Herod. Frank Slaughter. 26.95 (*0-89190-284-8*) Amereon Ltd.

*__Sins of Honor.__ Bill Bonanno. 1998. pap. 24.95 (*0-525-94203-3*) NAL-Dutton.

Sins of Israel. Stanley Yalkowsky. ix, 392p. 1996. 30.00 (*0-9620984-5-0*) Crucible Pubns.

Sins of Madame Eglentyne: And Other Essays on Chaucer. Richard Rex. LC 94-48358. 208p. 1995. 35.00 (*0-87413-567-2*) U Delaware Pr.

Sins of New York. Edward Van Every. LC 70-177502. (Illus.). 1972. reprint ed. 30.95 (*0-405-09038-2*, Pub. by Blom Pubns UK) Ayer.

Sins of Omission. Fern Michaels. 512p. 1989. mass mkt. 5.99 (*0-345-34120-1*) Ballantine.

Sins of Omission. Fern Michaels. 1994. reprint ed. lib. bdg. 22.00 (*0-7278-4670-1*) Severn Hse.

Sins of Omission: Critical Studies of CBC Television News. Barry Cooper. 224p. (C). 1994. 29.95 (*0-8020-0597-7*) U of Toronto Pr.

Sins of Our Fathers: A Profile of Pennsylvania Attorney General LeRoy S. Zimmerman & a Historical Explanation of the Suicide of State Treasurer R. Budd Dwyer. William Keisling & Richard Kearns. Ed. by Cecil Brooks. (Illus.). 108p. (Orig.). 1988. pap. 7.95 (*0-9620251-0-0*) Yardbird Bks.

Sins of Our Sons. Sonny Girard. Ed. by Doug Grad. 384p. (Orig.). 1995. mass mkt. 5.99 (*0-671-74515-8*) PB.

Sins of Philip Fleming. Irving Wallace. 228p. 1993. reprint ed. pap. 7.95 (0-8119-0754-6) LIFETIME.

Sins of Saint Anthony: Tales of the Theatre. Charles W. Collins. LC 72-116948. (Short Story Index Reprint Ser.). 1977. 20.95 (0-8369-3450-4) Ayer.

Sins of Severac Bablon. Sax Rohmer. 1967. 10.00 (0-685-22714-6) Bookfinger.

Sins of Summer. Dorothy Garlock. 416p. (Orig.). 1994. mass mkt. 5.99 (0-446-36414-2) Warner Bks.

Sins of Summer. large type ed. Dorothy Garlock. LC 94-25462. 515p. 1994. lib. bdg. 23.95 (0-8161-7461-X, GK Hall) Thorndike Pr.

Sins of Sumuru. Sax Rohmer. 1977. reprint ed. 8.50 (0-685-88227-6) Bookfinger.

Sins of the Blood. Kristine K. Rusch. 400p. 1994. mass mkt. 5.50 (0-440-21540-4) Dell.

Sins of the Cities of the Plain. 2nd ed. 1995. mass mkt. 5.95 (1-56333-322-8, Badboy) Masquerade.

Sins of the Father. Allan Massie. 304p. 1992. 19.95 (0-88184-849-2) Carroll & Graf.

Sins of the Father. Marianne Morris. LC 92-42184. 1993. pap. 9.99 (0-8163-1146-3) Pacific Pr Pub Assn.

***Sins of the Father: A Novel.** Will Cunningham. 288p. 1997. pap. 12.99 (0-7852-8129-0) Nelson.

Sins of the Father: Joseph P. Kennedy & the Dynasty He Founded. Ronald Kessler. (Illus.). 496p. 1996. 24.95 (0-446-51884-0) Warner Bks.

Sins of the Father: Joseph P. Kennedy & the Dynasty He Founded. Ronald Kessler. 432p. 1997. mass mkt. 6.99 (0-446-60384-8) Warner Bks.

Sins of the Fathers. (Chief Inspector Wexford Ser.). 1986. mass mkt. 5.99 (0-345-34253-4) Ballantine.

Sins of the Fathers. Lawrence Block. 192p. 1991. mass mkt. 5.99 (0-380-76363-X) Avon.

Sins of the Fathers. Sam Chupp. (World of Darkness: Wraith Ser.). 272p. 1995. mass mkt. 4.99 (0-06-105472-0) HarpC.

Sins of the Fathers. Susan Howatch. 1985. mass mkt. 6.99 (0-449-20798-6, Crest) Fawcett.

***Sins of the Fathers.** Jane Jenson. 1997. pap. 5.99 (0-451-45607-6, ROC) NAL-Dutton.

Sins of the Fathers. Ruth Rendell. 1994. reprint ed. lib. bdg. 29.95 (1-56849-322-3) Buccaneer Bks.

***Sins of the Fathers: An Anthology of Clerical Crime.** Mark Bryant. 246p. 1997. 26.00 (0-575-06384-X, Pub. by V Gollancz UK) Trafalgar.

Sins of the Fathers: Hawthorne's Psychological Themes. Frederick Crews. 1989. pap. 14.95 (0-520-06817-3) U CA Pr.

Sins of the Fathers Vol. IV: The Church & the World - The West & the Wider World. Lillian C. Harris. (Church & the World Ser.: Vols. 4 & 4). 193p. 1989. 28.85 (0-940121-08-5) Cross Cultural Pubns.

Sins of the Flesh. Don Davis & Jay Davis. 416p. 1989. mass mkt. 4.50 (0-8125-1679-6) Tor Bks.

Sins of the Flesh. Fern Michaels. 448p. (Orig.). 1990. mass mkt. 5.99 (0-345-34122-8) Ballantine.

Sins of the Flesh. Fern Michaels. 1994. pap. 8.95 (0-345-38662-0) Ballantine.

Sins of the Flesh. Fern Michaels. 448p. 1995. reprint ed. 22.00 (0-7278-4754-6) Severn Hse.

Sins of the Mother. Maria Eftimiades. 1995. mass mkt. 5.50 (0-312-95658-4) St Martin.

***Sins of the Mother.** Cheryl Saban. 256p. 1997. pap. 22.95 (0-7871-1268-2, Dove Bks) Dove Audio.

Sins of the Mother. B. Webster. Date not set. 3.98 (0-8317-8202-1) Smithmark.

Sins of the Mothers. Brenda Webster. LC 93-70943. 364p. 1993. 21.00 (1-880909-05-7) Baskerville.

Sins of the Son. Carlton Stowers. LC 95-2636. (Illus.). 256p. 1995. 22.95 (0-7868-6091-X) Hyperion.

Sins of the Sons. Dominick Dunne. 1997. 25.00 (0-517-58387-9) Random Hse Value.

Sins of the Wolf. Anne Perry. 1995. mass mkt. 6.99 (0-8041-1383-1) Ivy Books.

Sins of the Wolf. large type ed. Anne Perry. 720p. 1994. lib. bdg. 24.95 (0-7862-0319-6) Thorndike Pr.

Sins That Crucify. Howard W. Roberts. 112p. (Orig.). 1994. pap. 10.95 (1-880837-84-6) Smyth & Helwys.

Sinsemilla Technique. 120p. 1982. 24.95 (0-86719-328-X) Last Gasp.

***Sinsemilla Technique.** Kayo. 132p. 1997. pap. 24.95 (0-86719-303-4) Last Gasp.

Sinsemilla Tips: The Best of. 3rd rev. ed. Tom Alexander. Ed. by Trisha Coene. (Illus.). 288p. 1996. pap. 21.95 (0-944557-02-3) New Moon Pub.

Sintered Machine Elements. B. Kubicki. 1995. text ed. 105.00 (0-13-812637-2) P-H.

Sintering. M. B. Waldron & B. L. Daniell. LC 79-307614. (Monographs in Powder Science & Technology). 118p. reprint ed. pap. 33.70 (0-317-10497-7, 2019651) Bks Demand.

Sintering, Vol. 3. 480p. 1992. 120.00 (1-878954-22-9) Metal Powder.

Sintering & Plastic Deformation: Proceedings of the Fundamental Phenomena in the Materials Science Symposium, 1st, Boston, 1963. Fundamental Phenomena in the Materials Science Symposium Staff. Ed. by L. J. Bonis & H. H. Hausner. LC 64-20752. (Fundamental Phenomena in the Material Sciences Ser.: Vol. 1). 146p. reprint ed. pap. 41.70 (0-317-09858-6, 2003371) Bks Demand.

Sintering Processes. Ed. by G. C. Kuczynski. LC 79-25813. (Materials Science Research Ser.: Vol. 13). 586p. 1980. 135.00 (0-306-40336-6, Plenum Pr) Plenum.

Sintering Technology. Randall M. German et al. LC 96-26522. 524p. 1996. 185.00 (0-8247-9775-2) Dekker.

Sintering Theory & Practice. Randall M. German. LC 95-20223. 568p. 1996. text ed. 74.95 (0-471-05786-X) Wiley.

Sintering '85. Ed. by Hayne Palmour, III et al. 442p. 1987. 105.00 (0-306-42541-6, Plenum Pr) Plenum.

Sintesis de Distancia e Immersion en Cuatro Obras de Antonio Buero Vallejo. Mary K. Rice. LC 91-3802. (American University Studies: Romance Languages & Literature: Ser. II, Vol. 169). 112p. (C). 1992. text ed. 35.95 (0-8204-1555-3) P Lang Pubng.

Sintesis de Doctrina Biblica. Charles C. Ryrie. 208p. (SPA.). 1979. pap. 8.99 (0-8254-1636-1, Edit Portavoz) Kregel.

***Sintesis del Nuevo Testamento Tomo I.** Charles Porter. (TEE Ser.). 221p. (SPA.). 1991. 6.95 (1-879892-01-4) Editorial Bautista.

***Sintesis del Nuevo Testamento Tomo II.** Charles Porter. (TEE Ser.). 222p. (SPA.). 1978. 6.95 (1-879892-16-2) Editorial Bautista.

Sintomas, Sus Causas y Curas - Symptoms, Their Causes & Cures: How to Understand & Treat 265 Health Concerns. Prevention Magazine Editors. 1996. 29.95 (0-87596-366-8) Rodale Pr Inc.

Sintra Museum of Art. Berardo Collection Staff. 304p. 1996. pap. 60.00 (1-881616-72-X) Dist Art Pubs.

Sinus Disease: Current Therapy. Kennedy. 1997. write for info. (0-7216-5406-1) Saunders.

***Sinus Handbook: A Self-Help Guide.** Muriel K. MacFarlane. LC 96-61828. (Illus.). 312p. 1997. pap. 14.95 (1-887053-08-5) United Res CA.

Sinus Node: Structure, Function, & Clinical Relevance. Felix I. Bonke. 1978. lib. bdg. 165.00 (90-247-2064-8) Kluwer Ac.

Sinus Node Inhibitors: A New Concept in Angina Pectoris. Ed. by A. Hjalmarson & W. I. Remme. 72p. 1992. 29.00 (0-387-91393-9) Spr-Verlag.

***Sinus Sourcebook.** Deborah F. Rosin. Date not set. 25.00 (1-56565-643-1) Contemp Bks.

Sinus Survival: The Holistic Medical Treatment for Allergies, Asthma, Bronchitis, Colds, & Sinus. 3rd expanded rev. ed. Robert S. Ivker. LC 95-17371. 240p. (Orig.). 1995. pap. 12.95 (0-87477-807-7, Tarcher Putnam) Putnam Pub Group.

Sinuses. Ed. by Paul J. Donald et al. LC 94-13768. 688p. 1994. text ed. 199.00 (0-7817-0041-8) Lppncott-Raven.

Sinusitis: Pathogenesis & Treatment. Ed. by Howard M. Druce. LC 93-20821. (Clinical Allergy & Immunology Ser.: Vol. 1). 360p. 1993. 125.00 (0-8247-8845-1) Dekker.

Siobhan: A Memoir of an Actress. Michael OhAodha. (Illus.). 190p. 1995. 31.95 (0-86322-188-2, Pub. by Brandon Bk Pubs IE) Irish Bks Media.

Siobhan's Journey: A Belfast Girl Visits the United States. Barbara Beirne. (Photo Bks.). (Illus.). 48p. (J). (ps-5). 1993. lib. bdg. 19.95 (0-87614-728-7, Carolrhoda) Lerner Group.

Siolence: Essays on Women, Violence, & Silence. Susan McMaster. 1996. pap. text ed. 14.95 (1-55082-158-X, Pub. by Quarry Pr CN) LPC InBook.

SIOR Industrial Real Estate Market Survey: 1986 Review-1987 Forecast. National Association of Realtors, Economics & Research Division Staff. 24p. 1987. per. 50.00 (0-939623-06-4) Soc Industrial Realtors.

Siouan Tribes of the East. James Mooney. LC 73-108504. (American Indian History Ser.). (Illus.). 1970. reprint ed. 39.00 (0-403-00348-2) Scholarly.

Siouuan Tribes of the East. James Mooney. (Bureau of American Ethnology Bulletins Ser.). 101p. 1995. lib. bdg. 79.00 (0-7812-4022-0) Rprt Serv.

Sioux. B. Brooks. (Native American People Ser.). (Illus.). 32p. (J). (gr. 5-8). 1989. 11.95 (0-685-58585-9); lib. bdg. 15.94 (0-86625-382-3) Rourke Corp.

Sioux. Irene Handl. Ed. by Robert Gottlieb. LC 84-48795. 1985. 15.95 (0-394-54444-7) Knopf.

Sioux. Elaine Landau. LC 89-5654. (First Bks.). (Illus.). 64p. (J). (gr. 4-6). 1989. lib. bdg. 21.00 (0-531-10754-X) Watts.

Sioux. Elaine Landau. (Illus.). 64p. (J). (gr. 3 up). 1991. pap. 6.95 (0-531-15606-0) Watts.

Sioux. Robert Nicholson. (Journey into Civilization Ser.). (Illus.). 32p. (J). (gr. 3-7). 1994. lib. bdg. 15.95 (0-7910-2708-2) Chelsea Hse.

Sioux. Robert Nicholson. (Journey into Civilization Ser.). (Illus.). 32p. (J). (gr. 3-7). 1994. pap. 7.95 (0-7910-2732-5) Chelsea Hse.

Sioux. Alice Osinski. LC 84-7629. (New True Bks.). (Illus.). 48p. (J). (gr. k-4). 1984. pap. 5.50 (0-516-41929-3); lib. bdg. 19.00 (0-516-01929-5) Childrens.

Sioux. Hawk Sneve & Virginia Driving. (Illus.). (J). (gr. 2-6). 1995. pap. 6.95 (0-8234-1171-0) Holiday.

Sioux: A First American's Book. Virginia D. Sneve. LC 92-23946. (Illus.). 32p. (J). (gr. 2-6). 1993. lib. bdg. 16.95 (0-8234-1017-X) Holiday.

Sioux: Life & Customs of a Warrior Society. Royal B. Hassrick et al. LC 64-11331. (Civilization of the American Indian Ser.: No. 72). (Illus.). 400p. 1988. reprint ed. pap. 18.95 (0-8061-2140-8) U of Okla Pr.

Sioux & Other Native American Cultures of the Dakotas: An Annotated Biography. Ed. by Karen P. Zimmerman & Christopher J. Hoover. LC 93-25004. (Bibliographies & Indexes in Anthropology Ser.: No. 8). 320p. 1993. text ed. 69.50 (0-313-29093-8, GR9093, Greenwood Pr) Greenwood.

Sioux Chronicle. George E. Hyde. LC 56-11233. 1993. pap. 16.95 (0-8061-2483-0) U of Okla Pr.

Sioux Dawn. 1994. pap. 16.95 (0-7871-0094-3, Dove Bks) Dove Audio.

Sioux Dog Dance. Richard Red Hawk. (CSU Poetry Ser.: No. XXXV). 60p. (Orig.). 1991. pap. 8.00 (0-914946-90-0) Cleveland St Univ Poetry Ctr.

Sioux Falls: The City & The People. William J. Reynolds. LC 94-28677. (Illus.). (Orig.). 1994. pap. 5.95 (1-56037-070-X) Am Wrld Geog.

Sioux Indian Religion: Tradition & Innovation. Ed. by Raymond J. DeMallie & Douglas R. Parks. LC 86-40527. (Illus.). 240p. 1989. pap. 14.95 (0-8061-2166-1) U of Okla Pr.

***Sioux Indians.** Bill Lund. LC 97-6394. (Native Peoples Ser.). (J). 1998. write for info. (1-56065-563-1) Capstone Pr.

Sioux Indians: A Socio-Ethnological History. G. Mallery et al. (Illus.). 1897. 24.50 (0-914074-06-7, J M C & Co) Amereon Ltd.

Sioux Music. William N. Fenton. 1991. lib. bdg. 59.00 (0-403-08975-1) Scholarly.

Sioux of the Rosebud: A History in Pictures. Henry W. Hamilton & Jean T. Hamilton. LC 78-145506. (Civilization of the American Indian Ser.: Vol. 111). (Illus.). 320p. 1980. pap. 21.95 (0-8061-1622-6) U of Okla Pr.

***Sioux Slaughter.** David Thompson. (Davy Crockett Ser.: No. 2). 176p. (Orig.). 1997. mass mkt. 3.99 (0-8439-4157-X) Dorchester Pub Co.

Sioux Splendor. F. Rosanne Bittner. 448p. 1995. mass mkt. 4.99 (0-8217-5157-3, Zebra Kensgtn) Kensgtn Pub Corp.

Sioux Sunrise. Veronica Blake. 1994. pap. 4.50 (0-8217-4718-5) NAL-Dutton.

Sioux Uprising in Minnesota, 1862: Jacob Nix's Eyewitness History. Jacob Nix. Ed. by Don H. Tolzmann from GER. Tr. by Gretchen Steinhauser & Eberhard Reichmann from GER. (Illus.). xxii, 165p. (ENG & GER.). 1994. reprint ed. pap. text ed. 12.80 (1-880788-02-0) MKGAC & IGHS.

Sioux Uprising of 1862. rev. ed. Kenneth Carley. LC 76-16499. (Illus.). v, 102p. 1976. pap. 8.50 (0-87351-103-4) Minn Hist.

Sip of Aesop. Aesop. LC 94-41002. (Illus.). 32p. (J). (gr. k-5). 1995. 14.95 (0-590-47895-8, Blue Sky Press) Scholastic Inc.

***Sip, Slurp, Soup, Soup Caldo, Caldo, Caldo.** Diane G. Bertrand. (Illus.). (J). 1997. 14.95 (1-55885-183-6, Pinata Bks) Arte Publico.

Sip Through Time: A Collection of Old Brewing Recipes, in a Single Illustrated Volume, Containing Hundreds of Old Recipes for Ale, Beer, Mead, Metheglin, Cider, Perry, Brandy, Liqueurs, Distilled Waters, Hypocras, Wines, etc., Dating from 1800 B. C. to Modern Times. Cindy Renfrow. (Illus.). 335p. (Orig.). 1995. pap. 22.00 (0-9628598-3-4) C Renfrow.

Sip to Shore. Jan Robinson. 128p. 1986. pap. 10.95 (0-9612686-2-X) Ship-Shore.

Sipapu Odyssey. 2nd ed. Dorvshka Maerd. (Illus.). 128p. 1995. reprint ed. pap. 6.00 (1-56935-045-0) Phoenix Source.

Siphonaptera of the Indian Subregion. Ravi Iyenger. (Oriental Insects Monographs: No. 3). 1973. pap. 30.00 (1-877711-13-6) Assoc Pubs FL.

***Siphonini: (Diptera: Tachinidae) of Europe.** Stig Andersen. (Fauna Entomologica Scandinavica Ser.: Vol. 33). (Illus.). 192p. 1996. text ed. 93.00 (90-04-10731-2, NLG145) E J Brill.

Sippar-Amnanum Pt. 1: The Ur-Utu Archive: Transliterations, Translations. K. Van Lerberghe & G. Voet. (Texts Ser.: Series 3, Vol. 1). xii, 194p. 1991. pap. 65.00 (0-614-96324-9, Pub. by Recherches et Pubns SZ) Eisenbrauns.

Sippin' Bill Padgett. (Illus.). 52p. 1988. 12.95 (0-934073-04-X) Rountree Pub NC.

Sippurim, 5 pts. in 2, Set. Ed. by Wolf Pascheles. (Volkskundliche Quellen Ser.: No. IV). 1976. reprint ed. write for info. (3-487-06035-3) G Olms Pubs.

SIPRI Yearbook, 1979: World Armaments & Disarmament. Stockholm International Peace Research Institute Staff. 698p. 1979. 90.00 (0-85066-181-1) Taylor & Francis.

SIPRI Yearbook, 1980. Stockholm International Peace Research Institute Staff. 514p. 1980. 90.00 (0-85066-201-X) Taylor & Francis.

SIPRI Yearbook, 1982: World Armaments & Disarmament. Stockholm International Peace Research Institute Staff. 516p. 1982. 90.00 (0-85066-230-3) Taylor & Francis.

SIPRI Yearbook, 1983. Stockholm International Peace Research Institute Staff. 682p. 1983. 90.00 (0-8002-3084-1) Taylor & Francis.

SIPRI Yearbook, 1983: World Armaments & Disarmament. 14th ed. Stockholm International Peace Research Institute Staff. 500p. 1983. 90.00 (0-85066-247-8) Taylor & Francis.

SIPRI Yearbook, 1984: World Armaments & Disarmament. Stockholm International Peace Research Institute Staff. LC 83-643843. (Peace Studies). (Illus.). 650p. 1984. 90.00 (0-85066-263-X) Taylor & Francis.

SIPRI Yearbook, 1990: World Armaments & Disarmament. Stockholm International Peace Research Institute Staff. (Illus.). 752p. 1990. 75.00 (0-19-827862-4) OUP.

SIPRI Yearbook, 1991: World Armaments & Disarmament. Stockholm International Peace Research Institute Staff. (Illus.). 782p. 1991. 85.00 (0-19-829145-0, 12318) OUP.

SIPRI Yearbook, 1993: World Armaments & Disarmament. Stockholm International Peace Research Institute Staff. 600p. 1993. 75.00 (0-19-829166-3) OUP.

SIPRI Yearbook, 1994: World Armaments & Disarmaments. Stockholm International Peace Research Institute Staff. 800p. 1994. 79.00 (0-19-829182-5) OUP.

SIPRI Yearbook 1995: Armaments, Disarmaments, & International Security. Stockholm International Peace Research Institute Staff. (SIPRI Yearbook Ser.). (Illus.). 800p. 1995. 95.00 (0-19-829193-0) OUP.

SIPRI Yearbook 1996: Armaments, Disarmament & International Security. Stockholm International Peace Research Institute Staff. (SIPRI Yearbook Ser.). (Illus.). 752p. 1996. 110.00 (0-19-829202-3) OUP.

***SIPRI Yearbook 1997: Armaments, Disarmament & International Security.** Stockholm International Peace Research Institute Staff. (SIPRI Yearbook). (Illus.). 816p. 1997. 115.00 (0-19-829312-7) OUP.

SIPRI Yearbooks, 1968-1979 Cumulative Index: World Armaments & Disarmament. Stockholm International Peace Research Institute Staff. 90p. 1980. 25.00 (0-85066-189-7) Taylor & Francis.

***Sips from Foreign Shores.** Mary L. Friesz et al. (Illus.). 60p. (Orig.). 1997. per. 9.95 (0-9650788-7-6) Mustard Seed CA.

Sips of Living Water. Friends of East Bay Crisis Pregnancy Center Staff. 44p. 1993. pap. 4.95 (0-939513-78-1) Joy Pub SJC.

Sips of Wein. Anna M. Weinreis. (Illus.). 48p. 1984. pap. 4.00 (0-9610130-2-8, Wein Cellar) Melius Pub.

Sipuncula: Their Systematics, Biology, & Evolution. Edward B. Cutler. (Comstock Bk.). (Illus.). 480p. 1994. 69.95 (0-8014-2843-2) Cornell U Pr.

SiQueiros. D. Anthony White. (Illus.). 450p. (ENG & SPA.). 1990. 35.00 (0-915745-20-8) Floricanto Pr.

Siqueiros: His Life & Works. Philip Stein. Ed. by Ann Warren. (Illus.). 416p. 1994. 49.50 (0-7178-0709-6); pap. 29.95 (0-7178-0706-1) Intl Pubs Co.

Siquiatria de Dios. Charles L. Allen. 176p. 1975. 3.95 (0-88113-280-2) Edit Betania.

Sir A. Sherley His Relation of Travels into Persia. Anthony Sherley. LC 74-80232. (English Experience Ser.: No. 695). 140p. 1974. reprint ed. 15.00 (90-221-0695-0) Walter J Johnson.

Sir Alec Douglas-Home. Kenneth Young. LC 76-167748. (Illus.). 282p. 1971. 40.00 (0-8386-1041-2) Fairleigh Dickinson.

Sir Alexander Fleming: Man of Penicillin. John Malkin. 92p. 1985. 40.00 (0-907526-06-3, Pub. by Alloway Pub UK) St Mut.

Sir Alexander Mackenzie, Explorer & Fur Trader. Humphrey H. Wrong. (BCL1 - History - Canada Ser.). 171p. 1991. reprint ed. lib. bdg. 69.00 (0-7812-6373-5) Rprt Serv.

Sir Archibald. Wolo. LC 91-73411. (Illus.). 56p. (J). (ps-1). 1991. reprint ed. 14.95 (0-944439-22-5) Clark City Pr.

Sir Arthur Conan Doyle: Interviews & Recollections. Ed. by Harold Orel. LC 90-44945. 296p. 1991. text ed. 45.00 (0-312-05374-6) St Martin.

Sir Arthur Conan Doyle at the Cinema: A Critical Study of the Film Adaptations. Scott A. Nollen. (Illus.). 384p. 1996. lib. bdg. 45.00 (0-7864-0269-5) McFarland & Co.

***Sir Arthur Evans & the Minoans: An Archaeology of Myth & Ideals.** J. A. MacGillivray. 320p. 1997. 25.00 (0-06-017392-0) HarpC.

***Sir Arthur Newsholme & State Medicine 1885-1935.** John M. Eyler. (History of Medicine Ser.). (Illus.). 464p. (C). 1997. text ed. 64.95 (0-521-48186-4) Cambridge U Pr.

Sir Arthur Pinero's Plays & Players. Henry H. Fyfe. LC 78-6207. (Illus.). 319p. 1978. reprint ed. text ed. 59.75 (0-313-20391-1, FYSR, Greenwood Pr) Greenwood.

Sir Arthur Pinero's Plays & Players. Henry H. Fyfe. (BCL1-PR English Literature Ser.). 311p. 1992. reprint ed. lib. bdg. 89.00 (0-7812-7620-9) Rprt Serv.

Sir Arthur Sullivan. Arthur Lawrence. LC 79-27876. (Music Reprint Ser.: 1980). (Illus.). 340p. 1980. reprint ed. lib. bdg. 39.50 (0-306-76029-0) Da Capo.

Sir Arthur Sullivan. Arthur Lawrence. LC 72-3244. (English Biography Ser.: No. 31). 1972. reprint ed. lib. bdg. 66.95 (0-8383-1522-4) M S G Haskell Hse.

Sir Arthur Sullivan: A Resource Book. Philip H. Dillard. LC 96-10157. (Illus.). 424p. 1996. 49.50 (0-8108-3157-0) Scarecrow.

Sir Arthur Sullivan: His Life & Music. Benjamin W. Findon. 1976. reprint ed. 44.50 (0-404-12913-7) AMS Pr.

Sir Aurel Stein's Central Asia, 12 vols., Set. Prints India Staff. (C). 1988. 4,000.00 (0-7855-0048-0, Pub. by Print Hse II) St Mut.

Sir Bartle Frere & His Times. Rekha Ranande. (C). 1990. text ed. 18.50 (81-7099-222-2, Pub. by Mittal II) S Asia.

Sir Beves of Hamtoun: A Metrical Romance. Ed. by W. B. Turnbull. LC 72-144415. (Maitland Club, Glasgow, Publications: No. 44). reprint ed. 44.50 (0-404-53022-2) AMS Pr.

Sir Cadian Weight Management: Sir Cadian...It's about Time. Larry A. Richardson. LC 93-92672. (Illus.). 198p. (Orig.). 1993. pap. text ed. 20.00 (0-9636840-0-0) L A Richardson.

Sir Cedric. Roy Gerrard. LC 84-6111. (Illus.). 32p. (J). (ps up). 1984. 14.95 (0-374-36959-3) FS&G.

Sir Cedric. Roy Gerrard. (Sunburst Ser.). (Illus.). 32p. (J). (gr. k up). 1986. pap. 4.95 (0-374-46659-9) FS&G.

Sir Cedric Rides Again. Roy Gerrard. (Illus.). 32p. (J). (ps up). pap. 4.95 (0-374-46662-9, Sunburst Bks) FS&G.

Sir Cedric Rides Again. Roy Gerrard. (Illus.). 32p. (J). (ps up). 1986. 15.00 (0-374-36961-5, Sunburst Bks) FS&G.

Sir Charles. Charles Barkley. 1994. 10.00 (1-57042-121-8) Warner Bks.

Sir Charles: The Wit & Wisdom of Charles Barkley. Charles Barkley & Rick Reilly. 144p. 1995. mass mkt. 4.99 (0-446-60230-2) Warner Bks.

Sir Charles God Damn: The Life of Sir Charles G. D. Roberts. John C. Adams. 264p. 1986. 30.00 (0-8020-2595-1) U of Toronto Pr.

Sir Charles Grandison: The Compleat Conduct Book. Sylvia K. Marks. LC 85-47800. 176p. 1986. 36.50 (0-8387-5090-7) Bucknell U Pr.

Sir Charles Grey, First Earl Grey: Royal Soldier, Family Patriarch. Paul D. Nelson. LC 95-26341. (Illus.). 256p. 1996. 37.50 (0-8386-3673-X) Fairleigh Dickinson.

An Asterisk (*) at the beginning of an entry indicates that the title is appearing in BIP for the first time.

Sir Charles Lyell's Scientific Journals on the Species Question. Charles Lyell. Ed. by Leonard G. Wilson. LC 77-99848. (Yale Studies in the History of Science & Medicine: No. 5). (Illus.). 636p. reprint ed. pap. 180.00 (*0-8357-8322-7*, 2033922) Bks Demand.
Sir Charles Sedley, 1639-1701. Vivian De Sola Pinto. 1988. reprint ed. lib. bdg. 49.00 (*0-7812-0173-X*) Rprt Serv.
Sir Charles Sedley, 1639-1701. Vivian De Sola Pinto. (Illus.). 1971. reprint ed. 27.00 (*0-403-01150-7*) Scholarly.
Sir Charles Sedley, 1639-1701: A Study in the Life & Literature of the Restoration. Vivian de Sola Pinto. LC 76-85904. reprint ed. 49.50 (*0-404-05056-5*) AMS Pr.
Sir Charles V. Stanford. J. F. Porte. LC 76-12570. (Music Reprint Ser.). 1976. reprint ed. lib. bdg. 25.00 (*0-306-70790-X*) Da Capo.
Sir Claude MacDonald, the Open Door, & British Informal Empire in China, 1895-1900. Mary H. Wilgus. (Modern European History Ser.). 344p. 1987. text ed. 15.00 (*0-8240-7837-3*) Garland.
Sir Cleges: Sir Libeaus. Tr. by Jessie L. Weston. LC 72-141787. reprint ed. 22.50 (*0-404-00476-8*) AMS Pr.
Sir Cornelius Vermuyden: The Lifework of a Great Anglo-Dutchman in Land-Reclamation & Drainage, with Some Notes by the Author on the Present Condition of Drainage in England & a Resume of the Drainage Legislation in Holland. J. Korthals-Altes. Ed. by Mira Wilkins. LC 76-29751. (European Business Ser.). (Illus.). 1977. reprint ed. lib. bdg. 25.95 (*0-405-09767-0*) Ayer.
Sir Cumference. (J). 1998. pap. 3.99 (*0-679-88378-9*) Random.
***Sir Cumference.** (J). 1998. lib. bdg. 11.99 (*0-679-98378-3*) Random.
***Sir Cumference & the First Round Table: A Math Adventure.** Cindy Neuschwander. LC 97-5820. (Illus.). (J). 1997. pap. write for info. (*1-57091-152-5*) Charlesbridge Pub.
Sir Dana - A Knight: As Told by His Trusty Armor. Dana Fradon. LC 88-3968. (Illus.). 32p. (J). (gr. 3-7). 1988. pap. 13.95 (*0-525-44424-6*) Dutton Child Bks.
Sir David Lyndesay: The Historie of Squyer William Meldrum. Ed. by F. Hall. (EETS Original Ser.: Vol. 35). 1963. reprint ed. 20.00 (*0-19-722035-5*, Pub. by EETS UK) Boydell & Brewer.
Sir David Wilkie of Scotland (1785-1841) William J. Chiego et al. LC 86-63234. (Illus.). xix, 370p. 1987. pap. 24.95 (*0-88259-953-4*) NCMA.
Sir Day the Knight. Daniel T. Marsano. (Illus.). 48p. (J). (gr. k-6). 1993. 15.00 (*1-883960-11-8*) Henry Quill.
Sir De Villiers Graaff. Barnard. 1990. 36.95 (*0-86984-973-5*) Buttrwrth-Heinemann.
Sir Edmund Gosse. James D. Woolf. LC 79-125822. (English Authors Ser.). pap. text ed. 6.95 (*0-8290-2024-1*); lib. bdg. 17.95 (*0-89197-937-9*) Irvington.
Sir Edmund Hillary: To Everest & Beyond. Whitney Stewart. LC 95-23028. (YA). (gr. 5 up). 1996. lib. bdg. 23.95 (*0-8225-4927-1*, Lerner Publctns) Lerner Group.
Sir Edward Burne-Jones. Russell Ash. LC 93-3218. 1993. 29.95 (*0-8109-3126-5*) Abrams.
Sir Edward Burne-Jones: A Record & Review. Malcolm Bell. reprint ed. 37.50 (*0-404-00733-3*) AMS Pr.
Sir Edward Coke & "The Grievances of the Commonwealth," 1621-1628. Stephen D. White. LC 78-16418. (Studies in Legal History). xv, 327p. 1979. text ed. 45.00 (*0-8078-1335-4*) U of NC Pr.
Sir Edward Coke & "The Grievances of the Commonwealth", 1621-1628. Stephen D. White. LC 78-16418. (Studies in Legal History). 344p. 1979. reprint ed. pap. 98.10 (*0-608-02063-X*, 2062716) Bks Demand.
Sir Edward Elgar. John F. Porte. LC 75-107827. (Select Bibliographies Reprint Ser.). (Illus.). 1977. reprint ed. 21.95 (*0-8369-5194-8*) Ayer.
Sir Edward Elgar. John F. Porte. 214p. 1990. reprint ed. lib. bdg. 69.00 (*0-7812-9061-9*) Rprt Serv.
Sir Edward Seaward's Narrative of His Shipwreck, 3 Vols., Set. Edward Seaward. Ed. by Jane Porter. LC 79-164393. (Black Heritage Library Collection). 1977. reprint ed. 65.95 (*0-8369-8852-3*) Ayer.
Sir Edwyn Hoskyns As a Biblical Theologian. Richard E. Parsons. LC 85-25038. 152p. 1986. text ed. 29.95 (*0-312-72647-3*) St Martin.
Sir Eglamour of Artois. Ed. by F. E. Richardson. (EETS Original Ser.: Vol. 256). 1965. 30.00 (*0-19-722256-0*, Pub. by EETS UK) Boydell & Brewer.
Sir Ernest MacMillan: The Importance of Being Canadian. Ezra Schabas. (Illus.). 374p. 1996. 35.00 (*0-8020-2849-7*); pap. 18.95 (*0-8020-7871-0*) U of Toronto Pr.
Sir Francis Bacon's Cipher Story. Orville W. Owen. 218p. 1996. reprint ed. pap. 19.95 (*1-56459-591-9*) Kessinger Pub.
Sir Francis Drake. Roy Gerrard. pap. 3.95 (*0-374-46688-2*) FS&G.
Sir Francis Drake. Julian S. Corbett. LC 77-105513. (BCL Ser. II). reprint ed. 29.50 (*0-404-01725-8*) AMS Pr.
Sir Francis Drake. Julian S. Corbett. LC 68-25228. (English Biography Ser.: No. 31). 1969. reprint ed. lib. bdg. 75.00 (*0-8383-0932-1*) M S G Haskell Hse.
Sir Francis Drake: His Daring Deeds. Roy Gerrard. (Illus.). 32p. (J). (gr. 3 up). 1988. 15.00 (*0-374-36962-3*) FS&G.
Sir Francis Drake & the Struggle for an Ocean Empire. Alice Smith. Ed. by William H. Goetzmann. (World Explorers Ser.). (Illus.). 112p. (YA). (gr. 5 up). 1993. lib. bdg. 19.95 (*0-7910-1302-2*) Chelsea Hse.
Sir Francis Hincks: A Study of Canadian Politics, Railways, & Finance in the Nineteenth Century. Ronald S. Longley. Ed. by Stuart Bruchey. LC 80-1326. (Railroads Ser.). 1981. reprint ed. lib. bdg. 44.95 (*0-405-13800-8*) Ayer.
***Sir Galahad, Mr. Longfellow & Me.** Betty F. Horvath. LC 96-43460. (J). 1998. 15.00 (*0-689-81470-4*, Atheneum Bks Young) S&S Childrens.
Sir Gardner Wilkinson & His Circle. Jason Thompson. LC 91-47636. (Illus.). 326p. 1992. 29.95 (*0-292-77643-8*) U of Tex Pr.
Sir Garfield Todd & the Making of Zimbabwe. Ruth Weiss. (Illus.). 224p. 1993. text ed. 55.00 (*1-85043-693-2*, Pub. by I B Tauris UK) St Martin.
Sir Gawain: Eleven Romances & Tales. Ed. by Thomas Hahn. (Teams Middle English Text Ser.). 1995. pap. 16.00 (*1-879288-59-1*) Medieval Inst.
Sir Gawain & the Green Knight. Tr. by Marie Borroff. (Orig.). (C). 1967. pap. text ed. 7.95 (*0-393-09754-4*) Norton.
Sir Gawain & the Green Knight. Ed. by J. A. Burrow. Tr. by Brian Stone. (Classics Ser.). 176p. 1987. pap. 9.95 (*0-14-042295-1*, Penguin Bks) Viking Penguin.
Sir Gawain & the Green Knight. Selina Hastings. LC 80-85379. (Illus.). 32p. (J). (gr. 3-7). 1981. 16.00 (*0-688-00592-6*) Lothrop.
Sir Gawain & the Green Knight. Ed. by James R. Kreuzer. LC 59-6208. (Rinehart Editions Ser.). 167p. (C). 1959. pap. text ed. 20.00 (*0-03-008880-1*) HB Coll Pubs.
Sir Gawain & the Green Knight. Richard H. Osberg. LC 89-13304. (American University Studies: English Language & Literature: Ser. IV, Vol. 112). 274p. 1990. text ed. 45.95 (*0-8204-1160-4*) P Lang Pubng.
Sir Gawain & the Green Knight. Intro. by Burton Raffel. (Orig.). 1970. pap. 2.50 (*0-451-62456-4*, ME2312, Ment) NAL-Dutton.
Sir Gawain & the Green Knight. Tr. by Burton Raffel. (Orig.). 1970. pap. 2.95 (*0-451-62624-9*) NAL-Dutton.
Sir Gawain & the Green Knight. Tr. by Burton Raffel. 1970. mass mkt. 5.99 (*0-451-62823-3*) NAL-Dutton.
Sir Gawain & the Green Knight. Dennis Scott. (J). (gr. k up). 1978. 6.00 (*0-87602-202-6*) Anchorage.
Sir Gawain & the Green Knight. Dennis Scott. (Illus.). 1979. 9.95 (*0-930970-01-2*); pap. 4.95 (*0-930970-02-0*) O'Neill Pr.
Sir Gawain & the Green Knight. Tr. & Intro. by Brian Stone. 176p. 1959. pap. 7.95 (*0-14-044092-5*, Penguin Classics) Viking Penguin.
Sir Gawain & the Green Knight. J. R. R. Tolkien. 176p. 1980. mass mkt. 5.99 (*0-345-27760-0*) Ballantine.
Sir Gawain & the Green Knight. Tr. by James Winny. 200p. 1992. 27.95 (*0-921149-94-8*); pap. 9.95 (*0-921149-92-1*) Broadview Pr.
Sir Gawain & the Green Knight. 2nd ed. Ed. by J. R. R. Tolkien & E. V. Gordon. 262p. 1968. pap. 15.95 (*0-19-811486-9*) OUP.
Sir Gawain & the Green Knight. Ed. by Israel Gollancz. (EETS Original Ser.: Vol. 210). 1963. reprint ed. 20.00 (*0-19-722210-2*, Pub. by EETS UK) Boydell & Brewer.
Sir Gawain & the Green Knight. Intro. by R. A. Waldron. LC 75-129568. (York Medieval Texts Ser). (C). 1993. reprint ed. 15.95 (*0-8101-0328-1*) Northwestern U Pr.
Sir Gawain & the Green Knight. Tr. by Jessie L. Weston. LC 70-135732. reprint ed. 22.50 (*0-404-00471-7*) AMS Pr.
Sir Gawain & the Green Knight: A Reference Guide. Ed. by Robert J. Blanch. LC 82-50412. 298p. 1984. 22.50 (*0-87875-244-7*) Whitston Pub.
Sir Gawain & the Green Knight: A Secondary Bibliography, 1978-1989. Meg Stainsby. LC 91-36810. (Medieval Bibliographies Ser.: Vol. 13). 218p. 1992. text ed. 15.00 (*0-8153-0504-4*, 91-36810) Garland.
Sir Gawain & the Green Knight: Sources & Analogues. Elisabeth Brewer. (Arthurian Studies: No. XXVII). 192p. (C). 1992. pap. 23.00 (*0-85991-359-7*) Boydell & Brewer.
Sir Gawain & the Green Knight: Sources & Analogues. Ed. by Elisabeth Brewer. (Arthurian Studies: No. XXVII). 192p. (C). 1993. 53.00 (*0-85991-358-9*) Boydell & Brewer.
Sir Gawain & the Green Knight & the French Arthurian Romance. Ad Putter. 288p. 1995. 60.00 (*0-19-818253-8*) OUP.
Sir Gawain & the Green Knight & the Idea of Righteousness. Gerald Morgan. (Dublin Studies in Medieval Renaissance Literature). 192p. 1991. 14.95 (*0-7165-2470-8*, Pub. by Irish Acad Pr IE) Intl Spec Bk.
Sir Gawain & the Green Knight Notes. John C. Gardner. 1967. pap. 3.95 (*0-8220-0515-8*) Cliffs.
Sir Gawain & the Green Knight, Pearl, Cleanness & Patience. rev. ed. Ed. by J. J. Anderson. (Everyman Paperback Classics Ser.). 288p. (C). 1996. pap. 6.95 (*0-460-87510-8*, Everyman's Classic Lib) C E Tuttle.
Sir Gawain & the Lady of Lys. Tr. by Jessie L. Weston. LC 70-141789. reprint ed. 22.50 (*0-404-00478-4*) AMS Pr.
Sir Gawain & the Loathly Lady. Illus. by Juan Wijngaard. LC 85-63. 32p. (J). (gr. k up). 1987. reprint ed. pap. 4.95 (*0-688-07046-9*, Mulberry) Morrow.
Sir Gawain & the Loathly Lady - Sir Gawain y la Abominable Dama. Selina Hastings. (SPA.). (J). 14.95 (*84-372-6604-1*) Santillana.
Sir Gawain at the Grail Castle. Tr. by Jessie L. Weston. LC 76-141788. reprint ed. 22.50 (*0-404-00477-6*) AMS Pr.
Sir George Alexander & the St. James' Theatre. Alfred E. Mason. LC 72-84520. (Illus.). 1972. 24.95 (*0-405-08762-4*, Pub. by Blom Pubns UK) Ayer.
Sir George Beaumont: A Collector of Genius. Felicity Owen & David Brown. LC 87-26114. 248p. (C). 1988. text ed. 47.50 (*0-300-04183-7*) Yale U Pr.
Sir George Etienne Cartier, Bart. His Life & Times. John R. Boyd. LC 74-164590. (Select Bibliographies Reprint Ser.). 1977. reprint ed. 48.95 (*0-8369-5874-8*) Ayer.
Sir George Etienne Cartier, Bart: His Life & Times: A Political History of Canada from 1814 until 1873. John Boyd. (BCL1 - History - Canada Ser.). 1991. reprint ed. text ed. 99.00 (*0-7812-6361-1*) Rprt Serv.
Sir George Goldie, Founder of Nigeria: A Memoir. Dorothy Violet Wellington. Ed. by Mira Wilkins. LC 76-29765. (European Business Ser.). (Illus.). 1977. reprint ed. lib. bdg. 20.95 (*0-405-09779-4*) Ayer.
Sir Gibbie. George MacDonald. 1989. 27.50 (*0-940652-55-2*) Sunrise Bks.
Sir Gibbie. George MacDonald. (George MacDonald Original Works: Series I). 450p. 1992. reprint ed. 18.00 (*1-881084-01-9*) Johannesen.
Sir Giles Goosecap. LC 70-133738. (Tudor Facsimile Texts. Old English Plays Ser.: No. 112). reprint ed. 49.50 (*0-404-53412-0*) AMS Pr.
Sir Grumpalot. (Loony Balloonies Ser.). (Illus.). 8p. (J). (gr. k-3). 1992. pap. 3.95 (*1-56680-605-4*) Mad Hatter Pub.
Sir Hans Sloane & the British Museum. Gavin R. De Beer. LC 74-26258. (History, Philosophy & Sociology of Science Ser.). (Illus.). 1975. reprint ed. 24.95 (*0-405-06586-8*) Ayer.
Sir Harry: The Number One International Chauvinist of the Year. John H. Braccio. (Illus.). 112p. 1994. pap. 5.95 (*0-9637854-2-7*) Reg Psychol.
Sir Harry Gibbs: Without Fear Or Favour. Joan Priest. 207p. 1995. 43.00 (*0-646-23693-8*); pap. 32.00 (*0-614-07153-4*) Gaunt.
Sir Harry Hotspur of Humblethwaite. Anthony Trollope. Ed. by N. John Hall. LC 80-1891. (Selected Works of Anthony Trollope). 1981. reprint ed. lib. bdg. 38.95 (*0-405-14158-0*) Ayer.
Sir Harry Hotspur of Humblethwaite. Anthony Trollope. 248p. 1985. reprint ed. pap. 6.95 (*0-486-24953-0*) Dover.
Sir Harry Hotspur of Humblewaite. Anthony Trollope. Ed. by N. John Hall. (World's Classics Ser.). 288p. 1992. pap. 7.95 (*0-19-282205-5*, 12513) OUP.
Sir Harry Lauder Discography. Darryl Baker & Larry F. Kiner. LC 90-49631. (Illus.). 222p. 1990. 42.50 (*0-8108-2384-5*) Scarecrow.
Sir Harry Parkes: British Representative in Japan, 1865-1883. Gordon Daniels. (Meiji Ser.: No. 2). 264p. (C). 1995. text ed. 45.00 (*1-873410-36-0*, Pub. by Curzon Press UK) UH Pr.
Sir Henry. Robert Nathan. LC 79-12787. vi, 187p. 1979. reprint ed. pap. 21.00 (*0-89370-236-6*); reprint ed. lib. bdg. 31.00 (*0-89370-136-X*) Borgo Pr.
Sir Henry Bessemer, F. R. S. An Autobiography. Henry Bessemer. 496p. 1989. text ed. 33.90 (*0-901462-49-7*, Pub. by Inst Materials UK) Ashgate Pub Co.
Sir Henry Maine: A Brief Memoir of His Life. Mountstuart E. Grant Duff. Ed. by Whitley Stokes. 451p. 1979. reprint ed. lib. bdg. 35.00 (*0-8377-0609-2*) Rothman.
Sir Henry Maine: A Study in Victorian Jurisprudence. Raymond Cocks. (Cambridge Studies in English Legal History). 248p. 1989. text ed. 59.95 (*0-521-35343-2*) Cambridge U Pr.
Sir Henry Morgan, the Buccaneer, 3 vols. in 2, Set. Edward G. Howard. LC 79-8136. reprint ed. 84.50 (*0-404-61923-1*) AMS Pr.
***Sir Henry Pottinger.** Pottinger. 1997. text ed. 35.00 (*0-312-16506-4*) St Martin.
Sir Henry Vane, Theologian: A Study in Seventeenth-Century Religious & Political Discourse. David Parnham. LC 95-9478. 368p. 1997. 46.50 (*0-8386-3681-0*) Fairleigh Dickinson.
Sir Humphrey Davy's Published Works. June Z. Fullmer. LC 69-18029. 124p. 1969. 17.95 (*0-674-80961-0*) HUP.
Sir, I Represent Christian Salesmanship. William E. Cox. pap. 3.99 (*0-87377-036-6*) GAM Pubns.
SIR Industrial Real Estate Market Survey, Fall-Winter 1983. Society of Industrial Realtors Staff & National Association of Realtors Staff. 213p. 1984. per. 35.00 (*0-939623-12-9*) Soc Industrial Realtors.
SIR Industrial Real Estate Market Survey, Fall-Winter 1984. Society of Industrial Realtors Staff & National Association of Realtors Staff. 234p. 1984. per. 35.00 (*0-939623-14-5*) Soc Industrial Realtors.
SIR Industrial Real Estate Market Survey, Fall-Winter 1985. Society of Industrial Realtors Staff & National Association of Realtors Staff. 226p. 1985. per. 35.00 (*0-939623-16-1*) Soc Industrial Realtors.
SIR Industrial Real Estate Market Survey, Fall 1981. Society of Industrial Realtors Staff & National Association of Realtors Staff. 106p. 1981. per. 35.00 (*0-939623-09-9*) Soc Industrial Realtors.
SIR Industrial Real Estate Market Survey, Fall 1980. Society of Industrial Realtors Staff & National Association of Realtors Staff. 92p. 1980. per. 35.00 (*0-939623-18-8*) Soc Industrial Realtors.
SIR Industrial Real Estate Market Survey, Fall 1982. Society of Industrial Realtors Staff & National Association of Realtors Staff. 186p. 1982. per. 35.00 (*0-939623-27-7*) Soc Industrial Realtors.
SIR Industrial Real Estate Market Survey, May 1980. Society of Industrial Realtors Staff & National Association of Realtors Staff. 69p. 1980. 35.00 (*0-939623-07-2*) Soc Industrial Realtors.
SIR Industrial Real Estate Market Survey, Spring-Summer 1983. Society of Industrial Realtors Staff & National Association of Realtors Staff. 218p. 1983. per. 35.00 (*0-939623-11-0*) Soc Industrial Realtors.
SIR Industrial Real Estate Market Survey, Spring-Summer 1984. Society of Industrial Realtors Staff & National Association of Realtors Staff. 196p. 1984. per. 35.00 (*0-939623-13-7*) Soc Industrial Realtors.
SIR Industrial Real Estate Market Survey, Spring-Summer 1985. Society of Industrial Realtors Staff & National Association of Realtors Staff. 236p. 1985. per. 35.00 (*0-939623-15-3*) Soc Industrial Realtors.
SIR Industrial Real Estate Market Survey, Spring-Summer 1986. Society of Industrial Realtors Staff & National Association of Realtors Staff. 220p. 1986. per. 35.00 (*0-939623-17-X*) Soc Industrial Realtors.
SIR Industrial Real Estate Market Survey, Spring 1981. Society of Industrial Realtors Staff & National Association of Realtors Staff. 102p. 1981. per. 35.00 (*0-939623-08-0*) Soc Industrial Realtors.
SIR Industrial Real Estate Market Survey, Spring 1982. Society of Industrial Realtors Staff & National Association of Realtors Staff. 120p. 1982. per. 35.00 (*0-939623-10-2*) Soc Industrial Realtors.
Sir Isaac Newton. Deborah Hitzeroth & Sharon Leon. LC 93-38680. (Importance of Ser.). 112p. (J). (gr. 5-8). 1994. lib. bdg. 17.96 (*1-56006-046-8*) Lucent Bks.
Sir Isaac Newton. Edward N. Andrade. LC 79-15162. 140p. 1979. reprint ed. text ed. 59.75 (*0-313-22022-0*, ANNE, Greenwood Pr) Greenwood.
Sir Isaac Newton: A Catalogue of Manuscripts & Papers. Ed. by Peter Jones. (C). 1992. lib. bdg. 105.00 (*0-85964-226-7*) Chadwyck-Healey.
***Sir Israel Gollancz Memorial Lectures in Old English: Beowulf: The Monsters & the Critics.** J. R. Tolkien. 1977. 3.98 (*0-85672-003-8*) David Brown.
Sir Jack Hobbs: Test Match Career. Spellmount Ltd. Publishers Staff. (C). 1986. 80.00 (*0-946771-61-8*, Pub. by Spellmount UK) St Mut.
Sir James Douglas & British Columbia. Walter N. Sage. (BCL1 - History - Canada Ser.). 398p. 1991. reprint ed. lib. bdg. 89.00 (*0-7812-6375-1*) Rprt Serv.
Sir James Frazer & the Literary Imagination: Essays in Affinity & Influence. Ed. by Robert G. Fraser. LC 90-8880. 256p. 1991. text ed. 49.95 (*0-312-05321-5*) St Martin.
Sir James Gowans: Romantic Rationalist. Duncan McAra. 1977. 14.95 (*0-8464-0851-1*) Beekman Pubs.
Sir James Mackintosh: The Whig Cicero. Patrick O'Leary. 224p. 1989. text ed. 29.95 (*0-08-034531-X*, Pub. by Aberdeen U Pr) Macmillan.
Sir James Martin. Sara Sharman. 1996. 42.95 (*1-85260-551-0*, Pub. by J H Haynes & Co UK) Motorbooks Intl.
Sir James Pennethorne & the Making of Victorian London. Geoffrey Tyack. (Studies in the History of Architecture). (Illus.). 333p. (C). 1993. text ed. 150.00 (*0-521-39434-1*) Cambridge U Pr.
***Sir James Steuart's Principles of Political Economy, 4 vols.** Ed. by Andrew S. Skinner et al. (Pickering Masters Ser.). 2000p. 1997. 475.00 (*1-85196-246-8*, Pub. by Pickering & Chatto UK) Ashgate Pub Co.
Sir John: The Many Faces of Gielgud. Clive Francis. (Illus.). 158p. 1995. 29.95 (*0-86051-903-1*, Robson-Parkwest) Parkwest Pubns.
***Sir John A. Macdonald: The Man & the Politician.** Donald Swainson. (Illus.). 170p. 1989. pap. 12.95 (*0-919627-29-3*, Pub. by Quarry Pr CN) LPC InBook.
***Sir John Aubrey, Sixth Baronet of Llantrithyd (1739-1826)** John Aubrey-Fletcher. 376p. 1988. 18.00 (*0-904920-15-1*, Pub. by Leopards Head Pr UK) David Brown.
Sir John Betjeman: A Bibliography of Writings by & about Him. Margaret L. Stapleton. (Author Bibliographies Ser.: No. 21). 149p. 1974. 20.00 (*0-8108-0758-0*) Scarecrow.
Sir John Beverley Robinson: Bone & Sinew of the Compact. Patrick Brode. (Publications of the Osgoode Society). 344p. 1984. pap. 17.95 (*0-8020-3419-5*) U of Toronto Pr.
Sir John Beverley Robinson: Bone & Sinew of the Compact. Patrick Brode. LC 85-133805. (Illus.). 342p. reprint ed. pap. 97.50 (*0-7837-0538-7*, 2040866) Bks Demand.
Sir John Chardin's Travels in Persia. John Chardin. LC 76-181928. (BCL Ser.: No. I). reprint ed. 44.50 (*0-404-01449-6*) AMS Pr.
Sir John Dodderidge: Celebrated Barrister of Britain, 1555-1628. Elizabeth D. Wheeler. LC 91-37395. (Illus.). 252p. 1992. lib. bdg. 89.95 (*0-7734-9888-5*) E Mellen.
***Sir John Everett Millais.** Russell Ash. (Illus.). 96p. 1996. 45.00 (*1-85793-792-9*, Pub. by Pavilion UK) Trafalgar.
Sir John Falstaff Knight. Rupin W. Desai. Ed. by John E. Westburg. LC 75-5210. (Comparative Literature Studies). (Illus.). 133p. pap. 10.00 (*0-87423-013-6*) Westburg.
***Sir John Fortescue: On the Laws & Governance of England.** Ed. by Shelley Lockwood. (Cambridge Texts in the History of Political Thought Ser.). 204p. (C). 1997. text ed. 59.95 (*0-521-43445-9*); pap. text ed. 18.95 (*0-521-58996-7*) Cambridge U Pr.
Sir John Harington's Translation of Orlando Furioso. Ludovico Ariosto. (Centaur Classics Ser.). 591p. reprint ed. pap. 168.50 (*0-8357-6653-5*, 2035322) Bks Demand.
Sir John Hawkins, the Time & the Man. James A. Williamson. LC 77-110885. 542p. 1970. reprint ed. text ed. 75.00 (*0-8371-4569-4*, WIJH, Greenwood Pr) Greenwood.
Sir John Hicks: Critical Assessments, 4 vols., Set. John Cunningham & Ronald N. Woods. (Critical Assessments Ser.). 1136p. (C). 1989. boxed, text ed. 650.00 (*0-415-01272-4*) Routledge.
Sir John Mandeville. M. C. Seymour. (Authors of the Middle Ages Ser.). 64p. 1993. pap. 15.00 (*0-86078-371-5*, Pub. by Variorum UK) Ashgate Pub Co.
Sir John Mandeville: John Trevisa, William Langland, Thomas Hoccleve. M. C. Seymour et al. LC 94-22615. (Authors of the Middle Ages, 1-4, English Writers of the Late Middle Ages Ser.). 1994. 72.50 (*0-86078-466-5*, Pub. by Variorum UK) Ashgate Pub Co.
Sir John Mandeville: The Man & His Book. Malcolm Letts. LC 70-161957. 192p. 1949. reprint ed. 25.00 (*0-403-01318-6*) Scholarly.
Sir John Medley: A Memoir. Geoffrey Serle. 160p. 1993. 29.95 (*0-522-84540-1*, Pub. by Melbourne Univ Pr AT) Paul & Co Pubs.

S

An Asterisk (*) at the beginning of an entry indicates that the title is appearing in BIP for the first time.

Sir John Oldcastle. Michael Drayton et al. LC 72-133657. (Tudor Facsimile Texts. Old English Plays Ser.: No. 89). reprint ed. 59.50 (*0-404-53389-2*) AMS Pr.

Sir John Paston's Grete Boke: A Descriptive Catalogue with an Introduction, of British Library Ms. Lansdowne 285. G. A. Lester. 197p. 1984. 71.00 (*0-85991-161-6*) Boydell & Brewer.

Sir John Pritchard: His Life in Music. Helen Conway. (Illus.). 434p. 1994. 45.00 (*0-233-98845-9*, Pub. by A Deutsch UK) Trafalgar.

***Sir John Randolph's King's Bench Reports.** John Randolph. Ed. by W. Hamilton Bryson. LC 96-35586. 104p. 1996. 45.00 (*1-57588-125-X*, 310720) W S Hein.

Sir John Richardson, FRS (Seventeen Eighty-Seven to Eighteen Sixty-Five) Arctic Explorer, Natural Historian, Naval Surgeon. Robert E. Johnson. 300p. 1976. 55.00 (*0-85066-074-2*) Taylor & Francis.

Sir John Robert Seeley: A Study of the Historian. Gustav A. Rein. LC 82-18662. 155p. 1987. text ed. 25.00 (*0-89341-550-2*, Longwood Academic) Hollowbrook.

Sir John Soane: Enlightenment Thought & the Royal Academy Lectures. David Watkin. (Studies in the History of Architecture). (Illus.). 675p. (C). 1996. text ed. 125.00 (*0-521-44091-2*) Cambridge U Pr.

Sir John Soane's Museum. Susan F. Millenson. LC 86-24926. (Architecture & Urban Design Ser.: No. 18). (Illus.). 202p. reprint ed. pap. 57.60 (*0-8357-1766-6*, 2070611) Bks Demand.

Sir John Tenniel: Alice's White Knight. Rodney Engen. 164p. 1991. text ed. 77.95 (*0-85967-872-5*, Pub. by Scolar Pr UK) Ashgate Pub Co.

Sir John Tenniel: Aspects of His Work. Roger Simpson. LC 92-58943. 1994. 55.00 (*0-8386-3493-1*) Fairleigh Dickinson.

Sir John Vanbrugh: A Reference Guide. Frank G. McCormick. LC 92-13099. (Reference Bks.). 200p. 1992. 50.00 (*0-8161-8990-0*, Hall Reference) Macmillan.

Sir John Vanbrugh: The Playwright as Architect. Frank G. McCormick. (Illus.). 224p. 1991. 32.50 (*0-271-00723-0*) Pa St U Pr.

Sir John's Diary: The Fun-Tome of Opera. John Van Kestern. LC 94-36843. (Illus.). 225p. 1994. pap. 14.95 (*1-56825-022-3*) Rainbow Books.

Sir Jonas Moore: Practical Mathematics & Restoration Science. Frances Willmoth. (Illus.). 256p. (C). 1993. 63.00 (*0-85115-321-6*) Boydell & Brewer.

***Sir Joseph Banks: A Global Perspective.** Ed. by R. E. Banks et al. (Illus.). ii, 235p. 1994. pap. 24.00 (*0-947643-61-3*, Pub. by Royal Botnic Grdns UK) Balogh.

Sir Joseph Banks & Iceland. Halldor Hermannsson. LC 28-11080. (Islandica Ser.: Vol. 18). 1928. 25.00 (*0-527-00348-4*) Periodicals Srv.

Sir Joseph Banks, 1743-1820: A Guide to Biographical & Bibliographical Sources. Harold B. Carter. (Illus.). 328p. 1987. 48.00 (*0-906795-45-1*) Oak Knoll.

Sir Joseph Ward: A Political Biography. Michael Bassett. (Auckland University Press Book). (Illus.). 368p. (C). 1993. 39.95 (*1-86940-079-8*, 14466) OUP.

***Sir Joseph Whitworth.** Norman Atkinson. (Illus.). 320p. 1996. 44.95 (*0-7509-1211-1*, Pub. by Sutton Pubng UK) Bks Intl VA.

***Sir Joseph Whitworth: The World's Best Mechanician.** Norman Atkinson. (Illus.). 352p. (Orig.). 1997. pap. 26.95 (*0-7509-1648-6*, Pub. by Sutton Pubng UK) Bks Intl VA.

Sir Joshua, Himself. Sandy Ray. Ed. by Cheryle Sytsma. LC 90-63622. (Illus.). 30p. (Orig.). (J). (gr. k-5). 1991. pap. write for info. (*1-879068-02-8*) Ray-Ma Natsal.

Sir Joshua Reynolds: The Painter in Society. Richard Wendorf. (Illus.). 328p. 1996. 49.95 (*0-674-80966-1*) HUP.

Sir Joshua Reynolds: The Subject Pictures. Martin J. Postle. LC 93-28687. (Illus.). 328p. (C). 1995. text ed. 80.00 (*0-521-42066-0*) Cambridge U Pr.

Sir Joshua Reynolds: Discourses on Art. Robert R. Wark. LC 74-17647. (Paul Mellon Centre for Studies in British Art). (Illus.). 384p. 1981. pap. 25.00 (*0-300-02775-3*, Y-411) Yale U Pr.

Sir Kenelm Digby, F.R.S. An Annotated Bibliography. Davida Rubin. (Illus.). 130p. 1991. 95.00 (*0-930405-29-3*) Norman SF.

Sir Lacksalot & the Two Headed Dragon. Lenerd Thomas & Janis Thomas. (Illus.). (J). (gr. k-6). 1990. 16.95 (*1-879480-00-X*) L T Pub.

Sir Lacksalot & the Two Headed Dragon Meet the Savage Sea Serpent. Janis Thomas & Lenerd Thomas. LC 91-61114. (Sir Lacksalot & the Two Headed Dragon Ser.). (Illus.). 48p. (J). (gr. k-5). 1991. 16.95 (*1-879480-01-8*) L T Pub.

***Sir Lancelot.** Sophie Windham. Date not set. pap. 5.95 (*0-399-21413-5*) Putnam Pub Group.

Sir Laughalot. (Loony Balloonies Ser.). (Illus.). 8p. (J). (gr. k-3). 1992. pap. 3.95 (*1-56680-604-6*) Mad Hatter Pub.

***Sir Lawerence Alma Tadema.** Barroes. LC 96-30853. 1997. 65.00 (*0-8478-2001-7*) Rizzoli Intl.

Sir Lawrence Alma-Tadema. Russell Ash. 1990. 29.95 (*0-8109-1898-6*) Abrams.

Sir Leslie Martin: Architecture, Education, Research. Ed. by Peter Carolin & Trevor Dannatt. (Illus.). 144p. 1996. 45.00 (*1-85490-441-8*) Academy Ed UK.

Sir Lionel. Fred Archer. (Illus.). 339p. 1980. 12.95 (*0-86595-005-9*) Gift Pubns.

Sir Macfarlane Burnet: A Biography. Christopher Sexton. (Illus.). 300p. 1992. 45.00 (*0-19-553274-0*) OUP.

Sir Maggie, the Mighty. Michael P. Waite. LC 87-35527. (Building Christian Character Ser.). (Illus.). 32p. (J). (ps-2). 1988. 9.99 (*1-55513-616-8*, Chariot Bks) Chariot Victor.

Sir Matthew Hale, 1609-1676: Law, Religion & Natural Philosophy. Alan Cromartie. (Studies in Early Modern British History). 328p. (C). 1995. text ed. 59.95 (*0-521-45043-8*) Cambridge U Pr.

Sir Michael Tippett: A Bio-Bibliography. Compiled by Gordon Theil. LC 89-17185. (Music Reference Collection: No. 21). 357p. 1989. text ed. 59.95 (*0-313-24270-4*, TMT/, Greenwood Pr) Greenwood.

Sir Mistake & Mister Blunder: Collection of Satires & Parodies. Maksymilian B. Necker. 122p. (Orig.). 1989. pap. 13.50 (*1-877582-07-7*) Ardor Pub.

Sir! More Sir! The Joy of S&M. Master Jackson. 192p. (Orig.). 1992. pap. 14.95 (*0-943595-39-8*) Leyland Pubns.

Sir Nevill Mott: 65 Years in Physics. Ed. by N. F. Mott & A. S. Alexandrov. LC 95-18277. (Series in 20th Century Physics: Vol. 12). 750p. 1995. pap. text ed. 51.00 (*981-02-2252-1*) World Scientific Pub.

Sir Nevill Mott: 65 Years in Physics. Ed. by Nevill F. Mott & A. S. Alexandrov. LC 95-18277. (Series in 20th Century Physics: Vol. 12). 750p. 1995. text ed. 99.00 (*981-02-2237-8*) World Scientific Pub.

Sir Oliver Lodge: Psychical Researcher & Scientist. W. P. Jolly. LC 74-24803. 256p. 1975. 35.00 (*0-8386-1703-4*) Fairleigh Dickinson.

Sir Oliver Mowat. A. Margaret Evans. (Ontario Historical Studies). (Illus.). 544p. 1992. 50.00 (*0-8020-3392-X*); pap. 19.95 (*0-8020-3471-3*) U of Toronto Pr.

Sir Oliver Mowat: A Biographical Sketch, 2 vols., Set. Charles R. Biggar. LC 71-136404. (BCL Ser. I). reprint ed. 105.00 (*0-404-00858-5*) AMS Pr.

Sir Oliver Mowat: A Biographical Sketch, 2 vols., Set. Charles R. Biggar. (BCL1 - History - Canada Ser.). 1991. reprint ed. lib. bdg. 150.00 (*0-7812-6360-3*) Rprt Serv.

Sir Perceval of Galles & Ywain & Gawain. Ed. by Mary F. Braswell. (Teams Middle English Text Ser.). 1995. pap. 10.00 (*1-879288-60-5*) Medieval Inst.

Sir Percy & the Dragon. Helen Leetham. (Illus.). 32p. (J). (ps-1). 1994. 17.95 (*0-86264-273-6*, Pub. by Andersen Pr UK) Trafalgar.

Sir Peter Scott: Champion for the Environment & Founder of the World Wildlife Fund. Julia Courtney. LC 88-2076. (People Who Have Helped the World Ser.). (Illus.). 68p. (J). (gr. 5-6). 1989. lib. bdg. 23.93 (*1-55532-819-9*) Gareth Stevens Inc.

Sir Philip Sidney. Philip Sidney. Ed. by Katherine Duncan-Jones. (Oxford Authors Ser.). (Illus.). 446p. 1989. pap. 22.00 (*0-19-282024-9*) OUP.

Sir Philip Sidney. John A. Symonds. 1972. 59.95 (*0-8490-1055-1*) Gordon Pr.

Sir Philip Sidney: A Study in Conflict. C. Henry Warren. LC 67-30823. (English Biography Ser.: No. 31). 1969. reprint ed. lib. bdg. 75.00 (*0-8383-0737-X*) M S G Haskell Hse.

Sir Philip Sidney: An Annotated Bibliography of Texts & Criticism. Donald V. Stump et al. LC 93-12829. (Reference Ser.). 864p. 1994. 75.00 (*0-8161-8238-8*, Hall Reference) Macmillan.

Sir Philip Sidney: An Anthology of Modern Criticism. Ed. by Dennis Kay. 352p. 1988. 90.00 (*0-19-811204-1*) OUP.

Sir Philip Sidney: An Apology for Poetry. Ed. by Visvanath Chatterjee. 96p. (C). 1975. pap. 3.95 (*0-86125-617-4*, Pub. by Orient Longman Ltd II) Apt Bks.

Sir Philip Sidney: Courtier Poet. Katherine Duncan-Jones. (Illus.). 320p. 1991. text ed. 37.50 (*0-300-05099-2*) Yale U Pr.

Sir Philip Sidney: Selected Prose & Poetry. 2nd ed. Ed. by Robert Kimbrough. LC 82-51093. 576p. 1983. pap. 10.95 (*0-299-09134-1*) U of Wis Pr.

Sir Philip Sidney & Arcadia. Joan Rees. LC 89-46411. 1991. 32.50 (*0-8386-3406-0*) Fairleigh Dickinson.

Sir Philip Sidney & the Poetics of Protestantism: A Study of Contexts. Andrew D. Weiner. LC 78-25559. 243p. 1978. reprint ed. pap. 69.30 (*0-7837-2907-3*, 2057547) Bks Demand.

***Sir Philip Sidney (1554-1586) Selected Writings.** Ed. by Richard Dutton. pap. write for info. (*0-85635-625-5*, Pub. by Carcanet Pr UK) Paul & Co Pubs.

Sir Philip Sidney's Achievements. Ed. by M. J. Allen et al. LC 89-45860. (Studies in the Renaissance: No. 28). 1990. 42.50 (*0-404-62298-4*) AMS Pr.

Sir Philip Sidney's Defense of Poesy. Philip Sidney. Ed. by Lewis Soens. LC 74-108900. (Regents Critics Ser.). 137p. reprint ed. pap. 39.10 (*0-7837-5903-7*, 2045700) Bks Demand.

Sir Philip Sydney: 1586 & the Creation of a Legend. Jan A. Van Dorsten et al. (Publications of the Sir Thomas Browne Institute, Leiden, New Ser.: No. 9). (Illus.). x, 246p. 1986. 60.00 (*90-04-07923-8*) E J Brill.

Sir Philip's Folly. large type ed. Marion Chesney. LC 94-17132. 223p. 1994. lib. bdg. 17.95 (*0-8161-7414-8*, GK Hall) Thorndike Pr.

Sir Philip's Folly Vol. 1. Marion Chesney. 1994. mass mkt. 3.99 (*0-312-95336-4*) St Martin.

Sir Pompey & Madame Juno: And Other Tales. Martin D. Armstrong. LC 75-163021. (Short Story Index Reprint Ser.). 1977. reprint ed. 19.95 (*0-8369-3935-2*) Ayer.

Sir Ralph Esher. Leigh Hunt. LC 78-162913. (Bentley's Standard Novels Ser.: No. 118). reprint ed. 42.50 (*0-404-54518-1*) AMS Pr.

Sir Randal Cremer: His Life & Writings. Howard Evans. 1976. lib. bdg. 59.95 (*0-8490-2609-1*) Gordon Pr.

Sir Raymond Unwin: Architect, Planner & Visionary. Frank Jackson. Ed. by Peter Willis. (Architects in Perspective Ser.). (Illus.). 208p. 1986. pap. 29.95 (*0-302-00591-9*, Pub. by Zwemmer Bks UK) Sothebys Pubns.

Sir Reginald Blomfield: An Edwardian Architect. Richard A. Fellows. Ed. by Peter Willis. (Architects in Perspective Ser.). (Illus.). 184p. 1986. 29.95 (*0-302-00590-0*, Pub. by Zwemmer Bks UK) Sothebys Pubns.

Sir Rhys Ap Thomas. David Rees. 92p. 1992. pap. 21.00 (*0-86383-744-1*, Pub. by Gomer Pr UK) St Mut.

Sir Richard & the Dragon. Steven Leske. 14p. (J). (gr. k-6). 1992. pap. text ed. 5.99 (*1-881617-01-7*) Teapot Tales.

Sir Richard Blackmore. Solomon. 1980. 22.95 (*0-8057-6782-7*, Twayne) Scribnrs Ref.

Sir Richard Burton's Travels in Arabia & Africa: Four Lectures from a Huntington Library Manuscript. Richard Burton. LC 90-44363. (Illus.). 128p. 1990. 24.95 (*0-87328-131-4*) Huntington Lib.

Sir Richard F. Burton: A Biobibliographical Study. James A. Casada. 256p. 1990. 55.00 (*0-8161-9082-8*, Hall Reference) Macmillan.

Sir Richard Roos C., Lancastrian, 1410-1482. Ethel Seaton. 1988. reprint ed. lib. bdg. 99.00 (*0-7812-0063-6*) Rprt Serv.

Sir Richard Roos, Lancastrian Poet, c. 1410-1482. Ethel Seaton. LC 78-161959. reprint ed. 69.00 (*0-403-01322-4*) Scholarly.

Sir Richard Steele. M. P. The Later Career. Calhoun Winston. LC 75-112616. 283p. reprint ed. pap. 80.70 (*0-317-42062-3*, 2025882) Bks Demand.

Sir Richard Westmacott, Sculptor. Marie Busco. LC 93-28689. (Studies in the History of Art). (Illus.). 232p. (C). 1995. text ed. 115.00 (*0-521-39065-6*) Cambridge U Pr.

Sir Robert Chambers: Law, Literature, & Empire in the Age of Johnson. Thomas M. Curley. LC 96-33813. (Illus.). 640p. 1997. 87.50 (*0-299-15150-6*) U of Wis Pr.

Sir Robert Cotton As Collector. Ed. by Christopher Wright. (Illus.). 384p. 1996. 120.00 (*0-7123-0358-8*, Pub. by Brit Library UK) U of Toronto Pr.

Sir Robert Falconer: A Biography. James G. Greenlee. (Illus.). 432p. 1988. 40.00 (*0-8020-2655-9*) U of Toronto Pr.

Sir Robert Filmer & English Political Thought. James Daly. LC 78-25913. 228p. reprint ed. pap. 65.00 (*0-8357-8323-5*, 2033982) Bks Demand.

Sir Robert Heath, 1575-1649: Window on an Age. Paul E. Kopperman. (Royal Historical Society: Studies in History). 345p. 1989. 71.00 (*0-86193-213-7*) Boydell & Brewer.

Sir Robert Peel. Anna A. Ramsay. LC 72-95076. (Select Bibliographies Reprint Ser.). 1977. 24.95 (*0-8369-5076-3*) Ayer.

Sir Robert Peel. Anna A. Ramsay. LC 72-95076. (Select Bibliographies Reprint Ser.). 1982. reprint ed. lib. bdg. 21.50 (*0-8290-0839-X*) Irvington.

Sir Robert Peel: Statesmanship, Power & Party. Eric J. Evans. (Lancaster Pamphlets Ser.). 128p. (C). 1991. pap. text ed. 11.95 (*0-415-06049-4*, A6174) Routledge.

Sir Robert Peel, 1788-1850: A Bibliography. Compiled by Leonard W. Cowie. LC 95-41985. (Bibliographies of British Statesmen Ser.: No. 13). 160p. 1996. text ed. 65.00 (*0-313-29447-X*, Greenwood Pr) Greenwood.

***Sir Robert Walpole: A Political Life.** Robert Giddings. (Illus.). 224p. 1997. 35.95 (*0-7509-1090-9*, Pub. by Sutton Pubng UK) Bks Intl VA.

Sir Robert's Little Outing. Horacio Madinaveitia. (Illus.). 32p. (J). (gr. k-4). 1991. pap. text ed. 7.95 (*1-879567-00-8*, Valeria Bks); lib. bdg. 13.95 (*1-879567-01-6*, Valeria Bks) Wonder Well.

Sir Roger L'Estrange: A Contribution to the History of the Press in the 17th Century. George Kitchin. LC 74-120325. (English Book Trade Ser.). xv, 440p. 1971. reprint ed. 49.50 (*0-678-00703-9*) Kelley.

Sir Samuel Ferguson. Malcom Brown. (Irish Writers Ser.). 101p. 1973. pap. 1.95 (*0-8387-1208-8*) Bucknell U Pr.

Sir Sayyid Ahmad Khan & Muslim Modernization in India & Pakistan. Hafeez Malik. LC 80-13905. (Illus.). 288p. 1980. text ed. 57.50 (*0-231-04970-6*) Col U Pr.

***Sir Siddiq Abubakar III, 17th Sultan of Sokoto: The Sokoto Caliphate in Perspective.** Shehu Malami. LC 89-584. 1989. write for info. (*0-7146-3173-6*, Pub. by F Cass Pubs UK); pap. write for info. (*0-7146-4068-9*, Pub. by F Cass Pubs UK) Intl Spec Bk.

Sir Siddiq Abubakar the Third: Seventeenth Sultan of Sokoto. Alhaji S. Malami. (Kenya People Ser.). (Illus.). 240p. 1991. 22.95 (*0-237-51196-7*, Pub. by Evans Bros Ltd UK) Trafalgar.

Sir Small & the Dragonfly. Jane O'Connor. LC 87-35309. (Step into Reading Bks.). (Illus.). 32p. (Orig.). (J). (ps-1). 1988. pap. 3.99 (*0-394-89625-4*) Random Bks Yng Read.

Sir. Squirrel Starts a Business. (Oak Tree Tales Ser.). (Illus.). (J). (ps-1). 1.98 (*0-517-45740-7*) Random Hse Value.

Sir Stephen Powle of Court & Country: Memorabilia of a Government Agent for Queen Elizabeth the First, Chancery Official, & English Country Gentleman. Virginia F. Stern. LC 90-50632. (Illus.). 248p. 1992. 46.50 (*0-945636-22-9*) Susquehanna U Pr.

Sir T. Overbury His Observations in His Travailes. Thomas Overbury. LC 70-26399. (English Experience Ser.: No. 154). 28p. 1969. reprint ed. 25.00 (*90-221-0154-1*) Walter J Johnson.

Sir Thomas Beecham Discography. Beecham, Sir Thomas, Society Staff. LC 78-2261. 77p. 1978. reprint ed. text ed. 49.75 (*0-313-20367-9*, STBD, Greenwood Pr) Greenwood.

Sir Thomas Browne. Edmund W. Gosse. (BCL1-PR English Literature Ser.). 214p. 1992. reprint ed. lib. bdg. 79.00 (*0-7812-7325-0*) Rprt Serv.

Sir Thomas Browne: Selected Poems. Ed. by Claire Preston. 192p. 1995. pap. 18.95 (*1-85754-052-2*, Pub. by Carcanet Pr UK) Paul & Co Pubs.

Sir Thomas Browne, a Study in Religious Philosophy. 2nd ed. William P. Dunn. LC 50-10370. 192p. reprint ed. pap. 54.80 (*0-8357-7022-2*, 2033219) Bks Demand.

Sir Thomas Browne & Robert Burton: A Reference Guide. Dennis G. Donovan et al. (C). 1981. 60.00 (*0-8161-8018-0*, Hall Reference) Macmillan.

Sir Thomas Elyot & Renaissance Humanism. John M. Major. LC 64-11351. 292p. reprint ed. pap. 83.30 (*0-7837-6020-5*, 2045832) Bks Demand.

Sir Thomas Gresham, Founder of the Royale Exchange. Charles Knight. 245p. 1997. pap. 25.00 (*0-87556-366-X*) Saifer.

Sir Thomas Lawrence: Portraits of an Age, 1790-1830. Kenneth Garlick. LC 92-27654. 1993. pap. 29.95 (*0-88397-104-6*) Art Srvc Intl.

Sir Thomas Lewis: Pioneer Cardiologist & Clinical Scientist. A. Hollman. LC 96-9462. 300p. 1996. 75.00 (*3-540-76049-0*) Spr-Verlag.

Sir Thomas Malory. Catherine La Farge. 1990. 40.00 (*0-7463-0714-4*, Pub. by Northcote UK) St Mut.

Sir Thomas Malory. Ed. by Marylyn Parins. 424p. (C). 1996. text ed. 130.00 (*0-415-13400-5*) Routledge.

Sir Thomas Malory. George L. Kittredge. (BCL1-PR English Literature Ser.). 12p. 1992. reprint ed. lib. bdg. 59.00 (*0-7812-7187-8*) Rprt Serv.

Sir Thomas Malory: An Anecdotal Bibliography of Editions, 1485-1985. Barry Gaines. LC 85-48067. (Studies in the Middle Ages: No. 10). 1990. 42.50 (*0-404-61440-X*) AMS Pr.

Sir Thomas Malory: His Turbulent Career; A Biography. Edward Hicks. (BCL1-PR English Literature Ser.). 118p. 1992. reprint ed. lib. bdg. 69.00 (*0-7812-7186-X*) Rprt Serv.

Sir Thomas Malory: Views & Re-Views. Thomas Malory. Ed. by D. Hanks, Jr. LC 91-11928. (Studies in the Middle Ages: No. 19). 1991. 39.50 (*0-404-61449-3*) AMS Pr.

Sir Thomas Malory & the Cultural Crisis of the Late Middle Ages. Robert Merrill. LC 86-27318. (American University Studies: English Language & Literature: Ser. IV, Vol. 39). 469p. (C). 1987. text ed. 59.00 (*0-8204-0303-2*) P Lang Pubng.

Sir Thomas Malory & the Morte D'Arthur: A Survey of Scholarship & Annotated Bibliography. Page W. Life. LC 80-16180. 297p. 1980. text ed. 28.50 (*0-8139-0868-X*) U Pr of Va.

***Sir Thomas More.** (Tower of London Ser.). Date not set. pap. text ed. write for info. (*0-582-39684-0*, Pub. by Longman UK) Longman.

Sir Thomas More. Anthony Munday & William Shakespeare. LC 74-133715. (Tudor Facsimile Texts. Old English Plays Ser.: No. 65). reprint ed. 59.50 (*0-404-53365-5*) AMS Pr.

Sir Thomas More. Leslie Paul. LC 75-128882. (Select Bibliographies Reprint Ser.). 1977. reprint ed. 18.95 (*0-8369-5502-1*) Ayer.

Sir Thomas More: Selected Letters. Thomas More. LC 61-14944. (Yale Edition of the Works of St. Thomas More: Modernized Ser.). reprint ed. pap. 74.00 (*0-317-28285-9*, 2022022) Bks Demand.

Sir Thomas More in the English Renaissance: An Annotated Catalogue. Jackson C. Boswell. (Medieval & Renaissance Texts & Studies: Vol. 83). 364p. 1994. 30.00 (*0-86698-093-8*, MR83) MRTS.

***Sir Thomas More in the English Renaissance: An Annotated Catalogue.** Ed. by Jackson C. Boswell. (Medieval & Renaissance Texts & Studies: Vol. 83). 400p. 1994. 30.00 (*0-86698-094-6*, MR83) MRTS.

Sir Thomas More Reader Vol. 1: Merry Tales, Fables, Essays from the English Works (1557) Rudolph E. Habenicht. 463p. (Orig.). 1995. pap. 19.00 (*0-9651502-0-8*) Chelsea Pr HI.

Sir Thomas Overbury's Vision (1616) & Other English Sources of Nathaniel Hawthorne's "The Scarlet Letter." Richard Niccols. LC 57-6417. 1979. 50.00 (*0-8201-1239-9*) Schol Facsimiles.

Sir Thomas Urquhart of Cromarty (1611-1660), Adventurer, Polymath, & Translator of Rabelais. R. J. Craik. LC 93-15151. 248p. 1993. text ed. 89.95 (*0-7734-9269-0*, Mellen Univ Pr) E Mellen.

Sir Thomas Wyatt. Thomas Dekker & John Webster. LC 75-133655. (Tudor Facsimile Texts. Old English Plays Ser.: No. 122). reprint ed. 59.50 (*0-404-53422-8*) AMS Pr.

Sir Thomas Wyatt: A Literary Portrait. Ed. by H. A. Mason. 344p. 1987. 37.50 (*0-8453-4512-5*, Pub. by Brstl Class Pr UK) Assoc Univ Prs.

Sir Thomas Wyatt & Some Collected Studies. Edmund K. Chambers. (BCL1-PR English Literature Ser.). 227p. 1992. reprint ed. lib. bdg. 79.00 (*0-7812-7010-3*) Rprt Serv.

Sir Thomas Wyatt, the Complete Poems. Thomas Wyatt. Ed. by R. A. Rebholz. LC 80-53980. (English Poets Ser.: No. 5). 558p. 1981. pap. 159.10 (*0-7837-3316-X*, 2057719) Bks Demand.

Sir Walter: A Four-Part Study in Biography. Donald Carswell. (BCL1-PR English Literature Ser.). 292p. 1992. reprint ed. lib. bdg. 79.00 (*0-7812-7644-6*) Rprt Serv.

Sir Walter Ralegh & the New World. John W. Shirley. (America's 400th Anniversary Ser.). (Illus.). xii, 129p. (Orig.). 1985. pap. 5.00 (*0-86526-206-3*) NC Archives.

Sir Walter Raleigh. Henry David Thoreau. 1976. 250.00 (*0-87968-442-9*) Gordon Pr.

Sir Walter Raleigh. Williamson H. Ross. LC 78-17033. 215p. 1978. reprint ed. text ed. 35.00 (*0-313-20577-9*, ROSI, Greenwood Pr) Greenwood.

Sir Walter Raleigh. Henry David Thoreau. Ed. by Franklin B. Sanborn. LC 80-2523. reprint ed. 24.50 (*0-404-19071-5*) AMS Pr.

An Asterisk (*) at the beginning of an entry indicates that the title is appearing in BIP for the first time.

Sir Walter Raleigh: A Reference Guide. Jerry L. Miles. (Reference Guides to Literature Ser.). 148p. (C). 1986. 45.00 (*0-8161-8596-4*, Hall Reference) Macmillan.

***Sir Walter Raleigh: An Annotated Bibliography.** Christopher M. Armitage. LC 87-40134. 252p. 1987. reprint ed. pap. 71.90 (*0-608-03183-6*, 2063636) Bks Demand.

Sir Walter Raleigh, an Annotated Bibliography. Ed. by Christopher M. Armitage. LC 87-40134. xiii, 236p. 1988. 22.50 (*0-8078-1757-0*) U of NC Pr.

***Sir Walter Raleigh & His Reader.** Beer. LC 97-3277. 1997. text ed. 55.00 (*0-312-17610-4*) St Martin.

Sir Walter Raleigh, His Family & Private Life. Alfred L. Rowse. LC 73-21492. (Illus.). 348p. 1975. reprint ed. text ed. 38.50 (*0-8371-6388-9*, ROWR, Greenwood Pr) Greenwood.

Sir Walter Raleigh's Ghost or Englands Forewarner. Thomas Scott. LC 74-80222. (English Experience Ser.: No. 693). 42p. 1974. reprint ed. 15.00 (*90-221-0693-4*) Walter J Johnson.

Sir Walter Raleigh's Speech from the Scaffold: A Translation of the 1619 Dutch Edition, & Comparison with English Texts. Walter Raleigh. Ed. by John Parker & Carol A. Johnson. Tr. & Intro. by Carol A. Johnson. (Illus.). 80p. (C). 1995. text ed. 15.00 (*0-9601798-5-2*) Assocs James Bell.

Sir Walter Scott. William Ker. LC 74-7282. (Sir Walter Scott Ser.: No. 73). 1974. lib. bdg. 29.95 (*0-8383-1937-8*) M S G Haskell Hse.

Sir Walter Scott. H. Grierson. LC 72-95427. (English Biography Ser.: No. 31). 1969. reprint ed. lib. bdg. 75.00 (*0-8383-0977-1*) M S G Haskell Hse.

Sir Walter Scott. Richard H. Hutton. Ed. by John Morley. LC 68-58381. (English Men of Letters Ser.). reprint ed. lib. bdg. 29.50 (*0-404-51713-7*) AMS Pr.

Sir Walter Scott, an Index, Placing the Short Poems in His Novels & His Long Poems & Dramas. Ed. by Allston Burr. LC 76-148632. vi, 130p. 1974. reprint ed. text ed. 38.50 (*0-8371-5994-6*, BUSW, Greenwood Pr) Greenwood.

Sir Walter Scott & the Border Minstrelsy. Andrew Lang. LC 68-59266. reprint ed. 37.50 (*0-404-03869-7*) AMS Pr.

Sir Walter Scott & the Gothic Novel. Robert Letellier. LC 94-38897. (Salzburg University Studies). 236p. 1994. text ed. 89.95 (*0-7734-1276-X*) E Mellen.

Sir Walter Scott, Baronet. Herbert J. Grierson. LC 76-153326. reprint ed. 20.00 (*0-404-02914-0*) AMS Pr.

***Sir Walter Scott (1771-1832) Selected Poems.** Ed. by James Reed. pap. write for info. (*0-85635-958-0*, Pub. by Carcanet Pr UK) Paul & Co Pubs.

Sir Walter Scott's Edinburgh Annual Register. Kenneth Curry. LC 77-8136. 227p. reprint ed. 64.70 (*0-685-16060-2*, 2027563) Bks Demand.

Sir Walter Scott's First Love. Adam Scott. LC 72-2013. (English Literature Ser.: No. 33). 1972. reprint ed. lib. bdg. 75.00 (*0-8383-1450-3*) M S G Haskell Hse.

Sir Wilfred Laurier & the Romance of Canada. Laurier LaPierre. 512p. 1996. 29.95 (*0-7737-2979-8*, Pub. by Stoddart Pubng CN) Genl Dist Srvs.

***Sir Wilfred Laurier & the Romance of Canada.** Laurier LaPierre. 512p. 1997. 17.95 (*0-7737-5916-6*, Pub. by Stoddart Pubng CN) Genl Dist Srvs.

***Sir Wilfrid Laurier: The Great Conciliator.** Barbara Robertson. (Illus.). 164p. 1991. pap. 12.95 (*0-919627-95-1*, Pub. by Quarry Pr CN) LPC InBook.

Sir William Arrol: The Great Scottish Bridge Builder. (Illus.). 1995. pap. 9.99 (*0-9639687-3-4*) J Arrol.

Sir William Chambers: Architect to George III. John Harris & Michael Snodin. LC 96-21636. (Illus.). 234p. 1996. 55.00 (*0-300-06940-5*); pap. write for info. (*0-300-06941-3*) Yale U Pr.

Sir William Davenant: The Siege of Rhodes: A Critical Study. Ann-Mari Hedback. (Studia Anglistica Upsaliensia Ser.: No. 14). (Illus.). 121p. (Orig.). 1973. pap. 18.75 (*0-317-65800-X*) Coronet Bks.

Sir William Dawson: A Life in Science & Religion. Charles F. O'Brien. LC 71-153381. (American Philosophical Society, Memoirs Ser.: Vol. 84). 217p. reprint ed. pap. 61.90 (*0-317-20673-7*, 2025140) Bks Demand.

Sir William Dunch's Pavan & Galliard for Five Viols. Virginia Brookes. (Charney Manor Ser.: No. 6). i, 15p. 1993. pap. text ed. 10.00 (*1-56571-073-8*, CM006) PRB Prods.

Sir William Gilbert. Isaac Goldberg. 1973. 59.95 (*0-8490-2610-5*) Gordon Pr.

Sir William Gregory of Coole: A Biography. Brian Jenkins. LC 86-63638. (Illus.). 339p. 8700. 65.00 (*0-86140-175-1*, Pub. by Colin Smythe Ltd UK) Dufour.

Sir William Johnson: The Man & His Influence. David S. Igneri. LC 94-31216. 175p. 1995. 15.95 (*0-944957-49-8*) Rivercross Pub.

Sir William Jones. Michael J. Franklin. 137p. 1996. pap. 9.95 (*0-7083-1295-0*, Pub. by Univ Wales Pr UK) Paul & Co Pubs.

Sir William Jones: A Bibliography of Primary & Secondary Sources. Garland Cannon. (Library & Information Sources in Linguistics: No. 7). xiv, 73p. 1979. 29.00 (*90-272-0998-7*) Benjamins North Am.

Sir William Jones: A Reader. William Jones. Ed. by Satya S. Pachori. 250p. (C). 1993. 32.00 (*0-19-562928-0*, 14344) OUP.

Sir William Jones: A Study in Eighteenth-Century British Attitudes to India. S. N. Mukherjee. 184p. 1987. text ed. 22.50 (*0-86131-581-2*, Pub. by Orient Longman Ltd II) Apt Bks.

Sir William Jones: His Mind & Art. Janardan P. Singh. 324p. 1987. 35.00 (*0-317-52155-1*) St Mut.

Sir William Jones: Selected Poetical & Prose Works. Ed. by Michael J. Franklin. 448p. 1995. 85.00 (*0-7083-1294-2*) Paul & Co Pubs.

Sir William Jones, Orientalist: An Annotated Bibliography of His Works. Garland H. Cannon. LC 52-7595. (Pacific Area Bibliographies Ser.). 106p. reprint ed. pap. 30.30 (*0-317-09239-1*, 2001352) Bks Demand.

Sir William Osler: An Annotated Bibliography with Illustrations. Richard L. Golden & Charles G. Roland. LC 87-12209. (Bibliography Ser.: No. 1). (Illus.). 214p. 1988. 125.00 (*0-930405-00-5*) Norman SF.

Sir William Rowan Hamilton. Thomas L. Hankins. LC 80-10627. (Illus.). 496p. reprint ed. pap. 141.40 (*0-8357-4332-2*, 2037132) Bks Demand.

Sir William Scott, Lord Stowell, Judge of the High Court of Admirality, 1798-1828. Henry J. Bourguignon. LC 87-6377. (Cambridge Studies in English Legal History). 320p. 1987. text ed. 69.95 (*0-521-34076-4*) Cambridge U Pr.

Sir William the Worm. Gary Hogg. (Happy Hawk Golden Thought Ser.). (Illus.). 24p. (J). 1994. pap. 4.95 (*0-930771-06-0*); lib. bdg. 12.95 (*0-930771-05-2*) Buckaroo UT.

***Sir William Waller: The Campaigns of a Roundhead General.** John Adair. (Illus.). 1997. 45.00 (*0-7509-1312-6*, Pub. by Sutton Pubng UK) Bks Intl VA.

Sir William Watson. James G. Nelson. LC 66-28912. (Twayne's English Authors Ser.). 1966. pap. text ed. 6.95 (*0-8290-2025-X*); lib. bdg. 17.95 (*0-89197-938-7*) Irvington.

Sir William Wedderburn & Indian Freedom Movement. Virendra P. Rakesh. 1989. 26.00 (*0-8364-2538-3*, Commonwealth) S Asia.

Sir Williams Gregory K. C. M. G. An Autobiography. 3rd ed. Ed. by Isabella A. Gregory. (Coole Edition of the Collected Works of Lady Gregory Ser.). write for info. (*0-19-520282-1*) OUP.

Sir Willie Winkle. David M. Weiss. LC 95-68258. (Illus.). 24p. (Orig.). (J). (gr. k-4). 1995. pap. 6.95 (*0-9645762-3-6*) Reach Star Pub.

Sir Winston Churchill: His Life & Times. 2nd ed. Maxwell P. Schoenfeld. LC 85-5245. 124p. (C). 1986. pap. text ed. 10.50 (*0-89874-858-5*) Krieger.

Sir Winston Walrus & the Great Rescue. Langley, William, Studios Staff. (Shamu & His Crew Adventure Ser.). (Illus.). 32p. (J). (gr. k-3). 1994. 5.95 (*1-884506-06-2*) Third Story.

Sirach. John E. Rybolt. Ed. by Dianne Bergant. (Old Testament Ser.). pap. 3.95 (*0-8146-1478-7*) Liturgical Pr.

Sirague City. Photos by Vilem Kriz. LC 75-14371. 64p. 1975. 25.00 (*0-915756-00-5*); pap. 10.00 (*0-915756-01-3*) D McPhail.

Sirat Al Masih: The Life of the Messiah in Classical Arabic with English Translation. 443p. 1992. pap. text ed. 9.95 (*1-882464-00-1*) Global GA.

Sirat un-Nabi, 2 vol. set. Allama Shibli Numani. Tr. by M. Tayyib Bakhsh Budayuni. 500p. (C). 1985. text ed. 39.00 (*1-56744-376-1*) Kazi Pubns.

***Sirdar: Sir Reginald Wingate & the British Empire in the Middle East.** Martin W. Daly, Jr. LC 96-79457. (Memoirs Ser.: Vol. 222). (Illus.). 577p. 1977. write for info. (*0-87169-222-8*, M222-dam) Am Philos.

Sirdar's Sabre: Being for the Most Part the Adventures of Sirdar Bahadur Mohammed Khan. Louis Tracy. LC 74-37568. (Short Story Index Reprint Ser.). 1977. reprint ed. 21.95 (*0-8369-4127-6*) Ayer.

Sire de Maletroit's Door. Robert Louis Stevenson. Ed. by Ann A. Redpath. (Creative's Classic Short Stories Ser.). (Illus.). 58p. (J). (gr. 6 up). 1985. lib. bdg. 13.95 (*0-87191-967-2*) Creative Ed.

Sire Ratings 1996-97: For Exploring Pedigree. Mike Helm. 72p. 1996. per. 35.00 (*0-933944-17-9*) City Miner Bks.

***Sire Ratings 1997-1998: An Update to Exploring.** Mike Helm. 85p. 1997. pap. 35.00 (*0-933944-20-9*) City Miner Bks.

Siren. Linda C. Gray. 1989. pap. 3.95 (*0-8125-1838-1*) Tor Bks.

Siren, 3 Vols. Thomas A. Trollope. LC 75-32787. (Literature of Mystery & Detection Ser.). 1976. reprint ed. 71.95 (*0-405-07902-8*) Ayer.

Siren: And Selected Writings. Giuseppe T. Di Lampedusa. Tr. by Archibald Colquhoun et al. 192p. 1996. 24.00 (*1-86046-021-6*) HarperColl Wrld.

Siren & the Seashell: And Other Essays on Poets & Poetry by Octavio Paz. Octavio Paz. Tr. by Lysander Kemp & Margaret S. Peden. (Texas Pan American Ser.). 1991. pap. 9.95 (*0-292-77652-7*) U of Tex Pr.

***Siren City.** William Bailey. 280p. 1997. 19.95 (*0-9656241-0-2*) Halcyon Days.

***Siren Feasts: History of Food & Gastronomy in Greece.** Andrew Dalby. 336p. 1997. pap. 19.95 (*0-415-15657-2*) Routledge.

Siren Song: A Story Stranger Than Fiction. Gordon Honeycombe. 388p. 1993. 39.95 (*0-09-174855-0*, Pub. by Hutchnson UK) Trafalgar.

Siren Songs: Gender, Audiences, & Narrators in the Odyssey. Lillian E. Doherty. LC 95-19532. 1995. 39.50 (*0-472-10597-3*) U of Mich Pr.

Siren Songs & Classical Illusions. Jascha Kessler. LC 92-6642. 256p. (Orig.). 1992. pap. 12.00 (*0-929701-22-4*) McPherson & Co.

Siren Sparks. Rose M. Poole. 203p. 1984. 7.95 (*0-89697-173-2*) Intl Univ Pr.

Siren Years: A Canadian Diplomat Abroad. Charles M. Ritchie. 216p. 1987. pap. 4.95 (*0-7715-9269-8*) Genl Dist Srvs.

Sirena of Salado. Jackie Mills. (Illus.). 32p. (J). (gr. 2-7). 1991. 10.95 (*0-9629284-0-2*) Indian Trail.

Sirena Varada. Los Arboles Mueren de Pie. Alejandro Casona. Ed. by Carmen Diaz Castanon. (Nueva Austral Ser.: Vol. 121). (SPA.). 1991. pap. text ed. 24.95 (*84-239-1921-8*) Elliots Bks.

Sirene du Mississippi. William Irish. 384p. (FRE.). 1973. pap. 11.95 (*0-7859-2329-2*, 2070365077) Fr & Eur.

Sirene et l'Aventurier. Ann Major. (Rouge Passion Ser.). (FRE.). 1994. pap. 3.50 (*0-373-37291-4*, 1-37291-1) Harlequin Bks.

Sirenian Evolution in the North Pacific Ocean. Daryl P. Domning. LC 77-83099. (University of California Publications in Social Welfare: No. 118). (Illus.). 208p. reprint ed. pap. 59.30 (*0-685-20475-8*, 2029874) Bks Demand.

Sirenita. deluxe ed. (Golden Sound Story Bks.). (Illus.). 24p. (ESP.). (J). 1995. bds. 9.95 (*0-307-94014-4*, Golden Pr) Western Pub.

Sirenita - The Little Mermaid. (Spanish Classics Ser.). 96p. (J). (ps-4). 1994. 7.98 (*1-57082-056-2*) Mouse Works.

Sirenita - The Little Mermaid. Hans Christian Andersen. (J). (ps-3). 1994. pap. 2.95 (*0-486-28001-2*) Dover.

Sirens. Bernard Evslin. (Monsters of Mythology Ser.). (Illus.). 85p. 1988. lib. bdg. 19.95 (*1-55546-258-8*) Chelsea Hse.

***Sirens.** Marco Glaviano. Ed. by Andrea Danese. (Illus.). 296p. (Orig.). 1997. pap. 29.95 (*0-446-91245-X*) Warner Bks.

Sirens. Steve Pett. LC 89-40601. 401p. 1990. pap. 9.95 (*0-394-75712-2*, Vin) Random.

***Sirens.** Donald Rawley. 76p. (Orig.). 1996. pap. 8.95 (*1-882550-21-8*) Quiet Lion Pr.

Sirens. Sheri C. Sinykin. LC 93-77099. (J). 1993. 13.00 (*0-688-12309-0*) Lothrop.

Sirens. Eric Van Lustbader. 576p. 1986. mass mkt. 5.95 (*0-449-21152-5*, Crest) Fawcett.

Sirens. Richard Wesley. 1975. pap. 5.25 (*0-8222-1033-9*) Dramatists Play.

***Sirens: Symbols of Seduction.** Meri Lao. LC 97-15688. (Illus.). 224p. 1997. 40.00 (*0-89281-653-8*) Inner Tradit.

***Sirens & Other Demon Lovers.** Ed. by Ellen Datlow & Windling. mass mkt. 5.99 (*0-06-105782-7*, HarperPrism) HarpC.

***Sirens & Other Demon Lovers.** Ed. by Ellen Datlow & Windling. 1997. pap. 14.00 (*0-06-105372-4*, HarperPrism) HarpC.

***Siren's Lullaby.** William P. Kennedy. LC 96-40469. 1997. 22.95 (*0-312-15658-8*) St Martin.

Sirens of Titan. Kurt Vonnegut, Jr. 320p. 1970. mass mkt. 6.50 (*0-440-17948-3*) Dell.

Sirens Sang of Murder. Sarah L. Caudwell. 288p. 1990. mass mkt. 5.50 (*0-440-20745-2*) Dell.

Siren's Song. Cathy Forsythe. 192p. 1994. 17.95 (*0-8034-9050-X*) Bouregy.

Siren's Song. Constance O'Banyon. 336p. (Orig.). 1996. mass mkt. 5.99 (*0-06-108228-7*) HarpC.

Sirens' Song: For Brian Des Roches. Stephen Thomas. (Illus.). 14p. (Orig.). 1991. pap. 5.00 (*0-9638199-1-7*) Red Sky Pr.

Sires & Dams of Stakes Winners, 1925-1985. Ed. by Blood-Horse, Inc. Staff. 2000p. 1986. 95.00 (*0-936032-98-7*) Blood-Horse.

Sires of 1992. 160p. 1993. pap. 16.95 (*0-939049-53-8*) Blood-Horse.

Sires of 1993. Ed. by Raymond S. Paulick & Dan Mearns. (Illus.). 190p. (Orig.). 1994. pap. 16.95 (*0-939049-58-9*) Blood-Horse.

Sires of 1994: Annual Supplement to the Blood-Horse. Ed. by Raymond S. Paulick & Dan Mearns. (Blood-Horse Supplement Ser.). (Illus.). 180p. (Orig.). 1995. pap. 24.95 (*0-939049-66-X*) Blood-Horse.

Sires of 1995. Ed. by Raymond S. Paulick & Dan Mearns. (Illus.). 170p. (Orig.). 1996. pap. 24.95 (*0-939049-72-4*) Blood-Horse.

***Sires of 1996.** Ed. by Raymond S. Paulick & Dan Mearns. (Illus.). 170p. (Orig.). 1997. pap. 24.95 (*0-939049-83-X*) Blood-Horse.

Sirga. Rene Guillot. LC 59-12198. (Illus.). (J). (gr. 6-9). 1959. 24.95 (*0-87599-046-0*) S G Phillips.

Siri Sampige: A Play in Sixteen Scenes. Chandrasekhar Kambar. (C). 1992. pap. 7.00 (*81-7046-089-1*, Pub. by Seagull Bks II) S Asia.

Siringo. Ben E. Pingenot. LC 88-29511. (Centennial Series of the Association of Former Students: No. 31). (Illus.). 268p. 1989. 29.50 (*0-89096-381-9*) Tex A&M Univ Pr.

***Sirius.** M. Temple Richmond. LC 96-53578. 448p. (Orig.). 1997. pap. 19.95 (*0-9635766-2-3*) Source.

Sirius: A Volume of Fiction. Ellen T. Fowler. LC 73-150543. (Short Story Index Reprint Ser.). 1977. reprint ed. 24.95 (*0-8369-3840-2*) Ayer.

***Sirius Connection.** Lazaris. 144p. (Orig.). 1996. pap. 12.95 (*1-55638-301-0*, NPN Pub) Concept Synergy.

Sirius Connection: Unlocking the Secrets of Ancient Egypt. Murry Hope. 256p. 1996. pap. 24.95 (*1-85230-818-4*) Element MA.

***Sirius Connection: Unlocking the Secrets of Ancient Egypt.** Murry Hope. 1997. pap. 14.95 (*1-86204-102-4*) Element MA.

Sirius Mystery. Robert K. Temple. 292p. (Orig.). 1987. pap. 16.95 (*0-89281-163-3*, Destiny Bks) Inner Tradit.

***Sirk on Sirk.** Ed. by John Halliday. (Illus.). (Orig.). 1997. pap. 15.95 (*0-571-19098-7*) Faber & Faber.

Sirko & the Wolf: A Ukrainian Tale. Illus. by Robert Sauber. LC 96-33913. 32p. (J). (ps-3). 1997. lib. bdg. 15.95 (*0-8234-1257-1*) Holiday.

Siro. David Ignatius. 464p. 1993. mass mkt. 4.99 (*0-380-71820-0*) Avon.

Siro. David Ignatius. 448p. 1991. 19.95 (*0-374-26506-2*) FS&G.

SIRS Digest: Alcohol. Ed. by Eleanor C. Goldstein. (Digest Ser.). 1990. ring bd. 40.00 (*0-89777-114-1*) Sirs Inc.

SIRS Digest: Drugs. Ed. by Eleanor C. Goldstein. (Digest Ser.). 1990. ring bd. 40.00 (*0-89777-112-5*) Sirs Inc.

SIRS Digest: Energy. Ed. by Eleanor C. Goldstein. (Digest Ser.). 1990. ring bd. 40.00 (*0-89777-115-X*) Sirs Inc.

SIRS Digest: Family. Ed. by Eleanor C. Goldstein. (Social Issues Resources Ser.). 1990. 40.00 (*0-89777-116-8*) Sirs Inc.

SIRS Digest: Food. Ed. by Eleanor C. Goldstein. (Digest Ser.). 1990. ring bd. 40.00 (*0-89777-113-3*) Sirs Inc.

SIRS Digest: Pollution. Ed. by Eleanor C. Goldstein. (Social Issues Resources Ser.). 1991. 40.00 (*0-89777-143-5*) Sirs Inc.

Sirviendo al Senor, No. 2: La Organizacion de la Iglesia. Richard De Ridder. Tr. by Mariano Avila. (SPA.). 1990. 2.00 (*1-55955-111-9*) CRC Wrld Lit.

Sirviendo al Senor, No. 3: El Lugar y Funcion de los Miembros. Richard De Ridder. Tr. & Adapted by Mariano Avila. (SPA.). 2.00 (*1-55955-112-7*) CRC Wrld Lit.

Sirviendo al Senor, No. 4: Llamamiento y Ordenacion. Richard De Ridder. Tr. & Adapted by Mariano Avila. (SPA.). 2.00 (*1-55955-113-5*) CRC Wrld Lit.

Sirviendo al Senor, No. 5: Asambleas de la Iglesia. Richard De Ridder. Tr. by Elaine Hutt. (SPA.). 2.00 (*1-55955-114-3*) CRC Wrld Lit.

Sirviendo al Senor, No. 6: La Visitacion Familiar. Richard De Ridder. (SPA.). 2.00 (*1-55955-115-1*) CRC Wrld Lit.

Sirviendo al Senor, No. 7: Conflicto en la Iglesia. Louis Tamminga. Tr. & Adapted by Mariano Avila. (SPA.). 2.00 (*1-55955-116-X*) CRC Wrld Lit.

***Sirviendo Alenviar Obreros: Como Apoyar a Sus Misioneros Mientras Se Preparan para Salir, Mientras Estan en el Campo, Cuardo Regresan a Casa.** Neal Pirolo. Tr. by Manuel Lopez & Ruth Lopez. 206p. (Orig.). (SPA.). 1996. pap. 7.95 (*1-880185-05-9*) Emmaus Rd Intl.

Sirviendo Alimentos Sanos: Una Guia Para Empleados de la Industria Gastronomica. National Restaurant Association, Educational Foundation Staff. (ServSafe Ser.). (Illus.). 52p. (Orig.). (SPA.). (C). 1990. pap. text ed. 5.95 (*0-915452-55-3*) Educ Found.

***Sirviendo Como Enviadores - Serving As Senders.** Neal Pirolo. 180p. (SPA.). 1995. write for info. (*1-56063-720-X*) Editorial Unilit.

Sis & Chris & the Knowbots in "We Don't Need Drugs to Be O. K." Educational Coloring Book. Mary L. Pringle & Joseph Ellis. (J). (gr. k-5). 1994. reprint ed. pap. 1.95 (*0-935847-03-0*) Inst Subs Abuse Res.

Sis the Candy Kid-Paperdolls. Bill Woggon. 16p. 1989. spiral bd. 5.95 (*0-87588-347-8*) Hobby Hse.

Siskind, Aaron: Photographs 1932-1978. Text by Aaron Siskind & Peter Turner. (Illus.). 1979. pap. 21.00 (*0-905836-16-2*, Pub. by Museum Modern Art UK) St Mut.

***Siskiyou Line - an Adventure in Railroading: Includes: Yreka Western Railroad, Jacksonville Railroad, the W. C. T. U., Oregon's Great Train Holdup, & Others.** Bert Webber & Margie Webber. (Illus.). (Orig.). 1997. pap. write for info. (*0-936738-04-9*) Webb Research.

***Siskiyou Line, an Adventure in Railroading Documentary.** Bert Webber & Margie Webber. (Illus.). 1997. write for info. (*0-936738-49-9*) Webb Research.

Sisley. Raymond Cogniat. (CAL Art Ser.). (Illus.). 1984. 14.95 (*0-517-53321-9*, Crown) Crown Pub Group.

Sisley. Richard Shone. (Color Library). (Illus.). 128p. 1994. pap. 14.95 (*0-7148-3051-8*, Pub. by Phaidon Press UK) Chronicle Bks.

***Sisley.** Richard Stone. (Illus.). 240p. Date not set. 55.00 (*0-7148-2687-1*, Pub. by Phaidon Press UK) Chronicle Bks.

Sisley: Landscapes. (Rhythm & Color One Ser.). 1970. 9.95 (*0-8288-9507-4*) Fr & Eur.

Sisley & the Thames. Nicholas Reed. 1992. pap. 29.95 (*0-9515258-5-9*, Pub. by Lilburne Pr UK) St Mut.

Sismo. Marcia Biederman. LC 93-1866. 210p. 1993. 21.95 (*0-8027-3243-7*) Walker & Co.

Sissano, Movements of Migration Within & Through Melanesia. William Churchill. LC 16-23055. (Carnegie Institution of Washington Publication Ser.: No. 244). (Illus.). 89p. reprint ed. pap. 25.40 (*0-317-10107-2*, 2015706) Bks Demand.

Sissie. John A. Williams. (Classic Reprint Ser.). 278p. 1988. pap. 12.95 (*0-938410-66-0*) Thunders Mouth.

Sissinghurst: Portrait of a Garden. Jane Brown. (Illus.). 144p. 1994. pap. 19.95 (*0-297-83350-2*) Trafalgar.

Sisson Report on the German Bolshevik Conspiracy. Edgar Sisson & George Creel. 1980. lib. bdg. 59.95 (*0-8490-3097-8*) Gordon Pr.

Sisson. Yankee Heritage: A Sisson Ancestry (with 257 Connecting Lines) Brian J. Berry. (Illus.). 549p. 1995. reprint ed. pap. 83.00 (*0-8328-4892-1*); reprint ed. lib. bdg. 93.00 (*0-8328-4891-3*) Higginson Bk Co.

Sisson's Word & Expression Locater. A. F. Sisson. 371p. 1966. text ed. 27.95 (*0-13-810671-1*, Busn) P-H.

Sisson's Word & Expression Locater. 2nd ed. A. F. Sisson. LC 94-12091. 1994. 27.95 (*0-13-814088-X*); pap. 14.95 (*0-13-814096-0*) P-H.

Sissy & Gugenheimer. Barbara B. Baker & Donna Wysinger. (Pre-Readers Ser.: Vol. 3). (Illus.). 12p. (Orig.). (J). (gr. k-1). 1994. pap. 3.00 (*1-57812-015-2*) Learng Crew.

Sissy Cloud: A Potawatomi Fable. Jack Wooldridge. (Potawatomi Fables Ser.). (Illus.). 40p. (J). (gr. k-7). 1995. pap. 7.50 (*1-887963-04-9*) Pota Pr.

Sista' Women in the Tapestry of Life. Lorene Garrett-Browder. LC 94-96412. 136p. (Orig.). 1994. pap. 14.95 (*0-9642617-2-3*) L G B Ent.

Sista' Girlfren' Breaks it Down When You Need Advice & Mom's Not Around. Francheska Ahmed-Cawthorne. 160p. 1996. pap. 9.00 (*0-684-81899-X*, Fireside) S&S Trade.

***Sistah's Rules.** Denene Millner. LC 97-21792. 1997. pap. write for info. (*0-688-15689-4*, Quill) Morrow.

Sistema Alimentario Mexicano (SAM) Elements of a Program of Accelerated Production of Basic Foodstuffs in Mexico. Cassio Luiselli. (Research Reports: No. 22). 24p. (Orig.). (C). 1982. pap. 5.00 (*0-935391-21-5*, RR-22) UCSD Ctr US-Mex.

S

An Asterisk (*) at the beginning of an entry indicates that the title is appearing in BIP for the first time.

Sistema De Caja De Conversion: Hacia una Autentica Reforma Monetaria. Steve H. Hanke & Kurt Schuler. 94p. 1992. pap. 10.00 (*0-9639638-0-5*) Atlas Econ Res.

Sistema de Clasificacion Decimal Dewey, 4 vols., Set. 20th ed. Melvil Dewey. Ed. by G. Octavio & L. Rojas. Tr. by Margarita A. De Heredia. 3300p. (SPA.). 1995. text ed. 180.00 (*958-9121-03-9*) OCLC Online Comp.

Sistema de Manejo para Maestros: Guia - Guidebook. National School Services Staff. (SPA.). (C). 1994. student ed. 25.00 (*0-932957-70-6*) Natl School.

Sistema de Manejo para Maestros - Leaders Manual. National School Services Staff. (SPA.). (C). 1991. teacher ed. 125.00 (*0-932957-79-X*) Natl School.

Sistema de Produccion de Canon: Participacion Creativa Del Personal. Ed. by Constance Dyer. (Illus.). 276p. (Orig.). 1991. pap. 40.00 (*84-87022-69-3*) Prod Press.

Sistema de Produccion Toyota: Desde el Punto de Vista de la Ingenieria. 2nd ed. Shigeo Shingo. (Illus.). 316p. (SPA.). 1990. reprint ed. pap. 55.00 (*84-87022-04-9*) Prod Press.

S

Sistema de Produccion Toyota: Mas Alla de la Produccion de Toyota. Taiichi Ohno. (Illus.). 172p. (Orig.). (SPA.). 1991. pap. 40.00 (*84-87022-52-9*) Prod Press.

Sistema Expresivo de Ricardo Guiraldes. Miriam Curet De Anda. LC 76-8166. (Coleccion Mente y Palabra). 383p. (Orig.). (SPA.). 1976. 5.00 (*0-8477-0532-3*); pap. 4.00 (*0-8477-0533-1*) U of PR Pr.

Sistema Interamericano a Treaves de Tratados, Convenciones y Otros Documentos: Vol. I, Asuntos Juridicos Politicos. OAS, General Secretariat for Juridical Affairs. (Sistema Interamericano Ser.). 1040p. (C). 1981. text ed. 60.00 (*0-8270-1426-0*) OAS.

Sistema Judicial de Puerto Rico. Jose Trias-Monge. LC 77-10936. 1978. 15.00 (*0-8477-3014-X*) U of PR Pr.

Sistema Metrico (Modulo) Fe Acosta de Gonzalez. (UPREX, Pedagogia Ser.: No. 57). (SPA.). 1980. pap. text ed. 2.80 (*0-8477-2743-2*) U of PR Pr.

Sistemas de Datos de Industrias de Primer Nivel Mundial: Un Modelo Para Empresas Avanzadas. Brian H. Maskell. (Illus.). 407p. (Orig.). (SPA.). 1995. pap. 55.00 (*84-87022-15-4*) Prod Press.

Sister. A. Manette Ansay. LC 95-52672. 224p. 1996. 24.00 (*0-688-14449-7*) Morrow.

***Sister.** A. Manette Ansay. 1997. pap. 12.00 (*0-380-72976-8*) Avon.

Sister. Eloise Greenfield. LC 73-22182. (Illus.). 96p. (J). (gr. 5-12). 1974. 15.00 (*0-690-00497-4*, Crowell Jr Bks) HarpC Child Bks.

Sister. Elleston Trevor. 288p. 1994. mass mkt. 4.99 (*0-8125-3337-2*) Tor Bks.

Sister. Eloise Greenfield. LC 73-22182. (Trophy Bk.). (Illus.). 96p. (J). (gr. 5-8). 1992. reprint ed. pap. 3.95 (*0-06-440199-5*, Trophy) HarpC Child Bks.

Sister: A Novel. Jim Lewis. LC 92-34194. 216p. 1993. 20.00 (*1-55597-178-4*) Graywolf.

Sister - Stranger: Lesbians Loving Across the Lines. Intro. by Jan Hardy. 176p. (Orig.). 1993. pap. 11.95 (*0-9617406-3-9*) Sidewalk Revolution.

Sister Act: Highlights from the Motion Picture Sound Track. 48p. 1992. pap. 12.95 (*0-7935-1898-9*, 00312482) H Leonard.

Sister Act 2. 88p. 1994. otabind 14.95 (*0-7935-3160-8*, 00312497) H Leonard.

***Sister Adames' Dilemma.** large type ed. Jane Burdall. (Dales Large Print Ser.). 275p. 1997. pap. 18.99 (*1-85389-714-0*) Ulverscroft.

Sister Age. M. F. K. Fisher. LC 82-48880. 1983. 12.95 (*0-394-53066-7*) Knopf.

Sister Age. M. F. K. Fisher. 1984. pap. 12.00 (*0-394-72385-6*, Vin) Random.

Sister Aimee: The Life of Aimee. Daniel M. Epstein. 1994. pap. 14.95 (*0-15-600093-8*) HarBrace.

Sister Aimee: The Life of Aimee Semple McPherson. Daniel M. Epstein. 1993. 27.95 (*0-15-182688-9*) HarBrace.

Sister & the Surgeon. large type ed. Lynne Collins. (Linford Romance Library). 336p. 1993. pap. 15.99 (*0-7089-7406-6*, Linford) Ulverscroft.

Sister Arts: The Tradition of Literary Pictorialism & English Poetry from Dryden to Gray. Jean H. Hagstrum. LC 58-11948. (Illus.). xxii, 394p. (C). 1987. pap. text ed. 16.00 (*0-226-31298-4*) U Ch Pr.

Sister at Rivermead. large type ed. Clare A. Cavendish. 244p. 1994. pap. 17.99 (*1-85389-453-2*, Dales) Ulverscroft.

Sister Bear's Jewelry Box. Stan Berenstain & Jan Berenstain. (J). 1996. write for info. (*0-679-87327-9*) Random Bks Yng Read.

Sister Bernadette: Cowboy Nun from Texas. Mary B. Muller & Elizabeth H. Neeld. (Illus.). 256p. (Orig.). 1991. pap. 14.95 (*0-937897-98-1*) Centerpoint Pr.

Sister Blood. Karen Haber=. 1996. mass mkt. 5.99 (*0-88677-708-9*) DAW Bks.

Sister Bond: A Feminist View of a Timeless Connection. Ed. by Toni A. McNaron. (Athene Ser.: No. 6). (Illus.). 142p. 1985. text ed. 35.00 (*0-08-032367-7*, Pergamon Pr); pap. text ed. 14.95 (*0-08-032366-9*, Pergamon Pr) Elsevier.

Sister Bond: A Feminist View of a Timeless Connection. Ed. by Toni A. McNaron. (Athene Ser.). 146p. (C). 1985. pap. text ed. 14.95 (*0-8077-6232-6*) Tchrs Coll.

***Sister Brother: Gertrude & Leo Stein.** Brenda Wineapple. LC 97-17852. 1997. pap. text ed. 24.95 (*0-8018-5807-0*) Johns Hopkins.

Sister Brother: Gertrude & Leo Stein. Brenda Wineapple. LC 95-19523. (Illus.). 514p. 1996. 35.00 (*0-399-14103-0*, Putnam) Putnam Pub Group.

Sister Carrie. Theodore Dreiser. (Airmont Classics Ser.). (YA). (gr. 11 up). mass mkt. 2.95 (*0-8049-0147-3*, CL-147) Airmont.

Sister Carrie. Theodore Dreiser. 1976. 27.95 (*0-8488-0993-9*) Amereon Ltd.

Sister Carrie. Theodore Dreiser. 432p. 1982. pap. 4.50 (*0-553-21374-1*, Bantam Classics) Bantam.

***Sister Carrie.** Theodore Dreiser. LC 97-10452. 480p. 1997. 18.50 (*0-385-48724-X*) Doubleday.

Sister Carrie. Theodore Dreiser. 474p. (C). 1957. pap. text ed. 20.00 (*0-03-009075-X*) HB Coll Pubs.

Sister Carrie. Theodore Dreiser. Ed. by Claude Simpson. LC 59-1819. (YA). (gr. 9 up). 1972. pap. 11.56 (*0-395-05134-7*, RivEd) HM.

Sister Carrie. Theodore Dreiser. 1962. pap. 4.95 (*0-451-52273-7*, Sig Classics) NAL-Dutton.

Sister Carrie. Theodore Dreiser. (World's Classics Ser.). 512p. 1991. pap. 9.95 (*0-19-282742-1*, 9673) OUP.

***Sister Carrie.** Theodore Dreiser. LC 96-37888. 1997. 19.50 (*0-679-60250-X*, Modern Lib) Random.

Sister Carrie. Theodore Dreiser. (American Library). 488p. 1981. pap. 7.95 (*0-14-039002-2*, Penguin Classics) Viking Penguin.

Sister Carrie. Theodore Dreiser. 496p. 1994. pap. 11.95 (*0-14-018828-2*, Penguin Classics) Viking Penguin.

Sister Carrie. Lauren Fairbanks. LC 93-18998. 208p. 1993. 19.95 (*1-56478-035-X*) Dalkey Arch.

Sister Carrie. Lauren Fairbanks. (Illus.). 208p. 1995. pap. 10.95 (*1-56478-070-8*) Dalkey Arch.

***Sister Carrie.** large type ed. Theodore Dreiser. 632p. 1997. reprint ed. lib. bdg. 25.00 (*0-939495-16-3*) North Bks.

***Sister Carrie.** unabridged ed. Theodore Dreiser. 297p. 1997. reprint ed. pap. 14.95 (*1-57002-041-8*) Univ Publng Hse.

Sister Carrie. 2nd ed. Theodore Dreiser. Ed. by Donald Pizer. (Critical Editions Ser.). 600p. (C). 1991. pap. text ed. 14.95 (*0-393-96042-0*) Norton.

Sister Carrie. Theodore Dreiser. 557p. 1980. reprint ed. lib. bdg. 25.95 (*0-89968-207-3*, Lghtyr Pr) Buccaneer Bks.

Sister Carrie. Theodore Dreiser. LC 78-183140. 472p. 1971. reprint ed. lib. bdg. 20.00 (*0-8376-0401-X*) Bentley.

Sister Carrie, Jennie Gerhardt, Twelve Men. Theodore Dreiser. Ed. by Richard Lehan. LC 86-27583. 1168p. 1987. 35.00 (*0-940450-41-0*) Library of America.

Sister Carrie Notes. Frederick J. Balling. 1967. pap. 3.95 (*0-8220-1201-4*) Cliffs.

"Sister Carrie" Portfolio. James L. West, III. LC 85-5370. (Bibliographical Society Ser.). viii, 87p. 1985. text ed. 25.00 (*0-8139-1067-6*) U Pr of Va.

Sister Cat. Felix Gould. LC 94-46920. 224p. 1995. 12.00 (*1-56980-043-X*) Barricade Bks.

Sister CEO: The Black Woman's Guide to Starting Her Own Business. Cheryl Broussard. 1997. pap. 21.95 (*0-670-87144-3*) Viking Penguin.

***Sister CEO: The Black Woman's Guide to Starting Your Own Business.** Cheryl D. Broussard. 1998. pap. 11.95 (*0-14-025302-5*) Viking Penguin.

Sister Cities: A World of Difference. Leslie Burger & Debra L. Rahm. LC 95-3424. (International Cooperation Ser.). (J). 1996. lib. bdg. 21.50 (*0-8225-2697-2*, Lerner Publctns) Lerner Group.

Sister City & Other Tales. Norway Leif. (Illus.). 22p. (Orig.). 1971. pap. 2.50 (*0-932264-18-2*) Trask Hse Bks.

Sister Creeks Site Mounds: Middle Woodland Mortuary Practices in the Illinois River Valley, Vol. 2. Michael C. Meinkoth. LC 95-44995. (Transportation Archaeological Research Reports: Vol. 2). (Illus.). 148p. (C). 1995. pap. 8.00 (*0-9644881-1-6*) ITARP.

Sister Dressed Me Funny. Anthony Buccino. LC 95-92578. 64p. 1996. pap. 14.95 (*0-9629824-1-5*) Cherry Blossom.

Sister Earth: Creation, Ecology, & the Spirit. Helder Camara. LC 95-16784. (Illus.). 112p. 1995. pap. 7.95 (*1-56548-031-7*) New City.

Sister Feelgood: A Year of Health & Fitness for Our Bodies & Our Souls. Donna Williams. 384p. 1996. pap. 12.00 (*0-517-88488-7*, Crown) Crown Pub Group.

Sister Fly Goes to Market. Melissa Cannon. LC 80-21120. (Illus.). (Orig.). 1980. pap. 1.95 (*0-937212-01-6*) Truedog.

Sister Gin. June Arnold. LC 89-7926. 240p. 1989. pap. 8.95 (*1-55861-010-3*) Feminist Pr.

***Sister Harriet.** large type ed. Marjorie Curtis. (Dales Large Print Ser.). 212p. 1997. pap. 18.99 (*1-85389-749-3*, Dales) Ulverscroft.

Sister Hollywood. large type ed. C. K. Stead. 1991. 25.99 (*0-7089-2507-3*) Ulverscroft.

Sister Ignatia: Angel of Alcoholics Anonymous. Mary C. Darrah. 300p. 1992. pap. 12.95 (*0-8294-0712-X*) Loyola Pr.

Sister Images: Guided Meditations from the Stories of Biblical Women. Mary Zimmer. LC 93-18259. 128p. 1993. Alk. paper. pap. 7.95 (*0-687-38556-3*) Abingdon.

Sister in the Shadow. Anne W. Smith. 176p. (YA). (gr. 7-12). 1988. pap. 2.75 (*0-380-70378-5*, Flare) Avon.

Sister Is a Very Special Friend. Ed. by Robin Andrews. LC 91-73571. (Illus.). 64p. 1991. pap. 7.95 (*0-88396-348-5*) Blue Mtn Pr CO.

Sister Jamaica: A Study of Women, Work, & Households in Kingston. A. Lynn Bolles. LC 95-46006. 150p. (C). 1996. lib. bdg. 32.50 (*0-7618-0211-8*) U Pr of Amer.

Sister Jane: Her Friends & Acquaintances. Joel C. Harris. (Notable American Authors Ser.). 1992. reprint ed. lib. bdg. 75.00 (*0-7812-3024-1*) Rprt Serv.

Sister Jennie's Shaker Desserts. Arthur P. Tolve & James Bisseland, III. (Illus.). 48p. 1983. pap. 3.95 (*0-911861-00-9*) Gabriels Horn.

Sister Light, Sister Dark. Jane Yolen. 256p. 1995. 3.95 (*0-8125-0249-3*) Tor Bks.

Sister March's Secret. large type ed. Jane Lester. (Linford Romance Library). 296p. 1984. pap. 15.99 (*0-7089-6047-2*) Ulverscroft.

Sister Margarita. large type ed. Alex Stuart. 336p. 1988. 25.99 (*0-7089-1749-6*) Ulverscroft.

***Sister Marguerite.** Crown Publishing Group Staff. 1997. write for info. (*0-609-60113-X*) Crown Pub Group.

***Sister Mary Ignatius Explains It All for You & The Actor's Nightmare.** rev. ed. Christopher Durang. 1996. pap. 5.25 (*0-8222-1576-4*) Dramatists Play.

Sister Mask. Scholastic Staff. (Mask Ser.). (J). (ps-3). 1996. pap. text ed. 3.99 (*0-590-50203-4*) Scholastic Inc.

***Sister of Mercy.** Wilma Sulivan. Ed. by Pam Cretion. (Illus.). 100p. (Orig.). 1997. pap. 7.99 (*1-889893-11-0*) Emerald House Group Inc.

Sister of Mine: A Heartwarming Collection of Letters, Writings & Poetry. Ed. by Elizabeth Belew. (Illus.). 96p. 1996. boxed 13.95 (*1-889116-08-4*) Penbrooke Pub.

Sister of Serenity Ward. large type ed. Lynne Collins. (Linford Romance Library). 1995. pap. 15.99 (*0-7089-7779-0*, Linford) Ulverscroft.

Sister of the Bride. Beverly Cleary. 240p. (J). (gr. 6). 1992. mass mkt. 4.50 (*0-380-70928-7*, Flare) Avon.

Sister of the Bride. Beverly Cleary. (J). (gr. 4-7). 1996. pap. 4.50 (*0-380-72807-9*) Avon.

Sister of the Bride. Beverly Cleary. LC 63-8802. (Illus.). 256p. (J). (gr. 7 up). 1963. lib. bdg. 16.93 (*0-688-31742-1*, Morrow Junior) Morrow.

***Sister of the Bride.** Carol Quinto. 224p. 1997. mass mkt. 4.99 (*0-8217-5673-7*, Zebra Kensgtn) Kensgtn Pub Corp.

Sister of the Road: The Autobiography of Box Car Bertha. Bertha Thompson. (American Biography Ser.). 314p. 1991. reprint ed. lib. bdg. 79.00 (*0-7812-8384-1*) Rprt Serv.

Sister of Wisdom: St. Hildegard's Theology of the Feminine. Barbara Newman. LC 86-16094. 288p. (C). 1987. pap. 12.95 (*0-520-06615-4*) U CA Pr.

***Sister of Wisdom: St. Hildegard's Theology of the Feminine.** Barbara Newman. 1997. pap. text ed. 14.95 (*0-520-21162-6*) U CA Pr.

Sister Outsider: Essays & Speeches. Audre Lorde. LC 84-1844. (Feminist Ser.). 192p. 1984. pap. 10.95 (*0-89594-141-4*) Crossing Pr.

Sister Philomene. Edmond L. De Goncourt & Jules De Goncourt. Tr. by L. Ensor. 292p. 1975. reprint ed. 22.00 (*0-86527-304-9*) Fertig.

Sister Power: How Phenomenal Black Women Are Rising to the Top. Patricia Reid-Merritt. LC 96-4208. 304p. 1996. text ed. 22.95 (*0-471-10461-2*) Wiley.

***Sister Power: How Phenomenal Black Women Are Rising to the Top.** Patricia Reid-Merritt. 1997. pap. text ed. 14.95 (*0-471-19355-0*) Wiley.

Sister Radiance. David A. Clark. 1994. mass mkt. 6.95 (*1-56333-215-9*, Rhinoceros) Masquerade.

Sister Republics: Switzerland & the United States from 1776 to the Present. James H. Hutson. LC 91-6605. 68p. 1991. 7.95 (*0-8444-0716-X*) Lib Congress.

Sister Republics: Switzerland & the United States from 1776 to the Present. 2nd ed. James H. Hutson. LC 92-28579. 1992. write for info. (*0-8444-0762-3*) Lib Congress.

Sister Republics: The Origins of French & American Republicanism. Patrice L. Higonnet. LC 88-880. 336p. 1988. 36.50 (*0-674-80982-3*) HUP.

Sister Safety Pin. Lorrie Sprecher. LC 94-36114. 256p. (Orig.). 1994. pap. 9.95 (*1-56341-050-8*); lib. bdg. 20.95 (*1-56341-051-6*) Firebrand Bks.

Sister Sarah: A New Baby Can Be Fun. Carol Guzzy Kudeviz. LC 94-66126. (Illus.). 24p. (J). (ps-3). 1995. pap. 3.95 (*0-9639779-0-3*) Pigtail Pubng.

***Sister Schubert's Secret Bread Recipes.** Schubert. 128p. 1996. 14.95 (*0-8487-1517-9*, 102573) Oxmoor Hse.

Sister Secret (Family Ties) Jessica Steele. 1995. mass mkt. 2.99 (*0-373-03385-0*) Harlequin Bks.

***Sister Set.** Emily Gwathmey. LC 97-11913. 1997. write for info. (*0-688-15331-3*) Morrow.

Sister Shako & Kolo the Goat: Memories of My Childhood in Turkey. Vedat Dalokay. Tr. by Guner Ener. (YA). (gr. 5 up). 1994. 14.00 (*0-688-13271-5*) Lothrop.

Sister Sister. Eric J. Dickey. LC 96-17303. 272p. 1996. pap. 22.95 (*0-525-94126-6*) NAL-Dutton.

***Sister Sister.** Eric J. Dickey. 1997. mass mkt. 5.99 (*0-451-18802-0*, Sig) NAL-Dutton.

***Sister, Sister.** Eric J. Dickey. 1996. 22.95 (*0-614-25355-1*, Dutton) NAL-Dutton.

Sister, Sister: Cool in School. Janet Quin-Harkin. (J). (gr. 3-6). 1996. pap. 3.99 (*0-671-00176-0*) PB.

Sister Sister: One Crazy Christmas, No. 3. Quin Harkin. (J). (gr. 3-6). 1996. mass mkt. 3.99 (*0-671-00283-X*) PB.

Sister Sister: You Read My Mind. Quin Harkin. (J). (gr. 3-6). 1996. mass mkt. 3.99 (*0-671-00177-9*) PB.

Sister Slater's Secret. large type ed. Holly North. 271p. 1993. 25.99 (*0-7505-0433-1*) Ulverscroft.

***Sister Songs: A Poetic Voyage.** Linda F. Lewis. 66p. 1994. pap. 10.00 (*1-888077-00-X*) Akosua Visions.

Sister, Stay Out! Misty Taggart. LC 94-25681. (Angel Academy Ser.: Vol. 2). (Illus.). (J). 1994. pap. 3.99 (*0-8499-5017-1*) Word Pub.

Sister Stew, Fiction & Poetry by Women. Ed. by Juliet S. Kono & Cathy Song. LC 91-11471. (Bamboo Ridge Ser.: Nos. 50-51). 330p. (YA). (gr. 9-12). 1991. pap. 10.00 (*0-910043-22-1*) Bamboo Ridge Pr.

Sister Stories. Brenda Peterson. 1997. pap. 12.95 (*0-14-023299-0*) Viking Penguin.

***Sister Stories: Daily Inspiration from the Lives of Ruth & Esther.** Willy Nywening. LC 96-18732. 85p. 1997. pap. 9.50 (*1-56212-248-7*, 1701-0630) CRC Pubns.

Sister Stories: Taking the Journey Together. Brenda Peterson. LC 95-4771. 291p. 1996. pap. 23.95 (*0-670-85296-1*, Viking) Viking Penguin.

Sister Suzie Cinema: Collected Poems & Performances 1967-1986. Lee Breuer. LC 87-1955. (Illus.). 190p. 1987. pap. 10.95 (*0-930452-60-7*) Theatre Comm.

Sister Swap. Susan Napier. (Presents Ser.). 1996. mass mkt. 3.25 (*0-373-11788-4*, 1-11788-6) Harlequin Bks.

Sister Swap. large type ed. Susan Napier. 1995. 20.95 (*0-263-14287-6*, Pub. by Mills & Boon UK) Thorndike Pr.

***Sister Syd.** Harriet Gilmore. Date not set. write for info. (*0-688-04726-2*) Morrow.

Sister Sylvan. large type ed. Fay Chandos. 352p. 1988. 25.99 (*0-7089-1796-8*) Ulverscroft.

Sister to Jane. large type ed. Beatrice May. (Historical Romance Ser.). 320p. 1992. 25.99 (*0-7089-2696-7*) Ulverscroft.

Sister to Scheherazade. Assia Djebar. Tr. by Dorothy S. Blair. LC 92-42699. 116p. (C). 1993. pap. 12.95 (*0-435-08622-7*, 08622) Heinemann.

Sister to Scheherazade. Assia Djebar. 170p. 1991. 19.95 (*0-7043-2670-1*, Pub. by Quartet UK) Interlink Pub.

Sister to Sister: Devotion for & from African American Women. Ed. by Suzan D. Cook. 256p. 1995. pap. 10.00 (*0-8170-1221-4*) Judson.

Sister to Sister: Women Write about the Unbreakable Bond. Ed. by Patricia Foster. LC 95-10486. 400p. 1995. 22.95 (*0-385-47128-9*, Anchor NY) Doubleday.

Sister to Sister: Women Write about the Unbreakable Bond. Ed. by Patricia Foster. 368p. 1997. pap. 12.95 (*0-385-47129-7*, Anchor NY) Doubleday.

Sister to Sister Together at Death: Together During Sickness, Dying, Death & Funeral. Yuhaayaa L. Kaahena. Ed. by Latifa Ismail. 67p. (Orig.). 1994. pap. 5.00 (*1-883781-08-6*) Yuhaaya.

Sister to the Sioux: The Memoirs of Elaine Goodale Eastman, 1885-91. Elaine G. Eastman. Ed. by Kay Graber. LC 77-25018. (Pioneer Heritage Ser.: Vol. 7). (Illus.). xiii, 185p. 1978. pap. 7.95 (*0-8032-6713-4*, Bison Books) U of Nebr Pr.

Sister Vayda's Song. Wilma E. McDaniel. 1982. pap. 6.00 (*0-914610-27-9*) Hanging Loose.

Sister Water. Nancy Willard. 247p. 1994. mass mkt. 5.99 (*0-8041-0876-5*) Ivy Books.

Sister Wendy's Grand Tour: Discovering Europe's Great Art. Wendy Beckett. (Illus.). 166p. 1996. 24.95 (*1-55670-509-3*) Stewart Tabori & Chang.

Sister Wendy's Story of Painting. Wendy Beckett. LC 94-6322. (Illus.). 400p. 1997. 39.95 (*1-56458-615-4*) DK Pub Inc.

Sister Woman. Charlotte Barr. 96p. (Orig.). 1990. pap. 11.95 (*0-9624100-0-4*) Bell Buckle.

Sister Woman. Mary A. Barr. Ed. by Maggi Vaughn & Ron York. 94p. (Orig.). 1988. pap. write for info. (*0-318-65749-X*) Bell Buckle.

Sisterfire. C. Sherman. LC 94-795. 256p. 1994. pap. 13.00 (*0-06-095018-8*) HarpC.

***Sisterfriends: Motivational Empowerment for Women & a Celebration of Sisterhood.** Jewel D. Taylor. 200p. (Orig.). 1997. pap. 12.00 (*1-884743-06-4*) Quiet Time Pubng.

Sisterhood. Michael Palmer. 368p. 1991. mass mkt. 6.50 (*0-553-27570-4*) Bantam.

Sisterhood. large type ed. Michael Palmer. (Niagara Large Print Ser.). 390p. 1996. 27.99 (*0-7089-5820-6*) Ulverscroft.

Sisterhood & Solidarity: Feminism & Labor in Modern Times. Diane Balser. LC 87-4733. 248p. (Orig.). 1987. 35.00 (*0-89608-278-4*); pap. 10.00 (*0-89608-277-6*) South End Pr.

Sisterhood, Brotherhood & Equality of the Sexes in the Restoration Comedies of Manners. Nancy L. Tippetts. LC 93-2279. (Sociocriticism Ser.: Vol. 5). 224p. (C). 1995. text ed. 48.95 (*0-8204-2255-X*) P Lang Pubng.

Sisterhood Denied: Race, Gender, & Class in a New South Community. Dolores Janoewski. 1992. pap. 16.95 (*1-56639-006-0*) Temple U Pr.

***Sisterhood, Feminisms & Power: From Africa to the Diaspora.** Obioma Nnaemeka. LC 97-19965. 1997. write for info. (*0-86543-438-7*) Africa World.

Sisterhood, Feminisms, & Power in Africa. Ed. by Obioma Nnaemeka. LC 97-19965. 1995. pap. 16.95 (*0-86543-439-5*) Africa World.

Sisterhood Is Global: The International Women's Movement Anthology. Ed. by Robin Morgan. LC 96-38456. 832p. 1996. pap. 24.95 (*1-55861-160-6*) Feminist Pr.

Sisterhood Is Powerful: An Anthology of Writings from the Women's Liberation Movement. Ed. by Robin Morgan. 1970. pap. 16.00 (*0-394-70539-4*, Vin) Random.

Sisterhood of Steel. Marx & Allison C. Ledger. (Illus.). 1990. pap. 8.95 (*0-913035-23-8*) Eclipse Bks.

Sisterhood of the Night: A True Story. Becky Usry. 304p. 1995. 22.95 (*0-88282-134-2*) New Horizon NJ.

Sistermony. Richard Stern. 1995. pap. 17.50 (*1-55611-427-3*) D I Fine.

Sistermony. 2nd ed. Richard Stern. LC 95-46857. (Illus.). 121p. 1996. reprint ed. pap. 9.95 (*1-55611-476-1*, Primus) D I Fine.

***Sisters.** Ariel Books Staff. 1996. 3.95 (*0-8362-0973-7*, Arie Bks) Andrews & McMeel.

Sisters. Debbie Bailey. (Talk About Ser.). (Illus.). 14p. (J). 1993. text ed. 4.95 (*1-55037-275-0*, Pub. by Annick CN) Firefly Bks Ltd.

***Sisters.** Illus. by Katharine Barnwell. (Charming Petites Ser.). 80p. 1997. 4.95 (*0-88088-815-6*) Peter Pauper.

Sisters. Pat Booth. 416p. 1988. mass mkt. 5.99 (*0-345-34789-7*) Ballantine.

***Sisters.** Anita Bunkley. 1996. mass mkt. 5.99 (*0-451-19100-5*, Sig) NAL-Dutton.

Sisters. Ed. by Helen Exley. (Miniature Square Bks.). (Illus.). 64p. 1995. 6.00 (*1-85015-691-3*) Exley Giftbooks.

Sisters. Lisa Gregory. 1991. mass mkt. 4.99 (*0-446-35747-2*) Warner Bks.

Sisters. James Joyce. Ed. by Setlok. (Joyce Ser.). 1993. 16.95 incl. audio (*1-883049-00-8*) Commuters Lib.

An Asterisk (*) at the beginning of an entry indicates that the title is appearing in BIP for the first time.

Sisters. James Joyce. 1993. lib. bdg. 18.95 incl. audio (*1-883049-19-9*) Commuters Lib.

Sisters. Hilda McKenzie. 384p. 1994. pap. 11.95 (*0-7472-4116-3*, Pub. by Headline UK) Trafalgar.

Sisters. David McPhail. LC 84-3775. (Illus.). 32p. (J). (ps-3). 1984. 14.00 (*0-15-275319-2*, HB Juv Bks) HarBrace.

Sisters. David McPhail. LC 84-3775. (Illus.). 32p. (J). (ps-3). 1990. pap. 5.00 (*0-15-275320-6*, Voyager Bks) HarBrace.

***Sisters.** Carol Saline & Sharon J. Wohlmuth. 1997. pap. 17.95 (*0-7624-0089-7*) Running Pr.

Sisters. Tricia Tusa. LC 94-39047. (Illus.). 32p. (J). 1995. 15.00 (*0-517-70032-8*) Crown Pub Group.

Sisters. Tricia Tusa. LC 94-39047. (Illus.). 32p. (J). (gr. k-2). 1995. lib. bdg. 16.99 (*0-517-70033-6*) Crown Pub Group.

Sisters. Emily Wheeler. 1994. pap. 6.95 (*1-885061-00-5*) Adventure Pubns.

Sisters. Rose G. Willinger & Victoria Hinton. 1995. 8.95 (*0-533-11408-X*) Vantage.

Sisters. Photos by Sharon J. Wohlmuth. (Illus.). 136p. 1994. 27.50 (*1-56138-450-X*) Running Pr.

Sisters. large type ed. Hilda McKenzie. 1994. 25.99 (*0-7089-3170-7*) Ulverscroft.

***Sisters: A Shared Childhood, a Shared Friendship.** Lil Copan. LC 97-15008. 1997. pap. text ed. 5.99 (*0-87788-744-6*) Shaw Pubs.

Sisters: Devoted or Divided. Susan Ripps. 320p. 1994. 22.50 (*0-8217-4679-0*, Zebra Kensgtn) Kensgtn Pub Corp.

***Sisters: Miniature Edition.** Illus. by Jackie Pardo. 128p. 1997. 4.95 (*0-7624-0111-7*, Running Pr Mini Edtns) Running Pr.

Sisters: Photographic Portraits - An Exhibition. Birgitta Ralston. LC 88-51842. 32p. (Orig.). 1989. pap. 7.00 (*0-9621886-0-3*) Univ WI Art Gal.

Sisters: Relation & Rescue in Nineteenth-Century British Novels & Paintings. Michael Cohen. LC 94-14414. 1995. 60.00 (*0-8386-3555-5*) Fairleigh Dickinson.

Sisters: Shared Histories, Lifelong Ties. rev. ed. Elizabeth Fishel. 304p. 1994. reprint ed. pap. 12.95 (*0-943233-70-4*) Conari Press.

Sisters: Shared Histories, Lifelong Ties. rev. ed. Elizabeth Fishel. 300p. 1994. lib. bdg. 35.00 (*0-8095-5879-3*) Borgo Pr.

***Sisters: Shared Histories, Lifelong Ties.** rev. ed. Elizabeth Fishel. LC 97-5273. (Illus.). 304p. 1997. pap. 14.95 (*1-57324-092-3*) Conari Press.

Sisters: So Much We Share. (Little Ribbons of Love Ser.). (Illus.). 1995. pap. 4.99 (*1-57051-051-2*) Brownlow Pub Co.

Sisters: The Poetry of Women. Ed. & Intro. by Carole J. Heffley. (Illus.). 156p. (Orig.). 1994. pap. write for info. (*1-883331-04-8*) Anderie Poetry.

Sisters: The Story Goes On. Janice Chaffee. 192p. 1995. pap. 12.99 (*0-7852-7601-7*) Nelson.

Sisters & Brothers. Judy Dunn. LC 84-19343. (Developing Child Ser.). (Illus.). 192p. 1985. pap. text ed. 6.95 (*0-674-80981-5*) HUP.

Sisters & Brothers. Judy Dunn. LC 84-19343. (Developing Child Ser.). (Illus.). 192p. 1985. 23.50 (*0-674-80980-7*) HUP.

Sisters & Brothers. Gretchen Super. (Your Family Album Ser.). (Illus.). 48p. (J). (gr. k-3). 1992. lib. bdg. 15.98 (*0-8050-2219-8*) TFC Bks NY.

Sisters & Brothers: Reclaiming a Biblical Idea of Community. Verna J. Dozier & James R. Adams. LC 93-2755. 149p. 1993. Alk. paper. pap. 10.95 (*1-56101-076-6*) Cowley Pubns.

Sisters & Brothers: Resolving Your Adult Sibling Relationships. Patti McDermott. 240p. 1993. pap. 14.95 (*1-56565-083-2*, Legcy) Lowell Hse.

Sisters & Friends: A Resource Guide. Jocelyn Riley. 114p. 1995. 20.00 (*1-877933-45-7*) Her Own Words.

***Sisters & Lovers.** Connie Briscoe. 1996. pap. 12.00 (*0-345-40969-8*) Ballantine.

Sisters & Lovers. Connie Briscoe. 416p. 1995. mass mkt. 6.99 (*0-8041-1334-3*) Ivy Books.

Sisters & Lovers. large type ed. Connie Briscoe. (Niagara Large Print Ser.). 437p. 1995. 27.99 (*0-7089-5805-2*) Ulverscroft.

Sisters & Lovers. Brenda Clarke. 416p. 1992. reprint ed. mass mkt. 4.99 (*1-55817-655-1*, Pinncle Kensgtn) Kensgtn Pub Corp.

Sisters & Prophets. Mary L. Sleevi. LC 93-71540. (Illus.). 120p. (Orig.). 1993. pap. 12.95 (*0-87793-514-9*) Ave Maria.

Sisters & Quilts: Threads That Bind. Ann Seely & Joyce Stewart. Ed. by Sharon Holmes. (Illus.). 112p. 1992. pap. 19.95 (*1-880972-02-6*) Pssblts Denver.

Sisters & Strangers. Eileen Curtis. 368p. 1996. mass mkt. 5.50 (*0-06-101013-8*, Harp PBks) HarpC.

Sisters & Strangers. Nina Lambert. 416p. 1995. 26.00 (*0-7126-5564-6*, Pub. by Century UK) Trafalgar.

Sisters & Strangers: Women in the Shanghai Cotton Mills, 1919-1949. Emily Honig. LC 84-51711. 320p. 1986. 45.00 (*0-8047-1274-3*); pap. 14.95 (*0-8047-2012-6*) Stanford U Pr.

Sisters & Wives: The Past & Future of Sexual Equality. Karen Sacks. LC 78-75241. (Contributions in Women's Studies: No. 10). 274p. 1979. text ed. 45.00 (*0-313-20983-9*, SPA/, Greenwood Pr) Greenwood.

Sisters & Wives: The Past & Future of Sexual Equality. Karen Sacks. LC 82-13491. 288p. 1982. reprint ed. pap. text ed. 11.95 (*0-252-01004-3*) U of Ill Pr.

Sisters & Workers in the Middle Ages. Ed. by Judith M. Bennett et al. 344p. 1989. pap. 17.50 (*0-226-04248-0*); lib. bdg. 36.00 (*0-226-04247-2*) U Ch Pr.

Sisters Are Forever. Adventure Staff. (Small Wonders Ser.). 120p. 1995. spiral bd. 4.99 (*1-879127-53-9*) Lighten Up Enter.

Sisters' Arts: The Writing & Painting of Virginia Woolf & Vanessa Bell. Diane F. Gillespie. LC 88-2086. (Illus.). 360p. (C). 1991. reprint ed. text ed. 39.95 (*0-8156-2430-1*); reprint ed. pap. text ed. 17.95 (*0-8156-2529-4*) Syracuse U Pr.

***Sisters at Heart.** Susan Bowden. 1997. mass mkt. 5.99 (*0-451-19220-6*, Sig) NAL-Dutton.

Sisters at the Well. Jeni B. Holzapfel & Richard N. Holzapfel. 1993. 11.95 (*0-88494-896-X*) Bookcraft Inc.

***Sisters at War.** Created by Francine Pascal. (Sweet Valley Twins Ser.: No. 111). 144p. (Orig.). (J). (gr. 3-7). 1997. pap. 3.50 (*0-553-48442-7*) BDD Bks Young Read.

***Sisters, Brothers, & Disability: A Family Album.** Lydia Gans. LC 97-24862. (Illus.). 160p. (J). (gr. 3 up). 1997. pap. 12.95 (*1-57749-044-4*) Fairview Press.

Sister's Choice: Traditions & Change in American Women's Writing. Elaine Showalter. (Clarendon Lectures in Economics). (Illus.). 208p. 1991. 25.00 (*0-19-812383-3*) OUP.

Sister's Choice: Traditions & Change in American Women's Writing. Elaine Showalter. (Illus.). 208p. 1995. reprint ed. pap. 11.95 (*0-19-282417-1*) OUP.

Sisters in Arms: Catholic Nuns Through Two Millennia. Jo A. McNamara. 768p. 1996. 35.00 (*0-674-80984-X*) HUP.

Sisters in Crime. Carolyn Keene. (Nancy Drew Files Ser.: No. 19). 160p. (Orig.). (YA). (gr. 6 up). pap. 3.99 (*0-671-67957-0*, Archway) PB.

Sisters in Crime, No. 2. Ed. by Marilyn Wallace. (Sisters in Crime Ser.: 2). 1990. mass mkt. 4.99 (*0-425-11966-1*) Berkley Pub.

Sisters in Crime, No. 3. Marilyn Wallace. (Sisters in Crime Ser.: 3). 1990. mass mkt. 4.99 (*0-425-12214-X*) Berkley Pub.

Sisters in Crime, No. 4. Marilyn Wallace. (Sisters in Crime Ser.: 4). 1991. mass mkt. 5.99 (*0-425-13074-6*) Berkley Pub.

***Sisters in Crisis: The Tragic Unraveling of Women's Religious Communities.** Ann Carey. 1997. 19.95 (*0-614-27535-0*) Our Sunday Visitor.

***Sisters in Crisis: The Tragic Unravelling of Women's Religious Communities.** Ann Carey. 300p. 1997. 19.95 (*0-87973-655-0*) Our Sunday Visitor.

Sisters in Fantasy. Ed. by Susan Shwartz & Martin H. Greenberg. 336p. (Orig.). 1995. mass mkt. 4.99 (*0-451-45292-5*, ROC) NAL-Dutton.

Sisters in Fantasy 2. Ed. by Susan Shwartz & Martin H. Greenberg. 336p. 1996. mass mkt. 5.99 (*0-451-45503-7*, ROC) NAL-Dutton.

***Sisters in Law: Women Lawyers in Modern American History.** Virginia G. Drachman. LC 97-23490. 1997. write for info. (*0-674-80991-2*) HUP.

***Sisters in Rain.** Cecily Markham. 24p. (Orig.). 1996. pap. 6.00 (*1-877801-32-1*) Still Waters.

Sisters in Solitude: Two Traditions of Buddhist Monastic Ethics for Women. A Comparative Analysis of the Chinese Dharmagupta & the Tibetan Mulasarnisti Bhiksura Pratimoska Sutrar. Karma L. Tsomo. LC 96-24709. (SUNY Series, Feminist Philosophy). 198p. (C). 1996. text ed. 59.50 (*0-7914-3089-8*); pap. text ed. 19.95 (*0-7914-3090-1*) State U NY Pr.

Sisters in Spirit: Mormon Women in Historical & Cultural Perspective. Ed. by Maureen U. Beecher & Lavina F. Anderson. LC 86-30757. 304p. (C). 1992. pap. text ed. 14.95 (*0-252-06296-5*) U of Ill Pr.

Sisters in Struggle. Barnett. 224p. (C). Date not set. text ed. 55.00 (*0-415-91434-5*, Routledge NY) Routledge.

Sisters in Struggle. Bernice M. Barnett. 224p. Date not set. pap. 17.95 (*0-415-91435-3*, Routledge NY) Routledge.

Sisters in the Resistance: How Women Fought to Free France, 1940-1945. Margaret C. Weitz. LC 95-7632. (Illus.). 352p. 1995. text ed. 30.00 (*0-471-12676-4*) Wiley.

Sisters in the Sky, Vol. 1: The WAFS. Adela R. Scharr. LC 86-25321. (Illus.). ix, 531p. 1986. 27.95 (*0-935284-46-X*) Patrice Pr.

Sisters in the Sky, Vol. 2: The WASP. Adela R. Scharr. Ed. by Gregory M. Franzwa. LC 86-25321. (Illus.). x, 765p. 1988. 29.95 (*0-935284-55-9*) Patrice Pr.

***Sisters in the Storm.** Anna Eilenberg. LC 92-82715. (Illus.). 314p. (YA). (gr. 9-12). Date not set. 21.95 (*1-56062-156-7*) CIS Comm.

Sisters in the Wilderness: The Challenge of Womanist God-Talk. Delores S. Williams. LC 93-10654. 287p. (Orig.). 1995. pap. 15.00 (*1-57075-026-2*) Orbis Bks.

Sisters in Time: Imagining Gender in Nineteenth-Century British Fiction. Susan Morgan. 272p. 1989. 48.00 (*0-19-505822-4*) OUP.

Sisters Keeper. Randye Lordon. 320p. 1996. pap. 9.95 (*0-312-14134-3*) St Martin.

Sisters Listening to Sisters: Women of the World Share Stories of Personal Empowerment. Peggy Andrews. LC 96-15355. 208p. 1996. text ed. 55.00 (*0-89789-475-8*, Bergin & Garvey); pap. text ed. 18.95 (*0-89789-476-6*, Bergin & Garvey) Greenwood.

Sisters Long Ago. Peg Kehret. Ed. by Patricia MacDonald. 160p. (J). 1992. reprint ed. mass mkt. 3.99 (*0-671-73433-4*) PB.

Sisters of a Different Dawn. Darcy Williamson. LC 88-50760. 309p. 1988. pap. 10.95 (*1-55523-158-6*) Winston-Derek.

***Sisters of Caliban: Anthology of Women Poets of the Caribbean.** Ed. by M. M. Fenwick. LC 96-86065. 434p. (C). 1996. pap. 18.95 (*1-885214-09-X*) Azul Edits.

Sisters of Charity of New York, 1809-1959, Vol. 1. Marie D. Walsh. LC 60-10735. 396p. reprint ed. pap. 107.00 (*0-7837-5707-7*, 2045366) Bks Demand.

Sisters of Charity of New York, 1809-1959, Vol. 2. Marie D. Walsh. LC 60-10735. 365p. reprint ed. pap. 104.10 (*0-7837-5708-5*) Bks Demand.

Sisters of Charity of New York, 1809-1959, Vol. 3. Marie D. Walsh. LC 60-10735. 373p. reprint ed. pap. 106.40 (*0-7837-5709-3*) Bks Demand.

Sisters of Fortune: Being the True Story of How Three Motherless Sisters Saved Their Home in New England & Raised Their Younger Brother While Their Father Went Fortune Hunting in the California Gold Rush. Nancy C. Heffernan & Ann Page Stecker. LC 93-19716. (Illus.). 303p. 1993. pap. 17.95 (*0-87451-651-X*) U Pr of New Eng.

Sisters of Gore: Seven Gothic Melodramas by British Women, 1790-1843. Ed. by John C. Franceschina. LC 96-24213. 480p. 1996. text ed. 65.00 (*0-8153-1781-6*) Garland.

Sisters of Liberty: Marseille, Lyon, Paris, & the Reaction to a Centralized State, 1868-1871. Louis M. Greenberg. LC 70-134952. (Historical Monographs: No. 62). 405p. 1971. 27.50 (*0-674-81000-7*) HUP.

Sisters of Maryknoll: Through Troubled Waters. Mary De Paul Cogan. LC 72-167329. (Essay Index Reprint Ser.). 1977. reprint ed. 20.95 (*0-8369-2764-8*) Ayer.

Sisters of Mercy: Spirituality in America, 1843-1900. Ed. by Kathleen Healy. LC 91-42119. (Sources of American Spirituality Ser.). 416p. 1992. 24.95 (*0-8091-0453-9*) Paulist Pr.

Sisters of Orleans: A Tale of Race & Social Conflict. LC 72-2025. (Black Heritage Library Collection). 1977. reprint ed. 20.95 (*0-8369-9063-3*) Ayer.

Sisters of the Black Moon. F. J. Pesando. 432p. (Orig.). 1994. pap. 4.99 (*0-451-40440-8*, Onyx) NAL-Dutton.

***Sisters of the Brush: Their Family, Art, Life & Letters 1797-1833.** Ramsay MacMullen. (Illus.). 550p. 1997. 29.00 (*0-9658780-0-7*) R MacMullen.

Sisters of the Brush: Women's Artistic Culture in Late Nineteenth-Century Paris. Tamar Garb. LC 93-43147. (Illus.). 224p. (C). 1994. 55.00 (*0-300-05903-5*) Yale U Pr.

Sisters of the Earth: Women's Prose & Poetry about Nature. Loraine Anderson. LC 90-55686. 446p. 1991. pap. 14.00 (*0-679-73382-5*, Vin) Random.

***Sisters of the Great Lakes: Art of American Indian Women.** Marsha MacDowell & Janice Reed. (Illus.). 68p. (Orig.). 1996. pap. 24.95 (*0-944311-08-3*) MSU Museum.

Sisters of the Hawk. 42p. 1994. pap. 5.95 (*1-885405-03-0*) IOC Pr.

Sisters of the Hawk. Beverly Antaeus et al. 45p. 1994. pap. text ed. 5.95 (*1-885405-01-4*) IOC Pr.

Sisters of the Heart. Miriam Neff. 176p. 1995. 14.99 (*0-7852-7744-7*) Nelson.

Sisters of the Lone Star: Comanche Woman. Joan Johnston. 1989. pap. 4.95 (*0-671-62899-2*) S&S Trade.

Sisters of the Night. Ed. by Barbara Hambly & Martin H. Greenberg. (Orig.). 1995. pap. write for info. (*0-446-60052-0*, Aspect) Warner Bks.

Sisters of the Road. Barbara Wilson. LC 86-20367. 202p. (Orig.). 1986. pap. 9.95 (*1-878067-24-9*) Seal Pr WA.

Sisters of the Shadow. Maxine Harris. LC 90-49624. 372p. 1991. 19.95 (*0-8061-2324-9*) U of Okla Pr.

Sisters of the Shadow. Maxine Harris. LC 90-49624. 1993. pap. 12.95 (*0-8061-2502-0*) U of Okla Pr.

Sisters of the Spirit: Three Black Women's Autobiographies of the Nineteenth Century. Ed. by William L. Andrews. LC 85-42544. (Religion in North America Ser.). 256p. 1986. 31.50 (*0-253-35260-6*); pap. 11.95 (*0-253-28704-9*) Ind U Pr.

Sisters of the Wind: Voices of Early Women Aviators. Elizabeth S. Bell. (Illus.). 208p. (Orig.). 1994. pap. 14.95 (*0-9623879-4-0*) Trilogy Bks.

Sisters of the Wolf. Ernest Herndon. LC 96-24625. (Eric Sterling, Secret Agent Ser.: Bk. 5). 128p. (YA). (gr. 8-12). 1996. pap. 5.99 (*0-310-20729-0*) Zondervan.

Sisters of the Yam: Black Women & Self-Recovery. Bell Hooks. LC 93-22112. 200p. 1993. 30.00 (*0-89608-457-4*); pap. 14.00 (*0-89608-456-6*) South End Pr.

***Sisters of the 13 Moons: Rituals Celebrating Women's Lives.** Jeanne B. Grinnan et al. 69p. (Orig.). 1996. pap. 14.95 (*1-890662-03-8*) Prism Coll.

***Sisters on a Journey: Portraits of American Midwives.** Penfield Chester. (Illus.). 288p. (C). 1997. pap. 19.95 (*0-8135-2408-3*); text ed. 50.00 (*0-8135-2407-5*) Rutgers U Pr.

Sisters or Citizens? Women & Socialism in France since 1876. Charles Sowerwine. LC 81-7692. 266p. reprint ed. pap. 75.90 (*0-685-16128-5*, 2027253) Bks Demand.

Sisters Rondoli, & Other Stories: Collected Novels & Stories, Vol. 5. Guy De Maupassant. Ed. by Ernest A. Boyd. LC 79-157792. (Short Story Index Reprint Ser.). 1977. reprint ed. 23.95 (*0-8369-3904-2*) Ayer.

Sisters Rosensweig. Wendy Wasserstein. 1997. pap. 5.25 (*0-8222-1348-6*) Dramatists Play.

Sisters Rosensweig. Wendy Wasserstein. LC 93-224. 1993. 17.95 (*0-15-182692-7*) HarBrace.

Sisters Rosensweig. Wendy Wasserstein. 1994. pap. 9.00 (*0-15-600013-X*) HarBrace.

Sisters, Seeds & Cedars: Rediscovering Nineteenth-Century Life Through Correspondence from Rural Arkansas & Alabama. Ed. by Sarah M. Fountain. LC 94-34372. 1997. 45.00 (*0-944436-14-5*) Pelican.

Sisters (That Special Woman!) Penny Richards. 1996. mass mkt. 3.99 (*0-373-24015-5*, 1-24015-9) Silhouette.

Sisters under the Sari. Ruth G. Armstrong. LC 63-22164. 508p. reprint ed. pap. 144.80 (*0-317-11036-5*, 2022765) Bks Demand.

***Sister's View of the Million Man March.** Dianne Dale. (Illus.). (Orig.). 1996. mass mkt. 10.00 (*0-9655158-0-X*) D Dale.

Sister's Wish. Kate Jacobs. LC 94-24496. (Illus.). 32p. (J). (gr. k-2). 1996. 14.95 (*0-7868-0138-7*); lib. bdg. 14.89 (*0-7868-2112-4*) Hyprn Child.

***Sisters Without Color: A Celebration of Love.** Joice Fairchild & Judy Lamb. LC 96-70926. 96p. 1997. 14.95 (*1-56167-336-6*) Noble Hse MD.

Sisters/Hermanas. Gary Paulsen. 144p. (YA). (gr. 7 up). 1993. 11.00 (*0-15-275323-0*, HB Juv Bks) HarBrace.

***Sisters/Hermanas.** Gary Paulsen. 144p. (YA). (gr. 7 up). 1993. pap. 6.00 (*0-15-275324-9*, HB Juv Bks) HarBrace.

Sistine Cartoons. 2nd ed. L. C. Phillips. LC 68-59442. 84p. 1970. 19.95 (*0-912282-00-2*) Pulse-Finger.

Sistine Ceiling see Michelangelo

Sistine Ceiling Restored. Michael Hirst. LC 93-39787. 1994. 75.00 (*0-8109-3840-5*) Abrams.

***Sistine Chapel.** Fabrizio Mancinelli. (Illus.). 96p. 1996. pap. 25.00 (*0-614-24667-9*) Sheed & Ward MO.

***Sistine Chapel.** Fabrizio Mancinelli. (Illus.). 111p. 1995. pap. 25.00 (*88-86921-01-2*, Pub. by Musei Vaticani IT) Treasures Inc.

Sistine Chapel. Ed. by William E. Wallace. LC 95-4441. (Michelangelo: Selected Scholarship in English Ser.: Vol. 2). (Illus.). 616p. 1995. text ed. 99.00 (*0-8153-1825-1*) Garland.

Sistine Chapel: The Art, the History, & the Restoration. Carlo Pietrangeli et al. (Illus.). 272p. 1986. 24.99 (*0-517-05119-2*) Random Hse Value.

Sistine Chapel Walls & the Roman Liturgy. Carol F. Lewine. (Illus.). 192p. (C). 1993. 45.00 (*0-271-00792-3*) Pa St U Pr.

Sistuh's Sermon on the Mount: The Blood Still Boils. Tamara Madison-Shaw. LC XLittlebook. 42p. (Orig.). 1993. 6.00 (*0-940880-43-1*) Open Hand.

***Sisu.** Sue Harrison. (Illus.). 198p. (YA). (gr. 7-12). 1997. 16.95 (*1-882376-40-4*); pap. 11.95 (*1-882376-39-0*) Thunder Bay Pr.

Sisu: Even Through a Stone Wall. Oskari Tokoi. 9.95 (*0-8315-0008-5*) Speller.

Sisyphus: The Old Stone, a New Way: A Jungian Approach to Midlife Crisis. Verena Kast. 214p. 1995. pap. 15.00 (*3-85630-527-0*, Pub. by Daimon Pubs SZ) Continuum.

Sisyphus & Sycamore & Other Songs of Survival & Endurance. T. P. Daly. Ed. by New York Society for General Semantics Staff. 65p. (Orig.). 1988. pap. 12.50 (*0-9621550-0-4*) NY Genl Semantics.

Sisyphus in the Hayfield: Views of a Berkshire Farmer. Walter Howard. (Illus.). 128p. (Orig.). 1988. pap. 10.00 (*0-9621205-0-2*) Cobble Pr.

Sit! The Dog Portraits of Thierry Poncelet. Thierry Poncelet. (Illus.). 96p. 1993. 19.95 (*1-56305-380-2*, 3380) Workman Pub.

Sit: Zen Teachings of Master Taisen Deshimaru. Taisen Deshmaru. Ed. by Philip Coupey. LC 95-51033. (Illus.). 375p. (Orig.). 1996. pap. 19.95 (*0-934252-61-0*) Hohm Pr.

Sit By Me. Francis H. Wise & Joyce M. Wise. (Phonetic Readers Ser.: No. 13). (Illus.). (J). (ps-1). 1975. pap. text ed. 1.50 (*0-915766-33-7*) Wise Pub.

Sit Down! Mary & Martha. Mary M. Simon. (Hear Me Read Ser.). (Illus.). 24p. (Orig.). (J). (ps-1). 1991. pap. 2.49 (*0-570-04701-3*, 56-1660) Concordia.

Sit-Down: The General Motors Strike of 1936-1937. Sidney Fine. LC 73-83455. (C). 1969. 34.50 (*0-472-32948-0*) U of Mich Pr.

***Sit down & Listen.** Ellen Kuzwayo. pap. 9.95 (*0-7043-4230-8*, Pub. by Womens Press UK) Trafalgar.

Sit Down & Pay Attention: Coping with Attention-Deficit Disorder Throughout the Life Cycle. Ronald Goldberg. 144p. (Orig.). 1991. pap. 8.95 (*0-929162-41-2*) PIA Pr.

Sit Down & Play. Elsa J. Baker. Ed. by Kenneth W. Baker. LC 87-90545. (Illus.). 203p. (Orig.). 1987. pap. 9.95 (*0-9620178-0-9*) Sycamore WA.

Sit Down & Shape Up: Sit & Exercise? Yes You Can. Fairfax Stephenson. LC 78-62586. 1979. pap. 4.95 (*0-931490-04-9*) Gotuit Ent.

***Sit Down, God...I'm Angry.** R. F. Smith, Jr. LC 97-30. 176p. (Orig.). 1997. pap. 12.00 (*0-8170-1258-3*) Judson.

***Sit down, Shut up & Hang On: A Biker's Guide to Life.** Chuck Hayes & Penny Powers. LC 96-41583. (Illus.). 128p. 1997. pap. 7.95 (*0-87905-781-5*) Gibbs Smith Pub.

***Sit et Contextes.** 2nd ed. Siskin. (FRE.). (C). 1994. lab manual ed., wbk. ed. write for info. (*0-15-500637-1*) HB Coll Pubs.

Sit Free or Die: John Stark, Clear Thinking, Daniel Webster, & New Hampshire's Outhouse Heritage. Ed. by M. J. Beagle. (Illus.). 50p. (Orig.). 1994. pap. text ed. 4.95 (*0-9642213-0-6*) Moose Cntry.

Sit-In: Mini-Play. (Black Americans Ser.). (J). (gr. 5 up). 1977. 6.50 (*0-89550-309-3*) Stevens & Shea.

Sit Still! Nancy Carlson. LC 95-46307. (Illus.). 32p. (J). (ps-2). 1996. pap. 13.99 (*0-670-85721-1*) Viking Child Bks.

Sit Tight, & I'll Swing You a Tail: Using & Writing Stories with Young People. Gregory A. Denman. LC 91-271. (Illus.). 184p. (Orig.). 1991. pap. text ed. 21.00 (*0-435-08548-4*, 08548) Heinemann.

Sit, Walk, Stand. Watchman Nee. 1991. pap. 4.95 (*0-87508-419-2*) Chr Lit.

Sit, Walk, Stand. Watchman Nee. 77p. 1977. mass mkt. 4.99 (*0-8423-5893-5*) Tyndale.

Sit, Walk, Stand see Sentaos, Andad, Estad Firmes

Sita, Speak! Marilyn Turkovich. (Passages to India Ser.). (C). 1989. spiral bd. 20.00 (*1-56709-018-4*) Indep Broadcast.

Sitanka: The Full Story of Wounded Knee. Forrest W. Seymour. 1981. 10.75 (*0-8158-0399-0*) Chris Mass.

Sitar Technique in Nibaddha Forms. Stephen Slawek. (Illus.). 264p. 1987. 47.50 (*81-208-0200-4*, Pub. by Motilal Banarsidass II) S Asia.

Sita's Daughters: Coming Out of Purdah. Leigh Minturn & Swaran Kapor. LC 92-22147. 392p. (C). 1993. 47.95 (*0-19-507823-3*); pap. 23.00 (*0-19-508035-1*) OUP.

Sita's Kitchen: A Testimony of Faith & Inquiry. Ramchandra Gandhi. (C). 1994. text ed. 20.00 (*81-224-0593-2*) S Asia.

Sita's Kitchen: A Testimony of Faith & Inquiry. Ramchandra Gandhi. LC 91-34438. 127p. 1992. text ed. 57.50 (*0-7914-1153-2*); pap. text ed. 18.95 (*0-7914-1154-0*) State U NY Pr.

Sitayana. K. R. Iyengar. 706p. 1989. reprint ed. 39.95 (*0-910261-13-X*, Pub. by Samata Bks II) Lotus Light.

SITE: Buildings & Spaces. LC 80-16394. (Illus.). 48p. (Orig.). 1970. pap. 1.00 (*0-917046-10-2*) Va Mus Arts.

Site: Narrative Architecture. (Architecture & Urbanism Extra Edition Ser.). (Illus.). 232p. (Orig.). (ENG & JPN.). (C). pap. text ed. 75.00 (*4-900211-16-8*, Pub. by Japan Architect JA) Gingko Press.

Site Agent's Handbook: Construction under the ICE Conditions. Tom Redshaw. 183p. 1990. text ed. 58.50 (*0-7277-1540-2*, Pub. by T Telford UK) Am Soc Civil Eng.

Site Analysis & Evaluation: A Programmed Course. 1971. pap. 60.00 (*0-88329-016-2*) IAAO.

Site & the Expedition. Ed. by Bruce T. Dahlberg & Kevin G. O'Connell. LC 80-21724. (Joint Archaeological Expedition to Tell el-Hesi Ser.: No. 4). xix, 214p. 1989. 47.50 (*0-931464-57-9*) Eisenbrauns.

***Site & the Memory: Landscape as Contemporary Experience.** Flamino Gualdoni. 1997. pap. 19.95 (*88-8158-081-0*, Pub. by Charta IT) Dist Art Pubs.

Site Assessment: Preliminary Edition. R. Barth. 1993. pap. text ed. write for info. (*0-07-005146-1*) McGraw.

***Site-Based Management & Decision Making.** Linda Chion-Kenney. 83p. 1994. 4.75 (*0-87652-183-9*, 021-0348) Am Assn Sch Admin.

Site-Based Management & the School Business Administrator. 60p. 1993. pap. 20.00 (*0-910170-62-2*) Assn Sch Busn.

Site-Based Management in Education: How to Make It Work in Your School. I. Carl Candoli. LC 94-62043. 235p. 1995. pap. text ed. 34.95 (*1-56676-223-5*) Technomic.

Site Book: A Field Guide to Commercial Real Estate Evaluation. Richard M. Fenker. LC 95-81587. 176p. (Orig.). 1995. pap. 17.99 (*0-940352-10-9*) Mesa Hse.

Site Carpentry & Joinery. Peter Brett. (Illus.). 128p. 1993. pap. 27.50 (*0-7487-1298-4*, Pub. by Stanley Thornes UK) Trans-Atl Phila.

Site Characterization & Exploration. Ed. by C. H. Dowding. 401p. 1979. pap. 16.00 (*0-87262-186-3*) Am Soc Civil Eng.

***Site Characterization Sampling & Analysis.** (Environmental Engineering Ser.). (C). 1998. pap. 49.95 (*0-442-02604-8*) Van Nos Reinhold.

Site Cleanup under Superfund, DOD & DOE Markets: High Growth Potential. Market Intelligence Staff. 268p. 1993. 1,495.00 (*1-56753-458-9*) Frost & Sullivan.

Site Design & Construction Detailing. 3rd ed. Theodore D. Walker. (Illus.). 512p. 1992. text ed. 62.95 (*0-442-23778-2*) Van Nos Reinhold.

***Site Design Tips & Techniques.** Robert A. Stephen & James Jacobs. (Illus.). 56p. 1995. pap. 10.00 (*0-933885-08-3*) Arcade Pubs.

Site Details from Architectural Graphic Standards. 8th ed. Charles G. Ramsey & Harold R. Sleeper. LC 91-43622. (Ramsey-Sleeper Architectural Graphic Standards Ser.: No. 1955). 336p. 1992. text ed. 125.00 (*0-471-57060-5*) Wiley.

***Site Development, Landscaping & Amenities Provision: Snip III-10-75.** Russia's Minstroy Staff. (Snip Building Codes of Russia Ser.). (Illus.). iv, 48p. (Orig.). 1996. ring bd. 199.95 (*1-57937-019-5*) Snip Register.

Site-Directed Mutagenesis & Protein Engineering: Proceedings of the International Symposium, Tromso, 27-30 Aug., 1990. Ed. by M. R. El-Gewely. 216p. 1991. 134.50 (*0-444-81431-0*) Elsevier.

Site Engineering for Landscape Architects. 2nd ed. Steven Strom & Kurt Nathan. (Illus.). 256p. 1993. text ed. 64.95 (*0-442-00224-6*) Van Nos Reinhold.

Site Engineering For Landscape Architecture. Storm. (Landscape Architecture Ser.: 3). 1996. text ed. 64.95 (*0-442-02270-0*) Van Nos Reinhold.

***Site Engineering Practice.** Rougier. 1984. pap. text ed. write for info. (*0-582-41236-6*, Pub. by Longman UK) Longman.

Site Evaluation Workbook. John W. Schafer & Harry James. 1994. spiral bd. 16.00 (*0-88252-170-5*) Paladin Hse.

Site Grading Workbook. Robert Stephen & James Jacobs. (Illus.). 48p. 1996. wbk. ed., spiral bd. 28.00 (*0-933885-21-0*) Arcade Pubs.

Site Guides: La Ruta Maya: A Guide to the Best Birding Locations in the Yucatan, Belize, Guatemala, Honduras & El Salvador. Rogers. (Illus.). 60p. 1994. pap. 8.95 (*0-9637765-3-3*) Cinclus Pubns.

***Site Guides: Costa Rica & Panama: A Guide to the Best Birding Locations.** Dennis Rogers. (Illus.). 183p. (Orig.). 1996. pap. 19.95 (*0-9637765-6-8*) Cinclus Pubns.

Site Guides Venezuela: A Guide to the Best Birding Locations. Dennis Rogers. 54p. 1993. spiral bd. 14.50 (*0-9637765-0-9*) Cinclus Pubns.

Site Handling Equipment: Construction Guide. J. R. Illingworth. 69p. 1982. 10.00 (*0-7277-0141-X*, Pub. by T Telford UK) Am Soc Civil Eng.

Site Histories Documenting Hazards for Environmental Site Assessments Contents: The Historical Imperative of Site Assessments. Pollution Engineering Staff. 156p. 1993. 29.95 (*0-934165-45-9*) Gulf Pub.

Site Impact Traffic Assessment: Problems & Solutions, Proceedings of the Conference Sponsored by the Urban Transportation Division of the American Society of Civil Engineers in Cooperation with Institute of Transportation Engineers, Urban Land Institute, National Association of Regional Councils. Ed. by Robert E. Paaswell et al. LC 92-13902. 256p. 1992. pap. text ed. 29.00 (*0-87262-870-1*) Am Soc Civil Eng.

Site Index Curves for Gmelina Arborea. A. Greaves. 1978. 35.00 (*0-85074-043-6*) St Mut.

Site Investigation. Noel E. Simons et al. LC 94-44383. 1995. 99.95 (*0-632-02908-0*) Blackwell Sci.

Site Investigation & the Law. Jack Cottington & Robert Akenhead. 184p. 1984. 34.00 (*0-7277-0188-6*, Pub. by T Telford UK) Am Soc Civil Eng.

Site Investigations & Foundations Explained. M. Carter & M. V. Symons. 342p. 1989. pap. text ed. 33.50 (*0-7273-1907-8*, PP03) Am Soc Civil Eng.

Site Kit: Field Guide & Software for Commercial Real Estate Evaluation. 1995. pap. 89.00 (*0-940352-11-7*) Mesa Hse.

***Site Management: Handbook & Workbook.** D. Miles et al. (Improve Your Construction Business Ser.: Vol. 2). 112p. 1996. pap. 24.75 (*92-2-109315-8*) Intl Labour Office.

***Site Management of Building Services Contractors.** Wild. (Illus.). 312p. 1996. text ed. 64.50 (*0-419-20450-4*, E & FN Spon) Routledge Chapman & Hall.

Site of Our Lives: The Self & the Subject from Emerson to Foucault. James S. Hans. LC 94-20966. (SUNY Series, The Margins of Literature). 385p. (C). 1995. text ed. 59.50 (*0-7914-2431-6*); pap. text ed. 19.95 (*0-7914-2432-4*) State U NY Pr.

Site on McDonalds: The American Landscape. Thomas W. Sokolowski. LC 84-73328. (Illus.). 12p. 1984. pap. 1.00 (*0-940744-49-X*) Chrysler Museum.

Site Plan for Architectural Working Drawings. George T. Clayton. (Illus.). 42p. (C). 1973. pap. text ed. 5.80 (*0-87563-252-1*) Stipes.

Site Plan Reviewer. Jack Rudman. (Career Examination Ser.: C-3251). 1994. pap. 34.95 (*0-8373-3251-6*) Nat Learn.

Site Planning. R. G. Brooks. (Illus.). 512p. 1987. text ed. 64.60 (*0-13-811258-4*) P-H.

Site Planning. 3rd ed. Kevin Lynch & Gary Hack. (Illus.). 450p. (C). 1984. 52.50 (*0-262-12106-9*) MIT Pr.

Site Planning & Community Design for Great Neighborhoods. Frederick D. Jarvis. Ed. by Diana Rich et al. (Illus.). 133p. (Orig.). 1993. pap. 24.50 (*0-86718-384-5*) Home Builder.

Site Planning & Design for the Elderly. Diane V. Carstens. 1993. pap. 32.95 (*0-442-01351-5*) Van Nos Reinhold.

Site Planning for Affordable Housing: Four Case Studies in Falmouth, Massachusetts. Bunker Stimson Solien & Jacob, Inc. Staff. (Illus.). (Orig.). (C). 1988. pap. text ed. write for info. (*0-929072-00-6*) Bunker Stimson.

***Site Planning for Solar Access: A Guidebook for Residential Developers & Site Planners.** Duncan Erley & Martin Jaffe. (Illus.). 149p. (C). 1997. reprint ed. pap. text ed. 40.00 (*0-7881-4154-6*) DIANE Pub.

***Site Planning Vignette Preview & Mock Exam.** Robert A. Stephen & James Jacobs. (Illus.). 48p. (Orig.). 1997. pap. 40.00 (*0-933885-26-1*) Arcade Pubs.

Site Profites: Western Hemisphere Shorebird Reserve Network. 75p. 1993. pap. text ed. 10.00 (*1-883861-02-0*) Wetlnds Amer.

Site Reconnaissance & Engineering. H. C. Landphair. 1985. text ed. 74.00 (*0-13-500737-2*) P-H.

Site Reconnaissance & Engineering: An Introduction for Architects, Landscape Architects & Planners. H. C. Landphair & J. L. Motloch. xxi, 300p. 1985. 45.00 (*0-444-00900-0*) P-H.

Site Reconnaissance in the Yemen Arab Republic, 1984: The Stratigraphic Probe at Hajar Ar-Rayhani. William D. Glanzman & Abdu O. Ghaleb. (Wadi al-Jubah Archaeological Project Ser.: Vol. 3). 1989. text ed. 40.00 (*0-685-46080-0*, Am Foun Study) Eisenbrauns.

Site Remediation. Richard K. Miller & Marcia E. Rupnow. (Survey on Technology & Markets Ser.: No. 227). 50p. 1994. pap. text ed. 200.00 (*1-55865-258-2*) Future Tech Surveys.

***Site Remediation.** Richard K. Miller & Christy H. Gunter. (Market Research Survey Ser.: No. 286). 50p. 1996. 200.00 (*1-55865-311-2*) Future Tech Surveys.

Site Safety. J. Carl Laney. LC 81-19540. (Site Practice Ser.). (Illus.). 226p. reprint ed. pap. 64.50 (*0-8357-3536-2*, 2034484) Bks Demand.

Site Seeing the Internet Plain & Simple: For Teachers, Parents & Kids. Gary M. Garfield & Suzanne McDonough. 160p. (YA). (gr. k-8). 1996. spiral bd. 16.00 (*1-895411-81-5*) Peguis Pubs Ltd.

Site Selection. John Thompson. 1986. pap. 29.95 (*0-86730-524-X*) Lebhar Friedman.

Site Selection: Finding & Developing Your Best Location. Kay Whitehouse. (Illus.). 208p. 1989. 21.95 (*0-8306-3053-8*, Liberty Hse) TAB Bks.

Site Selection & Investigation. Dan Lampert & Douglas R. Woodley. 170p. 1991. text ed. 64.95 (*0-566-09090-2*, Pub. by Gower UK) Ashgate Pub Co.

Site Selection Factors for Repositories of Solid High-Level & Alpha Bearing Wastes in Geological Formations. (Illus.). 64p. 1977. pap. 25.00 (*92-0-125177-7*, IDC177, Pub. by IAEA AU) Bernan Associates.

Site Selection for New Hazardous Waste Management Facilities. W. M. Sloan. (WHO Regional Publications, European Ser.: No. 46). xiv, 118p. 1993. pap. text ed. 21.00 (*92-890-1309-5*, 1310046) World Health.

Site Specific Assessment of Mobile Jack-up Units. 1994. 70.00 (*0-614-06717-0*) Soc Naval Arch.

Site-Specific Management for Agricultural Systems: Proceedings. Ed. by P. C. Robert et al. 993p. 1995. pap. 39.00 (*0-89118-127-X*) Am Soc Agron.

Site Specific Risk Assessment. Jones. 1997. write for info. (*0-87371-334-6*, L334) Lewis Pubs.

***Site-Specific Strong Ground Motion Estimates for the Salt Lake Valley.** Ivan G. Wong & W. J. Silva. (Miscellaneous Publication of the Utah Geological Survey Ser.: Vol. 93-9). (Illus.). 34p. (Orig.). 1993. pap. 5.50 (*1-55791-327-7*, MP93-9) Utah Geological Survey.

Site Surveying. 2nd ed. John Muskett. LC 95-1472. 1995. 39.95 (*0-632-03848-9*) Blackwell Sci.

***Site Surveying Level 3.** Neal. 1985. pap. text ed. write for info. (*0-582-41291-9*, Pub. by Longman UK) Longman.

Site Surveying & Levelling: Level 2. H. Rawlinson. LC 81-8122. (Longman Technician Series, Construction & Civil Engineering). (Illus.). 173p. reprint ed. pap. 49.40 (*0-685-20303-4*, 2030342) Bks Demand.

Site Symmetry in Crystals: Theory & Applications. R. A. Evarestov & V. P. Smirnov. LC 92-33793. (Solid-State Sciences Ser.: Vol. 108). 1993. 149.95 (*0-387-56052-1*) Spr-Verlag.

***Site Symmetry in Crystals: Theory & Applications, Vol. 108.** 2nd ed. R. A. Evarestov & V. P. Smirnov. LC 96-36380. (Springer Series in Solid-State Sciences). 1997. pap. 119.00 (*3-540-61466-4*) Spr-Verlag.

Site Unseen: The Politics of Siting a Nuclear Waste Repository. Gerald Jacob. LC 89-40582. (Series in Policy & Institutional Studies). 255p. 1990. 49.95 (*0-8229-3640-2*) U of Pittsburgh Pr.

Site Unseen: The Politics of Siting a Nuclear Waste Repository. Gerald Jacob. (Policy & Institutional Studies). 255p. 1990. pap. 19.95 (*0-8229-5461-3*) U of Pittsburgh Pr.

Site World. H. McKinley Conway. (Illus.). 608p. 1991. 95.00 (*0-910436-30-4*) Conway Data.

SiteNet World Guide. H. McKinley Conway et al. (Illus.). 530p. 1989. 95.00 (*0-910436-28-2*) Conway Data.

Sites, No. 25. Dennis L. Dollens. 1993. pap. 15.00 (*0-930829-33-6*) Lumen Inc.

Sites: A Third Memoir. Wallace Fowlie. LC 86-19760. v, 179p. 1986. text ed. 25.95 (*0-8223-0700-6*) Duke.

Sites & Insights: The Special Event Location & Resource Directory for Southern California. Deni Presley. Ed. by Kathryn E. Berry. (Illus.). 208p. (Orig.). 1994. pap. text ed. 24.95 (*0-9640791-0-0*) Site Network.

***Sites & Monuments.** Carsten Larsen. (Illus.). 250p. 1992. 49.50 (*87-89364-02-3*) David Brown.

***Sites & Sights of the Iron Age.** Ed. by Barry Raftery et al. (Monographs in Archaeology: Vol. 56). (Illus.). 180p. 1996. pap. 48.00 (*1-900188-00-7*, Pub. by Oxbow Bks UK) David Brown.

Sites & Solutions: Recent Public Art. Judith E. Tannenbaum. LC 85-80210. (Illus.). 36p. (Orig.). 1985. pap. text ed. 8.00 (*0-941972-02-X*) Freedman.

Sites & Sounds of Savannah Jazz. Julius Horstein. LC 93-42791. 1994. 45.00 (*0-913720-91-7*) Beil.

Sites, No. 24. Ed. by Dennis Dollens. 120p. (Orig.). 1992. pap. 15.00 (*0-930829-22-0*) Lumen Inc.

Sites of Action for Neurotoxic Pesticides. Ed. by Robert M. Hollingworth & Maurice B. Green. LC 87-27047. (Symposium Ser.: No. 356). (Illus.). ix, 334p. 1987. 76.95 (*0-8412-1436-0*) Am Chemical.

***Sites of Action for Neurotoxic Pesticides.** Ed. by Robert M. Hollingworth & Maurice B. Green. LC 87-27047. (ACS Symposium Ser.: Vol. 356). 344p. 1987. reprint ed. pap. 98.10 (*0-608-03879-2*, 2064326) Bks Demand.

Sites of Concealment. (Illus.). 144p. 1993. 55.00 (*3-8030-2807-8*, Pub. by Verlag E Wasmuth) Dist Art Pubs.

***Sites of Desire, Economies of Pleasure: Sexualities in Asia & the Pacific.** Lenore Manderson & Margaret Jolly. LC 96-40938. (Chicago Series on Sexuality, History, & Society). 1996. pap. text ed. 19.95 (*0-226-50304-6*) U Ch Pr.

***Sites of Desire, Economies of Pleasure: Sexualities in Asia & the Pacific.** Lenore Manderson & Margaret Jolly. LC 96-40938. (Chicago Series on Sexuality, History, & Society). 1997. lib. bdg. 54.00 (*0-226-50303-8*) U Ch Pr.

Sites of Drug Action in the Human Brain. Ed. by Anat Biegon & Nora D. Volkow. LC 94-25232. 208p. 1995. 157.95 (*0-8493-7653-X*, 7653) CRC Pr.

Sites of Memory, Sites of Mourning: The Great War in European Cultural History. Jay Winter. (Studies in the Social & Cultural History of Modern Warfare: No. 1). (Illus.). 304p. (C). 1995. text ed. 34.95 (*0-521-49682-9*) Cambridge U Pr.

Sites of Memory, Sites of Mourning: The Great War in European Cultural History. Jay Winter. (Studies in the Social & Cultural History of Modern Warfare Ser.: No. 1). (Illus.). 320p. 1996. pap. text ed. 18.95 (*0-521-57453-6*) Cambridge U Pr.

Sites of Oahu. Compiled by Elspeth P. Sterling & Catherine C. Summers. LC 78-73981. (Special Publication-Anthropology Ser.). 372p. 1993. reprint ed. pap. 29.95 (*0-910240-73-6*) Bishop Mus.

Sites of Recollection: Four Altars & a Rap Opera. Julia B. Mandle & Deborah M. Rothschild. LC 92-50560. (Illus.). 112p. (Orig.). 1993. pap. 22.95 (*0-913697-15-X*) U of Pa Pr.

***Sites of Vision: The Discursive Construction of Sight in the History of Philosophy.** Ed. by David M. Levin. 520p. 1997. 50.00 (*0-262-12203-0*) MIT Pr.

Sites Perception & the Nonvisual Experience: Designing & Manufacturing Mobility Maps. Anne M. Kidwell & Peter S. Greer. 210p. reprint ed. pap. 59.90 (*0-7837-0139-X*, 2040428) Bks Demand.

Sites Twenty-Six. Dennis L. Dollens. 1995. pap. text ed. 20.00 (*0-930829-37-9*) Lumen Inc.

Sites 11: Essays on Jujol & Gaudi. Ed. by Dennis Dollens & Ronald Christ. 58p. 1983. pap. 5.00 (*0-930829-25-5*) Lumen Inc.

Sites 23. Koji Taki et al. (Illus.). 127p. 1990. pap. 10.00 (*0-930829-23-9*) Lumen Inc.

Sitescapes. Gregory M. Pierceall. 272p. 1990. text ed. 65.20 (*0-13-812066-8*) P-H.

SiteSpec Handbook Version Two: The Designers Manual of Site Specifications & Details. 400p. 1992. text ed. 300.00 (*0-685-59662-1*, JBA1) Am Soc Civil Eng.

Siting Culture: The Anthropological Object on the Move. Ed. by Karen F. Olwig & Kirsten Hastrup. 328p. (C). 1996. pap. write for info. (*0-415-15002-7*); text ed. write for info. (*0-415-15001-9*) Routledge.

Siting Handbook for Small Wind Energy Conversion Systems. rev. ed. James V. Ramsdell et al. Ed. by Harry L. Wegley. (Illus.). 100p. 1997. pap. 29.95 (*0-88016-003-9*) WindBks.

Siting Hazardous Waste Facilities: Guiding Principles. W. Victoria Becker. Ed. by Gerry Feinstein. 40p. (Orig.). 1993. pap. text ed. 15.00 (*1-55877-209-X*) Natl Governor.

Siting Hazardous Waste Management Facilities. J. Bloom. 71p. 1983. 3.00 (*0-318-20482-7*) Natl Resources Defense Coun.

Siting Hazardous Waste Treatment Facilities: The Nimby Syndrome. Kent E. Portney. LC 90-1217. 192p. 1991. text ed. 45.00 (*0-86569-016-2*, T016, Auburn Hse) Greenwood.

Siting in Earthquake Zones. J. G. Wang & K. T. Law. (Illus.). 176p. (C). 1994. text ed. 75.00 (*90-5410-092-3*, Pub. by A A Balkema NE) Ashgate Pub Co.

Siting Low-Level Radioactive Waste Disposal Facilities: The Public Policy Dilemma. Mary R. English. LC 91-42774. 304p. 1992. text ed. 59.95 (*0-89930-560-1*, EPV/, Quorum Bks) Greenwood.

Siting New Treatment & Disposal Facilities. Mary Houghton. Ed. by Karen Glass. (Hazardous Waste Management in the States Ser.). 50p. (Orig.). 1989. pap. text ed. 15.00 (*1-55877-071-2*) Natl Governor.

Siting of Hazardous Waste Disposal Facilities in Texas. Susan G. Hadden. LC 82-85620. (Policy Research Project Report: No. 53). 128p. 1982. pap. 7.50 (*0-89940-655-6*) LBJ Sch Pub Aff.

Siting of Locally Unwanted Land Uses: Towards a Cooperative Approach. Ed. by Audrey M. Armour. (Progress in Planning Ser.: No. 35). (Illus.). 80p. 1991. pap. 57.00 (*0-08-040788-9*, Pergamon Pr) Elsevier.

Siting of Low Level Flue Terminals. G. R. King. 1993. 300.00 (*0-86022-347-7*, Pub. by Build Servs Info Assn UK) St Mut.

Siting Translation: History, Post-Structuralism, & the Colonial Context. Tejaswini Niranjana. LC 91-21487. 216p. 1992. 40.00 (*0-520-07450-5*) U CA Pr.

Siting Translation: History, Post-Structuralism, & the Colonial Context. Tejaswini Niranjana. LC 91-21487. 216p. 1992. pap. 14.95 (*0-520-07451-3*) U CA Pr.

Sitings: Aycock, Fleischner, Miss, Trakas. Hugh M. Davies & Ronald J. Onorato. Ed. by Sally Yard. LC 86-80303. (Illus.). 150p. (Orig.). 1986. per. 19.50 (*0-934418-25-X*) Mus Contemp Art.

Sitio de Mascaras. Milton M. Martinez. LC 87-72348. (Coleccion Caniqui). (Illus.). 208p. (Orig.). (SPA.). 1987. pap. 9.95 (*0-89729-460-2*) Ediciones.

Sitio de Nadie. 3rd ed. Hilda Perera. 329p. (Orig.). (SPA.). 1973. 15.00 (*84-320-5271-X*) Ediciones.

Sitio en el Corazon. Arnaldo Salas. LC 89-81550. (Coleccion Caniqui). 64p. (Orig.). (SPA.). 1990. pap. 7.95 (*0-89729-557-9*) Ediciones.

Sitka. Louis L'Amour. 245p. 1984. mass mkt. 4.99 (*0-553-27881-9*) Bantam.

Sitka: A Short History. 2nd rev. ed. Jack Calvin. (Illus.). 48p. 1983. pap. 10.00 (*0-9615529-0-5*) Old Harbor Pr.

Sitka Man. Al Brookman, Sr. LC 84-6430. 180p. (Orig.). 1984. pap. 7.95 (*0-88240-263-3*) Alaska Northwest.

Sitka Spring. Gary Lawless. (Illus.). 32p. (Orig.). 1991. pap. 5.00 (*0-942396-63-4*) Blackberry ME.

Sitka (Travel Guide) Penny Rennick & L. J. Campbell. LC 95-40004. (Alaska Geographic Guides Ser.). (Illus.). 144p. 1995. pap. 15.95 (*1-56661-029-X*) Alaska Geog Soc.

Sitkum Siwash. Helen K. Smith. LC 74-33825. (Western Americana Bks.). (Illus.). 104p. (Orig.). 1976. pap. 15.00 (*0-931636-29-5*) S S S Pub Co.

Sitosterol. David Kritchevsky & O. J. Pollak. (Monographs on Atherosclerosis: Vol. 10). (Illus.). vii, 220p. 1981. pap. 118.50 (*3-8055-0568-X*) S Karger.

Sitsiy Yugh Noholnik Ts'in: As My Grandfather Told It. Catherine Attla. (Illus.). 258p. (Orig.). 1983. pap. 18.00 (*0-933769-07-5*) Alaska Native.

Sitt Marie-Rose. 3rd ed. Etel Adnan. Tr. by Georgina Kleege from FRE. (Novel Ser.). 105p. (Orig.). 1990. pap. 9.95 (*0-942996-18-6*) Post Apollo Pr.

***Sitt Marie-Rose.** 4th ed. Etel Adnan. Tr. by Georgina Kleege from FRE. (Novel Ser.). 105p. (Orig.). 1997. pap. 11.00 (*0-942996-27-5*) Post Apollo Pr.

Sittaford Mystery. Agatha Christie. 240p. 1987. pap. 4.99 (*0-425-01040-6*) Berkley Pub.

Sitti & the Cats: A Tale of Friendship. Sally Bahous. LC 98-80262. 32p. (J). (gr. 3-6). 1993. 13.95 (*1-879373-61-0*) R Rinehart.

***Sitti & the Cats: A Tale of Friendship.** Sally Bahous. (Illus.). 32p. (J). (gr. 1-5). 1997. pap. 7.95 (*1-57098-171-X*) R Rinehart.

Sittin' & a Thinkin' Glenn M. Chaffin, Jr. & Ernst Peterson. 1952. pap. 1.50 (*0-87517-036-6*) Dietz.

Sitting at His Feet. Martha Borth. (Illus.). 85p. (Orig.). 1985. pap. 5.95 (*0-935993-00-2*) Clar Call Bks.

An Asterisk (*) at the beginning of an entry indicates that the title is appearing in BIP for the first time.

Sitting at the Feet of Jesus. Stephen D. Eyre & Jacalyn Eyre. (Spiritual Encounter Guides Ser.). 96p. (Orig.). 1993. wbk. ed., pap. 4.99 (*0-8308-1178-8*, 1178) InterVarsity.

Sitting at the Feet of the Past: Retelling the North American Folktale for Children. Ed. by Gary D. Schmidt & Donald R. Hettinga. LC 92-9317. 256p. 1992. text ed. 55.00 (*0-313-27635-8*, SVK, Greenwood Pr) Greenwood.

*__Sitting Bull.__ (North American Indians Ser.). (Illus.). (YA). (gr. 6 up). 21.95 (*0-614-21962-0*) Smithmark.

Sitting Bull. Sheila Black. Ed. by Nancy Furstinger. (Alvin Josephy's Biography of the American Indians Ser.). (Illus.). 144p. (J). (gr. 5-7). 1989. pap. 7.95 (*0-382-09761-0*, Silver Pr NJ); lib. bdg. 12.95 (*0-382-09572-3*, Silver Pr NJ) Silver Burdett Pr.

Sitting Bull. Steven Bodow. LC 92-16518. (American Troublemakers Ser.). (Illus.). 128p. (J). (gr. 7-10). 1992. lib. bdg. 27.11 (*0-8114-2328-X*) Raintree Steck-V.

Sitting Bull. George Custer. (Buckaroos Ser.). (Illus.). 32p. (Orig.). (J). (gr. 2 up). 1996. pap. 1.50 (*1-55709-365-2*) Applewood.

Sitting Bull. Houghton Mifflin Company Staff. (J). (gr. 5). 1992. pap. 9.16 (*0-395-61807-X*) HM.

Sitting Bull. McDade. (War Chiefs Ser.). 320p. 1994. mass mkt. 4.99 (*0-06-100660-2*, Harp PBks) HarpC.

Sitting Bull. Lucille R. Penner. LC 94-46766. (All Aboard Reading Ser.: Level 2). (Illus.). 48p. (J). (gr. 1-3). 1995. 13.99 (*0-448-40938-0*, G&D); pap. 3.95 (*0-448-40937-2*, G&D) Putnam Pub Group.

*__Sitting Bull.__ Darlene Resling & Albert Lindel. (Our Changing Lives Ser.). (Illus.). 64p. (YA). (gr. 4-12). 1997. pap. text ed. 7.95 (*1-55596-173-8*, LW2050) Learning Well.

Sitting Bull. Kathie B. Smith. (Great Americans Ser.). (Illus.). 32p. (J). (gr. k-5). 1987. pap. 2.25 (*0-671-64027-5*, Litl Simon S&S) S&S Childrens.

Sitting Bull. Herman J. Viola. (American Indian Stories Ser.). (Illus.). 32p. (J). (gr. 3-6). 1990. lib. bdg. 21.40 (*0-8172-3401-2*) Raintree Steck-V.

Sitting Bull. Herman J. Viola. (Raintree-Rivilo American Indian Stories Ser.). (Illus.). 32p. (J). (gr. 3-6). 1990. pap. 4.95 (*0-8114-4088-5*) Raintree Steck-V.

Sitting Bull: A Story of Bravery. Peter Murray. LC 95-42267. (J). 1998. lib. bdg. write for info. (*1-56766-230-7*) Childs World.

Sitting Bull: And the Paradox of American Biography. Gary C. Anderson. (Library of American Biography). 192p. 1996. pap. 15.95 (*1-886746-55-9*) Talman Pub.

*__Sitting Bull: Courageous Sioux Chief.__ Diane Shaughnessy. LC 97-220. (Famous Native Americans Ser.). (J). 1997. write for info. (*0-8239-5109-X*) Rosen Group.

Sitting Bull: Dakota Boy. Augusta Stevenson. LC 95-37306. (Childhood of Famous Americans Ser.). (Illus.). 192p. (J). (gr. 2-6). 1996. pap. 4.99 (*0-689-80628-0*, Aladdin Paperbacks) S&S Childrens.

*__Sitting Bull: Sioux Leader.__ Elizabeth Schleichert. LC 96-25592. (Native American Biographies Ser.). (Illus.). 112p. (YA). (gr. 6 up). 1997. lib. bdg. 18.95 (*0-89490-868-5*) Enslow Pubs.

Sitting Bull: Sioux Warrior. William R. Sanford. LC 93-42255. (Native American Leaders of the Wild West Ser.). (Illus.). 48p. (J). (gr. 4-10). 1994. lib. bdg. 14.95 (*0-89490-514-7*) Enslow Pubs.

Sitting Bull & the Paradox of Lakota Nationhood. Anderson. (Library of American Biography Ser.). 208p. (C). 1996. text ed. 16.95 (*0-06-501033-7*) Addison-Wesley Educ.

Sitting Bull, Champion of the Sioux: A Biography. Stanley Vestal. LC 57-5961. (Civilization of the American Indian Ser.: Vol. 46). (Illus.). 392p. 1989. pap. 16.95 (*0-8061-2219-6*) U of Okla Pr.

Sitting Bull: Chief of the Sioux see North American Indians of Achievement

Sitting Bull: Chief of the Sioux see North Americans Indians of Achievement

Sitting Bull, Warrior of the Sioux. Jane Fleischer. LC 78-18047. (Illus.). 48p. (J). (gr. 4-6). 1979. pap. 3.50 (*0-89375-144-8*); lib. bdg. 11.89 (*0-89375-154-5*) Troll Communs.

*__Sitting Bull's Story: There Are No Indians Left but Me!__ Don Diessner. (Native American Leaders Ser.: Vol. 1). (Illus.). 183p. 1993. 35.00 (*0-912783-13-3*) Upton & Sons.

Sitting Down Hug. Marion D. Cohen. LC 88-26851. (Contemporary American Poets Ser.: Vol. 2). 150p. (Orig.). 1988. pap. 9.00 (*0-934659-14-1*) Liberal Pr.

Sitting down to Eat. Bill Harley. LC 95-53738. (Illus.). 32p. (J). 1996. 15.95 (*0-87483-460-0*) August Hse.

Sitting Duck. large type ed. Margaret A. Carr. (Linford Mystery Library). 240p. 1988. pap. 15.99 (*0-7089-6617-9*, Linford) Ulverscroft.

Sitting In: Selected Writings on Jazz, Blues, & Related Topics. Hayden Carruth. LC 93-1813. 239p. 1993. pap. 13.95 (*0-87745-423-X*) U of Iowa Pr.

Sitting in Circles. Dennis Maloney. Tr. by Yusuke Keida. 112p. (ENG & JPN.). 1987. pap. 8.00 (*0-934834-87-3*) White Pine.

Sitting in Judgment: The Sentencing of White-Collar Criminals. Stanton Wheeler et al. LC 88-3196. (C). 1988. 35.00 (*0-300-03983-2*) Yale U Pr.

Sitting in Judgment: The Sentencing of White-Collar Criminals. Stanton Wheeler et al. 211p. (C). 1992. reprint ed. pap. text ed. 16.00 (*0-300-05475-0*) Yale U Pr.

Sitting in My Box. Dee Lillegard. LC 89-31609. (Illus.). 32p. (J). (ps-2). 1989. pap. 12.95 (*0-525-44528-5*) Dutton Child Bks.

Sitting in My Box. Dee Lillegard. (Illus.). 32p. (J). (ps-2). 1992. pap. 4.99 (*0-14-054819-X*, Puff Unicorn) Puffin Bks.

Sitting in My Box. Dee Lillegard. (Giant Bk. Ser.). (Illus.). 32p. (J). (ps-2). 1993. pap. 17.99 (*0-14-054886-6*, Puff Unicorn) Puffin Bks.

Sitting in Our Treehouse Waiting for the Apocalypse. Leonard Terr. LC 75-319625. 63p. 1975. 3.50 (*0-87886-064-9*, Greenfld Rev Pr) Greenfld Rev Lit.

Sitting in the Club Car Drinking Rum & Karma Kola. Paulette Jiles. 112p. (Orig.). 1986. pap. 10.95 (*0-919591-13-2*, Pub. by Polestar Bk Pubs CN) Orca Bk Pubs.

Sitting in the Earth & Laughing: A Handbook of Humor. A. Roy Eckardt. 192p. (C). 1991. text ed. 34.95 (*1-56000-001-5*) Transaction Pubs.

Sitting in the Fire: Large Group Transformation Using Conflict & Diversity. Arnold Mindell. LC 95-78176. 268p. (Orig.). 1995. pap. 15.95 (*1-887078-00-2*) Lao Tse Pr.

Sitting in the Hot Seat: Leadership for Critical Incidents. Rhona Flin. LC 96-12076. 1996. text ed. 35.95 (*0-471-95796-8*) Wiley.

Sitting on a Wall: Selected Writings of Mon Roes. Mon Roes. 194p. 1993. 18.00 (*0-685-67895-4*) M M Fain.

Sitting on Moving Steel. deluxe limited ed. Michael Ventura. 32p. 1992. 10.00 (*0-930324-29-3*) Wings Pr.

Sitting on the Dynamite: The Revolutionary Teachings of Jesus. David Kirk. LC 93-60739. 191p. 1994. pap. 4.95 (*1-55523-632-4*) Winston-Derek.

*__Sitting on the Farm.__ Bob King & Bill Slavin. (FRE.). (J). pap. 7.99 (*0-590-73949-2*) Scholastic Inc.

*__Sitting on the Farm.__ Bob King & Bill Slavin. (FRE.). (J). pap. 13.99 incl. audio (*0-590-73991-3*) Scholastic Inc.

Sitting on the Farm. 95th ed. HB Staff. (J). (gr. 1). 1995. text ed., lib. bdg., pap. text ed. 9.00 (*0-15-303634-6*) HB Coll Pubs.

Sitting on the Farm Mac Lab Pack. Sanctuary Woods Staff. (Sanctuary Woods CD ROM Ser.). 1993. teacher ed. 200.00 incl. cd-rom (*0-201-87811-9*) Addison-Wesley.

Sitting on the Job: A Practical Survival Guide for People Who Earn Their Living While Sitting. Scott W. Donkin. Ed. by Joseph J. Sweere. LC 86-90503. (Illus.). 137p. 1987. pap. 8.95 (*0-9617281-0-8*) Parallel Integ.

Sitting on the Job: How to Survive the Stresses of Sitting Down to Work - a Practical Handbook. Scot W. Donkin. (Illus.). 1989. pap. 13.00 (*0-395-50089-3*) HM.

Sitting on Top of Your World: Confidence & Courage for the Crises of Life. George H. Harris. Ed. by Valerie M. Bailey. (Illus.). 112p. (Orig.). 1992. pap. 6.95 (*0-945641-05-2*) Castle Hills.

*__Sitting Posture, Comfort & Pressure.__ H. A. Staarink. (Series Physical Ergonomics: Vol. 5). (Illus.). 258p. (Orig.). 1995. pap. 47.50 (*90-407-1196-8*, Pub. by Delft U Pr NE) Coronet Bks.

Sitting Pretty. Al Young. LC 75-21461. 272p. 1986. reprint ed. pap. 8.95 (*0-88739-017-X*) Creat Arts Bk.

Sitting Still: An Encounter with Christian Zen. Patricia H. Clifford. 96p. 1995. pap. 5.95 (*0-8091-3617-1*) Paulist Pr.

Sitting Still see Sendero Luminoso: Evolucion de una Secta Estalinista

Sittings with Eusapai Palladino & Other Studies. Everard Feilding. (Illus.). 1963. 10.00 (*0-8216-0153-9*, Univ Bks) Carol Pub Group.

Sitti's Secrets. Naomi S. Nye. LC 93-19742. (Illus.). 32p. (J). (gr. 2-6). 1994. lib. bdg. 15.00 (*0-02-768460-1*, Four Winds Pr) S&S Childrens.

*__Sittis Secrets.__ Naomi S. Nye. (J). 1997. pap. text ed. 5.99 (*0-689-81706-1*, Aladdin Paperbacks) S&S Childrens.

Situacion del Escritor en la Obre de Manuel Galvez (1916-1935) Ricardo Szmetan. LC 91-872. (American Univ. Studies II, Romance Lang. & Lits.: Vol. 189). 257p. (C). 1994. text ed. 43.95 (*0-8204-1746-7*) P Lang Pubng.

Situacion Humana: Spanish Translation. Harvey Jackins. Tr. by Francisco Lopez-Bustos. 1984. pap. 7.00 (*0-911214-29-1*) Rational Isl.

Situacion Mundial Y La Direccion Del Mover Del Senor. Witness Lee. 65p. (SPA.). 2.25 (*0-87083-593-9*, 04017002) Living Stream Ministry.

*__Situaciones.__ 2nd annot. ed. Jean-Paul Valette et al. (SPA.). (C). 1994. teacher ed., text ed. 37.44 (*0-669-32281-4*) HM College Div.

Situaciones. 2nd ed. Jean-Paul Valette et al. 465p. (SPA.). 1994. pap. text ed. 37.08 (*0-669-32280-6*) McDougal-Littell.

*__Situaciones.__ 2nd ed. Jean-Paul Valette et al. (SPA.). (C). 1994. wbk. ed., text ed. 14.28 (*0-669-32282-2*) HM College Div.

*__Situaciones.__ 2nd ed. Jean-Paul Valette et al. (SPA.). (C). 1994. lab manual ed., text ed. 12.84 (*0-669-32283-0*) HM College Div.

Situado & Sabana: Spain's Support System for the Presido & Mission Provinces of Florida. Amy T. Bushnell. 1995. pap. text ed. 26.95 (*0-8203-1712-8*) U of Ga Pr.

Situated Actions & Vocabularies of Motive. C. Wright Mills. (Reprint Series in Sociology). (C). 1993. reprint ed. pap. text ed. 1.90 (*0-8290-2668-1*, S-200) Irvington.

*__Situated Cognition: On Human Knowledge & Computer Representations.__ William J. Clancey. (Learning in Doing: Social, Cognitive & Computational Perspectives Ser.). (Illus.). 375p. (C). 1997. text ed. 69.95 (*0-521-44400-4*); pap. text ed. 27.95 (*0-521-44871-9*) Cambridge U Pr.

Situated Cognition Theory: Social, Semiotic, & Neurological Perspectives. Ed. by David Kirshner & James A. Whitson. LC 96-34120. 360p. 1997. 69.95 (*0-8058-2037-X*); pap. 34.50 (*0-8058-2038-8*) L Erlbaum Assocs.

Situated Learning: Legitimate Peripheral Participation. Jean Lave & Etienne Wenger. (Learning in Doing: Social, Cognitive & Computational Perspectives Ser.). 100p. (C). 1991. text ed. 39.95 (*0-521-41308-7*); pap. text ed. 13.95 (*0-521-42374-0*) Cambridge U Pr.

Situated Learning Perspectives. Ed. by Hilary McLellan. LC 95-10925. 310p. 1996. 44.95 (*0-87778-289-X*) Educ Tech Pubns.

Situated Meaning: Inside & Outside in Japanese Self, Society, & Language. Ed. by Jane M. Bachnik & Charles J. Quinn, Jr. 368p. 1994. text ed. 55.00 (*0-691-06965-4*); pap. text ed. 17.95 (*0-691-01538-4*) Princeton U Pr.

Situated Order: Studies in the Social Organization of Talk & Embodied Activities. Ed. by Paul Ten Have & George Psathas. (Studies in Ethnomethodology & Conversation Analysis). 284p. (C). 1994. pap. text ed. 34.50 (*0-8191-9626-6*); lib. bdg. 59.50 (*0-8191-9625-8*) U Pr of Amer.

Situating College English: Lessons from an American University. Ed. by Evan Carton & Alan W. Friedman. LC 95-44323. (Series in Language & Ideology). 256p. 1996. text ed. 65.00 (*0-89789-460-X*, Bergin & Garvey) Greenwood.

Situating College English: Lessons from an American University. Ed. by Evan Carton & Alan W. Friedman. LC 95-44323. (Series in Language & Ideology). 1996. pap. write for info. (*0-89789-480-4*, Bergin & Garvey) Greenwood.

Situating College English: Lessons from an American University. Ed. by Evan Carton & Alan W. Friedman. LC 95-44323. 256p. 1996. pap. text ed. 19.95 (*0-89789-481-2*, Bergin & Garvey) Greenwood.

Situating Feminism: From Thought to Action. Sondra Farganis. LC 94-7489. (Contemporary Social Theory Ser.: Vol. 2). 192p. 1994. 42.00 (*0-8039-4649-X*); pap. 21.50 (*0-8039-4650-3*) Sage.

Situating Indian History. R. Thapar. 463p. 1986. 49.95 (*0-318-36973-7*) Asia Bk Corp.

Situating Medieval Indian State. Ed. by R. L. Hangloo. (C). 1995. 20.00 (*81-7169-322-9*, Pub. by Commonwealth II) S Asia.

*__Situating Portfolios: Four Perspectives.__ Ed. by Irwin H. Weiser & Karen B. Yancy. LC 96-45774. (Illus.). 416p. (Orig.). 1997. pap. 21.95 (*0-87421-220-0*) Utah St U Pr.

Situating Readers: Students Making Meaning of Literature. Harold A. Vine, Jr. & Mark A. Faust. 157p. 1993. 12.95 (*0-8141-4476-4*) NCTE.

Situating Selves: The Communication of Social Identities in American Scenes. Donal Carbaugh. LC 95-16183. (SUNY Series, Human Communication Processes). 238p. (C). 1996. text ed. 59.50 (*0-7914-2827-3*); pap. text ed. 19.95 (*0-7914-2828-1*) State U NY Pr.

Situating Social Theory. Tim May. LC 96-23676. 208p. 1996. 69.95 (*0-335-19287-4*, Open Univ Pr); pap. 19.95 (*0-335-19286-6*, Open Univ Pr) Taylor & Francis.

Situating the Self: Gender, Community, & Postmodernism in Contemporary Ethics. Seyla Benhabib. 280p. (C). 1992. pap. 17.95 (*0-415-90547-8*, A6805, Routledge NY) Routledge.

*__Situation Analysis Approach to Assessing Family Planning & Reproductive Health Services: A Handbook.__ Robert Miller & Population Council Staff. LC 97-5428. 1997. write for info. (*0-87834-090-4*) Population Coun.

Situation & Human Existance: Freedom, Subjectivity & Society. Sonia Kruks. (Problems in Modern European Thought Ser.). 192p. 1990. pap. text ed. 15.95 (*0-04-445457-0*) Routledge Chapman & Hall.

Situation Barnegat Light. Bradford Honigsberg. LC 94-70774. (Illus.). 235p. 1995. 26.50 (*0-9649342-0-5*); pap. 6.75 (*0-9649342-1-3*) ACT Publns.

Situation Cognition & Coherence in Personality: An Individual-Centered Approach. Barbara Krahe. (European Monographs in Social Psychology). 224p. (C). 1990. text ed. 64.95 (*0-521-35295-9*) Cambridge U Pr.

Situation de la Poesie. 2nd ed. Jacques Maritain. 144p. (FRE.). 1964. 10.95 (*0-8288-9912-6*, F16911) Fr & Eur.

Situation de la Terre. Jules Romains. 244p. (FRE.). 1958. pap. 10.95 (*0-7859-1405-6*, 2080506242) Fr & Eur.

Situation des Menschen: German Translation. Harvey Jackins. Tr. by Dietmar Kreuer from ENG. 1984. pap. 7.00 (*0-911214-75-5*) Rational Isl.

Situation et Signification. Ivan Fonagy. (Pragmatics & Beyond Ser.: III: 1). vi, 160p. (Orig.). (FRE.). 1982. pap. 47.00 (*90-272-2504-4*) Benjamins North Am.

*__Situation Ethics.__ Joseph Fletcher. 1997. pap. 15.00 (*0-664-25761-5*) Westminster John Knox.

Situation Ethics: The New Morality. Joseph Fletcher. LC 66-11917. 176p. 1966. pap. 13.00 (*0-664-24691-5*, Westminster) Westminster John Knox.

Situation in Flushing. Edmund G. Love. LC 87-17769. (Great Lakes Bks.). 272p. 1987. reprint ed. 29.95 (*0-8143-1916-5*); reprint ed. pap. 16.95 (*0-8143-1917-3*) Wayne St U Pr.

Situation in Logic. Jon Barwise. LC 88-38961. (CSLI Lecture Notes Ser.: No. 17). 337p. 1989. 44.95 (*0-937073-33-4*); pap. 17.95 (*0-937073-32-6*) CSLI.

Situation Is Hopeless, but Not Serious: The Pursuit of Unhappiness. Paul Watzlawick. 128p. 1993. pap. 10.95 (*0-393-31021-3*) Norton.

Situation Normal. Jared Carter. 8p. 1991. pap. 2.00 (*1-880649-26-8*) Writ Ctr Pr.

Situation of Poetry: Contemporary Poetry & Its Traditions. Robert Pinsky. LC 76-3015. (Essays in Literature Ser.). 200p. 1976. pap. 14.95 (*0-691-01352-7*) Princeton U Pr.

Situation of the Story: Short Fiction in Contemporary Perspective. Ed. by Diane Young. LC 92-52521. 792p. (C). 1992. pap. text ed. 24.00 (*0-312-04473-9*, Bedford Bks) St Martin.

Situation of Youth in the 1980s & Prospects & Challenges for the Year 2000. 106p. 1987. 11.00 (*92-1-130117-3*, E.86.IV.10) UN.

Situation-Reaction Drills for Offensive Basketball. Richard W. Harvey. LC 83-4084. 228p. 1983. 18.95 (*0-13-811273-8*, Parker Publishing Co) P-H.

Situation Reader, Unit A. Deakin University Press Staff. 89p. (C). 1988. 48.00 (*0-7300-0570-4*, Pub. by Deakin Univ AT) St Mut.

Situation Red, The UFO Siege. Leonard H. Stringfield. 1978. pap. 1.75 (*0-449-23654-4*, Crest) Fawcett.

Situation Story. Young. 1992. teacher ed., pap. text ed. 5.00 (*0-312-05258-8*) St Martin.

Situation Theory & Applications, Vol. 2. Ed. by Jon Barwise et al. (Center for the Study of Language & Information-Lecture Notes Ser.). xii, 625p. 1992. 64.95 (*0-937073-71-7*); pap. 27.95 (*0-937073-70-9*) CSLI.

Situation Theory & Its Applications, Vol. 1. Ed. by Robin Cooper et al. LC 90-82189. (CSLI Lecture Notes Ser.: No. 22). 515p. (Orig.). 1990. 64.95 (*0-937073-55-5*); pap. 24.95 (*0-937073-54-7*) CSLI.

Situation Theory & Its Applications, Vol. 3. Ed. by Peter Aczel et al. (CSLI Lecture Notes Ser.: No. 37). 430p. 1993. 54.95 (*1-881526-09-7*); pap. 20.95 (*1-881526-08-9*) CSLI.

Situation to Sentence: An Evolutionary Method for Descriptive Linguistics. Anoop Chandola. LC 78-7125. 1979. 32.50 (*0-404-16038-7*) AMS Pr.

Situational Awareness in Complex Systems. Ed. by R. D. Gilson et al. (Aviation Human Factors Ser.). 325p. (C). 1994. 45.00 (*1-884099-02-5*) Embry-Riddle Aeronaut.

Situational Crime Prevention. Ed. by Ronald V. Clarke. LC 91-43240. 287p. (C). 1992. text ed. 49.50 (*0-911577-22-X*); pap. text ed. 21.50 (*0-911577-21-1*) Harrow & Heston.

*__Situational Crime Prevention: Successful Case Studies.__ 2nd ed. Ronald V. Clarke. LC 97-20375. (Illus.). 280p. (C). 1997. pap. text ed. 25.50 (*0-911577-38-6*) Harrow & Heston.

*__Situational Crime Prevention: Successful Case Studies.__ 2nd rev. ed. Ronald V. Clarke. LC 97-20375. (Illus.). 280p. (C). 1997. text ed. 62.50 (*0-911577-39-4*) Harrow & Heston.

*__Situational Dialogues.__ Ockenden. Date not set. pap. text ed. write for info. (*0-582-52172-6*, Pub. by Longman UK); pap. text ed. write for info. (*0-582-74409-1*, Pub. by Longman UK) Longman.

Situational Leader. Paul Hersey. LC 84-40659. 126p. (Orig.). 1985. 13.00 (*0-446-51342-3*) Ctr Leadership.

Situational Leadership for Principals: The School Administrator in Action. Kenneth J. Dunn & Rita S. Dunn. LC 82-11211. 228p. 1983. 18.95 (*0-686-84595-1*, Parker Publishing Co) P-H.

*__Situational Problem Solving: 44 Conflict-Resolution Role-Play Situations for Grades 5-9.__ Cammie McDaniel. 1995. 7.95 (*1-884063-68-3*) Mar Co Prods.

Situational Russian, Pt. 1. Klara K. Lewis. (Illus.). (ENG & RUS.). 1995. pap. 17.95 incl. audio (*1-886821-26-7*) Pavleen.

Situational Russian, Pt. 2. Klara K. Lewis. (Illus.). (ENG & RUS.). 1995. pap. 17.95 incl. audio (*1-886821-27-5*) Pavleen.

Situational Sales. Bill Breon. 140p. 1994. pap. 10.95 (*1-882185-20-X*) Crnrstone Pub.

Situational Selling: An Approach for Increasing Sales Effectiveness. Paul Hersey. LC 85-72476. (Illus.). 169p. 1985. 29.95 (*0-931619-00-9*) Ctr Leadership.

Situational Selling: Six Keys to Mastering the Complex Business Sale. Paul J. Kelly. LC 87-47844. (Illus.). 208p. reprint ed. pap. 59.30 (*0-7837-4235-5*, 2043924) Bks Demand.

Situational Tensions of Critic-Intellectuals: Thinking Through Literary Politics with Edward W. Said & Frank Lentricchia. Ben Xu. LC 91-854. (Sociocriticism: Literature, Society & History Ser.: Vol. 2). 207p. (C). 1992. text ed. 43.95 (*0-8204-1749-1*) P Lang Pubng.

*__Situationism: Art Politics Urbanism.__ T. McDonough et al. 180p. 1997. pap. 32.00 (*84-89698-14-7*) Dist Art Pubs.

*__Situationist City.__ Simon Sadler. 1998. 35.00 (*0-262-19392-2*) MIT Pr.

Situationist International Anthology. Situationist International Staff. Ed. by Ken Knabb. LC 81-69735. 406p. (Orig.). 1981. pap. 15.00 (*0-939682-00-1*) Bur Public Secrets.

Situationist Scrapbook. 1991. lib. bdg. 79.95 (*0-8490-4613-0*) Gordon Pr.

Situationists & May '68: Revolutionary Theory & Practice, 1966-1972. Pascal Dumontier. (C). 1997. pap. 16.50 (*1-899438-22-X*, Pub. by Porcupine Bks UK) Humanities.

Situations. Charles Peguy. (FRE.). pap. 4.50 (*0-685-37040-2*) Fr & Eur.

Situations, Vol. 2. Jean-Paul Sartre. 336p. (FRE.). 1948. pap. 32.95 (*0-7859-1320-3*, 2070257630) Fr & Eur.

Situations, Vol. 3. Jean-Paul Sartre. 320p. (FRE.). 1949. pap. 32.95 (*0-7859-1321-1*, 2070257657) Fr & Eur.

Situations: A Casebook of Virtual Realities for the English Teacher. Betty J. Wagner & Mark K. Larson. LC 94-28627. 280p. 1994. pap. text ed. 25.00 (*0-86709-345-5*, 0345) Boynton Cook Pubs.

Situations: Autour de 1968, Vol. 8. Jean-Paul Sartre. 481p. (FRE.). 1972. pap. 29.95 (*0-7859-1337-8*, 2070279979) Fr & Eur.

Situations: Colonialisme et Neo-Colonialism, Vol. 5. Jean-Paul Sartre. 256p. (FRE.). 1964. pap. 19.95 (*0-7859-1323-8*, 2070257754) Fr & Eur.

Situations: Melanges, Vol. 9. Jean-Paul Sartre. 369p. (FRE.). 1972. pap. 45.00 (*0-7859-1338-6*, 2070280888) Fr & Eur.

S

An Asterisk (*) at the beginning of an entry indicates that the title is appearing in BIP for the first time.

Situations: Politique et Autobiographie, Vol. 10. Jean-Paul Sartre. 232p. (FRE.). 1976. pap. 18.95 (0-7859-1347-5, 2070293734) Fr & Eur.

Situations: Portraits, Vol. 4. Jean-Paul Sartre. 464p. (FRE.). 1964. pap. 19.95 (0-7859-1322-X, 2070257746) Fr & Eur.

Situations: Problemes du Marxisme, Pt. 1, Vol. 6. Jean-Paul Sartre. 352p. (FRE.). 1965. pap. 18.95 (0-686-54997-X, 2070257770) Fr & Eur.

Situations: Problemes du Marxisme, Pt. 2, Vol. 7. Jean-Paul Sartre. 352p. (FRE.). 1964. pap. 39.95 (0-7859-1324-6, 2070257762) Fr & Eur.

Situations: Textes Divers du Monde Francophone. Patricia De Meo. 292p. (FRE.). 1995. pap. text ed. write for info. (0-201-42389-8) Addison-Wesley.

Situations & Strategies in American Land-Use Planning. Thomas K. Rudel. (ASA Rose Monograph Ser.). (Illus.). 176p. (C). 1989. text ed. 52.95 (0-521-36186-9) Cambridge U Pr.

Situations et Contextes. H. Jay Siskin & Jo A. Recker. 576p. (FRE.). (C). 1992. text ed. 45.25 (0-03-076993-0); 232.75 (0-03-020733-9); audio write for info. (0-03-026412-X); vhs write for info. (0-318-69151-5) HB Coll Pubs.

Situations et Contextes. 2nd ed. H. Jay Siskin & JoAnn M. Reck. (Illus.). 480p. (FRE.). (C). 1993. teacher ed. write for info. (0-15-500683-5); text ed. 43.00 (0-15-500592-8) HB Coll Pubs.

Situations, Language & Logic. Ed. by Jens E. Fenstad et al. (C). 1987. lib. bdg. 115.50 (1-55608-048-4) Kluwer Ac.

Situations Philosophique. Jean-Paul Sartre. (FRE.). 1990. pap. 25.95 (0-7859-2944-4) Fr & Eur.

Situations Study Guide, Unit A. Ed. by Deakin University Press Staff. 144p. (C). 1988. 51.00 (0-7300-0569-0, Pub. by Deakin Univ AT) St Mut.

Situations, Tense, & Aspect: Dynamic Discourse Ontology & the Semantic Flexibility of Temporal System in German & English. Ranate Bartsch. (Groningen-Amsterdam Studies in Semantics: No. 13). 1995. 113.85 (0-614-08071-1) Mouton.

Situations, Tense, & Aspect: Dynamic Discourse Ontology & the Semantic Flexibility of Temporal System in German & English. Renate Bartsch. (Groningen-Amsterdam Studies in Semantics: No. 13). x, 289p. (C). 1995. lib. bdg. 113.85 (3-11-014584-7) Mouton.

Sitwells & the Art of the 1920s & 1930s. Sarah H. Bradford et al. (Literary Modernism Ser.). (Illus.). 240p. 1996. pap. 34.95 (0-292-77711-6) U of Tex Pr.

Sitwells on the Making of Gardens. George Sitwell. (Illus.). 144p. 1995. 14.95 (1-883145-06-6) Ursus Press.

Sitzungsberichte. 1995. 127.23 (3-540-58552-4) Spr-Verlag.

SIU 101: Special Investigation Units: Guidelines, Formats, Procedures, Forms, & Philosophy for Investigators & Adjustors. Bill Kizorek & Scott Finger. LC 94-31384. 1994. write for info. (1-884230-03-2) InPhoto Surv.

Siva: The Erotic Ascetic. Wendy D. O'Flaherty. (Illus.). 400p. 1981. reprint ed. pap. 14.95 (0-19-520250-3) OUP.

Siva & Buddha. Nivedita. pap. 1.00 (0-87481-116-3, Pub. by Advaita Ashrama II) Vedanta Pr.

Siva & Her Sisters: Gender, Caste, & Class in Rural South India. Karin Kapadia. (Studies in Ethnographic Imagination). 1995. text ed. 59.50 (0-8133-8158-4) Westview.

Siva in Art: A Study of Saiva Iconography & Miniatures. O. C. Handa. (C). 1992. 54.00 (81-85182-65-5, Pub. by Indus Pub II) S Asia.

Siva in Art, Literature & Thought. Shanti L. Nagar. (C). 1995. 125.00 (81-7387-019-5, Pub. by Indus Pub II) S Asia.

Siva in Dance, Myth & Iconography. Anne-Marie Gaston. (Illus.). 254p. 1983. 65.00 (0-19-561354-6) OUP.

Siva Mahimna Stotram. Pushpanjal. pap. 1.00 (0-87481-075-2) Vedanta Pr.

Siva Purana, Pt. I. Ed. by J. L. Shastri. (Ancient Indian Tradition & Mythology Ser.: Vol. 1). 1986. 26.00 (81-208-0269-1, Pub. by Motilal Banarsidass II) S Asia.

Siva Purana, Pt. II. Ed. by J. L. Shastri. (Ancient Indian Tradition & Mythology Ser.: Vol. 2). 1987. 26.00 (81-208-0312-4, Pub. by Motilal Banarsidass II) S Asia.

Siva Purana, Pt. III. Ed. by J. L. Shastri. (Ancient Indian Tradition & Mythology Ser.: Vol. 3). 1988. 26.00 (81-208-0338-8, Pub. by Motilal Banarsidass II) S Asia.

Siva Purana, Pt. IV. Tr. by N. A. Deshpande. (Ancient Indian Tradition & Mythology Ser.: Vol. 4). 1990. 26.00 (0-685-35376-1, Pub. by Motilal Banarsidass II) S Asia.

Siva Samhita. Tr. by Rai B. Vasu. 1990. 9.50 (0-685-40171-5, Pub. by Munshiram Manoharial II) S Asia.

Siva Samhita. Sivasamhita. Tr. by Srisa Chandra Vasu. LC 73-3803. (Sacred Books of the Hindus: Vol. 15, Pt. 1). reprint ed. 18.00 (0-404-57815-2) AMS Pr.

Siva! Siva! Cresent & Heart: Selected Poetry of Murshid Samuel L. Lewis. Samuel L. Lewis. (Bismillah Bks.: No. 1). (Illus.). 112p. (Orig.). 1980. pap. 8.95 (0-915424-04-5) PeaceWks Intl Ntwrk.

Sivalaya: Explorations of the Eight-Thousand Metre Peaks of the Himalaya. Louis Baume. LC 79-20964. 348p. 1979. reprint ed. pap. 9.95 (0-916890-71-6) Mountaineers.

Sivananda Companion to Yoga. Sivananda Yoga Center Staff & Lucy L. Narayani. 1983. pap. 14.00 (0-671-47088-4) S&S Trade.

Sivananda Lahari of Sri Sankara. Shankara. Tr. by Tapasyananda from SAN. 87p. 1987. pap. 3.95 (0-87481-545-2, Pub. by Ramakrishna Math II) Vedanta Pr.

Sivapithecus Palate see New Siwalik Primates: Their Bearing on the Question of Evolution of Man & the Anthropoidea

Siva's Warriors: The Basava Purana of Palkuriki Somanatha. Tr. by Velcheru N. Rao & Gene H. Roghair from TEL. 325p. 1990. text ed. 57.50 (0-691-05591-2) Princeton U Pr.

Sivastotravali of Utpaladeva. N. K. Kotru. 173p. 1986. 17.00 (0-317-53535-8, Pub. by Motilal Banarsidass II) S Asia.

Sivasvamin's Kapphinabhyudaya or Exaltation of King Kapphina. Ed. by Gauri Shankar. (C). 1989. 68.50 (81-85179-10-7, Pub. by Aditya Prakashan II) S Asia.

***Sivena.** Chronicle Books Staff. 1997. spiral bd. 9.95 (0-8118-1653-2) Chronicle Bks.

Siviculture: Concepts & Applications. Ralph D. Nyland. (Illus.). 576p. 1996. text ed. 44.00 (0-07-056999-1) McGraw.

Siviendo al Senor, No. 1: Que es la Iglesia? Richard De Ridder. Tr. by Mariano Avila. (SPA.). 1990. 2.00 (1-55955-110-0) CRC Wrld Lit.

Siwa Oasis. Ahmed Fakhry. 1992. pap. text ed. 15.00 (977-424-123-1, Pub. by Am Univ Cairo Pr UA) Col U Pr.

Siwash: Their Life, Legends, & Tales. J. A. Costello. 178p. 1977. 19.95 (0-87770-398-1) Ye Galleon.

Siwiti - a Whale's Story: A Whale's Story. Alexandra Morton. (Illus.). 48p. (Orig.). (YA). (gr. 8-12). 1991. pap. 9.95 (0-920501-97-4) Orca Bk Pubs.

***Si'wren of the Patriarchs.** Roland Cheney. 259p. (Orig.). 1997. mass mkt. 4.99 (1-55197-619-6, Pub. by Comnwlth Pub CN) Partners Pubs Grp.

Six. David Meltzer. LC 76-40038. (Illus.). 130p. (Orig.). 1976. pap. 4.00 (0-87685-270-3) Black Sparrow.

Six. Rudolf Rocker. 1972. 250.00 (0-87700-079-4) Revisionist Pr.

***6, 2.** Nicieza. 1997. mass mkt. 3.99 (0-671-01174-X) PB.

Six: Islam & Muslim Civilization. IIIT (Douglass) Staff. 192p. 1995. ring bd. 29.95 (0-8403-9942-1) Kendall-Hunt.

Six: The Versewagon Poetry Manual. Intro. & Selected by Ian McMillan. 128p. (C). 1988. 50.00 (0-947612-13-0, Pub. by Rivelin Grapheme Pr); pap. 40.00 (0-947612-14-9, Pub. by Rivelin Grapheme Pr) St Mut.

Six Acts on a Flying Trapeze. Ellen Clarkson. (Illus.). 160p. (C). 1986. pap. text ed. 11.00 (0-13-811308-4) P-H.

Six Adventure Theatre Plays. Ed. by Patricia Whitton. (Illus.). 212p. pap. 12.95 (0-932720-65-X) New Plays Inc.

Six Airs Varies for Violin & Piano, Op. 89. Charles Dancla. (Carl Fischer Music Library: No.125). 1911. pap. 7.50 (0-8258-0027-7, L125) Fischer Inc NY.

Six Airs Varies Opus 89: Violin & Piano. L. Dancla. 36p. 1986. pap. 7.95 (0-7935-5436-5) H Leonard.

Six American Colonists - Thomas Newbold, William Rodney, George Hufford, Eberhard Ream, Edward Painter, Richard Bridgeford - & Their Descendants, Vol. 1. Eunice N. Clark. LC 95-69865. (Illus.). 836p. 1995. lib. bdg. 40.00 (0-9614199-1-1) E N Clark.

Six American Poets. Ed. by Joel Conarroe. 256p. 1991. 27.50 (0-679-40689-1) Random.

Six American Poets: An Anthology. Joel Connaroe. LC 92-50624. 320p. 1993. pap. 13.00 (0-679-74525-4, Vin) Random.

Six American Poets from Emily Dickinson to the Present: An Introduction. Allen Tate. LC 70-172932. 273p. 1969. reprint ed. pap. 77.90 (0-7837-2916-2, 2057538) Bks Demand.

***Six American Stories.** Wymer. Date not set. pap. text ed. write for info. (0-17-557045-0) Addison-Wesley.

Six & Higher-Membered Monocarbocyclic Compounds see Rodd's Chemistry of Carbon Compounds

Six Anthems see Old English Edition

Six Architects. Reginald T. Blomfield. LC 78-99682. (Essay Index Reprint Ser.). 1977. 18.95 (0-8369-1340-X) Ayer.

Six Armies in Normandy: From D-Day to the Liberation of Paris. John Keegan. (Illus.). 392p. 1983. pap. 9.95 (0-14-005293-3, Penguin Bks) Viking Penguin.

Six Armies in Normandy: From D-Day to the Liberation of Paris. rev. ed. John Keegan. 416p. 1994. pap. 12.95 (0-14-023542-6, Penguin Bks) Viking Penguin.

Six Attitudes for Winners. Norman Vincent Peale. 88p. 1989. pap. 3.99 (0-8423-5906-0) Tyndale.

Six Award Winning Plays. Norman Beim. 251p. 1995. pap. 17.95 (0-931231-06-X) Newconcept Pr.

Six Axle Quartet: An Essay of Diesel Portraiture. Lowell Amrine. LC 86-2246. 96p. 1986. reprint ed. lib. bdg. 25.00 (0-89370-553-5) Borgo Pr.

Six Black Presidents: Black Blood, White Masks: A Little Bit of Melanin: The Six Black President (U. S. A.) Auset BaKhufu. LC 91-90486. 365p. (C). 1993. per. 19.95 (1-880187-00-0) PIKK Pubns.

Six Blind Men & the Elephant Pop up Book. 10p. (J). (gr. 4-7). 1991. 9.95 (0-8167-2199-8) Troll Communs.

Six Blue Horses. Yvonne Escoula. LC 70-103044. (J). (gr. 5-9). 1970. 24.95 (0-87599-162-9) S G Phillips.

Six Blues Roots Pianists. Eric Kriss. (Illus.). 104p. pap. 14.95 (0-8256-0144-4, OK62752, Oak) Music Sales.

Six Bookes of Commonweale. Jean Bodin. Ed. by J. P. Mayer. LC 78-67335. (European Political Thought Ser.). 1980. reprint ed. lib. bdg. 73.95 (0-405-11680-2) Ayer.

Six Brandenburg Concertos & the Four Orchestral Suites in Full Score. Johann Sebastian Bach. 273p. 1976. reprint ed. pap. 10.95 (0-486-23376-6) Dover.

Six Brave Explorers. Kees Moerbeek & Carla Dijs. (Triangle Pop-up Ser.). (Illus.). 12p. (J). (ps up). 1988. 9.95 (0-8431-2253-6) Price Stern Sloan.

Six Brave Explorers: Mini-Triangles Pop-Up. Kees Moerbeek. (Illus.). (J). 1992. 4.95 (0-8431-3449-6) Price Stern Sloan.

Six Breeds. Ralph G. Kirk. LC 70-125225. (Short Story Index Reprint Ser.). (Illus.). 1977. 19.95 (0-8369-3592-6) Ayer.

Six Brides of Dilston. A. R. Bolton. 100p. (C). 1988. 35.00 (0-7212-0745-6, Pub. by Regency Press UK) St Mut.

Six Bridges of Humphrey the Whale. Toni Knapp. LC 89-8417. (Illus.). 48p. (J). (gr. 4 up). 1993. pap. 9.95 (1-879373-64-5) R Rinehart.

Six Bridges of Humphrey the Whale. Ed. by Toni Knapp. LC 89-8417. (Illus.). 48p. (J). (gr. 8 up). 1989. 15.95 (1-882092-01-5) Travis Ilse.

Six Brothers from Hinsdale: The Bell Family History. George E. Bell. Ed. by Linda V. Bell. (Illus.). 350p. (C). 1990. text ed. write for info. (0-9623275-1-4) Wayne Ridge.

Six Busy Days. Mary Erickson. LC 88-11803. (Illus.). 32p. (J). (ps-2). 1988. 9.99 (1-55513-699-0, Chariot Bks) Chariot Victor.

Six by Lewis, 6 vols. C. S. Lewis. 1978. boxed, pap. 27.95 (0-02-086770-0) Macmillan.

Six by Lewis. C. S. Lewis. 1996. boxed, pap. 34.95 (0-684-83119-8, S&S) S&S Trade.

Six by Seuss. Dr. Seuss, pseud. (J). 1995. 25.00 (0-679-87921-8) Random Bks Yng Read.

Six Canterbury Tales. Eberle Thomas & Barbara Redmond. (Orig.). (YA). 1993. pap. 6.00 (0-87602-322-7) Anchorage.

***Six Cartesian Meditations.** Anders Jeffner. 45p. 1993. pap. 14.95 (90-390-0044-1, Pub. by KOK Pharos NE) Eisenbrauns.

Six Cent Sam's. Julian Hawthorne. LC 70-101283. (Short Story Index Reprint Ser.). 1977. 21.95 (0-8369-3220-X) Ayer.

Six Centuries in East Asia: China, Japan & Korea from the 14th Century to 1912. Peter Lum. LC 72-12582. (Illus.). 288p. 1973. 36.95 (0-87599-183-1) S G Phillips.

Six Centuries of Great Poetry. Robert Penn Warren. 608p. 1992. mass mkt. 6.50 (0-440-21383-5, LLL BDD) BDD Bks Young Read.

Six Centuries of the Provincial Book Trade in Britain. Ed. by Isaac Peter. 212p. 1990. 28.00 (0-906795-96-6) Oak Knoll.

Six Centuries of Verse. Selected by Anthony Thwaite. (Illus.). 224p. (Orig.). 1985. pap. 9.95 (0-423-00960-5, NO. 9410) Routledge Chapman & Hall.

Six Chapbook Romances. Ed. by John Simons. (Illus.). 160p. 1995. pap. text ed. 24.95 (0-85989-445-2, Pub. by Univ Exeter Pr UK) Northwestern U Pr.

Six Chaplet Rosary. Ed. by Alan Robinson. 80p. 1994. pap. 30.00 (0-85439-473-7, Pub. by St Paul Pubns UK) St Mut.

Six Chapters from My Life "Downunder" Jonathan D. Spence. LC 84-2228. (Renditions Bks.). (Illus.). 128p. 1984. pap. 9.95 (0-295-96644-0) U of Wash Pr.

***6 Chapters in Design: Saul Bass, Ivan Chermayeff, Milton Glaser, Paul Rand, Ikko Tanaka, Henryk Tomaszewski.** Philip B. Meggs. LC 97-12598. 1997. pap. write for info. (0-8118-1722-9) Chronicle Bks.

***Six Chapters of Canada's Prehistory.** J. V. Wright. (Canadian Prehistory Ser.). (Illus.). 118p. 1976. pap. 16.95 (0-660-00005-9, Pub. by Can Mus Civil CN) U of Wash Pr.

Six Characters in Search of an Author see Naked Masks: Five Plays

Six Characters in Search of an Author & Other Plays. Luigi Pirandello. 224p. 1996. pap. 11.95 (0-14-018922-X) Viking Penguin.

Six Children Draw. Ed. by S. Paine. LC 81-69580. 1982. text ed. 39.00 (0-12-543950-4) Acad Pr.

Six Christian One-Act Plays for Young Adults. Arthur Wise & Sarah Wise. 52p. (YA). (gr. 7-12). 1978. reprint ed. pap. 5.00 (0-88680-178-8) I E Clark.

Six Christmas Plays. Noelene Martin. 1993. pap. 9.50 (0-85819-850-9, Pub. by JBCE AT) Morehouse Pub.

Six Circles, One Dewdrop: The Religo-Aesthetic World of Komparu Zenchiku. Arthur H. Thornhill, III. (Illus.). 252p. 1992. text ed. 39.95 (0-691-07352-X) Princeton U Pr.

Six Classic American Writers: An Introduction. Paul Sherman. LC 71-120808. 277p. reprint ed. pap. 79.00 (0-318-39684-X, 2033279) Bks Demand.

***Six Color World: Color, Cloth, Quilts & Wearables.** Yvonne Porcella. Ed. by Lee Jonsson. LC 97-3062. (Illus.). 144p. (Orig.). 1997. pap. 26.95 (1-57120-035-5, 10159) C & T Pub.

Six Comedies. W. Somerset Maugham. LC 75-25391. (Works of W. Somerset Maugham). 1977. reprint ed. 35.95 (0-405-07849-8) Ayer.

Six Concert Etudes, Opus 35 see Three Piano Works

Six Contemporary Chinese Women Artists. Lucy Lim. LC 91-74138. (Illus.). 102p. 1993. pap. 24.95 (0-9609784-1-0) CCF San Francisco.

***Six Contemporary Chinese Women Writers, Vol. IV.** Pref. by Chen Meilan. 374p. 1995. pap. 8.95 (0-8351-3175-0) China Bks.

***Six Contemporary Dramatists.** Wu. 1997. text ed. 18.95 (0-312-16567-6) St Martin.

Six Contemporary Dramatists: Bennett, Potter, Gray, Brenton, Hare Ayckbourn. Duncan Wu. LC 94-26330. 1994. text ed. 49.95 (0-312-12360-4) St Martin.

***Six Contemporary French Women Poets: Theory, Practice & Pleasures.** Serge Gavronsky. LC 96-41759. 1997. pap. 16.95 (0-8093-2115-7) S Ill U Pr.

Six Core Theories of Modern Physics. Charles F. Stevens. (Illus.). 196p. 1995. 32.50 (0-262-19359-0, Bradford Bks) MIT Pr.

Six Core Theories of Modern Physics. Charles F. Stevens. (Illus.). 248p. 1996. reprint ed. pap. 12.50 (0-262-69188-4, Bradford Bks) MIT Pr.

Six-Cornered Snowflake & Other Poems. John F. Nims. LC 90-33222. 64p. 1990. 18.95 (0-8112-1143-6); pap. 9.95 (0-8112-1144-4, NDP700) New Directions.

Six Counties Walks. Joe Taylor & Chas Cook. (C). 1988. pap. 29.00 (0-946328-10-2, Pub. by Thornhill Pr UK) St Mut.

Six Creepy Sheep. Judith R. Enderle & Stephanie G. Tessler. LC 91-77609. (Illus.). 24p. (J). (ps-1). 1992. lib. bdg. 12.95 (1-56397-092-9) Boyds Mills Pr.

Six Creepy Sheep. Judith R. Enderle & Stephanie G. Tessler. LC 93-7140. (Illus.). 26p. (J). (ps-1). 1993. pap. 4.99 (0-14-054994-3, Puffin) Puffin Bks.

Six Criminal Women. Elizabeth Jenkins. LC 76-148222. (Biography Index Reprint Ser.). 1977. 20.95 (0-8369-8069-7) Ayer.

Six Crises. Richard M. Nixon. 1990. pap. 12.95 (0-671-70619-5) S&S Trade.

Six Crises. Richard M. Nixon. 1994. lib. bdg. 24.95 (1-56849-499-8) Buccaneer Bks.

Six Crows. Leo Lionni. LC 87-3141. (Illus.). 32p. (J). (ps-2). 1988. lib. bdg. 16.99 (0-394-99572-4) Knopf Bks Yng Read.

Six Cups! Six Bowls! Six Spoons! Humorous Hints from a Formerly Frazzled Mom on How to Get Your House in Order & Keep It That Way. Dana McGuinn. (Illus.). 48p. 1993. pap. 6.95 (1-880163-06-3); vhs 18.95 (1-880163-07-1) Firefly Pub.

Six Dances for Paper Piano. Coco Gordon. (Intimate Ser.: No. 8). 112p. (Orig.). 1987. 35.00 (0-943375-08-8) W Space.

***Six Dangerous Questions: To Transform Your View of the World.** Paul Borthwick. 144p. (Orig.). 1997. pap. 8.99 (0-8308-1685-2, 1685) InterVarsity.

Six-Day War: A Retrospective. Ed. by Richard B. Parker. LC 95-43804. (Illus.). 400p. 1996. lib. bdg. 49.95 (0-8130-1383-6) U Press Fla.

Six Days. Halim I. Barakat. Tr. by Bassam Frangieh & Scott McGhee. LC 90-11283. 128p. 1990. 22.00 (0-89410-661-9, Three Contnts); pap. 12.00 (0-89410-662-7, Three Contnts) Lynne Rienner.

Six Days & a Day. Marvin Byers. 252p. (Orig.). 1996. pap. 14.99 (1-56043-263-2) Destiny Image.

Six Days & the Seven Gates. Yitzhak Navon. 1980. 6.00 (0-930832-57-4); pap. 4.00 (0-686-70336-7) Herzl Pr.

Six Days in Havana. James A. Michener & John Kings. (Illus.). 144p. 1989. 24.95 (0-292-77629-2) U of Tex Pr.

Six Days in St. Petersburg: A Chronicle of Return - Poems. Alla R. Bozarth. LC 93-3566. 1993. pap. 9.95 (1-883230-03-9) Purple Iris Pr.

Six Days of Creation. Thomas M. Sennott. 1984. pap. 9.95 (0-911218-22-X) Ravengate Pr.

Six Days or Forever? Tennessee vs. John Thomas Scopes. Ray Ginger. 270p. 1974. pap. 10.95 (0-19-519784-4) OUP.

Six Days to Better Golf. Orbitz. 1995. 7.98 (0-88365-896-8) Galahad Bks.

Six Days to Swim-Jeff Farrell: A Story of Olympic Courage. Jean M. Henning. LC 71-103031. (Illus.). (J). (gr. 6-12). 1970. 3.50 (0-911822-02-X) Swimming.

Six Deadly Demons. DC Comics Staff. 1992. mass mkt. 3.95 (0-316-17767-9) Little.

***Six Degrees of Kevin Bacon.** Craig Fass. 1996. pap. 7.95 (0-452-27844-9, Plume) NAL-Dutton.

Six Degrees of Separation. John Guare. 1990. pap. 10.00 (0-679-73481-3) McKay.

Six Degrees of Separation. John Guare. 1992. pap. 5.25 (0-8222-1034-7) Dramatists Play.

Six Degrees of Separation. John Guare. 128p. 1990. 19.95 (0-679-40161-X) Random.

Six Dinner Sid. Inga Moore. LC 90-42749. (J). (gr. k-3). 1991. pap. 15.00 (0-671-73199-8, S&S Bks Young Read) S&S Childrens.

Six-Dinner Sid. Inga Moore. LC 90-42749. (Illus.). 32p. (J). (ps-3). 1993. pap. 5.95 (0-671-79613-5, S&S Bks Young Read) S&S Childrens.

Six Directions: Haiku & Field Notes. Jim Kacian. (Illus.). 112p. (Orig.). 1997. pap. 12.00 (0-9631909-4-6) La Alameda Pr.

Six Disciplines of Man's Being & Man's Relation to Government. rev. ed. Melvin Gorham. 128p. 1983. pap. 7.00 (0-914752-16-2) Sovereign Pr.

Six Drown Saving Chicken: And Other Stories from Reuters's "Oddly Enough File" Reuters America Staff. Ed. by Robert Basler. (Illus.). 160p. 1996. pap. 8.95 (0-7867-0369-5) Carroll & Graf.

Six Duets Opus 20 - 2 Violins. G. B. Viotti. 20p. 1986. pap. 8.95 (0-7935-5113-7) H Leonard.

Six Dynasties Poetry. Kang-i Sung Chang. LC 85-43274. 240p. 1986. 39.50 (0-691-06669-8) Princeton U Pr.

Six Early Blues Guitarists. Woody Mann. (Illus.). 112p. 1973. pap. 15.95 (0-8256-0135-5, OK62703, Oak) Music Sales.

Six Early Stories. Thomas Mann. Ed. by Burton Pike. Tr. by Peter Constantine from GER. (Classics Ser.: No. 82). 136p. 1997. 22.95 (1-55713-298-4) Sun & Moon CA.

Six Easy Pieces. Richard P. Feynman. (C). 1995. 49.95 incl. audio (0-201-40956-9) Addison-Wesley.

Six Easy Pieces. Richard P. Feynman. 176p. (YA). 1996. pap. 12.00 (0-201-40825-2) Addison-Wesley.

Six Easy Pieces: Essentials of Physics, Explained by Its Most Brilliant Teacher. Richard P. Faynman. (C). 1995. 22.00 (0-201-40955-0) Addison-Wesley.

Six Easy Steps to Millions in Grants: A Grant-Writing Manual. rev. ed. Debra M. Winn. (Illus.). 106p. 1996. 19.95 (0-9638480-0-3) Maldon Enter.

Six Easy Violin Duets. Pleyel. pap. 11.95 (0-685-69310-4, WH02927) Shawnee Pr.

Six Ecclesiastical Satires. Ed. by James Dean. (TEAMS Middle English Text Ser.). 1991. pap. 9.00 (1-879288-05-2) Medieval Inst.

Six Eight Zero Three Zero Assembly Language Reference: Includes the 60820. Steven Williams. 600p. 1989. pap. 29.95 (0-201-08876-2) Addison-Wesley.

An Asterisk (*) at the beginning of an entry indicates that the title is appearing in BIP for the first time.

***688 (1) Hunter/Killer: The Official Strategy Guide.** 240p. 1997. per. 19.99 (0-7615-1036-2) Prima Pub.

Six Elizabethan Plays. Incl. Tamburlaine, Pt. 1. Christopher Marlowe. LC 63-4440. 1959. (0-318-53425-8); Shoemaker's Holiday. Thomas Dekker. LC 63-4440. (0-318-53426-6); Knight of the Burning Pestle. Francis Beaumont & John Fletcher. LC 63-4440. 1959. (0-318-53427-4); Epicoene. Ben Jonson. LC 63-4440. (0-318-53428-2); Duchess of Malfi. John Webster. LC 63-4440. (0-318-53429-0); Broken Heart. John Ford. LC 63-4440. 1959. (0-318-53430-4); LC 63-4440. (YA). (gr. 9-p). 1959. pap. 11.56 (0-395-05135-5, RivEd) HM.

***Six Empty Pockets.** Matt Curtis. LC 96-49441. (Rookie Reader Ser.). (Illus.). (J). 1997. write for info. (0-516-20399-1) Childrens.

Six English Towns. Alec Clifton-Taylor. (Illus.). 176p. (Orig.). 1987. pap. 14.95 (0-563-20490-7, Pub. by BBC UK) Parkwest Pubns.

Six Essays on Desighn & New Media see Six Plus Two Essays on Design & New Media

Six Essays on Design & New Media. Jessica Helfand. 72p. 1996. 30.00 (1-884381-08-1); pap. 12.00 (1-884381-09-X) W Drenttel NY.

Six Essays on Erasmus & a Translation of Erasmus' Letter to Carondelet 1523. John C. Olin. LC 76-18467. (Illus.). xiv, 125p. 1977. pap. 17.50 (0-8232-1024-3) Fordham.

Six Essays on Johnson. Walter Raleigh. (BCL1-PR English Literature Ser.). 184p. 1992. reprint ed. lib. bdg. 69.00 (0-7812-7368-4) Rprt Serv.

Six Etudes de Psychologie. Jean Piaget. (FRE.). 1987. pap. 12.95 (0-7859-2805-7) Fr & Eur.

Six Etudes for Piano. L. Talma. 28p. 1991. pap. 8.95 (0-7935-1165-8, 50330060) H Leonard.

Six Exceptional Women. James Lord. LC 93-42384. 1994. 27.50 (0-374-26553-4) FS&G.

Six Existential Heroes: The Politics of Faith. Lucio P. Ruotolo. LC 72-86386. 161p. reprint ed. pap. 45.90 (0-7837-4187-1, 2059037) Bks Demand.

Six Existentialist Thinkers. H. J. Blackham. 179p. 1983. pap. 13.95 (0-7100-4611-1, RKP) Routledge.

***Six Existentialist Thinkers.** H. J. Blackham. 190p. (C). 1983. pap. text ed. 15.95 (0-415-05098-7) Routledge.

Six Faces of Mexico: History, People, Geography, Government, Economy, Literature & Art. Ed. by Russell C. Ewing. LC 66-18533. 334p. reprint ed. pap. 95.20 (0-317-28563-7, 2055251) Bks Demand.

Six Fairy Variations. Marius Petipa et al. Orig. Title: Sleeping Beauty Prologue. (Illus.). 44p. 1961. pap. text ed. 15.00 (0-932582-66-4, Pub. by Dance Bks UK) Princeton Bk Co.

Six Famous Living Poets. Coulson Kernahan. LC 68-8475. (Essay Index Reprint Ser.). 1977. reprint ed. 20.95 (0-8369-0593-8) Ayer.

***Six Fantasias for Four Viols, 2 vols.** 2nd ed. John Ward. Ed. by Virginia Brookes. Incl. Score & Parts. 2nd rev. ed. iv, 42p. (Orig.). 1996. pap. text ed. Not sold separately (1-56571-142-4); Organ Part. ii, 13p. (Orig.). 1996. pap. text ed. 8.00 (1-56571-143-2); (Viol Consort Ser.). 1996. Set pap. text ed. 25.00 (0-614-23618-5) PRB Prods.

***Six Fantasias for Six Viols.** William Cranford. Ed. by Virginia Brookes. (Viol Consort Ser.: Vol. VC027). v, 71p. (Orig.). 1996. pap. text ed. 28.00 (1-56571-128-9) PRB Prods.

Six Fantasias for Six Viols (Two Trebles, Two Tenors, Two Basses) Richard Dering. Ed. by Virginia Brookes. (Viol Consort Ser.: No. 24). ii, 60p. 1994. pap. text ed. 27.00 (1-56571-117-3) PRB Prods.

Six Fantasias on Sephardic Themes for Solo Bass Viol. David Loeb. (Contemporary Instrumental Ser.: No. 6). 12p. 1992. pap. text ed. 9.00 (1-56571-058-4, CI006) PRB Prods.

Six Feet of Country. Nadine Gordimer. 1986. pap. 8.95 (0-14-006559-8, Penguin Bks) Viking Penguin.

***Six Feet Under.** D. B. Borton. 240p. 1997. mass mkt. 5.99 (0-425-15700-8, Prime Crime) Berkley Pub.

Six Feet Under. large type ed. Dorothy Simpson. 1983. 15.95 (0-7089-1047-5) Ulverscroft.

***Six-Figure Consulting: How to Have a Great Second Career.** Gary S. Goodman. LC 97-2066. 176p. (Orig.). 1997. pap. 16.95 (0-8144-7958-8) AMACOM.

Six Fillious. B. P. Nichol et al. 1978. pap. 10.00 (0-87924-032-6) Membrane Pr.

***Six Fishermen.** San Souci. 1999. 14.95 (0-7868-2335-6) Hyprn Child.

***Six Fishrmen.** San Souci. (J). 1999. 14.95 (0-7868-0385-1) Hyprn Child.

Six-Five: A Different Shade of Blue. Steven Herberts. LC 96-26635. (Illus.). 186p. (Orig.). 1996. 19.95 (1-56072-338-6) Nova Sci Pubs.

6' 1" Grinch. Tiffany White. 1996. pap. 3.50 (0-373-44009-X, 1-44009-8) Harlequin Bks.

Six Foot Under. Katherine John. 384p. 1996. 23.95 (0-312-14416-4) St Martin.

***Six Foot Under.** large type ed. Katherine John. (Large Print Ser.). 752p. 1996. 25.99 (0-7089-3554-0) Ulverscroft.

Six for Heaven. large type ed. Lucy Walker. 377p. 1981. 25.99 (0-7089-0650-8) Ulverscroft.

Six French Poets: Studies in Contemporary Literature. Amy Lowell. LC 67-28737. (Essay Index Reprint Ser.). 1977. 22.95 (0-8369-0626-8) Ayer.

Six French Poets of Our Time: A Critical & Historical Study. Robert W. Greene. LC 78-70297. (Princeton Essays in Literature Ser.). 212p. 1979. reprint ed. pap. 60.50 (0-7837-8589-5, 2049404) Bks Demand.

Six from Sirius. Moench & Gulacy. 128p. 1988. pap. 8.95 (0-87135-334-2) Marvel Entmnt.

Six Galleons for the King of Spain: Imperial Defense in the Early Seventeenth Century. Carla R. Phillips. LC 86-45444. (Softshell Bks.). (Illus.). 332p. 1992. pap. text ed. 24.95 (0-8018-4513-0) Johns Hopkins.

Six Generations: The Story of German Village. Constance Walley. LC 91-76460. (Illus.). 120p. (Orig.). 1991. pap. 15.95 (0-9631389-0-1) German Vill Stories.

Six Generations Here: A Farm Family Remembers. Marjorie L. McLellan. LC 95-37595. 1996. pap. write for info. (0-87020-283-9) State Hist Soc Wis.

Six German Romantic Tales. Heinrich Von Kleist et al. LC 85-73377. 176p. (Orig.). 8600. pap. 15.95 (0-946162-17-4, Pub. by Angel Bks UK) Dufour.

Six German Romantic Tales. Heinrich Von Kleist et al. Tr. & Intro. by Ronald Taylor. LC 92-17745. 146p. 9300. pap. 13.95 (0-8023-1295-0) Dufour.

Six Grand Etudes: Piano. N. Paganini. 60p. 1986. pap. 8.95 (0-7935-4533-1) H Leonard.

***Six Great Advocates.** Norman Birkett. 109p. 1972. 11.95 (0-8369-8132-4) Ayer.

Six Great American Plays. Ed. & Intro. by Allan G. Halline. LC 83-42951. 419p. 1978. 16.00 (0-394-60457-1, Modern Lib) Random.

***Six Great American Poets, 6 vols., Set.** Dover Staff. boxed, pap. 6.00 (0-486-27425-X) Dover.

Six Great Ideas. Adler. 1996. pap. 10.00 (0-684-82681-X) S&S Trade.

Six Great Ideas: Truth, Goodness, Beauty, Liberty, Equality, Justice. Mortimer J. Adler. 243p. 1984. pap. 7.95 (0-02-072020-3, Collier S&S) S&S Trade.

Six Great Modern Plays. Incl. Three Sisters: Three Sisters (Tri Sewiry). Anton P. Chekhov. 1956. (0-318-51680-2); Master Builder. Henrik Ibsen. 1956. (0-318-51681-0); Mrs. Warren's Profession. George Bernard Shaw. (0-318-51682-9); Glass Menagerie. Tennessee Williams. (0-318-51684-5); All My Sons. Arthur Miller. (0-318-51685-3); 512p. 1956. mass mkt. 6.50 (0-440-37984-9, LE) Dell.

Six Great Modern Short Novels. Incl. Dead. James Joyce. (0-318-51686-1); Billy Budd, Foretopman. Herman Melville. (0-318-51687-X); Noon Wine. Katherine Anne Porter. 1954. (0-318-51688-8); Overcoat. Nikolai V. Gogol. 1954. (0-318-51689-6); Pilgrim Hawks. Glenway Wescott. 1954. (0-318-51690-X); Bear. William Faulkner. 1954. (0-318-51691-8); 448p. 1954. mass mkt. 6.99 (0-440-37996-2, LE) Dell.

Six Great Poets: Chaucer, Pope, Wordsworth, Shelley, Tennyson, the Brownings. Aubrey De Selincourt. 1988. reprint ed. lib. bdg. 49.00 (0-7812-0106-3) Rprt Serv.

Six Great Poets: Chaucer, Pope, Wordsworth, Shelley, Tennyson, the Brownings. Aubrey De Selincourt. reprint ed. 26.00 (0-403-04283-6) Somerset Pub.

Six Great Russian Composers. Donald Brook. LC 73-136643. (Biography Index Reprint Ser.). 1977. reprint ed. 27.95 (0-8369-8038-7) Ayer.

Six Great Russian Composers: Music Book Index. Donald Brook. 193p. 1993. reprint ed. lib. bdg. 69.00 (0-7812-9570-X) Rprt Serv.

Six Great Secular Cantatas in Full Score. Johann Sebastian Bach. 288p. (Orig.). 1980. pap. 11.95 (0-486-23934-9) Dover.

Six Great Sherlock Holmes Stories. Arthur Conan Doyle. (Thrift Editions Ser.). 112p. (Orig.). 1992. pap. 1.00 (0-486-27055-6) Dover.

Six Great Themes of Western Metaphysics & the End of the Middle Ages. Heinz Heimsoeth. Tr. & Intro. by Ramon J. Betanzos. LC 93-33894. 272p. 1994. text ed. 39.95 (0-8143-2477-0); pap. text ed. 19.95 (0-8143-2478-9) Wayne St U Pr.

Six Greek Sculptors. Ernest A. Gardner. LC 67-26744. (Essay Index Reprint Ser.). 1977. 22.95 (0-8369-0468-0) Ayer.

Six Group Therapies. Ed. by S. Long. LC 87-7187. 358p. 1987. 70.00 (0-306-42642-0, Plenum Pr) Plenum.

Six-Gun Bride of the Teton Bunch, & Seven Other Action-Packed Stories of the Wild West. Les Savage, Jr. Ed. by Martin H. Greenberg & Bill Pronzini. LC 94-45787. 220p. 1995. pap. 12.00 (1-56980-035-9) Barricade Bks.

Six-Gun Justice. Kit Dalton. (Buckskin Ser.). 368p. (Orig.). 1996. mass mkt. 5.99 (0-8439-3960-5) Dorchester Pub Co.

Six-Gun Ladies: Tales of the Range. Talmage Powell. LC 96-2825. 1996. pap. text ed. 9.95 (1-57090-029-9) Alexander Bks.

Six Gun Mystique. 2nd ed. John G. Cawelti. LC 84-72052. 155p. 1984. 18.95 (0-87972-313-0); pap. 9.95 (0-87972-314-9) Bowling Green Univ Popular Press.

Six-Gun Shootout. Kit Dalton. (Buckskin Giant Ser.). 368p. (Orig.). 1993. mass mkt., pap. text ed. 4.50 (0-8439-3383-6) Dorchester Pub Co.

Six Gun Wedding: Larry & Stretch. large type ed. Marshall Grover. (Linford Western Library). 288p. 1994. pap. 15.99 (0-7089-7502-X, Linford) Ulverscroft.

Six Guns. David Chorlton et al. Ed. by Angi Lowery & Charlie Mehrhoff. 54p. 1990. pap. text ed. 5.00 (0-9626890-0-9) Dark West Pub.

***Six Haunted Hairdos.** Gregory Maguire. 1997. 15.00 (0-395-78626-6, Clarion Bks) HM.

***Six Haunted Hairdos.** Gregory Maguire. LC 97-237. (J). 1997. 19.00 (0-395-74654-X, Clarion Bks) HM.

***Six Heritage Tours of the Lower East Side: A Walking Guide.** Ruth Limmer. LC 97-2074. (Illus.). 176p. 1997. pap. 12.95 (0-8147-5130-X) NYU Pr.

Six Hidden Picture Postcards. Anna Pomaska. (Illus.). (J). (gr. k-3). 1994. pap. 1.00 (0-486-27926-X) Dover.

Six Hidden Views of Japanese Music. William P. Malm. (Ernest Bloch Lectures: No. 6). 1986. 47.50 (0-520-05045-2) U CA Pr.

6 HO Railroads You Can Build. Model Railroader Magazine Staff. LC 93-28560. (Model Railroad Handbook Ser.: No. 38). (Illus.). 144p. 1993. per. 16.95 (0-89024-189-9, 12131) Kalmbach.

***Six Honest Serving Men.** Paul Muldoon. 50p. 1995. 22.95 (1-85235-169-1); pap. 12.95 (1-85235-168-3) Dufour.

Six-Horse Hitch. Janice H. Giles. 1976. 29.95 (0-8488-1011-2) Amereon Ltd.

Six Horses. William Banning. 1992. reprint ed. lib. bdg. 75.00 (0-7812-5006-4) Rprt Serv.

Six-Hour Mystery. Beverley Lewis. LC 93-35020. (Illus.). 64p. (J). (gr. 4 up). 1993. pap. 3.99 (0-8066-2666-6, 9-2666) Augsburg Fortress.

Six Hour Quilt: A Reversible Quilt. Kaye Wood. (Illus.). 12p. (Orig.). 1994. pap. 5.95 (0-944588-28-X, KWB20) K Wood.

Six Hours One Friday. Max Lucado. 240p. 1995. pap. 12.99 (0-88070-827-1, Multnomah Bks) Multnomah Pubs.

Six Hours One Friday. Max Lucado. 240p. 1995. 18.99 (0-88070-793-3, Multnomah Bks) Multnomah Pubs.

Six Hours One Friday. Max Lucado. 1989. audio 12.99 (0-88070-849-2, Multnomah Bks) Multnomah Pubs.

Six Hours One Friday: Anchoring to the Power of the Cross. large type ed. Max Lucado. 280p. 1996. pap. 13.95 (0-8027-2696-8) Walker & Co.

***600 Best Selling Home Plans.** Garlinghouse Company Staff. (Illus.). 448p. 1997. pap. text ed. 8.95 (0-938708-74-0) L F Garlinghouse Co.

611 Ways to Boost Your Self Esteem. Bryan E. Robinson & Jamie McCullers. 160p. (Orig.). 1994. pap. 8.95 (1-55874-297-2, 2972) Health Comm.

Six Hundred Endings. Lajos Portisch & Balazs Sarkozy. Tr. by Sandor Eszenyi et al. (Chess Ser.). (Illus.). 198p. 1981. 21.90 (0-08-024137-9, Pergamon Pr) Elsevier.

Six Hundred Low-Cost Electronic Circuits. David M. Gauthier. (Illus.). 350p. (Orig.). 1989. 27.95 (0-8306-9219-3); pap. 18.95 (0-8306-3219-0) McGraw-Hill Prof.

Six Hundred Low Cost Electronic Circuits. David M. Gauthier. 1989. text ed. 27.95 (0-07-156923-5) McGraw.

600 Manipulatives. 1991. pap. 19.95 (0-590-49132-6) Scholastic Inc.

Six Hundred MCQs in Anaesthesia: Basic Sciences. 2nd ed. Neville W. Goodman & Chris Johnson. LC 93-12699. 264p. 1993. pap. text ed. 29.00 (0-443-04831-2) Churchill.

Six Hundred MCQS in Anaesthesia: Clinical Practice. P. J. Simpson & N. W. Goodman. LC 86-14728. 256p. (Orig.). 1987. pap. text ed. 29.95 (0-443-03155-X) Churchill.

600 MCQs in Anaesthesia: Clinical Practice. 2nd ed. Neville W. Goodman & Chris Johnson. LC 95-20318. 1995. write for info. (0-443-04835-5) Churchill.

Six Hundred Mile Stretch. Jim Miller. Ed. by Doug Grad. (Ex-Rangers Ser.: No. 6). 224p. (Orig.). 1992. pap. 3.50 (0-671-74824-6) PB.

***600 Mulla Nasreddin Tales: 600 Dast An-E Mull A Nasreddin.** Mohammad Ramazani. LC 97-2753. (Popular Persian Texts Ser.: Vol. 1). (PER.). 1997. reprint ed. pap. 16.00 (0-936347-09-0) Iran Bks.

Six Hundred Ninety-Six Silly School Jokes & Riddles. Joseph Rosenbloom. (Illus.). 128p. (J). (gr. 2 up). 1986. pap. 4.95 (0-8069-6392-1) Sterling.

***601 Ways to Be a Good Parent: A Practical Handbook for Raising Children Ages 4-12.** Michele Elliott. 1997. pap. text ed. 14.95 (0-8065-1931-2, Citadel Pr) Carol Pub Group.

***601 Words You Need to Know to Pass Your Exam.** 3rd ed. Murray Bromberg & Julius Liebb. LC 96-28700. 1997. pap. 9.95 (0-8120-9645-2) Barron.

***600 Scout Knives.** Joseph R. Kerr. (Illus.). 180p. (Orig.). 1997. pap. 10.00 (1-57502-512-4, P01519) Morris Pubng.

Six Hundred Sixty-Six: Pictoral Format. Salem Kirban. 1980. pap. 4.95 (0-912582-33-2) Kirban.

666: The United States of Europe & the New World Order. 7.00 incl. audio (1-884137-82-2) J Van Impe.

666 & 1000. Salem Kirban. LC 71-109942. (Prophecy Studies). (Illus.). 480p. 1970. pap. 8.99 (0-912582-05-7) AMG Pubs.

613th Commandment: An Analysis of the Mitzvah to Write a Sefer Torah. J. Simcha Cohen. LC 94-9226. 172p. 1996. pap. 19.95 (1-56821-249-6) Aronson.

Six Hundred Thirty-Seven Best Things Anybody Ever Said. Robert Byrne. 1983. mass mkt. 5.99 (0-449-20375-1, Crest) Fawcett.

633 Squadron: Operation Cobra. large type ed. Frederick E. Smith. 448p. 1995. 25.99 (0-7089-3421-8) Ulverscroft.

633 Squadron: Operation Crucible. large type ed. Frederick E. Smith. 1995. 25.99 (0-7089-3353-X) Ulverscroft.

***633 Squadron: Operation Titan.** large type ed. Frederick E. Smith. 432p. 1996. 25.99 (0-7089-3620-2) Ulverscroft.

633 Squadron: Operation Valkyrie. large type ed. Frederick E. Smith. (General Ser.). 1993. 21.95 (0-7089-2815-3) Ulverscroft.

Six Ingredients or Less Chicken Cookbook. Carlean Johnson. (Six Ingredients or Less Ser.). (Illus.). 224p. (Orig.). 1989. pap. 12.95 (0-942878-02-7) C J Bks.

Six Images of Human Nature. Norman Chaney. 175p. (C). 1994. pap. text ed. 12.50 (1-57074-232-4) Greyden Pr.

Six Imaginary Letters of Young Caesar, 81 BC. Paul Mariah. 1988. 1.50 (0-318-41328-0) Man-Root.

6 Imperatives of Marketing: Lessons from the World's Best Companies. Allan J. Magrath. 208p. 1992. 22.95 (0-8144-5042-3) AMACOM.

Six in a Bath. Pam Adams. (Soap Opera Ser.). (J). (gr. 4 up). 1990. 6.99 (0-85953-443-X) Childs Play.

***Six in the Bed: Dealing with Parents, In-Laws & Their Impact on Your Marriage.** Nancy W. Cocola. LC 96-53676. 224p. 1997. pap. 12.00 (0-399-52343-X, Perigee Bks) Berkley Pub.

Six in the Easy Chair. Ed. by John Fischer. LC 73-76273. 279p. reprint ed. pap. 79.60 (0-317-29089-4, 2020227) Bks Demand.

Six Ingredients or Less Cookbook. rev. ed. Carlean Johnson. (Illus.). 224p. 1989. pap. 12.95 (0-942878-01-9) C J Bks.

Six Ingredients or Less Cooking Light & Healthy Cookbook. Carlean Johnson. (Illus.). 224p. (Orig.). 1992. pap. 12.95 (0-942878-03-5) C J Bks.

Six Ingredients or Less Pasta. C. Johnson. 1996. pap. text ed. 14.95 (0-942878-04-3) C J Bks.

Six Iron Spiders. Phoebe A. Taylor. (Asey Mayo Cape Cod Mystery Ser.). 288p. pap. 6.95 (0-88150-230-8) Countryman.

Six Islands on Two Wheels: A Cycling Guide to Hawaii. Tom Koch. LC 89-82129. (Illus.). 224p. (Orig.). 1990. pap. 11.95 (0-935848-79-7) Bess Pr.

Six Journeys: A Canadian Pattern. Charles Taylor. 254p. 1977. 11.95 (0-88784-057-4, Pub. by Hse of Anansi Pr CN) Genl Dist Srvs.

Six Keyboard Sonatas. Baldassare Galuppi. Ed. by Mary L. Serafine. 62p. 1980. pap. 10.95 (0-8258-0059-5, 05052) Fischer Inc NY.

Six Keyboard Sonatas from the Classical Era Score. William S. Newman. 67p. reprint ed. pap. 25.00 (0-317-09725-3, 2004336) Bks Demand.

Six Keys to a Happy Marriage. Tim LaHaye. 54p. 1978. mass mkt. 3.99 (0-8423-5895-1) Tyndale.

Six Keys to Recruiting, Orienting & Involving Nonprofit Board Members: A Guide to Building Your Board, No. 42. Judith G. Nelson. 64p. (Orig.). (C). 1992. reprint ed. pap. text ed. 26.00 (0-925299-11-1) Natl Ctr Nonprofit.

Six Kings of the American Pulpit. Clarence E. Macartney. LC 75-152192. (Essay Index Reprint Ser.). 1977. reprint ed. 18.95 (0-8369-2323-5) Ayer.

***Six Ladders of Learning: 1867: About How Things Are Made, Country, City & Rural.** Marcus London. 250p. 1996. reprint ed. pap. 25.00 (0-87556-835-1) Saifer.

Six Laws of Business Success: The Parable of American Entrepreneurship. J. W. Dicks. LC 95-16189. 1995. write for info. (1-881209-01-6) Crown Oak Pub.

Six Lectures Concerning Cryptography & Cryptanalysis. William F. Friedman. (Illus.). 282p. 1994. pap. 34.80 (0-89412-246-0) Aegean Park Pr.

Six Lectures Delivered at the International Congress of Mathematicians in Stockholm, 1962. E. B. Dynkin et al. LC 51-5559. (Translations Ser.: Series 2, Vol. 31). 84p. 1963. 23.00 (0-8218-1731-0, TRANS2/31) Am Math.

Six Lectures on Architecture. Ralph A. Cram et al. LC 68-57314. (Essay Index Reprint Ser.). 1977. 18.95 (0-8369-0348-X) Ayer.

***Six Lectures on Dynamical Systems.** 324p. 1996. 38.00 (981-02-2548-2) World Scientific Pub.

Six Lectures on Modern Natural Philosophy. Clifford A. Truesdell. (Illus.). 1966. 34.00 (0-387-03684-9) Spr-Verlag.

Six Lectures on Political Economy. William Whewell. LC 66-21701. (Reprints of Economic Classics Ser.). xii, 102p. 1967. reprint ed. 35.00 (0-678-00225-8) Kelley.

***Six Lectures on the Ante-Nicene Fathers.** Fenton J. Hort. Date not set. 138.00 (0-8369-2596-3) Ayer.

Six-Legged Science: Insects in the Classroom. Gary A. Dunn. (YES Special Publication Ser.). 51p. 1991. pap. text ed. 5.95 (1-884256-06-6) Yng Entomol.

Six Lessons in Crystal Gazing. Thessalonia DePrince. 122p. 1986. pap. 4.95 (0-935611-04-5) United Spirit.

Six Lessons in Crystal Gazing. Anna Riva. 32p. (Orig.). 1993. pap. text ed. 2.95 (0-943832-18-7) Intl Imports.

Six LF 21: A Paleo-Indian Site in Western Ct. Roger W. Moeller. LC 80-65186. (Occasional Papers: No. 2). (Illus.). 160p. 1980. pap. 12.50 (0-89488-010-1) Inst Amer Indian.

***Six Lies the Devil Uses to Destroy Marriages.** John Osteen. Date not set. mass mkt. 2.25 (0-912631-98-8) J O Pubns.

Six Life Studies of Famous Women. Matilda B. Edwards. LC 73-39701. (Essay Index Reprint Ser.). 1977. reprint ed. 23.95 (0-8369-2746-X) Ayer.

Six Lighted Windows: Memoirs of Swamis in the West. Swami Vogeshananda. Ed. by Peter Schneider. 300p. 1996. pap. 14.95 (0-87481-410-3) Vedanta Ctr.

Six Literary Lives: The Shared Impiety of Adams, London, Sinclair, Williams, Dos Passos, & Tate. Reed Whittemore. 248p. 1992. text ed. 34.95 (0-8262-0874-6) U of Mo Pr.

Six Little Cooks: or Aunt Jane's Cooking Class. Elizabeth S. Kirkland. LC 72-9796. (Cookery Americana Ser.). 1973. reprint ed. pap. 13.95 (0-405-05049-6) Ayer.

Six Little Ducks Big Book. Illus. by Bryce Kimberling. (J). (ps-2). 1994. pap. text ed. 14.00 (0-922053-34-0) N Edge Res.

Six Lives-Six Deaths. Robert J. Lifton. LC 78-11926. 1979. 17.00 (0-300-02266-2) Yale U Pr.

Six Love Poems. R. C. Kennedy. 15p. 1977. pap. 3.00 (0-940066-05-X) Dalmas & Ricour.

Six Loves. Mark Dunster. (Rin Ser.: Pt. 5). 1978. pap. 4.00 (0-89642-046-9) Linden Pubs.

Six Madrigals to Four Voices, 1597 see Old English Edition

Six Madrigals to Six Voices, 1597 see Old English Edition

Six Major Prophets. Edwin E. Slosson. LC 71-167421. (Essay Index Reprint Ser.). 1977. reprint ed. 25.95 (0-8369-2571-8) Ayer.

S

An Asterisk (*) at the beginning of an entry indicates that the title is appearing in BIP for the first time.

Six Makers of English Religion, Fifteen Hundred to Seventeen Hundred. Ernest G. Rupp. (Essay Index Reprint Ser.). 1977. reprint ed. 19.95 (*0-518-10159-2*) Ayer.

Six Masters of the Spanish Sonnet: Francisco de Quevedo, Sor Juana Ines de la Cruz, Antonia Machado, Federico Garcia Lorca, Jorge Luis Borges, Miguel Hernandez. Ed. & Tr. by Willis Barnstone. (Illus.). 272p. (C). 1992. 24.95 (*0-8093-1772-9*) S Ill U Pr.

***Six Masters of the Spanish Sonnet: Francisco De Quevedo, Sor Juana Ines de la Cruz, Antonia Machado, Federico Garcia Lorca, Jorge Luis Borges, Miguel Hernandez.** Tr. by Willis Barnstone from SPA. LC 92-12099. (Illus.). 272p. 1997. pap. 19.95 (*0-8093-2127-0*) S Ill U Pr.

***Six Measures of JSL Pragmatics.** Sayoko O. Yamashita. (Technical Reports: No. 14). 240p. 1997. pap. text ed. 15.00 (*0-8248-1914-4*) Sec Lang Tching.

Six Membered Heterocyclic Compounds with a Single Atom in the Rind, Pyridine, Polymethyl-Epyridines, Quinoline, Isoquinoline & Their Derivatives see Rodd's Chemistry of Carbon Compounds, Vol. 4, Pts. B & F

***Six-Membered Monoheterocyclic Compounds with a Hetero-Atom from Groups IV, VI, or VII of the Periodic Table.** R. Livingstone. 682p. 453.25 (*0-444-82753-6*) Elsevier.

S

Six-Membered Tellurium-Containing Heterocycles, Vol. 4. I. D. Sadekov et al. 52p. 1985. pap. text ed. 56.00 (*3-7186-0284-9*) Gordon & Breach.

Six Memos for the Next Millennium. Italo Calvino. Tr. by Patrick Creagh. LC 87-26025. (Charles Eliot Norton Lectures). (Illus.). 144p. 1988. text ed. 16.00 (*0-674-81040-6*) HUP.

Six Memos for the Next Millennium. Italo Calvino. LC 92-50641. 1993. pap. 10.00 (*0-679-74237-9*, Vin) Random.

Six Men. E. Radford & M. A. Radford. 184p. 1995. 18.50 (*0-7451-8657-2*, Black Dagger) Chivers N Amer.

Six Men: Charlie Chaplin, Edward VIII, H. L. Mencken, Humphrey Bogart, Adlai Stevenson, Bertrand Russell. Alistair Cooke. LC 95-10944. (Illus.). 208p. 1995. pap. 11.95 (*1-55970-317-2*) Arcade Pub Inc.

Six Men: Charlie Chaplin, Edward VIII, H.L. Mencken, Humphrey Bogart, Adlai Stevenson, Bertrand Russel. Alistair Cooke. LC 95-10944. (Illus.). 208p. 1995. 21.95 (*1-55970-324-5*) Arcade Pub Inc.

Six Men of Yale. Francis Parsons. LC 72-156702. (Essay Index Reprint Ser.). 1977. reprint ed. 20.95 (*0-8369-2329-4*) Ayer.

Six Messiahs. Mark Frost. 432p. 1996. mass mkt. 6.99 (*0-380-72229-1*) Avon.

Six Messiahs. Mark Frost. 1995. pap. 24.95 (*0-7871-0399-3*, Dove Bks) Dove Audio.

Six MicMac Stories. Illus. by Harold McGee. 51p. 1992. pap. 5.95 (*0-919680-35-6*, Pub. by Nimbus Publishing Ltd CN) Chelsea Green Pub.

Six Middle English Romances: The Sege of Melayne, Emare, Octavian, Sir Isumbras, Sir Gowther, Sir Amadace. Ed. by Maldwyn Mills. 256p. 1993. pap. 9.95 (*0-460-87225-7*, Everyman's Classic Lib) C E Tuttle.

Six Miles at Sea: A Pictorial History of Long Beach Island. John B. Lloyd. Ed. by Margaret T. Buchholz. (Illus.). 176p. (Orig.). 1990. 35.00 (*0-945582-03-X*) Down the Shore Pub.

Six Miles Out. Barbara Smith. 104p. 1981. pap. 3.50 (*0-941092-06-2*) Mtn St Pr.

Six Million Dollar Man's Trading Advice: The Secrets of Successfully Trading Futures & Stocks. Michel M. Arimoto. (Illus.). 140p. (Orig.). (C). 1993. pap. 39.12 (*0-317-05741-3*) Clermont NY.

Six Million Lost & Found. Richard Harwood. (Illus.). 28p. 1978. pap. 4.00 (*0-911038-61-2*) Legion Survival.

Six Minnesinger Songs. W. D. Snodgrass. (Burning Deck Poetry Ser.). (Illus.). 40p. (Orig.). 1983. pap. 5.00 (*0-930901-05-3*) Burning Deck.

Six-Minute Fraternity: The Rise & Fall of NCAA Tournament Boxing, 1932-60. E. C. Wallenfeldt. LC 94-8563. 432p. 1994. text ed. 59.95 (*0-275-94867-6*, Praeger Pubs) Greenwood.

Six-Minute Science Experiments. Faith H. Brynie. LC 95-24478. (Illus.). 80p. (J). 1996. 17.95 (*0-8069-0624-3*) Sterling.

***Six-Minute Science Experiments.** Faith H. Brynie. (Illus.). 80p. (J). 1997. pap. 9.95 (*0-8069-0623-5*) Sterling.

***Six-Minute Science Experiments Book & Kit.** Faith H. Brynie. (Illus.). 80p. 1997. pap. 19.95 (*0-8069-9588-2*) Sterling.

Six Minutes a Day to Perfect Spelling. Harry Shefter. 1989. mass mkt. 4.99 (*0-671-68896-0*) PB.

Six Missions of Texas. Lon Tinkle et al. (Illus.). 194p. 1965. 20.00 (*0-87244-002-8*) Texian.

Six Modern American Plays. Incl. Emperor Jones. Eugene O'Neill. LC 51-8900. (Orig.). (*0-318-54377-X*); Winterset: Acting Edition. Maxwell Anderson. 1966. (*0-318-54378-8*); Man Who Came to Dinner. George S. Kaufman & Moss Hart. LC 51-8900. (*0-318-54379-6*); Little Foxes. Lillian Hellman. LC 51-8900. 1966. (*0-318-54380-X*); Glass Menagerie. Tennessee Williams. LC 51-8900. (*0-318-54381-8*); Mister Roberts. Thomas Heggen & Joshua Logan. LC 51-8900. (*0-318-54382-6*); LC 51-8900. (Modern Library College Editions). (C). 1966. pap. text ed. write for info. (*0-07-553660-9*, T85) McGraw.

Six Modern American Plays. Ed. by Allan G. Halline. 1951. 7.95 (*0-685-04241-3*) Random.

Six Modern British Novelists. Ed. by George Stade. LC 74-6141. 336p. 1974. text ed. 60.00 (*0-231-03846-1*) Col U Pr.

Six Modern British Novelists. Ed. by George Stade. LC 74-6141. 336p. 1980. pap. text ed. 19.50 (*0-231-08374-2*) Col U Pr.

Six Months after the U. N. Verdict: An Update on Impunity in the Mexican Federal Judicial Police. Alicia Ely-Yamin. (North America Project Special Report Ser.). 20p. 1993. pap. 5.00 (*0-911646-56-6*) World Policy.

Six Months among Indians. 5th ed. Darius B. Cook. (Illus.). 1983. pap. 10.95 (*0-932212-30-1*) Avery Color.

Six Months among Indians. Darius B. Cook. (Illus.). 101p. 1974. reprint ed. 4.50 (*0-915056-03-8*) Hardscrabble Bks.

***Six Months Before Christmas.** David Walker. (Illus.). 28p. (J). (gr. k-2). 1996. 14.95 (*1-880092-35-2*) Bright Bks TX.

***Six Months Before Christmas: A Christmas Story in July.** David R. Walker. 1996. 14.95 (*1-880092-37-9*) Bright Bks TX.

Six Months in a Convent: The Narrative of Rebecca Theresa Reed & Supplement. Rebecca T. Reed. LC 76-46097. (Anti-Movements in America Ser.). 1977. reprint ed. lib. bdg. 39.95 (*0-405-09970-3*) Ayer.

Six Months in Hawaii. Isabella L. Bird. pap. 19.95 (*0-7103-0232-0*, 02320) Routledge Chapman & Hall.

Six Months in Kansas, by a Lady. Hannah A. Ropes. LC 76-38020. (Black Heritage Library Collection). 1977. reprint ed. 23.95 (*0-8369-8987-2*) Ayer.

Six Months in the Federal States. Edward Dicey. 1977. text ed. 29.95 (*0-8369-9221-0*, 9075) Ayer.

Six Months in the Sandwich Islands. Isabella L. Bird. LC 73-77575. (Illus.). 348p. 1973. pap. 9.95 (*0-8048-1112-1*) C E Tuttle.

Six Months Off: An American Family's Australian Adventure. large type ed. Lamar Alexander. (General Ser.). (Illus.). 504p. 1989. lib. bdg. 17.95 (*0-8161-4846-5*, GK Hall) Thorndike Pr.

Six Months Off: An American Family's Australian Adventure. Lamar Alexander. Ed. by Pat Golbitz. LC 89-39531. 320p. 1995. reprint ed. pap. 15.00 (*0-688-09510-0*, Quill) Morrow.

Six Months Off: How to Plan, Negotiate, & Take the Break You Need Without Burning Bridges or Going Broke. Hope Dlugozima et al. LC 95-37728. 1996. pap. 12.95 (*0-8050-3745-4*, Owl) H Holt & Co.

Six Months on the Plains: A Guide to Cheyenne & Rocky Mountains. E. B. Tuttle. Date not set. pap. write for info. (*0-87770-584-4*) Ye Galleon.

Six Months Rent. Anne F. Walker. 1991. pap. 10.95 (*0-88753-220-9*, Pub. by Black Moss Pr CN) Firefly Bks Ltd.

Six Months to Live. Lurlene McDaniel. 144p. (J). (gr. 5-8). 1985. pap. 2.99 (*0-87406-007-9*) Willowisp Pr.

Six Months to Live. Lurlene McDaniel. 144p. (YA). (gr. 7 up). 1995. mass mkt. 3.99 (*0-553-56760-8*, Starfire BDD) BDD Bks Young Read.

Six Months to Oblivion: The Defeat of the Luftwaffe over the Western Front 1944-1945. rev. ed. Werner Girbig. Tr. by David Johnston & Richard Simpkin from GER. LC 91-67054. (Illus.). 280p. 1992. 29.95 (*0-88740-348-4*) Schiffer.

Six Months Tour Through the North of England: Containing an Account of the Present State of Agriculture, Manufactures & Population in Several Counties of This Kingdom, 4 Vols, Set. 2nd ed. Arthur Young. LC 67-29461. (Reprints of Economic Classics Ser.). 1967. reprint ed. 250.00 (*0-678-00332-7*) Kelley.

Six-Moon Trail: Canada to Mexico along the Pacific Crest. Tom Marshburn. Ed. by Robert K. Leishman. LC 85-50297. (Illus.). 224p. 1985. 15.95 (*0-9614526-0-9*) R Leishman.

Six Moral Tales from Jules Laforgue. Jules Laforgue. Ed. by Frances Newman. LC 77-10275. 296p. reprint ed. 49.50 (*0-404-16327-0*) AMS Pr.

Six More English Towns. Alec Clifton-Taylor. (Illus.). 207p. (Orig.). 1987. pap. 14.95 (*0-563-20439-7*, Pub. by BBC UK) Parkwest Pubns.

Six Mystical Points. Jacob Boehme. 1989. pap. 4.95 (*1-55818-113-X*) Holmes Pub.

Six Myths of Our Time. Marina Warner. 1995. pap. 10.00 (*0-679-75924-7*, Vin) Random.

Six Nations of New York: Cayugas, Mohawks (St. Regis), Oneidas, Onondagas, Senecas, Tuscaroras, the 1892 United States Extra Census Bulletin. Robert W. Venables. (Documents in American Social History Ser.). (Illus.). 1996. pap. 15.95 (*0-8014-8317-4*) Cornell U Pr.

Six Nations of New York: Extra Census Bulletin. Indians. Thomas Donaldson. (Illus.). (C). reprint ed. pap. text ed. 22.00 (*0-916141-01-2*) NY Hist Soc.

Six Nations of New York: The 1892 United States Extra Census Bulletin. Robert W. Venables. (Documents in American Social History Ser.). (Illus.). 148p. 1996. 50.00 (*0-8014-3226-X*) Cornell U Pr.

***Six Nations Series.** Carol Correlius. (Illus.). 40p. (Orig.). Date not set. teacher ed., pap. 15.00 (*0-614-29684-6*) Akwe Kon Pr.

***Six Nations Series.** Carol Correlius. (Illus.). 38p. (Orig.). Date not set. student ed., pap. 4.00 (*0-614-29685-4*) Akwe Kon Pr.

Six... Nc6 in the Saemisch Variation, King's Indian Defense. John L. Watson. (Illus.). 109p. (Orig.). 1982. pap. 6.00 (*0-931462-18-5*) Chess Ent.

Six New Gospels: New Testament Women Tell Their Stories. Margaret Hebblethwaite. LC 93-51006. 154p. 1994. pap. 10.95 (*1-56101-087-1*) Cowley Pubns.

Six Nights with the Wasingtonians. Timothy S. Arthur. (Works of Timothy Shay Arthur). 1989. reprint ed. lib. bdg. 79.00 (*0-685-27473-X*) Rprt Serv.

Six Non-Lectures. e. e. Cummings. LC 53-10472. (Charles Eliot Norton Lectures: 1952-1953). 118p. 1953. pap. text ed. 8.95 (*0-674-44010-2*) HUP.

***Six Not So Easy Pieces: Lectures on Synnetry Relativity & Space Time.** Richard P. Feynmar. Ed. by Jeffrey Robbins. 87p. (C). 1997. 49.95 incl. cd-rom (*0-201-15026-3*) Addison-Wesley.

***Six Not So Easy Pieces: Lectures on Synnetry Relativity & Space Time.** Richard P. Feynmar. Ed. by Jeffrey Robbins. LC 96-47811. 87p. (C). 1997. 25.00 (*0-201-15025-5*) Addison-Wesley.

Six Novelists: Stendhal, Dostoevski, Tolstoy, Hardy, Dreiser & Proust. Ed. by Carnegie Institute of Technology, Department of English Staff. LC 72-1311. (Essay Index Reprint Ser.). 1977. reprint ed. 18.95 (*0-8369-2837-7*) Ayer.

Six Novelists Look at Society. John Atkins. 288p. (Orig.). 1983. pap. 11.95 (*0-7145-3863-9*) Riverrun NY.

Six O'Clock Man. John C. Armor. 272p. (Orig.). 1988. pap. 12.95 (*0-87651-995-8*) Southern U Pr.

Six O'Clock President: A Theory of Presidential Press Relations in the Age of Television. Fredric T. Smoller. LC 90-31180. 176p. 1990. text ed. 49.95 (*0-275-93598-1*, C3598, Praeger Pubs) Greenwood.

Six of Cups: A Circle of Stories. Erika B. Makino. LC 92-70849. (Illus.). 160p. (Orig.). 1992. pap. 8.50 (*0-929151-05-4*) Earth Bks.

Six of One. Rita Mae Brown. 368p. 1983. mass mkt. 6.50 (*0-553-27887-8*, Bantam Classics) Bantam.

Six Old English Chronicles. Ed. by J. A. Giles. LC 68-57866. (Bohn's Antiquarian Library). reprint ed. 59.00 (*0-404-50010-2*) AMS Pr.

Six Old Icelandic Sagas. Tr. by W. Bryant Bachman, Jr. & Gudmundur Erlingsson from ICE. 134p. (Orig.). (C). 1993. pap. text ed. 26.50 (*0-8191-9157-4*); lib. bdg. 49.50 (*0-8191-9156-6*) U Pr of Amer.

Six Old Time St. Patrick's Day Postcards. 1.00 (*0-486-26504-8*) Dover.

Six One-Day Walks in the Pecos Wilderness. rev. ed. Carl Overhage. LC 80-20061. 60p. 1984. pap. 4.95 (*0-86534-044-7*) Sunstone Pr.

Six Ottawa Poets: An Anthology. 96p. 1995. lib. bdg. 35.00 (*0-8095-4582-9*) Borgo Pr.

Six Out Seven. Jess Mowry. LC 93-15676. 1993. 22.00 (*0-374-22083-2*) FS&G.

Six out Seven. Jess Mowry. LC 94-20252. 512p. 1994. pap. 13.95 (*0-385-47534-9*, Anchor NY) Doubleday.

***Six Pack: Plays for Scotland.** John McGrath. 1996. pap. 26.00 (*0-7486-6201-4*, Pub. by Polygon UK) Subterranean Co.

Six Painters: Mondrian, DeKooning, Guston, Kline, Pollock, Rothko. Thomas B. Hess & Morton Feldman. LC 67-30452. (Illus.). 1968. pap. 7.95 (*0-914412-22-1*) Inst for the Arts.

Six Papers in Analysis. B. M. Levitan et al. LC 73-15614. (Translations Ser.: Series 2, Vol. 101). 250p. 1973. 59.00 (*0-8218-3051-1*, TRANS2/101) Am Math.

Six Papers on Partial Differential Equations. A. I. Koselev et al. LC 51-5559. (Translations Ser. 2: Vol. 20). 364p. 1962. 42.00 (*0-8218-1720-5*, TRANS2/20) Am Math.

Six Papers on the Size Distribution of Wealth & Income. Ed. by Lee Soltow. (Studies in Income & Wealth: No. 33). 281p. 1969. 73.90 (*0-87014-488-X*) Natl Bur Econ Res.

Six Perfectly Different Pigs. Adrienne Geoghegan. (Illus.). 32p. (J). (gr. k up). 1994. lib. bdg. 18.60 (*0-8368-1148-8*) Gareth Stevens Inc.

Six Personnages en Quete d'Auteur, la Volupte de l'Honneur. Luigi Pirandello. (FRE.). 1978. pap. 10.95 (*0-7859-4105-3*) Fr & Eur.

Six Perspectives on New Religions: A Case Study Approach. Anson D. Shupe, Jr. LC 81-9464. (Studies in Religion & Society: Vol. 1). 246p. (C). 1981. 89.95 (*0-88946-983-0*) E Mellen.

Six Perspectives on Theory for the Practice of Occupational Therapy see Perspectives on Theory for the Practice of Occupational Therapy

Six Philosophical Songs. William Dickey. 16p. 1983. 10.00 (*0-931757-13-4*) Pterodactyl Pr.

Six Pillars of Self-Esteem. Nathaniel Branden. 368p. 1995. pap. 13.95 (*0-553-37439-7*) Bantam.

Six Plays. Eugene O'Neill. 1976. 24.95 (*0-8488-0600-X*) Amereon Ltd.

Six Plays by Ken Dashow see Da-Show Must Go On: Six Short Plays

Six Plays by Lillian Hellman: The Children's Hour, Days to Come, the Little Foxes, Watch on the Rhine, Another Part of the Forest, the Autumn Garden. Lillian Hellman. LC 79-2160. 464p. 1979. pap. 15.00 (*0-394-74112-9*, Vin) Random.

Six Plays by Mavor Moore. Moore. (NFS Canada Ser.). 1993. pap. 13.95 (*0-88922-271-1*) Genl Dist Srvs.

Six Plays for Young People from the Federal Theatre Project (1936-1939) An Introductory Analysis & Six Representative Plays. Ed. by Lowell Swortzell. LC 85-21974. (Documentary Reference Collections). (Illus.). 258p. 1986. text ed. 42.95 (*0-313-24780-3*, SYO/) Greenwood.

Six Plays of the Yiddish Theatre. Ed. by Isaac Goldberg. 1977. lib. bdg. 59.95 (*0-8490-2611-3*) Gordon Pr.

***Six Plus Two Essays on Design & New Media.** 2nd rev. ed. Jessica Helfand. Orig. Title: Six Essays on Designn & New Media. 100p. 1997. pap. 12.00 (*1-884381-13-8*) W Drenttel NY.

Six Poets. Charles Bukowski et al. 1979. 5.00 (*0-912824-21-2*) Vagabond Pr.

Six Point Six Images of the Los Angeles Earthquake. James Hillman. 1994. pap. 12.95 (*1-883792-03-7*) LA Times.

Six Point Two Diesel Engine Explained. Daniel Ash. (Orig.). 1985. student ed. write for info. (*0-8064-0201-6*, 476); audio, vhs 239.00 (*0-8064-0202-4*) Bergwall.

Six-Pointed Star. O. J. Graham. LC 84-60276. 1995. pap. text ed. 4.00 (*0-932050-24-7*) New Puritan.

Six Political Discourses. Hugh H. Brackenridge. (Works of Hugh Henry Brackenridge). 1989. reprint ed. lib. bdg. 79.00 (*0-7812-2046-7*) Rprt Serv.

Six Portraits. John M. Bennett. 1975. pap. 2.00 (*0-935350-90-X*) Luna Bisonte.

Six Portraits. Isabel C. Clarke. LC 67-26725. (Essay Index Reprint Ser.). 1977. 23.95 (*0-8369-0309-9*) Ayer.

Six Possible Meanings of "Overvaluation" The 1981-85 Dollar. Jeffrey A. Frankel. LC 85-23827. (Essays in International Finance Ser.: No. 159). 46p. 1985. pap. 8.00 (*0-88165-066-8*) Princeton U Int Finan Econ.

Six Practical Lessons for an Easier Childbirth. 3rd rev. ed. Elisabeth D. Bing. LC 93-26507. (Illus.). 176p. 1994. pap. 10.95 (*0-553-37369-2*) Bantam.

Six Preludes & Fugues, Opus 61. D. Kabalevsky. 28p. 1985. pap. 8.95 (*0-7935-2731-7*, 00123066) H Leonard.

Six Presents of God. Gary Houston. (Orig.). 1988. pap. 4.75 (*1-55673-072-1*, 8869) CSS OH.

Six Principal Ragas: With a Brief View of Hindu Music. Sourindro M. Tagore. (C). reprint ed. 10.00 (*0-685-39097-7*, Pub. by Low Price II) S Asia.

Six Psychological Studies. Jean Piaget. Ed. by David Elkind. Tr. by Anita Tenzer. (Orig.). 1968. pap. 10.00 (*0-394-70462-2*, Vin) Random.

Six Puppy Feet: Bridge for Kids. Carole Marsh. (Quantum Leap Ser.). (Illus.). (J). (gr. k-12). 1994. 29.95 (*1-55609-157-5*); pap. 19.95 (*0-935326-13-8*) Gallopade Pub Group.

***Six Questions: Acting Techniques for Dance Performance.** Daniel Nagrin. LC 96-51277. (Illus.). 300p. 1997. 45.00 (*0-8229-3974-6*); pap. 19.95 (*0-8229-5624-1*) U of Pittsburgh Pr.

Six Quintets see Music of the Moravians in America from the Archives of the Moravian Church at Bethlehem Pa.

Six Racy Madams of Colorado. Caroline Bancroft. (Illus.). 64p. 1965. pap. 3.95 (*0-933472-22-6*) Johnson Bks.

Six Radical Thinkers: Bentham, J.S. Mill, Codden, Carlyle, Massine, T.H. Green. John MacCunn. Ed. by J. P. Mayer. LC 78-67370. (European Political Thought Ser.). 1979. reprint ed. lib. bdg. 21.95 (*0-405-11720-5*) Ayer.

Six Records of a Floating Life. Shen Fu. Ed. by Chiang Su-Hui. Tr. by Leonard Pratt & Chiang Su-Hui. 176p. 1983. pap. 9.95 (*0-14-044429-7*, Penguin Classics) Viking Penguin.

Six Red Months in Russia: An Observer's Account of Russia Before & During the Proletarian Dictatorship. Louise Bryant. LC 70-115578. (Russia Observed, Series I). 1978. reprint ed. 29.95 (*0-405-03006-1*) Ayer.

Six Religions in the Twentieth Century. W. Owen Cole & Peggy Morgan. (Illus.). 320p. (Orig.). 1984. pap. 27.50 (*0-7487-1290-9*, Pub. by Stanley Thornes UK) Trans-Atl Phila.

Six Religions in the Twentieth Century. W. Owen Cole & Peggy Morgan. 320p. (Orig.). (C). 1993. pap. 39.00 (*0-7175-1290-8*, Pub. by Stanley Thornes UK) Trans-Atl Phila.

***Six Renaissance Tragedies.** Gibson. LC 97-9607. 1997. pap. 19.95 (*0-312-17550-7*); text ed. 49.95 (*0-312-17549-3*) St Martin.

Six Reports from the Select Committee on Artizans & Machinery, 23 February - 21 May 1824. Great Britain, Parliament, House of Commons Staff. LC 68-110405. 620p. 1968. reprint ed. lib. bdg. 95.00 (*0-678-05229-8*) Kelley.

Six Restoration Plays. Incl. Country Wife. William Wycherley. LC 59-1770. (*0-318-53431-2*); Man of Mode. George Etherege. LC 59-1770. (*0-318-53432-0*); All for Love: The World Well Lost. John Dryden. LC 59-1770. (Orig.). (*0-318-53433-9*); Venice Preserved. Thomas Otway. LC 59-1770. (*0-318-53434-7*); Way of the World. William Congreve. LC 59-1770. 1959. (*0-318-53435-5*); Beaux Stratagem. George Farquhar. LC 59-1770. 1959. (*0-318-53436-3*); LC 59-1770. (YA). (gr. 9-p). 1959. pap. 11.56 (*0-395-05136-3*, RivEd) HM.

Six Roads from Newton: Great Discoveries in Physics. Edward Speyer. 196p. 1994. text ed. 22.95 (*0-471-30503-0*) Wiley.

Six Roads from Newton: Great Discoveries in Physics. Edward Speyer. 1996. pap. text ed. 14.95 (*0-471-15964-6*) Wiley.

Six Roundtable Discussions of Corporate Finance with Joel Stern. Ed. by Donald H. Chew, Jr. LC 86-12382. 345p. 1986. text ed. 55.00 (*0-89930-162-2*, SFV/, Quorum Bks) Greenwood.

Six Rural Problem Areas: Relief-Resources-Rehabilitation. P. G. Beck & M. C. Forster. LC 71-165679. (Research Monographs: Vol. 1). 1971. reprint ed. lib. bdg. 22.50 (*0-306-70333-5*) Da Capo.

***Six Sandy Sheep.** Judy Enderle & Stephanie Tessler. LC 96-83919. (Illus.). 24p. (J). (ps-1). 1997. 14.95 (*1-56397-582-3*) Boyds Mills Pr.

Six Satirists. Carnegie Institute of Technology, Department of English Staff. LC 72-1315. (Essay Index Reprint Ser.). 1977. reprint ed. 15.95 (*0-8369-2838-5*) Ayer.

Six Scandinavian Novelists: Lie, Jacobsen, Heidenstam, Selma Lagerlof, Hamsun, Sigrid Undset. Alrik Gustafson. LC 69-19835. 1968. reprint ed. 30.00 (*0-8196-0230-2*) Biblo.

***Six Screenplays by Robert Riskin: Platinum Bonde, American Madness, It Happened One Night, Mr. Deeds Goes to Town, Lost Horizon, Meet John.** Robert Riskin. Ed. by Pat McGilligan. LC 96-34595. (Illus.). 1997. pap. 35.00 (*0-520-20525-1*) U CA Pr.

***Six Screenplays by Robert Riskin: Platinum Bonde, American Madness, It Happened One Night, Mr. Deeds Goes to Town, Lost Horizon, Meet John.** Robert Riskin. Ed. by Patrick McGilligan. LC 96-34595. (Illus.). 1997. 65.00 (*0-520-20305-4*) U CA Pr.

Six Seconds to True Calm: Thriving Skills for 21st Century Living. Robert S. Siegel. (Illus.). 288p. 1996. 22.95 (*0-9648702-0-7*) Little Sun.

An Asterisk (*) at the beginning of an entry indicates that the title is appearing in BIP for the first time.

***Six Secret Teachings on the Way of Strategy: A Manual from Ancient China.** Tr. by Ralph D. Sawyer. LC 96-32871. 240p. (Orig.). 1997. pap. 12.00 (*1-57062-247-7*) Shambhala Pubns.

***Six Secular Philosophers.** Lewis W. Beck. (Key Texts). 126p. 1997. reprint ed. pap. 15.95 (*1-85506-518-5*) Thoemmes Pr.

Six Servants. Jacob W. Grimm & Wilhelm K. Grimm. Tr. by Anthea Bell. LC 95-45953. (Illus.). 32p. (J). (ps-3). Date not set. 15.95 (*1-55858-475-7*); lib. bdg. 15.88 (*1-55858-476-5*) North-South Bks NYC.

Six Servants. Thompson. (J). 15.00 (*0-671-73958-1*, S&S Bks Young Read) S&S Childrens.

Six Servants. Thomson. (J). Date not set. 15.00 (*0-689-80555-1*) S&S Childrens.

Six Short Pieces-Classic Gtr. John Mills. 4.95 (*0-7866-0063-2*, 94224) Mel Bay.

Six Short Plays. R. Cary Bynum. LC 93-29396. 1993. 12.95 (*1-878282-12-3*) St Johann Pr.

Six Short Plays of Eugene O'Neill. Incl. Dreamy Kid. Eugene O'Neill. 1965. pap. (*0-318-55467-4*); Before Breakfast. Eugene O'Neill. 1965. pap. (*0-318-55468-2*); Diff'rent. Eugene O'Neill. 1965. pap. (*0-318-55469-0*); Welded. Eugene O'Neill. 1965. pap. (*0-318-55470-4*); Straw. Eugene O'Neill. 1965. pap. (*0-318-55471-2*); Gold. (*0-318-55472-0*); (Orig.). 1965. pap. 10.00 (*0-394-70276-X*, Vin) Random.

***Six Short Stories & Seven Short Poems.** Mike Topp. 1997. 5.00 (*0-9605626-6-4*) Low-Tech.

Six Sick Sheep. Joanna Cole. LC 92-5715. (J). 1993. pap. 6.95 (*0-688-11068-1*) Morrow.

Six Sick Sheep: One Hundred One Tongue Twisters. Joanna Cole & Stephanie Calmenson. LC 92-5715. (Illus.). 64p. (J). (gr. 3 up). 1993. reprint ed. lib. bdg. 14.93 (*0-688-11140-8*, Morrow Junior) Morrow.

Six Sigma Approach to Designing with Screws. Ravi Bhatla. LC 92-25877. (Six Sigma Research Institute Ser.). 1993. write for info. (*0-201-63420-1*) Addison-Wesley.

Six Sigma Design of a Wideband Digital Communication System. Robert R. Glick & Joseph M. McQuade. LC 92-1740. (Six Sigma Research Institute Ser.). 1992. pap. write for info. (*0-201-63423-6*) Addison-Wesley.

Six Sigma Mechanical Design Tolerancing. 2nd ed. Mikel J. Harry & Reigle Stewart. 60p. (C). 1988. pap. 15.00 (*1-56946-016-7*) Motorola Univ.

Six Sigma Metrics. Jack Prins & Mikel J. Harry. LC 92-37809. (Six Sigma Research Institute Ser.). 1993. write for info. (*0-201-63405-8*) Addison-Wesley.

Six Sigma Producibility Analysis & Process Characterization. Mikel J. Harry & Ronald Lawson. (Illus.). 160p. 1992. pap. 33.95 (*0-201-63412-0*) Addison-Wesley.

Six Sigma Quality Control Charts. Jack Prins. LC 92-37808. (Six Sigma Research Institute Ser.). 1993. write for info. (*0-201-63403-1*) Addison-Wesley.

***Six Silent Killers: Management's Newest & Greatest Challenge.** James R. Fisher, Jr. (Illus.). 300p. 1997. 32.50 (*1-57444-152-3*) St Lucie Pr.

***Six Silent Men: 101st LRP/Rangers, Bk. 1.** Reynel Martinez. 1997. mass mkt. 5.99 (*0-8041-1566-4*) Ivy Books.

***Six Silent Men: 101st LRP//Rangers, Bk. 2.** Kenn Miller. 1997. mass mkt. 5.99 (*0-8041-1564-8*) Ivy Books.

***Six Silly Plays.** Groves. Date not set. pap. text ed. write for info. (*0-582-24379-3*, Pub. by Longman UK) Longman.

Six Silver Bullets. large type ed. George Flynn. (Linford Western Library). 320p. 1992. pap. 15.99 (*0-7089-7254-3*, Linford) Ulverscroft.

Six Silver Moonbeams: The Life & Times of Agustin Barrios Mangore. Richard D. Stover. LC 92-80182. (Illus.). 271p. (Orig.). 1992. pap. 29.95 (*0-9632233-1-3*) Querico Pubns.

Six Simple Pumps. Ed. by Margaret Crouch. 94p. 1983. pap. 9.50 (*0-86619-166-6*, E-11075) Vols Tech Asst.

Six Simple Steps to Stop Sexual Harassment. Susan L. Webb. 16p. (Orig.). 1990. pap. 4.00 (*1-878269-05-4*) Pacific Resource.

***Six Six Six: The Antichrist Speaks.** unabridged ed. Robert Spira. 93p. (Orig.). 1996. pap. 11.95 (*0-911455-05-1*) Quartz Pr.

Six Six Six - The True Identity of the Antichrist. Daniel D. Sikorsky. LC 92-90706. (Illus.). 73p. (Orig.). 1992. pap. 5.00 (*0-9632438-8-8*) W Lion Pub.

666 Terror the Day After. Ammu George. (Illus.). 56p. 1996. 7.95 (*0-9655881-0-6*) A George. 666 TERROR THE DAY AFTER is prophesy in a nutshell. Prophesies are relevant to present-day mankind & his inevitable future. It specifically reveals the rapture of the church (the resurrection of the dead in Christ & the transfiguration of the living believers). The eternal plan of God for man, for whom all things were created, is found in the Bible only. Biblical truths such as the signs of the end of time, world events, rapture, anti-Christ, tribulation, armageddon, second coming of Christ, & millennium are clearly & thoroughly explained in this book, to rid all confusion & complexity. The ultimate purpose of 666 TERROR THE DAY AFTER is to prepare even the worst critics & even atheists, to understand the mystery of God's love for man, who is called his bride, for whom he was manifest in the flesh & died to redeem them. It also serves as a self-guide manual to those that will be left behind. In this time of global turmoil & terror, 666 TERROR THE DAY AFTER & the Holy Bible will provide answers for those who are spiritually endangered. Follow the instructions to the letter if you will go through the tribulation time!** ***Publisher Provided Annotation.

Six Six Six the Final Warning. rev. ed. Gary D. Blevins. (Illus.). 512p. (Orig.). 1990. pap. 14.95 (*0-9626841-1-2*) Vision Res.

666/1000. Salem Kirban. (Illus.). 1976. pap. 8.95 (*0-912582-09-X*) Kirban.

Six-Sixty-Six: The Number of a Man. Marvin H. Banta. LC 87-91121. 64p. (Orig.). 1987. pap. 7.95 (*0-937139-01-7*) Grasshopper Pubns.

Six Sketches. Tony Caramia. Ed. by Frances Clark & Louise Goss. (Frances Clark Presents Ser.). 12p. 1985. pap. text ed. 2.95 (*0-913277-17-7*) New Schl Mus Study.

***Six Sketches.** Tony Caramia. 12p. 1985. pap. text ed. 3.50 (*0-614-23646-0*) Summy-Birchard.

Six Sketches of Kentucky: From the Pamphlets of J. Winston Coleman, Jr. J. Winston Coleman, Jr. Ed. & Intro. by Edward T. Houlihan. (Bluegrass Bookshelf Ser.: Vol. 1). (Illus.). 128p. 1996. 12.95 (*0-87642-014-5*) Henry Clay.

Six Sleepy Sheep. Jeffie R. Gordon. LC 90-85728. (Illus.). 24p. (J). (ps-1). 1991. 12.95 (*1-878093-06-1*) Boyds Mills Pr.

Six Snowy Sheep. Judith R. Enderle & Stephanie G. Tessler. LC 93-73307. (Illus.). 24p. (J). (ps-1). 1994. 14.95 (*1-56397-138-0*) Boyds Mills Pr.

Six Snowy Sheep. Judith R. Enderle & Stephanie G. Tessler. (Illus.). 24p. (J). (ps-3). 1995. pap. 4.99 (*0-14-055704-0*) Puffin Bks.

Six Sonatas for Cello or Double Bass & Piano: Score Parts for Both Instruments. B. Marcello. 40p. 1986. pap. 10.95 (*0-7935-5180-3*, 50262690) H Leonard.

Six Sonatas for Solo Viola Da Gamba & Violoncello. Andreas Lidl. Ed. by Hazelle Miloradovitch. (Baroque Ser.: No. 5). 1997. pap. text ed. 25.00 (*1-56571-095-9*) PRB Prods.

***Six Sonatas for Two Persons at One Keyboard: Franz Seydelmann.** Ed. by Bernard Brauchli. (Music Archive Publications Ser.). 1997. text ed. 74.00 (*90-5702-062-9*, Harwood Acad Pubs); pap. text ed. 29.00 (*90-5702-063-7*, Harwood Acad Pubs) Gordon & Breach.

Six Sonatas for Unaccompanied Violin. Johann Sebastian Bach. Ed. by Leopold Auer. (Carl Fischer Music Library: No. 788). 1917. pap. 9.95 (*0-8258-0088-9*, L788) Fischer Inc NY.

Six Sonatas for Violin & Piano. George F. Handel. Ed. by Leopold Auer & Carl Friedberg. (Carl Fischer Music Library: No. 846). 51p. 1919. pap. 10.95 (*0-8258-0091-9*, L 846) Fischer Inc NY.

Six Sonatas Opus 36: Piano. M. Clementi. 32p. 1986. pap. 4.95 (*0-7935-2569-1*) H Leonard.

Six Sonatinas: Violin & Piano. G. Telemann. 32p. 1991. pap. 9.95 (*0-7935-0497-X*) H Leonard.

Six Songs see Old English Edition

Six Songs from Amphion Anglicus, 1700 see Old English Edition

Six Songs from the "Orpheus Britannicus" see Old English Edition

Six Soviet Plays. Ed. by Eugene Lyons. LC 68-8937. 468p. 1968. reprint ed. text ed. 65.00 (*0-8371-0154-9*, LYSP, Greenwood Pr) Greenwood.

Six Spiritual Dynamics. Donald O. Clendaniel. 176p. (Orig.). 1994. pap. 9.95 (*1-56167-155-X*) Am Literary Pr.

Six Stages of Parenthood. Ellen Galinsky. LC 87-1800. 384p. 1987. pap. 17.00 (*0-201-10529-2*) Addison-Wesley.

***Six Stages of Parenthood.** Ellen Galinsky. 364p. 1987. pap. 16.00 (*0-614-22692-9*, V87-01) Families & Work.

Six Stars. Nelson M. Lloyd. LC 75-125229. (Short Story Index Reprint Ser.). 1977. 20.95 (*0-8369-3596-9*) Ayer.

Six States Super Centennial Celebration Book. Al Dempsey. 1989. pap. 1.95 (*0-8125-0015-6*) Tor Bks.

***Six-Step Economic-Justification Process for Tester Selection.** Stephen F. Scheiber. (Illus.). 48p. (Orig.). 1997. pap. write for info. (*0-9656161-0-X*) Quale Pr.

***Six Steps for Reforming America's Schools: A Guidebook for Change.** Sim O. Wilde. LC 97-7404. 1997. pap. 12.95 (*1-56825-059-2*) Rainbow Books.

Six Steps in Mental Mastery. Henry H. Brown. 105p. 1972. reprint ed. spiral bd. 7.00 (*0-7873-0123-X*) Hlth Research.

Six Steps in the Treatment of Borderline Personality Organization. Vamik D. Volkan. LC 87-19475. 250p. 1987. 30.00 (*0-87668-753-2*) Aronson.

Six Steps in the Treatment of Borderline Personality Organization. Vamik D. Volkan. 1995. pap. text ed. 30.00 (*1-56821-726-9*) Aronson.

Six Steps to a Sustainable Society. Lester Brown & Pamela Shaw. 1982. pap. write for info. (*0-916468-47-X*) Worldwatch Inst.

***Six Steps to Excellence in Ministry.** Kenneth Copeland. 64p. 1987. pap. 4.95 (*1-57562-104-5*) K Copeland Pubns.

Six Steps to Excellence in Selling: The Step-by-Step Guide to Effective Selling. Warren Wechsler. Ed. by Kristine Ellis. LC 94-96734. 192p. (Orig.). 1995. pap. 14.95 (*1-886656-06-1*) Better Books.

Six Steps to Free Publicity: And Dozens of Others Ways to Win Free Media Attention for You or Your Business. Marcia Yudkin. LC 94-13410. 1994. pap. 10.95 (*0-452-27192-4*, Plume) NAL-Dutton.

Six Steps to Intercultural Communication. Janice C. Hepworth. 15p. 1992. 45.00 incl. sl. (*1-881313-02-6*) Univ Centers.

***Six Steps to Quality: How to Plan & Implement a Continuous Quality Improvement Program for Colleges & Universities.** Robert A. Cornesky. (Illus.). 84p. (C). 1996. pap. text ed. 15.00 (*1-881807-13-4*) Cornesky & Assocs.

Six Steps to Quality Child Care. Cynthia M. Murphy. 244p. 1995. pap. 19.95 (*1-887931-00-7*); wbk. ed., pap. 15.95 (*1-887931-03-1*) Fam Care Netwrk.

Six Steps to Quality Elder Care. Cynthia M. Murphy. 244p. 1995. pap. 19.95 (*1-887931-01-5*); wbk. ed., pap. 15.95 (*1-887931-02-3*) Fam Care Netwrk.

Six Steps to Successful Interviewing: How to Build Your Reputation by Picking the Winners. 1986. 14.95 (*0-317-64342-8*) Coll Placement.

***Six Steps to the Fountain of Youth: How to Slay the Dragons of Aging Without Drawing the Sword.** Dennis Kelly. Ed. by Carol Adler. LC 94-12045. (Illus.). 250p. (Orig.). 1997. pap. 21.95 (*1-890243-01-9*) Trineurogenics.

***Six Sticks.** Molly Coxe. LC 97-7972. (Early Step into Reading & Math Ser.). (J). 1998. pap. write for info. (*0-679-88689-3*); lib. bdg. write for info. (*0-679-98689-8*) Random.

Six Stories of Jesus. Peter Enns & Glen Forsberg. (Stories that Live Ser.: Bk. 5). (Illus.). 24p. (J). (ps-5). 1985. 4.95 (*0-936215-05-4*); audio (*0-318-60185-0*) STL Intl.

***Six Stories of Murder & Suspense.** Peter Ferrell. LC 96-68829. 224p. (Orig.). 1996. pap. 15.95 (*1-57197-028-2*) Pentland Pr.

Six Studies in Quarrelling. Vincent Brome. LC 72-6176. 197p. 1973. reprint ed. text ed. 52.50 (*0-8371-6484-2*, BRSQ, Greenwood Pr) Greenwood.

Six Subjects of Reformation Art: A Preface to Rembrandt. William H. Halewood. (Illus.). 167p. 1982. pap. 16.95 (*0-8020-6491-4*) U of Toronto Pr.

Six Subjects of Reformation Art: A Preface to Rembrandt. William H. Halewood. LC 82-175730. 168p. reprint ed. pap. 47.90 (*0-685-16088-2*, 2026410) Bks Demand.

6 Success Strategies for Winning at Life, Love & Business. Wolf J. Rinke. 300p. 1996. pap. 12.95 (*1-55874-390-1*, 3901) Health Comm.

6 Sure Ways to Solve Any Problem, No Matter What. William J. Diehm. LC 93-38554. 160p. 1994. 14.99 (*0-8054-6089-6*, 4260-89) Broadman.

Six Swift Sisters & Related Families Vol. 1: A Swift Family History. George E. Bell. Ed. by Jean P. Bell. LC 96-60261. 600p. 1996. write for info. (*0-9623275-6-5*) Wayne Ridge.

Six Systems of Indian Philosophy. Friedrich M. Mueller. LC 73-18829. reprint ed. 44.50 (*0-404-11459-8*) AMS Pr.

Six Tales of the Jazz Age & Other Stories. F. Scott Fitzgerald. 192p. 1966. reprint ed. pap. 10.00 (*0-684-71762-X*) S&S Trade.

Six Talks on Jung's Psychology. Robert A. Clark. (Orig.). 1953. pap. 4.50 (*0-910286-07-8*) Boxwood.

Six Teddy Bear Postcards. Ann L. Cummings. (Illus.). (J). (gr. 4-7). 1993. pap. 1.00 (*0-486-27759-3*) Dover.

Six Theories of Child Development: Revised Formulations & Current Issues. Ed. by Ross Vasta. LC 92-235357. 304p. 1992. reprint ed. pap. 33.00 (*1-85302-137-7*) Taylor & Francis.

Six Theories of Justice: Perspectives from Philosophical & Theological Ethics. Karen Lebacqz. LC 86-26457. 144p. (Orig.). (C). 1986. pap. 15.99 (*0-8066-2245-8*, 10-5820, Augsburg) Augsburg Fortress.

Six Theosophic Points (an Open Gate of All the Secrets of Life Wherein the Causes of All Beings Become Known) Six Mystical Points on the Earthly & Heavenly Mystery on the Divine Intuition. Jacob Boehme. Tr. by John R. Earle. 220p. 1992. pap. 19.95 (*1-56459-240-5*) Kessinger Pub.

Six Thick Thumbs: A Tongue-Twisting Tale. Steve Charney. LC 94-20734. (Illus.). 32p. (J). (gr. k-2). 1994. lib. bdg. 12.50 (*0-8167-3594-8*, Whistlstop) Troll Communs.

Six Things Satan Uses to Rob You of God's Abundant Blessings. Peter Popoff. Ed. by Don Tanner. LC 81-86521. (Illus.). 96p. 1982. pap. 2.00 (*0-938544-11-X*) Faith Messenger.

Six Thinking Hats. Edward De Bono. 216p. pap. 25.00 (*0-9615400-5-2*) Intl Ctr Creat Think.

Six Thinking Hats: An Essential Approach to Business Management from the Creator of Lateral Thinking. Edward De Bono. 1986. 21.95 (*0-316-17791-1*) Little.

Six Thousand Miles of Fence: Life on the XIT Ranch of Texas. Cordia S. Duke & Joe B. Frantz. (M. K. Brown Range Life Ser.: No. 1). (Illus.). 285p. (C). 1992. reprint ed. pap. 13.95 (*0-292-77564-4*) U of Tex Pr.

Six Thousand Names for Your Baby. 176p. (Orig.). 1983. mass mkt. 4.50 (*0-440-17956-4*) Dell.

6001 Food Facts & Chef's Secrets. Myles H. Bader. (Illus.). 504p. 1995. pap. 18.95 (*0-9646741-0-6*) Northstar NV.

6194: Denali Solo. Ed Darack. 168p. (Orig.). 1995. pap. 12.00 (*1-884980-80-5*) E Darack Photo.

Six Thousand Sermon Illustrations: An Alphabetical Collection from Leaders & Writers of the Ages. Elon Foster. (gr. 10). 1952. reprint ed. pap. 29.99 (*0-8010-3455-8*) Baker Bks.

Six Thousand Soundalikes, Look-Alikes & Other Words Often Confused. Mary L. Gilman. 200p. 1992. pap. text ed. 12.50 (*1-881859-00-2*) Natl Ct Report.

Six Thousand Year Old Space Suit. Vaughn M. Greene. (Illus.). 116p. 1985. 5.95 (*0-317-00917-6*) V Greene.

Six Thousand Year-Old Spacesuit. Vaughn M. Greene. (Illus.). 104p. (Orig.). 1982. pap. 7.95 (*0-317-03151-1*) Merlin Engine Wks.

***Six Thousand Years of Bread.** H. E. Jacob. LC 97-3216. (Cook's Classic Library). (Illus.). 416p. 1997. reprint ed. pap. 16.95 (*1-55821-575-1*, 15751) Lyons & Burford.

Six Thumbnail Sketches for Two Alto Recorders. Freda Burford. (Contemporary Consort Ser.: No. 16). 6p. 1991. pap. text ed. 2.00 (*1-56571-033-9*) PRB Prods.

Six Timeless Marketing Blunders. William L. Shanklin. 154p. pap. 13.95 (*0-669-24816-9*, Lexington) Jossey-Bass.

Six to Five: The Six to Five Exercise Almanac-a Lunch, or other Hour Guide to Fitness & a Longer Life. 4th rev. ed. Harvest Staff. 1997. pap. 22.00 (*0-939074-05-2*) Harvest Pubns.

Six Transcendent Events: Using the Lord's Model to Solve Life's Problems. Stephen R. Covey. LC 96-22574. 1996. write for info. (*1-57345-187-8*) Deseret Bk.

Six Treatises Attributed to Maimonides. Tr. & Anno. by Fred Rosner. LC 89-18590. 280p. 1991. 40.00 (*0-87668-804-0*) Aronson.

Six Trees. Mary E. Wilkins Freeman. LC 74-94721. (Short Story Index Reprint Ser.). 1977. 20.95 (*0-8369-3100-9*) Ayer.

Six Trials of Jesus. John W. Lawrence. 240p. 1996. pap. 10.99 (*0-8254-3152-2*) Kregel.

Six-Twelve Plan: Reslicing the Work Pie. Alan M. Courtright. 168p. (Orig.). 1989. pap. 9.95 (*0-9624078-0-1*) Sharebooks Pub.

***Six Victorian & Edwardian Board Games.** Olivia Bristol. (Illus.). 12p. (J). 1995. bds. write for info. (*1-85479-713-1*, Pub. by M OMara UK) Assoc Pubs Grp.

S

Six Vignettes. Robert L. Merriam. (Illus.). 38p. 1981. 2.00 (*0-686-32492-7*) R L Merriam.

Six Vital Ingredients of Self-Esteem: And How to Develop Them in Your Students. Bettie B. Youngs. 208p. (Orig.). 1992. teacher ed. 19.95 (*0-915190-72-9*, JP9072-9) Jalmar Pr.

Six Vital Ingredients of Self-Esteem: How To Develop Them in Young People. Bettie B. Youngs. 188p. (Orig.). 1990. teacher ed. 49.95 (*0-685-35566-7*); student ed. 49.95 (*0-685-35567-5*); audio 49.95 (*0-940221-07-1*) Lrng Tools-Bilicki Pubns.

Six Voices: Contemporary Australian Poets. Ed. by Chris Wallace-Crabbe. LC 79-4265. 108p. 1979. reprint ed. text ed. 35.00 (*0-313-21250-3*, WCSV, Greenwood Pr) Greenwood.

Six Voyages of Pleasant Field Mouse. Jan Wahl. (Orig.). (J). 1994. pap. 3.99 (*0-8125-2403-9*) Tor Bks.

Six Walks in the Fictional Woods. Umberto Eco. LC 93-33605. (Charles Eliot Norton Lectures). 159p. (Orig.). 1994. 18.95 (*0-674-81050-3*) HUP.

Six Walks in the Fictional Woods. Umberto Eco. (Charles Eliot Norton Lectures). (Illus.). 153p. (Orig.). (C). 1995. pap. 10.00 (*0-674-81051-1*) HUP.

Six Wars at a Time. Audrey K. Shaff. LC 85-70296. 1985. 18.95 (*0-931170-27-3*); pap. 12.95 (*0-931170-26-5*) Ctr Western Studies.

Six Wars at a Time. rev. ed. Howard Shaff & Audrey K. Shaff. (Illus.). 379p. 1985. reprint ed. pap. 13.95 (*0-932195-06-7*) Permelia Pub.

Six Wasted Years. Len Williamson. (C). 1989. 35.00 (*0-86303-432-2*) St Mut.

Six-Way Paragraphs: Advanced Level. Walter Pauk. 240p. pap. 13.30 (*0-89061-303-6*, 731) Jamestown Pubs.

Six-Way Paragraphs: Advanced Level. large type ed. (YA). (gr. 6-12). Date not set. pap. 17.96 (*0-89061-463-6*) Jamestown Pubs.

Six-Way Paragraphs: Middle Level. Walter Pauk. 240p. (YA). (gr. 6-12). pap. 12.97 (*0-89061-302-8*, 730) Jamestown Pubs.

Six-Way Paragraphs: Middle Level. large type ed. Jamestown Publishers Staff. (J). 1995. student ed., pap. 17.96 (*0-89061-462-8*) Jamestown Pubs.

Six Ways of Being Religious: A Framework for Comparative Studies of Religion. Dale W. Cannon. LC 95-16047. 402p. 1996. pap. 32.95 (*0-534-25332-6*) Wadsworth Pub.

Six Ways to Better Manage Your Town Government: What Every Small Town Government Official Needs to Know. National Center for Small Communities Staff. LC 93-45605. 1994. 14.95 (*0-925532-10-X*) Natl Assn Town & Twps.

Six Ways to Pray from Six Great Saints. Gloria Hutchinson. (Illus.). 152p. 1982. pap. 6.95 (*0-86716-007-1*) St Anthony Mess Pr.

Six-Week Fat-to-Muscle Makeover. Ellington Darden. 176p. 1990. pap. 10.95 (*0-399-51562-3*, Perigee Bks) Berkley Pub.

Six Weeks in the Sioux Teepees. Sarah F. Wakefield. 1985. 19.95 (*0-87770-215-2*) Ye Galleon.

***Six Weeks in the Sioux Tepees: A Narrative of Indian Captivity.** Sarah F. Wakefield & June Namias. LC 97-2380. (Illus.). 192p. 1997. 27.95 (*0-8061-2975-1*) U of Okla Pr.

Six Weeks to a Simpler Lifestyle. Barbara DeGrote-Sorensen & David A. Sorensen. LC 94-33426. 128p. 1994. pap. 9.99 (*0-8066-2751-4*, Augsburg) Augsburg Fortress.

Six Weeks to a Toxic-Free Body. Dean Kimmel. 146p. (Orig.). 1992. pap. 9.95 (*0-9621446-2-2*) Corbin Hse.

Six Weeks to Better Parenting. Caryl W. Krueger. 1984. pap. 8.95 (*0-938632-05-1*) Belleridge.

Six Weeks to Better Parenting. Caryl W. Krueger. LC 85-6489. 1985. reprint ed. pap. 11.95 (*0-88289-482-X*) Pelican.

Six Weeks to Words of Power. Wilfred Funk. 1990. mass mkt. 4.99 (*0-671-73283-8*, PB Trade Paper) PB.

***6 Wild Adventures.** Sarah Albee. (Lunch Box Library). (J). 1997. pap. text ed. 6.95 (*0-7611-0678-2*) Workman Pub.

***6 Wild Adventures & 9 Puzzling Mysteries.** Workman Publishing Staff. (Lunch Box Library). 1997. pap. text ed. 83.40 (*0-7611-0863-7*) Workman Pub.

Six Wings: Men of Science in the Renaissance. George Sarton. LC 56-11998. (Patten Lectures). (Illus.). 334p. reprint ed. pap. 95.20 (*0-8357-6694-2*, 2056874) Bks Demand.

Six Wives of Henry VIII. Alison Weir. (Illus.). 656p. 1993. pap. 12.50 (*0-345-38072-X*, Ballantine Trade) Ballantine.

Six Women Novelists. Merryn Williams. LC 88-6435. (Modern Novelists Ser.). 140p. 1988. text ed. 29.95 (*0-312-02089-9*) St Martin.

Six Women's Slave Narratives. Intro. by William L. Andrews. (Schomburg Library of Nineteenth-Century Black Women Writers). 384p. 1989. reprint ed. pap. 12.95 (*0-19-506083-0*) OUP.

Six Women's Slave Narratives, 1831-1909. Mary Prince et al. (Schomburg Library of Nineteenth-Century Black Women Writers). 384p. 1988. 29.95 (*0-19-505262-5*) OUP.

Six-Won: The Nineteen Eighty-Six Literary Magazine Writers' Awards. 95p. 1986. pap. 6.95 (*0-942332-11-3*) Coord Coun Lit Mags.

***Six Words, Many Turtles & Three Days in Hong Kong.** Patricia McMahon. LC 96-44191. (J). 1997. 16.00 (*0-395-68621-0*) HM.

Six Wrinkled Woos. Lois R. Czarnecki. (Illus.). 32p. (J). (gr. k-3). 1992. 17.95 (*0-9627275-0-4*) Ohana Pr.

Six-Year-Old-Man. Stanley Elkin. LC 86-73201. 140p. 1987. 18.00 (*0-917453-16-6*); 25.00 (*0-917453-17-4*); pap. 10.00 (*0-917453-15-8*) Bamberger.

Six-Year Rural High School: A Comparative Study of Small & Large Units in Alabama. John I. Riddle. LC 70-177191. (Columbia University. Teachers College. Contributions to Education Ser.: No. 737). reprint ed. 37.50 (*0-404-55737-6*) AMS Pr.

Six-Year Sequence see Language Learner

***Six Years: The Dematerialization of the Art Object from 1966 to 1972.** Contrib. by Lucy Lippard. LC 96-47552. (Illus.). 1997. pap. 18.95 (*0-520-21013-1*) U CA Pr.

Six Years after D-Day: Cycling Through Europe. Marie B. Alsmeyer. LC 94-48004. 176p. (Orig.). 1995. pap. 14.95 (*0-929398-82-3*) UNTX Pr.

Six Years in Hell: A Returned Vietnam POW Views Captivity, Country & the Future. rev. ed. Jay R. Jensen. (Illus.). 176p. 1989. reprint ed. pap. 10.00 (*1-877898-05-8*) Pubns Of Worth.

Six Years of Educational Progress in Nepal. University of Oregon Contract Staff. 76p. (ENG & NEP.). 1959. 4.00 (*0-318-12885-3*, 17) Am-Nepal Ed.

Six Years of Hell: Harpers Ferry During the Civil War. Chester G. Hearn. LC 96-21738. (Illus.). 328p. 1996. 29.95 (*0-8071-2090-1*) La State U Pr.

Six Years on the West Coast of America, 1856-1862. Louis S. Rossi. Tr. by W. Victor Wortley. (Illus.). 376p. 1983. 19.95 (*0-87770-293-4*) Ye Galleon.

Six Years That Shook the World: Perestroika - The Impossible Project. Rachel Walker. LC 92-38069. 1993. text ed. 69.95 (*0-7190-3286-5*, Pub. by Manchester Univ Pr UK); text ed. 19.95 (*0-7190-3287-3*, Pub. by Manchester Univ Pr UK) St Martin.

Six Years with the Texas Rangers, 1875 to 1881. James B. Gillett. Ed. & Intro. by Milo M. Quaife. LC 76-4495. (Illus.). xxxvi, 279p. 1976. pap. 9.95 (*0-8032-5844-5*, Bison Books) U of Nebr Pr.

Six Yuan Plays. Tr. & Intro. by Liu Jung-En. (Classics Ser.). 288p. 1972. pap. 10.95 (*0-14-044262-6*, Penguin Classics) Viking Penguin.

Sixe Bookes of Politickes or Civil Doctrine. Justus Lipsius. Tr. by W. Jones. LC 79-25633. (English Experience Ser.: No. 287). 1970. reprint ed. 22.00 (*90-221-0287-4*) Walter J Johnson.

Sixgun Cartridges & Loads. Elmer Keith. 1985. reprint ed. 24.95 (*0-88227-024-9*) Gun Room.

Sixgun Duo. Ernest Haycox. 1990. mass mkt. 2.95 (*1-55817-404-4*, Pinncle Kensgtn) Kensgtn Pub Corp.

***Sixgun Showdown.** large type ed. Art Flynn. (Linford Western Library). 240p. 1997. pap. 16.99 (*0-7089-5006-X*, Linford) Ulverscroft.

Sixguns. Elmer Keith. 1955. 34.95 (*1-879356-09-0*) Wolfe Pub Co.

Sixguns: The Standard Reference Work. Elmer Keith. 335p. 1991. 35.00 (*1-884849-10-5*) R&R Bks.

Sixguns & Masons. Joseph E. Bennett. (Illus.). 133p. 1991. 12.00 (*0-935633-12-X*) Anchor Comm.

Sixguns & Society: A Structural Study of the Western. Will Wright. 1975. pap. 14.95 (*0-520-03491-0*) U CA Pr.

Sixieme Jour. Andree Chedid. (FRE.). 1989. pap. 10.95 (*0-7859-3278-X*, 2277225290) Fr & Eur.

***Sixieme Reunion du Sous-Comite Ouest & Centre Africain de Correlation des Sols pour la Mise en Valeur des Terres, Niamey, 1984.** 291p. (FRE.). 1985. 35.00 (*92-5-202277-5*, Pub. by FAO IT) Bernan Associates.

Six.Six: The Nineteen Ninety-Four Killer Quake. Ed. by J. Bruce Baumann. (Illus.). 80p. (Orig.). 1994. pap. 12.95 (*1-884850-01-4*) Scripps Howard.

Sixsport: Dealers Certified Price Guide, Issue 1, Vol. 1, Sept./Oct. '94. Alan Hager. 160p. pap. 20.00 (*1-883622-01-8*) A Hager Grp.

Sixteen: Short Stories by Outstanding Young Adult Writers. Ed. by Donald R. Gallo. 192p. (J). (gr. 5-12). 1985. mass mkt. 4.99 (*0-440-97757-6*, LLL BDD) BDD Bks Young Read.

Sixteen & Dying. Lurlene McDaniel. (One Last Wish Ser.: No. 5). 144p. (YA). 1992. pap. 3.99 (*0-553-29932-8*) Bantam.

Sixteen Authors to One: Intimate Sketches of Leading American Storytellers. David Karsner. LC 68-16944. (Essay Index Reprint Ser.). 1977. 20.95 (*0-8369-0584-9*) Ayer.

Sixteen Bananas. Hugh Gross. 192p. (Orig.). 1995. pap. 12.00 (*0-922811-21-0*) Mid-List.

Sixteen-Bit & Thirty-Two-Bit Microprocessors: Architecture, Software, & Interfacing Techniques. Walter A. Triebel & Avtar Singh. 656p. 1990. text ed. 91.00 (*0-13-812157-5*) P-H.

Sixteen-Bit Microprocessor Systems. T. Flik & H. Liebig. 300p. 1985. 52.95 (*0-387-15164-8*) Spr-Verlag.

Sixteen-Character Solution: Negotiations Between the United Kingdom & the People's Republic of China over the Future of Hong Kong, September 1982-September 1984. Martin Staniland. (Pew Case Studies in International Affairs). 152p. (C). 1987. pap. text ed. 3.50 (*1-56927-411-8*) Geo U Inst Dplmcy.

Sixteen Contemporary Violin Etudes for Study & Performance. Blank et al. Ed. by Gratovich. 9.95 (*0-318-18104-5*) Am String Tchrs.

Sixteen Cowries: Yoruba Divination from Africa to the New World. William R. Bascom. LC 78-3239. (Illus.). 800p. 1980. 49.95 (*0-253-35280-0*) Ind U Pr.

Sixteen Cowries: Yoruba Divination from Africa to the New World. William R. Bascom. LC 78-3239. (Illus.). 800p. 1993. pap. 24.95 (*0-253-20847-5*) Ind U Pr.

Sixteen Dances in Sixteen Rhythms. Ted Shawn. 64p. 1985. reprint ed. pap. 15.95 (*0-9510779-0-2*) Princeton Bk Co.

Sixteen Days at Mungol-li. James H. Dill. 1993. 24.00 (*0-943099-11-0*) M&M Pr.

Sixteen Famous European Plays. Bennett Cerf. 1976. 48.95 (*0-8488-0957-2*) Amereon Ltd.

Sixteen First Studies for Piano. Louis Koehler. (Carl Fischer Music Library: No. 370). (Illus.). 1904. pap. 4.00 (*0-8258-0114-1*) Fischer Inc NY.

Sixteen Hand Horse. Fred Gwynne. LC 79-13284. (Illus.). (J). (gr. 1-6). 1987. pap. 5.95 (*0-671-66968-0*, S&S Bks Young Read) S&S Childrens.

Sixteen Hundred & One: Conversation As it Was by the Social Fireside in the Times of the Tudors. Mark Twain. 16.95 (*0-8488-0058-3*) Amereon Ltd.

Sixteen Hundred & One: Tudor Bits. Mark Twain. 9.95 (*0-685-22111-3*) Wehman.

Sixteen Hundred Lines to Pilgrims: National Society of the Sons & Daughters of the Pilgrims. Ed. by Mary E. Mayo. 1048p. 1996. reprint ed. 75.00 (*0-8063-1499-0*) Genealog Pub.

Sixteen Hundred One. Mark Twain. 80p. 1990. reprint ed. lib. bdg. 16.95 (*0-89966-756-2*) Buccaneer Bks.

Sixteen Hundred One. Mark Twain, pseud. (Works of Samuel Clemens). 1989. reprint ed. lib. bdg. 79.00 (*0-685-28386-0*) Rprt Serv.

***1601 & Is Shakespeare Dead?** Mark Twain. Ed. by Fishkin. (Oxford Mark Twain Ser.). 256p. 1997. lib. bdg. 28.00 (*0-19-511426-4*) OUP.

Sixteen in Nome. large type ed. Max Brand. 267p. 1996. lib. bdg. 20.95 (*0-7862-0718-3*, Thorndike Lrg Prnt) Thorndike Pr.

Sixteen in Nome: A North-Western Story. Max Brand. LC 95-9438. (Five-Star Western Ser.). 200p. 1995. 16.95 (*0-7862-0509-1*) Thorndike Pr.

Sixteen Is Spelled O-U-C-H! unabridged ed. Joan Weir. 144p. (YA). (gr. 7 up). 1995. mass mkt. 4.95 (*0-7736-7290-7*, Pub. by Stoddart Kids CN) Genl Dist Srvs.

Sixteen Italian Songs & Arias: High. pap. 12.95 incl. audio (*0-7935-3419-4*, 00747074) H Leonard.

Sixteen Italian Songs & Arias: Low. pap. 12.95 incl. audio (*0-7935-3420-8*, 00747075) H Leonard.

Sixteen Millimeter Film Cutting. John Burder. (Media Manuals Ser.). 160p. 1976. pap. 24.95 (*0-240-50857-2*) Buttrwrth-Heinemann.

Sixteen Modern American Authors: A Survey of Research & Criticism. Ed. by Jackson R. Bryer. LC 73-97454. xx, 673p. 1973. text ed. 49.95 (*0-8223-0297-7*) Duke.

Sixteen Modern American Authors, Vol. 2: A Survey of Research & Criticism since 1972. Ed. by Jackson R. Bryer. LC 89-11789. 810p. (C). 1989. text ed. 64.95 (*0-8223-0976-9*); pap. text ed. 29.95 (*0-8223-1018-X*) Duke.

***Sixteen Modern Short Stories.** 2nd ed. Jennings. 1992. pap. text ed. write for info. (*0-582-87540-4*, Pub. by Longman UK) Longman.

Sixteen Months at the Gold Diggings. Daniel B. Woods. LC 72-9473. (Far Western Frontier Ser.). 204p. 1973. reprint ed. 19.95 (*0-405-05000-3*) Ayer.

Sixteen Months of Indecision: Slovak American Viewpoints Toward Compatriots & the Homeland from 1914 to 1915 as Viewed by the Slovak Language Press in Pennsylvania. Gregory C. Ference. (Illus.). 264p. 1995. 39.50 (*0-945636-59-8*) Susquehanna U Pr.

Sixteen Myhological Stories of IFA (Itan Ifa Merindinlogun) Fama A. Somadhi. 178p. 1996. pap. 14.95 (*0-9644247-2-X*) ILE Orunmila.

Sixteen New Testament Principles for World Evangelism. B. E. Underwood. 1991. teacher ed. 12.95 (*0-911866-15-9*) LifeSprings Res.

Sixteen-Nineteen Changes in Education & Training. Ed. by Tom Whiteside et al. 144p. 1992. pap. 29.95 (*1-85346-204-7*, Pub. by D Fulton UK) Taylor & Francis.

Sixteen Ninety-Two Witch Hunt: The Layman's Guide to the Salem Witchcraft Trials. George M. Yool. 165p. 1992. pap. 15.50 (*1-55613-565-3*) Heritage Bk.

Sixteen on Sixteen: Irish Writers on the Easter Rising. Ed. by Dermot Bolger. 48p. 1988. pap. 7.95 (*1-85186-051-7*) Dufour.

Sixteen Papers on Differential & Difference Equations, Functional Analysis, Games & Control. M. A. Aizerman et al. LC 51-5559. (Translations Ser.: Series 2, Vol. 87). 303p. 1970. 50.00 (*0-8218-1787-6*, TRANS2/87) Am Math.

Sixteen Papers on Differential Equations. J. V. Egorov et al. LC 82-20595. (AMS Translations Ser.: Series 2, Vol. 118). 339p. 1982. 101.00 (*0-8218-3073-2*, TRANS2/118) Am Math.

Sixteen Papers on Logic & Algebra. V. A. Baranskii et al. LC 51-5559. (Translations Ser.: Series 2, Vol. 94). 276p. 1970. 45.00 (*0-8218-1794-9*, TRANS2/94) Am Math.

Sixteen Papers on Number Theory & Algebra. A. P. Birjukov et al. LC 51-5559. (Translations Ser.: Series 2, Vol. 82). 264p. 1969. 49.00 (*0-8218-1782-5*, TRANS2/82) Am Math.

Sixteen Papers on Topology & One on Game Theory. Chow Sho-Kwan et al. LC 51-5559. (Translations Ser.: Series 2, Vol. 38). 340p. 1964. 38.00 (*0-8218-1738-8*, TRANS2/38) Am Math.

Sixteen PF: Personality in Depth. Heather B. Cattell. 1989. pap. 19.95 (*0-918296-20-X*) Inst Personality & Ability.

Sixteen PF Fifth Edition: Administrator's Manual. Mary T. Russell & Darcie L. Karol. 162p. (Orig.). 1994. pap. 20.00 (*0-918296-21-8*) Inst Personality & Ability.

Sixteen PF Fifth Edition Technical Manual. Ed. by Steven R. Conn & Mark L. Rieke. 324p. (Orig.). (C). 1994. pap. 50.00 (*0-918296-22-6*) Inst Personality & Ability.

Sixteen Pleasures. Robert Hellenga. 384p. 1995. pap. 11.95 (*0-385-31469-8*, Delta) Dell.

Sixteen Pleasures. Robert R. Hellenga. LC 93-43537. 327p. 1994. 22.00 (*1-56947-006-5*) Soho Press.

Sixteen Plus English. Michael Baber. (C). 1982. 48.00 (*0-85950-325-9*, Pub. by S Thornes Pubs UK) St Mut.

Sixteen Poems. Vittorio Sereni. Tr. by Paul Vangelisti from ITA. 1971. 2.00 (*0-88031-001-4*) Invisible-Red Hill.

Sixteen Principles for World Evangelization. B. E. Underwood. 1988. pap. 9.95 (*0-911866-06-X*) LifeSprings Res.

Sixteen Reasons Why I Killed Richard M. Nixon. L. A. Heberlein. 160p. (C). 1996. 19.95 (*0-942979-29-X*); pap. 9.95 (*0-942979-30-3*) Livingston U Pr.

Sixteen Satires. Juvenal. Tr. & Intro. by Peter Green. (Classics Ser.). 320p. (Orig.). 1967. pap. 10.95 (*0-14-044194-8*, Penguin Classics) Viking Penguin.

1676: The End of American Independence. Stephen S. Webb. (Illus.). 460p. 1995. pap. 17.95 (*0-8156-0361-4*) Syracuse U Pr.

Sixteen Seventy-Six: The End of American Independence. Stephen S. Webb. LC 85-8431. (Illus.). 493p. reprint ed. pap. 140.60 (*0-7837-1735-0*, 2057265) Bks Demand.

Sixteen Short Plays for Young Actors. 226p. (YA). 1996. pap. 16.95 (*0-8442-5133-X*) NTC Pub Grp.

Sixteen, Six Configurations & Geometry of Kummer Surfaces in P 3. Maria R. Gonzalez-Dorrego. LC 93-39029. (Memoirs of the American Mathematical Society Ser.: No. 512). 116p. 1994. pap. 29.00 (*0-8218-2574-7*, MEMO/107/512) Am Math.

Sixteen SR Book: A Guide to the System. Jon Fauer. Ed. by Stephen C. Chamberlain. LC 85-73871. (Illus.). 125p. (Orig.). 1986. pap. 19.95 (*0-936763-00-0*) Arriflex.

Sixteen-Thirteen Print of Juan Esquivel Barahona. Robert J. Snow. LC 78-70021. (Detroit Monographs in Musicology: No. 7). 91p. 1978. 20.00 (*0-911772-92-8*) Info Coord.

Sixteen Times Round Cape Horn. Isaac N. Hibberd. (Illus.). vi, 44p. 1980. pap. 5.95 (*0-913372-15-3*) Mystic Seaport.

Sixteen to Sixty: Memoirs of a Collector. Louisine W. Havemeyer. Ed. by Susan A. Stein. 364p. 1995. 35.00 (*1-883145-00-7*) Ursus Press.

Sixteen to Sixty: Memoirs of a Collector. Louisine W. Havemeyer & Susan A. Stein. 1995. pap. 19.95 (*1-883145-01-5*) Ursus Press.

Sixteen Toes: Anthology. Ed. by Gigi Bradford & Michael Moos. (Illus.). (J). (gr. 2-7). 1978. pap. 2.50 (*0-930970-00-4*) O'Neill Pr.

Sixteen Top Hits for Easy Piano. (Easy Play Ser.). 80p. 1993. pap. 8.95 (*0-7935-2367-2*, 00222565) H Leonard.

Sixteen Top Hits of 1995. 96p. 1995. pap. 10.95 (*0-7935-4932-9*, 00310082) H Leonard.

1628 Country Shortcuts from 1628 Country People. Reiman Publications Staff. 1996. pap. text ed. 12.95 (*0-89821-172-7*) Reiman Pubns.

Sixteen Voices: Poets: Survivors of Incest & Sexual Abuse. rev. ed. 80p. (Orig.). (C). 1994. pap. 12.00 (*0-933553-10-2*) Mariposa Print Pub.

16 Ways to Love Your Love: Understanding the 16 Personality Types So You Can Create a Love That Lasts Forever. Otto Kroeger & Janet M Thuesen. 288p. 1997. pap. 12.95 (*0-440-50666-2*, Dell Trade Pbks) Dell.

Sixteen Ways to Love Your Lover: How to Use Type Talk to Find a Love That Lasts Forever. Otto Kroeger & Janet M. Thuesen. LC 93-21511. 288p. 1994. 19.95 (*0-385-31031-5*) Delacorte.

16PF Couple's Counseling Report User's Guide. Mary T. Russell. 66p. (Orig.). (C). 1995. pap. 25.00 (*0-918296-24-2*) Inst Personality & Ability.

16th & 17th - Century Dutch & Flemish Paintings in the Springfield Museum of Fine Arts. Text by Alice I. Davies. (Illus.). 160p. 1993. 26.95 (*0-916746-17-8*) Springfield Lib & Mus.

16th Annual BDA International Design Awards. Supon Design Group Staff. (Illus.). viii, 208p. 1995. 45.00 (*0-9644038-1-1*) Design Ed.

16th Annual Institute on Computer Law: Understanding the Business & Legal Aspects of the Internet. (Patents, Copyrights, Trademarks, & Literry Property Course Handbook, 1995-96 Ser.). Date not set. pap. 99.00 (*0-614-17249-7*, G4-3966) PLI.

Sixteenth Annual Symposium on Computer Applications in Medical Care. American Medical Informatics Association Staff. 859p. 1993. pap. text ed. 65.00 (*0-07-055023-9*) McGraw.

Sixteenth Application of Computers & Operations Research in the Mineral Industry. fac. ed. Society of Mining Engineers of AIME Staff. Ed. by Thomas J. O'Neil. LC 79-52273. (Illus.). 661p. 1979. reprint ed. pap. 180.00 (*0-7837-7845-7*, 2047604) Bks Demand.

Sixteenth Biennial Conference Proceedings. ICHCA Staff. (C). 1988. 350.00 (*0-685-37350-9*, Pub. by ICHCA UK) St Mut.

Sixteenth Biennial Topical Meeting on Reactor Operating Experience, Long Island, NY August 15-19, 1993. 390p. 1994. 70.00 (*0-89448-181-9*, 700184) Am Nuclear Soc.

Sixteenth Census of the United States, 1940. U. S. Bureau of the Census Staff. LC 75-22861. (America in Two Centuries Ser.). 1976. reprint ed. 20.95 (*0-405-07727-0*) Ayer.

Sixteenth Century. Charles W. Oman. LC 75-25517. 247p. 1976. reprint ed. text ed. 59.75 (*0-8371-8118-6*, OMSIC, Greenwood Pr) Greenwood.

Sixteenth Century: Skelton Through Hooker. John L. Lievsay. LC 68-15229. (Goldentree Bibliographies Series in Language & Literature). (C). 1968. pap. text ed. write for info. (*0-88295-520-9*) Harlan Davidson.

Sixteenth Century see History of Magic & Experimental Science

Sixteenth Century Britain. Ed. by Boris Ford. (Cultural History of Britain Ser.). (Illus.). 336p. (C). 1992. pap. 24.95 (*0-521-42883-1*) Cambridge U Pr.

Sixteenth Century British Non-Dramatic Writers: 3rd Series. Mary Bruccoli et al. (Dictionary of Literary Biography Ser.: Vol. 167). 1996. 140.00 (*0-8103-9362-X*) Gale.

Sixteenth Century Counterpoint. H. Gilbert Trythall. 272p. (C). 1993. spiral bd. write for info. (*0-697-14350-3*) Brown & Benchmark.

Sixteenth-Century English Poetry. Ed. by Norman E. McClure. LC 73-139767. (Granger Index Reprint Ser.). 1977. 36.95 (*0-8369-6221-4*) Ayer.

Sixteenth Century Europe: Expansion & Conflict. Richard Mackenney. 1993. text ed. 18.95 (*0-312-06739-9*) St Martin.

Sixteenth-Century French Poetry. Ed. by Victor E. Graham. LC 65-1886. 146p. reprint ed. pap. 41.70 (*0-8357-2600-2*, 2014227) Bks Demand.

16th Century Galleon. Richard Humble. LC 94-42444. (Inside Story Ser.). (Illus.). 48p. (YA). (gr. 5 up). 1995. lib. bdg. 18.95 (*0-87226-372-X*) P Bedrick Bks.

Sixteenth Century Imprints in Libraries of the University of Pennsylvania. M. A. Shaaber. (Haney Foundation Ser.). 668p. 1976. 39.95 (*0-8122-7698-1*) U of Pa Pr.

Sixteenth Century Ireland: The Incomplete Conquest. Colm Lennon. LC 94-32460. 1995. text ed. 45.00 (*0-312-12462-7*) St Martin.

Sixteenth-Century Italian Drawings in New York Collections. William M. Griswold & Linda Wolk-Simon. LC 93-30679. 1993. write for info. (*0-8109-6436-8*) Abrams.

Sixteenth-Century Italian Drawings in New York Collections. William M. Griswold & Linda Wolk-Simon. LC 93-30679. 284p. 1993. 45.00 (*0-87099-688-6*); pap. 35.00 (*0-87099-689-4*) Metro Mus Art.

Sixteenth-Century Italian Prints. Marcus S. Sopher & Claudia Lazzaro-Bruno. LC 78-67093. (Illus.). 72p. 1978. 5.00 (*0-915478-12-9*) Montgomery Gallery.

Sixteenth Century Italian Schools. Cecil Gould. (Illus.). 1991. pap. text ed. 25.00 (*0-300-06141-2*) Yale U Pr.

Sixteenth-Century Maiolica Pottery in the Valley of Mexico. Florence C. Lister & Robert H. Lister. LC 81-16203. (Anthropological Papers: No. 39). 110p. 1982. 14.95 (*0-8165-0748-1*) U of Ariz Pr.

Sixteenth Century Mosque. Fiona MacDonald. LC 94-20008. (Inside Story Ser.). (Illus.). 48p. (YA). (gr. 5 up). 1994. lib. bdg. 18.95 (*0-87226-310-X*) P Bedrick Bks.

***16th Century Mosque.** Fiona MacDonald. 58p. (J). 1996. pap. 14.95 (*0-614-20979-X*, 1648) Kazi Pubns.

Sixteenth Century Physician & His Methods. Richard L. Sutton, Jr. LC 85-82669. (Illus.). 276p. 1986. 37.50 (*0-932845-12-6*) Lowell Pr.

Sixteenth-Century Polyphony: A Basis for the Study of Counterpoint. Arthur T. Merritt. LC 39-25128. (Illus.). 232p. 1939. reprint ed. pap. 66.30 (*0-7837-6086-8*, 2059132) Bks Demand.

***Sixteenth-Century St. Augustine: The People & Their Homes.** Albert C. Manucy. LC 96-31964. (Illus.). 136p. 1997. 24.95 (*0-8130-1484-0*) U Press Fla.

Sixteenth-Century Spanish Bookstore: The Inventory of Juan de Junta. William Pettas. LC 94-78553. (Transactions Ser.: Vol. 85, Pt. 1). 200p. (C). 1995. pap. 20.00 (*0-87169-851-X*, T851-pew) Am Philos.

Sixteenth Conference Proceedings. ICHCA Staff. (C). 1988. 210.00 (*0-685-46523-3*, Pub. by ICHCA UK) St Mut.

Sixteenth Edition IEE Wiring Regulations. Brian Scaddan. 144p. 1995. pap. 18.95 (*0-7506-2136-2*) Buttrwrth-Heinemann.

16th IEEE - NPSS Symposium Fusion Engineering. IEEE Nuclear & Plasma Sciences Society Staff. Ed. by IEEE Staff. LC 85-653749. 1746p. 1996. pap. text ed. 222.00 (*0-7803-2969-4*, 95CH35852); lib. bdg. 222.00 (*0-7803-2970-8*, 95CB35852); fiche 222.00 (*0-7803-2971-6*, 95CM35852) Inst Electrical.

Sixteenth Maine Regiment in the War of the Rebellion Vol. I, Vol. I. rev. ed. Abne R. Small. Ed. by Peter Dalton & Cynthia Dalton. (Illus.). 225p. 1995. reprint ed. pap. 12.95 (*0-9642029-1-3*) Union Pubng.

***Sixteenth Myres Memorial Lecture: Financial Documents & Geographical Knowledge in the Roman World.** Claude Nicolet. (Myres Memorial Lectures: Vol. 16). 24p. 1997. pap. 9.00 (*0-904920-32-1*, Pub. by Leopards Head Pr UK) David Brown.

Sixteenth Note Patterns for the Drumset. Lionel Hedden. LC 94-96405. 156p. 1994. pap. text ed. 25.00 (*0-9643479-0-3*) L Hedden.

Sixteenth Oil Shale Symposium Proceedings. Ed. by James H. Gary. (Illus.). 600p. 1983. pap. text ed. 25.00 (*0-918062-56-X*) Colo Sch Mines.

***XVI Olympiad, Melbourne 1956 & Squaw Valley 1960.** (Olympic Century Ser.). (Illus.). 1996. 21.95 (*1-888383-14-3*, Wrld Spt) Wld Sport Resch.

XVIth Rolf Nevanlinna Colloquium: Proceedings of the International Conference Held in Joensuu, Finland, August 1-5, 1995. Ed. by Ilpo Laine et al. LC 96-28630. ix, 353p. (C). 1996. lib. bdg. 158.95 (*3-11-014746-7*) De Gruyter.

Sixteenth Space Simulation Conference: Confirming Spaceworthiness into the Next Millennium. 466p. 1990. 95.00 (*0-685-63215-6*) Inst Environ Sci.

Sixteenth Virginia Cavalry. Jack L. Dickinson. (Virginia Regimental Histories Ser.). (Illus.). 123p. 1989. 19.95 (*0-685-57637-X*) H E Howard.

Sixteenth Virginia Infantry. Benjamin H. Trask. (Virginia Regimental Histories Ser.). (Illus.). 128p. 1986. 19.95 (*0-930919-26-2*) H E Howard.

6th Air Force. Turner Publishing Company Staff. LC 94-60848. 144p. 1995. 48.00 (*1-56311-153-5*) Turner Pub KY.

Sixth Airborne Division: A Story Untold. H. M. Harclerode. (C). 1990. 99.00 (*1-85563-009-5*, Pub. by Quoin Pub Ltd UK) St Mut.

Sixth Amendment in Modern American Jurisprudence: A Critical Perspective. Alfredo Garcia. LC 91-44047. (Contributions in Legal Studies: No. 67). 256p. 1992. text ed. 59.95 (*0-313-27877-6*, GAQ/, Greenwood Pr) Greenwood.

Sixth Amendment to the Constitution of the United States: A Study in Constitutional Development. Francis H. Heller. LC 69-13931. 195p. 1969. reprint ed. text ed. 35.00 (*0-8371-0471-8*, HESI, Greenwood Pr) Greenwood.

Sixth & Seventh Book of Moses: Or Moses' Magical Spirit - Art Known As the Wonderful Arts of the Old Wise Hebrews, Taken from the Mosaic Books of the Cabaca & the Talmud for the Good of Mankind. Egyptian Publishing Co. Staff. 190p. 1996. pap. 17.95 (*1-56459-857-8*) Kessinger Pub.

Sixth & Seventh Books of Moses. Horst. 9.95 (*0-685-22112-1*) Wehman.

Sixth & Seventh Books of Moses: Moses' Magical Spirit Art Known As the Wonderful Arts. 190p. 1972. reprint ed. spiral bd. 9.00 (*0-7873-0003-9*) Hlth Research.

Sixth & Seventh Books of Moses, Or, Moses' Magical Spirit Art from the Talmud & Cabala. 1991. lib. bdg. 250.00 (*0-8490-4549-5*) Gordon Pr.

Sixth Annual Digest of Law School Transfer Policies. 1996. 27.50 (*0-614-03507-4*) Graduate Group.

Sixth Annual Directory of Graduate Law Programs in the United States. 1997. 27.50 (*0-938609-15-7*) Graduate Group.

Sixth Annual Directory of Law School Summer Programs in the United States & Abroad. 1994. 27.50 (*0-685-71240-0*) Graduate Group.

Sixth Annual Institute on Corporate Law Department Management. (Corporate Law & Practice Course Handbook, 1985-86 Ser.: Vol. 796). 573p. 1992. 70.00 (*0-685-65498-2*, B4-7020) PLI.

Sixth Annual International Help Desk Conference & Expo. Ed. by Patrick Bultema et al. (Illus.). 1144p. (Orig.). pap. write for info. (*1-57125-021-2*) Help Desk Inst.

Sixth Annual Internship in Federal Government. 1992. 27.50 (*0-685-53122-8*) Graduate Group.

Sixth Annual Internships in State Government. 1995. 27.50 (*0-685-71247-8*) Graduate Group.

Sixth Annual Internships Leading to Careers. Date not set. 27.50 (*0-614-10255-3*) Graduate Group.

Sixth Annual Labor & Employment Law Institute, School of Law, University of Louisville: Evolving Applications & Consequences of Labor & Employment Law, June 29-30, 1989. Ed. by Marlin M. Volz. LC 93-25749. vi, 221p. 1994. 57.50 (*0-8377-1240-8*) Rothman.

Sixth Annual Meeting, New York, 1960 see Advances in the Astronautical Sciences

Sixth Annual Report of the Secretaries of State, 1988: Foreign Policy Choices for the New Administration. 1990. 5.00 (*0-685-34506-8*) Southern Ctr Intl Stud.

Sixth Annual Report on Carcinogens (1991) 461p. (Orig.). (C). 1994. pap. text ed. 65.00 (*0-7881-0423-3*) DIANE Pub.

Sixth Annual Women Artists & the West Show & Sale. (Illus.). 40p. 1996. 10.00 (*0-317-65206-0*) Tucson Mus Art.

Sixth Assembling. Ed. by Richard Kostelanetz & Henry J. Korn. 288p. 1975. pap. 18.00 (*0-915066-16-5*) Assembling Pr.

Sixth Book of Junior Authors & Illustrators. Ed. by Sally H. Holtze. 356p. 1989. 48.00 (*0-8242-0777-7*) Wilson.

Sixth Book of Virgil's Aeneid, Translated & Commented on by Sir John Harrington (1604) John Harington. 238p. 1991. 90.00 (*0-19-812512-7*) OUP.

***Sixth Canadian Conference on General Relativity & Relativistic Astrophysics.** Braham, Stephen P. E. on General Relativity & Relativistic Astrophysics et al. LC 97-11371. (Fields Institute Communications Ser.). 1997. write for info. (*0-8218-0523-1*) Am Math.

Sixth Canon: Belletristic Rhetorical Theory & Its French Antecedents. Barbara Warnick. LC 93-20266. (Studies in Rhetoric & Communication). 188p. (C). 1993. text ed. 34.95 (*0-87249-892-1*) U of SC Pr.

Sixth Cartesian Meditation: The Idea of a Transcendental Theory of Method. Eugen Fink. Tr. by Ronald Bruzina. LC 94-34. (Studies in Continental Thought). 352p. (GER.). 1995. 35.00 (*0-253-32273-1*) Ind U Pr.

Sixth Century Monastery at Beth-Shan (Scythopolis) G. M. FitzGerald. (Publications of the Palestine Section Ser.: Vol. 4). (Illus.). xiv, 66p. 1939. 30.00 (*0-686-24094-4*) U PA Mus Pubns.

***Sixth Circuit Federal Practice Manual.** 2nd ed. Michael I. Cioffi et al. 212p. (Orig.). 1993. pap. 27.00 (*0-87084-787-2*) Anderson Pub Co.

***Sixth Column.** Robert A. Heinlein. lib. bdg. 22.95 (*0-8488-1982-9*) Amereon Ltd.

Sixth Column. Robert A. Heinlein. 256p. 1990. reprint ed. mass mkt. 5.99 (*0-671-72026-0*) Baen Bks.

Sixth Commandment. Lawrence Sanders. 368p. (Orig.). 1987. reprint ed. mass mkt. 6.99 (*0-425-10430-3*) Berkley Pub.

Sixth Complement Genetics Workshop & Conference, Main, July 1989: Proceedings - Journal: Complement & Inflammation, Vol. 7, Nos. 4-6, 1990. Ed. by G. Hauptmann et al. (Illus.). vi, 150p. 1990. pap. 113.25 (*3-8055-5324-2*) S Karger.

Sixth Congress of the International Society for Rock Mechanics Montreal, Canada. 1987: Proceedings, 3 vols., Set. Ed. by G. Herget & S. Vongpaisal. 2000p. 1988. text ed. 695.00 (*90-6191-711-5*, Pub. by A A Balkema NE) Ashgate Pub Co.

Sixth Day. Andree Chedid. 176p. 1992. pap. 9.95 (*1-85242-111-8*) Serpents Tail.

Sixth Day of Creation: A Discourse on Post Biblical, Post Modern Thought. Roberta Kalechofsky. (Illus.). 24p. 1986. 10.00 (*0-916288-20-X*) Micah Pubns.

Sixth E. C. Photovoltaic Solar Energy Conference. Ed. by Wolfgang Palz & F. C. Treble. 1985. lib. bdg. 334.00 (*90-277-2104-1*) Kluwer Ac.

Sixth Extinction: Patterns of Life & the Future of Humankind. Richard Leakey & Roger Lewin. (Illus.). 288p. 1996. pap. 14.00 (*0-385-46809-1*, Anchor NY) Doubleday.

Sixth Extinction: The Impact of the Living World on Human Life. Eldredge. 1998. 40.00 (*0-684-80284-8*) S&S Trade.

***Sixth Ezra: The Text & Origin.** Theodore A. Bergren. 304p. 1997. 52.00 (*0-19-511201-6*) OUP.

Sixth Form Choices. Helen Handley. (Core Business Studies). 1990. pap. 21.00 (*0-7463-0658-X*, Pub. by Northcote UK) St Mut.

64 Great Songs of the 40's & 50's. Ed. by Tony Esposito. 160p. (YA). 1995. pap. text ed. 14.95 (*0-89724-717-5*, MF9537) Warner Brothers.

Sixth Garfield Treasury. Jim Davis. (Illus.). 128p. 1991. pap. 10.95 (*0-345-37367-7*, Ballantine Trade) Ballantine.

***Sixth General Programme of Work Covering a Specific Period (1978-1983)** WHO Staff. (Official Publication Ser.). 109p. 1976. 3.00 (*92-4-156056-8*) World Health.

Sixth Global Warming International Conference & Expo, April 3-6, 1995, San Francisco USA: Abstracts. Sinyan Shen. (Global Warming International Center Ser.). (Illus.). 120p. (C). 1995. pap. 105.00 (*1-884736-00-9*) Supcon Intl.

Sixth Grade. B. K. Hixson. (Utah Core-Science Ser.). 113p. 1990. pap. text ed. 19.99 (*1-57156-017-3*) Wild Goose UT.

Sixth-Grade Book. Grace Burton et al. Ed. by Miriam A. Leiva. LC 92-16924. (Curriculum & Evaluation Standards for School Mathematics Addenda Ser.: Grades K-6). (Illus.). 32p. (Orig.). (J). (gr. k-6). 1992. pap. 11.50 (*0-87353-316-X*) NCTM.

Sixth Grade Can Really Kill You. Barthe DeClements. 160p. (J). 1995. pap. 3.99 (*0-14-037130-3*) Puffin Bks.

Sixth-Grade Crush. Sherry Shahan. 144p. (J). (gr. 3-5). 1993. pap. 2.50 (*0-87406-647-6*) Willowisp Pr.

Sixth Grade Math Review. Frank Schaffer Publications, Inc. Staff. (Skill Builders Ser.). (Illus.). 128p. 1996. wbk. ed. 10.95 (*0-86734-921-2*, FS-32073) Schaffer Pubns.

Sixth Grade Math TAAS Instructional Packet. Patricia Enselek & Susan Griffin. (TAAS Instructional Packets (TIPs) Ser.). 91p. 1991. 19.95 (*1-883396-10-7*) Educ Etc.

***Sixth Grade Mutants Meet the Slime.** 1997. pap. 3.50 (*0-440-41317-6*) Dell.

***Sixth Grade Popularity Cream.** Stephany A. Poce. 100p. (Orig.). (J). (gr. 6). 1997. mass mkt. 5.99 (*1-55197-808-3*, Pub. by Comnwlth Pub CN) Partners Pubs Grp.

Sixth Grade Reading TAAS Instructional Packet. Patricia Enselek & Susan Griffin. (TAAS Instructional Packets (TIPs) Ser.). 68p. 1990. 19.95 (*1-883396-08-5*) Educ Etc.

Sixth Grade Review. Frank Schaffer Publications, Inc. Staff. (Skill Builders Ser.). (Illus.). 128p. 1996. wbk. ed. 10.95 (*0-86734-917-4*, FS-32061) Schaffer Pubns.

Sixth Grade Secrets. Louis Sachar. 208p. (J). (gr. 4-6). 1992. pap. 3.99 (*0-590-46075-7*, Apple Paperbacks) Scholastic Inc.

Sixth-Grade Star. Constance Hiser. LC 92-52856. 96p. (J). (gr. 3-7). 1992. 13.95 (*0-8234-0967-8*) Holiday.

Sixth Grade Star. Constance Hiser. (J). (gr. 3-6). 1996. mass mkt. 3.99 (*0-671-87116-1*) PB.

***Sixth-Grade Star.** Constance Hiser. (J). (gr. 3-6). Date not set. pap. 3.99 (*0-614-19322-2*) PB.

Sixth Grade Was a Nightmare, & Seventh Is Worse. Haw Cheng. Ed. by Joann M. Thurman. (Illus.). 128p. (J). (gr. 3-9). Date not set. 11.95 (*0-89896-335-4*) Larksdale.

Sixth Grade Was a Nightmare, & Seventh Is Worse. Haw Cheng. Ed. by Joann M. Thurman. (Illus.). 128p. (J). (gr. 3-9). 1996. pap. 7.95 (*0-89896-336-2*) Larksdale.

Sixth Grade Writing Instructional Packet. Patricia Enselek & Susan Griffin. (TAAS Instructional Packets (TIPs) Ser.). 67p. 1990. 19.95 (*1-883396-09-3*) Educ Etc.

Sixth Grandfather: Black Elk's Teachings Given to John G. Neihardt. Ed. by Raymond J. DeMallie. LC 83-14452. (Illus.). xxix, 462p. 1984. pap. 15.00 (*0-8032-6564-6*, Bison Books) U of Nebr Pr.

Sixth HGH Symposium. Ed. by J. S. Christiansen & J. Girard. (Journal Ser.: Vol. 45, Nos. 1 & 2, 1996). (Illus.). 112p. 1996. pap. 88.75 (*3-8055-6280-2*) S Karger.

Sixth Infantry Division. Turner Publishing Company Staff. LC 88-51132. 88p. 1989. 48.00 (*0-938021-71-0*) Turner Pub KY.

Sixth Infantry Division in World War II 1939-1945. Ed. by Sixth Infantry Division, Public Relation Section Staff. (Divisional Ser.: No. 24). (Illus.). 180p. 1983. reprint ed. 39.95 (*0-89839-073-7*) Battery Pr.

***6th International Conference on Intelligent Systems.** 215p. (C). 1997. write for info. (*1-880843-20-X*) Int Soc Comp App.

Sixth International Conference on AC & DC Power Transmission, No. IC423. 297p. 1996. pap. 148.00 (*0-85296-654-7*) Inst Elect Eng.

Sixth International Conference on Accounting Education: Proceedings, Kyoto, Japan 1987. International Conference on Accounting Education Staff. LC 88-31757. 913p. 1988. text ed. 125.00 (*0-89930-420-6*, ISP/, Quorum Bks) Greenwood.

Sixth International Conference on Collective Phenomena: Reports from the Moscow Refusnik Seminar. Inga Fischer-Hjalmars & Joel L. Lebowitz. (Annals Ser.: Vol. 452). 411p. 1985. text ed. 94.00 (*0-89766-298-9*); pap. text ed. 94.00 (*0-89766-299-7*) NY Acad Sci.

Sixth International Conference on Cyclic Nucleotides, Calcium & Protein Phosphorylation, Bethesda, MD, September 2-7, 1986. Sixth International Conference on Cyclic Nucleotides, Calcium & Protein Phosphorylation Staff. Ed. by Robert S. Adelstein et al. (Advances in Second Messenger & Phosphoprotein Research Ser.: No. 21). (Illus.). 240p. 1988. reprint ed. pap. 68.40 (*0-608-00668-8*, 2061255) Bks Demand.

Sixth International Conference on Expansive Soils (6eme Conference Internationale des Sols Expansifs: Proceedings, New Delhi, 1-4 December 1987, 2 vols. 700p. 1988. text ed. 210.00 (*90-6191-923-1*, Pub. by A A Balkema NE) Ashgate Pub Co.

Sixth International Conference on Industrial & Engineering Applications of Artificial Intelligence & Expert Systems: The City Chambers, Edinburgh, Scotland, June 1-4, 1993, Sponsored by International Society of Applied Intelligence. Ed. by P. W. Chung et al. LC 93-1469. 546p. 1993. pap. text ed. 105.00 (*2-88124-604-4*) Gordon & Breach.

Sixth International Conference on Radio Receivers & Associated Systems. 217p. 1995. pap. 86.00 (*0-85296-643-1*, IC415) Inst Elect Eng.

6th International Conference on the Conservation of Earthen Architecture, Adobe Conference Preprints. Ed. by Kirsten Grimstad. (Illus.). 489p. 1990. 49.95 (*0-89236-181-6*, Getty Conservation Inst) J P Getty Trust.

Sixth International Report on the Prevention & Suppression of Dust in Mining, Tunnelling, & Quarrying, 1973-1977. (Occupational Safety & Health Ser.: No. 48). viii, 152p. 1982. pap. 15.75 (*92-2-103006-7*) Intl Labour Office.

***Sixth International Symposium on Environmental Concerns in Rights-of-Way Management: 24-26 February 1997, New Orleans, Louisiana.** James R. Williams et al. LC 97-15931. 1997. write for info. (*0-08-043198-4*) Elsevier.

Sixth International Symposium on Environmental Degradation of Materials in Nuclear Power Systems: Water Reactors. Ed. by R. E. Gold & E. P. Simonen. LC 93-80614. (Illus.). 943p. 1994. 40.00 (*0-87339-258-2*, 2582) Minerals Metals.

Sixth International Symposium on Pediatric Neuro-Oncology, Marseille, June 1993: Abstracts. Ed. by M. Choux. (Journal: Pediatric Neurosurgery: Vol. 19, No. 6, 1993). (Illus.). 62p. 1993. pap. 48.00 (*3-8055-5883-X*) S Karger.

6th International Symposium on Vulcanospeleology. Ed. by G. Thomas Rea. (Illus.). 286p. 1991. pap. 11.00 (*1-879961-02-4*) Natl Speleological.

Sixth International Visual Field Symposium. Ed. by A. Heijl & Erik L. Greve. (Documenta Ophthalmologica Proceedings Ser.). 1985. lib. bdg. 304.00 (*90-6193-524-5*) Kluwer Ac.

Sixth International Workshop on Photon-Photon Collision. Ed. by R. L. Lander. 520p. 1985. 89.00 (*9971-978-22-9*) World Scientific Pub.

Sixth Marcel Grossman Meeting on General Relativity, 2 vols., Set. H. Sato. 1500p. 1993. text ed. 260.00 (*981-02-0950-9*) World Scientific Pub.

Sixth Marine Division Association History. Sixth Marine Division Association Staff. LC 87-50368. 128p. 1987. 48.00 (*0-938021-12-5*) Turner Pub KY.

Sixth Merry Adventure of Robin Hood. Howard Pyle. 1986. pap. 2.95 (*0-317-38208-X*, Sig Classics) NAL-Dutton.

Sixth National Space Symposium Proceedings Report. Ed. by Diane L. Nitschke et al. (Illus.). 198p. 1990. pap. 50.00 (*0-9616962-4-9*) US Space Found.

Sixth National Symposium on Vacuum Technology Transactions, Sheraton Hotel, Philadelphia, October, 1959: Cumulative Index of 1954-1959 Symposia. American Vacuum Society Inc. Staff & C. Meissner. LC 59-1422. 1960. 153.00 (*0-08-009119-9*, Pub. by Pergamon Repr UK) Franklin.

Sixth Palenque Round Table, Nineteen Eighty-Six. Ed. by Merle G. Robertson. LC 90-12171. (Illus.). 368p. 1990. 68.50 (*0-8061-2277-3*) U of Okla Pr.

Sixth Patriarch's Sutra: Great Master Hui Neng. Tr. by Buddhist Text Translation Society Staff from CHI. (Illus.). 235p. (Orig.). 1977. 15.00 (*0-917512-33-2*); pap. 10.00 (*0-917512-19-7*) Buddhist Text.

Sixth Precinct. Christopher Newman. 320p. (Orig.). 1987. mass mkt. 5.99 (*0-449-13174-2*, GM) Fawcett.

Sixth Quantum 1/f Noise & Other Low Frequency Fluctuations in Electronic Devices Symposium. Peter H. Handel & Alma L. Chung. (AIP Press Conference Proceedings Ser.: No. 371). (Illus.). 176p. 1996. boxed 130.00 (*1-56396-410-4*, CP 371, AIP) Am Inst Physics.

Sixth Reader see McGuffey's Revised Eclectic Readers

Sixth Refinement Workshop. Ed. by D. Till & C. J. Van Rijsbergen. (Workshops in Computing Ser.). 307p. 1994. 68.95 (*0-387-19886-5*) Spr-Verlag.

Sixth Seal. Mary Wesley. 194p. (YA). (gr. 7 up). 1993. 14.95 (*0-87951-506-6*) Overlook Pr.

Sixth Sense. Laurie Nadel et al. 304p. 1992. reprint ed. mass mkt. 4.99 (*0-380-71503-1*) Avon.

***Sixth Sense: Intuition.** Sue Hurwitz. LC 96-29963. (Library of the Five Senses (Plus the Sixth Sense)). (J). 1997. write for info. (*0-8239-5057-3*) Rosen Group.

Sixth Sense: Its Cultivation & Use. Charles H. Brent. 1993. reprint ed. pap. 16.95 (*1-872736-47-5*, Pub. by Mandrake Pr UK) Holmes Pub.

Sixth Sense: Practical Tips for Everyday Safety. Joseph Niehaus. (Illus.). (Orig.). 1990. pap. 11.95 (*0-933025-19-X*) Blue Bird Pub.

Sixth Sense: Psychic Powers & Your Five Senses. Jenny Randles. 240p. (C). 1987. 75.00 (*0-7090-2802-4*) St Mut.

Sixth Sense & Other Stories. Margaret S. Hopkins. LC 71-110199. (Short Story Index Reprint Ser.). 1977. 21.95 (*0-8369-3350-8*) Ayer.

***Sixth Sense...Faith.** John Osteen. Date not set. mass mkt. 1.99 (*0-912631-12-0*) J O Pubns.

***Sixth Sin.** David Michel. 274p. (Orig.). 1997. pap. 9.95 (*0-9656483-0-3*) Highland Pub Hse.

Sixth Stellation of the Icosahedron. Gerald Jenkins & Magdalen Bear. (Tarquin Polyhedra Ser.). 24p. (Orig.). (J). (gr. 5-9). 1986. pap. 4.95 (*0-906212-46-4*, Pub. by Tarquin UK) Parkwest Pubns.

Sixth Symposium by the 5 Winners of the Grants from Sandoz Foundation for Gerontological Research: Annual Meeting of the Japan Gerontological Society, Tokyo, Japan, September 1994. Ed. by H. Orimo. (Journal: Gerontology Ser.: Vol. 41, Suppl. 1, 1995). (Illus.). iv, 34p. 1995. pap. 21.75 (*3-8055-6235-7*) S Karger.

Sixth Symposium, Microdosimetry, 2, Vol. 1. Ed. by J. Booz & H. G. Ebert. (Commission of the European Communities Ser.). 688p. 1978. text ed. 274.00 (*0-906346-02-9*) Gordon & Breach.

Sixth Symposium, Microdosimetry, 2, Vol. 2. Ed. by J. Booz & H. G. Ebert. (Commission of the European Communities Ser.). 572p. 1978. text ed. 274.00 (*0-906346-03-7*) Gordon & Breach.

Sixth Symposium on a Long Term Clinical Care of Parkinson's Disease, Tokyo, October 1991. Ed. by T. Nakanishi. (Journal: European Neurology: Vol. 32, Suppl. 1, 1992). (Illus.). vi, 54p. 1992. pap. 26.25 (*3-8055-5664-0*) S Karger.

Sixth Trumpeter Swan Society Conference: Proceedings & Papers. Trumpeter Swan Society Staff. Ed. by David K. Weaver. 101p. (Orig.). 1981. pap. 4.00 (*0-9619936-1-8*) Trumpeter Swan Soc.

***Sixth USENIX Security Symposium Proceedings.** Ed. by Greg Rose. 222p. 1996. pap. 35.00 (*1-880446-79-0*) USENIX Assn.

Sixth Virginia Cavalry. Michael P. Musick. (Virginia Regimental Histories Ser.). (Illus.). 177p. 1990. 19.95 (*0-685-57636-1*) H E Howard.

Sixth Virginia Infantry. Michael A. Cavanaugh. (Virginia Regimental Histories Ser.). (Illus.). 143p. 1988. 19.95 (*0-930919-57-2*) H E Howard.

***Sixth Vision.** Bobbi Sinha-Morey. 78p. (Orig.). 1990. pap. 9.95 (*0-614-24115-4*) Cedar Bay Pr.

Sixth Workshop on Grand Unification: Proceedings of the Workshop held at Minneapolis, April, 1985. Ed. by S. Rudaz & T. Walsh. 500p. 1986. pap. 55.00 (*9971-978-84-9*); text ed. 124.00 (*9971-978-83-0*) World Scientific Pub.

Sixth Workshop on Parallel & Distributed Simulation (PADS '92) Newport Beach, California. Ed. by Marc Abrams & Paul Reynolds, Jr. 212p. 1992. 66.00 (*1-56555-008-0*, SS-24-3) Soc Computer Sim.

Sixties. Ed. by Peter Stine. LC 95-22000. (Illus.). 288p. (C). 1996. pap. 17.95 (*0-8143-2558-0*) Wayne St U Pr.

Sixties. Edmund Wilson. 1994. pap. 19.00 (*0-374-52414-9*, Noonday) FS&G.

Sixties. rev. ed. John Javna & Gordon Javna. (Illus.). 240p. 1988. pap. 15.95 (*0-312-01725-1*) St Martin.

Sixties, No. 4. Ed. by Robert Bly & William Duffy. 1982. reprint ed. pap. 5.95 (*0-934888-06-X*) Hobart & Wm Smith.

Sixties, No. 5. Ed. by Robert Bly & William Duffy. 1982. reprint ed. pap. 5.95 (*0-934888-07-8*) Hobart & Wm Smith.

Sixties, No. 6. Ed. by Robert Bly & William Duffy. 1982. reprint ed. pap. 5.95 (*0-934888-08-6*) Hobart & Wm Smith.

Sixties, No. 7. Ed. by Robert Bly & William Duffy. 1982. reprint ed. pap. 5.95 (*0-934888-09-4*) Hobart & Wm Smith.

Sixties, No. 8. Ed. by Robert Bly & William Duffy. 1982. reprint ed. pap. 5.95 (*0-934888-10-8*) Hobart & Wm Smith.

Sixties, No. 9. Ed. by Robert Bly & William Duffy. 1982. reprint ed. pap. 5.95 (*0-934888-11-6*) Hobart & Wm Smith.

Sixties, No. 10. Ed. by Robert Bly & William Duffy. 1982. reprint ed. pap. 5.95 (*0-934888-12-4*) Hobart & Wm Smith.

Sixties: (Poppy Chronicles VI) large type ed. Claire Rayner. (Charnwood Ser.). 432p. 1994. 27.99 (*0-7089-8751-6*, Charnwood) Ulverscroft.

Sixties: A Black Chronology. Norman Harris. 116p. (C). 1990. pap. text ed. 9.70 (*1-878531-00-X*) Black Res Ctr.

S

Sixties: Art, Politics, & the Media of Our Most Explosive Decade. Ed. by Gerald Howard. 1995. pap. 14.95 (*1-56924-824-9*) Marlowe & Co.

Sixties: Biographies of the Love Generation. Alan K. Gorg. LC 94-78291. 145p. (Orig.). 1995. pap. 8.95 (*0-9642754-1-4*) Media Associates.

Sixties: From Memory to History. Ed. by David Farber. LC 93-40102. 360p. 1994. pap. 15.95 (*0-8078-4462-4*); lib. bdg. 39.95 (*0-8078-2153-5*) U of NC Pr.

Sixties: From Notebooks & Diaries of the Period. Edmund Wilson. LC 92-16642. 1993. 35.00 (*0-374-26554-2*) FS&G.

Sixties: Recollections of the Decade fom Harper's Magazine. Katharine Wittemore. 1995. pap. 14.95 (*1-879957-20-5*) Harpers Mag Found.

Sixties: Years of Hope, Days of Rage. rev. ed. Todd Gitlin. 544p. 1993. pap. 16.95 (*0-553-37212-2*) Bantam.

Sixties' & Seventies' Designs & Memorabilia: Identification & Price Guide. Anne Gilbert. (Illus.). 432p. (Orig.). 1994. pap. 12.50 (*0-380-77089-X*, Confident Collect) Avon.

Sixties & Seventies Rock Score. (Illus.). 80p. 1990. pap. 14.95 (*0-8256-1303-5*, AM72620) Music Sales.

Sixties & the End of Modern America. David Steigerwald. 320p. 1994. pap. text ed. 20.00 (*0-312-09007-2*) St Martin.

Sixties & the End of Modern America Vol. 1. David Steigerwald. 1994. text ed. 39.95 (*0-312-12303-5*) St Martin.

Sixties Art Scene in London. David Mellor. (Illus.). 240p. (C). 1993. pap. 35.00 (*0-7148-2910-2*, Pub. by Phaidon Press UK) Chronicle Bks.

Sixties British Cinema. Robert Murphy. (Illus.). 320p. 1992. pap. 25.95 (*0-85170-324-0*, Pub. by British Film Inst UK); text ed. 59.95 (*0-85170-309-7*, Pub. by British Film Inst UK) Ind U Pr.

Sixties' Children. Leo Clarin. Ed. by Anita Pearson & W. B. Knox. (Illus.). 300p. (Orig.). 1996. pap. 12.95 (*1-881116-68-9*) Black Forest Pr.

***Sixties Design.** Philippe Garner. (Big Architecture & Design Ser.). 1996. pap. text ed. 24.99 (*3-8228-8934-2*) Taschen Amer.

Sixties Experience: Hard Lessons about Modern America. Edward P. Morgan. 1992. pap. 19.95 (*1-56639-014-1*) Temple U Pr.

60's Flashback. Greg Paul. LC 94-35574. 1995. pap. 19.95 (*0-86636-279-7*) PBC Intl Inc.

Sixties Going on Seventies. rev. ed. Nora Sayre. 400p. 1995. pap. 18.95 (*0-8135-2193-9*) Rutgers U Pr.

***Sixties London.** Amanda Hopkinson. 1997. 49.95 (*0-85331-699-6*) Antique Collect.

Sixties Papers: Documents of a Rebellious Decade. Ed. by Judith C. Albert & Stewart E. Albert. 336p. 1984. text ed. 55.00 (*0-275-91116-0*, C1116, Praeger Pubs); pap. text ed. 24.95 (*0-275-91781-9*, B1781, Praeger Pubs) Greenwood.

60s Pop Hits. (Easy Piano Ser.). 12.95 (*0-7935-4894-2*, 00310074) H Leonard.

Sixties Radicals, Then & Now: Candid Conversations with Those Who Shaped the Era. Ron Chepesiuk. LC 94-37664. (Illus.). 334p. 1995. lib. bdg. 39.95 (*0-89950-778-6*) McFarland & Co.

Sixties Source Book. Nigel Cawthorne. 25.98 (*1-55521-529-7*) Bk Sales Inc.

Sixties Spiritual Awakening. Robert Ellwood. LC 93-44227. 350p. (C). 1994. 24.95 (*0-8135-2093-2*) Rutgers U Pr.

Sixties, Without Apology. Ed. by Sohnya Sayres et al. LC 84-2274. (Illus.). 399p. 1984. pap. text ed. 17.95 (*0-8166-1337-0*) U of Minn Pr.

60th Anniversary Journal: House of Prayer Church of God. Ed. by Evelyn M. Taylor. (Illus.). 125p. (Orig.). 1996. pap. 10.00 (*1-877971-17-0*, 01-60) Mid Atl Reg Pr.

Sixtieth of a Second: Portraits of Women 1961-1981. Sue Ford. (C). 1990. 60.00 (*0-949836-19-2*, Pub. by Pascoe Pub AT) St Mut.

Sixtonian. Geraldo Guirty. 1991. 13.95 (*0-533-09473-9*) Vantage.

***60 - Deal with It.** Jan B. King. Ed. by Cliff Carle. (Illus.). 64p. (Orig.). 1997. pap. 5.95 (*1-57644-023-0*) CCC Pubns.

Sixty Art Projects for Children: Painting, Clay, Puppets, Paints, Masks, & More. Jeanette M. Baumgardner. (Illus.). 128p. 1993. pap. 12.00 (*0-517-88008-3*, C P Pubs) Crown Pub Group.

Sixty Bokes Olde & Newe: Manuscripts & Early Printed Books from Libraries in & Near Philadelphia Illustrating Chauncer's Sources, His Works, & Their Influence. Ed. by David Anderson. 123p. 1986. pap. text ed. 9.95 (*0-933784-08-2*) U Pr of Va.

Sixty Crocheted Snowflakes. Barbara Christopher. 32p. (Orig.). 1987. pap. 3.50 (*0-486-25393-7*) Dover.

Sixty-Day Diet Diary. Karen Kreps & Richard Smith. 144p. (Orig.). 1987. pap. 5.95 (*0-440-57946-5*, Dell Trade Pbks) Dell.

***60-Day Fully Financed Fortune Kit: How to Make Money Raising Money for People.** 9th ed. Tyler G. Hicks. 150p. 1998. pap. 29.50 (*1-56150-215-4*) Intl Wealth.

60-Day Fully Financed Fortune Kit: How to Make Money Raising Money for People, 3 bks., Set. 8th ed. Tyler G. Hicks. 150p. 1996. pap. 29.50 (*1-56150-165-4*) Intl Wealth.

Sixty Days of Low-Fat, Low-Cost Meals in Minutes: Over 150 Delicious, Healthy Recipes & Menus That Fit Your Budget. M. J. Smith. LC 92-26421. 1992. pap. 12.95 (*1-56561-010-5*) Chronimed.

***Sixty Days under the Influence: A Photo Journal Through France.** Billy Cone. LC 97-65961. (Illus.). 128p. (Orig.). 1997. pap. write for info. (*1-57197-064-9*) Pentland Pr.

6800 Microprocessor. I. Scott MacKenzie. LC 94-32687. 578p. 1995. 84.00 (*0-02-373654-2*, Macmillan Coll) P-H.

Sixty-Eight Hundred Microprocessor. Quinn. 526p. (C). 1990. text ed. 86.00 (*0-675-20515-8*, Merrill Coll) P-H.

Sixty-Eight Hundred Microprocessor: Architecture, Software & Interfacing Techniques. Walter A. Triebel & Avtar Singh. (Illus.). 384p. 1987. Motorola edition. text ed. 21.97 (*0-13-811290-8*) P-H.

Sixty-Eight Hundred Nine Microprocessor. Andrew C. Staugaard, Jr. (Illus.). 421p. (C). 1982. 99.95 (*0-87119-092-3*, EE-3404); teacher ed. 9.95 (*0-685-09158-9*); pap. text ed. 24.95 (*0-87119-081-8*, EB-6404) Heathkit-Zenith Ed.

Sixty-Eight Hundred Nine Primer: Assembly Language & Subroutines for the TRS-80 Color Computer. Kenneth Skier. 280p. 1983. pap. 16.95 (*0-07-057862-1*, BYTE Bks) McGraw.

Sixty-Eight Popular Children's Songs. Brimhall. 1990. 5.95 (*0-685-32154-1*, O450) Hansen Ed Mus.

Sixty-Eight Scientific & Engineering Programs for the Apple II & IIe. Joseph J. Carr. 1984. 22.00 (*0-8359-6920-7*, Reston) P-H.

Sixty-Eight, Seventy-Eight, Eighty-Eight: From Women's Liberation to Feminism. Amanda Sebestyen. 1989. pap. write for info. (*1-85327-022-9*, Pub. by Prism Pr UK) Assoc Pubs Grp.

Sixty-Eight Thousand & Sixty-Eight Thousand Twenty Microprocessors: Architecture, Software & Interfacing Techniques. Walter A. Triebel & Avtar Singh. 544p. 1991. text ed. 91.00 (*0-13-812132-X*) P-H.

Sixty-Eight Thousand Assembly Language. Alan Clements. 768p. 1994. text ed. 67.95 (*0-534-93275-4*) PWS Pubs.

68000 Family Microprocessor. 2nd ed. Miller. 1992. text ed. 86.00 (*0-02-381560-4*, Macmillan Coll) P-H.

Sixty-Eight Thousand Microcomputer Systems: Designing & Troubleshooting. Alan D. Wilcox. (Illus.). 512p. (C). 1987. text ed. 88.00 (*0-13-811399-8*) P-H.

Sixty-Eight Thousand Microprocessor: Hardware & Software Principles & Applications. 2nd ed. James L. Antonakos. LC 92-31742. (Merrill's International Series in Electrical & Electronics Technology). 512p. (C). 1992. text ed. 74.00 (*0-02-303603-6*, Macmillan Coll) P-H.

68000 Microprocessor: Hardware & Software Principles & Applications. 3rd ed. James L. Antonakos. 1995. text ed. 82.00 (*0-02-303617-6*, Macmillan Coll) P-H.

Sixty-Eight Thousand Sourcebook. Alan Clements. 1990. pap. text ed. 70.00 (*0-07-011321-1*) McGraw.

Sixty Eight Thousand User Guide. Fleetwood. 182p. 1985. 19.90 (*1-85058-001-4*, Pub. by Sigma Pr UK) Bk Clearing Hse.

Sixty-Eight Thousand User's Manual. Joseph J. Carr. write for info. (*0-318-59643-1*) S&S Trade.

Sixty Etudes for Violin, Op. 45, 2 bks., Bk. 1. (Carl Fischer Music Library: Nos. 122 & 123). (FRE & GER.). pap. 6.95 (*0-8258-0026-9*, L122) Fischer Inc NY.

Sixty Etudes for Violin, Op. 45, 2 bks., Bk. 2. (Carl Fischer Music Library: Nos. 122 & 123). (FRE & GER.). pap. 6.95 (*0-8258-0141-9*, L123) Fischer Inc NY.

Sixty Fairy Tales of the Brothers Grimm. Illus. by Arthur Rackham. (Fairy Tales & Fables Ser.). (J). (gr. 2-7). 8.98 (*0-517-28525-8*) Random Hse Value.

Sixty-Fifth Infantry Division. Turner Publishing Company Staff. LC 93-61017. 104p. 1993. 48.00 (*1-56311-118-7*) Turner Pub KY.

***Sixty Fingers, Sixty Toes: See How the Dilley Family Grows!** Becki Dilley et al. LC 97-23087. (Illus.). (J). 1998. write for info. (*0-8027-8613-8*); lib. bdg. write for info. (*0-8027-8614-6*) Walker & Co.

Sixty-First Art Directors Annual. Art Directors Club of New York Staff. Ed. by Miriam L. Solomon. (Illus.). 672p. 1982. 39.95 (*0-937414-02-6*) ADC Pubns.

Sixty-First Virginia Infantry. Benjamin H. Trask. (Virginia Regimental Histories Ser.). (Illus.). 120p. 1988. 19.95 (*0-930919-64-5*) H E Howard.

65 Golden Years. 1994. pap. 16.95 (*0-89724-224-6*, XW1515) Astor Bks.

65 Hits of the 90's: Alto Sax. 12.95 (*0-7935-4258-8*, 00849013) H Leonard.

65 Hits of the 90's: Clarinet. 12.95 (*0-7935-4257-X*, 00849012) H Leonard.

65 Hits of the 90's: Flute. 12.95 (*0-7935-4256-1*, 00849011) H Leonard.

65 Hits of the 90's: Trumpet. 12.95 (*0-7935-4259-6*, 00849014) H Leonard.

65 Hits of the 90's Fake Book: C Edition. limited ed. 80p. 1995. otabind 10.95 (*0-7935-4410-6*, 00240035) H Leonard.

Sixty-Five Little Pieces in Progressive Order for Beginner Flutists. L. Moyse. 80p. 1988. pap. 12.95 (*0-7935-4814-4*, 50488965) H Leonard.

Sixty-Five Pearls. Manohar Kelkar. LC 87-42906. 59p. 1988. 6.95 (*1-55523-116-0*) Winston-Derek.

***Sixty-Five Plus.** 1997. lib. bdg. 250.95 (*0-8490-8206-4*) Gordon Pr.

Sixty-Five Plus in America. (Illus.). 159p. (Orig.). (C). 1994. pap. text ed. 30.00 (*1-56806-268-0*) DIANE Pub.

Sixty-Five Plus in Pennsylvania. Pennsylvania State Data Center Staff. 25p. (Orig.). 1993. pap. 10.00 (*0-939667-32-0*) Penn State Data Ctr.

***65 Plus in the United States.** Frank B. Hobbs & Bonnie L. Damon. (Illus.). 185p. (Orig.). 1996. pap. 35.00 (*0-7881-3319-5*) DIANE Pub.

Sixty-Five Valiants. Alice H. Luiggi. LC 65-28692. (Illus.). 213p. reprint ed. pap. 60.80 (*0-7837-4930-9*, 2044596) Bks Demand.

Sixty-Five Ways to Give Evangelistic Invitations. Faris D. Whitesell. LC 84-11269. 128p. 1984. reprint ed. pap. 5.99 (*0-8254-4021-1*) Kregel.

Sixty-Five-Year Index to Physical Therapy. 1987. pap. 13.00 (*0-912452-65-X*, C-11) Am Phys Therapy Assn.

Sixty-Five Years of Progress & a Record of New York City Banks. Ed. by Stuart Bruchey. LC 80-1189. (Rise of Commercial Banking Ser.). (Illus.). 1981. reprint ed. lib. bdg. 15.95 (*0-405-13674-9*) Ayer.

65 Years of the Oscar: The Official History of the Academy Awards. Robert Osborne. (Illus.). 352p. 1994. 65.00 (*1-55859-715-8*) Abbeville Pr.

Sixty Folk-Tales from Exclusively Slavonic Sources. Ed. by Richard M. Dorson. Tr. by Albert H. Wratislaw. LC 77-70629. (International Folklore Ser.). 1977. reprint ed. lib. bdg. 26.95 (*0-405-10133-3*) Ayer.

Sixty for You: New Monologues for & about Actresses & Actors. Ken Friedman. 79p. (Orig.). (C). 1994. pap. 8.95 (*0-9641946-0-0*) Wagon Pr.

***64 Beds.** Sally Jacques. (Illus.). 64p. 1994. 12.95 (*0-911051-82-1*) Plain View.

64 Intruder. Gregory T. Glading. LC 95-90132. 152p. (Orig.). 1996. pap. 8.00 (*1-56002-557-3*, Univ Edtns) Aegina Pr.

64 Missing Years of Torture: The Twist to Slavery. Ricardo A. Scott. (Ras Cardo Speaks Ser.). (Illus.). 75p. (Orig.). Date not set. pap. write for info. (*1-883427-73-8*) Crnerstone GA.

Sixty-four to 256-Megabit Reticle Generation: Technology Requirements & Approaches. Ed. by Gregory K. Hearn & Robert J. Naber. LC 93-46150. (Critical Reviews of Optical Science & Technology Ser.: Vol. CR51). 1994. 40.00 (*0-8194-1357-7*); pap. 40.00 (*0-8194-1358-5*) SPIE.

Sixty-Four Yard & Garden Projects You Can Build Yourself. Monte Burch. Ed. by John Matthews & Deborah Balmuth. LC 94-13330. (Illus.). 192p. 1994. 28.95 (*0-88266-834-X*, Storey Pub); pap. 17.95 (*0-88266-846-3*, Storey Pub) Storey Comm Inc.

64 Years to Make a Negro: Willie Lynch Speech to the American Slave Owners in 1712. Alfred Ali. 190p. (Orig.). pap. 12.95 (*0-9636025-3-5*) A Ali Lit Wrks.

Sixty-Fourth Parallel Alaska Ice Postcard Collection, Vol. 1: New Ice Carving from Fairbanks, Alaska. Douglas Yates. (Illus.). 46p. (Orig.). 1990. pap. 12.00 (*0-9625711-0-5*) Sixtyfourth Parallel.

Sixty-Fourth Parallel Alaska Ice Postcard Collection, Vol. 1: New Ice Carving from Fairbanks, Alaska, Set. Douglas Yates. (Illus.). 46p. (Orig.). 1990. pap. write for info. (*0-9625711-1-3*) Sixtyfourth Parallel.

Sixty-Fourth Virginia Infantry. Jeffrey C. Weaver. (Virginia Regimental Histories Ser.). (Illus.). 175p. 1993. write for info. (*1-56190-041-9*) H E Howard.

Sixty Glorious Years: A Tribute to the Douglas DC-3. Arthur Pearcy. (Illus.). 168p. 1995. 34.95 (*0-7603-0192-1*) Motorbooks Intl.

Sixty Great Founders. G. Hanks. Date not set. 19.99 (*1-85792-140-2*, Pub. by Christian Focus UK) Spring Arbor Dist.

Sixty Great Room Fireplaces: Collection A104. (Illus.). (Orig.). 1995. pap. 20.00 (*0-922070-13-X*, COLLECTION A104) M Tecton Pub.

***Sixty Greatest Conspiracies of All Time: History's Biggest Mysteries, Cover-Ups & Cabals.** Jonathan Vankin. LC 96-43145. 1996. pap. text ed. 16.95 (*0-8065-1833-2*, Citadel Pr) Carol Pub Group.

Sixty Hiking Trails, Central Oregon Cascades. Don Lowe & Roberta Lowe. Ed. by Thomas K. Worcester. (Illus.). 128p. (Orig.). 1992. pap. 12.95 (*0-911518-51-7*) Touchstone Oregon.

Sixty Hits of the Nineties: "C" Edition. (Limited Edition Fake Book Ser.). 112p. 1991. pap. 12.95 (*0-7935-0745-6*, 00240037) H Leonard.

Sixty Is Just Extreme Middle Age: And Other Absurdities. Sally Bennett. (Illus.). 64p. (Orig.). 1993. pap. text ed. 5.95 (*0-9636600-0-4*) Twiga Pub.

Sixty Jane. John L. Long. LC 76-103524. (Short Story Index Reprint Ser.). 1977. 19.95 (*0-8369-3266-8*) Ayer.

Sixty Machine Quilting Patterns. Pat Holly & Sue Nickels. LC 93-50914. (Illus.). 96p. (Orig.). 1994. pap. 5.95 (*0-486-28013-6*) Dover.

Sixty Miles from Contentment: Traveling the Nineteenth-Century American Interior. M. H. Dunlop. 288p. 1996. pap. text ed. 15.00 (*0-465-03366-0*) Basic.

Sixty Miles to Glory. large type ed. Steven Gray. (Dales Large Print Ser.). 208p. 1996. pap. 17.99 (*1-85389-617-9*, Dales) Ulverscroft.

Sixty-Minute Estate Planner: Fast & Easy Illustrated Plans to Save Taxes, Avoid Probate, & Maximize Inheritance. Sandy F. Kraemer. LC 94-1360. 279p. 1994. text ed. 34.95 (*0-13-147323-9*); pap. text ed. 18.95 (*0-13-147315-8*) P-H.

Sixty Minute Father. Rob Parsons. LC 96-1357. 112p. 1996. pap. 7.99 (*0-8054-6289-9*, 4262-89) Broadman.

***60 Minute Financial Planner.** Dana Shilling. LC 97-16982. 1997. 34.95 (*0-13-489098-1*); pap. 19.95 (*0-13-489535-5*) P-H.

***60 Minute Guide to Internet Explorer 3.** J. W. Olsen. 1996. pap. 24.99 (*0-7645-3028-3*) IDG Bks.

60 Minute Guide to Lotus Script 3.0. Robert Beyer. 1996. pap. 19.99 (*1-56884-779-3*) IDG Bks.

***60 Minute Guide to Netscape Navigator 3.** Craig Witherspoon & Coletta Witherspoon. 312p. 1997. pap. 24.99 (*0-7645-3030-5*) IDG Bks.

60 Minute Guide to Shockwave. Ed Tittel. 1996. pap. text ed. 24.99 incl. cd-rom (*0-7645-8002-7*) IDG Bks.

Sixty-Minute Low-Calorie Gourmet. Pierre Franey. pap. 9.95 (*0-318-42742-7*, Times Bks) Random.

***60 Minute Museum Visits: Washington, D. C.** JoAnn Bright. Ed. by Museum Curators & PR Associates Staff. (Illus.). 180p. 1998. pap. 17.95 (*0-9650580-4-2*) Quick View.

60-Minute Museum Visits Bk. 1: New York City. JoAnn Bright. Ed. by Zeke Wigglesworth & Museum Curators, P. R. Assocs. Staff. (Illus.). 164p. (Orig.). Date not set. pap. 14.95 (*0-9650580-3-4*) Quick View.

***Sixty-Minute Shakespeare: A Midsummer Night's Dream.** Cass Foster. (YA). 1997. pap. 5.95 (*1-877749-22-2*) Five Star AZ.

***Sixty-Minute Shakespeare: Hamlet.** Cass Foster. (YA). 1997. pap. 5.95 (*1-877749-26-5*) Five Star AZ.

***Sixty-Minute Shakespeare: Macbeth.** Cass Foster. (YA). 1997. pap. 5.95 (*1-877749-25-7*) Five Star AZ.

***Sixty-Minute Shakespeare: Much Ado about Nothing.** Cass Foster. (YA). 1997. pap. 5.95 (*1-877749-23-0*) Five Star AZ.

Sixty-Minute Shakespeare: Romeo & Juliet. Cass Foster. Ed. by Mary E. Hawkins. LC 89-82072. 136p. (J). 1990. pap. 4.95 (*0-9619853-8-0*); 5.00 (*1-877749-00-1*) Five Star AZ.

***Sixty-Minute Shakespeare: Romeo & Juliet.** rev. ed. Cass Foster. (YA). 1997. pap. 5.95 (*1-877749-27-3*) Five Star AZ.

***Sixty-Minute Shakespeare: Twelfth Night.** Cass Foster. (YA). 1997. pap. 5.95 (*1-877749-24-9*) Five Star AZ.

60 Minute Software: Strategies for Accelerating the Information Systems Delivery Process. Ernst & Young LLP Staff & John Parkinson. LC 95-45677. (Ernst & Young Information Management Ser.: Vol. 4). 320p. 1995. text ed. 45.00 (*0-471-11503-7*) Wiley.

Sixty Minutes: 25 Years of Television's Finest Hour. Frank Coffey. Ed. by Murray Fisher. LC 93-35829. (Illus.). 304p. 1993. 29.99 (*1-881649-04-0*) Genl Pub Grp.

Sixty Minutes & the Assassination of Werner Erhard: How America's Top Rated Television Show Was Used in an Attempt to Destroy a Man Who Was Making a Difference. Jane Self. (Illus.). 180p. 1992. 19.95 (*0-942540-23-9*) Breakthru Pub.

Sixty Minutes & the News: A Mythology for Middle America. Richard Campbell. (Illinois Studies in Communications). (Illus.). 304p. 1991. 29.95 (*0-252-01777-3*) U of Ill Pr.

Sixty Minutes for St. George. large type ed. Alexander Fullerton. 480p. 1988. 25.99 (*0-7089-1761-5*) Ulverscroft.

Sixty Minutes Verbatim. CBS, Inc. Staff. LC 80-23836. (Illus.). 1981. lib. bdg. 23.95 (*0-405-13723-0*) Ayer.

69. Ryu Murakami. LC 93-28815. 192p. 1995. pap. 10.00 (*4-7700-1951-3*) Kodansha.

***69 Simple Science Fair Projects for Model Rockets: Aeronautics.** Timothy S. Van Milligan. (Illus.). 104p. (J). (gr. 4 up). 1996. per. 11.95 (*0-9653620-0-0*) Apogee Compnts.

69 Uses for a Dead Politician. Michael Kuhn et al. (Illus.). 140p. (Orig.). 1994. 8.95 (*0-9643264-1-8*) Image Prntng.

Sixty-Nine Ways to a Sexcessful Romance for Him-Her. Mary Travis. 40p. (Orig.). 1992. pap. 4.95 (*1-56411-124-5*) Untd Bros & Sis.

Sixty-Nine Ways to Play the Blues. Jurg Laederach. Tr. by Peter Wortsmann from GER. (Foreign Agents Ser.). 192p. (Orig.). (C). 1990. pap. 6.00 (*0-936756-62-4*) Autonomedia.

Sixty-Ninth Infantry Division. Turner Publishing Company Staff. LC 90-71722. 136p. 1991. 48.00 (*1-56311-012-1*) Turner Pub KY.

60 of the Funkiest Keyboard Riffs Known to Mankind. Andrew D. Gordon. Date not set. pap. 22.95 (*1-882146-48-4*) A D G Prods.

60 of the World's Easiest to Play Songs with 3 Chords 27. 96p. 1990. pap. 7.95 (*0-7935-4424-6*, 00001236) H Leonard.

Sixty One-Minute Family Builders. Dave Arp & Claudia Arp. LC 93-12445. 1993. 7.99 (*0-8407-4136-7*) Nelson.

Sixty One-Minute Marriage Builders. Dave Arp & Claudia Arp. LC 93-12447. 1993. 8.99 (*0-8407-4137-5*) Nelson.

Sixty One-Minute Memory Makers. Dave Arp & Claudia Arp. LC 93-12446. 1993. 7.99 (*0-8407-4138-3*) Nelson.

Sixty-One Psalms of David. Tr. by David R. Slavitt. LC 96-8719. (Illus.). 144p. 1996. 18.95 (*0-19-510711-X*) OUP.

Sixty-One Talks for Orthodox Funerals. Anthony M. Coniaris. 1969. pap. 10.95 (*0-937032-02-6*) Light&Life Pub Co MN.

Sixty-One Ways to Cut Gas Consumption see Up Your Gas: Sixty-One Ways to Cut Gas Consumption, Increase Your Mileage, Chop Costs & Minimize Waiting in Gas Lines! Plus Eleven Ways to Find a Good Mechanic & Save Money!

60 Patterns for Santa Carvers. Al Streetman. (Illus.). 64p. 1996. pap. 12.95 (*0-88740-996-2*) Schiffer.

Sixty-Plus & Fit Again: Exercises for Older Men & Women. Magda Rosenberg & Isadore Rossman. LC 76-49130. (Illus.). 156p. 1977. 12.95 (*0-87131-224-7*) M Evans.

Sixty-Plus in California. rev. ed. William R. Wishard & Laurie Wishard. LC 81-2823. 1981. 12.95 (*0-89666-013-3*); pap. 6.95 (*0-89666-014-1*) Cragmont Pubns.

Sixty-Plus in Massachusetts: The Guide to Benefits, Bargains & Better Living for People over Sixty. 2nd ed. Priscilla H. Claman & Victor N. Claman. (Illus.). 92p. 1985. pap. 8.95 (*0-939532-01-8*) Ctr Info Sharing.

60 Progressive Piano Pieces You Like to Play. 188p. 1986. otabind 11.95 (*0-7935-2573-X*, 50327360) H Leonard.

60 Role Plays for Management & Supervisory Training. David Turner. 300p. 1996. ring bd. 99.95 (*0-07-913049-6*) McGraw.

Sixty Saints for Boys. Joan Windham. 416p. (J). (gr. 1-6). 1988. reprint ed. pap. 13.95 (*0-87061-149-6*) Chr Classics.

Sixty Saints for Girls. Joan Windham. 384p. (J). (gr. 1-6). 1988. reprint ed. pap. 13.95 (*0-87061-150-X*) Chr Classics.

Sixty-Second Art Directors Annual. Art Directors Club of New York Staff. Ed. by Miriam L. Solomon. (Illus.). 816p. 1983. 39.95 (*0-937414-03-4*) ADC Pubns.

60 Second Chronic Pain Relief: The Quickest Way to Soften the Throb, Cool the Burn, Ease the Ache. Peter G. Lehndorff & Brian Tarcy. 160p. 1996. pap. 13.95 (0-88282-151-2) New Horizon NJ.

Sixty Second Ent. 2nd ed. Gideon Bosker. 256p. (gr. 13). 1995. pap. text ed. 22.95 (0-8016-7812-9) Mosby Yr Bk.

***Sixty Second Father: Ideas for Making Lifelong Memories with Your Child.** Rob Parsons. LC 97-6305. 1997. pap. write for info. (0-8054-6353-4) Broadman.

Sixty Second Impression: What Have You Said Before You Say "Hello"? Marilyn B. Subach. (Illus.). 48p. (Orig.). 1985. pap. 3.95 (0-935499-00-8) Classic Cons.

60 Second Menopause Management: The Quickest Ways to Handle Problems & Discomfort. Carol R. Schulz. 240p. 1995. pap. 13.95 (0-88282-137-7) New Horizon NJ.

60-Second Net Finder: Your Key to the Unlimited Potential of the Internet. Affinity Communications Corporation Staff & Knowledge Exchange Editorial Board Staff. LC 97-850. 432p. 1997. pap. text ed. 24.95 (1-888232-26-9) Knowldge Exchange.

Sixty Second Sells: Ninety-Nine Hot Radio Spots for Retail Businesses. Michael Redmond. LC 92-56684. 109p. 1993. lib. bdg. 23.50 (0-89950-792-1) McFarland & Co.

60-Second Shiatzu: The Natural Way to Energize, Erase Pain & Conquer Tension in One Minute. Eva Shaw. LC 95-15189. (Illus.). 1995. pap. 9.95 (0-8050-4068-4, Owl) H Holt & Co.

***60-Second Shrink: 101 Strategies for Staying Sane in a Crazy World.** Arnold A. Lazarus & Clifford N. Lazarus. LC 96-53590. 176p. (Orig.). 1997. pap. 12.95 (1-886230-04-8) Impact Pubs CA.

Sixty Second Stress Management: The Quickest Way to Relax & Ease Anxiety. rev. ed. Andrew Goliszek. LC 92-60614. 288p. 1992. reprint ed. pap. 13.95 (0-88282-115-6) New Horizon NJ.

Sixty Second System of Success: It's Simple, Yet It's Powerful! Jim Gentil. 83p. (Orig.). 1989. pap. write for info. (0-9621531-0-9) Banyan Pr TX.

Sixty-Second Virginia Infantry. Roger U. Delauter. (Illus.). 121p. 1988. write for info. (0-930919-53-X) H E Howard.

Sixty Seconds. Maxwell Bodenheim. LC 73-18549. (BCL Ser.: I). reprint ed. 20.00 (0-404-11364-8) AMS Pr.

Sixty Seconds & You're Hired! Robin Ryan. 117p. 1994. pap. 9.95 (1-57023-009-9) Impact VA.

Sixty Selected Poems. Joseph P. Brennan. LC 84-62734. (Illus.). 80p. 1985. 15.00 (0-932445-11-X); pap. 5.00 (0-932445-10-1) Ganley Pub.

Sixty-Seven Feet in the Air. Jack Dotson. 54p. (Orig.). 1994. pap. text ed. 7.00 (0-9641454-0-5) Pleiades Pr.

67 Good Ways to Sleep: A People's Medical Society Book. Charles B. Inlander & Cynthia K. Moran. 96p. 1995. 14.95 (0-8027-1306-8); pap. 7.95 (0-8027-7448-2) Walker & Co.

Sixty-Seven Seconds. 1992. write for info. (0-87135-864-6) Marvel Entmnt.

67 Ways to Good Sleep. Charles B. Inlander & Cynthia K. Moran. 1996. mass mkt. 4.99 (0-449-22473-2) Fawcett.

Sixty-Seven Years of Barber Family Reunions. Gary E. Swinson. 182p. 1990. pap. 22.50 (0-9629573-1-3) G E Swinson.

Sixty-Seventh Annual Convention of the National Council on Teacher Retirement: Proceedings, Directory, Committee Roster. Ed. & Illus. by Silent Partners, Inc. Staff. 166p. (Orig.). 1989. pap. 10.00 (1-878353-01-2) Silent Partners.

Sixty-Six, a Story of World War II. Siinto Wessman. (Divisional Ser.: No. 3). (Illus.). 1978. reprint ed. 39.95 (0-89839-012-5) Battery Pr.

Sixty-Six Contemporary Standards. (Piano-Vocal-Guitar Pop-Rock Ser.). 318p. (Orig.). 1990. pap. 16.95 (0-7935-0098-2, 00490501) H Leonard.

Sixty-Six Contemporary Standards. (Easy Piano Ser.). (Illus.). 301p. (Orig.). 1991. pap. 14.95 (0-7935-0754-5, 00490502) H Leonard.

Sixty-Six Year Round Crafts for Preschoolers. Carolyn S. Collins. 1994. pap. 7.00 (0-517-88066-0) Crown Pub Group.

Sixty-Six Years in Custer's Shadow. Henry Weibert. LC 85-71156. 31.95 (0-8488-0232-2, J M C & Co) Amereon Ltd.

Sixty-Six Years in Custer's Shadow. limited ed. Don L. Weibert. LC 85-71156. 174p. 1985. 50.00 (0-916027-04-X) D L Weibert.

Sixty-Sixth Annual Convention of the National Council on Teacher Retirement: Proceedings, Directory, Committee Roster. Ed. & Illus. by Silent Partners, Inc. Staff. 142p. (Orig.). 1988. pap. 10.00 (1-878353-02-0) Silent Partners.

***60 Small Farm Ideas.** rev. ed. 1997. per. 8.75 (0-9614126-8-2) Natl Lilac Pub.

Sixty Sonatas Vol. 1: Piano. D. Scarlatti. 132p. 1986. per. 9.95 (0-7935-2611-6, 50261610) H Leonard.

Sixty Sonatas Vol. 2: Piano. D. Scarlatti. 132p. 1986. per. 9.95 (0-7935-4396-7, 50261630) H Leonard.

Sixty Songs. Gabriel Faure. 1990. pap. 13.95 (0-486-26534-X) Dover.

60 Stories. Donald Barthelme. 1993. pap. 13.95 (0-14-015300-4, Viking) Viking Penguin.

***60 Stories.** Donald Barthelme. 1982. pap. 11.95 (0-525-48453-1, Obelisk) NAL-Dutton.

Sixty Studies Opus 45 Bk. 1: Violin Nos. 1-30. Franz Wohlfahrt. 24p. 1986. pap. 3.95 (0-7935-2570-5) H Leonard.

Sixty Studies Opus 45 Bk. 2: Violin Nos. 31-60. Franz Wohlfahrt. 32p. 1986. pap. 3.95 (0-7935-2595-0) H Leonard.

60 Super Hits, Vol. 160. 144p. 1983. per. 12.95 (0-7935-0953-X, 00101993) H Leonard.

60 Super Simple Crafts. Holly Herbert. LC 96-1771. (Sixty Super Simple Ser.). (Illus.). 80p. (YA). (gr. 8-12). 1996. pap. 5.95 (1-56565-385-8) Lowell Hse Juvenile.

60 Super Simple Magic Tricks. Shawn McMaster. LC 96-390. (Sixty Super Simple Ser.). (Illus.). 80p. (YA). (gr. 8-12). 1996. pap. 5.95 (1-56565-384-X) Lowell Hse Juvenile.

***60 Super Simple Travel Games.** Jill Smolinski. LC 97-9012. 1997. pap. 6.95 (1-56565-584-2) Contemp Bks.

Sixty Things God Said about Sex. Lester Sumrall. 162p. 1993. mass mkt. 4.99 (0-88368-316-4) Whitaker Hse.

Sixty-Third Art Directors Annual. Art Directors Club of New York Staff. Ed. by Miriam L. Soloman. (Illus.). 516p. 1984. 39.95 (0-937414-04-2) ADC Pubns.

Sixty-Third Virginia Infantry. Jeffrey C. Weaver. (Virginia Regimental Histories Ser.). (Illus.). 158p. 1991. 19.95 (1-56190-017-6) H E Howard.

Sixty-Three: Dream Palace, Selected Stories, 1956-1987. James Purdy. LC 91-27119. 356p. (Orig.). 1991. pap. 15.00 (0-87685-844-2) Black Sparrow.

Sixty-Two Home Remote Control & Automation Projects. Delton T. Horn. (Illus.). 294p. 1986. pap. 16.95 (0-8306-2735-9, NO. 2735) McGraw-Hill Prof.

Sixty-Two Minutes That Will Change Your Life. Larry Mullins. (Illus.). 40p. 1983. pap. 4.95 (0-912137-02-9) Actionizing.

Sixty-Two Poems That Sing. Helen Webb. 40p. 1986. pap. 2.95 (0-9615859-0-0) H Webb.

Sixty-Two Select Studies for Violoncello, Bk. 2. J. J. Dotzauer. Ed. by F. Girard. (Carl Fischer Music Library: No. 456). 1914. pap. 8.50 (0-8258-0181-8, L456) Fischer Inc NY.

Sixty-Two Sonnets & Definitions: Poems & Prosepoems. Tanikawa Shuntaro. Ed. by Thomas Fitzsimmons. Tr. by William I. Elliott & Kawamura Kazuo from JPN. (Asian Poetry in Translation: Japan Ser.: No. 14). 152p. (Orig.). (C). 1992. pap. text ed. 15.00 (0-942668-35-9) Katydid Bks.

Sixty-Two Ways to Create Change in the Lives of Troubled Children. 128p. 1991. pap. 9.95 (0-938586-47-5) Whole Person.

Sixty-Two Years of Uncertainty: Historical, Philosophical & Physical Inquiries into the Foundations of Quantum Mechanics. Ed. by A. I. Miller. (NATO ASI, Series B: Physics: Vol. 226). (Illus.). 320p. 1990. 95.00 (0-306-43608-6, Plenum Pr) Plenum.

62 Years Studying the Art & Science of Putting. Ray Cook. (Illus.). 136p. (Orig.). 1995. 20.00 (0-9644252-1-1) R Cook.

Sixty Voices: Celebrities Recall the Golden Age of British Cinema. Ed. by Brian McFarlane. (Illus.). 272p. (C). 1993. 60.00 (0-85170-353-4, Pub. by British Film Inst UK); pap. 29.95 (0-85170-349-6, Pub. by British Film Inst UK) Ind U Pr.

Sixty Walks in Central Victoria's Goldfields & Spa Country. Tyrone Thomas. (Hill of Content Walking Guides Ser.). (Illus.). 251p. (Orig.). 1994. pap. 15.95 (0-85572-241-X, Pub. by Hill Content Pubng AT) Seven Hills Bk.

60 Ways to Assure Success for Your Gifted Children. Jerry Chris. (Orig.). 1994. pap. 9.99 (0-88092-197-8) Royal Fireworks.

Sixty Ways to Make Stress Work for You. Andrew E. Slaby. (Illus.). 64p. 1987. reprint ed. pap. 4.50 (0-929162-02-1) PIA Pr.

Sixty Ways to Relieve Stress in Sixty Seconds. Manning Rubin. LC 92-50932. (Illus.). 128p. 1993. pap. 5.95 (1-56305-338-1, 3338) Workman Pub.

Sixty with Sizzle. Herbert I. Kavet. 96p. 1994. pap. 5.95 (0-88032-443-0) Ivory Tower Pub.

Sixty Women Poets: Poetry Book Society Special Commendation. Ed. by Linda France. 288p. 9400. pap. 18.95 (1-85224-252-3, Pub. by Bloodaxe Bks UK) Dufour.

Sixty Word Grand Canyon Series, 6 bks., Set. Julia Allen. (Illus.). (J). (gr. k-3). 1994. pap. 23.70 (0-89868-240-1, Read Res) ARO Pub.

Sixty Word Grand Canyon Series, 6 bks., Set. Bob Reese. (Illus.). (J). (gr. k-6). 1987. 59.70 (0-89868-241-X) ARO Pub.

Sixty Works: The Peggy Guggenheim Collection. Thomas M. Messer. (Illus.). 68p. 1982. pap. 5.95 (0-89207-037-4) S R Guggenheim.

Sixty Year Comprehensive Index of Pasque Petals (1926-1986) Ed. by Janet Leih et al. 328p. (Orig.). 1987. per. 5.00 (0-945124-00-7) Tesseract SD.

Sixty Year Index of the United States Specialist. Richard T. Hall. 380p. 1990. 35.00 (0-930412-17-6) Bureau Issues.

Sixty Year Steel Joist Manual: A Compilation of SJI Specifications & Load Tables from 1928-1988. 1992. 59.00 (0-318-04232-0) Steel Joist Inst.

Sixty Years a Builder. Henry Ericsson. (American Autobiography Ser.). 388p. 1995. reprint ed. lib. bdg. 89.00 (0-7812-8511-9) Rprt Serv.

Sixty Years a Builder: The Autobiography of Henry Ericsson. Henry Ericsson. LC 72-5046. (Technology & Society Ser.). (Illus.). 388p. 1972. reprint ed. 25.95 (0-405-04698-7) Ayer.

***60 Years an Alcoholic 50 Years Without a Drink.** Freeman Carpenter. LC 96-90221. 416p. (Orig.). 1996. pap. 17.95 (0-9651618-4-6) Unique Educ.

Sixty Years Behind the Mast, the Fox on the Water. Gordon K. Douglass. 288p. 1986. 19.95 (0-9617502-0-0) McClain.

Sixty Years in Cuba: Reminiscences of Edwin F. Atkins. Edwin F. Atkins. Ed. by Stuart Bruchey. LC 80-555. (Multinational Corporations Ser.). (Illus.). 1981. reprint ed. lib. bdg. 48.95 (0-405-13352-9) Ayer.

***Sixty Years in Search of Cures: An Herbalist's Success with Chinese Herbs.** Fung Fung & John Fung. 174p. Date not set. pap. 15.95 (0-9638285-1-7) Get Well Fnd.

Sixty Years in Southern California, 1853-1913. Harris Newmark. Ed. by Maurice H. Newmark & Marco R. Newmark. 744p. 1984. 25.00 (0-87093-186-5) Dawsons.

Sixty Years in Southern California, 1853-1913. Harris Newmark. 1992. reprint ed. lib. bdg. 75.00 (0-7812-5071-4) Rprt Serv.

Sixty Years in Waifdom: The Ragged School Movement in English History. C. J. Montague. LC 79-5721. (Social History of Education 1st Ser.: No. 7). (Illus.). xv, 459p. 1969. reprint ed. 49.50 (0-678-08450-5) Kelley.

Sixty Years in Waifdom or, the Ragged School Movement in English History. C. J. Montague. LC 70-108225. (Criminology, Law Enforcement, & Social Problems Ser.: No. 108). 1970. reprint ed. 18.00 (0-87585-108-8) Patterson Smith.

Sixty Years-MacMorris: Art Book & Autobiography. Ed. by Jeanne R. Simpson. LC 74-24737. (Illus.). 80p. (C). 1974. write for info. (0-9611558-0-9) J R Simpson.

Sixty Years of American Poetry: Celebrating the Anniversary of the Academy of American Poets. expanded rev. ed. Illus. by Barry Moser. LC 96-10854. 360p. 1996. 35.00 (0-8109-4464-2) Abrams.

Sixty Years of Biology: Essays on Evolution & Development. John T. Bonner. LC 95-25638. 168p. 1996. text ed. 24.95 (0-691-02130-9) Princeton U Pr.

***Sixty Years of Great Fiction from Partisan Review.** Ed. by William Phillips. LC 96-50882. 448p. (Orig.). 1997. 24.95 (0-9644377-5-9); pap. 14.95 (0-9644377-4-0) Partisan Rev Pr.

Sixty Years of Journalism by James M Cain. Ed. & Intro. by Roy Hoopes. LC 85-70856. 240p. 1986. 30.95 (0-87972-327-0); pap. 13.95 (0-87972-328-9) Bowling Green Univ Popular Press.

Sixty Years of Life & Adventure in the Far East, 2 vols., Set. John D. Ross. (Illus.). 1968. reprint ed. 85.00 (0-7146-2024-6, Pub. by F Cass Pubs UK) Intl Spec Bk.

60 Years of Photography the Discovering Eye. Photos by Ferenc Berko. (Illus.). 128p. 1995. 45.00 (3-905514-39-7, Pub. by Edit Stemmle SZ) Dist Art Pubs.

Sixty Years of Rifles. Paul Matthews. 1991. 19.50 (1-879356-03-1) Wolfe Pub Co.

Sixty Years of Siffords at Drakesbad. Roy D. Sifford. (Illus.). 166p. 1994. 16.95 (0-938373-14-5) Lahontan Images.

***Sixty Years of the Citroen 2CV 1937-1997.** John Reynolds. (Illus.). 192p. 1997. 29.95 (0-7509-1350-9, Pub. by A Sutton UK) Motorbooks Intl.

Sixty Years on the Brazos: The Life & Letters of Dr. John Washington Lockhart, 1824-1900. Jonnie L. Wallis. LC 65-27183. 384p. 1971. reprint ed. 23.95 (0-405-03685-X) Ayer.

Sixty Years with Men & Machines. Fred H. Colvin. 298p. reprint ed. pap. 14.95 (0-917914-86-4) Lindsay Pubns.

Sixty Years with Men & Machines: American Autobiography. Fred Colvin. 297p. 1995. lib. bdg. 79.00 (0-7812-8487-2) Rprt Serv.

Siyaghat al 'Ulum al Ijtima'iyah: Siyaghah Islamiyah: (The Formulation of the Social Sciences - An Islamic Formulation) Isma'il A. Faruqi. (Silsilat Rasa'il Islamiyat al Ma'rifah Ser.: No. 5). 30p. (Orig.). (ARA.). 1989. pap. 2.00 (1-56564-164-7) IIIT VA.

***Siz.** limited ed. James Humphrey. 90p. 1997. pap. 16.00 (0-936641-21-5) Poets Alive Pr.

Size. (My First Learning Ser.). (Illus.). 24p. (J). (gr. k-2). 1995. text ed. write for info. (1-56144-738-2) Modern Pub NYC.

Size. Henry Pluckrose. (Math Counts Ser.). 32p. (J). 1995. lib. bdg. 17.80 (0-516-05457-0) Childrens.

Size. Henry Pluckrose. (Math Counts Ser.). (J). 1995. pap. 4.95 (0-516-45457-9) Childrens.

Size. Brenda Walpole. LC 95-21852. (Measure up with Science Ser.). (Illus.). (J). 1995. lib. bdg. 18.60 (0-8368-1361-8) Gareth Stevens Inc.

Size & Cycle: An Essay on the Structure of Biology. John T. Bonner. LC 65-14306. (Illus.). 265p. 1965. reprint ed. pap. 75.60 (0-7837-8162-8, 2047867) Bks Demand.

Size & Democracy. Robert A. Dahl & Edward R. Tufte. LC 72-97200. xii, 148p. 1973. 24.50 (0-8047-0834-7) Stanford U Pr.

Size & Efficiency Debate: Public Library Authorities in a Time of Change. A. Midwinter & M. McVicar. 90p. 1994. pap. 45.00 (1-85604-148-4, LAP1484, Pub. by Library Association UK) Bernan Associates.

***Size & Growth of the Nutritionally Improved Farm Market.** Elizabeth Frazao & Jane E. Allshouse. (Illus.). 41p. (Orig.). (C). 1997. pap. text ed. 25.00 (0-7881-3699-2) DIANE Pub.

***Size & Growth Trends of the Information Industry: 1975-1987.** 3rd unabridged ed. Derrick C. Huang. 23p. (Orig.). 1990. reprint ed. pap. text ed. write for info. (1-879716-35-6, I-90-1) Ctr Info Policy.

Size & Scaling in Primate Biology. Ed. by William L. Jungers. LC 84-16099. (Advances in Primatology Ser.). 508p. 1985. 110.00 (0-306-41560-7, Plenum Pr) Plenum.

Size & Survival: The Politics of Security in the Small Island & Enclave Developing States of the Caribbean & the Pacific. Ed. by Paul Sutton & Anthony Payne. LC 93-7279. 200p. 1993. 35.00 (0-7146-4532-X, Pub. by F Cass Pubs UK) Intl Spec Bk.

Size, Composition & Growth of the Population of Mainland China. John S. Aird. LC 76-38047. (China Classic & Contemporary Works in Reprint Ser.). reprint ed. 41.50 (0-404-56901-3) AMS Pr.

Size, Distribution, & Growth of the Texas Population, 1980 to 2030. Robert K. Holz. (Research Monograph Ser.: No. 1987-4). (Illus.). 50p. (Orig.). 1987. pap. 10.00 (0-87755-307-6) Bureau Busn TX.

Size Effects in Concrete Structures. H. Mihashi. 1994. 112.00 (0-419-19040-6, E & FN Spon) Routledge Chapman & Hall.

Size, Efficiency, & Community Enterprise. Barry A. Stein. 129p. 1974. pap. text ed. 21.95 (0-87855-775-X) Transaction Pubs.

Size Enlargement by Agglomeration. Wolfgang Pietsch. LC 90-26875. 532p. 1991. text ed. 354.00 (0-471-92991-3) Wiley.

Size Exclusion Chromatography: Methodology & Characterization of Polymers & Related Materials. Ed. by Theodore J. Provder. LC 83-27515. (ACS Symposium Ser.: No. 245). 391p. 1984. lib. bdg. 72.95 (0-8412-0826-3) Am Chemical.

***Size Exclusion Chromatography: Methodology & Characterization of Polymers & Related Materials.** Ed. by Theodore J. Provder. LC 83-27515. (ACS Symposium Ser.: Vol. 245). 401p. 1984. reprint ed. pap. 114.30 (0-608-03125-9, 2063578) Bks Demand.

Size Exclusion Chromatography (GPC) Ed. by Theodore J. Provder. LC 80-22015. (ACS Symposium Ser.: No. 138). 1980. 41.95 (0-8412-0586-8) Am Chemical.

***Size Exclusion Chromatography (GPC)** Ed. by Theodore J. Provder. LC 80-22015. (ACS Symposium Ser.: No. 138). (Illus.). 320p. 1980. reprint ed. pap. 91.20 (0-608-03227-1, 2063746) Bks Demand.

Size Fourteen Is Not a Sin: How to Stop Yo Yo-ing, Get to & Maintain Your Right Weight, Eat Right & Look Great. Meg Whitcomb. (Illus.). 145p. 1993. pap. 8.00 (0-9638883-0-7) M Whitcomb.

Size, Function & Life History. unabridged ed. William A. Calder, 3rd. LC 83-22815. (Illus.). 448p. reprint ed. pap. 13.95 (0-486-69191-8) Dover.

Size Measurement & Characterisation of Weld Defects by Ultrasonic Testing Pt. 1: Non-Planar Defects in Ferritic Steels. (Illus.). 84p. 1979. pap. 115.00 (0-85300-130-8, Pub. by Woodhead Pubng UK) Am Educ Systs.

Size Measurement & Characterisation of Weld Defects by Ultrasonic Testing Pt. 2: Planar Defects in Ferritic Steels. (Illus.). 154p. 1982. pap. 135.00 (0-85300-161-8, Pub. by Woodhead Pubng UK) Am Educ Systs.

Size Measurement & Characterisation of Weld Defects by Ultrasonic Testing Pt. 3: The Effect of Metallurgical Features in Ferritic Steels. (Illus.). 34p. 1982. pap. 65.00 (0-85300-162-6, Pub. by Woodhead Pubng UK) Am Educ Systs.

***Size of the Crime Problem in Australia.** 2nd ed. S. Mukherjee & D. Dagger. 128p. 1990. pap. 25.00 (0-642-14935-6, Pub. by Aust Inst Criminology) Willow Tree NY.

Size of the Slave Population of Athens. Rachel S. Robinson. LC 73-10760. 136p. 1974. reprint ed. text ed. 57.50 (0-8371-7034-6, ROSP, Greenwood Pr) Greenwood.

Size of the Soul: Principles of Revival & Spiritual Growth. Aiden W. Tozer. LC 92-73704. 180p. (Orig.). 1992. pap. 8.99 (0-87509-497-X) Chr Pubns.

Size of the World: A Global Odyssey - Once Around Without Leaving the Ground. Jeff Greenwald. LC 95-39755. (Illus.). 400p. 1995. 22.95 (1-56440-623-7) Globe Pequot.

Size of the World: Once Around Without Leaving the Ground. 1997. pap. 12.95 (0-345-40551-X) Ballantine.

Size of Thoughts: Essays & Other Lumber. Nicholson Baker. 256p. 1996. 25.00 (0-679-43932-3) Random.

Size of Thoughts: Essays & Other Lumber. Nicholson Baker. 1997. pap. 13.00 (0-679-77624-9) Random.

***Size-Scale Effects in the Failure Mechanisms of Materials & Structures.** Ed. by A. Carpinteri. (Illus.). 608p. 1995. text ed. 146.50 (0-419-20520-9, E & FN Spon) Routledge Chapman & Hall.

Size-Structured Populations: Ecology & Evolution. Ed. by B. E. Benman & L. Persson. (Illus.). 310p. 1989. 97.00 (0-387-50188-6) Spr-Verlag.

***Size Wise.** Judy Sullivan. LC 96-36904. 336p. (Orig.). 1997. pap. 12.00 (0-380-78711-3) Avon.

***Size 6 1/2 EEE.** (Illus.). 28p. (ENG & SPA.). (J). 1997. pap. 5.95 (0-964574-2-3) Shoeless Pub.

Sizes. (Sticker Activity Ser.). (Illus.). 16p. (J). (ps-1). 1993. pap. 6.95 (1-56458-397-X) DK Pub Inc.

Sizes. Jan Pienkowski. (Nursery Board Bks.). (Illus.). 24p. (J). (ps). 1991. pap. 2.95 (0-671-72844-X, Litl Simon S&S) S&S Childrens.

Sizes. Sian Tucker. (Nursery Board Bks.). (Illus.). 24p. (J). (ps). 1992. pap. 2.95 (0-671-76909-X, Litl Simon S&S) S&S Childrens.

***Sizes.** Nicola Tuxworth. (Let's Look Ser.). (Illus.). 24p. (J). (ps). 1997. 3.95 (1-85967-412-7, Lorenz Bks) Anness Pub.

Sizes. J. Tyler & G. Round. (First Learning Ser.). (Illus.). 24p. (J). (ps up). 1989. pap. 3.95 (0-7460-0269-6, Usborne) EDC.

Sizes. Beth A. Wise. (Toddler Time Ser.). (Illus.). 16p. (J). 1992. student ed., pap. 2.95 (1-56293-187-3) McClanahan Bk.

***Sizesaurus.** Stephen Strauss. 256p. (Orig.). 1997. pap. 13.00 (0-380-72849-4) Avon.

Sizesaurus: From Hectares to Decibels to Calories, a Witty Compendium of Measurements. Stephen Strauss. Ed. by Philip Turner. LC 95-32176. (Illus.). 272p. 1995. 25.00 (1-56836-110-6) Kodansha.

Sizing & Estimating Software in Practice: Making MK II Function Points Work. Stephen Treble & Neil Douglas. LC 95-6972. 1996. pap. text ed. 35.00 (0-07-707620-6) McGraw.

Sizing & Selecting Air Pollution Control Systems. Ed. by Frank L. Cross & Howard E. Hesketh. LC 93-61892. 170p. 1994. text ed. 69.95 (1-56676-126-3) Technomic.

Sizing Down: Chronicle of a Plant Closing. Louise M. Illes. LC 95-37620. 240p. 1996. 29.95 (0-87546-351-7, ILR Press) Cornell U Pr.

S

*Sizing Down: Chronicle of a Plant Closing.** Louise M. Illes. (ILR Press Book). 240p. 1997. pap. 13.95 (*0-8014-8434-0*) Cornell U Pr.

Sizing-Keystone to Quality Fabrics. (Symposium Papers). 67p. 1985. 10.00 (*0-318-12169-7*) AATCC.

Sizing of Paper. 2nd ed. Ed. by Walter F. Reynolds. 170p. reprint ed. pap. 44.20 (*0-8357-6343-9*, 2035615) Bks Demand.

Sizing of Paper. 2nd ed. Ed. by Walter F. Reynolds. 156p. 1989. 73.00 (*0-89852-051-7*, 0102B051) TAPPI.

Sizing Short Course, Nineteen Eighty-Seven: Notes of TAPPI, Hyatt Regency, Atlanta, GA, April 8-10. Technical Association of the Pulp & Paper Industry Staff. 109p. pap. 31.10 (*0-685-20521-5*, 2029981) Bks Demand.

Sizing Short Course, 1992: Opryland Hotel, Nashville, TN, April 8-10. Technical Association of the Pulp & Paper Industry Staff. (TAPPI Notes Ser.). reprint ed. pap. 38.70 (*0-7837-2447-0*, 2042596) Bks Demand.

Sizing the Protection of Motors & Control Circuits No. 637: Video Booklet/Workbook. L. A. Bryan & E. A. Bryan. Ed. by L. B. Thompson. (Illus.). 28p. (Orig.). 1995. pap. 22.95 (*0-944107-16-8*) Indust Text.

Sizing up the Soviet Army. Jeffrey Record. LC 75-26941. (Studies in Defense Policy). 61p. reprint ed. pap. 25.00 (*0-685-23652-8*, 2027971) Bks Demand.

Sizing Up U. S. Export Disincentives. J. David Richardson. LC 92-37854. 182p. 1993. pap. 19.95 (*0-88132-107-9*) Inst Intl Eco.

Sizing up Your School System: The District Effectiveness Audit. Joan L. Buttram et al. 219p. 1989. reprint ed. pap. 35.95 (*1-56602-028-X*) Research Better.

Sizing Water Service Lines & Meters, No. M22. 112p. 1989. pap. 40.00 (*0-89867-080-2*, 30022) Am Water Wks Assn.

Sizzle. Jennifer Crusie. (Great Escapes Ser.). 1994. pap. 1.99 (*0-373-83271-0*, 1-83271-6) Harlequin Bks.

Sizzle: Barbecuing & Grilling. Ed. by Cole Group Staff. (Cooking Companion Ser.). 96p. (Orig.). 1995. pap. 7.95 (*1-56426-801-2*) Cole Group.

***Sizzle & Substance.** Eric Jensen. 1997. write for info. (*0-9637832-9-7*) Turn Pt Teach.

***Sizzle Cleans Up.** Elizabeth Anders. (Puzzle Place Ser.). (Illus.). 32p. (Orig.). (J). (ps-1). 1997. pap. 4.95 (*0-448-41300-0*, G&D) Putnam Pub Group.

Sizzlemanship. Elmer Wheeler. 294p. 1983. pap. 6.95 (*0-13-811505-2*, Reward) P-H.

Sizzling Monogamy: How to Have a Lifetime of Romance & Passion. 3rd rev. ed. Earl Smith & Rose Smith. LC 92-74746. Orig. Title: Secrets of a Mistress. 160p. 1997. pap. 12.95 (*1-882401-26-3*) W Havens Pub.

Sizzling Pops. pap. 14.95 incl. audio compact disk (*0-7935-4387-8*, 00290005) H Leonard.

Sizzling Pops: Late Elementary Piano Solos. 16p. 1991. pap. 5.95 (*0-7935-0594-1*, 00290268) H Leonard.

Sizzling Southwest Cuisine. Victoria Leigh. 48p. 1993. pap. 4.95 (*0-9642805-0-7*) Victoria Leigh.

Sizzling Southwestern Cookbook. Lynn Nusom. LC 94-35379. 192p. 1995. 25.00 (*1-56565-210-X*) Lowell Hse.

Sizzling Southwestern Cookbook: Hot & Zesty, Light & Healthy Chile Cuisine. Lynn Nusom. 224p. 1996. pap. 16.00 (*1-56565-430-7*) Lowell Hse.

***Sizzling Stir-Fries.** Kay Fairfax. LC 96-71423. (Illus.). 160p. 1997. 15.95 (*0-8478-2019-X*) Rizzoli Intl.

Sjahrir: Politics & Exile in Indonesia. Rudolf Mrazek. (Studies on Southeast Asia: No. 14). (Orig.). 1994. pap. text ed. 24.25 (*0-87727-713-3*) Cornell SE Asia.

Sjeca Svecenika U Hrvatskoj. Ivo Omrcanin. 72p. (Orig.). (CRO.). 1995. pap. 7.00 (*0-614-10151-4*) Ivor Pr.

Sjem' Vsjeljenskikh Soborov. 143p. 1968. reprint ed. pap. 5.00 (*0-317-30292-2*) Holy Trinity.

Sjogren's Syndrome: Model for Understanding Autoimmunity. Ed. by Norman Talal. (Second International Symposium Ser.). 275p. 1989. pap. text ed. 79.00 (*0-12-682345-6*) Acad Pr.

Sjogren's Syndrome: State of the Art. T. Tojo. LC 94-15740. (Illus.). xxxviii, 620p. 1994. text ed. 187.50 (*90-6299-107-6*) Kugler Pubns.

Sjogren's Syndrome Handbook. Elaine K. Harris & Steven Caroons. 1988. 24.95 (*0-9621157-0-3*) Sjogrens Syndrome.

Sjogren's Syndrome Handbook: An Authoritative Guide for Patients Prepared by Specialists in the Diagnosis & Treatment of Sjogren's Syndrome. Ed. by Steven Carsons & James J. Sciubba. (Illus.). 295p. 1988. 24.95 (*0-685-44313-2*) Sjogrens Syndrome.

Sjovold Site: A River Crossing Campsite in the Northern Plains. Ian Dyck & Richard E. Morlan. (Mercury Ser.: No. 642). (Illus.). 642p. 1995. pap. 39.95 (*0-660-14033-0*, Pub. by Can Mus Civil CN) U of Wash Pr.

SJ's Winners: An Exceptional Approach to Round-the-World Wining & Dining in the San Francisco Bay Area. Serena Jutkovitz. LC 82-99898. 278p. (Orig.). 1982. pap. 8.50 (*0-9608968-0-5*) Russian Hill.

Skadden: Legal Power Money & the Rise of a Empire. Lincoln Caplan. 1993. 25.00 (*0-374-26566-6*) FS&G.

Skadden: Power, Money, & the Rise of a Legal Empire. Lincoln Caplan. 350p. 1994. pap. 12.00 (*0-374-52424-6*, Noonday) FS&G.

Skadevergoedingsreg. J. Visser & J. M. Potgieter. 576p. 1992. pap. write for info. (*0-7021-2804-X*, Pub. by Juta SA) Gaunt.

Skagit-Sauk, WA. Dec Hogan. (River Journal Ser.: Vol. 2, No. 4). (Illus.). 48p. 1996. pap. 15.95 (*1-57188-031-3*) F Amato Pubns.

Skagit Valley Fare: A Cookbook Celebrating Bounty & Beauty in the Pacific Northwest. Lavone Newell. (Illus.). 240p. (Orig.). 1995. pap. 19.95 (*0-9615580-5-9*) Island Pubs WA.

Skagway: A Legacy of Gold. L. J. Campbell. Ed. by Penny Rennick. LC 72-92087. (Illus.). 96p. 1992. pap. 19.95 (*1-56661-000-1*); lib. bdg. 24.95 (*1-56661-001-X*) Alaska Geog Soc.

Skagway Kids: Alaska Christmas. Carl Nord. (Illus.). (J). 1994. 10.95 (*0-533-10931-0*) Vantage.

Skagway Kids: Alaska Snowstorm. Carl Nord. LC 96-90104. (Illus.). (J). (gr. 1-3). 1996. 13.95 (*0-533-11892-1*) Vantage.

Skagway Story: A History of Alaska's Most Famous Gold-Rush Town & of Some of the People Who Made That History. rev. ed. Howard Clifford. LC 75-13918. (Illus.). 180p. (Orig.). 1975. pap. 11.95 (*0-88240-330-3*) Alaska Northwest.

Skanda. Hilda Charlton. Ed. by Golden Quest Staff. (Golden Quest Ser.: Vol. 2). (Illus.). 126p. (Orig.). 1992. pap. 7.95 (*0-927383-03-9*) Golden Quest.

Skanda Purana, Pt. 1. Tr. by G. V. Tagare. (C). 1992. text ed. 18.50 (*81-208-0966-1*, Pub. by Motilal Banarsidass II) S Asia.

***Skaneateles: History of Its Earliest Settlement & Reminiscences of Later Times.** Edmund N. Leslie. (Illus.). 477p. 1997. reprint ed. lib. bdg. 49.00 (*0-8328-6241-X*) Higginson Bk Co.

Skansen: Traditional Swedish Style. Ralph Edenheim. (Museum Ser.). (Illus.). 150p. 30.00 (*1-85759-053-8*) Scala Books.

Skara Brae: A Pictish Village in Orkney. Vere G. Childe et al. LC 77-86427. reprint ed. 24.50 (*0-404-16633-4*) AMS Pr.

***Skate: 100 Years of Figure Skating.** Steve Milton. (Illus.). 208p. 1996. 29.95 (*1-57076-056-X*, Trafalgar Sq Pub) Trafalgar.

Skate Boarding. Gavin Hills. LC 92-8433. (All Action Ser.). (Illus.). 48p. (J). (gr. 4 up). 1993. lib. bdg. 9.50 (*0-8225-2483-X*, Lerner Publctns) Lerner Group.

Skate Expectations, Vol. 4. Bill Myers & Ken Johnson. (McGee & Me! Ser.: Vol. 4). (J). (gr. 3-7). 1989. pap. 5.99 (*0-8423-4165-X*) Tyndale.

Skate, Kate, Skate. Patty Carratello. Ed. by Darlene Spivak. (Easy Rainbow Reader Ser.). (Illus.). 16p. (J). (gr. k-2). 1988. student ed. 1.95 (*1-55734-380-2*) Tchr Create Mat.

Skate, Kate Skate: Easy Phonics Reader. Carratello. (Illus.). 16p. (J). (ps-1). 1996. pap. 2.49 (*1-57690-010-X*) Tchr Create Mat.

Skate Sailing. Richard Friary. LC 96-32308. (Illus.). 256p. (Orig.). 1996. pap. 19.95 (*1-57028-098-3*) Masters Pr IN.

Skateboard Champion. Edward Packard. (Choose Your Own Adventure Ser.: No. 112). 128p. (YA). 1991. pap. 3.50 (*0-553-28898-9*) Bantam.

Skateboard Champion, Vol. 112. large type ed. Edward Packard. LC 95-21670. (Choose Your Own Adventure Ser.: Vol. 112). (Illus.). 128p. (J). (gr. 4 up). 1995. lib. bdg. 15.93 (*0-8368-1406-1*) Gareth Stevens Inc.

Skateboard Fun. Stephen Caitlin. LC 87-19179. (First-Start Easy Readers Ser.). (J). (ps-1). 1988. lib. bdg. 9.79 (*0-8167-1233-6*) Troll Communs.

Skateboard Monsters. Daniel Kirk. 1992. 12.95 (*0-8478-1464-5*) Rizzoli Intl.

Skateboard Monsters. Daniel Kirk. (Illus.). 32p. (J). (ps-3). 1995. pap. 4.99 (*0-14-055553-6*) Puffin Bks.

Skateboard Practice: Addition & Subtraction. Mary Laycock et al. (Illus.). 63p. (J). (gr. 1-3). 1978. pap. text ed. 8.50 (*0-918932-55-6*, A-1570) Activity Resources.

Skateboard Practice: Multiplication & Division. Mary Laycock & Peggy McLean. (Illus.). 64p. (J). (gr. 2-6). 1979. pap. text ed. 8.50 (*0-918932-65-3*, A-1596) Activity Resources.

Skateboard Shakedown. 2nd rev. ed. Lesley Choyce. 124p. (J). (gr. 6-9). 1989. reprint ed. 16.95 (*0-88780-074-2*, Pub. by Formac Pubng CN); reprint ed. pap. 6.95 (*0-88780-232-X*, Pub. by Formac Pubng CN) Formac Dist Ltd.

Skateboard Tough. Matt Christopher. (J). (gr. 4-7). 1991. 15.95 (*0-316-14247-6*) Little.

Skateboard Tough. Matt Christopher. (Illus.). (J). (gr. 3-6). 1994. pap. text ed. 3.95 (*0-316-14241-7*) Little.

Skateboard Workbook. S. Kane. 1989. pap. 13.95 (*0-7156-2324-9*, Pub. by Duckworth UK) Focus Pub-R Pullins.

Skateboarding. Jeremy Evans. LC 93-18165. (Adventurers Ser.). (Illus.). 48p. (J). (gr. 5-6). 1994. lib. bdg. 13.95 (*0-89686-822-2*, Crstwood Hse) Silver Burdett Pr.

Skateboarding. Marilyn Gould. (Action Sports Ser.). 48p. (J). (gr. 3-4). 1991. lib. bdg. 17.80 (*1-56065-048-6*) Capstone Pr.

***Skateboarding.** Gutman. 1997. 13.95 (*0-312-86153-2*) St Martin.

Skateboarding. Bill Gutman. 128p. (YA). 1995. pap. 7.99 (*0-8125-1938-8*) Tor Bks.

***Skateboarding.** Bill Gutman. (YA). (gr. 3 up). 1997. 12.95 (*0-614-29124-0*) Tor Bks.

Skateboarding. Marty Nabham. LC 93-23317. (Pro-Am Sports Ser.). (J). 1993. write for info. (*0-86593-346-4*) Rourke Corp.

Skateboarding Basics. Jackson Jay. LC 95-44719. (New Action Sports Ser.). 48p. (J). (gr. 3-9). 1996. 17.80 (*1-56065-374-4*) Capstone Pr.

***Skateboarding Basics.** Jackson Jay. (New Action Sports Ser.). 48p. (J). (gr. 3-7). 1996. 18.40 (*0-516-20097-6*) Childrens.

Skateboarding Streetstyle. Joel Schoemaker. (Action Sports Ser.). 48p. (J). (gr. 3-9). 1995. lib. bdg. 17.80 (*1-56065-261-6*) Capstone Pr.

***Skateboarding Streetstyle.** Joel Shoemaker. (Action Sports Ser.). (Illus.). 48p. (J). (gr. 3-4). 1995. 18.40 (*0-516-35261-X*) Childrens.

***Skateland: California Portraits.** Edward L. Beggs. LC 96-92583. (Illus.). 250p. (Orig.). (YA). 1997. pap. 14.95 (*1-889607-01-0*) Self-Reliance Pr.

Skater's Edge Sourcebook: Ice Skating Resource Guide. Alice Berman. (Illus.). 336p. (Orig.). 1997. pap. 39.95 (*0-9643027-0-5*) Skaters Edge. Dubbed "The Whole Earth Catalog of Skating," The SKATER'S EDGE SOURCEBOOK compiles extensive resource information for the popular sport of ice skating. (Second edition scheduled for release 1/98, 336 pp, ISBN 0-9643027-1-3). Book includes detailed listings of more than 400 companies that make or sell skating-related products (apparel, boots, blades, accessories, etc.); that design or build skating rinks; or that serve as consultants to the industry. All companies cross-referenced by the type of services provided. Book also profiles close to 1,000 skating rinks in the U.S. [address, phone, # of ice surfaces, whether enclosed, months open, etc.] Other sections include listings of skating books, videos, associations, organizations, federations, training centers, summer skating schools, & more. Book includes consumer articles on such topics as GUIDE TO FITTING SKATES, SKATE BOOTS (makes, models, manufacturers), GUIDE TO BLADES (makes, specifications, uses), LACING SKATES, CHOOSING A PRO, & more. The SKATER'S EDGE SOURCEBOOK is published by SKATER'S EDGE, the world's leading "how-to" skating magazine with instructional articles & tips by the world's top coaches & pros. SKATER'S EDGE is published 5 times a year; the SOURCEBOOK is updated every three years. For more information, contact: SKATER'S EDGE, Box 500, Kensington, MD 20895. Phone/FAX: (301) 946-1971; e-mail: Skateredge@aol.com. The SKATER'S EDGE SOURCEBOOK is available direct from the publisher, or from Koen Book Distributors or Baker & Taylor. ***Publisher Provided Annotation.***

***Skater's Edge Sourcebook: Ice Skating Resource Guide.** 2nd rev. ed. Alice Berman. (Illus.). 336p. (Orig.). 1998. write for info. (*0-9643027-1-3*) Skaters Edge.

Skates & Grapes see Phonics Is My Way Series

Skates of Uncle Richard. Carol Fenner. LC 78-55910. (Illus.). (J). (gr. 2-5). 1978. lib. bdg. 9.99 (*0-394-93553-5*) Random Bks Yng Read.

Skates of Uncle Richard. Carol Fenner. LC 78-55910. (Stepping Stone Book & Cassette Library). (Illus.). 64p. (J). (gr. 2-4). 1995. pap. 3.50 (*0-679-84923-8*) Random Bks Yng Read.

Skateway to Freedom. Ann Alma. 160p. (Orig.). (J). (gr. 4-8). 1993. pap. 5.95 (*0-920501-89-3*) Orca Bk Pubs.

***Skating.** (Illus.). 64p. (YA). (gr. 6-12). 1996. pap. 2.40 (*0-8395-5006-5*, 35006) BSA.

Skating. Donna Bailey. LC 90-36525. (Sports World Ser.). (Illus.). 32p. (J). (gr. 1-4). 1990. pap. 3.95 (*0-8114-4715-4*); lib. bdg. 21.40 (*0-8114-2854-0*) Raintree Steck-V.

Skating Book. Ginny L. Winter. (Illus.). (J). (gr. k-3). 1963. 8.95 (*0-8392-3035-4*) Astor-Honor.

Skating Camp. Melissa Lowell. (Silver Blades Ser.: No. 6). 144p. (J). (gr. 4-7). 1994. pap. 3.50 (*0-553-48198-3*) Dell.

Skating for Cross-Country Skiers. Audun Endestad & John Teaford. LC 86-21298. (Illus.). 160p. (Orig.). 1987. pap. 15.95 (*0-88011-282-4*, PEND0282) Human Kinetics.

***Skating for Gold.** Lovitt. (YA). 1997. mass mkt. 3.99 (*0-671-01679-2*) PB.

Skating in the Arts of Seventeenth Century Holland. Laurinda S. Dixon. LC 87-50001. (Illus.). 44p. (Orig.). 1987. pap. 8.00 (*0-915577-12-7*) Taft Museum.

Skating on Skis. Dick Mansfield. LC 87-14563. (Illus.). 144p. 1988. pap. 9.95 (*0-937921-37-8*) Acorn Pub.

Skating on Thin Ice. Louise Everett. LC 86-30857. (Illus.). 32p. (J). (gr. k-2). 1988. lib. bdg. 9.79 (*0-8167-0992-0*) Troll Communs.

Skating on Thin Ice. Louise Everett. LC 86-30857. (Illus.). 32p. (J). (gr. k-2). 1997. pap. 2.50 (*0-8167-0993-9*) Troll Communs.

Skating Rink. Date not set. pap. 1.95 (*0-590-05185-7*) Scholastic Inc.

Skating Superstars. Allison Gertridge. (Illus.). 40p. (Orig.). (J). (gr. k up). 1996. pap. 4.95 (*1-55209-009-4*) Firefly Bks Ltd.

***Skating Superstars II.** Allison Gertridge. 1997. pap. text ed. 5.95 (*1-55209-158-9*) Firefly Bks Ltd.

Skating System: Scrutineering Ballroom Dance Competitions. Imperial Society of Teachers of Dancing Staff. (Ballroom Dance Ser.). 1986. lib. bdg. 69.95 (*0-8490-3360-8*) Gordon Pr.

Skating System: Scrutineering Ballroom Dance Competitions. Ed. by Imperial Society of Teachers of Dancing Staff. (Ballroom Dance Ser.). 1985. lib. bdg. 79.95 (*0-87700-869-8*) Revisionist Pr.

***Skating Whiz.** Claudette C. Mitchell et al. (Visions: African-American Experiences: Vol. 25). (Illus.). 8p. (Orig.). (J). (gr. k-1). 1996. pap. text ed. 3.00 (*1-57518-067-7*) Arborlake.

Skating with Katie. Kaitlin M. Smith. (Illus.). 15p. (J). (gr. k-3). 1992. pap. 17.95 (*1-895583-19-5*) MAYA Pubs.

Skazanie o Chudesakh: Vladimirskoi Ikony Bozh'ei Materi. Intro. by Vasily O. Kliuchevsky. (Monuments of Early Russian Literature Ser.: Vol. 7). 57p. (C). 1993. reprint ed. pap. 10.00 (*0-933884-92-3*) Berkeley Slavic.

Skazanije o Khrista Radi Jurodivoj - Pelagiji Ivanovna Serebrennikva. 183p. reprint ed. pap. 7.00 (*0-317-29280-3*) Holy Trinity.

Skazanije o zhizni i Podvigakh Ieroskimanakha Parthenija, startsa Kievo-Petcherskoj-Lavri. 104p. reprint ed. pap. 4.00 (*0-317-29270-6*) Holy Trinity.

Skazka o Zaichonke Pete-The Tale of Peter Rabbit. Beatrix Potter & Anna Pomaska. Tr. by Elvira Maler. (Illus.). 32p. (RUS.). (J). 1996. reprint ed. pap. text ed. 1.00 (*0-486-28717-3*) Dover.

Skedadle Skunk & Friends Say I Love You. Diane M. Stortz. (Illus.). 12p. (J). (ps). 1995. bds. 4.99 (*0-7847-0297-7*, 03437) Standard Pub.

Skeena, BC. Rob Brown. (River Journal Ser.: Vol. 3, No. 1). (Illus.). 48p. 1996. pap. 15.95 (*1-57188-032-1*) F Amato Pubns.

Skeeter. K. Smith. (J). (gr. 4-7). 1992. pap. 4.95 (*0-395-61621-2*) HM.

Skeeter: Hoglegs, Hipshots, & Jalapenos: Selected Works of Skeeter Skelton, Vol. II. 2nd ed. Ed. by Jim Bequette. (Illus.). 288p. 1991. 19.95 (*0-9621148-6-3*) PJS Pubns.

***Skeeter: The Wildly Wacky Raccoon.** Veralee Wiggins. LC 97-234. (J). 1997. write for info. (*0-8163-1388-1*) Pacific Pr Pub Assn.

SKEETS: The New Frankenstein Chronicles, 2 vols. deluxe limited ed. Artemis Smith. Ed. by Alana Collos & Judith Hebert. (Illus.). 330p. 1997. 5,000.00 (*1-878998-10-2*) Savant Garde.

SKEETS: The New Frankenstein Chronicles. 2nd limited ed. Artemis Smith, pseud. Ed. by Alana Collos et al. 310p. 1991. reprint ed. pap. 200.00 (*1-878998-11-0*) Savant Garde.

SKEETS: The New Frankenstein Chronicles, 2 vols., Set. Artemis Smith. Ed. by Alana Collos & Judith Hebert. (Illus.). 330p. 1997. boxed 1,000.00 (*1-878998-16-1*) Savant Garde.

***Skeff: Owen Sheehy Skeffington.** Andree S. Skeffington. 1996. 32.95 (*0-946640-60-2*, Pub. by Lilliput Pr Ltd IE) Irish Bks Media.

Skein of Legends Around Chopin. Adam Harasowski. LC 77-28829. (Music Reprint Ser.: 1978). (Illus.). 1980. reprint ed. lib. bdg. 39.50 (*0-306-77525-5*) Da Capo.

***Skeletal & Muscular Systems: A Laboratory Manual.** Deloris Johns. 152p. (C). 1996. pap. text ed. 16.80 (*0-7872-2914-8*) Kendall-Hunt.

Skeletal Biology in the Great Plains: Migration, Warfare, Health, & Subsistence. Ed. by Douglas W. Owsley & Richard L. Jantz. LC 91-14388. (Illus.). 408p. (C). 1994. text ed. 45.00 (*1-56098-093-1*) Smithsonian.

Skeletal Biology of CA-ALA-342. fac. ed. Ed. by Robert Jurmain. (Illus.). 71p. (C). 1983. reprint ed. pap. text ed. 6.50 (*1-55567-512-3*) Coyote Press.

Skeletal Biology of Earlier Human Populations. Don R. Brothwell. LC 68-14720. (Symposia of the Society for the Study of Human Biology Ser.: Vol. 8). 1968. 137.00 (*0-08-013187-5*, Pub. by Pergamon Repr UK) Franklin.

Skeletal Biology of Past Peoples: Advances in Research Methods. Shelley R. Saunders & M. Anne Katzenberg. 270p. 1992. text ed. 82.50 (*0-471-56138-X*, Wiley-L) Wiley.

Skeletal Biomineralization: Patterns, Processes, & Evolutionary Trends, 2 vols., Set. Joseph G. Carter. (Illus.). 700p. (gr. 13). 1990. text ed. 115.50 (*0-442-00667-5*) Chapman & Hall.

Skeletal Biomineralization: Patterns, Processes, & Evolutionary Trends, 2 vols., Vol. I. Joseph G. Carter. (Illus.). 832p. (gr. 13). 1990. text ed. 90.50 (*0-442-00620-9*) Chapman & Hall.

Skeletal Biomineralization: Patterns, Processes, & Evolutionary Trends, 2 vols., Vol. II. Joseph G. Carter. (Illus.). 301p. (gr. 13). 1990. text ed. 73.00 (*0-442-00666-7*) Chapman & Hall.

Skeletal Dysplasia Syndromes. Kazimierz Kozlowski. 150p. 1984. pap. 40.50 (*0-387-12825-5*) Spr-Verlag.

Skeletal Dysplasias. Ed. by Daniel Bergsma. (March of Dimes Ser.: Vol. 10, No. 8). 12.95 (*0-686-10015-8*) March of Dimes.

Skeletal Growth of Aquatic Organisms: Biological Records of Environmental Change. Ed. by Donald C. Rhoads & Richard A. Lutz. LC 79-25825. (Topics in Geobiology Ser.: Vol. I). (Illus.). 762p. 1980. 140.00 (*0-306-40259-9*, Plenum Pr) Plenum.

Skeletal Injury in the Child. 2nd ed. Ogden. 960p. 1989. text ed. 229.00 (*0-7216-2955-5*) Saunders.

Skeletal Material from San Jose Ruin, British Honduras. W. D. Hambly. Incl. Anthropometry of the Ovimbundu, Angola. 1940. (*0-318-54038-X*); Craniometry of New Guinea. 1940. (*0-318-54039-8*); (Field Museum of Natural History Ser.: Vol. 25). 1940. 55.00 (*0-527-01885-6*) Periodicals Srv.

***Skeletal Material from San Jose Ruin, British Honduras, Field Museum-Carnegie Institution Expeditions to British Honduras.** Wilfrid D. Hambly. LC 37-22773. (Field Museum of Natural History Anthropological Ser.: Vol. 25, No. 1). (Illus.). 19p. 1937. reprint ed. pap. 25.00 (*0-608-02712-X*, 2063377) Bks Demand.

Skeletal Mosaic. Marykay Gaines. Ed. by Mary K. Gaines. (Illus.). 195p. (Orig.). 1995. pap. 6.99 (*0-9641822-1-1*) O W L Press.

Skeletal Muscle. 133p. 1994. 21.00 (*0-912452-93-5*, P-105) Am Phys Therapy Assn.

Skeletal Muscle. H. Schalmbruch. (Handbuch der Mikroskopischen Anatomie Des Menschen Ser.: Vol. 2, Pt. 6). (Illus.). 500p. 1985. 464.00 (*0-387-15608-9*) Spr-Verlag.

An Asterisk (*) at the beginning of an entry indicates that the title is appearing in BIP for the first time.

Skeletal Muscle Form & Function. Alan J. McComas. LC 95-24525. (Illus.). 416p. 1996. text ed. 49.00 (*0-87322-780-8*, BMCC0780) Human Kinetics.

Skeletal Muscle in Health & Disease: A Textbook of Muscle Physiology. Dorothy A. Jones & J. M. Round. 1990. text ed. 27.95 (*0-7190-3164-8*, Pub. by Manchester Univ Pr UK) St Martin.

Skeletal Muscle Microcirculation. Ed. by K. Messmer & F. Hammersen. (Mikrozirkulation in Forschung und Klinik; Progress in Applied Microcirculation Ser.: Vol. 5). (Illus.). vii, 148p. 1984. pap. 59.25 (*3-8055-3920-7*) S Karger.

Skeletal Muscle Pathology. 2nd ed. Ed. by John Walton & Frank L. Mastaglia. (Illus.). 803p. 1992. text ed. 225.00 (*0-443-04241-1*) Churchill.

Skeletal Muscle Structure & Function. Richard E. Lieber. (Illus.). 314p. 1992. pap. 37.00 (*0-683-05026-5*) Williams & Wilkins.

Skeletal Muscle Toxicity of 6-Mercaptopurine, Vol. 11, 14. Ed. by C. P. Bianchi et al. LC 86-61951. (Toxicology & Industrial Health Ser.: Vol. 2, No. 2). (Illus.). 144p. 1986. 24.00 (*0-911131-95-7*) Princeton Sci Pubs.

Skeletal Musculature in Larval Phases of the Beetle Epicauta Segmenta, (Coleoptera, Meloidae) A. Berrios-Ortiz & R. B. Selandev. (Entomologica Ser.: Vol. 16). (Illus.). 1979. lib. bdg. 70.50 (*90-6193-126-6*) Kluwer Ac.

Skeletal Nuclear Medicine. Ed. by B. David Collier, Jr. et al. 000576p. (C). (gr. 13). 1996. text ed. 179.00 (*0-8151-3273-5*) Mosby Yr Bk.

Skeletal Radiology. Martin H. Reed. (Illus.). 696p. 1991. 150.00 (*0-683-07212-9*) Williams & Wilkins.

Skeletal Radiology. Ed. by Donald Resnick & Holger Pettersson. (Nicer Series on Diagnostic Imaging). (Illus.). 674p. 1992. 52.00 (*1-873413-45-9*) Merit Pub Intl.

Skeletal Radiology: The Bare Bones. Felix S. M. Chew. 262p. 1989. text ed. 75.00 (*0-8342-0071-6*) Lppncott-Raven.

***Skeletal Radiology: The Bare Bones.** 2nd ed. Felix S. M. Chew. LC 96-28914. 340p. 1996. 89.00 (*0-683-01680-6*) Williams & Wilkins.

Skeletal Radiology: The Bare Bones Teaching Collection. Felix S. M. Chew. (C). 1991. 500.00 incl. disk (*1-56815-001-6*) Mosby Yr Bk.

Skeletal Remains from Santa Barbara, California: I. Craniology. Bruno Oetteking. LC 76-43795. (MAI. Indian Notes & Monographs: No. 39). reprint ed. 49.50 (*0-404-15651-7*) AMS Pr.

Skeletal Remains of the Central Eskimos. Knud Fischer-Moller. Tr. by W. E. Calvert. LC 76-22524. (Thule Expedition, 5th, 1921-1924 Ser.: Vol. 3, No. 1). reprint ed. 41.50 (*0-404-58311-3*) AMS Pr.

Skeletal Remains Suggesting Or Attributed to Early Man in North America. Ales Hrdlicka. (Bureau of American Ethnology Bulletins Ser.). 113p. 1995. lib. bdg. 79.00 (*0-7812-4033-6*) Rprt Serv.

Skeletal System. (Invisible World Ser.). (Illus.). 32p. (J). (gr. 4 up). 1995. lib. bdg. 15.95 (*0-7910-3151-9*) Chelsea Hse.

Skeletal System. Virginia B. Silverstein. (Human Body Systems Ser.). (Illus.). 96p. (J). (gr. 5-8). 1994. lib. bdg. 16.98 (*0-8050-2837-4*) TFC Bks NY.

Skeletal Trauma. Nance. 1998. text ed. write for info. (*0-7216-5993-4*) Saunders.

***Skeletal Trauma: Fractures, Dislocations, Ligamentous Injuries, 2 vols.** Ed. by Bruce D. Browner et al. (Illus.). 2184p. 1992. write for info. (*0-7216-2726-9*) Saunders.

Skeletal Trauma: Fractures, Dislocations, Ligmaentous Injuries, 2 vols., Set. 2nd ed. Bruce D. Browner et al. Ed. by Richard Lampert. LC 96-50086. (Illus.). 2400p. 1997. text ed. write for info. (*0-7216-6884-4*) Saunders.

Skeletal Trauma in Children. Ed. by Neil E. Green & Marc F. Swiontkowski. LC 92-11622. (Illus.). 560p. 1993. text ed. 147.00 (*0-7216-5129-1*) Saunders.

Skeletal Trauma in Children, Vol. 3. 2nd ed. Neil E. Green & Marc F. Swiontkowski. Ed. by Richard Lampert. LC 96-49870. (Illus.). 608p. 1997. text ed. write for info. (*0-7216-6735-X*) Saunders.

Skeletal Trauma in Old Age. Ed. by David I. Rowley & Benedict Clift. LC 94-70928. 223p. (gr. 13). 1994. text ed. 68.95 (*0-412-48750-0*) Chapman & Hall.

Skeleton. Steve Parker. LC 87-26314. (Eyewitness Bks.). (Illus.). 64p. (J). (gr. 5 up). 1988. 19.00 (*0-394-89620-3*) Knopf Bks Yng Read.

Skeleton. Steve Parker. LC 87-26314. (Eyewitness Bks.). (Illus.). 64p. (J). (gr. 5 up). 1988. lib. bdg. 20.99 (*0-394-99620-8*) Knopf Bks Yng Read.

Skeleton. Steve Parker. LC 96-7962. (Look at Your Body Ser.). (Illus.). 32p. (J). (gr. 4-6). 1996. lib. bdg. 15.40 (*0-7613-0529-7*, Copper Beech Bks) Millbrook Pr.

Skeleton & Movement. (How Our Bodies Work Ser.). (Illus.). 48p. (J). (gr. 5-8). 1988. text ed. 12.95 (*0-382-09702-5*) Silver Burdett Pr.

Skeleton & Movement. rev. ed. Steve Parker. LC 88-51608. (Human Body Ser.). (Illus.). 48p. (J). (gr. 5-7). 1989. lib. bdg. 20.60 (*0-531-10709-4*) Watts.

***Skeleton & Muscular System: The Human Body.** Steve Parker. LC 96-29688. (J). 1997. 24.26 (*0-8172-4805-6*) Raintree Pr.

Skeleton & That Man. 2nd rev. ed. Amrita Pritam. Tr. by Khushwant Singh. 97p. 1992. pap. 5.95 (*81-207-0243-3*, Pub. by Sterling Pubs II) Apt Bks.

Skeleton at the Feast: The Day of the Dead in Mexico. Elizabeth Carmichael & Chloe Sayer. LC 91-66304. (Illus.). 192p. (Orig.). 1991. pap. 29.95 (*0-292-77658-6*) U of Tex Pr.

***Skeleton Canyon: A Joanna Brady Mystery.** J. A. Jance. 1997. 23.00 (*0-614-27899-6*) Avon.

***Skeleton Canyon: A Joanna Brady Mystery.** Judith A. Jance. LC 97-3217. (A Joanna Brady Mystery Ser.). 384p. (Orig.). 1997. pap. 23.00 (*0-380-97395-2*) Avon.

Skeleton Clocks. F. B. Royer-Collard. (Illus.). 165p. 1981. 49.50 (*0-7198-0110-9*, Pub. by NAG Press UK) Antique Collect.

Skeleton Closet: A Spooky Pop-Up Book. Steven Guarnaccia. LC 94-73440. (Illus.). 14p. (J). (ps up). 1996. 12.95 (*0-7868-0007-0*) Hyprn Child.

Skeleton Construction in Buildings. William H. Birkmire. LC 72-5035. (Technology & Society Ser.). (Illus.). 200p. 1978. reprint ed. 21.95 (*0-405-04688-X*) Ayer.

Skeleton Crew. Allan Ahlberg. LC 91-39161. (Illus.). 32p. (J). (ps-6). 1992. 16.00 (*0-688-11436-9*) Greenwillow.

***Skeleton Crew.** Janet Lorimer. LC 95-76741. (Ten-Minute Thrillers Ser.). 32p. (YA). (gr. 6-12). 1995. pap. 2.95 (*0-7854-1069-4*, 40817) Am Guidance.

Skeleton Crew. Stephen King. 576p. 1986. reprint ed. pap. 6.99 (*0-451-16861-5*, Sig) NAL-Dutton.

***Skeleton Crew Readalong.** Janet Lorimer. (Ten-Minute Thrillers Ser.). 32p. 1995. pap. 12.95 incl. audio (*0-7854-1080-5*, 40819) Am Guidance.

Skeleton Detective. Don Lessem. (J). 1997. 16.00 (*0-517-70932-5*); lib. bdg. write for info. (*0-517-70933-3*) Random Hse Value.

Skeleton from Mesa House. Bruno Oetteking. (Illus.). 48p. 1970. reprint ed. pap. 3.50 (*0-916561-61-5*) Southwest Mus.

Skeleton in God Closet. Paul L. Maier. 1996. mass mkt. 5.99 (*0-7852-7537-1*) Nelson.

Skeleton in God's Closet. Paul L. Maier. LC 93-28203. 1993. pap. 12.99 (*0-8407-3424-7*) Nelson.

Skeleton in the Closet. Clarence Darrow. 3.95 (*0-8283-1438-1*) Branden Pub Co.

Skeleton in the Closet, Vol 12. J. R. Black. (J). 1995. pap. 3.99 (*0-679-87171-3*) Random.

Skeleton in the Skateboard. Tom B. Stone. (Graveyard School Ser.: No. 2). 128p. (J). (gr. 4-7). 1994. pap. 3.50 (*0-553-48224-6*) Bantam.

Skeleton in the Wardrobe: C. S. Lewis's Fantasies: A Phenomenological Study. David Holbrook. LC 89-46400. 304p. 1991. 42.50 (*0-8387-5183-0*) Bucknell U Pr.

Skeleton-in-Waiting. Peter Dickinson. 1989. 16.95 (*0-394-58002-8*) Pantheon.

Skeleton-in-Waiting. large type ed. Peter Dickinson. LC 90-34615. 281p. 1990. lib. bdg. 8.95 (*1-56054-004-4*) Thorndike Pr.

Skeleton Inside You. Philip Balestrino. LC 85-42982. (Trophy Let's-Read-&-Find-Out Bk.). (Illus.). 40p. (J). (ps-3). 1986. pap. 4.95 (*0-06-445039-2*, Trophy) HarpC Child Bks.

Skeleton Inside You. rev. ed. Philip Balestrino. LC 88-24600. (Trophy Let's-Read-&-Find-Out Bk.). (Illus.). 32p. (J). (gr. k-3). 1989. pap. 4.95 (*0-06-445087-2*, Trophy) HarpC Child Bks.

Skeleton Inside You. rev. ed. Philip Balestrino. LC 88-23672. (Let's-Read-&-Find-Out Science Bk.). (Illus.). 32p. (J). (gr. k-3). 1989. lib. bdg. 14.89 (*0-690-04733-9*, Crowell Jr Bks) HarpC Child Bks.

Skeleton Key. E. L. Flood. LC 94-22762. (Welcome Inn Ser.: No. 03). 144p. (J). (gr. 4-7). 1996. teacher ed., pap. 3.50 (*0-8167-3429-1*, Rainbow NJ) Troll Communs.

***Skeleton Key.** John Moat. 68p. 1997. 45.00 (*0-930126-53-X*) Typographeum.

Skeleton Key: A Dictionary for Deadheads. David Shenk & Steve Silberman. LC 94-9192. 416p. 1994. pap. 14.95 (*0-385-47402-4*) Doubleday.

Skeleton Key to Finnegans Wake. Joseph Campbell & Henry M. Robinson. 1993. reprint ed. lib. bdg. 28.95 (*1-56849-168-9*) Buccaneer Bks.

Skeleton Keys: An Introduction to Human Skeletal Morphology, Development, & Analysis. Jeffrey H. Schwartz. (Illus.). 432p. 1995. text ed. 52.95 (*0-19-505638-8*) OUP.

Skeleton Man. Jay Bennett. 128p. 1988. mass mkt. 3.95 (*0-449-70284-7*, Juniper) Fawcett.

Skeleton of a Bridge. Robert Mirabal. 116p. (Orig.). 1994. pap. 10.00 (*1-883968-02-X*) Blinking Yellow.

Skeleton of Chaucer's Canterbury Tales. Henry Bradshaw. LC 70-39518. reprint ed. 32.50 (*0-404-00929-8*) AMS Pr.

Skeleton of the Boraphaginae (Carnivora, Canidae) Morphology & Function. Kathleen Munthe. 1990. pap. 20.00 (*0-520-09724-6*) U CA Pr.

Skeleton Warrior Tattoo. (J). write for info. (*0-679-87453-4*) Random.

Skeleton Woman. Alberto Villardo & Yoshi. (J). (gr. 4 up). 1995. 15.00 (*0-671-89728-4*, S&S Bks Young Read) S&S Childrens.

Skeletons. (Information Ser.). 32p. (J). 3.50 (*0-7214-1742-6*, Ladybrd) Penguin.

Skeletons. 1999. pap. 4.99 (*0-7214-5656-1*, Ladybrd) Penguin.

Skeletons: An Inside Look at Animals. Jinny Johnson. LC 94-62. (Illus.). 48p. (YA). (gr. 6 up). 1994. 16.95 (*0-89577-604-9*) Rdrs Dgst Yng Fam.

Skeletons Don't Play Tubas. Debbie Dadey. 96p. (J). (gr. 4-7). 1994. pap. 2.99 (*0-590-48113-4*) Scholastic Inc.

Skeletons from Our Closet. Tom Tyner. 84p. (Orig.). 1995. pap. 8.95 (*0-9645813-0-2*) Wendell & Lunar Pub.

Skeletons from the Opera Closet. David Groover & C. C. Conner. (Illus.). 256p. 1994. reprint ed. pap. 12.95 (*1-55921-104-0*) Moyer Bell.

***Skeletons in Her Cupboard: Festschrift for Juliet Clutton-Brock.** Ed. by Anneke Clason et al. (Oxbow Monographs in Archaeology: No. 34). (Illus.). 259p. 1993. pap. 55.00 (*0-946897-64-6*, Pub. by Oxbow Bks UK) David Brown.

Skeletons in the Closet. William J. Pomidor. 1997. pap. 5.50 (*0-451-18418-1*, Sig) NAL-Dutton.

Skeletons in the Closet: A Collection of Short Stories. Joseph Vollaro. Ed. by Joseph Paretta. (Illus.). 208p. (Orig.). (YA). (gr. 9-12). 1993. pap. 13.95 (*0-9633309-3-4*) Rightway Educ.

Skeleton's Knee. Archer Mayor. 320p. 1993. 18.95 (*0-89296-470-7*) Mysterious Pr.

Skeleton's Knee. Archer Mayor. 320p. 1994. mass mkt. 5.99 (*0-446-40099-8*, Mysterious Paperbk) Warner Bks.

Skeleton's Knees. large type ed. Archer Mayor. LC 94-5669. 1994. lib. bdg. 21.95 (*0-7862-0227-0*) Thorndike Pr.

Skeletons of a Course of Theological Lectures see Heart of Truth: Finney's Outlines of Theology

***Skeleton's Revenge.** Tom B. Stone. (Graveyard School Ser.: No. 21). 112p. (Orig.). (J). (gr. 3-7). 1997. pap. 3.99 (*0-553-48524-5*) BDD Bks Young Read.

Skelligside. Michael Kirby. (Illus.). 176p. 1990. pap. 13.95 (*0-946640-53-X*, Pub. by Lilliput Pr Ltd IE) Irish Bks Media.

Skelter. Michael R. Perry. Ed. by Jane Chellus. 560p. (Orig.). 1994. mass mkt. 5.99 (*0-671-73496-2*, Pocket Star Bks) PB.

Skelton. H. L. Edwards. LC 77-148879. (Select Bibliographies Reprint Ser.). 1977. 21.95 (*0-8369-5673-7*) Ayer.

Skelton. rev. ed. Mark Dunster. (Henry the Eighth Ser.). 13p. (Orig.). 1988. pap. 4.00 (*0-89642-156-2*) Linden Pubs.

Skelton: The Skeltons of Paxton, Pawhatan County, Va., Including Sketches of the Families of Skelton, Gifford & Crane. P. H. Baskervil. (Illus.). 119p. 1992. reprint ed. pap. 22.00 (*0-8328-2727-4*); reprint ed. lib. bdg. 32.00 (*0-8328-2726-6*) Higginson Bk Co.

Skelton, the Life & Times of an Early Tudor Poet. H. L. Edwards. 1988. reprint ed. lib. bdg. 75.00 (*0-7812-0060-1*) Rprt Serv.

Skepsis, Dogma, & Belief: Uses & Abuses in Medicine. Edmond A. Murphy. LC 80-8870. 176p. 1981. text ed. 30.00 (*0-8018-2510-5*) Johns Hopkins.

***Skepsis oder Furcht Gottes? Studien zur Komposition & Theologie des Buches Kohelet.** Alexander A. Fischer. (Beihefte zur Zeitschrift fuer die Alttestamentliche Wissenschaft Ser.: Vol. 247). x, 289p. (GER.). (C). 1997. lib. bdg. 117.05 (*3-11-015458-7*) De Gruyter.

Skeptic Among Scholars: August Fruge on University Publishing. August Fruge. LC 93-13477. 1993. 40.00 (*0-520-07733-4*); pap. 12.95 (*0-520-08426-8*) U CA Pr.

Skeptic Disposition: Deconstruction, Demystification, Ideology, & Other Matters. Eugene Goodheart. 196p. 1991. pap. text ed. 13.95 (*0-691-01519-8*) Princeton U Pr.

***Skeptic in the House.** James Kelley. LC 97-2377. 208p. (C). 1997. 29.95 (*0-8135-2427-X*) Rutgers U Pr.

Skeptic Way: Sextus Empiricus's Outlines of Pyrrhonism. Benson Mates. 352p. (C). 1996. text ed. 57.00 (*0-19-509212-0*); pap. text ed. 24.95 (*0-19-509213-9*) OUP.

Skeptical Biochemist. Joseph S. Fruton. 330p. (C). 1992. 34.50 (*0-674-81077-5*) HUP.

Skeptical Essays. Benson Mates. LC 80-19553. xii, 188p. (C). 1981. 20.50 (*0-226-50986-9*) U Ch Pr.

Skeptical Heart. Teresa Desjardien. 256p. 1996. mass mkt. 4.50 (*0-8217-5355-X*, Zebra Kensgtn) Kensgtn Pub Corp.

Skeptical Scenographer: Essays on Theatrical Design & Human Nature. Beeb Salzer. (Illus.). 192p. (Orig.). (C). 1995. pap. 19.95 (*0-911747-36-2*) Broadway Pr.

Skeptical Selves: Empiricism & Modernity in the French Novel. Elena Russo. 244p. 35.00 (*0-8047-2465-2*) Stanford U Pr.

Skeptical Selves: Empiricism & Modernity in the French Novel. Elena Russo. LC 95-18188. 1996. write for info. (*0-8047-2466-0*) Stanford U Pr.

Skepticism. Ernest Sosa. (Focus Ser.). 110p. 1996. 33.50 (*0-8133-0797-X*); pap. text ed. 11.95 (*0-8133-0798-8*) Westview.

***Skepticism about the External World.** Panayot Butchvarov. 224p. 1997. 45.00 (*0-19-511719-0*) OUP.

Skepticism & Dissent: Selected Journalism, 1898-1901. Ambrose Bierce. Ed. by Lawrence I. Berkove. LC 85-24588. (Nineteenth-Century Studies). 336p. reprint ed. 96.10 (*0-8357-1727-5*, 2070465) Bks Demand.

Skepticism & Ideology: Shelley's Political Prose & Its Philosophical Context from Bacon to Marx. Terence A. Hoagwood. LC 88-17270. 271p. 1988. text ed. 35.00 (*0-87745-218-0*) U of Iowa Pr.

Skepticism & Modern Enmity: Before & After Eliot. Jeffrey M. Perl. LC 89-11057. 256p. 1989. text ed. 39.95 (*0-8018-3853-3*) Johns Hopkins.

Skepticism & Naturalism: Some Varieties. P. F. Strawson. (Woodbridge Lectures Ser.: No. 12). 98p. 1987. reprint ed. pap. text ed. 13.50 (*0-231-05917-5*, King's Crown Paperbacks) Col U Pr.

Skepticism & Political Participation. Aryeh Botwinick. 256p. (C). 1990. 34.95 (*0-87722-657-1*) Temple U Pr.

Skepticism & the Basis of Morality, Vol. 6. Thomas L. McClintock. (New Perspectives in Philosophical Scholarship Ser.). 224p. (C). 1995. text ed. 48.95 (*0-8204-2761-6*) P Lang Pubng.

Skepticism & the Definition of Knowledge. Gilbert Harman. (Harvard Dissertations in Philosophy Ser.). 184p. 1990. reprint ed. text ed. 15.00 (*0-8240-5089-4*) Garland.

***Skepticism, Belief, & the Modern: Maimonides to Nietzsche.** Aryeh Botwinick. LC 97-19770. 264p. 1997. 39.95 (*0-8014-3208-1*) Cornell U Pr.

Skepticism in Cervantes. Maureen Ihrie. (Monagrafias A Ser.: Vol. LXXXVI). 122p. (C). 1982. 35.00 (*0-7293-0119-2*, Pub. by Tamesis Bks Ltd UK) Boydell & Brewer.

Skepticism in Ethics. Panayot Butchvarov. LC 88-45103. 238p. 1989. 37.50 (*0-253-35321-1*); pap. 15.95 (*0-253-20522-0*, MB-522) Ind U Pr.

Skepticism of Anatole France. Helen B. Smith. 1972. 35.00 (*0-8490-1057-8*) Gordon Pr.

***Skeptics Answered.** D. James Kennedy. LC 97-22501. 240p. 1997. 18.99 (*1-57673-148-0*, Multnomah Bks) Multnomah Pubs.

Skeptic's Guide to the Twelve Steps. Z. Phillip. 242p. (Orig.). 1990. pap. 11.00 (*0-89486-722-9*, 5130A) Hazelden.

Skeptic's Handbook of Parapsychology. Ed. by Paul Kurtz. LC 85-43082. 727p. 1985. pap. 24.95 (*0-87975-300-5*) Prometheus Bks.

Skeptic's Notebook. David Rigsbee. 80p. (Orig.). 1996. pap. 10.00 (*1-879934-46-9*) St Andrews NC.

Skeptics of the French Renaissance. John Owen. 1972. 59.95 (*0-8490-1058-6*) Gordon Pr.

Skeptics of the Italian Renaissance. John Owen. 1972. 59.95 (*0-8490-1059-4*) Gordon Pr.

Skeptics Who Demanded a Verdict. Josh McDowell. 96p. 1989. pap. 3.99 (*0-8423-5925-7*) Tyndale.

Sketch: A 1905 Bio of Joshua L. Chamberlain. Brian L. Higgins. Ed. by Larry Johnson. (Illus.). 33p. (Orig.). 1995. pap. 15.00 (*0-9649433-0-1*) NPS.

Sketch - with a Bibliography. Joseph Conrad. 1976. 16.95 (*0-8488-0463-5*) Amereon Ltd.

S

Sketch & Draw Today. Henry J. Filson. (Illus.). 120p. 1976. lib. bdg. 9.60 (*0-685-03710-X*); spiral bd. 12.00 (*0-918554-00-4*) Old Violin.

Sketch Book of Geoffrey Crayon, Gent. Washington Irving. 24.95 (*0-8488-0539-9*) Yestermorrow.

Sketch Book of Geoffrey Crayon, Gent. Washington Irving. Ed. by Malcom Bradbury. 400p. 1993. pap. 6.95 (*0-460-87151-X*, Everyman's Classic Lib) C E Tuttle.

Sketch Book of Geoffrey Crayon, Gent. Washington Irving. 389p. 1961. pap. 5.95 (*0-451-52495-0*, Sig Classics) NAL-Dutton.

Sketch Book of Geoffrey Crayon, Gent. Washington Irving. LC 81-9085. (Illus.). 512p. 1981. reprint ed. 23.95 (*0-912882-47-6*) Sleepy Hollow.

Sketch Book of Geoffrey Crayon, Gent. Washington Irving. (BCL1-PS American Literature Ser.). 487p. 1992. reprint ed. lib. bdg. 99.00 (*0-7812-6755-2*) Rprt Serv.

Sketch Book of Liberty VA: 1887 People & Trade. Edward Pollock. (Illus.). 144p. 1993. reprint ed. pap. 14.00 (*0-9608598-7-X*) Hamiltons.

Sketch-Books: Explore & Store. Gillian Robinson. 160p. 1996. pap. text ed., pap. 21.50 (*0-435-07018-5*) Heinemann.

Sketch for a Portrait of Rimbaud. Humphrey Hare. LC 74-7105. (Studies in French Literature: No. 45). 1974. lib. bdg. 49.95 (*0-8383-1922-X*) M S G Haskell Hse.

Sketch Map History of East Africa. J. C. Ssekamwa. (Illus.). (C). 1984. 45.00 (*0-7175-1135-9*, Pub. by S Thornes Pubs UK) St Mut.

Sketch Map History of East Africa. rev. ed. J. C. Ssekamwa. (Illus.). 276p. 1981. pap. 13.95 (*0-7175-0757-2*) Dufour.

Sketch Map History of West Africa. Norah Latham. 96p. (C). 1978. 39.00 (*0-685-33807-X*, Pub. by S Thornes Pubs UK) St Mut.

Sketch of a Migrating Family to California in 1848. Richard M. May. 66p. 1991. 14.95 (*0-87770-494-5*); pap. 9.95 (*0-87770-499-6*) Ye Galleon.

Sketch of a Plan: Method of Education. Joseph Neef. LC 79-89211. (American Education: Its Men, Institutions, & Ideas. Series 1). 1977. reprint ed. 18.95 (*0-405-01450-3*) Ayer.

***Sketch of a Plan & Method of Education: 1808 Edition.** Joseph Neef. Ed. & Intro. by Jeffrey Stern. (Classics in Education Ser.). 176p. 1996. reprint ed. write for info. (*1-85506-299-2*) Bks Intl VA.

Sketch of a System of the Philosophy of the Human Mind. Thomas Brown. Bd. with Logic of Condillac. LC 77-72191. LC 77-72191. (Contributions to the History of Psychology Ser.: Pt. A, Orientations). 510p. 1977. reprint ed. Set text ed. 69.50 (*0-313-26925-4*, U6925, Greenwood Pr) Greenwood.

Sketch of a Trip from Omaha to Salmon River. Daniel McLaughlin. 23p. 1976. pap. 4.95 (*0-87770-159-8*) Ye Galleon.

Sketch of Chester A. Harding, Artist. Chester A. Harding. Ed. by Margaret E. White. LC 70-87681. (Library of American Art). (Illus.). 1970. reprint ed. lib. bdg. 37.50 (*0-306-71711-5*) Da Capo.

Sketch of Chinese History, Pt. 1. rev. ed. Henry C. Fenn. (Mirror Ser.). 181p. (CHI.). 1983. pap. text ed. 11.95 (*0-88710-091-0*) Yale Far Eastern Pubns.

Sketch of Comparative Dravidian Phonology, Pt. 1. Kamil V. Zvelebil. (Janua Linguarum, Ser. Practica: No. 180). 1977. pap. text ed. 30.00 (*90-279-7646-5*) Mouton.

Sketch of Coptic Grammar: Adapted for Self-Tuition. William B. MacDonald. 1987. reprint ed. pap. 12.95 (*0-89979-047-X*) British Am Bks.

Sketch of English Legal History. Frederic W. Maitland. LC 75-41185. 1976. reprint ed. 34.50 (*0-404-14684-8*) AMS Pr.

Sketch of Glenn G. MacNutt. Karen L. MacNutt. (Illus.). 24p. 1989. 9.52 (*0-9622534-0-5*) MacNutt Art Trust.

Sketch of Grand Canyon Prehistory. A. Trinkle Jones & Robert Euler. 14p. 1979. pap. 4.95 (*0-938216-02-3*) GCA.

Sketch of Irish Musical History. W. H. Grattan-Flood. 99p. 1991. reprint ed. lib. bdg. 59.00 (*0-7812-9360-X*) Rprt Serv.

Sketch of Owen Biddle. H. D. Biddle. (Illus.). 87p. 1988. reprint ed. pap. 17.50 (*0-8328-0251-4*); reprint ed. lib. bdg. 25.50 (*0-8328-0250-6*) Higginson Bk Co.

Sketch of Pendleton. Michael G. Booth. (Illus.). 134p. 1993. pap. write for info. (*1-888236-12-4*) Art Wise.

An Asterisk (*) at the beginning of an entry indicates that the title is appearing in BIP for the first time.

Sketch of Recent Shakespearean Investigation, 1893-1923. Charles H. Herford. LC 70-153327. reprint ed. 29.50 (*0-404-03246-X*) AMS Pr.

***Sketch of Sam Bass: The Bandit.** Charles L. Martin. LC 96-35363. (Western Frontier Library Ser.: Vol. 6). (Illus.). 192p. 1997. pap. 9.95 (*0-8061-2915-8*) U of Okla Pr.

Sketch of Sam Bass, the Bandit: A Graphic Narrative of His Various Train Robberies, His Death, & Accounts of the Deaths of His Gang & Their History (with an Introduction by Ramon F. Adams) Charles L. Martin. LC 56-5991. (Western Frontier Library: Vol. 6). 190p. reprint ed. pap. 54.20 (*0-317-42394-0*, 2052166) Bks Demand.

Sketch of Sills Family. Louise J. Sills. 1969. pap. 8.00 (*0-686-05559-4*) L C Bryant.

***Sketch of the Early History of the Town of Nelson.** S. G. Griffith. (Illus.). 54p. 1997. reprint ed. pap. 11.00 (*0-8328-6014-X*) Higginson Bk Co.

Sketch of the Evolution of Our Native Fruits. Liberty H. Bailey. LC 72-89072. (Rural America Ser.). 1973. reprint ed. 39.00 (*0-8420-1473-X*) Scholarly Res Inc.

Sketch of the Flora of British India. J. D. Hooker. 60p. 1973. 45.00 (*0-685-21747-7*, Pub. by Intl Bk Distr II) St Mut.

Sketch of the Flora of British India. J. D. Hooker. (C). 1973. text ed. 50.00 (*0-89771-640-X*, Pub. by Intl Bk Distr II) St Mut.

Sketch of the History of Attleborough, Massachusetts. John Daggett. 136p. 1993. reprint ed. lib. bdg. 23.00 (*0-8328-3137-9*) Higginson Bk Co.

Sketch of the History of Flemish Literature from the Twelfth Century Down to the Present Time. Octave Delepiere. LC 72-3215. (Studies in European Literature: No. 56). 1972. reprint ed. lib. bdg. 75.00 (*0-8383-1521-6*) M S G Haskell Hse.

Sketch of the History of Key West, Florida. Walter C. Maloney. Ed. & Intro. by Thelma B. Peters. LC 68-21658. (Floridiana Facsimile & Reprint Ser.). xxi, 85p. 1968. reprint ed. 16.95 (*0-8130-0157-9*) U Press Fla.

Sketch of the Laws Relating to Slavery in the Several States of the United States of America. George M. Stroud. 300p. reprint ed. 40.00 (*0-933121-87-3*) Black Classic.

***Sketch of the Life & Character of Daniel Boone.** Peter Houston. Ed. by Ted F. Belue. LC 96-42539. 1997. 15.95 (*0-8117-1522-1*) Stackpole.

Sketch of the Life & Times of Sydney Smith. Stuart J. Reid. 1972. 59.95 (*0-8490-1060-8*) Gordon Pr.

Sketch of the Life & Writings of Sidney Lanier. C. West. 1972. 75.00 (*0-8490-1061-6*) Gordon Pr.

Sketch of the Life of Apollonius of Tyana: Founder of Christianity. Daniel M. Tredwell. 1991. lib. bdg. 79.95 (*0-8490-4258-5*) Gordon Pr.

Sketch of the Life of Thomas Skidmore. Amos Gilbert. (Young America Ser.: No. 2). 64p. pap. 5.95 (*0-88286-060-7*) C H Kerr.

Sketch of the Modern Languages of the East Indies. R. N. Cust. (Illus.). 198p. 1986. reprint ed. 24.00 (*0-8364-1689-9*, Pub. by Abhinav II) S Asia.

Sketch of the Negro in Politics, Especially in South Carolina & Mississippi. Frederic Bancroft. LC 70-160007. reprint ed. 39.50 (*0-404-00003-7*) AMS Pr.

Sketch of the Politics, Relations & Statistics of the Western World. Benjamin Chew. LC 77-128427. reprint ed. 55.00 (*0-404-01489-5*) AMS Pr.

Sketch of the Resources of the City of New York: With a View of Its Municipal Government, Population, Etc. John A. Dix. LC 79-112538. (Rise of Urban America Ser.). 1976. reprint ed. 19.95 (*0-405-02447-9*) Ayer.

Sketch of Trukese Grammar. Isidore Dyen. (American Oriental Society Essays Ser.: 4). 1964. pap. 3.00 (*0-685-00308-6*) Am Orient Soc.

Sketch of Twelfth Alabama Infantry. R. E. Park. 26.95 (*0-8488-0218-7*, J M C & Co) Amereon Ltd.

Sketch, the Original 1905 Biography of Joshua Lawerence Chamberlain. Chamberlain Corp. Staff. (Illus.). 70p. Date not set. text ed. write for info. (*0-9649433-1-X*) NPS.

***Sketchbook.** Boston Mills Press Staff. (Day in the Country Ser.). 1997. pap. text ed. 24.00 (*1-55046-225-3*, Pub. by Boston Mills Pr CN) Genl Dist Srvs.

Sketchbook. Washington Irving. Ed. by Susan Manning. (World's Classics Ser.). 368p. 1996. pap. 8.95 (*0-19-283212-3*) OUP.

Sketchbook: A Memoir of the 1930s & the Northwest School. William Cumming. LC 84-40324. (Illus.). 288p. 1984. 19.95 (*0-295-96156-2*) U of Wash Pr.

Sketchbook, Nineteen Seventeen. J. E. MacDonald. Ed. by Hunter Bishop. 134p. 1979. 9.95 (*0-920806-07-4*, Pub. by Penumbra Pr CN) U of Toronto Pr.

Sketchbook of Byron B. Wolfe. Byron B. Wolfe. LC 72-93802. (Illus.). 120p. 1972. 20.00 (*0-913504-12-2*) Lowell Pr.

Sketchbook of Villard de Honnecourt. Villard De Honnecourt. Ed. by Theodore Bowie. LC 82-15540. (Illus.). 144p. (C). 1982. text ed. 43.75 (*0-313-23747-6*, VISK, Greenwood Pr) Greenwood.

Sketchbook, Seventy-Six. R. L. Klinger & R. A. Wilder. 1967. 6.00 (*0-913150-22-3*) Pioneer Pr.

***Sketchbook Travels.** Illus. by Sari Mercedes. 200p. (Orig.). 1999. pap. write for info. (*0-614-29376-6*) Sari.

Sketchbooks of George Grosz. Ed. by Peter Nisbet. LC 93-32084. (Illus.). 191p. 1995. pap. 24.95 (*0-916724-83-2*, 4882) Harvard Art Mus.

***Sketchbooks of Picasso: Je Suis le Cahier.** Arnold Glimcher & Mark Pollard. 1996. pap. text ed. 37.50 (*0-87113-672-4*, Atlntc Mnthly) Grove-Atltic.

Sketchbooks of the Romantics. Robert Upstone. 1991. 29.98 (*1-55521-738-9*) Bk Sales Inc.

Sketches: Cultural Resource Directory. Cultural Alliance of Greater Hampton Roads Staff. (Illus.). 81p. (Orig.). 1993. pap. 10.00 (*0-943133-05-X*) Cultural Alliance.

Sketches: Cultural Resource Directory, 1989-90. Cultural Alliance of Greater Hampton Roads Staff. (Illus.). 190p. 1989. pap. 10.00 (*0-943133-02-5*) Cultural Alliance.

Sketches: Cultural Resource Directory, 1992-93. 8th ed. Cultural Alliance of Greater Hampton Roads Staff. (Illus.). 75p. (Orig.). 1992. pap. 10.00 (*0-943133-04-1*) Cultural Alliance.

Sketches: Historical, Literary, Biographical, Economic. Thomas E. Watson. (Studies in Populism). 1980. lib. bdg. 75.00 (*0-87700-323-8*) Revisionist Pr.

Sketches: New & Old. Mark Twain, pseud. 1981. reprint ed. lib. bdg. 69.00 (*0-685-38423-3*) Scholarly.

Sketches after "Pete's Beer" David Kresh. (Illus.). 24p. (Orig.). 1986. pap. 5.00 (*0-914473-03-4*) Stone Man Pr.

Sketches & Eccentricities of Colonel David Crockett of West Tennessee. David Crockett. LC 74-15735. (Popular Culture in America Ser.). 214p. 1975. reprint ed. 23.95 (*0-405-06370-9*) Ayer.

Sketches & Incidents from the Saddlebag of an Itinerant. George Peck. 1988. pap. 10.99 (*0-88019-237-2*) Schmul Pub Co.

Sketches & Measurings: Danish Architects in Greece 1818-1862. Margit Bendtsen. (Illus.). 383p. (C). 1993. text ed. 60.00 (*87-7288-500-9*, Pub. by Aarhus Univ Pr DK) David Brown.

Sketches & Reviews. Walter H. Pater. LC 77-99718. (Essay Index Reprint Ser.). 1977. 19.95 (*0-8369-1371-X*) Ayer.

Sketches by Boz. Charles Dickens. Ed. & Intro. by Dennis Walder. (Illus.). 1996. pap. 12.95 (*0-14-043345-7*) Viking Penguin.

Sketches by Boz: Illustrative of Every-Day Life & Every-Day People see Oxford Illustrated Dickens

Sketches by Edwin Lutyens: Drawings from the Collection of the Royal Institute of British Artifacts. Margaret Richardson. (Illus.). 120p. 1995. pap. 35.00 (*1-85490-377-2*) Academy Ed UK.

Sketches for a Life of Wassilly. Lydia Davis. 32p. 1981. pap. 3.50 (*0-930794-45-1*) Station Hill Pr.

Sketches for "The North American Review" by Henry Adams. Ed. by Edward Chalfant. LC 86-10901. (Illus.). xiii, 262p. (C). 1986. lib. bdg. 35.00 (*0-208-02115-9*, Archon Bks) Shoe String.

Sketches for Thirteen Sonnets. Gerard Boar. 1969. pap. 1.00 (*0-685-04673-7*) Oyez.

Sketches from a Hunter's Album. Ivan S. Turgenev. (Orig.). 22.95 (*0-8488-1210-7*) Amereon Ltd.

Sketches from a Hunter's Album. Ivan S. Turgenev. Tr. by Richard Freeborn. (Classics Ser.). (Orig.). 1967. mass mkt. 4.95 (*0-14-044186-7*, Penguin Classics) Viking Penguin.

Sketches from a Hunter's Album: The Complete Edition. Ivan S. Turgenev. (Illus.). 416p. 1990. pap. 10.95 (*0-14-044522-6*, Penguin Classics) Viking Penguin.

Sketches from a Library Window. Basil Anderton. LC 68-16903. (Essay Index Reprint Ser.). 1977. 18.95 (*0-8369-0154-1*) Ayer.

Sketches from a Life. George F. Kennan. 1990. pap. 12.95 (*0-679-72877-5*) Pantheon.

Sketches from Church History. S. M. Houghton. Ed. by Iain H. Murray. (Illus.). 256p. (Orig.). 1981. pap. 17.99 (*0-85151-317-4*) Banner of Truth.

Sketches from Eastern History. T. Noldeke. 292p. 1985. 220.00 (*1-85077-065-4*, Pub. by Darf Pubs Ltd UK) St Mut.

***Sketches from Hickory Hill.** William T. Roberts, Jr. & John W. Roberts. LC 96-36999. (Illus.). 168p. 1997. 14.95 (*1-883911-13-3*) Brandylane.

Sketches from My Life. Natalia Sats. Tr. by Sergei Syrovatkin. (Illus.). 438p. 1985. 17.95 (*0-912483-21-0*) Pro-Am Music.

Sketches from My Past: Encounters with India's Oppressed. Mahadevi Varma. Tr. by Merra K. Sohoni. (Women's Life Writings from Around the World Ser.). 208p. 1994. text ed. 24.95 (*1-55553-198-9*) NE U Pr.

Sketches from Texas Siftings. Alexander E. Sweet & J. A. Knox. LC 72-166896. (Illus.). 1971. reprint ed. 19.00 (*0-403-01414-X*) Scholarly.

Sketches, Historical & Descriptive, of Louisiana. Amos Stoddard. LC 72-956. reprint ed. 49.50 (*0-404-06278-4*) AMS Pr.

Sketches, Historical & Descriptive of Louisiana. M. A. Stoddard. 1974. reprint ed. 25.00 (*0-87511-117-3*) Claitors.

Sketches in Color: Seven Pieces for Piano, Set 1. Robert Starer. 12p. 1985. pap. 3.95 (*0-7935-0697-2*, 00121249) H Leonard.

Sketches in History & Poetry. John C. Shairp. Ed. by John Veitch. LC 72-4693. (Essay Index Reprint Ser.). 1977. reprint ed. 25.95 (*0-8369-2977-2*) Ayer.

Sketches in Lavender, Blue & Green. Jerome K. Jerome. LC 72-37274. (Short Story Index Reprint Ser.). 1977. reprint ed. 24.95 (*0-8369-4085-7*) Ayer.

Sketches in Nineteenth Century Biography. Keith G. Feiling. LC 73-107698. (Essay Index Reprint Ser.). 1977. 19.95 (*0-8369-1501-1*) Ayer.

Sketches in Spain & Morocco, Vol. 1. A. D. Brooke. 400p. 1987. 320.00 (*1-85077-153-7*, Pub. by Darf Pubs Ltd UK) St Mut.

Sketches in Spain & Morocco, Vol. 2. A. D. Brooke. 416p. 1987. 320.00 (*1-85077-154-5*, Pub. by Darf Pubs Ltd UK) St Mut.

Sketches in the History of the Underground Railroad. Eber M. Pettit. LC 73-149875. (Black Heritage Library Collection). 1977. 25.95 (*0-8369-8755-1*) Ayer.

Sketches in Winter: A Beijing Postscript. Charles Foran. 210p. (Orig.). 1993. pap. 12.00 (*0-00-637921-4*, Pub. by HarpC CN) HarpC.

Sketches in Winter, with Crows. Peter Blue Cloud. 30p. (Orig.). 1984. pap. 4.00 (*0-936574-11-9*) Strawberry Pr NY.

***Sketches, New & Old (1875)** Mark Twain. Ed. by Shelley F. Fishkin. (Oxford Mark Twain Ser.). 400p. 1997. lib. bdg. 25.00 (*0-19-511404-3*) OUP.

Sketches of a Growing Town: Episodes & People of Dallas from Early Days to Recent Times. Ed. by Darwin Payne. 208p. 1991. pap. 12.95 (*0-9631492-0-2*) S Meth U Mstr Lib Arts.

Sketches of a History of Literature. Robert Alves. LC 67-18714. 1967. reprint ed. 50.00 (*0-8201-1002-7*) Schol Facsimiles.

Sketches of a Journey on Two Oceans & to the Interior of America & of a Civil War in Northern Lower California. Abbe H. Alric. Ed. by Doyce B. Nunis. Tr. by Norah E. Jones. (Baja California Travels Ser.: No. 24). 215p. (FRE.). 1971. 30.00 (*0-87093-224-1*) Dawsons.

Sketches of a Tour to the Lakes. Thomas L. McKenney. (Illus.). 1959. reprint ed. 25.00 (*0-87018-042-8*) Ross.

Sketches of Allied Families: Knickerbacker-Viele, to Which Is Added an Appendix Containing Family Data. Kathlyne K. Viele. (Illus.). 134p. 1988. reprint ed. lib. bdg. 22.00 (*0-8328-0021-X*) Higginson Bk Co.

Sketches of America. 2nd ed. Henry B. Fearon. LC 70-100124. xi, 454p. 1970. reprint ed. 49.50 (*0-678-00584-2*) Kelley.

Sketches of America. Henry B. Fearon. LC 68-56487. 454p. 1972. reprint ed. 34.95 (*0-405-08497-8*, Pub. by Blom Pubns UK) Ayer.

Sketches of an Excursion to Southern Alaska. fac. ed. A. L. Lindsley. (Shorey Historical Ser.). 76p. pap. 4.95 (*0-8466-0091-9*, S91) Shorey.

Sketches of Bermuda. Susette H. Lloyd. (Illus.). 1977. text ed. 18.95 (*0-8369-9228-8*, 9082) Ayer.

***Sketches of Bible Child Life.** M. A. Steward. 144p. 1995. pap. 8.95 (*0-614-30877-1*) Hartland Pubns.

Sketches of Book Sellers of Other Days. J. Marsten. 1976. lib. bdg. 99.95 (*0-8490-2612-1*) Gordon Pr.

Sketches of Border Adventures in the Life & Times of Major Moses Van Campen. J. Niles Hubbard. Ed. by John S. Minard. (Illus.). 337p. 1992. reprint ed. lib. bdg. 26.00 (*1-880484-03-X*) Zebrowski Hist.

Sketches of Brooks History. Seth W. Norwood. (Illus.). 454p. 1995. reprint ed. lib. bdg. 46.50 (*0-8328-4666-X*) Higginson Bk Co.

***Sketches of Carmel by the Sea: An Artistic Souvenir Guide with Maps & Personal Journal.** Lisa Bryan-Day & Ashley M. Day. Ed. by John Livingstone. (Sketches Collection: Vol. SKI). (Illus.). 26p. 1997. 27.00 (*0-9655874-0-1*) Sketches-Wildreach.

Sketches of Central Asia Additional Chapters on My Travels, Adventures, & on the Ethnology of Central Asia. Arminius Vambery. LC 77-115593. (Russia Observed Ser., No. 1). 1970. reprint ed. 25.95 (*0-405-03069-X*) Ayer.

Sketches of Ceylon History. P. Arunachalam. (C). 1993. reprint ed. text ed. 10.00 (*81-206-0800-3*, Pub. by Asian Educ Servs II) S Asia.

Sketches of Contemporary Authors, 1828. Frederick D. Maurice. Ed. by A. J. Hartley. LC 74-106555. 182p. reprint ed. 51.90 (*0-8357-9585-3*, 2011080) Bks Demand.

Sketches of Eighteenth Century America. Michel-Guillaume Jean De Crevecoeur. (Works of Michel-Guillaume Jean De Crevecoeur Ser.). 1990. reprint ed. lib. bdg. 79.00 (*0-685-44773-1*) Rprt Serv.

Sketches of Eighteenth Century America. St. John De Crevecoeur. Ed. by H. L. Boudin et al. LC 72-83505. 1972. reprint ed. 29.95 (*0-405-08406-4*) Ayer.

Sketches of Eighteenth Century America: More Letters from an American Farmer. Michel G. Crevacoeur. Ed. by Henri L. Bourdin et al. (BCL1 - U. S. History Ser.). 342p. 1991. reprint ed. lib. bdg. 89.00 (*0-7812-6005-1*) Rprt Serv.

Sketches of Etruscan Places. D. H. Lawrence. Ed. by Simonetta De Filippis. LC 91-34290. (Cambridge Edition of the Works of D. H. Lawrence). 462p. (C). 1992. text ed. 125.00 (*0-521-25253-9*) Cambridge U Pr.

Sketches of Florida. Barbara V. Peterson & Wayne L. Peterson. (Illus.). 74p. (Orig.). 1996. 29.95 (*0-9651256-1-0*); pap. 14.95 (*0-9651256-0-2*) Peterson Publng.

Sketches of God. Carlos G. Valles. 172p. 1987. 9.95 (*0-8294-0584-4*) Loyola Pr.

Sketches of Great Painters. Edwin W. Chubb. LC 68-55843. (Essay Index Reprint Ser.). 1977. 23.95 (*0-8369-0304-8*) Ayer.

Sketches of Hayti from the Expulsion of the French to the Death of Christophe. William W. Harvey. 416p. 1972. reprint ed. 47.50 (*0-7146-2708-9*, Pub. by F Cass Pubs UK) Intl Spec Bk.

***Sketches of Historic Bennington.** John V. Merrill & Caroline E. Merrill. (Illus.). 99p. 1997. reprint ed. lib. bdg. 28.50 (*0-8328-6499-4*) Higginson Bk Co.

***Sketches of Historic Bennington.** John V. Merrill & Caroline E. Merrill. (Illus.). 99p. 1997. reprint ed. pap. 18.50 (*0-8328-6500-1*) Higginson Bk Co.

Sketches of History, Life, & Manners in the West. James A. Hall. (Notable American Authors Ser.). 1992. reprint ed. lib. bdg. 75.00 (*0-7812-2986-3*) Rprt Serv.

Sketches of Indian Life in the Pacific Northwest. Alexander Diomedi. 96p. 1978. 14.95 (*0-87770-199-7*) Ye Galleon.

Sketches of Jewish Social Life. Alfred Edersheim. 274p. 1994. 19.95 (*1-56563-138-2*); pap. 12.95 (*1-56563-005-X*) Hendrickson MA.

***Sketches of Landscapes: Philosophy by Example.** Avrum Stroll. LC 97-18852. 1997. write for info. (*0-262-19391-4*) MIT Pr.

***Sketches of Life: A Book of Poems.** Patricia Cruzan. (Illus.). viii, 42p. (Orig.). 1996. pap. 7.95 (*0-9653543-0-X*) Clear Creek Pubs.

Sketches of Life in Little Rock: Eighteen Thirty-Six to Eighteen Fifty Based on the F. W. Trapnalls. Rita P. Wooley. LC 81-68284. (Illus.). 48p. (Orig.). pap. 3.95 (*0-9606278-2-0*) AR Commemorative.

Sketches of Mexico. J. Butler. 1976. lib. bdg. 59.95 (*0-8490-2613-X*) Gordon Pr.

Sketches of Mission Life among the Indians of Oregon. Zachariah A. Mudge. 1983. 12.50 (*0-87770-308-6*) Ye Galleon.

Sketches of Montgomery Place. Alexander J. Davis. (Illus.). 9.95 (*0-912882-74-3*) Sleepy Hollow.

Sketches of My Own Times. David Turpie. LC 75-177581. reprint ed. 39.50 (*0-404-04636-3*) AMS Pr.

Sketches of Nature from Maine. Brian L. Willson. 196p. 1989. pap. 10.95 (*0-685-25670-7*) Three Islands.

Sketches of Nebraska. Robert Hanna. LC 84-3722. 144p. reprint ed. pap. 41.10 (*0-7837-6458-8*, 2046462) Bks Demand.

***Sketches of Old Bristol.** Charles O. Thompson. (Illus.). 418p. 1997. reprint ed. lib. bdg. 45.00 (*0-8328-6476-5*) Higginson Bk Co.

Sketches of Old Warrenton, North Carolina: Traditions & Reminiscences of the Town & People Who Made It. Lizzie W. Montgomery. (Illus.). 488p. 1984. reprint ed. 27.50 (*0-87152-393-0*, 83-23120) Reprint.

Sketches of Orleans, Vermont (Originally Barton Landing) An Informal History. Darrell Hoyt. Ed. by James Hayford. (Illus.). 97p. (Orig.). 1985. pap. 8.00 (*0-9610860-2-5*) Orleans.

Sketches of Places & People Abroad. William W. Brown. LC 71-133149. (Black Heritage Library Collection). 1977. 28.95 (*0-8369-8705-5*) Ayer.

Sketches of Reforms & Reformers of Great Britain & Ireland. Henry B. Stanton. LC 75-89446. (Black Heritage Library Collection). 1977. 19.95 (*0-8369-8654-7*) Ayer.

Sketches of Representative New England Women. Julia W. Howe. (Notable American Authors Ser.). 1992. reprint ed. lib. bdg. 75.00 (*0-7812-3224-4*) Rprt Serv.

Sketches of Scenery & Manners in the United States. Theodore Dwight. LC 82-10258. 1983. 50.00 (*0-8201-1383-2*) Schol Facsimiles.

Sketches of Shakers & Shakerism. Giles Avery. 50p. 1993. reprint ed. lib. bdg. 69.00 (*0-7812-5306-3*) Rprt Serv.

Sketches of Southern Mystery, Treason, & Murder. James Brewster. LC 70-39529. reprint ed. 39.50 (*0-404-00006-1*) AMS Pr.

Sketches of Springfield in 1856. fac. ed. Daily Nonpareil Office. (Annual Monograph). 96p. 1973. reprint ed. pap. 3.00 (*0-686-29090-9*) Clark County Hist Soc.

Sketches of St. Augustine, with a View of Its History & Advantages As a Resort for Invalids. Rufus K. Sewall. LC 75-44177. (Floridiana Facsimile & Reprint Ser.). 1976. reprint ed. 12.95 (*0-8130-0419-5*) U Press Fla.

Sketches of Summerland: Nassau & the Bahama Islands. G. J. Northcroft. 1976. lib. bdg. 59.95 (*0-8490-2614-8*) Gordon Pr.

Sketches of Tennessee's Pioneer Baptist Preachers: History of Baptist Beginnings in the Several Associations in the State. J. J. Burnett. (Illus.). 576p. 1985. reprint ed. 21.95 (*0-932807-11-9*) Overmountain Pr.

Sketches of the Christian Life & Public Labors of William Miller. James White. LC 70-134376. reprint ed. 54.00 (*0-404-08424-9*) AMS Pr.

Sketches of the Civil & Military Services of William Henry Harrison. Charles S. Todd & Benjamin Drake. LC 75-128. (Mid-American Frontier Ser.). 1975. reprint ed. 16.95 (*0-405-06893-X*) Ayer.

Sketches of the Dynasties of Southern India. Robert Sewell. 138p. reprint ed. text ed. 20.00 (*0-685-13380-X*) Coronet Bks.

Sketches of the Early Catholic Missions of Kentucky, from Their Commencement in 1787 to the Jubilee of 1826-7. Martin J. Spalding. LC 70-38548. (Religion in America, Ser. 2). 328p. 1972. reprint ed. 24.95 (*0-405-04087-3*) Ayer.

***Sketches of the Early Settlement & Present Advantages of Princeton, Including Valuable Statistics & a Brief Sketch of Bureau County & a Business Directory.** Isaac B. Smith. (Illus.). 96p. 1997. reprint ed. pap. 17.50 (*0-8328-5784-X*) Higginson Bk Co.

***Sketches of the First Emigrant Settlers on Newton Township, Old Gloucester County, West New Jersey.** John Clement. (Illus.). 444p. 1997. reprint ed. lib. bdg. 47.50 (*0-8328-6066-2*) Higginson Bk Co.

Sketches of the Higher Classes of Colored Society in Philadelphia. Joseph Willson. (Illus.). 1977. text ed. 12.95 (*0-8369-9227-X*, 9081) Ayer.

***Sketches of the History of Chautauque County.** Emory F. Warren. (Illus.). 159p. 1997. reprint ed. lib. bdg. 25.00 (*0-8328-6112-X*) Higginson Bk Co.

Sketches of the History of Man, 4 vols., Set. Henry Home. (Anglistica & Americana Ser.: No. 8). 1968. reprint ed. 258.70 (*0-685-66480-5*, 05101975) G Olms Pubs.

***Sketches of the History of Ogle County & the Early Settlement of the Northwest.** (Illus.). 88p. 1997. reprint ed. lib. bdg. 25.00 (*0-8328-5777-7*) Higginson Bk Co.

***Sketches of the History of Ogle County & the Early Settlement of the Northwest.** (Illus.). 88p. 1997. reprint ed. pap. 15.00 (*0-8328-5778-5*) Higginson Bk Co.

Sketches of the Island of Negros. Robustiano Echau. Tr. by Donn V. Hart. (Papers in International Studies: Southeast Asia Ser.: No. 50). 183p. reprint ed. pap. 52.20 (*0-317-09574-9*, 2007466) Bks Demand.

An Asterisk (*) at the beginning of an entry indicates that the title is appearing in BIP for the first time.

Sketches of the Judicial History of Massachusetts from 1630 to the Revolution in 1775. Emory Washburn. LC 74-6427. (American Constitutional & Legal History Ser). 407p. 1974. reprint ed. lib. bdg. 49.50 (*0-306-70616-4*) Da Capo.

Sketches of the Life & Character of Patrick Henry. William Wirt. LC 72-130568. (Select Bibliographies Reprint Ser.). 1977. 25.95 (*0-8369-5541-2*) Ayer.

Sketches of the Life, Times, - Character of Right Reverend Benedict Joseph Flaget, First Bishop of Louisville. Martin J. Spalding. LC 71-83441. (Religion in America, Ser. 1). 1970. reprint ed. 23.95 (*0-405-00266-1*) Ayer.

Sketches of the Lives, Times & Judicial Services of the Chief Justices of the Supreme Court of the United States. George Van Santvoord. LC 76-52304. (Classics in Legal History Ser.: Vol. 30). xii, 740p. 1994. 75.00 (*1-57588-362-7*, 308880) W S Hein.

***Sketches of the Master's Heart.** 88p. Date not set. 8.50 (*0-8341-1586-7*) Nazarene.

Sketches of the Origin, Process & Effects of Music. R. Eastcott. LC 70-159680. (Music Ser.). 1971. reprint ed. lib. bdg. 37.50 (*0-306-70184-7*) Da Capo.

Sketches of the Philosophy of Apparitions: Or, an Attempt to Trace Such Illusions to Their Physical Causes. Samuel Hibbert. LC 75-7387. (Perspectives in Psychical Research Ser.). 1975. reprint ed. 37.95 (*0-405-07035-7*) Ayer.

Sketches of the Pioneers in Burke County History, North Carolina. Thomas G. Walton. 96p. 1984. pap. 12.50 (*0-89308-538-3*) Southern Hist Pr.

Sketches of the Pioneers of Methodism in North Carolina & Virginia. M. H. Moore. 314p. 1977. reprint ed. 12.50 (*0-87921-039-7*) Attic Pr.

Sketches of the Royal Society & Royal Society Club. John Barrow. 216p. 1971. reprint ed. 30.00 (*0-7146-2405-5*, Pub. by F Cass Pubs UK) Intl Spec Bk.

Sketches of the Sixties. Bret Harte & Mark Twain. Ed. by John Howell. LC 77-92173. (Illus.). reprint ed. 34.50 (*0-404-03151-X*) AMS Pr.

Sketches of the Sixties: Being Forgotten Material Now Collected for the First Time from the Californian, 1864-1867. Bret Harte & Mark Twain, pseud. (BCL1-PS American Literature Ser.). 228p. 1992. reprint ed. lib. bdg. 79.00 (*0-7812-6720-X*) Rprt Serv.

Sketches of the Sixties: Being Forgotten Material Now Collected for the First Time from "The Californian" 1864-67 see California Sketches

***Sketches of the Town of Old Town, Penobscot Co., from Its Earliest Settlement to 1879, with Biographical Sketches.** David Norton. (Illus.). 152p. 1997. reprint ed. pap. 19.50 (*0-8328-5883-8*) Higginson Bk Co.

Sketches of Thought. Vinod Goel. (Illus.). 320p. 1995. 37.50 (*0-262-07163-0*, Bradford Bks) MIT Pr.

Sketches of Travel in Oregon & Idaho. Angelo C. Aubrey. 1988. reprint ed. 19.95 (*0-87770-427-9*) Ye Galleon.

Sketches of Urban & Cultural Life in North America. Ed. & Tr. by Stewart A. Stehlin. (Illus.). 288p. (C). 1988. text ed. 40.00 (*0-8135-1327-8*); pap. text ed. 16.95 (*0-8135-1328-6*) Rutgers U Pr.

Sketches of War History, Vol. II: Ohio. (Military Order of the Loyal Legion of the United States Ser.: Vol. 2). (Illus.). 411p. 1991. reprint ed. 50.00 (*1-56837-157-8*) Broadfoot.

Sketches of War History, 1861-1865: A Compilation of Miscellaneous Papers Compiled for the Ohio Commandery. (Military Order of the Loyal Legion of the United States Ser.: Vol. 7). (Illus.). 475p. 1993. 50.00 (*1-56837-162-4*) Broadfoot.

Sketches of War History, 1861-1865 Index to Ohio Volumes I-IX: A Compilation of Miscellaneous Papers Read Before the Ohio Commandery April 1912-April 1916. (Military Order of the Loyal Legion of the United States Ser.: Vol. 9). 466p. 1993. 100.00 (*1-56837-164-0*) Broadfoot.

Sketches of War History, 1861-1865, Vol. I: Ohio. (Military Order of the Loyal Legion of the United States Ser.: Vol. 1). (Illus.). 422p. 1991. reprint ed. 50.00 (*1-56837-156-X*) Broadfoot.

Sketches of War History 1861-1865, Vol. III: Ohio. Ed. by Robert Hunter. (Military Order of the Loyal Legion of the United States Ser.: Vol. 3). (Illus.). 452p. 1991. reprint ed. 50.00 (*1-56837-158-6*) Broadfoot.

Sketches of War History 1861-1865, Vol. IV: Ohio. Ed. by William H. Chamberlin. (Military Order of the Loyal Legion of the United States Ser.: Vol. 4). (Illus.). 443p. 1991. reprint ed. 50.00 (*1-56837-159-4*) Broadfoot.

Sketches of War History 1861-1865, Vol. V: Ohio. Ed. by William H. Chamberlin et al. (Military Order of the Loyal Legion of the United States Ser.: Vol. 5). (Illus.). 530p. 1992. reprint ed. 50.00 (*1-56837-160-8*) Broadfoot.

Sketches of War History 1861-1865, Vol. VI: Ohio. Ed. by Theodore F. Allen et al. (Military Order of the Loyal Legion of the United States Ser.: Vol. 6). (Illus.). 304p. 1992. reprint ed. 50.00 (*1-56837-161-6*) Broadfoot.

Sketches of Western Adventure. John A. M'Clung. LC 76-90184. (Mass Violence in America Ser.). 1969. reprint ed. 16.95 (*0-405-01326-4*) Ayer.

Sketches of Western Methodism: Biographical, Historical & Miscellaneous Illustrative of Pioneer Life. James B. Finley. LC 79-83419. (Religion in America, Ser. 1). 1977. reprint ed. 33.95 (*0-405-00244-0*) Ayer.

Sketches of Western North Carolina. xiv, 359p. 1996. pap. 28.00 (*0-7884-0382-6*) Heritage Bk.

Sketches of Yesterday & Today in Nevada County. Juanita K. Browne. LC 88-22584. (Illus.). xii, 92p. (Orig.). 1988. pap. 17.50 (*0-915641-02-X*) Nevada County Hist Society.

***Sketches on the History of Man: 1778 Edition, 4 vols., Set.** Henry Home. 1896p. 1996. reprint ed. write for info. (*1-85506-419-7*) Bks Intl VA.

Sketches Plus: Cultural Resource Directory Addendum. Cultural Alliance of Greater Hampton Roads Staff. (Illus.). 52p. (Orig.). 1990. pap. 10.00 (*0-943133-03-3*) Cultural Alliance.

Sketching & Drawing. Cathy Johnson. LC 95-10607. (First Steps Ser.). (Illus.). 128p. (Orig.). 1995. pap. 18.99 (*0-89134-615-5*, North Lght Bks) F & W Pubns Inc.

Sketching & Rendering for Design Presentations. Janet Shen & Theodore D. Walker. LC 92-3369. (Illus.). 208p. 1992. pap. 37.95 (*0-442-00414-1*) Van Nos Reinhold.

Sketching & Rendering Interior Spaces. Ivo Drpic. (Illus.). 176p. 1988. pap. 27.50 (*0-8230-4853-5*, Whitney Lib) Watsn-Guptill.

Sketching at Home & Abroad: British Landscape Drawings, 1750-1850. Evelyn J. Phimister et al. LC 92-80446. (Illus.). 64p. 1994. pap. 17.50 (*0-87598-094-5*) Pierpont Morgan.

Sketching Country. Roland Hilder. (Illus.). 128p. 1992. 30.00 (*1-871569-35-4*) New Amsterdam Bks.

Sketching Drawing for Children. Genevieve Vaughan & Jackson. (J). 1990. pap. 8.95 (*0-399-51619-0*, Perigee Bks) Berkley Pub.

Sketching in the Greek Kitchen: A Family Cookbook. Penelope D. Gregory & Ann S. Wiseman. (Sketching Around the World Ser.). (Illus.). 87p. (Orig.). 1989. pap. 7.95 (*0-937369-03-9*) Ansayre Pr.

Sketching in the San Juans & a Bit Beyond: And a Bit Beyond. Barbara M. Meyer. 100p. 1996. pap. 24.95 (*1-888345-01-2*) Paper Jam.

Sketching Made Easy. 1996. 12.99 (*0-517-14297-X*) Random Hse Value.

***Sketching Outdoors in Autumn.** (J). write for info. (*0-8317-3073-0*) Smithmark.

Sketching Outdoors in Autumn. Jim Arnosky. LC 88-1244. (Illus.). 48p. (J). (gr. 5 up). 1988. 12.95 (*0-688-06288-1*) Lothrop.

Sketching Outdoors in Spring. Jim Arnosky. LC 86-21308. (Illus.). 48p. (J). (gr. 4 up). 1987. 12.95 (*0-688-06284-9*) Lothrop.

Sketching Outdoors in Summer. Jim Arnosky. LC 87-29728. (J). (gr. 5 up). 1988. 12.95 (*0-688-06286-5*) Lothrop.

***Sketching Outdoors in Winter.** (J). write for info. (*0-8317-3088-9*) Smithmark.

Sketching Outdoors in Winter. Jim Arnosky. LC 88-2202. (Illus.). 48p. (J). (gr. 5 up). 1988. 12.95 (*0-688-06290-3*) Lothrop.

Sketching Stories, Stretching Minds. Phyllis Whitin. LC 95-40134. 137p. 1996. pap. text ed. 18.50 (*0-435-08870-X*, 08870) Heinemann.

Sketching the Concept. Harold Linton & Scott Sutton. (Illus.). 160p. 1992. 45.95 (*0-8306-4070-3*, 3858, Design Pr) TAB Bks.

Sketching with a Pencil: For Those Who Are Just Beginning. John Hamilton. 1991. pap. 9.95 (*0-7137-2284-3*, Pub. by Blandford Pr UK) Sterling.

Sketching with Markers II. C. K. Wang. 1993. pap. 25.95 (*0-442-00491-5*) Van Nos Reinhold.

Sketching Your Favorite Subjects in Pen & Ink. Claudia Nice. (Illus.). 144p. 1993. 22.95 (*0-89134-472-1*, 30473, North Lght Bks) F & W Pubns Inc.

Sketch's Sketch Book: TerraTopia. Ed. by Vicki Dobbs. (Illus.). 60p. (YA). (gr. 3 up). 1994. pap. 12.95 (*1-883871-03-4*) Nature Co.

Skew Fields. Peter K. Draxl. LC 82-22036. (London Mathematical Society Lecture Note Ser.: No. 81). 194p. 1983. pap. 38.95 (*0-521-27274-2*) Cambridge U Pr.

Skew Fields: Theory of General Division Rings. P. M. Cohn. (Encyclopedia of Mathematics & Its Applications Ser.: No. 57). 550p. (C). 1995. text ed. 95.00 (*0-521-43217-0*) Cambridge U Pr.

Skew Linear Groups. M. Shirvani & B. Wehrfritz. (London Mathematical Society Lecture Note Ser.: No. 118). 275p. 1987. pap. text ed. 47.95 (*0-521-33925-1*) Cambridge U Pr.

Skewed Sherlock. Violet Hunter & David L. Hammer. (Illus.). 112p. (Orig.). 1992. pap. 12.95 (*0-938501-15-1*) Wessex.

Skewer Cooking on the Grill. Bob Simmons & Coleen Simmons. (Illus.). 176p. (Orig.). 1995. pap. 8.95 (*1-55867-122-6*, Nitty Gritty Ckbks) Bristol Pub Ent CA.

Ski! (J). (ps). 1995. 5.95 (*1-885751-06-0*) Wee Venture.

Ski. Oliver C. Armitage. LC 95-90312. 136p. (Orig.). 1996. pap. 8.50 (*1-56002-566-2*, Univ Edtns) Aegina Pr.

***Ski British Columbia.** Heather Doughty. 1991. pap. 9.95 (*0-919433-94-4*) Lone Pine.

Ski Camping: A Guide to the Delights of Back-Country Skiing. rev. ed. Ron Watters. LC 89-85444. (Illus.). 154p. 1989. reprint ed. 14.95 (*1-877625-00-0*) Great Rift.

Ski Colorado: Complete Skiing & Snowboarding Guide. Global Inc. Staff & James D. Durdy. (Colorado Recreation Guides Ser.). 180p. (Orig.). 1995. pap. 7.95 (*1-887430-09-1*) Global Inc.

Ski Colorado: Complete Skiing & Snowboarding Guide. limited ed. Global Inc. Staff & James D. Durdy. (Colorado Recreation Guides Ser.). 180p. (Orig.). 1995. pap. write for info. (*0-614-06796-0*) Global Inc.

Ski Country: Nordic Skiers Guide to the Minnesota Arrowhead. Robert Beymer. LC 86-81167. 224p. (Orig.). 1986. pap. 8.95 (*0-933287-01-1*) Fisher Co.

Ski Country Western United States Access. 2nd ed. (Access Travel Guides Ser.). (Illus.). 244p. (Orig.). 1995. pap. 18.50 (*0-06-277174-4*, PL) HarpC.

Ski Doo, 1985-1989. (Illus.). Date not set. reprint ed. pap. 29.95 (*0-89287-521-6*, S829) Intertec Pub.

***Ski Doo, 1990-1995.** (Illus.). (Orig.). 1996. pap. 29.95 (*0-89287-663-8*, S830) Intertec Pub.

Ski Europe. 10th ed. Charles Leocha. Ed. by Diane S. Scholfield. (Illus.). 428p. (Orig.). 1995. pap. 17.95 (*0-915009-41-2*) World Leis Corp.

***Ski Europe.** 11th ed. Charles Leocha. 384p. (Orig.). 1997. pap. 19.95 (*0-915009-59-5*) World Leis Corp.

Ski Europe: Les Trois Vallees. Emily Sutherland. (C). 1990. 50.00 (*0-9589059-5-9*, Pub. by Pascoe Pub AT) St Mut.

Ski Games: A Fun-Filled Approach to Teaching Nordic & Alpine Skills. Laurie Gullion. LC 89-30437. (Illus.). 192p. 1990. pap. 15.95 (*0-88011-367-7*, PGUL0367) Human Kinetics.

Ski Japan! T. R. Reid. Ed. by Meagan Calogeras. (Illus.). 240p. 1994. pap. 20.00 (*4-7700-1680-8*) Kodansha.

Ski Lodge-Millers Idlewild Inn: Adventures in Snow Business. Virginia M. Cornell. (Illus.). 240p. 1993. 23.95 (*0-9627896-6-6*); pap. 14.95 (*0-9627896-7-4*) Manifest Pubns.

Ski Lodge Mystery. Joan Weir. 128p. (J). (gr. 3-6). 1991. pap. 4.95 (*0-7736-7322-9*, Pub. by Stoddart Pubng CN) Genl Dist Srvs.

***Ski Lodge Mystery.** Joan Weir. 1996. mass mkt. 4.95 (*0-7736-7325-3*) General Publishing Co Ltd.

Ski Minnesota: A Cross Country Skier's Guide to Trails Within Sixty Miles of the Twin Cities. Anders Noren. (Illus.). 160p. 1995. pap. 10.95 (*0-931714-65-6*) Nodin Pr.

Ski Now. Stephen L. Paul. (Spalding Sports Library). (Illus.). (Orig.). 1995. pap. 12.95 (*1-57028-017-7*) Masters Pr IN.

Ski Pioneers: Ernie Blake, His Friends, & the Making of Taos Ski Valley. Ed. by Rick Richards. LC 92-73483. (Illus.). 235p. 1992. 39.95 (*1-56044-157-7*) Falcon Pr MT.

Ski Powder. Martin Epp. (C). 1990. text ed. 59.00 (*0-906754-34-8*, Pub. by Fernhurst Bks UK) St Mut.

Ski Skating with Champions: How to Ski with Least Energy. Einar Svensson. LC 94-92442. (Illus.). 273p. (Orig.). (C). 1994. pap. text ed. 39.95 (*0-9641941-0-4*) E Svensson.

Ski Slope Mystery. Carolyn Keene. (Nancy Drew Notebooks Ser.: No. 16). (YA). 1997. pap. 3.50 (*0-671-56860-4*, PB Trade Paper) PB.

Ski Taos Style: How to Ski Better in Six Days - the Secrets of Super Ski Week. Jerome S. Gladysz. (Illus.). 288p. (Orig.). 1993. pap. 12.95 (*0-9638841-0-7*) Market Relations.

Ski Terminology in Six Languages: Spanish, English, French, German, Czech, Polish. 2nd ed. H. Abraham. (Illus.). 136p. 1986. pap. 25.25 (*3-85423-056-7*) IBD Ltd.

Ski the High Trail: World War Two Ski Troopers in the High Colorado Rockies. Harris Dusenbery. LC 91-70989. (Illus.). 176p. 1991. pap. 12.95 (*0-8323-0485-9*) Binford Mort.

Ski the Rockies. Photos by Marc Muench. 144p. 1994. 39.95 (*1-55868-196-5*) Gr Arts Ctr Pub.

Ski Tips. Andy Steggall. 28p. (C). 1990. 45.00 (*1-85283-282-7*, Pub. by Boxtree Ltd UK) St Mut.

Ski Touring Guide to New England. 4th ed. Ed. by Katey Ziegler. (Illus.). 1979. pap. 7.95 (*0-910146-23-3*) Eastern Mount.

Ski Touring the Eastern High Sierra. Don Douglass & Chris Lombardo. 1990. 8.95 (*0-938665-08-1*) Fine Edge Prods.

Ski Tours in Lassen Volcanic National Park. Marcus Libkind. LC 89-92069. (Illus.). 128p. (Orig.). 1989. pap. 10.95 (*0-931255-04-X*) Bittersweet Pub.

Ski Tours in the Sierra Nevada: Carson Pass, Bear Valley, Pinecrest, Vol. 2. Marcus Libkind. LC 84-73452. (Illus.). 132p. (Orig.). 1985. pap. 11.95 (*0-931255-01-5*) Bittersweet Pub.

Ski Tours in the Sierra Nevada: East of Sierra Crest, Vol. 4. Marcus Libkind. LC 84-73452. (Illus.). 184p. (Orig.). 1986. pap. 13.95 (*0-931255-03-1*) Bittersweet Pub.

Ski Tours in the Sierra Nevada: Yosemite, Kings Canyon, Sequoia, Vol. 3. Marcus Libkind. LC 84-73452. (Illus.). 136p. (Orig.). 1985. pap. 11.95 (*0-931255-02-3*) Bittersweet Pub.

Ski Tours in the Sierra Nevada Vol. 1: Lake Tahoe. Marcus Libkind. (Illus.). 266p. 1995. pap. 16.95 (*0-931255-08-2*) Bittersweet Pub.

Ski Train. Steve Patterson & Kenton Forrest. LC 95-83297. (Illus.). 80p. 1995. 29.95 (*0-918654-54-8*); pap. 19.95 (*0-918654-53-X*) CO RR Mus.

Ski Vacation. Don Patterson. (Illus.). 40p. (J). (gr. k-6). 1991. 13.95 (*0-9629093-3-5*) MyndSeye.

Ski Vacations with Kids in the U. S. & Canada. Candyce H. Stapen. LC 96-35450. 432p. 1996. per. 16.00 (*0-7615-0319-6*) Prima Pub.

Ski Weekend. R. L. Stine. Ed. by Patricia MacDonald. (Fear Street Ser.). 160p. (YA). (gr. 7 up). mass mkt. 3.99 (*0-671-72480-0*, Archway) PB.

***Skibereen.** David Hanly. Date not set. write for info. (*0-688-04840-4*) Morrow.

Skibo. Joseph F. Wall. (Illus.). 192p. 1984. 29.95 (*0-19-503450-3*) OUP.

Skid. Ed. by Milton Okun. pap. 14.95 (*0-89524-667-8*) Cherry Lane.

Skid: Drum. Ed. by Milton Okun. pap. 16.95 (*0-89524-601-5*) Cherry Lane.

Skid: Easy Guitar. Ed. by Milton Okun. pap. 9.95 (*0-89524-656-2*) Cherry Lane.

Skid: Play-It-Like-It-Is-Bass. Ed. by Milton Okun. pap. 14.95 (*0-89524-579-5*) Cherry Lane.

Skid: Play-It-Like-It-Is-Guitar. Ed. by Milton Okun. pap. 19.95 (*0-89524-578-7*) Cherry Lane.

Skid Marks: Common Jokes about Lawyers. Ed. by Michael Rafferty. 96p. 1988. pap. 3.95 (*0-89815-283-6*) Ten Speed Pr.

Skid Resistance of Highway Pavements. American Society for Testing & Materials Staff. LC 72-97870. (American Society for Testing & Materials Special Technical Publication Ser.: No. 530). 165p. reprint ed. pap. 47.10 (*0-317-11157-4*, 2016438) Bks Demand.

Skid Road: An Informal Portrait of Seattle. rev. ed. Murray Morgan. LC 81-11701. (Illus.). 296p. 1982. reprint ed. pap. text ed. 14.95 (*0-295-95846-4*) U of Wash Pr.

Skid Row: A Wide-Ranging Bibliography. J. Randolph Gregson. 1977. 2.50 (*0-686-19107-2*, 1249, Sage Prdcls Pr) Sage.

Skid Row: An Institutional Analysis. William R. McSheehy. 160p. 1975. pap. 11.95 (*0-87073-181-5*) Schenkman Bks Inc.

Skid Row - Slave to the Grind: Play-It-Like-It-Is-Bass. pap. 17.95 (*0-89524-721-6*) Cherry Lane.

Skid Row - Slave to the Grind: Play-It-Like-It-Is-Guitar. pap. 19.95 (*0-89524-644-9*) Cherry Lane.

Skidmarks in the Sky: An Irreverent Look at Aviation History. Ed Markin & Christian Beloit. Ed. by Pamela Sload. LC 85-807. (Illus.). 152p. (Orig.). 1986. pap. 4.95 (*0-9615223-0-5*) Flaming Hooker Pr.

Skidmore: A Genealogical & Biographical Records of the Pioneer Thomas Skidmore, Scudamore, of the Mass. & Conn. Colonies in New England, & of Huntington, L.I., & of His Descendants. E. C. Hawley. (Illus.). 359p. 1992. reprint ed. pap. 57.50 (*0-8328-2729-0*); reprint ed. lib. bdg. 67.50 (*0-8328-2728-2*) Higginson Bk Co.

Skidmore, Owings & Merrill. (Master Architect Ser.: No. 7). (Illus.). 256p. 1995. 69.95 (*1-875498-20-6*, Pub. by Images Publ AT) Bks Nippan.

Skidmore's Portland: His Fountain & Its Sculptor. Eugene E. Snyder. LC 73-85142. (Illus.). 152p. 1973. pap. 5.95 (*0-8323-0229-5*) Binford Mort.

***Skidrow, Death Row.** Pat Martino. 196p. (Orig.). 1997. mass mkt. 4.99 (*1-55237-006-2*, Pub. by Comnwlth Pub CN) Partners Pubs Grp.

Skier's Guide to California, Vol. 1: Northern California & Lake Tahoe. Nadine Davidson. 240p. 1990. pap. 15.95 (*0-87201-795-8*) Gulf Pub.

Skier's Guide to California, Vol. 2: Central Sierras & Southern California. Nadine Davidson. 242p. 1991. pap. 15.95 (*0-87201-811-3*) Gulf Pub.

Skier's Guide to Colorado. Curtis W. Casewit. LC 93-8518. 240p. 1993. 15.95 (*0-88415-046-1*) Gulf Pub.

Skier's Guide to North America. Ed. by Brent K. Pickard. LC 88-50618. (Illus.). 256p. (Orig.). 1988. pap. 11.95 (*0-944982-01-8*) Wise Guide Pub.

Skier's Guide to Utah. Michael Jenson. LC 95-3343. (Illus.). 210p. 1995. pap. 16.95 (*0-88415-823-3*, 5823) Gulf Pub.

Skiers' Song Book. Ed. by David Kemp. (Illus.). 1950. 8.95 (*0-87015-022-7*) Pacific Bks.

***Skies Here.** Rachel Barenblat. (Illus.). 65p. 1995. pap. 9.95 (*1-877603-31-7*) Pecan Grove.

Skies of Such Valuable Glass. Art Homer. 1990. pap. 9.00 (*0-937669-40-7*) Owl Creek Pr.

***Skiffy.** Cappie Townsend. (Illus.). 24p. (Orig.). (J). (gr. 3-7). 1998. mass mkt. 6.99 (*1-889501-91-3*, Candy Apple) Sovereign.

Skiing. (Illus.). 56p. (J). (gr. 6-12). 1980. pap. 2.40 (*0-8395-3364-0*, 33365) BSA.

Skiing. (Take up Sports! Ser.). (Illus.). 64p. pap. 4.95 (*1-56757-053-4*) Appleton Comms.

Skiing. Donna Bailey. LC 90-36125. (Sports World Ser.). (Illus.). 32p. (J). (gr. 1-4). 1990. pap. 3.95 (*0-8114-4710-3*); lib. bdg. 21.40 (*0-8114-2856-7*) Raintree Steck-V.

Skiing. Henry Beard & Roy McKie. LC 89-40369. (Illus.). 96p. (Orig.). 1989. pap. 5.95 (*0-89480-650-5*, 1650) Workman Pub.

***Skiing.** Larry D. Brimner. LC 97-12829. (True Book Ser.). (J). 1997. write for info. (*0-516-20449-1*) Childrens.

Skiing. Michele Dieterich. (All Action Ser.). (Illus.). 48p. (J). (gr. 4 up). 1992. lib. bdg. 9.50 (*0-8225-2478-3*, Lerner Publctns) Lerner Group.

Skiing. Jeremy Evans. LC 91-32025. (Adventurers Ser.). (Illus.). 48p. (J). (gr. 5-6). 1992. lib. bdg. 13.95 (*0-89686-681-5*, Crstwood Hse) Silver Burdett Pr.

Skiing. Kate Haycock. LC 91-670. (Olympic Sports Ser.). (Illus.). 48p. (J). (gr. 6). 1991. lib. bdg. 13.95 (*0-89686-669-6*, Crstwood Hse) Silver Burdett Pr.

Skiing. Herbert I. Kavet. 64p. 1993. 8.95 (*0-88032-362-0*) Ivory Tower Pub.

Skiing. Hal Rogers. LC 93-23410. (Pro-Am Sports Ser.). (J). 1993. write for info. (*0-86593-348-0*) Rourke Corp.

Skiing. John Shedden. LC 95-16949. (Know the Sport Ser.). (Illus.). 48p. 1996. pap. 5.95 (*0-8117-2828-5*) Stackpole.

Skiing: An Art.....a Technique. Georges Joubert. Ed. by Doug Smith. Tr. by James Major from FRE. LC 79-90394. (Illus.). (Orig.). 1980. pap. 19.95 (*0-935240-01-2*) Poudre Pr.

Skiing: Faceplants, Eggbeaters, & Snowsnakes. Carol Poster. LC 95-32767. (Illus.). 1995. 11.95 (*1-57034-030-7*) ICS Bks.

Skiing: Step by Step to Success with Alpine Skiing, Snowboarding & Telemarking. Robert Reichenfeld & Anna M. Bruechert. (Illus.). 160p. 1993. pap. 24.95 (*1-85223-707-4*, Pub. by Crowood Pr UK) Trafalgar.

Skiing: Technique, Tactics, Training. Fred Foxon. (Crowood Sports Guides Ser.). (Illus.). 128p. 1992. pap. 22.95 (*1-85223-571-3*, Pub. by Crowood Pr UK) Trafalgar.

Skiing America '97. 9th ed. Charles Leocha. (Illus.). 512p. 1996. pap. 18.95 (*0-915009-54-4*) World Leis Corp.

***Skiing America '98.** 10th ed. Charles Leocha. 512p. 1997. pap. 19.95 (*0-915009-58-7*) World Leis Corp.

***Skiing & the Art of Carving.** Ellen P. Foster. 1997. pap. text ed. 17.95 (*0-9647390-3-8*) Turning Pt Ski Found.

S

Skiing Colorado: A Complete Guide to America's Number 1 Ski State. Curtis W. Casewit. LC 75-21060. 160p. 1975. pap. 4.95 (*0-85699-123-6*) Chatham Pr.

***Skiing Everyone.** 3rd ed. Cottrell. 112p. 1996. pap. text ed. 13.95 (*0-88725-226-5*) Hunter Textbks.

***Skiing for Fun & Profit.** Leigh Gieringer. (Illus.). 350p. 1997. pap. 24.95 (*1-56559-911-X*) HGI Mrktng.

Skiing for Women. Pamela Ammons et al. (Illus.). 1979. 12.95 (*0-88280-052-3*); pap. 12.95 (*0-88280-053-1*) ETC Pubns.

Skiing in the Berkshire Hills. Lauren Stevens. LC 90-81449. (Berkshire Outdoors Ser.). (Illus.). 226p. (Orig.). 1991. pap. 8.95 (*0-936399-08-2*) Berkshire Hse.

Skiing in the East: Ski Trails & How to Get There. Federal Writers' Project Staff. 334p. 1993. reprint ed. lib. bdg. 89.00 (*0-7812-5263-6*) Rprt Serv.

Skiing in the U. S. A.: The Insider's Guide: Where to Ski, Where to Stay, Where to Eat in the 30 Best U. S. Ski Resorts. Fodor's Staff. (Illus.). 1995. pap. 17.00 (*0-679-02648-7*) Fodors Travel.

Skiing in Utah: A History. Alexis Kelner. 256p. (Orig.). 1980. pap. 14.95 (*1-884744-05-2*) Wasatch Tours.

Skiing into Wisconsin: A Celebration of Winter. Jerry Apps. (Illus.). 270p. (Orig.). 1985. pap. 10.95 (*0-9606240-7-4*) Pearl-Win.

Skiing Literature: A Bibliographical Catalogue. Gary H. Schwartz. Ed. by Allen H. Adler. LC 95-1309. (Illus.). 266p. 1995. 49.95 (*0-9623000-5-5*); disk 149.95 (*0-9623000-6-3*) Wood River CA.

Skiing Mechanics. John G. Howe. 1983. 24.95 (*0-935240-02-0*) Poudre Pr.

Skiing on a Budget. Claire Walter. LC 96-7628. 160p. 1996. pap. 15.99 (*1-55870-403-5*, Betrwy Bks) F & W Pubns Inc.

Skiing Out of Your Mind: The Psychology of Peak Performance. Leonard A. Loudis et al. Ed. by Kenneth M. Singer. LC 85-18210. (Illus.). 256p. (Orig.). 1986. pap. 16.95 (*0-88011-268-9*, PLOU0268) Human Kinetics.

Skiing Tales of Terror. William Nealy. 144p. 1990. pap. 6.95 (*0-89732-106-5*) Menasha Ridge.

***Skiing the Pioneer Valley: 8 Cross-Country Ski Centers, 22 Backcountry Tours, & 4 Downhill Ski Areas in the Connecticut River Valley Region of Western Massachusetts.** Bruce Scofield et al. Ed. by Valerie Vaughan. (Illus.). 168p. (Orig.). 1997. pap. 10.95 (*1-889787-01-9*) NE Cartographics.

***Skiing Trauma & Safety, Vol. 10.** Ed. by Mote, Jr. et al. 408p. 1996. 149.00 (*0-8031-2022-2*) ASTM.

Skiing Trauma & Safety: Fifth International Symposium - STP 860. Ed. by Robert J. Johnson & C. Daniel Mote. LC 85-3897. (Illus.). 500p. 1985. text ed. 62.00 (*0-8031-0429-4*, 04-860000-47) ASTM.

Skiing Trauma & Safety: International Symposium, STP 1104, 8th. C. Daniel Mote. LC 89-14984. (Special Technical Publication Ser.). (Illus.). 463p. 1991. pap. text ed. 113.00 (*0-8031-1405-2*, 04-011040-47) ASTM.

Skiing Trauma & Safety: Seventh International Symposium. Ed. by Robert J. Johnson et al. LC 89-14984. (Special Technical Publication Ser.: No. 1022). (Illus.). 410p. 1989. text ed. 79.00 (*0-8031-1197-5*, 04-010220-47) ASTM.

Skiing Trauma & Skiing Safety: Sixth International Symposium. Ed. by Robert J. Johnson & C. Daniel Mote, Jr. LC 87-1826. (Special Technical Publication Ser.: No. 938). (Illus.). 378p. 1987. text ed. 79.00 (*0-8031-0936-9*, 04-938000-47) ASTM.

***Skiing USA: The Insider's Guide.** 2nd ed. Fodors Travel Staff. 1997. pap. 17.50 (*0-679-03534-6*) Fodors Travel.

Skiing Utah. Alexis Kelner. (Illus.). 1979. pap. write for info. (*0-318-50121-X*) A Kelner.

Skiing with Kids. Christi M. Northrop. LC 76-18486. (Illus.). 160p. (Orig.). 1976. pap. 8.95 (*0-85699-136-8*) Chatham Pr.

Skiing with the Whole Body: Your Ticket to the Expert Slopes. Jack Heggie. (Illus.). 176p. (Orig.). 1993. pap. 12.95 (*1-55643-140-6*) North Atlantic.

Skijor with Your Dog. Mari Hoe-Raitto & Carol Kaynor. (Illus.). 200p. 1992. pap. 14.95 (*0-9630854-0-9*) OK Pub.
Skijoring is the fast-growing winter sport of being pulled on skis by a dog in harness. Now, a Norwegian champion dog driver & an Alaskan writer have teamed up to produce the first comprehensive, full-length book on this exciting sport. SKIJOR WITH YOUR DOG is a clear, concise, well-written source of information on teaching your dog to pull, skijoring equipment, winter camping with dogs, caring for the working dog, competition, skijoring with children & the disabled, & more. "This book provides easily understood information on the ins & outs of skijoring...SKIJOR WITH YOUR DOG gives you all the information you need to get started."--Susan Butcher, four-time Iditarod Sled Dog Race champion. "An excellent job of covering all aspects of skijoring & dog care. (The authors') emphasis on the proper socialization, training & care of their 'working friends' is especially noteworthy."--Richard E. Burrows, DVM. More than 70 illustrations & photographs in 12 chapters. Bibliography, index, glossary, resources.
Publisher Provided Annotation.

***Skilful Physician.** Jonathon Erlen et al. 266p. 1997. text ed. 69.00 (*90-5702-531-0*, Harwood Acad Pubs) Gordon & Breach.

***Skilful Physician.** Jonathon Erlen et al. 266p. 1997. pap. text ed. 29.95 (*90-5702-532-9*, Harwood Acad Pubs) Gordon & Breach.

Skilful Rugby Union. Geoff Cooke. (Illus.). 96p. 1992. pap. 14.95 (*0-7136-3444-8*, Pub. by A&C Black UK) Talman.

Skilful Soccer. Peter Treadwell. (Skilful Ser.). (Illus.). 96p. 1991. pap. 14.95 (*0-7136-3254-2*, Pub. by A&C Black UK) Talman.

Skilful Weight Lifting. John Lear. (Skilful Ser.). (Illus.). 96p. 1991. pap. 14.95 (*0-7136-3396-4*, Pub. by A&C Black UK) Talman.

Skill Acquisition & Human Performance. Robert W. Proctor & Addie Dutta. (Advanced Psychology Texts Ser.: Vol. 1). 400p. 1994. 52.00 (*0-8039-5010-1*) Sage.

Skill Acquisition Rates & Patterns. N. E. Lane. (Recent Research in Psychology Ser.). (Illus.). 170p. 1987. 56.95 (*0-387-96579-3*) Spr-Verlag.

Skill & Education: Reflection & Experience. Ed. by Bo Goranzon et al. LC 92-16598. (Artificial Intelligence & Society Ser.). xxviii, 291p. 1992. 71.95 (*0-387-19758-3*) Spr-Verlag.

Skill & Occupational Change. Ed. by Roger Penn et al. (Social Change & Economic Life Initiative Ser.). (Illus.). 336p. 1994. 69.00 (*0-19-827914-0*) OUP.

Skill & Style on the Harpsichord: A Reference Manual for the Developing Harpsichordist. Jean Nandi. LC 88-92719. (Illus.). 147p. (Orig.). (C). 1990. pap. 22.95 (*0-9622023-2-0*) Bon Gout Pub.

***Skill Based Automated Production.** Peter Kopacek & R. Genser. (IFAC Symposia Ser.: Vol. 9016). 250p. 1990. 120.50 (*0-08-037024-1*, Pergamon Pr) Elsevier.

Skill Builders. 3rd ed. Ronald D. Johnson. LC 95-25820. (TA - Typing/Keyboarding Ser.). 1997. pap. 18.95 (*0-538-64455-9*) S-W Pub.

Skill Builders: Course Code 392-1. Jill Anderson & Susan Weinman. Ed. by Bonnie Schroeder & Catherine Doheny. (Illus.). 86p. 1989. reprint ed. pap. text ed. 5.95 (*0-917531-87-6*) CES Compu-Tech.

Skill Builders: Course Code 392-2. Jill Anderson & Susan Weinman. Ed. by Bonnie Schroeder & Catherine Doheny. (Illus.). 90p. (J). (gr. 4). 1989. reprint ed. pap. text ed. 5.95 (*0-917531-88-4*) CES Compu-Tech.

Skill Builders: Grammar. Constance Immel & Sacks. (C). 1993. text ed. 7.00 (*0-06-501496-0*) Addson-Wesley Educ.

Skill Builders: Lab Pack 1. Jill Anderson et al. Ed. by Bonnie Schroeder & Cathy Doheny. (Illus.). student ed., teacher ed. 229.95 incl. disk (*1-56177-068-X*, L392-1); teacher ed. 19.95 (*1-56177-070-1*, T392-1); disk 15.95 (*1-56177-066-3*, D392-1) CES Compu-Tech.

Skill Builders: Lab Pack 1. Marilyn Mossman. Ed. by Bonnie Schroeder. (Illus.). student ed., teacher ed. 199.95 incl. disk (*1-56177-121-X*, L492-1); teacher ed. 19.95 (*1-56177-123-6*, TE492-1); student ed. 5.95 (*1-56177-117-1*, 492-1) CES Compu-Tech.

Skill Builders: Lab Pack 2. Jill Anderson et al. Ed. by Bonnie Schroeder & Cathy Doheny. (Illus.). student ed., teacher ed. 229.95 incl. disk (*0-685-45804-0*, L392-2); teacher ed. 19.95 (*1-56177-071-X*, TE392-2); disk 15.95 (*1-56177-067-1*, D392-2) CES Compu-Tech.

Skill Builders: Lab Pack 2. Marilyn Mossman. Ed. by Bonnie Schroeder. (Illus.). student ed., teacher ed. 199.95 incl. disk (*1-56177-122-8*, L492-2); teacher ed. 19.95 (*1-56177-124-4*, TE492-2); student ed. 5.95 (*1-56177-118-X*) CES Compu-Tech.

Skill Builders: Spelling Workout. Crosby & Edwin Emery. (C). 1994. text ed. 10.95 (*0-06-501554-1*) Addson-Wesley Educ.

Skill Builders Using Action Math Level A. Caryl K. Pierson et al. 150p. 1987. pap. 29.95 (*0-933383-23-1*) Math Teachers Pr.

Skill Builders Using Action Math Level D. Caryl K. Pierson & Vicki De Voss. (Illus.). 208p. 1988. pap. 29.95 (*0-933383-29-0*) Math Teachers Pr.

Skill Building for Begining Golf. Folio & Nichols. 224p. 1997. pap. 21.00 (*0-205-16006-9*) Allyn.

Skill Building for Drug Education. Carson Bates & James Wigtil. 100p. 1993. pap. text ed. 25.00 (*0-86720-757-4*) Jones & Bartlett.

Skill Building for Interpersonal Competence. Sharon A. Ratliffe & David D. Hudson. 320p. (C). 1988. pap. text ed. 18.00 (*0-03-012602-9*) HB Coll Pubs.

Skill Building for Professionals. 2nd ed. Dorothy H. Oberhaus. (C). 1995. pap. text ed. 19.75 (*0-03-015859-1*) HB Coll Pubs.

Skill-Building for Self-Directed Team Members: A Complete Course. rev. ed. Ann Harper & Bob Harper. LC 91-90570. 211p. 1995. pap. text ed. 29.95 (*1-880859-02-5*) MW Corp.

Skill Building Manual. Corrine R. Livesay. 160p. (C). 1995. per. 27.50 (*0-256-18494-1*) Irwin.

Skill-Building System: Complete Set of Six Books & Tape, 6 bks., 1 cass. Bertie Ryan Synowiec. (Successful Living Ser.). 1997. Set of 8 books & 2 tapes. pap. 149.95 incl. audio (*1-885335-10-5*) Positive Support.

Skill Checklists: Birth Through 5's. rev. ed. 1986. 6.00 (*0-939418-06-1*) Ferguson-Florissant.

Skill Checklists & Criteria for Kindergarten: Language. 1981. 5.00 (*0-939418-09-6*) Ferguson-Florissant.

Skill Checklists & Criteria for Kindergarten: Math. 1981. 5.00 (*0-939418-10-X*) Ferguson-Florissant.

***Skill Development for International Competitiveness.** Ed. by Martin Godfrey. LC 96-48953. 352p. 1997. 95.00 (*1-85898-551-X*) E Elgar.

Skill Formation in Japan & Southeast Asia. Ed. by Kazuo Koike & Takenori Inoki. 260p. 1990. 49.50 (*0-86008-464-7*, Pub. by U of Tokyo JA) Col U Pr.

***Skill in Communication: A Vital Element in Effective Management.** 1997. lib. bdg. 250.95 (*0-8490-7633-1*) Gordon Pr.

Skill in Communication - A Vital Element in Effective Management. David D. Acker. (Illus.). 129p. (Orig.). (C). 1994. pap. text ed. 25.00 (*1-56806-189-7*) DIANE Pub.

Skill in Communication - A Vital Element in Effective Management. David D. Acker. (Illus.). 140p. (Orig.). 1990. per. 6.00 (*0-16-024439-0*, 008-020-01218-1) USGPO.

Skill in Means (Upayakausalya) Sutra. Tr. by Mark Tatz. (C). 1994. 15.00 (*81-208-0915-7*, Pub. by Motilal Banarsidass II) S Asia.

Skill in Trials: Containing a Variety of Civil & Criminal Cases Won by the Art of Advocates; J. W. Donovan. 173p. 1982. reprint ed. lib. bdg. 20.00 (*0-8377-0515-0*) Rothman.

Skill Master for Reading Today & Tomorrow Level 3: End of Book Test. Beck. (Reading Ser.). (J). (gr. 3). 1989. teacher ed., pap. 17.00 (*0-15-718027-1*) HB Schl Dept.

Skill Master for Reading Today & Tomorrow Level 6: End of Book Tests. Beck. (Reading Ser.). (J). (gr. 6). 1989. teacher ed., pap. 17.00 (*0-15-718057-3*) HB Schl Dept.

Skill Master for Reading Today & Tomorrow Level 7: End of Book Test. Beck. (Reading Ser.). (J). (gr. 7). 1989. teacher ed., pap. 17.00 (*0-15-718067-0*) HB Schl Dept.

Skill Master for Reading Today & Tomorrow Level 8: End of Book Test. Beck. (Reading Ser.). (J). (gr. 8). 1989. teacher ed., pap. 17.00 (*0-15-718077-8*) HB Schl Dept.

Skill Master for Reading Today & Tomorrow Level 9: End of Book Test. Beck. (Reading Ser.). (YA). (gr. 9). 1989. teacher ed., pap. 17.00 (*0-15-718087-5*) HB Schl Dept.

Skill Master for Reading Today & Tomorrow Level 11: End of Book Test. Beck. (Reading Ser.). (YA). 1989. teacher ed., pap. 17.00 (*0-15-718107-3*) HB Schl Dept.

Skill Master for Reading Today & Tomorrow Level 12: End of Book Test. Beck. (Reading Ser.). (YA). (gr. 12). 1989. teacher ed., pap. 17.00 (*0-15-718117-0*) HB Schl Dept.

Skill Master for Reading Today & Tomorrow Level 13: End of Book Test. Beck. (Reading Ser.). (J). 1989. teacher ed., pap. 17.00 (*0-15-718127-8*) HB Schl Dept.

Skill Master for Reading Today & Tomorrow Level 14: End of Book Test. Beck. (Reading Ser.). (J). 1989. teacher ed., pap. 17.00 (*0-15-718137-5*) HB Schl Dept.

Skill Master Reading Today & Tomorrow Level 2: End of Book Test. Beck. (Reading Ser.). (J). (gr. 2). 1989. teacher ed., pap. 17.00 (*0-15-718017-4*) HB Schl Dept.

Skill Master Reading Today & Tomorrow Level 5: End of Book Test. Beck. (Reading Ser.). (J). (gr. 5). 1989. teacher ed., pap. 17.00 (*0-15-718047-6*) HB Schl Dept.

Skill of Happiness: Creative Daily Ecstacy with Vivation. Jim Leonard. 200p. (Orig.). 1996. pap. 12.95 (*1-881952-09-6*) Three Blue Herons.

***Skill of Reading Between the Lines.** Ellis. 1992. pap. text ed. write for info. (*0-17-555399-8*) Addison-Wesley.

***Skill of Speaking: Say the Word.** Hall & Foley. 1992. student ed., pap. text ed. write for info. (*0-17-555670-9*) Addison-Wesley.

***Skill of Writing: In a Word.** Hedge. 1992. pap. text ed. write for info. (*0-17-555395-5*) Addison-Wesley.

***Skill Progressions for Player & Coach.** Val Belmonte. Ed. by Darryl Seibel. (Illus.). 100p. (Orig.). 1997. pap. 1.00 (*1-890617-01-6*) USA Hockey.

Skill Qualification & Turbulence in the Army National Guard & Army Reserve. Richard Buddin & David Grissmer. LC 93-25652. 1994. pap. 15.00 (*0-8330-1422-6*, MR-289-RA) Rand Corp.

***Skill Reinforcers.** Robert Bell. Ed. by Anne Buckingham. (Thinking Skill Library). (Illus.). 104p. (Orig.). (J). (gr. 2-5). 1997. teacher ed., pap. 9.95 (*1-56784-706-4*) Newbridge Comms.

Skill Sharpener: Training for the Front Line. Customer Service Group Editors. (Illus.). 78p. (Orig.). 1993. student ed. 39.95 (*0-915910-35-7*) Downtown Res.

Skill Sharpeners, No. 1. 2nd ed. J. DeFilippo. (Illus.). 128p. 1991. pap. text ed. 10.25 (*0-201-51325-0*) Addison-Wesley.

Skill Sharpeners, No. 2. 2nd ed. J. DeFilippo. (Illus.). 128p. 1991. pap. text ed. 10.25 (*0-201-51326-9*) Addison-Wesley.

Skill Sharpeners, No. 4. 2nd ed. J. DeFilippo. (Illus.). 129p. 1991. pap. text ed. 10.25 (*0-201-51328-5*) Addison-Wesley.

Skill Sharpeners Level 1. Judy Defilippo. 1984. text ed. 10.45 (*0-201-15623-7*) Addison-Wesley.

Skill Sharpeners Level 2. Judy Defilippo. 1984. text ed. 10.45 (*0-201-15628-8*) Addison-Wesley.

Skill Sharpeners Level 3. John Losse. 1984. text ed. 10.45 (*0-201-15633-4*) Addison-Wesley.

Skill Sharpeners Level 4. Judy Defilippo. 1984. 10.45 (*0-201-15638-5*) Addison-Wesley.

Skill Shortages: Causes & Consequences. Derek Bosworth et al. 218p. 1992. 68.95 (*1-85628-320-8*, Pub. by Avebury Pub UK) Ashgate Pub Co.

Skill Standards & Skill Formation: Cross-National Perspectives on Alternative Training Strategies. Margaret Vickers. 57p. 1994. pap. 10.00 (*1-887410-63-5*) Jobs for Future.

Skill Standards Systems in Germany, Japan, & Canada: Implications for a U. S. Skill Standards System. Robert G. Sheets. 44p. (Orig.). 1994. pap. text ed. 15.00 (*1-55877-187-5*) Natl Governor.

Skill, Technology, & Enlightenment: On Practical Philosophy. Ed. by Bo G. Oranzon. LC 94-43443. (Artificial Intelligence & Society Ser.). 1994. 53.95 (*3-540-19920-9*) Spr-Verlag.

Skill with People. Les T. Giblin. 32p. (Orig.). (C). reprint ed. pap. 2.50 (*0-9616416-0-6*) L Giblin.

Skillbooster Series, Level B. Kravitz & Dramer. Incl. Building Word Power. pap. text ed. 4.99 (*0-8136-1202-0*); Increasing Comprehension. pap. text ed. 4.99 (*0-8136-1209-8*); Organizing Information. pap. text ed. 3.04 (*0-8136-1223-3*); Set pap. text ed. write for info. (*0-318-54346-X*) Modern Curr.

Skillbooster Series Level C. Incl. Building Wordpower. Alvin Kravitz & Dan Dramer. 1978. pap. text ed. 4.99 (*0-8136-1203-9*); Increasing Comprehension. 1978. pap. text ed. 4.99 (*0-8136-1210-1*); Organizing Information. 1978. pap. text ed. 4.99 (*0-8136-1224-1*); Using References. Alvin Kravitz & Dan Dramer. 1978. pap. text ed. 4.99 (*0-8136-1231-4*); Working with Facts & Details. Alvin Kravitz & Dan Dramer. 1978. pap. text ed. 4.99 (*0-87895-343-4*); 48p. (J). (gr. 3). write for info. (*0-318-54347-8*) Modern Curr.

Skillbooster Series, Level E. Incl. Building Word Power. pap. text ed. 4.99 (*0-8136-1205-5*); Increasing Comprehension. pap. text ed. 4.99 (*0-8136-1212-8*); Organizing Information. pap. text ed. 4.99 (*0-8136-1226-8*); Using References. pap. text ed. 3.04 (*0-8136-1233-0*); Working with Facts & Details. pap. text ed. 4.99 (*0-8136-1219-5*); (gr. 5). 1976. Set pap. write for info. (*0-318-54348-6*) Modern Curr.

Skillbooster Series, Level F. Incl. Building Word Power. pap. text ed. 4.99 (*0-8136-1206-3*); Increasing Comprehension. pap. text ed. 4.99 (*0-8136-1213-6*); Organizing Information. pap. text ed. 4.99 (*0-8136-1227-6*); Using References. pap. text ed. 4.99 (*0-8136-1234-9*); Working with Facts & Details. pap. text ed. 4.99 (*0-8136-1220-9*); (gr. 6). 1976. Set pap. write for info. (*0-318-54349-4*) Modern Curr.

Skillbuilding: Building Speed & Accuracy on the Keyboard. Carole H. Eide et al. LC 95-7152. 1995. write for info. incl. disk (*0-02-801936-9*); pap. 13.00 (*0-02-801935-0*); teacher ed., pap. write for info. (*0-02-801938-5*); disk write for info. (*0-02-801937-7*) Glencoe.

Skilled Consultant. Richard D. Parsons. 1995. text ed. 61.00 (*0-205-16119-7*) Allyn.

Skilled Facilitator: Practical Wisdom for Developing Effective Groups. Roger M. Schwarz. LC 93-48662. (Management Ser.). 336p. text ed. 29.95 (*1-55542-638-7*) Jossey-Bass.

***Skilled Helper.** 6th ed. Egan. (Counseling Ser.). (C). 1998. text ed. 53.95 (*0-534-34948-X*) Brooks-Cole.

Skilled Helper: A Problem-Management Approach to Helping. 5th ed. Gerard Egan. LC 93-4291. 358p. 1994. text ed. 53.95 (*0-534-21294-8*) Brooks-Cole.

Skilled Helper: A Systematic Approach to Effective Helping. 4th ed. Gerard Egan. LC 89-38002. (Psychology Ser.). 432p. (C). 1990. boxed 38.95 (*0-534-12138-1*) Brooks-Cole.

Skilled Interviewing. Daphne Keats. (C). 1992. 75.00 (*0-86431-119-2*, Pub. by Aust Council Educ Res AT) St Mut.

Skilled Labor Shortages in the United Kingdom: With Particular Reference to the Engineering Industry. Gerry Eastwood. (British-North American Committee Ser.). 52p. 1976. 3.00 (*0-902594-28-1*) Natl Planning.

Skilled Labour Supply Imbalances: The Canadian Experience. William Dodge. LC 77-93071. (British-North American Committee Ser.). 56p. 1977. 3.00 (*0-902594-31-1*) Natl Planning.

Skilled Metalworkers of Nuremberg: Craft & Class in the Industrial Revolution. Michael J. Neufeld. LC 88-23875. (Class & Culture Ser.). 240p. (C). 1989. text ed. 45.00 (*0-8135-1394-4*) Rutgers U Pr.

Skilled Nursing Facility Management: Cost Reporting. Michael E. Lesnick. LC 97-13983. 250p. 1995. 175.00 (*1-55738-637-4*) Irwin Prof Pubng.

Skilled Nursing Facility Management: Coverage Issues. Michael E. Lesnick. 200p. 1995. 175.00 (*1-55738-638-2*) Irwin Prof Pubng.

Skilled Nursing Facility Management: New Directions in Long Term Care. Michael E. Lesnick. 250p. 1995. 50.00 (*1-55738-639-0*) Irwin Prof Pubng.

Skilled Nursing Facility Management: Optimizing Reimbursement. Michael E. Lesnick. 300p. 1995. 175.00 (*1-55738-636-6*) Irwin Prof Pubng.

Skilled Pastor: Counseling as the Practice of Theology. Charles W. Taylor. LC 91-13455. 160p. 1991. pap. 13.00 (*0-8006-2509-9*, 1-2509, Fortress Pr) Augsburg Fortress.

Skilled Workers in Britain & America. Roger Penn. 220p. 1990. text ed. 49.95 (*0-312-03726-0*) St Martin.

Skillet & Trophy Fishing Texas. Curtis Morris. (Illus.). 256p. (Orig.). 1989. pap. text ed. 10.95 (*1-877740-00-4*) Nel-Mar Pub.

Skillful Field Athletics. Johnson. pap. 13.95 (*0-7136-5769-3*, 91945, Pub. by A&C Black UK) Talman.

Skillful Judo. Caffary & Marwood. pap. 14.95 (*0-7136-3604-1*, 92779, Pub. by A&C Black UK) Talman.

Skillful Karate. McLatchie. pap. 13.95 (*0-7136-5779-0*, 91944, Pub. by A&C Black UK) Talman.

Skillful Means. 2nd rev. ed. Tarthang Tulku. LC 78-73688. 158p. 1991. pap. 12.95 (*0-89800-231-1*) Dharma Pub.

Skillful Mind: An Introduction of Cognitive Psychology. Ed. by Angus Gellatly. LC 86-8622. 160p. 1986. 85.00 (*0-335-15336-4*, Open Univ Pr); pap. 29.00 (*0-335-15335-6*, Open Univ Pr) Taylor & Francis.

Skillful Movers: Lesson Plans T/A Developmental Physical Education for Today's Children. 3rd ed. David L. Gallahue et al. 336p. (C). 1995. per. write for info. (*0-697-25611-1*) Brown & Benchmark.

Skillful Reading: A Text & Workbook for Students of English as a Second Language. A. Sonka. 1980. pap. text ed. 20.10 (*0-13-812404-3*) P-H.

Skillful Show Jumping. Jane Holderness-Roddam. pap. 14.95 (*0-7136-3255-0*, 92255, Pub. by A&C Black UK) Talman.

An Asterisk (*) at the beginning of an entry indicates that the title is appearing in BIP for the first time.

Skillful Squash. Ian Robinson. pap. 13.95 (*0-7136-5749-9*, 91943, Pub. by A&C Black UK) Talman.
Skillful Teacher: Building Your Teaching Skills. Jon Saphier & Robert Gower. 402p. (Orig.). 1987. pap. text ed. 21.95 (*1-886822-00-X*) Res Better Teach.
Skillful Teacher: On Technique, Trust, & Responsiveness in the Classroom. Stephen D. Brookfield. LC 90-40387. (Higher Education Ser.). 255p. text ed. 29.95 (*1-55542-267-5*) Jossey-Bass.
Skillful Teacher's Handbook: Effectively Teaching Regular & Special Education Students. Rosanne M. Manus. (Illus.). 416p. (C). 1990. spiral bd., pap. 56.95 (*0-398-05702-8*) C C Thomas.
Skillful Track Athletics. Nick Whitehead. pap. 13.95 (*0-7136-5759-6*, 91946, Pub. by A&C Black UK) Talman.
Skills: Grammar & Usage. Ed. by Kellman. 1982. wbk. ed., pap. 7.06 (*0-8092-5814-5*) Contemp Bks.
Skills: Pre-Test Starter. Frechette et al. 1992. pap. 29.65 (*0-8092-3879-9*) Contemp Bks.
Skills: Pre-Tests Book. Contemporary Editors, Staff. 1992. pap. 16.95 (*0-8092-3864-0*) Contemp Bks.
Skills: Progress. Contemporary Editors, Staff. 1992. pap. 12.70 (*0-8092-3876-4*) Contemp Bks.
Skills: Progress Starter. Yoon. 1992. pap. 29.65 (*0-8092-3875-6*) Contemp Bks.
Skills: Progress Test. Frechette et al. 1992. pap. 3.00 (*0-8092-3878-0*) Contemp Bks.
Skills: Progress Tests. Contemporary Editors, Staff. 1992. wbk. ed., pap. 16.95 (*0-8092-3863-2*) Contemp Bks.
Skills: Scoring. Contemporary Editors, Staff. 1992. pap. 6.35 (*0-8092-3874-8*) Contemp Bks.
Skills: Sentence Structure. Ed. by Kellman. 1983. wbk. ed., pap. 7.06 (*0-8092-5812-9*) Contemp Bks.
Skills: Spelling, Capitals, Punctuation. Ed. by Kellman. 1982. wbk. ed., pap. 7.06 (*0-8092-5813-7*) Contemp Bks.
Skills Acquisitions in Microenterprises: Evidence from West Africa. OECD Staff. 92p. (Orig.). 1994. pap. 11.00 (*92-64-14182-0*) OECD.
Skills Advantage: Identify Your Skills for School, Work, & Life. J. Michael Farr & Susan Christophersen. Ed. by Sara Hall. (Illus.). 64p. (YA). (gr. 6 up). 1994. student ed., pap. 5.95 (*1-56370-093-X*, SKAD) JIST Works.
Skills & Assignments in Communication Studies. Jacqueline Tuson. Ed. by Alwyn Jones. 112p. (C). 1988. 60.00 (*0-85950-455-7*, Pub. by S Thornes Pubs UK) St Mut.
Skills & Ethics in the Practice of Law. LC 93-71289. xxi, 250p. 1993. pap. 39.95 (*0-8318-0710-5*, B710) Am Law Inst.
Skills & Knowledge for AIDS & Pregnancy Prevention. Children's Hospital of Los Angeles Staff. 1995. 45.00 (*1-56071-503-0*) ETR Assocs.
Skills & Knowledge of Cost Engineering. 3rd rev. ed. Ed. by Donald F. McDonald, Jr. 164p. 1992. pap. 32.50 (*0-930284-50-X*) AACE Intl.
Skills & Procedures of Emergency & General Medicine. Harvey W. Meislin & Stephen J. Dresnick. 250p. 1981. text ed. 31.50 (*0-8359-7009-4*, Reston) P-H.
Skills & Processes in Science Education: A Critical Analysis. Ed. by Jerry Wellington. 200p. 1989. 49.50 (*0-415-01287-2*) Routledge.
Skills & Strategies for Coaching Soccer. Alan Hargreaves. LC 89-35783. (Illus.). 384p. (Orig.). 1990. pap. 19.95 (*0-88011-328-6*, PHAR0328) Human Kinetics.
Skills & Strategies for Winning Racquetball see Winning Raquetball: Skills, Drills, & Strategies
Skills & Techniques for Group Work with Children & Adolescents. Rosemarie Smead. LC 95-69455. 300p. (Orig.). 1995. pap. text ed. 21.95 (*0-87822-352-5*, 4849) Res Press.
Skills & Vocationalism. Maurice Holt. 172p. 1987. 85.00 (*0-335-10290-5*, Open Univ Pr); pap. 32.00 (*0-335-10289-1*, Open Univ Pr) Taylor & Francis.
Skills Assessment, Job Placement, & Training: What Can Be Learned from the Temporary Help-Staffing Industry? An Overview of the Industry & a Case Study of Manpower, Inc. Dorie Seavey & Richard Kazis. 60p. 1994. pap. 10.00 (*1-887410-65-1*) Jobs for Future.
***Skills Collaborative Learning.** Edwina Stoll & James Luotto. 256p. (C). 1996. per., pap. text ed. 25.26 (*0-7872-2624-6*) Kendall-Hunt.
Skills Competencies for the Dental Assistant. Charline M. Dofka. LC 94-24642. (Illus.). 576p. 1996. text ed. 26.95 (*0-8273-6685-X*) Delmar.
Skills Development Handbook for Busy Managers. Pat O'Reilly. LC 92-45730. 1993. write for info. (*0-07-707682-6*) McGraw.
Skills Drills: A Self-Correcting Math Proficiency Game. Fredi Munger & Holly Shader. (Technical Notes Ser.: Vol. 28). 36p. (Orig.). 1989. pap. 2.00 (*0-932288-81-2*) Ctr Intl Ed U of MA.
Skills Drills, Vol. 1: Reading Level 4.5. Ed. by Edward Spargo. (Skills Drills Ser.). 100p. 1983. 162.26 (*0-89061-324-9*, 121) Jamestown Pubs.
Skills Drills, Vol. 1: Reading Level 4.5, Set. Ed. by Edward Spargo. (Skills Drills Ser.). 100p. 1983. 295.00 (*0-89061-352-4*, 125) Jamestown Pubs.
Skills Drills, Vol. 2: Reading Level 5.5. Ed. by Edward Spargo. (Skills Drills Ser.). 100p. 1983. 162.26 (*0-89061-350-8*, 122) Jamestown Pubs.
Skills Drills, Vol. 3: Reading Level 6.5. Ed. by Edward Spargo. (Skills Drills Ser.). 100p. 1983. 162.26 (*0-89061-351-6*, 123) Jamestown Pubs.
Skills For Adolescence. Ed. by Hank Resnik. (Illus.). 436p. 1985. student ed. 4.85 (*0-933419-05-8*); student ed. 4.85 (*0-933419-09-0*) Quest Intl.
Skills for Adolescence: Teachers Manual. rev. ed. Hank Resnik et al. Ed. by Linda Barr. (Skills for Adolescence Ser.). (Illus.). 531p. 1988. 110.00 (*0-933419-23-6*) Quest Intl.
Skills for Consumer Success. 2nd ed. Donnelly. (HM - Consumer Education Ser.). 1987. wbk. ed., pap. 19.95 (*0-538-08110-4*) S-W Pub.
Skills for Consumer Success. 3rd ed. Donnelly. (HM - Consumer Education Ser.). 1993. 3.95 (*0-538-61090-5*); wbk. ed., pap. 17.95 (*0-538-61089-1*) S-W Pub.
Skills for Direct Practice in Social Work. Ruth R. Middleman & Gale G. Wood. 176p. 1990. text ed. 39.50 (*0-231-05508-0*); pap. text ed. 16.50 (*0-231-05509-9*) Col U Pr.
Skills for Effective Human Services Management. Ed. by Richard L. Edwards. LC 91-16322. (Illus.). 386p. (C). 1991. 34.95 (*0-87101-195-6*) Natl Assn Soc Wkrs.
Skills for Geography. Stanley Thornes. (C). 1989. 60.00 (*0-85950-929-X*, Pub. by S Thornes Pubs UK) St Mut.
Skills for Life. Educational Assessment Publishing Co. Staff. (Discover Ser.). (Illus.). 240p. (J). (gr. 7). 1992. Spanish. text ed. 18.95 (*0-7854-0092-3*, 15371); Bilingual tchr's. ed., 256p. 41.95 (*0-7854-0223-3*, 15372); Bilingual total tchr. support system, 396p. 220.95 (*0-7854-0224-1*, 15373) Am Guidance.
Skills for Life. Educational Assessment Publishing Company Staff. (Discover Ser.). (Illus.). 48p. (J). (gr. k). 1992. Spanish. text ed. 11.95 (*0-7854-0071-0*, 15301); Spanish big bk. text ed. 87.95 (*0-7854-0171-7*, 15304) Am Guidance.
Skills for Life. Educational Assessment Publishing Company Staff. (Discover Ser.). (Illus.). 48p. (J). (gr. 1). 1992. Spanish. text ed. 11.95 (*0-7854-0074-5*, 15311); Spanish big bk., 64p. text ed. 87.95 (*0-7854-0172-5*, 15314) Am Guidance.
Skills for Life. Educational Assessment Publishing Company Staff. (Discover Ser.). (Illus.). 64p. (J). (gr. 2). 1992. Spanish. text ed. 11.95 (*0-7854-0077-X*, 15321) Am Guidance.
Skills for Life. Educational Assessment Publishing Company Staff. (Discover Ser.). (Illus.). 80p. (J). (gr. 3). 1992. Spanish. text ed. 12.95 (*0-7854-0080-X*, 15331) Am Guidance.
Skills for Life. Educational Assessment Publishing Company Staff. (Discover Ser.). (Illus.). 116p. (J). (gr. 4). 1992. Spanish. text ed. 12.95 (*0-7854-0083-4*, 15341) Am Guidance.
Skills for Life. Educational Assessment Publishing Company Staff. (Discover Ser.). (Illus.). 128p. (J). (gr. 5). 1992. Spanish. text ed. 13.95 (*0-7854-0086-9*, 15351) Am Guidance.
Skills for Life. Educational Assessment Publishing Company Staff. (Discover Ser.). (Illus.). 144p. (J). (gr. 6). 1992. Spanish. text ed. 14.95 (*0-7854-0089-3*, 15361) Am Guidance.
Skills for Life. Educational Assessment Publishing Company Staff. (Discover Ser.). (Illus.). 240p. (J). (gr. 8). 1992. Spanish. text ed. 18.95 (*0-7854-0093-1*, 15381) Am Guidance.
Skills for Life. Educational Assessment Publishing Company Staff. (Discover Ser.). (Illus.). (YA). (gr. 9-12). 1993. 41.95 (*0-7854-0147-4*, 15092); text ed. 18.95 (*0-7854-0146-6*, 15091); Total tchr. support system. 220.95 (*0-7854-0148-2*, 15093) Am Guidance.
Skills for Life. Merita L. Thompson & Johanna Strange. (Discover Ser.). (Illus.). 168p. (J). (gr. 6). 1991. 33.95 (*0-7854-0094-X*, 15062) Am Guidance.
***Skills for Life.** 11th ed. Couch. (CA - Career Development Ser.). 1997. wbk. ed., pap. 13.95 (*0-314-20332-X*) S-W Pub.
Skills for Life: Library Information Literacy for Grades K-6. Ed. by Linworth Publishing, Inc. Staff. LC 93-21178. (Professional Growth Ser.). 299p. 1993. student ed., ring bd. 36.95 (*0-938865-19-6*) Linworth Pub.
Skills for Life: Library Information Literacy for Grades 6-8. Ed. by Linworth Publishing, Inc. Staff. LC 93-33733. (Professional Growth Ser.). 292p. 1993. student ed., ring bd. 36.95 (*0-938865-20-X*) Linworth Pub.
Skills for Life: Library Information Literacy for Grades 9-12. Ed. by Linworth Publishing, Inc. Staff. LC 93-39622. (Professional Growth Ser.). 328p. 1993. student ed., ring bd. 36.95 (*0-938865-21-8*) Linworth Pub.
Skills for Life: Student's Book. L. Kaye-Besley & D. Byles. (C). 1984. 55.00 (*0-85950-204-X*, Pub. by S Thornes Pubs UK) St Mut.
Skills for Life: Tutor's Book. L. Kaye-Besley & D. Byles. (C). 1984. 70.00 (*0-85950-205-8*, Pub. by S Thornes Pubs UK) St Mut.
Skills for Living. rev. ed. Frances B. Parnell & Joyce H. Wooten. 622p. 1997. 46.60 (*1-56637-287-9*) Goodheart.
Skills for Living: Group Counseling Activities for Elementary Students. Rosemarie S. Morganett. LC 94-65700. 238p. (Orig.). 1994. pap. text ed. 25.95 (*0-87822-347-9*, 4761) Res Press.
Skills for Living: Group Counseling Activities for Young Adolescents. Rosemarie S. Morganett. LC 89-61588. 240p. (Orig.). 1989. pap. text ed. 25.95 (*0-87822-318-5*, 3184) Res Press.
Skills for Management Effectiveness, Set 6. Roger Burgraff. 28p. 1991. 79.50 incl. audio (*0-88432-437-0*, S03050) Audio-Forum.
Skills for Managerial Excellence. Robert E. Bidwell. 250p. 1995. pap. 32.25 (*0-536-58877-5*) Ginn Pr.
Skills for Managerial Success: Theory, Experience, & Practice. Laird W. Mealiea & Gary P. Latham. LC 95-12121. 544p. (C). 1995. per. 41.50 (*0-256-12454-X*) Irwin.
Skills for Managers & Leaders. Gary A. Yukl. 1990. pap. text ed. 37.60 (*0-13-556564-2*) P-H.
Skills for Managers in Organizations. Laird W. Mealiea. LC 94-1347. (C). 1994. per. 21.50 (*0-256-15948-3*) Irwin.
Skills for Practical Writing: A Workbook for Training in Work-Related Writing. 2nd ed. Ed. by Susan Dakin. (Illus.). 326p. 1994. student ed. 30.00 (*1-883314-01-1*) NC Writers Network.
Skills for Preschool Teachers. 5th ed. Janice J. Beaty. LC 95-750. 1995. pap. text ed. 30.00 (*0-02-307691-7*, Macmillan Coll) P-H.
Skills for Radio Broadcasters. 3rd ed. Curtis R. Holsopple. (Illus.). 208p. 1988. pap. 14.95 (*0-8306-2930-0*, 2930) McGraw-Hill Prof.
Skills for Simple Living: How-to Letters from the Home Front for Tomorrow's World. Betty Tillotson. LC 91-39934. (Illus.). 224p. (Orig.). 1992. pap. 14.95 (*0-88179-035-4*) Hartley & Marks.
Skills for Success. Adele M. Scheele. 208p. 1987. mass mkt. 4.99 (*0-345-35371-4*) Ballantine.
***Skills for Success.** Adele M. Scheele. 1996. pap. 11.00 (*0-345-41044-0*) Ballantine.
Skills for Successful School Leaders. 2nd ed. John R. Hoyle et al. 279p. (Orig.). 1995. 22.00 (*0-87652-083-2*, 021-0132) Am Assn Sch Admin.
Skills for Survival - How Families Can Prepare. Esther Dickey. LC 78-52124. 224p. 1989. 16.98 (*0-88290-093-5*) Horizon Utah.
Skills for the Changing Workplace, 4 vols. Incl. Marketing Educator's Guide. Marilyn J. Gordon & Catherine P. Warmbrod. 86p. 1985. (*0-318-60104-4*, RD253); Business & Office Educator's Guide. Frieda Bennett et al. 93p. 1985. (*0-318-60105-2*, RD254); Electronics Instructor's Guide. Robert D. Bhaerman & Larry Oliver. 81p. 1985. (*0-318-60106-0*, RD255); Automotive Repair Instructor's Guide. Robert D. Bhaerman & Ricke A. North. 78p. 1985. (*0-318-60107-9*, RD256); 1985. 8.00 (*0-317-05980-7*) Ctr Educ Trng Employ.
Skills for the Future. Robert Dilts. LC 93-84504. 1993. 29.95 (*0-916990-27-3*) META Pubns.
Skills Formation & Gender Relations: The Politics of Who Knows What. N. Jackson. 1992. pap. 59.00 (*0-7300-1358-8*, Pub. by Deakin Univ AT) St Mut.
Skills Fun, 6 bks., Set. Highlights for Children Staff. (Illus.). (J). (ps-3). 1991. pap. text ed. 14.95 (*0-87534-195-0*) Highlights.
Skills Fun: Critters. Highlights for Children Staff. (Illus.). (J). (ps-3). 1991. pap. text ed. 2.95 (*0-87534-192-6*) Highlights.
Skills Fun: Free Time. Highlights for Children Staff. (Illus.). (J). (ps-3). 1991. pap. text ed. 2.95 (*0-87534-193-4*) Highlights.
Skills Fun: Mystery. Highlights for Children Staff. (Illus.). (J). (ps-3). 1991. pap. text ed. 2.95 (*0-87534-194-2*) Highlights.
Skills Fun: Outdoors. Highlights for Children Staff. (Illus.). (J). (ps-3). 1991. pap. text ed. 2.95 (*0-87534-198-5*) Highlights.
Skills Fun: Space. Highlights for Children Staff. (Illus.). (J). (ps-3). 1991. pap. text ed. 2.95 (*0-87534-199-3*) Highlights.
Skills Fun: Trips. Highlights for Children Staff. (Illus.). (J). (ps-3). 1991. pap. text ed. 2.95 (*0-87534-200-0*) Highlights.
Skills in Action. D. R. Sellen. (C). 1982. text ed. 85.00 incl. audio (*0-7175-1015-8*, Pub. by S Thornes Pubs UK) St Mut.
Skills in Action. Stanley Thornes. (C). 1982. 70.00 (*0-7175-0973-7*, Pub. by S Thornes Pubs UK) St Mut.
Skills in Advanced Biology Vol. 2: Observing, Recording & Interpreting. J. W. Garvin & J. D. Boyd. 92p. (C). 1994. 42.00 (*0-85950-817-X*, Pub. by Stanley Thornes UK) Trans-Atl Phila.
Skills in Advanced Biology Series Vol. 1: Dealing with Data. J. W. Garvin. 176p. (C). 1994. 33.00 (*0-614-03936-3*, Pub. by Stanley Thornes UK) Trans-Atl Phila.
Skills in Advanced Biology Series - Dealing with Data-Worksheet Copymasters. Stanley, Thornes, Publishers Ltd. Staff. (C). 1986. text ed. 215.00 (*0-85950-589-8*, Pub. by S Thornes Pubs UK) St Mut.
Skills in Advanced Biology Series - Observing, Recording & Interpreting, Teacher's Guide. J. W. Garvin & J. D. Boyd. (C). 1989. text ed. 50.00 (*0-7487-0043-9*, Pub. by S Thornes Pubs UK) St Mut.
Skills in Advanced Biology Series, Vol. 1: Dealing with Data. J. W. Garvin. (C). 1986. text ed. 65.00 (*0-85950-588-X*, Pub. by S Thornes Pubs UK) St Mut.
Skills in Advanced Biology Two, Teacher's Book. G. Garvin. (C). 1989. text ed. 45.00 (*0-85950-818-8*, Pub. by S Thornes Pubs UK) St Mut.
Skills in Collaborative Classroom Consultation. Anne Jordan. 192p. (C). 1994. pap. 15.95 (*0-415-03864-2*, B0810) Routledge.
Skills in Collaborative Classroom Consultation. Anne Jordan. LC 93-5800. 192p. (C). (gr. 13). 1994. text ed. 49.95 (*0-415-03863-4*, B0806) Routledge.
Skills in Focus: Writing, Rewriting, Proofreading. Thomas Friedmann. LC 87-60509. 320p. (C). 1988. pap. text ed. 25.50 (*0-312-00291-2*); teacher ed., pap. text ed. 0.60 (*0-312-00292-0*) St Martin.
Skills in Geography. J. P. Harte & C. Dunbar. LC 93-27487. (J). 1994. pap. 18.95 (*0-521-44635-X*) Cambridge U Pr.
Skills in Language, 2 bks., Bk. 1. (Skill Power Ser.). 1988. pap. text ed. 7.80 (*0-8428-9336-9*); pap. text ed. 1.40 (*0-8428-9337-7*) Cambridge Bk.
Skills in Language, 2 bks., Bk. 2. (Skill Power Ser.). 1988. pap. text ed. 7.50 (*0-8428-9338-5*) Cambridge Bk.
Skills in Neighbourhood Work. Ed. by Paul Henderson & David Thomas. 1980. 90.00 (*0-317-05806-1*, Pub. by Natl Inst Soc Work) St Mut.
Skills Life Academics. Couch. (Skills Life & Living Now Ser.). Date not set. write for info. (*0-314-09789-9*) West Pub.
Skills Life Careers. Couch. (Skills Life & Living Now Ser.). Date not set. write for info. (*0-314-09787-2*) West Pub.
Skills Life Health. Couch. (Skills Life & Living Now Ser.). Date not set. write for info. (*0-314-09788-0*) West Pub.
Skills Life Work & Family. Couch. (Skills Life & Living Now Ser.). Date not set. write for info. (*0-314-09791-0*) West Pub.
Skills Manual for the EMT. Faught. pap. text ed. write for info. (*0-7216-6386-9*) Saunders.
Skills of Analysis. 2nd ed. Watson. 1993. pap. text ed. write for info. (*0-07-068492-8*) McGraw.
Skills of Appraisal. John Slater & Peter Packard. LC 87-22388. 1989. pap. text ed. 69.95 (*0-566-02729-1*, Pub. by Gower UK) Ashgate Pub Co.
Skills of Argument. Deanna Kuhn. (Illus.). 250p. (C). 1991. text ed. 69.95 (*0-521-40451-7*); pap. text ed. 25.95 (*0-521-42349-X*) Cambridge U Pr.
***Skills of Clinical Supervision for Nurses: A Practical Guide for Supervisees, Clinical Supervisors & Managers.** Meg Bond & Stevie Holland. LC 97-15164. (Supervision in Context Ser.). 1997. pap. write for info. (*0-335-19660-8*, Open Univ Pr) Taylor & Francis.
Skills of Cricket: The Skills of the Game. Keith Andrew. (Illus.). 144p. 1989. pap. 19.95 (*1-85223-237-4*, Pub. by Crowood Pr UK) Trafalgar.
Skills of Dictation. Eva Roman. (Illus.). 128p. 1990. pap. text ed. 11.95 (*0-566-02908-1*, Pub. by Gower UK) Ashgate Pub Co.
Skills of Encouragement: Bringing Out the Best in Yourself & Others. Don Dinkmeyer & Lewis E. Losoncy. 235p. 1995. pap. 18.95 (*1-57444-004-7*) St Lucie Pr.
Skills of Helping. Richard D. Parsons. LC 94-6038. 1994. pap. text ed. 35.00 (*0-205-14713-5*) Allyn.
Skills of Helping Individuals, Families, & Groups. 3rd ed. Lawrence Shulman. LC 91-67827. 740p. (C). 1992. boxed 52.00 (*0-87581-363-1*) Peacock Pubs.
Skills of Interviewing: A Guide for Managers & Trainers. Leslie Rae. 222p. 1989. pap. text ed. 15.95 (*0-7045-0620-3*, Pub. by Gower UK) Ashgate Pub Co.
Skills of Management. A. N. Welsh. 196p. (C). 1989. 111.00 (*0-685-36138-1*, Pub. by Inst Pur & Supply UK) St Mut.
Skills of Multicultural Competence. Garcia. (Counseling Ser.). Date not set. pap. 28.95 (*0-534-34301-5*) Brooks-Cole.
Skills of Negotiating. Bill Scott. 230p. (C). 1981. 105.00 (*0-685-39927-3*, Pub. by Inst Pur & Supply UK) St Mut.
***Skills of Persuasion: Speak with Verbal Fireworks.** Vandye J. Forrester, III. 128p. (Orig.). 1997. pap. 39.98 (*0-9656988-0-7*) Power Speakers.
Skills of Primary School Management. Les Bell & Chris Rhodes. LC 95-36545. 232p. (C). 1996. pap. text ed. 24.95 (*0-415-09757-6*) Routledge.
Skills of Supervision & Staff Management. Lawrence Shulman. LC 81-83338. 372p. reprint ed. pap. 106.10 (*0-7837-1433-5*, 2041810) Bks Demand.
Skills of Training. 2nd ed. Leslie Rae. 220p. 1990. text ed. 49.95 (*0-566-02902-2*, Pub. by Gower UK) Ashgate Pub Co.
Skills Practice Manual for Health Unit Coordinating. 3rd ed. Myrna W. LaFleur & Patricia Schneider. (Illus.). 272p. 1993. pap. text ed. 20.95 (*0-7216-4303-5*) Saunders.
Skills That Work: Communication Skills 1. Stein. 1991. pap. 11.93 (*0-8092-4122-6*) Contemp Bks.
Skills That Work: Communication Skills 2. Romanek. 1991. pap. 11.93 (*0-8092-4121-8*) Contemp Bks.
Skills That Work: Math Skills 2. Mitchell. 1991. pap. 11.93 (*0-8092-4123-4*) Contemp Bks.
Skills That Work: Reading 1. Echaore-Yoon. 1991. pap. 11.93 (*0-8092-4126-9*) Contemp Bks.
Skills That Work: Reading 2. Echaore-Yoon. 1991. pap. 11.93 (*0-8092-4125-0*) Contemp Bks.
***Skills to Thrive: Career Education Handbook.** Lila Cabbil et al. 260p. 1997. pap. 34.95 (*0-89128-943-7*) Am Foun Blind.
Skills Training for Children with Behavior Disorders: A Parent & Therapist Guidebook. Michael L. Bloomquist. 272p. 1996. pap. text ed. 29.95 (*1-57230-080-9*) Guilford Pr.
Skills Training for Counselling. Francesca Inskipp. LC 95-30562. (Counselor, Trainer, & Supervisor Ser.). (Illus.). 160p. 1995. 70.00 (*0-304-32920-7*); pap. 19.95 (*0-304-32918-5*) Cassell.
Skills Training for Productivity: Vocational Education & Training in Developing Countries. John Middleton et al. (World Bank Publication Ser.). (Illus.). 376p. 1993. 39.95 (*0-19-520887-0*, 60887) OUP.
Skills Training for Tomorrow's Work Force. Laurie Field. LC 94-66915. 270p. 1994. pap. text ed. 29.95 (*0-88390-433-0*, Pfffr & Co) Jossey-Bass.
Skills Training Manual for Treating Borderline Personality Disorder. Marsha M. Linehan. LC 93-15216. (Diagnosis & Treatment of Mental Disorders Ser.). 180p. (Orig.). 1993. student ed., pap. text ed. 26.95 (*0-89862-034-1*) Guilford Pr.
Skillstreaming in Early Childhood: Teaching Prosocial Skills to the Preschool & Kindergarten Child. Ellen McGinnis & Arnold P. Goldstein. LC 90-60925. (Illus.). 200p. (Orig.). 1990. pap. text ed. 15.95 (*0-87822-320-7*, 4423); Program forms. pap. text ed. 13.95 (*0-87822-321-5*, 4424) Res Press.
Skillstreaming the Adolescent: A Structured Learning Approach to Teaching Prosocial Skills. Arnold P. Goldstein et al. LC 79-66179. (Illus.). 232p. (Orig.). (C). 1979. pap. text ed. 15.95 (*0-87822-205-7*, 2057) Res Press.
***Skillstreaming the Adolescent: New Strategies & Perspectives for Teaching Prosocial Skills.** Arnold P. Goldstein & Ellen McGinnis. 260p. (Orig.). 1997. pap. text ed. write for info. (*0-87822-369-X*) Res Press.

S

S

***Skillstreaming the Adolescent: New Strategies & Perspectives for Teaching Prosocial Skills - Program Forms.** Arnold P. Goldstein & Ellen McGinnis. 60p. (Orig.). 1997. pap. text ed. write for info. (0-87822-371-1) Res Press.

***Skillstreaming the Adolescent: Student Manual.** Arnold P. Goldstein & Ellen McGinnis. 100p. (Orig.). (YA). (gr. 6-12). 1997. student ed., pap. text ed. write for info. (0-87822-370-3) Res Press.

***Skillstreaming the Elementary School Child: New Strategies & Perspectives for Teaching Prosocial Skills.** rev. ed. Ellen McGinnis & Arnold P. Goldstein. 260p. (Orig.). 1997. pap. text ed. write for info. (0-87822-372-X) Res Press.

***Skillstreaming the Elementary School Child: New Strategies & Perspectives for Teaching Prosocial Skills - Program Forms.** rev. ed. Ellen McGinnis & Arnold P. Goldstein. 60p. (Orig.). 1997. pap. text ed. write for info. (0-87822-374-6) Res Press.

***Skillstreaming the Elementary School Child: Student Manual.** Ellen McGinnis & Arnold P. Goldstein. 100p. (Orig.). (J). (gr. 1-5). 1997. student ed., pap. text ed. write for info. (0-87822-373-8) Res Press.

Skim. Thomas Henege. 272p. 1986. reprint ed. pap. 6.00 (0-89733-190-7) Academy Chi Pubs.

Skim the Fat. American Dietetic Association Staff. 192p. 1995. 10.95 (1-56561-062-8) Chronimed.

***Skimmin' Stones.** Nicholas P. Murray. LC 96-90488. (Orig.). 1997. pap. 12.95 (0-533-12072-1) Vantage.

Skimming & Scanning: Advanced Level. (YA). (gr. 7-10). Date not set. pap. 13.30 (0-89061-674-4) Jamestown Pubs.

Skimming & Scanning: Intermediate Level. (gr. 4-8). Date not set. pap. 12.64 (0-89061-673-6) Jamestown Pubs.

Skimming the Cream: Fifty Years with "Peggy of the Flint Hills" Zula B. Greene. 214p. 1983. 14.95 (0-941974-04-9) Baranski Pub Co.

Skimming the Fat: A Practical Food Guide. Maureen Callahan. LC 92-40300. 1992. pap. 9.95 (0-88091-112-3) Am Dietetic Assn.

Skin. (Looking Good Ser.). (Illus.). (J). (gr. 5 up). 1987. 11.95 (0-685-73924-4); lib. bdg. 15.94 (0-86625-276-2) Rourke Corp.

Skin. Barbara Hamby. Ed. by Rodger Moody. pap. 6.00 (1-878851-07-1) Silverfish Rev Pr.

***Skin.** Catharine Heller. 1997. pap. 8.95 (0-614-27325-0) Carroll & Graf.

Skin. Curzio Malaparte. LC 87-63048. 1988. pap. 12.95 (0-910395-37-3) Marlboro Pr.

Skin. Peter Milligan. 1996. pap. text ed. 8.95 (1-85809-000-8) Kitchen Sink.

Skin. Ed. by Elaine Palmer. (Illus.). 126p. (Orig.). (YA). (gr. 10). 1995. pap. 13.00 (1-899571-00-0, Pub. by Pulp Faction UK) AK Pr Dist.

Skin. C. E. Poverman. LC 92-9249. 279p. 1992. 19.95 (0-86538-076-7) Ontario Rev NJ.

Skin. 2nd ed. Brian C. Hamilton. 36p. (Orig.). 1995. pap. 4.00 (1-882550-15-3) Quiet Lion Pr.

Skin. 3rd ed. Ed. by W. S. Symmers & D. Weedon. (Systemic Pathology Ser.: Vol. 9). (Illus.). 1095p. 1992. text ed. 210.00 (0-443-03201-7) Churchill.

Skin: Drug Application & Evaluation of Environmental Hazards, Proceedings of the Oholo Biological Conference, 22nd, Ma'alot, March 1977. Oholo Biological Conference Staff. Ed. by J. W. Mali et al. (Current Problems in Dermatology Ser.: Vol. 7). (Illus.). 1977. 79.25 (3-8055-2797-7) S Karger.

***Skin: Sensual Tales.** Catharine Hiller. LC 97-2041. 176p. 1997. pap. 8.95 (0-7867-0435-7) Carroll & Graf.

Skin: Talking about Sex, Class & Literature. Dorothy Allison. LC 94-15071. 208p. (Orig.). 1994. pap. 14.95 (1-56341-044-3); lib. bdg. 28.95 (1-56341-045-1) Firebrand Bks.

Skin: Your Owner's Manual. William Montagna et al. (Illus.). xiii, 187p. 1990. 33.00 (88-7810-049-8) Micelle Pr.

Skin & Aging Processes. Barbara A. Gilchrest. 136p. 1984. 137.95 (0-8493-5472-2, RL73) CRC Pr.

Skin & Bones. Georges Hyvernaud. Tr. by Dominic Di Bernardi from FRE. LC 93-79808. 160p. 1994. 18.95 (1-56897-000-5) Marlboro Pr.

Skin & Bones. Thorne Smith. 24.95 (0-8488-1175-5) Amereon Ltd.

Skin & Coat Care for Cats. Lowell Ackerman. (Illus.). 192p. 1996. 29.95 (0-7938-0633-X, TS-250) TFH Pubns.

***Skin & Coat Care for Dogs.** Contrib. by Herbert Axelrod. (Cats & Dogs). (Illus.). (YA). (gr. 3 up). 1998. lib. bdg. 19.95 (0-7910-4815-2) Chelsea Hse.

Skin & Coat Care for Your Dog. Lowell Ackerman. (Illus.). 224p. 1996. 34.95 (0-7938-2099-5, TS249) TFH Pubns.

Skin & Infection: A Color Atlas & Text. Ed. by Charles V. Sanders & Lee T. Nesbitt, Jr. LC 94-26490. (Illus.). 325p. 1995. 139.00 (0-683-07539-X) Williams & Wilkins.

Skin & Its Troubles. Compiled by Health Research Staff. 88p. 1994. reprint ed. spiral bd. 8.50 (0-7873-1119-7) Hlth Research.

***Skin & Liars.** Dennis Foon. 1997. pap. text ed. 10.95 (0-88754-468-1, Pub. by Playwrights CN Pr CN) Theatre Comm.

Skin & Scuba Diving. Albert A. Tillman. (Physical Education Activities Ser.). 78p. (C). 1966. per. write for info. (0-697-07022-0) Wm C Brown Pubs.

Skin & Systemic Disease. Mark G. Lebwohl. (Illus.). 239p. 1995. text ed. 99.00 (0-443-08739-3) Churchill.

Skin Barrier: Principles of Percutaneous Absorption. H. Schaefer & T. E. Redelmeier. (Illus.). xvi, 310p. 1996. 191.50 (3-8055-6326-4) S Karger.

Skin Camouflage: A Guide to Remedial Techniques. Joyce Allsworth. (Illus.). 120p. (Orig.). 1985. pap. 39.00 (0-85950-151-5, Pub. by S Thornes Pubs UK) St Mut.

Skin Cancer. Ed. by J. A. Bishop et al. (Cancer Surveys Ser.: Vol. 26). (Illus.). 300p. (C). 1996. text ed. 80.00 (0-87969-483-1) Cold Spring Harbor.

Skin Cancer. R. A. Schwartz. (Illus.). 1005p. 1988. 120.00 (0-387-96612-9) Spr-Verlag.

Skin Cancer: Basic Science, Clinical Research, & Treatment. Ed. by C. Garbe et al. (Recent Results in Cancer Research Ser.: Vol. 139). 1995. 137.00 (0-387-57630-4) Spr-Verlag.

Skin Cancer: Mechanisms & Human Relevance. Mukhtar. 464p. 1994. 132.00 (0-8493-7358-1) CRC Pr.

***Skin Cancer & UV-Radiation.** Ed. by P. Altmeyer et al. LC 97-10068. (Illus.). 1300p. 1997. 225.00 (3-540-62723-5) Spr-Verlag.

Skin Carcinogenesis in Man & in Experimental Models. Ed. by Erich Hecker et al. LC 92-48377. (Recent Results in Cancer Research Ser.: Vol. 128). 1993. 168.00 (3-540-56321-0); 152.00 (0-387-56321-0) Spr-Verlag.

***Skin Care: Clear & Simple.** Ligaya H. Buchbinder. Ed. by Erica Orloff. LC 96-93067. 192p. (Orig.). 1997. pap. 12.95 (1-885843-05-4) Saturn Press.

Skin Care & Cosmetic Ingredients Dictionary. Natalia Michalun & M. Varinia Michalun. LC 93-33822. 328p. 1993. pap. 26.95 (1-56253-125-5) Milady Pub.

***Skin Care Book: Simple Herbal Recipes.** Kathlyn Quatrochi. LC 96-29747. 96p. 1997. pap. 10.95 (1-883010-24-1) Interweave.

***Skin Care for Cats.** Contrib. by Herbert Axelrod. (Cats & Dogs). (Illus.). (YA). (gr. 3 up). 1998. lib. bdg. 19.95 (0-7910-4807-1) Chelsea Hse.

***Skin Care in Health, Disease, Wounds, Cosmetics & Management Variations Including Products: Index of New Information.** James K. Tullar. 150p. 1997. 47.50 (0-7883-1360-6); pap. 44.50 (0-7883-1361-4) ABBE Pubs Assn.

Skin Changes & Diseases in Pregnancy. Harahap & Wallach. (Basic & Clinical Dermatology Ser.: Vol. 11). 416p. 1996. 155.00 (0-8247-9401-X) Dekker.

Skin Cleansing with Synthetic Detergents: Chemical, Ecological, & Clinical Aspects. Griesbach Conference Staff. Ed. by O. Braun-Falco & H. C. Korting. LC 92-13632. (Illus.). 264p. 1992. write for info. (3-540-55409-2); 70.95 (0-387-55409-2) Spr-Verlag.

Skin Cover in the Injured Hand. Ed. by David M. Evans. (Hand & Upper Limb Ser.: No. 9). (Illus.). 207p. 1992. text ed. 110.00 (0-443-03799-X) Churchill.

Skin Crawlers. Cathy E. Dubowski. (J). 1996. pap. 5.99 (0-679-87514-X) Random.

Skin Deep. Amanda Dewees. LC 90-55245. 110p. (Orig.). 1991. pap. 7.00 (1-56002-054-7) Aegina Pr.

***Skin Deep.** Guy Garcia. LC 96-34570. 1997. pap. 11.95 (0-520-20836-6) U CA Pr.

***Skin Deep.** John R. Gordon. 224p. (Orig.). 1997. pap. 14.95 (0-85449-246-1, Pub. by Gay Mens Pr UK) LPC InBook.

Skin Deep. Carol Gorman. LC 93-20230. (Tree House Kids Ser.: Vol. 6). (Illus.). 64p. (J). (gr. 2-4). 1993. pap. 3.99 (0-570-04747-1, 56-1766) Concordia.

Skin Deep. Carol D. Luce. 1990. mass mkt. 4.50 (1-55817-398-6, Pinncle Kensgtn) Kensgtn Pub Corp.

Skin Deep. Nora Roberts. 1995. mass mkt. 4.99 (1-55166-050-4, 1-66050-5, Mira Bks) Harlequin Bks.

Skin Deep. Lois Ruby. LC 93-13707. 224p. (YA). (gr. 7-9). 1994. 14.95 (0-590-47699-8) Scholastic Inc.

Skin Deep. Lois Ruby. (J). 1996. pap. text ed. 4.99 (0-590-47700-5) Scholastic Inc.

Skin Deep. Bob Vickery. (Orig.). 1994. mass mkt. 4.95 (1-56333-265-5, Badboy) Masquerade.

***Skin Deep.** Diana Wagman. LC 96-53362. 1997. write for info. (0-87805-982-2) U Pr of Miss.

Skin Deep. Susan Wallach. LC 89-39936. (Smart Talk Ser.). (Illus.). 128p. (J). (gr. 5-9). 1996. pap. 2.95 (0-8167-1998-5) Troll Communs.

Skin Deep. Rosemary Zarro. (Illus.). 32p. (J). 1994. 12.95 (0-8059-3552-5) Dorrance.

Skin Deep. large type ed. Hugh Miller. 293p. 1993. 25.99 (0-7505-0446-3) Ulverscroft.

Skin Deep. Timothy Hallinan. (Simeon Grist Suspense Novel Ser.). 336p. 1992. reprint ed. pap. 4.99 (0-451-40309-6, Onyx) NAL-Dutton.

Skin Deep: A Mind-Body Program for Healthy Skin. Ted A. Grossbart & Carl Sherman. LC 92-23697. 288p. 1992. pap. 14.95 (0-929173-11-2) Health Press.

Skin Deep: An A-Z of Skin, Skin Disorders, Treatments & Health. Carol A. Turkington & Jeffrey S. Dover. LC 95-10187. 404p. (YA). 1996. 40.00 (0-8160-3071-5) Facts on File.

Skin Deep: Black Women & White Women Write about Race. Ed. by Marita Golden & Susan R. Shreve. 272p. 1996. pap. 14.00 (0-385-47410-5, Anchor NY) Doubleday.

Skin Deep: Designer Clothes by God. Mary H. Kelley. (Illus.). 192p. (Orig.). 1990. pap. 10.00 (0-942971-25-6) His Way.

Skin Deep: Natural Recipes for Healthy Skin & Hair. Margaret Dinsdale. (Illus.). 128p. 1994. 27.95 (0-921820-88-7, Pub. by Camden Hse CN); pap. 15.95 (0-921820-81-X, Pub. by Camden Hse CN) Firefly Bks Ltd.

Skin Deep: Natural Treatments for Disorders, Discomforts & Diseases of the Skin. Linda Watson. LC 89-90109. 62p. (Orig.). 1989. pap. 5.00 (0-685-26156-5) L Watson.

Skin Deep: The Story of Black Models in America & Abroad. Barbara Summers. (Illus.). 452p. 1994. 35.00 (1-56743-031-7) Amistad Pr.

Skin Deep, Blood Red. Robert Skinner. 288p. 1997. 19.95 (1-57566-092-X, Knsington) Kensgtn Pub Corp.

***Skin Deep, Blood Red.** Robert Skinner. 256p. 1998. mass mkt. 5.99 (1-57566-254-X, Knsington) Kensgtn Pub Corp.

Skin Deep Is Fatal: A New Dan Kruger Detective Novel. Michael Cormany. 224p. 1992. 15.95 (1-55972-110-3, Birch Ln Pr) Carol Pub Group.

***Skin Disease: Diagnosis & Treatment.** Habif. (Illus.). 565p. (C). (gr. 13). 1998. text ed. 139.95 (0-8151-2886-X, 30735, Yr Bk Med Pubs) Mosby Yr Bk.

***Skin Disease: Diagnosis & Treatment.** Habif. (Illus.). 565p. (C). (gr. 13). 1998. text ed. 49.00 (0-8151-3762-1, 30735, Yr Bk Med Pubs) Mosby Yr Bk.

Skin Disease in Childhood & Adolescence. Elisabeth Higgins & Anthony Du Vivier. LC 95-6273. (Illus.). 256p. 1996. 125.00 (0-86542-835-2) Blackwell Sci.

Skin Diseases & Disorders Sourcebook. Ed. by Allan Cook. LC 97-6570. (Health Reference Ser.: Vol. 21). 1996. lib. bdg. 75.00 (0-7808-0080-X) Omnigraphics Inc.

Skin Diseases in the Dog & Cat. 2nd ed. D. Grant. 240p. 1995. pap. 44.95 (0-632-02935-8) Blackwell Sci.

Skin Diseases of Dogs & Cats: A Guide for Pet Owners & Professionals. Steven A. Melman et al. LC 94-94063. 250p. 1994. pap. 29.99 (0-9640295-0-2) DermaPet.

Skin Diseases of the Feet. Richard C. Gibbs. LC 96-176169. (Illus.). 238p. 1974. 27.60 (0-87527-105-7) Green.

Skin Disorders: Journal: Pediatrician, Vol. 18, No. 3, 1991. Ed. by David W. Kaplan. (Illus.). 72p. 1991. pap. 40.00 (3-8055-5460-5) S Karger.

Skin Disorders (CNS) Marcia Hill. 320p. (C). (gr. 13). 1994. text ed. 36.00 (0-8016-8055-7) Mosby Yr Bk.

Skin Endpoint Titration. 2nd ed. Richard L. Mabry. LC 93-50108. (AAOA Monographs). (Illus.). 104p. 1994. text ed. 22.00 (0-86577-525-7) Thieme Med Pubs.

Skin Flaps. Bennett. 1998. text ed. write for info. (0-7216-3414-1) Saunders.

Skin Flaps. Ed. by William C. Grabb & M. Bert Myers. LC 74-20219. 440p. 1975. 130.00 (0-316-32267-9) Little.

Skin Flicks. Philip Caveney. 512p. 1996. pap. 11.95 (0-7472-4419-7, Pub. by Headline UK) Trafalgar.

Skin for Skin. 152p. 1985. 30.00 (0-317-38811-8, Pub. by Redcliffe Pr Ltd) St Mut.

Skin for Thought: Interviews with Gilbert Tarrab on Psychology & Psychoanalysis. Didier Anzieu. 176p. 1990. pap. text ed. 30.95 (0-946439-86-9, Pub. by Karnac Bks UK) Brunner-Mazel.

Skin Game. Michael Brodin. 1990. mass mkt. 4.50 (0-8217-3214-5, Zebra Kensgtn) Kensgtn Pub Corp.

Skin Grafting. Ross Rudolph et al. 1979. 42.95 (0-316-76109-5) Little.

Skin Grafting. John W. Skouge. (Practical Manuals in Dermatologic Surgery Ser.). (Illus.). 81p. 1991. pap. text ed. 32.00 (0-443-08706-7) Churchill.

Skin, Hair & Teeth. Briget Ardley & Neil Ardley. (How Our Bodies Work Ser.). (Illus.). 48p. (J). (gr. 5-8). 1988. lib. bdg. 12.95 (0-382-09706-8) Silver Burdett Pr.

Skin Healthy: Everyone's Guide to Great Skin. Norman Levine. LC 95-9070. 184p. 1995. pap. 12.95 (0-87833-900-0) Taylor Pub.

***Skin Immune System.** 2nd ed. Ed. by Jan D. Bos. LC 96-41754. 736p. 1997. 170.00 (0-8493-4016-0) CRC Pr.

Skin Immune System (SIS) Bos. 520p. 1990. 217.00 (0-8493-4945-1, RL97) CRC Pr.

Skin in Diabetes. Ed. by J. E. Jelinek. LC 85-6901. 259p. reprint ed. pap. 73.90 (0-7837-2718-6, 2043098) Bks Demand.

Skin Langerhans (Dendritic) Cells in Virus Infections & AIDS. Ed. by Yechiel Becker. (Developments in Medical Virology Ser.). (C). 1990. lib. bdg. 172.00 (0-7923-1015-2) Kluwer Ac.

Skin Manifestations in Visceral Cancer. V. C. Andreev. (Current Problems in Dermatology Ser.: Vol. 8). (Illus.). 1978. pap. 79.25 (3-8055-2878-7) S Karger.

***Skin Manifestations of AIDS.** Neal S. Penneys. LC 89-80849. reprint ed. pap. 62.70 (0-608-04706-6, 2065427) Bks Demand.

Skin Microflora & Microbial Skin Disease. Ed. by W. C. Noble. (Illus.). 500p. (C). 1993. text ed. 110.00 (0-521-40198-4) Cambridge U Pr.

Skin of a Fish, Bones of a Bird. Helen Frost. LC 93-71217. 1993. pap. 10.00 (0-935331-15-8) Ampersand RI.

Skin of Glass. Nancy Garruba. (Illus.). 28p. (Orig.). 1989. pap. text ed. 45.00 (0-9624400-0-0); boxed 125.00 (0-9624400-1-9) Blue Hse Pr.

Skin of Our Teeth see Three Plays

Skin of Vertebrates. Ed. by R. I. Spearman & P. A. Riley. (Linnean Society Symposium Ser.: No. 9). 1981. text ed. 269.00 (0-12-656950-9) Acad Pr.

***Skin of Your Back: Sexy - Jewish - Punchy - Funny - Political.** Michael Rosen. 64p. 1996. pap. 11.95 (0-907123-66-X, Pub. by Five Leaves UK) AK Pr Dist.

Skin on My Teeth. Mike Elison. (Illus.). 75p. (Orig.). (YA). (gr. 12). Date not set. pap. 10.00 (0-9524592-3-X, Pub. by Dear Rorschach UK) AK Pr Dist.

Skin Painting Techniques & in vivo Carcinogenesis Bioassays. Ed. by F. Homburger. (Progress in Experimental Tumor Research Ser.: Vol. 26). (Illus.). vi, 314p. 1983. 176.00 (3-8055-3556-2) S Karger.

Skin Palace. Jack O'Connell. 416p. 1996. 21.95 (0-89296-547-9) Mysterious Pr.

Skin Palace. Jack O'Connell. 464p. 1996. mass mkt. 5.99 (0-446-40357-1) Warner Bks.

Skin Penetration: Hazardous Chemicals at Work. Philippe Grandjean. 220p. 1990. 71.00 (0-85066-834-4, Pub. by Tay Francis Ltd UK) Taylor & Francis.

Skin Permeability. Hans Schaefer et al. (Illus.). 360p. 1983. 115.00 (0-387-11797-0) Spr-Verlag.

Skin Pharmacology & Toxicology: Recent Advances. Ed. by Corrado L. Galli et al. LC 89-26614. (NATO ASI Series A, Life Sciences: Vol. 181). (Illus.). 326p. 1990. 95.00 (0-306-43404-0, Plenum Pr) Plenum.

Skin Problems of the Amputee. William S. Levy. LC 78-50196. (Illus.). 324p. 1983. 49.95 (0-87527-181-2) Green.

Skin, Scales, Feathers, & Fur. Mark J. Rauzon. LC 90-409858. (J). (ps-3). 1993. lib. bdg. 12.93 (0-688-10233-6) Lothrop.

Skin Sense. Gary Gweirtzman. 1993. pap. 12.95 (0-8119-0777-5) LIFETIME.

Skin Shows: Gothic Horror & the Technology of Monsters. Judith Halberstam. LC 95-948. (Illus.). 240p. 1995. text ed. 45.95 (0-8223-1651-X); pap. text ed. 15.95 (0-8223-1663-3) Duke.

Skin Shows: The Art of Tattoo. Chris Wroblewski. (Illus.). 118p. 1991. pap. 19.95 (0-86369-272-9, Pub. by W H Allen UK) Carol Pub Group.

Skin Shows II: The Art of Tattoo. Chris Wroblewski. (Illus.). 130p. pap. 19.95 (0-86369-517-5, Pub. by W H Allen UK) Carol Pub Group.

***Skin Shows III: The Art of Tattoo.** Chris Wroblewski. pap. 19.95 (0-86369-677-5, Pub. by W H Allen UK) Carol Pub Group.

Skin Shows IV. Chris Wroblewski. (Illus.). 112p. (Orig.). 1996. pap. 21.95 (0-86369-948-0, Pub. by Virgin Pub UK) London Brdge.

Skin Signs of Systemic Disease. 3rd ed. Irwin M. Braverman. Ed. by Judy Fletcher. LC 96-6572. (Illus.). 704p. 1997. text ed. write for info. (0-7216-3745-0) Saunders.

***Skin Substitute Production by Tissue Engineering.** Mahmoud Rouabhia. (Medical Intelligence Unit Ser.). 214p. 1997. 89.95 (1-57059-447-3) R G Landes.

Skin Surgery. Marwali Harahap. (Illus.). 1032p. 1985. 125.00 (0-87527-317-3) Green.

Skin, Teeth, & Hair. Anna Sandeman. LC 96-12646. (Body Bks.). (Illus.). 32p. (J). (gr. k-3). 1996. lib. bdg. 14.40 (0-7613-0489-4, Copper Beech Bks) Millbrook Pr.

Skin Therapy. Ed. by Ronald Marks & W. J. Cunliffe. 1994. 29.95 (1-85317-137-9, M Dunitz) Scovill Paterson.

Skin Tight. Carl Hiaasen. (Florida Mysteries Ser.). 1990. mass mkt. 6.99 (0-449-21941-0) Fawcett.

Skin Tight. large type ed. Carl Hiaasen. 24.95 (0-7838-1648-0, GK Hall) Thorndike Pr.

Skin Tight Orbit. Elaine Lee et al. 52p. 1995. pap. 9.95 (1-56163-118-3, Amerotica) NBM.

Skin Tight Orbit. deluxe ed. Elaine Lee et al. 52p. 1995. 45.00 (1-56163-119-1, Amerotica) NBM.

Skin Tight Orbit, 2. Elaine Lee et al. 52p. 1995. pap. 10.95 (1-56163-132-9, Amerotica) NBM.

Skin Tight Orbit, Vol. 2. Elaine Lee et al. 52p. 1995. 50.00 (1-56163-137-X, Amerotica) NBM.

Skin Trade. Ann DuCille. LC 96-16061. 240p. 1996. 29.95 (0-674-81081-3) HUP.

Skin Trade. Ann DuCille. 240p. 1996. pap. 16.95 (0-674-81084-8) HUP.

Skin Trades. Bruce Boston. (Booklet Ser.: No. 31). 64p. 1988. pap. text ed. 3.50 (0-936055-39-1) C Drumm Bks.

***Skin Tumors: Experimental & Clinical Aspects.** Ed. by Claudio J. Conti et al. LC 88-26435. (Carcinogenesis - a Comprehensive Survey Ser.: Vol. 11). 407p. 1989. reprint ed. pap. 116.00 (0-608-03399-5, 2064096) Bks Demand.

Skin Tumors of the Dog & Cat. M. H. Goldschmidt & F. Shofer. (Illus.). 232p. 1992. text ed. 105.00 (0-08-040823-0, Pergamon Pr) Elsevier.

Skin Wise: A Guide to Healthy Skin for Women. Ed. by Annette Callan. (Illus.). 208p. (C). 1996. pap. 22.95 (0-19-553745-9) OUP.

Skinflick. Joseph Hansen. LC 79-11077. 208p. 1980. pap. 5.95 (0-8050-0197-2, Owl) H Holt & Co.

Skinhead. Jay Bennett. 192p. 1992. mass mkt. 4.50 (0-449-70397-5, Juniper) Fawcett.

Skinhead. Jay Bennett. LC 90-13087. 144p. (YA). (gr. 7-12). 1991. lib. bdg. 22.70 (0-531-11001-X) Watts.

Skinhead. Nick Night. (Illus.). 86p. pap. 13.95 (0-7119-0052-3, OP 41599) Omnibus NY.

Skinhead International. ADL. 1995. pap. 7.50 (0-88464-166-X) ADL.

***Skinhead Nation.** George Marshall. 156p. 1996. pap. 26.95 (1-898927-45-6, Pub. by S T Pubng UK) AK Pr Dist.

Skinhead Street Gangs. Loren Christensen. (Illus.). 240p. 1993. pap. 20.00 (0-87364-756-4) Paladin Pr.

Skinheads Shaved for Battle: A Cultural History of American Skinheads. Jack Moore. LC 93-70440. (Illus.). 200p. 1993. 37.95 (0-87972-582-6); pap. 14.95 (0-87972-583-4) Bowling Green Univ Popular Press.

Skink. Ed. by Bruce Glassman. LC 94-28249. (What on Earth Is...? Ser.). 32p. (J). (gr. 2-5). 1994. lib. bdg. 14.95 (1-56711-096-7) Blackbirch.

Skinks. J. Walls. (Illus.). 1995. pap. text ed. 9.95 (0-7938-0257-1, RE111) TFH Pubns.

***Skinks.** large type ed. Erik Stoops. Ed. by Graphic Arts & Production Staff. (Young Explorer Series I: Vol. 3). (Illus.). 32p. (J). (gr. 3-7). 1997. lib. bdg. 12.95 (1-890475-02-5) Faulkners Pub.

Skinned: Activists Condemn the Horrors of the Fur Trade. John A. Livingston et al. 256p. (Orig.). (C). 1989. pap. text ed. 6.95 (0-685-26109-3) Intl Wildlife.

Skinned Alive. Edmund White. 272p. 1996. pap. 12.00 (0-679-75475-X) Random.

Skinned Alive: Stories. Edmund White. 1995. 23.00 (0-679-43476-3) Knopf.

Skinner Untitled # 2. Skinner. (J). Date not set. 14.00 (0-689-80556-X) S&S Childrens.

Skinner's Directory, 1992-1993. R. Walsh. 1992. per. 112.00 (1-879346-09-5) Walkers Research.

Skinner's Rules. Quintin Jardine. LC 94-419. 320p. 1994. 21.95 (0-312-11066-9, Thomas Dunne Bks) St Martin.

Skinner's Trail. Quintin Jardine. 320p. 1996. 22.95 (0-312-14417-2) St Martin.

An Asterisk (*) at the beginning of an entry indicates that the title is appearing in BIP for the first time.

Skinny. Robert Burch. LC 89-28225. (Brown Thrasher Bks.). 128p. (J). (gr. 4-6). 1990. reprint ed. 19.95 (*0-8203-1223-1*) U of Ga Pr.

Skinny Angel. Thelma Jones. 1970. 6.95 (*0-87018-035-5*) Ross.

Skinny Annie Blues. Neal Barrett, Jr. 256p. 1996. 21.95 (*1-57566-058-X*, Knsington) Kensgtn Pub Corp.

***Skinny Annie Blues.** Neal Barrett, Jr. 304p. 1997. mass mkt. 5.50 (*1-57566-134-9*, Knsington) Kensgtn Pub Corp.

Skinny Chicken: Over One Hundred Low-Fat High-Taste Ways to Make Chicken Absolutely Delicious. Erica L. Klein. LC 94-8528. (Skinny Cookbook Ser.). 200p. (Orig.). 1994. pap. 12.95 (*0-940625-84-9*) Surrey Bks.

Skinny Comfort Foods: Over 100 Easy, Low-Fat Recipes for the Foods You Remember: Chicken & Dumplings, Macaroni & Cheese, Meatloaf, Crispy Fries, Boston Cream Pie & Lots More. Sue Spitler. LC 96-24480. (Skinny Cookbook Ser.). 170p. 1996. pap. 12.95 (*1-57284-006-4*) Surrey Bks.

Skinny Dipping. Marian F. White. 1996. pap. 10.95 (*0-921881-39-8*, Pub. by Gynergy-Ragweed CN) LPC InBook.

Skinny-Dipping: And Other Immersions in Water, Myth & Being Human. Janet Lembke. LC 94-15378. 192p. 1994. 21.95 (*1-55821-274-4*) Lyons & Burford.

Skinny Dynamite & Other Short Stories. Jack Micheline. Ed. by A. D. Winans. LC 79-63969. 96p. (Orig.). 1980. pap. 10.00 (*0-915016-27-3*) Second Coming.

Skinny Italian Cooking. Ruth Glick & Nancy Baggett. LC 96-1578. (Skinny Cookbook Ser.). 205p. 1996. pap. 12.95 (*0-940625-98-9*) Surrey Bks.

Skinny Legs & All. Tom Robbins et al. 432p. 1995. reprint ed. pap. 10.95 (*0-553-37788-4*) Bantam.

Skinny Malinky Leads the War for Kidness. Stanley Kiesel. 176p. (J). (gr. 7 up). 1985. pap. 2.50 (*0-380-69875-7*, Flare) Avon.

Skinny Man. James Colbert. 224p. 1991. text ed. 18.95 (*0-689-12098-2*, Atheneum S&S) S&S Trade.

***Skinny Mexican Cooking.** Sue Spitler. (Skinny Cooking Ser.). 162p. (Orig.). 1996. pap. 12.95 (*0-614-30916-6*) Surrey Bks.

Skinny Mexican Cooking Vol. 16: Over 100 Low-Fat, Easy, Delicious Recipes from Nachos & Tamales to Chicken Mole, Snapper Vera Cruz & Caramel Flan. Sue Spitler. (Skinny Cookbook Ser.: No. 16). 155p. (Orig.). 1996. pap. 12.95 (*0-940625-97-0*) Surrey Bks.

Skinny One - Pot Meals: Over 100 Delicious, Easy to Make Main Dishes, Soups, & Salads. 2nd rev. ed. Ruth Glick. (Skinny Cookbook Ser.). 205p. 1997. pap. 12.95 (*1-57284-003-X*) Surrey Bks.

Skinny Pasta: Over 100 Delicious & Low-Fat Ways to Prepare & Embellish Pasta from Angel Hair to Ziti. 2nd ed. Sue Spitler. LC 96-32650. (Skinny Cookbook Ser.). 176p. 1996. pap. 12.95 (*1-57284-008-0*) Surrey Bks.

Skinny Pizzas: Over 100 Low-Fat, Easy to Make Delicious Pizzas from the Traditional Roman Pizza to Trendy California-Style Dishes. 2nd ed. Barbara Grunes. LC 95-49904. (Skinny Cookbook Ser.). 176p. 1996. reprint ed. pap. 12.95 (*1-57284-002-1*) Surrey Bks.

Skinny Scotty: The Adventurous Life of Rosa Ellen Scott. June E. Bussard. (Illus.). 200p. (Orig.). 1996. pap. 10.95 (*0-9652014-0-6*) J&J Books.

Skinny Soups: Over 100 Healthy, Low-Fat, Nutrition-Rich, Calorie Wise Soups. 2nd ed. Ruth Glick & Nancy Baggett. LC 97-16863. (Skinny Cookbook Ser.). 260p. 1997. pap. 12.95 (*1-57284-004-8*) Surrey Bks.

Skinny Vegetarian Entrees: Over 100 Delicious, Low-Fat, Quick & Easy Meatless Main Dishes from Soups, Stews, Casseroles & Ethnic Specialties to Bean, Grain & Dairy Delights. 2nd ed. Phyllis Magida & Sue Spitler. LC 96-24481. (Skinny Cookbook Ser.). (Illus.). 205p. 1996. pap. 12.95 (*1-57284-007-2*) Surrey Bks.

Skinnybones. Barbara Park. LC 81-20791. 128p. (J). (gr. 3-6). 1982. lib. bdg. 13.99 (*0-394-94988-9*) Knopf Bks Yng Read.

***Skinnybones.** Barbara Park. (J). 1997. pap. 3.99 (*0-679-88792-X*, Bullseye Bks) Random Bks Yng Read.

Skinnybones. Anne Spencer. Ed. by J. Friedland & R. Kessler. (Novel-Ties Ser.). 1992. student ed., pap. text ed. 15.95 (*0-88122-723-4*) Lrn Links.

Skinnybones. large type ed. Barbara Park. 1993. 30.50 (*0-614-09855-6*, L-34135-00) Am Printing Hse.

Skinnybones. Barbara Park. LC 81-20791. 112p. (J). (gr. 3-6). 1989. reprint ed. pap. 3.99 (*0-394-82596-9*) Knopf Bks Yng Read.

***Skinrolling.** Jerry Harvey. Date not set. write for info. (*0-688-04845-5*) Morrow.

Skins. Adrian C. Louis. 304p. 1995. 23.00 (*0-517-79958-8*, Crown) Crown Pub Group.

Skins. Gavin Watson. (Illus.). 128p. (Orig.). 1994. pap. 19.95 (*1-898927-05-7*, Pub. by S T Pubng UK) AK Pr Dist.

Skins & Bones. Paula G. Allen. 69p. (Orig.). 1988. pap. 8.95 (*0-931122-50-3*) West End.

***Skins & Grins: The Plight of the Black American Golfer.** Lenwood Robinson, Jr. (Illus.). 144p. (Orig.). 1997. pap. write for info. (*1-886094-67-5*) Chicago Spectrum.

Skins of Possible Lives. Renee Gregorio. (Illus.). 120p. (Orig.). 1994. pap. text ed. 9.00 (*1-883968-05-4*) Blinking Yellow.

Skinwalkers. Tony Hillerman. 320p. 1990. mass mkt. 5.99 (*0-06-100017-5*, Harp PBks) HarpC.

Skip. Mark Dunster. LC 74-281770. (Rin Ser.: Pt. 27). 1973. 4.00 (*0-89642-033-7*) Linden Pubs.

Skip. Alex N. Holland. (Illus.). 12p. (J). (gr. 1-3). 1992. pap. 6.95 (*1-895583-02-0*) MAYA Pubs.

Skip-a-Star: The Legend of the Christmas Snow. 2nd ed. Carolyn Graves. (Skip-a-Star Ser.: Bk. 1). (J). (gr. 2-4). 1993. reprint ed. digital audio 5.00 (*1-882716-04-3*) PAVE.

Skip-a-Star: The Legend of the Christmas Snow. 2nd ed. Carolyn E. Graves. (Skip-a-Star Ser.: Bk. 1). (Illus.). 32p. (J). (gr. 2-4). 1993. reprint ed. Set, audio cass. & bk. pap. text ed. 9.95 incl. digital audio (*1-882716-03-5*); reprint ed. Bk. pap. text ed. 4.95 (*1-882716-05-1*) PAVE.

Skip Across the Ocean: Nursery Rhymes from Around the World. Illus. by Sheila Moxley. LC 94-48739. 48p. (J). (ps-1). 1996. 15.95 (*0-531-09455-3*) Orchard Bks Watts.

Skip Bombing in Rabaul Harbor. James T. Murphy. LC 92-43434. 200p. 1993. text ed. 49.95 (*0-275-94540-5*, C4540, Praeger Pubs) Greenwood.

Skip Count Song. Rozanne L. Williams. (Emergent Reader Bks.). (Illus.). 8p. (Orig.). (J). (gr. k-2). 1995. pap. 1.59 (*0-916119-99-8*) Creat Teach Pr.

Skip Count Song. Rozanne L. Williams. (Emergent Reader Big Bks.). (Illus.). 8p. (Orig.). (J). (gr. k-2). 1996. pap. 7.98 (*1-57471-103-2*) Creat Teach Pr.

***Skipped Parts.** Tim Sandlin. LC 96-41566. 400p. 1997. pap. 12.00 (*1-57322-601-7*, Riverhd Trade) Berkley Pub.

Skipper: Confessions of a Fighter Squadron Commander. T. H. Winters. (Illus.). 160p. 1986. 16.95 (*0-912173-07-6*) Champlin Museum.

Skipper & Jade: A Love Story. Beverly Hoffman. LC 90-71859. 44p. (J). 1991. pap. 6.95 (*1-55523-411-9*) Winston-Derek.

***Skipper Secrets.** Martin Luray & M. Badham. Date not set. write for info. (*0-688-11010-X*) Hearst Bks.

Skipper's Birthday Surprise. (Favorite Sound Story Bks.). (Illus.). 24p. (J). 1995. bds. 9.95 (*0-307-70908-6*, Golden Pr) Western Pub.

Skipper's Safe Boating Course. US Coast Guard Auxiliary national Board Staff. 160p. (gr. 13). 1996. pap. text ed. 13.95 (*0-8151-4589-6*) Mosby Yr Bk.

Skipping a Beat. Carolyn Keene. (Nancy Drew Files Ser.: No. 117). (J). 1996. mass mkt. 3.99 (*0-671-56875-2*) PB.

Skipping a Grade Can Be Fun. Francine Cristel. 1984. pap. 5.00 (*0-89824-037-9*) Trillium Pr.

Skipping School. Jessie Haas. LC 91-37642. (J). (gr. 6-12). 1992. 14.00 (*0-688-10179-8*) Greenwillow.

Skipping Stones. Ed. by Dianne M. Henderson et al. Date not set. write for info. (*1-889463-07-8*) Golden Apple.

Skipping Stones: Ripple Effects of Mental Illness on the Family. Mona Wasow. LC 94-69598. 224p. 1995. pap. 16.95 (*0-8314-0082-X*) Sci & Behavior.

***Skipping Stones Through the Cosmos.** Robin Stiles. 72p. 1997. pap. 9.95 (*0-9654753-1-X*) Circle of Vsns.

Skippy Peanut Butter Birthday Party Book. Brokaw. 1993. pap. 5.00 (*0-671-88649-5*, Fireside) S&S Trade.

***Skippy Peanut Butter Cookbook.** Best Foods Staff. Date not set. write for info. (*0-688-12891-2*) Morrow.

Skippy Squirrel's Balloon Journey to the Land of Zogg. Andrew L. Traynor. (Illus.). (Orig.). (J). (gr. 3-5). 1996. pap. 12.95 (*0-533-11683-X*) Vantage.

Skiriki. Ed Calandro. Ed. by Carolyn Moore. 386p. 1994. 22.00 (*1-884520-02-2*); pap. write for info. (*1-884520-03-0*) Pierpont Pubng.

Skirmish Wargaming. Dale R. Ridder. 130p. (Orig.). 1995. pap. write for info. (*1-57502-034-3*) Morris Pubng.

Skirmishes. Catherine Hayes. 1983. pap. 5.25 (*0-8222-1037-1*) Dramatists Play.

***Skirmishes at the Edge of the Empire: The United States & International Terrorism.** David Tucker. LC 96-41391. 240p. 1997. text ed. 55.00 (*0-275-95762-4*, Praeger Pubs) Greenwood.

Skirt. Soto Gary. 80p. (J). (gr. 4-7). 1994. pap. 3.50 (*0-440-40924-1*) Dell.

Skirt. Duncan Searl. Ed. by J. Friedland & R. Kessler. (Novel-Ties Ser.). 1995. student ed., pap. text ed. 15.95 (*1-56982-277-8*) Lrn Links.

Skirt. large type ed. Gary Soto. (Illus.). 1995. pap. 21.00 (*0-614-09609-X*, L-34792-00) Am Printing Hse.

Skirt Tag: You're It. Juliet Freefoam, pseud. (Adult Poetry Ser.). (Illus.). 96p. (Orig.). 1987. pap. 6.95 (*0-915199-05-X*) Pen-Dec.

Skirted Garden: Nineteen Seventy to Nineteen Ninety. Bea Nettles. (Illus.). 80p. (Orig.). 1990. pap. 5.00 (*0-930810-04-X*) Inky Pr.

Skirting the Issue: Essays in Literary Theory. Mary Lydon. LC 94-27062. 1995. 48.00 (*0-299-14460-7*); pap. 24.95 (*0-299-14464-X*) U of Wis Pr.

Skirts. Mimi Albert. 259p. 1994. 19.00 (*1-880909-13-8*) Baskerville.

Skirts. Akbar Del Piombo. (Orig.). 1993. mass mkt. 4.95 (*1-56333-115-2*) Masquerade.

Skirts & More Skirts. Fiora Gandolfi. (Twentieth Century-Histories of Fashion Ser.). (Illus.). 143p. 1996. 29.95 (*0-89676-212-2*, Costume & Fashion Pr) QSMG Ltd.

Skirts & Pants Patterns: Minott Method. 4th ed. Jan Minott. 183p. 1992. pap. 17.00 (*0-9633880-5-3*) Minott Method.

Skis Against the Atom: The Exciting, First Hand Account of Heroism & Daring Sabotage During the Nazi Occupation of Norway. rev. ed. Knut Haukelid. LC 89-62268. (Illus.). 254p. 1989. reprint ed. pap. 11.95 (*0-942323-07-6*) N Amer Heritage Pr.

Skit Book: One Hundred & One Skits from Kids. Margaret R. MacDonald. LC 89-29654. 152p. (J). (gr. 1-9). 1990. pap. 16.50 (*0-208-02283-X*, Linnet Bks); lib. bdg. 25.00 (*0-208-02258-9*, Linnet Bks) Shoe String.

Skitch. Mark Dunster. 50p. (Orig.). 1982. pap. 4.00 (*0-89642-092-2*) Linden Pubs.

Skit'omatic. Compiled by Judith Roth. 128p. 1991. teacher ed., pap. 14.99 (*0-8307-1686-6*) Gospel Lght.

Skitops: Ski Tour Operators Association Annual Business Survey 1996. Charles R. Goeldner. 30p. 1994. pap. text ed. 25.00 (*0-89478-072-7*) U CO Busn Res Div.

Skits, 2 vols., Set. 8.95 (*0-685-61260-0*) Young Life.

Skits for Children. Sheila M. Kitchens. (Illus.). 1996. 11.95 (*1-887750-21-5*) Rutledge Bks.

Skits for Seniors Only. Jane L. Reynolds. 20p. 1980. The Yellow Book. write for info. (*0-932320-06-6*); The Green Book. write for info. (*0-932320-07-4*); The Orange Book. write for info. (*0-932320-05-8*) Solar Studio.

Skits for the Young in Heart. Clay Franklin. 1977. pap. 3.00 (*0-686-38386-9*) Eldridge Pub.

Skits in English. Mary E. Hines. (Illus.). 121p. (gr. 9-12). 1987. pap. text ed. 8.00 (*0-13-812397-1*, 18854); audio 74.00 (*0-13-812421-3*, 58855) Prentice ESL.

Skitterbrain. Irene B. Brown. LC 78-18349. (Sunflower Editions Ser.). 128p. (J). (gr. 4 up). 1992. reprint ed. pap. 6.95 (*0-936085-21-5*) Blue Heron OR.

SkiWriter II. write for info. (*0-318-58255-4*) P-H.

Skizze der Geschichte und Geographie Arabiens Von den Altesten Zeiten Bis Zum Propheten Muhammad. Eduard Glaser. 575p. 1976. reprint ed. write for info. (*3-487-05858-8*) G Olms Pubs.

Sklansky on Poker. 2nd ed. David Sklansky. 215p. 1994. pap. text ed. 29.95 (*1-880685-06-X*) Two Plus NV.

Sklaven in Den Rollen Von Dienern und Vertrauten Bei Euripides. Herwig Brandt. (Altertumswissenschaftliche Texte und Studien: No. 1). iv, 148p. 1973. 30.00 (*3-487-04777-2*) G Olms Pubs.

***Skoda Heavy Guns: 24cm Cannon, 38cm Howitzer, 42cm Howitzer & Others.** Michal Prasil. 144p. 1997. pap. 19.95 (*0-7643-0288-4*) Schiffer.

Skolni Rusko-Cesky Slovnik. Kopeckij. 1152p. (CZE & RUS.). 1983. 35.00 (*0-8288-1082-6*, M 14014) Fr & Eur.

Skolt Lapp Community Suenjelsijd During the Year 1938. Karl Nickul. LC 77-87728. (Acta Lapponica Ser.: 5). (Illus.). 160p. 1983. reprint ed. 79.50 (*0-404-16504-4*) AMS Pr.

***Skookum.** Shannon Applegate. 1996. 22.95 (*1-884961-09-6*) LEO Prods.

Skookum Sam - Spar Tree Man. Heather Kellerhals-Stewart. (Illus.). 24p. (J). (gr. 1-4). 1992. 7.95 (*0-919591-16-7*, Pub. by Polestar Bk Pubs CN) Orca Bk Pubs.

***Skorba.** D. H. Trump. (Illus.). 1966. 10.00 (*0-85431-202-1*, Pub. by Soc Antiquaries UK) David Brown.

Skoryi v Peterburg. Sergei Iur'enen. (Orig.). 1990. pap. 15.95 (*0-87501-071-7*) Ardis Pubs.

***Skorzeny's Special Missions: The Memoirs of the Most Dangerous Man in Europe.** Otto Skorzeny. LC 97-15642. 1997. write for info. (*1-85367-291-2*, Pub. by Greenhill Bks UK) Stackpole.

Skottowe Manuscript: Volumes I & II. Ed. by Tim Bonyhady. 190p. 1989. 385.00 (*0-7103-0362-9*, A3936) Routledge Chapman & Hall.

***Skowhegan, ME.** P. Dickey. (Images of America Ser.). 1997. pap. 16.99 (*0-7524-0568-3*, Arcdia) Chalford.

Skowhegan on the Kennebec (Maine), Vol. I. Louise H. Coburn. (Illus.). 460p. 1993. reprint ed. lib. bdg. 46.00 (*0-8328-2954-4*) Higginson Bk Co.

Skowhegan on the Kennebec (Maine), Vol. II. Louise H. Coburn. (Illus.). 590p. 1993. reprint ed. lib. bdg. 59.00 (*0-8328-2955-2*) Higginson Bk Co.

***Skrabble Dictionary for Losers.** 96p. 1996. pap. 7.00 (*1-887317-11-2*) Bad Dog Pr.

Skriker. Caryl Churchill. LC 94-17131. 64p. (Orig.). 1994. pap. 9.95 (*1-55936-097-6*) Theatre Comm.

Skruggs & Friends. Glen Hausladen. (Illus.). 100p. (Orig.). 1986. pap. 3.95 (*0-9617130-0-3*) Hausladen Pub.

SKS Carbine. Steve Kehaya & Joe Poyer. (For Collectors Only Ser.). (Illus.). 151p. (Orig.). 1997. pap. 16.95 (*1-882391-14-4*) N Cape Pubns.

Skua & Penguin: Predator & Prey. Euan Young. (Studies in Polar Research). (Illus.). 450p. (C). 1994. text ed. 105.00 (*0-521-32251-0*) Cambridge U Pr.

Skuas. Robert W. Furness. 336p. 1990. text ed. 37.00 (*0-85661-046-1*, 784646, Pub. by Poyser UK) Acad Pr.

***Skuas & Jaegers.** Klaus M. Olsen. 1997. 35.00 (*0-300-07269-4*) Yale U Pr.

Skulking Way of War. Patrick M. Malone. 1991. 29.95 (*0-8191-8067-X*) Madison Bks UPA.

Skulking Way of War: Technology & Tactics among the New England Indians. Patrick M. Malone. LC 92-22740. (Illus.). 160p. 1993. reprint ed. pap. 13.95 (*0-8018-4554-8*) Johns Hopkins.

Skull & Cross Bones. Tom McNamara. 1995. pap. 10.95 (*0-9625632-7-7*) NUVENTURES Pub.

Skull & Dog Bones. Melissa Cleary. (Orig.). 1994. mass mkt. 4.99 (*0-425-14541-7*) Berkley Pub.

Skull Base Surgery: Anatomy, Biology, & Technology. Ed. by Ivo P. Janecka & Klaus Tiedemann. 432p. 1996. text ed. 150.00 (*0-397-51716-5*) Lppncott-Raven.

Skull Base Surgery: Anatomy, Diagnosis & Treatment. Ed. by Madjid Samii. (Illus.). xx, 1276p. 1994. 574.00 (*3-8055-5967-4*) S Karger.

Skull Base Surgery Update: Update I: Proceedings of the First Congress of the European Skull Base Society, Held in Riva del Garda, Italy, September 25-30, 1993. European Skull Base Society Staff. Ed. by A. Mazzoni & Mario Sanna. LC 94-46322. (Illus.). xii, 504p. 1995. pap. text ed. 162.50 (*90-6299-115-7*, Pub. by Kugler NE) Kugler Pubns.

Skull Beneath the Skin. P. D. James. 432p. 1988. mass mkt. 6.50 (*0-446-35372-8*) Warner Bks.

Skull Beneath the Skin: The Achievement of John Webster. Charles R. Forker. LC 85-26144. (Illus.). 626p. (C). 1986. text ed. 49.95 (*0-8093-1279-4*) S Ill U Pr.

Skull Fractures: Medical Research Subject Analysis with Bibliography. Harriet D. Jakhovsky. LC 84-45733. 150p. 1986. 37.50 (*0-88164-244-4*); pap. 29.50 (*0-88164-245-2*) ABBE Pubs Assn.

Skull in Salop & Other Poems. Geoffrey Grigson. LC 68-8309. 6900. 15.95 (*0-8023-1183-0*) Dufour.

Skull Juices. Doug Blazek. (Orig.). 1970. pap. 8.00 (*0-912136-22-7*) Twowindows Pr.

***Skull Measurer's Mistake: And Other Portraits of Men & Women Who Spoke Out Against Racism.** Sven Lindqvist. LC 96-40902. 1997. write for info. (*1-56584-363-0*) New Press NY.

***Skull of Charlotte Corday, & Other Stories.** Leslie Dick. LC 97-2204. 1997. 22.00 (*0-684-83439-1*, Scribners PB Fict) S&S Trade.

Skull of Sinanthropus Pekinensis. Franz Weidenreich. (Paleontologia Sinica Ser.). (Illus.). 1943. pap. 25.00 (*0-934454-88-4*) Lubrecht & Cramer.

Skull of "Sinanthropus Pekinensis" A Comparative Study on a Primitive Hominid Skull. Franz Weidenreich. LC 77-86450. (China. Geological Survey. Palaeontologia Sinica. New Ser. D.: No. 10. Whole Ser. No. 127). (Illus.). reprint ed. 59.00 (*0-404-16693-8*) AMS Pr.

Skull of Swift. Shane Leslie. LC 79-169767. (Select Bibliographies Reprint Ser.). 1977. reprint ed. 26.95 (*0-8369-5987-6*) Ayer.

***Skull of Truth.** Bruce Coville. LC 97-9264. (Illus.). (J). 1997. write for info. (*0-15-275457-1*) HarBrace.

***Skull Sessions, 3 vols.** Prod. by Fire Pubns., Inc. Staff. Incl. Vol. I. . (Illus.). 100p. 1980. 40.00 (*0-614-29657-9*, 35185); Vol. II. . (Illus.). 100p. 1986. 40.00 (*0-614-29658-7*, 35287); Vol. III. . (Illus.). 100p. 1996. 40.00 (*0-614-29659-5*, 35938); 110.00 (*0-614-29753-2*, 35710) Fire Pubns.

***Skull Sessions.** Daniel Hecht. 1998. pap. write for info. (*0-670-87661-5*) Viking Penguin.

Skull, Spine & Contents: Part 1: Procedures & Indications. Ed. by H. J. Kaufmann. (Progress in Pediatric Radiology Ser.: Vol. 5). 300p. 1976. 103.25 (*3-8055-1382-8*) S Karger.

Skull, Spine & Contents: Part 2: Clinical Aspects. Ed. by H. J. Kaufmann. (Progress in Pediatric Radiology Ser.: Vol. 6). (Illus.). 1977. 129.00 (*3-8055-2337-8*) S Karger.

Skull, Vol. 1: Development. Ed. by James Hanken & Brian K. Hall. (Illus.). 608p. (C). 1993. pap. text ed. 37.50 (*0-226-31567-3*); lib. bdg. 82.50 (*0-226-31566-5*) U Ch Pr.

Skull, Vol. 2: Patterns of Structural & Systematic Diversity. Ed. by James Hanken & Brian K. Hall. (Illus.). 592p. (C). 1993. pap. text ed. 34.95 (*0-226-31570-3*); lib. bdg. 82.50 (*0-226-31568-1*) U Ch Pr.

Skull, Vol. 3: Functional & Evolutionary Mechanisms. Ed. by James Hanken & Brian K. Hall. (Illus.). 468p. (C). 1993. pap. text ed. 29.95 (*0-226-31573-8*) U Ch Pr.

Skull, Vol. 3: Functional & Evolutionary Mechanisms. Ed. by James Hanken & Brian K. Hall. (Illus.). 480p. (C). 1993. lib. bdg. 77.00 (*0-226-31571-1*) U Ch Pr.

Skull Worship. Connie Fox. 64p. 1988. 14.95 (*0-930090-37-3*); pap. 6.95 (*0-930090-38-1*); 20.00 (*0-930090-36-5*) Applezaba.

Skullcaps n Switchblades. David B. Lazerson. (Illus.). 204p. (C). 1988. 14.95 (*0-935063-30-7*, Bristol Rhein) CIS Comm.

Skulls & Bones: A Guide to the Skeletal Structures & Behavior of North American Mammals. Glenn Searfoss. LC 94-26504. (Illus.). 1995. pap. 19.95 (*0-8117-2571-5*) Stackpole.

Skulls Are Forever: A Book of Secret Truths. Mary H. Nash. (Illus.). (Orig.). 1986. pap. 12.95 (*0-9618893-0-6*) Ichthys VA.

Skulpturen vom 5. Jahrhundert bis in die Roemische zeit see Kerameikos: Ergebnisse der Ausgrabungen (Deutsches Archaeologisches Institut)

Skungpoomery. Ken Campbell. 47p. (J). 1988. pap. 5.95 (*0-413-33910-6*, A0263, Pub. by Methuen UK) Heinemann.

Skunk. Ed. by Lynn Saul & Ellen Basso. 113p. 1995. pap. 9.95 (*1-884106-03-X*) Jumping Cholla.

S.K.U.N.K. & the Ozone Conspiracy. Margrit Cruickshank. 235p. (YA). 1990. pap. 8.95 (*1-85371-067-9*, Pub. by Poolbeg Pr IE) Dufour.

Skunk at Hemlock Circle. Victoria Sherrow. LC 93-35511. (Illus.). 32p. (J). (ps-2). 1994. 19.95 incl. audio (*1-56899-047-2*); audio write for info. (*1-56899-045-6*) Soundprints.

Skunk at Hemlock Circle. Victoria Sherrow. LC 93-35511. (Illus.). 32p. (J). (ps-2). 1994. 15.95 (*1-56899-031-6*) Soundprints.

Skunk at Hemlock Circle, Incl. toy. Victoria Sherrow. LC 93-35511. (Illus.). 32p. (J). (ps-2). 1994. 32.95 (*1-56899-046-4*) Soundprints.

Skunk at Hemlock Circle: Mini-Sized Book. Victoria Sherrow. LC 93-35511. (Illus.). 32p. (J). (ps-2). 1994. 4.95 (*1-56899-032-4*) Soundprints.

Skunk at Hemlock Circle: Mini-Sized Book, Incl. toy. Victoria Sherrow. LC 93-35511. (Illus.). 32p. (J). (ps-2). 1994. 12.95 (*1-56899-048-0*) Soundprints.

Skunk Camp Promises. Tom Peters. 1987. 9.95 (*0-317-56480-3*) Knopf.

Skunk in the House. Constance T. Colby. 1976. 18.95 (*0-8488-0967-X*) Amereon Ltd.

Skunk Missal see NEA Series

Skunk River Anthology. Gene Olson. (Illus.). 166p. 1992. pap. 9.95 (*1-878488-59-7*) Quixote Pr IA.

Skunk Works. Ben R. Rich & Leo Janos. 1996. pap. 13.95 (*0-316-74300-3*) Little.

Skunk Works: A Personal Memoir from the U-2 to the Stealth Fighter. Ben R. Rich & Leo Janos. LC 94-8732. (Illus.). 416p. 1994. 24.95 (*0-316-74330-5*) Little.

***Skunked Again!** Peter Rehnberg. (Illus.). 96p. 1996. pap. 7.95 (*0-9654253-0-4*, C-101) Osprey Isl.

Skunks. Wyatt Blassingame. 1981. pap. text ed. 8.95 (*0-396-07909-1*) WC Stone PMA.

Skunks. Emilie U. Lepthien. LC 93-3410. (New True Bks.). (Illus.). 48p. (J). (gr. k-4). 1993. pap. 5.50 (*0-516-41197-7*); lib. bdg. 19.00 (*0-516-01197-9*) Childrens.

S

An Asterisk (*) at the beginning of an entry indicates that the title is appearing in BIP for the first time.

Skunks. Lynn M. Stone. (North American Animal Discovery Library). (Illus.). 24p. (J). (gr. k-5). 1990. lib. bdg. 11.94 (0-86593-046-5); lib. bdg. 8.95 (0-685-36341-4) Rourke Corp.

Skunks & Their Relatives. Timothy L. Biel. (Zoobooks Ser.). 24p. (J). (gr. 1-7). 1995. 13.95 (1-888153-03-2) Wildlife Educ.

Skunks & Their Relatives. Timothy L. Biel. (Zoobooks Ser.). (Illus.). 24p. (J). (gr. 3 up). 1996. lib. bdg. 14.95 (0-88682-779-5) Creative Ed.

Skunks & Their Relatives. Wildlife Education, Ltd. Staff. (Illus.). 20p. (Orig.). 1985. pap. 2.75 (0-937934-38-0) Wildlife Educ.

Skunk's Surprise: (A Modern Fable for Language Arts & Science Education in Grades K-6) Flora Joy. (Storytelling in Education Funbooks Ser.). (Illus.). 48p. (Orig.). 1994. pap. text ed. 7.00 (1-884624-01-4) Intl Storytelling.

Skunny Wundy: Seneca Indian Tales. Arthur C. Parker. (Iroquois & Their Neighbors Ser.). (Illus.). 224p. (C). 1994. reprint ed. pap. 14.95 (0-8156-0292-8) Syracuse U Pr.

Skutarevsky. Leonid M. Leonov. Tr. by Alec Brown. LC 76-135250. 444p. 1971. reprint ed. text ed. 79.50 (0-8371-5170-8, LESK, Greenwood Pr) Greenwood.

Skutky Tela. Vladimir Uhri. 50p. (Orig.). (SLO.). 1996. pap. 2.40 (1-56983-027-4) New Creat WI.

Sky. (World of Knowledge Ser.). (Illus.). 48p. (J). (gr. 1-6). 1995. text ed. 8.95 (1-56144-610-6) Modern Pub NYC.

Sky. Blaise Cendrars. (Illus.). 307p. 1994. 22.95 (1-56924-960-1) Marlowe & Co.

Sky. Blaise Cendrars. 307p. 1996. pap. 12.95 (1-56924-767-6) Marlowe & Co.

Sky. Deirdre Purcell. 1997. pap. 5.99 (0-451-19089-0, Sig) NAL-Dutton.

Sky: A True Story of Resistance During World War II. Hanneke Ippisch. LC 95-44065. 128p. (YA). (gr. 6 up). 1996. 17.00 (0-689-80508-X) S&S Childrens.

Sky: A User's Guide. Ed. by David H. Levy. (Illus.). 300p. (C). 1991. text ed. 34.95 (0-521-39112-1) Cambridge U Pr.

Sky: A User's Guide. David H. Levy. (Illus.). 313p. (C). 1993. pap. text ed. 17.95 (0-521-45958-3) Cambridge U Pr.

Sky: Air & Wind. Jean-Pierre Verdet. Date not set. 5.95 (0-944589-33-2) Young Discovery Lib.

Sky: All about Planets, Stars, Galaxies, Eclipses & More. David Alley. (Illus.). 32p. (J). 1993. pap. 5.95 (1-895688-04-3, Pub. by Greey dePencier CN) Firefly Bks Ltd.

Sky: Mystery, Magic, & Myth. Jean-Pierre Verdet. Tr. by Anthony Zielonka. (Discoveries Ser.). (Illus.). 200p. 1992. pap. 12.95 (0-8109-2873-6) Abrams.

Sky: Stars & Night. Jean-Pierre Verdat. Tr. by Vicki Bogard from FRE. LC 90-50776. (Young Discovery Library). (Illus.). 38p. (J). (gr. k-5). 1991. 5.95 (0-944589-32-4, 324) Young Discovery Lib.

Sky: Sun & Day. Jean-Pierre Verdet. Date not set. 5.95 (0-944589-31-6) Young Discovery Lib.

Sky above Earth Below. Joanna Cotler. LC 89-26743. (Charlotte Zolotow Bk). (Illus.). 32p. (J). (ps). 1990. 14.95 (0-06-021365-5) HarpC Child Bks.

Sky Above Us. Kate Petty. (Around & About Ser.). (Illus.). 32p. (J). (gr. 2-4). 1993. pap. 5.95 (0-8120-1234-8) Barron.

***Sky Adventures.** James Palmieri. Ed. by Maggie Palmieri. (Illus.). 260p. (Orig.). 1996. pap. 14.99 (1-57502-268-0, P0955) Morris Pubng.

Sky & Earth. (Child's First Library of Learning). (Illus.). 88p. (J). (gr. 1-4). 1990. 14.95 (0-8094-4837-8) Time-Life.

Sky & Earth. (Child's First Library of Learning). (Illus.). 88p. (J). (ps-3). 1990. lib. bdg. 21.27 (0-8094-4838-6) Time-Life.

Sky & Island Light. Brendan Galvin. 64p. 1996. pap. 9.95 (0-8071-2109-6); text ed. 16.95 (0-8071-2108-8) La State U Pr.

Sky & Telescope Monthly Star Charts: 24 All-Sky Charts for Star Watchers Worldwide. George Lovi. 56p. 1994. spiral bd. 24.95 (0-933346-69-7) Sky Pub.

Sky & Water in Pastel. (Leisure Arts Ser.: No. 21). (Illus.). 32p. pap. 4.95 (0-85532-531-3, 531-3, Pub. by Search Pr UK) A Schwartz & Co.

Sky & Weather. Alan Ward. LC 92-369. (Project Science Ser.). 32p. (J). 1993. lib. bdg. 20.00 (0-531-14176-4) Watts.

Sky at Ashland. Michael Anania. 80p. (Orig.). 1986. pap. 7.95 (0-918825-32-6) Moyer Bell.

Sky at Night Ten. Patrick Moore. LC 92-36620. 182p. (Orig.). 1993. pap. text ed. 19.95 (0-471-93763-0) Wiley.

Sky Atlas for Small Telescopes & Binoculars: The Beginners Guide to Successful Deep Sky Observing. David S. Chandler & Billie E. Chandler. (Illus.). 24p. (Orig.). 1996. pap. 17.95 (0-9613207-2-9) D Chandler.

Sky Atlas 2000.0 Companion. Robert A. Strong. 221p. 1994. spiral bd. 24.95 (0-9644393-0-1) R A Strong.

Sky Atlas 2000.0 Deluxe. Wil Tirion. 1981. spiral bd. 44.95 (0-933346-33-6) Sky Pub.

Sky Atlas 2000.0 Desk: Black Stars on White Background. Wil Tirion. (Illus.). 1981. 24.95 (0-933346-31-X) Sky Pub.

Sky Atlas 2000.0 Field: White Stars on Black Background. Wil Tirion. (Illus.). 1981. 24.95 (0-933346-32-8) Sky Pub.

Sky Babies. Judy Delton. (Pee Wee Scouts Ser.: No. 15). 96p. (J). (ps-3). 1991. mass mkt. 3.99 (0-440-40530-0, YB BDD) BDD Bks Young Read.

Sky Battles Sky Warriors: Stories of Exciting Air Combat. Alfred Price. (Illus.). 384p. 1996. pap. 19.95 (1-85409-335-5, Pub. by Arms & Armour UK) Sterling.

Sky Bear. Cami Berg. (Illus.). 40p. (J). (ps up). 1994. 15.95 (1-879244-87-X) Windom Bks.

***Sky Behind the Forest: Selected Poems.** Liliana Ursu. 96p. 1996. pap. 16.95 (1-85224-386-4, Pub. by Bloodaxe Bks UK) Dufour.

***Sky Below.** Ned Condini. 1997. mass mkt. 4.99 (1-55197-369-3, Pub. by Comnwlth Pub CN) Partners Pubs Grp.

***Sky Below: 18 Paintings by Gregory Amenoff.** Gregory Amenoff. LC 97-19467. (Illus.). 1997. 39.95 (1-889097-06-3) Hard Pr MA.

Sky Blew Blue. Cora Brooks. LC 87-60700. 80p. (C). 1987. pap. text ed. 4.95 (0-934678-13-8) New Victoria Pubs.

Sky Blue. Alexander M. Grace. (Association of the U. S. Army Book Ser.). 256p. 1995. 21.95 (1-57488-019-5) Brasseys Inc.

Sky Blue Frame. Franklin W. Dixon. (Hardy Boys Ser.: No. 89). 160p. (Orig.). (J). (gr. 3-6). pap. 3.99 (0-671-64974-4, Minstrel Bks) PB.

Sky Blue, Grass Green. Susan Kropa. 128p. (J). (gr. 1-3). 1986. student ed. 12.99 (0-86653-355-9, GA 698) Good Apple.

***Sky Break: Nebesen Sriv - Poems.** L. I. Levchev et al. LC 97-7225. (BUL & ENG.). 1997. pap. write for info. (1-57889-034-9) Passeggiata.

Sky Break: Poems by Lyubomir Levchev. limited ed. Lyubomir Levchev. 60p. 1995. 95.00 (0-9646958-1-2) Griffis Art Ctr.

Sky Bridges & Other Poems: Reading Level 1-3 & Above. Ruth Radin. LC 92-46291. 1993. 3.50 (0-88336-038-1); audio 9.95 (0-88336-620-7) New Readers.

Sky Burial: An Eyewitness Account of China's Brutal Crackdown in Tibet. Blake Kerr. LC 92-51080. 206p. 1993. 21.95 (1-879360-26-8) Noble Pr.

Sky Burial: An Eyewitness Account of China's Brutal Crackdown in Tibet. Blake Kerr. LC 92-51080. 1994. pap. 12.95 (1-879360-27-6) Noble Pr.

Sky Catalogue 2000, Vol. 1. 2nd ed. Alan Hirshfeld et al. 704p. 1991. 59.95 (0-933346-64-6); pap. 39.95 (0-933346-63-8) Sky Pub.

Sky Catalogue 2000, Vol. 2. Ed. by Roger W. Sinnott & Alan Hirshfeld. 448p. 1983. 54.95 (0-933346-39-5) Sky Pub.

Sky Catalogue 2000.0 Vol. 1: Stars to Magnitude 8.0. 2nd ed. Alan Hirshfeld et al. 702p. (C). 1991. text ed. 69.95 (0-521-41743-0); pap. text ed. 47.95 (0-521-42736-3) Cambridge U Pr.

Sky Catalogue 2000.0 Vol. 2: Galaxies, Double & Variable Stars, & Star Clusters. Alan Hirshfeld & Roger W. Sinnott. LC 81-17975. 512p. (C). 1985. Vol. 2, 1985. pap. text ed. 39.95 (0-521-27721-3) Cambridge U Pr.

Sky Changes: A Novel. Raji Narasimhan. 1991. 8.00 (81-7018-664-1, Pub. by BR Pub II) S Asia.

Sky Clears: Poetry of the American Indians. A. Grove Day. LC 83-1576. 204p. 1983. text ed. 59.75 (0-313-23883-9, Greenwood Pr) Greenwood.

Sky Clears: Poetry of the American Indians. A. Grove Day. LC 65-38538. xiv, 204p. (C). 1964. reprint ed. pap. 7.95 (0-8032-5047-9, DASK, Bison Books) U of Nebr Pr.

Sky Cops. Richard Rosenthal. Ed. by Eric Tobias. 384p. (Orig.). 1994. mass mkt. 5.50 (0-671-79516-3) PB.

***Sky Daddy.** Canaan Parker. 220p. (Orig.). 1997. pap. 9.95 (1-55583-398-5) Alyson Pubns.

Sky Dancer. Jack Bushnell. (Illus.). 1996. lib. bdg. 15.93 (0-688-05289-4) Lothrop.

Sky Dancer. Jack Bushnell. (Illus.). (J). 1996. 16.00 (0-688-05288-6) Lothrop.

Sky Dancer: The Secret Life & Songs of the Lady Yeshe Tsogyel. Keith Dowman. (Illus.). 28p. (Orig.). 1996. reprint ed. pap. 18.95 (1-55939-065-4) Snow Lion Pubns.

Sky Dancers: The Amazing World of North American Birds. Diane Swanson. LC 95-4920. (Illus.). 84p. (J). 1995. pap. 4.95 (0-89658-319-8) Voyageur Pr.

Sky Determines: An Interpretation of the Southwest. Ross Calvin. LC 48-6466. (Illus.). 350p. 1993. reprint ed. pap. 13.95 (0-944383-19-X) High-Lonesome.

Sky Diggers: Aces of the R.A.A.F. Stanley Brogden. 1944. 15.00 (0-913076-02-3) Beachcomber Bks.

***Sky Diving-to the Extreme-'Chute Roll.** LC 96-38593. (Short Cuts Ser.). (J). 1997. pap. 3.99 (0-8499-3953-4) Tommy Nelson.

Sky Dogs. Jane Yolen. LC 89-26960. (Illus.). 32p. (J). (ps-3). 1990. 16.00 (0-15-275480-6) HarBrace.

Sky Dogs. Jane Yolen. LC 89-26960. 32p. (J). (ps-3). 1995. pap. 5.00 (0-15-200776-8, Voyager Bks) HarBrace.

Sky Dogs. deluxe limited ed. Jane Yolen. LC 89-26960. (Illus.). 32p. (J). (ps-3). 1990. 100.00 (0-15-275481-4) HarBrace.

***Sky Dragon Chronicles: The Sound of Unheard Voices. Aaron Braswell. LC 97-91593. 200p. (Orig.). 1997. pap. 14.95 (0-9656730-0-6) Dragons Dream.**
SKY DRAGON CHRONICLES: THE SOUND OF UNHEARD VOICES is a collection of sobering stories from an eclectic blend of young authors. These writers offer unique perspectives on some of societies most relevant issues, ranging from rape to drug addiction. The reader is immediately enthralled by the startling realism of these writings, able to see the truth, free from the embellishment, prejudices or personal politics of a second-hand source. 2/3 of this book was written by Aaron Braswell, & as the twenty-one year old owner of Dragon's Dream Publishing, he is the youngest publisher in the country. Yet, every writer in this collection shines with a blinding light. These writers are not passive participants of their world, but real people who lived every line of these powerful pages, & though the stories seem tragic at times, each Sky Dragon writer "rises above" this tragedy & emerges with a renewed sense of hope. The authors range in age from 16 to 25. Read the book that was born of truth, to warn others of the wild wicked winds that sometimes blow through every life, & how to "rise above" these troubles with the Sky Dragon style. To order: Dragon's Dream Publishing, 341-11 S. College Rd., Suite 232, Wilmington, NC 28403. ***Publisher Provided Annotation.***

Sky Drift. David Dunn. LC 80-80806. (Illus.). 90p. 1979. 13.50 (0-939044-27-7) Lingua Pr.

Sky Edge: Mountaintop Meditations. W. Phillip Keller. LC 92-16139. (Illus.). 208p. 1992. reprint ed. pap. 10.99 (0-8254-3052-6) Kregel.

Sky Fighters of France: Aerial Warfare, Nineteen Fourteen to Nineteen Eighteen. Henry Farre. Ed. by James B. Gilbert. Tr. by Catharine Rush. LC 79-7252. (Flight: Its First Seventy-Five Years Ser.). (Illus.). 1980. reprint ed. lib. bdg. 21.95 (0-405-12164-4) Ayer.

Sky Fisherman. Craig Lesley. LC 94-47493. 320p. 1995. 22.95 (0-395-67724-6, Marc Jaffe Bk) HM.

Sky Fisherman. Leslie. LC 96-16227. 304p. 1996. pap. 13.00 (0-312-14738-4) St Martin.

Sky Full of Babies. R. Thompson. (Illus.). 24p. (J). (ps-8). 1987. 12.95 (0-920303-93-5, Pub. by Annick CN); pap. 4.95 (0-920303-92-7, Pub. by Annick CN) Firefly Bks Ltd.

Sky Full of Kites. Osmond Molarsky. LC 95-41082. (Illus.). 32p. (J). (gr. k-2). 1996. 12.95 (1-883672-26-0) Tricycle Pr.

***Sky Ghost.** Mack Maloney. 384p. 1997. mass mkt. 4.99 (0-7860-0452-5, Pinncle Kensgtn) Kensgtn Pub Corp.

Sky Giants of the Brass Stair. Thomas Kane. Ed. by John D. Ruemmler. (Shadow World Ser.). (Illus.). 64p. (Orig.). (C). 1990. pap. 12.00 (1-55806-089-8, 6012) Iron Crown Ent Inc.

Sky Giants over Japan. Chester Marshall. (Illus.). 214p. (Orig.). 1984. pap. 12.95 (0-942397-15-0) Buckeye Aviat Bk.

Sky Giants over Japan. Chester Marshall. (Illus.). 220p. (Orig.). 1994. 15.50 (1-885353-00-6) Global Press.

Sky Goes on Forever. Molly MacGregor. 165p. Date not set. pap. 5.95 (0-929929-00-4) MM Pr.

Sky Hangs Low. Jens Rosing. Tr. by Naomi J. Groves. 60p. 1986. 14.95 (0-920806-86-4, Pub. by Penumbra Pr CN) U of Toronto Pr.

Sky High. Franklin W. Dixon. (Hardy Boys Casefiles Ser.: No. 113). (YA). (gr. 6 up). 1996. mass mkt. 3.99 (0-671-50454-1) PB.

Sky High Faith. Ken Gaub. 176p. (Orig.). 1995. pap. 9.95 (0-89221-295-0) New Leaf.

***Sky-High Hopes: Coloring & Puzzle Book.** Alexandra Reid. (Sky Dancer Ser.). (Illus.). 64p. (J). (ps up). 1996. 4.95 (0-694-00941-5, Festival) HarpC Child Bks.

***Sky-High Love.** Winfield Blackwell. Ed. by Jane Kelly. x, 86p. 1996. reprint ed. write for info. (0-9621194-1-5) Stratford NC.

Sky Hooks & Track Shoes. Gruber. Date not set. pap. 12.95 (0-931790-86-7) Brick Hse Pub.

Sky in Mayan Literature. Anthony F. Aveni. 320p. 1992. 48.00 (0-19-506844-0) OUP.

Sky in Narrow Streets. Dannie Abse. (QRL Poetry Bks.: Vol. XXVII). (WEL.). 1987. 35.00 (0-614-06419-8) Quarterly Rev.

Sky in Silver Lace. R. Klein. 184p. (J). (gr. 5-7). 1996. 13.99 (0-670-86266-5) Viking Child Bks.

Sky in Silver Lace. Robin Klein. (J). 1996. pap. 13.99 (0-670-86692-X) Viking Penguin.

Sky Is a Long Way to Jump! Poem Exchange by City & Suburban Kids. City & Suburban Kids Staff. Ed. by Mary N. Woodrich. (Illus.). 60p. (Orig.). (J). (gr. 3-6). 1995. pap. 8.00 (0-913678-29-5) New Day Pr.

Sky Is Always in the Sky. Karla Kuskin. LC 95-45275. (Illus.). (J). 1997. write for info. (0-06-027083-7); lib. bdg. write for info. (0-06-027084-5) HarpC.

***Sky Is Blue.** Lorna Read. (Illus.). 12p. (J). (ps). 1997. bds. 3.98 (1-85854-559-5) Brimax Bks.

Sky Is Blue with Clouds Like Fishbones. Michelle Mee. (Storybridge Ser.). 64p. (J). (gr. 1-4). 1995. pap. 9.95 (0-7022-2707-2, Pub. by Univ Queensland Pr AT) Intl Spec Bk.

Sky Is Falling. Barbara Corcoran. 192p. (J). 1990. pap. 2.95 (0-380-70837-X, Camelot) Avon.

***Sky Is Falling.** Miles. LC 97-17351. (J). 1998. mass mkt. 3.99 (0-689-81791-6) S&S Childrens.

Sky Is Falling. Kit Pearson. 256p. (J). (gr. 5-9). 1995. pap. 3.99 (0-14-037652-6) Puffin Bks.

Sky Is Falling: Understanding & Coping with Phobias, Panic & Obsessive-Compulsive Disorders. Raeann Dumont. 352p. 1995. 25.00 (0-393-03848-3) Norton.

***Sky Is Falling: Understanding & Coping with Phobias, Panic & Obsessive-Compulsive Disorders.** Raeann Dumont. 320p. (C). 1997. pap. 13.00 (0-393-31603-3) Norton.

Sky Is Falling! Why Buildings Fail. Marvin Hornstein. LC 82-72602. (Illus.). 120p. (Orig.). 1982. pap. 7.95 (0-89708-106-4) And Bks.

Sky Is Full of Stars. Franklyn M. Branley. LC 81-43037. (Let's-Read-&-Find-Out Science Bk.). (Illus.). 40p. (J). (gr. k-3). 1981. lib. bdg. 14.89 (0-690-04123-3, Crowell Jr Bks) HarpC Child Bks.

Sky Is Full of Stars. Franklyn M. Branley. LC 81-43037. (Trophy Let's Read-&-Find-Out Science Bk.). (Illus.). 40p. (J). (gr. k-3). 1983. pap. 4.95 (0-06-445002-3, Trophy) HarpC Child Bks.

Sky Is Home. 2nd ed. John C. McCollister. LC 96-5562. 1996. 15.00 (0-8246-0386-9) Jonathan David.

Sky Is My Tipi. Ed. by Mody C. Boatright. LC 49-1690. (Texas Folklore Society Publications: No. 22). (Illus.). 243p. 1966. reprint ed. 13.95 (0-87074-010-5) UNTX Pr.

Sky Is Not So Far Away. Margaret Hillert. LC 92-83167. (Illus.). 32p. 1996. 15.95 (1-56397-223-9) Boyds Mills Pr.

***Sky Is Not the Limit: Breakthrough Leadership.** Robert Barthelemy. 200p. (Orig.). 1997. pap. 17.95 (1-57444-106-X) St Lucie Pr.

Sky Is Red. Giuseppe Berto. Tr. by Angus Davidson from ITA. LC 76-138575. 397p. 1971. reprint ed. text ed. 75.00 (0-8371-5774-9, BESR, Greenwood Pr) Greenwood.

Sky Island. L. Frank Baum. (Illus.). 288p. (J). (gr. 3 up). 1988. 24.95 (0-929605-02-0); pap. 12.95 (0-929605-01-2) Books Wonder.

Sky-Jam! Edward Packard. (Choose Your Own Adventure Ser.: No. 158). 128p. (J). (gr. 4-7). 1995. pap. 3.50 (0-553-56623-7) Bantam.

Sky Juice & Flying Fish: Traditional Caribbean Cooking. Jessica B. Harris. (Illus.). 256p. (Orig.). 1991. pap. 12.95 (0-671-68165-6, Fireside) S&S Trade.

***Sky Kings: Black Pioneers of Professional Basketball.** Bijan Bayne. LC 96-38708. (African-American Experience Ser.). 1997. lib. bdg. write for info. (0-531-11308-6) Watts.

***Sky Knife.** Sands. LC 97-14292. 1997. 22.95 (0-312-86126-5) St Martin.

Sky Legends of Vietnam. Lynette D. Vuong. LC 92-38345. (Illus.). 96p. (J). (gr. 4 up). 1993. lib. bdg. 13.89 (0-06-023001-0) HarpC Child Bks.

Sky-Liners. Louis L'Amour. 208p. 1982. pap. 3.99 (0-553-27687-5) Bantam.

Sky-Liners. large type ed. Louis L'Amour. (Special Ser.). 264p. 1993. reprint ed. 18.95 (1-56054-650-6) Thorndike Pr.

Sky Lord. Emma Harrington. 368p. 1994. mass mkt. 4.99 (0-06-108203-1) HarpC.

Sky Man. Stacie Johnson. (Eighteen Pine Street Ser.: No. 5). 160p. (YA). 1993. 3.50 (0-553-29723-6) Bantam.

Sky Masters. Dale Brown. 496p. 1992. mass mkt. 6.99 (0-425-13262-5) Berkley Pub.

Sky My Kid! Dictionnaire de l'Anglais Branche. Jean-Loup Chiflet. 153p. (FRE.). 1993. pap. 12.95 (0-7859-7628-0, 2020159945) Fr & Eur.

***Sky My Kingdom.** Hanna Reitsch. LC 97-5033. 1997. pap. write for info. (1-85367-262-9, Pub. by Greenhill Bks UK) Stackpole.

Sky Never Changes: Testimonies from the Guatemalan Labor Movement. Thomas F. Reed & Karen Brandow. (ILR Press Book). (Illus.). 200p. 1996. 35.00 (0-87546-354-1); pap. 14.95 (0-87546-355-X) Cornell U Pr.

Sky Observer's Guide. rev. ed. R. Newton Mayall et al. (Golden Guide Ser.). (Illus.). (YA). (gr. 9 up). 1985. pap. 5.50 (0-307-24009-6, Golden Pr) Western Pub.

Sky Observer's Guidebook. Charles E. Roth. (Phalarope Bk.). (Illus.). 256p. 1986. 17.95 (0-13-812793-X) P-H.

Sky of Now. Chaim Potok. (J). 1995. write for info. (0-679-96021-X) Random.

Sky of Scattered Roads: Poems, Essays & Short Stories. Louis D. Scalzetto. LC 92-93371. 46p. (Orig.). 1993. pap. 6.50 (1-879008-02-5) L D Scalzetto.

Sky of the Heart: Jewels of Wisdom from Nityananda. M. U. Hatengdi & Swami Chetanananda. 209p. (Orig.). 1996. pap. 14.95 (0-915801-63-9) Rudra Pr.

Sky on Fire: The First Battle of Britain, 1917-1918. Raymond H. Fredette. LC 90-45774. (History of Aviation Ser.). (Illus.). 304p. (Orig.). (C). 1991. reprint ed. pap. 17.95 (1-56098-016-8) Smithsonian.

***Sky Open Again.** Gian Lombardo. 80p. (Orig.). 1997. pap. 10.00 (0-940475-92-8) Dolphin-Moon.

Sky over El Nido. C. M. Mayo. LC 95-9961. 176p. 1995. 22.95 (0-8203-1766-7) U of Ga Pr.

Sky People. John Emery. LC 87-26525. 357p. 1988. 18.95 (0-939149-10-9) Soho Press.

Sky People. Jack Nisbet. LC 84-61542. (Illus.). 128p. (Orig.). 1984. 12.95 (0-931849-00-4); pap. 5.95 (0-931849-01-2) Quartzite Bks.

***Sky People: A History of Parachuting.** Peter Hearn. 1997. pap. 26.95 (1-85310-869-3) Specialty Pr.

Sky Phantom. Carolyn Keene. (Nancy Drew Ser.: Vol. 53). 180p. (gr. 3-7). 1975. 5.95 (0-448-09553-X, G&D) Putnam Pub Group.

Sky Phenomena: A Guide to Naked-eye Observation of the Stars: with Sections on Poetry in Astronomy, Constellation Mythology, & the Southern Hemisphere Sky. Norman Davidson. LC 92-43572. (Renewal of Education Ser.). 1993. pap. 19.95 (0-940262-56-8) Lindisfarne Bks.

Sky Pilot see Thomas Skyler: Foothills Preacher

Sky Pilot, a Tale of the Foothills. Ralph Connor. 1976. lib. bdg. 14.25 (0-89968-019-4, Lghtyr Pr) Buccaneer Bks.

Sky Pilot in No Man's Land. Ralph Connor. 1976. lib. bdg. 15.75 (0-89968-018-6, Lghtyr Pr) Buccaneer Bks.

Sky Pilot in No Man's Land. Ralph Connor. 1976. 16.95 (0-8488-1270-0) Amereon Ltd.

Sky Pilot, Tale of the Foothills. Ralph Connor. 1976. 15.95 (0-8488-1271-9) Amereon Ltd.

***Sky Pioneer: A Photobiography of Amelia Earhart.** Corrine Szabo. LC 96-32763. (J). 1997. write for info. (0-7922-3737-4) Natl Geog.

An Asterisk (*) at the beginning of an entry indicates that the title is appearing in BIP for the first time.

Sky Pioneering: Arizona in Aviation History. Ruth M. Reinhold. LC 81-11514. (Illus.). 232p. 1982. 32.00 (*0-8165-0737-6*); pap. 16.95 (*0-8165-0757-0*) U of Ariz Pr.

Sky Pirates! Dave Stone. (Dr. Who New Adventures Ser.). 1995. mass mkt. 5.95 (*0-426-20446-8*, Pub. by Virgin Pub UK) London Brdge.

***Sky Pirates & Other Tales.** (Indiana Jones Roleplaying Game Ser.). 15.00 (*0-87431-437-2*, 45015) West End Games.

Sky Point & Vivane: An Earthdawn Campaign Set. FASA Staff. (EarthDawn Ser.). (Illus.). 1995. boxed, pap. 25.00 (*1-55560-268-1*, 6108) FASA Corp.

Sky Pond. Marta Knobloch. LC 92-50362. 64p. 1992. pap. 9.95 (*0-930526-18-X*) SCOP Pubns.

Sky Ranch: The Denton Years. Melvin E. Brewer. 250p. (Orig.). 1996. pap. 9.95 (*0-9643885-4-5*) Personal Profiles.

Sky Ranch Engineering Manual. John Schwaner. 516p. 19. 95 (*0-614-13194-4*, 21-13049) EAA Aviation.

Sky River. Nan Hannon. Ed. by Tom Trusky. LC 89-80860. (Ahsahta Press Modern & Contemporary Poets of the West Ser.). 50p. (Orig.). 1991. pap. 6.95 (*0-916272-42-7*) Ahsahta Pr.

Sky Sash So Blue. Hathorn. LC 96-53144. (J). 1998. 17.00 (*0-689-81090-3*) S&S Childrens.

Sky Scanner. 2nd ed. Eppler Nowell. (Illus.). 17p. (Orig.). 1980. pap. text ed. 4.95 (*0-9611454-0-4*) E Nowell.

Sky Scrape, City Scape: Poems of City Life. Jane Yolen. LC 92-61940. 32p. (J). 1996. 15.95 (*1-56397-179-8*, Wordsong) Boyds Mills Pr.

Sky, Sea, Birds, Trees, Earth, House, Beast. 2nd ed. Kenneth Rexroth. LC 76-134750. (Illus.). 30p. 1973. 17. 50 (*0-87775-044-0*); pap. 7.95 (*0-87775-048-3*) Unicorn Pr.

Sky Songs. Myra C. Livingston. LC 83-12955. (Illus.). 32p. (J). (ps-4). 1984. lib. bdg. 14.95 (*0-8234-0502-8*) Holiday.

Sky Spirit: The American Bald Eagle. Michael Furtman. (Illus.). 144p. 1994. 29.95 (*1-55971-428-X*); pap. 19.95 (*1-55971-429-8*) NorthWord.

Sky Storming Yankee: Life of Glenn Curtis. Clara Studer. LC 76-169438. (Literature & History of Aviation Ser.). 1972. reprint ed. 29.95 (*0-405-03780-5*) Ayer.

***Sky Strike! Great U. S. Combat Aircraft.** Windrow & Greene Staff. 1997. 29.95 (*1-85915-054-3*, Pub. by Windrow & Green UK) Motorbooks Intl.

***Sky Surfing.** Pat Ryan. LC 97-11337. (Extreme Sports Ser.). (J). 1998. write for info. (*1-56065-537-2*) Capstone Pr.

Sky Surveys: Protostars to Protogalaxies. Ed. by B. T. Soifer. (ASP Conference Series Proceedings: Vol. 43). 314p. 1993. 28.00 (*0-937707-62-7*) Astron Soc Pacific.

***Sky, the Stars, & the Wilderness.** Bass. 1997. 23.00 (*0-395-71758-2*) HM.

***Sky, The Stars, The Wilderness.** Rick Bass. LC 97-24379. 1997. write for info. (*0-395-77015-7*) HM.

Sky Their Battlefield: The Complete List of Allied Air Casualties from Enemy Action in WWI. Trevor Henshaw. (Illus.). 416p. 1995. 69.95 (*1-898697-30-2*, Pub. by Grub St Pubns UK) Seven Hills Bk.

Sky Tonight: A Guided Tour of the Stars over Hawai'i. Sam Rhoads. 1994. spiral bd. 29.95 (*0-930897-75-7*) Bishop Mus.

Sky Tree: Seeing Science Through Art. Thomas Locker. LC 94-38342. (Illus.). 40p. (J). (gr. k-4). 1995. 15.95 (*0-06-024883-1*); lib. bdg. 15.89 (*0-06-024884-X*) HarpC Child Bks.

Sky Trillium. Julian May. LC 96-19001. 1997. pap. 12.95 (*0-345-38000-2*) Ballantine.

***Sky Warriors.** Cody Grant. 804p. (Orig.). 1997. mass mkt. 5.99 (*1-55237-058-5*, Pub. by Comnwlth Pub CN) Partners Pubs Grp.

Sky Was Blue. Charlotte Zolotow. LC 62-13328. (Charlotte Zolotow Bk.). (Illus.). (J). (gr. k-3). 1963. lib. bdg. 14.89 (*0-06-027001-2*) HarpC Child Bks.

Sky Watcher's Handbook: The Expert Reference Source for the Non-Professional Astronomer. Ed. by James Muirden. LC 92-32996. 1995. text ed. write for info. (*0-7167-4502-X*) W H Freeman.

Sky with Its Mouth Wide Open. Rocco Scotellaro. 1975. pap. 3.00 (*0-88031-024-3*) Invisible-Red Hill.

Sky Woman: Legends of the Iroquois. Joanne Shenandoah-Tek-Ya-Wha-Wha et al. LC 96-32488. (Illus.). 128p. (J). (gr. 3-12). 1997. 14.95 (*0-940666-99-5*) Clear Light.

Sky Words. Marilyn Singer. LC 92-3765. (Illus.). 32p. (J). (gr. k-3). 1994. lib. bdg. 14.95 (*0-02-782882-4*, Mac Bks Young Read) S&S Childrens.

Skyblue's Essays. Dallas Wiebe. (Fiction Ser.). 160p. (Orig.). 1995. pap. 8.95 (*1-886224-02-1*) Burning Deck.

Skyblue's Essays. limited ed. Dallas Wiebe. (Fiction Ser.). 160p. (Orig.). 1995. pap. 15.00 (*1-886224-03-X*) Burning Deck.

Skybowl. Melanie Rawn. (Dragon Star Ser.: Bk. 3). 776p. 1994. mass mkt. 6.99 (*0-88677-595-7*) DAW Bks.

Skybusters. Campbell Morris. 40p. (gr. 4-6). 1995. pap. 2.99 (*0-590-22285-6*) Scholastic Inc.

Skydancing. Manley Fredlund. (Illus.). 174p. (Orig.). 1990. pap. 14.95 (*0-88839-252-4*) Hancock House.

***Skydark.** 1997. mass mkt. 5.50 (*0-373-62536-7*, 1-62536-7, Wrldwide Lib) Harlequin Bks.

Skydive! Gary Paulsen. (World of Adventure Ser.: No. 11). 80p. (J). (gr. 3-7). 1996. mass mkt. 3.99 (*0-440-41049-5*, YB BDD) BDD Bks Young Read.

Skydiver Driver. 2nd ed. Mike Fischer. 265p. (Orig.). 1994. pap. 14.95 (*0-9639984-4-7*) Eastern Dakota.

Skydiving. Christopher Meeks. (Action Sports Ser.). 48p. (J). (gr. 3-4). 1991. lib. bdg. 17.80 (*1-56065-051-6*) Capstone Pr.

Skydiving: A Dictionary for the Sport Parachutist. Bill FitzSimons. LC 90-84620. (Illus.). 96p. (Orig.). 1990. reprint ed. pap. 7.95 (*1-878177-01-X*) Bandit Bks.

Skydiving Logbook Program: Computerized Jump Record. Gary Peek. 1992. 14.95 incl. disk (*0-915516-89-6*, PR-204) Para Pub.

Skydiving on Christopher Street. Stan Leventhal. (Orig.). 1995. mass mkt. 6.95 (*1-56333-287-6*, Hard Candy) Masquerade.

Skye. Lauran Paine. 192p. 1987. pap. 2.75 (*0-380-70186-3*) Avon.

Skye: The Island. James Hunter. (Illus.). 192p. 1996. pap. 29.95 (*1-85158-827-2*, Pub. by Mnstream UK) Trafalgar.

Skye & North West Highlands Walks. Ordnance Survey Pathfinder Guild Staff. 1996. pap. text ed. 16.95 (*0-7117-0850-9*, Pub. by Jarrold Pub UK) Seven Hills Bk.

Skye Lakota. Krista Janssen. 1996. pap. 5.99 (*0-671-51908-5*) S&S Trade.

***Skye Legacy.** Krista Janssen. 1997. mass mkt. 5.99 (*0-671-00217-1*) PB.

Skye O'Malley. Bertrice Small. 1984. mass mkt. 4.99 (*0-345-32364-5*) Ballantine.

Skye Terrier Champions, 1952-1987. Camino E. E. & Bk. Co. Staff. 175p. 1989. pap. 36.95 (*0-940808-92-7*) Camino E E & Bk.

Skye's West, No. 8. Richard S. Wheeler. (Orig.). 1994. pap. 4.99 (*0-8125-2144-7*) Forge NYC.

Skyfire. Frank Asch. LC 88-3193. (Illus.). 32p. (J). (ps-2). 1988. pap. 4.95 (*0-671-66861-7*, Litl Simon S&S) S&S Childrens.

Skyfire. Mack Maloney. (Wingman Ser.: No. 8). (gr. k). 1990. mass mkt. 3.95 (*0-8217-3121-1*, Zebra Kensgtn) Kensgtn Pub Corp.

Skyguide. Mark R. Chartrand. LC 81-70086. (Golden Field Guide Ser.). (Illus.). 280p. 1982. pap. 11.95 (*0-307-13667-1*) Western Pub.

Skyhook in the Midnight Sun. Fiona Cooper. (Masks Ser.). 272p. (Orig.). 1995. pap. 14.99 (*1-85242-357-9*) Serpents Tail.

Skyla. Benjamin Manaster. Ed. by Adolfo Caso. LC 94-43023. 246p. 1995. 21.95 (*0-8283-2002-0*) Branden Pub Co.

Skylab & Pioneer Report: Proceedings of the 12th Goddard Memorial Symposium. Ed. by Paul B. Richards & Philip H. Bolger. (Science & Technology Ser.: Vol. 36). (Illus.). 160p. 1975. lib. bdg. 20.00 (*0-87703-071-5*) Univelt Inc.

Skylab Results. Ed. by W. C. Schneider & T. E. Hanes. 1975. write for info. (*0-87703-072-3*) Am Astronaut.

***Skylab Results.** Ed. by W. C. Schneider & T. E. Hanes. (Advances in the Astronautical Sciences Microfiche Ser.: Vol. 22). 1975. 60.00 incl. fiche (*0-87703-143-6*) Am Astronaut.

Skylance. Don Pendleton. (Stony Man Ser.: No. 52). 1996. mass mkt. 5.50 (*0-373-61909-X*, 1-61909-7, Wrldwide Lib) Harlequin Bks.

***Skylar.** Gregory McDonald. 1997. mass mkt. 5.99 (*0-380-72524-X*) Avon.

Skylar in Yankeeland. Gregory Mcdonald. LC 96-18639. 1997. 23.00 (*0-688-14164-1*) Morrow.

Skylark. Dezso Kosztolanyi. Tr. by Richard. (Central European Classics Ser.). 240p. (C). 1996. pap. 14.95 (*1-85866-059-9*) OUP.

Skylark. Patricia MacLachlan. LC 93-33211. 64p. (J). (gr. 3-5). 1994. 12.95 (*0-06-023328-1*); lib. bdg. 12.89 (*0-06-023333-8*) HarpC Child Bks.

Skylark. Patricia MacLachlan. LC 93-33211. 96p. (J). (gr. 3-5). 1997. pap. 4.50 (*0-06-440622-9*, Trophy) HarpC Child Bks.

***Skylark.** Patricia MacLachlan. (J). (gr. 5). 1995. 8.64 (*0-395-73258-1*) HM.

Skylark. Sheila Simonson. 1994. mass mkt. 3.99 (*0-373-26145-4*, 1-26145-2) Harlequin Bks.

***Skylark.** large type ed. Patricia MacLachlan. 118p. (J). (gr. 5). 29.50 (*0-614-20620-0*, L-38193-00 APHB) Am Printing Hse.

Skylark: A Study Guide. Merrily Hansen. Ed. by J. Friedland & R. Kessler. (Novel-Ties Ser.). (J). (gr. 4-5). 1996. pap. text ed. 15.95 (*1-56982-624-2*) Lrn Links.

Skylark: Manuscript Edition. Samson Raphelson. 1942. pap. 13.00 (*0-8222-1319-2*) Dramatists Play.

Skylark's Song. Harriet Segal. 512p. 1995. pap. 5.99 (*0-380-72380-8*) Avon.

Skylark's Song: A Novel. large type ed. Harriet Segal. LC 93-38682. 1994. lib. bdg. 24.95 (*0-7862-0113-4*) Thorndike Pr.

Skyler Gabriel. Lierre Keith. LC 95-60878. 1995. pap. 10. 95 (*0-9632660-2-0*) Fighting Wds.

Skylight. David Hare. 96p. (Orig.). 1995. pap. 9.95 (*0-571-17612-7*) Faber & Faber.

Skylight. Carol Muske. (Classic Contemporaries Ser.). 96p. (C). 1996. pap. 12.95 (*0-88748-229-5*) Carnegie-Mellon.

Skylight Cave Mystery. Steve Prince. LC 93-79312. 187p. (Orig.). (YA). (gr. 9 up). 1993. pap. 9.95 (*0-939116-36-7*) Frontier OR.

Skyline: Chicago: The Series. Per. vol. 6.95 (*1-880005-10-7*) Perspectvs Intl.

Skyline: Israel from Above. Duby Tal & Moni Haramati. 208p. 1990. 38.00 (*965-05-0534-2*, Pub. by Israel Ministry Def IS) Gefen Bks.

Skyliners, Vol. 1: North America Mainliners, Falcons & Flagships. George W. Hamlin. 1992. 24.95 (*0-9626730-1-3*) World Transport.

Skyliners 2. George W. Hamlin. 1994. 24.95 (*0-9626730-2-1*) World Transport.

Skylines. Ethel R. Fuller. 92p. 1978. pap. 4.95 (*0-8323-0333-X*) Binford Mort.

Skymaze. Gillian Rubinstein. Ed. by Patricia MacDonald. 240p. (J). (gr. 5 up). 1993. reprint ed. pap. 2.99 (*0-671-76988-X*, Archway) PB.

Skyo. Martha Hardy. (American Autobiography Ser.). 256p. 1995. reprint ed. lib. bdg. 79.00 (*0-7812-8549-6*) Rprt Serv.

Skypirate. Justine Davis. 384p. (Orig.). 1995. pap. 4.99 (*0-451-40491-2*, Topaz) NAL-Dutton.

Skyrealms of Jorune: The Role Playing Game. 3rd ed. Andrew Leker et al. (Illus.). 216p. 1992. pap. text ed. 20.00 (*1-883240-00-X*) Chessex.

Skyriders: History of the 327-401 Glider Infantry. James L. McDonough & Richard S. Gardner. LC 80-67956. (Airborne Ser.: No. 11). (Illus.). 176p. 1980. 29.95 (*0-89839-034-6*) Battery Pr.

Skyripper. David Drake. 1992. mass mkt. 3.99 (*0-8125-2004-1*) Tor Bks.

Skyrme Model: Fundamentals, Methods, Applications. Vladimir G. Makhankov et al. LC 92-28266. (Series in Nuclear & Particle Physics). 1993. 107.95 (*0-387-54905-6*) Spr-Verlag.

Skyrmions & Anomalies: Proceedings of the Workshop. Ed. by M. Jezabek & M. Prassatowics. 544p. (C). 1987. text ed. 138.00 (*9971-5-0350-6*) World Scientific Pub.

Skyrocket Your Sales. Raymond A. Slesinski. LC 85-28452. 207p. 1986. 16.95 (*0-88289-485-4*) Pelican.

Sky's the Limit. Jill Bloom. 1986. pap. 2.25 (*0-373-25205-6*) Harlequin Bks.

Sky's the Limit. Wayne Dyer. 1990. mass mkt. 6.99 (*0-671-72565-3*) PB.

Sky's the Limit. John Nichols. 1990. pap. 14.95 (*0-393-30717-4*) Norton.

Sky's the Limit! Alexandra Reid. (Sky Dancer Ser.). (Illus.). 80p. (J). (ps up). 1996. 7.95 (*0-694-00943-1*, Festival) HarpC Child Bks.

Sky's the Limit. rev. ed. (J). (gr. 5-9). 1994. 16.95 (*1-881431-44-4*, 1303) AIMS Educ Fnd.

***Sky's the Limit, Vol. 6.** Jean Green. (Illus.). 44p. (Orig.). 1996. pap. 9.50 (*1-56770-372-0*) S Scheewe Pubns.

Sky's the Limit: The History of the Airlines. Charles J. Kelly, Jr. LC 70-169423. (Literature & History of Aviation Ser.). 1979. reprint ed. 27.95 (*0-405-03766-X*) Ayer.

Skyscape. Michael Cadnum. 368p. 1994. 21.95 (*0-7867-0135-8*) Carroll & Graf.

Skyscraper: The Making of a Building. Karl Sabbagh. (Illus.). 320p. 1991. pap. 19.95 (*0-14-015284-9*, Penguin Bks) Viking Penguin.

Skyscraper, Bioclimatically Considered: A Design Primer. Kenneth Yeang. (Illus.). 200p. 1996. 50.00 (*1-85490-431-0*) Academy Ed UK.

Skyscraper Book. James C. Giblin. LC 81-43038. (Illus.). 96p. (J). (gr. 3-6). 1981. lib. bdg. 14.89 (*0-690-04155-1*, Crowell Jr Bks) HarpC Child Bks.

Skyscraper in American Art, 1890-1931. Merrill Schleier. (Quality Paperbacks Ser.). (Illus.). 312p. 1990. pap. 12. 95 (*0-306-80385-2*) Da Capo.

Skyscraper Lullaby: The Life & Music of John Alden Carpenter. Howard Pollack. LC 93-46447. (Studies of American Musicians). (Illus.). 544p. 1994. text ed. 59.00 (*1-56098-400-7*) Smithsonian.

Skyscraper Ted & Other Zany Verse: Introduce Kids to Crazy Wacky Verse-to Poetry-to Fun! Margot Bosonnet et al. (Illus.). 96p. (J). (gr. 3-6). 1995. pap. 6.95 (*0-86327-406-4*) Dufour.

Skyscrapers. J. Cooper. (Man-Made Wonders Ser.). (J). 1991. 8.95 (*0-86592-637-9*) Rourke Enter.

***Skyscrapers.** Anne MacGregor. (J). Date not set. write for info. (*0-688-00960-3*) Lothrop.

Skyscrapers. Joy Richardson. (Picture Science Ser.). (Illus.). 32p. (J). (gr. 2-4). 1994. lib. bdg. 20.00 (*0-531-14291-4*) Watts.

Skyscrapers. Philip Sauvain. Ed. by Rebecca Stefoff. LC 90-40358. (How We Build Ser.). (Illus.). 48p. (J). (gr. 4-7). 1990. lib. bdg. 17.26 (*0-944483-78-X*) Garrett Ed Corp.

***Skyscrapers.** Charles Sheppard. (Architectural Masterpieces Ser.). 1996. 10.98 (*0-7651-9940-8*) Smithmark.

Skyscrapers: A History of the World's Most Famous & Important Skyscrapers. Judith Dupre. (Illus.). 128p. 1996. 22.98 (*1-884822-45-2*) Blck Dog & Leventhal.

Skyscrapers: A Social History of the Very Tall Building in America. George H. Douglas. LC 95-39761. (Illus.). 280p. 1996. lib. bdg. 35.00 (*0-7864-0082-X*) McFarland & Co.

Skyscrapers: Form & Function. David Bennett. LC 95-1018. 1995. 35.00 (*0-684-80318-6*) S&S Trade.

***Skyscrapers: Higher & Higher.** Ed. by Caroline Microp & Frances Faure. (Illus.). 224p. 1996. 65.00 (*2-909283-20-8*) Gingko Press.

Skyscrapers, & Other Essays. Lewis B. Namier. LC 68-22113. (Essay Index Reprint Ser.). 1977. 18.95 (*0-8369-0734-5*) Ayer.

Skyscrapers & Towers. Chris Oxlade. LC 96-5166. (Superstructures Ser.). (Illus.). (J). 1996. lib. bdg. 24.26 (*0-8172-4329-1*) Raintree Steck-V.

Skyscrapers, Celadon & Kimchee: A Korean Notebook. Cristina P. Hidalgo. 132p. (C). 1994. pap. text ed. 12.00 (*971-542-025-7*, Pub. by U of Philippines Pr PH) UH Pr.

Skyscrapers Hide the Heavens: A History of Indian-White Relations in Canada. J. R. Miller. (Illus.). 408p. 1991. pap. text ed. 22.95 (*0-8020-6869-3*) U of Toronto Pr.

Skyshooting: Photography for Amateur Astronomers. rev. ed. Robert N. Mayall & Margaret W. Mayall. reprint ed. pap. 5.95 (*0-486-21854-6*) Dover.

***Skystone.** Jack Whyte. 1996. mass mkt. 6.99 (*0-8125-5138-9*) Tor Bks.

Skystone: The Forging of Arthur's Britain. Jack Whyte. LC 95-41358. 352p. 1996. 22.95 (*0-312-86091-9*) Tor Bks.

Skytalk: English for Air Communication, Set 3. L. F. Leveson. (C). 1984. text ed. 330.00 incl. audio (*0-85950-163-9*, Pub. by S Thornes Pubs UK) St Mut.

Skytalk: English for Air Communication Teacher's Notes. Stanley Thornes. (C). 1984. 60.00 (*0-85950-186-8*, Pub. by S Thornes Pubs UK) St Mut.

Skythen. Alexej P. Smirnov. 216p. (GER.). 1979. 30.00 (*0-317-57347-0*) St Mut.

Skytrap. large type ed. John Smith. 464p. 1988. 25.99 (*0-7089-1872-7*) Ulverscroft.

Skywalking: The Life & Films of George Lucas. rev. ed. Dale Pollock. LC 90-37372. (Illus.). 304p. 1990. reprint ed. pap. 14.95 (*0-573-60606-4*) S French Trade.

Skyward Trend of Thought: The Metaphysics of the American Skyscraper. Thomas A. Van Leeuwen. 192p. 1990. reprint ed. pap. 16.95 (*0-262-72016-7*) MIT Pr.

Skywatch: The Western Weather Guide. Richard A. Keen. LC 87-11871. (Illus.). 168p. 1987. pap. 18.95 (*1-55591-019-X*) Fulcrum Pub.

Skywatch East: A Weather Guide. Richard A. Keen. LC 91-58490. (Illus.). 224p. (Orig.). 1992. pap. 19.95 (*1-55591-091-2*) Fulcrum Pub.

Skywatchers Handbook. Colin A. Ronan. 1989. pap. 16.00 (*0-517-57326-1*, Crown) Crown Pub Group.

Skywatchers of Ancient Mexico. Anthony F. Aveni. (Texas Pan American Ser.). (Illus.). 369p. 1980. pap. 24.95 (*0-292-77578-4*) U of Tex Pr.

Skywatchers, Shamans, & Kings: Astronomy & the Archaeology of Power. Edwin C. Krupp. LC 96-12997. (Popular Science Ser.). 1996. text ed. 27.95 (*0-471-04863-1*) Wiley.

Skywatching. David H. Levy. Ed. by John O'Byrne. LC 95-8609. (Nature Company Guide Ser.). (Illus.). 288p. (J). (gr. 3 up). 1995. 29.95 (*0-7835-4751-X*) Time-Life.

Skywatching: The Nature Company Journals. Time-Life Books Editors. 192p. 1996. 14.95 (*0-8094-9381-0*) Time-Life.

Skywriting. Margarita Engle. 320p. 1996. reprint ed. pap. 11.95 (*0-553-37775-2*) Bantam.

Skywriting by Word of Mouth & Other Writings, Including The Ballad of John & Yoko. John Lennon. 208p. 1996. reprint ed. 35.00 (*0-8095-9075-1*) Borgo Pr.

SL Two (IR) Serge A. Lang. (Graduate Texts in Mathematics Ser.: Vol. 105). (Illus.). xiv, 428p. 1985. reprint ed. 49.95 (*0-387-96198-4*) Spr-Verlag.

SL(2) Representations of Finitely Presented Groups. Gregory W. Brumfiel & H. M. Hilden. LC 95-15002. (Contemporary Mathematics Ser.: Vol. 187). 1995. 49.00 (*0-8218-0416-2*, CONM/187) Am Math.

SLA Biennial Salary Survey 1995: A Research Publication. Special Libraries Association Staff. 76p. 1994. reprint ed. pap. 25.00 (*0-608-02391-4*, 2063032) Bks Demand.

***SLA Biennial Salary Survey, 1996.** Ed. by Liana Sayer. 89p. 1996. pap. 45.00 (*0-87111-458-5*) SLA.

***SLA Government Relations: Improving the Flow of Information.** SLA Staff. 1997. 12.50 (*0-87111-462-3*) SLA.

Slabs on Grade. 80p. 14.95 (*0-317-39818-0*, CCS-1) ACI.

Slabs on Grade. rev. ed. (Concrete Craftman Ser.). 80p. 1994. pap. 14.95 (*0-614-02511-7*, CCS1BOW6) ACI.

Slab's Tavern & Other Uncanny Tales. John G. Betancourt. LC 90-81728. (Illus.). 96p. 1990. 15.00 (*0-932445-41-1*); 35.00 (*0-932445-42-X*) Ganley Pub.

Slack Family, More Particularly an Account of the Family of Eliphalet Slack & His Wife Abigail Cutter: Their Ascendants, Descendants & Relations. W. W. Slack. (Illus.). 252p. 1993. reprint ed. pap. 39.50 (*0-8328-3407-6*); reprint ed. lib. bdg. 49.50 (*0-8328-3406-8*) Higginson Bk Co.

Slack Line Strategies for Fly Fishing. John Judy. LC 93-8315. (Illus.). 208p. 1994. 19.95 (*0-8117-1549-3*) Stackpole.

Slacker. Richard Linklater. 1992. pap. 14.95 (*0-312-07797-1*) St Martin.

Slackers & Other Plays. Peter Turrini. Tr. & Afterword by Richard S. Dixon. (Studies in Austrian Literature, Culture, & Thought. Translation Ser.). 228p. 1992. pap. 21.50 (*0-929497-48-1*) Ariadne CA.

Slacks & Tops. Harry Kondoleon. 1983. pap. 3.25 (*0-8222-1038-X*) Dramatists Play.

Slacks for Perfect Fit: Sew-Fit Method. Ruth Oblander. LC 81-50280. (Illus.). 64p. 1981. pap. 5.95 (*0-933956-07-X*) Sew-Fit.

***Slackware Linux Unleashed.** 3rd ed. Kamran Hussain & Tim Parker. 1300p. 1997. 49.99 (*0-672-31012-0*) Mac Comp Pub.

Slade Range Detective. large type ed. Gene Tuttle. (Linford Western Library). 256p. 1995. pap. 15.99 (*0-7089-7771-5*, Linford) Ulverscroft.

Slade Short Course. 2nd ed. Slade Schuster. (Orig.). (J). 1982. pap. text ed. 8.25 (*0-88334-161-1*, 76128) Longman.

Slade Short Course. 2nd ed. Slade Schuster. 77p. (Orig.). (gr. 8-11). 1982. pap. text ed. 5.95 (*0-88334-111-5*) Longman.

Slade's Marauder. large type ed. Steven Cade. 352p. 1983. 27.99 (*0-7089-8150-X*) Ulverscroft.

Slag Atlas. 2nd ed. Ed. by German Iron & Steel Institute Staff. (Illus.). 636p. 1995. boxed 455.00 (*3-514-00457-9*, Pub. by Woodhead Pubng UK) Am Educ Systs.

Slag-Iron & Steel. (Metals & Minerals Ser.). 1993. lib. bdg. 250.95 (*0-8490-8966-2*) Gordon Pr.

Slag Like Me. Barry B. Longyear. Ed. by Kevin Ryan. (Alien Nation Ser.: No. 5). 320p. (Orig.). 1994. mass mkt. 5.50 (*0-671-79514-7*) PB.

Slag of Creation. Richard Grossinger. 256p. (Orig.). 1975. pap. 5.00 (*0-913028-32-0*) North Atlantic.

Slagging & Fouling Due to Impurities in Combustion Gases. Ed. by Richard E. Barrett. LC 89-84355. 869p. 1990. 50.00 (*0-939204-36-3*) Eng Found.

Slain by the Doones, & Other Stories. Richard D. Blackmore. LC 74-86137. (Short Story Index Reprint Ser.). 1977. 19.95 (*0-8369-3041-X*) Ayer.

S

An Asterisk (*) at the beginning of an entry indicates that the title is appearing in BIP for the first time.

Slain in the Spirit. Ezra M. Coppin. LC 75-36001. 96p. 1976. pap. 2.95 (*0-89221-010-9*) New Leaf.

Slake's Limbo. Felice Holman. LC 74-11675. 126p. (J). (gr. 4-8). 1974. lib. bdg. 16.00 (*0-684-13926-X*, C Scribner Sons Young) S&S Childrens.

Slake's Limbo. large type ed. Felice Holman. 1995. pap. 33.00 (*0-614-09610-3*, L-81905-00) Am Printing Hse.

Slake's Limbo. Felice Holman. LC 85-26795. 128p. (YA). (gr. 6 up). 1986. reprint ed. pap. 3.95 (*0-689-71066-6*, Aladdin Paperbacks) S&S Childrens.

Slake's Limbo: A Study Guide. Joyce Friedland & Rikki Kessler. (Novel-Ties Ser.). 1982. student ed., teacher ed., pap. text ed. 15.95 (*0-88122-009-4*) Lrn Links.

***Slam!** Dean Myers. 1996. 15.95 (*0-614-25384-5*) Scholastic Inc.

Slam! Walter D. Myers. LC 95-46647. (J). 1996. write for info. (*0-590-48668-3*) Scholastic Inc.

Slam! Walter D. Myers. 240p. (YA). (gr. 7 up). 1996. 15.95 (*0-590-48667-5*) Scholastic Inc.

***Slam.** Lewis Shiner. 1998. pap. text ed. 12.95 (*1-888869-28-3*) HardWired.

SLAM-Addition, 30 wkbks., Set. 15.95 (*0-86624-031-4*, LWB6536TB) Bilingual Ed Serv.

Slam & Scream: And Other Powerful Strategies & Career Moves for Secretaries, Assistants, & Anyone Else Who Has Had Enough. Carole Fungaroli. 288p. 1996. pap. text ed. 12.00 (*0-374-52474-2*, Noonday) FS&G.

Slam Bidding for You. Andrew Kambites. 128p. 1993. 24.95 (*0-575-05368-2*, Pub. by V Gollancz UK) Trafalgar.

Slam Book. Ann M. Martin. LC 87-45335. 160p. (YA). (gr. 7 up). 1987. 12.95 (*0-8234-0666-0*) Holiday.

Slam Book Fever. Francine Pascal. (Sweet Valley High Ser.: No. 48). 160p. (Orig.). (YA). 1988. pap. 3.50 (*0-553-27416-3*) Bantam.

Slam Dunk! Hank Herman. (Super Hoops Ser.: No. 7). 96p. (YA). 1996. mass mkt. 3.50 (*0-553-48429-X*, Skylark BDD) BDD Bks Young Read.

Slam Dunk. Illus. by Bill James. LC 94-14620. 64p. (J). 1995. 15.89 (*0-7868-2042-X*) Hyprn Child.

Slam Dunk. Illus. by Bill James. LC 94-14620. 64p. (J). (gr. k-6). 1997. pap. 5.95 (*0-7868-1060-2*) Hyprn Child.

Slam Dunk. Kim Sandy. (J). 1996. 4.99 (*1-85792-162-3*, Pub. by Christian Focus UK) Spring Arbor Dist.

Slam Dunk: A Young Boy's Struggle with Attention Defecit Disorder. Roberta N. Parker. (Illus.). 55p. (Orig.). (J). (gr. 3-8). 1993. pap. 11.00 (*0-9621629-4-9*) Spec Pr FL.

Slam Dunk: Winning Players Talk about Basketball, Family, & Faith. Dave Branon. 250p. (YA). 1994. pap. 11.99 (*0-8024-7894-8*) Moody.

Slam Dunk Vol. 1: Poems about Basketball. Lillian Morrison. LC 94-14620. (J). 1995. 15.95 (*0-7868-0054-2*) Hyprn Child.

***Slam Dunk Cover Letters That Score Every Time.** Mark Rowh. LC 97-1853. 1997. pap. text ed. 7.95 (*0-8442-8198-0*) NTC Pub Grp.

Slam Dunk Mad Libs. Roger Price & Leonard Stern. (Mad Libs Ser.). 48p. (Orig.). (J). (gr. 2 up). 1994. bds., pap. 3.50 (*0-8431-3722-3*) Price Stern Sloan.

***Slam Dunk Marketing: From Rim Shots to Results.** Phil Roberts & Christopher O'Donnell. (Illus.). 196p. (Orig.). 1997. pap. 16.95 (*1-879239-14-0*) Pencom.

***Slam Dunk Marketing: From Rim Shots to Results.** Phil Roberts & Christopher O'Donnell. (Illus.). 196p. 1997. 19.95 (*1-879239-15-9*) Pencom.

Slam Dunk Resumes. Steven A. Provenzano. Ed. by Sarah Kennedy. LC 93-45862. 160p. (Orig.). 1994. pap. 7.95 (*0-8442-8191-3*, VGM Career Bks) NTC Pub Grp.

Slam Dunk Sabotage. Franklin W. Dixon. (Hardy Boys Ser.: No. 140). (J). 1996. pap. 3.99 (*0-671-50526-2*) PB.

Slam Dunk Saturday. Jean Marzollo. (Stepping Stone Bks.). (Illus.). 64p. (Orig.). (J). (gr. 2-4). 1994. pap. 3.99 (*0-679-82366-2*) Random Bks Yng Read.

Slam Dunk Saturday. Jean Marzollo. (Stepping Stone Bks.). (Illus.). 64p. (Orig.). (J). (gr. 2-4). 1994. lib. bdg. 11.99 (*0-679-92366-7*) Random Bks Yng Read.

Slam II: Network Models for Decision Support. Pritsker. (QM - Quantitative Methods Ser.). 1994. text ed. 67.95 (*0-89426-248-3*) S-W Pub.

Slam II-Network Models for Decision Support. Alan B. Pritsker. 704p. 1989. text ed. 50.00 (*0-13-812819-7*) P-H.

Slam the Big Door. John D. MacDonald. 272p. 1987. mass mkt. 4.95 (*0-449-13275-7*, GM) Fawcett.

Slam the Door Gently: The Making & Unmaking of a Female Scientist. Ruth A. Glater. LC 96-19361. (Illus.). 240p. (Orig.). 1997. pap. 12.95 (*1-56474-187-7*) Fithian Pr.

***Slam the Door on Employee Lawsuits: Keep Your Business Out of Court.** Paul M. Lusky. 1997. pap. text ed. 12.99 (*1-56414-311-2*) Career Pr Inc.

Slam the Door Softly. Clare Booth Luce. 1970. pap. 3.25 (*0-8222-1039-8*) Dramatists Play.

Slama Jama in the Jungle. Dennis J. Byrd. 60p. (J). (gr. 4-5). 1994. pap. text ed. 9.95 (*1-886114-00-5*) Arrow Pubns.

Slammer. Marron Kevin. 352p. 1996. 34.95 (*0-385-25534-9*) Doubleday.

***Slammer.** Kevin Marron. 320p. 1997. pap. 19.95 (*0-385-25616-7*) Doubleday.

Slammers. Krista Bell. (Illus.). 64p. (Orig.). (J). (gr. 3-5). 1996. pap. 4.95 (*1-86373-836-3*, Pub. by Allen & Unwin Aust Pty AT) IPG Chicago.

***Slammin' Skits.** 1996. 12.95 (*1-57405-183-0*) CharismaLife Pub.

***Slammin' Starters.** 1996. 12.95 (*1-57405-182-2*) CharismaLife Pub.

Slamming It Down. Douglas Goodwin. 100p. 1993. pap. 10.00 (*1-883657-01-6*) Earth Rose Pr.

Slan. Ed. by Manuel Alvarado & Richard Collins. 1993. reprint ed. lib. bdg. 18.95 (*0-89968-380-0*, Lghtyr Pr) Buccaneer Bks.

Slander. Linda Le. Tr. & Afterword by Esther Allen. LC 96-33816. (European Women Writers Ser.). v, 160p. 1996. pap. 14.00 (*0-8032-7963-9*, Bison Books); text ed. 30.00 (*0-8032-2913-5*) U of Nebr Pr.

***Slander Most Savage.** large type ed. Rose Meadows. (Large Print Ser.). 320p. 1997. 27.50 (*0-7089-3688-1*) Ulverscroft.

Slanderer. Said Salah. (Dual Language Ser.). 28p. 1995. pap. 12.00 (*1-887584-33-1*) Intl Prom Art.

Slang! expanded rev. ed. Dickson. 1997. 28.00 (*0-671-54920-0*); pap. 17.00 (*0-671-54919-7*) PB.

Slang! The Topic-by-Topic Dictionary of Contemporary American Lingoes. Paul Dickson. Ed. by Paul McCarthy. 320p. pap. 10.00 (*0-671-67251-7*) S&S Trade.

Slang American Style. Ed. by Richard A. Spears. 460p. 1996. pap. 12.95 (*0-8442-0907-4*) NTC Pub Grp.

Slang & Euphemism: A Dictionary of Oaths, Curses, Insults, Racial Slurs, Sexual Slang & Metaphor Drug Talk Homosexual Lingo & Related Matters. 2nd abr. ed. Richard A. Spears. 544p. 1991. pap. 6.99 (*0-451-16554-3*, Sig) NAL-Dutton.

Slang & Euphemism: A Dictionary of Oaths, Curses, Insults, Racial Slang & Metaphor, Racial Slurs, Drug Talk, Homosexual Lingo, & Related Matters. Richard A. Spears. LC 80-18714. 1981. 24.95 (*0-8246-0259-5*); pap. 12.95 (*0-8246-0273-0*) Jonathan David.

Slang & Its Analogues, Past & Present, 7 Vols. in 3, Set. John S. Farmer & W. E. Henley. LC 05-16232. 1974. reprint ed. 300.00 (*0-527-28300-2*) Periodicals Srv.

Slang & Jargon of Drugs & Drink. Richard A. Spears. LC 85-26277. 601p. 1986. 42.50 (*0-8108-1864-7*) Scarecrow.

Slang & Sociability: In-Group Language among College Students. Connie Eble. LC 95-47512. 224p. (C). 1996. lib. bdg. 29.95 (*0-8078-2279-5*) U of NC Pr.

Slang & Sociability: In-Group Language among College Students. Connie Eble. LC 95-47512. 224p. (C). 1996. pap. 14.95 (*0-8078-4584-1*) U of NC Pr.

Slang Dictionary: Useful Slang, Colloquialism, Idioms, & Other Expressions to Be Remembered for Living in the U. S. Dan Kikuchi. 334p. (JPN.). 1993. pap. 27.95 (*0-9637566-0-5*) Daian Intl.

Slang Dictionary of Spanish: Diccionario del Argot Espanol. V. Leon. 157p. (SPA.). 1983. pap. 9.95 (*0-8288-2050-3*, S33020) Fr & Eur.

Slang-Lexikon. Peter Wendling. 500p. (GER.). 1994. 55.00 (*0-7859-8569-7*, 3927930180) Fr & Eur.

Slang Thesaurus. Jonathon Green. 304p. 1990. pap. 13.95 (*0-14-051205-5*, Penguin Bks) Viking Penguin.

Slang Through the Ages. Ed. by Jonathon Green. 400p. 1996. pap. 12.95 (*0-8442-0834-5*) NTC Pub Grp.

Slang U. Pamela Munro. 1991. pap. 10.00 (*0-517-58243-0*, Harmony) Crown Pub Group.

Slangin', Packin', Livin' & Dyin' Henry Hardee. 15p. 1994. pap. text ed. 5.00 (*1-884978-04-5*) Black Boys Dream.

Slanguage. John Artman. 80p. (J). (gr. 4 up). 1980. 9.99 (*0-916456-60-9*, GA 175) Good Apple.

***Slant.** Greg Bear. Date not set. 24.95 (*0-312-85517-6*) St Martin.

***Slant.** Greg Bear. 1997. 23.95 (*0-614-27875-9*) Tor Bks.

Slant - Six: New Theater from Minnesota's Playwrights' Center. Ed. by Morgan Jenness et al. (Illus.). 192p. (Orig.). (C). 1990. pap. 9.95 (*0-89823-120-5*) New Rivers Pr.

Slant Book. Peter Newell. LC 67-12304. (Illus.). 50p. (J). (gr. k-4). 1967. reprint ed. 16.95 (*0-8048-0532-6*) C E Tuttle.

Slant-Stack Processing. Ed. by G. H. Gardner & L. Lu. (Geophysics Reprint Ser.: No. 14). (Illus.). 528p. (C). 1991. pap. text ed. 75.00 (*1-56080-054-2*, 474) Soc Expl Geophys.

***Slanted Truths: Essays on Gaia, Symbiosis & Evolution.** Lynn Margulis & Dorion Sagan. LC 97-2160. 1997. write for info. (*0-387-94927-5*) Spr-Verlag.

Slap. 2nd ed. Karen Blomain. Ed. by Roy Zarucchi. (Illus.). 32p. (Orig.). 1993. pap. 5.00 (*1-879205-40-8*) Nightshade Pr.

Slap in the Farce & A Matter of Wife & Death. Eugene Labiche. (Farce Ser.: Vol. 2). 1987. pap. 7.95 (*0-936839-82-1*) Applause Theatre Bk Pubs.

Slap Style Techniques. (Four Bass Superchops Ser.). 1992. pap. 12.95 incl. audio (*0-7935-1025-2*, 00660300) H Leonard.

Slap Style Techniques. (Four Bass Superchops Ser.). 1992. pap. 14.95 incl. audio compact disk (*0-7935-1026-0*, 00660301) H Leonard.

***Slapdashes: Poems from Hollywood.** Mark Dunster. 20p. (Orig.). (YA). (gr. 9-12). 1997. pap. 5.00 (*0-89642-376-X*) Linden Pubs.

SLAPPS: Getting Sued for Speaking Out. George W. Pring & Penelope Canan. LC 95-13610. (C). 1996. pap. text ed. 24.95 (*1-56639-369-8*); lib. bdg. 59.95 (*1-56639-368-X*) Temple U Pr.

Slapshots. Kevin Nelson. 1995. pap. 10.00 (*0-684-81075-1*, Fireside) S&S Trade.

Slapstick: or Lonesome No More! Kurt Vonnegut, Jr. 256p. 1992. mass mkt. 6.50 (*0-440-18009-0*) Dell.

Slash. Jeannette C. Armstrong. 256p. (Orig.). (YA). (gr. 8-12). 1985. pap. 8.95 (*0-919441-29-7*, Pub. by Theytus Bks Ltd CN) Orca Bk Pubs.

Slash - Twenty-Five Great Solos. Ed. by Jon Chappell. 54p. (Orig.). pap. 14.95 (*0-89524-888-3*, 02506317) Cherry Lane.

Slash & Thrust. John Sanchez. (Illus.). 72p. 1980. pap. 10.00 (*0-87364-188-4*) Paladin Pr.

***Slash in the Night.** Goodman. (Mystery Files of Shelby Woo Ser.: No. 2). (J). 1997. mass mkt. 3.99 (*0-671-01153-7*) PB.

Slash IRS Back Taxes, Negotiate IRS Back Taxes for As Little As Ten Cents on the Dollar: A Guide to the IRS Offer in Compromise Process. Stuart Heaslet. LC 93-60000. (Illus.). 192p. (Orig.). 1993. pap. 19.95 (*0-9635928-0-7*) WP Pubns.

Slash of Scarlet. Nancy B. Jacobs. Ed. by Julie Rubenstein. 256p. 1993. reprint ed. mass mkt. 4.99 (*0-671-86504-8*) PB.

Slash of Waking. Stephen R. Roberts. Ed. by Alana Sherman. 20p. (Orig.). 1995. pap. text ed. 5.95 (*0-939689-19-7*) Alms Hse Pr.

Slash Your Advertising Costs Now! An Easy-Access Guide to Spending Less & Getting More for Your. James Mantice. 209p. 1991. pap. 32.95 (*0-85013-172-3*) Dartnell Corp.

Slash Your Mortgage in Half. Tag Powell. Ed. by Judith L. Powell & Yvonne Fawcett. LC 91-2643. (Illus.). 96p. 1991. pap. 10.00 (*0-914295-91-8*) Top Mtn Pub.

***Slash Your Workers' Comp Costs.** Thomas Lundberg & Lynn Tylczak. LC 97-2281. 192p. 1997. 27.95 (*0-8144-0347-6*) AMACOM.

Slashback. Paul Levine. 336p. 1995. mass mkt. 5.99 (*0-380-72162-7*) Avon.

Slashing Utility Costs Handbook. John M. Studebaker. LC 92-32927. 1993. write for info. (*0-88173-152-8*) Fairmont Pr.

Slash/Mulch Systems: Neglected Sustainable Tropical Agroecosystems. H. David Thurston. LC 96-46962. (C). 1996. text ed. 45.00 (*0-8133-8820-1*) Westview.

***Slate & Willis's Rivers Atlas.** William E. Trout, III. (Illus.). 53p. 1994. spiral bd. 8.00 (*1-888838-05-1*) VA Canals & Navigat.

Slate Blues. Sheri C. Sinykin. LC 92-14039. (J). 1993. 12.00 (*0-688-11212-9*) Lothrop.

Slate Industry. Merfyn Williams. 1989. pap. 35.00 (*0-7478-0124-X*, Pub. by Shire UK) St Mut.

Slate of Life: More Contemporary Stories by Women Writers of India. Kali for Women Staff. 176p. (Orig.). 1994. pap. 12.95 (*1-55861-088-X*) Feminist Pr.

Slate of Life: More Contemporary Stories by Women Writers of India. Kali for Women Staff. 176p. (Orig.). 1994. text ed. 35.00 (*1-55861-087-1*) Feminist Pr.

***Slate Roof Bible: Everything You Wanted to Know about Slate Roofs Including How to Keep Them Alive for Centuries.** Joseph Jenkins. (Illus.). 300p. (Orig.). 1997. pap. 30.00 (*0-9644258-0-7*) Jenkins Pubng.

Slate Waste Tips & Workings in Britain. 144p. 1995. pap. 75.00 (*0-11-752971-0*, HM29710, Pub. by Stationery Ofc UK) Bernan Associates.

Slater Creed. Larry D. Names. (Illus.). 352p. Date not set. 22.50 (*0-938313-12-6*) E B Houchin.

***Slater Mill, RI.** Leavitt & Slater Mill Staff. (Images of America Ser.). 1997. pap. 16.99 (*0-7524-0567-5*, Arcdia) Chalford.

SLATTER Fundamentals of Veterinary Ophthalmology. 2nd ed. (Illus.). 576p. 1990. pap. text ed. 65.00 (*0-7216-2463-4*) Saunders.

Slattery Stands Alone. large type ed. Steven C. Lawrence. LC 96-20885. (Orig.). 1996. pap. 20.00 (*0-7838-1848-3*, GK Hall) Thorndike Pr.

Slaughter. Elmer Kelton. 464p. 1994. mass mkt. 5.50 (*0-553-56547-8*, Bantam Domain) Bantam.

Slaughter. large type ed. Elmer Kelton. LC 94-37738. 1995. 22.95 (*0-7862-0354-4*) Thorndike Pr.

Slaughter among Neighbors: Political Origins of Communal Violence. Human Rights Watch Staff. LC 95-23132. 1995. 30.00 (*0-300-06496-9*) Yale U Pr.

Slaughter Among Neighbors: Political Origins of Communal Violence. Human Rights Watch Staff. LC 95-23132. 1995. pap. text ed. 15.00 (*0-300-06544-2*) Yale U Pr.

Slaughter at Detour's End. Melvin O. Swasey. LC 92-91200. 264p. (Orig.). 1994. pap. 10.00 (*1-56002-293-0*, Univ Edtns) Aegina Pr.

Slaughter by Product: Winning the Products Liability Case with 1992 Cumulative Supplement. Edward M. Swartz. 593p. 1986. 80.00 (*0-930273-54-0*) MICHIE.

Slaughter by Product: Winning the Products Liability Case with 1992 Cumulative Supplement. Edward M. Swartz. 593p. 1992. suppl. ed. 35.00 (*0-87473-970-5*) MICHIE.

***Slaughter City.** Naomi Wallace. (Orig.). 1997. pap. 10.95 (*0-571-17812-X*) Faber & Faber.

Slaughter-House of Mammon: An Anthology of Victorian Social Protest Literature. Ed. by Sharon A. Winn & Lynn M. Alexander. LC 92-7269. (Locust Hill Literary Studies: No. 8). 344p. (C). 1992. lib. bdg. 32.00 (*0-933951-41-8*) Locust Hill Pr.

Slaughter in Carolina. Frances S. Hall. Ed. by Frann Dykes. (Illus.). 220p. 1990. 14.95 (*0-685-46227-7*) Hmmngbird SC.

***Slaughter in the Ashes, No. 23.** William W. Johnstone. 288p. 1997. mass mkt. 5.99 (*0-7860-0380-4*, Pinncle Kensgtn) Kensgtn Pub Corp.

Slaughter Music. Russell James. 296p. 20.00 (*0-88150-333-9*) Countryman.

Slaughter of Poultry for Human Consumption. W. N. Scott. 1978. 30.00 (*0-317-43887-5*) St Mut.

Slaughter of Terrified Beasts: A Biblical Basis for the Humane Treatment of Animals. J. R. Hyland. LC 88-50200. 82p. (Orig.). 1988. pap. 6.95 (*0-945703-00-7*) Viatoris Ministries.

Slaughter of the Croatians. 1992. lib. bdg. 75.00 (*0-8490-5449-4*) Gordon Pr.

Slaughter of the Innocent. Hans Ruesch. 446p. 1992. reprint ed. pap. 4.95 (*0-9610016-0-7*) CIVIS-Civitas.

Slaughter of the Innocents. David Bakan. LC 78-155168. (Jossey-Bass Behavioral Science Ser.). 142p. reprint ed. pap. 40.50 (*0-7837-6507-X*, 2045619) Bks Demand.

Slaughter of the Innocents: A Study of the Battered Child Phenomenon. David Bakan. LC 78-155168. (Social & Behavioral Science Ser.). 136p. 1971. 30.95 (*0-87589-093-8*) Jossey-Bass.

Slaughter of the Innocents: Child Abuse through the Ages. S. J. Breiner. LC 89-29451. (Illus.). 325p. 1990. 23.50 (*0-306-43459-8*, Plenum Pr) Plenum.

Slaughter of the Innocents: Coercive Birth Control in China. John Aird. 150p. 1990. 24.75 (*0-8447-3703-8*, AEI Pr) Am Enterprise.

Slaughter on Second Street. David Kent. LC 93-77909. 100p. 1993. 15.00 (*0-9614811-6-1*) King Philip Pub.

Slaughterhouse: Bosnia & the Failure of the West. David Rieff. 240p. 1996. pap. 12.00 (*0-684-81903-1*, Touchstone Bks) S&S Trade.

***Slaughterhouse: The Shocking Story of Greed, Neglect & Inhumane Treatment Inside th U. S. Meat.** Gail A. Eisnitz. 1997. 25.95 (*1-57392-166-1*) Prometheus Bks.

***Slaughterhouse & Slaughterslab Design & Construction.** 97p. 1978. 12.00 (*92-5-100543-5*, Pub. by FAO IT) Bernan Associates.

Slaughterhouse Five. Kurt Vonnegut, Jr. (Book Notes Ser.). 1985. pap. 3.95 (*0-8120-3539-9*) Barron.

Slaughterhouse-Five: Or, the Children's Crusade. Kurt Vonnegut, Jr. 224p. 1991. mass mkt. 6.50 (*0-440-18029-5*) Dell.

***Slaughterhouse Five Notes.** Dennis S. Smith. 72p. (Orig.). 1997. pap. text ed. 4.25 (*0-8220-1205-7*) Cliffs.

Slaughterhouse-Five: or the Children's Crusade: Twenty-Fifth Anniversary Edition. Kurt Vonnegut. 224p. 1994. 22.95 (*0-385-31208-3*) Delacorte.

Slaughterhouse Province: An American Diplomat's Report on the Armenian Genocide of 1915-17. Leslie A. Davis. Ed. & Intro. by Susan K. Blair. (Illus.). viii, 216p. 1989. 30.00 (*0-89241-458-8*) Caratzas.

***Slav.** Sadler. 1997. pap. 19.95 (*1-901259-00-5*) Macmillan.

Slav for the Tournament Player. Glenn Flear. (Illus.). 128p. 1989. pap. 10.95 (*0-7134-5635-3*, Pub. by Batsford UK) Trafalgar.

Slav Soul, & Other Stories. Alexander I. Kuprin. LC 78-150547. (Short Story Index Reprint Ser.). 1977. reprint ed. 19.95 (*0-8369-3844-5*) Ayer.

Slave. Sara Adamson. (Orig.). 1994. mass mkt. 6.95 (*1-56333-173-X*, Rhinoceros) Masquerade.

Slave. Isaac B. Singer. Tr. by Cecil Hemley from YID. 311p. 1988. pap. 12.00 (*0-374-50680-9*) FS&G.

Slave: Or, Memoirs of Archy Moore, 2 vols in 1. Richard Hildreth. (Illus.). 1972. reprint ed. lib. bdg. 36.00 (*0-8422-8076-6*) Irvington.

Slave Ancestral Research: It's Something Else. Mary L. Fears. (Illus.). 269p. (Orig.). 1995. pap. text ed. 37.50 (*0-7884-0200-5*) Heritage Bk.

Slave Ancestral Research in Seven Steps Within the Jackson-Moore Family History & Genealogy: Family History & Genealogy. Mary L. Fears. (Illus.). 457p. (Orig.). 1996. pap. 66.00 (*0-7884-0414-8*, F107) Heritage Bk.

Slave & Citizen. Frank Tannenbaum. LC 91-21434. 160p. 1992. reprint ed. pap. 13.00 (*0-8070-0913-X*) Beacon Pr.

Slave & Citizen: The Life of Frederick Douglass. Nathan I. Huggins. (Library of American Biography). (C). 1980. text ed. 16.95 (*0-673-39342-9*) Addson-Wesley Educ.

Slave & Citizen: The Life of Frederick Douglass. Nathan I. Huggins. (Library of American Biography). 196p. reprint ed. pap. 15.95 (*1-886746-22-2*, 93470) Talman.

Slave & Freeman: The Autobiography of George L. Knox. George L. Knox. Ed. by Willard B. Gatewood, Jr. LC 78-21058. 256p. 1979. 28.00 (*0-8131-1384-9*) U Pr of Ky.

Slave & Soldier: The Military Impact of Blacks in the Colonial Americas. Peter M. Voelz. LC 93-18022. (Studies in African American History & Culture). 544p. 1993. Alk. paper. text ed. 112.00 (*0-8153-1009-9*) Garland.

Slave by Marriage. Dorothy Michell. 179p. (C). 1990. 39.00 (*0-947333-15-0*, Pub. by Pascoe Pub AT) St Mut.

Slave Catchers: Enforcement of the Fugitive Slave Law. Stanley W. Campbell. LC 79-109463. 246p. reprint ed. pap. 70.20 (*0-8357-3863-9*, 2036595) Bks Demand.

Slave Children of Thomas Jefferson. Samuel H. Sloan. 320p. (Orig.). (C). 1992. pap. 14.95 (*1-881373-02-9*) Orsden Pr.

Slave Coast of West Africa, 1550-1750: The Impact of the Atlantic Slave Trade on an African Society. Robin Law. (Oxford Studies in African Affairs). (Illus.). 392p. 1991. 95.00 (*0-19-820228-8*) OUP.

Slave Community: Plantation Life in the Ante-Bellum South. 2nd enl. rev. ed. John W. Blassingame. (Illus.). 432p. 1979. pap. text ed. 18.95 (*0-19-502563-6*) OUP.

Slave Culture: Nationalist Theory & the Foundations of Black America. Sterling Stuckey. 416p. 1988. reprint ed. pap. 14.95 (*0-19-505664-7*) OUP.

Slave Cultures & the Cultures of Slavery. Ed. by Stephan Palmie. LC 95-4374. 336p. 1996. text ed. 35.00 (*0-87049-903-3*) U of Tenn Pr.

Slave Dancer. Paula Fox. 128p. (YA). (gr. 7 up). 1975. mass mkt. 3.99 (*0-440-96132-7*, LLL BDD) BDD Bks Young Read.

Slave Dancer. Paula Fox. (Illus.). 192p. (J). (gr. 5-8). 1982. lib. bdg. 16.00 (*0-02-735560-8*, LLL BDD) BDD Bks Young Read.

Slave Dancer. Paula Fox. 160p. (J). (gr. k-6). 1991. pap. 4.99 (*0-440-40402-9*) Dell.

***Slave Dancer.** Paula Fox. 1997. mass mkt. 2.69 (*0-440-22739-9*) Dell.

Slave Dancer. Barbara Reeves. Ed. by J. Friedland & R. Kessler. (Novel-Ties Ser.). 1993. pap. text ed. 15.95 (*0-88122-905-9*) Lrn Links.

Slave Dancer & Book Club. (J). 1991. mass mkt. 3.50 (*0-440-80201-6*) Dell.

Slave Day. Thomas. LC 96-24617. (J). 1997. 16.00 (*0-689-80206-4*, S&S Bks Young Read) S&S Childrens.

Slave Dreads Her Work. Nathan Whiting. 1980. pap. 6.00 (*0-914610-15-5*) Hanging Loose.

An Asterisk (*) at the beginning of an entry indicates that the title is appearing in BIP for the first time.

Slave Drivers: Black Agricultural Labor Supervisors in the Antebellum South. William L. Van Deburg. LC 78-59261. (Contributions in Afro-American & African Studies: No. 43). 202p. 1979. text ed. 49.95 (*0-313-20610-4*, VSD/, Greenwood Pr) Greenwood.

Slave Economy of the Old South: Selected Essays in Economic & Social History. fac. ed. Ulrich B. Phillips. Ed. by Eugene D. Genovese. LC 68-21806. 318p. 1968. reprint ed. pap. 90.70 (*0-7837-7814-7*, 2047570) Bks Demand.

Slave Emancipation in Cuba: The Transition to Free Labor, 1860-1899. Rebecca J. Scott. LC 85-42703. (Illus.). 352p. 1986. pap. text ed. 21.95 (*0-691-10157-4*) Princeton U Pr.

Slave for a Day. Jana Ellis. LC 89-34375. (Merivale Mall Ser.). 160p. (YA). (gr. 7 up). 1989. pap. text ed. 2.50 (*0-8167-1610-2*) Troll Communs.

Slave Genealogy: A Research Guide with Case Studies. David H. Streets. iv, 87p. (Orig.). 1986. pap. 10.00 (*0-917890-63-9*) Heritage Bk.

Slave Girl. Buchi Emecheta. LC 79-25651. 179p. 1977. pap. 9.95 (*0-8076-0952-8*) Braziller.

Slave Girls. Wensley Clarkson. 1996. mass mkt. 5.99 (*0-312-95870-6*) St Martin.

***Slave Girls of Rome.** Don Winslow. (Orig.). 1997. mass mkt. 6.95 (*1-56333-577-8*) Masquerade.

Slave in the Empty Grave. Raymond J. Libert. 32p. 1994. pap. 6.95 (*0-8059-3478-2*) Dorrance.

Slave Insurrections "Selected Documents" Ed. by Al I. Obaba. (Illus.). 176p. (Orig.). 1990. pap. text ed. 15.00 (*0-916157-26-1*) African Islam Miss Pubns.

Slave Island. 3rd ed. Paul Little. 1996. mass mkt. 5.95 (*1-56333-441-0*) Masquerade.

Slave Law in the Americas. Alan Watson. LC 89-4958. 224p. 1990. 25.00 (*0-8203-1179-0*) U of Ga Pr.

Slave Laws in Virginia. Philip J. Schwarz. LC 96-1010. (Studies in the Legal History of the South). 1996. 40.00 (*0-8203-1831-0*) U of Ga Pr.

Slave Life in America: A Historiography & Selected Bibliography. James S. Olson. 128p. (Orig.). (C). 1983. lib. bdg. 47.50 (*0-8191-3285-3*) U Pr of Amer.

Slave Life in Georgia. John Brown. Ed. by L. A. Chamerovzow. LC 77-168512. (Black Heritage Library Collection). 1977. reprint ed. 27.95 (*0-8369-8865-5*) Ayer.

Slave Life in Georgia: A Narrative of the Life, Sufferings, & Escape of John Brown, a Fugitive Slave. John Brown. 218p. 1991. 25.00 (*0-88322-007-5*) Beehive GA.

Slave Life in Rio De Janerio, 1808-1850. Mary C. Karasch. LC 85-43290. 448p. 1986. text ed. 95.00 (*0-691-07708-8*) Princeton U Pr.

Slave Lover. Marco Vassi. 192p. 1993. pap. 16.95 (*0-933256-89-2*) Second Chance.

Slave Master's Religion: Breaking the Last Bonds of Slavery. Glenn Royster. 152p. 1993. pap. 7.00 (*0-9638214-4-X*) Kabila Communs.

Slave Narrative: It's Place in American History. Marion W. Starling. 400p. 1988. pap. 14.95 (*0-88258-165-1*) Howard U Pr.

***Slave Narrative of Frederick Douglass.** 176p. 1997. mass mkt. 5.99 (*0-440-22228-1*) Dell.

Slave Narratives: A Folk History of Slavery in the U. S. from Interviews with Former Slaves, 17 vols. Federal Writers' Project Staff. 1941. 49.00 (*0-318-55752-5*) Somerset Pub.

Slave Narratives: A Folk History of Slavery in the U. S. from Interviews with Former Slaves, 17 vols., Set. Federal Writers' Project Staff. (American Guidebook Ser.). 1941. 1,995.00 (*0-403-02211-8*) Somerset Pub.

Slave Narratives: A Folk History of Slavery in the United States, from Interviews with Former Slaves, 17 vols., Set. Federal Writers' Project Staff & Writers Program-WPA Staff. (American Guide Ser.). 1989. reprint ed. text ed. 1,495.00 (*0-7812-1071-2*, 1071) Rprt Serv.

Slave Narratives of Texas. Ed. by Ron C. Tyler & Lawrence R. Murphy. (Illus.). 192p. 1997. 24.95 (*1-880510-35-9*) State House Pr.

Slave Narratives of Texas. Ed. by Ron C. Tyler & Lawrence R. Murphy. (Illus.). 192p. 1997. pap. 16.95 (*1-880510-36-7*) State House Pr.

Slave of Catiline. Paul L. Anderson. LC 57-9446. 255p. (J). (gr. 7-11). 1930. pap. 19.00 (*0-8196-0101-2*) Biblo.

***Slave of My Thirst.** Tom Holland. 1997. 23.00 (*0-671-54052-1*, PB Hardcover) PB.

Slave of Passion. Katherine Tobias. (Orig.). 1978. mass mkt. 2.25 (*0-89083-425-3*, Zebra Kensgtn) Kensgtn Pub Corp.

Slave: or Memoirs of Archy Moore. Richard Hildreth. (Notable American Authors Ser.). 1992. reprint ed. lib. bdg. 75.00 (*0-7812-3120-5*) Rprt Serv.

Slave Population & Economy in Jamaica, 1807-1834. B. W. Higman. LC 75-28627. 334p. reprint ed. pap. 95.20 (*0-317-27994-7*, 2025586) Bks Demand.

Slave Populations of the British Caribbean, 1807-1834. B. W. Higman. LC 83-22203. (Johns Hopkins Studies in Atlantic History & Culture Ser.). (Illus.). 815p. reprint ed. pap. 180.00 (*0-7837-4779-9*, 2044534) Bks Demand.

Slave Power. Theodore Parker. LC 74-82209. (Anti-Slavery Crusade in America Ser.). 1970. reprint ed. 27.95 (*0-405-00647-0*) Ayer.

Slave Power Conspiracy & the Paranoid Style. fac. ed. David B. Davis. LC 79-96257. (Walter Lynwood Fleming Lectures in Southern History). 109p. 1969. reprint ed. pap. 31.10 (*0-7837-7729-9*, 2047485) Bks Demand.

Slave Prince. Vince Gilman. (Orig.). 1994. mass mkt. 4.95 (*1-56333-199-3*, Badboy) Masquerade.

Slave Rebellion in Brazil: The Muslim Uprising of 1835 in Bahia. Joao J. Reis. Tr. by Arthur Brakel from POR. (Studies in Atlantic History & Culture). (Illus.). 320p. 1995. reprint ed. pap. text ed. 15.95 (*0-8018-5250-1*) Johns Hopkins.

Slave Rebellion in Brazil: The Muslim Uprising of 1853 in Bahia. Joao J. Reis. Tr. by Arthur Brakel from POR. LC 92-27067. (Studies in Atlantic History & Culture). (Illus.). 320p. 1993. text ed. 48.00 (*0-8018-4462-2*) Johns Hopkins.

Slave Rebels, Abolitionists, & Southern Courts: The Pamphlet Literature, 2 vols. Ed. by Paul Finkelman. LC 87-29290. (Slavery, Race & the American Legal System, 1700-1872 Ser.: Vol. 4). 1134p. 1988. text ed. 130.00 (*0-8240-6721-5*) Garland.

Slave Religion: The Invisible Institution in the Antebellum South. Albert J. Raboteau. (Illus.). 400p. 1980. pap. 14.95 (*0-19-502705-1*) OUP.

Slave Ship: The Story of the Henrietta Marie. George Sullivan. LC 93-47653. (Illus.). 80p. (J). (gr. 5 up). 1994. pap. 15.99 (*0-525-65174-8*, Cobblehill Bks) Dutton Child Bks.

Slave Ships & Slaving. George F. Dow. LC 68-57116. (Illus.). 424p. reprint ed. pap. 120.90 (*0-7837-6849-4*, 2046678) Bks Demand.

Slave Society in Cuba During the Nineteenth Century. Franklin W. Knight. LC 76-121770. (Illus.). 250p. 1970. 25.00 (*0-299-05790-9*) U of Wis Pr.

Slave Society in Cuba During the Nineteenth Century. Franklin W. Knight. LC 76-121770. (Illus.). 250p. 1974. pap. 10.95 (*0-299-05794-1*) U of Wis Pr.

Slave Society in the Danish West Indies: St. Thomas, St. John, & St. Croix. Neville A. Hall. Ed. by B. W. Higman. (Atlantic History & Culture Ser.). (Illus.). 320p. 1992. text ed. 48.50 (*0-8018-4473-8*) Johns Hopkins.

Slave Soldiers & Islam: The Genesis of a Military System. Daniel Pipes. LC 80-23969. 276p. reprint ed. pap. 78.70 (*0-7837-2990-1*, 2043193) Bks Demand.

Slave Songs. Compiled by Jerry Silverman. (Traditional Black Music Ser.). (Illus.). 80p. (YA). (gr. 5 up). 1994. pap. 9.95 (*0-7910-1853-9*); lib. bdg. 18.95 (*0-7910-1837-7*) Chelsea Hse.

Slave Songs of the Georgia Sea Islands. Lydia A. Parrish. 256p. reprint ed. lib. bdg. 39.00 (*0-685-43693-4*) Rprt Serv.

Slave Songs of the Georgia Sea Islands. Intro. by Art Rosenbaum. LC 91-22948. (Brown Thrasher Bks.). (Illus.). 312p. 1992. reprint ed. 24.95 (*0-8203-1397-1*); reprint ed. pap. 19.95 (*0-8203-1389-0*) U of Ga Pr.

Slave Songs of the United States. Ed. by William F. Allen et al. 1960. 14.50 (*0-8446-1411-4*) Peter Smith.

Slave Songs of the United States. Ed. by William F. Allen et al. 176p. 1995. pap. text ed. 6.95 (*0-486-28573-1*) Dover.

Slave Songs of the United States. Ed. by William F. Allen et al. LC 72-138330. (Black Heritage Library Collection). 1980. reprint ed. 25.95 (*0-8369-8722-5*) Ayer.

Slave Songs of the United States. William F. Allen et al. LC 95-81112. 168p. (Orig.). 1996. reprint ed. pap. 9.95 (*1-55709-434-9*) Applewood.

Slave Soul of Russia: Moral Masochism & the Cult of Suffering. Daniel Rancour-Laferriere. 330p. (C). 1995. 45.00 (*0-8147-7458-X*) NYU Pr.

Slave Soul of Russia: Moral Masochism & the Cult of Suffering. Daniel Rancour-Laferriere. 330p. (C). 1996. pap. 19.95 (*0-8147-7482-2*) NYU Pr.

Slave States in the Presidential Election of 1860. Ollinger Crenshaw. 1990. 14.50 (*0-8446-1138-7*) Peter Smith.

Slave States in the Presidential Election of 1860. Ollinger Crenshaw. LC 78-64199. (Johns Hopkins University. Studies in the Social Sciences. Thirtieth Ser. 1912: 3). reprint ed. 37.50 (*0-404-61305-5*) AMS Pr.

Slave States in the Presidential Election of 1860. Ollinger Crenshaw. (History - United States Ser.). 332p. 1993. reprint ed. lib. bdg. 89.00 (*0-7812-4824-8*) Rprt Serv.

Slave Systems of Greek & Roman Antiquity. W. L. Westermann. LC 54-9107. (Memoirs Ser.: Vol. 40). 180p. 1984. reprint ed. pap. 25.00 (*0-87169-040-3*, M040-WEW) Am Philos.

Slave Testimony: Two Centuries of Letters, Speeches, Interviews, & Autobiographies. Ed. by John W. Blassingame. LC 75-18040. (Illus.). lxvi, 777p. 1977. pap. text ed. 19.95 (*0-8071-0273-3*) La State U Pr.

Slave to Love. Michelle Reid. 1995. mass mkt. 3.25 (*0-373-11776-0*) Harlequin Bks.

Slave to Love. large type ed. Michelle Reid. (Harlequin Romance Ser.). 1995. 20.95 (*0-263-14288-4*, Pub. by Mills & Boon UK) Thorndike Pr.

Slave Trade. Hugh Thomas. LC 97-17234. 1997. 35.00 (*0-684-81063-8*, S&S) S&S Trade.

Slave Trade. David Killingray. Ed. by Malcolm Yapp et al. (World History Program Ser.). (Illus.). (YA). (gr. 6-11). 1980. reprint ed. pap. text ed. 4.72 (*0-89908-124-X*) Greenhaven.

Slave Trade Set: Reports of the Select Committees on the Slave Trade, 1810-30. (British Parliamentary Papers: Vols. 1-95). Date not set. 12,090.00 (*0-7165-1499-0*, Pub. by Irish Acad Pr IE) Intl Spec Bk.

Slave Trade & Migration. Ed. by Paul Finkelman. (Articles on American Slavery Ser.). 488p. 1990. reprint ed. text ed. 40.00 (*0-8240-6782-7*) Garland.

Slave Trade Domestic & Foreign: Why It Exists & How It May Be Extinguished. Henry C. Carey. LC 67-18574. (Reprints of Economic Classics Ser.). 426p. 1967. reprint ed. 49.50 (*0-678-00248-7*) Kelley.

Slave Trades, 1500-1800: Globalization of Forces Labour. Ed. by Patrick Manning. LC 96-3760. (Expanding World Ser.: Vol. 15). 400p. 1996. text ed. 115.95 (*0-86078-512-2*, Pub. by Variorum UK) Ashgate Pub Co.

Slave Trading in the Old South. Frederic Bancroft. (Southern Classics Ser.). (Illus.). 464p. 1996. pap. text ed. 18.95 (*1-57003-103-7*) U of SC Pr.

Slave Trail. Alain Gerber. Tr. by Jeremy Leggatt from FRE. LC 88-7844. 148p. 1989. 18.95 (*0-916515-51-6*) Mercury Hse Inc.

Slave Women in Caribbean Society, 1650-1832. Barbara Bush. (Illus.). 198p. 1990. 31.50 (*0-253-31284-1*); pap. 13.95 (*0-253-21251-0*) Ind U Pr.

Slaveholder Abroad: A Series of Letters from Dr. Pleasant Jones to Major Joseph Jones. Ebenezer Starnes & William T. Thompson. 1977. 26.95 (*0-8369-9176-1*, 9049) Ayer.

Slaveholder's Daughter. Belle Kearney. (American Biography Ser.). 269p. 1991. reprint ed. lib. bdg. 69.00 (*0-7812-8226-8*) Rprt Serv.

Slaveholders' Dilemma: Freedom & Progress in Southern Conservative Thought, 1820-1860. Eugene D. Genovese. pap. text ed. 12.95 (*0-87249-995-2*) U of SC Pr.

Slaveholding Indians, 3 vols., Set. Annie H. Abel. 1988. reprint ed. lib. bdg. 145.00 (*0-317-90022-6*) Rprt Serv.

Slaveholding Indians, 3 vols., Set. Annie H. Abel. LC 70-116268. 1925. reprint ed. 200.00 (*0-403-00471-3*) Scholarly.

Slaveholding Indians, Vol 1: The American Indian As Slaveholder. Annie H. Abel. LC 70-116268. 1919. reprint ed. 69.00 (*0-685-26252-9*) Scholarly.

Slaveholding Indians, Vol. 2: The American Indian As Participant in the Civil War. Annie H. Abel. LC 70-116268. 1919. reprint ed. 69.00 (*0-685-26253-7*) Scholarly.

Slaveholding Indians, Vol. 3: The American Indian under Reconstruction. Annie H. Abel. LC 70-116268. 1919. reprint ed. 69.00 (*0-685-26254-5*) Scholarly.

Slaveholding Not Sinful. Samuel B. How. LC 70-152922. (Black Heritage Library Collection). 1977. 23.95 (*0-8369-8766-7*) Ayer.

Slavers in Paradise: The Peruvian Slave Trade in Polynesia, 1862-1864. H. E. Maude. LC 81-51203. (Illus.). 264p. 1981. 37.50 (*0-8047-1106-2*) Stanford U Pr.

***Slavery.** Christine Hatt. (History Sourcebook Ser.). (Illus.). 61p. (YA). (gr. 6 up). 1997. 19.95 (*0-87226-552-8*) P Bedrick Bks.

Slavery. William E. Channing. LC 71-82180. (Anti-Slavery Crusade in America Ser.). 1970. reprint ed. 24.95 (*0-405-00620-9*) Ayer.

Slavery. William E. Channing. (Works of William Ellery Channing II). 1990. reprint ed. lib. bdg. 79.00 (*0-685-27699-6*) Rprt Serv.

Slavery: A Problem in American Institutional & Intellectual Life. Stanley M. Elkins. LC 76-615. 328p. 1976. pap. text ed. 14.95 (*0-226-20477-4*) U Ch Pr.

Slavery: A World History. Milton Meltzer. (Illus.). 584p. 1993. reprint ed. pap. 22.50 (*0-306-80536-7*) Da Capo.

Slavery: And Other Forms of Unfree Labour. Leonie Archer. 288p. (C). 1988. pap. text ed. 19.95 (*0-415-00204-4*) Routledge.

Slavery: History & Historians. Peter J. Parish. LC 88-45541. 1990. pap. 12.00 (*0-06-430182-6*, Icon Edns) HarpC.

Slavery: Letters & Speeches. Horace Mann. LC 79-81126. (Black Heritage Library Collection). 1977. 32.95 (*0-8369-8623-7*) Ayer.

Slavery: Opposing Viewpoints. Ed. by William Dudley. LC 92-21796. (American History Ser.). 312p. (YA). 1992. pap. 12.96 (*1-56510-012-3*); lib. bdg. 20.96 (*1-56510-013-1*) Greenhaven.

Slavery Agitation in Virginia, 1829-1832. Theodore M. Whitfield. LC 30-23216. 162p. 1930. write for info. (*0-685-65090-1*) VA Bk.

Slavery Agitation in Virginia: 1829-1832. Theodore M. Whitfield. LC 78-64281. (Johns Hopkins University. Studies in the Social Sciences. Thirtieth Ser. 1912: 10). reprint ed. 37.50 (*0-404-61381-0*) AMS Pr.

Slavery & Abolition, Eighteen Thirty-One to Eighteen Forty-One. Albert B. Hart. LC 68-55891. (Illus.). 360p. 1969. reprint ed. text ed. 38.50 (*0-8371-0466-1*, HAS&, Greenwood Pr) Greenwood.

Slavery & Abolition, Eighteen Thirty-One to Eighteen Forty-One. Albert B. Hart. LC 68-24982. (Studies in Black History & Culture: No. 54). 1969. reprint ed. lib. bdg. 75.00 (*0-8383-0953-4*) M S G Haskell Hse.

Slavery & Abolition in Early Republican Peru. Peter Blanchard. LC 92-4999. (Latin American Silhouettes Ser.). 248p. 1992. 40.00 (*0-8420-2400-X*, SR Bks); pap. text ed. 15.95 (*0-8420-2429-8*, SR Bks) Scholarly Res Inc.

***Slavery & Abolition in the Ottoman Middle East.** Ehud R. Toledano. LC 97-9571. (Publications on the Near East). 208p. 1997. pap. 16.95 (*0-295-97642-X*) U of Wash Pr.

Slavery & Abolition, Part 1 see Millennium in America: From the Puritan Migration to the Civil War

Slavery & Abolition, Part 2 see Millennium in America: From the Puritan Migration to the Civil War

Slavery & Abolition, 1831-1841. Albert B. Hart. (History - United States Ser.). 360p. 1992. reprint ed. lib. bdg. 89.00 (*0-7812-6160-0*) Rprt Serv.

Slavery & Abolitionists. Suzanne M. Coil. (Illus.). 64p. (J). (gr. 5-8). 1997. lib. bdg. 15.98 (*0-8050-2984-2*) TFC Bks NY.

Slavery & African Life: Occidental, Oriental & African Slave Trades. Patrick Manning. (African Studies: No. 67). (Illus.). 264p. (C). 1990. pap. text ed. 20.95 (*0-521-34867-6*) Cambridge U Pr.

Slavery & Anti-Slavery in Mauritius: 1810-1833. Anthony J. Barker. 230p. 1996. text ed. 65.00 (*0-312-15920-X*) St Martin.

Slavery & Beyond: The African Impact on Latin America & the Caribbean. Ed. by Darien J. Davis. (Jaguar Books on Latin America: No. 5). 325p. 1994. 40.00 (*0-8420-2484-0*) Scholarly Res Inc.

Slavery & Beyond: The African Impact on Latin America & the Caribbean. Ed. by Darien J. Davis. (Jaguar Books on Latin America: No. 5). 301p. 1995. pap. 16.95 (*0-8420-2485-9*) Scholarly Res Inc.

Slavery & Four Years of War, 2 Vols. Joseph W. Keifer. LC 78-83948. (Black Heritage Library Collection). 1977. 70.95 (*0-8369-8616-4*) Ayer.

Slavery & Four Years of War: A Political History of Slavery in the United States, 2 Vols., Vol. 1. Joseph W. Keifer. LC 78-83948. 1977. reprint ed. 35.95 (*0-8369-9669-0*) Ayer.

Slavery & Four Years of War: A Political History of Slavery in the United States, 2 Vols., Vol. 2. Joseph W. Keifer. LC 78-83948. 1977. reprint ed. 35.95 (*0-8369-9670-4*) Ayer.

Slavery & Freedom: An Interpretation of the Old South. James Oakes. 1990. 22.95 (*0-394-53677-0*) Knopf.

***Slavery & Freedom among Early American Workers.** Hodges Graham. 208p. (C). (gr. 13). 1997. text ed. 59.95 (*0-7656-0112-5*) M E Sharpe.

***Slavery & Freedom among Early American Workers.** Graham Hodges. 208p. 1997. pap. text ed. 19.95 (*0-7656-0113-3*) M E Sharpe.

Slavery & Freedom in Delaware, 1639-1865: 1639-1865. William H. Williams. LC 96-13735. (Illus.). 270p. 1996. 50.00 (*0-8420-2594-4*) Scholarly Res Inc.

Slavery & Freedom in the Age of the American Revolution. Ed. by Ira Berlin & Ronald Hoffman. LC 86-11232. (Blacks in the New World Ser.). (Illus.). 352p. 1986. pap. text ed. 12.95 (*0-252-01363-8*) U of Ill Pr.

Slavery & Freedom in the Rural North: African Americans in Monmouth County, New Jersey, 1665-1865. Graham R. Hodges. LC 96-19334. (Illus.). 256p. 1996. 29.95 (*0-945612-43-5*) Madison Hse.

Slavery & Freedom on the Middle Ground. Barbara J. Fields. LC 84-20949. 287p. 1987. pap. 17.00 (*0-300-04032-6*, Y-680) Yale U Pr.

Slavery & Freedom on the Middle Ground: Maryland During the Nineteenth Century. Barbara J. Fields. LC 84-20949. (Yale Historical Publications: Misc. 123). 296p. 1985. 42.00 (*0-300-02340-5*) Yale U Pr.

Slavery & Historiography. Ed. by Paul Finkelman. (Articles on American Slavery Ser.: Vol. 1). 652p. 1990. reprint ed. text ed. 55.00 (*0-8240-6781-9*) Garland.

Slavery & Human Progress. David B. Davis. 400p. 1984. 40.00 (*0-19-503439-2*) OUP.

Slavery & Human Progress. David B. Davis. 400p. 1986. pap. 13.95 (*0-19-503733-2*) OUP.

Slavery & Its Consequences: The Constitution, Equality, & Race. Robert A. Goldwin & Art Kaufman. LC 88-10359. (AEI Studies: No. 469). 200p. (C). 1988. pap. 9.95 (*0-8447-3650-3*, AEI Pr) Am Enterprise.

Slavery & Methodism: A Chapter in American Morality, 1780-1845. Donald G. Mathews. LC 78-13249. 329p. 1978. reprint ed. text ed. 35.00 (*0-313-21045-4*, MASAM, Greenwood Pr) Greenwood.

Slavery & Plantation Growth in Antebellum Florida, 1821-1860. Julia F. Smith. LC 70-150656. (Illus.). 259p. 1973. reprint ed. pap. 73.90 (*0-7837-6069-8*, 2059115) Bks Demand.

Slavery & Race in American Popular Culture. William L. Van Deburg. LC 83-40272. 280p. 1984. pap. 14.50 (*0-299-09634-3*) U of Wis Pr.

Slavery & Rebellion in the Roman World, 140 B.C.-70 B.C. Keith R. Bradley. LC 88-45757. 202p. 1989. 31.50 (*0-253-31259-0*) Ind U Pr.

Slavery & Rice Culture in Low Country Georgia, 1750-1860. Julia F. Smith. LC 84-27063. (Illus.). 280p. 1985. text ed. 38.00 (*0-87049-462-7*) U of Tenn Pr.

Slavery & Rice Culture in Low Country Georgia, 1750-1860. Julia F. Smith. LC 84-27063. (Illus.). 280p. (C). 1985. pap. text ed. 18.00 (*0-87049-731-6*) U of Tenn Pr.

Slavery & Servitude in the Colonies of North Carolina. John S. Bassett. LC 78-63849. (Johns Hopkins University. Studies in the Social Sciences. Thirtieth Ser. 1912: 4-5). reprint ed. 37.50 (*0-404-61106-0*) AMS Pr.

Slavery & Social Death: A Comparative Study. Orlando Patterson. LC 82-1072. (Illus.). 528p. 1982. 39.95 (*0-674-81082-1*) HUP.

Slavery & Social Death: A Comparative Study. Orlando Patterson. 528p. 1985. pap. 19.95 (*0-674-81083-X*) HUP.

Slavery & Society at Rome. Keith Bradley. LC 93-42802. (Key Themes in Ancient History Ser.). (Illus.). 208p. (C). 1994. 54.95 (*0-521-37287-9*); pap. text ed. 18.95 (*0-521-37887-7*) Cambridge U Pr.

Slavery & Society in Medieval Scandinavia. Ruth M. Karras. LC 87-32167. (C). 1988. text ed. 45.00 (*0-300-04121-7*) Yale U Pr.

Slavery & the American West: The Eclipse of Manifest Destiny & the Coming of the Civil War. Michael A. Morrison. LC 96-23855. 448p. (C). (gr. 13). 1997. pap. 49.95 (*0-8078-2319-8*) U of NC Pr.

Slavery & the Catholic Tradition: Rights in the Balance. Stephen F. Brett. LC 93-42798. (Am. Univ. Studies, Series V: Vol. 157). 240p. (C). 1994. text ed. 42.95 (*0-8204-2358-0*) P Lang Pubng.

Slavery & the Church. William Hosmer. LC 78-133156. (Black Heritage Library Collection). 1977. 21.95 (*0-8369-8711-X*) Ayer.

Slavery & the Church. William Hosmer. LC 70-82465. 200p. 1970. reprint ed. text ed. 52.50 (*0-8371-1646-5*, HOS&, Greenwood Pr) Greenwood.

***Slavery & the Coming War.** Gary C. Walker. (Illus.). 280p. 1996. 32.95 (*0-9617898-3-2*) A & W Enterprises.

Slavery & the Domestic Slave Trade in the U. S. Ethan A. Andrews. LC 74-92412. 1836. 12.00 (*0-403-00148-X*) Scholarly.

Slavery & the Domestic Slave-Trade in the United States. Ethan A. Andrews. LC 76-138331. (Black Heritage Library Collection). 1977. 22.95 (*0-8369-8723-3*) Ayer.

Slavery & the Evolution of Cherokee Society, 1540-1866. Theda Perdue. LC 78-16284. 222p. 1979. 28.00 (*0-87049-259-4*); pap. 14.95 (*0-87049-530-5*) U of Tenn Pr.

Slavery & the Founders: Race & Liberty in the Age of Jefferson. Paul Finkelman. LC 95-22359. 300p. (C). 1995. pap. 19.95 (*1-56324-591-4*) M E Sharpe.

Slavery & the Founders: Race & Liberty in the Age of Jefferson. Paul Finkelman. LC 95-22359. 300p. (C). (gr. 13). 1995. 55.00 (*1-56324-590-6*) M E Sharpe.

Slavery & the French Revolutionists, 1788-1805. Anna J. Cooper. Ed. & Tr. by Frances R. Keller from FRE. LC 87-24704. (French Civilization Ser.: Vol. 1). (Illus.). 220p. 1988. lib. bdg. 89.95 (*0-88946-637-8*) E Mellen.

Slavery & the Internal Slave Trade in the United States of North America. Ed. by Theodore D. Weld. LC 79-82229. (Anti-Slavery Crusade in America Ser.). 1975. reprint ed. 25.95 (*0-405-00668-3*) Ayer.

Slavery & the Law. Ed. by Paul Finkelman. LC 96-8917. 544p. (C). 1997. 44.95 (*0-945612-36-2*) Madison Hse.

Slavery & the Literary Imagination. Ed. by Deborah E. McDowell & Arnold Rampersad. LC 88-45405. (Selected Papers from the English Institute; 1982-83, New Ser.: No. 13). 184p. 1989. reprint ed. pap. text ed. 13.95 (*0-8018-3948-3*) Johns Hopkins.

Slavery & the Rise of the Atlantic System. Ed. by Barbara L. Solow. (Illus.). 350p. (C). 1991. 54.95 (*0-521-40090-2*) Cambridge U Pr.

Slavery & the Rise of the Atlantic System. Ed. by Barbara L. Solow. (Illus.). 365p. (C). 1993. pap. text ed. 19.95 (*0-521-45737-8*) Cambridge U Pr.

Slavery & the Slave Trade: A Short Illustrated History. James Walvin. LC 82-24833. (Illus.). 168p. 1983. pap. 16.95 (*0-87805-181-3*) U Pr of Miss.

***Slavery & the South, 1852-1857.** Frederick L. Olmsted. Ed. by Charles E. Beveridge & Charles C. McLaughlin. LC 80-8881. (Papers of Frederick Law Olmsted: Vol. 2). 527p. 1981. reprint ed. pap. 150.20 (*0-608-03669-2*, 2064495) Bks Demand.

Slavery As It Relates to the Negro or African Race: The Light of Circumstances History & the Holy Scriptures. Josiah Priest. Ed. by Gerald Grob. LC 76-46096. (Anti-Movements in America Ser.). (Illus.). 1977. reprint ed. lib. bdg. 29.95 (*0-405-09969-X*) Ayer.

Slavery as Salvation: The Metaphor of Slavery in Pauline Christianity. Dale B. Martin. 272p. (C). 1990. text ed. 30.00 (*0-300-04735-5*) Yale U Pr.

Slavery at Monticello. Lucia C. Stanton. (Monticello Monographs). (Illus.). 58p. (Orig.). 1996. pap. 6.95 (*1-882886-02-X*) T J Mem Fnd.

Slavery Attacked: Southern Slaves & Their Allies, 1619-1865. Merton L. Dillon. LC 90-6067. 328p. 1990. pap. text ed. 16.95 (*0-8071-1653-X*) La State U Pr.

Slavery, Capitalism & Politics in the Antebellum Republic Vol. 1: Commerce & Compromise, 1820-1850. John Ashworth. (Illus.). 532p. (C). 1996. pap. text ed. 19.95 (*0-521-47994-0*) Cambridge U Pr.

Slavery, Capitalism & Politics in the Antebellum Republic Vol. 1: Commerce & Compromise, 1820-1850. John Ashworth. (Illus.). 532p. (C). 1996. text ed. 64.95 (*0-521-47487-6*) Cambridge U Pr.

Slavery Days in Old Kentucky. Isaac Johnson. Ed. & Intro. by Cornell Reinhart. (Illus.). 66p. (C). 1994. reprint ed. pap. text ed. 14.95 (*0-9634028-2-X*) Frnds O D Young Lib.

Slavery Discussed in Occasional Essays, from 1833-1846. Leonard Bacon. LC 72-82167. (Anti-Slavery Crusade in America Ser.). 1970. reprint ed. 22.95 (*0-405-00607-1*) Ayer.

Slavery During the Third Dynasty of Ur. Bernard J. Siegel. LC 48-8755. (American Anthropological Association Memoirs Ser.). 1947. pap. 25.00 (*0-527-00565-7*) Periodicals Srv.

Slavery Examined in the Light of the Bible. Luther Lee. 1988. reprint ed. lib. bdg. 75.00 (*0-7812-0277-9*) Rprt Serv.

Slavery Examined in the Light of the Bible. Luther Lee. LC 76-92434. 185p. 1855. reprint ed. 39.00 (*0-403-00166-8*) Scholarly.

Slavery from Roman Times to the Early Transatlantic Trade. William D. Phillips. LC 84-10470. 299p. 1985. reprint ed. pap. 85.30 (*0-608-00794-3*, 2059343) Bks Demand.

Slavery Illustrated in Its Effects upon Woman & Domestic Society. George Bourne. LC 72-6480. (Black Heritage Library Collection). 1977. reprint ed. 16.95 (*0-8369-9174-5*) Ayer.

Slavery, Imperialism, & Freedom: Studies in English Radical Thought. Gordon Lewis. LC 78-2826. 346p. 1979. pap. 10.00 (*0-85345-501-5*) Monthly Rev.

Slavery in Africa: Historical & Anthropological Perspectives. Ed. by Suzanne Miers & Igor Kopytoff. LC 76-53653. (Illus.). 494p. 1977. 35.00 (*0-299-07330-0*) U of Wis Pr.

Slavery in Africa: Historical & Anthropological Perspectives. Ed. by Suzanne Miers & Igor Kopytoff. LC 76-53653. (Illus.). 494p. 1979. pap. 16.50 (*0-299-07334-3*) U of Wis Pr.

Slavery in Alabama. James B. Sellers. LC 93-43412. (Library of Alabama Classics). 456p. 1994. pap. 24.95 (*0-8173-0594-7*) U of Ala Pr.

Slavery in America. Thomas Price. LC 71-92449. 1837. 15.00 (*0-403-00170-6*) Scholarly.

Slavery in American Society. 3rd ed. Ed. by Lawrence B. Goodheart et al. (Problems in American Civilization Ser.). 306p. (C). 1993. pap. text ed. 16.76 (*0-669-24446-5*) HM College Div.

Slavery in Ancient Greece. Yvon Garlan. Tr. by Janet Lloyd from FRE. LC 87-47963. 310p. 1988. 42.50 (*0-8014-1841-0*); pap. 16.95 (*0-8014-9504-0*) Cornell U Pr.

Slavery in Ancient Rome. M. Massey. (Inside the Ancient World Ser.). pap. 14.95 (*0-17-439745-3*) Focus Pub-R Pullins.

Slavery in Babylonia. Muhammad A. Dandamaev. Ed. by Marvin A. Powell & David B. Weisberg. Tr. by Victoria A. Powell from RUS. LC 84-10225. 836p. 1984. 55.00 (*0-87580-104-8*) N Ill U Pr.

Slavery in China During the Former Han Dynasty, 206 B. C.-A.D. 25. Clarence M. Wilbur. (Field Museum of Natural History Ser.: Vol. 34). 1943. 40.00 (*0-527-01894-5*) Periodicals Srv.

Slavery in Classical Greece. Fisher. (Classical World Ser.). 128p. 1993. pap. 14.95 (*1-85399-134-1*, Pub. by Brstl Class Pr UK) Focus Pub-R Pullins.

Slavery in Early Medieval England from the Reign of Alfred to the Twelfth Century. David A. Pelteret. (Studies in Anglo-Saxon History: Vol. 7). 390p. (C). 1995. 81.00 (*0-85115-399-2*) Boydell & Brewer.

Slavery in Kerala. Adoor Nair. 1986. 18.00 (*0-8364-1914-6*, Pub. by Mittal II) S Asia.

Slavery in Missouri, Eighteen Four to Eighteen Sixty-Five. Harrison A. Trexler. LC 78-63948. (Johns Hopkins University. Studies in the Social Sciences. Thirtieth Ser. 1912: 2). reprint ed. 37.50 (*0-404-61197-4*) AMS Pr.

Slavery in North Carolina, 1748-1775: Slavery in North Carolina, 1748-1775. Marvin L. Kay & Lorin L. Cary. LC 94-29751. 420p. 1995. text ed. 45.00 (*0-8078-2197-7*) U of NC Pr.

Slavery in the Americas: A Comparative Study of Virginia & Cuba. Herbert S. Klein. 288p. 1989. reprint ed. pap. text ed. 8.95 (*0-929587-04-9*, Elephant Paperbacks) I R Dee.

Slavery in the Ancient Near East: A Comparative Study of Slavery in Babylonia, Assyria, Syria & Palestine, from the Middle of the Third Millennium to the End of the First Millenium. Isaac Mendelsohn. LC 78-6962. 162p. 1978. reprint ed. text ed. 45.00 (*0-313-20499-3*, MESA) Greenwood.

Slavery in the Arab World. Murray Gordon. 272p. 1991. reprint ed. pap. 14.95 (*1-56131-023-9*) New Amsterdam Bks.

Slavery in the Circuit of Sugar: Martinique & the World Economy, 1830-1848. Dale W. Tomich. LC 89-26678. (Studies in Atlantic History & Culture). 368p. 1990. text ed. 52.00 (*0-8018-3918-1*) Johns Hopkins.

Slavery in the Cities: The South, Eighteen Twenty to Eighteen Sixty. Richard C. Wade. 352p. 1967. pap. 11.95 (*0-19-500755-7*) OUP.

Slavery in the Colonial Chesapeake. David B. Davis. (Foundations of America Ser.). (Illus.). 42p. (Orig.). 1986. pap. 9.95 (*0-87935-115-2*) Colonial Williamsburg.

Slavery in the Danish West Indies: A Bibliography. Ed. by Arnold R. Highfield & George F. Tyson. 73p. (Orig.). 1992. pap. write for info. (*0-916611-14-0*) Antilles Pr.

Slavery in the North & the West. Ed. by Paul Finkelman. (Articles on American Slavery Ser.: Vol. 5). 520p. 1990. reprint ed. text ed. 44.00 (*0-8240-6785-1*) Garland.

Slavery in the Ottoman Empire & Its Demise, 1800-1909. Hakan Erdem. LC 96-7125. 248p. 1997. text ed. 59.95 (*0-312-16209-X*) St Martin.

Slavery in the State of North Carolina. John S. Bassett. LC 79-161726. (Johns Hopkins University. Studies in the Social Sciences. Thirtieth Ser. 1912: No. 1899: 7-8). reprint ed. 37.50 (*0-404-00246-3*) AMS Pr.

Slavery in the Twentieth Century. Roger Sawyer. 400p. 1986. text ed. 39.95 (*0-7102-0475-2*, 04752, RKP) Routledge.

Slavery in the U. S. A. Henry Sherman. LC 79-92440. 1858. 14.00 (*0-403-00172-2*) Scholarly.

Slavery in the United States. William C. Hine. 1990. 24.95 (*1-56696-020-7*); student ed. 32.00 (*0-614-07316-2*) Golden Owl NY.

Slavery in the United States: A Narrative of the Life & Adventures of Charles Ball, a Black Man. Charles Ball. LC 71-92414. 1970. reprint ed. 11.00 (*0-403-00178-1*) Scholarly.

Slavery in the United States: Four Views. James C. Morgan. LC 84-43220. 214p. 1985. lib. bdg. 32.50 (*0-89950-162-1*) McFarland & Co.

***Slavery in the United States Today.** Max. 50p. (Orig.). 1997. pap. 30.00 (*0-922070-76-8*) M Tecton Pub.

Slavery Inconsistent with Justice & Good Policy. David Rice. LC 70-82216. (Anti-Slavery Crusade in America Ser.). 1970. reprint ed. 11.95 (*0-405-00655-1*) Ayer.

Slavery Is Alive - & We Are Not Well: How to Recognize & Escape Inter-Personal Control. Hugh W. Savage & Ethel F. Quiring. LC 95-60207. 186p. (Orig.). (C). 1995. pap. 12.95 (*0-932796-69-9*) Ed Media Corp.

Slavery, Law, & Politics: The Dred Scott Case in Historical Perspective. Don E. Fehrenbacher. (Illus.). 326p. 1981. pap. 12.95 (*0-19-502883-X*) OUP.

Slavery, Letters & Speeches. Horace Mann. LC 70-82205. (Anti-Slavery Crusade in America Ser.). 1970. reprint ed. 32.95 (*0-405-00643-8*) Ayer.

Slavery of Sex: Feminist-Abolitionists in America. Blanche G. Hersh. LC 78-14591. 296p. reprint ed. pap. 84.40 (*0-7837-0118-7*, 2040395) Bks Demand.

Slavery on Louisiana Sugar Plantations. Vernie A. Moody. LC 74-22753. (Labor Movement in Fiction & Non-Fiction Ser.). reprint ed. 29.50 (*0-404-58505-1*) AMS Pr.

Slavery on the Spanish Frontier: The Colombian Choco, 1680-1810. William F. Sharp. LC 76-18767. (Illus.). 1976. pap. 9.95 (*0-8061-1759-1*) U of Okla Pr.

Slavery Ordained by God. Frederick A. Ross. LC 74-83876. (Black Heritage Library Collection). 1977. 17.95 (*0-8369-8647-4*) Ayer.

Slavery Ordained of God. Frederick A. Ross. LC 70-95445. (Studies in Black History & Culture: No. 54). 1970. reprint ed. lib. bdg. 75.00 (*0-8383-1202-0*) M S G Haskell Hse.

Slavery Question. John T. Lawrence. 1977. 18.95 (*0-8369-9168-0*, 9043) Ayer.

Slavery Remembered: A Record of Twentieth-Century Slave Narratives. Paul D Escott. LC 78-12198. xv, 221p. 1979. pap. 10.95 (*0-8078-1343-5*) U of NC Pr.

Slavery Revisited: Blacks & the Southern Convict Lease System 1865-1933. Milfred C. Fierce. 260p. 1994. per., pap. text ed. write for info. (*0-9643248-0-6*) ASC-BC.

Slavery, Revolutionary America, & the New Nation. Ed. by Paul Finkelman. (Articles on American Slavery Ser.: Vol. 4). 512p. 1990. reprint ed. text ed. 44.00 (*0-8240-6784-3*) Garland.

Slavery, Sabbath, War & Women: Case Issues in Biblical Interpretation. Willard M. Swartley. LC 82-23417. (Conrad Grebel Lecture Ser.). 368p. (Orig.). 1983. pap. 16.99 (*0-8361-3330-7*) Herald Pr.

Slavery, the Civil Law, & the Supreme Court of Louisiana. Judith K. Schafer. LC 94-11801. (Illus.). 396p. 1994. text ed. 47.50 (*0-8071-1845-1*) La State U Pr.

***Slavery, the Civil Law, & the Supreme Court of Louisiana.** Judith K. Schafer. (Illus.). 329p. 1997. pap. text ed. 16.95 (*0-8071-2165-7*) La State U Pr.

Slavery, the Civil War, & Reconstruction. Eric Foner. (New American History Essays Ser.). 30p. (C). 1997. reprint ed. pap. 5.00 (*0-87229-054-9*) Am Hist Assn.

Slavery, the Civil War, & the Reintegration of American History. William W. Freehling. LC 93-32698. 336p. 1994. pap. 14.95 (*0-19-508808-5*) OUP.

Slavery, the Mere Pretext for the Rebellion. John P. Kennedy. 20p. 1967. reprint ed. pap. 3.65 (*0-910120-02-1*) Americanist.

***Slavery Time When I Was Chillun.** Belinda Hurmence. LC 96-37479. (Illus.). 144p. (YA). (gr. 4 up). 1997. 17.95 (*0-399-23048-3*, Putnam) Putnam Pub Group.

***Slavery Time When I Was Chillun.** Belinda Hurmence. LC 96-37479. (Illus.). 144p. (YA). (gr. 4 up). 1997. pap. 8.95 (*0-399-23194-3*) Putnam Pub Group.

Slavery Time When I Was Chillun down on Marster's Plantation: Interviews with Georgia Slaves. Ed. by Ronald Killion & Charles Waller. (Illus.). 169p. 1990. 20.00 (*0-88322-008-3*) Beehive GA.

Slavery Unmasked: Being a Truthful Narrative of A Three Year's Residence & Journeying in Eleven Southern States. Philo Tower. LC 74-104585. (Illus.). 432p. reprint ed. lib. bdg. 18.50 (*0-8398-1971-4*) Irvington.

Slavery Unmasked: Being a Truthful Narrative of a Three Years' Residence & Journeying in Eleven Southern States. Philo Tower. (Illus.). 432p. (C). 1986. reprint ed. pap. text ed. 7.95 (*0-8290-2005-5*) Irvington.

Slavery Versus English Justice: The Trial of Arthur Hodge. John H. Andrew. 306p. 1995. 25.95 (*0-932831-15-X*) Eastern Caribbean Inst.

Slavery Without Chains, & Other Selected Poems. Tonia R. Lee. LC 87-9058. (Orig.). 1988. pap. 5.00 (*0-942029-00-3*) Lee Price.

Slavery's End in Tennessee, 1861-1865. John Cimprich. LC 84-16200. (Illus.). 202p. 1985. reprint ed. pap. 57.60 (*0-608-01663-2*, 2062318) Bks Demand.

Slaves & Freedmen in Civil War Louisiana. fac. ed. C. Peter Ripley. LC 75-18043. 253p. 1976. reprint ed. pap. 72.20 (*0-7837-7819-8*, 2047575) Bks Demand.

Slaves & Masters in the Roman Empire: A Study in Social Control. Keith R. Bradley. 160p. 1987. pap. text ed. 15.95 (*0-19-520607-X*) OUP.

Slaves & Slavery: The British Colonial Experience. James Walvin. 192p. 1992. text ed. 59.95 (*0-7190-3750-6*, Pub. by Manchester Univ Pr UK); text ed. 17.95 (*0-7190-3751-4*, Pub. by Manchester Univ Pr UK) St Martin.

Slaves & Slavery in Ancient Rome. Zvi Yavetz. Tr. by Adam Vital. 206p. 1987. 39.95 (*0-88738-128-6*) Transaction Pubs.

Slaves & Slavery in Muslim Africa, 2 vols., Vol. 1. Ed. by John R. Willis. 1985. 47.50 (*0-7146-3142-6*, Pub. by F Cass Pubs UK) Intl Spec Bk.

Slaves & Slavery in Muslim Africa, 2 vols., Vol. 2. Ed. by John R. Willis. 1985. Vol. 1: Islam & the Ideology of Slavery. 47.50 (*0-7146-3201-5*, Pub. by F Cass Pubs UK) Intl Spec Bk.

***Slaves by Choice.** Sterling Sims. (Illus.). 156p. (Orig.). 1997. pap. 11.95 (*1-57502-517-5*, P01536) Morris Pubng.

Slave's Dream & Other Stories. Nabil N. Gorgy. Tr. by Denys Johnson-Davies from ARA. 176p. 1991. 19.95 (*0-7043-2776-7*, Pub. by Quartet UK) Interlink Pub.

Slaves' Economy: Independent Production by Slaves in the Americas. Ed. by Ira Berlin & Philip D. Morgan. 213p. 1995. pap. 24.00 (*0-7146-4172-3*, Pub. by F Cass Pubs UK) Intl Spec Bk.

Slave's Gambit. 2nd ed. Larry Townsend. 133p. 1993. reprint ed. pap. 8.95 (*1-881684-02-4*) L T Pubns CA.

Slaves I Claibourne County, Mississippi. Brenda Terry. 217p. (Orig.). pap. 16.50 (*0-7884-0269-2*) Heritage Bk.

Slaves in Red Coats: The British West India Regiments, 1795-1815. Rober N. Buckley. LC 78-16830. (Illus.). 1979. 32.00 (*0-300-02216-6*) Yale U Pr.

***Slaves in the Family.** Edward Ball. 1998. 30.00 (*0-374-26582-8*) FS&G.

Slaves into Workers: Emancipation & Labor in Colonial Sudan. Ahmad Sikainga. LC 95-37530. (Modern Middle East Ser.). (Illus.). 264p. 1955. text ed. 35.00 (*0-292-77694-2*) U of Tex Pr.

Slave's Narrative. Ed. by Charles T. Davis & Henry L. Gates, Jr. (Illus.). 384p. 1985. reprint ed. 40.00 (*0-19-503276-4*) OUP.

Slave's Narrative. Ed. by Charles T. Davis & Henry L. Gates, Jr. (Illus.). 384p. 1991. reprint ed. pap. 18.95 (*0-19-506656-1*) OUP.

Slaves No More: Letters from Liberia, 1833-1869. Ed. by Bell I. Wiley. LC 79-4015. 357p. reprint ed. pap. 101.80 (*0-7837-5776-X*, 2045441) Bks Demand.

Slaves No More: Three Essays on Emancipation & the Civil War. Ira Berlin et al. (Illus.). 240p. (C). 1992. text ed. 54.95 (*0-521-43102-6*); pap. text ed. 14.95 (*0-521-43692-3*) Cambridge U Pr.

Slaves Obey Your Masters: What the Bible Really Says about Slavery. Elreta Dodds. LC 94-61593. 247p. 1995. per., pap. 10.95 (*1-55523-734-7*) Winston-Derek.

Slaves of Cameroon. rev. ed. Paul Little. (Orig.). 1992. mass mkt. 4.95 (*1-56333-026-1*) Masquerade.

Slaves of New York. Tama Janowitz. 1991. pap. 8.95 (*0-671-74524-7*) S&S Trade.

Slaves of Shoanna. Mercedes Kelly. (Orig.). 1994. mass mkt. 4.95 (*1-56333-164-0*) Masquerade.

Slaves of Sleep & the Masters of Sleep. L. Ron Hubbard. (L. Ron Hubbard Fiction Classic Ser.). 392p. 9.98 (*0-88404-655-9*) Bridge Pubns Inc.

Slaves of Sumuru. Sax Rohmer. (Sumuru Ser.). 1979. 8.50 (*0-686-65266-5*) Bookfinger.

Slaves of the Depression: Workers' Letters about Life on the Job. Ed. by Gerald E. Markowitz & David Rosner. LC 87-6671. 272p. 1987. 45.00 (*0-8014-1956-5*); pap. 15.95 (*0-8014-9464-8*) Cornell U Pr.

Slaves of the Empire. Aaron Travis. 1992. reprint ed. mass mkt. 4.95 (*1-56333-054-7*, Badboy) Masquerade.

Slaves of the Harvest. Barbara B. Torey. 1978. 10.00 (*0-685-10101-0*) Tanadgusix Corp.

***Slaves of the Machine: The Quickening of Computer Technology.** Gregory J. Rawlins. LC 97-4013. (Illus.). 240p. 1997. 25.00 (*0-262-18183-5*, Bradford Bks) MIT Pr.

Slaves of the White God: Blacks in Mexico, 1570-1650. Colin A. Palmer. LC 75-34054. 246p. reprint ed. pap. 70.20 (*0-8357-8324-3*, 2033938) Bks Demand.

Slaves, Peasants, & Capitalists in Southern Angola, 1840-1926. Wilhelm G. Clarence-Smith. LC 78-67805. (African Studies Ser.: No. 27). 142p. reprint ed. pap. 40.50 (*0-318-34773-3*, 2031633) Bks Demand.

Slaves, Peasants, & Rebels: Reconsidering Brazilian Slavery. Stuart B. Schwartz. (Blacks in the New World Ser.). 192p. 1992. text ed. 34.95 (*0-252-01874-5*) U of Ill Pr.

Slaves, Peasants, & Rebels: Reconsidering Brazilian Slavery. Stuart B. Schwartz. 192p. 1996. pap. text ed. 14.95 (*0-252-06549-2*) U of Ill Pr.

Slaves, Spices & Ivory in Zanzibar: Integration of An East African Commercial Empire into the World Economy 1770-1873. Abdul Sheriff. LC 87-12339. (Illus.). 297p. 1987. text ed. 29.95 (*0-8214-0871-2*); pap. text ed. 15.95 (*0-8214-0872-0*) Ohio U Pr.

Slaves, Sugar, & Colonial Society: Travel Accounts of Cuba, 1801-1899. Ed. by Louis A. Perez, Jr. LC 91-44977. (Latin American Silhouettes Ser.). 259p. 1992. 40.00 (*0-8420-2354-2*, SR Bks); pap. 14.95 (*0-8420-2415-8*, SR Bks) Scholarly Res Inc.

Slaves to Duty. John Badcock, Jr. LC 72-77199. (Libertarian Broadsides Ser.: No. 2). 36p. 1972. reprint ed. pap. 0.85 (*0-87926-013-0*) R Myles.

***Slaves to Soldiers: African-American Fighting Men in the Civil War.** Wallace B. Black. LC 96-31630. (First Bks.). (J). 1997. lib. bdg. write for info. (*0-531-20252-6*) Watts.

Slaves Today: A Story of Liberia. George S. Schuyler. LC 72-99887. 1969. reprint ed. 39.50 (*0-404-00209-9*) AMS Pr.

Slaves Without Masters: The Free Negro in the Antebellum South. Ira Berlin. LC 92-1631. 448p. 1992. pap. 14.95 (*1-56584-028-3*) New Press NY.

Slavesong: The Art of Singing. Kweli Smith. LC 89-85170. (Illus.). 70p. (Orig.). 1989. pap. 8.00 (*0-9624092-0-0*) Anacostia Rep.

Slavianovedenie v SSSR: Izuchenie Iuzhnykh I Zapadnykh Slavian: Biobibliograficheskii Slovar' - A Biobibliographical Dictionary of Slavicists in the U. S. S. R. Specializing in Southern & Western Slavic Studies. Ed. by Iulian V. Bromlei & Vladimir A. D'Iakov. LC 92-60509. xii, 528p. (RUS.). 1993. lib. bdg. 90.00 (*0-88354-356-7*) N Ross.

Slavianskie Bogi. A. Kondrat'jev. 73p. (Orig.). 1990. reprint ed. 10.00 (*1-878445-53-7*) Antiquary CT.

Slavic Accentuation: A Study in Relative Chronology. F. H. Kortlandt. xiv, 94p. 1975. pap. 20.00 (*0-685-53314-X*) Benjamins North Am.

Slavic & Baltic Library Resources at the New York Public Library: A First History & Practical Guide. Robert H. Davis. 176p. 1994. pap. 12.95 (*0-87104-438-2*) NY Pub Lib.

Slavic Books & Bookmen: Papers & Essays. Edward Kasinec. LC 83-60970. (Russica Bibliography Ser.: No. 3). 180p. (Orig.). 1984. pap. 20.00 (*0-89830-069-X*) Russica Pubs.

Slavic Element in the Old Prussian Elbing Vocabulary. Jules F. Levin. LC 72-619636. (U. C. Publ. in Linguistics Ser.: Vol. 77). 124p. reprint ed. 35.40 (*0-8357-9639-6*, 2015116) Bks Demand.

Slavic Epic: Gundulic's Osman. Zdenko Zlatar. LC 93-45754. (Balkan Studies: Vol. 4). 632p. (C). 1995. text ed. 74.95 (*0-8204-2380-7*) P Lang Pubng.

Slavic Epic Studies see Selected Writings

Slavic Excursions: Essays on Russian & Polish Literature. Donald Davie. LC 90-34525. 312p. 1990. pap. text ed. 17.00 (*0-226-13759-7*) U Ch Pr.

An Asterisk (*) at the beginning of an entry indicates that the title is appearing in BIP for the first time.

Slavic Forum: Essays in Linguistics & Literature. Michael S. Flier. LC 72-88178. (Slavistic Printings & Reprintings Ser.: No. 277). 169p. 1974. text ed. 49.25 (90-279-2713-8) Mouton.

Slavic History & Literatures, 4 Vols, Set. Harvard University Library Staff. LC 69-10588. (Widener Library Shelflist: Nos. 28-31). 2996p. 1971. text ed. 200.00 (0-674-81090-2) HUP.

Slavic Literary Languages: Formation & Development. Ed. by Alexander M. Schenker & Edward Stankiewicz. LC 80-51031. (Russian & East European Publications: No. 1). 287p. 1980. 18.50 (0-936586-00-1) Yale Russian.

Slavic Poetics: Essays in Honor of Kiril Taranovsky. Roman Jakobson et al. LC 72-88184. (Slavistic Printings & Reprintings Ser.: Vol. 267). (Illus.). 1973. 161.55 (90-279-2526-7) Mouton.

***Slavic Sorcery: A Personal Journey.** Kenneth Johnson. (Illus.). 224p. (Orig.). 1998. pap. 12.95 (1-56718-374-3) Llewellyn Pubns.

***Slavic Specialties.** Ed. by Miriam Canter et al. 158p. 1996. 5.95 (1-57216-025-X) Penfield.

Slavic Structuralism. Endre Bojtar. LC 85-4291. (Linguistic & Literary Studies in Eastern Europe: No. 11). 160p. 1985. 55.00 (90-272-1507-3) Benjamins North Am.

***Slavic Studies.** Ed. by Alexander Kaun & Ernest J. Simmons. Date not set. write for info. (0-8369-7239-2) Ayer.

Slavic Studies: A Guide to Bibliographies, Encyclopedias, & Handbooks, 2 vols., Set. Ed. by Murlin Croucher. LC 92-28912. 980p. 1993. 150.00 (0-8420-2374-7) Scholarly Res Inc.

Slavic World & Scandinavia: Cultural Relations. Ed. by Kjeld Bjornager et al. 191p. (C). 1987. pap. 23.00 (87-7288-173-9, Pub. by Aarhus Univ Pr DK) David Brown.

Slavik Water Stress in Plants. 1965. lib. bdg. 64.50 (90-6193-251-3) Kluwer Ac.

***Slavische Lenworter im Albanischen.** Gunnar Svane. 352p. 1996. pap. 47.00 (87-7288-419-3, Pub. by Aarhus Univ Pr DK) David Brown.

***Slavischen Sprachen in Gegenwart und Geschichte: Sprachstrukturen und Verwandstschaft 2., Erweiterte und Verbesserte Auflage.** Baldur Panzer. (Heidelberger Publikationen zur Slavistick Ser.: Bd. 3). (Illus.). xiv, 464p. (GER.). 1996. 63.95 (3-631-49315-0) P Lang Pubng.

Slavonic & Western Music: Essays for Gerald Abraham. Ed. by Malcolm H. Brown & Roland J. Wiley. LC 84-2625. (Russian Music Studies: No. 12). 322p. reprint ed. 94.40 (0-8357-1594-9, 2070329) Bks Demand.

Slavonic Europe: A Political History of Poland & Russia from 1447 to 1796. R. Nisbet Bain. LC 76-135790. (Eastern Europe Collection). 1971. reprint ed. 25.95 (0-405-02732-X) Ayer.

Slavonic Europe: A Political History of Russia & Poland, 1447-1796. R. N. Bain. 1976. lib. bdg. 59.95 (0-8490-2615-6) Gordon Pr.

Slavonic Fairy Tales: From the Russian, Polish, Serbian & Bohemian. John T. Naake. 1972. 59.95 (0-8490-1062-4) Gordon Pr.

Slavonic Languages. Ed. by Bernard Comrie & Greville G. Corbett. LC 91-39221. (Language Family Descriptions Ser.). 512p. (C). (gr. 13). 1993. text ed. 150.00 (0-415-04755-2, A7038) Routledge.

Slavonic Mutual & Benevolent Society: One Hundred Twenty-Five Years in San Francisco 1857-1985. Adam S. Eterovich. LC 82-62215. 205p. 1984. 20.00 (0-918660-23-8) Ragusan Pr.

Slavonic Pioneers of California. Vjekoslav Meler. LC 68-57133. 1968. reprint ed. pap. 10.00 (0-88247-121-X) Ragusan Pr.

***Slavonic Translation of the Apocryphal Infancy Gospel of Thomas.** Thomas Rosen. (Acta Universitatis Upsaliensis Ser.: Vol. 39). 173p. 1997. pap. 44.50 (91-554-3964-0, Pub. by Almqvist & Wiksell SW) Coronet Bks.

Slavophile Controversy: History of a Conservative Utopia in Nineteenth Century Russian Thought. Andrzej Walicki. (C). 1989. pap. text ed. 23.00 (0-268-01734-4) U of Notre Dame Pr.

Slavs. Francis Conte. 250p. 1995. 35.00 (0-88033-310-3, E European Monographs) Col U Pr.

Slavs in European History & Civilization. Francis Dvornik. (Illus.). 696p. 1975. text ed. 24.95 (0-8135-0799-5) Rutgers U Pr.

Slavs in European History & Civilization. Francis Dvornik. (Illus.). 696p. 1986. pap. text ed. 20.00 (0-8135-0403-1) Rutgers U Pr.

Slavs in the Eyes of the Occident: The Occident in the Eyes of the Slavs. Ed. by Maria Ciesla-Korytowska. 200p. (C). 1993. text ed. 29.50 (0-88033-252-2, 355) Col U Pr.

Slay Ride. Dick Francis. 272p. 1987. reprint ed. mass mkt. 5.95 (0-449-21271-8, Crest) Fawcett.

Slayer: Just the Riffs. 65p. 1995. pap. 9.95 (0-89524-893-X) Cherry Lane.

Slayer - Divine Intervention. (Orig.). (YA). 1994. pap. 19.95 (0-89524-886-7, 02501244) Cherry Lane.

Slayer - Haunting the Chapel: Play-It-Like-It-Is-Guitar. 1994. pap. 14.95 (0-89524-824-7) Cherry Lane.

Slayer - Hell Awaits: Play-It-Like-It-Is-Guitar. pap. 19.95 (0-89524-720-8) Cherry Lane.

Slayer - Just the Riffs. Ed. by Jon Chappell & Steve Gorenberg. 31p. pap. 9.95 (0-614-04266-6) Cherry Lane.

Slayer - Reign in Blood: Play-It-Like-It-Is-Guitar. pap. 19.95 (0-89524-775-5) Cherry Lane.

Slayer - Seasons in the Abyss: Play-It-Like-It-Is-Bass. pap. 14.95 (0-89524-705-4) Cherry Lane.

Slayer - Seasons in the Abyss: Play-It-Like-It-Is-Guitar. pap. 19.95 (0-89524-671-6) Cherry Lane.

Slayer - Show No Mercy: Play-It-Like-It-Is-Guitar. pap. 19.95 (0-89524-678-3) Cherry Lane.

Slayer - South of Heaven: Play-It-Like-It-Is-Guitar. pap. 19.95 (0-89524-746-1) Cherry Lane.

Slayer-Decade of Aggression. Slayer. 161p. (YA). per., pap. 19.95 (0-89524-878-6, 02501246) Cherry Lane.

Slayer of Souls. Robert W. Chambers. Ed. by R. Reginald & Douglas Melville. LC 77-84207. (Lost Race & Adult Fantasy Ser.). 1978. reprint ed. lib. bdg. 29.95 (0-405-10963-6) Ayer.

Slayer of the Sacred Cow: A Contemporary Freethought Novel. Carl Shapiro. 186p. (Orig.). 1986. pap. 10.00 (0-914937-07-3) Ind Pubns.

Slayer of the Soul: Child Sexual Abuse & the Catholic Church. Stephen J. Rossetti. LC 90-70990. 224p. (Orig.). 1990. pap. 14.95 (0-89622-452-X) Twenty-Third.

Slayers of Moses: The Emergence of Rabbinic Interpretation in Modern Literary Theory. Susan A. Handelman. LC 81-16522. (SUNY Series in Modern Jewish Literature & Culture). 284p. (C). 1983. text ed. 64.50 (0-87395-576-5); pap. text ed. 21.95 (0-87395-577-3) State U NY Pr.

***Slaying the Dragon.** Michael Johnson. 1996. 22.00 (0-06-039218-5) HarpC.

Slaying the Dragon: Mythmaking in the Biblical Tradition. Bernard F. Batto. 176p. (Orig.). 1992. pap. 16.00 (0-664-25353-9) Westminster John Knox.

Slaying the English Jargon. Fern Rock. 116p. 1992. pap. text ed. 20.00 (0-914548-43-3, 147-92) Soc Tech Comm.

Slaying the Giant: Practical Help for Understanding Preventing & Overcoming Depression. French O'Shields. 145p. (Orig.). 1994. pap. 7.99 (0-9641901-0-9) Hem Of His Garment.

Slaying the Law School Dragon: How to Survive & Thrive in First Year Law School. 2nd ed. George Roth. LC 90-23358. 182p. 1991. pap. text ed. 15.95 (0-471-54298-9) Wiley.

***Slaying the Nimby Dragon.** Herbert Inhaber. LC 97-15480. 1997. write for info. (1-56000-219-0) Transaction Pubs.

***Slaying the Software Dragon: Practice Guide.** Benmenachem. (ITCP-UK Computer Science Ser.). 1997. pap. 39.99 (1-85032-326-7) ITCP.

***Slaying the Virus Villian: A 4-Lesson Program to be Used with Red Balloons Fly High in the Sky.** Cindy D. Holms. LC 96-79859. 16p. (Orig.). (J). 1997. pap. 4.95 (1-57543-024-X) Mar Co Prods.

SLCCS: Gale's Library of Congress Classification Schedules Combined with Addition & Changes Through 1995: Class C. Auxiliary Sciences of History. 95th ed. Kathleen Droste et al. 1996. 62.00 (0-8103-2573-X) Gale.

SLCCS: Gale's Library of Congress Classification Schedules Combined with Additions & Changes Through 1995, 47 Vols. 95th ed. Kathleen Droste et al. 1995. 3,150.00 (0-8103-2567-5) Gale.

SLCCS: Gale's Library of Congress Classification Schedules Combined with Additions & Changes Through 1995: Class A, General Works. 95th ed. Kathleen Droste et al. 1996. 56.00 (0-8103-2568-3) Gale.

SLCCS: Gale's Library of Congress Classification Schedules Combined with Additions & Changes Through 1995: Class B, Subclass BX. Religion: Christian Denominations. 95th ed. Kathleen Droste et al. 1996. 59.00 (0-8103-2572-1) Gale.

SLCCS: Gale's Library of Congress Classification Schedules Combined with Additions & Changes Through 1995: Class B, Subclasses B-BJ. Philosophy. Psychology. 95th ed. Kathleen Droste et al. 1996. 103.00 (0-8103-2569-1) Gale.

SLCCS: Gale's Library of Congress Classification Schedules Combined with Additions & Changes Through 1995: Class B, Subclasses BL-BQ. Religion, Hinduism, Judaisism, Islam, Buddhism. 95th ed. Kathleen Droste et al. 1996. 76.00 (0-8103-2570-5) Gale.

SLCCS: Gale's Library of Congress Classification Schedules Combined with Additions & Changes Through 1995: Class B, Subclasses BR-BV. Religion: Christianity, Bible. 95th ed. Kathleen Droste et al. 308p. 1996. 54.00 (0-8103-2571-3) Gale.

SLCCS: Gale's Library of Congress Classification Schedules Combined with Additions & Changes Through 1995: Class D, Subclasses DL-DR. History of Europe, Part 2. 95th ed. Kathleen Droste et al. 1996. 59.00 (0-8103-4297-9) Gale.

SLCCS: Gale's Library of Congress Classification Schedules Combined with Additions & Changes Through 1995: Class U. Military Science. 95th ed. Kathleen Droste et al. 119p. 1996. 57.00 (0-8103-4530-7) Gale.

SLCCS: Gale's Library of Congress Classification Schedules Combined with Additions & Changes Through 1995: Classes E-F. History: America. 95th ed. Kathleen Droste et al. 1996. 179.00 (0-8103-4473-4) Gale.

Sleaze Creatures: An Illustrated Guide to Obscure Hollywood Horror Movies 1956-1959. D. Earl Worth. Ed. by Larry Chidsey. (Illus.). 254p. (Orig.). 1995. pap. 19.95 (0-9634982-6-6) Fantasma Bks.

Sleaze Merchants: Adventures in Exploitation Filmmaking. John McCarty. 1995. pap. 16.95 (0-312-11893-7) St Martin.

Sleazy Business: A Pictorial History of Exploitation Tabloids 1959-1974. Alan Betrock. (Illus.). 128p. (Orig.). 1996. pap. 12.95 (0-9626833-8-8) Shake Bks.

Sleazy Cartoons of Bill Plympton. Bill Plympton. (Illus.). 80p. 1996. pap. 15.00 (0-9652075-0-1) B Plympton.

***Sled.** Judith Thompson. 1997. pap. text ed. 12.95 (0-88754-517-3, Pub. by Playwrights CN Pr CN) Theatre Comm.

Sled Dog for Moshi. Jeanne Bushey. LC 93-13568. (Illus.). 40p. (J). (gr. k-3). 1994. 14.95 (1-56282-631-X) Hyprn Child.

Sled Dog for Moshi. Jeanne Bushey. LC 93-13568. (Illus.). 40p. (J). (gr. 3-7). 1994. lib. bdg. 14.89 (1-56282-632-8) Hyprn Child.

***Sled Dog for Moshi.** large type ed. Jeanne Bushey. (Illus.). 40p. (J). (ps-3). 1994. 14.95 (0-920534-85-6, Pub. by Hyperion Pr Ltd CN) Sterling.

Sled Dog Trails. Mary Shields. (Illus.). 127p. 1984. pap. 11.00 (0-88240-258-7) Pyrola Pub.

Sled Dogs of Denali. Sandy Kogl. Ed. by Charles Gilbert. (Illus.). 20p. 1981. pap. 2.00 (0-9602876-3-9) Alaska Natural.

Sled Driver: Flying the World's Fastest Jet. 2nd ed. Brian Shul. (Illus.). 151p. 1992. 40.00 (0-929823-08-7) Mach One.

Sled Surprise. Gina C. Erickson. (Get Ready...Get Set... Read! Ser.). (Illus.). 24p. (J). (ps-2). 1991. pap. 3.50 (0-8120-4677-3) Barron.

Sled Surprise: A First Book. Kelli C. Foster & Gina C. Erickson. (Get Ready...Get Set...Read! Ser.: Set 1). (Illus.). 26p. (J). lib. bdg. 11.95 (1-56674-113-0) Forest Hse.

Sledding. Elizabeth Winthrop. LC 89-1761. (Illus.). 32p. (J). (ps-2). 1989. lib. bdg. 14.89 (0-06-026566-3) HarpC Child Bks.

Sleek for the Long Flight. William Matthews. 1988. pap. 8.00 (0-934834-22-9) White Pine.

***Sleep.** J. Paul Caldwell. (Your Personal Health Ser.). (Illus.). 222p. (Orig.). 1997. pap. 14.95 (1-55209-122-8) Firefly Bks Ltd.

Sleep. Ed. by Rosemary Cooper. LC 93-3996. 702p. (gr. 13). 1994. Acid-free paper. text ed. 143.95 (0-412-39150-3) Chapman & Hall.

Sleep. William Dement. Date not set. pap. 22.95 (0-670-85367-4) Viking Penguin.

Sleep. Edward Edelson. (Encyclopedia of Health Ser.). (Illus.). 112p. (YA). (gr. 7 up). 1992. lib. bdg. 19.95 (0-7910-0092-3) Chelsea Hse.

Sleep. J. Allan Hobson. LC 88-37027. (Scientific American Library). 213p. 1995. text ed. 32.95 (0-7167-5050-3) W H Freeman.

Sleep. J. Allan Hobson. LC 88-37027. (Illus.). 213p. 1996. pap. text ed. 19.95 (0-7167-6014-2) W H Freeman.

Sleep. 3rd rev. ed. ASET Staff et al. (Illus.). iv, 102p. 1994. spiral bd. 18.00 (1-57797-015-2) ASET.

Sleep: An Unobserved Element in Education. Audrey E. McAllen. 68p. 1990. pap. 14.95 (1-869890-03-5, 619, Pub. by Hawthorn Press UK) Anthroposophic.

Sleep: Fifteen Poems. Peter W. Katsirubas. 1986. pap. 2.65 (0-9616166-0-1) Aeolus Pr VA.

Sleep: How to Teach Your Child to Sleep Like a Baby. Tamara Eberlein. 1996. mass mkt. 5.99 (0-671-88038-1) PB.

Sleep: Neurotransmitters & Neuromodulators. Ed. by Albert Wauquier et al. LC 85-10800. 362p. 1985. reprint ed. pap. 103.20 (0-608-00364-6, 2061081) Bks Demand.

Sleep: The Gentle Tyrant. 2nd ed. Wilse B. Webb. 200p. (C). 1992. pap. 22.95 (0-9627042-2-9) Anker Pub.

***Sleep: The Secret of Problem-Free Nights.** Beatrice Hollyer & Lucy Smith. (Positive Parenting Ser.). 128p. 1997. pap. 10.95 (0-7063-7504-1, Pub. by Ward Lock UK) Sterling.

Sleep, Aging & Related Disorders. Ed. by W. Emser et al. (Interdisciplinary Topics in Gerontology Ser.: Vol. 22). (Illus.). x, 166p. 1987. 100.00 (3-8055-4451-0) S Karger.

Sleep & Aging: A Research-Based Guide to Sleep in Later Life. Kevin Morgan. LC 87-45486. 160p. 1987. text ed. 37.50 (0-8018-3564-X) Johns Hopkins.

Sleep & Alertness: Chronobiological, Behavioral, & Medical Aspects of Napping. Ed. by David F. Dinges & Roger J. Broughton. 335p. 1989. text ed. 109.50 (0-88167-524-5, 1959) Lppncott-Raven.

Sleep & Biological Rhythms: Basic Mechanisms & Applications to Psychiatry. Ed. by Jacques Montplaisir & Roger Godbout. (Illus.). 256p. 1990. 49.95 (0-19-505825-9) OUP.

Sleep & Breathing. 2nd ed. Ed. by Nicholas A. Saunders & Colin E. Sullivan. LC 93-28482. (Lung Biology in Health & Disease Ser.: Vol. 71). 1002p. 1993. 235.00 (0-8247-8877-X) Dekker.

Sleep & Cognition. Ed. by Richard Bootzin et al. 205p. 1990. pap. text ed. 19.95 (1-55798-262-7) Am Psychol.

Sleep & Cognition. Daniel L. Schacter. 205p. 1990. text ed. 39.95 (1-55798-083-7) Am Psychol.

Sleep & Dreaming. 2nd ed. Jacob Empson. 256p. 1994. pap. text ed. 39.95 (0-13-302118-1) P-H.

Sleep & Dreams. J. Allan Hobson. Ed. by J. J. Head. (Carolina Biology Readers Ser.). (Illus.). 16p. (Orig.). (YA). (gr. 10 up). 1992. pap. text ed. 2.75 (0-89278-117-3, 45-9617) Carolina Biological.

Sleep & Dreams. Duane Michals. (Illus.). 64p. 1984. pap. 11.95 (0-912810-46-7) Lustrum Pr.

Sleep & Health Risk. Ed. by J. H. Peter et al. (Illus.). 560p. 1991. pap. 126.00 (0-387-53083-5) Spr-Verlag.

Sleep & Its Derangements. W. A. Hammond. (Hypnosis & Altered States of Consciousness Ser.). 318p. 1982. reprint ed. lib. bdg. 35.00 (0-306-76160-2) Da Capo.

Sleep & Its Disorders. J. D. Parkes. (Major Problems in Neurology Ser.). (Illus.). 430p. 1986. text ed. 92.00 (0-7216-1858-8) Saunders.

Sleep & Its Secrets: The River of Crystal Light. M. S. Aronoff. (Illus.). 290p. 1991. 24.50 (0-306-43968-9, Plenum Insight) Plenum.

Sleep & Wakefulness. Nathaniel Kleitman. LC 63-17845. x, 560p. (C). 1987. pap. text ed. 39.00 (0-226-44073-7) U Ch Pr.

Sleep Apnea & Rhonchopathy. Ed. by K. Togawa et al. (Illus.). x, 178p. 1993. 214.00 (3-8055-5611-X) S Karger.

Sleep, Arousal, & Performance. Robert D. Ogilvie. Ed. by Roger J. Broughton. (Illus.). xvi, 286p. 1991. 109.50 (0-8176-3518-1) Birkhauser.

Sleep, Baby, Sleep: Lullabies & Night Poems. Illus. & Compiled by Michael Hague. LC 93-27119. 80p. (J). 1994. 18.00 (0-688-10877-6, Morrow Junior) Morrow.

Sleep Book for Tired Parents: A Practical Guide to Solving Children's Sleep Problems. Rebecca Huntley. LC 90-62673. 104p. 1991. pap. 14.95 (0-943990-34-3); lib. bdg. 19.95 (0-943990-35-1) Parenting Pr.

***Sleep Deep.** Leslie Kenton. 1997. mass mkt. 1.99 (0-8041-1627-X) Ivy Books.

Sleep Deprivation Chamber. Adam Kennedy & Adrienne Kennedy. LC 96-35079. 112p. (Orig.). 1996. pap. 10.95 (1-55936-126-3) Theatre Comm.

***Sleep Disorder Sourcebook.** Kenneth Fisher. Date not set. 25.00 (1-56565-645-8) Contemp Bks.

***Sleep Disorder Sourcebook.** Kenneth Fisher. 1997. 25.00 (0-614-28325-6) Lowell Hse.

Sleep Disorders: America's Hidden Nightmare. Roger Fritz. Ed. by Carol Haralson. 180p. (Orig.). 1993. pap. 12.95 (0-9635137-0-2) Nat Sleep Alert.

Sleep Disorders & Insomnia in the Elderly. Ed. by J. L. Albarede et al. 232p. 1993. 39.95 (0-8261-8171-6) Springer Pub.

Sleep Disorders in Childhood & Adolescence. Ed. by David W. Kaplan. (Journal: Pediatrician: Vol. 17, No. 1). (Illus.). 52p. 1990. pap. text ed. 29.75 (3-8055-5151-7) S Karger.

Sleep Disorders in Old Age. David A. Smith. (Geriatric Psychopathology Ser.). 52p. (Orig.). 1995. pap. 39.95 (1-884937-28-4) Manisses Communs.

Sleep Disorders Medicine: Basic Science, Technical Considerations, & Clinical Aspects. Sudhansu Chokroverty. (Illus.). 504p. 1993. text ed. 135.00 (0-7506-9002-X) Buttrwrth-Heinemann.

Sleep Disorders of Older People. 1992. lib. bdg. 250.00 (0-8490-5543-1) Gordon Pr.

Sleep Disturbances in Early Childhood. O'Neil & Brown. 20p. 1993. 2.95 (1-56456-085-6, 283) W Gladden Found.

Sleep, Divine & Human, in the Old Testament. Thomas H. McAlpine. pap. 19.95 (0-905774-99-X, Pub. by Sheffield Acad UK) CUP Services.

Sleep, Dreaming, & Sleep Disorders: An Introduction. 2nd ed. William H. Moorcroft. 508p. (Orig.). (C). 1993. pap. text ed. 39.50 (0-8191-9251-1); lib. bdg. 64.50 (0-8191-9250-3) U Pr of Amer.

Sleep 'Eighty-Six. Ed. by W. P. Koella et al. LC 87-36156. 466p. 1988. lib. bdg. 200.00 (0-89574-252-7) G F Verlag.

Sleep Handbook. Nancy Lagomarsino. LC 86-72477. 72p. (Orig.). (C). 1987. 15.95 (0-914086-68-5); pap. 9.95 (0-914086-69-3) Alicejamesbooks.

Sleep Has His House. Anna Kavan. LC 79-26730. 182p. 1980. pap. 10.95 (0-935576-01-0) Kesend Pub Ltd.

Sleep Has His House. Anna Kavan. LC 79-26730. 1980. reprint ed. 11.95 (0-935576-00-2) Kesend Pub Ltd.

Sleep in a Ditch. large type ed. Maisie Birmingham. (Linford Mystery Library). 320p. 1987. pap. 15.99 (0-7089-6452-4, Linford) Ulverscroft.

Sleep Is for Everyone. Paul Showers. LC 72-83785. (Let's-Read-&-Find-Out Science Bk.). (Illus.). 40p. (J). (ps-3). 1974. lib. bdg. 14.89 (0-690-01118-0, Crowell Jr Bks) HarpC Child Bks.

***Sleep Is for Everyone.** Paul Showers. LC 96-49375. (Let's-Read-&-Find-Out Science Ser.: Level 1). (Illus.). 32p. (J). (ps-1). 1997. 14.95 (0-06-025392-4) HarpC Child Bks.

***Sleep Is for Everyone.** Paul Showers. LC 96-49375. (Let's-Read-&-Find-Out Science Ser.: Stage 1). (Illus.). 32p. (J). (ps-1). 1997. pap. 4.95 (0-06-445141-0, Trophy) HarpC Child Bks.

***Sleep Is for Everyone.** Paul Showers. LC 96-49375. (Let's-Read-&-Find-Out Ser.: Vol. 1). (Illus.). 32p. (J). (ps-1). 1997. lib. bdg. 14.89 (0-06-025393-2) HarpC Child Bks.

Sleep It Off Lady. Jean Rhys. 176p. 1995. pap. 10.95 (0-14-018345-0, Penguin Classics) Viking Penguin.

Sleep Long, My Love. Hillary Waugh. 1989. pap. 3.95 (0-88184-552-3) Carroll & Graf.

***Sleep Long My Love.** Hillary Waugh. 3.95 (0-7867-0552-3) Carroll & Graf.

Sleep Matters: The Yawn of a New Day. JoAnn Friedrich. 250p. (Orig.). 1996. pap. 12.95 (0-9617317-1-0) Bright Bks CA.

Sleep My Child, Forever. John Coston. 320p. (Orig.). 1995. pap. 5.99 (0-451-40335-5, Onyx) NAL-Dutton.

***Sleep My Sweet Baby (A Lullaby)** Dolly Braida. Ed. & Contrib. by Christine Vaughan. (Illus.). 24p. (J). (ps-1). 1997. pap. 7.95 (0-9658113-0-1) Jo-Eric.

Sleep Nineteen Eighty: Proceedings of the European Congress on Sleep Research, 5th, Amsterdam, September 1980. European Congress on Sleep Research Staff. Ed. by W. P. Koella. (Illus.). xiv, 466p. 1981. 198.50 (3-8055-2045-X) S Karger.

Sleep Nineteen Eighty-Eight: Proceedings of the 9th European Congress on Sleep Research, Jerusalem, September 4-9, 1988. Ed. by Jim Horne. 310p. 1990. text ed. 150.00 (0-89574-301-9) G F Verlag.

Sleep Nineteen Eighty-Two: Sixth European Congress on Sleep Research, Zurich, March 1982. Ed. by W. P. Koella. (Illus.). xiv, 438p. 1983. 252.00 (3-8055-3577-5) S Karger.

Sleep Nineteen Seventy-Eight: Proceedings of the European Congress on Sleep Research, 4th, Tirgu-Mures, September 1978. European Congress on Sleep Research Staff. Ed. by L. Popoviciu et al. 1980. 157.75 (3-8055-0778-X) S Karger.

S

An Asterisk (*) at the beginning of an entry indicates that the title is appearing in BIP for the first time.

Sleep Nineteen Seventy-Four: Instinct, Neurophysiology, Endocrinology, Episodes, Dreams, Epilepsy & Intracranialpathology: Proceedings of the European Congress on Sleep Research, 2nd, Rome, April 8-11, 1974. European Congress on Sleep Research Staff. Ed. by W. P. Koella et al. 400p. 1975. 151.25 (*3-8055-2069-7*) S Karger.

Sleep Nineteen Seventy-Six: Proceedings of the European Congress on Sleep Research, 3rd, Montpellier, September 1976. European Congress on Sleep Research Staff. Ed. by W. P. Koella & P. Levin. 1977. 148.00 (*3-8055-2663-6*) S Karger.

Sleep No More: Railway, Canal & Other Stories of the Supernatural. L. T. Rolt. (Pocket Classics Ser.). 144p. 1996. pap. 8.95 (*0-7509-1157-3*, Pub. by Sutton Pubng UK) Bks Intl VA.

Sleep, Nutrition, & Mood. Edward Stonehill. LC 75-16121. (Illus.). 183p. reprint ed. pap. 52.20 (*0-685-20735-8*, 2030372) Bks Demand.

Sleep of Prisoners. Christopher Fry. 1953. pap. 5.25 (*0-8222-1040-1*) Dramatists Play.

***Sleep of Reason.** Hoberman. Date not set. 22.50 (*0-8050-4380-2*) St Martin.

Sleep of Reason. Ed. by Jonathan Williams. LC 74-76880. (Illus.). 120p. 1974. 25.00 (*0-912330-04-X*, Gnomon Pr); pap. 15.00 (*0-912330-23-6*, Gnomon Pr) Jargon Soc.

Sleep of Reason: Primitivism in Modern European Art & Aesthetics. Frances S. Connelly. 176p. 1995. 35.00 (*0-271-01305-2*) Pa St U Pr.

Sleep of Reason: Primitivism in Modern European Art & Aesthetics, 1725-1907. Frances S. Connelly. LC 93-27552. (Illus.). 154p. 1995. 35.00 (*0-271-01105-X*) Pa St U Pr.

Sleep of the Innocents. Carole Fernandez. LC 90-38831. 244p. (Orig.). 1991. pap. 9.50 (*1-55885-025-2*) Arte Publico.

Sleep on It! Kevin Kelly & Erin Jaeb. LC 95-12107. (World of Difference Ser.). 32p. (J). (gr. 3-7). 1995. lib. bdg. 19.50 (*0-516-08175-6*) Childrens.

Sleep on It! Kevin Kelly. (World of Difference Ser.). (Illus.). 32p. (J). (gr. 3-7). 1996. reprint ed. pap. 6.95 (*0-516-48175-4*) Childrens.

Sleep on It! The Practical Side of Dreaming. Janice Baylis. LC 77-74164. 254p. 1977. pap. 10.00 (*0-917738-04-7*) Sun Man Moon.

Sleep Onset: Normal & Abnormal Processes. Ed. by John Harsh & Robert D. Ogilvie. (Illus.). 397p. 1994. text ed. 39.95 (*1-55798-266-X*, 431-8320) Am Psychol.

Sleep Out. Carol Carrick. LC 72-88539. (Illus.). 32p. (J). (gr. 1-3). 1982. pap. 6.95 (*0-89919-083-9*, Clarion Bks) HM.

Sleep-over Mouse. Mary Packard. (My First Reader Ser.). (Illus.). 28p. (J). (ps-2). 1994. pap. 3.95 (*0-516-45367-X*); lib. bdg. 15.50 (*0-516-05367-1*) Childrens.

Sleep Psychologically Considered. Blanchard Fosgate. (Hypnosis & Altered States of Consciousness Ser.). 188p. 1982. reprint ed. lib. bdg. 22.50 (*0-306-76165-3*) Da Capo.

Sleep Related Breathing Disorders. Ed. by Hartmut Zwick. LC 92-24922. 100p. 1992. 30.95 (*0-387-82376-X*); pap. 25.00 (*3-211-82376-X*) Spr-Verlag.

***Sleep Research & Polysomnography: Index of New Information.** rev. ed. Ruth M. De Vecchia. 180p. 1997. 47.50 (*0-7883-1596-X*) ABBE Pubs Assn.

***Sleep Research & Polysomnography: Index of New Information.** rev. ed. Ruth M. De Vecchia. 180p. 1997. pap. 44.50 (*0-7883-1597-8*) ABBE Pubs Assn.

Sleep Restfully & Peacefully. 3.00 (*0-686-40910-8*, SR16) Transitions.

Sleep Rhymes Around the World. Ed. by Jane Yolen. LC 93-60244. (Illus.). 40p. (J). (ps-5). 1994. 16.95 (*1-56397-243-3*, Wordsong) Boyds Mills Pr.

Sleep Right in Five Nights: A Clear & Effective Guide for Conquering Insomnia. James Perl. 320p. 1995. pap. 10.00 (*0-688-14064-5*, Quill) Morrow.

Sleep Rx: 75 Proven Ways to Get a Good Night's Sleep. Norman D. Ford. LC 94-33844. 1994. pap. 9.95 (*0-13-143918-9*) P-H.

Sleep Rx: 75 Proven Ways to Get a Good Night's Sleep. Norman D. Ford. LC 94-33844. 1994. text ed. 24.95 (*0-13-143900-6*) P-H.

***Sleep Safe, Little Whale.** Miriam Schlein. LC 96-36899. (Illus.). 24p. (J). (ps up). 1997. 14.95 (*0-688-14757-7*) Greenwillow.

***Sleep Science: Integrating Basic Research & Clinical Practice.** Ed. by William J. Schwartz. (Monographs in Clinical Neuroscience: Vol. 15, 1997). (Illus.). viii, 200p. 1997. 174.00 (*3-8055-6537-2*) S Karger.

Sleep Secrets for Shift Workers & People with Off-Beat Schedules. David Morgan. LC 96-9961. 176p. (Orig.). 1996. pap. 12.95 (*1-57025-118-5*) Whole Person.

Sleep, Sleep, Sleep: A Lullaby for Little Ones Around the World. Nancy Van Laan. LC 93-44484. (Illus.). (J). (ps). 1994. 15.95 (*0-316-89732-9*) Little.

Sleep, Sleepiness & Performance. Ed. by Timothy H. Monk. LC 91-7466. (Series on Studies in Human Performance & Cognition: No. 1507). 325p. 1991. text ed. 125.00 (*0-471-93002-4*) Wiley.

Sleep Song. Karen Ray. LC 94-24859. (Illus.). 32p. (J). (ps). 1995. 15.95 (*0-531-06878-1*); lib. bdg. 16.99 (*0-531-08728-X*) Orchard Bks Watts.

Sleep Sound in Jesus. Michael Card. 32p. 1990. 15.99 (*0-89081-792-8*) Harvest Hse.

Sleep Talk. large type ed. Gillian Brown. 1990. pap. 15.99 (*0-7089-6872-4*, Traitree Bookshop) Ulverscroft.

Sleep-Talking: Psychology & Psychophysiology. Arthur M. Arkin. LC 81-3300. (Illus.). 640p. 1982. text ed. 89.95 (*0-89859-031-0*) L Erlbaum Assocs.

Sleep, Tantrums & Goodbyes. Child Magazine Staff. 1996. pap. write for info. (*0-614-98087-9*, Pocket Books) PB.

Sleep Therapy in Neuroses. Boris V. Andreev. Tr. by Basil Haigh. LC 60-13947. (International Behavioral Science Ser.). 121p. reprint ed. pap. 34.50 (*0-317-09869-1*, 2020659) Bks Demand.

***Sleep Thief, Restless Legs Syndrome.** Virginia N. Wilson. Ed. by Arthur S. Walters. (Illus.). 316p. 1996. 22.95 (*0-9652682-1-7*); pap. 16.95 (*0-9652682-0-9*) Galaxy Bks.

***Sleep Thieves.** Coren. 1997. pap. 12.00 (*0-684-83184-8*, Free Press) Free Pr.

Sleep Thieves: An Eye-Opening Exploration into the Science & Mysteries of Sleep. Stanley Coren. 320p. 1996. 24.00 (*0-684-82304-7*) Free Pr.

Sleep Tight. Matthew J. Costello. 1987. mass mkt. 3.95 (*0-8217-2121-6*, Zebra Kensgtn) Kensgtn Pub Corp.

Sleep Tight. B. G. Hennessy. (Illus.). 32p. (J). (ps-1). 1992. pap. 14.00 (*0-670-83567-6*) Viking Child Bks.

Sleep Tight. B. G. Hennessy. (Illus.). (J). (ps-1). 1995. pap. 4.99 (*0-14-054325-2*) Puffin Bks.

Sleep Tight! Sesame Street. Constance Allen. (Golden Super Shape Bks.). (Illus.). 24p. (J). 1991. pap. 1.95 (*0-307-10026-X*, Golden Pr) Western Pub.

Sleep Tight, Little Bear. Ingrid Huber. (Illus.). 32p. (J). 1994. 9.95 (*1-55859-887-1*, Abbeville Kids) Abbeville Pr.

Sleep Tight Mrs. Ming. 1993. pap. 5.95 (*1-55037-325-0*, Pub. by Annick CN); lib. bdg. 15.95 (*1-55037-322-6*, Pub. by Annick CN) Firefly Bks Ltd.

Sleep Tight, Pete. Ellen Schecter. LC 94-9790. (Bank Street Ready-to-Read Ser.). (J). 1995. pap. 3.99 (*0-553-37570-9*) Bantam.

Sleep Well, Little Bear. Quinn Buchholz. Tr. by Peter F. Neumeyer. (Illus.). 32p. (J). (ps up). 1994. 14.00 (*0-374-37026-5*) FS&G.

Sleep While I Sing. Laurali R. Wright. 240p. 1988. mass mkt. 6.99 (*0-7704-2300-0*) Bantam.

Sleep with the Angels. Mary Fisher. 224p. 1994. 24.95 (*1-55921-105-9*); pap. 12.95 (*1-55921-103-2*) Moyer Bell.

Sleep Without Drugs. Moses Wong. 135p. (Orig.). 1994. pap. 12.95 (*0-85572-190-1*, Pub. by Hill Content Pubng AT) Seven Hills Bk.

***Sleep Without Morning.** Rae Foley. LC 96-45512. 1997. 21.95 (*0-7838-8051-0*) G K Hall.

Sleeper. Woody Allen. 1978. 7.95 (*0-394-50051-2*) Random.

Sleeper. Louis Grachos et al. (Illus.). 40p. (Orig.). 1995. pap. text ed. 9.95 (*0-934418-46-2*) Mus Contemp Art.

Sleeper. Ray Nelson. (Illus.). 105p. (YA). 1995. pap. 9.95 (*0-9623068-1-9*) Raynel.

Sleeper. Gordon Stevens. 480p. 1994. mass mkt. 5.50 (*0-06-109241-X*, Harp PBks) HarpC.

Sleeper. large type ed. Eric Clark. 432p. 1987. 25.99 (*0-7089-1623-6*) Ulverscroft.

Sleeper. large type ed. Eileen Dewhurst. 1990. 25.99 (*0-7089-2188-4*) Ulverscroft.

***Sleeper Agent in Havana.** Frank Belsito. 160p. (Orig.). 1997. pap. 9.95 (*1-57502-459-4*, P01373) Morris Pubng.

Sleeper at Harvest Time. Leonid Latynin. Tr. by Andrew Bromfield from RUS. (Illus.). 288p. 1994. 21.00 (*0-939010-36-4*); pap. 11.00 (*0-939010-37-2*) Zephyr Pr.

Sleeper Awakes: A Journey to Sleep-Awareness. Jim Perry. 138p. 1992. pap. 11.95 (*0-945806-06-X*) Summit CA.

Sleeper Spy. William Safire. LC 95-8482. 480p. (YA). 1995. 24.00 (*0-679-43447-X*) Random.

***Sleeper Spy.** William Safire. 1997. mass mkt. 6.99 (*0-312-96156-1*) St Martin.

Sleeper Wakes: Harlem Renaissance Stories by Women. Intro. by Marcy Knopf. LC 92-30446. 250p. (C). 1993. pap. 14.95 (*0-8135-1945-4*); text ed. 40.00 (*0-8135-1944-6*) Rutgers U Pr.

Sleeper, You Wake: Poems. Bertha Rogers. Ed. by Patricia Schultz. LC 91-29832. (Poetry Ser.: Vol. 17). (Illus.). 84p. 1991. pap. 12.95 (*0-7734-9669-6*) E Mellen.

Sleepers. Lorenzo Carcaterra. LC 95-14039. 432p. 1995. 23.00 (*0-345-39606-5*) Ballantine.

Sleepers. Lorenzo Carcaterra. 1996. mass mkt. 6.99 (*0-345-40411-4*) Ballantine.

***Sleepers.** Lorenzo Carcaterra. 1996. pap. 6.99 (*0-345-90999-2*) Ballantine.

Sleepers. Dayal K. Khalsa. (Illus.). 24p. (J). (ps-1). 1988. lib. bdg. 7.95 (*0-517-56917-5*, Clarkson Potter) Crown Bks Yng Read.

Sleepers of Erin. Jonathan Cash. (Crime Monthly Ser.). 224p. 1984. pap. 5.95 (*0-14-006970-4*, Penguin Bks) Viking Penguin.

Sleepers of Erin. large type ed. Jonathan Gash. 1985. 15.95 (*0-7089-1363-6*) Ulverscroft.

Sleepers, Wake. Paul S. Jacobs. 192p. (J). (gr. 4-7). 1994. pap. 2.95 (*0-590-42398-3*) Scholastic Inc.

Sleepers Wake. Caroline Knox. LC 94-20317. 70p. 1994. pap. 11.00 (*0-943221-20-X*) Timken Pubs.

Sleepers, Wake! Technology & the Future of Work. 4th ed. Barry Jones. (Illus.). 304p. 1996. pap. 29.95 (*0-19-553756-4*) OUP.

***Sleeping Alone.** Barbara Bretton. 320p. 1997. mass mkt. 5.99 (*0-425-15717-2*) Berkley Pub.

Sleeping & the Dead. Anne Quinton. 1994. lib. bdg. 20.00 (*0-7278-4668-X*) Severn Hse.

Sleeping Arrangements. Laura Cunningham. 208p. 1991. pap. 10.95 (*0-452-26557-6*, Plume) NAL-Dutton.

***Sleeping at the Magnolia.** Lisa Brown. 464p. 1997. mass mkt. 5.99 (*0-06-108214-7*) HarpC.

Sleeping at the Starlite Motel. Bailey White. 1996. pap. 11.00 (*0-614-12569-3*, Vin) Random.

Sleeping at the Starlite Motel: And Other Adventures on the Way Back Home. Bailey White. 224p. 1995. 20.00 (*0-201-62670-5*) Addison-Wesley.

Sleeping at the Starlite Motel: And Other Adventures on the Way Back Home. Bailey White. 1996. pap. 12.00 (*0-679-77015-1*, Vin) Random.

Sleeping at the Starlite Motel: And Other Adventures on the Way Back Home. large type ed. Bailey White. LC 95-37987. 266p. 1996. 23.95 (*0-7862-0555-5*, Thorndike Lrg Prnt) Thorndike Pr.

Sleeping Bear: Its Legends, Lore & First People. George Weeks & William P. Mott, Jr. (Illus.). 58p. (Orig.). 1988. pap. 7.95 (*0-9614344-6-5*) Historical Soc MI.

Sleeping Beauties. Ken Haak. 1991. pap. 17.95 (*0-312-06015-7*) St Martin.

Sleeping Beauties. Susanna Moore. 1994. pap. 11.00 (*0-679-75539-X*, Vin) Random.

Sleeping Beauties. large type ed. Susanna Moore. LC 94-2973. 1994. lib. bdg. 19.95 (*0-7862-0198-3*) Thorndike Pr.

Sleeping Beauties: The Jerome L. Joss Collection of African Headrests at UCLA. William J. Dewey. LC 92-82945. (Illus.). 214p. 1993. 45.00 (*0-930741-27-7*); pap. 27.00 (*0-930741-28-5*) UCLA Fowler Mus.

Sleeping Beauty. (FRE & SPA.). (J). (gr. k-3). Span. ed. 6.25 (*0-685-28438-7*); Fr. ed. 9.95 (*0-685-28439-5*) Fr & Eur.

Sleeping Beauty. (Fun-to-Read Fairy Tales Ser.: Vol. 2). (Illus.). 24p. (J). (gr. k-3). 1992. pap. 2.50 (*1-56144-172-4*, Honey Bear Bks) Modern Pub NYC.

Sleeping Beauty. (Treasury of Fairy Tales Ser.). (Illus.). 24p. (J). (gr. 2-5). 1993. pap. 3.95 (*1-56144-362-X*, Honey Bear Bks) Modern Pub NYC.

Sleeping Beauty. (First Fairy Tales Ser.: No. S852-7). (Illus.). (J). (ps-2). 3.95 (*0-7214-5100-4*, Ladybrd) Penguin.

Sleeping Beauty. (Diamond Series Pop-Ups). (Illus.). (J). (ps-1). 1.29 (*0-517-47347-X*) Random Hse Value.

Sleeping Beauty. (Derrydale Fairytale Library). (Illus.). (J). (ps-3). 1985. 1.98 (*0-517-28811-7*) Random Hse Value.

Sleeping Beauty. (Disney Animated Ser.). (Illus.). 48p. (J). (ps-6). 1989. 5.99 (*0-517-67009-7*) Random Hse Value.

Sleeping Beauty. (J). 1996. pap. 1.25 (*0-8167-1513-0*) Troll Communs.

Sleeping Beauty. (Disney Collection). (Illus.). 24p. (J). (ps-2). 1995. bds. 1.59 (*0-307-02025-8*, Golden Books) Western Pub.

Sleeping Beauty. 32p. (J). (ps-2). 1996. pap. 2.50 (*0-7214-5646-4*, Ladybrd) Penguin.

Sleeping Beauty. (Cherished Fairytale Ser.). 32p. (J). (ps-3). Date not set. spiral bd. 4.95 (*1-56987-233-3*) Landoll.

Sleeping Beauty. 1996. 7.98 (*1-57082-329-4*) Mouse Works.

***Sleeping Beauty.** Sheilah Beckett & Charles Perrault. LC 97-19552. (J). 1997. pap. write for info. (*0-486-29915-5*) Dover.

***Sleeping Beauty.** Ann Braybrooks. LC 97-65590. (J). 1997. 4.95 (*0-7868-4179-6*) Disney Pr.

Sleeping Beauty. Stanley Burns. (Illus.). 96p. 1990. 75.00 (*0-942642-32-5*) Twelvetrees Pr.

Sleeping Beauty. Illus. by Lynn Bywaters. 32p. (J). (ps-3). 1992. 6.95 (*0-8362-4915-1*) Andrews & McMeel.

Sleeping Beauty. Charlotte B. Chorpenning. (J). (gr. 1-7). 1947. 5.00 (*0-87602-203-4*) Anchorage.

***Sleeping Beauty.** Disney Staff. (Little Library). (J). 1997. 5.98 (*1-57082-608-0*) Mouse Works.

Sleeping Beauty. Retold by Margaret Early. (Illus.). 32p. 1993. 17.95 (*0-8109-3835-9*) Abrams.

Sleeping Beauty. C. S. Evans. (J). 1993. 12.95 (*0-679-42814-3*, Everymans Lib) Knopf.

Sleeping Beauty. Naomi Fox. (Illus.). 24p. (J). (ps-1). 1992. Incl. cassette. pap. 9.95 (*1-882179-13-7*) Confetti Ent.

Sleeping Beauty. Charl Fromme. (Storytime Classics Ser.). (Illus.). 24p. (J). (ps-2). 1995. pap. 1.29 (*1-56293-560-7*) McClanahan Bk.

Sleeping Beauty. Mary J. Fulton. (Illus.). 24p. (J). (ps-3). 1995. pap. 2.25 (*0-307-12881-4*, Golden Books) Western Pub.

***Sleeping Beauty.** Golden Books Staff. (J). 1997. pap. text ed. 1.09 (*0-307-08719-0*, Golden Books) Western Pub.

Sleeping Beauty. Jacob W. Grimm & Wilhelm K. Grimm. 32p. (J). (gr. k-3). 1994. pap. 2.99 (*0-87406-714-6*) Willowisp Pr.

Sleeping Beauty. Retold by Carol A. Hanshaw. (Comes to Life Bks.). 16p. (J). (ps-2). 1993. write for info. (*1-883366-20-8*) YES Ent.

Sleeping Beauty. Retold by Carol A. Hanshaw. (Comes to Life Bks.). 16p. (J). (ps-2). 1994. write for info. (*1-883366-77-1*) YES Ent.

Sleeping Beauty. Margaret A. Hughes. Ed. by Ken Forsse & Mary Becker. (Talking Mother Goose Ser.). (Illus.). 26p. (J). (ps). 1986. 9.95 (*0-934323-27-5*) Alchemy Comms.

Sleeping Beauty. Ed. & Retold by Trina S. Hyman. LC 75-43769. (Illus.). (J). (gr. 1 up). 1983. mass mkt. 6.95 (*0-316-38708-8*) Little.

***Sleeping Beauty.** Ladybird Books Staff. (J). 1997. pap. 3.50 (*0-7214-5791-6*, Ladybrd) Penguin.

Sleeping Beauty. Illus. by Kerry Martin & Diana Wakeman. LC 92-53435. (Pop-up Bks.). 12p. (J). (ps-k). 1993. 11.95 (*1-56282-369-8*) Disney Pr.

Sleeping Beauty. Judith Michael. 1994. pap. 6.99 (*0-671-89959-7*) PB.

Sleeping Beauty. Robert Newby. (Awareness & Caring - Sign Language Storybook Ser.). (Illus.). 64p. (J). (gr. k-3). 1992. lib. bdg. 16.95 (*1-56674-035-5*) Forest Hse.

Sleeping Beauty. G. Nuebacher. (Traditional Fairy Tales Ser.). (Illus.). 32p. (J). (gr. 1-4). 1989. 6.95 (*0-88625-220-2*) Durkin Hayes Pub.

Sleeping Beauty. Illus. by Arthur Rackham. 110p. (J). (gr. k-4). 1920. pap. 4.95 (*0-486-22756-1*) Dover.

***Sleeping Beauty.** Christine San Jose. LC 96-80398. (Illus.). 32p. (J). (ps up). 1997. 14.95 (*1-56397-636-6*) Boyds Mills Pr.

Sleeping Beauty. Laurence Senelick. (J). (gr. 1-9). 1992. pap. 4.95 (*0-88388-045-8*) Bellerophon Bks.

Sleeping Beauty. Catherine Storr. (Easy Piano Picture Bks.). (Illus.). 32p. 1989. pap. 9.95 (*0-571-10097-X*) Faber & Faber.

***Sleeping Beauty.** Swan. Date not set. pap. text ed. write for info. (*0-582-02568-0*, Pub. by Longman UK) Longman.

Sleeping Beauty. Illus. by Van Gool Studio Staff. (Classic Ser.). 64p. (J). (ps-1). 1994. 4.98 (*0-8317-1666-5*) Smithmark.

Sleeping Beauty. Walt Disney Company Staff. 96p. (FRE.). (J). (gr. k-5). pap. 9.95 (*0-7859-8854-8*) Fr & Eur.

Sleeping Beauty. Jane Yolen. 1986. 12.95 (*0-394-55433-7*) Knopf.

Sleeping Beauty. rev. ed. Hayden Carruth. LC 90-81353. 144p. 1990. reprint ed. pap. 10.00 (*1-55659-033-4*) Copper Canyon.

Sleeping Beauty. Judith Michaels. Ed. by Bill Grose. 640p. 1992. reprint ed. mass mkt. 5.99 (*0-671-78252-5*) PB.

Sleeping Beauty, Vol. 518. rev. ed. Alfred Lipton. Ed. & Illus. by Janice Caban. (Once upon a Tale Ser.). 10p. (J). (gr. k). 1989. pap. 2.00 (*1-878501-04-6*) Ntrl Science Indus.

Sleeping Beauty: A Fairy Tale. Jacob W. Grimm & Wilhelm K. Grimm. Tr. by Anthea Bell. LC 94-34651. (Illus.). 32p. (J). (gr. k-3). Date not set. lib. bdg. 14.88 (*1-55858-400-5*) North-South Bks NYC.

Sleeping Beauty: A Retold Story. Fred Crump, Jr. LC 89-51788. (Illus.). 44p. (J). (gr. k-2). 1991. pap. 6.95 (*1-55523-300-7*) Winston-Derek.

***Sleeping Beauty: A Sky Dancers Sky-High Fairy Tale.** Alexandra Reid. (Sky Dancers Ser.). (Illus.). 24p. (J). (ps). 1997. 2.50 (*0-694-01014-6*, Festival) HarpC Child Bks.

***Sleeping Beauty: Behind the Scenes at the Ballet.** Leslie E. Spatt. (Illus.). (J). 19.99 (*0-590-24536-8*) Scholastic Inc.

Sleeping Beauty: Fairy Tale Fun. Katy Rhodes. 1996. 4.95 (*0-8120-6610-3*) Barron.

Sleeping Beauty: Perform Your Very Own Ballet with Cassette, Tiara, Book, & Poster. Linda Griffith. (Illus.). 36p. (J). 1993. 16.95 incl. audio (*0-8362-4215-7*) Andrews & McMeel.

Sleeping Beauty: Stand-Up Fairy Tale House. Dial Books for Young Readers Staff. (Illus.). (J). 1995. pap. 6.95 (*0-8037-1868-3*) Dial Bks Young.

Sleeping Beauty: The Ballet Story. Illus. by Todd L. Doney. LC 93-14399. 32p. (J). 1994. text ed. 14.95 (*0-689-31885-5*, Pub. by Ctrl Bur voor Schimmel NE) Macmillan.

Sleeping Beauty: The Story of the Ballet. Becker & Mayer Staff. (Illus.). 36p. (J). 1995. 6.95 (*0-8362-0640-1*) Andrews & McMeel.

Sleeping Beauty: Walt Disney. (Big Golden Bks.). (Illus.). 24p. (J). (ps-1). 1986. write for info. (*0-307-10408-7*) Western Pub.

Sleeping Beauty: With Selected Sentences in American Sign Language. Robert Newby. LC 91-29729. (Illus.). 64p. (J). (gr. 1-7). 1992. 38.20 incl. vhs (*1-56368-009-2*, Pub. by K Green Pubns) Gallaudet Univ Pr.

Sleeping Beauty: With Selected Sentences in American Sign Language. Robert Newby. LC 91-29729. (Illus.). 64p. (J). (gr. 1-7). 1992. 14.95 (*0-930323-97-1*, Pub. by K Green Pubns); vhs 29.95 (*0-930323-98-X*, Pub. by K Green Pubns) Gallaudet Univ Pr.

Sleeping Beauty - Mini: Illustrated Classic. A. L. Singer. LC 94-74960. (Disney Press Miniature Classics Ser.). (Illus.). 96p. (J). 1996. 5.95 (*0-7868-3075-1*) Disney Pr.

Sleeping Beauty & Bluebeard. Ed. by Ronald Storer. (J). (gr. k-6). 1983. pap. 3.50 (*0-19-421746-9*) OUP.

Sleeping Beauty & Other Classic French Fairy Tales. Charles Perrault. (J). 1991. 12.99 (*0-517-03706-8*) Random Hse Value.

Sleeping Beauty & Other Fairy Tales. Jacob W. Grimm & Wilhelm K. Grimm. (Illus.). 96p. (Orig.). (J). 1992. pap. 1.00 (*0-486-27084-X*) Dover.

Sleeping Beauty & Other Stories. Charles Perrault. LC 88-43558. (Miniature Editions Ser.). 96p. (J). 1989. 4.95 (*0-89471-721-9*) Running Pr.

Sleeping Beauty & Smoke. Laurence Klavan. 1985. pap. 5.25 (*0-8222-1041-X*) Dramatists Play.

Sleeping Beauty & The Frog Prince. Jacob W. Grimm & Wilhelm K. Grimm. (Illus.). 24p. (J). 1990. 5.99 (*0-517-05385-3*) Random Hse Value.

Sleeping Beauty-Art Now. Pontus Hulten & Oystein Hjort. LC 82-60793. (Illus.). 136p. 1982. pap. 9.00 (*0-89207-036-6*) S R Guggenheim.

Sleeping Beauty Coloring Book. Jacob W. Grimm & Wilhelm K. Grimm. (Illus.). (J). (gr. k-3). 1992. pap. 2.95 (*0-486-27318-0*) Dover.

Sleeping Beauty in the Wood. Carol Heyer. LC 96-16133. (Illus.). 32p. (J). (gr. k-3). 1996. 14.95 (*1-57102-094-2*, Ideals Child) Hambleton-Hill.

Sleeping Beauty Novels: The Claiming of Sleeping Beauty; Beauty's Punishment; Beauty's Release, Set. A. N. Roquelaure, pseud. 1991. Boxed set. pap. 32.85 (*0-452-15298-4*, Plume) NAL-Dutton.

Sleeping Beauty of Loreland. Frances Homer. 1962. pap. 3.45 (*0-87129-233-5*, S39) Dramatic Pub.

Sleeping Beauty: or The Famous Rose Taboo. Barbara Fried. 63p. (J). 1965. pap. 4.95 (*0-87129-667-5*, S01) Dramatic Pub.

Sleeping Beauty Prologue see Six Fairy Variations

Sleeping Beauty-Sticker Book. 1990. 3.99 (*0-517-69690-8*) Random Hse Value.

Sleeping Bread. Stefan Czernecki & Timothy Rhodes. LC 91-75422. (Illus.). 40p. (J). (gr. k-4). 1992. 14.95 (*1-56282-183-0*) Hyprn Child.

Sleeping Bread. Stefan Czernecki & Timothy Rhodes. LC 91-75422. (Illus.). 40p. (J). (gr. k-4). 1993. pap. 4.95 (*1-56282-519-4*) Hyprn Child.

***Sleeping Bread.** large type ed. Stefan Czernecki & Timothy Rhodes. (Illus.). 40p. (J). (gr. k-4). 1992. 14.95 (0-920534-84-8, Pub. by Hyperion Pr Ltd CN) Sterling.

***Sleeping Bride.** Dorothy Eden. LC 96-53225. 291p. 1997. pap. 20.95 (0-7838-8077-4, GK Hall) Thorndike Pr.

Sleeping Bride. Dorothy Eden. 192p. 1996. reprint ed. 22.00 (0-7278-4843-7) Severn Hse.

***Sleeping Car Murders.** Sebastien Japrisot. LC 96-50249. 1997. pap. 11.95 (0-452-27778-7, Plume) NAL-Dutton.

Sleeping Dogs. Neal Bell. 1989. pap. 5.25 (0-8222-1042-8) Dramatists Play.

Sleeping Dogs. Sonya Hartnett. (Illus.). 129p. (YA). (gr. 9 up). 1995. pap. 12.99 (0-670-86503-6) Viking Child Bks.

Sleeping Dogs. William Paul. LC 95-34245. 192p. 1995. 19.95 (0-312-13603-X) St Martin.

Sleeping Dogs: A Novel of Suspense. Thomas Perry. 1993. mass mkt. 5.99 (0-8041-1160-X) Ivy Books.

Sleeping Dogs & Popsicles: The Vatican Versus the KGB - The Memoirs of an American. Eugene H. Van Dee. 234p. 1996. lib. bdg. 42.00 (0-7618-0381-5) U Pr of Amer.

Sleeping Dragon. Joel Rosenberg. (Guardians of the Flame Ser.: Bk. 1). 256p. 1986. pap. 3.50 (0-451-14833-9, Sig) NAL-Dutton.

Sleeping Dragon. Joel Rosenberg. (Guardians of the Flame Ser.: No. 1). 256p. 1986. pap. 3.95 (0-451-16213-7, ROC) NAL-Dutton.

Sleeping Dragon. Joel Rosenberg. (Guardians of the Flame Ser.). 256p. 1993. pap. 4.99 (0-451-45350-6, ROC) NAL-Dutton.

Sleeping Dragons All Around. Sheree Fitch. (Illus.). 32p. 1992. pap. 5.95 (0-385-25398-2) Doubleday.

***Sleeping, Dreaming, & Dying: An Exploration of Consciousness.** Dalai Lama. Ed. by Francisco J. Varela. LC 97-2448. (Illus.). 224p. (Orig.). 1997. pap. 16.95 (0-86171-123-8) Wisdom MA.

***Sleeping Fires.** George Gissing. LC 83-12402. 105p. pap. 30.00 (0-608-04822-4, 2065479) Bks Demand.

***Sleeping Giant.** Paul E. Pepe. (Illus.). 324p. 1993. pap. 6.95 (0-614-26411-1) Purple Mnt Pr.

Sleeping Giant: American Armed Forces Between the Wars. J. E. Kaufmann & H. W. Kaufmann. LC 95-43727. 216p. 1996. text ed. 55.00 (0-275-95256-8, Praeger Pubs) Greenwood.

Sleeping Giant Reading Program. Kathlyn Messina. LC 82-83558. (Illus.). 160p. (Orig.). 1983. pap. 12.95 (0-910569-00-2) Hampton Court Pub.

Sleeping Handsome: The Untold Story. Catherine Heller. LC 96-5334. (Illus.). (J). 1996. 13.95 (1-55972-331-9, Birch Ln Pr) Carol Pub Group.

Sleeping in Flames. Jonathan Carroll. LC 89-40549. 288p. 1990. pap. 12.00 (0-679-72777-9, Vin) Random.

Sleeping in the Blood. large type ed. Robert Richardson. 348p. 1992. 25.99 (0-7505-0428-5) Ulverscroft.

***Sleeping in Velvet.** Thaisa Frank. 250p. 1997. pap. 15.00 (1-57423-043-3) Black Sparrow.

***Sleeping in Velvet.** Thaisa Frank. 250p. 1997. 27.50 (1-57423-044-1) Black Sparrow.

***Sleeping in Velvet.** limited ed. Thaisa Frank. 250p. 1997. 35.00 (1-57423-045-X) Black Sparrow.

Sleeping It Off. Clive Faust. (Illus.). 34p. (C). 1992. 8.00 (0-9624658-2-8) Landside Pr.

Sleeping Lady. Ann Dixon. LC 94-9157. (Illus.). 32p. (J). (ps-5). 1994. 15.95 (0-88240-444-X) Alaska Northwest.

Sleeping Lady. Sue Henry. 320p. 1996. 22.00 (0-688-13747-4, Morrow Junior) Morrow.

***Sleeping Lady.** Sue Henry. 320p. 1997. reprint ed. mass mkt. 5.99 (0-380-72407-3) Avon.

Sleeping Lady: The Trailside Murders above the Golden Gate. Robert Graysmith. (Illus.). 496p. 1991. pap. 5.99 (0-451-40255-3, Onyx) NAL-Dutton.

***Sleeping Life.** Ruth Rendell. lib. bdg. 19.95 (0-8488-2019-3) Amereon Ltd.

Sleeping Lord. David Jones. 112p. 1995. pap. 14.95 (0-571-17449-3) Faber & Faber.

Sleeping Moon. David L. Atwell. LC 94-270. (Illus.). (J). 1994. 14.95 (0-395-68677-6) HM.

Sleeping Mountain. large type ed. John Harris. 1976. 25.99 (0-85456-486-1) Ulverscroft.

Sleeping Murder. Agatha Christie. 224p. 1992. mass mkt. 4.99 (0-06-100380-8, Harp PBks) HarpC.

Sleeping Neighbors: Stories & Quick Takes. William Hester. Ed. by Ken Aaron. 276p. (Orig.). 1989. pap. 12.50 (0-945665-05-9) Cole & Sherwood.

Sleeping Neighbors: Stories & Quick Takes. rev. ed. William Hester. Ed. by James McDonald. LC 91-77104. 165p. (Orig.). (C). 1991. pap. 12.00 (0-945665-11-3) Cole & Sherwood.

Sleeping on a Wire. David Grossman. Tr. by Chaim Watzman. 1993. 22.00 (0-374-17788-0) FS&G.

Sleeping on a Wire: Conversations with Palestinians in Israel. David Grossman. 288p. 1994. pap. 10.00 (0-374-52400-9, Noonday) FS&G.

Sleeping on the Wing: An Anthology of Modern Poetry with Essays on Reading & Writing. Kenneth Koch & Kate Farrell. 336p. 1982. pap. 11.00 (0-394-74364-4) Random.

Sleeping Over. Molly See. 19p. (Orig.). 1979. pap. 3.00 (0-89924-021-6) Lynx Hse.

***Sleeping Palace.** M. Orlando. (Orig.). 1997. mass mkt. 6.95 (1-56333-582-4) Masquerade.

***Sleeping Partner.** William Paul. LC 96-44845. 1997. 19.95 (0-312-15208-6) St Martin.

Sleeping Partners. Charlotte Lamb. (Presents Ser.). 1993. mass mkt. 2.99 (0-373-11560-1, 1-11560-9) Harlequin Bks.

***Sleeping Partners.** large type ed. Pauline Bell. (Magna Large Print Ser.). 375p. 1997. 27.50 (0-7505-1076-5) Ulverscroft.

Sleeping Porch. Karen Ackerman. LC 94-16645. (Illus.). 40p. (J). (gr. k up). 1995. 15.00 (0-688-12822-X, Morrow Junior); lib. bdg. 14.93 (0-688-12823-8, Morrow Junior) Morrow.

Sleeping Porch. Justin Caldwell. LC 78-17912. (Lost Roads Poetry Ser.: No. 16). 1979. pap. 4.00 (0-918786-17-7) Lost Roads.

Sleeping Porch. Virginia Gross. Date not set. pap. write for info. (0-14-034869-7, Viking) Viking Penguin.

Sleeping Porch. Virginia T. Gross. Date not set. pap. write for info. (0-670-84145-5) Viking Penguin.

Sleeping Preacher. Julia Kasdorf. LC 92-50199. (Poetry Ser.). 80p. 1992. 19.95 (0-8229-3720-4); pap. 10.95 (0-8229-5480-X) U of Pittsburgh Pr.

Sleeping Pretty. William Paul. 192p. 1996. 19.95 (0-312-14418-0) St Martin.

Sleeping Prince. Knut Faldbakken. 208p. 8800. 30.00 (0-7206-0710-8, Pub. by P Owen Ltd UK) Dufour.

Sleeping Prince. Terence Rattigan. 126p. 1954. 12.95 (0-910278-44-X) Boulevard.

Sleeping Retrospect of Desire. Lynne Savitt. LC 93-7010. 44p. (Orig.). 1993. pap. 7.00 (0-914134-10-8) Konocti Bks.

Sleeping Rough: Stories of the Night. Tina Dunhill et al. 162p. (C). 1991. pap. 14.95 (0-413-45401-0, A0637, Pub. by Methuen UK) Heinemann.

Sleeping Sinning Falling. Mutsuo Takahashi. Tr. by Hiroaki Sato from JPN. 144p. (Orig.). 1992. pap. text ed. 8.95 (0-87286-268-2) City Lights.

Sleeping Sphinx. John D. Carr. (Dr. Fell Detective Ser.). 199p. pap. 4.95 (0-930330-24-2) Intl Polygonics.

Sleeping the Good Sleep: The Life & Times of John Gotti. Douglas Feiden. 1998. 19.95 (0-394-56379-4) Random.

***Sleeping Through the Night: How Infants, Toddlers & Their Parents Can Get a Good Night's Sleep.** Jodi A. Mindell. LC 96-39372. 1997. write for info. (0-06-273409-1) HarpC.

Sleeping Tiger. Rosamunde Pilcher. 288p. 1989. mass mkt. 5.50 (0-440-20247-7) Dell.

***Sleeping Tiger.** Rosamunde Pilcher. 1996. mass mkt. 5.99 (0-312-96125-1) St Martin.

Sleeping Tigers. Sandra Dark. 1994. mass mkt. 3.50 (0-373-27044-5, 1-27044-6) Harlequin Bks.

***Sleeping Ugly.** Jane Yolen. (Illus.). (J). (gr. 3). 1995. 7.56 (0-395-73227-1) HM.

Sleeping Ugly. Jane Yolen. (Break-of-Day Book). 64p. (J). (gr. 1-4). 1984. pap. 7.95 (0-698-20617-7, Coward) Putnam Pub Group.

***Sleeping Ugly.** Jane Yolen. (Illus.). 64p. (J). (gr. 2-5). 1997. pap. 5.95 (0-698-11560-0, Paperstar) Putnam Pub Group.

***Sleeping Ugly.** large type ed. Jane Yolen. (Illus.). 78p. (J). (gr. 3). 19.50 (0-614-20621-9, L-38220-00 APHB) Am Printing Hse.

***Sleeping Weather.** Cary Fagan. 128p. 1997. pap. 15.95 (0-88984-188-8, Pub. by Porcupines Quill CN) Genl Dist Srvs.

Sleeping with a Stranger: How I Survived Marriage to a Child Molester. Patricia Wiklund. 1995. pap. 9.95 (1-55850-443-5) Adams Media.

Sleeping with a Sunflower: A Treasury of Old-Time Gardening Lore. Louise Riotte. Ed. by Deborah Burns. LC 87-45008. (Illus.). 224p. (Orig.). 1987. pap. 11.95 (0-88266-502-2, Garden Way Pub) Storey Comm Inc.

Sleeping with Bread: Holding What Gives You Life. Dennis Linn et al. LC 95-2305. (Illus.). 80p. (Orig.). 1995. pap. 12.95 (0-8091-3579-5) Paulist Pr.

Sleeping with Extra-Terrestrials. Wendy Kaminer. 0001. pap. write for info. (0-679-75886-0) McKay.

Sleeping with Ghosts: A Life's Work in Photography. Donald McCullin. (Illus.). 208p. 1996. 45.00 (0-89381-684-1) Aperture.

Sleeping with Ghosts: A Life's Work in Photography. Donald McCullin. (Illus.). 208p. 1996. 45.00 (0-89381-659-0) Aperture.

***Sleeping with Literary Lions: The Booklover's Guide to Bed & Breakfasts.** Peggy Van Hulsteyn. LC 97-25068. (Illus.). 288p. (Orig.). 1997. pap. 16.95 (1-55591-319-9) Fulcrum Pub.

Sleeping with Monsters: Conversations with Scottish & Irish Women Poets. Rebecca Wilson & Gillean S. Arjat. 1990. pap. 13.95 (0-7486-6027-5, Pub. by Edinburgh U Pr UK) Col U Pr.

Sleeping with Moscow: The Authorized Account of the K. G. B.'s Bungled in Filtration of FBI by Two of the Soviet Union's Most Unlikely Operatives. Anatoile Verbitsky. LC 87-9692. 184p. 1987. 14.95 (0-933503-07-5) Sure Seller.

Sleeping with Our Sons & Daughters. Patrick Cauchi & Joyce Carbone. LC 92-90015. (Orig.). 1992. pap. 8.95 (1-878116-12-6) JVC Bks.

***Sleeping with Random Beasts.** Karin Goodwin. LC 97-22559. 1997. 22.95 (0-8118-1989-2) Chronicle Bks.

Sleeping with Sylvia Plath. Robert Novak. 1983. 4.00 (0-686-43216-9) Windless Orchard.

***Sleeping with the Boss: Female Subjectivity & Narrative Pattern in Robert Penn Warren.** Lucy Ferriss. LC 96-35464. (Southern Literary Studies). 253p. 1997. text ed. 28.50 (0-8071-2139-8) La State U Pr.

***Sleeping with the Buffalo: And Other Stories.** Christina Adam. LC 96-85607. (Orig.). 1996. pap. 15.00 (1-881090-24-8) Confluence Pr.

***Sleeping with the Crawfish: An Andy Broussard & Kit Franklyn Mystery.** D. J. Donaldson. LC 97-20036. 1997. write for info. (0-312-17025-4) St Martin.

Sleeping with the Devil. Suzanne Finstad. 400p. 1992. mass mkt. 5.99 (0-380-71932-0) Avon.

Sleeping with the Enemy. Myrna Temte. 1994. mass mkt. 3.99 (0-373-50167-6, 1-50167-5) Harlequin Bks.

Sleeping with the Enemy. Christine Zawadiwsky. 32p. (Orig.). 1980. pap. 5.00 (0-912449-02-0) Floating Island.

Sleeping with the FBI: Sex, Booze, Russians, & the Saga of an American Counterspy Who Couldn't. Russell W. Howe. 416p. 1993. 23.95 (0-915765-62-4) Natl Pr Bks.

***Sleeping with the Mayor: A True Story.** John Jiler. 1997. 25.00 (1-886913-14-5) Hungry Mind.

***Sleeping with the President: My Intimate Years with Bill Clinton.** Gennifer Flowers. pap. text ed. 9.95 (1-889801-00-3) Anonymous Pr.

Sleepless Beauty. Frances Minters. 32p. (J). (ps-3). 1996. pap. 14.99 (0-670-87033-1) Viking Penguin.

***Sleepless in Seattle: Soundtrack.** Ed. by Carol Cuellar. 48p. (Orig.). (C). 1993. pap. text ed. 14.95 (0-89898-690-7, P1019SMX) Warner Brothers.

Sleepless Night in a Soundproof Motel. Michael C. Ford. (Rockbook Ser.: No. 6). 16p. (Orig.). 1978. pap. 3.00 (0-930012-36-4) J Mudfoot.

Sleepless Nights. Elizabeth Hardwick. LC 89-40112. 1990. pap. 8.95 (0-679-72426-5, Vin) Random.

Sleepless Nights: Verses for the Wakeful. Wen-Siang. Tr. by Thomas Cleary from CHI. LC 94-24048. (Illus.). 108p. (Orig.). (C). 1995. pap. 9.95 (1-55643-200-3) North Atlantic.

Sleepless Nights in the Procrustean Bed: Essays. Harlan Ellison. Ed. by Marty Clark. LC 83-27543. (I. O. Evans Studies in the Philosophy & Criticism of Literature: No. 5). 192p. 1984. reprint ed. pap. 21.00 (0-89370-270-6, 10322376); reprint ed. lib. bdg. 31.00 (0-89370-170-X, 10322376) Borgo Pr.

Sleepless Sleepover. (Spider Tales Ser.). (J). (gr. 3-7). 1995. 14.00 (0-922242-92-5) Bepuzzled.

Sleepless Souls: Suicide in Early Modern England. Michael MacDonald & Terence R. Murphy. (Oxford Studies in Social History). (Illus.). 400p. 1991. 95.00 (0-19-822919-4) OUP.

Sleepless Souls: Suicide in Early Modern England. Michael MacDonald & Terence R. Murphy. (Oxford Studies in Social History). (Illus.). 400p. 1994. reprint ed. pap. 26.00 (0-19-820450-7) OUP.

***Sleepover.** Lara Bergen. (J). 1996. pap. 7.00 (0-448-41332-9) Putnam Pub Group.

***Sleepover.** Cullinan. 1994. 11.00 (0-15-302438-0) HarBrace.

***Sleepover.** Laura E. Williams. (Let's Have a Party Ser.: No. 3). (Illus.). (J). 1997. pap. 3.99 (0-380-78924-8) Avon.

Sleepover! For the Coolest Night of Your Life. Lara R. Bergen. (Books & Stuff). (Illus.). 32p. (J). (gr. 1 up). 1996. pap. text ed. 9.95 (0-448-40956-9, G&D) Putnam Pub Group.

***Sleepover Birthday Party.** Golden Books Staff. (Barbie Ser.). (Illus.). (J). 1997. pap. text ed. 2.29 (0-307-03416-X, Golden Books) Western Pub.

Sleepover Madness. Quin. (TGIF Ser.: No. 1). (J). (gr. 3-6). 1995. pap. 3.50 (0-671-51017-7) PB.

Sleepwalk. John Saul. 464p. 1990. mass mkt. 6.99 (0-553-28834-2) Bantam.

Sleepwalker. R. L. Stine. (Fear Street Ser.). 160p. (Orig.). (J). (gr. 6-9). mass mkt. 3.99 (0-671-74652-9, Archway) PB.

Sleepwalker in a Fog. Tatyana Tolstaya. Tr. by Jamey Gambrell from RUS. LC 92-50613. 1993. pap. 11.00 (0-679-73063-X, Vin) Random.

Sleepwalker in a Fog: Stories. Tatyana Tolstaya. 1992. 19.00 (0-394-58731-6) Knopf.

Sleepwalker with Eyes of Clay. Jean-Jacques Celly. Tr. by Katherine Gallagher from FRE. LC 93-71943. (Illus.). 79p. (ENG & FRE.). 1994. pap. 14.95 (1-85610-029-4, Pub. by Forest Bks UK) Dufour.

Sleepwalkers: A History of Man's Changing Vision of the Universe. Arthur Koestler. 624p. 1990. pap. 13.95 (0-14-019246-8, Penguin Bks) Viking Penguin.

Sleepwalkers: A Trilogy. Hermann Broch. Tr. by Willa Muir & Edwin Muir. LC 95-35201. 656p. 1996. pap. 16.00 (0-679-76406-2) Random.

Sleepwalker's Fate: New & Selected Poems 1965-1991. Tom Clark. LC 92-4317. 212p. (Orig.). 1992. 25.00 (0-87685-870-1); pap. 12.50 (0-87685-869-8) Black Sparrow.

Sleepwalker's Fate: New & Selected Poems 1965-1991. deluxe ed. Tom Clark. LC 92-4317. 212p. (Orig.). 1992. 30.00 (0-87685-871-X) Black Sparrow.

Sleepwalker's World. Gordon R. Dickson. 256p. (Orig.). 1993. mass mkt. 4.99 (0-671-72161-5) Baen Bks.

Sleepwalking: A Novel. Julie Myerson. LC 95-46712. 208p. 1996. pap. 12.00 (0-06-097685-3) HarpC.

***Sleepwalking Beauty.** Lynn K. Emerson. (Loveswept Ser.: No. 835). 240p. 1997. mass mkt. 3.50 (0-553-44583-9, Loveswept) Bantam.

Sleepwalking Beneath the Stars. Howard Schwartz. LC 91-26708. 64p. 1992. 9.50 (0-933532-82-2) BkMk.

Sleepwalking Nights Vol. II: Poems. August Strindberg. Tr. by Arvid Paulsen. LC 78-56420. 8.95 (0-88238-078-8) Law Arts.

Sleepwalking on the Borders of the Apocylapse. Bruce Braunstein. (Orig.). 1986. 19.95 (0-685-14666-9) Tetragrammaton.

Sleepwalking Through. Haynes B. Johnson. 544p. 1992. pap. 14.95 (0-385-42259-8, Anchor NY) Doubleday.

Sleepwalking with Mayakovsky. Robert Brown. LC 93-35960. (Wick Poetry Chapbook Ser.: No. 2). 46p. (Orig.). 1994. pap. 4.75 (0-87338-502-0) Kent St U Pr.

***Sleepwatcher's.** William C. Dement. 234p. (C). 1996. pap. text ed. 16.95 (0-9649338-0-2) Nychthemeron Pr.

Sleepy. Kate Orman. (Dr. Who New Adventures Ser.). 272p. (Orig.). 1996. mass mkt. 5.95 (0-426-20465-4) London Brdge.

Sleepy ABC. Margaret Wise Brown. LC 93-36398. (Illus.). 40p. (J). (ps-2). 1994. 14.95 (0-06-024284-1) HarpC Child Bks.

Sleepy Bear. Stewart Cowley. LC 93-77347. (Magic Window Bks.). (Illus.). (J). (ps). 1993. 6.99 (0-89577-513-1, Random) RD Assn.

Sleepy Bear. Lydia Dabcovich. (Unicorn Paperbacks Ser.). (Illus.). 32p. (J). (ps-2). 1985. pap. 4.95 (0-525-44196-4) Dutton Child Bks.

Sleepy Bear. Lydia Dabcovich. (Illus.). 32p. (J). (ps-1). 1993. pap. 19.99 (0-14-054937-4, Puff Unicorn) Puffin Bks.

Sleepy Bear. Dabcovivh. 1993. pap. 5.99 (0-14-054785-1) NAL-Dutton.

Sleepy Book. Little Golden Books Staff. (J). (ps-2). 1.59 (0-307-03010-5, Golden Pr) Western Pub.

Sleepy Book. Charlotte Zolotow. LC 87-45861. (Charlotte Zolotow Bk.). (Illus.). 32p. (J). (ps-1). 1988. lib. bdg. 14.89 (0-06-026968-5) HarpC Child Bks.

***Sleepy Bunnie.** Brown. (J). 1900. pap. 5.95 (0-7868-1257-5) Hyprn Child.

***Sleepy Bunnie.** Brown. (J). 1999. 14.95 (0-7868-0371-1); lib. bdg. 14.89 (0-7868-2321-6) Hyprn Child.

Sleepy Dog: A Step One Book. Harriet Ziefert. LC 84-4775. (Step into Reading Bks.). (Illus.). (J). (ps-2). 1984. pap. 3.99 (0-394-86877-3); lib. bdg. 11.99 (0-394-96877-8) Random Bks Yng Read.

Sleepy Dormouse. Mark Ezra. LC 94-5686. (Illus.). 32p. (J). (ps-3). 1994. 14.95 (1-56656-153-1, Crocodile Bks) Interlink Pub.

Sleepy Dormouse. Mark Ezra. LC 94-5686. (Illus.). 32p. (J). (ps-3). 1995. pap. 7.95 (1-56656-192-2, Crocodile Bks) Interlink Pub.

Sleepy Hallow: No Guns Allowed. Edwin W. Holden. 1991. 13.95 (0-533-09231-0) Vantage.

Sleepy Hollow Moon. Richard DuVall. (Illus.). 55p. 1993. per. 5.00 (0-914546-93-7) Rose Pub.

Sleepy Hollow Restorations: A Cross-Section of the Collection. Joseph T. Butler. LC 82-16774. (Illus.). 344p. 1983. 39.95 (0-912882-57-3) Sleepy Hollow.

***Sleepy Little Owl.** Howard Goldsmith. 1997. text ed. 14.95 (0-07-024543-6, Lrning Triangle) McGraw.

Sleepy Men. Margaret Wise Brown. LC 94-41939. (Illus.). 32p. (J). (ps-2). 1996. 14.95 (0-7868-0154-9); pap. text ed. 14.89 (0-7868-2126-4) Hyprn Child.

Sleepy on Sunday. (Language of Mathematics Ser.). 1989. 35.92 (0-8123-6475-9); pap. 5.36 (0-8123-6476-7); pap. 5.28 (0-8123-6477-5); audio 7.92 (0-8123-6478-3) McDougal-Littell.

Sleepy Time. Gyo Fujikawa. (Illus.). 16p. (J). (ps). 1989. reprint ed. bds. 6.95 (1-55987-001-X, Sunny Bks) J B Comns.

Sleepy-Time Moon. Suzy McPartland. (Pee Wee Pops Ser.). (Illus.). 12p. (J). (ps). 1994. bds. 4.95 (0-689-71748-2, Aladdin Paperbacks) S&S Childrens.

Sleepy Willie. Horace Mungin. Ed. by Charlotte Orange. LC 90-82440. 128p. (Orig.). (YA). (gr. 8-12). 1991. pap. 8.95 (0-936026-24-3) R&M Pub Co.

***Sleepyhead.** Barbara Mariconda. (J). 1999. 12.95 (0-7868-0330-4) Hyprn Child.

Sleepyhead Tale. Jeremy Eaton. 1993. pap. 6.95 (1-56097-019-7) Fantagraph Bks.

Sleepyheads - Block Book. Snapshot Staff. 22p. (J). 1996. 3.95 (0-7894-0623-3) DK Pub Inc.

Sleepytime: Poems Prayers & Lullabies. Joan W. Anglund. 24p. (J). 1996. pap. 11.95 (0-689-80055-X, Atheneum Bks Young) S&S Childrens.

***Sleepytime Anytime with God.** (Kids-Life Ser.). 384p. (J). 1998. pap. write for info. (0-7814-3022-4, Chariot Bks) Chariot Victor.

Sleepytime, Anytime with God. Ed. by Julie Smith. LC 94-4610. (Illus.). 384p. (J). (ps-2). 1994. 15.99 (0-7814-0174-7, Chariot Bks) Chariot Victor.

Sleepytime for Baby Mouse. Margaret Hopkins. (Teddy Board Bks.). (Illus.). 12p. (J). (ps-3). 1985. 3.95 (0-448-40875-9, G&D) Putnam Pub Group.

Sleepytown Days. Col. 1986. 19.95 (0-02-621560-8) Macmillan.

Sleeze Brothers. Carnell et al. 128p. 1990. pap. 14.95 (1-85400-242-2) Marvel Entmnt.

Sleigh Ride to Russia: The Quaker Mission to Russia to Try to Avert the Crimean War. Griselda F. Mason. (C). 1988. 60.00 (0-900657-99-5, Pub. by W Sessions UK) St Mut.

Sleight of Hand. large type ed. Vivien Armstrong. 383p. 1993. 25.99 (0-7505-0518-4) Ulverscroft.

Sleight of Hand: A Practical Manual of Legerdemain for Amateurs & Others. Edwin T. Sachs. (Illus.). 1980. reprint ed. pap. 7.95 (0-486-23911-X) Dover.

Sleight of Hand: Conversations with Walter Satterthwait. Walter Satterthwait & Ernie Bulow. LC 93-29925. (Illus.). 170p. (C). 1993. 24.95 (0-8263-1466-X) U of NM Pr.

Sleightly Guilty. Patrick A. Kelley. 192p. 1988. pap. 3.50 (0-380-75240-9) Avon.

Sleights of Mind: One & Multiples of One. Harold N. Boris. LC 93-3833. 400p. 1994. 40.00 (1-56821-082-5) Aronson.

Sleipnir. Linda Evans. 352p. (Orig.). 1994. mass mkt. 4.99 (0-671-87594-9) Baen Bks.

Sleisenger & Fordtran Gastrointestinal Disease: Review & Assessment. Richard A. Weisiger & Lyman Bihartz. 304p. 1995. pap. text ed. 41.00 (0-7216-6068-1) Saunders.

***Sleisenger & Fordtran's Gastrointestinal & Liver Disease: Pathophysiology/Diagnosis/Management.** 6th ed. Mark Feldman et al. Ed. by Richard Zorab. LC 96-21131. (Illus.). 1920p. 1997. text ed. 195.00 (0-7216-6291-9) Saunders.

Slektin - The Family. Leila Comstock. 132p. 1988. 14.95 (0-87770-457-0) Ye Galleon.

***Slender Ella & Her Fairy Hogfather.** Vivian Sathre. LC 97-11837. (Illus.). (J). Date not set. pap. write for info. (0-440-41397-4) Dell.

S

An Asterisk (*) at the beginning of an entry indicates that the title is appearing in BIP for the first time.

***Slender Ella & Her Fairy Hogfather.** Vivian Sathre. LC 97-11837. (Illus.). (J). Date not set. write for info. (0-385-32516-9) Doubleday.

Slender Human Word: Emerson's Artistry in Prose. William J. Scheick. LC 77-27020. 176p. reprint ed. pap. 50.20 (0-8357-7023-0, 2033369) Bks Demand.

Slender Is the Thread. Harry Caudill. LC 87-1983. 192p. (C). 1987. reprint ed. pap. 14.95 (0-8131-0811-X) U Pr of Ky.

Slender Is the Thread: Tales from a Country Law Office. Harry M. Caudill. LC 87-1983. 192p. (C). 1987. reprint ed. 21.00 (0-8131-1611-2) U Pr of Ky.

Slender Me Naturally. Bernard Jensen. 1986. pap. 9.95 (0-932615-00-7) B Jensen.

Slender Means. 3rd ed. Michael Hannon. 16p. 1986. pap. 25.00 (0-918824-41-9) Turkey Pr.

Slender Thread. Aubrey R. McKinney. LC 84-80635. (Illus.). 384p. 1985. 24.95 (0-914587-00-5) Helix Pr.

Slender Thread. Lee Scofield. 368p. 1995. mass mkt. 4.50 (0-06-108273-2, Harp PBks) HarpC.

Slender Thread: Crisis, Healing & Nature. Diane Ackerman. 294p. 1997. 24.00 (0-679-44877-2) Random.

***Slender Thread: Stories of Pioneer Girls' First 25 Years.** Eunice R. Schatz. 288p. (Orig.). 1996. pap. 15.00 (1-883893-49-6) WinePress Pub.

Slender Thread Totem, Bk. 3. Lewis Koch. 1993. 15.00 (0-932526-45-4) Nexus Pr.

Slenderness of Prestressed Concrete Columns. (PCI Journal Reprints Ser.). 30p. 1983. pap. 18.00 (0-318-19797-9, JR286) P-PCI.

Sleuth. 2nd ed. Anthony Shaffer. (Illus.). 92p. 1985. reprint ed. pap. 8.95 (0-7145-0763-6) M Boyars Pubs.

Sleuth & the Scholar: Origins, Evolution, & Current Trends in Detective Fiction. Ed. by Barbara A. Rader & Howard G. Zettler. LC 87-24958. (Contributions to the Study of Popular Culture Ser.: No. 19). 151p. 1988. text ed. 39.95 (0-313-26036-2, ZSS/) Greenwood.

Sleuthing Fossils: The Art of Investigating Past Life. Alan M. Cvancara. (Illus.). 203p. 1990. text ed. 24.95 (0-471-51046-7) Wiley.

Sleuths, Sidekicks & Stooges: An Annotated Bibliography of Detectives, Their Assistants & Their Rivals in Crime, Mystery & Adventure Fiction, 1795-1995. Joseph Green & Jim Finch. LC 95-49334. 880p. 1997. 119.95 (1-85928-192-3, Pub. by Scolar Pr UK) Ashgate Pub Co.

***Slew of Stupid Criminals: Plus Some Spectacular Misspellings & Other Atrocious Crimes.** Paul E. Lindholm. LC 96-71108. 94p. (Orig.). 1996. pap. 7.95 (0-9653027-2-5) Paper Moon Pub.

Slewfoot Sally & the Flying Mule: And Other Tales from Cotton County. Ardath Mayhar. Ed. by J. Richards. LC 95-76456. (Illus.). 226p. (Orig.). (YA). (gr. 7-12). 1995. pap. 12.00 (1-887303-00-6) Blu Lantern Pub.

***SLF Album: An Informal History of Notre Dame's Sophomore Literary Festival 1967-1996.** Linda DeCicco. 200p. (Orig.). 1997. pap. text ed. 12.95 (0-268-01481-7) U of Notre Dame Pr.

Slib, Schlamm, Sludge. 320p. 1990. pap. 64.00 (0-89867-532-4, 90575) Am Water Wks Assn.

Slice of Country Life, 1902-1915. George F. Walker. LC 83-9279. (Illus.). 192p. (Orig.). 1984. pap. 7.95 (0-89407-037-1) Strawberry Hill.

Slice of Life. Ludvig L. Lumholtz. 220p. (C). 1989. text ed. 65.00 (1-872795-51-X, Pub. by Pentland Pr UK) St Mut.

Slice of Life: A Personal Story of Healing Through Cancer. Lee Sturgeon-Day. 160p. (Orig.). 1991. pap. 10.95 (0-9628760-0-3) Lifeways.

***Slice of Life: Selected Documents of Medieval English Peasant Experience.** Edwin B. Dewindt & Consortium for the Teaching of the Middle Ages Staff. LC 96-45726. 1996. pap. write for info. (1-879288-73-7) Medieval Inst.

Slice of Life-Reflections. Claire Schneider. (Illus.). 48p. (Orig.). 1978. pap. 2.95 (0-9601982-1-0) Greenwood Hse.

***Slice of Orange: Favorite Vols Recipes.** University of Tennessee Staff. 1995. 19.95 (0-87197-421-5) Favorite Recipes.

Slice of Paradise. Naples Community Hospital, Hospital Service League Staff. LC 93-72352. 1993. 14.95 (0-87197-385-5) Favorite Recipes.

***Slice of Paradise: Fresh & Inviting Flavors from the Junior League of Palm Beaches.** Junior League of Palm Beaches Inc. Staff. LC 96-78698. (Illus.). 288p. 1996. 19. 95 (0-9608090-1-5) JL Palm Beaches.

Slice of Santa Barbara: California Riviera Cuisine. Junior League Staff. 1991. 15.95 (0-89951-084-1) Santa Barb Mus Art.

Slice of Suffolk. Bob Roberts. 112p. 1990. pap. 22.00 (0-86138-020-7, Pub. by T Dalton UK) St Mut.

Slice of the Big Apple. American Cancer Society Staff. 192p. 1982. pap. 6.00 (0-686-31486-7) Am Cancer Forest Hills.

Slice of the Cake. large type ed. William Newton. (Linford Mystery Library). 1991. pap. 15.99 (0-7089-7087-7) Ulverscroft.

Slice of the Times: Kansas City 1875-1880. Brad Finch. 258p. 1994. pap. text ed. 6.00 (0-9645325-0-6) KC Hist Res.

Slice of Time: A Carolinas Album, Nineteen Fifty to Nineteen Ninety. Don Sturkey. Ed. by Jerry Bledsoe. LC 90-62196. (Illus.). 141p. 1990. pap. 19.95 (0-9624255-7-5) Down Home NC.

Slice of Wry. Anne E. Edge. (Illus.). 1981. pap. 10.00 (0-918824-27-3) Turkey Pr.

Slice Through a City. Peter Kent. (Illus.). 32p. (J). (gr. 3-6). 1996. lib. bdg. 17.90 (0-7613-0039-2) Millbrook Pr.

Sliced. Eric Weiner. (Cliffhangers Ser.: No. 5). 128p. (YA). 1996. mass mkt. 3.99 (0-425-15641-9) Berkley Pub.

Sliced: State-of-the-Art Nutrition for Building Lean Body Mass. Bill Reynolds & Negrita Jayde. (Illus.). 320p. (Orig.). 1991. pap. 14.95 (0-8092-4116-1) Contemp Bks.

Sliced Dog. Frederic Will. LC 84-26135. 40p. (Orig.). 1985. pap. 5.95 (0-934332-40-1) LEpervier Pr.

Sliced Heather on Toast. Lissa H. Johnson. (China Tate Ser.: No. 1). 1994. pap. 5.99 (1-56179-281-0) Focus Family.

***Sliceforms.** John Sharp. 1996. pap. 9.95 (1-899618-06-6, Pub. by Tarquin UK) Parkwest Pubns.

Slices. McCullough & Baker. 1980. pap. 8.95 (0-937816-08-6) Tech Data.

Slices, Bites & Other Facts of Life. Iris Pastor & Bev Levine. (Illus.). 384p. (Orig.). 1996. pap. 12.95 (0-9652832-0-8) Ladies Ink.

Slices of Chocolate Lives. Linda F. Waters. 176p. (Orig.). (YA). 1993. pap. 4.95 (0-9630887-0-X) Ethnic Bks.

Slices of Life: Writing from North America. Thalia Rubio. 256p. 1993. text ed. 17.50 (0-13-813296-8) P-H.

Slices of Orange. Ed. by Nancy B. Rayl. 96p. 1994. pap. 14.00 (0-9632702-9-5) Lightning.

Slices of the Peach: A Portrait of Georgia: Selected from Atlanta Weekly, The Atlanta Journal & Constitution Magazine. Photos by Floyd Jillson. LC 88-18636. (Illus.). 264p. (Orig.). 1990. pap. 16.95 (0-87797-161-7) Larlin Corp.

***Slichos.** 144p. (HEB.). 1955. pap. 4.00 (0-8266-0285-1, Merkos LInyonei Chinuch) Kehot Pubn Soc.

Slicing Eggplant. Phyllis S. Prestia. 32p. 1984. pap. 3.50 (0-913719-72-2) High-Coo Pr.

Slicing, Hooking, & Cooking. Jackie Eddy. Ed. by Nancy D. Dominitz. (Illus.). 224p. 1987. pap. 9.95 (0-914629-05-0) Prima Pub.

Slicing the Pie: A Federal Budget Game, 5 booklets, Set. Close Up Foundation Staff. (YA). (gr. 9-12). 1994. pap. 24.95 (0-932765-51-3, 1382-94) Close Up Fnd.

Slicing Through Your Emotional Luggage. 3rd ed. Yuvonne C. Brooks. 64p. (C). 1996. per., pap. text ed. 15.69 (0-7872-1906-1) Kendall-Hunt.

Slick. Camarin Grae. 304p. 1990. pap. 9.95 (0-941483-74-6) Naiad Pr.

***Slick: The Silver & Black Life of Al Davis.** Mark Rivowsky. 358p. 4.98 (0-8317-3506-6) Smithmark.

***Slick - the Master Mainstreamer.** Warren E. Gerlach. LC 96-90466. 1997. 15.95 (0-533-12060-8) Vantage.

Slick Italian Hand. William Murray. 1995. 22.50 (0-8050-2972-9) H Holt & Co.

Slick Money. Giles Tippette. Ed. by Doug Grad. 256p. (Orig.). 1993. mass mkt. 4.50 (0-671-79346-2) PB.

Slick Spins & Fractured Facts: How Cultural Myths Distort the News. Caryl Rivers. LC 95-42313. 288p. 1996. 24.95 (0-231-10152-X) Col U Pr.

Slick Willie: Why America Cannot Trust Bill Clinton. Floyd G. Brown. (Illus.). 200p. 1992. pap. 8.95 (0-9634397-0-3) Annapolis-Wash Bk Pubs.

Slick Willie, Vol. 2: Why America Still Cannot Trust Bill Clinton. Deborah J. Stone & Christopher Manion. (Illus.). 264p. 1994. pap. 9.95 (0-9634397-2-3) Annapolis-Wash Bk Pubs.

***Slicky Boys.** Martin Limon. LC 96-47108. 1997. 21.95 (0-553-10443-8) Bantam.

***Slide Area.** Gavin Lambert. (Midnight Classics Ser.). 211p. (Orig.). Date not set. pap. 11.99 (1-85242-441-9) Serpents Tail.

Slide Area: Film Book Reviews 1989-1991. Anthony Slide. 260p. 1992. 29.50 (0-8108-2614-3) Scarecrow.

Slide Atlas of Endovascular Surgery: Interventional Techniques in Vascular Disease. R. White & G. White. (Illus.). 176p. 1992. ring bd. 595.00 (0-442-31556-2) Chapman & Hall.

Slide Atlas of Essential Immunology. Ivan M. Roitt. 236p. 1992. 995.00 incl. sl. (0-632-03273-1) Blackwell Sci.

Slide Atlas of Strabismus Surgery. R. Richards. (Illus.). 240p. 1991. ring bd. 895.00 (0-442-31557-0) Chapman & Hall.

Slide Collection Management in Libraries & Information Units. Glyn Sutcliffe. 232p. 1995. 74.95 (0-566-07580-6) Irwin.

Slide Interpretation. H. L. Beynon et al. (Complete MRCP Ser.). (Illus.). 232p. (Orig.). 1991. pap. text ed. 32.00 (0-443-04309-4) Churchill.

Slide Interpretation from the MRCP. Hugh J. Kennedy et al. (Illus.). 224p. (Orig.). 1987. pap. text ed. 30.00 (0-443-03638-1) Churchill.

Slide, Kelly, Slide: The Wild Life & Times of Mike "King" Kelly, Baseball's First Superstar. Marty Appel. LC 94-49546. (American Sports History Ser.: No. 3). 246p. 1996. 32.50 (0-8108-2997-5) Scarecrow.

Slide Mountain: Or the Folly of Owning Nature. Theodore Steinberg. LC 94-25476. 212p. 1995. 24.00 (0-520-08763-1) U CA Pr.

Slide Mountain: or The Folly of Owning Nature. Theodore Steinberg. (Illus.). 224p. (C). 1996. pap. 13.95 (0-520-20709-2) U CA Pr.

***Slide Preparation & Staining of Blood Films for the Laboratory Diagnosis of Parasitic Diseases: Tentative Guideline (1992)** Contrib. by Lynne S. Garcia. 1992. 75.00 (1-56238-161-X, M15-T) Natl Comm Clin Lab Stds.

***Slide Presentation for the Basic Critical Incident Stress Management Program.** Jeffrey T. Mitchell & George S. Everly, Jr. (Illus.). 80p. (Orig.). 1996. 295.00 incl. sl. (1-883581-04-4) Chevron Pub.

Slide Rule for Sea & Air Navigation. P. C. Podmore. (C). 1987. 40.00 (0-85174-213-0, Pub. by Brwn Son Ferg) St Mut.

Slide Rule Handbook. James O. Perrine. 112p. (C). 1965. 45.00 (0-677-01060-5) Gordon & Breach.

Slide Rule in a Nutshell. Stan L. Schirmacher. 1960. pap. 1.55 (0-686-08956-1) Azirona Agency.

Slide Rule Simplified. 3rd ed. Charles O. Harris. LC 78-183979. 352p. reprint ed. pap. 100.40 (0-317-08654-5, 2004578) Bks Demand.

Slide Rules & Submarines: American Scientists & Subsurface Warfare in World War II. (Illus.). 295p. (Orig.). (C). 1994. pap. text ed. 35.00 (0-7881-1199-X) DIANE Pub.

Slide Rules & Submarines: American Scientists & Subsurface Warfare in World War 2. Montgomery C. Meigs. LC 90-5793. (Illus.). 295p. 1990. per. 12.00 (0-16-018591-2, 008-020-01193-2) USGPO.

***Slide Set for Biochemistry.** Robert Roskoski, Jr. (Text & Review (STAR) Ser.). (Illus.). 24p. 1996. ring bd. write for info. incl. sl. (0-7216-6527-6) Saunders.

Slide Set for Primary: Care of the Anterior Segment. 2nd ed. Catania. (C). 1994. ring bd. 130.00 (0-8385-8092-0, A8092-7) Appleton & Lange.

Slide Set to Accompany Magnetic Resonance Imaging Atlas of Extremities. Kang & Donald Resnick. 1990. 895.00 (0-7216-3320-X) Saunders.

Slide Shows on a Shoe String. Nancy Macduff. Ed. by Janie Millgard. (Illus.). 54p. (C). 1986. pap. 10.00 (0-945795-02-5) MBA Pub.

Sliders: The Novel. Brad Linaweaver. (Orig.). (J). 1996. mass mkt. 5.50 (1-57297-098-7) Blvd Books.

***Sliders: The Ultimate Episode Guide.** Brad Linaweaver. (Illus.). (Orig.). 1997. pap. 16.95 (1-57500-053-9) TV Bks.

Slides. Roger A. Kueter & Janeen Miller. Ed. by James E. Duane. LC 80-21335. (Instructional Media Library: Vol. 13). (Illus.). 112p. 1981. 27.95 (0-87778-173-7) Educ Tech Pubns.

Slides: Planning & Producing Slide Programs. Ann Bishop. LC 81-67828. (Illus.). 159p. (Orig.). (C). 1993. pap. 19. 95 (0-87985-238-0, S-30, Kodak) Saunders Photo.

Slides from Transparencies to Accompany "Marketing: Principles & Strategy" 2nd ed. Henry Assael. 175p. (C). 1993. 133.00 incl. sl. (0-03-097819-X) Dryden Pr.

Slides in Human Arthrology. B. N. Tillman. (Illus.). 32p. 1985. 463.00 (0-387-00350-9) Spr-Verlag.

Slides to Sectional Anatomy Learning Section. Applegate. 1991. 495.00 (0-7216-3239-4) Saunders.

Sliding Bearings. V. N. Constantinescu et al. xx, 543p. 1984. 80.00 (0-89864-011-3) Allerton Pr.

Sliding Modes in Control & Optimization. V. I. Utkin. (Communications & Control Engineering Ser.). (Illus.). xvi, 286p. 1992. 119.95 (0-387-53516-0) Spr-Verlag.

Sliding Surprise see Haunted House: A Slide-&-Peek Book

Sliding Surprise see Tell Me a Toy Riddle: Sneak-&-Peek Book

Sliding Surprise Books: Who Plays This Sport? Charles Reasoner. (Sliding Surprise Bks.). (Illus.). 12p. (J). 1996. 9.95 (0-8431-7991-0) Price Stern Sloan.

Sliding Surprise Books: Whose Tale Is This? Charles Reasoner. (Sliding Surprise Bks.). (Illus.). 12p. (J). 1996. 9.95 (0-8431-7992-9) Price Stern Sloan.

Slight Case of Murder. Damon Runyon. 17.95 (0-8488-1143-7) Amereon Ltd.

Slight Momentary Affliction. Stories. Lawrence Dorr. LC 86-34424. 160p. 1987. 15.95 (0-8071-1346-8) La State U Pr.

Slightly Beyond Skepticism: Social Science & the Search for Morality. Leonard W. Doob. LC 86-22400. (Illus.). 329p. reprint ed. pap. 93.80 (0-7837-4555-9, 2080346) Bks Demand.

***Slightly Crazy.** LC 96-85317. (Illus.). 60p. (Orig.). 1996. pap. 20.00 (0-9652993-0-9) Enso Pr.

Slightly Off Center. Neal Barrett, Jr. (Illus.). 160p. (Orig.). 1992. pap. 9.50 (1-883722-00-4) Swan Pr TX.

Slightly Offshore: More Reflections on Contemporary Life from a Small Maine Island. Caskie Stinnett. LC 92-74425. (Illus.). 224p. 1992. 14.95 (0-89272-321-1) Down East.

Slightly Older Guy. Bruce J. Friedman. 1995. 16.95 (0-684-80206-6) S&S Trade.

***Slightly Older Guy.** Bruce J. Friedman. 1998. pap. 9.95 (1-55611-522-9) D I Fine.

Slightly Out of Focus. Robert Capa. (American Autobiography Ser.). 243p. 1995. reprint ed. lib. bdg. 79. 00 (0-7812-8472-4) Rprt Serv.

Slightly Scary Campfire Stories. Michael Teitelbaum. (J). 1994. 5.98 (0-8317-1171-X) Smithmark.

Slightly Skewed Computer Dictionary. Doug Mayer. LC 94-19285. 1994. pap. 8.95 (1-55958-432-7) Prima Pub.

Slightly Skewed Vignettes: Confessions of an Incorrigible Kid. Karl E. Rohnke. 144p. 1992. pap. text ed. 9.95 (0-8403-7852-1) Kendall-Hunt.

Slim: Memories of a Rich & Imperfect Life. Slim Keith. 1991. mass mkt. 5.99 (0-446-36196-8) Warner Bks.

Slim & Healthy Italian Cooking. Polvay. 1990. pap. 10.95 (0-942084-33-0) SeaSide Pub.

Slim & Healthy Recipes. (Favorite All Time Recipes Ser.). (Illus.). 96p. 1993. spiral bd. 3.50 (1-56173-609-0, 2111100) Pubns Intl Ltd.

Slim & Healthy Vegetarian: Delicious Recipes & Diet Plans for a Healthy Lifestyle. Judith Wills. 1996. 12.99 (0-517-14236-8) Random Hse Value.

Slim & Trim. P. Dutery. 36p. (Orig.). 1982. pap. 3.25 (0-940844-11-7) Wellspring.

Slim Book of Liposuction. Alan M. Engler. 1993. 10.95 (0-533-10604-4) Vantage.

Slim Buttes Battle. Fred H. Werner. 1981. pap. 7.95 (0-933147-01-5) Werner Pubn.

Slim Buttes, 1876: An Episode of the Great Sioux War. Jerome A. Greene. LC 81-40291. (Illus.). 208p. 1990. pap. 12.95 (0-8061-2261-7) U of Okla Pr.

Slim Chef: A Cookbook for the Healthy Gourmet. Arlyn Hackett. (Illus.). 190p. 1987. pap. 12.95 (0-8184-0449-3) Carol Pub Group.

Slim Deception-Fat Reflection: One Woman's Struggle with Bulimia. Deborah Yelinek. 96p. 1987. pap. 2.50 (0-919797-61-X) Kindred Prods.

Slim Fingers Beckon. Arch Merrill. LC 86-33602. (Arch Merrill's New York Ser.: Vol. 10). (Illus.). 204p. 1987. reprint ed. pap. 12.95 (0-932334-86-5, NY36044, Empire State Bks) Hrt of the Lakes.

Slim for Him: Biblical Devotions on Diet. Patricia B. Kreml. LC 78-53422. 163p. 1978. pap. 5.95 (0-88270-300-5) Bridge-Logos.

Slim Gauge Cars. Harold H. Carstens. (Hobby Bks.: No. C-72). (Illus.). 116p. 1991. 19.95 (0-911868-72-0, C72) Carstens Pubns.

Slim Gourmet Cookbook. Barbara Gibbons. 1993. 8.98 (0-88365-843-7) Galahad Bks.

Slim Gourmet's Soup Book: A Complete Book of Soups. Martin Lederman. 1974. lib. bdg. 69.95 (0-685-51364-5) Revisionist Pr.

Slim the Vegetarian Way. rev. ed. Leah Leneman. 144p. 1988. pap. 8.00 (0-7225-2807-8) Thorsons SF.

Slim to Shore: Recipes for a Healthy Lifestyle. Jan Robinson. Ed. by Jan Martin. (Illus.). 288p. 1994. pap. 14.95 (0-9612686-5-4) Ship-Shore.

Slim Ways with Pasta: From the Kitchens of Weight Watchers. LC 92-53538. 1993. 15.00 (0-453-01028-8) NAL-Dutton.

Slime: Slugs Have Feelings Too. Carol Olsen. (Left-over Louie Ser.: 1). (Illus.). 26p. (Orig.). (J). (k-6). 1994. pap. 6.95 (1-883078-80-6) Gig Harbor Pr.

***Slime Bag! & Other Tasteless Tales.** James Charbonneau. (Stomach Turners Ser.). 1997. pap. text ed. 5.95 (1-56565-613-X) Lowell Hse.

Slime Lake. Tom B. Stone. (Graveyard School Ser.: No. 7). 112p. (J). (gr. 3-7). 1995. pap. 3.50 (0-553-48333-1) Bantam.

Slime Lives! And Other Weird Facts That Will Amaze You: And Other Strange Facts. Robin Keats. LC 94-18503. (Illus.). 80p. (Orig.). (J). 1995. pap. 3.50 (0-380-77304-X, Camelot) Avon.

Slime Molds of Ohio. E. L. Fullmer. (Bulletin Ser.: No. 11). 1921. 3.00 (0-86727-010-1) Ohio Bio Survey.

Slime Time. Jane O'Connor et al. LC 89-77324. (Stepping Stone Bks.). (Illus.). 64p. (Orig.). (J). (gr. 2-4). 1990. pap. 2.50 (0-679-80714-4) Random Bks Yng Read.

***Slimetime: A Guide to Sleazy, Mindless, Movie Entertainment.** Steve Puchalski. (Illus.). 200p. (Orig.). 1996. pap. 19.95 (0-9523288-5-2, Pub. by Headpress UK) AK Pr Dist.

Slimming Down: The Numbers Game. ECRS Institute Staff. 78p. (Orig.). 1987. pap. 4.95 (0-9618644-1-9) Prof Homzons Pr.

Slimming Down & Growing Up. Neva Coyle & Marie Chapian. LC 85-15028. 176p. (Orig.). (J). (gr. 4-7). 1985. pap. 5.99 (0-87123-833-0) Bethany Hse.

Slimming Partner. Donald S. Fitch. (Illus.). 186p. (Orig.). 1988. pap. 9.95 (0-9620454-0-3) MicroSkills.

Slimming Your Hips & Thighs. Consumer Guide Editors & Ann Dugan. (Illus.). 64p. 1993. spiral bd. 5.98 (0-88176-083-8, 3200000) Pubns Intl Ltd.

Slim's Table. Mitchell Duneier. (C). Date not set. pap. text ed. write for info. (0-393-10080-4) Norton.

Slim's Table: Race, Respectability, & Masculinity. Mitchell Duneier. (Illus.). 200p. 1992. 19.95 (0-226-17030-6) U Ch Pr.

Slim's Table: Race, Respectability, & Masculinity. abr. ed. Mitchell Duneier. (Illus.). viii, 192p. (C). 1994. pap. 9.95 (0-226-17031-4) U Ch Pr.

***Slimy Science.** 1997. pap. 19.95 (0-8069-9887-3) Sterling.

Sling: For Sport & Survival. Cliff Savage. LC 84-81630. (Illus.). 72p. (Orig.). 1984. pap. 8.95 (0-915179-19-9) Loompanics.

***Sling Blade: A Screenplay.** Billy Bob Thornton. 160p. 1996. pap. 9.95 (0-7868-8250-6) Hyperion.

Slingerland Book. Rob Cook. (Illus.). vi, 292p. (Orig.). 1996. pap. 34.95 (1-888408-00-6) Rebeats Pubns.

Slings & Arrows: Narcissistic Injury & Its Treatment. Jerome D. Levin. LC 93-13285. 336p. 1993. 40.00 (0-87668-550-5) Aronson.

Slings & Arrows: Theatre in My Life. Robert Lewis. (Illus.). 384p. 1996. pap. 19.95 (1-55783-244-7) Applause Theatre Bk Pubs.

Slingshot. Jack Hunter. 1996. mass mkt. 6.99 (0-8125-2457-8) Forge NYC.

Slingshot of Hell: Holocaust Journal. Yechezkel Harfenes. 29p. 1989. 15.95 (0-944070-07-8) Targum Pr.

***Slinky & His Friend, Peanut.** Darlene Orsini. (Illus.). 11p. (J). (gr. k-3). 1996. pap. 6.00 (0-8059-3826-5) Dorrance.

***Slinky Inkermann & the Crazy Contest.** Dave Webb. (Illus.). 100p. (Orig.). (J). (gr. 3-6). 1996. pap. 3.95 (1-57502-290-7, PO1000) Morris Pubng.

***Slinky Inkermann's Superfreaky Summer.** Dave Webb. 98p. (Orig.). (J). 1997. pap. write for info. (1-57502-546-9, P01600) Morris Pubng.

Slinky Malinki. Lynley Dodd. LC 90-44686. (Gold Star First Readers Ser.). (Illus.). 32p. (J). (gr. 1-2). 1991. lib. bdg. 18.60 (0-8368-0197-0) Gareth Stevens Inc.

Slinky Malinki, Open the Door. Lynley Dodd. LC 93-21180. (Gold Star First Readers Ser.). (J). 1994. lib. bdg. 18.60 (0-8368-1074-0) Gareth Stevens Inc.

Slinky Snakes. D. M. Souza. (Creatures All Around Us Ser.). (Illus.). 40p. (J). (gr. 1-4). 1992. lib. bdg. 19.95 (0-87614-711-2, Carolrhoda) Lerner Group.

***Slip & Fall Practice.** 2nd ed. Charles E. Turnbow. 1994. write for info. (1-58012-007-5) James Pub Santa Ana.

Slip Bobbering. 3rd ed. Greg Bohn. (Secrets of a Northwoods Walleye Guide Ser.). (Illus.). 64p. 1990. 6.95 (0-685-48129-8) Fishing Hot.

***Slip Casting.** Sasha Wardell. (Illus.). 128p. Date not set. 26.00 (1-889250-06-6) Gentle Br.

Slip Form Techniques. T. A. Dinescu & C. Radulescu. (Abacus Bks.). (Illus.). 488p. 1984. text ed. 190.00 (0-85626-307-9) Gordon & Breach.

An Asterisk (*) at the beginning of an entry indicates that the title is appearing in BIP for the first time.

Slip in Time: An Historic Adventure at the Benton Harbor Ship Canal. Kathryn S. Zerler. Ed. by Joann Phillips & Nancy Watts-Stiles. (Illus.). 160p. 1993. 15.95 (*0-9627532-2-X*) Sleeping Cat.
Slip of Bamboo: A Collection of Haiku from Maui. Victor C. Pellegrino. LC 95-94392. (Illus.). 136p. 1996. pap. 7.95 (*0-945045-04-2*) Maui Arthoughts.
Slipcover Chic: Designing & Sewing Elegant Slipcovers at Home. Carol C. Garey & Catherine Revland. (Illus.). 144p. 1992. 23.00 (*0-688-11433-4*) Hearst Bks.
Slipcover Magic. Dorothea Hall & Ron Caralissen. 128p. 1995. pap. 21.95 (*0-8019-8631-1*) Chilton.
***Slipcovers.** Cowles Creative Publishing Staff. LC 97-14622. (Creative Textiles Ser.). (Illus.). 112p. 1997. pap. 16.95 (*0-86573-411-9*) Cowles Creative.
***Slipcovers & Bedspreads.** Sunset Staff. 1997. pap. text ed. 12.99 (*0-376-01514-4*, Sunset) Sunset Bks Inc.
Sliphammer. Brian Garfield. 1979. pap. 1.75 (*0-449-24215-3*, Crest) Fawcett.
Slipp' Away: The Loss of Black-Owned Farms. Ed. by David A. Dybiec. LC 88-81218. (Illus.). 80p. (Orig.). 1988. pap. 6.00 (*0-914422-16-2*) Glenmary Res Ctr.
Slippage. limited ed. Harlan Ellison. write for info. (*0-614-01287-2*) Mark Ziesing.
Slippage: Previously Uncollected, Precariously Poised Stories. Harlan Ellison. 288p. 1997. 22.00 (*0-395-35341-6*) HM.
Slipped Disc. James Cyriax. 1986. 5.95 (*0-684-16646-1*) S&S Trade.
Slipper Orchids. Catherine Cash. LC 90-39595. (Illus.). 304p. 1991. 49.95 (*0-88192-183-1*) Timber.
Slippery & Other Stories. R. A. Lafferty. (Booklet Ser.: No. 19). 39p. (Orig.). 1985. pap. 2.00 (*0-936055-18-9*) C Drumm Bks.
Slippery Customers: Estate Agents, the Public & Regulation. Michael Clarke et al. 1994. text ed. 44.00 (*1-85431-377-0*, Pub. by Blackstone Pr UK) Gaunt.
Slippery Earth: Nahua-Christian Moral Dialogue in Sixteenth-Century Mexico. Louise M. Burkhart. LC 88-38673. 242p. 1989. 44.50 (*0-8165-1088-1*) U of Ariz Pr.
Slippery, Slimy, Silly Mazes. S. Guastella & J. Strong. (J). 1997. pap. 2.95 (*0-8167-3204-3*) Troll Communs.
Slippery Slope: The Long Road to the Breakup of AT&T. Fred W. Henck. LC 87-28043. (Contributions in Economics & Economic History Ser.: No. 80). 288p. 1988. text ed. 59.95 (*0-313-26025-7*, HKO/, Greenwood Pr) Greenwood.
Slippery, Splendid Sea Creatures. Madelyn W. Carlisle. LC 92-45206. (Let's Investigate Ser.). (Illus.). 32p. (J). (gr. 2-6). 1996. lib. bdg. 13.95 (*1-56674-134-3*) Forest Hse.
Slippery Step. large type ed. Rae Foley. 1979. 25.99 (*0-7089-0365-7*) Ulverscroft.
Slippin' into Darkness. Norman Partidge. 304p. 1996. mass mkt. 4.99 (*1-57566-004-0*) Kensgtn Pub Corp.
***Slipping-down Life.** Anne Tyler. 1997. pap. 11.00 (*0-449-00102-4*) Fawcett.
Slipping-Down Life. Anne Tyler. 192p. 1992. reprint ed. mass mkt. 5.99 (*0-8041-0886-2*) Ivy Books.
Slipping Honey In. Audrey Hargreaves & Shirley Windward. 130p. (Orig.). 1995. pap. 9.95 (*1-881168-35-2*) Red Dancefir.
Slipping into Darkness. Norman Partridge. 1996. pap. 4.99 (*0-8217-5189-1*) NAL-Dutton.
Slipping Through the Cracks: The Status of Black Women. Ed. by Margaret C. Simms & Julianne M. Malveaux. 224p. 1986. pap. 21.95 (*0-88738-662-8*) Transaction Pubs.
Slipping, Tripping & Falling Accidents. Ed. by P. R. Davis. (Ergonomics Special Issue Ser.: Vol. 28). 168p. 1985. pap. 23.00 (*0-85066-950-2*) Taylor & Francis.
SLIP/PPP Connection: The Essential Guide to Graphical Internet Access. Paul Glister. LC 95-7398. 480p. 1995. pap. text ed. 24.95 (*0-471-11712-9*) Wiley.
Slippy Cleans Up. Sherii Parrett & Sylvia Brown. (Tub Tales of Slippy Jr. Ser.). (Illus.). 24p. (Orig.). (J). (ps-6). 1992. pap. 5.99 (*1-56722-002-9*) Word Aflame.
Slips & Slipware. Anthony Phillips. Ed. by Emmanuel Cooper. (Complete Potter Ser.). (Illus.). 96p. 1995. pap. 19.95 (*0-7134-7713-X*, Pub. by Batsford UK) Trafalgar.
Slips of Speech. John H. Bechtel. LC 77-159889. 217p. 1998. reprint ed. 40.00 (*1-55888-225-1*) Omnigraphics Inc.
Slips of the Tongue & Language Production. Ed. by Anne Cutler. 293p. 1982. pap. 30.80 (*90-279-3120-8*) Mouton.
Slips, Stumbles, & Falls: Pedestrian Footwear & Surfaces. Ed. by B. Everett Gray. LC 90-48899. (Special Technical Publication Ser.: No. 1103). (Illus.). 173p. 1990. text ed. 38.00 (*0-8031-1408-7*, 04-011030-47) ASTM.
***Slips, Trips & Falls: Safety Engineering Guidelines for the Prevention of Falls.** William English. (Illus.). 170p. (Orig.). Date not set. pap. text ed. write for info. (*0-9653462-1-8*) W English.
Slipware. David Barker. 1989. pap. 25.00 (*0-7478-0221-1*, Pub. by Shire UK) St Mut.
Slither McCreep & His Brother. Tony Johnston. 1996. pap. 5.00 (*0-15-201387-3*) HarBrace.
Slither, Swoop, Swing. Alex Ayliffe. (Illus.). 32p. (J). 1996. pap. 4.99 (*0-14-055604-4*) Puffin Bks.
Slitherfoot Snake. Bob Reese. (Grand Canyon Ser.). (Illus.). (J). (gr. k-6). 1987. 9.95 (*0-89868-191-X*); pap. 3.95 (*0-89868-192-8*) ARO Pub.
Slithering Around Texas. Jim Dunlap. (Illus.). 208p. 1993. pap. 12.95 (*1-55622-313-7*, Rep of TX Pr) Wordware Pub.
***Slithers Buy a Boa.** U. B. Gross. (J). 1997. pap. 3.99 (*0-679-88509-9*) Random.
Slithy Toves & Borogoves & Other Beasties. George Conklin. 1995. pap. 6.95 (*0-533-11381-4*) Vantage.
Sliver: A Novel. large type ed. Ira Levin. LC 93-40533. 1994. pap. 18.95 (*0-8161-5939-4*, GK Hall) Thorndike Pr.
Sliver of Glass & Other Uncommon Tales. Anne Mazer. LC 95-45992. (Illus.). 80p. (YA). (gr. 5-9). 1996. 13.95 (*0-7868-0197-2*); lib. bdg. 13.89 (*0-7868-2165-5*) Hyprn Child.
Slivers: A Poem. Philip Miller. Ed. by Gloria V. Hickok. 6p. (Orig.). 1994. pap. 2.50 (*1-884235-07-7*) Helicon Nine Eds.
Slivers from the Cross. Brad Hill. 1990. 8.95 (*0-910452-71-7*) Covenant.
Slivers of Jade. Albert E. Fitzwarren, pseud. 30p. 1986. pap. 3.00 (*0-942788-14-1*) Iris Visual.
Slivers of Light. Kathleen Bufford. 1994. pap. 7.95 (*1-55673-800-5*) CSS OH.
***Sloan: A Paleoindian Dalton Cemetery in Arkansas.** Dan F. Morse. LC 96-54013. (Series in Archaeological Inquiry). (Illus.). 208p. 1997. text ed. 70.00 (*1-56098-712-X*) Smithsonian.
Sloane-Dorland Annotated Medical-Legal Dictionary. Richard Sloane. (Illus.). 787p. 1987. text ed. 164.25 (*0-314-93512-6*) West Pub.
Sloane-Dorland Annotated Medical-Legal Dictionary: 1992 Supplement. Richard Sloane. LC 92-5676. 1992. pap. text ed. 64.75 (*0-314-00807-1*) West Pub.
Sloane's Column. George B. Sloane. Ed. by George T. Turner. 1979. reprint ed. 40.00 (*0-930412-09-5*) Bureau Issues.
Sloane's Complete Book of All-Terrain Bicycles: Revised & Updated for the Nineties. Eugene A. Sloane. 352p. 1991. pap. 14.95 (*0-671-67587-7*, Fireside) S&S Trade.
Sloane's New Bicycle Maintenance Manual. Eugene A. Sloane. 336p. 1991. pap. 14.95 (*0-671-61947-0*, Fireside) S&S Trade.
Sloan's Green Guide to Antiquing in New England: A Traveler's Guide. 5th ed. Susan P. Sloan. (Illus.). 550p. 1994. pap. 16.95 (*0-929233-05-0*) Globe Pequot.
***Sloan's Green Guide to Antiquing in New England: A Traveler's Guide.** 6th ed. Sloan. 1997. pap. text ed. 17.95 (*0-7627-0162-5*) Globe Pequot.
***Sloan's Quest: A J. D. Sloan Mystery.** Britt Jewell. LC 95-91029. 208p. (Orig.). 1996. pap. 8.00 (*1-56002-645-6*, Univ Edtns) Aegina Pr.
Sloan's Victorian Buildings: Illustrations & Floor Plans for 60 Residences & Other Structures, 2 vols. in 1. Samuel Sloan. (Illus.). 400p. 1981. reprint ed. pap. 21.95 (*0-486-24009-6*) Dover.
Sloboda. 2nd ed. Vladimir Uhri. 40p. (SLO.). 1996. pap. 2.00 (*1-56983-037-1*) New Creat WI.
Sloboda Od Strachu. Vladimir Uhri. 42p. (Orig.). (SLO.). 1996. pap. 2.20 (*1-56983-014-2*) New Creat WI.
Slobodan Jovanovic: An Unsentimental Approach to Politics. Aleksandar Pavkovic. 231p. 1993. 47.00 (*0-88033-268-9*, 371) East Eur Monographs.
Slocum No. 205: The Lady Gambler. Jake Logan. 192p. 1996. pap. text ed. 4.50 (*0-515-11827-3*) Jove Pubns.
***Slocum No. 220: Slocum's Inheritence, Vol. 220.** Jake Logan. (Jake Logan Ser.). 192p. 1997. mass mkt. 4.99 (*0-515-12103-7*) Jove Pubns.
***Slocum No. 224: Louisiana Lovely.** Jake Logan. 192p. 1997. mass mkt. 4.99 (*0-515-12176-2*) Jove Pubns.
***Slocum No. 225.** Jake Logan. 192p. 1997. mass mkt. 4.99 (*0-515-12190-8*) Jove Pubns.
***Slocum No. 226.** Jake Logan. 192p. 1998. mass mkt. 4.99 (*0-515-12208-4*) Jove Pubns.
***Slocum No. 227.** Jake Logan. 192p. 1998. mass mkt. 5.99 (*0-515-12229-7*) Jove Pubns.
***Slocum & Doc Holliday, Vol. 221.** Jake Logan. (Jake Logan Ser.). 192p. 1997. mass mkt. 4.99 (*0-515-12131-2*) Jove Pubns.
Slocum & the Apache Ransom. Jake Logan. (Jake Logan Ser.: No. 209). 192p. 1996. mass mkt. 4.99 (*0-515-11894-X*) Jove Pubns.
***Slocum & the Aztec Priestess No. 222.** Jake Logan. 192p. 1997. mass mkt. 4.99 (*0-515-12143-6*) Jove Pubns.
Slocum & the Bear Lake Monster, No. 204. Jake Logan. (Jake Logan Ser.: No. 204). 192p. (Orig.). 1996. mass mkt. 4.50 (*0-515-11806-0*) Jove Pubns.
***Slocum & the Colorado Riverboat No. 219.** Jake Logan. (Jack Logan Ser.). 192p. 1997. mass mkt. 4.99 (*0-515-12081-2*) Jove Pubns.
***Slocum & the Comanche Rescue No. 223.** Jake Logan. 192p. 1997. mass mkt. 4.99 (*0-515-12161-4*) Jove Pubns.
Slocum & the Cow Town Kill. Jake Logan. (Jake Logan Ser.: No. 184). 192p. (Orig.). 1994. mass mkt. 3.99 (*0-425-14255-8*) Berkley Pub.
Slocum & the Dirty Game. Jake Logan. (Slocum Ser.: No. 202). 192p. (Orig.). 1995. pap. text ed. 4.50 (*0-515-11764-1*) Jove Pubns.
Slocum & the Fort Worth Ambush. Jake Logan. (Slocum Ser.: No. 190). 192p. (Orig.). 1994. mass mkt. 3.99 (*0-425-14496-8*) Berkley Pub.
***Slocum & the Frisco Killers.** Jake Logan. (Slocum Ser.: No. 212). 192p. 1996. mass mkt. 4.99 (*0-515-11967-9*) Jove Pubns.
***Slocum & the Great Southern Hunt.** Jake Logan. (Slocum Ser.: No. 213). 192p. 1996. mass mkt. 4.99 (*0-515-11983-0*) Jove Pubns.
Slocum & the Invaders, No. 182. Jake Logan. 192p. (Orig.). 1994. mass mkt. 3.99 (*0-425-14182-9*) Berkley Pub.
***Slocum & the Irish Lass.** Jake Logan. 256p. 1997. mass mkt. 5.99 (*0-515-12155-X*) Jove Pubns.
***Slocum & the Lady in Blue No. 217.** Jake Logan. (Slocum Ser.: No. 217). 192p. 1997. mass mkt. 4.99 (*0-515-12049-9*) Jove Pubns.
Slocum & the Lady 'Niners. Jake Logan. (Slocum Ser.: No. 194). 192p. (Orig.). 1995. mass mkt. 3.99 (*0-425-14684-7*) Berkley Pub.
Slocum & the Mountain of Gold. Jake Logan. (Slocum Ser.: No. 183). 192p. (Orig.). 1994. mass mkt. 3.99 (*0-425-14231-0*) Berkley Pub.
Slocum & the Pirates, No. 196. Jake Logan. 192p. (Orig.). 1995. mass mkt. 3.99 (*0-515-11633-5*) Berkley Pub.
***Slocum & the Powder River Gamble No. 218, Vol. 218.** Jake Logan. (Jake Logan Ser.). 192p. 1997. mass mkt. 4.99 (*0-515-12070-7*) Jove Pubns.
Slocum & the Spotted Horse. Jake Logan. (Slocum Ser.: No. 198). 192p. (Orig.). 1995. mass mkt. 3.99 (*0-515-11679-3*) Jove Pubns.
***Slocum & the Town Boss.** Jake Logan. (Slocum Ser.: No. 216). 192p. 1997. mass mkt. 4.99 (*0-515-12030-8*) Jove Pubns.
Slocum & the Walapai War. Jake Logan. (Jake Logan Ser.: No. 210). 1996. mass mkt. 4.99 (*0-515-11924-5*) Jove Pubns.
***Slocum at Dead Dog.** Jake Logan. (Slocum Ser.: No. 215). 192p. 1997. mass mkt. 4.99 (*0-515-12015-4*) Jove Pubns.
Slocum at Dog Leg Creek, No. 199. Jake Logan. 192p. (Orig.). 1995. mass mkt. 3.99 (*0-515-11701-3*) Jove Pubns.
Slocum in Paradise, No. 206. Jake Logan. 192p. (Orig.). 1996. mass mkt. 4.50 (*0-515-11841-9*) Jove Pubns.
Slocum's Folly. Jake Logan. (Jake Logan Ser.: No. 211). 1996. mass mkt. 4.99 (*0-515-11940-7*) Jove Pubns.
***Slocum's Grubstake.** Jake Logan. (Slocum Ser.: No. 212). 1996. mass mkt. 5.50 (*0-515-11955-5*) Jove Pubns.
Slocum's Silver. Jake Logan. (Slocum Silver Ser.: No. 200). 192p. (Orig.). 1995. mass mkt. 3.99 (*0-515-11729-3*) Jove Pubns.
Slogans. Ed. by Laurence Urdang & Ceila D. Robbins. 560p. 1984. 82.00 (*0-8103-1549-1*) Gale.
Slogans. 2nd ed. Urdang Staff. 1905. 82.00 (*0-8103-5480-2*) Gale.
Slogans. 3rd ed. Urdang Staff. 1920. 82.00 (*0-8103-5481-0*) Gale.
Slogans or Distinctives: Reforming Christian Higher Education. David L. Wolfe & Harold Heie. LC 92-41860. 1993. 37.00 (*0-8191-8988-X*); pap. 16.50 (*0-8191-8989-8*) U Pr of Amer.
Slogum House. Mari Sandoz. LC 80-22077. 336p. 1981. reprint ed. text ed. 32.00 (*0-8032-4126-7*) U of Nebr Pr.
Slogum House. Mari Sandoz. LC 80-22077. 336p. 1981. reprint ed. pap. 16.95 (*0-8032-9123-X*, Bison Books) U of Nebr Pr.
***Slonimsky: Thesaurus of Scales & Melodic Patterns.** 256p. 1997. pap. 29.95 (*0-8256-1449-X*, GS 10018) Music Sales.
Sloop of War. Alexander Kent. 1992. reprint ed. lib. bdg. 25.95 (*0-89966-974-3*) Buccaneer Bks.
Sloops of the Hudson. William Verplanck & Moses W. Collyer. (Illus.). 50p. 1984. reprint ed. pap. 10.00 (*0-935796-06-1*) Purple Mnt Pr.
Sloops of the Hudson. William Verplanck. 171p. 1993. reprint ed. lib. bdg. 69.00 (*0-7812-5223-7*) Rprt Serv.
Sloops of the Hudson River: A Historical & Design Survey. Paul E. Fontenoy. (Illus.). xi, 130p. 1994. pap. 19.95 (*0-913372-71-4*) Mystic Seaport.
***Slop! A Welsh Folktale.** Margaret R. MacDonald. (Illus.). 24p. (J). (gr. k-6). 1997. 15.95 (*1-55591-352-0*) Fulcrum Pub.
Slop Goes the Soup. Pamela Edwards. LC 94-48809. (Illus.). (J). 1996. 9.95 (*0-06-026257-5*, HarpT); lib. bdg. 9.89 (*0-06-026262-1*, HarpT) HarpC.
Slope Instability. Ed. by Denys Brunsden & David B. Prior. LC 83-16923. (Landscape Systems Ser.). (Illus.). 646p. reprint ed. pap. 180.00 (*0-7837-6161-9*, 2045883) Bks Demand.
Slope of the Wind. Adrian Seligman. (Illus.). 232p. 1994. pap. 16.50 (*0-85036-443-4*) Sheridan.
***Slope Stability: Geotechnical Engineering & Geomorphology.** Ed. by M. G. Anderson & K. S. Richards. LC 86-4063. (Illus.). 656p. 1987. reprint ed. pap. 180.00 (*0-608-03996-9*, 2064733) Bks Demand.
Slope Stability & Stabilization Methods. Lee W. Abramson et al. LC 95-16406. 656p. 1995. text ed. 84.95 (*0-471-10622-4*) Wiley.
Slope Stability Engineering. Ed. by R. J. Chandler. 443p. 1992. text ed. 137.00 (*0-7277-1660-3*) Am Soc Civil Eng.
Slope Stabilization & Erosion Control: A Bioengineering Approach. Ed. by Royston P. Morgan & R. J. Rickson. 274p. 1995. 79.95 (*0-419-15630-5*, E & FN Spon) Routledge Chapman & Hall.
Slopes. Caroline Rush. LC 96-18785. (Simple Science Ser.). (J). 1997. lib. bdg. 18.54 (*0-8172-4502-2*) Raintree Steck-V.
***Slopes.** Young. 1976. pap. text ed. write for info. (*0-582-48433-2*, Pub. by Longman UK) Longman.
Slopes & Weathering. John Small & Michael Clark. LC 81-18025. (Cambridge Topics in Geography Second Ser.). 112p. 1982. 18.50 (*0-521-23340-2*) Cambridge U Pr.
Slopes of Lebanon. Amos Oz. 1992. pap. 11.00 (*0-679-73144-X*, Vin) Random.
Slopes of War. N. A. Perez. (Illus.). 224p. (J). (gr. 7 up). 1990. pap. 5.95 (*0-395-54979-5*) HM.
Slopes to the River. Beth A. Bassein. 72p. 1996. pap. 12.95 (*0-7734-2753-8*, Mellen Poetry Pr) E Mellen.
Sloppy Joe's: The Tradition Continues. Carol Shaughnessy. Ed. by Market Share Company Staff. 60p. (Orig.). 1995. pap. 7.50 (*0-9647728-9-2*) Market Share.
Sloppy Monster. Susan Kracht. LC 92-60289. (Illus.). 44p. (J). (ps-3). 1992. 5.95 (*1-55523-527-1*) Winston-Derek.
Sloshing, Fluid-Structure Interaction & Structural Response due to Shock & Impact Loads 1994: Proceedings of the Pressure Vessels & Piping Conference, Minneapolis, MN, 1994. Ed. by D. C. Ma. LC 94-71745. (PVP Ser.: Vol. 272). 233p. 1994. pap. 60.00 (*0-7918-1195-6*) ASME.
Sloss Furnaces & the Rise of the Birmingham District: An Industrial Epic. David Lewis. LC 93-48178. (History of American Science & Technology Ser.). 672p. 1994. text ed. 39.95 (*0-8173-0708-7*) U of Ala Pr.
Slot Machine. Chris Lynch. LC 94-48235. 256p. (YA). (gr. 7 up). 1995. 14.95 (*0-06-023584-5*); lib. bdg. 14.89 (*0-06-023585-3*) HarpC Child Bks.
Slot Machine. Chris Lynch. LC 94-48235. (Trophy Bk.). 256p. (YA). (gr. 7 up). 1996. pap. 4.50 (*0-06-447140-3*, Trophy) HarpC Child Bks.
Slot Machine, a Broken Test Tube: An Autobiography. Luria. 1985. pap. 6.95 (*0-465-07831-1*) Basic.
Slot Machine Buyer's Handbook: Consumer's Guide to Slot Machines. 2nd ed. David L. Saul. LC 90-91665. (Illus.). 322p. (Orig.). 1995. pap. 19.95 (*0-934422-02-8*, BKS160028) Mead Pub Corp.
***Slot Machine Magic: How to Be a Slot Wizard & Beat the One-Armed Bandits with Insider Slot Secrets.** Donald Currier. 32p. (Orig.). 1996. pap. 10.00 (*1-890030-04-X*) Las Vegas Insider.
Slot Machine Mania. Dwight Crevelt. 256p. 1989. pap. 6.99 (*0-914839-13-6*) Gollehon Pr.
Slot Machines. Dieter Ladwig. 1994. 12.98 (*0-7858-0072-7*) Bk Sales Inc.

S

Slot Machines: A Pictorial History of the First 100 Years. 4th rev. ed. Marshall Fey. Ed. by Douglas McDonald et al. (Illus.). 652p. 1994. reprint ed. 29.95 (*0-9623852-7-1*) Liberty Belle.

Slot Machines & Coin-Op Games. William Kurtz. 1991. 12.98 (*1-55521-731-1*) Bk Sales Inc.
Slot Machines on Parade. Robert N. Geddes & Daniel R. Mead. LC 79-89443. (Illus.). 200p. 1980. 39.95 (*0-934422-16-8*) Mead Pub Corp.
Slot Smarts: Winning Strategies at the Slot Machine. Claude Halcombe. 1996. pap. write for info. (*0-8184-0584-8*) Carol Pub Group.
Sloth. Ruth Hayes. (Illus.). 104p. (Orig.). 1988. pap. 4.95 (*0-941104-34-6*) Real Comet.
Slots. Tony Korfman. (Playing to Win Ser.). 48p. (Orig.). 1985. pap. text ed. 2.50 (*0-934047-04-9*) Gaming Bks Intl.
***Slots!** Ann Poyas. LC 96-72064. 336p. (Orig.). 1997. 21.95 (*0-9656167-0-3*) Book Creek.
***Slots!** Ann Poyas. LC 96-72064. 336p. (Orig.). 1997. pap. 12.95 (*0-9656167-1-1*) Book Creek.
***Slots for Profit: Yes, Slot Machines Can Be Beat & You Hold the Key!** Brian Smith. (Illus.). 32p. Date not set. pap. 9.95 (*0-9653440-0-2*) Indiv Advant.
***Slots for Profit: Yes Slot Machines Can Be Beat, & You Hold the Key.** Brian S. Smith. Ed. by Barb Chilletti. (Illus.). 32p. (Orig.). 1996. pap. write for info. (*0-614-30231-5*) Indiv Advant.
***Slouch in the Couch.** Stephen Hemenway. (Illus.). 32p. (J). (gr. k-2). 1997. 16.00 (*0-8059-4163-0*) Dorrance.
Slouching Towards Bethlehem. Joan Didion. 238p. 1990. pap. 10.00 (*0-374-52172-7*, Noonday) FS&G.
Slouching Towards Bethlehem... & Further Psychoanalytic Explorations. Nina Coltart. LC 92-1557. 200p. 1992. lib. bdg. 32.00 (*0-89862-134-8*) Guilford Pr.
***Slouching Towards Gomorrah.** Robert Bork. 1997. pap. 13.00 (*0-614-28103-2*, ReganBooks) HarpC.
Slouching Towards Gomorrah: Modern Liberalism & American Decline. Robert H. Bork. 382p. 1996. 25.00 (*0-06-039163-4*, ReganBooks) HarpC.
***Slouching Towards Gomorrah: Modern Liberalism & American Decline.** Robert H. Bork. 1997. pap. text ed. 14.00 (*0-06-098719-7*) HarpC.
Slovak: Beginning, Set 8. Sylvia Galova-Lorinc & Oscar E. Swan. 522p. 1992. pap. text ed. 185.00 incl. audio (*0-88432-521-0*, AFSL10) Audio-Forum.
Slovak: Hippocrene Handy Dictionary. Joseph P. Malatinsky. 200p. (ENG & SLO.). 1996. pap. 12.95 (*0-7818-0101-X*) Hippocrene Bks.
***Slovak & English Technical Dictionary.** A. Caforio. 919p. (ENG & SLO.). 1996. 95.00 (*0-7859-9368-1*) Fr & Eur.
Slovak Autonomy Movement, Nineteen Thirty-Five to Nineteen Thirty-Nine. Dorothea H. El Mallakh. (East European Monographs: No. 55). 1979. text ed. 58.00 (*0-914710-49-4*) East Eur Monographs.
Slovak-English Dictionary. J. Vilikovska & Jan Vilkovsky. (ENG & SLO.). 42.50 (*0-87559-041-1*); 47.50 (*0-87559-042-X*) Shalom.
Slovak-English, English-Slovak Compact Dictionary. (Hippocrene Compact Dictionaries Ser.). 360p. (Orig.). (ENG & SLO.). 1996. pap. 8.95 (*0-7818-0501-5*) Hippocrene Bks.
Slovak-English English-Slovak Dictionary. Nina Trnka. (Language Dictionaries Ser.). 360p. (Orig.). 1992. pap. 11.95 (*0-87052-115-2*) Hippocrene Bks.
Slovak for You: Slovak for Speakers of English. Ada Bohmerova. (Illus.). 143p. (SLO.). 1996. pap. 30.00 (*0-86516-331-6*) Bolchazy-Carducci.
Slovak-Hungarian Concise Dictionary. 2nd ed. A. Stelczer & I. Vendegh. 870p. (HUN & SLO.). 1983. 39.95 (*0-8288-1670-0*, M 8580) Fr & Eur.
Slovak-Hungarian Pocket Dictionary. T. M. Gobel. 480p. 1988. 15.00 (*963-205-220-X*, Pub. by Akad Kiado HU) St Mut.
***Slovak Lutheran Social Ethics.** Vasil Gluchman. LC 97-950. (Studies in Religion & Society: Vol. 37). 168p. 1997. text ed. 79.95 (*0-7734-8651-8*) E Mellen.
Slovak National Awakening: An Essay in the Intellectual History of East Central Europe. Peter Brock. LC 75-42013. 114p. reprint ed. pap. 32.50 (*0-317-55660-6*, 2029326) Bks Demand.

Slovak Phrase Book. Sylvia Galova-Lorinc & Stephen R. Hoferka, Jr. Ed. by John M. Lorinc. (Illus.). 82p. (Orig.). 1991. pap. 9.50 (*0-9644998-0-0*); pap. 18.00 incl. audio (*0-9644998-2-7*); audio 9.50 (*0-9644998-1-9*) Lor-Hof Pub.

Slovak Politics: Essays on Slovak History in Honour of Joseph M. Kirschbaum. Stanislav J. Kirschbaum. LC 83-80380. xviii, 381p. 1983. 18.00 (*0-9610908-0-4*) Slov Ins.

Slovak-Russian Dictionary. D. Kollar et al. 768p. (RUS & SLO.). 1976. 49.95 (*0-8288-5754-7*, M9076) Fr & Eur.

***Slovak World Congress Cookbook: A Culinary Collection of Our Slovak Heritage.** Slovak World Congress Staff. Ed. by Anne Z. Sarosy & Sandra S. Duve. 352p. 1997. 16.00 (*0-917909-00-3*) K & K Hse.

Slovakia: Restructuring for Recovery. World Bank Staff. LC 94-35172. (Country Study). 182p. 1994. 10.95 (*0-8213-3066-7*, 13066) World Bank.

Slovakia: The Heart of Europe. Olga Drobna et al. Tr. by Martin C. Styan & Zuzana Paulikova from SLO. (Illus.). 56p. 1997. lib. bdg. 30.00 (*0-86516-319-7*) Bolchazy-Carducci.

Slovakia - Decorations & Insignia 1939-1945. Juray Shoviera. Ed. by Marian Furlan. (Illus.). 62p. (Orig.). (ENG, GER & SLO.). 1994. pap. 10.00 (*0-929757-45-9*, Pub. by Militaria Hse CN) Regt QM.

Slovakia in Pictures. Lerner Publications, Department of Geography Staff. LC 94-45803. (Visual Geography Ser.). (Illus.). 64p. (YA). (gr. 5 up). 1995. lib. bdg. 14.96 (*0-8225-1912-7*) Lerner Group.

Slovakia 1918-1938. Owen V. Johnson. 1985. text ed. 75.50 (*0-88033-072-4*, 180) Col U Pr.

Slovar Slovenskega Knjiznega Jezika, 4 vols., Set. Janko Jurancic. 4075p. (SLV.). 1987. 350.00 (*0-8288-2088-0*, F78660) Fr & Eur.

Slovene - French Dictionary: Dictionnaire Francais-Slovene. Anton Grad. 748p. (FRE & SLV.). 1987. 59.95 (*0-8288-1134-2*, M9693) Fr & Eur.

Slovene - Italian Dictionary. G. Tomat. (ITA & SLV.). 1991. 95.00 (*0-8288-8506-0*) Fr & Eur.

Slovene-English Dictionary. Janko Kotnik. 831p. (ENG & SLV.). 1987. 49.95 (*0-8288-0551-2*, M9694) Fr & Eur.

Slovene-English Dictionary. 5th ed. Janko Kotnik. (ENG & SLV.). 37.50 (*0-87559-035-7*); 42.00 (*0-87559-036-5*) Shalom.

Slovene-English, English-Slovene Modern Dictionary. Dasa Komac. 935p. (ENG & SLV.). 1994. pap. 24.95 (*0-7818-0252-0*) Hippocrene Bks.

Slovene-Latin Dictionary: Slovensko-Latinski Slovar. Fran Bradac. 347p. (LAT & SLV.). 1986. 65.00 (*0-8288-1138-5*, M2039) Fr & Eur.

Slovene Medieval History: Selected Studies. Aloysius L. Kuhar. LC 65-2942. 143p. 1962. 12.00 (*0-686-28376-7*); pap. 8.00 (*0-686-28377-5*) Studia Slovenica.

Slovenes in the United States & Canada: A Bibliography. Ed. by Joseph D. Dwyer. LC 81-83551. (IHRC Ethnic Bibliography Ser.: No. 3). (Illus.). xiv, 196p. 1981. pap. text ed. 8.95 (*0-932833-02-0*) Immig His Res.

Slovenes of Carinthia. Thomas M. Barker & Andreas Moritsch. LC 84-80620. (East European Monographs: No. 169). 415p. 1984. text ed. 79.00 (*0-88033-061-9*) East Eur Monographs.

Slovenes of Carinthia. 2nd ed. Thomas M. Barker & Andreas Moritsch. LC 79-15399. (Eastern European Studies of Columbia University). 59.00 (*0-685-42094-9*) East Eur Monographs.

***Slovenia.** Compiled by Cathie Carmichael. (World Bibliographical Ser.: Vol. 186). 176p. Date not set. 85.00 (*1-85109-239-0*, DR1375) ABC-CLIO.

***Slovenia: A Study of the Educational System of the Republic of Slovenia.** (Working Papers Ser.). 126p. 1995. 25.00 (*0-614-23472-7*, 5343) Am Assn Coll Registrars.

Slovenia: A Study of the Educational System of the Republic of Slovenia. Karlene N. Dickey. LC 95-15013. (PIER World Education Ser.: Working Papers). 1995. 25.00 (*0-929851-47-1*) Am Assn Coll Registrars.

Slovenia: Travel Survival Kit. Steve Fallon. (Illus.). 336p. 1995. pap. 13.95 (*0-86442-309-8*) Lonely Planet.

Slovenia, Republika-Army Insignia & Decorations 1918-1992. Marian Furlan. (Illus.). 88p. (Orig.). 1993. pap. 10.00 (*0-929757-44-0*, Pub. by Militaria Hse CN) Regt QM.

Slovenia under Nazi Occupation, Nineteen Forty-One to Nineteen Forty-Five. Helga H. Harriman. LC 76-151284. 94p. 1977. 8.00 (*0-686-28385-6*) Studia Slovenica.

Slovenia, Vol. 1: A Bibliography in Foreign Languages. Valentin Leskovsek. 105p. 1990. 12.00 (*0-685-34712-5*) Studia Slovenica.

Slovenia, Vol. 2: A Bibliography in Foreign Languages. Valentin Leskorsek. 115p. 1991. 12.00 (*0-685-41046-3*) Studia Slovenica.

Slovenian Community in Bridgeport, Conn. John A. Arnez. LC 73-170467. (Studia Slovenica, Special Ser.). 96p. 1971. 7.00 (*0-686-28388-0*) Studia Slovenica.

Slovenian-Italian Dictionary: Slovensko-Italijanski Slovar. Janko Kotnik. 799p. (ITA & SLV.). 1986. 49.95 (*0-8288-1137-7*, F79240) Fr & Eur.

Slovenian Lands & Their Economies, 1848-1873. John A. Arnez. LC 83-116220. (Studia Slovenica Ser.: No. 15). 321p. 1983. pap. 20.00 (*0-938616-16-1*) Studia Slovenica.

Slovenian Letters by Missionaries in America, 1851-1874. Intro. by John A. Arnez. (Studia Slovenica, Special Ser.: No.4). 230p. 1984. pap. 12.00 (*0-318-01454-8*) Studia Slovenica.

Slovenian Russian Phraseology Dictionary. R. I. Jarancev. 304p. (RUS & SLV.). 1981. 24.95 (*0-8288-2003-1*, M15166) Fr & Eur.

Slovenian Village: Zerovnica. Irene P. Winner. LC 77-127367. 289p. reprint ed. pap. 82.40 (*0-685-15801-2*, 2027530) Bks Demand.

Slovenly Betsy. Henry Hoffman. LC 95-20328. (Wee Books for Wee Folks). (Illus.). 96p. (J). 1995. 7.95 (*1-55709-408-X*) Applewood.

Slovenly Peter: Cheerful Stories. Henry Hoffmann. 1976. 16.95 (*0-8488-1369-3*) Amereon Ltd.

Slovenly Peter: or Cheerful Stories & Funny Pictures for Good Little Folks. Henry Hoffmann. (Illus.). 88p. (J). 1991. reprint ed. lib. bdg. 25.95 (*0-89966-765-1*) Buccaneer Bks.

Slovensko-Angleski Slovar. Ed. by A. Grad & H. Leeming. 848p. 1994. 55.00 (*86-341-0984-4*) OUP.

***Slovensko Moje.** Olga Drobna & Eduard Drobny. (Illus.). 56p. (SLO.). 30.00 (*0-86516-318-9*) Bolchazy-Carducci.

Slovesa Tsarei I Dnei. Iurii Kashkarov. 250p. (Orig.). (RUS.). pap. 15.00 (*0-89830-112-2*) Russica Pubs.

***Slovnik Spisovneho Jazyka Ceskeho, 8 vols.** Cintr J. Belic. 1989. 196.00 (*0-614-25058-7*) Szwede Slavic.

Slovo: The Unfinished Autobiography of ANC Leader Joe Slovo. Joe Slovo. (Illus.). 293p. 1997. pap. 18.95 (*1-875284-95-8*) Ocean Pr NY.

Slovo O Polku Igoreve/Prince Igor in Search of Glory: Kniaz' Igor' v Poiskakh Slavy. A. V. Riasanovsky & Vera Zubarev. Tr. by Fred Patton. LC 96-10583. 110p. (Orig.). (ENG & RUS.). 1996. pap. 12.00 (*1-55779-088-4*) Hermitage.

Slow Amassing Light. Tony Compagno. 67p. pap. write for info. (*0-9636625-0-3*) T Compagno.

Slow & Easy Waltz. (Ballroom Dance Ser.). 1986. lib. bdg. 74.95 (*0-8490-3293-8*) Gordon Pr.

Slow & Easy Waltz. (Ballroom Dance Ser.). 1985. lib. bdg. 74.00 (*0-87700-785-3*) Revisionist Pr.

Slow & Steady, Get Me Ready: A How-to Book That Grows with the Child. rev. ed. June R. Oberlander. Ed. by Clyde G. Oberlander. (Illus.). 324p. (Orig.). 1992. pap. 17.95 (*0-9622322-1-1*) Bio-Alpha.

Slow & Steady, Get Me Ready - Despacio y Constantemente, Preparenme: El Libro de Instrucciones que Crece Con Su Nino. Jose G. Roig. (Illus.). 344p. (Orig.). (SPA.). 1994. pap. 17.95 (*0-9622322-4-6*) Bio-Alpha.

Slow & Sure. Horatio Alger, Jr. (Works of Horatio Alger Jr.). 1989. reprint ed. lib. bdg. 79.00 (*0-685-27555-8*) Rprt Serv.

Slow Boat Through Germany. Hugh McKnight. (Illus.). 228p. 1993. 37.50 (*0-7136-3778-1*) Sheridan.

Slow Burn. (Orig.). 1992. mass mkt. 4.95 (*1-56333-042-3*, Badboy) Masquerade.

Slow Burn. Eleanor T. Bland. 336p. 1994. pap. 4.99 (*0-451-17944-7*, Sig) NAL-Dutton.

Slow Burn. Marten Claridge. 352p. 1995. pap. 11.95 (*0-7472-4495-2*, Pub. by Headline UK) Trafalgar.

***Slow Burn.** Leslie Esdaile. 320p. 1997. mass mkt. 4.99 (*0-7860-0424-X*, Pinncle Kensgtn) Kensgtn Pub Corp.

Slow Burn. Eileen Goudge. Date not set. pap. 3.50 (*0-14-036075-1*, Viking) Viking Penguin.

Slow Burn. Elizabeth Hurst. Ed. by Edward Mycue. (Took Modern Poetry in English Ser.: No. 42). 32p. (Orig.). 1993. pap. write for info. (*1-879457-44-X*) Norton Coker Pr.

Slow Burn. Roxanne Longstreet. 320p. 1996. pap. 5.50 (*0-7860-0241-7*, Pinncle Kensgtn) Kensgtn Pub Corp.

Slow Burn. Heather G. Pozzessere. 1994. pap. 5.99 (*1-55166-000-8*, 1-66000-0, Mira Bks) Harlequin Bks.

Slow Burn: A Marti MacAlister Mystery. Eleanor T. Bland. 224p. 1993. 17.95 (*0-312-09237-7*) St Martin.

Slow Burn: A Photodocument of Centralia, Pennsylvania. Renee Jacobs. LC 86-19212. (Illus.). 168p. 1986. pap. 34.95 (*0-8122-1235-5*) U of Pa Pr.

***Slow Burn, a Photodocument of Centralia, Pennsylvania.** Photos & Text by Renee Jacobs. LC 86-19212. (Illus.). 172p. 1986. reprint ed. pap. 49.10 (*0-608-04096-7*, 2064828) Bks Demand.

***Slow Burning Love of God.** Harold Klemp. LC 97-8007. (Mahanta Transcripts Ser.). 1997. write for info. (*1-57043-130-2*) ECKANKAR.

Slow Burning Love of God Bk. 13: The Mahanta Transcripts. Harold Klemp. (Illus.). (Orig.). 1997. pap. 14.00 (*1-57043-111-6*) ECKANKAR.

***Slow Christmas.** 2nd ed. Jeff Brown. 77p. 1996. reprint ed. pap. 9.95 (*1-890069-00-0*, 862, Brownflower Pr) Brownflower Creat.

***Slow Chrysanthemums.** Kim Jong-Gil. 126p. 1987. 21.95 (*0-85646-162-8*, Pub. by Anvil Press UK); pap. 14.95 (*0-85646-163-6*, Pub. by Anvil Press UK) Dufour.

***Slow Coins.** Julia Fields. LC 80-53380. 220p. 1981. 12.00 (*1-57889-008-X*); pap. 8.00 (*1-57889-007-1*) Passeggiata.

Slow Cooking: For Crock Enthusiasts. Ed. by G & R Publishing Staff. (Uni-Bks.). 160p. (Orig.). 1994. pap. text ed. 3.00 (*1-56383-013-2*, 1600) G & R Pub.

Slow Cooking: In Crock-Pot, Slow Cooker, Oven & Multi-Cooker. Joanna White. (Illus.). 160p. (Orig.). 1994. pap. 8.95 (*1-55867-100-5*, Nitty Gritty Ckbks) Bristol Pub Ent CA.

Slow-Crock Cookery. Karen Plageman. LC 74-24590. (Illus.). 1974. pap. 2.95 (*0-915942-02-X*) SF Design.

Slow Dance. Donna Julian. 384p. (Orig.). 1995. mass mkt. 5.50 (*0-451-18671-0*, Sig) NAL-Dutton.

Slow Dance: A Story of Discovery. Date not set. write for info. (*0-394-28161-6*) Random.

Slow Dance for Slow Blues or Ballads. 1986. write for info. (*0-318-61015-9*) Gordon Pr.

Slow Dance for Slow Blues or Ballads. (Ballroom Dance Ser.). 1985. lib. bdg. 60.00 (*0-87700-834-5*) Revisionist Pr.

***Slow Dance Heartbreak.** Arnold Adoff. Date not set. lib. bdg. write for info. (*0-688-10570-X*) Lothrop.

Slow Dance Heartbreak Blues. Arnold Adoff. LC 94-48242. (Illus.). 80p. (YA). (gr. 6 up). 1995. 14.00 (*0-688-10569-6*) Lothrop.

Slow Dance in Autumn. Philip L. Williams. 240p. 1988. 15.95 (*0-934601-56-9*) Peachtree Pubs.

Slow Dance on the Killing Ground. Lenox Cramer. LC 89-81582. (Illus.). 274p. 1990. 19.95 (*0-939427-57-5*, 14001) Alpha Pubns OH.

Slow Dance on the Killing Ground. Lenox Cramer. 272p. 1991. pap. 3.95 (*0-380-71445-0*) Avon.

Slow Dance on the Killing Ground. William Hanley. 1965. pap. 5.25 (*0-8222-1043-6*) Dramatists Play.

Slow Dance to Pearl Harbor: A Tin Can Ensign in Prewar America. William J. Ruhe. LC 95-8906. 224p. 1995. 23.95 (*1-57488-020-9*) Brasseys Inc.

Slow Dancer. Joseph Millar. 1992. pap. 10.00 (*0-916156-89-3*) Cherry Valley.

***Slow Dancing.** Joan E. Lloyd. LC 97-4260. 224p. 1997. pap. 9.95 (*0-7867-0436-5*) Carroll & Graf.

***Slow Dancing on Dinosaur Bones.** Witt. 1997. pap. 12.00 (*0-671-89122-7*, PB Trade Paper) PB.

Slow Dancing on Dinosaur Bones. Lana Witt. LC 95-32326. 416p. 1996. 22.00 (*0-684-81535-4*) S&S Trade.

Slow Dancing Through Time. Gardner Dozois et al. 270p. 1990. 22.00 (*0-942681-03-7*) Ursus Imprints.

Slow Dancing Through Time. deluxe ed. Gardner Dozois et al. 270p. 1990. Signed & boxed ed. boxed 60.00 (*0-942681-04-5*) Ursus Imprints.

Slow Dancing with the Angel of Death. Helen Chappell. 1996. mass mkt. 5.50 (*0-449-14983-8*, GM) Fawcett.

Slow Death. Stewart Home. (High Risk Ser.). 160p. (Orig.). 1996. 12.99 (*1-85242-519-9*) Serpents Tail.

Slow Death for Slavery: The Course of Abolition in Northern Nigeria, 1897- 1936. Paul E. Lovejoy & Jan S. Hogendorn. (African Studies: No. 76). (Illus.). 408p. (C). 1993. text ed. 60.00 (*0-521-37469-3*); pap. text ed. 21.95 (*0-521-44702-X*) Cambridge U Pr.

Slow Deformation & Transmission of Stress in the Earth, IUGG 4. Ed. by S. V. Cohen & P. Vantcek. (Geophysical Monograph Ser.: Vol. 49). 148p. 1989. 25.00 (*0-87590-453-X*) Am Geophysical.

Slow down ... & Get More Done. Marshall Cook. 192p. (Orig.). 1993. pap. 12.99 (*1-55870-270-9*, Betrwy Bks) F & W Pubns Inc.

Slow Down & Simplify Your Life. Mark Thurston. (Life-Changing Principles from the Edgar Cayce Readings Ser.). 87p. (Orig.). 1991. pap. 3.50 (*0-87604-274-4*, 360) ARE Pr.

Slow-down Therapy. Linus Mundy. LC 90-81236. (Illus.). 72p. (Orig.). 1990. pap. 4.95 (*0-87029-229-3*) Abbey.

Slow Dynamics in Condensed Matter. Ed. by K. Kawasaki. (Conference Proceeding Ser.: No. 256). 624p. 1992. 110.00 (*0-88318-938-0*) Am Inst Physics.

Slow Exposures. John Wheatcroft. LC 85-47910. 184p. 1986. 15.95 (*0-8453-4735-7*, Cornwall Bks) Assoc Univ Prs.

***Slow Fade.** Rudolph Wurlitzer. (Midnight Classics Ser.). 211p. (Orig.). 1997. pap. 11.99 (*1-85242-411-7*) Serpents Tail.

Slow Fade to Black: The Negro in American Film, 1900-1942. Thomas Cripps. (Illus.). 464p. 1977. pap. 14.95 (*0-19-502130-4*) OUP.

Slow for a Mania Fast for a Waltz. Peter Tenney. 1995. pap. 3.00 (*0-929730-52-6*) Zeitgeist Pr.

Slow Funeral. Rebecca Ore. 320p. 1995. 4.99 (*0-8125-1604-4*) Tor Bks.

Slow Fuse. Masako Togawa. Tr. by Simon Prentice from JPN. LC 95-11771. 208p. 1995. 21.00 (*0-679-41862-8*) Pantheon.

Slow Fuse: New Poems. Theodore Weiss. 96p. 1984. pap. 8.95 (*0-685-08862-6*) Macmillan.

Slow Hand: Women Writing Erotica. Ed. by Michele B. Slung. LC 91-58375. 256p. 1993. pap. 12.00 (*0-06-092236-2*, PL) HarpC.

Slow Heat. 1990. mass mkt. 4.95 (*0-445-77155-0*, Mysterious Paperbk) Warner Bks.

Slow Heat in Heaven. Sandra Brown. 464p. (Orig.). 1991. mass mkt. 6.99 (*0-446-36173-9*) Warner Bks.

Slow Heat in Heaven. large type ed. Sandra Brown. LC 94-20367. 680p. (Orig.). 1994. 22.95 (*1-56054-791-X*) Thorndike Pr.

Slow Homecoming. Peter Handke. Tr. by Ralph Manheim. LC 84-28597. 278p. 1985. 16.95 (*0-374-26635-2*) FS&G.

Slow Horses & Fast Women. Damon Runyon. (Illus.). reprint ed. lib. bdg. 22.95 (*0-89190-439-5*, Rivercity Pr) Amereon Ltd.

Slow Infections of the Central Nervous System: The Legacy of Dr. Bjorn Sigurdsson. Ed. by Johannes Bjornsson. LC 94-12040. (Annals Ser.: Vol. 724). 1994. write for info. (*0-89766-843-X*); pap. write for info. (*0-89766-844-8*) NY Acad Sci.

Slow Inward Current. Douglas P. Zipes. 1980. lib. bdg. 175.00 (*90-247-2380-9*, Pub. by M Nijhoff NE) Kluwer Ac.

***Slow Isn't Bad, Fast Isn't Better, Different Isn't Wrong.** Bertie R. Synowiec. (Illus.). 1996. pap. 9.95 (*1-885335-14-8*) Positive Support.

Slow Joe. April Kassel. (Illus.). 36p. (Orig.). (J). (gr. k-8). 1993. text ed. 12.95 (*1-56763-067-7*); pap. text ed. 2.95 (*1-56763-068-5*) Ozark Pub.

Slow Joy. Stefanie Marlis. LC 89-40260. (Brittingham Prize in Poetry Ser.). 90p. 1989. pap. 10.95 (*0-299-12304-9*) U of Wis Pr.

Slow Joy. Stefanie Marlis. LC 89-40260. (Brittingham Prize in Poetry Ser.). 90p. (C). 1990. 17.95 (*0-299-12300-6*) U of Wis Pr.

Slow Juggling. Karen Brodine. 48p. (Orig.). 1975. pap. 5.95 (*0-917658-02-7*) BPW & P.

Slow Learner: Early Stories. Thomas Pynchon. LC 84-934. 208p. 1985. reprint ed. pap. 13.95 (*0-316-72443-2*) Little.

Slow Learner in the Classroom. 2nd ed. Newell C. Kephart. LC 77-158613. (Slow Learner Ser.). (Illus.). 448p. reprint ed. pap. 127.70 (*0-685-44480-5*, AU00362) Bks Demand.

Slow Learners: A Break in the Circle. Diane Griffin. (Illus.). 225p. 1978. teacher ed., text ed. 25.00 (*0-7130-0137-2*, Pub. by Woburn Pr UK); teacher ed., pap. text ed. 10.75 (*0-7130-4003-3*, Pub. by Woburn Pr UK) Intl Spec Bk.

Slow Marches. Ed. by John C. Moon. LC 75-19259. (Music of the Fifes & Drums Ser.: Vol. 2). 24p. 1977. pap. 7.95 (*0-87935-046-6*) Colonial Williamsburg.

Slow Memories. Barry Litvak. 1972. pap. 3.25 (*0-8222-1044-4*) Dramatists Play.

Slow Miracles: Urban Women Fighting for Liberation. G. F. Thompson. LC 94-43246. 96p. (Orig.). 1996. pap. 11.95 (*1-880913-12-7*) Innisfree Pr.

***Slow Mirror & Other Stories: New Fiction by Jewish Writers.** Ed. by Sonja Lyndon & Sylvia Paskin. 240p. (Orig.). 1997. pap. 15.00 (*0-907123-81-3*, Pub. by Five Leaves UK) AK Pr Dist.

Slow Moe. John G. Pedicini. Ed. by John Serino. (Nantucket Nanny & Friends Ser.). (Illus.). 32p. (J). (gr. k-2). 1991. 9.95 (*0-9627436-7-4*) Je Suis Derby.

Slow Motion: Changing Masculinities, Changing Men. Lynne Segal. 396p. (Orig.). (C). 1990. pap. 15.95 (*0-8135-1620-X*); text ed. 45.00 (*0-8135-1619-6*) Rutgers U Pr.

Slow Motion Riot. Peter Blauner. 384p. 1992. mass mkt. 4.99 (*0-380-71306-3*) Avon.

Slow of Heart. Marvenea Rainwater. 1989. pap. 10.00 (*0-941179-19-2*) Latitudes Pr.

Slow Plague: A Geography of the AIDS Pandemic. Peter Gould. LC 92-38653. 1993. pap. 27.95 (*1-55786-419-5*) Blackwell Pubs.

Slow Play: Fast Solutions. unabridged ed. (NGF Info Pacs Ser.). (Illus.). 156p. (Orig.). 1995. pap. 45.00 (*0-9638647-1-8*) Natl Golf.

Slow Positron Beam Techniques for Solids & Surfaces. Ed. by Eric Ottewitte & Alex Weiss. LC 94-71036. (AIP Conference Proceedings Ser.: No. 303). 640p. 1994. pap. text ed. 165.00 (*1-56396-267-5*) Am Inst Physics.

Slow Potential Changes in the Brain. Ed. by Wolfgang Haschke et al. LC 92-48777. (Brain Dynamics Ser.). xxii, 288p. 1992. 127.50 (*0-8176-3583-1*) Birkhauser.

Slow Potential Changes in the Human Brain. Ed. by W. Cheyne McCallum & S. Hutch Curry. LC 93-26280. (NATO ASI Ser.: Series A, Life Sciences: Vol. 254). 1994. 95.00 (*0-306-44596-4*, Plenum Pr) Plenum.

Slow Potentials, & Microprocessor Applications. Ed. by Hansjoerg E. Kolder. (Documenta Ophthalmologica Proceedings Ser.). 1983. 451.00 (*90-6193-733-7*) Kluwer Ac.

Slow Reign of Calamity Jane. Gillian Robinson. 1995. pap. 10.95 (*1-55082-117-2*) LPC InBook.

Slow River. Nicola Griffith. 352p. 1996. pap. 11.00 (*0-345-39537-9*, Del Rey) Ballantine.

Slow Sand Filtration. L. Huisman & W. E. Wood. 1974. pap. text ed. 16.00 (*92-4-154037-0*, 1150144) World Health.

Slow Sand Filtration. Ed. by Gary S. Logsdon. LC 91-28171. 227p. 1991. pap. text ed. 21.00 (*0-87262-847-7*) Am Soc Civil Eng.

Slow Sand Filtration: An International Compilation of Recent Scientific & Operational Developments. (Illus.). 336p. 1994. pap. 45.00 (*0-89867-754-8*, 20330) Am Water Wks Assn.

Slow Settles the Dust in Oregon: A Memoir. Norris H. Perkins. (Illus.). 131p. 1993. pap. 24.95 (*0-9638442-0-2*) Four Mntn Prods.

Slow Squeeze: An Iris Thorne Mystery. Dianne G. Pugh. 1995. mass mkt. 5.99 (*0-671-77844-7*) PB.

Slow Stirring Spoon. Al Ortolani. 16p. 1981. pap. 2.00 (*0-913719-49-8*) High-Coo Pr.

Slow Strain Rate Testing for the Evaluation of Environmentally Induced Cracking: Research & Engineering Applications. Ed. by Russell D. Kane. LC 93-19461. (Special Technical Publication Ser.: No. 1210). (Illus.). 300p. 1993. 73.00 (*0-8031-1870-8*, 04-012100-27) ASTM.

Slow Surrender. Bronwyn Williams. (Historical Romance Ser.). 384p. 1995. pap. 5.50 (*0-451-40643-5*, Onyx) NAL-Dutton.

Slow to Understand: The Disciples in Synoptic Perspective. Bertram L. Melbourne. LC 88-22771. 224p. (Orig.). (C). 1988. lib. bdg. 41.50 (*0-8191-7154-9*) U Pr of Amer.

Slow Train to Cincinnati. P. J. Blumenthal. 1975. pap. 3.00 (*0-915572-51-6*) Panjandrum.

Slow Train to Paradise: How Dutch Investors Helped Build American Railroads. Augustus J. Veenendaal, Jr. LC 95-11959. (Illus.). 400p. 1996. 45.00 (*0-8047-2517-9*) Stanford U Pr.

***Slow Turtle Saves the Day.** (Ready Readers Series II Stage II). (Illus.). 32p. (J). (gr. 1-3). 1996. pap. write for info. (*1-56144-950-4*, Honey Bear Bks) Modern Pub NYC.

Slow Virus Diseases. Ed. by J. Hotchin. (Progress in Medical Virology Ser.: Vol. 18). 380p. 1974. 109.00 (*3-8055-1700-9*) S Karger.

Slow Virus Infections of the Central Nervous System. Ed. by V. Ter Meulen & M. B. Katz. LC 77-1570. 1977. 136.00 (*0-387-90188-4*) Spr-Verlag.

Slow Waking at Jenner-by-the-Sea. David Watts. (Wind Room Ser.). 16p. (Orig.). 1996. pap. 4.00 (*1-887853-04-9*) Radiolarian.

Slow Waltz in Cedar Bend. Robert J. Waller. 240p. 1994. mass mkt. 4.99 (*0-446-60164-0*) Warner Bks.

Slow Waltz in Cedar Bend. large type ed. Robert J. Waller. LC 93-24250. 1993. lib. bdg. 21.95 (*0-7862-0017-0*) Thorndike Pr.

S

An Asterisk (*) at the beginning of an entry indicates that the title is appearing in BIP for the first time.

Slow Waltz in Cedar Bend. large type ed. Robert J. Waller. LC 93-24250. 184p. 1995. lib. bdg. 13.95 (*0-7862-0018-9*) Thorndike Pr.

Slow-Wave Propagation in Plasma Waveguides. A. W. Trivelpiece. (Illus.). 1967. 12.50 (*0-911302-02-6*) San Francisco Pr.

***Slow Wolf & Dan Fox: Larry & Stretch.** large type ed. Marshall Grover. (Linford Western Large Print Ser.). 288p. 1997. pap. 16.99 (*0-7089-5040-X*) Ulverscroft.

Slow Work to the Rhythm of Cicadas. Rebecca Gonzales. (Illus.). 64p. (Orig.). 1985. pap. 9.95 (*0-933384-13-0*); lib. bdg. 13.95 (*0-933384-14-9*) Prickly Pear.

Slowdown: Global Economic Maladies. Andrew Brody. LC 84-15040. (Studies in Economic Development & Planning: Vol. 36). 151p. 1985. reprint ed. pap. 43.10 (*0-608-00816-8*, 2061604) Bks Demand.

Slowdowns, Recessions, & Inflation: Some Issues & Answers. Geoffrey H. Moore. (Explorations in Economic Research Two Ser.: No. 2). 42p. 1975. reprint ed. 35.00 (*0-685-61382-8*) Natl Bur Econ Res.

Slower Runner's Guide. Arthur J. Amchan. (Illus.). 62p. (Orig.). 1985. pap. 5.95 (*0-9617132-0-8*) Amchan Pubns.

Slower Than a Snail. Anne Schreiber. (J). 1995. 3.50 (*0-590-18074-6*) Scholastic Inc.

Slower Than a Snail. Anne Schreiber. (Hello Math Reader Ser.: Level 1). (Illus.). 32p. (J). 1995. pap. 2.95 (*0-590-26599-7*, Cartwheel) Scholastic Inc.

Slowhand: The Life & Music of Eric Clapton. Marc Roberty. 192p. 1993. pap. 19.00 (*0-517-88118-7*, Crown) Crown Pub Group.

Slowhand: The Life & Music of Eric Clapton. Mark Roberty. 1991. 30.00 (*0-517-58351-8*, Harmony) Crown Pub Group.

Slowing Down in a Speeded up World. Adair Lara. 171p. (Orig.). 1994. pap. 8.95 (*0-943233-57-7*) Conari Press.

Slowing down in a Speeded-up World. Adair Lara. 150p. 1994. lib. bdg. 27.00 (*0-8095-5878-5*) Borgo Pr.

***Slowing Down to Speed of Life.** Carlson. LC 97-5358. 1997. pap. 12.00 (*0-06-251454-7*) HarpC.

***Slowing Down to the Speed of Life.** Richard Carlson. 1997. 20.00 (*0-06-251453-9*) Harper SF.

Slowing Global Warming: A Worldwide Strategy. Christopher Flavin. (Orig.). (C). 1989. pap. 5.00 (*0-916468-92-5*) Worldwatch Inst.

Slowly by Slowly, Teaching English As a Second Language in Kenya's Harambee Schools. Ray Stratton. 1989. pap. 7.00 (*0-8196-3866-8*) Biblo.

Slowly, Out of Stones. Edward Zuckrow. LC 80-53432. (Illus.). 80p. (Orig.). 1980. pap. 6.00 (*0-912292-64-4*) Smith.

Slowmotional Meditation. Colin F. Howard. LC 85-60092. (Illus.). 359p. (Orig.). 1987. per. 8.95 (*0-916222-24-1*) OLAM.

Slowness: A Novel. Milan Kundera. Tr. by Linda Asher. 156p. 1996. 21.00 (*0-06-017369-6*) HarpC.

***Slowness: A Novel.** Milan Kundera. 160p. 1997. pap. 12.00 (*0-06-092841-7*, PL) HarpC.

***Slownik Geograficzno-Krajoznawczy Polski.** Ed. by Maria I. Milewska. (Illus.). 896p. (POL.). 1994. 26.00 (*83-01-09822-8*) Szwede Slavic.

Slownik Geograficzny Krolestwa Polskiego, 16 vols. reprint ed. 2,000.00 (*0-318-23348-7*) Szwede Slavic.

Slownik Gwar Polskich, 6 vols. Jan Karlowicz. reprint ed. 450.00 (*0-318-23362-2*) Szwede Slavic.

Slownik Idiomow Amerykanskich dla Polakow: Essential American Idioms for Polish Speakers. Richard A. Spears. LC 97-15349. 256p. (ENG & POL.). 1997. pap. 12.95 (*0-8442-4207-1*) NTC Pub Grp.

Slownik Lotniczo-Kosmonautyczny. Sergiusz Czerni. 123p. (ENG, GER, POL & RUS.). 1984. 49.95 (*0-8288-0024-3*, M15567) Fr & Eur.

Slownik Mitologiczny, 3 vols. A. Osinski. reprint ed. 280.00 (*0-318-23358-4*) Szwede Slavic.

***Slownik Nazwisk Wspolczesnie w Polsce Uzywanych, 10 vols.** Kazimierz Rymut. (POL.). 1994. pap. 400.00 (*83-85579-25-7*) Szwede Slavic.

Slownik Staropolskich Nazw Osobowych, 7 vols. Ed. by W. Taszycki. reprint ed. 800.00 (*0-318-23363-0*) Szwede Slavic.

Slowpitch Tips. Glen D. Eley. (Illustrated Instructions Ser.). 1983. pap. 7.95 (*0-940934-07-8*) GDE Pubns OH.

Slowth: The Changing Economy & How You Can Successfully Cope. Martin Kupferman & Maurice D. Levi. LC 80-18863. 264p. reprint ed. pap. 75.30 (*0-317-09675-3*, 2022246) Bks Demand.

SLP & the U. S. S. R. Socialist Labor Party Staff. 1978. pap. 0.75 (*0-935534-26-1*) NY Labor News.

SLR 87: Papers from the Fourth International Symposium on Sign Language Research. Ed. by W. H. Edmondson & F. Karlsson. (International Studies on Sign Language & the Communication of the Deaf: Vol. 10). 288p. 1990. pap. text ed. 34.95 (*3-927731-06-4*, Pub. by Signum-Verlag GW) Gallaudet Univ Pr.

Sludge: Handling & Disposal. 164p. 1989. pap. 45.00 (*0-89867-476-X*, 20034) Am Water Wks Assn.

Sludge Conditioning. Water Pollution Control Federation Staff. 144p. 1988. pap. 37.50 (*0-943244-29-3*, MFD14) Water Environ.

Sludge Dewatering. Water Pollution Control Federation Staff. (Manual of Practice Ser.: 20). (Illus.). 164p. (C). 1983. pap. text ed. 35.50 (*0-943244-42-0*, MOO16PA) Water Environ.

Sludge Digest. 200p. 1992. pap. 55.00 (*1-881369-16-1*) Water Environ.

Sludge Disinfection: A Review of the Literature. Water Pollution Control Federation Staff. (Manual of Practice Ser.: No. P0040). 50p. 1984. pap. 30.00 (*0-943244-55-2*) Water Environ.

Sludge Incineration: Thermal Destruction of Residues. Water Pollution Control Federation Staff. (MOP Ser.: No. 19). (Illus.). 250p. 1991. pap. 45.00 (*0-943244-34-X*) Water Environ.

Sludge Incineration Thermal Destruction of Residues: MFD-19. (Illus.). 419p. 1992. pap. 50.00 (*0-943244-95-1*) Water Environ.

Sludge Management: Proceedings of the IAWPRC Conference on Sludge Management, Loyola Marymount University, Los Angeles, California, USA, 8-12 January 1990. Ed. by W. F. Garber & D. R. Anderson. (Water Science & Technology Ser.: No. 22). (Illus.). 368p. 1991. pap. 139.00 (*0-08-041138-X*, Pergamon Pr) Elsevier.

Sludge Management & Disposal for the Practicing Engineer. Aarne Vesiland et al. 350p. 1986. 197.00 (*0-87371-060-6*, TD767, CRC Reprint) Franklin.

Sludge Management Equipment. Richard K. Miller & Marcia E. Rupnow. LC 90-83900. (Survey on Technology & Markets Ser.: No. 196). 50p. 1991. pap. text ed. 200.00 (*1-55865-220-5*) Future Tech Surveys.

Sludge Management Symposia, Vol. 4: WEF 1992 Annual Conference. 1992. pap. 150.00 (*1-881369-07-2*) Water Environ.

Sludge Management Symposium, Vol. 4: WEF Annual Conference, 1993. 364p. 1993. pap. 150.00 (*1-881369-44-7*) Water Environ.

Sludge Stabilization. Water Pollution Control Federation Staff. LC 85-51397. (Manual of Practice, Facilities Development Ser.: No. 9). 106p. (Orig.). 1985. pap. 35.00 (*0-943244-63-3*, MOPFD9) Water Environ.

Sludge Stabilization: Processes & Technology for Bioslids Production. Prod. by Task Force on Sludge Stabilization Staff. LC 95-14028. (Manual of Practice Ser.: Vol. FD-9). 1995. 95.00 (*1-881369-94-3*) Water Environ.

Sludge Thickening ('80) Water Pollution Control Federation Staff. (Manual of Practice, Facilities Development Ser.: No. 1). 189p. 1980. pap. 19.00 (*0-943244-18-8*, MFD1PA) Water Environ.

Sludge Treatment. fac. ed. Ed. by W. Wesley Eckenfelder, Jr. & Chakre J. Santhanam. LC 80-28050. (Pollution Engineering & Technology Ser.: No. 14). (Illus.). 607p. 1981. pap. 173.00 (*0-7837-7718-3*, 2047480) Bks Demand.

Sluff of History's Boot Soles: An Anecdotal History of Dayton's Bench & Bar. David C. Greer. LC 95-70436. (Illus.). 592p. 1996. text ed. 35.00 (*1-882203-08-9*) Orange Frazer.

***Slug.** Jacky Robb & Berny Stringle. (Bang on the Door Ser.). (Illus.). 30p. (J). (ps up). 1997. 4.95 (*0-8431-7931-7*) Price Stern Sloan.

Slug & Nettle Caterpillars: The Biology, Taxonomy & Control of the Limacodidae of Economic Importance on Palms in South-East Asia. Ed. by M. J. Cock et al. 322p. 1987. 115.00 (*0-85198-600-5*, Pub. by CAB Intntl UK) OUP.

Slug Bread & Beheaded Thistles: Amusing & Useful Techniques for Non-Toxic Gardening & Housekeeping. Ellen Sandbeck. (Illus.). 80p. (Orig.). 1995. pap. 7.95 (*0-9646164-0-8*) De la Terre Pr.

Sluggers! Twenty-Seven of Baseball's Greatest. George Sullivan. LC 90-45817. (Illus.). 80p. (J). (gr. 3 up). 1991. lib. bdg. 18.00 (*0-689-31566-X*, Atheneum Bks Young) S&S Childrens.

Sluggers Club: A Sports Mystery. Paul R. Walker. LC 92-28201. 160p. (J). (gr. 3-7). 1993. 14.00 (*0-15-276163-2*) HarBrace.

Slugging It Out in Japan. Warren Cromartie & Robert Whiting. 336p. 1992. pap. 5.99 (*0-451-17076-8*, Sig) NAL-Dutton.

Slugs. David Greenberg. LC 82-10017. (Illus.). 32p. (J). (gr. k-5). 1983. 13.95 (*0-316-32658-5*, Joy St Bks); mass mkt. 4.95i (*0-316-32659-3*, Joy St Bks) Little.

Slugs: Pet Slug & Book. David Greenburg. (Illus.). (J). 1995. pap. 12.95 (*0-316-32756-5*) Little Brown Yemanja Sings.

***Slugs, Bugs & Salamanders: Discovering Animals in Your Garden.** Sally S. Kneidel. LC 96-48161. (Illus.). 128p. (Orig.). 1997. pap. 15.95 (*1-55591-313-X*) Fulcrum Pub.

Slum & Squatter Settlements in Sub-Saharan Africa: Toward a Planning Strategy. Ed. by Robert A. Obudho & Constance C. Mhlanga. LC 87-11705. 448p. 1988. text ed. 75.00 (*0-275-92309-6*, C2309, Praeger Pubs) Greenwood.

Slum & the Ghetto: Immigrants, Blacks, & Reformers in Chicago, 1880-1930. 2nd ed. Thomas L. Philpott. 437p. (C). 1991. pap. 26.95 (*0-534-14742-9*) Wadsworth Pub.

Slum Children of India. S. D. Singh & K. P. Pothen. 110p. 1982. 19.95 (*0-318-36934-6*) Asia Bk Corp.

Slum Habitat. H. U. Bijlani & Prodipto Roy. 1990. text ed. 30.00 (*0-7069-5324-X*, Pub. by Vikas II) S Asia.

Slum Housing & Residential Renewal: The Case in Urban Britain. David Kirby. LC 77-30748. (Topics in Applied Geography Ser.). 112p. reprint ed. pap. 32.00 (*0-317-20813-6*, 2025275) Bks Demand.

Slum Silouette. Leela Dharmaraj. 8.00 (*0-89253-551-2*); 4.00 (*0-89253-552-0*) Ind-US Inc.

Slumber Boat. Alice C. Riley. (Illus.). 24p. (J). (ps). 1995. 14.95 (*0-9642944-2-7*) Starry Night.

***Slumber Mountain: A Western Trio.** Max Brand. (Sagebrush Large Print Westerns Ser.). 1997. 18.95 (*1-57490-109-5*, Beeler LP Bks) T T Beeler.

Slumber of Apollo: Reflections on Recent Art, Literature, Language & the Individual Consciousness. John Holloway. LC 83-14279. (Illus.). 150p. 1984. text ed. 69.95 (*0-521-24804-3*) Cambridge U Pr.

Slumber Party! Judith Caseley. LC 95-963. (Illus.). 32p. (J). (ps up). 1996. 15.00 (*0-688-14015-7*); lib. bdg. 14.93 (*0-688-14016-5*) Greenwillow.

Slumber Party. Christopher Pike. 176p. (Orig.). (J). (gr. 7-9). 1985. pap. 3.50 (*0-590-43014-9*) Scholastic Inc.

Slumber Party Secret. Carolyn Keene. Ed. by Anne Greenberg. (Nancy Drew Notebooks Ser.: No. 1). (Illus.). 80p. (Orig.). (J). (gr. 2-4). pap. 3.50 (*0-671-87945-6*, Minstrel Bks) PB.

Slumbering Giant of the Past. Rodman J. Bethel & Louise White. (Illus.). 91p. (Orig.). 1984. pap. 11.95 (*0-9614702-0-8*) Slumbering.

Slumbering Giant of the Past. 2nd ed. Rodman J. Bethel. Ed. by Louise White. (Illus.). 91p. (Orig.). 1985. lib. bdg. 19.95 (*0-9614702-1-6*) Slumbering.

***Slumbering Volcano: American Slave Ship Revolts & the Production of Violent Masculinities.** Maggie Sale. LC 97-7610. 256p. 1997. text ed. 49.95 (*0-8223-1983-7*); pap. text ed. 15.95 (*0-8223-1992-6*) Duke.

Slumgullion, the Executive Pig. Matt Cibula. (Illus.). 32p. (J). (gr. k-4). 1994. 14.95 (*1-55933-149-6*) Zino Pr.

Slumps, Grunts, & Snickerdoodles: What Colonial America Ate & Why. Lila Perl. LC 75-4894. (Illus.). 128p. (J). (gr. 6 up). 1979. 14.95 (*0-395-28923-8*, Clarion Bks) HM.

Slums. Thomas Akare. (African Writers Ser.). 192p. (Orig.). (C). 1981. pap. 7.95 (*0-435-90241-5*, 90241) Heinemann.

Slums. Ed. by Martin Gaskell. 300p. 1990. text ed. 49.00 (*0-7185-1293-6*) St Martin.

Slums & Blighted Areas in the United States. Edith E. Wood. Date not set. write for info. (*0-8434-0068-4*, Pub. by McGrath NH) Ayer.

Slums & Redevelopment. James A. Yelling. LC 92-27872. 220p. 1993. text ed. 59.95 (*0-312-09078-1*) St Martin.

Slums & Slum Clearance in Victorian London. James A. Yelling. (London Research Series in Geography: No. 10). 176p. 1986. text ed. 55.00 (*0-04-942192-1*) Routledge Chapman & Hall.

Slums & Urbanization. S. D. Pillai. (C). 1990. 45.00 (*81-7154-259-X*, Pub. by Popular Prakashan II) S Asia.

Slums As Urban Villages. Rajesh Gill. (C). 1995. 18.00 (*81-7033-219-2*, Pub. by Rawat II) S Asia.

Slums of Baltimore, Chicago, New York, & Philadelphia: Seventh Special Report of the Commissioner of Labor. Carroll D. Wright. LC 71-112587. (Rise of Urban America Ser.). 1978. reprint ed. 51.95 (*0-405-02489-4*) Ayer.

Slums, Projects & People. Kurt W. Back. LC 73-19572. 123p. (C). 1974. reprint ed. text ed. 57.50 (*0-8371-7289-6*, BASL, Greenwood Pr) Greenwood.

Slums, Projects, & People: Social Psychological Problems of Relocation in Puerto Rico. LC 62-15369. (Duke Univeristy Press, a Sociological Monograph Ser.). 137p. reprint ed. pap. 39.10 (*0-317-41840-8*, 2026184) Bks Demand.

Slums, Urban Decline & Revitalization. C. S. Yadav. 1987. 40.00 (*0-8364-2309-7*, Pub. by Concept II) S Asia.

Slums Within Slums. Sabir Ali. 1990. text ed. 22.50 (*0-685-37407-6*, Pub. by Vikas II) S Asia.

Slurry Erosion: Uses, Applications, & Test Methods. Ed. by J. E. Miller & F. E. Schmidt, Jr. LC 87-920. (Special Technical Publication Ser.: No. 946). (Illus.). 274p. 1987. text ed. 48.00 (*0-8031-0941-5*, 04-946000-29) ASTM.

Slurry Flow Technology. Ed. by Nicholas P. Cheremisinoff. LC 85-9742. (Encyclopedia of Fluid Mechanics Ser.: Vol. 5). (Illus.). 1446p. 1986. 195.00 (*0-87201-517-3*, 1517) Gulf Pub.

Slurry Transportation & Pneumatic Handling. Ed. by E. Hay. 104p. 1983. pap. text ed. 10.00 (*0-317-03527-4*, H00256) ASME.

Slurry Walls: Design, Construction, & Quality Control. Ed. by David B. Paul et al. LC 92-32908. (Special Technical Publication Ser.: 1129). (Illus.). 430p. 1992. text ed. 47.00 (*0-8031-1427-3*, 04-011290-38) ASTM.

Slurry Walls As Structural Systems. 2nd ed. Petros P. Xanthakos. LC 93-31724. 1993. text ed. 90.00 (*0-07-072216-1*) McGraw.

Sly Fox & the Little Red Hen in Arabic. (Ladybird Bks.). (Illus.). (J). (gr. 4-6). 1987. 4.50 (*0-86685-224-7*) Intl Bk Ctr.

Sly Fox (Playscript) C. A. Shepherd et al. (Orig.). (J). (gr. 3-12). 1985. pap. 8.00 (*0-88734-503-4*) Players Pr.

Sly Spy. large type ed. Marjorie W. Sharmat. 1993. 13.50 (*0-614-09856-4*, L-34093-00) Am Printing Hse.

S/M Futures: Erotica on the Edge. Ed. by Cecilia Tan. (Illus.). 182p. (Orig.). 1995. pap. 12.95 (*1-885865-02-3*) Circlet Pr.

SM Murder. Elizabeth Oliver. (Orig.). 1995. mass mkt. 5.95 (*1-56333-353-8*, Rosebud) Masquerade.

S/M Pasts. Ed. by Cecilia Tan. (Illus.). 192p. (Orig.). 1995. pap. 12.95 (*1-885865-06-6*) Circlet Pr.

SM Visions: Best of Circlet. Ed. by Cecilia Tan. (Orig.). 1995. pap. 10.95 (*1-56333-339-2*, R Kasak Bks) Masquerade.

Sm-Z see Milton Encyclopedia

***SM 101: A Realistic Introduction.** Jay Wiseman. (Illus.). 384p. (Orig.). 1996. pap. 24.95 (*0-9639763-8-9*) Greenery Pr.

Smack. Drury Pifer. (Contemporary Drama Ser.). 1979. 6.95 (*0-912262-58-3*); pap. 2.95 (*0-912262-59-1*) Proscenium.

Smack Goddess. Richard Stratton. 1990. 18.95 (*1-55972-046-8*, Birch Ln Pr) Carol Pub Group.

Smacks & Bawleys. John Leather. 160p. (C). 1990. 45.00 (*0-86138-079-7*, Pub. by T Dalton UK) St Mut.

Sm'algyax: A Reference Dictionary & Grammar of the Coast Tsimshian Language. Ed. by John A. Dunn. LC 94-31488. 255p. 1995. pap. text ed. 22.50 (*0-295-97419-2*) U of Wash Pr.

Small- & Medium-Size Enterprises. Ed. by Arnaldo Bagnasco & Charles F. Sabel. LC 95-8062. (Social Change in Western Europe Ser.). 1995. 19.95 (*1-85567-308-8*); pap. 45.95 (*1-85567-309-6*) St Martin.

Small AC Generator Service Manual. 1991. 24.95 (*0-87288-467-8*, GSM-3) Intertec Pub.

***Small Actors.** Stephen Gregg. 31p. 1997. pap. 3.50 (*0-87129-768-X*, SB8) Dramatic Pub.

Small Acts: Thoughts on the Politics of Black Cultures. Paul Gilroy. 1994. pap. 16.99 (*1-85242-298-X*) Serpents Tail.

Small Acts of Kindness. James Vollbracht. LC 95-36334. (Illus.). 32p. (J). (ps-4). 1996. pap. 5.95 (*0-8091-6629-1*) Paulist Pr.

***Small African Towns - Between Rural Networks & Urban Hierarchies.** Poul O. Pedersen. (Making of Modern Africa Ser.). (Illus.). 234p. 1997. text ed. 68.95 (*1-85972-589-9*, Pub. by Ashgate UK) Ashgate Pub Co.

Small Agency Survival Manual: How to Emerge Victorious from the Advertising Battleground. Anthony P. Mikes. 515p. (Orig.). 1995. pap. 79.95 (*0-9626971-3-3*) Second Wind.

***Small Air-Cooled Engine Service Manual Vol. 2: 1990-94.** LC 94-75604. (Illus.). (Orig.). 1995. pap. 26.95 (*0-87288-569-0*, SES2-1) Intertec Pub.

Small Air-Cooled Engines Service Manual, Vol. 1. 17th ed. Intertec Publishing Staff. LC 89-45330. (Illus.). 432p. 1989. pap. text ed. 24.95 (*0-87288-489-9*, SES-17) Intertec Pub.

Small Airport Management Handbook. Jerry A. Singer. 176p. (Orig.). 1985. pap. 15.95 (*0-89854-099-2*) U of GA Inst Govt.

Small Airport Managers Handbook. Earl Seay. LC 92-33593. (Aviation Management Ser.). 76p. 1980. 10.95 (*0-89100-140-9*, EA-140-9) IAP.

Small Alpine Form: Studies in Nabokov's Short Fiction. Ed. by Charles Nicol & Gennady Barabtarlo. LC 92-22715. 264p. 1992. text ed. 42.00 (*0-8153-0857-4*, H1580) Garland.

S

***Small Amish Quilt Patterns.** rev. ed. Rachel T. Pellman. LC 85-70280. (Illus.). 128p. 1997. pap. 14.95 (*1-56148-236-6*) Good Bks PA.

Small Anaya Spanish Dictionary: Pequeno Diccionario Anaya de la Lengua. Anaya Staff. 644p. (SPA.). 1984. pap. 14.95 (*0-8288-2024-4*, S60163) Fr & Eur.

Small & Exciting Woodturning Projects. James A. Jacobson. LC 94-16843. (Illus.). 168p. 1994. pap. 14.95 (*0-8069-0822-X*) Sterling.

Small & Large Air-Cooled Engine Flat Rate Pricing Guide. 10th ed. 1989. pap. 24.95 (*0-87288-327-2*, SEF10) Intertec Pub.

Small & Large Animal Physiology. Ruckebusch et al. (Illus.). 688p. (C). 1990. 69.95 (*1-55664-136-2*) Mosby Yr Bk.

Small & Medium Enterprises: Technology Policies & Options. Ed. by A. S. Bhalla. LC 91-11403. (Contributions in Economics & Economic History Ser.: No. 124). 296p. 1991. text ed. 65.00 (*0-313-27594-7*, BHV, Greenwood Pr) Greenwood.

Small & Medium Industries in Hong Kong. V. F. Sit. 162p. (C). 1989. pap. text ed. 35.00 (*962-209-229-2*, Pub. by Hong Kong U Pr HK) St Mut.

Small & Medium Size Enterprises & Regional Development. Ed. by Maria Giaoutzi et al. 256p. (C). 1989. text ed. 79.95 (*0-415-00415-2*) Routledge.

Small & Medium Sized Enterprises. Kenneth H. Dyson. (Spicers European Policy Reports). 192p. (C). 1990. pap. text ed. 185.00 (*0-415-03829-4*, A4390) Routledge.

Small & Medium-Sized Restaurant Chains. Peter Allen. 250p. 1987. 1,250.00 (*0-941285-10-3*) FIND-SVP.

Small & Micro Enterprise Credit: Recommendations & Case Studies Presented at the Best Practices Workshop. Community Economics Corporation Staff & Jim Cotter. 138p. 1993. pap. text ed. 25.00 (*0-9637044-2-7*) PACT Pubns.

Small & New Business Development: An Action Guide for State Governments. Roger Vaughan. LC 83-179220. 29p. 1983. pap. text ed. 5.00 (*0-914193-02-3*) Coalition NE Govn.

Small & Successful in Japan: A Study of 30 British Firms in the World's Most Competitive Market. Simon Collinson. 160p. 1996. 55.95 (*1-85628-921-4*, Pub. by Avebury Pub UK) Ashgate Pub Co.

Small Angle Scattering: Perspectives in Crystallography at Atomic Resolution. American Crystallographic Association Staff. (American Crystallographic Association Program & Abstracts Ser. 2). 1983. pap. 10.00 (*0-686-45047-7*) Polycrystal Bk Serv.

Small Animal Allergy: A Practical Guide. Edward Baker. LC 90-5615. (Illus.). 144p. 1990. pap. 42.50 (*0-8121-1240-7*) Williams & Wilkins.

Small Animal Anaesthesia. Bedford. 1991. pap. text ed. 40.00 (*0-7020-1501-6*) HarBrace.

Small Animal Anesthesia. McKelvey & Hollingshead. (Fundamentals Ser.: Vol. II). 352p. (C). (gr. 13). 1994. pap. text ed. 32.00 (*0-8016-7961-3*) Mosby Yr Bk.

***Small Animal Behavior Problems.** O'Farrell. 1997. text ed. write for info. (*0-7020-1789-2*, Bailliere-Tindall) Saunders.

Small Animal Cardiology. Keene. 1998. text ed. write for info. (*0-7216-5497-5*) Saunders.

Small Animal Cardiovascular Medicine. Kittleson & Pion. 480p. (gr. 13). 1998. text ed. 99.00 (*0-8151-5140-3*) Mosby Yr Bk.

Small Animal Care & Management. Dean Warren. LC 94-17075. (Illus.). 560p. (J). 1992. text ed. 37.25 (*0-8273-4557-7*) Delmar.

Small Animal Care & Management. 2nd ed. Dean Warren. 64p. 1992. teacher ed., pap. 12.75 (*0-8273-4558-5*) Delmar.

Small Animal Care & Management CTB. Dean Warren. (Agriculture Ser.). 1995. text ed. 105.95 (*0-8273-7076-8*) Delmar.

Small Animal Care & Management Training. Dean Warren. 268p. 1995. teacher ed., pap. 89.95 (*0-8273-7326-0*) Delmar.

Small Animal Clinical Diagnosis by Laboratory Methods. 2nd ed. Michael D. Willard et al. LC 93-31784. (Illus.). 416p. 1994. pap. text ed. 47.50 (*0-7216-5202-6*) Saunders.

Small Animal Clinical Oncology. 2nd ed. Stephen J. Withrow & E. Gregory MacEwen. (Illus.). 480p. 1995. text ed. 89.00 (*0-7216-5592-0*) Saunders.

Small Animal Dentistry. Harvey & Emily. (Illus.). 408p. (gr. 13). 1993. text ed. 69.00 (*0-8016-6076-9*) Mosby Yr Bk.

Small Animal Diagnosis. 2nd ed. Ed. by Michael D. Lorenz & Larry M. Cornelius. LC 92-46032. 651p. 1993. pap. text ed. 49.50 (*0-397-51200-7*) Lppncott-Raven.

Small Animal Emergency Radiology. Farrow. (Illus.). 375p. (C). 1988. 49.95 (*1-55664-031-5*) Mosby Yr Bk.

Small Animal Endocrinology. Drazner. 1986. text ed. 86.00 (*0-7216-5927-6*) Saunders.

Small Animal Endoscopy. Tams. (Illus.). 400p. (gr. 13). 1990. text ed. 117.95 (*0-8016-4899-8*) Mosby Yr Bk.

*__Small Animal Formulary.__ 2nd ed. Bryn Tennant. 288p. 1997. spiral bd. 35.00 (*0-905214-44-7*) OUP.

Small Animal Gastroenterology. 2nd ed. Donald R. Strombeck & W. Grant Guilford. (Illus.). 744p. 1990. 85.00 (*0-685-35384-2*) Stonegate Rancho.

*__Small Animal Internal Medicine.__ Darcy H. Shaw & Sherri L. Ihle. LC 97-3958. (National Veterinary Medical Ser.). 1997. write for info. (*0-683-07670-1*) Williams & Wilkins.

*__Small Animal Internal Medicine.__ 2nd ed. Nelson & Couto. 1250p. (gr. 13). 1998. text ed. 99.95 (*0-8151-6351-7*) Mosby Yr Bk.

*__Small Animal Internal Medicine Case Management Test Booklet.__ Darcy H. Shaw & Sherri L. Ihle. LC 97-8339. (National Veterinary Medical Series for Independent Study). 1997. write for info. (*0-683-30348-1*) Williams & Wilkins.

Small Animal Medical Therapeutics. Michael D. Lorenz et al. (Illus.). 656p. 1991. pap. text ed. 49.50 (*0-397-50994-4*) Lppncott-Raven.

Small Animal Medicine. Dana Allen. (Illus.). 1184p. 1991. text ed. 139.00 (*0-397-51025-X*) Lppncott-Raven.

Small Animal Nutrition. F. A. Kallfelz. 400p. 1998. write for info. (*0-632-03041-0*) Blackwell Sci.

*__Small Animal Ophthalmology: A Problem Oriented Approach.__ 2nd ed. 205p. 1997. write for info. (*0-7020-2017-6*, Pub. by W B Saunders UK) Saunders.

Small Animal Oral Medicine & Surgery. Mark A. Tholen. LC 88-32647. (Illus.). 270p. 1989. text ed. 79.50 (*0-8121-1205-9*) Williams & Wilkins.

Small Animal Orthopedics. Olmstead. (Illus.). 700p. (gr. 13). 1995. text ed. 78.00 (*0-8016-5874-8*) Mosby Yr Bk.

Small Animal Physical Diagnosis & Clinical Procedures. Dennis M. McCurnin & Poffenbarger. (Illus.). 244p. 1990. text ed. 51.00 (*0-7216-5931-4*) Saunders.

Small Animal Practice. Boden. 1993. pap. text ed. 52.50 (*0-7020-1685-3*) HarBrace.

Small Animal Radiology: A Diagnostic Atlas & Text. Ronald L. Burk & Norman Ackerman. LC 86-12994. (Illus.). 390p. reprint ed. pap. 111.20 (*0-7837-1616-8*, 2041908) Bks Demand.

Small Animal Radiology & Ultrasonography: A Diagnostic Atlas & Text. 2nd ed. Ronald L. Burk & Norman Ackerman. Ed. by Ray Kersey. (Illus.). 560p. 1996. text ed. 115.00 (*0-7216-5270-0*) Saunders.

*__Small Animal Surgery.__ Fossum. (Illus.). 928p. (C). (gr. 13). 1997. text ed. 139.00 (*0-8151-3238-7*, 24202) Mosby Yr Bk.

Small Animal Surgery. Ed. by Joseph Harari. (National Veterinary Medical Series for Independent Study). 1995. write for info. (*0-683-03910-5*) Williams & Wilkins.

Small Animal Surgery. Harvey et al. (Illus.). 800p. 1990. text ed. 98.00 (*0-397-50852-2*) Lppncott-Raven.

Small Animal Surgery. Saunders. 1995. text ed. 67.00 (*0-7020-1688-8*) Saunders.

Small Animal Surgical Nursing, Vol. 2. 2nd ed. Tracy & McBride. 375p. (gr. 13). 1994. pap. text ed. 31.00 (*0-8016-6813-1*) Mosby Yr Bk.

Small Animal Ultrasound. Ed. by Ronald W. Green. 400p. 1995. text ed. 79.95 (*0-397-51387-9*) Lppncott-Raven.

Small Animal Wound Management. Steven F. Swaim & Ralph A. Henderson. LC 89-12383. (Illus.). 252p. 1990. pap. text ed. 49.50 (*0-8121-1239-3*) Williams & Wilkins.

*__Small Animal Wound Management.__ 2nd ed. Steven F. Swaim & Ralph A. Henderson. LC 96-29668. 1997. write for info. (*0-683-30276-0*) Williams & Wilkins.

Small Animals. LC 91-60533. (What's Inside? Ser.). (Illus.). 24p. (J). (ps-3). 1991. 8.95 (*1-879431-09-2*) DK Pub Inc.

*__Small Animals.__ Jane Burton. LC 77-18623. (Color Nature Library). 1997. write for info. (*0-517-27809-X*) Crown Pub Group.

Small Animals. Paul Sterry. (Animal Stars Ser.). (Illus.). 24p. (J). (gr. 1-3). 1994. pap. 1.99 (*1-884628-16-8*) Flying Frog.

*__Small Animals, Bk. 4.__ Jim Arnosky. Date not set. write for info. (*0-688-05453-6*); lib. bdg. write for info. (*0-688-05454-4*) Lothrop.

Small Animals of America Coloring Book. McClelland. (Illus.). (J). (gr. k-3). 1976. pap. 2.95 (*0-486-24217-X*) Dover.

Small Animals Thoracic Surgery. Orten & McCracken. 1994. 79.00 (*0-683-06670-6*) Williams & Wilkins.

Small Antennas. K. Fujimoto et al. LC 86-26198. (Antenna Ser.). 300p. 1987. text ed. 198.00 (*0-471-91413-4*) Wiley.

Small-Aperture Radio Direction-Finding. Herndon H. Jenkins. (Artech House Radar Library). 290p. 1991. text ed. 47.00 (*0-89006-420-2*) Artech Hse.

Small Appliance Industry. Ed. by Peter Allen. 400p. (Orig.). 1983. pap. 295.00 (*0-931634-30-X*) FIND-SVP.

Small Appliances. (Fix-It-Yourself Ser.). (Illus.). 144p. 1988. 17.27 (*0-8094-6256-5*); lib. bdg. 23.27 (*0-8094-6257-3*) Time-Life.

Small Apt. Jim Nisbet. (Thumbscrew Press Ser.). (Illus.). 68p. (Orig.). 1992. pap. 8.95 (*0-926664-12-3*) Bay Area Ctr Art & Tech.

Small Area Statistics: An International Symposium. Carl-Erik Sarndal. 294p. (C). 1990. reprint ed. lib. bdg. 47.95 (*0-471-84456-X*) Krieger.

Small Arms: Pistols & Rifles. Ian V. Hogg. LC 93-39620. (Greenhill Military Manuals Ser.). (Illus.). 160p. 1994. 19.95 (*1-85367-175-4*, 5635) Stackpole.

Small Arms & Cannons. D. J. Marchant-Smith & P. R. Haslem. (Brassey's Battlefield Weapons Systems & Technology Ser.: Vol. 5). 160p. 1982. text ed. 30.00 (*0-08-028330-6*, Pergamon Pr); pap. text ed. 18.95 (*0-08-028331-4*, Pergamon Pr) Elsevier.

Small Arms & Intra-State Conflicts. (UNDIR Research Papers: No. 34). 52p. Date not set. pap. 12.00 (*92-9045-102-5*, E.GV.95.0.7) UN.

Small Arms Identification & Operation Guide-Submachine Guns. 1986. lib. bdg. 79.95 (*0-8490-3576-7*) Gordon Pr.

Small Arms Identification & Operations Guide: Pistols. 1986. lib. bdg. 79.95 (*0-8490-3575-9*) Gordon Pr.

Small Arms Training: Sten Machine Carbine, Vol. 1. 1983. pap. text ed. 5.00 (*0-86663-990-X*) Ide Hse.

Small Arms 1856: Reports of Experiments with Small Arms for the Military Service. Officers of the U. S. Army Ordnance Dept. (Illus.). 168p. (C). 1984. reprint ed. 14.95 (*0-939631-01-6*) Thomas Publications.

Small As a Resurrection. Honor Johnson. LC 82-82498. (Lost Roads Ser.: No. 20). 60p. (C). 1982. pap. 5.95 (*0-918786-23-1*) Lost Roads.

Small Astronomical Observatories: Amateur & Professional Designs & Constructions. Ed. by Patrick Moore. LC 96-13224. (Practical Astronomy Ser.). 227p. 1996. pap. 32.95 (*3-540-19913-6*) Spr-Verlag.

Small Bachelor. P. G. Wodehouse. 208p. 1991. pap. 8.95 (*0-14-008506-8*, Penguin Bks) Viking Penguin.

Small Basket of Poetry. Carrina Whitney. 60p. Date not set. pap. text ed. write for info. (*1-57553-016-3*) Watermrk Pr.

Small Basket of Poetry. Corrina Whitney. (Orig.). 1995. pap. write for info. (*1-57553-080-5*) Watermrk Pr.

Small Bear Lost. Martin Waddell. LC 95-41009. (Illus.). 32p. (J). (ps). 1996. 15.99 (*1-56402-871-2*) Candlewick Pr.

*__Small Bees' Honey.__ George Clark. 208p. (Orig.). 1997. pap. 14.00 (*1-877727-74-1*) White Pine.

*__Small Beginnings: First Steps to Prepare Your Child for Lifelong Learning.__ Barbara Curtis. LC 96-30264. 160p. 1997. pap. 9.99 (*0-8054-6287-2*, 4262-87) Broadman.

Small Bequest. Edmund G. Love. LC 87-16202. (Great Lakes Bks.). 238p. 1987. 28.50 (*0-8143-1925-4*); pap. 14.95 (*0-8143-1926-2*) Wayne St U Pr.

Small Bird, Tell Me: Stories of Greek Immigrants. Helen Z. Papanikolas. LC 93-8426. 208p. 1993. 24.95 (*0-8040-0974-0*) Swallow.

Small Bird, Tell Me: Stories of Greek Immigrants. Helen Papanikolas. LC 93-8426. 208p. 1994. reprint ed. pap. 15.95 (*0-8040-0982-1*) Swallow.

Small Bit of Bread & Butter: Letters from the Dakota Territory 1832-1869. Ed. by Maida L. Riggs. LC 96-83698. 350p. (Orig.). 1996. pap. 17.95 (*1-886172-22-6*) Ash Grove Pr.

Small Bites of Love, & Life, & Some Crazy Places. Peter Kuntz. 1996. 11.95 (*0-533-11489-6*) Vantage.

Small-Block Chevy Performance. Dave Emanuel. 176p. (Orig.). 1996. pap. 15.95 (*0-614-17504-6*, HP Books) Berkley Pub.

Small Block Chevy Performance Vol. 2. (Illus.). 144p. 1994. pap. 18.95 (*0-931472-14-8*) Motorbooks Intl.

Small Block Chevy Performance 1955-81. John Michelsen. 1981. 18.95 (*0-931472-07-5*) Motorbooks Intl.

Small Board-&-Care Homes: Residential Care in Transition. Leslie A. Morgan et al. LC 94-38059. (Illus.). 264p. 1995. text ed. 47.50 (*0-8018-4996-9*) Johns Hopkins.

Small Boat. Michael Hettich. 72p. 1990. pap. 10.95 (*0-8130-1015-2*); lib. bdg. 19.95 (*0-8130-1009-8*) U Press Fla.

Small Boat Building. H. W. Patterson. 144p. 1985. reprint ed. pap. 20.00 (*0-87556-691-X*) Saifer.

Small Boat Building see How to Build Wooden Boats: With Sixteen Small-Boat Designs

Small Boat Design. Ed. by Johanna M. Reinhart. (Illus.). 79p. 1983. pap. text ed. 12.00 (*0-89955-393-1*, Pub. by ICLARM PH) Intl Spec Bk.

Small Boat Diving. Steven M. Barsky. LC 94-79808. (Illus.). 208p. (Orig.). 1994. 14.95 (*0-941332-43-8*, D727) Best Pub Co.

*__Small Boat Guide to Cases Bay.__ Curtis Rindlaub. (SmallBoat Guides to the Maine Coast Ser.: Vol. 2). (Illus.). 288p. (Orig.). Date not set. pap. write for info. (*0-9649246-2-5*) Diamond Pass.

Small Boat Guide to Electronics Afloat. Tim Bartlett. 96p. (C). 1990. text ed. 59.00 (*0-906754-72-0*, Pub. by Fernhurst Bks UK) St Mut.

Small Boat Guide to Radar. Tim Bartlett. 96p. (C). 1990. text ed. 65.00 (*0-906754-58-5*, Pub. by Fernhurst Bks UK) St Mut.

Small Boat Guide to the Rules of the Road: The Collision Regulations Simplified. John Mellor. 64p. (C). 1990. text ed. 59.00 (*0-906754-54-2*, Pub. by Fernhurst Bks UK) St Mut.

Small Boat in the Midi. Roger Pilkington. 210p. (C). 1989. 110.00 (*0-907864-44-9*, Pub. by Imray Laurie Norie & Wilson UK) St Mut.

Small Boat Law. Herbert L. Markow. LC 77-154289. (Illus.). 435p. (Orig.). (C). 1977. pap. 40.00 (*0-934108-00-5*) H L Markow.

Small Boat Law: Nineteen Seventy-Eight Supplement. Herbert L. Markow. LC 79-88475. 144p. (C). 1979. pap. 20.00 (*0-934108-01-3*) H L Markow.

Small Boat Law: 1981-1983 Supplement. Herbert L. Markow. LC 77-154289. 274p. (C). 1984. pap. text ed. 36.00 (*0-934108-03-X*) H L Markow.

*__Small-Boat Sailing.__ (Illus.). 80p. (YA). (gr. 6-12). 1995. pap. 2.40 (*0-8395-3356-X*, 33356) BSA.

Small Boat Sailor Certification Record Book. John Kantor. Ed. by Steve Colgate. 16p. (Orig.). pap. 1.00 (*1-882502-32-9*) US Sail Assn.

Small Bones, Little Eyes. Nila Northsun & Jim Sagel. Ed. by Kirk Robertson. (Windriver Ser.). 72p. (Orig.). (C). 1982. pap. 5.00 (*0-916918-17-3*) Duck Down.

Small Bones Stretching. Toni Swanson. (Illus.). 82p. (Orig.). 1995. pap. 8.95 (*0-935711-32-6*) Tecolote Pubns.

Small Book. Jack Trimpey. 320p. 1996. reprint ed. pap. 12.95 (*0-440-50725-1*, Dell Pr) Dell.

*__Small Book about God.__ Roy Hicks. 176p. 1997. 12.99 (*1-57673-072-7*, Multnomah Bks) Multnomah Pubs.

Small Book of Angels. Eugene Stiles. LC 95-52942. (Illus.). 96p. 1996. pap. 12.95 (*0-87654-595-9*) Pomegranate Calif.

Small Book of Black & White Lies. Dave McKean. Ed. by Clare Haythornthwaite. (Illus.). 56p. 1995. 25.00 (*0-9642069-0-0*) A Spiegel Fine Arts.

Small Book of Fairies. Eugene Stiles. LC 95-24184. (Illus.). 96p. 1995. pap. 12.95 (*0-87654-476-6*) Pomegranate Calif.

Small Book of Herbs. Karen Feinberg. LC 83-90112. (Illus.). 64p. 1984. 22.00 (*0-88014-071-2*) Mosaic Pr OH.

Small Book of Tales. Helen Bramos & Ann A. Bramos. (Illus.). 77p. (Orig.). (J). (ps-7). 1995. pap. 8.00 (*0-9635333-3-9*) A S Bramos.

Small Book of Unicorns. Josephine Bradley. LC 94-49450. (Illus.). 96p. 1995. pap. 12.95 (*0-87654-358-1*) Pomegranate Calif.

Small Books & Pleasant Histories: Popular Fiction & Its Readership in Seventeenth-Century England. Margaret Spufford. (Past & Present Publications). 296p. 1985. pap. 22.95 (*0-521-31218-3*) Cambridge U Pr.

Small Bowel Enterocyte Culture & Transplantation. F. C. Campbell. (Medical Intelligence Unit Ser.). 116p. 1994. 89.95 (*1-57059-004-4*, LN9004) R G Landes.

Small Bowel Radiology. G. Antes & F. Eggemann. (Illus.). 210p. 1988. 139.00 (*0-387-15263-6*) Spr-Verlag.

Small Bowel Transplantation. Ed. by David Grant & Richard F. Wood. 176p. 1994. 95.00 (*0-340-57322-8*, Pub. by Ed Arnold UK) OUP.

Small Bronze Sculpture from the Ancient World. Ed. by Marion True & Jerry Podany. LC 90-5002. (Illus.). 284p. 1990. pap. 49.95 (*0-89236-176-X*, J P Getty Museum) J P Getty Trust.

Small Buildings. Michael Cadwell. (Pamphlet Architecture Ser.: No. 17). (Illus.). 64p. (Orig.). 1996. pap. 11.95 (*1-56898-055-8*) Princeton Arch.

Small Bulk Installation for Domestic Purposes Pt. 2. William Culross & Son Ltd. Staff. (C). 1988. 95.00 (*0-900323-87-6*, Pub. by W Culross & Son Ltd UK) St Mut.

Small Business. LC 93-41994. (Business Strategy Ser.: Vol. 10). 1993. 26.00 (*0-88406-266-X*) GA St U Busn Pr.

Small Business. Hatten. (C). 1996. text ed. 70.00 (*0-13-180340-9*) P-H.

*__Small Business: A Comparison of SBA's 7(A) Loans & Borrowers with Other Loans & Borrowers.__ (Illus.). 60p. (Orig.). (C). 1996. pap. 25.00 (*0-7881-3583-X*) DIANE Pub.

Small Business: An Entrepreneur's Plan. 3rd ed. Lee A. Eckert et al. LC 92-71877. 388p. (C). 1993. pap. text ed. 43.00 (*0-03-096585-3*) Dryden Pr.

Small Business: An Entrepreneur's Plan. 4th ed. Ryan. (C). 1995. teacher ed., pap. text ed. 30.00 (*0-03-017613-1*) HB Coll Pubs.

Small Business: Analysis of SBA's Preferred Lenders Program. (Illus.). 53p. (Orig.). (C). 1993. pap. text ed. 25.00 (*1-56806-962-6*) DIANE Pub.

Small Business: Developing the Winning Management Team. George W. Rimler & Neil J. Humphreys. LC 79-54848. 190p. reprint ed. pap. 54.20 (*0-317-26901-1*, 2023562) Bks Demand.

Small Business: Entrepreneurs. 4th ed. Ryan. (C). 1995. pap. text ed. 47.75 (*0-03-012894-3*) HB Coll Pubs.

*__Small Business: Information on SBA's Small Business Investment Company Programs.__ (Illus.). 40p. (Orig.). (C). 1996. pap. 25.00 (*0-7881-3484-1*) DIANE Pub.

Small Business: Its Place & Problems. Abraham D. Kaplan. Ed. by Stuart Bruchey & Vincent P. Carosso. LC 78-18965. (Small Business Enterprise in America Ser.). (Illus.). 1979. reprint ed. lib. bdg. 23.95 (*0-405-11469-9*) Ayer.

Small Business: Planning & Management. 2nd ed. Peggy Lambing & Charles R. Kuehl. 560p. (C). 1990. text ed. 52.00 (*0-03-030024-X*) Dryden Pr.

Small Business: Planning & Management. 3rd ed. Peggy A. Lambing & Charles R. Kuehl. LC 93-72828. 851p. (C). 1993. text ed. 51.00 (*0-03-097578-6*) Dryden Pr.

Small Business: Responses to Survey on Construction Firms' Access to Surety Bonds. 92p. (Orig.). (C). 1995. pap. text ed. 30.00 (*0-7881-2486-2*) DIANE Pub.

Small Business Accountant. Hamilton & West. (C). 1994. pap. 48.95 (*0-538-82040-3*, AI61AB) S-W Pub.

*__Small Business Accounting.__ Melvin A. Montgomery. LC 97-11601. 1998. 34.67 (*0-13-628793-X*) P-H.

Small Business Agenda: Trends in a Global Economy. Galen S. Hull. 138p. (Orig.). (C). 1986. pap. text ed. 18.00 (*0-8191-5164-5*); lib. bdg. 44.50 (*0-8191-5163-7*) U Pr of Amer.

Small Business Analysis: A Business Planning Tool Kit Using Lotus 1-2-3. Norman M. Scarborough. 144p. (C). 1990. pap. write for info. (*0-675-21349-5*, Merrill Coll) P-H.

Small Business & Pattern Bargaining. Walter H. Carpenter, Jr. & Edward Handler. Ed. by Stuart Bruchey & Vincent P. Carosso. LC 78-18953. (Small Business Enterprise in America Ser.). 1979. reprint ed. lib. bdg. 21.95 (*0-405-11461-3*) Ayer.

Small Business & Public Policy. Ed. by William Greenwood et al. 172p. (Orig.). 1985. pap. 15.00 (*0-918592-83-6*) Pol Studies.

*__Small Business & the Big Banks.__ Susan Bellan. pap. 19.95 (*1-55028-448-7*, Pub. by J Lorimer CN) Formac Dist Ltd.

*__Small Business & the Big Banks.__ Susan Bellan. bds. 29.95 (*1-55028-449-5*, Pub. by J Lorimer CN) Formac Dist Ltd.

*__Small Business & the Law.__ 62p. 8.95 (*0-644-43004-4*, Pub. by Aust Gov Pub AT) Aubrey Bks.

Small Business & Venture Capital. Rudolph L. Weissman. Ed. by Stuart Bruchey & Vincent P. Carosso. LC 78-18153. (Small Business Enterprise in America Ser.). 1979. reprint ed. lib. bdg. 17.95 (*0-405-11510-5*) Ayer.

Small Business at the Crossroad. Wilfred Lumer. Ed. by Stuart Bruchey & Vincent P. Carosso. LC 78-18967. (Small Business Enterprise in America Ser.). (Illus.). 1979. reprint ed. lib. bdg. 15.95 (*0-405-11471-0*) Ayer.

Small Business Audit Manual, 3 vols., Vol. 1. George Marthinuss & Larry L. Perry. (AICPA Integrated Practice System Ser.). (Illus.). 234p. reprint ed. pap. 66.70 (*0-7837-4869-8*, 2044399) Bks Demand.

Small Business Audit Manual, 3 vols., Vol. 2. George Marthinuss & Larry L. Perry. (AICPA Integrated Practice System Ser.). (Illus.). 243p. reprint ed. pap. 69.30 (*0-7837-4870-1*, 2044399) Bks Demand.

Small Business Audit Manual, 3 vols., Vol. 3. George Marthinuss & Larry L. Perry. (AICPA Integrated Practice System Ser.). (Illus.). 368p. reprint ed. pap. 104.90 (*0-7837-4871-X*, 2044399) Bks Demand.

Small Business Audit Manual Vol. 2. Larry L. Perry. 344p. 1987. 140.00 (*0-13-813155-4*) P-H.

Small Business Audit Manual Vol. 2. fac. ed. George Marthinuss & Larry L. Perry. (AICPA Integrated Practice System Ser.). 610p. 1992. pap. 173.90 (*0-7837-8241-1*, 2049008) Bks Demand.

Small Business Audit Manual Vol. 2, Vol. 1. fac. ed. George Marthinuss & Larry L. Perry. (AICPA Integrated Practice System Ser.). 140p. 1992. pap. 39.90 (*0-7837-8240-3*, 2049008) Bks Demand.

Small Business Audit Manual Documentation. Larry L. Perry. 176p. 1987. pap. 50.00 (*0-13-813106-6*) P-H.

Small Business Bankruptcy Kit. Robert L. Davidson. 160p. 1992. pap. text ed. 12.95 (*0-471-57649-2*) Wiley.

Small Business Bankruptcy Reorganization. Ed. by James A. Pusateri et al. LC 94-20896. (Bankruptcy Practice Library). 672p. 1994. pap. text ed. 130.00 (*0-471-10228-8*) Wiley.

Small Business, Banks, & SBA Loan Guarantees: Subsidizing the Weak or Bridging a Credit Gap? Elisabeth H. Rhyne. LC 87-36098. 188p. 1988. text ed. 55.00 (*0-89930-256-4*, RSB/, Quorum Bks) Greenwood.

Small Business Barriers & Battlefields: Adding Reality to the American Dream. Robert E. Fleury. Ed. by Paul Halvey. (Illus.). 220p. (Orig.). pap. 15.95 (*0-9642814-1-4*) Matahari Pubng.

Small Business Barriers & Battlefields: Adding Reality to the American Dream. Robert E. Fleury. Ed. by Paul Halvey. (Illus.). 220p. (Orig.). 1995. 27.95 (*0-9642814-0-6*) Matahari Pubng.

Small Business Basics. Benedetto. 352p. (C). 1991. per. 39.84 (*0-8403-6387-7*) Kendall-Hunt.

Small Business Bible: The Make-or-Break Factors for Survival & Success. Paul Resnick. LC 88-17207. 230p. 1988. pap. text ed. 22.95 (*0-471-62985-5*) Wiley.

Small Business Bibliography. University of Pittsburgh, Bureau of Business Research Staff. Ed. by Stuart Bruchey. LC 78-19003. (Small Business Enterprise in America Ser.). 1979. reprint ed. lib. bdg. 25.95 (*0-405-11507-5*) Ayer.

Small Business, Big Politics: What Entrepreneurs Need to Know to Use Their Growing Political... Charles A. Riley. 271p. 1996. pap. text ed. 14.95 (*1-56079-707-X*) Petersons.

Small Business Case Book. I. A. Fleming. 144p. 1985. text ed. 69.95 (*0-566-00841-6*, Pub. by Avebury Pub UK) Ashgate Pub Co.

Small Business Challenge. Dennis D. Wahler. 300p. (C). 1992. pap. text ed. 35.00 (*0-9634216-0-3*) Mary-Joe.

Small Business Computer Guide. Joseph S. Beckman. LC 94-46815. (Illus.). 368p. 1995. pap. 31.95 (*1-55558-136-6*, Digital DEC) Buttrwrth-Heinemann.

Small Business Computer Systems. 2nd ed. Mayur Mehta & Gary Vieira. 144p. 1993. ring bd. 13.59 (*0-8403-7908-0*) Kendall-Hunt.

*__Small Business Computing for Dummies.__ 1997. pap. 24.99 (*0-7645-0287-5*) IDG Bks.

Small Business Computing Made Easy: Everything You Need to Know to Get Started with a Computer. Linda Rohrbough. Ed. by Mark Rohrbough. (Illus.). 240p. 1989. pap. 24.95 incl. disk (*1-877855-00-6*) SoftServe Pr.

Small-Business Consulting. Hugh Arnold. 110p. (Orig.). (C). 1994. pap. text ed. 16.00 (*0-9639974-0-8*) Arnold Bks.

Small Business Controller. 84.00 (*0-685-69584-0*, COAC) Warren Gorham & Lamont.

Small Business Coordinator. (Career Examination Ser.: C-3688). pap. 34.95 (*0-8373-3688-0*) Nat Learn.

Small Business Credit & Collection Guide. Gini G. Scott. 216p. 1995. pap. 9.95 (*0-8065-1621-6*, Citadel Pr) Carol Pub Group.

An Asterisk (*) at the beginning of an entry indicates that the title is appearing in BIP for the first time.

Small Business Development: Some Current Issues. Kent O'Neill. 280p. 1987. text ed. 59.95 (0-566-05382-9, Pub. by Avebury Pub UK) Ashgate Pub Co.

Small Business Directory. 1992. lib. bdg. 79.95 (0-8490-5522-9) Gordon Pr.

***Small Business Edition, MS Office 97 for Dummies.** 1997. pap. 24.99 (0-7645-0290-5) IDG Bks.

Small Business Enterprise: An Economic Analysis. Gavin C. Reid. LC 92-37256. 368p. (C). (gr. 13). 1993. text ed. 79.95 (0-415-05681-0, B0708, Routledge NY) Routledge.

Small Business Enterprise: Economic Analysis. Gavin C. Reid. 352p. (C). 1996. pap. 24.95 (0-415-13207-X, Routledge NY) Routledge.

Small Business Enterprise in America Series, 42 bks. Ed. by Stuart Bruchey & Vincent P. Carosso. (Illus.). 1979. lib. bdg. 1,049.50 (0-405-11457-5) Ayer.

Small Business Entrepreneural Services - Suggestions for a Small Business Entrepreneural Service Center: A Business Workbook. rev. ed. Bibliotheca Press Staff. 70p. 1992. ring bd. 26.95 (0-939476-95-9, Biblio Pr) Prosperity & Profits.

***Small Business Entrepreneurs in Asia & Europe: Towards a Comparative Perspective.** Mario Rutten & Carol Upadhya. LC 97-11575. 1997. write for info. (0-8039-9381-1) Sage.

Small Business Expense Planner. LaVerne H. Ireland. 49p. (Orig.). 1984. pap. 10.00 (0-943932-00-9) Petervin Pr.

***Small Business Finance.** Adelman & Marks. LC 97-8385. 1997. pap. text ed. 36.00 (0-13-812983-5) P-H.

Small Business Finance, 2 vols., Set. Ed. by Paul M. Horvitz & R. Richardson Pettit. LC 83-48089. (Contemporary Studies in Economic & Financial Analysis: Vol. 42). 1984. 146.50 (0-89232-471-6) Jai Pr.

Small Business Financing. Ed. by Charlotte Weisman. LC 87-5534. (Special Collection from the Journal of Commercial Bank Lending). 132p. 1987. pap. text ed. 45.00 (0-936742-40-2) Robt Morris Assocs.

Small Business Guide to Direct Mail: Build Your Customer Base & Boost Profits. Lin Grensing. (Business Ser.). 192p. (Orig.). 1991. pap. 9.95 (0-88908-976-0) Self-Counsel Pr.

Small Business Guide to Doing Big Business on the Internet. Brian Hurley & Peter Birkwood. 192p. (Orig.). 1996. pap. 14.95 (1-55180-029-2) Self-Counsel Pr.

***Small Business Guide to Doing Big Business on the Internet.** 2nd rev. ed. Brian Hurley & Peter Birkwood. 216p. 1997. pap. 14.95 (1-55180-119-1) Self-Counsel Pr.

Small Business Guide to Employee Selection: Finding, Interviewing, & Hiring the Right People. 2nd ed. Lin Grensing. (Business Ser.). 176p. 1991. pap. 7.95 (0-88908-959-0) Self-Counsel Pr.

Small Business Guide to Environmental Management. (Illus.). 75p. (Orig.). (C). 1994. pap. text ed. 25.00 (0-7881-0349-0) DIANE Pub.

Small Business Guide to Hazardous Materials Management. Jacqueline Maher et al. 200p. 1988. ring bd. 48.00 (0-9621718-0-8) WSOS Cmnt Action Com.

Small Business Guide to Internet Marketing see Smart Business Guide to Internet Marketing: Version 2.1

***Small Business Guide to Payroll.** 128p. 1995. pap. 20.00 (0-8080-0070-5, 14595BLS02) Commerce.

***Small Business Handbook.** 3rd ed. Burstiner. LC 97-20330. 1997. pap. 20.00 (0-684-83022-1, Fireside) S&S Trade.

Small Business Handbook: A Comprehensive Guide to Starting & Running Your Own Business. rev. ed. Irving Burstiner. 368p. 1994. pap. 18.00 (0-671-88108-6, Fireside) S&S Trade.

Small Business Handbook: Laws, Regulations & Technical Assistance Services - U. S. Department of Labor. Ed. by Mario DiStasio et al. 87p. (Orig.). (C). 1994. pap. text ed. 25.00 (0-7881-1479-4) DIANE Pub.

Small Business in a Regulated Economy: Issues & Policy Implications. Ed. by Richard J. Judd et al. LC 87-32611. 255p. 1988. text ed. 55.00 (0-89930-343-9, JSL/, Quorum Bks) Greenwood.

Small Business in America: The Year 2000 & Beyond. Naisbitt Group Staff. (Illus.). 20p. (Orig.). 1986. pap. 6.00 (0-940791-00-5) NFIB Found.

***Small Business in Indonesia.** Peter Van Dierman. (Illus.). 252p. 1997. text ed. 63.95 (1-85972-592-9, Pub. by Ashgate UK) Ashgate Pub Co.

Small Business in the American Economy. 1992. lib. bdg. 77.95 (0-8490-5486-9) Gordon Pr.

Small Business in the American Economy. LC 88-600350. (Illus.). 1988. pap. 6.50 (0-16-004557-6, 045-000-00252-7) USGPO.

Small Business in the American Economy. 1995. lib. bdg. 251.95 (0-8490-6772-3) Gordon Pr.

***Small Business in the American Economy.** 1997. lib. bdg. 250.95 (0-8490-6082-6) Gordon Pr.

Small Business in the Clinton Years: What Your Company Must Do to Survive & Succeed. Ed. by S. Jackson Faris. 208p. (Orig.). 1993. pap. 9.95 (0-9635489-0-5) Hammock Pub.

Small Business in the Modern Economy. Ed. & Intro. by P. H. Admiraal. (Illus.). 200p. 1996. 52.95 (0-631-20018-5) Blackwell Pubs.

Small Business in the Third World: Guidelines for Practical Assistance. Malcolm Harper. 228p. (Orig.). 1984. pap. 24.95 (0-471-90474-0, Pub. by Intermed Tech UK) Women Ink.

Small Business in the Third World: Guidelines for Practical Assistance. fac. ed. Malcolm Harper. LC 83-25960. 225p. (Orig.). 1984. reprint ed. pap. 64.20 (0-608-00962-8, 2061810) Bks Demand.

***Small Business in Transition: Entering the 21st Century.** Benjamin P. Gerding. 262p. 1997. lib. bdg. 34.00 (1-56072-461-7) Nova Sci Pubs.

Small Business in Transition Economies: Promoting Enterprise in Central & Eastern Europe & the Former Soviet Union. Ed. by Jacob Levitsky. 160p. (Orig.). 1996. pap. 18.95 (1-85339-343-6, Pub. by Intermed Tech UK) Women Ink.

Small Business Incorporation Kit. Robert L. Davidson. LC 92-14054. 160p. 1992. pap. text ed. 15.95 (0-471-57652-2) Wiley.

Small Business Innovation Research: Abstracts of Phase I Awards, Dept. of Energy 1993. 106p. (Orig.). (C). 1994. pap. text ed. 35.00 (0-7881-0376-8) DIANE Pub.

Small Business Innovation Research: Abstracts of Phase I Awards, 1992. 119p. (Orig.). (C). 1993. pap. text ed. 40.00 (1-56806-644-9) DIANE Pub.

Small Business Innovation Research: Abstracts of Phase I Awards (1995) 124p. (Orig.). (C). 1996. pap. text ed. 35.00 (0-7881-2659-8) DIANE Pub.

Small Business Innovation Research: Program Solicitation (1996) 96p. (Orig.). (C). 1996. pap. text ed. 35.00 (0-7881-2660-1) DIANE Pub.

Small Business Innovation Research Program: The First Decade. (Illus.). 313p. (Orig.). (C). 1993. pap. text ed. 45.00 (1-56806-427-6) DIANE Pub.

***Small Business Innovation Research (SBIR) Program Development Blueprint.** James R. Atchison. LC 97-16574. 1997. lib. bdg. 49.00 (1-56072-409-9) Nova Sci Pubs.

***Small Business Insider's Guide to Bankers.** Suzanne Caplan & Thomas M. Nunnally. LC 97-13597. (Illus.). 176p. (Orig.). 1997. pap. 18.95 (1-55571-400-5) Oasis Pr OR.

***Small Business Internet Connections for Dummies.** 1997. pap. 24.99 (0-7645-0288-3) IDG Bks.

Small Business Investment Companies. Commerce Clearing House, Inc. Ed. by Stuart Bruchey & Vincent P. Carosso. LC 78-18958. (Small Business Enterprise in America Ser.). 1979. reprint ed. lib. bdg. 17.95 (0-405-11462-1) Ayer.

Small Business Investment Company Directory & Handbook. 150p. 1996. 35.00 (0-685-55415-5) B Klein Pubns.

Small Business Investment Company Directory & Handbook. 8th ed. Tyler G. Hicks. 150p. 1996. pap. 15.00 (1-56150-151-4) Intl Wealth.

***Small Business Investment Company Directory & Handbook.** 9th ed. Tyler G. Hicks. 150p. 1998. pap. 15.00 (1-56150-201-4) Intl Wealth.

Small Business Leave Policies: Excerpts from a Small Business Administration Report. (BNA Special Report Series on Work & Family: No. 40). 32p. 1991. 35.00 (1-55871-218-6, BSP212) BNA Plus.

Small Business Legal Guide. Barbara S. Shea & Jennifer Haupt. 320p. 1996. text ed. 39.95 (0-471-11950-4); pap. text ed. 19.95 (0-471-11951-2) Wiley.

Small Business Legal Guide: The Critical Legal Matters Affecting Your Business. Lynne A. Frasier. LC 95-36914. (Small Business Sourcebooks Ser.). 188p. 1995. pap. 9.95 (1-57071-060-0) Sourcebks.

***Small Business Legal Guide: The Critical Legal Matters Affecting Your Business.** 2nd rev. ed. Lynne A. Frasier. 176p. 1997. pap. 12.95 (1-57071-216-6) Sourcebks.

Small Business Legal Kit: 300 Forms, Agreements, & Contracts for Any Small Business. J. W. Dicks. (Business Advisor Ser.). 300p. (Orig.). 1995. pap. 17.95 (1-55850-487-7) Adams Media.

Small Business Management. Ames. Date not set. teacher ed., pap. text ed. write for info. (0-314-71074-4) West Pub.

Small Business Management. Michael D. Ames & Norval L. Wellsfry. (Illus.). 492p. (C). 1983. text ed. 60.75 (0-314-69631-8) West Pub.

***Small Business Management.** Neil Marriott. (C). 1998. pap. text ed. write for info. (0-201-40390-0) Addison-Wesley.

Small Business Management. Robert C. Ronstadt. (GC - Principles of Management Ser.). 1996. text ed. write for info. (0-538-81940-5) S-W Pub.

Small Business Management, 5 Vols. Nicholas C. Siropolis. (C). 1994. suppl. ed., teacher ed., pap. 7.96 (0-395-69316-0) HM.

Small Business Management, 6 Vols. Nicholas C. Siropolis. (C). 1996. text ed. 68.76 (0-395-80887-1) HM.

Small Business Management, 6 Vols. Nicholas C. Siropolis. (C). 1996. teacher ed., pap. 11.96 (0-395-80888-X) HM.

Small Business Management, 5 Vols. Nicholas C. Siropolis. (C). 1994. teacher ed., pap. 5.96 (0-395-67657-6) HM.

Small Business Management, 5 Vols. Nicholas C. Siropolis. (C). 1993. student ed., pap. 18.76 (0-395-67656-8) HM.

Small Business Management, 5 Vols. Nicholas C. Siropolis. (C). 1993. text ed. 68.76 (0-395-47207-5) HM.

Small Business Management. D. Stokes. 416p. 1995. pap. 59.95 (1-85805-129-0, Pub. by DP Publns UK) St Mut.

Small Business Management. 4th ed. William D. Hailes, Jr. & Raymond T. Hubbard. 1988. pap. 42.95 (0-8273-3128-2); teacher ed., pap. 15.95 (0-8273-3129-0) Delmar.

Small Business Management, 5 Vols. 4th ed. Nicholas C. Siropolis. (C). 1994. 76.36 (0-395-52998-0) HM.

Small Business Management. 5th ed. Hubbard. (General Business & Business Education Ser.). 1993. teacher ed. 15.95 (0-8273-5140-2); pap. 37.95 (0-8273-5139-9) Delmar.

Small Business Management. 5th ed. Hal B. Pickle & Royce L. Arahamson. LC 89-36239. 736p. 1990. Net. text ed. 39.50 (0-471-50071-2) Wiley.

***Small Business Management.** 6th ed. Hodgetts. (C). 1997. teacher ed., pap. text ed. 26.75 (0-03-024926-0) HB Coll Pubs.

Small Business Management. 8th ed. Longnecker. (GC - Principles of Management Ser.). 1991. pap. 30.95 (0-538-80791-1) S-W Pub.

Small Business Management. 9th ed. Longnecker et al. (C). 1994. text ed. 54.50 (0-538-83045-X, GG70IA) S-W Pub.

Small Business Management. 9th ed. Longnecker. (GC - Principles of Management Ser.). 1994. student ed., pap. 18.50 (0-538-83047-6) S-W Pub.

Small Business Management. 10th ed. Longnecker & Carlos W. Moore. (GG - Small Business Management Ser.). 1997. pap. 62.95 (0-538-85077-9) S-W Pub.

Small Business Management. Hal B. Pickle & Royce L. Abrahamson. LC 86-19198. (Wiley Series in Management). (Illus.). 649p. reprint ed. pap. 180.00 (0-7837-3507-3, 2057840) Bks Demand.

Small Business Management: A Planning Approach. Joel Corman & Robert N. Lussier. LC 95-21713. 464p. (C). 1995. text ed. 64.95 (0-256-14517-2) Irwin Prof Pubng.

Small Business Management: A Planning Approach. Larry D. Redinbaugh & Clyde W. Neu. (Illus.). 475p. 1980. text ed. 56.00 (0-314-52971-3); teacher ed., pap. text ed. write for info. (0-314-52998-5) West Pub.

Small Business Management: An Entrepreneur's Guide to Success. William L. Megginson et al. LC 93-6704. 576p. (C). 1993. per. 47.95 (0-256-14094-4) Irwin.

Small Business Management: An Entrepreneur's Guide to Success. 2nd ed. William L. Megginson. 576p. (C). 1996. per. 47.95 (0-256-21893-5) Irwin.

Small Business Management: Cases & Incidents: Canadian Version. D. Balderson. (C). 1989. text ed. 36.95 (0-256-07834-3) Irwin.

Small Business Management: Testbank, 6 Vols. Nicholas C. Siropolis. (C). 1996. suppl. ed., pap. 11.96 (0-395-80889-8) HM.

Small Business Management: Tools for Success. Jim Carland & JoAnn Carland. 696p. (C). 1990. text ed. 50.50 (0-534-92036-5) S-W Pub.

Small Business Management & Entrepreneurship. Curtis E. Tate, Jr. et al. 859p. (C). 1992. text ed. 69.95 (0-534-92357-7) S-W Pub.

Small Business Management Exam, 5 Vols. Nicholas C. Siropolis. (C). Date not set. text ed. write for info. (0-395-69242-3) HM.

Small Business Management Fundamentals. 6th ed. Daniel Steinhoff & John F. Burgess. LC 92-20046. 1993. pap. text ed. write for info. (0-07-061221-8) McGraw.

Small Business Management in Australia. 2nd ed. Gary Meredith. 352p. 1982. 18.50 (0-07-451006-1) McGraw.

Small Business Marketing: A Selected & Annotated Bibliography. William H. Brannen. LC 78-15082. (American Marketing Association Bibliography Ser.: No. 31). 87p. reprint ed. pap. 25.00 (0-317-39650-1, 2023352) Bks Demand.

Small Business Matters: Topics, Procedures & Strategies. Mary F. McVicker. LC 87-47977. 320p. 1988. pap. 14.95 (0-8019-7813-0) Chilton.

Small Business Money Source Directory, 1989. Sammy S. Jenkins, Sr. 183p. 1989. pap. 49.95 (0-9620989-2-2) All States Pub.

Small Business Partnership Kit. Robert L. Davidson. 160p. 1992. text ed. 55.00 (0-471-57653-0); pap. text ed. 16.95 (0-471-57654-9) Wiley.

Small Business Planning & Management for the First-Time Entrepreneur. Donald F. Connelly & William H. Hamilton. Ed. by Jacqueline A. Stuts. 160p. (Orig.). (C). 1996. student ed., wbk. ed., pap. text ed. 11.95 (1-56502-012-X, 8004W) Ohio Agri Educ.

Small Business Planning & Management for the First-Time Entrepreneur. D. Howard Doster et al. Ed. by Jacqueline A. Stuts. (Illus.). 268p. (Orig.). (C). 1996. pap. text ed. 18.95 (1-56502-010-3, 8003M) Ohio Agri Educ.

***Small Business Planning & Management for the First-Time Entrepreneur: Instructor's Resource Manual.** William H. Hamilton & Donald F. Connelly. Ed. by Jacqueline A. Stuts. 325p. (Orig.). 1996. pap. text ed. 16.95 (1-56502-013-8, 8005G) Ohio Agri Educ.

Small Business Planning Workbook. John Wisdom. 1990. 95.00 (0-685-31932-6) Clark Boardman Callaghan.

***Small Business Policy in Japan & the United States: A Comparative Analysis of Objectives & Outcomes.** Yuko Aoyama & Michael B. Teitz. LC 96-77878. (Policy Papers in International Affairs). (Illus.). (Orig.). 1996. pap. 8.25 (0-87725-544-X) U of Cal IAS.

Small Business Possibilities for At Your Own Pace Research. Center for Self Sufficiency, Research Division Staff. 60p. 1984. ring bd. 25.95 (0-317-03486-3) Ctr Self Suff.

Small Business Possibility Encyclopaedia: Word Mapping Edition. Center for Self Sufficiency Staff. Orig. Title: The A to Z Small Business Reference Encyclopaedia: Word Mapping Edition. 100p. (C). 1991. ring bd. 149.00 (0-910811-17-2) Ctr Self Suff.

Small Business, Principles of Marketing. Lewison. (SB - Marketing Education Ser.). 1998. student ed., text ed. 13.95 (0-538-85138-4) S-W Pub.

Small Business Problems & Priorities. William J. Dennis, Jr. 117p. (Orig.). 1986. pap. 6.00 (0-940791-02-1) NFIB Found.

Small Business Problems in Urban Areas. U. S. House of Representatives Select Committee on Small Business. Ed. by Stuart Bruchey & Vincent P. Carosso. LC 78-18998. (Small Business Enterprise in America Ser.). (Illus.). 1979. reprint ed. lib. bdg. 17.95 (0-405-11506-7) Ayer.

***Small Business Profiles.** 3rd ed. 1998. 95.00 (0-8103-9326-3, 00002624, Gale Res Intl) Gale.

Small Business Profiles, 2 vols., Set. 1994. lib. bdg. 600.00 (0-8490-8568-3) Gordon Pr.

Small Business Profiles: A Guide to Today's Top Opportunities for Entrepreneurs. Suzanne M. Bourgoin. 350p. 1994. 95.00 (0-8103-9178-3) Gale.

Small Business Profiles Vol. 2: A Guide to Today's Top Opportunities for Entrepreneurs. 2nd ed. Ed. by Jennifer A. Mast. 361p. 1995. 95.00 (0-8103-9325-5, 102052) Gale.

***Small-Business Profit Guide.** 1996. pap. text ed. 24.95 (0-15-606568-1) Profess Pubns.

Small Business Reference Guide For: Home-Based Business, Small Manufacturers, Self-Publishers, Entrepreneurs, Craftsmen, Retailers, Writers, Artists. Belle M. Biebel. 63p. pap. 12.95 (0-941825-02-7) Bluechip Bks.

Small Business Regulatory Compliance Manual. James Newton. 450p. 1995. ring bd. 70.00 (1-888555-05-X) MGR Pr.

***Small Business Resource Guide to the Web 1997.** Suzanne Cross et al. 528p. 1997. 39.99 (0-7897-1058-7) Mac Comp Pub.

Small Business Safety & Health Manual. LC 84-60340. 80p. 1984. pap. 19.95 (0-87912-120-3, 13021-000) Natl Safety Coun.

***Small Business Schedule C&F Expenses.** Debra J. Risik. 196p. (Orig.). (C). 1996. pap. 40.00 (0-926709-63-1) MicroMash.

Small Business Services Possibilities. Alpha Pyramis Research Division Staff. 38p. 1948. ring bd. 49.95 (0-913597-45-7) Prosperity & Profits.

Small Business Sourcebook. 2nd ed. Ed. by Robert J. Elster. 1837p. 1986. 185.00 (0-8103-1597-1) Gale.

Small Business Sourcebook, 2 vols. 3rd ed. Ed. by Charity A. Dorgan. 2000p. 1988. 189.00 (0-8103-2648-5) Gale.

Small Business Sourcebook, 2 vols. 5th ed. Carol A. Schwartz. 1991. 210.00 (0-8103-5482-9) Gale.

Small Business Sourcebook, 2 vols. 6th ed. Carol A. Schwartz. 1992. 220.00 (0-8103-8076-5) Gale.

Small Business Sourcebook, 2 Vols. 7th ed. Ed. by Kathleen E. Maki. 3000p. 1993. 235.00 (0-8103-8904-5, 004802) Gale.

Small Business Sourcebook, 2 vols. 8th ed. Ed. by Kathleen E. Maki. 2971p. 1994. 260.00 (0-8103-5668-6) Gale.

Small Business Sourcebook, 2 Vol. 10th ed. Emrich. 1996. 295.00 (0-8103-5798-4) Gale.

***Small Business Sourcebook, 2 vols.** 12th ed. 1998. 295.00 (0-7876-1253-7, 00156430, Gale Res Intl) Gale.

Small Business Sourcebook, 2 vols., Set. 9th ed. Emrich. 1995. 280.00 (0-8103-5672-4) Gale.

Small Business Sourcebook, Vol. 1. 6th ed. Carol A. Schwartz. 1992. write for info. (0-8103-8077-3) Gale.

Small Business Sourcebook, Vol. 2. 6th ed. Carol A. Schwartz. 1992. write for info. (0-8103-8078-1) Gale.

Small Business Sourcebook: Supplement. 2nd ed. Ed. by Robert J. Elster. 235p. 1987. 80.00 (0-8103-2512-8) Gale.

Small Business Sourcebook: The Entrepreneur's Resource, 2 vols. 4th ed. Ed. by Carol A. Schwartz. 2000p. 1990. 199.00 (0-8103-6850-1) Gale.

***Small Business Sourcebook: The Entrepreneur's Resource, 2 vols.** 11th ed. Ed. by Yolanda Johnson. 1997. 295.00 (0-7876-1121-2, 00156267, Gale Res Intl) Gale.

Small Business Sourcebook: 3rd Edition Supplement. 3rd ed. Gale Research, Inc., Staff. Ed. by Charity A. Dorgan. 180p. 1989. 85.00 (0-8103-1832-6) Gale.

Small Business Sourcebook Supplement. 4th ed. 1991. 90.00 (0-8103-7440-4) Gale.

Small Business Sourcebook Supplement. 5th ed. Carol A. Schwartz. 1992. 94.00 (0-8103-7441-2) Gale.

***Small Business Specialists to Assist Small Business, Small Disadvantaged Business, Women-Owned Small Business & Labor Surplus Area Business Firms.** 1996. lib. bdg. 253.00 (0-8490-6066-4) Gordon Pr.

***Small Business Start-Up Guide: A Surefire Blueprint to Successfully Launch Your Own Business.** 2nd rev. ed. Hal Root & Steve Koenig. 152p. 1997. pap. 12.95 (1-57071-221-2) Sourcebks.

Small Business Start-up Guide: Make or Break Factors to Successfully Launch Your Own Business. Hal Root & Steve Koenig. LC 93-31432. (Small Business Sourcebooks Ser.). 152p. 1993. 17.95 (0-942061-70-5) Sourcebks.

Small Business Start-up Guide: Make or Break Factors to Successfully Launch Your Own Business. Hal Root & Steve Koenig. LC 93-31432. (Small Business Sourcebooks Ser.). 152p. 1994. pap. 9.95 (0-942061-67-5) Sourcebks.

***Small Business Start-up Guide: Practical Advice on Starting & Operating a Small Business.** 2nd ed. Robert Sullivan. LC 97-93259. (Illus.). 280p. 1998. pap. 16.95 (1-882480-05-8) Info Intl.

Small Business Start-Up Index, Issue 3. 90th ed. Ed. by Michael Madden. 400p. 1990. Annual volume. 95.00 (0-8103-7721-7) Gale.

Small Business Start-Up Index, 1990, Nos. 1-3. 90th ed. Ed. by Michael Madden. 1990. Set. 125.00 (0-8103-7718-7, 030300) Gale.

Small Business Start up Index 1991, Issue 3. 91th ed. 1991. 130.00 (0-8103-7990-2) Gale.

Small Business Start up Index 1991, Issue 3. 91th ed. Michael Madden. 1991. 95.00 (0-8103-7993-7) Gale.

Small Business Start up Index 1992 ISS 1, 2 Vols., Vol. 1. 3rd ed. Michael Madden. 1995. 600.00 (0-8103-8240-7) Gale.

Small Business Start up Manual. John B. Walton. LC 81-50038. (Illus.). 228p. 1981. 29.95 (0-939356-00-7) Weybridge.

Small Business Startup Guide: Practical Advice on Selecting, Starting, & Operating a Small Business. Robert Sullivan. LC 95-95245. 260p. 1996. pap. 15.95 (1-882480-22-8) Info Intl.

Small Business Subcontracting Directory. 1990. lib. bdg. 250.00 (0-8490-4031-0) Gordon Pr.

Small Business Success Secrets. Donald M. Dible. 1982. pap. 21.95 (0-8359-7010-8, Reston) P-H.

S

An Asterisk (*) at the beginning of an entry indicates that the title is appearing in BIP for the first time.

Small Business Success Through TQM: Practical Methods to Improve Your Organization's Performance. Terry Ehresman. LC 94-21676. 255p. 1994. 30.00 (0-87389-309-3, H0864) ASQC Qual Pr.

Small Business Survival. Roger Bennett. 268p. 1991. pap. 36.00 (0-273-03624-6, Pub. by Pitman Pubng UK) St Mut.

Small Business Survival Guide: How to Manage Your Cash, Profits & Taxes. Robert E. Fleury. LC 95-11371. 237p. 1992. 29.95 (0-942061-11-X); pap. 17.95 (0-942061-12-8) Sourcebks.

Small Business Survival Guide: How to Manage Your Cash, Profits & Taxes. 3rd rev. ed. Robert E. Fleury. LC 95-11371. 1995. pap. 17.95 (1-57071-045-7) Sourcebks.

Small Business Survival Guide for the '90s. Blaise Matz. 80p. (Orig.). 1995. pap. write for info. (1-57502-039-4) Morris Pubng.

Small Business Survival Kit. John Ventura. 224p. 1994. pap. 19.95 (0-7931-0608-7, 56140701) Dearborn Finan.

Small Business Survival Manual: Applied Management for Small Non-Profit. Selma H. Lamkin. (Orig.). (C). 20.00 (0-686-32947-3) Nikmal Pub.

Small Business Tax Advisor: Understanding the New Tax Law. Cliff Roberson. 176p. (Orig.). 1987. pap. 12.95 (0-8306-3024-4, 30024) McGraw-Hill Prof.

Small Business Tax Guide: Guide to Small Business Tax. Andrew J. Lynn. (Illus.). (Orig.). 1992. pap. 24.95 (1-877983-04-7) Data-Lynn Bk.

***Small Business Taxation Update.** Maydew. 56p. 1994. pap. 22.00 (0-614-26815-X, BLS-3330) Commerce.

Small Business Taxaton: Planning & Practice. Maydew. 464p. 1994. 60.00 (0-685-67145-3, 4975) Commerce.

Small Business Technology Transfer: Abstracts of Phase I Awards 1994. 25p. (Orig.). (C). 1995. pap. text ed. 25.00 (0-7881-1749-1) DIANE Pub.

Small Business Technology Transfer: Program Solicitation. 46p. (Orig.). (C). 1995. pap. text ed. 25.00 (0-7881-1743-2) DIANE Pub.

Small Business Toolkit-Marketing for the Self Employed. Martin Edic. LC 96-41172. 368p. 1997. pap. 15.00 (0-7615-0592-X) Prima Pub.

Small Business Toolkit-Sales. Martin Edic. LC 96-50056. 336p. 1997. pap. 15.00 (0-7615-0593-8) Prima Pub.

Small Business Troubleshooter. Roger Fritz. 224p. (Orig.). 1995. pap. 16.99 (1-56414-191-8) Career Pr Inc.

Small Business under Siege. Ed. by Jack Faris. 208p. (Orig.). 1994. pap. 9.95 (0-9635489-1-3) Hammock Pub.

Small Business Valuation Book: Easy to Use Techniques for Determining Fair Price, Resolving Disputes, & Minimizing Taxes. Lawrence W. Tuller. LC 94-8708. (Business Advisors Ser.). 1994. 29.95 (1-55850-356-0); pap. 10.95 (1-55850-355-2) Adams Media.

Small Businesses & Small Business Development, 2 vols., Set. Ed. by European Research Pr. Ltd. Staff. (C). 1991. 210.00 (1-872677-01-0, Pub. by European Res Pr UK) St Mut.

***Small Businesses in Singapore: Case Studies in Entrepreneurship & Strategic Management.** Lai Y. Poh et al. 288p. 1992. pap. write for info. (981-210-009-1, Pub. by Times Academic SI) Intl Spec Bk.

Small Businesses That Grow & Grow & Grow. 2nd ed. Patricia A. Woy. (Illus.). 264p. 1989. pap. 9.95 (1-55870-126-5, Betrwy Bks) F & W Pubns Inc.

Small Businesses with an Investment of 100 Dollars or Less. 1991. lib. bdg. 75.95 (0-8490-4793-5) Gordon Pr.

Small But Powerful - A Review Guide to Small Alternative Energy Projects for California's Local Decisionmaakers. 66p. 1987. 8.00 (0-317-05647-6, P87001NRG) Assn Bay Area.

Small Buys, Great Deals. Richard Russill. LC 97-10149. 1996. pap. text ed. 36.00 (0-13-442625-8) P-H.

Small Canvas: An Introduction to Dreiser's Short Stories. Joseph Griffin. LC 83-49347. 176p. 1985. 29.50 (0-8386-3217-3) Fairleigh Dickinson.

Small Cap Stocks: Investment & Portfolio Strategies for the Institutional Investor. Jess Lederman & Richard A. Klein. 1993. text ed. 70.00 (1-55738-518-1) Irwin Prof Pubng.

Small Cats. Markus Kappeler. LC 92-10655. (Animal Families Ser.). (J). 1992. lib. bdg. 19.93 (0-8368-0843-6) Gareth Stevens Inc.

Small Cats. Susan Lumpkin. LC 92-26837. (Great Creatures of the World Ser.). (Illus.). 72p. (YA). (gr. 6-9). 1993. 17.95 (0-8160-2848-6) Facts on File.

Small Caucasian Woman. Elaine F. Palencia. 176p. (C). 1993. pap. 16.95 (0-8262-0943-2) U of Mo Pr.

Small Cell Lung Cancer: Proceedings of the International Conference on Small Cell Lung Cancer, Ravenna, Italy, 27-28 March, 1987. Ed. by M. Marangolo & G. Fiorentini. (Advances in the Biosciences Ser.: Vol. 72). (Illus.). 182p. 1988. 92.00 (0-08-036631-7, Pergamon Pr) Elsevier.

Small Ceremonies. Carol Shields. LC 95-30647. 192p. 1996. pap. 10.95 (0-14-025145-6, Penguin Bks) Viking Penguin.

Small Ceremonies. large type ed. Carol Shields. 241p. 1996. lib. bdg. 24.95 (0-7838-1830-0, GK Hall) Thorndike Pr.

***Small Change.** Elizabeth Hay. 208p. 1997. pap. 16.95 (0-88984-187-X, Pub. by Porcupines Quill CN) Genl Dist Srvs.

Small Change. Vassar Miller. Ed. by Joseph F. Lomax & J. Whitebird. LC 77-77-20728. 1977. pap. 10.00 (0-930324-00-5) Wings Pr.

Small Change. Francois Truffaut. Tr. by Anselm Hollo from FRE. (Illus.). 192p. 1986. pap. 6.95 (0-936839-51-1) Applause Theatre Bk Pubs.

Small Change: A Life of Tom Waits. Patrick Humphries. (Illus.). 128p. (Orig.). 1990. pap. 9.95 (0-312-04582-4) St Martin.

Small Change: Domestic Policy under the Clinton Presidency. David Stoesz. 240p. (Orig.). (C). 1996. pap. text ed. 25.95 (0-8013-1515-8, 76849) Longman.

Small Change: The Economics of Child Support. Andrea Beller & John W. Graham. LC 92-39623. (Illus.). 392p. 1993. 40.00 (0-300-05362-2) Yale U Pr.

Small Change: The Economics of Child Support. Andrea H. Beller. 1996. pap. text ed. 18.00 (0-300-06659-7) Yale U Pr.

Small Change & Kick for Touch: Two Plays. Peter Gill. 128p. 1985. pap. 8.95 (0-7145-2826-9) M Boyars Pubs.

Small Change for the Long Haul. Jonathan Greene. 64p. (Orig.). 1984. pap. 4.95 (0-88268-009-9) Open Bk Pubns.

Small Changes. Marge Piercy. 544p. 1985. mass mkt. 5.95 (0-449-21083-9, Crest) Fawcett.

***Small Changes.** Marge Piercy. 1997. pap. 12.00 (0-449-00093-1) Fawcett.

Small Christian Communities: A Pastoral Companion. rev. ed. James O'Halloran. LC 96-10160. Orig. Title: Signs of Hope. 187p. (Orig.). 1996. pap. 13.00 (1-57075-077-7) Orbis Bks.

Small Christian Communities & the Parish. John P. Vandenakker. 260p. (Orig.). 1994. pap. 14.95 (1-55612-709-X) Sheed & Ward MO.

Small Church, Big Vision. Lynn Green. 1995. pap. 10.50 (0-551-02904-8) Zondervan.

Small Church Is Different. Lyle E. Schaller. LC 82-1830. 192p. (Orig.). 1982. pap. 13.95 (0-687-38717-5) Abingdon.

Small Church Is Different: Leader's Guide. Lyle E. Schaller & Joe Iaquinta. 1990. pap. 11.95 (0-911866-20-5) LifeSprings Res.

Small Church with a Big Mission: The History of the First 50 Years of Seigle Avenue Presbyterian Church. Margaret G. Bigger & Katherine M. Dunlap. LC 95-79297. (Illus.). 128p. (Orig.). 1995. pap. 12.95 (0-9640606-2-0) A Borough Bks.

Small Circle Jujitsu. Wally Jay. Ed. by Mike Lee. LC 89-42904. 256p. 1989. pap. 14.95 (0-89750-122-5, 462) Ohara Pubns.

Small City & Regional Community: Conference Proceedings, 1986, Vol. VII. Ed. by Robert P. Wolensky & Edward J. Miller. LC 79-644450. viii, 500p. 1987. pap. text ed. 19.00 (0-932310-08-7) U of Wis-Stevens Point.

Small City & Regional Community: Proceedings of the 1979 Conference, Vol. II. Ed. by Edward J. Miller & Robert P. Wolensky. (Orig.). 1979. pap. text ed. 16.50 (0-932310-01-X) U of Wis-Stevens Point.

Small City & Regional Community: Proceedings of the 1980 Conference, Vol. III. Ed. by Robert P. Wolensky & Edward J. Miller. viii, 450p. (Orig.). 1980. pap. text ed. 16.50 (0-932310-02-8) U of Wis-Stevens Point.

Small City & Regional Community: Proceedings of the 1981 Conference, Vol. IV. Ed. by Edward J. Miller & Robert P. Wolensky. LC 79-644450. viii, 550p. (Orig.). (C). 1981. pap. text ed. 16.50 (0-932310-03-6) U of Wis-Stevens Point.

Small City & Regional Community: Proceedings of the 1982 Conference, Vol. V. Robert P. Wolensky & Edward J. Miller. LC 79-644450. viii, 450p. (C). 1982. pap. text ed. 16.50 (0-932310-04-4) U of Wis-Stevens Point.

Small City & Regional Community: Proceedings of the 1984 Conference, Vol. VI. Ed. by Edward J. Miller & Robert P. Wolensky. LC 79-644450. viii, 450p. (Orig.). (C). 1985. pap. text ed. 16.50 (0-932310-06-0) U of Wis-Stevens Point.

Small City & Regional Community, Vol. 8: Proceedings of the 1988 Conference. Ed. by Nancy S. Lind & Ann Elder. vii, 295p. 1988. pap. text ed. 19.00 (0-932310-10-9, 79-644450) U of Wis-Stevens Point.

Small City in France. Francoise Gaspard. Tr. by Arthur Goldhammer. LC 94-12460. (Illus.). 208p. 1995. text ed. 32.50 (0-674-81096-1, GASSMA); pap. text ed. 15.95 (0-674-81097-X, GASSMX) HUP.

Small Civil War. John Neufeld. 1996. 16.00 (0-689-80770-8, S&S Bks Young Read) S&S Childrens.

***Small Civil War.** John Neufeld. 1996. pap. 3.99 (0-689-80771-6, S&S Bks Young Read) S&S Childrens.

***Small Claims: Step-by-Step.** Ted Rothstein. LC 97-17748. (Legal-Ease Ser.). 1997. pap. text ed. 14.95 (0-7641-0237-0) Barron.

Small Claims & Traffic Courts: Case Management Procedures, Case Characteristics, & Outcomes in 12 Urban Jurisdictions. John Goerdt. 188p. 1992. pap. 6.95 (0-89656-118-6, R-140) Natl Ctr St Courts.

Small Claims Court. 111p. (Orig.). 1995. pap. text ed. 14.95 (1-56382-409-4) E-Z Legal.

Small Claims Court. I. M. Bredenkamp. 115p. 1986. pap. 41.00 (0-409-01336-6, SA) MICHIE.

Small Claims Court. David W. Felder. 44p. 1996. pap. text ed. 8.95 (0-910959-96-X) Wellington Pr.

Small Claims Court. Theresa M. Rudy. (Random House Practical Law Manual Ser.). 160p. 1990. pap. write for info. (0-679-72950-X) HALT DC.

Small Claims Court Guide for Florida: What You Really Need to Know. Luke S. Brown. (Legal Ser.). 240p. 1993. pap. 15.95 (0-88908-780-6) Self-Counsel Pr.

Small Claims Court Guide for Ontario. 7th ed. Jennifer Young. (Legal Ser.). 232p. 1993. Canadian Edition. pap. 10.95 (0-88908-380-0) Self-Counsel Pr.

Small Claims Court Guide for Washington: How to Win Your Case! 2nd ed. Donald D. Stuart. (Legal Ser.). 168p. 1989. pap. 8.95 (0-88908-740-7) Self-Counsel Pr.

Small Claims Court Without a Lawyer. W. Kelsea Wilber. LC 91-28539. 218p. 1992. pap. 18.95 (0-942061-32-2) Sourcebks.

Small Claims Kit. 40p. (Orig.). 1995. pap. 19.95 (1-56382-109-5) E-Z Legal.

Small Claims, Large Encounters. Sonya Jones. 64p. 1995. 17.95 (0-9646230-0-5) Brito & Lair.

Small Claims Litigation. 2nd ed. James L. Kenkel & D. R. Chalmers. 192p. 1991. pap. 33.00 (0-409-89776-0) MICHIE.

Small Claims Procedure in the Sheriff Court. David Kelbie. 1994. pap. text ed. 44.00 (0-406-11710-1, UK) MICHIE.

Small Clauses in English: The Non-Verbal Types. Bas Aarts. LC 92-13313. (Topics in English Linguistics Ser.: No. 8). xi, 228p. (C). 1992. lib. bdg. 86.15 (3-11-013487-X) Mouton.

Small Cloud. Ariane & Ashley Wolff. LC PZ7.W821234On 1996. (Illus.). 24p. (J). (gr. k-3). 1996. reprint ed. pap. 5.95 (0-8027-7490-3) Walker & Co.

Small Collection. Garry B. Trudeau. 1989. pap. 6.95 (0-8050-1021-1) H Holt & Co.

Small Collections from Fort Shalmaneser see Ivories from Nimrud

Small College & Rugby Football Scorebook. Kenneth N. Carlson. (Illus.). 816p. (Orig.). 1995. pap. 19.75 (0-938428-14-4) Rain Belt.

Small College in Maine: Two Hundred Years of Bowdoin. Charles C. Calhoun. LC 93-79513. (Illus.). 275p. (Orig.). (C). 1994. pap. 21.95 (0-916606-24-4) Bowdoin Coll.

Small Colonial War. Robert Frezza. 304p. 1990. mass mkt. 4.99 (0-345-36200-4, Del Rey) Ballantine.

Small Comforts: More Comments & Comic Pieces. Tom Bodett. 160p. 1988. pap. 12.00 (0-201-13689-9) Addison-Wesley.

Small Commercial Garden: How to Make 10,000 Dollars a Year in Your Backyard. Dan Haakenson. 208p. 1995. pap. 17.95 (0-9642861-0-6) PC Services.

Small Community: Foundation of Democratic Life. Arthur E. Morgan & Donald Harrington Szantho. LC 83-73240. 336p. 1984. reprint ed. pap. 10.00 (0-910420-28-9) Comm Serv OH.

Small Community, Population & the Economic Order. rev. ed. Griscom Morgan. 1975. pap. 2.00 (0-910420-22-X) Comm Serv OH.

Small Community Water & Wastewater Treatment: Summary Report. (Illus.). 92p. (Orig.). (C). 1994. pap. text ed. 35.00 (0-7881-0684-8) DIANE Pub.

Small Computer Theory & Applications. Denton J. Dailey. (Illus.). 448p. (C). 1988. text ed. 27.95 (0-07-050409-1) McGraw.

Small Computers in Construction: Proceedings of a Symposium Sponsored by the Construction Division. Wayne C. Moore. 89p. 1984. 16.00 (0-87262-400-5) Am Soc Civil Eng.

Small Concrete Dams. rev. ed. 50p. 1980. pap. 15.00 (0-89312-047-2, EB002W) Portland Cement.

Small Conference. Margaret Mead & Paul Byers. 1968. text ed. 21.55 (90-279-6049-6) Mouton.

Small Congregations: New & Selected Poems. Thylias Moss. 1994. pap. 12.00 (0-88001-363-X) Ecco Pr.

Small Congregations New & Selected Poems. Thylias Moss. 1993. 22.95 (0-88001-289-7) Ecco Pr.

Small Cookbook - Beef. Wei Chuan Publishing Staff. Ed. by Huang Su-Huei & Sophia Lin. Tr. by Wynne Chang. (Illus.). 64p. (CHI & ENG.). 1993. pap. 6.95 (0-941676-41-2) Wei-Chuan Pub.

Small Cookbook - Chicken. Wei Chuan Publishing Staff. Ed. by Huang Su-Huei & Sophia Lin. Tr. by Wynne Chang. (Illus.). 64p. 1993. pap. 6.95 (0-941676-40-4) Wei-Chuan Pub.

Small Cookbook - Soup! Soup! Soup! 80p. (CHI & ENG.). 1994. pap. 7.95 (0-941676-50-1) Wei-Chuan Pub.

Small Cookbook - Tofu! Tofu! Tofu! 80p. (CHI & ENG.). 1994. pap. 7.95 (0-941676-49-8) Wei-Chuan Pub.

Small Cookbook - Vegetables. Wei Chuan Publishing Staff. Ed. by Huang Su-Huei & Sophia Lin. Tr. by Wynne Chang. (Illus.). 64p. 1993. pap. 6.95 (0-941676-39-0) Wei-Chuan Pub.

Small Cookbook - Very! Very! Vegetarian! 80p. (CHI & ENG.). 1994. pap. 7.95 (0-941676-51-X) Wei-Chuan Pub.

***Small Countries, Big Lessons: Governance & the Rise of East Asia.** Hilton Root. (Illus.). 216p. 1997. 19.95 (0-19-590026-X) OUP.

Small Countries Facing Technological Revolution. Ed. by Chris Freeman & Bengt-Ake Lundvall. 260p. 1988. text ed. 54.00 (0-86187-978-3) St Martin.

Small Country. Sian James. LC 89-82033. 192p. (Orig.). 1990. pap. 13.95 (1-85411-016-0, Pub. by Seren Bks UK) Dufour.

Small-Crack Test Methods. Ed. by James M. Larsen & John E. Allison. LC 92-10509. (STP Ser.: Vol. 1149). (Illus.). 230p. 1992. text ed. 72.00 (0-8031-1469-9, 04-011490-30) ASTM.

Small Craft Advisory: A Book about the Building of a Boat. Louis D. Rubin, Jr. LC 91-19545. 394p. 1991. pap. 12.00 (0-87113-533-7, Atlntc Mnthly) Grove-Atltic.

Small Craft Handling. (Illus.). 1995. pap. 1.00 (0-916682-48-X) Outdoor Empire.

Small Craft Owner's Manual. Ken Cook Company Staff. (Illus.). 96p. (Orig.). 1996. 3.95 (0-9652491-0-7) Ken Cook.

***Small Craft Safety.** American Red Cross Staff. 96p. (gr. 13). 1997. pap. text ed. write for info. (0-8151-7956-1) Mosby Yr Bk.

Small Craft Warnings. Tennessee Williams. LC 72-80978. 1972. 7.95 (0-8112-0461-8, NDP348) New Directions.

Small Criminology Dictionary: Kleines Kriminologisches Woerterbuch. 3rd ed. Gunther Kaiser. 615p. (GER.). 1993. pap. 75.00 (0-8288-1321-3, M7501) Fr & Eur.

***Small, Dark Place: A Novel.** Martin Schenk. LC 97-18666. 1997. 23.00 (0-375-50074-X, Villard Bks) Random.

Small Dark Room of the Soul: And Other Stories. Matthew J. Pallamary. 150p. (Orig.). 1994. pap. 14.95 (1-885516-00-2) SD Writs Mnthly.

Small Deceit. large type ed. Margaret Yorke. LC 91-36826. 376p. 1992. reprint ed. lib. bdg. 20.95 (1-56054-280-2) Thorndike Pr.

Small Details. Marjorie Everitt. 1993. 17.95 (0-8034-9006-2) Bouregy.

Small Dictionary of Chemistry & Chemical Engineering: Kleines Woerterbuch der Chemie und Chemischen Technik, Vol. 2: German-English. H. W. Gross & Wolfgang Borsdorf. 95p. (ENG & GER.). 1980. pap. 24.95 (0-8288-0166-5, M8009) Fr & Eur.

Small Dictionary of Japanology: Kleines Woerterbuch der Japanologie. 2nd ed. B. Lewin & Bruno. 596p. (GER & JPN.). 1981. 85.00 (0-8288-1019-2, M7512) Fr & Eur.

Small Dictionary of Philosophy: Kleines Philosophisches Woerterbuch. 12th ed. Max Muller & Alois Halder. 343p. (GER.). 1985. pap. 19.95 (0-8288-2279-4, M7506) Fr & Eur.

Small Dictionary of Textile Terms. June W. Barnett. 73p. (Orig.). 1987. pap. 4.00 (0-9624960-0-6) J W Barnett.

Small Diesel Engine Service Manual. Intertec Publishing Staff. (Orig.). 1991. 24.95 (0-87288-448-1, SDS-3) Intertec Pub.

Small Differences: Irish Catholics & Irish Protestants, 1815-1922, An International Perspective. Donald H. Akenson. (Studies in the History of Religion). 256p. (C). 1988. 55.00 (0-7735-0636-5, Pub. by McGill CN) U of Toronto Pr.

Small Differences: Irish Catholics & Irish Protestants, 1815-1922, An International Perspective. Donald H. Akenson. (McGill-Queen's Studies in the History of Religion). 256p. (C). 1991. reprint ed. pap. text ed. 22.95 (0-7735-0858-9, Pub. by McGill CN) U of Toronto Pr.

Small Differences That Matter: Labor Markets & Income Maintenance in Canada & the United States. Ed. by David Card & Richard B. Freeman. LC 93-10513. (National Bureau of Economic Research Comparative Labor Markets Ser.: Vol. 1). (Illus.). 288p. 1993. Alk. paper. 29.95 (0-226-09283-6) U Ch Pr.

Small Districts, Big Problems: Making School Everbody's House. Richard A. Schmuck & Patricia A. Schmuck. LC 92-12420. 200p. 1992. 47.95 (0-8039-6025-5); pap. 21.95 (0-8039-6026-3) Corwin Pr.

Small Dogs. Armin Kriechbaumer. (Pet Owner's Manuals Ser.). 96p. (Orig.). 1994. pap. 6.95 (0-8120-1951-2) Barron.

Small Dogs Bark Cartoons. Doug Knott. (Illus.). 1991. pap. 11.00 (0-9627387-0-0) Seven Wolves.

***Small Dolls.** Benzell et al. (Illus.). 47p. 1996. pap. 12.95 (0-614-23847-1, N4444) Hobby Hse.

Small Dreams Have No Magic: The Key to Success. Roger F. Johnsrud. 88p. 1994. pap. 6.95 (0-8059-3676-9) Dorrance.

Small Ecological Garden. Sue Strickland. (Illus.). 48p. 1996. pap. 15.95 (0-85532-773-1, 27731, Pub. by Search Pr UK) A Schwartz & Co.

Small Ecstasies. Moya Costello. 1994. pap. 14.95 (0-7022-2600-9, Pub. by Univ Queensland Pr AT) Intl Spec Bk.

Small Eichborn: Der Kleine Eichborn. 2nd ed. Reinhart V. Eichborn. 978p. (ENG & GER.). 1981. 250.00 (0-8288-0093-6, M15058) Fr & Eur.

Small Electric Motors. 2nd ed. Rex Miller. 436p. 1993. 30.00 (0-02-584975-1) Macmillan.

Small Electrical Appliances in Europe 1980-1990. Euromonitor Staff. 150p. 1986. 825.00 (0-86338-208-8, Pub. by Euromonitor Pubns UK) Gale.

Small Elegies. David Mason. 1990. 2.50 (0-941127-09-5) Dacotah Terr Pr.

Small Embroidery Gifts. Ondori Publishing Company Staff. (Illus.). 124p. (Orig.). 1989. pap. 13.95 (0-87040-819-4) Japan Pubns USA.

Small Employer Health Insurance Reform: Minnesota Department of Commerce Study. (Illus.). 62p. (Orig.). (C). 1995. pap. text ed. 20.00 (0-7881-2610-5) DIANE Pub.

Small Encyclopedia of Mathematics: Kleine Enzyklopaedie der Mathematik. 2nd ed. W. Gellert. 820p. (GER.). 1980. 75.00 (0-8288-1898-3, M7498) Fr & Eur.

Small Endearments: Nineteenth-Century Quilts for Children & Dolls. rev. ed. Sandi Fox. LC 94-11327. (Illus.). 209p. 1994. pap. 24.95 (1-55853-313-3) Rutledge Hill Pr.

Small Endearments: Nineteenth-Century Quilts for Children & Dolls. 2nd rev. ed. Sandi Fox. LC 94-11327. (Illus.). 224p. 1994. 32.95 (1-55853-312-5) Rutledge Hill Pr.

Small Engine Explained. Bruce Hunter. LC 77-731128. (Orig.). 1977. student ed. 7.00 (0-8064-0163-X, 450); audio, vhs 499.00 (0-8064-0164-8) Bergwall.

Small Engine Mechanics. 2nd ed. William H. Crouse & Donald L. Anglin. LC 79-4658. (Illus.). 1979. text ed. 27.95 (0-07-014795-7) McGraw.

Small Engine Mechanics. 3rd ed. William H. Crouse & Donald L. Anglin. 304p. 1986. pap. text ed. 27.95 (0-07-014803-1) McGraw.

Small Engine Repair. Jack Rudman. (Occupational Competency Examination Ser.: OCE-32). 1994. pap. 27.95 (0-8373-5732-2) Nat Learn.

Small Engine Repair for Pathfinders: A Basic Youth Enrichment Skill Honor Packet. L. S. Gattis, III. (Illus.). 20p. (Orig.). (J). (gr. 5 up). 1987. teacher ed., pap. 5.00 (0-936241-19-5) Cheetah Pub.

Small Engine Repair 0-20hp, 1982-92. Chilton Automotives Editorial Staff. 728p. 1994. pap. 19.95 (0-8019-8325-8) Chilton.

Small Engine Repair 13-20hp, 1989-92. 400p. 1993. pap. 19.95 (0-8019-8324-X) Chilton.

Small Engine Repair 2-12hp, 1989-92. 576p. 1993. pap. 19.95 (0-8019-8323-1) Chilton.

Small Engine Technology. William A. Schuster. LC 92-35113. 348p. 1993. pap. 24.50 (0-8273-4928-9) Delmar.

An Asterisk (*) at the beginning of an entry indicates that the title is appearing in BIP for the first time.

Small Engine Technology. William A. Schuster. LC 92-35113. 348p. 1993. text ed. 31.00 (*0-8273-4927-0*) Delmar.
Small Engine Technology. 2nd ed. Schuster. (Automotive Technology Ser.). 1998. teacher ed. 16.50 (*0-8273-7700-2*) Delmar.
Small Engine Technology. 2nd ed. Shuster. (Automotive Technology Ser.). 1998. text ed. 33.95 (*0-8273-7699-5*) Delmar.
Small Engine Technology: Instructor's Guide. William A. Schuster. 34p. 1994. pap. 13.50 (*0-8273-4929-7*) Delmar.
Small Engine Technology Conference Proceedings. 468p. 1989. 17.00 (*0-89883-487-2*, P224) Soc Auto Engineers.
Small Engines. (Home Repair & Improvement Ser.). (Illus.). 136p. 1982. 14.60 (*0-8094-3510-1*); lib. bdg. 20.60 (*0-8094-3511-X*) Time-Life.
Small Engines. 19p. (YA). (gr. 10 up). student ed. 7.00 (*0-8064-0386-1*, A15) Bergwall.
***Small Engines.** R. Bruce Radcliff & R. T. Miller. LC 96-45663. 1997. 44.96 (*0-8269-0008-9*) Am Technical.
***Small Engines.** Stagner. LC 97-5240. 1997. pap. text ed. 46.67 (*0-13-454539-7*) P-H.
Small Enginge Technology. 2nd ed. Schuster. (Automotive Technology Ser.). 1998. 33.95 (*0-8273-7778-9*) Delmar.
Small Enterprise & Oligopoly. Harold G. Vatter. Ed. by Stuart Bruchey & Vincent P. Carosso. LC 78-18152. (Small Business Enterprise in America Ser.). 1979. reprint ed. lib. bdg. 15.95 (*0-405-11508-3*) Ayer.
Small Enterprise Development. Kevin Caley et al. 208p. 1993. 85.00 (*1-85396-215-5*, Pub. by Paul Chapman UK) Taylor & Francis.
Small Enterprise Development: Policies & Programmes. 2nd rev. ed. Ed. by Philip A. Neck & Robert E. Nelson. (Management Development Ser.: No. 14). xiii, 282p. (Orig.). 1987. pap. 31.50 (*92-2-105699-6*) Intl Labour Office.
Small Enterprises Adjusting to Liberalization in Five African Contries. Ronald L. Parker et al. LC 95-191. (Discussion Papers: Africa Technical Department Ser.: Vol. 271). 106p. 1995. 8.95 (*0-8213-3154-X*, 13154) World Bank.
Small Enterprises & Changing Policies: Structural Adjustment, Financial Policy & Assistance Programmes in Africa. Ed. by A. H. Helmsing & Th. Kolstee. 284p. (Orig.). 1993. pap. 32.50 (*1-85339-185-9*, Pub. by Intermed Tech UK) Women Ink.
Small Entrepreneurial Firm. Gavin C. Reid & Lowell R. Jacobsen. (David Hume Papers). 100p. 1988. pap. text ed. 19.95 (*0-08-036577-9*, Pub. by Aberdeen U Pr) Macmillan.
Small Exotic Mammals: A to Z. 2nd rev. ed. Pat Storer. 344p. (Orig.). 1995. pap. 33.00 (*1-888144-05-X*, R Zu Two U) Country Storer Ent.
Small Faces. Gary Soto. 144p. (Orig.). (J). (gr. 4-7). 1993. mass mkt. 3.50 (*0-440-21553-6*) Dell.
Small Family Business. Alan Ayckbourn. 90p. (Orig.). 1987. pap. 8.95 (*0-571-14970-7*) Faber & Faber.
Small Farm Grain Storage, Vol. I. Carl Lindblad & Laurel Druben. (Illus.). 204p. 1976. 12.50 (*0-86619-052-X*) Vols Tech Asst.
Small Farm Grain Storage, Vol. II. Carl Lindblad & Laurel Druben. (Illus.). 170p. 1976. 12.50 (*0-86619-053-8*) Vols Tech Asst.
Small Farm Grain Storage, Vol. III. Carl Lindblad & Laurel Druben. (Illus.). 148p. 1976. 12.50 (*0-86619-054-6*) Vols Tech Asst.
Small Farm Grain Storage: Almaceniamento del Grano. Carl Lindblad & Laurel Druben. (Illus.). 331p. (SPA.). 1976. Spanish. 19.95 (*0-86619-072-4*) Vols Tech Asst.
Small Farm Handbook. Ed. by Shirley Humphrey & Eric C. Mussen. 190p. 1995. pap. 25.00 (*1-879906-23-6*, SFP001) ANR Pubns CA.
Small Farm Mechanization for Developing Countries. Peter Crossley & John Kilgour. LC 83-5935. (Illus.). 269p. reprint ed. pap. 76.70 (*0-685-66682-4*, 2036034) Bks Demand.
Small Farmer Credit: Cultural & Social Factors Affecting Small Farmer Participation in Formal Credit Programs & the Political Economy of Distributing Agricultural Credit & Benefits. Cynthia Gillette et al. (Occasional Paper Ser.: No. 3). 57p. (Orig.). (C). 1973. pap. text ed. 4.85 (*0-86731-016-2*) Cornell CIS RDC.
***Small Farmer Development in Asia & the Pacific: Some Lessons for Strategy Formulation & Planning.** 105p. 1990. 14.00 (*92-5-102895-8*, Pub. by FAO IT) Bernan Associates.
Small Farmer Development Programme in Thailand - Post Project Study. Food & Agriculture Organization Staff. (People's Participation Ser.: No. 4). 64p. 1994. pap. 10.00 (*92-5-103467-2*, F34672, Pub. by FAO IT) Bernan Associates.
Small Farmers & Institutional Credit India. S. Gunasekaran. 1985. 16.00 (*0-317-40616-7*, Pub. by Ashish II) S Asia.
Small Farmers, Big Business: Contract Farming & Rural Development. David Glover & Ken Kusterer. LC 90-8112. (International Political Economy Ser.). 195p. 1990. text ed. 49.95 (*0-312-04631-6*) St Martin.
Small Farms Appropriate Technology: Research, Production, Hardware, & Animal Traction. Oleen Hess. 175p. 1985. 20.00 (*0-318-18269-6*) Brandon-Lane-Pr.
Small Favor. Elizabeth August. (Romance Ser.: No. 809). 1991. pap. 2.50 (*0-373-08809-4*) Silhouette.
Small Favors. James R. Mayes. LC 94-19573. 303p. 1994. 19.95 (*1-55583-258-X*) Alyson Pubns.
Small Field. Huw Jones. 106p. (C). 1985. pap. 20.00 (*0-86383-194-X*, Pub. by Gomer Pr UK) St Mut.
Small Finds from Tell Basta in the Collection of F. G. Hilton Price. Charles C. Van Siclen, III. 140p. 1985. pap. text ed. 25.00 (*0-933175-03-5*) Van Siclen Bks.
Small Firm Finance: An Entrepreneurial Analysis. Jerome S. Osteryoung et al. 416p. (C). 1997. pap. text ed. write for info. (*0-03-098220-0*) Dryden Pr.
Small Firm Formation & Regional Economic Development. Ed. by Michael W. Danson. LC 95-34494. (Small Business Ser.). 272p. (C). 1996. text ed. 69.95 (*0-415-12970-2*) Routledge.
Small Firm Management: Ownership, Finance & Performance. Kevin Keasey & Robert Watson. 256p. 1993. pap. 33.95 (*0-631-17981-X*) Blackwell Pubs.
***Small Firms: Contributions to Economic Regeneration.** Ed. by Robert Blackburn & Peter Jennings. 208p. 1996. pap. 74.00 (*1-85396-339-9*, Pub. by Paul Chapman UK) Taylor & Francis.
Small Firms: Partnerships for Growth. Ed. by Francis Chittenden et al. 240p. 1995. text ed. 75.00 (*1-85396-288-0*, Pub. by Paul Chapman UK) Taylor & Francis.
Small Firms & Economic Growth. Ed. by Zoltan J. Acs. LC 95-36670. (International Library of Critical Writings in Economics Ser.: Vol. 61). 1376p. 1996. 420.00 (*1-85898-116-6*) E Elgar.
Small Firms & Entrepreneurship: An East-West Perspective. Ed. by Zoltan J. Acs & David B. Audretsch. 232p. (C). 1993. text ed. 54.95 (*0-521-43115-8*) Cambridge U Pr.
Small Firms & Industrial Development in Italy. Edward Goodman et al. 228p. 1989. 72.50 (*0-415-03563-5*, A3503) Routledge.
Small Firms & Local Economic Developments: Entrepreneurship in Southern Europe & Turkey. Gul B. Ozcan. 240p. 1995. 59.95 (*1-85972-117-6*, Pub. by Avebury Pub UK) Ashgate Pub Co.
***Small Firms As Foreign Investors: Case Studies from Transition Economies.** OECD Staff. 228p. (Orig.). 1996. pap. 38.00 (*92-64-14812-4*, 14-96-05-1) OECD.
Small Firms in Global Competition. Ed. by Tamir Agmon & Richard Drobnick. LC 92-40074. 160p. 1994. 39.95 (*0-19-507825-X*) OUP.
Small Firms in Regional Economic Development: Britain, Ireland & the United States. Ed. by David J. Storey. 256p. 1985. text ed. 59.95 (*0-521-30198-X*) Cambridge U Pr.
***Small Firms in the Japanese Economy.** D. H. Whittaker. 248p. (C). 1997. text ed. 49.95 (*0-521-58152-4*) Cambridge U Pr.
Small Firms Informally Financed: Studies from Bangladesh. Ed. by Reazul Islam et al. LC 94-32838. (World Bank Discussion Papers: 253). 1994. 13.95 (*0-8213-2969-3*, 12969) World Bank.
Small-Fly Adventures in the West: Angling for Larger Trout. Neale Streeks. LC 96-3315. (Illus.). 226p. (Orig.). 1996. pap. 22.50 (*0-87108-870-3*) Pruett.
Small Folk Quilters. Ingrid Rogler. Ed. by Pamela M. Watts. LC 89-60974. (Illus.). 66p. (Orig.). (J). (gr. 3-10). 1989. pap. 9.95 (*0-9622565-0-1*) Chitra Pubns.
Small Format Television Production see Video Field Production & Editing
Small Fractional Parts of Polynomials. Wolfgang M. Schmidt. LC 77-8028. (CBMS Regional Conference Series in Mathematics: No. 32). 41p. 1977. 21.00 (*0-8218-1682-9*, CBMS/32) Am Math.
Small Fragment Set Manual: Technique Recommended by the ASIF Group. 2nd ed. U. Heim & K. M. Pfeiffer. Tr. by R. L. Batten. (Illus.). 400p. 1982. 100.00 (*0-387-11143-3*) Spr-Verlag.
Small French & English Lexicon of Animal Physiology & Nutrition: Petit Lexique de Physiologie et de Nutrition Animales. Alice Daifuku. 52p. (ENG & FRE.). 1986. pap. 27.95 (*0-8288-0749-3*, F25160) Fr & Eur.
Small Fruit Crop Management. Gene J. Galletta. 1994. pap. text ed. 105.00 (*0-13-185455-0*) P-H.
***Small Fruits in the Home Garden.** Ed. by Robert E. Gough & E. Barclay Poling. 295p. 1996. pap. 19.95 (*1-56023-086-X*) Haworth Pr.
***Small Fruits in the Home Garden.** Ed. by Robert E. Gough & E. Barclay Poling. LC 94-41094. 272p. 1996. 39.95 (*1-56022-054-6*) Haworth Pr.
***Small Fruits in the Home Garden.** Ed. by Robert E. Gough & E. Barclay Poling. LC 94-41094. 272p. 1996. pap. 19.95 (*1-56022-057-0*) Haworth Pr.
Small Fry, Big Spender. Toerpe. 1996. 22.50 (*0-226-80672-3*) U Ch Pr.
Small-Game & Varmint Hunter's Bible. Lea Lawrence. LC 94-1637. 192p. 1994. pap. 12.00 (*0-385-46836-9*) Doubleday.
Small Garden. Thomas Cooper. 1996. 35.00 (*0-8050-4916-9*) H Holt & Co.
Small Garden. Roger Grounds. (Illus.). 64p. 1994. 7.98 (*1-55859-661-5*) Abbeville Pr.
***Small Garden.** Lance Hattatt. 1996. 9.98 (*0-7651-9697-2*) Smithmark.
Small Garden: A Practical Guide to Planning & Planting. Julie Toll. LC 95-18313. (Wayside Gardens Collection). (Illus.). 128p. 1995. 19.95 (*0-8069-3833-1*) Sterling.
Small Garden Book. John Brookes. (Illus.). 223p. 1991. 15.99 (*0-517-05607-0*) Random Hse Value.
Small Garden Book. Peter McHoy. 160p. 1995. 15.98 (*0-8317-7995-0*) Smithmark.
Small Gardens. (Essential Tips Ser.). 1996. pap. write for info. (*0-614-97864-2*) DK Pub Inc.
***Small Gardens: Inspired Plantings for Diminutive Spaces.** Rebecca G. Davis. LC 96-35753. 1997. 25.00 (*1-56799-429-6*) M Friedman Pub Grp Inc.
Small Gardens & Backyards. David Stevens. (Illus.). 80p. 1996. pap. 9.95 (*1-85029-065-2*, Pub. by Conrad Octopus) Trafalgar.
Small Gardens with Style. Jill Billington. (Illus.). 144p. (Orig.) 1996. pap. 16.95 (*0-7063-7475-4*, Pub. by Ward Lock UK) Sterling.
Small Gas Engine Repair. 2nd ed. Paul Dempsey. 1993. text ed. 24.95 (*0-07-016341-3*); pap. text ed. 12.95 (*0-07-016342-1*) McGraw.
Small Gas Engines. rev. ed. Alfred C. Roth. (Illus.). 352p. (YA). 1992. text ed. 31.96 (*0-87006-919-5*) Goodheart.
***Small Gas Engines: Fundamentals, Service, Troubleshooting, Repair & Applications.** Alfred C. Roth. LC 97-8119. 512p. 1998. 35.96 (*1-56637-379-4*) Goodheart.
Small Gas Engines: How to Repair & Maintain Them. Paul Weissler. (Orig.). 1991. 15.95 (*1-55654-020-5*) Times Mir Mag Bk Div.
Small Gas Engines: Maintenance, Troubleshooting & Repair. George R. Drake. 500p. 1981. teacher ed. write for info. (*0-8359-7015-9*, Reston) P-H.
Small Gasoline Engines. 3rd ed. Rex Miller. 681p. 1993. 30.00 (*0-02-584991-3*) Macmillan.
Small Gasoline Engines. 4th ed. George Stephenson. (Illus.). 288p. (C). 1984. teacher ed. 8.95 (*0-8273-2243-7*) Delmar.
Small Gasoline Engines. 4th ed. George Stephenson. (Illus.). 288p. (C). 1984. text ed. 28.95 (*0-8273-2242-9*) Delmar.
Small Gasoline Engines, Operation & Maintenance. rev. ed. Harry J. Hoerner & W. Forrest Bear. (Illus.). 176p. 1995. pap. 12.95 (*0-913163-26-0*, 473) Hobar Pubns.
Small Gasoline Engines Student's Workbook. 2nd ed. K. L. MacDonald. 1973. pap. write for info. (*0-672-97632-3*) Macmillan.
Small Gathering of Bones. Patricia Powell. (Caribbean Writers Ser.). 144p. 1994. pap. 9.95 (*0-435-98936-7*, 98936) Heinemann.
Small Georgian Houses & Their Details 1750-1820. Stanley C. Ramsey & J. D. Harvey. (Illus.). 256p. 1977. pap. 61.95 (*0-85139-248-2*) Buttrwrth-Heinemann.
Small Georgian Houses in England & Virginia: Origins & Development Through the 1750s. Daniel Reiff. LC 83-40521. (Illus.). 352p. 1986. 85.00 (*0-87413-254-1*) U Delaware Pr.
Small Glimmer of Light: Reflections on the Book of Genesis. Steven Saltzman. LC 96-1750. 1996. write for info. (*0-88125-549-1*) Ktav.
Small Gods: A Novel of Discworld. Terry Pratchett. 352p. 1994. mass mkt. 4.99 (*0-06-109217-7*, Harp PBks) HarpC.
Small Golden Key to the Treasure of the Various Essential Necessities of General & Extraordinary Buddhist Dharma. Thinley Norbu. Tr. by Lisa Anderson. LC 92-56459. 120p. 1993. reprint ed. pap. 11.00 (*0-87773-856-4*) Shambhala Pubns.
Small Golden Shrine from the Tomb of Tutankhamun. Eaton-Krauss. 1986. 50.00 (*0-900416-43-2*, Pub. by Aris & Phillips UK) David Brown.
Small Green Snake. Libba M. Gray. LC 93-49396. (Illus.). 32p. (J). (ps-1). 1994. 14.95 (*0-531-06844-7*); lib. bdg. 15.99 (*0-531-08694-1*) Orchard Bks Watts.
***Small Green Snake.** Libba M. Gray. LC 93-49396. (Illus.). 32p. (J). (ps-1). 1997. pap. 5.95 (*0-531-07090-5*) Orchard Bks Watts.
Small Group Book: The Practical Guide for Nurturing Christians & Building Churches. Dale E. Galloway & Kathi Mills. LC 95-2892. 160p. (Orig.). (YA). (gr. 10). 1995. pap. 8.99 (*0-8007-5570-7*) Revell.
***Small Group Communication.** Thomas E. Harris & John Sherblom. 385p. (C). 1998. pap. text ed. write for info. (*0-614-24122-7*) Gorsuch Scarisbrick.
Small Group Communication. Arthur D. Jensen & Joseph C. Chilberg. 430p. (C). 1991. pap. 37.95 (*0-534-13140-9*) Wadsworth Pub.
Small Group Communication: A Reader. 6th ed. Robert Cathcart & Larry A. Samovar. 608p. (C). 1991. per. write for info. (*0-697-08644-5*) Brown & Benchmark.
Small Group Communication: A Reader. 7th ed. Robert Cathcart. 432p. (C). 1995. per. write for info. (*0-697-20437-5*) Brown & Benchmark.
Small Group Communication in Organizations. 2nd ed. H. Lloyd Goodall. 368p. (C). 1989. per. write for info. (*0-697-04891-8*) Brown & Benchmark.
Small Group Decision Making: Communication & the Group Process. 4th ed. Donald G. Ellis & B. Aubrey Fisher. LC 93-27420. 1993. text ed. write for info. (*0-07-021212-0*) McGraw.
***Small Group Discussion.** 2nd ed. Pavitt & Curtis. 1990. pap. text ed. 42.00 (*0-13-776659-9*) P-H.
Small Group Discussion: A Theoretical Approach. 2nd ed. Charles Pavitt. Ed. by Ellen Curtis. LC 93-21097. 450p. (Orig.). 1993. pap. text ed. 35.95 (*0-89787-350-5*) Gorsuch Scarisbrick.
Small Group Fitness Kit. Thom Corrigan. 1996. pap. 7.00 (*0-89109-939-5*) NavPress.
Small Group Idea Book: Resources to Enrich Community, Worship & Prayer, Nurture & Outreach. Ed. by Cindy Bunch. LC 95-26744. 120p. (Orig.). 1996. pap. 7.99 (*0-8308-1167-2*, 1167) InterVarsity.
Small Group Leaders Handbook: The Next Generation. 2nd ed. Ann Beyerlein et al. LC 95-43636. 192p. 1995. pap. 10.99 (*0-8308-1139-7*, 1139) InterVarsity.
Small Group Leaders Training Course: Everything You Need to Organize & Launch a Successful Small Group Ministry in Your Church, Participant's Manual. Judy Hamlin. LC 90-61779. 208p. (Orig.). 1990. student ed., pap. 10.00 (*0-89109-304-4*) NavPress.
Small Group Leaders Training Course: Everything You Need to Organize & Launch a Successful Small Group Ministry in Your Church, Training Manual. Judy Hamlin. LC 90-61778. 208p. (Orig.). 1990. teacher ed., pap. 29.00 (*0-89109-308-7*) NavPress.
Small Group Learning in the Classroom. JoAnne Reid et al. LC 90-35956. 95p. 1990. pap. text ed. 16.50 (*0-435-08542-5*, 08542) Heinemann.
Small Group Member's Commentary. Lawrence O. Richards. 656p. 1992. pap. 18.99 (*0-89693-055-6*, 6-1055, Victor Bks) Chariot Victor.
Small Group Ministry with Youth. David R. Veerman. LC 92-10254. (Orig.). 1992. pap. 10.99 (*0-89693-919-7*, 6-1919, Victor Bks) Chariot Victor.
Small Group Problem Solving: An Aid to Organizational Effectiveness. L. Nathanson et al. 1981. pap. write for info. (*0-201-05203-2*) Addison-Wesley.
Small Group Research: A Handbook. A. Paul Hare et al. 592p. (C). 1994. pap. 49.50 (*0-89391-952-7*) Ablex Pub.
Small Group Research: A Handbook. Ed. by A. Paul Hare et al. 592p. (C). 1994. text ed. 125.00 (*0-89391-692-7*) Ablex Pub.
Small Group Resources Vol. 2: High Participation & Experiential Discipleship for High School Students. Student Impact Team Staff & Bo Boshers. (Student Impact Ser.). (Illus.). 112p. (Orig.). 1997. pap. 14.99 (*0-310-20126-8*) Zondervan.
Small Group Resources Vol. 3: High Participation & Experiential Discipleship for High School Students. Student Impact Team Staff & Bo Boshers. (Student Impact Ser.). (Illus.). 112p. (Orig.). 1997. pap. 14.99 (*0-310-20127-6*) Zondervan.
Small Group Resources Vol. 4: High Participation & Experiential Discipleship for High School Students. Student Impact Team Staff & Bo Boshers. (Student Impact Ser.). (Illus.). 112p. (Orig.). 1997. pap. 14.99 (*0-310-20128-4*) Zondervan.
Small Group Starter Guide on Community. Thom Corrigan. 1996. pap. 6.00 (*0-89109-938-7*) NavPress.
***Small Group Starter Kit.** (Nineteen Ninety-Seven 50-Day Spiritual Adventure Ser.). 1996. 39.00 (*1-57849-013-8*) Chapel of Air.
Small Group Starter Kit. Jeffrey Arnold. (LifeGuide Bible Studies). 64p. (Orig.). 1995. wbk. ed., pap. 4.99 (*0-8308-1073-0*, 1073) InterVarsity.
Small Group Trainer's Survival Guide. Birge D. Reichard & Christiane M. Siewers. Ed. by Paul Rodenhauser. 168p. (C). 1992. text ed. 42.00 (*0-8039-4740-2*); pap. text ed. 19.50 (*0-8039-4757-7*) Sage.
Small Groups: An Introduction. A. Paul Hare et al. LC 96-15329. 280p. 1996. text ed. 45.00 (*0-275-94896-X*, Praeger Pubs) Greenwood.
Small Groups & Social Interaction, Vol. 1. Ed. by Herbert H. Blumberg et al. LC 82-8558. 477p. reprint ed. pap. 124.10 (*0-8357-7541-0*, 2036264) Bks Demand.
Small Groups & Social Interaction, Vol. 2. Ed. by Herbert H. Blumberg et al. LC 82-8558. 609p. reprint ed. pap. 173.60 (*0-8357-7542-9*) Bks Demand.
Small Groups in Counseling and Therapy: Process & Leadership. 2nd ed. Barbara W. Posthuma. 1995. pap. text ed. 41.50 (*0-205-16169-3*) Allyn.
Small Groups in the Church: A Handbook for Creating Community. Thomas G. Kirkpatrick. (Church Leader's Core Library). 1995. pap. 15.75 (*1-56699-151-X*, AL161) Alban Inst.
Small Groups in Writing Workshops: Invitations to A Writer's Life. Robert E. Brooke et al. LC 94-16963. 206p. 1994. 19.95 (*0-8141-4483-7*) NCTE.
Small Handbook for the Heart: The Adoption Poems. Jim Sorcic. 100p. 1995. pap. 20.00 (*1-880723-06-9*) Morgan Pr WI.
Small Hands, Big Ideas. Tony Hart. 1988. text ed. 19.95 (*1-85219-007-8*, Pub. by Bishopsgte Pr UK) Intl Spec Bk.
Small Helpings: A Complete Guide to Feeding Babies, Toddlers & Schoolchildren. Annabel Karmel. 1996. 14.95 (*1-56426-077-1*) Cole Group.
Small High Efficiency Antennas: The Loop. 2nd ed. Ted Hart. Ed. by Jack L. Stone. (Illus.). 1989. pap. 19.95 (*0-685-28859-5*) Franklin-Belle.
Small High School. John Rufi. LC 70-177214. (Columbia University. Teachers College. Contributions to Education Ser.: No. 236). reprint ed. 37.50 (*0-404-55236-6*) AMS Pr.
Small High Technology Firms in Developing Countries: The Case of Biotechnology. Regina M. Galhardi. 251p. 1994. 59.95 (*1-85628-658-4*, Pub. by Avebury Pub UK) Ashgate Pub Co.
***Small Home Plans.** 7th unabridged ed. LC 96-77245. (Illus.). 256p. 1996. pap. 6.95 (*0-938708-70-8*) L F Garlinghouse Co.
Small Home Repairs Made Easy. Robert L. Berko. write for info. (*0-318-61890-7*) Consumer Ed Res.
Small, Honest Hollows. Galen Malicoat. 32p. (Orig.). 1992. pap. 10.00 (*0-911623-11-6*) I Klang.
Small Hotels & Restaurants in Northern France & Belgium. Marc Millon & Kim Millon. (Illus.). 192p. 1995. pap. 19.95 (*1-85793-148-3*, Pub. by Pavilion UK) Trafalgar.
Small Hours. George S. Kaufman. 1951. pap. 13.00 (*0-8222-1045-2*) Dramatists Play.
***Small Hours of the Morning.** Margaret Yorke. 1975. 6.95 (*0-8027-5331-0*) Walker & Co.
Small Hours of the Night: Selected Poems of Roque Dalton. Rogue Dalton. Ed. by Hardie St. Martin. Tr. by Jonathan Cohen et al. 228p. 1996. pap. 14.95 (*1-880684-35-7*) Curbstone.
***Small House at Allington.** Anthony Trollope. 1997. 22.50 (*0-375-40067-2*, Everymans Lib) Knopf.
Small House at Allington. Anthony Trollope. (Barsetshire Chronicles Ser.: No. 5). (Illus.). 752p. 1996. pap. 8.95 (*0-14-043332-5*, Penguin Classics) Viking Penguin.
Small House at Allington. Anthony Trollope. Ed. & Intro. by Julian Thompson. 752p. 1991. pap. 7.95 (*0-14-043325-2*, Penguin Classics) Viking Penguin.
Small House at Allington. Anthony Trollope. Ed. by James R. Kincaid. (World's Classics Ser.). 688p. 1981. reprint ed. pap. 6.95 (*0-19-281552-0*) OUP.
Small House at Allington see Barsetshire Novels

S

S

Small House at Allington (1864) Anthony Trollope. 624p. 1993. 8.95 (*0-14-043816-5*, Penguin Classics) Viking Penguin.

***Small House Designs.** Ed. by Lawrence Von Bamford & Kenneth R. Tremblay. LC 96-47252. 1997. 27.95 (*0-88266-854-4*); pap. 19.95 (*0-88266-966-4*) Storey Comm Inc.

Small House for the Next Century. 2nd ed. D. Dickinson. 1995. text ed. 39.95 (*0-07-016828-8*) McGraw.

Small Houses. (Great Houses Ser.). (Illus.). 160p. 1995. pap. 17.95 (*1-56158-106-2*) Taunton.

***Small Hydraulic Structures, Vol. 1.** 422p. 1982. 41.00 (*92-5-100160-X*, F996, Pub. by FAO IT) Bernan Associates.

***Small Hydraulic Structures, Vol. 2.** 308p. 1982. 31.00 (*92-5-100161-8*, F996, Pub. by FAO IT) Bernan Associates.

Small Hydro-Power Fluid Machinery: Presented at the Winter Annual Meeting of the American Society of Mechanical Engineers, Chicago, Illinois, November 16-21, 1980. American Society of Mechanical Engineers Staff. Ed. by D. R. Webb & C. N. Papadakis. LC 80-68343. 116p. reprint ed. pap. 33.10 (*0-8357-6996-8*, 2039049) Bks Demand.

***Small in the Saddle.** Louise Marley. 50p. (Orig.). 1996. mass mkt. 2.99 (*0-9654318-1-9*) Atomic Wstrn.

Small-Incision Cataract Surgery: Foldable Lenses, One Stitch Surgery, Sutureless Surgery, Asigmatic Keratotomy. Ed. by James P. Gills & Donald Sanders. LC 90-53312. 271p. 1990. 95.00 (*1-55642-184-2*) SLACK Inc.

Small Indulgences. Susan Rieke. LC 89-17928. (Target Poetry Ser.). 64p. (Orig.). 1990. pap. 6.50 (*0-933532-72-5*) BkMk.

Small Industries in Development: India's Experience, & Lessons for Other Developing Countries. Daniel S. Sisken. Ed. by Victoria Cuffel. (MacArthur Scholar Ser.: No. 3). 56p. (Orig.). 1991. pap. 1.85 (*1-881157-01-6*) In Ctr Global.

Small Industry: Challenges & Perspectives. Nirmal K. Gupta. 224p. 1992. 88.00 (*81-7041-611-6*, Pub. by Scientific Pubs II) St Mut.

Small Industry Bulletin for Asia & the Pacific, No. 22. 106p. 1988. 13.50 (*92-1-119460-1*, 88.II.F.4) UN.

Small Industry Bulletin for Asia & the Pacific, No. 23. 13.50 (*92-1-119537-3*, 89.II.F.9) UN.

Small Industry Bulletin for Asia & the Pacific, No. 24. 104p. 1990. 12.00 (*92-1-119565-9*) UN.

Small Industry Bulletin for Asia & the Pacific, No. 28. 69p. 1994. 12.00 (*92-1-119632-9*) UN.

Small Industry Bulletin for Asia & the Pacific, No. 29. 180p. 1995. 15.00 (*92-1-119679-5*) UN.

Small Intarsia: Woodworking Projects You Can Make. Judy G. Roberts & Jerry Booher. 72p. 1996. pap. 14.95 (*1-56523-062-0*) Fox Chapel Pub.

***Small Intestine.** Lawrence R. Schiller. LC 97-5655. (Gastroenterology & Hepatology Ser.). 1997. write for info. (*0-443-07865-3*) Churchill.

Small Inventions That Make a Big Difference. Ed. by Donald J. Crump. LC 83-23770. (Books for World Explorers Series 5: No. 2). 104p. (J). (gr. 3-8). 1984. 8.95 (*0-87044-498-0*); lib. bdg. 12.50 (*0-87044-503-0*) Natl Geog.

Small Investor: A Beginner's Guide to Stocks, Bonds, & Mutual Funds. Jim Gard. 160p. (Orig.). 1996. pap. 11.95 (*0-89815-825-7*) Ten Speed Pr.

Small Investor's Guide to Making Money in Canadian Real Estate. Gary Weiss. 224p. 1990. pap. 16.95 (*0-7737-5345-1*) Genl Dist Srvs.

Small Investor's Guide to Making Money in Canadian Real Estate. Gary Weiss. 192p. 1992. pap. 16.95 (*0-7737-5553-5*) Genl Dist Srvs.

Small Iowa Plates. Illus. by David J. Donovan, II. 9p. (Orig.). 1989. 100.00 (*1-877886-00-9*) dG Printers.

Small Is Beautiful: Economics As If People Mattered. E. F. Schumacher. 352p. 1989. reprint ed. pap. 13.00 (*0-06-091630-3*, PL) HarpC.

Small is Beautiful: Economics As If People Mattered. E. F. Schumacher. 347p. 1991. reprint ed. lib. bdg. 35.00 (*0-8095-9115-4*) Borgo Pr.

Small Is Not Always Beautiful: The Story of Equatorial Guinea. Max Liniger-Goumaz. 200p. (C). 1989. lib. bdg. 50.00 (*0-389-20861-2*, N8419) B&N Imports.

Small Is Powerful: The Future As if People Really Mattered. John Papworth. LC 95-22714. (Praeger Studies on the 21st Century). 248p. 1995. text ed. 59.95 (*0-275-95424-2*, Praeger Pubs); pap. text ed. 18.95 (*0-275-95425-0*, Praeger Pubs) Greenwood.

Small Island, Big Politics: The Tonbs & Uba Musa in Iranian Foreign Policy. Hooshang Amirahmadi. 262p. 1996. text ed. 45.00 (*0-312-15910-2*) St Martin.

Small Island Economics: Structure & Performance in the English-Speaking Caribbean Since 1970. DeLisle Worrell. LC 87-12495. 303p. 1987. text ed. 65.00 (*0-275-92795-4*, C2795, Praeger Pubs) Greenwood.

***Small Islands: Marine Science & Sustainable Development.** George A. Maul & American Geophysical Union Staff. LC 96-29237. (Coastal & Estaurine Studies). 467p. 1996. 65.00 (*0-87590-265-0*) Am Geophysical.

Small Islands, Large Questions: Society, Culture & Resistance in the Post-Emancipation Caribbean. Ed. by Karen Fog-Olwig. LC 95-14437. (Studies in Slave & Post-Slave Societies & Cultures). 200p. 1995. 39.50 (*0-7146-4576-1*, Pub. by F Cass Pubs UK); pap. 19.50 (*0-7146-4225-8*, Pub. by F Cass Pubs UK) Intl Spec Bk.

Small Italian - Polish, Polish - Italian Dictionary. G. Tomat. 1991. 59.95 (*0-8288-8507-9*) Fr & Eur.

Small Japanese-German Form Lexicon: Kleines Formlexikon Japanisch-Deutsch. Florian Coulmas et al. 216p. (GER & JPN.). 1983. 59.95 (*0-8288-1017-6*, M15780) Fr & Eur.

Small Kid Time Hawaii. Ed. by Eric Chock. (Bamboo Ridge Ser.: No. 12). 204p. (J). (gr. k-12). 1981. pap. 8.00 (*0-910043-03-5*) Bamboo Ridge Pr.

Small Killing. Alan Moore. (Illus.). 96p. (Orig.). 1993. pap. 11.95 (*1-878574-45-0*) Dark Horse Comics.

Small Korean-German Dictionary: Koreanisch-Deutsches Kleinwoerterbuch. K. Kuh. 289p. (GER & KOR.). 1985. 65.00 (*0-8288-0473-7*, M15802) Fr & Eur.

Small Latin. Beth Halifax. (C). 1982. pap. text ed. 39.00 (*0-685-44232-2*, Pub. by Old Vicarage UK) St Mut.

Small Lexicon of Micro-Accounting Terms, English, German & Serbocroatian: Mali Leksikon Mikroracunarskih Izraza. Dusan Petkovic. 202p. (ENG, GER & SER.). 1987. 35.00 (*0-8288-0273-4*, F44460) Fr & Eur.

Small Libraries: A Handbook for Successful Management. Sally G. Reed. LC 90-50813. 156p. 1991. lib. bdg. 28.50 (*0-89950-596-1*) McFarland & Co.

Small Libraries: Organization & Operation. 2nd ed. Donald J. Sager. LC 96-25850. (Highsmith Press Handbook Ser.). 1996. 13.00 (*0-917846-79-6*) Highsmith Pr.

Small Libraries: Organization & Operation, a Reference List. 1992. lib. bdg. 79.95 (*0-8490-8771-6*) Gordon Pr.

Small Library Cataloging. 2nd ed. Herbert H. Hoffman. LC 86-15504. (Illus.). 226p. 1986. 23.50 (*0-8108-1910-4*) Scarecrow.

Small Local Governments & Information Management. Donald F. Morris. 17p. (Orig.). 1984. pap. 2.00 (*1-55719-078-X*) U NE CPAR.

Small Log Sawmills: Profitable Product Selection, Process Design & Operation. Ed. by Ed M. Williston. LC 80-84893. (Forest Industries Book). (Illus.). 368p. 1981. pap. 53.00 (*0-87930-091-4*) Miller Freeman.

Small Lullabies. Michel & Company Staff. (Illus.). 80p. 1994. 4.95 (*0-8362-3082-5*) Andrews & McMeel.

Small Magellanic Cloud. Paul W. Hodge & Frances W. Wright. LC 76-49159. (Illus.). 80p. 1978. boxed 65.00 (*0-295-95387-X*) U of Wash Pr.

Small Mammals. Anita Ganeri. LC 92-32706. (Nature Detective Ser.). 32p. (J). 1993. lib. bdg. 18.60 (*0-531-14249-3*) Watts.

Small Mammals Are Where You Find Them. Helen D. Tee-Van. (Illus.). (J). (gr. 3-7). 1967. lib. bdg. 5.99 (*0-394-91643-3*) Knopf Bks Yng Read.

Small Mammals (Excluding Bats) Ed. by Adrian Barnett. (C). 1992. 21.00 (*0-907649-51-3*, Pub. by Expedit Advisory Centre UK) St Mut.

Small Mammals of the Yellowstone Ecosystem. Donald Streubel. 168p. 1989. 22.50 (*0-911797-60-2*); pap. 12.50 (*0-911797-59-9*) R Rinehart.

***Small Mammals of West Africa.** Booth. Date not set. pap. text ed. write for info. (*0-582-60848-1*, Pub. by Longman UK) Longman.

Small Manufacturing Enterprises: A Comparative Study of India & Other Economies. Ian M. Little et al. (World Bank Research Publications Ser.). 376p. 1989. reprint ed. pap. 18.95 (*0-19-520779-3*) OUP.

Small Manufacturing Reprints: Tools for the Small Manufacturer. American Production & Inventory Control Society Staff. 110p. 1992. 16.50 (*1-55822-089-5*) Am Prod & Inventory.

Small Manufacturing SIG Annotated Bibliography. Ed. by Martha L. Howard. 62p. 1990. 10.00 (*1-55822-025-9*) Am Prod & Inventory.

Small Matter of a Horse: The Life of "Nongoloza" Mathebula, 1867-1948. Charles Van Onselen. 72p. 1984. pap. text ed. 8.95 (*0-86975-239-1*, Pub. by Ravan Pr ZA) Ohio U Pr.

Small Matter of Programming: Perspectives on End User Computing. Bonnie A. Nardi. (Illus.). 257p. 1993. pap. 30.00 (*0-262-14053-5*) MIT Pr.

Small Media Big Revolution: Communication, Culture & the Iranian Revolution. Annabelle Sreberny-Mohammadi & Ali Mohammadi. LC 93-46191. (C). 1994. pap. text ed. 17.95 (*0-8166-2217-5*) U of Minn Pr.

Small Medical Encyclopedia (Petite Encyclopedie Medicale) 17th ed. J. Hamburger. 1600p. (FRE.). 1987. 195.00 (*0-7859-4745-0*, M15436) Fr & Eur.

Small Membership Church: Scenarios for Tomorrow. Lyle E. Schaller. (Ministry for the Third Millennium Ser.). 144p. (Orig.). 1995. pap. 12.95 (*0-687-38718-3*) Abingdon.

Small Mercies. Elizabeth Weber. (Poetry Chapbook Ser.). 57p. (Orig.). 1983. write for info. (*0-937669-09-1*) Owl Creek Pr.

Small Mercies. limited ed. Elizabeth Weber. (Poetry Chapbook Ser.). 57p. (Orig.). 1983. Hardbound, sign & Ltd. number ed. of 50 copies 15.00. 5.00 (*0-937669-10-5*) Owl Creek Pr.

Small Michaelis English-Portuguese, Portuguese-English Dictionary: Pequeno Dicionario Michaelis: Ingles-Portugues, Portugues-Ingles. Michaelis. 642p. (ENG & POR.). 1980. pap. 22.95 (*0-8288-0496-6*, M9282) Fr & Eur.

Small Michell (Banki) Turbine: A Construction Manual. 58p. 1985. per. 11.50 (*0-86619-244-1*, 11045-BK) Vols Tech Asst.

Small Millets. K. Riley et al. (C). 1989. 50.00 (*81-204-0434-3*) S Asia.

***Small Miracle.** Peter Collington. LC 96-53916. (J). 1997. lib. bdg. 19.99 (*0-679-98725-8*, Vin) Random.

***Small Miracle.** Peter Collington. LC 96-53916. (J). 1997. 18.00 (*0-679-88725-3*) Random Bks Yng Read.

Small Miracle. Paul Gallico. 1976. 16.95 (*0-8488-0494-5*) Amereon Ltd.

Small Miracle: South Africa's Negotiated Settlement. Ed. by Steven Friedman & Doreen Atkinson. (South African Studies: No. 7). 360p. (Orig.). (C). 1995. pap. text ed. 24.95 (*0-86975-453-X*, Pub. by Ravan Pr ZA) Ohio U Pr.

***Small Miracles: Extraordinary Coincidences from Everyday Life.** Yitta H. Mandelbaum & Judith Leventhal. LC 96-43249. 1997. pap. 7.95 (*1-55850-646-2*) Adams Media.

Small Miracles: The Extraordinary Stories of Ordinary People. Tom Sheridan. 192p. 1996. 14.99 (*0-310-20793-2*) Zondervan.

***Small Miracles: The Precious Gift of Children.** Illus. by Sandra Kuck. 32p. (Orig.). 1997. 12.99 (*1-56507-555-2*) Harvest Hse.

***Small Motor Play.** Mary A. Hodge. (101 Tips for Toddler Teachers Ser.). (Illus.). 24p. (Orig.). 1997. pap. 3.95 (*1-57029-156-X*, 4017, Totline Bks) Warren Pub Hse.

Small Motors & Transformers: Design & Construction. Ed. by Edward Molloy. LC 54-32875. 176p. reprint ed. pap. 50.20 (*0-317-10064-5*, 2051335) Bks Demand.

Small Mouth Bass. Al Lindner. 1994. pap. text ed. 11.95 (*0-929384-50-4*) In-Fisherman.

Small Nation's Contribution to the World: Essays on Anglo-Irish Literature & Language. Ed. by Donald E. Morse et al. (Irish Literary Studies Ser.). 250p. (C). 1994. lib. bdg. 59.00 (*0-86140-375-4*, Pub. by C Smythe Ltd UK) B&N Imports.

Small Nations, Giant Firms. Louis W. Goodman. LC 87-42. 181p. (C). 1987. 37.50 (*0-8419-0996-2*); pap. 19.75 (*0-8419-1112-6*) Holmes & Meier.

Small Nations in Times of Crisis & Confrontation. Yohanan Cohen. Tr. by Naftali Greenwood from HEB. LC 88-24871. 399p. 1989. text ed. 74.50 (*0-7914-0018-2*); pap. text ed. 24.95 (*0-7914-0019-0*) State U NY Pr.

***Small Notebook.** Boston Mills Press Staff. (Day in the Country Ser.). 1997. pap. text ed. 14.50 (*1-55046-223-7*, Pub. by Boston Mills Pr CN) Genl Dist Srvs.

Small Obligation & Other Stories of Hilo. Susan Nunes. LC 82-72555. (Bamboo Ridge Ser.: No. 16). 88p. (Orig.). 1982. pap. 8.00 (*0-910043-00-0*) Bamboo Ridge Pr.

***Small Office/Home Office E-Mail Directory.** Ed. by Ron Perkins. pap. 8.95 (*0-9627185-5-6*) Newport Media.

Small One. Alex Walsh. LC 95-67083. (Illus.). 32p. (J). (ps-1). 1995. 12.95 (*0-7868-3087-5*) Disney Pr.

***Small One.** Alex Walsh. 1997. bds. 4.95 (*0-7868-3139-1*) Disney Pr.

Small Paintings That Sell. Lola Ades. (How to Draw & Paint Ser.). (Illus.). 32p. (Orig.). 1989. pap. 6.95 (*0-929261-46-1*, HT201) W Foster Pub.

Small Particles & Inorganic Clusters. Ed. by C. Chapon et al. (Illus.). xii, 612p. 1989. 159.95 (*0-387-51390-6*) Spr-Verlag.

***Small Particles & Inorganic Clusters: Proceedings of the Eighth International Symposium on Small Particles & Inorganic Clusters, ISSPIC 8, Copenhagen, Denmark, 1-6, July, 1996.** Hans H. Andersen. LC 97-22211. 1997. write for info. (*3-540-63157-7*) Springer Pub.

Small Particles & Inorganic Clusters, Pts. 1-2: Proceedings of the International Meeting, ISSPIC 5, 5th, University of Konstanz, Germany, September 10-14, 1990. Ed. by O. Echt & E. Recknagel. xxii, 928p. 1991. 350.95 (*0-387-53304-4*) Spr-Verlag.

Small Parties in Western Europe: Comparative & National Perspectives. Ed. by Ferdinand Muller-Rommel & Geoffrey Pridham. (Illus.). 240p. 1991. 55.00 (*0-8039-8261-5*); pap. 19.95 (*0-8039-8262-3*) Sage.

Small Party. large type ed. Lillian Beckwith. 1991. 25.99 (*0-7089-2274-0*) Ulverscroft.

Small Patchwork Projects. Barbara Brondolo. (Illus.). 64p. (Orig.). 1981. pap. 4.95 (*0-486-24030-4*) Dover.

Small Patriot. Betty McPherson. (Pocket Tales Ser.: Bk. 2). (Illus.). 32p. (J). (ps-1). 1987. 6.00 (*0-918823-01-3*) Boyce-Pubns.

Small Peptides: Chemistry, Biology, & Clinical Studies. A. S. Dutta. LC 93-11629. (Pharmacochemistry Library: Vol. 19). 632p. 1993. 307.00 (*0-444-88655-9*) Elsevier.

***Small Percentage: A Dark Tale of Alien Invasion.** James H. Cline. 544p. 1997. 21.95 (*0-9653210-0-2*) Timberwolf Pr.

***Small Pet Handbook.** David Taylor. LC 96-29778. 1997. 11.95 (*0-7641-5033-2*) Barron.

Small Piece of Paradise. large type ed. Geoffrey Morgan. (Dales Large Print Ser.). 1996. pap. 17.99 (*1-85389-634-9*, Dales) Ulverscroft.

Small Pig. Arnold Lobel. LC 69-10213. (Harper I Can Read Bk.). (Illus.). 64p. (J). (gr. k-3). 1969. lib. bdg. 14.89 (*0-06-023932-8*) HarpC Child Bks.

Small Pig. Arnold Lobel. LC 69-10213. (Trophy I Can Read Bk.). (Illus.). 64p. (J). (gr. k-3). 1988. pap. 3.50 (*0-06-444120-2*, Trophy) HarpC Child Bks.

Small Place. Jamaica Kincaid. LC 88-34575. 96p. 1989. pap. 9.95 (*0-452-26235-6*, Plume) NAL-Dutton.

Small Place in Galilee: Religion & Social Conflict in an Israeli Village. Zvi Sobel. (New Perspectives: Jewish Life & Thought Ser.). 274p. 1994. 39.95 (*0-8419-1342-0*) Holmes & Meier.

***Small Place in Italy.** Eric Newby. 225p. (Orig.). 1995. pap. 15.95 (*0-330-33818-8*, Pub. by Picador UK) Trans-Atl Phila.

Small Plasma Physics Experiments: Proceedings of Symposium on Small Scale Lab Plasma Number Exp. Spring College. Ed. by S. Lee & Paulo H. Sakanaka. 396p. 1988. text ed. 89.00 (*9971-5-0768-4*) World Scientific Pub.

Small Plasma Physics Experiments II: Proceedings of the Symposium on Small Scale Laboratory Plasma Physics Experiments. Ed. by S. Lee & Paulo H. Sakanaka. 384p. (C). 1990. text ed. 101.00 (*981-02-0285-7*) World Scientific Pub.

Small Plate of Olives & Other Mediterranean First Courses. Joanne Weir. LC 93-30139. 1994. 27.50 (*0-517-58962-1*, Crown) Crown Pub Group.

Small Plays for Special Days. Sue Alexander. LC 76-28424. (Illus.). 64p. (J). (ps-1). 1988. pap. 6.95 (*0-89919-798-1*, Clarion Bks) HM.

Small Pleasure. C. B. Christiansen. 128p. (YA). (gr. 7 up). 1989. pap. 2.95 (*0-380-70699-7*, Flare) Avon.

Small Pleasure. C. B. Christiansen. LC 87-19313. 144p. (YA). (gr. 7 up). 1988. lib. bdg. 13.95 (*0-689-31369-1*, Atheneum Bks Young) S&S Childrens.

Small Poems Again. Valerie Worth. LC 85-47513. (Illus.). 48p. (J). (gr. 3 up). 1986. 11.00 (*0-374-37074-5*) FS&G.

Small Potatoes. Ralph G. Martell. 194p. 19.95 (*0-9634828-1-5*) Pan Pr NY.

Small Power Loads. M. Hejab. (C). 1992. 110.00 (*0-86022-340-X*, Pub. by Build Servs Info Assn UK) St Mut.

Small Powers at Sea: Scandinavia & the New International Marine Order. Finn Laursen. LC 93-10952. 336p. (C). 1993. lib. bdg. 125.00 (*0-7923-2341-6*) Kluwer Ac.

Small Press: An Annotated Guide. Loss P. Glazier. LC 92-15482. 138p. 1992. text ed. 55.00 (*0-313-28310-9*, GZP, Greenwood Pr) Greenwood.

Small Press Center Directory. annot. ed. Ed. by Karin Taylor. (Illus.). 360p. (Orig.). 1992. pap. 19.95 (*0-9622769-4-4*) Small Pr Ctr.

Small Press Publishers Workbook. Ed. by Bibliotheca Press Research Division Staff. 70p. 1991. reprint ed. student ed., ring bd. 29.95 (*0-939476-77-0*) Prosperity & Profits.

Small Press Publishing Techniques: Desktop (Word) Publishing. George A. Swiftwater. LC 89-91063. (Illus.). 160p. (Orig.). 1989. pap. 15.95 (*0-922958-11-4*) H W Parker.

Small Press Record of Bks-94-5. Fulton. 1994. 55.00 (*0-916685-46-2*) Dustbooks.

Small Privatization: The Transformation of Retail Trade & Consumer Services in the Czech Republic, Hungary, & Poland. John S. Earle et al. (Central European University Press Bk.: Vol. 3). (Illus.). 256p. 1994. 59.00 (*1-85866-006-8*); pap. 14.95 (*1-85866-007-6*) OUP.

Small Problem. A. R. Plumb. LC 94-72228. (Further Adventures of Aladdin Ser.: Bk. 3). (Illus.). 64p. (J). (gr. 1-4). 1995. pap. 3.50 (*0-7868-4023-4*) Disney Pr.

Small Programs for Small Machines: Computers & Education. Jurg Nievergelt et al. LC 84-28338. 240p. 1985. pap. write for info. (*0-201-11129-2*) Addison-Wesley.

Small Project Automation for Libraries & Information Centers. Jane Mandelbaum. (Supplement to Small Computers in Libraries Ser.: No. 28). 350p. 1992. lib. bdg. 42.50 (*0-88736-731-3*) Mecklermedia.

Small Projects for Small Hands: Arts & Crafts for Beginning Skills Programs. Lynn Brisson. (Illus.). 80p. (Orig.). 1991. pap. text ed. 9.95 (*0-86530-187-5*, IP 193-4) Incentive Pubns.

Small Property Versus Big Government: Social Origins of the Property Tax Revolt. Clarence Y. Lo. 1990. 40.00 (*0-520-05971-9*) U CA Pr.

Small Property vs. Big Government: Expanded & Updated Edition. Clarence Y.H. Lo. 306p. 1995. pap. 14.00 (*0-520-20028-4*) U CA Pr.

Small Public Library: Design Guide, Site Selection, & Design Case Study. Ann B. Hill. (Publications in Architecture & Urban Planning: No. R80-3). (Illus.). vi, 120p. 1987. reprint ed. 12.00 (*0-938744-13-5*) U of Wis Ctr Arch-Urban.

Small Publisher. Audrey Ward & Philip Ward. (Illus.). 1979. 35.00 (*0-900891-59-9*) Oleander Pr.

Small Publishers Handbook of Creative Finance: How to Finance Your Publishing Company. Gary L. Clark. 200p. 1996. ring bd. 24.95 (*1-887585-59-1*) James & Gordon.

Small Quantity Generator Handbook: The Smarter Neighbor Quest. Robin Brack-Schorner. (Illus.). (Orig.). (C). 1989. pap. write for info. (*0-318-65928-X*) Amer Hazmat.

Small Quilting Projects. Linda Seward. (Illus.). 144p. (C). 1989. reprint ed. lib. bdg. 35.00 (*0-8095-7532-9*) Borgo Pr.

Small Quilts, Vol. 1. Vanessa-Ann Collection Staff. 1989. 19.95 (*0-8487-0735-4*) Oxmoor Hse.

Small Railroads You Can Build. 2nd ed. Model Railroader Magazine Staff. (Illus.). 64p. 1996. per., pap. 10.95 (*0-89024-225-9*, 12146) Kalmbach.

Small Rain: A Novel. Madeleine L'Engle. LC 84-47839. 371p. (J). (gr. 7 up). 1984. 14.95 (*0-374-26637-9*) FS&G.

Small Rain: A Novel. Madeleine L'Engle. LC 84-47839. 371p. (J). (gr. 7 up). 1985. pap. 13.00 (*0-374-51912-9*) FS&G.

Small Rain: Eight Poets from San Diego. Ed. by Kate Watson. LC 96-60298. 206p. (Orig.). 1996. pap. write for info. (*0-9651267-0-6*) D G Wills.

Small Reef Aquarium Basics. rev. ed. Albert J. Thiel. (Illus.). 276p. reprint ed. pap. write for info. (*0-945777-10-8*) Aardvark Pr.

Small Reef Aquarium Basics: The Optimum Aquarium for the Reef Hobbyist. Albert J. Thiel. (Illus.). 176p. (Orig.). 1989. pap. text ed. 14.95 (*0-945777-02-7*) Aardvark Pr.

Small Ring Compounds in Organic Synthesis, Vol. IV. (Topics in Current Chemistry Ser.: Vol. 155). (Illus.). viii, 160p. 1990. 119.95 (*0-387-52422-3*) Spr-Verlag.

An Asterisk (*) at the beginning of an entry indicates that the title is appearing in BIP for the first time.

Small Ring Compounds in Organic Synthesis, I. Ed. by Armin De Meijere. (Topics in Current Chemistry Ser.: Vol. 133). (Illus.). 170p. 1986. 93.95 (*0-387-16307-7*) Spr-Verlag.

Small Ring Compounds in Organic Synthesis II. Ed. by Armin De Meijere. (Topics in Current Chemistry Ser.: Vol. 135). (Illus.). 160p. 1986. 108.95 (*0-387-16662-9*) Spr-Verlag.

Small Ring Compounds in Organic Synthesis III. A. De Meijere. (Topics in Current Chemistry Ser.: Vol. 144). (Illus.). 210p. 1988. 141.95 (*0-387-18368-X*) Spr-Verlag.

Small Ring Compounds in Organic Synthesis V. Ed. by A. de Meijere. (Topics in Current Chemistry Ser.: Vol. 178). (Illus.). x, 182p. 1996. 139.00 (*3-540-60495-2*) Spr-Verlag.

Small, Robust & Updated Computer Program for Lowry Type Models. A. Rodriguez-Bachiller. (C). 1979. 29.00 (*0-685-30301-2*, Pub. by Oxford Polytechnic UK) St Mut.

***Small Ruminant Production & the Small Ruminant Genetic Resource in Tropical Africa.** 250p. 1991. 30.00 (*92-5-102998-9*, F0299, Pub. by FAO IT) Bernan Associates.

Small-Rural Community Colleges: Report of the Commission on Small and-or Rural Community Colleges. American Association of Community & Junior Colleges Staff. LC 88-152947. (Illus.). 70p. reprint ed. pap. 25.00 (*0-7837-2481-0*, 2042637) Bks Demand.

Small Rural Parish. Bernard Quinn. LC 79-56508. (Orig.). 1980. pap. 3.50 (*0-914422-11-1*) Glenmary Res Ctr.

Small Rural Primary School: A Matter of Quality. Adrian Bell & Alan Sigsworth. 225p. 1987. 65.00 (*1-85000-155-3*, Falmer Pr); pap. 33.00 (*1-85000-156-1*, Falmer Pr) Taylor & Francis.

Small Sacrifice. Ellen Hart. LC 94-9481. 300p. 1994. 20.95 (*1-878067-55-9*) Seal Pr WA.

Small Sacrifice. Ellen Hart. 1996. mass mkt. 5.99 (*0-345-39113-6*) Ballantine.

Small Sacrifices. Ann Rule. 496p. 1988. pap. 5.99 (*0-451-16660-4*, Sig); pap. 5.99 (*0-451-18779-2*, Sig) NAL-Dutton.

***Small Sacrifices: Religious Change & Cultural Identity among the Ngaju of Indonesia.** Anne Schiller. (Illus.). 192p. 1997. 45.00 (*0-19-509557-X*); pap. 19.95 (*0-19-509558-8*) OUP.

Small Salvations. Patricia Dienstfrey. LC 87-14028. (Illus.). 36p. (Orig.). 1987. pap. 8.00 (*0-932716-22-9*) Kelsey St Pr.

Small Sample Asymptotics. Christopher A. Field & Elvezio Ronchetti. LC 90-84215. (IMS Lecture Notes - Monograph Ser.: Vol. 13). vi, 151p. 1990. pap. 25.00 (*0-940600-18-8*) Inst Math.

Small-Sample Reactivity Measurements in Nuclear Reactors. Wesley K. Foell. LC 74-144051. (ANS Monographs). 272p. 1972. 23.50 (*0-89448-003-0*, 300005) Am Nuclear Soc.

Small Sawmill Handbook: Doing It Right & Making Money. Joseph Denig. (Illus.). 192p. (Orig.). 1993. pap. 37.00 (*0-87930-286-0*) Miller Freeman.

Small Scale Bibliographic Databases. Peter J. Judge & Brenda Gerrie. 1986. text ed. 60.00 (*0-12-391970-3*) Acad Pr.

Small-Scale Biomass Gasifiers for Heat & Power: A Global Review, Vol. 296. Hubert E. Stassen. LC 95-35168. (World Bank Technical Paper Ser.). 80p. 1995. text ed. 7.95 (*0-8213-3371-2*, 13371) World Bank.

Small Scale Crayfish Farming for Food & Profit. rev. ed. Don R. Wilson. (Illus.). 50p. (Orig.). 1992. lib. bdg. 8.95 (*0-9631526-1-0*) Atlas Pubns.

Small-Scale Fisheries of San Miguel Bay, Philippines: Biology & Stock Assessment. Ed. by Daniel Pauly & Antonio N. Mines. (ICLARM Technical Reports: No. 7). (Illus.). 124p. (Orig.). 1983. pap. 16.00 (*0-89955-394-X*, Pub. by ICLARM PH) Intl Spec Bk.

Small-Scale Fisheries of San Miguel Bay, Philippines: Economics of Production & Marketing. Ed. by Ian R. Smith & Antonio N. Mines. (ICLARM Technical Reports: No. 8). (Illus.). 143p. (Orig.). 1982. pap. text ed. 25.00 (*0-89955-395-8*, Pub. by ICLARM PH) Intl Spec Bk.

Small-Scale Fisheries of San Miguel Bay, Philippines: Occupational & Geographical Mobility. Conner Bailey. (ICLARM Technical Reports: No. 10). (Illus.). 57p. (Orig.). 1983. pap. 11.50 (*0-89955-396-6*, Pub. by ICLARM PH) Intl Spec Bk.

***Small-Scale Fisheries of San Miguel Bay, Philippines: Options for Management & Research.** Daniel Pauly et al. (ICLARM Technical Reports: No. 11). 80p. 1983. per. write for info. (*971-10-2208-7*, Pub. by ICLARM PH) Intl Spec Bk.

Small-Scale Fisheries of San Miguel Bay, Philippines: Social Aspects of Production & Marketing. Ed. by Conner Bailey. (ICLARM Technical Reports: No. 9). (Illus.). 57p. (Orig.). 1982. pap. text ed. 14.00 (*0-89955-397-4*, Pub. by ICLARM PH) Intl Spec Bk.

Small-Scale Fishery Development: Sociocultural Perspectives. Ed. by Richard B. Pollnac. (Illus.). 158p. 1991. pap. 11.00 (*1-882027-04-3*) URI ICMRD.

Small Scale Gas Producer - Engine Systems. Albrecht Kaupp & John R. Goss. (GATE Ser.). (Illus.). 284p. 1984. pap. 40.00 (*3-528-02001-6*, Pub. by Vieweg & Sohn GW) Informatica.

Small-Scale Gold Mining: A Manual for Suriname. E. H. Dahlberg. 54p. (Orig.). 1984. pap. 13.50 (*1-85339-049-6*, Pub. by Intermed Tech UK) Women Ink.

Small-Scale Gold Mining: Processing Techniques in Developing Countries. Michael Priester & Thomas Hentschel. Ed. by Deutsches Zentrum fur Entwicklungstechnologien GATE In: Deutsche Gesellschaft fur Technische Zusammenarbeit (GTZ) GmbH Staff. (Illus.). 96p. (C). 1992. pap. text ed. 14.00 (*3-528-02066-0*) Informatica.

***Small-Scale Hatchery for Common Carp.** B. A. Costa-Pierce et al. (ICLARM Education Ser.: No. 8). (Illus.). 42p. 1989. write for info. (*971-10-2273-7*, Pub. by ICLARM PH) Intl Spec Bk.

Small-Scale Horn Processing. International Labour Office Staff. (Illus.). 90p. (Orig.). 1988. pap. 12.00 (*92-2-105358-X*, ILO358X) Intl Labour Office.

Small-Scale Hydroelectric Power Development: Potential Sources of Federal Financial Support for Low-Income Communities. Vanessa C. Cones & Gregory P. Malinowski. (Illus.). 267p. 1980. ring bd. 25.00 (*0-936130-00-8*) Intl Sci Tech.

Small-Scale Industries in Kenya, Set. (Toward a Better World Ser.). (YA). (gr. 9-12). 1981. student ed., teacher ed., text ed. 60.00 incl. flmstrp (*0-8213-0072-5*, 10072) World Bank.

Small-Scale Industry in the Soviet Union. Adam Kaufman. (Occasional Papers: No. 80). 111p. 1962. reprint ed. 28.90 (*0-87014-394-8*); reprint ed. mic. film 20.00 (*0-685-61333-X*) Natl Bur Econ Res.

Small Scale Irrigation: A Manual of Low-Cost Water Technology. Peter Stern. 152p. (Orig.). (C). 1988. 160.00 (*0-685-54218-1*, Pub. by Scientific UK) St Mut.

Small Scale Maize Milling. 2nd ed. (Technical Memorandum, Technology Ser.: No. 7). xi, 143p. 1992. pap. 15.75 (*92-2-103640-5*) Intl Labour Office.

Small-Scale Manufacture of Burned Building Brick. D. W. Thomas. 22p. 1990. 6.25 (*0-86619-019-8*); French, 20p. 6.25 (*0-86619-020-1*); Portuguese, 12p. 6.25 (*0-86619-022-8*) Vols Tech Asst.

Small-Scale Manufacture of Footwear. (Technical Memorandum, Technology Ser.: No. 2). xvi, 207p. 1989. pap. 22.50 (*92-2-103079-2*) Intl Labour Office.

Small-Scale Master Builder: Selected Readings on Professional Practice as an Architectural Designer-Builder-Investor at the Personal Scale. Donald P. Grant. LC 83-60946. 198p. (Orig.). 1986. pap. 19.00 (*0-911215-04-2*) Small Master.

Small-Scale Milling: A Guide for Development Workers. L. O. Jonsson et al. 166p. (Orig.). 1994. pap. 28.50 (*1-85339-219-7*, Pub. by Intermed Tech UK) Women Ink.

Small-Scale Mining: A Global Overview. Ajoy K. Ghose. (Illus.). 380p. (C). 1994. text ed. 75.00 (*90-5410-231-4*, Pub. by A A Balkema NE) Ashgate Pub Co.

Small-Scale Model Railroads. S. Blackwell Duncan. (Illus.). 160p. 1990. pap. 12.95 (*0-8306-3518-1*, 3518) McGraw-Hill Prof.

Small-Scale Municipal Solid Waste Energy Recovery Systems. Gershman et al. (Illus.). 250p. 1986. text ed. 62.95 (*0-442-22778-7*) Chapman & Hall.

Small-Scale Oil Extraction from Groundnuts & Copra. (Technical Memorandum, Technology Ser.: No. 5). vii, 111p. 1992. pap. 15.75 (*92-2-103503-4*) Intl Labour Office.

Small Scale Oil Extraction from Groundnuts & Copra. (C). 1991. pap. 15.00 (*81-204-0549-8*, Pub. by Oxford IBH II) S Asia.

Small-Scale Pig Raising. Dirk Van Loon. LC 78-12938. (Illus.). 272p. 1978. pap. 14.95 (*0-88266-136-1*, Garden Way Pub) Storey Comm Inc.

Small-Scale Poultry Keeping: A Guide to Free-Range Poultry Production. Ray Feltwell. (Illus.). 176p. (Orig.). 1992. pap. 10.95 (*0-571-16699-7*) Faber & Faber.

Small-Scale Process for Manufacturing Woodwool-Cement Slabs in Developing Countries. Ed. by A. J. Hawkes & D. R. Cox. 1993. pap. 35.00 (*0-85954-330-7*, Pub. by Nat Res Inst UK) St Mut.

Small-Scale Processing of Beef. Intro. by A. S. Bhalla. (Technical Memorandum, Technology Ser.: No. 10). vi, 121p. (Orig.). 1985. pap. 18.00 (*92-2-105050-5*) Intl Labour Office.

Small-Scale Processing of Fish. (Technical Memorandum, Technology Ser.: No. 3). xi, 118p. 1989. pap. 15.75 (*92-2-103205-1*) Intl Labour Office.

Small Scale Processing of Oilfruits & Oilseeds. Hans-Jurgen Wiemer et al. Ed. by Deutsches Zentrum fur Entwicklungs-technologien-GATE. (GATE Ser.). (Illus.). 100p. 1989. pap. 17.50 (*3-528-02046-6*, Pub. by Vieweg & Sohn GW) Informatica.

Small-Scale Production: Strategies for Industrial Restructuring. Ed. by F. Uribe-Echevarria et al. 256p. (Orig.). 1991. text ed. 56.95 (*1-85339-107-7*, Pub. by Intermed Tech UK) Women Ink.

Small Scale Production of Lime for Building. John Spiropoulos. (GATE Ser.). (Illus.). 80p. 1985. pap. 15.00 (*3-528-02016-4*, Pub. by Vieweg & Sohn GW) Informatica.

Small Scale Property in a Socialist Economy. Katalin Falus-Szikra. 214p. (C). 1989. pap. 42.00 (*963-05-5303-1*, Pub. by Akad Kiado HU) St Mut.

Small Scale Quiltmaking: Precision, Proportion, & Detail. Sally Collins. Ed. by Joyce E. Lytle & Diana Roberts. LC 95-46104. (Illus.). 112p. (Orig.). 1996. 24.95 (*1-57120-009-6*) C & T Pub.

Small Scale Refining of Jewelers Wastes. Roland Loewen. 1995. 34.95 (*0-931913-19-5*) Met-Chem Rsch.

Small-Scale Sacred Concertato in the Early Seventeenth Century, 2 vols., 1. Anne Kirwan-Mott. LC 81-13026. (Studies in British Musicology). 417p. reprint ed. pap. 118.90 (*0-8357-1263-X*, 2070260) Bks Demand.

Small-Scale Sacred Concertato in the Early Seventeenth Century, 2 vols., 2. Anne Kirwan-Mott. LC 81-13026. (Studies in British Musicology). 271p. reprint ed. pap. 77.30 (*0-8357-1264-8*, 2070260) Bks Demand.

***Small-Scale Sheep-Keeping.** Jeremy Hunt. (Orig.). 1997. pap. 12.95 (*0-571-17893-6*) Faber & Faber.

Small Scale Structures: Proceedings of Symposium A on Microstructuring & Symposium B on Microsystems. Ed. by H. Schmidt et al. (European Materials Research Society Symposia Proceedings Ser.: Vol. 52). 556p. 1996. text ed. 293.25 (*0-444-82312-3*, North Holland) Elsevier.

Small-Scale Structures in Three-Dimensional Hydrodynamic & Magnetohydrodynamic Turbulence: Proceedings of a Workshop, Held at Nice, France 10-13 January 1995. Ed. by Maurice Meneguzzi et al. LC 95-44629. (Lecture Notes in Physics Ser.: Vol. 462). 420p. 1995. 101.95 (*3-540-60486-3*) Spr-Verlag.

Small Scale Synthesis. Murray Zanger & James R. McKee. 576p. (C). 1994. spiral bd. write for info. (*0-697-20957-1*) Wm C Brown Pubs.

Small-Scale Turbulence & Mixing in the Ocean: Proceeding of the 19th Liege Colloquium on Ocean Hydrodynamics, Liege, Belgium, 4-9 May, 1987. Ed. by J. C. Nihoul & B. M. Jamart. (Oceanography Ser.: 46). 542p. 1988. 219.75 (*0-444-42987-5*) Elsevier.

Small Scale Turkey Growing for the Beginner. David Podoll. (Shorey Lost Arts Ser.). 26p. 1975. reprint ed. pap. 2.95 (*0-8466-6044-X*, U44) Shorey.

Small Scale Urban Enterprises in Tanzania: Results from a 1991 Survey. Mboya S. Bagachwa et al. (Working Papers: No. 44). 48p. 1993. pap. 7.00 (*1-56401-144-5*) Cornell Food.

Small-Scale Vegetable Oil Extraction. S. W. Head et al. 107p. 1995. pap. 38.00 (*0-85954-387-0*, Pub. by Nat Res Inst UK) St Mut.

***Small Schools & Democratic Practice.** Clive Harber. 1996. pap. 14.95 (*0-9518022-9-1*, Pub. by Drake Intl Serv UK) Intl Spec Bk.

Small Sea Creatures. Jason Cooper. LC 92-16073. (Sea Discovery Library). (J). 1992. 12.67 (*0-86593-230-1*); 9.50 (*0-685-59715-6*) Rourke Corp.

Small Secretary's Lexicon: Kleines Sekretaerinnenlexikon. Christa Bruhn-Jade. 517p. (GER.). 1986. 75.00 (*0-8288-1276-4*, M7086) Fr & Eur.

Small Shadow on the Earth. S. Woods. 19.95 (*0-06-017962-7*, HarpT) HarpC.

***Small Shadow on the Earth.** Stuart Woods. mass mkt. write for info. (*0-06-109088-3*, Harp PBks) HarpC.

Small Ship, Big Sea. Robin Adams. LC 94-90555. (Illus.). 264p. (Orig.). 1995. pap. 14.95 (*1-56002-520-4*, Univ Edtns) Aegina Pr.

***Small Ships: A Book of Study Plans of Tugs, Freighters, Ferries, Excursion Boats, Trawler Yachts, Houseboats & Fishing Vessels.** 3rd ed. Benford Design Group Staff. 1996. pap. text ed. 25.00 (*0-07-006001-0*) McGraw.

Small Signal Analysis: By Computer, By Inspection. Joel H. Levitt. LC 82-83970. (Illus.). 184p. (C). 1983. pap. text ed. 11.25 (*0-9609892-0-X*) Haywood Pr.

Small Silent Ordeal. Larry Kimmel. LC 92-91108. 104p. (Orig.). 1994. pap. 9.00 (*1-56002-273-6*, Univ Edtns) Aegina Pr.

Small Silver Tableware. Stephen Helliwell. (Christie's Collectibles Ser.). 1996. 12.95 (*0-614-96827-5*) Bulfinch Pr.

Small-Size Economics: Lessons for the Primary Grades K-3. Dorothy J. Skeel. (Illus.). 28p. (Orig.). 1988. pap. 6.95 (*0-673-18768-3*, GoodYrBooks) Addson-Wesley Educ.

Small Sound of the Trumpet: Women in Medieval Life. Margaret W. Labarge. LC 86-47509. (Illus.). 288p. 1988. reprint ed. pap. 18.00 (*0-8070-5627-8*) Beacon Pr.

Small Sounds in the Night. Eric Sevareid. 1994. lib. bdg. 21.95 (*1-56849-469-6*) Buccaneer Bks.

Small Sounds in the Night: A Collection of Capsule Commentaries on the American Scene. Eric Sevareid. LC 76-56347. 305p. 1977. reprint ed. text ed. 38.50 (*0-8371-9421-0*, SESM, Greenwood Pr) Greenwood.

Small Space - Big Bucks: Converting Home Space into Profits. Jack P. Jones. 1994. pap. text ed. 16.95 (*0-07-033022-0*) McGraw.

Small Space - Big Bucks: Converting Home Space into Profits. Jack P. Jones. LC 93-2169. 1993. text ed. 26.95 (*0-8306-3960-8*); pap. text ed. 16.95 (*0-8306-3961-6*) McGraw-Hill Prof.

Small Space, Big Harvest: Turn Your Small Garden into a Vegetable Factory - Naturally. Duane G. Newcomb. LC 92-39921. 272p. (Orig.). 1993. pap. 14.95 (*1-55958-289-8*) Prima Pub.

Small Space Living Design. Norman Smith. 128p. 1995. 24.99 (*1-56496-118-4*) Rockport Pubs.

Small Space Living Design. Norman Smith. (Illus.). 225p. 1995. 39.95 (*1-55835-128-0*) AIA Press.

Small Spaces: Stylish Ideas for Making More of Less in the Home. Azby Brown. (Illus.). 96p. 1996. pap. 25.00 (*4-7700-2084-8*) Kodansha.

Small Spaces: Stylish Ideas for Making More of Less in the Home. Ed. by Barry Lancet. LC 92-36529. (Illus.). 96p. 1993. 27.00 (*4-7700-1495-3*) Kodansha.

Small Spaces Between Emergencies. Alison Moore. LC 91-30614. 1992. 18.95 (*1-56279-022-6*) Mercury Hse Inc.

Small Specimen Test Techniques Applied to Nuclear Reactor Vessel Thermal Annealing & Plant Life Extension, STP 1204. Ed. by William R. Corwin et al. LC 93-20768. (Special Technical Publication Ser.). (Illus.). 470p. 1993. text ed. 125.00 (*0-8031-1869-4*, 04-012040-35) ASTM.

Small Stage Sets on Tour: A Practical Guide to Portable Stage Sets. 2nd ed. James H. Miller. Ed. by Arthur L. Zapel & Theodore O. Zapel. LC 87-42872. 128p. (Orig.). 1987. pap. 12.95 (*0-916260-46-1*, B102) Meriwether Pub.

Small-State Security in the Balkans. Aurel Braun. LC 82-6639. (Studies in Russian & East European History). 346p. (C). 1983. text ed. 38.50 (*0-389-20288-6*, 07110) B&N Imports.

Small States & Security Regimes: The International Politics of Nuclear Non-Proliferation in Nordic Europe & the South Pacific. John S. Masker. LC 94-46781. 172p. (C). 1995. lib. bdg. 32.50 (*0-8191-9846-3*) U Pr of Amer.

Small States & Territories: Status & Problems. Jacques Rapaport et al. LC 72-140128. (UNITAR Studies). 1971. 65.95 (*0-405-02237-9*) Ayer.

Small States & the Security Challenge in the New Europe. Ed. by Armand Clesse et al. (Atlantic Commentaries Ser.: No. 8). 272p. 1996. pap. 24.00 (*1-85753-153-1*, Pub. by Brasseys UK) Brasseys Inc.

Small States in World Markets: Industrial Policy in Europe. Peter J. Katzenstein. LC 84-45796. (Cornell Studies in Political Economy). 288p. (C). 1985. pap. 14.95 (*0-8014-9326-9*) Cornell U Pr.

Small States, Open Markets & the Organization of Business Interests. Dermott McCann. (Illus.). 216p. 1995. text ed. 62.95 (*1-85521-513-6*, Pub. by Dartmth Pub UK) Ashgate Pub Co.

Small Steel Craft. Ian Nicolson. (Illus.). 208p. 1971. 34.95 (*0-8464-1296-9*) Beekman Pubs.

Small Steps: The Year I Got Polio. Peg Kehret. 184p. (J). (gr. 3-8). 1996. lib. bdg. 14.95 (*0-8075-7457-0*) A Whitman.

Small Store Survival: Success Strategies for Retailers. Arthur Andersen. LC 96-24438. 384p. 1996. text ed. 34.95 (*0-471-16468-2*) Wiley.

***Small, Strong Congregations.** Callahan. 20.00 (*0-06-061261-4*) HarpC.

Small Sweaters: Colorful Knits for Kids. Lise Kolstad & Tone Takle. 152p. 1996. pap. text ed. 21.95 (*1-883010-22-5*) Interweave.

Small Talk. Jan Pienkowski. (Pop-up Ser.). (Illus.). 10p. (J). (ps up). 1983. 9.95 (*0-8431-0982-3*) Price Stern Sloan.

Small Talk. Jan Pienkowski. (Pienkowski Mini Pop-Up Ser.). (Illus.). 10p. (J). (ps up). 1991. 4.95 (*0-8431-2966-2*) Price Stern Sloan.

Small Talk. Donna L. Thomas. Ed. by Liz McGehee. LC 90-48053. (Illus.). 88p. (Orig.). 1991. pap. 18.95 (*0-943574-74-9*, B117) That Patchwork.

Small Talk. Harold G. Nicolson. LC 72-152206. (Essay Index Reprint Ser.). 1977. reprint ed. 19.95 (*0-8369-2420-7*) Ayer.

Small Talk: A Book of Short Poems. Ed. by Lee B. Hopkins. LC 94-7601. (Illus.). 48p. (J). (ps-7). 1995. 14.00 (*0-15-276577-8*) HarBrace.

Small Talk: More Jazz Chants. 1993. 12.95 (*0-88336-155-8*, OX1); audio 17.50 (*0-685-65862-7*); audio 17.50 (*0-685-65863-5*, OX2) OUP.

Small Talk about Great Books. Herman Liebaers. pap. 3.00 (*0-89073-062-8*) Boston Public Lib.

Small Talk, Big Names: Forty Years of Rock Quotes 1953-1993. Myles Palmer. 192p. 1994. pap. 13.95 (*1-85158-573-7*, Pub. by Mnstream UK) Trafalgar.

Small Talk Resource Guide. 2nd ed. Steve Mann. 225p. (Orig.). 1994. pap. 40.00 (*0-9642181-0-0*) Creat Digital.

Small Talk Stinks. Josh Kirsch. 52p. 1994. pap. 8.95 (*0-9643723-0-4*) O Press.

Small Talks about God: Devotions for Young Children. Kenneth N. Taylor. (J). (gr. 1-4). 1995. text ed. 9.99 (*0-8024-7911-1*) Moody.

Small Target, Vol. 1. Christine Andreae. LC 96-20047. 1996. 21.95 (*0-312-14543-8*) Thomas Dunne Bks.

Small Theatre Handbook: A Guide to Management & Production. Joann Green. LC 81-6730. (Illus.). 192p. (Orig.). 1981. pap. 9.95 (*0-916782-20-4*) Harvard Common Pr.

Small Theological Dictionary: Kleines Theologisches Woerterbuch. 15th ed. Karl Rahner & Herbert Vorgrimler. 460p. (GER.). 1985. pap. 24.95 (*0-8288-2310-3*, M7508) Fr & Eur.

Small Thing Like-a-Breath. Anthony S. Abbott. 93p. Date not set. pap. 8.95 (*1-879934-16-7*) St Andrews NC.

***Small Things Screaming.** Jim Shugrue. 26p. 1995. reprint ed. 5.00 (*0-614-30120-3*) Skydog OR.

Small Thoughts. W. H. Hawley, Jr. (Illus.). 112p. (Orig.). 1993. pap. 4.95 (*0-9638131-0-2*) McClain.

***Small Time Operator: How to Start Your Own Small Business, Keep Your Books, Pay Your Taxes... Fifth Edition.** 5th ed. Bernard Kamoroff. 1997. pap. 16.95 (*0-917510-14-3*) Bell Springs Pub.

***Small Time Operator: Start Your Own Business.** Bernard Kamoroff. 1997. 16.95 (*0-614-28336-1*) Bell Springs Pub.

Small Time Operator: The Computer Edition. Steve Steinke & Bernard Kamoroff. (Illus.). 160p. (Orig.). 1989. pap. 14.95 (*0-89708-180-3*) And Bks.

Small-Time Operator: The Software. rev. ed. Bernard Kamoroff et al. LC 89-80503. 184p. 1992. reprint ed. pap. 29.95 incl. disk (*0-89708-205-2*) And Bks.

***Small Time Smirker: (Or in Nevada, I Was Rabbity) & Fluffy Clouds.** Gilmore Tamny. 56p. (Orig.). 1997. pap. 7.00 (*1-882811-09-7*) Skyline Pubns.

Small Town: Reflections on People, History, Religion & Nature in Central New England. Thomas Mattson. (Illus.). 366p. 1992. pap. 12.95 (*0-9633929-0-5*) Northfld Pr.

Small Town America. Photos & Text by David Plowden. LC 93-35961. (Illus.). 1994. 49.50 (*0-8109-3842-1*) Abrams.

Small Town America: The Missouri Photo Workshops, 1949-1991. Cliff Edom et al. LC 92-23715. (Illus.). 248p. 1993. 39.95 (*1-55591-167-6*); pap. 10.99 (*1-55591-168-4*) Fulcrum Pub.

Small Town & Rural Police. Victor H. Sims. (Illus.). 226p. 1988. pap. 27.95 (*0-398-06431-8*) C C Thomas.

Small Town & Rural Police. Victor H. Sims. (Illus.). 226p. (C). 1988. text ed. 41.95 (*0-398-05405-3*) C C Thomas.

Small Town & the Nation: The Conflict of Local & Translocal Forces. Don Martindale & R. Galen Hanson. LC 79-90793. (Contributions in Sociology Ser.: No. 3). 211p. 1970. text ed. 38.50 (*0-8371-1854-9*, MAT/, Greenwood Pr) Greenwood.

Small Town Bound. John Clayton. LC 96-21270. 224p. (Orig.). 1996. pap. 11.99 (*1-56414-251-5*) Career Pr Inc.

Small Town Called Hibiscus. Gu Hua. 260p. 1995. lib. bdg. 29.00 (*0-8095-4519-5*) Borgo Pr.

***Small Town Called Hibiscus.** Gu Hua. Tr. by Gladys Yang. 9.95 (*0-8351-1074-5*) China Bks.

Small Town Children's Easter. P. K. Hallinan. (Illus.). 24p. (J). (ps-3). 1989. pap. 3.95 (*0-8249-8319-X*, Ideals Child) Hambleton-Hill.

Small Town D.A. John Voelker. 253p. 1992. reprint ed. pap. 12.95 (*1-878005-48-0*) Northmont Pub.

Small Town Destiny: The Story of Five Small Towns Along the Potomac Valley. Gilbert Gude. LC 89-80275. 130p. (Orig.). 1989. 29.95 (*0-912338-69-5*); pap. 19.50 (*0-912338-71-7*) Lomond.

Small Town England: Population Change among Small to Medium Sized Urban Areas, 1971-81. Ed. by John Shepherd & Peter Congdon. (Progress in Planning Ser.: No. 33). (Illus.). 112p. 1990. pap. 41.50 (*0-08-040168-6*, Pergamon Pr) Elsevier.

Small Town, Giant Corporation: Japanese Manufacturing Investment & Community Economic Development in the U. S. James F. Hettinger & Stanley D. Tooley. 212p. (C). 1994. pap. text ed. 19.50 (*0-8191-9612-6*); lib. bdg. 47.50 (*0-8191-9611-8*) U Pr of Amer.

***Small Town Girl.** LaVryle Spencer. LC 96-45510. 1997. write for info. (*0-7838-8049-9*) G K Hall.

***Small Town Girl.** LaVyrle Spencer. LC 96-24317. 384p. 1997. 24.95 (*0-399-14249-5*, Putnam) Putnam Pub Group.

***Small Town Girl.** large type ed. LaVyrle Spencer. LC 96-45510. (Core Ser.). 536p. 1997. 28.95 (*0-7838-8048-0*, GK Hall) Thorndike Pr.

***Small-Town Heroes: Images of Minor League Baseball.** Hank Davis. LC 96-41937. (Illus.). 396p. 1997. 34.95 (*0-87745-579-1*) U of Iowa Pr.

Small Town in America: A Multidisciplinary Revisit. Ed. by Hans Bertens & Theo D'Haen. (European Contributions to American Studies: Vol. 32). 250p. 1995. pap. 30.00 (*90-5383-385-4*) Paul & Co Pubs.

Small Town in American Drama. Ima H. Herron. LC 69-11729. (Illus.). 610p. reprint ed. pap. 173.90 (*0-8357-7024-9*, 2033422) Bks Demand.

Small Town in American Literature. Ima Herron. (BCL1-PS American Literature Ser.). 477p. 1993. reprint ed. lib. bdg. 99.00 (*0-7812-6572-X*) Rprt Serv.

Small Town in American Literature. Irma H. Herron. LC 70-92967. (Studies in Fiction: No. 34). 1970. reprint ed. lib. bdg. 75.00 (*0-8383-0980-1*) M S G Haskell Hse.

Small Town in Mass Society: Class, Power & Religion in a Rural Community. rev. ed. Arthur J. Vidich & Joseph Bensman. 348p. 1968. pap. text ed. 19.95 (*0-691-02807-9*, 131) Princeton U Pr.

Small Town in Modern Times: Alexandria, Ontario. David M. Rayside. 360p. (C). 1991. text ed. 49.95 (*0-7735-0826-0*, Pub. by McGill CN) U of Toronto Pr.

Small Town Law Practice. Philip C. Williams. LC 96-12699. (Illus.). 1996. pap. write for info. (*1-57073-290-6*) Amer Bar Assn.

Small Town Nurse. large type ed. Jeanne Bowman. (Romance Ser.). 1994. pap. 15.99 (*0-7089-7602-6*, Linford) Ulverscroft.

Small Town Planning Handbook. 2nd ed. Thomas L. Daniels et al. LC 94-71489. (Illus.). 312p. (Orig.). 1995. pap. 34.95 (*1-884829-02-3*); lib. bdg. 50.00 (*1-884829-03-1*) Planners Pr.

Small Town Renaissance: A Story of the Montana Study. Richard W. Poston. LC 76-109300. 231p. 1971. reprint ed. text ed. 55.00 (*0-8371-3843-4*, POST, Greenwood Pr) Greenwood.

Small Town Secrets. Andrea Parnell. 320p. 1993. mass mkt. 4.50 (*0-8217-4264-7*, Zebra Kensgtn) Kensgtn Pub Corp.

Small-Town Sports Heroes. (Illus.). 96p. (Orig.). (YA). (gr. 7-12). 1996. pap. 12.00 (*0-9616367-3-4*) Michael Paul.

***Small Town Tales: A Brookline Boyhood.** Sidney Hall, Jr. 174p. (Orig.). 1997. pap. 12.95 (*0-9636413-3-6*) Hobblebush Bks.

Small Town Teacher. Gertrude H. McPherson. LC 71-188349. 259p. 1972. reprint ed. pap. 73.90 (*0-7837-4170-7*, 2059019) Bks Demand.

Small Towns Book: Show Me the Way to Go Home. James Robertson & Carolyn Robertson. LC 76-23813. 208p. reprint ed. pap. 59.30 (*0-317-29958-1*, 2051722) Bks Demand.

***Small Towns, Detroit's Crown: A Perspective of 20th Century Small Towns.** (Illus.). 128p. 1996. pap. 19.95 (*0-9655344-0-5*) Spring Times.

Small Towns in Early Modern Europe. Ed. by Peter Clark. (Themes in International Urban History Ser.: No. 3). (Illus.). 309p. (C). 1995. text ed. 64.95 (*0-521-46463-3*) Cambridge U Pr.

Small Towns of Roman Britain. Barry Burnham & John Wacher. LC 90-41007. (Illus.). 388p. 1991. 55.00 (*0-520-07303-7*) U CA Pr.

Small Tractor Shop Service Set, 16 vols. 1991. ring bd. 149.95 (*0-87288-295-0*, STSS) Intertec Pub.

Small Treasures. Kathleen Kane. (Homespun Ser.). 336p. (Orig.). 1993. mass mkt. 4.99 (*1-55773-866-1*) Diamond.

Small Treasures. Lass Small. 560p. 1993. 9.98 (*0-8317-7866-0*) Smithmark.

Small Treasures. large type ed. Kathleen Kane. LC 93-26077. (Orig.). 1993. lib. bdg. 16.95 (*0-7862-0023-5*) Thorndike Pr.

***Small Treasury of Christmas Poems & Prayers.** Susan Spellman. LC 97-70362. (Illus.). 32p. (J). (ps-1). 1997. 8.95 (*1-56397-680-3*) Boyds Mills Pr.

***Small Treasury of Easter Poems & Prayers.** Illus. by Susan Spellman. LC 96-79428. 32p. (J). (ps-1). 1997. 8.95 (*1-56397-647-1*) Boyds Mills Pr.

Small Treatise on Large Virtues. Andre Compte-Sponville. 1997. 4.95 (*0-8050-4555-4*) H Holt & Co.

Small Treatise on Large Virtues. Andre Compte-Sponville. Date not set. pap. write for info. (*0-8050-4556-2*) H Holt & Co.

Small Tree Resource: A Materials Handling Challenge. 135p. 1983. 24.00 (*0-8403-3072-3*) Forest Prod.

Small Unit Action in Vietnam: Summer 1966. Francis I. West. 133p. 1967. pap. 12.95 (*0-405-00018-9*) Ayer.

Small Unit Actions During the German Campaign in Russia. 1995. lib. bdg. 260.75 (*0-8490-6575-5*) Gordon Pr.

***Small Unit Actions in World War II in France, Italy & Saipan.** (Illus.). 212p. 1997. reprint ed. pap. text ed. 50.00 (*0-7881-3985-1*) DIANE Pub.

Small Unit Leadership: A Commonsense Approach. Dandridge M. Malone. LC 83-4268. (Illus.). 180p. (Orig.). 1983. pap. 12.95 (*0-89141-173-9*) Presidio Pr.

Small Upright Spinning Wheel Construction Manual. Richard Schneider & Myrna Schneider. (Spinster-Helper Ser.). (Illus.). 58p. (Orig.). 1984. pap. 4.95 (*0-936984-06-6*) Schneider Pubs.

***Small Vices.** Robert B. Parker. 1997. pap. 29.95 incl. audio (*0-7871-1133-3*, Dove Bks) Dove Audio.

***Small Vices.** Robert B. Parker. LC 96-9827. 320p. 1997. 21.95 (*0-399-14244-4*, Putnam) Putnam Pub Group.

***Small Vices.** large type ed. Robert B. Parker. LC 97-23289. (Large Print Book Ser.). 1997. write for info. (*1-56895-466-2*) Wheeler Pub.

Small Victories. Sallie Bingham. LC 91-66474. 312p. 1993. 20.95 (*0-944072-20-8*) Zoland Bks.

Small Victories. Sallie Bingham. LC 91-66474. 312p. 1993. pap. 9.95 (*0-944072-25-9*) Zoland Bks.

Small Victories. 2nd ed. Victoria Rivas. (Illus.). 32p. (Orig.). 1995. reprint ed. 4.00 (*1-889289-01-9*) Ye Olde Font Shoppe.

Small Victories: The Real World of a Teacher, Her Students, & Their High School. Samuel G. Freedman. LC 89-45654. 448p. 1991. pap. 13.00 (*0-06-092087-4*, PL) HarpC.

Small Voice. Elise McGehee. 76p. 1982. 12.50 (*0-88289-375-0*) Pelican.

Small Voices: Heralds of Wonder in Everyday Life. James M. Apel. LC 94-68164. 208p. (Orig.). 1994. pap. 8.95 (*0-9642782-9-4*) Sparrow Press.

Small War on Murray Hill. Robert E. Sherwood. 1957. pap. 5.25 (*0-8222-1046-0*) Dramatists Play.

Small Wars. Ed. by William J. Olson. LC 94-68309. (Annals of the American Academy of Political & Social Science Ser.: Vol. 541). 1995. 28.00 (*0-8039-7124-9*); pap. 18.00 (*0-8039-7125-7*) Am Acad Pol Soc Sci.

Small Wars: Their Principles & Practice. 3rd ed. C. E. Callwell. LC 95-25837. xviii, 579p. 1996. pap. 25.00 (*0-8032-6366-X*, Bison Books) U of Nebr Pr.

Small Wars: Their Principles & Practices. C. E. Callwell. (Illus.). 1977. reprint ed. 35.00 (*0-7158-1200-9*) Charles River Bks.

Small Wars, Big Defense: Paying for the Military after the Cold War. Murray L. Weidenbaum. 256p. 1992. 25.00 (*0-19-507248-0*) OUP.

Small Wars Manual: United States Marine Corps, 1940. Intro. by Ronald Schaffer. (Illus.). 469p. reprint ed. pap. text ed. 26.95 (*0-89745-112-0*) Sunflower U Pr.

Small Wastewater Treatment Plants. Ed. by H. Odegaard. (Water Science & Technology Ser.: No. 22). (Illus.). 374p. 1990. pap. 139.00 (*0-08-040764-1*, Pergamon Pr) Elsevier.

Small Water System Operation & Maintenance. 3rd ed. Kenneth D. Kerri. (Illus.). 576p. (C). 1993. pap. text ed. 20.00 (*1-884701-15-9*) CA St U Ofc Water.

Small-Water Trout Fishing. Charles Jardine. (Illus.). 176p. 1995. 50.00 (*0-7134-6942-0*, Pub. by Batsford UK) Trafalgar.

Small Wolf. Nathaniel Benchley. LC 93-26717. (I Can Read Bk.). (Illus.). 64p. (J). (ps-3). 1972. 14.95 (*0-06-020491-5*); lib. bdg. 14.89 (*0-06-020492-3*) HarpC Child Bks.

Small Wolf. Nathaniel Benchley. LC 93-26717. (I Can Read Bk.). (Illus.). 64p. (J). 1994. pap. 3.75 (*0-06-444180-6*) HarpC Child Bks.

Small Woman. large type ed. Alan Burgess. 486p. 1973. 25.99 (*0-85456-166-8*) Ulverscroft.

Small Woman. Alan Burgess. 1993. reprint ed. lib. bdg. 27.95 (*1-56849-184-0*) Buccaneer Bks.

Small Wonder: How to Answer Your Child's Impossible Questions About Life. Jean G. Fitzpatrick. 256p. 1995. pap. 10.95 (*0-14-017344-7*, Penguin Bks) Viking Penguin.

Small Wonder: Worlds in a Box. David Levinthal. LC 95-25368. (Illus.). 156p. 1995. pap. 35.00 (*1-881616-39-8*) Dist Art Pubs.

Small Wonder Complete Program. Merle B. Karnes. 1981. 329.95 (*0-913476-62-5*, 7899) Am Guidance.

Small Wonders. TV Associates Frendship Staff. (Simply Grand Quigley's Band Ser.: Vol. 5). 1995. pap. 12.99 (*0-310-24449-8*) Zondervan.

Small Wonders: Hands-on Science Activities for Young Children. Peggy K. Perdue. (Illus.). 66p. (Orig.). 1988. pap. 8.95 (*0-673-38198-6*, GoodYrBooks) Addson-Wesley Educ.

Small Wonders: New Stories by Twelve Distinguished Canadian Authors. Ed. by Robert Weaver. 176p. 1982. pap. 9.95 (*0-88794-104-4*) Genl Dist Srvs.

Small Wonders: The Funny Animal Art of Frank Frazetta. Frank Frazetta. Ed. by Dave Schreiner & Greg Theakston. LC 91-9719. (Illus.). 80p. (Orig.). 1991. pap. 9.95 (*0-87816-146-5*) Kitchen Sink.

Small Wonders: Year-Round-Alaska. Mary Shields. (Illus.). 96p. (Orig.). 1987. pap. 14.00 (*0-9618348-0-3*) Pyrola Pub.

Small Works: Selections from the Richard Brown Baker Collection of Contemporary Art. LC 73-75996. 123p. 1973. pap. 3.50 (*0-911517-38-3*) Mus of Art RI.

Small Works in Fiber: The Mildred Constantine Collection. LC 92-43062. (Illus.). 84p. 1993. pap. 12.95 (*0-940717-20-4*) Cleveland Mus Art.

***Small Works, Repairs & Maintenance.** (Laxton's Trade Price Bks.). 436p. 1996. pap. write for info. (*0-7506-2978-9*, Pub. by Laxtons UK) Buttrwrth-Heinemann.

Small World. Tabitha King. 1982. pap. 3.95 (*0-451-13633-0*, AE1408, Sig); pap. 5.99 (*0-451-15631-5*) NAL-Dutton.

Small World. David Lodge. 400p. 1995. pap. 11.95 (*0-14-024486-7*, Penguin Bks) Viking Penguin.

Small World. Photos by Martin P. Simon. (Illus.). 96p. 39.95 (*1-899235-05-1*) Dist Art Pubs.

Small World: A Volume of Recent Research Commemorating Ithiel de Sola Pool, Stanley Milgram, & Theodore Newcombe. Ed. by Manfred Kochen & Brenda Dervin. LC 88-7460. (Communication & Information Science Ser.). 432p. 1989. text ed. 78.50 (*0-89391-479-7*) Ablex Pub.

Small World: An Academic Romance. David Lodge. 1991. pap. 10.99 (*0-446-39327-4*) Warner Bks.

Small World Celebrations: Multi-Cultural Holidays to Celebrate with Young Children. Jean Warren & Elizabeth S. McKinnon. LC 88-50594. (Celebration Ser.). (Illus.). 160p. (Orig.). (J). (ps-1). 1988. pap. 14.95 (*0-911019-19-7*, WPH 0701) Warren Pub Hse.

Small World of Millie McIvor. Ronald Burke. 1974. 3.00 (*0-87129-506-7*, S41) Dramatic Pub.

Small World of Our Own: Authentic Pioneer Stories of the Pacific Northwest from the Old Settlers Contest of 1892. Ed. by Robert A. Bennett. 382p. 1985. pap. 10.95 (*0-936546-10-7*) Pioneer Pr Bks.

Small Worlds. Mary L. Edgren. 216p. (Orig.). 1989. pap. 7.95 (*0-9622981-0-7*) Petite Publishing.

Small Worlds: A Novel. Allen Hoffman. LC 96-5768. 280p. 1996. 24.95 (*0-7892-0129-1*) Abbeville Pr.

Small Worlds: Children & Adolescents in America, 1850-1950. Ed. by Elliott West & Paula Petrik. LC 91-40586. (Illus.). 400p. 1992. 29.95 (*0-7006-0510-X*); pap. 17.95 (*0-7006-0511-8*) U Pr of KS.

Small Worlds: Sixty Moons of Our Solar System. Joseph W. Kelch. Ed. by Jane Steltenpohl. (Illus.). 128p. (YA). (gr. 6-8). 1990. lib. bdg. 16.95 (*0-671-70013-8*, Julian Messner) Silver Burdett Pr.

***Small Worlds: 60 Moons of the Solar System.** Joseph W. Kelch. LC 87-2424. 1987. write for info. (*0-13-814369-2*) P-H.

Small Worlds, Large Questions: Explorations in Early American Social History, 1600-1850. Darrett B. Rutman & Anita H. Rutman. LC 94-7440. 448p. (C). 1994. text ed. 55.00 (*0-8139-1529-5*); pap. text ed. 17.95 (*0-8139-1530-9*) U Pr of Va.

Small Yachts: Their Design & Construction. C. P. Kunhardt. 1987. pap. text ed. 20.00 (*0-07-155751-2*) McGraw.

Smallboat Fishing with the Experts. William A. Muller. (With the Experts Ser.). (Illus.). 213p. 1988. text ed. 16.95 (*0-9625187-2-7*) Wavecrest Comns.

***Smallcap 600 Guide.** Standard & Poor's Staff. (Standard & Poor's Ser.). 1997. pap. 24.95 (*0-07-052613-3*) McGraw.

Smaller Academic Library: A Management Handbook. Ed. by Gerard B. McCabe. LC 87-23655. (Library Management Collection). (Illus.). 391p. 1988. text ed. 65.00 (*0-313-25027-8*, MMH/, Greenwood Pr) Greenwood.

Smaller Church in a Super Church Era. Ed. by Jon Johnston & Bill M. Sullivan. 152p. 1983. pap. 7.99 (*0-8341-0895-X*) Beacon Hill.

***Smaller Perennials: A Comprehensive A-Z.** Jack Elliott. LC 96-44009. (Illus.). 176p. 1997. 29.95 (*0-88192-383-4*) Timber.

Smaller Rhododendrons. Peter A. Cox. (Illus.). 216p. 1985. 29.95 (*0-88192-014-2*) Timber.

Smaller Slang Dictionary. Eric Partridge. 1976. reprint ed. pap. 13.95 (*0-7100-8331-9*, RKP) Routledge.

Smaller Solar System Bodies & Orbits. Ed. by S. K. Runcorn et al. (Advances in Space Research Ser.: No. 10). (Illus.). 434p. 1989. pap. 190.25 (*0-08-040163-5*, Pergamon Pr) Elsevier.

Smallest. David Armentrout. LC 96-20858. (Fascinating Facts Ser.). 1996. write for info. (*1-57103-130-8*) Rourke Pr.

Smallest Cow. Laurie Diamond. Ed. by J. Friedland & R. Kessler. (Novel-Ties Ser.). 1995. student ed., pap. text ed. 15.95 (*1-56982-254-9*) Lrn Links.

Smallest Cow in the World. Katherine Paterson. LC 90-30521. (I Can Read Bks.). (Illus.). 64p. (J). (ps-3). 1996. pap. 7.95 incl. audio (*0-694-70036-3*) HarpC.

Smallest Cow in the World. Katherine Paterson. LC 90-30521. (Trophy I Can Read Bk.). (Illus.). 64p. (J). (gr. k-3). 1993. pap. 3.75 (*0-06-444164-4*, Trophy) HarpC Child Bks.

Smallest Stegosaurus. Lynn Sweat & Louis Phillips. (Illus.). 32p. (J). 1995. pap. 4.99 (*0-14-054389-9*) Puffin Bks.

Smallest Stegosaurus. Lynn Sweat. 1994. pap. write for info. (*0-14-050228-9*) Viking Penguin.

Smallest Turtle. Lynley Dodd. LC 85-9771. (Gold Star First Readers Ser.). (Illus.). 29p. (J). (gr. 1-2). 1985. lib. bdg. 18.60 (*0-918831-07-5*) Gareth Stevens Inc.

***Smallholders & Political Voice in Zimbabwe.** Stephen F. Burgess. LC 97-7904. 238p. 1997. 39.50 (*0-7618-0741-1*) U Pr of Amer.

Smallholders, Householders: Farm Families & the Ecology of Intensive, Sustainable Agriculture. Robert M. Netting. (Illus.). 416p. (C). 1993. 49.50 (*0-8047-2061-4*); pap. 16.95 (*0-8047-2102-5*) Stanford U Pr.

Smallmouth: "How to Fish" Dan D. Gapen, Sr. (Illus.). 129p. (Orig.). 1987. pap. text ed. 7.95 (*0-932985-05-X*) Whitewater Pubns.

Smallmouth Bass. Dick Sternberg. LC 86-16617. (Hunting & Fishing Library). (Illus.). 160p. 1986. 19.95 (*0-86573-017-2*) Cowles Creative.

Smallmouth Bass: An In-Fisherman Handbook of Strategies. Al Lindner et al. (Illus.). 246p. (Orig.). 1984. pap. 11.95 (*0-9605254-3-2*) In-Fisherman.

Smallmouth Strategies. LC 90-62350. (Complete Angler's Library). 378p. 1990. write for info. (*0-914697-32-3*) N Amer Outdoor Grp.

Smallmouth Strategies for the Fly Rod. Will Ryan. (Illus.). 240p. 1996. 25.00 (*1-55821-343-0*, 13430) Lyons & Burford.

Smallpox: When Should Routine Vaccination Be Discontinued. J. C. Frauenthal. 55p. 1981. pap. text ed. 10.95 (*0-8176-3042-2*) Birkhauser.

Smallpox & Its Eradication. Frank Fenner et al. (Illus.). 1500p. 1988. text ed. 140.00 (*92-4-156110-6*, 1150277) World Health.

Smallpox & the American Indian. Arthur Diamond. LC 91-23066. (World Disasters Ser.). (Illus.). 64p. (J). (gr. 5-8). 1991. lib. bdg. 15.96 (*1-56006-018-2*) Lucent Bks.

Smallpox & the Iroquois Wars: An Ethnohistorical Study of the Influence of Disease & Demographic Change in Iroquoian Culture History, 1630-1700. Stephen Clark. (Illus.). vi, 121p. 1981. reprint ed. pap. text ed. 12.00 (*1-55567-027-X*) Coyote Press.

Smallpox Eradication: Proceedings of the WHO Scientific Group, Geneva, 1967. WHO Staff. (Technical Report Ser.: No. 393). 52p. 1968. pap. text ed. 5.00 (*92-4-120393-5*, 1100393) World Health.

Smallpox in Colonial America: An Original Anthology. Ed. by Barbara G. Rosenkrantz. LC 76-40353. (Public Health in America Ser.). (Illus.). 1977. reprint ed. lib. bdg. 23.95 (*0-405-09880-4*) Ayer.

Smallpox Story: In Words & Pictures. Abbas M. Behbehani. LC 88-20846. (Illus.). (Orig.). (C). 1988. pap. text ed. 15.95 (*0-685-24022-3*) Univ KS Med Ctr.

***Smallpox Vaccination: A Survey of Recent Legislation.** WHO Staff. (International Digest of Health Legislation Offprints: Vol. 5, No. 3). 42p. 1954. 3.00 (*92-4-169052-6*) World Health.

Smalltalk. Glass & Ian S. Larman. (C). 1996. pap. text ed. 22.75 (*0-13-455817-0*) P-H.

Smalltalk. Nicola. (C). 1996. pap. text ed. 29.25 (*0-13-206145-7*) P-H.

Smalltalk: An Introduction to Application Development Using VisualWorks. 2nd ed. Trevor Hopkins. LC 95-7583. (Object-Oriented Ser.). 408p. (C). 1995. pap. text ed. 38.60 (*0-13-318387-4*) P-H.

***Smalltalk & Object-Orientation: An Introduction.** John Hunt. 1997. write for info. (*3-540-76115-2*) Spr-Verlag.

***Smalltalk Best Practice Patterns.** Kent Beck. LC 96-2941. 1996. pap. 30.60 (*0-13-476904-X*) P-H.

Smalltalk by Example. Alec Sharp. LC 96-47061. (Illus.). 320p. 1997. pap. text ed. 42.00 (*0-07-913036-4*) McGraw.

Smalltalk Developer's Guide to VisualWorks. Tim Howard. LC 95-16526. (Advances in Object Technology Ser.: Vol. 9). (Illus.). 645p. (Orig.). 1995. pap. 45.00 (*1-884842-11-9*) SIGS Bks & Multimedia.

SmallTalk Developers Guide to VisualWorks. Timothy G. Howard & Howard & Sigs Books, Inc., Staff. 1995. pap. 45.00 incl. disk (*0-13-442526-X*) P-H.

Smalltalk in Action. Wilf R. Lalonde & John R. Pugh. 185p. (C). 1993. pap. text ed. 44.00 (*0-13-814039-1*) P-H.

Smalltalk Object & Design. Chamond Liu. 1996. text ed. 44.00 (*0-13-268335-0*) P-H.

Smalltalk Programming for Windows. Dan Shafer. LC 92-31893. 400p. 1993. pap. 39.95 (*1-55958-237-5*) Prima Pub.

Smalltalk Resource Guide. 3rd ed. Steve Mann. 300p. 1995. pap. write for info. (*0-9642181-1-9*) Creat Digital.

Smalltalk with Style. Suzanne Skublics. (C). 1995. pap. text ed. 20.00 (*0-13-165549-3*) P-H.

Smalltalk-80: A Practical Introduction. Ed. by Phil D. Gray & Ramzan Mohamed. 224p. (C). 1990. pap. text ed. 90.00 (*0-273-03105-8*, Pub. by Pitman Pubng UK) St Mut.

Smalltalk-80: The Language. Adele Goldberg & David Robson. (Illus.). 608p. (C). 1989. pap. text ed. 33.50 (*0-201-13688-0*) Addison-Wesley.

Smalltalk-80: The Language. Adele Goldberg & David Robson. (Computer Science Ser.). (Illus.). 608p. (C). 1989. pap. text ed. write for info. (*0-201-11370-8*) Addison-Wesley.

***Smalltime.** Jerry Raine. (Bloodlines Ser.). 184p. 9700. pap. 12.95 (*1-899344-13-6*) Dufour.

Smara: The Forbidden City. Michel Vieuchange. 276p. 1987. pap. 9.50 (*0-88001-146-7*) Ecco Pr.

Smarandache Class of Paradoxes. Ilie Mitroiescu. Ed. by R. Muller. (Illus.). 75p. (C). pap. 9.99 (*1-879585-46-4*) Erhus Univ Pr.

Smarandache Function Number Theory. Constantin Dumitrescu & Marcela Popescu. Ed. by Homer Tilton. (Illus.). 100p. (Orig.). (C). 1996. pap. 9.99 (*1-879585-47-2*) Erhus Univ Pr.

Smarandache Geometries. Charles Ashbacher. (Illus.). 100p. (Orig.). (C). 1996. pap. text ed. 13.95 (*1-879585-53-7*) Erhus Univ Pr.

An Asterisk (*) at the beginning of an entry indicates that the title is appearing in BIP for the first time.

Smart Actors, Foolish Choices: A Self-Help Guide to Coping with the Emotional Stresses. Katherine Mayfield. 1996. pap. text ed. 16.95 (*0-8230-8424-8*) Watsn-Guptill.

Smart Alecs Knock Knock Jokes. 240p. 1988. mass mkt. 3.99 (*0-345-35196-7*) Ballantine.

***Smart Art.** (Mad Jack Bks.). (Illus.). (J). 1996. 13.95 (*0-7894-1146-6*) DK Pub Inc.

Smart Art: Learning to Classify & Critique Art. Patricia Hollingsworth & Stephen F. Hollingsworth. (Illus.). 112p. (Orig.). (J). (gr. 3-8). 1989. pap. 20.00 (*0-913705-31-4*) Zephyr Pr AZ.

***Smart Assets: Turning You & Your Business into a Wealth Machine.** George D. Brenner. 1997. pap. text ed. 14.95 (*0-07-007645-6*) McGraw.

Smart Assets: Turning Your Business into a Wealth Machine. Stanfield Hill et al. 250p. 1996. text ed. 24.95 (*0-7863-0457-X*) Irwin Prof Pubng.

Smart Attorney's Guide to Accounting Documents for Discovery & Evidence. William N. McNairn. (Illus.). 100p. 1987. pap. text ed. 14.95 (*0-932621-02-3*) Quotamus Pr.

Smart Autoclave Cure of Composites. Peter R. Ciriscioli & George S. Springer. LC 90-71382. 172p. 1990. 49.95 (*0-87762-802-5*) Technomic.

Smart Bomb. David Alexander. (Nomad Ser.). 1993. mass mkt. 4.99 (*0-373-62117-5*, 1-62117-6) Harlequin Bks.

Smart Bombs: Advanced Weapons Systems & Improvised Sensory Detonation Techniques. 1991. lib. bdg. 75.00 (*0-8490-4233-X*) Gordon Pr.

Smart Bombs: Improvised Sensory Detonation Techniques & Advanced Weapons System. Lawrence W. Myers. (Illus.). 112p. 1990. pap. 12.00 (*0-87364-548-0*) Paladin Pr.

***SmART Book: The Smart Mart to the Arts.** 3rd ed. Jan Patterson & Jim Patterson. Date not set. pap. 24.95 (*0-9643197-2-1*) Patterson Mktg.

Smart Bread Machine Recipes: Healthy, Wholegrain & Delicious. Sandra L. Woodruff. LC 94-27252. (Illus.). 128p. 1994. pap. 6.95 (*0-8069-0690-1*) Sterling.

Smart Breakfasts: 101 Delicious, Healthy Ways to Start the Day. Jane Kinderlehrer. LC 89-12610. (Smart Cookbooks Ser.). (Illus.). 192p. (Orig.). 1991. pap. 11.95 (*1-55704-045-1*) Newmarket.

Smart Buildings & Technology-Enhanced Real Estate, Vols. I & II. Dean Schwanke. LC 85-51319. 136p. (Orig.). 1985. pap. 61.95 (*0-87420-640-5*, H02) Urban Land.

***Smart Business Guide for African-Americans.** Boston Media, Inc. Staff. 1998. pap. write for info. (*0-399-52380-4*, Perigee Bks) Berkley Pub.

Smart Business Guide to Internet Marketing: Electronic Version 2.0, ASCII Text. Alfred R. Bredenberg. 70p. 1996. 12.00 (*1-889213-02-0*, SBGIM 2.0) A Bredenberg.

***Smart Business Guide to Internet Marketing: Version 2.1.** Alfred R. Bredenberg. Orig. Title: The Small Business Guide to Internet Marketing. (Illus.). 70p. 1997. 20.00 (*1-889213-03-9*, SBGIM 2.1) A Bredenberg.

Smart Business Strategies: The Guide to Small Business Marketing Excellence. Richard Tyler. 185p. 1996. pap. 19.95 (*0-318-22759-2*) Guardian Pr.

Smart Business Travel: How to Stay Safe When You're on the Road. Stacey R. Abarbanel. 128p. (Orig.). 1994. pap. 12.95 (*0-912301-23-6*) First Bks.

Smart but Feeling Dumb. Harold N. Levinson. LC 84-40090. 256p. 1988. pap. 10.95 (*0-446-38841-6*) Warner Bks.

Smart But Feeling Dumb. rev. ed. Harold N. Levinson. 320p. 1994. pap. 12.99 (*0-446-39545-5*) Warner Bks.

Smart Capacitive Sensors: Physical, Geometrical & Electronic Aspects. G. W. De Jong. 316p. (Orig.). 1994. pap. 67.50 (*90-6275-975-0*, Pub. by Delft U Pr NE) Coronet Bks.

***Smart Car Buying & Leasing 101.** Charles R. Devorak. (Illus.). 166p. (Orig.). 1997. pap. 8.95 (*1-890172-00-6*) Vehicle Info.

Smart Car Buying Sense. David J. Gibbs. (Illus.). 68p. (Orig.). 1990. pap. write for info. (*0-318-68204-4*) Trends & Events.

***Smart Card: New Directions.** (Report Ser.: No. G-100N). 196p. 1996. 2,850.00 (*1-56965-077-2*) BCC.

Smart Card: The Global Information Passport. Jack Kaplan. (Illus.). 250p. 1996. text ed. 44.95 (*1-85032-212-0*) ITCP.

Smart Card - Update, No. G-100R. Business Communications Co., Inc. Staff. 175p. 1991. 2,350.00 (*0-89336-809-1*) BCC.

Smart Card Handbook. Wolfgang Rankl & Wolfgang Effing. LC 97-1037. 1997. text ed. write for info. (*0-471-96720-3*) Wiley.

Smart Card Two Thousand. David Chaum. 1991. 110.00 (*0-444-89266-4*) Elsevier.

Smart Cards. Richard K. Miller & Terri C. Walker. LC 88-80899. (Survey on Technology & Markets Ser.: No. 15). 50p. 1989. pap. text ed. 200.00 (*1-55865-014-8*) Future Tech Surveys.

Smart Cards. Jose M. Oton. LC 94-7671. 1994. 67.00 (*0-89006-687-6*) Artech Hse.

Smart Cards: Seizing Strategic Business Opportunities. Catherine Allen. LC 96-41903. 312p. 1996. text ed. 37.50 (*0-7863-1108-8*) Irwin Prof Pubng.

Smart Casino Gambling: How to Win More & Lose Less. Olaf Vancura. LC 95-81308. (Illus.). 360p. (Orig.). 1996. pap. 24.95 (*1-56866-424-9*) Index Pub Grp.

Smart Chicken: One Hundred One Tasty & Healthy Poultry Dishes, Plus Stuffings & Accompaniments. Jane Kinderlehrer. LC 90-27453. (Jane Kinderlehrer Smart Food Ser.). (Illus.). 192p. 1991. pap. 11.95 (*1-55704-073-7*) Newmarket.

Smart Choices. Victor Craig. LC 81-70755. (Illus.). 112p. 1982. pap. 9.95 (*0-941156-00-1*) Clear View Pubns.

Smart Choices, Small Changes: The Healthy Lifestyle Planning Kit. Judith D. Grillo. (Illus.). 125p. (Orig.). 1995. pap. text ed. 9.95 (*0-9643606-0-8*) Cricket Commun.

Smart, Clean Pigs. Allan Fowler. LC 92-36365. (Rookie Read-about Science Ser.). (Illus.). 32p. (J). (ps-2). 1993. pap. 3.95 (*0-516-46013-7*); lib. bdg. 17.30 (*0-516-06013-9*) Childrens.

Smart, Clean Pigs, Big bk. Allan Fowler. LC 92-36365. (Rookie Read-about Science Big Bks.). (Illus.). 32p. (J). (ps-2). 1993. 32.40 (*0-516-49644-1*) Childrens.

Smart Comebacks to Stupid Questions. Richard Porteus & Charles Goll. 1996. pap. 5.95 (*0-918259-92-4*) CCC Pubns.

***Smart Comebacks to Stupid Questions.** Richard Porteus. 1996. pap. 5.95 (*1-57644-040-0*) CCC Pubns.

***Smart Companies; Smart Tools.** Thomas M. Koulopoulos. 1997. write for info. (*0-614-28297-7*) Van Nos Reinhold.

***Smart Companies, Smart Tools: Transforming Business Processes into Business Assets.** Thomas Koubpoulos. LC 97-19345. 250p. 1997. text ed. 29.95 (*0-442-02496-7*) Van Nos Reinhold.

Smart Composites. Ed. by P. Gardiner. 144p. 1993. 120.00 (*1-85573-144-4*, Pub. by Woodhead Pubng UK) Am Educ Systs.

Smart Consumer: A Legal Guide to Your Rights in the Marketplace. Wesley J. Smith. (Orig.). 1994. write for info. (*0-910073-20-1*) HALT DC.

Smart Consumer's Book of Questions. Linda M. Ross. LC 96-3241. 224p. (Orig.). 1996. pap. 14.95 (*1-55652-265-7*) Chicago Review.

Smart Cookies: Eighty Recipes for Heavenly, Healthful Snacking. Jane Kinderlehrer. 176p. (Orig.). 1992. pap. 11.95 (*1-55704-111-3*) Newmarket.

***Smart Cookies Don't Crumble.** 1989. mass mkt. 4.95 (*0-671-69580-0*) PB.

Smart Cookies Don't Crumble: A Modern Woman's Guide to Living & Loving Her Own Life. Sonya Friedman. pap. 3.95 (*0-317-61748-6*) PB.

Smart Crockery Cooking: Over 100 Delicious Recipes. Carol H. Munson. (Illus.). 144p. 1996. pap. 9.95 (*0-8069-6106-6*) Sterling.

***Smart Culture.** Hayman. 1997. 24.95 (*0-8147-3533-9*) NYU Pr.

***Smart Cycling.** Baker. LC 96-18734. 1997. pap. 14.00 (*0-684-82243-1*, Fireside) S&S Trade.

Smart-Daaf Boys: The Inventors of Radio & Television & Nathan B. Stubblefield, 4 vols., II. Troy Stubblefield-Cory et al. 1994. write for info. (*1-883644-02-X*) TV Int Pubs.

Smart-Daaf Boys: The Inventors of Radio & Television & Nathan B. Stubblefield, 4 vols., III. Troy Stubblefield-Cory et al. 1994. write for info. (*1-883644-03-8*) TV Int Pubs.

Smart-Daaf Boys: The Inventors of Radio & Television & Nathan B. Stubblefield, 4 vols., IV. Troy Stubblefield-Cory et al. 1994. write for info. (*1-883644-04-6*) TV Int Pubs.

Smart-Daaf Boys: The Inventors of Radio & Television & Nathan B. Stubblefield, 4 vols., Set. Troy Stubblefield-Cory et al. 1994. 80.00 (*1-883644-00-3*) TV Int Pubs.

Smart-Daaf Boys: The Inventors of Radio & Television & Nathan B. Stubblefield, 4 vols., Vol. 1. Troy Stubblefield-Cory et al. 1994. pap. 49.00 (*1-883644-24-0*); lib. bdg. 49.00 (*1-883644-07-0*) TV Int Pubs.

Smart Dating: A Guide for Men & Women to Dating, Romance, & Sex. Donald Black. Ed. by Werner A. Riefling. LC 93-87561. (Illus.). (Orig.). 1994. pap. 14.95 (*1-879706-62-8*) Paper Chase.

Smart Dating: Workshop Workbook. Donald Black. Ed. by Jennifer L. Osborn. 112p. (Orig.). 1996. wbk. ed., pap. 9.95 (*1-879706-66-0*) Paper Chase.

***Smart Discipline: A Workbook for Parents.** Larry Koenig. 36p. 1988. pap. 12.00 (*1-886901-01-5*) Up With Youth.

Smart Discipline for the Classroom: Respect & Cooperation Restored. rev. ed. Larry Koenig. (1-Off Ser.). 128p. 1995. pap. 19.95 (*0-8039-6341-6*) Corwin Pr.

Smart Dog. Ralph Leemis. (Illus.). 32p. (J). (ps-3). 1993. 14.95 (*1-56397-109-7*) Boyds Mills Pr.

Smart Dragons, Foolish Elves. Alan Dean Foster. Ed. by Martin H. Greenberg. 1991. mass mkt. 4.95 (*0-441-18481-2*) Ace Bks.

***Smart Drinks: Alcohol-Free Natural Beverages.** Bob Schwiers. (Illus.). 64p. 1997. pap. 7.95 (*0-8069-9614-5*) Sterling.

Smart Drugs: Food for Thought. rev. ed. Jimmy Magahem. 1997. pap. 0.50 (*0-89230-246-1*) Do It Now.

Smart Drugs & Nutrients: How to Improve Your Memory & Increase Your Intelligence Using the Latest Discoveries in Neuroscience. Ward Dean & John Morgenthaler. LC 90-84066. (Smart Drugs Ser.: Vol. 1). (Illus.). 224p. (Orig.). 1991. reprint ed. pap. 12.95 (*0-9627418-9-2*) Smart Pubns CA.

Smart Drugs II: The New Generation: New Drugs & Nutrients to Improve Your Memory & Increase Your Intelligence. Ward Dean et al. LC 93-78074. 350p. 1993. pap. 14.95 (*0-9627418-7-6*) Smart Pubns CA.

***Smart Eating.** Bailey. 1996. pap. 9.95 (*0-395-85492-X*) HM.

Smart Eating. Covert Bailey. 1996. 19.95 (*0-614-15494-4*) HM.

Smart Eating: Choosing Wisely, Living Lean. Covert Bailey & Ronda Gates. LC 95-37876. 288p. 1996. 19.95 (*0-395-75283-3*) HM.

***Smart Eats, Smart Supplements, & Smart Exercise.** Dusty R. Green. Ed. by Joe Norton et al. (Illus.). 200p. (Orig.). 1997. pap. 19.95 (*0-9655254-0-6*) Natl Hlth Solutions.

Smart English: The Easy-to-Use, Instant-Access Guide to Proper Written & Spoken English. Annette Francis. 368p. 1995. pap. 5.99 (*0-451-18510-2*, Sig) NAL-Dutton.

Smart Exercise: Burning Fat, Getting Fat. Covert Bailey. 1994. 19.95 (*0-395-47043-9*) HM.

Smart Exercise: Burning Fat, Getting Fit. Covert Bailey. 288p. 1996. pap. 9.95 (*0-395-66114-5*) HM.

Smart Eyes. Jamie Marron. write for info. (*0-318-59574-5*) Addison-Wesley.

***Smart Finances for Your 20s & 30s.** 1997. 15.95 (*0-02-862216-2*) Macmillan.

Smart Fish Cookbook: One Hundred & One Healthful Recipes for Main Courses, Soups, & Salads. Jane Kinderlehrer. 192p. 1993. 18.95 (*1-55704-164-4*); pap. 9.95 (*1-55704-163-6*) Newmarket.

Smart Gardener's Guide to Growing Fruits. Bob Gough. (Illus.). 224p. 1997. pap. 16.95 (*0-8117-2925-7*) Stackpole.

Smart Gardener's Guide to Growing Vegetables. Bob Gough. (Illus.). 224p. 1997. pap. 16.95 (*0-8117-3087-5*) Stackpole.

Smart Girl. Sandy Miller. 160p. (YA). (gr. 7 up). 1982. pap. 2.25 (*0-451-11887-1*, Sig Vista) NAL-Dutton.

***Smart Girls: A New Psychology of Girls, Women & Giftedness.** 3rd rev. ed. Barbara A. Kerr. LC 97-23100. Orig. Title: Smart Girls, Gifted Women; Smart Girls Two. (Illus.). 290p. 1997. pap. 22.00 (*0-910707-26-X*) Gifted Psych Pr.

Smart Girls, Gifted Women; Smart Girls Two see Smart Girls: A New Psychology of Girls, Women & Giftedness

***Smart Girl's Guide to College: A Serious Book Written by Women in College to Help You Make the Perfect College Choice.** Christina Page. LC 97-12833. 1997. pap. write for info. (*0-374-52514-5*, Noonday) FS&G.

Smart Girls Two: A New Psychology of Girls, Women & Giftedness. enl. rev. ed. Barbara A. Kerr. LC 94-45864. 340p. (Orig.). (C). 1995. pap. 22.00 (*0-910707-25-1*) Gifted Psych Pr.

Smart Golf. Charles F. Kemp. LC 74-82856. (Illus.). 200p. (Orig.). 1974. pap. 3.85 (*0-87706-057-6*) Branch-Smith.

***Smart Golf.** Kirchenbaum. LC 97-17208. 1997. 21.00 (*0-7879-1062-7*) Jossey-Bass.

Smart Growth: Critical Choices for Business Continuity & Prosperity. Ernesto J. Poza. LC 89-8191. (Management Ser.). 233p. 28.95 (*1-55542-170-9*) Jossey-Bass.

***Smart Guys.** Prescott Hill. LC 95-76743. (Ten-Minute Thrillers Ser.). 32p. (YA). (gr. 6-12). 1995. pap. 2.95 (*0-7854-1070-8*, 40820) Am Guidance.

***Smart Guys Readalong.** Prescott Hill. (Ten-Minute Thrillers Ser.). 32p. (YA). (gr. 6-12). 1995. pap. 12.95 incl. audio (*0-7854-1081-3*, 40822) Am Guidance.

Smart Handicapping Made Easy. William Bauman. 1979. pap. 5.00 (*0-87980-270-7*) Wilshire.

Smart Hearts in the City. Barbara P. Solomon. LC 92-17762. 1992. 21.95 (*0-15-183157-2*) HarBrace.

Smart Highways, Smart Cars. Richard Whelan. 1994. 59.00 (*0-89006-765-1*) Artech Hse.

Smart Hiring: The Complete Guide for Recruiting Employees. Robert W. Wendover. (Illus.). 170p. 1989. pap. 17.95 (*0-9623289-0-1*) Leadership Res.

Smart Hiring: The Complete Guide to Finding & Hiring the Best Employees. Robert W. Wendover. LC 93-14722. (Small Business Sourcebooks Ser.). 200p. 1993. pap. 9.95 (*0-942061-56-X*) Sourcebks.

***Smart Hiring: The Complete Guide to Finding & Hiring the Best Employees.** 2nd rev. ed. Robert W. Wendover. 200p. 1997. pap. 12.95 (*1-57071-213-1*) Sourcebks.

Smart Hiring for Your Business: Everything You Need to Know to Find & Hire the Best Employees. Robert W. Wendover. LC 93-14722. 200p. 1993. 17.95 (*0-942061-57-8*) Sourcebks.

Smart Homes & Home Automation. Richard K. Miller & Terri C. Walker. LC 88-80904. (Survey on Technology & Markets Ser.: No. 20). 50p. 1989. pap. text ed. 200.00 (*1-55865-019-9*) Future Tech Surveys.

Smart Homeseller's Sale by Owner Kit. J. R. Paine. 1986. 19.95 (*0-8187-0065-3*) Harlo Press.

Smart Hospital: A Case Study in Hospital Computerization. Matthew M. Person, III. LC 88-71149. 244p. 1988. lib. bdg. 29.95 (*0-89089-338-1*) Carolina Acad Pr.

Smart House: Control Your Home with Your PC. Gregory H. Plesur. 1994. pap. 27.95 incl. disk (*0-8306-4506-3*, Windcrest) TAB Bks.

Smart House Wiring. H. Brooke Stauffer & Ray C. Mullin. LC 92-13283. 1993. pap. 35.95 (*0-8273-5489-4*) Delmar.

Smart House Wiring: Instructor's Guide. H. Brooke Stauffer & Ray C. Mullin. 1993. teacher ed. 13.50 (*0-8273-5490-8*) Delmar.

Smart in Everything ... Except School. G. N. Getman. Ed. by Sally M. Corngold. (Illus.). 250p. 1992. lib. bdg. 15.00 (*0-929780-03-5*) VisionExtension.

Smart Interviewer. Bradford D. Smart. LC 89-37359. 205p. 1990. pap. text ed. 19.95 (*0-471-51332-6*) Wiley.

Smart Investors: Picking the Right Stock Broker for Maximum Profits. Francis W. Miller. LC 96-18822. 1996. pap. text ed. 16.95 (*0-935016-43-0*) Zinn Communs.

Smart Investor's Guide to Distressed Property. Thomas J. Lucier. Ed. by Frank Reuter. 200p. (Orig.). 1990. per. 29.95 (*0-945343-05-1*) Home Eq.

Smart Jews: The Construction of the Image of Jewish Superior Intelligence. Sander L. Gilman. LC 95-45639. (Abraham Lincoln Lectures). ix, 246p. 1996. text ed. 35.00 (*0-8032-2158-4*) U of Nebr Pr.

***Smart Jews: The Construction of the Image of Jewish Superior Intelligence.** Sander L. Gilman. LC 95-45639. (Abraham Lincoln Lecture Ser.). ix, 246p. 1997. pap. 15.00 (*0-8032-7069-0*, Bison Books) U of Nebr Pr.

Smart Job Search: A Guide to Proven Methods for Finding a Great Job. Marc L. Makos. LC 91-31232. 297p. 1991. pap. 18.95 (*0-9630394-8-2*) HD Pub.

Smart Jobs Training Plan: A Strategy for Texas. 174p. (Orig.). (C). 1994. pap. text ed. 30.00 (*0-7881-0192-7*) DIANE Pub.

Smart Kids: How Academic Talents Are Developed & Nurtured in America. William G. Durden & Arne E. Tangherlini. LC 92-40190. 336p. 1994. text ed. 27.50 (*0-88937-112-1*) Hogrefe & Huber Pubs.

Smart Kids Allowance System. Rob Berry & Kathleen Duey. (Family Skill Builders Ser.). (J). (gr. k-6). Date not set. pap. 9.95 (*1-883761-34-4*) Fmly Life Prods.

Smart Kids Solve Double Meanings. Jean G. DeGaetano & Geraldine A. Rosone. 43p. 1988. pap. text ed. 16.95 (*1-886143-24-2*) Grt Ideas Tching.

Smart Kids with School Problems: Things to Know & Ways to Help. Priscilla L. Vail. 1989. pap. 12.95 (*0-452-26242-9*, Plume) NAL-Dutton.

Smart Lamb-Wave Sensor System for the Determination of Fluid Properties. M. J. Vellekoop. 148p. 1994. pap. 57.50 (*90-407-1036-8*, Pub. by Delft U Pr NE) Coronet Bks.

***Smart Leadership.** Michael Podlinsky. (Smart Tapes Ser.). 28p. 1996. pap. 19.95 incl. audio (*1-55678-063-X*) Learn Inc.

Smart Learning: A Study Skills Guide for Teens. William Christen & Thomas Murphy. Ed. by Deborah B. Strother & William C. Strother. LC 91-48274. (Illus.). 111p. (Orig.). (J). (gr. 6 up). 1992. pap. 10.95 (*0-9628556-5-0*) Grayson Bernard Pubs.

Smart Like Me: High School Age Writers 1966-1988. Dick Lourie & Mark Pawlak. 200p. 1988. pap. 10.00 (*0-914610-58-9*) Hanging Loose.

Smart Like Me: High School Age Writing Form the Sixties to Now. Ed. by Dick Lourie & Mark Pawlak. 1988. 20.00 (*0-914610-59-7*) Hanging Loose.

Smart Litigating with Computers. Patricia S. Eyres. (Paralegal Law Library). 432p. 1992. pap. text ed. 65.00 (*0-471-59228-5*) Wiley.

Smart Little Cat. (Illus.). (J). (ps-2). 1991. lib. bdg. 7.95 (*0-8136-5172-7*, TK3879) Modern Curr.

Smart Love. Jody Hayes & Maureen Redl. 208p. (Orig.). 1989. pap. 10.95 (*0-87477-472-1*, Tarcher Putnam) Putnam Pub Group.

Smart Magazines: 50 Years of Literary Revelry & High Jinks at "Vanity Fair," "The New Yorker," "Life," "Esquire" & "The Smart Set" George H. Douglas. LC 91-15036. (Illus.). vi, 229p. (C). 1991. lib. bdg. 32.50 (*0-208-02309-7*, Archon Bks) Shoe String.

Smart Manager's Guide to Effective CAD Management. 3rd ed. Roy L. Wysack & CAD Report Staff. (Illus.). 448p. 1995. ring bd. 125.00 (*0-934869-10-3*) Cad-Cam Pub.

Smart Maneuvers: Taking Control of Your Career & Personal Success in the Information Age. Carl W. Battle. LC 94-70296. 224p. 1994. pap. 12.95 (*1-880559-16-1*) Allworth Pr.

Smart Manufacturing with Artificial Intelligence. Ed. by Jake Krakauer. LC 87-60008. (Manufacturing Update Ser.). (Illus.). 272p. reprint ed. pap. 77.60 (*0-7837-6275-5*, 2045990) Bks Demand.

***Smart Material Structures: Modeling, Estimation & Control.** H. T. Banks et al. 1996. pap. text ed. 78.00 (*0-471-97024-7*) Wiley.

Smart Materials: A Technology Assessment. 182p. 1992. 1,500.00 (*0-89336-909-8*, GB-154) BCC.

***Smart Materials & Structures.** Ed. by Friend. (Illus.). 320p. 1997. text ed. 92.00 (*0-412-64030-9*, Chap & Hall NY) Chapman & Hall.

***Smart Materials & Structures.** Gandhi & Thompson. (Illus.). 309p. (C). (gr. 13 up). Date not set. text ed. 75.50 (*0-412-37010-7*, Chap & Hall NY) Chapman & Hall.

Smart Materials Fabrication & Materials for Micro-Electro-Mechanical Systems. Ed. by A. P. Jardine et al. (Materials Research Society Symposium Proceedings Ser.: Vol. 276). 317p. 1992. text ed. 62.00 (*1-55899-171-9*) Materials Res.

Smart Materials, Structures & Mathematical Issues: Selected Papers from the U. S. Army Research Office Workshop, Smart Materials, Structures & Mathematical Issues, September 1988. Craig A. Rogers. LC 89-85344. 244p. 1989. pap. 49.95 (*0-87762-682-0*) Technomic.

Smart Medicine. Bruce Hensel. 1996. mass mkt. 6.50 (*0-425-15447-5*) Berkley Pub.

Smart Medicine for a Healthier Child: A Practical A-to-Z Reference to Natural & Conventional Treatments for Infants & Children. Janet Zand et al. LC 94-16594. 464p. pap. 19.95 (*0-89529-545-8*) Avery Pub.

Smart Medicine for Menopause: Hormone Replacement Therapy & Its Natural Alternatives. Sandra Cabot. (Illus.). 176p. pap. 9.95 (*0-89529-628-4*) Avery Pub.

Smart Medicine for Your Eyes: A Concise Guide to Nutritional Therapies for Eye Disorders. Todd. 96p. 1995. pap. 10.95 (*0-89529-661-6*) Avery Pub.

Smart Money. Lia Matera. 192p. (Orig.). 1991. mass mkt. 4.95 (*0-345-37127-5*) Ballantine.

Smart Money. Lia Matera. (Laura Di Palma Ser.). 224p. (Orig.). 1991. mass mkt. 4.99 (*0-345-37126-7*) Ballantine.

Smart Money. Jerry Tuma. 284p. 1994. 16.99 (*0-88070-664-3*, Multnomah Bks) Multnomah Pubs.

Smart Money: How to Be Your Own Financial Manager. Ken Dolan. 1990. pap. 12.00 (*0-425-12179-8*, Berkley Trade) Berkley Pub.

Smart Money: The Intelligent Guide to Financial Planning. Carl M. Heintz. 1995. 34.95 (*0-89447-310-7*) Cypress.

S

Smart Money: The Story of Bill Gates. Aaron Boyd. LC 94-48273. (Notable Americans Ser.). (Illus.). 112p. (YA). (gr. 6 up). 1995. lib. bdg. 17.95 (*1-883846-09-9*) M Reynolds.

Smart Money: Understanding & Successfully Controlling Your Financial Behavior. Jerry Tuma et al. 284p. 1994. pap. 11.99 (*0-88070-787-9*, Multnomah Bks) Multnomah Pubs.

Smart Money Financial Planner. Ken Dolan & Daria Dolan. 208p. (Orig.). 1992. pap. 10.95 (*0-425-13477-6*) Berkley Pub.

Smart Money Guide to Bargain Homes: How to Find & Buy Foreclosures. James T. Wiedemer. 232p. (Orig.). 1994. pap. 15.95 (*0-7931-0747-4*, 19132001, Real Estate Ed) Dearborn Finan.

***Smart Money Moves for African-Americans.** Kelvin Boston & Dennis Kimbro. 336p. 1997. pap. 12.00 (*0-399-52262-X*, Perigee Bks) Berkley Pub.

Smart Money Moves For African Americans. Kelvin E Boston. LC 95-37409. 336p. 1996. 21.95 (*0-399-14028-X*, Putnam) Putnam Pub Group.

Smart Moves. Sam Deep. 1990. pap. 11.00 (*0-201-51812-0*) Addison-Wesley.

Smart Moves. Stuart M. Kaminsky. 224p. 1996. mass mkt., pap. 5.99 (*0-446-40438-1*, Mysterious Paperbk) Warner Bks.

Smart Moves. National Dairy Council Staff & Dairy Council of California Staff. (Illus.). (YA). 1990. teacher ed. write for info. (*1-55647-172-6*); student ed. write for info. (*1-55647-173-4*); write for info. (*1-55647-174-2*); vhs write for info. (*1-55647-171-8*) Natl Dairy Coun.

***Smart Moves.** 2nd ed. Sam Deep ac. 1997. pap. write for info. (*0-201-32812-7*) Addison-Wesley.

Smart Moves: A Crash Course on Merger Integration Management. Price Pritchett & Ron Pound. (Orig.). 1989. pap. 5.95 (*0-944002-03-X*) Pritchett Assocs.

Smart Moves: A Kid's Guide to Self-Defense. Christopher J. Goedecke & Rosmarie Hausherr. (Illus.). 96p. (J). (gr. 3-9). 1995. 16.00 (*0-689-80294-3*, S&S Bks Young Read) S&S Childrens.

Smart Moves: How to Succeed in School, Sports, Career & Life. Dick DeVenzio. (Young Readers Ser.). 293p. (YA). (gr. 6-12). 1989. pap. 15.95 (*0-87975-546-6*) Prometheus Bks.

Smart Moves: Why Learning Is Not All in Your Head. Carla Hannaford. (Illus.). 240p. 1995. 24.95 (*0-915556-26-X*); pap. 15.95 (*0-915556-27-8*) Great Ocean.

***Smart Moves: Your Guide Through the Emotional Maze of Relocation.** Stuart Copans et al. LC 96-24012. 224p. (Orig.). 1996. pap. 16.95 (*1-57525-079-9*) Smith & Kraus.

Smart Moves for People in Charge: 130 Checklists to Help You Be a Better Leader. Sam Deep & Lyle Sussman. LC 95-9571. 304p. 1995. pap. 15.00 (*0-201-48328-9*) Addison-Wesley.

***Smart Moves for Selling.** Sam Deep. 1998. pap. write for info. (*0-201-77298-1*) Addison-Wesley.

Smart Moves Manual: The Step by Step Guide on How to Move Your Company. B. Alan Whitson. LC 90-90352. (Corporate Real Estate Ser.: Vol. 3). 114p. 1990. 119.95 incl. disk (*0-9627392-2-7*); ring bd. 89.95 (*0-9627392-0-0*) B A Whitson.

Smart Moves Manual: The Step by Step Guide on How to Move Your Company. B. Alan Whitson. LC 90-90352. (Corporate Real Estate Ser.: Vol.3). 114p. 1990. lib. bdg. 89.95 (*0-9627392-3-5*) B A Whitson.

Smart Muffins: Eighty-Three Recipes for Heavenly, Healthful Eating. Jane Kinderlehrer. (Illus.). 176p. (Orig.). 1991. pap. 11.95 (*1-55704-107-5*) Newmarket.

Smart Muffins, Cookies, Biscuits & Breads: Heavenly, Healthy Cookbook for High-Fiber, Low-Fat, No-Sugar Baked Goods. Jane Kinderlehrer. 1996. 19.95 (*1-55704-281-0*) Newmarket.

Smart Negotiating: How to Make Good Deals in the Real World. James C. Freund. 272p. 1993. pap. 12.00 (*0-671-86921-3*, Fireside) S&S Trade.

***Smart Networking: How to Turn Contacts into Cash, Clients, & Career Success.** Baber & Waymon. 208p. 1997. per. 18.00 (*0-7872-3612-8*) Kendall-Hunt.

Smart Nutrients: A Guide to Nutrients That Can Prevent & Reverse Senility. Abram Hoffer & Morton Walker. LC 93-39554. 208p. pap. 9.95 (*0-89529-562-8*) Avery Pub.

***Smart Organization: Creating Value Through Strategic.** Harvard Business School Press Staff. 1997. text ed. 29.95 (*0-07-105054-X*) McGraw.

***Smart Organization: Creating Value Through Strategic R & D.** James Matheson & David Matheson. LC 97-10776. 1997. write for info. (*0-87584-793-5*) Harvard Busn.

***Smart Organization: Creating Value Through Strategic R&D.** David Matheson & Jim Matheson. 304p. 1997. 29.95 (*0-87584-765-X*, HBS Pr) Harvard Busn.

Smart Parenting: A Guide to Child Assessment & Therapeutic Interventions. Bill J. Duke. 352p. (Orig.). 1996. pap. 19.95 (*0-9648838-3-X*) DCC Pubng.

Smart Parents Guide to College: The 10 Most Important Factors for Students & Parents to Know When Choosing a College. Ernest L. Boyer & Paul Boyer. 256p. (Orig.). 1996. pap. 16.95 (*1-56079-591-3*) Petersons.

Smart Parent's Guide to Kids' TV. Milton Chen. LC 94-20570. (Illus.). 224p. (Orig.). 1994. pap. 8.95 (*0-912333-47-2*) BB&T Inc.

***Smart Parents, Safe Kids: Everything You Need to Protect Your Family in the Modern World.** Robert Struber & Jeff Bradley. (Illus.). 256p. 1997. 19.95 (*0-8362-3533-9*) Andrews & McMeel.

Smart Patient, Good Medicine: Working with Your Doctor to Get the Best Medical Care. Richard L. Sribnick & Wayne B. Sribnick. 144p. 1994. 19.95 (*0-8027-1287-8*); pap. 8.95 (*0-8027-7414-8*) Walker & Co.

Smart Plays: A Story about Safety for Young People. Frances S. Dayee. (Illus.). 80p. (YA). (gr. 3-7). 1989. pap. 9.95 (*0-89106-039-1*, 7383) Davies-Black.

Smart Power Chips. Richard K. Miller & Terri C. Walker. LC 88-81670. (Survey on Technology & Markets Ser.: No. 79). 50p. 1989. pap. text ed. 200.00 (*1-55865-078-4*) Future Tech Surveys.

Smart Power ICs: Technologies & Application. Ed. by B. Murari et al. 496p. 1995. 163.95 (*3-540-60332-8*) Spr-Verlag.

***Smart Practice Development.** Manaktala. 192p. 1995. pap. 27.00 (*0-614-26816-8*) Commerce.

***Smart Pressure Cooker Cookbook.** Carlol Munson. Date not set. write for info. (*0-8069-9985-3*) Sterling.

Smart Profile: A Qualitative Approach of Describing Learners & Designing Instruction. Lynda Miller. 94p. 1993. pap. 24.00 (*0-9636140-0-2*) Smart Alternat.

Smart Questions. Dorothy Leeds. 1988. mass mkt. 5.99 (*0-425-11132-6*) Berkley Pub.

***Smart Questions Regarding Finances.** Dorothy Leeds. mass mkt. write for info. (*0-06-104279-X*, Harp PBks) HarpC.

***Smart Questions to Ask about Financial Advisors.** Lynn Brenner. 1997. 19.95 (*1-57660-015-7*) Bloomberg NJ.

Smart Runner's Handbook. 2nd rev. ed. Matt Greenwald. (Illus.). 160p. 1996. pap. 9.95 (*1-883323-35-5*) Open Rd Pub.

Smart Salespeople Sometimes Wear Plaid: Dare to Be Extraordinary in a Mediocre World. Barry G. Munro. LC 93-34369. 1994. pap. 12.95 (*1-55958-422-X*) Prima Pub.

Smart Schools. Perkins. 1995. pap. text ed. 16.00 (*0-205-19554-7*) Allyn.

Smart Schools: From Training Memories to Educating Minds. David Perkins. 1995. pap. 13.00 (*0-02-874018-1*) Free Pr.

Smart Schools, Smart Kids: Why Do Some Schools Work? Edward B. Fiske. 304p. 1992. pap. 11.00 (*0-671-79212-1*, Touchstone Bks) S&S Trade.

Smart Selection & Management of Association Computer Systems. Thomas J. Orlowski. 85p. 1995. pap. 34.95 (*0-88034-098-3*) Am Soc Assn Execs.

Smart Self-Publishing: An Author's Guide for Producing a Marketable Book. Jim Salisbury & Linda G. Salisbury. LC 95-35376. (Illus.). 176p. 1995. pap. 12.95 (*1-881539-03-2*) Tabby Hse Bks.

***Smart Self-Publishing: An Author's Guide to Producing a Marketable Book.** 2nd rev. ed. Jim Salisbury & Linda G. Salisbury. LC 96-44431. (Illus.). 192p. Date not set. pap. 14.95 (*1-881539-14-8*) Tabby Hse Bks.

Smart Selling: Successful Sales Techniques for Bankers. Judith A. Pennington. 1991. text ed. 35.00 (*1-55520-162-8*) Irwin Prof Pubng.

Smart Sensors. Paul W. Chapman. LC 95-36234. 1995. 65.00 (*1-55617-575-2*) ISA.

Smart Sensors. Richard K. Miller & Terri C. Walker. LC 88-81654. (Survey on Technology & Markets Ser.: No. 63). 50p. 1989. pap. text ed. 200.00 (*1-55865-062-8*) Future Tech Surveys.

Smart Sentencing: The Emergence of Intermediate Sanctions. Ed. by James M. Byrne et al. (Illus.). 320p. (C). 1992. 49.95 (*0-8039-4164-1*); pap. 24.00 (*0-8039-4165-X*) Sage.

***Smart Shopper in Hong Kong: Your Guide to Factory Outlets & Other Useful Information.** Carolyn Radin. (Illus.). 130p. (Orig.). 1996. mass mkt. 10.95 (*0-9655110-0-6*) Black Hawk Prods.

Smart Shopper's Guide to the Best Buys for Kids. Sue Robinson. 1996. 12.95 (*0-02-861287-6*) Macmillan.

Smart Shopping: A Guide to Discount Stores in Utah. Timothy P. Aebi & Carolyn E. Kenney. LC 94-69844. xxi, 327p. (Orig.). 1995. pap. 11.99 (*0-87579-834-9*, Shadow Mount) Deseret Bk.

Smart Simple Design: A Guide to Variety Effectiveness Planning. Gwen D. Galsworth. 300p. (C). 1994. 102.00 (*0-939246-62-7*) Wiley.

Smart, Simple Design: Using Variety Effectiveness to Reduce Total Cost & Maximize Customer Selection. Gwen D. Galsworth. 256p. 1995. text ed. 39.95 (*0-471-13185-7*) Wiley.

Smart Simplified. Jean E. Gutmann. (Illus.). (Orig.). 1989. pap. 22.95 (*0-8306-3223-9*, Windcrest) TAB Bks.

Smart Snacks: Groups Size Snacks for Kids of All Ages. Betsy Rhein & Sandy Drummond. 121p. (Orig.). 1995. pap. 9.95 (*0-9647228-0-1*) TBM Pubns.

Smart Snips: Hands-on Adventures in Thinking, Reading & Direction-Following. Greta Rasmussen & Ted Rasmussen. 112p. 1993. pap. 11.95 (*0-936110-15-5*) Tin Man Pr.

Smart Speaking: Sixty-Second Strategies for More Than 100 Speaking Problems & Fears. Laurie Schloff & Marcia Yudkin. 256p. 1992. reprint ed. pap. 11.95 (*0-452-26777-3*, Plume) NAL-Dutton.

Smart Spending: A Consumer's Guide. Lois Schmitt. LC 88-29524. 112p. (J). (gr. 5-9). 1989. lib. bdg. 13.95 (*0-684-19035-4*, C Scribner Sons Young) S&S Childrens.

Smart Squash: How to Win at Soft Ball. Austin M. Francis. (Illus.). 160p. 1995. pap. 16.95 (*1-55821-341-4*) Lyons & Burford.

Smart Start: Elementary Education for the Twenty-First Century. Ruth Mitchell & Patte Barth. LC 92-60659. (Illus.). 224p. 1992. 21.95 (*1-55591-908-1*) Fulcrum Pub.

Smart Start: Elementary Education for the Twenty-First Century. Ruth Mitchell & Patte Barth. LC 92-60659. (Illus.). 224p. 1992. pap. 14.95 (*1-55591-909-X*) Fulcrum Pub.

***Smart Start: The Parents' Complete Guide to Preschool Education.** Marian E. Borden. LC 97-11599. 1997. write for info. (*0-8160-3604-7*); pap. write for info. (*0-8160-3677-2*) Facts on File.

Smart Steps to Smart Choices: Testing Your Business Idea. David H. Bangs, Jr. 144p. 1996. pap. 22.95 (*1-57410-021-1*, 6100-9301) Upstart Pub.

Smart Structures & Materials. Brian Culshaw. LC 95-48914. 1995. 67.00 (*0-89006-681-7*) Artech Hse.

Smart Structures, Nonlinear Dynamics & Control. Ardeshin Guran & Daniel J. Inman. LC 95-6171. (C). 1995. text ed. 81.00 (*0-13-434457-X*) P-H.

***Smart Student Trap.** Kaplan Staff. LC 97-15766. 1997. pap. 10.00 (*0-684-84169-X*) S&S Trade.

Smart Studying Four Hundred. Edward Chappie. 97p. (Orig.). 1992. pap. text ed. 9.95 (*0-9630832-0-1*) Stoneycreek.

Smart Survivors. Sneed Collard. LC 93-19650. (J). (gr. 1-5). 1994. 9.95 (*1-55971-224-4*) NorthWord.

***Smart Take from the Strong.** Carril. LC 96-50904. 1997. 21.00 (*0-684-83510-X*) S&S Trade.

Smart Talk: The Art of Savvy Business Conversation. Roberta Roesch. LC 89-45455. 256p. 1989. pap. 14.95 (*0-8144-7713-5*) AMACOM.

***Smart Talk for Achieving Your Potential: 5 Steps to Get You from Here to There.** Lou Tice. 304p. pap. 15.00 (*0-9634917-6-8*) Exec Excell.

Smart Talk for Achieving Your Potential: 5 Steps to Get You from Here to There. Louis E. Tice. 280p. 1995. 25.00 (*0-9634917-9-2*) Exec Excell.

***Smart Tax Write-Offs: Hundreds of Tax Deduction Ideas for Home-Based Businesses, Independent Contractors, All Entrepreneurs.** Norman H. Ray. (Illus.). 112p. 1996. pap. 12.95 (*1-877810-20-7*) Rayve Prodns.

Smart Thermal Flow Sensors. Huibert-Jan Verhoeven. (Illus.). 196p. (Orig.). 1995. pap. 87.50 (*90-407-1223-9*, Pub. by Delft U Pr NE) Coronet Bks.

Smart Tracks: Systems Management for Orthopaedic Rehabilitation. James Hoyme et al. 300p. (Orig.). 1996. text ed. 249.95 (*0-9643582-1-2*) Learn Pubns.

***Smart Trainers: Brilliant Dogs.** Janet R. Lewis. (Illus.). 192p. (Orig.). 1997. pap. 19.95 (*1-888119-01-2*) Canine Spts.

Smart Traveler: Ready-Set-Go. Carol L. Walker & Carol J. Farr. (Illus.). 50p. (Orig.). 1997. mass mkt. 6.95 (*0-9652347-0-3*) CnC Publns.

Smart Trust Deed Investment in California. 2nd ed. George Coats. LC 87-33370. (Illus.). 292p. (Orig.). 1988. pap. 23.50 (*0-934581-01-0*) Barr-Randol Pub.

Smart Trust Deed Investor's Formsbook. George Coats. LC 93-21655. 224p. (Orig.). 1993. spiral bd. 67.50 (*0-934581-02-9*) Barr-Randol Pub.

Smart Tutor/Smart Tester. Milady Publishing Company Staff. (Standard Texts of Cosmetology Ser.). 1989. teacher ed. 10.00 (*0-87350-806-8*) Van Nos Reinhold.

Smart Tutor/Smart Tester Revision. 2nd ed. Jeans. (Cosmetology Ser.). 1995. 599.00 (*1-56253-272-3*) Van Nos Reinhold.

Smart Vacations: The Traveler's Guide to Learning Adventures Abroad. Council on International Educational Exchange Staff & Priscilla M. Torey. LC 92-43173. 320p. (Orig.). 1993. pap. 14.95 (*0-312-08823-X*) St Martin.

Smart Vehicles. Ed. by J. P. Pauwelussen & Hans B. Pacejka. xii, 472p. 1995. 94.25 (*90-265-1456-5*) Swets.

Smart Verse: The Owl Flies amid the Woodwind Hooting. Ninian Smart. 128p. (Orig.). 1996. pap. 9.50 (*1-56474-171-0*) Fithian Pr.

***Smart Way to Buy Information Technology: How to Maximize Value & Avoid Costly Pitfalls.** Brad L. Petersen & Diane M. Carco. 304p. 1997. 35.00 (*0-8144-0387-5*) AMACOM.

Smart Ways to Pay For a College Education: Saturday Morning Planner. Craig Smith & Anita Jay. LC 90-85517. (Illus.). 112p. (Orig.). 1990. pap. text ed. 9.50 (*0-9628583-0-7*) Blue Sky Pub.

Smart Ways to Save Money During & after Divorce. Victoria Felton-Collins & Ginita Wall. 200p. 1994. pap. 14.95 (*0-87337-214-X*) Nolo Pr.

Smart Ways to Stay Young & Healthy. Bradley Gascoigne & Julie Irwin. 128p. (Orig.). 1992. pap. 7.95 (*0-914171-49-6*) Ronin Pub.

***Smart Woman's Guide.** Diane Pearl & Ellie Clinton. 192p. 1997. mass mkt. 5.99 (*0-06-101200-9*, Harp PBks) HarpC.

Smart Woman's Guide to Career Success. Janet Hauter. 160p. (Orig.). 1993. pap. 11.95 (*1-56414-056-3*) Career Pr Inc.

***Smart Woman's Guide to Career Success.** Janet Hauter. (Smart Woman's Guides Ser.). 160p. (Orig.). 1996. lib. bdg. 19.95 (*0-7910-4472-6*) Chelsea Hse.

Smart Woman's Guide to Interviewing & Salary Negotiation. 2nd ed. Julie A. King. 224p. (Orig.). 1995. pap. 12.99 (*1-56414-206-X*) Career Pr Inc.

***Smart Woman's Guide to Interviewing & Salary Negotiations.** Julie A. King. (Smart Woman's Guides Ser.). 224p. (Orig.). 1996. lib. bdg. 19.95 (*0-7910-4437-8*) Chelsea Hse.

Smart Woman's Guide to Networking. Betsy Sheldon & Joyce Hadley. 224p. (Orig.). 1995. pap. 12.99 (*1-56414-207-8*) Career Pr Inc.

***Smart Woman's Guide to Networking.** Betsy Sheldon & Joyce Hadley. (Smart Woman's Guides Ser.). 192p. (Orig.). 1996. lib. bdg. 19.95 (*0-7910-4473-4*) Chelsea Hse.

***Smart Woman's Guide to Resumes & Job Hunting.** Julie A. King & Betsy Sheldon. (Smart Woman's Guides Ser.). 216p. 1996. lib. bdg. 19.95 (*0-7910-4474-2*) Chelsea Hse.

Smart Woman's Guide to Resumes & Job Hunting. 3rd ed. Julie A. King & Betsy Sheldon. 224p. (Orig.). 1995. pap. 9.99 (*1-56414-205-1*) Career Pr Inc.

***Smart Woman's Guide to Spending, Saving & Managing Money.** Diane Pearl & Ellie Williams. (Smart Woman's Guides Ser.). 192p. 1996. lib. bdg. 19.95 (*0-7910-4488-2*) Chelsea Hse.

Smart Womans Guide to Spending, Saving & Managing Money. Ellie Williams & Diane Pearl. 192p. (Orig.). 1994. pap. text ed. 11.95 (*1-56414-136-5*) Career Pr Inc.

Smart Woman's Guide to Starting a Business. Vickie Montgomery. 216p. (Orig.). 1994. pap. 14.95 (*1-56414-129-2*) Career Pr Inc.

***Smart Woman's Guide to Starting a Business.** Vickie Montgomery. (Smart Woman's Guides Ser.). 216p. 1996. lib. bdg. 19.95 (*0-7910-4487-4*) Chelsea Hse.

Smart Women. Judy Blume. 1985. mass mkt. 6.50 (*0-671-72758-3*) PB.

Smart Women, Foolish Choices. Connell Cowan & Melvyn Kinder. 1986. pap. 5.99 (*0-451-15885-7*, Sig) NAL-Dutton.

Smart Women Keep It Simple. Annie Chapman & Maureen Rank. 192p. (Orig.). 1992. pap. 8.99 (*1-55661-236-2*) Bethany Hse.

Smart Work. Syntax Staff. 176p. 1995. per., pap. text ed. 19.95 (*0-7872-0491-9*) Kendall-Hunt.

Smart Yard: The Guide to 60-Minute Lawn Care. Jeff Ball & Liz Ball. (Illus.). 208p. (Orig.). 1995. pap. 16.95 (*1-55591-138-2*) Fulcrum Pub.

***Smartass Answers to Stupid Interview Questions.** Barry Shamis. (Illus.). 96p. 1996. pap. 12.95 (*0-9653930-0-3*) Leverage Pr.

Smartcuts: One Hundred Plus User Friendly Shortcuts for the Mac Keyboard & Mouse. Todd Corleto. 1993. pap. 7.95 (*1-879682-47-8*) Earth Works.

Smarte Date Pak. John R. Craig. 144p. (Orig.). 1992. pap. text ed. 5.95 (*0-9614423-1-X*) Rite Bks Pub.

Smarten Up. Roger B. Yepsen. (J). (gr. 4-7). 1990. 13.95 (*0-316-96864-1*) Little.

Smarter Board Meetings: For Effective Nonprofit Governance. Robert K. Mueller. (Nonprofit Governance Ser.: No. 12). 22p. (Orig.). (C). 1993. reprint ed. pap. text ed. 12.00 (*0-925299-18-9*) Natl Ctr Nonprofit.

Smarter Business Finance. Dileep Rao. 298p. 1993. pap. write for info. (*1-884147-00-3*) InterFinance.

Smarter Charters. Chris Caswell. (Illus.). 256p. (Orig.). 1994. pap. 14.95 (*0-312-10550-9*) St Martin.

Smarter Company's Guide to Managing Your Banking: Techniques to Gain Maximum Value at Minimum Cost. Hunter Clark Associates Staff. (Financial Times Management Ser.). 240p. 1994. 77.50 (*0-273-60471-6*, Pub. by Pitman Pub Ltd UK) Trans-Atl Phila.

***Smarter Insurance Solutions.** Janet Bamford. LC 96-84216. (Bloomberg Personal Bookshelf Ser.). (Illus.). 256p. 1996. 19.95 (*1-57660-003-3*) Bloomberg NJ.

Smarter Kids: At Home & School. Ed. by Elinor Katz. (Professional Development Ser.). (Illus.). 100p. (Orig.). 1996. pap. text ed. 15.45 (*0-9638228-2-9*) Open Space Comn.

Smarter Organization: How to Build a Business That Learns & Adapts to Marketplace Needs. Michael McGill & John W. Slocum. 288p. 1994. text ed. 32.50 (*0-471-59846-1*) Wiley.

***Smarter than You Think: A Revolutionary Approach to Teaching & Understanding Your Dog in Just a Few Hours.** Paul Loeb. 1997. 22.00 (*0-671-00172-8*, PB Hardcover) PB.

Smarter Trading: Improving Performance in Changing Markets. Perry J. Kaufman. 1995. text ed. 29.95 (*0-07-034002-1*) McGraw.

***Smarter Vehicle Leasing Vol. 1: A Consumers Guide to Understanding the System.** Nick Santangelo & Steven Anthony. (Illus.). 74p. (Orig.). 1996. pap. 9.95 (*0-9653048-0-9*) Scarlet Gypsy.

Smartest Man in Ireland. Mollie Hunter. (J). 1996. pap. 5.00 (*0-15-200993-0*) HarBrace.

SmartJobs. 1995. 199.95 incl. audio compact disk (*0-614-08836-4*, 315010) Busn Legal Reports.

SmartMoves for the SmartKid in All of Us. Margaret Danson. (Illus.). 88p. (Orig.). 1996. pap. write for info. (*0-9651529-0-1*) SmartMoves.

SmartMoves Training Manual: A Manual for Pre-Employment Training for the Homeless. Spring Institute for International Studies Staff. 122p. 1995. ring bd. write for info. (*0-940723-11-5*) SIIS.

Smartparenting: A New Approach to Raising Happy, Well-Adjusted Kids. Peter Favaro. 288p. 1995. pap. 14.95 (*0-8092-3431-9*) Contemp Bks.

SmartPolicies. 1995. 199.95 incl. cd-rom (*0-614-08861-5*, 315004/315005) Busn Legal Reports.

SMARTS is Never Letting a Computer Get You a Date: Advice from FELIX the Cat. Frank Hill. LC 82-74028. (Illus.). 1984. 3.95 (*0-915696-61-4*) Determined Prods.

SMARTS (Studying, Memorizing, Active Listening, Reviewing, Test-Taking, & Survival SKills) A Study Skills Resource Guide. 2nd ed. Susan H. Custer et al. (Illus.). 116p. 1995. teacher ed., pap. text ed. 19.50 (*1-57035-045-0*, 10SMARTS) Sopris.

Smartstart Custom Binding 1. 1994. 68.00 (*1-56529-941-8*) Que.

***SmartStart Your Arizona Business.** PSI Research Staff. 300p. (Orig.). 1997. pap. 19.95 (*1-55571-409-9*) Oasis Pr OR.

***SmartStart Your California Business.** PSI Research Staff. 300p. (Orig.). 1997. pap. 19.95 (*1-55571-416-1*) Oasis Pr OR.

***SmartStart Your Colorado Business.** PSI Research Staff. 300p. (Orig.). 1997. pap. 19.95 (*1-55571-411-0*) Oasis Pr OR.

***SmartStart Your Florida Business.** PSI Research Staff. 300p. (Orig.). 1997. pap. 19.95 (*1-55571-415-3*) Oasis Pr OR.

An Asterisk (*) at the beginning of an entry indicates that the title is appearing in BIP for the first time.

***SmartStart Your Kentucky Business.** PSI Research Staff. 300p. (Orig.). 1997. pap. 19.95 (*1-55571-407-2*) Oasis Pr OR.
***SmartStart Your Massachusetts Business.** PSI Research Staff. 300p. (Orig.). 1997. pap. 19.95 (*1-55571-408-0*) Oasis Pr OR.
***SmartStart Your New Jersey Business.** PSI Research Staff. 300p. (Orig.). 1997. pap. 19.95 (*1-55571-419-6*) Oasis Pr OR.
***SmartStart Your New York Business.** PSI Research Staff. 300p. (Orig.). 1997. pap. 19.95 (*1-55571-414-5*) Oasis Pr OR.
***SmartStart Your North Carolina Business.** PSI Research Staff. 300p. (Orig.). 1997. pap. 19.95 (*1-55571-410-2*) Oasis Pr OR.
***SmartStart Your Texas Business.** PSI Research Staff. 300p. (Orig.). 1997. pap. 19.95 (*1-55571-417-X*) Oasis Pr OR.
***SmartStart Your Washington Business.** PSI Research Staff. 300p. (Orig.). 1997. pap. 19.95 (*1-55571-418-8*) Oasis Pr OR.
SmartSuit Desktop Companion. Patrick J. Burns et al. (Illus.). 784p. 1994. 24.95 (*1-56604-184-8*) Ventana Communs.
Smartsuite 3 for Dummies. Jan Weingarten. 384p. 1995. pap. 19.99 (*1-56884-367-4*) IDG Bks.
SmartSuite 97 for Windows for Dummies. (Illus.). 400p. (Orig.). 1997. pap. 19.99 (*1-56884-610-X*) IDG Bks.
***SmartSuite 97 Visual Learning Guide: Fast & Easy.** Sharon Podlin. 400p. 1997. per. 16.99 (*0-7615-1192-X*) Prima Pub.
SmartWare: A Beginners Guide. Ed. by Dexter Booth. 358p. (C). 1989. pap. text ed. 160.00 (*0-273-03185-6*, Pub. by Pitman Pubng UK) St Mut.
Smarty Arty: Art Play for You & Your Preschooler. Linda Allison & Martha Weston. LC 93-24556. (Brown Paper Preschool Ser.). 1994. 8.95 (*0-316-03465-7*) Little.
Smartype---A Keyboard Program. C. Daiute. 1986. 39.95 (*0-07-838066-9*) McGraw.
Smarty's New Friend. Joseph C. Dennie & Joseph Weathers. Ed. by Charlotte A. Bonnette. LC 93-39652. (Illus.). 20p. (Orig.). (J). (gr. 1-4). 1994. pap. 7.95 incl. audio (*1-877971-11-1*) Mid Atl Reg Pr.
Smash. Jeffrey Hatcher. 1997. pap. 5.25 (*0-8222-1553-5*) Dramatists Play.
Smash Caps: The Official Milk-Cap Manual. Lawrence Paros & Ben J. Paros. (Illus.). 55p. (Orig.). (J). (gr. 3-6). 1995. pap. 7.99 (*0-380-78459-9*, Camelot) Avon.
Smash Cut. Womack. Date not set. 3.98 (*0-8317-4629-7*) Smithmark.
Smash the Pyramid. William Doyle & William Perkins. 320p. 1996. mass mkt. 6.99 (*0-446-60367-8*) Warner Bks.
Smash the Pyramid: One Hundred Career Secrets from America's Fastest Rising Executives. William Doyle & William Perkins. 256p. 1994. 19.95 (*0-446-51760-7*) Warner Bks.
Smash-up Crash-up Derby. Tres Seymour. LC 94-24857. (Illus.). 32p. (J). (ps-2). 1995. 15.95 (*0-531-06881-1*); lib. bdg. 16.99 (*0-531-08731-X*) Orchard Bks Watts.
Smashed Potatoes & Other Thanksgiving Disasters. Carol W. Murphy. LC 94-15001. 128p. (J). (gr. 3-6). 1994. pap. 2.95 (*0-8167-3518-2*, Rainbow NJ) Troll Communs.
***Smasher: The Ugly Puppy.** Dick King-Smith. LC 96-53137. (J). 1997. pap. 3.99 (*0-679-88330-4*); lib. bdg. 11.99 (*0-679-98330-9*) Random Bks Yng Read.
Smashing Pots: Works of Clay from Africa. Nigel Barley. LC 94-65294. (Illus.). 176p. (Orig.). 1994. pap. 29.95 (*1-56098-419-8*) Smithsonian.
***Smashing Pumpkins.** (Photo Bks.). (Illus.). 1996. 11.95 (*1-870049-92-6*, OB 11016, Pub. by Oliver Bks UK) Music Sales.
***Smashing Pumpkins.** (Interview CD Bks.). (Illus.). 14.99 (*1-57899-007-6*, Pub. by Sound & Media UK) Mus Bk Servs.
Smashing Pumpkins. Jim Stapleton. (CD Bks.). (Illus.). 120p. 1995. pap. 7.99 (*1-886894-05-1*, MBS Paperbk) Mus Bk Servs.
***Smashing Pumpkins: Mellon Collie & the Infinite Sadness.** Ed. by Aaron Stang. 240p. (Orig.). (YA). 1996. pap. text ed. 29.95 (*1-57623-339-1*, PG9602) Warner Brothers.
Smashing Pumpkins: Siamese Dream. Ed. by Aaron Stang. 128p. (Orig.). (YA). 1994. pap. text ed. 22.95 (*0-89898-825-X*, P1027GTX) Warner Brothers.
Smashing the Gates of Hell: In the Last Days. David A. Lewis. LC 86-65887. 240p. 1987. pap. 9.95 (*0-89221-143-1*) New Leaf.
Smashing the Idols: A Jewish Inquiry into the Cult Phenomenon. Ed. by Gary D. Eisenberg. LC 88-10202. 360p. 1988. 40.00 (*0-87668-974-8*) Aronson.
***Smashing the Wall of Fear: Dynamic Strategies to Overcome the Obstacles in Your Life.** unabridged ed. Sean Hockensmith. Ed. by Gina Leis et al. LC 96-86670. (Illus.). 256p. 1997. 19.99 (*0-9651246-5-7*); pap. 12.99 (*0-9651246-8-1*) Dynamic Life.
Smashing Thru Language Barriers. Karl A. Krippes. 106p. (Orig.). 1996. pap. 12.00 (*0-9651505-0-X*) Hierogly Pr.
***Smashmouth: Attitude Between the Lines.** Roland Lazenby. Ed. by Susan Storey. 144p. 1997. pap. 14.95 (*1-886110-26-3*) Addax Pubng.
Smastykker Til Daglig Andakt see God's Word for Today: A Daily Devotional for the Whole Year
Smattering of Monsters: A Kind of Memoir. George C. Greenfield. 324p. 1995. 39.95 (*1-57113-071-3*) Camden Hse.
***Smau Sightings.** Linda Opyr. 1996. pap. 5.00 (*1-878173-46-4*) Birnham Wood.
***SMDS Market.** 300p. 1991. 2,800.00 (*0-614-18363-4*, IGIC-53) Info Gatekeepers.
SME Mining Engineering Handbook, 2 vols., Set. 2nd ed. Ed. by Howard L. Hartman. LC 92-61198. (Illus.). 2342p. (C). 1992. 136.50 (*0-87335-100-2*) SMM&E Inc.
Smear Terror. John T. Flynn. 1982. lib. bdg. 59.95 (*0-87700-367-X*) Revisionist Pr.
Smeatonians: The Society of Civil Engineers. Garth Watson. 197p. 1989. text ed. 31.00 (*0-7277-1526-7*, Pub. by T Telford UK) Am Soc Civil Eng.
Smedley Butler & the Plot to Take over the White House. 1991. lib. bdg. 79.95 (*0-8490-4250-X*) Gordon Pr.
Smedvig Production Unit. R. Arnfinn Nergaard. 1989. 150.00 (*90-6314-520-9*, Pub. by Lorne & MacLean Marine) St Mut.
Smell. Illus. by Miguel Ferron. LC 95-17488. (Five Senses of the Animal World Ser.). (J). 1996. lib. bdg. 15.95 (*0-7910-3492-5*) Chelsea Hse.
***Smell.** Sue Hurwitz. LC 96-29964. (Library of the Five Senses (Plus the Sixth Sense)). (J). 1997. write for info. (*0-8239-5053-0*) Rosen Group.
Smell. J. M. Parramon & J. J. Puig. (Five Senses Ser.). (Illus.). 32p. (J). (ps). 1985. pap. 6.95 (*0-8120-3565-8*); pap. 6.95 (*0-8120-3607-7*) Barron.
***Smell.** Maria Rius et al. (Five Senses Ser.). (J). 1985. 6.95 (*0-8120-5738-4*) Barron.
Smell. Mandy Suhr. LC 93-44189. (I'm Alive Ser.). (Illus.). (J). (ps-1). 1993. lib. bdg. 14.21 (*0-87614-835-6*, Carolrhoda) Lerner Group.
***Smell: The Secret Seducer.** Piet Vroon. LC 97-2299. 1997. 24.00 (*0-374-25704-3*) FS&G.
Smell & Taste in Health & Disease. Ed. by Thomas V. Getchell. (Illus.). 906p. 1991. text ed. 182.50 (*0-88167-798-1*) Lppncott-Raven.
Smell It Like It Is: Tales from the Garlic Capital of the World. Kathryn M. Nichols. LC 91-36046. (Illus.). 112p. (Orig.). 1992. pap. 8.95 (*1-56474-008-0*) Fithian Pr.
***Smell It... Touch It!** Thomas-Cochran. (What a Wonderful World Intro Ser.). 1993. pap. text ed. write for info. (*0-582-91082-X*, Pub. by Longman UK) Longman.
***Smell of Apples.** Behr. 1997. pap. 12.00 (*0-312-15209-4*) St Martin.
Smell of Apples: A Novel. Mark Behr. LC 95-21658. 1995. 21.95 (*0-312-13604-8*) St Martin.
Smell of Books: A Cultural-Historical Study of Olfactory Perception in Literature. Hans J. Rindisbacher. 300p. (C). 1992. text ed. 52.50 (*0-472-10383-0*) U of Mich Pr.
Smell of Burning & Then: Two Plays. David Campton. 1969. pap. 3.25 (*0-8222-1047-9*) Dramatists Play.
Smell of Humans: A Memoir of the Holocaust in Hungary. Erno Szep. Tr. by John Batki. (Central European University Press Bk.). 208p. 1995. 45.00 (*1-85866-014-9*); pap. 18.95 (*1-85866-011-4*) OUP.
Smell of Leaves & Summer: Collected Stories. Hagger. 1995. pap. 35.00 (*1-85230-650-5*) Element MA.
Smell of Matches. Poems. John Stone. 77p. 1988. pap. 6.95 (*0-8071-1477-4*) La State U Pr.
Smell of Money. large type ed. William Newton. 1990. pap. 15.99 (*0-7089-6996-8*, Trailtree Bookshop) Ulverscroft.
***Smell of the Rain.** Cullinan. 1994. 11.00 (*0-15-302384-8*) HarBrace.
Smell, Taste & Touch. Jenny Bryan. (Body Talk Ser.). (Illus.). 48p. (J). (gr. 5). 1994. lib. bdg. 13.95 (*0-87518-590-8*, Dillon Silver Burdett) Silver Burdett Pr.
***Smell the Rain.** Cullinan. (J). 1994. 17.00 (*0-15-302204-3*, HB Juv Bks) HarBrace.
Smelling. Kathie B. Smith & Victoria Crenson. LC 87-5887. (Question Bks.). (Illus.). 24p. (J). (gr. k-3). 1988. lib. bdg. 11.89 (*0-8167-1010-4*) Troll Communs.
***Smelling a Rat.** Mike Leigh. 80p. (Orig.). 1996. pap. 14.95 (*1-85459-316-1*, Pub. by N Hern Bks UK) Theatre Comm.
Smelling & Tasting. Lesley Sims. (What about...? Ser.). (J). 1995. pap. text ed. 4.95 (*0-8114-7997-8*) Raintree Steck-V.
Smelling & Tasting. Lillian Wright. (What about...? Ser.). (Illus.). 32p. (J). (gr. 2-4). 1994. lib. bdg. 21.40 (*0-8114-5518-1*) Raintree Steck-V.
Smelling of Roses: A Rugby Life. Stuart Barnes. (Illus.). 206p. 1995. 34.95 (*1-85158-640-7*, Pub. by Mnstream UK) Trafalgar.
Smelling Things. Allan Fowler. LC 90-22123. (Rookie Read-about Science Ser.). (Illus.). 32p. (J). (ps-2). 1991. pap. 3.95 (*0-516-44912-5*); lib. bdg. 17.30 (*0-516-04912-7*) Childrens.
Smelling Things Big Book. Allan Fowler. (Rookie Read-about Science Big Bks.). (Illus.). 32p. (J). (ps-2). 1991. pap. 32.40 (*0-516-49472-4*) Childrens.
***Smells.** Luann Colombo. (Gross But True Ser.). (J). 1997. 8.99 (*0-689-81496-8*, Litl Simon S&S) S&S Childrens.
***Smelt Fly Patterns.** Donald A. Wilson. (Illus.). 61p. 1996. 19.95 (*1-57188-071-2*) F Amato Pubns.
Smelter Process Gas Handling & Treatment: Proceedings of an International Symposium Sponsored by the Pyrometallurgy Committee, Held at the Annual Meeting of the Minnerals, Metals & Materials Society in San Diego, CA, March 1-5, 1992. Minerals, Metals & Materials Society Staff. Ed. by Tim J. Smith & Chris J. Newman. LC 91-51053. 1991. reprint ed. pap. 78.40 (*0-608-00769-2*, 2061567) Bks Demand.
Smelting & Forging. Kizu. 1991. pap. 4.95 (*0-910704-27-9*) Hawley.
Smerkli & the Booger Picker. Rhyk Gilbar. (Illus.). 32p. (J). (gr. k-7). 1996. pap. 6.95 (*0-614-17773-1*); lib. bdg. 14.95 (*0-614-17772-3*) Positive Press.
SME's: Internationalization, Networks & Strategy. Ed. by Jose MaVeciana. 736p. 1994. 105.95 (*1-85628-696-7*, Pub. by Avebury Pub UK) Ashgate Pub Co.
Smetana. Brian Large. LC 84-1825. (Music Reprint Ser.). (Illus.). 524p. 1985. reprint ed. lib. bdg. 52.50 (*0-306-76243-9*) Da Capo.
Smidgen of Honey: A Cookbook. Maxine Wilhelm. LC 86-80962. (Illus.). 86p. 1986. pap. 12.00 (*0-934188-21-1*) Evans Pubns.
***Smidgen the Miniature Hose.** Virginia M. Bennack. (Illus.). 51p. (Orig.). (J). (gr. k-5). 1996. pap. 4.95 (*0-9655446-0-5*) Agarita Press.
Smiffy Blue: Ace Crime Detective: the Case of the Missing Ruby & Other Stories. Walter D. Myers. LC 95-21820. (Illus.). 96p. (J). (gr. 3-6). 1996. 14.95 (*0-590-67665-2*) Scholastic Inc.
Smiffy Blue: Ace Crime Detective: The Case of the Missing Ruby & Other Stories. Walter D. Myers. (Illus.). (J). (gr. 3-6). 1996. 14.95 (*0-614-15761-7*) Scholastic Inc.
Smile. Ray Bradbury. (Classic Short Stories Ser.). (J). 1991. lib. bdg. 13.95 (*0-88682-466-4*) Creative Ed.
Smile. David Campton. 31p. 1991. pap. 3.00 (*0-87129-088-X*, S96) Dramatic Pub.
Smile! Denise Duhamel. LC 92-91159. 100p. (Orig.). 1993. pap. 10.00 (*1-879294-04-4*) Warm Spring Pr.
***Smile!** Roberta G. Intrater. (Baby Faces Ser.). (J). 1997. 4.95 (*0-590-05899-1*, Cartwheel) Scholastic Inc.
Smile: A Picture History of Olympic Park, 1887-1965. Alan A. Siegel. (Illus.). 176p. (C). 1995. pap. 19.95 (*0-8135-2255-2*) Rutgers U Pr.
Smile! Twenty-Five Happy Reminders. (Miniature Pop-up Bks.). (Illus.). 12p. 1995. 4.95 (*1-56138-556-5*, Running Pr Mini Edtns) Running Pr.
***Smile, a Chuckle or a Loud Guffaw: or What Happened When I Wasn't Looking.** Marguerite L. Dye. 84p. (Orig.). 1996. pap. 12.95 (*1-890175-00-5*) Armadillo Poetry.
Smile & Be a Villain: The Autobiography of Ireland's Beloved Comic Actor. Niall Toibin. LC 96-67078. 336p. 1996. pap. text ed. 16.95 (*1-57098-086-1*) R Rinehart.
Smile & Say Murder. Carolyn Keene. (Nancy Drew Files Ser.: No. 4). (YA). (gr. 7 up). 1991. pap. 3.75 (*0-671-73659-0*, Archway) PB.
Smile & Say Murder. large type ed. Carolyn Keene. (Nancy Drew Files Ser.). (J). (gr. 5-10). 1988. 9.50 (*0-942545-26-5*); lib. bdg. 10.50 (*0-942545-30-3*) Grey Castle.
Smile at the Foot of the Ladder. Henry Miller. LC 58-11829. (Illus.). 64p. 1975. pap. 6.95 (*0-8112-0556-8*, NDP386) New Directions.
***Smile, Baby! Level 2.** Catherine Peters. (Special Times, Little Readers Ser.). (J). 1997. pap. text ed. 2.50 (*0-395-88311-3*) HM.
Smile, Be True to Your Teeth & They'll Never Be False to You. 2nd rev. ed. Robert S. Rauch. (Illus.). 105p. 1991. pap. 9.95 (*0-9624076-0-7*) R S Rauch.
Smile Connection: How to Use Humor in Dealing with People. Esther Blumenfeld & Lynne Alpers. 300p. 1985. 14.95 (*0-13-525783-2*); pap. 7.95 (*0-13-525775-1*) P-H.
Smile for Sammy. S. Stern. 1993. 11.99 (*0-89906-984-3*); 8.99 (*0-89906-985-1*) Mesorah Pubns.
Smile for Toto. Jill Barnes & Ken Asuka. Ed. by Caroline Rubin. Tr. by Japan Foreign Rights Centre Staff from JPN. LC 90-37747. (Dragonfly Tales Ser.). (Illus.). 32p. (J). (gr. k-4). 1990. lib. bdg. 14.60 (*0-944483-87-9*) Garrett Ed Corp.
Smile from Andy. Nan Holcomb. (Illus.). 32p. (J). (ps-2). 1989. pap. 7.95 (*0-944727-04-2*) Jason & Nordic Pubs.
Smile from Andy. Nan Holcomb. (Illus.). 32p. (J). (ps-3). 1992. reprint ed. lib. bdg. 13.95 (*0-944727-15-8*) Jason & Nordic Pubs.
Smile from Katie Hattan & Other Natural Wonders. Leon Hale. LC 82-60563. 288p. 1982. 13.95 (*0-940672-07-3*) Shearer Pub.
Smile, Honey. Anabel Donald. LC 89-32144. 256p. 1989. pap. 8.95 (*0-916515-88-5*) Mercury Hse Inc.
Smile in a Mad Dog's I. 2nd ed. Richard Stine. 1977. 6.95 (*0-916860-02-7*) Healthy Planet Prods.
Smile in the Mind. Beryl McAlhone & David Stuart. (Illus.). 240p. 1996. 69.95 (*0-7148-3328-2*, Pub. by Phaidon Press UK) Chronicle Bks.
Smile Increases Your Face Value. Ed. by Mac Anderson. (Illus.). 78p. (Orig.). 1991. pap. 7.95 (*1-56245-011-5*) Great Quotations.
Smile is the Beginning: Operation Smile International the First Ten Years. Operation Smile International Staff. 196p. 1993. 50.00 (*0-9635271-0-X*) Oper Smile Intl.
***Smile! It Improves Your Face Value.** Reiman Publications Staff. 1997. 11.95 (*0-89821-212-X*) Reiman Pubns.
Smile! Let's Play "Political Dissident" American Style. (Analysis Ser.). 12.50 (*0-686-45489-8*) Inst Analysis.
Smile Makes a Lousy Umbrella. Charles M. Schulz. LC 77-71352. (Peanuts Parade Bks.: No. 17). 192p. 1977. pap. 5.00 (*0-03-021406-8*, Owl) H Holt & Co.
Smile Makes a Lousy Umbrella. Charles M. Schulz. (Peanuts Classics Ser.). 128p. 1991. pap. 7.95 (*0-8050-1896-4*, Owl) H Holt & Co.
***Smile Method: How to Avoid Gum Surgery & Dentures.** 2nd rev. ed. Vasilios Gardiakos. Orig. Title: The Z Mile Treatment - How to Avoid Gum Surgery & Dentures. (Illus.). 160p. 1997. pap. 12.95 (*0-9646271-1-6*, Enosis Pr) Albrite FL.
Smile of Eros: A Novel. John Coriolan. 192p. (Orig.). 1984. pap. 7.95 (*0-917342-39-9*) Gay Sunshine.
Smile of the Gods: A Thematic Study of Cesare Pavese's Works. Gian-Paolo Biasini. LC 68-9748. 337p. 1968. 20.00 (*0-915042-19-3*) Lib Soc Sci.
Smile of the Lamb. David Grossman. 1991. 19.95 (*0-374-26639-5*) FS&G.
Smile of the Unknown Mariner. Vincenzo Consolo. Tr. by Joseph Farrell from ITA. 128p. 1995. 27.95 (*1-85754-051-4*, Pub. by Carcanet Pr UK) Paul & Co Pubs.
Smile of the World. Garson Kanin. 1949. pap. 1.50 (*0-8222-1048-7*) Dramatists Play.
Smile of Truth: The French Satirical Eulogy & Its Antecedents. Annette H. Tomarken. 368p. 1990. text ed. 49.50 (*0-691-06791-0*) Princeton U Pr.
Smile on Your Face Money in Your Pocket: Do-It-Yourself Hypnosis. Shelley L. Stockwell. pap. 14.95 (*0-912559-17-9*) Creativity Unltd Pr.
Smile or Die! J. Shafer. LC 94-65460. 272p. 1994. pap. 11.00 (*1-884847-24-2*) Peasant Bks.
Smile, Please! Illus. by Peter Rutherford. (You Can Read It Ser.). 24p. (J). (ps-1). 1996. 3.49 (*1-85854-420-3*) Brimax Bks.
Smile Please: An Unfinished Autobiography. Jean Rhys. 176p. 1995. pap. 9.95 (*0-14-018405-8*, Penguin Classics) Viking Penguin.
Smile Power: Look Good - Feel Great. Donald E. Vollmer. Ed. by Charles A. Corriere. (Illus.). 80p. (Orig.). 1993. pap. 4.95 (*1-881976-02-5*) Bridge Pub CO.
Smile Pretty & Say Jesus: The Last Great Days of PTL. Hunter James. LC 92-39494. 216p. (C). 1993. 22.95 (*0-8203-1529-X*) U of Ga Pr.
Smile, Says Little Crocodile. Jane B. Moncure. LC 87-13833. (Magic Castle Readers Ser.). (Illus.). 32p. (J). (ps-2). 1987. lib. bdg. 21.36 (*0-89565-401-6*) Childs World.
***Smile So Big.** Abel. LC 97-2313. 1998. write for info. (*0-15-200671-0*) HarBrace.
***Smile When the Raindrops Fall: The Story of Charley Chase.** Brian Anthony & Andy Edmonds. LC 97-25443. (Filmmakers Ser.). 1997. write for info. (*0-8108-3377-8*) Scarecrow.
Smile Wise. Woody Young. (Kit-Cat-Wise Ser.). (Illus.). 48p. (Orig.). (YA). 1986. pap. text ed. 4.95 (*0-939513-21-8*) Joy Pub SJC.
***Smileage: Fun for the Highway Hypnotized.** Michael Nolan. LC 97-6312. 192p. (Orig.). 1997. pap. 8.95 (*1-888952-43-1*) Cumberland Hse.
Smiles: Lovable, Livable, Laughable Lines. Marcia Kaplan & David Kaplan. (Illus.). 96p. (Orig.). 1982. reprint ed. 6.95 (*0-9617744-1-X*) Cheers.
Smiles Level 5: HBJ Reading 1987. Early. (J). 1987. student ed., pap. 27.25 (*0-15-330505-3*) HB Schl Dept.
Smiles & Frowns - Ups & Downs with the Alphabet Pals: Rainy Days & Rainbows. LC 89-51291. (Illus.). 20p. (J). (ps). 1989. lib. bdg. write for info. (*0-7166-1903-2*) World Bk.
***Smiles Are for Mornings.** Andrea Ross. LC 96-61516. (Illus.). 44p. (J). (ps-4). 1997. pap. 6.95 (*1-55523-851-3*) Winston-Derek.
***Smiles for Seniors: Growing Old Is a Laughing Matter.** J. LC 97-17777. 1997. pap. 7.95 (*1-56980-117-7*) Barricade Bks.
Smiles, Giggles & Frowns. Christopher Carrie. (Crayola So Big Bks.). (Illus.). 40p. (Orig.). (J). (ps up). 1989. pap. 1.99 (*0-86696-223-9*) Binney & Smith.
Smiles Journal. John McPherson. 1995. pap. 9.00 (*0-687-05028-6*) Abingdon.
Smiles Notations Database. Howard. 16p. 1992. 112.00 (*0-87371-783-X*, L783) Lewis Pubs.
Smiles Notes. Valerie Coursen. (Notes Ser.). 1996. pap. text ed. 3.95 (*1-56138-757-6*) Running Pr.
Smiles on Washington Square. Raymond Federman. (Sun & Moon Classics Ser.: No. 60). 152p. (Orig.). 1995. pap. 10.95 (*1-55713-181-3*) Sun & Moon CA.
Smiles Yoked with Sighs. Robert J. Burdette. LC 76-139757. (Granger Index Reprint Ser.). 1977. 19.95 (*0-8369-6211-7*) Ayer.
Smiley Dictionary. Seth Godin. (Illus.). 96p. (Orig.). (C). 1993. pap. text ed. 6.95 (*1-56609-008-3*) Peachpit Pr.
Smiley Snake. Bob Reese & Nancy Reese. Ed. by Alton Jordan. (I Can Read Ser.). (Illus.). (J). (gr. k-3). 1984. 7.95 (*0-89868-010-7*, Read Res); pap. 3.95 (*0-89868-043-3*, Read Res) ARO Pub.
Smiley Snake's Adventure. Phyllis N. Barber. Ed. by Alton Jordan. (Buppet Bks.). (Illus.). (J). (gr. 1-4). 1980. 9.95 (*0-89868-098-0*, Read Res); pap. 3.95 (*0-89868-109-X*, Read Res) ARO Pub.
Smileys. David W. Sanderson. (Nutshell Handbook Ser.). (Illus.). 93p. (Orig.). 1993. pap. 5.95 (*1-56592-041-4*) OReilly & Assocs.
Smiley's People. John Le Carre. LC 79-2299. 1980. 25.00 (*0-394-50843-2*) Knopf.
***Smilin' Tim.** Larry Grab. (Illus.). ii, 8p. (J). (ps-6). 1996. ring bd. write for info. incl. audio (*0-9656652-0-8*) GRABB.
Smiling At Yourself: Educating Young Children About Stress & Self Esteem. Etrw. 1991. pap. 17.95 (*0-941816-90-7*) ETR Assocs.
Smiling Charlie. Max Brand. LC 95-2908. iv, 315p. (C). 1995. pap. 12.00 (*0-8032-6124-1*, Bison Books) U of Nebr Pr.
Smiling Charlie. large type ed. Max Brand. (General Ser.). 364p. 1992. lib. bdg. 20.95 (*0-8161-5086-9*, GK Hall) Thorndike Pr.
Smiling Country. Sally Portman. (Illus.). 1993. pap. 12.95 (*0-9636921-0-0*) Pack & Paddle.
Smiling Dan: Structure & Function at a Middle Woodland Settlement in the Illinois Valley. Ed. by Barbara D. Stafford & Mark B. Sant. LC 85-7861. (Kampsville Archeological Center Research Ser.: No. 2). (Illus.). 513p. (Orig.). 1985. pap. 12.95 (*0-942118-19-7*) Ctr Amer Arche.
Smiling Dog. Robert Hardie. 1995. 16.95 (*0-533-11206-0*) Vantage.
Smiling Each Day. Abraham J. Twerski. 1993. 21.99 (*0-89906-581-3*); 17.99 (*0-89906-582-1*) Mesorah Pubns.
***Smiling Gunman.** large type ed. J. D. Kincaid. (Dales Large Print Ser.). 207p. 1997. pap. 18.99 (*1-85389-689-6*) Ulverscroft.
Smiling Hill Farm. Miriam E. Mason. (Illus.). (J). 1995. reprint ed. lib. bdg. 24.95 (*1-56849-616-8*) Buccaneer Bks.

S

Smiling Inside, Smiling Outside: Learning to Care for Myself, My Family, My World. Susanna Palomares. Ed. by Dianne Schilling. (Illus.). 96p. (J). (gr. k-3). 1993. teacher ed. 12.95 (*1-56499-014-1*) Innerchoice Pub.

Smiling Muse: Victoriana in the Periodical Press. Jerold J. Savory & Patricia Marks. LC 82-46024. (Illus.). 256p. 1985. 50.00 (*0-87982-501-4*) Art Alliance.

Smiling Response. Rene A. Spitz & K. M. Wolf. LC 72-345. (Facial Expression in Children). 1972. pap. write for info. (*0-318-50818-4*) Ayer.

Smiling Response see Facial Expression in Children: Three Surveys

***Smiling Sam's Joke Plan.** (Ready Readers Series II Stage II). (Illus.). 32p. (J). (gr. 1-3). 1996. pap. write for info. (*1-56144-952-0*, Honey Bear Bks) Modern Pub NYC.

Smiling Spleen. W. Pagel. (Illus.). x, 214p. 1984. 122.50 (*3-8055-3707-7*) S Karger.

Smiling Through; or Institute Afters. Illus. by Ron Woodward. (C). 1992. 40.00 (*1-85609-036-1*, Pub. by Witherby & Co UK) St Mut.

***Smiling Through Tears.** Pamela Freyd & Eleanor C. Goldstein. LC 97-13345. 1997. write for info. (*0-89777-125-7*, Upton Bks) Sirs Inc.

Smiling Through the Apocalypse. Bonnie McCafferty. 248p. 1992. pap. 14.95 (*0-9634142-0-8*) Loose Canons.

Smilla's Sense of Snow. Peter Hoeg. 512p. 1994. mass mkt. 6.99 (*0-7704-2618-2*) Bantam.

Smilla's Sense of Snow. Peter Hoeg. 512p. 1994. mass mkt. 6.99 (*0-440-21853-5*) Dell.

Smilla's Sense of Snow. Peter Hoeg. Tr. by Tiina Nunnally from DAN. LC 93-17742. 1993. 21.00 (*0-374-26644-1*) FS&G.

Smilla's Sense of Snow. Peter Hoeg. 456p. 1993. 24.95 (*0-385-25442-3*) Doubleday.

Smilla's Sense of Snow. Peter Hoeg. 488p. 1995. reprint ed. pap. 9.95 (*0-385-31514-7*, Delta) Dell.

***Smilla's Sense of Snow: The Making of a Film by Bille August.** Karin Trolle. 1997. pap. text ed. 18.00 (*0-374-52512-9*) FS&G.

Smith: A Memorial of Rev. Thomas Smith & His Descendants. S. A. Smith. 146p. 1991. reprint ed. pap. 23.00 (*0-8328-2169-1*) Higginson Bk Co.

Smith: A Novel. Geoff Hill. 176p. 9400. pap. 12.95 (*0-85640-485-3*, Pub. by Blackstaff Pr IE) Dufour.

Smith: Complete Genealogy of the Descendants of Matthew Smith of East Haddam, Ct., with Mention of His Ancestors, 1637-1890. Sophia S. Martin. 269p. 1994. reprint ed. pap. 42.00 (*0-8328-4381-4*); reprint ed. lib. bdg. 52.00 (*0-8328-4380-6*) Higginson Bk Co.

Smith: Family Gatherings Relating to the Smith & Blanchard Families, with a Memoir of Rev. Elias Smith of Middleton, Mass. Ed. by W. C. Endicott. (Illus.). 170p. 1992. reprint ed. pap. 35.00 (*0-8328-2731-2*); reprint ed. lib. bdg. 25.00 (*0-8328-2730-4*) Higginson Bk Co.

Smith: Family Tree Book, Genealogical & Biographical, Listing the Relatives of General William Alexander Smith & of W. Thomas Smith. Compiled by W. Thomas Smith. (Illus.). 304p. 1993. reprint ed. lib. bdg. 57.00 (*0-8328-6584-2*) Higginson Bk Co.

Smith: Lt. Samuel Smith. J. W. Hook. 381p. 1991. reprint ed. pap. 59.50 (*0-8328-2172-1*); reprint ed. lib. bdg. 69.50 (*0-8328-2171-3*) Higginson Bk Co.

Smith: Notes & Illustrations Concerning the Family History of James Smith. Lady Durning-Lawrence. (Illus.). 156p. 1991. reprint ed. pap. 24.00 (*0-8328-2170-5*) Higginson Bk Co.

Smith: The Smith & the Chamberlains; Also the Wilsons, Walters, Warfields, Van Sitterts. Clifford E. Smith. (Illus.). 184p. 1995. reprint ed. pap. 29.50 (*0-8328-4842-5*); reprint ed. lib. bdg. 39.50 (*0-8328-4841-7*) Higginson Bk Co.

Smith: Wills of the Smith Families of NY & Long Island, 1664-1794, with Genealogy & History Notes. William S. Pelletreau. 151p. 1991. reprint ed. pap. 27.50 (*0-8328-1832-1*); reprint ed. lib. bdg. 37.50 (*0-8328-1831-3*) Higginson Bk Co.

Smith - Fiction: Anthology. LC 64-9367. 264p. 1972. 10.50 (*1-882986-10-5*); pap. 6.50 (*1-882986-11-3*) Smith.

Smith - Seventeen: Eleven Young Poets. LC 64-9367. 176p. 1975. pap. 5.00 (*0-912292-36-9*) Smith.

Smith & Allied Families History: Beaty - Bowers - Hull. Jack Masters. (Illus.). 250p. 1991. 35.00 (*0-9622761-1-1*) J Masters.

***Smith & Hawken: The Tool Book.** William B. Logan. 1997. 40.00 (*0-7611-0855-6*) Workman Pub.

***Smith & Hawken Composting.** Liz Ball. 1998. pap. 10.95 (*0-7611-0732-0*) Workman Pub.

***Smith & Hawken Hands-on Gardener Pruning.** Robert Kourik. LC 97-8881. 1997. pap. text ed. 10.95 (*0-7611-0806-8*) Workman Pub.

***Smith & Hawken Hands-on Gardener Seeds & Propagation.** Susan A. McClure. 1997. pap. text ed. 10.95 (*0-7611-0733-9*) Workman Pub.

Smith & Hawken the Book of Outdoor Gardening. Smith & Hawkin Editors. (Illus.). 432p. 1996. 28.95 (*0-7611-0231-0*, 10231); pap. 18.95 (*0-7611-0110-1*, 10110) Workman Pub.

***Smith & Hawken 100 English Roses for the American Garden.** Clair G. Martin. LC 97-71. 1997. pap. text ed. 16.95 (*0-7611-0185-3*) Workman Pub.

Smith & Keenan's English Law. 11th ed. Denis Keenan. 800p. (Orig.). 1995. pap. 59.50 (*0-273-61407-X*, Pub. by Pitman Pub Ltd UK) Trans-Atl Phila.

***Smith & Kraus Guide to Over 2000 Performing Arts WEB Sites.** Jocelyn A. Beard. 1996. pap. text ed. 19.95 (*1-57525-063-2*) Smith & Kraus.

Smith & Kraus Monologue Index. Ed. by Karen Morris. 208p. 1995. pap. 14.95 (*1-880399-75-X*) Smith & Kraus.

Smith & Nephew in the Health Care Industry. James Foreman-Peck. 304p. 1995. 80.00 (*1-85898-085-2*) E Elgar.

Smith & Other Events: Tales of the Chilcotin. Paul H. St. Pierre. 1984. 16.95 (*0-8253-0209-9*) Beaufort Bks NY.

Smith & Other Events: Tales of the Chilcotin. Paul H. St. Pierre. LC 94-9391. 332p. (Orig.). 1994. pap. 12.95 (*0-8061-2677-9*) U of Okla Pr.

***Smith & Robards.** Shane Hensley. (Illus.). 128p. (Orig.). 1997. pap. 25.00 (*1-889546-04-6*) Pinnacle Ent.

Smith & Roberson's Business Law. 9th ed. Richard A. Mann & Barry S. Roberts. Ed. by Bruckner. LC 93-21510. 1250p. (C). 1993. text ed. 71.25 (*0-314-02712-2*) West Pub.

***Smith & Roberson's Business Law.** 10th ed. Mann. (LA - Business Law Ser). (C). 1997. text ed. 67.95 (*0-314-14080-8*) Wadsworth Pub.

***Smith & Roberson's Business Law.** 10th ed. Richard A. Mann et al. LC 96-38398. 1996. write for info. (*0-314-20227-7*) West Pub.

***Smith & Roberson's Business Law.** 10th ed. Robert Mannroberts. (LA - Business Law Ser.). (C). 1997. student ed., pap. 22.95 (*0-314-22062-3*) Wadsworth Pub.

Smith & Son: An Expedition into Africa. large type ed. Anthony Smith. 464p. 1986. 27.99 (*0-7089-8335-9*, Charnwood) Ulverscroft.

Smith & Telfer Photographic Collection of the New York State Historical Association. 1978. pap. 14.50 (*0-917334-10-8*) Fenimore Hse Mus.

Smith & Wesson Hand Guns. Roy C. McHenry & Walter F. Roper. 1994. reprint ed. 32.00 (*1-879356-35-X*) Wolfe Pub Co.

Smith & Wesson Revolvers Price List of Parts Catalogue P-2. reprint ed. 9.00 (*1-877704-06-7*) Pioneer Pr.

Smith & Williams' Introduction to the Principles of Drug Design. 2nd ed. H. J. Smith. (Illus.). 384p. 1988. 54.50 (*0-318-39850-8*, Yr Bk Med Pubs) Mosby Yr Bk.

Smith Brothers-Boston Mass: 1888 Barbers Supplies Catalog. (Illus.). pap. 3.50 (*0-686-20764-5*) Sand Pond.

Smith Collects Contemporary. Smith College Museum of Art Staff. LC 91-60788. (Illus.). 92p. (Orig.). 1991. pap. 20.00 (*0-87391-044-3*) Smith Coll Mus Art.

Smith College. Photos by Tom Sobolik. (Illus.). 112p. 1991. 39.00 (*0-916509-73-7*) Harmony Hse Pub.

Smith College Classical Jazz Review. (C). 1987. 60.00 (*0-393-99150-4*) Norton.

Smith College Jazz Record Review. (C). 1988. 55.00 (*0-393-99342-6*) Norton.

Smith College Stories. Josephine D. Bacon. LC 70-94701. (Short Story Index Reprint Ser.). 1977. 21.95 (*0-8369-3079-7*) Ayer.

Smith, Currie & Hancock's Common Sense Construction Law. Ed. by Neal J. Sweeney et al. LC 96-27813. 400p. 1996. text ed. 54.95 (*0-471-01031-6*) Wiley.

Smith Family: Being a Popular Account of Most Branches of the Names - However Spelt. C. Reade. (Illus.). 324p. 1990. reprint ed. pap. 48.00 (*0-8328-1537-3*); reprint ed. lib. bdg. 56.00 (*0-8328-1536-5*) Higginson Bk Co.

Smith, Grant & Irons Families of New Jersey's Shore Counties, Including the Related Families of Willets & Birdsall. J. W. Hook. (Illus.). 280p. 1994. reprint ed. pap. 47.50 (*0-8328-4238-9*); reprint ed. lib. bdg. 57.50 (*0-8328-4237-0*) Higginson Bk Co.

Smith-Hurd Illinois Annotated Statutes. write for info. (*0-318-57494-2*) West Pub.

Smith Island: Chesapeake Bay. Frances W. Dize. LC 89-40301. 222p. 1990. pap. 17.95 (*0-87033-492-1*, Tidewtr Pubs) Cornell Maritime.

Smith Kline-Beecham Collaborates with NIH. Michael Ryan et al. (Pew Case Studies in International Affairs). 50p. (C). 1995. pap. text ed. 3.50 (*1-56927-712-5*, GU Schl Foreign) Geo U Inst Dplmcy.

Smith-Morra Accepted: A Game Collection. Ken Smith & Bill Wall. 118p. (Orig.). 1992. pap. 7.95 (*0-945470-22-3*) Chess Ent.

Smith-Morra Declined: A Game Collection. Ken Smith & Bill Wall. 120p. 1993. pap. 7.95 (*0-945470-25-8*) Chess Ent.

Smith of Smiths Being the Life, Wit & Humor of Sydney Smith. Hesketh Pearson. 1988. reprint ed. lib. bdg. 49.00 (*0-7812-0197-7*) Rprt Serv.

Smith of Smiths Being the Life, Wit & Humor of Sydney Smith. Hesketh Pearson. LC 73-145230. (Literature Ser.). (Illus.). 338p. 1972. reprint ed. 49.00 (*0-403-01146-9*) Scholarly.

Smith of Wooton Major & Farmer Giles of Ham. J. R. R. Tolkien. 160p. 1986. mass mkt. 5.99 (*0-345-33606-2*) Ballantine.

***Smith-Parcell Effect.** V. P. Shestopalev. 310p. (C). 1997. lib. bdg. 89.00 (*1-56072-446-3*) Nova Sci Pubs.

Smith Poets (The Smith - Twelve) LC 70-94633. 262p. 1970. 15.00 (*1-882986-12-1*); pap. 7.50 (*1-882986-13-X*) Smith.

***Smith Rock State Park.** Alan Watts. (Classic Rock Climbs Ser.: Vol. 14). (Illus.). (Orig.). 1997. pap. 10.95 (*1-57540-039-1*) Chockstone Pr.

Smith Teleserv via Satellite. 1979. lib. bdg. 93.50 (*90-286-0708-0*) Kluwer Ac.

***Smith Wigglesworth.** Smith Wigglesworth. (Living Classics Ser.). mass mkt. 5.99 (*0-89274-986-5*) Harrison Hse.

Smith Wigglesworth: A Life Ablaze with the Power of God. W. Hacking. 96p. 1995. pap. 5.99 (*0-89274-785-4*, HH-785) Harrison Hse.

Smith Wigglesworth: A Man who Walked with God. George Stormont. 176p. (Orig.). 1989. pap. 6.99 (*0-89274-595-9*, HH-595) Harrison Hse.

Smith Wigglesworth: Apostle of Faith. Stanley H. Frodsham. 158p. 1948. pap. 3.95 (*0-88243-586-8*, 02-0586) Gospel Pub.

***Smith Wigglesworth: The Complete Collection of His Life Teachings.** Compiled by Roberts Liardon. 1997. 29.99 (*0-614-27170-3*) Albury Pub.

***Smith Wigglesworth: The Complete Collection of His Life Teachings.** Roberts Liardon. 1997. 29.99 (*1-57778-024-8*) Albury Pub.

Smith Wigglesworth: The Secret of His Power. Albert Hibbert. 112p. 1982. pap. 5.99 (*0-89274-211-9*, HH-211) Harrison Hse.

Smith Wigglesworth on Faith. Ed. by Larry Keefauver. (Thirty Day Devotional Ser.). 48p. (Orig.). 1996. pap. 3.99 (*0-88419-437-X*) Creation House.

Smith Wigglesworth on Healing. Ed. by Larry Keefauver. (Thirty Day Devotional Ser.). 1996. pap. 3.99 (*0-88419-438-8*) Creation House.

Smith Wigglesworth on Prayer. Ed. by Larry Keefauver. (Thirty Day Devotional Ser.). 1996. pap. 3.99 (*0-88419-439-6*) Creation House.

Smith Wildman Brookhart: Iowa's Renegade Republican. George W. McDaniel. LC 95-12116. (Illus.). 320p. 1995. text ed. 29.95 (*0-8138-2107-X*) Iowa St U Pr.

Smithells Metals Reference Book. 7th ed. E. A. Brandes & G. B. Brook. (Illus.). 1783p. 1992. 315.00 (*0-7506-1020-4*) Buttrwrth-Heinemann.

Smithereens. Susan T. Chehak. 1996. pap. 10.00 (*0-614-97794-0*, WSP) PB.

Smithereens: A Novel. Susan T. Chehak. 320p. 1996. pap. 10.00 (*0-671-56779-9*) S&S Trade.

Smithereens - Especially for You: Play-It-Like-It-Is-Guitar. pap. 19.95 (*0-89524-569-8*) Cherry Lane.

Smithfield Bargain. Rachelle Edwards. 224p. 1981. pap. 1.50 (*0-449-50203-1*, Coventry) Fawcett.

Smithfield Bargain. Jo Ann Ferguson. 320p. 1994. mass mkt. 3.99 (*0-8217-4536-0*, Zebra Kensgtn) Kensgtn Pub Corp.

Smithfield Bargain. large type ed. Rachelle Edwards. (Linford Romance Library). 272p. 1995. pap. 15.99 (*0-7089-7680-8*, Linford) Ulverscroft.

Smithfield Lutheran Register, 1792-1826, Middleway, Jefferson County, WV. Ed. by Klaus Wust. Tr. by Ilse Martin & George M. Smith. 60p. 1993. pap. 10.95 (*0-917968-16-6*) Shenandoah Hist.

Smithfield Militia, 1776-1781. Patricia G. Johnson. LC 91-92830. (Illus.). 22p. (Orig.). 1991. pap. text ed. 6.00 (*1-878188-01-1*) Walpa Pub.

Smiths. Johnny Rogan. (Illus.). 120p. (Orig.). (C). pap. 7.95 (*0-7119-4900-X*, OP 47768) Omnibus NY.

Smiths: All Men Have Secrets. Tom Gallagher et al. 256p. 1995. pap. 9.95 (*0-86369-874-3*, Pub. by Virgin Pub UK) London Brdge.

Smiths: The Complete Story. rev. ed. Mick Middles. (Illus.). 128p. 1996. 14.95 (*0-7119-0693-9*, OP 43389) Omnibus NY.

Smiths: The Visual Documentary. Johnny Rogan. (Illus.). 160p. pap. 19.95 (*0-7119-3337-5*, OP 47284) Omnibus NY.

Smith's Anesthesia for Infants & Children. 6th ed. Motoyama & Davis. 1024p. (C). (gr. 13). 1995. text ed. 135.00 (*0-8151-5937-4*) Mosby Yr Bk.

Smith's Bible Dictionary. William Smith. (Bible Reference Library). (Illus.). 352p. 1988. pap. 3.97 (*1-55748-017-6*) Barbour & Co.

Smith's Bible Dictionary. William Smith. 1991. lib. bdg. 79.95 (*0-8490-4270-4*) Gordon Pr.

Smith's Bible Dictionary. William Smith. 912p. 1988. 16.95 (*0-917006-24-0*) Hendrickson MA.

Smith's Bible Dictionary. William Smith. Ed. by F. N. Peloubet & M. A. Peloubet. LC 86-5281. (Illus.). 768p. 1986. 14.99 (*0-8407-5542-2*); pap. 9.99 (*0-8407-3085-3*) Nelson.

Smith's Bible Dictionary. rev. ed. William Smith. (Illus.). 800p. (C). 1979. 14.99 (*0-87981-033-5*, 4690-25); 24.99 (*0-87981-035-1*, 4690-26) Broadman.

Smith's Bible Dictionary. rev. ed. William Smith. (Illus.). 800p. (C). 1981. pap. 12.99 (*0-87981-489-6*, 4691-02) Broadman.

Smith's Bible Dictionary. Ed. by William Smith. (Reference Library Edition). 912p. 1989. reprint ed. 15.99 (*0-529-06676-9*) World Publng.

***Smiths Bible Dictionary: Supersaver.** Smith. 1988. 9.97 (*0-7852-1222-1*) Nelson.

Smith's Bible Dictionary see Bible Reference Library: Value Pack

***Smith's Canyon.** large type ed. Larry Chatham. (Dales Large Print Ser.). 224p. 1996. pap. 17.99 (*1-85389-654-3*, Dales) Ulverscroft.

Smith's General Urology. 4th ed. Emil A. Tanagho & Jack W. MacAninch. (Illus.). 743p. (C). 1994. pap. text ed. 43.95 (*0-8385-8612-0*, A8612-2) Appleton & Lange.

Smith's Illustrated Astronomy. A. Smith. (Illus.). 79p. 1984. reprint ed. pap. text ed. 25.00 (*0-87556-396-1*) Saifer.

Smiths of Sandy Pond Road. Sumner Smith. (Illus.). 95p. (Orig.). 1983. pap. 15.00 (*0-944856-07-1*) Lincoln Hist Soc.

Smith's Recognizable Patterns of Human Deformation. 2nd ed. Graham. 208p. 1988. text ed. 55.00 (*0-7216-2338-7*) Saunders.

Smith's Recognizable Patterns of Human Malformation. 5th ed. Kenneth L. Jones. Ed. by Judy Fletcher. 832p. 1996. text ed. 59.00 (*0-7216-6115-7*) Saunders.

Smiths' Sea Fishes. 6th ed. Ed. by M. M. Smith & Phillip C. Heemstra. (Illus.). 1200p. 1986. 249.95 (*0-387-16851-6*) Spr-Verlag.

Smith's Textbook of Endourology, 2 vols., Set. Ed. by Arthur D. Smith et al. (Illus.). 1300p. 1996. 395.00 (*0-942219-81-3*) Quality Med Pub.

Smith's the Critically Ill Child: Diagnosis & Medical Management. 3rd ed. Joseph D. Dickerman & Jerold F. Lucey. (Illus.). 352p. 1985. text ed. 80.00 (*0-7216-8386-X*) Saunders.

Smithsburg. deluxe ed. Michael Brondoli. (Treacle Story Ser.: No. 2). (Illus.). 48p. 1976. 12.50 (*0-914232-09-6*) McPherson & Co.

Smithsonian. Michael Wetzenbach. 1992. write for info. (*0-679-41240-9*) McKay.

Smithsonian: Octopus on the Mall. Geoffrey T. Hellman. LC 77-16190. 224p. 1978. reprint ed. text ed. 55.00 (*0-313-20019-X*, HESM, Greenwood Pr) Greenwood.

Smithsonian: 150 Years of Adventure, Discovery, & Wonder. James Conaway. (Illus.). 432p. 1995. 60.00 (*0-679-44175-1*) Random.

Smithsonian: 150 Years of Adventure, Discovery, & Wonder. James Conaway. Date not set. write for info. (*0-614-13118-9*) Knopf.

Smithsonian & the American Indian: Making a Moral Anthropology in Victorian America. Curtis M. Hinsley. LC 80-20193. Orig. Title: Savages & Scientists. (Illus.). 320p. (C). 1994. pap. text ed. 17.95 (*1-56098-409-0*) Smithsonian.

Smithsonian Book of Books. Michael Olmert. LC 91-39590. (Illus.). 320p. 1992. 49.95 (*0-89599-030-X*) Smithsonian Bks.

Smithsonian Book of First Ladies: Their Lives, Times, & Issues. Edith P. Mayo. (Illus.). 352p. (J). (gr. 6-9). 1996. 24.95 (*0-8050-1751-8*) H Holt & Co.

Smithsonian Book of Flight. Walter J. Boyne. Ed. by Joseph Goodwin. (Illus.). 288p. 1987. 35.00 (*0-89599-020-2*) Smithsonian Bks.

Smithsonian Book of Flight. Walter J. Boyne. LC 94-16740. 1996. reprint ed. 24.99 (*0-517-11850-5*) Random Hse Value.

Smithsonian Book of North American Indians: Before the Coming of the Europeans. Philip Kopper. Ed. by Alexis Doster, III. (Illus.). 288p. 1986. 39.95 (*0-89599-018-0*, Abrams) Smithsonian Bks.

Smithsonian Connection, Vol. 2. Daryl J. Lucas. (Choice Adventures Ser.: Vol. 2). (J). (gr. 3-7). 1991. pap. 4.99 (*0-8423-5026-8*) Tyndale.

Smithsonian Experience. Smithsonian Staff. 1986. 25.00 (*0-89599-000-8*) Smithsonian Bks.

Smithsonian Folklife Cookbook. Katherine S. Kirlin & Thomas M. Kirlin. LC 91-268. (Illus.). 336p. (C). 1991. pap. 19.95 (*1-56098-089-3*) Smithsonian.

Smithsonian Frontiers of Flight. Jeffrey L. Ethell. LC 92-28336. 1992. write for info. (*0-89599-033-4*) Smithsonian Bks.

Smithsonian Guide: Aviation. Lopez & Collins. (Illus.). 256p. 1995. pap. 18.00 (*0-671-50549-1*) S&S Trade.

Smithsonian Guide: Spaceflight. Neal & Collins. 1995. pap. 18.00 (*0-671-50548-3*) S&S Trade.

Smithsonian Guide to Historic America: The Mid-Atlantic States: New York, New Jersey, Pennsylvania. Michael Durham. Ed. by Roger G. Kennedy. LC 88-16001. (Smithsonian Guide to Historic America Ser.). (Illus.). 496p. 1989. 24.95 (*1-55670-060-1*) Stewart Tabori & Chang.

Smithsonian Guide to Natural America: Northern New England. Walter D. Wetherell. (Illus.). 304p. 1995. pap. 19.95 (*0-679-76153-5*) Random.

Smithsonian Guide to Natural America: The Northern Rockies--Idaho, Montana & Wyoming. Jeremy C. Schmidt. LC 95-5255. (Illus.). 304p. 1995. pap. 19.95 (*0-679-76312-0*) Random.

Smithsonian Guide to Natural America: The Pacific. Steve Barth & Kim Heacox. (Illus.). 304p. 1995. pap. 19.95 (*0-679-76155-1*) Random.

Smithsonian Guide to Natural America: The Southwest. Jake Page. (Illus.). 304p. 1995. pap. 19.95 (*0-679-76154-3*) Random.

Smithsonian Guide to Seaside Plants of the Gulf & Atlantic Coast: From Louisiana to Massachusetts, Exclusive of Lower Peninsular Florida. Wilbur H. Duncan & Marion B. Duncan. LC 85-22095. (Illus.). 410p. 1987. pap. 29.95 (*0-87474-387-7*) Smithsonian.

Smithsonian Guides: Untitled. Smith. 1996. pap. 18.00 (*0-671-50609-9*) S&S Trade.

Smithsonian Guides: Untitled, No. 3. Smith. 1995. pap. 18.00 (*0-671-50608-0*) S&S Trade.

Smithsonian Guides: Untitled, No. 4. Smith. 1995. pap. 18.00 (*0-671-50607-2*) S&S Trade.

Smithsonian Guides: Untitled, No. 5. Smith. 1996. pap. 18.00 (*0-671-50605-6*) S&S Trade.

Smithsonian Guides to Natural America: Northern New England -- Vermont, New Hampshire & Maine. Photos by Len Jenshel. LC 94-32174. 1995. pap. write for info. (*0-89599-046-6*) Smithsonian Bks.

Smithsonian Guides to Natural America: Southern New England - Connecticut, Rhode Island, & Massachusetts. Photos by Jonathan Wallen. (Illus.). 1996. pap. 19.95 (*0-679-76475-5*) Smithsonian Bks.

Smithsonian Guides to Natural America: The Appalachians: West Virginia, Kentucky, Tennessee. Photos by Willard Clay. 1996. pap. 19.95 (*0-679-76474-7*) Smithsonian Bks.

Smithsonian Guides to Natural America: The Atlantic Coast & Blue Ridge-Maryland, Washington, D. C., Virginia, & North Carolina. Photos by Bates Littlehales. LC 95-1486. (Illus.). 304p. 1995. pap. 19.95 (*0-679-76314-7*) Smithsonian Bks.

Smithsonian Guides to Natural America: The Far West--California & Nevada. Photos by Len Jenscbel. (Illus.). 304p. 1996. pap. 19.95 (*0-679-76473-9*) Random.

Smithsonian Guides to Natural America: The Great Lakes - Ohio, Indiana, Michigan, Wisconsin. Photos by Gary Irving. (Illus.). 1996. pap. 19.95 (*0-679-76476-3*) Smithsonian Bks.

Smithsonian Guides to Natural America: The Heartland - Nebraska, Iowa, Illinois, Missouri, Kansas. Photos by Michael Forsberg et al. (Illus.). 1997. pap. 19.95 (*0-679-76481-X*) Random.

An Asterisk (*) at the beginning of an entry indicates that the title is appearing in BIP for the first time.

Smithsonian Guides to Natural America: The Mid-Atlantic States - New York, Pennsylvania, New Jersey. Photos by Jonathan Wallen. (Illus.). 1996. pap. 19.95 (0-679-76478-X) Random.

Smithsonian Guides to Natural America: The Northern Plains - Minnesota, North Dakota, South Dakota. Photos by Tom Bean. (Illus.). 1996. pap. 19.95 (0-679-76477-1) Random.

Smithsonian Guides to Natural America: The Pacific Northwest--Washington & Oregon. Photos by Tim Thompson. LC 95-1485. (Illus.). 304p. 1995. pap. 19.95 (0-679-76313-9) Random.

Smithsonian Guides to Natural America: The Southeast - South Carolina, Georgia, Alabama, Florida. Photos by Tony Arruza. (Illus.). 1997. pap. 19.95 (0-679-76480-1) Random.

Smithsonian Guides to Natural America: The Southern Rockies - Colorado & Utah. Susan Lamb. LC 95-9041. 304p. 1996. pap. 19.95 (0-679-76472-0) Smithsonian Bks.

Smithsonian Guides to Natural America the South Central States: Texas, Oklahoma, Arkansas, Louisana, Mississippi. Photos by Jim Bones & Tria Giovan. (Illus.). 1996. pap. 19.95 (0-679-76479-8) Random.

Smithsonian Institution: A World of Discovery. LC 93-14987. (Illus.). 128p. (Orig.). 1993. pap. 10.00 (1-56098-314-0) Smithsonian.

Smithsonian Institution: Bugs! Alice Jablonsky. (Pop 'N Hear Ser.). 12p. (J). (ps-2). 1994. write for info. (1-883366-57-7) YES Ent.

Smithsonian Institution: Deep in the Rain Forest. Alice Jablonsky. (Pop 'N Hear Ser.). 12p. (J). (ps-2). 1994. write for info. (1-883366-56-9) YES Ent.

Smithsonian Institution: Documents Relative to Its History, 2 Vols. William J. Rhees. Ed. by I. Bernard Cohen. LC 79-8405. (Three Centuries of Science in America Ser.). (Illus.). 1980. lib. bdg. 86.00 (0-686-65997-X) Ayer.

Smithsonian Institution: Documents Relative to Its History, 2 Vols., Set. William J. Rhees. Ed. by I. Bernard Cohen. LC 79-8405. (Three Centuries of Science in America Ser.). (Illus.). 1980. lib. bdg. 189.95 (0-405-12583-6) Ayer.

Smithsonian Institution: Documents Relative to Its History, 2 Vols., Vol. 1. William J. Rhees. Ed. by I. Bernard Cohen. LC 79-8405. (Three Centuries of Science in America Ser.). (Illus.). 1980. 94.95 (0-405-12597-6) Ayer.

Smithsonian Institution: Documents Relative to Its History, 2 Vols., Vol. 2. William J. Rhees. Ed. by I. Bernard Cohen. LC 79-8405. (Three Centuries of Science in America Ser.). (Illus.). 1980. lib. bdg. 94.95 (0-405-12599-2) Ayer.

Smithsonian Institution Eighteen Hundred Forty-Six to Eighteen Hundred Ninety-Six: The History of Its First Half Century. George B. Goode. Ed. by I. Bernard Cohen. LC 79-3119. (Three Centuries of Science in America Ser.). (Illus.). 1980. reprint ed. lib. bdg. 83.95 (0-405-12584-4) Ayer.

Smithsonian Meteorological Tables, Vol. 114. 6th rev. ed. Smithsonian Institution Staff. (Smithsonian Miscellaneous Collections). 540p. reprint ed. pap. 153.90 (0-317-08606-5, 2051196) Bks Demand.

Smithsonian Science Activity Book. Megan Stine et al. Ed. by Cheryl Solimini. (Science Activity Book Ser.). (Illus.). 100p. (J). (gr. 2-6). 1987. pap. text ed. 8.95 (0-939456-51-6) Galison.

Smithsonian Studies in Air & Space, No. 7 see United States Women in Aviation, 1940-1985

Smithsonian Studies in Air & Space Number 5 see United States Women in Aviation 1919-1929

Smithsonian Studies in Air & Space Number 6 see United States Women in Aviation 1930-1939

Smithsonian Timelines of the Ancient World: A Visual Chronology from the Origins of Life to A. D. 1500. Christopher Scarre. LC 93-18480. (Illus.). 256p. 1993. 49.95 (1-56458-305-8) DK Pub Inc.

Smithsonian Visual Timeline of Inventions. Richard Platt. LC 94-21429. (Illus.). 64p. (J). (gr. 3 up). 1994. 16.95 (1-56458-675-8) DK Pub Inc.

Smithsonian's Great Battles & Battlefields of the Civil War: A Field Guide Based on the Award-Winning Video Series by Mastervision. Jay Wertz & Edwin C. Bearss. 408p. 1997. 42.00 (0-688-13549-8) Morrow.

Smithsonian's New Zoo. Jake Page. LC 89-29626. (Illus.). 208p. 1990. 29.95 (0-87474-734-1) Smithsonian.

Smithson's Island: The Necessity of Solitude. Judith A. Smithson. LC 95-81508. (Illus.). 122p. (Orig.). 1997. reprint ed. pap. 9.95 (1-883477-08-5) Lone Oak MN.

***Smithtown, New York, 1669-1929: Looking Back Through the Lens.** Noel Gish. LC 96-34811. 1996. write for info. (0-89865-980-9) Donning Co.

***Smitten with Kittens.** Ariel Books Staff. LC 96-85916. 80p. 1997. 4.95 (0-8362-2652-6, Arie Bks) Andrews & McMeel.

Smitty. Bill Gutman. (YA). (gr. 7-12). 1988. pap. 4.25 (0-89872-301-9) Turman Pub.

Smitty II: The Olympics. Bill Gutman. 82p. (Orig.). (YA). (gr. 7-12). 1990. pap. 4.25 (0-89872-303-5) Turman Pub.

***Smitty's Stories: Adventures in Pacific County.** Lorrie Haight. Ed. by Harrison Smith. LC 96-96221. (Illus.). 250p. 1996. 19.95 (1-887153-02-0) Floating Pr.

Smitty's Stories: Growing up in Lowell. Lorrie Haight. LC 95-60594. 186p. 1996. 17.95 (1-887153-00-4) Floating Pr.

***Smitty's Stories: The Fishing Poet in Alaska.** Lorrie Haight & Harrison Smith. (Illus.). 1997. write for info. (1-887153-03-9) Floating Pr.

SMM7 - The Standard Method of Measurement of Building Works. RICS Staff & Building Employers Confederation Staff. 190p. (C). 1988. text ed. 125.00 (0-85406-360-9, Pub. by R-I-C-S Bks UK) St Mut.

SMM7 Measurement Code. RICS Staff & Building Employers Confederation Staff. (C). 1988. pap. text ed. 75.00 (0-85406-361-7, Pub. by R-I-C-S Bks UK) St Mut.

Smocking. Madeline Bird & Margie Prestedge. (C). 1989. 30.00 (1-85368-077-X, Pub. by New Holland Pubs UK) St Mut.

Smocking: Techniques, Projects & Designs. Dianne Durand. (Illus.). 1979. pap. 3.50 (0-486-23788-5) Dover.

Smocking & Gathering for Fabric Manipulation. Nelle W. Link. Ed. by Jules Kliot & Kaethe Kliot. (Illus.). 112p. 1987. pap. 10.00 (0-916896-25-0) Lacis Pubns.

Smocking Design. Jean Hodges. (Illus.). 144p. 1996. pap. 29.95 (0-7134-6344-9, Pub. by Batsford UK) Trafalgar.

Smocks. Maggie Hall. 1989. pap. 25.00 (0-85263-477-3, Pub. by Shire UK) St Mut.

Smofcon Three Record. Pref. by Aron K. Insinga. ii, 68p. 1987. spiral bd. 5.00 (0-9603146-5-2) MA Convent Fandom.

***Smog: The Ozone Myth.** Stephen E. Blewett. (Illus.). 142p. (Orig.). 1996. pap. 15.00 (0-9640565-0-X) Ozone Resch.

Smog Alert. Derek Elsom. 192p. 1996. pap. 23.00 (1-85383-192-1, Pub. by Erthscan Pubns UK) Island Pr.

Smoke. John E. Bradley. 416p. 1995. pap. 10.95 (0-14-024759-9, Penguin Bks) Viking Penguin.

Smoke. Dawn Richardson. 112p. (YA). (gr. 9-12). 1985. 7.95 (0-920806-73-2, Pub. by Penumbra Pr CN) U of Toronto Pr.

Smoke. Ivan S. Turgenev. LC 94-61775. 190p. (Orig.). 1995. pap. 12.95 (1-885983-00-X) Turtle Point Pr.

Smoke. Donald E. Westlake. 448p. 1996. mass mkt. 6.50 (0-446-40344-X, Mysterious Paperbk) Warner Bks.

***Smoke.** Donald E. Westlake. 1996. mass mkt. 5.99 (0-614-20513-1) Mysterious Pr.

***Smoke: A Wolf's Story.** Melaine J. Banner. (Illus.). 128p. (YA). 1997. pap. 8.95 (1-896867-08-1, Pub. by Moulin Pub CN) Genl Dist Srvs.

Smoke: It's Chemistry, Physics & Control by Engineering. 1984. 32.50 (0-318-02520-5, 84-9) Society Fire Protect.

Smoke & Ashes: The Story of the Holocaust. Barbara Rogasky. LC 87-28617. (Illus.). 192p. (YA). (gr. 5 up). 1988. 19.95 (0-8234-0697-0) Holiday.

Smoke & Ashes: The Story of the Holocaust. Barbara Rogasky. LC 87-28617. (Illus.). 192p. (YA). (gr. 5 up). 1991. pap. 12.95 (0-8234-0878-7) Holiday.

Smoke & Blue in the Face: Two Films, 2 bks. in 1. Paul Auster. (Illus.). 304p. 1995. pap. 12.95 (0-7868-8098-8) Hyperion.

Smoke & Draft-Control Door Assemblies. National Fire Protection Association Staff. 1993. 16.75 (0-317-63312-0, 105-89) Natl Fire Prot.

Smoke & Fire. Carroll F. Terrell. LC 85-61183. (Collected Poems Ser.). 132p. 1985. 8.95 (0-915032-47-3); pap. 5.00 (0-915032-48-1) Natl Poet Foun.

Smoke & Heat Venting. (Two Hundred Ser.). 22p. 1991. pap. 20.25 (0-685-58165-9, 204M-91) Natl Fire Prot.

Smoke & Mirrors. Jane M. Lindskold. 256p. (Orig.). 1996. mass mkt. 5.50 (0-380-78290-1, AvoNova) Avon.

Smoke & Mirrors. Barbara Michaels. 1990. mass mkt. 6.99 (0-425-11911-4, Berkley Trade) Berkley Pub.

***Smoke & Mirrors.** Ken Silverstein. 27p. (Orig.). 1996. pap. 10.00 (0-937188-48-4) Pub Citizen Inc.

Smoke & Mirrors: A Helen Black Mystery. Pat Welch. 224p. (Orig.). 1996. pap. 10.95 (1-56280-143-0) Naiad Pr.

Smoke & Mirrors: How Science Reflects Reality. James R. Brown. LC 93-25307. (Philosophical Issues in Science Ser.). 224p. (C). 1994. pap. 17.95 (0-415-09181-0) Routledge.

Smoke & Mirrors: How Science Reflects Reality. James R. Brown. LC 93-25307. (Philosophical Issues in Science Ser.). 224p. (C). 1994. text ed. 62.95 (0-415-09180-2) Routledge.

Smoke & Mirrors: The Magical World of Chemical Dependency. Dorothy M. England. (Illus.). 96p. (Orig.). 1995. pap. 5.95 (0-88028-166-9, 1341) Forward Movement.

Smoke & Mirrors: The War on Drugs & the Politics of Failure. Dan Baum. 416p. 1996. 24.95 (0-316-08412-3) Little.

***Smoke & Mirrors: The War on Drugs & the Politics of Failure.** Dan Baum. 1997. pap. 13.95 (0-316-08446-8) Little.

***Smoke & Mirrors: Violence, Television, & Other American Cultures.** John Leonard. 290p. 1996. 23.00 (0-614-19285-4) New Press NY.

Smoke & Other Early Stories. 2nd rev. ed. Djuna Barnes. Ed. by Douglas Messerli. (Sun & Moon Classics Ser.: No. 2). 184p. 1988. pap. 10.95 (1-55713-014-0) Sun & Moon CA.

Smoke & Spice: Cooking with Smoke The Real Way to Barbecue on Your Charcoal Grill, Water Smoker, or Wood Burning Pit. Cheryl A. Jamison & Bill Jamison. Ed. by Andrea Chessman. LC 94-1963. (Illus.). 432p. 1994. 29.95 (1-55832-060-1); pap. 16.95 (1-55832-061-X) Harvard Common Pr.

Smoke Away: Quit Smoking Now. Jay Burchett. 31p. (Orig.). 1989. pap. 4.95 (0-929013-04-2) Newport Pub Hse.

***Smoke Bellew.** Jack London. lib. bdg. 27.95 (0-8488-1996-9) Amereon Ltd.

Smoke Bellew. unabridged ed. Jack London. LC 92-16275. (Illus.). 240p. 1992. reprint ed. pap. text ed. 7.95 (0-486-27364-4) Dover.

Smoke Bellew. Jack London. 1992. reprint ed. lib. bdg. 19.95 (0-89966-952-2) Buccaneer Bks.

Smoke Control in Buildings: An Annotated Bibliography. Ed. by S. R. Loyd. (C). 1988. 105.00 (0-86022-221-7, Pub. by Build Servs Info Assn UK) St Mut.

Smoke Eaters: The Story of a Fire Crew. Harvey J. O'Higgins. 1977. 21.95 (0-8369-4249-3, 6059) Ayer.

Smoke Fired Pottery. Jane Perryman. (Illus.). 128p. 1995. reprint ed. 39.95 (0-9650786-7-1) Gentle Br.

Smoke-Free Guide: How to Eliminate Tobacco Smoke from Your Environment. Arlene Galloway. (Illus.). 160p. (Orig.). 1988. pap. 14.95 (0-921348-02-9) Gordon Soules Bk.

Smoke-Free Workplace. William L. Weis & Bruce W. Miller. LC 85-62780. 196p. 1985. pap. 19.95 (0-87975-309-9) Prometheus Bks.

Smoke from Auschwitz Chimneys. (Illus.). 112p. 1989. 19.50 (0-317-93562-3) Ardor Pub.

Smoke from the Fires. Michael D. Browne. LC 84-72533. (Poetry Ser.). 80p. 1985. 20.95 (0-88748-006-3); pap. 11.95 (0-88748-007-1) Carnegie-Mellon.

***Smoke from Their Fires: The Life of a Kwakiutl Chief.** rev. ed. Clellan S. Ford. (Illus.). 264p. (C). 1996. reprint ed. pap. text ed. 10.95 (0-88133-915-6) Waveland Pr.

Smoke from This Altar. Louis L'Amour. 96p. 1990. 12.95 (0-553-07349-4) Bantam.

Smoke in Food Processing. Joseph A. Maga. LC 87-24231. 176p. 1988. 101.00 (0-8493-5155-3, TP371, CRC Reprint) Franklin.

Smoke in the Canyon: My Steam Days in Dunsmuir. Dick Murdock. Ed. by Jayne Murdock. LC 85-90443. (Illus.). 144p. (Orig.). 1986. pap. 15.95 (0-932916-10-4) May-Murdock.

***Smoke in the Valley: An Original Gold Medal Novel.** Steve Frazee. LC 96-48191. (Nightingale Ser.). 1997. pap. 17.95 (0-7838-2046-1) G K Hall.

Smoke Jokes. Eugene Hamilton & Daniel McFeeley. 112p. 1991. pap. 8.95 (0-918805-22-8) Pac Aero Pr.

Smoke Jumpers. Paul Freeman. LC 91-77073. 258p. 1992. 18.00 (0-9627509-1-3) Baskerville.

***Smoke of Satan: Conservative & Traditionalist Dissent in Contemporary American Catholicism.** Michael W. Cuneo. LC 96-34719. 256p. 1997. 27.50 (0-19-511350-0) OUP.

Smoke of Summer. I. Yevish. LC 91-90875. 266p. (Orig.). 1991. 15.95 (0-9626330-3-8); pap. 11.95 (0-9626330-2-X) I Yevish Bks.

Smoke of the Snake. Carl Jacobi. 288p. (C). 1993. 25.00 (1-878252-10-0) Fedogan & Bremer.

Smoke on the Horizon. Jerry Spafford. 243p. (Orig.). 1996. mass mkt. 4.99 (1-55197-197-6, Pub. by Comnwlth Pub CN) Partners Pubs Grp.

Smoke on the Mountain: An Interpretation of the Ten Commandments. Joy Davidman. LC 85-7622. 144p. 1985. pap. 12.00 (0-664-24680-X, Westminster) Westminster John Knox.

Smoke on the River. large type ed. Anne T. Brooks. (Historical Romance Ser.). 496p. 1992. 25.99 (0-7089-2655-X) Ulverscroft.

Smoke over Birkenau. Liana Millu. Tr. by Lynne Sharon Schwartz from ITA. LC 91-22973. 208p. 1991. 19.95 (0-8276-0398-3) JPS Phila.

Smoke Ring. Larry Niven. 336p. 1988. mass mkt. 5.99 (0-345-30257-5, Del Rey) Ballantine.

Smoke Ring: Politics & Tobacco in the Third World. Ed. by Maxine Alexander et al. (Southern Exposure Ser.). (Illus.). 64p. (Orig.). (C). 1984. pap. 4.00 (0-943810-26-4) Inst Southern Studies.

Smoke Rings. Gladys B. Stern. LC 72-10810. (Short Story Index Reprint Ser.). 1977. reprint ed. 23.95 (0-8369-4229-9) Ayer.

Smoke Rising: The Native North American Literary Companion. Ed. by Joseph Bruchac et al. LC 95-10006. (Illus.). 492p. 1995. 17.95 (0-7876-0479-8) Visible Ink Pr.

***Smoke Screen.** Vincent Patrick. Date not set. write for info. (0-688-15536-7) Morrow.

Smoke Screen: Women, Smoking & Identity. Lorraine Greaves. 1996. pap. text ed. 14.95 (1-85727-058-4, Pub. by Scarlet Pr UK) LPC InBook.

Smoke Screen Mystery. Franklin W. Dixon. Ed. by Ann Greenberg. (Hardy Boys Mystery Stories Ser.: No. 105). 160p. (Orig.). (J). (gr. 3-6). pap. 3.99 (0-671-69274-7, Minstrel Bks) PB.

***Smoke Signals.** Brodsky. Date not set. text ed. 39.50 (1-86064-150-4, Pub. by I B Tauris UK) St Martin.

Smoke Signals: A Directory of American Indian & Alaska Native Businesses in Indian Country, USA. Gregory W. Frazier. 225p. 1989. lib. bdg. 24.95 (0-935151-25-7) Arrowstar Pub.

Smoke Signals: Cigarettes, Advertising & the American Way of Life. Jane W. Smith. Ed. by Nancy G. Brooks. LC 90-70405. (Illus.). 52p. (C). 1990. pap. 9.55 (1-878719-00-9) Valentine Mus.

Smoke Signals: Smoking & You. rev. ed. Christina Dye. 1996. pap. 0.50 (0-89230-208-9) Do It Now.

Smoke Stack Cleanup: Technologies, Markets. 1993. 2,450.00 (0-89336-939-X, E-063) BCC.

Smoke the Burning Body Makes. Steve Schutzman. LC 78-2256. (Illus.). 64p. 1978. pap. 6.00 (0-915572-28-1) Panjandrum.

***Smoke to Flame: September 1935 to December 1938.** Victoria Sherrow. LC 96-52206. (Holocaust Ser.). (Illus.). 80p. (J). (gr. 7 up). 1997. lib. bdg. 18.95 (1-56711-201-3) Blackbirch.

Smoke Tree. Margaret Holley. 82p. 1991. 16.50 (1-878325-05-1); pap. 8.50 (1-878325-04-3) Bluestem Press.

Smoke Without Fire. large type ed. Elizabeth X. Ferrars. 290p. 1991. reprint ed. lib. bdg. 17.95 (1-56054-210-1) Thorndike Pr.

Smokechaser. Warren Yahr. (Living the West Ser.). (Illus.). 224p. (Orig.). 1995. pap. 18.95 (0-89301-180-0) U of Idaho Pr.

Smoked & Cured Seafood Guide. Ian Dore. 250p. 1993. 69.00 (1-881693-03-1) Urner Barry Pubns.

Smoked-Foods Cookbook: How to Flavor, Cure, & Prepare Savory Meats, Game, Fish, Nuts, & Cheese. Lue Park & Ed Park. LC 92-7047. 224p. 1992. 18.95 (0-8117-0116-6) Stackpole.

Smoked Glass. Robert H. Newell. LC 70-171060. reprint ed. 32.50 (0-404-03663-5) AMS Pr.

Smoked Yankees & the Struggle for Empire: Letters from Negro Soldiers, 1898-1902. Willard B. Gatewood, Jr. LC 86-19352. 342p. 1987. pap. 18.00 (0-938626-88-4) U of Ark Pr.

Smoked Yankees & the Struggle for Empire: Letters from Negro Soldiers, 1898-1902. Willard B. Gatewood, Jr. LC 78-146006. 339p. reprint ed. pap. 96.70 (0-317-27556-9, 2014922) Bks Demand.

SmokeFree - How to Stop Smoking in Nine Easy Steps. Harold H. Dawley, Jr. (Illus.). 127p. (Orig.). 1987. pap. 9.95 (0-9617202-0-4) Wellness Inst.

SmokeFree - Worksite Smoking Control, Discouragement, & Cessation. Harold H. Dawley, Jr. (Illus.). 90p. (Orig.). 1987. pap. 14.95 (0-9617202-1-2) Wellness Inst.

Smokehouse Five. Sergio Aragones. 1992. pap. 9.95 (1-56398-024-X) Malibu Comics Ent.

Smokejumper: A Summer in the American Wilderness. Dale L. Schmaljohn. (Illus.). 163p. (gr. 6-12). 1982. 9.95 (0-9608454-0-2); pap. 6.95 (0-9608454-1-0) Hyde Park Pr.

Smokejumper: Firefighter from the Sky. Keith Greenberg. Ed. by Bruce Glassman. LC 94-23658. (Risky Business Ser.). (Illus.). 32p. (J). (gr. 2-5). 1995. lib. bdg. 14.95 (1-56711-153-X) Blackbirch.

Smokejumpers. Charles W. Sasser. 1996. mass mkt. 5.99 (0-671-52713-4, PB Trade Paper) PB.

Smokejumpers, '49: Brothers in the Sky: With Photos by Peter Stackpole. Starr Jenkins. LC 95-94011. (Illus.). 282p. 1995. 23.95 (1-886659-09-5) M Starr Bks.

Smokeless Coal Fields of West Virginia. W. P. Tams, Jr. LC 63-62525. 107p. 1963. 12.50 (0-937058-18-1) West Va U Pr.

Smokeless Side: Humor to Reverse Your Urge to Smoke & the Effects of Ads & Peer Pressure. The Original Cartoon Book for Smoking Cessation, Vol. 1. Peter Migaly. LC 95-94397. 112p. 1995. pap. 15.95 (0-9647363-0-6) P Migaly.

***Smokeless Tobacco Control: Report of a WHo Study Group, 1988.** (Technical Report Ser.: No. 773). 81p. 1988. pap. text ed. 11.00 (92-4-120773-6, 1100773) World Health.

Smokeless Tobacco in the Western World. Jan Rogozinski. 194p. 1990. 25.00 (0-8159-6856-6) Devin.

Smokeless Tobacco in the Western World, 1550-1950. Jan Rogozinski. LC 90-6899. 208p. 1990. text ed. 49.95 (0-275-93600-7, C3600, Praeger Pubs) Greenwood.

Smokeless Tobacco or Health: An International Perspective. (Illus.). 389p. (Orig.). (C). 1995. pap. text ed. 50.00 (0-7881-2067-0) DIANE Pub.

Smokerama: Classic Tobacco Accoutrements. Philip Collins. (Illus.). 132p. 1992. pap. 17.95 (0-8118-0119-5) Chronicle Bks.

***Smokers & Quitters: What Smoking Means to People & How They Manage to Quit.** Erli Gronberg & Katherine Sub. 149p. 1997. pap. 17.95 (1-56072-473-0) Nova Sci Pubs.

Smokers Are People Too. Timothy Neat. 96p. 1995. pap. 5.95 (0-88032-462-7) Ivory Tower Pub.

Smoker's Cough. large type ed. Alan Sewart. (Linford Mystery Library). 1990. pap. 15.99 (0-7089-6898-8) Ulverscroft.

Smokers Guide to Dining Out in New York City. Alan Yeck. 112p. 1995. pap. 9.95 (0-9647912-0-X) Salmeri Pubng.

Smoker's Heaven: You Don't Have to Die to Go There. Martin Ehde, Jr. LC 79-57444. (Illus.). 132p. (Orig.). 1980. pap. 4.95 (0-936188-01-4) Ehde Pub Co.

***Smokers' Tobacco Poisoning.** Max. 50p. (Orig.). 1997. pap. 30.00 (0-922070-74-1) M Tecton Pub.

Smokescreen. Dick Francis. 1993. mass mkt. 5.99 (0-449-22111-3) Fawcett.

Smokescreen: The Truth Behind the Tobacco Industry Cover-Up. Philip J. Hilts. Ed. by Henning Gutmann. 288p. (C). 1996. 22.00 (0-201-48836-1) Addison-Wesley.

***Smokescreen Secrets, Vol. 1.** Marianne Hering. (Lights, Camera, Action! Mysteries Ser.). (J). 1997. pap. text ed. 4.99 (1-56476-564-4, Chariot Bks) Chariot Victor.

Smokescreens. Jack T. Chick. (Illus.). 93p. 1982. pap. 3.95 (0-937958-14-X) Chick Pubns.

Smokestack Iron. large type ed. Lee Thomas. (Linford Western Library). 352p. 1993. pap. 15.99 (0-7089-7376-0, Linford) Ulverscroft.

Smokestack Lightning: Adventures in the Heart of Barbecue Country. Lolis E. Elie. LC 94-40211. 240p. 1996. 35.00 (0-374-26646-8) FS&G.

***Smokestack Lightning: Adventures in the Heart of Barbecue Country.** Lolis E. Elie. 1997. pap. text ed. 25.00 (0-86547-517-2) FS&G.

Smokestack Lightning: Adventures in the Heart of Barbecue Country. Lolis E. Elie. LC 94-40211. 1997. pap. text ed. 20.00 (0-374-52438-6) FS&G.

Smokestacks Allegro: The Story of Solvay, a Remarkable Industrial - Immigrant Village (1880-1920) Rita Cominolli. 250p. 1990. 19.50 (0-934733-50-3); pap. text ed. 14.50 (0-934733-51-1) CMS.

Smoketree. Margarita Engle. 20p. 1983. pap. 2.00 (0-913719-63-3) High-Coo Pr.

Smokey. Bill Peet. (Illus.). (J). (gr. k-3). 1962. 14.95 (0-395-15992-X) HM.

S

An Asterisk (*) at the beginning of an entry indicates that the title is appearing in BIP for the first time.

Smokey. Bill Peet. (Illus.). 48p. (J). (gr. k-3). 1983. reprint ed. pap. 6.95 (*0-395-34924-9*) HM.

Smokey Bear & the Great Wilderness. Elliott S. Barker. LC 82-19373. (Illus.). 150p. (Orig.). 1982. pap. 12.95 (*0-86534-017-X*) Sunstone Pr.

Smokey Bear Story. Ellen E. Morrison. LC 94-73401. (Illus.). 64p. (J). (gr. 1 up). 1995. lib. bdg. 15.95 (*0-9622537-4-X*) Morielle Pr.

Smokey Bear 20252: A Biography. William C. Lawter, Jr. LC 94-5997. 1994. write for info. (*0-9640017-0-5*) L Smith Pubs.

Smokey O. Celia Cohen. 160p. 1994. pap. 9.95 (*1-56280-057-4*) Naiad Pr.

Smokey the Bear. (J). 1998. pap. 14.99 (*0-525-45596-5*) NAL-Dutton.

***Smokey the Bear: Guide & Diary.** Ladybird Staff. Date not set. pap. 7.99 (*0-7214-5639-1*, Ladybrd) Penguin.

***Smokey the Bear Nature Diary.** Ladybird Staff. Date not set. pap. 4.99 (*0-7214-5642-1*, Ladybrd) Penguin.

***Smokey the Bear Ranger Guide.** Ladybird Staff. 1998. pap. 7.99 (*0-7214-5641-3*, Ladybrd) Penguin.

***Smokey the Bear's Little Story Book.** Ladybird Staff. 1996. pap. 1.49 (*0-7214-5662-6*, Ladybrd) Penguin.

Smokey, the Horse Who Ate Too Much. large type ed. William O. Beazley. (Illus.). 36p. (Orig.). (J). (gr. k-5). 1993. spiral bd., pap. 7.95 (*1-884758-06-1*) W O Beazley.

***Smokey Yunick's Track Tech: Thirty Years of Rule Bend.** Smokey Yunick. (Illus.). 140p. 1995. pap. 19.95 (*1-85520-319-7*, Pub. by Brooklands Bks UK) Motorbooks Intl.

Smokin' Joe: The Autobiography of the Former Heavyweight Champion of the World, Smokin' Joe Frazier. Joe Frazier & Phil Berger. 256p. 1996. 23.95 (*0-02-860847-X*) Macmillan.

Smoking. Bosworth et al. (Body Awareness Resource Network Ser.). (YA). (gr. 7-12). 120.00 incl. disk (*0-912899-56-5*) Lrning Multi-Systs.

Smoking. David Pietrusza. LC 96-35444. (Overview Ser.). (Illus.). (J). (gr. 4-12). 1996. lib. bdg. 17.96 (*1-56006-186-3*) Lucent Bks.

Smoking. Laurence Pringle. (Save the Earth Ser.). (Illus.). (J). 1996. 16.00 (*0-688-13039-9*, Morrow Junior) Morrow.

Smoking. Pete Sanders & Steve Myers. LC 96-12647. (What Do You Know About...Ser.). (Illus.). 32p. (J). (gr. 4-6). 1996. lib. bdg. 15.40 (*0-7613-0536-X*, Copper Beech Bks) Millbrook Pr.

Smoking. Ed. by Carol Wekesser. LC 96-36098. (Current Controversies Ser.). 192p. (J). (gr. 5-12). 1996. pap. 12.96 (*1-56510-533-8*) Greenhaven.

Smoking. Ed. by Carol Wekesser. LC 96-36098. (Current Controversies Ser.). (J). (gr. 5-12). 1996. lib. bdg. 20.96 (*1-56510-534-6*) Greenhaven.

Smoking: A Risky Business. Laurence Pringle. (Save the Earth Ser.). (Illus.). (J). (gr. 3 up). Date not set. lib. bdg. 16.00 (*0-688-13040-2*, Morrow Junior) Morrow.

Smoking: At Issue. Ed. by Karin L. Swisher. (At Issue Ser.). 80p. (C). 1995. pap. text ed. 8.96 (*1-56510-268-1*) Greenhaven.

Smoking: At Issue. Ed. by Karin L. Swisher. (At Issue Ser.). 80p. 1995. lib. bdg. 14.96 (*1-56510-301-7*) Greenhaven.

Smoking: Facilitator's Manual. Sabina M. Dunton & Melody S. Fanning. Ed. by Richard A. McNeely. (Well Aware About Health Risk Reduction Ser.). (Illus.). 186p. (Orig.). 1982. 29.95 (*0-943562-51-1*) Well Aware.

Smoking: Individual Differences, Psychopathology, & Emotion. David G. Gilbert. (Series in Health Psychology & Behavioral Medicine). 307p. 1995. 49.95 (*1-56032-171-7*) Taylor & Francis.

Smoking: Making the Choice under Uncertainty. W. Kip Viscusi. (Illus.). 208p. 1992. 32.00 (*0-19-507486-6*) OUP.

Smoking: Medical Subject Analysis & Research Guide with Bibliography. Jorge S. Reginald. LC 84-45743. 150p. 1987. 44.50 (*0-88164-270-3*); pap. 39.50 (*0-88164-271-1*) ABBE Pubs Assn.

Smoking: Psychology & Pharmacology. Heather Ashton & Rod Stepney. LC 81-18829. 250p. 1982. pap. 14.95 (*0-422-77710-2*, NO. 3836, Pub. by Tavistock UK) Routledge Chapman & Hall.

Smoking: The Artificial Passion. David Krough. 1995. pap. text ed. write for info. (*0-7167-2347-6*) W H Freeman.

Smoking: The Health Consequences of Tobacco Use. Cecilia M. Schmitz & Richard A. Gray. (Science & Social Responsibility Ser.: No. 2). 320p. 1995. pap. 30.00 (*0-87650-343-1*) Pierian.

***Smoking: The Story Behind the Haze.** Edward L. Koven. 277p. 1996. 39.00 (*1-56072-401-3*) Nova Sci Pubs.

Smoking: Third World Alert. Nath U. Ram. (Illus.). 270p. 1986. 29.95 (*0-19-261402-9*) OUP.

Smoking: To Be or Not to Be. Robert Horning. LC 93-85796. 144p. (Orig.). 1993. pap. 6.95 (*0-9637330-0-1*) Portage Pub.

Smoking: Workbook. Sabina M. Dunton & Melody S. Fanning. Ed. by Richard A. McNeely. (Well Aware About Health Risk Reduction Ser.). (Illus.). 109p. (Orig.). 1982. pap. 8.50 (*0-943562-52-X*) Well Aware.

Smoking & Arterial Disease. Ed. by R. M. Greenhalgh. 315p. 1981. 62.95 (*0-8464-1215-2*) Beekman Pubs.

***Smoking & Health: Report of a Regional Seminar.** (SEARO Technical Publications Ser.: No. 7). 57p. 1985. pap. text ed. 8.00 (*92-9022-146-1*) World Health.

Smoking & Health in the Americas: A 1992 Report of the Surgeon General, in Collaboration with the Pan American Health Organization. 213p. (Orig.). (C). 1995. pap. text ed. 50.00 (*0-7881-2310-6*) DIANE Pub.

Smoking & Hormone-Related Disorders. Ed. by Nicholas J. Wald & John Baron. (Illus.). 304p. 1990. 89.00 (*0-19-261935-7*) OUP.

Smoking & Hospitals Are a Bad Match! American Hospital Association Staff. (Illus.). 47p. 1988. 35.00 (*0-87258-517-4*, 166901) Am Hospital.

Smoking & Human Behavior. Ed. by Tara Ney & Anthony Gale. LC 88-33844. 395p. reprint ed. pap. 112.60 (*0-7837-5874-X*, 2045594) Bks Demand.

Smoking & Politics: Policy Making & the Federal Bureaucracy. 5th ed. A. Lee Fritschler & James M. Hoefler. LC 95-5578. (C). 1995. pap. text ed. 27.20 (*0-13-435801-5*) P-H.

Smoking & Reproduction: A Comprehensive Bibliography. Ernest L. Abel. LC 82-15660. xviii, 163p. 1982. text ed. 49.95 (*0-313-23663-1*, ASR/, Greenwood Pr) Greenwood.

Smoking & Reproduction: An Annotated Bibliography. Ernest L. Abel. 160p. 1984. 98.00 (*0-8493-6481-7*, Z6671, CRC Reprint) Franklin.

Smoking & Reproductive Health. Michael J. Rosenberg. 352p. (gr. 13). 1989. 44.95 (*0-88416-549-3*, Yr Bk Med Pubs) Mosby Yr Bk.

Smoking & the Workplace: Issues & Answers for Human Resources Professionals. William M. Timmins & Clark B. Timmins. LC 88-39742. 145p. 1989. text ed. 49.95 (*0-89930-423-0*, TSP, Quorum Bks) Greenwood.

Smoking As a Cardiovascular Risk Factor: New Strategies for Smoking Cessation. Ed. by Lars Wilhelmsen. LC 91-20878. (Illus.). 75p. 1992. text ed. 16.00 (*0-88937-069-9*) Hogrefe & Huber Pubs.

Smoking Behavior from Pre-Adolescence to Young Adulthood. Anthony V. Swan & Michael Murray. Ed. by Linda Jarrett. 254p. 1991. text ed. 63.95 (*1-85628-033-0*, Pub. by Avebury Pub UK) Ashgate Pub Co.

***Smoking Cessation: Clinical Practice Guideline.** Michael C. Fiore et al. (Illus.). 125p. (Orig.). (C). 1996. pap. 30.00 (*0-7881-3050-1*) DIANE Pub.

Smoking Cessation: HP 609 Study Guide. Patricia Scheiderman. 15p. (C). 1989. student ed., spiral bd. write for info. (*0-931657-18-0*) Learning Proc Ctr.

Smoking Cigarettes - The Unfiltered Truth: Understanding Why & How to Quit. Janet Benner. LC 87-80270. 144p. (Orig.). 1987. pap. 10.95 (*0-942723-12-0*) Joelle Pub.

***Smoking Collectibles.** 2nd rev. ed. Neil S. Wood. (Illus.). 112p. 1996. pap. 24.95 (*0-89538-070-6*) L-W Inc.

Smoking Control among Women: Risk Reduction Programs. 1991. lib. bdg. 79.95 (*0-8490-4368-9*) Gordon Pr.

***Smoking Control Strategies in Developing Countries.** (Technical Report Ser.). 92p. 1983. pap. text ed. 10.00 (*92-4-120695-0*) World Health.

***Smoking Drinking, & Drug Use in Young Adulthood: The Impact of New Freedoms & New Responsibilities.** Jerald G. Bachman et al. LC 96-45203. (Research Monographs in Adolescence Ser.). 256p. 1997. 59.95 (*0-8058-2547-9*) L Erlbaum Assocs.

Smoking Flax. Hallie E. Rives. LC 72-2026. (Black Heritage Library Collection). 1977. reprint ed. 26.95 (*0-8369-9057-9*) Ayer.

Smoking Handbook. Ian Dore. 1994. text ed. write for info. (*0-442-00211-4*) Van Nos Reinhold.

Smoking Hopes. Victoria N. Alexander. 208p. 1996. 22.00 (*1-877946-69-9*) Permanent Pr.

Smoking in the Workplace. (ASPA-BNA Survey Ser.: No. 51). 1987. 30.00 (*0-87179-977-4*) BNA.

Smoking-Is It a Sin? Tom McDevitt. 80p. (Orig.). 1981. pap. 5.00 (*0-933046-03-0*) Little Red Hen.

Smoking Leg, & Other Stories. John Metcalfe. LC 74-152950. (Short Story Index Reprint Ser.). 1977. reprint ed. 20.95 (*0-8369-3828-3*) Ayer.

***Smoking Life: What Do You Think Was in Those Peace Pipes?** Ilene Barth. 1997. 29.95 (*1-885478-22-4*) Genesis Press.

Smoking Mirror. Brian Henderson. (Illus.). 64p. (C). 1990. pap. 12.00 (*1-55022-105-1*, Pub. by ECW Press CN) Genl Dist Srvs.

Smoking Out the Barons: The Campaign Against the Tobacco Industry. British Medical Association Staff. LC 85-2641. 192p. 1986. pap. text ed. 59.95 (*0-471-90937-8*, Wiley-Interscience) Wiley.

Smoking, Personality & Stress: Psychosocial Factors in the Prevention of Cancer & Coronary Heart Disease. Hans J. Eysenck. (Illus.). ix, 130p. 1995. 48.95 (*0-387-97493-8*) Spr-Verlag.

Smoking Policy: Law, Politics, & Culture. Ed. by Robert L. Rabin & Stephen D. Sugarman. LC 92-33045. 256p. 1993. 45.00 (*0-19-507231-6*) OUP.

Smoking Poster. David Krough. 1995. text ed. write for info. (*0-7167-2495-2*) W H Freeman.

Smoking Salmon & Trout. Jack Whelan. (Illus.). 230p. (Orig.). 1982. pap. 19.95 (*0-919807-00-3*) Gordon Soules Bk.

Smoking Scare De-Bunked. W. T. Whitby. 118p. 1990. 9.50 (*0-9595564-1-9*) Green.

Smoking Technology of the Aborigines of the Iroquois Area of New York State. Edward S. Rutsch. LC 73-92558. 252p. 1975. 39.50 (*0-8386-7568-9*) Fairleigh Dickinson.

Smoking Yokadokas: HeartPower! Student Reader Level 6-8. American Heart Association Staff. (HeartPower! American Heart Association Schoolsite Program Ser.). (Illus.). 48p. (J). (gr. 1-3). 1996. pap. write for info. (*0-87493-307-2*) Am Heart.

Smoky God: A Voyage to the Inner World. Willis G. Emerson. 186p. 1965. reprint ed. spiral bd. 10.50 (*0-7873-0315-1*) Hlth Research.

Smoky God or, A Voyage to the Inner World. W. G. Emerson. 1991. lib. bdg. 75.00 (*0-8490-5000-6*) Gordon Pr.

Smoky-House. Elizabeth Goudge. 1976. 18.95 (*0-8488-1345-6*) Amereon Ltd.

Smoky-House. Elizabeth Goudge. 391p. 1983. reprint ed. lib. bdg. 17.95 (*0-89966-108-4*) Buccaneer Bks.

Smoky Mountain Black Bear: Spirit of the Hills. Jeff Rennicke. Ed. by Steve Kemp. (Illus.). 60p. (Orig.). 1991. pap. 7.95 (*0-937207-04-7*) GSMNH.

***Smoky Mountain Cage Bird Society: And Other Magical Tales from Everyday Life.** John Skoyles. LC 97-2762. 192p. 1997. 15.00 (*1-56836-181-5*) Kodansha.

***Smoky Mountain Fly Fishing.** Don Kirk. LC 96-48482. (Illus.). 224p. (Orig.). 1997. pap. 17.95 (*0-89732-235-5*) Menasha Ridge.

***Smoky Mountain Girl.** Joshua Noonon. 427p. (Orig.). 1997. mass mkt. 5.99 (*1-55197-827-X*, Pub. by Comnwlth Pub CN) Partners Pubs Grp.

Smoky Mountain Hiking & Camping: A Guide to the Great Smoky Mountains National Park. Lee Barnes. (Illus.). 163p. 1994. pap. 12.95 (*0-89732-126-X*) Menasha Ridge.

Smoky Mountain Journal. 1995. pap. text ed. 10.95 (*0-9630682-9-6*) Panther TN.

Smoky Mountain Magic. Junior League Staff. 1995. 18.95 (*0-9642075-1-6*) Jr Leag Johnson Cty.

Smoky Mountain Memories: Stories from the Hearts of the Parton Family. Willadeene Parton. LC 96-13776. 229p. 1996. pap. text ed. 14.95 (*1-55853-404-0*) Rutledge Hill Pr.

Smoky Mountain Rose: An Appalachian Cinderella. Alan Schroeder & Charles Perrault. LC 92-1250. (J). 1997. pap. 14.99 (*0-8037-1733-4*); pap. 14.89 (*0-8037-1734-2*) Dial Bks Young.

Smoky Mountain Voices: A Lexicon of Southern Appalachian Speech Based on the Research of Horace Kephart. Ed. by Harold Farwell & J. Karl Nicholas. LC 93-19156. 200p. 1993. 19.00 (*0-8131-1823-9*) U Pr of Ky.

Smoky Mountains Trout Fishing Guide. Don Kirk. LC 83-61709. (Illus.). 160p. 1985. pap. 10.95 (*0-89732-036-0*) Menasha Ridge.

Smoky Night. Eve Bunting. LC 93-14885. (Illus.). 32p. (J). (ps-3). 1994. 15.00 (*0-15-269954-6*) HarBrace.

Smoky the Cow Horse. 2nd ed. Will James. LC 92-28753. (Illus.). 324p. (J). (gr. 3-7). 1993. reprint ed. pap. 4.50 (*0-689-71682-6*, Aladdin Paperbacks) S&S Childrens.

Smoky, the Cow Horse. Will James. 1993. reprint ed. lib. bdg. 35.95 (*1-56849-236-7*) Buccaneer Bks.

***Smoky Years.** large type ed. Alan LeMay. LC 96-36880. 1996. lib. bdg. 17.95 (*1-57490-052-8*, Sagebrush LP West) T T Beeler.

***Smoky Years.** Alan MeMay. 304p. 1997. reprint ed. mass mkt. 4.99 (*0-8439-4333-5*, Leisure Bks) Dorchester Pub Co.

Smoky's Special Easter Present. Dorothea Lachner. Tr. by Marianne Martens. LC 95-52220. (Illus.). 32p. (J). (ps-3). Date not set. 15.95 (*1-55858-573-7*); lib. bdg. 15.88 (*1-55858-574-5*) North-South Bks NYC.

Smoldering City: Chicagoans & the Great Fire, 1871-1874. Karen Sawislak. LC 95-4677. (Historical Studies of Urban America). 408p. 1995. pap. text ed. 15.95 (*0-226-73548-6*) U Ch Pr.

Smoldering City: Chicagoans & the Great Fire, 1871-1874. Karen Sawislak. LC 95-4677. (Historical Studies of Urban America). 408p. 1995. lib. bdg. 42.50 (*0-226-73547-8*) U Ch Pr.

***Smoldering Embers: The True Story of a Serial Murderer & Three Courageous Women.** Joy Wellman et al. 366p. 1997. 23.95 (*0-88282-154-7*) New Horizon NJ.

Smoldering Wick: Never Too Late for New Life. John L. O'Reilly. (Illus.). 144p. (Orig.). 1990. write for info. (*0-9625748-0-5*); write for info. (*0-9625748-1-3*); teacher ed. write for info. (*0-9625748-6-4*); student ed. write for info. (*0-9625748-7-2*); student ed. write for info. (*0-9625748-8-0*); write for info. (*0-9625748-9-9*); pap. 12.00 (*0-9625748-4-8*); text ed. write for info. (*0-9625748-3-X*); pap. text ed. write for info. (*0-9625748-5-6*); lib. bdg. write for info. (*0-9625748-2-1*) J L OReilly.

***Smolensk Oblast: Economy, Industry, Government, Business.** 2nd rev. ed. Russian Information & Business Center, Inc. Staff. (Russian Regional Business Directories Ser.). (Illus.). 200p. 1997. pap. 99.00 (*1-57751-414-9*) Russ Info & Busn Ctr.

Smoley's Four Combined Tables. rev. ed. C. K. Smoley. Ed. by E. R. Smoley & N. G. Smoley. 1612p. 1980. 61.95 (*0-911390-00-6*, QA) Smoley.

Smoley's Metric Four Combined Tables. C. K. Smoley. Ed. by E. R. Smoley & N. G. Smoley. 1400p. 1976. 72.95 (*0-911390-08-1*, QA) Smoley.

Smoley's Parallel Tables of Slopes & Rises. E. R. Smoley & N. G. Smoley. 528p. 1980. 41.95 (*0-911390-03-0*) Smoley.

Smoley's Three Combined Tables. rev. ed. C. K. Smoley. Ed. by E. R. Smoley & N. G. Smoley. 1112p. 1974. 51.95 (*0-911390-01-4*) Smoley.

Smollet's Women: A Study in an Eighteenth-Century Masculine Sensibility. Robert D. Spector. LC 93-49538. (Contributions to the Study of World Literature Ser.: No. 56). 208p. 1994. text ed. 55.00 (*0-313-28790-2*, Greenwood Pr) Greenwood.

Smollett: Author of the First Distinction. Ed. by Alan Bold. (Critical Studies). 240p. 1982. text ed. 44.00 (*0-389-20240-1*, 07097) B&N Imports.

Smollett Studies. Claude E. Jones. LC 70-128188. 128p. (C). 1970. reprint ed. 40.00 (*0-87753-048-3*) Phaeton.

Smoochy Poochy-Hettie's Apfel Tree. (Book on Amish Ser.). 1981. 15.00 (*0-9609624-2-5*) Bookworm Rochester NY.

Smooth & Round in the Ground. Susan B. Morgan. 1989. 1.98 (*0-945603-04-5*) Dinnerman Bks.

***Smooth as Silk.** Rebecca Rosenblat. 1996. mass mkt. 4.99 (*1-55197-517-3*, Pub. by Comnwlth Pub CN) Partners Pubs Grp.

Smooth Compactification of Locally Symmetric Varieties. A. Ash et al. LC 75-38142. (Lie Groups: History, Frontiers & Applications Ser.: No. 4). 340p. 1975. 35.00 (*0-915692-12-0*, 991600061) Math Sci Pr.

Smooth Ergodic Theory of Random Dynamical Systems. P. D. Liu & Min Qian. Ed. by A. Dold & F. Takens. (Lecture Notes in Mathematics Ser.: Vol. 1606). xi, 221p. 1995. pap. 44.95 (*3-540-60004-3*) Spr-Verlag.

Smooth Ergodic Theory of Random Dynamical Systems. Pei-Dong Liu & Min Qian. LC 95-21996. (Lecture Notes in Mathematics Ser.: Vol. 1606). 1995. write for info. (*0-387-60004-3*) Spr-Verlag.

Smooth Four-Manifolds & Complex Surfaces. John Friedman & John Morgan. LC 93-34949. (Ergebnisse der Mathematik und Ihrer Grenzgebiete Ser.: No. 3). 1994. 142.95 (*0-387-57058-6*) Spr-Verlag.

Smooth Invariant Manifolds & Normal Forms. I. U. Bronstein & A. Ya Kopanskii. 396p. 1994. text ed. 74.00 (*981-02-1572-X*) World Scientific Pub.

Smooth Move. Berniece Rabe. Ed. by Kathleen Tucker. LC 87-2099. (Albert Whitman Concept Bks.). (Illus.). (J). (gr. 1-4). 1987. lib. bdg. 12.95 (*0-8075-7486-4*) A Whitman.

Smooth Muscle Cells in Atherosclerosis. J. C. Geer. Ed. by M. Daria Haust et al. (Monographs on Atherosclerosis: Vol. 2). 1972. 45.75 (*3-8055-1377-1*) S Karger.

Smooth Muscle Contraction. Ed. by Newman L. Stephens. LC 83-21076. 583p. reprint ed. pap. 166.20 (*0-7837-0930-7*, 2041235) Bks Demand.

Smooth Muscle Contraction: New Regulatory Modes. Ed. by K. Saida & Kazuhiro Kohama. (Illus.). xvi, 160p. 1995. 172.25 (*3-8055-6123-7*) S Karger.

Smooth Muscle Excitation. Ed. by T. B. Bolton & Tadao Tomita. (Illus.). 560p. 1996. text ed. 120.00 (*0-12-112360-X*) Acad Pr.

Smooth Muscle Regeneration: A Review & Experimental Study. J. McGeachie. (Monographs in Developmental Biology: Vol. 9). (Illus.). vii, 90p. 1975. 44.00 (*3-8055-2058-1*) S Karger.

Smooth Sailing: Navigating Life's Challenges. Sarah C. Radcliffe. (Illus.). 191p. 1994. 17.95 (*1-56871-039-9*) Targum Pr.

Smooth Stones from Ancient Brooks: The Sayings of Thomas Brooks. Compiled by Charles H. Spurgeon. 269p. 1995. 24.95 (*1-57358-027-9*) Soli Deo Gloria.

Smooth Talkers: The Linguistic Performance of Auctioneers & Sportscasters. Koenraad Kuiper. (Everyday Communication Ser.). 120p. 1996. pap. 16.50 (*0-8058-1720-4*); text ed. 29.95 (*0-8058-1719-0*) L Erlbaum Assocs.

Smooth Tests of Goodness of Fit. J. C. Rayner & D. J. Best. (Oxford Statistical Science Ser.). (Illus.). 176p. 1989. 49.95 (*0-19-505610-8*) OUP.

Smoother Journey. Simon Schrock. LC 94-67321. 192p. 1994. pap. 9.95 (*0-89221-267-5*) New Leaf.

***Smoothies: 22 Frosty Fruit Drinks.** Anne A. Johnson. (Illus.). 18p. (J). (gr. k up). 1997. 6.95 (*1-57054-101-9*) Klutz Pr.

***Smoothies: 50 Recipes for High-Energy Refreshment.** Mary C. Barber. LC 97-1124. 1997. pap. 15.95 (*0-8118-1648-6*) Chronicle Bks.

Smoothing Methods in Statistics. Jeffrey S. Simonoff. LC 96-11742. (Series in Statistics). (Illus.). 352p. 1996. student ed. 57.95 (*0-387-94716-7*) Spr-Verlag.

Smoothing of Time Series. Frederick R. Macaulay. (General Ser.: No. 19). 172p. 1931. reprint ed. 44.80 (*0-87014-018-3*); reprint ed. mic. film 22.40 (*0-685-61151-5*) Natl Bur Econ Res.

Smoothing Techniques in Theory: With Implementation in S. W. Hardel. Ed. by David R. Brillinger et al. (Series in Statistics). (Illus.). xi, 261p. 1990. 54.95 (*0-387-97367-2*) Spr-Verlag.

***Smoothness & Reenormings in Banach Spaces.** R. Deville. 1993. pap. 167.40 (*0-582-07250-6*, Pub. by Longman UK) Longman.

Smoothness & Roughness. Yang Zeng Guang. (CHI.). pap. 9.95 (*7-80005-257-5*, Pub. by China Intl Bk CH) Distribks Inc.

Smoothness Priors Analysis of Time Series, Vol. 116. G. Kitagawa & Will Gersch. LC 96-22800. (Lecture Notes in Statistics Ser.). 280p. 1996. pap. 39.95 (*0-387-94819-8*) Spr-Verlag.

Smoothstitch Four Seasons Jacket. Roxi Eppler. Ed. by Barbara Weiland. LC 91-25066. (Illus.). 20p. 1991. pap. 4.95 (*0-943574-90-0*, L607) That Patchwork.

***Smoothstitch Quilts: Easy Machine Applique.** Roxi Eppler. (Illus.). 64p. (Orig.). pap. text ed. 9.95 (*0-486-29471-4*) Dover.

S'more Firehouse Jokes. unabridged ed. 128p. 1996. pap. 6.00 (*0-9641530-1-7*) Evans & Assocs.

Smorgasbord Cookbook. (Hippocrene International Cookbooks Ser.). 158p. 1995. pap. 14.95 (*0-7818-0407-8*) Hippocrene Bks.

Smouldering Charcoal. Tiyambe Zeleza. (African Writers Ser.). 183p. (C). 1992. pap. 9.95 (*0-435-90583-X*, 90583) Heinemann.

Smouldering Fire. Martin Israel. 191p. (C). 1993. 49.00 (*0-85305-328-6*, Pub. by J Arthur Ltd UK) St Mut.

***Smouldering Souls.** Randall E. Osborne. 244p. (Orig.). 1997. mass mkt. 4.99 (*1-55237-168-9*, Pub. by Comnwlth Pub CN) Partners Pubs Grp.

***SMPS Simulation with SPICE3.** Steven M. Sandler. (Illus.). 275p. 1996. text ed. 55.00 incl. disk (*0-07-913227-8*) McGraw.

SMPTE Standards for Advanced Television. SMPTE Staff. Ed. & Pref. by Mark Hyman. (Illus.). 188p. (Orig.). 1996. pap. 55.00 (*0-940690-31-4*) Soc Motion Pic & TV Engrs.

An Asterisk (*) at the beginning of an entry indicates that the title is appearing in BIP for the first time.

SMPTE Standards for Motion Picture Production & Presentation. SMPTE Staff. Ed. & Pref. by Mark Hyman. (Illus.). 91p. (Orig.). 1996. pap. 30.00 (0-940690-32-2) Soc Motion Pic & TV Engrs.

SMS: A Program Package for Simulation & Gaming of Stochastic Market Processes & Learning Behavior. J. Perski & Ulrich Witt. (Lecture Notes in Economics & Mathematical Systems Ser.: Vol. 202). (Illus.). 266p. 1982. 38.00 (0-387-11551-X) Spr-Verlag.

SM/SD. Victor Terry. (Orig.). 1996. mass mkt. 5.95 (1-56333-406-2, Badboy) Masquerade.

SMT Advance Design Techniques. James C. Blankenhorn. 268p. (C). 1988. text ed. 199.95 (1-882812-01-8) SMT Plus.

SMT Area Analysis Program. James C. Blankenhorn. (C). 1992. 295.00 incl. disk (1-882812-10-7) SMT Plus.

SMT Design Rules & Standards. James C. Blankenhorn. 175p. (C). 1991. text ed. 299.95 (1-882812-03-4) SMT Plus.

SMT Designing for Testability. James C. Blankenhorn. 119p. (C). 1991. text ed. 99.95 (1-882812-02-6) SMT Plus.

SMT Fundamentals of Product Design. James C. Blankenhorn. 235p. (C). 1990. text ed. 99.95 (1-882812-00-X) SMT Plus.

*SMTP, X.500, X.400: An Introduction. John Rhoton. LC 97-14875. 1997. pap. text ed. 34.95 (1-55558-165-X) Buttrwrth-Heinemann.

*Smudge. John A. Rowe. LC 97-8737. (J). 1997. write for info. (1-55858-789-6); write for info. (1-55858-788-8) North-South Bks NYC.

Smudge, the Little Lost Lamb. James Herriot. (Illus.). 32p. (J). 1991. 12.95 (0-312-06404-7) St Martin.

Smudge, the Little Lost Lamb. James Herriot. (Illus.). 32p. (J). 1994. pap. 6.95 (0-312-11067-7) St Martin.

Smudgkin Elves & Other Lame Excuses. Dotsey Welliver. 81p. 1981. pap. 3.95 (0-89367-058-8) Light & Life Comm.

Smuggler see Heinemann Guided Readers

Smugglers, Vol. 1. Lord Teignmouth & Charles G. Harper. 1976. reprint ed. 17.50 (0-85409-899-2) Charles River Bks.

*Smugglers & Sailors: The Customs History of Australia 1788-1901. David Day. 564p. lib. bdg. 194.95 (0-644-25239-1, Pub. by Aust Gov Pub AT) Aubrey Bks.

*Smuggler's Forecast. Jay Young. 480p. (Orig.). 1997. pap. 14.95 (1-56883-071-8) Colonial Pr AL.

Smuggler's Island. Avi. LC 93-35964. Orig. Title: Shadrach's Crossing. 192p. (J). (gr. 5 up). 1994. pap. 4.95 (0-688-12797-5, Morrow Junior) Morrow.

Smuggler's Island. Avi. LC 93-35964. Orig. Title: Shadrach's Crossing. 192p. (J). (gr. 5 up). 1994. 16.00 (0-688-12796-7, Morrow Junior) Morrow.

Smuggler's Island. Archibald S. Cox. (Oxford Graded Readers Ser.). 1983. pap. 3.25 (0-19-421767-1) OUP.

Smuggler's Lady. Jane Feather. 416p. 1986. mass mkt. 3.95 (0-8217-1948-3, Zebra Kensgtn) Kensgtn Pub Corp.

Smuggler's Lady. Jane Feather. 464p. 1996. mass mkt. 5.99 (0-8217-5401-7, Zebra Kensgtn) Kensgtn Pub Corp.

Smuggler's Love. Emma Goldrick. (Presents Ser.). 1992. pap. 2.89 (0-373-11488-5, 1-11488-3) Harlequin Bks.

Smugglers on Grizzly Mountain. Ernest Herndon. (Eric Sterling, Secret Agent Ser.: Vol. 4). 128p. (J). 1994. pap. 5.99 (0-310-38281-5) Zondervan.

Smugglers Paradise. Brian Wyant & Eric Wyant. (Illus.). 64p. 1997. pap. 7.50 (1-883788-18-8) Event Horzn.

Smuggler's Road. Date not set. pap. 1.95 (0-590-04503-2) Scholastic Inc.

Smuggler's Secret. Sandra G. Garrett & Philip C. Williams. LC 93-31884. (Screech Owl Mysteries Ser.). (YA). (gr. 6 up). 1994. write for info. (0-86625-501-X) Rourke Pubns.

Smuggler's Summer. Carola Dunn. 1987. 16.95 (0-8027-0976-1) Walker & Co.

Smuggler's Trail. Evan Evans, pseud. 241p. 1976. reprint ed. lib. bdg. 20.95 (0-89190-209-0, Rivercity Pr) Amereon Ltd.

Smugglers Woods. Arthur D. Pierce. 322p. (C). 1984. reprint ed. pap. 14.95 (0-8135-0444-9) Rutgers U Pr.

Smuggling. Philip Steele. LC 92-13611. (Past & Present Ser.). (Illus.). 48p. (YA). (gr. 6 up). 1993. lib. bdg. 12.95 (0-02-786884-2, Mac Bks Young Read) S&S Childrens.

Smuggling: The Wicked Trade. John Douch. 1984. 25.00 (0-906124-05-0, Pub. by Regency Press UK) St Mut.

Smuggling-Flogging Joey's Warriors. Ed. by John Douch. 165p. (C). 1988. 35.00 (0-906124-08-5, Pub. by Regency Press UK) St Mut.

Smuggling in East Anglia. Stan Jarvis. 192p. 1987. 30.00 (0-905392-86-8) St Mut.

Smuggling in Hampshire & Dorset: 1700-1850. Geoffrey Morley. 224p. 1987. pap. 30.00 (0-905392-24-8) St Mut.

Smuggling in Kent & Sussex 1700-1840. Mary Waugh. 192p. 1987. 30.00 (0-905392-48-5) St Mut.

*Smuggling in the American Colonies at the Outbreak of the Revolution: With Special Reference to the West Indies Trade. William S. McClellan. xx, 105p. 1997. reprint ed. pap. 15.00 (0-7884-0639-6, M111) Heritage Bk.

Smuggling-Rough, Rude Men. John Douch. 150p. (C). 1988. 35.00 (0-906124-07-7, Pub. by Regency Press UK) St Mut.

Smuggling Villages of North East Essex. George Pluckwell. 1993. pap. 13.00 (0-86025-403-8, Pub. by Ian Henry Pubns UK) Empire Pub Srvs.

Smugtown U. S. A. Curt Gehring. 236p. 1993. reprint ed. pap. write for info. (1-55787-093-4) Plaza Pubs.

Smurf Collectibles: A Handbook & Price Guide. Jan Lindenberger & Joel Martone. LC 96-17120. (Illus.). 160p. 1996. pap. 19.95 (0-7643-0031-8) Schiffer.

Smut: American Sex Slang: Over Four Thousand Five Hundred Entries. Walt S. Stanchfield. LC 92-26396. (Illus.). 254p. 1993. 12.00 (0-933380-22-4); lib. bdg. 14.00 (0-933380-23-2) Olive Pr Pubns.

Smut: Erotic Reality-Obscene Ideology. Murray S. Davis. LC 82-16061. 342p. (C). 1985. pap. 17.95 (0-226-13792-9) U Ch Pr.

Smut Peddlers. James J. Kilpatrick. LC 72-7506. (Illus.). 323p. 1973. reprint ed. text ed. 38.50 (0-8371-6515-6, KISP, Greenwood Pr) Greenwood.

Smuts: A Reappraisal. Bernard Friedman. LC 75-21835. 200p. 1976. text ed. 29.95 (0-312-73045-4) St Martin.

*Smutter! Vince Marsden. (Illus.). 24p. (J). (gr. 1-3). 1997. 8.00 (1-85854-535-8) Brimax Bks.

*Smyrna: Early Years in Smyrna & Our First Old Home Week, Chenango County, New York. George A. Munson. Ed. by Shirley B. Goerlich. (Illus.). 245p. 1997. reprint ed. pap. 28.00 (1-887530-13-4) RSG Pub.

Smyslov's 125 Selected Games. Vasily V. Smyslov. 256p. 1995. pap. 19.95 (1-85744-028-5, Pub. by Cadogan Books UK) Macmillan.

*Smyth & Hawk'Em: A Parody. Tom Connor. 1997. pap. text ed. 12.50 (0-06-095239-3, PL) HarpC.

Smyth County History & Traditions (Virginia) Goodridge Wilson. (Illus.). 397p. 1993. reprint ed. lib. bdg. 41.00 (0-8328-2958-7) Higginson Bk Co.

Smyth County Marriages, Eighteen Thirty-Two to Eighteen Fifty. John Vogt & T. William Kethley, Jr. (Virginia Historic Marriage Register Ser.). (Illus.). viii, 89p. (Orig.). 1984. pap. 6.00 (0-935931-19-8) Borgo Pr.

Smyth County Marriages, Eighteen Thirty-Two to Eighteen Fifty. John Vogt & T. William Kethley, Jr. (Virginia Historic Marriage Register Ser.). viii, 89p. (Orig.). (C). 1984. reprint ed. lib. bdg. 25.00 (0-8095-8233-3) Borgo Pr.

*Smythe & Hawk 'Em. Tom Connor & Jim Downey. (Orig.). 1997. pap. 12.50 (0-614-27410-9, PL) HarpC.

SN Distribution Study of Grocery Store Sales 1996. 320p. 1996. pap. 85.00 (1-56367-098-4) Fairchild.

Sn-Organotin Compounds. 1980. 465.00 (0-387-93424-3) Spr-Verlag.

*Sn Organotin Compounds Vol. XIV, Pt. 24: Dinuclear Compounds Containing Only Tin-Carbon Bonds: R3Sn-G-SnR3 with Various Organic G Units & R = Alkyl, Cycloalkyl, & Alenyl. (Illus.). 292p. 1996. 1,239.00 (3-540-93738-2) Spr-Verlag.

SN Select - Electronic Database & Directory. ring bd. 995.00 incl. disk (1-56367-093-3) Fairchild.

Sn3 Modeling. (Illus.). 1989. pap. 12.95 (0-911581-18-9) Heimburger Hse Pub.

Sn Tin: Compounds with Bounds Between Tin & Main Group IV to Main Group I Elements, Vol. 20. 193p. 1993. 850.00 (0-387-93667-X) Spr-Verlag.

Sn Tin: Organotin Compounds, 21. 8th ed. Gmelin Institute for Inorganic Chemistry Staff. 309p. 1994. 1,375.00 (0-387-93690-4) Spr-Verlag.

SNA: Architecture, Protocols, & Implementation. Atul Kapoor. 480p. 1992. text ed. 60.00 (0-07-033727-6) McGraw.

SNA: IBM's Networking Solution. James Martin & Kathleen K. Chapman. (Illus.). 384p. 1987. text ed. 91.00 (0-13-815143-1) P-H.

SNA: IBM's System Network Architecture. Stephen J. Randesi & Donald H. Czubek. (Illus.). 384p. 1992. pap. 44.95 (0-442-00504-0) Van Nos Reinhold.

SNA: Theory & Practice. Guruge. 1984. 36.00 (0-08-028584-8, Pergamon Pr) Elsevier.

SNA: Theory & Practice. A. Guruge. (Illus.). 200p. 1984. 94.00 (0-08-028583-X, Pergamon Pr) Elsevier.

SNA, APPN, & TCP/IP: Integration & Management. David G. Matusow. (Illus.). 452p. 1996. text ed. 55.00 (0-07-041051-8) McGraw.

SNA Interconnections: Routing SNA in Hierarchial, Peer, & High-Speed Networks. John A. Chiong. 1996. text ed. 55.00 (0-07-011486-2) McGraw.

SNA Internetworking Handbook. Dan Lynch. LC 97-25853. 1997. 44.25 (0-13-127168-7) P-H.

SNA (Systems Network Architecture) Helmut De Meulen & Werner Schafer. (Illus.). 232p. (C). 1992. text ed. 33.50 (0-201-56533-1) Addison-Wesley.

Snack Attack. Brenda C. Ward & Jane C. Jarrell. LC 95-11645. (Teachable Moments Cookbook Ser.: Vol. 3). 80p. 1995. pap. 9.99 (0-8499-3670-5) Word Pub.

Snack Attack: How to Stick to a Diet, Eat Lots of Snacks, & Still Lose Weight. Kitty O'Neill. LC 94-60670. 100p. (Orig.). 1994. pap. 12.95 (0-9641463-4-7) Ctr for Design.

Snack Attack Mystery. Elizabeth Levy. (Invisible Inc. Ser.). (Illus.). 32-48p. (J). (gr. 2-4). 1996. pap. 3.99 (0-590-60289-6, Cartwheel) Scholastic Inc.

Snack Food. R. G. Booth. 416p. (gr. 13). 1990. text ed. 89.95 (0-442-23745-6) Chapman & Hall.

*Snack Food Technology. 2nd ed. Samuel A. Matz. (Ellis Horwood Series in Food Science & Technology). (Illus.). 415p. (C). 1987. text ed. 131.95 (0-7476-0016-3) Van Nos Reinhold.

Snack Food Technology. 3rd ed. Samuel A. Matz. 415p. (gr. 13). 1993. text ed. 137.50 (0-442-30893-0) Chapman & Hall.

Snack Food Technology. 3rd rev. ed. Samuel A. Matz. LC 92-31152. (Illus.). 450p. (C). 1993. text ed. 79.00 (0-942849-08-6) Pan Tech Intl.

Snack Pak. Edmon J. Rodman. 1995. 8.95 (0-316-15241-2) Little.

Snack Sneak! 1993. pap. 9.95 (1-55037-332-3, Pub. by Annick CN) Firefly Bks Ltd.

*Snacking Habits: Up to Date Advice from the World's Foremost Nutrition Experts. American Dietetic Association Staff. (Nutrition Now Ser.). 120p. (Orig.). 1997. pap. 6.95 (1-56561-122-5) Chronimed.

*Snacks & Appetizers: A Giving Christmas Idea Book, Vol. 6. Bargain Books Staff. (Little Library). 1997. pap. 0.99 (1-57748-109-7) Barbour & Co.

Snacks 'n Stuff: Recipes for Kids. Ed. by Elaine M. Myers. (Illus.). 48p. (Orig.). 1993. pap. 5.40 (0-944943-27-6, CODE 21154-0) Current Inc.

SNAFU: Great American Military Disasters. Geoffrey B. Regan. 296p. (Orig.). 1993. pap. 10.00 (0-380-76755-4) Avon.

Snafu: The Littlest Clown. Lillian B. Pennington. LC 73-90113. (Illus.). 32p. (J). (gr. 1-6). 1972. lib. bdg. 9.95 (0-913532-00-2); audio 7.94 (0-87783-225-0) Oddo.

Snagged. Carol H. Clark. 320p. 1994. mass mkt. 5.99 (0-446-60076-8, Mysterious Paperbk) Warner Bks.

Snaggle Doodles. Patricia R. Giff. (Kids of the Polk Street School Ser.: No. 8). (Illus.). 80p. (J). (gr. 1-4). 1985. mass mkt. 3.99 (0-440-48068-X, YB BDD) BDD Bks Young Read.

*Snaggletooth in Ocean Park. Frances D. Smith. LC 96-72099. 80p. (Orig.). 1996. pap. 10.00 (0-9652048-3-9) Sacred Beverage.

Snagharakshita: A New Voice in the Buddhist Tradition. Subhuti. 323p. (Orig.). (C). 1996. pap. 19.95 (0-904766-68-3) Windhorse Pubns.

*Snail. Lynda P. Halley. (Beasty Bks.). (Illus.). 12p. (J). (ps-k). 1997. 14.95 (0-7613-0243-3) Millbrook Pr.

Snail. Jens Olesen. LC 86-10084. (Stopwatch Ser.). (Illus.). 25p. (J). (gr. k-4). 1986. pap. 3.95 (0-382-24019-7, Silver Pr NJ); lib. bdg. 9.95 (0-382-09289-9, Silver Pr NJ) Silver Burdett Pr.

*Snail. Nancy Shaw. (Illus.). 32p. (J). (gr. 1-4). 1998. lib. bdg. write for info. (0-88682-966-6) Creative Ed.

Snail & Buffalo. Jim Latimer. LC 95-4276. (Illus.). 32p. (J). (ps-3). 1995. lib. bdg. 16.99 (0-531-08790-5) Orchard Bks Watts.

Snail & Buffalo. Jim Latimer. LC 95-4276. (Illus.). 32p. (J). (ps-3). 1995. 15.95 (0-531-09490-1) Orchard Bks Watts.

Snail Hut. Barry Gifford. 1978. pap. 4.95 (0-87922-125-9) Christophers Bks.

Snail in My Prime: New & Selected Poems. Paul Durcan. LC 95-11466. 288p. 1995. pap. 14.95 (0-14-058720-9, Penguin Bks) Viking Penguin.

Snail Lady/The Magic Vase. Duance Vorhees & Mark Mueller. (Korean Folk Tales for Children Ser.: Vol. 6). (Illus.). 46p. (J). (gr. 2-5). 1990. lib. bdg. 10.95 (0-930878-89-2) Hollym Intl.

Snail River. James Bertolino. (QRL Poetry Bks.: Vol. XXXIV). 1995. 20.00 (0-614-06462-7) Quarterly Rev.

*Snail Started It! Katja Reider. LC 96-44944. (Illus.). 32p. (J). (gr. k-3). 1997. 15.95 (1-55858-706-3); lib. bdg. 15.88 (1-55858-707-1) North-South Bks NYC.

Snail Trails & Tadpole Tails: Nature Education for Young Children. Richard Cohen et al. Ed. by Rosemary Wallner & Eileen Nelson. LC 93-5850. (Illus.). 96p. (Orig.). (J). (ps-1). 1993. pap. text ed. 13.95 (0-934140-78-2, 4570) Redleaf Pr.

Snail Transmitted Parasitic Diseases, 2 vols., Vol. 1. Emile A. Malek. 352p. 1980. 193.00 (0-8493-5269-X, RC119, CRC Reprint) Franklin.

Snail Transmitted Parasitic Diseases, 2 vols., Vol. 2. Emile A. Malek. 344p. 1980. 188.00 (0-8493-5270-3, CRC Reprint) Franklin.

Snailology. Michael E. Ross. LC 95-30900. (Illus.). 48p. (J). (gr. 1-4). 1996. lib. bdg. 14.96 (0-87614-894-1, Carolrhoda) Lerner Group.

Snails. Enid Fisher. LC 95-54171. (New Creepy Crawly Collection). (Illus.). (J). 1996. lib. bdg. 18.60 (0-8368-1581-5) Gareth Stevens Inc.

Snails. Sylvia A. Johnson. LC 82-10086. (Lerner Natural Science Bks.). (Illus.). 48p. (J). (gr. 4 up). 1982. lib. bdg. 21.50 (0-8225-1475-3, Lerner Publctns) Lerner Group.

*Snails. Peter Murray. LC 97-1044. (J). 1997. write for info. (1-56766-382-6) Childs World.

Snails & Slugs. Lynn M. Stone. LC 95-18458. (Creepy Crawlers Ser.). (J). 1995. write for info. (1-55916-159-0) Rourke Bk Co.

*Snails, Bats & Bathtub Drivers: 14 Stories. Calef Brown. LC 97-12011. (J). 1998. write for info. (0-395-85403-2) HM.

*Snails, Flies & Butterflies. Steven Jones. 176p. 1997. write for info. (0-465-07841-9) Basic.

*Snails, Flies & Butterflies. Steven Jones. 176p. 1998. pap. write for info. (0-465-07842-7) Basic.

Snail's Spell. Joan Ryder. (Illus.). (J). (gr. 3-8). 1988. pap. 4.99 (0-14-050891-0, Puffin) Puffin Bks.

Snail's Spell. Joanne Ryder. (Illus.). 32p. (J). (ps-3). 1992. pap. 14.00 (0-670-84385-7) Viking Child Bks.

Snailsleap Lane. Beshlie. (Illus.). 14.95 (0-8464-0854-6) Beekman Pubs.

*Snak Posse. David Pettigrew. Ed. by Robert Orchanian. (Illus.). 136p. Date not set. pap. 9.95 (0-9658108-1-X) HCom.

Snake. Caroline Arnold. LC 90-22591. (Illus.). 48p. (J). (gr. 2 up). 1991. 13.95 (0-688-09409-0, Morrow Junior); lib. bdg. 13.88 (0-688-09410-4, Morrow Junior) Morrow.

Snake. Michael Chinery. LC 90-10951. (Life Story Ser.). (Illus.). 32p. (J). (gr. 4-6). 1991. pap. 4.95 (0-8167-2107-6); lib. bdg. 12.95 (0-8167-2106-8) Troll Communs.

Snake. Sabrina Crewe. LC 96-4827. (Life Cycles Bks.). (Illus.). (J). 1996. lib. bdg. 21.40 (0-8172-4372-0) Raintree Steck-V.

*Snake. Kate Jennings. LC 96-41698. 157p. 1997. 21.00 (0-88001-538-1) Ecco Pr.

Snake. Kwok Man-Ho. LC 93-48006. (Chinese Horoscopes Library). (Illus.). 48p. 1994. pap. 8.95 (1-56458-610-3) DK Pub Inc.

Snake. Susin Nielsen. (Degrassi Book Ser.). (J). (gr. 6-9). 1995. pap. 4.95 (1-55028-368-5) Formac Dist Ltd.

Snake. Susin Nielsen. (Degrassi Book Ser.). (J). (gr. 6-9). 1995. bds. 16.95 (1-55028-370-7) Formac Dist Ltd.

Snake. Stephen Ray & Kathleen Murdoch. LC 92-21453. (Illus.). (J). 1993. 4.25 (0-383-03653-4) SRA McGraw.

*Snake. Nancy Shaw. (Illus.). 32p. (J). (gr. 1-4). 1998. lib. bdg. write for info. (0-88682-967-4) Creative Ed.

*Snake. Rebecca Stefoff. LC 96-39106. (Living Things Ser.). (Illus.). 32p. (J). (gr. 1 up). 1997. lib. bdg. 14.95 (0-7614-0412-0, Benchmark NY) Marshall Cavendish.

Snake: A Very Long Love Story. Bernard Waber. (Illus.). (J). (ps-1). 1978. lib. bdg. 7.95 (0-685-02310-9) HM.

Snake: An Owner's Guide to a Happy, Healthy Pet. Lenny Flauk. LC 96-23745. 1996. 12.95 (0-87605-490-4) Howell Bk.

*Snake Alley Band. Elizabeth Nygaard. LC 97-15544. (Illus.). (J). 1998. write for info. (0-385-32323-9, DD Bks Yng Read) BDD Bks Young Read.

Snake & Lizard. Rod Theodorou & Carole Telford. LC 96-7227. (Discover the Difference Ser.). (Illus.). (J). 1996. write for info. (1-57572-106-6) Rigby Interact Libr.

Snake & Other Stories. Premendra Mitra. 1990. 17.50 (81-7046-073-5, Pub. by Seagull Bks II) S Asia.

Snake & the Spider: A Real-Life Case of Abduction & Murder in Daytona Beach. Karen Kingsbury. 400p. 1995. mass mkt. 5.99 (0-440-21792-X) Dell.

Snake & Wings. Jorge E. Oliva. 40p. (J). (gr. 1-6). 1990. pap. 5.00 (0-9629756-0-5, Wings Books) Random.

Snake-Back Solos. Quincy Troupe. LC 78-65598. 1979. pap. 5.95 (0-918408-11-3) Reed & Cannon.

Snake Bites & Their Treatment. Wee Y. Chin et al. 1991. pap. 19.95 (9971-69-151-5, Pub. by Singapore Univ Pr SI) Intl Spec Bk.

Snake Blossoms. Belden. 64p. (Orig.). 1976. pap. 5.95 (0-917658-06-X) BPW & P.

*Snake Book. Christopher Mattison. LC 96-38294. (Illus.). 32p. (J). 1997. 12.95 (0-7894-1526-7) DK Pub Inc.

Snake Book of India with Many Plates & Diagrams. Ed. by T. S. Murthy. (C). 1987. 150.00 (81-7089-049-7, Pub. by Intl Bk Distr II) St Mut.

Snake Called George. Mary A. Brittain. (Illus.). 32p. (Orig.). (gr. 1-12). 1987. pap. 3.00 (0-917134-13-3) NC Natl Sci.

Snake Ceremonials at Walpi. Jesse W. Fewkes et al. LC 76-17497. (Journal of American Ethnology & Archaeology: Vol. 4). reprint ed. 37.50 (0-404-58044-0) AMS Pr.

Snake Charm. Marilyn Nissenson & Susan Jonas. LC 94-42669. (Illus.). 160p. 1995. 29.95 (0-8109-4456-1) Abrams.

Snake Charmers Are Made Not Born. Richard E. Petitti. (Self Realization Bks.: Bk. V). (Illus.). 100p. 1986. pap. 10.00 (0-938582-09-7) Sensitive Man.

Snake Country. James McEuen. 60p. (Orig.). 1990. pap. 8.00 (0-915380-26-9) Word Works.

Snake Country Expedition of 1830-1831: John Work's Field Journal. John Work. LC 70-145501. (American Exploration & Travel Ser.: Vol. 59). 208p. reprint ed. pap. 59.30 (0-317-26309-9, 2052150) Bks Demand.

Snake Dance of the Hopi Indians. Earle R. Forrest. LC 61-15835. (Illus.). 175p. 18.95 (0-87026-018-9) Westernlore.

Snake-Dance of the Moquis of Arizona. John G. Bourke. LC 84-16379. (Illus.). 371p. 1984. reprint ed. pap. 18.95 (0-8165-0872-0) U of Ariz Pr.

Snake Discovery Library, 6 bks., Set I, Reading Level 2. Sherie Barger & Johnson. (Illus.). 144p. (J). (gr. k-5). 1986. Set. lib. bdg. 71.60 (0-86592-954-8); lib. bdg. 53.70 (0-685-58804-1) Rourke Corp.

Snake Discovery Library, 6 bks., Set II, Reading Level 2. (Illus.). 144p. (J). (gr. k-5). 1987. Set. lib. bdg. 71.60 (0-86592-243-8); lib. bdg. 53.70 (0-685-58806-8) Rourke Corp.

Snake Driver! Cobras in Vietnam. Bob Rosenburgh. 1993. mass mkt. 5.99 (0-8041-0538-3) Ivy Books.

Snake Eater! From Infantry to Special Forces. William T. Craig. 1994. mass mkt. 5.99 (0-8041-0688-6) Ivy Books.

Snake Eater: Tales of U. S. Army Special Forces in the Vietnam War. Don Bendell. 176p. 1994. mass mkt. 5.99 (0-440-21141-7) Dell.

Snake Eyes. Girard. 1996. pap. 6.50 (0-671-78500-1) PB.

Snake Eyes. Richard Hoyt. 256p. 1995. 21.95 (0-312-85805-1) Forge NYC.

*Snake Eyes. Richard Hoyt. 1996. mass mkt. 5.99 (0-8125-5072-2) Forge NYC.

Snake Eyes Two. Ed. by Glenn Head & Kaz. (Illus.). 100p. pap. 9.95 (1-56097-075-8) Fantagraph Bks.

Snake Gulch Swindlers. Jake Logan. (Slocum Ser.: No. 192). 192p. (Orig.). 1995. mass mkt. 3.99 (0-425-14570-0) Berkley Pub.

Snake Hill. Norman Julian. LC 92-91180. (Orig.). 1993. pap. 12.00 (0-9635248-0-1) Trillium Pubng.

Snake Hunt. Jill Kastner. LC 92-32601. (Illus.). 32p. (J). (ps-2). 1993. lib. bdg. 14.95 (0-02-749395-4, Four Winds Pr) S&S Childrens.

*Snake in Gambling. M. Dora Riboni. (Illus.). 112p. 1996. 19.95 (1-880470-38-1) Creative Des.

*Snake in Her Mouth: Poems 1974-96. Nila Northsun. 80p. (Orig.). 1997. pap. 8.95 (0-931122-87-2) West End.

Snake in His Bosom & Other Stories. R. A. Lafferty. (Booklet Ser.: No. 13). 44p. (Orig.). 1983. pap. 2.00 (0-936055-10-3) C Drumm Bks.

Snake in the Heart. Henrik Stangerup. Tr. by Anne Born. 256p. (DAN.). 1996. 24.95 (0-7145-2996-6) M Boyars Pubs.

Snake in the House. Faith McNulty. LC 92-27939. (Illus.). 32p. (J). (ps-3). 1994. 14.95 (0-590-44758-0) Scholastic Inc.

Snake in the Parsonage: Award-Winning Poetry. Jean Janzen. LC 95-19505. 73p. 1995. pap. 9.95 (1-56148-177-7) Good Bks PA.

Snake in the Sandtrap & Other Misadventures on the Golf Tour. Lee Trevino & Sam Blair. LC 85-8463. 176p. 1987. pap. 9.95 (0-8050-0368-1, Owl) H Holt & Co.

S

Snake Lovers' Lifelist & Journal. Chris Scott. (Illus.). 288p. (Orig.). 1996. 19.95 (*0-292-77698-5*) U of Tex Pr.

Snake Music. Kenneth Sherman. 48p. 1995. lib. bdg. 25.00 (*0-8095-4583-7*) Borgo Pr.

***Snake of God: A Story of Memory & Imagination.** Bard Young. LC 96-39168. (Illus.). 176p. 1996. 25.00 (*1-881320-86-3*, Black Belt) Black Belt Comm.

Snake-Oil Syndrome: Patent Medicine Advertising. A. Walker Bingham. LC 93-72216. (Illus.). 1994. 40.00 (*0-8158-0484-9*) Chris Mass.

***Snake Pit.** Gerald Seymour. 368p. 1997. mass mkt. 5.99 (*0-06-101196-7*, HarperPrism) HarpC.

Snake Pit. Sigird Undset. 1994. pap. 12.00 (*0-679-75554-3*, Vin) Random.

Snake Pit. Mary J. Ward. 23.95 (*0-8488-1215-8*) Amereon Ltd.

Snake Pit. Mary J. Ward. 278p. 1981. reprint ed. lib. bdg. 21.95 (*0-89966-260-9*) Buccaneer Bks.

***Snake River.** Judy Katschke. 1997. pap. text ed. 3.95 (*0-8114-9310-5*) Raintree Steck-V.

Snake River: Window to the West. Tim Palmer. LC 91-8585. (Illus.). 320p. (Orig.). 1991. 34.95 (*0-933280-59-9*); pap. 17.95 (*0-933280-60-2*) Island Pr.

Snake River Country. Bill Gulick. LC 71-140117. (Illus.). 1971. 39.95 (*0-87004-215-7*) Caxton.

Snake River Country: Flies & Waters. Bruce Staples. (Illus.). 96p. 1992. 29.95 (*1-878175-09-2*); pap. 19.95 (*1-878175-08-4*) F Amato Pubns.

Snake River, of Hells Canyon. Cort Conley & John Carrey. LC 79-55450. (Orig.). 1979. pap. 12.95 (*0-9603566-0-6*) Backeddy Bks.

Snake River Plain - Yellowstone Volcanic Province. Ed. by Ruebelman. (IGC Field Trip Guidebooks Ser.). 1989. 28.00 (*0-87590-627-3*, T305) Am Geophysical.

Snake River Secrets. Lanny Harward. (Illus.). 96p. 1996. pap. 15.95 (*1-57188-049-6*) F Amato Pubns.

Snake Secrets. Joan M. Roever. LC 78-4318. (Illus.). (J). (gr. 5 up). 1979. lib. bdg. 11.85 (*0-8027-6333-2*) Walker & Co.

Snake Song. Sheila Farr. (Illus.). 68p. (Orig.). 1994. pap. write for info. (*0-936563-16-8*) Signpost.

Snake Stew. Patti Cakes & Tammy Hunt. 32p. (J). 1995. pap. 9.95 (*0-9649800-0-2*) Cozy Bks.

***Snake Stomper.** large type ed. Wayne D. Overholser. LC 96-35733. (Nightingale Ser.). 1997. pap. 18.95 (*0-7838-1975-7*) G K Hall.

Snake-Stone. Berlie Doherty. LC 95-36070. 176p. (J). (gr. 6 up). 1996. lib. bdg. 16.99 (*0-531-08862-6*) Orchard Bks Watts.

Snake-Stone. Berlie Doherty. LC 95-36070. 176p. (J). (gr. 6 up). 1996. 15.95 (*0-531-09512-6*) Orchard Bks Watts.

***Snake Stone.** Berlie Doherty. 1998. pap. 4.99 (*0-14-038392-1*) Viking Penguin.

Snake Stone. Margaret James. 304p. 1994. 20.00 (*0-7278-4566-7*) Severn Hse.

Snake Stone. large type ed. Margaret James. (Magna Large Print Ser.). 1994. pap. 17.99 (*1-85389-516-4*, Pub. by Magna Print Bks UK) Ulverscroft.

Snake Supper. Alan Durant. LC 94-27637. (Illus.). 32p. (J). (ps-1). 1995. 9.95 (*0-307-17519-7*) Western Pub.

Snake Tattoo. Linda Barnes. 208p. 1990. mass mkt. 5.99 (*0-449-21759-0*, Crest) Fawcett.

Snake Tattoo. large type ed. Linda Barnes. (General Ser.). 350p. 1990. lib. bdg. 19.95 (*0-8161-4866-X*, GK Hall) Thorndike Pr.

Snake, the Crocodile & the Dog. Elizabeth Peters. 448p. 1994. mass mkt. 5.99 (*0-446-36478-9*) Warner Bks.

Snake, the Crocodile, & the Dog. large type ed. Elizabeth Peters. LC 92-35900. (General Ser.). 555p. 1993. 24.95 (*0-8161-5681-6*, GK Hall) Thorndike Pr.

Snake, the Crocodile, & the Dog. large type ed. Elizabeth Peters. LC 92-35900. (General Ser.). 555p. 1994. pap. 17.95 (*0-8161-5682-4*, GK Hall) Thorndike Pr.

Snake Toxins. A. L. Harvey. (International Encyclopedia of Pharmacology & Therapeutics Ser.). (Illus.). 476p. 1991. 173.00 (*0-08-040294-1*, Pub. by PPI UK) Elsevier.

Snake Tree. Uwe Timm. Tr. by Peter Tegel from GER. LC 89-14496. 1990. 19.95 (*0-8112-1101-0*); pap. 10.95 (*0-8112-1121-5*, NDP686) New Directions.

Snake Trouble. William Whisenant. 15p. (J). (ps-3). 1996. pap. text ed. 1.95 (*1-56763-169-X*) Ozark Pub.

Snake Twin & Other Stories. Edilberto K. Tiempo. 152p. (Orig.). 1992. pap. 12.50 (*971-10-0490-9*, Pub. by New Day Pub PH) Cellar.

Snake Venom Poisoning. rev. ed. Findlay Russell. LC 83-3134. (Illus.). 576p. 1983. text ed. 57.50 (*0-87936-015-1*) Scholium Intl.

Snake Who Was Afraid of People. Barry L. Polisar. (Illus.). 32p. (J). (ps-2). 1993. reprint ed. 14.95 (*0-938663-16-X*) Rainbow Morn.

***Snake...& Amy-Tsosie: A Navajo Sandpainting Story.** June Behrens. Ed. by Pauline Brower. LC 96-61103. (All Americans Series: Vol. 1). (Illus.). 32p. (Orig.). (J). (gr. 2-5). 1996. pap. text ed. 6.95 (*1-889121-04-5*) York Hse Pubs.

Snakebite: Lives & Legends of Central Pennsylvania. James Y. Glimm. LC 90-49473. 268p. (C). 1991. 19.95 (*0-8229-3667-4*); pap. 14.95 (*0-8229-5444-3*) U of Pittsburgh Pr.

Snakebite Assessment & Treatment in the Eastern United States: A Merging of the Methods of Top Experts into a Guidebook for Nurses & Physicians, Including Comprehensive Protocols Plus Patient Assessment & Treatment Records Designed for Photocopying. Jon E. Soskis. LC 94-80125. (Illus.). 107p. 1995. student ed., spiral bd. 95.00 (*0-9639911-5-9*) Snakebite.

Snakebite First Aid. Thomas G. Glass, Jr. (Illus.). 41p. 1981. reprint ed. pap. 9.95 (*0-9614759-0-0*) Glass Pub Co.

Snakebite Letters: Devilishly Devious Secrets for Subverting Society As Taught in Tempter's Training School. Peter J. Kreeft. 123p. 1993. pap. 8.95 (*0-89870-449-9*) Ignatius Pr.

Snakebite Protocols/Consultant Directory. Jon E. Soskis. 32p. 1994. spiral bd. 30.00 (*0-9639911-7-5*) Snakebite.

Snakebite Sonnet: A Novel. Max Phillips. LC 95-43249. 320p. 1996. 22.95 (*0-316-70620-5*) Little.

Snakedreams. Barbara Presnell. Ed. by L. D. Zarucchi. (Illus.). 36p. (Orig.). 1994. pap. 6.95 (*1-879205-54-8*) Nightshade Pr.

Snakefoot: The Making of a Champion. Robert G. Wehle. (Illus.). 256p. 1996. 50.00 (*0-913174-06-8*) Country Pr NY.

Snakefoot: The Making of a Champion. deluxe limited ed. Robert G. Wehle. (Illus.). 256p. 1996. 150.00 (*0-913174-05-X*) Country Pr NY.

Snakehunter. Chuck Kinder. LC 91-917788. 224p. 1991. reprint ed. pap. 13.50 (*0-917788-50-8*) Gnomon Pr.

***Snakes.** (Eyes on Nature Ser.). (Illus.). 32p. (J). (gr. 1 up). write for info. (*1-56156-461-3*) Kidsbks.

Snakes. Donna Bailey. LC 89-26078. (Animal World Ser.). (Illus.). 32p. (J). (gr. 1-4). 1990. pap. 4.95 (*0-8114-4613-1*); lib. bdg. 21.40 (*0-8114-2636-X*) Raintree Steck-V.

Snakes. Ray Broekel. LC 81-38487. (New True Bks.). (Illus.). 48p. (J). (gr. k-4). 1982. pap. 5.50 (*0-516-41649-9*); lib. bdg. 19.00 (*0-516-01649-0*) Childrens.

***Snakes.** John Coborn. (Illus.). 64p. 1997. 6.95 (*0-7938-2022-7*, RE-166) TFH Pubns.

Snakes. Patricia Demuth. LC 92-24466. (All Aboard Reading Ser.). (Illus.). 4832p. (J). (gr. 1-3). 1993. pap. 3.95 (*0-448-40513-X*, G&D) Putnam Pub Group.

Snakes. James E. Gerholdt. LC 94-7795. (Remarkable Reptiles Ser.). (J). 1994. lib. bdg. 14.98 (*1-56239-307-3*) Abdo & Dghtrs.

Snakes. Eric S. Grace. (Wildlife Library). (Illus.). 64p. (J). (gr. 3-6). 1994. 15.95 (*0-87156-490-4*) Sierra Club Childrens.

Snakes. Eric S. Grace. (Wildlife Library). (Illus.). 64p. (J). (gr. 3-6). 1996. pap. 7.95 (*0-87156-863-2*) Sierra Club Childrens.

Snakes. Klaus Griehl. (Pet Care Ser.). 1984. pap. 6.95 (*0-8120-2813-9*) Barron.

Snakes. Sylvia A. Johnson. LC 87-7162. (Natural Science Bks.). (Illus.). 48p. (J). (gr. 4 up). 1986. pap. 5.95 (*0-8225-9503-6*, First Ave Edns) Lerner Group.

***Snakes.** Claudette C. Mitchell et al. (Visions: African-American Experiences: Vol. 38). (Illus.). 8p. (Orig.). (J). (gr. k-1). 1996. pap. text ed. 3.00 (*1-57518-080-4*) Arborlake.

***Snakes.** Arthur Morton. (Illus.). (J). (gr. k-3). 1996. write for info. (*1-57842-082-2*) Delmas Creat.

***Snakes.** Arthur Morton. (J). 1996. write for info. (*0-614-22154-4*) Delmas Creat.

Snakes. Peter Murray. (Nature Bks.). 32p. (J). (gr. 2-6). 1992. lib. bdg. 22.79 (*0-89565-849-6*) Childs World.

Snakes. Alan Rickard. 1991. pap. 7.00 (*0-936128-26-7*) De Young Pr.

Snakes. Mervin F. Roberts. (Illus.). 80p. 1990. pap. 6.95 (*0-86622-784-9*, PB126) TFH Pubns.

Snakes. Seymour Simon. LC 91-15948. (Illus.). 32p. (J). (gr. 2-5). 1992. 16.00 (*0-06-022529-7*); lib. bdg. 15.89 (*0-06-022530-0*) HarpC Child Bks.

Snakes. Seymour Simon. LC 91-15948. (Trophy Nonfiction Bk.). (Illus.). 32p. (J). (gr. 2-5). 1994. pap. 5.95 (*0-06-446165-3*, Trophy) HarpC Child Bks.

Snakes. Erik D. Stoops & Annette T. Wright. (Illus.). 80p. (J). 1994. pap. 9.95 (*0-8069-8483-X*) Sterling.

Snakes. John B. Wexo. (Zoobooks Ser.). (J). 1991. lib. bdg. 14.95 (*0-88682-331-5*) Creative Ed.

Snakes. Wildlife Education, Ltd. Staff. (Zoobooks Ser.). (Illus.). 20p. (Orig.). (YA). (gr. 5 up). 1981. pap. 2.75 (*0-937934-05-4*) Wildlife Educ.

Snakes. Herbert S. Zim. LC 49-10266. (Illus.). 64p. (J). (gr. 3-7). 1949. lib. bdg. 12.93 (*0-688-31549-6*, Morrow Junior) Morrow.

Snakes. 2nd ed. Ruth B. Gross. LC 89-38254. (Illus.). 64p. (J). (ps-3). 1990. reprint ed. lib. bdg. 14.95 (*0-02-737022-4*, Four Winds Pr) S&S Childrens.

Snakes: A Natural History. Ed. by Roland Bauchot. LC 93-43892. (Illus.). 220p. 1994. 39.95 (*0-8069-0654-5*) Sterling.

***Snakes: A Natural History.** Roland Bauchot. 1997. write for info. (*0-8069-0653-7*) Sterling.

Snakes: Ecology & Behavior. Ed. by Richard A. Seigel & Joseph T. Collins. LC 93-18568. 464p. 1993. pap. text ed. 27.95 (*0-07-056056-0*) McGraw.

Snakes: Look & Learn. William P. Mara. (Illus.). 64p. 1993. 9.95 (*0-7938-0074-9*, KD003) TFH Pubns.

Snakes: Silent Hunters. Claudia Schnieper. (Illus.). 48p. (J). (gr. 4-6). 1995. pap. 5.95 (*0-87614-952-2*) Lerner Group.

Snakes: The Evolution of Mystery in Nature. Harry W. Green. LC 96-21928. 1997. 45.00 (*0-520-20014-4*) U CA Pr.

***Snakes: The Evolution of Mystery in Nature.** Harry W. Greene. 1997. 45.00 (*0-614-28267-5*) U CA Pr.

Snakes: The Keeper & the Kept. Carl Kauffeld. LC 94-41162. 286p. (C). 1995. reprint ed. 29.95 (*0-89464-936-1*) Krieger.

Snakes: The Silent Hunters. Claudia Schnieper. LC 94-42329. (Nature Watch Bks.). (Illus.). 48p. (J). (gr. 4-6). 1995. 19.95 (*0-87614-881-X*, Carolrhoda) Lerner Group.

Snakes: The Snakes, Vol. 1. rev. ed. Ray Eashton, Jr. & Patricia S. Ashton. Ed. by Sandra Romashko. LC 81-51066. (Handbook of Reptiles & Amphibians of Florida Ser.: Pt. 1). (Illus.). 176p. (Orig.). 1998. pap. 18.95 (*0-89317-033-X*) Windward Pub.

Snakes: Their Place in the Sun. Robert M. McClung. LC 91-692. (Illus.). 64p. (J). (gr. 2-4). 1993. pap. 5.95 (*0-8050-2893-5*, Bks Young Read) H Holt & Co.

Snakes, A Photo-Fact Book. S. Tropea. (Illus.). 24p. (Orig.). (J). 1988. pap. 1.95 (*0-942025-15-6*) Kidsbks.

Snakes Alive! Its Reptile Clive! Chodkowski. (Reading Well Ser.). (J). 1990. pap. 6.00 (*0-88335-799-2*) Milliken Pub Co.

Snakes Alive! Jokes about Snakes. Diane L. Burns. (Make Me Laugh! Joke Bks.). (Illus.). (J). (gr. 1-4). 1988. pap. 2.95 (*0-8225-9543-5*, First Ave Edns); lib. bdg. 6.95 (*0-8225-0996-2*, Lerner Publctns) Lerner Group.

***Snakes & Ladders: Glimpses of Modern India.** Gita Mehta. LC 96-49004. 256p. 1997. 22.95 (*0-385-47495-4*, N A Talese) Doubleday.

Snakes & Ladders: The Development Game. Jay Dubashi. 299p. 1985. 24.95 (*0-317-39861-X*, Pub. by Allied Pubs II) Asia Bk Corp.

***Snakes & Ladders (& Hundreds of Mice) A Weird & Wonderful Tower Maze.** Piers Harper. LC 96-45005. (Illus.). (J). 1997. 14.99 (*0-7636-0333-3*) Candlewick Pr.

Snakes & Lizards. (Super Tough Hidden Pictures Ser.). (Illus.). 48p. (J). (gr. k-2). 1993. pap. 3.95 (*0-8431-3539-5*) Price Stern Sloan.

***Snakes & Lizards.** (Eye-to-Eye Bks.). (J). (gr. 1-7). 1997. 9.99 (*0-614-28833-9*, Ladybrd) Penguin.

Snakes & Lizards. Tom Langton. (Illus.). 128p. text ed. 19.95 (*0-905483-77-4*, Pub. by Whittet Bks UK) Diamond Farm Bk.

Snakes & Lizards: A Golden Junior Guide. George S. Fichter. (Illus.). 36p. (J). (ps-3). 1993. 5.50 (*0-307-11432-5*, Golden Pr) Western Pub.

Snakes & Lizards: Their Care & Breeding in Captivity. John Corbin. (Illus.). 208p. 21.95 (*3-89356-036-X*, 16047) Tetra Pr.

Snakes & Other Reptiles of the Southwest. Erik D. Stoops. LC 92-35815. (Orig.). 1992. pap. 9.95 (*0-914846-79-5*) Golden West Pub.

Snakes & Reptiles: A Portrait of the Animal World. Andrew Cleave. 1995. 10.98 (*0-8317-0964-2*) Smithmark.

Snakes & Snake Hunting. Carl Kauffeld. LC 94-41066. (Illus.). 274p. (C). 1995. reprint ed. 29.95 (*0-89464-931-0*) Krieger.

Snakes & Snakebite: Venomous Snakes & Management of Snakebite in Southern Africa. John Visser & David S. Chapman. 176p. (C). 1989. 180.00 (*1-85368-032-X*, Pub. by New Holland Pubs UK) St Mut.

Snakes & the Boy Who Was Afraid of Them. Barry L. Polisar. (Illus.). 32p. (J). (ps-3). 1993. reprint ed. 14.95 (*0-938663-15-1*) Rainbow Morn.

Snakes Are Hunters. Patricia Lauber. LC 87-47695. (Let's-Read-&-Find-Out Science Bk.). (Illus.). 32p. (J). (ps-3). 1988. lib. bdg. 14.89 (*0-690-04630-8*, Crowell Jr Bks) HarpC Child Bks.

Snakes Are Hunters. Patricia Lauber. LC 87-47695. (Trophy Let's-Read-&-Find-Out Science Bk.). (Illus.). 32p. (J). (ps-4). 1989. pap. 4.95 (*0-06-445091-0*, Trophy) HarpC Child Bks.

Snakes Are Nothing to Sneeze At. Gabrielle Charbonnet. LC 89-26919. (Illus.). 80p. (J). (gr. 2-4). 1991. pap. 4.95 (*0-8050-1842-5*, Bks Young Read) H Holt & Co.

Snakes As a Hobby. Thomas Leetz. (Illus.). 99p. 1991. pap. 8.95 (*0-86622-415-7*, TT001) TFH Pubns.

Snakes As a New Pet. Jake Oberon. (Illus.). 64p. (Orig.). 1990. pap. 6.95 (*0-86622-623-0*, TU-015) TFH Pubns.

***Snake's Daughter: The Roads in & Out of War.** Gail H. Gilberg. LC 96-49229. (Singular Lives Ser.). (Illus.). 272p. 1997. 32.95 (*0-87745-585-6*); pap. 16.95 (*0-87745-586-4*) U of Iowa Pr.

Snakes for Those Who Care. Anmarie Barrie. (Illus.). 32p. 1994. pap. 4.95 (*0-7938-1389-1*, B111) TFH Pubns.

Snakes from Around the World. Scott Wiedensaul. 1991. 12.98 (*1-55521-733-8*) Bk Sales Inc.

Snakes in Question: The Smithsonian Answer Book. Carl H. Ernst & George R. Zug. (Illus.). 264p. (Orig.). 1996. pap. 24.95 (*1-56098-649-2*) Smithsonian.

Snakes in Question: The Smithsonian Answer Book. Carl H. Ernst & George R. Zug. (Illus.). 264p. (Orig.). 1996. text ed. 49.00 (*1-56098-648-4*) Smithsonian.

Snakes in the Eagle's Nest: A History of Ground Attacks on Air Bases. Alan Vick. LC 95-3051. (Illus.). 189p. (Orig.). 1995. pap. 15.00 (*0-8330-1629-6*, MR-553-AF) Rand Corp.

Snakes in the Garden. L. S. Whiteley. 280p. 1990. 19.95 (*0-8027-1113-8*) Walker & Co.

Snakes in the Outhouse, & Other Causes for Wonder. Jay Shuler. (Illus.). 119p. (Orig.). 1994. pap. 15.00 (*1-882966-02-3*) McClellanville Arts.

Snakes in the Zoo. Roland Smith. LC 91-45588. (New Zoo Ser.). (Illus.). 64p. (J). (gr. 3-6). 1992. lib. bdg. 16.40 (*1-56294-211-5*) Millbrook Pr.

Snakes, Lizards & Turtles of the Lake Mead Region. Russell K. Grater. LC 81-50464. (Illus.). 48p. (Orig.). 1981. pap. 4.95 (*0-911408-58-4*) SW Pks Mnmts.

Snakes, Lizards, Turtles, Frogs, Toads & Salamanders of New Mexico: A Field Guide. Michael A. Williamson et al. LC 94-27383. (Illus.). 180p. (Orig.). 1994. pap. text ed. 19.95 (*0-86534-233-4*) Sunstone Pr.

Snake's Marble. Mehry M. Reid. 1995. 21.95 (*0-533-11387-3*) Vantage.

Snakes' Nest. Ledo Ivo. 144p. 1990. 25.00 (*0-7206-0737-X*) Dufour.

Snakes' Nest or a Tale Badly Told. Ledo Ivo. Tr. by Kern Krapohl. LC 81-3956. 144p. 1981. 12.95 (*0-8112-0806-0*); pap. 5.95 (*0-8112-0807-9*, NDP521) New Directions.

Snakes of Australia: Dangerous & Harmless. Peter Mirtschin & Richard Davis. (Illus.). 216p. (Orig.). 1994. pap. 19.95 (*0-85572-209-6*, Pub. by Hill Content Pubng AT) Seven Hills Bk.

Snakes of Eastern North America. Carl H. Ernst & Roger W. Barbour. (Illus.). 290p. (C). 1989. lib. bdg. 108.00 (*0-913969-24-9*, G Mason Univ Pr) Univ Pub Assocs.

Snakes of India. P. J. Deoras. (Illus.). 152p. 1990. 11.95 (*0-318-36997-4*) Asia Bk Corp.

Snakes of Iran. Latifi. LC 90-63908. 1991. write for info. (*0-916984-22-2*) SSAR.

Snakes of Medical Importance: Asia-Pacific Region. Ed. by P. Gopalkrishnakone & L. M. Chou. 675p. 1996. 150.00 (*9971-62-217-3*, Pub. by Singapore Univ Pr SI) Intl Spec Bk.

Snakes of Medical Importance & Snake-Bite Treatment. Indramani Jena & Akulananada Sarangi. (Illus.). xxxv, 293p. 1993. 38.00 (*81-7024-577-X*, Pub. by Ashish Pub Hse II) Nataraj Bks.

Snakes of Nyasaland. R. C. Sweeney. (Illus.). 1971. reprint ed. 37.50 (*90-6123-242-2*) Lubrecht & Cramer.

Snakes of Ontario. Eugene B. Logier. LC 67-110673. (Canadian University Paperbooks Ser.: No. 64). (Illus.). 106p. reprint ed. pap. 30.30 (*0-8357-6384-6*, 2035739) Bks Demand.

***Snakes of Sumatra: An Annotated Checklist & Key with Natural History Notes.** Patrick David & Gernot Vogel. (Illus.). 264p. (Orig.). 1996. pap. 39.95 (*3-930612-08-9*, Pub. by Edition Chimaira GW) Bibliomania.

Snakes of Thailand & Their Husbandry. Merel J. Cox. 564p. (C). 1991. 82.50 (*0-89464-437-8*) Krieger.

Snakes of the "Agkistrodon" Complex. Gloyd & Conant. LC 89-50342. 1990. write for info. (*0-916984-20-6*) SSAR.

Snakes of the Catskill Mountains. 1988. pap. 3.00 (*0-939166-08-9*) Outdoor Pubns.

***Snakes of the Catskills: A Guide to Their Recognition.** James E. Lawrence. (Illus.). 36p. 1953. 2.50 (*0-614-26408-1*) Purple Mnt Pr.

Snakes of the Orient: A Checklist. Kenneth R. Welch. LC 86-27298. 192p. 1988. lib. bdg. 28.50 (*0-89464-203-0*) Krieger.

Snakes of the Southwest: Southwestern Snakes. (Illus.). 32p. 1994. pap. 1.25 (*0-935810-17-X*) Primer Pubs.

Snakes of the United States & Canada: Keeping Them Healthy in Captivity, 2 vols., Set. John V. Rossi & Roxanne Rossi. 566p. 1995. 110.00 (*0-89464-956-6*) Krieger.

Snakes of the United States & Canada Vol. II: Keeping Them Healthy in Captivity: Western Area. 2nd ed. John V. Rossi & Roxanne Rossi. LC 91-2199. 342p. 1995. 74.50 (*0-89464-808-X*) Krieger.

Snakes of the United States & Canada, Vol. One, Eastern Area: Keeping Them Healthy in Captivity. John V. Rossi. 224p. (Orig.). 1992. lib. bdg. 54.50 (*0-89464-590-0*) Krieger.

Snakes of the World. Chris Mattison. (Illus.). 190p. 1986. 25.95 (*0-8160-1082-X*) Facts on File.

Snakes of the World, Vol. 1, Synopsis of Living & Extinct Species. Kenneth L. Williams & Van Wallach. LC 88-1. 244p. 1989. Vol. 1, 1988 ed., Synopsis of Living & Extinct Species. 15.75 (*0-89464-215-4*) Krieger.

Snakes of Utah. Douglas C. Cox & Wilmer W. Tanner. (Illus.). 1995. write for info. (*0-8425-2331-6*) Frnds of the Libry.

Snakes of Virginia. Donald W. Linzey & Michael J. Clifford. LC 81-12951. (Illus.). 224p. (C). 1995. pap. 24.95 (*0-8139-0826-4*) U Pr of Va.

Snakes of Virginia. Donald W. Linzey & Michael J. Clifford. LC 81-12951. 207p. reprint ed. pap. 59.00 (*0-7837-1244-8*, 2041381) Bks Demand.

Snakes or Ladders? The Ambitious Executive's Guide to Headhunters & How to Handle Them. Graham Perkins. 240p. 1991. pap. 60.00 (*0-273-03285-2*, Pub. by Pitman Pubng UK) St Mut.

Snake's Pass. Bram Stoker. 256p. 1990. reprint ed. pap. 9.95 (*0-86322-119-X*, Pub. by Brandon Bk Pubs IE) Irish Bks Media.

Snakes, Salamanders, & Lizards. Diane L. Burns. LC 95-15127. (Take-Along Guide Ser.). (Illus.). 48p. (J). (gr. 3-7). 1995. 9.95 (*1-55971-478-6*) NorthWord.

Snake's Spit. Darr Anderson. 325p. 1989. text ed. 17.95 (*0-9620810-1-9*) B Deviladog & Co.

Snakeskin. Carmen A. Fiore. (Illus.). 112p. (J). (gr. 3-7). 1991. 14.95 (*0-939219-07-7*) Townhouse Pub.

Snaketrack. large type ed. Frank Bonham. LC 93-31599. 1994. lib. bdg. 16.95 (*0-8161-5854-1*, GK Hall) Thorndike Pr.

Snaketrack. Frank Bonham. 160p. 1989. reprint ed. pap. 2.95 (*0-380-70845-0*) Avon.

Snakey Riddles. Katy Hall & Lisa Eisenberg. (Illus.). 48p. (J). (ps-3). 1993. pap. 3.99 (*0-14-054588-3*) Puffin Bks.

Snakey Riddles Level 3, Yellow. Katy Hall & Lisa Eisenberg. (Easy-to-Read Ser.). (Illus.). (J). (gr. 1-4). 1994. pap. 3.50 (*0-14-037141-9*) Puffin Bks.

Snap! Marcia Vaughan. LC 95-11773. (Illus.). 32p. (J). 1996. 14.95 (*0-590-60377-9*) Scholastic Inc.

Snap! Charlie Gets the Whole Picture: Getting the Main Idea. Monica Weiss. LC 91-16499. (Frimble Family First Learning Adventures Ser.). (Illus.). (J). (gr. k-2). 1992. lib. bdg. 10.95 (*0-8167-2494-6*) Troll Communs.

Snap Fashion Sketchbook. Sharon L. Tate. 224p. 1995. pap. text ed. 52.00 (*0-13-057423-6*) P-H.

***Snap Happy.** John Light. (ITA). (J). 1991. pap. 3.99 (*0-85953-607-6*) Childs Play.

Snap Happy. John Light. LC 91-36610. (Light Reading Ser.). (J). (gr. 4 up). 1991. 3.99 (*0-85953-504-5*) Childs Play.

Snap Judgement. Sandra Canfield. (Superromance Ser.). 1993. mass mkt. 3.39 (*0-373-70545-X*, 1-70545-8) Harlequin Bks.

Snap Judgments. Young Playwrights at the Walden Theatre Staff. 1992. pap. 5.00 (*0-87129-136-3*, S17) Dramatic Pub.

An Asterisk (*) at the beginning of an entry indicates that the title is appearing in BIP for the first time.

Snap Revolution--James Fenton in the Philippines: Granta Eighteen. Ed. by Bill Buford. 1986. pap. 6.95 (*0-14-008596-3*, Penguin Bks) Viking Penguin.
Snap! Snap! Buzz Buzz: Set Is Called Snappy Sounds. Rich Cowley. (Snappy Sounds Ser.). (Illus.). 24p. (J). (ps). 1996. 3.95 (*1-55209-032-9*, Pub. by Annick CN) Firefly Bks Ltd.
Snap Your Fingers, Slap Your Face & Wake Up! Ma D. Sarito. LC 84-43011. (Initiation Talks Ser.). 256p. (Orig.). 1984. pap. 3.95 (*0-88050-632-6*) Osho America.
Snapdragon. Desmond Egan. Ed. by Stanley H. Barkan. (Review Chapbook Ser.: No. 31: Irish Poetry 1). 16p. 1989. 15.00 (*0-89304-971-9*); pap. 5.00 (*0-89304-972-7*) Cross-Cultrl NY.
Snapdragon. Ed. by Kathleen L. Mendel. (Illus.). 24p. (Orig.). 1995. pap. 6.10 (*1-878142-44-5*) Telstar FL.
Snapdragon, Mini. Desmond Egan. Ed. by Stanley H. Barkan. (Review Chapbook Ser.: No. 31: Irish Poetry 1). 16p. 1989. 15.00 (*0-89304-973-5*); pap. 5.00 (*0-89304-974-3*) Cross-Cultrl NY.
***Snapp, Snurr & the Yellow Sled.** Maj Lindman. Date not set. lib. bdg. 11.95 (*0-614-25288-1*) Amereon Ltd.
***Snapped.** Ed Assoline. 1997. pap. 14.95 (*2-908228-90-4*, Pub. by Assouline FR) Rizzoli Intl.
Snapper. Roddy Doyle. 224p. 1992. pap. 10.95 (*0-14-017167-3*, Penguin Bks) Viking Penguin.
***Snapper Bible.** Joe Richard. (Illus.). 128p. (Orig.). 1996. pap. 17.95 (*0-9649317-1-0*) Saltwater Spec.
Snapping: America's Epidemic of Sudden Personality Change. 2nd expanded rev. ed. Flo Conway & Jim Siegelman. LC 95-69831. 400p. 1995. pap. 14.95 (*0-9647650-0-4*) Stillpt Pr NY.
Snappy Jazzy Jewelry. Katie Gayle. LC 95-21848. (Illus.). 48p. (J). (gr. 5-8). 1995. 14.95 (*0-8069-3854-4*) Sterling.
***Snappy, Jazzy Jewelry.** Katie Gayle. (Illus.). 48p. (J). 1997. pap. 9.95 (*0-8069-3855-2*) Sterling.
***Snappy, Jazzy Jewelry Book & Kit.** Katie Gayle. (Illus.). 48p. 1996. pap. 19.95 (*0-8069-9631-5*) Sterling.
***Snappy Stories.** Paul E. Holdcraft. pap. 4.15 (*0-687-38777-9*) Abingdon.
Snaps. Ellen Von Unwerth. LC 94-11786. 1994. 35.00 (*0-8212-2124-8*) Little.
***Snaps, Vol. 4.** Jim Percelay. Date not set. pap. write for info. (*0-688-15014-4*, Quill) Morrow.
Snaps: Ellen Von Unwerth. Ellen Von Unwerth. (Illus.). 124p. 1994. 60.00 (*0-944092-29-2*) Twin Palms Pub.
Snaps: Poetry & Prose from a Family Album. Frank Pommersheim. 125p. 1994. pap. 7.95 (*0-9636224-1-2*) Rose Hill Bks.
Snaps: The African American Art of Verbal Warfare. James Percelay et al. LC 93-34484. 1994. pap. 8.95 (*0-688-12896-3*) Morrow.
Snapshot. Ruairi McCormac, pseud. 345p. 1995. pap. 25.00 (*1-898162-30-1*, Pub. by IMMEL Pubng UK) St Mut.
Snapshot. Ted Morris. 345p. (C). 1990. pap. 35.00 (*0-318-71718-2*, Pub. by IMMEL Pubng UK) St Mut.
Snapshot. large type ed. Linda Barnes. LC 93-11280. 1993. lib. bdg. 21.95 (*1-56054-761-8*) Thorndike Pr.
Snapshot. large type ed. Linda Barnes. LC 93-11280. 1994. lib. bdg. 14.95 (*1-56054-878-9*) Thorndike Pr.
Snapshot. large type ed. A. J. Quinnell. (Adventure Suspense Ser.). 432p. 1984. 27.99 (*0-7089-8178-X*) Ulverscroft.
Snapshot: A Carlotta Carlyle Mystery. Linda Barnes. 400p. 1994. mass mkt. 5.99 (*0-440-21220-0*) Dell.
***Snapshot of America's Nonprofit Boards: Results of the NCNB Nonprofit Governance Survey, Vol. 146.** 2nd ed. Richard L. Moyers & Kathleen P. Enright. 24p. 1997. pap. 19.00 (*0-925299-74-X*) Natl Ctr Nonprofit.
Snapshot Poetics: Allen Ginsberg's Photographic Memoir of the Beat Era. Allen Ginsberg. LC 92-40516. 96p. 1993. pap. 12.95 (*0-8118-0372-4*) Chronicle Bks.
Snapshot Versions of Life. Richard Chalfen. LC 87-70258. (Illus.). 213p. 1987. 23.95 (*0-87972-387-4*); pap. 11.95 (*0-87972-388-2*) Bowling Green Univ Popular Press.
Snapshot View of Communication Patterns: The New Hampshire Division of Vocational Rehabilitation. Michael Nyhan et al. 67p. 1982. 7.50 (*0-318-19197-0*, R-55) Inst Future.
Snapshots. Marv Bondarowicz. (Illus.). 1977. pap. 5.00 (*0-89439-000-7*) Printed Matter.
***Snapshots.** Cynthia Mercati. 1996. pap. 5.00 (*0-614-18963-2*) Bakers Plays.
Snapshots. Reader's Digest Editors et al. (New Writers' Voices Ser.). (Illus.). 64p. (Orig.). 1993. pap. text ed. 3.50 (*1-56853-004-8*, Signal Hill) New Readers.
Snapshots. Alain Robbe-Grillet. 72p. (C). 1995. pap. 11.95 (*0-8101-1328-7*) Northwestern U Pr.
Snapshots: A Collection of Readings for Adults. Incl. Reading Level 5. Ed. by Brian Schenk et al. 1988. pap. text ed. 5.50 (*0-8428-9550-7*); Reading Level 6. Ed. by Brian Schenk et al. 1988. pap. text ed. 5.50 (*0-8428-9551-5*); Reading Level 7. Ed. by Brian Schenk et al. 1988. pap. text ed. 5.50 (*0-8428-9552-3*); 144p. Set pap. write for info. (*0-318-58324-0*) Cambridge Bk.
***Snapshots: The People Called Free Methodist.** Donald E. Demaray. (Illus.). 310p. (Orig.). (C). 1985. pap. text ed. 4.95 (*0-89367-110-X*) Light & Life Comm.
Snapshots: True-Color Photo Images Using the Fractal Formatter. Iterated Systems, Inc. Staff. 32p. (C). 1992. student ed. 119.95 incl. disk (*0-86720-299-8*) AK Peters.
Snapshots & Portraits: A Two-Act Play about the Family. Paul McCusker. 1989. 8.99 (*0-8341-9298-5*, MP-652) Lillenas.
Snapshots for a Serial Killer: A Fiction & a Play. Robert Peters. 125p. (Orig.). 1992. pap. 10.95 (*1-879194-07-4*) GLB Pubs.
Snapshots from Hell: The Making of an MBA. Peter Robinson. 304p. 1995. pap. 11.99 (*0-446-67117-7*) Warner Bks.
Snapshots from the Underground. Milford H. Wolpoff. 1994. 24.95 (*0-02-935595-8*) S&S Trade.
Snapshots from the Wedding. Gary Soto. LC 95-5793. (Illus.). (J). 1997. 15.95 (*0-399-22808-X*, Putnam) Putnam Pub Group.
***Snapshots of Service in the Disciplines.** 51p. 1996. pap. 5.00 (*0-614-30592-6*) Ed Comm States.
Snapshots of the Carolinas: Landscapes & Cultures. Association of American Geographers Staff. Ed. by D. Gordon Bennett. (Illus.). 280p. (Orig.). (C). 1996. pap. 15.00 (*0-89291-225-1*) Assn Am Geographers.
Snapshots of the Past. Brian Fagan. (Illus.). 160p. 1995. 32.00 (*0-7619-9108-5*); pap. 14.95 (*0-7619-9109-3*) AltaMira Pr.
Snapshots of the Presidential Campaign, 1988, 3 vols., Set. Contrib. by Michael L. Gillette. (Presidential Election Studies). 1992. pap. 30.00 (*0-89940-316-6*) LBJ Sch Pub Aff.
Snapshots of the Presidential Campaign, 1988, 3 vols., Vol. 1: The Bush Campaign. Contrib. by Michael L. Gillette. (Presidential Election Studies). 157p. 1992. pap. 12.50 (*0-89940-312-3*) LBJ Sch Pub Aff.
Snapshots of the Presidential Campaign, 1988, 3 vols., Vol. 2: The Dukakis Campaign. Contrib. by Michael L. Gillette. (Presidential Election Studies). 145p. 1992. pap. 12.50 (*0-89940-313-1*) LBJ Sch Pub Aff.
Snapshots of the Presidential Campaign, 1988, 3 vols., Vol. 3: The Jackson Campaign. Contrib. by Michael L. Gillette. (Presidential Election Studies). 73p. 1992. pap. 8.50 (*0-89940-314-X*) LBJ Sch Pub Aff.
Snare. large type ed. Gwen Moffat. 1990. 25.99 (*0-7089-2128-0*) Ulverscroft.
Snare. Elizabeth Spencer. LC 93-30728. (Banner Bk.). 448p. 1993. reprint ed. pap. 16.95 (*0-87805-666-1*) U Pr of Miss.
Snare Drum Pocketbook. William J. Schinstine & Fred A. Hoey. pap. 0.95 (*0-87166-556-5*, 93747) Mel Bay.
Snare Drum Rudiment Dictionary. Sandy Feldstein. (Alfred Handy Guides Ser.). 32p. (Orig.). 1980. pap. text ed. 4.95 (*0-88284-212-9*, 1893) Alfred Pub.
Snare in the Dark. large type ed. Frank Parrish. (Mystery Ser.). 320p. 1983. 25.99 (*0-7089-1007-6*) Ulverscroft.
Snare of Serpents. Victoria Holt. 1991. mass mkt. 5.99 (*0-449-21928-3*, Crest) Fawcett.
Snare of Serpents. large type ed. Victoria Holt. LC 93-36327. (General Ser.). 1994. pap. 19.95 (*0-8161-5800-2*, GK Hall) Thorndike Pr.
Snares. Will Weaver. (Winter Book Ser.). (Illus.). 52p. 1992. 75.00 (*1-879832-03-8*) MN Ctr Book Arts.
Snares, Deadfalls & Other Traps of the Northern Algonquians & Northern Athapaskans. John M. Cooper. LC 76-43683. (Catholic University of America Anthropological Ser.: No. 5). reprint ed. 37.50 (*0-404-15516-2*) AMS Pr.
Snares of Death. Kate Charles. 368p. 1993. 18.95 (*0-89296-498-7*) Mysterious Pr.
Snares of Death. Kate Charles. 352p. 1994. mass mkt. 5.50 (*0-446-40195-1*, Mysterious Paperbk) Warner Bks.
Snares Without End. Olympe Bhely-Quenum. Ed. by A. J. Arnold & K. Drame. Tr. by Dorothy Blair from FRE. LC 87-7301. (CARAF Bks.). 204p. (Orig.). 1988. pap. text ed. 12.95 (*0-8139-1189-3*) U Pr of Va.
Snaring Heaven. Christopher Meredith. 80p. 1990. pap. 13.95 (*1-85411-026-8*, Pub. by Seren Bks UK) Dufour.
Snark Puzzle Book. Martin Gardner. (Young Readers Ser.). (Illus.). 124p. (J). (gr. 3 up). 1990. reprint ed. 16.95 (*0-87975-583-0*) Prometheus Bks.
Snarkout Boys & the Avocado of Death. Daniel Pinkwater. (J). 1995. pap. 12.95 (*0-7871-0248-2*, Dove Bks) Dove Audio.
Snarkout Boys & the Avocado of Death. Daniel M. Pinkwater. Bd. with Avocado of Death. 160p. 1983. pap. 2.50 (*0-451-15852-0*, Sig Vista) NAL-Dutton.
Snarkout Boys & the Baconburg Horror. Daniel Pinkwater. (J). 1995. pap. 12.95 (*0-7871-0249-0*, Dove Bks) Dove Audio.
Snarkout Boys & the Baconburg Horror. Daniel M. Pinkwater. (J). 1985. pap. 2.50 (*0-451-13581-4*, Sig Vista) NAL-Dutton.
***Snarl of the Lynx.** large type ed. Robert Charles. (Linford Mystery Library). 368p. 1996. pap. 15.99 (*0-7089-7943-2*, Linford) Ulverscroft.
Snarling Citizen. Barbara Ehrenreich. 1995. 20.00 (*0-374-26648-4*) FS&G.
Snarling Citizen: Essays. Barbara Enrenreich. LC 95-54202. 256p. 1996. pap. 12.00 (*0-06-097688-8*) HarpC.
Snatch. David Champion. LC 93-81067. 266p. 1994. 19.95 (*0-9627297-2-8*) A A Knoll Pubs.
Snatch a Falling Star. Craig Alpaugh. 62p. 1991. pap. 5.00 (*0-87129-025-1*, S93) Dramatic Pub.
***Snatch & Grab.** Groves. (J). Date not set. pap. text ed. write for info. (*0-582-18303-0*, Pub. by Longman UK) Longman.
Snatched Away: Raptured. Phillip G. Goudeaux. 83p. 1992. pap. text ed. 9.95 (*1-56550-002-4*) Vis Bks Intl.
Snatched Before the Storm! Richard L. Mayhue. 1980. pap. 1.50 (*0-88469-124-1*) BMH Bks.
Snatched from Oblivion: A Cambridge Memoir. Marian C. Schlesinger. (Illus.). 243p. 1984. reprint ed. pap. 12.00 (*0-9645809-0-X*) Gale Hill Bks.
Snatches. Alec Cairncross. 44p. 8000. pap. 6.95 (*0-86140-051-8*, Pub. by Colin Smythe Ltd UK) Dufour.
Snax from Maxine: Recipes for Entertaining from Country Cuisine, Vol. 2. 2nd large type ed. Maxine Henderson. (Illus.). 273p. (Orig.). 1996. pap. 9.95 (*0-9625024-0-5*) Ctry Cuisine Cookbks.
Snax from Maxine: Recipes for Entertaining from Country Cuisine, Vol. 2. 2nd large type ed. Maxine Henderson. (Illus.). 273p. (Orig.). 1996. lthr. 9.95 (*0-9625024-1-3*) Ctry Cuisine Cookbks.
***Snazaroo Zoo: Great Faces & Easy Costumes to Bring Out the Animal in You.** LC 96-38024. 1997. write for info. (*0-8019-8940-X*) Chilton.
Snazzy Aunties. Nick Sharratt. LC 92-47087. (Illus.). 24p. (J). (ps). 1994. 8.95 (*1-56402-214-5*) Candlewick Pr.
Snazzy Aunties. Nick Sharratt. LC 92-47087. (Illus.). (J). 1996. pap. 3.99 (*1-56402-685-X*) Candlewick Pr.
SNCC: The New Abolitionists. Howard Zinn. LC 84-27925. x, 286p. 1985. reprint ed. text ed. 79.50 (*0-313-24801-X*, ZIAB, Greenwood Pr) Greenwood.
Sneak Attack! Nathan Aaseng. LC 94-44807. (Grubstake Adventures Ser.). 80p. (J). 1995. pap. 5.99 (*0-8066-2787-5*, Augsburg) Augsburg Fortress.
Sneak It Through. Michael Connor. (Illus.). 112p. 1984. pap. 12.50 (*0-87364-282-1*) Paladin Pr.
***Sneakers: Musical.** Judith Weinstein & Arnold Somers. 67p. (YA). (gr. 7 up). 1983. pap. 5.00 (*0-87129-722-1*, S07) Dramatic Pub.
Sneakers: The Shoes We Choose. Robert Young. LC 90-26473. (Illus.). 64p. (J). (gr. 3 up). 1991. lib. bdg. 14.95 (*0-87518-460-X*, Dillon Silver Burdett) Silver Burdett Pr.
Sneaking Inmates down the Alley: Problems & Prospects in Jail Management. David B. Kalinich & John Klofas. (Illus.). 220p. 1986. pap. 24.95 (*0-398-05264-6*) C C Thomas.
***Sneaking Inmates down the Alley: Problems & Prospects in Jail Management.** David B. Kalinich & John Klofas. (Illus.). 220p. 1986. 38.95 (*0-398-06610-8*) C C Thomas.
Sneaking Out. Francine Pascal. (Sweet Valley Twins Ser.: No. 5). 112p. (J). 1987. pap. 3.50 (*0-553-15659-4*) Bantam.
Sneaking Out. large type ed. Jamie Suzanne. (Sweet Valley Twins Ser.: No. 5). 106p. (YA). (gr. 7-12). 1990. reprint ed. 9.95 (*1-55905-068-3*) Grey Castle.
Sneaky Pete. Rita Milios. LC 89-34666. (Rookie Reader Ser.). (Illus.). 32p. (J). (ps-2). 1989. pap. 3.50 (*0-516-42092-5*); lib. bdg. 15.00 (*0-516-02092-7*) Childrens.
Sneaky Pete Almanac & Encyclopedia of Numbers 1995. SPG Inc. Staff & Calvin P. Kline. 85p. pap. 4.95 (*0-944149-05-7*) Sneaky Pete.
Sneaky Pete Big Book. (Rookie Readers Big Bks.). (Illus.). 32p. (J). (ps-2). 1990. pap. 32.40 (*0-516-49455-4*) Childrens.
Sneaky Square & Other Math Activities for Kids. 2nd expanded ed. Richard M. Sharp & Seymour Metzner. (J). 1995. pap. text ed. 12.95 (*0-07-057232-1*) McGraw.
Sneaky Square & 113 Other Math Activities For Kids. Richard M. Sharp & Seymour Metzner. (Illus.). 126p. (J). (ps up). 1990. 15.95 (*0-8306-8474-3*, 3474); pap. 8.95 (*0-8306-3474-6*) McGraw-Hill Prof.
Sneaky Square & 113 Other Math Activities for Kids. Richard M. Sharp & Seymour Metzner. 1990. pap. text ed. 10.95 (*0-07-157270-8*) McGraw.
SNEAP XXVIII - Symposium of the North Eastern Accelerator Personnel - 1994. S. M. Ferguson & E. D. Berners. 300p. 1995. text ed. 90.00 (*981-02-2256-4*) World Scientific Pub.
Sneap '92: Proceedings of the Symposium of North Eastern Accelerator Personnel, 1992. J. W. McKay. 260p. 1995. text ed. 78.00 (*981-02-1885-0*) World Scientific Pub.
Sneathen & Gonne. Chris Barry. (Orig.). 1994. lib. bdg. 15.00 (*0-88092-190-0*) Royal Fireworks.
Sneathen & Gonne. Christopher Barry. (Orig.). 1992. pap. 5.00 (*0-88092-189-7*) Royal Fireworks.
Sneetches & Other Stories. Dr. Seuss. (Illus.). (J). (gr. k-4). 1966. lib. bdg. 15.99 (*0-394-90089-8*) Random Bks Yng Read.
Sneetches & Other Stories. Dr. Seuss. (Illus.). (J). (gr. k-4). 1966. 14.00 (*0-394-80089-3*) Random Bks Yng Read.
Sneetches Are Sneetches: Dr. Seuss Beginner Fun Book. Dr. Seuss. 1995. pap. 3.99 (*0-679-86841-0*) Random.
***Sneeze on Monday.** Lou Kassem. 1997. pap. 3.99 (*0-380-78646-X*) Avon.
Sneeze on Sunday. Andre Norton & Grace A. Hogarth. 256p. 1992. reprint ed. mass mkt. 4.99 (*0-8125-1697-4*) Tor Bks.
Sneezing Your Head Off? Learning to Live with Your Allergic Nose. Peter B. Boggs. (Illus.). 274p. 1994. pap. 10.00 (*0-9642569-0-8*) Patient Ed Pubns.
Snellen Sel Papers Electrocard. 1977. lib. bdg. 112.00 (*90-6021-420-X*) Kluwer Ac.
Snellings: Minnesota's First First Family. Barbara K. Luecke & John C. Luecke. (Illus.). 298p. (Orig.). 1993. pap. 21.95 (*0-9621020-3-2*) Grenadier Pubns.
SNES Compendium. Wallace Poulter. 12.99 (*1-56686-352-X*) Brady Pub.
SNG Fact Book: Synthetic Pipeline Gas from Coal. 58p. 1978. pap. 2.50 (*0-318-12700-8*, F00683) Am Gas Assn.
Snicker Doodle. Stephen Cosgrove. (Treasure Trolls Ser.). (Illus.). 32p. (J). (gr. k-5). 1993. lib. bdg. 12.95 (*1-56674-044-4*, HTS Bks) Forest Hse.
Snicker Doodle. Stephen Cosgrove. (J). (ps-3). 1992. pap. 3.95 (*0-307-13452-0*) Western Pub.
Snicker-Snees. Lynda Holland. LC 90-71710. 44p. (J). 1991. 5.95 (*1-55523-403-8*) Winston-Derek.
Snickers. Charles Ghigna. 1994. pap. 5.95 (*0-9624032-8-8*) Best Times Inc.
Sniffles (Relaunch) Stephen Cosgrove. 32p. (J). (ps-3). 1995. 3.95 (*0-8431-3827-0*) Price Stern Sloan.
***Sniffy: The Virtual Rat: Version 4.5 for Windows.** Lester Krames et al. 105p. 1996. 51.95 incl. disk (*0-534-26702-5*, BF201) Brooks-Cole.
Sniggles, Squirrels & Chicken Pox: Forty Original Songs with Activities for Early Childhood, Vol. I. Jackie Weissman. 64p. (J). (ps-5). 1984. audio 10.95 (*0-685-09112-0*) Miss Jackie.
Sniggles, Squirrels & Chicken Pox: Forty Original Songs with Activities for Early Childhood, Vol. II. Jackie Weissman. 64p. (J). (ps-5). 1984. audio 10.95 (*0-685-09114-7*) Miss Jackie.
***Snip, Snip, Little Lambs.** Tomie Depaola. 1997. pap. 2.95 (*0-8167-4065-8*) Troll Communs.
***Snip, Snip...Snow!** Nancy Poydar. LC 97-9052. (Illus.). 32p. (J). (ps-3). 1997. lib. bdg. 15.95 (*0-8234-1328-4*) Holiday.
Snipe & Woodcock: Sport & Conservation. Colin McKelvie. (Illus.). 224p. 1996. 34.95 (*1-85310-713-1*, Pub. by Swan Hill UK) Voyageur Pr.
Sniper. Adrian Gilbert. 1996. mass mkt. 6.99 (*0-312-95766-1*) Tor Bks.
Sniper. Eric Helm. (Super Vietnam: Ground Zero Ser.: No. 5). 1990. mass mkt. 4.50 (*0-373-60505-6*) Harlequin Bks.
Sniper. Anthony V. LaPenta, Jr. LC 75-16563. 1976. 21.95 (*0-87949-042-X*) Ashley Bks.
Sniper. Theodore Taylor. 240p. (YA). 1991. mass mkt. 4.50 (*0-380-71193-1*, Flare) Avon.
Sniper. Theodore Taylor. LC 89-7415. 256p. (YA). (gr. 7 up). 1989. 16.00 (*0-15-276420-8*) HarBrace.
Sniper - Counter Sniper. (Illus.). 180p. 1986. 15.00 (*0-939235-00-5*) Spec Trning Unit.
Sniper II. (Illus.). 250p. 1992. 20.00 (*0-939235-05-6*) Spec Trning Unit.
***Sniper in the Tower: The Charles Whitman Murders.** Gary M. Lavergne. LC 96-50411. (Illus.). 324p. 1997. pap. 18.95 (*1-57441-029-6*) UNTX Pr.
Sniper One-on-One. Adrian Gilbert. (Illus.). 288p. (Orig.). 1995. pap. 17.95 (*0-330-34425-0*, Pub. by Sidgwick & Jackson UK) Trans-Atl Phila.
Snipe's Castle. Gomer Press Staff. 89p. (C). 1979. pap. 20.00 (*0-85088-741-0*, Pub. by Gomer Pr UK) St Mut.
Snipe's Index to Economic Geography. 3rd ed. Ronald H. Snipe. Ed. by Elizabeth J. Snipe. 159p. 1980. 19.00 (*0-938740-01-6*) Snipe.
Snipe's Index to Geographical Review. 3rd ed. Ronald H. Snipe. Ed. by Elizabeth J. Snipe. 200p. 1980. 19.00 (*0-938740-02-4*) Snipe.
Snipe's Index to the Annals of the Association of American Geographers. 3rd ed. Ronald H. Snipe. Ed. by Elizabeth J. Snipe. 137p. 1979. 19.00 (*0-938740-00-8*) Snipe.
Sniping in France: How the British Army Won the Sniping War in the Trenches. H. Hesketh Prichard. 211p. 1993. 25.00 (*1-884849-08-3*) R&R Bks.
Sniping in France: With Notes on the Scientific Training of Scouts, Observers & Snipers. H. Hesketh-Prichard. (Illus.). 224p. 1993. reprint ed. 24.95 (*0-935856-09-9*) Lancer.
Snipp, Snapp, Snurr & Gingerbread. Maj Lindman. 1976. 11.95 (*0-8488-1413-4*) Amereon Ltd.
Snipp, Snapp, Snurr & the Big Farm. Maj Lindman. (Illus.). 32p. (J). 1993. reprint ed. lib. bdg. 14.95 (*1-56849-004-6*) Buccaneer Bks.
Snipp, Snapp, Snurr & the Big Surprise. Maj Lindman. LC 96-2706. (Snipp, Snapp, Snurr Ser.). (Illus.). 32p. (J). (ps-2). 1996. pap. 6.95 (*0-8075-7490-2*) A Whitman.
Snipp, Snapp, Snurr & the Big Surprise. Maj Lindman. (Illus.). 32p. (J). 1993. reprint ed. lib. bdg. 14.95 (*1-56849-003-8*) Buccaneer Bks.
Snipp, Snapp, Snurr & the Buttered Bread. Maj Lindman. (J). (ps-3). 1995. pap. 6.95 (*0-8075-7491-0*) A Whitman.
Snipp, Snapp, Snurr & the Buttered Bread. Maj Lindman. (Illus.). 32p. (J). 1993. reprint ed. lib. bdg. 14.95 (*1-56849-002-X*) Buccaneer Bks.
Snipp, Snapp, Snurr & the Gingerbread. Maj Lindman. (Albert Whitman Prairie Bks.). (Illus.). 32p. (J). (ps-2). 1994. pap. 6.95 (*0-8075-7493-7*) A Whitman.
Snipp, Snapp, Snurr & the Gingerbread. Maj Lindman. (Illus.). 30p. (J). 1991. reprint ed. pap. 10.95 (*0-89966-829-1*) Buccaneer Bks.
Snipp, Snapp, Snurr & the Magic Horse. Maj Lindman. (Illus.). 32p. (J). 1993. reprint ed. lib. bdg. 14.95 (*1-56849-001-1*) Buccaneer Bks.
Snipp, Snapp, Snurr & the Red Shoes. Maj Lindman. (Albert Whitman Prairie Bks.). (Illus.). 32p. (J). (ps-2). 1994. pap. 6.95 (*0-8075-7496-1*) A Whitman.
Snipp, Snapp, Snurr & the Red Shoes. Maj Lindman. (Illus.). 32p. (J). 1993. reprint ed. lib. bdg. 14.95 (*1-56849-000-3*) Buccaneer Bks.
Snipp, Snapp, Snurr & the Reindeer. Maj Lindman. LC 95-1048. (Illus.). (J). (ps-2). 1995. pap. 6.95 (*0-8075-7497-X*) A Whitman.
Snipp, Snapp, Snurr & the Reindeer. Maj Lindman. (Illus.). 32p. (J). 1993. reprint ed. lib. bdg. 14.95 (*1-56849-005-4*) Buccaneer Bks.
Snipp, Snapp, Snurr & the Seven Dogs. Maj Lindman. (Illus.). 32p. (J). 1993. reprint ed. lib. bdg. 14.95 (*1-56849-007-0*) Buccaneer Bks.
Snipp, Snapp, Snurr & the Yellow Sled. Maj Lindman. LC 95-1049. (J). (ps-2). 1995. pap. 6.95 (*0-8075-7499-6*) A Whitman.
Snipp, Snapp, Snurr & the Yellow Sled. Maj Lindman. (Illus.). 30p. (J). 1991. reprint ed. pap. 10.95 (*0-89966-828-3*) Buccaneer Bks.
Snipp, Snapp, Snurr Learn to Swim. Maj Lindman. (J). (ps-3). 1995. pap. 6.95 (*0-8075-7494-5*) A Whitman.
Snipp, Snapp, Snurr Learn to Swim. Maj Lindman. (Illus.). 32p. (J). 1993. reprint ed. lib. bdg. 14.95 (*1-56849-006-2*) Buccaneer Bks.
***Snippet Sensations: Fast, Fusible Fabric Art.** Cindy Walter. 88p. 1996. pap. 26.95 (*0-945169-20-5*) Doheny Pubns.
Snippets. Tom Carl, pseud. 173p. 1993. pap. 5.95 (*0-9640554-0-6*) Southern Source.
Snippets. Susan Crandell. Ed. by Robert L. Crowe. 96p. (Orig.). 1995. pap. write for info. (*0-9644681-1-5*) Consortium IL.
Snips & Snails & Walnut Whales. Phyllis Fiarotta. LC 75-9574. (Illus.). 288p. (J). (gr. 1-5). 1975. pap. 9.95 (*0-911104-49-6*, 065) Workman Pub.
Snitch. Jimmy Graham. 1995. pap. 10.95 (*0-533-11417-9*) Vantage.

***Snitch.** Bob Leuci. LC 96-34917. 1997. 24.95 (*0-312-14739-2*) St Martin.

Snitch: A Handbook for Informers. Jack Luger. LC 91-62782. 152p. (Orig.). 1991. pap. 16.95 (*1-55950-076-X*, 40072) Loompanics.

Snitch Factory. Peter Plate. 180p. (Orig.). 1996. pap. 13.00 (*1-888277-02-5*) Incommcdo San Diego.

SNMP: Simple Network Management Protocol, Versions 1 & 2. Mathias Hein & David Griffiths. 600p. 1995. pap. 59.95 (*1-85032-139-6*) ITCP.

SNMP - Application Developers Guide. Robert L. Townsend. (B & F - Computer Science Ser.). 238p. 1995. pap. 46.95 (*0-442-01874-6*) Van Nos Reinhold.

SNMP a Guide to Network Management. Sidnie Feit. 1994. text ed. 65.00 (*0-07-020359-8*) McGraw.

SNMP, SNMPV2, & CMIP: The Practical Guide to Network Management Standards. William Stallings. LC 92-38220. 1993. 51.95 (*0-201-63331-0*) Addison-Wesley.

Sno-Jobs of America: America's Handbook of Snowjobs. Larry Caputo. Ed. by Clay Blanchard. 314p. (Orig.). 1995. pap. text ed. 8.00 (*0-9646991-0-9*) Brookdale Pub.

Snobbery with Violence. Colin Watson. 1988. 8.95 (*0-89296-934-2*) Mysterious Pr.

Snobissimo. Pierre Daninos. 256p. (FRE.). 1964. 11.95 (*0-8288-9179-6*, M3361); pap. 3.95 (*0-686-55575-9*) Fr & Eur.

S

SNOBOL Programming for the Humanities. Susan Hockey. 190p. 1986. pap. 29.95 (*0-19-824676-5*) OUP.

Snodgrass Site of the Powers Phase of Southeast Missouri. James E. Price & James B. Griffin. (Anthropological Papers: No. 66). (Illus.). (Orig.). 1979. pap. 3.00 (*0-932206-77-8*) U Mich Mus Anthro.

Snodgrass Small Mound & Middle Tennessee Valley Prehistory. Richard A. Krause. LC 88-24959. (Publications in Anthropology: Vol. 52). (Illus.). 117p. (Orig.). 1988. pap. write for info. (*0-87077-002-0*) TVA.

SnoDrift Ice Cream Company In-Basket. Richard H. Wirth. (Illus.). 160p. 1983. text ed. 10.48 (*0-07-071145-3*) McGraw.

***Snohomish County Street Guide & Directory: 1998 Edition.** Thomas Bros. Maps Staff. 112p. 1997. pap. 16.95 (*0-88130-915-X*) Thomas Bros Maps.

Snollygosters, Airheads & Wimps: John Clay's Dictionary of Presidential Words. John E. Clay. 275p. (Orig.). 1995. pap. 10.00 (*0-9647638-0-X*) Logolept Pr.

Snook Book: Complete Angler's Guide. Frank Sargeant. LC 90-63532. (Inshore Ser.). (Illus.). 160p. 1991. pap. 11.95 (*0-936513-13-6*) Larsens Outdoor.

Snooker. Ted Lowe. (EP Sports Ser.). (Illus.). 1977. 6.95 (*0-7158-0585-1*) Charles River Bks.

Snooker & Billiards: Techniques, Tactics, Training. Clive Everton. (Illus.). 128p. 1992. pap. 22.95 (*1-85223-480-6*, Pub. by Crowood Pr UK) Trafalgar.

Snooperman. Mel Cebulash. (Author's Signature Collection). (J). (gr. 3-8). 1992. lib. bdg. 12.79 (*0-89565-879-8*) Childs World.

Snoopers. Fred S. Howell. 1991. 14.95 (*0-533-08896-8*) Vantage.

Snoopy: Droles D'Oiseau. Charles M. Schulz. (Peanuts Ser.). 128p. (FRE.). (J). 1975. 9.95 (*0-8288-4557-3*) Fr & Eur.

Snoopy: Not Your Average Dog. Charles M. Schulz. (Illus.). 80p. (J). 1996. 19.95 (*0-00-225188-4*) Collins SF.

Snoopy: Vocal Selections. Ed. by Michael Lefferts. (Illus.). 64p. (Orig.). (C). 1997. pap. text ed. 12.95 (*0-88188-111-2*, 00312382) H Leonard.

Snoopy & His Sopwith Camel. Charles M. Schulz. LC 78-91065. (Illus.). 64p. (J). (gr. 5 up). 1969. pap. 2.95 (*0-03-083177-6*, Bks Young Read) H Holt & Co.

Snoopy & the Gang Out West. June Dutton & Charles M. Schulz. LC 82-71284. (Illus.). (J). 1983. 6.95 (*0-915696-55-X*); pap. 4.95 (*0-915696-82-7*) Determined Prods.

Snoopy & the Red Baron. Charles M. Schulz. LC 66-22569. (Illus.). 64p. (J). (gr. 5 up). 1966. pap. 2.95 (*0-03-060560-1*, Bks Young Read) H Holt & Co.

Snoopy & the Twelve Days of Christmas. Charles M. Schulz. (J). (gr. 1 up). 9.95 (*0-317-13662-3*) Determined Prods.

Snoopy Arbitre. Charles M. Schulz. (Peanuts Ser.). (FRE.). (J). 1984. 14.95 (*0-8288-4559-X*) Fr & Eur.

Snoopy au Cirque. Charles M. Schulz. (Peanuts Ser.). 50p. (FRE.). 1983. 14.95 (*0-8288-4560-3*) Fr & Eur.

Snoopy Come Home. (Peanuts Storybook & Dramatized Tape Ser.). 24p. 1993. pap. 5.98 (*1-57007-003-2*, XU1003) Astor Bks.

Snoopy Connait La Musique. Charles M. Schulz. (Peanuts Ser.). 128p. (FRE.). (J). 1974. 9.95 (*0-8288-4561-1*) Fr & Eur.

Snoopy Counts to Ten. American. 1994. 3.95 (*1-56189-257-2*) Amer Educ Pub.

Snoopy Delire. Charles M. Schulz. (Peanuts Ser.). 50p. (FRE.). (J). 1983. 14.95 (*0-8288-4562-X*) Fr & Eur.

Snoopy Detective. Charles M. Schulz. (Peanuts Ser.). 50p. (FRE.). (J). 1983. 14.95 (*0-8288-4563-8*) Fr & Eur.

Snoopy Doghouse Cookbook. Evelyn Shaw. LC 78-68776. (Illus.). 1979. pap. 4.95 (*0-915696-12-6*) Determined Prods.

Snoopy Escritor. Charles M. Schulz. (Peanuts Ser.). 64p. (SPA.). (J). 1971. 4.95 (*0-8288-4503-4*) Fr & Eur.

Snoopy Et la Culture. Charles M. Schulz. (Peanuts Ser.). (FRE.). (J). 1975. 9.95 (*0-8288-4565-4*) Fr & Eur.

Snoopy et la St-Valentin. Charles M. Schulz. (Peanuts Ser.). (FRE.). (J). 1984. 14.95 (*0-8288-4566-2*) Fr & Eur.

Snoopy Et Ses Freres. Charles M. Schulz. (Peanuts Ser.). 128p. (FRE.). (J). 1974. 9.95 (*0-8288-4567-0*) Fr & Eur.

Snoopy Et Son Copain Linus. Charles M. Schulz. (Peanuts Ser.). 128p. (FRE.). (J). 1975. 9.95 (*0-8288-4568-9*) Fr & Eur.

Snoopy Festival. Charles M. Schulz. LC 74-4809. (Peanuts Parade Bks.). 224p. 1980. pap. 7.95 (*0-03-057503-6*, Owl) H Holt & Co.

Snoopy Grand Coeur. Charles M. Schulz. (Peanuts Ser.). (FRE.). (J). 1975. 9.95 (*0-8288-4569-7*) Fr & Eur.

Snoopy Omnibus. Monica Bayley & Charles M. Schulz. LC 82-71285. (Illus.). (J). 1983. 6.95 (*0-915696-54-1*); pap. 4.95 (*0-915696-81-9*) Determined Prods.

Snoopy Patineur. Charles M. Schulz. (Peanuts Ser.). (FRE.). (J). 1984. 14.95 (*0-8288-4570-0*) Fr & Eur.

Snoopy Prestidigitateur. Charles M. Schulz. (Peanuts Ser.). 50p. (FRE.). (J). 1983. 14.95 (*0-8288-4571-9*) Fr & Eur.

Snoopy S'En Va-T-En Guerre. Charles M. Schulz. (Peanuts Ser.). 128p. (FRE.). (J). 1974. 9.95 (*0-8288-4572-7*) Fr & Eur.

Snoopy's ABC. American Education Publishing Staff. (J). (ps). 1994. 3.95 (*1-56189-258-0*) Amer Educ Pub.

Snoopy's All My Things. American Education Publishing Staff. (J). (ps). 1994. 3.95 (*1-56189-264-5*) Amer Educ Pub.

Snoopy's Christmas Tree. Charles M. Schulz. (Peanuts Ser.). (Illus.). 10p. (J). (ps). 1996. 5.95 (*0-694-00907-5*, Festival) HarpC Child Bks.

Snoopy's Crayons. American Education Publishing Staff. (J). (ps). 1994. 3.95 (*1-56189-259-9*) Amer Educ Pub.

Snoopy's Easy Piano Album. John Welch. (Peanuts Piano Course Ser.). (Illus.). 38p. (Orig.). (J). (gr. 1-6). 1989. pap. 5.50 (*1-56516-052-5*) H Leonard.

Snoopy's Facts & Fun Book about Planes. Charles M. Schulz. LC 79-674. (Snoopy's Facts & Fun Bks.). (Illus.). (J). (ps-1). 1979. lib. bdg. 3.99 (*0-685-04263-4*) Random Bks Yng Read.

Snoopy's Favorite Piano Solos. John Welch. (Peanuts Piano Course Ser.). (Illus.). 38p. (Orig.). (J). (gr. 1-6). 1989. pap. 5.50 (*1-56516-053-3*) H Leonard.

Snoopy's Friends. American Education Publishing Staff. (J). (ps). 1994. 3.95 (*1-56189-265-3*) Amer Educ Pub.

Snoopy's Love Book. Charles M. Schulz. 1994. 6.95 (*0-8050-3146-4*) H Holt & Co.

Snoopy's Make Believe. American Education Publishing Staff. (J). (ps). 1994. 3.95 (*1-56189-263-7*) Amer Educ Pub.

Snoopy's Tennis Book. Charles M. Schulz. LC 78-14169. (Peanuts Parade Bks.). (Illus.). 104p. 1979. pap. 4.95 (*0-03-050585-2*, Owl) H Holt & Co.

Snoopy's Very First Christmas Songs. June Edison. (Peanuts Piano Course Ser.). (Illus.). 32p. (Orig.). (J). (gr. 1-6). 1989. pap. 5.50 (*1-56516-046-0*) H Leonard.

Snoopy's Very First Christmas Songs: Clavinova Software. June Edison. (Peanuts Piano Course for Clavinova Ser.). (Illus.). 32p. (Orig.). (J). (gr. 1-6). 1992. pap. 34.95 (*1-56516-020-7*) H Leonard.

Snooty Baronet. Wyndham Lewis. LC 83-22472. (Illus.). 350p. (Orig.). 1984. 25.00 (*0-87685-600-8*); pap. 14.00 (*0-87685-599-0*) Black Sparrow.

Snooty Baronet. deluxe ed. Wyndham Lewis. LC 83-22472. (Illus.). 350p. (Orig.). 1984. 30.00 (*0-87685-601-6*) Black Sparrow.

Snooty Baronet. Wyndham Lewis. LC 77-176492. (English Literature Ser.: No. 33). (Orig.). 1971. reprint ed. lib. bdg. 59.95 (*0-8383-1359-0*) M S G Haskell Hse.

Snooty the Fox. Rosemary M. Metzler. 28p. (J). 1993. pap. write for info. (*0-9637381-0-0*) Snooty Prods.

Snooty the Fox Meets Dead-Eye Dick. Rosemary M. Metzler. (Illus.). 48p. (J). (gr. 3-4). 1995. lib. bdg. 6.95 (*0-9637381-1-9*) Snooty Prods.

Snooze: The Best of Our Magazine. Ed. by Alfred Gingold & John Buskin. LC 86-40198. (Illus.). 272p. (Orig.). 1986. pap. 10.95 (*0-89480-118-X*, 1118) Workman Pub.

Snopp on the Sidewalk & Other Poems. Jack Prelutsky. LC 76-46323. (Illus.). 32p. (J). (gr. 3 up). 1977. lib. bdg. 15.93 (*0-688-84084-1*) Greenwillow.

Snoqualmie Pass: From Indian Trail to Interstate. Yvonne Prater. (Illus.). 167p. (Orig.). 1996. reprint ed. pap. 9.95 (*0-89886-015-6*) Mountaineers.

***Snore No More.** Jeffrey Hausfield. 1997. pap. write for info. (*0-609-80154-6*) Crown Pub Group.

Snore No More. James L. Mosley. (Modern Technology & Information Ser.). (Illus.). 80p. 4.95 (*0-685-51586-9*) Son Rise Pubns.

***Snore or Roar, I've Got the Cure.** unabridged ed. Lewis B. Newberg. (Illus.). 250p. 1997. 31.00 (*0-9656368-0-1*) Snore or Roar.

Snoring. Marcus Boulware. LC 73-94369. 1974. 6.95 (*0-912834-02-1*) Am Faculty Pr.

Snoring & Obstructive Sleep Apnea. 2nd ed. Ed. by David N. Fairbanks & Shiro Fujita. LC 94-2841. 272p. 1994. text ed. 79.00 (*0-7817-0196-1*) Lppncott-Raven.

Snoring & Sleep Apnea: Personal & Family Guide to Diagnosis & Treatment. 2nd ed. Ralph A. Pascualy & Sally W. Soest. LC 95-46517. (Illus.). 238p. 1996. pap. 24.95 (*0-939957-82-5*) Demos Vermande.

Snoring As a Fine Art & Twelve Other Essays. Albert J. Nock. LC 74-121493. (Essay Index Reprint Ser.). 1977. 12.95 (*0-8369-2007-4*) Ayer.

***Snoring from A to Zzzz.** Derek Lipman. 256p. 1997. pap. 12.95 (*0-9650708-1-6*) Spencer Press.

Snoring from A to ZZZZ: Proven Cures for the Night's Worst Nuisance, Vol. 1. unabridged ed. Derek S. Lipman. LC 95-72633. 256p. 1996. 24.95 (*0-9650708-0-8*) Spencer Press.

Snoring Log Mystery: Wilderness Adventures of a Young Naturalist. Todd Lee. (Illus.). 96p. (Orig.). (J). (gr. 4-8). 1993. pap. 8.95 (*0-919591-76-0*, Pub. by Polestar Bk Pubs CN) Orca Bk Pubs.

Snorkel Hawaii: Maui & Lana'i: Guide to the Underwater World. Judy Malinowski & Mel Malinowski. LC 96-95140. (Illus.). 160p. (Orig.). 1996. pap. 14.95 (*0-9646680-1-7*) Indigo CA.

Snorkel Hawaii the Big Island: Guide to the Underwater World. Judy Malinowski & Mel Malinowski. LC 96-94357. 128p. 1996. pap. 14.95 (*0-9646680-0-9*) Indigo CA.

Snorkeling. Mike Holbrook. LC 92-45219. (Adventurers Ser.). (Illus.). 48p. (J). (gr. 5-6). 1994. lib. bdg. 13.95 (*0-89686-823-0*, Crstwood Hse) Silver Burdett Pr.

Snorkeling: A Complete Guide to the Underwater Experience. John R. Clark. LC 85-9397. 191p. 1986. 18.95 (*0-13-815192-X*) P-H.

Snorkeling: Here's How. 2nd ed. Bob French. 1994. pap. 5.95 (*1-55992-083-1*, Pisces Bks) Gulf Pub.

Snorkeling Adventures: A Guide to the Bahamas, Bermuda, Caribbean, Hawaii & Florida Keys. Joyce Huber & Jon Huber. (Illus.). 240p. (Orig.). 1997. pap. 15.95 (*0-9643844-1-8*) Photograph Pub.

Snorkeling for Kids. 2nd ed. Judith Jennet. 56p. (J). (ps-9). 1992. pap. text ed. 5.95 (*0-916974-50-2*, 10501) NAUI.

Snorkeling for Kids Kit. (J). Date not set. text ed. 24.95 incl. vhs (*0-916974-65-0*, 90504) NAUI.

Snorkeling Guide to Marine Life: Florida, Caribbean, Bahamas. Paul Humann & Ned Deloach. (Illus.). (Orig.). 1995. pap. 12.95 (*1-878348-10-8*) New World FL.

***Snorkeling Guide to Michigan Inland Lakes.** Nancy Washburne. (Illus.). 286p. 1997. per. 16.95 (*0-9658570-0-X*) Nanmar Intl.

***Snorkeling Instructor Manual.** 14p. 1992. pap. text ed. write for info. (*1-880229-13-7*) Concept Sys.

***Snorkeling Manual.** 48p. 1992. pap. text ed. write for info. (*1-880229-11-0*) Concept Sys.

Snorkeller's Guide to the Coral Reef: From the Red Sea to the Pacific Ocean. Paddy Ryan. 1994. pap. 19.95 (*0-8248-1605-6*) UH Pr.

Snorkels for Tadpoles. Rob Morrison & Penelope Morrison. LC 93-28967. (Voyages Ser.). (Illus.). (J). 1994. 4.25 (*0-383-03775-1*) SRA McGraw.

Snort of Kings. large type ed. Ron Ellis. (Linford Mystery Library). 336p. 1989. pap. 15.99 (*0-7089-6739-6*, Linford) Ulverscroft.

Snot Stew. Bill Wallace. LC 88-31976. (Illus.). 96p. (J). (gr. 3-7). 1989. 15.95 (*0-8234-0745-4*) Holiday.

Snot Stew. Bill Wallace. (Illus.). 96p. (J). (gr. 4-6). pap. 3.50 (*0-671-69335-2*, Minstrel Bks) PB.

Snotball Rock. Al Blair. 6p. 1990. pap. 3.95 (*0-930366-53-0*) Northcountry Pub.

Snots Plus. Jarc Savenns. 230p. 1995. 14.95 (*0-9645446-0-1*) J Savenns.

Snout to Snout. Daniel Kaminsky. (Cleveland Poets Ser.: No. 9). 26p. (Orig.). 1974. pap. 10.00 (*0-914946-49-8*) Cleveland St Univ Poetry Ctr.

Snouters: Form & Life of the Rhinogrades. Harald Stumpke. Tr. by Leigh Chadwick. LC 81-10429. (Illus.). 118p. 1981. pap. 8.50 (*0-226-77895-9*) U Ch Pr.

Snouters Revisited: A Sequel. Charles C. Davis. 40p. 1995. 10.95 (*0-533-11316-4*) Vantage.

Snouts in the Trough: European Farmers, The Common Agricultural Policy & the Public Purse. Michael Atkin. 192p. 1993. 69.95 (*1-85573-114-2*, Pub. by Woodhead Pubng UK) Am Educ Systs.

Snow. Lisbeth Mark & Babs Lefrak. LC 95-14811. 128p. (Orig.). 1995. pap. 10.00 (*0-399-52166-6*, Perigee Bks) Berkley Pub.

Snow. Roy McKie & Philip D. Eastman. LC 62-15114. (Illus.). 72p. (J). (gr. 1-2). 1962. lib. bdg. 11.99 (*0-394-90027-8*) Beginner.

Snow. Roy McKie & Philip D. Eastman. LC 62-15114. (Illus.). 72p. (J). (gr. 1-2). 1966. 7.99 (*0-394-80027-3*) Beginner.

Snow. Nancy E. Wallace. (Illus.). 32p. (J). (ps-1). 1995. 11.95 (*0-307-17562-6*) Western Pub.

Snow: A Big Song Kid Book. Kemp Harris. (Illus.). 32p. (J). (ps-2). 1993. 16.95 incl. audio (*1-883181-03-8*); audio 4.95 (*1-883181-04-6*) Big Song Bk.

***Snow: A Novel.** Betsy Howie. 1998. 20.00 (*0-15-100273-8*) HarBrace.

Snow: Causes & Effects. Philip Steele. LC 90-45020. (Weather Watch Ser.). (Illus.). 32p. (J). (gr. 4-6). 1991. lib. bdg. 20.00 (*0-531-10990-9*) Watts.

Snow: Learning for the Fun of It. John Bianchi & Frank B. Edwards. (Illus.). 48p. (J). (gr. 5 up). 1992. pap. 7.95 (*0-921285-09-4*, Pub. by Bungalo Bks CN); lib. bdg. 17.95 (*0-921285-15-9*, Pub. by Bungalo Bks CN) Firefly Bks Ltd.

Snow: When Will It Fall? Janet Riehecky. LC 89-28084. (Discovery World Ser.). (Illus.). 32p. (J). (ps-2). 1990. lib. bdg. 21.36 (*0-89565-560-8*) Childs World.

Snow & Ice. Kay Davies & Wendy Oldfield. LC 95-6007. (See for Yourself Ser.). (Illus.). (J). 1995. lib. bdg. 19.97 (*0-8172-4042-X*) Raintree Steck-V.

Snow & Ice. Stephen Krensky. (Illus.). 32p. (Orig.). (J). (gr. k-3). 1994. pap. 2.95 (*0-590-41449-6*) Scholastic Inc.

Snow & Ice. Joy A. Palmer. LC 92-38438. (What About...? Ser.). (Illus.). 32p. (J). (gr. 2-3). 1992. lib. bdg. 21.40 (*0-8114-3414-1*) Raintree Steck-V.

Snow & Ice. Joy A. Palmer. (J). (ps-3). 1994. pap. 4.95 (*0-8114-7775-4*) Raintree Steck-V.

Snow & Steel. Girolamo Sommi-Picenardi. Tr. by Rudolph Altrocchi. LC 77-130072. (Short Story Index Reprint Ser.). 1977. 20.95 (*0-8369-3653-1*) Ayer.

Snow & Summers. Solveig Von Schoultz. Tr. by Anne Born from SWE. LC 89-81661. 107p. (Orig.). 9000. pap. 17.95 (*0-948259-52-3*, Pub. by Forest Bks UK) Dufour.

Snow Angel. Debby Boone. (Illus.). 32p. (J). (ps-1). 1991. 14.99 (*0-89081-871-1*) Harvest Hse.

Snow Angel. Isolde Evans. (Stolen Moments Ser.). 1993. pap. 1.99 (*0-373-83285-0*, 1-83285-6) Harlequin Bks.

Snow Angel. Penny Ives. (J). 1995. 4.95 (*0-689-80333-8*, Litl Simon S&S) S&S Childrens.

Snow Angel. Jean Marzollo. LC 94-31997. (Illus.). 32p. (J). (ps-2). 1995. 14.95 (*0-590-48748-5*, Scholastic Hardcover) Scholastic Inc.

***Snow Angel.** Angela McAllister & Claire Fletcher. (Illus.). 26p. (J). 3.98 (*0-8317-3091-9*) Smithmark.

Snow Angel. Thom Racina. 304p. 1996. pap. 23.95 (*0-525-94030-8*) NAL-Dutton.

***Snow Angel.** Thom Racina. 1997. mass mkt. 167.76 (*0-451-98410-2*, Onyx) NAL-Dutton.

Snow Angel. Suzanne Weyn. (Forever Angels Ser.). 216p. (Orig.). (J). (gr. 3-7). 1996. pap. 3.50 (*0-8167-4119-0*) Troll Communs.

Snow Angels: A Novel. Stewart O'Nan. 320p. 1995. pap. 10.95 (*0-14-025096-4*, Penguin Bks) Viking Penguin.

Snow-Avalanche Hazard Analysis for Land-Use Planning & Engineering. Arthur I. Mears. (Bulletin Ser.: No. 49). (Illus.). 55p. (Orig.). 1992. pap. 12.00 (*1-884216-10-2*) Colo Geol Survey.

Snow Avalanche Hazards & Mitigation in the United States. National Research Council Staff. 96p. 1990. pap. text ed. 15.00 (*0-309-04335-2*) Natl Acad Pr.

Snow Babies, Santas & Elves: Collecting Christmas Bisque Figures. Mary Morrison. LC 95-85213. (Illus.). 160p. 1993. pap. 29.95 (*0-88740-493-6*) Schiffer.

Snow Baby. Margaret Hillert. (Illus.). (J). (ps). 1969. pap. 5.10 (*0-8136-5555-2*, TK2364); lib. bdg. 7.95 (*0-8136-5055-0*, TK2363) Modern Curr.

Snow Ball. A. R. Gurney. (Illus.). 120p. 1994. 8.99 (*1-56865-074-4*, GuildAmerica) Dblday Direct.

Snow Ball. A. R. Gurney. LC 84-10971. 1992. pap. 5.25 (*0-8222-1318-4*) Dramatists Play.

***Snow Birds & Other Birds.** Thomas Plante. 90p. 1997. 20.00 (*1-890193-02-X*) Red Dragonfly.

Snow Birds & Other Stories. Dan Boles. 302p. (Orig.). 1994. pap. 12.95 (*0-938711-23-7*) Tecolote Pubns.

***Snow Booklet: A Guide to the Science, Climatology & Measurement of Snow in the United States.** Nolan J. Doesken & Arthur Judson. (Illus.). 84p. (Orig.). (C). 1996. pap. text ed. 10.00 (*0-9651056-1-X*) CSU Pub & Printing.

***Snow Booklet: A Guide to the Science, Climatology, & Measurement of Snow in the United States.** 2nd rev. ed. Nolan J. Doesken & Arthur Judson. (Illus.). 88p. (C). 1997. pap. text ed. write for info. (*0-9651056-2-8*) CSU Pub & Printing.

Snow Bound. Harry Mazer. 144p. (J). (gr. 5 up). 1975. mass mkt. 3.99 (*0-440-96134-3*, LLL BDD) BDD Bks Young Read.

Snow Bound. Harry Mazer. 1987. 17.75 (*0-8446-6240-2*) Peter Smith.

Snow Bride. Dallas Schulze. (Intimate Moments Ser.). 1994. mass mkt. 3.50 (*0-373-07584-7*, 1-07584-5) Harlequin Bks.

***Snow Bride.** Dallas Schulze. (Silhouette Romance Ser.). 1996. 20.95 (*0-373-59749-5*) Thorndike Pr.

Snow Bugs. Susan Schade. 1996. 7.99 (*0-679-87913-7*) Random.

Snow Bugs, Go Bugs. Susan Schade. 1997. lib. bdg. 11.99 (*0-679-97913-1*) Random.

***Snow Bunnies.** Created by Francine Pascal. (Unicorn Club Ser.: No. 21). 144p. (Orig.). (J). (gr. 3-7). 1997. pap. 3.50 (*0-553-48449-4*) BDD Bks Young Read.

Snow Calf. Vesta M. Rundle. (Illus.). 36p. (Orig.). (J). (gr. 4-8). 1993. pap. 4.50 (*1-882672-01-1*) V M Rundle.

Snow Camp Lookout: View with a Room...Mouse Included. David Calahan. LC 96-76155. (Illus.). xx, 172p. (Orig.). 1996. pap. 14.00 (*0-9619808-1-8*) In-Forms Pub Hse.

Snow Camping. Ed. by Wordic World Staff. 1974. pap. 3.95 (*0-02-499790-0*, Macmillan Coll) P-H.

Snow Camping: The Complete Guide to Enjoying the Back Country. Jo A. Creore. 1992. pap. text ed. 11.95 (*1-55105-011-0*) Lone Pine.

Snow Cat. Dayal K. Khalsa. LC 92-8988. (Illus.). 32p. (J). (ps-2). 1992. 14.00 (*0-517-59183-9*, Clarkson Potter) Crown Bks Yng Read.

Snow Cats. Phyllis J. Perry. LC 96-25873. (First Bks.). (J). 1997. lib. bdg. 21.00 (*0-531-20267-4*) Watts.

***Snow Cats.** Phyllis J. Perry. (First Books). 1997. pap. text ed. 6.95 (*0-531-15859-4*) Watts.

Snow Caves for Fun & Survival. rev. ed. Ernest Wilkinson. LC 92-70048. (Illus.). 108p. 1992. pap. 9.95 (*1-55566-095-9*) Johnson Bks.

Snow Child. Illus. by Barbara Lavallee & Leon Shtainmets. 32p. (J). (gr. 2-5). 1989. pap. 2.50 (*0-590-42141-7*) Scholastic Inc.

Snow Clinging to the Window Panes: Some Thoughts about Living. Joseph M. Vles. 36p. (Orig.). 1989. pap. 6.95 (*0-9624549-0-7*) Maurits Pub.

Snow Country. Yasunari Kawabata. 192p. 1996. pap. 11.00 (*0-679-76104-7*) Random.

Snow Country: Fragments for Radio. Laird Hunt. 60p. (Orig.). 1995. pap. 5.00 (*1-887289-07-0*) Rodent Pr.

Snow Country Tales: Life in the Other Japan. Suzuki Bokushi. (Illus.). 400p. 1986. 32.50 (*0-8348-0210-4*) Weatherhill.

Snow Cover & Climate in the Sierra Nevada, California. David H. Miller. LC 55-9597. (University of California Publications in Social Welfare: Vol. 11). 226p. reprint ed. pap. 64.50 (*0-317-29516-0*, 2021271) Bks Demand.

Snow Crash. Neal Stephenson. 480p. 1993. mass mkt. 6.50 (*0-553-56261-4*, Spectra) Bantam.

Snow Creatures & Other Stories. Christoph Meckel. Tr. by Carol Bedwell from GER. LC 90-37811. (Studies in German Language & Literature: Vol. 3). (Illus.). 104p. 1991. lib. bdg. 59.95 (*0-88946-581-9*) E Mellen.

Snow Crystals. W. A. Bentley & W. J. Humphreys. (Illus.). 1931. pap. 15.95 (*0-486-20287-9*) Dover.

Snow Crystals. W. A. Bentley & W. J. Humphreys. (Illus.). (J). (gr. 5 up). 1990. 26.75 (*0-8446-1660-5*) Peter Smith.

Snow Dance. Lezlie Evans. LC 95-43099. (Illus.). (J). 1997. 16.00 (*0-395-77849-2*) HM.

An Asterisk (*) at the beginning of an entry indicates that the title is appearing in BIP for the first time.

Snow Day. M. T. Coffin. (Spinetinglers Ser.: No. 7). 160p. (Orig.). (J). 1996. pap. 3.50 (*0-380-78157-3*, Camelot) Avon.

Snow Day. Moira Fain. 1996. 15.95 (*0-8027-8409-7*) Walker & Co.

Snow Day. Moira Fain. 1996. lib. bdg. 16.85 (*0-8027-8410-0*) Walker & Co.

Snow Day! Barbara M. Joosse. LC 94-17012. (Illus.). 32p. (J). (ps-3). 1900. 14.95 (*0-395-66588-4*, Clarion Bks) HM.

Snow Day. Betsy Meastro. 32p. (J). (ps-3). 1992. pap. 4.95 (*0-590-46083-8*) Scholastic Inc.

Snow Day. Strasser. (J). 1998. 17.00 (*0-689-81113-6*) S&S Childrens.

***Snow Day Colors.** Mary Hogan. (J). 1997. 3.50 (*1-57719-217-6*) GT Pubng Corp.

Snow Demo. large type ed. Nicola A. West. 271p. 1993. 25.99 (*0-7505-0572-9*, Pub. by Magna Print Bks UK) Ulverscroft.

Snow Dog. Jim Kjelgaard. 176p. (J). 1983. pap. 4.50 (*0-553-15560-1*) Bantam.

Snow Dome. Teresa A. O'Shaughnessy. LC 94-70626. (Illus.). 32p. (J). 1995. 17.95 (*0-9636274-4-9*) Coming Age Pr.

Snow Dreams: Flute Guitar Score. J. Tower. 16p. 1987. pap. 6.95 (*0-7935-3721-5*, 50507800) H Leonard.

Snow Eagle. Frank F. Bell. (Illus.). 337p. (Orig.). 1990. pap. 8.95 (*0-934959-00-5*) Western Horizons Bks.

***Snow Engineering - Recent Advances: Proceedings of the International Conference, Sendai, Japan, 26-31 May 1997.** Ed. by M. Izumi et al. (Illus.). 650p. (C). 1997. text ed. 110.00 (*90-5410-865-7*, Pub. by A A Balkema NE) Ashgate Pub Co.

Snow Faculty Studies: The Journal of the Faculty of Snow College, Vol. 1. Ed. by Roger G. Baker. 101p. (C). 1991. text ed. 14.95 (*1-886632-01-4*) Snow Coll Eng.

Snow Faculty Studies: The Journal of the Faculty of Snow College, Vol. 2. Ed. by Roger G. Baker. 99p. (C). 1992. text ed. 14.95 (*1-886632-02-2*) Snow Coll Eng.

Snow Faculty Studies: The Journal of the Faculty of Snow College, Vol. 3. Ed. by Roger G. Baker. 84p. (C). 1993. text ed. 14.95 (*1-886632-03-0*) Snow Coll Eng.

Snow Faculty Studies: The Journal of the Faculty of Snow College, Vol. 4. Ed. by Roger G. Baker. 113p. (C). 1994. text ed. 14.95 (*1-886632-04-9*) Snow Coll Eng.

Snow Faculty Studies: The Journal of the Faculty of Snow College, Vol. 5. Ed. by David Rosier. 101p. (C). 1995. text ed. 14.95 (*1-886632-05-7*) Snow Coll Eng.

Snow Falcon. Craig Thomas. 544p. 1990. mass mkt. 5.99 (*0-06-100076-0*, Harp PBks) HarpC.

Snow Falling on Cedars. David Guterson. LC 94-7535. 1994. 21.95 (*0-15-100100-6*) HarBrace.

Snow Falling on Cedars. David Guterson. LC 95-11457. (Vintage Contemporaries Ser.). 1995. pap. 12.00 (*0-679-76402-X*, Vin) Random.

***Snow Falling on Cedars.** David Guterson. 1996. 25.95 (*0-7862-0841-4*) Thorndike Pr.

Snow Flurries. A. C. Snow. Ed. by Judy Bolch. LC 85-72570. (Illus.). 212p. 1985. 12.95 (*0-935400-12-5*) News & Observer.

Snow for Christmas. Charnan Simon. (J). 1989. pap. 2.95 (*0-8167-1882-2*) Troll Communs.

Snow Geese of La Perouse Bay: Natural Selection in the Wild. Fred Cooke et al. (Oxford Ornithology Ser.). (Illus.). 312p. 1995. 65.00 (*0-19-854064-7*) OUP.

***Snow Ghost.** Al Lacy. LC 97-11834. (Journeys of the Stranger Ser.: No. 7). 300p. 1997. pap. 9.99 (*1-57673-047-6*, Multnomah Bks) Multnomah Pubs.

Snow Glistens on the Great Wall: The Complete Poetical Works of Mao Tse-Tung. Mao Tse-tung. Ed. by Ma Wen-yee. Tr. by Ma Wen-Yee. (Illus.). 208p. (Orig.). 1985. 17.95 (*0-915520-78-8*); pap. 9.95 (*0-915520-79-6*) Santa Barb Pr.

Snow Goose. Paul Gallico. (YA). (gr. 9 up). 1941. 15.00 (*0-394-44593-7*) Knopf Bks Yng Read.

Snow Goose. Paul Gallico. 1976. 16.95 (*0-8488-0495-3*) Amereon Ltd.

Snow Hill Remembered: A History of the Harris Family of Maryland, Ohio, & Kentucky. Richard E. Stevens. (Illus.). 293p. (Orig.). 1994. pap. text ed. 40.00 (*0-7884-0018-5*) Heritage Bk.

Snow How: St. Moritz, Switzerland. Sochitl S. Cotman. Ed. & Photos by Jacqueline N. Cotman. LC 96-96409. (Illus.). 26p. (Orig.). (J). 1996. pap. 9.00 (*0-9652390-1-2*) J N Cotman.

Snow, Ice, & Cold. Bernard Stonehouse. LC 92-26298. (Repairing the Damage Ser.). (Illus.). 48p. (YA). (gr. 6 up). 1993. lib. bdg. 13.95 (*0-02-788530-5*, Mac Bks Young Read) S&S Childrens.

Snow Image, & Other Twice-Told Tales. Nathaniel Hawthorne. LC 75-116954. (Short Story Index Reprint Ser.). 1977. 18.95 (*0-8369-3457-1*) Ayer.

Snow Image & Other Twice-Told Tales. Nathaniel Hawthorne. (Notable American Authors Ser.). 1992. reprint ed. lib. bdg. 75.00 (*0-7812-3044-6*) Rprt Serv.

Snow-Image, & Uncollected Tales. Nathaniel Hawthorne. Ed. by William Charvat et al. LC 73-5365. (Centenary Edition of the Works of Nathaniel Hawthorne: Vol. 11). 500p. 1974. 67.50 (*0-8142-0204-7*) Ohio St U Pr.

***Snow in America.** Bernard Mergen. LC 97-12247. (Illus.). 336p. 1997. 24.95 (*1-56098-780-4*) Smithsonian.

Snow in April. Rosamunde Pilcher. 256p. 1989. mass mkt. 5.50 (*0-440-20248-5*) Dell.

***Snow in April.** Rosamunde Pilcher. 1997. mass mkt. 5.99 (*0-312-96129-4*) St Martin.

***Snow in August: A Novel.** Peter Hamill. LC 96-36043. 327p. 1997. 23.95 (*0-316-34094-4*) Little.

***Snow in July.** (Get Ready...Get Set...Read! Ser.: Set 5). (J). 1996. lib. bdg. 11.95 (*1-56674-164-5*) Forest Hse.

Snow in July. Gina Erikson. 1996. pap. text ed. 3.95 (*0-8120-9336-4*) Barron.

Snow in May: An Anthology of Modern Finnish Writing 1945-1972. Ed. by Richard Dauenhauer & Philip Binham. LC 74-4967. (Illus.). 389p. 1978. 40.00 (*0-8386-1583-X*) Fairleigh Dickinson.

Snow in South Texas. Cynthia J. Harper. 63p. (Orig.). pap. write for info. (*1-877603-26-0*) Pecan Grove.

Snow in the Cities: A History of America's Urban Response. Blake McKelvey. (Illus.). 248p. (C). 1995. 39.00 (*1-878822-54-3*) Univ Rochester Pr.

Snow in the River. Carol R. Brink. LC 92-46243. (Washington State University Press Reprint Ser.). 308p. 1993. reprint ed. pap. 17.95 (*0-87422-097-1*) Wash St U Pr.

Snow in Us. David P. Reiter. (Illus.). 64p. (C). 1989. 39.00 (*0-9587972-3-4*, Pub. by Five Islands Pr AT) St Mut.

Snow in Winter. Margaret Bacon. 352p. 1996. 23.95 (*0-312-14419-9*) St Martin.

***Snow Inside the House.** Sean Diviny. LC 96-30723. (Illus.). (J). 1998. write for info. (*0-06-027354-2*); lib. bdg. write for info. (*0-06-027355-0*) HarpC Child Bks.

Snow Is Falling. rev. ed. Franklyn M. Branley. LC 85-48256. (Trophy Let's-Read-&-Find-Out Bk.). (Illus.). 32p. (J). (ps-3). 1986. reprint ed. pap. 4.95 (*0-06-445058-9*, Trophy) HarpC Child Bks.

Snow Job. Annis Oetinger. (Illus.). 192p. (Orig.). 1992. pap. 10.95 (*0-9634757-0-3*) A Oetinger.

Snow-Job. large type ed. Basil Copper. (Linford Mystery Library). 260p. 1989. pap. 15.99 (*0-7089-6636-5*, Linford) Ulverscroft.

Snow Job: An Anamnesis. Barbara F. Graham. 348p. (Orig.). 1995. pap. 20.00 (*0-9647175-0-6*) Hang On To Hat.
Written in a spirited first-person voice, SNOW JOB tells the story of a Boston-area mother & her children who choose to survive the hell of substance abuse in the family--only to find an even greater hell & danger awaiting them in the U.S. legal system. This nonfiction novel describes THE ACTUAL LEGAL, SPIRITUAL, & FINANCIAL CONSEQUENCES that befall family members as they strive to move forward & rebuild their lives. In contrast to most books on substance abuse, SNOW JOB takes readers into lawyers' offices, judges' chambers, bank mortgage departments, & medical settings where conversation is not a matter of public record. Elements of this story will ring true with anyone whose life has been touched by divorce, substance abuse, domestic violence in all its forms (physical, emotional, financial) & a legal system that devalues the important job of nurturing the next generation. Recommended by FCD Educational Services Inc., The Domestic Violence Training & Resource Institute Inc., & The National Coalition for Family Justice, Inc. $20. 00 plus shipping ($3/book in U.S.; MA orders add 5% sales tax). Check & Money Orders: direct from Hang On To Your Hat! Press, P.O. Box 320, Princeton, NJ 08542-0320 (609-279-2776, FAX 609-279-2778 or http://www.hatpress.com). Credit card orders: contact Book Stacks Unlimited (http://www.books.com). ***Publisher Provided Annotation.***

Snow Job: Canada, the United States & Vietnam (1954-1973) Charles Taylor. 209p. (Orig.). 1974. pap. 7.95 (*0-88784-619-X*, Pub. by Hse of Anansi Pr CN) Genl Dist Srvs.

Snow Job? On Controlling Cocaine at the Source. Kevin J. Riley. 252p. (C). 1996. text ed. 34.95 (*1-56000-242-5*) Transaction Pubs.

Snow Joe. Carol Greene. LC 82-9403. (Rookie Reader Ser.). (Illus.). 32p. (J). (ps-2). 1982. pap. 3.50 (*0-516-42035-6*); lib. bdg. 15.00 (*0-516-02035-8*) Childrens.

***Snow Kisses.** Diana Palmer. (Mira Bks.). 1997. 5.50 (*1-55166-262-0*, 1-66262-6, Mira Bks) Harlequin Bks.

Snow Laced Rainbows. Marla Hess. LC 85-51962. 85p. 1986. 6.95 (*0-938232-96-7*) Winston-Derek.

Snow Lambs. Debi Gliori. 32p. (J). (ps-2). 1996. 15.95 (*0-590-20304-5*) Scholastic Inc.

Snow Leopard. Tua Forsstrom. Tr. by David McDuff from FIN. 64p. (Orig.). 9000. pap. 15.95 (*1-85224-111-X*, Pub. by Bloodaxe Bks UK) Dufour.

Snow Leopard. Edward Hoagland. (Penguin Nature Classics Ser.). 352p. 1987. pap. 12.95 (*0-14-025508-7*, Penguin Bks) Viking Penguin.

Snow Leopard. Peter Matthiessen. 352p. 1987. pap. 12.95 (*0-14-010266-3*, Penguin Bks) Viking Penguin.

Snow Leopard. Alison Tibbitts & Alan Roocroft. (Animals, Animals, Animals Ser.). (Illus.). 24p. (J). (ps-2). 1992. lib. bdg. 17.80 (*1-56065-106-7*) Capstone Pr.

Snow Lion. (Parents Magazine Press Read-Aloud Library). (Illus.). 42p. (J). (ps-3). 1992. lib. bdg. 17.27 (*0-8368-0888-6*) Gareth Stevens Inc.

Snow Lion. David McPhail. LC 82-8119. (Illus.). 48p. (J). (ps-3). 1987. 5.95 (*0-8193-1097-2*); lib. bdg. 5.95 (*0-8193-1098-0*) Parents.

***Snow Lion & the Dragon: China, Tibet & the Dalai Lama.** Melvyn C. Goldstein. LC 97-2562. 1998. write for info. (*0-520-21254-1*) U CA Pr.

Snow Lion's Turquoise Mane: Wisdom Tales from Tibet. Surya Das. LC 90-55787. 1992. pap. 17.00 (*0-06-250849-0*) Harper SF.

Snow Load Analysis for Washington. 2nd ed. Snow Load Committee Staff & David Golden. 70p. 1995. spiral bd., pap. 25.00 (*1-886982-00-7*) SEAW.

Snow Lotus: Exploring the Eternal Moment. Peter M. Leschak. LC 95-52674. (C). 1996. 17.95 (*0-8166-2820-3*) U of Minn Pr.

Snow Man. large type ed. Valerie Kershaw. (Linford Mystery Library). 320p. 1994. pap. 15.99 (*0-7089-7557-7*, Linford) Ulverscroft.

***Snow Man: John Hornby in the Barren Lands.** Malcolm Waldron. LC 97-25484. 320p. 1997. pap. 15.00 (*1-56836-183-1*) Kodansha.

Snow Melting Calculation & Installation (S-40) rev. ed. Hydronics Institute Staff. (Illus.). 46p. (C). 1993. reprint ed. pap. 5.50 (*0-942711-05-X*) Hydronics Inst.

Snow Monkeys. Lynn M. Stone. (Monkey Discovery Library). (Illus.). 24p. (J). (gr. k-5). 1990. lib. bdg. 11.94 (*0-86593-066-X*); lib. bdg. 8.95 (*0-685-36320-1*) Rourke Corp.

Snow Monkeys. Mae Woods. LC 96-11385. (Monkeys Ser.). (J). 1997. lib. bdg. 13.95 (*1-56239-601-3*) Abdo & Dghtrs.

Snow Moon. Laura Beheler. 1986. 20.00 (*0-946270-30-9*, Pub. by Pentland Pr UK) St Mut.

Snow on Lake Como. Laura Brylawski-Miller. LC 90-25997. (Series Fifteen). 72p. (Orig.). 1991. pap. 9.00 (*0-931846-38-2*) Wash Writers Pub.

Snow on Snow. Maura Stanton. (Classic Contemporaries Ser.). 1993. pap. 12.95 (*0-88748-159-0*) Carnegie-Mellon.

Snow on Snow. Maura Stanton. LC 74-21349. (Yale Series of Younger Poets: No. 70). 78p. reprint ed. pap. 25.00 (*0-7837-2792-5*, 2043184) Bks Demand.

Snow on Snow on Snow. Cheryl Chapman. (Illus.). (J). 1994. pap. 14.99 (*0-8037-1456-4*); pap. 14.89 (*0-8037-1457-2*) Dial Bks Young.

Snow on the Backs of Animals & Other Poems. Dan Gerber. (Illus.). 88p. (Orig.). 1985. write for info. (*0-916947-07-6*); pap. 6.95 (*0-916947-08-4*) Winn Bks.

Snow on the Ben. large type ed. Ian Stuart. (Linford Mystery Library). 272p. 1988. pap. 15.99 (*0-7089-6503-2*) Ulverscroft.

Snow on the Cane Fields: Women's Writing & Creole Subjectivity. Judith Raiskin. 368p. 1995. text ed. 49.95 (*0-8166-2300-7*); pap. text ed. 19.95 (*0-8166-2301-5*) U of Minn Pr.

Snow on the Roses: A Garth Ryland Mystery. John R. Riggs. LC 95-51078. 272p. 1996. 17.95 (*1-56980-072-3*) Barricade Bks.

Snow Orchid. Joe Pintauro. 1996. pap. 5.25 (*0-8222-1546-2*) Dramatists Play.

Snow over Judaea. Kenneth Radu. 212p. (Orig.). 1994. pap. 13.95 (*1-55065-056-4*, Pub. by Vehicule Pr CN) Genl Dist Srvs.

***Snow Paws.** unabridged ed. Mary A. Downie. (Illus.). 24p. (J). (ps-3). 1996. 12.95 (*0-7737-2968-2*, Pub. by Stoddart Kids CN) Genl Dist Srvs.

Snow Poems. Marshall Brooks & Harry Smith. 12p. 1985. 15.00 (*0-933292-15-5*, Baguette Bks); pap. 3.50 (*0-933292-14-7*, Baguette Bks) Arts End.

Snow Pony. Anne E. Crompton. (J). (gr. 3-6). 1994. pap. 3.99 (*0-671-78507-9*) S&S Trade.

Snow Prince Poems & Collages. Harold Witt. (Illus.). 120p. (Orig.). 1982. pap. 8.75 (*0-9608574-1-9*) Blue Unicorn.

Snow Probe for In Situ Determination of Wetness & Density Technical Report. John R. Kendra et al. (University of Michigan Reports: No. 029721-1-T). 51p. reprint ed. pap. 25.00 (*0-7837-6288-7*, 2046003) Bks Demand.

***Snow Problem: Fisher Price Great Adventure.** Roger Befler. (Illus.). (Orig.). 1997. pap. 2.99 (*0-88743-452-5*) Sch Zone Pub Co.

Snow Queen. (J). 1993. pap. 8.98 (*1-879496-24-0*) Lightyear Entrtnmnt.

Snow Queen. (J). 1993. pap. 8.98 incl. audio (*1-879496-25-9*) Lightyear Entrtnmnt.

***Snow Queen.** Hans Christian Andersen. 1997. pap. text ed. 7.95 (*1-55858-779-9*) North-South Bks NYC.

Snow Queen. Hans Christian Andersen. LC 83-71172. (Creative's Collection of Fairy Tales). (Illus.). 48p. (J). (gr. 6 up). 1984. lib. bdg. 13.95 (*0-87191-950-8*) Creative Ed.

Snow Queen. Hans Christian Andersen. LC 82-70199. (Pied Piper Bks.). (Illus.). 40p. (J). (gr. k up). 1982. pap. 4.95 (*0-8037-0692-8*); lib. bdg. 12.89 (*0-8037-8029-X*) Dial Bks Young.

Snow Queen. Hans Christian Andersen. LC 93-42711. (Illus.). 48p. (J). (gr. 1-5). 1994. 17.00 (*0-15-200874-8*, Gulliver Bks) HarBrace.

Snow Queen. Hans Christian Andersen. LC 87-1518. (Illus.). 32p. (J). (gr. k-3). Date not set. 14.95 (*1-55858-053-0*) North-South Bks NYC.

Snow Queen. Hans Christian Andersen. LC 68-17218. (Illus.). 32p. (J). (ps-5). 9.95 (*0-87592-048-9*) Scroll Pr.

Snow Queen. Hans Christian Andersen. 29p. (Orig.). (J). (gr. 3-8). 1990. pap. 3.00 (*1-57514-230-9*, 1099) Encore Perform Pub.

***Snow Queen.** Anne Avery. 400p. (Orig.). 1996. mass mkt. 5.99 (*0-505-52151-2*) Dorchester Pub Co.

Snow Queen. Joan D. Vinge. 480p. 1989. mass mkt. 5.99 (*0-445-20529-6*, Aspect) Warner Bks.

Snow Queen. Hans Christian Andersen. Tr. by Naomi Lewis. LC 92-54412. (Illus.). 48p. (J). (gr. 2-6). 1996. reprint ed. pap. 6.99 (*1-56402-979-4*) Candlewick Pr.

Snow Queen: A Christmas Pageant. Richard Kennedy. LC 95-52211. (Laura Geringer Bk.). (Illus.). 96p. (J). (ps up). 1996. 16.95 (*0-06-027115-9*) HarpC Child Bks.

Snow Queen: A Christmas Pageant. Richard Kennedy. LC 95-52211. (Laura Geringer Bk.). (Illus.). 96p. (J). (ps up). 1996. lib. bdg. 16.89 (*0-06-027116-7*) HarpC Child Bks.

Snow Queen - with Incidental Music. Stuart Paterson & Savourna Stevenson. 86p. 1990. pap. 5.00 (*0-87129-065-0*, S84) Dramatic Pub.

Snow Queen & the Goblin. Martha B. King. 48p. 1956. pap. 3.45 (*0-87129-069-3*, S90) Dramatic Pub.

Snow Removal & Ice Control in Urban Areas. (Special Reports: No. 30). (Illus.). 128p. 1965. 15.00 (*0-917084-23-3*) Am Public Works.

Snow Ride. Bonnie Bryant. (Saddle Club Ser.: No. 20). 144p. (J). 1992. mass mkt. 3.99 (*0-553-15907-0*) Bantam.

Snow Riders. Constance W. McGeorge. LC 94-47214. (Illus.). 32p. (J). 1995. 13.95 (*0-8118-0873-4*) Chronicle Bks.

Snow Sense: A Guide to Evaluating Snow Avalanche Hazard. rev. ed. Jill Fredston & Doug Fesler. 116p. 1994. pap. 7.95 (*0-9616003-0-6*) State AK Dept Nat Res.

Snow Sky. large type ed. Cameron Judd. (General Ser.). 289p. 1991. lib. bdg. 19.95 (*0-8161-5198-9*, GK Hall) Thorndike Pr.

Snow Speaks. Nancy W. Carlstrom. (Illus.). (J). (ps-3). 1992. 15.95 (*0-316-12861-9*) Little.

Snow Speaks. Nancy W. Carlstrom. (J). (ps-3). 1995. pap. 4.95 (*0-316-12830-9*) Little.

Snow Spider. Jenny Nimmo. 136p. (J). (gr. 5-9). 1997. pap. 2.95 (*0-8167-2264-1*) Troll Communs.

Snow Storm. Aleksandr Pushkin. Ed. by Ann A. Redpath. (Creative's Classic Short Stories Ser.). 40p. (YA). (gr. 6 up). 1983. lib. bdg. 13.95 (*0-87191-923-0*) Creative Ed.

Snow Story. Melvin J. Leavitt. LC 94-21532. (Illus.). (J). (gr. k-3). 1995. 15.00 (*0-02-754633-0*, S&S Bks Young Read) S&S Childrens.

Snow Story. Melvin J. Leavitt. (J). (ps-2). 1995. 15.00 (*0-689-80296-X*, S&S Bks Young Read) S&S Childrens.

***Snow Swan.** Barbara J. Hicks. LC 97-968. 286p. 1997. pap. 8.99 (*1-57673-107-3*, Palisades OR) Multnomah Pubs.

Snow Toward Evening: A Year in a River Valley. Josette Frank. (Illus.). 32p. (J). 1995. pap. 5.99 (*0-14-055582-X*) Puffin Bks.

Snow Toward Evening, a Year in a River Valley. Illus. by Thomas Locker. LC 89-48307. 32p. (J). 1990. pap. 16.99 (*0-8037-0810-6*); lib. bdg. 15.89 (*0-8037-0811-4*) Dial Bks Young.

Snow Treasure. Marie McSwigan. 160p. (J). (gr. 4-6). 1986. pap. 3.50 (*0-590-42537-4*) Scholastic Inc.

Snow Treasure: A Study Guide. Marvin Bachelder. Ed. by Joyce Friedland & Rikki Kessler. (Novel-Ties Ser.). (J). (gr. 5-7). 1991. pap. text ed. 15.95 (*0-88122-582-7*) Lrn Links.

***Snow Tree.** Caroline Repchuk. (J). 1997. pap. 13.99 (*0-525-45903-0*) Dutton Child Bks.

Snow Trouble: Neighborhood Stories from Highlights. Highlights Staff. (Illus.). 96p. (J). (gr. 2-5). 1996. pap. 3.95 (*1-56397-607-2*) Boyds Mills Pr.

Snow Walker. Farley Mowat. 224p. 1984. mass mkt. 5.99 (*0-7704-2209-8*) Bantam.

Snow Walker. Charles M. Wetterer & Margaret K. Wetterer. LC 94-44131. (Carolrhoda On My Own Bks.). (Illus.). 48p. (J). (gr. 1-3). 1995. lib. bdg. 11.96 (*0-87614-891-7*, Carolrhoda) Lerner Group.

Snow Walker. Margaret Wetterer. (J). 1996. pap. 5.95 (*0-87614-959-X*) Lerner Group.

Snow Walker's Companion: Winter Trail Skills from the Far North. Garrett Conover & Alexandra Conover. LC 94-3374. (Illus.). 272p. 1994. pap. text ed. 19.95 (*0-07-022892-2*, Ragged Mntn) Intl Marine.

***Snow War.** Ann M. Martin. (Kids in Ms. Coleman's Class Ser.: No. 5). (J). 1997. mass mkt. 2.99 (*0-590-69201-1*) Scholastic Inc.

***Snow Watch: Experiments, Activities & Things to Do with Snow.** unabridged ed. Cheryl Archer. (Illus.). 56p. (J). (gr. 3-6). 1994. pap. 7.95 (*1-55074-190-X*, Pub. by Kids Can Pr CN) Genl Dist Srvs.

Snow Water Cove. Jeanne Savard. LC 87-34590. (University of Utah Press Poetry Ser.). 73p. (Orig.). reprint ed. pap. 25.00 (*0-7837-5541-4*, 2045315) Bks Demand.

Snow Whale. Caroline Pitcher. 24p. (J). (PS-3). 1996. 15.95 (*0-87156-915-9*) Sierra Club Childrens.

Snow White. (Play - a - Sound Ser.). (Illus.). 24p. (J). 1993. 12.98 (*0-7853-0130-5*) Pubns Intl Ltd.

Snow White. (Classic Fairytales Pop-Ups Ser.). (Illus.). (J). (ps-1). 1.98 (*0-517-39465-0*); 1.29 (*0-318-12084-4*) Random Hse Value.

Snow White. (J). 1990. 5.99 (*0-517-05143-5*) Random Hse Value.

Snow White. (Little Library). 8p. (J). (ps-1). 1994. 4.98 (*0-8317-5528-8*) Smithmark.

Snow White. (J). 3.39 (*0-307-03781-9*) Western Pub.

Snow White. (J). 2.59 (*0-307-08316-0*) Western Pub.

Snow White. Donald Barthelme. LC 67-14324. 192p. 1972. pap. 7.95 (*0-689-70331-7*, Bobbs) Macmillan.

Snow White. Donald Barthelme. LC 67-14324. 192p. 1996. pap. 10.00 (*0-684-82479-5*) S&S Trade.

Snow White. Rebecca Bondor. (Storytime Classics Ser.). (Illus.). 24p. (J). (ps-2). 1995. pap. 1.29 (*1-56293-540-2*) McClanahan Bk.

Snow White. Jacob W. Grimm & Wilhelm K. Grimm. (Children's Classics Ser.). (Illus.). 32p. (J). 1991. 6.95 (*0-8362-4906-2*) Andrews & McMeel.

Snow White. Jacob W. Grimm & Wilhelm K. Grimm. Tr. by Paul Heins. (Illus.). (J). (ps-3). 1979. mass mkt. 6.95 (*0-316-35451-1*, Joy St Bks) Little.

Snow White. Richard Hack. 1996. pap. 24.99 (*0-7871-0504-X*, Dove Bks) Dove Audio.

Snow White. Sharon Holland. (Enchanted Tales Ser.: No. 2). 96p. 1996. mass mkt. 3.50 (*0-06-106332-0*, Harp PBks) HarpC.

S

An Asterisk (*) at the beginning of an entry indicates that the title is appearing in BIP for the first time.

***Snow White.** Charles Santore. (J). 1997. 18.00 (0-679-88759-8) Random Bks Yng Read.

Snow White. Marilyn J. Shearer. LC 90-60396. (Illus.). 16p. (Orig.). (J). (ps-6). 1990. pap. 10.95 (1-878389-00-9) L Ashley & Joshua.

Snow White. Marilyn J. Shearer. LC 90-60396. (Illus.). 16p. (Orig.). (J). (ps-6). 1990. 19.95 (0-685-33066-4) Perma-Bound.

Snow White: A Tale from the Brothers Grimm. Illus. by Charles Santore. LC 95-33734. 48p. (J). 1996. 20.00 (0-517-20071-6, Park Ln Pr) Random.

Snow White: Full-Color Picture Book. Sheilah Beckett. LC 94-48705. (Little Activity Bks.). (Illus.). 12p. (Orig.). (ENG & GER.). (J). 1995. pap. text ed. 1.00 (0-486-28516-2) Dover.

Snow White: Hidden Picture Fairy Tales. Illus. & Retold by Kit Wray. LC 90-85902. 32p. (J). (gr. k-5). 1991. 7.95 (1-878093-26-6) Boyds Mills Pr.

Snow White: Stand-Up Fairy Tale House. Illus. by Susan Rowe. LC 94-37520. (J). 1995. pap. 6.95 (0-8037-1869-1) Dial Bks Young.

Snow White: The Untold Story. Catherine Heller. LC 95-19221. (Upside Down Tales Ser.). (Illus.). (J). 1995. 13.95 (1-55972-326-2, Birch Ln Pr) Carol Pub Group.

Snow White: U. K. English. Adapted by Sarah Harris. (Comes to Life Bks.). 16p. (J). (ps-2). 1995. write for info. (1-57234-025-8) YES Ent.

***Snow White & Other Fairy Tales.** unabridged ed. Jacob W. Grimm & Wilhelm K. Grimm. LC 94-32381. (Children's Thrift Classics Ser.). (Illus.). 96p. (J). 1994. pap. text ed. 1.00 (0-486-28327-5) Dover.

Snow White & Rose Red. (Ladybird Bks.). (Illus.). 52p. (ARA.). 4.50 (0-86685-225-5, LDL181, Pub. by Librairie du Liban FR) Intl Bk Ctr.

Snow White & Rose Red. (Ladybird Bks.). (Illus.). (ARA.). 14.95 incl. audio (0-614-09208-6, LDL121C, Pub. by Librairie du Liban FR) Intl Bk Ctr.

Snow White & Rose Red. 1982. pap. 3.50 (0-19-421751-5) OUP.

Snow White & Rose Red. Jacob W. Grimm & Wilhelm K. Grimm. (Creative's Collection of Fairy Tales). (Illus.). 32p. (YA). (gr. 6 up). 1984. lib. bdg. 13.95 (0-87191-938-9) Creative Ed.

Snow White & Rose Red. Jacob W. Grimm & Wilhelm K. Grimm. LC 87-72036. (Illus.). 32p. (J). (gr. k-3). 1988. 14.95 (1-55858-054-9) North-South Bks NYC.

***Snow White & Rose Red.** Jacob W. Grimm & Wilhelm K. Grimm. (Illus.). 32p. (J). (gr. k-3). 1997. pap. 7.95 (1-55858-696-2) North-South Bks NYC.

***Snow White & Rose Red.** Jacob W. Grimm & Wilhelm K. Grimm. (Illus.). 32p. (J). (ps-3). 1997. pap. 4.95 (0-698-11585-6, Paperstar) Putnam Pub Group.

Snow White & Rose Red. Jacob W. Grimm & Wilhelm K. Grimm. LC 78-18074. (Illus.). 32p. (J). (gr. k-3). 1979. lib. bdg. 11.89 (0-89375-136-7) Troll Communs.

Snow White & Rose Red. Jacob W. Grimm & Wilhelm K. Grimm. LC 78-18074. (Illus.). 32p. (J). (gr. k-3). 1996. pap. 3.95 (0-89375-114-6) Troll Communs.

Snow White & Rose Red. Ed McBain. 256p. 1994. mass mkt. 5.99 (0-446-60133-0) Warner Bks.

Snow White & Rose Red. Patricia C. Wrede. 288p. 1993. mass mkt. 4.99 (0-8125-3497-2) Tor Bks.

Snow White & Rose Red. Ed McBain. 256p. 1986. reprint ed. mass mkt. 4.99 (0-445-40513-9, Mysterious Paperbk) Warner Bks.

***Snow White & Rose Red: A Modern Fairy Tale.** Regina Doman. 280p. (Orig.). (YA). (gr. 9 up). 1997. 15.95 (1-883937-23-X, 23-X) Bethlehem ND.

Snow White & the Little Men. William Springer. 1979. pap. 1.75 (0-686-38381-8) Eldridge Pub.

Snow White & the Seven Dwarfs. (Recorder Fun! Ser.). 24p. (J). 1992. 9.95 (0-7935-1500-9, 00710358) H Leonard.

Snow White & the Seven Dwarfs. (Ladybird Stories Ser.). (Illus.). 52p. (ARA.). (J). (gr. 1-12). 1987. pap. 4.50 (0-86685-268-9, LDL202); audio 12.00 (0-86685-636-6) Intl Bk Ctr.

Snow White & the Seven Dwarfs. (Fun-to-Read Fairy Tales Ser.). (Illus.). 24p. (J). 1992. pap. 2.50 (1-56144-092-2) Modern Pub NYC.

Snow White & the Seven Dwarfs. (First Fairy Tales Ser.: No. S852-5). (Illus.). (J). (ps-2). 3.95 (0-7214-5062-8, Ladybrd) Penguin.

Snow White & the Seven Dwarfs. (Derrydale Fairytale Library). (Illus.). (J). (ps-3). 1985. 2.98 (0-517-28812-5) Random Hse Value.

Snow White & the Seven Dwarfs. 32p. (J). (ps-2). 1996. pap. 2.50 (0-7214-5619-7, Ladybrd) Penguin.

Snow White & the Seven Dwarfs. (Disney Collection). 24p. (J). (ps-2). 1995. bds. 1.59 (0-307-01036-8, Golden Books) Western Pub.

Snow White & the Seven Dwarfs. (Classics Ser.). 96p. (J). 1994. 7.98 (1-57082-026-0) Mouse Works.

Snow White & the Seven Dwarfs. (Little Library). 126p. (J). 1994. 5.98 (1-57082-027-9) Mouse Works.

Snow White & the Seven Dwarfs. (Once Upon a Time Ser.). (J). (ps-1). 1995. 3.98 (1-85854-281-2) Brimax Bks.

Snow White & the Seven Dwarfs. Berthe Amoss. (Illus.). 10p. (J). (ps-7). 1989. pap. 2.95 (0-922589-01-1) More than Card.

Snow White & the Seven Dwarfs. Disney Studios Staff. (Disney Animated Ser.). (Illus.). (J). 1988. 5.99 (0-517-66196-9) Random Hse Value.

Snow White & the Seven Dwarfs. Illus. by Mimi Everett. (Happytime Storybks.). 24p. (J). (ps-1). 1991. pap. 1.25 (0-7214-5306-6, S9016-7, Ladybrd) Penguin.

Snow White & the Seven Dwarfs. Jacob W. Grimm & Wilhelm K. Grimm. (Illus.). (FRE.). (J). (gr. 3-8). 8.95 (0-685-11566-6) Fr & Eur.

Snow White & the Seven Dwarfs. Jacob W. Grimm & Wilhelm K. Grimm. LC 92-44516. (Illus.). (J). (ps-2). 1994. pap. 2.50 (0-679-84347-7) Random Bks Yng Read.

Snow White & the Seven Dwarfs. Jacob W. Grimm & Wilhelm K. Grimm. LC 85-12158. (Illus.). 40p. (J). (gr. 1 up). 1991. pap. 15.95 (0-88708-012-X, Picture Book Studio) S&S Childrens.

Snow-White & the Seven Dwarfs. Jacob W. Grimm & Wilhelm K. Grimm. Tr. by Randall Jarrell from GER. LC 28-1489. (Illus.). 32p. (J). (ps up). 1972. 17.00 (0-374-37099-0) FS&G.

Snow-White & the Seven Dwarfs. Jacob W. Grimm & Wilhelm K. Grimm. Tr. by Randall Jarrell from GER. (Illus.). 32p. (J). (ps up). 1987. pap. 5.95 (0-374-46868-0, Sunburst Bks) FS&G.

Snow White & the Seven Dwarfs. Judith Kase-Baker. (J). (ps-6). 1984. pap. 5.00 (0-87602-256-5) Anchorage.

Snow White & the Seven Dwarfs. Teddy S. Margulies. (J). 1993. 12.60 (0-307-62686-5, Golden Pr) Western Pub.

Snow White & the Seven Dwarfs. Illus. by Franc Mateu. (Golden Sound Story Book). 24p. (J). (ps up). 1991. 9.95 (0-307-74018-8, 64018) Western Pub.

Snow White & the Seven Dwarfs. Illus. by Franc Mateu & Franc Mateo. LC 92-53432. (Pop-up Bks.). 12p. (J). (ps-k). 1993. 11.95 (1-56282-365-5) Disney Pr.

***Snow White & the Seven Dwarfs.** Laura Rossiter. (My Favorite Sound Story Bks.). (Illus.). 32p. (J). 1996. write for info. (0-307-71135-8, 61135-30, Golden Books) Western Pub.

Snow White & the Seven Dwarfs. Raymond Sibley. (Favorite Tales Ser.). (Illus.). 28p. (J). 1994. 2.99 (0-7214-5454-2, Ladybrd) Penguin.

Snow White & the Seven Dwarfs. Walt Disney Company Staff. 96p. (FRE.). (J). (gr. k-5). pap. 9.95 (0-7859-8853-X) Fr & Eur.

***Snow-White & the Seven Dwarfs: A Grimm's Fairy Tale.** Illus. by Elisabeth Wagner-Koch. 32p. (J). 1994. write for info. (0-904693-59-7, Pub. by Temple Ldge Pub UK) Anthroposophic.

Snow White & the Seven Dwarfs: An Off-the-Wall Fairy Tale. Jacob W. Grimm & Wilhelm K. Grimm. 48p. (J). (ps-2). 1996. pap. 17.95 incl. audio (0-7871-0431-0) Dove Audio.

Snow White & the Seven Dwarfs: It's Time to Wash! Illus. by Isidre Mones. LC 94-71695. (Surprise Lift-the-Flap Ser.). 18p. (J). (ps-k). 1995. 9.95 (0-7868-3030-1) Disney Pr.

Snow White & the Seven Dwarfs: Suppertime. Illus. by Fred Marvin. LC 93-71376. (Tiny Changing Pictures Bks.). 10p. (J). (ps-1). 1994. 4.95 (1-56282-600-X) Disney Pr.

Snow White & the Seven Dwarfs: Walt Disney. (Big Golden Bks.). (Illus.). 24p. (J). (ps). 1986. 3.50 (0-307-10205-X, Golden Pr) Western Pub.

Snow White & the Seven Dwarfs: Walt Disney. Teddy S. Margulies. (Look-Look Bks.). (Illus.). 24p. (J). (ps-3). 1993. pap. 2.25 (0-307-12686-2, 12686, Golden Pr) Western Pub.

Snow White & the Seven Dwarfs: Walt Disney. Illus. by Don Williams. (Golden Super Shape Bks.). 24p. (J). (ps). 1992. pap. 1.95 (0-307-10037-5, 10037, Golden Pr) Western Pub.

Snow White & the Seven Dwarfs - Coloring Book. Nina Barbaresi. (J). 1989. pap. 1.00 (0-486-25911-0) Dover.

Snow White & the Seven Dwarfs - Str. Marian Jonson. 67p. 1957. reprint ed. pap. 3.45 (0-87129-017-0, S91) Dramatic Pub.

***Snow White & the Seven Dwarfs (a Play in Eleven Scenes)** Ken Pickering. (Illus.). 38p. (Orig.). 1996. pap. 4.50 (0-88680-425-6) I E Clark.

Snow White & the Seven Dwarfs Whistle While You Work: A Musical Pop-up Book. Illus. by Franc Mateu. LC 92-53432. 10p. (J). (ps-1). 1994. 11.95 (1-56282-514-3) Disney Pr.

***Snow White & the 7 Dwarfs: Snow White, the Rottweiler Version.** (Illus.). 36p. (J). (gr. 2-4). 1996. 29.95 (1-886123-06-3) Geyers Garten.

Snow White & the 7 Dwarfs - Musical. Adapted by Carol Weiss. 1995. 5.00 (0-87129-446-X, SA7) Dramatic Pub.

Snow White & the 7 Dwarfs of the Black Forest. June W. Rogers. 1969. 3.75 (0-87129-440-0, S42) Dramatic Pub.

***Snow White & the 7 Dwarfs, the German Shepherd Version.** (Illus.). 36p. (J). (gr. 2-4). 1996. 29.95 (1-886123-07-1) Geyers Garten.

Snow White, Blood Red. Ed. by Ellen Datlow & Terri Windling. 432p. 1993. mass mkt. 5.99 (0-380-71875-8, AvoNova) Avon.

Snow White in New York. Fiona French. (Illus.). 32p. (J). (gr. 1-4). 1987. bds. 18.95 (0-19-279808-1) OUP.

Snow White in New York. Fiona French. (Illus.). 32p. (J). 1990. pap. 8.95 (0-19-272210-7) OUP.

Snow White-Pop Up. (J). 1989. pap. 9.95 (0-8167-0898-3) Troll Communs.

Snow White-Sticker Book. 1990. 3.99 (0-517-69696-7) Random Hse Value.

Snow White's Escape. (Slide-n-Show Ser.). 20p. (J). 1994. 9.98 (1-57082-153-4) Mouse Works.

Snow Wife. Illus. by Stephen T. Johnson. LC 92-28966. 32p. (J). (ps-3). 1993. pap. 14.99 (0-8037-1409-2) Dial Bks Young.

Snow Wolf. Roberta Debono. 243p. (Orig.). 1989. pap. 8.95 (0-9613901-0-7) Ankh Pr CA.

Snow Wolf. Glenn Meade. 432p. 1996. 24.95 (0-312-14421-0) St Martin.

***Snow Wolf.** Glenn Meade. 1997. mass mkt. 6.99 (0-312-96211-8) St Martin.

Snow Wolf. large type ed. Glenn Meade. LC 96-12113. 855p. 1996. 26.95 (0-7838-1791-6, GK Hall) Thorndike Pr.

Snow Woman. David Monobe. 165p. 1984. 7.95 (0-89697-167-8) Intl Univ Pr.

Snow World. Kevin Urick. LC 82-51026. 477p. 1983. 16.95 (0-917976-16-9, White Ewe Pr) Thunder Baas Pr.

Snowball. Jennifer Armstrong. LC 94-48883. (Early Step into Reading Ser.). (J). 1996. pap. 3.99 (0-679-86444-X) Random.

Snowball. Jennifer Armstrong. LC 94-48883. (Early Step into Reading Ser.). (J). 1996. lib. bdg. 11.99 (0-679-96444-4) Random.

***Snowball.** Nina Crews. LC 96-48180. (Illus.). 24p. (J). (ps up). 1997. 15.00 (0-688-14928-6); lib. bdg. 14.93 (0-688-14929-4) Greenwillow.

Snowball. Meng Wang. Tr. by Cathy Silber & Deirdre Huang. (Selected Works of Wang Meng: No. 2). (Illus.). 464p. (Orig.). 1989. pap. 14.95 (0-8351-2162-3) China Bks.

***Snowball & Other Plays: A Collection of Short, Zany, Wild, Absurd, Mysterious, Thought-Provoking, & Fun Plays for Kids.** Paul Sedgwick. 80p. 1996. pap. 4.00 (0-87440-027-9) Bakers Plays.

***Snowball Class Set.** Jennifer Armstrong. 1996. pap. write for info. (0-676-73733-1) Random.

Snowball Quilt. Patricia Knoechel. (Illus.). 96p. 1993. 8.95 (0-922705-41-0) Quilt Day.

***Snowballs.** Ehlert. (J). 1996. 15.00 (0-15-201626-0, HB Juv Bks) HarBrace.

Snowballs. Lois Ehlert. LC 94-47183. (Illus.). 32p. (J). (ps-3). 1995. 15.00 (0-15-200074-7, HB Juv Bks) HarBrace.

Snowbear Whittington: An Appalachian Beauty & the Beast. William H. Hooks. LC 93-8691. (Illus.). 56p. (J). 1994. text ed. 15.95 (0-02-744355-8) Macmillan.

Snowbeast. Peter Tremayne. 224p. 1992. reprint ed. 19.00 (0-7278-4333-8) Severn Hse.

Snowbelt Cities: Metropolitan Politics in the Northeast & Midwest since World War II. Ed. by Richard M. Bernard. LC 89-19931. 284p. 1990. 35.00 (0-253-31177-2) Ind U Pr.

Snowbird. Patricia Calvert. 192p. (YA). (gr. 7 up). 1982. pap. 1.95 (0-451-13353-6, AE1354, Sig Vista) NAL-Dutton.

Snowbird. Stef A. Holm. Ed. by Caroline Tolley. 384p. (Orig.). 1994. mass mkt. 5.50 (0-671-79734-4) PB.

Snowbird: The Story of Anne Murray. Barry Grills. 1996. pap. text ed. 14.95 (1-55082-153-9, Pub. by Quarry Pr CN) LPC InBook.

Snowbird & Winter Texan Guide: How to Escape Winter's Chill in Your RV & Discover Adventures in America's Sunbelt! Bill Farlow. 152p. 1996. pap. 14.95 (0-937877-19-0) Cottage Pubns Inc.

Snowbird Cherokees: People of Persistence. Sharlotte Neely. LC 90-11308. (Brown Thrasher Bks.). (Illus.). 192p. 1993. pap. 14.95 (0-8203-1575-3) U of Ga Pr.

Snowbird Gravy & Dishpan Pie: Mountain People Recall. Patsy M. Ginns. LC 81-16296. 223p. reprint ed. pap. 63.60 (0-8357-4421-3, 2037241) Bks Demand.

Snowbird Mating Season. large type ed. Bernita J. Brown. Ed. by Jerra Davis & Jean Long. (Illus.). 200p. (Orig.). 1992. pap. 10.95 (0-9632555-0-9) Snowbird Pub.

***Snowblind.** Cheryl-Lynn Braun. 1996. mass mkt. 3.99 (1-55197-486-X, Pub. by Comnwlth Pub CN) Partners Pubs Grp.

Snowblind: One Man's Career in the Coedine Trade. Robert Sabbag. LC 75-32691. 256p. 1976. 8.95 (0-672-52079-6, Bobbs) Macmillan.

Snowblind Moon. John B. Cooke. 864p. 1993. mass mkt. 5.99 (0-8125-2461-6) Tor Bks.

***Snowboard Maverick.** Matt Christopher. LC 97-18916. (J). 1997. 15.95 (0-316-14261-1); pap. 3.95 (0-316-14203-4) Little.

Snowboard Racer. Anson Montgomery. (Choose Your Own Adventure Ser.: No. 165). (Illus.). 128p. (YA). (gr. 5 up). 1995. mass mkt. 3.50 (0-553-56620-2, Choose) BDD Bks Young Read.

Snowboarder's Start-Up: A Beginner's Guide to Snowboarding. Doug Werner. 128p. (Orig.). 1993. lib. bdg. 29.00 (0-8095-5917-X) Borgo Pr.

Snowboarder's Start-Up: A Beginner's Guide to Snowboarding. Doug Werner. LC 93-30926. (Start-Up Sports Ser.: Vol. 2). (Illus.). 128p. (Orig.). 1993. pap. 9.95 (0-934793-53-0) Tracks Pubng.

***Snowboarding.** David Armentrout. LC 97-12418. (Sports Challenge Ser.). (J). 1997. write for info. (1-55916-220-1) Rourke Bk Co.

***Snowboarding.** Larry D. Brimner. LC 97-8962. (First Bks.). 1997. write for info. (0-531-20313-1) Watts.

***Snowboarding.** Gutman. Date not set. pap. 13.95 (0-312-86255-5) St Martin.

Snowboarding. Bill Gutman. 128p. (Orig.). 1995. pap. 7.99 (0-8125-1936-1) Tor Bks.

***Snowboarding.** Lowell Hart. Date not set. pap. 18.95 (0-393-31692-0) Norton.

***Snowboarding.** Howe. Date not set. pap. write for info. (0-312-17026-2) St Martin.

Snowboarding. Robert Reichenfeld & Anna M. Bruechert. LC 94-28366. (Outdoor Pursuits Ser.). (Illus.). 144p. (Orig.). 1994. pap. 13.95 (0-87322-677-1, PREI0677) Human Kinetics.

Snowboarding. George Sullivan. 1999. pap. 13.99 (0-525-45579-5) NAL-Dutton.

***Snowboarding.** George Sullivan. 1997. pap. 5.99 (0-14-056181-1) Viking Penguin.

Snowboarding: A Complete Guide for Beginners. George Sullivan. LC 96-22756. 1997. pap. 14.99 (0-525-65235-3) NAL-Dutton.

***Snowboarding: A Guide to the Ultimate Freeride.** Mike Fabbro. (Illus.). 112p. (YA). (gr. 7 up). 1996. pap. 12.99 (0-7710-3122-X) McCland & Stewart.

***Snowboarding: All You Ever Wanted to Know about Surfing the Snow.** Paul Davies. 1996. 9.98 (0-7651-9699-9) Smithmark.

Snowboarding Basics. Jackson Jay. LC 95-44718. (New Action Ser.). 48p. (J). (gr. 3-9). 1996. 17.80 (1-56065-401-5) Capstone Pr.

***Snowboarding Basics.** Jackson Jay. (New Action Sports Ser.). (Illus.). 48p. (J). (gr. 3-7). 1996. 18.40 (0-516-20099-2) Childrens.

Snowboarding Know-How. Christof Weiss. LC 93-4748. 128p. (YA). (gr. 10-12). 1993. pap. 12.95 (0-8069-0502-6) Sterling.

***Snowboarding to Nirvana.** Lenz. Date not set. pap. write for info. (0-312-18179-5) St Martin.

***Snowboarding to Nirvana: A Novel.** Frederick Lenz. LC 96-45535. 1997. 16.95 (0-312-15293-0) St Martin.

Snowboarding...to the Extreme - Rippin. Sigmund Brouwer. LC 96-18646. (Short Cuts Ser.: No. 1). 64p. (YA). 1996. mass mkt. 3.99 (0-8499-3951-8) Word Pub.

***Snowbound.** Ladd Hamilton. LC 97-18694. 1997. write for info. (0-87422-153-6); pap. write for info. (0-87422-154-4) Wash St U Pr.

***Snowbound.** Keene. (Nancy Drew on Campus Ser.: No. 25). (J). 1998. mass mkt. 3.99 (0-671-00779-3) PB.

Snowbound. Ann M. Martin. (Baby-Sitters Club Super Special Ser.: No. 7). 256p. (J). (gr. 4-6). 1991. pap. 4.50 (0-590-44963-X) Scholastic Inc.

Snowbound. Bill Pronzini. 256p. 1994. pap. 4.95 (0-7867-0108-0) Carroll & Graf.

Snowbound: Shotgun Wedding, Murder by the Book, On a Wing & a Prayer. Charlotte Lamb et al. 1998. mass mkt. 5.99 (0-373-20143-5, 1-20143-3) Harlequin Bks.

Snowbound: The Tragic Story of the Donner Party. David Lavender. (J). (gr. 4-7). 1996. 16.95 (0-8234-1231-8) Holiday.

Snowbound Hidden Valley. pap. 1.95 (0-590-05414-7) Scholastic Inc.

Snowbound Mystery. Gertrude C. Warner. LC 68-9124. (Boxcar Children Mysteries Ser.: No. 13). (Illus.). (J). (gr. 2-7). 1968. pap. 3.95 (0-8075-7516-X); lib. bdg. 13.95 (0-8075-7517-8) A Whitman.

Snowbound Weekend: Gambler's Love, 2 bks. in 1. Amii Lorin. 368p. 1994. mass mkt., pap. text ed. 4.99 (0-505-51935-6, Love Spell) Dorchester Pub Co.

Snowbrother. S. M. Stirling. 304p. 1992. reprint ed. mass mkt. 4.99 (0-671-72119-4) Baen Bks.

Snowcap. Peggy Merritt. 117p. (Orig.). 1994. pap. 3.95 (0-943861-17-9) Lone Tree.

***Snowcat.** Dayal K. Khalsa. Date not set. 3.99 (0-517-17646-7) Random Hse Value.

Snowcat Poems, 1980-1981, to the Photographs of Robert Frank. Simon Perchik. LC 90-80827. (Illus.). 64p. 1989. reprint ed. pap. 7.95 (0-943512-24-7) Linwood Pub.

Snowchild. Illus. by Deborah K. Ray. (Pudgy Pal Board Bks.). 18p. (J). (ps). 1995. bds. 3.95 (0-448-40883-X, G&D) Putnam Pub Group.

Snowdomes. Nancy McMichael. (Illus.). 96p. 1990. 27.50 (1-55859-036-6) Abbeville Pr.

***Snowdon on Stage: A Personal View of the British Theatre.** Snowdon. (Illus.). 158p. 1997. 50.00 (0-8478-2026-2) St Martin.

Snowdonia Leisure Guide. (Automobile Assoc. Guides Ser.). (Illus.). 128p. (Orig.). 1995. pap. 17.95 (0-86145-802-8) Hunter NJ.

Snowdonia Walks: (Including Anglesey & the Lleyn Peninsula) (Ordnance Survey Pathfinder Guides Ser.). (Illus.). 80p. 1993. pap. 14.95 (0-7117-0550-X) Seven Hills Bk.

Snowdon's Global International Protocols: Asia-Pacific Rim. Sondra Snowdon. 352p. 1996. 25.00 (0-7863-0130-9) Irwin Prof Pubng.

Snowdon's Global International Protocols: Europe. Sondra Snowdon. LC 95-7943. 544p. 1995. 25.00 (0-7863-0145-7) Irwin Prof Pubng.

Snowdon's Global Protocols: The Americas. Sondra Snowdon. LC 94-29876. 304p. 1994. text ed. 25.00 (0-7863-0131-7) Irwin Prof Pubng.

Snowdon's Official International Protocols: The Definitive Guide to Business & Social Customs of the World. Sondra Snowdon. LC 94-28790. 864p. 1996. 75.00 (0-7863-0118-X) Irwin Prof Pubng.

***Snowdrops & Scandalbroth.** Barbara Metzger. 1997. mass mkt. 4.50 (0-449-22506-2, Crest) Fawcett.

Snowdrops for a Bride. Grace Green. 1994. mass mkt. 2.99 (0-373-11694-2, 1-11694-6) Harlequin Bks.

Snowed In. Alan Gettis. 20p. 1978. pap. 2.00 (0-913719-33-1) High-Coo Pr.

***Snowed In.** Uthman Hutchinson. LC 95-80044. (Children Stories Project Ser.). (Illus.). (Orig.). (J). (gr. 1 up). 1995. pap. 3.95 (0-915957-51-5) amana pubns.

Snowed in at Pokeweed Public School. John Bianchi. (Illus.). 24p. (J). (gr. 6-9). 1991. 14.95 (0-921285-07-8, Pub. by Bungalo Bks CN); pap. 4.95 (0-921285-05-1, Pub. by Bungalo Bks CN) Firefly Bks Ltd.

Snowed Under. Baltimore Sun Company Staff. (Orig.). 1996. pap. 8.95 (0-9649819-1-2) Baltimore Sun.

Snowfall. large type ed. Hester Rowan. 352p. 1985. 25.99 (0-7089-1395-4) Ulverscroft.

Snowfields: The War on Cocaine in the Andes. Clare Hargreaves. (Illus.). 245p. 1992. text ed. 47.95 (0-8419-1327-7); pap. text ed. 18.00 (0-8419-1328-5) Holmes & Meier.

Snowfire. Noel Monahan. 61-p. 9600. pap. 12.95 (1-897648-41-3, Pub. by Poolbeg Pr IE) Dufour.

Snowfire. Heather G. Pozzessere. (Intimate Moments Ser.: No. 386). 1991. mass mkt. 3.25 (0-373-07386-0) Silhouette.

Snowfire. Phyllis A. Whitney. 1987. mass mkt. 5.99 (0-449-21448-6) Fawcett.

Snowfire. large type unabridged ed. (Harlequin Ser.). 1993. lib. bdg. 19.95 (0-263-13579-9, Pub. by Mills & Boon UK) Thorndike Pr.

Snowflake. J. Nichols. LC 89-90662. 64p. (Orig.). (C). 1989. pap. 7.95 (0-9622423-0-6) Snowflake Pr.

An Asterisk (*) at the beginning of an entry indicates that the title is appearing in BIP for the first time.

***Snowflake: Another Greyhound's Story.** Ginny A. Folkman. (Illus.). 30p. (J). 1997. pap. 10.95 (0-9644470-1-0) Emerald Press.

***Snowflake Bentley.** Martin. LC 97-12458. 1998. write for info. (0-395-86162-4) HM.

***Snowflake, Come Home.** John A. Giegling. (Illus.). 122p. (J). 1992. per. 4.95 (0-614-24785-3) Tesseract SD.

Snowflake Come Home: A Wolf's Story. John A. Giegling. (Illus.). 124p. (Orig.). (J). (gr. 7-9). 1992. pap. 4.95 (0-912661-12-7) Woodsong Graph.

Snowflake in My Hand. large type ed. Samantha Mooney. LC 95-17990. (Large Print Bks.). 1995. pap. 19.95 (1-56895-227-9) Wheeler Pub.

Snowflake on the Belfry: Dogma & Disquietude in the Critical Arena. Anna A. Balakian. LC 93-7762. 1994. 39.95 (0-253-31132-2) Ind U Pr.

Snowflake the Ghost Kitten. Zeno Zeplin. (J). (gr. 2-4). 1993. 11.95 (1-877740-14-4); pap. 6.95 (1-877740-15-2) Nel-Mar Pub.

***Snowflake Wishes.** Lydia Browne. 336p. 1997. mass mkt. 5.99 (0-515-12181-9) Jove Pubns.

Snowflaker. Bill Kachler. 112p. 1993. pap. 16.95 (1-880365-38-3) Prof Pr NC.

Snowflakes. Etienne Delessert. LC 93-27457. (Yok-Yok Ser.). (Illus.). 32p. (J). (gr. 1-8). 1994. lib. bdg. 10.95 (0-88682-647-0, 97935-098) Creative Ed.

Snowflakes. Illus. by Ruth Heller. (Designs for Coloring Ser.). 64p. (J). 1990. pap. 3.95 (0-448-03145-0, G&D) Putnam Pub Group.

Snowflakes see Set 1

Snowflakes & Flowers. Bill Padgett. 52p. 1995. 12.95 (0-614-06924-6) Rountree Pub NC.

Snowflakes & Other Stories. Shambhunath Verma. xi, 132p. 1992. text ed. 18.95 (81-220-0265-X, Pub. by Konark Pubs Pvt Ltd II) Advent Bks Div.

Snowflakes & Quartz. 2nd rev. ed. Louis Wyman. (Illus.). 140p. 1993. reprint ed. pap. 13.95 (0-9632028-1-2) Simpler Way.

Snowflakes & Snowdrifts: Individualism & Sexuality in America. David Bertelson. 294p. (Orig.). (C). 1986. pap. text ed. 25.50 (0-8191-5579-9); lib. bdg. 48.00 (0-8191-5578-0) U Pr of Amer.

Snowflakes in September: Stories about God's Mysterious Ways. LC 91-42389. 96p. (Orig.). 1992. pap. 8.00 (0-687-38782-5) Dimen for Liv.

***Snowflakes in the Sun.** Jean Buffong. 180p. 1997. pap. 13.95 (0-7043-4423-8, Pub. by Womens Press UK) Trafalgar.

Snowflakes Made Easy & Fun. Cindy Higham. (Illus.). 32p. 1995. pap. 5.95 (0-9651163-2-8) Harkness Pubng.

Snowflakes on the Sea. Linda L. Miller. 1994. mass mkt. 4.50 (0-373-48303-1, 5-48303-7) Silhouette.

Snowflakes Stained Glass Coloring Book. John Green. (Illus.). (J). (gr. k-3). 1993. pap. 1.00 (0-486-27531-0) Dover.

Snowflakes, Sugar, & Salt: Crystals up Close. Chu Maki. LC 92-18538. (Science All Around You Ser.). (Illus.). 24p. (J). (gr. 1-3). 1993. lib. bdg. 18.95 (0-8225-2903-3, Lerner Publctns) Lerner Group.

Snowflame. large type ed. Christa Merlin. 304p. 1995. 25.99 (0-7089-3224-X) Ulverscroft.

Snowflower for Six Viols. Susan Ross. (Contemporary Consort Ser.: No. 10). i, 14p. 1990. pap. text ed. 11.00 (1-56571-005-3) PRB Prods.

Snowharry Takes a Vacation (with Arctic Friends) Sherry C. Miller. (Molly Character - Color Me Ser.: No. 4). (Illus.). 32p. (J). (gr. k-5). 1985. pap. write for info. (0-913379-03-4) Double M Pub.

Snowhite. (Illus.). 16p. (J). 1991. audio write for info. (1-880459-04-3) Arrow Trad.

Snowing at Delphi. Catherine Butterfield. 1994. pap. 5.25 (0-8222-1377-X) Dramatists Play.

Snowing Whistling. Karen E. Lotz. 1997. pap. 4.99 (0-14-055865-9) Viking Penguin.

Snowjob. Ted Wood. (Mystery Ser.). 1995. mass mkt. 3.99 (0-373-26182-9, 1-26182-5, Wrldwide Lib) Harlequin Bks.

Snowmaiden. Stephen Lambert. (Illus.). 32p. (J). (gr. 1-3). 1992. 15.95 (0-09-173861-X, Pub. by Hutchnson UK) Trafalgar.

Snowman. Howard Blake. (Easy Piano Picture Bks.). (Illus.). 32p. 1987. pap. 9.95 (0-571-10074-0) Faber & Faber.

Snowman. Raymond Briggs. LC 78-55904. (Illus.). 32p. (Orig.). (J). (ps-3). 1978. 17.00 (0-394-83973-0) Random Bks Yng Read.

Snowman. Raymond Briggs. LC 78-55904. (Illus.). 32p. (Orig.). (J). (ps-2). 1986. pap. 5.95 (0-394-88466-3) Random Bks Yng Read.

Snowman. Raymond Briggs. LC 90-60078. (Illus.). 32p. (Orig.). (J). (ps-8). 1990. 4.95 (0-679-80906-6) Random Bks Yng Read.

Snowman. Raymond Briggs. (J). 1995. 3.99 (0-679-87273-6) Random.

Snowman. Alfredo Castelli. Ed. by Bernd Metz. Tr. by Stefano Gaudiano from ITA. (Illus.). 49p. (Orig.). 1990. pap. 9.95 (0-87416-124-X) Catalan Communs.

Snowman. Reader's Digest Editors. (J). 1995. 4.99 (0-89577-814-9) RD Assn.

Snowman. R. L. Stine. 192p. (YA). (gr. 7-9). 1991. pap. 3.99 (0-590-43280-X) Scholastic Inc.

Snowman. Francis H. Wise & Joyce M. Wise. (Dr. Wise Learn to Read Bk.: No. 16). (Illus.). (J). (gr. 1). 1976. pap. 1.50 (0-915766-37-X) Wise Pub.

Snowman, No. 8612-4. Raymond Briggs. (Illus.). (Orig.). (J). (ps-4). 1990. 3.50 (0-7214-1109-6, Ladybrd) Penguin.

Snowman: A Young Boy Deals with the Death of His Father. Robin H. Vogel. Ed. by Joy Johnson. (Illus.). 24p. (J). (gr. 2-6). 1994. pap. 4.00 (1-56123-068-5) Centering Corp.

***Snowman: Col. Tom Parker.** Alanna Nash. Date not set. write for info. (0-688-15627-4) Morrow.

Snowman: Songbook. Raymond Briggs. (J). 1987. pap. 7.95 (0-7935-1831-8, 50489170) H Leonard.

Snowman Board Books. Incl. Building the Snowman. 1985. pap. (0-316-10813-8); Dressing up. Raymond Briggs. 1985. pap. 3.95 (0-316-10814-6); Walking in the Air. Raymond Briggs. 1985. pap. 3.95 (0-316-10815-4); (Illus.). (J). (ps-k). 1985. Set pap. 3.95 (0-685-73726-8) Little.

Snowman Cuddle Cloth Book. Raymond Briggs. (Cuddle Cloth Bks.). (Illus.). 12p. (J). (ps). 1993. 4.99 (0-679-82696-3) Random Bks Yng Read.

Snowman on Sycamore Street. C. B. Christiansen. (Illus.). (J). (gr. 1-3). 1996. 15.00 (0-689-31927-4, Atheneum Bks Young) S&S Childrens.

Snowman, Snowman: Fables & Fantasies. Janet Frame. 182p. 1993. pap. 10.95 (0-8076-1304-5) Braziller.

Snowman Storybook. Raymond Briggs. LC 90-8029. (Just Right Bks.). (Illus.). 24p. (J). (ps). 1990. 6.00 (0-679-80840-X) Random Bks Yng Read.

Snowman Storybook. Raymond Briggs. LC 96-16076. (Pictureback Bks.). (J). 1997. pap. 3.25 (0-679-88343-6) Random.

***Snowman Storybook.** Raymond Briggs. (Pictureback Ser.). 1997. lib. bdg. 8.99 (0-679-98343-0) Random Bks Yng Read.

Snowman Who Wanted to See July. Nicole B. Estvanik. (Publish-a-Book Contest Ser.). (Illus.). 32p. (J). 1989. lib. bdg. 22.83 (0-8172-2779-2) Raintree Steck-V.

Snowman Who Wanted to See July. Nicole B. Estvanik. (J). (ps-3). 1993. pap. 4.95 (0-8114-5210-7) Raintree Steck-V.

Snowman's Christmas Surprise. 12p. (J). (ps). 1996. pap. 2.95 (0-8167-2190-4) Troll Communs.

Snowman's Christmas Surprise. Lucinda McQueen. (Sparkling Christmas Tree Bks.). (Illus.). 10p. (J). (ps). 1994. bds. 4.95 (0-590-48042-1, Cartwheel) Scholastic Inc.

Snowman's Dream. Molly Kates. (J). 1996. 3.99 (0-679-87010-5) Random Bks Yng Read.

Snowman's Squeaky Song. Funworks Staff. 18p. (J). 1996. 6.98 (1-57082-339-1) Mouse Works.

Snowmobile Accident Reconstruction: A Technical & Legal Guide. Richard Hermance. (Illus.). 732p. 1995. text ed. 99.00 (0-913875-02-3, 5023) Lawyers & Judges.

Snowmobile Atlas of Maine. M. Keim. Ed. & Illus. by Gannet Keim. 71p. 1994. pap. 9.95 (0-9642055-2-1) Hiking Ctr.

Snowmobile Revolution: Technology & Social Change in the Arctic. Pertti J. Pelto. (Illus.). 225p. (C). 1987. reprint ed. pap. text ed. 11.50 (0-88133-287-9) Waveland Pr.

Snowmobile Safety & You. (Illus.). 1992. teacher ed. 2.95 (0-916682-32-3) Outdoor Empire.

Snowmobile Safety & You. (Illus.). 1995. student ed. 1.95 (0-916682-33-1) Outdoor Empire.

Snowmobile Service Manual. (Illus.). 512p. 1991. 24.95 (0-87288-461-9, SMS-11) Intertec Pub.

Snowprints: A Grandmother's Glimpses of New Life & Old Art. Robbie De Vries. LC 90-91420. (Lifeprints Ser.: Vol. I). (Illus.). (Orig.). pap. write for info. (0-9627886-0-0) R R P de Vries.

Snows of Jaspre. Houghton Mifflin Company Staff. (Literature Experience 1991 Ser.). (J). (gr. 8). 1990. pap. 9.84 (0-395-55186-2) HM.

Snows of Kilimanjaro. Ernest Hemingway. (Hudson River Editions Ver.). 154p. 1987. 35.00 (0-02-550940-3) S&S Trade.

Snows of Kilimanjaro. Ernest Hemingway. 1995. pap. 5.00 (0-87129-255-6, S95) Dramatic Pub.

Snows of Kilimanjaro. Ernest Hemingway. 1995. pap. 9.00 (0-684-80444-1) S&S Trade.

Snows of Nazareth. Judy L. Vernon. 100p. (Orig.). 1987. pap. 7.95 (0-9617776-2-1) J Vernon.

Snows of Olympus: A Garden on Mars. Arthur C. Clarke. (Illus.). 120p. 1995. 25.00 (0-393-03911-0) Norton.

Snows of Springtime. large type ed. Stewart. 1995. 25.99 (0-7505-0752-7, Pub. by Magna Print Bks UK) Ulverscroft.

Snows of Yesteryear. Gregor Von Rezzori. LC 90-50158. (Vintage International Ser.). (Illus.). 304p. 1991. pap. 12.00 (0-679-73181-4, Vin) Random.

Snows of Yesteryear: Portraits for an Autobiography. Gregor Von Rezzori. Tr. by H. F. De Rothermann. 1989. 19.95 (0-685-28838-2) Knopf.

Snowshoe & Earmuff Go North. Carole Marsh. (Serendipity Travel Series for Young People). (Illus.). (J). (ps-4). 1994. 29.95 (1-55609-646-1); pap. 19.95 (1-55609-758-1) Gallopade Pub Group.

Snowshoe & Earmuff Go West. Carole Marsh. (Serendipity Travel Series for Young People). (Illus.). (J). (ps-3). 1994. 29.95 (1-55609-304-7); pap. 19.95 (1-55609-303-9) Gallopade Pub Group.

Snowshoe Story: Business, Politics & the Judiciary in West Virginia. S. Franklin Burford. 178p. 1992. 19.95 (0-9633805-0-8) Kerens Hill Pubns.

Snowshoe Thompson. Nancy S. Levinson. LC 90-37401. (I Can Read Bk.). (Illus.). 64p. (J). (gr. k-3). 1992. lib. bdg. 15.89 (0-06-023802-X) HarpC Child Bks.

Snowshoe Thompson. Nancy S. Levinson. LC 90-37401. (Trophy I Can Read Bk.). (Illus.). 64p. (J). (gr. k-3). 1996. pap. 3.75 (0-06-444206-3, Trophy) HarpC Child Bks.

Snowshoeing. Sally Edwards & Melissa McKenzie. LC 94-40482. (Outdoor Pursuits Ser.). (Illus.). 128p. (Orig.). 1995. pap. 13.95 (0-87322-767-0, PEDW0767) Human Kinetics.

***Snowshoeing.** Trailside. LC 97-22846. 1997. pap. 17.95 (0-393-31720-X) Norton.

***Snowshoeing.** 4th ed. Gene Prater. 1997. pap. text ed. 16.95 (0-89886-497-6) Mountaineers.

Snowshoeing: Adventures in New York City, New Jersey, & Philadelphia. Michael A. Rockland. LC 94-10145. 165p. (C). 1994. 21.95 (0-8135-2115-7) Rutgers U Pr.

Snowshot. Douglas McBriarty. LC 88-14406. 192p. 1989. 17.95 (0-8027-5717-0) Walker & Co.

Snowskate Goes for Gold. Sherry C. Miller. (Molly Character - Color Me Ser.: No. 3). (Illus.). 32p. (Orig.). (J). (gr. k-5). 1984. pap. 1.95 (0-913379-02-6) Double M Pub.

Snowsong Whistling. Karen E. Lotz. LC 92-47117. (Illus.). 32p. (J). (ps-2). 1993. pap. 14.99 (0-525-45145-5) Dutton Child Bks.

Snowstorm. Richard Scarry. (J). 1995. 3.25 (0-689-80368-0); pap. 2.95 (0-689-80746-5) S&S Childrens.

Snowstorm Surprise. Golden Books Staff. (Little Golden Bks.). (Illus.). 24p. (J). (ps-2). 1995. 1.49 (0-307-30212-1, Golden Pr) Western Pub.

Snowthrower Service Manual. Intertec Publishing Staff. (Orig.). 1990. pap. 24.95 (0-87288-409-0, SSM-3) Intertec Pub.

Snowtime. Dave Saunders & Julie Saunders. LC 90-42565. (Illus.). 32p. (J). (ps-1). 1991. lib. bdg. 14.95 (0-02-781075-5, Bradbury S&S) S&S Childrens.

***Snowy.** Berlie Doherty & Keith Bowen. 32p. (J). 4.98 (0-8317-4559-2) Smithmark.

Snowy. Sheila Lavelle. 32p. (J). Date not set. write for info. (0-19-279909-6) OUP.

Snowy Day. Ezra J. Keats. (Illus.). 15p. (J). (ps). 1996. pap. 6.99 (0-670-86733-0) Viking Child Bks.

Snowy Day. Ezra J. Keats. (J). Date not set. pap. 1.95 (0-590-03031-0) Scholastic Inc.

Snowy Day. Ezra J. Keats. (SPA.). (J). (ps-3). 1993. pap. 19.95 (0-590-72632-3) Scholastic Inc.

Snowy Day. Ezra Jack Keats. (J). (ps-3). 1993. pap. 19.95 (0-590-73323-0) Scholastic Inc.

Snowy Day. Ezra Jack Keats. (Picture Puffins Ser.). (Illus.). (J). (ps). 1976. pap. 4.99 (0-14-050182-7, Puffin) Puffin Bks.

Snowy Day. Ezra Jack Keats. LC 62-15441. (Illus.). 40p. (J). (ps-1). 1962. pap. 14.99 (0-670-65400-0) Viking Child Bks.

Snowy Day: Stories & Poems. Ed. by Caroline Feller Bauer. LC 85-45858. (Illus.). 80p. (J). (gr. 2-5). 1986. lib. bdg. 14.89 (0-397-32177-5, Lipp Jr Bks) HarpC Child Bks.

***Snowy Day: Stories & Poems.** Margot Tomes. Ed. by Caroline Feller Bauer. (Illus.). (J). (gr. 2-5). 14.89 (0-397-32176-7, 097259, Lipp Jr Bks) HarpC Child Bks.

***Snowy Days: With Antique Changing Pictures.** Piggytoes Press Staff. (Ernest Nister's Mini Christmas Books Ser.). 1997. 4.95 (1-888443-35-9, Piggytoes Pr) Intervisual Bks.

Snowy Days Activity & Game Book. Elvira Gamiello. (Illus.). (Orig.). (J). (gr. 4-6). 1989. pap. 1.95 (0-942025-36-9) Kidsbks.

Snowy Days & Sunny Days. Marjorie Stith. Ed. by Karen Gross. (Illus.). 24p. (Orig.). (J). 1993. pap. text ed. 6.95 (1-56309-094-5, New Hope) Womans Mission Union.

Snowy Earth Comes Gliding. Evelyn Eaton. 1974. pap. 5.95 (0-943404-02-9) Bear Tribe.

Snowy Owls. Wendy Pfeffer. LC 96-16961. (Creatures in White Ser.). (J). 1996. pap. 5.95 (0-382-39322-8, Silver Pr NJ) Silver Burdett Pr.

Snowy Owls. Wendy Pfeffer. LC 96-16961. (Creatures in White Ser.). (J). 1996. lib. bdg. 15.95 (0-382-39323-6, Silver Pr NJ) Silver Burdett Pr.

Snowy Owls & Battered Bulbuls. Richard Brigham. (Illus.). 128p. 1996. 29.95 (1-873580-27-4, Pub. by Whittet Bks UK) Diamond Farm Bk.

Snowy Path: A Christmas Journey. Lark Carrier. LC 89-8449. (Illus.). 28p. (J). (ps up). 1991. pap. 15.95 (0-88708-121-5, Picture Book Studio) S&S Childrens.

Snowy Range Gang. Mike Blakely. 1996. mass mkt. 4.99 (0-8125-6357-3) Forge NYC.

Snowy Range Gang. Mike Blakely. LC 91-43639. 192p. 1992. 16.95 (0-87131-670-6) M Evans.

***Snowy Ride.** Lee Davis. LC 97-10701. (P. B. Bear Ser.). (J). 1997. write for info. (0-7894-1414-7) DK Pub Inc.

Snowy Road & Other Stories: An Anthology of Korean Fiction. Tr. by Hyunjae Y. Sallee. 1992. pap. 12.00 (1-877727-19-9) White Pine.

***Snowy, the Story of a Reluctant Snowflake.** large type ed. Phil Cisneros. (Illus.). 22p. (Orig.). (J). (gr. k-4). 1993. pap. 8.00 (0-9651804-0-9, 101) New Horizons Unlimited.

Snowy Torrents: Avalanche Accidents in the United States, 1972-1979. 3rd ed. Knox Williams & Betsy Armstrong. (Illus.). 221p. 1984. pap. 14.95 (0-933160-13-5) Teton Bkshop.

SNT-TC-1A Questions & Answers: Inquiries to & Responses from ASNT's SNT-TC-1A Interpretation Panel. American Society for Nondestructive Testing (ASNT) Staff. 11p. (Orig.). 1991. pap. 18.75 (0-931403-76-6, 2040) Am Soc Nondestructive.

Snubber Design Applications & Minimization Methods: Presented at the Joint Conference of the Pressure Vessels & Piping, Materials, Nuclear Engineering, Solar Energy Divisions, Denver, Colorado, June 21-25, 1981. Joint Conference of the Pressure Vessels & Piping, Materials, Nuclear Engineering, Solar Energy Divisions Staff. Ed. by Floyd Fredrickson. LC 81-65620. (PVP Ser.: Vol. 55). (Illus.). 81p. reprint ed. pap. 25.00 (0-8357-2841-2, 2039076) Bks Demand.

Snuff. Ursula Bourne. 1989. pap. 25.00 (0-7478-0089-8, Pub. by Shire UK) St Mut.

Snuff. Kirby Farrell. 232p. 1991. 19.95 (0-8027-5782-0) Walker & Co.

Snuff Bottles from China. Helen White. (Illus.). 292p. 1990. 450.00 (1-870076-10-9, Pub. by Bamboo Pub UK) Antique Collect.

Snuff Bottles in the National Palace Museum. (Illus.). 382p. 1991. 85.00 (957-562-060-7) Heian Intl.

Snuffed Out. Myron M. Streeter. 1969. 14.95 (0-318-19129-6) SWAC Pr.

Snuffles. Joan Anson-Weber. LC 94-38154. (Illus.). 32p. (J). (ps-7). 1994. 14.95 (0-87797-262-1) Cherokee.

Snuffles & Snouts. Illus. by Steven Kellogg. LC 94-9209. 40p. (J). (gr. k-4). 1995. pap. 14.99 (0-8037-1597-8) Dial Bks Young.

Snuffles & Snouts. Illus. by Steven Kellogg. LC 94-9209. 40p. (J). (gr. k-4). 1995. pap. 14.89 (0-8037-1598-6) Dial Bks Young.

Snuffles Makes a Friend. Mary L. Donovan. LC 95-10693. (Gund Children's Library). (Illus.). (J). (ps up). 1995. 9.99 (1-56402-497-0) Candlewick Pr.

Snuffles Makes a Friend. Mary L. Donovan. LC 95-10693. (Gund Children's Library). (Illus.). 32p. (J). (ps up). 1997. reprint ed. pap. 3.99 (0-7636-0096-2) Candlewick Pr.

Snuffling Hedgehog. Jean T. Fredeking. (J). 1987. pap. 20.00 (0-317-59264-5, Pub. by A H S Ltd UK) St Mut.

Snuffs & Butters. Ellen N. La Motte. LC 74-125226. (Short Story Index Reprint Ser.). 1977. 19.95 (0-8369-3593-4) Ayer.

Snuffy. Barbara A. Hench. (J). 1994. 7.95 (0-533-10603-6) Vantage.

Snug. Hanson. LC 96-44996. (J). 1998. 16.00 (0-689-81164-0) S&S Childrens.

Snug Bug. Cathy E. Dubowski & Mark Dubowski. LC 94-22489. (All Aboard Reading Ser.). 32p. (J). (ps-1). 1995. pap. 3.95 (0-448-40849-X, G&D) Putnam Pub Group.

***Snug Bugs Play Day.** Cathy E. Dubowski. LC 97-8290. (J). 1997. pap. 3.95 (0-448-41623-9) Putnam Pub Group.

***Snug Bug's Play Day.** Cathy E. Dubowski. LC 97-8290. (All Aboard Reading Ser.). (Illus.). (J). 1997. write for info. (0-448-41642-5, G&D) Putnam Pub Group.

Snug Harbor. Richard Katrovas. LC 84-20851. (Wesleyan Poetry Ser.). 87p. 1986. pap. 11.95 (0-8195-6125-8, Wesleyan Univ Pr); text ed. 25.00 (0-8195-5134-1, Wesleyan Univ Pr) U Pr of New Eng.

Snug House, Bug House. Susan Schade & Jon Buller. LC 93-34058. (Bright & Early Bks.). (Illus.). 48p. (J). (ps-1). 1994. 7.99 (0-679-85300-6); lib. bdg. 11.99 (0-679-95300-0) Random Bks Yng Read.

Snug in Their Mouldy Cells: University Life in Eighteenth-Century Oxford. Graham Midgley. LC 96-19288. 1996. 30.00 (0-300-06813-1) Yale U Pr.

Snug Little Purchase: How Richard Henderson Bought Kaintuckee from the Cherokees in 1775. Charles Brashers. LC 78-74150. (Illus.). 1979. 7.95 (0-933362-01-3) Assoc Creative Writers.

Snuggle Up: A Gift of Songs for Sweet Dreams. Ed. by J. Aaron Brown. (Illus.). 8p. (J). (ps). 1992. 12.95 incl. audio (0-927945-06-1) Someday Baby.

Snuggle Up: A Gift of Songs for Sweet Dreams. Ed. by J. Aaron Brown. (Illus.). 8p. (J). (ps). 1995. 15.95 incl. cd-rom (0-927945-11-8) Someday Baby.

Snuggle Up with Winnie the Pooh. (Squeeze Me Ser.). (J). 1996. 6.98 (1-57082-389-8) Mouse Works.

***Snurps.** Steitz. Date not set. 1.20 (0-7167-9279-6) W H Freeman.

Snyder & Slinn: International Law of Development - Comparative Perspectives. Ed. by Francis G. Snyder & Peter Slinn. 1987. pap. 42.00 (0-86205-240-8) MICHIE.

***Snyder County Marriages, 1835-1899, with Index of Surnames.** Compiled by George W. Wagenseller. (Illus.). 266p. 1997. reprint ed. pap. 27.50 (0-8328-6453-6) Higginson Bk Co.

Snyders Mounds & Five Other Mound Groups in Calhoun County, Illinois. David P. Braun et al. LC 82-622498. (University of Michigan, Museum of Anthropology, Anthropological Papers: No. 8). 192p. reprint ed. pap. 54.80 (0-685-15334-7, 2026235) Bks Demand.

So-- You Want to Be a Travel Agent: An Introduction to Domestic Travel. Douglas A. Payette. LC 94-33705. 224p. 1994. pap. text ed. 44.00 (0-13-326000-3) P-H.

So--You Want to Be an Innkeeper. 3rd ed. Mary E. Davies et al. LC 95-37028. 240p. 1996. pap. 14.95 (0-8118-1226-X) Chronicle Bks.

***So All Is Not Lost: The Poetics of Print in Nuevomexicano Communities, 1834-1958.** A. Gabriel Melendez. LC 97-4583. (Paso por Aqui Ser.). 1997. 50.00 (0-8263-1776-6); pap. 24.95 (0-8263-1806-1) U of NM Pr.

***So Amazing, So Divine: A Guide to Living Prayer.** Isaac Watts. LC 97-21466. Orig. Title: A Guide to Prayer. 210p. (Orig.). 1997. pap. 10.95 (1-55725-182-7) Paraclete MA.

So Away I Went! William B. Stout. Ed. by James B. Gilbert. LC 79-7299. (Flight: Its First Seventy-Five Years Ser.). (Illus.). 1980. reprint ed. lib. bdg. 35.95 (0-405-12205-5) Ayer.

So Beautiful De Swatches. Marva Cooper. 48p. (Orig.). 1991. pap. 6.95 (1-56411-011-7) Untd Bros & Sis.

So Beloved Cousins: The Life & Times of Solon B. Cousins, Jr. Joseph E. Nettles. LC 82-23986. x, 178p. 1983. 12.95 (0-86554-070-5, MUP/H053) Mercer Univ Pr.

So Bewirbt Man Sich. Wolfgang Manekeller. 160p. (GER.). 1980. pap. 8.95 (3-581-66255-8) Langenscheidt.

So Big. Christopher Carrie. (Crayola Crayons Ser.). (Illus.). 32p. (J). 1988. 2.70 (0-86696-205-0) Binney & Smith.

So Big. Edna Ferber. 1976. 23.95 (0-8488-0799-5) Amereon Ltd.

So Big. Edna Ferber. (Prairie State Bks.). 232p. 1995. 14.95 (0-252-06376-7) U of Ill Pr.

So Big. Edna Ferber. 1992. reprint ed. lib. bdg. 29.95 (0-89968-280-4, Lghtyr Pr) Buccaneer Bks.

So Blow Ye Winds: A Diary of Oscar Rice. Ed. by Lois R. McWilliams. (Illus.). 85p. (Orig.). 1990. pap. 9.95 (0-9625505-1-5) SOS Pubns NJ.

S

So-Called Dollars. E. Kenney. 1984. reprint ed. pap. 6.00 (*0-942666-26-7*) S J Durst.

So-Called Peleus & Thetis Sarcophagus in the Villa Albani. Frank G. Muller. (Iconological Studies in Roman Art: Vol. 1). (Illus.). xii, 208p. 1994. lib. bdg. 57.00 (*90-5063-246-7*, Pub. by Gieben NE) Benjamins North Am.

So Circles the Eagle: The Bold Adventures of Jedediah Smith & His Love for a Native American Woman, an American Saga. Erin King. LC 91-61885. (Illus.). 343p. (Orig.). 1992. pap. 19.95 (*0-945437-09-9*) MacDonald-Sward.

So Close. Nancy Adams & Patricia Carter. 80p. (Orig.). 1996. pap. 10.00 (*0-932616-55-0*, NPS100) Brick Hse Bks.

So Close & No Closer. Penny Jordan. (Presents Ser.: No. 1353). 1991. pap. 2.75 (*0-373-11353-6*) Harlequin Bks.

So Close to Heaven: The Vanishing Buddhist Kingdoms of the Himalayas. Barbara Crossette. (Illus.). 297p. 1995. 25.00 (*0-615-00757-0*) Knopf.

So Close to Heaven: The Vanishing Buddhist Kingdoms of the Himalayas. Barbara Crossette. 1996. pap. 13.00 (*0-679-74363-4*) Random.

So Comes Tomorrow. Essie Summers. 224p. 1996. 22.00 (*0-7278-4882-8*) Severn Hse.

***So Comes Tomorrow.** large type ed. Essie Summers. (Ulverscroft Large Print Ser.). 336p. 1997. 27.50 (*0-7089-3800-0*) Ulverscroft.

So Cranes May Dance: A Rescue from the Brink of Extinction. Barbara Katz. LC 92-44904. (Illus.). 300p. 1993. 19.95 (*1-55652-171-5*) Chicago Review.

***So Dark a Shadow.** large type ed. Freda Hurt. (Linford Mystery Library). 320p. 1996. pap. 15.99 (*0-7089-7935-1*) Ulverscroft.

So Dear to Their Hearts. large type ed. Lilian Woodward. 1989. 25.99 (*0-7089-2115-9*) Ulverscroft.

So Dear to Wicked Men, Vol. 1. Takis Iakovou. 320p. 1996. 22.95 (*0-312-14740-6*) Thomas Dunne Bks.

So Deep, So Wide, So High see **Hewitt Early Readers: Level II**

So Doth, So Is Religion: John Donne & Diplomatic Contexts in the Reformed Netherlands, 1619-1620. Paul R. Sellin. LC 87-19124. (Illus.). 312p. 1988. text ed. 37.50 (*0-8262-0666-2*) U of Mo Pr.

So ein Dackel! Bildband. Ed. by I. Schuessler & R. Tzschoppe. (Illus.). 49p. (GER.). (C). 1972. pap. text ed. 13.75 (*3-12-558600-3*, Pub. by Klett Edition GW) Intl Bk Import.

So Far. Kelsey Grammar. (Illus.). 320p. 1995. pap. 22.95 (*0-525-94041-3*, Dutton) NAL-Dutton.

So Far... Kelsey Grammer. 1996. pap. 6.99 (*0-451-18605-2*, Sig) NAL-Dutton.

So Far. Kelsey Grammer. 1999. pap. 17.95 (*0-7871-0742-5*, Dove Bks) Dove Audio.

So Far. Kelsey Grammer. 1995. pap. 22.95 (*0-670-86671-7*) Viking Penguin.

So Far. Fred Wah. 112p. 1991. pap. 10.95 (*0-88922-290-8*) SPD-Small Pr Dist.

So Far. deluxe ed. Cid Corman. 1973. 6.00 (*0-685-36864-5*); 8.00 (*0-685-36865-3*) Elizabeth Pr.

So Far: The Autobiography of Meyer Weisgal 1894-1977. Meyer Weisgal. (Illus.). 404p. 1978. 34.95 (*0-394-47594-1*) Transaction Pubs.

***So Far from Bamboo Grove.** Yoko K. Watkins. Date not set. lib. bdg. write for info. (*0-688-06111-7*) Lothrop.

So Far from God: A Novel. Ana Castillo. LC 93-45382. 258p. 1994. pap. 11.95 (*0-452-27209-2*, Plume) NAL-Dutton.

So Far from God: A Novel. Ana Castillo. LC 92-34362. 256p. 1993. 19.95 (*0-393-03490-9*) Norton.

So Far from God: The U. S. War with Mexico, 1846-1848. John D. Eisenhower. 464p. 1990. pap. 14.95 (*0-385-41214-2*, Anchor NY) Doubleday.

So Far from God: The U. S. War with Mexico, 1846-48. John S. Eisenhower. LC 88-42675. (Illus.). 704p. 1989. 24.95 (*0-394-56051-5*) Random.

So Far from Heaven: David Alfaro Siqueiros' The March of Humanity & Mexican Revolutionary Politics. Leonard Folgarait. (Cambridge Iberian & Latin American Studies). (Illus.). 185p. 1987. text ed. 57.95 (*0-521-33061-0*) Cambridge U Pr.

So Far from Home. James Mitchell. 480p. 1996. pap. 10.95 (*0-7472-4881-8*, Pub. by Headline UK) Trafalgar.

***So Far from Home.** large type ed. James Mitchell. (Charnwood Large Print Ser.). 512p. 1997. 29.50 (*0-7089-8896-2*, Charnwood) Ulverscroft.

So Far from Home: An Army Bride on the Western Frontier, 1865-69. Julia S. Gilliss. Ed. by Priscilla Knuth. (Illus.). 360p. 1993. pap. 14.95 (*0-87595-135-X*) Oregon Hist.

***So Far from Home: Manila's Santo Tomas Internment Camp, 1942-1945.** Bruce E. Johansen. LC 96-70185. (Illus.). 224p. (Orig.). 1997. pap. 16.00 (*1-57579-037-8*) Pine Hill Pr.

***So Far from Home: The Diary of Mary Driscoll, an Irish Mill Girl.** Barry Denenberg. LC 97-5846. (Dear America Ser.). (J). 1997. write for info. (*0-590-92667-5*) Scholastic Inc.

So Far from Spring: A Novel of the American West. Peggy S. Curry. LC 83-21179. 356p. 1993. pap. 16.95 (*0-87108-840-1*) Pruett.

So Far From the Bamboo Grove. Yoko K. Watkins. 1995. 18.75 (*0-8446-6810-9*) Peter Smith.

So Far From the Bamboo Grove. Yoko K. Watkins. (J). (gr. 5-9). reprint ed. pap. 3.95 (*0-317-62272-2*, Puffin) Puffin Bks.

So Far From the Bamboo Grove. Yoko K. Watkins. (Illus.). 192p. (YA). (gr. 5 up). 1994. reprint ed. pap. 4.95 (*0-688-13115-8*) Morrow.

So Far from the Bamboo Grove: A Study Guide. Mary Quinn. Ed. by J. Friedland & R. Kessler. (Novel-Ties Ser.). (YA). (gr. 6-10). 1996. pap. text ed. 15.95 (*1-56982-654-4*) Lrn Links.

***So Far Gone.** Cody. Date not set. write for info. (*0-312-18180-9*) St Martin.

***So Far, So Good!** Grampa Gray. 48p. (Orig.). 1996. pap. 7.50 (*1-885631-22-7*, 22-7) G F Hutchison.

So Far, So Good. Gil Scott-Heron. 1990. 8.00 (*0-88378-133-6*) Third World.

So Far, So Good: A Memoir. Burgess Meredith. 1994. 22.95 (*0-316-56717-5*) Little.

***So Far So Good: Roy R. Neuberger - An Autobiography.** Roy R. Neuberger. LC 97-14193. 224p. 1997. 29.95 (*0-471-17186-7*) Wiley.

So Far, So Good: The Autobiography. Paul Eddington. (Illus.). 256p. 1996. 35.00 (*0-340-63837-0*, Pub. by H & S UK) Trafalgar.

So Far, So Good, So What? Women's Studies in the U. K. Ed. by Renate Duelli-Klein. 100p. 1984. pap. 19.25 (*0-08-030816-3*, Pergamon Pr) Elsevier.

So Fat, Low Fat, No Fat. Betty Rohde. 94p. 1993. 9.00 (*0-9637239-0-1*) Be Ro Pub.

***So Fat, Low Fat, No Fat.** Betty Rohde. 144p. 1995. pap. 12.00 (*0-671-89813-2*, Fireside) S&S Trade.

So Favored by Grace: Education in the Time of John Baptist de La Salle. Ed. by Lawrence Colhocker. LC 90-62775. (Illus.). 193p. 1990. pap. 15.00 (*0-944808-06-9*) Lasallian Pubns.

So Fine a Prospect: Historic New England Gardens. Alan Emmet. LC 95-36320. (Illus.). 256p. 1996. 49.95 (*0-87451-749-4*) U Pr of New Eng.

***So Fine a Prospect: Historic New England Gardens.** Alan Emmet. LC 95-36320. (Illus.). 256p. 1996. pap. 29.95 (*0-87451-774-5*) U Pr of New Eng.

So Forth: Poems. Joseph Brodsky. 132p. 1996. 18.00 (*0-374-26641-7*) FS&G.

***So Fruitful a Fish: Ecology, Conservation & Aquaculture of the Amazon's Tambaqui.** Carlos Araujo-Lima & Michael Goulding. LC 96-45658. (Biology & Resource Management in the Tropics Ser.). 1997. write for info. (*0-231-10830-3*) Col U Pr.

So Gifted Education. Spicker. (C). 1997. pap. text ed. write for info. (*0-8013-0225-0*) Addison-Wesley.

So Glad to Know You. Jubilee Staff. 40p. 1996. pap. 15.00 (*1-884920-04-7*) Jubilee Christian Ctr.

So Go on & Sing: Celebrating Faith in the Carolinas. Ken Garfield. 192p. (Orig.). 1994. pap. 12.95 (*1-880837-63-3*) Smyth & Helwys.

So Going Around Cities: New & Selected Poems, 1958-1979. deluxe limited ed. Ted Berrigan. LC 80-10185. (Selected Works Ser.: No. 4). (Illus.). 1980. boxed 150.00 (*0-912652-63-2*) Blue Wind.

So Good. Venise Berry. LC 95-53068. 256p. 1996. pap. 21.95 (*0-525-93885-0*, Dutton) NAL-Dutton.

So Good a Cause: A Decade of Southern Partisan. Ed. by Oran P. Smith. 376p. 1993. 29.95 (*0-9623842-5-9*) Fndtn Amer Ed.

So Great a Cloud of Witnesses. David O. Rankin. LC 78-2584. (Illus.). 208p. (Orig.). 1978. pap. 6.95 (*0-89407-014-2*) Strawberry Hill.

So Great an Honor: On Becoming a Baha'i. National Spiritual Assembly of the Baha'is of the United States Staff. 81p. 1995. pap. 4.95 (*0-87743-248-1*) Bahai.

So Great Salvation. Charles G. Finney. LC 65-25844. (Charles G. Finney Memorial Library). 128p. 1975. pap. 6.99 (*0-8254-2621-9*) Kregel.

So Great Salvation. Charles C. Ryrie. 168p. 1990. pap. 9.99 (*0-89693-127-7*, 6-1127, Victor Bks) Chariot Victor.

So Great Salvation: Understanding God's Redemptive Plan. John F. Strombeck. LC 91-39322. 160p. 1992. pap. 8.99 (*0-8254-3780-6*) Kregel.

***So Great Salvation: What It Means to Believe in Jesus Christ.** Charles C. Ryrie. 155p. 1997. pap. 11.99 (*0-8024-7818-2*) Moody.

So Grows the Willow. Sylvia L. Leong. (Orig.). 1996. pap. 11.95 (*0-533-11628-7*) Vantage.

***So Hakase No Kampoh: Dr. Tsung's Chinese Medicine.** unabridged ed. Pi-Kwang Tsung. 116p. (Orig.). (JPN.). 1996. pap. 14.95 (*0-9655166-0-1*) Am Inst Chinese Herbs.

So Happy/So Sad. Julie Paschkis. LC 94-41654. 32p. (J). (ps-1). 1995. 12.95 (*0-8050-3862-0*) H Holt & Co.

So Hard the Stones: Lucy Poate Stebbins & Her Life in Literature. Richard P. Stebbins. LC 91-40081. (American University Studies: History: Ser. IX, Vols. 110). 350p. (C). 1992. text ed. 52.95 (*0-8204-1597-9*) P Lang Pubng.

***So Hard to Forget.** Evelyn A. Crowe. 1997. mass mkt. 3.99 (*0-373-70745-2*, 1-70745-4) Harlequin Bks.

So Have I Heard: Iti Maya Srutam. Axel Fredenholm. Tr. by Thord Fredenholm from SWE. LC 89-62537. 112p. (Orig.). 1989. pap. 7.00 (*1-878398-00-8*) Blue Note Pubns.

***So He Says.** Larry Woiwode. 1998. pap. 24.95 (*0-670-87398-5*) Viking Penguin.

So Help Me God: The U. S. Presidents in Perspective. Daniel E. White. LC 96-23829. (Illus.). 161p. (Orig.). 1996. 16.95 (*1-56072-334-3*) Nova Sci Pubs.

***So Help Me God: The U. S. Presidents in Perspective.** Daniel E. White. 217p. 1996. lib. bdg. 39.00 (*1-56072-376-9*) Nova Sci Pubs.

So Here I Am! But Where Did I Come From? An Adoptee's Search for Identity. Mary R. Wotherspoon. LC 93-85595. (Illus.). 206p. 1994. 19.95 (*0-9638488-0-1*) Pate Pubng.

At age 50, once her adoptive parents had died, the author started a search for her natural parents & her heritage. With the help of a private detective, a genealogist, her daughter, a psychic & kind individuals, she found two sisters & a brother. She discovered a town full of people with the same name & a newfound compassion when her first husband was critically ill. SO HERE I AM! BUT WHERE DID I COME FROM? is about the irrepressible 10-year search for identity that time, obstacles & bureaucracies couldn't defeat. Hear the author tell in her own words the joy of seeing her birth mother's photograph for the first time. It's the story of linking families, the old, the new & the children yet to come. For anyone who has wanted to know more about themselves but didn't have the courage to explore, this book describes the rewards that come with each revelation. SO HERE I AM! BUT WHERE DID I COME FROM? contains a list of sources to help adoptees streamline their search. $19.95 (USA); $25.50 (Can). Mary Ruth Wotherspoon is an oil & pastel portrait artist. She resides with her husband in Sante Fe, New Mexico. Book available through Pate Publishing, 20247 Kelly Rd., Detroit, MI 48225. Phone: 313-521-3300, FAX: 313-521-0760. $19.95 plus postage & handling charge, $3.50. ***Publisher Provided Annotation.***

So Human a Brain: Knowledge & Values in the Neurosciences. Ed. by A. Harrington. (Illus.). 355p. 1992. 98.00 (*0-8176-3540-8*) Spr-Verlag.

***So Humble the Heart.** John R. McKinney. 160p. (Orig.). 1997. pap. 12.95 (*0-9656192-0-6*) Humble Heart.

So Hungry! Harriet Ziefert. LC 87-4763. (Step into Reading Bks.). (Illus.). 32p. (J). (ps-1). 1987. pap. 3.99 (*0-394-89127-9*) Random Bks Yng Read.

So I Can Read. Dandi D. Mackall. (J). (ps-3). 1993. pap. 4.99 (*0-8066-2686-0*, Augsburg) Augsburg Fortress.

So I Said to the Little Old Man. Joseph Neri. Ed. by Kristen Edwards. (Illus.). 96p. (Orig.). (J). (gr. k-6). 1994. pap. 12.95 (*0-9639428-3-2*); lib. bdg. 14.99 (*0-9639428-1-6*) Tympanon Prods.

So I Shall Tell You a Story: The Magic World of Beatrix Potter. Ed. by Judy Taylor. (Illus.). 224p. (J). 1993. pap. 24.95 (*0-7232-4025-6*) Warne.

So Idle a Rogue: The Life & Death of Lord Rochester. Jeremy Lamb. (Illus.). 336p. 1995. 21.95 (*0-7490-0291-3*, Pub. by A & B UK) London Brdge.

So I'm Not Perfect: A Psychology of Humility. Robert J. Furey. LC 86-3301. 143p. (Orig.). 1986. pap. 6.95 (*0-8189-0499-2*) Alba.

***So in the Meantime, 3 vols.** Katherine E. Anderson. Incl. What Do I Do?: Patient's Guide. large type ed. (Illus.). 100p. (Orig.). 1997. spiral bd., pap. 12.95 (*1-57876-925-6*); How Do I Help?: Caregiver's Guide. large type ed. (Illus.). 100p. (Orig.). 1997. spiral bd., pap. 12.95 (*1-57876-927-2*); What Do I Tell Them?: Doctor's Guide. (Illus.). 100p. (Orig.). 1997. spiral bd., pap. 12.95 (*1-57876-928-0*); 32.95 (*1-57876-929-9*) Triple U Prods.

***So In the Meantime, What Do I Do? Patient Guide.** large type ed. Katherine E. Anderson. (Illus.). 150p. (Orig.). 1997. spiral bd., pap. 15.95 (*1-57876-926-4*) Triple U Prods.

So Incredibly Idaho! Seven Landscapes That Define the Gem State. Carlos A. Schwantes. LC 95-26340. (Illus.). 141p. 1996. 49.95 (*0-89301-193-2*) U of Idaho Pr.

So Ist Es! 2nd ed. Kimberly Sparks et al. (Illus.). 134p. (GER.). (C). 1983. pap. text ed. 18.75 (*0-15-582390-6*) HB Coll Pubs.

So It Goes. Eamon Grennan. LC 95-77950. 88p. (Orig.). 1995. pap. 14.00 (*1-55597-232-2*) Graywolf.

So It Is: In the Image of God He Created Them (Poems) Aminta Marks. LC 90-82231. (Illus.). 179p. (Orig.). 1990. pap. 12.00 (*0-9626898-0-7*) Grindstone Pr.

So Late into the Night: Eighteen Fifteen to Eighteen Eighteen see **Byron's Letters & Journals**

So Laudable an Undertaking: The Wilmington Library, 1788-1988. Claudia L. Bushman. LC 88-51846. (Illus.). 150p. (Orig.). 1989. pap. 7.95 (*0-924117-00-1*) Delaware HP.

So Like Sleep. Jeremiah Healy. 1991. mass mkt. 4.50 (*0-671-74328-7*) PB.

So Little Done: The Testament of a Serial Killer. Theodore Dalrymple. 144p. 1996. 17.95 (*0-233-98959-5*, Pub. by A Deutsch UK) Trafalgar.

So Little Time. Doreen Roberts. (Intimate Moments Ser.). 1995. mass mkt. 3.75 (*0-373-07653-3*, 1-07653-8) Silhouette.

So Little to Die For. Lucretia Grindle. Ed. by Dana Issacson. 256p. (Orig.). 1994. mass mkt. 4.99 (*0-671-74846-7*) PB.

So Long: Stories 1987-1992. Lucia Berlin. LC 93-6659. 214p. (Orig.). (C). 1993. 25.00 (*0-87685-894-9*); pap. 13.00 (*0-87685-893-0*) Black Sparrow.

So Long: Stories 1987-1992, signed ed. deluxe ed. Lucia Berlin. LC 93-6659. 214p. (Orig.). (C). 1993. 30.00 (*0-87685-895-7*) Black Sparrow.

So Long a Letter. Mariama Ba. Tr. by Modupe' Bode'-Thomas from FRE. (African Writers Ser.). 96p. (Orig.). (C). 1989. pap. 8.95 (*0-435-90555-4*, 90555) Heinemann.

So Long & Thanks for All the Fish. Douglas Adams. 1985. mass mkt. 5.99 (*0-671-74553-0*) PB.

So Long & Thanks for All the Fish. Douglas Adams. 1998. pap. write for info. (*0-345-39183-7*) Ballantine.

So Long at the Fair. Hadley Irwin. 160p. 1990. pap. 2.95 (*0-380-70858-2*, Flare) Avon.

So Long at the Fair. Hadley Irwin. LC 88-12813. 208p. (YA). (gr. 9 up). 1988. lib. bdg. 16.00 (*0-689-50454-3*, McElderry) S&S Childrens.

So Long, Cowboys of the Open Range. Truman M. Cheney & Roberta C. Cheney. LC 90-91858. (Illus.). 143p. (Orig.). 1990. pap. 9.95 (*1-56044-048-1*) Falcon Pr MT.

So Long, Farewell: From the Sound of Music. Richard Rodgers & Oscar Hammerstein. (Piano-Vocal-Guitar Ser.). 8p. 1981. 3.95 (*0-7935-0821-5*, 00305099) H Leonard.

So Long Partner. 1987. 4.95 (*0-317-55309-7*) United Elec R&M.

So Long, Scout, & Other Stories. Gerald E. Lewis. LC 87-7104. (Illus.). 161p. (Orig.). 1988. pap. 9.95 (*0-945432-00-3*) Nrth Country Pr.

So Long, See You Tomorrow. William Maxwell. 160p. 1996. pap. 10.00 (*0-679-76720-7*) Random.

So Long the Night. LaJoyce Martin. LC 94-48229. 196p. (Orig.). (YA). 1995. pap. 7.99 (*1-56722-032-0*) Word Aflame.

So Loud a Silence. Lyll De Jenkins. 160p. (YA). (gr. 7 up). 1996. pap. 16.99 (*0-525-67538-8*) NAL-Dutton.

***So Love Me Now.** Oukah. 74p. (Orig.). 1989. pap. 7.95 (*1-890174-00-9*) Triskelion Pr.

So Many Bridges. large type ed. Contrib. by Ned Peggy. 1994. 25.99 (*0-7089-3209-6*) Ulverscroft.

***So Many Candles, So Little Cake.** Illus. by Jenny Faw. (Charming Petites Ser.). 80p. 1997. 4.95 (*0-88088-811-3*) Peter Pauper.

So Many Cats. Beatrice S. De Regniers. LC 85-3739. (Illus.). 32p. (J). (ps-3). 1988. pap. 6.95 (*0-89919-700-0*, Clarion Bks) HM.

***So Many Circles, So Many Squares.** Tana Hoban. LC 97-10110. 32p. (J). (ps up). 1998. 15.00 (*0-688-15165-5*); lib. bdg. 14.93 (*0-688-15166-3*) Greenwillow.

So Many Crossroads. Alannah Van Boven. LC 87-72493. 1990. 11.95 (*0-8158-0443-1*) Chris Mass.

So Many Dynamos! And Other Palindromes. Jon Agee. (Illus.). 80p. (J). (ps up). 1994. 13.31 (*0-374-22473-0*) FS&G.

***So Many Dynamos! And Other Palindromes.** Jon Agee. (Illus.). 80p. 1997. pap. 6.96 (*0-374-46905-9*, Sunburst Bks) FS&G.

So Many Gifts. Anne M. Pierce. (Illus.). (J). (gr. k-6). 1992. audio 8.00 (*0-9623937-1-1*) Forword MN.

So Many Gifts. Anne M. Pierce. (Illus.). 32p. (J). (gr. k-6). 1993. reprint ed. 15.95 (*0-9623937-0-3*) Forword MN.

So Many Gifts, Miniature edition. Anne M. Pierce. (Illus.). 32p. (J). (gr. k-6). 1994. 7.95 (*0-9623937-2-X*) Forword MN.

So Many Heroes. rev. ed. Alan Levy. LC 80-65002. Orig. Title: Rowboat to Prague. 384p. 1980. reprint ed. pap. 16.00 (*0-933256-16-7*) Second Chance.

So Many Heroes. 2nd rev. ed. Alan Levy. LC 80-65002. Orig. Title: Rowboat to Prague. 384p. 1980. reprint ed. 22.00 (*0-933256-12-4*) Second Chance.

So Many Hungers! Bhabani Bhattacharya. 205p. 1978. pap. 2.95 (*0-86578-092-7*) Ind-US Inc.

So Many Mornings. 2nd ed. Yvonne F. Georg. 400p. 1995. 20.00 (*0-9648521-0-1*) DYG Inc.

So Many Pups. 6p. (J). 1996. 9.98 (*1-57082-421-5*) Mouse Works.

So Many Songs: Es Zog Manch Lied a Cappalla from in the World of Nature. Antonin Dvorak. 8p. 1986. pap. 1.25 (*0-7935-5505-1*, 50319370) H Leonard.

***So Many Sweet Flowers: A Seventeenth-Century Florilegium.** Illus. by Johann Walther. 104p. 1997. 27.50 (*1-85793-353-2*, Pub. by Pavilion UK) Trafalgar.

So Many Things to See. (Illus.). 1977. 0.50 (*0-685-57764-3*) Am Dental.

So Many Tomorrows. large type ed. Nancy John. (Romance Ser.). 400p. 1993. 25.99 (*0-7089-2899-4*) Ulverscroft.

So Many Worlds, Vol. 1. Magris. 1996. 60.00 (*0-8212-2324-0*) Little.

***So Many Worlds: Leroy Hill Invention, Management, Philosophy & Risk.** Craig Miner. LC 97-11191. (Illus.). 224p. 1997. 29.95 (*0-89672-380-1*) Tex Tech Univ Pr.

So Moses Was Born. Joan Grant. 312p. 1990. pap. 9.95 (*0-89804-149-X*) Ariel GA.

So Moses Was Born. Joan M. Grant. 1980. 23.95 (*0-405-11791-4*) Ayer.

So Mote It Be! Christian Bernard. 172p. (Orig.). 1995. pap. text ed. 12.95 (*0-9526420-0-X*, 510214) RO AMORC.

So Mote It Be. Robin L. Stratton. 1992. pap. 10.95 (*0-9626541-3-2*) Mockngbrd Square.

So, Mrs. Smith, You Say You're 35 & You Still Like to Play with Blocks: A Book of Quilting Blocks & Humor. John W. Shimp. (Illus.). 64p. (Orig.). 1991. pap. 17.95 (*1-879844-04-4*) Boyd Pub.

So Much. Trish Cooke. LC 94-13435. 32p. (J). (ps up). 1994. 16.99 (*1-56402-344-3*) Candlewick Pr.

***So Much.** Trish Cooke. LC 94-13435. (Illus.). 48p. (J). (ps-1). 1997. reprint ed. pap. 6.99 (*0-7636-0296-5*) Candlewick Pr.

So Much for Illusion. Deborah McClatchey. 150p. (Orig.). 1996. spiral bd. 6.95 (*1-888038-06-3*) Rubenesque.

So Much in Common. Laurie A. Jacobs. LC 92-73995. (Illus.). 32p. (J). (ps-3). 1994. 14.95 (*1-56397-115-1*) Boyds Mills Pr.

So Much More Than a Sing-a-Long: Music Activities for Group Leaders. Neta Wenrick. LC 94-70728. (Illus.). 150p. (C). 1995. pap. 16.95 (*0-943873-38-X*) Elder Bks.

So Much Sky. Jan W. Schulte Nordholt. (Illus.). 1994. pap. 10.00 (*0-8028-0831-X*) Eerdmans.

So Much to Be Done: Women Settlers on the Mining & Ranching Frontier. Ed. by Ruth B. Moynihan et al. LC 89-22549. (Women in the West Ser.). (Illus.). xxii, 326p. 1990. text ed. 40.00 (*0-8032-3134-2*) U of Nebr Pr.

An Asterisk (*) at the beginning of an entry indicates that the title is appearing in BIP for the first time.

So Much to Be Done: Women Settlers on the Mining & Ranching Frontier. Ed. by Ruth B. Moynihan et al. LC 89-22549. (Women in the West Ser.). (Illus.). xxii, 326p. 1990. pap. 13.95 (*0-8032-8165-X*, Bison Books) U of Nebr Pr.

So Much to Live For. Lurlene McDaniel. 160p. (J). (gr. 5-8). 1991. pap. 2.99 (*0-685-57448-2*) Willowisp Pr.

So Much to Live For. Lurlene McDaniel. 160p. (YA). 1996. mass mkt. 4.50 (*0-553-56763-2*) Bantam.

So Much to See, So Little Time: Travelling the U. S. A. Charles B. Ferguson. LC 96-90058. (Orig.). 1996. pap. 12.95 (*0-533-11868-9*) Vantage.

So Much to Tell You. John Marsden. 128p. (YA). (gr. 7 up). 1990. mass mkt. 5.50 (*0-449-70374-6*, Juniper) Fawcett.

So Near & Yet So Far: Rome, Canterbury & ARCIC. Hugh Montefiore. 160p. (C). 1986. pap. text ed. 11.95 (*0-334-01517-0*, SCM Pr) TPI PA.

So Noble a Captain: The Life & Times of Ferdinand Magellan. Charles M. Parr. LC 75-31439. (Illus.). 423p. 1975. reprint ed. text ed. 49.75 (*0-8371-8521-1*, PASN, Greenwood Pr) Greenwood.

So Now You Own a Food Processor. Dona Reynolds & Ricki Older. (Illus.). 285p. 1984. pap. text ed. 10.95 (*0-931955-00-9*) East-West Pub.

So-o You Are Going to the Hospital. Carol Zimet. (Illus.). 24p. 1993. pap. write for info. (*0-9639659-0-5*) C Zimet.

So-o You Are Going to the Hospital, Men's Version. Carol Zimet. (Illus.). 32p. 1994. pap. 8.00 (*0-8059-3651-3*) Dorrance.

So-o You Are Going to the Hospital, Women's Version. Carol Zimet. (Illus.). 32p. 1994. pap. 8.00 (*0-8059-3648-3*) Dorrance.

So Ordered: Making Partner the Hard Way. Ann B. Hopkins. LC 96-19645. 432p. (C). 1996. 34.95 (*1-55849-051-5*) U of Mass Pr.

So Proudly He Served: The Sam Bird Story. Ronald W. Reinhold et al. 412p. 24.95 (*0-9635542-4-7*); audio 29.95 (*0-9635542-7-1*) Okarche Bks.

So Reckless a Love. Eileen Winwood. 304p. (Orig.). 1995. mass mkt. 4.99 (*0-7865-0079-4*) Diamond.

So Red the Rose. Stark Young. LC 92-82381. (Southern Classics Ser.). 450p. 1992. reprint ed. pap. 11.95 (*1-879941-12-0*) J S Sanders.

So Rich a Tapestry: The Sister Arts & Cultural Studies. Ed. by Ann Hurley & Kate Greenspan. LC 94-35071. (Illus.). 408p. 1995. 57.50 (*0-8387-5282-9*) Bucknell U Pr.

So Say the Little Monkeys. Nancy Van Laan. LC 95-17360. (Illus.). (J). 1997. write for info. (*0-679-87784-3*, Apple Soup Bks); lib. bdg. write for info. (*0-679-97784-8*, Apple Soup Bks) Knopf Bks Yng Read.

So Say the Little Monkeys. Nancy Van Laan. (J). 1998. 16.00 (*0-689-81038-5*) S&S Childrens.

So schreibt man Briefe besser. Waltraud Freiberger & Brigitte B. Gschwind. 128p. (GER.). 1977. pap. 8.00 (*3-581-66301-5*) Langenscheidt.

So schreibt man Geschaeftsbriefe. Wolfgang Manekeller. 160p. (GER.). 1982. pap. 8.95 (*3-581-66229-9*) Langenscheidt.

So Send I You - Workmen of God. Oswald Chambers. 1993. pap. 10.95 (*0-87508-308-0*) Chr Lit.

So Send I You, &, Workmen of God: Recognizing & Answering God's Call to Service. Oswald Chambers. LC 93-395. 240p. 1993. pap. 10.99 (*0-929239-74-1*) Discovery Hse Pubs.

So Shall You Reap: Farming & Crops in Human Affairs. Otto T. Solbrig & Dorothy J. Solbrig. LC 93-43330. (Illus.). 304p. 1996. reprint ed. 29.95 (*1-55963-308-5*); reprint ed. pap. 16.95 (*1-55963-309-3*) Island Pr.

So Sick. Harriet Ziefert. LC 85-1957. (Step into Reading Bks.: Step 1). 32p. (J). (ps-1). 1985. pap. 3.99 (*0-394-87580-X*) Random Bks Yng Read.

So Simple So Good! Selma Raskin. 1989. write for info. (*0-938509-05-5*) Pretty Penny Pr.

So Simply Means the Rain. Ronald Moran. 1965. pap. 4.95 (*0-87511-086-X*); text ed. 6.95 (*0-87511-087-8*) Claitors.

So Sings the Blue Deer. Charmayne McGee. LC 93-26580. 160p. (J). (gr. 3-7). 1994. lib. bdg. 14.95 (*0-689-31888-X*, Atheneum Bks Young) S&S Childrens.

So Sleepy. Susan T. Hall. (Illus.). (J). (ps). 1989. pap. text ed. 5.95 (*0-927106-01-9*) Prod Concept.

***So Sleepy/Wide Awake.** Julie Paschkis. 1997. pap. text ed. 4.95 (*0-8050-5157-0*, Owlet BYR) H Holt & Co.

So Small a Pocket. Mary Plutchak. 68p. 1991. pap. 10.95 (*0-9630322-0-8*) Carrousel Pr.

So Soft Kitty. Hitz Demi. (Soft & Furry Board Bks.). (Illus.). 12p. (J). (ps). 1986. bds. 6.95 (*0-448-18986-0*, G&D) Putnam Pub Group.

So Soon Done For. Marian Babson. LC 88-23. 1988. 15.95 (*0-8027-5694-8*) Walker & Co.

So Speaks Higher Power. Isaac Shamaya. 72p. 1989. pap. 7.00 (*0-89540-179-7*, SB-179) Sun Pub.

So Speaks My Sea. Theta Burke. 80p. (Orig.). 1995. pap. 7.95 (*0-916872-10-6*) Delafield Pr.

***So Speaks the Heart.** Joyce Carlow. 304p. 1997. mass mkt. 4.99 (*0-8217-5785-7*, Zebra Kensgtn) Kensgtn Pub Corp.

So Speaks the Heart. Johanna Lindsey. 384p. 1983. mass mkt. 6.99 (*0-380-81471-4*) Avon.

So Speaks the Heart. large type ed. Johanna Lindsey. (Romance-Hall Ser.). 466p. 1996. 25.95 (*0-7838-1838-6*, Thorndike Lrg Prnt) Thorndike Pr.

So Spoke the Uncle. 2nd ed. Jean Price-Mars. Tr. by Magdaline W. Shannon from FRE. LC 82-74251. (Illus.). xxviii, 252p. 1990. pap. 15.00 (*0-89410-390-3*, Three Contnts) Lynne Rienner.

So Strange My Path: A Spiritual Pilgrimage. rev. ed. Abraham Carmel. LC 93-1282. 296p. 1993. pap. 9.95 (*0-8197-0040-1*) Bloch.

So Strong This Bond. Blanche Jefferson. 1995. pap. 11.95 (*0-935016-35-X*) Zinn Communs.

So Sue Me. Joe Kohut. 160p. (Orig.). 1993. pap. 7.95 (*0-9628362-2-2*) Black Tooth Pr.

So Sue Me! Cartoons on the Law. Sidney Harris. LC 93-9215. (Illus.). 150p. (C). 1993. pap. 9.95 (*0-8135-1964-0*) Rutgers U Pr.

So Sweet an Enemy. large type ed. Cora Mayne. 304p. 1996. 25.99 (*0-7089-3469-2*) Ulverscroft.

So Swift the Storm. LaJoyce Martin. LC 90-35201. (Illus.). 232p. (Orig.). 1990. pap. 7.99 (*0-932581-66-8*) Word Aflame.

So That His Death Will Have Not Been in Vain: The Sickel Cell Trait: A Serious Factor to Be Observed by the Military. Peggy D. Friend. LC 92-50578. 675p. (Orig.). 1994. pap. 19.95 (*0-936026-77-4*) R&M Pub Co.

So That Others May Live: Caroline Hebard & Her Search & Rescue Dogs. Hank Whittemore & Caroline Hebard. 336p. 1996. mass mkt. 5.99 (*0-553-57483-3*) Bantam.

So That Others May Live: The Caroline Hebard Story. Hank Whittemore & Caroline Hebard. LC 95-35308. (Illus.). 320p. 1995. 21.95 (*0-553-09951-5*) Bantam.

***So That You May Be One.** Joa Bolendas. Tr. & Intro. by John Hill. LC 96-40526. 416p. (Orig.). 1997. pap. 24.95 (*0-940262-85-1*) Lindisfarne Bks.

So That Your Values Live On: Ethical Wills & How to Prepare Them. Ed. by Jack Riemer & Nathaniel Stampfer. 272p. 1993. pap. 17.95 (*1-879045-34-6*) Jewish Lights.

So That's How I Was Born. Robert Brooks. LC 81-20859. (Illus.). 48p. (J). (ps-2). 1993. pap. 5.95 (*0-671-78344-0*, S&S Bks Young Read) S&S Childrens.

So That's How the Moon Changes Shape. Allan Fowler. LC 91-3142. (Rookie Read-about Science Ser.). (Illus.). 32p. (J). (ps-2). 1991. pap. 3.95 (*0-516-44917-6*); lib. bdg. 17.30 (*0-516-04917-8*) Childrens.

So That's How the Moon Changes Shape, Big bk. Allan Fowler. LC 91-3142. (Rookie Read-about Science Big Bks.). (Illus.). 32p. (J). (ps-2). 1991. pap. text ed. 32.40 (*0-516-49477-5*) Childrens.

***So That's How They Do It: Tricks & Illusions of the World's Greatest Magicians.** Herbert Becker. 1996. pap. text ed. 9.95 (*0-8065-1839-1*, Citadel Pr) Carol Pub Group.

So That's How They're Spending Our Money! Your Federal Taxes at Work. Dale Neseman & Jack Thebo. (Illus.). 144p. (Orig.). 1991. pap. 6.95 (*0-9629343-0-5*) Neseman Enter.

***So That's in the Bible?** Broadman & Holman Staff. LC 97-6436. 1997. pap. 14.99 (*1-55819-474-6*) Broadman.

***So That's What a Christian Is! 12 Pictures of the Dynamic Christian Life.** Warren W. Wiersbe. 168p. (YA). (gr. 10). 1996. pap. 9.99 (*0-8010-5732-9*) Baker Bks.

So That's What They're For: Breastfeeding Basics. Janet Tamaro-Natt. (Illus.). 256p. 1996. pap. 10.95 (*1-55850-611-X*) Adams Media.

***So That's Where They Came From! An Oliphant Collection.** Pat Oliphant. (Illus.). 160p. (Orig.). 1997. pap. 10.95 (*0-8362-3687-4*) Andrews & McMeel.

So That's Who You Used to Be! A Reunion Planning Guide. Patricia M. Bauer. LC 95-94014. (Illus.). 176p. (Orig.). 1995. pap. 18.95 (*0-9646152-0-7*) P M Bauer.

So the People May Know: A Guide to Water Utility Public Information Practices. (Illus.). 196p. 1993. pap. 45.00 (*0-89867-670-3*, 20302) Am Water Wks Assn.

"So the Witch Won't Eat Me" Fantasy & the Child's Fear of Infanticide. Dorothy Bloch. LC 94-70895. 256p. 1994. pap. 30.00 (*1-56821-259-3*) Aronson.

So the Woman Went Her Way: A Personal Journey. Lynne Bundesen. 176p. (Orig.). 1993. pap. 10.00 (*0-671-67702-0*, Touchstone Bks) S&S Trade.

So, There Are Laws about Sex! Answers on Legal Sex for Canadian Children & Youth. Harvey & McGuire. 48p. (YA). 1989. pap. 10.00 (*0-409-88936-9*) MICHIE.

***So They Burned the Black Churches.** Shelia P. Moses. Ed. by Marcia Jackson. 1996. 5.00 (*0-9644197-3-4*) M-Promotions.

So This Is Africa! Betty Kilgour. (Illus.). 120p. (Orig.). 1987. pap. 10.95 (*0-920490-73-5*) Temeron Bks.

So This Is Depravity. Russell Baker. pap. 4.95 (*0-317-56882-5*) PB.

***So This Is Ecstasy?** Bernard O'Mahoney. (Illus.). 192p. 1997. pap. 17.95 (*1-85158-896-5*, Pub. by Mnstream UK) Trafalgar.

So This Is Farming: A Journal. Dean Carlson. (Illus.). 184p. (Orig.). 1988. 14.95 (*0-934860-51-3*); pap. 8.95 (*0-934860-50-5*) Adventure Pubns.

So This Is Jazz. Henry O. Osgood. LC 77-17859. (Roots of Jazz Ser.). (Illus.). 1978. reprint ed. lib. bdg. 32.50 (*0-306-77540-9*) Da Capo.

So This Is Love. E. Coffman. Date not set. pap. 8.95 (*0-449-91265-5*) Fawcett.

So This Is Love. Elaine Coffman. (Orig.). 1993. reprint ed. mass mkt. 5.99 (*0-449-14860-2*, GM) Fawcett.

So This Is Normal Too? Teachers & Parents Working Out Developmental Issues in Young Children. Deborah J. Hewitt. LC 95-34645. 141p. (Orig.). 1995. pap. 14.95 (*1-884834-07-8*, 1539) Redleaf Pr.

So Vast So Beautiful a Land: Louisiana & the Purchase. Marshall Sprague. LC 90-19573. (Illus.). 416p. 1991. reprint ed. pap. 19.95 (*0-8040-0943-0*); reprint ed. text ed. 39.95 (*0-8040-0944-9*) Swallow.

So Very English. Fay Weldon et al. Ed. by Marsha Rowe. LC 90-60287. 288p. (Orig.). 1992. pap. 14.95 (*1-85242-179-7*) Serpents Tail.

***So Vile a Son.** Ben Aaronovitch. (Dr. Who New Adventures Ser.). 280p. 1996. mass mkt. 5.95 (*0-426-20484-0*, Pub. by Virgin Pub UK) London Brdge.

So We Believe, So We Pray. George A. Buttrick. (Abingdon Classics Ser.). 256p. 1992. reprint ed. pap. 1.79 (*0-687-39049-4*) Abingdon.

So We're Growing Older. John E. Biegert. (Looking up Ser.). 1982. pap. 1.95 (*0-8298-0436-6*) Pilgrim OH.

So What. (Choices & Decisions Ser.). (J). (gr. k-1). 1990. pap. 5.28 (*0-8123-6442-2*); audio 7.92 (*0-8123-6444-9*) McDougal-Littell.

So What. Lewis Anderson. LC 89-80861. 280p. (Orig.). 1989. pap. 9.95 (*0-9623580-4-5*) Avalanche Pr.

So What about Sewing, 2 vols., Set. large type ed. Adele Brown. pap. 15.00 (*0-317-01861-2*) Cath Guild Blind.

So What Do I Do about Me? Kirk Hill, pseud. xxi, 136p. (Orig.). 1993. pap. text ed. 19.00 (*1-56308-048-6*) Teacher Ideas Pr.

***So What Do You Do?** Douglas Evans. LC 96-54055. 112p. (J). 1997. 14.95 (*1-886910-20-0*) Front Str.

So What! (For the White Dude Who Said This Ain't Poetry) Kenneth Carroll. 60p. 1995. pap. 10.00 (*0-938572-10-5*) Bunny Crocodile.

So What if I'm 50? Straight Talk & Proven Strategies for Getting Hired in the Toughest Job Market Ever. Bob Weinstein. 224p. 1995. pap. text ed. 12.95 (*0-07-069189-4*) McGraw.

So What If You Can't Chew, Eat Hearty! Recipes & a Guide for the Healthy & Happy Eating of Soft & Pureed Foods. Phyllis Z. Goldberg. (Illus.). 152p. 1980. spiral bd., pap. 24.95 (*0-398-04065-6*) C C Thomas.

So, What Is Assertiveness? An Assertiveness Training Course. Chrissie Whitehead. LC 94-12124. 72p. 1994. reprint ed. teacher ed., pap. 29.95 (*0-89390-296-9*) Resource Pubns.

So What's It to Me? Sexual Assault Information for Guys. Gayle M. Stringer & Deanna Rants-Rodriguez. (Illus.). 35p. (Orig.). 1987. pap. 4.50 (*0-941953-05-X*) KCSA Res Ctr.

So What's New? (Illus.). 88p. (Orig.). 1992. pap. 8.00 (*0-9631618-1-4*) Highgrove Pr.

So, What's Next? T. Bathgate. 6.99 (*1-871676-84-3*, Pub. by Christian Focus UK) Spring Arbor Dist.

So What's Wrong with a Big Nose? Building Self-Esteem. Fran Sciacca & Jill Sciacca. (Lifelines Ser.). 64p. (YA). 1992. pap. 4.99 (*0-310-48051-5*) Zondervan.

So, What's Your Point? A Practical Guide to Learning & Applying Effective Techniques for Interpersonal Communication. 2nd ed. James C. Wetherbe & Bond Wetherbe. (Illus.). 192p. 1996. reprint ed. 25.00 (*1-883096-01-4*) Mead Pub MN.

So Where's My Apple? Diary of a First-Year Teacher. Glen Walter. (Illus.). 180p. (Orig.). (C). 1988. pap. text ed. 9.95 (*0-943274-03-6*) SC Ed Comm Inc.

So Where's the Dawn? A Journey of Emotional Healing. Leland Baggett. LC 88-32154. 100p. (Orig.). 1989. pap. 8.95 (*0-929153-01-4*) Royal Pub NC.

So Who Says I Have to Act My Age? Making the Jump to Adulthood Without Leaving All the Fun Behind. Kevin Johnson. (Junior High Devotions Ser.). 112p. (YA). (gr. 7-10). 1994. pap. 6.99 (*1-55661-414-4*) Bethany Hse.

So Who the Heck Was Oscar Mayer? The Real People Behind Those Brand Names. Doug Gelbert. LC 96-21037. 400p. (Orig.). 1996. pap. 12.00 (*1-56980-082-0*) Barricade Bks.

So, Who's Dr. Rabbit? Patricia C. McKissack & Roberta L. Duyff. (Illus.). 32p. (J). (gr. 2-4). 1994. pap. text ed. write for info. (*0-9642684-0-X*) JMH Communs.

So Wide a Sea: Essays on Biblical & Systematic Theology. Ed. by Ben C. Ollenburger. (Text-Reader Ser.: No. 4). 145p. (Orig.). 1991. pap. text ed. 10.00 (*0-936273-18-6*) Inst Mennonite.

***So Wide the Sky.** Elizabeth Grayson. 384p. (Orig.). 1997. mass mkt. 5.99 (*0-380-77846-7*) Avon.

So Wise Were Our Elders: Mythic Narratives from the Kamsa. John H. McDowell. LC 93-5083. 296p. 1994. text ed. 45.00 (*0-8131-1826-3*) U Pr of Ky.

***So Worthy My Love.** Kathleen Woodiwiss. Date not set. write for info. (*0-688-12498-4*) Morrow.

So Worthy My Love. Kathleen E. Woodiwiss. 1989. pap. 10.95 (*0-380-89817-9*) Avon.

So Worthy My Love. Kathleen E. Woodiwiss. 672p. 1990. mass mkt. 6.50 (*0-380-76148-3*) Avon.

So Ya Wanna Be a Private Investigator, Huh Binky? Greg Hauser. 19.95 (*1-882852-00-1*) Marinelli Publishing.

So You Are a Church Member. rev. ed. Robert T. Fauth. LC 95-17956. 64p. 1995. pap. 3.95 (*0-8298-1101-X*) Pilgrim OH.

So, You Can't Believe You're Dead? Robert D. Gidel & Kathryn B. Bostwick. LC 92-74513. 156p. (Orig.). 1993. pap. 12.95 (*0-9623887-2-6*) Andaraeon.

So You Can't Stand Evangelism? A Thinking Person's Guide to Church Growth. James R. Adams. LC 94-21573. 192p. 1994. pap. 12.95 (*1-56101-096-0*) Cowley Pubns.

So, You Got Talent - Now What? A Musician's Guide to the Music Business. Randy S. Cierley. (Illus.). (Orig.). 1989. pap. text ed. write for info. (*0-318-66597-2*) Strlng Pub CA.

So You Have High Blood Cholesterol. 1990. lib. bdg. 75.00 (*0-8490-3996-7*) Gordon Pr.

So You Have High Blood Cholesterol. (Illus.). 26p. (Orig.). (C). 1995. pap. text ed. 12.00 (*0-7881-2170-7*) DIANE Pub.

So, You Have to Go to Court! A Child's Guide to Testifying As a Witness in Child Abuse Cases. 3rd ed. Harvey & Watson-Russell. 48p. (J). 1991. pap. 10.00 (*0-409-90611-5*) MICHIE.

***So, You Have to Write a Story.** Cindy Iutzi. (Illus.). 20p. (Orig.). 1996. pap. 15.95 (*1-56490-025-8*) G Grimm Assocs.

So You Have to Write an Economics Term Paper. Lawrence H. Officer et al. LC 80-80313. x, 149p. (Orig.). 1985. reprint ed. pap. 7.50 (*0-87013-229-6*) Mich St U Pr.

So You Have to Write an Essay. Chris Morris. 88p. (C). 1995. spiral bd. 16.74 (*0-7872-0821-3*) Kendall-Hunt.

So, You Love Animals: An Action-Packed, Fun-Filled Book to Help Kids Help Animals. Zoe Weil. (Illus.). 192p. (Orig.). (J). (gr. 2-7). 1994. pap. 14.95 (*1-881699-01-3*) Am Anti-Viv Soc.

So You Mean to Read the Bible: Some Tips for Absolute Beginners. Gerard S. Sloyan. 68p. (Orig.). 1992. pap. 3.95 (*0-8146-2044-2*) Liturgical Pr.

So You Think Nobody Loves You. Robert Kelly & Peter J. Kreeft. 115p. 1992. pap. 9.95 (*1-85390-144-X*) Ignatius Pr.

***So You Think So Know Sports? The Ultimate Playbook of Trivia, Teasers, Puzzles & Puzzlers.** Ron Smith. (Illus.). 312p. (Orig.). 1997. write for info. (*0-614-30990-5*) Sporting News.

So! You Think You Are Coaching Your Employees: Creating a Total Quality Culture. Linda Seifert. 72p. 1995. text ed. 25.00 (*0-8059-3800-1*) Dorrance.

So You Think You Know...? Quiz Book. Ed. by IAP, Inc. Staff. (Aviation Training Ser.). (Illus.). 297p. (C). 1985. pap. 8.95 (*0-89100-071-2*, EA-QB) IAP.

So You Think You Want to Be a Crop-Duster. rev. ed. Miles E. Gibson. (Illus.). 140p. 1978. pap. 9.95 (*0-942306-00-7*) Diversified Pub Co.

So You Think You're a Sports Fan! 802 Questions to Challenge Your Knowledge. Ed. by Shepard Long. LC 94-31927. 160p. 1994. pap. 8.95 (*0-8027-7439-3*) Walker & Co.

So You Think You're Good at Trivia: Take the Official NTN Trivia Challenge. Patrick Downs & Debra Weiss. LC 94-21256. 432p. mass mkt. 6.95 (*0-89529-631-4*) Avery Pub.

So You Think You're Irish. Margaret Kelleher. 176p. 1991. reprint ed. 7.99 (*0-517-05224-5*) Random Hse Value.

***So You Think You're Macho.** Jerry Cooper. 24p. (Orig.). 1996. pap. 3.95 (*1-889419-10-9*) J Cooper.

So You Think You're Not Religious: A Thinking Person's Guide to the Church. James R. Adams. LC 88-37625. 208p. (Orig.). 1989. pap. 9.95 (*0-936384-69-7*) Cowley Pubns.

So You Think You're Smart: One Hundred Fifty Fun & Challenging Brain Teasers. Pat Battaglia. 1988. pap. text ed. 9.95 (*0-07-155543-9*) McGraw.

So You Think You're Smart - One Hundred Fifty Fun & Challenging Brain Teasers. Pat Battaglia. (Illus.). 114p. 1988. 14.95 (*0-8306-9406-4*, 3106H); pap. 8.95 (*0-8306-3106-2*, 3106) McGraw-Hill Prof.

So You Thought You Couldn't Draw: Drawing Basics. Sandra Angelo. (Illus.). 150p. (YA). (gr. 9-12). 1994. pap. 24.95 (*1-887882-32-4*) Discover Art.

So You Thought You Couldn't Draw Vol. I: Easy Art Lessons for People Who Can't Draw a Straight Line. 2nd rev. ed. Illus. by Tiko Youngdale & Gre Hann. LC 95-78792. 150p. 1995. pap. text ed. 24.95 incl. vhs (*1-887823-24-7*) Discover Art.

***So You Wanna Be a Gambler: Advanced Craps.** John Patrick. 589p. 1994. pap. 29.95 (*0-614-31094-6*) Gambler.

***So You Wanna Be a Gambler: Advanced Roulette.** John Patrick. 406p. 1987. pap. 19.95 (*0-614-31092-X*) Gambler.

So You Wanna Be a Gambler: Baccarat. John Patrick. (Illus.). 246p. (Orig.). 1985. pap. 14.95 (*0-930911-03-2*) Gambler.

So You Wanna Be a Gambler: Blackjack. John Patrick. (Illus.). 188p. (Orig.). 1983. pap. 14.95 (*0-930911-01-6*) Gambler.

So You Wanna Be a Gambler: Card Counting. John Patrick. (Illus.). 371p. (Orig.). 1986. pap. 19.95 (*0-317-61500-9*) Gambler.

So You Wanna Be a Gambler: Craps. John Patrick. (Illus.). 371p. (Orig.). 1984. pap. 19.95 (*0-930911-00-8*) Gambler.

So You Wanna Be a Gambler: Roulette-Slots. John Patrick. (Illus.). 234p. (Orig.). 1983. pap. 14.95 (*0-930911-02-4*) Gambler.

***So You Wanna Be a Gambler: Slots.** John Patrick. 465p. 1992. pap. 19.95 (*0-614-31093-8*) Gambler.

***So You Wanna Be a Gambler: Sports Handicapping.** John Patrick. 586p. 1996. pap. 29.95 (*0-614-31095-4*) Gambler.

So You Wanna Buy a Car... Insider Tips for Saving Money & Your Sanity. Bruce Fuller & Tony Whitney. 248p. (Orig.). 1996. pap. 10.95 (*1-55180-061-6*) Self-Counsel Pr.

So You Want a Divorce: How to Do It Yourself in the State of Washington, an Explanation of the State of Washington Divorce Law with Forms You Will Need to Obtain Your Own Divorce. 7th rev. ed. Daniel W. Giboney. LC 79-128750. (Illus.). 272p. 1986. 12.95 (*0-9606396-0-8*) D Giboney.

***So You Want to Be a Brain Surgeon? A Medical Careers Guide.** Ed. by Simon Eccles & Christopher Ward. LC 96-53435. (Illus.). 208p. 1997. pap. 19.50 (*0-19-262746-5*) OUP.

So You Want to Be a Channel! 2nd ed. Arthur C. Lytle. LC 87-83572. 256p. (Orig.). 1988. pap. 12.95 (*1-56184-106-4*) New Falcon Pubns.

So You Want to Be a Comics Retailer: A Step-by-Step Guide on Opening & Operating a Successful & Profitable Comic Book Store. Rick Boal. 208p. (Orig.). 1995. pap. text ed. 12.95 (*0-9645094-0-7*) RBM Pr.

So You Want to Be a Consultant. Kabis. 1993. 59.95 (*1-881116-26-3*) Black Forest Pr.

So You Want to Be a Corporate Pilot. L. G. Keilberg. LC 85-9045. 1985. 29.95 (*0-9615732-0-1*) Petrleum Resch.

So You Want to Be a Doctor. Stuart C. Zeman. LC 92-11876. 280p. 1992. pap. 9.95 (*0-89815-502-9*) Ten Speed Pr.

S

So You Want to Be a Federal Agent. Louis C. Rodriguez, Jr. 84p. 1992. Career Book. 8.95 (0-9634286-0-8) Ancur Comms.

So You Want to Be a Goalkeeper: The No. 1 Handbook for Soccer Coaches & Players. Joe Machnik & Paul Harris. (Illus.). 62p. 1980. pap. 7.95 (0-916802-18-3) Soccer for Am.

***So You Want to Be a Lawyer.** Date not set. pap. 13.95 (0-553-06889-X) Broadway BDD.

So You Want to Be a Lawyer. Kaplan Staff. 160p. 1996. 16.00 (0-385-32343-3) Law Schl Admission.

So You Want to Be a Lesbian. Liz Tracey & Sydney Pokorny. 272p. 1996. pap. 12.95 (0-312-14423-7) St Martin.

So You Want to Be a Manager? Francis J. Bridges. LC 93-8230. 123p. (Orig.). 1993. pap. 9.95 (0-9623126-2-2) ESM Bks.

So You Want to Be a Mortgage Banker. 66p. 1986. 25.00 (0-929097-27-0, 18283) Sav & Comm Bank.

***So, You Want to Be a Slave?** John E. Birch. Ed. by David A. Miley. (Illus.). 48p. 1997. pap. 12.95 (0-9631226-1-4) Selective Pub.

***So You Want to Be a Snowbird.** Paul Chevalier. Ed. by Jim Ciano. 180p. (Orig.). 1997. pap. 14.95 (1-888672-16-1) J Ciano Pubng.

So, You Want to Be a Teacher. Charles J. Mertz. Ed. by M. L. Jones. LC 95-78284. 198p. 1996. pap. 9.95 (0-9636072-7-8) J Honea Pubs.

So You Want to Be a Teacher? Jannay Valdez. (Illus.). 100p. write for info. (1-886709-05-X) Outlaw Publ.

So You Want to Be a Tennis Pro? A Practical & Mental Guide for Players, Parents & Coaches. Noel Blundell. (Illus.). 192p. (Orig.). 1995. pap. 14.95 (0-85091-666-6, Pub. by Lothian Pub AT) Seven Hills Bk.

So You Want to Be a Witch. Keith Morgan. (Orig.). 1993. pap. 7.95 (1-872189-51-2, Pub. by Mandrake Pr UK) Holmes Pub.

So You Want to Be a Wizard. Diane Duane. LC 95-33451. 384p. (J). (gr. 7-9). 1996. reprint ed. pap. 6.00 (0-15-201239-7) HarBrace.

So You Want to Be an Executive. Elton T. Reeves. LC 73-138569. 254p. reprint ed. pap. 72.40 (0-317-09942-6, 2050398) Bks Demand.

So You Want to Be an Interpreter? An Introduction to Sign Language Interpreting. 2nd rev. ed. Janice H. Humphrey & Bob J. Alcorn. 423p. 1995. pap. text ed. 49.95 (0-9640367-3-8) H&H Pubng.

***So You Want to Be Beautiful? How to Be Beautiful When Your Mirror Says "Ho-Hum"** Florence E. Parkes. 92p. 1997. 18.99 (0-9657988-0-1) LongView Press.

So You Want to Be in Business! Barbara Massie. 52p. 1992. pap. text ed. 6.00 (1-884053-01-7) Magnolia AR.

So You Want to Be President. Everett Blackman. 88p. 1972. 4.00 (0-86690-060-8, B1024-014) Am Fed Astrologers.

***So You Want to Be Sophisticated.** A. K. Belkaoui. Ed. by Kelly O'Donnell. (Illus.). 126p. 1997. mass mkt. 8.95 (1-57532-075-4) Press-Tige Pub.

So You Want to Be the Boss. J. W. Mclean. 1990. pap. 15.95 (0-13-815432-5) P-H.

So You Want to Become a Paralegal. Starkman. 1990. pap. 13.00 (0-409-27113-6) MICHIE.

So You Want to Build a Live Steam Locomotive. Joseph F. Nelson. LC 74-75879. (Illus.). 164p. 1978. reprint ed. 20.95 (0-914104-01-2) Wildwood Pubns MI.

So You Want to Buy a Diamond: A No-Nonsense Guide. Greg Becker. Ed. by Don Becker & Bill Hines. (Illus.). (Orig.). 1994. pap. 3.95 (0-9639712-1-2) High Adventure.

So You Want to Buy a Handgun! Read This Before Going Any Further. Michael F. Mangiaracina. Ed. by Kathleen M. Garrison. (Illus.). 91p. (Orig.). 1995. pap. text ed. 11.95 (0-9644837-1-8) Garrison Desktop.

So You Want to Buy a Resort. Larren Wood. LC 93-93940. 186p. 1993. pap. text ed. 9.95 (0-9636546-0-8) Woodstock North.

So, You Want to Do Bread Dough Art. Diane Morizio. 1992. student ed. 8.95 (0-9632807-6-7) J&D Ent.

So You Want to Do Ministry? 2nd ed. John J. Walsh & James DiGiacomo. 110p. 1993. reprint ed. pap. 11.50 (0-88344-914-5) Orbis Bks.

***So You Want to Get a Degree.** Bell. 1984. pap. text ed. write for info. (0-582-49714-0, Pub. by Longman UK) Longman.

So You Want to Get into the Race. Chuck Klein. 95p. (YA). 1980. student ed., pap. 5.99 (0-8423-6082-4) Tyndale.

So You Want to Go into Business. Herman Clements. 32p. 1995. pap. 5.00 (0-8059-3744-7) Dorrance.

So You Want to Go Racing? John Webb. (Illus.). 80p. (Orig.). 1984. pap. text ed. 11.95 (0-936834-42-0) S S Autosports.

So You Want to Go to College? 50 Questions to Ponder. large type unabridged ed. Burton O. Witthuhn et al. (Illus.). 204p. (Orig.). (YA). (gr. 10-12). 1997. pap. 22.50 (1-881807-16-9) Cornesky & Assocs.

So You Want to Have a Long-Range Plan. rev. ed. William W. Simmons. 36p. 1987. pap. 10.00 (0-912841-25-7, 02) Planning Forum.

So, You Want to Lead a Jazz Band? Here's One Way to Do It: For the Teacher, Student & Dilettante. Roger Schueler. (Illus.). 131p. (Orig.). (C). 1992. pap. 24.00 (1-56516-063-0) H Leonard.

So, You Want to Learn How to Double Dutch? How to Jump, Judge & Make Adjustments. Judy Roberson-Williams. (Illus.). 72p. 1994. pap. 8.00 (0-8059-3606-8) Dorrance.

So You Want to Learn How to Type. rev. ed. J. Robbins Barrett. (Illus.). 1990. pap. 9.50 (0-9619019-5-0); pap. text ed. 8.95 (0-9619019-2-6) J R Barrett.

So You Want to Meet the Family. 1991. pap. 4.94 (0-87162-525-3) Warner Pr.

So You Want to Meet the Family. Jeff Hayes. 1991. spiral bd. 4.95 (0-87162-523-7, D8310) Warner Pr.

So You Want to Open a Profitable Day Care Center: Everything You Need to Know to Plan, Organize & Implement a Successful Program. rev. ed. Patricia C. Gallagher. 128p. (C). 1993. pap. 19.95 (0-943135-53-2) Young Sparrow Pr.

So You Want to Open a Restaurant: Making Your Favorite Fantasy Real. rev. ed. Charles Robbins. Ed. by Susan Suffes. 240p. 1986. pap. 11.95 (0-685-17757-2) Beaufort Bks NY.

So You Want to Open a Restaurant: The Complete Guide to Owning & Operating Your Business Successfully. Charles Robbins. 1987. pap. 11.95 (0-8253-0451-2) Beaufort Bks NY.

So You Want to Open a Tea Shop: Let Me Tell You about It. Martha J. Jones. LC 92-97277. (Illus.). 72p. (Orig.). 1993. pap. 10.95 (0-9635241-0-0) Proper Tea.

So, You Want to Own a Restaurant? The Dream, The Steps, The Reality. Monty Campbell & Fabrizio Gruppioni. 110p. (C). 1989. pap. 7.50 (1-877718-03-3) Archangel Pr.

So You Want to Own a Yacht. Frank D. Simons. (Illus.). 200p. (Orig.). Date not set. pap. write for info. (0-685-26970-1) Tippicanoe Import Export.

So You Want to Own the Store. Brown. LC 97-6705. 1996. pap. write for info. (0-8092-3236-7) Contemp Bks.

So You Want to Produce a Picture. Leon Chooluck. Ed. by Ivan J. Rado. (Illus.). 204p. (Orig.). (C). 1992. pap. 20.00 (0-9633948-0-0) I J Rado.

So You Want to Quit. Jean Kirkpatrick. 18p. 1983. pap. 2.00 (0-318-19527-5) WFS.

So You Want to Restore a Vintage Home: A Buyer's Guide. Diane Haugen. LC 90-70304. (Illus.). 96p. (Orig.). 1990. pap. 14.95 (0-9625756-0-7) Whiskey Creek.

So You Want to Run for Political Office: A Practical Guide for Aspiring Politicians. Robert D. England, Jr. 120p. 1992. pap. 12.95 (0-9633671-0-2) Greenfield Ctr.

So You Want to See a Psychiatrist? Ed. by Bruce L. Danto et al. LC 79-23225. 170p. 1980. lib. bdg. 18.95 (0-405-12622-0) Ayer.

***So You Want to Self-Publish: How to Avoid the Pitfalls, Experience the Joys & Make Money at Self-Publishing.** Steve Meyer. (Illus.). 224p. (Orig.). 1997. pap. 14.95 (0-9630284-6-4) Meyer Pub.

So You Want to Take Physics. Cole. (C). 1993. teacher ed., pap. text ed. 32.00 (0-03-096021-5) HB Coll Pubs.

So You Want to Take Physics. Cole. (C). 1994. teacher ed., pap. text ed. 33.75 (0-03-097216-7) HB Coll Pubs.

So You Want to Take Physics: A Preparatory Course. Rodney Cole. LC 92-25836. 1993. write for info. (0-03-096020-7) SCP.

So You Want to Take Physics: A Preparatory Course with Algebra & Trigonometry. Rodney Cole. LC 92-41426. 1993. text ed. 25.50 (0-03-097215-9) SCP.

So You Want to Write a Book. 1990. pap. 5.00 (0-930061-50-0) Interspace Bks.

So You Want to Write a Cookbook. Judy Rehmel. LC 83-61899. (Illus.). 100p. 1983. pap. 4.95 (0-915216-88-4) Marathon Intl Bk.

So, You Want to Write a Cookbook! Judy Rehmel. (Illus.). 52p. 1982. pap. 8.95 (0-913731-04-8) J Rehmel.

So You Want to Write a Novel. Lou W. Stanek. LC 94-14334. 208p. (Orig.). 1994. pap. 10.00 (0-380-77688-X) Avon.

So You Want to Write Your Family History. Norma P. Evans. LC 83-82903. (Illus.). 47p. (Orig.). 1983. pap. text ed. 6.50 (0-937418-09-9) N P Evans.

***So, You Wanted America: One DP's Story.** Alfons Hering. LC 95-96143. 222p. 1996. 16.95 (0-9650678-0-7) Evrgreen Press.

So, You Wish to Learn All about Economics? A Text on Elementary Mathematical Economics. Lyndon H. LaRouche, Jr. 192p. (Orig.). 1995. pap. 10.00 (0-933488-35-1) Exec Intel Review.

So, You Wish to Learn All about Economics? A Text on Elementary Mathematical Economics. 2nd ed. Lyndon H. LaRouche, Jr. Ed. by Christina Huth. (Illus.). 192p. (Orig.). 1995. pap. 10.00 (0-943235-13-8) Exec Intel Review.

So Young to Die: The Story of Hannah Senesh. Candice F. Ransom. (J). (gr. 4-7). 1993. pap. 2.95 (0-685-65620-9) Scholastic Inc.

So Your Child Has a Learning Problem: Now What? 2nd ed. Fred H. Wallbrown & Jane D. Wallbrown. LC 90-84016. 171p. (Orig.). 1991. pap. 19.95 (0-88422-015-X) Clinical Psych.

So Your Daughter Is Engaged: or Why the Mother of the Bride Oughtn't Be in Pictures. Kay D. Quain. LC 89-51256. (Illus.). 64p. (Orig.). 1989. pap. write for info. (0-9623646-0-6) Wales Pub.

So Your Home is Built on Expansive Soils... A Discussion of How Expansive Soils Affect Buildings. Ed. by Warren K. Wray. LC 95-34322. 88p. 1995. 20.00 (0-7844-0109-8) Am Soc Civil Eng.

***So You're a Step-Parent.** Bill Adler Books Staff. Date not set. write for info. (0-688-11739-2) Hearst Bks.

So You're a Teenage Girl. rev. ed. Jill Renich-Meyers. 144p. 1989. pap. 10.99 (0-310-31801-7) Zondervan.

***So, You're Getting Married.** Fred Sahner. Ed. by Cliff Carle. (Illus.). 72p. (Orig.). 1997. pap. 5.95 (1-57644-044-3) CCC Pubns.

***So You're Going to Be a House Daddy: A Survival Manual for Happiness & Sanity in the Home.** John M. Lacson & Scott Carrothers. Ed. & Illus. by Christopher Lacson. (House Daddy Bks.). 64p. (Orig.). 1996. pap. 16.95 (0-9656632-0-5) HouseDaddies.

So You're Going to Be a Mother: Taking Control of Your Pregnancy. Karla Morales & Charles B. Inlander. LC 95-31205. 240p. 1995. pap. 14.95 (1-882606-23-X) Peoples Med Soc.

So You're Going to Court: The Law & You. Robert W. Smedley. 302p. 8.00 (0-685-41739-5) Fountainhead.

So You're Going to Haiti? Tom C. McKenney. LC 88-50163. (Illus.). 56p. (Orig.). 1990. pap. 3.00 (0-934527-08-3) Words Living Minis.

So You're Going to Have Puppies. Mari Stein. (Illus.). 1973. pap. 3.95 (0-918546-03-6) Quarterdeck.

***So, You're Going to Plan a Family Reunion.** Frances M. Keitt. (Illus.). 62p. (Orig.). 1997. write for info. (0-9656816-0-2) F Keitt.

So You're Going to Run a Library: A Library Management Primer. Dave Sutton. xvi, 190p. 1995. pap. text ed. 22.50 (1-56308-306-X) Libs Unl.

So You're Having an Operation: A Step-by-Step Guide to Controlling Your Hospital Stay. Karen R. Williams & Janet K. Stensaas. LC 85-6324. 228p. 1986. 19.95 (0-13-823949-5) P-H.

So You're Injured, What's Next? L. Royal James. Ed. by M. Sammye Miller. (Illus.). 75p. (Orig.). 1995. text ed. 12.75 (0-9635708-2-X); pap. text ed. 8.75 (0-9635708-3-8) Royal Pub DE.

So You're Looking for a New Preacher: A Guide for Pulpit Nominating Committees. Elizabeth Achtemeier. 64p. (Orig.). 1991. pap. 5.00 (0-8028-0596-5) Eerdmans.

So You're off to Summer Camp: A Trunk Load of Tips for a Fun-Filled Camp Adventure. Margaret M. Queen. LC 93-77129. (Illus.). 136p. (J). (gr. 2-12). 1993. 14.95 (1-882959-55-8); per. 6.95 (1-882959-50-7) Foxglove TN.

So You're "On Disability"...& You Think You Might Want to Get Back into Action: Thoughts & Stories That May Help Some People Who Are Receiving "Long Term Disability" Benefits. Daniel T. McAneny. 124p. (Orig.). 1995. pap. 7.95 (0-9646490-0-4) D T McAneny.

So You're on the Council. National Community Education Association Staff. Ed. by Mary R. Boo. (Illus.). 20p. 1987. student ed. 2.50 (0-932399-02-9) Natl Comm Ed.

So You're on the Council: Facilitator's Guide. Guy Faust. Ed. by Mary R. Boo. 24p. 1987. 5.00 (0-932399-03-7) Natl Comm Ed.

So You're on the Hospital Board! 4th ed. Richard J. Umbdenstock. LC 92-29099. 49p. (Orig.). 1992. pap. 62.50 (1-55648-095-4, 196115) AHPI.

So You're on the Search Committee. Bunty Ketcham. pap. 6.95 (1-56699-015-7) Alban Inst.

So You're the Safety Director. Michael V. Manning. 200p. 1995. pap. text ed. 49.00 (0-86587-481-6) Gov Insts.

***So You're Thinking about Contemporary Worship.** Tim Carson & Kathy Carson. LC 97-19597. 104p. (Orig.). 1997. pap. 9.99 (0-8272-3437-6) Chalice Pr.

So You're Thinking about Starting a Business: A Comprehensive Business Start up Manual. Business of Your Own Staff. 240p. 1988. 59.95 (0-943267-00-5) Busn Your Own.

So You're Thinking of Going to a Chiropractor. Robert Dryburgh. 160p. 1984. 12.95 (0-87983-345-9); pap. 3.95 (0-87983-355-6) Keats.

So You've Been Asked to Pray: An Easy to Use Self-Guide for Public Prayer. John Toay. (Illus.). 128p. (Orig.). (C). 1990. pap. 9.95 (0-939513-40-4) Joy Pub SJC.

***So You've Been Asked to Speak? A Practical Guide to Preaching & Public Speaking.** Marvin Hunt. 96p. (Orig.). 1996. pap. 5.95 (1-57847-000-5) MAGCOS-DA.

So, You've Been Busted! A Guide to Court Procedures for Adolescents Charged under the Young Offenders Act. Watson-Russell & Harvey. 48p. (YA). 1989. pap. 10.00 (0-409-80985-3) MICHIE.

***So You've Been "Integrated" Now What.** Richard E. Thompson. LC 96-85548. 94p. (Orig.). 1996. pap. 38.00 (0-924674-46-6) Am Coll Phys Execs.

So You've Got a Great Idea. Steve Fiffer. LC 85-26701. 211p. 1986. pap. 14.00 (0-201-11536-0) Addison-Wesley.

So You've Got Gout! Bryan Emmerson. (Illus.). 160p. 1996. pap. 19.95 (0-19-553748-3) OUP.

Soakercise: Exercises for the Hot Tub, Pool & Spa. Sharon R. Hines. (Illus.). 27p. (Orig.). 1981. pap. 3.00 (0-941904-03-2) Hot Water Pubs.

Soaking the Yule Log: Biographical Sketches of the Brown, Cheshier, Sain & Allied Families, 1749-1995. Katie B. Bennett. 542p. 1995. text ed. 42.00 (0-9649853-1-4) R L Bennett.

Soap: Making It, Enjoying It. Ann Bramson. LC 75-7286. (Illus.). 120p. 1975. pap. 6.95 (0-911104-57-7, 073) Workman Pub.

Soap Book: Simple Herbal Recipes. Sandy Maine. LC 95-4865. 96p. 1995. pap. 9.95 (1-883010-14-4) Interweave.

Soap Bubble Magic. Seymour Simon. LC 84-4432. (Illus.). 48p. (J). (ps-3). 1985. lib. bdg. 13.93 (0-688-02685-0) Lothrop.

Soap Bubbles. 3rd ed. Charles V. Boys. (Illus.). 1959. pap. 3.95 (0-486-20542-8) Dover.

Soap Fans: Pursuing Pleasure & Making Meaning in Everyday Life. C. Lee Harrington & Denise D. Bielby. (Illus.). (Orig.). (C). 1995. pap. text ed. 19.95 (1-56639-330-2); lib. bdg. 49.95 (1-56639-329-9) Temple U Pr.

Soap Films & Bubbles. Ann Wiebe. (J). (gr. 4-9). 1990. 16.95 (1-881431-25-8, 1209) AIMS Educ Fnd.

***Soap Opera.** Muriel G. Cantor & Suzanne Pingree. LC 83-11057. (Sage Commtext Ser.: Vol. 12). 167p. 1983. reprint ed. pap. 47.60 (0-608-02990-4, 2059630) Bks Demand.

Soap Opera: The Dark Side of Proctor & Gamble-The Company That Brings You Crest, Ivory, Pampers & Tide. Alecia Swasy. 416p. 1994. pap. 14.00 (0-671-89781-0, Touchstone Bks) S&S Trade.

Soap Opera & Women's Talk: The Pleasure of Resistance. Mary E. Brown. (Communication & Human Values Ser.: Vol. 14). 280p. (C). 1994. text ed. 52.00 (0-8039-4392-X); pap. text ed. 24.95 (0-8039-4393-8) Sage.

Soap Opera Book: Who's Who in Daytime Drama. Ed. by Ellen Buckley & Nancy E. Rout. 320p. 1993. pap. 20.00 (0-915344-23-8) Todd Pubns.

Soap Opera Book of Lists. Gerard J. Waggett. LC 95-48028. 240p. 1996. pap. 10.00 (0-06-100985-7, Harp PBks) HarpC.

***Soap Opera Cafe: The Skinny on Food from a Daytime Star.** Robin Mattson. (Illus.). 1997. 20.00 (0-446-52056-X) Warner Bks.

***Soap Opera Encyclopedia.** Gerard J. Waggett. 1997. mass mkt. 10.00 (0-06-101157-6, Harp PBks) HarpC.

***Soap Opera Puzzle Book.** Gerard J. Waggett. 1997. mass mkt. 5.99 (0-06-101156-8) HarpC.

Soap Operas for Social Change: Toward a Methodology for Entertainment-Education Television. Heidi N. Nariman. LC 92-36547. (Media & Society Ser.). 184p. 1993. text ed. 49.95 (0-275-94389-5, C4389, Praeger Pubs) Greenwood.

Soap Operas of the Sky. Jeannie Kuich. (Illus.). (Orig.). 1994. pap. 10.00 (0-944428-23-1) Cruising Guide.

Soap, Polishes, Leather, Resilient Floor Coverings see 1997 Annual Book of ASTM Standards: General Products, Chemical Specialties, & End Use Products, Section 15

Soap Recipes: Seventy Tried & True Ways to Make Modern Soap with Herbs, Beeswax & Vegetable Oils. Elaine C. White. LC 94-90605. (Illus.). 224p. 1995. pap. 23.95 (0-9637539-5-9) Valley Hills.

Soap, Sex, & Cigarettes: A Cultural History of American Advertising. Juliann Sivulka. (Mass Communication Ser.). (C). 1997. pap. text ed. 20.95 (0-534-51593-2) Wadsworth Pub.

Soap! Soap! Don't Forget the Soap! An Appalachian Folktale. Illus. by Andrew Glass. LC 92-11295. 32p. (J). (ps-3). 1993. lib. bdg. 15.95 (0-8234-1005-6) Holiday.

Soap! Soap! Don't Forget the Soap! An Appalachian Folktale. Illus. by Andrew Glass. 32p. (J). (ps-3). 1996. pap. 6.95 (0-8234-1230-X) Holiday.

Soap Soup: And Other Verses. Karla Kuskin. LC 91-22947. (Charlotte Zolotow Bk.). (Illus.). 64p. (J). (gr. k-3). 1992. 14.95 (0-06-023571-3) HarpC Child Bks.

Soap Soup: And Other Verses. Karla Kuskin. LC 91-22947. (Charlotte Zolotow Bk.). (Illus.). 64p. (J). (ps-3). 1994. pap. 3.50 (0-06-444174-1, Trophy) HarpC Child Bks.

***Soap, Water, & Sex: A Lively Guide to the Benefits of Sexual Hygiene & to Coping with...** Jacob Lipman. 1998. pap. text ed. 18.95 (1-57392-193-9) Prometheus Bks.

***Soapmaker's Companion: A Comprehensive Guide with Recipes, Techniques & Know-How.** Susan M. Cavitch. LC 97-5139. (Illus.). 256p. (Orig.). 1997. pap. 18.95 (0-88266-965-6) Storey Comm Inc.

Soaps: Scene Stealing Scenes for Actors. Karen Dent. Ed. by Arthur L. Zapel. LC 89-37760. 128p. (Orig.). 1989. pap. text ed. 9.95 (0-916260-60-7, B123) Meriwether Pub.

Soaps & Detergents: A Theoretical & Practical Review. Ed. by Luis Spitz. 464p. 1996. 105.00 (0-935315-72-1) AOCS Pr.

Soaps & Surface Active Agents: Index of New Information with Authors & Subjects. rev. ed. Vivian J. Samperstone. 123p. 1994. 47.50 (0-7883-0388-0); pap. 44.50 (0-7883-0389-9) ABBE Pubs Assn.

Soap's On: A Soap Opera Celebrity Chefs Cookbook. Diedre Hall. 220p. (Orig.). 1989. pap. text ed. 12.95 (0-89716-324-9) P B Pubng.

***Soapy Smith: Uncrowned King of Skagway.** Howard Clifford. (Illus.). 148p. 1997. pap. 11.95 (0-911803-03-3) Sourdough.

Soapy Smith Tragedy. 4th ed. Shea & Patton. (Illus.). 28p. 1997. reprint ed. pap. 5.95 (0-911803-01-7) Sourdough.

Soar - A Cognitive Architecture in Perspective: A Tribute to Allen Newell. Ed. by John A. Michon. (Studies in Cognitive Systems). 260p. (C). 1992. lib. bdg. 117.50 (0-7923-1660-6) Kluwer Ac.

***Soar Like an Eagle.** Jenniffer Ringquist. 220p. (Orig.). 1998. mass mkt. 7.99 (1-889501-66-2, Sherlock Pr) Sovereign.

Soar Papers: Research on Integrated Intelligence, 2 vols. Paul S. Rosenbloom. (Artificial Intelligence Ser.). (Illus.). 1300p. (C). 1993. 95.00 (0-262-18152-5); pap. 65.00 (0-262-68071-8) MIT Pr.

Soar Up on Wings of Morning. Diana Goure. (Illus.). 48p. (Orig.). 1994. pap. 7.00 (0-934852-62-6) Lorien Hse.

Soar with the Eagles. Charles S. Lauer. LC 91-73259. 236p. 1991. 24.95 (0-8163-1061-0) CCI Bks WA.

Soar with the Eagles: A Challenge to Excellence. Charles S. Lauer. LC 93-83849. 236p. 1993. pap. 11.95 (1-881802-01-9) CCI Bks WA.

Soar with Your Strengths. Donald O. Clifton & Paula Nelson. 208p. 1996. reprint ed. pap. 11.95 (0-440-50564-X, Dial Pr) Dell.

***Soares Book on Grounding.** 6th ed. J. Philip Simmons. LC 96-77947. (Illus.). ix, 246p. 1996. per., pap. 20.00 (1-890659-00-2, 357003) Intl Assn Elec Inspect.

***Soares Geostatistics Environment.** 1997. text ed. write for info. (0-7923-4590-8) Kluwer Ac.

Soar...If You Dare: How to Use Your Secret Powers for Success to Make Your Dreams Come True. James R. Ball. Ed. by Vicki Shannon. (Illus.). 288p. 1992. 21.95 (0-9633184-9-7) Goals Inst.

Soaring. Vujka Andrich. 1993. write for info. (0-9638160-0-4) Happy Hands.

***Soaring.** Phyllis J. Perry. LC 96-41075. (First Bk.). (J). 1997. lib. bdg. 21.00 (0-531-20258-5) Watts.

An Asterisk (*) at the beginning of an entry indicates that the title is appearing in BIP for the first time.

***Soaring.** Phyllis J. Perry. (First Bks.). 1997. pap. text ed. 6.95 (*0-531-15852-7*) Watts.

Soaring: The Diary & Letters of a Denishawn Dancer in the Far East, 1925-1926. Jane Sherman. LC 75-34445. (Illus.). 288p. reprint ed. pap. 82.10 (*0-685-20343-3*, 2029784) Bks Demand.

Soaring above Setbacks: The Autobiography of Janet Harmon Bragg, African American Aviator. Janet H. Bragg. Ed. by Marjorie M. Kriz. LC 95-41126. (History of Aviation Ser.). (Illus.). 160p. 1996. 19.95 (*1-56098-458-9*) Smithsonian.

***Soaring above Setbacks: The Autobiography of Janet Harmon Bragg African American Aviator.** Marjorie M. Kriz. (Illus.). 141p. (Orig.). 1997. pap. 12.95 (*1-56098-755-3*) Smithsonian.

Soaring & Above the Problems of Life. Jack Hartman. 187p. 1986. pap. text ed. 6.95 (*0-915445-05-0*) Lamplight FL.

Soaring Eagle. Mary Pearce Finley. LC 92-38263. (YA). (gr. 6 up). 1993. pap. 16.00 (*0-671-75598-6*, S&S Bks Young Read) S&S Childrens.

Soaring Eagle. Stephanie G. Whitson. LC 95-39368. (Prairie Winds Ser.: Bk. 2). 312p. 1996. pap. 10.99 (*0-7852-7617-3*) Nelson.

Soaring Eagle: Alfred Marshall 1842-1924. Peter Groenewegen. 832p. 1995. 95.00 (*1-85898-151-4*) E Elgar.

Soaring Fells. Kay Stephens. (Illus.). 392p. 1993. 24.95 (*0-7126-5072-5*, Pub. by Century UK) Trafalgar.

Soaring Gulls & Bowing Trees: The History of the Islands above Niagara Falls. Paul Gromosiak. (Illus.). 96p. (Orig.). 1989. pap. 9.95 (*0-9620314-6-1*) Meyer Enter.

Soaring in Self Respect. Virginia G. Kite. 144p. (Orig.). (YA). (gr. 8 up). 1995. pap. 7.95 (*0-942847-03-2*) Nugget Truth Minist.

***Soaring into the Storm: A Book about Those Who Triumph over Adversity.** large type ed. Alison Asher. (Illus.). 160p. (Orig.). 1996. pap. 17.95 (*1-887703-00-4*) LifeSkills WA.

Soaring on a Grasshopper's Back. Mary Lane. Ed. by Christine Wilson & Austin Wilson. (Illus.). 141p. 1983. 9.95 (*0-9612144-0-6*) Vireo Pr.

Soaring on Broken Wings: A Story of Triumph in Tragedy. Kathy Bartalsky. 1990. pap. 9.99 (*0-8024-2316-7*) Moody.

Soaring Spirit: Thirty-Five Years of Ford Thunderbird. John F. Katz. LC 89-81296. (Illus.). 64p. 19.95 (*0-915038-67-6*, 3-AQ-0055) Auto Quarterly.

Soaring Spirit, (600-400 Hundred BC) (Time Frame Ser.). (Illus.). 176p. 1988. 19.93 (*0-8094-6408-X*); lib. bdg. 25.93 (*0-8094-6409-8*) Time-Life.

Soaring Spirits: Conversations with Native American Teenagers. Karen Gravelle. LC 95-6822. (American Indian Experience Ser.). (Illus.). 128p. (YA). (gr. 7-12). 1995. lib. bdg. 22.00 (*0-531-11221-7*) Watts.

Soaring Straight Ahead. Susie Shellenberger. 32p. 1991. pap. 3.25 (*0-8341-1396-1*) Beacon Hill.

Soaring to New Heights on the Wings of Eagles: A Treasure Book of Affirmations for Personal Fulfillment, Set 4. Carleen Franklin & Sarah LaPlant. 120p. 1992. pap. text ed. 39.00 incl. audio (*0-9640867-4-3*) Excel Speaking.

Soaring to New Heights on the Wings of Eagles: A Treasury of Affirmations & Quotations for Personal Achievement. Carleen Franklin & Sarah LaPlant. 112p. 1995. pap. 9.00 (*0-9640867-1-9*) Excel Speaking.

Soaring Twenties: Babe Ruth & the Home Run Decade. Tom W. Gilbert. LC 96-14464. (American Game Ser.). 160p. (YA). (gr. 9-12). 1996. lib. bdg. 22.70 (*0-531-11279-9*) Watts.

Soaring Underground: A Young Fugitive's Life in Nazi Berlin. Larry Orbach & Vivien O. Smith. 300p. 1996. 24.95 (*0-929590-15-5*) Compass Pr.

Soaring with Eagles. Billy J. Daugherty. 32p. (Orig.). 1993. pap. 0.50 (*1-56267-091-3*) Victory Ctr OK.

Soaring with Eagles. Ed. by Ronald W. Vinson & Jack Payan. 1993. write for info. (*0-9624449-0-1*) Ind Insurance.

***Soaring with the Eagles.** Kenneth E. Hagin. 1996. pap. 2.95 (*0-89276-734-0*) Hagin Ministries.

***Soaring with the Spirit.** Janet Baughman. 100p. (Orig.). 1997. pap. 5.50 (*1-57502-377-6*, P01199) Morris Pubng.

S.O.B. The Handbook for Handling Super Difficult People. R. K. Tucker. LC 95-69595. 367p. 1996. pap. 14.95 (*0-9647375-0-7*) OptimAm.

Sob Sister Journalism. Phyllis L. Abramson. LC 90-36637. (Contributions to the Study of Mass Media & Communications Ser.: No. 23). 144p. 1990. text ed. 47.95 (*0-313-26513-5*, AST, Greenwood Pr) Greenwood.

***Soba: Archaeological Research at a Medieval Capital on the Blue Nile.** C. M. Daniels & Derek A. Welsby. (Illus.). 363p. 1991. 72.00 (*1-872566-02-2*, Pub. by Brit Inst Estrn Africa UK) David Brown.

Sobayid Atlas. Joseph S. Coleman & Andrew Leker. Ed. by Janice Sellers. (Skyrealms of Jorune Ser.). (Illus.). 64p. (Orig.). 1994. pap. text ed. 16.00 (*1-883240-03-4*) Chessex.

Sober Alcoholic: An Organizational Analysis of Alcoholics Anonymous. Irving P. Gellman. 1964. 24.95 (*0-8084-0279-X*) NCUP.

Sober & Free: Making Your Recovery Work for You. Guy Kettelhack. LC 95-24801. 176p. 1996. pap. 11.00 (*0-684-81120-0*, Fireside) S&S Trade.

Sober As a Judge see **Henry Cecil Reprint Series**

***Sober, but Stuck.** Dan F. 1991. pap. 11.00 (*1-56838-078-X*) Hazelden.

Sober But Stuck: Issues Most Often Encountered Which Keep Us from Growing in Recovery. Dan F. Ed. by Jane T. Noland. 204p. 1991. pap. 11.00 (*0-89638-246-X*) Hazelden.

Sober Days, Golden Years: Alcoholism & the Older Person. 48p. 1982. pap. 4.95 (*0-935908-06-4*, P109) Johnsn Inst.

Sober Generation: A Topology of Competent Adolescent Coping in Modern Puerto Rico. R. Fernandez Marina et al. 798p. 1969. 7.50 (*0-8477-2475-1*); pap. 6.00 (*0-8477-2476-X*) U of PR Pr.

Sober Living Workbook. Rip O'Keefe. 240p. 1980. pap. 12.00 (*0-89486-093-3*, 1098A) Hazelden.

Sober on a Small Plane. Dina Ben-Lev. 31p. (Orig.). 1995. pap. 6.95 (*0-9636545-5-1*) Wind Pubns.

Sober Spring: One Family's Battle with Addiction. Robert F. Bollendorf. 170p. (Orig.). 1988. pap. 5.95 (*0-915388-32-4*, 114, Buckley Pubns) ACTA Pubns.

***Sober Women, Sober Sex.** Pauline Falstrom. 272p. (Orig.). 1997. pap. 12.95 (*0-939339-14-5*, 14) AFCOM Pub.

Soberania de Dios. 3rd ed. Arthur W. Pink. Tr. by Jose M. Blanch from ENG. 215p. (Orig.). (SPA.). 1995. reprint ed. pap. 5.99 (*0-85151-416-2*) Banner of Truth.

***Sobering Questions.** G. N. Wright. 47p. (Orig.). 1987. pap. 2.00 (*0-940999-23-4*, C-2132) Star Bible.

Sobering Tales: Narratives of Alcoholism & Recovery. Edmund B. O'Reilly. LC 96-20323. 256p. (C). 1997. 50.00 (*1-55849-064-7*); pap. 16.95 (*1-55849-065-5*) U of Mass Pr.

Sobering Up: From Temperance to Prohibition in Antebellum America, Eighteen Hundred to Eighteen Sixty. Ian R. Tyrrell. LC 78-22132. (Contributions in American History Ser.: No. 82). 350p. 1979. text ed. 59.95 (*0-313-20822-0*, TYT/, Greenwood Pr) Greenwood.

Sobesednik (Conversationalist) Poems. Valery Petrochenkov. LC 92-81982. 160p. (Orig.). 1992. pap. 28.00 (*0-911971-77-7*) Effect Pub.

Sobolev Spaces. V. G. Maz'ya. Tr. by T. O. Saposnikova from RUS. (Soviet Mathematics Ser.). (Illus.). 510p. 1985. 225.00 (*0-387-13589-8*) Spr-Verlag.

***Sobolev Spaces of Fractional Order, Nemytskij Operators, & Nonlinear Partial Differential Equations.** Thomas Runst & Winfried Sickel. LC 96-31730. (Nonlinear Analysis & Applications Ser.). x, 547p. (C). 1996. text ed. 158.95 (*3-11-015113-8*) De Gruyter.

Sobolev Spaces of Infinite Order & Differential Equations. Julii A. Dubinskii. 1986. lib. bdg. 89.00 (*90-277-2147-5*) Kluwer Ac.

***Sobolev Spaces on Riemannian Manifolds.** Emmanuel Hebey. LC 96-36418. (Lecture Notes in Mathematics Ser.: Vol. 1635). 116p. 1996. pap. 29.00 (*3-540-61722-1*) Spr-Verlag.

Sobotta Atlas of Human Anatomy, 2 vols., Set. 12th ed. Ed. by R. Putz et al. Tr. by Anna N. Taylor. LC 96-10269. (Illus.). 1996. write for info. (*0-683-30030-X*) Williams & Wilkins.

Sobotta Atlas of Human Anatomy, Vol. 1, Head, Neck, Upper Limbs. 12th ed. Ed. by R. Putz et al. Tr. by Anna N. Taylor. LC 96-10269. (Illus.). 1996. write for info. (*0-683-18209-9*) Williams & Wilkins.

Sobotta Atlas of Human Anatomy, Vol. 2, Thorax, Abdomen, Pelvis, Lower Limb. 12th ed. Ed. by R. Putz et al. Tr. by Anna N. Taylor. LC 96-10269. (Illus.). 1996. write for info. (*0-683-18210-2*) Williams & Wilkins.

Sobranie Russkikh Vorovskikh Slovarei. (RUS.). 1983. pap. write for info. (*1-56541-160-9*) Chalidze.

Sobranie Sochinenii, Vol. 10: Lolita. Vladimir Nabokov. (Collected Works). 312p. (RUS.). 1989. 25.00 (*0-88233-535-9*) Ardis Pubs.

Sobranie Sochinenii, Vol. 2: Stat'i i Retsenzii, 1905-1926. Vladislav F. Khodasevich. Ed. by Robert Hughes & John E. Malmstad. (Illus.). 560p. (RUS.). (C). 1990. 37.50 (*0-88233-687-8*) Ardis Pubs.

Sobranie Stikhotvorenii v Dvukh Tomakh, Vol. 2. Boris B. Bozhnev. Ed. by Lazar Fleishman. (Modern Russian Literature & Culture, Studies & Texts: Vol. 24). (Illus.). 296p. (RUS.). 1989. pap. 16.00 (*0-933884-67-2*) Berkeley Slavic.

Sobranie Stikhotvorenii v Dvukh Tomakh, Vol. 1. Boris B. Bozhnev. Ed. by Lazar Fleishman. (Modern Russian Literature & Culture, Studies & Texts: Vol. 23). 177p. (Orig.). (RUS.). 1987. pap. 9.00 (*0-933884-53-2*) Berkeley Slavic.

***Sobranie Stikhov.** Nikolai Morshen. (Modern Russian Literature & Culture, Studies & Text: Vol. 37). 269p. (Orig.). (RUS.). 1996. pap. 20.00 (*1-57201-024-X*) Berkeley Slavic.

Sobranie Stikhov. Vladislav F. Khodasevich. LC 78-65602. 1978. reprint ed. pap. 7.95 (*0-89830-000-2*) Russica Pubs.

Sobranie Stikhov I Pesen V Trekh Tomakh, 3 vols. Vladimir Vysotskii. Ed. by Arkady A. Lvov & Alexander Sumerkin. LC 88-60720. (Illus.). 1000p. (Orig.). (RUS.). 1988. 150.00 (*0-89830-115-7*); pap. 85.00 (*0-89830-116-5*) Russica Pubs.

Sobre Critica y Criticos (Historia de la Literatura Espanola: Parentesis Teorico Que Apenas Tiene Que Ver Con la Presente Historia. J. L. Alborg. 1006p. (SPA.). 1993. 200.00 (*84-249-1465-1*) Elliots Bks.

Sobre el Amor. Plutarco. Ed. & Tr. by Antonio Guzman Guerra. (Nueva Austral Ser.: Vol. 127). (SPA.). 1991. pap. text ed. 24.95 (*84-239-1927-7*) Elliots Bks.

***Sobre el Sermon del Monte.** Charles R. Wood. (Bosquejos de Sermones Ser.). (SPA.). 1996. pap. 2.99 (*0-8254-1902-6*, Edit Portavoz) Kregel.

***Sobre el Yunque - On the Anvil.** Lucado. (SPA.). 1995. write for info. (*1-56063-924-5*) Editorial Unilit.

Sobre Esta Dificil Tierra. Felix C. Iturregui. LC 93-73104. 121p. (Orig.). 1993. pap. 6.95 (*0-929157-26-5*) Ediciones Huracan.

Sobre Esta Praia: Eight Meditations on the Coast of the Pacific. Jorge De Sena. Tr. by Jonathan Griffin. LC 79-114869. (Inklings Ser.: No. 1). 28p. (ENG & POR.). 1979. pap. 5.00 (*0-930012-31-3*) J Mudfoot.

Sobre Esta Roca Edificare Mi Iglesia. Raul C. Yoccou. 226p. (SPA.). 1991. pap. 6.99 (*1-56063-083-3*, 498487) Editorial Unilit.

Sobre Jose Lezama Lima y Sus Lectores: Guia y Compendio Bibliografico. Justo C. Ulloa. LC 87-60111. 101p. (SPA.). 1987. pap. 25.00 (*0-89295-049-8*) Society Sp & Sp-Am.

Sobre la Esencia del Hombre. Angel J. Casares. LC 78-15645. 104p. 1979. pap. 5.00 (*0-8477-2818-8*) U of PR Pr.

Sobre la Libertad & Comentarios a Tocqueville. John S. Mill. Ed. by Pavon D. Negro. Tr. by Cristina Garcia Cay. (Nueva Austral Ser.: Vol. 183). (SPA.). 1991. pap. text ed. 24.95 (*84-239-1983-8*) Elliots Bks.

Sobre la Vida y la Politica: Dialogo Con Vargas Llosa: Y Ensayos y Conferencias. 2nd ed. Ricardo A. Setti. (Illus.). 271p. (SPA.). 1989. pap. 9.95 (*968-6330-01-1*, Pub. by Kosmos Edit SA MX) Ediciones.

***Sobre las Alas del Viento.** Mizraim Esquilin. 284p. Date not set. pap. 9.99 (*0-88113-444-9*) Edit Betania.

***Sobre los Proverbios.** Charles R. Wood. (Bosquejos de Sermones Ser.). (SPA.). 1996. pap. 2.99 (*0-8254-1898-4*, Edit Portavoz) Kregel.

***Sobreponiendose Problemas Financieros - Avoiding Common Financial Problems.** Ron Blue. 119p. (SPA.). 1995. write for info. (*0-7899-0005-X*) Editorial Unilit.

Sobreproteccion Error de los Padres: La Error de los Padres. James C. Dobson. (Serie Enfoque a la Familia - Focus on the Family Ser.). 55p. (SPA.). 1992. pap. 1.79 (*1-56063-257-7*, 497428) Editorial Unilit.

Sobrino Del Mago - The Magician's Nephew. C. S. Lewis. 1995. pap. text ed. 11.95 (*84-204-4510-X*) Santillana.

Sobstvennye Rasskazy, Stikhi i Pesni Detei. 2nd rev. ed. Ed. by Aleksei Druchenykh. 29p. (RUS.). 1995. pap. 7.00 (*1-57201-020-7*) Berkeley Slavic.

Sobukwe & Apartheid. Benjamin Pogrund. 416p. (C). 1991. pap. 16.95 (*0-8135-1693-5*); text ed. 45.00 (*0-8135-1692-7*) Rutgers U Pr.

Socalist Thought: A Documentary History. rev. ed. Robert Sanders. Ed. by Albert Fried. LC 92-44881. 570p. (C). 1993. pap. 20.00 (*0-231-08265-7*, Mrngside); text ed. 49.50 (*0-231-08264-9*, Mrngside) Col U Pr.

Soccer. (Sportscene Ser.). 1992. 24.95 (*0-7134-6783-5*, Pub. by Batsford UK) Trafalgar.

Soccer! (J). (ps). 1995. 5.95 (*1-885751-05-2*) Wee Venture.

Soccer. 8.95 (*0-86685-707-9*, LDL65E, Pub. by Librairie du Liban FR) Intl Bk Ctr.

Soccer. (Take up Sports! Ser.). (Illus.). 64p. pap. 4.95 (*1-56757-054-2*) Appleton Comms.

***Soccer.** LC 97-11911. (Know the Sport Ser.). (Illus.). 48p. 1997. pap. 5.95 (*0-8117-2838-2*) Stackpole.

***Soccer.** (Composite Guide to...Ser.). (YA). (gr. 3 up). 1998. lib. bdg. 15.95 (*0-7910-4718-0*) Chelsea Hse.

Soccer. Tony Book. (Skills of the Game Ser.). (Illus.). 144p. 1995. pap. 19.95 (*1-85223-557-8*, Pub. by Crowood UK) Trafalgar.

Soccer. Paul Joseph. LC 96-1633. (How to Sports Ser.). (Illus.). (J). 1996. lib. bdg. 13.98 (*1-56239-649-8*) Abdo & Dghtrs.

Soccer. Mark Littleton. (Sports Heroes Ser.). 112p. 1996. pap. 4.99 (*0-310-20264-7*) Zondervan.

Soccer. David Marshall. (Successful Sports Ser.). (J). 1996. lib. bdg. write for info. (*1-57572-069-8*) Rigby Interact Libr.

Soccer. Antony Mason. (Butterfly Bks.). (Illus.). 31p. (ARA.). 11.95 (*0-86685-606-4*, LDL6064, Pub. by Librairie du Liban FR) Intl Bk Ctr.

Soccer. Stephen Negoesco. 144p. (C). 1992. per. write for info. (*0-697-10059-6*) Brown & Benchmark.

***Soccer.** Penny Nye. (Illus.). 16p. (Orig.). (J). (ps-4). 1997. pap. 10.00 (*1-890703-07-9*) Penny Laine.

Soccer. David Smale. (The Summer Olympics Ser.). 32p. (J). (gr. 4-8). 1995. 14.79 (*1-887068-02-3*) Smart Apple.

Soccer. Barry Wilner. LC 93-1525. (How to Play the All-Star Way Ser.). (J). 1993. lib. bdg. 24.26 (*0-8114-5777-X*) Raintree Steck-V.

Soccer. Barry Wilner. (J). 1995. pap. 6.95 (*0-8114-6343-5*) Raintree Steck-V.

Soccer. rev. ed. Ken Goldman & Peter Dunk. (Play the Game Ser.). (Illus.). 80p. 1994. pap. 8.95 (*0-7137-2419-6*, Pub. by Blandford Pr UK) Sterling.

Soccer. rev. ed. Bert Rosenthal. LC 95-16449. (New True Bks.). 48p. (J). (gr. k-4). 1995. lib. bdg. 19.00 (*0-516-01084-0*) Childrens.

***Soccer, 3 vols., Vol. 3.** unabridged ed. Laurie Wark. (Basics for Beginners Ser.). (Illus.). 24p. (J). (gr. k-3). 1994. pap. 3.50 (*1-55074-188-8*, Pub. by Kids Can Pr CN) Genl Dist Srvs.

Soccer: A Guide for Parents & Coaches. Cooper Publishing Group Staff. (U. S. O. C. Sports Education Ser.). (Illus.). 128p. (Orig.). 1996. pap. 30.00 (*1-884125-54-9*) Cooper Pubng.

***Soccer: An Intimate History of the World's Most Popular Game.** Mark Stewart. LC 97-17201. (Watts History of Sports Ser.). (J). 1998. write for info. (*0-531-11456-2*) Watts.

***Soccer: Attacking.** Barbara Bonney. LC 97-8096. (Play It Like a Pro Ser.). (J). 1997. write for info. (*1-57103-135-9*) Rourke Pr.

***Soccer: Defending.** Barbara Bonney. LC 97-8097. (Play It Like a Pro Ser.). (J). 1997. write for info. (*1-57103-136-7*) Rourke Pr.

Soccer: Easy Sports Reader. Burt & Hog. (Illus.). 16p. (J). (ps-1). 1996. pap. 2.49 (*1-55734-894-4*) Tchr Create Mat.

Soccer: Steps to Success. 2nd ed. Joseph A. Luxbacher. LC 95-44483. (Steps to Success Activity Ser.). (Illus.). 168p. (Orig.). 1996. pap. 14.95 (*0-87322-763-8*, PLUX0763) Human Kinetics.

Soccer: Technique, Tactics & Training. Sean Gallery. (Crowood Sports Guides Ser.). (Illus.). 128p. 1992. pap. 22.95 (*1-85223-542-X*, Pub. by Crowood Pr UK) Trafalgar.

Soccer: The Complete Player. Dan Herbst. 1993. pap. 10.95 (*1-56800-005-7*, Sports Illus Bks) Natl Bk Netwk.

Soccer: The Game & How to Play It. rev. ed. Gary Rosenthal. LC 72-129116. (Illus.). 256p. (J). (gr. 3-9). 1978. lib. bdg. 14.95 (*0-87460-258-0*) Lion Bks.

Soccer: The Universal Game: A Comprehensive Technical Casebook Valuable to All. Orazio Z. Buttafuoco. (Illus.). 200p. 1994. pap. 16.95 (*0-8059-3448-0*) Dorrance.

Soccer: What's It All about Diving Headers, Selling a Dummy, & Everything Else about the Game. Dick Howard. (Illus.). 120p. 1996. pap. text ed. 8.95 (*1-895629-56-X*, Pub. by Warwick Pub CN) Firefly Bks Ltd.

Soccer: Wilson Sports Book. Wilson Editors. 1995. pap. 10.00 (*0-671-88831-5*) S&S Trade.

Soccer: Winning Techniques. 2nd ed. Joseph A. Luxbacher. (Illus.). 162p. (Orig.). 1992. pap. 13.95 (*0-945483-11-2*) E Bowers Pub.

Soccer: Winning Through Technique & Tactics. Richard Alagich. 1995. pap. text ed. 29.95 (*0-07-470228-9*), McGraw.

Soccer - the Game & How to Play It. Gary Rosenthall. 1981. pap. 7.00 (*0-87980-310-X*) Wilshire.

Soccer - The International Training Guide. Jerzy Wrzos. 1991. 25.00 (*0-533-08904-2*) Vantage.

Soccer Around the World. Dale E. Howard. (World Cup Soccer Ser.). (Illus.). 48p. (J). (gr. 4-9). 1994. lib. bdg. 21.00 (*0-516-08046-6*) Childrens.

Soccer Around the World. Dale E. Howard. (World Cup Soccer Ser.). (Illus.). 48p. (J). (gr. 4-9). 1994. pap. 6.95 (*0-516-48046-4*) Childrens.

Soccer Basics. Sellin. 1987. pap. 3.95 (*0-02-499800-1*, Macmillan Coll) P-H.

Soccer Circus. Jamie Gilson. LC 92-9716. (J). 1993. 15.00 (*0-688-12021-0*) Lothrop.

Soccer Circus. Jamie Gilson. (J). 1996. pap. 4.95 (*0-688-14746-1*) Morrow.

Soccer Coaching Handbook. Martin Bidzinski. (Illus.). 224p. 1996. pap. 29.95 (*1-85223-973-5*, Pub. by Crowood Pr UK) Trafalgar.

Soccer Coaching Methods. Bill Thomson. (Illus.). 154p. 1984. reprint ed. pap. 8.95 (*0-943752-02-7*) Soccer Pubns Inc.

Soccer Coach's Guide to Practices, Drills & Skill Training. Butch Lauffer & Sandy Davie. LC 92-44087. (Illus.). 160p. 1993. pap. 13.95 (*0-8069-8219-5*) Sterling.

Soccer Cousins. Jean Marzollo. (Hello Reader! Ser.). (Illus.). 1997. write for info. (*0-590-74254-X*) Scholastic Inc.

***Soccer Czars.** Jason Tomas. (Illus.). 192p. 1996. 34.95 (*1-85158-774-8*, Pub. by Mnstream UK) Trafalgar.

Soccer Drills for Individual & Team Play. James P. McGettigan. 276p. 1986. 21.95 (*0-13-815309-4*, Parker Publishing Co) P-H.

Soccer Drills for Individual & Team Play. James P. McGettigan. 240p. 1989. 9.95 (*0-13-815366-3*) P-H.

Soccer Duel. Thomas J. Dygard. 224p. (J). (gr. 4 up). 1990. pap. 4.99 (*0-14-034116-1*, Puffin) Puffin Bks.

***Soccer Equipment.** Barbara Bonney. LC 97-8098. (Play It Like a Pro Ser.). (J). 1997. write for info. (*1-57103-137-5*) Rourke Pr.

Soccer Everyone. Pronk & Gorman. 160p. 1991. pap. text ed. 14.95 (*0-88725-137-4*) Hunter Textbks.

Soccer Fit: Training & Health for Soccer Players. Mervyn Beck. (Illus.). 96p. 1992. pap. 22.95 (*1-85223-472-5*, Pub. by Crowood Pr UK) Trafalgar.

Soccer for Beginners: How to Understand & Play the Game of Soccer. Julius Abangma. (Illus.). 128p. (YA). (gr. 7-12). 1994. pap. 10.95 (*1-885392-07-9*) Allied Publishers.

Soccer for Juniors. Bruce Pollock. (J). 1980. 9.95 (*0-684-16487-6*) S&S Trade.

Soccer for Juniors: A Guide for Players, Parents, & Coaches. Robert Pollock. (Illus.). 208p. 1985. pap. 9.95 (*0-684-18369-2*) S&S Trade.

Soccer Fundamentals. John Learmouth. LC 94-12571. 1994. pap. 7.95 (*0-312-11532-6*) St Martin.

Soccer Fundamentals: Basic Techniques & Training for Beginning Players. John Learmouth. LC 78-19415. (Illus.). 1979. pap. 4.95 (*0-312-73133-7*) St Martin.

Soccer Fundamentals for Players & Coaches. Wiel Coerver. 184p. 1986. 19.95 (*0-13-815226-8*, Busn); pap. 10.95 (*0-13-815218-7*, Busn) P-H.

Soccer Game! Grace Maccarone. LC 93-43742. (Illus.). 32p. (J). 1994. 2.95 (*0-590-48369-2*) Scholastic Inc.

Soccer Games Book. J. Malcolm Simon & John A. Reeves. LC 82-81817. (Illus.). 176p. (Orig.). 1982. pap. 13.95 (*0-88011-064-3*, PSIM0064) Human Kinetics.

Soccer Goalkeeper. 2nd ed. Joseph A. Luxbacher & Gene Klein. LC 93-6290. 176p. 1993. pap. 14.95 (*0-87322-397-7*, PLUX0397) Human Kinetics.

Soccer Goalkeeping: The First Line of Attack, the Last Line of Defense. Lincoln Phillips. (Illus.). 160p. (Orig.). 1996. pap. 12.95 (*1-57028-077-0*) Masters Pr IN.

Soccer Halfback. Matt Christopher. (Illus.). (J). (gr. 4-6). 1978. 15.95 (*0-316-13946-7*) Little.

Soccer Halfback. Matt Christopher. (Illus.). (J). (gr. 4-6). 1985. mass mkt. 3.95 (*0-316-13981-5*) Little.

Soccer Handbook. Paul Harris. (Spalding Sports Library). (Illus.). 128p. (Orig.). 1992. pap. 9.95 (*0-940279-46-0*) Masters Pr IN.

Soccer Handbook. David Keith. (Illus.). 66p. pap. 6.95 (*0-88839-048-3*) Hancock House.

Soccer Handbook for Players, Coaches & Parents. Albert M. Luongo. LC 96-27651. (Illus.). 212p. 1996. pap. 22.50 (*0-7864-0159-1*) McFarland & Co.

S

Soccer in Latin America. Tony Mason. (Critical Studies in Latin American Culture). 224p. 1995. pap. 18.00 (0-86091-667-7, B3633, Pub. by Vrso UK) Norton.

Soccer Injuries: Prevention & First Aid. Alan G. Smith. (Illus.). 96p. 1995. pap. 22.95 (1-85223-186-6, Pub. by Crowood UK) Trafalgar.

***Soccer Is Fun No. 1: A Workbook for 6, 7 & 8 Year Olds.** Tony Waiters & Jane Cowan. Ed. by Bob Dunn. (Soccer Activity Book Ser.: No. 1). (Illus.). 48p. (Orig.). (J). (gr. 1-3). 1991. wbk. ed., pap. 7.95 (1-896466-05-2) T Waiters.

***Soccer Is Fun No. 2: A Workbook for 6, 7 & 8 Year Olds.** Tony Waiters & Jane Cowan. Ed. by Dunn Communications, Ltd. (Soccer Activity Book Ser.: No. 2). (Illus.). 48p. (Orig.). (J). (gr. 1-3). 1995. pap. 7.95 (1-896466-09-5) T Waiters.

***Soccer is Fun No. 3: A Workbook for 6, 7, & 8 Year Olds.** Tony Waiters & Jane Cowan. Ed. by Dunn Communications, Ltd. (Soccer Activity Book Ser.: No. 3). (Illus.). 48p. (Orig.). (J). (gr. 1-3). 1997. wbk. ed., pap. 7.95 (1-896466-13-3) T Waiters.

Soccer Made Simple: A Spectator's Guide. P.J. Harari. 125p. 1994. pap. 7.95 (1-884309-01-1) First Base Spts.

Soccer Made Simple for Parents & Spectators: A Quick Guide for Understanding Terminology & Rules. Dennis H. Reid. 100p. 1996. write for info. (0-9645562-1-9) Habilit Mgt Consult.

Soccer Madness: Brazil's Passion for the World's Most Popular Sport. rev. ed. Janet Lever. (Illus.). 200p. (C). 1995. pap. text ed. 10.95 (0-88133-843-5) Waveland Pr.

Soccer Mania! Erika Tamar. (Stepping Stone Bks.). 64p. (Orig.). (J). (gr. 2-4). 1993. pap. 3.99 (0-679-83396-X); lib. bdg. 11.99 (0-679-93396-4) Random Bks Yng Read.

***Soccer Mystery.** Created by Gertrude C. Warner. LC 97-25386. (Boxcar Children Mysteries Ser.: Vol. 60). (Illus.). 128p. (J). (gr. 2-7). 1997. pap. 3.95 (0-8075-7527-5); lib. bdg. 13.95 (0-8075-7528-3) A Whitman.

Soccer, Play Like a Pro. Anthony Ventura. LC 89-27292. (Be the Best! Ser.). (Illus.). 64p. (J). (gr. 4-8). 1990. lib. bdg. 11.89 (0-8167-1933-0) Troll Communs.

Soccer, Play Like a Pro. Anthony Ventura. LC 89-27292. (Be the Best! Ser.). (Illus.). 64p. (J). (gr. 4-8). 1996. pap. 3.95 (0-8167-1934-9) Troll Communs.

Soccer Practice Games. Joseph A. Luxbacher. LC 94-12525. 160p. 1994. pap. 14.95 (0-87322-554-6, PLUX0554) Human Kinetics.

Soccer Referee's Manual. David Ager. pap. 17.95 (0-7136-3988-1, 93167, Pub. by A&C Black UK) Talman.

Soccer Restart Plays. Ed. by J. Malcolm Simon & John A. Reeves. LC 93-24693. (Illus.). 152p. 1994. pap. 13.95 (0-87322-521-X, PSIM0521) Human Kinetics.

Soccer Rules: A Player's Guide. Ken Goldman. (Illus.). 80p. 1996. pap. 9.95 (0-7137-2474-9, Pub. by Blandford Pr UK) Sterling.

Soccer Sam. Jean Marzollo. LC 86-47533. (Step into Reading Bks.). (Illus.). 48p. (J). (gr. 1-3). 1987. pap. 3.99 (0-394-88406-X) Random Bks Yng Read.

Soccer Sam. Jean Marzollo. LC 86-47533. (Step into Reading Bks.). (Illus.). 48p. (J). (gr. 1-3). 1987. lib. bdg. 7.99 (0-394-98406-4) Random Bks Yng Read.

***Soccer School: Bind-Up.** Gill Harvey & Richard Dungworth. (Soccer School Ser.). 128p. (Orig.). (YA). (gr. 3 up). 1997. pap. 14.95 (0-7460-2915-2, Usborne) EDC.

***Soccer School: Bind-Up.** Gill Harvey & Richard Dungworth. (Soccer School Ser.). 128p. (J). (gr. 3 up). 1997. lib. bdg. 22.95 (0-88110-943-6, Usborne) EDC.

***Soccer Scoop, 57 Vols., Vol. 57.** Matt Christopher. (Matt Christopher Sports Classics Ser.). 1997. 15.95 (0-316-14206-9); pap. text ed. 3.95 (0-316-18896-4) Little.

Soccer Sense: Terms, Tips & Techniques. Paul S. Delson. LC 93-90052. (Illus.). 97p. (Orig.). (J). (gr. 8). 1993. pap. 9.95 (0-9634669-0-9) Excalibur CA.

Soccer Shock. Donna J. Napoli. LC 91-20706. (Illus.). 192p. (J). (gr. 4-7). 1991. pap. 13.95 (0-525-44827-6) Dutton Child Bks.

Soccer Shock. Donna J. Napoli. LC 93-7483. (Illus.). 192p. (J). (gr. 3-7). 1993. pap. 3.99 (0-14-036482-X, Puffin) Puffin Bks.

Soccer Shoe Clue. Carolyn Keene. Ed. by Anne Greenberg. (Nancy Drew Ser.: No. 5). 80p. (Orig.). (J). (gr. 2-4). 1995. pap. 3.50 (0-671-87949-9, Minstrel Bks) PB.

Soccer Shots. Werner Quies. LC 95-60070. (Illus.). 125p. (Orig.). (YA). 1995. pap. 10.95 (0-939116-37-5) Frontier OR.

***Soccer Skills.** Barbara Bonney. LC 97-8100. (Play It Like a Pro Ser.). (J). 1997. write for info. (1-57103-139-1) Rourke Pr.

Soccer Skills. P. Woods. (Superskills Ser.). (Illus.). 48p. (YA). (gr. 6-10). 1987. pap. 5.95 (0-7460-0167-3) EDC.

Soccer Skills & Drills. Gary Rosenthal. (Illus.). 224p. (gr. 7 up). 1984. pap. 14.00 (0-684-18217-3) S&S Trade.

Soccer Skills & Drills. rev. ed. Gary Rosenthal. LC 93-32462. 262p. 1994. pap. 14.00 (0-02-036435-0) Macmillan.

Soccer Star. Edward Packard. (Young Readers Ser.: No. 146). 128p. (J). 1994. pap. 3.50 (0-553-56011-5) Bantam.

Soccer Stars. Dale E. Howard. (World Cup Soccer Ser.). (Illus.). 48p. (J). (gr. 4-9). 1994. lib. bdg. 21.00 (0-516-08047-4) Childrens.

Soccer Stars. Dale E. Howard. (World Cup Soccer Ser.). (Illus.). 48p. (J). (gr. 4-9). 1994. pap. 6.95 (0-516-48047-2) Childrens.

***Soccer Tactics: Top Team Strategies Explained.** W. H. Wilkinson. (Illus.). 128p. 1997. pap. 22.95 (1-85223-984-0, Pub. by Crowood Pr UK) Trafalgar.

Soccer Techniques in Pictures. Michael Brown. (Techniques in Pictures Ser.). (Illus.). 80p. (Orig.). (YA). 1991. pap. 8.95 (0-399-51701-4, Perigee Bks) Berkley Pub.

Soccer Techniques, Tactics & Teamwork. Gerhard Bauer. 160p. 1994. lib. bdg. 39.00 (0-8095-7621-X) Borgo Pr.

Soccer Techniques, Tactics & Teamwork. Gerhard Bauer. (Illus.). 160p. 1993. pap. 14.95 (0-8069-8730-8) Sterling.

Soccer Training. Mervyn Beck et al. (Illus.). 128p. 1996. pap. 22.95 (1-85223-896-8, Pub. by Crowood Pr UK) Trafalgar.

Soccer Training. 4th ed. Whitehead & Cook. pap. 19.95 (0-7136-3832-X, 92981, Pub. by A&C Black UK) Talman.

Soccer War. Ryszard Kapuscinski. 1992. pap. 13.00 (0-679-73805-3, Vin) Random.

***Sochineniia.** Elena Guro. Ed. by Gareth K. Perkins. (Modern Russian Literature & Culture, Studies & Text: Vol. 34). (Illus.). 394p. (Orig.). (RUS.). 1996. pap. 30.00 (0-933884-96-6) Berkeley Slavic.

Sociability & Intoxication: Alcohol & Drinking in Kenya, Africa & the Modern World. J. Partanen. (Finnish Foundation for Alcohol Studies: Vol. 39). 1991. pap. 35.00 (951-9192-48-4) Rutgers Ctr Alcohol.

Social Action with Children & Families: A Community Development Approach to Child & Family Welfare. Ed. by Crescy Cannan & Chris Warren. (State of Welfare Ser.). 240p. (C). 1997. pap. write for info. (0-415-13151-0); text ed. write for info. (0-415-13150-2) Routledge.

Social Acceptance of Weather Modification. Barbara C. Farhar & Julia Mewes. (Program on Environment & Behavior Monograph Ser.: No. 23). 194p. (Orig.). (C). 1976. pap. 8.00 (0-685-28100-0) Natural Hazards.

Social Accountability Budget: A Process for Planning & Reporting Community Service in a Time of Fiscal Constraint. 119p. 1989. pap. 20.00 (0-87125-179-5, 813) Cath Health.

Social Accountability in Communication. Richard Buttny. 208p. (C). 1993. text ed. 59.95 (0-8039-8306-9); pap. text ed. 19.95 (0-8039-8307-7) Sage.

Social Accountability Program: Continuing the Community Benefit Tradition of Not-for-Profit Homes & Services for the Aging. 98p. 1993. pap. 9.95 (0-943774-47-0, 812) Cath Health.

Social Accounting for Development Planning with Special Reference to Sri Lanka. F. Graham Pyatt & Alan Roe. LC 76-30553. 222p. reprint ed. pap. 63.30 (0-317-30419-4, 2024943) Bks Demand.

Social Accounting Framework for Development: Concepts, Construction & Applications. Jorge Alarcon et al. 290p. 1991. text ed. 68.95 (1-85628-164-7, Pub. by Avebury Pub UK) Ashgate Pub Co.

Social Accounting Matrix for Cameroon. Madeleine Gauthier & Steven Kyle. (Working Papers). (C). 1991. pap. text ed. 7.00 (1-56401-104-6) Cornell Food.

Social Accounting Matrix for Madagascar: Methodology & Results. Paul A. Dorosh et al. (Working Papers). (C). 1991. pap. text ed. 7.00 (1-56401-106-2) Cornell Food.

Social Accounting Matrix for Niger: Methodology & Results. CFNPP Staff et al. (Working Papers). (C). 1991. pap. text ed. 7.00 (1-56401-118-6) Cornell Food.

Social Accounting Matrix for Tanzania. Alexander H. Sarris. (Working Papers: No. 62). 38p. (C). Date not set. pap. 7.00 (1-56401-162-3) Cornell Food.

Social Accounting Matrix for the Gambia. CFNPP Staff et al. (Working Papers). (C). 1992. pap. text ed. 7.00 (1-56401-120-8) Cornell Food.

Social Action. Gottfried Seebass & Raimo Tuomela. 1985. lib. bdg. 132.00 (90-277-1871-2) Kluwer Ac.

Social Action & Human Nature. Axel Honneth & Hans Joas. 175p. 1989. 65.00 (0-521-32683-4); pap. text ed. 19.95 (0-521-33935-9) Cambridge U Pr.

Social Action & Social Change. Ed. by C. Lakshmanna et al. 1990. 37.00 (0-685-40054-9, Pub. by Ajanta II) S Asia.

Social Action Collections at the State Historical Society of Wisconsin: A Guide. Menzi L. Behrnd-Klodt & Carolyn J. Mattern. LC 85-5007. 158p. 1983. pap. 12.00 (0-87020-220-0) State Hist Soc Wis.

Social Action in Group Work. Ed. by Ave Vinik & Morris Levin. LC 91-39986. (Social Work with Groups Ser.). 208p. 1992. pap. text ed. 19.95 (1-56024-212-4); lib. bdg. 39.95 (1-56024-211-6) Harrington Pk.

Social Action Progress & Social Funds: A Review of Design & Implementation in Sub-Saharan Africa. Alexandre Marc et al. LC 94-48191. (Discussion Paper Ser.: No. 274). 174p. 1995. 10.95 (0-8213-3167-1, 13167) World Bank.

Social Action Through Law: Partnership for Social Justice. P. K. Gandhi. (C). 1990. 75.00 (0-89771-318-4) St Mut.

Social Actors & Designing the Civil Society of Eastern Europe. Ed. by Alberto Gasparini & Vladimir Yadov. LC 95-37796. (Foundations in International Social Structures Ser.: Vol. 1). 1995. 73.25 (1-55938-965-6) Jai Pr.

Social Adaptation to Food Stress: A Prehistoric Southwestern Example. Paul E. Minnis. LC 84-28103. (Prehistoric Archeology & Ecology Ser.). (Illus.). 250p. 1985. pap. text ed. 10.00 (0-226-53024-8) U Ch Pr.

Social Adjustment of Young Children: A Cognitive Approach to Solving Real-Life Problems. George Spivack & Myrna B. Shure. LC 73-10942. (Jossey-Bass Behavioral Science Ser.). 232p. reprint ed. pap. 66.20 (0-317-08624-3, 2021090) Bks Demand.

Social Administration: A Client-Centered Approach. Charles A. Rapp & John Poertner. 308p. (C). 1992. teacher ed. write for info. (0-8013-0450-4, 78262); pap. text ed. 54.50 (0-8013-0435-0, 78244) Longman.

Social Administration: The Management of the Social Services. Ed. by Simon Slavin. LC 77-88090. 579p. 1978. 49.95 (0-917724-01-1) Haworth Pr.

***Social Administration Vol. 1: An Introduction to Human Services.** Ed. by Simon Slavin. 1985. 49.95 (0-86656-343-1); pap. 24.95 (0-86656-344-X) Haworth Pr.

***Social Administration Vol. 2: Managing Finances, Personnel, & Information in Human Services.** Ed. by Simon Slavin. 1985. 49.95 (0-86656-345-8); pap. 24.95 (0-86656-346-6) Haworth Pr.

Social Agency: Dilemmas & Education. Ed. by Wojciech W. Gasparski et al. (Praxiology Ser.: Vol. 4). 351p. (C). 1996. text ed. 49.95 (1-56000-240-9) Transaction Pubs.

Social Agency Policy. 2nd ed. John P. Flynn. LC 84-25561. 323p. 1992. pap. text ed. 25.95 (0-8304-1272-7) Nelson-Hall.

Social Agendas & the Corruption of Criticism. John Ellis. (Rethinking Theory Ser.). 29.95 (0-8101-1104-7) Northwestern U Pr.

Social Amnesia: A Critique of Contemporary Psychology. Russell Jacoby. 200p. 1996. pap. text ed. 24.95 (1-56000-892-X) Transaction Pubs.

Social Analysis: A Marxist Critique & Alternative. Victor L. Allen. LC 75-327627. 338p. reprint ed. pap. 96.40 (0-317-09619-2, 2010049) Bks Demand.

Social Analysis: Linking Faith & Justice. enl. rev. ed. Joe Holland & Peter Henriot. LC 83-6259. 118p. 1983. pap. 13.50 (0-88344-462-3) Orbis Bks.

Social Analysis in the Time of AIDS: Theory, Method, & Action. Gilbert Herdt & Shirley Lindenbaum. (Illus.). 408p. 1992. 58.00 (0-8039-4372-5); pap. 26.50 (0-8039-4373-3) Sage.

Social Analysis of Education: After the New Sociology. Philip Wexler. (Critical Social Thought Ser.). 192p. 1987. 29.95 (0-7100-9964-9, RKP) Routledge.

Social Analysis of Education: After the New Sociology. Philip Wexler. (Critical Social Thought Ser.). 240p. (C). 1990. pap. 15.95 (0-415-90340-8, A4777, Routledge NY) Routledge.

Social Anarchism or Lifestyle Anarchism: An Unbridgeable Chasm. Murray Bookchin. 96p. (Orig.). 1996. pap. 11.95 (1-873176-83-X, AK Pr San Fran) AK Pr Dist.

Social & Applied Aspects of Perceiving Faces. Ed. by Thomas R. Alley. (Wm Mace Ser.). 304p. 1988. text ed. 69.95 (0-8058-0163-4) L Erlbaum Assocs.

Social & Behavioral Aspects of AIDS, Vol. 3. Ed. by Gary L. Albrecht & Rick Zimmerman. (Advances in Medical Sociology Ser.). 227p. 1993. 73.25 (1-55938-439-5) Jai Pr.

Social & Behavioral Aspects of Female Alcoholism: An Annotated Bibliography. Compiled by H. Paul Chalfant & Brent S. Roper. LC 80-1021. xvi, 145p. 1980. text ed. 49.95 (0-313-20947-2, CAL/, Greenwood Pr) Greenwood.

Social & Behavioral Aspects of Pharmaceutical Care. Ed. by Mickey C. Smith & Albert I. Wertheimer. (Illus.). 838p. 1996. lib. bdg. 89.95 (1-56024-952-8, Pharmctl Prods) Haworth Pr.

Social & Behavioral Science Research: A New Framework for Conceptualizing, Implementing, & Evaluating Research Studies. David R. Krathwohl. LC 84-43028. (Social & Behavioral Science Ser.). 347p. 40.95 (0-87589-637-5) Jossey-Bass.

Social & Behavioral Sciences: Report of the Project 2061 Phase I. Mortimer H. Appley & Winifred B. Maher. LC 89-101. 56p. 1989. pap. 7.50 (0-87168-346-6, 89-05S) AAAS.

Social & Biological Aspects of Ethnicity. Ed. by Malcolm Chapman. LC 93-22091. (Biosocial Society Ser.: No. 4). 144p. 1993. 45.00 (0-19-852280-0) OUP.

Social & Biological Aspects of Mental Disease. Benjamin Malzberg. Ed. by Gerald N. Grob. LC 78-22573. (Historical Issues in Mental Health Ser.). (Illus.). 1980. reprint ed. lib. bdg. 28.95 (0-405-11926-7) Ayer.

Social & Built Environment in an Older Society. Institute of Medicine Staff. (America's Aging Ser.). 304p. 1988. pap. text ed. 29.95 (0-309-03780-8) Natl Acad Pr.

Social & Ceremonial Organization of Cochiti. Esther S. Goldfrank. LC 28-11444. (American Anthropological Association Memoirs Ser.). 1927. 25.00 (0-527-00532-0) Periodicals Srv.

***Social & Cognitive Approaches to Interpersonal Communication.** Ed. by Susan R. Fussell & Roger J. Kreuz. LC 97-21638. 1997. write for info. (0-8058-2269-0) L Erlbaum Assocs.

***Social & Cognitive Approaches to Interpersonal Communication.** Ed. by Susan R. Fussell & Roger J. Kreuz. LC 97-21638. 1997. pap. write for info. (0-8058-2270-4) L Erlbaum Assocs.

Social & Cognitive Aspects of Normal & Atypical Language Development. Ed. by S. Von Tetzchner et al. (Cognitive Development Ser.). (Illus.). 195p. 1989. 124.95 (0-387-96882-2) Spr-Verlag.

Social & Cognitive Treatment of Children & Adolescents: Practical Strategies for Problem Behaviors. Richard P. Barth. LC 85-45899. (Social & Behavioral Science Ser.). 549p. text ed. 85.00 (0-87589-675-8) Jossey-Bass.

Social & Cultural Aspects of VCR Use. Ed. by Julia Dobrow. 232p. (C). 1990. text ed. 65.00 (0-8058-0499-4) L Erlbaum Assocs.

Social & Cultural Change. Bryce F. Ryan. LC 79-84081. 506p. reprint ed. pap. 144.30 (0-317-09616-8, 2012534) Bks Demand.

Social & Cultural Change: Social Science for a Dynamic World. Jay A. Weinstein. LC 96-11694. 464p. 1996. 57.00 (0-02-425333-2, Macmillan Coll) P-H.

Social & Cultural Contexts of New Ceramic Technologies. Ed. by W. D. Kingery. LC 93-10029. (Ceramics & Civilization Ser.: Vol. VI). 298p. 1993. 69.00 (0-944904-61-0, CCV6) Am Ceramic.

Social & Cultural Dynamics. abr. ed. Pitirim A. Sorokin. LC 57-14120. (Extending Horizons Ser.). (Illus.). 720p. (C). 1985. 10.00 (0-87558-029-7) Porter Sargent.

Social & Cultural Dynamics: A Study of Change in Major Systems of Art, Truth, Ethics, & Social Relationships. Pitirim A. Sorokin. 718p. (C). 1981. pap. 29.95 (0-87855-787-3) Transaction Pubs.

Social & Cultural Foundations of Education: Scholar's Study Guide. Jeanne Ewing & Jack London. 500p. (Orig.). pap. 30.00 (1-884690-02-5) Owl Press.

Social & Cultural History of Ancient India. M. L. Bose. 1990. 24.00 (81-7022-287-7, Pub. by Concept II) S Asia.

Social & Cultural History of the Soviet Union: The Lenin & Stalin Years. Ed. by William Rosenberg. LC 91-44186. (Articles on Russian & Soviet History, 1500-1991 Ser.: Vol. 6). 536p. 1992. text ed. 25.00 (0-8153-0563-X) Garland.

Social & Cultural Issues of the New International Economic Order. Ed. by Jorge A. Lozoya. (Policy Studies). 1981. 52.00 (0-08-025123-4, Pergamon Pr) Elsevier.

Social & Cultural Life of Nagas: (The Tangkhul Nagas) M. Horam. (C). 1992. reprint ed. 8.00 (81-85418-94-2, Pub. by Low Price II) S Asia.

Social & Cultural Roots of Linear Perspective. Leonard Goldstein. LC 87-3547. (Studies in Marxism: Vol. 22). 181p. 1988. 26.95 (0-930656-51-2); pap. 12.95 (0-930656-52-0) MEP Pubns.

Social & Cultural Selections from Contemporary Persian. Ed. by Michel M. Mazzaoui & William G. Millward. LC 73-569. 128p. (C). 1973. text ed. 15.00 (0-88206-100-3) Caravan Bks.

Social & Demographic Accounting. Ed. by Geoffrey J. Hewings & Moss Madden. 256p. (C). 1995. text ed. 54.95 (0-521-46572-9) Cambridge U Pr.

Social & Ecological Aspects of Irrigation & Drainage: Selected Papers. American Society of Civil Engineers Staff. LC 75-30807. 381p. reprint ed. pap. 108.60 (0-317-10978-2, 2007865) Bks Demand.

Social & Economic Adjustment of the Croatian Displaced Persons in Cleveland Compared with That of the Earlier Croatian Immigrants. Joseph C. Brentar. LC 77-155331. 1971. pap. 10.00 (0-88247-099-X) Ragusan Pr.

Social & Economic Aspects of Radioactive Waste Disposal: Considerations for Institutional Management. National Research Council Staff. 175p. 1984. pap. text ed. 19.95 (0-309-03444-2) Natl Acad Pr.

Social & Economic Aspects of the Chain Store Movement. Harold M. Haas. Ed. by Stuart Bruchey & Vincent P. Carosso. LC 78-18962. (Small Business Enterprise in America Ser.). 1979. lib. bdg. 25.95 (0-405-11466-4) Ayer.

Social & Economic Aspects of the Islam of Mohammad. S. A. Ali. LC 93-7498. 184p. 1993. 79.95 (0-7734-9279-8) E Mellen.

Social & Economic Aspects of Water Resources Development: Proceedings of the Symposium, Ithaca, NY, 1971. Social & Economic Aspects of Water Resources Development Symposium Staff. Ed. by Leonard B. Dworsky et al. LC 73-79332. (Proceedings of American Water Resources Association Ser.: No. 9). 267p. reprint ed. pap. 76.10 (0-317-09865-9, 2003128) Bks Demand.

Social & Economic Atlas of India. (Illus.). 253p. 1988. 75.00 (0-19-562041-0) OUP.

Social & Economic Change among the Northern Ojibwa. R. W. Dunning. LC 60-50269. 1959. pap. 9.95 (0-8020-6131-1) U of Toronto Pr.

Social & Economic Change in Assam: Middle Class Hegemony. Manorama Sharma. 1990. 21.50 (81-202-0261-9, Pub. by Ajanta II) S Asia.

***Social & Economic Characteristics, U. S. (1990)** (Illus.). 550p. (C). 1996. pap. 50.00 (0-7881-3045-5) DIANE Pub.

Social & Economic Conditions under the Imperial Rashtrakutas. Jayashri Mishra. (C). 1992. 28.50 (81-7169-171-4, Pub. by Commonwealth II) S Asia.

Social & Economic Consequences of Deregulation: The Transportation Industry in Transition. Paul S. Dempsey. LC 89-3168. 293p. 1989. text ed. 59.95 (0-89930-380-3, DYE, Quorum Bks) Greenwood.

Social & Economic Development. Baha'i Publishing Trust (Australia) Staff. 48p. 1989. pap. 3.95 (0-909991-31-6) Bahai.

Social & Economic Development: A Baha'i Approach. Holly H. Vick. (Global Transformation Ser.). 148p. (Orig.). (C). 1990. pap. 9.50 (0-85398-293-7) G Ronald Pub.

Social & Economic Development: An Introduction. Tony Barnett. LC 88-28394. 232p. (Orig.). 1989. pap. text ed. 19.95 (0-89862-511-4); lib. bdg. 47.95 (0-89862-784-2) Guilford Pr.

Social & Economic Development of Crewe, Seventeen Eighty to Nineteen Twenty-Three. W. H. Chaloner. LC 73-1616. xx, 326p. 1973. reprint ed. 45.00 (0-678-00754-3) Kelley.

Social & Economic Dimensions in Project Evaluation. Ed. by Hugh H. Schwartz & Richard Berney. 338p. 1977. write for info. (0-940602-02-4) IADB.

Social & Economic Effects of Petroleum Development in Non-OPEC Developing Countries: Synthesis Report. Jon McLin. xiii, 104p. (Orig.). 1986. pap. 18.00 (92-2-105505-1) Intl Labour Office.

Social & Economic Factors Affecting Morality: Confluence 5. Bernard Benjamin. 1965. text ed. 10.00 (3-11-000279-5) Mouton.

Social & Economic Foundations of Association Among the Silk Weavers of Lyons, 1852-1870. George J. Sheridan, Jr. Ed. by Stuart Bruchey. LC 80-2829. (Dissertations in European Economic History Ser.). (Illus.). 1981. lib. bdg. 78.95 (0-405-14013-4) Ayer.

An Asterisk (*) at the beginning of an entry indicates that the title is appearing in BIP for the first time.

Social & Economic History of Central European Jewry. Ed. by Yehuda Don & Victor Karady. 248p. 1989. 44.95 (*0-88738-211-8*) Transaction Pubs.

Social & Economic History of Early Deccan: Some Interpretations. Ed. by Aloka Parasher-Sen. (C). 1993. 29.50 (*81-7304-053-2*, Pub. by Manohar II) S Asia.

***Social & Economic History of Industrial Britain.** Robottom. Date not set. pap. text ed. write for info. (*0-582-22332-6*, Pub. by Longman UK) Longman.

Social & Economic History of Jammu & Kashmir State 1885-1925 AD: 1885 to 1925 A.D. M. L. Kapur. (C). 1992. 32.00 (*81-7041-629-9*, Pub. by Anmol II) S Asia.

Social & Economic History of Prerevolutionary Russia. Ed. by Daniel T. Orlovsky. LC 91-44282. (Articles on Russian & Soviet History, 1500-1991 Ser.: Vol. 4). 696p. 1992. text ed. 35.00 (*0-8153-0561-3*) Garland.

Social & Economic History of the Roman Empire. M. Rostovtzeff. 695p. 1926. pap. 40.00 (*0-8196-2164-1*) Biblo.

Social & Economic History of the Twentieth-Century Europe. Gerald Ambrosius & William H. Hubbard. LC 89-1750. (Illus.). 384p. 1989. 50.00 (*0-674-81340-5*); pap. 23.00 (*0-674-81341-3*) HUP.

Social & Economic Impact of Earthquakes on Utility Lifelines: Seismic Considerations in Lifelines Planning, Siting & Design. Ed. by J. Isenberg. LC 80-69153. 250p. 1981. pap. 23.00 (*0-87262-254-1*) Am Soc Civil Eng.

Social & Economic Impact of New Technology, 1978-1984. Ed. by Leslie Grayson. (IFI Data Base Library). 90p. 1984. 95.00 (*0-306-65209-9*, IFI-Plenum) Plenum.

Social & Economic Inequality in the Soviet Union: Six Studies. Murray Yanowitch. LC 77-71634. 215p. reprint ed. pap. 61.30 (*0-317-41979-X*, 2027628) Bks Demand.

Social & Economic Modernization in Eastern Germany: From Honecker to Kohl. Mike Dennis. LC 93-8747. 252p. 1993. 45.00 (*0-86187-166-9*) St Martin.

Social & Economic Perspectives on Irrigation. Ed. by Ian Carruthers. 100p. 1981. pap. 26.00 (*0-08-026780-7*, Pergamon Pr) Elsevier.

Social & Economic Reform in Ecuador: Life & Work in Guyaquil. Ronn F. Pineo. LC 95-45919. (Illus.). 256p. (C). 1996. lib. bdg. 49.95 (*0-8130-1437-9*) U Press Fla.

Social & Economic Rights in the Soviet Union & East Europe. Sophia M. Miskiewicz & Aaron Trehub. 256p. 1988. 44.95 (*0-88738-186-3*) Transaction Pubs.

Social & Economic Status of College Students. Ora E. Reynolds. LC 71-177189. (Columbia University. Teachers College. Contributions to Education Ser.: No. 272). reprint ed. 37.50 (*0-404-55272-2*) AMS Pr.

Social & Economic Structure of the City of New York, 1695-1796. Bruce M. Wilkenfeld. LC 77-14797. (Dissertations in American Economic History Ser.). 1978. 28.95 (*0-405-11062-6*) Ayer.

Social & Economic Views of Mr. Justice Brandeis. Alfred Lief. 1996. reprint ed. 110.00 (*0-614-14969-X*) Gaunt.

Social & Economic Works of John Ruskin, 6 vols., Set. Peter Cain. (Modern Economics Ser.). 1540p. (C). (gr. 13 up). 1994. boxed, text ed. 495.00 (*0-415-11350-4*, Routledge NY) Routledge.

Social & Educational Thought of Harold Rugg. Peter F. Carbone. LC 75-36176. 238p. reprint ed. pap. 67.90 (*0-317-20094-1*, 2023374) Bks Demand.

Social & Emotional Adjustment & Family Relations in Ethnic Minority Families. Ed. by Ronald D. Taylor & Margaret C. Wang. LC 96-22744. 400p. (C). 1996. 55.00 (*0-8058-2155-4*); pap. 27.50 (*0-8058-2156-2*) L Erlbaum Assocs.

Social & Emotional Development of Exceptional Students: Handicapped & Gifted. Carroll J. Jones. 218p. 1992. pap. 27.95 (*0-398-06194-7*); text ed. 39.95 (*0-398-05781-8*) C C Thomas.

Social & Environmental Objectives in Water Resources Planning & Management. 49p. 1984. 13.00 (*0-87262-404-8*) Am Soc Civil Eng.

Social & Environmental Objectives in Water Resources Planning & Management, No. II. Ed. by Warren Viessman, Jr. & Kyle E. Schilling. (Conference Proceedings Ser.). 336p. 1986. 31.00 (*0-87262-559-1*) Am Soc Civil Eng.

Social & Ethical Effects of the Computer Revolution. Ed. by Joseph M. Kizza. LC 95-49868. 347p. 1996. lib. bdg. 38.50 (*0-7864-0205-9*) McFarland & Co.

Social & Ethical Interpretations in Mental Development. 2nd ed. James M. Baldwin. LC 73-2960. (Classics in Psychology Ser.). 1977. reprint ed. 40.95 (*0-405-05133-6*) Ayer.

Social & Ethnic Dimensions of Matthean Salvation History: "Go Nowhere among the Gentiles..." (Matt. 10. 5b) Amy J. Levine. LC 88-12701. (Studies in the Bible & Early Christianity: Vol. 14). 319p. 1989. lib. bdg. 99.95 (*0-88946-614-9*) E Mellen.

Social & Functional Approaches to Language & Thought. Ed. by Maya Hickman. 328p. 1987. text ed. 73.00 (*0-12-347225-3*) Acad Pr.

***Social & Health Aspects of Sexually Transmitted Diseases Principles of Control Measures.** (Public Health Papers: No. 65). 56p. 1977. pap. text ed. 8.00 (*92-4-130065-5*, 1110065) World Health.

Social & Historical Change: An Islamic Perspective. Ayatullah M. Mutahhari. Ed. by Hamid Algar. Tr. by R. Campbell from PER. LC 85-28554. (Contemporary Islamic Thought, Persian Ser.). 156p. (C). 1986. 19.95 (*0-933782-18-7*); pap. 9.95 (*0-933782-19-5*) Mizan Pr.

Social & Industrial Conditions in the North During the Civil War. Emerson D. Fite. LC 74-22742. 328p. 1983. reprint ed. 39.50 (*0-404-58493-4*) AMS Pr.

Social & Industrial Conditions in the North During the Civil War. Emerson D. Fite. 318p. 1976. reprint ed. 26.95 (*0-87928-070-0*) Corner Hse.

Social & Industrial Problems of Shanghai. Eleanor M. Hinder. LC 75-30059. reprint ed. 32.50 (*0-404-59529-4*) AMS Pr.

Social & Interactional Dimensions of Human-Computer Interfaces. Ed. by Peter Thomas. (Series in Human-Computer Interaction: No. 10). (Illus.). 300p. (C). 1995. text ed. 54.95 (*0-521-45302-X*) Cambridge U Pr.

Social & International Ideals: Being Studies in Patriotism. Bernard Bosanquet. LC 67-23181. (Essay Index Reprint Ser.). 1977. reprint ed. 23.95 (*0-8369-0225-4*) Ayer.

Social & Labor Practices of Multinational Enterprises in the Petroleum Industry. vi, 100p. 1977. pap. 14.00 (*92-2-101806-7*, ILO218) Intl Labour Office.

Social & Labour Market Policies in Hungary. OECD Staff. 190p. (Orig.). 1995. pap. 48.00 (*92-64-14525-7*, Pub. by Org for Econ FR) OECD.

Social & Labour Practices of Multinational Enterprises in the Textiles, Clothing & Footwear Industries. xii, 184p. (Orig.). 1984. pap. 15.75 (*92-2-103882-3*) Intl Labour Office.

Social & Labour Practices of Some European-Based Multinationals in the Metal Trades. vi, 143p. 1981. 22.50 (*92-2-101474-6*) Intl Labour Office.

Social & Legal Status of Women: A Global Perspective. Winnie Hazou. LC 89-72096. 240p. 1990. text ed. 55.00 (*0-275-93362-8*, C3362, Praeger Pubs) Greenwood.

Social & Literary Papers. Charles C. Shackford. LC 72-335. (Essay Index Reprint Ser.). 1977. reprint ed. 23.95 (*0-8369-2825-3*) Ayer.

Social & Medical Aspects of Drug Abuse. Ed. by George Serban. 288p. 1984. text ed. 40.00 (*0-88331-201-8*) Luce.

Social & Mental Traits of the Negro. Howard W. Odum. LC 68-56677. (Columbia University. Studies in the Social Sciences: No. 99). reprint ed. 29.50 (*0-404-51099-X*) AMS Pr.

Social & Moral Reform, Vol. 17, Pt. I see History of Women in the United States: Topically Arranged Articles on the Evolution of Women's History in the United States

Social & Moral Values: Individual & Societal Perspectives. Ed. by Nancy Eisenberg et al. 392p. 1989. 79.95 (*0-89859-956-3*) L Erlbaum Assocs.

Social & Organizational Context of Management Accounting. A. G. Puxty. (Advanced Management Accounting & Finance Ser.). (Illus.). 163p. 1993. pap. text ed. 17.00 (*0-12-568660-9*) Acad Pr.

Social & Personal Ethics. William H. Shaw. 480p. (C). 1993. pap. 33.75 (*0-534-17886-3*) Wadsworth Pub.

Social & Personal Ethics. 2nd ed. William H. Shaw. LC 95-17017. (C). 1996. pap. 43.95 (*0-534-25458-6*) Wadsworth Pub.

Social & Personality Development. 2nd ed. David R. Shaffer. LC 87-10958. 516p. (C). 1987. Test items also avail. text ed. 50.95 (*0-534-08412-5*) Brooks-Cole.

Social & Personality Development. 3rd ed. David R. Shaffer. LC 93-18915. 1994. text ed. 63.95 (*0-534-20760-X*) Brooks-Cole.

Social & Personality Development: An Evolutionary Synthesis. K. B. MacDonald. (Perspectives in Developmental Psychology Ser.). (Illus.). 340p. 1988. 60.00 (*0-306-42891-1*, Plenum Pr) Plenum.

Social & Personality Development: Essays on the Growth of the Child. William Damon. 504p. (C). 1983. pap. text ed. 24.95 (*0-393-95307-6*) Norton.

Social & Personality Development: From Infancy Through Adolescence. William Damon. (Illus.). (C). 1983. pap. text ed. 26.95 (*0-393-95248-7*) Norton.

Social & Personality Development: From Infancy through Adolescence. 2nd ed. William Damon. (C). Date not set. pap. text ed. write for info. (*0-393-96331-4*) Norton.

Social & Political Body. Theodore R. Schatzki & Wolfgang Natter. LC 96-19771. (Multidisciplinary Studies in Social Theory Ser.). 228p. 1996. pap. text ed. 18.95 (*1-57230-140-6*); lib. bdg. 42.95 (*1-57230-139-2*) Guilford Pr.

Social & Political Change in Literature & Film: Selected Papers from the Sixteenth Annual Florida State University Conference on Literature & Film. Ed. by Richard L. Chapple. LC 93-35010. (Florida State University Annual Conference on Literature & Film Ser.). 120p. (C). 1994. pap. 19.95 (*0-8130-1286-4*) U Press Fla.

Social & Political Contexts of Family Therapy. Marsha P. Mirkin. 407p. 1990. text ed. 76.00 (*0-205-12455-0*, H24557) Allyn.

***Social & Political Dynamics of the Informal Economy in African Cities: Nairobi & Harare.** Kinuthia MacHaria. LC 97-13284. 1997. write for info. (*0-7618-0840-X*); pap. write for info. (*0-7618-0841-8*) U Pr of Amer.

Social & Political Economy of the Household. Ed. by Michael Anderson et al. (Social Change & Economic Life Initiative Ser.). (Illus.). 280p. 1995. 68.00 (*0-19-827938-8*) OUP.

Social & Political France. (Yale French Studies: No. 15). 1955. pap. 25.00 (*0-527-01723-X*) Periodicals Srv.

Social & Political History of Nepal. B. D. Sanwal. (C). 1993. 24.00 (*81-7304-021-4*, Pub. by Manohar Bk Srv II) S Asia.

Social & Political History of Texas. Lewis Newton. 1993. reprint ed. lib. bdg. 75.00 (*0-7812-5946-0*) Rprt Serv.

Social & Political History of the Jews in Poland, 1919-1939. Joseph Marcus. LC 82-22420. (New Babylon Studies in the Social Sciences: No. 37). xviii, 569p. 1983. 115.40 (*90-279-3239-5*) Mouton.

Social & Political Ideas of Bipin Chandra Pal. Amalendu P. Mookerjee. LC 75-901635. 1974. 11.00 (*0-88386-473-8*) S Asia.

Social & Political Ideas of Some Great Thinkers of the Renaissance & the Reformation. Ed. by Fossey J. Hearnshaw. LC 85-7662. 216p. 1985. text ed. 59.75 (*0-313-23862-6*, HREN, Greenwood Pr) Greenwood.

Social & Political Ideas of Some Representative Thinkers of the Victorian Age: A Series of Lectures Delivered at King's College University of London during the Session 1931-32. Ed. by Fossey J. Hearnshaw. LC 83-1517. 271p. (C). 1983. reprint ed. text ed. 59.75 (*0-313-23864-2*, HVIC) Greenwood.

Social & Political Ideas of the Muckrakers. David M. Chalmers. LC 70-117765. (Essay Index Reprint Ser.). 1977. 18.95 (*0-8369-1745-6*) Ayer.

Social & Political Implications of the 1984 Jesse Jackson Presidential Campaign. Ed. by Lorenzo Morris. LC 89-27476. (Praeger Series in Political Economy). 288p. 1990. text ed. 59.95 (*0-275-92785-7*, C2785, Praeger Pubs) Greenwood.

Social & Political Philosophy. John Arthur & William H. Shaw. 560p. (C). 1991. pap. text ed. 46.00 (*0-13-753799-9*) P-H.

Social & Political Philosophy. William L McBride. LC 92-44094. (Issues in Philosophy Ser.). 144p. (C). 1993. pap. text ed. 16.95 (*1-55778-220-2*) Paragon Hse.

Social & Political Philosophy. Ed. by Peter A. French et al. LC 82-1996. (Midwest Studies in Philosophy: No. 7). 553p. 1982. reprint ed. pap. 157.70 (*0-7837-2959-6*, 2057495) Bks Demand.

Social & Political Philosophy: Classical Western Texts in Feminist & Multicultural Perspectives. James P. Sterba. LC 94-35333. 539p. 1995. text ed. 41.95 (*0-534-24726-1*) Wadsworth Pub.

***Social & Political Philosophy: Classical Western Texts in Feminist & Multicultural Perspectives.** 2nd ed. James P. Sterba. LC 97-20171. (Philosophy Ser.). (C). 1997. pap. text ed. 41.95 (*0-534-52744-2*) Wadsworth Pub.

Social & Political Philosophy: Readings from Plato to Gandhi. Ed. by Ronald Santoni & John Somerville. LC 63-18039. 560p. 1963. pap. 14.00 (*0-385-01238-1*, Anchor NY) Doubleday.

Social & Political Study of Modern Hindi Cinema. Ram A. Agnihotri. (C). 1990. 48.00 (*0-8364-2486-7*) S Asia.

Social & Political Study of Modern Hindi Cinema. Atvar A. Ram. 1990. 48.50 (*81-7169-049-1*, Commonwealth) S Asia.

Social & Political Thought of Bertrand Russell: The Development of an Aristocratic Liberalism. Philip Ironside. (Ideas in Context Ser.: No. 37). 292p. (C). 1995. text ed. 52.95 (*0-521-47383-7*) Cambridge U Pr.

Social & Political Thought of Dr. S. Radhakrishnan. Clarissa Rodrigues. 1993. text ed. 30.00 (*81-207-0389-8*, Pub. by Sterling Pubs II) Apt Bks.

Social & Political Thought of Karl Marx. Shlomo Avineri. LC 68-12055. (Studies in the History & Theory of Politics). 278p. 1970. pap. text ed. 28.95 (*0-521-09619-7*) Cambridge U Pr.

Social & Political Thought of Leon Trotsky. Baruch Knei-Paz. 652p. 1980. pap. 32.00 (*0-19-827234-0*) OUP.

Social & Political Thought of Michael Bakunin. Richard B. Saltman. LC 82-9348. (Contributions in Political Science Ser.: No. 88). xiii, 199p. 1983. text ed. 55.00 (*0-313-23378-0*, SPB/, Greenwood Pr) Greenwood.

***Social & Political Thought of R. G. Collingwood.** 312p. 1989. text ed. 80.00 (*0-521-36384-5*) Cambridge U Pr.

Social & Political Thought of the French Revolution, 1788-1796: An Anthology of Original Thought. Ed. by Marc A. Goldstein. LC 93-46669. 1994. write for info. (*0-8204-2405-6*) P Lang Pubng.

Social & Polity Formations in Pre-Colonial North-East India. J. B. Bhattacharjee. 1991. text ed. 35.00 (*0-7069-5464-5*, Pub. by Vikas II) S Asia.

***Social & Preventive Health Administration.** R. Kumar. (C). 1992. 42.00 (*81-7024-454-4*, Pub. by Ashish II) S Asia.

Social & Private Life at Rome in the Time of Plautus & Terence. Georgia W. Leffingwell. LC 18-17902. (Columbia University. Studies in the Social Sciences: No. 188). reprint ed. 20.00 (*0-404-51188-0*) AMS Pr.

Social & Psychological Aspects of Aging. Ed. by Clark Tibbitts et al. LC 79-8691. (Growing Old Ser.). 1980. reprint ed. lib. bdg. 88.95 (*0-405-12787-1*) Ayer.

Social & Psychological Contexts of Language. Ed. by Robert N. St. Clair & Howard Giles. LC 79-28232. 352p. 1980. text ed. 69.95 (*0-89859-021-3*) L Erlbaum Assocs.

Social & Psychological Foundations of Rehabilitation. Robert A. Chubon. 274p. (C). 1994. text ed. 51.95 (*0-398-05920-9*); pap. text ed. 35.95 (*0-398-06042-8*) C C Thomas.

Social & Psychological Problems of Women: Prevention & Crisis Intervention. Ed. by Annette U. Rickel et al. LC 83-18423. (Clinical & Community Psychology Ser.). 352p. 1984. text ed. 51.95 (*0-89116-330-1*) Hemisp Pub.

Social & Psychological Research in Community Settings. Ricardo F. Munoz et al. LC 79-88107. (Jossey-Bass Social & Behavioral Science Ser.). 416p. reprint ed. pap. 118.60 (*0-8357-6881-3*, 2037933) Bks Demand.

Social & Religious Aspects in Bengal Inscriptions. RK Tripathi. (C). 1987. 40.00 (*0-8364-2129-9*, KL Mukhopadhyay) S Asia.

Social & Religious Designs of J. S. Bach's Brandenburg Concertos. Michael Marissen. LC 94-28688. 160p. 1995. text ed. 26.95 (*0-691-03739-6*) Princeton U Pr.

Social & Religious History of the Jews. 2nd enl. rev. ed. Salo W. Baron. LC 92-25418. (C). 1993. 79.00 (*0-231-08856-6*) Col U Pr.

Social & Religious History of the Jews, 18 vols. 2nd enl. rev. ed. Salo W. Baron. Incl. Vol. 1. Ancient Times to the Beginning of the Christian Era. LC 52-404. 1958. text ed. 75.00 (*0-231-08838-8*); Vol. 2. Ancient Times: Christian Era: the First Five Centuries. LC 52-404. 1952. text ed. 75.00 (*0-231-08839-6*); Vol. 3. High Middle Ages: Heirs of Rome & Persia. LC 52-404. 1957. text ed. 75.00 (*0-231-08840-X*); Vol. 4. High Middle Ages: Meeting of the East & West. LC 52-404. 1957. text ed. 75.00 (*0-231-08841-8*); Vol. 5. High Middle Ages: Religious Controls & Dissensions. LC 52-404. 1957. text ed. 75.00 (*0-231-08842-6*); Vol. 6. High Middle Ages: Laws, Homilies & the Bible. LC 52-404. 1958. text ed. 75.00 (*0-231-08843-4*); Vol. 7. High Middle Ages: Hebrew Language & Letters. LC 52-404. 1958. text ed. 75.00 (*0-231-08844-2*); Vol. 8. High Middle Ages: Philosophy & Science. LC 52-404. 1958. text ed. 75.00 (*0-231-08845-0*); Vol. 9. Late Middle Ages & Era of European Expansion, 1200-1650: Under Church & Empire. LC 52-404. 1965. text ed. 75.00 (*0-231-08846-9*); Vol. 10. Late Middle Ages & Era of European Expansion, 1200-1650: On the Empire's Periphery. LC 52-404. 1965. text ed. 65.00 (*0-231-08847-7*); Vol. 11. Late Middle Ages & Era of European Expansion, 1200-1650: Citizen or Alien Conjurer. LC 52-404. 1967. text ed. 65.00 (*0-231-08848-5*); Vol. 12. Late Middle Ages & Era of European Expansion, 1200-1650: Economic Catalyst. LC 52-404. 1967. text ed. 65.00 (*0-231-08849-3*); Vol. 13. Late Middle Ages & Era of European Expansion, 1200-1650: Inquisition, Renaissance & Reformation. LC 52-404. 1970. text ed. 65.00 (*0-231-08850-7*); Vol. 14. Late Middle Ages & Era of European Expansion, 1200-1650: Catholic Restoration & Wars of Religion. LC 52-404. 1970. text ed. 65.00 (*0-231-08851-5*); Vol. 15. Late Middle Ages & Era of European Expansion, 1200-1650: Resettlement & Exploration. LC 52-404. 1973. text ed. 65.00 (*0-231-08852-3*); LC 52-404. write for info. (*0-318-51413-3*) Col U Pr.

Social & Religious History of the Jews, Vol. 16. Salo W. Baron. 1976. text ed. 75.00 (*0-231-08853-1*) Col U Pr.

Social & Religious History of the Jews, Vols. 5-8. Salo W. Baron. 1960. text ed. 55.00 (*0-231-08877-9*) Col U Pr.

Social & Religious Life of Italians in the United States. Enrico C. Sartorio. LC 73-13520. xiv, 149p. 1974. reprint ed. 29.50 (*0-678-01364-0*) Kelley.

Social & Religious Philosophy of Martin Buber: Alienation & the Search for Meaning. Laurence J. Silberstein. (Reappraisals in Jewish Social & Intellectual History Ser.). 256p. (C). 1989. text ed. 40.00 (*0-8147-7886-0*) NYU Pr.

Social & Religious Philosophy of Martin Buber: Alienation & the Search for Meaning. Laurence J. Silberstein. (Reappraisals in Jewish Social & Intellectual History Ser.). 256p. (C). 1990. pap. 20.00 (*0-8147-7910-7*) NYU Pr.

Social & Religious Plays of Strindberg. John Ward. 337p. (C). 1980. text ed. 46.50 (*0-485-11183-7*, Pub. by Athlone Pr UK) Humanities.

Social & Religious Thought of William Jennings Bryan. Willard H. Smith. 270p. 1975. 15.00 (*0-87291-076-8*) Coronado Pr.

Social & Ritual Life of the Ambo of Northern Rhodesia. Bronislaw Stefaniszyn. Ed. by Raymond Apthorpe. LC 64-1310. 193p. reprint ed. pap. 55.10 (*0-8357-6970-4*, 2039030) Bks Demand.

Social & Secure? Politics & Culture of the Welfare State: a Comparative Inquiry. Ed. by Hans Bak et al. 400p. 1996. pap. 50.00 (*90-5383-458-3*, Pub. by VU Univ Pr NE) Paul & Co Pubs.

***Social & Sexual Revolution.** Bertell Ollman. 228p. 41.99 (*0-919618-85-5*, Pub. by Black Rose Bks CN); pap. 12.99 (*0-919618-84-7*, Pub. by Black Rose Bks CN) Consort Bk Sales.

Social & Sexual Revolution: Essays on Marx & Reich. Bertell Ollman. LC 78-71204. 228p. 1979. 20.00 (*0-89608-081-1*); pap. 7.50 (*0-89608-080-3*) South End Pr.

Social & State Structure of the U. S. S. R. Viacheslav A. Karpinsky. LC 79-98775. 181p. 1970. reprint ed. text ed. 35.00 (*0-8371-3116-2*, KASU, Greenwood Pr) Greenwood.

Social Animal. 7th ed. Elliot Aronson. (C). 1995. pap. text ed. write for info. (*0-7167-2618-1*) W H Freeman.

Social Animal. 7th ed. Elliot Aronson. teacher ed. write for info. (*0-7167-2687-4*) W H Freeman.

Social Animal. 7th ed. Elliot Aronson. write for info. (*0-7167-2733-1*) W H Freeman.

***Social Animal Text & Readings, Vol. 1.** Aronson. 1991. 30.40 (*0-7167-2304-2*) W H Freeman.

Social Anthropology. Edward E. Evans-Pritchard. LC 84-19811. 144p. 1987. text ed. 43.75 (*0-313-24680-7*, EVSA, Greenwood Pr) Greenwood.

Social Anthropology: Alternative Introduction. Anagela P Cheater. 336p. (C). 1989. pap. 24.95 (*0-415-07885-7*, Routledge NY) Routledge.

Social Anthropology see Handbook of Middle American Indians

Social Anthropology & Development Policy. Ed. by Ralph Grillo & Alan Rew. (ASA Monographs). 240p. (C). 1985. pap. text ed. 16.95 (*0-422-79620-4*, 9525, Pub. by Tavistock UK) Routledge Chapman & Hall.

Social Anthropology & Public Policy in Northern Ireland. Hastings Donnan & Graham McFarlane. 165p. 1989. text ed. 59.95 (*0-566-05594-5*, Pub. by Avebury Pub UK) Ashgate Pub Co.

An Asterisk (*) at the beginning of an entry indicates that the title is appearing in BIP for the first time.

Social Anthropology & the Lonely Crowd: A Comparative Approach to the Problems of Modern Society. Jan Brogger. Ed. by Mario D. Zamora & Michael Bradshaw. (Anthropological Persepectives: Resources for Teaching Anthropology Ser.: No. 3). 1993. 15.95 (0-685-65103-7, Pub. by Reliance Pub Hse II) Apt Bks.

Social Anthropology in India: Contemporary Perspectives. Ed. by Ratish Srivastava. xx, 257p. 16.00 (0-88065-194-6, Messers Today & Tomorrow) Scholarly Pubns.

Social Anthropology in Perspective: The Relevance of Social Anthropology. 2nd ed. I. M. Lewis. 400p. 1986. pap. text ed. 17.95 (0-521-31351-1) Cambridge U Pr.

Social Anthropology in Polynesia: A Review of Research. Felix M. Keesing. LC 80-17490. x, 126p. 1980. reprint ed. text ed. 49.75 (0-313-22498-6, KESO, Greenwood Pr) Greenwood.

Social Anthropology of Complex Societies. Ed. by Michael P. Banton. (Orig.). 1968. pap. 15.95 (0-422-72520-X, NO. 2069, Pub. by Tavistock UK) Routledge Chapman & Hall.

Social Anthropology of Pilgrimmage. Ed. by Makhan Jha. (C). 1991. 54.00 (81-210-0265-6, Pub. by Inter-India Pubns) S Asia.

Social Anxieties of Progressive Reform: Atlantic City, 1854-1920. Martin Paulsson. LC 93-47416. (American Social Experience Ser.). (Illus.). 245p. (C). 1994. 45.00 (0-8147-6620-X) NYU Pr.

Social Anxieties of Progressive Reform: Atlantic City, 1854-1920. Martin Paulsson. (Illus.). 245p. (C). 1996. pap. 20.00 (0-8147-6643-9) NYU Pr.

Social Anxiety. Robert E. Kowalski. (Emotions & Social Behavior Ser.). 244p. 1995. lib. bdg. 27.95 (1-57230-007-8) Guilford Pr.

Social Applications & Issues in Psychology, Vol. 8: Proceedings of the 24th International Congress of Psychology of the International Union of Psychological Science, Sydney, Australia, Aug. 28-Sept. 2, 1988. Ed. by R. C. King & J. K. Collins. 380p. 1989. 87.25 (0-444-88526-9, North Holland) Elsevier.

Social Approaches to Communication. Ed. by Wendy Leeds-Hurwitz. LC 95-18761. (Guilford Communication Ser.). 260p. 1995. pap. text ed. 19.95 (0-89862-873-3); lib. bdg. 42.50 (0-89862-867-9) Guilford Pr.

Social Approaches to Sport. Ed. by Robert M. Pankin. LC 81-65466. (Illus.). 360p. 1982. 39.50 (0-8386-3015-4) Fairleigh Dickinson.

Social Approaches to Viking Studies. Ed. by Ross Samson. 254p. (C). 1993. 45.00 (1-873448-00-7, Pub. by Cruithne Pr UK) Boydell & Brewer.

Social Archaeology of Houses. Ed. by Ross Samson. (Illus.). 282p. 1992. 42.50 (0-7486-0290-9, Pub. by Edinburgh U Pr UK) Col U Pr.

Social Areas in Cities: Past & Future. Harold Carter. (Urban Studies: No. 3). 28p. 1984. pap. 3.00 (0-913749-01-X) U MD Urban Stud.

Social Areas in Cities: Spatial Processes & Form, Vol. 1. Ed. by David T. Herbert & R. J. Johnston. LC 75-30943. 295p. reprint ed. pap. 84.10 (0-318-34686-9, 2031758) Bks Demand.

Social Art: Language & Its Uses. Ronald K. Macaulay. 256p. 1996. pap. 12.95 (0-19-510657-1) OUP.

Social Art: Language & Its Uses. Ronald K. Macauley. (Illus.). 256p. 1994. 30.00 (0-19-508382-2) OUP.

Social Aspects & Country Reviews of Population Aging: Europe & North America. Ed. by George J. Stolnitz. 377p. 1994. pap. 55.00 (92-1-100687-2) UN.

Social Aspects of a Verb Form: Native Atlanta Fifth-Grade Speech - The Present Tense of Be. Howard G. Dunlap. (Publications of the American Dialect Society: Nos. 61 & 62). 96p. 1974. pap. text ed. 10.50 (0-8173-0661-7) U of Ala Pr.

Social Aspects of AIDS. Ed. by Peter Aggleton & Hilary Homans. 250p. 1988. 65.00 (1-85000-363-7, Falmer Pr); pap. 30.00 (1-85000-364-5, Falmer Pr) Taylor & Francis.

Social Aspects of Democracy. M. S. Gore. 1986. 27.50 (81-7033-010-6, Pub. by Rawat II) S Asia.

Social Aspects of Development. M. S. Gore. vi, 232p. 1985. 19.00 (0-685-58185-3, Pub. by Rawat Pubns II) Nataraj Bks.

Social Aspects of Interaction & Transportation. Frederick P. Stutz. Ed. by Salvatore J. Natoli. LC 76-19932. (Resource Papers for College Geography). 1976. pap. text ed. 15.00 (0-89291-117-4) Assn Am Geographers.

Social Aspects of Mining Towns of the Tribal Regions, Pt. I. Maheshwari Prasad. 196p. 1986. 21.00 (1-55528-082-X, Pub. by Today & Tomorrows P & P II) Scholarly Pubns.

Social Aspects of Mining Towns of the Tribal Regions, Pt. II. Maheshwari Prasad. (Illus.). 60p. 1986. 12.00 (1-55528-083-8, Pub. by Today & Tomorrows P & P II) Scholarly Pubns.

Social Aspects of Obesity. Ed. by Igor De Garine. 1995. pap. text ed. 25.00 (2-88449-186-4) Gordon & Breach.

Social Aspects of Obesity, Vol. 1. Ed. by Igor De Garine. 304p. 1995. text ed. 50.00 (2-88449-185-6) Gordon & Breach.

Social Aspects of Retirement. Otto Pollak. (C). 1956. 5.50 (0-256-00675-X) Irwin.

Social Aspects of Sustainable Dryland Management. Ed. by Daniel Stiles. 313p. 1995. text ed. 95.00 (0-471-95633-3) Wiley.

Social Aspects of the Banana Industry. Charles D. Kepner. LC 36-20189. (Columbia University. Studies in the Social Sciences: No. 414). reprint ed. 27.50 (0-404-51414-6) AMS Pr.

Social Aspects of the Italian Revolution, in a Series of Letters from Florence. Theodosia Trollope. LC 71-37728. (Women of Letters Ser.). reprint ed. 55.00 (0-404-56855-6) AMS Pr.

Social Aspects of Urban Development. H. D. Kopardekar. 1986. 38.50 (0-86132-132-4, Pub. by Popular Prakashan II) S Asia.

Social Assessment of High Technology: The Superconducting Super Collider in Southeast Michigan. Richard W. Stoffle et al. LC 87-2902. 120p. (Orig.). 1987. pap. text ed. 15.00 (0-87944-321-9) Inst Soc Res.

Social Assessment of High Technology: The Superconducting Super Collider in Southeast Michigan. Richard W. Stoffle et al. LC 87-2902. (Institute for Social Research, Research Report Ser.). 115p. (Orig.). reprint ed. pap. 32.80 (0-7837-5244-X, 2044978) Bks Demand.

***Social Assumptions, Medical Categories.** Barbara Hansen. (Advances in Medical Sociology Ser.: Supplement 1). 1997. 73.25 (0-7623-0243-7) Jai Pr.

Social Attitudes & Psychophysical Measurement. Bernd Wegener. 512p. 1982. text ed. 99.95 (0-89859-083-3) L Erlbaum Assocs.

Social Attitudes in Northern Ireland. Gillian Robinson & Peter Stringer. (Illus.). 240p. (Orig.). 1992. pap. 24.00 (0-85640-483-7, Pub. by Blackstaff Pr IE) Dufour.

Social Attitudes in Northern Ireland: The Third Report 1992-93, Vol. 3. Peter Stringer. 177p. 9300. pap. 40.00 (0-85640-512-4, Pub. by Blackstaff Pr IE) Dufour.

Social Attitudes in Northern Ireland 1990-91, Vol. 3. Ed. by Peter Stringer & Gillian Robinson. (Illus.). 216p. (Orig.). 9200. pap. 21.00 (0-85640-477-2, Pub. by Blackstaff Pr IE) Dufour.

Social Attitudes of American Generals, Eighteen Ninety-Eight to Nineteen Forty. Richard C. Brown. Ed. by Richard H. Kohn. LC 78-22413. (American Military Experience Ser.). 1980. lib. bdg. 31.95 (0-405-11887-2) Ayer.

Social Audit for Management: Problems & Possibilities. Clark C. Abt. 1976. 30.00 (0-89011-489-7, REM-107) Abt Bks.

Social Awareness: Serving God in the World. Mary R. Power. (J). (ps-5). 1986. 16.25 (1-881678-33-4) CRIS.

Social Background & Activities of Teachers College Students. M'Ledge Moffett. LC 79-177077. (Columbia University. Teachers College. Contributions to Education Ser.: No. 375). reprint ed. 37.50 (0-404-55375-3) AMS Pr.

Social Background of Indian Nationalism. A. R. Desai. 1986. reprint ed. 10.00 (0-86132-086-7, Pub. by Popular Prakashan II) S Asia.

Social Background of Political Leadership in India. G. Narayana Pillai. 1984. 18.50 (0-8364-1060-2, Pub. by Uppal Pub Hse II) S Asia.

Social Badger: Ecology & Behaviour of a Group-Living Carnivore (Meles meles) Hans Kruuk. (Illus.). 180p. 1989. 38.00 (0-19-858703-1) OUP.

Social Bases of City Politics: Atlanta, Eighteen Sixty-Five to Nineteen Hundred Three. Eugene J. Watts. LC 77-94756. (Contributions in American History Ser.: No. 73). 188p. 1978. text ed. 55.00 (0-313-20322-9, WTS/, Greenwood Pr) Greenwood.

Social Bases of West German Politics, 1953. UNESCO Staff. 1974. write for info. (0-89138-110-4) ICPSR.

Social Basis Ethnic Enterprise: Greeks in the Pizza Business. Ed. by Lawrence A. Lovell-Troy. LC 90-42045. (European Immigrants & American Society Ser.). 264p. 1990. reprint ed. text ed. 20.00 (0-8240-7426-2) Garland.

Social Basis of American Communism. Nathan Glazer. LC 74-4658. 244p. 1974. reprint ed. text ed. 35.00 (0-8371-7476-7, GLAC, Greenwood Pr) Greenwood.

Social Basis of Community Care. Martin Bulmer. LC 87-988. 247p. 1987. 55.00 (0-04-361072-2); pap. 18.95 (0-04-361073-0) Routledge Chapman & Hall.

Social Basis of European Fascist Movements. Ed. by Detlef Muhlberger. LC 87-14093. 384p. 1987. lib. bdg. 49.95 (0-7099-3585-4, Pub. by Croom Helm UK) Routledge Chapman & Hall.

Social Basis of Health & Healing in Africa. Ed. by Steven Feierman & John M. Janzen. LC 90-44243. (Comparative Studies of Health Systems & Medical Care: Vol. 30). (C). 1992. 65.00 (0-520-06680-4); pap. 18.00 (0-520-06681-2) U CA Pr.

Social Basis of the Microelectronics Revolution. Alfonso H. Molina. 1990. pap. text ed. 22.00 (0-85224-605-6, Pub. by Edinburgh U Pr UK) Col U Pr.

Social Behavior: Psycho-Medical Subject Analysis & Research Index with Bibliography. Rosalie F. Zoltano. LC 83-71674. 150p. 1984. 37.50 (0-88164-060-3); pap. 34.50 (0-88164-061-1) ABBE Pubs Assn.

Social Behavior & Culture. Harry C. Triandis. 320p. 1993. pap. text ed. write for info. (0-07-065110-8) McGraw.

Social Behavior & Medicine: Subject Analysis with Reference Bibliography. Rosalie F. Zoltano. LC 85-48188. 150p. 1986. 37.50 (0-88164-510-9); pap. 34.50 (0-88164-511-7) ABBE Pubs Assn.

Social Behavior & Organization among Vertebrates. William Etkin. LC 64-13947. (Illus.). 319p. reprint ed. pap. 91.00 (0-685-23871-7, 2056655) Bks Demand.

Social Behavior & Personality. Arnold H. Buss. 244p. (C). 1986. text ed. 49.95 (0-89859-812-5) L Erlbaum Assocs.

Social Behavior & Personality: Contributions of W. I. Thomas to Theory & Social Research. William I. Thomas. Ed. by Edmund H. Volkart. LC 80-29525. (Illus.). ix, 338p. 1981. reprint ed. text ed. 59.75 (0-313-22778-0, THSB, Greenwood Pr) Greenwood.

Social Behavior As Exchange. George C. Homans. (Reprint Series in Social Sciences). (C). 1993. reprint ed. pap. text ed. 1.00 (0-8290-2665-7, S-122) Irvington.

Social Behavior in Animals. 2nd ed. Nikolaas Tinbergen. (Illus.). 184p. (gr. 13). 1990. pap. text ed. 34.95 (0-412-36920-6, A4618) Chapman & Hall.

Social Behavior in Autism. Ed. by Eric Schopler & Gary B. Mesibov. (Current Issues in Autism Ser.). 402p. 1986. 55.00 (0-306-42163-1, Plenum Pr) Plenum.

Social Behavior in Fluctuating Populations. Andrew Cockburn & John Lazarus. (Studies in Behavioral Adaptation Ser.). 272p. 1987. lib. bdg. 69.50 (0-7099-3426-2, Pub. by Croom Helm UK) Routledge Chapman & Hall.

Social Behavior of the Bees. Charles D. Michener. LC 73-87379. 464p. 1974. 45.00 (0-674-81175-5) Belknap Pr.

Social Being. Rom Harre. LC 92-29854. 1993. pap. 24.95 (0-631-18782-0) Blackwell Pubs.

Social Being & Time. Chris Gosden. (Social Archaeology Ser.). (Illus.). 256p. 1994. pap. 22.95 (0-631-19023-6) Blackwell Pubs.

Social Beliefs, Cultural Practices in Health & Disease. K. L. Pokarna. (C). 1994. 28.00 (81-7033-254-0, Pub. by Rawat II) S Asia.

***Social Benefits of Education.** Ed. by Jere R. Behrman & Nevzer G. Stacey. LC 96-43405. (Economics of Education Ser.). (C). 1997. 49.50 (0-472-10769-0) U of Mich Pr.

Social Biology Enlightenment. Roe. 1993. lib. bdg. 34.95 (0-226-72363-1) U Ch Pr.

Social Biology of Wasps. Ed. by Kenneth G. Ross & Robert W. Matthews. LC 90-44178. (Illus.). 688p. 1991. 85.00 (0-8014-2035-0); pap. 36.50 (0-8014-9906-2) Cornell U Pr.

Social Blunder. Tim Sandlin. LC 94-43193. 281p. 1995. 22.50 (0-8050-1628-7) H Holt & Co.

Social Blunders. Tim Sandlin. LC 96-16059. 336p. 1997. reprint ed. pap. 12.00 (1-57322-588-6, Riverhd Trade) Berkley Pub.

Social Bodies: Science, Reproduction & Italian Modernity. David G. Horn. LC 94-19052. (Studies in Culture - Power - History). 200p. 1995. text ed. 45.00 (0-691-03721-3); pap. text ed. 15.95 (0-691-03720-5) Princeton U Pr.

Social Bonds & Teen Pregnancy. LaWanda Ravoira & Andrew L. Cherry, Jr. LC 92-9821. 200p. 1992. text ed. 45.00 (0-275-94179-5, C4179, Praeger Pubs) Greenwood.

Social Bonds in Later Life: Aging & Interdependence. Ed. by Warren A. Peterson & Jill S. Quadagno. LC 85-1830. (Illus.). 477p. reprint ed. pap. 136.00 (0-7837-4566-4, 2044095) Bks Demand.

Social Cage: Human Nature & the Evolution of Society. Alexandra Maryanski & Jonathan H. Turner. LC 92-17311. 323p. (C). 1992. 42.50 (0-8047-2002-9); pap. 12.95 (0-8047-2003-7) Stanford U Pr.

Social Capability & Long-Term Economy Growth. Ed. by Bon-Ho Koo & Dwight H. Perkins. LC 94-30587. 356p. 1995. text ed. 69.95 (0-312-12438-4) St Martin.

Social Capitalism: A Study of Christian Democracy & the Welfare State. Kees Van Kersbergen. LC 95-7804. 304p. (C). (gr. 13). 1995. text ed. 74.95 (0-415-11670-8) Routledge.

Social Care in a Mixed Economy. Gerald Wistow et al. LC 93-32694. (Public Policy & Management Ser.). 1994. 85.00 (0-335-19044-8, Open Univ Pr); pap. 32.00 (0-335-19043-X, Open Univ Pr) Taylor & Francis.

Social Care in Europe. Ed. by Brian Munday & Peter Ely. LC 95-34018. 240p. (C). 1996. pap. text ed. 36.00 (0-13-354193-2) P-H.

Social Care Markets: Progress & Prospects. Gerald Wistow et al. 208p. 1996. 89.00 (0-335-19547-4, Open Univ Pr) Taylor & Francis.

Social Care Markets: Progress & Prospects. Gerald Wistow et al. 208p. 1996. pap. 29.00 (0-335-19546-6, Open Univ Pr) Taylor & Francis.

***Social Care Services: The Key to the Scandinavian Welfare Model.** Ed. by Jorma Sipila. 208p. 1997. text ed. 34.95 (1-85972-403-5, Pub. by Avebury Pub UK) Ashgate Pub Co.

Social Caricature in the Eighteenth-Century. George Paston. LC 67-12467. (Illus.). 1972. reprint ed. 54.95 (0-405-08840-X) Ayer.

Social Cartography: Mapping Ways of Seeing Social & Educational Change. Rolland Paulston. Ed. by Edward R. Beauchamp. LC 96-22198. (Garland Reference Library of Social Science: Vol. 1024). (Illus.). 456p. 1996. text ed. 70.00 (0-8153-1994-0) Garland.

Social Case Work, Generic & Specific: An Outline: a Report of the Milford Conference. Milford Conference Staff. LC 74-83097. (Studies in the Practice of Social Work: No. 2). 102p. reprint ed. pap. 29.10 (0-7837-5365-9, 2045129) Bks Demand.

Social Case Worker. Jack Rudman. (Career Examination Ser.: C-795). 1994. pap. 23.95 (0-8373-0795-3) Nat Learn.

Social Casework: A Behavioral Approach. Arthur Schwartz et al. LC 75-2298. 336p. 1975. text ed. 45.00 (0-231-03778-3) Col U Pr.

Social Casework: A Problem-Solving Process. Helen H. Perlman. LC 57-6270. 283p. 1957. lib. bdg. 14.50 (0-226-66033-8) U Ch Pr.

Social Casework: Cumulative Index Nineteen Twenty to Nineteen Seventy-Nine. Compiled by Katherine A. Kendall. 704p. 1981. 95.00 (0-89232-194-6) Jai Pr.

Social Casework: Cumulative Index, 1920-1989, Vols. 1-70. rev. ed. Compiled by Katherine A. Kendall. LC 92-39020. 704p. 1992. 143.50 (1-55938-526-X) Jai Pr.

Social Casework: Principles & Techniques in Social Casework. Ed. by Cora Kasius. LC 75-142321. 433p. 1972. reprint ed. text ed. 75.00 (0-8371-5924-5, SCPT, Greenwood Pr) Greenwood.

Social Causality. Jerald Hage & Barbara Meeker. 236p. (C). 1988. pap. text ed. 18.95 (0-04-312030-X) Routledge Chapman & Hall.

Social Causality. Jerald Hage & Barbara Meeker. 236p. 1988. 55.00 (0-04-312029-6) Routledge Chapman & Hall.

Social Causation. Robert M. MacIver. 1990. 14.50 (0-8446-2504-3) Peter Smith.

Social Causes of Environmental Destruction in Latin America. Ed. by Michael Painter & William H. Durham. (Linking Levels of Analysis Ser.). (Illus.). 350p. 1994. text ed. 59.50 (0-472-09560-9); pap. text ed. 23.95 (0-472-06560-2) U of Mich Pr.

Social Causes of Husband-Wife Violence. Ed. by Murray A. Straus & Gerald T. Hotaling. LC 79-27071. 282p. 1980. pap. 80.40 (0-7837-2918-9, 2057536) Bks Demand.

Social Causes of Psychological Distress. John Mirowsky & Catherine E. Ross. (Social Institutions & Social Change Ser.). 224p. (Orig.). (C). 1989. pap. text ed. 24.95 (0-202-30355-1) Aldine de Gruyter.

Social Causes of Violence: Crafting a Science Agenda. Felice J. Levine & Katherine J. Rosich. LC 96-83435. x, 114p. (Orig.). 1996. pap. 15.00 (0-912764-26-0) Am Sociological.

Social Challenge of Job Creation: Combating Unemployment in Europe. Ed. by Jordi Gual. LC 96-15145. (Illus.). 240p. (C). 1996. text ed. 80.00 (1-85898-459-9) E Elgar.

Social Challenge to Business. Robert W. Ackerman. LC 75-8921. 363p. reprint ed. pap. 103.50 (0-7837-3833-1, 2043654) Bks Demand.

Social Change. 3rd ed. Steven Vago. LC 95-19437. 1995. text ed. 49.33 (0-13-186560-9) P-H.

Social Change: Social Theory & Historical Processes. Anthony D. Smith. LC 75-42477. (Aspects of Modern Sociology: Social Processes Ser.). 192p. reprint ed. pap. 54.80 (0-317-09554-4, 2019611) Bks Demand.

Social Change among Malsa: An Ex-Untouchable Caste in South India. K. Rathnaiah. (C). 1991. 24.50 (81-7141-137-1) S Asia.

Social Change & Aging in the Twentieth Century. Southern Conference on Gerontology Staff. Ed. by Daniel E. Allegar. LC 72-190955. (Institute of Gerontology Ser.: No. 13). 124p. reprint ed. pap. 35.40 (0-7837-5035-8, 2044708) Bks Demand.

***Social Change & Continuity: England 1550-1750.** Barry Coward. LC 97-4237. (Seminar Studies in History). 1997. write for info. (0-582-29442-8) Longman.

Social Change & Continuity in Early Modern England 1550-1750. Barry Coward. (C). 1988. pap. text ed. 13.50 (0-582-35453-6) Addison-Wesley.

Social Change & Corporate Strategy: The Expanding Role of Public Affairs. Andrew B. Gollner. Ed. by W. Howard Chase. LC 83-81612. (Illus.). 205p. 1984. 29.95 (0-913869-00-7) Issue Action Pubns.

Social Change & Cultural Crisis. Richard Lowenthal. LC 84-4964. (European Perspectives Ser.). 224p. 1984. text ed. 39.50 (0-231-05644-3) Col U Pr.

Social Change & Cultural Transformation in Australia. Adam Jamrozik et al. (Illus.). 272p. (C). 1995. text ed. 57.95 (0-521-41462-8) Cambridge U Pr.

Social Change & Development: Modernization, Dependency & World-Systems Theory. Alvin Y. So. (Library of Social Research: Vol. 178). (Illus.). 288p. (C). 1990. pap. 24.95 (0-8039-3547-1); text ed. 54.00 (0-8039-3546-3) Sage.

Social Change & Education. M. R. Paliwal. 1985. 30.00 (0-8364-1255-9, Pub. by Uppal Pub Hse II) S Asia.

Social Change & Educational Problems in Japan, Singapore & Hong Kong. W. O. Lee. LC 90-44166. 304p. 1991. text ed. 49.95 (0-312-05371-1) St Martin.

Social Change & Images of the Future. James Mau. 192p. 1968. 18.95 (0-87073-048-7) Schenkman Bks Inc.

Social Change & Modernity. Ed. by Hans Haferkamp. 1991. 58.00 (0-520-06554-9); pap. 18.00 (0-520-06828-9) U CA Pr.

Social Change & Modernization: Lessons from Eastern Europe. Ed. by Bruno Grancelli. LC 95-16611. (Studies in Organization: Vol. 65). xii, 314p. (C). 1995. lib. bdg. 71.95 (3-11-014490-5) De Gruyter.

Social Change & Personality: Essays in Honor of Nevitt Sanford. Ed. by M. B. Freedman. (Recent Research in Psychology Ser.). vii, 231p. 1987. 64.95 (0-387-96485-1) Spr-Verlag.

Social Change & Political Discourse in India Vol. 2: Structures of Power, Movement of Resistance: Industry & Agriculture in India since Independence. Ed. by T. V. Sathamurthy. 352p. 1995. 32.00 (0-19-563457-8) OUP.

Social Change & Political Discourse in India - Structures of Power, Movements of Resistance, Class Formation & Political Transformation in Post-Colonial India. T. V. Sathyamurthy. 592p. 1997. text ed. 39.95 (0-19-563459-4) OUP.

Social Change & Political Discourse in India - Structures of Power, Movements of Resistance: Region, Religion, Caste, Gender & Culture in Contemporary India, Vol. 3. T. V. Sathyamurthy. 616p. 1996. text ed. 45.00 (0-19-563458-6) OUP.

Social Change & Political Transformation: A New Europe? Ed. by Chris Rootes & Howard Davis. 224p. 1994. 75.00 (1-85728-147-0, Pub. by UCL Pr UK); pap. 27.50 (1-85728-148-9, Pub. by UCL Pr UK) Taylor & Francis.

Social Change & Political Violence in Colonial Nigeria. Bernard Nkemdirim. 160p. (C). 1990. 35.00 (0-7223-0693-8, Pub. by A H S Ltd UK) St Mut.

Social Change & Scientific Organization: The Royal Instutution, 1799-1844. Morris Berman. LC 77-79702. (Illus.). 249p. 1978. 45.00 (0-8014-1093-2) Cornell U Pr.

Social Change & Social Issues in the Former U. S. S. R. Ed. by Walter Joyce. LC 92-3479. (Selected Papers from the Fourth World Congress for Soviet & East European Studies, Harrogate, 1990). 176p. 1992. text ed. 59.95 (0-312-07994-X) St Martin.

An Asterisk (*) at the beginning of an entry indicates that the title is appearing in BIP for the first time.

Social Change & Social Policy in Contemporary China. Ed. by Linda Wong & Stewart MacPherson. 272p. 1995. 59.95 (*1-85628-853-6*, Pub. by Avebury Pub UK) Ashgate Pub Co.

Social Change & Social Research: An Indian Perspective. R. S. Mann. (C). 1988. 38.00 (*81-7022-200-1*, Pub. by Concept II) S Asia.

Social Change & Social Work Practice: Writings of Fred Berl. Fred Berl. 243p. (C). 1988. 24.95 (*0-9620785-0-6*) D Berl.

Social Change & Status Protest: An Essay on the Marginal Man. Everett C. Hughes. (Reprint Series in Social Sciences). (C). 1993. reprint ed. pap. text ed. 1.00 (*0-8290-3543-5*, S-129) Irvington.

Social Change & the Experience of Unemployment. Ed. by Duncan Gallie et al. (Social Change & Economic Life Initiative Ser.). 352p. 1994. 65.00 (*0-19-827782-2*) OUP.

Social Change & the Family in Taiwan. Arland Thornton & Hui-Sheng Lin. LC 94-8973. (Population & Development Ser.). (Illus.). 480p. 1994. 29.95 (*0-226-79858-5*) U Ch Pr.

Social Change & the Labouring Poor: Antwerp, 1770-1860. Catharina Lis. LC 85-52070. 224p. 1986. 35.00 (*0-300-03610-8*) Yale U Pr.

Social Change & the Life Course. Ed. by Matilda W. Riley. (American Sociological Association Presidential Ser.). 560p. 1988. 74.95 (*0-8039-3432-7*) Sage.

Social Change & the Life Course, Set, Vols. 1 & 2. Ed. by Matilda W. Riley. (American Sociological Association Presidential Ser.). 560p. 1988. Set. pap. 34.90 (*0-8039-3433-5*) Sage.

Social Change & the Life Course Vol. 1: Social Structures & Human Lives. Ed. by Matilda W. Riley et al. 368p. 1988. pap. 104.90 (*0-7837-8966-1*, 2049747) Bks Demand.

Social Change & the Life Course Vol. 2: Sociological Lives. Ed. by Matilda W. Riley. LC 87-37658. (American Sociological Association Presidential Ser.). 192p. 1988. reprint ed. pap. 54.80 (*0-608-01727-2*, 2062384) Bks Demand.

Social Change & the Middle Classes. Ed. by Tim Butler & Mike Savage. 352p. 1995. 85.00 (*1-85728-271-X*, Pub. by UCL Pr UK); pap. 29.95 (*1-85728-272-8*, Pub. by UCL Pr UK) Taylor & Francis.

Social Change & Violence: The Indian Experience. P. R. Rajgopal. 227p. (C). 1987. 35.00 (*81-85024-27-8*, Pub. by Uppal Pub Hse II) S Asia.

Social Change & Women's Reproductive Health Care: A Guide to Physicians & Their Patients. Nada L. Stotland. LC 87-27591. 288p. 1988. text ed. 65.00 (*0-275-92570-6*, Praeger Pubs) Greenwood.

Social Change, Crime & Victimization in Tunisia. 1994. 20.00 (*92-9078-029-0*) UN.

Social Change, Development, & Dependency: Modernity, Colonialism & the Development of the West. Tony Spybey. LC 92-20938. 272p. 1993. 44.95 (*0-7456-0729-2*); pap. 22.95 (*0-7456-0730-6*) Blackwell Pubs.

Social Change, Differentiation & Evaluation. S. N. Eisenstadt. (Reprint Series in Social Sciences). (C). 1993. reprint ed. pap. text ed. 1.00 (*0-8290-3441-2*, S-576) Irvington.

Social Change Environmental Change: EDRA Proceedings: Nineteen Eighty-Five. Ed. by Stephan Klein et al. 450p. 1985. 35.00 (*0-939922-08-8*) EDRA.

Social Change in a Hostile Environment: The Crusador's Kingdom of Jerusalem. Aharon Ben-Ami. LC 68-27412. (Princeton Studies on the Near East). 201p. reprint ed. pap. 57.30 (*0-685-23407-X*, 2032631) Bks Demand.

Social Change in a Late Colonial Metropolis: Manila Nineteen Hundred to Nineteen Forty-One. Daniel F. Doeppers. LC 84-50326. (Monograph Ser.: No. 27). (Illus.). 194p. 1985. pap. 14.00 (*0-938692-06-2*) Yale U SE Asia.

Social Change in a Metropolitan Community. Otis D. Duncan et al. LC 73-76764. 136p. 1973. pap. 14.95 (*0-87154-216-1*) Russell Sage.

Social Change in a Spanish Village. Joseph Aceves. (Illus.). 144p. 1971. pap. 11.95 (*0-87073-755-4*) Schenkman Bks Inc.

Social Change in a Yemeni Highlands Town. Thomas B. Stevenson. LC 85-5322. (Illus.). 214p. reprint ed. pap. 61.00 (*0-7837-5534-1*, 2045307) Bks Demand.

Social Change in an Industrial Town: Patterns of Progress in Warren, Pennsylvania from Civil War to World War I. Michael P. Weber. LC 75-1634. 1975. 30.00 (*0-271-01201-3*) Pa St U Pr.

Social Change in Brazil, 1945-1985: The Incomplete Transition. Ed. by Edmar L. Bacha & Herbert S. Klein. LC 88-19895. 355p. (Orig.). 1989. pap. 12.95 (*0-8263-1111-3*) U of NM Pr.

Social Change in India. B. Kuppuswamy. (C). 1993. 24.00 (*81-220-0311-7*, Pub. by Konark Pubs II) S Asia.

Social Change in India. 4th rev. ed. B. Kuppuswamy. 1992. pap. 15.95 (*81-220-0160-2*, Pub. by Konark Pubs Pvt Ltd II) Advent Bks Div.

Social Change in Modern Africa: Studies Presented & Discussed. International African Seminar Staff. Ed. by Aiden Southall. LC 61-4358. 349p. reprint ed. pap. 99.50 (*0-8357-3225-8*, 2057119) Bks Demand.

Social Change in Modern France: Towards a Cultural Anthropology of the Fifth Republic. Henri Mendras. 256p. (C). 1991. 49.95 (*0-521-39108-3*); pap. text ed. 18.95 (*0-521-39998-X*) Cambridge U Pr.

Social Change in Nigeria. Ed. by Tola O. Pearce & Simi Abonja. 262p. (Orig.). (C). 1986. pap. text ed. 13.95 (*0-582-64434-8*) Longman.

Social Change in Nigeria. Ed. by Simi Afonja & Tola O. Pearce. LC 84-800. 269p. reprint ed. pap. 76.70 (*0-8357-2962-1*, 2039224) Bks Demand.

Social Change in Soviet Russia. Alex Inkeles. LC 68-54020. (Russian Research Center Studies: No. 57). 493p. 1968. 39.95 (*0-674-81196-8*) HUP.

Social Change in the Age of the Enlightenment: Edinburgh 1660-1760. Rab A. Houston. (Illus.). 420p. 1995. 75.00 (*0-19-820438-8*) OUP.

Social Change in the Industrial Revolution: An Application of Theory to the British Cotton Industry. Neil J. Smelser. (Modern Revivals in Economic & Social History Ser.). 456p. (C). 1994. text ed. 76.95 (*0-7512-0163-4*, Pub. by Gregg Revivals UK) Ashgate Pub Co.

Social Change in the Law of Trusts. George W. Keeton. LC 73-9374. 128p. 1974. reprint ed. text ed. 49.75 (*0-8371-7011-7*, KELT, Greenwood Pr) Greenwood.

Social Change in the Modern Era. Daniel Chirot & Robert E. Merton. 330p. (C). 1986. pap. text ed. 22.75 (*0-15-581421-4*) HB Coll Pubs.

Social Change in the Pacific Islands. Ed. by Albert B. Robillard. 320p. (C). 1990. text ed. 74.00 (*0-7103-0400-5*, A5632) Routledge Chapman & Hall.

***Social Change in the Royal Navy 1924-70: Admiral Sir Frank Twiss.** Ed. by Chris H. Bailey. (Illus.). 256p. 1996. 25.00 (*0-7509-0610-3*, Pub. by Sutton Pubng UK) Bks Intl VA.

Social Change in the Southwest, 1350-1880. Thomas D. Hall. LC 88-14250. (Studies in Historical Social Change). xvi, 288p. 1989. 35.00 (*0-7006-0374-3*); pap. 14.95 (*0-7006-0497-9*) U Pr of KS.

Social Change in Village India. Sachchidananda. (C). 1988. 35.00 (*81-7022-206-0*, Pub. by Concept II) S Asia.

Social Change in 19th Century Ceylon. Patrick Peebles. (C). 1995. 30.00 (*81-7013-141-3*, Pub. by Navrang) S Asia.

Social Change Philanthropy in America. Alan Rabinowitz. LC 89-24362. 248p. 1990. text ed. 55.00 (*0-89930-536-9*, RSD/, Greenwood Pr) Greenwood.

Social Change, Social Welfare, & Social Science. Peter Taylor-Gooby. 256p. (Orig.). 1992. 45.00 (*0-8020-2680-X*); pap. 18.95 (*0-8020-7696-3*) U of Toronto Pr.

Social Change, Social Work & the Adoption of Children. Alan Teague. (Illus.). 155p. 1989. lib. bdg. 63.95 (*0-566-07056-1*, Pub. by Gower UK) Ashgate Pub Co.

Social Changes, Crime & the Police. Louise I. Shelley. 208p. 1995. text ed. 42.00 (*3-7186-5684-1*); pap. text ed. 18.00 (*3-7186-5691-4*, Harwood Acad Pubs) Gordon & Breach.

Social Changes During Depression & Recovery. Ed. by William F. Ogburn. LC 72-2381. (FDR & the Era of the New Deal Ser.). 117p. 1974. reprint ed. lib. bdg. 22.50 (*0-306-70483-8*) Da Capo.

Social Changes in England in the Sixteenth-Century As Reflected in Contemporary Literature. Edward P. Cheyney. LC 76-168055. (Illus.). reprint ed. 36.50 (*0-404-01523-9*) AMS Pr.

Social Changes in Indian Society. R. Sinha. 208p. 1978. 16.50 (*0-318-36863-3*) Asia Bk Corp.

Social Character in a Mexican Village. Erich Fromm & Michael Maccoby. 303p. 1996. reprint ed. pap. text ed. 24.95 (*1-56000-876-8*) Transaction Pubs.

Social Character of Learning. Krishna Kumar. 140p. 1989. text ed. 20.00 (*0-8039-9589-X*) Sage.

Social Characteristics of Cities: A Basis for New Interpretations of the Role of the City in American Life. William F. Ogburn. LC 73-11940. (Metropolitan America Ser.). 80p. 1979. reprint ed. 18.95 (*0-405-05409-2*) Ayer.

Social Charter & the Single European Market: Towards a Socially Responsible Community. John Hughes. 78p. 1991. pap. 23.50 (*0-85124-524-2*, Pub. by Spokesman Bks UK) Coronet Bks.

Social Chaucer. 1994. pap. 16.95 (*0-674-81199-2*) HUP.

Social Chauncer. Paul Strohm. LC 89-30655. 280p. 1989. 36.00 (*0-674-81198-4*) HUP.

Social Choice. Bernhardt Lieberman. LC 75-132954. (Monographs & Texts in the Behavioral Sciences). (Illus.). xii, 426p. 1971. text ed. 194.00 (*0-677-14770-8*) Gordon & Breach.

Social Choice: A Framework for Collective Decisions & Individual Judgements. John Craven. (Illus.). 160p. (C). 1992. text ed. 54.95 (*0-521-32536-6*); pap. text ed. 17.95 (*0-521-31051-2*) Cambridge U Pr.

Social Choice & Bargaining Perspectives on Distributive Justice. W. Gaertner & M. Klemisch-Ahlert. LC 92-24420. (Lecture Notes in Economics & Mathematical Systems Ser.: Vol. 387). viii, 131p. 1992. 39.95 (*0-387-55815-2*) Spr-Verlag.

Social Choice & Individual Values. 2nd ed. Kenneth J. Arrow. (Cowles Foundation Monograph Ser.: No. 12). 1970. pap. 12.00 (*0-300-01364-7*, Y233) Yale U Pr.

Social Choice Re-Examined: Proceedings of the IEA Conference Held at Schloss Hernstein, Berndorf, Near Vienna, Austria, 2 vols, Vol. 2. Ed. by Kenneth J. Arrow et al. LC 95-11796. (IEA Conference Ser.: No. 116-117). 1997. text ed. 65.00 (*0-312-12741-3*) St Martin.

Social Choice Re-Examined: Proceedings of the IEA Conference Held at Schoss Hernstein, Berndorf, near Vienna, Austria. Amartya K. Sen. LC 95-11796. (IEA Conference Ser.: No. 116). 1995. text ed. 65.00 (*0-312-12739-1*) St Martin.

Social Choice Theory. J. S. Kelly. (Illus.). 190p. 1987. 42.00 (*0-387-17634-9*) Spr-Verlag.

Social Choice Theory, 3 vols. Ed. by Charles K. Rowley. (International Library of Critical Writings in Economics Ser.: Vol. 27). 1716p. 1993. 485.00 (*1-85278-159-9*) E Elgar.

Social Choice Theory & Soviet National Security Decisionmaking. Jeffrey T. Richelson. (CISA Working Papers: No. 37). 43p. (Orig.). 1982. pap. 15.00 (*0-86682-048-5*) Ctr Intl Relations.

Social Choice, Welfare & Ethics: Proceedings of the Eighth International Symposium in Economic Theory & Econometrics. Ed. by William A. Barnett et al. (International Symposia in Economic Theory & Econometrics Ser.: No. 8). (Illus.). 432p. (C). 1995. text ed. 64.95 (*0-521-44340-7*) Cambridge U Pr.

Social Christian Novel. Robert G. Wright. LC 88-25106. (Contributions in American Studies: No. 93). 206p. 1989. text ed. 49.95 (*0-313-24661-0*, WGO/, Greenwood Pr) Greenwood.

Social Citizenship for Whom? Thomas Faist. 264p. 1995. 59.95 (*1-85972-208-3*, Pub. by Avebury Pub UK) Ashgate Pub Co.

Social Citizenship Rights: A Critique of F. A. Hayek & Raymond Plant. Joao C. Espada. 240p. 1996. text ed. 65.00 (*0-312-15976-5*) St Martin.

Social Class & Church Participation. Erich Goode. Ed. by Harriet Zuckerman & Robert K. Merton. LC 79-9001. (Dissertations on Sociology Ser.). 1980. lib. bdg. 24.95 (*0-405-12970-X*) Ayer.

Social Class & Democratic Leadership: Essays in Honor of E. Digby Baltzell. Harold J. Bershady. LC 89-4845. 316p. (C). 1989. text ed. 44.95 (*0-8122-8158-6*) U of Pa Pr.

Social Class & Marxism: Defences & Challenges. Ed. by Neville Kirk. LC 95-25341. (Illus.). 256p. 1996. 79.95 (*1-85928-142-7*, Pub. by Scolar Pr UK) Ashgate Pub Co.

Social Class & Social Change in Puerto Rico. Melvin M. Tumin & Arnold S. Feldman. LC 70-145756. 1971. 39.50 (*0-672-61375-1*) Irvington.

***Social Class & Stratification: Classic Statements & Theoretical Debates.** Ed. by Rhonda F. Levine. 1998. 62.50 (*0-8476-8542-X*) Rowman.

***Social Class & Stratification: Classic Statements & Theoretical Debates.** Ed. by Rhonda F. Levine. 1998. pap. 17.95 (*0-8476-8543-8*) Rowman.

***Social Class in Modern Britain.** Gordon Marshall & David Rose. 336p. 1989. pap. text ed. 22.95 (*0-415-09876-9*) Routledge.

Social Class in Modern Britain. Gordon Marshall et al. 336p. (C). 1989. pap. text ed. 22.95 (*0-04-445416-3*) Routledge Chapman & Hall.

Social Class in Modern Britain. Gordon Marshall et al. 336p. 1989. 49.95 (*0-09-167940-0*) Routledge Chapman & Hall.

Social Class in Urban India: Essays on Cognitions & Structures. Edwin D. Driver & Aloo E. Driver. (Illus.). x, 159p. 1987. pap. 40.00 (*90-04-08106-2*) E J Brill.

Social Classes & Social Credit in Alberta. Edward Bell. 224p. (C). 1994. 47.95 (*0-7735-1168-7*, Pub. by McGill CN); pap. text ed. 18.95 (*0-7735-1169-5*, Pub. by McGill CN) U of Toronto Pr.

Social Classes & Social Relations in Britain, 1850-1914. Alastair J. Reid. (New Studies in Economic & Social History: No. 19). 77p. (C). 1995. text ed. 34.95 (*0-521-55278-8*); pap. text ed. 10.95 (*0-521-55775-5*) Cambridge U Pr.

Social Climbers: Heaven for High Tea. Chris Darwin & John Amy. (Illus.). 272p. pap. 22.95 (*1-85158-463-3*, Pub. by Mnstream UK) Trafalgar.

Social Cognition. 2nd ed. Susan T. Fiske & Shelley E. Taylor. 746p. 1991. pap. text ed. write for info. (*0-07-021191-4*) McGraw.

Social Cognition, Vol. 1. Ed. by E. Tory Higgins et al. (Ontario Symposia on Personality & Social Psychology Ser.: Vol. I). 448p. 1981. text ed. 79.95 (*0-89859-049-3*) L Erlbaum Assocs.

Social Cognition: An Integrated Perspective. Martha Augoustinos & Lain Walker. 304p. (C). 1995. 65.00 (*0-8039-8989-X*); pap. 19.95 (*0-8039-8990-3*) Sage.

Social Cognition: Impact on Social Psychology. Ed. by Patricia G. Devine et al. (Illus.). 403p. 1994. text ed. 69.00 (*0-12-213630-6*) Acad Pr.

Social Cognition & Clinical Psychology: A Synthesis. Ed. by Lyn Y. Abramson. LC 86-18453. 372p. 1988. lib. bdg. 46.95 (*0-89862-011-2*) Guilford Pr.

Social Cognition & Communication. Ed. by Michael E. Roloff & Charles R. Berger. LC 82-10715. 328p. reprint ed. pap. 93.50 (*0-8357-4850-2*, 2037781) Bks Demand.

Social Cognition & Consumer Behavior. M. Joseph Sirgy. 256p. 1983. text ed. 55.00 (*0-275-91081-4*, C1081, Praeger Pubs) Greenwood.

Social Cognition & Development: Studies of the Development of Understanding. George E. Butterworth & Paul C. Light. LC 81-24075. 282p. (C). 1982. 24.00 (*0-226-08609-7*) U Ch Pr.

Social Cognition & Individual Change: A Cognitive-Ecological Approach to Practice. Aaron M. Brower. LC 93-29475. (Sourcebooks for the Human Services Ser.: Vol. 26). 1993. 52.00 (*0-8039-3883-7*); pap. 24.95 (*0-8039-3884-5*) Sage.

Social Cognition, Inference, & Attribution. Robert S. Wyer & D. E. Carlston. 400p. 1979. 89.95 (*0-89859-499-5*) L Erlbaum Assocs.

***Social Cognitive Psychology: History & Current Domains.** David F. Barone et al. LC 97-1614. (Series in Social/Clinical Psychology). 490p. (C). 1997. 85.00 (*0-306-45474-2*); pap. 42.50 (*0-306-45475-0*) Plenum.

Social Cohesion: Essays Toward a Sociophysiological Perspective. Ed. by Patricia R. Barchas & Sally P. Mendoza. LC 83-22594. (Contributions in Sociology Ser.: No. 49). (Illus.). xvi, 219p. 1984. text ed. 55.00 (*0-313-24395-6*, BCH/) Greenwood.

Social Commentary 1969-1989: From University Troubles to a California Earthquake. Ed. by Heinz-Dietrich Fischer & Erika J. Fischer. (Pulitzer Prize Archive: Vol. 5). 448p. 1992. lib. bdg. 98.00 (*3-598-30175-8*) K G Saur.

Social Communication: Activities for Improving Peer Interactions & Self-Esteem. M. Ann Marquis & Elaine Addy-Trout. LC 92-21826. 1992. pap. 37.00 (*0-930599-75-6*) Thinking Pubns.

Social Communication & Movement: Studies of Interaction & Expression in Man & Chimpanzee. Ed. by Mario Von Cranach & Ian Vine. (European Monographs in Social Psychology). 1974. text ed. 247.00 (*0-12-724750-5*) Acad Pr.

Social Communication in Advertising: Persons, Products & Images of Well-Being. William Leiss et al. (Illus.). 327p. 1986. pap. 14.95 (*0-415-90084-0*, 9685, Routledge NY) Routledge.

Social Communication in Advertising: Persons, Products & Images of Well-Being. 2nd ed. William Leiss et al. 340p. (C). 1990. pap. 15.95 (*0-415-90354-8*, A4785, Routledge NY) Routledge.

Social Communication in Nutrition: A Methodology for Intervention. Michel Andrien. 107p. 1994. pap. 25.00 (*92-5-103367-6*, F33676, Pub. by FAO IT) Bernan Associates.

Social Comparison: Contemporary Theory & Research. Jerry Suls. 432p. (C). 1990. pap. 49.95 (*0-8058-0550-8*); text ed. 99.95 (*0-8058-0549-4*) L Erlbaum Assocs.

Social Comparison, Social Justice, & Relative Deprivation: Theoretical, Empirical, & Policy Perspectives. Ed. by John C. Masters & William P. Smith. (Greenwald & Krauss Ser.). 320p. 1987. text ed. 59.95 (*0-89859-632-7*) L Erlbaum Assocs.

Social Competence & Employability Skills Curriculum. Robert A. Weisgerber. LC 88-35070. 586p. 1989. 149.00 (*0-8342-0057-0*) Aspen Pub.

Social Competence in Developmental Perspective. Ed. by Barry H. Schneider et al. (C). 1989. lib. bdg. 185.00 (*0-7923-0400-4*) Kluwer Ac.

Social Competence of Children with Disabilities: Nature, Development, & Intervention. Ed. by Samuel L. Odom et al. 352p. (Orig.). (C). 1992. pap. text ed. 32.00 (*1-55766-085-9*) P H Brookes.

Social Competency in Adolescence. Ed. by Thomas P. Gullotta et al. (Advances in Adolescent Development Ser.: Vol. 3). (Illus.). 264p. (C). 1990. 55.00 (*0-8039-3898-5*); pap. 24.95 (*0-8039-3899-3*) Sage.

Social Complexity & the Development of Towns in Iberia: From the Copper Age to the Second Century A. D. Ed. by Barry Cunliffe & Simon Keay. (Proceedings of the British Academy Ser.: No. 86). (Illus.). 480p. 1995. 65.00 (*0-19-726157-4*) OUP.

Social Composition of Boards of Education. George S. Counts. LC 79-89167. (American Education: Its Men, Institutions, & Ideas. Series 1). 1975. reprint ed. 12.95 (*0-405-01405-8*) Ayer.

Social Composition of Political Leadership: Genesee County, New York 1821-1860. Kathleen S. Kutolowski. (Nineteenth Century American Political & Social History Ser.). 341p. 1989. reprint ed. 25.00 (*0-8240-4068-6*) Garland.

Social Compulsions of Ideas: Toward a Sociological Analysis of Knowledge. Gerard DeGre. Ed. by Cyril Levitt. 264p. 1984. 44.95 (*0-88738-003-4*) Transaction Pubs.

Social Concept Cards: Primary Education. Hegeman. 1982. 40.00 (*0-89824-032-8*) Trillium Pr.

Social Concern in Calvin's Geneva. William C. Innes. LC 83-23640. (Pittsburgh Theological Monographs, New Ser.: No. 7). 1983. pap. 15.00 (*0-915138-33-6*) Pickwick.

Social Concern, Universalism & the New Novel see New History of Spanish-American Fiction

Social Condition & Education of the People in England & Europe: Showing the Result of the Primary Schools & of the Division of Landed Property, 2 vols., Set. Joseph Kay. LC 72-141318. 1973. reprint ed. lib. bdg. 125.00 (*0-678-00144-8*) Kelley.

***Social Conditions & Education of the People in England & Europe: 1850 Edition, 2 vols.** Joseph Kay. Ed. & Intro. by Jeffrey Stern. (Classics in Education Ser.). 1156p. 1996. reprint ed. write for info. (*1-85506-290-9*) Bks Intl VA.

Social Conditions in an American City. Shelby M. Harrison. LC 75-22821. (America in Two Centuries Ser.). (Illus.). 1976. reprint ed. 39.95 (*0-405-07693-2*) Ayer.

Social Conditions in Britain Nineteen Eighteen to Nineteen Thirty-Nine. Steven Constantine. (Lancaster Pamphlet Ser.). 55p. (C). 1984. pap. text ed. 4.95 (*0-416-36010-6*, NO. 3983) Routledge Chapman & Hall.

Social Conditions in Industrial Rhode Island Eighteen Twenty to Eighteen Sixty. Joseph Brennan. LC 78-14597. (Perspectives in American History Ser.: No. 41). ix, 181p. 1978. reprint ed. lib. bdg. 35.00 (*0-87991-365-7*) Porcupine Pr.

***Social Conditions, Status & Community c. 1860-1920.** Ed. by Keith Laybourn. (Studies in Modern British History). 224p. 1997. 72.00 (*0-7509-1070-4*, Pub. by Sutton Pubng UK) Bks Intl VA.

***Social Conditions, Status & Community c. 1860-1920.** Ed. by Keith Laybourn. (Studies in Modern British History). 224p. 1997. pap. 22.95 (*0-7509-1501-3*, Pub. by Sutton Pubng UK) Bks Intl VA.

Social Conduct & Attitudes of Movie Fans see Motion Pictures & the Social Attitudes of Children

Social Conflict. Ed. by N. Jayaram & Satish Saberwal. (Oxford in India Readings in Sociology & Social & Cultural Anthropology Ser.). (Illus.). 528p. 1997. 32.00 (*0-19-563690-2*) OUP.

S

S

Social Conflict: Escalation, Stalemate, & Settlement. 2nd ed. Jeffrey Z. Rubin et al. LC 93-24557. 1993. pap. text ed. write for info. (*0-07-054211-2*) McGraw.

Social Conflict & Populist Policies in Latin America. Jeffrey Sachs. LC 89-77542. 36p. 1990. pap. 6.95 (*1-55815-099-4*) ICS Pr.

***Social Conflict & Television News.** Akiba A. Cohen et al. LC 90-38951. (Sage Library of Social Research: Vol. 183). 258p. 1990. reprint ed. pap. 73.60 (*0-608-03372-3*, 2059636) Bks Demand.

Social Conflict & the City. Enzo Mingione. 1981. text ed. 32.50 (*0-312-73163-9*) St Martin.

Social Conflict & the Theory of Social Change. Lewis A. Coser. (Reprint Series in Social Sciences). (C). 1993. reprint ed. pap. text ed. 1.00 (*0-8290-3839-6*, S-51) Irvington.

***Social Conflicts in Manohar Malgonkar's Fiction.** B. P. Engade. 1995. 24.00 (*81-7018-827-X*, Pub. by BR Pub II) S Asia.

Social Conflicts in the Roman Republic. P. A. Brunt. (Ancient Culture & Society Ser.). (Illus.). 176p. (C). 1974. reprint ed. pap. text ed. 8.95 (*0-393-00586-0*) Norton.

Social Consciousness & Career Awareness: Emerging Link in Higher Education. Ed. by John S. Swift, Jr. LC 91-65607. (ASHE-ERIC Higher Education Reports: No. 8). 97p. 1990. pap. 17.00 (*1-878380-05-2*) GWU Grad Schl E&HD.

Social Consequences of Genetic Engineering: Proceedings of the Sixth Boehringer Ingelheim Symposium, Kronberg, Taunus, 12-14 June, 1988. Ed. by D. J. Weatherall & J. H. Shelley. (International Congress Ser.: No. 820). 224p. 1989. 167.50 (*0-444-81069-2*, Excerpta Medica) Elsevier.

Social Consequences of Modernization in Communist Societies. Ed. by Mark G. Field. LC 76-169. 288p. reprint ed. pap. 82.10 (*0-317-42071-2*, 2025888) Bks Demand.

Social Consequences of the Big Con in the Reading & Writing Game. Bernard A. Goldberg. 74p. (Orig.). 1994. pap. text ed. 15.00 (*0-9624348-2-5*) B A Goldberg.

Social Construction of American Realism. Amy Kaplan. LC 88-10834. 200p. 1992. pap. text ed. 13.95 (*0-226-42430-8*) U Ch Pr.

Social Construction of Context Through Play. M. Nawal Lutfiyya. 238p. (Orig.). 1987. pap. text ed. 23.00 (*0-8191-6135-7*) U Pr of Amer.

Social Construction of Democracy, 1870-1990. Ed. by George R. Andrews & Herrick Chapman. 432p. (C). 1995. 45.00 (*0-8147-1508-7*) NYU Pr.

Social Construction of Democracy, 1870-1990. Ed. by George R. Andrews & Herrick Chapman. 432p. (C). 1997. pap. 20.00 (*0-8147-1506-0*) NYU Pr.

Social Construction of Expertise: The English Civil Service & Its Influence, 1919-1939. Gail Savage. (Pitt Series in Policy & Institutional). 238p. (C). 1996. pap. 22.95 (*0-8229-5596-2*); text ed. 49.95 (*0-8229-3904-5*) U of Pittsburgh Pr.

Social Construction of Gender. Ed. by Judith Lorber & Susan A. Farrell. (Illus.). 400p. (C). 1990. text ed. 52.00 (*0-8039-3956-6*); pap. text ed. 24.00 (*0-8039-3957-4*) Sage.

Social Construction of Lesbianism. Celia Kitzinger. (Inquiries in Social Construction Ser.: Vol. 1). 288p. (C). 1988. text ed. 45.00 (*0-8039-8116-3*); pap. text ed. 19.95 (*0-8039-8117-1*) Sage.

Social Construction of Markets & Industries. Porac & Ventresca. (Tourism Social Science Ser.). 352p. Date not set. text ed. 71.00 (*0-08-042587-9*, Pergamon Pr) Elsevier.

Social Construction of Nature: A Sociology of Ecological Enlightenment. Klaus Eder. (Theory, Culture & Society Ser.). 256p. 1996. 75.00 (*0-8039-7848-0*); pap. 26.95 (*0-8039-7849-9*) Sage.

Social Construction of Reality: A Treatise in the Sociology of Knowledge. Peter L. Berger & Thomas Luckmann. LC 66-14925. 240p. 1967. pap. 10.95 (*0-385-05898-5*, Anchor NY) Doubleday.

Social Construction of Reality: A Treatise in the Sociology of Knowledge. Peter L. Berger & Thomas Luckmann. LC 66-14925. reprint ed. write for info. (*0-89197-578-0*) Irvington.

Social Construction of Reform: Crime Prevention & Community Organization. Dan A. Lewis et al. 192p. 1988. 34.95 (*0-88738-138-3*) Transaction Pubs.

Social Construction of Science. Tom Jagtenberg. 1983. lib. bdg. 129.50 (*90-277-1498-3*) Kluwer Ac.

Social Construction of Social Policy: Methodologies, Racism, Citizenship & the Environment. Ed. by Colin Samson & Nigel South. LC 95-13607. 1996. text ed. 59.95 (*0-312-12717-0*) St Martin.

Social Construction of Technological Systems: New Directions in the Sociology & History of Technology. Ed. by Wiebe E. Bijker et al. LC 86-27600. (Illus.). 424p. 1989. pap. 19.00 (*0-262-52137-7*) MIT Pr.

Social Construction of the Past: Representation as Power. Ed. by George C. Bond & Angela Gilliam. LC 93-40053. (One World Archaeology Ser.). 256p. (C). (gr. 13). 1994. 45.00 (*0-415-09045-8*, B4676) Routledge.

***Social Construction of the Past: Representation As Power.** Ed. by George C. Bond & Angela Gilliam. (One World Archaeology Ser.). 256p. (C). 1997. pap. 19.95 (*0-415-15224-0*) Routledge.

Social Construction of the Person. Ed. by Kenneth J. Gergen & K. E. Davis. (Social Psychology Ser.). (Illus.). 300p. 1985. 94.95 (*0-387-96091-0*) Spr-Verlag.

***Social Construction of Thomas Carlyle's New England Reputation, 1834-36.** Leon Jackson. 23p. 1997. reprint ed. pap. 6.00 (*0-944026-73-7*) Am Antiquarian.

Social Construction of Urban Schooling: Situating the Crisis. Louis Miron. Ed. by William T. Pink & George W. Noblit. LC 96-21375. (Understanding Education & Policy Ser.). 272p. (C). 1996. text ed. 55.00 (*1-57273-074-9*); pap. text ed. 22.95 (*1-57273-075-7*) Hampton Pr NJ.

Social Construction of Virtue: The Moral Life of Schools. George W. Noblit et al. LC 95-39477. 192p. (C). 1996. text ed. 57.50 (*0-7914-3079-0*); pap. text ed. 18.95 (*0-7914-3080-4*) State U NY Pr.

Social Construction of Western Women's Rhetoric Before 1750. Yvonne D. Merrill. LC 95-46894. (Women's Studies: Vol. 9). 284p. 1996. 89.95 (*0-7734-8851-0*) E Mellen.

Social Construction of Written Communication. Ed. by Bennett A. Rafoth et al. LC 88-22347. (Writing Research Ser.: Vol. 17). 336p. (C). 1988. pap. 39.50 (*0-89391-549-1*); text ed. 73.25 (*0-89391-436-3*) Ablex Pub.

Social Context & Proclamation: A Socio-Cognitive Study in Proclaiming the Gospel Cross-Culturally. David Filbeck. LC 84-28539. (Illus.). 181p. 1985. pap. text ed. 9.95 (*0-87808-199-2*) William Carey Lib.

Social Context & Relationships. Steve Duck. (Understanding Relationship Processes Ser.: Vol. 3). (Illus.). 184p. (C). 1993. text ed. 36.00 (*0-8039-5377-1*); pap. text ed. 16.95 (*0-8039-5378-X*) Sage.

Social Context & Values: Perspectives of the Americas. Ed. by George F. McLean & Olinto Pegoraro. LC 88-37080. (Cultural Heritage & Contemporary Life Series I. Culture & Values). 215p. (Orig.). 1989. 45.00 (*0-8191-7354-1*); pap. 17.50 (*0-8191-7355-X*) Coun Res Values.

Social Context of AIDS. Ed. by Joan Huber & Beth E. Schneider. LC 91-7433. (American Sociological Association Presidential Ser.). 215p. 1992. reprint ed. pap. 61.30 (*0-608-01618-7*, 2059597) Bks Demand.

Social Context of AIDS: Sociological Contributions to Research & Policy. Joan Huber & Beth E. Schneider. (American Sociological Association Presidential Ser.). (Illus.). 240p. 1992. text ed. 39.95 (*0-8039-4329-6*); pap. text ed. 19.50 (*0-8039-4330-X*) Sage.

Social Context of an Ideology: Ambedkar's Political & Social Thought. M. S. Gore. LC 93-25689. 364p. (C). 1994. text ed. 38.95 (*0-8039-9136-3*) Sage.

***Social Context of Art in Northern New Ireland.** Phillip H. Lewis. LC 71-83764. (Field Museum of Natural History, Publication 184, Anthropological Ser.: Vol. 58). 1969. reprint ed. pap. 55.30 (*0-608-03767-2*, 2064590) Bks Demand.

Social Context of Child Abuse & Neglect. Ed. by Leroy H. Pelton. LC 80-13922. 331p. 1981. 45.95 (*0-87705-504-1*) Human Sci Pr.

Social Context of Conduct: Psychological Writings of Theodore R. Sarbin. Ed. by Vernon L. Allen & Karl E. Scheibe. LC 81-5864. 288p. 1982. text ed. 65.00 (*0-275-90752-X*, C0752, Praeger Pubs) Greenwood.

Social Context of Coping. Ed. by J. Eckenrode. (Stress & Coping Ser.). (Illus.). 290p. 1991. 45.00 (*0-306-43783-X*, Plenum Pr) Plenum.

Social Context of Innovation: Bureaucrats, Families, & Heros in the Early Industrial Revolution, As Foreseen in Bacon's New Atlantis. Anthony F. Wallace. LC 81-47956. (Illus.). 191p. 1982. reprint ed. pap. 54.50 (*0-7837-9471-1*, 2060213) Bks Demand.

Social Context of Language. Ed. by Ivena Markova. LC 77-3861. 251p. reprint ed. pap. 71.60 (*0-685-20650-5*, 2030436) Bks Demand.

Social Context of Literacy. Kenneth Levine. (Language, Education & Society Ser.). 247p. (C). 1986. text ed. 42.50 (*0-7100-9745-X*, RKP); pap. text ed. 19.95 (*0-685-12291-3*, RKP) Routledge.

Social Context of Literacy. Kenneth Levine. 272p. (C). 1986. pap. 19.95 (*0-7102-1391-3*, RKP) Routledge.

Social Context of Pastoral Care: Defining the Life Situation. George M. Furniss. LC 94-8766. 212p. (Orig.). 1994. pap. 20.00 (*0-664-25436-5*) Westminster John Knox.

Social Context of Paul's Ministry: Tentmaking & Apostleship. Ronald F. Hock. LC 79-7381. 112p. reprint ed. pap. 32.00 (*0-685-24165-3*, 2033041) Bks Demand.

Social Context of the Chronic Pain Sufferer. Ranjan Roy. 176p. 1992. 50.00 (*0-8020-2860-8*); pap. 19.95 (*0-8020-7360-3*) U of Toronto Pr.

Social Context of the New Information & Communication Technologies: A Bibliography. Elia T. Zureik. (American University Studies: Communications: Ser. XV, Vol. 2). 310p. (C). 1987. text ed. 35.00 (*0-8204-0413-6*) P Lang Pubng.

Social Context Schooling. M. Cole. 240p. 1989. 75.00 (*1-85000-450-1*, Falmer Pr); pap. 33.00 (*1-85000-451-X*, Falmer Pr) Taylor & Francis.

Social Contexts of American Ethnology, 1840-1984. Ed. by June Helm. (Proceedings of the American Ethnological Society Ser.). 1985. 15.00 (*0-942976-06-1*) Am Anthro Assn.

Social Contexts of Criminal Sentencing. Talarico Myers. LC 87-4771. (Research in Criminology Ser.). 245p. 1987. 114.95 (*0-387-96483-5*) Spr-Verlag.

Social Contexts of Tribal Education. V. P. Shah & Tara Patel. 212p. 1985. 34.95 (*0-318-36827-7*) Asia Bk Corp.

Social Contours of an Industrial City. D. N. Majumdar. LC 73-13863. (Illus.). 247p. 1975. reprint ed. text ed. 59.75 (*0-8371-6762-0*, MASD, Greenwood Pr) Greenwood.

Social Contract. Jean-Jacques Rousseau. 20.95 (*0-8488-0840-1*) Amereon Ltd.

Social Contract. Jean-Jacques Rousseau. Ed. by Charles Frankell. (Library of Classics: No. 1). 160p. 1970. pap. 13.95 (*0-02-851150-6*) Hafner.

Social Contract. Jean-Jacques Rousseau. Tr. by G. D. Cole. LC 88-60152. (Great Books in Philosophy). 150p. (C). 1988. pap. 5.95 (*0-87975-444-3*) Prometheus Bks.

Social Contract. Jean-Jacques Rousseau. Tr. & Intro. by Maurice Cranston. LC . (Classics Ser.). 192p. 1968. pap. 7.95 (*0-14-044201-4*, Penguin Classics) Viking Penguin.

Social Contract: A Critical Study of Its Development. 2nd ed. John W. Gough. LC 78-6099. 259p. 1978. reprint ed. text ed. 35.00 (*0-313-20494-2*, GOSO, Greenwood Pr) Greenwood.

Social Contract: Essays by Locke, Hume & Rousseau. Ed. by Ernest Barker. 352p. 1962. pap. 16.95 (*0-19-500309-8*) OUP.

Social Contract: Essays by Locke, Hume, & Rousseau. Ed. by Ernest Barker. LC 80-22006. xliv, 307p. 1980. reprint ed. text ed. 35.00 (*0-313-22409-9*, BACT, Greenwood Pr) Greenwood.

Social Contract & Discourse on the Origin of Inequality. Jean-Jacques Rousseau. Ed. by Lester G. Crocker. 288p. mass mkt. 5.99 (*0-671-68956-8*, WSP) PB.

Social Contract & Discourses. Jean-Jacques Rousseau. Ed. by J. H. Brumfitt. Tr. by G. D. Cole. 422p. 1993. pap. 6.95 (*0-460-87357-1*, Everyman's Classic Lib) C E Tuttle.

***Social Contract & Other Later Political Writings.** Ed. by Victor Gourevitch. (Cambridge Texts in the History of Political Thought Ser.). 336p. (C). 1997. text ed. 44.95 (*0-521-41382-6*); pap. text ed. 12.95 (*0-521-42446-1*) Cambridge U Pr.

Social Contract & the Islamic State. Ilyas Ahmad. 203p. 1981. 9.95 (*0-318-36777-7*) Asia Bk Corp.

Social Contract Bridge Made Easy: The Myths of Contract Bridge Exposed. R. F. Jacka. 1994. pap. 14.95 (*0-533-10719-9*) Vantage.

Social Contract, Discourse on the Virtue Most Necessary for a Hero, Political Fragments, & Geneva Manuscript. Jean-Jacques Rousseau. Ed. by Roger D. Masters & Christopher Kelly. Tr. by Christopher Kelly et al. from FRE. LC 94-4496. (Collected Writings of Rousseau: Vol. 4). (Illus.). 306p. (C). 1994. 45.00 (*0-87451-646-3*) U Pr of New Eng.

Social Contract, Free Ride: A Study of the Public Goods Problem. Anthony De Jasay. 264p. 1991. pap. 26.00 (*0-19-823912-2*) OUP.

Social Contract from Hobbes to Rawls. Ed. by David Boucher & Paul Kelly. LC 94-4918. 336p. (C). 1994. pap. 19.95 (*0-415-10846-2*, B4681) Routledge.

Social Contract Law & European Integration. Ed. by Thomas Wilhelmsson. LC 94-42386. 1995. 59.95 (*1-85521-623-X*, Pub. by Dartmth Pub UK) Ashgate Pub Co.

Social Contract Revisited: Aims & Outcomes of President Reagan's Welfare Policy. Ed. by D. Lee Bawden. LC 84-7209. (Changing Domestic Priorities Ser.). 250p. (Orig.). 1984. lib. bdg. 57.00 (*0-87766-362-9*) Urban Inst.

Social Contract; The Discourses. Jean-Jacques Rousseau. Tr. by G. D. Cole. LC 93-22368. 1993. 17.00 (*0-679-42302-8*, Everymans Lib) Knopf.

Social Contract Theories. Vincente Medina. 150p. (C). 1990. lib. bdg. 43.50 (*0-8476-7624-2*) Rowman.

Social Contract Theory. M. Lessnoff. 330p. (C). 1990. pap. 17.50 (*0-8147-5055-9*); text ed. 36.00 (*0-8147-5054-0*) NYU Pr.

Social Contract Theory of Organizations. Michael Keeley. LC 87-40621. (Soundings: A Series in Ethics, Economics & Business: Vol. 2 of Soundings). 288p. 1988. text ed. 38.00 (*0-268-01730-1*) U of Notre Dame Pr.

Social Contracts & Economic Markets. Judith R. Blau. (Illus.). 206p. (C). 1993. 37.50 (*0-306-44391-0*, Plenum Pr) Plenum.

Social Contribution by the Aging. Ed. by Clark Tibbitts & Leon Stein. LC 79-8690. (Growing Old Ser.). (Illus.). 1980. reprint ed. lib. bdg. 19.95 (*0-405-12806-1*) Ayer.

Social Control: Aspects of Non-State Justice. Ed. by Stuart Henry. (International Library of Criminology & Criminal Justice). 372p. 1994. 99.95 (*1-85521-354-0*, Pub. by Dartmth Pub UK) Ashgate Pub Co.

Social Control: The Production of Deviance in the Modern State. Nanette J. Davis & Bo Anderson. LC 83-136. 364p. 1983. text ed. 19.95 (*0-8290-0727-X*) Irvington.

Social Control: The Production of Deviance in the Modern State. Nanette J. Davis & Bo Anderson. LC 83-136. 364p. (C). 1986. reprint ed. pap. text ed. 14.95 (*0-8290-2010-1*) Irvington.

Social Control: Views from the Social Sciences. Ed. by Jack P. Gibbs. LC 82-5774. (Sage Focus Editions Ser.: No. 51). (Illus.). 288p. 1982. reprint ed. pap. 82.10 (*0-8357-4797-2*, 2037734) Bks Demand.

Social Control & Deviance in Cuba. Luis Salas. LC 79-19597. (Praeger Special Studies). (Illus.). 416p. 1979. text ed. 75.00 (*0-275-90417-2*, C0417, Praeger Pubs) Greenwood.

Social Control & Multiple Discovery in Science: The Opiate Receptor Case. Susan E. Cozzens. LC 88-15983. (SUNY Series in Science, Technology, & Society). 236p. 1989. text ed. 64.50 (*0-88706-935-5*); pap. text ed. 21.95 (*0-88706-936-3*) State U NY Pr.

Social Control & Political Change. David H. Bayley. LC 86-201513. (Center for International Studies, Woodrow Wilson School of Public & International Affairs: Vol. 49). (Illus.). 139p. pap. 39.70 (*0-8357-7025-7*, 2033372) Bks Demand.

Social Control & Political Change. David H. Bayley. LC 86-201513. (Research Monograph: No. 49). 134p. 1985. 8.00 (*0-685-17694-0*) Princeton CIS.

Social Control & Political Order: European Perspectives at the End of the Century. Roberto Bergalli & Colin Sumner. 176p. 1996. 65.00 (*0-8039-7558-9*); pap. 22.95 (*0-8039-7559-7*) Sage.

Social Control & Social Change. Ed. by John P. Scott & Sarah F. Scott. LC 74-147822. 248p. 1971. lib. bdg. 11.50 (*0-226-74295-4*) U Ch Pr.

Social Control for the Nineteen Eighties: A Handbook for Order in a Democratic Society. Joseph S. Roucek. LC 77-91112. (Contributions in Sociology Ser.: No. 31). 386p. 1978. text ed. 65.00 (*0-313-20048-3*, RSC/, Greenwood Pr) Greenwood.

***Social Control in Canada: Issues in the Social Construction of Deviance.** Ed. by Bernard Schissel & Linda Mahood. (Illus.). 432p. 1996. pap. 29.95 (*0-19-540919-1*) OUP.

Social Control in China: A Study of Chinese Work Units. Victor N. Shaw. LC 96-2204. 304p. 1996. text ed. 59.95 (*0-275-95599-0*, Praeger Pubs) Greenwood.

Social Control in Slave Plantation Societies: A Comparison of St. Domingue & Cuba. Gwendolyn M. Hall. LC 95-50414. 184p. (C). 1996. pap. 11.95 (*0-8071-2083-9*) La State U Pr.

Social Control in Slave Plantation Societies: A Comparison of St. Dominique & Cuba. Gwendolyn M. Hall. LC 79-163195. (Johns Hopkins University Studies in Historical & Political Science: Ser. 89, No. 1). 175p. reprint ed. pap. 49.90 (*0-7837-4776-4*, 2044531) Bks Demand.

Social Control in the Colonial Economy. Jonathan R. Hughes. LC 75-17630. 188p. reprint ed. pap. 53.60 (*0-7837-4353-X*, 2044063) Bks Demand.

Social Control in the People's Republic of China. Ed. by Ronald J. Troyer et al. LC 88-37570. 231p. 1989. text ed. 55.00 (*0-275-93176-5*, C3176, Praeger Pubs) Greenwood.

Social Control of Business. 2nd ed. John M. Clark. LC 68-55508. (Reprints of Economic Classics Ser.). (Illus.). xvi, 537p. 1969. reprint ed. 57.50 (*0-678-00526-5*) Kelley.

Social Control of Deviance. Nanette J. Davis & C. Stasz. 1990. text ed. write for info. (*0-07-015930-0*) McGraw.

Social Control of Religious Zeal: A Study of Organizational Contradictions. Jon Miller. LC 93-6030. (Arnold & Caroline Rose Monograph Series of the American Sociological Association). 240p. (C). 1994. text ed. 48.00 (*0-8135-2060-6*) Rutgers U Pr.

***Social Control of Technology in North Africa: Information in the Global Economy.** Andrea L. Kavanaugh. 1997. text ed. write for info. (*0-275-94815-3*, Praeger Pubs) Greenwood.

Social Control of the Drinking Driver. Michael D. Laurence et al. (Studies in Crime & Justice). xxx, 482p. 1988. pap. text ed. 24.00 (*0-226-46954-9*) U Ch Pr.

Social Control of the Mentally Deficient. Stanley P. Davies. LC 75-17215. (Social Problems & Social Policy Ser.). (Illus.). 1976. reprint ed. 35.95 (*0-405-07486-7*) Ayer.

Social Control of the Welfare State. Morris Janowitz. LC 75-35903. 192p. reprint ed. pap. 54.80 (*0-685-15411-4*, 2026262) Bks Demand.

Social Control Through Law. Roscoe Pound. LC 96-2793. 160p. (Orig.). 1996. pap. text ed. 21.95 (*1-56000-916-0*) Transaction Pubs.

Social Corporatism: A Superior Economic System? Ed. by Jukka Pekkarinen et al. (WIDER Studies in Development Economics). (Illus.). 416p. 1992. 105.00 (*0-19-828380-6*) OUP.

Social Correlates of Infant & Reproductive Mortality in the United States: A Reference Guide. Ann Creighton-Zollar. LC 92-41215. 224p. 1993. text ed. 37.00 (*0-8153-0221-5*, SS766) Garland.

Social Cost-Benefit Analysis: An Introduction to Financial & Economic Appraisal of Projects. Krishan Chawla. 1987. 24.00 (*81-7099-022-X*, Pub. by Mittal II) S Asia.

Social Cost of Small Families & Land Reform: A Case Study of the Wataita of Kenya. C. C. Mkangi. (International Population Ser.: Vol. 2). (Illus.). 180p. 1983. text ed. 83.00 (*0-08-028952-5*, Pub. by Pergamon Repr UK) Franklin.

Social Costs & Rewards of Caring. Dermot Clifford. 261p. 1990. text ed. 59.95 (*1-85628-074-8*, Pub. by Avebury Pub UK) Ashgate Pub Co.

***Social Costs & Sustainability: Valuation & Implementation in the Energy & Transport Sector.** Olav Hohmeyer et al. LC 96-35868. 1996. 139.50 (*3-540-60177-5*) Spr-Verlag.

Social Costs in Modern Society: A Qualitative & Quantitative Assessment. Ed. by John E. Ullmann. LC 82-18590. (Illus.). xiv, 268p. 1983. text ed. 55.00 (*0-89930-019-7*, USC/, Quorum Bks) Greenwood.

Social Costs of Business Enterprise. 3rd ed. K. William Kapp. 348p. 1978. 37.50 (*0-85124-174-3*, Pub. by Spokesman Bks UK) Coronet Bks.

Social Costs of Economic Restructuring in Asia & the Pacific. 568p. 1994. 35.00 (*92-1-119617-5*, E.94.II.F2) UN.

***Social Costs of Economic Transformation in Central Europe.** Ed. by Janos M. Kovacs. (International Review of Comparative Public Policy Ser.: Vol. 7). 264p. 1996. 73.25 (*0-7623-0153-8*) Jai Pr.

Social Costs of Energy - Present Status & Future Trends: Proceedings of an International Conference, Held at Racine, Wisconsin, September 8-11, 1982. Ed. by Olav Hohmeyer & Richard L. Ottinger. LC 94-16187. 1994. 127.95 (*0-387-57841-2*) Spr-Verlag.

Social Costs of Energy Consumption. Olav Hohmeyer. (Illus.). 140p. 1989. pap. 38.00 (*0-387-19350-2*) Spr-Verlag.

Social Costs of Genetic Welfare. Marque-Luisa Miringoff. 200p. (C). 1991. text ed. 35.00 (*0-8135-1706-0*); pap. text ed. 15.00 (*0-8135-1707-9*) Rutgers U Pr.

Social Costs, Public Policy, & Freedom of Choice. Norman B. Ture. 32p. 1992. pap. 4.95 (*0-614-04373-5*) IRET.

An Asterisk (*) at the beginning of an entry indicates that the title is appearing in BIP for the first time.

Social Courts in Theory & Practice: Yugoslav Workers' Courts in Comparative Perspective. Robert M. Hayden. LC 90-40821. (Law in Social Context Ser.). 204p. (C). 1991. text ed. 33.50 (*0-8122-8259-0*) U of Pa Pr.

Social Creation of Nature. Neil Evernden. 192p. 1992. text ed. 38.00 (*0-8018-4396-0*); pap. text ed. 13.95 (*0-8018-4548-3*) Johns Hopkins.

Social Credit. C. H. Douglas. 1974. 250.00 (*0-87968-107-1*) Gordon Pr.

Social Credit: An Impact. Ezra Pound. 1983. lib. bdg. 250.00 (*0-87700-457-9*) Revisionist Pr.

Social Credit: One Hundred & Sixty Questions & Answers. 1991. lib. bdg. 250.00 (*0-8490-4472-3*) Gordon Pr.

Social Credit: One Hundred Sixty Questions & Answers. 1984. lib. bdg. 79.95 (*0-87700-571-0*) Revisionist Pr.

Social Credit: The English Origins. John L. Finlay. 1972. 44.95 (*0-7735-0111-8*, Pub. by McGill CN) U of Toronto Pr.

Social Credit & Catholicism. George H. Levesque. 1979. lib. bdg. 39.95 (*0-8490-3006-4*) Gordon Pr.

Social Credit Movement in Alberta. John A. Irving. LC 60-1477. (Social Credit in Alberta: Its Background & Development Ser.: No. 10). 383p. reprint ed. pap. 109.20 (*0-685-15374-6*, 2026528) Bks Demand.

Social Credit Phenomenon in Alberta. Alvin Finkel. xii, 285p. 1989. 40.00 (*0-8020-5821-3*); pap. 18.95 (*0-8020-6731-X*) U of Toronto Pr.

Social Crisis & Educational Research. Ed. by Len Barton & Stephen Walker. 347p. 1984. 28.00 (*0-7099-3235-9*, Pub. by Croom Helm UK); pap. 14.50 (*0-7099-3248-0*, Pub. by Croom Helm UK) Routledge Chapman & Hall.

Social Crisis of Our Time. Wilhelm Roepke. 290p. (C). 1991. pap. text ed. 24.95 (*1-56000-580-7*) Transaction Pubs.

***Social Criticism & Nineteenth-Century American Fictions.** Robert Shulman. 344p. 1989. pap. 16.95 (*0-8262-0726-X*) U of Mo Pr.

Social Criticism of Stephen Leacock: The Unsolved Riddle of Social Justice & Other Essays. Stephen Leacock. LC 73-79860. (Social History of Canada Ser.). 193p. reprint ed. pap. 55.10 (*0-8357-3766-7*, 2036495) Bks Demand.

Social Currents in Eastern Europe: The Sources & Consequences of the Great Transformation. 2nd ed. Sabrina P. Ramet. LC 94-28352. 624p. 1994. text ed. 65.00 (*0-8223-1551-3*); pap. text ed. 23.95 (*0-8223-1548-3*) Duke.

Social Currents in Eastern Europe: The Sources & Meaning of the Great Transformation. Sabrina P. Ramet. LC 90-24049. 447p. 1991. pap. text ed. 24.95 (*0-8223-1148-8*); lib. bdg. 52.95 (*0-8223-1129-1*) Duke.

Social Dance. W. Pillich. (Ballroom Dance Ser.). 1986. lib. bdg. 79.95 (*0-8490-3345-4*) Gordon Pr.

Social Dance. W. Pillich. (Ballroom Dance Ser.). 1985. lib. bdg. 74.00 (*0-87700-688-1*) Revisionist Pr.

Social Dance: A Short History. A. H. Franks. (Ballroom Dance Ser.). 1986. lib. bdg. 79.95 (*0-8490-3318-7*) Gordon Pr.

Social Dance: A Short History. A. H. Franks. (Ballroom Dance Ser.). 1985. lib. bdg. 64.00 (*0-87700-761-6*) Revisionist Pr.

Social Dance: Steps to Success. Judy P. Wright. LC 91-31230. (Steps to Success Activity Ser.). (Illus.). 176p. (Orig.). 1992. pap. 15.95 (*0-88011-449-5*, PWRI0449) Human Kinetics.

Social Dance Instruction: Steps to Success. Judy P. Wright. LC 95-44481. (Steps to Success Activity Ser.). (Illus.). 168p. (Orig.). 1995. pap. 19.95 (*0-87322-830-8*, PWRI0830) Human Kinetics.

Social Dance Rhythms. Alma Heaton. (Ballroom Dance Ser.). 1985. lib. bdg. 79.95 (*0-8490-3250-4*) Gordon Pr.

Social Dances from the American Revolution. Charles C. Hendrickson & Kate Van Winkle Keller. (Illus.). 48p. (Orig.). 1992. pap. 5.95 (*1-877984-15-9*) Hendricksn Group.

Social Dancing. Arthur Murray. (Ballroom Dance Ser.). 1986. lib. bdg. 79.95 (*0-8490-3255-5*) Gordon Pr.

Social Dancing. Arthur Murray. (Ballroom Dance Ser.). 1985. lib. bdg. 79.95 (*0-87700-694-6*) Revisionist Pr.

Social Dancing. A. P. Wright & D. J. Dexter. (Ballroom Dance Ser.). 1986. lib. bdg. 79.95 (*0-8490-3388-8*) Gordon Pr.

Social Dancing. A. P. Wright & D. J. Dexter. (Ballroom Dance Ser.). 1985. lib. bdg. 79.00 (*0-87700-723-3*) Revisionist Pr.

Social Darwinism: Science & Myth. rev. ed. Robert C. Bannister. LC 79-615. (American Civilization Ser.). 292p. (C). 1989. 16.95 (*0-87722-566-4*) Temple U Pr.

Social Darwinism in American Thought. Richard Hofstadter. LC 91-45525. 284p. 1992. pap. 16.00 (*0-8070-5503-4*) Beacon Pr.

***Social Darwinism in European & American Thought, 1860-1945: Nature As Model & Nature As Threat.** Mike Hawkins. 360p. (C). 1997. text ed. 69.95 (*0-521-57400-5*); pap. text ed. 27.95 (*0-521-57434-X*) Cambridge U Pr.

Social Darwinism in France. Linda L. Clark. LC 82-21795. 275p. 1984. pap. 78.40 (*0-7837-8366-3*, 2059176) Bks Demand.

Social Decision Methodology for Technological Projects. Ed. by Charles Vlek & George Cvetkovich. (C). 1989. lib. bdg. 145.00 (*0-7923-0371-7*) Kluwer Ac.

Social Defense: The Future of Penal Reform. Marc Ancel. Ed. by Edward P. Wise. LC 86-15458. (Publications of the Comparative Criminal Law Project: Vol. 16). xxi, 314p. 1987. 47.50 (*0-8377-0219-4*) Rothman.

Social Democracy & Population. Alvan A. Tenney. LC 68-56689. (Columbia University. Studies in the Social Sciences: No. 71). reprint ed. 24.50 (*0-404-51071-X*) AMS Pr.

Social Democracy & Rational Choice: The Scandanavian (sic) Experience & Beyond. Henry Milner. LC 94-15094. (Illus.). 312p. (C). (gr. 13). 1994. 49.95 (*0-415-11699-6*, B4762) Routledge.

Social Democracy & the Rule of Law. Otto Kirchheimer et al. LC 86-32198. 1987. 55.00 (*0-04-301300-7*) Routledge Chapman & Hall.

Social Democracy & the St. Petersburg Labor Movement, 1885-97. 2nd ed. Richard Pipes. LC 85-27842. xviii, 107p. (C). 1985. 20.00 (*1-884445-13-6*) C Schlacks Pub.

Social Democracy in a Post-Communist Europe. Ed. by Michael Waller et al. LC 93-36936. (Illus.). 203p. 1994. 37.50 (*0-7146-4522-2*, Pub. by F Cass Pubs UK); pap. 18.50 (*0-7146-4092-1*, Pub. by F Cass Pubs UK) Intl Spec Bk.

Social Democracy in the Austrian Provinces, 1918-1934: Beyond Red Vienna. Charlie Jeffery. 256p. 1996. write for info. (*0-8386-3629-2*) Fairleigh Dickinson.

Social Democracy in Transition: Northern, Southern & Eastern Europe. Lauri Karvonen & Jan Sundberg. 332p. 1991. 59.95 (*1-85521-111-4*, Pub. by Dartmth Pub UK) Ashgate Pub Co.

Social Democracy of the Austrian. Jeffrey. Date not set. 59.95 (*0-7185-1398-3*) St Martin.

Social Democratic Image of Society: A Study of the Achievements & Origins of Scandinavian Social Democracy in Comparative Perspective. Francis G. Castles. 1978. 22.50 (*0-7100-8870-1*, RKP) Routledge.

Social Democratic Parties in Europe. Anton Pelinka. LC 82-18940. 208p. 1983. text ed. 55.00 (*0-275-91057-1*, C1057, Praeger Pubs) Greenwood.

Social Democratic State: Bureaucracy & Social Reforms in Swedish Labor Market & School Policy. Bo Rothstein. LC 95-2869. (Pitt Series in Policy & Institutional). 272p. 1996. 39.95 (*0-8229-3881-2*) U of Pittsburgh Pr.

Social Democrats: Those Who Went & Those Who Stayed, the Forward March of Labour Halted? Ken Coates. 116p. 1983. 42.50 (*0-85124-357-6*, Pub. by Spokesman Bks UK) Coronet Bks.

Social Democrats -U. S. A. in the Service of Reaction: A Record of Racism, Low Wages, Bureaucracy & Betrayal of Socialism. George Morris. 1976. pap. 0.50 (*0-87898-119-5*) New Outlook.

Social Democrats in Imperial Germany: A Study in Working-Class Isolation & National Integration. Guenther Roth. Ed. by Lewis A. Coser & Walter W. Powell. LC 79-7018. (Perennial Works in Sociology). 1980. reprint ed. lib. bdg. 29.95 (*0-405-12117-2*) Ayer.

Social-Demokraten & Internationalism: The Copenhagen Social Democratic Newspaper's Coverage of International Labor Affairs, 1871-1958. Gerd Callesen & John Logue. LC 79-121967. (University of Gothenburg (Sweden), Research Section Post-War History Publications Ser.: No. 8). (Illus.). 73p. 1979. pap. 4.95 (*0-933522-00-2*) Kent Popular.

Social Desirability Variable in Personality Assessment & Research. Allen L. Edwards. LC 81-20141. vii, 108p. 1982. reprint ed. text ed. 49.75 (*0-313-23245-8*, EDSD, Greenwood Pr) Greenwood.

Social Destiny of Man: Or Association & Reorganization of Industry. Albert Brisbane. LC 68-18217. (Reprints of Economic Classics Ser.). xiv, 480p. 1969. reprint ed. 57.50 (*0-678-00471-4*) Kelley.

Social Destiny of Mankind. Albert Brisbane. 1972. 300.00 (*0-87968-025-3*) Gordon Pr.

Social Determinants of Labour Productivity in West Africa. Austin N. Isamah. (African Social Challenges Ser.: No. 3). 189p. 1991. lib. bdg. 55.00 (*0-905450-48-5*, Pub. by H Zell Pubs UK) Bowker-Saur.

Social Devaluation & Special Education: The Right to Full Mainstream Inclusion & an Honest Statement. John Hall. 192p. 1996. pap. text ed. 26.95 (*1-85302-354-X*, Pub. by J Kingsley Pubs UK) Taylor & Francis.

Social Development. Ed. by Nancy Eisenberg. (Review of Personality & Social Psychology Ser.: Vol. 15). 352p. 1994. 54.00 (*0-8039-5684-3*) Sage.

Social Development. Ed. by Nancy Eisenberg. (Review of Personality & Social Psychology Ser.: Vol. 15). 352p. 1994. pap. 24.95 (*0-8039-5685-1*) Sage.

Social Development. J. E. Grusec & H. Lytton. (Illus.). 500p. 1996. 54.00 (*0-387-96591-2*) Spr-Verlag.

Social Development. James Midgley. 192p. (C). 1995. 69.95 (*0-8039-7772-7*) Sage.

Social Development. James Midgley. 192p. (C). 1995. pap. 21.95 (*0-8039-7773-5*) Sage.

Social Development. David G. Perry & Kay Bussey. (Illus.). 416p. (C). 1983. text ed. 64.00 (*0-13-816034-1*) P-H.

Social Development: A New Role for the Organizational Sciences. Ed. by Pradip N. Khandwalla. 360p. (C). 1989. text ed. 27.50 (*0-8039-9574-1*) Sage.

Social Development: An Introduction. H. Rudolph Schaffer. 1996. pap. 29.95 (*0-631-18574-7*) Blackwell Pubs.

Social Development: An Introduction. H. Rudolph Schaffer. 438p. 1996. 59.95 (*0-631-18573-9*) Blackwell Pubs.

Social Development: Conceptual, Methodological & Policy Issues. John T. Jones & Rama S. Pandey. 1981. text ed. 19.95 (*0-312-73201-5*) St Martin.

Social Development: Psychological Growth & the Parent-Child Relationship. Eleanor E. Maccoby. 436p. (C). 1980. pap. text ed. 24.00 (*0-15-581422-2*) HB Coll Pubs.

Social Development & Absolute Poverty in Asia & Latin America. Willy De Geyndt. LC 96-27954. (World Bank Technical Paper Ser.: No. 328). 56p. 1996. 7.95 (*0-8213-3695-9*, 13695) World Bank.

Social Development & Demographic Changes in South India: Focus on Kerala 1994. Ed. by V. Balakrishnan Nair. (C). 1994. 70.00 (*81-85880-50-6*, Pub. by Print Hse II) St Mut.

Social Development & Justice in India. R. G. Singh & R. D. Gadkar. (C). 1995. 32.00 (*81-7027-206-8*, Pub. by Radiant Pubs II) S Asia.

***Social Development & Social Welfare: Asian Experiences.** Ed. by Jacqueline Ismael. 260p. (Orig.). (C). 1997. pap. text ed. 19.95 (*1-55059-153-3*, Pub. by Detselig CN) Temeron Bks.

Social Development, Cultural Change, & Fertility Decline: A Study of Fertility Change in Kerala. Kuttan Mahadevan & M. Sumangala. 160p. (C). 1989. text ed. 17.95 (*0-8039-9536-9*) Sage.

Social Development in Africa: Strategies, Policies & Programs since the Lagos Plan. S. Bedrani & E. Chole. (African Social Challenges Ser.: No. 4). 224p. 1991. lib. bdg. 65.00 (*0-905450-28-0*, Pub. by H Zell Pubs UK) Bowker-Saur.

Social Development in Africa Today: Some Radical Proposals. Stephen Chan. Ed. by Jonathan Alner. LC 91-37447. 136p. 1992. lib. bdg. 69.95 (*0-7734-9637-8*) E Mellen.

Social Development in Africa, 1950-1985: Methodological Perspectives & Future Prospects. Arega Yimam. (Illus.). 384p. 1990. text ed. 76.95 (*0-566-07136-3*, Pub. by Avebury Pub UK) Ashgate Pub Co.

Social Development in Childhood: Day-Care Programs & Research. Ed. by Roger A. Webb. LC 77-4778. (Hyman Blumberg Symposium Ser.: No.4). 224p. 1977. pap. text ed. 12.95 (*0-8018-1947-4*) Johns Hopkins.

Social Development in Childhood: Day-Care Programs & Research. Hyman Blumberg Symposium on Research in Early Childhood Education Staff. LC 77-4778. 220p. reprint ed. pap. 62.70 (*0-317-09807-1*, 2020543) Bks Demand.

Social Development in the Third World: Level of Living Indicators & Social Planning. Ed. by J. G. Hilhorst & M. Klatter. LC 84-23747. 233p. 1985. 34.50 (*0-685-09643-2*, Pub. by Croom Helm UK) Routledge Chapman & Hall.

Social Development in Young Children: A Study of Beginners. Susan S. Isaacs. LC 75-41153. reprint ed. 32.50 (*0-404-14557-4*) AMS Pr.

Social Development of Canada. Samuel D. Clark. LC 75-41060. reprint ed. 49.50 (*0-404-14655-4*) AMS Pr.

Social Development of English Quakerism, 1655-1755. Richard T. Vann. LC 79-78524. 277p. 1969. reprint ed. pap. 79.00 (*0-7837-4195-2*, 2059045) Bks Demand.

Social Development of Learning Disabled Persons: Examining the Effects & Treatments of Inadequate Interpersonal Skills. Doreen Kronick. LC 81-81960. (Jossey-Bass Social & Behavioral Science Ser.). 272p. reprint ed. pap. 77.60 (*0-7837-0178-0*, 2040475) Bks Demand.

Social Deviance. Ed. by Erich Goode. LC 95-15294. 1995. pap. text ed. 39.00 (*0-205-16583-4*) Allyn.

Social Deviance: Readings in Theory & Research. 2nd ed. Ed. by Henry N. Pontell. LC 95-14296. 456p. (C). 1995. pap. text ed. 33.33 (*0-13-148719-1*) P-H.

Social Deviancy & Adolescent Personality. John C. Ball. LC 72-12308. (Illus.). 119p. 1973. reprint ed. text ed. 45.00 (*0-8371-6687-X*, BASD, Greenwood Pr) Greenwood.

Social Diagnosis. Mary E. Richmond. 512p. 1917. 45.00 (*0-87154-703-1*) Russell Sage.

Social Dialectics: Nation & Revolution, Vol. 2. Anouar Abdel-Malek. Tr. by M. Gonzalez from FRE. LC 80-25061. 214p. 1981. text ed. 54.50 (*0-87395-501-3*) State U NY Pr.

Social Differences in Contemporary America. James A. Davis. 196p. (C). 1987. pap. text ed. 17.50 (*0-15-581425-7*, DAV) HB Coll Pubs.

Social Differentiation & Social Inequality: Essays in Honor of John Pock. David Grusky et al. Ed. by James Baron. (Social Inequality Ser.). 381p. (C). 1996. text ed. 58.00 (*0-8133-8883-X*) Westview.

Social Dilemmas. Samuel S. Komorita & Craig Parks. 190p. (C). 1993. pap. write for info. (*0-697-15026-7*) Brown & Benchmark.

Social Dilemmas. Samuel S. Komorita & Graig D. Parks. LC 96-463. (Social Psychology Ser.). (C). 1996. pap. text ed. 19.00 (*0-8133-3003-3*) Westview.

Social Dilemmas: Perspectives on Individuals & Groups. David A. Schroeder. LC 94-22648. 240p. 1995. text ed. 59.95 (*0-275-92392-4*, Praeger Pubs) Greenwood.

Social Dilemmas: Theoretical Issues & Research Findings. Ed. by W. G. Liebrand et al. (International Series in Experimental Social Psychology). 242p. 1992. 57.95 (*0-08-037775-0*, Prgamon Press) Buttrwrth-Heinemann.

Social Dilemmas & Cooperation. Ed. by Ulrich Schulz et al. LC 94-8967. (Illus.). x, 541p. 1994. 143.95 (*0-387-57757-2*) Spr-Verlag.

Social Dimension: Ethics, Policy, Law, Management, Development, Economics, Education. Ed. by David Ehrenfeld. LC 94-46715. (Readings from Conservation Biology Ser.). 234p. 1995. 24.95 (*0-86542-455-1*) Blackwell Sci.

Social Dimension: European Developments in Social Psychology, 2 Vols., 1. Henri Tajfel. (European Studies in Social Psychology). 384p. 1984. text ed. 69.95 (*0-521-23972-9*); pap. text ed. 25.95 (*0-521-28383-3*) Cambridge U Pr.

Social Dimension: European Developments in Social Psychology, 2 Vols., 2. Henri Tajfel. (European Studies in Social Psychology). 388p. 1984. text ed. 74.95 (*0-521-23979-8*) Cambridge U Pr.

***Social Dimension: European Developments in Social Psychology, Vol. 2.** 388p. 1984. pap. text ed. 25.95 (*0-521-28387-6*) Cambridge U Pr.

Social Dimension of Nineteen Ninety-Two: Europe Faces a New EC. Beverly Springer. LC 91-24930. 184p. 1992. text ed. 49.95 (*0-313-27400-2*, SIZ/, Praeger Pubs); pap. text ed. 17.95 (*0-275-94182-5*, B4182, Praeger Pubs) Greenwood.

Social Dimensions of Adjustment: World Bank Experience, 1980-93. Carl A. Jayarajah et al. LC 96-14517. (Operations Evaluation Study Ser.). 240p. 1996. 13.95 (*0-8213-3610-X*) World Bank.

Social Dimensions of Adjustment in Africa: A Policy Agenda. 32p. 1990. 6.95 (*0-8213-1462-9*, 11462) World Bank.

Social Dimensions of Adjustment in Africa: A Policy Agenda. 32p. (FRE.). 1990. 6.95 (*0-8213-1466-1*, 11466) World Bank.

Social Dimensions of AIDS: Method & Theory. Ed. by Douglas A. Feldman & Thomas M. Johnson. LC 86-9491. 256p. 1986. text ed. 55.00 (*0-275-92110-7*, C2110, Praeger Pubs) Greenwood.

Social Dimensions of Development: Social Policy & Planning in the Third World. Margaret Hardiman & James Midgley. LC 81-22006. (Social Development in the Third World Ser.). 325p. reprint ed. pap. 92.70 (*0-685-20352-2*, 2029799) Bks Demand.

***Social Dimensions of Early Buddhism.** Uma Chakravarti. 1996. 22.50 (*81-215-0749-9*, Pub. by M Manoharial II) Coronet Bks.

Social Dimensions of Health: The Israeli Experience. Judith T. Shuval. LC 92-14557. 224p. 1992. text ed. 55.00 (*0-275-93495-0*, C3495, Praeger Pubs) Greenwood.

Social Dimensions of International Business: An Annotated Bibliography. Jon P. Alston. LC 92-29466. (Bibliographies & Indexes in Economics & Economic History Ser.: No. 12). 352p. 1992. text ed. 69.50 (*0-313-28029-0*, ACR, Greenwood Pr) Greenwood.

Social Dimensions of Law & Justice. Julius Stone. LC 73-168258. 933p. 1976. reprint ed. 94.00 (*0-912004-01-0*) Gaunt.

Social Dimensions of Mental Illness, Alcoholism, & Drug Dependence. Don Martindale & Edith Martindale. LC 72-133499. 332p. 1971. text ed. 59.95 (*0-8371-5175-9*, MAM/, Greenwood Pr) Greenwood.

Social Dimensions of Science. Ed. by Ernan McMullin. LC 91-50577. (Studies in Science & the Humanities from the Reilly Center for Science, Technology, & Values: Vol. III). (C). 1992. text ed. 44.00 (*0-268-01741-7*); pap. text ed. 23.00 (*0-268-01742-5*) U of Notre Dame Pr.

Social Dimensions of Soviet Industrialization. Ed. by William G. Rosenberg & Lewis H. Siegelbaum. LC 92-19627. (Indiana-Michigan Series in Russian & East European Studies). 320p. 1993. 39.95 (*0-253-34993-1*); pap. 15.95 (*0-253-20772-X*) Ind U Pr.

Social Disability: Alcoholism, Drug Addiction, Crime, & Social Disadvantage. Ed. by David Malikin. LC 72-96468. 256p. (C). 1973. text ed. 32.00 (*0-8147-5361-2*) NYU Pr.

Social Discipline in the Reformation: Central Europe, 1550-1750. R. Po-chia Hsia. (Christianity & Society in the Modern World Ser.). (Illus.). 224p. (C). 1992. pap. 15.95 (*0-415-01149-3*, A6634) Routledge.

Social Discourse & Moral Judgment. Ed. by Daniel N. Robinson. (Illus.). 260p. 1992. text ed. 42.00 (*0-12-590155-0*) Acad Pr.

Social Discrimination & Prejudice: Index of Modern Authors & Subjects with Guide for Rapid Research. John V. Grainger. LC 90-56320. 160p. 1991. 44.50 (*1-55914-438-6*); pap. 39.50 (*1-55914-439-4*) ABBE Pubs Assn.

Social Disease. Paul Rudnick. 1986. 14.95 (*0-394-55270-9*) Knopf.

***Social Disease.** Paul Rudnick. 1997. pap. 11.95 (*0-312-15659-6*) St Martin.

***Social Disgraces: Etiquette for the Socially Impaired.** Sherrie Weaver. Ed. by Patrick Caton. LC 97-71655. 168p. 1997. pap. 5.95 (*1-56245-305-X*) Great Quotations.

Social Diversity & Social Justice: Diversity & Oppression: Conceptual Frameworks. Maurianne Adams. 64p. (C). 1995. 10.50 (*0-7872-1688-7*) Kendall-Hunt.

Social Division. Alan Carling. 360p. 1991. 59.95 (*0-86091-341-4*, A4514, Pub. by Verso UK); pap. 18.95 (*0-86091-553-0*, A4518, Pub. by Verso UK) Routledge Chapman & Hall.

Social Division. Alan Carling. 464p. (C). 1992. pap. text ed. 23.00 (*0-86091-506-9*, Pub. by Vrso UK) Norton.

Social Division, Economy & Schooling. Ed. by Peter J. Dwyer et al. 126p. (C). 1985. 65.00 (*0-7300-0336-1*, Pub. by Deakin Univ AT) St Mut.

Social Divisions: Economic Decline & Social Structural Change. Lydia Morris. 224p. 1995. 65.00 (*1-85728-201-9*, Pub. by UCL Pr UK) Taylor & Francis.

Social Divisions: Economic Decline & Social Structural Change. Lydia Morris. 224p. 1995. pap. 24.95 (*1-85728-202-7*, Pub. by UCL Pr UK) Taylor & Francis.

Social Doctrine of the Sermon on the Mount. Charles Gore. 1972. 59.95 (*0-8490-1063-2*) Gordon Pr.

Social Documentary in Latin America. Ed. by Julianne Burton. LC 89-4831. (Latin American Ser.). (Illus.). 468p. 1990. 49.95 (*0-8229-3621-6*); pap. 25.95 (*0-8229-5419-2*) U of Pittsburgh Pr.

Social Dynamics of Adolescent Fertility in Sub-Saharan Africa. National Research Council Staff. Ed. by Caroline H. Bledsoe & Barney Cohen. (Population Dynamics of Sub-Saharan Africa Ser.). 224p. (Orig.). (C). 1993. pap. text ed. 33.00 (*0-309-04897-4*) Natl Acad Pr.

Social Dynamics of Deforestation: A Case Study from Nepal. John Soussan et al. LC 95-18144. (Illus.). 210p. 1995. 62.00 (*1-85070-654-9*) Prthnon Pub.

Social Dynamics of Financial Markets, Vol. 2. Ed. by Patricia A. Adler et al. LC 84-4340. (Contemporary Studies in Applied Behavioral Science: Vol. 2). 212p. 1984. 73.25 (*0-89232-435-X*) Jai Pr.

Social Dynamics of Gelada Baboons. R. Dunbar & Patsy Dunbar. (Contributions to Primatology Ser.: Vol. 6). (Illus.). 176p. 1975. 71.25 (*3-8055-2137-5*) S Karger.

S

Social Dynamics of Pottery Style in the Early Puebloan Southwest. Michelle Hegmon et al. LC 95-322. (Occasional Paper Ser.: No. 5). (Illus.). 292p. (Orig.). 1996. pap. 22.95 (0-9624640-7-4) Crow Canyon Archaeol.

Social Dynamics of Schooling: Participants, Structures & Strategies. F. J. Hunt. 240p. 1990. 70.00 (1-85000-747-0, Falmer Pr); pap. 33.00 (1-85000-748-9, Falmer Pr) Taylor & Francis.

Social Dynamics of Self-Esteem: Theory to Theory. R. A. Steffenhagen & Jeff D. Burns. LC 87-2421. 258p. 1987. text ed. 59.95 (0-275-92325-8, C2325, Praeger Pubs) Greenwood.

Social Dynamics of the IT Field: The Case of Denmark. Finn Borum et al. LC 92-19766. (Studies in Organization: No. 39). xvi, 328p. 1992. lib. bdg. 69.95 (3-11-012981-7) De Gruyter.

Social Ecological Psychology & the Psychology of Women see International Congress of Psychology of the International Union of Psychological Science, XXIII, Acapulco, Mexico, 2-7 September 1984: Proceedings

Social Ecology. Ram Guha. (Oxford in India Readings in Sociology & Social & Cultural Anthropology Ser.). 300p. 1994. 29.95 (0-19-563113-7) OUP.

Social Ecology: Exploring Post-Industrial Society. Martin Large. 224p. 1990. pap. 8.95 (0-9507062-2-1, 660, Pub. by Hawthorn Press UK) Anthroposophic.

Social Ecology, a Critical Analysis. Milla A. Alihan. LC 64-24804. 267p. reprint ed. 55.50 (0-8154-0008-X) Cooper Sq.

Social Ecology of Crime. James M. Byrne & Robert J. Sampson. LC 85-27823. (Research in Criminology Ser.). (Illus.). 216p. 1986. 77.95 (0-387-96231-X) Spr-Verlag.

Social Ecology of Religion. Vernon Reynolds & Ralph Tanner. (Illus.). 304p. (C). 1995. 41.95 (0-19-506973-0); pap. text ed. 19.95 (0-19-506974-9) OUP.

Social, Economic & Biological Aspects of Global Warming: Bibliography. Rama K. Rao. (Bibliographies Ser.: No. 3). 15p. (C). 1992. 6.00 (1-883215-02-1) Ramdil.

Social, Economic & Political Implications of Green Revolution in India. B. S. Hansra. (C). 1991. 21.00 (81-7054-135-2, Pub. by Classical Pub II) S Asia.

Social, Economic & Religious Beliefs among the Maryland Catholic Laboring People During the Period of the English Civil War, 1639-1660. Edward F. Terrar. LC 93-36580. 1996. 64.95 (1-883255-21-X); pap. 44.95 (1-883255-20-1) Intl Scholars.

Social-Economic Movements: An Historical & Comparative Survey of Socialism. Harry W. Laidler. (Essay Index Reprint Ser.). 1977. reprint ed. 48.95 (0-518-10149-5) Ayer.

Social-Economic-Statistical Dictionary. 464p. (RUS.). 1981. 19.95 (0-8288-1282-9, M 15491) Fr & Eur.

Social Economics. Friedrich Von Wieser. Tr. by A. F. Hinrichs. LC 67-20930. (Reprints of Economic Classics Ser.). xxii, 470p. 1967. reprint ed. 49.50 (0-678-00274-6) Kelley.

Social Economics: Premises, Findings & Policies. Edward J. O'Boyle. LC 95-35434. (New Directions in Social Economics Ser.). 224p. (C). 1996. text ed. 59.95 (0-415-13721-7) Routledge.

Social Economics: Retrospect & Prospect. Ed. by Mark A. Lutz. (C). 1989. lib. bdg. 91.00 (0-7923-9004-0) Kluwer Ac.

Social Economics of Human Material Need. Ed. by John B. Davis & Edward J. O'Boyle. LC 93-8620. (Political & Social Economy Ser.). 304p. (C). 1994. 39.95 (0-8093-1921-7) S Ill U Pr.

Social Economics of Old Age: Strategies to Maintain Income in Later Life in the Netherlands, 1880-1940. E. Bulder. (Tinbergen Institute Ser.). 281p. 1993. pap. 26.50 (90-5170-186-1, Pub. by Thesis Pubs NE) IBD Ltd.

Social Economy: The Logic of Capitalist Development. Clark Everling. LC 96-2020. (Frontiers of Political Economy Ser.). 208p. (C). 1996. text ed. write for info. (0-415-15336-0) Routledge.

Social Economy & the Democratic State. Ed. by Alcock. (C). 1989. pap. 19.95 (0-85315-718-9, Pub. by Lawrence & Wishart UK) NYU Pr.

Social Economy of the Himalayas. S. D. Pant. (C). 1988. 31.50 (0-8364-2431-X, Pub. by Mittal II) S Asia.

Social Education & Personal Development. Eva Tattum & Delwyn P. Tattum. (Illus.). 224p. (Orig.). 1991. pap. text ed. 34.95 (0-8464-1494-5) Beekman Pubs.

Social Education & Personal Development. Eva Tattum & Delwyn P. Tattum. (Studies in Primary Education Ser.). 192p. (Orig.). 1992. pap. 29.95 (1-85346-110-5, Pub. by D Fulton UK) Taylor & Francis.

Social Education & Personal Development in Primary Schools. Delwyn P. Tattum & Eva Tattum. 224p. (Orig.). 1990. 34.95 (0-8464-1443-0) Beekman Pubs.

Social Education of Bulgarian Youth. Peter J. Georgeoff. LC 68-22364. 339p. reprint ed. pap. 96.70 (0-317-39709-5, 2055870) Bks Demand.

Social, Educational, & Religious State of the Manufacturing Districts. Edward Baines. LC 75-5885. (Social History of Education Ser.). iv, 76p. 1969. reprint ed. 25.00 (0-678-08454-8) Kelley.

Social Effectiveness Therapy. Samuel M. Turner et al. 127p. 1994. pap. 39.00 (1-886344-00-0) Turndel.

Social Effectiveness Therapy: A Patient Guide. Samuel M. Turner & Deborah C. Beidel. 100p. 1995. pap. write for info. (1-886344-01-9) Turndel.

***Social Effects of Economic Adjustment in the Arab World.** T. Ahir KanAn & International Monetary Fund Staff. LC 97-2497. 1997. write for info. (1-55775-605-8) Intl Monetary.

***Social Effects of Electronic Interactive Games: An Annotated Bibliography.** Ed. by Joel Federman et al. 150p. (Orig.). 1996. pap. write for info. (1-889162-01-9) Mediascope.

Social Effects of Free Market Policies: An International Text. Ed. by Ian Taylor. 416p. 1991. text ed. 55.00 (0-312-05771-7) St Martin.

Social Effects of Inflation. Ed. by Marvin E. Wolfgang & Richard D. Lambert. (Annals of the American Academy of Political & Social Science Ser.: No. 456). 250p. (C). 1981. 28.00 (0-87761-264-1); pap. 18.00 (0-87761-265-X) Am Acad Pol Soc Sci.

***Social Effects of Mass Media in India.** N. Bhaskara Rao & G. N. Raghavan. 1996. 40.00 (81-212-0521-2, Pub. by Gian Publng Hse II) S Asia.

Social Elements in English Prose Fiction Between 1700 & 1832. C. B. Proper. LC 68-1013. 1970. reprint ed. 75.00 (0-8383-0612-8) M S G Haskell Hse.

***Social Engagement of Social Science: A Tavistock Anthology, Vol. III: The Socio-Ecological Perspective.** Ed. by Eric Trist et al. 736p. 1997. text ed. 69.95 (0-8122-8194-2) U of Pa Pr.

Social Engagement of Social Science, Vol. II: A Tavistock Anthology: the Socio-Technical Perspective. Ed. by Eric Trist et al. (Innovations in Organizations Ser.). 712p. (C). 1993. text ed. 49.95 (0-8122-8193-4) U of Pa Pr.

Social Engineering in Family Matters. Burton Mindick. LC 85-6595. 240p. 1985. text ed. 55.00 (0-275-90040-1, C0040, Praeger Pubs) Greenwood.

Social Engineering in the Philippines: The Aims, Execution & Impact of American Colonial Policy, 1900-1913. Glenn A. May. LC 79-7467. (Contributions in Comparative Colonial Studies: No. 2). 268p. 1980. text ed. 59.95 (0-313-20978-2, MAE, Greenwood Pr) Greenwood.

Social England under the Regency, Vol. I. John Aston. (Illus.). 1976. 25.00 (0-7158-1110-X) Charles River Bks.

Social Entertainment of the Nineteenth Century (What Shall We Do Tonight?) Leger D. Mayne. 366p. 1996. pap. 35.00 (0-87556-821-1) Saifer.

Social Entrepreneurship of Change. Leonard J. Duhl. LC 95-10815. 172p. (C). 1995. pap. text ed. 25.00 (0-944473-24-5) Pace Univ Pr.

Social Entropy Theory. Kenneth D. Bailey. LC 88-30109. 310p. 1990. pap. text ed. 24.95 (0-7914-0057-3) State U NY Pr.

Social Entropy Theory. Kenneth D. Bailey. LC 88-30109. 310p. 1990. text ed. 74.50 (0-7914-0056-5) State U NY Pr.

Social Environment: Open Systems Applications. Patricia Y. Martin & Gerald G. O'Connor. 320p. (C). 1989. pap. text ed. 33.50 (0-582-29014-7, 71713) Longman.

Social Environment & Health. Stewart G. Wolf. LC 80-50868. (Jessie & John Danz Lectures). (Illus.). 112p. 1981. 20.00 (0-295-95777-8) U of Wash Pr.

Social Environment & Human Behavior: A Multicultural Perspective. Magaly Queralt. LC 95-11989. 1995. text ed. 63.00 (0-02-397191-6, Macmillan Coll) P-H.

Social Environment of India. S. D. Maurya & Gayatri Devi. (C). 1989. 34.00 (81-85076-65-0, Pub. by Chugh Pubns II) S Asia.

Social Epistemology. Steve Fuller. LC 87-31056. (Science, Technology, & Society Ser.). 332p. (Orig.). 1988. 35.00 (0-253-35227-4) Ind U Pr.

Social Epistemology. Steve Fuller. LC 87-31056. (Science, Technology, & Society Ser.). 332p. (Orig.). 1991. reprint ed. pap. 13.95 (0-253-20693-6, MB-693) Ind U Pr.

Social Equality. Rudolf Dreikurs. LC 83-72318. 1971. pap. 9.95 (0-918560-30-6) Adler Sch Prof Psy.

Social Equality: The Constitutional Experiment in India. Maju Kumar. 264p. 1982. 22.95 (0-318-36857-9) Asia Bk Corp.

Social Equality: The Constitutional Experiment in India. Maju Kumar. 1982. text ed. 23.00 (0-685-14100-4) Coronet Bks.

Social Equality in Indian Society. P. A. Augustine. (C). 1991. text ed. 21.50 (81-7022-303-2, Pub. by Concept II) S Asia.

Social Equity & Changing Production Patterns: An Integrated Approach. 252p. Date not set. pap. 17.50 (92-1-121172-7, E.92.II.G.5) UN.

Social, Ergonomic & Stress Aspects of Work with Computers, Vol. 1: Proceedings of the Second International Conference, Honolulu, HI, August 10-14, 1987. Ed. by Gavriel Salvendy et al. (Advances in Human Factors-Ergonomics Ser.: No. 10A). 374p. 1987. 180.00 (0-444-42847-X); 219.50 (0-685-19275-X) Elsevier.

Social Ethics: A Student's Guide. Jenny Teichman. LC 96-6455. 224p. 1996. 54.95 (0-631-19608-0); pap. 21.95 (0-631-19609-9) Blackwell Pubs.

Social Ethics: An Examination of American Moral Traditions. Roger G. Betsworth. 224p. (Orig.). (C). 1990. pap. 17.00 (0-664-25092-0) Westminster John Knox.

Social Ethics: Morality & Social Policy. 5th ed. Thomas A. Mappes & Jane S. Zembaty. LC 96-7924. 1996. pap. text ed. write for info. (0-07-040143-8) McGraw.

Social Ethics & the Return to Cosmology: A Study of Gibson Winter. Moni McIntyre. LC 92-10251. (American University Studies: Theology & Religion: Ser. VII, Vol. 131). 191p. (C). 1993. 38.95 (0-8204-1846-3) P Lang Pubng.

***Social Ethos of Corinthian Correspondence: Interests & Ideology from 1 Corinthians to 1 Clement.** David A. Horrell. (Studies of the New Testament & Its World). 304p. 1996. 47.95 (0-567-08528-7, Pub. by T & T Clark UK) Bks Intl VA.

Social Europe. Joe Bailey. (C). 1992. text ed. 45.00 (0-582-06801-0) Addison-Wesley.

Social Europe. Joe Bailey. (C). 1992. pap. text ed. 29.95 (0-582-06809-6) Addison-Wesley.

***Social Europe: Employee Representatives in Europe & Their Economic Prerogatives.** Commission of the European Communities. 146p. 1996. suppl. ed., pap. 25.00 (92-827-6312-9, CENC-96-003-ENC, Pub. by Europ Com UK) Bernan Associates.

***Social Europe, Agreements on Information & Consultation in European Multinationals, 5/1995.** 146p. 1996. suppl. ed., pap. 25.00 (92-827-6929-1, CENC-95-005-ENC, Pub. by Europ Com UK) Bernan Associates.

***Social Europe, New Activities, New Jobs, 1/1996: Which Development Strategies?** 146p. 1996. suppl. ed., pap. 25.00 (92-827-0026-7, CENC-96-001-ENC, Pub. by Europ Com UK) Bernan Associates.

***Social Europe, Strategies for Gender Democracy, 4/1995: Women & the European Social Dialogue.** 146p. 1996. suppl. ed., pap. 25.00 (92-827-5917-2, CENC-95-004-ENC, Pub. by Europ Com UK) Bernan Associates.

***Social Europe (Supplements Only) 5/1996 Work & Childcare: Implementing the Council Recommendation on Childcare.** Commission of the European Communities. 146p. 1996. pap. 25.00 (92-827-6318-8, CE-NC-96-005ENC, Pub. by Europ Com UK) Bernan Associates.

Social Evil in Chicago: A Study of Existing Conditions with Recommendations by the Vice Commission of Chicago. Vice Commission of Chicago. LC 78-112578. (Rise of Urban America Ser.). (Illus.). 1976. reprint ed. 34.95 (0-405-02479-7) Ayer.

Social Evolution. Robert Trivers. (C). 1985. pap. text ed. 34.50 (0-8053-8507-X) Benjamin-Cummings.

Social Evolution & Political Theory. Leonard T. Hobhouse. LC 67-27584. 1978. reprint ed. lib. bdg. 15.00 (0-89824-004-2) Trillium Pr.

Social Evolution & Sociological Categories. Paul Q. Hirst. LC 76-5413. 140p. 1976. 19.75 (0-8419-0257-7) Holmes & Meier.

Social Evolution in Ants. Andrew F. Bourke & Nigel R. Franks. LC 95-5959. 550p. 1995. text ed. 79.50 (0-691-04427-9); pap. text ed. 32.50 (0-691-04426-0) Princeton U Pr.

Social Evolution of Indonesia: The Asiatic Mode of Production & Its Legacy. Fritjov Tichelman. (Studies in Social History: No. 5). 314p. 1980. lib. bdg. 104.50 (90-247-2389-2) Kluwer Ac.

Social Exchange: Advances In Theory & Research. Ed. by Kenneth J. Gergen et al. LC 80-18170. 324p. 1980. 55.00 (0-306-40395-1, Plenum Pr) Plenum.

Social Exchange, Dramaturgy & Ethnomethodology: Toward a Paradigmatic Synthesis. Jack N. Mitchell. LC 78-13198. 187p. 1981. text ed. 35.00 (0-444-99057-7, MSX/) Greenwood.

Social Exchange Theory. Ed. by Karen S. Cook. LC 86-6613. 248p. reprint ed. pap. 70.70 (0-7837-6589-4, 2046154) Bks Demand.

***Social Exclusion: Rhetoric, Reality, Responses: A Contribution to the World Summit for Social Development.** Ed. by Gerry Rodgers et al. xii, 311p. 1995. pap. 36.00 (92-9014-537-4) Intl Labour Office.

***Social Exclusion & Inequality in Peru.** Adolfo Figueroa et al. x, 96p. 1996. pap. 15.75 (92-9014-572-2) Intl Labour Office.

***Social Exclusion from a Welfare Rights Perspective in India.** Paul Appasamy et al. x, 133p. 1996. pap. 20.25 (92-9014-575-7) Intl Labour Office.

Social Experience. 2nd ed. James W. Vander Zanden. 1990. text ed. write for info. (0-07-557190-0) McGraw.

Social Experience: Study Guide with Classic Readings. 2nd ed. James W. Vander Zanden. 1990. student ed., pap. text ed. write for info. (0-07-066977-5) McGraw.

Social Experience & Anthropological Knowledge. Kirsten Hastrup & Peter Hervik. LC 93-44330. (European Association of Social Anthropologists Ser.). 224p. (C). 1994. pap. 17.95 (0-415-10658-3, B4383, Routledge NY) Routledge.

Social Experience & Anthropological Knowledge. Kirsten Hastrup & Peter Hervik. LC 93-44330. (European Association of Social Anthropologists Ser.). 224p. (C). (gr. 13). 1994. text ed. 62.95 (0-415-10657-5, B4379, Routledge NY) Routledge.

Social Experiment in Program Administration: The Housing Allowance Administration Agency Experiment. William L. Hamilton. (Illus.). 318p. (C). 1984. reprint ed. lib. bdg. 62.00 (0-8191-4114-3) U Pr of Amer.

Social Experimentation. Jerry A. Hausman & David A. Wise. LC 84-8825. (National Bureau of Economic Research Conference Report Ser.). (Illus.). 304p. 1985. lib. bdg. 40.00 (0-226-31940-7) U Ch Pr.

Social Experimentation & Economic Policy. Robert Ferber & Werner Z. Hirsch. LC 81-6146. (Cambridge Surveys of Economic Literature Ser.). (Illus.). 224p. 1981. pap. 15.95 (0-521-28507-0) Cambridge U Pr.

***Social Experimentation & Manpower Policy: The Rhetoric & the Reality.** Sar A. Levitan & Robert Taggart, 3rd. LC 78-153557. (Policy Studies in Employment & Welfare: Vol. 9). 124p. 1971. reprint ed. pap. 35.40 (0-608-03718-4, 2064543) Bks Demand.

***Social Experiments: Methods for Design & Evaluation.** Leonard M. Saxe. LC 81-13606. (Sage Library of Social Research: Vol. 131). 267p. 1981. reprint ed. pap. 76.10 (0-608-02992-0, 2059632) Bks Demand.

Social Experiments with Information Technology & the Challenges of Innovation. Ed. by Lars Qvortrup et al. (C). 1987. lib. bdg. 152.00 (90-277-2488-1) Kluwer Ac.

Social Explorations. 2nd ed. Daudistel. Date not set. pap. text ed. 15.50 (0-314-03620-2) West Pub.

Social Fabric, 2 vols., I. 6th ed. Cary & Weinberg. (C). 1991. pap. text ed. 19.50 (0-673-52043-9) Addison-Wesley Educ.

Social Fabric, 2 vols., II. 6th ed. Cary & Weinberg. (C). 1991. pap. text ed. 19.50 (0-673-52044-7) Addison-Wesley Educ.

Social Fabric: Dimensions & Issues. Ed. by James F. Short, Jr. LC 86-1191. 366p. 1986. reprint ed. pap. 104.40 (0-608-01505-9, 2059549) Bks Demand.

Social Fabric Vol. 1: American Life from 1607 to 1877. 7th ed. Ed. by John H. Cary. LC 94-6210. (C). 1995. text ed. 31.50 (0-673-52391-8) Addson-Wesley Educ.

Social Fabric Vol. 1: To 1877, Vol. I. 7th ed. Thomas L. Hartshorne et al. 352p. reprint ed. pap. 29.00 (1-886746-03-6, 93364) Talman.

Social Fabric Vol. 2: American Life from the Civil War to the Present. 7th ed. Ed. by John H. Cary et al. LC 94-6210. (C). 1995. text ed. 31.50 (0-673-52392-6) Addson-Wesley Educ.

Social Fabric Vol. 2: Civil War to the Present, Vol. II. 7th ed. Thomas L. Hartshorne et al. 365p. reprint ed. pap. 29.00 (1-886746-04-4, 93365) Talman.

Social Fabric & Spatial Structure in Colonial Latin America. Ed. by David J. Robinson. LC 79-15744. (Dellplain Latin American Studies: No. 1). 496p. reprint ed. pap. 141.40 (0-317-28161-5, 2022589) Bks Demand.

Social Fabric South Carolina Traditional Quilts. 1993. pap. 11.95 (0-87249-957-X) U of SC Pr.

Social Fabrics of the Mind. Ed. by Michael R. Chance & Donald R. Omark. 360p. 1989. text ed. 79.95 (0-86377-097-5) L Erlbaum Assocs.

***Social Faces of Humour: Practices & Issues.** Ed. by George Patron et al. (Popular Culture Studies). 368p. 1996. pap. 25.95 (1-85742-270-8, Pub. by Arena UK) Ashgate Pub Co.

***Social Faces of Humour: Practices & Issues.** Ed. by Stephen Wagg et al. (Popular Culture Studies). 368p. 1996. text ed. 56.95 (1-85742-269-4, Pub. by Arena UK) Ashgate Pub Co.

Social Facilitation. Bernard Guerin. LC 92-11487. (European Monographs in Social Psychology). (Illus.). 250p. (C). 1993. text ed. 64.95 (0-521-33358-X) Cambridge U Pr.

Social Factors in Medical Progress. Bernhard J. Stern. LC 68-57582. (Columbia University. Studies in the Social Sciences: No. 287). reprint ed. 20.00 (0-404-51287-9) AMS Pr.

Social Factors in Social Forestry. R. R. Prasad & M. P. Jahagirdar. (C). 1992. 21.50 (81-85613-64-8, Pub. by Chugh Pubns II) S Asia.

Social Factors in the Personality Disorders: A Biopsychosocial Approach to Etiology & Treatment. Joel Paris. (Studies in Social & Community Psychiatry). (Illus.). 244p. (C). 1996. text ed. 57.95 (0-521-47224-5) Cambridge U Pr.

Social Facts & Fabrications: Customary Law on Kilimanjaro, Eighteen Eighty to Nineteen Eighty. Sally F. Moore. LC 85-7897. 413p. 1986. pap. text ed. 35.95 (0-521-31201-9) Cambridge U Pr.

***Social Feeding Behavior of Birds.** Austin L. Rand. LC 54-1522. (Chicago Natural History Museum, Publication 814, Fieldiana, Anthropology Ser.: Vol. 36, No. 1). 71p. 1954. reprint ed. pap. 25.00 (0-608-03785-0, 2064639) Bks Demand.

Social Feminism. Naomi Black. LC 88-47937. 416p. 1988. pap. 18.95 (0-8014-9573-3) Cornell U Pr.

Social Ferment in India. Alexandra George. LC 86-17257. 388p. (C). 1986. text ed. 39.95 (0-485-11287-6, 51660, Pub. by Athlone Pr UK) Humanities.

Social Figures: George Eliot, Social History & Literary Representation. Daniel Cottom. LC 86-19249. (Theory & History of Literature Ser.: Vol. 44). 265p. 1987. pap. text ed. 15.95 (0-8166-1548-9) U of Minn Pr.

***Social Focus on Ethnic Minorities.** Stationery Office. 68p. 1997. pap. 50.00 (0-11-620793-0, HM207930, Pub. by Stationery Ofc UK) Bernan Associates.

Social Focus on Women. H. M. S. O. Staff. 68p. 1995. pap. 55.00 (0-11-620713-2, HM07132, Pub. by Stationery Ofc UK) Bernan Associates.

Social Force in Politics: Study of U. P. M. F. Chandel. 1990. 17.50 (81-7099-193-5, Pub. by Mittal II) S Asia.

Social Forces & Aging: An Introduction to Social Gerontology. 6th ed. Robert C. Atchley. 578p. (C). 1991. text ed. 42.95 (0-534-14670-8) Wadsworth Pub.

Social Forces & Aging: An Introduction to Social Gerontology. 7th ed. Robert C. Atchley. 607p. 1994. text ed. 44.75 (0-534-18948-2) Wadsworth Pub.

Social Forces & Aging: An Introduction to Social Gerontology. 8th ed. Robert C. Atchley. (Sociology Ser.). (C). 1997. text ed. 60.95 (0-534-50460-4) Wadsworth Pub.

Social Forces in American History. A. M. Simons. 1976. lib. bdg. 59.95 (0-8490-2616-4) Gordon Pr.

Social Forces in German Literature. Kuno Francke. 1972. 59.95 (0-8490-1064-0) Gordon Pr.

Social Forces in Southeast Asia. Cora A. Du Bois. LC 59-2120. (Smith College Lectures Ser.: No. 1947). (Illus.). 82p. 1959. reprint ed. pap. 25.00 (0-7837-4143-X, 2057991) Bks Demand.

Social Forces in the Middle East. Ed. by Sydney N. Fisher. LC 68-23289. (Illus.). 282p. 1968. reprint ed. text ed. 59.75 (0-8371-0074-7, FIME, Greenwood Pr) Greenwood.

Social Forecasting Methodology: Suggestions for Research. Doniel P. Harrison. LC 75-41511. (Social Science Frontiers Ser.). 97p. 1977. pap. 9.95 (0-87154-376-1) Russell Sage.

Social Forestry & Environment. M. P. Singh et al. 322p. 1993. pap. 175.00 (0-7855-0402-8, Pub. by Intl Bks & Periodicals II) St Mut.

Social Forestry for Rural Development. Bhawdeep Singh. (C). 1992. 36.00 (0-685-59775-X, Pub. by Anmol II) S Asia.

Social Forestry for Rural Development. K. M. Tiwari. 108p. (C). 1983. text ed. 125.00 (0-89771-667-1, Pub. by Intl Bk Distr II) St Mut.

S

An Asterisk (*) at the beginning of an entry indicates that the title is appearing in BIP for the first time.

Social Forestry for Rural Development. Ed. by K. M. Tiwari. (C). 1983. 125.00 (*0-685-21817-1*, Pub. by Intl Bk Distr II) St Mut.

***Social Forestry in India: Experience over a Decade.** Ram Prasad. 235p. 1995. pap. 99.00 (*81-7089-231-7*, Pub. by Intl Bks & Periodicals II) St Mut.

Social Forestry in India: Problems & Prospects. N. D. Bachkheti. 115p. 1987. text ed. 22.50 (*81-7027-103-7*, Pub. by Radiant Pubs II) S Asia.

***Social Formation & Symbolic Landscape.** Denis E. Cosgrove. (Illus.). 320p. (Orig.). 1998. pap. 16.95 (*0-299-15514-5*) U of Wis Pr.

Social Foundations of American Education. Robert C. Serow. LC 94-71945. 464p. (C). 1994. pap. 26.95 (*0-89089-584-8*) Carolina Acad Pr.

Social Foundations of Contemporary Economics. Georges Sorel. Ed. by John L. Stanley. 270p. 1983. reprint ed. 44.95 (*0-87855-482-3*) Transaction Pubs.

Social Foundations of Education. 2nd ed. Richard D. Van Scotter et al. (Illus.). 432p. (C). 1985. text ed. write for info. (*0-13-815887-8*) P-H.

Social Foundations of Industrial Powers: A Comparison of France & Germany. Marc Maurice et al. Tr. by Arthur Goldhammer. 400p. 1986. 42.50 (*0-262-13213-3*) MIT Pr.

Social Foundations of Meaning. E. Von Savigny. 160p. 1988. pap. 37.00 (*0-387-19006-6*) Spr-Verlag.

Social Foundations of Thought & Action: A Social Cognitive Theory. Albert Bandura. (Illus.). 544p. 1985. text ed. 84.00 (*0-13-815614-X*) P-H.

Social Fragmentation & Political Hostility: An Austrian Case Study. G. Bingham Powell, Jr. LC 74-83119. xvi, 208p. 1970. 35.00 (*0-8047-0715-4*) Stanford U Pr.

Social Framework of Agriculture. Harold H. Mann. LC 67-29802. xxx, 501p. 1967. 49.50 (*0-678-08007-0*) Kelley.

Social Framework of Agriculture. Harold H. Mann. Ed. by Daniel Thorner. (Illus.). 501p. 1968. 37.50 (*0-7146-2333-4*, Pub. by F Cass Pubs UK) Intl Spec Bk.

Social France at the Time of Philip Augustus. Achille Luchaire. 1976. lib. bdg. 59.95 (*0-8490-2617-2*) Gordon Pr.

Social France in the XVII Century. Cecile Hugon. 1977. 23.95 (*0-8369-7140-X*, 7973) Ayer.

Social Freedom: The Responsibility View. Kristjan Kristjansson. 216p. (C). 1996. text ed. 52.95 (*0-521-56092-6*) Cambridge U Pr.

Social Frontier, Nineteen Thirty-Four to Nineteen Forty-Three: A Journal of Educational Criticism & Reconstruction, 5 Vols. Progressive Education Assn. Staff. LC 70-168564. 1971. reprint ed. 198.00 (*0-405-03723-6*) Ayer.

Social Function in Psychiatry: The Hidden Axis of Classification Exposed. Ed. by Peter Tyrer & Patricia Casey. LC 93-28470. 176p. 1993. 55.00 (*1-871816-23-8*, Pub. by Wrightson Biomed UK) Taylor & Francis.

Social Function of Social Science. Duncan MacRae, Jr. LC 75-32282. 376p. 1976. 45.00 (*0-300-01921-1*) Yale U Pr.

Social Functioning Patterns in Families of Offspring Receiving Treatment for Drug Abuse. Sharol Cannon. LC 75-42602. 1975. 10.95 (*0-87212-040-6*) Libra.

Social Functions & Economic Aspects of Health Insurance. William A. Rushing. (S. S. Huebner International Ser.). 1987. lib. bdg. 72.00 (*0-89838-219-X*) Huebner Foun Insur.

Social Functions of Avoidances & Taboos among the Zulu. Otto F. Raum. (Illus.). (C). 1973. 211.55 (*3-11-003460-3*) De Gruyter.

Social Functions of Iranian Education: An Historical Survey Related to the Current Political Crisis. David C. Woolman. (TWEC World Education Monographs). 29p. 1979. 2.50 (*0-685-05158-7*) I N Thut World Educ Ctr.

Social Functions of Language in a Mexican-American Community. George C. Barker. LC 70-186238. (Anthropological Papers: No. 22). 56p. 1972. pap. 7.95 (*0-8165-0317-6*) U of Ariz Pr.

Social Functions of Literature: Alexander Pushkin & Russian Culture. Paul Debreczeny. LC 96-16591. 1997. write for info. (*0-8047-2662-0*) Stanford U Pr.

Social Future. rev. ed. Rudolf Steiner. Tr. by Henry B. Monges from GER. LC 72-87742. 151p. 1972. pap. text ed. 9.95 (*0-910142-34-3*) Anthroposophic.

Social Futures, Global Visions. Ed. & Intro. by Cynthia Hewitt. 256p. (Orig.). (C). 1996. 62.95 (*0-631-20230-7*); pap. 20.95 (*0-631-20229-3*) Blackwell Pubs.

Social Gains from Female Education: A Cross-National Study. K. Subbarao & Laura Raney. LC 93-6970. (Discussion Paper Ser.: No. 194). 58p. 1993. 6.95 (*0-8213-2387-3*, 12387) World Bank.

***Social Geography.** write for info. (*0-340-66281-6*, Pub. by E Arnold UK) Routledge Chapman & Hall.

***Social Geography.** pap. write for info. (*0-340-66282-4*, Pub. by E Arnold UK) Routledge Chapman & Hall.

***Social Geography: A Reader.** Ed. by Chris Hamnett. 1996. pap. text ed. 29.95 (*0-470-23639-6*) Halsted Pr.

***Social Geography: A Reader.** Ed. by Chris Hamnett. 1996. text ed. 54.95 (*0-470-23640-X*) Wiley.

Social Geography: An Introduction to Contemporary Issues. John Cater & Trevor Jones. 256p. 1989. 49.50 (*0-7131-6486-7*, Pub. by E Arnold UK); pap. 18.95 (*0-7131-6474-3*, Pub. by E Arnold UK) Routledge Chapman & Hall.

Social Geography: An Introduction to Contemporary Issues. John Cater & Trevor Jones. 260p. 1995. pap. text ed. 29.95 (*0-470-24967-6*) Wiley.

Social Geography: Progress & Prospect. Ed. by Michael Pacione. LC 87-506. 328p. 1987. 57.50 (*0-7099-4026-2*, Pub. by Croom Helm UK) Routledge Chapman & Hall.

Social Geography of British Elections, 1885-1910. Henry Pelling. (Modern Revivals in History Ser.). 488p. (C). 1994. text ed. 80.95 (*0-7512-0278-9*, Pub. by Gregg Revivals UK) Ashgate Pub Co.

Social Geography of the City. David Ley. 449p. (C). 1982. pap. text ed. 58.50 (*0-06-384875-9*) Addson-Wesley Educ.

Social Germany in Luther's Time: Being the Memoirs of Bartholomew Sastrow. Bartholomaus Sastrow. Tr. by Albert D. Vandam. LC 83-45674. reprint ed. 39.50 (*0-404-19863-5*) AMS Pr.

Social Gerontology: A Multidisciplinary Perspective. 2nd ed. Nancy R. Hooyman & H. Asuman Kiyak. 656p. 1991. pap. text ed. 42.00 (*0-205-12793-2*, H27931) Allyn.

Social Gerontology: A Multidisciplinary Perspective. 4th ed. Nancy R. Hooyman & H. Asuman Kiyak. LC 95-33032. 1995. text ed. 61.00 (*0-205-16776-4*) Allyn.

Social Gerontology: New Directions. Ed. by Silvana Di Gregorio. 300p. 1987. lib. bdg. 49.95 (*0-7099-3894-2*, Pub. by Croom Helm UK) Routledge Chapman & Hall.

***Social Gerontology: Selected Readings.** Ed. by David E. Redburn & Robert P. McNamara. 1998. text ed. write for info. (*0-86569-264-5*, Auburn Hse) Greenwood.

Social Goals & Educational Reform: American Schools in the Twentieth Century. Ed. by Charles V. Willie & Inabeth Miller. LC 88-217. (Contributions to the Study of Education Ser.: No. 27). 184p. 1988. text ed. 45.00 (*0-313-24781-1*, WIE/) Greenwood.

Social Goals & Social Organization: Essays in Memory of Elisha Pazner. Ed. by Leonid Hurwicz et al. 416p. 1985. text ed. 80.00 (*0-521-26204-6*) Cambridge U Pr.

Social Goals, Social Programs, & the Aging. Southern Conference on Gerontology Staff. LC 75-44462. (Center for Gerontological Studies & Programs Ser.: No. 24). 184p. reprint ed. pap. 52.50 (*0-7837-4899-X*, 2044564) Bks Demand.

Social Good: A Guide to Responsible Investing, Purchasing, & Banking. 36p. 1992. pap. 2.00 (*0-87125-211-2*, 820) Cath Health.

Social Gospel for Millions! The Religious Bestsellers of Charles Sheldon, Charles Gordon, & Harold Bell Wright. John Ferre. LC 88-70596. 114p. (C). 1988. 25.95 (*0-87972-437-4*); pap. 13.95 (*0-87972-438-2*) Bowling Green Univ Popular Press.

Social Gospel in Black & White: American Racial Reform, 1885-1912. Ralph E. Luker. LC 91-50257. (Studies in Religion). (Illus.). xvi, 446p. (C). 1991. text ed. 16.95 (*0-8078-1978-6*) U of NC Pr.

Social Gospel in the South: The Woman's Home Mission Movement in the Methodist Episcopal Church, South, 1886-1939. John P. McDowell. LC 82-15292. x, 167p. (C). 1982. text ed. 27.50 (*0-8071-1022-1*) La State U Pr.

Social Gospel Liberalism & the Ministry of Ernest Fremont Tittle: A Theology for the Middle Class. Christopher H. Evans. LC 96-26620. 252p. 1996. text ed. 89.95 (*0-7734-8778-6*, Mellen Univ Pr) E Mellen.

***Social Gospel of E. Nicholas Comfort: Founder of the Oklahoma School of Religion.** Robert C. Cottrell. LC 96-36293. (Illus.). 360p. 1997. 34.95 (*0-8061-2931-X*) U of Okla Pr.

Social Graces. deluxe limited ed. Larry Fink. (Illus.). 80p. 1984. 500.00 (*0-89381-159-9*) Aperture.

Social Group in French Thought. Robert A. Nisbet. Ed. by Harriet Zuckerman & Robert K. Merton. LC 79-9017. (Dissertations on Sociology Ser.). 1980. lib. bdg. 23.95 (*0-405-12985-8*) Ayer.

Social Group Work: A Helping Process. 3rd ed. Gisela Konopka. 256p. 1983. text ed. write for info. (*0-13-815787-1*) P-H.

Social Group Work: Competence & Values in Practice. Ed. by Joseph Lassner et al. LC 86-32012. (Social Work with Groups Supplement Ser.: No. 2). 230p. 1987. text ed. 49.95 (*0-86656-643-0*) Haworth Pr.

Social Group Work Today & Tomorrow: Moving from Theory to Advanced Training & Practice. Ed. by Benj L. Stempler & Marilyn S. Glass. LC 96-359. 146p. 1996. 29.95 (*0-7890-6023-X*) Haworth Pr.

Social Group Work with Older People. National Association of Social Workers Staff. Ed. by Leon Stein. LC 79-8684. (Growing Old Ser.). 1980. reprint ed. lib. bdg. 18.95 (*0-405-12801-0*) Ayer.

Social Groups & Identities: Developing the Legacy of Henri Tajfel. W. Peter Robinson. LC 96-7631. (International Series in Social Psychology). 256p. 1996. pap. 28.95 (*0-7506-3083-3*) Buttrwrth-Heinemann.

Social Groupwork & Alcoholism. Ed. by Marjorie Altman & Ruth Crocker. LC 82-2998. (Social Work with Groups Ser.: Vol. 5, No. 1). 92p. 1982. text ed. 32.95 (*0-917724-94-1*) Haworth Pr.

Social Groupwork & Alcoholism. Ed. by Marjorie Altman & Ruth Crocker. LC 82-2998. (Social Work with Groups Ser.: Vol. 5, No. 1). 92p. 1985. pap. text ed. 14.95 (*0-86656-439-X*) Haworth Pr.

Social Health Insurance: A Guidebook for Planning. C. Normand & A. Weber. vii, 136p. 1994. pap. text ed. 12.60 (*0-614-08025-8*, 1930057) World Health.

Social Health Investigator. Jack Rudman. (Career Examination Ser.: C-2970). 1994. pap. 29.95 (*0-8373-2970-1*) Nat Learn.

Social Hierarchies: Essays Toward a Sociophysiological Perspective. Ed. by Patricia R. Barchas. LC 83-22600. (Contributions in Sociology Ser.: No. 47). (Illus.). xvi, 160p. 1984. text ed. 45.00 (*0-313-23165-6*, BSH/, Greenwood Pr) Greenwood.

Social Historians. H. A. Toulmin. 1972. 34.95 (*0-8490-1065-9*) Gordon Pr.

Social History. 2nd ed. Alice Kessler-Harris. (New American History Essays Ser.). 30p. (C). 1997. reprint ed. pap. 5.00 (*0-87229-058-1*) Am Hist Assn.

Social History, 135 vols., Set. (British Parliamentary Papers). Date not set. 11,750.00 (*0-614-16206-8*, Pub. by Irish Acad Pr IE) Intl Spec Bk.

Social History & Human Experience. Asa Briggs. (Grace A. Tanner Lecture in Human Values Ser.). 22p. 1984. 7.50 (*0-910153-02-7*) E T Woolf.

Social History & Issues in Human Consciousness. Andrew E. Barnes & Peter N. Stearns. 272p. (C). 1989. text ed. 36.00 (*0-8147-1130-8*) NYU Pr.

Social History & Issues in Human Consciousness. Andrew E. Barnes & Peter N. Stearns. 272p. (C). 1990. pap. 22.50 (*0-8147-1144-8*) NYU Pr.

Social History & the Dynamics of Belief. James H. Parker. LC 94-9254. (Illus.). 130p. (Orig.). (C). 1994. pap. text ed. 24.50 (*0-8191-9518-9*) U Pr of Amer.

Social History & Theoretical Analyses of the Economy of Ethiopia. Daniel Teferra. LC 90-45341. (Studies in African Economic & Social Development: Vol. 4). 140p. 1990. lib. bdg. 69.95 (*0-88946-517-7*) E Mellen.

Social History Approach to Research in Distance Education. Louise Moran. (C). 1991. pap. 24.00 (*0-7300-1350-2*, IDE806, Pub. by Deakin Univ AT) St Mut.

Social History in Museums: A Manual of Curatorship. Ed. by J. Rhodes et al. 344p. 1992. 80.00 (*0-11-290529-3*, HM05293, Pub. by Stationery Ofc UK) Bernan Associates.

Social History of American Agriculture. Joseph Schafer. LC 70-99471. (American Scene Ser.). 1970. reprint ed. lib. bdg. 37.50 (*0-306-71857-X*) Da Capo.

Social History of American Education. Ed. by B. Edward McClellan & William J. Reese. LC 87-5893. 381p. 1988. pap. text ed. 15.95 (*0-252-01462-6*) U of Ill Pr.

Social History of American Family Sociology, Eighteen Sixty-Five to Nineteen Forty. Ronald L. Howard. Ed. by John H. Mogey & Louis Van Leeuwen. LC 80-1790. (Contributions in Family Studies: No. 4). xiii, 150p. 1981. text ed. 45.00 (*0-313-22767-5*, MOA/) Greenwood.

***Social History of American Technology.** Ruth S. Cowan. (Illus.). 320p. 1997. 45.00 (*0-19-504606-4*); pap. 18.95 (*0-19-504605-6*) OUP.

Social History of an Indian Caste: The Kayasths of Hyderabad. Karen I. Leonard. (C). 1995. 16.00 (*81-250-0032-1*, Pub. by UBS Pubs Dist II) S Asia.

Social History of an Indian Caste: The Kayasths of Hyderabad. Karen I. Leonard. LC 76-52031. (Illus.). 371p. reprint ed. pap. 105.80 (*0-7837-4846-9*, 2044493) Bks Demand.

Social History of an Indonesian Town. Clifford Geertz. LC 75-29282. (Illus.). 217p. 1975. reprint ed. text ed. 50.00 (*0-8371-8431-2*, GEIT, Greenwood Pr) Greenwood.

Social History of Ancient Ireland, 2 vols. Patrick W. Joyce. LC 68-56473. (Illus.). (C). 1972. reprint ed. 60.95 (*0-405-08677-6*, Pub. by Blom Pubns UK) Ayer.

Social History of Ancient Ireland, 2 vols, Vol. 1. Patrick W. Joyce. LC 68-56473. (Illus.). (C). 1972. reprint ed. 30.95 (*0-405-08678-4*, Pub. by Blom Pubns UK) Ayer.

Social History of Ancient Ireland, 2 vols, Vol. 2. Patrick W. Joyce. LC 68-56473. (Illus.). (C). 1972. reprint ed. 30.95 (*0-405-08679-2*, Pub. by Blom Pubns UK) Ayer.

***Social History of Ancient Ireland: Manners, Customs, & Domestic Life of the Ancient Irish, 2 vols.** unabridged ed. P. W. Joyce. (Illus.). 1283p. 1997. reprint ed. 150.00 (*0-940134-24-1*) Irish Genealog.

Social History of Andhra Pradesh. N. K. Reddy. 1991. 44.00 (*0-685-48716-4*, Pub. by Agam Kala Prakashan) S Asia.

Social History of Art, Vol. 1. Arnold Hauser. 267p. 1957. pap. 14.00 (*0-394-70114-3*) Random.

Social History of Art, Vol. 2. Arnold Hauser. 240p. 1957. pap. 14.00 (*0-394-70115-1*) Random.

Social History of Art, Vol. 3. Arnold Hauser. 240p. 1966. pap. 12.95 (*0-394-70116-X*) Random.

Social History of Art, Vol. 4. Arnold Hauser. 272p. 1958. pap. 12.95 (*0-394-70117-8*) Random.

***Social History of Art: From Prehistoric Times to the Middle Ages, Vol. 1.** Arnold Hauser. 259p. (C). 1963. pap. text ed. 22.95 (*0-415-04578-9*) Routledge.

***Social History of Art: Naturalism Impressionism the Film Age, Vol. 4.** A. Hauser. 278p. (C). 1963. pap. text ed. 22.95 (*0-415-04581-9*) Routledge.

***Social History of Art: Renaissance Mannerism Baroque, Vol. 2.** Arnold Hauser. 243p. (C). 1963. pap. text ed. 22.95 (*0-415-04579-7*) Routledge.

***Social History of Art: Rococo Classicism & Romanticism, Vol. 3.** A. Hauser. 244p. (C). 1963. pap. text ed. 22.95 (*0-415-04580-0*) Routledge.

Social History of Art, Vol. 1: Prehistoric Times Ancient-Oriental Urban Cultures Greece & Rome Middle Ages. Arnold Hauser. 1985. pap. 6.95 (*0-685-09925-3*, Vin) Random.

Social History of Art, Vol. 2: Renaissance Mannerism & Baroque. Arnold Hauser. 1985. pap. 6.95 (*0-685-09926-1*, Vin) Random.

Social History of Art, Vol. 3: Rococco Classicism & Romanticism. Arnold Hauser. 1985. pap. 6.95 (*0-685-09927-X*, Vin) Random.

Social History of Art, Vol. 4: Naturalism Impressionism & the Film Age. Arnold Hauser. 1985. pap. 6.95 (*0-685-09928-8*, Vin) Random.

Social History of Assam. M. L. Bose. (C). 1989. 17.00 (*81-7022-224-9*, Pub. by Concept II) S Asia.

Social History of British Broadcasting, Vol 1, 1922-1939: Serving the Nation. Paddy Scannell & David Cardiff. 400p. 1991. text ed. 77.95 (*0-631-17543-1*) Blackwell Pubs.

Social History of British Labour, 1870-1970. Kenneth Lunn. 224p. 1993. pap. 19.95 (*0-7131-6478-6*, A3400, Pub. by E Arnold UK) Routledge Chapman & Hall.

Social History of Economic Decline: Business, Politics, & Work in Trenton. John T. Cumbler. LC 88-15809. (Class & Culture Ser.). 285p. (C). 1989. text ed. 42.00 (*0-8135-1373-1*); pap. text ed. 16.95 (*0-8135-1374-X*) Rutgers U Pr.

Social History of England. Asa Briggs. (Illus.). 352p. 1995. 45.00 (*0-297-83262-X*, Weidenfeld) Trafalgar.

Social History of England 1851-1990. Francois Bedarida. LC 90-44716. (Illus.). 384p. (C). 1991. pap. 18.95 (*0-415-01614-2*, A1963) Routledge.

Social History of English. Dick Leith. (Language & Society Ser.). 224p. 1983. pap. 14.95 (*0-7100-9261-X*, RKP) Routledge.

***Social History of English.** 2nd ed. Dick Leith. 304p. (Orig.). (C). 1997. pap. 18.95 (*0-415-09797-5*) Routledge.

***Social History of English.** 2nd ed. Dick Leith. 304p. (C). 1997. text ed. 65.00 (*0-415-16456-7*) Routledge.

Social History of English Law. A. Harding. 1990. 21.75 (*0-8446-2204-4*) Peter Smith.

Social History of English Music. Eric D. Mackerness. LC 75-40994. (Illus.). 307p. 1976. reprint ed. text ed. 38.50 (*0-8371-8705-2*, MAHEM, Greenwood Pr) Greenwood.

Social History of English Rowing. Neil Wigglesworth. 1992. text ed. 36.00 (*0-7146-3415-8*, Pub. by F Cass Pubs UK) Intl Spec Bk.

Social History of Ethiopia. Richard Pankhurst. LC 92-14746. (Illus.). 385p. 1992. 49.95 (*0-932415-85-7*); pap. 16.95 (*0-932415-86-5*) Red Sea Pr.

***Social History of Flatbush, & Manners & Customs of the Cutch Settlers in Kings County.** Gertrude L. Vanderbilt. (Illus.). 391p. 1997. reprint ed. lib. bdg. 44.00 (*0-8328-6136-7*) Higginson Bk Co.

***Social History of Fleeting Attraction: American Servicemen in Western Australia During the Second World War.** Anthony J. Barker & Lisa Jackson. 296p. 1996. pap. 29.95 (*1-875560-74-2*, Pub. by Univ of West Aust Pr AT) Intl Spec Bk.

Social History of France in the 19th Century. Christophe Charle. Tr. by Miriam Kochan. 352p. 1994. 45.95 (*0-85496-906-3*) Berg Pubs.

Social History of France in the 19th Century. Matthew Jefferies. Tr. by Christophe Charle. 284p. 1995. pap. 19.95 (*0-85496-913-6*) Berg Pubs.

Social History of France, 1780-1880. Peter McPhee. (Social History of the Modern World Ser.). 360p. (C). 1993. pap. 18.95 (*0-415-01616-9*, B2473) Routledge.

Social History of French Catholicism 1789-1914. Ralph Gibson. 352p. 1989. 39.95 (*0-415-01619-3*, A3551) Routledge.

Social History of Greece & Rome. Michael Grant. (Illus.). 208p. 1993. reprint ed. 20.00 (*0-684-19309-4*) S&S Trade.

Social History of Imperial Russia, 1700-1917. Boris N. Mironov. (C). 1998. pap. text ed. 14.95 (*0-8133-8599-7*) Westview.

Social History of Irish Traditional Music. Colin Hamilton. 320p. 1997. 45.00 (*1-85182-243-7*, Pub. by Four Cts Pr IE) Intl Spec Bk.

Social History of Kamarupa, 3 vols. in 1. Nagendra N. Vasu. 1990. reprint ed. 23.50 (*81-85395-51-9*, Pub. by Low Price II) S Asia.

Social History of Labor in the Middle East. Ed. by Ellis J. Goldberg. LC 95-45132. (Social History of the Modern Middle East Ser.). 8p. (C). 1996. text ed. 75.00 (*0-8133-8495-8*) Westview.

Social History of Lancashire, 1558-1939. John K. Walton. LC 88-21659. (Illus.). 406p. 1988. text ed. 39.95 (*0-7190-1701-7*, Pub. by Manchester Univ Pr UK) St Martin.

Social History of Language. Ed. by Peter Burke & Roy Porter. (Cambridge Studies in Oral & Literate Culture: No. 12). (Illus.). 208p. 1987. pap. text ed. 19.95 (*0-521-31763-0*) Cambridge U Pr.

Social History of Leisure since 1600. Gary Cross. LC 90-70208. (Illus.). 297p. 1990. 27.95 (*0-910251-35-5*) Venture Pub PA.

Social History of Modern Art, Vol. 1: Art in the Age of Revolution, 1750-1800. Albert Boime. LC 87-5944. (Illus.). xxx, 550p. 1990. pap. text ed. 24.00 (*0-226-06334-8*) U Ch Pr.

Social History of Modern Art, Vol. 2: Art in an Age of Bonapartism, 1800-1815. Albert Boime. LC 89-20201. (Illus.). 736p. 1990. 59.95 (*0-226-06335-6*) U Ch Pr.

Social History of Modern Art, Vol. 2: Art in an Age of Bonapartism, 1800-1815. Albert Boime. LC 89-20201. (Illus.). xxviii, 734p. (C). 1993. pap. text ed. 33.00 (*0-226-06336-4*) U Ch Pr.

Social History of Modern Spain. Adrian Shubert. 352p. (C). 1990. pap. text ed. 22.95 (*0-04-445459-7*) Routledge Chapman & Hall.

Social History of Modern Spain. Adrian Shubert. 352p. (C). (gr. 13). 1990. text ed. 85.00 (*0-04-445458-9*) Routledge Chapman & Hall.

Social History of Modern Spain. Adrian Shubert. (Illus.). 304p. (C). 1990. pap. 25.00 (*0-415-09083-0*, Routledge NY) Routledge.

Social History of Nepal. Tulasi R. Vaidya. (C). 1993. 34.00 (*81-7041-799-6*, Pub. by Anmol II) S Asia.

Social History of Nineteenth-Century France. Roger Price. LC 87-22684. (Illus.). 370p. (C). 1988. 49.50 (*0-8419-1165-7*); pap. 29.95 (*0-8419-1166-5*) Holmes & Meier.

Social History of Palestine in the Herodian Period: The Land is Mine. David A. Fiensy. LC 90-22673. (Studies in the Bible & Early Christianity: Vol. 20). 248p. 1991. lib. bdg. 89.95 (*0-88946-272-0*) E Mellen.

Social History of Politics: Critical Perspectives in West German Historical Writing since 1945. Georg Iggers. LC 85-22349. 1986. text ed. 39.95 (*0-312-73295-3*) St Martin.

S

Social History of Puerto Rico. Ed. by Raoul Gordon. 1976. lib. bdg. 59.95 (*0-8490-1066-7*) Gordon Pr.

Social History of Religion in Modern Scotland. Callum Brown. Ed. by Hugh McLeod & Bob Scribner. (Christianity & Society in the Modern World Ser.). 288p. 1987. lib. bdg. 65.00 (*0-416-36980-4*) Routledge Chapman & Hall.

Social History of Rome. Geza Alfoldy. Tr. by David Braund & Frank Pollock from GER. LC 87-36082. (Ancient Society & History Ser.). 256p. 1988. reprint ed. pap. text ed. 15.95 (*0-8018-3701-4*) Johns Hopkins.

Social History of Scandinavian Immigration, Washington State, 1895-1910. Jorgen Dahlie. LC 80-849. (American Ethnic Groups Ser.). 1981. lib. bdg. 23.95 (*0-405-13412-6*) Ayer.

*__Social History of the American Family from Colonial Times to the Present.__ Arthur W. Calhoun. Date not set. write for info. (*0-405-03886-0*) Ayer.

Social History of the American Negro. Benjamin G. Brawley. LC 70-37233. reprint ed. 20.00 (*0-404-00138-6*) AMS Pr.

Social History of the Chinese in Singapore & Malaya, 1800-1911. Ching-Hwang Yen. (Illus.). 433p. 1986. 49. 95 (*0-19-582666-3*) OUP.

Social History of the Domestic Chaplain. William Gibson. LC 96-17178. 288p. 1997. text ed. 65.00 (*0-7185-0093-8*, Pub. by Leicester Univ Pr) Bks Intl VA.

Social History of the English Countryside. G. E. Mingay. 272p. (C). (gr. 13). 1991. text ed. 62.95 (*0-415-03408-6*, A4689) Routledge.

Social History of the French Revolution. Norman Hampson. LC 64-20652. 1963. pap. 19.95 (*0-8020-6060-9*) U of Toronto Pr.

Social History of the Hungarian Intelligentsia in the "Long Nineteenth Century," 1825-1914. Janos Mazsu. (Atlantic Studies on Society in Change: No. 89). 300p. 1996. 42.00 (*0-88033-362-6*) East Eur Monographs.

Social History of the Huntington Wildlife Forest: Which Includes Rich Lake & the Pendleton Settlement. Raymond Masters. LC 93-12342. 96p. 1993. pap. 9.95 (*0-925168-13-0*) North Country.

Social History of the Jewish East End in London, 1914-1939: A Study of Life, Labour & Liturgy. J. Green. LC 91-39460. (Studies in British History: Vol. 28). 540p. 1992. lib. bdg. 119.95 (*0-7734-9770-6*) E Mellen.

Social History of the Machine Gun. John A. Ellis. 1981. 19.95 (*0-405-14209-9*) Ayer.

Social History of the Machine Gun. John Ellis. LC 74-26204. (Illus.). 186p. reprint ed. 53.10 (*0-8357-9483-0*, 2013992) Bks Demand.

Social History of the Machine Gun. John Ellis. LC 86-45457. (Illus.). 200p. 1986. reprint ed. pap. 13.95 (*0-8018-3358-2*) Johns Hopkins.

Social History of the Minor Tranquilizers: The Quest for Small Comfort in the Age of Anxiety. Ed. by Mickey C. Smith. 1991. reprint ed. pap. 19.95 (*1-56024-142-X*) Haworth Pr.

Social History of the Scotch-Irish. Carlton Jackson. LC 92-26455. 224p. 1993. 22.95 (*0-8191-8071-8*) Madison Bks UPA.

Social History of the Sea Islands, with Special Reference to St. Helena Island, South Carolina. Guion G. Johnson. LC 69-16573. (Illus.). 245p. 1969. reprint ed. text ed. 52.50 (*0-8371-1143-9*, JOS&, Greenwood Pr) Greenwood.

Social History of the Tamils 1707-1947. P. Subramanian. (C). 1996. 62.00 (*81-246-0045-7*, Pub. by DK Pubs Dist II) S Asia.

Social History of the Unconscious. George Frankl. (Psychoanalysis & Society Ser.). 416p. 1989. 39.95 (*1-871871-00-X*, Pub. by Open Gate Pr UK) Paul & Co Pubs.

Social History of the United States: A Guide to Information Sources. Ed. by Donald F. Tingley. LC 78-13196. (American Government & History Information Guide Ser.: Vol. 3). 272p. 1979. 68.00 (*0-8103-1366-9*) Gale.

Social History of the Western World. Harry E. Barnes. 1971. 399.99 (*0-87700-035-2*) Revisionist Pr.

Social History of Truth: Civility & Science in Seventeenth-Century England. Steven Shapin. (Illus.). xxx, 482p. 1995. pap. text ed. 16.95 (*0-226-75019-1*) U Ch Pr.

Social History of Truth: Gentility, Credibility, & Scientific Knowledge in Seventeenth-Century England. Steven Shapin. LC 93-41950. (Science & Its Conceptual Foundations Ser.). 1994. 29.95 (*0-226-75018-3*) U Ch Pr.

Social History of Twentieth Century Russia. Vladimir Andrle. 384p. 1995. text ed. 19.95 (*0-340-52515-0*, Pub. by E Arnld UK) St Martin.

Social History of Western Civilization, 2. 3rd ed. Golden. 1995. pap. text ed. 20.00 (*0-312-09646-1*) St Martin.

Social History of Western Civilization: Readings from the Ancient World to the Seventeenth Century, Vol. 1. 3rd ed. Golden. 1995. pap. text ed. 20.00 (*0-312-09645-3*) St Martin.

Social History of Western Civilization, Vol. 2: Readings from the Seventeenth Century to the Present. 2nd ed. Richard M. Golden. 352p. (C). 1992. pap. text ed. write for info. (*0-318-68815-8*) St Martin.

Social History of Wet Nursing in America: From Breast to Bottle. Janet Golden. (History of Medicine Ser.). (Illus.). 288p. (C). 1996. text ed. 54.95 (*0-521-49544-X*) Cambridge U Pr.

*__Social History of Women & the Family in the Middle East.__ Judith Tucker. Ed. by Margaret L. Meriwether. (Social History Of The Modern Middle East). (C). 1998. pap. text ed. 18.00 (*0-8133-2101-8*) Westview.

Social Holiness: John Wesley's Thinking on Christian Community & Its Relationship to the Social Order. R. George Eli. LC 92-39451. (American University Studies: Theology & Religion: Ser. VII, Vol. 151). 133p. (C). 1994. text ed. 38.95 (*0-8204-2117-0*) P Lang Pubng.

Social Housekeepers: Women Shaping Public Policy in New Mexico, 1920-1940. Sandra Schackel. LC 91-26105. (Illus.). 224p. 1992. 11.95 (*0-8263-1324-8*) U of NM Pr.

Social Humanities: Toward an Integrative Discipline of Science & Values. Raymond D. Gastil. LC 76-52580. (Jossey-Bass Behavioral Science Ser.). 332p. reprint ed. pap. 94.70 (*0-317-41968-4*, 2025673) Bks Demand.

Social Hygiene in Twentieth Century Britain. Greta Jones. (Wellcome Institute Ser.). 192p. 1987. 57.50 (*0-7099-1481-4*, Pub. by Croom Helm UK) Routledge Chapman & Hall.

Social Ideals of Alfred Tennyson As Related to His Times. William C. Gordon. LC 68-812. (Studies in Tennyson: No. 27). 1969. reprint ed. lib. bdg. 75.00 (*0-8383-0661-6*) M S G Haskell Hse.

Social Ideas of American Physicians, 1776-1976: Studies of the Humanitarian Tradition in Medicine. Eugene P. Link. LC 91-50603. (Illus.). 320p. 1993. 46.50 (*0-945636-34-2*) Susquehanna U Pr.

Social Identifications: A Social Psychology of Intergroup Relations & Group Processes. Michael Hogg & Dominic Abrams. 200p. (C). 1988. lib. bdg. 62.00 (*0-415-00694-5*) Routledge.

Social Identifications: A Social Psychology of Intergroup Relations & Group Processes. Michael Hogg & Dominic Abrams. 200p. (C). 1990. pap. 22.95 (*0-415-00695-3*) Routledge.

Social Identity. Richard Jenkins. LC 96-7863. 248p. (C). 1997. pap. 16.95 (*0-415-12053-5*); text ed. 45.00 (*0-415-12052-7*) Routledge.

*__Social Identity in Imperial Russia.__ Elise K. Wirtschafter. LC 97-3293. 1997. write for info. (*0-87580-231-1*) N Ill U Pr.

Social Identity of Women. Ed. by Suzanne Skevington & Deborah Baker. 210p. (C). 1989. text ed. 45.00 (*0-8039-8205-4*); pap. text ed. 17.95 (*0-8039-8206-2*) Sage.

Social Identity Theory: Constructive & Critical Advances. Ed. by Dominic Abrams & Michael Hogg. 1990. 72.95 (*0-387-91389-0*) Spr-Verlag.

Social Impact Assessment Methods. Ed. by Kurt Finsterbusch et al. LC 83-17721. 318p. 1983. reprint ed. pap. 90.70 (*0-608-01490-7*, 2059534) Bks Demand.

Social Impact of AIDS in the United States. National Research Council, Panel on Monitoring the Social Impact of the AIDS Epidemic Staff. 336p. 1993. 39.95 (*0-309-04628-9*) Natl Acad Pr.

Social Impact of Bomb Destruction. Fred C. Ikle. LC 58-11611. 280p. reprint ed. pap. 79.80 (*0-317-08300-7*, 2005840) Bks Demand.

Social Impact of Computers. Richard S. Rosenberg. (Illus.). 375p. 1992. pap. text ed. 48.00 (*0-12-597130-3*) Acad Pr.

*__Social Impact of Computers.__ 2nd ed. Richard S. Rosenberg. LC 97-8076. 1997. write for info. (*0-12-597131-1*) Acad Pr.

Social Impact of Energy Development in the West. Ed. by Charles F. Cortese. text ed. write for info. (*0-8290-0235-9*); pap. text ed. write for info. (*0-8290-1083-1*) Irvington.

Social Impact of Land Development: An Initial Approach for Estimating Impacts on Neighborhood Usages & Perceptions. Kathleen Christensen. (Land Development Impact Ser.). 144p. (Orig.). 1976. pap. text ed. 13.50 (*0-87766-171-5*) Urban Inst.

Social Impact of the Chernobyl Disaster. David R. Marples. 316p. 1988. pap. 16.95 (*0-312-02513-0*) St Martin.

Social Implications of Bioengineering. Elisabeth Beck-Gernsheim. Tr. by Laimdota Mazzarins. LC 95-12912. 144p. (C). 1995. pap. 15.00 (*0-391-03842-7*); text ed. 45. 00 (*0-391-03841-9*) Humanities.

Social Implications of Early Negro Music in the United States: With over 150 of the Songs, Many of Them with Their Music. Bernard Katz. 1979. 20.95 (*0-405-01875-4*, 16393) Ayer.

Social Implications of Industrialization & Urbanization in Africa South of the Sahara. International African Institute Staff. LC 72-12557. (Illus.). 743p. 1973. reprint ed. text ed. 65.00 (*0-8371-6720-5*, SIIU, Greenwood Pr) Greenwood.

Social Implications of Spina Bifida. Woodburn. (Education Ser.). 1975. pap. 20.00 (*0-85633-061-2*) NFER UK.

Social Importance of Self-Esteem. Ed. by John Vasconcellos et al. 1989. pap. 14.00 (*0-520-06709-6*) U CA Pr.

Social Indicator Models. Ed. by Kenneth C. Land & Seymour Spilerman. LC 74-79447. 412p. 1975. 45.00 (*0-87154-505-5*) Russell Sage.

Social Indicators: An Aid to Public Policy Evaluation in State Government. C. Kenneth Meyer et al. 1979. 1.00 (*1-55614-114-9*) U of SD Gov Res Bur.

Social Indicators of Development: 1995 Edition. World Bank Staff. (World Bank Ser.). 400p. (Orig.). 1995. pap. text ed. 24.95 (*0-8018-5021-5*) Johns Hopkins.

Social Indicators of Development: 1996 Edition. Ed. by World Bank Staff. (World Bank Ser.). 412p. (Orig.). 1996. pap. text ed. 26.95 (*0-8018-5274-9*, 45274) Johns Hopkins.

Social Indicators of Well-Being: Americans' Perception of Life Quality. Frank M. Andrews & Stephen B. Withey. LC 76-26179. (Illus.). 476p. 1976. 59.50 (*0-306-30935-1*, Plenum Pr) Plenum.

Social Inequality: Features, Forms & Functions. Pajendra Randey. 317p. 1982. 34.95 (*0-317-13625-9*, Pub. by Anuj Pubns India) Asia Bk Corp.

Social Inequality: Forms, Causes, & Consequences. 2nd ed. Charles E. Hurst. LC 94-18159. 1994. text ed. 57.00 (*0-205-15616-9*) Allyn.

*__Social Inequality: Forms, Causes & Consequences.__ 3rd ed. LC 96-53202. 1997. 56.00 (*0-205-26484-0*) Allyn.

Social Inequality & Political Structures: Studies in Class Formation & Interest Articulation in an Indian Coalfield & Its Rural Hinterland. Ed. by John P. Neelsen. 1983. 27.50 (*0-8364-1071-8*, Pub. by Manohar II) S Asia.

Social Inequality in a Portuguese Hamlet: Land, Late Marriage, & Bastardy, 1870-1978. Brian J. O'Neill. (Cambridge Studies in Social & Cultural Anthropology: No. 63). (Illus.). 464p. 1987. text ed. 89.95 (*0-521-32284-7*) Cambridge U Pr.

Social Inequality in India. Ed. by K. L. Sharma. (C). 1995. 50.00 (*81-7033-274-5*, Pub. by Har-Anand Pubns II) S Asia.

Social Inequality in Oaxaca: A History of Resistance & Change. Arthur D. Murphy & Alex Stepick. (Conflicts in Urban & Regional Development Ser.). (Illus.). 300p. (Orig.). (C). 1991. 54.95 (*0-87722-868-X*); pap. 19.95 (*0-87722-869-8*) Temple U Pr.

Social Influence. John C. Turner. (Mapping Social Psychology Ser.). 224p. (C). 1991. pap. 26.95 (*0-534-16950-3*) Brooks-Cole.

*__Social Influence.__ John C. Turner. Ed. by Anthony S. Manstead. (Mapping Social Psychology Ser.). 224p. 1991. pap. 13.99 (*0-335-15340-2*, Open Univ Pr) Taylor & Francis.

Social Influence, Vol. 5. Ed. by Peter Herman et al. (Ontario Symposia on Personality & Social Psychology Ser.: Vol. V). 312p. (C). 1987. text ed. 59.95 (*0-89859-678-5*) L Erlbaum Assocs.

Social Influence Processes & Prevention. Ed. by J. Edwards et al. LC 89-23236. (Social Psychological Applications to Social Issues Ser.: Vol. 1). (Illus.). 368p. 1990. 59.50 (*0-306-43293-5*, Plenum Pr) Plenum.

Social Influences Affecting the Behavior of Young Children. Ruth P. Koshuk. (SRCD M Ser.: Vol. 6, No. 2). 1941. pap. 25.00 (*0-527-01518-0*) Periodicals Srv.

Social Influences & Socialization in Infancy. Ed. by M. Lewis & Saul Feinman. LC 90-14308. (Genesis of Behavior Ser.: Vol. 6). (Illus.). 330p. 1990. 60.00 (*0-306-43632-9*, Plenum Pr) Plenum.

Social Influences on Behavior: Student Booklet. American Psychological Association Staff. (Human Behavior Curriculum Project Ser.). 80p. (Orig.). (gr. 9-12). 1981. pap. text ed. 3.95 (*0-8077-2619-2*) Tchrs Coll.

Social Influences on Behavior: Teachers Handbook. American Psychological Association Staff. (Human Behavior Curriculum Project Ser.). 48p. (Orig.). (gr. 9-12). 1981. pap. 9.95 (*0-8077-2620-6*) Tchrs Coll.

*__Social Influences on Vocal Development.__ Ed. by Charles T. Snowdon & Martine Hausberger. (Illus.). 324p. (C). 1997. text ed. 90.00 (*0-521-49526-1*) Cambridge U Pr.

Social Information for Developing Countries. Ed. by Itzhal Galnoor & Richard D. Lambert. LC 72-148004. (Annals of the American Academy of Political & Social Science Ser.: No. 393). 1971. 28.00 (*0-87761-135-1*); pap. 18.00 (*0-87761-134-3*) Am Acad Pol Soc Sci.

Social Information Processing & Statistical Systems-Change & Reform. Edgar S. Dunn. LC 74-5289. 256p. reprint ed. pap. 73.00 (*0-317-10338-5*, 2051570) Bks Demand.

Social Information Processing & Survey Methodology. Ed. by H. J. Hippler et al. (Recent Research in Psychology Ser.). (Illus.). 230p. 1988. pap. 49.00 (*0-387-96570-X*) Spr-Verlag.

Social Information Science: Love, Health & the Information Society the Challenge of the 21st Century. Shifra Baruchson-Arbib. 124p. 1996. pap. 22.95 (*1-898723-36-2*, Pub. by Sussex Acad Pr UK) Intl Spec Bk.

Social Infrastructure Construction in the Sahel: Options for Improving Current Practices. Bernard Abeille & Jean-Marie Lantran. LC 93-10137. (Discussion Paper Ser.: No. 200). 54p. 1993. 6.95 (*0-8213-2418-7*, 12418) World Bank.

Social Innovation in the City: New Enterprises for Community Development, A Collection of Working Papers. Ed. by Richard S. Rosenbloom & Robin Marris. LC 69-72560. (Studies in Technology & Society). 212p. 1969. pap. 4.00 (*0-674-81350-2*) HUP.

Social Innovations: A Compendium. Ed. by Institute of Social Innovations Staff. 1993. pap. 60.00 (*0-948826-30-4*, Pub. by Inst Social Invent UK) St Mut.

Social Inquiry: Instructional Manual to Accompany Mark. Matthew Lipman & Ann M. Sharp. 396p. 1980. teacher ed. 45.00 (*0-916834-15-8*, TX 758-975) Inst Advncmnt Philos Child.

Social Inquiry: Needs, Possibilities, Limits. Eugene J. Meehan. LC 93-39678. 224p. (Orig.). (C). 1994. pap. text ed. 29.95 (*1-56643-006-2*) Chatham Hse Pubs.

Social Inquiry Reports: A Framework for Practice Development. Anthony Bottoms & Andrew Stelmar. (Community Care Practice Handbook Ser.: No. 29). 1988. text ed. 19.95 (*0-7045-0579-7*, Pub. by Gower UK) Ashgate Pub Co.

Social Insects. Ed. by W. Engels. 265p. 1990. 71.95 (*0-387-50812-0*) Spr-Verlag.

Social Insects & the Environment: Proceedings of the 11th International Congress of IUSSI, 1990 (International Union for the Study of Social Insects) Ed. by G. K. Veeresh et al. LC 90-43582. (Illus.). xxi, 765p. 1991. 107.00 (*90-04-09316-8*) E J Brill.

Social Insecurities. Rosalind Welcher. (Illus.). 72p. (Orig.). 1989. pap. 5.95 (*0-939775-05-0*) West Hill Pr.

Social Institutions: Ibn Khaldun's Social Thought. Fuad Baali. LC 92-14020. 1992. 36.50 (*0-8191-8726-7*) U Pr of Amer.

Social Institutions: Their Emergence, Maintenance, & Effects. Ed. by Michael Hechter et al. LC 89-17836. (Sociology & Economics: Controversy & Integration Ser.). (Illus.). 349p. 1990. lib. bdg. 57.95 (*0-202-30409-4*) Aldine de Gruyter.

Social Institutions & Economic Performance: Industrial Relations in Advanced Capitalist Economies. Wolfgang Streeck. (Illus.). 256p. (C). 1992. 69.95 (*0-8039-8475-8*); pap. 24.95 (*0-8039-8775-7*) Sage.

Social Institutions in an Era of World Upheaval. Harry E. Barnes. LC 77-6677. 927p. 1977. reprint ed. text ed. 145.00 (*0-8371-9654-X*, BASO, Greenwood Pr) Greenwood.

Social Institutions of France. P. Laroque. xxii, 802p. 1983. text ed. 813.00 (*0-677-30970-8*) Gordon & Breach.

Social Insurance. Isaac M. Rubinow. LC 76-89761. (American Labor, from Conspiracy to Collective Bargaining Ser., No. 1). 525p. 1974. reprint ed. 30.95 (*0-405-02146-1*) Ayer.

Social Insurance & Economic Security. 2nd ed. George E. Rejda. (Illus.). 512p. (C). 1984. 33.00 (*0-13-815845-2*) P-H.

Social Insurance & Economic Security. 5th ed. George E. Rejda. LC 93-11492. 500p. (C). 1994. text ed. 76.00 (*0-13-834359-4*) P-H.

Social Insurance Claims Representative. Jack Rudman. (Career Examination Ser.: C-3372). 1994. pap. 27.95 (*0-8373-3372-5*) Nat Learn.

Social Insurance in Germany, Eighteen Eighty-Three to Nineteen Eleven. William H. Dawson. LC 78-32002. (Illus.). xi, 283p. 1979. reprint ed. text ed. 59.75 (*0-8371-5446-4*, DASI, Greenwood Pr) Greenwood.

Social Insurance Issues '90s. NASI Staff. 240p. 1992. 34.95 (*0-8403-7409-7*) Kendall-Hunt.

Social Integration & Narrative Structure: Patterns of Realism in Auerbach, Freytag, Fontane, & Raabe. Nancy A. Kaiser. (New York University Ottendorfer Ser.: Vol. 23). 229p. 1986. text ed. 27.25 (*0-8204-0327-X*) P Lang Pubng.

Social Integration of American Cities of More Than 100, 000 Population. Robert C. Angell. (Reprint Series in Social Sciences). (C). 1993. reprint ed. pap. text ed. 1.00 (*0-8290-2810-2*, S-3) Irvington.

Social Integration of People with Schizophrenia. Lesley Cotterill. (Studies of Care in the Community). 154p. 1994. 51.95 (*1-85628-841-2*, Pub. by Avebury Pub UK) Ashgate Pub Co.

Social Intelligence & Cognitive Assessments of Personality: Advances in Social Cognition, Vol. 2. Ed. by Robert S. Wyer & Thomas K. Srull. 225p. (C). 1989. pap. 22.00 (*0-8058-0500-1*); text ed. 49.95 (*0-8058-0506-0*) L Erlbaum Assocs.

Social Intelligence & Interaction: Expressions & Implications of the Social Bias in Human Intelligence. Ed. by Esther N. Goody. (Illus.). 328p. (C). 1995. text ed. 59.95 (*0-521-45329-1*) Cambridge U Pr.

Social Intelligence & Interaction: Expressions & Implications of the Social Bias in Human Intelligence. Ed. by Esther N. Goody. (Illus.). 328p. (C). 1995. pap. text ed. 19.95 (*0-521-45949-4*) Cambridge U Pr.

Social Inter-Personal Interactions: Index of Modern Authors & Subjects with Guide for Rapid Research. Marcus R. Soviero. LC 90-56318. 165p. 1991. 44.50 (*1-55914-442-4*); pap. 39.50 (*1-55914-443-2*) ABBE Pubs Assn.

Social Interaction. Michael Argyle. 1973. pap. 16.95 (*0-422-75480-3*, Pub. by Tavistock UK) Routledge Chapman & Hall.

Social Interaction. 4th ed. Clark. 1992. teacher ed., pap. text ed. 5.00 (*0-312-06849-2*) St Martin.

*__Social Interaction, Vol. 1.__ 5th ed. Robboy. Date not set. pap. text ed. write for info. (*0-312-09644-5*) St Martin.

Social Interaction: Readings in Sociology. 4th ed. Candace Clark & Howard Robboy. LC 90-63538. 608p. (C). 1992. pap. text ed. 17.50 (*0-312-05665-6*) St Martin.

Social Interaction Analysis: Methodological Issues. Ed. by Michael E. Lamb et al. LC 78-53287. (Illus.). 336p. 1979. 32.50 (*0-299-07590-7*) U of Wis Pr.

Social Interaction & Cognitive Development in Children. Anne N. Perret-Clermont. (European Monographs in Social Psychology: No. 19). 1980. text ed. 132.00 (*0-12-551950-8*) Acad Pr.

Social Interaction & Consciousness. Peter D. Ashworth. LC 78-27252. 237p. reprint ed. pap. 67.60 (*0-8357-4608-9*, 2037541) Bks Demand.

Social Interaction & Its Management. Judy Gahagan. Ed. by Peter Herriot. LC 83-15129. (New Essential Psychology Ser.). 187p. 1984. pap. 7.50 (*0-416-33780-5*, NO. 4043) Routledge Chapman & Hall.

*__Social Interaction & Personal Relationships.__ Ed. by Dorothy Miell & Rudi Dallos. 392p. 1996. 79.95 (*0-7619-5035-4*); pap. 27.95 (*0-7619-5036-2*) Sage.

Social Interaction & the Development of Children's Understanding. Ed. by Lucien T. Winegar. LC 89-31305. 232p. (C). 1989. text ed. 73.25 (*0-89391-533-5*) Ablex Pub.

Social Interaction As Drama: Applications from Conflict Resolution. Alexander P. Hare. LC 84-26275. 183p. reprint ed. pap. 52.20 (*0-7837-1126-3*, 2041656) Bks Demand.

Social Interaction in Chinese Society. Sidney L. Greenblat. Ed. by Richard L. Wilson & Amy A. Wilson. LC 82-15019. 272p. 1982. text ed. 65.00 (*0-275-90810-0*, C0810, Praeger Pubs) Greenwood.

Social Interaction in Individual Development. Willem Doise & Augusto Palmonari. (European Studies in Social Psychology). 287p. 1984. 69.95 (*0-521-25024-2*) Cambridge U Pr.

An Asterisk (*) at the beginning of an entry indicates that the title is appearing in BIP for the first time.

Social Interaction, Social Context, & Language: Essays in Honor of Susan Ervin-Tripp. Ed. by Dan I. Slobin et al. LC 96-18567. 672p. 1996. 89.95 (0-8058-1498-1); pap. 45.00 (0-8058-1499-X) L Erlbaum Assocs.

Social Interest & Categorical Structure: Conceptions of History & Social Change. Jeffers Chertok. LC 89-13612. (American University Studies: Anthropology & Science: Ser. XI, Vol. 44). 185p. (C). 1990. text ed. 43.95 (0-8204-1128-0) P Lang Pubng.

Social Interpretation of the French Revolution. Alfred B. Cobban. LC 64-21535. 190p. 1968. reprint ed. pap. text ed. 16.95 (0-521-09548-4) Cambridge U Pr.

Social Intervention: Potential & Constraints. Ed. by Klaus Hurrelmann et al. (Prevention & Intervention in Childhood & Adolescence Ser.: Vol. 1). xii, 399p. (C). 1987. lib. bdg. 72.95 (3-11-011256-6) De Gruyter.

Social Intervention: Theory & Practice. Edward M. Bennett. LC 87-24005. (Studies in Health & Human Services: Vol. 11). (Illus.). 432p. (C). 1987. lib. bdg. 109.95 (0-88946-136-8) E Mellen.

Social Investigator. Jack Rudman. (Career Examination Ser.: C-743). 1994. pap. 27.95 (0-8373-0743-0) Nat Learn.

Social Investigator Trainee. Jack Rudman. (Career Examination Ser.: C-744). 1994. pap. 23.95 (0-8373-0744-9) Nat Learn.

Social Investing. Ed. by Dan M. McGill. LC 83-82624. (Pension Research Council Publications). 184p. (C). 1984. text ed. 36.95 (0-256-03170-3) U of Pa Pr.

Social Investing in the Life & Health Insurance Industry. (Illus.). 61p. (Orig.). (C). 1994. pap. text ed. 20.00 (0-7881-0535-3) DIANE Pub.

Social Investing on Campus. Carolyn Mathiasen. 13p. (Orig.). 1993. pap. 15.00 (1-879775-10-7) IRRC Inc DC.

Social Issues: Meditative Thinking & the Threefold Social Order. Rudolf Steiner. Tr. by Joe Reuter & Sabine H. Seiler from GER. LC 91-29399. Orig. Title: Vom Einheitsstaat zum Driegliedrigen Sozialen Organismus. 152p. 1991. 24.95 (0-88010-359-0); pap. 12.95 (0-88010-358-2) Anthroposophic.

***Social Issues: The Ethics & Economics of Taxes & Public Programs.** John C. Winfrey. 256p. (C). 1997. pap. text ed. 19.95 (0-19-511433-7) OUP.

***Social Issues: The Ethics & Economics of Taxes & Public Programs.** John C. Winfrey. 256p. (C). 1997. text ed. 45.00 (0-19-511432-9) OUP.

Social Issues & Education: Challenge & Responsibility. fac. ed. Ed. by Alex Molnar. LC 86-72697. (Illus.). 149p. 1987. reprint ed. pap. 42.50 (0-608-01031-6, 2082507) Bks Demand.

***Social Issues & Problems.** (Information Guide Ser.). 1978. 62.00 (0-8103-4392-4, 00000575, Gale Res Intl) Gale.

Social Issues & Service at the Middle Level. Ed. by Samuel Totten & Jon E. Pedersen. LC 96-13392. 384p. 1996. 35.95 (0-205-15093-4) Allyn.

***Social Issues for Carers.** write for info. (0-340-53598-9, Pub. by E Arnold UK) Routledge Chapman & Hall.

Social Issues in Business: Strategy & Public Policy Perspectives. 6th rev. ed. Fred Luthans & Richard M. Hodgetts. 672p. (C). 1989. text ed. 80.00 (0-02-372971-6, Macmillan Coll) P-H.

Social Issues in Computing: Putting Computing in Its Place. Ed. by Charles Huff & Thomas Finholt. LC 93-49600. 1994. pap. text ed. write for info. (0-07-030863-2) McGraw.

Social Issues in Contemporary Sport: A Resource Guide. Suzanne Wise. LC 93-29608. 808p. 1994. text ed. 130.00 (0-8240-6046-6, SS595) Garland.

Social Issues in Regional Policy & Regional Planning. Antoni Kuklinski. (New Babylon Ser.: No. 27). 1977. text ed. 73.85 (90-279-7601-5) Mouton.

***Social Issues in Sport.** Sleap. LC 97-8879. 1997. text ed. 65.00 (0-312-17602-3) St Martin.

Social Issues in Technology: A Format for Investigation. 2nd ed. Paul A. Alcorn. LC 95-44968. 320p. (C). 1996. text ed. 55.00 (0-13-459876-8) P-H.

Social Issues in the English Classroom. Ed. by C. Mark Hurlbert & Samuel Totten. LC 92-14843. 356p. 1992. 18.95 (0-8141-4504-3) NCTE.

***Social Judgement Theory: A Special Double Issue of "Thinking & Reasoning", Vol. 2, Nos. 2 & 3, 1997.** Doherty. 1997. pap. 45.00 (0-86377-951-4) L Erlbaum Assocs.

Social Judgment. J. Richard Eiser. (Mapping Social Psychology Ser.). 192p. (C). 1991. pap. 37.95 (0-534-16116-2) Brooks-Cole.

***Social Judgment.** J. Richard Eiser. Ed. by Anthony S. Manstead. (Mapping Social Psychology Ser.). 184p. 1990. 42.50 (0-335-09868-1, Open Univ Pr); pap. 13.99 (0-335-09867-3, Open Univ Pr) Taylor & Francis.

Social Judgment: Assimilation & Contrast Effects in Communication & Attitude Change. Muzafer Sherif & Carl I. Hovland. LC 80-21767. (Yale Studies in Attitude & Communication: Vol. 4). xii, 218p. 1981. reprint ed. text ed. 45.00 (0-313-22438-2, SHSO) Greenwood.

Social Judgment & Intergroup Relations: Essays in Honor of Muzafer Sherif. Ed. by D. Granberg & G. Sarup. x, 280p. 1992. 87.95 (0-387-97725-2) Spr-Verlag.

Social Justice. Jeremy J. Waldron. (C). 1998. text ed. 44.00 (0-8133-1452-6) Westview.

Social Justice. Jeremy J. Waldron. (C). 1998. pap. text ed. 14.95 (0-8133-1453-4) Westview.

Social Justice: Opposing Viewpoints. Ed. by Carol Wekesser & Karin L. Swisher. LC 90-42855. (Opposing Viewpoints Ser.). (Illus.). 264p. (YA). (gr. 10 up). 1990. pap. text ed. 12.96 (0-89908-457-5); lib. bdg. 20.96 (0-89908-482-6) Greenhaven.

Social Justice: The Teachings of Catholics, Protestants, Jews, & Muslims. Ed. by James J. Horgan & Lucy Fuchs. LC 92-81090. 184p. 1992. pap. 15.95 (0-945759-04-5) St Leo Col Pr.

Social Justice - Sunset or Dawn. Ed. by V. R. Iyer. (C). 1989. 70.00 (0-89771-750-3, Pub. by Eastern Book II) St Mut.

Social Justice Agenda: Justice, Ecology, Power, & the Church. Donal Dorr. LC 90-49049. 1991. pap. 13.50 (0-88344-722-3) Orbis Bks.

Social Justice & Deuteronomy: The Case of Deuteronomy 15. Jeffries M. Hamilton. LC 92-25380. (Society of Biblical Literature Dissertation Ser.). 182p. 1992. 31.95 (1-55540-747-1, 062136); pap. 20.95 (1-55540-748-X) Scholars Pr GA.

Social Justice & Individual Responsibility in the Welfare State: Proceedings of the 11th World Congress on Philosophy of Law & Social Philosophy, Helsinki. Ed. by Jan M. Broekman. 299p. (Orig.). 1985. pap. 58.50 (3-515-04459-0) Coronet Bks.

Social Justice & Its Enemies: A Normative Approach to Social Problems. Thomas F. Hoult. 500p. 1975. pap. 15.95 (0-87073-252-8) Schenkman Bks Inc.

Social Justice & Local Development Policy. Robert Mier. (Illus.). 256p. 1993. 52.00 (0-8039-4947-2); pap. 24.50 (0-8039-4948-0) Sage.

Social Justice & Political Change: Public Opinion in Capitalist & Post-Communist Nations. Ed. by James R. Kluegel et al. (Social Institutions & Social Change Ser.). 373p. 1995. lib. bdg. 55.95 (0-202-30503-1) Aldine de Gruyter.

Social Justice & Political Change: Public Opinion in Capitalist & Post-Communist Nations. Ed. by James R. Kluegel et al. (Social Institutions & Social Change Ser.). 373p. 1995. pap. text ed. 27.95 (0-202-30504-X) Aldine de Gruyter.

Social Justice & Political Safeguards for Depressed Classes. Bhimrao R. Ambedkar. (C). 1991. 26.00 (81-7071-106-1, Pub. by Manohar II) S Asia.

Social Justice & Popular Rule: Essays, Addresses, & Public Statements of the Progressive Movement, 1910-1916. Theodore Roosevelt, Jr. LC 73-19173. (Politics & People Ser.). (Illus.). 604p. 1974. reprint ed. 44.95 (0-405-05909-4) Ayer.

Social Justice & Public Policy. A. B. Atkinson. 480p. 1982. 47.50 (0-262-01067-4) MIT Pr.

***Social Justice & the City.** David Harvey. Date not set. 25.95 (0-631-16476-6) Blackwell Pubs.

Social Justice & the City. David Harvey. LC 73-7183. (Johns Hopkins Studies in Urban Affairs). 336p. reprint ed. pap. 95.80 (0-7837-4486-2, 2044263) Bks Demand.

Social Justice & Third World Education. Timothy Scrase. Ed. by Edward R. Beauchamp. LC 96-20094. (Reference Books in International Education: Vol. 37). 245p. 1996. text ed. 45.00 (0-8153-1168-0) Garland.

Social Justice for Women: The International Labor Organization & Women. Carol R. Lubin & Anne Winslow. LC 90-2003. (Duke Press Policy Studies). 348p. (C). 1990. text ed. 49.95 (0-8223-1062-7) Duke.

Social Justice in a Diverse Society. Rita C. Manning & Rene Trujillo. LC 95-34562. 553p. 1996. pap. text ed. 36.95 (1-55934-411-3, 1411) Mayfield Pub.

***Social Justice in a Diverse Society.** Tom R. Tyler. LC 96-49150. (C). 1997. pap. text ed. 24.00 (0-8133-3215-X) Westview.

***Social Justice in a Diverse Society.** Tom R. Tyler. 1997. pap. 24.00 (0-8133-2312-6) Westview.

Social Justice in Ancient Israel & in the Ancient Near East. Moshe Weinfeld. LC 95-4329. 1995. 34.00 (0-8006-2596-X, Fortress Pr) Augsburg Fortress.

Social Justice in Human Relations, Vol. 1: Societal & Psychological Origins of Justice. Ed. by R. Vermunt & H. Steensma. LC 90-25382. (Critical Issues in Social Justice Ser.). (Illus.). 310p. 1990. 60.00 (0-306-43625-6, Plenum Pr) Plenum.

Social Justice in Human Relations, Vol. 2: Societal & Psychological Consequences at Justice & Injustice. Ed. by R. Vermunt & H. Steensma. (Critical Issues in Social Justice Ser.). (Illus.). 270p. 1990. 60.00 (0-306-43626-4, Plenum Pr) Plenum.

Social Justice in Islam. Sayyid Qutb. 1993. pap. 12.50 (0-915597-87-X) Amana Bks.

Social Justice in the Ancient World. K. D. Irani & Morris Silver. LC 94-30932. (Contributions in Political Science Ser.: Vol. 349). 240p. 1995. text ed. 57.95 (0-313-29144-6, Greenwood Pr) Greenwood.

Social Justice in the Hebrew Bible: What Is New & What Is Old. Bruce V. Malchow. LC 95-37823. 104p. (Orig.). 1996. pap. text ed. 8.95 (0-8146-5523-8, M Glazier) Liturgical Pr.

Social Justice of Dr. B. R. Ambedkar. K. L. Bhatia et al. (C). 1995. 28.00 (81-7100-809-7, Pub. by Deep II) S Asia.

Social Justice Reconsidered: The Problem of Appropriate Precision in a Theory of Justice. David Mapel. LC 88-30131. 184p. 1989. text ed. 24.95 (0-252-01598-3) U of Ill Pr.

Social Ladder. May K. Van Rensselaer. LC 75-911. (Leisure Class in America Ser.). (Illus.). 1975. reprint ed. 25.95 (0-405-06937-5) Ayer.

Social Language for Teens: Tracking Real Life Situations. Gloria N. Turnbow & Deborah M. Proctor. student ed., spiral bd. 31.95 (1-55999-263-8) LinguiSystems.

Social Laws: An Outline of Sociology. Gabriel Tarde. Tr. by Howard C. Warren from FRE. LC 73-14183. (Perspectives in Social Inquiry Ser.). 230p. 1974. reprint ed. 18.95 (0-405-05527-7) Ayer.

Social Laws of the Qoran: Considered & Compared with Those of the Hebrew & Other Ancient Codes. Robert Roberts. LC 89-27402. 136p. 1990. pap. 15.00 (0-391-03661-0) Humanities.

Social Learning: Psychological & Biological Perspectives. Ed. by Thos Zentall & Bennett G. Galef, Jr. (Roitblat-Bever-Olton: Comparative Cognition & Neuroscience Ser.). 368p. 1988. text ed. 79.95 (0-89859-921-0); pap. text ed. 39.95 (0-8058-0104-9) L Erlbaum Assocs.

Social Learning & Career Decision Making. Ed. by Anita M. Mitchell et al. LC 78-8930. 1979. 18.50 (0-910328-21-8); pap. 14.00 (0-910328-22-6) Sulzburger & Graham Pub.

Social Learning & Change: A Cognitive Approach to Human Services. Howard Goldstein. 514p. 1984. pap. 15.95 (0-422-79120-2, NO. 9168) Routledge Chapman & Hall.

Social Learning & Imitation. Neal E. Miller & John Dollard. LC 78-23728. (Illus.). 341p. 1979. reprint ed. text ed. 35.00 (0-313-20714-3, MISL, Greenwood Pr) Greenwood.

***Social Learning & Social Structure: A General Theory of Crime & Deviance.** Ronald L. Akers. LC 97-10291. 1997. write for info. (1-55553-310-8) NE U Pr.

Social Learning in Animals: The Roots of Culture. Ed. by Cecilia M. Heyes & Bennett G. Galef, Jr. (Illus.). 411p. 1996. text ed. 54.95 (0-12-273965-5) Acad Pr.

Social Learning Theory. Albert Bandura. 1976. pap. text ed. 44.00 (0-13-816744-3) P-H.

Social Legacies of Communism. Ed. by James R. Millar & Sharon L. Wolchik. (Woodrow Wilson Center Press Ser.). 350p. (C). 1994. text ed. 74.95 (0-521-46182-0); pap. text ed. 20.95 (0-521-46748-9) Cambridge U Pr.

Social Legislation. 2nd ed. Helen I. Clarke. LC 57-6100. 1957. 29.50 (0-8290-1656-2) Irvington.

***Social Legislation & Status of Hindu Women.** Shailly Sahai. 1996. 30.00 (0-614-25274-1, Pub. by Rawat II) S Asia.

Social Legislation in the Contemporary Middle East. Ed. by Laurence O. Michalak & Jeswald W. Salacuse. LC 86-18613. (Research Ser.: No. 64). (Illus.). xii, 381p. (C). 1986. pap. text ed. 15.50 (0-87725-164-9) U of Cal IAS.

Social Legislation of the Primitive Semites. Henry Schaeffer. LC 70-174369. 1972. reprint ed. 18.95 (0-405-08929-5) Ayer.

Social Legislations & Civil Rights of Scheduled Castes in India. Mumtaz Ali Khan. (C). 1993. 22.00 (81-85565-26-0, Pub. by Uppal Pub Hse II) S Asia.

Social Life see Gros Ventre of Montana

Social Life in Ancient India: Studies in Vatsyasyana's Kama Sutra. Haran C. Chakladar. 1990. 20.00 (81-206-0524-1, Pub. by Asian Educ Servs II) S Asia.

Social Life in Ancient India: 800 B. C. - 183 B. C. Swaswati Das. (C). 1994. 20.00 (81-7018-759-1, Pub. by BR Pub II) S Asia.

Social Life in Early England: Historical Association Essays. Historical Association, London Staff. Ed. by Geoffrey Barraclough. LC 79-16998. (Illus.). xi, 264p. 1980. reprint ed. text ed. 59.75 (0-313-21298-8, HASL, Greenwood Pr) Greenwood.

Social Life in Egypt: A Description of the Country & Its People. Stanley Lane-Poole. LC 77-87653. (Illus.). reprint ed. 32.50 (0-404-16414-5) AMS Pr.

Social Life in Medieval Karnataka. Jyotsna Kamat. 1980. 21.00 (0-8364-0554-4, Pub. by Abhinav II) S Asia.

Social Life in Old New Orleans: Being Recollections of My Girlhood. Eliza Ripley. LC 75-1867. (Leisure Class in America Ser.). (Illus.). 1975. reprint ed. 26.95 (0-405-06933-2) Ayer.

Social Life in Old Virginia Before the War. Thomas N. Page. (Illus.). 80p. 1994. pap. 9.95 (0-939218-02-X) Chapman Billies.

Social Life in Old Virginia Before the War. Thomas N. Page. LC 73-130560. (Select Bibliographies Reprint Ser.). (Illus.). 1977. reprint ed. 13.95 (0-8369-5533-1) Ayer.

Social Life in Stuart England. Mary Coate. LC 77-109721. (Illus.). 188p. 1971. reprint ed. text ed. 35.00 (0-8371-4211-3, COSL, Greenwood Pr) Greenwood.

Social Life in the Early Republic. Anne H. Wharton. LC 74-81516. (Illus.). 1972. reprint ed. 24.95 (0-405-09064-1) Ayer.

Social Life in the Early Republic. Anne H. Wharton. (Illus.). 346p. 1970. reprint ed. 26.95 (0-87928-015-8) Corner Hse.

Social Life in the Insect World. Jean H. Fabre. Tr. by Bernard Miall. LC 78-179517. (Select Bibliographies Reprint Ser.). 1977. reprint ed. 25.95 (0-8369-6646-5) Ayer.

Social Life in the Middle East. Chadirji. 1995. text ed. 40.00 (1-85043-837-4, Pub. by I B Tauris UK) St Martin.

Social Life in the Middle East Vol. 1. Chadirji. 1995. text ed. 24.95 (1-85043-860-9, Pub. by I B Tauris UK) St Martin.

Social Life in the Reign of Queen Anne. John Ashton. (Works of John Ashton). xix, 474p. 1985. reprint ed. 69.00 (0-685-10447-8) Rprt Serv.

Social Life, Local Politics, & Nazism: Marburg, 1880-1935. Rudy Koshar. LC 85-28958. xviii, 395p. (C). 1990. reprint ed. pap. 17.95 (0-8078-4287-7) U of NC Pr.

Social Life of a Modern Community. William L. Warner & Paul S. Lunt. LC 73-8152. (Illus.). 460p. 1973. reprint ed. text ed. 35.00 (0-8371-6958-5, WASL, Greenwood Pr) Greenwood.

Social Life of Animals. Warder C. Allee. LC 75-41008. reprint ed. 52.50 (0-404-14639-2) AMS Pr.

Social Life of Children in a Changing Society. K. M. Borman. (Illus.). 320p. (C). 1982. text ed. 69.95 (0-89859-187-2) L Erlbaum Assocs.

Social Life of Children in a Changing Society. Ed. by Kathryn M. Borman. LC 82-11557. 296p. (C). 1982. text ed. 73.25 (0-89391-165-8) Ablex Pub.

***Social Life of Numbers: A Quechua Ontology of Numbers & Philosophy of Arithmetic.** Gary Urton. Ed. by Primitivo N. Llanos. LC 97-598. (Illus.). 264p. 1997. 35.00 (0-292-78533-X); pap. 17.95 (0-292-78534-8) U of Tex Pr.

Social Life of Scotland in the Eighteenth Century. 2nd ed. Henry G. Graham. LC 73-173169. 560p. 1972. reprint ed. 33.95 (0-405-08569-9, Pub. by Blom Pubns UK) Ayer.

Social Life of Small Urban Spaces. William H. Whyte. LC 79-56569. (Illus.). 125p. (Orig.). 1980. pap. 9.50 (0-89164-057-6) World Wildlife Fund.

Social Life of the Crow Indians. Robert H. Lowie. LC 74-7987. reprint ed. 32.50 (0-404-11875-5) AMS Pr.

Social Life of the Navajo Indians. Gladys A. Reichard. LC 76-82350. (Columbia Univ. Contributions to Anthropology Ser.: Vol. 7). reprint ed. 31.00 (0-404-50557-0) AMS Pr.

Social Life of the Owikeno. fac. ed. Ronald L. Olson. Ed. by R. F. Heizer et al. (University of California Publications: No. 14:3). (Illus.). 54p. (C). 1954. reprint ed. pap. 4.95 (1-55567-136-5) Coyote Press.

Social Life of Things: Commodities in Cultural Perspective. Ed. by Arjun Appadurai. (Illus.). 384p. 1986. 69.95 (0-521-32351-7) Cambridge U Pr.

Social Life of Things: Commodities in Cultural Perspective. Ed. by Arjun Appadurai. (Illus.). 384p. 1988. pap. text ed. 20.95 (0-521-35726-8) Cambridge U Pr.

Social Life of Virginia in the Seventeenth-Century. Philip A. Bruce. 268p. 1968. reprint ed. 23.95 (0-87928-002-6) Corner Hse.

Social Life Reader. Newman. Date not set. teacher ed., pap. text ed. 19.00 (0-314-01715-1) West Pub.

Social Life under the Abbasids. M. M. Ahsan. 315p. 1979. 42.00 (0-86685-592-0) Intl Bk Ctr.

Social Limits of Art. John Manfredi. LC 82-8661. (Illus.). 208p. 1982. lib. bdg. 27.50 (0-87023-372-6) U of Mass Pr.

Social Limits to Economic Theory. Jon Mulberg. LC 94-47651. (Modern Economics Ser.). 224p. (C). 1995. pap. 19.95 (0-415-12386-0); text ed. 74.95 (0-415-09298-1) Routledge.

Social Limits to Growth. Fred Hirsch. (Twentieth Century Fund Study). 200p. 1976. 24.00 (0-674-81365-0) HUP.

Social Linguistics & Literacies: Ideology in Discourses. James P. Gee. (Critical Perspectives on Literacy & Education Ser.). 224p. 1991. 65.00 (1-85000-829-9, Falmer Pr); pap. 26.00 (1-85000-830-2, Falmer Pr) Taylor & Francis.

Social Linguistics & Literacies: Ideology in Discourses. 2nd ed. James P. Gee. (Critical Perspectives on Literacy & Education Ser.). 226p. 1996. 75.00 (0-7484-0499-6); pap. 25.95 (0-7484-0500-3) Taylor & Francis.

Social Literacies: Critical Approaches to Literacy Development, Ethnography, & Education. Brian V. Street. (Real Language Ser.). 1995. pap. text ed. 22.00 (0-582-10221-9) Longman.

Social Literacies: Critical Approaches to Literacy Development, Ethnography, & Education. Brian V. Street. (Real Language Ser.). 1995. write for info. (0-582-10220-0) Longman.

Social Logic of Health. Will Wright. LC 94-34212. 239p. 1994. pap. 17.95 (0-8195-6283-1, Wesleyan Univ Pr) U Pr of New Eng.

Social Logic of Space. Bill Hillier & Julienne Hanson. LC 83-15004. 320p. 1989. pap. text ed. 29.95 (0-521-36784-0) Cambridge U Pr.

Social, Managerial, & Economic Issues. Jacques Vallee et al. (Group Communication Through Computers Ser.: Vol. 4). 222p. 1978. 15.00 (0-318-14421-2, R40) Inst Future.

Social Marketing: Strategies for Changing Public Behavior. Philip Kotler & Eduardo L. Roberto. 352p. 1989. 40.00 (0-02-918461-4, Free Press) Free Pr.

***Social Marketing: Theoretical & Practical Perspectives.** Ed. by Marvin Goldberg et al. LC 96-36833. (Advertising & Consumer Psychology Ser.). 456p. 1997. 99.95 (0-8058-2499-5) L Erlbaum Assocs.

Social Maturity Scale for Blind Preschool Children: A Guide to Its Use. Kathryn E. Maxfield & Sandra Bucholz. 57p. 1957. pap. 9.95 (0-89128-059-6) Am Foun Blind.

Social Meaning of Civic Space: Studying Political Authority Through Architecture. Charles T. Goodsell. LC 87-21466. (Illus.). xviii, 230p. 1988. 25.00 (0-7006-0347-6) U Pr of KS.

Social Meaning of Death. Ed. by Renee C. Fox & Richard D. Lambert. LC 79-53669. (Annals of the American Academy of Political & Social Science Ser.: No. 447). 1980. 28.00 (0-87761-246-3); pap. 18.00 (0-87761-247-1) Am Acad Pol Soc Sci.

Social Meaning of Mental Retardation. Robert Bogdan & Steven Taylor. (Special Education Ser.). 256p. (C). 1994. pap. text ed. 18.95 (0-8077-3343-1) Tchrs Coll.

Social Meaning of Modern Biology: From Social Darwinism to Sociobiology. Howard L. Kaye. 210p. 1996. pap. text ed. 19.95 (1-56000-914-4) Transaction Pubs.

***Social Meaning of Money: Pin Money, Paychecks, Poor Relief & Other Currencies.** Viviana A. Zelizer. LC 97-19216. 1997. pap. write for info. (0-691-04821-5) Princeton U Pr.

Social Meaning of Surgery. Nicholas J. Fox. 192p. 1991. 90.00 (0-335-09943-2, Open Univ Pr); pap. 32.00 (0-335-09942-4, Open Univ Pr) Taylor & Francis.

***Social Meanings of News: A Text-Reader.** Ed. by Daniel A. Berkowitz. LC 96-51208. 400p. (C). 1997. 62.00 (0-7619-0075-6, 00756); pap. 29.95 (0-7619-0076-4, 00764) Sage.

Social Meanings of Suicide. Jack D. Douglas. LC 67-14408. 412p. 1973. reprint ed. pap. 117.50 (0-7837-8166-0, 2047871) Bks Demand.

S

***Social Mechanisms: An Analytical Approach to Social Theory.** Ed. by Peter Hedstrom & Richard Swedberg. (Studies in Rationality & Social Change). (Illus.). 300p. (C). 1997. text ed. 59.95 (0-521-59319-0) Cambridge U Pr.

***Social Mechanisms: An Analytical Approach to Social Theory.** Ed. by Peter Hedstrom & Richard Swedberg. (Studies in Rationality & Social Change). (Illus.). 300p. (C). 1997. pap. text ed. 19.95 (0-521-59687-4) Cambridge U Pr.

Social Medicine in Eastern Europe: The Organization of Health Services & the Education of the Medical Personnel in Czechoslovakia, Hungary, & Poland. Richard E. Weinerman & Shirley B. Weinerman. LC 72-78525. (Commonwealth Fund Publications). (Illus.). 217p. 1960. 23.50 (0-674-81380-4) HUP.

Social Medicine of Old Age: Report of an Inquiry in Wolverhampton. J. H. Sheldon. LC 79-8688. (Growing Old Ser.). 1980. reprint ed. lib. bdg. 24.95 (0-405-12804-5) Ayer.

***Social Medicine Reader.** Gail E. Henderson. Ed. by Nancy M. King et al. LC 96-50376. (Illus.). 632p. 1997. 79.95 (0-8223-1957-8); pap. 29.95 (0-8223-1965-9) Duke.

Social Metaphor: Essays in Structural Epistemology. Robert N. St. Clair. 592p. (Orig.). (C). pap. text ed. 44.50 (0-8191-9559-6) U Pr of Amer.

Social Method & Social Life. Ed. by Michael Brenner. 1981. text ed. 101.00 (0-12-131550-9) Acad Pr.

Social Mind: Language, Ideology, & Social Practice. James P. Gee. LC 91-36812. (Language & Ideology Ser.). 192p. 1992. text ed. 49.95 (0-89789-248-8, H248, Bergin & Garvey); pap. text ed. 14.95 (0-89789-249-6, G249, Bergin & Garvey) Greenwood.

***Social Mindscapes: An Invitation to Cognitive Sociology.** Eviatar Zerubavel. LC 97-22037. 1997. 24.95 (0-674-81391-X) HUP.

Social Ministry. rev. ed. Dieter T. Hessel. 256p. 1992. pap. 16.00 (0-664-25241-9) Westminster John Knox.

Social Misconstruction of Reality: Validity & Verification in the Scholarly Community. Richard F. Hamilton. 289p. 1996. 32.50 (0-300-06345-8) Yale U Pr.

Social Mobility Among Scheduled Caste Women in India: A Study of Kerala. Leela Viswanath. (C). 1993. 28.00 (81-85565-33-3, Pub. by Uppal Pub Hse II) S Asia.

Social Mobility & Caste Dynamics. K. K. Mohanti. (C). 1993. 18.00 (81-7033-211-7, Pub. by Rawat II) S Asia.

Social Mobility & Class Structure in Modern Britain. 2nd ed. John H. Goldthorpe. (Illus.). 398p. 1987. pap. 24.00 (0-19-827285-5) OUP.

Social Mobility & Controlled Fertility. H. Y. Tien. 1965. 23.95 (0-8084-0280-3) NCUP.

Social Mobility & Political Attitudes: Comparative Perspectives. Ed. by Frederick C. Turner. 324p. (C). 1991. 44.95 (0-88738-347-5) Transaction Pubs.

Social Mobility & Social Structure. Ed. by Ronald L. Breiger. (Structural Analysis in the Social Sciences Ser.: No. 3). (Illus.). 458p. (C). 1990. 59.95 (0-521-34043-8) Cambridge U Pr.

Social Mobility & Social Structure. Bogdan W. Mach & Wlodzimierz Weslowski. 180p. 1987. text ed. 47.50 (0-7100-9982-7, RKP) Routledge.

Social Mobility in Contemporary Japan. Hiroshi Ishida. LC 91-68446. 320p. (C). 1993. 45.00 (0-8047-2087-8) Stanford U Pr.

Social Mobility in Contemporary Japan. Hiroshi Ishida. 332p. (C). 1995. pap. 15.95 (0-8047-2523-3) Stanford U Pr.

Social Mobility in Industrial Society. Seymour M. Lipset & Reinhard Bendix. 316p. (C). 1991. pap. text ed. 24.95 (1-56000-606-4) Transaction Pubs.

Social Mobility in Industrializing Society. Suresh Kumar. 1986. 24.00 (81-7033-015-7, Pub. by Rawat II) S Asia.

Social Mobility in Israeli Society. Moshe Lissak. 136p. 1969. 39.95 (0-87855-176-X) Transaction Pubs.

Social Mobility in the Nineteenth & Twentieth-Centuries. Hartmut Kaelble. LC 85-13415. 324p. 1986. text ed. 39.95 (0-312-73448-4) St Martin.

Social Mobility in the United States: Historiography & Methods. Susan C. Boyle. (Studies in Historical Demography). 254p. 1990. reprint ed. text ed. 25.00 (0-8240-4696-X) Garland.

Social Mobility of Women: Beyond Male Mobility Models. Geoff Payne & Pamela Abbott. 224p. 1990. 60.00 (1-85000-845-0, Falmer Pr); pap. 30.00 (1-85000-846-9, Falmer Pr) Taylor & Francis.

Social Mode of Restoration Comedy. Kathleen M. Lynch. LC 65-23483. 1926. pap. 21.00 (0-8196-0164-0) Biblo.

Social Mode of Restoration Comedy. Kathleen M. Lynch. (BCL1-PR English Literature Ser.). 242p. 1992. reprint ed. lib. bdg. 79.00 (0-7812-7109-6) Rprt Serv.

Social Motivation: Understanding Children's School Adjustment. Ed. by Jaana Juvonen & Kathryn R. Wentzel. (Cambridge Studies in Social & Emotional Development Ser.). (Illus.). 350p. (C). 1996. pap. text ed. 29.95 (0-521-56442-5) Cambridge U Pr.

Social Motivation: Understanding Children's School Adjustment. Ed. by Jaana Juvonen & Kathryn R. Wetzel. (Cambridge Studies in Social & Emotional Development Ser.). (Illus.). 350p. (C). 1996. text ed. 74.95 (0-521-47324-1) Cambridge U Pr.

Social Motivations for Codeswitching: Evidence from Africa. Carol Myers-Scotton. (Oxford Studies in Language Contact). (Illus.). 192p. 1995. pap. 21.00 (0-19-823923-8) OUP.

***Social Movement & Their Support.** LC 96-43974. 1997. text ed. 65.00 (0-312-17245-1) St Martin.

Social Movement Organizations: A Guide to Insurgent Realities. John Lofland. (Social Problems & Social Issues Ser.). 424p. 1996. pap. text ed. 24.95 (0-202-30553-8); lib. bdg. 49.95 (0-202-30552-X) Aldine de Gruyter.

***Social Movement Society: Comparative Perspectives.** Ed. by David Meyer & Sidney Tarrow. (Illus.). 288p. (Orig.). 1997. pap. 22.95 (0-8476-8541-1); text ed. 65.00 (0-8476-8540-3) Rowman.

Social Movement Theory. Johnston. 1996. 26.95 (0-8057-3889-4); pap. 15.95 (0-8057-3890-8) Macmillan.

Social Movement Theory & Research: An Annotated Bibliographical Guide. Roberta Garner & John Tenuto. LC 96-26900. (Magill Bibliographies Ser.). 288p. 1996. pap. 39.50 (0-8108-3197-X) Scarecrow.

***Social Movements.** Lyman. 1997. pap. 29.95 (0-333-62019-4) St Martin.

Social Movements: A Cognitive Approach. Ron Eyerman & Andrew Jamison. 200p. 1991. 35.00 (0-271-00752-4); pap. text ed. 14.95 (0-271-00756-7) Pa St U Pr.

Social Movements: An Introduction to Political Sociology. Rudolf Heberle. (Century Sociology Ser.). (Illus.). 1951. 12.95 (0-89197-414-8); pap. text ed. 8.95 (0-89197-415-6) Irvington.

Social Movements: Critiques, Concepts, Case Studies. Ed. by Stanford M. Lyman et al. (Main Trends of the Modern World Ser.). 340p. (C). 1994. 50.00 (0-8147-5085-0); pap. 17.50 (0-8147-5086-9) NYU Pr.

Social Movements: Ideologies, Interests & Identities. Anthony Oberschall. 402p. 1996. pap. text ed. 29.95 (1-56000-868-7) Transaction Pubs.

Social Movements: Perspectives & Issues. Steven M. Buechler & F. Kurt Cylke, Jr. LC 96-7995. 578p. (Orig.). (C). 1996. pap. text ed. 27.95 (1-55934-569-1, 1569) Mayfield Pub.

Social Movements: Readings on Their Emergence, Mobilization, & Dynamics. Ed. by Doug McAdam & David S. Snow. LC 96-19801. 557p. (Orig.). (C). 1997. pap. text ed. 32.95 (0-935732-86-1) Roxbury Pub Co.

Social Movements among Tribals. Prakash C. Jain. (C). 1991. 12.50 (0-685-59787-3, Pub. by Rawat II) S Asia.

***Social Movements & American Political Institutions.** Ed. by Anne Costain & Andrew S. McFarland. 320p. (Orig.). 1997. 65.00 (0-8476-8357-5); pap. 22.95 (0-8476-8358-3) Rowman.

Social Movements & Cultural Change: The First Abolition Campaign Revisited. Leo D'Anjou. (Sociological Imagination & Structural Change Ser.). 304p. 1996. pap. text ed. 23.95 (0-202-30522-8); lib. bdg. 47.95 (0-202-30521-X) Aldine de Gruyter.

Social Movements & Culture. Ed. by Hank Johnston & Bert Klandermans. LC 94-43723. (Social Movements, Protest & Contention Ser.: Vol. 4). 1995. pap. text ed. 19.95 (0-8166-2575-1) U of Minn Pr.

Social Movements & Political Power: Emerging Forms of Radicalism in the West. Carl Boggs. LC 86-6045. 304p. 1989. pap. 18.95 (0-87722-622-9) Temple U Pr.

Social Movements & Social Change. Ed. by Robert H Lauer. LC 76-18747. 320p. 1976. 19.95 (0-8093-0771-5) S Ill U Pr.

Social Movements & Social Classes. Louis Maheu. 272p. 1995. text ed. 65.00 (0-8039-7952-5) Sage.

***Social Movements & Social Classes: The Future of Collective Action.** Ed. by Louis Maheu. (Studies in International Sociology: Vol. 46). 296p. 1995. pap. 21.95 (0-8039-7953-3) Sage.

Social Movements & Social Structure: A Study in the Princely State of Mewar. Pushpendra Surana. 1983. 20.00 (0-8364-1003-3, Pub. by Manohar II) S Asia.

Social Movements & Social Transformation. M. S. Rao. (C). 1987. reprint ed. 27.50 (0-8364-2133-7, Pub. by Manohar II) S Asia.

Social Movements for Development. S. K. Srivastava. (C). 1987. 35.00 (81-85076-34-0, Pub. by Chugh Pubns II) S Asia.

Social Movements in an Organizational Society. Mayer N. Zald & John D. McCarthy. 436p. 1989. pap. 24.95 (0-88738-802-7) Transaction Pubs.

***Social Movements in Britain.** Paul Byrne. (Theory & Practice in British Politics Ser.). 224p. (C). 1997. pap. 19.95 (0-415-07123-2); text ed. 65.00 (0-415-07122-4) Routledge.

***Social Movements in Development: The Challenge of Globalization & Democratization.** Staffan Lindberg & Arni Sverrisson. LC 96-9721. (International Political Economy Ser.). 1997. text ed. 59.95 (0-312-16472-6) St Martin.

Social Movements in India: Peasant & Backward Classes Movements, Vol. 1. Ed. by M. B. Rao. 1980. 17.50 (0-8364-0199-9) S Asia.

Social Movements in India: Tribal, Sectarian & Women's Movements, Vol. 2. Ed. by M. S. Rao. 1981. 17.50 (0-8364-0787-3, Pub. by Manohar II) S Asia.

Social Movements in Latin America: The Experience of Peasants, Workers, Women, the Urban Poor, & the Middle Sectors. Intro. by Jorge I. Dominguez. LC 93-42736. (Essays on Mexico, Central & South America Ser.: Vol. 4). 400p. 1994. text ed. 70.00 (0-8153-1488-4) Garland.

Social Movements in Manipur (1917-1951) N. Joykumar Singh. (C). 1992. 19.00 (81-7099-340-7, Pub. by Mittal II) S Asia.

***Social Movements in Politics.** Cyrus E. Zirakzadeh. LC 96-53294. (C). 1997. pap. text ed. 19.95 (0-582-20946-3) Addison-Wesley.

***Social Movements in Politics: A Comparative Study.** LC 96-53294. (Perspectives in Contemporary Politics Ser.). 1997. write for info. (0-582-20947-1) Longman.

Social Movements, Political Violence, & the State: A Comparative Analysis of Italy & Germany. Donatella Della Porta. (Studies in Comparative Politics). (Illus.). 288p. (C). 1995. text ed. 59.95 (0-521-47396-9) Cambridge U Pr.

Social Needs Versus Economic Efficiency in China: Sun Yefang's Critique of Socialist Economics. Yeh-fang Sun. Ed. & Tr. by K. K. Fung. LC 82-10265. 179p. 1982. reprint ed. pap. 51.10 (0-7837-9974-8, 2060701) Bks Demand.

Social Network Analysis: A Handbook. John Scott. 210p. 1992. 69.95 (0-8039-8480-4) Sage.

Social Network Analysis: A Handbook. John Scott. LC 91-50803. 210p. 1992. pap. 19.95 (0-8039-8481-2) Sage.

Social Network Analysis: Methods & Applications. Stanley Wasserman & Katherine Faust. (Structural Analysis in the Social Sciences Ser.: No. 8). (Illus.). 780p. (C). 1994. pap. text ed. 32.95 (0-521-38707-8) Cambridge U Pr.

Social Network Analysis: Methods & Applications. Stanley Wasserman & Katherine Faust. (Structural Analysis in the Social Sciences Ser.: No. 8). (Illus.). 780p. (C). 1995. text ed. 80.00 (0-521-38269-6) Cambridge U Pr.

Social Network Research: Substantive Issues & Methodological Questions. C. P. Knipscheer & Antonuc. 1990. 41.50 (90-265-1068-3) Swets.

Social Networks among Biological Scientists. Nicholas C. Mullins. Ed. by Harriet Zuckerman & Robert K. Merton. LC 79-6270. (Dissertations on Sociology Ser.). 1980. lib. bdg. 25.95 (0-405-12983-1) Ayer.

Social Networks & Health of the Frail Elderly. Michal E. Mor-Barak. LC 91-28275. (Studies on Elderly in America). 192p. 1991. text ed. 57.00 (0-8153-0515-X) Garland.

Social Networks & Marital Interaction. Charles E. Grantham. Ed. by Robert D. Reed. LC 81-83621. (Illus.). 125p. (C). 1982. pap. 11.00 (0-88247-617-3) R & E Pubs.

Social Networks & Mental Health: An Annotated Bibliography. David E. Biegel. LC 84-23585. 391p. 1985. reprint ed. pap. 111.50 (0-608-01475-3, 2059519) Bks Demand.

Social Networks & Social Influences in Adolescence. John Cotterell. (Adolescence in Society Ser.). 256p. (C). 1996. pap. 19.95 (0-415-10974-4); text ed. 65.00 (0-415-10973-6) Routledge.

Social Networks & Social Support. Benjamin H. Gottlieb. LC 81-9351. (Sage Studies in Community Mental Health: No. 4). 304p. 1981. reprint ed. pap. 86.70 (0-608-01476-1, 2059520) Bks Demand.

Social Networks & Social Support in Childhood & Adolescence. Ed. by Frank Nestmann & Klaus Hurrelman. LC 94-544. (Prevention & Intervention in Childhood & Adolescence Ser.: Vol. 16). xii, 441p. (C). 1994. lib. bdg. 84.95 (3-11-014360-7) De Gruyter.

***Social Networks, Drug Abuse, & HIV Transmission.** 1997. lib. bdg. 250.99 (0-8490-6077-5) Gordon Pr.

Social Networks of Older People: A Cross-National Analysis. Ed. by Howard Litwin. LC 96-16265. 264p. 1996. text ed. 59.95 (0-275-95327-0, Praeger Pubs) Greenwood.

Social New York under the Georges 1717-1776. Esther Singleton. LC 68-26018. (Illus.). 1972. reprint ed. 30.95 (0-405-08973-2, Pub. by Blom Pubns UK) Ayer.

Social Norms & Economic Institutions. Ed. by Jeffrey Miller & Kenneth J. Koford. 300p. (C). 1991. text ed. 49.50 (0-472-10242-7) U of Mich Pr.

Social Nudism in America. Fred Ilfeld, Jr. & Roger Lauer. 1964. pap. 17.95 (0-8084-0281-1) NCUP.

Social Odours in Mammals, 2 vols., 2. Ed. by Richard E. Brown & David W. MacDonald. (Illus.). 340p. (C). 1985. 89.00 (0-19-857617-X) OUP.

Social Ontology of Karl Barth. Paul E. Stroble, Jr. LC 94-3883. 156p. 1994. 64.95 (1-883255-49-X); pap. 44.95 (1-883255-48-1) Intl Scholars.

Social Oppression. Adam Podgorecki. LC 93-7712. (Contributions in Sociology Ser.: No. 106). 152p. 1993. text ed. 49.95 (0-313-29024-5, GM9024, Greenwood Pr) Greenwood.

Social Order - Mental Disorder: Anglo-American Psychiatry in Historical Perspective. Andrew T. Scull. (Medicine & Society Ser.: Vol. 3). (C). 1992. pap. 16.00 (0-520-07889-6) U CA Pr.

Social Order & Entrepreneurship: Proceedings of the Second Fuji Conference/International Conference on Business History. International Conference on Business History Staff. Ed. by Keiichiro Nakagawa. LC 79-319892. 344p. 1977. reprint ed. pap. 98.10 (0-608-01252-1, 2061940) Bks Demand.

Social Order & Political Change: Constitutional Governments among the Cherokee, the Choctaw, the Chickasaw, & the Creek. Duane Champagne. LC 91-27600. 328p. (C). 1992. 45.00 (0-8047-1995-0) Stanford U Pr.

***Social Order & Political Change: Constitutional Governments among the Cherokee, the Choctaw, the Chickasaw, & the Creek.** Duane Champagne. LC 91-27600. 328p. 1992. reprint ed. pap. 30.00 (0-608-03978-0, 2064707) Bks Demand.

Social Order & the General Theory of Strategy. Alexander Atkinson. LC 81-17906. 305p. (Orig.). 1982. pap. 18.95 (0-7100-0907-0, RKP) Routledge.

Social Order in Child Communication: A Study in Microethnography. Juergen Streeck. (Pragmatics & Beyond: An Interdisciplinary of Language Studies: Vol. IV, No. 8). vii, 130p. (Orig.). 1983. pap. 44.00 (0-915027-30-5) Benjamins North Am.

Social Order-Mental Disorder: Anglo-American Psychiatry in Historical Perspective. Andrew T. Scull. (Medicine & Society Ser.: Vol. 3). 1989. 35.00 (0-520-06406-2) U CA Pr.

Social Order of a Frontier Community: Jacksonville, Illinois, 1825-70. Don H. Doyle. LC 78-5287. (Illus.). 304p. 1978. text ed. 29.95 (0-252-00685-2) U of Ill Pr.

Social Order of a Frontier Community: Jacksonville, Illinois, 1825-70. Don H. Doyle. LC 78-5287. (Illus.). 304p. 1983. pap. text ed. 11.95 (0-252-01036-1) U of Ill Pr.

Social Order of the Slum. Gerald D. Suttles. (Studies of Urban Society). 266p. 1970. pap. text ed. 12.95 (0-226-78192-5, P363) U Ch Pr.

Social Orders & Social Classes in Europe since 1500. Michael L. Bush. (Studies in Social Stratification). 320p. (C). 1991. pap. text ed. 30.50 (0-582-08343-5, 78916) Longman.

***Social Orders & Social Classes Since 1500.** Bush. 1991. text ed. write for info. (0-582-08344-3, Pub. by Longman UK) Longman.

Social Organisation of Death: Medical Discourse & Social Practices in Belfast. Lindsay Prior. LC 88-15868. 240p. 1989. text ed. 45.00 (0-312-02374-X) St Martin.

Social Organization. William H. Rivers. LC 76-44785. reprint ed. 29.50 (0-404-15968-0) AMS Pr.

Social Organization: A Study of the Larger Mind. Charles H. Cooley. LC 80-15746. (Social Science Classics Ser.). 457p. (C). 1983. pap. 29.95 (0-87855-824-1) Transaction Pubs.

Social Organization: Essays Presented to Raymond Firth. Ed. by Maurice Freedman. 300p. 1967. reprint ed. 35.00 (0-7146-1059-3, Pub. by F Cass Pubs UK) Intl Spec Bk.

Social Organization & Behavior of the Acorn Woodpecker in Central Coastal California. Michael H. MacRoberts & Barbara R. MacRoberts. 115p. 1976. 7.50 (0-943610-21-4) Am Ornithologists.

***Social Organization & Cultural Aesthetics: Essays in Honor of William H. Davenport.** William H. Davenport et al. Ed. by William W. Donner & James G. Flanagan. LC 97-19969. 160p. 1997. 48.00 (0-7618-0783-7); pap. 26.50 (0-7618-0784-5) U Pr of Amer.

Social Organization & Development Anthropology. Michael M. Cernea. (Environmentally Sustainable Development Occasional Papers: Vol. 6). 46p. 1996. 7.95 (0-8213-3462-X, 13462) World Bank.

Social Organization & Ritualistic Ceremonies of the Blackfoot Indians, 2 parts in 1 vol. Clark Wissler. LC 74-9020. (Anthropological Papers of the American Museum of Natural History: Vol. 7). (Illus.). reprint ed. 49.50 (0-404-11917-4) AMS Pr.

Social Organization & Social Process: Essays in Honor of Anselm Strauss. Ed. by David R. Maines. (Communication & Social Order Ser.). 408p. 1991. lib. bdg. 67.95 (0-202-30390-X) Aldine de Gruyter.

Social Organization in an Indian Slum. Ratna N. Rao. 1990. 37.50 (81-7099-186-2, Pub. by Mittal II) S Asia.

Social Organization in South China, 1911-1949: The Case of the Kuan Lineage in K'ai-P'ing County. Yuen-fong Woon. (Michigan Monographs in Chinese Studies: No. 48). 158p. (C). 1984. text ed. 30.00 (0-89264-051-0) Ctr Chinese Studies.

Social Organization of Disputes & Dispute Processing & Methods for the Investigation of Their Social, Legal & Interactive Properties. Philip Wilkinson. LC 81-196937. 64p. 1980. write for info. (0-86226-035-3) Soc Sci Res.

Social Organization of Doctor-Patient Communication. 2nd ed. Sue Fisher & Alexandra D. Todd. 320p. (C). 1993. pap. 39.50 (0-89391-699-4); text ed. 73.25 (0-89391-694-3) Ablex Pub.

Social Organization of Early Industrial Capitalism. Michael B. Katz et al. LC 81-7044. (Illus.). 464p. 1982. 50.00 (0-674-81445-2) HUP.

Social Organization of Immigration: The Italians in Philadelphia. Richard N. Juliani. Ed. by Francesco Cordasco. LC 80-868. (American Ethnic Groups Ser.). 1981. lib. bdg. 30.95 (0-405-13430-4) Ayer.

Social Organization of Juvenile Justice. Aaron V. Cicourel. LC 94-17406. 362p. (C). 1994. reprint ed. pap. 24.95 (1-56000-779-6) Transaction Pubs.

***Social Organization of Medical Work.** Anselm L. Strauss. LC 96-53073. 1997. pap. 24.95 (1-56000-968-3) Transaction Pubs.

Social Organization of Mental Illness. Lindsay Prior. (Illus.). 240p. (C). 1993. text ed. 69.95 (0-8039-8499-5) Sage.

Social Organization of Mental Illness. 2nd ed. Jodi O'Brien et al. (Illus.). 240p. (C). 1996. pap. 19.95 (0-8039-8500-2) Sage.

Social Organization of Schools: New Conceptualizations of the Learning Process. Ed. by Maureen T. Hallinan. LC 86-30577. 246p. 1987. 49.50 (0-306-42428-2, Plenum Pr) Plenum.

Social Organization of Sexuality: Sexual Practices in the United States. Edward O. Laumann et al. (Illus.). 742p. 1994. lib. bdg. 49.95 (0-226-46957-3) U Ch Pr.

Social Organization of the Alas People of Northern Sumatra. Akifumi Iwabuchi. (Oxford Studies in Social & Cultural Anthropology). (Illus.). 332p. 1995. 69.00 (0-19-827902-7) OUP.

Social Organization of the Haisla of British Columbia. fac. ed. Ronald L. Olson. Ed. by A. L. Kroeber & Robert H. Lowie. (University of California Publications: No. 2:5). 37p. (C). 1940. reprint ed. pap. 3.35 (1-55567-124-1) Coyote Press.

Social Organization of the Manchus: A Study of the Manchu Clan Organization. Sergei M. Shirokogorov. LC 77-38082. (China Ser.). reprint ed. 37.50 (0-404-56946-3) AMS Pr.

Social Organization of the Papago Indians. Ruth M. Underhill. LC 74-82347. (Columbia Univ. Contributions to Anthropology Ser.: Vol. 30). 1969. reprint ed. 32.50 (0-404-50580-5) AMS Pr.

An Asterisk (*) at the beginning of an entry indicates that the title is appearing in BIP for the first time.

Social Organization of the Tewa of New Mexico. Elsie C. Parsons. LC 30-5855. (American Anthropological Association Memoirs Ser.). 1929. 35.00 (*0-527-00535-5*) Periodicals Srv.

***Social Organization of the Western Apache.** Grenville Goodwin. 724p. 1969. write for info. (*0-8165-1742-8*) U of Ariz Pr.

Social Organization of Work. Randy Hodson & Teresa A. Sullivan. 481p. (C). 1990. text ed. 47.95 (*0-534-12564-6*) Wadsworth Pub.

Social Organization of Work. 2nd ed. Randy Hodson & Teresa A. Sullivan. 514p. 1995. text ed. 58.95 (*0-534-20982-3*) Wadsworth Pub.

Social Organization of Zen Practice: Constructing Transcultural Reality. David L. Preston. (Illus.). 240p. 1988. text ed. 69.95 (*0-521-35000-X*) Cambridge U Pr.

Social Organizations. Istvan Szentpeteri. Tr. by J. Decsenyi from HUN. 278p. (C). 1986. 81.00 (*963-05-4210-2*, Pub. by Akad Kiado HU) St Mut.

Social Organizations: Interaction Inside, Outside & Between Organizations. Goran Ahrne. 160p. 1994. 55.00 (*0-8039-8920-2*) Sage.

Social Organizations: Interaction Inside, Outside & Between Organizations. Goran Ahrne. 1994. pap. 18.95 (*0-8039-8921-0*) Sage.

Social Origins & Career Lines of Three Generations of American Business Leaders. Suzanne I. Keller. Ed. by Harriet Zuckerman & Robert K. Merton. LC 79-9008. (Dissertations on Sociology Ser.). 1980. lib. bdg. 21.95 (*0-405-12976-9*) Ayer.

Social Origins of a Labor Elite: French Engine-Drivers, 1837-1917. Margot B. Stein. (Modern European History Ser.). 560p. 1987. text ed. 15.00 (*0-8240-8043-2*) Garland.

***Social Origins of Christian Architecture Vol. 1: Building God's House in the Roman World: Architectural Adaptation among Pagans, Jews & Christians.** L. Michael White. LC 96-38709. (Harvard Theological Studies: Vol. 42). (Illus.). 224p. (C). 1996. reprint ed. pap. 17.00 (*1-56338-180-X*) TPI PA.

***Social Origins of Christian Architecture Vol. 2: Texts & Monuments for the Christian Domus Ecclesiae in Its Environment.** L. Michael White. LC 96-38709. (Harvard Theological Studies: Vol. 42). (Illus.). 520p. (Orig.). (C). 1996. pap. 30.00 (*1-56338-181-8*) TPI PA.

Social Origins of Democratic Collapse: The First Portuguese Republic in the Global Economy. Kathleen C. Schwartzman. LC 89-37218. (Studies in Historical Social Change). xxii, 226p. 1989. 29.95 (*0-7006-0410-3*) U Pr of KS.

Social Origins of Democratic Socialism in Jamaica. Nelson W. Keith & Novella Z. Keith. 485p. (C). 1992. 59.95 (*0-87722-906-6*) Temple U Pr.

Social Origins of Depression: A Study of Psychiatric Disorder in Women. George W. Brown & Tirril O. Harris. LC 78-3209. 1978. 50.00 (*0-02-904890-7*, Free Press) Free Pr.

Social Origins of Dictatorship & Democracy: Lord & Peasant in the Making of the Modern World. Barrington Moore, Jr. LC 93-17802. 592p. 1993. pap. 20.00 (*0-8070-5073-3*) Beacon Pr.

Social Origins of Distress & Disease: Depression, Neurasthenia, & Pain in Modern China. Arthur Kleinman. LC 85-29597. 276p. 1986. pap. 78.80 (*0-7837-8652-2*, 2082328) Bks Demand.

Social Origins of Educational Systems: The University Edition. abr. ed. Margaret S. Archer. LC 83-51281. (Illus.). 238p. reprint ed. pap. 67.90 (*0-8357-4738-7*, 2037658) Bks Demand.

Social Origins of Egyptian Expansionism During the Muhammad Ali Period. Frederick H. Lawson. 224p. 1992. text ed. 42.00 (*0-231-07632-0*) Col U Pr.

Social Origins of Korean Immigration to the United States from 1965-Present. In-Jin Yoon. LC 93-36357. (Papers of the Program on Population: No. 121). 1993. write for info. (*0-86638-160-0*) EW Ctr HI.

Social Origins of Mental Ability. Gary Collier. LC 93-3625. (Series on Personality Processes). 300p. 1993. text ed. 65.00 (*0-471-30407-7*) Wiley.

Social Origins of Nationalist Movements: The Contemporary West European Experience. John Coakley. (Modern Politics Ser.: Vol. 31). 288p. (C). 1992. text ed. 65.00 (*0-8039-8572-X*) Sage.

Social Origins of Private Life: A History of American Families, 1600-1900. Stephanie Coontz. (C). 1988. pap. text ed. 19.00 (*0-86091-907-2*, Pub. by Vrso UK) Norton.

Social Origins of the French Revolution: The Debate on the Roles of the Middle Classes. Ralph W. Greenlaw. 259p. (C). 1975. pap. text ed. 16.76 (*0-669-91116-X*) HM College Div.

Social Origins of the Iran-Iraq War. W. Thom Workman. LC 93-29380. 182p. 1994. lib. bdg. 36.00 (*1-55587-460-6*) Lynne Rienner.

Social Origins of the Iranian Revolution. Misagh Parsa. LC 88-31285. (Social Foundations of the Policy Process Ser.). 256p. (C). 1989. pap. text ed. 17.95 (*0-8135-1412-6*) Rutgers U Pr.

Social Origins of the New South: Alabama, 1860-1885. fac. ed. Jonathan M. Wiener. LC 78-6596. 254p. 1978. reprint ed. pap. 72.40 (*0-7837-7749-3*, 2047505) Bks Demand.

Social Origins of Violence in Uganda, 1964-1985. A. B. Kasozi. 376p. 1994. 55.00 (*0-7735-1218-7*, Pub. by McGill CN) U of Toronto Pr.

Social Overload. Henri-Pierre Jeudy. 143p. Date not set. 7.00 (*1-57027-016-3*) Autonomedia.

Social Paralysis & Social Change: British Working-Class Education in the Nineteenth Century. Neil J. Smelser. LC 91-6384. (Illus.). 540p. 1991. 38.00 (*0-520-07529-3*) U CA Pr.

Social Participation in Urban Society. Ed. by John Edwards & Alan Booth. LC 72-135339. 283p. 1972. pap. text ed. 15.95 (*0-87073-040-1*) Schenkman Bks Inc.

Social Partnership: The Austrian System of Industrial Relations & Social Insurance. Theodor Tomandl & Karl Fuerboeck. LC 85-14344. (Cornell International Industrial & Labor Relations Reports: No. 12). 176p. 1986. 25.00 (*0-87546-116-6*, ILR Press) Cornell U Pr.

Social Passion: Religion & Social Reform in Canada 1914-1928. Richard Allen. 416p. 1990. pap. 20.95 (*0-8020-6199-0*) U of Toronto Pr.

Social Passion: Religion & Social Reform in Canada, 1914-1928. Richard Allen. LC 71-151352. (Illus.). 412p. reprint ed. pap. 117.50 (*0-8357-8325-1*, 2034018) Bks Demand.

Social Pathology in Comparative Perspective: The Nature & Psychology of Civil Society. Ed. by Jerome Braun. LC 95-3332. 304p. 1995. text ed. 62.95 (*0-275-94796-3*, Praeger Pubs) Greenwood.

Social Patterns in Australian Literature. Tom I. Moore. LC 71-133027. 360p. reprint ed. pap. 102.60 (*0-318-34920-5*, 2031441) Bks Demand.

Social Patterns in Normal Aging: Findings from the Duke Longitudinal Studies. Frwd. by George L. Maddox. LC 81-9800. xii, 135p. 1981. text ed. 29.95 (*0-8223-0458-9*) Duke.

Social Pediatrics. Ed. by Bengt Lindstrom & Nick Spencer. (Illus.). 550p. 1995. 135.00 (*0-19-262179-3*) OUP.

Social Pediatrics. Ed. by Robert J. Schlegel. LC 81-80987. (Illus.). 81p. (Orig.). 1981. pap. 12.50 (*0-934314-03-9*) Intl Found Biosocial Dev.

Social Perception. Leslie Zebrowitz. 256p. (C). 1991. pap. 37.95 (*0-534-15631-2*) Brooks-Cole.

***Social Perception.** Leslie Zebrowitz. Ed. by Anthony S. Manstead. (Mapping Social Psychology Ser.). 248p. 1990. pap. 13.99 (*0-335-09860-6*, Open Univ Pr) Taylor & Francis.

***Social Perception.** Leslie Zebrowitz. Ed. by Anthony S. Manstead. (Mapping Social Psychology Ser.). 248p. 1990. 42.50 (*0-335-09861-4*, Open Univ Pr) Taylor & Francis.

Social Perception in Clinical & Counseling Psychology. J. H. Harvey et al. Ed. by R. P. McGlynn et al. (Interfaces in Psychology Ser.: No. 2). 185p. 1984. 29.95 (*0-89672-127-2*); pap. 17.95 (*0-89672-126-4*) Tex Tech Univ Pr.

Social Perception in Infants. Ed. by Tiffany M. Field & Nathan Fox. LC 84-28462. 352p. 1985. text ed. 73.25 (*0-89391-231-X*) Ablex Pub.

Social Perceptions, Impressions & Mental Actions: Research Bible with New Information. Michael A. Gaspari. 150p. 1994. 44.50 (*0-7883-0072-5*); pap. 39.50 (*0-7883-0073-3*) ABBE Pubs Assn.

Social Perplexities. Allan A. Hunter. LC 68-58797. (Essay Index Reprint Ser.). 1977. 18.95 (*0-8369-0119-3*) Ayer.

Social Perspective of Development of Science & Technology in India. Ed. by B. V. Rangarao & N. P. Chaubey. 1983. 22.00 (*0-8364-0931-0*, Pub. by Heritage IA) S Asia.

***Social Perspectives in Lesbian & Gay Studies: A Reader.** Peter M. Nardi & Beth E. Schneider. LC 97-2918. 656p. (C). 1997. pap. write for info. (*0-415-16709-4*); text ed. write for info. (*0-415-16708-6*) Routledge.

Social Perspectives on Emotion, Vol. 1. Ed. by David D. Franks. 1988. 73.25 (*0-89232-759-6*) Jai Pr.

Social Perspectives on Emotions, Vol. 1. Ed. by David D. Franks. 269p. 1986. 73.25 (*1-892327-59-7*) Jai Pr.

Social Perspectives on Emotions, Vol. 2. Ed. by David D. Franks. 308p. 1994. 73.25 (*1-55938-136-1*) Jai Pr.

Social Perspectives on Emotions, Vol. 4. Ed. by David D. Franks et al. 1996. 73.25 (*0-7623-0050-7*) Jai Pr.

Social Philosophy. Joel Feinberg. 1973. pap. text ed. 12.20 (*0-13-817254-4*) P-H.

Social Philosophy. Hans Fink. 128p. (C). 1981. pap. text ed. 8.50 (*0-416-72000-5*, NO. 3475) Routledge Chapman & Hall.

Social Philosophy & Ecological Scarcity. Lee Keekok. 432p. 1989. 55.00 (*0-415-03220-2*, A3505) Routledge.

Social Philosophy & Policy No. 13:2: Scientific Innovation, Philosophy, & Public Policy. Ed. by Ellen F. Paul et al. 344p. (C). 1996. pap. text ed. 21.95 (*0-521-58994-0*) Cambridge U Pr.

Social Philosophy of Athletics. Hans Lenk. 1979. pap. text ed. 9.60 (*0-87563-165-7*) Stipes.

Social Philosophy of Carlyle & Ruskin. Frederick W. Roe. LC 76-116555. 342p. (C). 1970. reprint ed. 60.00 (*0-87752-095-X*) Gordian.

Social Philosophy of Carlyle & Ruskin. Frederick W. Roe. (BCL1-PR English Literature Ser.). 335p. 1992. reprint ed. lib. bdg. 89.00 (*0-7812-7493-1*) Rprt Serv.

Social Philosophy of John Taylor of Carolina. Eugene T. Mudge. LC 76-181960. reprint ed. 20.00 (*0-404-04515-4*) AMS Pr.

Social Philosophy of John Taylor of Caroline: A Study in Jeffersonian Democracy. Eugene T. Mudge. (BCL1 - U. S. History Ser.). 227p. 1992. reprint ed. lib. bdg. 79.00 (*0-7812-6131-7*) Rprt Serv.

Social Philosophy of Mahatama Gandhi. K. S. Bharathi. (C). 1991. 17.50 (*81-7022-362-8*, Pub. by Concept II) S Asia.

Social Philosophy of Sri Aurobindo & the New Age. 2nd enl. rev. ed. Kishor Gandhi. 413p. 15.00 (*81-7058-258-X*) Aurobindo Assn.

Social Philosophy of the St. Louis Hegelians. Frances A. Harmon. LC 75-3159. 1976. reprint ed. 20.00 (*0-404-59164-7*) AMS Pr.

Social Philosophy of Vedanta. P. George Victor. (C). 1991. 19.50 (*81-7074-101-7*) S Asia.

***Social Phobia: A Guide.** John H. Greist et al. 61p. 1997. pap. 4.50 (*1-890802-09-3*) Dean Fnd for HRE.

Social Phobia: Clinical & Research Perspectives. Ed. by Murray B. Stein. 384p. 1995. text ed. 48.00 (*0-88048-653-8*, 8653) Am Psychiatric.

Social Phobia: Diagnosis, Assessment, & Treatment. Ed. by Richard Heimberg et al. LC 95-34091. 435p. 1995. lib. bdg. 45.00 (*1-57230-012-4*, 0012) Guilford Pr.

Social Phobia: From Shyness to Stage Fright. John R. Marshall. 240p. 1995. pap. 13.00 (*0-465-07896-6*) Basic.

Social Planning & Human Service Delivery in the Voluntary Sector. Ed. by Gary A. Tobin. LC 84-25307. (Studies in Social Welfare Policies & Programs: No. 1). (Illus.). xxx, 290p. 1985. text ed. 59.95 (*0-313-23892-8*, TOP/, Greenwood Pr) Greenwood.

Social Planning Process: Conceptualization & Methods. Janet Scheff. LC 76-5840. (Planning Ser.: No. S-2). (Illus.). 124p. (Orig.). 1976. pap. 4.00 (*0-8477-2432-8*) U of PR Pr.

Social Plays, 4 vols. Arthur W. Pinero. (BCL1-PR English Literature Ser.). 1992. reprint ed. lib. bdg. 300.00 (*0-7812-7618-7*) Rprt Serv.

Social Plays, 4 vols., Set. Arthur W. Pinero. Ed. by Clayton Hamilton. LC 79-18169. reprint ed. 325.00 (*0-404-05080-8*) AMS Pr.

Social Pluralism & Literary History: The Literature of Italian Immigration. Ed. by Francesco Loriggio. (Essay Ser.: No. 22). 300p. 1995. 20.00 (*1-55071-018-4*) Guernica Editions.

***Social Poetry of the Georgics.** Edweirtl W. Spofford. Date not set. write for info. (*0-88143-024-2*) Ayer.

Social Poetry of the Georgics. rev. ed. Edward W. Spofford. Ed. by W. R. Connor. LC 80-2668. (Monographs in Classical Studies). 1981. lib. bdg. 12.00 (*0-405-14051-7*) Ayer.

Social Polarization in Post-Industrial Metropolises. Ed. by John O'Loughlin & Juergen Friedrichs. (Illus.). xiv, 335p. (C). 1996. lib. bdg. 49.95 (*3-11-013728-3*, 111/96) De Gruyter.

Social Policies & Population Growth in Mauritius. Richard M. Titmuss & Brian Abel-Smith. 308p. 1968. reprint ed. 39.50 (*0-7146-1254-5*, Pub. by F Cass Pubs UK) Intl Spec Bk.

Social Policies for Children. Ed. by Irwin Garfinkel et al. 350p. (C). 1995. 42.95 (*0-8157-3666-5*) Brookings.

Social Policies for Children. Ed. by Irwin Garfinkel et al. 200p. (C). 1995. pap. 18.95 (*0-8157-3665-7*) Brookings.

Social Policies for the Elderly in the Third World. Martin B. Tracy. LC 90-45605. (Contributions to the Study of Aging Ser.: No. 22). 200p. 1991. text ed. 45.00 (*0-313-26377-9*, TET, Greenwood Pr) Greenwood.

***Social Policy.** Outram. 1990. pap. text ed. write for info. (*0-582-35533-8*, Pub. by Longman UK) Longman.

***Social Policy.** 3rd ed. Jansson. (Social Work Ser.). 1999. text ed. 51.95 (*0-534-35520-X*) Brooks-Cole.

Social Policy: A Comparative Analysis. Michael Hill. LC 95-42457. 1996. pap. 24.95 (*0-13-353905-9*) P-H.

***Social Policy: A Conceptual & Theoretical Introduction.** Ed. by Michael Lavalette & Alan Pratt. 304p. 1997. 69.95 (*0-8039-7532-5*) Sage.

***Social Policy: A Conceptual & Theoretical Introduction.** Ed. by Michael Lavalette & Alan Pratt. 304p. 1997. pap. 23.95 (*0-8039-7533-3*) Sage.

Social Policy: A Feminist Analysis. Gillian Pascall. 250p. 1986. text ed. 47.50 (*0-422-78660-8*, 1026, Pub. by Tavistock UK); pap. text ed. 15.95 (*0-422-78670-5*, 1043, Pub. by Tavistock UK) Routledge Chapman & Hall.

Social Policy: A New Feminist Analysis. 2nd ed. Gillian Pascall. LC 96-21372. 272p. (C). 1996. pap. 19.95 (*0-415-09928-5*); text ed. 65.00 (*0-415-09927-7*) Routledge.

Social Policy: From Theory to Policy Practice. 2nd ed. Bruce S. Jansson. LC 93-37936. 447p. 1994. text ed. 53.95 (*0-534-20520-8*) Brooks-Cole.

Social Policy: Institutional Context of Social Development & Human Services. Demetrius Iatridis. LC 93-24327. 211p. 1994. pap. 50.95 (*0-534-19212-2*) Brooks-Cole.

Social Policy: Issues of Choice & Change. abr. ed. Martin Rein. LC 82-19676. 384p. 1983. reprint ed. pap. 109.50 (*0-7837-9981-0*, 2060708) Bks Demand.

***Social Policy: Reform, Research, & Practice.** Patricia L. Ewalt et al. LC 97-6110. 448p. (Orig.). (C). 1997. pap. text ed. 38.95 (*0-87101-279-0*, 2790) Natl Assn Soc Wkrs.

Social Policy: Themes & Approaches. Paul Spicker. LC 94-46375. 1995. write for info. (*0-13-354762-0*) P-H.

Social Policy - A Critical Introduction: Issues of Race, Gender & Class. Fiona Williams. (Illus.). 240p. 1989. pap. text ed. 24.95 (*0-7456-0150-2*) Blackwell Pubs.

Social Policy & Administration in Britain: A Bibliography. Tessa Blackstone & Peter Vines. 130p. 1975. 27.00 (*0-87471-811-2*) Rowman.

Social Policy & Administration Revised Studies in the Development of Social Services at the Local Level. David Donnison. 1970. 30.00 (*0-317-05808-8*, Pub. by Natl Inst Soc Work) St Mut.

Social Policy & Missionary Organizations in Ceylon, 1840-1855. K. M. De Silva. 318p. 1965. 69.50 (*0-614-01826-9*) Elliots Bks.

Social Policy & Social Justice: The NDP Government in Saskatchewan During the Blakeney Years. Ed. by Jim Harding. xii, 484p. (C). 1995. pap. 29.95 (*0-88920-240-0*) Wilfrid Laurier.

Social Policy & Social Programs: A Method for the Practical Public Policy Analyst. 2nd ed. Donald E. Chambers. LC 92-8351. 336p. (C). 1992. pap. text ed. 53.00 (*0-02-320582-2*, Macmillan Coll) P-H.

Social Policy & Social Responsibility: Record of a Study Day, Nineteen Seventy-Nine. 1979. 30.00 (*0-317-05770-7*, Pub. by Natl Inst Soc Work) St Mut.

Social Policy & Social Services. 2nd ed. Alfred J. Kahn. 1979. pap. text ed. write for info. (*0-318-55409-7*) Random.

Social Policy & Social Welfare. Ed. by Martin Loney et al. 352p. 1983. pap. 27.00 (*0-335-10408-8*, Open Univ Pr) Taylor & Francis.

Social Policy & Social Work: Critical Essays on the Welfare State. Robert M. Moroney. (Modern Applications of Social Work Ser.). 270p. 1991. pap. text ed. 27.95 (*0-202-36062-8*); lib. bdg. 49.95 (*0-202-36061-X*) Aldine de Gruyter.

Social Policy & the City. Ed. by Helen Jones & John Lansley. 176p. 1995. 51.95 (*1-85628-891-9*, Pub. by Avebury Pub UK) Ashgate Pub Co.

***Social Policy & the Conservative Agenda.** Ed. by Clarence Y. Lo & Michael Schwartz. 416p. 1998. text ed. 64.95 (*1-57718-119-0*) Blackwell Pubs.

***Social Policy & the Conservative Agenda.** Ed. by Clarence Y. Lo & Michael Schwartz. 416p. 1998. pap. text ed. 29.95 (*1-57718-120-4*) Blackwell Pubs.

***Social Policy & the Labour Market: Issues at Stake Across the World.** Ed. by Peter R. De Jong & Theodore R. Marmor. (International Studies on Social Security). (Illus.). 420p. 1997. text ed. 68.95 (*1-84014-156-5*, Pub. by Avebury Pub UK) Ashgate Pub Co.

Social Policy & the Third Reich: The Working Class & the National Community, 1918-1939. Tim Mason. Ed. by Jane Kaplan. Tr. by John A. Bradwin. 432p. 1993. pap. 22.95 (*0-85496-410-X*); text ed. 45.95 (*0-85496-621-8*) Berg Pubs.

S

Social Policy Beyond Borders: Essays on the Global Social Question. Ed. by Abram De Swaan. 150p. (Orig.). (C). 1995. pap. 34.50 (*90-5356-069-6*, Pub. by Amsterdam U Pr NE) U of Mich Pr.

Social Policy, Crime & Punishment: Essays in Memory of Jane Morgan. Ed. by Ieuan G. Jones & Glanmor Williams. 160p. 1994. 49.95 (*0-7083-1258-6*, Pub. by Univ Wales Pr UK) Paul & Co Pubs.

Social Policy for Nurses & the Caring Professions. Louise Ackers & Pamela Abbott. LC 95-49768. (Social Science for Nurses & the Caring Professions Ser.). 192p. (C). 1996. 79.00 (*0-335-19360-9*, Open Univ Pr); pap. 23.95 (*0-335-19359-5*, Open Univ Pr) Taylor & Francis.

Social Policy in a Changing World: The ILO Response: Selected Speeches by Wilfred Jenks, Director-General of the ILO, 1970-1973. 270p. 1976. 18.00 (*92-2-101445-2*) Intl Labour Office.

***Social Policy in Aotearoa/New Zealand: A Critical Introduction.** Christine Cheyne et al. 224p. 1997. pap. text ed. 49.95 (*0-19-558334-5*) OUP.

Social Policy in Britain: Themes & Issues. Peter Alcock. 272p. 1996. text ed. 49.95 (*0-312-16201-4*) St Martin.

Social Policy in Britain, 1914-1939. 2nd ed. Anne Crowther. (New Studies in Economic & Social History: No. 5). (Illus.). 96p. (C). 1997. text ed. 27.95 (*0-521-55264-8*); pap. text ed. 9.95 (*0-521-55789-5*) Cambridge U Pr.

Social Policy in Germany. Jochen Clasen. 1995. pap. 36.00 (*0-13-342767-6*) P-H.

Social Policy in the European Union. Linda Hantrais. LC 95-7830. 1995. text ed. 55.00 (*0-312-12700-6*) St Martin.

Social Policy in the Third World: The Social Dilemmas of Underdevelopment. Stewart MacPherson. LC 82-6837. 220p. (C). 1983. pap. text ed. 20.00 (*0-86598-090-X*, R3890) Rowman.

Social Policy in the United States: Future Possibilities in Historical Perspective. Theda Skocpol. 328p. 1995. pap. text ed. 16.95 (*0-691-03785-X*) Princeton U Pr.

Social Policy in Transition: Anglo-German Perspectives in the New European Community. Ed. by John Ferris & Robert Page. 215p. 1994. 50.95 (*1-85628-365-8*, Pub. by Avebury Pub UK) Ashgate Pub Co.

Social Policy in Transition Adjusting to the Needs of the 1990s. 138p. 1989. 30.00 (*92-1-130137-8*, E.89.IV.8) UN.

Social Policy in Western Europe & the U. S. A., Nineteen Fifty to Nineteen Eighty: An Assessment. Ed. by Roger Girod et al. LC 84-17747. 128p. 1985. text ed. 29.95 (*0-312-73376-3*) St Martin.

Social Policy, Law & Protection of Weaker Sections of Society. D. N. Saraf. (C). 1989. 175.00 (*0-89771-763-5*, Pub. by Eastern Book II) St Mut.

Social Policy of Nazi Germany. C. W. Guillebaud. LC 71-80553. 1971. reprint ed. 35.00 (*0-86527-183-6*) Fertig.

Social Policy of the Economic State & Community Care in Chinese Culture: Aging, Family, Urban Change & the Socialist Welfare Pluralism. Sheying Chen. 352p. 1996. 68.95 (*1-85972-294-6*, Pub. by Avebury Pub UK) Ashgate Pub Co.

Social Policy, Social Justice & Citizenship in Eastern Europe. Ed. by Bob Deacon. (Studies in the Social Policy of Eastern Europe & Soviet Union). 1992. 59.95 (*1-85628-243-0*, Pub. by Avebury Pub UK) Ashgate Pub Co.

Social Policy Towards 2000: Squaring the Welfare Circle. Ed. by Victor George & Stewart Miller. LC 93-15045. 256p. (C). 1993. pap. text ed. 22.95 (*0-415-08707-4*) Routledge.

Social, Political, & Economic Concepts & Contexts in Public Relations: Theory & Cases. Hugh M. Culbertson et al. (Communication Textbook (Public Relations) Ser.). 328p. 1993. pap. 34.50 (*0-8058-1288-1*); text ed. 69.95 (*0-8058-1013-7*) L Erlbaum Assocs.

Social, Political, & Economic Issues in Black America, Vol. IV. Ed. by Wornie L. Reed. (Assessment of the Status of African-Americans Ser.). 150p. (Orig.). (C). 1990. pap. 8.95 (*1-878358-03-0*) U MA W M Trotter Inst.

An Asterisk (*) at the beginning of an entry indicates that the title is appearing in BIP for the first time.

S

Social, Political, & Economic Life in Contemporary Oaxaca. Ed. by Aubrey Williams & J. Corbett. (Publications in Anthropology: No. 24). (Illus.). 179p. 1979. pap. 8.95 (0-935462-13-9) VUPA.

Social Politics in the United States. Frederick E. Haynes. LC 70-126648. reprint ed. 37.50 (0-404-03168-4) AMS Pr.

Social Portrait of Europe. H. Christophersen & V. Papandreou. 142p. 1991. pap. 14.00 (92-826-1747-5, CA-57-89-241-EN-C, Pub. by Commiss Europ Commun BE) Bernan Associates.

Social Portrait of the South at the Turn of the Eighteenth Century. George C. Rogers, Jr. 14p. 1988. reprint ed. pap. 4.00 (0-944026-03-6) Am Antiquarian.

Social Postmodernism: Beyond Identity Politics. Ed. by Linda J. Nicholson & Steven Seidman. (Cultural Social Studies). 416p. (C). 1995. 59.95 (0-521-47516-3) Cambridge U Pr.

Social Postmodernism: Beyond Identity Politics. Ed. by Linda J. Nicholson & Steven Seidman. (Cultural & Social Studies). 416p. (C). 1995. pap. text ed. 19.95 (0-521-47571-6) Cambridge U Pr.

Social Power: Social Psychological Models & Theories. Allen H. Henderson. LC 81-15354. (Illus.). 128p. 1981. text ed. 49.95 (0-275-90644-2, C0644, Praeger Pubs) Greenwood.

Social Power & Political Freedom. Gene Sharp. LC 80-81479. (Extending Horizons Ser.). 456p. (C). 1980. pap. 8.95 (0-87558-093-9) Porter Sargent.

Social Power & Political Freedom. Gene Sharp. LC 80-81479. (Extending Horizons Ser.). 456p. (C). 1980. 15.95 (0-87558-091-2) Porter Sargent.

Social Power of Ideas. Ed. by Yeager Hudson & W. Creighton Peden. LC 94-24826. 400p. 1995. text ed. 99.95 (0-7734-9043-4) E Mellen.

Social Practice of Symbolization: An Anthropological Analysis. Ivo Strecker. LC 88-707. (London School of Economics Monographs on Social Anthropology: No. 60). 240p. (C). 1988. text ed. 35.00 (0-485-19557-7, Pub. by Athlone Pr UK) Humanities.

Social Practices: A Wittgensteinian Approach to Human Activity & the Soul. Theodore R. Schatzki. 350p. (C). 1996. text ed. 49.95 (0-521-56022-5) Cambridge U Pr.

Social Pressures in Informal Groups: A Study of Human Factors in Housing. Leon Festinger et al. x, 197p. 1950. reprint ed. 29.50 (0-8047-0173-3); reprint ed. pap. 12.95 (0-8047-0174-1) Stanford U Pr.

Social Prevention & the Social Sciences: Theoretical Controversies, Research Problems, & Evaluation Strategies. Ed. by Gunter Albrecht & Hans-Uwe Otto. (Prevention & Intervention in Childhood & Adolescence Ser.: No. 11). xii, 638p. (C). 1991. lib. bdg. 99.95 (3-11-012387-8, 148-91) De Gruyter.

Social Problem. J. A. Hobson. (Key Texts Ser.). 303p. 1996. pap. 24.95 (1-85506-429-4) Bks Intl VA.

Social Problem America: Alienation & Discontinuity. John Wildeman. 291p. 1985. pap. text ed. 19.95 (0-8290-1467-5) Irvington.

Social Problem-Solving Interventions: Individual, Group, Classroom & Organizational Approaches. Maurice J. Elias & Steven E. Tobias. LC 95-53954. (School Practitioner Ser.). 1996. lib. bdg. 26.95 (1-57230-072-8, 0072) Guilford Pr.

Social Problems. Ed. by Craig Calhoun & George Ritzer. 1992. text ed. write for info. (0-07-152746-X) McGraw.

***Social Problems.** Ed. by Chambliss. (C). Date not set. text ed. write for info. (0-321-01373-5) Addson-Wesley Educ.

Social Problems. Doob. (C). 1994. pap. text ed. 43.75 (0-15-500636-3) HB Coll Pubs.

Social Problems. Doob. (C). 1995. teacher ed., pap. text ed. 32.00 (0-15-501865-5) HB Coll Pubs.

Social Problems. Amitai Etzioni. (Foundations of Modern Sociology Ser.). 192p. 1976. pap. text ed. write for info. (0-13-817403-2) P-H.

***Social Problems.** Ed. by Glick. (C). 1998. text ed. write for info. (0-321-01211-9) Addson-Wesley Educ.

***Social Problems.** Jones. (C). 1997. pap. text ed. 28.00 (0-15-505749-9) HarBrace.

Social Problems. Jones. (C). 1997. text ed. write for info. (0-15-501431-5) HB Coll Pubs.

***Social Problems.** Jones. (C). 1997. teacher ed., pap. text ed. 28.00 (0-15-505740-5) HB Coll Pubs.

Social Problems. Mooney. Date not set. student ed. write for info. (0-314-06719-1) West Pub.

Social Problems. Joan W. Moore & Burton M. Moore. (Illus.). 464p. (C). 1982. text ed. write for info. (0-13-817387-7) P-H.

Social Problems. Ron E. Roberts. 310p. 1978. pap. 12.95 (0-8016-4143-8) Schenkman Bks Inc.

***Social Problems.** Ed. by Schambliss. (C). Date not set. student ed., pap. text ed. write for info. (0-321-01374-3) Addson-Wesley Educ.

Social Problems. 2nd ed. George Ritzer. (Illus.). 608p. (C). 1986. pap. text ed. write for info. (0-07-554947-6) McGraw.

Social Problems. 2nd ed. Frank R. Scarpitti & Margaret L. Andersen. (C). 1992. text ed. 58.95 (0-06-500475-2); pap. text ed. 16.50 (0-06-500476-0) Addson-Wesley Educ.

***Social Problems.** 3rd ed. Ed. by Scarpitti. (C). 1996. student ed., pap. text ed. 16.50 (0-673-99312-4) Addison-Wesley.

Social Problems. 3rd ed. Frank R. Scarpitti et al. LC 96-8951. (C). 1997. text ed. 58.95 (0-673-99307-8) Longman.

Social Problems. 4th ed. Curran & Claire M. Renzetti. 1995. student ed., pap. text ed. 20.00 (0-205-17889-8) Allyn.

Social Problems. 4th ed. James M. Henslin. LC 95-19488. 1995. text ed. 56.00 (0-13-186578-1) P-H.

Social Problems. 4th ed. Korda. 1995. student ed., pap. text ed. 19.00 (0-13-442401-8) P-H.

Social Problems. 4th ed. Kenneth J. Nuebeck & Mary A. Neubeck. LC 96-22208. 1996. pap. text ed. write for info. (0-07-046372-7) McGraw.

Social Problems. 5th ed. James W. Coleman & Donald R. Cressey. LC 92-24775. (C). 1992. 53.00 (0-06-500144-3) Addson-Wesley Educ.

Social Problems. 5th ed. Feagin. 1996. pap. text ed. 49.33 (0-13-651084-1) P-H.

Social Problems. 6th ed. James W. Coleman & Donald R. Cressey. (C). 1995. teacher ed. write for info. (0-673-97070-1) Addson-Wesley Educ.

Social Problems. 6th ed. James W. Coleman & Donald R. Cressey. LC 95-21569. 592p. (C). 1996. text ed. 51.50 (0-673-99079-6); student ed., pap. text ed. 17.50 (0-673-99653-0) Addson-Wesley Educ.

Social Problems. 7th ed. Meyers. 1996. student ed., pap. text ed. 16.00 (0-205-26245-7) Allyn.

Social Problems. 7th ed. Maxine B. Zinn. 640p. 1996. 55.00 (0-205-17567-8) Allyn.

Social Problems. 8th ed. Gottfried. 1995. student ed., pap. text ed. 20.00 (0-13-121625-2) P-H.

Social Problems. 8th ed. William Kornblum & Joseph Julian. LC 94-18152. 603p. 1994. text ed. 56.00 (0-13-101148-0) P-H.

***Social Problems.** 9th ed. Kornblum & Julian. 1997. text ed. 54.67 (0-13-608480-X) P-H.

Social Problems. Henry George. (Notable American Authors Ser.). 1992. reprint ed. lib. bdg. 75.00 (0-7812-2916-2) Rprt Serv.

Social Problems. Henry George. LC 81-11896. 310p. 1992. reprint ed. pap. 8.00 (0-911312-52-8) Schalkenbach.

Social Problems. Henry George. LC 81-11896. 310p. 1996. reprint ed. 15.00 (0-911312-17-X) Schalkenbach.

Social Problems: A Critical Approach. 3rd ed. Kenneth J. Neubeck. 1991. pap. text ed. write for info. (0-07-557741-0) McGraw.

Social Problems: A Critical Thinking Approach. 2nd ed. Paul J. Baker et al. 530p. (C). 1993. pap. 41.95 (0-534-19014-6) Wadsworth Pub.

Social Problems: A World at Risk. Michael P. Soroka & George J. Bryjak. LC 94-31405. 1994. pap. text ed. 48.00 (0-205-14128-5) Allyn.

***Social Problems: Brief Version.** Ed. by Coleman. LC 97-23113. (C). 1998. text ed. write for info. (0-321-01249-6) Addison-Wesley Educ.

Social Problems: Causes, Consequences, Interventions. Richard Bourne & Jack Levin. (Illus.). 422p. (C). 1983. pap. text ed. 45.25 (0-314-69661-X); Tchr's. manual. teacher ed., pap. text ed. write for info. (0-314-71081-7) West Pub.

***Social Problems: Causes, Consequences, Interventions.** 2nd rev. ed. Jack Levin et al. (Illus.). 450p. (C). 1998. pap. text ed. write for info. (0-935732-96-9) Roxbury Pub Co.

Social Problems: Issues & Solutions. 4th ed. Charles H. Zastrow. 672p. 1996. text ed. 45.95 (0-8304-1444-4) Nelson-Hall.

Social Problems: Issues & Solutions. 4th ed. Charles H. Zastrow. 620p. 1996. teacher ed. write for info. (0-8304-1448-7) Nelson-Hall.

Social Problems: Issues, Opinions, & Solutions. Brian J. Jones et al. 1988. text ed. write for info. (0-07-022766-7) McGraw.

Social Problems: Issues, Opinions, & Solutions. Brian J. Jones et al. 1988. pap. text ed. write for info. (0-07-022772-1) McGraw.

Social Problems: Society in Crisis. 2nd ed. Daniel J. Curran & Claire M. Renzetti. 600p. 1990. pap. text ed. 43.00 (0-205-12252-3, H22528) Allyn.

Social Problems: Society in Crisis. 4th ed. Daniel J. Curran & Claire M. Renzetti. LC 95-33100. 1995. text ed. 59.00 (0-205-16793-4) Allyn.

Social Problems: The Search for Solutions: An Anthology. Ed. by Frank R. Scarpitti & F. Kurt Cylke, Jr. LC 94-11038. (Illus.). 200p. (Orig.). (C). 1995. pap. text ed. write for info. (0-935732-59-4) Roxbury Pub Co.

Social Problems: 1996-1997. annuals 24th ed. Widdison. 256p. (C). 1996. per. write for info. (0-697-31732-3) Brown & Benchmark.

Social Problems - Social Processes: Selected Papers from the Proceedings of the American Sociological Society, 1932. American Sociological Society Staff. Ed. by Emory S. Bogardus. LC 67-23173. (Essay Index Reprint Ser.). 1977. 19.95 (0-8369-0151-7) Ayer.

Social Problems & Mental Health. Ed. by Jessica Kuper. (Social Science Lexicons Ser.). 176p. 1987. pap. text ed. 14.95 (0-7102-1170-8, RKP) Routledge.

Social Problems & Social Contexts in Adolescence: Perspectives Across Boundaries. Ed. by Klaus Hurrelmann & Stephen F. Hamilton. 320p. (Orig.). 1996. pap. text ed. 24.95 (0-202-36101-2) Aldine de Gruyter.

Social Problems & Social Movements: An Exploration into the Sociological Construction of Alternative Realities. Harry H. Bash. LC 93-28775. 280p. (C). 1995. text ed. 49.95 (0-391-03844-3) Humanities.

Social Problems & Social Policy Series, 51 Vols. Ed. by Gerald N. Grob. (Illus.). 1975. 1,799.50 (0-405-07474-3) Ayer.

Social Problems & the City: New Perspectives. 2nd ed. Ed. by David T. Herbert & David M. Smith. (Illus.). 416p. 1989. 75.00 (0-19-874145-6) OUP.

Social Problems & the Family. Ed. by Rudi Dallos & Eugene McLaughlin. (Illus.). 320p. (C). 1993. text ed. 69.95 (0-8039-8836-2); pap. text ed. 25.95 (0-8039-8837-0) Sage.

Social Problems & the Mores. Willard Waller. (Reprint Series in Social Sciences). (C). 1993. reprint ed. pap. text ed. 1.00 (0-8290-3090-5, S-300) Irvington.

Social Problems & the Quality of Life. 5th ed. Robert H. Lauer. 624p. (C). 1991. per. write for info. (0-697-11133-4) Brown & Benchmark.

Social Problems & the Quality of Life. 6th ed. Robert H. Lauer. 672p. (C). 1994. per. write for info. (0-697-21352-8) Brown & Benchmark.

***Social Problems & the Quality of Life.** 7th ed. Robert H. Lauer. 688p. (C). 1997. per. write for info. (0-697-24455-5) Wm C Brown Pubs.

Social Problems & the Sociological Imagination: A Paradigm for Analysis. David R. Simon. LC 94-30656. 1995. pap. text ed. write for info. (0-07-057623-8) McGraw.

Social Problems & Welfare in India. Jogan Shankar. (Illus.). xxvii, 387p. (C). 1992. 42.00 (81-7024-492-7, Pub. by Ashish Pub Hse II) Nataraj Bks.

***Social Problems in Focus.** Ed. by Thompson. (C). 1998. text ed. write for info. (0-321-01177-5); student ed., pap. text ed. write for info. (0-321-01178-3) Addson-Wesley Educ.

Social Problems in India. Ram Ahuja. (C). 1992. 35.00 (81-7033-138-2, Pub. by Rawat II) S Asia.

Social Problems in Puerto Rico. Fred K. Fleagle. LC 74-14233. (Puerto Rican Experience Ser.). (Illus.). 152p. 1975. reprint ed. 15.95 (0-405-06222-2) Ayer.

Social Problems in the Asia Pacific Region. Sandra Sewell & Anthony Kelly. 353p. (C). 1990. pap. 65.00 (0-86439-114-5, Pub. by Boolarong Pubns AT) St Mut.

Social Problems in the Philosophy of Rousseau. John Charvet. LC 73-88311. (Cambridge Studies in the History & Theory of Politics). 158p. reprint ed. pap. 45.10 (0-317-26041-3, 2024436) Bks Demand.

Social Problems in the United States. J. Kenneth Morland. LC 74-22542. (Illus.). 694p. reprint ed. pap. 180.00 (0-317-09589-7, 2012515) Bks Demand.

Social Problems of an Industrial Civilization. Elton Mayo. Ed. by Leon Stein. LC 77-70516. 1977. reprint ed. lib. bdg. 22.95 (0-405-10185-6) Ayer.

Social Problems of Contemporary India. Rajendra Pandey. (Illus.). vi, 373p. 1994. 43.00 (81-7024-604-0, Pub. by Ashish Pub Hse II) Nataraj Bks.

Social Problems of the Industrial Revolution. Peter F. Speed. 160p. 1975. pap. 5.90 (0-08-018883-4, Pergamon Pr) Elsevier.

Social Problems Today. Henslin. 1990. pap. text ed. 37.60 (0-13-815523-2) P-H.

Social Process in Hawaii: A Reader. Manicas. 1993. pap. text ed. write for info. (0-07-040029-6) McGraw.

Social Process of Aging & Old Age. 2nd ed. Arnold S. Brown. LC 95-19370. 1995. pap. text ed. 36.00 (0-13-449604-3) P-H.

Social Process Revisited: Achieving Human Interests Through Alliance & Opposition. Harold Fallding. LC 90-35969. (American University Studies: Anthropology & Science: Ser. XI, Vol. 49). 336p. (C). 1990. 59.95 (0-8204-1280-5) P Lang Pubng.

Social Processes & Mental Abilities in Non-Human Primates: Evidences from Longitudinal Field Studies. Ed. by Frances D. Burton. LC 92-11041. 308p. 1992. 99.95 (0-7734-9537-1) E Mellen.

Social Processes in Clinical & Counseling Psychology. Ed. by J. E. Maddux et al. (Illus.). 392p. 1987. 52.00 (0-387-96533-5) Spr-Verlag.

Social Processes in Early Number Development. Geoffrey B. Saxe et al. (CDM 216 Ser.: Vol. 52, No. 2). viii, 170p. 1987. pap. text ed. 15.00 (0-226-73550-8) U Ch Pr.

Social Production of Art. Janet Wolff. 208p. (C). 1984. pap. 17.50 (0-8147-9201-4) NYU Pr.

Social Production of Art. 2nd ed. Janet Wolff. LC 93-7703. 250p. (C). 1993. pap. 17.50 (0-8147-9270-7); text ed. 36.00 (0-8147-9269-3) NYU Pr.

Social Production of Indifference: Exploring the Symbolic Roots of Western Bureaucracy. Michael Herzfeld. LC 91-37678. (Global Issues Ser.). 217p. 1992. 29.95 (0-85496-638-2) Berg Pubs.

Social Production of Indifference: Exploring the Symbolic Roots of Western Bureaucracy. Michael Herzfeld. LC 93-1674. ix, 224p. 1993. pap. text ed. 12.95 (0-226-32908-9) U Ch Pr.

Social Production of Merit: Education, Psychology & Politics in Australia, 1900-1950. David McCallum. 224p. 1990. 55.00 (1-85000-859-0, Falmer Pr); pap. 26.00 (1-85000-864-7, Falmer Pr) Taylor & Francis.

Social Production of Merit: Education, Psychology & Politics in Australia 1900-1950. David McCallum. 224p. 1990. 50.00 (1-85000-922-8, Falmer Pr); pap. 22.00 (1-85000-923-6, Falmer Pr) Taylor & Francis.

Social Production of Scientific Knowledge. Ed. by Everett I. Mendelsohn et al. (Sociology of the Sciences Yearbook Ser.: Vol. 1). 1977. lib. bdg. 88.00 (90-277-0775-8) Kluwer Ac.

Social Production of Technical Work: The Case of British Engineers. Peter Whalley. LC 85-14813. (SUNY Series in the Sociology of Work). 237p. 1985. text ed. 29.50 (0-88706-252-0) State U NY Pr.

Social Production of Urban Space. 2nd ed. M. Gottdiener. LC 93-39444. 336p. (C). 1994. pap. 17.95 (0-292-72772-0) U of Tex Pr.

Social Profile of Tarakeswar. Prafulla Chakrabarti. 1984. 14.00 (0-8364-1244-3, Pub. by Mukhopadhyaya II) S Asia.

Social Programs in Sweden: A Search for Security in a Free Society. Albert H. Rosenthal. LC 67-27098. 213p. reprint ed. pap. 60.80 (0-317-29497-0, 2055906) Bks Demand.

***Social Protection.** Schoukens. 1994. pap. text ed. 40.50 (90-6544-826-8) Kluwer Ac.

***Social Protection & the European Economic & Monetary Union.** Jozef Pacolet. 320p. 1996. text ed. 67.95 (1-85628-581-2, Pub. by Avebury Pub UK) Ashgate Pub Co.

Social Protection Code: A New Model of Criminal Justice. Tadeusz Grygier. (American Series of Foreign Penal Codes: Vol. 22). xxiv, 96p. 1977. text ed. 15.00 (0-8377-0605-X) Rothman.

Social Protection in the Member States of the European Union: Situation on 1 July 1994 & Evolution. M.I.S.S. O.C. Staff. 453p. 1995. pap. text ed. 16.00 (92-826-9973-0, CE-83-94-555-EN, Pub. by Commiss Europ Commun BE) Bernan Associates.

***Social Protection in the Member States of the European Union: Situation on 1 July 1995 & Evolution.** 453p. 1996. pap. 40.00 (92-827-7162-8, CE94-96-518-ENC, Pub. by Europ Com UK) Bernan Associates.

Social Protection vs. Economic Flexibility: Is There a Tradeoff? Ed. by Rebecca M. Blank. (National Bureau of Economic Research Comparative Labor Markets Ser.). (Illus.). 386p. 1994. 50.00 (0-226-05678-3) U Ch Pr.

Social Protest & Popular Culture in Eighteenth-Century Japan. Anne Walthall. LC 85-24647. (Monographs: No. 43). xviii, 286p. 1986. 23.00 (0-8165-0961-1) Assn Asian Studies.

Social Protest from the Left in Canada, 1870-1970. Peter Weinrich. LC 82-192529. 651p. reprint ed. pap. 180.00 (0-7837-1228-6, 2041364) Bks Demand.

Social Protest in an Urban Barrio: A Study of the Chicano Movement, 1966-1974. Marguerite V. Marin. Ed. by Sethard Fisher. (Class, Ethnicity, Gender, & the Democratic Nation Ser.). 320p. (C). 1990. lib. bdg. 53.00 (0-8191-7962-0) U Pr of Amer.

Social Protest in India: British Protestant Missionaries & Social Reforms, Eighteen Fifty to Nineteen Hundred. G. A. Oddie. 1979. 17.50 (0-8364-0195-6) S Asia.

Social Protest in the Eighteenth-Century English Novel. Mona Scheuermann. LC 84-27157. 256p. 1985. pap. 27.50 (0-8142-0403-1) Ohio St U Pr.

Social Protest in the Eighteenth-Century English Novel. Mona Scheuermann. LC 84-27157. 256p. 1985. 47.50 (0-8142-0381-7) Ohio St U Pr.

Social Psychiatry: Eighteen Essays. Ed. by Ari Kiev. 1970. 32.95 (0-8464-0855-4) Beekman Pubs.

Social Psychiatry: Theory, Methodology, & Practice. Ed. by Paul E. Bebbington. 420p. (C). 1991. 49.95 (0-88738-403-X) Transaction Pubs.

Social Psychiatry Across Cultures: Studies from North America, Asia, Europe & Africa. Ed. by Rumi K. Price et al. (Topics in Social Psychiatry Ser.). (Illus.). 226p. 1995. 42.50 (0-306-44971-4, Plenum Pr) Plenum.

***Social Psychiatry & Community Attitudes.** (Technical Report Ser.: No. 177). 42p. 1959. pap. text ed. 3.00 (92-4-120177-0) World Health.

Social Psychiatry & World Accords. Ed. by Jules H. Masserman & Christine M. Masserman. 244p. 1995. 34.95 (0-916147-63-0) Regent Pr.

Social Psychiatry in the Late Twentieth Century: Selected Proceedings - XII World Congress of Social Psychiatry. Ed. by Eliot Sorel et al. LC 92-48296. 1993. pap. write for info. (1-881901-02-5) LEGAS.

Social, Psychological & Situational Factors in Wife Abuse. Kathleen H. Hofeller. Ed. by Robert D. Reed. LC 81-83618. (Illus.). 125p. (C). 1982. spiral bd. 15.95 (0-88247-620-3) R & E Pubs.

Social Psychological Foundations: Readings from the Internationist Perspective. Ed. by Harvey A. Farberman et al. 306p. 1993. pap. 25.75 (1-55938-540-5) Jai Pr.

Social Psychological Foundations for School Services. Ed. by Merl E. Bonney et al. 318p. (C). 1986. 45.95 (0-89885-282-X); pap. 24.95 (0-89885-283-8) Human Sci Pr.

Social-Psychological Perspective on Food-Related Behavior. M. L. Axelson & D. Brinberg. (Recent Research in Psychology Ser.). (Illus.). viii, 190p. 1989. 70.95 (0-387-97095-9) Spr-Verlag.

Social Psychological Study of Widespread Beliefs. Ed. by Colin Fraser & George Gaskell. (Illus.). 256p. 1990. 75.00 (0-19-852134-0) OUP.

Social Psychologists: Research Adventures. Ed. by Gary G. Brannigan & Matther R. Merrins. LC 94-16599. (Social Psychology Ser.). 1994. pap. text ed. write for info. (0-07-007234-5) McGraw.

Social Psychology. 1986. 59.95 (0-387-96246-8) Spr-Verlag.

Social Psychology. Date not set. student ed., pap. text ed. 17.25 (0-314-03708-X) West Pub.

Social Psychology. Ed. by Michael Argyle & Andrew M. Colman. LC 95-18119. (Essential Psychology Ser.). 110p. (C). 1995. pap. text ed. 11.95 (0-582-27804-X, Pub. by Longman UK) Longman.

Social Psychology. Elliot Aronson et al. LC 93-43017. (C). 1994. text ed. 57.50 (0-06-040294-6) Addson-Wesley Educ.

Social Psychology. Elliot Aronson et al. LC 93-43017. (C). 1994. 18.50 (0-06-500618-6) Addson-Wesley Educ.

Social Psychology, 3 vols. Ed. by Elliot Aronson & Anthony R. Pratkanis. (International Library of Critical Writings in Economics Ser.). 1993. Set. 426.95 (1-85278-422-9) E Elgar.

Social Psychology, 3 vols. Ed. by Elliot Aronson & Anthony R. Pratkanis. (International Library of Critical Writings in Business History). 1800p. (C). 1993. 510.00 (0-8147-0609-6) NYU Pr.

Social Psychology, 3 Vols. Brehm. (C). Date not set. suppl. ed., teacher ed., text ed. 59.96 (0-395-76069-0) HM.

Social Psychology, 3 Vols. Brehm. (C). 1995. student ed., pap. 17.96 (0-395-74527-6) HM.

Social Psychology, 3 Vols. Brehm. (C). 1995. suppl. ed., teacher ed., pap. 11.96 (0-395-74526-8) HM.

Social Psychology. Sharon S. Brehm & Saul M. Kassin. (C). 1989. trans. write for info. (0-318-66707-X) HM.

Social Psychology. Marilynn B. Brewer & William D. Crano. Ed. by Schonebaum. LC 93-41156. 625p. (C). 1993. text ed. 54.25 (*0-314-02840-4*) West Pub.
Social Psychology. Byers & Leonard. 1995. pap. text ed. write for info. (*0-205-16147-2*) Allyn.
Social Psychology. Robert S. Feldman. LC 94-17697. 578p. 1994. text ed. 67.00 (*0-13-830514-5*) P-H.
Social Psychology. Donelson R. Forsyth. LC 86-17102. (Psychology Ser.). 651p. (C). 1986. boxed 48.95 (*0-534-06744-1*) Brooks-Cole.
Social Psychology. Stephen L. Franzio. 640p. (C). 1995. text ed. write for info. (*0-697-17472-7*) Brown & Benchmark.
Social Psychology. Stephen L. Franzio. 640p. (C). 1995. student ed., per. write for info. (*0-697-17473-5*) Brown & Benchmark.
***Social Psychology.** Stephen L. Franzoi. 672p. (C). 1997. text ed. write for info. (*0-07-114233-9*) McGraw.
Social Psychology. Irwin A. Horowitz & Kenneth S. Bordens. (C). 1994. vhs write for info. (*0-614-02762-4*) Mayfield Pub.
Social Psychology. Irwin A. Horowitz & Kenneth S. Bordens. LC 94-16772. 793p. (C). 1994. text ed. 55.95 (*0-87484-976-4*, 976) Mayfield Pub.
Social Psychology. Kenrick & Neuberg. 1997. text ed. 66.00 (*0-205-16521-4*) Allyn.
***Social Psychology.** Kenrick & Neuberg. 1997. pap. text ed. 20.00 (*0-205-27426-9*) P-H.
***Social Psychology.** Ed. by Lennon. (C). 1998. text ed. write for info. (*0-321-01152-X*) Addson-Wesley Educ.
Social Psychology. Lord. (C). 1997. pap. text ed. 28.00 (*0-03-019104-1*) HarBrace.
Social Psychology. Charles G. Lord. 738p. (C). 1996. text ed. 60.00 (*0-03-055133-1*) HB Coll Pubs.
Social Psychology. Charles G. Lord. 302p. (C). 1996. student ed., pap. text ed. 20.75 (*0-03-019108-4*) HB Coll Pubs.
Social Psychology. Alan Marks. 194p. 1994. student ed., pap. text ed. 14.95 (*0-87901-749-X*) Worth.
Social Psychology. H. Andrew Michener & John D. DeLamater. (Illus.). 688p. (C). 1993. text ed. 51.00 (*0-15-500760-2*) HB Coll Pubs.
Social Psychology. Nash. Date not set. teacher ed., pap. text ed. write for info. (*0-314-87237-X*) West Pub.
Social Psychology. Regan. 1995. student ed., pap. text ed. 23.00 (*0-13-831330-X*) P-H.
Social Psychology. Leonard M. Saxe. (Illus.). 540p. (C). 1991. text ed. 48.00 (*0-03-021523-4*) HB Coll Pubs.
Social Psychology. Sandra Scarry et al. 168p. (C). 1996. teacher ed., pap. text ed. 28.00 (*0-03-019107-6*) HB Coll Pubs.
Social Psychology. Elliott Smith & Diane Mackie. 645p. 1994. text ed. 61.95 (*0-87901-719-8*) Worth.
***Social Psychology.** Wilder. (Psychology Ser.). (C). Date not set. text ed. 52.95 (*0-534-35457-2*) Brooks-Cole.
Social Psychology. 2nd ed. Elliot Aronson et al. LC 96-2311. (C). 1997. text ed. 57.50 (*0-673-99929-7*) Addson-Wesley Educ.
Social Psychology. 2nd ed. Roger Brown. 720p. (C). 1985. 35.00 (*0-02-908300-1*, Free Press) Free Pr.
***Social Psychology.** 2nd ed. Feldman. LC 97-12803. 1997. text ed. 56.00 (*0-13-660739-X*) P-H.
***Social Psychology.** 2nd ed. Franzoi. 1998. text ed. 41.50 (*0-697-35596-9*) McGraw.
***Social Psychology.** 2nd ed. Franzoi. 1998. student ed., pap. text ed. 12.00 (*0-697-35597-7*) McGraw.
Social Psychology. 2nd ed. H. Andrew Michener et al. 664p. (C). 1990. text ed. 46.75 (*0-15-581446-X*) HB Coll Pubs.
Social Psychology. 2nd ed. Susan Rakowitz. (C). Date not set. suppl. ed., teacher ed., pap. write for info. (*0-393-96668-2*) Norton.
Social Psychology. 2nd ed. John Sabini. (C). 1994. pap. text ed. write for info. (*0-393-96669-0*) Norton.
Social Psychology. 2nd ed. John Sabini. (C). Date not set. text ed. 61.95 (*0-393-96609-7*) Norton.
Social Psychology. 2nd ed. John Sabini. (C). Date not set. suppl. ed., teacher ed., pap. text ed. write for info. (*0-393-96612-7*) Norton.
Social Psychology. 2nd ed. Joseph Sabini. (C). Date not set. student ed., pap. text ed. 19.95 (*0-393-96667-4*) Norton.
***Social Psychology.** 3rd ed. Sharon S. Brehm & Saul M. Kassin. 551p. (C). 1996. text ed. write for info. (*0-395-73630-7*) HM.
Social Psychology. 3rd ed. H. Andrew Michener. (C). 1994. suppl. ed., teacher ed., pap. text ed. 33.75 (*0-15-500764-5*) HB Coll Pubs.
Social Psychology. 4th ed. H. Andrew Michener. (C). 1997. text ed. write for info. (*0-15-504128-2*); teacher ed., pap. text ed. 42.00 (*0-15-504129-0*) HarBrace.
Social Psychology. 4th ed. David G. Myers. LC 92-16358. 1992. Study guide. student ed., pap. text ed. 10.36 (*0-07-044298-3*) McGraw.
Social Psychology. 4th ed. James V. Zanden. 576p. (C). 1986. text ed. write for info. (*0-07-553945-4*) McGraw.
Social Psychology. 5th ed. David G. Myers. LC 95-39693. 1995. text ed. write for info. (*0-07-044377-7*) McGraw.
Social Psychology. 5th ed. David G. Myers. 1995. student ed., pap. text ed. write for info. (*0-07-044360-2*) McGraw.
Social Psychology. 5th ed. Joyce E. Salisbury. 1994. student ed., pap. text ed. write for info. (*0-07-026903-3*) McGraw.
Social Psychology. 5th rev. ed. James A. Wiggins et al. LC 93-27414. 1993. pap. text ed. write for info. (*0-07-066980-5*) McGraw.
Social Psychology. 6th ed. Alfred R. Lindesmith et al. (Illus.). 512p. (C). 1988. text ed. write for info. (*0-13-817990-5*) P-H.
Social Psychology. 8th ed. Baron & Byrne. 1996. student ed., pap. text ed. 19.00 (*0-205-26350-X*) Allyn.
Social Psychology. 8th ed. Robert A. Baron & Donn Byrne. LC 96-2476. 720p. 1996. 65.00 (*0-205-18944-X*) Allyn.
Social Psychology. 9th ed. Taylor & Letitia A. Peplau. LC 96-8786. 656p. (C). 1996. text ed. 66.33 (*0-13-449612-4*) P-H.
***Social Psychology.** 9th ed. Taylor. 1996. student ed., pap. text ed. 22.00 (*0-13-490293-9*) P-H.
Social Psychology. Ed. by Kurt W. Back. LC 76-30835. 512p. reprint ed. pap. 146.00 (*0-317-09548-X*, 2055188) Bks Demand.
Social Psychology. Edward A. Ross. LC 73-14178. (Perspectives in Social Inquiry Ser.). 394p. 1974. reprint ed. 25.95 (*0-405-05521-8*) Ayer.
Social Psychology, Vol. 1. Aronson. (C). 1992. 170.00 (*0-8147-0610-X*) NYU Pr.
Social Psychology, Vol. 2. Aronson. (C). 1992. 170.00 (*0-8147-0611-8*) NYU Pr.
Social Psychology, Vol. 3. Aronson. (C). 1992. 170.00 (*0-8147-0612-6*) NYU Pr.
Social Psychology: A Critical Agenda. Wendy S. Rogers et al. (Illus.). 300p. (C). 1995. text ed. 57.95 (*0-7456-1182-6*, Pub. by Polity Pr UK); pap. text ed. 22.95 (*0-7456-1183-4*, Pub. by Polity Pr UK) Blackwell Pubs.
Social Psychology: An Analysis of Human Behavior. Leonard W. Doob. LC 79-136063. 583p. 1971. reprint ed. text ed. 38.50 (*0-8371-5213-5*, DOSP, Greenwood Pr) Greenwood.
Social Psychology: An Introduction. Michael A. Hogg & Graham M. Vaughan. LC 94-38461. 1995. pap. write for info. (*0-7450-1625-1*) P-H.
Social Psychology: Attitudes, Cognition & Social Behaviour. 2nd ed. J. Richard Eiser. (Illus.). 450p. 1986. text ed. 74.95 (*0-521-32678-8*); pap. text ed. 24.95 (*0-521-33934-0*) Cambridge U Pr.
***Social Psychology: Exploring Universals Across Cultures.** Fathali M. Moghaddam. LC 97-25255. 1997. write for info. (*0-7167-2849-4*, Sci Am Yng Rdrs) W H Freeman.
Social Psychology: Forging Social Identities in a Changing Society. Catherine Campbell. (International Series in Experimental Social Psychology: Vol. 34). 250p. 1995. text ed. 68.01 (*0-08-042401-5*, Pergamon Pr) Elsevier.
Social Psychology: Handbook of Basic Principles. Ed. by E. Tory Higgins & Arie W. Kruglanski. LC 96-22623. 948p. 1996. lib. bdg. 100.00 (*1-57230-100-7*) Guilford Pr.
Social Psychology: Index of Modern Authors & Subjects with Guide for Rapid Research. Salvatore S. Pequeno. LC 90-56329. 160p. 1991. 44.50 (*1-55914-454-8*); pap. 39.50 (*1-55914-455-6*) ABBE Pubs Assn.
Social Psychology: International Edition. Kenneth J. Gergen & Mary M. Gergen. 570p. (C). 1981. International ed. write for info. (*0-318-52938-6*) HB Coll Pubs.
***Social Psychology: Professional.** 2nd ed. Aronson. (C). 1997. pap. text ed. 9.00 (*0-321-40170-0*) Addson-Wesley Educ.
Social Psychology: Shaping Identity, Thought, & Conduct. Michael C. Kearl & Chad Gordon. 608p. (C). 1991. text ed. 72.00 (*0-205-13268-5*) Allyn.
Social Psychology: Society & Self. Jeffrey E. Nash. (Illus.). 425p. (C). 1985. text ed. 52.00 (*0-314-85281-6*) West Pub.
Social Psychology: Sociological Perspectives. Ed. by Morris Rosenberg & Ralph H. Turner. 798p. (C). 1990. pap. 29.95 (*0-88738-854-X*) Transaction Pubs.
Social Psychology: Testbank. Brewer. Date not set. suppl. ed., teacher ed., pap. text ed. write for info. (*0-314-03326-2*) West Pub.
***Social Psychology: The Heart & the Mind.** 2nd ed. Ed. by Aronson. (C). 1997. student ed., pap. text ed. 17.50 (*0-673-99932-7*) Addison-Wesley.
Social Psychology A to Z. Elliott McGinnies. 356p. 1993. pap. text ed. 32.50 (*0-89876-210-3*) Gardner Pr.
Social Psychology Across Culturel: Analysis & Perspectives. Peter Smith. 1993. pap. text ed. 45.00 (*0-205-15326-7*) Allyn.
Social Psychology & Behavioral Medicine. Ed. by J. Richard Eiser. LC 80-42062. (Illus.). 602p. reprint ed. pap. 171.60 (*0-8357-3925-2*, 2036660) Bks Demand.
Social Psychology & Contemporary Society. 2nd ed. Edward E. Sampson. LC 75-30225. (Illus.). 577p. reprint ed. pap. 164.50 (*0-7837-3466-2*, 2057796) Bks Demand.
Social Psychology & Developing Countries. fac. ed. Ed. by Frank Blackler. LC 83-6560. 311p. 1983. reprint ed. pap. 88.70 (*0-7837-8283-7*, 2049065) Bks Demand.
Social Psychology & Dysfunctional Behavior. Mark R. Leary & R. S. Miller. (Social Psychology Ser.). (Illus.). 250p. 1986. 59.00 (*0-387-96325-1*) Spr-Verlag.
Social Psychology & Health. Wolfgang Stroebe & Margaret S. Stroebe. LC 95-3089. (Mapping Social Psychology Ser.). 290p. 1995. pap. 39.95 (*0-534-26004-7*) Brooks-Cole.
***Social Psychology & Health.** Wolfgang Stroebe & Margaret Stroebe. Ed. by Anthony S. Manstead. (Mapping Social Psychology Ser.). 304p. 1994. 42.50 (*0-335-09858-4*, Open Univ Pr); pap. 13.99 (*0-335-09857-6*, Open Univ Pr) Taylor & Francis.
Social Psychology & Health: European Perspectives. D. R. Rutter & Lyn Quine. 232p. 1994. 59.95 (*1-85628-562-6*, Pub. by Avebury Pub UK) Ashgate Pub Co.
Social Psychology & Human Values. M. Brewster Smith. 440p. 1988. reprint ed. text ed. 49.50 (*0-8290-0744-X*) Irvington.
Social Psychology & Organizational Behaviour. Ed. by Michael Gruneberg & Toby Wall. LC 83-19871. (Illus.). 293p. reprint ed. pap. 83.60 (*0-8357-3106-5*, 2039362) Bks Demand.
Social Psychology at the Crossroads: Conference on Social Psychology, University of Oklahoma, 1950. Ed. by John N. Rohrer & Muzafer Sherif. LC 73-111822. (Essay Index Reprint Ser.). 1977. 28.95 (*0-8369-1600-X*) Ayer.
Social Psychology at Work: Essays in Honour of Michael Argyle. Ed. by Peter Collett & Adrian Furnham. LC 94-18905. 304p. (C). (gr. 13). 1995. text ed. 74.95 (*0-415-09754-1*, B4386) Routledge.
Social Psychology: Conflicts & Continuities: An Introduction Textbook. Dennis Howitt et al. 208p. 1989. 80.00 (*0-335-09883-5*, Open Univ Pr); pap. 24.00 (*0-335-09882-7*, Open Univ Pr) Taylor & Francis.
***Social Psychology for Nurses.** write for info. (*0-7131-4577-3*, Pub. by E Arnold UK) Routledge Chapman & Hall.
Social Psychology for Nurses. Abraham. 286p. 1993. pap. 37.50 (*1-56593-552-7*, 0534) Singular Publishing.
Social Psychology for Social Work. Sheila Feld & Norma Radin. LC 81-17061. 544p. 1982. text ed. 39.50 (*0-231-04190-X*) Col U Pr.
Social Psychology in Athletics. Bryant J. Cratty. (Illus.). 320p. 1981. text ed. write for info. (*0-13-817650-7*) P-H.
Social Psychology in Cross-Cultural Perspective. Fathali M. Moghaddam et al. LC 92-23851. (C). 1995. text ed. write for info. (*0-7167-2354-9*); pap. text ed. write for info. (*0-7167-2355-7*) W H Freeman.
Social Psychology in Organizations: Advances in Theory & Research. J. Keith Murnighan. 416p. (C). 1992. text ed. 63.33 (*0-13-374059-5*) P-H.
Social Psychology in the '90s. 6th ed. Kay Deaux et al. 700p. (C). 1993. text ed. 65.95 (*0-534-10398-7*) Brooks-Cole.
Social Psychology in the 90's: Study Guide. 6th ed. Deaux & Dane. (Psychology Ser.). 1993. student ed., pap. 21.95 (*0-534-10400-2*) Brooks-Cole.
Social Psychology, Instructor's Resource Guide. Irwin A. Horowitz & Kenneth S. Bordens. 280p. (C). 1994. teacher ed., pap. text ed. write for info. (*0-87484-977-2*, 977) Mayfield Pub.
Social Psychology of Absenteeism. J. K. Chadwick-Jones & Colin Brown. LC 81-23395. 176p. 1982. text ed. 31.95 (*0-275-90771-6*, C0771, Praeger Pubs) Greenwood.
Social Psychology of Adolescent Delinquency. Nicholas Emler & Stephen Reicher. (Social Psychology & Society Ser.). 240p. (C). 1995. 57.95 (*0-631-13802-1*); pap. 24.95 (*0-631-16823-0*) Blackwell Pubs.
Social Psychology of Aging. Vern L. Bengtson. LC 73-4918. 1973. pap. 3.50 (*0-672-61339-5*, Bobbs) Macmillan.
Social Psychology of Aging. Ed. by Shirlynn Spacapan & Stuart Oskamp. (Claremont Symposium on Applied Social Psychology Ser.). 256p. (C). 1989. text ed. 36.00 (*0-8039-3555-2*); pap. text ed. 16.95 (*0-8039-3556-0*) Sage.
Social Psychology of Aging: A Cognitive Perspective. Michael W. Pratt & Joan E. Norris. (Understanding Aging Ser.). (Illus.). 272p. 1994. pap. 23.95 (*1-55786-492-6*) Blackwell Pubs.
Social Psychology of Clothing. 2nd rev. ed. Susan B. Kaiser. 640p. 1996. 56.00 (*1-56367-107-7*) Fairchild.
Social Psychology of Collective Action. Caroline Kelly & Sara Breinlinger. (European Monographs in Social Psychology Ser.). 224p. 1996. 72.95 (*0-7484-0510-0*); pap. 25.95 (*0-7484-0511-9*) Taylor & Francis.
Social Psychology of Developing Adults. Thomas O. Blank. LC 81-19835. (Wiley Series on Personality Processes). 343p. 1982. reprint ed. pap. 97.80 (*0-7837-2836-0*, 2057636) Bks Demand.
Social Psychology of Education: Current Research & Theory. Ed. by Robert S. Feldman. (Illus.). 375p. 1986. text ed. 74.95 (*0-521-30620-5*) Cambridge U Pr.
Social Psychology of Education: Current Research & Theory. Ed. by Robert S. Feldman. (Illus.). 375p. (C). 1990. pap. text ed. 30.95 (*0-521-39642-5*) Cambridge U Pr.
Social Psychology of Everyday Life. Michael Argyle. 352p. (Orig.). (C). 1992. pap. 18.95 (*0-415-01072-1*, A6660) Routledge.
Social Psychology of Facial Appearance. R. Bull & N. Rumsey. (Social Psychology Ser.). 400p. 1988. 124.95 (*0-387-96607-2*) Spr-Verlag.
Social Psychology of Gender. Shawn M. Burn. LC 95-15698. (Social Psychology Ser.). 1996. pap. text ed. write for info. (*0-07-009182-X*) McGraw.
Social Psychology of Group Cohesiveness: From Attraction to Social Identity. Michael A. Hogg. LC 92-22551. 300p. (C). 1992. 50.00 (*0-8147-3499-5*) NYU Pr.
Social Psychology of Groups. John W. Thibaut & Harold H. Kelley. 334p. 1986. pap. text ed. 24.95 (*0-88738-633-4*) Transaction Pubs.
Social Psychology of Groups: A Reader. Ed. by Edward J. Lawler & Barry Markovsky. LC 93-41124. 277p. 1993. pap. 25.75 (*1-55938-754-8*) Jai Pr.
Social Psychology of Health. Claremont Symposium on Applied Social Psychology Staff. Ed. by Shirlynn Spacapan & Stuart Oskamp. LC 87-35339. 251p. reprint ed. pap. 71.60 (*0-7837-6718-8*, 2046345) Bks Demand.
Social Psychology of Health & Illness. Jerry Suls. LC 82-1465. (Environment & Health Ser.). 368p. 1989. pap. text ed. 39.95 (*0-8058-0554-0*) L Erlbaum Assocs.
Social Psychology of HIV Infection. Ed. by John B. Pryor & Glenn Reeder. 376p. 1993. text ed. 75.00 (*0-8058-0991-0*) L Erlbaum Assocs.
Social Psychology of Identity & the Self Concept. Ed. by Glynis M. Breakwell. (Surrey Seminars in Social Psychology). (Illus.). 271p. 1992. text ed. 89.00 (*0-12-128685-1*) Acad Pr.
Social Psychology of Interaction. Jerold Heiss. (Biology Ser.). 400p. 1981. pap. text ed. write for info. (*0-13-817718-X*) P-H.
Social Psychology of Intergroup & International Conflict Resolution. R. J. Fisher. (Social Psychology Ser.). (Illus.). vii, 277p. 1989. 125.95 (*0-387-97073-8*) Spr-Verlag.
Social Psychology of Intergroup Conflict. Ed. by Wolfgang Stroebe et al. (Social Psychology Ser.). 240p. 1988. 120.00 (*0-387-17695-0*) Spr-Verlag.
Social Psychology of Interpersonal Discrimination. Ed. by Bernice Lott & Diane Maluso. LC 95-2851. 232p. 1995. lib. bdg. 30.00 (*1-57230-021-3*) Guilford Pr.
Social Psychology of Knowledge. Ed. by Daniel Bar-Tal & Arie W. Kruglanski. (Illus.). 425p. 1988. 69.95 (*0-521-32114-X*) Cambridge U Pr.
Social Psychology of Mental Health: Basic Mechanisms & Applications. Ed. by Diane N. Ruble et al. LC 92-1540. 365p. 1992. lib. bdg. 45.00 (*0-89862-136-4*) Guilford Pr.
***Social Psychology of Military Service.** Ed. by Nancy L. Goldman & David R. Segal. LC 76-2111. (Sage Research Progress Series on War, Revolution, & Peacekeeping: Vol. 6). 303p. 1976. reprint ed. pap. 86.40 (*0-608-03380-4*, 2059644) Bks Demand.
Social Psychology of Minority Influence. Gabriel Mugny & Juan A. Perez. Tr. by Vivian E. Lamongie. (European Monographs in Social Psychology). 216p. (C). 1991. 75.00 (*0-521-39054-0*) Cambridge U Pr.
Social Psychology of Modern Japan. Munesuke Mita. (Japanese Studies). 535p. 1993. 59.95 (*0-7103-0451-X*, A9864) Routledge Chapman & Hall.
***Social Psychology of Music.** Ed. by David Hargreaves & Adrian North. (Illus.). 336p. 1997. pap. 36.95 (*0-19-852383-1*) OUP.
***Social Psychology of Music.** Ed. by David Hargreaves & Adrian North. (Illus.). 336p. 1997. 85.00 (*0-19-852384-X*) OUP.
Social Psychology of Nonviolent Action: A Study of Three Satyagrahas. Amrot Nakhre. 1982. 15.00 (*0-8364-0897-7*, Pub. by Chanakya II) S Asia.
Social Psychology of Organizations. 2nd ed. Daniel Katz & Robert L. Kahn. 838p. 1978. Net. text ed. 63.50 (*0-471-02355-8*) Wiley.
Social Psychology of Organizing. 2nd ed. Karl E. Weick. LC 79-10015. (Topics in Social Psychology Ser.). 294p. (C). 1979. pap. text ed. write for info. (*0-07-554808-9*) McGraw.
***Social Psychology of Party Behaviour.** Anna Triandafyllidou. LC 96-43130. (Illus.). 256p. 1997. text ed. 63.95 (*1-85521-893-3*, Pub. by Dartmth Pub UK) Ashgate Pub Co.
Social Psychology of Political & Economic Cognition. Ed. by Glynis M. Breakwell. (Surrey Seminars in Social Psychology). (Illus.). 189p. 1991. text ed. 86.00 (*0-12-128680-0*) Acad Pr.
Social Psychology of Poverty. Annup K. Singh. (C). 1991. text ed. 14.50 (*81-7099-295-8*, Pub. by Mittal II) S Asia.
Social Psychology of Power. Sik Hung Ng. (European Monographs in Social Psychology). 1981. text ed. 124.00 (*0-12-518180-9*) Acad Pr.
Social Psychology of Prejudice. John Duckitt. LC 91-33889. 328p. 1992. text ed. 65.00 (*0-275-94241-4*, C4241, Praeger Pubs) Greenwood.
Social Psychology of Prejudice. John Duckitt. LC 91-33889. 328p. 1994. pap. text ed. 24.95 (*0-275-95099-9*, Praeger Pubs) Greenwood.
Social Psychology of Prejudice: A Systematic Theoretical Review & Propositional Inventory of the American Social Psychological Study of Preujdice. Howard J. Ehrlich. LC 72-10058. 222p. reprint ed. pap. 63.30 (*0-317-10314-8*, 2007633) Bks Demand.
Social Psychology of Procedural Justice. Ed. by E. A. Lind & T. R. Tyler. LC 87-38473. (Critical Issues in Social Justice Ser.). (Illus.). 280p. 1988. 39.50 (*0-306-42726-5*, Plenum Pr) Plenum.
Social Psychology of Protest. Bert Klandermans. (Illus.). 724p. (Orig.). (C). 1997. text ed. 52.95 (*0-631-18878-9*); pap. text ed. 21.95 (*0-631-18879-7*) Blackwell Pubs.
Social Psychology of Science. Ed. by William R. Shadish, Jr. & Steve Fuller. LC 93-18825. (Conduct of Science Ser.). 432p. 1993. lib. bdg. 52.50 (*0-89862-021-X*) Guilford Pr.
Social Psychology of Self-Referent Behavior. Howard B. Kaplan. 205p. 1987. 45.00 (*0-306-42356-1*, Plenum Pr) Plenum.
Social Psychology of Social Movements. Hans Toch. LC 64-66077. 1965. pap. 5.50 (*0-672-60847-2*, Bobbs) Macmillan.
Social Psychology of Sport. Gordon W. Russell. LC 92-34893. 336p. 1994. 43.95 (*0-387-97792-9*) Spr-Verlag.
Social Psychology of Stereotyping & Group Life. Ed. by Russell Spears et al. 288p. (C). 1996. pap. 29.95 (*0-631-19773-7*) Blackwell Pubs.
Social Psychology of Stereotyping & Group Life. Ed. by Russell Spears et al. 288p. (C). 1996. 74.95 (*0-631-19772-9*) Blackwell Pubs.
Social Psychology of Telecommunications. John Short et al. LC 75-44335. (Illus.). 205p. reprint ed. pap. 58.50 (*0-685-20752-8*, 2030393) Bks Demand.
Social Psychology of the Epileptic Child. Christopher Bagley. LC 79-142199. (Illus.). 1971. 15.95 (*0-87024-188-5*) U of Miami Pr.
Social Psychology of the Primary School. Ed. by Roger Colin & Peter Kutnick. 288p. (C). 1992. pap. text ed. 22.95 (*0-415-07197-6*, Routledge NY) Routledge.
Social Psychology of the Self-Concept. Ed. by Morris Rosenberg & Howard B. Kaplan. (Illus.). 576p. (C). 1982. text ed. write for info. (*0-88295-214-5*); pap. text ed. write for info. (*0-88295-215-3*) Harlan Davidson.
Social Psychology of Time: New Perspectives. Ed. by Joseph E. McGrath. (Focus Editions Ser.: Vol. 91). 320p. (C). 1988. text ed. 54.00 (*0-8039-2766-5*); pap. text ed. 24.95 (*0-8039-2767-3*) Sage.

S

An Asterisk (*) at the beginning of an entry indicates that the title is appearing in BIP for the first time.

***Social Psychology of Time: New Perspectives.** Ed. by Joseph E. McGrath. LC 87-37700. (Sage Focus Editions Ser.: Vol. 91). 271p. 1988. reprint ed. pap. 77.30 (*0-608-03009-0*, 2063459) Bks Demand.

Social Psychology of Tourist Behaviour. P. L. Pearce. (International Series in Experimental Social Psychology: Vol. 3). 142p. 1982. 80.00 (*0-08-025794-1*, Pub. by Pergamon Repr UK) Franklin.

Social Psychology of War & Peace. Mark A. May. 1943. 79.50 (*0-686-51314-2*) Elliots Bks.

Social Psychology, Past & Present: An Integrative Orientation. J. M. Jackson. 184p. 1993. pap. 22.50 (*0-8058-1572-4*) L Erlbaum Assocs.

Social Psychology Readings: A Century of Research. A. G. Halberstadt & S. L. Ellyson. 1990. pap. text ed. write for info. (*0-07-025543-1*) McGraw.

Social Psychology, Student Study Guide. Irwin A. Horowitz & Kenneth S. Bordens. (C). 1994. pap. text ed. 16.95 (*0-87484-978-0*, 978) Mayfield Pub.

***Social Psychology Test Bank.** Irwin A. Horowitz. 354p. (Orig.). (C). 1994. pap. text ed. write for info. (*1-55934-564-0*, 1564) Mayfield Pub.

***Social Psychology 97/98.** annuals Mark H. Davis. (Annual Ser.). (Illus.). 256p. (C). 1997. pap. text ed. 11.75 (*0-697-35425-3*) Dushkin Pub.

Social Psychophysiology: A Sourcebook. Ed. by John T. Cacioppo & Richard E. Petty. LC 82-15575. (Illus.). 796p. reprint ed. pap. 180.00 (*0-7837-0688-X*, 2041021) Bks Demand.

***Social Psycology.** 4th ed. Michener. (C). 1997. text ed. write for info. (*0-15-508312-0*) HB Coll Pubs.

Social Purpose & Schooling: Alternatives, Agendas & Issues. Jerry Paquette. 204p. 1991. 60.00 (*1-85000-920-1*, Falmer Pr); pap. 29.00 (*1-85000-921-X*, Falmer Pr) Taylor & Francis.

***Social Quality of Europe.** Wolfgang Beck et al. LC 97-25286. (Studies in Social Policy). 1997. write for info. (*90-411-0456-9*) Kluwer Law Tax Pubs.

Social Quest: The Expanded Vision of Four Women Travellers in the Era of the French Revolution. Sandra Adickes. LC 91-17514. (American University Studies: History: Ser. IX, Vol. 92). 164p. 1991. 35.95 (*0-8204-0657-0*) P Lang Pubng.

Social Questions. David M. Orenstein. Date not set. teacher ed., pap. text ed. write for info. (*0-314-77939-6*) West Pub.

Social Reading of the Old Testament: Prophetic Approaches to Israel's Communal Life. Walter Brueggemann. Ed. by Patrick D. Miller. LC 93-34115. 1994. pap. 18.00 (*0-8006-2734-2*, Fortress Pr) Augsburg Fortress.

Social Realism in the Argentine Narrative. David W. Foster. (Studies in the Romance Languages & Literatures: No. 227). 180p. (Orig.). 1986. pap. 24.95 (*0-8078-9231-9*) U of NC Pr.

Social Realism in the French-Canadian Novel. Ben-Zion Shek. LC 77-379601. 326p. reprint ed. pap. 93.00 (*0-317-30434-8*, 2024929) Bks Demand.

Social Realism in the Novels of John Steinbeck. Rajni Chadha. 1991. text ed. 30.00 (*81-85151-31-8*) Advent Bks Div.

Social Realities & Community Psychiatry. H. Warren Dunham. LC 74-10967. 252p. 1976. 42.95 (*0-87705-215-8*) Human Sci Pr.

***Social Reality.** Finn Collin. LC 96-48387. (Problems of Philosophy Ser.). 232p. (C). 1997. pap. write for info. (*0-415-14797-2*); text ed. write for info. (*0-415-14796-4*) Routledge.

Social Reality: Perspectives & Understanding. Ed. by Janak Pandey. (C). 1988. 19.00 (*81-7022-199-4*, Pub. by Concept II) S Asia.

***Social Reality & Early Christians.** Theissen. 47.95 (*0-567-09618-1*, Pub. by T & T Clark UK) Bks Intl VA.

Social Reality of Clinical Nursing in a Rural Hospital. Alan Pearson. 35p. (C). 1989. pap. 51.00 (*0-7300-0694-8*, NPR803, Pub. by Deakin Univ AT) St Mut.

Social Reality of Death... Kathleen C. Charmaz. (Sociology Ser.). 1980. text ed. write for info. (*0-201-01033-X*) Addison-Wesley.

Social Reconstruction of the Feminine Character. 2nd ed. Sondra Farganis. 320p. (C). 1996. pap. text ed. 21.95 (*0-8476-8019-3*); lib. bdg. 59.50 (*0-8476-8018-5*) Rowman.

Social Reconstruction Through Education: The Philosophy, History & Curricula of a Radical Idea. Susan F. Semel et al. (Social & Policy Issues in Education Ser.). (Illus.). 208p. 1995. text ed. 73.25 (*0-89391-924-1*) Ablex Pub.

Social Reconstruction Through Education: The Philosophy, History & Curricula of a Radical Idea. Susan F. Semel et al. (Social & Policy Issues in Education Ser.). (Illus.). 208p. 1995. pap. 39.50 (*1-56750-145-1*) Ablex Pub.

Social Reference Groups & Political Life. Jeffrey W. Koch. LC 94-48673. 148p. (C). 1995. pap. text ed. 24.50 (*0-8191-9874-9*); lib. bdg. 45.00 (*0-8191-9873-0*) U Pr of Amer.

Social Referencing & the Social Construction of Reality in Infancy. Ed. by Saul Feinman. LC 92-11922. (Illus.). 376p. 1992. 69.50 (*0-306-43850-X*, Plenum Pr) Plenum.

Social Reform & the Church. John R. Commons. LC 66-21663. (Illus.). x, 176p. 1967. reprint ed. 35.00 (*0-678-00286-X*) Kelley.

Social Reform & the Reformation. Jacob S. Schapiro. LC 74-127456. (Columbia University. Studies in the Social Sciences: No. 90). 1970. reprint ed. 34.50 (*0-404-51090-6*) AMS Pr.

Social Reform in Norway. John E. Nordskog. LC 72-13001. 184p. 1973. reprint ed. text ed. 35.00 (*0-8371-6736-1*, NOSR, Greenwood Pr) Greenwood.

Social Reform in the United States Navy, Seventeen Ninety-Eight to Eighteen Sixty-Two. Harold G. Langley. LC 67-10440. (Illus.). 323p. reprint ed. pap. 92.10 (*0-317-08240-X*, 2015037) Bks Demand.

Social Reform in the United States Navy, 1798-1862. Harold D. Langley. LC 67-10440. 323p. reprint ed. pap. 92.10 (*0-7837-5741-7*, 2045402) Bks Demand.

Social Reform Movement in Kerala: An Annotated Bibliography of Source Materials. G. Devarajan. (C). 1990. 16.00 (*0-8364-2642-8*, Pub. by Indian Doc Serv II) S Asia.

Social Reform Movements in India: A Historical Perspective. V. D. Divekar. (C). 1991. 17.50 (*81-7154-561-0*, Pub. by Vintage II) S Asia.

Social Reform, Sexuality, & the State. Ed. by Patricia Uberoi. LC 96-2603. 1996. 45.00 (*0-8039-9305-6*) Sage.

Social Reform to World Wars: Significant Events & the People Who Shaped Them, 8 vols. Joyce Moss & George Wilson. (Profiles in World History Ser.: Vol. 6). 228p. (J). 1995. 34.95 (*0-7876-0470-4*, 6 of 8, UXL) Gale.

Social Reformers in Urban China: The Chinese Y. M. C. A., Eighteen Ninety-Five to Nineteen Twenty-Six. Shirley Garrett. LC 74-133218. (East Asian Monographs: No. 56). 233p. 1970. 24.95 (*0-674-81220-4*) HUP.

Social Reforms in Maharashtra & V. N. Mandlik. Varsha S. Shirgaonkar. (C). 1989. 34.00 (*81-7013-055-7*) S Asia.

Social Register: Facsimile Edition of 1887 Books. 300p. 1986. 25.00 (*0-940281-00-7*) Social Reg Assn.

Social Register: 1995 Edition, 2 vols., Set. 1994. 105.00 (*0-940281-08-2*) Social Reg Assn.

Social Register: 1996 Edition, 2 vols., Set. 1996. 105.00 (*0-940281-09-0*) Social Reg Assn.

Social Regulation: Strategies for Reform. Ed. by Eugene Bardach & Robert A. Kagan. LC 81-85279. 420p. 1982. text ed. 39.95 (*0-917616-47-2*); pap. text ed. 24.95 (*0-917616-46-4*) Transaction Pubs.

Social Regulation in Markets for Consumer Goods & Services. David T. Scheffman & Elie Appelbaum. LC 82-216683. (Ontario Economic Council Research Studies: No. 25). 191p. reprint ed. pap. 54.50 (*0-7837-4285-1*, 2043977) Bks Demand.

Social Relation & Freedom. Benjamin R. Tucker & Thomas S. Robertson. 1980. lib. bdg. 59.95 (*0-8490-3084-6*) Gordon Pr.

Social Relations & Human Attributes. Paul Q. Hirst & Penny Woolley. 1982. pap. 14.95 (*0-422-77230-5*, NO. 3570) Routledge Chapman & Hall.

Social Relations & Ideas. T. H. Aston et al. LC 82-9727. (Past & Present Publications). 352p. 1984. 64.95 (*0-521-25132-X*) Cambridge U Pr.

Social Relations & Social Roles. Florian Znaniecki. (Reprint Series in Sociology). reprint ed. pap. 12.95 (*0-89197-940-9*); reprint ed. lib. bdg. 39.50 (*0-697-00219-5*) Irvington.

Social Relations in a Philippine Town. Robert J. Morais. (Special Reports: No. 19). (Illus.). 151p. (C). 1981. pap. 11.00 (*1-877979-69-4*) SE Asia.

Social Relations in Byron's Eastern Tales. Daniel P. Watkins. LC 85-46014. 1987. 32.50 (*0-8386-3287-4*) Fairleigh Dickinson.

Social Relations in Our Southern States. Daniel R. Hundley. Ed. by William J. Cooper, Jr. LC 78-23811. (Library of Southern Civilization). (Illus.). 1979. pap. text ed. 14.95 (*0-8071-0559-7*) La State U Pr.

Social Relations in Our Southern States. Daniel R. Hundley. LC 72-11344. (American South Ser.). 1973. reprint ed. 31.95 (*0-405-05060-7*) Ayer.

Social Relations in the Near East. 2nd enl. rev. ed. Stuart C Dodd. LC 75-180333. reprint ed. 110.00 (*0-404-56239-6*) AMS Pr.

Social Relations in the Urban Parish. Joseph H. Fichter. LC 54-11207. 272p. reprint ed. pap. 77.60 (*0-317-07856-9*, 2020061) Bks Demand.

Social Relations of Jonson's Theatre. Jonathan Haynes. 160p. (C). 1992. text ed. 59.95 (*0-521-41918-2*) Cambridge U Pr.

Social Relations of Physics, Mysticism & Mathematics. Sal P. Restivo. 318p. 1983. lib. bdg. 133.00 (*90-277-1536-X*, D Reidel) Kluwer Ac.

Social Relations of Physics, Mysticism & Mathematics. Sal P. Restivo. (Pallas Paperbacks Ser.). 308p. 1985. pap. text ed. 49.00 (*90-277-2084-3*, D Reidel) Kluwer Ac.

Social Relationships & Cognitive Development: A Fyssen Foundation Symposium. Robert A. Hinde. Ed. by Joan Stevenson-Hinde & Anne N. Perret-Clermont. (Illus.). 400p. 1986. 65.00 (*0-19-852155-3*); pap. 38.00 (*0-19-852167-7*) OUP.

Social Rented Housing in Europe: Policy Tenure & Design. B. Danermark & I. Elander. 192p. (Orig.). 1994. pap. 47.50 (*90-6275-942-4*, Pub. by Delft U Pr NE) Coronet Bks.

Social Representation & the Social Bases of Knowledge. Ed. by M. Cranach et al. (Illus.). 290p. 1992. pap. text ed. 36.00 (*0-88937-070-2*) Hogrefe & Huber Pubs.

Social Representations & the Development of Knowledge. Ed. by Gerard Duveen & Barbara Lloyd. 232p. (C). 1990. text ed. 59.95 (*0-521-36368-3*) Cambridge U Pr.

Social Representations of Intelligence. Gabriel Mugny & Felice Carugati. (European Monographs in Social Psychology). (Illus.). 225p. (C). 1989. text ed. 74.95 (*0-521-33348-2*) Cambridge U Pr.

Social Reproduction: The Political Economy of the Labour Market. Antonella Picchio. 208p. (C). 1992. text ed. 49.95 (*0-521-41872-0*) Cambridge U Pr.

Social Reproduction & History in Melanesia: Mortuary Ritual, Gift Exchange, & Custom in the Tanga Islands. Robert J. Foster. (Studies in Social & Cultural Anthropology: No. 96). (Illus.). 360p. (C). 1995. pap. text ed. 29.95 (*0-521-48332-8*) Cambridge U Pr.

Social Reproduction & History in Melanesia: Mortuary Ritual, Gift Exchange, & Custom in the Tanga Islands. Robert J. Foster. (Studies in Social & Cultural Anthropology: No. 96). (Illus.). 360p. (C). 1995. text ed. 69.95 (*0-521-48030-2*) Cambridge U Pr.

Social Research: Issues, Methods, & Process. Timothy May. LC 92-43089. 1993. pap. 23.00 (*0-335-19054-5*, Open Univ Pr) Taylor & Francis.

***Social Research: Issues, Methods & Process.** 2nd ed. Tim May. LC 97-20094. 1997. write for info. (*0-335-20006-0*, Open Univ Pr); pap. write for info. (*0-335-20005-2*, Open Univ Pr) Taylor & Francis.

Social Research: Philosophy, Politics & Practice. Martyn Hammersley. 304p. (C). 1993. text ed. 69.95 (*0-8039-8804-4*); pap. text ed. 22.95 (*0-8039-8805-2*) Sage.

Social Research: The Scientific Study of Human Interactions. Morton Hunt. LC 85-60759. (Russell Sage Foundation 75th Anniversary Ser.). 300p. (Orig.). 1986. pap. text ed. 14.95 (*0-87154-394-X*) Russell Sage.

Social Research & the Practicing Professions. Robert Merton. 1982. pap. 19.75 (*0-685-05493-4*); text ed. 30.00 (*0-89011-569-9*) Abt Bks.

Social Research & the Practicing Professions. Robert K. Merton. 300p. 1984. reprint ed. lib. bdg. 59.00 (*0-8191-4111-9*) U Pr of Amer.

Social Research Ethics. Ed. by Martin Bulmer. LC 81-4250. 304p. 1982. pap. 18.95 (*0-8419-0780-3*) Holmes & Meier.

Social Research for Consumers. Earl Babbie. 383p. (C). 1982. text ed. 44.95 (*0-534-01125-X*) Wadsworth Pub.

Social Research in Communication & Law. Ed. by Jeremy Cohen & Timothy Gleason. (CommText Ser.: Vol. 23). 160p. (C). 1990. 37.00 (*0-8039-3266-9*); pap. 16.95 (*0-8039-3267-7*) Sage.

Social Research in Developing Countries: Surveys & Censuses in the Third World. Ed. by Martin Bulmer & Donald P. Warwick. 383p. 1993. pap. 32.50 (*1-85728-137-3*, Pub. by UCL Pr UK) Taylor & Francis.

Social Research in Developing Countries: Surveys & Censuses in the Third World. Ed. by Martin Bulmer & Donald P. Warwick. LC 83-6970. (Social Development in the Third World Ser.). (Illus.). 401p. reprint ed. pap. 114.30 (*0-8357-7524-0*, 2036031) Bks Demand.

Social Research in Puerto Rico: Science, Humanism & Society. Ed. by Ronald J. Duncan. LC 83-12635. 255p. 1984. pap. 8.00 (*0-913480-57-6*) Inter Am U Pr.

Social Research Methods. D. Forcese & S. Richter. (Illus.). 1973. text ed. write for info. (*0-13-818237-X*) P-H.

Social Research Methods. Richard Hessler. Ed. by LaMarre. 400p. (C). 1992. text ed. 56.00 (*0-314-93107-4*) West Pub.

Social Research Methods. 3rd ed. David Dooley. LC 94-6044. 448p. 1994. text ed. 62.00 (*0-13-126161-4*) P-H.

Social Research Methods. 3rd ed. Neuman. 1996. text ed. 58.00 (*0-205-19356-0*) Allyn.

Social Research Methods & Statistics: A Computer-Assisted Introduction. William S. Bainbridge. 573p. (C). 1992. text ed. 60.95 (*0-534-13122-0*) Wadsworth Pub.

Social Research Methods, Feminist Perspectives. Shulamit Reinharz. (Athene Ser.). 1993. text ed. 50.01 (*0-08-032794-X*, Pub. by PPI UK); pap. text ed. 21.01 (*0-08-032793-1*, Pub. by PPI UK) Elsevier.

Social Research on Children & Adolescents: Ethical Issues. Ed. by Barbara Stanley & Joan E. Sieber. (Focus Editions Ser.: Vol. 133). 240p. (C). 1991. 54.00 (*0-8039-4333-4*); pap. 24.95 (*0-8039-4334-2*) Sage.

Social Responses to Handicap. Eda Topliss. LC 81-18602. (Social Policy in Modern Britain Ser.). 198p. reprint ed. pap. 56.50 (*0-685-44028-1*, 2030327) Bks Demand.

Social Responses to Large Technical Systems: Control or Anticipation. Ed. by Todd R. La Porte. (C). 1991. lib. bdg. 113.50 (*0-7923-1192-2*) Kluwer Ac.

Social Responses to Mexico's Economic Crisis of the 1980's. Ed. by Mercedes Gonzalez de la Rocha & Agustin Escobar-Latapi. (U. S. - Mexico Contemporary Perspectives Ser.: No. 1). 242p. 1991. pap. 21.95 (*1-878367-03-X*, CP-01) UCSD Ctr US-Mex.

Social Responses to Technological Change. Ed. by Augustine Brannigan & Sheldon Goldenberg. LC 84-27934. (Contributions in Sociology Ser.: No. 56). (Illus.). xi, 292p. 1985. text ed. 65.00 (*0-313-24727-7*, BNT/, Greenwood Pr) Greenwood.

Social Responsibilities of Business. Morrell Heald. 348p. 1988. 44.94 (*0-88738-231-2*) Transaction Pubs.

Social Responsibilities of Business: Concepts, Areas & Progress. K. M. Mital. (C). 1988. 32.00 (*81-7001-035-7*, Pub. by Chanakya II) S Asia.

Social Responsibilities of Business Corporations. LC 76-168378. 1971. pap. 5.00 (*0-87186-042-2*) Comm Econ Dev.

Social Responsibilities of Lawyers: Case Studies. Lance M. Liebman & Philip B. Heymann. (University Casebook Ser.). 354p. (C). 1988. text ed. 20.95 (*0-88277-645-2*) Foundation Pr.

Social Responsibility: A Selection of Passages for the Study of the Teachings of J. Krishnamurti. Jiddu Krishnamurti. Ed. by Douglas Evans & Frode Steen. 137p. 1992. per. write for info. (*1-888004-03-7*) Krishnamurti.

Social Responsibility & the Business Predicament. Ed. by James D. McKie. LC 74-23967. (Studies in the Regulation of Economic Activity). 361p. 1975. 42.95 (*0-8157-5608-9*); pap. 18.95 (*0-8157-5607-0*) Brookings.

Social Responsibility & the Place of the Artist in Society. Carol Becker. 22p. (C). 1990. pap. text ed. 3.00 (*0-941702-28-6*) Lake View Pr.

Social Responsibility in Farm Leadership. Walter W. Wilcox. LC 75-33001. 194p. 1975. reprint ed. text ed. 49.75 (*0-8371-8494-0*, WISR, Greenwood Pr) Greenwood.

Social Responsibility in Marketing: A Proactive & Profitable Marketing Management Strategy. A. Coskun Samli. LC 92-9810. 224p. 1992. text ed. 49.95 (*0-89930-628-4*, SYJ, Quorum Bks) Greenwood.

Social Responsibility in Marketing: A Selected & Annotated Bibliography. Ernest B. Uhr & Lance P. Jarvis. LC 77-5551. (American Marketing Association Bibliography Ser.: No. 27). 83p. reprint ed. pap. 25.00 (*0-317-39652-8*, 2023351) Bks Demand.

Social Responsibility in Science, Technology, & Medicine. Paul T. Durbin. LC 92-72013. 232p. (C). 1993. 31.50 (*0-934223-27-0*) Lehigh Univ Pr.

Social Responsibility of Gynecology & Obstetrics. Ed. by Allan C. Barnes. LC 65-24793. (Illus.). 224p. reprint ed. pap. 63.90 (*0-317-07931-X*, 2015431) Bks Demand.

Social Responsibility of the Historian. Francois Bedarida. 120p. (C). 1995. pap. 12.95 (*1-57181-896-0*) Berghahn Bks.

Social Responsiveness of Infants. Ed. by Evelyn B. Thoman & Sharland Trotter. (Pediatric Round Table Ser.: No. 2). 75p. 1978. 10.00 (*0-931562-01-5*) J & J Consumer Prods.

Social Revelation: Profound Challenge for Christian Spirituality. James Hug. 64p. (Orig.). 1987. pap. 5.95 (*0-934255-05-9*) Center Concern.

***Social Revolution in Comic Accents: A Modern Translation of Goldoni's Plays by L. Paris Saiko.** Tr. by L. Paris Saiko from ITA. LC 95-95199. (Illus.). xvii, 223p. (Orig.). 1997. pap. 12.00 (*0-9656886-1-5*) Timelight.

Social Revolution in Guatemala: The Carrera Revolt see Applied Enlightenment: Nineteenth Century Liberalism, 1800-1839

Social Revolution in Mexico. E. Ross. 1976. lib. bdg. 59.95 (*0-8490-2618-0*) Gordon Pr.

Social Revolutionaries & Secret Agents: The Carinthian Slovene Partisans & Britain's Special Operations Executive. Thomas M. Barker. (East European Monographs). 272p. 1990. text ed. 60.00 (*0-88033-173-9*) Col U Pr.

Social Revolutionist: Rising Sun Association. Greenville, Ohio, Jan. 1856-Dec. 1857, 23 nos. in 2 vols. (Free Love in America Ser.). 59.50 (*0-404-60979-1*) AMS Pr.

Social Revolutions in the Modern World. Theda Skocpol. (Cambridge Studies in Comparative Politics). 288p. (C). 1994. text ed. 54.95 (*0-521-40088-0*); pap. text ed. 18.95 (*0-521-40938-1*) Cambridge U Pr.

Social Rituals & the Verbal Art of Zora Neale Hurston. Lynda M. Hill. LC 96-14560. 269p. 1996. 29.95 (*0-88258-188-0*) Howard U Pr.

***Social Rituals & the Verbal Art of Zora Neale Hurston.** Lynda M. Hill. LC 96-14560. 1996. pap. 19.95 (*0-88258-189-9*) Howard U Pr.

Social Role of Higher Education: Comparative Perspectives. Ed. by Ken Kempner et al. LC 96-16423. (Studies in Higher Education: Vol. 7). (Illus.). 224p. 1996. text ed. 40.00 (*0-8153-1765-4*, SS0988) Garland.

Social Role of Sport in Caribbean Societies, Vol. 9. Ed. by Michael A. Malec. (Caribbean Studies). 256p. 1995. text ed. 45.00 (*2-88449-134-1*) Gordon & Breach.

Social Role of Sport in Caribbean Societies, Vol. 9. Ed. by Michael A. Malec. (Caribbean Studies). 256p. 1995. pap. text ed. 19.00 (*2-88449-135-X*) Gordon & Breach.

Social Role of the Man of Knowledge. Florian Znaniecki. Ed. by John Stanley. (Social Science Classics Ser.). 216p. 1986. reprint ed. pap. text ed. 24.95 (*0-88738-642-3*) Transaction Pubs.

***Social Role of the University Student.** Date not set. pap. text ed. 18.95 (*0-8385-0607-0*) U of Ill Pr.

Social Roles: Conformity, Conflict, & Creativity. Louis A. Zurcher. LC 83-9548. (Sociological Observations Ser.: No. 15). 395p. 1983. reprint ed. pap. 84.10 (*0-608-01477-X*, 2059521) Bks Demand.

Social Roles & Social Institutions: Essays in Honor of Rose Laub Coser. Ed. by Judith R. Blau & Norman Goodman. 296p. (C). 1994. pap. 24.95 (*1-56000-797-4*) Transaction Pubs.

Social Roots of Religion in Ancient India. Ramendra N. Nandi. 218p. (C). 1987. 22.00 (*81-7074-009-6*) S Asia.

Social Rules: Origin, Character, Logic, Change. Ed. by David Braybrooke. 290p. (C). 1996. text ed. 65.00 (*0-8133-2867-5*) Westview.

Social Safety Net Reexamined: FDR to Reagan. Richard T. McCulley. (Policy Research Project Report: No. 86). 240p. 1992. reprint ed. pap. 12.00 (*0-89940-693-9*) LBJ Sch Pub Aff.

Social Savvy. Judith Re & Meg F. Schneider. (Illus.). 208p. 1992. pap. 11.00 (*0-671-74198-5*, Fireside) S&S Trade.

Social Science: An Introduction to the Study of Society. 9th ed. Elgin F. Hunt & David C. Colander. LC 95-18017. 1995. pap. text ed. 49.00 (*0-205-17431-0*) Allyn.

Social Science Activities of Some Eastern European Academies of Science see Cinema & Social Sciences: A Survey of Ethnographic & Sociological Films

Social Science Agricultural Agendas & Strategies. Ed. by Glenn L. Johnson et al. LC 90-50847. 800p. (C). 1991. text ed. 35.00 (*0-87013-289-X*) Mich St U Pr.

Social Science & Institutional Change. Robert R. Mayer. LC 81-2705. 202p. 1982. text ed. 34.95 (*0-87855-432-7*) Transaction Pubs.

Social Science & Legal Occupations: A Guide to Employment for Economists, market Research Analysts, Psychologists, Sociologists, Urban & Regional Planners, Paralegals, Judges & Lawyers. 1991. lib. bdg. 79.95 (*0-8490-5084-7*) Gordon Pr.

Social Science & Medicine: Seventh International Conference Background Papers. Ed. by Peter J. McEwan. (Journal of Social Science & Medicine Ser.: Vol. 15A, No. 3). 100p. 1981. pap. 18.00 (*0-08-028130-3*, Pergamon Pr) Elsevier.

An Asterisk (*) at the beginning of an entry indicates that the title is appearing in BIP for the first time.

Social Science & National Policy. rev. ed. Ed. by Fred R. Harris. LC 72-87663. 152p. 1973. reprint ed. pap. text ed. 18.95 (*0-87855-544-7*) Transaction Pubs.

Social Science & National Policy. 2nd rev. ed. Ed. by Fred R. Harris. LC 72-87663. 152p. 1973. reprint ed. 29.95 (*0-87855-051-8*) Transaction Pubs.

Social Science & Political Theory. 2nd ed. Walter G. Runciman. LC 69-16286. 208p. reprint ed. pap. 59.30 (*0-317-26386-2*, 2024528) Bks Demand.

Social Science & Social Pathology. Barbara Wootton. Ed. by Vera G. Seal & Rosalind Chambers. LC 78-3616. 400p. 1978. reprint ed. text ed. 35.00 (*0-313-20339-3*, WOSO, Greenwood Pr) Greenwood.

Social Science & Social Policy. Martin Bulmer et al. (Contemporary Social Research Ser.: No. 12). 272p. (C). 1987. text ed. 49.95 (*0-04-312025-3*); pap. text ed. 19.95 (*0-04-312026-1*) Routledge Chapman & Hall.

Social Science & Social Policy. Ed. by R. Lance Shotland & Melvin M. Mark. LC 84-18196. 375p. 1985. reprint ed. pap. 105.50 (*0-608-01479-6*, 2059523) Bks Demand.

Social Science & the Arts Nineteen Eighty-Four: A State-of-the-Arts Review from the Tenth Annual Conference on Social Theory, Politics & the Arts University of Maryland, College Park, October 12-14, 1984. Ed. by John P. Robinson. (Illus.). 190p. (Orig.). 1986. pap. text ed. 20.00 (*0-8191-4926-8*); lib. bdg. 46.00 (*0-8191-4925-X*) U Pr of Amer.

Social Science & the Challenge of Relativism: A Wilderness of Mirrors, on Practices in a Gray Age, 06, 2 vols., Vol. 1. Lawrence E. Hazelrigg. 1989. lib. bdg. 49.95 (*0-8130-0890-5*) U Press Fla.

Social Science & the Challenge of Relativism: Claims of Knowledge, on the Labor of Making Found Worlds, 2 vols., Vol. 2. Lawrence E. Hazelrigg. 1989. lib. bdg. 49.95 (*0-8130-0873-5*) U Press Fla.

Social Science & the Challenge of Relativism Vol. III: Cultures of Nature, an Essay on the Production of Nature. Lawrence E. Hazelrigg. 362p. 1995. lib. bdg. 59.95 (*0-8130-1340-2*) U Press Fla.

Social Science & the Federal Government. Gene M. Lyons & Richard D. Lambert. LC 76-148005. (Annals of the American Academy of Political & Social Science Ser.: No. 394). 1971. 28.00 (*0-87761-137-8*); pap. 18.00 (*0-87761-136-X*) Am Acad Pol Soc Sci.

Social Science & the Self: Personal Essays on an Art Form. Susan Krieger. LC 90-28754. 256p. (C). 1991. text ed. 40.00 (*0-8135-1714-1*); pap. text ed. 16.00 (*0-8135-1715-X*) Rutgers U Pr.

Social Science Approaches to the Judicial Process. J. B. Grossman et al. LC 74-153371. (Symposia on Law & Society Ser.). 1971. reprint ed. lib. bdg. 19.50 (*0-306-70135-9*) Da Capo.

Social Science As Civic Discourse: Essays on the Invention, Legitimation & Uses of Social Theory. Richard H. Brown. 246p. 1989. 33.00 (*0-226-07624-5*) U Ch Pr.

Social Science Aspects of Dress: New Directions. Sharron J. Lennon et al. (ITAA Special Publication: No. 5). 211p. (C). 1993. pap. text ed. 35.00 (*1-885715-01-3*) Intl Textile.

***Social Science Chapters.** O'Hair. Date not set. pap. text ed. write for info. (*0-312-17144-7*) St Martin.

Social-Science Commentary on the Synoptic Gospels. Bruce J. Malina & Richard L. Rohrbaugh. LC 92-359. 432p. 1992. pap. 24.00 (*0-8006-2562-5*, 1-2562, Fortress Pr) Augsburg Fortress.

Social Science Concepts: A Systematic Analysis. Ed. by Giovanni Sartori. LC 83-19280. 455p. 1984. reprint ed. pap. 129.70 (*0-608-01478-8*, 2059522) Bks Demand.

Social Science Encyclopedia. 2nd ed. Adam Kuper & Jessica Kuper. 952p. (C). 1995. text ed. 99.95 (*0-415-10829-2*, Routledge NY) Routledge.

Social Science in Christian Perspective. Ed. by Paul A. Marshall & Robert E. VanderVennen. (Christian Studies Today). 357p. (Orig.). (C). 1988. lib. bdg. 55.00 (*0-8191-7103-4*, Inst Christ Stud) U Pr of Amer.

Social Science in Court: Mobilizing Experts in the School Desegregation Cases. Mark A. Chesler et al. LC 88-6088. 296p. 1988. text ed. 45.00 (*0-299-11620-4*); pap. text ed. 17.50 (*0-299-11624-7*) U of Wis Pr.

Social Science in Law: Cases & Materials. 3rd ed. John Monahan & Laurens Walker. LC 93-32890. (University Casebook Ser.). 609p. 1993. text ed. 40.95 (*1-56662-121-6*) Foundation Pr.

Social Science in Law: Cases & Materials, Revised Teachers Manual To. 2nd ed. John Monahan & Laurens Walker. 52p. (C). 1992. text ed. write for info. (*0-318-69339-9*) Foundation Pr.

Social Science in Southeast Asia: From Particularism to Universalism, Vol. 17. Nico S. Nordholt & Leontine E. Visser. 140p. 1996. pap. 15.00 (*90-5383-427-3*, Pub. by VUB Univ Pr BE) Paul & Co Pubs.

Social Science in the CGIAR: Proceedings of a Meeting of CGIAR Social Scientists Held at the Interanational Service for National Agricultural Research (ISNAR), the Hague, the Netherlands, August 1992. Ed. by Michael P. Collinson & Kerri Platis. (CGIAR Study Paper Ser.: No. 28). 160p. 1994. 9.95 (*0-8213-2798-4*, 12798) World Bank.

Social Science in the Crucible. Mark C. Smith. LC 94-7823. 344p. 1994. text ed. 49.95 (*0-8223-1484-3*); pap. text ed. 15.95 (*0-8223-1497-5*) Duke.

Social Science in the Making: Essays on the Russell Sage Foundation, 1907-1972. David C. Hammack & Stanton Wheeler. LC 94-36035. 176p. 1994. 65.00 (*0-87154-347-8*) Russell Sage.

Social Science Information & Documentation: Search for Relevance in India. Suren Agrowal. 1987. 30.00 (*0-8364-2313-5*, Pub. by Concept II) S Asia.

Social Science Information & Public Policy Making. Robert F. Rich. LC 79-92468. (Jossey-Bass Social & Behavioral Science Ser.). 231p. reprint ed. pap. 65.90 (*0-8357-6888-0*, 2037940) Bks Demand.

Social Science Law. 3rd ed. John Monahan. Date not set. teacher ed., pap. text ed. write for info. (*1-56662-143-7*) Foundation Pr.

Social Science, Law, & Public Policy. Stuart S. Nagel & Lisa A. Bievenue. 344p. (C). 1992. pap. text ed. 32.50 (*0-8191-8429-2*); lib. bdg. 57.50 (*0-8191-8428-4*) U Pr of Amer.

***Social Science Methodology.** Frank Lewins. pap. 16.95 (*0-7329-1331-4*) Paul & Co Pubs.

Social Science Methods in the Legal Process. Noreen L. Channels. LC 84-11527. (Illus.). 286p. 1985. 65.50 (*0-86598-013-6*) Rowman.

***Social Science Microsimulation.** Klaus G. Troitzsch. LC 96-33502. (Illus.). 471p. 1996. 139.00 (*3-540-61572-5*) Spr-Verlag.

Social Science of Play, Games & Sport: Learning Experiences. Glyn C. Roberts et al. LC 79-89695. 110p. reprint ed. pap. 31.40 (*0-317-55492-1*, 2029532) Bks Demand.

Social Science Organization & Policy, First Series: Belgium, Chile, Egypt, Hungary, Nigeria & Sri Lanka. Intro. by Albert B. Cherns. (New Babylon Studies in the Social Sciences: No. 17). 1974. pap. text ed. 30.75 (*90-279-7290-7*) Mouton.

Social Science Perspectives on Citizenship Education. Ed. by Richard E. Gross & Thomas L. Dynneson. 256p. (C). 1990. text ed. 41.00 (*0-8077-3052-1*); pap. text ed. 20.95 (*0-8077-3051-3*) Tchrs Coll.

***Social Science Perspectives on Citizenship Education.** Ed. by Richard E. Gross & Thomas L. Dynneson. LC 90-46620. 257p. pap. 73.30 (*0-608-05097-0*, 2065653) Bks Demand.

Social Science Perspectives on Medical Ethics. Ed. by George Weisz. 312p. (C). 1990. lib. bdg. 106.00 (*0-7923-0566-3*, Pub. by Klwr Acad Pubs NE) Kluwer Ac.

Social Science Perspectives on Medical Ethics. Ed. by George Weisz. LC 90-13026. 320p. (C). 1990. reprint ed. pap. text ed. 19.95 (*0-8122-1349-1*) U of Pa Pr.

***Social Science Projects for ESL.** Bassano. 1993. pap. text ed. 14.83 (*0-8013-0349-4*) Addison-Wesley.

Social Science Quotations. David L. Sills. 437p. 1992. 25.00 (*0-02-897397-6*) Macmillan.

Social Science Quotations: Supplement to the International Encyclopedia of the Social Sciences. Ed. by David L. Sills & Robert K. Merton. 464p. 1991. 110.00 (*0-02-928751-0*, Free Press) Free Pr.

Social Science Quotations: Supplement to the International Encyclopedia of the Social Sciences. Ed. by David L. Sills & Robert K. Merton. 464p. 1991. 110.00 (*0-02-897395-X*) Macmillan.

Social Science Reference Services. Ed. by Pam Baxter. (The Reference Librarian: Vol. 48). 253p. 1995. 39.95 (*1-56024-718-5*) Haworth Pr.

Social Science Reference Sources: A Practical Guide. 2nd enl. rev. ed. Tze-Chung Li. LC 90-2733. 624p. 1990. text ed. 85.00 (*0-313-25539-3*, Greenwood Pr) Greenwood.

Social Science Research. Weis & Michael J. Bucuvalas. 1980. text ed. 55.00 (*0-231-04676-6*) Col U Pr.

Social Science Research: A Cross Section of Journal Articles for Discussion & Evaluation. Ed. by Robert F. Szafran. 293p. (C). 1994. pap. text ed. 22.95 (*0-9623744-8-2*) Pyrczak Pub.

Social Science Research: A Handbook. Gerald S. Ferman & Jack Levin. 144p. 1977. pap. 9.95 (*0-87073-219-6*) Schenkman Bks Inc.

Social Science Research & Climate Change. Robert S. Chen et al. 1983. lib. bdg. 124.50 (*90-277-1490-8*) Kluwer Ac.

Social Science Research & Government: Comparative Essays on Britain & the United States. Ed. by Martin Bulmer. (Illus.). 400p. 1987. text ed. 80.00 (*0-521-32350-9*) Cambridge U Pr.

Social Science Research & Problem of Poverty. Ed. by Tarlok Singh. 1990. 56.00 (*81-7022-231-1*, Pub. by Concept II) S Asia.

Social Science Research for Agricultural Technology Development: Spatial & Temporal Dimensions. Ed. by Karen A. Dvorak. 260p. 1993. 75.00 (*0-85198-806-7*) CAB Intl.

***Social Science Research Methods.** Gordon Diem. 172p. (C). 1996. pap. text ed. 22.95 (*1-56226-345-5*) CT Pub.

Social Science Research on Higher Education & Universities, 3 pts. Incl. Pt. 1. Trend Report. Walter Weller. 1973. text ed. 30.40 (*90-279-7254-0*); Pt. 2. Annotated Bibliography. Wolfgang Nitsch. Ed. by Dietrich Goldschmidt. 1970. text ed. 88.50 (*90-279-6870-5*); 1973. write for info. (*0-318-54406-7*) Mouton.

***Social Science, Technical Systems & Cooperative Work: The Great Divide.** Ed. by Geoffrey Bowker et al. LC 96-40366. (Computers, Cognition, & Work Ser.). 412p. 1997. write for info. (*0-8058-2402-2*); pap. write for info. (*0-8058-2403-0*) L Erlbaum Assocs.

Social Science Tests & Reviews. Ed. by Oscar K. Buros. LC 75-8115. xxiii, 227p. 1975. 35.00 (*0-910674-22-1*) U of Nebr Pr.

Social Science Theory: Structure & Application. Herbert I. London. 375p. 1989. pap. text ed. 24.95 (*0-88738-774-8*) Transaction Pubs.

Social Sciences: A Cross-Disciplinary Guide to Selected Sources. 2nd ed. Ed. by Nancy L. Herron. LC 95-26359. (Library Science Text Ser.). 400p. 1996. lib. bdg. 43.00 (*1-56308-309-4*) Libs Unl.

Social Sciences: A Cross-Disciplinary Guide to Selected Sources. 2nd ed. Ed. by Nancy L. Herron. LC 95-26359. (Library Science Text Ser.). 400p. 1996. pap. text ed. 32.00 (*1-56308-351-5*) Libs Unl.

Social Sciences: An International Bibliography of Serial Literature, 1830-1985. Jan Wepsiec. 496p. 1992. text ed. 130.00 (*0-7201-2109-4*, Mansell Pub) Cassell.

Social Sciences see Comprehensive Dissertation Index 1861-1972

Social Sciences - Area Examination. Jack Rudman. (Graduate Record Examination Ser.: GRE-44). 1994. pap. 23.95 (*0-8373-5244-4*) Nat Learn.

Social Sciences & History. Jack Rudman. (College-Level Examination Series (General Examinations): ATS-9E). 1994. pap. 23.95 (*0-8373-5249-5*) Nat Learn.

Social Sciences & Humanities see Comprehensive Dissertation Index, 1988: Supplement

Social Sciences & Humanities see Comprehensive Dissertation Index, 1989: Supplement

Social Sciences & Humanities Index, Vols. 1968-69 to 1973-74. LC 17-4969. 1974. 126.00 (*0-685-22255-1*) Wilson.

Social Sciences & International Agricultural Research: Lessons from the CRSPs. Ed. by Constance M. McCorkle. LC 89-32083. 300p. 1989. lib. bdg. 44.00 (*1-55587-133-X*) Lynne Rienner.

Social Sciences & Modern States: National Experiences & Theoretical Crossroads. Ed. by Peter Wagner et al. (Advances in Political Science Ser.). (Illus.). 384p. (C). 1991. text ed. 65.00 (*0-521-38198-3*) Cambridge U Pr.

Social Sciences & New Testament Interpretation. Richard L. Rohrbaugh. 330p. (C). 1996. 19.95 (*1-56563-239-7*) Hendrickson MA.

***Social Sciences & the Churches.** Mitton. pap. 14.95 (*0-567-22305-1*, Pub. by T & T Clark UK) Bks Intl VA.

Social Sciences & the Government: The Asian Scene. Igbal Narain & Yogesh Atal. (C). 1987. 20.00 (*81-7062-032-5*, Pub. by Lancer II) S Asia.

Social Sciences & Their Interrelations. William F. Ogburn & Alexander Goldenweiser. LC 73-14173. (Perspectives in Social Inquiry Ser.). 518p. 1974. reprint ed. 33.95 (*0-405-05516-1*) Ayer.

Social Sciences at Harvard, 1860-1920: From Inculcation to the Open Mind. Robert L. Church et al. Ed. by Paul H. Buck. LC 65-22059. 336p. 1965. reprint ed. pap. 95.80 (*0-7837-4451-X*, 2057981) Bks Demand.

Social Sciences at Mid-Century. Minnesota University, Graduate School Staff. LC 68-55852. (Essay Index Reprint Ser.). 1977. 17.95 (*0-8369-0710-8*) Ayer.

Social Sciences in Secondary Schools see Survey on the Ways in Which States Interpret Their International Obligations

Social Sciences Index, 1974-89. write for info. (*0-318-56462-9*) Wilson.

Social Sciences Index, 1974-89, Vol. 19. 225.00 (*0-685-05425-X*) Wilson.

Social Sciences, Problems & Orientations: Selected Studies. (Studies in Behavioral Sciences: No. 4). 1968. text ed. 34.75 (*90-279-6026-7*) Mouton.

Social Sciences Research & Women in the Arab World. UNESCO Staff. 1992. text ed. 49.00 (*0-86187-387-4*) St Martin.

Social Sciences since the Second World War. Daniel Bell. LC 80-27957. 104p. (C). 1981. reprint ed. 32.95 (*0-87855-426-2*); reprint ed. pap. text ed. 21.95 (*0-87855-872-1*) Transaction Pubs.

Social Sciences Today. Ed. by Robert M. Hutchins & Mortimer J. Adler. LC 75-4299. (Great Ideas Anthologies Ser.). (Illus.). 618p. 1977. 23.95 (*0-405-07171-X*) Ayer.

Social Scientist As Innovator. Michael Young. (Illus.). 282p. 1984. reprint ed. lib. bdg. 58.50 (*0-8191-4084-8*) U Pr of Amer.

Social Scientists & Politics in Canada. Stephen Brooks & Alain G. Gagnon. 168p. (C). 1988. text ed. 49.95 (*0-7735-0663-2*, Pub. by McGill CN) U of Toronto Pr.

Social Scientists & the Physically Handicapped: An Original Anthology. Ed. by William R. Phillips & Janet Rosenberg. LC 79-6011. (Physically Handicapped in Society Ser.). 1980. lib. bdg. 35.95 (*0-405-13103-8*) Ayer.

Social Scientist's Bestiary: A Guide to Fabled Threats to, & Defences of, Naturalistic Social Science. D. C. Phillips. LC 92-21654. 280p. 1992. 42.95 (*0-08-040254-2*, Prgamon Press) Buttrwrth-Heinemann.

Social Scientists Meet the Media. Ed. by Cheryl Haslam & Alan Bryman. LC 93-24572. 256p. (C). 1994. pap. 18.95 (*0-415-08191-2*, Routledge NY) Routledge.

Social Scientists Meet the Media. Ed. by Cheryl Haslam & Alan Bryman. LC 93-24572. 256p. (C). (gr. 13). 1994. text ed. 62.95 (*0-415-08190-4*, Routledge NY) Routledge.

Social Scientists, Policy & the State. Stephen Brooks & Alain G. Gagnon. LC 89-22771. 193p. 1990. text ed. 55.00 (*0-275-93449-7*, C3449, Greenwood Pr) Greenwood.

Social Secretary. David G. Phillips. (Illus.). 1972. reprint ed. lib. bdg. 29.00 (*0-8422-8169-X*) Irvington.

Social Secretary. David G. Phillips. (Illus.). 1982. reprint ed. pap. text ed. 5.95 (*0-8290-1160-9*) Irvington.

Social Security. Peter G. Peterson. 19.95 (*0-394-53318-6*) Random.

Social Security. 2nd ed. Myers. (C). 1981. 44.95 (*0-256-02585-1*) Irwin Prof Pubng.

Social Security. 4th ed. Robert J. Myers. LC 92-30848. (Pension Research Council Publications). (Illus.). 968p. (C). 1993. text ed. 62.95 (*0-8122-3191-0*) U of Pa Pr.

***Social Security: A Commitment Worth Keeping: Ensuring a Healthy Social Security System for America: A Statement on National Policy.** Committee for Economic Development Staff. LC 96-40029. 1997. write for info. (*0-87186-124-0*) Comm Econ Dev.

Social Security: A Cross-Cultural Perspective. Robert P. Scheurell. (Orig.). 1993. pap. 15.00 (*0-944285-36-8*) Pol Studies.

Social Security: A Workers' Education Guide. International Labour Office Staff. (Illus.). 103p. 1992. pap. 13.50 (*92-2-108004-8*) Intl Labour Office.

Social Security: An Idea Whose Time Has Passed. 2nd ed. Helen P. Rogers. LC 85-51900. (Illus.). 150p. 1986. pap. 6.95 (*0-915915-04-9*) Wellington Pubns.

Social Security: Beyond the Rhetoric of Crisis. Ed. by Theodore R. Marmor & Jerry L. Mashaw. (Studies from the Project on the Federal Social Role). 272p. 1988. pap. text ed. 15.95 (*0-691-02285-2*) Princeton U Pr.

***Social Security: Disability Rolls Keep Growing, While Explanations Remain Elusive.** Ed. by Barry D. Tice et al. (Illus.). 56p. 1997. reprint ed. pap. text ed. 30.00 (*0-7881-4113-9*) DIANE Pub.

Social Security: How Social? How Secure? Ed. by Felicitas Hinman & Erin-Aine Miller. (Policy & Practice Publication). 108p. 1978. 5.00 (*0-89215-087-4*) U Cal LA Indus Rel.

Social Security: Index of Modern Information. rev. ed. Nicholas E. Grisholme. LC 88-47623. 150p. 1991. 44.50 (*1-55914-498-X*); pap. 39.50 (*1-55914-499-8*) ABBE Pubs Assn.

***Social Security: Inequality & the Third World.** James Midgley. LC 84-5188. (Social Development in the Third World Ser.). 235p. reprint ed. pap. 67.00 (*0-608-05265-5*, 2065803) Bks Demand.

Social Security: Lies, Myths & Reality: The Truth about Social Security, the Trust Funds & the National Debt. James Turk. (Illus.). 144p. (Orig.). (C). 1992. pap. 12.95 (*0-9615576-1-3*) Greenfield Bks.

Social Security: Perspectives on Preserving the System. Sylvester J. Schieber & Dallas L. Salisbury. LC 82-21046. (Illus.). 338p. (Orig.). 1982. 29.95 (*0-86643-029-6*); pap. 15.00 (*0-86643-028-8*) Empl Benefit Res Inst.

Social Security: Policy for the Seventies: Proceedings of the Social Security Conference, 7th. Social Security Conference Staff. Ed. by Philip Booth. LC 73-82218. 229p. 1973. 10.50 (*0-87736-319-6*) U of Mich Inst Labor.

Social Security: Promise & Reality. Rita Ricardo-Campbell. LC 77-83830. (Publication Ser.: No. 179). 351p. 1977. 6.38 (*0-8179-6791-5*) Hoover Inst Pr.

Social Security: Prospects for Real Reform. Ed. by Peter J. Ferrara. LC 85-9642. 228p. 1985. 5.00 (*0-932790-45-3*); pap. 3.00 (*0-932790-48-8*) Cato Inst.

Social Security: The Inherent Contradiction. Peter J. Ferrara. LC 80-18949. (Policy Bks.: No. 1). 484p. 1980. 5.00 (*0-932790-24-0*) Cato Inst.

***Social Security: The Inside Story.** 2nd rev. ed. Andrew Landis. (Professional Ser.). 250p. 1997. pap. 14.95 (*1-56052-452-9*) Crisp Pubns.

Social Security: Visions & Revisions. W. Andrew Achenbaum. LC 86-4145. (Twentieth Century Fund Study Ser.). 256p. 1986. text ed. 59.95 (*0-521-32866-7*) Cambridge U Pr.

Social Security: Visions & Revisions. W. Andrew Achenbaum. LC 86-4145. (Twentieth Century Fund Study Ser.). 256p. 1988. pap. text ed. 19.95 (*0-521-35766-7*) Cambridge U Pr.

Social Security: What Every Taxpayer Should Know. A. Haeworth Robertson. LC 92-80166. (Illus.). 352p. 1992. 40.00 (*0-9632345-4-4*) Retire Policy.

Social Security: What Every Taxpayer Should Know. A. Haeworth Robertson. 352p. 1992. pap. 14.95 (*0-9632345-5-2*) Retire Policy.

Social Security: What Role for the Future? Ed. by Peter Diamond et al. LC 95-41812. 1996. write for info. (*0-8157-1836-5*) Natl Acad.

Social Security: What Role for the Future? Ed. by Peter A. Diamond et al. LC 95-41812. 233p. 1996. pap. 19.95 (*0-8157-1835-7*) Brookings.

Social Security Act - Annotations. Welfare Rights Centre Staff & Peter Sutherland. 1992. pap. 68.00 (*1-86287-081-0*, Pub. by Federation Pr AU) Gaunt.

Social Security Administration's Decentralized Computer Strategy: Issues & Options. 1995. lib. bdg. 256.75 (*0-8490-7443-6*) Gordon Pr.

Social Security after Fifty: Successes & Failures. Ed. by Edward D. Berkowitz. LC 86-19383. (Studies in Social Welfare Policies & Programs: No. 5). 176p. 1987. text ed. 45.00 (*0-313-25542-3*, BZS/, Greenwood Pr) Greenwood.

Social Security & Individual Equity: Evolving Standards of Equity & Adequacy. Charles W. Meyer & Nancy Wolff. LC 92-25739. (Studies in Social Welfare Policies & Programs: No. 15). 208p. 1993. text ed. 49.95 (*0-313-26459-7*, MYC, Greenwood Pr) Greenwood.

Social Security & Medicare: A Policy Primer. Eric R. Kingson & Edward D. Berkowitz. LC 92-43384. 232p. 1993. text ed. 62.95 (*0-86569-200-9*, T200, Auburn Hse); pap. text ed. 18.95 (*0-86569-201-7*, R201, Auburn Hse) Greenwood.

Social Security & Medicare Answer Book. 1995. 106.00 (*1-56706-132-X*) Aspen Pub.

Social Security & Medicare with Medigap: Approved 1990 Guide to Your Benefits, What They Are - How to Get Them. Wm. J. Williams. LC 90-81879. 130p. (Orig.). 1990. 15.95 (*0-9626952-1-1*); pap. 10.95 (*0-9626952-0-3*) Gamala Pub Co.

Social Security & National Policy: Sweden, Yugoslavia, Japan. David E. Woodsworth. LC 77-371640. 168p. reprint ed. pap. 47.90 (*0-317-27200-4*, 2023862) Bks Demand.

Social Security & Private Pension Plans: Competitive or Complementary? Ed. by Dan M. McGill. 200p. (C). 1977. text ed. 20.95 (*0-256-01968-1*, U of Pa Pr) Irwin.

Social Security & Privatization Vol. I: Possible with "Mediscare" out of the Way. Rick Henderson. 10p. (Orig.). 1996. 10.00 (*1-886306-19-2*) Nevada Policy.

S

Social Security & Public Policy. Eveline M. Burns. LC 75-17211. (Social Problems & Social Policy Ser.). 1976. reprint ed. 23.95 (*0-405-07483-2*) Ayer.

Social Security & SSI. Bill McKee. 65p. pap. 6.25 (*0-685-23169-0*, 41,575S) NCLS Inc.

Social Security & the Budget: Proceedings of the First Conference of the National Academy of Social Insurance December 15th & 16th, 1988, Washington, D.C. Ed. by Henry J. Aaron. LC 89-22570. (Illus.). 160p. (Orig.). (C). 1990. pap. text ed. 22.50 (*0-8191-7602-8*); lib. bdg. 44.50 (*0-8191-7601-X*) U Pr of Amer.

Social Security & the Weaker Sections. Sobha B. Nair. 1990. 17.50 (*81-85199-38-8*, Pub. by Renaiss Publng Hse II) S Asia.

Social Security Applications: A Genealogical Resource. rev. ed. Desmond W. Allen & Carolyn E. Billingsley. (Illus.). 18p. 1995. pap. 5.95 (*1-56546-069-3*) Arkansas Res.

Social Security at the Crossroads: Public Opinion & Public Policy. Charles M. Brain. LC 91-5097. (Studies on Elderly in America). 320p. 1991. text ed. 76.00 (*0-8153-0511-7*) Garland.

Social Security Benefits - A Guide to Accessing Services for Persons with Traumatic Brain Injury. Ed. by Linda J. Courtney. 40p. 1994. pap. 6.50 (*1-882855-28-0*) HDI Pubs.

Social Security Benefits Handbook. Stanley A. Tomkiel, III. LC 96-67021. 212p. (Orig.). 1996. pap. 14.95 (*1-57248-033-5*, Leg Surv Guides) Sourcebks.

Social Security Benefits, 1993: Including Medicare January 1, 1993. 48p. 1993. pap. 4.00 (*0-685-67161-5*, 4709) Commerce.

Social Security Case Law, Digest of Commissioners' Decisions (Neligan) & Supples Supplement 28. 60p. 1995. pap. text ed. 25.00 (*0-11-762354-7*, HM23547, Pub. by Stationery Ofc UK) Bernan Associates.

Social Security Claims & Procedure, Vol. 1. 4th ed. Harvey L. McCormick. 549p. 1991. pap. write for info. (*0-318-67297-9*) West Pub.

Social Security Claims & Procedure, Vol. 2. 4th ed. Harvey L. McCormick. 706p. 1991. pap. write for info. (*0-318-67298-7*) West Pub.

Social Security Claims & Procedure, Vols. 1 & 2. 4th ed. Harvey L. McCormick. 1991. text ed. write for info. (*0-314-77340-1*) West Pub.

Social Security Contributions as a Fiscal Burden on Enterprises Engaged in International Activities. Ed. by International Fiscal Association Staff. 1984. 91.00 (*90-6544-175-1*) Kluwer Law Tax Pubs.

Social Security Disability. Charles T. Hall. 529p. (C). 1993. pap. text ed. write for info. (*0-314-02423-9*) West Pub.

Social Security Disability: A Comprehensive & Practical Guide to the Effective Representation of Claimants. William R. LaVere. 1995. write for info. (*1-877663-01-8*) Bydand.

Social Security Disability: A Comprehensive & Practical Guide to the Effective Representation of Claimants. 3rd ed. William R. LaVere. 357p. 1994. ring bd. 125.00 (*1-886335-00-1*) Bydand.

***Social Security Disability: Alternatives Would Boost Cost-Effectiveness of Continuing Disability Reviews.** Robert L. MacLafferty et al. (Illus.). 112p. (Orig.). (C). 1997. pap. text ed. 40.00 (*0-7881-4053-1*) DIANE Pub.

***Social Security Disability: Backlog Reduction Efforts under Way; Significant Challenges Remain.** (Illus.). 51p. (Orig.). (C). 1996. pap. 25.00 (*0-7881-3600-3*) DIANE Pub.

***Social Security Disability: Improvements Needed to Continuing Disability Review Process.** Robert L. MacLafferty et al. (Illus.). 112p. (Orig.). (C). 1997. pap. text ed. 40.00 (*0-7881-4050-7*) DIANE Pub.

Social Security, Disability & Rehabilitation: Conflicts in the Development of Social Policy 1914-1946. Helen Bolderson. 280p. 1991. 79.00 (*1-85302-517-8*) Taylor & Francis.

Social Security Disability Benefits: How to Get Them! How to Keep Them! rev. ed. James W. Ross. 104p. 1984. 29.95 (*0-9615202-6-4*); pap. 19.95 (*0-9615202-5-6*) Ross Pub Co.

Social Security Disability Claims, 2 vols. Ronald R. Gilbert & J. Douglas Peters. LC 82-84688. 1982. ring bd. 210.00 (*0-685-59859-4*) Clark Boardman Callaghan.

Social Security Disability Claims. North Carolina Bar Association Foundation Staff & Steven F. Blalock. 1983. write for info. (*0-318-58303-8*) NC Bar Found.

Social Security Disability Claims, 3 vols., Set. 2nd ed. Barbara Samuels. LC 94-69740. 1994. ring bd. 375.00 (*0-317-12004-2*) Clark Boardman Callaghan.

Social Security Disability Law & Procedure in Federal Court. Carolyn A. Kubitschek. LC 93-74199. 1994. 125.00 (*0-614-07298-0*) Clark Boardman Callaghan.

Social Security Disability Practice: 1995 Edition. Charles T. Hall. (West's Handbook Ser.). 560p. (C). 1995. pap. text ed. write for info. (*0-314-06543-1*) West Pub.

Social Security Disability Practice, 1994. Charles T. Hall. (Handbook Ser.). 625p. 1994. pap. text ed. write for info. (*0-314-04376-4*) West Pub.

Social Security Disability Practice, 1996 Edition. Charles T. Hall. (West's Handbook Ser.). 590p. 1996. pap. text ed. write for info. (*0-314-09749-X*) West Pub.

***Social Security Disability Practice 1997.** Charles T. Hall. (Handbook Ser.). 486p. 1997. pap. text ed. write for info. (*0-314-20463-6*) West Pub.

Social Security Disability Training Manual. Linda Christ. 511p. 1986. 35.00 (*0-685-23190-9*, 41,875) NCLS Inc.

Social Security Explained, 1997. 320p. 1997. pap. 26.00 (*0-685-67162-3*, 5418) Commerce.

Social Security Financing. Ed. by Felicity Skidmore. 312p. 1981. 45.00 (*0-262-19196-2*) MIT Pr.

Social Security for Young People. Neville Harris. 216p. 1989. text ed. 59.95 (*0-566-07029-4*, Pub. by Avebury Pub UK) Ashgate Pub Co.

Social Security Fraud. 2nd ed. Abraham Ellis. LC 96-84490. 211p. 1996. pap. 14.95 (*1-57246-053-9*) Foun Econ Ed.

Social Security Handbook. 1984. lib. bdg. 300.00 (*0-87700-535-4*) Revisionist Pr.

***Social Security Handbook.** 1997. lib. bdg. 300.00 (*0-8490-6071-0*) Gordon Pr.

Social Security Handbook. U. S. Dept. HHS Staff. 1993. pap. 20.00 (*0-87511-630-2*) Claitors.

***Social Security Handbook '95.** U. S. Department of HHS Staff. 1995. pap. 28.00 (*0-614-30815-1*, USO95P) Claitors.

Social Security in America. Philip Booth. LC 73-620091. (Policy Papers in Human Resources & Industrial Relations Ser.: No. 19). 180p. 1973. 10.00 (*0-87736-119-3*); pap. 5.00 (*0-87736-120-7*) U of Mich Inst Labor.

Social Security in Australia. Terry Carney & Peter Hanks. 360p. 1994. pap. 45.00 (*0-19-553562-6*) OUP.

Social Security in Britain: A History-A Greenwood Archival Edition. 2nd ed. Harold E. Raynes. LC 76-40057. 264p. 1977. reprint ed. text ed. 79.50 (*0-8371-9055-X*, RASSB, Greenwood Pr) Greenwood.

Social Security in Developing Countries. Ed. by Ehtisham Ahmad et al. (WIDER Studies in Development Economics). 496p. 1991. 105.00 (*0-19-823300-0*) OUP.

Social Security in Developing Countries: Operation & Dynamics of Social Security Mechanisms in Rural Swaziland. A. Leliveld. (Tinbergen Institute Research Ser.: No. 85). 442p. 1994. pap. 33.00 (*90-5170-305-8*, Pub. by Thesis Pubs NE) IBD Ltd.

Social Security in Europe: Development or Dismantlement? Niels Ploug & Jon Kvist. LC 95-45764. (Kluwer SOVAC Series on Social Security: No. 3). 100p. 1996. pap. 42.00 (*90-411-0160-8*) Kluwer Law Tax Pubs.

Social Security in Europe: Miscellanea of the Erasmus Programme of Studies Relating to Social Security in the European Communities. Ed. by Danny Pieters. 295p. 1991. pap. 93.00 (*90-6215-284-8*, Pub. by Maklu Uitgevers BE) Gaunt.

Social Security in International Perspective: Essays in Honor of Eveline M. Burns. Shirley Jenkins. LC 71-94628. (Social Work & Social Issues Ser.). 255p. 1969. text ed. 60.00 (*0-231-03294-3*) Col U Pr.

Social Security in Latin America: Pressure Groups, Stratification, & Inequality. Carmelo Mesa-Lago. LC 77-15732. (Pitt Latin American Ser.). 372p. reprint ed. pap. 106.10 (*0-7837-2474-8*, 2042628) Bks Demand.

Social Security in the Netherlands. Ministry of Social Affairs & Employment Staff. 192p. 1990. pap. 24.00 (*90-6544-493-9*) Kluwer Law Tax Pubs.

Social Security in the United Kingdom: Contracting Out of the System. John C. Goodman. LC 81-10927. (AEI Studies: No. 335). (Illus.). 80p. reprint ed. pap. 25.00 (*0-8357-4704-2*, 2037415) Bks Demand.

Social Security in the United States: An Analysis & Appraisal of the Federal Social Security Act. 2nd ed. Paul H. Douglas. LC 70-167847. (FDR & the Era of the New Deal Ser.). 1971. reprint ed. lib. bdg. 55.00 (*0-306-70323-8*) Da Capo.

Social Security in the United States: An Analysis & Appraisal of the Federal Social Security Act. Paul H. Douglas. LC 71-137164. (Poverty U. S. A. Historical Record Ser.). 1980. reprint ed. 23.95 (*0-405-03102-5*) Ayer.

Social Security in the 21st Century. Ed. by Eric R. Kingson & James H. Schulz. (Illus.). 336p. (C). 1996. text ed. 63.00 (*0-19-510424-2*); pap. text ed. 24.95 (*0-19-510425-0*) OUP.

Social Security Law. Ed. by Jef Van Langendonck. 1992. ring bd. write for info. (*0-318-68485-3*) Kluwer Law Tax Pubs.

Social Security Law & Practice, 9 vols. LC 86-82947. 1987. ring bd. 1,250.00 (*0-685-59857-8*) Clark Boardman Callaghan.

Social Security Law in Britain & Ireland: A Bibliography. M. Partington & Patrick O'Higgins. 446p. 1986. text ed. 120.00 (*0-7201-1794-1*, Mansell Pub) Cassell.

Social Security Laws, 3 vols., Set. 1994. lib. bdg. 1,555.95 (*0-8490-9051-2*) Gordon Pr.

Social Security Manual 1996. National Underwriters Staff. 1996. pap. text ed. 18.50 (*0-87218-155-3*) Natl Underwriter.

Social Security, Medicare & Pensions. large type ed. Joseph L. Matthews. 288p. 1991. lib. bdg. 14.95 (*1-56054-989-0*) Thorndike Pr.

Social Security, Medicare, & Pensions. 6th ed. Joseph L. Matthews & Dorothy M. Berman. 1996. pap. 19.95 (*0-87337-289-1*) Nolo Pr.

***Social Security, Medicare & Pensions: Get the Most Out of Your Retirement & Medical Benefits.** 6th large type ed. Joseph L. Matthews et al. LC 96-38562. 1997. pap. 20.00 (*0-7838-1984-6*) G K Hall.

***Social Security, Medicare & Pensions: Get the Most Out of Your Retirement & Medical Benefits.** 6th large type ed. Joseph L. Matthews et al. LC 96-38562. (Spec-Hall Ser.). 651p. 1996. lib. bdg. 25.95 (*0-7838-1983-8*, GK Hall) Thorndike Pr.

***Social Security, Medicare, Welfare Are Unconstitutional.** Max. 50p. (Orig.). 1997. pap. 30.00 (*0-922070-80-6*) M Tecton Pub.

Social Security Number Guide. 3rd ed. National Employment Screening Services Staff. 16p. reprint ed. write for info. (*0-318-69321-6*) Source Okla.

Social Security, Pensions & Medicare: A Guide for Those 55 & Over. 1992. lib. bdg. 300.00 (*0-8490-5286-6*) Gordon Pr.

Social Security Policies in Industrial Countries: A Comparative Analysis. Margaret S. Gordon. (Illus.). 416p. (C). 1989. text ed. 85.00 (*0-521-33311-3*) Cambridge U Pr.

Social Security Practice Guide, 4 vols. National Organization of Social Security Claimants' Representatives. 1984. Updates. ring bd. write for info. (*0-8205-1637-6*) Bender.

Social Security Programs: A Cross-Cultural Comparative Perspective. Robert P. Scheurell. Ed. by John Dixon. LC 95-7438. (Contributions in Political Science Ser.: Vol. 359). 248p. 1995. text ed. 59.95 (*0-313-29654-5*, Greenwood Pr) Greenwood.

***Social Security Programs in the U. S.** 82p. 1996. reprint ed. pap. 25.00 (*0-7881-3300-4*) DIANE Pub.

Social Security Programs in the United States: Old Age, Survivors, Disability Insurance, Medicare, Unemployment Insurance, Workers' Compensation & Temporary Disability. 1991. lib. bdg. 250.00 (*0-8490-5078-2*) Gordon Pr.

Social Security Programs in the United States & Throughout the World, 2 vols., Set. 1996. lib. bdg. 615.99 (*0-8490-5984-4*) Gordon Pr.

Social Security Reform in Chile. Mario Marcel & Alberto Arenas. 47p. 1992. pap. text ed. write for info. (*0-940602-46-6*) IADB.

Social Security Review & Women. Hilary Land & Sue Ward. 1986. 20.00 (*0-946088-26-8*, Pub. by NCCL UK) St Mut.

Social Security Rulings. 1992. lib. bdg. 250.00 (*0-8490-5502-4*) Gordon Pr.

Social Security Statistics 1994. HMSO Staff. (Social Security Statistics Ser.). 357p. 1994. pap. 60.00 (*0-11-762226-5*, HM22265, Pub. by Stationery Ofc UK) Bernan Associates.

***Social Security Statistics 1996.** HMSO Staff. 335p. 1996. pap. 70.00 (*0-11-762433-0*, HM24330, Pub. by Stationery Ofc UK) Bernan Associates.

***Social Security Statistics 1997.** TSO Staff. 335p. 1997. pap. 75.00 (*0-11-762535-3*, HM25353, Pub. by Stationery Ofc UK) Bernan Associates.

Social Security Swindle. Irwin A. Schiff. 254p. 1984. 24.95 (*0-8159-6857-4*) Devin.

Social Security Swindle: How Anyone Can Drop Out. Irwin A. Schiff. 1984. 16.00 (*0-930374-04-5*) Freedom Bks.

Social Security System of India. Najmul Hasan. 265p. 1972. text ed. 20.00 (*0-685-13746-5*) Coronet Bks.

Social Security Systems in Latin America. Ed. by Francisco E. Barreto de Oliveira. (Inter-American Development Bank Ser.). 228p. (Orig.). 1994. 18.50 (*0-940602-91-1*) IADB.

Social Security Taxation & Europe. J. Berghman et al. 89p. 1993. pap. 33.00 (*90-6215-349-6*, Pub. by Maklu Uitgevers BE) Gaunt.

Social Security, the Inside Story: An Expert Explains Your Rights & Benefits. Andy Landis. LC 92-63250. (Illus.). 270p. (Orig.). 1993. pap. 14.95 (*0-931213-09-6*) Mount Vernon Pr.

Social Security Today & Tomorrow. Robert Ball. 1978. text ed. 75.00 (*0-231-04254-X*) Col U Pr.

Social Security Update. Phil Philcox. LC 92-31316. 1992. 5.95 (*0-87576-162-3*) Pilot Bks.

Social Security's Looming Surpluses: Prospects & Implications. Ed. by Carolyn L. Weaver. 240p. 1990. 36.25 (*0-8447-3729-1*) Am Enterprise.

Social Self. George H. Mead. (Reprint Series in Sociology). (C). 1993. reprint ed. pap. text ed. 1.00 (*0-8290-2918-4*, S-187) Irvington.

***Social Self: Group Influences on Personal Identity.** Elisha Y. Babad et al. LC 82-21553. (Sage Library of Social Reserach: Vol. 144). 267p. 1983. reprint ed. pap. 76.10 (*0-608-02798-7*, 2063865) Bks Demand.

Social Self: Hawthorne, Howells, William James, & Nineteenth-Century Psychology. Joseph Alkana. LC 96-16404. 176p. 1997. text ed. 29.95 (*0-8131-1971-5*) U Pr of Ky.

***Social Self: Inquiries in Social Construction.** Ed. by David Bakhurst & Christine Sypnowich. 192p. 1995. pap. 21.95 (*0-8039-7597-X*) Sage.

***Social Self: Inquiries in Social Construction.** Ed. by David Bakhurst & Christine Sypnowich. 192p. 1995. 69.95 (*0-8039-7596-1*) Sage.

***Social Self, Global Culture: An Introduction to Sociological Ideas.** Ed. by Allen Kellehear. 352p. 1997. pap. 45.00 (*0-19-553740-8*) OUP.

Social Self in Zen & American Pragmatism. Steve Odin. LC 94-33404. (SUNY Series in Constructive Postmodern Thought). 482p. 1996. text ed. 74.50 (*0-7914-2491-X*); pap. text ed. 24.95 (*0-7914-2492-8*) State U NY Pr.

Social Selves: Theories of the Social Formation of Personality. Ian Burkitt. 240p. (C). 1992. 69.95 (*0-8039-8384-0*); pap. 19.95 (*0-8039-8385-9*) Sage.

Social Semigroups: A Unified Theory of Scaling & Blockmodeling. John P. Boyd. 280p. (C). 1991. lib. bdg. 49.50 (*0-913969-34-6*, G Mason Univ Pr) Univ Pub Assocs.

Social Semiotics. Robert Hodge & Gunther Kress. LC 87-47976. (Illus.). 280p. 1988. 52.50 (*0-8014-2195-0*); pap. 16.95 (*0-8014-9515-6*) Cornell U Pr.

Social Semiotics: Text, Meaning, & Nabokov's "Ada" Paul J. Thibault. (Theory & History of Literature Ser.: Vol. 74). (Illus.). 320p. (C). 1990. pap. text ed. 16.95 (*0-8166-1866-6*) U of Minn Pr.

Social Semiotics of Casual Conversation. Eggins. 1995. pap. 24.95 (*1-85567-218-9*) St Martin.

Social Semiotics of Mass Communications. Klaus B. Jensen. 256p. 1995. text ed. 69.95 (*0-8039-7809-X*); pap. text ed. 25.95 (*0-8039-7810-3*) Sage.

Social Sensitivity: A Study of Habit & Experience. James M. Ostrow. LC 89-35027. (SUNY Series in Philosophy of the Social Sciences). 137p. 1990. pap. text ed. 21.95 (*0-7914-0216-9*) State U NY Pr.

Social Sensitivity: A Study of Habit & Experience. James M. Ostrow. LC 89-35027. (SUNY Series in Philosophy of the Social Sciences). 137p. 1990. text ed. 64.50 (*0-7914-0215-0*) State U NY Pr.

Social Service & the Art of Healing. Richard C. Cabot. LC 73-84257. (NASW Classics Ser.). 192p. 1973. reprint ed. pap. text ed. 9.95 (*0-87101-062-3*) Natl Assn Soc Wkrs.

Social Service Careers, 5 vols. 89.00 (*0-685-23048-1*, CG370) Ready Ref Pr.

Social Service Delivery Systems: An Agenda for Reform. Ed. by Cristian Aedo & Osvaldo Larranaga. 160p. (Orig.). 1994. pap. text ed. 18.50 (*0-940602-76-8*) IADB.

***Social Service Entry Test.** Jack Rudman. (Career Examination Ser.: Vol. C-3824). 1997. pap. 23.95 (*0-8373-3824-7*) Nat Learn.

Social Service Gestapo: How the Government Can Legally Abduct Your Child. Janson Kauser. 224p. (Orig.). 1995. pap. 3.49 (*1-56384-104-5*) Huntington Hse.

Social Service in Hawaii. Margaret M. Catton. LC 58-14378. (Illus.). 1959. 21.95 (*0-87015-088-X*) Pacific Bks.

Social Service in Vermont: The Community & the State. Marshall True. (Occasional Papers: No. 5). 28p. (Orig.). 1981. pap. text ed. 3.50 (*0-944277-06-3*, T78) U VT Ctr Rsch VT.

Social Service Organizations, 2 vols. Ed. by Peter Romanofsky. LC 77-84754. (Encyclopedia of American Institutions Ser.: No. 2). 1978. text ed. 150.00 (*0-8371-9829-1*, RSS/) Greenwood.

Social Service Organizations, 2 vols., 1. Ed. by Peter Romanofsky. LC 77-84754. (Encyclopedia of American Institutions Ser.: No. 2). 1978. text ed. 95.00 (*0-8371-9902-6*, RSS/1) Greenwood.

Social Service Organizations, 2 vols., Vol. 2. Ed. by Peter Romanofsky. LC 77-84754. (Encyclopedia of American Institutions Ser.: No. 2). 1978. text ed. 95.00 (*0-8371-9903-4*, RSS/2) Greenwood.

Social Service Organizations & Agencies Directory. Ed. by Anthony T. Kruzas. 548p. 1982. 140.00 (*0-8103-0329-9*) Gale.

Social Service Organizations in California: A Directory. Ed. by Jennifer D. Trzyna. LC 83-72436. (California Information Guides Ser.). 72p. 1985. pap. 22.50 (*0-912102-66-7*) Cal Inst Public.

Social Service Policies & Procedures for Long Term Care Facilities. Marylou Hughes. 100p. (C). 1991. ring bd. 22.50 (*1-877735-33-7*, 181) M&H Pub Co TX.

Social Service Representative. Jack Rudman. (Career Examination Ser.: C-745). 1994. pap. 23.95 (*0-8373-0745-7*) Nat Learn.

Social Services: An Introduction. 4th ed. H. Wayne Johnson et al. LC 94-66867. 450p. (C). 1994. pap. text ed. 41.00 (*0-87581-387-9*) Peacock Pubs.

***Social Services: The Next Lap.** Ed. by Yap M. Teng. 232p. 1991. pap. write for info. (*981-210-011-3*, Pub. by Times Academic SI) Intl Spec Bk.

Social Services: What Happens to the Clients? Margo Koss et al. 150p. (Orig.). 1979. pap. text ed. 18.50 (*0-87766-272-X*) Urban Inst.

Social Services Administrative Planner. Jack Rudman. (Career Examination Ser.: C-3066). 1994. pap. 34.95 (*0-8373-3066-1*) Nat Learn.

Social Services Aide. Jack Rudman. (Career Examination Ser.: C-3319). 1994. pap. 23.95 (*0-8373-3319-9*) Nat Learn.

Social Services & the Ethnic Community. Rosina M. Becerra. LC 94-25718. 1994. pap. text ed. 33.00 (*0-205-15712-2*) Allyn.

Social Services by Government Contract. Kenneth R. Wedel et al. LC 79-19744. 142p. 1979. text ed. 49.95 (*0-275-90434-2*, C0434, Praeger Pubs) Greenwood.

Social Services Collection Representative. Jack Rudman. (Career Examination Ser.: C-3304). 1994. pap. 27.95 (*0-8373-3304-0*) Nat Learn.

Social Services Disability Aide. Jack Rudman. (Career Examination Ser.: C-3259). 1994. pap. 23.95 (*0-8373-3259-1*) Nat Learn.

Social Services Disability Analyst. Jack Rudman. (Career Examination Ser.: C-859). 1994. pap. 27.95 (*0-8373-0859-3*) Nat Learn.

Social Services Employment Specialist. Jack Rudman. (Career Examination Ser.: C-2816). 1994. pap. 29.95 (*0-8373-2816-0*) Nat Learn.

Social Services for Gay & Lesbian Couples. Intro. by Lawrence A. Kurdek. LC 93-40413. (Journal of Gay & Lesbian Social Services). (Illus.). 122p. 1993. pap. text ed. 10.95 (*1-56023-052-5*); lib. bdg. 24.95 (*1-56024-584-0*) Haworth Pr.

Social Services for Senior Gay Men & Lesbians. Ed. by Jean K. Quam. LC 96-52129. 115p. 1997. 39.95 (*1-56024-808-4*); pap. 12.95 (*1-56023-084-3*) Haworth Pr.

Social Services for Women in Eastern Europe. Bogdan Mieczkowski. (ASN Series in Issues Studies (U. S. S. R. & East Europe): No. 3). 128p. (Orig.). (C). 1982. pap. 9.50 (*0-910895-00-7*) Assn Study Nat.

Social Services Human Resources Development Specialist. Jack Rudman. (Career Examination Ser.: C-3189). 1994. pap. 34.95 (*0-8373-3189-7*) Nat Learn.

Social Services in International Perspective: The Emergence of the Sixth System. Alfred J. Kahn & Sheila B. Kamerman. LC 79-66434. 411p. 1980. pap. text ed. 24.95 (*0-87855-724-5*) Transaction Pubs.

Social Services in Nigeria: An Introduction. A. G. Onokerhoraye. LC 82-17156. 354p. 1983. pap. 18.50 (*0-7103-0042-5*) Routledge Chapman & Hall.

An Asterisk (*) at the beginning of an entry indicates that the title is appearing in BIP for the first time.

Social Services in the States: Profiles on State Use of Federal Title XX Social Services Block Grant Funds. Sunny Harris et al. 39p. reprint ed. pap. 25.00 (0-7837-5367-5, 2045131) Bks Demand.

Social Services Law. John Williams. 250p. 1987. 136.00 (1-85190-039-X, Pub. by Fourmat Pub UK) St Mut.

Social Services Law. 2nd ed. John Williams. 430p. 1995. 175.00 (0-85459-824-3, Pub. by Tolley Pubng UK) St Mut.

***Social Services Law: The Case for Reform.** Ed. by Tessa Harding. 1990. pap. 24.00 (1-899942-10-6, Pub. by Natl Inst Soc Work) St Mut.

Social Services Management Specialist. Jack Rudman. (Career Examination Ser.: C-1994). 1994. pap. 34.95 (0-8373-1994-3) Nat Learn.

Social Services Management Trainee. Jack Rudman. (Career Examination Ser.: C-1993). 1994. pap. 29.95 (0-8373-1993-5) Nat Learn.

Social Services Medical Assistance Specialist. Jack Rudman. (Career Examination Ser.: C-2431). 1994. pap. 34.95 (0-8373-2431-9) Nat Learn.

Social Services Program Coordinator. Jack Rudman. (Career Examination Ser.: C-3566). 1994. pap. 34.95 (0-8373-3566-3) Nat Learn.

Social Services Program Specialist. Jack Rudman. (Career Examination Ser.: C-2235). 1994. pap. 34.95 (0-8373-2235-9) Nat Learn.

Social Services Specialist. Jack Rudman. (Career Examination Ser.: No. C-3747). pap. 29.95 (0-8373-3747-X) Nat Learn.

Social Services Specialist Trainee. Jack Rudman. (Career Examination Ser.: C-3547). 1994. pap. 27.95 (0-8373-3547-7) Nat Learn.

Social Services Systems Manager. Jack Rudman. (Career Examination Ser.: C-2992). 1994. pap. 39.95 (0-8373-2992-2) Nat Learn.

***Social Services Year Book 1990-1991.** Longman Community Info Guide Staff. 1990. pap. text ed. write for info. (0-582-06040-0, Pub. by Longman UK) Longman.

***Social Services Yeark Book, 1994.** Longman Publishing Staff. 1994. pap. text ed. write for info. (0-582-21682-6, Pub. by Longman UK) Longman.

Social Setting of Pauline Christianity. Gerd Theissen. Ed. & Tr. by J. H. Schultz. 224p. 1995. pap. 24.95 (0-567-29183-9, Pub. by T & T Clark UK) Bks Intl VA.

Social Setting, Stigma & Communicative Competence: Explorations of the Conversational Interactions of Retarded Adults. Sharon Sabsay et al. LC 86-8240. (Pragmatics & Beyond Ser.: VI-6). vi, 137p. (Orig.). 1985. pap. 44.00 (0-915027-92-5) Benjamins North Am.

Social Settlement of Britain & the United States. Rose. Date not set. write for info. (0-7185-1390-8) St Martin.

Social Shakespeare: Aspects of Renaissance Dramaturgy & Contemporary Society. Peter J. Smith. LC 95-2957. 1995. text ed. 49.95 (0-312-12627-1) St Martin.

***Social Shaping of Information Superhighways: European & American Roads to the Information Society.** Ed. by Herbert Kubicek et al. 400p. 1997. text ed. 49.95 (0-312-16569-2) St Martin.

Social Shaping of Science: Institutions, Ideology, & Careers in Science. Roger G. Krohn. LC 75-90792. (Contributions in Sociology Ser.: No. 4). (Illus.). 280p. 1971. text ed. 38.50 (0-8371-1852-2, KRS/, Greenwood Pr) Greenwood.

Social Shaping of Technology. Ed. by Donald Mackenzie & Judy Wajcman. 336p. 1985. pap. 32.00 (0-335-15026-8, Open Univ Pr) Taylor & Francis.

Social Significance of Modern Drama. Emma Goldman. 304p. (Orig.). 1987. 24.95 (0-936839-62-7); pap. 8.95 (0-936839-61-9) Applause Theatre Bk Pubs.

Social Significance of Sport: An Introduction to the Sociology of Sport. Barry D. McPherson et al. LC 89-1975. (Illus.). 352p. (C). 1989. text ed. 36.00 (0-87322-235-0, BMCPO235) Human Kinetics.

Social Significance of Telematics: An Essay on the Information Society. Lars Qvortrup. Tr. by Philip Edmonds. LC 85-7493. (P&B Ser.: Vol. V, No. 7). xviii, 228p. (Orig.). 1984. pap. 78.00 (0-915027-04-6) Benjamins North Am.

Social Significance of the Modern Drama. Emma Goldman. 1972. 250.00 (0-8490-1067-5) Gordon Pr.

Social Silhouettes: Being the Impressions of Mr. Mark Manhattan. fac. ed. Edgar Fawcett. LC 75-1846. (Leisure Class in America Ser.). 1975. 26.95 (0-405-06913-8) Ayer.

Social Situation in India. B. L. Raina. 1990. 55.00 (81-7169-054-8, Commonwealth) S Asia.

Social Situation of Migrant Workers & Their Families, No. 2. 63p. 1986. 11.00 (92-1-130118-1, E.86.IV.11) UN.

Social Situations. Michael Argyle et al. (Illus.). 450p. 1981. pap. text ed. 28.95 (0-521-29881-4) Cambridge U Pr.

Social Skill Strategies (SSS) Bk. A: A Curriculum for Adolescents. Nancy Gajewski & Patty Mayo. 336p. (YA). (gr. 5-12). 1989. pap. 37.00 (0-930599-51-9) Thinking Pubns.

Social Skill Strategies (SSS) Bk. B: A Curriculum for Adolescents. Patty Mayo & Nancy Gajewski. (Illus.). 350p. (Orig.). (J). (gr. 5-12). 1989. pap. 37.00 (0-930599-52-7) Thinking Pubns.

Social Skills. Matson. (Applied Research in Mental Retardation). 1984. pap. 18.25 (0-08-030959-3, Pergamon Pr) Elsevier.

Social Skills Activities for Special Children. Darlene Mannix. LC 93-12222. (Illus.). 1993. spiral bd. 27.95 (0-87628-868-9) Ctr Appl Res.

Social Skills & the Speech Impaired. 2nd ed. Lena Rustin. 240p. 1997. 52.50 (1-56593-388-5, 0814) Singular Publishing.

Social Skills Assessment & Training with Children: An Empirically Based Handbook. Larry K. Michelson et al. 276p. 1983. 59.50 (0-306-41234-9, Plenum Pr) Plenum.

Social Skills at Work. David Fonana. (Problems in Practice Ser.). 128p. (C). 1990. pap. text ed. 15.95 (1-85433-015-2, A4842, Pub. by British Psy Soc UK) Routledge.

Social Skills at Work. David Fonana. (Problems in Practice Ser.). 128p. (C). (gr. 13). 1990. text ed. 39.95 (1-85433-016-0, A4838, Pub. by British Psy Soc UK) Routledge.

Social Skills Development: Practical Strategies for Adolescents & Adults with Developmental Disabilities. Stephen J. Antonello. LC 95-21050. 1995. pap. text ed. 52.50 (0-205-17411-6) Allyn.

Social Skills for Job Success: Teacher's Guide. Barbara L. McCombs & Linda Brannan. (Skills for Job Success Ser.). 150p. (Orig.). 1990. ring bd. 16.95 (1-56119-058-6) Educ Pr MD.

Social Skills for Mental Health: A Structured Learning Approach. Robert P. Sprafkin et al. LC 92-49061. (Practitioner Guidebook Ser.). 147p. 1993. text ed. 32.95 (0-205-14841-7, H48416, Longwood Div) Allyn.

Social Skills for Nursing Practice. Peter French. (Illus.). 272p. 1983. pap. 17.50 (0-7099-1009-6, Pub. by Croom Helm UK) Routledge Chapman & Hall.

Social Skills for Nursing Practice. 2nd ed. Peter French. LC 93-33906. 1993. write for info. (0-412-94740-4, Chap & Hall NY) Chapman & Hall.

Social Skills for Nursing Practice. 2nd ed. Peter French. 312p. 1994. pap. 44.75 (1-56593-228-5, 0571) Singular Publishing.

Social Skills for People with Learning Disabilities: A Social Capability Approach. M. Burton et al. 352p. 1995. pap. 44.75 (1-56593-194-7, 0509) Singular Publishing.

***Social Skills for Schizophrenia.** Alan S. Bellack et al. LC 96-52826. (Treatment Manuals for Practitioners Ser.). 250p. 1997. lib. bdg. 32.50 (1-57230-177-5) Guilford Pr.

Social Skills for Students with Autism. Richard L. Simpson et al. 22p. 1991. pap. text ed. 9.75 (0-86586-202-8, P343) Coun Exc Child.

Social Skills Game. Yvonne Searkle & Isabelle Streng. 1995. 39.95 (1-85302-336-1) Taylor & Francis.

Social Skills in Interpersonal Communication. 3rd ed. 384p. (C). (gr. 13). 1994. text ed. 74.95 (0-415-11830-1, B4763) Routledge.

Social Skills in Interpersonal Communication. 3rd ed. Owen Hargie et al. LC 93-23616. 384p. (C). 1994. pap. 19.95 (0-415-08137-8, B3731) Routledge.

Social Skills in the Classroom. 2nd rev. ed. Thomas M. Stephens. LC 91-42494. 434p. (C). 1992. 50.00 (0-911907-04-1, RO-1984) Psych Assess.

Social Skills in the School & Community. Laurence R. Sargent. 1991. pap. text ed. 18.00 (0-685-52087-0, D412) Coun Exc Child.

Social Skills on the Job Computer Software Manual. Macro Systems, Inc. Staff. (Social Skills on the Job Ser.). 1989. pap. text ed. 8.95 (0-88671-347-1, 4704) Am Guidance.

Social Skills on the Job Teacher's Guide. Macro Systems, Inc. Staff. (Social Skills on the Job Ser.). 1989. teacher ed. 10.95 (0-88671-346-3, 4703) Am Guidance.

Social Skills Planning Guide. Joni Alberg et al. 176p. 1994. teacher ed., ring bd. 47.50 (1-57035-029-9, 68GD) Sopris.

Social Skills Playbook: Why Be Shy? Jim Rohrbach. LC 90-91986. 96p. (Orig.). 1990. pap. 11.95 (0-9627754-0-1) J M Rohrbach.

Social Skills Speech Impairment. Rustin. 1988. 52.50 (1-56593-546-2, 0065) Singular Publishing.

Social Skills Stories. Anne Johnson & Jackie Susnik. (Illus.). 408p. (YA). 1995. spiral bd. 29.00 (1-884135-21-8) Mayer-Johnson.

Social Skills Training. Ed. by James Curran & Peter M. Monti. LC 85-32083. 447p. (C). 1986. pap. text ed. 20.00 (0-8147-1402-1) NYU Pr.

Social Skills Training: A Practical Handbook for Assessment & Treatment. Ed. by James P. Curran & Peter M. Monti. LC 81-6374. 459p. reprint ed. pap. 130.90 (0-7837-3882-X, 2043730) Bks Demand.

Social Skills Training: A Special Issue of Behavioral Counseling Quarterly. Ed. by Craig T. Twentyman. LC 81-84339. 104p. 1982. pap. 16.95 (0-89885-125-4) Human Sci Pr.

Social Skills Training & the Professional Helper. J. Collins & M. Collins. LC 91-29939. 210p. 1992. pap. text ed. 42.95 (0-471-93145-4) Wiley.

Social Skills Training for Children & Youth. Ed. by Craig W. LeCroy. LC 83-228. (Child & Youth Services Ser.: Vol. 5, Nos. 3 & 4). 152p. 1983. text ed. 39.95 (0-86656-184-6) Haworth Pr.

***Social Skills Training for Children & Youth.** Ed. by Craig W. LeCroy. 152p. 1983. pap. 19.95 (0-86656-229-X) Haworth Pr.

Social Skills Training for Psychiatric. Liberman. (C). 1992. text ed. 51.50 (0-205-14407-1, H4407) Allyn.

Social Skills Training for Psychiatric. Liberman. (C). 1992. pap. text ed. 31.50 (0-205-14406-3, H4406) Allyn.

Social Skills Training Manual: Assessment, Programme Design, & Management of Training. Jill Wilkinson & Sandra Canter. LC 81-12957. 160p. reprint ed. pap. 45.60 (0-7837-6398-0, 2046111) Bks Demand.

Social Skills Training Treatment. Becker. (C). 1987. pap. 19.95 (0-205-14273-7, H4273) Allyn.

***Social Skills Training with Adolescents: Assessment, Intervention & Evaluation.** Richard Bulkeley. pap. text ed. 30.00 (0-471-95116-1) Wiley.

Social Smarts: Manners for Today's Kids. Carol Barkin & Elizabeth James. LC 95-35613. (Illus.). (J). (gr. 4-8). 1996. 14.95 (0-395-66585-X, Clarion Bks) HM.

Social Smarts: Manners for Today's Kids. Elizabeth James & Carol Barkin. (Illus.). (J). 1996. pap. 6.95 (0-395-81312-3) HM.

Social Software of Accounting & Information Systems. Norman B. Macintosh. LC 84-10447. 249p. 1985. text ed. 85.00 (0-471-90543-7) Wiley.

Social Sources of Adjustment to Blindness. Irving F. Lukoff & Martin Whiteman. LC 73-84034. (American Foundation for the Blind Research Ser.: No. 21). 301p. reprint ed. pap. 85.80 (0-7837-2759-3, 2043142) Bks Demand.

Social Sources of Church Growth: Korean Churches in the Homeland & Overseas. Gil Soo Han. 222p. (C). 1994. lib. bdg. 46.50 (0-8191-9758-0) U Pr of Amer.

Social Sources of Denominationalism. Richard H. Niebuhr. 1984. 23.75 (0-8446-6150-3) Peter Smith.

Social Space: Human Spatial Behaviour in Dwellings & Settlements. Ed. by Ole Gron et al. (Odense University Studies in History & Social Sciences: No. 147). (Illus.). iv, 184p. (Orig.). 1991. pap. 57.50 (87-7492-842-2, Pub. by Odense Universitets Forlag DK) Coronet Bks.

Social Space for Domestic Animals. Ed. by R. Zayan. (Current Topics in Veterinary Medicine & Animal Science Ser.). 1985. lib. bdg. 157.50 (0-89838-773-6) Kluwer Ac.

Social Spending in Latin America: The Story of the 1980s. Margaret Grosh. (Discussion Paper Ser.: No. 106). 156p. 1990. 9.95 (0-8213-1691-5, 11691) World Bank.

Social Spirit in America. Charles R. Henderson. LC 77-39378. (Select Bibliographies Reprint Ser.). 1977. reprint ed. 21.95 (0-8369-9911-8) Ayer.

Social Star: General Interaction Skills, Bk. 1. Patty Mayo et al. LC 92-39097. 485p. 1993. pap. 39.00 (0-930599-79-9) Thinking Pubns.

Social Star: Peer Interaction Skills, Bk. 2. Nancy Gajewski et al. LC 92-39097. (Illus.). 478p. (Orig.). 1994. pap. text ed. 39.00 (0-930599-91-8) Thinking Pubns.

Social Statics. unexpurgated ed. Herbert Spencer. 430p. 1995. reprint ed. 15.00 (0-911312-33-1) Schalkenbach.

Social Statistics. 2nd ed. Hubert M. Blalock, Jr. 1979. text ed. write for info. (0-07-005752-4) McGraw.

Social Statistics: A User-Friendly Approach. Steven P. Schacht. LC 94-43560. 1995. pap. text ed. 38.00 (0-205-14004-1) Allyn.

***Social Statistics for a Diverse Society.** Chava Nachmias & Mark Rodeghier. LC 96-45371. (Pine Forge Press Series on Research Methods & Statistics). 1997. pap. write for info. (0-8039-9026-X) Pine Forge.

Social Statistics in Use. Philip M. Hauser. LC 74-24747. 400p. 1975. 45.00 (0-87154-375-3) Russell Sage.

Social Statistics Using MicroCase (with Doing Statistics Using MicroCase), Set. 2nd ed. William Fox. 280p. (C). 1995. pap. text ed. 37.00 (0-922914-12-5) MicroCase.

Social Statistics Using SPSS. Dometrius. (C). 1992. text ed. 31.95 (0-06-041714-5) Addson-Wesley Educ.

Social Status & Power in Java. L. H. Palmier. (London School of Economics Monographs on Social Anthropology: No. 20). 174p. (C). 1969. pap. 16.95 (0-485-19620-4, Pub. by Athlone Pr UK) Humanities.

Social Status & Psychological Disorder: A Casual Inquiry. Bruce P. Dohrenwend & Barbara S. Dohrenwend. LC 72-88310. (Personality Processes Ser.). 223p. (C). reprint ed. 63.60 (0-8357-9978-6, 2012570) Bks Demand.

Social Status in the City. Richard P. Coleman & Bernice L. Neugarten. LC 70-132820. (Jossey-Bass Behavioral Science Ser.). 338p. reprint ed. 96.40 (0-8357-9348-6, 2013782) Bks Demand.

Social Status of Women in Developing Countries. Ed. by Man Singh Das & Vijay Kumar Gupta. 175p. 1995. pap. 125.00 (81-85880-53-0, Pub. by Print Hse II) St Mut.

Social Stigma of Occupations. K. C. Saunders. 244p. 1981. text ed. 54.95 (0-566-00334-1, Pub. by Avebury Pub UK) Ashgate Pub Co.

***Social Stories: All New Stories Teaching Social Skills.** Carol Gray. Ed. by Sue Jonker. 209p. (Orig.). 1994. pap. 31.95 (1-885477-20-1) Fut Horizons.

Social Strategy & Corporate Structure. Chamberlin. 192p. 1982. 32.95 (0-02-905810-4, Free Press) Free Pr.

Social Stratification. Ed. by Dipankar Gupta. (Oxford in India Readings in Sociology & Social & Cultural Anthropology Ser.). 540p. (C). 1993. pap. 13.95 (0-19-563088-2, 14453) OUP.

Social Stratification, 3 vols., Set. Ed. by John Holmwood. LC 96-25430. (International Library of Critical Writings in Economics Ser.: Vol. 9). 1984p. 1996. 590.00 (1-85898-159-X) E Elgar.

Social Stratification: Canada. J. Curtis & W. Scott. 1972. write for info. (0-13-818625-1) P-H.

Social Stratification: Canada. 2nd ed. J. Curtis & W. Scott. 1979. pap. 16.00 (0-13-818633-2) P-H.

Social Stratification: Class, Race, & Gender in Sociological Perspective. Ed. by David B. Grusky. (Social Inequality Ser.). 750p. (C). 1994. pap. text ed. 34.00 (0-8133-1065-2) Westview.

Social Stratification: Research & Theory for the 1970's. Ed. by Edward O. Laumann. LC 77-135769. (Illus.). (Orig.). 1970. 8.50 (0-672-51402-8, Bobbs); pap. 6.95 (0-672-61195-3, Bobbs) Macmillan.

Social Stratification: The Forms & Functions of Inequality. 2nd ed. Melvin M. Tumin. (Illus.). 192p. (C). 1984. pap. text ed. 30.20 (0-13-818659-6) P-H.

Social Stratification: The Interplay of Class, Race, & Gender. 2nd ed. Daniel W. Rossides. 544p. (C). 1996. pap. text ed. 46.00 (0-13-192535-0) P-H.

Social Stratification & Change in India. Yogendra Singh. (C). 1989. reprint ed. 11.50 (0-685-45059-7, Pub. by Manohar II) S Asia.

Social Stratification & Inequality. 3rd ed. Harold R. Kerbo. 1996. text ed. write for info. (0-07-034258-X) McGraw.

Social Stratification & Mobility. K. L. Sharma. (C). 1995. 32.00 (81-7033-262-1, Pub. by Rawat II); pap. 32.00 (81-7033-263-X, Pub. by Rawat II) S Asia.

Social Stratification & Mobility in the U. S. S. R. Ed. by Murray Yanowitch & Wesley A. Fisher. LC 72-77202. (Illus.). 435p. reprint ed. pap. 124.00 (0-685-23747-8, 2032788) Bks Demand.

Social Stratification & Mobility in Urban India. W. S. Phillips. 1990. 23.00 (81-7033-084-X, Pub. by Rawat II) S Asia.

Social Stratification & Occupations. Alexander Stewart et al. Ed. by Ken Prandy & R. M. Blackburn. LC 80-16282. 320p. 1980. 45.00 (0-8419-0629-7) Holmes & Meier.

Social Stratification & Psychiatric Disorders. August B. Hollinghead & Frederick C. Redlich. (Reprint Series in Social Sciences). (C). 1993. reprint ed. pap. text ed. 1.00 (0-8290-3793-4, S-120) Irvington.

Social Stratification & Socioeconomic Inequality: Reproductive & Interpersonal Aspects of Dominance, Vol. 2. Ed. by Lee Ellis. LC 92-28546. 240p. 1994. text ed. 65.00 (0-275-94526-X, Praeger Pubs) Greenwood.

Social Stratification & Socioeconomic Inequality Vol. 1: A Comparative Biosocial Analysis. Ed. by Lee Ellis. LC 92-28546. 256p. 1993. text ed. 59.95 (0-275-93262-1, C3262, Praeger Pubs) Greenwood.

Social Stratification & Third World County: Mahatma Gandhi's Theory of Stratification. Ashwin Vyas. 125p. 1989. 15.00 (0-9623432-1-8) Folklore Inst.

Social Stratification in Contemporary Japan. Ed. by Kenji Kosaka. LC 93-11979. (Japanese Studies). 265p. 1994. 76.50 (0-7103-0467-6) Routledge Chapman & Hall.

Social Stratification in India. Ed. by K. L. Sharma. 343p. (C). 1986. 34.00 (81-85054-15-0, Pub. by Manohar II) S Asia.

***Social Stratification in India: Issues & Themes.** Kanhaiyalal Sharma. LC 97-3382. 1997. pap. write for info. (0-8039-9363-3) Sage.

***Social Stratification in India: Issues & Themes.** Kanhaiyalal L. Sharma. LC 97-3382. 200p. 1997. text ed. 26.50 (0-8039-9362-5) Sage.

Social Stratification in Poland: Eight Empirical Studies. Ed. by Tadeusz K. Krauze & Kazimierz M.. Slomcynski. LC 85-18387. (Illus.). 203p. 1986. reprint ed. pap. 57.90 (0-7837-9972-1, 2060699) Bks Demand.

Social Stratification in Polynesia. Marshall D. Sahlins. LC 84-45526. (American Ethnological Society Monographs: No. 29). 1988. reprint ed. 34.50 (0-404-62928-8) AMS Pr.

Social Stratification in the United States: The American Profile Poster. Stephen J. Rose. LC 92-18940. 48p. 1992. pap. 14.95 (1-56584-021-6) New Press NY.

Social Stratification of English in New York City. William Labov. LC 66-24073. 513p. reprint ed. pap. 146.30 (0-8357-3348-3, 2039581) Bks Demand.

Social Stress & Mental Health: Social Psychiatric Field Study of Calcutta Ser. Ajita Chakraborty. (Illus.). 200p. (C). 1990. 25.00 (0-8039-9633-0) Sage.

Social Stress & the Family: Advances & Developments in Family Stress Therapy & Research. Ed. by Hamilton I. McCubbin et al. LC 83-190. (Marriage & Family Review Ser.: Vol. 6, Nos. 1-2). 231p. 1983. text ed. 49.95 (0-86656-163-3) Haworth Pr.

Social Stress in Domestic Animals. Ed. by R. Zayan & R. Dantzer. (Current Topics in Veterinary Medicine & Animal Science Ser.). (C). 1990. lib. bdg. 162.50 (0-7923-0615-5) Kluwer Ac.

Social Stress in the United States: Links to Regional Patterns in Crime & Illness. Arnold S. Linsky & Murray A. Straus. LC 86-14192. 174p. 1986. text ed. 55.00 (0-86569-149-5, Auburn Hse) Greenwood.

Social Structure. Charles Crothers. LC 96-14318. 160p. 1996. text ed. 59.95 (0-415-14946-0) Routledge.

Social Structure: Sex, Gender, Marriage & Kinship in Cross-Cultural Perspectives. Burton Pasternak & Carol R. Ember. LC 96-41018. 352p. (C). 1996. pap. text ed. 28.40 (0-13-206533-9) P-H.

Social Structure & Aging: Psychological Processes. K. Warner Schaie & Carmi Schooler. (Social Structure & Aging Ser.). 280p. (C). 1988. 59.95 (0-8058-0093-X) L Erlbaum Assocs.

Social Structure & Anomie. Robert K. Merton. (Reprint Series in Social Sciences). (C). 1993. reprint ed. pap. text ed. 1.00 (0-8290-3491-9, S-194) Irvington.

Social Structure & Change. Ed. by A. M. Shah et al. 234p. 1995. 35.00 (0-8039-9261-0) Sage.

Social Structure & Change: Women in Indian Society. Ed. by A. M. Shah et al. (Social Structure & Change Ser.: Vol. 2). 214p. 1996. 27.50 (0-8039-9290-4) Sage.

***Social Structure & Change Vol. 4: Development & Ethnicity.** Ed. by A. M. Shah et al. 240p. 1997. text ed. 32.00 (0-8039-9360-9) Sage.

Social Structure & Culture. Ed. by Hans Haferkamp. viii, 340p. (C). 1989. lib. bdg. 70.00 (3-11-011310-4) De Gruyter.

Social Structure & Disaster. Ed. by Gary A. Kreps. LC 87-40545. 448p. 1989. 55.00 (0-87413-340-8) U Delaware Pr.

Social Structure & Fertility. Gomti Arora. (C). 1990. 27.50 (81-85135-50-9, National Bk Ctr) S Asia.

Social Structure & Law: Theoretical & Empirical Perspectives. William M. Evans. (Illus.). 272p. (C). 1990. text ed. 54.00 (0-8039-2881-5); pap. text ed. 24.95 (0-8039-2882-3) Sage.

Social Structure & Network Analysis. Ed. by Pater V. Marsden & Nan Lin. LC 82-10564. (Sage Focus Editions Ser.: No. 57). 319p. reprint ed. pap. 91.00 (0-7837-1115-8, 2041645) Bks Demand.

Social Structure & Personality. Talcott Parsons. LC 64-11218. 1964. 24.95 (0-02-924850-7, Free Press) Free Pr.

S

Social Structure & Personality Development: The Individual As a Productive Processor of Reality. Klaus Hurrelmann. (Illus.). 176p. 1988. text ed. 54.95 (0-521-35474-9); pap. text ed. 19.95 (0-521-35747-0) Cambridge U Pr.

Social Structure & Political Participation: Development Relationships, Pt. I. Norman H. Nie et al. (Reprint Series in Political Science). (C). 1993. reprint ed. pap. text ed. 1.00 (0-8290-2748-3, PS-519) Irvington.

Social Structure & Regional Development: A Social Geography Perspective. Ed. by Aijazuddin Ahmad. 1993. 52.00 (81-7033-182-X, Pub. by Rawat II) S Asia.

Social Structure & Rural Development. I. S. Chauhan & V. S. Bais. (C). 1995. 22.00 (0-614-13261-4, Pub. by Rawat II) S Asia.

Social Structure & Rural Development in the Third World. Guy Berger. (Illus.). 216p. (C). 1992. text ed. 54.95 (0-521-39258-6) Cambridge U Pr.

Social Structure & Self-Direction: A Comparative Analysis of the United States & Poland. Melvin L. Kohn & Kazimierz M. Slomcynski. 300p. 1994. pap. text ed. 26.95 (1-55786-529-9) Blackwell Pubs.

Social Structure & Social Mobility. Ed. & Intro. by Neil L. Shumsky. LC 95-36145. (American Cities Ser.: Vol. 7). (Illus.). 424p. 1995. reprint ed. text ed. 85.00 (0-8153-2192-9) Garland.

S

Social Structure & Social Relations. Ed. by Norman E. Whitten, Jr. (American Ethnologist Ser.: Vol. 11, No. 4). 1984. 12.50 (0-317-66329-1) Am Anthro Assn.

Social Structure & Social Thought. Norman Birnbaum. 304p. 1993. 45.00 (0-19-506889-0) OUP.

Social Structure & Testosterone: Explorations of the Socio-Bio-Social Chain. Theodore D. Kemper. LC 89-70040. 265p. (C). 1990. text ed. 40.00 (0-8135-1550-5); pap. text ed. 17.00 (0-8135-1551-3) Rutgers U Pr.

Social Structure & the German Reformation. Norman Birnbaum. Ed. by Harriet Zuckerman & Robert K. Merton. LC 79-8976. (Dissertation on Sociology Ser.). 1980. lib. bdg. 44.95 (0-405-12952-1) Ayer.

Social Structure & the Ruling Class, Pt. I. Raymond Aron. (Reprint Series in Sociology). (C). 1993. reprint ed. pap. text ed. 2.90 (0-8290-2779-3, S-4) Irvington.

Social Structure in Divided Germany: A Contribution to the Comparative Analysis of Social Systems. Jaroslav Krejci. LC 76-1338. 192p. 1976. text ed. 29.95 (0-312-73535-9) St Martin.

Social Structure of a Cape Coloured Reserve. W. Peter Carstens. LC 75-3985. (Illus.). 264p. 1975. reprint ed. text ed. 59.75 (0-8371-7431-7, CACR, Greenwood Pr) Greenwood.

Social Structure of Ancient Israel: The Institution of the Family (Beit'ab) from the Settlement to the End of the Monarchy. S. Bendor. 1996. pap. write for info. (0-614-96367-2, Pub. by Simor Ltd IS) Eisenbrauns.

Social Structure of Attention. Ed. by Michael R. Chance & Ray R. Larsen. LC 76-15675. (Illus.). 349p. reprint ed. pap. 99.50 (0-317-08030-X, 2017801) Bks Demand.

Social Structure of Early Christian Communities. Dimitris Kyrtatas & Geoffrey De Ste Croix. 224p. (C). 1987. text ed. 55.00 (0-86091-163-2, Pub. by Vrso UK) Norton.

Social Structure of Modern Britain. 3rd ed. E. A. Johns. 296p. 1979. pap. 28.50 (0-08-023342-2, Pergamon Pr) Elsevier.

Social Structure of Patidar Caste in India. Jayaprakash M. Trivedi. (C). 1992. 24.00 (81-85475-19-9, Pub. by Kanishka) S Asia.

Social Structure of Revolutionary America. Jackson T. Main. LC 65-17146. 340p. reprint ed. pap. 96.90 (0-317-08695-2, 2011969) Bks Demand.

Social Structure of Right & Wrong. Donald Black. (Illus.). 224p. 1993. text ed. 48.00 (0-12-102800-3) Acad Pr.

Social Structure of the Restaurant. William F. Whyte. (Reprint Series in Social Sciences). (C). 1993. reprint ed. pap. text ed. 1.00 (0-8290-3105-7, S-314) Irvington.

Social Structure of the U. S. S. R. Recent Soviet Studies. Ed. & Intro. by Murray Yanowitch. LC 85-18322. 288p. (gr. 13). 1986. pap. text ed. 35.95 (0-87332-468-4) M E Sharpe.

Social Structure Theory & Elements of Knowledge. unabridged ed. Ronald W. Cutburth. 220p. 1996. spiral bd. 26.00 (1-878291-24-6) Love From Sea.

Social Structures: A Network Approach. Ed. by Barry Wellman & S. D. Berkowitz. (Structural Analysis in the Social Sciences Ser.: No. 2). (Illus.). 528p. 1988. pap. 33.95 (0-521-28687-5) Cambridge U Pr.

***Social Structures: A Network Approach.** Barry Wellman & Stephen D. Berkowitz. LC 96-40930. 1996. pap. write for info. (1-56750-327-6) Ablex Pub.

***Social Structures: A Network Approach.** Barry Wellman & Stephen D. Berkowitz. LC 97-2551. (Contemporary Studies in Sociology). 1997. write for info. (0-7623-0290-9); pap. write for info. (0-7623-0291-7) Jai Pr.

Social Structures & Alignments: A Study of Rural India. Hetu K. Jha. 1985. 11.00 (0-8364-1410-1, Pub. by Usha II) S Asia.

Social Structures & Human Lives, Vol. 1: Social Change & the Life Course. Ed. by Matilda W. Riley et al. (American Sociological Association Presidential Ser.). 368p. (C). 1988. text ed. 48.00 (0-8039-3287-1); pap. text ed. 21.50 (0-8039-3288-X) Sage.

Social Structures in Moliere's Theater. James F. Gaines. (Illus.). 293p. 1984. 50.00 (0-8142-0358-2) Ohio St U Pr.

Social Structures of Accumulation: The Political Economy of Growth & Crisis. Ed. by David M. Kotz et al. (Illus.). 320p. (C). 1994. text ed. 59.95 (0-521-44250-8); pap. text ed. 19.95 (0-521-45904-4) Cambridge U Pr.

Social Structures of Indian Villages: A Study of Rural Bihar. Hetukar Jha. (Illus.). 204p. 1991. 27.50 (0-8039-9686-1) Sage.

Social Struggles & the City: The Case of Sao Paulo. Ed. by Lucio Kovarick. 352p. (C). 1993. text ed. 38.00 (0-85345-862-6); pap. text ed. 18.00 (0-85345-863-4) Monthly Rev.

Social Struggles in Archaic Rome: New Perspective on the Conflict of the Orders. Ed. by Kurt A. Raaflaub. 424p. (C). 1986. 70.00 (0-520-05528-4) U CA Pr.

Social Studies. (National Teacher Examination Ser.: NT-8). pap. 23.95 (0-8373-8418-4) Nat Learn.

Social Studies. 1986. 27.00 (0-03-001778-5) HB Schl Dept.

Social Studies. Howard D. Mehlinger. LC 80-83744. (National Society for the Study of Education Publication Ser.: No. 80, Pt II). 290p. (C). 1981. lib. bdg. 16.00 (0-226-60131-5) U Ch Pr.

Social Studies: Applications for a New Century. Sarah S. Pate. LC 95-34828. (Teaching Methods Ser.). 264p. 1996. text ed. 23.00 (0-8273-6637-X) Delmar.

Social Studies: Applications for a New Century. Sarah S. Pate. (Teaching Methods Ser.). 40p. (C). 1996. teacher ed., text ed. 14.95 (0-8273-6638-8) Van Nos Reinhold.

Social Studies: Economics, International Relations, & Political Science. William P. Glade & Emily Baldwin. (Latin American Curriculum Units for Junior & Community Colleges Ser.). v, 85p. (Orig.). (C). 1981. pap. text ed. 4.95 (0-86728-005-0) U TX Inst Lat Am Stud.

Social Studies: History. Richard Graham & Angela Goldston. (Latin American Curriculum Units for Junior & Community Colleges Ser.). v, 46p. 1981. pap. text ed. 3.95 (0-86728-008-5) U TX Inst Lat Am Stud.

Social Studies: In Search of a Rationale. Gerald L. Johnston. (C). 1992. 60.00 (0-86431-058-7, Pub. by Aust Council Educ Res AT) St Mut.

***Social Studies: Middle & High School.** Laughlin. (C). 1995. write for info. (0-15-500098-5) HB Coll Pubs.

***Social Studies: The Best of the Globe & Mail's Daily Miscellany of Information.** Michael Kesterton. 1996. pap. text ed. 19.99 (0-7710-4451-8) McCland & Stewart.

Social Studies: The World 1986. Cangemi. 1986. 46.25 (0-03-001809-9) HB Schl Dept.

Social Studies: Writing Essays & Using Your Textbook. Larry Tominberg & Sylvia Blake. 84p. 1991. student ed. 4.95 (0-560-78029-X) Comp Pr.

Social Studies - Elementary see Ideas for Teaching Gifted Students

Social Studies - Secondary see Ideas for Teaching Gifted Students

Social Studies & Social Sciences: A Fifty-Year Perspective. Stanley P. Wronski & Donald H. Bragaw. LC 86-61765. (Bulletin Ser.: No. 78). 205p. (Orig.). 1986. pap. text ed. 14.95 (0-87986-052-9) Nat Coun Soc Studies.

Social Studies & the Elementary-Middle School Student. Cynthia S. Sunal. 416p. (C). 1993. text ed. 45.25 (0-03-055042-4) HB Coll Pubs.

Social Studies & the Elementary School Child. 5th ed. George W. Maxim. LC 94-11830. 528p. (C). 1994. text ed. 65.00 (0-02-377940-3, Macmillan Coll) P-H.

Social Studies Brochure. Date not set. pap. text ed. write for info. (0-314-60087-6) West Pub.

Social Studies Communities 3. Cangemi. 1988. 34.25 (0-03-001784-X) HB Schl Dept.

Social Studies Content Picture Dictionary. Bonner. (Global ESL/ELT Ser.). (Illus.). 1997. pap. 12.95 (0-8384-6692-3); wbk. ed., pap. 12.95 (0-8384-6693-1) Heinle & Heinle.

Social Studies Curriculum. Mary A. Hepburn et al. (Illus.). 1973. pap. text ed. 14.95 (0-8422-0275-7) Irvington.

***Social Studies Curriculum: Purposes, Problems, & Possibilities.** Ed. by E. Wayne Ross. LC 96-36305. (SUNY Series in Theory, Research, & Practice). 288p. 1997. text ed. 56.50 (0-7914-3443-5) State U NY Pr.

***Social Studies Curriculum: Purposes, Problems, & Possibilities.** Ed. by E. Wayne Ross. LC 96-36305. (SUNY Series in Theory, Research, & Practice). 288p. 1997. pap. text ed. 18.95 (0-7914-3444-3) State U NY Pr.

Social Studies Curriculum Resource Handbook: A Practical Guide for K-12 Social Studies Curriculum. LC 92-20365. (Teacher Resource Handbook Ser.). (Illus.). 408p. 1992. pap. 29.95 (0-8039-6374-2) Corwin Pr.

Social Studies for Children: A Guide to Basic Instruction. 9th ed. John U. Michaelis. (Illus.). 448p. (C). 1988. text ed. write for info. (0-13-818832-7) P-H.

Social Studies for Children: A Guide to Basic Instruction. 11th ed. John U. Michaelis & Jesus Garcia. 1995. text ed. 64.00 (0-205-17537-6) Allyn.

Social Studies for Elementary School Children: Developing Young Citizens. Peter H. Martorella. 432p. (C). 1994. text ed. 64.00 (0-02-376792-8, Macmillan Coll) P-H.

***Social Studies for Elementary School Children: Developing Young Citizens.** 2nd ed. Martorella. (C). 1997. text ed. 60.33 (0-13-496506-X) P-H.

Social Studies for Our Times. Richard E. Gross. LC 78-2733. 401p. reprint ed. pap. 114.30 (0-317-29265-X, 2055517) Bks Demand.

***Social Studies for Secondary Schools: Teaching to Learn, Learning to Teach.** Alan J. Singer & Hofstra Social Studies Educators Staff. LC 97-7496. 1997. pap. write for info. (0-8058-2289-5) L Erlbaum Assocs.

Social Studies for the Eighties in Elementary & Middle Schools. 3rd ed. Leonard S. Kenworthy. LC 80-19096. 541p. (C). 1981. pap. write for info. (0-02-363070-1, Macmillan Coll) P-H.

Social Studies for the Preschool-Primary Child. 5th ed. Carol Seefeldt. LC 96-573. (Illus.). 1996. pap. text ed. 38.00 (0-13-457045-6, Merrill Pub Co) Macmillan.

Social Studies for the Twenty-First Century: Methods & Materials for Teaching in Middle & Secondary Schools. Jack Zevin. (C). 1992. text ed. 54.50 (0-8013-0231-5, 75887) Longman.

Social Studies for Understanding. Helen F. Darrow. LC 64-18225. (Practical Suggestions for Teaching Ser.). 103p. reprint ed. pap. 29.40 (0-317-42002-X, 2026003) Bks Demand.

Social Studies Guide on Korea for High School Teachers. Craig S. Coleman. Ed. by Carol Y. Matthieu. (Illus.). 100p. (Orig.). 1994. pap. 11.95 (0-9637888-1-7) Korea Soc LA.

Social Studies in a Bag. Hayes. (Illus.). 80p. (J). (gr. 1-3). 1995. wbk. ed., pap. text ed. 9.95 (1-55734-198-2) Tchr Create Mat.

Social Studies in a Global Society. Fred Stopsky et al. LC 93-25149. 464p. 1994. text ed. 52.50 (0-8273-5655-2) Delmar.

Social Studies in a Global Society. Fred Stopsky & Sharon Lee. 47p. 1994. teacher ed. 14.95 (0-8273-5656-0) Delmar.

***Social Studies in Elementary & Middle Schools.** Hirsch G. McEachron. (C). 1998. text ed. write for info. (0-8013-1640-5) Addison-Wesley.

Social Studies in Elementary Education. 10th ed. Walter C. Parker & John Jarolimek. LC 96-3433. (Illus.). 1996. text ed. 61.00 (0-13-470015-5, Merrill Pub Co) Macmillan.

Social Studies in England. Sarah K. Bolton. 1977. 13.95 (0-8369-7210-4, 8009) Ayer.

Social Studies in Schools: A History of the Early Years. David W. Saxe. LC 90-48101. (SUNY Series, Theory, Research, & Practice in Social Education). 310p. 1991. pap. text ed. 21.95 (0-7914-0776-4) State U NY Pr.

Social Studies in Schools: A History of the Early Years. David W. Saxe. LC 90-48101. (SUNY Series, Theory, Research, & Practice in Social Education). 310p. 1992. text ed. 64.50 (0-7914-0775-6) State U NY Pr.

Social Studies in the 1980s. fac. ed. Ed. by Irving Morrissett. LC 82-72766. (Report of Project SPAN Ser.). 159p. 1982. reprint ed. pap. 45.40 (0-608-01032-4, 2082508) Bks Demand.

Social Studies, Jr. H. S. Jack Rudman. (Teachers License Examination Ser.: T-54). 1994. pap. 27.95 (0-8373-8054-5) Nat Learn.

Social Studies (K-6) Essential Learning & Study Guide. Cecilia Kabisch. 180p. (C). 1995. per., pap. text ed. 18.37 (0-7872-1918-5) Kendall-Hunt.

Social Studies Learning Centers for the Primary Grades. Carol A. Poppe & Nancy A. Van Matre. 248p. 1989. pap. 27.95 (0-87628-795-X) Ctr Appl Res.

Social Studies, Literature & Fine Arts. (National Teacher Examination Ser.: NC-4). pap. 23.95 (0-8373-8404-4) Nat Learn.

Social Studies of Science. Bernard Barber. 265p. 1990. 44.95 (0-88738-329-7) Transaction Pubs.

Social Studies Readers Theatre for Children: Scripts & Script Development. Mildred K. Laughlin et al. xi, 189p. 1991. pap. text ed. 22.50 (0-87287-865-1) Teacher Ideas Pr.

Social Studies Readers Theatre for Young Adults: Scripts & Script Development. Kathy H. Latrobe et al. ix, 189p. 1991. pap. text ed. 21.50 (0-87287-864-3) Teacher Ideas Pr.

Social Studies Reading. Marilyn Hayes. (Reading Ser.). 24p. (gr. 2). 1980. student ed. 5.00 (0-8209-0195-4, RSS-2) ESP.

Social Studies Region 4. Cangemi. 1986. 45.50 (0-03-001793-9) HB Schl Dept.

***Social Studies Resource Guide.** Ed. by Joel Kupperstein. (Learn to Read Resource Guide Ser.). (Illus.). 80p. (Orig.). 1997. teacher ed., pap. 25.98 (1-57471-223-3, 3496) Creat Teach Pr.

Social Studies, Sr. H. S. Jack Rudman. (Teachers License Examination Ser.: T-55). 1994. pap. 27.95 (0-8373-8055-3) Nat Learn.

Social Studies Teachers Book. Ronald L. Partin. 1991. pap. 29.95 (0-13-824970-9) P-H.

Social Studies Teacher's Guide. (Spanish Storybooks Ser.). 38p. (Orig.). (ENG & SPA.). 1992. 12.00 (1-56334-146-8) Hampton-Brown.

Social Studies Teacher's Survival Kit: Ready-to-Use Activities for Teaching Specific Skills. Martha Lovett. 288p. 1988. spiral bd. 29.95 (0-87628-782-8) Ctr Appl Res.

Social Studies Through Children's Literature: An Integrated Approach. Anthony D. Fredericks. (Illus.). 192p. 1991. pap. text ed. 24.00 (0-87287-970-4) Teacher Ideas Pr.

Social Studies 1: Anthology. 1993. 10.00 (0-88336-115-9); teacher ed. 7.50 (0-88336-116-7); 31.99 (0-88336-117-5) New Readers.

Social Studies 1986: Neighbor Grade 2. Cangemi. 1986. 28.75 (0-03-001782-3) HB Schl Dept.

Social Studies 1991: Grade 1. Harcourt Brace. 1992. teacher ed. 53.00 (0-15-300829-6) HB Schl Dept.

Social Studies 2 Anthology. 1993. 10.00 (0-88336-118-3); teacher ed. 7.50 (0-88336-119-1); 31.99 (0-88336-120-5) New Readers.

Social Study of Judaism: Essays & Reflections, Vol. I. Jacob Neusner. LC 88-33664. (Brown Judaic Studies). 270p. 1989. 46.95 (1-55540-306-9, 14 01 60) Scholars Pr GA.

***Social Study of Judaism: Essays & Reflections, Vol. II.** Jacob Neusner. (Brown Judaic Studies). 162p. 1989. 46.95 (1-55540-332-8, 14 01 62) Scholars Pr GA.

Social Study of Lawyers in Maryland, 1660-1775. Alan F. Day. (Outstanding Studies in Early American History). 350p. 1990. reprint ed. 35.00 (0-8240-6177-2) Garland.

Social Study of One Hundred Fifty Chippewa Indian Families of the White Earth Reservation of Minnesota. Inez Hilger. LC 76-43741. reprint ed. 49.50 (0-404-15582-0) AMS Pr.

Social Study of the Russian German. Hattie P. Williams. LC 83-73458. (Illus.). 100p. (C). 1984. reprint ed. pap. text ed. 10.50 (0-914222-13-9) Am Hist Soc Ger.

Social Style/Management Style. Robert Bolton & Dorothy G. Bolton. LC 83-45959. 192p. 1984. pap. 15.95 (0-8144-7617-1) AMACOM.

Social Stylistics: Syntactic Variations in British Newspapers. Andreas H. Jucker. LC 91-45888. (Topics in English Linguistics Ser.: No. 6). xxii, 297p. (C). 1992. lib. bdg. 90.80 (3-11-012969-8) Mouton.

Social Subjects Within the Curriculum: Children's Social Learning in the National Curriculum. Ed. by John Ahier & Alistair Ross. LC 94-36897. 192p. 1995. 75.00 (0-7507-0381-4, Falmer Pr); pap. 24.95 (0-7507-0382-2, Falmer Pr) Taylor & Francis.

***Social Suffering.** Arthur Kleinman et al. LC 97-201. 1997. write for info. (0-520-20993-1); pap. write for info. (0-520-20995-8) U CA Pr.

Social Support: An International View. Barbara R. Sarason et al. LC 89-27301. (Personality Processes Ser.). 528p. 1990. text ed. 100.00 (0-471-60624-3) Wiley.

Social Support: Theory, Research & Intervention. Alan Vaux. LC 88-5888. 355p. 1988. text ed. 59.95 (0-275-92811-X, C2811, Praeger Pubs) Greenwood.

Social Support & Cardiovascular Disease. Ed. by S. A. Shumaker & S. M. Czajkowski. (Behavioral Psychophysiology & Medicine Ser.). (Illus.). 360p. 1994. 55.00 (0-306-43982-4, Plenum Pr) Plenum.

Social Support & Health: An Annotated Bibliography. John B. Bruhn et al. LC 87-17796. (Library of Sociology: Vol. 13). 528p. 1987. text ed. 82.00 (0-8240-8348-2, SS412) Garland.

Social Support & Motherhood: The Natural History of a Research Project. Ann Oakley. LC 92-14642. 416p. 1992. pap. 28.95 (0-631-18274-8) Blackwell Pubs.

Social Support & Motherhood: The Natural History of a Research Project. Ann Oakley. LC 92-14642. 416p. 1993. 56.95 (0-631-18273-X) Blackwell Pubs.

Social Support & Patient Adherence: Experimental & Survey Findings. Robert D. Caplan et al. 283p. (Orig.). 1980. pap. 16.00 (0-87944-260-3) Inst Soc Res.

Social Support & Psychiatric Disorder: Research Findings & Guidelines for Clinical Practice. Ed. by T. S. Brugha. (Studies in Social & Community Psychiatry). (Illus.). 400p. (C). 1995. text ed. 85.00 (0-521-44238-9) Cambridge U Pr.

Social Support in Couples: Marriage As a Resource in Times of Stress. Carolyn E. Cutrona. (Series in Close Relationships: Vol. 13). 150p. (C). 1996. pap. 16.95 (0-8039-4884-0); 38.00 (0-8039-4883-2) Sage.

Social Support Networks: A Bibliography. David Biegel et al. LC 88-32824. 347p. 1989. text ed. 75.00 (0-313-26604-2, BSX, Greenwood Pr) Greenwood.

Social Support Networks: Informal Helping in the Human Services. James K. Whittaker & James Garbarino. LC 83-11761. (Modern Applications of Social Work Ser.). 499p. (C). 1983. pap. text ed. 30.95 (0-202-36032-6) Aldine de Gruyter.

Social Support Strategies: Guidelines for Mental Health Practice. Benjamin H. Gottlieb. LC 83-6653. (Sage Studies in Community Mental Health: No. 7). 239p. 1983. reprint ed. pap. 68.20 (0-608-01480-X, 2059524) Bks Demand.

Social Support Systems for the Aged in Egypt. 145p. Date not set. pap. 30.00 (92-808-0765-X, E.91.III.A.2) UN.

Social Support Systems in Practice: A Generalist Approach. Lambert Maguire. LC 91-28008. 187p. (C). 1991. 21.95 (0-87101-189-1) Natl Assn Soc Wkrs.

Social Survey in Historical Perspective, 1880-1940. Ed. by Martin Bulmer et al. (Illus.). 304p. (C). 1992. 75.00 (0-521-36334-9) Cambridge U Pr.

Social Survey Methods: A Guide for Development Workers. Paul Nichols. 132p. (C). 1991. pap. 14.95 (0-85598-126-1, Pub. by Oxfam UK) Humanities.

Social Survey Methods for Mass Media Research. R. C. Adams. 192p. 1989. 29.95 (0-8058-0140-5) L Erlbaum Assocs.

Social Survey of Grand Gedah County. Svend E. Holsoe. 1979. 9.00 (0-686-33170-2) Arden Assocs.

Social Survey of the Kuting District of Taipei City. Lung Kwan-Hai. (Asian Folklore & Social Life Monographs: No. 65). 200p. (CHI.). 1975. 14.00 (0-89986-060-5) Oriental Bk Store.

Social System. Talcott Parsons. 1964. pap. 22.95 (0-02-924190-1, Free Press) Free Pr.

Social System Accounts. Fox. (Theory & Decision Library). 1985. lib. bdg. 86.50 (90-277-2020-7) Kluwer Ac.

Social System & Legal Process. Ed. by Harry M. Johnson. LC 77-93676. (Jossey-Bass Social & Behavioral Science Ser.). 370p. reprint ed. pap. 105.50 (0-317-41971-4, 2025675) Bks Demand.

Social System & the Dalit Identity. Ed. by Prakash Sangwan. (C). 1996. 54.00 (81-7169-367-9, Pub. by Commonwealth II) S Asia.

Social System of a Rural Yugoslav-American Community-Oysterville. Frank M. Lovrich. LC 79-155329. 1963. pap. 10.00 (0-88247-119-8) Ragusan Pr.

Social Systems. Niklas Luhmann. Tr. by John Bednarz, Jr. & Dirk Baecker from GER. (Writing Science Ser.). 570p. pap. 24.95 (0-8047-2625-6) Stanford U Pr.

Social Systems. Niklas Luhmann. Tr. by John Bednarz, Jr. & Dirk Baecker from GER. LC 94-46175. (Writing Science Ser.). 570p. (GER.). 1995. 69.50 (0-8047-1993-4) Stanford U Pr.

Social Systems & Family Patterns: A Propositional Inventory. William J. Goode et al. LC 75-158851. 1971. 49.50 (0-672-61151-1) Irvington.

Social Systems & Learning Systems. A. F. Hanken & H. A. Reuver. (Frontiers in Systems Research Ser.: Vol. 4). 240p. 1981. lib. bdg. 70.50 (0-89838-050-2) Kluwer Ac.

Social Systems & Population Cycles in Voles. R. H. Tamarin et al. (Advances in Life Sciences Ser.). 232p. 1991. 63.50 (0-8176-2437-6) Birkhauser.

An Asterisk (*) at the beginning of an entry indicates that the title is appearing in BIP for the first time.

Social Systems & Schizophrenia: Selected Papers. H. Warren Dunham. LC 80-14193. 332p. 1980. text ed. 65.00 (0-275-90472-5, C0472, Praeger Pubs) Greenwood.

Social Systems of American Ethnic Groups. William L. Warner. LC 75-31425. (Yankee City Ser.: Vol. 3). (Illus.). 318p. 1976. reprint ed. text ed. 65.00 (0-8371-8502-5, WAAE, Greenwood Pr) Greenwood.

Social Teaching of the Black Churches. Peter J. Paris. LC 84-47930. 162p. 1985. pap. 15.00 (0-8006-1805-X, 1-1805, Fortress Pr) Augsburg Fortress.

Social Teaching of the Christian Churches, 2 vols. Ernst Troeltsch. Tr. by Olive Wyon. (Library of Theological Ethics). 1024p. 1992. reprint ed. pap. 37.00 (0-664-25320-2) Westminster John Knox.

Social Teachings in the Episcopal Church. Robert E. Hood. LC 90-31394. 176p. (Orig.). 1990. pap. 9.95 (0-8192-1533-3) Morehouse Pub.

Social Teachings of James Connolly. Lambert McKenna. 104p. 1989. pap. 22.00 (1-85390-133-4, Pub. by Veritas IE) St Mut.

Social Teachings of Pope John Paul II. Ed. by Stephen H. Gratto. 168p. 1987. pap. 18.00 (0-318-37559-1); lib. bdg. 39.00 (0-318-37558-3) Catholic Charities.

Social Tensions in India. Govind S. Ghurye. 552p. 1968. 89.50 (0-614-01820-X) Elliots Bks.

Social Tensions, Job Creation, & Economic Policy in Latin America. 388p. (Orig.). 1995. pap. 45.00 (92-64-14403-X, Pub. by Org for Econ FR) OECD.

***Social Theories of Art.** Heywood. LC 97-15323. 1998. 50.00 (0-8147-3372-7); pap. 17.50 (0-8147-3531-2) NYU Pr.

Social Theories of Risk. Ed. by Sheldon Krimsky & Dominic Golding. LC 91-47739. 432p. 1992. text ed. 65.00 (0-275-94168-X, C4168, Praeger Pubs); pap. text ed. 22.95 (0-275-94317-8, B4317, Praeger Pubs) Greenwood.

Social Theories of Talcott Parsons: A Critical Examination. Ed. by Max Black. LC 75-40325. (Arcturus Books Paperbacks). 384p. 1976. reprint ed. pap. 12.95 (0-8093-0759-6) S Ill U Pr.

***Social Theories of the City, 10 vols.** Bryan S. Turner. (Making of Sociology Ser.). 4000p. (C). 1997. text ed. 25.00 (0-415-15386-7) Routledge.

Social Theories of the Middle Ages, Twelve Hundred to Twelve-Fifty. Bede Bartlett. 1976. lib. bdg. 59.95 (0-8490-2619-9) Gordon Pr.

Social Theories of the Press: Early German & American Perspectives. Hanno Hardt. LC 78-31588. (People & Communication Ser.: No. 6). 240p. reprint ed. pap. 68.40 (0-8357-8426-6, 2034689) Bks Demand.

Social Theory. John Wilson. (Illus.). 256p. (C). 1982. pap. text ed. 55.00 (0-13-819573-0) P-H.

Social Theory: A Guide to Central Thinkers. Ed. by Peter Beilharz. 256p. (Orig.). pap. 22.95 (1-86373-163-6, Pub. by Allen Unwin AT) Paul & Co Pubs.

Social Theory: Its Situation & Its Task: A Critical Introduction. Roberto M. Unger. 231p. 1987. pap. text ed. 16.95 (0-521-33862-X) Cambridge U Pr.

Social Theory: Its Situation & Its Task: A Critical Introduction. Roberto M. Unger. 231p. 1988. text ed. 54.95 (0-521-32974-4) Cambridge U Pr.

Social Theory: Multicultural & Classic Readings. Ed. by Charles C. Lemert. LC 93-1043. 672p. (C). 1993. pap. text ed. 28.00 (0-8133-1584-0) Westview.

Social Theory after Postmodernism: Rethinking Production, Law & Class. Anthony Woodiwiss. 205p. (C). 66.50 (0-7453-0387-0, Pub. by Pluto Pr UK); pap. 21.00 (0-7453-0472-9, Pub. by Pluto Pr UK) LPC InBook.

Social Theory & Education: A Critique of Theories of Social & Cultural Reproduction. Ed. by Raymond A. Morrow & Carlos A. Torres. LC 94-3956. (SUNY Series, Teacher Empowerment & School Reform). 517p. (C). 1995. text ed. 74.50 (0-7914-2251-8); pap. text ed. 24.95 (0-7914-2252-6) State U NY Pr.

Social Theory & Modern Sociology. Anthony Giddens. LC 86-63251. x, 310p. 1987. 45.00 (0-8047-1355-3); pap. 16.95 (0-8047-1356-1) Stanford U Pr.

Social Theory & Modernity: Critique, Dissent, & Revolution. Timothy W. Luke. 280p. (C). 1990. text ed. 49.95 (0-8039-3860-8); pap. text ed. 24.00 (0-8039-3861-6) Sage.

Social Theory & Political Practice. Brian Fay. (Controversies in Sociology Ser.). 1975. pap. text ed. 15.95 (0-04-300048-7) Routledge Chapman & Hall.

Social Theory & Psychoanalysis in Transition: Self & Society from Freud to Kristeva. Anthony Elliott. 220p. 1992. text ed. 56.95 (0-631-18327-2) Blackwell Pubs.

Social Theory & Public Policy. Ed. by J. Rogers Hollingsworth & Richard D. Lambert. LC 77-83259. (Annals of the American Academy of Political & Social Science Ser.: No. 434). 1977. pap. 18.00 (0-87761-221-8) Am Acad Pol Soc Sci.

Social Theory & Social Criticism: Essay for Tom Bottomore. Ed. by William Outhwaite & Michael Mulkay. (Modern Revivals in Sociology Ser.). 273p. 1992. 59.95 (0-7512-0073-5, Pub. by Gregg Revivals UK) Ashgate Pub Co.

Social Theory & Social Policy: Essays in Honor of James S. Coleman. Ed. by Aage B. Sorensen & Seymour Spilerman. LC 92-15683. 280p. 1993. text ed. 62.95 (0-275-94235-X, C4235, Praeger Pubs) Greenwood.

Social Theory & Social Structure. Robert K. Merton. LC 68-28789. 1968. 35.00 (0-02-921130-1, Free Press) Free Pr.

Social Theory & Sociology: The Classics & Beyond. Ed. by Stephen P. Turner. LC 96-3615. 320p. Date not set. 64.95 (0-631-19192-5); pap. 19.95 (0-631-19193-3) Blackwell Pubs.

Social Theory & the Crisis of State Socialism. Larry Ray. LC 95-42409. (Studies of Communism in Transition). 304p. 1996. 75.00 (1-85278-688-4) E Elgar.

Social Theory & the Global Environment. Ed. by Michael Redclift & Ted Benton. LC 93-44072. (Global Environmental Change Ser.). 256p. (C). 1994. pap. 18.95 (0-415-11170-6, B3823, Routledge NY) Routledge.

Social Theory & the Politics of Identity. Craig Calhoun. 352p. 1994. pap. text ed. 22.95 (1-55786-473-X) Blackwell Pubs.

Social Theory As Science. rev. ed. Russell Keat & John Urry. (International Library of Sociology). 288p. 1983. pap. 12.95 (0-7100-9431-0, RKP) Routledge.

Social Theory for Action: How Individuals & Organizations Learn to Change. William F. Whyte. (Illus.). 336p. 1991. 39.95 (0-8039-4166-8); pap. text ed. 21.95 (0-8039-4167-6) Sage.

***Social Theory for Action: How Individuals & Organizations Learn to Change.** William F. Whyte. LC 91-6941. (Illus.). 309p. 1991. reprint ed. pap. 88.10 (0-608-04326-5, 2065106) Bks Demand.

Social Theory of Georg Simmel. Nicholas J. Spykman. (Modern Revivals in Sociology Ser.). 330p. 1992. 61.95 (0-7512-0047-6, Pub. by Gregg Revivals UK) Ashgate Pub Co.

Social Theory of James Mark Baldwin. Vahan D. Sewny. LC 66-19695. vii, 93p. 1967. reprint ed. 25.00 (0-678-00211-8) Kelley.

Social Theory of Modern Societies: Anthony Giddens & His Critics. Ed. by David Held & John B. Thompson. (Illus.). 320p. (C). 1990. pap. text ed. 21.95 (0-521-27855-4) Cambridge U Pr.

Social Theory of Practices: Tradition, Tacit Knowledge & Presuppositions. Stephen P. Turner. LC 93-44989. (Illus.). 156p. 1994. pap. text ed. 14.95 (0-226-81738-5); lib. bdg. 39.95 (0-226-81737-7) U Ch Pr.

Social Theory of Religious Education. George A. Coe. LC 78-89164. (American Education: Its Men, Institutions, & Ideas. Series 1). 1977. reprint ed. 26.95 (0-405-01402-3) Ayer.

Social Theory Perspectives on Adult Education. B. Elsey. (C). 1986. 39.00 (1-85041-013-5, Pub. by Univ Nottingham UK) St Mut.

Social Theory Perspectives on Adult Education. Barry Elsey. 171p. (C). 1986. 75.00 (0-317-94047-3, Pub. by Univ Nottingham UK) St Mut.

Social Theory, Social Change & Social Work. Ed. by Nigel Parton. LC 95-31962. (State of Welfare Ser.). 256p. (C). 1996. pap. 18.95 (0-415-12698-3); text ed. 59.95 (0-415-12697-5) Routledge.

Social Theory Today. Ed. by Anthony Giddens & Jonathan H. Turner. 434p. 1987. 49.50 (0-8047-1397-9); pap. 19.95 (0-8047-1514-9) Stanford U Pr.

***Social Things: An Introduction to the Sociological Life.** Charles Lemert. 188p. 1997. 17.95 (0-8476-8538-1) Rowman.

***Social Things: An Introduction to the Sociological Life.** Charles Lemert. 188p. 1997. pap. 12.95 (0-8476-8539-X) Rowman.

Social Thought. George A. Kourvetaris. 572p. (Orig.). (C). 1994. pap. text ed. 42.50 (0-8191-9326-7); lib. bdg. 67.50 (0-8191-9325-9) U Pr of Amer.

Social Thought. Peter C. Phan. Ed. by Thomas Halton. LC 83-83156. (Message of the Fathers of the Church Ser.: Vol. 20). 268p. 1984. pap. 14.95 (0-8146-5331-6) Liturgical Pr.

Social Thought: From Hammurabi to Comte. Rollin Chambliss. LC 54-10267. 469p. 1982. reprint ed. pap. text ed. 19.95 (0-8290-0147-6) Irvington.

Social Thought from Lore to Science, Vols. 2 & 3, Each Volume. 3rd ed. Howard Becker & Harry E. Barnes. 1990. Vol. 2 & 3. 17.00 (0-8446-1620-6) Peter Smith.

Social Thought of Bernard Mandeville: Virtue & Commerce in Early Eighteenth Century England. Thomas A. Horne. LC 77-13573. 1978. text ed. 49.50 (0-231-04274-4) Col U Pr.

Social Thought of Jane Addams. Jane Addams. Ed. by Christopher Lasch. LC 65-22345. (Orig.). 1965. pap. 6.30 (0-672-60110-9, Bobbs) Macmillan.

Social Thought of Jane Addams. Jane Addams. Ed. by Christopher Lasch. LC 82-7135. 300p. (Orig.). 1982. reprint ed. pap. text ed. 16.95 (0-8290-0338-X) Irvington.

Social Thought of John Twenty-Third: Mater et Magistra. Jean Y. Calvez. Tr. by George J. McKenzie. LC 75-40992. 121p. 1977. reprint ed. text ed. 49.75 (0-8371-8711-7, CASCJ, Greenwood Pr) Greenwood.

Social Thought of Rabindranath Tagore: A Historical Analysis. Tapati Dasgupta. (C). 1993. 24.00 (81-7017-302-7, Pub. by Abhinav II) S Asia.

Social Thought of the Ancient Civilizations. Joyce O. Hertzler. 1973. 250.00 (0-87968-383-X) Gordon Pr.

Social Thought of Thomas Merton. David W. Givey. 135p. 1983. 4.49 (0-8199-0859-2, Frncscn Herld) Franciscan Pr.

Social Threat & Social Control. Ed. by Allen E. Liska. LC 91-7550. (SUNY Series in Deviance & Social Control). (Illus.). 288p. (C). 1992. text ed. 59.50 (0-7914-0903-1); pap. text ed. 19.95 (0-7914-0904-X) State U NY Pr.

***Social Ties & Economic Performance.** Frans Van Dijk. (Theory & Decision Library: Series C). 224p. 1997. lib. bdg. 110.00 (0-7923-9836-X) Kluwer Ac.

Social Transformation in India. Ed. by T. M. Dak. 1990. 29.50 (81-202-0284-8, Pub. by Ajanta II) S Asia.

Social Transformation of American Medicine. Paul Starr. LC 81-68412. 514p. 1984. pap. 22.00 (0-465-07935-0) Basic.

Social Transformations: A General Theory of Historical Development. Stephen K. Sanderson. (Illus.). 432p. (C). 1995. 67.95 (1-55786-403-9); pap. 25.95 (1-55786-404-7) Blackwell Pubs.

Social Traps. John Cross & Mel Guyer. (Illus.). 1980. pap. 16.95 (0-472-06315-4) U of Mich Pr.

Social Treatment: An Approach to Interpersonal Helping in Social Work Practice. 2nd ed. James K. Whittaker & Elizabeth M. Tracy. (Modern Applications of Social Work Ser.). 293p. (Orig.). (C). 1989. pap. text ed. 24.95 (0-202-36051-2); lib. bdg. 45.95 (0-202-36050-4) Aldine de Gruyter.

Social Treatment in Probation & Delinquency. 2nd ed. Pauline V. Young. LC 69-14955. (Criminology, Law Enforcement, & Social Problems Ser.: No. 47). 1969. reprint ed. 30.00 (0-87585-047-2) Patterson Smith.

Social Trend. Edward A. Ross. LC 72-117831. (Essay Index Reprint Ser.). 1977. 20.95 (0-8369-1680-8) Ayer.

Social Trends in Contemporary Russia: A Statistical Source-Book. Tr. & Compiled by Michael Ryan. LC 93-7913. 1993. text ed. 59.95 (0-312-10070-1) St Martin.

Social Trends in the Soviet Union from 1950. Michael Ryan & Richard Prentice. LC 86-33919. 120p. 1987. text ed. 45.00 (0-312-00543-1) St Martin.

Social Triumph of the Ancient Church. Shirley J. Case. LC 76-164596. (Select Bibliographies Reprint Ser.). 1977. reprint ed. 20.95 (0-8369-5880-2) Ayer.

Social Trust: Toward a Cosmopolitan Society. Timothy C. Earle & George T. Cvetkovich. LC 94-45265. 240p. 1995. text ed. 57.95 (0-275-94845-5, Praeger Pubs) Greenwood.

Social Typifications & the Elusive Other: Alfred Schutz's Phenomenology & the Sociology of Knowledge. Michael D. Barber. LC 86-73241. 144p. 1988. 32.50 (0-8387-5123-7) Bucknell U Pr.

Social Understanding Through Spiritual Scientific Knowledge. Rudolf Steiner. 20p. 1982. pap. 3.95 (0-88010-075-3) Anthroposophic.

Social Unrest in the Late Middle Ages: Papers of the Fifteenth Annual Conference of the Center for Medieval & Early Renaissance Studies. Ed. by Francis X. Newman. LC 85-28420. (Medieval & Renaissance Texts & Studies: Vol. 39). (Illus.). 160p. 1986. 20.00 (0-86698-071-7, MR39) MRTS.

Social Use of Information: Ownership & Access. Andrew E. Wessel. LC 76-18211. (Information Sciences Ser.). (Illus.). 264p. reprint ed. pap. 75.30 (0-317-10572-8, 2022496) Bks Demand.

Social Use of Metaphor: Essays on the Anthropology of Rhetoric. Ed. by J. David Sapir. LC 76-53200. 263p. reprint ed. pap. 75.00 (0-8357-3324-6, 2039548) Bks Demand.

Social Uses of Literacy. Ed. by Mastin Prinsloo & Mignonne Breier. LC 96-14789. (Studies in Written Language & Literacy: Vol. 4). 288p. 1996. pap. 24.95 (1-55619-321-1); lib. bdg. 69.00 (1-55619-320-3) Benjamins North Am.

Social Uses of Writing: Politics & Pedagogy. Thomas Fox. Ed. by George W. Noblit & William Pink. LC 89-78106. (Interpretive Perspectives on Education & Policy Ser.). 140p. (C). 1990. text ed. 73.25 (0-89391-601-3) Ablex Pub.

Social Value: A Study in Economic Theory Critical & Constructive. Benjamin M. Anderson, Jr. LC 65-26357. (Reprints of Economic Classics Ser.). xviii, 204p. 1966. reprint ed. 35.00 (0-678-00177-4) Kelley.

Social Value of Property According to St. Thomas Aquinas: A Study in Social Philosophy. William J. McDonald. 1972. 59.95 (0-8490-1068-3) Gordon Pr.

Social Values: Index of Modern Information with Bibliography. rev. ed. Duane C. Umbaugh. 150p. (Orig.). 1992. 47.50 (1-55914-836-5); pap. 44.50 (1-55914-837-3) ABBE Pubs Assn.

Social Values among Young Adults: A Changing Scenario. Ed. by Man Singh Das & Vijay Kumar Gupta. 187p. 1995. pap. 120.00 (81-85880-65-4, Pub. by Print Hse II) St Mut.

Social Values & Development: Asian Perspectives. Ed. by Durganand Sinha & S. R. Kao. 320p. (C). 1989. text ed. 27.50 (0-8039-9568-7) Sage.

Social Values & Poetic Acts: The Historical Judgment of Literary Work. Jerome J. McGann. LC 87-14649. 296p. 1988. 37.00 (0-674-81495-9) HUP.

Social Values & Public Policy. Ed. by William Dunn. (Orig.). (C). 1981. pap. 15.00 (0-918592-44-5) Pol Studies.

Social Values & Social Change: Adaptations to Life in America. Ed. by Lynn R. Kahle. LC 83-16074. 346p. 1983. text ed. 55.00 (0-275-91018-0, C1018, Praeger Pubs) Greenwood.

Social Values in Folklore. Deep Punia. (C). 1993. 19.50 (81-7033-193-5, Pub. by Rawat II) S Asia.

Social Viability of Money: Competitive Equilibria & the Core of Overlapping Generations Economies. J. Esteban. Ed. by Martin J. Beckmann & W. Krelle. (Lecture Notes in Economics & Mathematical Systems Ser.: Vol. 372). (Illus.). x, 202p. 1991. 44.00 (0-387-54649-9) Spr-Verlag.

***Social Vision of William Blake.** Michael Ferber. LC 85-522. 269p. 1985. reprint ed. pap. 76.70 (0-608-02519-4, 2063163) Bks Demand.

Social, Vol. 17, Pt. II see History of Women in the United States: Topically Arranged Articles on the Evolution of Women's History in the United States

Social Warfare, Special Weapons: Small Arms & Equipment of the U. S. Navy Seals & UDT. Kevin Dockery. (Illus.). 192p. 29.95 (1-883476-00-3) Emperors Pr.

Social Wasps of India & the Adjacent Countries (Hymenoptera: Vespidae) (An Illustrated Account of the Vespid Fauna of the Indian Subregion) Bina P. Das & Virendra K. Gupta. (Oriental Insects Monographs: No. 11). (Illus.). 300p. (C). 1989. 55.00 (1-877711-22-5) Assoc Pubs FL.

Social Web: An Introduction to Sociology. 6th ed. John A. Perry & Erna K. Perry. LC 92-28783. (C). 1993. text ed. 29.50 (0-06-501212-7) Addson-Wesley Educ.

***Social Welfare.** 2nd ed. Central Office of Info. (Aspects of Britain Ser.). (Illus.). 138p. 1997. pap. 13.00 (0-11-701931-3, Pub. by Stationery Ofc UK) Seven Hills Bk.

Social Welfare: A Helping Hand? Ed. by Norma Jones et al. (Compact Reference Ser.). (Illus.). 56p. (J). (gr. 6-9). 1995. pap. text ed. 11.95 (1-57302-000-1) Info Plus TX.

Social Welfare: A History of the American Response to Need. 3rd ed. June Axinn & Herman Levin. 368p. (C). 1992. pap. text ed. 34.50 (0-8013-0294-3, 75944) Longman.

Social Welfare: A History of the American Response to Need. 4th ed. June Axinn. LC 96-9085. (C). 1997. pap. text ed. 34.95 (0-8013-1700-2) Addison-Wesley.

Social Welfare: A Response to Human Need. 4th ed. Louise C. Johnson et al. LC 96-12679. 1996. text ed. 59.00 (0-205-19729-9) Allyn.

Social Welfare: A World View. Katherine. LC 96-10556. (Illus.). (Orig.). 1996. pap. text ed. 37.95 (0-8304-1435-5) Nelson-Hall.

***Social Welfare: Help or Hindrance?** rev. ed. Ed. by Jacquelyn F. Quiram. (Reference Ser.). 144p. 1996. pap. text ed. 22.95 (1-57302-030-3) Info Plus TX.

Social Welfare: Policy & Analysis. 2nd ed. Andrew W. Dobelstein. LC 96-4578. (Illus.). (Orig.). 1996. pap. text ed. 29.95 (0-8304-1428-2) Nelson-Hall.

Social Welfare: Politics & Public Policy. 4th ed. Diana M. DiNitto. LC 94-29493. 1994. text ed. 53.00 (0-13-063819-6) Allyn.

Social Welfare Abroad: Comparative Data on the Social Insurance & Public Assistance Programs of Selected Industrialized Democracies. Bette K. Fishbein. LC 75-9028. (Illus.). 35p. 1975. pap. 3.00 (0-915312-01-8) Inst Socioecon.

Social Welfare Alive! Stephen Moore. 256p. (Orig.). (C). 1993. pap. 42.50 (0-7487-1402-2, Pub. by Stanley Thornes UK) Trans-Atl Phila.

Social Welfare Alive! An Introduction to Issues & Policies in Health & Welfare. Stephen Moore. 256p. 1993. 60.00 (0-614-07519-X, Pub. by Stanley Thornes UK) Trans-Atl Phila.

Social Welfare & Social Development. Eugen Pusic. LC 79-189707. (Institute of Social Studies Publications: No. 5). (Illus.). 251p. (Orig.). 1972. pap. text ed. 19.25 (90-279-1969-0) Mouton.

Social Welfare & the Feminization of Poverty. Shirley A. Lord. LC 92-33245. (Children of Poverty Ser.). 112p. 1993. text ed. 39.00 (0-8153-1119-2) Garland.

Social Welfare Examiner. Jack Rudman. (Career Examination Ser.: C-2132). 1994. reprint ed. pap. 23.95 (0-8373-2132-8) Nat Learn.

Social Welfare Examiner (Spanish Speaking) Jack Rudman. (Career Examination Ser.: C-2136). 1994. reprint ed. pap. 27.95 (0-8373-2136-0) Nat Learn.

Social Welfare in America: An Annotated Bibliography. Ed. by Walter I. Trattner & W. Andrew Achenbaum. LC 83-10855. xxxiii, 324p. 1983. text ed. 69.50 (0-313-23002-1, TSW/, Greenwood Pr) Greenwood.

Social Welfare in Asia. Ed. by John Dixon & Hyung S. Kim. LC 85-21279. 432p. 1986. 49.95 (0-7099-0853-9, Pub. by Croom Helm UK) Routledge Chapman & Hall.

Social Welfare in Britain, Eighteen Eighty-Five to Nineteen Eighty-Five. Ed. by Rex Pope et al. 192p. (Orig.). (C). 1986. 37.50 (0-7099-4001-7, Pub. by Croom Helm UK) Routledge Chapman & Hall.

Social Welfare in Canada Revisited: Facing up to the Future. Andrew Armitage. 222p. 1996. pap. 35.00 (0-19-541204-4) OUP.

Social Welfare in Developed Market Countries. Robert P. Scheurell. (Comparative Social Welfare Ser.). 320p. (C). 1989. lib. bdg. 67.50 (0-415-00532-9) Routledge.

***Social Welfare in Global Context.** James Midgley. LC 96-51210. 1997. write for info. (0-7619-0787-4); pap. write for info. (0-7619-0788-2) Sage.

Social Welfare in India. Sumitra Gupta. (C). 1989. 34.00 (81-85076-60-X, Pub. by Chugh Pubns II) S Asia.

Social Welfare in India. Nalina Pranjpe. 1990. text ed. 18.95 (81-7045-051-9, Pub. by Associated Pub Hse II) Advent Bks Div.

Social Welfare in Society. George T. Martin & Mayer N. Zald. LC 81-3837. (Illus.). 576p. 1981. text ed. 69.00 (0-231-04922-6) Col U Pr.

Social Welfare in Society. Ed. by George T. Martin, Jr. & Mayer M. Zald. LC 81-3837. 614p. reprint ed. pap. 175.00 (0-8357-6866-X, 2035564) Bks Demand.

Social Welfare in the Middle East. Ed. by John Dixon. 256p. (C). 1986. 55.00 (0-7099-4502-7, Pub. by Croom Helm UK) Routledge Chapman & Hall.

Social Welfare in the South from Colonial Times to World War I. fac. ed. Elizabeth Wisner. LC 78-123206. 162p. 1970. reprint ed. pap. 46.20 (0-7837-7751-5, 2047507) Bks Demand.

Social Welfare in the Soviet Union. Bernice Q. Madison. xxvi, 298p. 1968. 42.50 (0-8047-0654-9) Stanford U Pr.

Social Welfare in Today's World. Ronald C. Federico. 1990. pap. text ed. write for info. (0-07-020374-1) McGraw.

Social Welfare in Today's World. 2nd ed. William H. Whitaker & Ronald C. Federico. LC 96-22609. 1996. pap. text ed. write for info. (0-07-069624-1) McGraw.

Social Welfare Law. David Pearl & Kevin Gray. 308p. 1981. 29.95 (0-85664-644-X, Pub. by Croom Helm UK); pap. 14.75 (0-7099-2004-0, Pub. by Croom Helm UK) Routledge Chapman & Hall.

Social Welfare of the Aging: Proceedings of the International Association of Gerontology, 5th Congress, Vol. 2. International Association of Gerontology Staff. Ed. by Jerome Kaplan & G. J. Aldridge. (Aging Around the World Ser.). 1962. text ed. 55.00 (0-231-08950-3) Col U Pr.

S

An Asterisk (*) at the beginning of an entry indicates that the title is appearing in BIP for the first time.

Social Welfare or Social Control? Some Historical Reflections on "Regulating the Poor" Ed. by Walter I. Trattner. LC 82-15901. 168p. 1983. text ed. 25.00 (0-87049-374-4); pap. text ed. 15.00 (0-87049-375-2) U of Tenn Pr.

Social Welfare Policy. Tice. (Social Work Ser.). Date not set. pap. 34.00 (0-534-34502-6) Course Tech.

Social Welfare Policy: A Research & Action Strategy. W. Joseph Heffernan. (C). 1992. text ed. 51.95 (0-8013-0546-2, 78452) Longman.

Social Welfare Policy: From Theory to Practice. Bruce S. Jansson. 469p. (C). 1989. text ed. 42.95 (0-534-12600-6) Brooks-Cole.

***Social Welfare Policy, Programs, & Practice.** Elizabeth A. Segal & Stephanie Brzuzy. 350p. (Orig.). (C). 1997. pap. text ed. write for info. (0-87581-411-5) Peacock Pubs.

Social Welfare Spending: Accounting for Changes from Nineteen Fifty to Nineteen Seventy-Eight. Robert J. Lampman. (Institute for Research on Poverty Policy Analysis Ser.). 1984. text ed. 57.00 (0-12-435260-X) Acad Pr.

Social Welfare with Indigenous Peoples. Ed. by John Dixon & Robert P. Scheurell. LC 94-8496. (Comparative Social Welfare Ser.). 320p. (C). (gr. 13). 1994. text ed. 89.95 (0-415-05564-4, B4387, Routledge NY) Routledge.

Social Will see Johns Hopkins University Psychology Laboratories: Studies

Social Withdrawal, Inhibition, & Shyness in Childhood. Ed. by Kenneth H. Rubin & Jens Asendorpf. 368p. 1993. pap. 39.95 (0-8058-1220-2); text ed. 79.95 (0-8058-1219-9) L Erlbaum Assocs.

Social Work. 2nd ed. Dinitto & C. Aaron McNeece. LC 96-23669. 432p. 1996. 53.00 (0-13-063827-7) P-H.

Social Work. 2nd ed. Heffernan. Date not set. teacher ed., pap. text ed. write for info. (0-314-88774-1) West Pub.

***Social Work.** 8th ed. Morales & Sheafor. 1997. text ed. 54.00 (0-205-27224-X) P-H.

Social Work: A Profession of Many Faces. 5th ed. Armando T. Morales & Bradford W. Sheafor. 740p. 1989. boxed 44.00 (0-205-11888-7, H18880) Allyn.

Social Work: A Profession of Many Faces. 7th ed. Armando T. Morales & Bradford W. Sheafor. LC 94-21177. 1994. text ed. 60.00 (0-205-16201-0) Allyn.

Social Work: Challenges & Directions: A Special Issue of Families in Society. 72p. 1995. pap. 8.95 (0-87304-277-8) Families Intl.

Social Work: Disabled People & Disabling Environments. Ed. by Michael Oliver. 160p. 1991. 57.00 (1-85302-042-7) Taylor & Francis.

Social Work: Disabled People & Disabling Environments. Ed. by Michael Oliver. 208p. 1992. pap. 27.50 (1-85302-178-4) Taylor & Francis.

Social Work: Essays on the Meeting-Ground of Doctor & Social Worker. Richard C. Cabot. LC 76-180561. (Medicine & Society in America Ser.). 224p. 1972. reprint ed. 18.95 (0-405-03940-9) Ayer.

Social Work: Search for Identity. Leslie Leighninger. LC 86-12155. (Studies in Social Welfare Policies & Programs: No. 4). 262p. 1987. text ed. 55.00 (0-313-24775-7, LSW/, Greenwood Pr) Greenwood.

Social Work: The Collected Writings of William Schwartz. Ed. by Toby Berman-Rossi. LC 93-87325. 725p. (C). 1994. boxed 55.00 (0-87581-385-2) Peacock Pubs.

Social Work: The Membership Perspective. Hans Falck. (Social Work Ser.). 224p. 1988. 29.95 (0-8261-4950-2) Springer Pub.

Social Work: The Social Organisation of an Invisible Trade. A. Pithouse. 1987. text ed. 55.95 (0-566-05378-0, Pub. by Avebury Pub UK) Ashgate Pub Co.

Social Work Administration: Dynamic Management & Human Relationships. 3rd ed. Rex A. Skidmore. LC 94-3502. 1994. text ed. 53.00 (0-13-669037-8) P-H.

Social Work Administration in Health Care. Ed. by Abraham Lurie & Gary Rosenberg. LC 84-799. 310p. 1984. pap. 39.95 (0-86656-314-8); text ed. 59.95 (0-917724-42-9) Haworth Pr.

Social Work Almanac. 2nd ed. Leon H. Ginsberg. LC 94-48860. 391p. (Orig.). (C). 1995. lib. bdg. 34.95 (0-87101-248-0, 2480) Natl Assn Soc Wkrs.

Social Work & Alzheimer's Disease: Practice Issues with Victims & Their Families. Ed. by Rose Dobrof. LC 85-220269. (Journal of Gerontological Social Work: Vol. 9, No. 2). 126p. 1986. text ed. 29.95 (0-86656-402-0) Haworth Pr.

Social Work & Assessment with Adolescents. David Berridge et al. 334p. 1996. pap. 38.50 (1-874579-56-3, Pub. by Natl Childrens Bur UK) Paul & Co Pubs.

Social Work & Child Abuse. Dave Merrick. LC 96-2573. (State of Welfare Ser.). 240p. (C). 1996. pap. 22.95 (0-415-13068-9); text ed. 69.95 (0-415-13067-0) Routledge.

Social Work & Child Sexual Abuse. Ed. by Jon R. Conte & David A. Shore. LC 82-11952. (Journal of Social Work & Human Sexuality: Vol. 1, Nos. 1-2). 184p. 1982. text ed. 39.95 (0-917724-98-4) Haworth Pr.

Social Work & Criminal Law in Scotland. George Moore & Chris Wood. 220p. 1982. text ed. 22.00 (0-08-025731-3, Pergamon Pr) Elsevier.

Social Work & Criminal Law in Scotland. 2nd ed. George Moore & Chris Wood. (Aberdeen University Press Bks.). 250p. 1991. text ed. 25.50 (0-08-041221-1, Pub. by Aberdeen U Pr) Macmillan.

Social Work & Criminal Law in Scotland: An Update. George Moore & Chris Wood. (Aberdeen University Press Bks.). 32p. 1987. pap. text ed. 8.00 (0-08-035069-0, Pub. by Aberdeen U Pr) Macmillan.

Social Work & Debt Problems. Martin Ryan. 180p. 1996. text ed. 55.95 (1-85972-011-0, Pub. by Avebury Pub UK) Ashgate Pub Co.

Social Work & Dialysis: The Medical & Psychosocial Aspects of Kidney Disease. Carrie L. Fortner-Frazier. LC 78-51754. 224p. 1981. 40.00 (0-520-03674-3) U CA Pr.

Social Work & Ethnicity. Ed. by Juliet Cheetham. 1982. 45.00 (0-317-05807-X, Pub. by Natl Inst Soc Work) St Mut.

Social Work & Genetics: A Guide to Practice. Ed. by Sylvia Schild & Rita B. Black. LC 84-560. (Social Work in Health Care Ser.: Supplement No. 1). 164p. 1984. text ed. 39.95 (0-86656-193-5) Haworth Pr.

Social Work & Health Sciences: Medical Analysis Index with Reference Bibliography. Paula N. Aggerholm. LC 85-47858. 150p. 1987. 44.50 (0-88164-392-0); pap. 39.50 (0-88164-393-9) ABBE Pubs Assn.

***Social Work & People with Mental Health Problems.** Ed. by Marion Ulas & Anne Connor. (Research Highlights in Social Work Ser.: No. 28). 250p. 1996. pap. 29.95 (1-85302-302-7, Pub. by J Kingsley Pubs UK) Taylor & Francis.

Social Work & Psychoanalysis. Margaret Yelloly. 1980. pap. 30.95 (0-442-30167-7) Chapman & Hall.

Social Work & Psychotropic Medicine. Bentley. (Social Work Ser.). 1996. text ed. 48.95 (0-534-34101-2) Brooks-Cole.

Social Work & Social Development. R. K. Nayak & H. Y. Siddiqui. 1989. 23.50 (81-85060-32-0, Pub. by Gitanjali Prakashan II) S Asia.

Social Work & Social Living: Explorations in Philosophy & Practice. Bertha C. Reynolds. LC 75-29534. (NASW Classics Ser.). 176p. 1975. reprint ed. pap. 8.95 (0-87101-071-2) Natl Assn Soc Wkrs.

Social Work & Social Order: The Settlement Movement in Two Industrial Cities, 1889-1930. Ruth H. Crocker. 364p. 1992. text ed. 39.95 (0-252-01790-0) U of Ill Pr.

Social Work & Social Welfare. 3rd ed. Joseph Heffernan et al. 550p. (C). 1997. text ed. write for info. (0-314-06715-9) West Pub.

Social Work & Social Welfare Yearbook, Vol. 1. Ed. by Pam Carter et al. 256p. 1989. 95.00 (0-335-15876-5, Open Univ Pr); pap. 39.00 (0-335-15875-7, Open Univ Pr) Taylor & Francis.

Social Work & Social Welfare Yearbook, Vol. 3. Ed. by Pam Carter et al. 224p. 1991. pap. 39.00 (0-335-09795-2, Open Univ Pr) Taylor & Francis.

Social Work & Terminal Care. Ed. by Lee H. Suszycki et al. LC 84-11615. (Foundation of Thanatology Ser.: Vol. 2). 176p. 1984. text ed. 29.95 (0-275-91280-9, C1280, Praeger Pubs) Greenwood.

Social Work & Thanatology. Ed. by Ben A. Orcutt et al. LC 79-22448. 300p. 1980. lib. bdg. 27.95 (0-405-12621-2) Ayer.

Social Work & the Black Experience. Joanne M. Martin & Elmer D. Martin. 291p. (Orig.). (C). 1995. lib. bdg. 32.95 (0-87101-257-X, 257x) Natl Assn Soc Wkrs.

***Social Work & the Courts: A Casebook.** Daniel Pollack. LC 96-44894. (Illus.). 296p. 1997. text ed. 49.00 (0-8153-2069-8, SS1046); pap. text ed. 17.95 (0-8153-2070-1, SS1046) Garland.

Social Work & the European Community. Ed. by Malcom Hill. (Research Highlights in Social Work Ser.: No. 23). 226p. 1991. 42.50 (1-85302-052-4) Taylor & Francis.

Social Work & the Law. 2nd ed. Donald Brieland & John A. Lemmon. (Illus.). 621p. 1985. text ed. 61.00 (0-314-77848-9) West Pub.

Social Work & the Unemployed. Katharine H. Briar. LC 87-34846. 222p. 1988. 21.95 (0-87101-153-0) Natl Assn Soc Wkrs.

Social Work & Transplantation of Human Organs. Surjit S. Dhooper. LC 93-14136. 256p. 1993. text ed. 57.95 (0-275-94338-0, C4338, Praeger Pubs) Greenwood.

Social Work & Welfare Yearbook, Vol. 2. Pam Carter et al. 1990. 95.00 (0-335-09424-4, Open Univ Pr); pap. 39.00 (0-335-09423-6, Open Univ Pr) Taylor & Francis.

***Social Work Approaches to Alcohol & Other Drug Problems: Case Studies & Teaching Tools.** Maryann Amodeo. LC 96-52842. (Orig.). 1997. pap. text ed. write for info. (0-87293-053-X) Coun Soc Wk Ed.

Social Work Approaches to Conflict Resolution: Making Fighting Obsolete, Incl. instr's. manual. Benyamin Chetkow-Yanoov. LC 96-13118. 174p. (C). 1996. 39.95 (0-7890-6035-3) Haworth Pr.

***Social Work Approaches to Conflict Resolution: Making Fighting Obsolete, Incl. instr's. manual.** Benyamin Chetkow-Yanoov. LC 96-13118. 174p. (C). 1996. pap. 19.95 (0-7890-0185-3) Haworth Pr.

Social Work as a Profession. 4th ed. Esther L. Brown. LC 75-17207. (Social Problems & Social Policy Ser.). 1976. reprint ed. 20.95 (0-405-07479-4) Ayer.

Social Work As Art: Making Sense for Good Practice. Hugh England. 176p. 1986. pap. text ed. 44.95 (0-04-360063-8); pap. text ed. 14.95 (0-04-360064-6) Routledge Chapman & Hall.

Social Work As Community Development: A Management Model for Social Change. Stephen Clarke. 288p. 1996. 59.95 (1-85972-098-6, Pub. by Avebury Pub UK) Ashgate Pub Co.

Social Work Assistant. Jack Rudman. (Career Examination Ser.: C-796). 1994. pap. 23.95 (0-8373-0796-1) Nat Learn.

***Social Work Care & Planning.** Webb. 1987. pap. text ed. write for info. (0-582-29601-3, Pub. by Longman UK) Longman.

***Social Work Career Development.** Carol N. Doellsng. (Orig.). (C). 1997. pap. text ed. write for info. (0-87101-282-0, NASW Pr) Natl Assn Soc Wkrs.

Social Work Case Management. Betsy S. Vourlekis & Roberta R. Greene. (Modern Applications of Social Work Ser.). 215p. 1992. pap. text ed. 22.95 (0-202-36076-8); lib. bdg. 43.95 (0-202-36075-X) Aldine de Gruyter.

Social Work Competences: Core Knowledge, Values & Skills. Ed. by Anthony A. Vass. (New Directions in Social Work Ser.). 240p. 1996. 65.00 (0-8039-7799-9); pap. 22.95 (0-8039-7800-6) Sage.

Social Work Competences in Practice. Ed. by Kieran O'Hagan. 200p. 1995. pap. 24.95 (1-85302-332-9, Pub. by J Kingsley Pubs UK) Taylor & Francis.

Social Work Day-To-Day: The Experience of Generalist Social Work Practice. 2nd ed. Carolyn C. Wells. 224p. (C). 1989. pap. text ed. 33.50 (0-8013-0041-X, 75705) Longman.

Social Work Dictionary. 3rd ed. Robert L. Barker. 448p. (C). 1995. lib. bdg. 34.95 (0-87101-253-7, 2537) Natl Assn Soc Wkrs.

Social Work Education. Hong-Chan Li. LC 77-19339. 359p. 1978. lib. bdg. 26.00 (0-8108-1108-1) Scarecrow.

Social Work Education & Public Human Services - a Technical Assistance Document: Report of a Ford Foundation-Funded Project. Norma J. Harris. 1996. pap. 1.50 (0-614-02477-3) Coun Soc Wk Ed.

Social Work Education II: A Bibliography, 1977-1987. Hong-Chan Li. LC 77-19339. 318p. 1989. 29.50 (0-8108-2195-8) Scarecrow.

Social Work Education in Conflict. Margaret Richards & Peter Righton. 1979. 25.00 (0-317-05763-4, Pub. by Natl Inst Soc Work) St Mut.

Social Work Education in the United States: The Report of a Study Made for the National Council on Social Work Education. Ernest V. Hollis & Alice L. Taylor. LC 75-136070. (Illus.). 422p. 1971. reprint ed. text ed. 75.00 (0-8371-5220-8, HOSW) Greenwood.

Social Work Ethics. Charles S. Levy. LC 75-11007. 266p. 1976. 42.95 (0-87705-254-9); pap. 20.95 (0-87705-493-2) Human Sci Pr.

Social Work Ethics Day to Day: Guidelines for Professional Practice. Carolyn C. Wells & M. Kathleen Masch. 167p. (C). 1991. reprint ed. pap. text ed. 15.95 (0-88133-546-0) Waveland Pr.

Social Work Ethics on the Line. Charles S. Levy. LC 92-3349. 130p. 1993. lib. bdg. 29.95 (1-56024-282-5) Haworth Pr.

Social Work Experience: An Introduction to the Profession. Mary A. Suppes & Carolyn C. Wells. 1991. text ed. write for info. (0-07-062607-3) McGraw.

Social Work Experience: An Introduction to the Profession & Its Relationship to Social Welfare Policy. 2nd ed. Mary A. Suppes & Carolyn C. Wells. LC 95-42321. 1996. text ed. write for info. (0-07-063094-1) McGraw.

Social Work Face to Face: Clients & Social Workers' Perceptions of the Content & Outcome of Their Meetings. Stuart Rees. 1979. text ed. 39.50 (0-231-04764-9) Col U Pr.

Social Work Field. Dean Schneck & Gayla Rogers. 560p. 1995. per., pap. text ed. 30.00 (0-7872-0971-6) Kendall-Hunt.

***Social Work Field Instruction in Post-Communist Societies.** Ed. by Robert Constable & Regina Kulys. 112p. (Orig.). (C). 1996. pap. 10.95 (0-925065-12-9) Lyceum IL.

Social Work in a Changing Europe. Walter Lorenz. 208p. (C). 1993. pap. text ed. 25.00 (0-415-07808-3, Routledge NY) Routledge.

Social Work in a Changing World: An International Perspective on Practice. Ed. by Mark Doel & Steven Shardlow. 232p. 1996. text ed. 59.95 (1-85742-343-7, Pub. by Arena UK) Ashgate Pub Co.

Social Work in a Multiracial Society. David Denney & Peter Ely. 144p. 1987. text ed. 54.95 (0-566-00939-0, Pub. by Avebury Pub UK) Ashgate Pub Co.

Social Work in a Turbulent World: Seventh NASW Symposium: Selected Papers, Seventh NASW Professional Symposium on Social Work, November 18-21, 1981, Philadelphia, PA. NASW Professional Symposium on Social Work Staff. Ed. by Miriam Dinerman. LC 82-8216. 220p. reprint ed. pap. 62.70 (0-7837-6548-7, 2045685) Bks Demand.

Social Work in Ambulatory Care: New Implications for Health & Social Services. Ed. by Gary Rosenberg & Andrew Weissman. (Social Work in Health Care Ser.). (Illus.). 108p. 1994. lib. bdg. 19.95 (1-56024-697-9) Haworth Pr.

Social Work in an Enterprise Society. Robert A. Pinker. 192p. (C). (gr. 13). 1991. text ed. 79.95 (0-415-04491-X, A5535) Routledge.

***Social Work in Contemporary Society.** 2nd ed. Garvin & Tropman. 1997. text ed. 53.33 (0-205-27166-9) P-H.

Social Work in Health Care: A Guide to Professional Practice. Neil F. Bracht. LC 78-7881. 346p. 1978. 39.95 (0-917724-04-6); pap. 24.95 (0-917724-05-4) Haworth Pr.

Social Work in Health Care: A Handbook for Practice. Ed. by Kay W. Davidson. LC 89-24535. 517p. (C). 1990. text ed. 89.95 (0-86656-846-8); pap. text ed. 49.95 (0-86656-907-3) Haworth Pr.

Social Work in Health Care: A Review of the Literature. Society for Hospital Social Work Directors Staff. 91p. (Orig.). 1988. pap. 27.00 (0-87258-477-1, 187902) Am Hospital.

***Social Work in Health Care in the 21st Century.** Surjit S. Dhooper. LC 96-45777. (Sourcebooks for the Human Serives Ser.). 416p. 1997. 55.00 (0-8039-5932-X); pap. 24.95 (0-8039-5933-8) Sage.

Social Work in Health Settings: Practice in Context. Ed. by Toba Schwaber Kerson & Associates Staff. LC 89-1684. (Social Work Practice Ser.: No. 4). 523p. 1989. text ed. 49.95 (0-86656-811-5); pap. text ed. 24.95 (0-86656-851-4) Haworth Pr.

***Social Work in Health Settings: Practice in Context.** 2nd ed. Ed. by Toba S. Kerson. LC 96-51915. (Illus.). 706p. (C). 1997. pap. text ed. 29.95 (0-7890-6019-1); lib. bdg. 59.95 (0-7890-6018-3) Haworth Pr.

***Social Work in Juvenile & Criminal Justice Settings.** 2nd ed. Albert R. Roberts. LC 96-19014. (Illus.). 474p. 1997. 87.95 (0-398-06758-9) C C Thomas.

***Social Work in Juvenile & Criminal Justice Settings.** 2nd ed. Albert R. Roberts. 1997. pap. write for info. (0-398-06759-7) C C Thomas.

Social Work in Pediatrics. Ed. by Ruth B. Smith & Helen G. Clinton. 130p. 1995. 24.95 (1-56024-765-7) Haworth Pr.

Social Work in Primary Care. Ed. by Matthew L. Henk. (Sourcebooks for the Human Services Ser.: Vol. 8). 256p. (C). 1989. text ed. 52.00 (0-8039-3035-6); pap. text ed. 24.95 (0-8039-3036-4) Sage.

***Social Work in Primary Care.** Ed. by Matthew L. Henk. LC 89-10237. (Sage Sourcebooks for the Human Services Ser.: No. 8). 204p. 1989. reprint ed. pap. 58.20 (0-608-04313-3, 2065092) Bks Demand.

Social Work in Private Practice. 2nd ed. Robert L. Barker. LC 91-35705. 209p. (C). 1991. 26.95 (0-87101-198-0) Natl Assn Soc Wkrs.

Social Work in Rural Communities. 2nd ed. Ed. by Leon H. Ginsberg. (C). 1993. pap. text ed. 13.00 (0-87293-037-8) Coun Soc Wk Ed.

Social Work in the Current Scene, Nineteen Fifty: Selected Papers of the National Conference of Social Work, 77th. National Conference of Social Work Staff. LC 72-3382. (Essay Index Reprint Ser.). 1977. reprint ed. 25.95 (0-8369-2915-2) Ayer.

Social Work in the Philippines: A Historical Overview. F. Landa Jocano. viii, 237p. 1980. pap. 15.00 (0-686-27945-X, Pub. by New Day Pub PH); pap. text ed. 15.00 (0-686-27946-8, Pub. by New Day Pub PH) Cellar.

Social Work in the Wake of Disaster. Ed. by Philip Seed. (Case Studies for Practice Ser.: No. 6). 128p. 1991. 17.95 (1-85302-060-5) Taylor & Francis.

Social Work in the Workplace. Ed. by Gary M. Gould & Michael L. Smith. (Social Work Ser.). 384p. 1988. 39.95 (0-8261-5380-1) Springer Pub.

***Social Work in the 21st Century.** Michael Reisch & Eileen Gambrill. LC 96-45367. 1997. pap. write for info. (0-8039-9091-X) Pine Forge.

Social Work Intervention in an Economic Crisis: The River Communities Project. Martha Baum & Pamela Twiss. LC 96-357. 220p. 1996. 29.95 (0-7890-6036-1) Haworth Pr.

***Social Work Intervention in Health Care: The Hong Kong Scene.** Ed. by Cecilia L. Chan & Nancy Rhind. 430p. (Orig.). 1997. pap. 42.50 (962-209-419-8, Pub. by Hong Kong Univ Pr HK) Coronet Bks.

Social Work Interventions: Helping People of Color. George Henderson. LC 93-40164. 256p. 1994. text ed. 55.00 (0-89789-382-4, Bergin & Garvey) Greenwood.

Social Work Interview. Alfred Kadushin. LC 82-23670. 368p. 1983. pap. text ed. 24.50 (0-231-04763-0) Col U Pr.

Social Work Interview. 2nd ed. Alfred Kadushin. LC 82-23670. 368p. 1983. text ed. 57.00 (0-231-04762-2) Col U Pr.

Social Work Interview: A Guide for Human Service Professionals. 3rd ed. Alfred Kadushin. 416p. 1990. pap. text ed. 27.50 (0-231-06791-7) Col U Pr.

***Social Work Interview: A Guide for Human Service Professionals.** 4th ed. Alfred Kadushin & Goldie Kadushin. LC 96-38296. 458p. 1997. 49.50 (0-231-09658-5); pap. write for info. (0-231-09659-3) Col U Pr.

Social Work Leadership in Healthcare: Directors' Perspectives. Ed. by Gary Rosenberg & Andrew Weissman. LC 95-23135. 116p. 1995. 24.95 (1-56024-764-9) Haworth Pr.

Social Work Macro-Practice. Ellen Netting et al. LC 92-18943. 279p. (C). 1993. text ed. 46.95 (0-8013-0464-4, 78281) Longman.

Social Work Macro Practice. 2nd ed. Ellen Netting. (C). 1998. text ed. write for info. (0-8013-1611-1) Addison-Wesley.

Social Work Malpractice & Liability: Strategies for Prevention. Frederic G. Reamer. LC 94-7628. 1994. pap. 22.50 (0-231-08263-0) Col U Pr.

Social Work Pioneers. Herbert W. Stroup. 320p. 1985. 32.95 (0-88229-212-9); pap. 20.95 (0-8304-1164-X) Nelson-Hall.

Social Work Practice. Ronda S. Connaway & Martha E. Gebtry. 240p. (C). 1987. text ed. 72.00 (0-13-819558-7) P-H.

***Social Work Practice.** 6th ed. Johnson. LC 97-24254. 1997. text ed. 54.00 (0-205-27055-7) P-H.

***Social Work Practice: A Critical Thinker's Guide.** Eileen Gambrill. (Illus.). 688p. (C). 1997. text ed. 59.95 (0-19-511332-2) OUP.

Social Work Practice: A Generalist Approach. 3rd ed. Louise C. Johnson. 464p. 1989. boxed 42.00 (0-205-11751-1, H17510) Allyn.

Social Work Practice: A Generalist Approach. 5th ed. Louise C. Johnson. LC 94-7156. 1994. text ed. 61.00 (0-205-15618-5) Allyn.

Social Work Practice: A Systems Approach. Benyamin Chetkow-Yanoov. LC 91-18004. (Illus.). 172p. 1992. lib. bdg. 29.95 (1-56024-175-6) Haworth Pr.

Social Work Practice: A Systems Approach. Benyamin Chetkow-Yanoov. LC 91-18004. 158p. 1992. pap. 19.95 (1-56024-176-4) Haworth Pr.

***Social Work Practice: A Systems Approach.** 2nd ed. Benyamin Chetkow-Yanoov. LC 91-18004. (Illus.). 172p. 1997. lib. bdg. 39.95 (0-7890-0137-3) Haworth Pr.

***Social Work Practice: A Systems Approach.** 2nd ed. Benyamin Chetkow-Yanoov. LC 91-18004. (Illus.). 172p. 1997. pap. text ed. 19.95 (0-7890-0246-9) Haworth Pr.

An Asterisk (*) at the beginning of an entry indicates that the title is appearing in BIP for the first time.

Social Work Practice: An Ecological Approach. Roland G. Meinert. LC 95-40691. 184p. 1996. text ed. 52.95 (0-86569-236-X, Auburn Hse) Greenwood.
Social Work Practice: Bridges to Change. Kay S. Hoffman & Alvin L. Sallee. LC 92-9217. 1993. text ed. 65.00 (0-205-13959-0) Allyn.
Social Work Practice: Cases & Principles. Cynthia Bisman. LC 93-23213. 314p. 1994. text ed. 43.95 (0-534-22230-7) Brooks-Cole.
Social Work Practice: People & Environments. Ed. by Carel B. Germain. LC 78-26351. 336p. 1979. text ed. 57.00 (0-231-04332-5); pap. text ed. 21.50 (0-231-04333-3) Col U Pr.
Social Work Practice: Toward a Child, Family, School, Community Perspective. Edith M. Freeman & Marianne Pennekamp. (Illus.). 354p. 1988. pap. 36.95 (0-398-06133-5) C C Thomas.
Social Work Practice: Toward a Child, Family, School, Community Perspective. Edith M. Freeman & Marianne Pennekamp. (Illus.). 354p. (C). 1988. text ed. 55.95 (0-398-05456-8) C C Thomas.
Social Work Practice & People of Color: A Process-Stage Approach. 2nd ed. Doman Lum. 336p. (C). 1992. pap. 25.75 (0-534-17040-4) Brooks-Cole.
Social Work Practice & People of Color: A Process-Stage Approach. 3rd ed. Doman Lum. LC 95-2871. 336p. 1996. pap. 36.95 (0-534-33854-2) Brooks-Cole.
Social Work Practice in Health Care: An Ecological View. Carel B. Germain. LC 83-48757. (Fields of Practice Ser.). 336p. (C). 1984. 35.00 (0-02-911660-0, Free Press) Free Pr.
Social Work Practice in Maternal & Child Health. Terri Combs-Orme. LC 89-26218. (Social Work Ser.: Vol. 15). 336p. 1990. 38.95 (0-8261-6370-X) Springer Pub.
Social Work Practice in Sexual Problems. Ed. by James Gripton & Mary Valentich. LC 85-21992. (Journal of Social Work & Human Sexuality: Vol. 4, Nos. 1-2). 139p. 1986. text ed. 39.95 (0-86656-485-3); pap. text ed. 29.95 (0-86656-526-4) Haworth Pr.
Social Work Practice in the Health Field. Harriett M. Bartlett. LC 61-17630. 285p. 1961. 12.95 (0-87101-035-6) Natl Assn Soc Wkrs.
Social Work Practice in the Nursing Home Setting: A Primer for Social Workers. Pat Gleason-Wynn & Karen Fonville. 104p. (Orig.). (C). 1993. pap. text ed. 13.00 (1-877735-43-4, 248) M&H Pub Co TX.
Social Work Practice with Asian Americans. Ed. by Sharlene M. Furuto et al. LC 92-7770. (Sourcebooks for the Human Services Ser.: Vol. 21). 1992. 52.00 (0-8039-3809-8); pap. 24.95 (0-8039-3810-1) Sage.
Social Work Practice with Black Families: A Culturally Specific Approach. Sadye L. Logan et al. 288p. (Orig.). (C). 1990. pap. text ed. 39.95 (0-8013-0012-6, 75678) Longman.
Social Work Practice with Children. LC 96-25483. (Child & Family Social Work Practice Ser.). 1996. lib. bdg. 35.00 (1-57230-149-X, 0149) Guilford Pr.
Social Work Practice with Families: A Diversity Model. Lonnie R. Helton & Maggie Jackson. LC 96-12687. 1996. pap. text ed. 37.00 (0-205-16704-7) Allyn.
Social Work Practice with Groups: A Clinical Perspective. Reid. 311p. (C). 1991. text ed. 59.95 (0-534-14820-4) Brooks-Cole.
Social Work Practice with Groups: A Clinical Perspective. 2nd ed. Kenneth E. Reid. (Miscellaneous/Catalogs Ser.). 306p. (C). 1997. pap. text ed. 38.95 (0-534-34548-4) Brooks-Cole.
Social Work Practice with Immigrants. Siegel & Greenspan. 1996. pap. text ed. write for info. (0-205-17329-2) Allyn.
Social Work Practice with Minorities. 2nd ed. David R. Burgest. LC 89-32068. 362p. 1989. 39.50 (0-8108-2207-5) Scarecrow.
Social Work Practice with the Frail Elderly & Their Families: The Auxiliary Function Model. Barbara Silverstone & Ann Burack-Weiss. (Illus.). 346p. 1983. pap. 29.95 (0-398-06430-X); text ed. 41.95 (0-398-04851-7) C C Thomas.
Social Work Practice with the Terminally Ill: A Transcultural Perspective. Ed. by Joan K. Parry. 250p. (C). 1990. text ed. 51.95 (0-398-05697-8) C C Thomas.
Social Work Practice with the Terminally Ill: A Transcultural Perspective. Ed. by Joan K. Parry. 250p. 1990. pap. 35.95 (0-398-06315-X) C C Thomas.
Social Work Practicum: An Access Guide. 2nd ed. Barbara Thomlison et al. 332p. (C). 1996. pap. text ed. 30.00 (0-87581-400-X) Peacock Pubs.
Social Work Processes. 4th ed. Beulah R. Compton & Burt Galaway. 773p. (C). 1989. pap. 48.95 (0-534-11096-7) Brooks-Cole.
Social Work Processes. 5th ed. Beulah R. Compton & Burt Galaway. LC 93-49529. 689p. 1994. pap. 58.95 (0-534-17364-0) Brooks-Cole.
Social Work Quality Assurance Programs: A Comparative Analysis. Claudia J. Coulton. LC 79-64947. 112p. reprint ed. pap. 32.00 (0-7837-5362-4, 2045125) Bks Demand.
Social Work Records. 2nd ed. Jill D. Kagle. (Illus.). 225p. (C). 1995. reprint ed. pap. text ed. 15.95 (0-88133-887-7) Waveland Pr.
Social Work Research: Methods for the Helping Professions. rev. ed. Ed. by Norman A. Polansky. LC 74-26798. (Illus.). 352p. 1975. lib. bdg. 21.00 (0-226-67219-0) U Ch Pr.
Social Work Research & Evaluation: Quantitative & Qualitative Approaches. 5th ed. Richard M. Grinnell, Jr. LC 96-69325. 650p. (C). 1997. boxed 52.00 (0-87581-402-6) Peacock Pubs.
Social Work Research in the Human Services. 2nd ed. Ed. by Henry Wechsler et al. LC 81-1760. 358p. 1981. pap. 26.95 (0-89885-039-8) Human Sci Pr.
Social Work Research Methods. York. 1996. pap. text ed. 44.00 (0-205-19357-9) Allyn.
Social Work Research on Prevention. Ed. by David Fanshel. 50p. reprint ed. pap. 25.00 (0-7837-6543-6, 2045680) Bks Demand.
***Social Work Response to the 1995 White House Conference on Aging: From Issues to Actions.** Ed. by Constance C. Saltz. LC 97-16058. 126p. 1997. 29.95 (0-7890-0332-5) Haworth Pr.
***Social Work Services.** Vicki Rust. 113p. 1996. spiral bd. 110.00 (1-879575-71-X) Acad Med Sys.
Social Work Services in Schools. 2nd ed. Betty L. Welsh et al. 1995. text ed. 51.00 (0-205-17330-6) Allyn.
Social Work Skills Workbook. Barry Cournoyer. 384p. (C). 1991. pap. 24.75 (0-534-14730-5) Brooks-Cole.
Social Work Skills Workbook. 2nd ed. Barry Cournoyer. LC 95-12973. 464p. 1996. pap. 37.95 (0-534-33875-5) Brooks-Cole.
Social Work, Social Welfare & American Society. Philip R. Popple & Leslie Leighninger. 600p. 1990. text ed. 44.00 (0-205-12270-1, H22700) Allyn.
Social Work Social Welfare & American Society. 3rd ed. Parkinson. 1995. student ed., pap. text ed. 23.00 (0-205-19403-6) Allyn.
Social Work, Social Welfare & American Society. 3rd ed. Philip R. Popple & Leslie Leighninger. LC 95-11219. 1995. text ed. 59.00 (0-205-16799-3) Allyn.
Social Work Speaks: NASW Policy Statements. 3rd ed. Ed. by NASW Staff. 304p. (C). 1994. pap. text ed. 31.95 (0-87101-234-0, 2340) Natl Assn Soc Wkrs.
***Social Work Speaks: NASW Policy Statements.** 4th ed. 300p. (C). 1997. pap. text ed. 36.95 (0-87101-273-1, 2731) Natl Assn Soc Wkrs.
Social Work Stress & Intervention. Stephen Fineman. LC 84-21268. 174p. 1985. text ed. 63.95 (0-566-00664-2, Pub. by Avebury Pub UK) Ashgate Pub Co.
Social Work Supervision: Classic Statements & Critical Issues. Ed. by Carlton E. Munson. LC 78-72149. 1979. pap. 22.95 (0-02-922280-X, Free Press) Free Pr.
Social Work Supervisor: Supervision in Community, Day Care & Residential Settings. Allan Brown & Iain Bourne. LC 95-14730. (Supervision in Context Ser.). 192p. 1995. 79.00 (0-335-19459-1, Open Univ Pr); pap. 23.95 (0-335-19458-3, Open Univ Pr) Taylor & Francis.
Social Work Theory & Practice with the Terminally Ill. Ed. by Joan K. Parry. LC 88-29623. (Social Work Practice Ser.: No. 3). (Illus.). 130p. 1989. 34.95 (0-86656-750-X) Haworth Pr.
Social Work Theory & Practice with the Terminally Ill. Ed. by Joan K. Parry. LC 88-29623. 130p. 1996. pap. 14.95 (0-7890-0084-9) Haworth Pr.
Social Work Training Director. Jack Rudman. (Career Examination Ser.: C-3476). 1994. pap. 39.95 (0-8373-3476-4) Nat Learn.
Social Work Treatment: Interlocking Theoretical Approaches. 4th ed. Ed. by Francis J. Turner. 738p. 1996. 49.95 (0-684-82994-0) S&S Trade.
Social Work Treatment of Alcohol Problems. Ed. by D. Cook et al. LC 82-620033. (NIAAA-RUCAS Alcoholism Treatment Ser.: No. 5). 1983. pap. 15.00 (0-911290-15-X) Rutgers Ctr Alcohol.
Social Work, Two Thousand: The Future of Social Work in a Changing Society. Ronald G. Walton. LC 82-12. 118p. reprint ed. pap. 33.70 (0-8357-3537-0, 2034501) Bks Demand.
Social Work Update. NISW Information Service Staff. (C). 1988. 90.00 (0-685-28594-4, Pub. by Natl Inst Soc Work) St Mut.
Social Work Values & Ethics. Frederic G. Reamer. LC 94-38229. 217p. 1995. 49.50 (0-231-09990-8); pap. 15.00 (0-231-09991-6) Col U Pr.
Social Work Values in an Age of Discontent. Ed. by Katherine A. Kendall. 1970. 3.30 (0-318-35366-0) Coun Soc Wk Ed.
Social Work with Abused & Neglected Children: A Manual of Interdisciplinary Practice. Kathleen C. Faller. 256p. 1981. 35.00 (0-02-910280-4, Free Press) Free Pr.
Social Work with Addictions. James G. Barber. LC 94-25331. (C). 1994. 40.00 (0-8147-1241-X); pap. 17.50 (0-8147-1242-8) NYU Pr.
Social Work with Children. Florence Lieberman. LC 78-23287. 344p. 1979. 45.95 (0-87705-255-7); pap. 26.95 (0-87705-257-3) Human Sci Pr.
***Social Work with Children: The Educational Perspective.** Eric Blyth & Judith Milner. LC 97-25031. 1997. write for info. (0-582-29308-1) Longman.
Social Work with Children & Adolescents. Paula Allen-Meares. 1994. write for info. (0-615-00078-9) Longman.
Social Work with Children & Adolescents. Paula Allen-Meares. 352p. (C). 1995. pap. text ed. 38.95 (0-8013-0211-0) Longman.
***Social Work with Children & Their Families: Pragmatic Foundations.** Christopher G. Petr. (Illus.). 448p. 1998. 45.00 (0-19-510607-5) OUP.
Social Work with Groups. Helen Northen. LC 69-19462. (C). 1969. text ed. 39.50 (0-231-02965-9) Col U Pr.
Social Work with Groups. 2nd ed. Helen Northen. 452p. 1988. text ed. 37.50 (0-231-06744-5) Col U Pr.
Social Work with Groups. 4th ed. Charles H. Zastrow. 620p. 1996. text ed. 43.95 (0-8304-1443-6) Nelson-Hall.
Social Work with Groups: A Process Model. Joseph Anderson. LC 96-15770. (C). 1997. text ed. 49.95 (0-8013-1837-8) Longman.
Social Work with Groups: Expanding Horizons. Ed. by Stanley Wenocur et al. LC 92-34708. (Social Work with Groups Ser.: Vol. 16, Nos. 1-2). (Illus.). 225p. 1993. lib. bdg. 39.95 (1-56024-296-5) Haworth Pr.
Social Work with Groups in Health Settings. Ed. by Abraham Lurie et al. LC 82-18151. 124p. 1982. pap. 7.95 (0-88202-137-0) Watson Pub Intl.
Social Work with Immigrants & Refugees. Ed. by Angela S. Ryan. LC 92-32667. (Journal of Multicultural Social Work: No. 2-1). (Illus.). 157p. 1993. pap. 19.95 (1-56024-355-4); lib. bdg. 39.95 (1-56024-354-6) Haworth Pr.
***Social Work with Multi-Family Groups.** Ed. by D. Rosemary Cassano. 107p. 1989. 29.95 (0-86656-882-4) Haworth Pr.
Social Work with Older People. 2nd ed. Hancock. 1990. text ed. 67.00 (0-13-816968-3) P-H.
***Social Work with People with Dementia.** Ed. by Susan Hunter. (Research Highlights in Social Work Ser.: No. 31). 200p. 1996. pap. 29.95 (1-85302-312-4, Pub. by J Kingsley Pubs UK) Taylor & Francis.
Social Work with the Aged & Their Families. Roberta R. Greene. Ed. by James K. Whittaker. (Modern Applications of Social Work Ser.). (Illus.). 272p. (C). 1986. pap. text ed. 26.95 (0-202-36044-X); lib. bdg. 49.95 (0-202-36043-1) Aldine de Gruyter.
Social Work with the Aging. rev. ed. Ed. by Carol H. Meyer. LC 75-27193. (Readings in Social Work Ser.). 257p. 1986. pap. text ed. 21.95 (0-87101-139-5) Natl Assn Soc Wkrs.
Social Work with the Aging: The Challenge & Promise of the Later Years. 2nd ed. Louis Lowy. 435p. (C). 1991. reprint ed. pap. text ed. 24.95 (0-88133-614-9) Waveland Pr.
***Social Work 2000.** Walton. Date not set. pap. text ed. write for info. (0-582-29622-6, Pub. by Longman UK) Longman.
Social Worker. Jack Rudman. (Career Examination Ser.: C-746). 1994. pap. 23.95 (0-8373-0746-5) Nat Learn.
Social Worker & Psychotropic Medication: Toward Effective Collaboration with Mental Health Clients, Families, & Providers. Kia J. Bentley & Joseph Walsh. LC 95-35303. 230p. 1996. pap. 32.95 (0-534-34004-0) Brooks-Cole.
***Social Worker As Manager.** 3rd ed. Weinbach. LC 97-14342. 1997. pap. text ed. 46.67 (0-205-26772-6) P-H.
Social Worker as Manager: Theory & Practice. 2nd ed. Robert W. Weinbach. LC 93-3618. 1993. text ed. 64.00 (0-205-14843-3) Allyn.
Social Worker Eligibility Worker Examination. Harry W. Koch. 1985. pap. 8.00 (0-910553-03-3) Ken-Bks.
Social Worker Empowerment in Child Protection Court. Barry Friesen. 206p. 1990. pap. 26.95 (0-398-06134-3) C C Thomas.
Social Worker Empowerment in Child Protection Court. Barry Friesen. 206p. (C). 1990. text ed. 39.95 (0-398-05690-0) C C Thomas.
Social Workers & Labor Unions. Howard J. Karger. LC 88-3127. (Contributions in Labor Studies: No. 26). 211p. 1988. text ed. 55.00 (0-313-25867-8, KSW/, Greenwood Pr) Greenwood.
Social Workers & Their Workloads. Vida Carver. Ed. by Les Edwards. 1972. 25.00 (0-317-42896-9, Pub. by Natl Inst Soc Work) St Mut.
Social Workers & Their Workloads in Northern Ireland Welfare Departments. Rae Walker et al. 1972. 25.00 (0-317-13359-4, Pub. by Natl Inst Soc Work) St Mut.
Social Worker's Guide to the Family Support Act Of 1988. NASW Legislative Affairs Department Staff. 30p. 1989. pap. 6.95 (0-87101-173-5) Natl Assn Soc Wkrs.
Social Workers in Health Care Management: The Move to Leadership. Ed. by Gary Rosenberg & Sylvia S. Clarke. LC 87-15026. (Social Work in Health Care Ser.: Vol. 12, No. 3). 159p. 1987. 39.95 (0-86656-672-4) Haworth Pr.
Social Workers in Health Care Management: The Move to Leadership. Ed. by Gary Rosenberg & Sylvia S. Clarke. LC 87-15026. (Social Work in Health Care Ser.: Vol. 12, No. 3). 159p. 1988. pap. text ed. 14.95 (0-86656-815-8) Haworth Pr.
Social Workers' Perceptions of Clients: A Study of the Caseload of a Social Agency. Edgar F. Borgatta et al. LC 80-27204. 92p. 1981. reprint ed. text ed. 59.75 (0-313-22812-4, BOSW, Greenwood Pr) Greenwood.
Social Workers' Theoretical Orientations. Carmelo L. Cocozzelli. 206p. (Orig.). (C). 1987. pap. text ed. 25.50 (0-8191-5695-7) U Pr of Amer.
***Social Working.** Carter. 1997. text ed. 19.95 (0-333-60911-5, Pub. by Macm UK) St Martin.
Social Working: An Ethnography of Front-Line Practice. Gerald A. De Montigny. 276p. 1995. pap. 19.95 (0-8020-7726-9) U of Toronto Pr.
Social World in Beowulf. John M. Hill. (Anthropological Horizons Ser.). 350p. 1994. 55.00 (0-8020-2981-7); pap. 19.95 (0-8020-7438-3) U of Toronto Pr.
Social World of Adolescents: International Perspectives. Ed. by Uwe Engel & Klaus Hurrelmann. (Prevention & Intervention in Childhood & Adolescence Ser.: Vol. 2). x, 406p. (C). 1989. lib. bdg. 62.95 (3-11-011996-X) De Gruyter.
Social World of an English Crown Court: Witness & Professionals in the Crown Court Centre at Wood Green. Paul E. Rock. LC 93-16309. (Oxford Socio-Legal Studies). (Illus.). 400p. 1993. 72.00 (0-19-825843-7) OUP.
Social World of Ancient Israel. Victor H. Matthews & Don C. Benjamin. LC 93-34183. 320p. 1993. 24.95 (0-913573-89-2) Hendrickson MA.
Social World of Batavia: European & Eurasian in Dutch Asia. Jean G. Taylor. LC 83-47772. (Illus.). 256p. 1984. text ed. 27.50 (0-299-09470-7) U of Wis Pr.
Social World of Children's Learning: Case Studies of Pupils from Four to Seven. Andrew Pollard & Ann Filer. (Cassell Education Ser.). (Illus.). 352p. 1996. 95.00 (0-304-32639-9); pap. 23.00 (0-304-32641-0) Cassell.
Social World of Drugs. Phyllis A. Langton. 450p. (C). 1996. pap. text ed. 37.00 (0-314-07165-2) West Pub.
Social World of Jesus & the Gospels. Bruce J. Malina. LC 96-12602. 255p. (C). 1996. pap. 22.95 (0-415-14629-1); text ed. write for info. (0-415-14628-3) Routledge.
Social World of Luke-Acts: Models for Interpretation. Ed. by Jerome H. Neyrey. LC 91-3333. 464p. 1991. 19.95 (0-943575-48-6) Hendrickson MA.
Social World of the Child. William Damon. LC 77-79480. (Jossey-Bass Behavioral Science Ser.). 377p. reprint ed. pap. 107.50 (0-7837-0165-9, 2040462) Bks Demand.
Social World of the First Christians: Essays in Honor of Wayne A. Meeks. Ed. by L. Michael White & O. Larry Yarbrough. LC 95-2033. 1995. 54.00 (0-8006-2585-4, Fortress Pr) Augsburg Fortress.
Social World of the Primary School. Pollard. 1987. pap. text ed. 24.95 (0-304-31445-5) Cassell.
Social Worlds of Children Learning to Write in an Urban Primary School. Anne H. Dyson. LC 93-25086. (Language & Literacy Ser.). 288p. (C). 1993. text ed. 43.00 (0-8077-3296-6); pap. text ed. 19.95 (0-8077-3295-8) Tchrs Coll.
***Social Worlds of Sentencing: Court Communities under Sentencing Guidelines.** Jeffrey T. Ulmer. LC 96-45351. (SUNY Series in New Directions in Crime & Justice Studies). 160p. 1997. text ed. 49.50 (0-7914-3497-4) State U NY Pr.
***Social Worlds of Sentencing: Court Communities under Sentencing Guidelines.** Jeffrey T. Ulmer. LC 96-45351. (SUNY Series in New Directions in Crime & Justice Studies). 1997. pap. text ed. 17.95 (0-7914-3498-2) State U NY Pr.
Social Worlds, Personal Lives: An Introduction to Social Psychology. Edward E. Sampson. 352p. (C). 1990. pap. text ed. 21.50 (0-15-581805-8) HB Coll Pubs.
Social Writings of Jack London. Philip S. Foner. 1984. reprint ed. pap. 8.95 (0-8065-0886-8, Citadel Pr) Carol Pub Group.
Socialisation. Graham E. White. LC 77-5792. (Aspects of Modern Sociology: Social Processes Ser.). 155p. reprint ed. pap. 44.20 (0-317-27707-3, 2025221) Bks Demand.
Socialisation, Education & Women: Explorations in Gender Identity. Ed. by Karuna Chanana. 311p. 1988. text ed. 35.00 (0-86131-829-3, Pub. by Orient Longman Ltd II) Apt Bks.
Socialisation of School Children & Their Education for Democratic Values & Human Rights. Ed. by Hugh Starkey. 224p. 1991. 38.50 (90-265-1148-5) Swets.
Socialising Contexts. P. W. Musgrave. 200p. 1987. pap. text ed. 21.95 (0-04-176011-5) Routledge Chapman & Hall.
***Socialism.** Bernard Crick. Ed. by Frank Parkin. (Concepts in the Social Sciences Ser.). 136p. 1987. pap. 9.99 (0-335-15387-9, Open Univ Pr) Taylor & Francis.
***Socialism.** Bernard Crick. Ed. by Frank Parkin. (Concepts in the Social Sciences Ser.). 136p. 1987. 32.50 (0-335-15388-7, Open Univ Pr) Taylor & Francis.
Socialism. Ludwig Von Mises. LC 79-21701. Orig. Title: Die Gemeinwirtschaft. 1981. 25.00 (0-913966-62-2); pap. 10.00 (0-913966-63-0) Liberty Fund.
Socialism: Crisis & Renewal. Ed. by Chronis Polychroniou. LC 92-36546. 272p. 1993. text ed. 57.95 (0-275-94089-6, C4089, Praeger Pubs) Greenwood.
Socialism: Ideals, Ideologies, & Local Practice. Ed. by C. M. Hann. LC 92-15337. (ASA Monographs). 288p. (C). 1993. pap. 24.95 (0-415-08322-2, A9867, Routledge NY) Routledge.
Socialism: Institutional, Philosophical & Economic Issues. Ed. by S Prejovich. (C). 1987. lib. bdg. 101.50 (90-247-3487-8) Kluwer Ac.
Socialism: Past & Future. Michael Harrington. 384p. 1992. pap. 5.99 (0-451-62854-3, Ment) NAL-Dutton.
Socialism: The Active Utopia. Zygmunt Bauman. LC 75-28243. (Controversies in Sociology Ser.: No. 3). 148p. 1976. 19.75 (0-8419-0240-2) Holmes & Meier.
Socialism: The State & Public in France. Ed. by Philip G. Cerny & Martin A. Schain. 220p. (Orig.). (C). pap. 12.95 (0-416-01161-6, 9416) Routledge Chapman & Hall.
Socialism: Utopian & Scientific-With an Essay on "The Mark" Friedric Engels. Tr. by Edward B. Aveling from GER. LC 77-4356. 93p. 1977. reprint ed. text ed. 59.75 (0-8371-9622-1, ENSO, Greenwood Pr) Greenwood.
Socialism - What Went Wrong? An Inquiry into the Theoretical & Historical Roots of the Socialist Crisis. Irwin Silber. LC 94-18170. (C). 66.50 (0-7453-0715-9, Pub. by Pluto Pr UK); pap. 18.95 (0-7453-0716-7, Pub. by Pluto Pr UK) LPC InBook.
Socialism After Communism: The New Market Socialism. Christopher Pierson. LC 94-47518. 260p. 1995. pap. 16.95 (0-271-01479-2) Pa St U Pr.
Socialism After Communism: The New Market Socialism. Christopher Pierson. LC 94-47518. 260p. 1995. 45.00 (0-271-01478-4) Pa St U Pr.
Socialism & America. Irving Howe. 240p. 1986. pap. 5.95 (0-15-683520-7, Harvest Bks) HarBrace.
Socialism & American Life: Bibliography - Descriptive & Critical, Vol. 2. Ed. by Donald D. Egbert & Stow Persons. LC 52-5828. (Princeton Studies in American Civilization: No. 4). 589p. reprint ed. pap. 167.90 (0-317-08565-4, 2015480) Bks Demand.
Socialism & Communism in Their Practical Application. Moritz Kaufman. LC 76-134403. reprint ed. 42.50 (0-404-08447-8) AMS Pr.
Socialism & Democracy: A Marxist Look at Socialist Democracy. B. Topornin & E. Machulsky. 221p. 1975. 18.95 (0-8464-0857-0) Beekman Pubs.
Socialism & Democracy in Czechoslovakia, 1945-1948. Martin R. Myant. LC 80-41951. (Soviet & East European Studies). 312p. reprint ed. pap. 89.00 (0-318-34842-X, 2031697) Bks Demand.
Socialism & Freedom. Bryan Gould. 135p. 1986. 22.50 (0-89341-538-3, Longwood Academic); pap. 12.50 (0-89341-539-1, Longwood Academic) Hollowbrook.

S

An Asterisk (*) at the beginning of an entry indicates that the title is appearing in BIP for the first time.

Socialism & History: The Political Essays of Henry Pachter. Henry Pachter. Ed. by Stephen E. Bronner. LC 83-18904. (Illus.). 300p. 1984. text ed. 54.00 (*0-231-05660-5*) Col U Pr.

Socialism & Individual Freedom. Harry Ring. 22p. 1982. reprint ed. pap. 2.50 (*0-87348-393-6*) Pathfinder NY.

Socialism & International Economic Order. Elisabeth Tamedly. 302p. 1986. 5.00 (*0-317-52990-0*, Noontide Pr) Legion Survival.

Socialism & Labor, & Other Arguments Social, Political & Patriotic. John L. Spalding. LC 67-28768. (Essay Index Reprint Ser.). 1977. 19.95 (*0-8369-0893-7*) Ayer.

Socialism & Man in Cuba. Ernesto C. Guevara & Fidel Castro. 1989. pap. 3.50 (*0-87348-577-7*) Pathfinder NY.

Socialism & Marginalism in Economics, 1870-1930. Ed. by Ian Steedman. LC 95-7771. (Studies in the History of Economics). 263p. (C). (gr. 13). 1995. text ed. 74.95 (*0-415-13079-4*) Routledge.

Socialism & Morality. Ed. by David McLellan & Sean Sayers. 224p. 1990. pap. 14.95 (*0-312-03701-5*); text ed. 45.00 (*0-312-03700-7*) St Martin.

Socialism & Nationalism in the Ottoman Empire. Erik J. Zurcher. 192p. 1994. text ed. 59.50 (*1-85043-787-4*, Pub. by I B Tauris UK) St Martin.

Socialism & Parliamentary Democracy. Geoff Hodgson. 183p. 1977. 32.50 (*0-85124-207-3*, Pub. by Spokesman Bks UK) Coronet Bks.

S

Socialism & Philosophy. Antonio Labriola. LC 79-90007. 223p. (C). 1980. 26.00 (*0-914386-21-2*); pap. 14.00 (*0-914386-22-0*) Telos Pr.

Socialism & Populism in Chile, 1932-52. Paul W. Drake. LC 77-17414. 416p. 1977. text ed. 34.95 (*0-252-00657-7*) U of Ill Pr.

Socialism & Saint-Simon (Le Socialisme) Emile Durkheim. Ed. by Alvin W. Gouldner. LC 58-8736. 282p. reprint ed. pap. 80.40 (*0-317-20142-5*, 2023199) Bks Demand.

Socialism & Self-Reliance in Tanzania. K. A. Okoko. 200p. 1985. 65.00 (*0-7103-0269-X*) Routledge Chapman & Hall.

Socialism & State. Rudolf Rocker. 1972. 250.00 (*0-8490-1069-1*) Gordon Pr.

Socialism & Superior Brains: The Political Thought of Bernard Shaw. Gareth Griffith. LC 92-19483. 320p. (C). (gr. 13). 1992. text ed. 69.95 (*0-415-08281-1*, A9883) Routledge.

Socialism & Superior Brains: The Political Thought of George Bernard Shaw. Gareth Griffith. 320p. (C). 1995. pap. 17.95 (*0-415-12473-5*, C0557) Routledge.

Socialism & the American Spirit. Nicholas P. Gilman. LC 70-150183. (Select Bibliographies Reprint Ser.). 1977. reprint ed. 25.95 (*0-8369-5696-6*) Ayer.

Socialism & the Challenge of War: Ideas & Politics in Britain, 1912-1918. J. M. Winter. (Modern Revivals in History Ser.). 320p. 1993. 59.95 (*0-7512-0155-3*, Pub. by Gregg Pub UK) Ashgate Pub Co.

Socialism & the Common Good. Ed. by Preston King. 336p. (C). 1995. pap. 22.50 (*0-7146-4255-X*, Pub. by F Cass Pubs UK) Intl Spec Bk.

Socialism & the Common Good: New Fabian Essays. Ed. by Preston King. LC 95-24863. 336p. (C). 1995. 47.50 (*0-7146-4655-5*, Pub. by F Cass Pubs UK) Intl Spec Bk.

Socialism & the Environment. 2nd ed. Ed. by Ken Coates. 116p. (Orig.). 1979. pap. 19.95 (*0-85124-242-1*, Pub. by Spokesman Bks UK) Coronet Bks.

Socialism & the Great State: Essays in Construction. H. G. Wells et al. LC 75-156719. (Essay Index Reprint Ser.). 1977. reprint ed. 27.95 (*0-8369-2863-6*) Ayer.

Socialism & the Individual: Notes on Joining the Labour Party. William A. Sinclair. LC 77-18930. 168p. 1978. reprint ed. text ed. 49.75 (*0-313-20199-4*, SISO, Greenwood Pr) Greenwood.

Socialism & the Intelligentsia: 1880-1914. Ed. by Carl Levy. (History Workshop Ser.). 224p. (C). 1988. pap. text ed. 22.00 (*0-7102-1257-7*, RKP); lib. bdg. 59.95 (*0-7102-0722-0*, RKP) Routledge.

Socialism & the Jews: The Dilemmas of Assimilation in Germany & Austria-Hungary. Robert S. Wistrich. (Littman Library of Jewish Civilization). 436p. 1984. 27.50 (*0-19-710053-8*) Bnai Brith Bk.

Socialism & the Literary Artistry of William Morris. Ed. by Florence S. Boos & Carole G. Silver. LC 89-4834. 192p. 1990. text ed. 27.50 (*0-8262-0725-1*) U of Mo Pr.

Socialism & the Literary Imagination: Essays on East German Writers. Ed. by Martin Kane. 267p. 1991. 19.95 (*0-85496-643-9*) Berg Pubs.

Socialism & the Newly Independent Nations: An Account of National Liberation Movements. R. Ulyanovsky. 562p. (C). 1975. 22.95 (*0-8464-0858-9*) Beekman Pubs.

Socialism & the NHS: Fabian Essays in Health Care. Ed. by John Carrier & Ian Kendall. (Illus.). 120p. 1990. text ed. 59.95 (*0-566-07110-X*, Pub. by Avebury Pub UK) Ashgate Pub Co.

Socialism & the Workers in Massachusetts, 1886-1912. Henry F. Bedford. LC 66-15794. (Illus.). 234p. 1966. 30.00 (*0-87023-010-7*) U of Mass Pr.

Socialism & under Development. Ken Post & Philip Wright. 242p. 1989. 39.95 (*0-415-01627-4*) Routledge.

Socialism & under Development. Ken Post & Philip Wright. 242p. (C). 1989. pap. text ed. 14.95 (*0-415-01628-2*) Routledge.

***Socialism & War: Essays, Doucments, Reviews, Vol. 10.** F. A. Hayek. 1997. 36.00 (*0-226-32058-8*) U Ch Pr.

Socialism & War: The Spanish Socialist Party in Power & Crisis, 1936-1939. Helen Graham. 332p. (C). 1991. text ed. 64.95 (*0-521-39257-8*) Cambridge U Pr.

Socialism & Wealth: The Creation & Distribution of Socialist Wealth. Y. Lazutkin. 217p. 1975. 22.95 (*0-8464-0859-7*) Beekman Pubs.

Socialism, Communism, & Liberation Theology in Brazil: An Opinion Survey Using Q-Methodology. N. Patrick Peritore. LC 90-36505. (Monographs in International Studies, Latin America Ser.: No. 15). 274p. reprint ed. pap. 78.10 (*0-7837-6474-X*, 2046478) Bks Demand.

Socialism, Economics & Development. Alec Nove. 280p. (C). 1986. text ed. 37.95 (*0-04-335054-2*); pap. text ed. 16.95 (*0-04-335055-0*) Routledge Chapman & Hall.

Socialism, Feminism & Philosophy: A Radical Philosophy Reader. Ed. by Sean Sayers & Peter Osborne. 256p. (C). 1991. pap. text ed. 18.95 (*0-415-05628-4*, A5087) Routledge.

Socialism, Feminism & Philosophy: A Radical Philosophy Reader. Ed. by Sean Sayers & Peter Osborne. 256p. (C). (gr. 13). 1991. text ed. 74.95 (*0-415-05627-6*, A5083) Routledge.

Socialism for a Skeptical Age. Miliband. 200p. (C). 1994. pap. text ed. 19.00 (*1-85984-057-4*, C0495, Pub. by Vrso UK) Norton.

Socialism for a Skeptical Age. Miliband. 200p. (C). (gr. 13). 1994. text ed. 65.00 (*1-85984-947-4*, C0494, Pub. by Vrso UK) Norton.

Socialism for Beginners. Anna Paczuska & Sophie Grillet. (Writers & Readers Documentary Comic Bks.). (Illus.). (C). 1986. pap. 6.95 (*0-906495-92-X*) Writers & Readers.

***Socialism, Historical Truth & the Crisis of Political Thought in the United States.** David North. 46p. (Orig.). 1996. pap. 3.50 (*0-929087-73-9*) Labor Pubns Inc.

Socialism in America from the Shakers to the Third International: A Documentary History. Compiled by Albert Fried. LC 92-32772. 618p. (C). 1993. pap. 19.00 (*0-231-08141-3*, Mrngside); text ed. 49.50 (*0-231-08140-5*, Mrngside) Col U Pr.

Socialism in Cuba. Leo Huberman & Paul M. Sweezy. LC 68-8078. (Modern Reader Ser.: No. PB-133). 221p. reprint ed. pap. 63.00 (*0-7837-3921-4*, 2043769) Bks Demand.

Socialism in England. Sidney Webb. 154p. 1987. text ed. 52.95 (*0-566-05144-3*, Pub. by Dartmth Pub UK) Ashgate Pub Co.

Socialism in Galicia: The Emergence of Polish Social Democracy & Ukrainian Radicalism, 1860-1890. Himka John-Paul. LC 83-47953. (Harvard Ukrainian Research Institute Monograph). xiii, 253p. (Orig.). 1990. pap. 17.00 (*0-916458-07-5*) Harvard Ukrainian.

Socialism in Greece. P. Z. Tzannatos. 125p. 1986. text ed. 53.95 (*0-566-05097-8*, Pub. by Dartmth Pub UK) Ashgate Pub Co.

Socialism in One Country see History of Soviet Russia

Socialism in One Zone: Stalin's Policy in Korea, 1945-47. Erik Van Ree. (Illus.). 320p. 1989. 19.95 (*0-85496-274-3*) Berg Pubs.

Socialism in Russia: Theory & Practice. Nodari A. Simonia. LC 93-15842. 208p. 1994. text ed. 59.95 (*0-313-28830-5*, Greenwood Pr) Greenwood.

Socialism in Sub-Saharan Africa: A New Assessment. Ed. by Carl G. Rosberg & Thomas M. Callaghy. LC 79-84635. (Research Ser.: No. 38). (Illus.). 1979. pap. text ed. 12.95 (*0-87725-138-X*) U of Cal IAS.

Socialism in the Chinese Countryside. Jurgen Domes. 1980. 42.95 (*0-7735-0532-6*, Pub. by McGill CN) U of Toronto Pr.

Socialism in the Crucible of History. Michel Beaud. Tr. by Tom Dickman from FRE. LC 92-15659. 232p. (C). 1993. text ed. 55.00 (*0-391-03770-6*) Humanities.

Socialism in the Heartland: The Midwestern Experience, 1900-1925. Ed. by Donald T. Critchlow. LC 85-40602. 221p. 1987. pap. text ed. 14.00 (*0-268-01720-4*) U of Notre Dame Pr.

Socialism in Theory & Practice. Morris Hillquit. 1977. 22.95 (*0-8369-7162-0*, 7994) Ayer.

Socialism, Liberalism, & Dictatorship in Paraguay. Paul H. Lewis. Ed. by Hoover Institution Press Staff & Robert Wesson. LC 81-21092. (Politics in Latin America, A Hoover Institution Ser.). 170p. 1982. text ed. 49.95 (*0-275-90847-X*, C0847, Praeger Pubs) Greenwood.

Socialism of a Different Kind: Reshaping the Left in France. Bernard E. Brown. LC 82-6125. (Contributions in Political Science Ser.: No. 85). xiv, 201p. 1982. text ed. 55.00 (*0-313-23377-2*, BFL/, Greenwood Pr) Greenwood.

Socialism of Fools: Anti-Semitism on the Left. Michael Lerner. (C). 1992. pap. 10.00 (*0-03-593305-4*) HB Coll Pubs.

Socialism of Fools: Anti-Semitism on the Left. Michael Lerner. 1992. pap. 10.00 (*0-935933-05-0*) Inst Labor & Mental.

Socialism of Jaharwalal Nehru. R. C. Dutt. 1981. 18.50 (*0-8364-0708-3*, Pub. by Abhinav II) S Asia.

Socialism of Jawaharlal Nehru. R. C. Dutt. 284p. 1981. 24.95 (*0-318-36638-X*) Asia Bk Corp.

Socialism of My Conception. M. K. Gandhi. Ed. by A. T. Hingorani. 290p. (Orig.). 1981. pap. 8.00 (*0-934676-29-1*) Greenlf Bks.

Socialism on Trial. 2nd ed. James P. Cannon. LC 73-86630. 192p. 1973. pap. 14.95 (*0-87348-317-0*) Pathfinder NY.

Socialism, Participation & Agricultural Development in Post-Revolutionary Ethiopia: A Study of Constraints. Makonen Getu. (Stockholm Studies in Economic History: No. 11). 225p. (Orig.). 1987. pap. 48.00 (*91-7146-477-8*, Pub. by Stockholms Universitet SW) Coronet Bks.

Socialism, Peace & Solidarity: Speeches of Olaf Palme. Ed. by E. S. Reddy. 1990. text ed. 25.00 (*0-7069-5316-9*, Pub. by Vikas II) S Asia.

Socialism, Radicalism & Nostalgia: Social Criticism in Britain 1775-1830. William Stafford. 250p. 1987. pap. 21.95 (*0-521-33989-8*) Cambridge U Pr.

Socialism Re-Examined. Norman M. Thomas. LC 84-12988. 280p. 1984. reprint ed. text ed. 59.75 (*0-313-24429-4*, THSR, Greenwood Pr) Greenwood.

Socialism Revised & Modernized: The Case for Pragmatic Market Socialism. James A. Yunker. LC 91-33764. 360p. 1992. text ed. 57.95 (*0-275-94134-5*, C4134, Praeger Pubs) Greenwood.

Socialism Since Eighteen Eighty-Nine: A Biographical History. James D. Young. LC 88-23588. 272p. (C). 1988. lib. bdg. 62.50 (*0-389-20813-2*, N8371) B&N Imports.

Socialism Today? The Changing Meaning of Socialism. Ed. by Ota Sik. 217p. 1991. text ed. 65.00 (*0-312-06023-8*) St Martin.

Socialism Today & Tomorrow. Michael Albert & Robin Hahnel. LC 81-50138. 406p. (C). 1981. 35.00 (*0-89608-078-1*); pap. 9.50 (*0-89608-077-3*) South End Pr.

Socialism Utopian & Scientific. Frederick Engels. 96p. (C). 1935. pap. text ed. 2.95 (*0-7178-0191-8*) Intl Pubs Co.

Socialism Utopian & Scientific. Frederick Engels. 64p. 1989. pap. 3.00 (*0-87348-579-3*) Pathfinder NY.

Socialism vs. Anarchism. Daniel De Leon. 1970. pap. 0.50 (*0-935534-39-3*) NY Labor News.

Socialisme Au Dix-Huitieme Siecle: Etudes Sur les Idees Socialistes Dans les Ecrivains Francais due XVIII Siecle Avant la Revolution. Andre Lichtenberger. LC 67-27835. viii, 471p. 1967. reprint ed. 57.50 (*0-678-00329-7*) Kelley.

Socialisme et l'Homme a Cuba - Socialism & Man in Cuba. Ernesto Che Guevara & Fidel Castro. 56p. 1989. pap. 4.00 (*0-87348-580-7*) Pathfinder NY.

Socialismo: Analisis Economico y Sociologico. Ludwig Von Mises. Tr. by Luis M. De Oca from ENG. 621p. (SPA.). (C). reprint ed. pap. 10.00 (*0-317-91166-X*) West Bks Found.

Socialismo y el Hombre en Cuba (Socialism & Man in Cuba) Ernesto C. Guevara. LC 92-64136. (Illus.). 152p. (SPA.). 1992. pap. 14.95 (*0-87348-578-5*) Pathfinder NY.

Socialisms: Old & New. 2nd ed. Anthony C. Wright. LC 96-26287. 176p. (C). 1996. pap. 15.95 (*0-415-15180-5*); text ed. 49.95 (*0-415-15179-1*) Routledge.

Socialism's Dilemmas: State & Society in the Soviet Bloc. Walter D. Connor. 320p. 1988. text ed. 49.50 (*0-231-06606-6*) Col U Pr.

Socialist Albania since Nineteen Forty-Four: Domestic & Foreign Developments. Peter R. Prifti. LC 78-1728. (Studies in Communism, Revisionism, & Revolution: No. 22). 1978. 40.00 (*0-262-16070-6*) MIT Pr.

Socialist & Labour Movement in Japan. Arthur M. Young. LC 79-65476. (Studies in Japanese History & Civilization). 145p. 1979. reprint ed. text ed. 59.95 (*0-313-26990-4*, U6990, Greenwood Pr) Greenwood.

Socialist, Anti-Semite, & Jew: German Social Democracy Confronts the Problem of Anti-Semitism, 1918-1933. Donald L. Niewyk. LC 79-137123. 264p. 1971. pap. 75.30 (*0-7837-8519-4*, 2049328) Bks Demand.

Socialist Authority: The Hungarian Experience. Peter A. Toma. LC 87-11775. 320p. 1988. text ed. 69.50 (*0-275-92602-8*, C2602, Praeger Pubs) Greenwood.

Socialist Cities: Municipal Politics & the Grass Roots of American Socialism. Richard W. Judd. LC 88-31321. (SUNY Series in American Labor History). 254p. (Orig.). 1989. text ed. 74.50 (*0-7914-0080-8*); pap. text ed. 24.95 (*0-7914-0081-6*) State U NY Pr.

Socialist City: Spatial Structure & Urban Policy. Ed. by Richard A. French & F. E. Hamilton. LC 78-16828. 559p. reprint ed. pap. 159.40 (*0-317-55679-7*, 2029261) Bks Demand.

Socialist Collective Agreement. Laszlo Nagy. 257p. (C). 1984. 70.00 (*963-05-3368-5*, Pub. by Akad Kiado HU) St Mut.

Socialist Commonwealth of Nations: Organizations & Institutions. Kazimierz Grzybowski. 1964. 79.50 (*0-685-26695-8*) Elliots Bks.

Socialist Communist Interactions in India. Madhu Limaye. (C). 1991. 36.00 (*81-202-0319-4*, Pub. by Ajanta II) S Asia.

Socialist Countries: General Features of Political, Economic, & Cultural Life. 2nd ed. Erwin Marquit. LC 83-9329. (Studies in Marxism: Vol. 3). 226p. 1983. 19.95 (*0-930656-31-8*); pap. 9.95 (*0-930656-32-6*) MEP Pubns.

Socialist Cuba: As Seen by a U. S. Communist Delegation. Joseph North. 1970. pap. 0.60 (*0-87898-073-3*) New Outlook.

Socialist Debate: Beyond Red & Green. Bogdan Denitch. 256p. 64.00 (*0-7453-0381-1*, Pub. by Pluto Pr UK) LPC InBook.

Socialist Debate: Beyond Red & Green. Bogdan Denitch. (C). pap. 18.95 (*0-7453-0382-X*, Pub. by Pluto Pr UK) LPC InBook.

Socialist Dilemmas. Ed. by Henryk Flakierski & Thomas T. Sekine. LC 90-8616. 162p. (gr. 13). 1990. text ed. 72.95 (*0-87332-687-3*) M E Sharpe.

Socialist Economic Integration. Jozef M. Van Brabant. LC 79-23766. (Soviet & East European Studies). (Illus.). 275p. 1980. 64.95 (*0-521-23046-2*) Cambridge U Pr.

Socialist Economies & the Transition to the Market: A Guide. Ian Jeffries. LC 92-36243. (Illus.). 464p. (C). 1993. pap. 29.95 (*0-415-07580-7*, B0147) Routledge.

Socialist Economies & the Transition to the Market: A Guide. Ian Jeffries. LC 92-36243. (Illus.). 464p. (C). (gr. 13). 1993. text ed. 125.00 (*0-415-07579-3*, B0143) Routledge.

Socialist Economies in Transition: A Primer on Semi-reformed Systems. Robert W. Campbell. LC 91-8653. (Illus.). 256p. 1991. 35.00 (*0-253-31301-5*); pap. 13.95 (*0-253-20670-7*, MB-670) Ind U Pr.

Socialist Economies in Transition: Appraisals of the Market Mechanism. Ed. by Mark Knell & Christine Rider. 256p. 1992. 75.00 (*1-85278-438-5*) E Elgar.

Socialist Economy: Theory & Practice. Thomas B. Bottomore. LC 90-36084. 160p. 1990. pap. text ed. 17.95 (*0-89862-453-3*); lib. bdg. 36.95 (*0-89862-449-5*) Guilford Pr.

Socialist Ensembles: Theater & State in Cuba & Nicaragua. Randy Martin. 208p. 1994. text ed. 44.95 (*0-8166-2480-1*); pap. text ed. 19.95 (*0-8166-2482-8*) U of Minn Pr.

Socialist Enterprise: Reclaiming the Economy. Diana Gilhespy et al. 230p. 1986. pap. 27.50 (*0-85124-470-X*, Pub. by Spokesman Bks UK) Coronet Bks.

Socialist Entrepreneurs: Embourgeoisement in Rural Hungary. Ivan Szelenyi. LC 87-16085. (Illus.). 320p. (C). 1988. text ed. 35.00 (*0-299-11360-4*); pap. text ed. 17.95 (*0-299-11364-7*) U of Wis Pr.

Socialist Europe & Revolutionary Russia: Perception & Prejudice, 1848-1923. Bruno Naarden. 424p. (C). 1993. text ed. 80.00 (*0-521-41473-3*) Cambridge U Pr.

Socialist Health-Capitalist Health: Is There a Difference?: A Special Issue of the Journal Medical Anthropology. Ed. by M. Singer & H. A. Baer. 126, iip. 1989. pap. text ed. 29.00 (*2-88124-343-6*) Gordon & Breach.

Socialist Humanism: The Outcome of Classical European Morality. Donald C. Hodges. LC 73-96983. 384p. 1974. 16.70 (*0-87527-042-5*) Green.

Socialist Ideology & the Struggle for Southern Africa. John S. Saul. LC 88-71175. 200p. (C). 1990. 35.00 (*0-86543-099-3*); pap. 11.95 (*0-86543-100-0*) Africa World.

Socialist in Congress: His Conduct & Responsibilities. 5th ed. Daniel De Leon. 1962. pap. 0.50 (*0-935534-41-5*) NY Labor News.

Socialist International at Gunpoint. Manos Haris. 144p. 1990. pap. 39.00 (*0-614-08412-1*, Pub. by Picton UK) St Mut.

Socialist International at Gunpoint: Did the CIA Murder Olaf Palme? Picton Publishing (Chippenham) Ltd. Staff. (C). 1987. 65.00 (*0-948251-40-9*, Pub. by Picton UK) St Mut.

Socialist Investment Cycles: Analysis in Retrospect. Peter Mihalyi. LC 92-31351. (International Studies in Economics & Econometrics). 1992. lib. bdg. 129.50 (*0-7923-1973-7*) Kluwer Ac.

Socialist Korea: A Case Study in the Strategy of Economic Development. Ellen Brun & Jacques Hersh. LC 76-1651. (Illus.). 432p. 1977. 16.50 (*0-85345-386-1*) Monthly Rev.

Socialist Labor & Politics in Weimar Germany: The General Federation of German Trade Unions. Gerard Braunthal. LC 77-29131. (Illus.). 253p. (C). 1978. lib. bdg. 33.50 (*0-208-01740-2*, Archon Bks) Shoe String.

Socialist Labor Party, 1876-1991: A Short History. Frank Girard & Ben Perry. 112p. 1991. pap. 8.00 (*0-9629315-0-0*) Livra Bks.

Socialist Landmarks. 2nd ed. Daniel De Leon. 1977. pap. 1.50 (*0-935534-29-6*) NY Labor News.

Socialist Legalism: Reform & Continuity in Post-Mao People's Republic of China. Ed. by Hungdah Chiu. (Occasional Papers-Reprints Series in Contemporary Asian Studies: No. 1). 35p. (Orig.). 1982. pap. text ed. 4.00 (*0-942182-45-6*) Occasional Papers.

Socialist Management & Planning: Topics in Comparative Socialist Economics. Nicolas Spulber. LC 73-126220. (International Development Research Center, Studies in Development: No. 2). (Illus.). 253p. reprint ed. 72.20 (*0-8357-9242-0*, 2015834) Bks Demand.

Socialist Mathematics Education. Ed. by Frank Swetz. LC 78-68025. 1979. pap. 30.00 (*0-917574-04-4*) Burgundy Pr.

Socialist Mayor: Bernard Sanders in Burlington, Vermont. Steven Soifer. LC 90-48954. 312p. 1991. text ed. 55.00 (*0-89789-219-4*, H219, Bergin & Garvey) Greenwood.

Socialist Models of Development. Ed. by Charles K. Wilber & K. P. Jameson. 240p. 1982. pap. 48.00 (*0-08-027921-X*, Pergamon Pr) Elsevier.

Socialist Movement in India. Hari D. Sharma & N. C. Mehrotra. 165p. 1993. text ed. 27.50 (*0-685-37818-7*, Pub. by Radiant Pubs II) S Asia.

Socialist Movement in Reading, Pennsylvania, Eighteen Thirty-Six to Nineteen Thirty-Six: A Study in Social Change. Henry G. Stetler. LC 73-16306. (Perspectives in American History Ser.: No. 21). (Illus.). viii, 198p. 1974. reprint ed. lib. bdg. 37.50 (*0-87991-333-9*) Porcupine Pr.

Socialist Movement in Turkey, 1960-1980. Igor P. Lipovsky. LC 92-18122. (Social, Economic & Political Studies of the Middle East: Vol. 45). 190p. 1992. 64.50 (*90-04-09582-9*) E J Brill.

Socialist Network. Nesta H. Webster. 1973. 250.00 (*0-8490-1070-5*) Gordon Pr.

Socialist Network. Nesta H. Webster. 163p. 1926. reprint ed. pap. 5.00 (*0-913022-06-3*) CPA Bk Pub.

Socialist Network. Nesta H. Webster. 163p. 1926. reprint ed. pap. 11.95 (*0-945001-05-3*) GSG & Assocs.

Socialist Novel in Britain: Towards the Recovery of a Tradition. H. Gustav Klaus. LC 81-18376. 190p. 1982. text ed. 35.00 (*0-312-73775-0*) St Martin.

Socialist Offensive: The Collectivization of Soviet Agriculture, 1929-1930. Richard W. Davies. LC 79-15263. (Industrialization of Soviet Russia Ser.: Vol. 1). (Illus.). 512p. 1980. 46.50 (*0-674-81480-0*) HUP.

Socialist Option in Central America: Two Reassessments. Shafik J. Handal & Carlos M. Vilas. 256p. (C). 1992. text ed. 26.00 (*0-85345-867-7*); pap. text ed. 17.00 (*0-85345-868-5*) Monthly Rev.

Socialist Orientation of Jawaharlal Nehru. Neelam Mishra. 200p. 1989. 13.00 (*81-212-0285-X*, Pub. by Gian Publng Hse II) S Asia.

An Asterisk (*) at the beginning of an entry indicates that the title is appearing in BIP for the first time.

Socialist Parties & the Question of Europe in the 1950s. Ed. by Richard T. Griffiths. LC 92-30546. (Contributions to the History of Labour & Society Ser.: Vol. 4). 1992. 89.25 (*90-04-09734-1*) E J Brill.

Socialist Parties in Postwar Japan. Allan Burnett Cole et al. LC 66-21511. (Illus.). 508p. reprint ed. pap. 144.80 (*0-317-09609-5*, 2021989) Bks Demand.

Socialist Party of Argentina, 1890-1930. Richard J. Walter. LC 77-620003. (Latin American Monographs: No. 42). 304p. 1977. pap. text ed. 8.95 (*0-292-77540-7*) U of Tex Pr.

Socialist Population Politics: The Political Implications of Demographic Trends in the U. S. S. R. & Eastern Europe. John F. Besemeres. LC 80-65260. 389p. reprint ed. pap. 110.90 (*0-685-23731-1*, 2032772) Bks Demand.

Socialist Price Theory & Price Policy. B. Csikos-Nagy. 372p. (C). 1975. 48.00 (*963-05-0357-3*, Pub. by Akad Kiado HU) St Mut.

Socialist Pyramid: Elites & Power in Yugoslavia. Lenard J. Cohen. 300p. 29.95 (*0-88962-386-4*); pap. 19.95 (*0-88962-385-6*) Mosaic.

Socialist Realism: An Impossible Aesthetic. Regine Robin. Tr. by Catherine Porter from FRE. 376p. 1992. 47.50 (*0-8047-1655-2*) Stanford U Pr.

Socialist Realism in Louis Atragon's Le Monde reel. A. M. Kimyongur. 135p. 1996. pap. 18.95 (*0-85958-642-1*, Pub. by Univ of Hull Pr UK) Paul & Co Pubs.

***Socialist Realism Without Shores.** Ed. by Thomas Lahusen & Evgeny Dobrenko. LC 96-43217. (Post-Contemporary Interventions Ser.). (Illus.). 392p. 1997. pap. text ed. 19.95 (*0-8223-1941-1*); lib. bdg. 59.95 (*0-8223-1935-7*) Duke.

Socialist Reasoning: An Inquiry into the Political Philosophy of Socialist China. Collier. 1995. 63.00 (*0-7453-0364-1*, Pub. by Pluto Pr UK) LPC InBook.

Socialist Reconstruction of Society. 20th ed. Daniel De Leon. 1977. pap. 0.50 (*0-935534-42-3*) NY Labor News.

Socialist Regimes of Eastern Europe: Their Establishment & Consolidation 1944-1967. Jerzy Tomaszewski. 192p. 1989. 75.00 (*0-415-02027-1*, A3583) Routledge.

Socialist Register: Annuals: Nineteen Seventy-Nine to Nineteen Ninety-One. John Saville. 1991. 35.00 (*0-87556-440-2*) Saifer.

Socialist Register: 1978. Ed. by Ralph Miliband & John Saville. 338p. 1978. pap. 10.00 (*0-85345-453-1*) Monthly Rev.

Socialist Register, 1980. Ed. by Ralph Miliband & John Saville. (C). 1980. pap. 7.50 (*0-85036-267-9*, Pub. by Merlin Pr UK); text ed. 12.95 (*0-85036-266-0*, Pub. by Merlin Pr UK) Humanities.

Socialist Register 1982. Ed. by Martin Eve & David Musson. (C). 1982. pap. 7.50 (*0-85036-293-8*, Pub. by Merlin Pr UK); text ed. 15.95 (*0-85036-292-X*, Pub. by Merlin Pr UK) Humanities.

Socialist Register 1983. Ed. by Ralph Miliband & John Saville. (C). 1983. pap. 8.50 (*0-85036-310-1*, Pub. by Merlin Pr UK); text ed. 15.95 (*0-85036-309-8*, Pub. by Merlin Pr UK) Humanities.

Socialist Register, 1988. Ed. by Ralph Miliband et al. 460p. (C). 1988. text ed. 60.00 (*0-85036-354-3*, Pub. by Merlin Pr UK) Humanities.

Socialist Register, 1989: Revolution Today: Aspirations & Realities. Ed. by Ralph Miliband et al. 320p. (C). 1989. text ed. 60.00 (*0-85036-376-4*, Pub. by Merlin Pr UK) Humanities.

Socialist Register, 1990: The Retreat of the Intellectuals. Ed. by Ralph Miliband & Leo Panitch. 384p. (C). 1990. text ed. 60.00 (*0-85036-395-0*, Pub. by Merlin Pr UK) Humanities.

Socialist Register, 1991: The Communist Experience & Its Lessons. Ed. by Ralph Miliband et al. 400p. (C). 1991. text ed. 60.00 (*0-85036-419-1*, Pub. by Merlin Pr UK) Humanities.

Socialist Register, 1992: New World Order? Ed. by Ralph Miliband & Leo Panitch. (Socialist Register Ser.). 400p. (C). 1992. text ed. 60.00 (*0-85036-427-2*, Pub. by Merlin Pr UK) Humanities.

Socialist Register, 1993. Ed. by Ralph Miliband & Leo Panitch. 256p. (C). 1993. text ed. 60.00 (*0-85036-431-0*, Pub. by Merlin Pr UK) Humanities.

Socialist Register 1994: Between Globalism & Nationalism. Ed. by Ralph Miliband & Leo Panitch. 356p. (C). 1994. text ed. 60.00 (*0-85036-441-8*, Pub. by Merlin Pr UK) Humanities.

Socialist Register, 1995: Why Not Capitalism? Ed. by Leo Panitch & Ellen Wood. 256p. 1995. 60.00 (*0-85036-449-3*, Pub. by Merlin Pr UK) Humanities.

Socialist Register 1995: Why Not Capitalism. Ed. by Leo Panitch & Ellen M. Wood. 304p. (Orig.). (C). 1995. pap. text ed. 18.00 (*0-85345-964-9*, Pub. by Merlin UK) Monthly Rev.

Socialist Register 1996: Are There Alternatives? Ed. by Leo Panitch. 280p. 1996. 60.00 (*0-85036-455-8*, Pub. by Merlin Pr UK) Humanities.

***Socialist Register 1997: Ruthless Criticism of All That Exists.** Ed. by Leo Panitch. 384p. 1997. 60.00 (*0-85036-465-5*, Pub. by Merlin Pr UK) Humanities.

***Socialist Republic of Rumania.** Stephen A. Fischer-Galati. LC 69-19468. (Integration & Community Building in Eastern Europe Ser.). 127p. 1969. reprint ed. pap. 36.20 (*0-608-04060-6*, 2064796) Bks Demand.

Socialist Revolutionaries & the Russian Anti-War Movement, 1914-1917. Michael Melancon. 368p. 1991. 50.00 (*0-8142-0528-3*) Ohio St U Pr.

Socialist Somalia: Rhetoric & Reality. Ahmed I. Samatar. LC 88-17248. 224p. (C). 1988. pap. 17.50 (*0-86232-589-7*, Pub. by Zed Bks Ltd UK); text ed. 49.95 (*0-86232-588-9*, Pub. by Zed Bks Ltd UK) Humanities.

Socialist States in the World-System. Ed. by Christopher K. Chase-Dunn. LC 82-10725. (Sage Focus Editions Ser.: No. 58). (Illus.). 304p. reprint ed. pap. 86.70 (*0-8357-8484-3*, 2034752) Bks Demand.

Socialist System: The Political Economy of Communism. Janos Kornai. 507p. 1992. pap. text ed. 19.95 (*0-691-00393-9*) Princeton U Pr.

Socialist Tradition: From Crisis to Decline. Carl Boggs. (Revolutionary Thought - Radical Movements Ser.). 320p. (C). 1994. pap. 17.95 (*0-415-90670-9*, B0751) Routledge.

Socialist Tradition: From Crisis to Decline. Carl Boggs. (Revolutionary Thought - Radical Movements Ser.). 256p. (C). (gr. 13). 1995. text ed. 62.95 (*0-415-90669-5*, B0747) Routledge.

Socialist Transformation in Peripheral Economies: Lessons from Grenada. Courtney D. Smith. 302p. 1995. 63.95 (*1-85972-050-1*, Pub. by Avebury Pub UK) Ashgate Pub Co.

Socialist Unemployment: The Political Economy of Yugoslavia. Susan L. Woodward. LC 94-46153. 443p. 1995. text ed. 55.00 (*0-691-08645-1*) Princeton U Pr.

Socialist Unemployment: The Political Economy of Yugoslavia, 1945-1990. Susan L. Woodward. 443p. (C). 1995. pap. text ed. 19.95 (*0-691-02551-7*) Princeton U Pr.

Socialist Utopia in the New South: The Ruskin Colonies in Tennessee & Georgia, 1894-1901. W. Fitzhugh Brundage. (C). 1996. text ed. 38.95 (*0-252-02244-0*); pap. text ed. 16.95 (*0-252-06548-4*) U of Ill Pr.

Socialist Visions. Ed. by Stephen R. Shalom. LC 82-61155. 300p. 1983. 35.00 (*0-89608-170-2*); pap. 9.00 (*0-89608-169-9*) South End Pr.

Socialist Women: European Socialist Feminism in the Nineteenth & Early Twentieth-Centuries. Ed. by Marilyn J. Boxer & Jean H. Quataert. LC 77-16618. 260p. 1981. text ed. 29.95 (*0-444-99042-9*, BSW/) Greenwood.

Socialist Workers Party in World War Two: Writings & Speeches, 1940-1943. James P. Cannon. Ed. by George Breitman & Les Evans. LC 75-20719. (Illus.). 446p. 1975. pap. 22.95 (*0-87348-457-6*); lib. bdg. 60.00 (*0-87348-456-8*) Pathfinder NY.

Socialist Zionism: Theory & Issues in Contemporary Jewish Nationalism. Allon Gal. 225p. 1973. pap. 21.95 (*0-87073-669-8*) Transaction Pubs.

Socialist-Zionism: Theory & Issues in Contemporary Jewish Nationalism. Allon Gal. LC 89-5468. (Brown Classics in Judaica Ser.). 242p. (C). 1989. reprint ed. pap. text ed. 26.00 (*0-8191-7275-8*) U Pr of Amer.

Socialists & Socialism. Thomas E. Watson. (Studies in Populism). 1980. lib. bdg. 69.95 (*0-87700-324-6*) Revisionist Pr.

Socialists & the Ballot Box: An Historical Analysis. Eric T. Chester. LC 85-6475. 192p. 1985. text ed. 49.95 (*0-275-90073-8*, C0073, Praeger Pubs) Greenwood.

Socialists & the Fight Against Anti-Semitism. Peter Seidman. 32p. 1973. pap. 3.00 (*0-87348-293-X*) Pathfinder NY.

Socialist's Budget (1907) see From Serfdom to Socialism (1907)

Socialists in the Recession: The Search for Solidarity. Giles Radice & Lisanne Radice. LC 86-14265. 200p. 1986. text ed. 35.00 (*0-312-73748-3*) St Martin.

Socialists of Rural Andalusia: Unacknowledged Revolutionaries of the Second Republic. George A. Collier. LC 87-9929. (Illus.). 264p. 1987. 37.50 (*0-8047-1411-8*) Stanford U Pr.

Sociality & Sympathy. J. W. Jones. Bd. with The Practice Curve. J. H. Bair. ; Psychology of Expectations. Clara M. Hitchcock. ; Motor, Visual & Applied Rhythms. J. B. Miner. ; Perception of Number. J. F. Messenger. ; Study of Memory. E. N. Henderson. (Psychology Monographs General & Applied: Vol. 5). 1974. reprint ed. 55.00 (*0-8115-1404-8*) Periodicals Srv.

Socialization & Communication in Primary Groups. Ed. by Thomas R. Williams. (World Anthropology Ser.). (Illus.). xii, 470p. 1975. 51.55 (*90-279-7730-5*) Mouton.

Socialization & Education: Essays in Conceptual Criticism. Wolfgang Brezinka. LC 93-47087. (Contributions to the Study of Education Ser.: No. 63). 232p. 1994. text ed. 55.00 (*0-313-29258-2*, Greenwood Pr) Greenwood.

***Socialization & Interaction: A Program Designed for Students with a Variety of Handicapping Conditions.** Doris Robinson & Wendy Mopsik. (Illus.). 28p. (Orig.). (J). (gr. k-6). 1991. pap. 7.95 (*1-57543-008-8*) Mar Co Prods.

Socialization & Schools. Talcott Parsons et al. LC 68-59278. (Reprint Ser.: No. 1). 90p. 1968. pap. 5.95 (*0-916690-00-8*) Harvard Educ Rev.

Socialization & Sex Education. Geraldine Rouse & Carol Birch. (C). 1991. pap. text ed. 99.00 (*1-56304-031-X*) J Stanfield.

Socialization & the Life Cycle. Ed. by Peter I. Rose. LC 78-65243. 1979. pap. text ed. 17.00 (*0-312-73800-5*) St Martin.

Socialization as Cultural Communication: Development of a Theme in the Work of Margaret Mead. Ed. by Theodore Schwartz. LC 75-17282. 1976. pap. 14.00 (*0-520-03955-6*) U CA Pr.

Socialization for Achievement: Essays on the Cultural Psychology of the Japanese. George A. De Vos. LC 78-132420. (Center for Japanese Studies, UC Berkeley: No. 7). 613p. 1973. 65.00 (*0-520-01827-3*); pap. 24.95 (*0-520-02893-7*) U CA Pr.

***Socialization Games for Persons with Disabilities: Structured Group Activities for Social & Interpersonal Development.** Nevalyn Nevil et al. LC 96-37683. (Illus.). 176p. 1997. 45.95 (*0-398-06749-X*) C C Thomas.

***Socialization Games for Persons with Disabilities: Structured Group Activities for Social & Interpersonal Development.** Nevalyn Nevil et al. LC 96-37683. (Illus.). 176p. 1997. pap. 32.95 (*0-398-06746-5*) C C Thomas.

Socialization in Drug Abuse. Ed. by Robert Coombs et al. LC 75-37067. 496p. 1976. pap. text ed. 24.95 (*0-87073-489-X*) Transaction Pubs.

Socialization into Physical Education: Learning to Teach. Thomas Templin & Paul G. Schempp. (Illus.). 340p. (C). 1989. per. write for info. (*0-697-14831-9*) Brown & Benchmark.

Socialization of Emotions. Ed. by Michael Lewis & Carolyn Saarni. (Genesis of Behavior Ser.: Vol. 5). 334p. 1985. 70.00 (*0-306-41851-7*, Plenum Pr) Plenum.

Socialization of Family Size Values: Youth & Family Planning in an Indian Village. Thomas Poffenberger & Kim Sebaly. LC 76-53996. (Michigan Papers on South & Southeast Asia: No. 12). (Illus.). xiv, 159p. (Orig.). 1976. pap. 3.00 (*0-89148-012-9*) Ctr S&SE Asian.

Socialization of Law Students: A Case Study in Three Parts. Wagner P. Thielens, Jr. Ed. by Harriet Zuckerman & Robert K. Merton. LC 79-9034. (Dissertation on Sociology Ser.). 1980. lib. bdg. 46.95 (*0-405-13001-5*) Ayer.

Socialization of Neophyte Nurses. Loretta C. Myers. LC 82-7014. (Studies in Nursing Management: No. 1). (Illus.). 156p. reprint ed. pap. 44.50 (*0-685-20336-0*, 2070022) Bks Demand.

Socialization of the New England Clergy Eighteen Hundred to Eighteen Sixty. Gordon A. Riegler. LC 79-13027. (Perspectives in American History Ser.: No. 37). 187p. 1979. reprint ed. lib. bdg. 35.00 (*0-87991-361-4*) Porcupine Pr.

Socialization, Sexism & Stereotyping: Women's Issues in Nursing. Janet Muff. (Illus.). 434p. (C). 1988. reprint ed. pap. text ed. 24.95 (*0-88133-372-7*) Waveland Pr.

Socialization to Old Age. Irving Rosow. LC 73-78540. 1975. pap. 12.00 (*0-520-03417-1*) U CA Pr.

***Socialization Trap: Protecting Your Children from Age Segregation & Other Pitfalls.** Rick Boyer & Marilyn Boyer. 150p. Date not set. lib. bdg. 7.99 (*0-9645396-2-4*, Home School Pr) GCB.

Socialized Agriculture of the U. S. S. R. Plans & Performance. Naum Jasny. xv, 837p. 1949. 85.00 (*0-8047-0401-5*) Stanford U Pr.

***Socializing.** Ellis & O'Driscoll. (Longman Business English Skills Ser.). 1992. pap. text ed. write for info. (*0-582-09308-2*, Pub. by Longman UK) Longman.

Socializing Capital: The Rise of the Large Industrial Corporation in America. William G. Roy. LC 96-8672. 338p. 1997. text ed. 35.00 (*0-691-04353-1*) Princeton U Pr.

Socializing Epistemology: The Social Dimensions of Knowledge. Ed. by Frederick F. Schmitt. 288p. 1994. pap. 23.95 (*0-8476-7959-4*); lib. bdg. 59.50 (*0-8476-7958-6*) Rowman.

Socializing Instinct: Individual, Family & Social Bonds. Andrew L. Cherry. LC 94-13726. 224p. 1994. text ed. 55.00 (*0-275-94626-6*, Praeger Pubs) Greenwood.

Socializing Security: Progressive-Era Economists & the Origins of American Social Policy. David A. Moss. LC 95-20652. 256p. (C). 1995. text ed. 39.95 (*0-674-81502-5*) HUP.

Socializing the Human - Computer Environment. Jerry J. Vaske & Charles E. Grantham. Ed. by Ben Shneiderman. LC 89-17745. (Human-Computer Interaction Ser.: Vol. 9). 312p. (C). 1990. text ed. 78.50 (*0-89391-471-1*) Ablex Pub.

Socially Critical View of the Self-Managing School. Ed. by John Smyth. 226p. 1993. 77.00 (*0-7507-0212-5*, Falmer Pr); pap. 31.00 (*0-7507-0213-3*, Falmer Pr) Taylor & Francis.

Socially Relevant Policy Analysis: Structuralist Computable General Equilibrium Models for the Developing World. Ed. by Lance Taylor. 388p. 1990. 39.95 (*0-262-20075-9*) MIT Pr.

Socially Responsible Accounting. M. R. Mathews. LC 92-38135. 260p. 1993. 26.95 (*0-412-47340-2*) Chapman & Hall.

Socially Responsible Investing. Harriet Tramer. 108p. (YA). (gr. 7-12). 1993. pap. 6.95 (*1-57515-027-1*) PPI Pubng.

Socially Responsible Investing: How to Invest with Your Conscience. Alan J. Miller. 250p. 1991. 19.95 (*0-13-156183-9*) NY Inst Finance.

Socially Responsible Stock Guide (With Supplement Insert, "How to Screen Traditional Investments for Social Factors") Ritchie P. Lowry. 48p. (Orig.). 1985. spiral bd. 2.50 (*0-933609-01-9*) Good Money Pubns.

Socially Responsive Portfolio: Balancing Politics & Profits in Institutional Money Management. James Melton & Matthew Keenan. 275p. 1993. text ed. 45.00 (*1-55738-501-7*) Irwin Prof Pubng.

Socially Responsive Self: Social Theory & Professional Ethics. Larry May. 216p. 1996. pap. text ed. 15.95 (*0-226-51172-3*); lib. bdg. 35.00 (*0-226-51171-5*) U Ch Pr.

Socialness of Things: Essays on the Socio-Semiotics of Objects. Ed. by Stephen H. Riggins. (Approaches to Semiotics Ser.: No. 115). 490p. (C). 1994. lib. bdg. 175.40 (*3-11-014133-7*, 226-94) Mouton.

Sociedad Colonial en Guatemala: Estudios Regionales y Locales. Ed. by Stephen Webre. LC 89-6011. (Monograph Ser.: No. 5). 312p. (SPA.). 1990. pap. 16.50 (*0-910443-07-6*) CIRMA.

Sociedad de Clases Medias. Salustiano Del Campo. (Nueva Austral Ser.: Vol. 85). (SPA.). 1991. pap. text ed. 24.95 (*84-239-1885-8*) Elliots Bks.

Sociedad, Derecho y Justicia. Jose T. Monge. LC 84-25862. 538p. (SPA.). 1986. lib. bdg. 25.00 (*0-8477-3020-4*) U of PR Pr.

Sociedad Enferma. Kittim Silva. 74p. (SPA.). 1995. 3.25 (*0-945792-20-4*, 498455) Editorial Unilit.

Sociedad Espanola: Desde 1500 Hasta Nuestros Dias. Fernando Diaz Plaja. (C). pap. 3.00 (*0-8477-3117-0*) U of PR Pr.

Sociedad Espanola En El Siglo de Oro, 2 vols. Manuel Fernandez Alvarez. 1070p. (SPA.). 1993. 200.00 (*84-249-1389-2*) Elliots Bks.

Sociedad Espanola en la Novela de la Postguerra. F. Carenas & Jose Ferrando. 1971. 10.95 (*0-88303-997-4*) E Torres & Sons.

Sociedad Hidraulica Zenu: Estudio Arqueologico de 2.000 Anos de Historia en las Llanuras del Caribe Colombiano. Clemencia Plazas et al. (Illus.). 308p. (Orig.). (SPA.). (C). 1993. pap. 22.00 (*958-9028-92-6*, Pub. by Banco de la Repub CK) UPLAAP.

Sociedad y Tipos en las Novelas de Ramon Meza y Suarez Inclan. Manuel A. Gonzales. LC 82-84334. (Coleccion Polymita). 184p. (Orig.). (SPA.). 1985. pap. 12.95 (*0-89729-326-6*) Ediciones.

Societa Italiana Di Fronte Alle Prime Migrazioni Di Massa: Italian Society at the Beginnings of the Mass Migrations. Ed. by Francesco Cordasco. LC 74-17954. (Italian American Experience Ser.). (Illus.). 524p. 1975. reprint ed. 35.95 (*0-405-06423-3*) Ayer.

Societal Change Between Market & Organization. John Child et al. (Public Policy & Social Welfare Ser.: Vol. 11). 228p. 1993. 38.95 (*1-85628-517-0*, Pub. by Avebury Pub UK) Ashgate Pub Co.

Societal Culture & Management. Ed. by Theodore D. Weinshall. (Studies in Organization: No. 44). xiv, 587p. (C). 1993. lib. bdg. 145.00 (*3-11-012211-1*) De Gruyter.

Societal Decision-Making: Democratic Challenges to State Technocracy. Tom Burns & Svein S. Andersen. 243p. 1992. 59.95 (*1-85521-269-2*, Pub. by Dartmth Pub UK) Ashgate Pub Co.

***Societal Development & Minority Rights.** Y. N. Kly. 272p. (Orig.). 1997. pap. 29.95 (*0-932863-23-X*) Clarity Pr.

Societal Dynamics. Olsen. 1994. pap. text ed. 55.00 (*0-13-157397-7*) P-H.

Societal Foundations of Education. (National Teacher Examination Ser.: NC-2). pap. 23.95 (*0-8373-8402-8*) Nat Learn.

Societal Impact on Aging: Historical Perspectives. Ed. by K. Warner Schaie & W. Andrew Achenbaum. LC 93-4292. 280p. 1993. 38.95 (*0-8261-8200-3*) Springer Pub.

Societal Influences, Vol. 5. Ed. by Helena Z. Lopata. (Current Research on Occupations & Professions Ser.). 187p. 1990. 73.25 (*0-89232-904-1*) Jai Pr.

Societal Issues - Scientific Viewpoints. Margaret A. Strom. LC 87-18822. 256p. (C). 1987. text ed. 50.00 (*0-88318-537-7*); pap. text ed. 31.25 (*0-88318-538-5*) Am Inst Physics.

***Societal Mechanisms for Maintaining Competence in Old Age.** Sherry L. Willis et al. LC 97-16310. (Societal Impact on Aging Ser.). 284p. 1997. write for info. (*0-8261-9690-X*) Springer Pub.

Societal Psychology. Ed. by Hilde T. Himmelweit & George Gaskell. (Focus Editions Ser.: Vol. 111). 288p. (C). 1990. text ed. 54.00 (*0-8039-3436-X*); pap. text ed. 24.95 (*0-8039-3437-8*) Sage.

***Societal Psychology.** Ed. by Hilde T. Himmelweit & George Gaskell. LC 89-27841. (Sage Focus Editions Ser.: Vol. 111). 287p. 1990. reprint ed. pap. 81.80 (*0-608-02993-9*, 2059633) Bks Demand.

Societal Risk Assessment: How Safe Is Safe Enough? Ed. by Richard C. Schwing & Walter A. Albers. LC 80-23833. (General Motors Research Symposia Ser.). 374p. 1980. 89.50 (*0-306-40554-7*, Plenum Pr) Plenum.

Societal Stratification: A Theoretical Analysis. Jonathan H. Turner. LC 83-7660. 216p. 1984. text ed. 55.00 (*0-231-05740-7*, King's Crown Paperbacks); pap. text ed. 19.50 (*0-231-05741-5*, King's Crown Paperbacks) Col U Pr.

Societal Subject: On Foundations of Mind; on Mind & Society; on Growing up in Society. Ed. by Niels Engelsted et al. (Illus.). 300p. (C). 1993. pap. 27.00 (*87-7288-113-5*, Pub. by Aarhus Univ Pr DK) David Brown.

Societal Systems. John N. Warfield. 490p. 1989. pap. text ed. 16.95 (*0-685-25892-0*) Intersystems Pubns.

Societal Systems: Planning, Policy, & Complexity. John N. Warfield. (Systems Inquiry Ser.). 516p. reprint ed. pap. 147.10 (*0-7837-6550-9*, AU00445) Bks Demand.

Societal Value of Geologic Maps. Richard L. Bernknopf et al. (Illus.). 53p. (Orig.). (C). 1994. pap. text ed. 35.00 (*0-7881-0728-3*) DIANE Pub.

Societas Ergophthalmologica Internationalis: 5th Symposium, Bordeux 1974. 6th Symposium, Hamburg 1976. 7th Symposium, Nagoya 1978. Ed. by H. J. Merte. (Problems of Industrial Medicine in Ophthalmology Ser.: Vol. 5-7). (Illus.). xx, 760p. 1982. pap. 199.25 (*3-8055-3003-X*) S Karger.

Societas et Fraternitas. Karl H. Schmid. 40p. (C). 1975. pap. text ed. 11.55 (*3-11-006580-0*) De Gruyter.

Societe Anonyme, Inc. Selected Publications, 3 vols. (Contemporary Art Ser.). (Illus.). 1972. reprint ed. #0-405-00771-X. 48.95 (*0-405-00770-1*) Ayer.

Societe Anonyme, Inc. Selected Publications, 3 vols, Set. (Contemporary Art Ser.). (Illus.). 1971. reprint ed. 88.95 (*0-685-27567-1*) Ayer.

Societe Anonyme, the First Museum of Modern Art, 1920-1944: Selected Publications, 3 Vols. Societe Anonyme Staff. 1972. 88.95 (*0-405-00798-1*, 11379) Ayer.

S

Societe Belge de Dermatologie et de Syphiligraphie: Belgische Vereniging voor Dermatologie en Syfiligrafie - Journal: Dermatologica, Vol. 158, No. 3. Ed. by R. Schuppli. (Illus.). 1979. pap. 26.50 (*3-8055-3018-8*) S Karger.

Societe de Consommation, ses Mythes, ses Structures. Jean Baudrillard. (Folio Essais Ser.: No. 35). 318p. (FRE.). 1970. pap. 11.95 (*2-07-032349-8*) Schoenhof.

Societe des Jacobins, 6 Vols, Set. Tr. by Francois V. Aulard. LC 78-161707. (Collection de documents relatifs a l'histoire de Paris pendant la Revolution francaise). reprint ed. 810.00 (*0-404-52560-1*) AMS Pr.

Societe et Demographie a Byzance et en Romaine Latine. David Jacoby. (Collected Studies: No. CS35). 372p. (C). 1975. reprint ed. lib. bdg. 74.95 (*0-902089-74-9*, Pub. by Variorum UK) Ashgate Pub Co.

Societe et Economie a Genes (XIVe-XVe Siecles) Jacques Heers. (Collected Studies: No. CS101). 362p. (FRE & ITA.). (C). 1979. reprint ed. lib. bdg. 97.95 (*0-86078-046-5*, Pub. by Variorum UK) Ashgate Pub Co.

Societe Feodale. Joseph L. Calmette. LC 80-1994. reprint ed. 30.00 (*0-404-18556-8*) AMS Pr.

Societe Feodale Allemande et Ses Institutions Du Xe Au XIIe Siecle. Charles E. Perrin. LC 80-2013. reprint ed. 38.50 (*0-404-18583-5*) AMS Pr.

Societe Francophone de Primatologie & the Primate Society of Great Britain, Scientific Meetings, Abstracts. (Journal Ser.: Vol. 62, No. 4, 1994). iv, 58p. 1994. pap. 38.50 (*3-8055-6100-8*) S Karger.

Societe Industrielle & Ses Musees 1890-1990: Demande Sociale & Choix Politiques. B. Schroeder-Gudehus. 324p. (FRE.). 1992. pap. text ed. 30.00 (*2-88124-857-8*) Gordon & Breach.

Societe, Politique, Individu: Les Formes Elementaires de la Vie Sociale en Inde Ancienne. fac. ed. Andreas Buss. 129p. (FRE.). reprint ed. pap. 36.80 (*0-7837-6952-0*, 2046781) Bks Demand.

Societe Rurale Au XIX Siecle: Les Paysans Du Calvados, Eighteen Fifteen to Eighteen Ninty-Five. Gabriel Desert. Ed. by Stuart Bruchey. LC 77-77166. (Dissertations in European Economic History Ser.). (Illus.). (FRE.). 1978. lib. bdg. 77.95 (*0-405-10780-3*) Ayer.

Societe Suisse de Gynecologie, Bericht ueber die Jahresversammlung, Genf, 1981. Ed. by E. Dreher. (Gynaekologische Rundschau Journal: Vol. 21, Suppl. 3). (Illus.). iv, 88p. 1981. pap. 23.25 (*3-8055-3479-5*) S Karger.

Societes Bantoues du Congo Belge et les Problemes de la Politique Indigene. Georges Van der Kerken. (B. E. Ser.: No. 173). (FRE.). 1920. 50.00 (*0-8115-3084-1*) Periodicals Srv.

***Societies: A Cultural Reader.** 2nd ed. Ed. by Thio. (C). 1994. text ed. 6.95 (*0-06-502164-9*) Addison-Wesley.

Societies & Cultures in World History, 5 vols. Incl. Vol. A. Through the Middle Ages: Chapters 1-11. Mark A. Kishlansky & Patrick J. Geary. 416p. (C). 1995. text ed. 39.50 (*0-06-500348-9*); Vol. B. 1100-1800: Chapters 1-23. Mark A. Kishlansky & Patrick J. Geary. 480p. (C). 1995. text ed. 39.50 (*0-06-500349-7*); Vol. C. 1789-Present: Chapters 22-35. Mark A. Kishlansky & Patrick J. Geary. 544p. (C). 1995. text ed. 40.95 (*0-06-500350-0*); Vol. 2. From 1350: Chapters 14-35. Mark A. Kishlansky & Patrick J. Geary. 784p. (C). 1995. text ed. 48.95 (*0-06-500352-7*); Vol. 2. From 1350. Bishoff. (C). 1995. student ed., pap. text ed. 20.95 (*0-06-501050-7*); Vol. 1. To 1650: World History Map. Wilson. (C). 1995. wbk. ed., pap. text ed. 20.95 (*0-06-502343-9*); Vol. 2. From 1350: World History Map. Wilson. (C). 1995. wbk. ed., pap. text ed. 20.95 (*0-06-502344-7*); Vol. 1. To 1650 Vol. 1. Bishoff. (C). 1995. student ed., pap. text ed. 19.95 (*0-06-500353-5*); Vols. 1-2. Societies & Cultures in World History. Bishoff. (C). Date not set. (*0-06-500355-1*); 1995. 61.50 (*0-06-500347-0*) Addson-Wesley Educ.

Societies & Cultures in World History see Societies & Cultures in World History

Societies & Languages of the Ancient Near East: Studies in Honour of I. M. Diakonoff. Ed. by Dandmayev. 1982. pap. 69.95 (*0-85668-205-5*, Pub. by Aris & Phillips UK) David Brown.

Societies & Military Power: India & Its Armies. Stephen P. Rosen. LC 96-11014. (Studies in Security Affairs). 296p. 1996. 39.95 (*0-8014-3210-3*) Cornell U Pr.

***Societies & Nature in the Sahel: Rethinking Environmental Degradation.** Claude Raynaut & Philippe L. Delville. (Routledge/Stockholm Environmental Institute Global Ser.: Vol. 1). 376p. (C). 1997. text ed. 74.95 (*0-415-14102-8*) Routledge.

Societies at Peace: Anthropological Perspectives. Ed. by Signe Howell & Roy Willis. 272p. 1989. 49.95 (*0-415-01824-2*, A3506); pap. 14.95 (*0-415-01825-0*, A3510) Routledge.

Societies, Cultures, & Kinship, 1580-1850: Cultural Provinces & English Local History. Intro. by Charles Phythian-Adams. LC 92-36511. (Illus.). 240p. 1993. 65.00 (*0-7185-1453-X*) St Martin.

Societies, Cultures & Kinships, 1580-1850: Cultural Provinces & English Local History. Ed. & Intro. by Charles Phythian-Adams. 230p. 1996. pap. 26.00 (*0-7185-0052-0*, Pub. by Leicester Univ Pr) Bks Intl VA.

***Societies in Space.** Alvin Rudoff. (American University Studies XI: Vol. 69). 224p. (C). 1996. text ed. 42.95 (*0-8204-3078-1*) P Lang Pubng.

Societies in Transition. Caroline Sweetman. (Focus on Gender Ser.). 64p. (C). 1995. pap. 12.95 (*0-85598-339-6*) Humanities.

Societies in Transition - East-Central Europe Today: Prague Papers on Social Responses to Transformation, Vol. 1. Claire Wallace & Stein Ringen. (Studies in the Social Policy of Eastern Europe & Soviet Union). 232p. 1994. 62.95 (*1-85628-698-3*, Pub. by Avebury Pub UK) Ashgate Pub Co.

Societies in Upheaval: Insurrections in France, Hungary, & Spain in the Early Eighteenth Century. Linda Frey & Marsha Frey. LC 86-25744. (Contributions to the Study of World History Ser.: No. 6). 154p. 1987. text ed. 45.00 (*0-313-25592-X*, FYU/) Greenwood.

Societies of Brains: A Neuroscience of Love & Hate. Walter J. Freeman. 216p. 1995. pap. 19.95 (*0-8058-2017-5*); text ed. 39.95 (*0-8058-2016-7*) L Erlbaum Assocs.

Societies of the Plains Indians, 13 pts. in 1 vol. Ed. by Clark Wissler. LC 74-9027. (Anthropological Papers of the American Museum of Natural History: Vol. 11). (Illus.). reprint ed. 160.00 (*0-404-11918-2*) AMS Pr.

Societies Registration Act, 1860. J. P. Bhatnagar. (C). 1993. 110.00 (*81-7012-457-3*, Pub. by Eastern Book II) St Mut.

Society. David Frisby & Derek Sayer. (Key Ideas Ser.). 150p. 1986. 19.95 (*0-85312-834-0*, 9708, Pub. by Tavistock-E Horwood UK); pap. 8.95 (*0-85312-852-9*, 9703, Pub. by Tavistock-E Horwood UK) Routledge Chapman & Hall.

Society. Bill Myers. LC 94-7014. (Forbidden Doors Ser.: Vol. 1). 1994. pap. 5.99 (*0-8423-5922-2*) Tyndale.

Society. 3rd ed. Borne. 1995. student ed., pap. text ed. 13.33 (*0-13-457078-2*) P-H.

***Society.** 4th ed. Macionis. 1997. pap. text ed. 37.33 (*0-13-653825-8*) P-H.

Society: A Brief Introduction. Ian Robertson. (Orig.). (C). 1988. pap. text ed. 36.95 (*0-87901-412-1*) Worth.

Society: A Brief Introduction. Ian Robertson. 264p. (Orig.). (C). 1989. student ed., pap. text ed. 14.95 (*0-87901-415-6*) Worth.

Society: A Brief Introduction. Ian Robertson. xvii, 416p. (Orig.). (C). 1990. text ed. 41.95 (*0-87901-548-9*) Worth.

Society: A Macroscopic View. Maurice N. Richter, Jr. 122p. 1980. pap. text ed. 11.95 (*0-87073-804-6*) Schenkman Bks Inc.

***Society: An Alaskan Perspective.** Sharon K. Araji. 512p. (C). 1996. pap. text ed. 30.39 (*0-7872-1898-7*) Kendall-Hunt.

Society: The Basics. 3rd annot. ed. John J. Macionis. LC 95-2839. 1995. teacher ed., pap. write for info. (*0-13-437906-3*) P-H.

Society: The Basics. 3rd ed. John J. Macionis. LC 95-2839. 512p. (C). 1995. pap. text ed. 36.00 (*0-13-435819-8*) P-H.

***Society: The Basics.** 4th ed. John J. Macionis. LC 97-9982. 1997. pap. write for info. (*0-13-621186-0*) P-H.

Society, Action & Space: An Alternative Human Geography. Benno Werlen. LC 92-6606. 272p. (C). 1992. pap. 17.95 (*0-415-06966-1*, A7761) Routledge.

Society, Action & Space: An Alternative Human Geography. Benno Werlen. LC 92-6606. 272p. (C). (gr. 13). 1992. text ed. 59.95 (*0-415-06965-3*, A7757) Routledge.

Society Against the State: Essays in Political Anthropology. Pierre Clastres. Tr. by Robert Hurley & Abe Stein from FRE. LC 87-50396. 218p. 1987. 24.95 (*0-942299-00-0*); pap. 12.95 (*0-942299-01-9*) Zone Bks.

Society & Change: A Sociological Introduction to Contemporary Australia. Brian Furze & Christine Stafford. 500p. 1994. 69.95 (*0-7329-1881-2*, Pub. by Macmill Educ AT); pap. 34.95 (*0-7329-1880-4*, Pub. by Macmill Educ AT) Paul & Co Pubs.

Society & Change: The Development of Canadian Sociology Through the Work of S. D. Clark. Harry H. Hiller. 200p. 1982. 30.00 (*0-8020-5540-0*) U of Toronto Pr.

Society & Civilization in Greece & Rome. Victor L. Ehrenberg. LC 64-19580. (Martin Classical Lectures: No. 18). (Illus.). 120p. 1964. 8.95 (*0-674-81510-6*) HUP.

Society & Community in India. R. K. Mukharjee. 155p. 1979. 12.95 (*0-318-36864-1*) Asia Bk Corp.

Society & Cosmos: Chewong of Peninsular Malaysia. Signe Howell. (Illus.). xvi, 320p. 1989. reprint ed. pap. text ed. 18.00 (*0-226-35505-5*) U Ch Pr.

Society & Cosmos: Their Interrelations or Their Coalescence in Melanesia. Ed. by Daniel De Coppet et al. (Explorations in Anthropology Ser.). 416p. 1995. 52.95 (*1-85973-037-X*); pap. 22.95 (*1-85973-042-6*) Berg Pubs.

Society & Culture During the Mughal Age. P. N. Chopra. 1987. 74.95 (*0-318-36978-8*) Asia Bk Corp.

Society & Culture in Early Modern France: Eight Essays by Natalie Zemon Davis. Natalie Z. Davis. LC 74-82777. (Illus.). xx, 364p. 1975. 49.50 (*0-8047-0868-1*); pap. 17.95 (*0-8047-0972-6*) Stanford U Pr.

Society & Culture in Northern India, 1850-1900. Shiva S. Dua. vi, 272p. 1985. 26.50 (*81-85004-04-8*) Nataraj Bks.

Society & Culture in the Himalayas. Ed. by K. Warikoo. (C). 1995. 28.00 (*81-241-0308-9*, Pub. by Har-Anand Pubns II) S Asia.

Society & Culture in the Slave South. Ed. by J. William Harris. LC 92-8841. (Re-writing Histories Ser.). 208p. (C). (gr. 13). 1992. text ed. 69.95 (*0-415-07054-6*, A6562) Routledge.

Society & Culture in the Slave South. J. William Harris. LC 92-8841. 208p. (C). 1992. pap. 17.95 (*0-415-07055-4*, Pub. by Tavistock UK) Routledge Chapman & Hall.

Society & Democracy in Germany. Ralf Dahrendorf. (Modern Revivals in Sociology Ser.). 496p. 1993. 69.95 (*0-7512-0117-0*, Pub. by Gregg Pub UK) Ashgate Pub Co.

Society & Democracy in Germany. Ralf Dahrendorf. LC 79-15142. 457p. 1980. reprint ed. text ed. 45.50 (*0-313-22027-1*, DASO, Greenwood Pr) Greenwood.

Society & Development in China & India. Ed. by Kuttan Mahadevan et al. (C). 1994. 48.00 (*81-7018-812-1*, Pub. by BR Pub II) S Asia.

Society & Development in Contemporary India. Ranjit Tirtha. LC 80-83157. (Illus.). 368p. 1980. 13.50 (*0-8187-0040-8*) Harlo Press.

Society & Deviance in Communist Poland: Attitudes Towards Social Control. Jerzy Kwasniewski. Tr. by Margaret Watson. LC 84-6803. 256p. 1984. text ed. 32.50 (*0-312-73803-X*) St Martin.

***Society & Documentation in Crusader Valencia.** Robert I. Burns. LC 84-17828. (Diplomatarium of the Crusader Kingdom of Valencia Ser.). reprint ed. pap. 81.80 (*0-608-04624-8*, 2065311) Bks Demand.

Society & Drugs: Social & Cultural Observations. Richard H. Blum et al. LC 73-75936. (Jossey-Bass Behavioral Science Ser.). 416p. reprint ed. pap. 118.60 (*0-8357-4697-6*, 2052352) Bks Demand.

Society & Economics in Islam. Sayyid M. Taleghani. Tr. by R. Campbell from PER. LC 82-2115. (Contemporary Islamic Thought, Persian Ser.). 225p. 1983. 17.95 (*0-933782-08-X*) Mizan Pr.

Society & Economy in Ancient India. Neeta Verma. (C). 1992. 27.50 (*0-7069-5953-1*, Pub. by Vikas II) S Asia.

Society & Economy in Colonial Connecticut. Jackson T. Main. LC 84-42892. 420p. 1985. text ed. 55.00 (*0-691-04726-X*) Princeton U Pr.

Society & Economy in Modern Britain 1700-1850. Richard Brown. 448p. (C). 1991. pap. text ed. 25.00 (*0-415-01121-3*, A4859) Routledge.

Society & Education. 9th ed. David U. Levine & Rayna F. Levine. 1995. text ed. 62.00 (*0-205-18935-0*) Allyn.

Society & Exchange in Nias. Andrew Beatty. (Oxford Studies in Social & Cultural Anthropology). (Illus.). 328p. 1992. 79.00 (*0-19-827865-9*) OUP.

Society & Family Strategy: Erie County, New York 1850-1920. Mark J. Stern. LC 86-23121. 172p. 1987. text ed. 64.50 (*0-88706-495-7*); pap. text ed. 21.95 (*0-88706-496-5*) State U NY Pr.

Society & Freedom. 2nd ed. Joseph A. Scimecca. 1994. pap. text ed. 25.95 (*0-8304-1376-6*) Nelson-Hall.

Society & Gender: An Introduction to Sociology. Gillian Lupton et al. 368p. 1994. 69.95 (*0-7329-1303-9*, Pub. by Macmill Educ AT) Paul & Co Pubs.

Society & Gender: An Introduction to Sociology. S. Sarantakos et al. 368p. pap. 34.95 (*0-7329-1302-0*, Pub. by Macmill Educ AT) Paul & Co Pubs.

Society & Gender Equity in Mathematics Education. Helen Forgasz. 105p. (C). 1995. pap. 38.00 (*0-7300-2086-X*, Pub. by Deakin Univ AT) St Mut.

Society & Government in Colonial Brazil, 1500-1822. A. J. Russell-Wood. (Collected Studies: No. 382). 352p. 1992. 94.95 (*0-86078-333-2*, Pub. by Variorum UK) Ashgate Pub Co.

Society & Health. Ed. by Benjamin Amick, III et al. (Illus.). 400p. 1995. 49.95 (*0-19-508506-X*) OUP.

Society & Health: An Introduction to Social Science for Health Professionals. Ed. by Graham Moon & Rosemary Gillespie. LC 94-45145. (Illus.). 196p. (C). 1995. text ed. 62.95 (*0-415-11021-1*, C0179) Routledge.

Society & Health: An Introduction to Social Science for Health Professionals. Ed. by Graham Moon & Rosemary Gillespie. LC 94-45145. (Illus.). 224p. (C). 1995. pap. text ed. 19.95 (*0-415-11022-X*, C0180) Routledge.

Society & Health in Guyana: The Sociology of Health Care in a Developing Nation. Marcel Fredericks et al. LC 84-70752. (Illus.). 189p. (Orig.). (C). 1986. pap. 12.50 (*0-89089-296-2*); lib. bdg. 29.95 (*0-89089-295-4*) Carolina Acad Pr.

Society & History: Essays in Honor of Karl August Wittogel. G. L. Ulmen. 1978. 184.60 (*90-279-7776-3*) Mouton.

Society & Homicide in Thirteenth-Century England. James B. Given. LC 76-23372. xiv, 262p. 1977. 39.50 (*0-8047-0939-4*) Stanford U Pr.

Society & Identity: Toward a Sociological Psychology. Andrew J. Weigert et al. (ASA Rose Monograph Ser.). 176p. 1986. text ed. 52.95 (*0-521-32325-8*) Cambridge U Pr.

Society & Ideology: An Inquiry into the Sociology of Knowledge. Gerard DeGre. Ed. by Lewis A. Coser & Walter W. Powell. LC 79-6991. (Perennial Works in Sociology). 1980. reprint ed. lib. bdg. 18.95 (*0-405-12091-5*) Ayer.

Society & Ideology: Essays in South Asian History Presented to Professor K. A. Ballhatchet. Ed. by Peter Robb. (SOAS Studies on South Asia). 276p. 1993. 29.95 (*0-19-563214-1*) OUP.

Society & Ideology in India: Essays in Honor of Professor R. S. Sharma. D. N. Jha. 458p. (C). 1996. 67.50 (*81-215-0639-5*, Pub. by M Manoharial II) Coronet Bks.

Society & Institutions in Early Modern France. Ed. by Mack P. Holt. LC 90-11247. 256p. 1991. pap. 20.00 (*0-8203-1328-9*) U of Ga Pr.

Society & Intellectual Life in Late Byzantium. Ihor Sevcenko. (Collected Studies: No. CS137). (Illus.). 374p. (C). 1981. reprint ed. lib. bdg. 109.95 (*0-86078-083-X*, Pub. by Variorum UK) Ashgate Pub Co.

Society & Knowledge. Vera G. Childe. LC 72-10690. 131p. 1973. reprint ed. text ed. 59.75 (*0-8371-6620-9*, CHSK, Greenwood Pr) Greenwood.

Society & Knowledge: Contemporary Perspectives on the Sociology of Knowledge. Ed. by Nico Stehr & Volker Meja. 430p. 1984. 44.95 (*0-87855-493-9*) Transaction Pubs.

Society & Literature, Nineteen Forty-Five to Nineteen Seventy. Ed. by Alan Sinfield. LC 83-12844. (Context of English Literature Ser.). 266p. (C). 1983. 36.00 (*0-8419-0903-2*); pap. 18.00 (*0-8419-0904-0*) Holmes & Meier.

Society & Medical Progress. Bernard F. Stern. LC 75-119215. 1941. 21.95 (*0-8434-0095-1*, Pub. by McGrath NH) Ayer.

Society & Medicine. New York Academy of Medicine Staff. Ed. by Iago Galdston. LC 74-142684. (Essay Index Reprint Ser.). 1977. 17.95 (*0-8369-2124-0*) Ayer.

Society & Milieu in the French Geographic Tradition. Anne Buttimer. LC 72-158112. (Monographs: No. 6). 1971. 15.00 (*0-89291-085-2*) Assn Am Geographers.

Society & Museum: A History of the Buffalo Society of Natural Sciences 1861-1993 & the Buffalo Museum of Science 1928-1993. George F. Goodyear. (Bulletin of the Buffalo Society of Natural Sciences Ser.: Vol. 34). (Illus.). 325p. (C). 1995. 35.00 (*0-944032-55-9*) Buffalo SNS.

Society & Nature. Peter Dickens. (C). 1992. 54.95 (*0-87722-968-6*); pap. 16.95 (*0-87722-969-4*) Temple U Pr.

Society & Nature: A Sociological Inquiry. Hans Kelsen. LC 73-14161. (Perspectives in Social Inquiry Ser.). 404p. 1974. reprint ed. 25.95 (*0-405-05507-2*) Ayer.

Society & Non-Timber Products in Tropical Asia. Pacific Science Congress Staff. Ed. by Jefferson Fox. LC 94-48590. (Occasional Papers: No. 19). 1995. write for info. (*0-86638-169-4*) EW Ctr HI.

Society & Personality: The Interactionist Approach to Social Psychology. Tamotsu Shibutani. 646p. 1987. pap. 29.95 (*0-88738-688-1*) Transaction Pubs.

Society & Politics in Ancient Rome: Essays & Sketches. Frank F. Abbott. LC 63-10767. 267p. (J). (gr. 7 up). 1909. 28.00 (*0-8196-0118-7*) Biblo.

Society & Politics in India: Essays in a Comparative Perspective. Andre Beteille. LC 91-23882. (London School of Economics Monographs on Social Anthropology: No. 63). 248p. (C). 1991. text ed. 35.00 (*0-485-19563-1*, Pub. by Athlone Pr UK) Humanities.

Society & Politics in Snorri Sturluson's "Heimskringla" Sverre Bagge. LC 91-2038. 434p. 1991. 50.00 (*0-520-06887-4*) U CA Pr.

Society & Politics in the Age of the Risorgimento: Essays in Honour of Denis Mack Smith. Ed. by John A. Davis & Paul Ginsborg. 262p. (C). 1991. text ed. 69.95 (*0-521-36592-9*) Cambridge U Pr.

Society & Politics in the Plays of Thomas Middleton. Swapan Chakravorty. (Oxford English Monographs). 256p. 1996. 55.00 (*0-19-818266-X*) OUP.

Society & Polity at Bronze Age Pella: An Annales Perspective. Bernard L. Knapp. (Journal for the Study of the Old Testament Supplement Ser.: No. 6). 116p. 35.00 (*1-85075-347-4*) CUP Services.

Society & Polity in Modern Sri Lanka. K. L. Sharma. 1988. 17.50 (*81-7003-089-7*) South Asia Pubns.

Society & Population. 3rd ed. David M. Heer & Jill Grigsby. 144p. (C). 1991. pap. text ed. 28.00 (*0-13-819707-5*) P-H.

Society & Power: Five New England Towns, 1800-1860. Robert Doherty. LC 77-73477. 128p. 1977. 20.00 (*0-87023-242-8*) U of Mass Pr.

Society & Prisons: With Intro. Added. Thomas M. Osborne. LC 72-172587. (Criminology, Law Enforcement, & Social Problems Ser.: No. 177). 1975. 22.00 (*0-87585-177-0*) Patterson Smith.

Society & Psyche: Social Theory & the Unconscious Dimension of the Social. Kanakis Leledakis. 256p. 1995. 49.95 (*1-85973-062-0*); pap. 19.95 (*1-85973-067-1*) Berg Pubs.

***Society & Puritanism in Pre-Revolutionary England.** Christopher Hill. 1997. 49.95 (*0-312-17431-4*); text ed. 18.95 (*0-312-17432-2*) St Martin.

***Society & Religion: From Rigveda to Puranas.** Jayant Gadkari. 1996. 30.00 (*81-7154-743-5*, Pub. by Popular Prakashan II) S Asia.

Society & Religion from Jahiliyya to Islam. M. J. Kister. (Collected Studies). 350p. 1990. text ed. 104.95 (*0-86078-277-8*, Pub. by Variorum UK) Ashgate Pub Co.

Society & Religion in Early Ottoman Egypt: Studies in the Writings of 'Abd al-Wahhab al-Sharani. Michael Winter. LC 81-3042. (Studies in Islamic Culture & History: No. 4). 355p. reprint ed. pap. 101.20 (*0-8357-7026-5*, 2033585) Bks Demand.

Society & Religion in Elizabethan England. Richard L. Greaves. LC 81-2530. 937p. reprint ed. pap. 180.00 (*0-685-15913-2*, 2056201) Bks Demand.

Society & Religion in Munster. R. Po-Chia Hsia. LC 83-14819. (Yale Historical Publications: No. 131). 320p. 1984. 40.00 (*0-300-03005-3*) Yale U Pr.

Society & Religion in the Grand Duchy of Lituania: A Reprint of the Seventeen Fifty-Four Nieswiez Edition of Pelnai Pieknej jak ksiezyc lask promieniami swiatu przyswiecajaca. Intro. by Maciej Siekierski. 118p. (POL.). 1985. pap. 9.50 (*0-933884-51-6*) Berkeley Slavic.

Society & Science: Decision-Making Episodes for Exploring Society, Science & Technology. Robert J. Stahl. 1994. pap. 32.00 (*0-201-49097-8*) Addison-Wesley.

Society & Self in the Novel see English Institute Essays

Society & Settlement: Jewish Land of Israel in the Twentieth Century. Aharon Kellerman. LC 91-47853. (SUNY Series in Israeli Studies). 321p. 1993. text ed. 64.50 (*0-7914-1295-4*); pap. text ed. 21.95 (*0-7914-1296-2*) State U NY Pr.

Society & Social Change in the Writings of St. Thomas, Ward, Sumner, & Cooley. Mary E. Healy. LC 75-156191. 159p. 1972. reprint ed. text ed. 52.50 (*0-8371-6140-1*, HESC, Greenwood Pr) Greenwood.

An Asterisk (*) at the beginning of an entry indicates that the title is appearing in BIP for the first time.

Society & Solitude. Emile Durkheim et al. LC 95-40641. (Lynchburg College Symposium Readings Ser.: Vol. 5). 1995. pap. text ed. write for info. (0-7618-0129-4) U Pr of Amer.
Society & Solitude. Ralph Waldo Emerson. (Notable American Authors Ser.). 1992. reprint ed. lib. bdg. 75.00 (0-7812-2814-X) Rprt Serv.
Society & Spirit: A Trinitarian Cosmology. Joseph A. Bracken. LC 90-50601. 192p. 1991. 32.50 (0-945636-21-0) Susquehanna U Pr.
Society & State Building in Nepal. R. S. Chauhan. 250p. 1988. text ed. 25.00 (81-207-0864-4, Pub. by Sterling Pubs II) Apt Bks.
Society & State Building in Nepal. R. S. Chauhan. 1989. 65.00 (0-7855-0297-1, Pub. by Ratna Pustak Bhandar) St Mut.
Society & State Building in Nepal. R. S. Chauhan. 163p. (C). 1989. 225.00 (0-89771-092-4, Pub. by Ratna Pustak Bhandar) St Mut.
Society & Technological Change. 3rd ed. Rudi Volti. 320p. 1995. pap. text ed. 19.00 (0-312-09642-9) St Martin.
Society & the Dance: The Social Anthropology of Process & Performance. Ed. by Paul Spencer. 208p. 1986. pap. text ed. 20.95 (0-521-31550-6) Cambridge U Pr.
Society & the Environment: A Swedish Research Perspective. Ed. by Uno Svedin & Britt H. Aniansson. LC 92-15406. (Ecology, Economy & Environment Ser.: Vol. 2). 336p. (C). 1992. lib. bdg. 153.00 (0-7923-1796-3) Kluwer Ac.
Society & the Healthy Homosexual. Gerry E. Studds. 150p. 1991. reprint ed. pap. 7.95 (1-55583-193-1) Alyson Pubns.
Society & the Holy in Late Antiquity. Peter Brown. LC 80-39862. 350p. 1982. 50.00 (0-520-04305-7); pap. 14.00 (0-520-06800-9) U CA Pr.
Society & the Homosexual. Gordon Westwood. LC 84-27933. 191p. 1985. reprint ed. text ed. 52.50 (0-313-24840-0, SCHO, Greenwood Pr) Greenwood.
Society & the Individual: Readings in Political & Social Philosophy. Ed. by Richard T. Garner & Andrew G. Oldenquist. 508p. (C). 1990. text ed. 50.95 (0-534-12210-8) Wadsworth Pub.
***Society & the Language Classroom.** Hywel Coleman. (Cambridge Language Teaching Library). (Illus.). 256p. (C). 1997. text ed. 49.95 (0-521-49616-0); pap. text ed. 19.95 (0-521-49949-6) Cambridge U Pr.
Society & the Official World: A Reintroduction to Sociology. John A. Denton. LC 89-80376. (Illus.). 200p. (Orig.). 1990. text ed. 35.95 (0-930390-95-4); pap. text ed. 22.95 (0-930390-94-6) Gen Hall.
Society & the Professions in Italy, 1860-1914. Ed. by Maria Malatesta. (Studies in Italian History & Culture). 348p. (C). 1996. text ed. 59.95 (0-521-46536-2) Cambridge U Pr.
***Society & the State in Interwar Japan.** Elise K. Tipton. LC 96-40109. (Nissan Institute-Routledge Japanese Studies). 256p. (C). 1997. text ed. write for info. (0-415-15069-8) Routledge.
Society & Trade in South Arabia. R. B. Serjeant. Ed. by G. Rex Smith. (Collected Studies: No. CS552). 320p. 1996. 98.95 (0-86078-603-X, Pub. by Variorum UK) Ashgate Pub Co.
Society As Educator in an Age of Transition: Eighty-Sixth Yearbook of the National Society for the Study of Education, Pt. II. Ed. by Kenneth D. Benne & Steven E. Tozer. xvi, 296p. (C). 1987. 26.00 (0-226-60145-5, Natl Soc Stud Educ) U Ch Pr.
Society As I Have Found It. Samuel W. McAllister. LC 75-1855. (Leisure Class in America Ser.). 1975. reprint ed. 34.95 (0-405-06921-9) Ayer.
Society As I Have Found It. Samuel W. McAllister. (American Biography Ser.). 469p. 1991. reprint ed. lib. bdg. 89.00 (0-7812-8280-2) Rprt Serv.
Society As Text: Essays on Rhetoric, Reason & Reality. Richard H. Brown. LC 86-30893. (Illus.). x, 264p. (C). 1987. 29.95 (0-226-07616-4) U Ch Pr.
Society As Text: Essays on Rhetoric, Reason, & Reality. Richard H. Brown. LC 86-30893. x, 262p. 1992. pap. text ed. 16.95 (0-226-07617-2) U Ch Pr.
Society at the Time of the Buddha. Narendra Wagle. (C). 1995. reprint ed. 28.00 (81-7154-553-X, Pub. by Popular Prakashan II) S Asia.
Society at War: The Militarisation of South Africa. Ed. by Jacklyn Cock & Laurie Nathan. LC 89-35155. 320p. 1989. text ed. 45.00 (0-312-03551-9) St Martin.
Society Ball Murders. Jack A. Anderson. 192p. 1990. 18.95 (0-8027-5766-9) Walker & Co.
Society Based on Work. Anthony P. Carnevale. 102p. 1984. 8.75 (0-318-22200-0, IN270) Ctr Educ Trng Employ.
Society, Caste & Factional Politics: Conflict & Continuity in Rural India. Masaaki Fukunaga. (C). 1993. 22.00 (81-7304-038-9, Pub. by Manohar II) S Asia.
Society, Culture, & Development. Ramkrishna Mukherjee. 272p. 1992. 29.95 (0-8039-9102-9) Sage.
Society, Culture, & Drinking Patterns Reexamined. David J. Pittman & Helene R. White. 824p. 1991. pap. 34.95 (0-911290-22-2) Rutgers Ctr Alcohol.
Society, Culture, & Mass Communication: Sociology of Journalism. Hema Agrawal. (C). 1995. 27.50 (81-7033-282-6, Pub. by Har-Anand Pubns II) S Asia.
Society, Culture & Military System. Leena Parmar. (C). 1995. 22.00 (81-7033-264-8, Pub. by Rawat II) S Asia.
Society, Culture & Population Policy in India. K. Raghavendra Rao. 1989. 19.50 (81-202-0241-4, Pub. by Ajanta II) S Asia.
Society, Culture, & the State in Germany, 1870-1930. Geoff Eley. LC 95-42516. (C). 1996. 59.50 (0-472-10627-9) U of Mich Pr.
Society, Culture, & Urbanization. Arie Shachar. LC 85-26249. 391p. 1987. reprint ed. pap. 111.50 (0-608-01481-8, 2059525) Bks Demand.
Society, Economics, & Philosophy: Selected Papers. Michael Polanyi. LC 96-42469. 335p. 1996. text ed. 44.95 (1-56000-278-6) Transaction Pubs.
Society, Economy & Religion in Late Medieval Castile. Angus MacKay. (Collected Studies: No. CS261). (Illus.). 334p. (ENG & SPA.). (C). 1987. reprint ed. lib. bdg. 98.95 (0-86078-209-3, Pub. by Variorum UK) Ashgate Pub Co.
***Society Fit for Human Beings.** E. M. Adams. LC 96-52316. (SUNY Series in Constructive Postmodern Thought). 206p. (C). 1997. text ed. 56.50 (0-7914-3523-7); pap. text ed. 16.95 (0-7914-3524-5) State U NY Pr.
Society for American Archaeology: Regional Conferences Summary Report (Conference on Cultural Resources Management Issues) Ed. by Cynthia Irwin-Williams & Don D. Fowler. (SAA Publication). 118p. 1986. pap. 7.00 (0-932839-10-X) Soc Am Arch.
Society for Community Service Recognition: Registry of Outstanding Northeast Firefighters, 1992. Ed. by Carolyn S. Zagury. LC 93-60030. (Illus.). 96p. 1992. 49.95 (1-880254-05-0) Vista.
Society for International Development: Prospectus 1984. Ed. by Ann Mattis. LC 83-16550. (Duke Press Policy Studies). xxi, 249p. (C). 1983. text ed. 35.95 (0-8223-0561-5); pap. text ed. 19.00 (0-8223-0562-3) Duke.
Society for Pure English, 6 vols., Set, Tracts 1-66. reprint ed. Set. 390.00 (0-404-19554-7) AMS Pr.
Society for the Propagation of the Faith: Its Foundation, Organization & Success (1822-1922) Edward J. Hickey. LC 73-3557. (Catholic University of America. Studies in Romance Languages & Literatures: No. 3). reprint ed. 37.50 (0-404-57753-9) AMS Pr.
Society for the Scientific Study of Sex: A Brief History. Vern L. Bullough. 44p. 1989. pap. write for info. (0-318-65755-4) FSS Sexuality.
Society for Vascular Surgery: A History, Nineteen Forty-Five to Nineteen Eighty-Three. Harris B. Shumacker. Ed. by James N. Rogers. LC 83-20450. (Illus.). 450p. 1984. text ed. 15.00 (0-9612978-0-8) Society Vascular Surgery.
Society Former FBI. Turner Publishing Company Staff. LC 95-60549. 175p. 1996. 48.00 (1-56311-205-1) Turner Pub KY.
Society from the Inside Out: Anthropological Perspectives of the South Asian Household. Ed. by John N. Gray & David J. Mearns. 264p. (C). 1989. text ed. 26.00 (0-8039-9609-8) Sage.
Society in Action: The Theory of Social Becoming. Piotr Sztompka. 224p. 1991. 40.50 (0-226-78815-6) U Ch Pr.
Society in America, 3 Vols. Harriet Martineau. LC 01-27890. reprint ed. write for info. (0-404-04260-0) AMS Pr.
Society in America. Harriet Martineau. Ed. by Seymour M. Lipset. LC 80-27647. (Social Science Classics Ser.). 357p. 1981. reprint ed. pap. 24.95 (0-87855-853-5) Transaction Pubs.
Society in Ancient India. Sures C. Banerji. (Reconstructing Indian History & Culture Ser.: No. 1). (C). 1993. text ed. 40.00 (81-246-0000-7, Pub. by DK Pubs Dist II) S Asia.
Society in Change: Studies in Honor of Bela K. Kiraly. Ed. by Steven B. Vardy. (East European Monographs: No. 132). 680p. 1983. text ed. 59.00 (0-88033-021-X) East Eur Monographs.
Society in Colonial North Carolina. rev. ed. Alan D. Watson. (Illus.). ix, 147p. (YA). (gr. 8-12). 1996. pap. 8.00 (0-86526-267-5) NC Archives.
Society in Focus. 2nd ed. Thompson. (C). 1996. 10.50 (0-673-97515-0) Addson-Wesley Educ.
Society in Focus: An Introduction to Sociology. William E. Thompson & Joseph V. Hickey. LC 93-8128. (C). 1994. 53.95 (0-673-38915-4); Study guide. student ed., pap. text ed. 19.95 (0-673-99026-5) Addson-Wesley Educ.
Society in Focus: An Introduction to Sociology. 2nd ed. William E. Thompson & Joseph V. Hickey. (C). 1995. teacher ed. write for info. (0-673-97230-5) Addson-Wesley Educ.
Society in Focus: An Introduction to Sociology. 2nd ed. William E. Thompson & Joseph V. Hickey. LC 95-20810. 624p. (C). 1996. text ed. 53.50 (0-673-99829-0); student ed., pap. text ed. 16.95 (0-673-98192-4) Addson-Wesley Educ.
Society in Focus: The Essentials. Lewis et al. (C). 1995. teacher ed., pap. text ed. write for info. (0-673-97519-3) Addson-Wesley Educ.
***Society in Focus: The Essentials.** Ed. by Thompson. (C). 1996. text ed. 33.95 (0-673-99092-3) Addison-Wesley.
Society in Imperial Rome: Selections from Juvenal, Martial, Petronius, Seneca, Tacitus & Pliny (Translations from Greek & Roman Authors) Michael Massey. LC 81-15490. 96p. 1982. pap. 10.50 (0-521-28036-2) Cambridge U Pr.
Society in India, Vol. I: Continuity & Change. David G. Mandelbaum. 392p. 1970. pap. 16.00 (0-520-01893-1) U CA Pr.
Society in India, Vol. II: Change & Continuity. David G. Mandelbaum. 408p. 1970. pap. 16.00 (0-520-01895-8) U CA Pr.
Society in Prehistory: The Origins of Human Culture. Tim Megarry. LC 95-37355. (Illus.). 400p. (C). 1995. 55.00 (0-8147-5537-2); pap. 20.00 (0-8147-5538-0) NYU Pr.
Society in the Elizabethan Age. Hubert Hall. 1976. lib. bdg. 59.95 (0-8490-2620-2) Gordon Pr.
Society in the Novel. Elizabeth Langland. LC 83-23597. 279p. reprint ed. pap. 79.60 (0-7837-2067-X, 2042342) Bks Demand.
Society in Transition: Impact on Nursing. Marian M. Pettengill & Lu A. Young. 150p. (Orig.). 1987. pap. 12.50 (0-942146-14-X) Midwest Alliance Nursing.
Society in War: Planning Perspectives. Per Molander. 141p. (Orig.). (C). 1994. pap. text ed. 30.00 (0-7881-1227-9) DIANE Pub.
***Society in Zimbabwe's Liberation War.** 1996. 62.00 (0-435-07411-3); pap. 27.95 (0-435-07412-1) Heinemann.
Society Islands Insects. Pacific Entomological Survey Publications Staff. (BMB Ser.). 1935. 21.00 (0-527-02219-5) Periodicals Srv.
Society, Language & Health. Richard Totman. 1985. text ed. 113.00 (0-12-696080-1) Acad Pr.
Society, Language, & the University. Sol Saporta. 1994. pap. 14.95 (0-533-10702-4) Vantage.
Society, Law & Trade in Medieval Montpellier. Kathryn L. Reyerson. (Collected Studies Ser.: No. CS475). 330p. 1995. 89.95 (0-86078-460-6, Pub. by Variorum UK) Ashgate Pub Co.
Society, Manners, & Politics in the United States: Being a Series of Letters on North America. Michel Chevalier. LC 66-21661. iv, 467p. 1966. reprint ed. 57.50 (0-678-00195-2) Kelley.
Society, Manners & Politics in the United States: Letters on North America. Michael Chevalier. Ed. by John W. Ward. Tr. by T. G. Bradford. 1990. 14.50 (0-8446-1111-5) Peter Smith.
Society of Accountants in Edinburgh, 1854-1914: A Study of Recruitment to a New Profession. Stephen P. Walker. LC 88-16322. (Foundations of Accounting Ser.). 416p. 1988. text ed. 10.00 (0-8240-6121-7) Garland.
Society of Arts & Crafts, Boston Exhibition Record Eighteen-Ninty-Seven to Nineteen Twenty-Seven. Compiled by Karen E. Ulehla. 1981. pap. 10.00 (0-685-09592-4) Boston Public Lib.
Society of Biblical Literature: Seminar Papers Nineteen Eighty-Three. Ed. by Kent H. Richards. 523p. 1986. 22.95 (1-55540-044-2, 06 09 25) Scholars Pr GA.
Society of Biblical Literature Nineteen Eighty-One: Seminar Papers. Ed. by Kent H. Richards. (Society of Biblical Literature Seminar Papers & Abstracts). 386p. 1981. pap. 22.95 (0-89130-548-3, 06-09-20) Scholars Pr GA.
Society of Captives: A Study of a Maximum Security Prison. Gresham M. Sykes. 164p. 1958. pap. text ed. 12.95 (0-691-02814-1) Princeton U Pr.
Society of Critical Care Medicine--Self-Assessment in Multidisciplinary Critical Care, Vol. 2: A Comprehensive Review. Ed. by R. Phillip Dellinger et al. 500p. (Orig.). 1989. pap. 47.00 (0-936145-29-3) SCCM Fullerton.
Society of Ethnic Conflict. Rex. Date not set. text ed. write for info. (1-85043-906-0, Pub. by I B Tauris UK) St Martin.
Society of Friends. rev. ed. Howard H. Brinton. (C). 1962. pap. 3.00 (0-87574-048-0) Pendle Hill.
Society of Gentlemen, Vol. 5, Encyclopaedia Britannica see Encyclopaedic Dictionary in the 18th Century: Architecture, Arts & Crafts
Society of Independent Artists: The Exhibition Record, 1917-1944. Clark S. Marlor. LC 84-14867. (Illus.). 600p. 1984. 64.00 (0-8155-5063-4) Sound View Pr.
Society of Jesus in Ireland, Scotland & England, 1541-1588: "Our Way of Proceeding" Thomas M. McCoog. LC 96-2790. (Studies in Medieval & Reformation Thought). 1996. 84.00 (90-04-10482-8) E J Brill.
Society of Logistics Engineers Annals. 30.00 (0-318-20628-5) Soc Logistics Engrs.
Society of Logistics Engineers Proceedings. Incl. . 139p. (0-318-16585-6); . 152p. (0-318-16586-4); . 154p. (0-318-16587-2); . 312p. (0-318-16588-0); 25.00 (0-685-73755-1) Soc Logistics Engrs.
Society of Man. Louis J. Halle. LC 78-31208. 203p. 1979. reprint ed. text ed. 55.00 (0-313-20942-1, HASM, Greenwood Pr) Greenwood.
Society of Mind. Marvin Minsky. 336p. 1988. pap. 14.95 (0-671-65713-5, Touchstone Bks) S&S Trade.
Society of Naval Architects & Marine Engineers: Transactions, Vol. 101. (Illus.). 1994. 45.00 (0-685-56499-1); 45.00 (0-939773-15-5) Soc Naval Arch.
Society of Petroleum Engineers Technical Papers: Cumulative Index to the Microfiche Collection, 1985-1989 Supplements. 1059p. 1991. lib. bdg. 160.00 (0-8357-2148-5) Univ Microfilms.
Society of Petroleum Engineers Technical Papers: Index to the Microfiche Collection, 2 vols., Set. LC 80-28727. 1981. 310.00 (0-8357-0217-0) Univ Microfilms.
Society of Petroleum Engineers Technical Papers: Index to the Microfiche Collection: 1990 Supplement. 258p. 1991. pap. 35.00 (0-8357-2122-1) Univ Microfilms.
Society of Petroleum Engineers Technical Papers: Index to the Microfiche Collection: 1991 Supplement. 351p. 1992. pap. 35.00 (0-8357-2208-2) Univ Microfilms.
***Society of Pleasures.** Hoffman. LC 96-37253. 1997. text ed. write for info. (0-312-16507-2) St Martin.
***Society of Publication Designers Annual, Vol. 32.** Compiled by Society of Publication Designers Staff. (Illus.). 256p. 1997. 49.99 (1-56496-387-X) Rockport Pubs.
Society of Publication Designers' Best of Magazine Publication Design, No. 29. Ed. by Rockport Publishers Editorial Staff. (Illus.). 240p. 1995. 49.99 (1-56496-152-4) Rockport Pubs.
Society of Renaissance Florence. Ed. by Gene A. Brucker. 1972. pap. text ed. 14.00 (0-06-131607-5, TB1607, Torch) HarpC.
Society of Salty Saints: Story & Prayer from the Street. Micheal Elliott. (Illus.). 128p. 1987. 7.95 (0-940989-14-X) Meyer Stone Bks.
Society of Signs? David. LC 95-31320. 216p. (C). 1996. pap. 18.95 (0-415-11129-3, Routledge NY); text ed. 65.00 (0-415-11128-5, Routledge NY) Routledge.
***Society of Six: California Colorists.** LC 96-37048. (Illus.). 1997. 65.00 (0-520-21054-9) U CA Pr.
***Society of Six: California Colorists.** Nancy Boas. (Illus.). 1997. pap. 35.00 (0-520-21055-7) U CA Pr.
Society of Southwest Archivists: Guide to Archival & Manuscript Repositories. Ed. by Kathryn Stallard et al. x, 258p. 1993. 15.00 (0-9640169-0-7) Soc SW Archivists.
Society of Subordinates: Inmate Organization in a Narcotic Hospital. Charles R. Tittle. LC 72-80669. (Indiana University Social Science Ser.: No. 30). 208p. reprint ed. pap. 59.30 (0-317-09051-8, 2015836) Bks Demand.
Society of Text: Hypertext, Hypermedia & the Social Construction of Information. Ed. by Edward Barrett. (Information Systems Ser.). 350p. 1989. 50.00 (0-262-02291-5) MIT Pr.
Society of Text: Hypertext, Hypermedia, & the Social Construction of Information. Ed. by Edward Barrett. (Illus.). 479p. 1991. reprint ed. pap. 26.50 (0-262-52161-X) MIT Pr.
Society of the Cincinnati: 1783-1935. William S. Thomas. LC 35-8178. (Illus.). 187p. 1935. 10.00 (0-318-16566-X) Anderson Hse Mus.
Society of the Enlightenment: The Rise of the Middle Class & Enlightenment Culture in Germany. Richard Van Dulmen. Tr. by Anthony Williams. 237p. (C). 1992. text ed. 55.00 (0-312-08454-4) St Martin.
Society of the Future. Raghavan N. Iyer. 1984. 8.75 (0-88695-018-X) Concord Grove.
Society of the Mind. Eric L. Harry. 1995. 25.00 (0-614-96260-9) HarpC.
***Society of the Mind.** Eric L. Harry. 672p. 1997. mass mkt. 6.99 (0-06-109615-6, Harp PBks) HarpC.
Society of the Mind: A Cyberthriller. Eric L. Harry. LC 96-1188. 432p. 1996. 25.00 (0-06-017694-6) HarpC.
***Society of the Muslim Brothers.** Richard P. Mitchell. 350p. 1996. pap. 16.95 (0-614-21499-8, 1144) Kazi Pubns.
Society of the Muslim Brothers. Richard P. Mitchell. 384p. 1993. pap. 19.95 (0-19-508437-3) OUP.
Society of the Ramayana. Ananda Guruge. (C). 1991. 57.50 (81-7017-265-9, Pub. by Abhinav II) S Asia.
Society of the Spectacle. Guy Debord. 1983. pap. 4.00 (0-934868-07-7) Black & Red.
Society of the Spectacle. Guy Debord. Tr. by Donald Nicholson-Smith from FRE. LC 89-39940. 154p. 1994. 21.95 (0-942299-80-9) Zone Bks.
Society of the Spectacle. Guy Debord. Tr. by Donald Nicholson-Smith from FRE. 154p. 1995. pap. 10.95 (0-942299-79-5) Zone Bks.
Society of the Spectacle Film Scripts. Guy Debord. (Illus.). 136p. (Orig.). pap. 12.00 (0-946061-06-8) Autonomedia.
Society of the 173rd Airborne Brigade (Separate) Turner Publishing Company Staff. LC 91-67153. (Illus.). 144p. 1992. 48.00 (1-56311-071-7) Turner Pub KY.
Society of Tomorrow. Gustavo De Molinari. 1973. 59.95 (0-8490-1071-3) Gordon Pr.
Society of Vacuum Coaters: Thirtieth Annual Technical Conference Proceedings, 1987. Ed. by Society of Vacuum Coaters Staff. 337p. (Orig.). 1987. pap. 50.00 (1-878068-06-7) Vacuum Coaters.
Society of Vacuum Coaters: Thirty-Fifth Annual Technical Conference Proceedings, 1992. Ed. by Society of Vacuum Coaters Staff. 444p. (Orig.). 1992. pap. 95.00 (1-878068-11-3) Vacuum Coaters.
Society of Vacuum Coaters: Thirty-First Annual Technical Conference Proceedings, 1988. Ed. by Society of Vacuum Coaters Staff. 425p. (Orig.). 1988. pap. 50.00 (1-878068-07-5) Vacuum Coaters.
Society of Vacuum Coaters: Thirty-Fourth Annual Technical Conference Proceedings. Society Of Vacuum Coaters Staff. 426p. (Orig.). 1991. pap. 95.00 (1-878068-10-5) Vacuum Coaters.
Society of Vacuum Coaters: Thirty-Sixth Annual Technical Conference Proceedings, 1993. Ed. by Society of Vacuum Coaters Staff. 1993. pap. 105.00 (1-878068-12-1) Vacuum Coaters.
Society of Vacuum Coaters: Twenty-Eighth Annual Technical Conference Proceedings, 1985. Ed. by Society of Vacuum Coaters Staff. 216p. (Orig.). 1985. pap. 50.00 (1-878068-05-9) Vacuum Coaters.
Society of Vacuum Coaters: Twenty-Fourth Annual Technical Conference Proceedings, 1981. Ed. by Society of Vacuum Coaters Staff. 91p. (Orig.). 1981. pap. 50.00 (1-878068-04-0) Vacuum Coaters.
Society of Vacuum Coaters, Thirty-Third Annual Technical Conference Proceedings, 1990. Ed. by Society of Vacuum Coaters Staff. 380p. (Orig.). 1990. pap. 75.00 (1-878068-09-1) Vacuum Coaters.
Society of Wine Educators Resource Manual. Ed. by Diane McComber & James J. Holsing. 82p. (Orig.). 1993. pap. text ed. 45.00 (0-614-13713-6) Soc Wine Educators.
Society of Wolves: National Parks & the Battle Over the Wolf. Rick McIntyre. LC 93-15918. (Illus.). 128p. 1993. 14.95 (0-89658-194-2) Voyageur Pr.
Society of Wolves: National Parks & the Battle over the Wolf. rev. ed. Rick McIntyre. LC 95-40898. (Illus.). 144p. 1996. pap. 19.95 (0-89658-325-2) Voyageur Pr.
Society on the Run: A European View of Life in America. Werner Peters. LC 95-25770. (Illus.). 312p. (C). (gr. 13). 1996. 65.95 (1-56324-585-X, HN59) M E Sharpe.
Society on the Run: A European View of Life in America. Werner Peters. LC 95-25770. (Illus.). 312p. (C). (gr. 13). 1996. pap. 23.95 (1-56324-586-8) M E Sharpe.
Society, Personality & Culture. Zevedei Barbu. (Blackwell's Sociology Ser.). 183p. (C). 1971. 14.95 (0-8464-1162-8) Beekman Pubs.
Society, Politics & Culture: Studies in Early Modern England. Mervyn James. (Past & Present Publications). (Illus.). 416p. 1988. pap. text ed. 29.95 (0-521-36877-4) Cambridge U Pr.

S

S

Society, Politics, & Economic Development: A Quantitative Approach. Irma Adelman & Cynthia T. Morris. 336p. 1972. reprint ed. pap. 15.95 (0-8018-1301-8) Johns Hopkins.

Society Politics, & the Market Revolution, 1815-1848. 2nd ed. Sean Wilentz. (New American History Ser.). 30p. (C). 1997. reprint ed. pap. 5.00 (0-87229-053-0) Am Hist Assn.

Society, Polity, & Economy of Bangladesh. S. R. Chakravarty. (C). 1994. text ed. 22.00 (81-241-0237-6, Pub. by Har-Anand Pubns II) S Asia.

***Society Reconsidered: A Debate on the Issues of Modern Times.** Robert DePaolo. 306p. (Orig.). 1996. pap. 12.95 (0-9654686-0-7) Ecclectic Bks.

Society, Schools & Progress in England. G. Baron. 1966. 111.00 (0-08-011594-2, Pub. by Pergamon Repr UK) Franklin.

Society, Schools & Progress in Tanzania. J. Cameron & W. A. Dodd. 1970. 127.00 (0-08-015564-2, Pub. by Pergamon Repr UK) Franklin.

Society, Schools & Progress in the West Indies. John J. Figueroa. 1971. 101.00 (0-08-016174-X, Pub. by Pergamon Repr UK) Franklin.

Society, Schools & Teacher Preparation. Donald E. Orlosky. LC 88-80932. 1988. pap. 6.25 (0-89333-050-7) Assn Tchr Ed.

Society, State & Nation in Twentieth-Century Europe. Roderick Phillips. LC 95-24431. 576p. (C). 1995. pap. text ed. 47.33 (0-13-103821-4) P-H.

Society, State, & Urbanism: Ibn Khaldun's Sociological Thought. Fuad Baali. LC 87-9925. 175p. 1988. text ed. 74.50 (0-88706-609-7); pap. text ed. 24.95 (0-88706-610-0) State U NY Pr.

Society, Stress, & Disease: Vol. 5: Old Age. Ed. by Lennart Levi. (Illus.). 410p. 1988. 180.00 (0-19-264422-X) OUP.

Society, Stress, & Disease, Vol. 4: Working Life. Ed. by Lennart Levi. 400p. 1982. text ed. 79.50 (0-19-264421-1) OUP.

Society, the Sacred & Scripture in Ancient Judaism: A Sociology of Knowledge. Jack N. Lightstone. (Studies in Christianity & Judaism: Vol. 3). 148p. (C). 1988. pap. 15.95 (0-88920-975-8) Wilfrid Laurier.

Society, Theory & the French Revolution: Studies in the Revolutionary Imaginary. Brian C. Singer. LC 85-25010. 240p. 1986. text ed. 32.50 (0-312-73924-9) St Martin.

Society to L & D, Stat! Murray A. Freedman. LC 88-62504. 128p. 1988. 11.95 (0-9614496-1-6) Marshwinds Advisory.

Society to Match the Scenery: Personal Visions of the Future of the American West. Ed. by Gary Holthaus et al. (C). 1993. pap. 22.50 (0-87081-300-5) Univ Pr Colo.

Society vs. the State. Pierre Clastres. 1991. lib. bdg. 78.95 (0-8490-4701-3) Gordon Pr.

Society Without Government. LC 74-172235. (Right Wing Individualist Tradition in America Ser.). 1972. reprint ed. 15.00 (0-405-00440-0) Ayer.

Society Women of Shakespeare's Time. Violet Wilson. 1973. 75.00 (0-8490-1072-1) Gordon Pr.

Society's Choices: Social & Ethical Decision Making in Biomedicine. Institute of Medicine Staff. Ed. by Harvey V. Feinberg et al. 550p. (C). 1995. text ed. 59.95 (0-309-05132-0) Natl Acad Pr.

***Society's Final Solution: A History & Discussion of the Death Penalty.** Ed. by Laura E. Randa. LC 97-1663. 288p. 1997. 44.50 (0-7618-0713-6) U Pr of Amer.

Society's Impact on Television: How the Viewing Public Shapes Television Programming. Gary W. Selnow & Richard R. Gilbert. LC 92-23455. 240p. 1993. text ed. 52.95 (0-275-94390-9, C4390, Praeger Pubs) Greenwood.

Society's Man - Fifty Posters. limited ed. Algimantas Kezys. (Illus.). 104p. 1994. 600.00 (1-886060-01-0); boxed 600.00 (1-886060-02-9) Galerija.

***Society's Response to the Violent Offender.** P. Grabosky. 68p. 1989. pap. 12.00 (0-642-14777-9, Pub. by Aust Inst Criminology) Willow Tree NY.

Society's Victims - The Police: An Analysis of Job Stress in Policing. 2nd ed. William H. Kroes. (Illus.). 202p. 1985. pap. text ed. 22.95 (0-398-06640-X) C C Thomas.

Society's Victims - The Police: An Analysis of Job Stress in Policing. 2nd ed. William H. Kroes. (Illus.). 202p. (C). 1985. text ed. 31.95 (0-398-05120-8) C C Thomas.

Socinenija Prinadle-Zascija K Grammatike Votskago Jazyka see First Votyak Grammar

Socio-Behavioral Approach & Applications to Social Work. 1967. 3.30 (0-318-35367-9) Coun Soc Wk Ed.

Socio-Behavioral Sciences & Public Health Practice. Rowitz et al. 300p. 39.95 (0-8342-0627-7) Aspen Pub.

Socio-Cultural Adjustment Question: The Role of Ghanaian Immigrant Ethnic Associations in America. Agyemang Attah-Poku. 185p. 1996. text ed. 55.95 (1-85972-392-6, Pub. by Avebury Pub UK) Ashgate Pub Co.

Socio-Cultural Dimension of Marriage in Rural India. N. Audinarayan. 1990. 32.50 (81-7099-188-9, Pub. by Mittal II) S Asia.

Socio-Cultural Factors in Modern Family Planning Methods in Tanzania. C. K. Omari. LC 88-9352. (Studies in African Health & Medicine: Vol. 3). 250p. 1989. lib. bdg. 89.95 (0-88946-189-9) E Mellen.

Socio-Cultural Foundations of Education & the Evolution of Education Policies in the U. S. Ed. by James J. Van Patten. LC 91-19074. (Studies in Education: Vol. 17). 252p. 1991. lib. bdg. 89.95 (0-7734-9727-7) E Mellen.

Socio-Cultural Matrix of Alcohol & Drug Use: A Sourcebook of Patterns & Factors. Ed. by Brenda Forster & Jeffrey C. Salloway. LC 89-13794. (Interdisciplinary Studies in Alcohol Use & Abuse: Vol. 4). 587p. 1990. lib. bdg. 119.95 (0-88946-285-2) E Mellen.

Socio-Cultural Study of a Minority Linguistic Group. Sudeshna Basak. (C). 1990. text ed. 28.00 (81-7018-627-7, Pub. by BR Pub II) S Asia.

Socio-Cultural Study of Scheduled Tribes: The Pardhans of Maharastra. S. R. Murkute. (Castes & Tribes of India Ser.: Vol. II). 1990. 28.00 (81-7022-262-1, Pub. by Concept II) S Asia.

Socio-Cultural Study of 118 Mexican Families Living in a Low-Rent Public Housing Project in San Antonio, Texas. Winifred Murray. Ed. by Carlos E. Cortes. LC 76-1275. (Chicano Heritage Ser.). 1977. reprint ed. lib. bdg. 17.95 (0-405-09515-5) Ayer.

***Socio-Cultural Transformation & Foodways in the Republic of Georgia.** Mary E. Chatwin. (Illus.). 295p. (C). 1997. lib. bdg. 59.00 (1-56072-440-4) Nova Sci Pubs.

Socio-Demographic Change & the Inner City. HMSO Staff. 131p. 1995. pap. 55.00 (0-11-753051-4, HM30514, Pub. by Stationery Ofc UK) Bernan Associates.

Socio-Economic Accounting. Ahmed R. Belkaoui. LC 83-17682. (Illus.). xii, 324p. 1984. text ed. 69.50 (0-89930-065-0, BSE, Quorum Bks) Greenwood.

Socio-Economic & Cultural Correlates of Infant Mortality: A Demographic Appraisal. S. Sandhya. (C). 1991. 14.00 (81-7022-372-5, Pub. by Concept II) S Asia.

Socio-Economic & Legal Implications of Urban Land Ceiling & Regulation. Gopal Bhargava. 1983. 12.00 (0-8364-1053-X, Pub. by Abhinav II) S Asia.

Socio-Economic Aspects of Migration. G. S. Mehta. (C). 1991. 20.00 (81-7100-362-1, Pub. by Deep II) S Asia.

Socio-Economic Aspects of Population Structures: Case Study of Uttar Pradesh, India. M. A. Jaipur. (C). 1988. 31.00 (81-7033-049-1, Pub. by Rawat II) S Asia.

Socio Economic Backwardness in Women. Arandita Mukherji. (C). 1987. 9.00 (81-7024-096-4, Pub. by Ashish II) S Asia.

Socio-Economic Change in India. K. Balan. (C). 1992. text ed. 11.00 (81-7024-474-9, Pub. by Ashish II) S Asia.

Socio-Economic Change in Kerala. K. E. Verghese. 1986. 27.00 (0-317-56200-2, Pub. by Ashish II) S Asia.

Socio-Economic Culture in Medieval India. M. P. Srivastava. (C). 1993. 27.00 (81-85613-71-0, Pub. by Chugh Pubns II) S Asia.

Socio-Economic Development & Fertility Decline. 125p. 1991. 35.00 (92-1-151235-2, 91.XIII.14) UN.

Socio-Economic Development & Population Control. Ed. by M. E. Khan & D. V. Sarma. (C). 1988. 28.00 (81-85054-51-7, Pub. by Manohar II) S Asia.

Socio-Economic Development in ASEAN: An International Perspective. Habibullah Khan. 104p. 1986. text ed. 30.00 (9971-68-123-4, Pub. by Chopmen Singapore SI); pap. text ed. 15.95 (9971-68-124-2, Pub. by Chopmen Singapore SI) Advent Bks Div.

Socio Economic Development in India. Ratnakar Gedam. 240p. 1992. 100.00 (81-7041-562-4, Pub. by Scientific Pubs II) St Mut.

Socio-Economic Differentials in Child Mortality in Developing Countries. 319p. 1986. 29.00 (92-1-151154-2, E.85.XIII.7) UN.

Socio-Economic Disparities in Israel. Fanny Ginor. 313p. 1979. 39.95 (965-216-000-8); pap. 21.95 (0-87855-332-0) Transaction Pubs.

Socio-Economic Dynamics in Rural Bangladesh: The Individual & Societal Effects of Opportunities & Obstacles. Dietmar Herbon. 392p. 1994. 72.95 (1-85628-681-9, Pub. by Avebury Pub UK) Ashgate Pub Co.

Socio-Economic Effects of Power Stations on Their Localities. Oxford Polytechnic Staff. (C). 1989. write for info. (0-318-66594-8, Pub. by Oxford Polytechnic UK) St Mut.

Socio-Economic Groups & Income Distribution in Mexico. Wouter Van Ginneken. 1980. text ed. 18.95 (0-312-73941-9) St Martin.

Socio-Economic Impact of Sati in Bengal & the Role of Raja Rammohun Roy. Benoy B. Roy. (C). 1987. 31.00 (81-85109-70-2, Pub. by Naya Prokash IA) S Asia.

Socio-Economic Impacts of Environment. Ed. by B. B. Dhar & N. C. Sexena. (Illus.). x, 296p. 1994. 30.00 (81-7024-603-2, Pub. by Ashish Pub Hse II) Nataraj Bks.

***Socio-Economic Indicators Relating to the Agricultural Sector & Rural Development.** 110p. 1984. 14.00 (92-5-101497-3, F2598, Pub. by FAO IT) Bernan Associates.

Socio-Economic Life of Northern India. Sukla Das. 1980. 22.50 (0-8364-0609-5) S Asia.

Socio-Economic Profile of Sri Lankan Repatriated in Kotagiri. L. Vedavalli. (C). 1994. text ed. 18.00 (81-220-0360-5, Pub. by Konark Pubs II) S Asia.

Socio-Economic Re-Evaluation of the Torts Law of Liability for Personal Injuries. S. M. Hasan. 115p. 1962. pap. 15.00 (0-317-54688-0) St Mut.

Socio-Economic Reforms in the U. S. S. R. V. D. Chopra et al. 1990. 150.00 (0-317-99589-8, Pub. by Patriot II) S Asia.

***Socio-Economic Status of Scavengers: A Study.** Sabir Ali. (C). 1994. 16.00 (81-241-0184-1, Pub. by Har-Anand Pubns II) S Asia.

Socio-Economic Survey of Recreational Boating & Fishing in the U. S. Virgin Islands. David Olsen. (Illus.). 80p. 1979. 12.00 (0-318-14618-5) Isl Resources.

Socio Economic Transformation of Soviet Central Asia. Ed. by R. G. Gidadhubli. 253p. 1988. text ed. 32.50 (0-317-90502-3, Pub. by Patriot Pubs II) Advent Bks Div.

Socio Economic Transformation of Soviet Central Asia. R. G. Gidadhubli. 1988. 30.00 (81-7050-050-8, Pub. by Patriot II) S Asia.

Socio-Economics: Toward a New Synthesis. Ed. by Amitai Etzioni & Paul R. Lawrence. LC 90-40462. (Studies in Socio-Economics). 288p. (gr. 13). 1991. text ed. 56.95 (0-87332-685-7) M E Sharpe.

Socio-Economics: Toward a New Synthesis. Ed. by Amitai Etzioni & Paul R. Lawrence. LC 90-40462. (Studies in Socio-Economics). 288p. (gr. 13). 1993. pap. text ed. 28.95 (0-87332-686-5) M E Sharpe.

Socio-Economics of Conversion from War to Peace. Ed. by Lloyd J. Dumas & Amitai Etzioni. LC 94-48186. (Studies in Socio-Economics Ser.). (Illus.). 354p. (C). 1995. pap. text ed. 27.95 (1-56324-529-9) M E Sharpe.

Socio-Economics of Conversion from War to Peace. Ed. by Lloyd J. Dumas & Amitai Etzioni. LC 94-48186. (Studies in Socio-Economics Ser.). (Illus.). 354p. (C). (gr. 13-13). 1995. text ed. 65.95 (1-56324-528-0) M E Sharpe.

Socio-Economics of Crime & Justice. Ed. by Brian Forst. LC 93-23797. (Studies in Socio-Economics). 344p. (gr. 13). 1993. text ed. 62.95 (1-56324-074-2); pap. text ed. 25.95 (1-56324-025-4) M E Sharpe.

Socio-Egocentrism: Theory, Research & Practice. James S. Peters, II. 76p. (Orig.). 1997. pap. 49.95 (1-57309-034-4); pap. 69.95 (1-57309-035-2) Intl Scholars.

Socio-Ethical Issues in Nigeria. Nwachukwuike S. Iwe. 270p. 1987. text ed. 33.35 (0-8204-0380-6) P Lang Pubng.

***Socio-Historicocultural Psychology: Lev-Semenovich Vygotsky: Bibliographical Notes.** Mohamed Elhammoumi. LC 96-49101. 244p. 1997. text ed. 42.50 (0-7618-0648-2) U Pr of Amer.

Socio-History of Ex-Criminal Communities OBCs. S. S. Shashi & P. S. Varma. (C). 1991. text ed. 30.00 (0-685-54665-9, Pub. by Sundeep Prakashan II) S Asia.

Socio-Intellectual History of the Isna Ashari Shi'is in India, 7th to 19th Century AD, Set, Vols. 1 & 2. Saiyid A. Rizvi. 1986. Set. 78.50 (81-215-0004-4, Pub. by Munshiram Manoharial II) S Asia.

Socio-Legal Foundations of Civil-Military Relations. James B. Jacobs. 231p. (C). 1986. 34.95 (0-88738-033-6) Transaction Pubs.

Socio-Legal Status of Muslim Women in India. Muniza R. Khan. 150p. 1992. text ed. 27.50 (0-685-37819-5, Pub. by Radiant Pubs II) S Asia.

***Socio-Legal Studies.** Philip A. Thomas. LC 96-52819. 250p. 1997. text ed. 64.95 (1-85521-717-1, K370.S65, Pub. by Dartmth Pub UK) Ashgate Pub Co.

***Socio-Legal Studies.** Ed. by Phillip A. Thomas. LC 96-52819. 250p. 1997. pap. text ed. 27.95 (1-85521-968-9, Pub. by Ashgate UK) Ashgate Pub Co.

Socio-Lifestyles Marketing: The New Science of Identifying, Classifying & Targeting. Bernard Cathelat. 1994. text ed. 47.50 (1-55738-818-0) Irwin Prof Pubng.

Socio-Medical Health Indicators. Ed. by Jack Elinson & Athilia E. Siegmann. LC 78-74484. 240p. (Orig.). 1979. pap. 24.95 (0-89503-013-6) Baywood Pub.

Socio (onto) logy: A Disciplinary Reading. Ben Agger. LC 88-10697. 440p. 1989. text ed. 34.95 (0-252-01558-4) U of Ill Pr.

Socio-Political & Economic Study of India. Jai N. Asopa. 336p. 1990. 120.00 (81-7158-101-3, Pub. by Scientific Pubs II) St Mut.

Socio-Political Dimensions of Modern India. N. M. Khilnani. 214p. (C). 1993. 75.00 (81-85880-06-9, Pub. by Print Hse II) St Mut.

***Socio-Political Framework in North-East India.** R. Gopalakrishnan. 1996. 28.00 (0-7069-9820-0, Pub. by Vikas II) S Asia.

Socio-Political Theatre in Nigeria. I. Peter Ukpokodu. LC 92-6687. 328p. 1992. lib. bdg. 99.95 (0-7734-9963-6) E Mellen.

Socio-Psychological Aspect of Public Administration. Padam N. Guatam. 1993. 25.00 (81-207-1457-1, Pub. by Sterling Pubs II) Apt Bks.

Socio-Religious & Political Analysis of the Judeo-Christian Concept of Prophetism & Modern Bakongo & Zulu African Prophet Movements. Samuel S. Simbandumwe. LC 92-30297. (African Studies: Vol. 28). 452p. 1993. text ed. 109.95 (0-7734-9182-1) E Mellen.

Socio-Religious Life of the Assamese Hindus: (A Study of the Fasts & Festivals of Kamrup District) Hemanta K. Sarma. (C). 1992. 28.00 (81-7035-084-0, Pub. by Daya Pub Hse II) S Asia.

Socio-Religious Movements in British India. Kenneth W. Jones. (New Cambridge History of India Ser.: III: 1). 255p. (C). 1990. text ed. 49.95 (0-521-24986-4) Cambridge U Pr.

Sociobiological Imagination. Ed. by Mary Maxwell. LC 90-10336. (SUNY Series in Philosophy & Biology). 376p. 1991. text ed. 59.50 (0-7914-0767-5); pap. text ed. 21.95 (0-7914-0768-3) State U NY Pr.

Sociobiological Perspectives on Human Development. K. Macdonald. (Illus.). 450p. 1987. 85.95 (0-387-96581-5) Spr-Verlag.

Sociobiology: A Book of Quotations. 1992. lib. bdg. 250.00 (0-8490-5445-1) Gordon Pr.

Sociobiology: Sense or Nonsense. rev. ed. Michael Ruse. (Episteme Ser.: No. 8). 244p. 1984. pap. text ed. 39.00 (90-277-1798-2, D Reidel) Kluwer Ac.

Sociobiology: Sense or Nonsense. 2nd rev. ed. Michael Ruse. (Episteme Ser.: No. 8). 248p. 1984. lib. bdg. 89.00 (90-277-1797-4, D Reidel) Kluwer Ac.

Sociobiology: The Abridged Edition. Edward O. Wilson. (Illus.). 375p. 1980. pap. text ed. 19.95 (0-674-81624-2) Belknap Pr.

Sociobiology: The New Synthesis. Edward O. Wilson. LC 74-83910. (Illus.). 698p. 1975. 55.00 (0-674-81621-8) Belknap Pr.

Sociobiology & Conflict: Evolutionary Perspectives on Competition, Cooperation, Violence & Warfare. Ed. by Johan M. Van der Dennen & Vincent S. Falger. 320p. (gr. 13). 1990. text ed. 108.95 (0-412-33770-3, A4380) Chapman & Hall.

Sociobiology & Epistemology. James H. Fetzer. 228p. 1985. pap. text ed. 53.00 (90-277-2006-1, D Reidel); lib. bdg. 122.00 (90-277-2005-3, D Reidel) Kluwer Ac.

Sociobiology & Human Nature: An Interdisciplinary Critique & Defense. Ed. by Michael S. Gregory et al. LC 78-62559. (Jossey-Bass Social & Behavioral Science Ser.). 348p. reprint ed. pap. 99.20 (0-8357-4978-9, 2037911) Bks Demand.

Sociobiology & Psychology: Ideas, Issues & Applications. Ed. by Charles Crawford et al. LC 87-6783. 446p. 1987. 89.95 (0-89859-580-0) L Erlbaum Assocs.

Sociobiology & the Law: The Biology of Altruism in the Courtroom of the Future. John H. Beckstrom. LC 84-16415. 160p. 1985. text ed. 24.95 (0-252-01171-6) U of Ill Pr.

Sociobiology & the Preemption of Social Science. Alexander Rosenberg. LC 80-8091. 240p. 1981. text ed. 38.00 (0-8018-2423-0) Johns Hopkins.

Sociobiology & the Social Sciences. Ed. by Robert W. Bell & Nancy J. Bell. LC 89-645312. (Interfaces in Psychology Ser.: No. 3). vi, 130p. (C). 1989. 25.00 (0-89672-161-2) Tex Tech Univ Pr.

Sociobiology of Ethnocentrism: Evolutionary Dimensions of Xenophobia, Discrimination, Racism & Nationalism. Ed. by Vernon Reynolds. 336p. 1986. 45.00 (0-7099-4222-2, Pub. by Croom Helm UK) Routledge Chapman & Hall.

Sociobiology of Homo Sapiens. Mark Shapiro. LC 78-60932. (C). 1978. 9.95 (0-9601858-0-1) Pinecrest Fund.

Sociobiology of Infant & Adult Male Baboons. David M. Stein. LC 84-338. (Monographs on Infancy: Vol. 5). 256p. 1984. text ed. 73.25 (0-89391-265-4) Ablex Pub.

Sociobiology of Sexual & Reproductive Strategies. Ed. by Anne E. Rasa et al. 300p. (gr. 13). 1989. text ed. 95.50 (0-412-33780-0, A3098) Chapman & Hall.

Sociobiology, Sex, & Science. Harmon R. Holcomb, III. LC 91-41478. (SUNY Series in Philosophy & Biology). 446p. (C). 1993. text ed. 74.50 (0-7914-1259-8); pap. text ed. 24.95 (0-7914-1260-1) State U NY Pr.

Sociocognitive Rhetoric of Meridel Le Sueur: Feminist Discourse & Reportage of the Thirties. James M. Boehnlein. LC 93-50868. 172p. 1994. text ed. 79.95 (0-7734-9136-8) E Mellen.

Sociocritique of Translation Theatre & Alterity in Quebec, 1968-1988. Annie Brisset. (Theory/Culture Ser.). 272p. 1996. 45.00 (0-8020-0533-0) U of Toronto Pr.

Sociocultural Approaches to Language & Literacy: An Interactionist Perspective. Ed. by Vera John-Steiner et al. LC 93-5495. (Illus.). 384p. (C). 1994. text ed. 59.95 (0-521-37301-8) Cambridge U Pr.

Sociocultural Changes in American Jewish Life As Reflected in Selected Jewish Literature. Bernard Cohen. LC 75-146162. 282p. 1975. 36.50 (0-8386-7848-3) Fairleigh Dickinson.

***Sociocultural Contexts of Language & Literacy.** Ed. by Bertha Perez. 256p. 1997. write for info. (0-8058-2256-9) L Erlbaum Assocs.

***Sociocultural Contexts of Language & Literacy.** Ed. by Bertha Perez. 256p. 1997. pap. write for info. (0-8058-2257-7) L Erlbaum Assocs.

***Sociocultural Differences Between America-Born & West Indian-Born Elderly Blacks: A Comparative Study of Health & Social Service Use.** Beverly P. Lyons. LC 97-22284. (Garland Studies on the Elderly in America). 1997. write for info. (0-8153-3042-1) Garland.

Sociocultural Dimensions of Mixtec Ceramics. Ronald M. Spores. (Publications in Anthropology: No. 33). (Illus.). 120p. (Orig.). 1987. pap. text ed. 13.85 (0-935462-24-4) VUPA.

Sociocultural Factors in the Industrialization of Korea. Bon H. Koo. LC 92-20694. 32p. 1992. pap. 6.95 (1-55815-220-2) ICS Pr.

***Sociocultural Implications in Treatment Planning in Occupational Therapy.** Ed. by Florence S. Cromwell. 171p. 1987. 37.95 (0-86656-612-0) Haworth Pr.

***Sociocultural Perspectives: Readings in Social Psychology.** Letitia A. Peplau & Shelley E. Taylor. LC 96-36173. 1996. pap. 29.40 (0-13-241860-6) P-H.

***Sociocultural Perspectives on Volatile Solvent Use.** Fred Beauvais & Joseph E. Trimble. LC 97-699. 1997. write for info. (1-56023-096-7) Harrington Pk.

Sociocultural Psychology: Theory & Practice of Doing & Knowing. Ed. by Laura M. Martin. (Learning in Doing: Social, Cognitive & Computational Perspectives Ser.). (Illus.). 400p. (C). 1995. text ed. 59.95 (0-521-46278-9) Cambridge U Pr.

Sociocultural Studies of Mind. James V. Wertsch. (Learning in Doing: Social, Cognitive & Computational Perspectives Ser.). (Illus.). 250p. (C). 1995. text ed. 54.95 (0-521-47056-0) Cambridge U Pr.

Sociocultural Studies of Mind. James V. Wertsch. (Learning in Doing: Social, Cognitive & Computational Perspectives Ser.). (Illus.). 250p. (C). 1995. pap. text ed. 17.95 (0-521-47643-7) Cambridge U Pr.

Sociocultural Theory in Anthropology. Merwyn S. Garbarino. 114p. (C). 1983. reprint ed. pap. text ed. 9.50 (0-88133-056-6) Waveland Pr.

Sociocybernetics: A Perspective for Living in Complexity. John A. Busch & Gladys M. Busch. 291p. (C). 1992. pap. 15.80 (0-935563-24-5) Social Sys Pr.

An Asterisk (*) at the beginning of an entry indicates that the title is appearing in BIP for the first time.

Sociocybernetics: Rethinking Social Organization. Ed. by John A. Busch & Gladys M. Busch. (Systems Inquiry Ser.). 139p. 1988. pap. text ed. 16.95 (*0-318-37715-2*) Intersystems Pubns.

Sociodemographic Factors in the Epidemiology of Multiple Sclerosis: An Annotated Bibliography. Compiled by George W. Lowis. LC 90-14016. (Bibliographies & Indexes in Medical Studies: No. 5). 256p. 1991. text ed. 59.95 (*0-313-26838-X*, LSY/, Greenwood Pr) Greenwood.

Sociodrama: An Interpretive Theory for the Practice of Public Relations. Thomas J. Mickey. 136p. (Orig.). (C). Date not set. lib. bdg. 42.00 (*0-7618-0027-1*) U Pr of Amer.

Sociodrama: An Interpretive Theory for the Practice of Public Relations. Thomas J. Mickey. 136p. (Orig.). (C). 1995. pap. text ed. 22.00 (*0-7618-0028-X*) U Pr of Amer.

Sociodrama: Who's in Your Shoes. Antonina Garcia. LC 89-33970. 224p. 1994. pap. text ed. 19.95 (*0-275-95098-0*, Praeger Pubs) Greenwood.

Sociodrama: Who's In Your Shoes? Patricia Sternberg & Antonina Garcia. LC 89-33970. 224p. 1989. text ed. 55.00 (*0-275-93053-X*, C3053, Praeger Pubs) Greenwood.

Socioecology & Psychology of Primates. Ed. by Russell H. Tuttle. (World Anthropology Ser.). (Illus.). xvi, 575p. 1975. 62.35 (*90-279-7709-7*) Mouton.

Socioeconomic Adjustments of Tribals: A Case Study of Tripura Jhumias (India) Bani P. Misra. LC 76-903504. 1976. 6.50 (*0-88386-700-1*) S Asia.

Socioeconomic & Political Influences on Industrial Production Decisions in East German Provinces. Robert C. Rickards. (Working Paper Ser.: No. 44). 36p. 1988. pap. 5.00 (*0-89940-525-8*) LBJ Sch Pub Aff.

Socioeconomic Aspects of Renewable Energy Technologies. Ed. by Ramesh Bhatia et al. LC 87-22890. 226p. 1988. text ed. 59.95 (*0-275-92851-9*, C2851, Praeger Pubs) Greenwood.

Socioeconomic Change & Individual Adaptation: Comparing East & West. Ed. by Avi Gottlieb et al. LC 94-44280. (Monographs in Organizational Behavior & Industrial Relations: Vol. 18). 333p. 1995. 73.25 (*1-55938-913-3*) Jai Pr.

Socioeconomic Characteristics & Nutritional Status of Nepalese Children in Chitawan. 81p. 1984. 10.00 (*0-318-23193-X*) Am-Nepal Ed.

***Socioeconomic Characteristics of Medical Practice 1996.** American Medical Association Staff. 175p. pap. 120.00 (*0-614-19678-7*, OP192696WE); pap. 175.00 incl. 3.5 ld (*0-614-19679-5*, OP192496WE) AMA.

Socioeconomic Conditions of the Tribal under British Rule (1803-1936) B. C. Padhi. (C). 1992. 30.00 (*0-685-61701-7*, Pub. by Punthi Pus II) S Asia.

Socioeconomic Determinants of Fertility in Mexico: Changing Perspectives. Jane R. Rubin-Kurtzman. (Monographs: No. 23). 66p. (Orig.). (C). 1987. pap. 7.50 (*0-935391-73-8*, MN-23) UCSD Ctr US-Mex.

Socioeconomic History of Argentina, 1776-1860. Jonathan C. Brown. LC 78-6800. (Cambridge Latin American Studies: No. 35). 318p. reprint ed. pap. 90.70 (*0-318-34763-6*, 2031623) Bks Demand.

***Socioeconomic Impact & Farmers Assessment of Nile Tilapia (Oreochromis Niloticus) Culture in Bangladesh.** M. V. Gupta et al. (ICLARM Technical Reports: No. 35). 50p. 1992. write for info. (*971-8709-23-1*, Pub. by ICLARM PH) Intl Spec Bk.

Socioeconomic Profile of South Africa. William R. Duggan. LC 72-91715. (Special Studies in International Economics & Development). 1973. 39.50 (*0-275-28653-3*) Irvington.

Socioeconomics of Sustainable Agriculture: An Annotated Bibliography. Gary A. Goreham et al. LC 92-16285. 360p. 1992. text ed. 58.00 (*0-8240-7127-1*, H1332) Garland.

Socioemotional Measures for Preschool & Kindergarten Children: A Handbook. Deborah K. Walker. LC 73-10937. (Jossey-Bass Behavioral Science Ser.). 376p. reprint ed. pap. 107.20 (*0-685-16110-2*, 2027772) Bks Demand.

Sociogenesis of Language & Human Conduct. Ed. by Bruce Bain. 580p. 1983. 110.00 (*0-306-41041-9*, Plenum Pr) Plenum.

Sociogenesis Reexamined: With 7 Figures. Ed. by Willibrord De Graaf & Robert Maier. LC 94-1169. 1994. 83.95 (*0-387-94276-9*) Spr-Verlag.

Sociogenetic Perspectives on Internalization. Ed. by Brian D. Cox & Cynthia Lightfoot. LC 96-39146. 264p. 1997. 49.95 (*0-8058-1708-5*) L Erlbaum Assocs.

***Sociolegal Control of Homosexuality: A Multi-Nation Comparison.** LC 97-20368. (Volume in Perspectives in Sexuality Ser.). (Illus.). 342p. (C). 1997. write for info. (*0-306-45532-3*, Plenum Pr) Plenum.

Sociolegal Status of Women in India. Rama Mehta. 192p. 1987. 24.00 (*0-8364-2080-2*, Pub. by Mittal II) S Asia.

Sociolinguistic Aspects of Assimilation: Puerto Rican English in New York City. Walt Wolfram. LC 73-89563. (Urban Language Ser.: No. 9). 257p. reprint ed. pap. 73.30 (*0-8357-3341-6*, 2039569) Bks Demand.

Sociolinguistic Aspects of French Liaison. Daan De Jong. (Topics in Sociolinguistics Ser.). (Orig.). (C). pap. write for info. (*90-6765-489-2*) Mouton.

Sociolinguistic Attitudes in India: An Historical Reconstruction. Madhav M. Deshpande. (Linguistica Extranea: Studia Ser.: No. 5). 178p. 1979. lib. bdg. 12.50 (*0-89720-007-1*) Karoma.

Sociolinguistic Description of Detroit Negro Speech. Walt Wolfram. LC 71-84378. (Urban Language Ser.: No. 5). 257p. reprint ed. pap. 73.30 (*0-8357-3349-1*, 2039582) Bks Demand.

Sociolinguistic Market of Cairo: Gender, Class & Education. Niloofar Haeri. (Library of Arabic Linguistics). 250p. 1996. 110.00 (*0-7103-0503-6*, Pub. by Kegan Paul Intl UK) Col U Pr.

Sociolinguistic Metatheory. Esther Figueroa. LC 94-14272. (Language & Communication Library: No. 14). 214p. 1994. text ed. 89.50 (*0-08-042399-X*, Pergamon Pr) Elsevier.

Sociolinguistic Patterns. William Labov. (Conduct & Communication Ser.). 362p. 1973. pap. 20.95 (*0-8122-1052-2*) U of Pa Pr.

Sociolinguistic Perspectives: Papers on Language in Society, 1959-1994. Charles A. Ferguson. Ed. by Thom Huebner. (Oxford Studies in Sociolinguistics). 360p. 1996. 75.00 (*0-19-509290-2*); pap. 35.00 (*0-19-509291-0*) OUP.

Sociolinguistic Perspectives on Bilingual Education. Christina B. Paulston. (Multilingual Matters Ser.: No. 84). 180p. 1992. 79.00 (*1-85359-147-5*, Pub. by Multilingual Matters UK); pap. 29.95 (*1-85359-146-7*, Pub. by Multilingual Matters UK) Taylor & Francis.

Sociolinguistic Perspectives on Register. Ed. by Douglas Biber & Edward Finegan. LC 92-44536. 400p. 1994. 70.00 (*0-19-508364-4*) OUP.

Sociolinguistic Perspectives on Soviet National Languages: Their Past, Present & Future. Ed. by Isabelle T. Kreindler. (Contributions to the Sociology of Language Ser.: No. 40). x, 381p. 1985. 138.00 (*0-89925-120-X*) Mouton.

Sociolinguistic Studies in Language Contact. Ed. by William F. Mackey & Jacob Ornstein. (Trends in Linguistics, Studies & Monographs: No. 6). 1979. text ed. 65.40 (*90-279-7866-2*) Mouton.

Sociolinguistic Theory: Linguistic Variation & Its Social Significance. J. K. Chambers. (Language in Society Ser.). 256p. 1995. pap. 22.95 (*0-631-18326-4*) Blackwell Pubs.

Sociolinguistic Variation: A Formal Model. Earl M. Herrick. LC 83-1295. (Illus.). 214p. 1984. pap. 61.00 (*0-7837-8380-9*, 2059190) Bks Demand.

Sociolinguistic Variation: Data, Theory, & Analysis. Ed. by Jennifer Arnold et al. 552p. (C). 1996. pap. text ed. 29.95 (*1-57586-038-4*) CSLI.

Sociolinguistic Variation: Data, Theory, & Analysis. Selected Papers from NWAV23 at Stanford. Ed. by Jennifer Arnold et al. 552p. (C). 1996. text ed. 80.00 (*1-57586-039-2*) CSLI.

***Sociolinguistics.** Coupland. LC 97-11315. 1997. text ed. 59.95 (*0-312-17572-8*); text ed. 24.95 (*0-312-17573-6*) St Martin.

Sociolinguistics. R. A. Hudson. LC 79-51824. (Textbooks in Linguistics Ser.). (Illus.). 256p. 1980. pap. text ed. 20.95 (*0-521-29668-4*) Cambridge U Pr.

Sociolinguistics. Peter Trudgill. 208p. 1983. pap. 9.95 (*0-14-013470-0*, Viking) Viking Penguin.

Sociolinguistics. 2nd ed. R. A. Hudson. (Textbooks in Linguistics Ser.). 295p. (C). 1996. text ed. 54.95 (*0-521-56349-6*); pap. text ed. 19.95 (*0-521-56514-6*) Cambridge U Pr.

Sociolinguistics: A Guide to Language Problems in India. Snehamoy Chaklader. 1990. 37.50 (*81-7099-194-3*, Pub. by Mittal II) S Asia.

Sociolinguistics: A Sociological Critique. Glyn Williams. LC 91-31695. 256p. (Orig.). (C). 1992. pap. 16.95 (*0-415-06514-3*, A6789) Routledge.

Sociolinguistics: An Introduction to Language & Society. rev. ed. Peter Trudgill. 208p. 1983. mass mkt. 6.95 (*0-14-022479-3*, Penguin Bks) Viking Penguin.

Sociolinguistics: An Introduction to Language & Society. 3rd rev. ed. Peter Trudjill. (Illus.). 208p. 1996. pap. 11.95 (*0-14-023926-X*, Penguin Bks) Viking Penguin.

Sociolinguistics - Soziolinguistik: An International Handbook of the Science of Language & Society - Ein Internationales Handbuch zur Wissenschaft von Sprache und Gesellschaft. Ed. by Norbert Dittmar et al. (Handbooks of Linguistics & Communication Science: Vol. 3/2). xix, 1058p. (GER.). 1988. lib. bdg. 534.65 (*3-11-011645-6*) De Gruyter.

Sociolinguistics & Contemporary French. Dennis Ager. 250p. (C). 1991. text ed. 59.95 (*0-521-39335-3*) Cambridge U Pr.

Sociolinguistics & Contemporary French. Dennis Ager. 250p. (C). 1991. pap. text ed. 19.95 (*0-521-39730-8*) Cambridge U Pr.

Sociolinguistics & Language Teaching. Ed. by Sandra L. McKay & Nancy F. Hornberger. (Applied Linguistics Ser.). (Illus.). 400p. (C). 1995. text ed. 54.95 (*0-521-48205-4*) Cambridge U Pr.

Sociolinguistics & Language Teaching. Ed. by Sandra L. McKay & Nancy F. Hornberger. (Applied Linguistics Ser.). (Illus.). 496p. (C). 1995. pap. text ed. 22.95 (*0-521-48434-0*) Cambridge U Pr.

Sociolinguistics in Cross-Cultural Analysis. David M. Smith & Roger W. Shuy. LC 72-186589. 133p. reprint ed. pap. 38.00 (*0-7837-6342-5*, 2046054) Bks Demand.

***Sociolinguistics in Deaf Communities, Vol. 4.** Ed. by Ceil Lucas. (C). 1998. text ed. 39.95 (*1-56368-066-1*) Gallaudet Univ Pr.

Sociolinguistics in Deaf Communities: x, Vol. 1. Ed. by Ceil Lucas. (Sociolinguistics in Deaf Communities Ser.: Vol. 1). 352p. 1995. text ed. 39.95 (*1-56368-036-X*) Gallaudet Univ Pr.

Sociolinguistics in Hindi Contexts. Raja R. Mehrotra. (Contributions to the Sociology of Language Ser.: No. 38). xii, 153p. 1985. 73.10 (*0-89925-139-0*) Mouton.

Sociolinguistics in the Low Countries. K. Deprez. LC 84-24240. (Studies in the Sciences of Language: No. 5). viii, 359p. (Orig.). 1984. pap. 78.00 (*90-272-2321-1*) Benjamins North Am.

Sociolinguistics of Language: Introduction to Sociolinguistics, Vol. II. Ralph Fasold. 384p. 1990. pap. text ed. 25.95 (*0-631-13825-0*) Blackwell Pubs.

Sociolinguistics of Society. Ralph Fasold. 352p. 1984. pap. 25.95 (*0-631-13462-X*) Blackwell Pubs.

Sociolinguistics of the Brazilian-Uruguayan Border. Frederik G. Hensey. (Janua Linguarum, Ser. Practica: No. 16). (Illus.). 115p. 1973. pap. text ed. 60.00 (*90-279-2326-4*) Mouton.

Sociolinguistics of the Deaf Community. Ed. by Ceil Lucas. 307p. 1989. text ed. 61.00 (*0-12-458045-9*) Acad Pr.

Sociolinguistics of the Spanish-Speaking World: Iberia, Latin America, United States. Ed. by Carol A. Klee & Luis A. Ramos-Garcia. LC 90-25750. 368p. 1991. pap. 28.00 (*0-927534-13-4*) Biling Rev-Pr.

Sociolinguistics of Urban Vernaculars: Case Studies & Their Evaluation. Ed. by Norbert Dittmar & Peter Schlobinski. (Sociolinguistics & Language Contact Ser.: Vol. 1). 276p. (C). 1988. lib. bdg. 125.95 (*3-11-010534-9*) De Gruyter.

Sociolinguistics of Urbanization: The Case of the Nordic Countries. Ed. by Bengt Nordberg. (Sociolinguistics & Language Contact Ser.: Vol. 7). viii, 290p. (C). 1994. lib. bdg. 129.25 (*3-11-011184-5*, 97-94) De Gruyter.

***Sociolinguistics Read, Vol. II.** Cheshire. LC 97-20091. 1997. text ed. 69.95 (*0-340-69182-4*); text ed. 23.95 (*0-340-69999-X*) St Martin.

Sociologia: Curso Introductorio. Roberto Agramonte. LC 77-5905. (Illus.). 1978. pap. 8.00 (*0-8477-2443-3*) U of PR Pr.

Sociologia Guatemalteca: El Problema Social del Indio. Miguel A. Asturias. Tr. by Maureen Ahern. LC 77-8270. 106p. 1977. 20.00 (*0-87918-035-8*); pap. 10.00 (*0-87918-037-4*) ASU Lat Am St.

Sociologia y Educacion. 5th ed. Jose A. Caceres. LC 76-10842. 478p. 1989. pap. 12.95 (*0-8477-2736-X*) U of PR Pr.

Sociologia y Servicios Sociales: Sociology & Social Services. Protase E. Woodford & Conrad J. Schmitt. 1992. pap. text ed. 10.95 (*0-07-056817-0*) McGraw.

Sociological Abstracts User's Reference Manual. 4th ed. Miriam Chall & Terry Owen. LC 89-63306. v, 175p. 1989. 60.00 (*0-930710-07-X*) Soc Abstracts.

Sociological Adventure: A Holistic Perspective. Peter Roche de Coppens. 348p. (C). 1996. per., pap. text ed. 31.50 (*0-7872-2002-7*) Kendall-Hunt.

Sociological Adventures: Earle Edward Eubank's Visits with European Sociologists. Dirk Kasler. 276p. (C). 1990. 39.95 (*0-88738-368-8*) Transaction Pubs.

Sociological Ambivalence & Other Essays. Robert K. Merton. LC 76-1033. (Illus.). 1976. pap. 19.95 (*0-02-921120-4*, Free Press) Free Pr.

Sociological Analysis of Southern Regionalism: The Contributions of Howard W. Odum. Paul Challen. LC 93-1724. 92p. 1993. 49.95 (*0-7734-9161-9*) E Mellen.

Sociological Analysis of the California Taxi-Dancer: The Hidden Halls. Mary V. Meckel. LC 94-38355. (Women's Studies: Vol. 8). 168p. 1995. text ed. 79.95 (*0-7734-9039-6*) E Mellen.

Sociological Analysis of the Theology of Quakers: The Silent Revolution. Pink Dandelion. LC 96-23943. (Studies in Religion & Society: No. 34). 456p. 1997. text ed. 109.95 (*0-7734-8807-3*) E Mellen.

Sociological & Economic Change in the Peasant Society of Troina, Sicily. Clifford J. Jansen & Anton J. Jansen. LC 92-907. 200p. 1992. lib. bdg. 79.95 (*0-7734-9469-3*) E Mellen.

Sociological & Medical Aspects of Nutrition. Ed. by G. H. Bourne. (World Review of Nutrition & Dietetics Ser.: Vol. 55). (Illus.). xii, 252p. 1988. 185.00 (*3-8055-4703-X*) S Karger.

***Sociological Applications of Health & Medicine.** Morgan & Calnan. 304p. (C). 1988. pap. text ed. 25.00 (*0-415-02556-7*) Routledge.

Sociological Approaches to Health & Medicine. Myfanwy Morgan et al. LC 85-48015. (Social Analysis Ser.). 297p. (C). 1985. 24.50 (*0-7099-1705-8*, Pub. by Croom Helm UK); pap. 11.50 (*0-7099-3514-5*, Pub. by Croom Helm UK) Routledge Chapman & Hall.

Sociological Aspects of the Church. Ken Lawrence. Ed. by Dale Sauls & James Hill. 144p. (Orig.). (C). 1997. pap. 6.95 (*0-910653-25-9*, Red River Pr) Archival Servs.

Sociological Backgrounds of Adult Education. Ed. by R. Burns. (Notes & Essays Ser.: No. 41). 1970. pap. text ed. 2.50 (*0-685-76690-X*, NES 41) Syracuse U Cont Ed.

Sociological Beginnings for Beginners: On the Origins of Key Ideas in Sociology. George Ritzer. LC 93-23915. 1993. pap. text ed. write for info. (*0-07-052974-4*) McGraw.

Sociological Concepts. George V. Zito. (Illus.). 1980. reprint ed. pap. text ed. 5.95 (*0-8290-0082-8*) Irvington.

Sociological Critique of Theories of Cognitive Development: The Limitations of Piaget & Kohlberg. Mathew J. Kanjirathinkal. LC 89-12484. (Studies in Sociology: Vol. 2). 232p. 1990. lib. bdg. 89.95 (*0-88946-632-7*) E Mellen.

Sociological Debates: Thinking about "The Social" Ed. by Floya Anthias & Michael P. Kelly. 454p. (C). 1996. pap. 29.00 (*1-874529-55-8*) NYU Pr.

Sociological Dynamics of Sport & Exercise. James E. Bryant & Mary McElroy. (Illus.). 312p. (Orig.). (C). 1997. pap. text ed. 36.95 (*0-89582-328-4*) Morton Pub.

Sociological Enterprise: A Discussion of Fundamental Concepts. C. C. Harris. LC 79-21637. 1980. text ed. 29.95 (*0-312-73968-0*) St Martin.

Sociological Eye: Selected Papers. Everett C. Hughes. 598p. 1984. pap. 29.95 (*0-87855-959-0*) Transaction Pubs.

Sociological Footprints. 7th ed. Cargan. LC 96-26098. (Sociology Ser.). 1997. pap. 27.95 (*0-534-50488-4*) Wadsworth Pub.

Sociological Footprints: Introductory Readings in Sociology. 5th ed. Ed. by Leonard Cargan & Jeanne H. Ballantine. 456p. (C). 1991. pap. 20.95 (*0-534-14652-X*) Wadsworth Pub.

Sociological Footprints: Introductory Readings in Sociology. 6th ed. Leonard Cargan & Jeanne H. Ballantine. 555p. 1994. pap. 20.50 (*0-534-20802-9*) Wadsworth Pub.

Sociological Foundations of Education in an Urban Society. John P. Sikula. (C). 1975. pap. text ed. 6.80 (*0-87563-085-5*) Stipes.

***Sociological Foundations of Human Movement.** David Kirk et al. 450p. 1997. 69.95 (*0-7329-3550-4*, Pub. by Macmill Educ AT) Paul & Co Pubs.

***Sociological Foundations of Human Movement.** David Kirk et al. 450p. 1997. pap. 34.95 (*0-7329-3551-2*, Pub. by Macmill Educ AT) Paul & Co Pubs.

Sociological Ideas: Concepts & Applications. 3rd ed. William C. Levin. 416p. (C). 1991. pap. 24.95 (*0-534-14646-5*) Wadsworth Pub.

Sociological Ideas: Concepts & Applications. 4th ed. William C. Levin. LC 93-3256. 473p. 1994. pap. 32.95 (*0-534-20856-8*) Wadsworth Pub.

Sociological Image of the City: Through Children's Eyes. Silvia B. Golombek. (American University Studies: Anthropology & Science: Ser. XI, Vol. 58). 140p. (C). 1993. text ed. 35.95 (*0-8204-1785-8*) P Lang Pubng.

Sociological Imagination. C. Wright Mills. 242p. 1967. reprint ed. pap. 9.95 (*0-19-500751-4*) OUP.

***Sociological Imagination: Introduction to Sociology (Telecourse Study Guide)** 3rd ed. Glenn Currier & Jane Penney. 368p. (C). 1996. pap. text ed. 20.75 (*0-15-504004-9*) HB Coll Pubs.

Sociological Impressionism: A Reassessment of Georg Simmel's Social Theory. 2nd ed. David Frisby. (International Library of Sociology). 240p. (C). 1992. pap. text ed. 17.95 (*0-415-05795-7*, A6136) Routledge.

***Sociological Inquiry.** Kooros Mahmoudi. 176p. (C). Date not set. per., pap. text ed. 23.95 (*0-7872-3319-6*) Kendall-Hunt.

Sociological Insight: An Introduction to Non-Obvious Sociology. 2nd ed. Randall Collins. 224p. (C). 1992. pap. text ed. 15.95 (*0-19-507442-4*) OUP.

Sociological Interpretation of Education. David Blackledge & Barry Hunt. LC 85-4145. (Social Analysis Ser.). 353p. 1985. pap. 18.95 (*0-7099-0676-5*, Pub. by Croom Helm UK) Routledge Chapman & Hall.

***Sociological Investigations.** 2nd ed. Cover. 1997. pap. text ed. 9.50 (*0-697-35634-5*) McGraw.

***Sociological Investigations.** 2nd ed. Dan Cover. 240p. 1993. 14.95 (*0-697-31043-4*) Dushkin Pub.

Sociological Justice. Donald Black. (Illus.). 192p. (C). 1993. reprint ed. pap. text ed. 15.95 (*0-19-508558-2*, 11141) OUP.

Sociological Literature South Asia, Vol. 1: 1992. Ed. by T. K. Oommen. (C). 1993. 62.00 (*81-900333-0-1*, Pub. by Deep II) S Asia.

Sociological Lives, Vol. 2: Social Change & the Life Course. Ed. by Matilda W. Riley. (American Sociological Association Presidential Ser.). 192p. (C). 1988. text ed. 42.00 (*0-8039-3285-5*); pap. text ed. 19.50 (*0-8039-3286-3*) Sage.

Sociological Methodology. Peter Marsden. 432p. 1994. text ed. 66.95 (*1-55786-592-2*) Blackwell Pubs.

***Sociological Methodology.** Peter Marsden. Date not set. 66.95 (*1-55786-682-1*) Blackwell Pubs.

Sociological Methodology, Vol. 19. Ed. by Clifford C. Clogg. 474p. 1990. 58.95 (*0-631-17052-9*) Blackwell Pubs.

***Sociological Methodology, Vol. 27.** Ed. by Adrian Raftery. 244p. (C). 1997. text ed. 84.95 (*1-57718-109-3*) Blackwell Pubs.

Sociological Methodology, Nineteen Eighty. Ed. by Karl F. Schuessler. LC 68-54940. 600p. reprint ed. pap. 171.00 (*0-317-26047-2*, 2023782) Bks Demand.

Sociological Methodology Nineteen Eighty-Eight, Vol. 18. Ed. by Clifford C. Clogg. (C). 1988. text ed. 40.00 (*0-912764-25-2*) Am Sociological.

Sociological Methodology, Nineteen Eighty-Five. Ed. by Nancy B. Tuma. LC 68-54940. (Jossey-Bass Social & Behavioral Science Ser.). 430p. reprint ed. pap. 122.60 (*0-7837-2537-X*, 2042696) Bks Demand.

Sociological Methodology, 1970. Ed. by Edgar F. Borgatta. LC 74-110635. (Jossey-Bass Behavioral Science Ser.). 352p. reprint ed. pap. 100.40 (*0-8357-4969-X*, 2037902) Bks Demand.

Sociological Methodology, 1976. Ed. by David R. Heise. LC 68-54940. (Jossey-Bass Behavioral Science Ser.). (Illus.). 317p. reprint ed. pap. 90.40 (*0-8357-4698-4*, 2052353) Bks Demand.

Sociological Methodology, 1977. Ed. by David R. Heise. LC 76-11879. (Jossey-Bass Behavioral Science Ser.). 336p. reprint ed. pap. 95.80 (*0-8357-4985-1*, 2037918) Bks Demand.

Sociological Methodology, 1978. Ed. by Karl F. Schuessler. LC 68-54940. (Jossey-Bass Behavioral Science Ser.). 302p. reprint ed. pap. 86.10 (*0-8357-6893-7*, 2037946) Bks Demand.

Sociological Methodology, 1979. Ed. by Karl F. Schuessler. LC 78-62564. (Jossey-Bass Social & Behavioral Science Ser.). 414p. pap. 118.00 (*0-8357-6895-3*, 2037947) Bks Demand.

Sociological Methodology, 1982. Ed. by Samuel Leinhardt. LC 68-54940. (Jossey-Bass Social & Behavioral Science Ser.). (Illus.). 406p. reprint ed. pap. 115.80 (*0-8357-4901-0*, 2037831) Bks Demand.

Sociological Methodology, 1983-1984. Ed. by Samuel Leinhardt. LC 68-54940. (Jossey-Bass Social & Behavioral Science Ser.). 383p. reprint ed. pap. 109.20 (*0-8357-4902-9*, 2037832) Bks Demand.

S

Sociological Outlook. 3rd ed. Reid Luhman. (Illus.). 525p. (C). 1992. pap. text ed. 35.90 (*0-939693-25-9*) Collegiate Pr.

***Sociological Outlook: A Text with Readings.** 5th rev. ed. Reid Luhman. LC 94-72319. (Illus.). (C). 1997. pap. text ed. 36.90 (*0-939693-40-2*) Collegiate Pr.

Sociological Perspective: A Down-to-Earth Approach. James M. Henslin. LC 95-38595. 1995. pap. text ed. 37.00 (*0-205-17480-9*) Allyn.

Sociological Perspective in Education: A Reader. S. Shukla & K. Kumar. 1986. 27.50 (*81-7001-007-1*, Pub. by Chanakya II) S Asia.

Sociological Perspective of Sport. 4th ed. Wilbert M. Leonard, II. LC 92-28102. 512p. (C). 1992. pap. text ed. 51.00 (*0-02-369871-3*, Macmillan Coll) P-H.

Sociological Perspectives on Modern Accountancy. Robin Roslender. LC 91-32486. 256p. (C). 1992. pap. text ed. 19.95 (*0-415-02576-1*, Routledge NY) Routledge.

Sociological Perspectives on Social Psychology. Ed. by Karen Cook et al. LC 94-1890. 1994. text ed. 66.00 (*0-205-13716-4*) Allyn.

Sociological Pilgrimage. Michael Mulkay. 1990. 65.00 (*0-335-09409-0*, Open Univ Pr); pap. 21.00 (*0-335-09404-X*, Open Univ Pr) Taylor & Francis.

Sociological Poetics & Aesthetic Theory. Alan Swingewood. LC 86-15633. 1987. pap. 11.95 (*0-312-00040-5*); text ed. 35.00 (*0-312-00039-1*) St Martin.

Sociological Portrait of the Homeless Population in a Moderate Sized City: Macon, Georgia. James E. Floyd. LC 94-9768. 192p. 1995. 79.95 (*0-7734-9090-6*) E Mellen.

Sociological Practice, Vol. 7. Ed. by Jan M. Fritz & Elizabeth J. Clark. 200p. 1989. 30.00 (*0-87013-271-7*) Mich St U Pr.

Sociological Practice, Vol. 10: Conflict Processing. Ed. by Maria R. Volpe & Peter R. Maida. 186p. (C). 1992. pap. 30.00 (*0-87013-307-1*) Mich St U Pr.

Sociological Practice, Vol. 8: Community. Ed. by Alvin Lackey. 246p. (C). 1990. pap. 30.00 (*0-87013-278-4*) Mich St U Pr.

Sociological Practice, Vol. 9: Health. Ed. by Jan Fritz & Elizabeth Clark. 211p. (C). 1991. pap. 30.00 (*0-87013-292-X*) Mich St U Pr.

Sociological Quest: An Introduction to the Study of Social Life. Evan Willis. 120p. 1993. pap. text ed. 14.95 (*1-86373-344-2*, Pub. by Allen Unwin AT) Paul & Co Pubs.

Sociological Quest: An Introduction to the Study of Social Life. 3rd ed. Evan Willis. LC 96-18233. 150p. (C). 1996. text ed. 45.00 (*0-8135-2366-4*); pap. text ed. 15.95 (*0-8135-2367-2*) Rutgers U Pr.

Sociological Quest: Principles of Sociology. David M. Orenstein. (Illus.). 415p. 1985. pap. text ed. 39.75 (*0-314-77938-8*) West Pub.

Sociological Readings & Re-Readings. Paul Atkinson. (Cardiff Papers in Qualitative Research: Vol. 4). 160p. 1996. 55.95 (*1-85628-578-2*, Pub. by Avebury Pub UK) Ashgate Pub Co.

Sociological Reality. Betty G. Yorburg. 544p. (C). 1995. per. 17.95 (*1-56134-313-7*) Dushkin Pub.

Sociological Reasoning. Stones. 1996. text ed. 49.95 (*0-312-16076-3*); text ed. 18.95 (*0-312-16077-1*) St Martin.

Sociological Research Methods. 2nd ed. Ed. by Martin Bulmer. 450p. (C). 1984. pap. 18.95 (*0-333-37346-4*) Transaction Pubs.

Sociological Slices: Introductory Readings from an Interactionist Perspective. Ed. by Gary A. Fine et al. 338p. 1993. pap. 25.75 (*1-55938-551-0*) Jai Pr.

Sociological Snapshots 2: Seeing Social Structure & Change in Everyday Life. 2nd ed. Jack Levin. LC 95-8239. 1995. pap. 12.95 (*0-8039-9075-8*) Pine Forge.

Sociological Spirit. 2nd ed. Earl Babbie. 241p. 1994. pap. 13.95 (*0-534-20202-0*) Wadsworth Pub.

***Sociological Spirit.** 3rd ed. Babbie. (Sociology Ser.). (C). Date not set. pap. 13.95 (*0-534-53379-5*) Wadsworth Pub.

Sociological Spirit: Critical Essays in a Critical Science. Earl Babbie. 186p. (C). 1988. pap. 10.95 (*0-534-08982-8*) Wadsworth Pub.

Sociological Studies. Jean Piaget. Ed. by Leslie Smith. LC 94-27215. 368p. (C). (gr. 13). 1995. 49.95 (*0-415-10780-6*, B4388) Routledge.

Sociological Studies in Roman Catholic Religion: Historical & Contemporary Perspectives. Ed. by Roger O'Toole. LC 89-37719. (Studies in Religion & Society: Vol. 24). 192p. 1989. lib. bdg. 79.95 (*0-88946-850-8*) E Mellen.

Sociological Studies of Children, Vol. 1. Ed. by Nancy Mandell. 303p. 1986. 73.25 (*0-89232-565-8*) Jai Pr.

Sociological Studies of Children, Vol. 2. Ed. by Nancy Mandell. 244p. 1987. 73.25 (*0-89232-760-X*) Jai Pr.

Sociological Studies of Children, Vol. 3. Ed. by Nancy Mandell. 264p. 1990. 73.25 (*0-89232-903-3*) Jai Pr.

Sociological Studies of Children, Vol. 4: Perspectives on & of Children. Ed. by Nancy Mandell. 248p. 1991. 73.25 (*1-55938-195-7*) Jai Pr.

Sociological Studies of Children, Vol. 5. Ed. by Nancy Mandell. 252p. 1993. 73.25 (*1-55938-480-8*) Jai Pr.

Sociological Studies of Children, Vol. 6: Macro-Micro Connections in the Pathways to. Ed. by Nancy Mandell. 219p. 1994. 73.25 (*1-55938-746-7*) Jai Pr.

Sociological Studies of Children, Vol. 7. Ed. by Nancy Mandell. 268p. 1995. 73.25 (*1-55938-900-1*) Jai Pr.

Sociological Studies of Children, Vol. 8. Ed. by Nancy Mandell. 1996. 73.25 (*0-7623-0051-5*) Jai Pr.

Sociological Study of a Texas Lynching. Durward Pruden. (Reprint Series in Sociology). (C). 1993. reprint ed. pap. text ed. 1.00 (*0-8290-2939-7*, S-479) Irvington.

Sociological Study of Secularization Trends in the American Catholic University: Decatholicizing the Catholic Religious Curriculum. Frank D. Schubert. LC 89-48984. (Studies in Religion & Society: Vol. 25). 144p. 1990. lib. bdg. 69.95 (*0-88946-242-9*) E Mellen.

Sociological Study of the Free-Lance Classical Musician: In the Pits. Jon Frederickson & James F. Rooney. LC 92-1094. 180p. 1993. text ed. 79.95 (*0-7734-9281-X*) E Mellen.

Sociological Task. Harold Fallding. LC 68-24428. 1968. 29.50 (*0-89197-416-4*) Irvington.

Sociological Theories in Progress: New Formulations. Ed. by Joseph Berger et al. (Illus.). 416p. (C). 1989. text ed. 44.00 (*0-8039-3525-0*) Sage.

Sociological Theories of Law. Ed. by Kahei Rokumoto. LC 93-27760. (International Library of Essays in Law & Legal Theory: Vol. 12). (C). 1994. 150.00 (*0-8147-7425-3*) NYU Pr.

Sociological Theories of Today. Pitirim A. Sorokin. Ed. by Lewis A. Coser & Walter W. Powell. LC 79-7022. (Perennial Works in Sociology). 1980. reprint ed. lib. bdg. 54.95 (*0-405-12121-0*) Ayer.

***Sociological Theory.** Richard Hadden. 180p. 1997. pap. 14.95 (*1-55111-095-4*) Broadview Pr.

Sociological Theory. William D. Perdue. LC 86-61124. 410p. (C). 1986. text ed. 47.95 (*0-87484-693-5*, 693) Mayfield Pub.

Sociological Theory. 4th ed. George Ritzer. 1996. text ed. write for info. (*0-07-053016-5*) McGraw.

Sociological Theory: A Book of Readings. 5th ed. Ed. by Lewis A. Coser & Bernard Rosenberg. 603p. (C). 1989. reprint ed. pap. text ed. 25.95 (*0-88133-457-X*) Waveland Pr.

Sociological Theory: An Introduction. Ed. by Walter L. Wallace. LC 68-8162. (Illus.). 311p. 1969. lib. bdg. 41.95 (*0-202-30091-9*) Aldine de Gruyter.

Sociological Theory: Classical Statements. 3rd ed. George Ritzer. 1994. text ed. 59.00 (*0-205-15626-6*) Allyn.

***Sociological Theory: Classical Statements.** 4th ed. Ashley & Orenstein. LC 97-19764. 1997. text ed. 56.00 (*0-205-27157-X*) P-H.

Sociological Theory: Contemporary Debates. John Scott. LC 94-40622. 320p. 1995. 80.00 (*1-85278-418-0*); pap. 25.00 (*1-85278-427-X*) E Elgar.

Sociological Theory: From the Enlightenment to the Present. Calvin J. Larson. LC 86-80124. 247p. (Orig.). 1987. pap. text ed. 22.95 (*0-930390-71-7*); lib. bdg. 38.95 (*0-930390-72-5*) Gen Hall.

Sociological Theory: What Went Wrong?: Diagnosis & Remedies. Nicos Mouzelis. LC 94-44296. 232p. (C). 1995. pap. 17.95 (*0-415-07694-3*, Routledge NY) Routledge.

Sociological Theory: What Went Wrong?: Diagnosis & Remedies. Nicos Mouzelis. LC 94-44296. 232p. (C). (gr. 13). 1995. text ed. 62.95 (*0-415-12720-3*, Routledge NY) Routledge.

Sociological Theory & Cognitive Science. Ed. by D. Heckathorn. iv, 120p. 1989. pap. text ed. 222.00 (*0-677-22280-7*) Gordon & Breach.

Sociological Theory & Collective Subjectivity. Jose M. Domingues. 1995. text ed. 59.95 (*0-312-12976-9*) St Martin.

Sociological Theory & Educational Reality: The Sociology of Education in Australia. Alan Barcan. 1992. pap. 46.95 (*0-86840-125-0*, Pub. by New South Wales Univ Pr AT) Intl Spec Bk.

Sociological Theory & Medical Sociology. Graham Scambler. 280p. 1988. text ed. 69.95 (*0-422-60630-8*, Pub. by Tavistock UK) Routledge Chapman & Hall.

Sociological Theory & Mental Disorder. Henry W. Dunham. LC 59-9323. (Illus.). 311p. reprint ed. pap. 88.70 (*0-7837-3597-9*, 2043462) Bks Demand.

Sociological Theory I: From the 1850s to the 1920s, 3 vols., Set. Richard Munch. LC 92-39833. (Sociology Ser.). 1994. pap. text ed. 24.95 (*0-8304-1255-7*) Nelson-Hall.

Sociological Theory II: From the 1920s to the 1960s, 2 vols., II. Richard Munch. LC 92-39833. (Sociology Ser.). 1994. pap. text ed. 24.95 (*0-8304-1338-3*) Nelson-Hall.

Sociological Theory III: Development since the 1960s. Richard Munch. (Sociology Ser.). 400p. 1994. pap. text ed. 24.95 (*0-8304-1342-1*) Nelson-Hall.

Sociological Theory in Research Practice. Elizabeth Freidheim. 325p. 1976. pap. text ed. 24.95 (*0-87073-015-0*) Transaction Pubs.

Sociological Theory in Transition. Stephen P. Turner. LC 85-18617. 224p. 1986. pap. text ed. 16.95 (*0-04-301206-X*) Routledge Chapman & Hall.

Sociological Theory of Law. Niklas Luhmann. Tr. by Elizabeth King-Utz & Martin Albrow. 448p. 1985. 59.95 (*0-7100-9747-6*, RKP) Routledge.

Sociological Theory, 1983. Ed. by Randall Collins. LC 83-187481. (Jossey-Bass Social & Behavioral Science Ser.). (Illus.). 381p. reprint ed. pap. 108.60 (*0-8357-4875-8*, 2037807) Bks Demand.

Sociological Theory, 1984. Ed. by Randall Collins. (Jossey-Bass Social & Behavioral Science Ser.). 452p. pap. 128.90 (*0-7837-0164-0*, 2040461) Bks Demand.

Sociological Thought: From Comte to Sorokin. Francis Abraham & John H. Morgan. LC 89-40442. 263p. (C). 1989. pap. text ed. 19.95 (*1-55605-104-2*) Wyndham Hall.

Sociological Tradition. rev. ed. Robert A. Nisbet. LC 92-35189. 365p. (C). 1993. pap. text ed. 24.95 (*1-56000-667-6*) Transaction Pubs.

Sociological Traditions from Generation to Generation: Glimpses of the American Experience. Ed. by Robert K. Merton & Matilda W. Riley. LC 79-26693. (Modern Sociology Ser.). (Illus.). 184p. (C). 1980. pap. 39.50 (*0-89391-061-9*); text ed. 73.25 (*0-89391-034-1*) Ablex Pub.

Sociological Value of Christianity. Georges Chatterton-Hill. LC 83-45605. reprint ed. 36.00 (*0-404-19873-2*) AMS Pr.

Sociological View of Sovereignty: A Series of Articles in the American Journal of Sociology, 1899-1900. John R. Commons. LC 64-17405. (Reprints of Economic Classics Ser.). xiv, 107p. 1967. reprint ed. 29.50 (*0-678-00090-5*) Kelley.

***Sociological Visions.** Ed. by Kai Erikson. LC 97-9429. 288p. (Orig.). 1997. pap. 19.95 (*0-8476-8509-8*); text ed. 60.00 (*0-8476-8508-X*) Rowman.

Sociological Wonderment: The Puzzles of Social Life. Paul Higgins. LC 93-46596. 230p. (Orig.). (C). 1994. pap. text ed. write for info. (*0-935732-55-1*) Roxbury Pub Co.

Sociological Worlds: Comparative & Historical Readings on Society. Ed. by Stephen K. Sanderson. LC 94-41021. (Illus.). (C). 1995. pap. text ed. write for info. (*0-935732-67-5*) Roxbury Pub Co.

Sociological Worldview. Sal P. Restivo. 224p. 1991. pap. 20.95 (*0-631-17781-7*) Blackwell Pubs.

Sociological Writings. Max Weber & Wolf Heydebrand. 324p. (C). 1993. 29.50 (*0-8264-0718-8*); pap. text ed. 16.95 (*0-8264-0719-6*) Continuum.

Sociologie De Proudhon. Celestin C. Bougle. Ed. by J. P. Mayer. LC 78-67336. (European Political Thought Ser.). (FRE.). 1980. reprint ed. lib. bdg. 28.95 (*0-405-11681-0*) Ayer.

Sociologie des Migrations aux Etats-Unis Societe, Mouvements Sociaux & Ideologies. Rene Duchac. (Premier Serie, Etudes: No. 15). 1974. pap. 49.25 (*90-279-7191-9*) Mouton.

Sociologie d'une Revolution. Frantz Fanon. (Petite Coll. Maspero Ser.). pap. 9.95 (*0-685-35635-3*) Fr & Eur.

Sociologies of Food & Nutrition. William A. McIntosh. LC 96-31303. (Environment, Development, & Public Policy: Public Policy & Social Ser.). (Illus.). 300p. (C). 1996. 45.00 (*0-306-45335-5*, Plenum Pr) Plenum.

Sociologische Erkenntnis: Sociological Knowledge: The Positive Philosophy of Social Life. Gustav Ratzenhofer. LC 74-25775. (European Sociology Ser.). 372p. 1975. reprint ed. 31.95 (*0-405-06529-9*) Ayer.

Sociologism & Existentialism: Two Perspectives on the Individual & Society. Edward A. Tiryakian. Ed. by Lewis A. Coser & Walter W. Powell. LC 79-7026. (Perennial Works in Sociology). 1980. reprint ed. lib. bdg. 22.95 (*0-405-12125-3*) Ayer.

Sociologist As Consultant. Ed. by Joyce M. Iutcovich & Mark Iutcovich. LC 86-30330. 302p. 1987. text ed. 59.95 (*0-275-92615-X*, C2615, Praeger Pubs) Greenwood.

Sociologists & Music: An Introduction to the Study of Music & Society Through the Later Writings of Paul Honigsheim. 2nd ed. Ed. by K. Peter Etzkorn. 375p. 1989. 44.95 (*0-88738-281-9*) Transaction Pubs.

Sociologists, Economists, & Democracy. Brian Barry. 208p. 1988. pap. text ed. 15.95 (*0-226-03824-6*, Midway Reprint) U Ch Pr.

Sociologists on Sociology. Ed. by Bob Mullan. 371p. 1996. 59.95 (*1-85972-316-0*, Pub. by Avebury Pub UK) Ashgate Pub Co.

Sociologist's Statistical Tools: Computer Based Data Analysis Using SPSS Windows. Henry W. Fischer, III. LC 96-15788. 242p. 1996. pap. text ed. 34.00 (*0-7618-0357-2*); lib. bdg. 54.00 (*0-7618-0356-4*) U Pr of Amer.

Sociologist's Training Manual for Historians. John Zito. 86p. (Orig.). (C). 1993. pap. text ed. 14.50 (*0-8191-9260-0*); lib. bdg. 34.50 (*0-8191-9259-7*) U Pr of Amer.

Sociology. (National Teacher Examination Ser.). pap. 23.95 (*0-8373-8481-8*, NT-61) Nat Learn.

Sociology. (C). 1995. teacher ed. write for info. (*0-06-500815-4*) Addson-Wesley Educ.

***Sociology.** write for info. (*0-340-66200-X*, Pub. by E Arnold UK) Routledge Chapman & Hall.

Sociology. Alix. Date not set. student ed., pap. text ed. 16.50 (*0-314-04775-1*) West Pub.

Sociology. Richard P. Appelbaum & Chambliss. 575p. (C). 1995. text ed. 40.00 (*0-06-500813-8*) Addson-Wesley Educ.

Sociology. Aulette. (Sociology Ser.). Date not set. pap. 30.95 (*0-534-24414-9*) Wadsworth Pub.

***Sociology.** William S. Bainbridge. LC 97-6360. (College Review Ser.). 1997. pap. 12.95 (*0-8120-9920-6*) Barron.

Sociology. Carter. (C). 1995. student ed., text ed. 12.75 (*0-06-502152-5*) Addson-Wesley Educ.

Sociology. John E. Farley. 672p. (C). 1989. Casebound. boxed write for info. (*0-13-816000-7*) P-H.

Sociology. Robert Hagedorn. 624p. (C). 1983. pap. text ed. write for info. (*0-697-07571-0*) Brown & Benchmark.

Sociology. Robert Hagedorn. 624p. (C). 1983. student ed. write for info. (*0-697-07573-7*) Brown & Benchmark.

Sociology. Hess. 1992. pap. text ed. 30.00 (*0-02-354386-8*, Macmillan Coll) P-H.

Sociology. Hugh Klein. (Barron's EZ-101 Study Keys Ser.). 144p. 1992. pap. 5.95 (*0-8120-4853-9*) Barron.

Sociology. Scott G. McNall & Sally A. McNall. 624p. (C). 1991. text ed. 63.00 (*0-13-497595-2*, 610802) P-H.

Sociology. Stephen Moore. 352p. 1995. pap. text ed. 12.95 (*0-8442-3649-7*, Teach Yourslf) NTC Pub Grp.

Sociology. T. K. Oommen & C. N. Venugopal. (C). 1988. 80.00 (*0-685-25674-X*) St Mut.

***Sociology.** Ed. by Orum. (C). 1998. text ed. write for info. (*0-321-01368-9*); student ed., pap. text ed. write for info. (*0-321-01369-7*) Addson-Wesley Educ.

Sociology. Ed. by Martin Pearce. 250p. (C). 1991. pap. 60.00 (*1-85352-929-X*, Pub. by HLT Pubns UK) St Mut.

Sociology. Jack Rudman. (Regents College Proficiency Examination Ser.: CPEP-14). 1994. pap. 23.95 (*0-8373-5414-5*) Nat Learn.

Sociology. Jack Rudman. (Graduate Record Examination (GRE) Ser.: Vol. GRE-18). 1994. pap. 23.95 (*0-8373-5218-5*) Nat Learn.

Sociology. Jack Rudman. (Undergraduate Program Field Tests (UPFT) Ser.: Vol. UPFT-23). 1994. pap. 23.95 (*0-8373-6023-4*) Nat Learn.

Sociology. Neil J. Smelser. (Illus.). 440p. 1993. text ed. 61.95 (*0-631-18915-7*); pap. text ed. 27.95 (*0-631-18916-5*) Blackwell Pubs.

Sociology. Achilles A. Theodorson. Date not set. student ed., pap. text ed. 19.00 (*0-314-53956-5*); teacher ed., pap. text ed. write for info. (*0-314-53999-9*) West Pub.

Sociology. Thomas. 1990. 57.90 (*0-15-371123-X*) HB Schl Dept.

Sociology. Ward. Date not set. pap. text ed. write for info. (*0-314-06442-7*); student ed., pap. text ed. 19.00 (*0-314-06443-5*) West Pub.

Sociology. David A. Ward & Lorene Stone. LC 95-36780. 600p. (C). 1996. text ed. 54.25 (*0-314-06438-9*) West Pub.

Sociology. abr. ed. Hess. 1991. pap. text ed. 30.00 (*0-02-354431-7*, Macmillan Coll) P-H.

***Sociology.** 2nd ed. Appelbaum. (C). 1997. student ed., pap. text ed. 17.95 (*0-673-98184-3*) Addison-Wesley.

Sociology. 2nd ed. Richard P. Appelbaum & William J. Chambliss. LC 96-24447. (C). 1997. text ed. 53.50 (*0-673-98140-1*) Longman.

Sociology. 2nd ed. Farley. 1992. student ed., pap. write for info. (*0-13-817461-X*) P-H.

Sociology. 2nd ed. John E. Farley. 704p. (C). 1992. text ed. 48.00 (*0-13-817420-2*) P-H.

Sociology. 2nd ed. Goode. 1987. text ed. 60.00 (*0-13-821448-4*) P-H.

Sociology. 2nd ed. Jon M. Shepard. 669p. 1983. text ed. 35.00 (*0-314-77794-6*) West Pub.

Sociology. 3rd ed. Brinkerhoff. Date not set. teacher ed., pap. text ed. 16.50 (*0-314-81739-5*); student ed., pap. text ed. 18.50 (*0-314-81740-9*) West Pub.

Sociology. 3rd ed. David B. Brinkerhoff & Lynne K. White. Ed. by Clyde Perlee. 681p. (C). 1991. text ed. 54.75 (*0-314-74128-3*) West Pub.

Sociology. 3rd ed. John E. Farley. LC 93-29493. 660p. (C). 1993. text ed. 58.00 (*0-13-042706-3*) P-H.

Sociology. 3rd ed. Henslin. 736p. 1996. 58.00 (*0-205-19141-X*) Allyn.

Sociology. 3rd ed. Henslin. 1996. student ed., pap. text ed. 19.00 (*0-205-26304-6*) Allyn.

Sociology. 3rd ed. Ian Robertson. 715p. (C). 1987. text ed. 54.95 (*0-87901-245-5*) Worth.

Sociology. 3rd ed. Ian Robertson. xvi, 558p. (C). 1987. student ed., pap. text ed. 14.95 (*0-87901-246-3*) Worth.

Sociology. 3rd ed. Michael P. Soroka. 1996. student ed., pap. text ed. 18.00 (*0-205-26241-4*) Allyn.

Sociology. 3rd ed. Sullivan. 1994. pap. text ed. 18.00 (*0-02-418404-7*, Macmillan Coll) P-H.

Sociology. 3rd large type ed. Joel M. Charon. 1991. pap. text ed. 57.00 (*0-205-13223-5*, H32238) Allyn.

Sociology. 4th ed. Borne. 1993. student ed., pap. write for info. (*0-13-818949-8*) P-H.

Sociology. 4th ed. Brinkerhoff. LC 96-26108. 1996. text ed. write for info. (*0-314-02562-6*) West Pub.

Sociology. 4th ed. Doob. (C). 1993. suppl. ed., teacher ed., pap. text ed. 33.75 (*0-15-500789-0*) HB Coll Pubs.

***Sociology.** 4th ed. Farley. LC 97-25935. 1997. text ed. 56.00 (*0-13-618067-1*) P-H.

Sociology. 4th ed. Jon M. Shepard. Date not set. pap. text ed. write for info. (*0-314-72415-X*) West Pub.

Sociology. 4th ed. Rodney Stark. 678p. (C). 1992. text ed. 45.95 (*0-534-16188-X*) Wadsworth Pub.

***Sociology.** 4th ed. Sullivan. 1997. pap. text ed. 29.33 (*0-205-26488-3*) P-H.

Sociology. 4th ed. Alex Thio. (C). 1995. teacher ed. write for info. (*0-673-55516-X*) Addson-Wesley Educ.

Sociology. 4th ed. Alex Thio. (C). 1996. student ed., pap. text ed. 19.95 (*0-673-99136-9*) Addson-Wesley Educ.

Sociology. 5th ed. Borne. 1994. student ed., pap. text ed. 20.00 (*0-13-118522-5*) P-H.

Sociology. 5th ed. Cohen. 1980. Study Guide. student ed., pap. text ed. write for info. (*0-07-030432-7*) McGraw.

Sociology. 5th ed. Beth B. Hess et al. 720p. (C). 1995. text ed. 58.00 (*0-02-354621-2*, Macmillan Coll) P-H.

Sociology. 5th ed. John J. MacIonis. LC 94-13021. 708p. 1994. text ed. 60.00 (*0-13-101155-3*) P-H.

Sociology. 5th ed. Helen Rosengarte. 1996. student ed., pap. text ed. 19.00 (*0-02-403655-2*, Macmillan Coll) P-H.

Sociology. 5th ed. Richard T. Schaefer & Robert P. Lamm. LC 94-13650. 1994. text ed. write for info. (*0-07-056959-2*) McGraw.

Sociology. 5th ed. Richard T. Schaefer. 1994. student ed., pap. text ed. write for info. (*0-07-057038-8*) McGraw.

Sociology. 5th ed. Jon M. Shepard. Ed. by Jucha. LC 92-29591. 560p. (C). 1993. text ed. 53.25 (*0-314-00728-8*) West Pub.

Sociology. 5th ed. Jon M. Shepard. Date not set. student ed., pap. text ed. 19.00 (*0-314-01690-2*) West Pub.

Sociology. 5th ed. Neil J. Smelser. 464p. 1994. pap. text ed. 40.00 (*0-13-063835-8*) P-H.

Sociology. 5th ed. Rodney Stark. 691p. (C). 1994. text ed. 40.75 (*0-534-20502-X*) Wadsworth Pub.

Sociology. 5th ed. Rodney Stark. (Sociology Ser.). 1994. student ed., pap. 13.25 (*0-534-20503-8*) Wadsworth Pub.

***Sociology.** 5th ed. Ed. by Thio. LC 97-21630. (C). 1998. text ed. write for info. (*0-321-01466-9*); student ed., pap. text ed. write for info. (*0-321-01496-0*) Addson-Wesley Educ.

Sociology. 6th ed. Craig Calhoun et al. LC 93-25016. 1993. text ed. write for info. (*0-07-037879-7*); Video. vhs write for info. (*0-07-037943-2*) McGraw.

An Asterisk (*) at the beginning of an entry indicates that the title is appearing in BIP for the first time.

Sociology. 6th ed. Paul B. Horton & Chester L. Hunt. (Illus.). 650p. (C). 1984. text ed. write for info. (0-07-030443-2); student ed., pap. text ed. 16.77 (0-07-030446-7) McGraw.
***Sociology.** 6th ed. Macionis. 1996. student ed., pap. text ed. 18.67 (0-13-465303-3) P-H.
Sociology. 6th ed. John J. Macionis. LC 96-22938. 736p. (C). 1996. text ed. 58.00 (0-13-237264-9) P-H.
***Sociology.** 6th ed. Richard T. Schaefer & Robert P. Lamm. LC 97-5063. 1997. text ed. write for info. (0-07-057771-4) McGraw.
Sociology. 6th ed. Jon M. Shepard. LC 95-30464. 700p. (C). 1996. text ed. 54.25 (0-314-06316-1) West Pub.
Sociology. 6th ed. Jon M. Shepard. Date not set. teacher ed., pap. text ed. write for info. (0-314-06317-X); student ed., pap. text ed. 19.00 (0-314-06318-8) West Pub.
Sociology. 6th ed. Stark. 1996. student ed., pap. 18.95 (0-534-25714-3) Wadsworth Pub.
Sociology. 6th ed. Rodney Stark. LC 95-19157. 711p. (C). 1996. text ed. 57.95 (0-534-25710-0) Wadsworth Pub.
Sociology. 7th ed. Craig Calhoun & Donald Light. 1996. text ed. write for info. (0-07-038069-4) McGraw.
***Sociology.** 7th ed. Landis. (C). 1998. student ed., pap. 18.95 (0-534-52867-8) Wadsworth Pub.
***Sociology.** 7th ed. Stark. (C). 1998. text ed. 57.95 (0-534-52866-X) Wadsworth Pub.
***Sociology.** 7th ed. Ted Wagner. 1996. student ed., pap. text ed. write for info. (0-07-038072-4) McGraw.
Sociology. 10th ed. Mark Kassop. 1994. student ed., pap. text ed. 17.33 (0-13-116114-8) P-H.
Sociology. 10th ed. David Popenoe. LC 94-20359. 580p. 1994. pap. text ed. 44.00 (0-13-101163-4) P-H.
Sociology. Jon M. Shepard et al. LC 77-4969. (Wiley Self-Teaching Guides Ser.). 239p. reprint ed. pap. 68.20 (0-8357-9979-4, 2011876) Bks Demand.
Sociology: A Brief but Critical Introduction. Anthony Giddens. 200p. (C). 1992. pap. text ed. write for info. (0-15-582002-8) HB Coll Pubs.
Sociology: A Brief but Critical Introduction. 2nd ed. Anthony Giddens. 192p. (C). 1987. pap. text ed. 16.00 (0-15-582001-X) HB Coll Pubs.
***Sociology: A Brief Introduction.** Appelbaum. (C). 1997. pap. text ed. 33.95 (0-673-98520-2) Addison-Wesley.
Sociology: A Brief Introduction. 2nd ed. Richard T. Schaefer & Robert P. Lamm. 1996. student ed., pap. text ed. write for info. (0-07-057242-9) McGraw.
***Sociology: A Brief Introduction.** 3rd ed. Ed. by Thio. (C). 1997. student ed., pap. text ed. 14.95 (0-673-98113-4) Addison-Wesley.
Sociology: A Brief Introduction. 3rd ed. Alex Thio. LC 96-16015. (C). 1997. text ed. 33.95 (0-673-98111-8) Addson-Wesley Educ.
***Sociology: A Brief Introduction Societies:A Multicultural Read.** 3rd ed. Thio. (C). 1997. pap. text ed. 9.50 (0-673-98114-2) Addison-Wesley.
Sociology: A Core Text with Adapted Readings. Leonard Broom et al. 388p. (C). 1990. pap. 37.95 (0-534-12000-8) Wadsworth Pub.
Sociology: A Core Text with Adapted Readings. Leonard Broom et al. 388p. (C). 1990. student ed., wbk. ed., pap. 12.95 (0-534-12001-6) Wadsworth Pub.
***Sociology: A Global Perpsective.** 3rd ed. Joan Ferrante. (Sociology Ser.). (C). 1998. student ed., pap. 18.95 (0-534-52552-0) Wadsworth Pub.
Sociology: A Global Perspective. Joan Ferrante. 534p. (C). 1992. pap. 33.95 (0-534-12738-X) Wadsworth Pub.
Sociology: A Global Perspective. 2nd ed. Joan Ferrante. LC 94-17688. 603p. 1995. pap. 41.95 (0-534-20976-9) Wadsworth Pub.
Sociology: A Global Perspective. 2nd ed. Joan Ferrante. (Sociology Ser.). 1995. student ed., pap. 18.95 (0-534-20977-7) Wadsworth Pub.
***Sociology: A Global Perspective.** 3rd ed. Joan Ferrante. LC 97-26146. (Sociology Ser.). (C). 1997. pap. text ed. 41.95 (0-534-52551-2) Wadsworth Pub.
Sociology: A Guide to Problems & Literature. 3rd ed. Thomas B. Bottomore. 368p. (C). 1986. text ed. 39.95 (0-04-300108-4); pap. text ed. 17.95 (0-04-300109-2) Routledge Chapman & Hall.
***Sociology: A Guide to Reference & Information Sources.** Stephen H. Aby. (Reference Sources in the Social Sciences Ser.). 225p. 1997. lib. bdg. 42.00 (1-56308-422-8) Libs Unl.
Sociology: A Text Reader. Brabant et al. 1991. 23.50 (0-536-57997-0) Ginn Pr.
Sociology: An Everyday Life Approach. Ernest K. Alix. LC 94-30526. 624p. (C). 1995. text ed. 53.25 (0-314-04435-3) West Pub.
Sociology: An Introduction. Christopher B. Doob. LC 93-79059. 565p. 1994. pap. 22.95 (0-15-500771-8) HarBrace.
Sociology: An Introduction. J. Ross Eshleman et al. (C). 1993. student ed., pap. text ed. 17.50 (0-673-52124-9) Addson-Wesley Educ.
Sociology: An Introduction. 2nd ed. Ed. by Neil J. Smelser. LC 72-11540. 810p. (C). reprint ed. pap. 180.00 (0-8357-9980-8, 2051232) Bks Demand.
Sociology: An Introduction. 4th ed. Michael S. Bassis & Richard J. Gelles. 1991. student ed., pap. text ed. write for info. (0-07-911031-2) McGraw.
Sociology: An Introduction. 4th ed. J. Ross Eshleman et al. LC 92-30198. (C). 1993. text ed. 55.95 (0-673-52123-0) Addson-Wesley Educ.
Sociology: An Introduction. 4th ed. Alex Thio. LC 95-24107. 640p. (C). 1996. text ed. 53.50 (0-673-99135-0) Addson-Wesley Educ.
***Sociology: An Introduction.** 5th ed. Doob. (C). 1996. pap. text ed. 42.00 (0-15-504051-0) HB Coll Pubs.
Sociology: An Introduction. 5th ed. Christopher B. Doob. 592p. (C). 1996. pap. text ed. 25.95 (0-15-503636-X) HB Coll Pubs.
Sociology: An Introduction. 5th ed. Richard J. Gelles & Ann Levine. 1994. student ed., pap. text ed. write for info. (0-07-911927-1) McGraw.
Sociology: An Introduction for Nurses, Midwives & Health Visitors. Caroline Cox, BSc, MSc, SRN. 228p. 1983. pap. 12.50 (0-7506-0305-4) Buttrwrth-Heinemann.
***Sociology: Australian Connections.** Ray Jureidini et al. 400p. 1997. pap. 35.00 (1-86448-275-3, Pub. by Allen Unwin AT) Paul & Co Pubs.
Sociology: Classification Schedule, Author & Title Listing, Chronological Listing, 2 vols., Set. Harvard University Library Staff. LC 72-83391. (Widener Library Shelflist: Nos. 45-46). 1304p. 1973. text ed. 85.00 (0-674-81625-0) HUP.
Sociology: Concepts & Applications for a Diverse World. 3rd ed. Thomas J. Sullivan. Orig. Title: Sociology - Concepts, Issues, & Applications. 528p. (C). 1994. reprint ed. pap. text ed. 40.00 (0-02-418400-4, Macmillan Coll) P-H.
Sociology: Concepts & Characteristics. 8th ed. Judson R. Landis. 483p. (C). 1992. pap. 30.95 (0-534-17256-3) Wadsworth Pub.
Sociology: Concepts & Characteristics. 9th ed. Judson R. Landis. LC 94-35558. 482p. 1995. pap. 37.95 (0-534-23754-1) Wadsworth Pub.
***Sociology: Concepts & Characteristics.** 10th ed. Judson R. Landis. (C). 1997. pap. text ed. 37.95 (0-534-52560-1) Wadsworth Pub.
Sociology: Concepts & Uses. Jonathan H. Turner. LC 93-28039. 1993. pap. text ed. write for info. (0-07-065596-0) McGraw.
***Sociology: Contours of Society.** Robert H. Laver & Jeanette C. Laver. LC 97-13296. (Illus.). 425p. (Orig.). (C). 1998. pap. text ed. write for info. (0-935732-01-2) Roxbury Pub Co.
Sociology: Cultural Diversity in a Changing World. 3rd ed. George J. Bryjak & Michael P. Soroka. 592p. 1996. pap. 43.00 (0-205-19155-X) Allyn.
***Sociology: CUNY Panel: Rethinking the Disciplines, Vol. 8G.** Margaret L. Andersen et al. (Women in the Curriculum Ser.). 65p. 1997. pap. 10.00 (1-885303-15-7) Towson St Univ.
***Sociology: Curriculum Unit.** Center for Learning Network Staff. (Social Studies Ser.). 201p. 1996. teacher ed. 37.95 (1-56077-494-0) Ctr Learning.
***Sociology: Discipline Analysis, Vol. 7O.** Jacqueline Johnson & Barbara Risman. (Women in the Curriculum Ser.). 26p. (Orig.). 1997. pap. 7.00 (1-885303-29-7) Towson St Univ.
Sociology: Discovering Society. Jean Stockard. (Sociology Ser.). (C). 1997. text ed. 57.95 (0-534-24060-7) Wadsworth Pub.
Sociology: Experiencing Changing Societies. 4th ed. Kenneth C. Kammeyer et al. 700p. 1989. text ed. 45.00 (0-205-12203-5, H22031) Allyn.
Sociology: Experiencing Changing Societies. 7th ed. Kenneth C. Kammeyer & George Ritzer. 752p. 1996. pap. 22.00 (0-205-16801-9) Allyn.
Sociology: Experiencing Changing Society. 7th ed. Kenneth C. Kammeyer & George Ritzer. 1996. student ed., pap. text ed. 17.00 (0-205-26622-3) Allyn.
***Sociology: Exploring the Architecture of Everyday Life.** 2nd ed. LC 96-45366. 1997. write for info. (0-7619-8518-2) Pine Forge.
***Sociology: Exploring the Architecture of Everyday Life: Readings.** 2nd ed. David M. Newman. LC 96-45391. 1997. write for info. (0-7619-8519-0) Pine Forge.
Sociology: From Concepts to Practice. Bernard S. Phillips. 1979. student ed., pap. text ed. write for info. (0-07-049793-1) McGraw.
Sociology: Guide to Critical Thinking. 5th ed. Richard T. Schaefer. 1994. pap. text ed. write for info. (0-07-057069-8) McGraw.
Sociology: Guide to Critical Thinking. 6th ed. Mark Kassop. 1993. pap. text ed. write for info. (0-07-037942-4) McGraw.
Sociology: Human Relationships. Thomas. 1990. wbk. ed., pap. text ed. 11.25 (0-15-371125-6) HR&W Schl Div.
Sociology: Human Relationships - Tests. Thomas. 1990. pap. 10.00 (0-15-371126-4) HR&W Schl Div.
Sociology: Human Society. 4th ed. Melvin L. DeFleur et al. 475p. (C). 1984. pap. text ed. write for info. (0-07-554593-4) McGraw.
Sociology: IBM PC. 6th ed. Paul B. Horton & Chester L. Hunt. 1984. Study Disk. student ed. write for info. incl. disk (0-07-030463-7) McGraw.
***Sociology: Insights in Health Care.** Ed. by Abbie Perry. (Illus.). 320p. (Orig.). 1996. pap. 38.25 (1-56593-770-8, 1498) Singular Publishing.
Sociology: Micro, Macro & Mega Sociology. Jones et al. (Orig.). (C). 1994. suppl. ed., teacher ed., pap. text ed. 12.50 (0-03-029644-7) HB Coll Pubs.
Sociology: Micro, Mega & Mega Sociology. Jones. (C). 1995. teacher ed., pap. text ed. 32.00 (0-03-029642-0) HB Coll Pubs.
Sociology: Or, the Reconstruction of Society, Government, & Property. Lewis Masquerier. LC 76-88504. (Illus.). 213p. 1971. reprint ed. text ed. 55.00 (0-8371-4967-3, MASO) Greenwood.
Sociology: Principles & Applications. James A. Inciardi & Robert A. Rothman. 692p. (C). 1990. pap. text ed. 46.00 (0-15-582290-X); disk, vhs write for info. (0-318-67032-1); disk write for info. (0-318-67031-3) HB Coll Pubs.
Sociology: Principles & Applications. George A. Theodorson. Ed. by Baxter. 627p. (C). 1990. text ed. 53.25 (0-314-48148-6) West Pub.
Sociology: Snapshots & Portraits of Society. Jack Levin & Arnold Arluke. LC 95-37238. 1996. pap. 18.95 (0-8039-9084-7) Pine Forge.
Sociology: Social Structure & Social Conflict. Harold R. Kerbo. 1056p. (C). 1988. pap. text ed. 57.00 (0-02-362741-7, Macmillan Coll) P-H.
Sociology: Social World Reader. 3rd ed. Ian Robertson. xvi, 360p. (C). 1987. 22.95 (0-87901-330-3) Worth.
Sociology: Study of Human Relations. Thomas. 1995. student ed., text ed. 57.00 (0-03-097589-1) H Holt & Co.
Sociology: Testbank. 5th ed. Jon M. Shepard. Date not set. suppl. ed., teacher ed., pap. text ed. write for info. (0-314-01857-3) West Pub.
Sociology: The Classic Statements. Ed. by Marcello Truzzi. (C). 1971. pap. text ed. write for info. (0-07-553680-3) McGraw.
Sociology: The Core. 3rd ed. Meg W. Karraker. 1993. student ed., pap. text ed. write for info. (0-07-067003-X) McGraw.
***Sociology: The Core.** 4th ed. Meg Wilkes Karraker. 1996. student ed., pap. text ed. write for info. (0-07-067028-5) McGraw.
Sociology: The Core. 4th ed. James W. Vander Zanden. LC 95-16831. 1996. pap. text ed. write for info. (0-07-067021-8) McGraw.
Sociology: The Discipline & Its Direction. William J. Chambliss & Thomas E. Ryther. (Illus.). 480p. (C). 1976. pap. text ed. write for info. (0-07-010466-2) McGraw.
Sociology: The Science of Human Organization. Jonathan H. Turner et al. LC 84-25368. (Illus.). 504p. 1984. text ed. 43.95 (0-8304-1112-7) Nelson-Hall.
Sociology: Traditional & Radical Perspectives. P. Hamilton. 384p. 1982. pap. 21.00 (0-335-09900-9, Open Univ Pr) Taylor & Francis.
***Sociology: Understanding a Diverse Society.** Ed. by Andersen. (C). 1998. student ed., pap. text ed. write for info. (0-321-01036-1) Addison-Wesley.
Sociology: Understanding Social Behavior. Alan P. Bates & Joseph Julian. (C). 1975. teacher ed., pap. 2.36 (0-395-18794-X); text ed. 45.16 (0-395-18652-8) HM.
Sociology: Understanding Society. Peter I. Rose et al. (gr. 11-12). 1978. text ed. 24.88 (0-13-821322-4) P-H.
Sociology: Windows on Society. 4th rev. ed. Ed. by John W. Heeren & Marylee Mason. LC 95-26273. (Illus.). 330p. (C). 1996. pap. text ed. write for info. (0-935732-72-1) Roxbury Pub Co.
Sociology: 1996-1997. annuals 25th ed. Kurt Finsterbusch. 256p. (C). 1996. per. write for info. (0-697-31727-7) Brown & Benchmark.
Sociology Study Guide. 3rd ed. Frank. 1994. pap. text ed. 20.00 (0-13-064395-5) P-H.
Sociology see Comprehensive Dissertation Index: Ten Year Cumulation, 1973-1982
Sociology - A Brief Introduction. 2nd ed. Richard T. Schaefer & Robert P. Lamm. LC 96-537. 1996. pap. text ed. write for info. (0-07-057234-8) McGraw.
Sociology - Concepts, Issues, & Applications see Sociology: Concepts & Applications for a Diverse World
Sociology - Technology: Foundations of Postacademic Social Science. Jay A. Weinstein. LC 80-24637. 383p. reprint ed. pap. 109.20 (0-7837-2125-0, 2042407) Bks Demand.
***Sociology after Postmodernism.** Ed. by David Owen. 224p. 1997. 69.95 (0-8039-7514-7) Sage.
***Sociology after Postmodernism.** Ed. by David Owen. 224p. 1997. pap. 22.95 (0-8039-7515-5) Sage.
Sociology after the Crisis. Charles Lemert. LC 95-15689. 304p. (C). 1995. pap. text ed. 19.95 (0-8133-2544-7) Westview.
Sociology Alive! Ed. by Stephen Moore. 288p. (C). 1987. pap. 45.00 (0-85950-661-4, Pub. by S Thornes Pubs UK) St Mut.
***Sociology Alive.** 2nd ed. Stephen Moore. 320p. (Orig.). 1996. pap. 34.50 (0-7487-1531-2, Pub. by Stanley Thornes UK) Trans-Atl Phila.
***Sociology, an Introduction.** 5th ed. Doob. (C). 1996. pap. text ed. 42.00 (0-15-503639-4) HB Coll Pubs.
Sociology & Christianity. David Mendez. 55p. (Orig.). 1989. pap. 8.00 (1-56428-003-9) Logos Intl Pub.
Sociology & Critical Inquiry: The Work, Tradition, & Purpose. 3rd ed. John Walton. 395p. (C). 1993. pap. 31.95 (0-534-20400-7) Wadsworth Pub.
Sociology & Development: The Impasse & Beyond. Ray Kiely. 224p. 1995. 65.00 (1-85728-195-0, Pub. by UCL Pr UK); pap. write for info. (1-85728-196-9, Pub. by UCL Pr UK) Taylor & Francis.
Sociology & Education: An Analysis of the Theories of Spencer & Ward. Elsa P. Kimball. LC 68-58599. (Columbia University. Studies in the Social Sciences: No. 369). reprint ed. 29.50 (0-404-51369-7) AMS Pr.
Sociology & Estrangement: Three Sociologists of Imperial Germany. Arthur Mitzman. 370p. (C). 1986. pap. 24.95 (0-88738-605-9) Transaction Pubs.
Sociology & Feminism. Harkess. 1997. pap. 14.95 (0-8057-9768-8, Twayne) Scribnrs Ref.
Sociology & Feminism. Harkess. 1997. 22.95 (0-8057-9753-X, Twayne) Scribnrs Ref.
Sociology & Health Care: An Introduction for the Health Care Professionals. 2nd ed. John Bond & Senga Bond. (Illus.). 280p. 1994. pap. text ed. 34.00 (0-443-04059-1) Churchill.
Sociology & Interpretation: From Weber to Habermas. Charles A. Pressler & Fabio B. Dasilva. LC 95-40977. 208p. 1996. text ed. 60.50 (0-7914-3043-X); pap. text ed. 22.95 (0-7914-3044-8) State U NY Pr.
***Sociology & Islam.** Muhammad Muslehuddin. 245p. 1996. pap. 3.50 (0-614-21524-2, 1145) Kazi Pubns.
Sociology & Its Publics: The Forms & Fates of Disciplinary Organization. Ed. by Terence C. Halliday & Morris B. Janowitz. LC 91-38024. (Heritage of Sociology Ser.). (Illus.). 448p. 1992. pap. text ed. 16.95 (0-226-31380-8) U Ch Pr.
Sociology & Its Publics: The Forms & Fates of Disciplinary Organization. Ed. by Terence C. Halliday & Morris B. Janowitz. LC 91-38024. (Heritage of Sociology Ser.). (Illus.). 448p. 1992. lib. bdg. 34.50 (0-226-31379-4) U Ch Pr.
Sociology & Jurisprudence of Leon Petrazycki. Ed. by Jan Gorecki. LC 75-38551. (Office of International Programs & Studies Ser.). 156p. 1975. text ed. 24.95 (0-252-00525-2) U of Ill Pr.
Sociology & Liturgy: Re-Presentations of the Holy. Kieran Flanagan. LC 91-24687. 304p. 1991. text ed. 65.00 (0-312-06874-3) St Martin.
Sociology & Meaning. 4th ed. Joel M. Charon & John J. Macionis. 1993. 71.40 (0-13-101312-2) P-H.
***Sociology & Nature.** Raymond Murphy. LC 97-3286. (C). 1997. text ed. 55.00 (0-8133-2865-9) Westview.
***Sociology & Nature.** Raymond Murphy. LC 97-3286. (C). 1998. pap. text ed. 22.00 (0-8133-2866-7) Westview.
Sociology & Organization Theory: Positivism, Paradigms & Postmodernity. John Hassard. LC 92-28988. (Cambridge Studies in Management: No. 20). (Illus.). 176p. (C). 1993. text ed. 54.95 (0-521-35034-4) Cambridge U Pr.
Sociology & Organization Theory: Positivism, Paradigms & Postmodernity. John Hassard. (Studies in Management: No. 20). (Illus.). 192p. (C). 1995. pap. text ed. 17.95 (0-521-48458-8) Cambridge U Pr.
Sociology & Philosophy. Emile Durkheim. Tr. by D. F. Pocock. LC 54-2835. 1974. pap. 13.95 (0-02-908580-2, Free Press) Free Pr.
Sociology & Political Theory. Harry E. Barnes. LC 74-185842. 1972. reprint ed. lib. bdg. 250.00 (0-87700-036-0) Revisionist Pr.
Sociology & Politics: The Soviet Case. Vladimir Shlapentokh. Ed. by Ben Armfield. 154p. (Orig.). 1985. pap. text ed. 75.00 (1-55831-043-6) Delphic Associates.
Sociology & Professionalization of Economics, Vol. II: British & American Economic Essays. A. W. Coats. LC 93-16563. 512p. (C). (gr. 13). 1993. text ed. 85.00 (0-415-06716-2, B0771, Routledge NY) Routledge.
Sociology & School Knowledge. Geoff Whitty. 224p. (C). 1986. pap. text ed. 15.95 (0-416-36970-7, 9942) Routledge Chapman & Hall.
Sociology & Scientism: The American Quest for Objectivity, 1880-1940. Robert C. Bannister. LC 86-24985. x, 302p. (C). 1991. reprint ed. 39.95 (0-8078-1733-3); reprint ed. pap. 16.95 (0-8078-4327-X) U of NC Pr.
Sociology & Social Welfare. Michael Sullivan. 172p. 1987. pap. text ed. 16.95 (0-04-301214-0) Routledge Chapman & Hall.
Sociology & Society of Japan. Nozomu Kawamura. LC 94-11715. (Japanese Studies). 260p. 1995. 76.50 (0-7103-0468-4) Routledge Chapman & Hall.
Sociology & Teaching: A New Challenge for the Sociology of Education. Ed. by Peter Woods & Andrew Pollard. 256p. 1988. lib. bdg. 59.00 (0-7099-3697-4, Pub. by Croom Helm UK) Routledge Chapman & Hall.
***Sociology & the Changing World Reader.** 4th ed. Kornblu. (C). 1997. suppl. ed. write for info. (0-15-504005-7) HB Coll Pubs.
Sociology & the Field of Public Health. Edward A. Suchman. LC 63-21228. 182p. 1963. pap. 9.95 (0-87154-864-X) Russell Sage.
Sociology & the Jesus Movement. Richard A. Horsley. 186p. 1994. pap. text ed. 15.95 (0-8264-0645-9) Continuum.
Sociology & the New Systems Theory: Toward a Theoretical Synthesis. Kenneth D. Bailey. LC 93-22318. 372p. (C). 1994. text ed. 64.50 (0-7914-1743-3); pap. text ed. 21.95 (0-7914-1744-1) State U NY Pr.
Sociology & the Public Agenda. William J. Wilson. (American Sociological Association Presidential Ser.). (Illus.). 365p. (C). 1993. text ed. 52.00 (0-8039-5082-9); pap. text ed. 24.95 (0-8039-5083-7) Sage.
Sociology & The Race Problem: The Failure of a Perspective. James B. McKee. LC 92-42293. 384p. 1993. text ed. 39.95 (0-252-02022-7); pap. text ed. 16.95 (0-252-06328-7) U of Ill Pr.
Sociology & the Religion: A Collection of Readings. Andrew M. Greeley. LC 94-7907. (C). 1995. text ed. 31.95 (0-06-501881-8) Addson-Wesley Educ.
Sociology & the Twilight of Man: Homocentrism & Discourse in Sociological Theory. Charles C. Lemert. LC 78-17146. 276p. 1980. pap. 9.95 (0-8093-0975-0) S Ill U Pr.
Sociology & Visual Representation. Elizabeth Chaplin. LC 94-5590. (Illus.). 336p. (C). 1994. pap. 19.95 (0-415-07363-4, B4384) Routledge.
Sociology & You: An Applied Approach. 3rd ed. Michael P. Nofz. (Illus.). 454p. (C). 1995. pap. text ed. 28.95 (0-87563-574-1) Stipes.
Sociology at San Jacinto College. 2nd ed. Henslin. 1995. pap. text ed. 55.00 (0-205-19394-3) P-H.
Sociology Before Comte. Harry E. Barnes. 1973. 250.00 (0-87700-202-9) Revisionist Pr.
***Sociology Brief.** Ed. by Appelbaum. (C). 1997. student ed., pap. text ed. write for info. (0-673-98395-1) Addison-Wesley.
Sociology Brief. 2nd ed. Alex Thio. (C). 1993. Incl. reader. text ed. 26.00 (0-06-502163-0) Addson-Wesley Educ.
Sociology Brief. 2nd ed. Alex Thio. (C). 1993. Study guide. student ed. 8.25 (0-06-502006-5) Addson-Wesley Educ.
Sociology Brief. 2nd ed. Alex Thio. (C). 1994. Text only. 36.00 (0-06-501359-X) Addson-Wesley Educ.

S

An Asterisk (*) at the beginning of an entry indicates that the title is appearing in BIP for the first time.

*__Sociology Brief: Reader.__ Ed. by Appelbaum. (C). 1997. 10. 50 (*0-673-97777-3*) Addison-Wesley.

Sociology by the Discovery Method: Cutting Costs & Teaching More. Gordon D. Morgan. LC 83-62300. 125p. (Orig.). (C). 1985. pap. text ed. 5.95 (*0-88247-726-9*) R & E Pubs.

Sociology Comprehensive Exam, 5 Vols. McKay. (C). Date not set. text ed. write for info. (*0-395-71719-1*) HM.

Sociology, Environmentalism, Globalization: Reinventing the Globe. Steven Yearley. (New Horizons in Sociology: International Perspectives Ser.: Vol. 1). 192p. 1996. 69.95 (*0-8039-7516-3*); pap. 22.95 (*0-8039-7517-1*) Sage.

*__Sociology Explained.__ Barnard Andy & Burgess Terry. 496p. 1997. pap. text ed. 33.95 (*0-521-42671-5*) Cambridge U Pr.

Sociology, Exploring the Architecture of Everyday Life. David M. Newman. LC 94-38140. 1995. pap. 29.95 (*0-8039-9004-9*) Pine Forge.

Sociology, Exploring the Architecture of Everyday Life: Readings. Ed. by David M. Newman. LC 94-38139. 1995. pap. 18.95 (*0-8039-9054-5*) Pine Forge.

Sociology for Business: A Practical Approach. Martin Joseph. (Illus.). 230p. 1990. pap. text ed. 25.95 (*0-7456-0434-X*) Blackwell Pubs.

Sociology for Canadians: Images of Society. Alexander Himelfarb & C. James Richardson. 512p. 1982. 26.95 (*0-07-548440-4*) McGraw.

Sociology for Everyone. 2nd ed. Martin Joseph. (Illus.). 350p. (C). 1990. pap. text ed. 36.95 (*0-7456-0708-X*) Blackwell Pubs.

Sociology for Law Students. T. K. Oommen & C. N. Venugogal. (C). 1993. 32.50 (*81-7012-375-5*, Pub. by Eastern Book II) St Mut.

Sociology for Life: Expanding Circles of Social Participation Through Scholarship, Community Service & Teaching. George K. Floro. LC 86-5509. 154p. (Orig.). (C). 1986. pap. text ed. 22.00 (*0-8191-5328-1*); lib. bdg. 46.00 (*0-8191-5327-3*) U Pr of Amer.

Sociology for Nurses. 3rd ed. Christine M. Chapman. (Illus.). 210p. 1987. pap. text ed. 18.50 (*0-7020-1188-6*, Bailliere-Tindall) Saunders.

Sociology for Nursing & Health Care. Martin Joseph. 256p. (C). 1994. pap. text ed. 22.95 (*0-7456-0906-6*) Blackwell Pubs.

*__Sociology for Pastoral Care: An Introduction for Students & Pastors.__ George Furniss. 208p. 1996. pap. 21.95 (*0-687-06617-4*) Abingdon.

Sociology for People: A Caring Profession. Alfred M. Lee. LC 88-9672. 259p. 1988. text ed. 39.95 (*0-8156-2442-5*) Syracuse U Pr.

Sociology for People: Toward a Caring Profession. Alfred M. Lee. 228p. (C). 1990. pap. text ed. 14.95 (*0-8156-2510-3*) Syracuse U Pr.

Sociology for the South: Or the Failure of Free Society. George Fitzhugh. LC 67-622. 312p. reprint ed. 21.00 (*0-8337-1141-5*) Ayer.

Sociology for the 21st Century. Curry & Jiobu. 560p. (C). 1996. pap. text ed. 36.00 (*0-13-184045-2*) P-H.

Sociology for Whom. 2nd ed. Alfred M. Lee. LC 85-26134. 280p. 1986. pap. text ed. 16.95 (*0-8156-2355-0*) Syracuse U Pr.

Sociology Full Circle. 5th ed. William Feigelman. 512p. (C). 1989. pap. text ed. 21.50 (*0-03-023229-5*) HB Coll Pubs.

Sociology Full Circle: Contemporary Readings on Society. 6th ed. Ed. by William Feigelman. LC 93-169512. 570p. pap. 21.75 (*0-15-500501-4*) HarBrace.

*__Sociology Game.__ Anderson. 1985. pap. text ed. write for info. (*0-582-29641-2*, Pub. by Longman UK) Longman.

Sociology Game: An Introduction to Sociological Reasoning. R. J. Anderson et al. LC 84-19442. 175p. reprint ed. pap. 49.90 (*0-7837-1601-X*, 2041893) Bks Demand.

*__Sociology, Ideology & Utopia: Socio-Political Philosophy of East & West.__ D. P. Chattopadhyaya. LC 97-14142. (Philosophy of History & Culture Ser.: Vol. 18). 248p. 1997. text ed. 90.00 (*90-04-10807-6*) E J Brill.

Sociology in a Changing World. William Kornblum. (C). 1997. teacher ed., pap. text ed. 28.00 (*0-15-501001-8*); pap. text ed. 17.75 (*0-15-501934-1*) HB Coll Pubs.

Sociology in a Changing World. 2nd ed. William Kornblum & Carolyn D. Smith. (Illus.). 720p. (C). 1990. write for info. (*0-318-68177-3*); text ed. write for info. (*0-03-054999-X*, HM51.K66) HB Coll Pubs.

Sociology in a Changing World. 3rd ed. William Kornblum & Carolyn D. Smith. LC 92-75764. 773p. 1994. 48.25 (*0-15-500497-2*) HarBrace.

Sociology in a Changing World. 4th ed. William Kornblum. 772p. (C). 1996. text ed. 59.00 (*0-15-503290-9*) HB Coll Pubs.

*__Sociology in a Changing World.__ 4th ed. William Kornblum. 772p. (C). 1996. text ed. write for info. (*0-614-20959-5*); teacher ed., pap. text ed. 28.00 (*0-15-503291-7*); student ed., pap. text ed. 24.00 (*0-15-503292-5*) HB Coll Pubs.

Sociology in America. Ed. by Herbert J. Gans. (American Sociological Association Presidential Ser.). (Illus.). 336p. (C). 1990. text ed. 52.00 (*0-8039-3826-8*); pap. text ed. 25.95 (*0-8039-3827-6*) Sage.

*__Sociology in America.__ Ed. by Herbert J. Gans. LC 90-8218. (American Sociological Association Presidential Ser.). 333p. 1990. reprint ed. pap. 95.00 (*0-608-04308-7*, 2065087) Bks Demand.

Sociology in Asia. Man S. Das. 201p. (C). 1989. 75.00 (*81-85453-02-0*, Pub. by Print Hse II) St Mut.

Sociology in Australia & New Zealand: Theory & Methods. Cora V. Baldock & James Lally. LC 72-778. (Contributions in Sociology Ser.: No. 16). (Illus.). 328p. 1974. text ed. 69.50 (*0-8371-6126-6*, BSA/, Greenwood Pr) Greenwood.

Sociology in Everyday Life. 2nd ed. David A. Karp & William C. Yoels. LC 92-61957. 320p. (C). 1993. pap. text ed. 35.00 (*0-87581-369-0*) Peacock Pubs.

Sociology in Government: The Galpin-Taylor Years in the U. S. Department of Agriculture, 1919-1953. Olaf F. Larson et al. (Rural Studies). (C). 1998. text ed. 59.85 (*0-8133-8793-0*) Westview.

Sociology in India: Perspectives & Trends 1986, 3 vols., Set. G. C. Hallen. (C). 1986. 500.00 (*0-685-36460-7*) St Mut.

Sociology in Israel. Leonard Weller. LC 72-849. (Contributions in Sociology Ser.: No. 11). 315p. 1974. text ed. 59.95 (*0-8371-6417-6*, WES/, Greenwood Pr) Greenwood.

Sociology in Latin America. Ed. by Man S. Das. 434p. (C). 1994. 210.00 (*81-85880-35-2*, Pub. by Print Hse II) St Mut.

Sociology in Medicine. 3rd ed. Mervyn W. Susser et al. (Illus.). 470p. 1985. 59.95 (*0-19-503444-9*) OUP.

*__Sociology in Our Times.__ Kendall. (C). 1998. student ed., pap. 17.95 (*0-534-52487-7*) Wadsworth Pub.

Sociology in Our Times. Diana Kendall. (Sociology Ser.). 1996. student ed., pap. 17.95 (*0-534-21027-9*) Wadsworth Pub.

Sociology in Our Times. Diana Kendall. LC 95-35125. (C). 1996. text ed. 57.95 (*0-534-21024-4*) Wadsworth Pub.

*__Sociology in Our Times: The Essentials.__ Diana Kendall. LC 97-8300. (Sociology Ser.). (C). 1997. pap. text ed. 34.95 (*0-534-52479-6*) Wadsworth Pub.

*__Sociology in the Changing World.__ William Kornblum. (C). 1997. pap. text ed. 28.00 (*0-15-501002-6*) HB Coll Pubs.

*__Sociology in the 21st Century.__ Nelson. 1996. student ed., pap. text ed. 13.33 (*0-13-476730-6*) P-H.

*__Sociology Net: Sociology on the Internet.__ Joan Ferrante. LC 96-46313. (Sociology Ser.). (C). 1997. pap. text ed. 25.95 (*0-534-52756-6*) Wadsworth Pub.

Sociology of a New York City Block. Thomas J. Jones. (Columbia University. Studies in the Social Sciences: No. 55). reprint ed. 29.50 (*0-404-51055-8*) AMS Pr.

Sociology of Adult & Continuing Education. Peter Jarvis. LC 85-4087. 278p. 1984. pap. 18.95 (*0-415-03977-0*, Routledge NY) Routledge Chapman & Hall.

Sociology of Adult Education. R. Kenneth Jones. LC 84-13591. 159p. 1984. text ed. 63.95 (*0-566-00663-4*, Pub. by Avebury Pub UK) Ashgate Pub Co.

Sociology of Aging. Matcha. 372p. 1996. pap. 44.00 (*0-205-16468-4*) Allyn.

Sociology of Aging. 2nd ed. Diana K. Harris. 480p. (C). 1990. text ed. 61.50 (*0-06-042655-1*) Addison-Wesley Educ.

Sociology of Agriculture. Frederick H. Buttel et al. LC 89-17099. (Contributions in Sociology Ser.: No. 88). 273p. 1990. text ed. 55.00 (*0-313-26444-9*, BUT/, Greenwood Pr) Greenwood.

Sociology of America: A Guide to Information Sources. Ed. by Charles Mark & Paula F. Mark. LC 73-17560. (American Studies Information Guide: Vol. 1). 468p. 1980. 68.00 (*0-8103-1267-0*) Gale.

Sociology of American Indians: A Critical Bibliography. Russell Thornton & Mary K. Grasmick. LC 82-19235. (Bibliographical Series - The Newberry Center for the History of the American Indian). 124p. reprint ed. pap. 36.00 (*0-685-23900-4*, 2056722) Bks Demand.

Sociology of an Industrial Complex. C. A. Somashekharappa. (Sociological Publications in Honour of Dr. K. Ishwaran: No. 7). 178p. 1990. text ed. 27.50 (*81-85047-64-2*, Pub. by Reliance Pub Hse II) Apt Bks.

Sociology of Andrew M. Greeley. Andrew M. Greeley. LC 93-32119. (USF South Florida - St. Louis - Rochester Studies on Religion & the Social Order: Vol. 4). 630p. 1994. 99.95 (*1-55540-910-5*, 245004) Scholars Pr GA.

Sociology of Canadian Mennonites, Hutterites & Amish Vol. I: A Bibliography with Annotations. Ed. by Donovan E. Smucker. 1991. pap. text ed. 29.95 (*0-88920-051-3*) Wilfrid Laurier.

Sociology of Change & Reaction in Latin America. Dale D. Johnson. LC 73-7794. (Studies in Sociology). 1973. pap. text ed. 3.50 (*0-672-61238-0*, Bobbs) Macmillan.

*__Sociology of Childhood.__ LC 96-45368. (Sociology for a New Century Ser.). 1997. 25.95 (*0-8039-9011-1*) Sage.

Sociology of Childhood: Essential Readings. Ed. by Chris Jenks. (Modern Revivals in Sociology Ser.). 299p. 1992. 67.95 (*0-7512-0044-1*, Pub. by Gregg Revivals UK) Ashgate Pub Co.

Sociology of Chiropractic. Saul Rosenthal. LC 86-8532. (Studies in Health & Human Services: Vol. 6). 1986. lib. bdg. 89.95 (*0-88946-130-9*) E Mellen.

Sociology of Communism. Jules Monnerot. Tr. by Jane Degras & Richard Rees. LC 76-46469. 1977. reprint ed. text ed. 55.00 (*0-8371-9309-5*, MOSO, Greenwood Pr) Greenwood.

Sociology of Community: A Collection of Readings. Ed. by Colin Bell & Howard Newby. 424p. 1974. 35.00 (*0-7146-2970-7*, Pub. by F Cass Pubs UK) Intl Spec Bk.

*__Sociology of Consumption: An Introduction.__ Peter Corrigan. 224p. 1997. 69.95 (*0-7619-5010-9*) Sage.

*__Sociology of Consumption: An Introduction.__ Peter Corrigan. 224p. 1997. pap. 23.95 (*0-7619-5011-7*) Sage.

Sociology of Contemporary India. Danesh A. Chekki. 216p. 1978. 18.95 (*0-318-36865-X*) Asia Bk Corp.

Sociology of Contemporary India. Danesh A. Chekki. 1978. 12.50 (*0-8364-0245-6*) S Asia.

Sociology of Correctional Management. Ed. by David A. Jones & Catherine M. Jones. 502p. 1976. pap. text ed. 12.50 (*0-8422-0468-7*) Irvington.

Sociology of Crime. Stephen Hester & Peter Eglin. LC 91-41468. 224p. (C). 1992. pap. 18.95 (*0-415-07370-7*, A6923) Routledge.

Sociology of Crime & Deviance: Selected Issues. Ed. by Susan Caffrey & Gary Mundy. 516p. (C). 1996. pap. 45. 00 (*1-874529-52-3*) NYU Pr.

*__Sociology of Crime, Law & Deviance, Vol. 1.__ Ed. by Jeffrey T. Ulmer. 1998. 73.25 (*0-7623-0282-8*) Jai Pr.

Sociology of Culture. Raymond Williams. LC 95-6963. xviii, 248p. 1995. pap. text ed. 14.95 (*0-226-89921-7*) U Ch Pr.

Sociology of Culture: Emerging Theoretical Perspectives. Ed. by Diana Crane. (Illus.). 352p. 1994. pap. 25.95 (*1-55786-463-2*) Blackwell Pubs.

Sociology of Death: Theory, Culture, Practice. David Clark. (Sociological Review Monograph Ser.). 224p. 1993. pap. 22.95 (*0-631-19057-0*) Blackwell Pubs.

*__Sociology of Development.__ Harris. Date not set. pap. text ed. write for info. (*0-582-35563-X*, Pub. by Longman UK) Longman.

Sociology of Development, 2 vols. Set. Ed. by Bryan R. Roberts et al. LC 95-24272. (International Library of Critical Writings in Sociology: No. 2). 1232p. 1995. 400. 00 (*1-85278-914-X*) E Elgar.

*__Sociology of Developmental Behavior.__ 9th ed. Clinard. (C). 1995. write for info. (*0-15-501616-4*) HB Coll Pubs.

Sociology of Deviance: An Obituary. Colin Summer. 352p. (C). 1994. 39.50 (*0-8264-0693-9*) Continuum.

*__Sociology of Deviance: An Obituary.__ Colin Sumner. 352p. 1994. pap. 14.99 (*0-335-09780-4*, Open Univ Pr) Taylor & Francis.

*__Sociology of Deviance: An Obituary.__ Colin Sumner. 352p. 1994. 45.00 (*0-335-09781-2*, Open Univ Pr) Taylor & Francis.

Sociology of Deviant Behavior. 7th ed. Marshall B. Clinard & Robert F. Meier. 464p. (C). 1989. text ed. 44.00 (*0-03-023097-7*) HB Coll Pubs.

Sociology of Deviant Behavior. 8th ed. Marshall B. Clinard. (C). 1992. text ed. 44.00 (*0-03-052867-4*) HB Coll Pubs.

Sociology of Deviant Behavior. 8th ed. Marshall B. Clinard & Robert F. Meier. 450p. (C). 1992. text ed. write for info. (*0-318-69131-0*) HB Coll Pubs.

Sociology of Deviant Behavior. 9th ed. Clinard. (C). 1994. teacher ed., pap. text ed. 33.75 (*0-15-502142-7*) HB Coll Pubs.

Sociology of Early Palestinian Christianity. Gerd Theissen. Tr. by John Bowden from GER. LC 77-15248. 144p. 1978. pap. 13.00 (*0-8006-1330-9*, 1-1330, Fortress Pr) Augsburg Fortress.

Sociology of Economic Life. Ed. by Mark S. Granovetter & Richard Swedberg. 399p. (C). 1991. pap. text ed. 24.50 (*0-8133-1033-4*) Westview.

Sociology of Educating. 2nd ed. Meighan et al. 448p. 1986. pap. text ed. 24.95 (*0-304-31587-7*) Cassell.

Sociology of Education: A Guide to Information Sources. Ed. by Francesco Cordasco & David N. Alloway. LC 78-10310. (Education Information Guide Ser.: Vol. 2). 280p. 1979. 68.00 (*0-8103-1436-3*) Gale.

Sociology of Education: A Systematic Analysis. 3rd ed. Jeanne H. Ballantine. 448p. 1993. text ed. 55.00 (*0-13-819095-X*) P-H.

*__Sociology of Education: A Systematic Analysis.__ 4th ed. Jeanne H. Ballantine. LC 96-42921. 1997. 48.00 (*0-13-476037-9*) P-H.

Sociology of Education: Beyond Equality. Philip Wexler. LC 75-35994. (Studies in Sociology). 64p. 1976. pap. text ed. 3.50 (*0-672-61338-7*, Bobbs) Macmillan.

Sociology of Education: Theoretical & Empirical Investigations. Lynn M. Mulkey. 450p. (C). 1993. text ed. 46.75 (*0-03-032343-6*) HB Coll Pubs.

Sociology of Elites, 3 vols. Ed. by John Scott. (Schools of Thought in Sociology Ser.: Vol. 1). 1471p. 1990. Set; Vol. 1 528p., Vol. 2 528p., Vol. 3 352p. text ed. 450.00 (*1-85278-170-X*) E Elgar.

Sociology of Emotions: An Annotated Bibliography. Beverly Cuthbertson-Johnson et al. LC 93-27205. (Library of Sociology: Vol. 28). 243p. 1994. text ed. 42. 00 (*0-8240-2321-8*) Garland.

Sociology of Emotions Vol. 9: Original Essays & Research Papers. Ed. by David D. Franks & E. Doyle McCarthy. LC 89-1783. (Contemporary Studies in Sociology). 328p. 1989. 73.25 (*1-55938-052-7*) Jai Pr.

Sociology of Fertility: Determinants of Fertility Differentials in South India. Kuttan Mahadevan. 1978. 11.00 (*0-8364-0293-6*) S Asia.

Sociology of Film: Studies & Documents. J. P. Mayer. LC 73-169334. (Literature of Cinema, Ser. 2). (Illus.). 398p. 1976. reprint ed. 26.95 (*0-405-03901-8*) Ayer.

Sociology of Food & Eating. Stephen Mennell et al. LC 92-50680. (Special Issue of Current Sociology Ser.). (Illus.). 160p. (C). 1993. text ed. 55.00 (*0-8039-8839-7*); pap. text ed. 19.95 (*0-8039-8838-9*) Sage.

Sociology of Formal Organizations. Ed. by Abha Chaturvedi & Anil Chaturvedi. (Oxford in India Readings in Sociology & Social & Cultural Anthropology Ser.). 356p. 1995. 35.00 (*0-19-563609-0*) OUP.

Sociology of Freedom. Krishna Chaitanya. 1978. 18.50 (*0-8364-0008-9*) S Asia.

Sociology of G. S. Ghurye. S. K. Pramanich. (C). 1995. 34. 00 (*81-7033-261-3*, Pub. by Rawat II) S Asia.

Sociology of Gender. Ed. by Sarah Franklin. LC 96-5875. (Schools of Thought in Sociology Ser.: Vol. 12). 488p. (C). 1996. text ed. 160.00 (*1-85278-755-4*) E Elgar.

Sociology of Gender: A Text-Reader. Laura Kramer. LC 89-63913. 464p. 1990. text ed. 45.00 (*0-312-05209-X*) St Martin.

Sociology of Gender: A Text-Reader. Ed. by Laura Kramer. LC 89-639. 499p. (C). 1990. pap. text ed. 24.50 (*0-312-03063-0*) St Martin.

*__Sociology of Gender Roles Across Races, Classes & Cultures.__ Barbara Mitrano et al. 81p. 1993. ring bd. 49. 95 (*1-890662-08-9*) Prism Coll.

*__Sociology of Gender Roles Across Races, Classes & Cultures: Scripture-Based Version.__ 2nd rev. ed. Barbara Mitrano et al. 81p. 1993. ring bd. 49.95 (*1-890662-09-7*) Prism Coll.

Sociology of Georg Simmel. Georg Simmel. Tr. by Kurt H. Wolff. 1964. pap. 15.95 (*0-02-928920-3*, Free Press) Free Pr.

Sociology of Good Works: Research in Catholic America. Joseph H. Fichter. LC 93-19779. 200p. (Orig.). 1993. pap. 13.95 (*0-8294-0751-0*) Loyola Pr.

Sociology of Health. 2nd ed. Andrew C. Twaddle & Richard M. Hessler. 427p. (C). 1987. text ed. 76.00 (*0-02-421870-7*, Macmillan Coll) P-H.

Sociology of Health & Healing. Margaret Stacey. 320p. (C). 1988. pap. text ed. 29.95 (*0-415-07872-5*, Routledge NY) Routledge.

Sociology of Health & Health Care: An Introduction for Nurses. Ed. by Steve Taylor & David Field. LC 93-7900. 1993. pap. 24.95 (*0-632-03402-5*) Blackwell Sci.

*__Sociology of Health & Health Care: An Introduction for Nurses.__ 2nd ed. Steve Taylor & David Field. LC 97-22077. 1997. write for info. (*0-632-04147-1*) Blackwell Sci.

Sociology of Health & Illness. Kenneth Jones. (Illus.). 494p. (C). 1991. pap. text ed. 57.50 (*0-7021-2441-9*, Pub. by Juta & Co SA) Intl Spec Bk.

Sociology of Health & Illness. Sarah Nettleton. 280p. (C). 1995. 60.95 (*0-7456-0893-0*); pap. 25.95 (*0-7456-0894-9*) Blackwell Pubs.

Sociology of Health & Illness. 2nd ed. Ed. by Gillian Lupton & Jake Najman. 420p. 1995. 69.95 (*0-7329-2800-1*); pap. 34.95 (*0-7329-2799-4*) Paul & Co Pubs.

Sociology of Health, Healing & Illness. 2nd ed. Weiss & Lynne E. Lonnquist. 1996. text ed. 49.00 (*0-13-476433-1*) P-H.

Sociology of Health, Illness, & Health Care: A Critical Approach. Rose Weitz. LC 95-303. 476p. (C). 1996. pap. 49.95 (*0-534-20742-1*) Wadsworth Pub.

Sociology of Health Promotion: Critical Analyses of Consumption, Lifestyle & Risk. Ed. by Robin Bunton et al. LC 94-47490. 224p. (C). (gr. 13). 1995. text ed. 62.95 (*0-415-11646-5*, C0099) Routledge.

Sociology of Health Promotion: Critical Analyses of Consumption, Lifestyle & Risk. Ed. by Robin Bunton et al. 224p. (C). 1995. pap. 19.95 (*0-415-11647-3*, C0100) Routledge.

Sociology of HIV Transmission. Michael Bloor. 176p. 1995. 65.00 (*0-8039-8749-8*); pap. 21.50 (*0-8039-8750-1*) Sage.

Sociology of Homosexuality. Ed. by Wayne R. Dynes & Stephen Donaldson. LC 92-13735. (Studies in Homosexuality: Vol. 13). (Illus.). 432p. 1992. text ed. 90.00 (*0-8153-0768-3*) Garland.

Sociology of Human Fertility: An Annotated Bibliography. Ronald Freedman. LC 73-12272. (Population & Demography Ser.). 283p. 1975. 26.00 (*0-8290-2302-X*) Irvington.

Sociology of Indian Culture. D. P. Mukharji. 239p. 1979. 18.95 (*0-318-36974-5*) Asia Bk Corp.

Sociology of Indian Intellectuals. U. B. Bhoite. 342p. (C). 1987. 36.00 (*81-7033-035-1*, Pub. by Rawat II) S Asia.

Sociology of Indian Literature. Sulochana R. Raghava. (C). 1987. lib. bdg. 26.00 (*81-7033-011-4*, Pub. by Rawat II) S Asia.

Sociology of Indian Sociology. Ramkrishna Mukherjee. 1980. write for info. (*0-8364-1453-5*, Pub. by Allied II) S Asia.

Sociology of Industrial Injury. Theo Nichols. LC 96-20534. 1997. write for info. (*0-7201-2255-4*, Mansell Pub) Cassell.

Sociology of Industry. 4th ed. S. R. Parker & R. K. Brown. 208p. (C). 1988. pap. text ed. 16.95 (*0-04-301129-2*) Routledge Chapman & Hall.

Sociology of International Relations. Marcel Merle. Tr. by Dorothy Parkin from FRE. LC 86-26360. 429p. 1987. 19.95 (*0-907582-44-3*); pap. 9.95 (*0-907582-45-1*) Berg Pubs.

Sociology of Invention. S. C. Gilfillan. 1970. pap. 5.95 (*0-262-57020-3*) MIT Pr.

*__Sociology of Johannine Christianity.__ Anthony J. Blasi. LC 96-41014. (Texts & Studies in Religion: Vol. 69). 456p. 1997. text ed. 109.95 (*0-7734-8753-0*) E Mellen.

Sociology of Juvenile Delinquency. 2nd ed. Ed. by Ronald J. Berger. LC 95-9129. 1995. 28.95 (*0-8304-1416-9*) Nelson-Hall.

Sociology of Knowledge. Jacques P. Maquet. Tr. by John F. Locke from FRE. LC 70-168963. 318p. 1973. reprint ed. text ed. 59.75 (*0-8371-6236-X*, MASK, Greenwood Pr) Greenwood.

Sociology of Knowledge: Theoretical Problems. M. Tavakol. 276p. 1990. text ed. 35.00 (*81-207-1127-0*, Pub. by Sterling Pubs II) Apt Bks.

Sociology of Knowledge: Toward a Deeper Understanding of the History of Ideas. Werner Stark. 365p. (C). 1991. pap. text ed. 24.95 (*1-56000-557-2*) Transaction Pubs.

Sociology of Language. Thomas Luckmann. LC 74-19085. (Studies in Sociology). 79p. 1975. pap. 3.00 (*0-672-61262-3*, Bobbs) Macmillan.

Sociology of Law. A. Javier Trevino. 1995. pap. text ed. 37. 00 (*0-312-07836-6*) St Martin.

Sociology of Law. 2nd ed. Roger Cotterrell. 398p. 1992. pap. text ed. 25.00 (*0-406-51770-3*, UK) MICHIE.

Sociology of Law: A Bibliography of Theoretical Literature. A. Javier Trevino. 105p. (C). 1994. 19.95 (*0-87047-100-7*) Schenkman Bks Inc.

Sociology of Legal Profession, Law & Legal Systems: The Indian Setting. J. S. Gandhi. (C). 1990. 65.00 (*0-89771-298-6*) St Mut.

Sociology of Leisure. John R. Kelly & Geoffrey Godbey. LC 92-85018. 550p. (C). 1992. text ed. 33.95 (*0-910251-56-8*) Venture Pub PA.

Sociology of Leisure. Ed. by Theodore B. Johannis & C. Neil Bull. LC 73-87853. (Sage Contemporary Social Science Issues Ser.: No. 1). 136p. reprint ed. pap. 38.80 (*0-317-29675-2*, 2021916) Bks Demand.

S

An Asterisk (*) at the beginning of an entry indicates that the title is appearing in BIP for the first time.

***Sociology of Leisure: A Reader.** Critcher et al. (Illus.). 304p. (Orig.). 1994. pap. text ed. 27.95 (*0-419-19420-7*, E & FN Spon) Routledge Chapman & Hall.

Sociology of Literature. Ed. by Peter Davison et al. LC 77-90614. (Literary Taste, Culture & Mass Communication Ser.: Vol. 6). 370p. 1978. lib. bdg. 105.00 (*0-85964-041-8*) Chadwyck-Healey.

Sociology of Literature. Robert Escarpit. Tr. by E. Pick. 104p. 1971. 32.50 (*0-7146-2729-1*, Pub. by F Cass Pubs UK) Intl Spec Bk.

Sociology of Literature. John Hall. LC 79-40138. 170p. reprint ed. pap. 48.50 (*0-317-28355-3*, 2022534) Bks Demand.

Sociology of Literature: A Study of Urdu Novels. Syed Fazle Rab. (C). 1992. text ed. 22.00 (*81-7169-191-9*, Commonwealth) S Asia.

Sociology of Malayan Peoples: Being Three Essays on Kinship, Marriage & Inheritance in Indonesia. George A. Wilken. Tr. by G. Hunt. LC 77-87034. reprint ed. 39.50 (*0-404-16879-5*) AMS Pr.

Sociology of Marriage & the Family: Gender, Love & Property. 4th ed. Randall Collins & Scott Coltrane. LC 94-15709. (Series in Sociology). 500p. 1995. text ed. 45.95 (*0-8304-1392-8*) Nelson-Hall.

Sociology of Marriage & the Family: Gender, Love & Property. 4th ed. Mark Eckel. LC 94-15709. (Series in Sociology). 500p. 1995. teacher ed. write for info. (*0-8304-1412-6*) Nelson-Hall.

Sociology of Marriage & the Family: Gender, Love & Property, Test Bank. 4th ed. Melinda Messineo. LC 94-15709. (Series in Sociology). 1995. write for info. (*0-8304-1418-5*) Nelson-Hall.

Sociology of Marx. Henri Lefebvre. LC 82-9539. (Morningside Bk.). 218p. 1982. text ed. 52.50 (*0-231-05580-3*); pap. text ed. 16.00 (*0-231-05581-1*) Col U Pr.

Sociology of Medicine. Ed. by William C. Cockerham. LC 95-24273. (International Library of Critical Writings in Sociology: No. 4). 672p. 1995. 210.00 (*1-85898-021-6*) E Elgar.

Sociology of Medicine. Renee C. Fox. 448p. (C). 1988. pap. text ed. 40.00 (*0-13-820507-8*) P-H.

***Sociology of Medicine: As Applied to Medicine.** 3rd ed. Ed. by Graham Scambler. (Illus.). 318p. 1991. pap. write for info. (*0-7020-1559-8*, Pub. by W B Saunders UK) Saunders.

Sociology of Mennonites, Hutterites & Amish Vol. II: A Bibliography with Annotations, 1977-1990. Ed. by Donovan E. Smucker. 232p. (C). 1991. text ed. 39.95 (*0-88920-999-5*) Wilfrid Laurier.

Sociology of Mental Disorder. 2nd ed. William C. Cockerham. (Sociology Ser.). 416p. (C). 1989. Casebound. boxed write for info. (*0-13-820499-3*) P-H.

Sociology of Mental Disorder. 4th ed. William C. Cockerham. LC 95-12725. 372p. (C). 1995. text ed. 50.00 (*0-13-125469-3*) P-H.

Sociology of Mental Disorders. 2nd ed. William E. Eaton. LC 85-19134. 250p. 1985. text ed. 49.95 (*0-275-90011-8*, C0011, Praeger Pubs); pap. text ed. 22.95 (*0-275-91458-5*, B1458, Praeger Pubs) Greenwood.

Sociology of Mental Health. Giri R. Gupta. LC 92-23282. 399p. 1992. text ed. 64.00 (*0-205-13960-4*) Allyn.

Sociology of Mental Health & Illness. Peter K. Manning & Martine Zucker. LC 76-16067. (Studies in Sociology). (C). 1976. pap. text ed. write for info. (*0-672-61265-8*, Bobbs) Macmillan.

Sociology of Mental Health & Illness. David Pilgrim & Anne Rogers. LC 93-18726. 1993. 79.00 (*0-335-19014-6*, Open Univ Pr); pap. 27.50 (*0-335-19013-8*, Open Univ Pr) Taylor & Francis.

Sociology of Mental Illness. Howard B. Kaplan. 1972. pap. 17.95 (*0-8084-0356-7*) NCUP.

Sociology of Mental Illness. 3rd ed. Bernard J. Gallagher, III & Corinne J. Rita. LC 94-35083. 496p. 1995. text ed. 54.00 (*0-13-014408-8*) P-H.

Sociology of Mental Illness: Basic Studies, 1981. Grusky & Pollner. 544p. (C). 1981. pap. text ed. 40.00 (*0-03-053211-6*) HB Coll Pubs.

Sociology of Migration. Ed. by Robin Cohen. LC 96-12607. (International Library of Studies on Migration: Vol. 3). 576p. (C). 1996. text ed. 170.00 (*1-85898-000-3*) E Elgar.

Sociology of Minority Groups Courses: Syllabi & Related Materials. Wilhelmina Perry. 145p. 1981. 9.50 (*0-317-36345-X*) Am Sociological.

Sociology of Modernity: Liberty & Discipline. Peter Wagner. LC 93-7362. 288p. (C). 1993. pap. 17.95 (*0-415-08186-6*) Routledge.

Sociology of Modernization: Studies on Its Historical & Theoretical Aspects with Special Regard to the Latin America Case. Gino Germani. LC 79-64855. 272p. (C). 1981. text ed. 39.95 (*0-87855-268-5*) Transaction Pubs.

Sociology of Modernization & Development. David Harrison. 224p. 1988. pap. text ed. 18.95 (*0-04-301221-3*) Routledge Chapman & Hall.

Sociology of Money: Economics, Reason & Contemporary Society. Nigel Dodd. LC 93-34177. 212p. 1994. 27.50 (*0-8264-0637-8*) Continuum.

Sociology of Music. Alphons Silbermann. Tr. by Corbet Stewart from GER. LC 76-58565. 216p. 1977. reprint ed. text ed. 55.00 (*0-8371-9455-5*, SISM, Greenwood Pr) Greenwood.

Sociology of North American Sport. 5th ed. D. Stanley Eitzen & George H. Sage. 432p. (C). 1992. per. write for info. (*0-697-12625-0*) Brown & Benchmark.

Sociology of North American Sport. 6th ed. D. Stanley Eitzen & George H. Sage. 432p. (C). 1996. per. write for info. (*0-697-25885-8*) Brown & Benchmark.

Sociology of Old Age. Graham Fennell et al. 224p. 1988. pap. 29.00 (*0-335-15860-9*, Open Univ Pr) Taylor & Francis.

Sociology of Opera: Organization, Production & Performance. Roseanne Martorella. 288p. 1982. text ed. 59.95 (*0-275-90857-7*, C0857, Praeger Pubs) Greenwood.

Sociology of Organizations: Basic Studies. 2nd ed. Ed. by Oscar Grusky & George A. Miller. LC 80-1060. (Illus.). 1981. pap. 19.95 (*0-02-912930-3*, Free Press) Free Pr.

Sociology of Physical Disability & Rehabilitation. Ed. by Gary L. Albrecht. LC 75-33544. (Contemporary Community Health Ser.). (Illus.). 319p. 1976. reprint ed. pap. 91.00 (*0-608-00895-8*, 2061689) Bks Demand.

Sociology of Post-Colonial Societies: Economic Disparity, Cultural Diversity & Development. J. E. Goldthorpe. 350p. (C). 1996. text ed. 54.95 (*0-521-57097-2*); pap. text ed. 17.95 (*0-521-57800-0*) Cambridge U Pr.

Sociology of Postmodernism. Scott Lash. LC 89-24184. (International Library of Sociology). 256p. (C). 1990. pap. 18.95 (*0-415-04785-4*, A4163) Routledge.

Sociology of Pottery in Ancient Palestine: The Ceramic Industry & the Diffusion of Ceramic Style in the Bronze & Iron Age. Bryant G. Wood. (Journal for the Study of the Old Testament Supplement Ser.: Vol. 103). 148p. 45.00 (*1-85075-269-9*, Pub. by Sheffield Acad UK) CUP Services.

Sociology of Poverty in the United States: An Annotated Bibliography, No. 3. H. Paul Chalfant. LC 84-25191. (Bibliographies & Indexes in Sociology Ser.). xxii, 187p. 1985. text ed. 59.95 (*0-313-23929-0*, CHS/, Greenwood Pr) Greenwood.

Sociology of Public Issues. Steven L. Nock & Paul W. Kingston. 256p. (C). 1990. pap. 26.95 (*0-534-12096-2*) Wadsworth Pub.

Sociology of Punishment & Correction. Norman B. Johnston et al. LC 79-101970. 859p. 1970. reprint ed. pap. 180.00 (*0-317-07760-0*, 2055149) Bks Demand.

Sociology of Race Relations: Reflection & Reform. Thomas F. Pettigrew. LC 79-54666. (Illus.). 1980. pap. 19.95 (*0-02-925110-9*, Free Press) Free Pr.

Sociology of Religion. Thomas F. O'Dea & Janet O. Aviad. 144p. (C). 1983. text ed. 26.00 (*0-13-821066-7*); pap. text ed. write for info. (*0-13-821058-6*) P-H.

Sociology of Religion. Max Weber. Tr. by Ephraim Fischoff from GER. LC 92-38884. 384p. 1993. pap. 17.00 (*0-8070-4205-6*) Beacon Pr.

Sociology of Religion. Max Weber. 1993. 22.50 (*0-8446-6693-9*) Peter Smith.

Sociology of Religion. Georg Simmel. Ed. by Lewis A. Coser & Walter W. Powell. Tr. by Curt Rosenthal from GER. LC 79-7021. (Perennial Works in Sociology). 1980. reprint ed. lib. bdg. 18.95 (*0-405-12120-2*) Ayer.

Sociology of Religion, 2 vols., Set. Ed. by Steve Bruce. (International Library of Critical Writings in Sociology: No. 3). 1240p. 1995. 385.00 (*1-85278-899-2*) E Elgar.

Sociology of Religion: A Bibliographical Survey. Compiled by Roger Homan. LC 86-18471. (Bibliographies & Indexes in Religious Studies: No. 9). 309p. 1986. text ed. 75.00 (*0-313-24710-2*, HOS/, Greenwood Pr) Greenwood.

Sociology of Religion: An Organizational Bibliography. Anthony J. Blasi & Michael W. Cuneo. LC 90-40684. 490p. 1990. text ed. 76.00 (*0-8240-2584-9*, SS612) Garland.

Sociology of Religion: Classical & Contemporary Approaches. 2nd ed. Barbara Hargrove. 386p. (C). 1989. pap. text ed. write for info. (*0-88295-218-8*) Harlan Davidson.

Sociology of Religion: Theoretical & Comparative Perspectives. Malcolm B. Hamilton. LC 94-9579. 272p. (C). 1994. pap. 17.95 (*0-415-10659-1*, B4385) Routledge.

***Sociology of Religious Movements.** William Sims Bainbridge. LC 96-37328. 472p. (C). 1996. pap. 24.95 (*0-415-91202-4*, Routledge NY); text ed. 74.95 (*0-415-91201-6*, Routledge NY) Routledge.

Sociology of Rural Communities, 2 vols., Set. Ed. by Graham Crow. LC 95-51132. (International Library of Critical Writings in Economics Ser.: Vol. 7). 1104p. 1996. 330.00 (*1-85898-240-5*) E Elgar.

Sociology of Sacred Texts. Ed. by Jon Davies & Isabel Wollaston. 193p. 37.50 (*1-85075-404-7*, Pub. by Sheffield Acad UK) CUP Services.

Sociology of School & Education. Ivan Reid. 320p. 1986. pap. 23.00 (*1-85396-183-3*, Pub. by P Chapman Pub UK) Taylor & Francis.

***Sociology of Science.** Mulkey & Catsambis. 1997. pap. text ed. 32.00 (*0-205-17435-3*) P-H.

Sociology of Science. Ed. by Jerry Gaston. LC 78-70090. (Jossey-Bass Social & Behavioral Science Ser.). 239p. reprint ed. pap. 68.20 (*0-685-16279-6*, 2027752) Bks Demand.

Sociology of Science: A Sociological Pilgrimage. Michael Mulkay. LC 90-5275. (Science, Technology, & Society Ser.). (Illus.). 248p. 1991. 39.95 (*0-253-33933-2*) Ind U Pr.

Sociology of Science: An Episodic Memoir. Robert K. Merton. LC 79-9962. (Arcturus Books Paperbacks). 164p. 1979. pap. 7.95 (*0-8093-0925-4*) S Ill U Pr.

Sociology of Science: Theoretical & Empirical Investigations. Robert K. Merton. Ed. by Norman W. Storer. LC 72-97623. 640p. 1979. pap. text ed. 22.00 (*0-226-52092-7*, P846) U Ch Pr.

Sociology of Sciences: An Annotated Bibliography on Invisible Colleges, 1972-1981. Daryl E. Chubin. LC 82-48773. 216p. 1983. text ed. 49.00 (*0-8240-9223-6*) Garland.

Sociology of Sex & Sexuality. Gail Hawkes. LC 95-26513. (Sociology & Social Change Ser.). 160p. (C). 1996. 79.00 (*0-335-19317-X*, Open Univ Pr); pap. 21.00 (*0-335-19316-1*, Open Univ Pr) Taylor & Francis.

Sociology of Shakespeare. George V. Zito. LC 90-15715. (American University Studies: Anthropology & Science: Ser. XI, Vol. 56). 233p. (C). 1991. text ed. 39.95 (*0-8204-1523-5*) P Lang Pubng.

Sociology of Shoplifting: Boosters & Snitches Today. Lloyd W. Klemke. LC 91-45609. (Criminology & Crime Control Policy Ser.). 184p. 1992. text ed. 45.00 (*0-275-94108-6*, C4108, Praeger Pubs) Greenwood.

Sociology of Slavery. Orlando Patterson. LC 70-84198. 310p. 1975. 35.00 (*0-8386-7469-0*) Fairleigh Dickinson.

Sociology of Social Change. Piotr Sztompka. LC 93-9824. (Illus.). 368p. 1994. pap. 25.95 (*0-631-18206-3*) Blackwell Pubs.

***Sociology of Social Problems.** 12th ed. Paul B. Horton et al. LC 96-39927. (Illus.). 496p. (C). 1997. pap. text ed. 49.33 (*0-13-657438-6*) P-H.

Sociology of Social Security. Ed. by Michael Adler et al. 1991. text ed. 50.00 (*0-7486-0258-5*, Pub. by Edinburgh U Pr UK) Col U Pr.

Sociology of Social Security. Ed. by Michael Adler et al. (Edinburgh Education & Society Ser.). 320p. 1992. pap. text ed. 30.00 (*0-7486-0325-5*, Pub. by Edinburgh U Pr UK) Col U Pr.

Sociology of Social Work. Ed. by Martin Davies. LC 94-5597. 272p. (C). 1994. pap. 17.95 (*0-415-11521-3*, B4693) Routledge.

Sociology of Sport. Howard L. Nixon, II & James H. Frey. LC 95-15353. 363p. 1996. pap. 42.95 (*0-534-24762-8*) Wadsworth Pub.

Sociology of Sport. John C. Phillips. LC 92-22181. 1992. pap. text ed. 46.00 (*0-205-13983-3*) Allyn.

Sociology of Sport: An Introduction. Conrad C. Vogler & Stephen Schwartz. LC 92-15512. 224p. (C). 1992. pap. text ed. 40.00 (*0-13-818451-8*) P-H.

Sociology of Suicide. Steve D. Taylor. LC 88-535. (Sociology in Focus Ser.). 102p. reprint ed. pap. 29.10 (*0-7837-5181-8*, 2044911) Bks Demand.

Sociology of Suicide: A Reader. Ed. by Anthony Giddens. 424p. 1971. 45.00 (*0-7146-2591-4*, Pub. by F Cass Pubs UK) Intl Spec Bk.

Sociology of Talcott Parsons. Francois Bourricaud. Tr. by Arthur Goldhammer. LC 81-1348. xvi, 340p. 1984. pap. text ed. 14.95 (*0-226-06756-4*) U Ch Pr.

Sociology of Taste. Jukka Gronow. LC 96-25692. 216p. (C). 1997. pap. write for info. (*0-415-13295-9*); text ed. write for info. (*0-415-13294-0*) Routledge.

Sociology of Teaching. Willard Waller. LC 32-20285. 484p. reprint ed. pap. 138.00 (*0-8357-4708-5*, 2017003) Bks Demand.

Sociology of the Absurd. 2nd ed. Stanford M. Lyman & Marvin B. Scott. LC 89-80378. 256p. 1989. text ed. 36.95 (*0-930390-86-5*); pap. text ed. 22.95 (*0-930390-85-7*) Gen Hall.

Sociology of the Black Experience. Daniel C. Thompson. LC 73-20974. (Contributions in Sociology Ser.: No. 14). 261p. 1974. text ed. 47.95 (*0-8371-7336-1*, TBE/, Greenwood Pr) Greenwood.

Sociology of the Caring Professions. Pamela Abbott & Claire Wallace. 200p. 1990. 55.00 (*1-85000-819-1*, Falmer Pr); pap. 29.00 (*1-85000-824-8*, Falmer Pr) Taylor & Francis.

Sociology of the Environment, 3 vols., Set. Ed. by Michael Redclift & Graham Woodgate. (International Library of Critical Writings in Sociology Ser.: No. 1). 2004p. 1995. 600.00 (*1-85278-902-6*) E Elgar.

Sociology of the Family. 2nd ed. Steven L. Nock. 432p. (C). 1991. text ed. 60.00 (*0-13-808593-5*, 610803) P-H.

Sociology of the Future. Ed. by Wendell Bell & James Mau. LC 72-158565. 464p. 1971. 55.00 (*0-87154-106-8*) Russell Sage.

Sociology of the Global System. 2nd ed. Sklair. 1996. pap. text ed. 19.95 (*0-13-432964-3*) P-H.

Sociology of the Global System. 2nd ed. Leslie Sklair. LC 95-17452. 352p. 1995. text ed. 45.00 (*0-8018-5210-2*); pap. text ed. 17.95 (*0-8018-5211-0*) Johns Hopkins.

Sociology of the Meal. Roy C. Wood. 139p. 1996. pap. 25.00 (*0-7486-0596-7*, Pub. by Edinburgh U Pr UK) Col U Pr.

Sociology of the Offbeat: Essays in the Science of Human Social Behavior. Ed. by Robert M. Khoury. LC 81-40726. (Illus.). 418p. (Orig.). (C). 1982. pap. text ed. 31.00 (*0-8191-2458-3*) U Pr of Amer.

Sociology of the Palestinians. Elia Zureik & Khalil Nakhleh. LC 79-12706. 1980. text ed. 35.00 (*0-312-74073-5*) St Martin.

Sociology of the Professions. Keith M. Macdonald. 224p. 1995. 69.95 (*0-8039-8633-5*) Sage.

Sociology of the Professions. Keith M. Macdonald. 224p. 1995. pap. 23.95 (*0-8039-8634-3*) Sage.

Sociology of the Renaissance. Alfred W. Von Martin. LC 83-45658. reprint ed. 29.50 (*0-404-19808-2*) AMS Pr.

Sociology of the School. Myles W. Rodehaver et al. LC 80-26021. x, 262p. (C). 1981. reprint ed. text ed. 59.75 (*0-313-22897-3*, ROSSC, Greenwood Pr) Greenwood.

Sociology of the Sciences, 2 vols., Set. Ed. by Helga Nowotny & Klaus Taschwer. LC 95-48335. (International Library of Critical Writings in Economics Ser.: Vol. 8). 1152p. 1996. 350.00 (*1-85278-911-5*) E Elgar.

Sociology of the State. Bertrand Badie & Pierre Birnbaum. Tr. by Arthur Goldhammer from FRE. LC 82-20249. 182p. (C). 1983. pap. text ed. 16.50 (*0-226-03549-2*) U Ch Pr.

Sociology of the Third World: Disparity & Development. 2nd ed. J. E. Goldthorpe. LC 83-13506. 320p. 1984. pap. text ed. 21.95 (*0-521-27293-9*) Cambridge U Pr.

***Sociology of Tourism: Theoretical & Empirical Investigations.** Ed. by Yiorgis Apostolopoulos & Stella Leivadi. 376p. 1996. text ed. 75.00 (*0-415-13508-7*) Routledge.

Sociology of Town Planning: A Bibliography, Nos. 1039-1040. James M. Simmie et al. 1976. 8.50 (*0-686-20396-8*, Sage Prdcls Pr) Sage.

Sociology of Tristan da Cunha: Results of the Norwegian Scientific Expedition to Tristan da Cunha, 1937-1938. Peter A. Munch. LC 77-87549. reprint ed. 30.00 (*0-404-16611-3*) AMS Pr.

Sociology of U. S. Agriculture: An Ecological Perspective. Don E. Albrecht & Steve H. Murdock. LC 89-77423. (Illus.). 257p. 1990. reprint ed. pap. 73.30 (*0-608-00040-X*, 2060806) Bks Demand.

Sociology of Urban Communities, 3 vols., Set. Ed. by Michael Harloe. LC 95-49262. (International Library of Critical Writings in Economics Ser.: Vol. 6). 1520p. (C). 1996. text ed. 450.00 (*1-85278-990-5*) E Elgar.

Sociology of Urban Life. Harry Gold. (Illus.). 416p. (C). 1982. text ed. write for info. (*0-13-821371-2*) P-H.

Sociology of Urban Women's Image in African Literature. Kenneth L. Little. 174p. 1980. 42.00 (*0-8476-6290-X*) Rowman.

***Sociology of Women.** 2nd ed. Ollenburger & Moore. LC 97-24490. 1998. pap. 28.00 (*0-13-671637-7*) P-H.

Sociology of Women: An Introduction. Sara Delamont. 256p. (Orig.). 1980. text ed. 29.95 (*0-04-301119-5*) Routledge Chapman & Hall.

Sociology of Women: The Intersection of Patriarchy, Capitalism & Colonization. Jane Ollenburger & Helan Moore. 240p. (C). 1991. pap. text ed. 37.33 (*0-13-818766-5*, 610702) P-H.

Sociology of Work. Theodore Caplow. LC 77-18112. (Illus.). 330p. 1978. reprint ed. text ed. 85.00 (*0-313-20111-0*, CASOW, Greenwood Pr) Greenwood.

Sociology of Work: A Critical Annotated Bibliography. Parvin Ghorayshi. LC 90-2840. (Library of Sociology). 240p. 1990. text ed. 39.00 (*0-8240-3438-4*, SS591) Garland.

Sociology of Work: An Introduction. Keith Grint. 320p. 1991. pap. 24.95 (*0-7456-0607-5*); text ed. 70.95 (*0-7456-0606-7*) Blackwell Pubs.

Sociology of Work: Concepts & Cases. Carol J. Auster. LC 95-20396. 1996. pap. 35.95 (*0-8039-9033-2*) Pine Forge.

Sociology of Work: Perspectives, Analyses, & Issues. Richard H. Hall. 488p. 1993. pap. 37.95 (*0-8039-9003-0*) Pine Forge.

Sociology of Yiddish: International Journal of the Sociology of Language, No. 24. Ed. by Joshua A. Fishman. 1980. pap. text ed. 60.00 (*90-279-3058-9*) Mouton.

Sociology on the Menu: An Invitation to the Study of Food & Society. Alan Beardsworth & Teresa Keil. LC 96-18305. 288p. (C). 1997. pap. write for info. (*0-415-11425-X*); text ed. write for info. (*0-415-11424-1*) Routledge.

Sociology: or The Reconstruction of Society, Government & Property. Lewis Masquerier. 1973. 59.95 (*0-8490-1073-X*) Gordon Pr.

Sociology, Phenomenology & Marxian Analysis: A Critical Discussion of the Theory & Practice of a Science of Society. Barry Smart. (International Library of Sociology). 1976. pap. 14.95 (*0-7100-8373-4*, RKP) Routledge.

Sociology, Race & Ethnicity: A Critique of American Ideological Intrusions Upon Sociological Theory. Harry H. Bash. (Monographs in Sociology). xii, 292p. 1979. text ed. 91.00 (*0-677-05390-8*) Gordon & Breach.

***Sociology Student Writer's Manual.** Johnson & Richard P. Rettig. (C). 1997. pap. text ed. 21.33 (*0-13-462961-2*) P-H.

***Sociology Study of Human Relations.** Thomas. 1995. teacher ed., pap. text ed. 37.50 (*0-03-098216-2*) HR&W Schl Div.

Sociology Text. 2nd ed. John J. Macionis. 704p. (C). 1989. Incl. audio cassette. write for info. incl. audio (*0-13-823832-4*) P-H.

***Sociology the Central Questions.** Kornblum. (C). 1997. pap. text ed. 32.25 (*0-15-500836-6*) HB Coll Pubs.

Sociology, the Core. 3rd ed. James W. Vander Zanden. LC 92-11222. 1993. pap. text ed. write for info. (*0-07-066996-1*) McGraw.

Sociology Through Humor. Joseph E. Faulkner. LC 86-26666. 301p. (Orig.). (C). 1987. pap. text ed. 35.50 (*0-314-28491-5*) West Pub.

Sociology Through the Eyes of Faith. Anthony Campolo & David A. Fraser. LC 91-55337. 336p. 1992. pap. 11.00 (*0-06-061315-7*) Harper SF.

Sociology Tomorrow: An Evaluation of Sociological Theories in Terms of Science. Peter Park. LC 68-27989. 1968. reprint ed. pap. 9.95 (*0-672-63596-8*) Irvington.

***Sociology Understanding.** Ed. by Andersen. (C). 1998. text ed. write for info. (*0-321-01035-3*) Addson-Wesley Educ.

Sociology Update. 4th ed. Hess. 1993. text ed. 58.00 (*0-02-354393-0*, Macmillan Coll) P-H.

Sociology Update. 4th ed. Beth B. Hess et al. 720p. (C). 1992. text ed. 58.00 (*0-02-354387-6*, Macmillan Coll) P-H.

Sociology, War & Disarmament: Studies in Peace Research. Johan Niezing. 131p. 1973. pap. text ed. 21.95 (*90-237-6223-1*) Transaction Pubs.

Sociology, Work & Industry. 2nd ed. Tony J. Watson. 272p. 1987. 49.50 (*0-7102-0962-2*, RKP); pap. 16.95 (*0-415-02545-1*, RKP) Routledge.

Sociology, Work & Industry. 3rd ed. Tony J. Watson. LC 95-19334. 440p. (C). 1996. pap. 24.95 (*0-415-13374-2*); text ed. 79.95 (*0-415-13373-4*) Routledge.

Sociology 1986 see International Bibliography of the Social Sciences

Sociology 1987 see International Bibliography of the Social Sciences

Sociology 1989. 250p. (C). 1989. text ed. 125.00 (*0-415-01779-3*, A3664) Routledge.

S

An Asterisk (*) at the beginning of an entry indicates that the title is appearing in BIP for the first time.

Sociology 5. Jon M. Shepard. Date not set. teacher ed., text ed. write for info. (*0-314-00729-6*) West Pub.

Sociology's Models of Man. W. L. Skidmore. xii, 204p. 1975. text ed. 117.00 (*0-677-04780-0*) Gordon & Breach.

Sociomedia: Multimedia, Hypermedia & the Social Construction of Knowledge. Ed. by Edward Barrett. (Technical Communications & Information Ser.). 600p. 1994. pap. 24.95 (*0-262-52193-8*) MIT Pr.

Sociomedia: Multimedia, Hypermedia, & the Social Creation of Knowledge. Edward Barrett. (Technical Communications & Info Systems Ser.). (Illus.). 360p. 1992. 55.00 (*0-262-02346-6*) MIT Pr.

Sociomedical Perspectives on Patient Care Relationships. Ed. by Jeffrey M. Clair & Richard M. Allman. LC 92-48516. 304p. (C). 1993. text ed. 36.00 (*0-8131-1815-8*); pap. text ed. 19.00 (*0-8131-0819-5*) U Pr of Ky.

Sociometry, Experimental Method & the Science of Society. J. L. Moreno. 16.00 (*0-685-06814-5*) Beacon Hse.

Sociometry in Group Relations. Helen Jennings. LC 72-9829. (Illus.). 105p. 1973. reprint ed. text ed. 59.75 (*0-8371-6483-4*, JESG, Greenwood Pr) Greenwood.

Sociophysics: A General Theory of Natural & Cultural Systems. P. Arnopoulos. 390p. (C). 1994. lib. bdg. 85.00 (*1-56072-108-1*) Nova Sci Pubs.

Sociophysiology. Ed. by W. M. Waid. (Social Psychology Ser.). (Illus.). 580p. 1984. 95.95 (*0-387-90861-7*) Spr-Verlag.

***Sociopolitical Aspects of International Marketing.** Ed. by Erdener Kaynak. 387p. 1996. pap. 24.95 (*1-56024-989-7*) Haworth Pr.

***Sociopolitical Ecology: Human Systems & Ecological Fields.** F. L. Bates. (Contemporary Systems Thinking Ser.). 300p. (C). 1997. write for info. (*0-306-45653-2*, Plenum Pr) Plenum.

Sociopolitics: Political Development in Postmodern Societies. Paris Amopoulous. (Essay Ser.: No. 18). 250p. 1995. 20.00 (*0-920717-99-3*) Guernica Editions.

Sociopsychological Aspects of Sexually Transmitted Diseases. Ed. by Margaret Rodway & Marianne Wright. LC 88-638. (Journal of Social Work & Human Sexuality: Vol. 6, No. 2). (Illus.). 162p. 1988. text ed. 32.95 (*0-86656-737-2*) Haworth Pr.

Sociosemiotic Theory of Theatre. Jean Alter. LC 90-41885. 296p. (C). 1990. text ed. 37.95 (*0-8122-3054-X*) U of Pa Pr.

Sociotherapy & Psychotherapy. Marshall Edelson. LC 73-94997. (Austen Riggs Center Monograph Ser.: No. 6). (Illus.). 284p. reprint ed. pap. 81.00 (*0-8357-7027-3*, 2056780) Bks Demand.

Socjologia Amerykanska: Wybor Prac 1950-1960. Ed. by Jerzy Kosinski. 211p. 1962. pap. 6.00 (*0-940962-41-1*) Polish Inst Art & Sci.

Sock Animals: Tiger's New Friends. Ann J. Mooney. LC 91-76359. (Sock Animals Ser.). (Illus.). 32p. (Orig.). (J). (ps-2). 1992. pap. 7.95 (*0-9631035-0-4*) Jamondas Pr.

Sock Bunnies: Christmas & Spring Edition. pap. 5.98 (*0-317-03192-9*) Gick.

Sock Club: Angry Feelings - Smart Choices. Cheryl Gross & Ed Werz. 16p. (J). (gr. k-4). 1992. 0.95 (*1-56688-053-X*) Bur For At-Risk.

Sock Club: Drugs Make You Do Bad Things. Cheryl Gross & Ed Werz. 16p. (J). (gr. k-4). 1992. 0.95 (*1-56688-050-5*) Bur For At-Risk.

Sock Club: How to Say No to Drugs! Cheryl Gross & Ed Werz. 16p. (J). (gr. k-4). 1992. 0.95 (*1-56688-052-1*) Bur For At-Risk.

Sock Club: Real & Fake. Cheryl Gross & Ed Werz. 16p. (J). (gr. k-4). 1992. 0.95 (*1-56688-049-1*) Bur For At-Risk.

Sock Club: What Could Happen. Cheryl Gross & Ed Werz. 16p. (J). (gr. k-4). 1992. 0.95 (*1-56688-051-3*) Bur For At-Risk.

Sock Doll Workshop: 30 Delightful Dolls to Create & Cherish. Cindy Crandall-Frazier. (Illus.). 112p. (Orig.). 1996. pap. 19.95 (*1-887374-08-6*) Lark Books.

Sock Puppets. June Ford. (You Can Do It! Ser.). (Illus.). 58p. (Orig.). (J). (ps up). 1994. pap. 12.95 (*1-56530-157-9*) Summit TX.

Sockets Source Code Secrets. Lynne G. Jolitz & William F. Jolitz. (Operating System Source Code Secrets Ser.: Vol. 3). 450p. 1997. 44.95 (*1-57398-003-X*) Peer-to-Peer Communications.

Sockeye Salmon: A Pictorial Tribute. Hiromi Naito & Stefani Paine. 1995. pap. 19.95 (*0-89886-458-5*) Mountaineers.

Socks. Beverly Cleary. 160p. (J). 1990. pap. 4.50 (*0-380-70926-0*, Camelot) Avon.

Socks. Beverly Cleary. LC 72-10298. (Illus.). 160p. (J). (gr. 3-7). 1973. 16.00 (*0-688-20067-2*, Morrow Junior); lib. bdg. 15.93 (*0-688-30067-7*, Morrow Junior) Morrow.

***Socks.** Jeri Dayle. (J). 1998. pap. 3.25 (*0-679-88643-5*) Random Bks Yng Read.

Socks: A Spin-off Special Publication for Knitters & Spinners. Ed. & Intro. by Deb Robson. 56p. pap. 7.95 (*0-934026-94-7*) Interweave.

Socks: A Study Guide. Joyce Friedland & Rikki Kessler. (Novel-Ties Ser.). 1983. student ed., teacher ed., pap. text ed. 15.95 (*0-88122-018-3*) Lrn Links.

Socks & Cretin: Two Democats Helping Bill with the Presidency. Socks Clinton et al. LC 95-30272. (Illus.). xii, 169p. 1995. pap. 15.00 (*0-86663-212-3*) Ide Hse.

Socks & Other Sorrows. Harry D. Hewitt. Ed. by Elizabeth R. Hewitt. 56p. (Orig.). 1996. pap. 10.00 (*0-9627244-4-0*) Penn Sounds.

Socks Changes His Mind: (The White House Cat), Bk. II. J. Abell-Grubbs. Ed. & Illus. by Joan Abell. (J). (gr. 1 up). 1993. pap. 28.00 (*1-56611-044-0*); lib. bdg. 32.00 (*1-56611-043-2*) Jones.

Socks for Supper. Jack Kent. LC 93-7771. (Parents Magazine Read Aloud Original Ser.). (J). 1993. lib. bdg. 17.27 (*0-8368-0975-0*) Gareth Stevens Inc.

Socks for Supper. Jack Kent. LC 78-6224. (Illus.). 40p. (J). (ps-3). 1978. 5.95 (*0-8193-0964-8*) Parents.

Socks for Supper. Jack Kent. LC 78-6224. (Illus.). 40p. (J). (ps-3). 1978. lib. bdg. 5.95 (*0-8193-0965-6*) Parents.

Socks Goes to Washington: The Diary of America's First Cat. Jean-Claude Suares. 78p. 1993. pap. 6.95 (*1-56566-042-0*) Lickle Pubng.

Socks on a Rooster - Louisiana's Earl K. Long. Richard McCaughan. 1967. 20.00 (*0-87511-081-9*) Claitors.

***Socks Revision.** Beverly Cleary. (J). Date not set. write for info. (*0-688-09820-7*, Morrow Junior); lib. bdg. write for info. (*0-688-09821-5*, Morrow Junior) Morrow.

Socks Says! Carolyn B. Finch. (Illus.). 40p. (Orig.). (J). 1993. pap. 8.95 (*1-882956-00-1*) Bogart Comm.

Socks, the Cat Who Moved to Washington. J. Grubbs. Ed. by J. Abell. (Illus.). 50p. (J). (gr. 1-4). 1993. pap. 28.00 (*1-56611-047-5*) Jones.

Socks, the Cat Who Moved to Washington. J. Grubbs. Ed. by Joan Abell. (Illus.). 50p. (J). (gr. 1-4). 1993. lib. bdg. 32.00 (*1-56611-022-X*) Jones.

Socksnatchers. Lorna Balian. (Illus.). 32p. (J). (ps-3). 1988. 14.95 (*0-687-39047-8*) Humbug Bks.

Socorro, Daughter of the Desert. Karen Papagapitos. Ed. by Estelle Kleinman. (JB Ser.). (Illus.). 64p. (J). (gr. 3-6). 1993. 6.95 (*0-9637328-0-3*) Kapa Hse Pr.

Socorro Slaughter. Jon Sharpe. (Trailsman Ser.: No. 169). 176p. 1996. mass mkt., pap. 4.99 (*0-451-18523-4*, Sig) NAL-Dutton.

Socotra: Island of Tranquillity. Brian Doe. 238p. (C). 1995. 150.00 (*0-907151-31-0*, Pub. by IMMEL Pubng UK) St Mut.

Socrates. R. Nicol Cross. LC 70-130546. (Select Bibliographies Reprint Ser.). 1977. 28.95 (*0-8369-5519-6*) Ayer.

Socrates. Rascal. LC 92-24120. (Illus.). 32p. (J). 1993. 13.95 (*0-8118-0314-7*) Chronicle Bks.

Socrates. Rascal. (Illus.). 32p. (J). (ps-3). 1995. pap. 6.95 (*0-8118-1047-X*) Chronicle Bks.

Socrates. Gerasimos X. Santas. 1982. pap. 15.95 (*0-7100-9327-6*, RKP) Routledge.

Socrates. Alfred E. Taylor. LC 73-1436. (Illus.). 192p. 1975. reprint ed. text ed. 49.75 (*0-8371-6793-0*, TASO, Greenwood Pr) Greenwood.

Socrates: Critical Assessments, 4 vols., Set. Ed. by William J. Prior. LC 95-51962. (Critical Assessments of Leading Philosophers Ser.: .). 1200p. (C). 1996. boxed, text ed. 660.00 (*0-415-10968-X*) Routledge.

Socrates: The Man & His Philosophy. Luis E. Navia. (Illus.). 376p. (Orig.). 1985. pap. text ed. 25.50 (*0-8191-4855-5*) U Pr of Amer.

Socrates: The Wisest & Most Just. Ed. by Meg Parker. LC 79-11761. (Translations from Greek & Roman Authors Ser.). (Illus.). 120p. 1980. pap. text ed. 12.95 (*0-521-22813-1*) Cambridge U Pr.

Socrates - An Approach. Mario Montuori. (Philosphica Ser.: Vol. 2). 235p. (C). 1988. 60.00 (*90-70265-89-3*, Pub. by Gieben NE) Benjamins North Am.

Socrates' - the Lost Dialogues. Charles Walters. LC 93-79265. 136p. 1994. pap. 12.00 (*0-911311-42-4*) Acres USA.

Socrates among the Corybantes: Dionysian Spirituality & the Philosophy of Plato. Carl Levenson. 176p. (Orig.). 1997. pap. 17.50 (*0-88214-226-7*) Spring Pubns.

Socrates' Ancestor: An Essay on Architectural Beginnings. Indra K. McEwen. LC 93-21863. (Illus.). 206p. 1993. pap. 16.50 (*0-262-63148-2*) MIT Pr.

Socrates & Aristophanes. Leo Strauss. x, 322p. 1996. pap. text ed. 15.95 (*0-226-77719-7*) U Ch Pr.

Socrates & Athens. M. Parker. (Inside the Ancient World Ser.). 88p. 1986. reprint ed. pap. 14.95 (*0-86292-185-6*, Pub. by Brstl Class Pr UK) Focus Pub-R Pullins.

Socrates & Christ. Robert M. Wenley. 1977. 75.00 (*0-8490-2621-0*) Gordon Pr.

Socrates & His Contemporaries see Classical Philosophy: Collected Papers

Socrates & Legal Obligation. Reginald E. Allen. LC 80-18193. 162p. 1980. reprint ed. pap. 46.20 (*0-7837-2981-2*, 2057473) Bks Demand.

Socrates & the Political Community: An Ancient Debate. Mary P. Nichols. LC 86-14421. (SUNY Series in Political Theory: Contemporary Issues). 237p. 1987. text ed. 74.50 (*0-88706-395-0*); pap. text ed. 24.95 (*0-88706-396-9*) State U NY Pr.

Socrates & the Sophistic Enlightenment: A Commentary on Plato's Protagoras. Patrick Coby. LC 86-47856. 216p. 1988. 35.00 (*0-8387-5109-1*) Bucknell U Pr.

Socrates & the State. Richard Kraut. LC 83-17113. (Illus.). 338p. 1984. pap. text ed. 17.95 (*0-691-02241-0*) Princeton U Pr.

Socrates, Buddha, Confucius & Jesus: Taken from Vol. 1 of the Great Philosophers. Karl Jaspers. Tr. by Ralph Manheim. 1966. pap. 7.00 (*0-15-683580-0*, Harvest Bks) HarBrace.

Socrates' Discursive Democracy: Logos & Ergon in Platonic Political Philosophy. Gerald M. Mara. LC 96-17779. 324p. (C). 1997. pap. text ed. 21.95 (*0-7914-3300-5*) State U NY Pr.

Socrates' Discursive Democracy: Logos & Ergon in Platonic Political Philosophy. Gerald M. Mara. LC 96-17779. 324p. (C). 1997. text ed. 65.50 (*0-7914-3299-8*) State U NY Pr.

***Socrates Dissatisfied: An Analysis of Plato's Crito.** Rosalyn Weiss. 208p. 1997. 45.00 (*0-19-511684-4*) OUP.

***Socrates' Education to Virtue: Learning the Love of the Noble.** Mark J. Lutz. LC 97-16696. 256p. (C). 1998. text ed. 59.50 (*0-7914-3653-5*) State U NY Pr.

***Socrates' Education to Virtue: Learning the Love of the Noble.** Mark J. Lutz. LC 97-16696. 256p. (C). 1998. pap. text ed. 19.95 (*0-7914-3654-3*) State U NY Pr.

Socrates in August: From Incondensable Complexity to Myth. Michael J. Katz. (American University Studies: Philosophy: Ser. V, Vol. 66). 193p. (C). 1989. text ed. 44.95 (*0-8204-0781-X*) P Lang Pubng.

Socrates in October: Dialogues on Incondensable Complexity. Michael J. Katz. (American University Studies: Philosophy: Ser. V, Vol. 64). 215p. (C). 1988. text ed. 42.95 (*0-8204-0544-2*) P Lang Pubng.

Socrates in September: The Entanglements of Complexity. Michael J. Katz. (American University Studies: Philosophy: Ser. V, Vol. 53). 256p. (C). 1989. text ed. 35.50 (*0-8204-0652-X*) P Lang Pubng.

Socrates in the Agora. Mabel L. Lang. (Excavations of the Athenian Agora Picture Bks.: No. 17). (Illus.). 32p. 1978. pap. 3.00 (*0-87661-617-1*) Am Sch Athens.

Socrates in the Apology: An Essay on Plato's Apology of Socrates. C. D. Reeve. LC 89-33069. (Illus.). 224p. 1989. 34.95 (*0-87220-089-2*); pap. 14.95 (*0-87220-088-4*) Hackett Pub.

***Socrates in 90 Minutes.** LC 96-40322. 1997. pap. 5.95 (*1-56663-148-3*) I R Dee.

***Socrates in 90 Minutes.** Paul Strathern. LC 96-40322. 1997. text ed. 12.95 (*1-56663-147-5*) I R Dee.

Socrates, Ironist & Moral Philosopher. Gregory Vlastos. LC 90-37095. (Cornell Studies in Classical Philology). 500p. 1991. pap. 18.95 (*0-8014-9787-6*) Cornell U Pr.

Socrates of Constantinople: Historian of Church & State. Theresa Urbainczyk. LC 96-10154. (C). 1996. 39.50 (*0-472-10737-2*) U of Mich Pr.

Socrates on Trial. Thomas C. Brickhouse & Nicholas D. Smith. 350p. 1989. pap. text ed. 17.95 (*0-691-01900-2*) Princeton U Pr.

Socrates Physiology of a Myth. Mario Montuori. (London Studies in Classical Philology: Vol. 6). viii, 246p. (Orig.). (C). 1981. pap. 47.00 (*90-70265-23-0*, Pub. by Gieben NE) Benjamins North Am.

Socrates, Plato & Their Tradition see Studies in Greek Philosophy

Socrates Poisoned Again after 25 Centuries. Rajneesh Osho Staff. Ed. by M. P. Lisa & M. D. Sarar. (Talks in Greece Ser.). 433p. 1988. 24.95 (*3-89338-018-3*, Pub. by Rebel Hse GW) Osho America.

Socrates Scholasticus, Ecclesiastica Historia, 3 vols. in 2, Set. Ed. by Robert Hussey. xlviii, 1496p. 1992. reprint ed. write for info. (*3-487-09559-9*) G Olms Pubs.

Socrates' Second Sailing: On Plato's Republic. Seth Benardete. LC 88-27909. (Illus.). x, 248p. 1992. pap. text ed. 16.95 (*0-226-04244-8*) U Ch Pr.

Socrates to Sartre: A History of Philosophy. 5th ed. Samuel E. Stumpf. LC 92-2454. 576p. (C). 1993. text ed. write for info. (*0-07-062469-0*) McGraw.

Socrates to Sartre: A History of Philosophy. 5th rev. ed. Samuel E. Stumpf. LC 93-48406. 1994. text ed. 22.25 (*0-07-062564-6*) McGraw.

Socratic Commentary. Plato. Ed. by B. A. Hubbard. LC 83-18122. xvi, 188p. 1984. lib. bdg. 24.00 (*0-226-67034-1*) U Ch Pr.

Socratic Humanism. Lazslo Versenyi. LC 78-23762. 187p. 1979. reprint ed. text ed. 35.00 (*0-313-20716-X*, VESH, Greenwood Pr) Greenwood.

***Socratic Method & Writing Instruction.** Robert D. Whipple, Jr. LC 96-41349. 122p. 1997. pap. text ed. 19.50 (*0-7618-0527-3*) U Pr of Amer.

Socratic Movement. Ed. by Paul A. Vander Waerdt. 416p. 1994. 47.50 (*0-8014-2585-9*); pap. 19.95 (*0-8014-9903-8*) Cornell U Pr.

Socratic Presence: A Study of the Sources. Luis E. Navia. LC 93-13758. (Illus.). 416p. 1993. text ed. 65.00 (*0-8153-1478-7*, H1787) Garland.

Socratic Problem: The History - Solutions. Mario Montuori. (Philosophica Ser.: Vol. IV). ix, 475p. 1992. 107.00 (*90-5063-048-0*, Pub. by Gieben NE) Benjamins North Am.

***Socratic Puzzles.** Robert Nozick. LC 96-39221. 1997. write for info. (*0-674-81653-6*) HUP.

Socratic Rationalism & Political Philosophy: An Interpretation of Plato's Phaedo. Paul Stern. LC 92-32010. 240p. (C). 1993. text ed. 57.50 (*0-7914-1573-2*); pap. text ed. 18.95 (*0-7914-1574-0*) State U NY Pr.

Socratic Satire: An Essay on Diderot & Le Neveu de Rameau. Stephen Werner. LC 87-62171. 124p. 1987. lib. bdg. 18.95 (*0-917786-59-9*) Summa Pubns.

Socratic Selling: How to Ask the Right Questions & Get the Sale. Kevin Daley & Emmett Wolfe. LC 95-20289. 228p. 1995. text ed. 19.95 (*0-7863-0455-3*) Irwin Prof Pubng.

Socratic Studies. Gregory Vlastos. Ed. by Myles F. Burnyeat. LC 92-47419. 172p. (C). 1994. pap. text ed. 16.95 (*0-521-44735-6*) Cambridge U Pr.

Socratic Testimonies. Luis E. Navia. (Illus.). 380p. (Orig.). 1987. pap. text ed. 31.00 (*0-8191-6115-2*) U Pr of Amer.

Sod & Stubble: The Story of a Kansas Homestead. John Ise. LC 37-10937. xvi, 340p. 1967. pap. 10.95 (*0-8032-5098-3*, Bison Books) U of Nebr Pr.

Sod & Stubble: The Unabridged & Annotated Edition. John Ise. LC 96-3722. (Illus.). 408p. 1996. 35.00 (*0-7006-0774-9*); pap. 12.95 (*0-7006-0775-7*) U Pr of KS.

Sod ha-Shabbat: The Mystery of the Sabbath. Elliot K. Ginsburg. LC 87-26765. (SUNY Series in Judaica: Hermeneutics, Mysticism, & Religion). 280p. 1989. text ed. 24.50 (*0-88706-780-8*) State U NY Pr.

Sod House. Cass G. Barns. LC 73-100812. 301p. 1970. reprint ed. pap. 85.80 (*0-608-00489-8*, 2061308) Bks Demand.

Sod-House Days: Letters from a Kansas Homesteader 1877-78. Howard Ruede. Ed. by J. Ise. LC 66-17858. 248p. reprint ed. 53.00 (*0-8154-0200-7*) Cooper Sq.

Sod-house Frontier, 1854-1890: A Social History of the Northern Plains from the Creation of Kansas & Nebraska to the Admission of the Dakotas. Everett N. Dick. LC 78-24204. (Illus.). 634p. reprint ed. pap. 180.00 (*0-8357-6601-2*, 2035231) Bks Demand.

Sod Houses on the Great Plains. Glen Rounds. LC 94-27390. (J). (ps-3). 1995. lib. bdg. 15.95 (*0-8234-1162-1*) Holiday.

Sod Houses on the Great Plains. Glen Rounds. (Illus.). (J). (ps-3). 1996. pap. 6.95 (*0-8234-1263-6*) Holiday.

Sod, the Mysteries of Adonai. Samuel F. Dunlap. LC 92-81766. (Secret Doctrine Reference Ser.). 240p. 1997. reprint ed. 16.00 (*0-913510-62-9*) Wizards.

Sod, the Son of Man. 2nd ed. Samuel F. Dunlap. LC 92-81768. (Secret Doctrine Reference Ser.). (Illus.). 185p. 1997. reprint ed. 16.00 (*0-913510-61-0*) Wizards.

Sod Walls. rev. ed. Roger Welsch. (Illus.). 208p. 1991. reprint ed. pap. 12.95 (*0-934904-27-8*) J & L Lee.

Soda Ash. (Metals & Minerals Ser.). 1993. lib. bdg. 250.95 (*0-8490-8975-1*) Gordon Pr.

Soda Ash. 1994. lib. bdg. 254.95 (*0-8490-9025-3*) Gordon Pr.

***Soda Bread on Sunday.** Elizabeth Nielsen. LC 97-3111. 1997. write for info. (*0-944957-69-2*) Rivercross Pub.

Soda Can Collectors Guide, 3 vols., Set. Paul Bates et al. (Illus.). 502p. (Orig.). 1992. reprint ed. pap. 29.95 (*1-56046-157-8*) Interact Pubs.

Soda Can Collectors Guide (A&P to Fyne Taste), Vol. 1. Paul Bates et al. (Illus.). 179p. (Orig.). 1992. pap. 10.00 (*1-56046-151-9*) Interact Pubs.

Soda Can Collectors Guide (Galaxy to Pussypop), Vol. 2. Paul Bates et al. (Illus.). 161p. (Orig.). 1987. pap. 10.00 (*1-56046-152-7*) Interact Pubs.

Soda Can Collectors Guide (Q-Tonic to Zippy), Vol. 3. Paul Bates et al. (Illus.). 162p. (Orig.). 1987. pap. 10.00 (*1-56046-153-5*) Interact Pubs.

Soda Glazing. Ruthanne Tudball. (Illus.). 96p. 1995. pap. text ed. 19.95 (*0-8122-1571-0*) U of Pa Pr.

Soda Jerk. Cynthia Rylant. LC 89-35654. (Illus.). 48p. (YA). (gr. 7 up). 1990. 15.95 (*0-531-05864-6*); lib. bdg. 16.99 (*0-531-08464-7*) Orchard Bks Watts.

Soda Jerk. Cynthia Rylant. (Illus.). 64p. (YA). (gr. 7 up). 1993. pap. 3.95 (*0-688-12654-5*) Morrow.

***Soda off Road Racing.** Prima Publishing Staff. 1997. pap. 19.99 (*0-7615-1118-0*) Prima Pub.

Soda Pop. Arlene Erlbach. LC 93-20106. (How It's Made Ser.). (Illus.). 48p. (J). (gr. 2-5). 1993. lib. bdg. 18.95 (*0-8225-2386-8*, Lerner Publctns) Lerner Group.

Soda Pop. Arlene Erlbach. (J). 1995. pap. 6.95 (*0-8225-9710-1*) Lerner Group.

***Soda Pop! From Medicine to "Po Ulture"** Gyvel Young-Witzel & Michael K. Witzel. 128p. 1998. 29.95 (*0-89658-368-6*, Town Sq) Voyageur Pr.

***Soda Pop! From Medicine to "Pop Culture"** Michael K. Witzel & Gyvel Y. Witzel. (Illus.). 128p. 1998. 29.95 (*0-89658-326-0*, Town Sq) Voyageur Pr.

Soda Pop: How to Make Your Own Soda Pop. 1996. lib. bdg. 249.75 (*0-8490-8306-0*) Gordon Pr.

Soda Pop Can & the Road Sign, Bk. 4. Ralph F. Parkison. Ed. by Marion O. Withrow. (Illus.). 13p. (Orig.). (J). (gr. 2-6). 1988. pap. text ed. 3.73 (*0-929949-03-X*) Little Wood Bks.

Soda Pop Science. B. K. Hixson. 104p. 1990. pap. text ed. 18.99 (*1-57156-006-8*) Wild Goose UT.

Soda Science: Designing & Testing Soft Drinks. Bernie Zubrowski. LC 96-23735. (Boston Children's Museum Activity Book). (J). 1997. pap. 6.95 (*0-688-13983-3*, Morrow Junior); lib. bdg. 14.93 (*0-688-13917-5*, Morrow Junior) Morrow.

Sodasangahrdayam: Essentials of Ayurveda. Priya V. Sharma. (C). 1993. 27.50 (*0-685-69770-3*, Pub. by Motilal Banarsidass II) S Asia.

Sodasi: An Anthology of Contemporary Sanskrit Poets. Ed. by Radhavallabh Tripathi. (C). 1992. 15.00 (*81-7201-200-4*, Pub. by Sahitya Akademi II) S Asia.

Sodbuster. David W. Toht. LC 94-43305. (American Pastfinder Ser.). (Illus.). 48p. (J). (gr. 4-7). 1996. lib. bdg. 19.95 (*0-8225-2977-7*, Lerner Publctns) Lerner Group.

***Sodbuster Poet: Poems.** Danny Smith. Ed. by Karen Smith. 48p. 1995. pap. 5.95 (*0-9652605-0-X*) Danny Smith.

Soddy Bear: The Persian Gulf War. Eliza Toussant. (Illus.). 76p. (Orig.). (J). (gr. 4 up). 1991. pap. 17.95 (*0-9630583-0-4*) E Toussant.

Soderberg Saga: Includes: The Bishop's Horse Race, Brother Brigham's Gold, Seven Days for Ruby, & In Search of Steenie Bergman. Blaine M. Yorgason & Brenton Yorgason. 1995. 17.95 (*0-87579-957-4*) Deseret Bk.

Soderini & the Medici: Power & Patronage in Fifteenth-Century Florence. Paula C. Clarke. 304p. 1991. 85.00 (*0-19-822992-5*, 8824) OUP.

***Sodic Soils: Distribution, Properties, Management, & Environmental Consequences.** Ed. by Malcolm E. Sumner & Ravendra Naidu. (Topics in Sustainable Agronomy Ser.). (Illus.). 256p. 1997. 75.00 (*0-19-509655-X*) OUP.

Sodium: Its Biological Significance. Solomon Papper. (CRC Uniscience Ser. on Cations of Biological Significance). 304p. 1981. 113.95 (*0-8493-5873-6*, RC632) CRC Pr.

Sodium-Calcium Exchange. Ed. by T. Jeff Allen et al. (Illus.). 344p. 1989. 85.00 (*0-19-854735-8*) OUP.

Sodium-Calcium Exchange. Ed. by Donald W. Hilgemann et al. LC 96-5419. (Annals of the New York Academy of Sciences Ser.: No. 779). 1996. write for info. (*1-57331-000-X*) NY Acad Sci.

Sodium-Calcium Exchange. Ed. by Donald W. Hilgemann et al. LC 96-5419. (Annals of the New York Academy of Sciences Ser.: No. 779). 593p. 1996. pap. 110.00 (*1-57331-001-8*) NY Acad Sci.

Sodium-Calcium Exchange: Proceedings of the Second International Conference. Ed. by Mordecai P. Blaustein et al. LC 91-44531. (Annals Ser.: Vol. 639). 671p. 1992. pap. 160.00 (*0-89766-694-1*, Q11) NY Acad Sci.

Sodium Chloride: The Production & Properties of Salt & Brine. Ed. by Dale W. Kaufmann. LC 60-10504. (ACS Monograph: No. 145). 1960. 90.95 (*0-8412-0251-6*) Am Chemical.

Sodium Content of Your Food. 1984. lib. bdg. 79.95 (*0-87700-547-8*) Revisionist Pr.

***Sodium Counter.** William Kaufman. 1990. pap. 2.95 (*0-425-12570-X*) Berkley Pub.

Sodium Counter. Annette B. Natow & Jo-Ann Hesun. Ed. by Sally Peters. 576p. (Orig.). 1993. mass mkt. 5.99 (*0-671-69566-5*) PB.

Sodium Glutamate (MSG) Index of New Information & Medical Research Bible. Morton N. Willette. LC 96-12485. 151p. 1997. 47.50 (*0-7883-1106-9*); pap. 44.50 (*0-7883-1107-7*) ABBE Pubs Assn.

Sodium Hunger: The Search for a Salty Taste. Jay Schulkin. (Illus.). 196p. (C). 1992. text ed. 59.95 (*0-521-35368-8*) Cambridge U Pr.

Sodium Hypochlorite - Uses & Importance: Index of New Information with Authors, Subjects, Research Categories & References. Gerald J. Howell. 160p. (Orig.). 1995. 47.50 (*0-7883-0734-7*); pap. 44.50 (*0-7883-0735-5*) ABBE Pubs Assn.

Sodium-Nak Engineering Handbook, Vol. 1. O. J. Foust. 340p. 1972. 159.00 (*0-677-03020-7*) Gordon & Breach.

Sodium-Nak Engineering Handbook, 5 vols., Vol. 5. O. J. Foust. 1979. Set. text ed. 1,103.00 (*0-677-03070-3*) Gordon & Breach.

Sodium-Proton Exchange in Cardiac Cells: Role in Mulations of Intracellular Sodium & Sodium-Dependent Processes. F. Bielen. No. 42. 169p. (Orig.). 1991. pap. 37.50 (*90-6186-450-X*, Pub. by Leuven Univ BE) Coronet Bks.

Sodium Pump: Structure Mechanism Hormonal Control & Its Role in Disease. Ed. by E. Bamberg & W. Schoner. 906p. 1994. 87.95 (*0-387-91466-8*) Spr-Verlag.

Sodium Sulfate. (Metals & Minerals Ser.). 1993. lib. bdg. 248.75 (*0-8490-8997-2*) Gordon Pr.

Sodium Sulfate. (Metals & Minerals Ser.). 1994. lib. bdg. 248.75 (*0-8490-5686-1*) Gordon Pr.

Sodium-Sulfur Battery. J. L. Sudworth & A. R. Tilley. 400p. (gr. 13). 1986. text ed. 189.95 (*0-412-16490-6*) Chapman & Hall.

Sodium Transport Inhibitors. Ed. by G. S. Stokes & J. F. Marwood. (Progress in Biochemical Pharmacology Ser.: Vol. 23). (Illus.). xiv, 162p. 1988. 119.25 (*3-8055-4707-2*) S Karger.

Sodom & Gomorrah. Tr. by C. K. Moncrieff & Terence Kilmartin. LC 92-27272. (In Search of Lost Time Ser.: Vol. 4). 700p. 1993. 18.50 (*0-679-60029-9*, Modern Lib) Random.

Sodom & Gomorrah: Tradition, Motif, & Message - a Traditio-Literary Study of Genesis 19 & Related Biblical Narratives. Weston W. Fields. (JSOTS Ser.: No. 210). 210p. 1996. 45.00 (*1-85075-633-3*, Pub. by Sheffield Acad UK) CUP Services.

Sodom Had No Bible. Leonard Ravenhill. 208p. 1979. reprint ed. pap. 8.99 (*0-87123-496-3*) Bethany Hse.

Sodome et Gomorrhe. Jean Giraudoux. pap. 9.95 (*0-685-33928-9*) Fr & Eur.

Sodome et Gomorrhe. Marcel Proust. 1966. write for info. (*0-318-63599-2*, 1641) Fr & Eur.

Sodome et Gomorrhe. Marcel Proust. (Folio Ser.: No. 2047). 599p. (FRE.). 1985. pap. 16.50 (*2-07-038135-8*, 1641) Schoenhof.

Sodome et Gomorrhe, Bk. 5: A la Recherche du Temps Perdu. Marcel Proust. (FRE.). 1972. pap. 18.95 (*0-8288-3765-1*, F119590) Fr & Eur.

Sodometries: Renaissance Texts, Modern Sexualities. Jonathan Goldberg. (Illus.). 288p. (C). 1992. 42.50 (*0-8047-2050-9*); pap. 15.95 (*0-8047-2051-7*) Stanford U Pr.

***Sodomite in Fiction & Satire, 1660-1750.** Cameron McFarlane. 1997. pap. text ed. 16.50 (*0-231-10895-8*) Col U Pr.

Sodoms in Eden: The City in American Fiction Before 1860. Janis P. Stout. LC 75-35356. (Contributions in American Studies: No. 19). 192p. 1976. text ed. 45.00 (*0-8371-8585-8*, SSE/, Greenwood Pr) Greenwood.

***Sodom's Seed in the Netherlands.** Van Der Meer. 1997. pap. text ed. 16.95 (*0-226-84730-6*); lib. bdg. 46.50 (*0-226-84729-2*) U Ch Pr.

Sodomy & Interpretation: Marlowe to Milton. Gregory W. Bredbeck. LC 91-55066. 256p. 1991. 39.95 (*0-8014-2644-8*); pap. 15.95 (*0-8014-9945-3*) Cornell U Pr.

Sodomy & the Perception of Evil see Sodomy & the Pirate Tradition: English Sea Rovers in the Seventeenth Century Caribbean

Sodomy & the Pirate Tradition: English Sea Rovers in the Seventeenth-Century Caribbean. B. R. Burg. 240p. (C). 1984. pap. text ed. 11.16 (*0-8147-1073-5*) NYU Pr.

Sodomy & the Pirate Tradition: English Sea Rovers in the Seventeenth Century Caribbean. rev. ed. B. R. Burg. LC 94-25521. Orig. Title: Sodomy & the Perception of Evil. (C). 1995. reprint ed. 37.50 (*0-8147-1235-5*); reprint ed. pap. 14.95 (*0-8147-1236-3*) NYU Pr.

Sodomy, U. S. A. B. Wilson. 65p. 1986. pap. 14.95 (*0-9617160-1-0*) B Wilson KY.

Sody Sallyratus. Illus. by Kenn Compton. LC 94-28261. (J). (ps-3). 1995. lib. bdg. 15.95 (*0-8234-1165-6*) Holiday.

Sody Sallyratus. Teri Sloat. LC 96-14688. 1997. pap. 15.99 (*0-525-45609-0*) NAL-Dutton.

SOE: The Special Operations Executive, 1940-46. M. R. Foot. LC 85-26568. 280p. 1984. text ed. 49.95 (*0-313-27014-7*, U7014, Greenwood Pr) Greenwood.

S.O.E. in France: An Account of the Work of the British Special Operations Executive in France, 1940-1944. M. R. Foot. LC 83-23438. 596p. 1984. text ed. 65.00 (*0-313-27001-5*, U7001, Greenwood Pr) Greenwood.

SOE Secret Operations Manual. (Illus.). 272p. 1993. pap. 20.00 (*0-685-70282-0*) Paladin Pr.

Soeben Erschienen, Band 3: Nordrhein-Westfalen A-I. 367p. (GER.). 1992. write for info. (*0-318-70547-8*) G Olms Pubs.

SOES Bandits' Guide - Day Trading in the 21st Century. rev. ed. (Illus.). 79p. (Orig.). pap. 29.95 (*0-9647872-0-2*) Kashan Litho.

Soeur. Rotrou. Ed. by Kite. (Exeter French Texts Ser.: No. 88). 136p. (FRE.). Date not set. pap. text ed. 19.95 (*0-85989-398-7*, Pub. by Univ Exeter Pr UK) Northwestern U Pr.

Soeurs Lacroix. Georges Simenon. (Folio Ser.: No. 1209). (FRE.). pap. 8.95 (*2-07-037209-X*) Schoenhof.

Soeurs Rondoli. Guy De Maupassant. 1992. pap. 10.95 (*0-7859-3171-6*, 2253060097) Fr & Eur.

Soeurs Vatard. Joris-Karl Huysmans. 9.95 (*0-686-54183-9*) Fr & Eur.

Sofer: The Story of a Torah Scroll. Eric Ray. LC 85-52420. (Illus.). 32p. (Orig.). (J). (ps-4). 1986. pap. 4.95 (*0-933873-04-2*) Torah Aura.

Sofer: The Story of a Torah Scroll. Eric Ray & Joel L. Grishaver. (Illus.). 32p. (Orig.). 1988. text ed. 12.95 (*0-933873-24-7*) Torah Aura.

Sofia. Ann Chamberlin. LC 95-36251. 368p. 1996. 23.95 (*0-312-86110-9*) Forge NYC.

Sofia: Portrait of a City. Philip Ward. (Travel Bks.: Vol. 20). (Illus.). 186p. (Orig.). 1992. pap. 19.95 (*0-906672-65-1*) Oleander Pr.

Sofia & the Heartmender. Marie Olofsdotter. LC 92-46200. (Illus.). 32p. (J). (gr. k up). 1993. 14.95 (*0-915793-50-4*) Free Spirit Pub.

Sofia Casanova (1861-1958) Spanish Woman Poet, Journalist, & Author. Ofelia Alayeto. LC 92-22741. (Scripta Humanistica Ser.: Vol. 89). 1992. 54.50 (*0-916379-95-7*) Scripta.

Sofia Petrovna. Lydia Chukovskaya. Tr. by Aline Werth from RUS. (European Classics Ser.). 126p. 1994. pap. text ed. 12.95 (*0-8101-1150-0*) Northwestern U Pr.

Sofia's Heart: American Dreams. Sharon Cadwallader. 192p. (Orig.). (YA). 1996. mass mkt. 3.99 (*0-380-78322-3*, Flare) Avon.

Sofie's Role. Amy Heath. LC 91-33488. (Illus.). 40p. (J). (gr. k-2). 1992. lib. bdg. 14.95 (*0-02-743505-9*, Mac Bks Young Read) S&S Childrens.

Sofonija's Tale of the Russian-Tatar Battle on the Kulikovo Field. Ed. by Roman Jakobson & Dean S. Worth. (S P R Ser.: No. 51). 1963. text ed. 41.55 (*90-279-0196-1*) Mouton.

SOFSEM '95 Theory & Practice of Informatics: Proceedings of the 22nd Seminar on Current Trends in Theory & Practice of Informatics, Milovy, Czech Republic, November 23-December 1, 1995. Ed. by Miroslav Bartosek et al. LC 95-46102. (Lecture Notes in Computer Science Ser.: Vol. 1012). 499p. 1995. 81.00 (*3-540-60609-2*) Spr-Verlag.

***Sofsem '96: Theory & Practice of Informatics: 23rd Seminar on Current Trends in Theory & Practice of Informatics, Milovy, Czech Republic, November 1996: Proceedings.** Keith Jeffery et al. LC 96-47542. (Lecture Notes in Computer Science Ser.: Vol. 1175). 491p. 1996. text ed. 81.00 (*3-540-61994-1*) Spr-Verlag.

***Soft & Easy Exercise for Everyone: Recommended for Fibromyalgia & Osteoporosis.** unabridged ed. Mary K. Bennett & Judy Palmquist. (Illus.). 160p. (Orig.). 1997. pap. 19.95 (*0-9658619-0-2*) Fitness Is Busn.

Soft & Hard Tissue Repair: Biological & Clinical Aspects. Ed. by Thomas K. Hunt et al. LC 83-24595. (Surgical Science Ser.: Vol. II). 624p. 1984. text ed. 95.00 (*0-275-91434-8*, C1434, Praeger Pubs) Greenwood.

Soft & Misty Paintings, Vol. 2. Kathy Snider. 100p. 1990. pap. text ed. 9.50 (*1-56770-229-5*) S Scheewe Pubns.

Soft & Noisy. Judy Hindley. LC 91-39110. (Illus.). 32p. (J). (ps-1). 1992. 13.95 (*1-56282-224-1*) Hyprn Child.

Soft Anvil Flexo Rotary Die Cutting Seminar, Chicago, October 29-30, 1987. Technical Association of the Pulp & Paper Industry Staff. (TAPPI Notes Ser.). (Illus.). 183p. reprint ed. pap. 52.20 (*0-685-23340-5*, 2032265) Bks Demand.

Soft as a Kitten. Illus. by Audean Johnson. (Touch-Me Bks.). 14p. (J). (ps). 1982. 9.00 (*0-394-85517-5*) Random Bks Yng Read.

Soft as the Voice of an Angel. (Little Treasures Ser.). (Illus.). 1994. 4.99 (*1-57051-011-3*) Brownlow Pub Co.

Soft Bottom Macrobenthic Community of Arthur Harbor, Antarctica: Paper 1 in Biology of the Antarctic Seas V. James K. Lowry. Ed. by David L. Pawson. LC 75-22056. (Antarctic Research Ser.: Vol. 23). (Illus.). 20p. 1975. pap. 5.20 (*0-87590-123-9*) Am Geophysical.

***Soft Budget Constraints & the Fate of Economic Reforms in Transition Economies & Developing Countries.** Martin Raiser. (C). 1997. 87.50 (*3-16-146708-6*) U of Mich Pr.

Soft Canopies. (Detail in Building Ser.). 1996. pap. 25.00 (*1-85490-440-X*) Academy Ed UK.

Soft Child: How Rattlesnake Got Its Fangs. Joe Hayes. LC 93-1641. (Illus.). 32p. (Orig.). (J). (ps-3). pap. 8.95 (*0-943173-89-2*, Harbinger CO) R Rinehart.

Soft Coal, Hard Choices: The Economic Welfare of Bituminous Coal Miners, 1890-1930. Price V. Fishback. 304p. 1992. 48.00 (*0-19-506725-8*) OUP.

Soft-Coated Wheaten Terrier Champions, 1973-1986. Camino E. E. & Bk. Co. Staff. (Illus.). 131p. 1988. pap. 36.95 (*0-940808-73-0*) Camino E E & Bk.

***Soft-Coated Wheaten Terriers.** Margaret A. O'Connor. (Illus.). 192p. 1997. pap. 9.95 (*0-7938-2382-X*, KW-177S) TFH Pubns.

***Soft Commutation.** Y. Cheron. (Illus.). 233p. (C). (gr. 13 up). Date not set. text ed. 92.50 (*0-412-39510-X*, Chap & Hall NY) Chapman & Hall.

***Soft Computing.** Ed. by Lin & Wildberger. 332p. 1995. pap. 80.00 (*1-56555-077-3*, SOFT-95) Soc Computer Sim.

Soft Computing: Art & Design. Brian Reffin-Smith. 192p. (C). 1986. pap. text ed. write for info. (*0-318-61094-9*) Addison-Wesley.

Soft Computing in Remote Sensing Data Analysis: Proceedings of the International Workshop, Milan Italy, Dec. 4-5, 1995. Elisabetta Binaghi et al. LC 96-8559. (Series in Remote Sensing). 276p. 1996. write for info. (*981-02-2757-4*) World Scientific Pub.

Soft Covers for Hard Times: Quiltmaking & the Great Depression. Merikay Waldvogel. LC 90-32002. (Illus.). 128p. (C). 1990. 22.95 (*1-55853-062-2*) Rutledge Hill Pr.

Soft Curve. Ethel Dunlop. LC 92-74836. (Illus.). 128p. (Orig.). 1993. pap. 11.95 (*0-9627680-5-7*) Inkwell CA.

Soft Day: A Miscellany of Contemporary Irish Writing. Ed. by Peter Fallon & Sean Golden. LC 78-63298. 244p. 1980. reprint ed. pap. 69.60 (*0-608-00884-2*, 2061678) Bks Demand.

Soft Drink Bottling: A History with Special Reference to Illinois. John R. Paul & Paul W. Parmalee. (Illus.). 121p. 1973. pap. 5.00 (*0-89792-079-1*) Ill St Museum.

Soft Drinks. Colin Emmins. 1989. pap. 30.00 (*0-7478-0125-8*, Pub. by Shire UK) St Mut.

Soft Drinks in West Germany. Euromonitor Staff. (C). 1988. 975.00 (*0-86338-285-1*, Pub. by Euromonitor Pubns UK) Gale.

***Soft Edge: A Natural History & Future of the Information Revolution.** Paul Levinson. LC 97-7248. 264p. 1997. write for info. (*0-415-15785-4*) Routledge.

Soft-Edge Piecing: Add the Elegance of Applique to Traditional-Style Patchwork Design. Jinny Beyer. LC 94-38483. (Illus.). 144p. 1995. pap. 24.95 (*0-914881-94-9*, 10112) C & T Pub.

Soft Ferrites: Properties & Applications. 2nd ed. E. C. Snelling. (Illus.). 412p. 1988. 275.00 (*0-408-02760-6*) Buttrwrth-Heinemann.

***Soft Furnishings.** Heather Luke. (Home Decorator Ser.). (Illus.). 96p. 1997. pap. 15.95 (*1-85368-617-4*, Pub. by New Holland Pubs UK) Sterling.

Soft Furnishings. Hilary More. (Pleasures of Home Ser.). (Illus.). 128p. 1997. 21.95 (*0-304-34629-2*, Pub. by Cassell UK) Sterling.

Soft Furnishings: Ideas & Fabrics by Designers Guild. Ed. by Elsie B. Donald. (Illus.). 159p. (Orig.). 1980. pap. 29.50 (*0-330-25915-6*, Pub. by Pan Books UK) Trans-Atl Phila.

***Soft Furnishings for Your Home.** Sharyn Skrabanich. (Illus.). 200p. 1997. pap. 22.95 (*1-56477-201-2*, B314) That Patchwork.

Soft Gardens: Make Flowers with Your Sewing Machine. Yvonne Perez-Collins. LC 92-28182. (Creative Machine Arts Ser.). 160p. 1993. pap. 17.95 (*0-8019-8327-4*) Chilton.

Soft Gold: The Fur Trade & Cultural Exchange on the Northwest Coast of America. 2nd rev. ed. Thomas Vaughan & Bill Holm. LC 82-81739. (North Pacific Studies: No. 14). (Illus.). 312p. 1990. pap. 25.00 (*0-87595-206-2*) Oregon Hist.

Soft Ground Improvement in Lowland Environment. D. T. Bergado et al. 440p. 1996. 48.00 (*0-7844-0151-9*) Am Soc Civil Eng.

Soft-Ground Tunnelling: Failures & Displacements. Ed. by Daniel Resendiz & Miguel P. Romo. 110p. (C). 1981. text ed. 70.00 (*90-6191-201-6*, Pub. by A A Balkema NE) Ashgate Pub Co.

Soft-Hackled Fly: A Trout Fisherman's Guide. Sylvester Nemes. LC 93-12705. (Illus.). 130p. 1993. reprint ed. 22.95 (*0-8117-1670-8*) Stackpole.

Soft-Hackled Fly Addict. Sylvester Nemes. LC 93-12707. (Illus.). 144p. 1993. reprint ed. 19.95 (*0-8117-1671-6*) Stackpole.

Soft Interfaces: The 1994 Dirac Memorial Lecture. Pierre Gilles De Gennes. LC 96-45963. (Dirac Memorial Lectures Ser.). (Illus.). 148p. (C). 1997. text ed. 19.95 (*0-521-56417-4*) Cambridge U Pr.

Soft Interior Architecture. John Kurtich. (Architecture Ser.). 1996. pap. 34.95 (*0-442-02139-9*) Van Nos Reinhold.

Soft Ionization Biological Mass Spectrometry: Proceedings of the Chemical Society Symposium on Advances in Mass Spectrometry Soft Ionization Methods, London, July, 1980. Symposium on Advances in Mass Spectrometry Soft Ionization Methods Staff. Ed. by H. R. Morris. (Illus.). 168p. reprint ed. pap. 47.90 (*0-8357-3054-9*, 2039311) Bks Demand.

Soft Is Hard: Barriers & Incentives in Canadian Energy Policy. P. S. Elder. 116p. (Orig.). 1984. pap. 10.95 (*0-920490-41-7*) Temeron Bks.

Soft Kites & Windsocks. Jim Rowlands. LC 92-26426. 1993. pap. 14.95 (*0-312-08966-X*) St Martin.

Soft Landing: Flights of Fantasy in Space & Time. Randy D. Daniel. LC 93-86888. 256p. (Orig.). 1993. pap. 15.00 (*1-884469-00-0*) Renegade Pr.

Soft Lepton Pair & Photon Production. Ed. by J. Thompson. 268p. 1992. 130.00 (*1-56072-015-8*) Nova Sci Pubs.

Soft Little Kitty. B. J. Johnson. (Illus.). 10p. (J). (ps). 1994. bds. 3.95 (*0-590-48394-3*, Cartwheel) Scholastic Inc.

Soft Little Puppy. (Illus.). 10p. (J). (ps). 1994. bds. 3.95 (*0-590-48395-1*, Cartwheel) Scholastic Inc.

***Soft-Logic: A Guide to Using a Personal Computer As a Programmable Logic Controller.** Robert S. Carrow. LC 97-22481. 1997. text ed. 60.00 (*0-07-014017-0*) McGraw.

Soft Machine. William S. Burroughs. LC 92-18811. 394p. (Orig.). 1992. pap. 9.95 (*0-8021-3329-0*, Grove) Grove-Atltic.

Soft Magnet Materials - Types, Processing, New Developments. 200p. 1992. 2,475.00 (*0-89336-946-2*, GB-149B) BCC.

***Soft Magnetic Materials.** (Report Ser.: No. GB-192). 230p. 1996. 2,950.00 (*1-56965-235-X*) BCC.

Soft Magnetism: Fundamentals for Powder Metallurgy & Metal Injection Molding. Chaman Lall. LC 92-19313. (Monographs in P-M Ser.: No. 2). (Illus.). (C). 1992. pap. 60.00 (*1-878954-17-2*) Metal Powder.

Soft Money: A Loophole for the 80's. Peter Lindstrom & Ellen Miller. 28p. (Orig.). (C). 1985. pap. text ed. 5.95 (*0-939715-03-1*) Ctr Politics.

Soft Order in Physical Systems. Ed. by Y. Rabin & R. Bruinsma. (NATO ASI Ser.: Series B, Physics: Vol. 323). (Illus.). 216p. (C). 1994. 75.00 (*0-306-44678-2*) Plenum.

Soft Parts of the Back. Daryl N. Chinn. (University of Central Florida Contemporary Poetry Ser.). 88p. 1989. 19.95 (*0-8130-0922-7*); pap. 10.95 (*0-8130-0938-3*) U Press Fla.

Soft Pawn. William Hartston. 1995. pap. 8.95 (*1-85744-145-1*) Macmillan.

Soft Petals. Georgia Bartlett. 48p. 1987. pap. text ed. 6.50 (*1-56770-171-X*) S Scheewe Pubns.

Soft Physics & Fluctuations: Cracow Workshop on Multiparticle Production. A. Bialas et al. 344p. 1994. text ed. 116.00 (*981-02-1588-6*) World Scientific Pub.

***Soft Power Negotiation Skills.** Ida Greene. 1997. pap. text ed. 7.00 (*0-614-30046-0*) People Skills.

***Soft Reply.** Barlow Packer. 1997. pap. 8.95 (*1-57008-316-9*) Bookcraft Inc.

Soft Rock. 1990. pap. 4.95 (*0-7935-0223-3*, 00001358) H Leonard.

Soft Rock 1992. rev. ed. 224p. 1992. otabind 14.95 (*0-7935-1838-5*, 00311596) H Leonard.

Soft Room. Summer Brenner. 1978. pap. 6.00 (*0-935724-80-X*) Figures.

Soft Room. deluxe ed. Summer Brenner. 1978. pap. 10.00 (*0-935724-55-9*) Figures.

Soft Running. David Gershon. (Chrysalis Bks.). 128p. (Orig.). 1986. pap. 9.95 (*0-916349-01-2*) Amity Hse Inc.

Soft Science of Road Racing Motorcycles. Keith Code. (Illus.). 144p. (Orig.). 1986. pap. 16.95 (*0-918226-11-2*) Acrobat.

Soft Scripts for Quiet Books: Old & New Testament. Caralee Workman. 75p. 1995. pap. 12.95 (*1-55517-169-9*) CFI Dist.

Soft Sculpture & Beyond: An International Perspective. Jutta Feddersen. 216p. 1993. text ed. 65.00 (*976-8097-38-8*) Gordon & Breach.

Soft Secret Word. Jane Aylott. (Illus.). 32p. (J). 1993. 12.95 (*0-9631440-0-6*) Winged Peoples.

Soft Sell: The New Art of Selling, Self-Empowerment, & Persuasion. 2nd ed. Tim Connor. LC 93-31118. 224p. 1994. pap. 9.95 (*0-942061-64-0*, Financial Sourcebks) Sourcebks.

Soft Selling in a Hard World: Plain Talk on the Art of Persuasion. Jerry Vass. LC 93-83458. 218p. 1993. 12.95 (*1-56138-298-1*) Running Pr.

***Soft Shells: Design & Technology of Tensile Architecture.** Hans-Joachim Schock. LC 97-12214. 1997. write for info. (*0-8176-5450-X*) Birkhauser.

***Soft Shells: Design & Technology of Tensile Architecture.** Hans-Joachim Schock. (Illus.). 152p. 1997. 71.00 (*3-7643-5450-X*) Birkhauser.

***Soft Shells: Design & Technology of Tensile Architecture.** Hans-Joachim Schock. (Illus.). 152p. (GER.). 1997. 71.00 (*3-7643-5449-6*) Birkhauser.

Soft, Shimmering Sand. Madelyn W. Carlisle. LC 92-44756. (Let's Investigate Ser.). (Illus.). 32p. (J). (gr. 2-6). 1996. lib. bdg. 13.95 (*1-56674-148-3*) Forest Hse.

Soft Side. Henry James. LC 77-140330. (Short Story Index Reprint Ser.). 1977. 18.95 (*0-8369-3722-8*) Ayer.

Soft Sighs of If. Judy Murray. (Illus.). 24p. (Orig.). 1992. pap. 3.00 (*0-926935-75-5*) Runaway Spoon.

***Soft Signature.** Lisa Downe. 80p. 1997. pap. 12.00 (*1-55022-314-3*, Pub. by ECW Press CN) Genl Dist Srvs.

Soft Soap. David Rogers. 1982. 5.00 (*0-87129-529-6*, S65) Dramatic Pub.

Soft Soap, Hard Sell: American Hygiene in an Age of Advertisement. Vincent Vinikas. LC 90-48686. (Illus.). 188p. (C). 1992. text ed. 34.95 (*0-8138-1788-9*) Iowa St U Pr.

Soft Soil Properties & Testing Methods. Ryszard B. Zeidler. (Selected Translations of Russian Geotechnical Literature Ser.). (Illus.). 192p. (C). 1993. text ed. 70.00 (*90-5410-134-2*, Pub. by A A Balkema NE) Ashgate Pub Co.

Soft Song. 2nd ed. Saundra Sharp. (Illus.). 64p. 1991. reprint ed. 18.95 (*0-86316-301-7*) Writers & Readers.

Soft Song. Saundra Sharp. (Illus.). 64p. 1991. reprint ed. pap. 8.95 (*0-86316-306-8*) Writers & Readers.

Soft Spring Night in Shillington. deluxe ed. John Updike. 60p. 1986. 50.00 (*0-935716-39-4*) Lord John.

Soft Steps to a Hard Body. Ellington Darden. LC 92-37452. (Illus.). 184p. 1993. pap. 9.95 (*0-87833-795-4*) Taylor Pub.

Soft Systems Methodology in Action. Peter B. Checkland & Jim Scholes. 329p. 1990. text ed. 75.00 (*0-471-92768-6*) Wiley.

Soft Targets. Dean Ing. 1996. mass mkt. 5.99 (*0-8125-1947-7*) Tor Bks.

Soft Targets. Simon Rae & Willie Rushton. 96p. 9100. pap. 15.95 (*1-85224-165-9*) Dufour.

Soft-Tec, Inc: Practice Case, 5 Vols. 5th ed. Belverd E. Needles, Jr. & McWhorter. (C). 1994. teacher ed., text ed. 18.76 (*0-395-71979-8*) HM.

S

An Asterisk (*) at the beginning of an entry indicates that the title is appearing in BIP for the first time.

Soft Technologies, Hard Choices. Colin Norman. 1978. pap. write for info. (*0-916468-20-8*) Worldwatch Inst.

Soft Tissue Changes in Contractures, Vol. 1. Gordon Cummings et al. (Orthopedic Physical Therapy Ser.). (Illus.). 1983. pap. 22.00 (*0-936030-02-X*) Stokesville Pub.

Soft Tissue Implant Markets: Manufacturers Address Regulations & Defend Against Litigation. Market Intelligence Staff. 221p. 1993. 1,895.00 (*1-56753-454-6*) Frost & Sullivan.

Soft Tissue Implants Market. (Market Research Reports: No. 224). (Illus.). 133p. 1991. 295.00 (*0-317-04150-9*) Theta Corp.

***Soft Tissue Injuries: Diagnosis & Treatment.** Robert E. Windsor & Dennis Lox. LC 97-13858. 1997. write for info. (*1-56053-212-2*) Hanley & Belfus.

Soft Tissue Injuries in Sports Medicine. Louis C. Almekinders. 288p. 1995. pap. 49.95 (*0-86542-382-2*) Blackwell Sci.

Soft-Tissue Manipulation. Leon Chaitow. 192p. (Orig.). 1988. text ed. 39.95 (*0-89281-276-1*) Inner Tradit.

Soft Tissue Pain & Disability. 3rd ed. Rene Cailliet. LC 95-39159. (Pain Ser.). (Illus.). 545p. (C). 1996. pap. text ed. 29.95 (*0-8036-0110-7*) Davis Co.

Soft Tissue Reconstruction in the Upper Extremity. LC 95-9478. (Illus.). 1995. write for info. (*0-614-07957-8*) Churchill.

Soft Tissue Rheumatic Pain: Recognition, Management, & Prevention. 3rd ed. Robert P. Sheon et al. (Illus.). 391p. 1996. 49.95 (*0-683-07678-7*) Williams & Wilkins.

Soft Tissue Roentgenography in Diagnosis of Thyroid Cancer: Detection of Psammoma Bodies by Spot-tangential Projection. Masayoshi Akisada & Yoshihide Fujimoto. LC 74-176722. 143p. reprint ed. pap. 40.80 (*0-317-27214-4*, 2024710) Bks Demand.

Soft Tissue Sarcomas. Ed. by Laurence H. Baker. (Cancer Treatment & Research Ser.). 1983. lib. bdg. 81.00 (*0-89838-584-9*) Kluwer Ac.

Soft Tissue Sarcomas: Histological Diagnosis. Artemis D. Nash. LC 88-26490. (Biopsy Interpretation Ser.). 285p. 1989. reprint ed. pap. 81.30 (*0-7837-8354-X*, 2049144) Bks Demand.

Soft Tissue Sarcomas: New Developments in the Multidisciplinary Approach to Treatment. Ed. by Herbert M. Pinedo et al. (C). 1991. lib. bdg. 132.00 (*0-7923-1139-6*) Kluwer Ac.

***Soft Tissue Sarcomas: Present Achievements & Future Prospects.** J. Verweij et al. LC 97-9988. (Cancer Treatment & Research Ser.). 1997. lib. bdg. write for info. (*0-7923-9913-7*) Kluwer Ac.

Soft Tissue Sarcomas in Adults. Ed. by D. K. Hossfeld et al. LC 94-22889. (Recent Results in Cancer Research Ser.: Vol. 138). (Illus.). xi,180p. 1994. 127.00 (*0-387-57629-0*) Spr-Verlag.

***Soft Tissue Tumors.** Brooks. 1998. text ed. write for info. (*0-7216-6696-5*) Saunders.

Soft Tissue Tumors. Ed. by Dieter Harms & Dietmar Schmidt. LC 94-29977. (Current Topics in Pathology Ser.: 89). 1994. write for info. (*3-540-55150-6*) Spr-Verlag.

***Soft Tissue Tumors.** Andrew Rosenberg. (Illus.). 1997. write for info. (*0-89640-323-8*) Igaku-Shoin.

Soft Tissue Tumors. Sharon W. Weiss & John S. Brooks. (International Academy of Pathology Monograph: Vol. 24). 259p. 1996. 79.00 (*0-683-08963-3*) Williams & Wilkins.

Soft Tissue Tumors. 3rd ed. Franz M. Enzinger & Sharon W. Weiss. LC 94-32118. 1104p. (C). (gr. 13). 1994. text ed. 225.00 (*0-8151-3132-1*) Mosby Yr Bk.

Soft Tissue Tumors, 89. Ed. by Dieter Harms & Dietmar Schmidt. LC 94-29977. (Current Topics in Pathology Ser.: Vol. 89). (Illus.). 360p. 1994. 199.00 (*0-387-55150-6*) Spr-Verlag.

Soft Tissue Tumours. Ed. by V. Eusebi. (Journal: Applied Pathology: Vol. 6, No. 3). (Illus.). 92p. 1988. pap. 46.50 (*3-8055-4794-3*) S Karger.

***Soft Tissues: Trauma & Sports Injuries.** Ed. by G. R. McLatchie & C. M. Lennox. 485p. 1996. pap. 60.00 (*0-7506-3065-5*, 71307) Buttrwrth-Heinemann.

Soft Tissues: Trauma & Sports Injuries. Ed. by Greg R. McLatchie & C. M. Lennox. (Illus.). 485p. 1993. 95.00 (*0-7506-0170-1*) Buttrwrth-Heinemann.

Soft Tissues of the Extremities: A Radiologic Study of Rheumatic Disease. W. J. Weston & D. G. Palmer. LC 77-7951. (Comprehensive Manuals in Radiology Ser.: Vol. 1). (Illus.). 1978. 115.00 (*0-387-90259-7*) Spr-Verlag.

Soft Touch. Alma Blair. 1995. 17.95 (*0-8034-9107-7*, 095112) Bouregy.

Soft Toys for Babies. Judi Maddigan. Ed. by Robbie Fanning. (Stitch & Enrich Ser.). (Illus.). 200p. (Orig.). 1991. pap. 17.95 (*0-932086-29-2*) Open Chain Pub.

Soft Toys Made Easy: A Step-by-Step Creative Guide to Making over Thirty Toys. Gail Attwell. (Illus.). 96p. 1995. pap. 16.95 (*1-85368-152-0*, Pub. by New Holland Pubs UK) Sterling.

Soft Toys Piece-by-Piece: Step-by-Step Instructions. Janette Zapirain. (Illus.). 84p. 1994. pap. 14.95 (*1-86351-115-6*, Pub. by S Milner AT) Sterling.

Soft Toys to Sew. Sheila McGraw. (Illus.). 160p. (Orig.). 1992. pap. 19.95 (*1-895565-11-1*) Firefly Bks Ltd.

***Soft Underbelly of Reason: The Passions in the Seventeenth Century.** Stephen Gaukroger. LC 97-24517. 1998. write for info. (*0-415-17054-0*) Routledge.

Soft Voice of the Rain. Deborah Redding-Stewart. LC 91-67097. 55p. 1992. pap. 5.95 (*1-55523-475-5*) Winston-Derek.

Soft War: The Uses & Abuses of U. S. Economic Aid in Central America. Tom Barry & Deb Preusch. LC 87-13238. 320p. 1988. reprint ed. pap. 91.20 (*0-7837-9240-9*, 2049991) Bks Demand.

Soft Whisper of the Dead. Charles L. Grant. (Illus.). 208p. 1983. 15.00 (*0-937986-55-0*) D M Grant.

Soft Workouts. (Fitness, Health & Nutrition Ser.). (Illus.). 144p. 1988. 17.27 (*0-8094-6195-1*); lib. bdg. 23.27 (*0-8094-6196-X*) Time-Life.

Soft X-Ray Cosmos ROSAT Science Symposium. Ed. by Eric M. Schlegel & Robert Petre. (AIP Conference Proceedings Ser.: No. 313). 496p. 1994. text ed. 135.00 (*1-56396-327-2*) Am Inst Physics.

Soft X-Ray Optics. Eberhard Spiller. LC 94-13107. 1994. 81.00 (*0-8194-1655-X*, PM15/HC); pap. 66.00 (*0-8194-1654-1*, PM15) SPIE.

Soft-X-Ray Projection Lithography. LC 92-80614. (Technical Digest Series, 1992: Vol. 8). 200p. (Orig.). 1992. pap. 66.00 (*1-55752-230-8*) Optical Soc.

Soft X-Ray Projection Lithography. Ed. by Jeffrey Bokor. LC 90-63176. (Proceedings Ser.: Vol. 12). 350p. 1991. lib. bdg. 69.00 (*1-55752-187-5*) Optical Soc.

Soft X-Ray Projection Lithography. Ed. by Andrew M. Hawryluk & Richard H. Stulen. LC 92-62915. (Proceedings Ser.: Vol. 18, 1993). 250p. 1994. text ed. 69.00 (*1-55752-304-5*) Optical Soc.

Softball. (Scorebooks Ser.). 1977. 4.50 (*0-88314-168-X*) AAHPERD.

Softball. Les Palmer & Dewayne J. Johnson. (Illus.). 54p. 1980. pap. text ed. 8.95 (*0-89641-044-7*) American Pr.

Softball: A Step-By-Step Guide. Dick Walker. LC 89-27290. (Be the Best! Ser.). (Illus.). 64p. (J). (gr. 4-8). 1990. lib. bdg. 11.89 (*0-8167-1937-3*) Troll Communs.

Softball: A Step-By-Step Guide. Dick Walker. LC 89-27290. (Be the Best! Ser.). (Illus.). 64p. (J). (gr. 4-8). 1997. pap. 3.95 (*0-8167-1938-1*) Troll Communs.

Softball: Fast & Slow Pitch. Mario Pagnoni & Gerald Robinson. (Spalding Sports Library). (Illus.). 156p. (Orig.). 1995. pap. 12.95 (*1-57028-025-8*) Masters Pr IN.

Softball: Slow & Fast Pitch. 5th ed. Marian E. Kneer & Charles L. McCord. 160p. (C). 1990. pap. write for info. (*0-697-10120-7*) Brown & Benchmark.

Softball: Slow & Fast Pitch. 6th ed. Marian E. Kneer & Charles L. McCord. 160p. (C). 1994. per. write for info. (*0-697-15255-3*) Brown & Benchmark.

Softball: Steps to Success. Diane L. Potter & Gretchen A. Brockmeyer. LC 88-34421. (Steps to Success Activity Ser.). (Illus.). 228p. (Orig.). 1989. pap. 14.95 (*0-88011-358-8*, PPOT0358) Human Kinetics.

Softball Everyone. 2nd ed. Reach & Schwartz. 174p. 1992. pap. text ed. 14.95 (*0-88725-162-5*) Hunter Textbks.

Softball for Girls. Margaret J. Dobson & Becky L. Sisley. LC 79-24256. 232p. 1980. reprint ed. lib. bdg. 15.50 (*0-89874-103-3*) Krieger.

Softball for Girls & Women. Gladys C. Meyer. (Illus.). 320p. 1984. pap. 11.00 (*0-684-18140-1*) S&S Trade.

Softball Handbook. Susan Craig & Ken Johnson. LC 84-12253. (Illus.). 160p. (Orig.). 1985. pap. 15.95 (*0-88011-260-3*, PCRA0260) Human Kinetics.

***Softball Skills Test Manual.** Ed. by Roberta E. Rikki. 64p. (Orig.). 1991. pap. 14.00 (*0-88314-494-8*, A4948) AAHPERD.

***Softball's Power Offense.** Susan Craig & Ken Johnson. 1997. 15.00 (*1-57167-141-2*) Sagamore Pub.

***Softbills: Care, Breeding & Conservation.** Martin Vince. 280p. (Orig.). 1996. pap. 24.95 (*0-88839-393-8*) Hancock House.

Softcops & Fen. Caryl Churchill. (Methuen Modern Plays Ser.). 98p. (Orig.). (C). 1988. pap. 9.95 (*0-413-41200-8*, A0266, Pub. by Methuen UK) Heinemann.

Softcore: Moral Crusades Against Pornography in Britain & America. Bill Thompson. (Sexual Politics Ser.). 224p. 1994. pap. 15.95 (*0-304-32793-X*, Pub. by Cassell Pubng UK) LPC InBook.

Softdesk Architecture 1 Certified Courseware. Softdesk Technical Resource Staff. 228p. 1996. pap. text ed. 34.95 incl. cd-rom (*1-56690-095-6*, 1001, OnWord Pr) High Mtn.

Softdesk Architecture 2 Certified Courseware. Softdesk Technical Resource Staff. LC 96-22905. 384p. 1996. pap. text ed. 34.95 (*1-56690-100-6*, 1003, OnWord Pr) High Mtn.

***Softdesk Civil: Using the Power of Softdesk.** Phillip Zimmerman. 512p. 1997. pap. 29.95 incl. disk (*0-8273-8440-8*) Delmar.

Softdesk Civil 1 Certified Courseware. Softdesk Technical Resource Staff. 294p. 1996. pap. text ed. 34.95 incl. cd-rom (*1-56690-096-4*, 1000, OnWord Pr) High Mtn.

Softdesk Civil 2 Certified Courseware. Softdesk Technical Resource Staff. 304p. 1996. pap. text ed. 34.95 incl. cd-rom (*1-56690-101-4*, 1002, OnWord Pr) High Mtn.

***Softdesk Primer.** Pfleiderer. 1997. pap. text ed. 33.33 (*0-13-617838-3*) P-H.

Softdesk Solutions: The Essential Guide to Auto-Architect w/CD-ROM. Dennis Neeley. LC 96-7187. 500p. 1996. pap. 32.95 (*0-471-15418-0*) Wiley.

Softening without Liberalization in the Soviet Union: The Case of Juri Kukk. Rein Taagepera. (Illus.). 254p. 1984. lib. bdg. 52.50 (*0-8191-3800-2*) U Pr of Amer.

Softer Side of the 60's. 16.95 (*0-7935-4983-3*, 00310083) H Leonard.

Softest, Warmest Bear in the Whole World. Chyng-Feng Sun. LC 92-9111. (Illus.). 1994. 14.95 (*0-395-63412-1*) HM.

***Softimage.** Barry Ruff & Gene Bodio. 1997. pap. 49.99 (*0-614-28449-X*) Coriolis Grp.

Softindex, 1982: Periodical Guide for Computerists Annual. 19.95 (*0-686-40865-9*) Applegate Comp Ent.

***Softly & Tenderly.** 1986. pap. 1.20 (*0-8341-9276-4*) Lillenas.

Softly & Tenderly: The Altar: A Place to Encounter God. Leslie Parrott. 228p. 1989. 15.99 (*0-8341-1304-X*) Beacon Hill.

Softly Call the Muster: The Evolution of a Texas Aggie Tradition. John A. Adams, Jr. LC 93-36982. (Centennial Series of the Association of Former Students: Vol. 52). (Illus.). 116p. (C). 1994. pap. 9.95 (*0-89096-586-2*) Tex A&M Univ Pr.

Softly in Silver Sandals: A Selection of Writings on Love. Flavia M. Weedn. (Illus.). 90p. reprint ed. 10.00 (*0-929632-06-0*) Applause Inc.

SoftPub Yellow Pages: Directory of Suppliers to the Software Publishing Industry. 150p. 1994. pap. 49.00 (*0-9643850-0-7*) SoftPub Grp.

Softstat 'Ninety-One: Advances in Statistical Software 3: The 6th Conference on the Scientific Use of Statistical Software, 7 April-12 April 1991 in Heidelberg. Ed. by Frank Faulbaum. LC 92-12540. 1992. 94.00 (*3-437-40280-3*, Pub. by G Fischer Verlag GW) Lubrecht & Cramer.

Softstat 'Ninety-One: Advances in Statistical Software 3: The 6th Conference on the Scientific Use of Statistical Software, 7 April-12 April 1991 in Heidelberg. Ed. by Frank Faulbaum. LC 92-12540. 536p. 1992. pap. 60.00 (*1-56081-348-2*, Pub. by G Fischer Verlag GW) Lubrecht & Cramer.

Software. Rudy Rucker. 176p. (Orig.). 1987. mass mkt. 5.99 (*0-380-70177-4*, AvoNova) Avon.

Software. rev. ed. Time-Life Books Editors. (Understanding Computers Ser.). (Illus.). 128p. 1990. write for info. (*0-8094-7554-5*); lib. bdg. write for info. (*0-8094-7555-3*) Time-Life.

Software: What's Hot! What's Not! Cheryl Currid. 512p. (Orig.). 1993. pap. 16.95 (*1-55958-386-X*) Prima Pub.

Software see Parallel Processing, 1996 International Conference

Software Acquisition Management: Managing the Acquisition of Custom Software Systems. John J. Marciniak & Donald J. Reifer. (Wiley Series in Software Engineering Practice). 290p. 1990. text ed. 59.95 (*0-471-50643-5*) Wiley.

***Software Agents.** Ed. by Jeffrey M. Bradshaw. LC 97-1553. (AAAI Press Ser.). (Illus.). 300p. (Orig.). 1997. pap. 40.00 (*0-262-52234-9*) MIT Pr.

Software Agents: Papers from the 1994 Spring Symposia. Ed. by Oren Etzioni. (Technical Reports). (Illus.). 130p. (Orig.). 1994. spiral bd. 25.00 (*0-929280-59-8*) AAAI Pr.

***Software Agents & Soft Computing: Toward Enhancing Machine Intelligence: Concepts & Applications.** Hyacinth S. Nwana & Nadar Azarmi. LC 97-878. (Lecture Notes in Artificial Intelligence Ser.: Vol. 119). 1997. 39.95 (*3-540-62560-7*) Spr-Verlag.

Software & Example Book for Reflector & Lens Antennas, Set. Ed. by Carlyle J. Sletten. (Antenna Software Library). 250p. 1988. student ed. 150.00 incl. disk (*0-89006-240-4*) Artech Hse.

Software & Hardware Applications of Microcomputers: Proceedings IASTED Symposium, Fort Collins, U. S. A., February 4-6, 1987. Ed. by G. K. Lee. 127p. 1987. 58.00 (*0-88986-102-1*, 108) Acta Pr.

Software & Hardware Applications of Microcomputers - MIMI '86: Proceedings, ISMM Symposium, Beverly Hills, U. S. A., February 5-7, 1986. Ed. by M. H. Hamza & G. K. Lee. 254p. 1986. 70.00 (*0-88986-085-8*, 097) Acta Pr.

Software & Hardware Dictionary: Italian - English, English - Italian. D. Roberto Lesina. (ENG & ITA.). 1991. 89.95 (*0-7859-3709-9*, 8808114880) Fr & Eur.

Software & Hardware Dictionary: Italian-English - English-Italian. D. Roberto Lesina. 416p. 1991. 85.00 (*88-08-11488-0*) IBD Ltd.

***Software & Hardware Engineering: The Motorola M68HC11.** Frederick M. Cady. (Illus.). 336p. (C). 1997. pap. text ed. 36.00 (*0-19-511046-3*) OUP.

Software & Intellectual Property Protection: Copyright and Patent Issues for Computer and Legal Professionals. Bernard A. Galler. LC 94-40353. 224p. 1995. text ed. 55.00 (*0-89930-974-7*, Quorum Bks) Greenwood.

***Software & Interface Design Guide for Delphi.** David Bowden et al. (Illus.). 600p. Date not set. pap. 49.95 (*1-55622-555-5*) Wordware Pub.

Software & Media for Anatomy & Physiology: Clip Art of the Human. 7th ed. Bastian. (C). 1995. text ed. 105.95 (*0-06-502466-4*) Addison-Wesley Educ.

Software & Services State Tax Report. Arthur Andersen. LC 95-95130. 303p. (Orig.). 1995. pap. text ed. 195.00 (*0-942319-49-4*) A Andersen.

Software & the Agile Manufacturer: Computer Systems & World Class Manufacturing. Brian H. Maskell. LC 93-33282. (Illus.). 424p. 1994. 50.00 (*1-56327-046-3*) Prod Press.

***Software Applications & Directory for Energy Analysis.** Anna F. Williams. (Illus.). 285p. 64.00 (*0-88173-132-3*, 0262) Fairmont Pr.

Software Applications for Mental Health. 40p. 1993. pap. 15.00 (*1-883066-00-X*) Natl Comm Mental.

Software Applications in Electrical Engineering. Ed. by P. P. Silvester & C. A. Brebbia. LC 93-71018. (Electrosoft Ser.: Vol. 2). 424p. 1993. 161.00 (*1-56252-169-1*) Computational Mech MA.

Software Architecture & Design. Witt. (C). 1994. pap. text ed. 44.95 (*1-85032-845-5*) ITCP.

Software Architecture & Design: Principles, Models, & Methods. Bernard I. Witt et al. LC 93-8489. 1994. pap. 44.95 (*0-442-01556-9*) Van Nos Reinhold.

Software Architecture & Iterative Development. Philippe Kruchten. (C). 1998. text ed. write for info. (*0-8053-0596-3*) Addison-Wesley.

***Software Architecture for Professionals.** Ken Bass. (C). 1998. pap. text ed. write for info. (*0-201-19930-0*) Addison-Wesley.

Software Architectures. Mary Shaw. 264p. (C). 1996. pap. text ed. 29.40 (*0-13-182957-2*) P-H.

***Software Architectures: A Practical Guide for Software Designers.** Robert Nord. (C). 1998. text ed. write for info. (*0-201-32571-3*) Addison-Wesley.

***Software As Captial: An Economic Perspective on Software Engineering.** Howard Baetjer. 175p. 1997. 25.00 (*0-8186-7779-1*, BP07779) IEEE Comp Soc.

***Software Assessment.** (VDT-2000 Ser.: Vol. 4). 1995. 2,995.00 (*0-614-18341-3*, IGIC-95) Info Gatekeepers.

Software Assessment: Reliability, Safety, Testability. Michael A. Friedman & Jeffrey M. Voas. LC 94-49676. 288p. 1995. text ed. 59.95 (*0-471-01009-X*) Wiley.

Software Assitance for Business Re-Engineering. Ed. by Kathy Spurr et al. 224p. 1994. text ed. 65.00 (*0-471-94240-5*) Wiley.

Software Bomb. Womack. Date not set. 3.98 (*0-8317-4632-7*) Smithmark.

***Software Boot Camp.** Advantage International Inc. Staff. Ed. & Photos by Exposure Unlimited Staff. (Illus.). 150p. 1996. wbk. ed., spiral bd. 29.99 (*1-56756-092-X*) Advant Intl.

Software Buyers Handbook: A Guide to Selecting Application Software. H. T. Wrobel. 320p. 1991. pap. 69.00 (*1-880271-00-1*) Tactical Techs.

Software by Design. Penny Bauersfeld. 1993. pap. 29.95 (*1-55828-296-3*) MIS Press.

Software Catalog, 1. 69.00 (*0-318-03637-1*) ISD.

Software Challenge. (Understanding Computers Ser.). (Illus.). 128p. 1989. 19.93 (*0-8094-6058-0*); lib. bdg. 25.93 (*0-8094-6059-9*) Time-Life.

Software Change Impact Analysis. Robert Arnold & Shawn. LC 95-52098. 392p. 1996. pap. 45.00 (*0-8186-7384-2*, BPO7384) IEEE Comp Soc.

Software Compatibility Journal of Research on Computing in Education Special Issue. Dennis W. Spuck. 208p. 1991. 20.00 (*0-924667-82-6*) Intl Society Tech Educ.

Software Components with Ada: Structures, Tools, & Subsystems. Grady Booch. (C). 1987. pap. 47.50 (*0-8053-0609-9*) Benjamin-Cummings.

Software Configuration Management. Wayne A. Babich. LC 85-22917. 140p. (C). 1986. pap. text ed. 26.95 (*0-201-10161-0*) Addison-Wesley.

Software Configuration Management. Ronald Berlack. LC 91-33348. (Series in Software Engineering Practice). 352p. 1991. text ed. 61.50 (*0-471-53049-2*) Wiley.

Software Configuration Management: ICSE SCM-4 & SCM-5 Workshops, Selected Papers. Ed. by Jacky Estublier. LC 95-45501. (Lecture Notes in Computer Science Ser.: Vol. 1005). 311p. 1995. 56.00 (*3-540-60578-9*) Spr-Verlag.

***Software Configuration Management: ICSE 96 SCM-6 Workshop, Berlin, Germany, March 1996: Selected Papers.** Ian Sommerville. LC 96-45249. (Lecture Notes in Computer Science Ser.: Vol. 1167). 291p. 1996. 49.00 (*3-540-61964-X*) Spr-Verlag.

***Software Configuration Management: ICSE '97 SCM-7 Workshop, Boston, Ma, U. S. A. May 18-19, 1997, Proceedings, Vol. 123.** Reidar O. Conradi. LC 97-14611. (Lecture Notes in Computer Science). 1997. pap. write for info. (*3-540-63014-7*) Spr-Verlag.

Software Construction & Data Structure with Ada 95. 2nd ed. Michael Feldman. 550p. (C). 1996. pap. text ed. 62.95 incl. disk (*0-201-87998-0*) Addison-Wesley.

Software Construction with Object-Oriented Pictures: Specifying Reactive & Interactive Systems. George W. Cherry. LC 89-51266. (Illus.). 156p. (C). 1989. pap. text ed. 28.95 (*0-9625003-0-5*) Thought-Tools.

Software Contract Forms: Nineteen Eighty-Seven Collection. American Bar Association, Science & Technology Staff. LC 87-70985. 1081p. 1987. pap. 37.50 (*0-89707-303-7*, 545-0006) Amer Bar Assn.

Software, Copyright, & Competition: The "Look & Feel" of the Law. Anthony L. Clapes. LC 89-10477. (Illus.). 247p. 1989. text ed. 49.95 (*0-89930-507-5*, CCJ/, Quorum Bks) Greenwood.

Software Copyright Law. 2nd ed. David Bainbridge. 1994. pap. write for info. (*0-406-04841-X*, U.K.) MICHIE.

Software Costing: An Objective Approach to Estimating & Controlling the Cost of Computer Science. Frank Wellman. 380p. 1992. pap. 39.00 (*0-685-61088-8*) P-H.

Software Design. David Budgen. (C). 1994. text ed. 37.75 (*0-201-54403-2*) Addison-Wesley.

Software Design & Data Structures in Turbo Pascal. Elliot B. Koffman & Bruce B. Maxim. LC 93-37679. (Illus.). 593p. (C). 1994. pap. text ed. 50.50 (*0-201-15624-5*) Addison-Wesley.

Software Design & Implementation for Distributed Systems. A. Fleischmann. (Illus.). 400p. 1994. 71.95 (*0-387-57382-8*) Spr-Verlag.

Software Design, Automated Testing, & Maintenence: A Practical Approach. Daniel Hoffman & Paul Strooper. 399p. 1996. text ed. 49.95 (*1-85032-206-6*) ITCP.

Software Design for Microcomputers. Carol A. Ogdin. LC 78-5801. (Illus.). 1978. 32.00 (*0-13-821744-0*) P-H.

Software Design for Real-Time Systems. Cooling. (Illus.). 528p. (C). 1991. pap. text ed. 39.95 (*1-85032-279-1*) ITCP.

Software Design in Organizations. Harold Salzman & Stephen R. Rosenthal. (Illus.). 224p. 1994. 49.95 (*0-19-508340-7*) OUP.

Software Design Methods for Concurrent & Real-Time Systems. Hassan Gomaa. LC 92-23216. (SEI Series in Software Engineering). (Illus.). 441p. (C). 1993. text ed. 47.50 (*0-201-52577-1*) Addison-Wesley.

Software Design Realtime Systems. Cooling. (C). 1990. text ed. 98.50 (*0-412-34180-8*) Chapman & Hall.

Software Design with C: Distributed & Imbedded Systems. Bruce Krell. (Illus.). 400p. 1995. pap. 39.95 (*0-12-426130-2*, AP Prof) Acad Pr.

An Asterisk (*) at the beginning of an entry indicates that the title is appearing in BIP for the first time.

Software Developer's & Marketer's Legal Companion: Protect Your Software & Your Business. Gene K. Landy. LC 93-19050. 560p. 1993. pap. 36.95 incl. disk (*0-201-62276-9*) Addison-Wesley.

Software Developer's Complete Legal Companion: The Combined Disk & Practical Handbook to Protect You & Your Creative Work. Thorne D. Harris, III. LC 93-50766. 1994. 39.95 (*1-55958-502-1*) Prima Pub.

Software Developer's Guide to Windows. Martin Heller. 608p. 1995. pap. text ed. 39.95 incl. disk (*0-471-07671-6*) Wiley.

Software Developer's Internet Directory. Jim Kyle. 1996. pap. 39.99 (*1-56884-821-8*) IDG Bks.

Software Development: A Legal Guide. Stephen Fishman. 300p. 1995. pap. 44.95 (*0-87337-209-3*) Nolo Pr.

***Software Development: A Legal Guide.** 2nd ed. Stephen Fishman. 1997. pap. text ed. 44.95 (*0-87337-397-9*) Nolo Pr.

Software Development: Fashioning the Baroque. Darrel C. Ince. (Illus.). 176p. 1989. 42.00 (*0-19-853757-3*) OUP.

***Software Development & Maintenance.** Benmenachem. (ITCP-UK Computer Science Ser.). (C). 1997. pap. 39.99 (*1-85032-329-1*) Van Nos Reinhold.

Software Development & Management for Microprocessor-Based Systems. Tomlinson G. Rauscher & Linda M. Ott. (Illus.). 256p. 1987. text ed. 32.95 (*0-317-56706-3*) P-H.

Software Development & Quality Assurance for the Healthcare Manufacturing Industries. Steven R. Mallory. 320p. 1994. 179.00 (*0-935184-58-9*) Interpharm.

***Software Development & Quality Assurance for the Healthcare Manufacturing Industry.** 2nd ed. Ed. by Steven R. Mallory. LC 97-5731. (Illus.). 340p. 1997. 179.00 (*1-57491-052-3*) Interpharm.

Software Development & Reality Construction. Ed. by C. Floyd et al. (Illus.). x, 477p. 1992. 59.00 (*0-387-54349-X*) Spr-Verlag.

Software Development Environments & CASE Technology: Proceedings of European Symposium, Konigswinter, FRG, June 17-19, 1991. Ed. by A. Endres & H. Weber. (Lecture Notes in Computer Science Ser.: Vol. 509). viii, 286p. 1991. 32.95 (*0-387-54194-2*) Spr-Verlag.

Software Development in C. Sartaj Sahni & Robert F. Cmelik. LC 94-30355. 1994. write for info. (*0-929306-16-3*) Silicon Pr.

Software Development in Chemistry 4: Proceedings of the 4th Workshop "Computers in Chemistry" Hochfilzen, Tirol, November 22-24, 1989. Ed. by J. Gasteiger. xii, 419p. 1990. 79.95 (*0-387-52173-9*) Spr-Verlag.

Software-Development in Chemistry 5: Proceedings of the Workshop "Computers in Chemistry", Oldenburg, 5th, November 21-23, 1990. Ed. by J. Gmehling. (Illus.). xiii, 235p. 1991. 79.95 (*0-387-53532-2*) Spr-Verlag.

Software Development in Pascal. Sartaj Sahni. 1985. text ed. 40.00 (*0-942450-01-9*) Camelot Pub FL.

Software Development Project & Management. Berkely. 1990. boxed write for info. (*0-318-68272-9*) P-H.

***Software Development to Government Standards.** 2nd ed. William Roetzheim. (C). 1996. text ed. 18.00 (*0-13-461690-1*) P-H.

Software Development Tools. 1986. lib. bdg. 79.95 (*0-8490-3745-X*) Gordon Pr.

Software Development with C Plus Plus: Maximizing Reuse with Object Technology. Kjell Nielsen. (Illus.). 450p. 1994. pap. text ed. 39.95 (*0-12-518420-4*, AP Prof) Acad Pr.

Software Development with Modula-2. D. Budgen. (Illus.). 256p. (C). 1989. pap. text ed. 33.50 (*0-201-18482-6*) Addison-Wesley.

Software Development with Z: A Practical Approach to Formal Methods in Software Engineering. J. B. Wordsworth. LC 92-15874. (C). 1992. pap. text ed. 32.25 (*0-201-62757-4*) Addison-Wesley.

Software Development Within Limits. John Boddie. (Orig.). 1986. pap. text ed. write for info. (*0-917072-59-6*, Yourdon) P-H.

Software Directory Apple: Business, Vol. 1. Widl. 1983. pap. 9.95 (*0-684-17931-8*) S&S Trade.

Software Directory Apple: Education, Vol. 3. Widl. 1983. pap. 9.95 (*0-684-17933-4*) S&S Trade.

Software Directory Apple: Games, Vol. 2. Widl. 1983. pap. 9.95 (*0-684-17932-6*) S&S Trade.

Software Directory for Automated Records Management Systems. Paul Tarrant & John T. Phillips. 336p. 1995. spiral bd. 47.00 (*0-933887-34-5*, A4568) ARMA Intl.

***Software Directory for Automated Records Management Systems.** Paul Tarrant & John T. Phillips. 298p. 1996. spiral bd. 55.00 (*0-933887-61-2*, A4568) ARMA Intl.

Software Directory for Home Builders & Remodelers, 1995. 4th ed. Home Builder Press of the National Association of Home Builders Staff. Ed. by John Tuttle. 144p. 1994. pap. 15.00 (*0-86718-399-3*) Home Builder.

Software Directory for Home Builders & Remodelers, 1996. 5th rev. ed. Jean Carmichael. 112p. 1995. pap. 18.75 (*0-86718-413-2*) Home Builder.

Software Directory for Retailers. 5th ed. Coopers & Lybrand Staff. 600p. 1995. pap. text ed. 125.00 (*0-471-13531-3*) Wiley.

Software Directory for the Classics. Rob Latousek. 95p. 1993. spiral bd. 10.00 (*0-939507-45-5*, W900) Amer Classical.

Software Diversity in Computerized Control Systems. Ed. by U. Voges. (Dependable Computing & Fault-Tolerant Systems Ser.: Vol. 2). (Illus.). 220p. 1988. 59.00 (*0-387-82014-0*) Spr-Verlag.

***Software Economy.** Ted Lewis. LC 97-13811. 256p. 1997. 25.00 (*0-88730-847-3*) Harper Busn.

Software Education Conference, 1994. LC 94-75251. 384p. 1995. pap. 60.00 (*0-8186-5870-3*, PR05870) IEEE Comp Soc.

***Software Encyclopedia 1997, Vol. 1.** Bowker, R. R., Staff. 1997. pap. write for info. (*0-8352-3918-7*) Bowker.

***Software Encyclopedia 1997, Vol. 2.** Bowker, R. R., Staff. 1997. pap. write for info. (*0-8352-3919-5*) Bowker.

Software Encyclopedia 1996, 2 vols. rev. ed. Bowker, R. R., Staff. 1996. pap. 245.00 (*0-8352-3735-4*) Bowker.

Software Encyclopedia 1996, Vol. 1. Bowker, R. R., Staff. 1996. pap. write for info. (*0-8352-3733-8*) Bowker.

Software Encyclopedia 1996, Vol. 2. Bowker, R. R., Staff. 1996. pap. write for info. (*0-8352-3734-6*) Bowker.

Software Engineering. Merlin Dorfman & Richard H. Thayer. LC 96-15910. 696p. 1996. pap. 60.00 (*0-8186-7609-4*) IEEE Comp Soc.

Software Engineering. R. E. Fairley. 1985. text ed. write for info. (*0-07-019902-7*) McGraw.

Software Engineering. Gregory Jones. 480p. 1990. Net. text ed. 37.50 (*0-471-60882-3*) Wiley.

Software Engineering. Roger S. Pressman. LC 87-35396. 1988. pap. text ed. write for info. (*0-07-050790-2*) McGraw.

Software Engineering. Ian Sommerville. 1982. write for info. (*0-201-13795-X*) Addison-Wesley.

Software Engineering. 2nd ed. Doug Bell et al. 350p. 1992. pap. text ed. 40.00 (*0-13-832536-7*) P-H.

Software Engineering. 2nd ed. Shari L. Pfleeger. 1991. text ed. 70.00 (*0-02-395115-X*, Macmillan Coll) P-H.

Software Engineering. 2nd ed. Stephen R. Schach. LC 92-31651. (Aksen Associates Series in Electrical & Computer Engineering). (Illus.). 521p. (C). 1993. text ed. 59.95 (*0-256-12998-3*, Q2998) Irwin.

Software Engineering. 2nd ed. Ian Sommerville. 318p. (C). 1985. pap. text ed. 25.75 (*0-201-14229-5*) Addison-Wesley.

Software Engineering. 3rd ed. Ian Sommerville. (International Computer Science Ser.). (Illus.). (C). 1989. text ed. 32.76 (*0-201-17568-1*) Addison-Wesley.

Software Engineering. 5th ed. Ian Sommerville. LC 95-38788. (International Computer Science Ser.). 742p. (C). 1996. text ed. 54.95 (*0-201-42765-6*) Addison-Wesley.

Software Engineering: A European Perspective. Richard H. Thayer & Andrew D. McGettrick. LC 92-17144. 696p. 1993. 55.00 (*0-8186-9117-4*, 2117) IEEE Comp Soc.

Software Engineering: A Holistic View. Bruce I. Blum. (Johns Hopkins Applied Physics Laboratory Series in Science & Engineering). (Illus.). 608p. (C). 1992. text ed. 57.00 (*0-19-507159-X*) OUP.

Software Engineering: A Practitioner's Approach. 3rd ed. Roger S. Pressman. 1992. text ed. write for info. (*0-07-050814-3*) McGraw.

***Software Engineering: A Practitioner's Approach.** 4th ed. Roger S. Pressman. (Illus.). 816p. 1996. text ed. 57.75 (*0-07-052182-4*) McGraw.

Software Engineering: A Systems Perspective. Brian Hambling. 1991. pap. 48.00 (*0-13-819715-6*, 270106) P-H.

Software Engineering: Analysis & Design. C. Easteal & G. Davies. 1989. pap. text ed. write for info. (*0-07-707202-2*) McGraw.

Software Engineering: Education & Practice. LC 95-81858. 375p. 1996. pap. 80.00 (*0-8186-7379-6*, PRO7379) IEEE Comp Soc.

Software Engineering: Methods & Management. Anneliese Von Mayrhauser. 896p. 1990. text ed. 61.00 (*0-12-727320-4*) Acad Pr.

Software Engineering: Methods, Management, & CASE Tools. Jag Sodhi. (Illus.). 400p. 1991. 39.95 (*0-8306-3442-8*, 3442, TAB/TPR) TAB Bks.

Software Engineering: Principles & Practice. J. C. Van Vliet. 558p. 1993. text ed. 44.95 (*0-471-93611-1*) Wiley.

Software Engineering: The Policy Challenge. (Information Computer Communications Policy Ser.: No. 26). 56p. (Orig.). 1991. pap. 17.00 (*92-64-13573-1*) OECD.

***Software Engineering: 1994 Edition.** 230.00 (*1-55937-442-X*, SH94213) IEEE Standards.

Software Engineering - ESEC '93: 4th European Software Engineering Conference, Garmisch-Partenkirchen, Germany, September 1993: Proceedings. Ed. by Ian Sommerville & Manfred Paul. LC 93-29537. (Lecture Notes in Computer Science Ser.: Vol. 717). 1993. 73.95 (*0-387-57209-0*) Spr-Verlag.

Software Engineering - ESEC '95: 5th European Software Engineering Conference, Sitges, Spain, September 25-28, 1995 - Proceedings. Ed. by W. Schafer et al. (Lecture Notes in Computer Science Ser.: Vol. 989). xii, 519p. 1995. pap. 81.00 (*3-540-60406-5*) Spr-Verlag.

Software Engineering & Environment: An Object-Oriented Perspective. Phillip C. Sheu. LC 96-47606. (Software Science & Engineering Ser.). (Illus.). 310p. (C). 1996. 59.50 (*0-306-45163-8*, Plenum Pr) Plenum.

Software Engineering & Human-Computer Interaction: ICSE '94 Workshop on SE-HCI : Joint Research Issues, Sorrento, Italy, May 16-17, 1994 : Proceedings. Ed. by Richard M. Taylor & Joelle Coutaz. LC 95-3824. (Lecture Notes in Computer Science Ser.: Vol. 896). x, 281p. 1995. 49.00 (*3-540-59008-0*) Spr-Verlag.

Software Engineering & Knowledge Engineering: Trends for the Next Decade. W. D. Hurley. 328p. 1995. text ed. 61.00 (*981-02-1911-3*) World Scientific Pub.

Software Engineering Economics. Barry W. Boehm. (Illus.). 768p. (C). 1981. text ed. 89.00 (*0-13-822122-7*) P-H.

Software Engineering Economics & Declining Budgets. Ed. by Pamela T. Geriner et al. (Illus.). vii, 223p. 1994. 95.95 (*0-387-57808-0*) Spr-Verlag.

Software Engineering Education. Ed. by G. A. Ford. (Lecture Notes in Computer Science Ser.: Vol. 327). (Illus.). v, 207p. 1988. 39.95 (*0-387-96854-7*) Spr-Verlag.

Software Engineering Education. Ed. by N. E. Gibbs & R. E. Fairley. (Illus.). 445p. 1986. 51.00 (*0-387-96469-X*) Spr-Verlag.

Software Engineering Education. Ed. by N. E. Gibbs. (Lecture Notes in Computer Science Ser.: Vol. 376). (Illus.). vii, 312p. 1989. 41.95 (*0-387-97090-8*) Spr-Verlag.

Software Engineering Education: Proceedings of the Eighth SEI CSEE Conference Held at New Orleans, Louisiana, U. S. A., March 29 - April 1, 1994. Eighth SEI CSEE Conference Staff. Ed. by Rosalind Ibrahim. LC 94-45980. (Lecture Notes in Computer Science: Vol. 895). xii, 449p. 1995. 75.00 (*3-540-58951-1*) Spr-Verlag.

Software Engineering Education: Proceedings of the Eighth SEI CSEE Conference Held at New Orleans, Louisiana, U. S. A., March 29-April 1, 1994. Eighth SEI CSEE Conference Staff. Ed. by Rosalind Ibrahim. LC 94-45980. (Lecture Notes in Computer Science: Vol. 895). 1995. write for info. (*0-387-58951-1*) Spr-Verlag.

Software Engineering Education: Proceedings of the IFIP WG3.4 - SEARCC SRIG on Education & Training Working Conference, Hong Kong, 28 September- 2 October 1993. Ed. by Ben-Zion Barta et al. LC 93-45542. (IFIP Transactions A: Computer Science & Technology Ser.: Vol. A-40). 350p. 1994. 126.75 (*0-444-81597-X*, North Holland) Elsevier.

Software Engineering Education: Proceedings of the Seventh SEI Conference, CSEE 1994, San Antonio, Texas, U. S. A., January 1994. Seventh SEI Conference on Software Engineering Education. Ed. by Jorge L. Diaz-Herrera. LC 93-41150. (Lecture Notes in Computer Science Ser.). 1993. 87.95 (*0-387-57461-1*) Spr-Verlag.

Software Engineering Education: SEI Conference 1990, Pittsburgh, Pennsylvania, U. S. A., April 2-3, 1990 Proceedings. Ed. by L. E. Deimel et al. (Lecture Notes in Computer Science Ser.: Vol. 423). vi, 164p. 1990. 29.95 (*0-387-97274-9*) Spr-Verlag.

Software Engineering Education: SEI Conference 1991 Pittsburgh, Pennsylvania, U. S. A., October 7-8, 1991 Proceedings. Ed. by J. E. Tomayko et al. (Lecture Notes in Computer Science Ser.: Vol. 536). viii, 296p. 1991. 35.95 (*0-387-54502-6*) Spr-Verlag.

Software Engineering Education: SEI Conference 1992, San Diego, California, U. S. A., October 1992, Proceedings. Ed. by C. Sledge. LC 92-30805. (Lecture Notes in Computer Science Ser.: Vol. 640). xi, 451p. 1992. pap. 67.00 (*0-387-55963-9*) Spr-Verlag.

Software Engineering Education Conference, 9th Conference On. LC 95-81859. 283p. 1996. 60.00 (*0-8186-7249-8*, PRO7249) IEEE Comp Soc.

***Software Engineering Education, 10th Conference.** 450p. 1997. 90.00 (*0-8186-7886-0*) IEEE Comp Soc.

Software Engineering Environments: Automated Support for Software Engineering. Alan W. Brown. (International Series in Software Engineering). 254p. 1993. pap. text ed. 38.00i (*0-07-707432-7*) McGraw.

Software Engineering Environments: Proceedings of the International Workshop in Environments Chinon, France, September 18-20, 1989. Ed. by F. W. Long. (Lecture Notes in Computer Science Ser.: Vol. 467). vi, 313p. 1990. 38.00 (*0-387-53452-0*) Spr-Verlag.

Software Engineering Environments, 7th Conference on (SEE '95) Ed. by Malcolm S. Verrall. LC 95-75657. 224p. 1995. pap. 50.00 (*0-8186-7093-2*, PR07093) IEEE Comp Soc.

***Software Engineering Environments, 8th International Conference.** 184p. 1997. pap. 70.00 (*0-8186-8019-9*) IEEE Comp Soc.

Software Engineering for Higher Education: Proceedings of the First International Conference. Ed. by G. King et al. LC 94-79237. (SEHE Ser.: Vol. 1). 496p. 1994. text ed. 219.00 (*1-56252-213-2*, 2890) Computational Mech MA.

Software Engineering for Higher Education II: Proceedings of the 2nd Conference. Ed. by J. L. Uso et al. LC 95-68885. (SEHE Ser.: Vol. 2). 416p. 1995. 190.00 (*1-56252-309-0*, 3854) Computational Mech MA.

***Software Engineering for Manufacturing Systems: Methods & Case-Tools.** A. Storr. 208p. 1996. text ed. write for info. (*0-412-78460-2*, Chap & Hall NY) Chapman & Hall.

Software Engineering for Microprocessor Systems. Ed. by P. Depledge et al. (Computing Ser.). 273p. 1984. boxed 53.00 (*0-86341-087-1*, CM002) Inst Elect Eng.

***Software Engineering for Parallel & Distributed Systems Conference (Pdse '97)** 300p. 1997. pap. 60.00 (*0-8186-8043-1*) IEEE Comp Soc.

Software Engineering Fundamentals. Ali Behforooz & Frederick J. Hudson. (Illus.). 688p. (C). 1996. 64.00 (*0-19-510539-7*) OUP.

Software Engineering in C. Philip E. Margolis & P. A. Darnell. (Books on Professional Computing). (Illus.). 500p. 1989. pap. 32.00 (*0-387-96574-2*) Spr-Verlag.

***Software Engineering in Medical Informatics.** T. Timmers & B. I. Blum. 548p. 1991. 181.50 (*0-444-89013-0*, North Holland) Elsevier.

Software Engineering Mathematics. Jim Woodcock & Martin J. Loomes. (Software Engineering Institute Ser.). (Illus.). 256p. (C). 1990. text ed. 32.25 (*0-201-50424-3*) Addison-Wesley.

Software Engineering Mathematics. Jim Woodcock & Martin J. Loomes. 292p. (C). 1988. pap. text ed. 150.00 (*0-273-02673-9*, Pub. by Pitman Pubng UK) St Mut.

Software Engineering Metrics, Vol. 1. Martin Shepperd. 1994. pap. text ed. 45.00 (*0-07-707410-6*) McGraw.

Software Engineering Metrics & Models. Samuel D. Conte et al. 500p. (C). 1986. text ed. 51.75 (*0-8053-2162-4*) Benjamin-Cummings.

Software Engineering on the Sun Workstation. Bill Cureton. 1993. 60.95 (*0-387-97480-6*) Spr-Verlag.

Software Engineering Productivity: A Practical Guide. C. Stevenson. 1994. text ed. 79.95 (*0-412-37840-X*) Chapman & Hall.

Software Engineering Productivity Handbook. Jessica Keyes. LC 92-23356. 608p. 1993. text ed. 59.50 (*0-07-911366-4*) McGraw.

Software Engineering Project Management. Richard H. Thayer. LC 87-71731. 512p. 1988. pap. 60.00 (*0-8186-0751-3*, 751) IEEE Comp Soc.

***Software Engineering Project Management.** 2nd ed. Ed. by Richard H. Thayer. LC 97-20500. 504p. 1997. pap. 60.00 (*0-8186-8000-8*) IEEE Comp Soc.

Software Engineering Risk Management. Dale Karolak. LC 95-36599. 184p. 1995. 40.00 (*0-8186-7194-7*, BP07194) IEEE Comp Soc.

***Software Engineering Standards: A User S Road Map.** James W. Moore. LC 97-19179. 1997. write for info. (*1-55937-925-1*) IEEE Standards.

Software Engineering Standards: An Annotated Index & Directory. S. Magee & Leonard Tripp. 250p. 1994. 79.50 (*0-912702-82-6*) Global Eng Doc.

Software Engineering Standards Symposium (SESS '95) LC 10-823670. 304p. 1995. pap. 50.00 (*0-8186-7137-8*, PR07137) IEEE Comp Soc.

***Software Engineering Standards, 3rd International Symposium: Experience & Practice.** LC 10-823670. 300p. 1997. pap. 80.00 (*0-8186-7837-2*) IEEE Comp Soc.

Software Engineering Strategies: A Guide for Instituting Technology for the 1990s. Roger S. Pressman. (Illus.). 288p. 1988. text ed. 38.00 (*0-13-823030-7*) P-H.

Software Engineering Technique. Coates. (ITCP-UK Computer Science Ser.). 1997. pap. 27.95 (*1-85032-224-4*) Van Nos Reinhold.

Software Engineering Tools for Professional Workstations: The Lilith Project. Gustav Pomberger. 1991. boxed 48.00 (*0-13-823485-X*) P-H.

Software Engineering with Abstractions. Valdis Berzins & Lucia Lugi. (Illus.). (C). 1991. text ed. 50.50 (*0-201-08004-4*) Addison-Wesley.

Software Engineering with Ada. 3rd rev. ed. Grady Booch et al. LC 93-5093. (Series in Object-Oriented Software Engineering). 560p. (C). 1994. pap. 45.25 (*0-8053-0608-0*) Benjamin-Cummings.

Software Engineering with B. John Wordsworth. 1996. pap. text ed. 39.75 (*0-201-40356-0*) Addison-Wesley.

Software Engineering with C++ & CASE. Michael Pont. 1996. pap. 39.75 incl. disk (*0-201-87718-X*) Addison-Wesley.

Software Engineering with Formal Metrics. Lem O. Ejiogu. 1991. 49.95 (*0-89435-329-2*) Wiley.

Software Engineering with Formal Metrics. Lem O. Ejiogu. 334p. 1993. text ed. 59.95 (*0-471-56155-X*) Wiley.

***Software Engineering with Java.** Stephen R. Schach. 640p. (C). 1996. text ed. 51.95 (*0-256-24167-8*) Irwin.

Software Engineering with MODULA-2 & Ada. Richard S. Wiener & Richard F. Sincovec. LC 83-21827. 451p. (C). 1984. Net. text ed. 47.50 (*0-471-89014-6*) Wiley.

Software Engineering with PERL. Carl Dichter & Mark Pease. (C). 1995. pap. text ed. 38.00 (*0-13-016965-X*) P-H.

***Software Engineering with Reusable Components.** LC 97-11976. 1997. write for info. (*3-540-62695-6*) Spr-Verlag.

Software Engineering with Systems Analysis & Design. Donald V. Steward. LC 86-26808. 414p. (C). 1987. text ed. 62.95 (*0-534-07506-1*) PWS Pubs.

Software Engineering with UNIX-C Environment. William B. Frakes et al. 368p. 1991. text ed. 60.00 (*0-13-829763-0*) P-H.

Software Engineering, 16th International Conference (ICSE-16) LC 80-640758. 392p. 1994. pap. 80.00 (*0-8186-5855-X*, 5855) IEEE Comp Soc.

Software Engineering, 18th International Conference on (ICSE-18) LC 02-705257. 400p. 1996. pap. 80.00 (*0-8186-7246-3*, PRO7246) IEEE Comp Soc.

***Software Engineer's Pocket Book.** Michael M. Tooley. LC 95-108939. 248p. pap. 70.70 (*0-608-04990-5*, 2065608) Bks Demand.

Software Engineer's Reference Book. Ed. by John A. McDermid. 1993. 86.00 (*0-8493-7766-8*, QA76) CRC Pr.

Software Error Analysis. Wendy W. Peng & Dolores R. Wallace. LC 94-24763. 1994. write for info. (*0-929306-18-X*) Silicon Pr.

S

Software Evaluation for Certification: Principles, Practice, & Legal Liability. Ed. by Andrew Rae et al. LC 94-29412. (Software Assurance Ser.). 1994. write for info. (*0-07-709042-X*) McGraw.

Software Evolution: A Software Maintenance Challenge. Lowell J. Arthur. LC 87-20972. 254p. 1988. text ed. 67.95 (*0-471-62871-9*) Wiley.

***Software Excellence: A Total Quality Management Guide.** Shigeichi Moriguchi. LC 96-50309. (Illus.). 640p. 1997. 90.00 (*1-56327-050-1*) Prod Press.

Software Factory: Managing Software Development & Maintenance. 2nd ed. James R. Johnson. 277p. 1993. text ed. 49.95 (*0-471-57225-X*) Wiley.

***Software Factory Challenge.** Ed. by H. Weber. LC 96-77817. 240p. (gr. 12). 1997. 89.00 (*90-5199-288-2*, 288-2) IOS Press.

Software Failure Risk: Measurement & Management. Susan A. Sherer. LC 92-29736. (Applications of Modern Technology in Business Ser.). (Illus.). 280p. (C). 1992. 49.50 (*0-306-44293-0*, Plenum Pr) Plenum.

Software Fault Tolerance. Ed. by Michael R. Lyu. LC 94-46435. (Trends in Software Ser.). 200p. 1995. pap. text ed. 46.95 (*0-471-95068-8*) Wiley.

Software Fault Tolerance: Achievement & Assessment Strategies. Ed. by M. Kersken & F. Saglietti. (Research Reports ESPRIT: Vol. 1). 243p. 1992. 47.95 (*0-387-55212-X*) Spr-Verlag.

Software Folklore. Robert L. Glass. 1991. 10.00 (*0-942337-04-2*) Computing Trends.

Software for Architects: The Guide to Computer Applications for the Architecture Profession. Douglas E. Noble & Karen M. Kenser. (Illus.). 472p. (Orig.). pap. 50.00 (*1-882352-00-9*) Ctr Architect Tech.

Software for Building Services: A Selection Guide. S. R. Loyd. 1993. 120.00 (*0-86022-354-X*, Pub. by Build Servs Info Assn UK) St Mut.

Software for Computer Control (SOCOCO 1988) Selected Papers from the Fifth IFAC-IFIP Symposium, Johannesburg, South Africa, 26-28 April, 1988. Ed. by I. M. Macleod & A. D. Heher. (IFAC Proceedings Ser.). (Illus.). 164p. 1989. 94.00 (*0-08-035724-5*) Elsevier.

Software for Electrical Engineering Analysis & Design III: Proceedings of the Third International Conference. Ed. by P. P. Silvester. LC 96-83665. (Electrosoft Ser.: Vol. 3). 528p. 1996. text ed. 221.00 (*1-85312-395-1*, 3951) Computational Mech MA.

Software for Engineering. Ed. by Robert A. Adey. (Progress in Engineering Ser.). 113p. 1985. pap. 46.00 (*0-931215-04-8*) Computational Mech MA.

Software for Engineering Problems III. Ed. by Robert A. Adey. LC 90-81260. (Progress in Engineering Ser.). 184p. 1993. pap. text ed. 75.00 (*0-945824-31-9*, 0480) Computational Mech MA.

Software for Engineering WorkStations: Finite Element Codes. Ed. by C. A. Brebbia. LC 87-70263. (Progress in Engineering Ser.). 102p. 1987. 46.00 (*0-931215-63-3*) Computational Mech MA.

Software for Industrial Automation. 1987. 35.00 (*92-1-116392-7*, E.87.II.E.19) UN.

***Software for Industrial Safety & Health.** Richard K. Miller et al. (Market Research Survey Ser.: No. 242). 50p. 1996. 200.00 (*1-55865-292-2*) Future Tech Surveys.

Software for Internists: Critical Evaluations from Medical Software Reviews & the Journal Literature. Ed. by Sue Frisch. LC 94-10259. 211p. 1994. 75.00 (*0-943126-32-0*) Amer Coll Phys.

Software for Parallel Computation: Proceedings of the NATO Advanced Research Workshop on Software for Parallel Computation, Held at Cetraro, Cosenza, Italy, June 22-26, 1992. NATO Advanced Research Workshop on Software for Parallel Computation. Ed. by Janusz S. Kowalik & Lucio Grandinetti. LC 93-16443. (NATO ASI Series F: Computer & Systems Sciences, Special Programme AET: Vol. 106). 1993. 100.95 (*0-387-56451-9*) Spr-Verlag.

Software for Parallel Computers. R. H. Perrott. (UNICOM Applied Information Technology Ser.: No. 9). (Illus.). 304p. 1991. text ed. 103.95 (*0-412-39960-1*) Chapman & Hall.

Software for Photometric Astronomy. Silvano Ghedini. LC 82-8574. (Illus.). 224p. 1982. pap. text ed. 19.95 (*0-943396-00-X*) Willmann-Bell.

***Software for Use: A Practical Guide to the Models & Methods of Usage-Centered Design.** Larry L. Constantine. (C). 1997. pap. text ed. 29.95 (*0-201-92478-1*) Addison-Wesley.

***Software Fur Den Fremdsprachenunterricht.** Ioanna Andreadou. (Sprache und Computer Ser.: Bd. 6). viii, 211p. (GER.). 1987. write for info. (*3-487-07826-0*) G Olms Pubs.

***Software Goes to School: Teaching for Understanding with New Technology.** Ed. by David N. Perkins et al. (Illus.). 304p. 1997. reprint ed. pap. text ed. 19.95 (*0-19-511577-5*) OUP.

Software Handbook. 1986. lib. bdg. 79.95 (*0-8490-3754-9*) Gordon Pr.

Software Handbook for DOS for IBM PC, XT, AT, PS2 & Compatibles. Ed. by Homer W. Parker, Sr. LC 88-92322. 240p. (Orig.). 1989. pap. 12.95 (*0-922958-00-9*) H W Parker.

Software Implementation. 2nd ed. Michael Marcotty. 300p. 1991. pap. 49.20 (*0-13-823493-0*) P-H.

Software Implementation Techniques: Open VMS, UNIX, OS-2 & Windows NT. 2nd ed. Donald E. Merusi. LC 95-14929. (Illus.). 680p. 1995. pap. 52.95 (*1-55558-134-X*, Digital DEC) Buttrwrth-Heinemann.

Software Important to Safety in Nuclear Power Plants. International Atomic Energy Agency Staff. (Technical Reports: No. 367). 169p. 1994. pap. 55.00 (*92-0-101594-1*, STI/DOC/367, Pub. by IAEA AU) Bernan Associates.

Software Industry. 1986. lib. bdg. 79.95 (*0-8490-3764-6*) Gordon Pr.

Software Industry: Current Trends & Implications for Developing Countries. (UNIDO General Studies). 243p. 1993. 49.00 (*92-1-106283-7*) UN.

Software Industry Accounting. J. M. Morris. 142p. 1994. suppl. ed., pap. 45.00 (*0-471-30398-4*) Wiley.

Software Industry Accounting. Joseph M. Morris et al. LC 92-21904. 320p. 1992. text ed. 130.00 (*0-471-55931-8*) Wiley.

***Software Industry Accounting, 1997 Cumulative Supplement.** Joseph M. Morris. 416p. 1997. pap. 65.00 (*0-471-16716-9*, AC32) Wiley.

Software Industry Factbook: The Software Industry's Annual Report. Jeff Silverstein et al. (Illus.). 580p. (Orig.). 1991. pap. 395.00 (*0-927252-05-8*) Digital Information.

Software Inspection. Tom Gilb et al. Ed. by Susannah Finzi. LC 93-1151. 471p. (C). 1993. pap. text ed. 43.25 (*0-201-63181-4*) Addison-Wesley.

Software Inspection: An Industry Best Practice. Ed. by David A. Wheeler et al. LC 95-41054. 312p. 1996. pap. 38.00 (*0-8186-7340-0*) IEEE Comp Soc.

Software Inspection Process. Susan H. Strauss. 1993. text ed. 47.00 (*0-07-062166-7*) McGraw.

Software Interface for CEMS Relative Accuracy Test Audit Data. 1995. pap. 30.00 (*1-55617-571-X*, S77.81.05) ISA.

***Software Law: A User Friendly Legal Guide for Software Developers.** Todd F. Bassinger. LC 97-8433. (Legal Survival Guides Ser.). 250p. (Orig.). 1997. pap. 29.95 incl. disk (*1-57071-163-1*) Sourcebks.

Software Law Primer. Frederic W. Neitzke. LC 83-23508. 176p. 1984. text ed. 37.95 (*0-442-26866-1*) Van Nos Reinhold.

Software Legal Book: 1997 Edition, 2 vols. rev. ed. Paul S. Hoffman. 998p. 1996. ring bd. 199.75 (*0-931687-00-4*) Shafer Bks.

Software Lifecycle Management: The Incremental Method. William C. Cave & Gilbert W. Maymon. LC 84-11264. (Atre Ser.). 300p. 1984. 34.95 (*0-02-949210-6*, Free Press) Free Pr.

Software Maintenance: Concepts & Practice. Penny Grubb & Armstrong Takang. (Illus.). 256p. 1996. 34.95 (*1-85032-192-2*) ITCP.

Software Maintenance: The Problems & Its Solutions. James Martin & Carma L. McClure. (Illus.). 512p. (C). 1983. text ed. 88.00 (*0-13-822361-0*) P-H.

Software Maintenance: The Small System Management Guide. David Bellin. 176p. 1990. pap. text ed. 30.00 (*0-685-40434-X*) P-H.

***Software Maintenance & Reengineering, 1st Euromicro Working Conference.** LC 96-80270. 250p. 1997. pap. 50.00 (*0-8186-7892-5*) IEEE Comp Soc.

Software Maintenance Guidebook. Robert L. Glass & Ronald A. Noiseux. (Illus.). 208p. 1981. text ed. 45.00 (*0-13-821728-9*) P-H.

Software Maintenance Management. 1986. lib. bdg. 79.95 (*0-8490-3739-5*) Gordon Pr.

Software Maintenance Management. Bennett P. Lientz & E. Burton Swanson. LC 80-12154. 160p. 1980. pap. text ed. write for info. (*0-201-04205-3*) Addison-Wesley.

Software Maintenance, 1994 Conference On. LC 94-76076. 472p. 1994. pap. 100.00 (*0-8186-6330-8*) IEEE Comp Soc.

Software Maintenance, 1995 Conference on (CSM '95) LC 10-636773. 392p. 1995. pap. 100.00 (*0-8186-7141-6*, PR07141) IEEE Comp Soc.

Software Maintenance, 1996 International Conference on (ICSM '96) LC 10-636773. 400p. 1996. pap. 80.00 (*0-8186-7677-9*) IEEE Comp Soc.

***Software Maintenance, 1997 International Conference.** 330p. 1997. pap. 80.00 (*0-8186-8013-X*) IEEE Comp Soc.

Software Management. 4th ed. Donald J. Reifer. LC 92-27322. 664p. 1993. 79.00 (*0-8186-3342-5*, 3342) IEEE Comp Soc.

***Software Management.** 5th ed. Donald J. Reifer. LC 97-20501. 550p. 1997. 70.00 (*0-8186-8001-6*) IEEE Comp Soc.

Software Management Resources: Issues, Answers, Industry Experience, Technology, & Resource Pointers for Managing a Software Portfolio. Nicholas Zvegintzov. 36p. 1994. pap. 35.00 (*1-884521-02-9*) Software Maint.

Software Management Technology Reference Guide: Release 4.2. Nicholas Zvegintzov. 274p. 1994. pap. 95.00 (*1-884521-01-0*) Software Maint.

Software Management Technology Reference Guide: 1994-95 European Edition. Nicholas Zvegintzov. 274p. 1994. pap. 95.00 (*1-884521-05-3*) Software Maint.

Software Measurement: Understanding Software Engineering. Melton. 1995. pap. (*0-412-55180-2*) Chapman & Hall.

Software Measurement: Understanding Software Engineering. Austin Melton. (Illus.). 288p. 1996. 39.95 (*1-85032-178-7*) ITCP.

Software Measurement Guidebook. John E. Gaffney, Jr. et al. 260p. 1995. pap. 39.95 (*0-442-02009-0*) VA Numismatic Assn.

Software Measurement Guidebook. Software Productivity Consortium Staff et al. LC 95-44144. 260p. 1996. pap. 39.95 (*1-85032-195-7*) ITCP.

Software Merging & Slicing. Ed. by Valdis Berzins. LC 95-7313. 248p. 1995. pap. 46.00 (*0-8186-6792-3*, PB06792) IEEE Comp Soc.

Software Methods for Business Reengineering. Alfs Berztiss. LC 95-19289. (Illus.). 320p. 1995. 54.95 (*0-387-94553-9*) Spr-Verlag.

Software Metrics. Ed. by Mary Shaw et al. (Computer Science Ser.). (Illus.). 350p. 1981. 50.00 (*0-262-16083-8*) MIT Pr.

Software Metrics: A Practical Guide. Jonathan R. Moller. (C). 1992. pap. text ed. 39.50 (*0-412-45900-0*) Chapman & Hall.

Software Metrics: A Rigorous & Practical Approach. 2nd ed. N. E. Fenton. 400p. 1996. pap. 36.95 (*1-85032-275-9*) ITCP.

Software Metrics: A Rigorous Approach. N. E. Fenton. (Illus.). 352p. 1991. pap. 36.95 (*0-412-40440-0*) Chapman & Hall.

Software Metrics: A Rigorous Approach. 2nd ed. Norman Fenton & Shari L. Pfleeger. (Computer Science Ser.). 320p. 1997. pap. 47.95 (*0-534-95600-9*) PWS Pubs.

Software Metrics: Establishing a Company-Wide Program. Robert B. Grady & Deborah L. Caswell. 1987. text ed. 56.00 (*0-13-821844-7*) P-H.

Software Metrics: Measurement for Software Process Improvement. Barbara Kitchenham. 241p. 1996. 74.95 (*1-85554-820-8*) Blackwell Pubs.

Software Metrics for Product Assessment. Richard Bache & Gualtiero Bazanna. LC 93-29406. (International Series in Software Assurance). 1993. write for info. (*0-07-707923-X*) McGraw.

Software Metrics Symposium, 2nd International. LC 94-75387. 120p. 1994. pap. 40.00 (*0-8186-5865-7*) IEEE Comp Soc.

Software Metrics Symposium, 3rd International: From Measurement to Empirical Results. LC 96-75874. 200p. 1996. pap. 50.00 (*0-8186-7364-8*, PRO7364) IEEE Comp Soc.

***Software Metrics Symposium, 4th International (Metrics '97)** 225p. 1997. pap. 80.00 (*0-8186-8093-8*) IEEE Comp Soc.

Software Numerical Analysis. 5th ed. Burden. (Mathematics Ser.). 1993. student ed., pap. 33.95 (*0-534-93221-5*) PWS Pubs.

Software of the Self: Technology & Culture. Anthony Smith. 144p. 1996. text ed. 22.00 (*0-19-503900-9*) OUP.

Software Package in Support of ASTM Standard Practice for Environmental Site Assessments: Transaction Screen Process, User's Guide, E1528-93. Ed. by Anthony J. Buonicore. (ASTM Manual Ser.: MNL24). 54p. 1995. text ed. 99.00 (*0-8031-2063-X*, 28-024094-65) ASTM.

Software Patents. Gregory A. Stobbs. LC 94-41806. (Business Practice Library). 350p. 1995. text ed. 135.00 (*0-471-06324-X*) Wiley.

***Software Patents - 1997 Cumulative Supplement.** Gregory A. Stobbs. pap. text ed. write for info. (*0-471-17959-0*) Wiley.

***Software Patterns: Management Briefings.** James O. Coplien. 61p. 1996. pap. 85.00 (*1-884842-50-X*) SIGS Bks & Multimedia.

Software Performability: From Concepts to Applications. Ann T. Tai et al. LC 95-39326. (International Series in Engineering & Computer Science, Natural Language Processing & Machine Translation: Vol. 347). 216p. (C). 1995. lib. bdg. 99.50 (*0-7923-9670-7*) Kluwer Ac.

Software Perspectives: The System Is the Message. Peter Freeman. LC 86-32135. 294p. (C). 1987. pap. text ed. 24.75 (*0-201-11969-2*) Addison-Wesley.

***Software Portability with Imake.** 2nd ed. Paul Dubois. Ed. by Gigi Estabrook. (Illus.). 410p. 1996. pap. 32.95 (*1-56592-226-3*) OReilly & Assocs.

Software Process Automation: The Technology & Its Adoption. A. M. Christie. 1995. 39.95 (*3-540-58414-5*) Spr-Verlag.

Software Process Automation: The Technology & Its Adoption. Alan M. Christie. LC 95-2780. 1995. write for info. (*0-387-58414-5*) Spr-Verlag.

Software Process Design. Jacqueline Holdsworth. LC 94-18466. (International Software Quality Assurance Ser.). 1994. text ed. 35.00 (*0-07-707842-X*) McGraw.

***Software Process Improvement: Successful Models & Strategies.** Sami Zahran. (C). 1997. text ed. 39.76 (*0-201-17782-X*) Addison-Wesley.

Software Process Modelling & Technology. Ed. by Anthony Finkelstein et al. LC 94-14996. (Research Studies Advanced Software Development). 362p. 1994. text ed. 94.95 (*0-471-95206-0*) Wiley.

Software Process Technology: Proceedings of Second European Workshop, Trondheim, Norway, September 7-8, 1992. Ed. by J. C. Derniame. LC 92-28845. (Lecture Notes in Computer Science Ser.: Vol. 635). ix, 253p. 1992. 47.00 (*0-387-55928-0*); pap. 43.00 (*3-540-55928-0*) Spr-Verlag.

Software Process Technology: Proceedings of the Third European Workshop EWSPT '94, Villard de Lans, France, February 7-8, 1994. Ed. by Brian C. Warboys. LC 93-49868. (Lecture Notes in Computer Science Ser.: Vol. 772). ix, 278p. 1994. 44.95 (*0-387-57739-4*) Spr-Verlag.

Software Process Technology: Proceedings of the 4th European Workshop, EWSPT '95, Noordwijkerhout, the Netherlands, April 3-5, 1995. Ed. by Wilhelm Schafer et al. LC 95-13006. (Lecture Notes in Computer Science Ser.: Vol. 913). ix, 261p. 1995. 49.00 (*3-540-59205-9*) Spr-Verlag.

Software Process Technology: Proceedings of the 4th European Workshop, EWSPT '95, Noordwijkerhout, the Netherlands, April 3-5, 1995. Ed. by Schafer Wilhelm & EWSPT '95 Staff. LC 95-13006. (Lecture Notes in Computer Science Ser.: Vol. 913). 1995. write for info. (*0-387-59205-9*) Spr-Verlag.

***Software Process Technology: 5th European Workshop, EWSPT '96, Nancy, France, October 8-11, 1996, Proceedings, Vol. 114.** Carlo Montangero. LC 96-43203. (Lecture Notes on Computer Science Ser.). 1996. 49.00 (*3-540-61771-X*) Spr-Verlag.

***Software Process Workshop, 10th International.** 160p. 1997. pap. 50.00 (*0-8186-7725-2*, PR07725) IEEE Comp Soc.

Software Process Workshop, 9th International. LC 94-61096. 160p. 1995. pap. 36.00 (*0-8186-6770-2*, PR06770) IEEE Comp Soc.

Software Process, 3rd International Conference On. LC 94-77791. 200p. 1994. pap. 40.00 (*0-8186-6695-1*) IEEE Comp Soc.

Software Product Assurance. Bryan. 1987. text ed. 87.00 (*0-13-500505-1*) P-H.

***Software Product Directory for Builders & Remodelers: Updated for 1997.** 6th rev. ed. Jean Carmichael. 84p. 1997. pap. 22.50 (*0-86718-422-1*) Home Builder.

Software Productivity. Harlan D. Mills. LC 88-5099. (Illus.). 288p. 1988. reprint ed. pap. 25.00 (*0-932633-10-2*) Dorset Hse Pub Co.

Software Productivity & Quality Today: The Worldwide Perspective. Capers Jones. 150p. 1993. ring bd. 180.00 (*1-56909-001-7*) Info Systs Mgmt.

***Software Productivity, Quality & Usability: Measurement, Prediction & Improvements.** Simmons & Newton C. Ellis. (C). 1997. text ed. 50.00 (*0-13-840695-2*) P-H.

***Software Project Cost & Schedule Estimating: Best Practices.** William H. Roetzheim & Reyna Beasley. (C). 1997. text ed. 33.75 incl. disk (*0-13-682089-1*) P-H.

Software Project Dynamics: An Integrated Approach. T. Abdel-Hamid. 1991. text ed. 69.00 (*0-13-822040-9*) P-H.

Software Project Management. Mike Cotterell & Robert Hughes. (Illus.). 336p. 1996. pap. 31.95 (*1-85032-190-6*) ITCP.

Software Project Management: A Practitioner's Approach. E. M. Bennatan. LC 92-9486. 1992. write for info. (*0-07-707437-8*) McGraw.

Software Project Management: Practitioner's Approach. E.M. Bennatan. LC 94-5319. 1994. write for info. (*0-07-707648-6*) McGraw.

Software Project Management: Readings & Cases. Chris Kemerer. LC 96-43010. 688p. (C). 1996. per. 62.95 (*0-256-18545-X*) Irwin.

Software Project Management - Step by Step. Marsha D. Lewin & Milton D. Rosenau, Jr. 313p. 1988. text ed. 35.00 (*0-9627022-0-X*) M D Lewin Assocs.

Software Project Management for Small to Medium Sized Projects. John Rakos. 1990. text ed. 69.33 (*0-13-826173-3*) P-H.

Software Project Planning. M. Cotterell. 1995. pap. (*0-412-60400-0*) Chapman & Hall.

***Software Project Survival Guide.** Steve McConnell. 1997. pap. text ed. 34.99 (*1-57231-621-7*) Microsoft.

***Software Projects: Evolutionary Versus Big Bang Theory.** Felix Redmill. 1997. 49.99 (*0-471-93343-0*) Wiley.

Software Prototyping, Formal Methods & VDM. Sharam Hekmatpour & Darrel C. Ince. (International Computer Science Ser.). (Illus.). 256p. (C). 1988. text ed. 31.25 (*0-201-17572-X*) Addison-Wesley.

Software Publishers Association Legal Guide to Multimedia. Thomas J. Smedinghoff. LC 94-12959. 1994. 44.95 incl. disk (*0-201-40931-3*) Addison-Wesley.

Software Quality. Ernest Wallmuller. 300p. 1994. pap. text ed. 42.00 (*0-13-819780-6*) P-H.

***Software Quality.** 2nd ed. Gilles. LC 96-49771. (ITCP-UK Computer Science Ser.). 1996. pap. 44.95 (*1-85032-312-7*) ITCP.

Software Quality: A Framework for Success in Software Development. Joc Sanders. (C). 1994. pap. text ed. 29.25 (*0-201-63198-9*) Addison-Wesley.

Software Quality: Concepts & Plans. Robert H. Dunn. 700p. 1989. text ed. 78.00 (*0-13-820283-4*) P-H.

Software Quality: Objective Quality: Second Symposium on Software Quality Techniques & Acquisition Criteria, Florence, Italy, May 28-30, 1995: Proceedings. Ed. by Paolo Nesi. (Lecture Notes in Computer Science Ser.: Vol. 926). 1995. write for info. (*0-387-59449-3*) Spr-Verlag.

Software Quality: Objective Quality: Second Symposium on Software Quality Techniques & Acquisition Criteria, Florence, Italy, May 28-30, 1995: Proceedings. Ed. by Paolo Nesi et al. (Lecture Notes in Computer Science Ser.: Vol. 926). 249p. 1995. 49.00 (*3-540-59449-3*) Spr-Verlag.

Software Quality: Theory & Management. Alan C. Gillies. 256p. 1992. pap. 39.95 (*0-442-31577-5*) Chapman & Hall.

Software Quality: Theory & Management. Alan C. Gillies. 272p. 1992. pap. 46.50 (*0-412-45130-1*) Chapman & Hall.

Software Quality: Theory & Management. 2nd ed. Alan C. Gillies. (ITCP-UK Computer Science Ser.). (Illus.). 300p. 1997. pap. 44.95 (*1-85032-270-8*) ITCP.

Software Quality & Copyright: Issues in Computer-Assisted Instruction. Virginia Helm. 152p. 1984. 16.00 (*0-89240-047-1*) Assn Ed Comm Tech.

***Software Quality & Productivity: Theory, Practice, Education & Training.** Ed. by Lee et al. (Illus.). 416p. (C). 1994. text ed. 103.95 (*0-412-62960-7*, Chap & Hall NY) Chapman & Hall.

Software Quality & Reliability. Ince. (C). 1991. text ed. 89.50 (*0-412-37810-8*) Chapman & Hall.

Software Quality & Reliability: Tools & Methods. Ed. by Darrel C. Ince. (UNICOM Applied Information Technology Ser.: No. 5). (Illus.). 180p. 1991. 76.95 (*0-442-31314-4*) Chapman & Hall.

***Software Quality Assurance: A Guide for Developers & Auditors.** Howard G. Smith. LC 97-3242. (Illus.). 380p. 1997. 189.00 (*1-57491-049-3*) Interpharm.

Software Quality Assurance: A Student Introduction. Darrel Ince. LC 95-7040. 1995. write for info. (*0-07-709096-9*) McGraw.

Software Quality Assurance: What It Buys You & What It Costs You. Peter Farrell-Vinay. (C). 1994. 190.00 (*0-946655-53-7*, Pub. by Stanley Thornes UK) Trans-Atl Phila.

Software Quality Assurance & Management. Michael W. Evans & John J. Marciniak. LC 86-1713. 352p. 1987. text ed. 65.00 (*0-471-80930-6*) Wiley.

Software Quality Assurance & Measurement: A Worldwide Perspective. Norman Fenton et al. 304p. 1995. pap. 49.95 (*1-85032-174-4*) ITCP.

***Software Quality Assurance SOPs for Healthcare Manufacturers.** Steven R. Mallory. LC 97-6739. 425p. 1997. 179.00 (*1-57491-038-8*) Interpharm.

Software Quality Control, Error Analysis, & Testing. Judith A. Clapp & Deborah A. Cerino. LC 94-35136. (Advanced Computing & Telecommunications Ser.). (Illus.). 392p. 1995. 54.00 (*0-8155-1363-1*) Noyes.

Software Quality Engineering. Ed. by C. Tasso et al. (SQE Ser.). 357p. 1997. text ed. 188.00 (*1-85312-403-6*, 4036) Computational Mech MA.

Software Quality Engineering: A Total Technical & Management Approach. Michael S. Deutsch & Ronald R. Willis. (Illus.). 416p. (C). 1988. text ed. 34.67 (*0-685-37792-X*) P-H.

Software Quality Engineering: A Total Technical & Management Approach. Michael S. Deutsch & Ronald R. Willis. LC 87-25712. 1988. text ed. 87.00 (*0-13-823204-0*) P-H.

Software Quality Management. Cooper. 1979. text ed. 25.95 (*0-89433-093-4*) Petrocelli.

Software Quality Management. TAB Books Staff. 1979. 25.95 (*0-07-155517-X*) McGraw.

Software Quality Management II: Proceedings of the Second International Conference, 2 vols., Set. Ed. by M. Ross et al. LC 94-70402. (SQM Ser.). 1592p. 1994. text ed. 491.00 (*1-56252-188-8*, 2645) Computational Mech MA.

Software Quality Management II Vol. 1: Managing Quality Systems. Ed. by C. A. Brebbia et al. LC 94-70402. (SQM Ser.: No. 2). 800p. 1994. 273.00 (*1-56252-277-9*, 3528) Computational Mech MA.

Software Quality Management II Vol. 2: Building Quality into Software. Ed. by C. A. Brebbia et al. LC 94-70402. (SQM Ser.: No. 2). 792p. 1994. 270.00 (*1-56252-278-7*, 3536) Computational Mech MA.

Software Quality Management III: Proceedings of the Third International Conference, 2 vols., Set. M. Ross. LC 95-67478. (SQM Ser.: Vol. 3). 952p. 1995. 336.00 (*1-56252-233-7*, 3099) Computational Mech MA.

Software Quality Management III Vol. 1: Quality Management, 2 vols., Set. Ed. by C. A. Brebbia et al. LC 95-67478. (SQM Ser.: Vol. 3). 494p. 1995. 190.00 (*1-56252-337-6*, 4168) Computational Mech MA.

Software Quality Management III Vol. 2: Measuring & Maintaining Quality, 2 vols., Set. Ed. by C. A. Brebbia et al. LC 95-67478. (SQM Ser.: Vol. 3). 458p. 1995. 176.00 (*1-56252-338-4*, 4176) Computational Mech MA.

Software Quality Mangement & ISO 9001: How to Make Them Work for You. Michael G. Jenner. LC 94-40487. 256p. 1995. pap. text ed. 39.95 (*0-471-11888-5*) Wiley.

Software Re-Engineering Symposium Proceedings: Fall, 1988. 1988. 250.00 (*0-318-41123-7*) Digit Consult MA.

Software Re-use, Utrecht 1989: Proceedings of the Software Re-use Workshop 23-24 November 1989, Utrecht, The Netherlands. Ed. by L. M. Dusink & P. A. Hall. 176p. 1991. 43.95 (*0-387-19652-8*) Spr-Verlag.

Software Reengineering. Robert S. Arnold. LC 92-41597. 688p. 1993. 79.00 (*0-8186-3272-0*, 3272) IEEE Comp Soc.

Software Reference Guide, 1996. Christine Ulrich. 348p. 1996. pap. text ed. 55.00 (*0-87326-101-1*) Intl City-Cnty Mgt.

Software Reliability: Measurement, Prediction, Application. John D. Musa. 621p. 1987. text ed. write for info. (*0-07-044093-X*) McGraw.

Software Reliability: Principles & Practices. Glenford J. Myers. (Business Data Processing Ser.). 360p. 1976. text ed. 60.00 (*0-471-62765-8*, Wiley-Interscience) Wiley.

Software Reliability: Professional Edition. John D. Musa. 1990. text ed. 50.00 (*0-07-044119-7*) McGraw.

Software Reliability & Testing (3-95) Ed. by Hoang Pham. LC 95-7582. 144p. 1995. pap. 39.00 (*0-8186-6852-0*, BP06852) IEEE Comp Soc.

Software Reliability Determination for Conventional & Logic Programming. Alireza Azem. (Programming Complex Systems Ser.: No. 7). xvi, 175p. (C). 1995. lib. bdg. 66.95 (*3-11-014807-2*) De Gruyter.

Software Reliability Engineering, 6th International Symposium on (ISSRE '95) LC 10-719458. 270p. 1996. pap. 80.00 (*0-8186-7131-9*, PR07131) IEEE Comp Soc.

***Software Reliability Engineering, 7th International Symposium on (ISSRE '96)** LC 10-719458. 270p. 1996. pap. 60.00 (*0-8186-7707-4*, PR07707) IEEE Comp Soc.

Software Reliability Modelling. Min Xie. 200p. (C). 1991. text ed. 48.00 (*981-02-0640-2*) World Scientific Pub.

Software Reliability Modelling & Identification. Ed. by S. Bittanti. (Lecture Notes in Computer Science Ser.: Vol. 341). vii, 209p. 1989. 34.00 (*0-387-50695-0*) Spr-Verlag.

Software Requirements: Objects, Functions & States. 2nd rev. ed. Davis, Alan M., BTG Inc. Staff & Marilyn D. Weidner. 478p. 1993. text ed. 68.00 (*0-13-805763-X*) P-H.

Software Requirements Analysis & Specification. Jag Sodhi. 1992. text ed. 45.00 (*0-07-157879-X*) McGraw.

Software Requirements & Specifications: A Lexicon of Practice, Principles & Prejudices. Michael Jackson. LC 95-22593. (C). 1995. pap. text ed. 24.95 (*0-201-87712-0*) Addison-Wesley.

Software Requirements Engineering. Pericles Loucopoulos & Vassilios Karakostas. LC 94-39117. (International Series in Software Engineering). 1995. pap. text ed. 40.00 (*0-07-707843-8*) McGraw.

***Software Requirements Engineering.** 2nd ed. Richard H. Thayer et al. LC 96-45235. ~600p. 1997. pap. 60.00 (*0-8186-7738-4*) IEEE Comp Soc.

Software Requirements Evaluation Guide for Manufacturing Planning Control Systems Symposium. APICS T. A. Sig. 50p. (Orig.). 1994. pap. 30.00 (*1-55822-115-8*) Am Prod & Inventory.

Software Reusability. Ted J. Biggerstaff. (Illus.). 450p. (C). 1989. text ed. 43.25 (*0-201-08017-6*) Addison-Wesley.

Software Reusability. Wilhelm Shafer & Diaz Prieto. 200p. 1993. text ed. 67.00 (*0-13-063918-4*) P-H.

Software Reusability, Vol. II: Applications & Experience. Ted J. Biggerstaff & Alan J. Perlis. (ACM Press Frontier Ser.). (Illus.). 448p. (C). 1989. text ed. 43.25 (*0-201-50018-3*) Addison-Wesley.

***Software Reuse.** Ivar Jacobson. (C). 1997. text ed. 40.95 (*0-201-92476-5*) Addison-Wesley.

Software Reuse. Roy Rada. 224p. (Orig.). 1994. pap. text ed. 29.95 (*1-871516-53-6*, Pub. by Intellect Bks UK) Cromland.

Software Reuse. Roy Rada. 167p. 1995. 42.50 (*1-56750-188-5*) Ablex Pub.

Software Reuse: A Holistic Approach. Ed. by Even-Andre Karlsson. (Software-Based Systems Ser.). 510p. 1995. pap. text ed. 75.00 (*0-471-95819-0*) Wiley.

Software Reuse: Guidelines & Methods. J. W. Hooper & R. O. Chester. (Software Science & Engineering Ser.). (Illus.). 196p. 1991. 49.50 (*0-306-43918-2*, Plenum Pr) Plenum.

Software Reuse: Methods, Models, & Costs. Ronald J. Leach. (Illus.). 352p. 1996. text ed. 45.00 (*0-07-036929-1*) McGraw.

Software Reuse & Reverse Engineering in Practice. Ed. by P. A. Hall. (UNICOM Applied Information Technology Ser.). 600p. 1992. 124.95 (*0-442-31409-4*) Chapman & Hall.

Software Reuse & Reversed Engineering Practice. Hall. 1992. text ed. 216.50 (*0-412-39980-6*) Chapman & Hall.

***Software Reuse Techniques.** McClure. 1997. text ed. 40.00 (*0-13-661000-5*) P-H.

Software Reuse, 4th International Conference on (ICSR-4) LC 10-859098. 253p. 1996. 60.00 (*0-8186-7301-X*, PRO7301) IEEE Comp Soc.

Software Reviews & Audits Handbook. Charles P. Hollocker. (Series in Industrial Software Engineering Practice). 240p. 1990. text ed. 59.95 (*0-471-51401-2*) Wiley.

Software Reviews on File. annuals (Monthly Service Ser.). 239.00 (*0-685-54353-6*) Facts on File.

Software Risk Management. Barry W. Boehm. LC 89-80295. 508p. 1989. 62.00 (*0-8186-8906-4*, 1906) IEEE Comp Soc.

***Software Runaways.** Glass. 1997. pap. 28.00 (*0-13-673443-X*) P-H.

***Software RX: Secrets of Engineering Quality Software.** Rodney C. Wilson. LC 96-2761. 1996. 24.95 (*0-13-472663-4*) P-H.

Software Safety Assessment. Phil Bennett. 216p. (C). 1990. pap. text ed. 210.00 (*0-273-03040-X*, Pub. by Pitman Pubng UK) St Mut.

Software Science & Engineering: Selected Papers from the Kyoto Symposia. Ed. by I. Nakata et al. (Computer Science Ser.: Vol. 31). 256p. (C). 1991. text ed. 74.00 (*981-02-0776-X*) World Scientific Pub.

Software Selection for Surveyors. Stephen Hargitay & Tim Dixon. (C). 1991. 175.00 (*0-333-57050-2*, Pub. by Surveyors Pubns) St Mut.

Software Selection...Law Firms. ALA Staff. 96p. 1993. per. 49.95 (*0-8403-8960-4*) Kendall-Hunt.

Software Shock: The Danger & the Opportunity. Roger S. Pressman & S. Russell Herron. LC 91-20988. (Illus.). 240p. (Orig.). 1991. pap. 18.95 (*0-932633-20-X*) Dorset Hse Pub Co.

Software Sifter: An Intelligent Shopper's Guide to Buying Computer Software. Philip Frankel & Ann Gras. 1986. pap. text ed. 28.95 (*0-07-021886-2*) McGraw.

Software Sizing & Estimating: MKII FPA (Function Point Analysis. Charles R. Symons. LC 91-13589. (Series in Software Engineering Practice: No. 1936). 200p. 1991. text ed. 90.00 (*0-471-92985-9*) Wiley.

Software Sleuth. Kaliski. (West - Engineering Ser.). 1991. student ed., pap. 8.75 (*0-534-93880-9*) PWS Pubs.

Software Sleuth. Burton S. Kaliski. (West - Engineering Ser.). 1991. text ed. 40.95 (*0-534-93826-4*) PWS Pubs.

***Software Smart, No. 6.** Princeton Review Staff. 1998. pap. write for info. (*0-679-77898-5*) Random.

***Software Smart, No. 8.** Princeton Review Staff. (Princeton Review Ser.). 1998. pap. write for info. (*0-679-77900-0*) Random.

***Software Smart, No. 9.** Princeton Review Staff. (Princeton Review Ser.). 1998. pap. write for info. (*0-679-77901-9*) Random.

***Software Smart, No. 10.** Princeton Review Staff. (Princeton Review Ser.). 1998. pap. write for info. (*0-679-77902-7*) Random.

***Software Smart, No. 11.** Princeton Review Staff. (Princeton Review Ser.). 1998. pap. write for info. (*0-679-77903-5*) Random.

***Software Smart, No.7.** Princeton Review Staff. 1998. pap. write for info. (*0-679-77899-3*) Random.

Software Soliloquies. Robert L. Glass. 1981. 10.00 (*0-686-31797-1*) Computing Trends.

Software Solutions: Concepts & Applications. Sharon Burton & Nelda Shelton. (C). 1991. 47.56 (*0-395-53249-3*) HM Soft Schl Col Div.

Software Solutions in C. Schumacher. 1995. pap. text ed. 17.00 (*0-12-784830-4*) Acad Pr.

Software Solutions in C. Ed. by Dale Schumacher. (Illus.). 463p. 1994. pap. text ed., pap. 44.95 incl. disk (*0-12-632360-7*, AP Prof) Acad Pr.

Software Solutions Using Java. John Lewis. LC 97-19400. (C). 1998. pap. text ed. write for info. (*0-201-57164-1*) Addison-Wesley.

Software Source Inc. Michael Gehling. 1983. 34.95 (*0-930241-00-2*) Soft Source.

Software Specification: A Comparison of Formal Methods. John D. Gannon et al. LC 94-50696. 264p. 1995. pap. 39.50 (*1-56750-034-X*); text ed. 78:50 (*1-56750-033-1*) Ablex Pub.

Software Specification & Design: Disciplined Approach for Real Time Systems. Kenneth C. Shumate & Marilyn M. Keller. LC 91-28911. (Series in Engineering & Technology Management: No. 1736). 432p. 1992. text ed. 55.00 (*0-471-53296-7*) Wiley.

Software Specification & Design, 8th International Workshop On. LC 10-636765. 200p. 1996. pap. 50.00 (*0-8186-7361-3*, PRO7361) IEEE Comp Soc.

Software Specification Techniques. Narain Gehani & Andrew D. McGettrick. 490p. 1986. text ed. 35.50 (*0-201-14230-9*) Addison-Wesley.

***Software Standards for Interoperability.** Abdelsalam Helal. 1997. 48.37 (*0-201-63447-3*) Addison-Wesley.

Software State-of-the-Art: Selected Papers. Ed. by Tom DeMarco & Timothy R. Lister. LC 89-83372. (Illus.). 584p. 1990. 45.00 (*0-932633-14-5*) Dorset Hse Pub Co.

Software Success Reference Book, 1992. David H. Bowen. 547p. (Orig.). 1992. pap. 9.95 (*0-9625967-1-X*) Software Success.

Software Synthesis from Dataflow Graphs. Shuvra S. Bhattacharyya et al. (Kluwer International Series in Engineering & Computer Science). 192p. (C). 1996. lib. bdg. 92.50 (*0-7923-9722-3*) Kluwer Ac.

Software System Design Methods. Ed. by J. K. Skwirzynski. (NATO Asi Series F: Vol. 22). xvi, 847p. 1986. 158.00 (*0-387-16765-X*) Spr-Verlag.

Software System Development: A Gentle Introduction. 2nd ed. Carol Britton & Jill Doake. LC 96-9028. (International Series In Software E). 1996. write for info. (*0-07-709224-4*) McGraw.

Software System Testing & Quality Assurance. Boris Beizer. (C). 1984. text ed. 55.95 (*1-85032-821-8*) ITCP.

Software Systems Construction with Examples in Ada. Bo Sanden. LC 93-2801. 443p. (C). 1993. text ed. 69.00 (*0-13-030834-X*) P-H.

Software Systems Development: A Gentle Introduction. Carol Britton & Jill Doake. LC 92-26809. (International Series in Software Engineering). 240p. 1993. pap. text ed. 30.00 (*0-07-707712-1*) McGraw.

Software Systems Engineering. Andrew P. Sage & James D. Palmer. LC 89-37350. (Systems Engineering Ser.). 520p. 1990. text ed. 95.95 (*0-471-61758-X*) Wiley.

Software Systems for Structural Optimization. Ed. by H. R. Hornlein & K. Schittkowski. LC 92-42808. (International Series of Numerical Mathematics: Vol. 110). viii, 283p. 1992. 109.50 (*0-8176-2836-3*) Birkhauser.

Software Systems in Engineering, Vol. 59. Ed. by M. M. Tanik et al. LC 93-74681. 428p. 1994. pap. 65.00 (*0-7918-1186-7*) ASME.

Software Systems in Engineering, 1995: Proceedings: The Energy & Environmental EXPO '95 - the Energy-Sources Technology Conference & Exhibition (1995: Houston, TX) Ed. by D. Cooke et al. LC 93-74681. (PD Ser.: Vol. 67). 249p. 1995. pap. 94.00 (*0-7918-1290-1*, H00922) ASME.

***Software Systems Using Java Preliminary Version.** John Lewis. (C). 1997. pap. text ed. write for info. (*0-201-69588-X*) Addison-Wesley.

Software Taxation & the OEM Agreement. Kutish Publications Inc Staff. LC 95-75307. 125p. (Orig.). 1995. pap. text ed. 125.00 (*1-880815-06-0*) Sftware Taxation.

***Software Technology & Engineering Practice, 8th International Workshop.** 480p. 1997. pap. 80.00 (*0-8186-7840-2*) IEEE Comp Soc.

***Software Test Engineering & Quality Assurance.** Jones. (ITCP-US Computer Science Ser.). 1997. pap. 49.95 (*1-85032-886-2*) ITCP.

Software Testing: A Craftsman's Approach. Paul C. Jorgensen. (Software Engineering Ser.). 352p. 1995. 65.00 (*0-8493-7345-X*, 7345) CRC Pr.

Software Testing & Evaluation: A Report. R. Martin et al. 537p. (C). 1987. text ed. 59.25 (*0-8053-2535-2*) Benjamin-Cummings.

Software Testing for Conventional & Logic Programming. Oliver Jack. LC 96-16969. (Programming Complex Systems Ser.: Vol. 10). xxi, 230p. (C). 1996. lib. bdg. 79.95 (*3-11-015071-9*) De Gruyter.

Software Testing in the Real World: Improving the Process. Edward Kit. Ed. by Susannah Finzi. LC 95-37212. (ACM Press Bks.). (C). 1995. text ed. 31.95 (*0-201-87756-2*) Addison-Wesley.

Software Testing Methods & Metrics: The Most Important Tests Methods. Marnie L. Hutcheson. (Illus.). 256p. 1997. pap. text ed. 45.00 incl. cd-rom (*0-07-912929-3*) McGraw.

Software Testing Techniques. 2nd ed. Boris Beizer. 1990. text ed. 52.95 (*0-442-20672-0*) Van Nos Reinhold.

Software Testing Techniques, 2/e. 2nd ed. Boris Beizer. 1990. text ed. 53.95 (*1-85032-880-3*) ITCP.

Software Testing Tools for C-C Plus Plus. Mark L. Murphy. 352p. (C). 1996. pap. text ed. 42.00 incl. disk (*0-13-445123-6*) P-H.

Software to Accompany Nonlinear Dynamics, Chaos, & Instability IBM & MAC Disks. William A. Brock et al. (Illus.). 1992. 15.00 incl. disk (*0-262-52173-3*) MIT Pr.

Software to Accompany Nonlinear Dynamics, Chaos, & Instability UNIX Disks. William A. Brock et al. (Illus.). 300p. 1992. 15.00 incl. disk (*0-262-52172-5*) MIT Pr.

***Software Tool Kit: Word 6 for Windows.** Tim Duffy & Cindy Barnes. (Illus.). 320p. 1994. teacher ed., text ed. write for info. incl. 3.5 ld (*0-534-30251-3*) Course Tech.

Software Tools. Brian W. Kernighan & P. L. Plauger. 286p. 1976. audio write for info. (*0-201-03668-1*) Addison-Wesley.

Software Tools. Brian W. Kernighan & P. L. Plauger. 286p. (C). 1976. pap. text ed. 34.50 (*0-201-03669-X*) Addison-Wesley.

Software Tools & Techniques for Electronic Engineers. Keith Jobes. LC 93-32582. (International Series in Software Engineering). 1993. pap. write for info. (*0-07-707720-2*) McGraw.

Software Tools & Techniques for Embedded Distributed Processing. Herbert C. Conn, Jr. et al. LC 85-28422. (Illus.). 684p. 1986. 72.00 (*0-8155-1062-4*) Noyes.

Software Tools for Business: An Information Systems Approach. Roger Hayen. 992p. 1993. Net. pap. text ed. 38.00 (*0-471-54694-1*) Wiley.

Software Tools for OS-2. Michael J. Young. 1989. pap. 22.95 (*0-201-51787-6*) Addison-Wesley.

***Software Tools for Quantitative Methods & Management Science, 5 1/4 Ibm Disk.** Willbann D. Terpening. 1993. text ed. write for info. (*0-07-832587-0*) McGraw.

Software Tools in Pascal. Brian W. Kernighan & P. L. Plauger. LC 81-3629. 1981. audio write for info. (*0-201-10343-5*) Addison-Wesley.

Software Tools in Pascal. Brian W. Kernighan & P. L. Plauger. LC 81-3629. (C). 1981. pap. text ed. 31.25 (*0-201-10342-7*) Addison-Wesley.

Software Trends for Executive Planning & Strategy Proceedings. George Schussel. 500p. 1986. pap. text ed. 250.00 (*0-318-21394-X*) Digit Consult MA.

***Software under Siege.** E. L. Leiss. vi, 136p. 1990. 105.00 (*0-946395-58-6*, Pub. by Elsvr Adv Tech UK) Elsevier.

Software User: Education & Qualification. Papers Presented at a Panel Discussion, Winter Annual Meeting of ASME, New York, NY, November 16, 1972. Sponsored by ASME Pressure Vessels & Piping Division. Ed. by Harry Kraus. LC 72-93670. 44p. reprint ed. pap. 25.00 (*0-317-08070-9*, 2016826) Bks Demand.

Software User Interface Compatibility after Lotus Development Corporation vs Paperback Software International, No. P-93-4. Richard A. Magnan. (Illus.). 49p. (Orig.). 1993. pap. text ed. write for info. (*1-879716-04-6*) Ctr Info Policy.

***Software User's Manual: Computer Application.** 11th ed. Paz. (DC - Introduction to Computing Ser.). (C). 1989. pap. 18.95 (*0-314-53950-6*) West Pub.

***Software Users Manual: Doing Business.** 11th ed. Paz. (DC - Introduction to Computers Ser.). 1990. pap. 30.95 (*0-314-53949-2*) S-W Pub.

***Software Verification & Validation: A Practitioner's Guide.** Steven R. Rakitin. LC 96-47264. 1997. 59.00 (*0-89006-889-5*) Artech Hse.

***Software Visualization.** 300p. 1996. lib. bdg. 56.00 (*981-02-2826-0*) World Scientific Pub.

***Software Visualization: Programming As a Multimedia Experience.** John Stasko. LC 97-23612. 1997. write for info. (*0-262-19395-7*) MIT Pr.

***Software Without Frontiers: A Multi-Platform, Multi-Cultural & Multi-National Approach.** Pat Hall. 1996. pap. text ed. 48.95 (*0-471-96478-6*) Wiley.

***Software Without Frontiers: A Multi-Platform, Multi-Cultural, Multi-National Approach.** Pat Hall. 1997. pap. text ed. 39.95 (*0-471-96974-5*) Wiley.

Software 2020. Robert L. Glass. 1996. pap. text ed. write for info. (*0-8186-7409-1*, BRO7409) IEEE Comp Soc.

***Software 2020.** Robert L. Glass. 140p. (Orig.). 1997. pap. 15.00 (*0-614-28418-X*) Computing Trends.

Softwars: The Legal Battles for Control of the Global Software Industry. Anthony L. Clapes. LC 92-24223. 336p. 1993. text ed. 49.95 (*0-89930-597-0*, CRX, Quorum Bks) Greenwood.

Softwood Lumber Dispute & Canada-U. S. Trade in Natural Resources. Michael B. Percy & Christian Yoder. 1989. pap. text ed. 20.00 (*0-88645-057-8*, Pub. by Inst Res Pub CN) Ashgate Pub Co.

Softy. John O'Brien. 18p. 1991. pap. 3.00 (*0-87129-098-7*, S94) Dramatic Pub.

Sog: The Secret Wars of America's Commandos in Vietnam. John L. Plaster. 1997. 25.00 (*0-684-81105-7*) S&S Trade.

Soggy Shrub Rides Again & Other Improbabilities. James Smart. (Illus.). 208p. (Orig.). 1995. pap. text ed. 16.95 (*0-9603924-9-1*, Enoch Flower) Blue Flower.

Soggy Sneakers: A Guide to Oregon Rivers. 3rd ed. Willamette Kayak & Canoe Club Staff. LC 93-45840. (Illus.). 320p. 1994. pap. 18.95 (*0-89886-330-9*) Mountaineers.

Soggy Sneakers Guide to Oregon Rivers. 2nd rev. ed. Williamette Kayak & Canoe Club Staff. (Illus.). 208p. 1986. pap. 9.00 (*0-9616257-0-8*) Willamette Kayak Canoe Club.

Sohar: Culture & Society in an Omani Town. Fredrik Barth. LC 82-9925. 304p. 1983. 45.00 (*0-8018-2840-6*) Johns Hopkins.

Sohn des Asterix. Rene De Goscinny & A. Uderzo. (GER.). 1992. 19.95 (*0-7859-1024-7*, 3770400275) Fr & Eur.

Sohne der Wuste. Carl R. Raswan. (Documenta Hippologica Ser.). (Illus.). 132p. 1977. write for info. (*3-487-08134-2*) G Olms Pubs.

SoHo. Helene Z. Seeman & Alanna Siegfried. LC 78-22225. (Illus.). 1979. pap. 14.95 (*0-918212-09-X*) Neal-Schuman.

Soho: Drawings on Drawings. Maris Bishofs. (Illus.). (Orig.). 1988. pap. 9.95 (*1-55774-040-2*) Hemed Bks.

S

Soho: Drawings on Drawings. limited ed. Maris Bishofs. (Illus.). (Orig.). 1988. 32.00 (*0-318-33428-3*) Hemed Bks.

SoHo Guide. Artist Consortium Staff. 118p. 1995. 10.00 (*1-886016-01-1*) SoHo Prtnship.

SoHo Guide 1996-1997. 3rd ed. Illus. by Robert M. Parker. 186p. 1996. 15.00 (*1-886016-04-6*) SoHo Prtnship.

Soho Journal. Ed. by Robert Beryman-Ungar. (Illus.). 200p. (Orig.). 1994. pap. 20.00 (*1-885957-00-9*) Map Pubns.

Soho Journal 1995-1996: Transcendence. Ed. by Gary Koepke. (Journal Ser.: No. 3). (Illus.). 176p. 1995. pap. 25.00 (*1-886016-02-X*) SoHo Prtnship.

Soho Journal 94-95. Artist Consortium Staff. Ed. by Robert Bergman-Ungar. (Journal Ser.). 176p. 1994. pap. 20.00 (*1-886016-00-3*) SoHo Prtnship.

SOHO Mission. Ed. by Bernhard Fleck. 544p. (C). 1996. lib. bdg. 277.00 (*0-7923-3894-4*) Kluwer Ac.

SOHO Windows 95. Michael Price. LC 96-297. 1995. pap. write for info. (*0-07-709199-X*) McGraw.

Sohrab & Rustem, the Epic Theme of a Combat Between Father & Son: A Study of Its Genesis & Use in Literature & Popular Tradition. Murray A. Potter. LC 75-144527. (Grimm Library: No. 14). reprint ed. 27.50 (*0-404-53557-7*) AMS Pr.

Soie et les Cendres. Myriam Anissimov. 438p. (FRE.). 1991. pap. 21.95 (*0-7859-2169-9*, 2070384047) Fr & Eur.

Soigner en Deux Langues (Nursing in Two Languages) French/English. Huguette Fizaine. 305p. (ENG & FRE.). 1995. pap. 82.00 (*2-87209-394-X*) IBD Ltd.

Soil. Photos by Barrie Watts. LC 95-33271. (See for Yourself Ser.). (Illus.). 30p. (J). 1996. lib. bdg. 19.97 (*0-8172-4213-9*) Raintree Steck-V.

Soil: A Portrait of Rural Life in Meiji Japan. Nagatsuka Takashi. Tr. by Anne Waswo from JPN. LC 93-1851. (Voices from Asia Ser.: Vol. 8). 222p. 1993. 12.00 (*0-520-08372-5*) U CA Pr.

Soil: How the Soil Is Made Up. (Better Farming Ser.: No. 4). (Illus.). 37p. 1976. pap. 5.00 (*92-5-100143-X*, F62, Pub. by FAO IT) Bernan Associates.

Soil: How to Conserve the Soil. (Better Farming Ser.: No. 5). (Illus.). 29p. 1976. pap. 5.00 (*92-5-100144-8*, F63, Pub. by FAO IT) Bernan Associates.

Soil: How to Improve the Soil. rev. ed. (Better Farming Ser.: No. 6). (Illus.). 29p. 1976. pap. 5.00 (*92-5-100145-6*, F64, Pub. by FAO IT) Bernan Associates.

Soil Acidity. Malcolm E. Sumner. (Illus.). 224p. 1991. 135.95 (*0-387-50782-5*) Spr-Verlag.

Soil Acidity & Liming. 2nd ed. Ed. by Fred Adams. 380p. 1984. 25.00 (*0-89118-080-X*) Am Soc Agron.

Soil Adsorption of Odorant Compounds. P. B. Tarman & H. R. Linden. (Research Bulletin Ser.: No. 33). iv, 28p. 1961. pap. 3.50 (*0-317-56881-7*) Inst Gas Tech.

Soil Aeration & Its Role for Plants. Ed. by J. Glinski & W. Stephiewski. 240p. 1985. 138.00 (*0-8493-5250-9*, S593, CRC Reprint) Franklin.

Soil Amendments: Impacts on Biotic Systems. Ed. by Jack E. Rechcigl. (Agriculture & Environment Ser.). 336p. 1994. 79.95 (*0-87371-860-7*, L860) Lewis Pubs.

Soil Amendments & Environmental Quality. Ed. by Jack E. Rechcigl. 528p. 1995. 95.00 (*0-87371-859-3*, L859) Lewis Pubs.

Soil Analysis: Modern Instrumental Techniques. 2nd expanded rev. ed. Ed. by Keith A. Smith. (Books in Soils, Plants & the Environment: Vol. 16). 672p. 1990. 195.00 (*0-8247-8355-7*) Dekker.

Soil Analysis: Physical Methods. Ed. by Keith A. Smith. (Books in Soils, Plants & the Environment: Vol. 17). 632p. 1990. 195.00 (*0-8247-8361-1*) Dekker.

***Soil & Environmental Science.** 7th ed. Henry Foth et al. 224p. (C). 1996. lab manual ed., spiral bd. write for info. (*0-697-38401-2*) Wm C Brown Pubs.

Soil & Immunity. Bernard Jensen. 1988. pap. 4.95 (*0-932615-17-1*) B Jensen.

***Soil & Plant Analysis in Sustainable Agriculture & Environment.** Ed. by Teresa Hood & J. Benton Jones. LC 96-47255. (Books in Soils, Plants & the Environment: Vol. 54). 880p. 1997. 195.00 (*0-8247-0054-6*) Dekker.

Soil & Rock Classification for the Design of Ground Coupled Heat Pump Systems: Field Manual. L. H. Salomone & J. I. Marlowe. Ed. by James E. Bose. (Illus.). (C). 1989. pap. 25.00 (*0-929974-02-6*) GSHP Pubns.

***Soil & Rock Construction Materials.** G. Mcnally. (Illus.). 272p. 1997. write for info. (*0-419-21420-8*, E & FN Spon) Routledge Chapman & Hall.

Soil & Rock Hydraulics: Fundamentals, Numerical Methods & Techniques of Electrical Analogs. Fernando O. Franciss. 184p. (C). 1985. text ed. 85.00 (*90-6191-550-3*, Pub. by A A Balkema NE); pap. text ed. 55.00 (*90-6191-555-4*, Pub. by A A Balkema NE) Ashgate Pub Co.

Soil & Rock (I): D 420-D 4914 see 1997 Annual Book of ASTM Standards: Construction, Section 4

Soil & Rock (III): D 4943-Latest; Geosynthetics see 1997 Annual Book of ASTM Standards: Construction, Section 4

Soil & Rocks. Ed Catherall. LC 90-10024. (Exploring Science Ser.). (Illus.). 48p. (J). (gr. 4-8). 1990. lib. bdg. 24.26 (*0-8114-2595-9*) Raintree Steck-V.

***Soil & Rocks.. Socks.** Thomas-Cochran. (What a Wonderful World Intro Ser.). 1993. pap. text ed. write for info. (*0-582-91077-3*, Pub. by Longman UK) Longman.

Soil & Sky: Mel Chin at the Fabric Workshop. Thomas McEvilley. (Illus.). 32p. 1993. pap. 15.00 (*0-9619760-3-9*) Fabric Workshop Inc.

Soil & Vegetation Systems. 2nd ed. Stephen T. Trudgill. (Contemporary Problems in Geography Ser.). (Illus.). 224p. 1988. 65.00 (*0-19-874139-1*); pap. 22.00 (*0-19-874138-3*) OUP.

Soil & Water Conservation. (Illus.). 96p. (J). (gr. 6-12). 1983. pap. 2.40 (*0-8395-3291-1*, 33291) BSA.

Soil & Water Conservation. 2nd ed. Frederick R. Troeh et al. 1991. text ed. 93.00 (*0-13-830324-X*, 510102) P-H.

Soil & Water Conservation Engineering. 4th ed. Glenn O. Schwab et al. LC 92-10953. 528p. 1992. Net. text ed. 51.00 (*0-471-57490-2*) Wiley.

Soil & Water Conservation in Semi-Arid Kenya. Ed. by R. M. Kiome & M. A. Stocking. 1993. pap. 30.00 (*0-85954-359-5*, Pub. by Nat Res Inst UK) St Mut.

Soil & Water Contamination & Remediation. Wright. 1996. text ed. write for info. (*0-442-01706-5*) Van Nos Reinhold.

***Soil & Water Management Strategies for Tidal Lowlands in Indonesia.** F. X. Suryadi. (IHE-Thesis Ser.). (Illus.). 262p. (C). 1996. text ed. 50.00 (*90-5410-406-6*, Pub. by A A Balkema NE) Ashgate Pub Co.

Soil & Water Management Systems. 4th rev. ed. Glenn O. Schwab et al. LC 95-25189. Orig. Title: Elementary Soil & Water Engineering. 371p. 1995. text ed. 52.00 (*0-471-10973-8*, S623) Wiley.

Soil & Water Quality: An Agenda for Agriculture. National Research Council Staff. 442p. (C). 1993. text ed. 54.95 (*0-309-04933-4*) Natl Acad Pr.

Soil & Water Science: Keys to Understanding Our Global Environment. Ed. by Ralph S. Baker et al. LC 94-31646. (SSSA Special Publications: No. 41). 1994. pap. 30.00 (*0-89118-816-9*) Soil Sci Soc Am.

Soil Bank Community. 117p. pap. 4.00 (*0-685-19150-8*) Hardin Pub Co.

Soil Behaviour & Critical State Mechanics. David M. Wood. (Illus.). 450p. (C). 1991. text ed. 90.00 (*0-521-33249-4*); pap. text ed. 38.95 (*0-521-33782-8*) Cambridge U Pr.

Soil Behaviour in Earthquake Geotechnics. Kenji Ishihara. (Oxford Engineering Science Ser.: Vol. 46). (Illus.). 360p. (C). 1996. 95.00 (*0-19-856224-1*) OUP.

Soil Biochemistry. Paul. (Books in Soils, Plants & the Environment: Vol. 8). 300p. 1975. pap. 125.00 (*0-8247-7023-4*) Dekker.

Soil Biochemistry. Ed. by G. Stotzky & Jean-Marc Bollag. (Books in Soils, Plants & the Environment: Vol. 50). 568p. 1996. 125.00 (*0-8247-9441-9*) Dekker.

Soil Biochemistry, Vol. 1. Ed. by A. Douglas McLaren & George H. Peterson. LC 66-27705. 523p. reprint ed. pap. 149.10 (*0-8357-3538-9*, 2027117) Bks Demand.

Soil Biochemistry, Vol. 2. Ed. by Arthur D. McLaren & George H. Peterson. LC 66-27705. (Books in Soil Science: Nos. 1 & 2). 547p. reprint ed. pap. 155.90 (*0-8357-3539-7*, 2027117) Bks Demand.

Soil Biochemistry, Vol. 5. Paul McLaren & Ladd. (Books in Soils, Plants & the Environment: Vol. 9). 504p. 1981. 199.00 (*0-8247-1131-9*) Dekker.

Soil Biochemistry, Vol. 6. G. Stotzky. (Books in Soils, Plants & the Environment: Vol. 15). 584p. 1990. 125.00 (*0-8247-8232-1*) Dekker.

Soil Biochemistry, Vol. 7. G. Stotzky. (Books in Soils, Plants & the Environment: Vol. 22). 432p. 1991. 125.00 (*0-8247-8575-4*) Dekker.

Soil Biochemistry, Vol. 8. G. Stotzky. (Books in Soils, Plants & the Environment: Vol. 27). 432p. 1993. 125.00 (*0-8247-9044-8*) Dekker.

Soil Biochemistry, Vol. 3. Ed. by Eldor A. Paul & A. Douglas McLaren. LC 66-27705. (Books in Soils & the Environment). 352p. reprint ed. pap. 100.40 (*0-8357-3540-0*, 2027833) Bks Demand.

Soil Biology: Effects on Soil Quality. Ed. by J. L. Hatfield & B. A. Stewart. 176p. 1993. 75.00 (*0-87371-927-1*, L927) Lewis Pubs.

Soil Biology Guide. Ed. by Daniel L. Dindal. LC 88-28016. 1349p. 1990. text ed. 165.00 (*0-471-04551-9*) Wiley.

Soil Biota & Nutrient Cycling Farming Systems. David C. Coleman et al. 336p. 1993. 89.95 (*0-87371-919-0*, L919) Lewis Pubs.

Soil Bioventing: Principles & Practice. Robert E. Hinchee. LC 96-43809. 300p. 1996. write for info. (*1-56670-126-0*, L1126) Lewis Pubs.

Soil-Borne Plant Pathogens. B. Schippers & W. Gams. 1979. text ed. 249.00 (*0-12-624850-8*) Acad Pr.

Soil-Cement Construction Handbook. rev. ed. 40p. 1995. pap. 12.00 (*0-89312-114-2*, EB003S) Portland Cement.

Soil-Cement Inspector's Manual. rev. ed. 64p. 1980. pap. 12.00 (*0-89312-049-9*, PA050S) Portland Cement.

Soil-Cement Laboratory Handbook. rev. ed. 60p. 1992. pap. 15.00 (*0-89312-116-9*, EB052S) Portland Cement.

Soil Changes Associated with Loblolly Pine Succession on Abandoned Agricultural Land of the Piedmont Plateau. Theodore S. Coile. (Duke University, School of Forestry Bulletin Ser.: No. 5). (Illus.). 85p. reprint ed. pap. 25.00 (*0-7837-6051-5*, 2045864) Bks Demand.

Soil Chemistry. D. S. Orlov. Ed. by V. S. Kothekar. (Russian Translation Ser.: No. 92). (Illus.). 402p. (RUS.). (C). 1992. text ed. 95.00 (*90-6191-915-0*, Pub. by A A Balkema NE) Ashgate Pub Co.

Soil Chemistry. 2nd ed. Hinrich L. Bohn et al. LC 85-3221. 360p. 1985. text ed. 74.95 (*0-471-82217-5*) Wiley.

Soil Chemistry & Its Applications. M. S. Cresser et al. (Cambridge Environmental Chemistry Ser.: No. 5). (Illus.). 250p. (C). 1993. text ed. 64.95 (*0-521-32269-3*); pap. text ed. 24.95 (*0-521-31134-9*) Cambridge U Pr.

***Soil Chemistry of Hazardous Materials.** 2nd ed. James Dragon. (Illus.). 800p. 1997. text ed. 59.95 (*1-884940-11-0*) Amherst Sci Pubs.

Soil Colloids & Their Associations in Soil Aggregates. Ed. by M. F. De Boodt et al. LC 89-71019. (NATO ASI Ser.: Series B, Physics: Vol. 215). (Illus.). 616p. 1990. 145.00 (*0-306-43419-9*, Plenum Pr) Plenum.

Soil Color: Proceedings of a Symposium Sponsored by Divisions S-5 & S-9 of the Soil Science Society of America in San Antonio, Texas, 21-26 Oct. 1990. Ed. by J. M. Bigham et al. LC 93-16678. (Special Publications: No. 31). 1993. write for info. (*0-89118-802-9*) Soil Sci Soc Am.

Soil Compaction & Regeneration: Proceedings of the Workshop on "Soil Compaction: Consequences, Structural Regeneration Processes", Avignon, 17-18 September 1985. Ed. by G. Monnier & M. J. Goss. 160p. (C). 1987. text ed. 70.00 (*90-6191-780-8*, Pub. by A A Balkema NE) Ashgate Pub Co.

Soil Compaction in Crop Production. Ed. by B. D. Soane & C. van Ouwerkerk. (Developments in Agricultural Engineering Ser.: Vol. 11). 682p. 1994. text ed. 285.25 (*0-444-88286-3*) Elsevier.

Soil Conditioners & Amendment Technologies Vol. I: Soil Amendments. Ed. by Arthur Wallace. 340p. 1995. text ed. 40.00 (*0-937892-12-2*) LL Co.

Soil Conservation. 3rd ed. Norman Hudson. 168p. 1995. pap. text ed. 34.95 (*0-8138-2372-2*) Iowa St U Pr.

Soil Conservation. Hugh H. Bennett. LC 74-125731. (American Environmental Studies). 1974. reprint ed. 56.95 (*0-405-02656-0*) Ayer.

Soil Conservation & Land Management. S. K. Datta. 337p. (C). 1976. text ed. 250.00 (*0-89771-592-6*, Pub. by Intl Bk Distr II) St Mut.

Soil Conservation & Management in the Humid Tropics. D. J. Greenland. 283p. 1989. 240.00 (*81-7089-103-5*, Pub. by Intl Bk Distr II) St Mut.

Soil Conservation & Management in the Humid Tropics. International Conference on Soil Conservation & Management in the Humid Tropics (1975: Ibadan, Nigeria) Staff. Ed. by D. J. Greenland & R. Lal. LC 76-56838. (Illus.). 325p. reprint ed. pap. 92.70 (*0-685-20348-4*, 2029795) Bks Demand.

Soil Conservation & Silviculture. Ed. by J. Dvorak & L. Novak. (Developments in Soil Science Ser.: Vol. 23). 420p. 1994. 257.50 (*0-444-98792-4*) Elsevier.

***Soil Conservation Extension: From Concepts to Adoption.** Ed. by S. Sombatpanit et al. (Illus.). 400p. (C). 1997. 65.00 (*1-886106-85-1*); pap. 39.00 (*1-886106-86-X*) Science Pubs.

***Soil Conservation for Small Farmers in the Humid Tropics.** 113p. 1989. 14.00 (*92-5-102869-9*, F8699, Pub. by FAO IT) Bernan Associates.

Soil Conservation for Survival. Ed. by Kebede Tato & Hans Hurni. (Illus.). 440p. (C). 1992. 35.00 (*0-935734-27-9*) Soil & Water Conserv.

Soil Conservation in Developing Countries: Project & Policy Intervention. Jock R. Anderson & Jesuthason Thampapillai. (Policy & Research Ser.: No. 8). 52p. 1990. 6.95 (*0-8213-1448-3*, 11448) World Bank.

Soil Conservation in Perspective. R. Burnell Held & Marion Clawson. LC 65-22946. 359p. reprint ed. pap. 102.40 (*0-7837-3036-5*, 2042890) Bks Demand.

Soil Conservation in the United States: Policy & Planning. Frederick R. Steiner. LC 89-71742. (Illus.). 288p. 1990. text ed. 45.00 (*0-8018-3997-1*); pap. text ed. 18.50 (*0-8018-3998-X*) Johns Hopkins.

Soil Conservation Policies: An Assessment. Pref. by William C. Moldenhauer. LC 80-406. 154p. (Orig.). 1980. pap. 7.50 (*0-935734-04-X*) Soil & Water Conserv.

Soil Conservation Policies, Institutions, & Incentives. Ed. by Harold G. Halcrow et al. LC 82-699. 330p. (C). 1982. text ed. 7.00 (*0-935734-06-6*) Soil & Water Conserv.

Soil Conservation Problems & Prospects. Royston P. Morgan. 576p. (C). 1992. write for info. (*0-318-69592-8*, Pub. by Intl Bk Distr II) St Mut.

Soil Conservation Problems & Prospects. M. T. Williams. 133p. (C). 1991. pap. 130.00 (*81-7089-121-3*, Pub. by Intl Bk Distr II) St Mut.

Soil Conservation Problems & Prospects: Proceedings of Conservation 80, the International Conference on Soil Conservation, Held at the National College of Agricultural Engineering, Silsoe, Bedford, U. K., 21st-25th July, 1980. International Conference on Soil Conservation & Management in the Humid Tropics (1975: Ibadan, Nigeria) Staff. Ed. by Royston P. Morgan. LC 80-42351. 592p. reprint ed. pap. 168.80 (*0-8357-6939-9*, 2037998) Bks Demand.

***Soil Conservation Strategies for Upland Areas of Indonesia.** Brian Carson. LC 89-12012. (East-West Environment & Policy Institute, Occasional Paper Ser.: Vol. 9). 134p. 1989. reprint ed. pap. 38.20 (*0-608-03575-0*, 2064398) Bks Demand.

Soil Conservation, Vol. 1: An Assessment of the National Resources Inventory. National Research Council Staff. 112p. 1986. pap. text ed. 14.95 (*0-309-03649-6*) Natl Acad Pr.

Soil Conservation, Vol. 2: An Assessment of the National Resources Inventory. National Research Council Staff. 314p. 1986. pap. text ed. 24.95 (*0-309-03675-5*) Natl Acad Pr.

Soil Conservationist. Jack Rudman. (Career Examination Ser.: C-1032). 1994. pap. 29.95 (*0-8373-1032-6*) Nat Learn.

Soil Crusting: Chemical & Physical Processes. Ed. by Malcolm E. Sumner & Bobby A. Stewart. (Advances in Soil Science Ser.). 384p. 1992. 89.95 (*0-87371-869-0*, L869) Lewis Pubs.

Soil Cutting & Tillage: Developments in Agricultural Engineering, No. 7. E. McKyes. 218p. 1985. 145.25 (*0-444-42548-9*) Elsevier.

Soil Degradation. Ed. by B. A. Stewart & Rattan Lal. (Advances in Soil Science Ser.: Vol. 11). (Illus.). 352p. 1989. 146.95 (*0-387-97126-2*) Spr-Verlag.

Soil Degradation: Proceedings of the Land Use Seminar on Soil Degradation, Wageningen, 13-15th October 1980. Ed. by D. Boels et al. 286p. (C). 1982. text ed. 95.00 (*90-6191-220-2*, Pub. by A A Balkema NE) Ashgate Pub Co.

Soil Description Handbook. P. L. Singleton et al. 1991. 35.50 (*0-477-02616-8*, Pub. by Manaaki Whenua NZ) Balogh.

Soil Dynamics. T. H. Wu. LC 79-117987. (Illus.). 1977. reprint ed. text ed. 30.00 (*0-918498-01-5*) T H Wu.

Soil Dynamics & Earthquake Engineering. Ed. by C. A. Brebbia et al. (SDEE Ser.: Vol. 2). 700p. 1985. 99.00 (*0-931215-54-4*) Computational Mech MA.

Soil Dynamics & Earthquake Engineering, 3 vols. Ed. by A. S. Cakmak & I. Herrera. LC 89-85630. (SDEE Ser.: Vol. 4). 1989. 305.00 (*1-85312-053-7*) Computational Mech MA.

Soil Dynamics & Earthquake Engineering: Proceedings of the Conference, Southampton, 13-15 July 1982, 2 vols., Set. Ed. by A. S. Cakmak et al. 1017p. (C). 1982. text ed. 292.00 (*90-6191-253-9*, Pub. by A A Balkema NE) Ashgate Pub Co.

Soil Dynamics & Earthquake Engineering Vol. III: Ground Motion & Engineering Seismology. Ed. by A. S. Cakmak. LC 87-70780. (SDEE Ser.: Vol. 3). 632p. 1987. 154.00 (*0-931215-87-0*, 1899) Computational Mech MA.

Soil Dynamics & Earthquake Engineering V. Ed. by IBF Staff. LC 91-74078. (SDEE Ser.: Vol. 5). 770p. 1991. 260.00 (*1-56252-081-4*) Computational Mech MA.

Soil Dynamics & Earthquake Engineering VI. Ed. by A. S. Cakmak & C. A. Brebbia. LC 92-75802. (SDEE Ser.: Vol. 6). 960p. 1993. 337.00 (*1-56252-154-3*, 2319) Computational Mech MA.

Soil Dynamics & Earthquake Engineering VII: Proceedings of the Seventh International Conference. Ed. by A. S. Cakmak et al. LC 95-67975. (SDEE Ser.: Vol.7). 680p. 1995. 302.00 (*1-56252-239-6*, 3153) Computational Mech MA.

Soil Dynamics & Earthquakes Engineering: Soil Dynamics & Liquefaction. Ed. by A. S. Cakmak. LC 87-70778. (SDEE Ser.: Vol. 3). 386p. 1987. 112.00 (*0-931215-57-9*) Computational Mech MA.

Soil Dynamics & Geotechnical Earthquake Engineering: Proceedings, Lisboa, Portugal, July 1992. Ed. by Pedro S. Seco & E. Pinto. (Illus.). 500p. 1993. text ed. 75.00 (*90-5410-310-8*, Pub. by A A Balkema NE) Ashgate Pub Co.

Soil Dynamics & Liquefaction Vol. 1, 3 vols., Vol. 2: Soil Dynamics & Liquefaction. Ed. by A. S. Cakmak. LC 89-85630. (SDEE Ser.: Vol. 4). 1989. 103.00 (*0-945824-35-1*) Computational Mech MA.

Soil Dynamics, Deep Stabilization, & Geotechnical Construction: Design Manual, No. 7.3. Scientific Publishers Staff. (C). 1985. 150.00 (*81-85046-38-7*, Pub. by Scientific UK) St Mut.

Soil Ecology. Ken Killham. LC 93-26150. (Illus.). 250p. (C). 1994. text ed. 74.95 (*0-521-43517-X*); pap. text ed. 28.95 (*0-521-43521-8*) Cambridge U Pr.

***Soil Ecology.** Spain & C. L. Lavelle. 256p. (C). (gr. 13 up). 1997. text ed. 89.95 (*0-412-28570-3*) Chapman & Hall.

***Soil Ecology in Sustainable Agricultural Systems.** L. Brussaard & Ronald Ferrara-Cerrato. LC 96-30093. 1997. write for info. (*1-56670-277-1*) Lewis Pubs.

***Soil Ecotoxicology.** J. Tarradellas et al. LC 96-27157. 1996. write for info. (*1-56670-134-1*) Lewis Pubs.

Soil Engineering. (Research Record Ser.: No. 1192). 119p. 1988. 15.50 (*0-309-04770-6*) Transport Res Bd.

***Soil Engineering, Vol. 1.** 5th ed. Handy. (C). 1998. write for info. (*0-321-01062-0*) Addson-Wesley Educ.

***Soil Engineering, Vol. 2.** 5th ed. Handy. (C). 1998. text ed. write for info. (*0-321-01063-9*) Addson-Wesley Educ.

Soil Engineering in Theory & Practice. Alam Singh. 742p. 1981. 62.95 (*0-318-37336-X*) Asia Bk Corp.

Soil Erosion: A Source Guide. 1991. lib. bdg. 75.00 (*0-8490-4860-5*) Gordon Pr.

Soil Erosion: Quiet Crisis in the World Economy. Lester Brown. LC 84-62062. (Worldwatch Papers). 1984. pap. 5.00 (*0-916468-60-7*) Worldwatch Inst.

Soil Erosion & Conservation. Ed. by S. A. El-Swaify et al. LC 85-2507. 793p. 1985. text ed. 35.00 (*0-935734-11-2*) Soil & Water Conserv.

Soil Erosion & Conservation. 2nd ed. Royston P. Morgan. (C). 1995. pap. text ed. 33.50 (*0-582-24492-7*) Addison-Wesley.

Soil Erosion & Conservation. International Conference on Soil Erosion & Conservation Staff. Ed. by S. A. El-Swaify et al. LC 85-2507. (Illus.). 821p. reprint ed. pap. 180.00 (*0-7837-4421-8*, 2044172) Bks Demand.

Soil Erosion & Conservation in the Tropics. Ed. by W. Kussow et al. (ASA Special Publication Ser.). 149p. (C). 1982. pap. 8.50 (*0-89118-068-0*) Am Soc Agron.

Soil Erosion & Crop Productivity. R. F. Follett & B. A. Stewart. 533p. 1985. 36.00 (*0-89118-087-7*) Am Soc Agron.

Soil Erosion & Its Control. Quincy C. Ayres. LC 72-2832. (Use & Abuse of America's Natural Resources Ser.). (Illus.). 382p. 1980. reprint ed. 33.95 (*0-405-04501-8*) Ayer.

Soil Erosion & Pollution. Darlene R. Stille. LC 89-25360. (New True Bks.). (Illus.). 48p. (J). (gr. k-4). 1990. pap. 5.50 (*0-516-41188-8*); lib. bdg. 19.00 (*0-516-01188-X*) Childrens.

Soil Erosion, Conservation, & Rehabilitation. Ed. by Menachem Agassi. LC 95-40716. (Soils, Plants, & the Environment Bks.: Vol. 46). 424p. 1995. 150.00 (*0-8247-8984-9*, S623) Dekker.

Soil Erosion in a Coastal River Basin: A Case Study from the Philippines. Random DuBois. (Research Papers). (Illus.). 145p. 1990. pap. 12.00 (*0-89065-139-6*) U Ch Pr.

An Asterisk (*) at the beginning of an entry indicates that the title is appearing in BIP for the first time.

Soil Erosion in the European Community--Impact of Changing Agriculture: Proceedings of a Seminar on Land Degradation Due to Hydrological Phenomena in Hilly Areas: Impact of Change of Land Use & Management, Cesena, 9-11 October 1985. Ed. by G. Chisci & Royston P. Morgan. 248p. (C). 1986. text ed. 75.00 (*90-6191-657-7*, Pub. by A A Balkema NE) Ashgate Pub Co.

Soil Erosion Research Methods. 2nd ed. Ed. by Rattan Lal. LC 93-45352. (Illus.). 352p. (Orig.). 1994. pap. text ed. 44.95 (*1-884015-09-3*) St Lucie Pr.

Soil Exhaustion As a Factor in the Agricultural History of Virginia & Maryland, 1606-1860. Avery O. Craven. 1926. 14.50 (*0-8446-1136-0*) Peter Smith.

Soil Factor in Nutrition: Animal & Human. Kenneth C. Beeson & Gennard Matrone. LC 76-18421. (Nutrition & Clinical Nutrition Ser.: No. 2). 168p. reprint ed. pap. 47.90 (*0-7837-0702-9*, 2041034) Bks Demand.

*****Soil Fertility.** 2nd ed. H. D. Foth & Boyd G. Ellis. LC 96-27155. 1996. write for info. (*1-56670-243-7*) Lewis Pubs.

Soil Fertility & Fertilizer Management in Semiarid Tropical India. Ed. by C. Bruce Christianson. LC 89-24489. (Special Publications: No. SP-11). (Illus.). 160p. (Orig.). 1989. pap. text ed. 20.00 (*0-88090-081-4*) Intl Fertilizer.

Soil Fertility & Fertilizers. 5th ed. Samuel L. Tisdale et al. (Illus.). 624p. (C). 1993. text ed. 90.00 (*0-02-420835-3*, Macmillan Coll) P-H.

Soil Fertility & Organic Matter As Critical Components of Production Systems. Ed. by R. F. Follett. 176p. 1987. 22.10 (*0-89118-782-0*) Soil Sci Soc Am.

Soil Fertility & the Ancient Maya. Ursula M. Cowgill. (Connecticut Academy of Arts & Sciences Ser., Trans.: Vol. 42). 1961. pap. 49.50 (*0-685-22891-6*) Elliots Bks.

Soil Fertility Evaluation & Control. Charles A. Black & Skip DeWall. 768p. 1993. 69.95 (*0-87371-834-8*, 2596, CRC Reprint) Franklin.

*****Soil Fertility Management for Sustainable Agriculture.** Rajendra Prasad & J. F. Power. LC 96-44795. 1997. write for info. (*1-56670-254-2*) Lewis Pubs.

Soil Food Web. Ingham. 1995. write for info. (*0-8493-5939-2*) CRC Pr.

Soil Fungicides, 2 vols., Vol. I. A. P. Sinha et al. 224p. 1988. 116.00 (*0-8493-4548-0*, SB951, CRC Reprint) Franklin.

Soil Fungicides, 2 vols., Vol. II. A. P. Sinha et al. 176p. 1988. 109.00 (*0-8493-4549-9*, SB951, CRC Reprint) Franklin.

Soil Gas & Related Methods for Natural Resource Exploration. Ronald W. Klusman. LC 92-45608. 483p. 1994. text ed. 275.00 (*0-471-93892-0*) Wiley.

Soil Genesis & Classification. 3rd ed. S. W. Buol et al. LC 88-34450. (Illus.). 460p. (C). 1989. text ed. 49.95 (*0-8138-1462-6*) Iowa St U Pr.

*****Soil Genesis & Classification.** 4th ed. S. W. Buol. LC 97-5055. 1997. 59.95 (*0-8138-1464-2*) Iowa St U Pr.

Soil Geomorphology. Raymond B. Daniels & Richard D. Hammer. LC 92-3789. 256p. 1992. text ed. 84.95 (*0-471-51153-6*) Wiley.

Soil Geomorphology. J. G. Gerrard. 240p. 1992. 99.95 (*0-412-44170-5*, A9492) Chapman & Hall.

Soil Geomorphology. J. G. Gerrard. 240p. (gr. 13). 1992. pap. text ed. 38.95 (*0-412-44180-2*, A9496) Chapman & Hall.

Soil Improvement: History, Capabilities, & Outlook: Report by the Committee on Placement & Improvement of Soils of the Geotechnical Engineering Division of the American Society of Civil Engineers. American Society of Civil Engineers Staff. LC 78-104862. (Illus.). 186p. reprint ed. pap. 53.10 (*0-317-08310-4*, 2019549) Bks Demand.

Soil Improvement by Preloading. Aris C. Stamatopoulos & Panaghiotis C. Kotzias. LC 85-5365. (Geotechnical Engineering Ser.). 261p. 1985. text ed. 95.00 (*0-471-81593-4*) Wiley.

Soil Improvement for Earthquake Hazard Mitigation: Proceedings of Sessions Sponsored by the Soil Improvement & Geosynthetics Committees, San Diego, October 22-26, 1995. Ed. by Roman D. Hryciw. LC 95-20623. (Geotechnical Special Publications: No. 49). 152p. 1995. 18.00 (*0-7844-0123-3*) Am Soc Civil Eng.

Soil Landscape Analysis. Francis D. Hole & James B. Campbell. LC 83-24418. (Illus.). 214p. (C). 1985. 61.50 (*0-86598-140-X*) Rowman.

*****Soil Liquefaction.** Ed. by Jefferies & Been. (Illus.). 320p. 1997. text ed. 129.00 (*0-7514-0250-8*, Pub. by Blackie Acad & Prof UK) Routledge Chapman & Hall.

Soil Management. Ed. by Deere & Company Staff. (Farm Business Management Ser.). 145p. (Orig.). (C). 1993. pap. text ed. 24.95 (*0-86691-145-6*, FBM11101B); Instr.'s guide. teacher ed., pap. text ed. 19.95 (*0-86691-185-5*, FBM11501T); Student guide. student ed., pap. text ed. 9.95 (*0-86691-186-3*, FBM11601W) Deere & Co.

Soil Management. 5th ed. D. B. Davies et al. (Illus.). 288p. 1993. 34.95 (*0-85236-238-2*, Pub. by Farming Pr UK) Diamond Farm Bk.

Soil Management: A World View of Conservation & Production. Ray L. Cook & Boyd G. Ellis. LC 91-38873. 428p. (C). 1992. reprint ed. 63.50 (*0-89464-682-6*) Krieger.

Soil Management: Experimental Basis for Sustainability. B. A. Stewart. (Advances in Soil Science Ser.). 576p. 1995. 79.95 (*1-55670-076-8*, L1076) Lewis Pubs.

Soil Management & Greenhouse Effect. Ed. by Rattan Lal. 400p. 1995. 79.95 (*1-56670-117-1*, L1117) Lewis Pubs.

Soil Management for Sustainability. Ed. by F. J. Pierce. (Illus.). 178p. (Orig.). (C). 1991. pap. text ed. 18.00 (*0-935734-23-6*) Soil & Water Conserv.

Soil Management in Tropical America, 2 Vols., Set. Elmer Bornemisza & Alfredo Alvarado. 1978. lib. bdg. 600.00 (*0-8490-2622-9*) Gordon Pr.

Soil Map of the World, 1: Legend. 59p. 1972. Incl. sheet & text. pap. 12.00 (*92-3-101125-1*, UM125X, Pub. by UNESCO FR) Bernan Associates.

Soil Map of the World, 10: Australasia. 221p. 1976. pap. text ed. 25.00 (*92-3-001359-5*, UM359X, Pub. by UNESCO FR) Bernan Associates.

Soil Map of the World, 2: North America. (Illus.). 1975. pap. text ed. 25.00 (*92-3-001126-6*, UM1260, Pub. by UNESCO FR) Bernan Associates.

Soil Map of the World, 3: Mexico & Central America. (Illus.). 1975. pap. text ed. 12.00 (*92-3-001127-4*, UM127X, Pub. by UNESCO FR) Bernan Associates.

Soil Map of the World, 6: Africa. 299p. 1975. pap. 35.00 (*92-3-001362-5*, UM362X, Pub. by UNESCO FR) Bernan Associates.

Soil Map of the World, 8: North & Central Asia. 165p. 1977. pap. 35.00 (*92-3-001345-5*, UM345X, Pub. by UNESCO FR) Bernan Associates.

Soil Map of the World, 9: South-East Asia. 149p. 1978. pap. 12.00 (*92-3-001363-3*, UM363X, Pub. by UNESCO FR) Bernan Associates.

Soil Mechanics. Alfreds R. Jumikis. LC 79-12978. 618p. 1983. lib. bdg. 66.50 (*0-88275-969-8*) Krieger.

Soil Mechanics. T. William Lambe & Robert V. Whitman. (Geotechnical Engineering Ser.). 553p. (C). 1969. text ed. 59.95 (*0-471-51192-7*) Wiley.

*****Soil Mechanics.** William T. Lambe & Robert V. Whitman. pap. text ed. write for info. (*0-471-18111-0*) Wiley.

*****Soil Mechanics.** Smith. 1988. pap. text ed. write for info. (*0-582-03380-2*, Pub. by Longman UK) Longman.

Soil Mechanics. 2nd ed. T. H. Wu. LC 75-26633. 440p. (C). 1982. reprint ed. text ed. 40.00 (*0-918498-02-3*) T H Wu.

*****Soil Mechanics.** 5th ed. Craig. (Illus.). 440p. (Orig.). (C). (gr. 13 up). Date not set. pap. text ed. 34.95 (*0-412-39590-8*, Chap & Hall NY) Chapman & Hall.

Soil Mechanics: Design Manual, No. 7.1. Scientific Publishers Staff. 348p. (C). 1985. 275.00 (*81-85046-16-6*, Pub. by Scientific UK) St Mut.

*****Soil Mechanics: Solutions Manual.** 5th ed. Craig. (Illus.). 88p. (Orig.). (C). (gr. 13 up). pap. text ed. 18.50 (*0-412-47230-9*, Chap & Hall NY) Chapman & Hall.

Soil Mechanics & Foundation Engineering. G. Petrasovits. 640p. (C). 1984. 405.00 (*0-569-08888-7*, Pub. by Collets) St Mut.

Soil Mechanics & Foundation Engineering: Proceedings of the 10th International Conference on Soil Mechanics & Foundation Engineering, Stockholm, 15-19th June 1981, 4 vols., Set. 3542p. (C). 1982. text ed. 995.00 (*90-6191-210-5*, Pub. by A A Balkema NE) Ashgate Pub Co.

Soil Mechanics & Foundation Engineering: Proceedings of the 7th Regional Conference for Africa, Accra, June 1980, 2 vols. Ed. by M. D. Gidigasu et al. 902p. (C). 1982. text ed. 305.00 (*90-6191-079-X*, Pub. by A A Balkema NE) Ashgate Pub Co.

Soil Mechanics & Foundation Engineering: Proceedings of the 8th Regional Conference for Africa, Harare, 4-7 June 1984, 2 vols., Set. Ed. by J. R. Boyce et al. 1000p. (C). 1987. text ed. 315.00 (*90-6191-531-7*, Pub. by A A Balkema NE) Ashgate Pub Co.

Soil Mechanics & Foundations Engineering: Proceedings of the 9th Regional Conference for Africa, Lagos, 15-18 Sept 1987, 2 vols. Ed. by J. O. Akinmusuru et al. 850p. 1987. text ed. 315.00 (*90-6191-717-4*, Pub. by A A Balkema NE) Ashgate Pub Co.

Soil Mechanics Considerations in Arid & Semiarid Areas. (Research Record Ser.: No. 1137). 89p. 1987. 13.00 (*0-309-04513-4*) Transport Res Bd.

Soil Mechanics for Unsaturated Soils. Delwyn G. Fredlund & Haianto Rahardjo. LC 92-30869. 544p. 1993. text ed. 95.00 (*0-471-85008-X*) Wiley.

Soil Mechanics, Foundations & Footings: Selected Translations of Russian Geotechnical Literature. Ryszard B. Zeidler. (Geotechnika Ser.: No. 3). (Illus.). 408p. (C). 1991. text ed. 130.00 (*90-6191-172-9*, Pub. by A A Balkema NE) Ashgate Pub Co.

Soil Mechanics in Engineering Practice. 3rd ed. Karl Terzaghi et al. LC 95-6166. 560p. 1996. text ed. 79.95 (*0-471-08658-4*) Wiley.

Soil Mechanics in the Light of Critical State Theories: An Introduction. J. A. Ortigao. (Illus.). 160p. (C). 1995. pap. 35.00 (*90-5410-195-4*, Pub. by A A Balkema NE); text ed. 65.00 (*90-5410-194-6*, Pub. by A A Balkema NE) Ashgate Pub Co.

*****Soil Mechanics Laboratory Manual.** 5th ed. Braja Das. (Illus.). 280p. (C). 1997. text ed. 29.50 (*1-57645-010-4*, 104) Engineering.

Soil Mechanics, Transient & Cyclic Loads: Constitutive Relations & Numerical Treatment. Ed. by G. N. Pande & O. C. Zienkiewicz. LC 81-16485. (Wiley Series in Numerical Methods in Engineering). (Illus.). 639p. reprint ed. pap. 180.00 (*0-318-39649-1*, 2033053) Bks Demand.

Soil Micro-Organism & Crop Growth. Ed. by L. L. Somani. (C). 1989. text ed. 135.00 (*0-7855-0110-X*, Pub. by Scientific Pubs II) St Mut.

Soil Microbial Associations: Control of Structures & Functions. Ed. by V. Vancura & F. Kunc. (Developments in Agricultural & Managed Forest Ecology Ser.: Vol.17). 498p. 1988. 257.00 (*0-444-98961-7*) Elsevier.

Soil Microbial Ecology: Applications in Agricultural & Environmental Management. Ed. by F. Blaine Metting. LC 92-26049. (Books in Soils, Plants & the Environment: Vol. 25). 648p. 1992. 185.00 (*0-8247-8737-4*) Dekker.

Soil Microbiology. Robert L. Tate. 424p. 1994. text ed. 69.95 (*0-471-57868-1*) Wiley.

Soil Microbiology: A Model of Decomposition. Michael J. Bazin & O. L. Smith. 272p. 1982. 161.00 (*0-8493-5952-X*, QR111, CRC Reprint) Franklin.

*****Soil Microbiology: Principles & Applications.** Sylvia & Fuhrmann. 1997. text ed. 91.00 (*0-13-459991-8*) P-H.

Soil Microbiology & Biochemistry. Ed. by E. A. Paul & F. E. Clark. 470p. 1988. text ed. 49.95 (*0-12-546805-9*) Acad Pr.

Soil Microbiology & Biochemistry. 2nd ed. Eldor A. Paul & Francis E. Clark. (Illus.). 340p. 1996. text ed. 39.95 (*0-12-546806-7*) Acad Pr.

Soil Micromorphology: A Basic & Applied Science: Proceedings of the VIIIth International Working Meeting, San Antonio, Texas, July 1988. Ed. by L. A. Douglas. (Developments in Soil Science Ser.: Vol. 19). 716p. 1990. 226.75 (*0-444-88302-9*) Elsevier.

Soil Micromorphology: Studies in Managment & Genesis. Ed. by A. J. Ringrose-Voase & G. S. Humphreys. LC 94-21731. (Development in Soil Science Ser.: 22). 900p. 1994. 264.25 (*0-444-89792-5*) Elsevier.

Soil Micromorphology & Soil Classification. Ed. by M. L. Thompson et al. 216p. 1985. pap. 19.00 (*0-89118-776-6*) Soil Sci Soc Am.

Soil Microorganisms & Crop Growth. L. L. Somani & S. C. Bhandari. 263p. (C). 1989. 135.00 (*81-85312-04-4*, Pub. by Scientific UK) St Mut.

Soil Microorganisms & Plant Growth. N. S. Rao. 350p. 1995. text ed. 29.95 (*1-886106-18-5*) Science Pubs.

Soil Microscopy & Micromorphology. E. A. FitzPatrick. LC 92-39763. 304p. 1993. text ed. 125.00 (*0-471-93859-9*) Wiley.

Soil Mineral Stresses: Approaches to Crop Improvement. Ed. by A. R. Yeo & T. J. Flowers. LC 93-46743. (Monographs on Theoretical & Applied Genetics: No. 21). (Illus.). 230p. 1994. 158.95 (*0-387-53115-7*) Spr-Verlag.

Soil Monitoring: Early Detection & Surveying of Soil Contamination & Degradation. Ed. by R. Schulin et al. LC 93-34474. (Monte Verita, Proceedings of the Centro Stefano Franciscini Ascona Ser.). 1993. 86.00 (*0-8176-2956-4*, Pub. by Birkhauser Vlg SZ) Birkhauser.

Soil Morphology Genesis & Classification. Devlin S. Fanning. LC 88-7930. 416p. 1989. Net. text ed. 78.95 (*0-471-89248-3*) Wiley.

Soil Nutrient Bioavailability: A Mechanistic Approach. 2nd ed. Stanley A. Barber. LC 94-22899. (Illus.). 414p. 1995. text ed. 69.95 (*0-471-58747-8*) Wiley.

Soil Organic Matter: Biological & Ecological Effects. Robert L. Tate, III. LC 92-15329. 304p. 1992. reprint ed. lib. bdg. 49.50 (*0-89464-765-2*) Krieger.

Soil Organic Matter Dynamics & the Sustainability of Tropical Agriculture. Ed. by K. Mulongoy & R. Merckx. 392p. 1993. text ed. 115.00 (*0-471-93915-3*) Wiley.

Soil Organic Matter in Temperate Agroecosystems: Long Term Experiments in North America. Eldor A. Paul et al. LC 96-23071. 528p. 1996. 89.95 (*0-8493-2802-0*) CRC Pr.

Soil Physical Chemistry. Ed. by Donald L. Sparks. 320p. 1986. 180.00 (*0-8493-5448-X*, S592, CRC Reprint) Franklin.

Soil Physical Conditions & Crop Growth. Ed. by L. L. Somani. (C). 1988. 130.00 (*81-85147-22-1*, Pub. by Scientific UK) St Mut.

Soil Physical Conditions & Plant Roots. Ed. by Jan Glinski & Jerzy Lipiec. 288p. 1989. 220.95 (*0-8493-6498-1*, S596) CRC Pr.

Soil Physical Properties & Crop Production in the Tropics. Rattan Lal. 551p. (C). 1989. 65.00 (*0-685-61469-7*, Pub. by Intl Bk Distr II); pap. 45.00 (*0-685-61470-0*, Pub. by Intl Bk Distr II) St Mut.

Soil Physical Properties & Crop Production in the Tropics. Ed. by Rattan Lal. 551p. 1989. 325.00 (*81-7089-104-3*, Pub. by Intl Bk Distr II) St Mut.

Soil Physical Properties & Crop Production in the Tropics. Rattan Lal. 551p. 1989. pap. 625.00 (*0-614-09641-3*, Pub. by Intl Bk Distr II) St Mut.

*****Soil Physical Properties & Crop Production in the Tropics.** Ed. by R. Lal & D. J. Greenland. LC 79-40583. reprint ed. pap. 163.40 (*0-608-04600-0*, 2065370) Bks Demand.

Soil Physics. A. Kezdi. LC 73-85223. (Handbook of Soil Mechanics Ser.: Vol. 1). 256p. 1974. 165.00 (*0-444-99890-X*) Elsevier.

Soil Physics. 2nd ed. T. J. Marshall & J. W. Holmes. (Illus.). 350p. 1988. pap. 37.95 (*0-521-35817-5*) Cambridge U Pr.

Soil Physics. 3rd ed. T. J. Marshall et al. (Illus.). 400p. (C). 1996. pap. text ed. 37.95 (*0-521-45766-1*) Cambridge U Pr.

Soil Physics. 3rd ed. T. J. Marshall et al. (Illus.). 400p. (C). 1996. text ed. 90.00 (*0-521-45151-5*) Cambridge U Pr.

Soil Physics. 5th ed. Wilford Gardner et al. LC 90-24351. 352p. 1991. text ed. 75.00 (*0-471-83108-5*) Wiley.

Soil Physics with Basic: Transport Models for Soil-Plant Systems. G. S. Campbell. (Developments in Soil Science Ser.: No. 14). 150p. 1985. 149.00 (*0-444-42557-8*) Elsevier.

Soil Plasticity: Theory & Implementation. Wai-Fah Chen & G. Y. Baladi. (Developments in Geotechnical Engineering Ser.: No. 38). 234p. 1985. 158.75 (*0-444-42455-5*) Elsevier.

Soil Pollution. S. G. Misra & Dinesh Mani. (C). 1991. text ed. 22.00 (*81-7024-431-5*, Pub. by Ashish II) S Asia.

Soil Pollution: Processes & Dynamics. Bruno Yaron et al. LC 96-10597. 310p. 1996. 149.50 (*3-540-60927-X*) Spr-Verlag.

Soil Pollution & Soil Organisms. P. C. Mishra. (C). 1989. 39.00 (*81-7024-258-4*, Pub. by Ashish II) S Asia.

Soil Processes: A Systematic Approach. S. Ross. (Illus.). 416p. 1989. text ed. 95.00 (*0-415-00205-2*) Routledge.

Soil Processes & Water Quality. Ed. by B. A. Stewart & Rattan Lal. (Advances in Soil Science Ser.). 416p. 1994. 69.95 (*0-87371-980-8*, L980) Lewis Pubs.

Soil Properties. 3rd ed. Liu & Evett. 365p. (C). 1996. text ed. 58.00 (*0-13-440462-9*) P-H.

Soil Properties Evaluation from Centrifugal Models & Field Performance. Ed. by Frank C. Townsend & G. M. Norris. (Sessions Proceedings Ser.). 164p. 1988. 19.00 (*0-87262-646-6*) Am Soc Civil Eng.

Soil Protozoa. J. F. Darbyshire. 224p. 1994. 80.00 (*0-85198-884-9*) CAB Intl.

Soil Reaction & Plant Distribution in the Sylene National Park, Norway. Erling Christophersen. (Connecticut Academy of Arts & Sciences Ser., Trans.: Vol. 27). 1925. pap. 75.00 (*0-685-22814-2*) Elliots Bks.

Soil Reclamation Processes: Microbiological Analyses & Applications. Tate & Klein. (Books in Soils, Plants & the Environment: Vol. 12). 368p. 1985. 175.00 (*0-8247-7286-5*) Dekker.

Soil Remediation for Petroleum Extraction Industry. Lloyd E. Deuel, Jr. & George H. Holliday. LC 94-28065. 1994. 84.95 (*0-87814-425-0*) PennWell Bks.

Soil Resilience & Sustainable Land Use. Ed. by D. J. Greenland & I. Szabolcs. 576p. 1994. 140.00 (*0-85198-871-7*) CAB Intl.

Soil Resource: Origin & Behavior. Hans Jenny. (Ecological Studies: Vol. 37). (Illus.). 377p. 1986. 77.00 (*0-387-90543-X*) Spr-Verlag.

Soil Responses to Climate Change. 1996. 149.50 (*3-540-58373-4*) Spr-Verlag.

Soil Responses to Climate Change. Ed. by Mark D. Rounsevell & Peter J. Loveland. LC 94-35237. (NATO ASI Series I: Global Environmental Change: Vol. 23). 1994. write for info. (*0-387-58373-4*) Spr-Verlag.

Soil Restoration. Ed. by B. A. Stewart & Rattan Lal. (Advances in Soil Science Ser.: Vol. 17). (Illus.). 440p. 1991. 156.95 (*0-387-97657-4*) Spr-Verlag.

Soil-Root Interface. Ed. by J. L. Harley. 1979. text ed. 99.00 (*0-12-325550-3*) Acad Pr.

*****Soil Salinity & Water Quality.** R. Chhabra. (Illus.). 300p. (C). 1996. text ed. 65.00 (*90-5410-727-8*, Pub. by A A Balkema NE) Ashgate Pub Co.

Soil Sampling & Methods of Analysis. Ed. by M. R. Carter. 864p. 1993. 77.95 (*0-87371-861-5*, L861) Lewis Pubs.

Soil Sampling, Preparation, & Analysis. Kim H. Tan. (Books in Soils, Plants & the Environment: Vol. 45). 432p. 1995. 99.75 (*0-8247-9675-6*) Dekker.

*****Soil Science.** Plaster. 1997. teacher ed., pap. text ed. 12.75 (*0-8273-8228-6*) Delmar.

Soil Science: An Introduction. G. W. Leeper & N. C. Uren. (Illus.). 260p. (Orig.). 1993. pap. 34.95 (*0-522-84464-2*, Pub. by Melbourne Univ Pr AT) Paul & Co Pubs.

Soil Science: Methods & Applications. D. L. Rowell. (C). 1994. pap. text ed. 54.50 (*0-582-08784-8*) Addison-Wesley.

Soil Science: Sustainable Production & Environmental Protection. 2nd ed. K. Cameron & R. G. McLaren. (Illus.). 336p. 1996. pap. 65.00 (*0-19-558345-0*) OUP.

Soil Science Analyses: A Guide to Current Use. Denis Baize. Tr. by Graham Cross. LC 93-2794. 192p. 1993. text ed. 105.00 (*0-471-93469-0*) Wiley.

Soil Science & Management. 2nd ed. Edward J. Plaster. 1991. teacher ed., pap. 12.75 (*0-8273-4051-6*); text ed. 45.95 (*0-8273-4050-8*) Delmar.

Soil Science & Management. 3rd ed. Edward F. Plaster. (Agriculture Ser.). 1997. lab manual ed. 18.95 (*0-8273-7864-5*) Delmar.

Soil Science & Management. 3rd ed. Edward J. Plaster. (Agriculture Ser.). 416p. 1996. text ed. 46.95 (*0-8273-7293-0*) Delmar.

Soil Science & Management. 3rd ed. Edward J. Plaster. (Agriculture Ser.). 1997. teacher ed. 13.95 (*0-8273-7294-9*) Delmar.

Soil Science & Sustainable Land Management in the Tropics. Ed. by J. K. Syers & D. L. Rimmer. 304p. 1994. 90.00 (*0-85198-874-1*, Pub. by CAB Intntl UK) OUP.

Soil Science Education: Philosophy & Perspectives: Proceedings of a Symposium Sponsored by Divisions S-1, S-2, S-3, S-4, S-5, S-6, S-7, S-8, S-9 of the Soil Science Society of America in Minneapolis, November 5, 1992. Ed. by Philippe Baveye et al. LC 94-17681. (SSSA Special Publications: No. 37). 1994. write for info. (*0-89118-809-6*) Soil Sci Soc Am.

Soil Science Simplified. Ed. by Milo I. Harpstead & Francis D. Hale. (C). 1988. 70.00 (*81-85046-72-7*, Pub. by Scientific UK) St Mut.

*****Soil Science Simplified.** 3rd ed. Milo I. Harpstead et al. LC 96-43802. 1997. 36.95 (*0-8138-1504-5*) Iowa St U Pr.

Soil Science Simplified. 4th rev. ed. Helmut Kohnke & D. P. Franzmeier. (Illus.). 162p. (C). 1995. pap. text ed. 7.50 (*0-88133-813-3*) Waveland Pr.

Soil Scientist. Jack Rudman. (Career Examination Ser.: C-1033). 1994. pap. 29.95 (*0-8373-1033-4*) Nat Learn.

Soil Screening Guidance. 1995. lib. bdg. 259.95 (*0-8490-8370-2*) Gordon Pr.

Soil Sediment Adsorption Constant Program. Howard. 78p. 1992. 548.00 (*0-87371-782-1*, L782) Lewis Pubs.

*****Soil Seed Banks of North West Europe: Methodology, Density & Longevity.** Ken Thompson et al. (Illus.). 286p. (C). 1996. text ed. 120.00 (*0-521-49519-9*) Cambridge U Pr.

*****Soil Settlement Effects on Buildings.** E. Dulacska. (Developments in Geotechnical Engineering Ser.: Vol. 69). 448p. 1992. 213.00 (*0-444-98689-8*) Elsevier.

Soil-Site Relations, Stand Structure, & Yields of Slash & Loblolly Pine Plantations in the Southern United States. Theodore S. Coile & F. X. Schumacher. LC 82-170983. (Illus.). 310p. reprint ed. pap. 88.40 (*0-7837-6225-9*, 2045939) Bks Demand.

Soil Slope Instability & Stabilisation: Proceedings of the Slope Stability Extension Course, Sydney, August 1987. Ed. by Bruce F. Walker & Robin Fell. 380p. (C). 1987. text ed. 140.00 (90-6191-730-1, Pub. by A A Balkema NE) Ashgate Pub Co.

Soil Solarization. Ed. by J. E. Devay et al. (Plant Production & Protection Papers: No. 109). 412p. 1991. pap. 35.00 (92-5-103057-X, F057X, Pub. by FAO IT) Bernan Associates.

Soil Solarization. Jaacov Katan & James E. Devay. (Illus.). 256p. 1991. 205.95 (0-8493-6868-5, SB732) CRC Pr.

Soil Solution Chemistry: Applications to Environmental Science & Agriculture. Jeffrey D. Wolt. 360p. 1994. text ed. 84.95 (0-471-58554-8) Wiley.

Soil Specimen Preparation for Laboratory Testing: A Symposium Presented at the Seventy-Eighth Annual Meeting, ASTM, Montreal, Canada, 22-27 June 1975. Symposium on Soil Specimen Preparation for Laboratory Testing Staff. LC 76-704. (ASTM Special Technical Publication Ser.: No. 599). 350p. reprint ed. pap. 99.80 (0-7837-4799-3, 2044843) Bks Demand.

Soil Stability & Deformation Due to Seepage. Milan Vukovic & Milenko Pusic. 100p. 1992. spiral bd. 35.00 (0-918334-78-0) WRP.

Soil-Steel Bridges: Design & Construction. George Abdel-Sayed et al. 500p. 1993. text ed. 60.00i (0-07-003021-9) McGraw.

Soil Structure: Its Development & Function. Ed. by K. H. Hartge & B. A. Stewart. (Advances in Soil Sciences Ser.). 448p. 1995. 75.00 (1-56670-173-2, L1173) Lewis Pubs.

Soil Structure - Soil Biota Interrelationships: Proceedings of the International Workshop on Methods of Research on Soil Structure Soil Biota Interrelationships, Wageningen, the Netherlands, November, 1991. Ed. by L. Brussaard & M. J. Kooistra. 846p. 1993. 352.00 (0-444-81490-6) Elsevier.

Soil Structure - Soil Biota Relationships: Proceedings of the International Workshop on Methods of Research on Soil Structure - Soil Biota Interrelationships, Held at the International Agricultural Centre, Wageningen, The Netherlands, 24-28 November 1991. Ed. by L. Brussaard & M. J. Kooistra. LC 93-15218. 508p. 1993. Alk. paper. 216.25 (0-444-81498-1) Elsevier.

Soil Structure & Fabric. R. Brewer & J. R. Sleeman. 1988. 50.00 (0-643-04859-6, Pub. by CSIRO AT) Aubrey Bks.

Soil Structure Assessment. Ed. by W. Burke et al. 99p. (C). 1986. text ed. 45.00 (90-6191-656-9, Pub. by A A Balkema NE) Ashgate Pub Co.

Soil-Structure Interaction. (Research Record Ser.: No. 1129). 67p. 1987. 10.50 (0-309-04510-X) Transport Res Bd.

Soil-Structure Interaction. Ed. by A. S. Cakmak. LC 87-70779. (SDEE Ser.: Vol. 3). 382p. 1987. 105.00 (0-931215-86-2) Computational Mech MA.

***Soil-Structure Interaction: Instruments for Monitoring of Soil Pressures.** George E. Lazebnik & Gregory P. Tsinker. LC 97-8343. 1997. write for info. (0-412-07431-1) Chapman & Hall.

***Soil-Structure Interaction: Numerical Analysis & Modelling.** Ed. by Bull. (Illus.). 744p. 1994. text ed. 117.95 (0-419-19070-8, E & FN Spon) Routledge Chapman & Hall.

Soil-Structure Interaction: The Real Behavior of Structures, NO. 5034. Institution of Structural Engineers Staff. 120p. 1989. pap. 73.50 (0-685-32920-8, S034, Pub. by Inst Civil Eng UK) Am Soc Civil Eng.

Soil-Structure-Interaction Analysis in Time Domain. John P. Wolf. (Illus.). 416p. (C). 1988. text ed. 52.00 (0-685-19509-0) P-H.

Soil Suction Applications in Geotechnical Engineering Practice: Proceedings of a Session Sponsored by the Committee on Shallow Foundations & Soil Properties, San Diego, October 22-26, 1995. Ed. by Warren K. Wray & Sandra L. Houston. (Geotechnical Special Publications: Vol. 48). 80p. 1995. 20.00 (0-7844-0117-9) Am Soc Civil Eng.

***Soil Survey Manual, 2 vols.** 1997. lib. bdg. 600.99 (0-8490-6175-X) Gordon Pr.

***Soil Survey Manual.** 3rd ed. (Illus.). xxi, 437p. 1997. pap. text ed. 60.00 (1-57979-216-2) BPI Info Servs.

Soil Survey Techniques. W. U. Reybold & G. W. Petersen. 112p. 1987. 15.00 (0-89118-783-9) Soil Sci Soc Am.

Soil Technicians' Handbook. K. H. Head. 158p. 1989. text ed. 61.95 (0-470-21443-0) Halsted Pr.

Soil Testing: Correlating & Interpreting the Analytical Results. Ed. by T. R. Peck et al. 117p. 1977. pap. 6.00 (0-89118-047-8) Soil Sci Soc Am.

Soil Testing: Prospects for Improving Nutrient Recommendations. David M. Kral. LC 94-31653. (Special Publications: Vol. 40). 1994. pap. 30.00 (0-89118-815-0) Soil Sci Soc Am.

Soil Testing: Sampling, Correlation, Calibration, & Interpretation. Ed. by J. R. Brown. 144p. 1987. 20.00 (0-89118-784-7) Soil Sci Soc Am.

Soil Testing: Soil Mechanics of Earthworks, Foundations, & Road Construction. A. Kezdi. (Handbook of Soil Mechanics Ser.: Vol. 2). 260p. 1980. 165.00 (0-444-99778-4) Elsevier.

Soil Testing & Plant Analysis. Ed. by L. M. Walsh & James D. Beaton. (Illus.). 491p. 1973. 10.00 (0-89118-755-3) Soil Sci Soc Am.

Soil Testing in Civil Engineering. J. N. Mandal & D. G. Divshikar. (Illus.). 256p. 1995. 85.00 (90-5410-233-0) Balkema RSA.

Soil Transmitted Helminths: Proceedings of the WHO Expert Committee on Helminthiasis, Rio de Janeiro, 1963. WHO Staff. (Technical Report Ser.: No. 277). 70p. (ENG, FRE, RUS & SPA.). 1964. pap. text ed. 5.00 (92-4-120277-7, 1100277) World Health.

***Soil Treatability Pilot Studies to Design & Model Soil Aquifer Treatment Systems.** Arizona State University Staff et al. LC 97-17617. 1997. write for info. (0-89867-911-7) Am Water Wks Assn.

Soil Vapor Extraction Technology. Tom A. Pedersen & James T. Curtis. LC 91-12465. (Pollution Technology Review Ser.: No. 204). (Illus.). 316p. 1991. 54.00 (0-8155-1284-8) Noyes.

Soil Viscoplasticity & Design of Structures: Including Appendices on Viscoplasticity of Ice & Frozen Ground Long Term Stability & Creep of Structures on Slopes. Ryszard B. Zeidler. (Selected Translations of Russian Geotechnical Literature Ser.). (Illus.). 512p. (C). 1993. text ed. 115.00 (90-6191-174-5, Pub. by A A Balkema NE) Ashgate Pub Co.

Soil Washing/Soil Flushing. Ed. by W. C. Anderson. (Innovative Site Remediation Technology Ser.: Vol. 3). 174p. 1995. 75.95 (3-540-59062-5) Spr-Verlag.

Soil Water & Ground Water Sampling. Neal Wilson. 208p. 1995. 49.95 (1-56670-073-6, L1073) Lewis Pubs.

Soil-Water & Nitrogen: In Mediterranean-Type Environments. John Monteith & Colin Webb. 1981. lib. bdg. 152.00 (90-247-2406-6) Kluwer Ac.

Soil Water Assessment by the Neutron Method. E. L. Greacen. (Illus.). 140p. 1981. pap. text ed. 20.00 (0-643-00414-9, Pub. by CSIRO AT) Aubrey Bks.

Soil, Water, Biology, & Belief in Prehistoric & Traditional Southwestern Agriculture. Ed. by H. Wolcott Toll. (NMAC Special Publications: No. 2). xvi, 373p. 1995. pap. 22.00 (0-9646931-1-9) NMex Archeol.

Soil-Water Engineering Field & Laboratory Manual. Thomas J. Trout et al. (C). 1987. 190.00 (0-317-62315-X, Pub. by Scientific UK) St Mut.

Soil-Water Interactions: Mechanisms & Applications. 2nd expanded rev. ed. Shingo Iwata et al. LC 94-22883. (Books in Soils, Plants & the Environment: Vol. 38). 464p. 1994. 175.00 (0-8247-9293-9) Dekker.

Soil Zoology: Proceedings. Easter School in Agricultural Science (21st: 1974: University of Nottingham) Staff. Ed. by D. Keith Kevan. 532p. reprint ed. pap. 151.70 (0-317-41863-7, 2025739) Bks Demand.

***Soilborne Diseases of Tropical Crops.** Ed. by R. J. Hillocks & J. M. Waller. 480p. 1997. 120.00 (0-85199-121-1, Pub. by CAB Intntl UK) OUP.

Soilborne Plant Pathogens: Management of Diseases with Macro- & Microelements. Ed. by Arthur W. Engelhard. LC 89-85115. (Illus.). 217p. (Orig.). 1989. pap. 30.00 (0-89054-101-9) Am Phytopathol Soc.

Soilborne Plant Pathogens (Management of Diseases with Macro & Microelements) Ed. by Arther W. Englehard. (C). 1993. text ed. 200.00 (81-7233-054-5, Pub. by Scientific Pubs II) St Mut.

Soiled Dove. Dirk Fletcher. (Spur Giant Ser.). 368p. (Orig.). 1995. mass mkt., pap. text ed. 4.99 (0-8439-3801-3) Dorchester Pub Co.

Soiled Doves: Prostitution in the Early West. Anne Seagraves. LC 93-94257. (Illus.). 176p. pap. 11.95 (0-9619088-4-X) Wesanne Pubns.

Soiling & Cleaning of Building Facades. Ed. by L. G. Verhoef. (RILEM Reports). 200p. 1988. 65.00 (0-412-30670-0) Chapman & Hall.

Soilless Culture Management. M. Schwarz. (Advanced Series in Agricultural Sciences: 24). 1995. 133.95 (0-387-58159-6) Spr-Verlag.

Soilless Culture Management. Meier Schwarz. (Advanced Series in Agricultural Sciences: No. 24). (Illus.). 197p. 1995. write for info. (3-540-58159-6) Spr-Verlag.

Soils. Ed. by John P. Bowles. (Plants & Gardens Ser.). (Illus.). 240p. 1990. per., pap. 7.95 (0-945352-43-3) Bklyn Botanic.

***Soils.** John W. Schafer. 1996. spiral bd. 30.00 (0-88252-201-9) Paladin Hse.

Soils: A New Global View. G. S. Humphreys et al. 1995. 40.00 (1-85728-464-X, Pub. by UCL Pr UK); pap. write for info. (1-85728-465-8, Pub. by UCL Pr UK) Taylor & Francis.

Soils: A New Global View. Thomas R. Patom. 1996. pap. text ed. 28.00 (0-300-06609-0) Yale U Pr.

Soils: A New Global View. Thomas R. Paton. 1996. 55.75 (0-300-06576-0) Yale U Pr.

Soils: An Introduction. 3rd ed. Michael J. Singer & Donald N. Munns. 1995. text ed. 86.00 (0-13-449174-2) P-H.

Soils: In Our Environment. 7th rev. ed. Raymond W. Miller & Roy L. Donahue. Ed. by Joyce U. Miller. LC 94-44096. Orig. Title: Soils. 649p. 1995. text ed. 89.00 (0-13-095803-4) P-H.

Soils: Science & Management. Edward Plaster. LC 85-4486. 352p. (C). 1985. text ed. 41.95 (0-8273-2406-5) Delmar.

Soils: Science & Management. Edward Plaster. LC 85-4486. 352p. (C). 1985. teacher ed. 12.00 (0-8273-2407-3) Delmar.

Soils see Soils: In Our Environment

Soils & Crops-Diagnostic Techniques. H. B. Kitchen. 308p. 1992. pap. 175.00 (0-7855-0391-9, Pub. by Intl Bks & Periodicals II) St Mut.

Soils & Environment. Steve Ellis & Tony Mellor. LC 94-23894. (Physical Environment Ser.). (Illus.). 256p. (C). 1995. pap. 25.00 (0-415-06888-6, C0477) Routledge.

Soils & Environment. Steve Ellis & Tony Mellor. LC 94-23894. (Physical Environment Ser.). (Illus.). 256p. (C). (gr. 13). 1995. text ed. 79.95 (0-415-06887-8, C0414) Routledge.

Soils & Environmental Quality. Gary M. Pierzynski et al. 336p. 1993. 69.95 (0-87371-680-9, L680) Lewis Pubs.

Soils & Foundations. 3rd ed. Cheng Liu & Jack B. Evett. 464p. 1991. text ed. 86.00 (0-13-816182-8, 510802) P-H.

***Soils & Foundations.** 4th ed. Liu & Evett. LC 97-9754. 1997. text ed. 56.00 (0-13-494949-8) P-H.

Soils & Foundations for Architects & Engineers. Chester I. Duncan. (Structural Engineering Ser.). (Illus.). 384p. (gr. 13). 1992. text ed. 60.95 (0-442-00604-7) Chapman & Hall.

Soils & Geomorphology. Peter W. Birkeland. (Illus.). 386p. 1984. pap. 35.00 (0-19-503435-X) OUP.

Soils & Global Change. Bobby A. Stewart. 464p. 1995. 89.95 (1-56670-118-X, L1118) Lewis Pubs.

Soils & Land Use. Sherwood. (C). Date not set. pap. text ed. write for info. (0-03-005933-X) HB Coll Pubs.

Soils & Land Use. Sherwood. (C). 1901. teacher ed., pap. text ed. write for info. (0-03-005934-8) HB Coll Pubs.

Soils & Landscape Evolution: Proceedings of the 21st Binghamton Symposium on Geomorphology, Binghamton, NY 6-7 Oct., 1990. Ed. by P. L. Knuepfer & L. D. McFadden. 379p. 1990. reprint ed. 168.75 (0-444-88692-3) Elsevier.

Soils & Micromorphology in Archaeology. Marie-Agnes Courty et al. (Cambridge Manuals in Archaeology Ser.). (Illus.). (C). 1990. 85.00 (0-521-32419-X) Cambridge U Pr.

Soils & Quaternary Geology: A Handbook for Field Scientists. J. A. Catt. (Monographs on Soil & Resources Survey: No. 11). (Illus.). 300p. 1986. 89.00 (0-19-854568-1) OUP.

Soils & Quaternary Landscape Evolution. Ed. by John Boardman. LC 84-20994. (Illus.). 401p. reprint ed. pap. 114.30 (0-7837-6369-7, 2046081) Bks Demand.

***Soils & Sediments: Mineralogy & Geochemistry.** Ed. by H. Paquet & N. Clauer. LC 97-8044. (Illus.). 260p. 1997. 115.00 (3-540-61599-7) Spr-Verlag.

Soils & Soil Fertility. 5th ed. Frederick R. Troeh & Louis M. Thompson. (Illus.). 512p. (C). 1993. text ed. 57.00 (0-19-508328-8) OUP.

Soils & Soil Management. 2nd ed. Charles D. Sopher & Jack V. Baird. (C). 1982. text ed. 97.00 (0-8359-7031-0, Reston) P-H.

Soils & the Environment: A Guide to Their Applications. Gerald W. Olson. 191p. 1982. pap. 19.95 (0-412-23760-1, 6587) Chapman & Hall.

Soils & the Environment: An Introduction. Alan Wild. LC 92-24680. (Illus.). 307p. (C). 1993. pap. text ed. 29.95 (0-521-43859-4) Cambridge U Pr.

Soils & the Greenhouse Effect: The Present Status & Future Trends Concerning the Effect of Soils & Their Cover on the Fluxes of Greenhouse Gases, the Surface Energy Balance & the Water Balance. Ed. by A. F. Bouwman. LC 89-21519. 575p. 1990. text ed. 185.00 (0-471-92395-8) Wiley.

Soils & Their Environment. John J. Hassett & Wayne L. Banwart. 432p. (C). 1991. text ed. 69.80 (0-13-484049-6) P-H.

Soils for Management of Organic Wastes & Waste Waters. Ed. by L. F. Elliott & F. J. Stevenson. (Illus.). 650p. 1977. 17.50 (0-89118-049-4) Am Soc Agron.

Soils in Archaeology: Landscape Evolution & Human Occupation. Ed. by Vance T. Holliday. LC 91-13686. (Illus.). 272p. (C). 1993. reprint ed. pap. text ed. 16.95 (1-56098-308-6) Smithsonian.

Soils in Construction. 4th ed. W. L. Schroeder & S. E. Dickenson. LC 95-16334. 1995. text ed. 73.00 (0-13-441031-9) P-H.

***Soils in Our Environment.** 8th ed. Raymond W. Miller & Duane T. Gardiner. LC 96-53481. 1997. 88.00 (0-13-610882-2) P-H.

Soils in the Urban Environment. P. Bullock & P. Gregory. 1991. 95.00 (0-632-02988-9) Blackwell Sci.

Soils in Waste Treatment & Utilization, Vol. I: Land Treatment. Ed. by W. H. Fuller & A. W. Warrick. 288p. 1985. 158.00 (0-8493-5151-0, TD760) CRC Pr.

Soils in Waste Treatment & Utilization, Vol. II. Ed. by W. H. Fuller & A. W. Warrick. 240p. 1985. 141.00 (0-8493-5152-9) CRC Pr.

Soils Manual. (Illus.). 260p. 1986. 16.00 (0-318-13398-9, MS-10) Asphalt Inst.

Soils of New Jersey. John C. Tedrow. LC 85-18226. 512p. 1986. text ed. 72.50 (0-89874-897-6) Krieger.

Soils of the Desert Southwest. Wallace H. Fuller. LC 74-79390. (Illus.). 120p. reprint ed. pap. 34.20 (0-8357-3175-8, 2039439) Bks Demand.

Soils of the Great Plains: Land Use, Crops, & Grasses. Andrew R. Aandahl. LC 81-7435. (Illus.). 334p. reprint ed. pap. 95.20 (0-8357-3787-X, 2036517) Bks Demand.

Soils of the Past: An Introduction to Paleopedology. Gregory J. Retallack. 300p. 1989. 100.00 (0-04-551128-4) Routledge Chapman & Hall.

***Soils of the Past: An Introduction to Paleopedology.** Gregory J. Retallack. (Illus.). 538p. (C). 1990. pap. text ed. 54.95 (0-04-445757-X) Routledge Chapman & Hall.

Soils of the Tropics: Properties & Appraisal. Armand V. Wambeke. 550p. 1992. text ed. 58.00 (0-07-067946-0) McGraw.

Soils of the World: Soil Families & Soil Types, Vol. 1. M. A. Glazovskaya. Tr. by C. M. Rao from RUS. 224p. (C). 1983. text ed. 85.00 (90-6191-419-1, Pub. by A A Balkema NE) Ashgate Pub Co.

Soils of the World: Soil Geography, Vol. 2. M. A. Glazovskaya. Tr. by C. M. Rao from RUS. 409p. (C). 1984. text ed. 85.00 (90-6191-420-5, Pub. by A A Balkema NE) Ashgate Pub Co.

Soils of Wisconsin. Francis D. Hole et al. LC 75-12209. (Geological & Natural History Survey Bulletin Ser.: No. 87). 263p. reprint ed. pap. 75.00 (0-8357-4987-8, 2037920) Bks Demand.

Soils on a Warmer Earth: Proceedings of an International Workshop on Effects of Expected Climate Change on Soil Processes in the Tropics & Sub-Tropics, Nairobi, 12-14 Feb., 1990. Ed. by H. W. Scharpenseel et al. (Developments in Soil Science: No. 20). 274p. 1990. 150.75 (0-444-88838-1) Elsevier.

Soils Response Spectrum. Ed. by A. S. Cakmak. LC 90-82732. (Progress in Engineering Ser.: Vol. 10). 1990. 54.00 (0-945824-63-7) Computational Mech MA.

Soils, Sustainability & the Natural Heritage. A. G. Taylor et al. 256p. 1995. pap. 140.00 (0-11-495270-1, Pub. by Stationery Ofc UK) Bernan Associates.

Soils under Cyclic & Transient Loading: Proceedings from the International Symposium, Swansea, 7-11th January 1980, 2 vols., Set. Ed. by G. N. Pande & O. C. Zienkiewicz. 894p. (C). 1980. text ed. 240.00 (90-6191-076-5, Pub. by A A Balkema NE) Ashgate Pub Co.

Soirees du Hameau. Nikolai V. Gogol. 288p. (FRE.). 1989. pap. 11.95 (0-7859-2566-X, 2070381250) Fr & Eur.

So...Is He Gay? The Single Woman's Guide to Whether He'd Make a Better Groom or Caterer at Your Wedding. Laurie Mitchell. (Illus.). 128p. 1996. pap. 8.95 (1-56352-328-0) Longstreet Pr Inc.

Sois Philosophe, Charlie Brown. Charles M. Schulz. (Peanuts Ser.). (FRE.). (J). 1985. 4.95 (0-8288-4517-4) Fr & Eur.

Soitiye: Almanac of Russian Erotic Literature. Ed. by Mikhail Armalinsky. LC 89-91401. 184p. (Orig.). (RUS.). 1991. pap. 6.00 (0-916201-06-6) M I P Co.

Soixante Ans de Ma Vie Litteraire. Andre Maurois. Incl. Role de l'ecrivain dans le monde d'aujourd'hui. 9.95 (0-685-36961-7); write for info. (0-318-52265-9) Fr & Eur.

Sojan. Michael Moorcock. 160p. (Orig.). 1980. pap. 11.95 (0-86130-000-9, Pub. by Savoy Bks UK) AK Pr Dist.

Sojourn. Molly Colton. 359p. (Orig.). 1996. mass mkt. 5.99 (1-55197-169-0, Pub. by Comnwlth Pub CN) Partners Pubs Grp.

Sojourn. Mary E. Croney. LC 93-29800. (Illus.). 214p. (Orig.). 1994. pap. 10.95 (0-9624209-2-1) Landmark ID.

Sojourn: Forgotten Realms. R. A. Salvatore. LC 90-71499. (Dark Elf Trilogy Ser.: Bk. 3). 320p. (Orig.). 1991. pap. 5.99 (1-56076-047-8) TSR Inc.

Sojourn in Gascony: Pleasures of the Palette. Erasmus H. Kloman. Ed. by Lynne Shaner. 96p. (Orig.). 1994. pap. 11.95 (0-9639596-3-8) Judd Pubng.

Sojourn in Gascony: Pleasures of the Palette. Erasmus H. Kloman. (Illus.). (Orig.). 1996. pap. 11.95 (0-614-17588-7) Judd Pubng.

Sojourn in Gascony: Pleasures of the Palette. limited ed. Erasmus H. Kloman. Ed. by Lynne Shaner. (Illus.). 108p. (Orig.). 1994. pap. 24.95 (0-9639596-4-6) Judd Pubng.

Sojourn in Israel. Inez S. Cooper. LC 89-50414. (Illus.). 77p. (Orig.). pap. 6.95 (0-935615-06-7) S Utah U Pr.

Sojourn with the Grand Sharif of Makkah. Charles Didier. Tr. by Richard Boulind from FRE. (Arabia Past & Present Ser.: Vol. 18). (Illus.). 176p. 1985. 45.00 (0-906672-11-2) Oleander Pr.

Sojourner. Marjorie K. Rawlings. 24.95 (0-8488-0616-6) Amereon Ltd.

Sojourner. Pat Sternberg & Dolly Beechman. 46p. (J). 1989. Playscript. 5.00 (0-87602-283-2) Anchorage.

Sojourner. Marjorie K. Rawlings. LC 90-27830. 336p. 1991. reprint ed. 29.95 (0-87797-228-1) Cherokee.

Sojourner Microcosms: New & Selected Poems, 1959-1977. Anselm Hollo. LC 77-21781. (Selected Works Ser.: No. 2). 1977. 49.95 (0-912652-39-X); pap. 19.95 (0-912652-38-1) Blue Wind.

Sojourner Microcosms: New & Selected Poems, 1959-1977. deluxe limited ed. Anselm Hollo. LC 77-21781. (Selected Works Ser.: No. 2). 1977. 75.00 (0-912652-40-3) Blue Wind.

***Sojourner, So to Speak: Poems.** Joe Somoza. 104p. (Orig.). 1997. pap. 12.00 (1-888809-04-3) La Alameda Pr.

***Sojourner Truth.** LC 96-37382. (Read & Discover Photo-Illustrated Biographies Ser.). (J). 1997. write for info. (1-56065-518-6) Capstone Pr.

Sojourner Truth. Mark Dunster. 12p. (Orig.). 1983. pap. 4.00 (0-89642-106-6) Linden Pubs.

***Sojourner Truth.** Margo Mcloone. (Read-&-Discover Biographies Ser.). (Illus.). (J). 1997. 13.25 (0-516-20540-4) Childrens.

***Sojourner Truth.** Nell Painter. Date not set. pap. 14.95 (0-393-31708-0) Norton.

***Sojourner Truth.** W. Terry Whalin. (Heroes of the Faith Ser.). 208p. (Orig.). (YA). (gr. 9 up). 1997. pap. 3.97 (1-55748-933-5) Barbour & Co.

Sojourner Truth. Peter Krass. (Black American Ser.). (Illus.). 192p. (Orig.). (YA). 1990. reprint ed. mass mkt. 3.95 (0-87067-559-1, Melrose Sq) Holloway.

Sojourner Truth. Susan Taylor-Boyd. LC 89-4345. (People Who Have Helped the World Ser.). (Illus.). 68p. (J). 1990. reprint ed. pap. 7.95 (0-8192-1541-4) Morehouse Pub.

Sojourner Truth: A Life, A Symbol. Nell I. Painter. LC 95-47595. 370p. 1996. 28.00 (0-393-02739-2) Norton.

Sojourner Truth: A Self-Made Woman. Victoria Ortiz. LC 73-22290. (Illus.). 160p. (YA). (gr. 7 up). 1986. lib. bdg. 13.89 (0-397-32134-1, Lipp Jr Bks) HarpC Child Bks.

Sojourner Truth: A Voice for Freedom. Patricia McKissack & Fredrick McKissack. LC 92-6190. (Great African Americans Ser.). (Illus.). 32p. (J). (gr. 1-4). 1992. lib. bdg. 12.95 (0-89490-313-6) Enslow Pubs.

Sojourner Truth: Ain't I a Woman? Fredrick McKissack, Jr. & Patricia C. McKissack. 192p. (YA). (gr. 4-6). 1994. pap. 3.50 (0-590-44691-6) Scholastic Inc.

Sojourner Truth: Ain't I a Woman. Patricia C. McKissack & Fredrick McKissack, Jr. 192p. (J). (gr. 4-6). 1992. 13.95 (0-590-44690-8, Scholastic Hardcover) Scholastic Inc.

Sojourner Truth: Antislavery Activist. Peter Krass. Ed. by Nathan I. Huggins. (Black Americans of Achievement Ser.). (Illus.). 112p. (Orig.). (YA). (gr. 5 up). 1988. lib. bdg. 19.95 (1-55546-611-7) Chelsea Hse.

An Asterisk (*) at the beginning of an entry indicates that the title is appearing in BIP for the first time.

Sojourner Truth: Crusader for Civil Rights. Norman L. Macht. (Junior Black Americans of Achievement Ser.). (Illus.). 80p. (J). (gr. 3-6). 1993. pap. 4.95 (*0-7910-1998-5*); lib. bdg. 15.95 (*0-7910-1754-0*) Chelsea Hse.

Sojourner Truth: Slave, Prophet, Legend. Carleton Mabee & Susan M. Newhouse. LC 93-9370. (Illus.). 320p. (C). 1993. 45.00 (*0-8147-5484-8*) NYU Pr.

Sojourner Truth: Slave, Prophet, Legend. Carleton Mabee & Susan M. Newhouse. LC 93-9370. (Illus.). 320p. (C). 1995. pap. 16.95 (*0-8147-5525-9*) NYU Pr.

Sojourner Truth: The Courageous Former Slave Who Led Others to Freedom. Susan Taylor-Boyd. LC 90-37992. (People Who Made a Difference Ser.). (Illus.). 64p. (J). (gr. 3-4). 1991. lib. bdg. 23.93 (*0-8368-0458-9*) Gareth Stevens Inc.

Sojourner Truth: The Courageous Former Slave Whose Eloquence Helped Promote Human Equality. Susan Taylor-Boyd. LC 89-4345. (People Who Have Helped the World Ser.). (Illus.). 68p. (J). (gr. 5-6). 1990. lib. bdg. 23.93 (*0-8368-0101-6*) Gareth Stevens Inc.

Sojourner Truth - God's Faithful Pilgrim. Arthur H. Fauset. (African Studies). reprint ed. 20.00 (*0-938818-93-7*) ECA Assoc.

Sojourner Truth & the Struggle for Freedom. Edward B. Clafin. LC 87-19325. (Henry Steele Commager's Americans Ser.). (Illus.). 144p. (J). (gr. 3-6). 1987. pap. 5.95 (*0-8120-3919-X*) Barron.

Sojourner Truth & the Voice of Freedom. Jane Shumate. (Gateway Civil Rights Ser.). (Illus.). 32p. (J). (gr. 2-4). 1991. pap. 4.95 (*1-878841-71-8*); lib. bdg. 15.40 (*1-56294-041-4*) Millbrook Pr.

Sojourner Truth Great Nubian Quiz. Al I. Obaba. (Great Nubian Quiz Bks.). (Illus.). 43p. (Orig.). (YA). 1989. pap. 3.95 (*0-916157-08-3*) African Islam Miss Pubns.

Sojourner Truth Guide. (J). 1995. pap. write for info. (*0-590-39311-1*) Scholastic Inc.

Sojourners: The Epic Story of China's Centuries-Old Relationship with Australia. Eric Rolls. (Orig.). 1992. 49.95 (*0-7022-2478-2*, Pub. by Univ Queensland Pr AT) Intl Spec Bk.

Sojourners: The Return of German Jews & the Question of Identity. John Borneman & Jeffrey M. Peck. LC 95-3125. (Texts & Contexts Ser.: Vol. 16). xi, 309p. 1995. text ed. 40.00 (*0-8032-1255-0*) U of Nebr Pr.

Sojourners & Settlers: Histories of Southeast Asia & the Chinese. Ed. by Anthony Reid. (Illus.). 232p. 1996. pap. 24.95 (*1-86373-990-4*, Pub. by Allen & Unwin Aust Pty AT) Paul & Co Pubs.

Sojourners & Settlers: The Macedonian Community in Toronto in 1940. Lillian Petroff. (Multicultural History Society of Ontario Ser.). (Illus.). 256p. 1995. 50.00 (*0-8020-0452-0*); pap. 19.95 (*0-8020-7240-2*) U of Toronto Pr.

Sojourners & Settlers: The Yemeni Immigrant Experience. Ed. by Jonathan Friedlander. LC 88-14377. (Illus.). 198p. reprint ed. pap. 56.50 (*0-7837-5547-3*, 2045322) Bks Demand.

Sojourners in Faith: The First 35 Years of Covenant Presbyterian Church, Madison, Wisconsin, 1954-1989. Robert F. Patton. 288p. 1994. 19.95 (*1-881576-25-6*) Providence Hse.

Sojourners in the Sun: Scottish Migrants in Jamaica & the Chesapeake, 1740-1800. Alan L. Karras. LC 92-52763. (Illus.). 256p. 1992. 37.50 (*0-8014-2691-X*) Cornell U Pr.

***Sojourners in the Wilderness: The Christian Right in Comparative Perspective.** Ed. by James M. Penning & Corwin E. Smidt. LC 97-18546. 224p. 1997. 58.00 (*0-8476-8644-2*); pap. 22.95 (*0-8476-8645-0*) Rowman.

***Sojourners No More: The Quakers in the New South, 1865-1920.** Damon D. Hickey. (Illus.). 192p. (Orig.). 1997. pap. write for info. (*0-942727-28-2*) NC Yrly Pubns Bd.

Sojourners of the Caribbean: Ethnogenesis & Ethnohistory of the Garifuna. Nancie L. Gonzalez. LC 87-6044. (Illus.). 272p. 1988. text ed. 29.95 (*0-252-01453-7*) U of Ill Pr.

Sojourner's Truth & Other Stories. Lee Maracle. 1995. pap. 10.95 (*0-88974-023-2*, Pub. by Press Gang CN) LPC InBook.

Sojourns. Cristina P. Hidalgo. 172p. (Orig.). 1984. pap. 10.75 (*971-10-0166-7*, Pub. by New Day Pub PH) Cellar.

Sojourns & Extremes of Stochastic Processes. Simeon M. Berman. (Advanced Statistics Ser.). 320p. (C). (gr. 13). 1992. text ed. 76.95 (*0-534-13932-9*) Chapman & Hall.

Sokagakkai & Mass Society. James W. White. LC 75-93498. xiv, 380p. 1970. 49.50 (*0-8047-0728-6*) Stanford U Pr.

Sokodae: A West African Dance. Drid Williams. 12p. 1971. pap. 4.00 (*0-9500029-5-X*, Pub. by Octagon Pr UK) ISHK.

Sokol Gymnastic Manual: New & Revised Version. Stephen Banjak. LC 93-83580. 364p. write for info. (*0-912981-23-7*) Hse BonGiovanni.

Sokolov Investigation into the Mysterious Disappearance of the Russian Imperial Family. Nicolai Sokolov. Tr. by John F. O'Conor. 1968. 14.95 (*0-8315-0110-3*) Speller.

Sokrascenija V'Greceskich' Rukopisjach' Preimuscestvenno Po Datirovannym' Rukopisjam' S. Petersburga i Moskvy. Grigorij F. Cereteli. lvii, 226p. 1969. reprint ed. 90.00 (*0-318-71750-6*) G Olms Pubs.

Sokuma. Mark Bessire et al. LC 96-38236. (Heritage Library of African Peoples: Set 3). (Illus.). 64p. (YA). (gr. 7-12). 1997. lib. bdg. 15.95 (*0-8239-1992-7*, D1992-7) Rosen Group.

***Sol a Sol.** Carlson. LC 97-18574. 1997. pap. 14.95 (*0-8050-4373-X*) St Martin.

***Sol de los Venados/The Sun of the Deer.** Gloria C. Diaz. 1996. pap. 6.95 (*84-348-3976-8*) Lectorum Pubns.

Sol de un Solo Dia. Ana R. Nunez. LC 92-75884. (Coleccion Espejo de Paciencia). 93p. (Orig.). (SPA.). 1993. pap. 9.95 (*0-89729-658-3*) Ediciones.

Sol de una Esperanza Nueva. Charles R. Swindoll. 43p. (SPA.). 1986. pap. 3.25 (*0-8423-6346-7*, 498525) Editorial Unilit.

Sol Ecce Surgit Igneus: A Commentary on the Morning & Evening Hymns of Prudentius. Marion M. Van Assendelft. vii, 275p. 1976. 51.00 (*90-6088-060-9*, Pub. by Boumas Boekhuis NE) Benjamins North Am.

Sol-Gel: Science & Technology. Ed. by M. Jafelicci, Jr. et al. 516p. (C). 1989. text ed. 151.00 (*9971-5-0890-7*) World Scientific Pub.

***Sol-Gel & Polymer Photonic Devices.** Mark P. Andrews & S. Iraj Najafi. LC 97-23157. 1997. pap. write for info. (*0-8194-2599-0*) SPIE.

Sol-Gel Optics: Processing & Applications. Ed. by Lisa C. Klein. LC 93-33696. (International Series in Engineering & Computer Science, VLSI, Computer Architecture, & Digital Screen Processing). 600p. (C). 1994. lib. bdg. 204.00 (*0-7923-9424-0*) Kluwer Ac.

***Sol-Gel Optics IV.** Ed. by Bruce S. Dunn et al. 67p. 1997. pap. 107.00 (*0-8194-2558-3*) SPIE.

Sol-Gel Processes for Ceramic Fuels. (Panel Proceedings Ser.). (Illus.). 179p. 1969. pap. 25.00 (*92-0-141068-9*, ISP207, Pub. by IAEA AU) Bernan Associates.

Sol-Gel Processing & Applications. Ed. by Y. A. Attia. (Illus.). 394p. (C). 1995. 115.00 (*0-306-44837-8*, Plenum Pr) Plenum.

***Sol-Gel Processing of Advanced Ceramics.** F. D. Ginanam. (Illus.). 260p. (C). 1996. 69.00 (*1-886106-87-8*) Science Pubs.

Sol-Gel Science: The Physics & Chemistry of Sol-Gel Processing. Ed. by C. Jeffrey Brinker & George W. Scherer. 928p. 1990. text ed. 201.00 (*0-12-134970-5*) Acad Pr.

Sol-Gel Science & Technology: Proceedings, International Symposium on Sol-Gel Science & Technology (1st: 1994: Los Angeles, CA) Ed. by Edward J. Pope et al. LC 95-24464. (Ceramic Transactions Ser.: No. 55). 402p. 1995. 83.00 (*0-944904-97-1*) Am Ceramic.

Sol-Gel Technology for Thin Films, Fibers, Preforms, Electronics, & Specialty Shapes. Ed. by Lisa C. Klein. LC 87-34780. (Illus.). 407p. 1988. 72.00 (*0-8155-1154-X*) Noyes.

***Sol Goldberg's Ithaca: The Journal Years.** Ed. by John Marcham. LC 96-71112. (Illus.). 96p. (Orig.). 1996. pap. 17.95 (*0-942690-38-9*) DeWitt Hist.

Sol Kit. Alma F. Ada. (Spanish Elementary Ser.). (Illus.). 1989. 161.50 (*0-201-12755-5*); audio 64.75 (*0-201-12756-3*) Addison-Wesley.

Sol, la Luna, y las Estrellas. Joy Evans & Jo E. Moore. Tr. by Liz Wolfe & Dora Ficklin from ENG. (Science Mini-Unit Ser.). (Illus.). 16p. (SPA.). (J). (gr. 1-3). 1992. pap. text ed. 5.95 (*1-55799-235-5*, EMC 037) Evan-Moor Corp.

***Sol Lewitt: Critical Texts.** Ed. by Adachiara Zevi. 497p. 1996. pap. 35.00 (*1-881616-78-9*, 620501) Dist Art Pubs.

Sol LeWitt: Twenty-Five Years of Wall Drawings, 1968-1993. Andrea M. Keller & Jock Reynolds. Ed. by Allison Kemmerer. LC 93-72778. (Illus.). 88p. (Orig.). 1993. pap. 29.95 (*1-879886-34-0*) Addison Gallery.

Sol Plaatje, South African Nationalist, 1876-1932. Brian Willan. LC 84-2471. (Perspectives on Southern Africa Ser.: No. 36). (Illus.). 430p. 1984. 65.00 (*0-520-05274-9*); pap. 17.00 (*0-520-05334-6*) U CA Pr.

Sol Power: The Evolution of Solar Architecture. Stephan Behling & Sophia Behling. (Illus.). 224p. 1996. 65.00 (*3-7913-1670-2*, Pub. by Prestel GW) te Neues.

Sol Siempre Brilla En Alguna Parte: The Sun Is Always Shining Somewhere. Allan Fowler. LC 90-2176. (Spanish Rookie Read-About Science Ser.). (Illus.). 32p. (SPA.). (J). (ps-2). 1992. lib. bdg. 15.30 (*0-516-34906-6*) Childrens.

Sol Siempre Brilla En Alguna Parte: The Sun Is Always Shining Somewhere. Allan Fowler. LC 90-2176. (Rookie Read-about Science Ser.). (Illus.). 32p. (SPA.). (J). (ps-2). 1992. pap. 3.95 (*0-516-54906-5*) Childrens.

Sol Solo Sololos. Rair Ennerg. 83p. (Orig.). 1988. pap. 16.95 (*0-926256-02-5*) Destnne Pub.

***Sol T. Plaatje: Select Writing.** Solomon T. Plaatje. Ed. by Brian Willan. 480p. (Orig.). 1997. pap. text ed. 29.95 (*0-8214-1186-1*) Ohio U Pr.

Sol Tiene Manchas. Rene Reyna. LC 92-71445. (Coleccion Caniqui). 177p. (Orig.). (SPA.). 1992. pap. 19.95 (*0-89729-643-5*) Ediciones.

Sol White's History of Colored Base Ball with Documents on the Early Black Game 1886-1936. Sol White. LC 94-20992. lxv, 190p. 1996. pap. 12.00 (*0-8032-9783-1*, Bison Books) U of Nebr Pr.

Sol White's History of Colored Base Ball, with Other Documents on the Early Black Game, 1886-1936. rev. ed. Sol White. LC 94-20992. Orig. Title: Sol White's Official Base Ball Guide. (Illus.). lxv, 190p. 1995. reprint ed. text ed. 30.00 (*0-8032-4771-0*) U of Nebr Pr.

Sol White's Official Base Ball Guide see Sol White's History of Colored Base Ball, with Other Documents on the Early Black Game, 1886-1936

Sol White's Official Baseball Guide. White. 16.95 (*0-8488-1588-2*) Amereon Ltd.

Sol White's Official Baseball Guide. Sol White. LC 83-73430. (Camden House Library of Baseball Classics: Vol. 2). (Illus.). vi, 128p. reprint ed. 39.95 (*0-938100-31-9*) Camden Hse.

Sol y Los De Abajo. Jose Montoya. (Illus.). 13p. (ENG & SPA.). 1992. 90.00 (*0-9614597-8-6*) Ninja Pr.

Sol y Sombra. 3rd ed. Paul Pimsleur et al. (Illus.). 224p. (Orig.). (SPA.). (C). 1983. pap. text ed. 20.00 (*0-15-582413-9*) HB Coll Pubs.

Sola en el Camino de la Fe. Marfa Cabrera. (Serie Actualidades - Actualities Ser.). 30p. (SPA.). 1992. pap. 1.99 (*1-56063-405-7*, 498180) Editorial Unilit.

Sola Scriptura: The Protestant Position on the Bible. Joel R. Beeke et al. Ed. by Don Kistler. 300p. (Orig.). 1996. pap. 14.95 (*1-57358-028-7*) Soli Deo Gloria.

Solace & Romance. Kenneth Levin. LC 95-70438. 341p. 1996. 24.95 (*0-9647566-0-9*) Sorenson Bks.

Solace of Food: A Life of James Beard. Robert Clark. 357p. 1996. pap. 16.00 (*1-883642-04-3*) Steerforth Pr.

Solace of Open Spaces. Gretel Ehrlich. 148p. 1986. pap. 10.95 (*0-14-008113-5*, Penguin Bks) Viking Penguin.

***Solace of the Mare.** Dan Stryk. (Illus.). (Orig.). (C). 1997. pap. text ed. 12.95 (*0-614-29883-0*) Dancng Jester.

Solace Paradigm: An Eclectic Search for Psychological Immunity. Paul C. Horton et al. 1988. 65.00 (*0-8236-6210-1*) Intl Univs Pr.

Solal. Albert Cohen. (FRE.). 1981. pap. 11.95 (*0-7859-1933-3*, 2070372693) Fr & Eur.

Solal. Albert Cohen. (Folio Ser.: No. 1269). (FRE.). pap. 10.95 (*2-07-037269-3*) Schoenhof.

Solamente por Gracia. Charles H. Spurgeon. 128p. (SPA.). 1982. mass mkt. 4.50 (*0-8254-1678-7*, Edit Portavoz) Kregel.

Solanaceae: Biology & Systematics. Ed. by W. G. D'Arcy. LC 85-17057. (Illus.). 608p. 1986. text ed. 112.00 (*0-231-05780-6*) Col U Pr.

***Solanaceae III - Taxonomy, Chemistry, Evolution.** Ed. by J. G. Hawkes et al. ix, 483p. 1991. pap. 60.00 (*0-947643-31-1*, Pub. by Royal Botnic Grdns UK) Balogh.

Solanaceae, Scrophulariaceae, Vol. 22. Ed. by B. K. Shishkin. (Flora of the USSR Ser.). (Illus.). (C). 1996. text ed. write for info. (*1-886106-40-1*) Science Pubs.

Solange's Daughter. large type ed. Nerina Thorne. (Linford Romance Library). 288p. 1993. pap. 15.99 (*0-7089-7403-1*, Linford) Ulverscroft.

Solano County Street Guide & Directory: 1997 Edition. (Illus.). 96p. 1996. pap. 16.95 (*0-88130-846-3*) Thomas Bros Maps.

Solar Access As a Property Right: Oregon & New Mexico. Marion S. Beaumont & Kathryn B. Imperati. (Tax Policy Roundtable Property Tax Papers: No. TPR 14). 36p. reprint ed. pap. 25.00 (*0-7837-2158-7*, 2042460) Bks Demand.

Solar Action: 27 Communities Boost Renewable Energy Use. 1981. pap. 9.00 (*0-686-84642-7*) Am Solar Energy.

Solar Active Region Ecolution: Comparing Models with Observations. Ed. by K. S. Balasubramaniam & George W. Simon. (ASP Conference Series Proceedings: Vol. 68). 448p. 1994. 28.00 (*0-937707-87-2*) Astron Soc Pacific.

Solar Active Regions: A Monograph from Skylab Solar Workshop III. Skylab Solar Workshop Staff. LC 79-56357. (Illus.). 360p. reprint ed. pap. 102.60 (*0-685-23653-6*, 2027912) Bks Demand.

Solar Air Conditioning & Refrigeration. Ed. by A. A. Sayigh & J. C. McVeigh. (Renewable Energy Ser.: No. 3). (Illus.). 298p. 1992. 121.75 (*0-08-040750-1*, Pergamon Pr) Elsevier.

Solar Alcohol: The Fuel Revolution. rev. ed. M. Mandeville et al. (Illus.). 128p. 1980. pap. 8.95 (*0-940828-00-6*) D Youra Studios.

Solar & Aeolian Energy: Proceedings of the International Seminar on Solar & Aeolean Energy held at Sounion, Greece, Sept. 4-15, 1961. International Seminar on Solar & Aeolian Energy Staff. Ed. by A. G. Spanides & Athan D. Hatzikakidis. LC 62-9965. 501p. reprint ed. pap. 142.80 (*0-317-08517-4*, 2019390) Bks Demand.

Solar & Astrophysical Magnetohydrodynamic Flows. Ed. by Kanaris C. Tsinganos. LC 96-13181. (NATO ASI Ser.: Series C, Vol. 481). 742p. 1996. lib. bdg. 330.00 (*0-7923-4054-X*) Kluwer Ac.

***Solar & Heliospheric Plasma Physics: Proceedings of the 8th European Meeting on Solar Physics, Held in Halkidiki, near Thessaloniki, Greece, 13-18 May, 1996.** G. M. Simnett et al. LC 97-20573. (Lecture Notes in Physics Ser.: Vol. 489). 1997. write for info. (*3-540-63072-4*) Springer Pub.

***Solar & Interplanetary Disturbances.** S. K. Alurkar. LC 96-49790. (Astronomy & Astrophysics Ser.). 1997. write for info. (*981-02-2925-9*) World Scientific Pub.

Solar & Interplanetary Dynamics. Ed. by Murray Dryer & Einar Tandberg-Hanssen. (International Astronomical Union Symposia Ser.: No. 91). 570p. 1980. pap. text ed. 78.00 (*90-277-1163-1*); lib. bdg. 165.00 (*90-277-1162-3*) Kluwer Ac.

***Solar & Middle Atmosphere Variability.** G. A. Chapman. (Advances in Space Research (RJ) Ser.: Vol. 8). 218p. 1989. 78.00 (*0-08-036889-1*, Pergamon Pr) Elsevier.

Solar & Planetary Dynamos. Ed. by M. R. Proctor et al. (Publications of the Newton Institute). (Illus.). 366p. (C). 1994. text ed. 52.95 (*0-521-45470-0*) Cambridge U Pr.

Solar & Planetary Longitudes for Years Minus 2500 to Plus 2000 by 10-day Intervals. William D. Stahlman et al. LC 63-10534. 596p. reprint ed. pap. 169.90 (*0-317-07758-9*, 2051912) Bks Demand.

Solar & Planetary Plasma Physics: Papers Presented at the Spring College on Plasma Physics. Ed. by B. Buti. 240p. (C). 1990. text ed. 92.00 (*981-02-0155-9*) World Scientific Pub.

Solar & Space Physics. National Research Council Staff. (Space Science in the Twenty-First Century Series: Imperatives for the Decades 1995 to 2015). 150p. 1988. pap. text ed. 17.95 (*0-309-03848-0*) Natl Acad Pr.

Solar & Stellar, ser. vol. 6. Francoise Praderie. (Advances in Space Research Ser.). 1988. pap. 63.00 (*0-08-036643-0*, Pergamon Pr) Elsevier.

Solar & Stellar Activity Cycles. Peter R. Wilson. LC 93-29835. (Astrophysics Ser.: Vol. 24). (Illus.). 320p. (C). 1994. text ed. 69.95 (*0-521-43081-X*) Cambridge U Pr.

Solar & Stellar Granulation. Ed. by Robert J. Rutten & Giuseppe Severino. (C). 1989. lib. bdg. 265.00 (*0-7923-0122-6*) Kluwer Ac.

Solar & Ultraviolet Radiation. WHO Staff. (IARC Monographs on the Evaluation of Carcinogenic Risks of Chemicals to Humans: Vol. 55). 316p. 1992. pap. text ed. 72.00 (*92-832-1255-X*, 1720055) World Health.

Solar & Wind Energy: An Economic Evaluation of Current & Future Technologies. Martin T. Katzman. LC 83-23044. 212p. 1984. 67.50 (*0-86598-152-3*, R3958) Rowman.

Solar Angel. Torkom Saraydarian. LC 89-83490. 1991. text ed. 25.00 (*0-911794-61-1*); pap. text ed. 20.00 (*0-911794-62-X*) Aqua Educ.

Solar Angular Velocity. Ed. by Bernard R. Durney & Sabatino Sofia. (C). 1987. lib. bdg. 160.50 (*90-277-2523-3*) Kluwer Ac.

Solar Applications see Alternative Energy Sources V: Energy Research

Solar Applications in Industry & Commerce. John D. Myers. (Illus.). 432p. (C). 1984. text ed. 43.00 (*0-13-822404-8*) P-H.

Solar Architecture in Europe: Design Performance & Evaluation. Commission of the European Union Staff. (Illus.). 178p. (Orig.). (C). 1991. pap. 22.95 (*1-85327-073-3*, Pub. by Prism Pr UK) Assoc Pubs Grp.

Solar Astronomy Handbook. Rainer Beck et al. LC 95-46338. 1995. write for info. (*0-943396-47-6*) Willmann-Bell.

Solar Astrophysics. Peter Foukal. LC 89-32525. 496p. 1990. text ed. 137.00 (*0-471-83935-3*) Wiley.

Solar Biology. Hiram E. Butler. 288p. 1996. pap. 25.00 (*0-89540-234-3*, SB-234, Sun Bks) Sun Pub.

Solar Biology: A Scientific Method of Delineating Character, Diagnosing Disease, Determining Mental, Physical & Business Qualifications & Conjugal Adaptability. Hiram E. Butler. 1991. lib. bdg. 250.00 (*0-8490-4256-9*) Gordon Pr.

Solar Building Architecture. Bruce Anderson. Ed. by Charles A. Bankston. (Solar Heat Technologies: Fundamentals & Applications Ser.). (Illus.). 340p. 1990. 52.50 (*0-262-01111-5*) MIT Pr.

***Solar Cells: An Introduction to Crystalline Photovoltaic Technology.** Jeffrey A. Mazer. LC 96-34491. 240p. (C). 1996. lib. bdg. 120.00 (*0-7923-9808-4*) Kluwer Ac.

Solar Cells: Their Optics & Metrology. M. M. Koltun. Ed. by N. S. Lidorenko. Tr. by S. Chomet from RUS. LC 88-4570. (Illus.). x, 336p. 1988. 65.00 (*0-89864-034-2*) Allerton Pr.

Solar Cells: Understanding & Using Photovoltaics. T. J. Byers. 256p. (Orig.). 1982. pap. 14.95 (*0-942412-04-4*) Micro Text Pubns.

Solar Cells & Optics for Photovoltaic Concentration. Antonio Luque. (Optics & Optoelectronics Ser.). (Illus.). 552p. 1989. 226.00 (*0-85274-106-5*) IOP Pub.

Solar Cells & Their Applications. Ed. by Larry D. Partain. LC 94-29987. 550p. 1995. text ed. 89.95 (*0-471-57420-1*) Wiley.

Solar Chromosphere & Corona: Quiet Sun. R. G. Athay. LC 75-33385. (Astrophysics & Space Science Library: No. 53). 540p. 1975. lib. bdg. 206.50 (*90-277-0244-6*) Kluwer Ac.

Solar Collector Manufacturing Activity. 1990. lib. bdg. 250.00 (*0-8490-4003-5*) Gordon Pr.

Solar Collector Manufacturing Activity. 1994. lib. bdg. 250.00 (*0-8490-8600-0*) Gordon Pr.

Solar Collector Manufacturing Activity. 1996. lib. bdg. 252.95 (*0-8490-6006-0*) Gordon Pr.

Solar Collector Manufacturing Activity (1992) (Illus.). 80p. (Orig.). (C). 1994. pap. text ed. 30.00 (*0-7881-0492-6*) DIANE Pub.

Solar Collector Manufacturing Activity (1993) (Illus.). 84p. (Orig.). (C). 1994. pap. text ed. 30.00 (*0-7881-1277-5*) DIANE Pub.

Solar Collectors: Test Methods & Design Guidelines. W. B. Gillett & J. E. Moon. 1985. lib. bdg. 122.00 (*90-277-2052-5*) Kluwer Ac.

Solar Collectors, Energy Storage & Materials. Francis De Winter. (Solar Heat Technologies: Fundamentals & Applications Ser.). (Illus.). 1104p. 1991. 90.00 (*0-262-04104-9*) MIT Pr.

Solar Collectors in Architecture: Integration of Photovoltaic & Thermal Collectors in New & Old Building Structures. Ed. by Wolfgang Palz et al. 320p. 1984. lib. bdg. 122.50 (*90-277-1784-2*) Kluwer Ac.

Solar Conscience/ Lunar Conscience: An Essay on the Psychological Foundations of Morality, Lawfulness, & the Sense of Justice. Murray Stein. LC 93-11414. 144p. (Orig.). 1993. pap. 19.95 (*0-933029-72-1*) Chiron Pubns.

Solar Control & Shading Devices. Aladar Olgyay. LC 57-5455. (Illus.). 208p. reprint ed. pap. 59.30 (*0-8357-3703-9*, 2036428) Bks Demand.

Solar Cookers in the Third World. K. Kuhnke. 220p. 1990. pap. 22.00 (*3-528-02056-3*) Informatica.

Solar Cookery Book see Cooking with the Sun: How to Make & Use Solar Cookers

Solar Cooking: A Primer - Cookbook. Harriet Kofalk. LC 95-1588. (Illus.). 96p. (Orig.). 1995. pap. 8.95 (*1-57067-007-2*) Book Pub Co.

Solar Cooking Naturally. 3rd ed. Virginia H. Gurley. (Illus.). 94p. (Orig.). 1995. pap. 12.00 (*0-9634694-0-1*) Sun Light Wks.

Solar Corona. A.H. Gabriel. (Advances in Space Research Ser.: No. 14/6). 218p. 1994. pap. 165.00 (*0-08-042478-3*, Pergamon Pr) Elsevier.

***Solar Corona.** Leon Golub & Jay M. Pasachoff. (Illus.). 400p. (C). 1997. text ed. 100.00 (*0-521-48082-5*) Cambridge U Pr.

***Solar Corona.** Leon Golub & Jay M. Pasachoff. (Illus.). 400p. (C). 1997. pap. text ed. 39.95 (*0-521-48535-5*) Cambridge U Pr.

S

An Asterisk (*) at the beginning of an entry indicates that the title is appearing in BIP for the first time.

Solar Corona & Solar Wind: Proceedings of Symposium 9 of the COSPAR Twenty-Eighth Plenary Meeting held in The Hague, The Netherlands, 25 June-6 July 1990. Boris V. Somov. (Advances in Space Research Ser.). (Illus.). 418p. 1991. pap. 147.00 (*0-08-041141-X*, Pergamon Pr) Elsevier.

Solar Crop Drying, 2 Vols. Mahendra S. Sodha et al. 1987. 165.00 (*0-317-60692-1*, CRC Reprint) Franklin.

Solar Crop Drying, 2 Vols., Set. Mahendra S. Sodha et al. 404p. 1987. 239.00 (*0-8493-6885-5*, SB129) CRC Pr.

Solar Crop Drying, 2 Vols., Vol. I. Mahendra S. Sodha et al. 208p. 1987. 91.00 (*0-8493-6883-9*, CRC Reprint) Franklin.

Solar Crop Drying, 2 Vols., Vol. II. Mahendra S. Sodha et al. 196p. 1987. Vol II 196 p. 105.00 (*0-8493-6884-7*, CRC Reprint) Franklin.

Solar Cycle. Ed. by K. Harvey. (ASP Conference Series Proceedings: Vol. 27). 562p. 1992. 28.00 (*0-937707-46-5*) Astron Soc Pacific.

Solar Design: Components, Systems, Economics. J. F. Kreider et al. 450p. 1988. 120.00 (*0-89116-406-5*) Hemisp Pub.

Solar Design & Energy in Building (C45) L. F. Jesch. 91p. (C). 1986. 105.00 (*0-685-30229-6*, Pub. by Interntl Solar Energy Soc UK) St Mut.

Solar Design & Energy in Buildings. L. F. Jesch. (C). 1986. 100.00 (*0-685-33088-5*, Pub. by Interntl Solar Energy Soc UK) St Mut.

Solar Designing: 1979. James Lambeth & John Delap. (Illus.). 1977. 22.95 (*0-9601678-1-1*); pap. 11.95 (*0-9601678-2-X*) Miami Dog Pr.

Solar Dish Systems. H. W. Braun. 1988. pap. 3.50 (*0-685-24746-5*) Research Analysts.

Solar Distillation. M. A. Malik. 1982. 22.00 (*0-08-028700-X*, Pergamon Pr) Elsevier.

Solar Distillation. M. A. Malik et al. 1982. 89.00 (*0-08-028679-8*, Pub. by Pergamon Repr UK) Franklin.

Solar Diversification: Proceedings of the International Solar Energy Society, American Section, Annual Meeting, Denver, 1978, 2 vols., Set. International Solar Energy Society, American Section Staff. Ed. by Karl W. Boer & Gregory E. Franta. 1978. pap. text ed. 115.00 (*0-89553-011-2*) Am Solar Energy.

Solar Drivers of Interplanetary & Terrestrial Disturbances. Ed. by K. S. Balasubramaniam et al. (ASP Conference Series Proceedings: Vol. 95). 628p. 1996. 44.00 (*1-886733-16-3*) Astron Soc Pacific.

Solar Education Home Plan Kits, Solar Related Companies & Information: A How to Find or Locate Reference Workbook. rev. ed. Center for Self-Sufficiency, Research Division Staff. 100p. 1993. ring bd. 26.95 (*0-910811-35-0*) Ctr Self Suff.

Solar Electric Book: How to Save Money Through Clean Solar Power - A Practical Guide. Gary Starr. LC 87-80925. (Illus.). 144p. 1987. 18.95 (*0-944891-08-X*); pap. 11.95 (*0-944891-09-8*) Solar Elec Pub.

Solar Electric House: Energy for the Environmentally-Responsive, Energy-Independent Home. 2nd rev. ed. Steven J. Strong & William G. Scheller. (Illus.). 288p. 1993. pap. 21.95 (*0-9637383-2-1*) Sustainability.

Solar Electric Independent Home Book. New England Solar Electric, Inc. Staff. (Illus.). 200p. (Orig.). 1994. pap. 16.95 (*1-879523-01-9*) Nw England Solar.

Solar Electricity. Ed. by Thomas Markvart. 228p. 1994. pap. text ed. 39.95 (*0-471-94161-1*) Wiley.

Solar Electricity: A Practical Guide to Small Photovoltaic Systems. Simon Roberts. 448p. 1991. boxed 35.00 (*0-13-826314-0*) P-H.

Solar Electricity: Its Current Role in Overseas Aid. Ed. by N. M. Pearsall. (C). 1987. 135.00 (*0-685-33091-5*, Pub. by Interntl Solar Energy Soc UK) St Mut.

Solar Electricity: Its Current Role in Overseas Aid (C48) N. M. Pearsall. (C). 1987. 100.00 (*0-685-30231-8*, Pub. by Interntl Solar Energy Soc UK) St Mut.

Solar Electricity for Development. E. B. McNeils & S. Saylgh. (C). 1989. 130.00 (*0-685-33096-6*, Pub. by Interntl Solar Energy Soc UK) St Mut.

Solar Energy. Bob Brooke. (Earth at Risk Ser.). (Illus.). (YA). (gr. 5 up). 1992. lib. bdg. 19.95 (*0-7910-1590-4*) Chelsea Hse.

Solar Energy. Graham Rickard. (Alternative Energy Ser.). (Illus.). 32p. (J). (gr. 4-6). 1991. lib. bdg. 18.60 (*0-8368-0709-X*) Gareth Stevens Inc.

Solar Energy. J. I. Wilson. (Wykeham Science Ser.: No. 56). 196p. 1979. pap. 18.00 (*0-85109-810-X*) Taylor & Francis.

Solar Energy. J. I. Wilson & H. G. Brown. LC 79-19525. (Wykeham Science Ser.: No. 56). 196p. (C). 1980. pap. 18.00 (*0-8448-1331-1*, Crane Russak) Taylor & Francis.

Solar Energy, Bk. 2. Ed. by Laurent Hodges. (Reprint Bks.). 144p. (Orig.). 1986. pap. text ed. 26.00 (*0-917853-16-4*, RB41) Am Assn Physics.

Solar Energy: A Resource Guide. 1991. lib. bdg. 250.00 (*0-8490-4807-9*) Gordon Pr.

Solar Energy: Chemical Conversion & Storage. Ed. by Richard R. Hautala et al. LC 79-87568. (Contemporary Issues in Science & Society Ser.). (Illus.). 419p. 1979. 79.50 (*0-89603-006-7*) Humana.

Solar Energy: Lessons from the Pacific Island Experience. Andres Liebenthal et al. LC 94-13345. (Technical Paper, Energy Ser.: No. 244). 72p. 1994. 7.95 (*0-8213-2802-6*, 12802) World Bank.

Solar Energy: Proceedings of the International Symposium on Solar Energy, Washington, D. C., 1976. International Symposium on Solar-Terrestial Physics Staff. Ed. by Joan B. Benkowitz. LC 76-9237. 370p. reprint ed. pap. 105.50 (*0-317-10962-6*, 2051566) Bks Demand.

Solar Energy: The Infinite Source. G. K. Ghosh. (C). 1991. text ed. 17.50 (*81-7024-420-X*, Pub. by Ashish II) S Asia.

Solar Energy & Building Design. L. F. Jesch. (C). 1985. 150.00 (*0-685-33083-4*, Pub. by Interntl Solar Energy Soc UK) St Mut.

Solar Energy & Building Design (C40) L. F. Jesch. 110p. (C). 1985. 100.00 (*0-685-30226-1*, Pub. by Interntl Solar Energy Soc UK) St Mut.

Solar Energy & Conservation: Technology, Commercialization, Utilization: Proceedings of the Symposium, Miami Beach, Florida, 1978. Solar Energy & Conservation Sympsium Staff. Ed. by T. Nejat Veziroglu. LC 79-19526. (Illus.). 2000p. 1980. 720.00 (*0-08-025551-5*, Pergamon Pr) Elsevier.

Solar Energy & Potentials for Minnesota. Spring Hill Center Staff. Ed. by Donna Hoel & John Ziegenhagen. 1978. pap. text ed. 2.50 (*0-932676-02-2*) Spring Hill.

Solar Energy & the Arab World. Ed. by H. Alawi et al. (Illus.). 502p. 1983. 30.00 (*0-08-030571-7*, Pergamon Pr) Elsevier.

Solar Energy Application in the Tropics. Bill B. Lim. 1982. lib. bdg. 146.00 (*90-277-1506-8*) Kluwer Ac.

Solar Energy Applications in the Design of Buildings. Ed. by Henry J. Cowan. (Illus.). x, 325p. 1980. 88.25 (*0-85334-883-9*, Pub. by Elsevier Applied Sci UK) Elsevier.

Solar Energy Applications to Buildings & Solar Radiation Data. Ed. by Theo C. Steemers. (C). 1987. lib. bdg. 110.00 (*90-277-2527-6*) Kluwer Ac.

Solar Energy Applications to Buildings & Solar Radiation Data. Ed. by Theo C. Steemers. (C). 1988. lib. bdg. 113.50 (*90-277-2715-5*) Kluwer Ac.

Solar Energy Applications to Dwellings. Ed. by Wolfgang Palz & Theo C. Steemers. 1982. lib. bdg. 88.00 (*90-277-1372-3*) Kluwer Ac.

Solar Energy Applications to Dwellings. Ed. by Theo C. Steemers & C. Den Ouden. 1983. lib. bdg. 198.00 (*90-277-1696-X*) Kluwer Ac.

Solar Energy Arab World: 1st Arab International Solar Energy Conference Kuwait 12/83. H. Alawi & A. Al-Jassar. LC 83-17410. 1983. reprint ed. 225.00 (*0-08-030570-9*, Pub. by Pergamon Repr UK) Franklin.

Solar Energy Calculations. Roderich W. Graeff. 280p. 1982. pap. text ed. 28.00 (*0-9604570-0-3*) Graeff.

Solar Energy Collection & Its Utilization for House Heating. Austin Whillier. Ed. by Stuart Bruchey. LC 78-22712. (Energy in the American Economy Ser.). (Illus.). 1979. lib. bdg. 18.95 (*0-405-12022-2*) Ayer.

Solar Energy Congress Nineteen Eighty-Three: International Solar Energy Society Congress, Proceedings, Perth, Australia, August 14-19, 1983, 4 Vols. Ed. by S. V. Szokolay. 3000p. 1984. 1,256.00 (*0-08-029947-4*, 15/5, 11/5, Pub. by Pergamon Repr UK) Franklin.

Solar Energy Conversion. Yu V. Pleskov. (Illus.). x, 163p. 1989. 174.95 (*0-387-51474-0*) Spr-Verlag.

Solar Energy Conversion: An Introductory Course. Solar Energy Conversion Course, 5th, University of Waterloo, Ontario, August 6-19, 1978. Ed. by A. E. Dixon & J. D. Leslie. LC 79-41159. (Illus.). 1979. 570.00 (*0-08-024744-X*, Pub. by Pergamon Repr UK) Franklin.

Solar Energy Conversion: The Solar Cell. 2nd ed. Richard C. Neville. LC 94-39734. 440p. 1995. 181.50 (*0-444-89818-2*) Elsevier.

Solar Energy Data. Ed. by Wolfgang Palz. 1983. lib. bdg. 123.50 (*90-277-1566-1*) Kluwer Ac.

Solar Energy for Developing Countries Power for Villages (C44) B. McNelis & J. Morton. 83p. (C). 1986. 95.00 (*0-685-30228-8*, Pub. by Interntl Solar Energy Soc UK) St Mut.

Solar Energy for Developing Countries...Power for the Villages. Ed. by B. McNelis & J. Morton. (C). 1986. 100.00 (*0-685-33087-7*, Pub. by Interntl Solar Energy Soc UK) St Mut.

Solar Energy for Development: Proceedings of the International Conference, Varese, Italy, March 26-29, 1979. Ed. by Commission of the European Communities, Directorate-General Telecommunications, Information Industries & Innovation Staff. 1979. pap. text ed. 73.00 (*90-247-2239-X*) Kluwer Ac.

Solar Energy Handbook. rev. ed. Ed. by Paul A. Fleck. (Illus.). 1976. 4.45 (*0-918826-01-2*) Time-Wise.

Solar Energy Handbook. 5th ed. Henry C. Landa. (Illus.). (C). 1977. pap. 12.00 (*0-931974-00-3*) FICOA.

Solar Energy Handbook, Special California Edition: How to Save Three Thousand Dollars on State Income Taxes with Solar Energy. Paul A. Fleck. (Illus.). 1977. 5.95 (*0-918826-03-9*) Time-Wise.

***Solar Energy Houses: Strategies, Technologies, Examples.** Ed. by Anne-Grete Hestnes et al. (Illus.). 320p. 1996. write for info. (*1-873936-69-9*, Pub. by J & J Sci Pubs UK) Bks Intl VA.

Solar Energy in Agriculture, Vol. 4. Ed. by B. F. Parker. (Energy in World Agriculture Ser.). 448p. 1991. 275.50 (*0-444-88622-2*) Elsevier.

Solar Energy in Agriculture: A European Perspective. J. Coombs. (C). 1983. 100.00 (*0-685-33079-6*, Pub. by Interntl Solar Energy Soc UK) St Mut.

Solar Energy in Agriculture: A European Perspective (C33) J. Coombs. 89p. (C). 1983. 125.00 (*0-685-30220-2*, Pub. by Interntl Solar Energy Soc UK) St Mut.

Solar Energy in Agriculture & Industry: Potential of Solar Heat in European Agriculture, an Assessment. Ed. by G. Schepens et al. 1986. lib. bdg. 112.00 (*90-277-2295-1*) Kluwer Ac.

Solar Energy in Architecture & Urban Planning. Ed. by Thomas Herzog. (Illus.). 200p. 1996. 65.00 (*3-7913-1652-4*, Pub. by Prestel GW) te Neues.

***Solar Energy in Architecture & Urban Planning: Proceedings of the Third European Conference on Architecture, Florence, Italy, May 1993.** Norman Foster & Hermann Scheer. 752p. 185.00 (*0-9521452-1-9*) Bks Intl VA.

***Solar Energy in Building Renovation, 4 bks.** Ed. by Chiel Boonstra. (Illus.). 1997. 25.00 (*1-873936-74-5*, Pub. by J & J Sci Pubs UK) Bks Intl VA.

Solar Energy Notebook. David A. Wilson & William H. Rankins. (Illus.). 56p. (Orig.). 1976. pap. 8.00 (*0-934852-15-4*) Lorien Hse.

Solar Energy Owner's Guide, No. 1. Ralph W. Ritchie. (Energy & Ecology "Do It" Bks.). (Illus.). 100p. (Orig.). 1981. pap. 6.00 (*0-939656-07-8*) Ritchie Unltd.

Solar Energy Phase Transfer Catalysis Transport Processes. W. D. Comper et al. (Advances in Polymer Science Ser.: Vol. 55). (Illus.). 170p. 1984. 74.00 (*0-387-12592-2*) Spr-Verlag.

Solar Energy Prospect in the Arab World: Proceedings of the 2nd Arab International Solar Energy Conference, Bahrain, 15-21 February, 1986. Ed. by H. Alawi & S. Ayyash. 1986. 208.00 (*0-08-032573-4*, Pub. by PPL UK) Franklin.

Solar Energy Research. Ed. by Farrington Daniels & John A. Duffie. LC 55-6325. 306p. reprint ed. pap. 87.30 (*0-317-10982-0*, 2002069) Bks Demand.

Solar Energy-Simplified. 3rd ed. Frank L. Bouquet. (Illus.). 125p. 1989. 49.00 (*0-937041-54-8*); text ed. 30.00 (*0-937041-55-6*) Systems Co.

Solar Energy Simplified. 4th ed. Frank L. Bouquet. (Illus.). 130p. 1991. text ed. 52.00 (*1-56216-053-2*); pap. text ed. 32.00 (*1-56216-054-0*) Systems Co.

Solar Energy Simplified. 5th ed. Frank L. Bouquet. (Illus.). 155p. 1994. 70.00 (*1-56216-122-9*); pap. 40.00 (*1-56216-123-7*) Systems Co.

Solar Energy Source Book. 2nd ed. Ed. by C. W. Martz. (Illus.). 1977. 30.00 (*0-686-23456-1*); pap. 15.00 (*0-686-23457-X*) United Tel.

Solar Energy Symposia: Bio-Chemistry, Physics, Wind, & "On the Rise", a Program on State & Local Government Initiatives. International Solar Energy Society, American Section Staff. Ed. by Karl W. Boer & Alec F. Jenkins. 1978. pap. text ed. 50.00 (*0-89553-014-7*) Am Solar Energy.

Solar Energy Technology. B. Norton. (Illus.). xvi, 279p. 1991. 130.00 (*0-387-19583-1*) Spr-Verlag.

Solar Energy Technology - 1992. Ed. by W. M. Worek & A. A. Pesaran. (SED Ser.: Vol. 13). 100p. 1992. 30.00 (*0-7918-1126-3*, G00770) ASME.

Solar Energy Technology Dissemination. Ed. by Werner Gocht et al. 439p. 1989. pap. 45.00 (*3-7890-1923-2*, Pub. by Nomos Verlags GW) Intl Bk Import.

Solar Energy Technology Handbook: Pt. B: Applications, System Designs & Economics. W. C. Dickinson. (Energy, Power & Environment Ser: Vol. 6). 848p. 1980. 275.00 (*0-8247-6927-9*) Dekker.

Solar Energy Technology 1991. Frank L. Bouquet. (Illus.). 125p. (Orig.). (C). 1991. text ed. 59.00 (*1-56216-023-0*); pap. text ed. 29.00 (*1-56216-024-9*) Systems Co.

Solar Energy Technology, 1992. 2nd ed. Frank L. Bouquet. (Illus.). 150p. 1992. pap. 32.00 (*1-56216-105-9*); text ed. 62.00 (*1-56216-104-0*) Systems Co.

Solar Energy Thermal Storage. H. P. Garg et al. 1985. lib. bdg. 216.50 (*90-277-1930-6*) Kluwer Ac.

Solar Energy Timetable. Denis Hayes. 1978. pap. write for info. (*0-916468-18-6*) Worldwatch Inst.

Solar Energy to Dwellings. Wolfgang Palz. 1982. lib. bdg. 146.00 (*90-277-1491-6*) Kluwer Ac.

Solar Energy-Utility Interface. Ed. by A. B. Cambel et al. 190p. 1982. pap. 26.00 (*0-08-028695-X*, Pergamon Pr) Elsevier.

Solar Energy Utilization: Fundamentals & Applications. Ed. by H. Yuncu & E. Paykoc. (C). 1987. lib. bdg. 323.50 (*90-247-3537-8*) Kluwer Ac.

Solar Engine & Its Influence of Terrestrial Atmosphere & Climate. Elizabeth Nesme-Ribes. LC 94-34430. 1994. 262.95 (*3-540-58417-X*) Spr-Verlag.

Solar Engineering: ASME - JSME - JSES International Solar Energy Conference, Maui, Hawaii, March 19-24, 1995, 2 vols., Set. W. B. Stine. 1995. 400.00 (*0-614-05627-6*, HX0932) ASME.

Solar Engineering Vol. 2: ASME - JSME - JSES International Solar Energy Conference, Maui, Hawaii, March 19-24, 1995. W. B. Stine. 584p. 1995. 400.00 (*0-614-05626-8*, H0932B) ASME.

Solar Engineering - 1994. 672p. 1994. 85.00 (*0-7918-1192-1*, G00837) ASME.

Solar Engineering for Domestic Buildings. William A. Himmelman. LC 80-18387. (Mechanical Engineering Ser.: No. 4). (Illus.). 454p. reprint ed. pap. 129.40 (*0-7837-0819-X*, 2041133) Bks Demand.

Solar Engineering of Thermal Processes. 2nd ed. John A. Duffie & William A. Beckman. LC 90-25202. 944p. 1991. text ed. 95.00 (*0-471-51056-4*) Wiley.

Solar Engineering Technology. Ted J. Jansen. (Illus.). 256p. (C). 1985. text ed. 48.00 (*0-13-822719-5*) P-H.

Solar Engineering, 1981: Proceedings of the ASME Solar Energy Division Third Annual Conference on Systems Simulation, Economic Analysis - Solar Heating & Cooling Operational Results, Reno, Nevada, April 27-May 1, 1981. Conference on Systems Simulation, Economic Analysis - Solar Heating & Cooling Operational Results Staff. Ed. by Robert L. Reid et al. LC 81-65532. (Illus.). 779p. reprint ed. pap. 180.00 (*0-8357-2890-0*, 2039126) Bks Demand.

Solar Engineering, 1983. Ed. by L. M. Murphy. 632p. 1983. pap. text ed. 25.00 (*0-317-02649-6*, H00253) ASME.

Solar Engineering, 1993. Ed. by A. Kirkpatrick & W. M. Worek. LC 81-65532. 540p. 1993. pap. 75.00 (*0-7918-0953-6*, H00785) ASME.

Solar Engineering, 1993: Presented at the ASME International Solar Energy Conference, Washington, D. C., April 4-9, 1993. American Society of Mechanical Engineers Staff. Ed. by Allan Kirkpatrick & William Worek. LC 93-155719. 548p. 1993. reprint ed. pap. 156.20 (*0-608-00283-6*, 2059311) Bks Demand.

Solar Engineering 1995; Proceedings Vol. 1: ASME-JSME-JSES International Solar Energy Conference (1995: Maui, Hawaii), 2 vols., Set. Ed. by William B. Stine et al. LC 81-65532. 1296p. 1995. pap. 400.00 (*0-7918-1300-2*, H0932A) ASME.

Solar Epoch - A New Astrological Thesis. A. Sepharial. 90p. 1991. pap. 11.00 (*0-89540-185-1*, SB-185, Sun Bks) Sun Pub.

***Solar Ethics.** Don Cupitt. 80p. (Orig.). 1995. pap. 17.00 (*0-334-02618-0*, SCM Pr) TPI PA.

Solar Failure. Kaiman Lee & Linda Donnelly. LC 80-130467. (Illus.). 1980. 30.00 (*0-915250-36-5*) Environ Design.

Solar Family. rev. ed. James P. Dilley. Ed. by Betty K. Craddock & Thomas E. Tigner. (Illus.). 471p. (C). 1996. pap. text ed. 30.00 (*0-9647223-3-X*) Ross Pub OH.

Solar Flames. Alan Goldberg. (Orig.). 1984. pap. 6.95 (*0-916939-01-4*) Red Leopard.

***Solar Flare.** Larry Burkett. Date not set. 18.99 (*0-8024-7917-0*) Moody.

***Solar Flare.** Larry Burkett. 350p. 1997. 18.99 (*1-881273-07-5*) Moody.

***Solar Flare, Coronal & Heliospheric Dynamics.** J. L. Culhane & E. Hiei. (Advances in Space Research (RJ) Ser.: Vol. 17). 392p. 1995. 194.50 (*0-08-042644-1*, Pergamon Pr) Elsevier.

Solar Flare Magnetohydrodynamics, Vol. 1. E. R. Priest. LC 80-67417. (Fluid Mechanics of Astrophysics & Geophysics Ser.). 564p. 1980. text ed. 413.00 (*0-677-05530-7*) Gordon & Breach.

Solar Flare Prediction. C. Sawyer et al. LC 85-73399. (Illus.). 191p. reprint ed. pap. 54.50 (*0-8357-5515-0*, 2035131) Bks Demand.

Solar Flares. Z. Svestka. LC 75-379339. (Geophysics & Astrophysics Monographs: No. 8). 1976. pap. text ed. 80.00 (*90-277-0663-8*) Kluwer Ac.

Solar Flares: A Monograph from Skylab Solar Workshop II. Skylab Solar Workshop Staff. Ed. by Peter W. Sturrock. LC 78-73437. (Illus.). 523p. reprint ed. pap. 149.10 (*0-8357-5516-9*, 2035132) Bks Demand.

***Solar Flares & Collisions Between Current-Carrying Loops: Types & Mechanisms of Solar Flares & Coronal Loop Heating.** Jun I. Sakai & C. D. Jager. LC 96-35780. 1996. lib. bdg. 110.00 (*0-7923-4218-6*) Kluwer Ac.

Solar Florida: A Sustainable Energy Future. John O. Blackburn. LC 93-71423. 237p. (Orig.). 1993. pap. 24.95 (*0-913207-07-1*) FL Conser Fnd.

Solar Four. Wright et al. 96p. 1981. pap. 14.95 (*0-9601678-7-0*) Miami Dog Pr.

Solar Fuel: How to Make Automotive Fuel Using Your Own Alcohol Solar Still. Dennis E. Smith. LC 80-80971. (Illus.). 96p. (Orig.). 1980. pap. 4.95 (*0-915216-53-1*) Marathon Intl Bk.

Solar Gamma-X & EUV Radiation: Proceedings of the Symposium, No. 68, Buenos Aires, Argentina, June 11-14, 1974. International Astronomical Union Staff. Ed. by S. R. Kane. LC 75-6545. (I.A.U. Symposia Ser.: No. 68). 439p. 1975. pap. text ed. 129.50 (*90-277-0577-1*); lib. bdg. 194.00 (*90-277-0576-3*) Kluwer Ac.

Solar Gardening: Growing Vegetables Year-Round the American-Intensive Way. Leandre Poisson & Gretchen V. Poisson. (Illus.). 288p. (Orig.). 1994. pap. 24.95 (*0-930031-69-5*) Chelsea Green Pub.

Solar Greenhouse Guide for the Pacific Northwest. 2nd ed. Tim Magee et al. Ed. by Annie Stewart & Richard Sassaman. (Illus.). 91p. 1979. pap. 6.00 (*0-934478-26-0*) Ecotope.

Solar Heat Storage--Latent Heat Materials: Vol. 1, Background & Scientific Principles. Ed. by George A. Lane. 288p. 1983. 143.00 (*0-8493-6585-6*, TJ810, CRC Reprint) Franklin.

Solar Heat Storage--Latent Heat Materials: Vol. 1, Background & Scientific Principles, II. Ed. by George A. Lane. 288p. 1986. 141.00 (*0-8493-6586-4*, TJ810, CRC Reprint) Franklin.

Solar Heating & Cooling of Buildings: Contains Sections 3 4.1 4.3. Karl W. Boer. (Sharing the Sun Solar Technology in the Seventies Ser.: Vol. 3). reprint ed. 187.00 (*0-08-021699-4*, Pub. by Pergamon Repr UK) Franklin.

Solar Heating & Cooling Systems: Design for Australian Conditions. E. Baker et al. (Illus.). 332p. 1984. pap. text ed. 46.00 (*0-08-029852-4*, Pergamon Pr) Elsevier.

Solar Heating in Cold Regions. Jean-Francois Rozis. 184p. (Orig.). 1996. pap. write for info. (*0-614-17100-8*, Pub. by Intermed Tech UK) Women Ink.

Solar Heating Using Rocks: A Solar Heating System for Homes Using Rock Storage. Hugh G. Stocker. (Illus.). 25p. (Orig.). 1993. 55.00 (*0-937041-84-X*) Systems Co.

Solar Heating Using Rocks: A Solar Heating System for Homes Using Rock Storage. Hugh G. Stocker. Ed. & Illus. by Frank L. Bouquet. 60p. (Orig.). 1993. pap. 26.00 (*0-937041-85-8*) Systems Co.

Solar Heating Using Rocks: A Solar Heating System for Homes Using Rock Storage. 2nd ed. Hugh G. Stocker. (Illus.). 28p. (Orig.). 1993. 60.00 (*1-56216-213-6*); pap. 30.00 (*1-56216-214-4*) Systems Co.

Solar Home: How to Design & Build a House You Heat with the Sun. Mark Freeman. (Illus.). 224p. 1994. pap. 14.95 (*0-8117-2446-8*) Stackpole.

Solar Hydrogen: Moving Beyond Fossil Fuels. Joan M. Ogden & Robert H. Williams. 100p. (Orig.). 1989. pap. 10.00 (*0-915825-38-4*) World Resources Inst.

An Asterisk (*) at the beginning of an entry indicates that the title is appearing in BIP for the first time.

Solar-Hydrogen Energy System. E. W. Justi. Tr. by W. Schuh & K. Claus from GER. LC 87-7009. (Illus.). 348p. 1987. 95.00 (*0-306-42150-X*, Plenum Pr) Plenum.

Solar-Hydrogen Energy System: An Authoritative Review of Water-Splitting Systems by Solar Beam & Solar Heat; Hydrogen Production, Storage & Utilization. Ed. by T. Ohta. LC 79-40694. (Illus.). 1979. 119.00 (*0-08-022713-9*, Pub. by Pergamon Repr UK) Franklin.

Solar Influences on Global Change. National Research Council, Board on Global Change Staff. 180p. (Orig.). (C). 1994. pap. text ed. 25.00 (*0-309-05148-7*) Natl Acad Pr.

Solar Insolator-Insulator TM. Richard L. Field. (Solar Energy Ser.: No. 580). (Illus.). (Orig.). 1978. pap. 3.95 (*0-931912-11-3*) Solpub.

Solar Interior & Atmosphere. Ed. by Arthur N. Cox et al. LC 91-34154. (Space Science Ser.). (Illus.). 1416p. 1992. 82.00 (*0-8165-1229-9*) U of Ariz Pr.

Solar Journal: Oecological Sections. Richard Grossinger. (Illus.). 130p. (Orig.). 1973. pap. 10.00 (*0-87685-011-5*) Black Sparrow.

Solar Kill. Charles Ingrid. (Sand Wars Ser.: Bk. 1). 304p. 1987. pap. 3.95 (*0-88677-391-1*) DAW Bks.

Solar Law. Sandy F. Kraemer. (Construction Law: Land Use-Environmental Publication). 364p. 1978. text ed. 95.00 (*0-07-035400-6*) Shepards.

Solar Livestock Housing Handbook. Midwest Plan Service Engineers Staff. LC 82-20889. (Illus.). 88p. (Orig.). 1983. pap. 7.00 (*0-89373-056-4*, MWPS-23) MidWest Plan Serv.

Solar Living: The Complete Guide to Renewable Energy Technologies & Sustainable Living. 8th ed. Real Goods Co. Staff & John Schaeffer. (Real Goods Independent Living Bks.). (Illus.). 672p. (Orig.). 1994. pap. 23.00 (*0-930031-68-7*) Real Goods Pub.

Solar Living Sourcebook: The Complete Guide to Renewable Energy Technologies & Sustainable Living. Douglas R. Pratt & John Schaeffer. (Illus.). 670p. (Orig.). 1996. pap. 30.00 (*0-930031-82-2*) Chelsea Green Pub.

Solar Logos. Coulson Turnbull. 66p. 4.95 (*0-86690-019-5*, T2438-034) Am Fed Astrologers.

Solar Logos or Studies in Arcane Mysticism. Coulson Turnbull. 157p. 1997. pap. 13.00 (*0-89540-241-6*, SB-241, Sun Bks) Sun Pub.

Solar Low Energy Houses of Task Thirteen. International Energy Agency Staff. (Illus.). 48p. (Orig.). (C). 1994. pap. 20.00 (*1-873936-37-0*, Pub. by J & J Sci Pubs UK) Bks Intl VA.

Solar Magnetic Fields. Ed. by Manfred Schussler & Wolfgang Schmidt. (Illus.). 432p. (C). 1994. text ed. 69.95 (*0-521-46119-7*) Cambridge U Pr.

Solar Magnetic Fields: Polarized Radiation Diagnostics. Jan O. Stenflo. LC 94-9736. (Astrophysics & Space Science Library: Vol. 189). 1994. lib. bdg. 134.00 (*0-7923-2793-4*) Kluwer Ac.

Solar Manifesto: The Need for a Total Solar Energy Supply...& How to Achieve It. Hermann Scheer. Tr. by Sara Hoffman & Peter Hoffman from GER. 240p. 1994. 35.00 (*1-873936-32-X*) Bks Intl VA.

Solar Maximum Analysis: Proceedings of Symposium 2 of the COSPAR 25th Plenary Meeting, Graz, Austria, 25 June-7 1984. Ed. by P. A. Simon. (Illus.). 412p. 1985. pap. 54.00 (*0-08-032735-4*, Pub. by PPL UK) Elsevier.

Solar Maximum Analysis: Proceedings of the SMA-SMY Workshop, Irkutsk, U. S. S. R., June, 1985. Ed. by V. E. Stepanov & V. N. Obdidko. 466p. 1986. lib. bdg. 172.00 (*90-6764-065-4*, Pub. by VSP NE) Coronet Bks.

***Solar Modeling.** 250p. 1995. 41.00 (*981-02-2489-3*) World Scientific Pub.

Solar Neutrinos: The First Thirty Years. John N. Bahcall. 464p. (C). 1995. 59.95 (*0-201-40791-4*) Addison-Wesley.

Solar Neutrinos & Neutrino Astronomy. Ed. by M. L. Cherry et al. LC 84-63143. (Conference Proceeding Ser.: No. 126). 320p. 1985. lib. bdg. 44.25 (*0-88318-325-0*) Am Inst Physics.

Solar Observations: Techniques & Interpretation. Ed. by F. Sanchez et al. (Illus.). 250p. (C). 1991. text ed. 80.00 (*0-521-40251-4*) Cambridge U Pr.

Solar Omens of Enuma Anu Enlil: Tablets 23 (24) - 29 (30) Wilfred H. Van Soldt. xii, 152p. 1995. pap. 40.75 (*90-6258-074-2*, Pub. by Netherlands Inst NE) Eisenbrauns.

Solar Optical Materials. M. G. Hutchins. (C). 1988. 100.00 (*0-685-33094-X*, Pub. by Interntl Solar Energy Soc UK) St Mut.

Solar Optical Materials (C51) M. G. Hutchins. 180p. (C). 1988. 100.00 (*0-685-30233-4*, Pub. by Interntl Solar Energy Soc UK) St Mut.

Solar Output & Climate During the Holocene. Ed. by Burkhard Frenzel et al. (Palaoklimaforschung/ Palaeoclimate Research & Man: Vol. 16). (Illus.). 200p. 1995. 50.00 (*3-437-30815-7*, Pub. by G Fischer Verlag GW) Lubrecht & Cramer.

Solar Output & Its Variation. Ed. by Oran R. White. LC 76-15773. (Illus.). 536p. reprint ed. pap. 152.80 (*0-8357-5518-5*, 2035134) Bks Demand.

Solar Phenomena in Stars & Stellar Systems. Ed. by Robert L. Bonnet & A. K. Dupree. 1981. lib. bdg. 158.50 (*90-277-1275-1*) Kluwer Ac.

Solar Photo Rates for Planetary Atmospheres & Atmospheric Pollutants. Ed. by W. F. Huebner et al. LC 92-30457. 292p. (C). 1992. lib. bdg. 149.00 (*0-7923-1999-0*) Kluwer Ac.

Solar Photoshere. Iaus & Jan O. Stenflo. 1989. pap. text ed. 88.00 (*0-7923-0530-2*) Kluwer Ac.

Solar Photosphere: Structure, Convection & Magnetic Fields: Proceedings of the 138th Symposium of the International Astronomical Union, Held in Kiev, U. S. S. R., May 15-20, 1989. Ed. by Jan O. Stenflo. (C). 1989. lib. bdg. 203.00 (*0-7923-0529-9*) Kluwer Ac.

Solar Photovoltaic Industry. 400p. 1995. 1,995.00 (*0-614-06123-7*, LE610) Lead Edge Reports.

Solar Physics: The Proceedings of NATO Advanced Study Institute on Solar Physics Held at Lagonissi, Athens, Greece, September 1965. fac. ed. NATO Advanced Study Institute on Solar Physics Staff. Ed. by John N. Xanthakis. LC 67-29173. (Illus.). 551p. pap. 157.10 (*0-7837-7365-X*, 2047174) Bks Demand.

Solar Physics in the 1990s. Ed. by D. F. Neidig & H. S. Hudson. (Advances in Space Research Ser.: Vol. 8). 286p. 1989. pap. 78.00 (*0-08-037371-2*, Pergamon Pr) Elsevier.

Solar Plexus. Theron Dumont. pap. 3.00 (*0-911662-40-5*) Yoga.

Solar Plexus: Abdominal Brain. Theron Q. Dumont. 64p. 1974. reprint ed. spiral bd. 5.00 (*0-7873-0302-X*) Hlth Research.

Solar Polarization: Proceedings of an International Workshop Held in St. Petersburg, Russia, 8-12 May, 1995. Ed. by Jan O. Stenflo & K. N. Nagendra. LC 96-7088. 448p. (C). 1996. lib. bdg. 245.00 (*0-7923-3985-1*) Kluwer Ac.

Solar Potpourri-All Our Shorter Works in One. Richard L. Field. (Solar Energy Ser.: No. 599). (Illus.). (Orig.). 1977. pap. 9.95 (*0-931912-03-2*) Solpub.

***Solar Power Satellites: A Space Energy System for Earth.** 2nd ed. Glaser, Peter E. Glaser et al. LC 96-28787. 1997. write for info. (*0-471-96817-X*) Wiley.

Solar Power Satellites: Proceedings of the International Symposium, Toulouse, France, June 1980. Ed. by J. W. Freeman. 200p. 1981. pap. 43.00 (*0-08-027592-3*, Pergamon Pr) Elsevier.

Solar Power Satellites: The Emerging Energy Option. Ed. by Peter E. Glaser et al. 300p. 1995. text ed. 98.00 (*0-471-95428-4*) Wiley.

Solar Products 'Eighty-Four Market Experience & Future Prospects for the UK Solarmarket (C36) UK-ISES Staff. 69p. (C). 1984. 100.00 (*0-685-30222-9*, Pub. by Interntl Solar Energy Soc UK) St Mut.

Solar Products 1984 Market Experience & Future Prospects for the U. K. Solar Market. U. K. ISES Staff. (C). 1984. 100.00 (*0-685-33081-8*, Pub. by Interntl Solar Energy Soc UK) St Mut.

Solar Prominences. Einar Tandberg-Hanssen. LC 73-88593. (Geophysics & Astrophysics Monographs: Vol. 12). 1974. lib. bdg. 80.00 (*90-277-0399-X*) Kluwer Ac.

Solar Pumping: An Introduction & Update on the Technology, Performance, Costs, & Economics. Roy Barlow et al. (Technical Paper Ser.: No. 168). 163p. 1993. 10.95 (*0-8213-2101-3*, 12101) World Bank.

Solar Radiation & Clouds. Ronald M. Welch et al. (Meteorological Monograph: Vol. 17, No. 39). (Illus.). 96p. 1980. 40.00 (*0-933876-49-1*) Am Meteorological.

***Solar Radiation & Daylight Models for Energy Efficient Design of Buildings.** T. Muneer & H. Kambezidis. LC 96-51639. 1997. write for info. (*0-7506-2495-7*) Buttrwrth-Heinemann.

Solar Radiation Atlas of Africa: Global & Diffuse Radiation Fluxes at Ground Level Derived from Imaging Data of the Geostationary Satellite METEOSAT 2. Ed. by Ehrhard Raschke et al. (Illus.). 172p. (C). 1991. text ed. 160.00 (*90-5410-109-1*, Pub. by A A Balkema NE) Ashgate Pub Co.

Solar Radiation Availability on Surfaces in the U. S. as Affected by Season, Orientation, Latitude, Altitude, & Cloudiness. Clarence F. Becker. Ed. by Stuart Bruchey. LC 78-22659. (Energy in the American Economy Ser.). (Illus.). 1979. lib. bdg. 17.95 (*0-405-11963-1*) Ayer.

Solar Radiation-Collection-Storage see Alternative Energy Sources V: Energy Research

Solar Radiation Data. Ed. by Wolfgang Palz. 1982. lib. bdg. 70.50 (*90-277-1387-1*) Kluwer Ac.

Solar Radiation Data from Satellite Images. Ed. by W. Gruter et al. 1986. lib. bdg. 69.00 (*90-277-2204-8*) Kluwer Ac.

Solar Radiation Measurements in Developing Countries. Ed. by B. B. Goldberg. 135p. 1983. pap. 25.00 (*0-08-030547-4*, Pergamon Pr) Elsevier.

Solar Radiophysics. N. R. Labrun. Ed. by Donald J. McLean. (Illus.). 550p. 1985. 95.00 (*0-521-25409-4*) Cambridge U Pr.

Solar Refrigeration & Space Conditioning. S. C. Kaushika. (C). 1989. text ed. 165.00 (*0-685-61672-X*, Pub. by Scientific Pubs II) St Mut.

Solar Resources. Ed. by Roland L. Hulstrum. (Solar Heat Technologies: Fundamentals & Applications Ser.: Vol. 2). 350p. 1989. 50.00 (*0-262-08184-9*) MIT Pr.

Solar Return Book of Prediction. Raymond A. Merriman. (Illus.). 132p. 1977. per. 5.95 (*0-930706-00-5*) Seek-It Pubns.

Solar Return Event Timing: Direction & Timing Methods. Martha Lang-Wescott. (Astrological Reference Text Ser.). 7.50 (*0-9619852-2-4*) Treehouse Mtn.

***Solar Returns in Your Face.** Marc Penfield. 1996. 18.95 (*0-86690-460-3*, P3618-014) Am Fed Astrologers.

***Solar Returns Through the Eyes of Horary.** Christina Wise. (Illus.). 126p. (Orig.). 1996. pap. 8.95 (*0-9651584-3-8*) Wise Astro.

Solar Revolution & the Prophet. Pierre Renard. (Testimonials Ser.). (Illus.). 193p. (Orig.). 1980. pap. 13.95 (*2-85566-135-8*, Pub. by Prosveta FR) Prosveta USA.

Solar Rising: Proceedings of the International Solar Energy Society, American Section, Annual Meeting, Philadelphia, 1981, 2 vols., Set. International Solar Energy Society, American Section Staff. Ed. by Barbara H. Glenn & Gregroy E. Franta. LC 77-79643. (Illus.). 1982. pap. text ed. 100.00 (*0-89553-030-9*) Am Solar Energy.

Solar Screen Window Films. Richard K. Miller & Marcia E. Rupnow. LC 90-83927. (Survey on Technology & Markets Ser.: No. 130). 50p. 1991. pap. text ed. 200.00 (*1-55865-153-5*) Future Tech Surveys.

Solar Selective Surfaces. O. P. Agnihotri & B. K. Gupta. LC 80-17392. 238p. (Orig.). 1981. 44.95 (*0-471-06035-6*, JW) Krieger.

Solar SNG: The Estimated Availability of Resources for Large-Scale Production of SNG by Anaerobic Digestion of Specially Grown Plant Material. REDEX Staff. 450p. 1979. pap. 15.00 (*0-318-12701-6*, M80779) Am Gas Assn.

Solar Space Heating for Free Heat see How to Find & Benefit from a "Passive Solor Collector" As a Space Heater

Solar-Space Observations & Stellar Prospects: Proceedings of the Topical Meeting of the COSPAR Interdisciplinary Scientific Commission E (Meetings E1, E2 & E6) of the COSPAR 25th Plenary Meeting, Graz, Austria, 25 June-7 July 1984. Ed. by J. W. Harvey et al. (Illus.). 184p. 1985. pap. 54.00 (*0-08-032743-5*, Pub. by PPL UK) Elsevier.

Solar Still. W. R. Breslin. 36p. 1979. 7.25 (*0-86619-030-9*) Vols Tech Asst.

Solar Storms. Linda Hogan. 1994. 21.00 (*0-689-12190-3*) S&S Trade.

Solar Storms. Linda Hogan. 1995. 22.00 (*0-684-81227-4*) S&S Trade.

***Solar Storms.** Linda Hogan. 1997. pap. 12.00 (*0-684-82539-2*) S&S Trade.

Solar Surface Magnetism: Proceedings of the NATO Advanced Research Workshop, Soesterberg, the Netherlands, November 1-5, 1993. Ed. by Robert J. Rutten. (NATO Advanced Science Institutes: C Mathematical & Physical Sciences Ser.). 552p. (C). 1994. lib. bdg. 271.00 (*0-7923-2845-0*) Kluwer Ac.

***Solar System.** (Doodle Art Travel Packs Ser.). (Illus.). 4p. (J). (gr. k up). 1996. boxed 8.00 (*0-8431-6555-3*, TP-9, Doodle Art) Price Stern Sloan.

***Solar System.** Brad Caudle & Melissa Caudle. (Illus.). 24p. (J). (gr. 2 up). 1997. pap. 9.95 incl. audio (*1-878489-60-7*, RL960) Rock n Learn.

Solar System. Colorprint Staff. 1989. pap. 4.95 (*0-8416-9572-5*) Am Map.

Solar System. T. Encrenaz et al. Ed. by Martin D. Harwit et al. (Astronomy & Astrophysics Library). (Illus.). 352p. 1991. 59.50 (*0-387-18910-6*) Spr-Verlag.

Solar System. Maura M. Gouck. LC 93-17027. (Vision Bks). 32p. (J). (gr. 2-6). 1993. lib. bdg. 22.79 (*1-56766-061-4*) Childs World.

Solar System. Robin Kerrod. LC 93-4339. (Let's Investigate Science Ser.). (Illus.). 64p. (YA). (gr. 5 up). 1993. lib. bdg. 17.95 (*1-85435-621-6*) Marshall Cavendish.

Solar System. A. E. Powell. 1991. lib. bdg. 250.00 (*0-87700-997-X*) Revisionist Pr.

***Solar System.** Paul B. Sipiera. LC 96-28556. (True Book Ser.). (J). 1997. 19.00 (*0-516-20339-8*) Childrens.

Solar System. Jane Walker. (Fascinating Facts Ser.). (Illus.). 32p. (J). (gr. 2-4). 1995. pap. 5.95 (*1-56294-899-7*) Millbrook Pr.

Solar System. Jane Walker. (Fascinating Facts Ser.). (Illus.). 32p. (J). (gr. 2-4). 1995. lib. bdg. 14.90 (*1-56294-609-9*) Millbrook Pr.

Solar System. Anne Welsbacher. (The Universe Ser.). (J). 1997. lib. bdg. 13.95 (*1-56239-717-6*) Abdo & Dghtrs.

Solar System. rev. ed. B. W. Jones & Milton Keynes. LC 83-2165. (Illus.). 400p. 1984. 158.00 (*0-08-026496-4*, Pub. by Pergamon Repr UK) Franklin.

Solar System. 2nd ed. Therese Encrenas. 1995. 59.95 (*3-540-58836-1*) Spr-Verlag.

Solar System. 2nd rev. ed. T. Encrenaz & J. P. Bibring. Tr. by S. Dunlop from FRE. LC 94-48499. (Astronomy & Astrophysics Library). (Illus.). 1995. write for info. (*0-387-58836-1*) Spr-Verlag.

Solar System. Powell. 371p. reprint ed. spiral bd. 34.50 (*0-7873-1153-7*) Hlth Research.

Solar System: A Practical Guide. Reidy & Wallace. pap. 19.95 (*0-04-442260-1*, Pub. by Allen Unwin AT) Paul & Co Pubs.

***Solar System: Chemistry as a Key to Its Origin.** 251p. 1989. text ed. 105.00 (*0-521-38006-5*) Cambridge U Pr.

Solar System: Earth As a Planet, Vol. 2. Gerard P. Kuiper. LC 54-7183. 769p. reprint ed. pap. 180.00 (*0-685-15752-0*, 2026779) Bks Demand.

Solar System: Facts & Exploration. Gregory L. Vogt. (Scientific American Sourcebooks Ser.). (Illus.). 96p. (J). (gr. 5-8). 1995. pap. 8.95 (*0-8050-3248-7*); lib. bdg. 18.98 (*0-8050-3249-5*) TFC Bks NY.

Solar System: Practical Guide. David Reidy & Ken Wallace. 1991. 29.95 (*0-04-442288-1*, Pub. by Allen Unwin AT) Paul & Co Pubs.

Solar System Pt. A: From the Renaissance to the Nineteenth Century. Ed. by Curtis Wilson. (General History of Astronomy Ser.: No. 2A). 300p. 1989. text ed. 64.95 (*0-521-24254-1*) Cambridge U Pr.

Solar System Astronomy in America: Communities, Patronage, & Interdisciplinary Science, 1920-1960. Ronald E. Doel. (Illus.). 320p. (C). 1996. text ed. 59.95 (*0-521-41573-X*) Cambridge U Pr.

Solar System Evolution: A New Perspective. Stuart R. Taylor. (Illus.). 325p. (C). 1992. text ed. 54.95 (*0-521-37212-7*) Cambridge U Pr.

Solar System Magnetic Fields. Ed. by E. R. Priest. 1985. lib. bdg. 109.50 (*90-277-2137-8*) Kluwer Ac.

Solar System Photometry Handbook. Ed. by Russell M. Genet. LC 83-21382. (Illus.). 224p. 1983. pap. text ed. 17.95 (*0-943396-03-4*) Willmann-Bell.

Solar System Plasma in Space & Time. Ed. by J. Burch & J. H. Waite, Jr. LC 94-25481. (Geophysical Monograph: Vol. 84). 295p. 1994. 57.00 (*0-87590-041-0*) Am Geophysical.

Solar System Plasma Physics. Ed. by J. H. Waite, Jr. et al. (Geophysical Monograph Ser.: Vol. 54). 465p. 1989. 58.00 (*0-87590-074-7*, GM0540747) Am Geophysical.

Solar-Terrestrial Energy Program: The Initial Results from STEP Facilities & Theory Campaigns. Ed. by D. N. Baker et al. LC 94-7968. (COSPAR Colloquia Ser.: Vol. 5). 844p. 1994. 272.25 (*0-08-042131-8*, Ed Skills Dallas) Elsevier.

Solar-Terrestrial Environment: An Introduction to Geospace-the Science of the Terrestrial Upper Atmosphere, Ionosphere, & Magnetosphere. J. K. Hargreaves. (Cambridge Atmospheric & Space Science Ser.: No. 5). (Illus.). 448p. (C). 1992. text ed. 85.00 (*0-521-32748-2*) Cambridge U Pr.

Solar-Terrestrial Physics: Proceedings of an International Symposium, Innsbruck, Austria, 1978. Ed. by Granville Beynon. (Illus.). 240p. 1979. pap. 52.00 (*0-08-025054-8*, Pergamon Pr) Elsevier.

Solar-Terrestrial Physics: Proceedings of the International Symposium, Leningrad, 1970, 4 vols. International Symposium on Solar-Terrestrial Physics Staff. Ed. by E. R. Dyer. LC 78-170337. (Astrophysics & Space Science Library). 914p. 1987. lib. bdg. 97.00 (*90-277-0209-8*) Kluwer Ac.

Solar Thermal & Photovoltaics, No. E-036R. Business Communications Co., Inc. Staff. 175p. 1996. 2,750.00 (*0-89336-806-7*, E-036N) BCC.

Solar Thermal Central Receiver Systems, Vol. 3: Performance Evaluation Standards for Solar Central Receivers. Ed. by M. Carasso & Martin Becker. 150p. 1991. 47.95 (*0-387-53270-6*) Spr-Verlag.

Solar Thermal Energy in Europe. D. Turrent & N. Baker. 1983. lib. bdg. 104.50 (*90-277-1592-0*) Kluwer Ac.

Solar Thermal Energy Utilization: German Studies on Technology & Applications, Vol. 6: Final Reports 1990. Ed. by Martin Becker et al. 350p. 1993. 89.95 (*0-387-54836-X*) Spr-Verlag.

Solar Thermal Energy Utilization German Studies on Technology & Applications, Vol. 7: Final Reports 1991. Martin Becker et al. 300p. 1993. 79.95 (*0-387-55666-4*) Spr-Verlag.

Solar Thermal Energy Utilization IV: Final Reports 1988. Ed. by Martin Becker & K. H. Funken. (German Studies on Technology & Applications). 460p. 1991. pap. 64.00 (*0-387-53268-4*) Spr-Verlag.

Solar Thermal Energy Utilization V: Final Reports 1989. Ed. by Martin Becker et al. (German Studies on Technology & Applications). 520p. 1991. pap. 77.00 (*0-387-53269-2*) Spr-Verlag.

Solar Thermal Power Plants: Achievements & Lessons Learned Exemplified by the SSPS Project in Almeria-Spain. F. G. Casal. (Illus.). 160p. 1987. 69.95 (*0-387-17458-3*) Spr-Verlag.

Solar Thermal Technology. Gupta. 1990. 132.00 (*1-56032-095-8*) Hemisp Pub.

Solar Transition Region. John T. Mariska. (Cambridge Astrophysics Ser.: No. 23). (Illus.). 275p. (C). 1993. text ed. 69.95 (*0-521-38261-0*) Cambridge U Pr.

***Solar Ultraviolet Radiation: Modelling, Measurements, & Effects.** C. S. Zerefos & Alkiviadis F. Bais. LC 97-7993. (NATO ASI Series). 1997. write for info. (*3-540-62711-1*) Spr-Verlag.

Solar Voltaic Cells. Wilbur D. Johnston. LC 80-14158. (Energy, Power, & Environment Ser.: No. 7). (Illus.). 223p. reprint ed. pap. 63.60 (*0-7837-0625-1*, 2040969) Bks Demand.

Solar Water Heater. 48p. 1988. 7.25 (*0-86619-025-2*) Vols Tech Asst.

Solar Water Heating Systems. H. P. Garg. 1985. lib. bdg. 178.50 (*90-277-2136-X*) Kluwer Ac.

Solar Wind: Magnetosphere Coupling ASSL. Ed. by Y. Kamide & J. A. Slavin. (ASSL Ser.: Vol. 126). 1986. lib. bdg. 358.00 (*90-277-2303-6*) Kluwer Ac.

Solar Wind & the Earth. Ed. by Syun-Ichi Akasofu & Y. Kamide. (C). 1987. lib. bdg. 204.50 (*90-277-2471-7*) Kluwer Ac.

***Solar Wind Eight: Proceedings of the Eighth International Solar Wind Conference Dana Point, California 1995.** Ed. by Daniel Winterhalter et al. (Conference Proceeding Ser.: Vol. 382). (Illus.). 700p. 1996. 185.00 (*1-56396-551-8*, AIP) Am Inst Physics.

Solar Wind Seven: Proceedings of the Third COSPAR Colloquium Held in Goslar, Germany, 16-20 September 1991. Ed. by E. Marsch & R. Schwenn. LC 92-20040. (COSPAR Colloquia Ser.: Vol. 3). 732p. 1992. 206.25 (*0-08-042049-4*, Pergamon Pr) Elsevier.

Solar Wind Sources of Magnetospheric Ultra-Low-Frequency Waves. Ed. by M. Engebretson et al. LC 94-2008. (Geophysical Monograph: Vol. 81). 424p. 1994. 80.00 (*0-87590-040-2*) Am Geophysical.

Solar World: Proceedings of the Annual Meeting of the International Solar Energy Society, 3 vols., Set. Ed. by Charles Beach & Edward Fordyce. 1977. pap. text ed. 115.00 (*0-89553-004-X*) Am Solar Energy.

Solar World Congress 1991: 1991 ISES Solar World Congress, 6 vols., Set. M. Arden & S. Burley. 1992. 1,586.00 (*0-08-041690-X*, Pub. by Pergamon Repr UK) Franklin.

Solar, 1987: Proceedings of the 1987 Annual Meeting, Portland Oregon, July 11-16, 1987. Ed. by John Hayes & Dennis A. Andrejko. (Illus.). 518p. 50.00 (*0-89553-160-7*) Am Solar Energy.

Solar, 1987: Twelfth National Passive Solar Conference Proceedings, July 11-16, 1987. 12th ed. Ed. by Dennis A. Andrejko & John Hayes. (Illus.). 574p. 50.00 (*0-89553-203-4*) Am Solar Energy.

Solar 90: Annual Conference Proceedings of the American Solar Energy Society. Ed. by M. A. Burley & M. J. Coleman. (Illus.). 515p. (Orig.). (C). 1990. per. 100.00 (*0-89553-163-1*) Am Solar Energy.

Solar 94: Annual Solar Energy Conference Proceedings. 497p. 1994. pap. 100.00 (*0-89553-166-6*) Am Solar Energy.

Solar 95: Minneapolis, MN. (Twentieth National Passive Solar Conference Proceedings Ser.: No. 20). 300p. 1995. 100.00 (*0-89553-167-4*) Am Solar Energy.

Solar 95: Minneapolis, MN 1995. (Annual Conference Proceedings Ser.). 400p. 1995. 100.00 (*0-89553-210-7*) Am Solar Energy.

Solaraust Microcomputer Solar Analysis Package. E. Baker. 1986. 41.50 (*0-08-029860-5*) Elsevier.

Solarex: Energy Sciences. 1991. 2.00 (*0-8306-5322-8*) McGraw-Hill Prof.

Solaria Binaria: Origins & History of the Solar System. Alfred De Grazia & Earl R. Milton. (Quantavolution Ser.). (Illus.). 292p. 1984. pap. 21.00 (*0-940268-04-3*) Metron Pubns.

Solarian Chronicles One. Michael Bell. 250p. 1993. pap. 8.95 (*0-912526-62-9*) Lib Res.

Solaris. Stanislaw Lem. 1987. pap. 9.00 (*0-15-683750-1*, Harvest Bks) HarBrace.

Solaris. Stanislaw Lem. 1993. reprint ed. lib. bdg. 18.95 (*0-89968-351-7*, Lghtyr Pr) Buccaneer Bks.

Solaris Advanced System Administrator's Guide. Janice Winsor. 512p. 1993. 29.95 (*1-56276-131-5*, Ziff-Davis Pr) Que.

Solaris Developer's Tool Kit. Kevin E. Leininger. LC 94-34427. (J. Ranade Workstation Ser.). 1995. pap. text ed. 49.95 (*0-07-911852-6*) McGraw.

Solaris Farm: A Story of the Twentieth Century. Milan C. Edson. LC 78-154440. (Utopian Literature Ser.). (Illus.). 1976. reprint ed. 34.95 (*0-405-03523-3*) Ayer.

Solaris for X86 Hardware Configuration Guide. Ron Ledesma. 352p. 1994. pap. text ed. 47.00 (*0-13-124678-X*) P-H.

Solaris Multithreaded Programming Guide. SunSoft Staff. (Illus.). 176p. (C). 1994. pap. text ed. 42.00 (*0-13-160896-7*) P-H.

Solaris Porting Guide. 2nd ed. Sunsoft. 1995. pap. text ed. 49.00 (*0-13-443672-5*) P-H.

Solaris Porting Guide for the Intel Processor. Anthony Brooks et al. pap. 40.00 (*0-13-030404-2*) P-H.

Solaris System Administrator's Guide. Janice Winsor. (Illus.). 320p. (Orig.). 1992. pap. 29.95 (*1-56276-080-7*, Ziff-Davis Pr) Que.

Solaris System Administrator's Implementation. SunSoft Inc. Staff et al. 300p. (C). 1995. pap. text ed. 42.00 (*0-13-353350-6*) P-H.

Solaris System Security. Casella & Sunsoft Books Staff. 1997. pap. text ed. 34.95 (*0-13-653650-6*) P-H.

Solaris 2 System Administrators Guide. Lee S. Henry. 1994. pap. text ed. 44.95 (*0-07-029368-6*) McGraw.

Solaris 2.x: Internals & Architecture. John R. Graham. LC 95-10087. 1995. pap. text ed. 44.00 (*0-07-911876-3*) McGraw.

***Solaris 2.X: Performance Management, Fine Tuning, & Capacity Planning.** H. Frank Cervone. (Illus.). 352p. 1997. pap. text ed. 45.00 (*0-07-011768-3*) McGraw.

***Solaris 2.X Managers & Administrators Guide.** 2nd ed. Kent Parkinson et al. 520p. 1997. pap. 39.95 (*1-56690-150-2*, OnWord Pr) High Mtn.

Solaris(TM) & Sparc(TM) Harvey M. Deitel. (Technical Perspective Ser.). (Illus.). 608p. (C). 1992. text ed. write for info. (*0-201-54310-9*) Addison-Wesley.

Solarize Your Hot Tub: Be Your Own Solar System & Plumbing Consultant. Sharon R. Hines. (Hot Tub & Spa Workbook Ser.: No. 4). (Illus.). 44p. (Orig.). 1982. pap. 7.50 (*0-941904-10-5*) Hot Water Pubs.

Solarize Your Spa: Be Your Own Solar System & Plumbing Consultant. Sharon R. Hines. (Hot Tub & Spa Workbook Ser.: No. 5). (Illus.). 44p. (Orig.). 1982. pap. 7.50 (*0-941904-11-3*) Hot Water Pubs.

SolarTrack. Karlyn Kamm & Gerald Chastain, Jr. (Solar Reading - Flight Two Ser.). (J). (gr. 5). 95.00 incl. disk (*0-912899-17-4*) Lrning Multi-Systs.

SolarWind: The Car That Runs on Free Energy You Can Build It. K. W. Krutz. (Illus.). 54p. (Orig.). 1986. pap. text ed. 10.00 (*0-9620932-0-3*) SolarWind.

Solas Amendments 1988-1989. International Maritime Organization Staff. 1989. text ed. 75.00 (*0-89771-856-9*, Pub. by Intl Maritime Org UK) St Mut.

Solas Amendments 1990-1991. International Maritime Organization Staff. 1990. text ed. 65.00 (*0-89771-860-7*, Pub. by Intl Maritime Org UK) St Mut.

Solas con Dios. 192p. (Orig.). (SPA.). 1990. pap. 4.95 (*0-88113-272-1*) Edit Betania.

Solcoderm. Ed. by M. Weiner & P. Hafner. (Journal: Dermatologica: Vol. 168, Suppl. 1). (Illus.). iv, 68p. 1984. pap. 25.75 (*3-8055-3890-1*) S Karger.

Sold. Henry Brown. 92p. (C). 1989. text ed. 32.00 (*0-902662-70-8*, Pub. by R K Pubns UK); pap. text ed. 21.00 (*0-902662-71-6*, Pub. by R K Pubns UK) St Mut.

Sold: A Biography by Legendary Auctioneer. Walter S. Britten & J. DeArman. (Illus.). 200p. 1988. 21.00 (*0-9619686-0-5*) Britten Trust.

Sold! The Origins of Money & Trade. Ed. by Lerner Geography Department Staff. LC 93-37782. (Buried Worlds Ser.). (Illus.). (YA). (gr. 6 up). 1994. lib. bdg. 22.95 (*0-8225-3206-9*, Runestone Pr) Lerner Group.

Sold! The Professional's Guide to Real Estate Auctions. Stephen Martin & Thomas Battles. 289p. 1991. pap. 32.95 (*0-7931-0211-1*, 1903-3101) Dearborn Finan.

Sold - the Inside Scoop on Selling a House. James C. Murray. 192p. 1996. pap. 14.95 (*0-9648287-0-7*) Pyramid Pr TN.

***Sold American: The Story of Alaska Natives & Their Land, 1867-1959 - The Army to Statehood.** Donald C. Mitchell. LC 96-41871. (Arctic Visions Ser.). (Illus.). 490p. 1997. 55.00 (*0-87451-800-8*); pap. 24.95 (*0-87451-748-6*) U Pr of New Eng.

Sold by Owner: A Professional Guide for Selling Your Home Successfully. 2nd ed. Alfred E. Wilson. (Illus.). 52p. (Orig.). 1969. pap. text ed. 3.00 (*0-685-24996-4*) Stoney Brook.

Sold for a Farthing. Clare Kipps. (Illus.). 1984. 15.00 (*0-8446-6161-9*) Peter Smith.

Sold in Dark Places. Kate Green. 320p. 1998. 20.00 (*0-06-017985-6*, HarpT) HarpC.

Sold Into Egypt: Joseph's Journey into Human Being. Madeleine L'Engle. LC 89-32030. (Wheaton Literary Ser.). 240p. 1989. 14.99 (*0-87788-766-7*) Shaw Pubs.

***Sold on Selling: Skills & Techniques.** Doug Malouf. LC 96-84567. (How-to Book Ser.). 86p. (Orig.). 1996. pap. 12.95 (*1-884926-54-1*, SOLDS) Amer Media.

***Sold Out.** Bill McCartney. 256p. 1997. 19.99 (*0-8499-1515-5*) Word Pub.

Sold Separately: Children & Parents in Consumer Culture. Ellen Seiter. 257p. 1995. pap. 15.95 (*0-8135-2198-X*) Rutgers U Pr.

Sold Separately: Parents & Children in Consumer Culture. Ellen Seiter. LC 92-44227. (Illus.). 280p. 1993. 35.00 (*0-8135-1988-8*) Rutgers U Pr.

Sold to Miss Seeton. Hamilton Crane. LC 95-6298. (Heron Carvic's Miss Seeton Ser.). 272p. 1995. 19.95 (*0-425-14936-6*, Prime Crime) Berkley Pub.

Sold to Miss Seeton. Hamilton Crane. 1996. mass mkt. 5.99 (*0-425-15462-9*) Berkley Pub.

Sold to the Highest Bidder. Norman E. Wymbs. 1991. 14.95 (*0-533-09335-X*) Vantage.

Sold to the Lady in the Green Hat. rev. ed. Emma Bailey. 228p. 1969. 8.95 (*0-914960-01-6*) Academy Bks.

Sold to the Surgeon. large type ed. Ann Jennings. (Linford Romance Library). 352p. 1996. pap. 15.99 (*0-7089-7843-6*, Linford) Ulverscroft.

Soldaderas in the Mexican Military: Myth & History. Elizabeth Salas. (Illus.). 201p. 1990. pap. 11.95 (*0-292-77638-1*); text ed. 25.00 (*0-292-77630-6*) U of Tex Pr.

Soldados: Chicanos in Viet Nam. Ed. by Charley Trujillo. 170p. (Orig.). (C). 1989. pap. 9.95 (*0-685-29369-6*) Chusma Hse.

Soldados: Chicanos in Viet Nam. Charley Trujillo. 1990. pap. 11.95 (*0-9624536-0-9*) Chusma Hse.

Soldat. Siegfried Knappe. 448p. 1993. mass mkt. 5.99 (*0-440-21526-9*, Dell Trade Pbks) Dell.

Soldat: Reflections of a German Soldier, 1936-1949. Siegfried Knappe & C. Brusaw. 1992. write for info. (*0-517-58895-1*) Random Hse Value.

Soldat: The World War II German Army Combat Uniform: Collections Handbook 1939-1942, Vol. 1. Cyrus A. Lee. LC 92-61981. (Illus.). 232p. (Orig.). 1992. pap. 12.95 (*0-929521-59-5*) Pictorial Hist.

Soldat: The WW II German Army Combat Uniform Collector's Handbook, Equipping the German Army Foot Soldier in Europe 1943, Vol. 2. Cyrus A. Lee. LC 88-90959. (Illus.). 88p. 1988. pap. 7.95 (*0-929521-01-3*) Pictorial Hist.

Soldat Vol. 3: Equipping the German Foot Soldier in Europe 1944-1945. Cyrus A. Lee. LC 90-64461. (Illus.). 196p. 1991. pap. 10.95 (*0-929521-46-3*) Pictorial Hist.

Soldat Vol. 5: The WW Two German Army Combat Uniform Collector's Handbook. Cyrus A. Lee. LC 88-90959. (Illus.). 218p. 1993. pap. 12.95 (*0-929521-76-5*) Pictorial Hist.

Solder Joint Reliability: Theory & Applications. Ed. by John H. Lau. LC 90-12968. (Illus.). 576p. 1991. text ed. 89.95 (*0-442-00260-2*) Van Nos Reinhold.

Solder Joint Reliability of BGA, CSP, & Flip Chip Assemblies. John H. Lau & Yi-Hsin Pao. LC 96-31361. (Illus.). 370p. 1996. text ed. 65.00 (*0-07-036648-9*) McGraw.

Solder Magic Book: Instructions & Patterns. Kay B. Weiner. (Illus.). 64p. (Orig.). (C). 1989. pap. text ed. 12.95 (*0-9625663-0-6*) Eastman Pub.

***Solder Mechanics: A State of the Art Assessment.** Ed. by D. R. Frear et al. LC 91-60213. (EMPMD Monograph Ser.: No. 1). (Illus.). 465p. pap. 132.60 (*0-608-04975-1*, 2065592) Bks Demand.

Solder Mechanics - A State of the Art Assessment. Ed. by D. R. Frear et al. (Illus.). 437p. 1991. 10.00 (*0-87339-166-7*, 1667) Minerals Metals.

Solder Paste Handbook. Colin C. Johnson & Joseph Kevra. (Illus.). 400p. 1989. 46.95 (*0-8306-3203-4*, TAB/TPR) TAB Bks.

Solder Paste Technology: Principles & Applications. Colin C. Johnson & Joseph Kevra. 1989. 46.95 (*0-07-156730-5*) McGraw.

Soldering & Brazing. Tubal Cain. (Workshop Practice Ser.: No. 9). (Illus.). 136p. (Orig.). 1985. pap. 18.50 (*0-85242-845-6*, Pub. by Nexus Special Interests UK) Trans-Atl Phila.

Soldering & Brazing. Jennifer Turpin. pap. 6.00 (*0-85344-098-0*) Apple Blossom.

***Soldering, Brazing & Welding: A Manual of Techniques.** Derek Pritchard. (Illus.). 160p. 1997. 35.00 (*1-85223-991-3*, Pub. by Crowood Pr UK) Trafalgar.

Soldering for Electronic Assemblies. Lambert. (Manufacturing Engineering & Materials Processing Ser.: Vol. 25). 368p. 1987. 130.00 (*0-8247-7681-X*) Dekker.

Soldering Handbook for Printed Circuits & Surface Mounting. Howard M. Manko. 1986. text ed. 74.95 (*0-442-26423-2*) Van Nos Reinhold.

Soldering Handbook for Printed Circuits & Surface Mounting. 2nd ed. Howard H. Manko. 1995. text ed. 74.95 (*0-442-01206-3*) Van Nos Reinhold.

Soldering in Electronics Assembly. Mike Judd & Keith Brindley. 286p. 1993. 94.95 (*0-7506-0589-8*) Buttrwrth-Heinemann.

Soldering Manual (SM) 2nd ed. 160p. 1978. 32.00 (*0-87171-151-6*) Am Welding.

Soldering Processes & Equipment. Michael G. Pecht. LC 92-3370. 312p. 1993. text ed. 79.95 (*0-471-59167-X*) Wiley.

Solders & Soldering: Materials, Design, Production, & Analysis for Reliable Bonding. 3rd ed. Howard M. Manko. 1992. text ed. 59.00 (*0-07-039970-0*) McGraw.

***Soldier.** Caroljean Ellis. (Tales of Little Angels: Bk. 2). (Illus.). 40p. (Orig.). (J). (gr. k-4). 1996. pap. 8.95 (*1-889383-01-5*) Angel Publns NJ.

Soldier: A Novel. R. C. Binstock. LC 95-26356. 288p. 1996. 24.00 (*1-56947-059-6*) Soho Press.

Soldier: Consolidated B-24 Liberator. Photos by Dan Patterson. (Living History Ser.: No. 2). (Illus.). 64p. 1993. pap. 15.95 (*0-943231-61-2*) Howell Pr VA.

Soldier, America & Me. Carol A. Osley. 1982. pap. 4.50 (*0-910119-00-7*) SOCO Pubns.

Soldier & Civilian in the Later Roman Empire. Ramsay MacMullen. LC 63-7591. (Historical Monographs: No. 52). (Illus.). 224p. 1963. 15.00 (*0-674-81690-0*) HUP.

Soldier & Peasant in Japan: The Origins of Conscription. E. Herbert Norman. LC 77-4281. (Illus.). 76p. 1977. text ed. 45.00 (*0-8371-9597-7*, NOSP, Greenwood Pr) Greenwood.

Soldier & Peasant in Japan: The Origins of Conscription. E. Herbert Norman. LC 75-33572. (Institute of Pacific Relations Ser.). reprint ed. 29.50 (*0-404-59549-9*) AMS Pr.

***Soldier & Scholar: Basil Lanneau Gildersleeve & the Civil War.** Basil L. Gildersleeve & Ward W. Briggs. LC 97-11292. (Publications of the Southern Texts Society). 1997. write for info. (*0-8139-1743-3*) U Pr of Va.

Soldier & Society in Roman Egypt: A Social History. Richard Alston. LC 95-13204. 280p. (C). (gr. 13). 1995. text ed. 62.95 (*0-415-12270-8*) Routledge.

Soldier & State in Africa: A Comparative Analysis of Military Intervention & Political Change. Ed. by Claude E. Welch. LC 74-98467. 330p. reprint ed. pap. 94.10 (*0-317-08199-3*, 2015312) Bks Demand.

***Soldier & State in Poland: Civil-Military Relations & Institutional Change after Communism.** Mark Kramer. 176p. 1997. 54.00 (*0-8476-8700-7*) Rowman.

***Soldier & State in Poland: Civil-Military Relations & Institutional Change after Communism.** Mark Kramer. 176p. 1997. pap. 21.95 (*0-8476-8701-5*) Rowman.

Soldier & the Baby. Anne Stuart. (American Romance Ser.). 1995. pap. 3.50 (*0-373-16573-0*, 1-16573-7) Harlequin Bks.

***Soldier & the Baby.** Anne Stuart. (Silhouette Ser.). 1997. 20.95 (*0-373-59769-X*, Pub. by Mills & Boon UK) Thorndike Pr.

***Soldier & the Citizen: The Role of the Military in Taiwan's Development.** Monte Bullard. LC 96-38663. (Taiwan in the Modern World Ser.). 250p. (C). (gr. 13). 1997. 62.95 (*1-56324-978-2*, East Gate Bk); pap. 24.95 (*1-56324-979-0*, East Gate Bk) M E Sharpe.

Soldier & the Lady. Barriss Mills. 1975. 16.00 (*0-685-56232-8*); pap. 8.00 (*0-685-56233-6*) Elizabeth Pr.

Soldier & the State: The Theory & Politics of Civil-Military Relations. Samuel P. Huntington. 550p. 1981. pap. 17.95 (*0-674-81736-2*) Belknap Pr.

Soldier & Tsar in the Forest: A Russian Tale. Uri Shulevitz. Tr. by Richard Lourie from RUS. LC 72-188254. (Illus.). 32p. (J). (ps-3). 1972. 16.00 (*0-374-37126-1*) FS&G.

Soldier, Ask Not. Gordon R. Dickson. 320p. 1993. mass mkt. 4.99 (*0-8125-0400-3*) Tor Bks.

***Soldier Bear.** large type ed. Geoffrey Morgan. (Magna Large Print Ser.). (Illus.). 200p. 1996. 25.99 (*0-7505-0961-9*) Ulverscroft.

Soldier Boy. Burks. LC 96-30289. (J). 1997. 12.00 (*0-15-201218-4*) HarBrace.

Soldier Boy. Burks. LC 96-30289. (J). 1997. pap. 5.00 (*0-15-201219-2*) HarBrace.

Soldier Boy. Frank A. Ucman. LC 94-45310. (Illus.). 240p. (Orig.). 1995. pap. 11.95 (*0-9633083-3-5*) Quixote Pubns.

Soldier Boy: The Civil War Letters of Charles O. Musser, 29th Iowa. Ed. by Barry Popchock. LC 95-17660. (Illus.). 272p. 1995. 24.95 (*0-87745-523-6*) U of Iowa Pr.

Soldier Boy: The Letters & Memoirs of Gunner W. J. Duffell 1915-1918. Ed. by Gilbert Mant. 192p. 1993. 24.95 (*0-86417-429-2*, Pub. by Kangaroo Pr AT); pap. 14.95 (*0-86417-418-7*, Pub. by Kangaroo Pr AT) Seven Hills Bk.

Soldier Boy Elvis. deluxe limited ed. Ira Jones & Bill E. Burk. LC 92-64067. (Illus.). 256p. 1992. 24.95 (*1-879207-23-0*) Propwash Pub.

Soldier Boys. Daniel Panger. LC 87-62533. 240p. (Orig.). (C). 1988. pap. 16.95 (*0-89390-102-4*) Resource Pubns.

Soldier Boy's Discovery. Gilbert Morris. (Bonnets & Bugles Ser.: No. 4). (J). (gr. 5-9). 1996. pap. 5.99 (*0-8024-0914-8*) Moody.

Soldier for Hire, No. 1: Zulu Blood. Robert Skimin. 1981. mass mkt. 2.50 (*0-89083-777-5*, Zebra Kensgtn) Kensgtn Pub Corp.

Soldier from the Wars Returning. Charles Carrington. (Modern Revivals in Military History Ser.). 287p. 1992. 54.95 (*0-7512-0031-X*, Pub. by Gregg Revivals UK) Ashgate Pub Co.

Soldier Heros: British Adventure, Empire, & the Imagining of Masculinity. Graham Dawson. LC 94-1523. 360p. (C). 1994. pap. 19.95 (*0-415-08882-8*, B2265) Routledge.

Soldier Heros: British Adventure, Empire, & the Imagining of Masculinity. Graham Dawson. LC 94-1523. 256p. (C). (gr. 13). 1994. text ed. 69.95 (*0-415-08881-X*, B2261) Routledge.

Soldier in Buckskin. Ray Hogan. (Five-Star Western Ser.). 296p. 1996. 16.95 (*0-7862-0619-5*) Thorndike Pr.

Soldier in Buckskin. large type ed. Ray Hogan. LC 95-47969. (Western Ser.). 435p. 1997. 19.95 (*0-7862-0620-9*) Thorndike Pr.

Soldier in the Rain. William Goldman. 1976. 22.95 (*0-8488-0506-2*) Amereon Ltd.

***Soldier King, Perseus.** (J). (ps-3). Date not set. 4.99 (*0-614-19190-4*) Scholastic Inc.

Soldier Life. Time-Life Books Editors. LC 96-2415. (Voices of the Civil War Ser.). 168p. 1996. 24.95 (*0-7835-4703-X*) Time-Life.

Soldier of Arete. Gene Wolfe. 1990. mass mkt. 4.95 (*0-8125-1155-7*) Tor Bks.

Soldier of Fortune. Ernest K. Gann. 1976. 21.95 (*0-8488-0496-1*) Amereon Ltd.

Soldier of Fortune. Diana Palmer. 1994. mass mkt. 4.50 (*0-373-48292-2*, 5-48292-2) Silhouette.

Soldier of France: Sebastien Le Prestre de Vauban, 1633-1707. John Hebbert & George A. Rothrock. LC 89-12331. (American University Studies: History: Ser. IX, Vol. 51). 274p. 1990. text ed. 59.95 (*0-8204-0890-5*) P Lang Pubng.

Soldier of God. Patricia Treece. 32p. (J). (gr. 1-8). 1982. pap. 1.00 (*0-913382-22-1*, 111-1) Marytown Pr.

***Soldier of Jerusalem.** Uzi Narkiss. LC 97-21946. 1997. write for info. (*0-7146-4800-0*, Pub. by F Cass Pubs UK); pap. write for info. (*0-7146-4372-6*, Pub. by F Cass Pubs UK) Intl Spec Bk.

Soldier of Lyons: A Tale of the Tuileries. Catherine G. Gore. LC 71-162906. (Bentley's Standard Novels Ser.: No. 82). reprint ed. 18.50 (*0-404-54482-7*) AMS Pr.

***Soldier of Manhattan.** Joseph A. Altsheler. Date not set. lib. bdg. 39.95 (*0-8488-1863-6*, 207) Amereon Ltd.

Soldier of the Cross: The Civil War Diary & Correspondence of Rev. Andrew Jackson Hartsock. Ed. by James Durham & Eleanor Durham. (Illus.). 275p. (Orig.). 1979. pap. 41.95 (*0-89126-076-5*) MA-AH Pub.

Soldier of the Great War. Mark Helprin. 752p. 1992. mass mkt. 7.50 (*0-380-71589-9*) Avon.

Soldier of the Great War. Mark Helprin. 1991. 24.95 (*0-15-183600-0*) HarBrace.

Soldier of the Great War. Mark Helprin. 800p. 1996. reprint ed. pap. 15.00 (*0-380-72736-6*) Avon.

Soldier of the Mist. Gene Wolfe. 352p. (Orig.). 1987. pap. 3.95 (*0-8125-5815-4*) Tor Bks.

Soldier of the Sixth. Jim Pickering. 200p. (C). 1989. text ed. 60.00 (*1-85821-010-0*, Pub. by Pentland Pr UK) St Mut.

Soldier of the South: General Pickett's War Letters to His Wife. George E. Pickett. Ed. by Arthur C. Inman. LC 78-160986. (Select Bibliographies Reprint Ser.). 1977. reprint ed. 25.95 (*0-8369-5854-3*) Ayer.

Soldier of the South: General Pickett's War Letters to His Wife. George E. Pickett. (American Biography Ser.). 157p. 1991. reprint ed. lib. bdg. 59.00 (*0-7812-8313-2*) Rprt Serv.

***Soldier of the Year.** John Underwood. 308p. (Orig.). 1997. mass mkt. 4.99 (*1-55197-796-6*, Pub. by Comnwlth Pub CN) Partners Pubs Grp.

Soldier of the Year. Jose Zuniga. Ed. by Tom Miller. 336p. 1995. pap. 12.00 (*0-671-88815-3*) PB.

Soldier of the Year: The Story of a Gay American Patriot. Jose Zuniga. Ed. by Tom Miller. 1994. 22.00 (*0-671-88814-5*) PB.

Soldier of Virginia. Burton E. Stevenson. 1993. reprint ed. lib. bdg. 89.00 (*0-7812-5837-5*) Rprt Serv.

Soldier Performance in Continuous Operations. 1995. lib. bdg. 250.95 (*0-8490-6558-5*) Gordon Pr.

Soldier Poetry of the Second World War. Ed. by Jane Morgan & Walter Morgan. 19.95 (*0-88962-473-9*); pap. 14.95 (*0-88962-470-4*) Mosaic.

Soldier Priest. John J. Morrett. Ed. by M. L. Jones. LC 92-83986. 304p. (Orig.). 1992. pap. 12.95 (*1-882270-01-0*) Old Rugged Cross.

Soldier Reports. William C. Westmoreland. (Quality Paperbacks Ser.). (Illus.). 488p. 1989. pap. 14.95 (*0-306-80376-3*) Da Capo.

Soldier Returns: A Long Tan Veteran Discovers the Other Side of Vietnam. Terry Burstall. 1990. pap. 16.95 (*0-7022-2252-6*, Pub. by Univ Queensland Pr AT) Intl Spec Bk.

Soldier, Sage, Saint. Robert C. Neville. LC 77-75798. 141p. 1989. reprint ed. pap. 15.00 (*0-8232-1036-7*) Fordham.

***Soldier, Sail North.** large type ed. James A. Pattinson. (Large Print Ser.). 448p. 1996. 25.99 (*0-7089-3577-X*) Ulverscroft.

Soldier-Scholars Vol. 121: Higher Education in the American Expeditionary Forces, 1917-1919. Alfred E. Cornebise. (Memoirs of the American Philosophical Society Ser.). (Illus.). 246p. 1997. 25.00 (*0-87169-121-3*) Am Philos.

***Soldier-Scholars Vol. 221: Higher Education in the American Expeditionary Forces, 1917-1919.** Alfred E. Cornebise. LC 96-84045. (Memoirs Ser.). (Illus.). 246p. 1977. 25.00 (*0-87169-221-X*, M221-coa) Am Philos.

Soldier Skills Manual. Alan E. Gonzalez. Ed. by Shannon Gonzalez. (R.A.I.D. Roleplaying Game System Ser.). (Illus.). 88p. 1992. 14.95 (*1-880798-01-8*) Centurion Pub & Mgt.

Soldier Spies. Baldwin. (Men at War Ser.: No. 3). 1989. mass mkt. 4.50 (*0-671-68444-2*) PB.

Soldier Statesman: Of the Age of Enlightenment: International Commission of Military History, No. 7. Ed. by Abigail T. Siddall. 535p. (Orig.). 1984. pap. 23.00 (*0-89745-073-6*) MA-AH Pub.

Soldier Stories. Rudyard Kipling. LC 70-110205. (Short Story Index Reprint Ser.). 1980. 18.95 (*0-8369-3356-7*) Ayer.

Soldier-Surgeon: The Crimean War Letters of Dr. Douglas A. Reid, 1855-1856. Ed. by Joseph O. Baylen & Alan Conway. LC 67-21109. (Illus.). 168p. reprint ed. 47.90 (*0-8357-9765-1*, 2016171) Bks Demand.

An Asterisk (*) at the beginning of an entry indicates that the title is appearing in BIP for the first time.

***Soldier Talk.** Simon Cullen. 1997. pap. text ed. 11.95 (*0-85052-459-8*, Pub. by L Cooper Bks UK) Trans-Atl Phila.

Soldier, the Athlete, the Farmer. Paul Chase. Ed. by Andrell Stevens. 1992. write for info. (*0-9628168-1-7*) Keys Freedom.

Soldier Who Walked Away: Autobiography of Andrew Pearson, a Peninsular War Veteran. Intro. & Notes by Arthur H. Haley. 1990. 59.00 (*0-9511427-1-2*, Pub. by Bullfinch Pubns UK) St Mut.

Soldier Who Wasn't. Charles J. Keating. LC 95-60333. (Illus.). 123p. 1995. 30.00 (*0-9635924-2-4*) Union Square.

Soldiering in Dakota: Among the Indians in 1863-5. Frank Myers. LC 77-160983. (Select Bibliographies Reprint Ser.). 1977. reprint ed. 15.95 (*0-8369-5851-9*) Ayer.

Soldiering in the Army of Tennessee: A Portrait of Life in a Confederate Army. Larry J. Daniel. LC 91-50250. (Illus.). xviii, 231p. (C). 1991. 24.95 (*0-8078-2004-0*) U of NC Pr.

Soldiering On. Hubert Gough. 9.95 (*0-8315-0010-7*) Speller.

Soldiers. Charles L. Convis. (True Tales of the Old West Ser.: Vol. 2). (Illus.). ii, 62p. (Orig.). 1996. pap. 7.95 (*0-9651954-2-2*) Athena Inst.

Soldiers. L. Matthews. (Wild West in American History Ser.). (Illus.). 32p. (J). (gr. 3-8). 1989. 13.50 (*0-685-67678-1*); lib. bdg. 18.00 (*0-86625-365-3*) Rourke Corp.

Soldiers: A Portrait of the United States Army. Kathleen D. Valenzi. LC 89-80795. (Illus.). 208p. 1991. 45.00 (*0-943231-22-1*) Howell Pr VA.

***Soldier's Aim.** Sigmund Brouwer. (Cyberquest Ser.: Vol. 5). 64p. (Orig.). (J). (gr. 5-8). 1998. mass mkt. 3.50 (*0-8499-4038-9*) Tommy Nelson.

Soldiers & Civilians: The Martial Spirit in America, 1775-1865. Marcus Cunliffe. (Modern Revivals in Military History Ser.). 512p. 1993. 84.95 (*0-7512-0126-X*, Pub. by Gregg Revivals UK) Ashgate Pub Co.

Soldiers & Civilians: The U. S. Army & the American People. Ed. by Garry D. Ryan & Timothy K. Nenninger. LC 86-21664. (Illus.). 210p. 1987. text ed. 25.00 (*0-911333-52-5*, 100011) National Archives & Recs.

Soldiers & Governments: Nine Studies in Civil-Military Relations. Michael E. Howard. LC 78-1468. 192p. 1978. reprint ed. text ed. 35.00 (*0-313-20303-2*, HOSG, Greenwood Pr) Greenwood.

Soldiers & Oil: The Transformation of Nigeria. Ed. by Keith Panter-Brick. (Studies in Commonwealth Politics & History: No. 5). 375p. 1978. 47.50 (*0-7146-3098-5*, Pub. by F Cass Pubs UK) Intl Spec Bk.

Soldiers & Politics in Eastern Europe, 1945-1990: The Case of Hungary. Zoltan D. Barany. LC 93-16624. 240p. 1993. text ed. 65.00 (*0-312-09722-0*) St Martin.

Soldiers & Politics in Southeast Asia: Cases & Comparisons in Civil Military Relations. Joseph J. Hoadley. 310p. 1975. 44.95 (*0-87073-306-0*) Transaction Pubs.

***Soldiers & Politics in Southeast Asia: Civil-Military Relations in Comparative Perspective.** J. Stephen Hoadley. LC 73-84739. 319p. reprint ed. pap. 91.00 (*0-608-05336-8*, 2065041) Bks Demand.

Soldiers & Scholars: The U. S. Army & the Uses of Military History, 1865-1920. Carol Reardon. LC 90-50111. (Modern War Studies). viii, 272p. 1990. 35.00 (*0-7006-0466-9*) U Pr of KS.

Soldiers & Society: The Effects of Military Service & War on American Life. Peter Karsten. LC 77-87973. (Grass Roots Perspectives on American History Ser.: No. 1). (Illus.). 339p. 1978. text ed. 45.00 (*0-313-20056-4*, KAM/, Greenwood Pr) Greenwood.

Soldiers & Statesmen, 2 vols., Set. William Robertson. (Modern Revivals in Military History Ser.). 685p. 1992. 87.50 (*0-7512-0035-2*, Pub. by Gregg Revivals UK) Ashgate Pub Co.

Soldiers & Statesmen: The General Council of the Army & Its Debates 1647-48. Austin Woolrych. 368p. 1987. 80.00 (*0-19-822752-3*) OUP.

Soldiers & the Soviet State: Civil-Military Relations from Brezhnev to Gorbachev. Ed. by Timothy J. Colton & Thane Gustafson. (Illus.). 377p. (C). 1990. pap. text ed. 17.95 (*0-691-02328-X*) Princeton U Pr.

Soldiers Are Coming. Fred H. Werner. (Western Americana Ser.). 1982. pap. 7.95 (*0-933147-05-8*) Werner Pubn.

Soldier's Art see Dance to the Music of Time: Third Movement

Soldiers Blue & Gray. James I. Robertson, Jr. Ed. by Thomas L. Connelly. (American Military History Ser.). 288p. 1988. 24.95 (*0-87249-572-8*) U of SC Pr.

***Soldier's Book.** Joanna Higgins. LC 97-4370. 1998. write for info. (*1-57962-009-4*) Permanent Pr.

Soldier's Bride & Other Tales. James A. Hall. (Notable American Authors Ser.). 1992. reprint ed. lib. bdg. 75.00 (*0-7812-2985-5*) Rprt Serv.

Soldier's Chronology. James W. Atkinson. LC 92-16454. 624p. 1993. text ed. 99.00 (*0-8153-0813-2*, H1577) Garland.

***Soldiers, Citizens & the Symbols of War: From Classical Greece to Republican Rome, 500-167 B. C.** Antonio Santosuosso. LC 97-7294. (History & Warfare Ser.). (C). 1997. text ed. 65.00 (*0-8133-3276-1*); pap. text ed. 21.00 (*0-8133-3277-X*) Westview.

Soldiers, Civilians, & Democracy: Post-Franco Spain in Comparative Perspective. Felipe Aguero. LC 95-3399. 336p. 1995. text ed. 48.50 (*0-8018-5085-1*) Johns Hopkins.

Soldiers Cry by Night. Ana M. Matute. Ed. by Yvette E. Miller. Tr. by Robert Nugent & Maria De la Camara from SPA. LC 94-25087. (Discoveries Ser.). 160p. 1995. pap. 16.95 (*0-935480-67-6*) Lat Am Lit Rev Pr.

Soldier's Delight Journal: Exploring a Globally Rare Ecosystem. Jack Wennerstrom. (Pitt Series in Nature & Natural History). 264p. (C). 1994. 34.95 (*0-8229-3870-7*) U of Pittsburgh Pr.

Soldier's Delight Journal: Exploring a Globally Rare Ecosystem. Jack Wennerstrom. (Pitt Series in Nature & Natural History). 264p. (C). 1994. pap. 16.95 (*0-8229-5550-4*) U of Pittsburgh Pr.

***Soldiers Do Reason Why...** Christopher C. Bell, Jr. 40p. 1996. pap. 7.00 (*0-8059-3867-2*) Dorrance.

***Soldier's Dream of Home: The Civil War Letters of John C. Hughes to His Wife, Harriet.** unabridged ed. Ed. by Grata J. Clark & Jeffrey S. Clark. (Illus.). 110p. 1996. 19.95 (*0-9619337-2-0*) Arcadia Clark Inc.

Soldiers Falling into Camp: The Battles at the Rosebud & the Little Big Horn. Robert Kammer et al. 240p. 1992. 19.95 (*1-879915-04-9*) Affil Writers America.

Soldiers for Peace. Ed. by Barbara Benton. (Illus.). 256p. 1996. 29.95 (*0-8160-3509-1*) Facts on File.

Soldiers for Peace. Ed. by Barbara Benton. (Illus.). 259p. 1996. pap. 14.95 (*0-8160-3510-5*) Facts on File.

Soldiers for Peace: An Operational Typology. Bruce R. Pirnie et al. LC 96-2897. (Illus.). 114p. 1996. pap. 15.00 (*0-8330-2396-9*, MR-582-OSD) Rand Corp.

Soldiers for Peace: Critical Operational Issues. Bruce R. Pirnie et al. LC 96-22855. (Illus.). 167p. 1996. pap. 15.00 (*0-8330-2412-4*, MR-583-OSD) Rand Corp.

Soldier's Guidebook. Raymond K. Bluhm & James B. Motley. (Association of the U. S. Army Book Ser.). (Illus.). 424p. 1995. 24.95 (*0-02-881035-X*) Brasseys Inc.

Soldier's Guidebook. 2nd rev. ed. Raymond K. Bluhm, Jr. & James B. Motley. (Illus.). 424p. 1998. 24.95 (*1-57488-070-5*) Brasseys Inc.

Soldier's Handbook for Defense Against Chemical & Biological Operations & Nuclear Warfare. 1986. lib. bdg. 79.95 (*0-8490-3525-2*) Gordon Pr.

Soldier's Heart. John E. Ames. 416p. 1996. mass mkt. 5.50 (*0-553-57378-0*) Bantam.

Soldier's Heart: Rita Winner. Kathleen Korbel. 1994. mass mkt. 3.50 (*0-373-07602-9*, 1-07602-5) Harlequin Bks.

Soldier's Heart: Survivors' Views of Combat Trauma. Ed. by Sarah Hansel et al. LC 94-69895. (Illus.). xii, 241p. (Orig.). 1995. pap. 19.95 (*0-9629164-6-3*) Sidran Pr.

Soldier's Hero: General Sir Archibald Hunter. Duncan H. Doolittle. (Illus.). 1991. text ed. write for info. (*0-9630635-0-2*) Anawan Pub.

Soldiers in a Narrow Land: The Pinochet Regime in Chile. Mary H. Spooner. LC 93-9910. 1994. 30.00 (*0-520-08083-1*) U CA Pr.

***Soldiers in King Philip's War.** George M. Bodge. (New World Ser.: Vol. 1). (Illus.). 496p. 1997. 34.95 (*1-58057-050-X*, SKPW001B) Digital Antiq.

Soldiers in King Philip's War, Containing Lists of the Soldiers of Massachusetts Colony Who Served in the Indian War of 1675-1677. George M. Bodge. 369p. 1992. reprint ed. lib. bdg. 39.00 (*0-8328-2369-4*) Higginson Bk Co.

***Soldiers in Politics: The Impact of the Military on Australian Political Life & Institutions.** Chris Coulthard-Clark. (Illus.). 256p. 1997. pap. 29.95 (*1-86448-185-4*, Pub. by Allen Unwin AT) Paul & Co Pubs.

Soldiers in the Proletarian Dictatorship: The Red Army & the Soviet Socialist State, 1917-1930. Mark Von Hagen. LC 89-36148. (Cornell Studies in Soviet History & Scoiety - Studies of the Harriman Institute). (Illus.). 408p. 1990. 42.50 (*0-8014-2420-8*) Cornell U Pr.

Soldiers in the Proletarian Dictatorship: The Red Army & the Soviet Socialist State, 1917-1930. Mark Von Hagen. LC 89-36148. (Cornell Studies in Soviet History & Society - Studies of the Harriman Institute). (Illus.). 408p. 1993. pap. 17.95 (*0-8014-8127-9*) Cornell U Pr.

Soldiers in the Son: An Adventure in Imperialism. William T. Sexton. LC 70-146872. (Select Bibliographies Reprint Ser.). 1977. reprint ed. 23.95 (*0-8369-5638-9*) Ayer.

Soldiers in Zimbabwe's Liberation War. Ed. by Terence O. Ranger & Ngwabi Bhebe. LC 95-4003. (Social History of Africa Ser.). 211p. 1995. 60.00 (*0-435-08974-9*, 08974); pap. 24.95 (*0-435-08972-2*) Heinemann.

Soldier's India. large type ed. Clifford Keates. (Illus.). 272p. 1988. 25.99 (*0-7089-1745-3*) Ulverscroft.

Soldier's Joy. Madison Smartt Bell. 480p. 1990. pap. 11.95 (*0-14-013359-3*, Penguin Bks) Viking Penguin.

Soldier's Legacy. Heinrich Boll. Tr. by Leila Vennewitz from GER. (European Classics Ser.). 131p. 1994. reprint ed. 35.00 (*0-8101-1198-5*); reprint ed. pap. 10.95 (*0-8101-1202-7*) Northwestern U Pr.

Soldier's Letters to Charming Nellie. J. B. Pollery. 21.95 (*0-8488-1128-3*) Amereon Ltd.

Soldier's Letters to Charming Nellie. J. B. Polley. 350p. 1984. reprint ed. 32.50 (*0-942211-91-X*) Olde Soldier Bks.

***Soldier's Life.** Andrew Robertshaw. LC 96-44309. (C). 1997. pap. 16.99 (*0-525-67550-7*) NAL-Dutton.

Soldier's Load. S. L. Marshall. 120p. reprint ed. 2.00 (*0-686-31001-2*) Marine Corps.

Soldiers' National Cemetery - Gettysburg: Revised Report of the Select Committee Relative to the Soldiers' National Cemetery. Edward G. Lee & W. M. Nelson. Ed. by Alfred Slack. (Illus.). 212p. (C). 1988. reprint ed. pap. 11.95 (*0-939631-08-3*) Thomas Publications.

Soldier's Note-Book, 1914-1918. Aleksiei A. Brusilov. LC 75-84265. 340p. 1971. reprint ed. text ed. 45.00 (*0-8371-5003-5*, BRSN, Greenwood Pr) Greenwood.

Soldiers of Christ: Preaching in Late Medieval & Reformation France. Larissa J. Taylor. 384p. 1992. 59.00 (*0-19-506993-5*) OUP.

Soldiers of Christ: Saints & Saint's Lives from Late Antiquity & the Early Middle Ages. Ed. by Thomas F. Moble & Thomas Head. LC 94-6757. 416p. 1995. 50.00 (*0-271-01344-3*); pap. 18.95 (*0-271-01345-1*) Pa St U Pr.

Soldiers of Colonial America. Ed. by Alan Quincannon. (Learning & Coloring Bks.). (Illus.). 24p. (Orig.). (J). (gr. k-6). 1992. pap. 3.95 (*1-878452-11-8*, Lrning & Coloring Bks) Tory Corner Editions.

Soldiers of Destruction: The SS Death's Head Division, 1933-1945. Charles W. Syndor, Jr. 400p. (Orig.). 1990. pap. text ed. 16.95 (*0-691-00853-1*) Princeton U Pr.

Soldiers of Fortune. Richard H. Davis. 1976. 19.95 (*0-8488-0258-6*) Amereon Ltd.

Soldiers of Fortune. Snyder Kirtland. (Illus.). 44p. 1993. pap. 25.00 (*0-911623-12-4*) I Klang.

Soldiers of Fortune. Richard H. Davis. LC 74-96880. (Illus.). 348p. reprint ed. lib. bdg. 15.00 (*0-8398-0356-7*) Irvington.

Soldiers of Fortune. Richard H. Davis. (Illus.). 348p. (C). 1986. reprint ed. pap. text ed. 7.95 (*0-8290-2027-6*) Irvington.

Soldiers of Fortune. Richard H. Davis. (BCL1-PS American Literature Ser.). 347p. 1992. reprint ed. lib. bdg. 89.00 (*0-7812-6702-1*) Rprt Serv.

***Soldiers of God.** Bushart et al. 320p. 1997. 22.95 (*1-57566-206-X*, Knsington) Kensgtn Pub Corp.

***Soldiers of Light.** 48p. 1988. 8.99 (*0-8341-9554-2*) Lillenas.

Soldiers of Light & Love: Northern Teachers & Georgia Blacks, 1865-1873. Jacqueline Jones. LC 79-27129. (Fred W. Morrison Series in Southern Studies). 287p. reprint ed. pap. 81.80 (*0-7837-0303-1*, 2040625) Bks Demand.

Soldiers of Light & Love: Northern Teachers & Georgia Blacks, 1865-1873. Jacqueline Jones. LC 91-41388. 288p. 1992. reprint ed. pap. 18.95 (*0-8203-1442-0*) U of Ga Pr.

Soldiers of Light & Other Sketches. Hicks & Cohagan. 1988. 8.99 (*0-685-68709-0*, MP-647) Lillenas.

Soldiers of Misfortune. James D. Sanders et al. 328p. 1994. mass mkt. 5.50 (*0-380-72144-9*) Avon.

Soldiers of Misfortune: Invoirien Tirailleurs of World War II. Nancy E. Lawler. LC 91-24369. (Illus.). 273p. (C). 1992. text ed. 35.00 (*0-8214-1012-1*) Ohio U Pr.

Soldiers of Misfortune: The Somervell & Mier Expeditions. Sam W. Haynes. LC 90-33976. (Illus.). 287p. 1990. 24.95 (*0-292-75118-4*) U of Tex Pr.

***Soldiers of Misfortune: The Somervell & Mier Expeditions.** Sam W. Haynes. (Illus.). 287p. 1997. pap. 15.95 (*0-292-73115-9*) U of Tex Pr.

Soldiers of Misfortune: Washington's Secret Betrayal of America's POWs in the Soviet Union. James D. Sanders et al. LC 92-23155. 1992. 23.95 (*0-915765-83-7*) Natl Pr Bks.

Soldiers of Oakham, in the Revolutionary War, the War of 1812, & the Civil War. Henry P. Wright. (Illus.). 325p. 1995. reprint ed. lib. bdg. 37.50 (*0-8328-4494-2*) Higginson Bk Co.

Soldiers of Paradise. Paul Park. 288p. 1990. pap. 3.95 (*0-380-70581-8*) Avon.

***Soldiers of the American Revolution of Lebanon.** George W. Chamberlain. (Illus.). 48p. 1997. reprint ed. pap. 10.00 (*0-8328-5866-8*) Higginson Bk Co.

Soldiers of the Cross: Flexible Voicings for Men's Choir or Ensemble. Des. by Joseph Linn. 1994. suppl. ed. 7.00 (*0-614-01737-8*, L-9170C) Lillenas.

Soldiers of the English Civil War: Cavalry. John Tincey. (Elite Ser.: No. 27). (Illus.). 64p. 1990. pap. 12.95 (*0-85045-940-0*, 9427) Stackpole.

Soldiers of the English Civil War, Vol. 1: Infantry. Keith Roberts. (Elite Ser.: No. 25). (Illus.). 64p. pap. 12.95 (*0-85045-903-6*, 9425, Pub. by Osprey UK) Stackpole.

Soldiers of the French Revolution. Alan Forrest. Ed. by Keith M. Baker & Steven L. Kaplan. LC 89-35875. (Bicentennial Reflections on the French Revolution Ser.). 207p. (C). 1989. text ed. 40.95 (*0-8223-0909-2*); pap. text ed. 12.95 (*0-8223-0935-1*) Duke.

Soldiers of the Mists: Minutemen of the Alaska Frontier. C. A. Salisbury. LC 92-80007. (Illus.). 128p. (Orig.). 1992. pap. 12.95 (*0-929521-38-2*) Pictorial Hist.

Soldiers of the Old Army. Victor Vogel. LC 89-20314. (Military History Ser.: No. 15). (Illus.). 136p. 1990. 23.95 (*0-89096-420-3*) Tex A&M Univ Pr.

Soldiers of the Queen: The History of the Queen's Regiment 1966-1992. J. P. Riley. 816p. 1990. 165.00 (*0-948251-65-4*, Pub. by Picton UK) St Mut.

Soldiers of the Revolutionary War Buried in Vermont: And Anecdotes & Incidents Relating to Some of Them. Walter H. Crockett. 77p. 1991. reprint ed. pap. 9.00 (*0-685-60362-8*, 1220) Clearfield Co.

Soldiers of the Sea. Robert D. Heinl, Jr. LC 90-49078. (Great War Stories Ser.). (Illus.). 768p. 1991. reprint ed. 32.95 (*1-877853-01-1*) Nautical & Aviation.

Soldiers of the Soil. Fay C. Johnson. 1995. pap. 8.95 (*0-533-11328-8*) Vantage.

Soldiers of the States. William H. Riker. Ed. by Richard H. Kohn. LC 78-22394. (American Military Experience Ser.). 1980. reprint ed. lib. bdg. 15.95 (*0-405-11870-8*) Ayer.

Soldiers of the Sun: The Rise & Fall of the Imperial Japanese Army. Meirion Harries & Susie Harries. 1992. 30.00 (*0-394-56935-0*) Random.

Soldiers of the Sun: The Rise & Fall of the Imperial Japanese Army. Meirion Harries & Susie Harries. 1994. pap. 17.00 (*0-679-75303-6*) Random.

Soldiers of the Virgin: The Moral Economy of a Colonial Maya Rebellion. Kevin Gosner. LC 91-42775. (Illus.). 228p. 1992. 33.50 (*0-8165-1293-0*) U of Ariz Pr.

Soldiers of 1814: American Enlisted Men's Memoirs of the Niagara Campaign. Ed. & Pref. by Donald E. Graves. (Illus.). 80p. (Orig.). 1995. pap. 6.50 (*0-941967-16-6*) Old Fort Niagara Assn.

Soldiers on Skis: A Pictorial Memoir of the 10th Mtn. Division. Flint Whitlock & Bob Bishop. (Illus.). 244p. 1992. text ed. 50.00 (*0-87364-676-2*) Paladin Pr.

Soldiers on the Steppe: Army Reform & Social Change in Early Modern Russia. Carol B. Stevens. LC 94-20855. (Illus.). 250p. 1995. lib. bdg. 35.00 (*0-87580-198-6*) N Ill U Pr.

Soldier's Pay: A Novel. William Faulkner. 320p. 1996. pap. 13.00 (*0-87140-166-5*) Liveright.

Soldier's Pay: Carbon Typescript. William Faulkner. Ed. by Blotner. (William Faulkner Manuscripts). 488p. 1987. text ed. 60.00 (*0-8240-6803-3*) Garland.

Soldiers, Peacekeepers & Disasters. Ed. by Leon Gordenker & Thomas G. Weiss. LC 91-3278. 105p. 1992. text ed. 65.00 (*0-312-06578-7*) St Martin.

Soldier's Recollections: Leaves from the Diary of a Confederate. Randolph McKim. 1983. reprint ed. 26.95 (*0-89201-104-1*) Zenger Pub.

Soldiers, Sailors, & Patriots of the Revolutionary War - Maine. Carleton E. Fisher & Sue G. Fisher. LC 82-73096. 933p. 1982. 45.00 (*0-9607188-3-4*, 1324) Picton Pr.

Soldiers, Scholars, Etc. Wright. 313p. 1992. 11.00 (*0-911541-19-5*) Gregory Pub.

***Soldiers Serving the Nation: The U. S. Army Art Collection.** Ed. by Gordon R. Sullivan & Marylou G. Jernes. (Illus.). 193p. (C). 1996. 60.00 (*0-7881-2705-5*) DIANE Pub.

Soldiers, Society, & National Security. Sam C. Sarkesian et al. 216p. 1994. lib. bdg. 45.00 (*1-55587-273-5*) Lynne Rienner.

Soldiers, Spies & the Rat Line: America's Undeclared War Against the Soviets. Patrick Brogan & James V. Milano. 264p. 1996. 23.95 (*1-57488-050-0*) Brasseys Inc.

Soldiers, Statesman & Heroes: America's Founding Presidents. Jay A. Parry. LC 88-21146. (Illus.). 250p. 1990. 15.95 (*0-88080-027-5*) Natl Ctr Constitutional.

Soldiers, Statesmen & Cold War Crises. Richard K. Betts. 330p. 1991. text ed. 52.50 (*0-231-07468-9*); pap. text ed. 18.00 (*0-231-07469-7*) Col U Pr.

Soldiers' Story. Anna Heinamaa et al. LC 94-20029. (Research Ser.: No. 90). 1994. pap. text ed. 12.50 (*0-87725-190-8*) U of Cal IAS.

Soldiers' Story: The Battle at Xa Long Tan Vietnam, August 18, 1966. Terry Burstall. (Illus.). 188p. (Orig.). 1987. pap. 16.95 (*0-7022-2047-7*, Pub. by Univ Queensland Pr AT) Intl Spec Bk.

***Soldier's Story: The Double Life of a Confederate Spy.** David Phillips. LC 97-12842. (Civil War Chronicles Ser.). 1997. 15.98 (*1-56799-425-3*, MetroBooks) M Friedman Pub Grp Inc.

Soldier's Story: The Life & Times of an Israeli War Hero. Raful Eitan. 320p. 1990. 17.95 (*1-56171-016-4*) Sure Seller.

Soldier's Story: The Life & Times of an Israeli War Hero. Raful Eitan. 1992. pap. 5.95 (*1-56171-094-6*) Sure Seller.

Soldier's Study Guide: How to Prepare for Promotion Boards & Advancement. 2nd ed. Walter J. Jackson. LC 92-27212. 128p. (Orig.). 1993. pap. 12.95 (*0-8117-3022-0*) Stackpole.

Soldiers Study Guide: How to Prepare for Promotion Boards & Advancement. 3rd ed. Walter J. Jackson. 128p. 1996. pap. 12.95 (*0-8117-3091-3*) Stackpole.

***Soldiers Such As We.** Frank E. Owens. 201p. (Orig.). 1997. mass mkt. 4.99 (*1-55237-198-0*, Pub. by Comnwlth Pub CN) Partners Pubs Grp.

Soldiers, Sutlers, & Settlers: Garrison Life on the Texas Frontier. Robert Wooster. LC 87-1948. (Clayton Wheat Williams Texas Life Ser.: No. 2). (Illus.). 250p. 1987. 29.50 (*0-89096-356-8*) Tex A&M Univ Pr.

Soldiers Tale: Bearing Witness to Modern War. Samuel Hynes. LC 96-25842. 1997. pap. 22.95 (*0-670-86585-0*) Viking Penguin.

Soldiers' Tale: Bearing Witness to Modern War. Samuel Hynes. 1997. pap. 24.95 (*0-7139-9190-9*) Viking Penguin.

Soldiers Three & In Black & White. Rudyard Kipling. (Illus.). 240p. 1993. pap. 9.95 (*0-14-018289-6*, Penguin Classics) Viking Penguin.

***Soldiers to the Rescue: Humanitarian Lessons from Rwanda.** Larry Minear & Philippe Guillot. 204p. (Orig.). 1996. pap. 30.00 (*92-64-14917-1*, 41-96-08-1) OECD.

Soldiers, Traders, & Slaves: State Formation & Economic Transformation in the Greater Nile Valley, 1700-1885. Janet J. Ewald. LC 90-50084. 288p. (Orig.). (C). 1990. text ed. 45.00 (*0-299-12600-5*); pap. text ed. 19.95 (*0-299-12604-8*) U of Wis Pr.

Soldiers' Voice: The Story of Ernie Pyle. Barbara O'Connor. LC 94-44283. (J). 1995. write for info. (*0-87614-942-5*, Carolrhoda) Lerner Group.

Soldiers West: Biographies from the Military Frontier. Paul A. Hutton. LC 86-19283. (Illus.). xiv, 276p. 1987. pap. 14.95 (*0-8032-7225-1*, Bison Books) U of Nebr Pr.

Soldiers with Little Feet. Dian Layton. 182p. (Orig.). 1992. pap. 7.99 (*0-914903-86-1*) Destiny Image.

Soldiers with Railways. A. A. Mains. 200p. 1990. pap. 51.00 (*0-948251-70-0*, Pub. by Picton UK) St Mut.

Soldiers/Viet-Nam. L. T. Wolf. LC 96-90327. 88p. (Orig.). 1996. pap. 8.95 (*0-9651683-0-1*) L T Wolf.

***Soldiery of West Virginia: In the French & Indian War; Lord Dunmore's War; the Revolution; the Later Indian Wars; the Whiskey Insurrection; the Second War with England; the War with Mexico.** Virgil A. Lewis. 227p. 1996. reprint ed. pap. 25.00 (*0-614-23590-1*, 3375) Clearfield Co.

Sole Proprietorship Merchandising Business Practice Set: Schier Furniture Company. 2nd ed. Horace R. Brock & Charles E. Palmer. (College Accounting Instructional System Ser.). (Illus.). 120p. (C). 1981. pap. text ed. 16.50 (*0-07-008106-9*) McGraw.

S

An Asterisk (*) at the beginning of an entry indicates that the title is appearing in BIP for the first time.

Sole Proprietorship Service Business Practice Set: Garden Real Estate. Horace R. Brock & Charles E. Palmer. (College Accounting Instructional System Ser.). (Illus.). 232p. (C). 1981. pap. text ed. 15.50 (*0-07-008104-2*) McGraw.

Sole Source: The Footwear Industry Directory. 350p. 1997. per. 45.00 (*0-318-20645-5*) Footwear Indus.

Sole Spokesman: Jinnah, the Muslim League & the Demand for Pakistan. Ayesha Jalal. (Illus.). 322p. (C). 1994. pap. text ed. 19.95 (*0-521-45850-1*) Cambridge U Pr.

*__Sole Survivor.__ (Shatterzone Ser.). 4.95 (*0-87431-226-4*, 21102) West End Games.

Sole Survivor. George H. Gay. (Illus.). 320p. 20.00 (*0-938300-08-3*) Midway Pubs.

Sole Survivor. Dean R. Koontz. 1997. 25.95 (*0-679-42526-8*) Knopf.

*__Sole Survivor.__ Dean R. Koontz. 1997. mass mkt. 7.99 (*0-345-38437-7*) Ballantine.

*__Sole Survivor.__ aut. ed. Dean R. Koontz. 1997. 25.95 (*0-676-52202-5*) Random.

*__Sole Survivor.__ large type ed. Dean R. Koontz. 1997. pap. 25.95 (*0-679-77415-7*) Random Hse Lrg Prnt.

*__Sole Survivor.__ large type ed. Dean R. Koontz. 1997. pap. 25.95 (*0-7838-8061-8*) Thorndike Pr.

*__Sole Survivor: Dennis Hale's Own Story.__ Dennis Hale et al. 143p. (Orig.). 1996. pap. 14.95 (*0-9627084-2-9*) Lakeshore Charters.

Sole Survivors of the Sea. James E. Wise, Jr. LC 93-48875. 1994. 22.95 (*1-877853-29-1*) Nautical & Aviation.

Soledad: Remedio Supremo. Arnoldo Canclini. (Serie Realidades - Realities Ser.). 88p. (SPA.). 1991. pap. 1.79 (*1-56063-047-7*, 498119) Editorial Unilit.

Soledad Absoluta: Diario Poetico. Josemilio Gonzales. (UPREX, Poesia Ser.: No. 3). 78p. (C). 1971. pap. 1.50 (*0-8477-0003-8*) U of PR Pr.

Soledad Brother: The Prison Letters of George Jackson. Frwd. by Jonathan Jackson, Jr. LC 94-28264. 368p. 1995. pap. 14.95 (*1-55652-230-4*) L Hill Bks.

*__Soledad de un Sacerdote - The Lonely Priest.__ Leon O. Narvaez. (SPA.). 1995. write for info. (*0-945792-31-X*) Editorial Unilit.

Soledad, or Solitudes. rev. ed. R. G. Vliet. LC 85-40826. (Texas Tradition Ser.: No. 6). 270p. 1986. 19.50 (*0-87565-063-5*) Tex Christian.

Soledad Women: Wives of Prisoners Speak Out. Lori B. Girshick. LC 95-45419. 160p. 1996. text ed. 49.95 (*0-275-95409-9*, Praeger Pubs) Greenwood.

Soledad y Compania. Jose M. Oviedo. 236p. (SPA.). 1988. pap. 12.00 (*0-910061-34-3*, 1118) Ediciones Norte.

Soleil Cou Coupe see Cadastre

Soleil de Nuit. Jacques Prevert. 310p. (FRE.). 1989. pap. 11.95 (*0-7859-2574-0*, 2070381757) Fr & Eur.

Soleil de Nuit. Jacques Prevert. (Folio Ser.). (FRE.). pap. 9.95 (*2-07-038175-7*) Schoenhof.

Soleil des Independences. Ahmadou Kourouma. (FRE.). 1990. pap. 11.95 (*0-7859-2721-2*) Fr & Eur.

Soleil Noir: Depression et Melancholie. Julia Kristeva. (FRE.). 1989. pap. 11.95 (*0-7859-2817-0*) Fr & Eur.

Soleil Noir. Depression et Melancolie. Julia Kristeva. (Folio Essais Ser.: No. 123). (Orig.). (FRE.). pap. 8.95 (*2-07-032515-6*) Schoenhof.

Soleil se Leve Aussi. Ernest Hemingway. 288p. (FRE.). 1972. pap. 10.95 (*0-7859-2284-9*, 2070362213) Fr & Eur.

Solemn Appeal. fac. ed. E. G. White. LC 96-60001. 88p. 1996. reprint ed. per. 5.95 (*1-57258-100-X*) Teach Servs.

Solemn Covenant: The Mormon Polygamous Passage. B. Carmon Hardy. (Illus.). 488p. 1991. 34.95 (*0-252-01833-8*) U of Ill Pr.

*__Solemn Duty.__ Leonard B. Scott. 1997. mass mkt. 5.99 (*0-345-41997-9*) Ballantine.

Solemn Exposition of the Holy Eucharist. Frwd. by Alan F. Detscher. (Liturgy Documentary Ser.: Vol. 11). 37p. (Orig.). 1996. pap. 5.95 (*1-57455-106-X*) US Catholic.

Solemn Review of the Custom of War: Showing That War Is the Effect of Popular Delusion & Proposing a Remedy. Noah Worcester. LC 73-137561. (Peace Movement in America Ser.). 25p. 1972. reprint ed. lib. bdg. 18.95 (*0-89198-093-8*) Ozer.

Solemn Silence: The Complete Guide to Hood Canal, by Land, & Sea. William H. Schweizer. (Illus.). 304p. (Orig.). (YA). 1992. pap. 19.95 (*0-925244-02-3*) EOS Pub.

Solemnidades. Hamid Galib. (UPREX, Poesia Ser.: No. 68). 88p. 1985. pap. 3.00 (*0-8477-0068-2*) U of PR Pr.

*__Solenoid-Actuated Directional Control Valves for Hydraulic Service.__ James E. Anders, Sr. (Illus.). 144p. 1997. spiral bd. 40.00 (*0-9636737-3-4*) Hydraulics.

Solent. Imray, Laurie, Norie & Wilson Ltd. Staff. (Illus.). (C). 1990. text ed. 70.00 (*0-685-40234-7*, Pub. by Imray Laurie Norie & Wilson UK) St Mut.

Solent: A Cruising Guide from Selsey Bill to the Needles. Derek Bowskill. (Illus.). 200p. (C). 1990. 90.00 (*0-85288-140-1*, Pub. by Imray Laurie Norie & Wilson UK) St Mut.

Solent Way. Barry Shurlock. 132p. 1987. 35.00 (*0-905392-40-X*) St Mut.

Solera Poems. Mary Burritt. LC 79-11408. 55p. 1979. pap. 3.75 (*0-934332-11-8*) LEpervier Pr.

Soles Emellis. Ed. by Rafael Catala & Roberto Lugo. LC 83-61864. 160p. (Orig.). (SPA.). 1983. pap. text ed. 6.95 (*0-910235-02-3*) Prisma Bks.

*__Soles of Your Feet.__ G. Yagu. LC 96-42113. (J). 1997. write for info. (*0-916291-72-3*) Kane-Miller Bk.

Solesmes & Dom Gueranger, 1805-1875. Dom L. Soltner. Tr. by Joseph O'Connor from FRE. LC 95-21549. (From Solesmes about the Chant Ser.). 224p. (Orig.). 1996. 8.95 (*1-55725-150-9*) Paraclete MA.

Solfege According to the Kodaly Concept, Vol. I. Erzsebet Hegyi. Tr. by Fred Macnicol from HUN. LC 75-21981. (Illus.). 429p. 1975. 42.00 (*0-913932-09-4*) Boosey & Hawkes.

Solfege According to the Kodaly Concept, Vol. 2. Erzsebet Hegyi. Tr. by Kata Ittzes from HUN. (Illus.). 563p. 1979. 36.00 (*963-330-274-9*, Pub. by Editio Musica Budapest HU) Boosey & Hawkes.

Solfege des Solfeges Bk. 1: Vocal. A. Danhauser. 68p. 1986. pap. 5.95 (*0-7935-5326-1*, 50258490) H Leonard.

Solfege, Ear Training, Rhythm, Dictation, & Music Theory: A Comprehensive Course. 2nd ed. Marta A. Ghezzo. LC 92-14152. 272p. (C). 1993. pap. text ed. 24.95 (*0-8173-0476-2*) U of Ala Pr.

Solfeo do Los Solfeos Libro: 1 Vocal. A. Danhauser. 68p. (SPA.). 1986. pap. 5.95 (*0-7935-5354-7*) H Leonard.

Solibo Magnifique. Patrick Chamoiseau. 243p. (FRE.). 1991. pap. 10.95 (*0-7859-2166-4*, 2070383911) Fr & Eur.

*__Solibo Magnifique.__ Patrick Chamoiseau. 1998. write for info. (*0-679-43236-1*) Pantheon.

Solicit, Remake & Resell: The Jeans & Denim Recycling Fundraising Project Workbook. Recycling Consortium Staff. 1991. ring bd. 23.95 (*0-318-03755-6*, Recycling Consort) Prosperity & Profits.

Solicit, Remake & Resell: The Panty Hose Recycling Fundraising Project Workbook. Recycling Consortium Staff. 1991. ring bd. 23.95 (*0-318-03754-8*, Recycling Consort) Prosperity & Profits.

Soliciting Interpretation: Literary Theory & Seventeenth-Century English Poetry. Ed. by Elizabeth D. Harvey & Katharine E. Maus. LC 89-20680. (Illus.). 352p. 1990. pap. text ed. 19.95 (*0-226-31876-1*); lib. bdg. 57.00 (*0-226-31875-3*) U Ch Pr.

Solicitor - Client Privilege in Canadian Law. Ronald D. Manes & Michael Silver. 256p. 1993. text ed. 77.50 (*0-409-80654-4*) MICHIE.

Solicitor General: The Politics of Law. Rebecca M. Salokar. 325p. (C). 1992. 59.95 (*0-87722-926-0*) Temple U Pr.

Solicitor General: The Politics of Law. Rebecca M. Salokar. 325p. 1994. pap. 22.95 (*1-56639-260-8*) Temple U Pr.

Solicitors' Accounts. Ed. by M. A. Nardone. 204p. (C). 1990. pap. 65.00 (*1-85352-897-8*, Pub. by HLT Pubns UK) St Mut.

Solicitors' Accounts: A Student's Guide. 4th ed. Janet Baker. x, 392p. 1992. 36.00 (*1-85431-238-3*, Pub. by Blackstone Pr UK) Gaunt.

Solicitors & Their Business Clients. Antony King & John Barlow. 308p. (C). 1990. 46.00 (*1-85431-016-X*, Pub. by Blackstone Pr UK) Gaunt.

Solicitors & VAT. John Phelps & Julian Gizzi. 1986. pap. 30.00 (*0-406-50360-5*) MICHIE.

Solicitor's Duty in Law & Conduct. P. M. Bird. (Practitioner's Library). 224p. 1989. 99.00 (*0-08-033073-8*, Waterlow) Macmillan.

Solicitor's Guide to Estate Practice in Ontario. 2nd ed. Rintoul. 288p. 1990. 65.00 (*0-409-89336-6*) MICHIE.

Solicitud. rev. ed. Jane B. Moncure. LC 80-27506. (Valores para la Vida Ser.). (Illus.). 32p. (SPA.). (J). (ps-2). 1991. lib. bdg. 21.36 (*0-89565-934-4*) Childs World.

Solid Analytic Geometry. Abraham A. Albert. 174p. reprint ed. pap. 49.60 (*0-317-09471-8*, 2016983) Bks Demand.

Solid & Liquid Lubricants for Extreme Environments: Papers Presented at Symposium Lubricants for Extreme Environments. 79p. 1984. 40.00 (*0-318-17679-3*, SP-15); 25.00 (*0-318-17680-7*) Soc Tribologists.

Solid & Liquid Wastes: Management, Methods & Socioeconomic Considerations. Ed. by Shyamal K. Majumdar & E. Willard Miller. LC 84-61472. (Illus.). xxii, 412p. 1984. 35.00 (*0-9606670-3-2*) Penn Science.

*__Solid Answers.__ James Dobson. 1997. 19.99 (*0-8423-0623-4*) Tyndale.

Solid As the Rock. 1992. 5.99 (*0-8341-9042-7*, MB-643) Lillenas.

Solid Body Guitar Construction. R. J. Gluck. 100p. pap. 24.95 (*1-882731-03-4*) Cactus Pub.

Solid Earth: An Introduction to Global Geophysics. C. M. Fowler. (Illus.). 448p. (C). 1990. 74.95 (*0-521-37025-6*); pap. text ed. 47.95 (*0-521-38590-3*) Cambridge U Pr.

Solid Earth Geomagnetism. Tsuneji Rikitake & Yoshimori Honkura. 1986. lib. bdg. 182.50 (*90-277-2120-3*) Kluwer Ac.

Solid Earth GeoPhysics, ser. vol. 6. Christoph Reigber. (Advances in Space Research Ser.). 1988. pap. 56.00 (*0-08-036644-9*, Pergamon Pr) Elsevier.

Solid Earth Geophysics & Geotechnology: Presented at the Winter Annual Meeting of the American Society of Mechanical Engineers, Chicago, Illinois, November 16-21, 1980. American Society of Mechanical Engineers Staff. Ed. by S. Nemat-Nasser. LC 78-59886. (AMD Ser.: Vol. 42). (Illus.). 95p. reprint ed. pap. 27.10 (*0-8357-2848-X*, 2039083) Bks Demand.

Solid-Earth Science & Society. 368p. 1993. text ed. 49.95 (*0-309-04739-0*) Natl Acad Pr.

Solid-Earth Sciences & Society. Status & Research Opportunities in the Solid-Earth Sciences Committee et al. LC 92-41781. 1993. 49.95 (*0-685-70086-0*) Natl Acad Sci.

Solid Electrolytes: Proceedings of the International Meeting on Solid Electrolytes, 2nd, University of St. Andrews, Sept. 20-22, 1978. International Meeting on Solid Electrolytes Staff. Ed. by R. D. Armstrong. (Illus.). 68p. 1979. pap. 33.00 (*0-08-025267-2*, Pergamon Pr) Elsevier.

Solid for Mulhooly: A Political Satire. Rufus E. Shavley. LC 76-112572. (Rise of Urban America Ser.). (Illus.). 1978. reprint ed. 23.95 (*0-405-02475-4*) Ayer.

Solid for Mulhooly... "I'm Fur 'im" A Sketch of Municipal Politics. Rufus E. Shavley. 179p. 1986. reprint ed. pap. text ed. 6.95 (*0-8290-2028-4*) Irvington.

Solid for Mulhooly..."I'm Fur 'im" A Sketch of Municipal Politics. Rufus E. Shavley. LC 76-96894. 179p. reprint ed. lib. bdg. 18.00 (*0-8398-1855-6*) Irvington.

*__Solid Freeform Fabrication: A New Direction in Manufacturing.__ Joseph J. Beaman. LC 96-47010. 344p. (C). 1996. lib. bdg. 125.00 (*0-7923-9834-3*) Kluwer Ac.

Solid Freeform Manufacturing: Advanced Rapid Prototyping. D. Kochan. LC 93-31067. (Manufacturing Research & Technology Ser.: Vol. 19). 226p. 1993. 166.75 (*0-444-89652-X*) Elsevier.

Solid Fuel Mineral Deposits: Proceedings of the 27th International Geological Congress, Vol. 14. International Geological Congress Staff. 288p. 1984. lib. bdg. 95.00 (*90-6764-023-9*, Pub. by VSP NE) Coronet Bks.

Solid-Gas Interface, 2 vols., Vol. 1. Ed. by E. Alison Flood. LC 66-11284. (Illus.). 532p. reprint ed. pap. 143.70 (*0-7837-0879-3*, 2041186) Bks Demand.

Solid-Gas Interface, 2 vols., Vol. 2. Ed. by E. Alison Flood. LC 66-11284. (Illus.). 676p. reprint ed. pap. 180.00 (*0-7837-0880-7*) Bks Demand.

Solid-Gas Interface: Proceedings of the 2nd International Conference on Surface Activity, 1957. International Congress of Surface Activity Staff. 356p. reprint ed. pap. 101.50 (*0-317-09040-2*, 2051336) Bks Demand.

Solid Gold, No. 10. 64p. 1985. pap. 6.95 (*0-7935-3218-3*, 00106938) H Leonard.

Solid Gold: The Popular Record Industry. R. Serge Denisoff. LC 74-20194. 504p. 1995. pap. 29.95 (*0-87855-586-2*) Transaction Pubs.

Solid Gold Buddha. large type ed. W. H. Canaway. 316p. 1981. 25.99 (*0-7089-0597-8*) Ulverscroft.

Solid Gold Cadillac. Howard Teichmann & George S. Kaufman. 1955. pap. 5.25 (*0-8222-1049-5*) Dramatists Play.

Solid Gold Cadillac see Best American Plays: Fourth Series, 1952-1957

Solid Gold Fund Raising Letters. Arthur L. Cone, Jr. LC 87-81191. (Illus.). 160p. 1987. 22.95 (*0-930807-04-9*, 600181) Fund Raising.

Solid Gold Illusion. Claire Burch. (Illus.). 116p. 1991. lib. bdg. 125.00 (*0-916147-15-0*) Regent Pr.

Solid Gold Kid. Harry Mazer & Norma F. Mazer. 224p. (YA). (gr. 7 up). 1989. pap. 3.99 (*0-553-27851-7*, Starfire BDD) BDD Bks Young Read.

Solid Gold Music: An Automated Accounting Simulation. 3rd ed. Dale H. Klooster. (BA - Accounting - First Year Ser.). 1993. pap. 11.95 (*0-538-61827-2*) S-W Pub.

Solid Gold Success Strategies for Your Business. Don Taylor. 192p. 1996. pap. 16.95 (*0-8144-7914-6*) AMACOM.

Solid Ground. Jill Briscoe. (Jill Briscoe Inductive Bible Study Ser.). 96p. 1992. pap. 7.99 (*0-89693-884-0*, 6-1884) SP Pubns.

Solid Helium Three. E. R. Dobbs. (Illus.). 196p. 1994. 69.00 (*0-19-851382-8*) OUP.

Solid Hydrogen: Theory of the Properties of Solid H2, HD, & D2. Jan Van Kranendonk. LC 82-18054. 322p. 1983. 95.00 (*0-306-41080-X*, Plenum Pr) Plenum.

*__Solid Investment: Making Full Use of the Nation's Human Capital.__ 1997. lib. bdg. 250.95 (*0-8490-6075-3*) Gordon Pr.

Solid-Liquid Dispersions. Ed. by Tharwat F. Tadros. 344p. 1987. text ed. 94.00 (*0-12-682178-X*) Acad Pr.

*__Solid-Liquid Electrochemical Interfaces, Vol. 656.__ Ed. by Gregory Jerkiewicz et al. LC 96-49774. (Symposium Ser.: No. 656). (Illus.). 355p. 1997. 110.95 (*0-8412-3480-9*) Am Chemical.

Solid-Liquid Equilibrium Data Collection: Binary Systems, Tables, Diagrams & Model Parameters. H. Knapp et al. (Dechema Chemistry Data Ser.: Vol. 8, Pt. 1). (Illus.). 555p. 1987. text ed. 275.00 (*3-921567-75-0*, Pub. by Dechema GW) Scholium Intl.

Solid-Liquid Filtration & Separation Technology & Introduction. A. Rushton et al. (Illus.). 538p. 1996. 185.00 (*3-527-28613-6*, VCH) Wiley.

Solid, Liquid, Gas! Fay Robinson. (Rookie Read-about Science Ser.). (Illus.). 32p. (J). (ps-2). 1996. reprint ed. pap. 3.95 (*0-516-46041-2*) Childrens.

Solid-Liquid Interface. D. P. Woodruff. LC 72-91362. (Cambridge Solid State Science Ser.). (Illus.). 150p. 1973. 37.95 (*0-521-20123-3*) Cambridge U Pr.

Solid, Liquid or Gas? Ray Robinson. LC 95-5563. (Rookie Read-About Science Ser.). 32p. (J). (ps-2). 1995. lib. bdg. 17.30 (*0-516-06041-4*) Childrens.

Solid-Liquid Separation Practice III. Ed. by Peter Snowdon et al. LC 89-15417. (European Federation of Chemical Engineering Ser.). 310p. 1989. 69.95 (*0-89116-971-7*) Hemisp Pub.

Solid-Liquid Separations: Waste Management & Productivity Enhancement. Ed. by H. S. Muralidhara. LC 89-17828. 584p. 1990. 87.50 (*0-935470-54-9*) Battelle.

Solid Materials. International Editorial Board Staff. (Structure & Bonding Ser.: Vol. 69). (Illus.). 135p. 1988. 103.95 (*0-387-18790-1*) Spr-Verlag.

Solid Mechanics: An Introduction. J. P. Ward. LC 92-18170. (Solid Mechanics & Its Applications Ser.: Vol. 15). 296p. (C). 1992. lib. bdg. 117.50 (*0-7923-1949-4*) Kluwer Ac.

*__Solid Mechanics 2.__ Urry. Date not set. pap. text ed. write for info. (*0-582-98812-8*, Pub. by Longman UK) Longman.

Solid Modeling: A State-of-the Art Report. 2nd rev. ed. Robert H. Johnson. Ed. by Jonathan Linden. (Illus.). 270p. 1986. ring bd. 495.00 (*0-932007-06-6*, SMB) Mgmt Roundtable.

Solid Modeling for Engineering & Manufacturing Applications: A Report & Buyer's Guide. Robert H. Johnson. 300p. 1988. ring bd. 595.00 (*0-932007-18-X*) Mgmt Roundtable.

Solid Modeling in Computer Graphics: The Technology, Its Applications, & Supply Sources. Illus. by John Kelley. 85p. (C). 1984. 129.00 (*0-914849-02-6*) TBC Inc.

Solid Modeling in Engineering. Josann Duane & Robert Wilke. (Illus.). 528p. (C). 1992. text ed. write for info. (*0-201-18344-7*) Addison-Wesley.

*__Solid Modeling with Autocad.__ Robert McFarlane. pap. text ed. write for info. (*0-470-23735-X*) Wiley.

Solid Modeling with AutoCAD, Release 12. 2nd ed. Ronald W. Leigh. 271p. 1991. 29.95 (*0-614-16834-1*, V75) Am Soc Civil Eng.

Solid Modeling with AutoCAD's AME. L. G. Bullard. (Illus.). 87p. 1992. pap. text ed. 14.80 (*0-87563-402-8*) Stipes.

Solid Modelling. Hiroaki Chiyokura. (Illus.). 256p. (C). 1988. pap. text ed. 41.95 (*0-201-19245-4*) Addison-Wesley.

*__Solid Modelling with AutoCAD.__ write for info. (*0-340-63204-6*, Pub. by E Arnold UK) Routledge Chapman & Hall.

Solid Modelling with Pro-Engineer. Clarence W. Mayott & Geraldine B. Milano. 336p. (C). 1993. ring bd. 40.89 (*0-8403-8729-6*) Kendall-Hunt.

Solid Organ Transplant Rejection: Mechanisms, Pathology, & Diagnosis. Ed. by Kim Solez et al. 656p. 1996. 195.00 (*0-8247-9510-5*) Dekker.

Solid Organ Transplantation Pathology. Ed. by Elizabeth H. Hammond. LC 93-36143. (Major Problems in Pathology Ser.: No. 30). (Illus.). 304p. 1994. text ed. 70.00 (*0-7216-4482-1*) Saunders.

Solid Oxide Fuel Cells: Fourth International Symposium. H. Tagawa et al. 1180p. 1995. 90.00 (*1-56677-095-5*, PV 95-1) Electrochem Soc.

*__Solid Oxide Fuel Cells V (SOFC-V)__ Ed. by U. Stimming et al. (Illus.). 1420p. 1997. 90.00 (*1-56677-145-5*, PV97-40) Electrochem Soc.

Solid Particle Erosion & Erosion-Corrosion of Materials. Alan V. Levy. (Illus.). 225p. 1995. 102.00 (*0-87170-519-2*, 6469) ASM.

Solid Particles in the Solar System. Ed. by Ian Halliday & Bruce A. McIntosh. (International Astronomical Union Symposia Ser.: No. 90). 432p. 1980. pap. text ed. 70.50 (*90-277-1165-8*); lib. bdg. 129.50 (*90-277-1164-X*) Kluwer Ac.

*__Solid Phase Extraction: Principles, Strategies & Applications.__ Ed. by Nigel Simpson. (Illus.). 300p. 1997. text ed. write for info. (*0-8247-0021-X*) Dekker.

Solid Phase Extraction Applications Guide & Bibliography: A Resource for Sample Preparation Methods Development. 6th ed. Ed. by Patrick D. McDonald & Edouard S. Bouvier. LC 95-60173. (Illus.). 646p. (Orig.). (C). 1995. pap. text ed. 75.00 (*1-879732-06-8*) Waters MA.

Solid Phase Extraction in Sample Preparation: An Applications Bibliography. 52p. (Orig.). (C). 1994. pap. text ed. 25.00 (*0-7881-1344-5*) DIANE Pub.

*__Solid Phase Microextraction: Theory & Practice.__ LC 96-45276. 1997. write for info. (*1-56081-963-4*, VCH) Wiley.

*__Solid Polymer Electrolytes: Fundamentals & Technological Applications.__ F. M. Gray. 1991. text ed. 69.95 (*0-471-18737-2*) Wiley.

Solid Polymer Electrolytes: Fundamentals & Technological Applications. Fiona M. Gray. 245p. 1991. text ed. 65.00 (*0-89573-772-8*, VCH) Wiley.

Solid Polyurethane Elastomers. P. Wright & A. P. Cumming. 318p. 1969. text ed. 288.00 (*0-677-61690-2*) Gordon & Breach.

Solid Propellant Rockets. Clayton Huggett et al. LC 60-12049. (Princeton Aeronautical Paperbacks Ser.: Vol. 2). (Illus.). 167p. reprint ed. pap. 47.60 (*0-685-23463-0*, 2056658) Bks Demand.

Solid Rocket Propulsion Technology. Ed. by Alain Davenas. (Illus.). 620p. 1992. 272.25 (*0-08-040999-7*, Pergamon Pr) Elsevier.

*__Solid Sense in Mathematics: Problem Solving, 3 bks.__ Mary Laycock & Margaret Smart. Incl. Level 1. rev. ed. (Illus.). 64p. (Orig.). (J). (gr. 4-6). 1993. pap. 8.50 (*0-614-25990-8*, A-1671); Level 2. rev. ed. (Illus.). 64p. (Orig.). (J). (gr. 6-8). 1993. pap. 8.50 (*0-614-25991-6*, A-1672); Level 3. rev. ed. (Illus.). 64p. (J). (gr. 7-9). 1993. pap. 8.50 (*0-614-25992-4*, A-1673); 25.50 (*0-918932-74-2*) Activity Resources.

Solid Shape. Jan J. Koenderink. (Artificial Intelligence Ser.). 750p. 1990. 90.00 (*0-262-11139-X*) MIT Pr.

*__Solid-Solid Interactions: Proceedings of the First Royal Society-Unilever Indo U. K. Forum in Materials Science.__ 448p. 1996. 61.00 (*1-86094-010-2*) World Scientific Pub.

Solid-Solid Phase Transformations: Proceedings of the International Conference on Solid-Solid Phase Transformations (1994: Farmington, Pennsylvania) Ed. by William C. Johnson et al. LC 94-73001. (Illus.). 1250p. 1995. 50.00 (*0-87339-278-7*, 2787) Minerals Metals.

Solid State: An Introduction to the Physics of Crystals for Students of Physics, Materials Science, & Engineering. 3rd ed. H. M. Rosenberg. (Oxford Physics Ser.: No. 9). (Illus.). 326p. (C). 1988. pap. text ed. 23.00 (*0-19-851870-6*) OUP.

Solid State: From Superconductors to Superalloys. Andre Guinier & Remi Jullien. (International Union of Crystallography Texts on Crystallography Ser.: No. 1). (Illus.). 288p. 1989. 80.00 (*0-19-855290-4*); pap. 32.00 (*0-19-855554-7*) OUP.

Solid State see Chemical Engineering Practice

Solid-State AC Motor Controls: Selection & Application. Campbell. (Mechanical Engineering Ser.: Vol. 56). 248p. 1987. 125.00 (*0-8247-7728-X*) Dekker.

An Asterisk (*) at the beginning of an entry indicates that the title is appearing in BIP for the first time.

Solid-State & Chemical Radiation Dosimetry in Medicine & Biology. (Proceedings Ser.). (Illus.). 471p. 1967. pap. 50.00 (*92-0-010167-4*, ISP138, Pub. by IAEA AU) Bernan Associates.

Solid-State & Molecular Theory: A Scientific Biography. John C. Slater. LC 74-22367. (Wiley-Interscience Publications). (Illus.). 367p. 1975. reprint ed. pap. 104.60 (*0-7837-3473-5*, 2057804) Bks Demand.

Solid State & Quantum Physics. Ed. by Alan D. Boardman. LC 80-40125. (Physics Programs Ser.: Vol. 3). (Illus.). 142p. reprint ed. pap. 40.50 (*0-685-20668-8*, 2030456) Bks Demand.

Solid State Astrophysics. Ed. by Nalin C. Wickramasinghe & D. J. Morgan. LC 75-34355. (Astrophysics & Space Science Library: No. 55). 1975. lib. bdg. 135.00 (*90-277-0653-0*) Kluwer Ac.

Solid State Astrophysics: Proc. of the Internat. School of Physics, Enrico Fermi, Course CXI, 27 June-7 July, 1989. Ed. by E. Bussoletti & G. Strazzulla. (Enrico Fermi International Summer School of Physics Ser.: Vol. 111). 440p. 1991. 200.00 (*0-444-89218-4*, North Holland) Elsevier.

Solid State Batteries: Materials Design & Optimization. Ed. by Christian Julien & Gholam-Abbas Nazri. LC 94-14426. (International Series in Engineering & Computer Science, VLSI, Computer Architecture, & Digital Screen Processing: Vol. 271). 648p. (C). 1994. lib. bdg. 204.00 (*0-7923-9460-7*) Kluwer Ac.

Solid State Cameras. Richard K. Miller & Terri C. Walker. LC 88-81662. (Survey on Technology & Markets Ser.: No. 71). 50p. 1989. pap. text ed. 200.00 (*1-55865-070-9*) Future Tech Surveys.

Solid State Chemistry. 1980. 11.00 (*0-910362-14-9*) Chem Educ.

Solid State Chemistry. R. A. Mashelkar & C. N. Rao. Ed. by S. K. Joshi. LC 94-34672. (Twentieth Century Chemistry Ser.). 740p. 1995. text ed. 86.00 (*981-02-1808-7*) World Scientific Pub.

Solid State Chemistry. Ed. by C. N. Rao. LC 73-82705. (Illus.). 923p. reprint ed. pap. 180.00 (*0-7837-0918-8*, 2041223) Bks Demand.

Solid-State Chemistry, Vol. 11. Ed. by M. E. Vol'pin. (Soviet Scientific Reviews Ser.: Section B, Chemistry). 256p. 1988. text ed. 630.00 (*3-7186-0410-8*) Gordon & Breach.

Solid State Chemistry: A Contemporary Overview. Ed. by Smith L. Holt et al. LC 80-17185. (Advances in Chemistry Ser.: No. 186). 1980. 65.95 (*0-8412-0472-1*) Am Chemical.

***Solid State Chemistry: A Contemporary Overview.** Ed. by Smith L. Holt et al. LC 80-17185. (Advances in Chemistry Ser.: Vol. 186). 447p. 1980. reprint ed. pap. 127.40 (*0-608-03858-X*, 2064305) Bks Demand.

Solid State Chemistry: An Introduction. Lesley Smart & Elaine Moore. (Illus.). 240p. (C). (gr. 13). 1992. pap. text ed. 36.95 (*0-412-40040-5*, A7074) Chapman & Hall.

***Solid State Chemistry: An Introduction.** 2nd ed. L. Smart & E. Moore. (Illus.). 384p. (Orig.). (C). 1995. pap. text ed. 32.50 (*0-412-62220-3*, Chap & Hall NY) Chapman & Hall.

Solid State Chemistry: Synthesis, Structure, & Properties of Selected Oxides & Sulfides. Aaron Wold & Kirby Dwight. LC 92-35607. 264p. (gr. 13). 1993. pap. text ed. 36.95 (*0-412-03621-5*) Chapman & Hall.

Solid State Chemistry: Synthesis, Structure, & Properties of Selected Oxides & Sulfides. Aaron Wold & Kirby Dwight. LC 92-35607. 264p. (gr. 13). 1993. text ed. 77.95 (*0-412-03611-8*) Chapman & Hall.

Solid-State Chemistry: Techniques. A. K. Cheetham & Peter Day. (Illus.). 412p. 1990. pap. 50.00 (*0-19-855286-6*) OUP.

Solid-State Chemistry see International Congress of Pure & Applied Chemistry, 24th, Hamburg, 1973: Proceedings

Solid State Chemistry & Its Applications. Alan West. LC 83-21607. 734p. 1987. pap. text ed. 69.95 (*0-471-90874-6*) Wiley.

Solid State Chemistry & Physics, Vol. 1: An Introduction. Ed. by Paul F. Weller. LC 73-85302. (Illus.). 518p. reprint ed. pap. 147.70 (*0-7837-0876-9*, 2041184) Bks Demand.

Solid State Chemistry & Physics, Vol. 2: An Introduction. Ed. by Paul F. Weller. LC 73-85302. (Illus.). 451p. reprint ed. pap. 128.60 (*0-7837-0539-5*, 2040867) Bks Demand.

***Solid State Chemistry in Catalysis.** Ed. by Robert K. Grasselli & James F. Brazdil. LC 85-9190. (ACS Symposium Ser.: Vol. 279). 376p. 1985. reprint ed. pap. 107.20 (*0-608-03910-1*, 2064357) Bks Demand.

Solid State Chemistry of Energy Conversion & Storage: A Symposium Sponsored by the Division of Inorganic Chemistry at the 71st Meeting of the American Chemical Society. Ed. by John B. Goodenough & M. Stanley Whittingham. LC 77-20011. (Advances in Chemistry Ser.: No. 163). 382p. reprint ed. pap. 108.90 (*0-317-08982-X*, 2015231) Bks Demand.

***Solid-State Chemistry of Inorganic Materials.** Ed. by A. Jacobson et al. LC 97-8050. (Materials Research Society Symposium Proceedings Ser.: No. 453). 1997. text ed. 75.00 (*1-55899-357-6*) Materials Res.

Solid State Chemistry, Vol. 2: Compounds. Ed. by A. K. Cheetham & Peter Day. (Illus.). 352p. 1992. 95.00 (*0-19-855166-5*) OUP.

Solid State Design for the Radio Amateur. 1986. pap. 15.00 (*0-87259-040-2*) Am Radio.

***Solid State Device Research '91.** M. Ilegems & M. Dutoit. xxiv, 698p. 1991. 275.75 (*0-444-89066-1*) Elsevier.

Solid State Device Research '92: Proceedings of the 22nd European Conference, ESSDERC '92, 14-17 September 1992, Leuven, Belgium. Ed. by H. E. Maes et al. LC 92-23521. 1992. 301.25 (*0-444-89478-0*) Elsevier.

Solid State Devices & Applications. Frederick F. Driscoll, Jr. & Robert F. Coughlin. (Illus.). 384p. 1975. text ed. 53.00 (*0-13-822106-5*) P-H.

Solid State Devices & Integrated Circuits. William Cooper & Henry Wiesbecker. (C). 1982. text ed. 40.00 (*0-8359-7045-0*, Reston); teacher ed. write for info. (*0-8359-7046-9*, Reston) P-H.

Solid State Diffusion. J. P. Stark. LC 80-11750. 252p. 1983. reprint ed. lib. bdg. 30.50 (*0-89874-145-9*) Krieger.

Solid-State Dosimetry. (Bibliographical Ser.: No. 23). 143p. 1967. pap. 15.00 (*92-0-114067-3*, ISP21 23, Pub. by IAEA AU) Bernan Associates.

Solid State Electrochemistry. Ed. by Peter G. Bruce. LC 93-42634. (Chemistry of Solid State Materials Ser.: No. 4). (Illus.). 300p. (C). 1995. text ed. 90.00 (*0-521-40007-4*) Cambridge U Pr.

***Solid State Electrochemistry.** Ed. by Peter G. Bruce. (Chemistry of Solid State Materials Ser.: No. 5). (Illus.). 360p. 1997. pap. text ed. 39.95 (*0-521-59949-0*) Cambridge U Pr.

Solid State Electrochemistry & Its Applications to Sensors & Electronic Devices. K. S. Goto. (Materials Science Monographs: Vol. 45). 454p. 1988. 211.25 (*0-444-42912-3*) Elsevier.

Solid State Electronic Controls in Air Conditioning & Refrigeration. Billy C. Langley. 304p. 1988. text ed. 76.00 (*0-13-823360-8*) P-H.

Solid State Electronic Devices. 4th ed. Ben G. Streetman. LC 94-37720. (Solid State Physical Electronics Ser.). 1995. text ed. 89.33 (*0-13-158767-6*) P-H Gen Ref & Trav.

Solid-State Electronics. Lawrence E. Murr. (Electrical Engineering & Electronics Ser.: Vol. 4). 432p. 1978. 125.00 (*0-8247-6676-8*) Dekker.

Solid-State Electronics. George B. Rutkowski. LC 77-131132. 1972. 17.90 (*0-672-20801-6*, Bobbs) Macmillan.

Solid-State Electronics: Principles & Applications. Timothy J. Maloney. 535p. (C). 1994. pap. text ed. 33.50 (*0-9639857-4-4*) Dirk Pubng.

Solid State Electronics - Towards the 21st Century. Nguyen T. Nghi & V. I. Fistual. 170p. 1997. text ed. 44.00 (*981-02-1605-X*) World Scientific Pub.

***Solid State Electronics & High Speed Devices.** Raven. 304p. 1997. text ed. write for info. (*0-412-78300-2*, Chap & Hall NY) Chapman & Hall.

Solid State Fundamentals for Electricians. 2nd ed. Gary Rockis. LC 93-5537. (Illus.). 232p. 1993. 34.96 (*0-8269-1631-7*) Am Technical.

Solid State Gas Sensors. Ed. by P. T. Moseley & B. C. Tofield. (Sensors Ser.). (Illus.). 264p. 1987. 116.00 (*0-85274-514-1*) IOP Pub.

Solid-State Imaging with Charge-Coupled Devices. Albert J. Theuwissen. LC 95-11945. (Solid-State Science & Technology Library). 416p. (C). 1995. lib. bdg. 192.00 (*0-7923-3456-6*) Kluwer Ac.

Solid State Industrial Electronics. Richard Pearman. (C). 1984. teacher ed. write for info. (*0-8359-7042-6*, Reston); text ed. 58.00 (*0-8359-7041-8*, Reston) P-H.

Solid State Ionic Devices. Ed. by B. V. Chowdari & S. Radhakrishna. 740p. (C). 1988. text ed. 138.00 (*9971-5-0626-2*) World Scientific Pub.

Solid State Ionic Materials: Proceedings of the 4th Asian Conference on Solid State Ionics. B. V. Rchowdari et al. 472p. 1994. text ed. 109.00 (*981-02-1861-3*) World Scientific Pub.

Solid State Ionics. Tetsuichi Kudo & Kazuo Fueki. 241p. 1990. 135.00 (*3-527-28166-5*, VCH) Wiley.

***Solid State Ionics: New Developments.** 550p. 1996. 66.00 (*981-02-3018-4*) World Scientific Pub.

Solid State Ionics: Symposium A2 on Solid State Ionics, Strasbourg, France, 1991. Ed. by M. Balkanski et al. LC 91-42719. 669p. 1992. 189.50 (*0-444-89354-7*, TK7871, North Holland) Elsevier.

Solid State Ionics: Third Asian Conference. B. V. Chowdari. 792p. 1992. text ed. 116.00 (*981-02-1138-4*) World Scientific Pub.

Solid State Ionics Vol. 135: Materials Research Society Symposium Proceedings. Ed. by D. F. Shriver et al. 621p. 1989. text ed. 30.00 (*1-55899-008-9*) Materials Res.

Solid State Ionics II Vol. 210: Materials Research Society Symposium Proceedings. Ed. by M. Balkanski et al. 722p. 1991. text ed. 58.00 (*1-55899-102-6*) Materials Res.

Solid State Ionics III. M. Armand. Ed. by Gholam-Abbas Nazri et al. (Materials Research Society Symposium Proceedings Ser.: Vol. 293). 471p. 1993. text ed. 79.00 (*1-55899-188-3*) Materials Res.

Solid State Ionics IV: 1994 MRS Fall Meeting, Boston, MA. Ed. by Gholam-Abbas Nazri et al. (MRS Symposium Proceedings Ser.: Vol. 369). 715p. 1995. 82.00 (*1-55899-271-5*) Materials Res.

Solid-State Laser Engineering. Walter Koechner. (Optical Sciences Ser.: Vol. 1). (Illus.). xii, 606p. 1988. 83.00 (*0-387-18747-2*) Spr-Verlag.

Solid-State Laser Engineering. Walter Koechner. LC 95-36479. (Springer Series in Optical Sciences). 656p. 1996. 79.00 (*3-540-60237-2*) Spr-Verlag.

Solid-State Laser Engineering. 3rd rev. ed. Walter Koechner. (Optical Sciences Ser.: Vol. 1). (Illus.). xii, 634p. 1992. 89.00 (*0-387-53756-2*) Spr-Verlag.

Solid State Lasers: New Developments & Applications. Ed. by M. Inguscio & R. Wallenstein. (NATO ASI Ser.: Series B, Physics: Vol. 317). (Illus.). 342p. 1994. 105.00 (*0-306-44598-0*, Plenum Pr) Plenum.

Solid State Lasers III. Ed. by G. J. Quarles. 1992. 20.00 (*0-8194-0773-9*, 1627) SPIE.

Solid State Luminescence: Theory, Materials, & Devices. Ed. by A. H. Kitai. LC 93-12191. 400p. (gr. 13). 1993. text ed. 88.95 (*0-412-43340-0*) Chapman & Hall.

Solid State Magnetic Sensors. Ed. by Chavdar S. Roumenin. LC 94-26842. 434p. 1994. 168.75 (*0-444-89401-2*) Elsevier.

Solid State Magnetism. John Crangle. (Illus.). 324p. (gr. 13). 1991. text ed. 41.95 (*0-442-30856-6*) Chapman & Hall.

Solid State Materials. Ed. by S. Radhakrishna et al. 400p. 1992. 75.95 (*0-387-54229-9*) Spr-Verlag.

Solid State Microbatteries. Ed. by J. R. Akridge & M. Balkanski. LC 90-6769. (NATO ASI Ser.: Series B, Physics: Vol. 217). (Illus.). 450p. 1990. 125.00 (*0-306-43505-5*, Plenum Pr) Plenum.

Solid-State Microwave Amplifier Design. Tri T. Ha. LC 90-46862. 344p. (C). 1991. reprint ed. lib. bdg. 56.50 (*0-89464-507-2*) Krieger.

Solid State Microwave Devices. Thomas S. Laverghetta. LC 87-19319. (Artech House Microwave Library). (Illus.). 208p. reprint ed. pap. 59.30 (*0-8357-3938-4*, 2036673) Bks Demand.

Solid-State Microwave Generation. J. Anastassiades et al. LC 92-18094. 288p. (gr. 13). 1992. text ed. 152.95 (*0-412-37440-4*) Chapman & Hall.

Solid State Microwave Oscillators. M. Odyniec. 1987. text ed. write for info. (*0-442-23708-1*) Van Nos Reinhold.

Solid-State Microwave Power Oscillator Design. Eric L. Holzman & Ralston S. Robertson. (Microwave Library). 454p. 1992. text ed. 88.00 (*0-89006-487-3*) Artech Hse.

Solid-State Microwave Power Oscillator Design. fac. ed. Eric L. Holzman & Ralston S. Robertson. LC 91-48225. (Artech House Microwave Library). (Illus.). 479p. 1992. reprint ed. pap. 136.60 (*0-608-00940-7*, 2061732) Bks Demand.

Solid State Motor Control. Richard Hunter. LC 73-254. (Orig.). 1984. student ed. 8.00 (*0-8064-0323-3*, 816); audio, vhs 369.00 (*0-8064-0324-1*) Bergwall.

Solid-State NMR: Methods & Applications of Solid-State NMR, Vol. 4. Ed. by P. Diehl et al. (NMR-Basic Principles & Progress Ser.: Vol.33). 214p. 1994. 174.95 (*0-387-58212-6*) Spr-Verlag.

Solid-State NMR: Organic Matter, Vol. 3. Ed. by P. Diehl et al. (NMR-Basic Principles & Progress Ser.: Vol.32). 223p. 1994. 174.95 (*0-387-57399-2*) Spr-Verlag.

Solid State NMR & X-Ray Crystallography: Complementary Tools for Structure Determination: Structure-Property Relationships in Sensors. Robert E. Newnham et al. Ed. by M. Moore. (Crystallography Reviews Ser.: Vol. 1, No. 4). 88p. 1988. pap. text ed. 61.00 (*2-88124-667-2*) Gordon & Breach.

Solid State NMR of Polymers. Ed. by Lon J. Mathias. (Illus.). 464p. 1991. 115.00 (*0-306-44015-6*, Plenum Pr) Plenum.

Solid State Nuclear Track Detectors: Proceedings of the International Conference on Solid Nuclear Track Detectors, 11th, Bristol, UK, Sept, 1981. International Conference on Solid State Nuclear Track Detectors Staff. Ed. by P. H. Fowler & V. M. Clapham. (Illus.). 991p. 1982. 285.00 (*0-08-026509-X*, C120, C140, Pergamon Pr) Elsevier.

Solid State Nuclear Track Detectors: Proceedings of the International Conference, 10th, Lyon, France, July 1979. International Conference on Solid State Nuclear Track Detectors Staff. Ed. by H. Francois et al. LC 79-41577. (Illus.). 1082p. 1980. 482.00 (*0-08-025029-7*, Pergamon Pr) Elsevier.

Solid State Nuclear Track Detectors: Proceedings of the 14th International Conference, Lahore, Pakistan, 2-6 April 1988. Ed. by H. A. Khan et al. (Nuclear Tracts Ser.: No. JNT 15). Orig. Title: Nuclear Tracks & Radiation Measurements, Vol. 15, Nos. 1-4. 800p. 1989. 195.00 (*0-08-036382-2*, Pergamon Pr) Elsevier.

Solid-State Optical Materials. Ed. by Allan J. Bruce & Basavaraj V. Hiremath. LC 92-27701. (Ceramic Transactions Ser.: Vol. 28). 724p. 1992. 69.00 (*0-944904-52-1*, TRANS028) Am Ceramic.

Solid State Phenomena: As Seen by Muons, Protons, & Excited Nuclei. Erik B. Karlsson. (Illus.). 320p. 1995. 105.00 (*0-19-853778-6*) OUP.

Solid State Physics. Neil W. Ashcroft & N. David Mermin. LC 74-9772. 826p. (C). 1976. text ed. 63.00 (*0-03-083993-9*) SCP.

Solid State Physics. Gerald Burns. (C). 1985. text ed. 56.00 (*0-12-146070-3*) Acad Pr.

Solid State Physics. H. E. Hall. (Manchester Physics Ser.). 351p. 1974. pap. text ed. 98.00 (*0-471-34281-5*) Wiley.

Solid State Physics. Stokes. 336p. 1986. text ed. write for info. (*0-205-10508-4*) P-H.

Solid State Physics. 2nd ed. J. S. Blakemore. (Illus.). 506p. 1985. pap. text ed. 49.95 (*0-521-31391-0*) Cambridge U Pr.

Solid State Physics. 2nd ed. J. R. Hook & H. E. Hall. LC 90-20571. (Manchester Physics Ser.). 474p. 1995. pap. text ed. 35.50 (*0-471-92805-4*) Wiley.

Solid State Physics, Vol. 49. Ed. by Henry Ehrenreich & Frans Spaepen. (Illus.). 436p. 1995. boxed 89.95 (*0-12-607749-5*) Acad Pr.

***Solid State Physics, Vol. 50.** Ed. by Henry Ehreinreich & Frans Spaepen. (Illus.). 403p. 1996. boxed 120.00 (*0-12-607750-9*) Acad Pr.

***Solid-State Physics: An Introduction to Principles of Materials Science.** Hans Luth & Harald Ibach. LC 96-3237. 1996. write for info. (*0-387-58573-7*) Spr-Verlag.

Solid-State Physics: An Introduction to Theory & Experiment. Harald Ibach & Hans Luth. Tr. by A. Lahee & K. Prince from GER. (Illus.). 360p. 1991. 49.50 (*0-387-52207-7*) Spr-Verlag.

Solid-State Physics: An Introduction to Theory & Experiment. 2nd ed. Harald Ibach & Hans Luth. (Illus.). 350p. 1993. 39.50 (*0-387-56841-7*) Spr-Verlag.

Solid-State Physics: An Introduction to Theory & Experiment. 2nd rev. ed. Harald Ibach & Hans Luth. LC 95-17872. 1995. 43.95 (*3-540-58573-7*) Spr-Verlag.

Solid State Physics: Problems & Solutions. Laszlo Mihaly & Michael C. Martin. LC 96-6184. 1996. pap. text ed. 29.95 (*0-471-15287-0*) Wiley.

Solid State Physics: Structure & Electron Related Properties. S. O. Pillai. 1994. write for info. (*81-224-0643-2*, Pub. by Wiley Estrn II) Franklin.

Solid State Physics Vol. 47: Advances in Research & Applications. Ed. by Henry Ehrenreich & David Turnbull. (Illus.). 494p. 1994. text ed. 94.00 (*0-12-607747-9*) Acad Pr.

Solid State Physics - One. Ed. by M. A. Dissanayake et al. 325p. (C). 1989. text ed. 112.00 (*0-941743-66-7*) Nova Sci Pubs.

Solid-State Physics & Engineering. Craig T. Van Degrift. (Technical Japanese Supplements Ser.). 104p. 1995. pap. 20.00 (*0-299-14734-7*) U of Wis Pr.

Solid-State Physics for Engineering & Materials Science. John P. McKelvey. LC 93-4226. 514p. (C). 1993. lib. bdg. 53.50 (*0-89464-436-X*) Krieger.

Solid State Physics Simulations: The Consortium for Upper Level Physics Software. Ian Johnston et al. LC 95-35660. 173p. 1995. pap. text ed., pap. write for info. incl. disk (*0-471-54885-5*) Wiley.

Solid State Physics Two. Ed. by M. A. Dissanayake et al. 292p. (C). 1993. pap. text ed. 125.00 (*1-56072-030-1*) Nova Sci Pubs.

Solid State Physics under Pressure. Ed. by S. Minomura. 1985. lib. bdg. 206.00 (*90-277-1897-0*) Kluwer Ac.

Solid State Physics, Vol. 44: Advances in Research & Applications. Ed. by Henry Ehrenreich & David Turnbull. (Illus.). 454p. 1991. text ed. 122.00 (*0-12-607744-4*); pap. text ed. 74.00 (*0-12-606044-4*) Acad Pr.

Solid State Physics, Vol. 46: Advances in Research & Applications. Ed. by Henry Ehrenreich & David Turnbull. (Illus.). 405p. 1992. text ed. 95.00 (*0-12-607746-0*) Acad Pr.

Solid State Physics, Vol. 48: Fullerene Fundamentals. Ed. by Henry Ehrenreich & Frans Spaepen. (Illus.). 434p. 1994. text ed. 84.00 (*0-12-607748-7*); pap. text ed. 53.00 (*0-12-606048-7*) Acad Pr.

***Solid State Powder Processing: Proceedings of a Symposium Sponsored by the TMS Powder Metallurgy Committee, & Held at the TMS Fall Meeting in Indianapolis, Indiana, October 1-5, 1989.** Minerals, Metals & Materials Society Staff. Ed. by Allan H. Clauer & John J. DeBarbadillo. LC 89-63258. (Illus.). 395p. 1990. reprint ed. pap. 112.60 (*0-608-02489-9*, 2063133) Bks Demand.

Solid State Power Conversion Handbook. Ralph E. Tarter. LC 92-18179. 738p. 1993. text ed. 113.00 (*0-471-57243-8*) Wiley.

Solid-State Radar Transmitters. E. D. Ostroff et al. 272p. (C). 1985. text ed. write for info. (*0-89006-169-6*) Artech Hse.

Solid-State Radar Transmitters. Edward D. Ostroff et al. LC 85-73318. 280p. 1985. reprint ed. pap. 79.80 (*0-608-01416-8*, 2062179) Bks Demand.

Solid State Radio Engineering. Herbert L. Krauss et al. LC 78-27797. 534p. 1980. Net. text ed. 61.00 (*0-471-03018-X*) Wiley.

Solid State Reactions. 2nd ed. Hermann Schmalzried. (Monographs in Modern Chemistry: Vol. 12). (Illus.). 254p. 1981. 105.00 (*3-527-25872-8*, VCH) Wiley.

Solid State Science: Past, Present & Predicted. Ed. by D. L. Weaire & C. G. Windsor. (Illus.). 328p. 1987. 131.00 (*0-85274-584-2*) IOP Pub.

Solid State Surface Science, 2 vols., Vol. 2. Ed. by Mino Green. LC 77-85241. (Illus.). 262p. reprint ed. pap. 70.80 (*0-7837-0714-2*, 2041043) Bks Demand.

Solid State Surface Science, 2 vols., Vol. 3. Ed. by Mino Green. LC 77-85241. (Illus.). 355p. reprint ed. pap. 101.20 (*0-7837-0715-0*) Bks Demand.

Solid State Theory. Walter A. Harrison. 1980. reprint ed. pap. text ed. 13.95 (*0-486-63948-7*) Dover.

Solid State Transformations. N. N. Sirota. Ed. by F. K. Gorskii. Tr. by Geoffrey D. Archard from RUS. LC 66-18733. 179p. reprint ed. pap. 51.10 (*0-317-08917-X*, 2020673) Bks Demand.

Solid Supports & Catalysts in Organic Synthesis. K. Smith. 300p. 1992. text ed. 97.00 (*0-13-639998-3*) P-H.

Solid Systems see Chemical Engineering Practice

Solid Tantalum Capacitors World Markets, Technologies & Opportunities: A 1994-1999 Technical-Economic Analysis. Dennis M. Zogbi. 118p. (Orig.). 1994. pap. 1,295.00 (*0-929717-24-4*) Paumanok Pubns.

Solid Tantalum Capacitors World Markets, Technologies & Opportunities: A 1995-2000 Technical-Economic Analysis. Dennis M. Zogbi. 182p. (Orig.). 1996. pap. 1,500.00 (*0-929717-33-3*) Paumanok Pubns.

Solid to Solid Phase Transformations: Proceedings of an International Conference. International Conference on Solid to Solid Phase Transformations Staff. Ed. by Hubert I. Aaronson et al. LC 82-62934. (Illus.). 1634p. reprint ed. pap. 180.00 (*0-8357-8523-8*, 2034820) Bks Demand.

Solid Tumor in Childhood. Norman S. Jaffe. 176p. 1983. 103.00 (*0-8493-5732-2*, RC281, CRC Reprint) Franklin.

Solid Waste: State & Federal Efforts to Manage Non-Hazardous Waste. (Illus.). 50p. (Orig.). (C). 1995. pap. text ed. 30.00 (*0-7881-2026-3*) DIANE Pub.

Solid Waste & Recycling. Hayder Erdogan. Ed. by J. J. Head. (Carolina Biology Readers Ser.: No. 189). 16p. (Orig.). (YA). (gr. 5 up). 1992. pap. text ed. 2.75 (*0-89278-189-0*, 45-9789) Carolina Biological.

Solid Waste As a Resource. Ed. by M. E. Henstock & M. W. Biddulph. LC 77-24726. 1978. 78.00 (*0-08-021571-8*, Pergamon Pr) Elsevier.

Solid Waste Collection Practice. (C). 1975. 28.00 (*0-917084-00-4*) Am Public Works.

S

Solid Waste Construction & Maintenance Supervisor. Jack Rudman. (Career Examination Ser.: C-3606). 1994. pap. 34.95 (*0-8373-3606-6*) Nat Learn.

Solid Waste Dilemma: An Agenda for Action. (Illus.). 70p. (Orig.). (C). 1993. pap. text ed. 30.00 (*1-56806-903-0*) DIANE Pub.

Solid Waste Disposal & Re-Use in the United States, Vol. I. Murarka. 200p. 1987. 110.00 (*0-8493-4647-9*) CRC Pr.

Solid Waste Disposal & Re-Use in the United States, Vol. II. Murarka. 168p. 1987. 101.00 (*0-8493-4648-7*) CRC Pr.

Solid Waste Disposal Facility Supervisor. (Career Examination Ser.: C-3772). pap. 34.95 (*0-8373-3772-0*) Nat Learn.

Solid Waste Education Recycling Directory. Teresa Jones et al. (Illus.). 128p. 1990. 70.00 (*0-87371-359-1*, L359) Lewis Pubs.

Solid Waste Generation Coefficients: Manufacturing Sectors. Gene Steiker. (Discussion Paper Ser.: No. 70). 1973. pap. 10.00 (*1-55869-113-8*) Regional Sci Res Inst.

Solid Waste Handbook: A Practical Guide. Ed. by William D. Robinson. LC 85-12454. 848p. 1986. text ed. 150.00 (*0-471-87711-5*) Wiley.

Solid Waste Landfill Engineering & Design. Edward A. McBean et al. LC 94-10676. 544p. 1994. text ed. 70.00 (*0-13-079187-3*) P-H.

Solid Waste Management. D. Joseph Hagerty et al. LC 73-10281. (Van Nostrand Reinhold Environmental Engineering Ser.). 316p. reprint ed. pap. 90.10 (*0-317-11224-4*, 2014903) Bks Demand.

Solid Waste Management: A Selected & Annotated Bibliography, No. 1295. Marilyn Gehr. 1977. 7.00 (*0-686-19695-3*, Sage Prdcls Pr) Sage.

Solid Waste Management: 1989-1990 State Legislation. 2nd ed. 95p. 1990. 15.00 (*1-55516-489-7*, 4623) Natl Conf State Legis.

Solid Waste Management in Minnesota: Economic Status & Outlook. Christine Leavitt & Robert J. McCarron. (Illus.). 101p. (Orig.). (C). 1994. pap. text ed. 35.00 (*0-7881-0222-2*) DIANE Pub.

***Solid Waste Management Legislation: Summary of State & Federal Legislation.** 31p. (Orig.). 1997. pap. text ed. 30.00 (*0-7881-3751-4*) DIANE Pub.

Solid Waste Management Specialist. (Career Examination Ser.: C-3477). 1994. pap. 34.95 (*0-8373-3477-2*) Nat Learn.

Solid Waste Mess. (Environmental Issues Forums Ser.: Vol. 1). (Illus.). 41p. (Orig.). 1992. pap. 6.00 (*1-884008-01-1*) NAAEE.

Solid Waste Recycling: The Complete Resource Guide. LC 90-25946. 600p. 1990. ring bd. 195.00 (*1-55871-188-0*, BSP 135) BNA Plus.

Solid Waste, Reduction, Reuse & Recycling: Building Sustainable Communities, an Environmental Guide for Local Government. Center for the Study of Law & Politics Staff. 144p. 1991. 40.00 (*1-880386-02-X*) Ctr Study Law.

Solid Waste Research & Development Needs for Emerging Coal Technologies: ASCE-PRC-EPRI Workshop Proceedings. Compiled by American Society of Civil Engineers Staff. 268p. 1979. pap. 23.00 (*0-87262-199-5*) Am Soc Civil Eng.

Solid Waste-Resource Recovery Management. International Research & Evaluation Staff. (Swm-1ser Ser.). 1978. 175.00 (*0-930318-06-4*) Intl Res Eval.

Solid Wastes: Factors Influencing Generation Rates. Douglas B. Cargo. LC 78-16823. (University of Chicago, Department of Geography, Research Paper Ser.: No. 174). 112p. 1978. reprint ed. pap. 32.00 (*0-608-02237-3*, 2062797) Bks Demand.

Solid Wastes: Origin, Collection, Processing, & Disposal. Charles L. Mantell. LC 74-26930. (Illus.). 1143p. reprint ed. pap. 180.00 (*0-685-23821-0*, 2056602) Bks Demand.

Solid Wastes Disposal & Control: Proceedings of the WHO Expert Committee, Debendorf, 1971. WHO Staff. (Technical Report Ser.: No. 484). 1971. pap. text ed. 5.00 (*92-4-120484-2*, 1100484) World Health.

Solid Wastes from Coal Fired Power Plants: Water Pollution Problems: Part of an IAWPRC International Conference on Coal Fired Power Plants & the Aquatic Environment, 16-18 August 1982, Copenhagen, Vol. 15/11. Ed. by S. H. Jenkins & P. Schjodtz Hansen. LC 83-19445. (Illus.). 258p. 1983. pap. 44.00 (*0-08-031026-5*, Pergamon Pr) Elsevier.

Solid Wood Cabinet Construction: Contemporary Designs with Details. Franz Karg. (Illus.). 144p. 1991. 26.95 (*0-942391-97-7*) Taunton.

Solidarite de la Famille Dans le Droit Criminel en Grece. Gustave Glotz. LC 72-7891. (Greek History Ser.). (FRE.). 1980. reprint ed. 47.95 (*0-405-04787-8*) Ayer.

***Solidarities of Strangers: The English Poor Laws & the People, 1700-1948.** Lynn H. Lees. (Illus.). 350p. (C). 1997. text ed. 54.95 (*0-521-57261-4*) Cambridge U Pr.

Solidarity. Denis MacShane. LC 81-16515. 8200. 40.00 (*0-85124-319-3*) Dufour.

***Solidarity: A Synthesis of Personalism & Communalism in the Thought of Karol Wojtyla/John Paul II.** Kevin Doran. (American University Studies: Vol. VII). 304p. (C). 1996. text ed. 47.95 (*0-8204-3071-4*) P Lang Pubng.

Solidarity: Poland's Independent Trade Union. Denis MacShane. LC 81-16515. 1982. 37.50 (*0-685-38820-4*, Pub. by Spkesman UK) Dufour.

Solidarity: The Analysis of a Social Movement; Poland 1980-1981. Alain Touraine et al. LC 83-1859. (Illus.). 256p. 1984. pap. 17.95 (*0-521-27595-4*) Cambridge U Pr.

Solidarity & Dissent: Union Member Attitudes & the Political Process. Peter Keisler. LC 84-82115. 76p. (Orig.). (C). 1984. pap. 11.75 (*0-942522-03-6*) Free Congr Res.

Solidarity & Fragmentation: Working People & Class Consciousness in Detroit, 1875-1900. Richard Oestreicher. LC 85-1030. (Working Class in American History Ser.). (Illus.). 296p. 1990. pap. text ed. 12.95 (*0-252-06120-9*) U of Ill Pr.

Solidarity & Poland: Impacts East & West. Ed. by Steve W. Reiquam. LC 87-29537. (Illus.). 72p. (Orig.). (C). 1988. pap. text ed. 9.00 (*0-943875-02-1*, Johns Hopkins); lib. bdg. 20.25 (*0-943875-05-6*, Johns Hopkins) W Wilson Ctr Pr.

Solidarity & Schism: The Problem of Disorder in Durkheimian & Marxist Sociology. David Lockwood. 472p. 1992. 95.00 (*0-19-827717-2*) OUP.

Solidarity & Survival: A Vision for Europe. John Lambert. 148p. 1994. 55.95 (*1-85628-871-4*, Pub. by Avebury Pub UK) Ashgate Pub Co.

Solidarity & Survival: An Oral History of Iowa Labor in the Twentieth Century. Shelton Stromquist. LC 93-13805. (Illus.). 360p. 1993. pap. 15.95 (*0-87745-431-0*); text ed. 39.95 (*0-87745-430-2*) U of Iowa Pr.

Solidarity & the Politics of Anti-Politics: Opposition & Reform in Poland since 1968. David Ost. (Labor & Social Change Ser.). 272p. (C). 1990. 39.95 (*0-87722-655-5*) Temple U Pr.

Solidarity & the Politics of Anti-Politics: Opposition & Reform in Poland since 1968. David Ost. (Labor & Social Change Ser.). 272p. (C). 1991. pap. 18.95 (*0-87722-900-7*) Temple U Pr.

Solidarity & the Soviet Worker. Elizabeth Teague. 400p. 1988. lib. bdg. 69.50 (*0-7099-4350-4*, Pub. by Croom Helm UK) Routledge Chapman & Hall.

Solidarity & Treason: Resistance & Exile, 1933-1940. Lisa Fittko. 1995. pap. text ed. 14.95 (*0-8101-1130-6*) Northwestern U Pr.

Solidarity & Treason: Resistance & Exile, 1933-40. Lisa Fittko. Tr. by Roslyn Theobald from GER. 150p. 1993. 22.50 (*0-8101-1129-2*) Northwestern U Pr.

Solidarity As Hermeneutics: A Revisionist Reading of the Theology of Walter Rauschenbusch. Darlene A. Peitz. LC 91-865. (American University Studies: Theology & Religion: Ser. VII, Vol. 122). 236p. (C). 1992. text ed. 46.95 (*0-8204-1753-X*) P Lang Pubng.

Solidarity Congress, Nineteen Eighty-One: The Great Debate. Ed. & Tr. by George Sanford. LC 89-70283. 175p. 1990. text ed. 45.00 (*0-312-04490-9*) St Martin.

Solidarity for Survival: The Don Thomson Reader on Trade Union Internationalism. Ed. by Mike Press & Don Thomson. 161p. 1989. 49.50 (*0-85124-510-2*, Pub. by Spokesman Bks UK) Coronet Bks.

Solidarity Forever: An Oral History of the I. W. W. Stewart Bird et al. LC 84-82491. (Illus.). 256p. 1985. 25.00 (*0-941702-11-1*); pap. 9.95 (*0-941702-12-X*) Lake View Pr.

Solidarity Forever: Rose Schneiderman & the Women's Trade Union League. Gary E. Endelman. 1981. 35.95 (*0-405-14079-7*) Ayer.

Solidarity in Economic Transactions: An Experimental Study of Framing Effects in Bargaining & Contracting. Paul E. Ligthart. 155p. 1995. pap. 25.00 (*90-5170-310-4*, Pub. by Thesis Pubs NE) IBD Ltd.

Solidarity in Poland, 1980-1981: And the Perspective of Political Revolution. Wolfgang Weber. Tr. by Bill Brust from GER. (Illus.). 157p. (Orig.). (C). 1989. pap. 11.95 (*0-929087-30-5*) Labor Pubns Inc.

Solidarity in the Conversation of Humankind: The Ungroundable Liberalism of Richard Rorty. Geras. 200p. (C). 1995. text ed. 65.00 (*0-86091-453-4*, C0530, Pub. by Vrso UK) Norton.

Solidarity in the Conversation of Humankind: The Ungroundable Liberalism of Richard Rorty. Norman Geras. LC 95-1097. 151p. (C). 1995. pap. text ed. 16.00 (*0-86091-659-6*, C0529, Pub. by Vrso UK) Norton.

Solidarity in the Heartland. Tom Frank & Dave Mulcahey. (Open Magazine Pamphlet Ser.). 30p. (Orig.). 1995. pap. text ed. 4.00 (*1-884519-17-2*) Open Media.

Solidarity of a Philosophe: Diderot, Russia & The Soviet Union. Peter H. Kaufman. LC 92-26546. (Age of Revolution & Romanticism Ser.: Vol. 4). 208p. (C). 1995. text ed. 49.95 (*0-8204-1997-4*) P Lang Pubng.

Solidarity of Strangers: Feminism after Identity Politics. Jodi Dean. LC 95-13906. 228p. 1996. pap. 16.00 (*0-520-20231-7*) U CA Pr.

Solidarity of Strangers: Feminism after Identity Politics. Jodi Dean. LC 95-13906. 228p. (C). 1996. 40.00 (*0-520-20230-9*) U CA Pr.

Solidarity or Egoism? The Economics of Sociotropic & Egocentric Influences on Political Behavior: Denmark in International & Theoretical Perspective. Douglas A. Hibbs, Jr. (Voters in Scandinavia Ser.: Vol. 1). (Illus.). 72p. (Orig.). (C). 1993. pap. 12.95 (*87-7288-452-5*, Pub. by Aarhus Univ Pr DK) David Brown.

Solidarity or Survival? American Labor & European Immigrants, 1830-1924. A. T. Lane. LC 86-25735. (Contributions in Labor Studies: No. 21). 242p. 1987. text ed. 55.00 (*0-313-25544-X*, LSV/, Greenwood Pr) Greenwood.

Solidarity, Solitude. Adam Zagajewski. Tr. by Lillian Vallee from POL. 240p. 1990. 19.95 (*0-88001-186-6*) Ecco Pr.

Solidarity Unionism. Contrib. by Mike Konopacki. 64p. (Orig.). 1992. pap. 9.00 (*0-88286-208-1*) C H Kerr.

Solidarity with the People of Nicaragua. James B. McGinnis. LC 84-27202. (Illus.). 176p. (Orig.). reprint ed. pap. 50.20 (*0-8357-8547-5*, 2034886) Bks Demand.

Solide maligne Tumoren im Kindesalter. E. Bern Rossi. (Paediatrische Fortbildungskurse fuer die Praxis Ser.: Vol. 39). (Illus.). 100p. 1974. 26.50 (*3-8055-1691-6*) S Karger.

***Solider of Freedom: Roosevelt.** James M. Burns. 1996. 14.98 (*0-7651-9919-X*) Smithmark.

Solidification. A. Ohno. (Illus.). 130p. 1987. 65.95 (*0-387-18233-0*) Spr-Verlag.

Solidification & Cast Structure. I. Minkoff. LC 85-9382. 240p. 1986. text ed. 299.00 (*0-471-90798-7*) Wiley.

Solidification & Stabilization of Wastes Using Portland Cement. rev. ed. 16p. 1991. pap. 12.00 (*0-89312-096-0*, EB071W) Portland Cement.

Solidification Characteristics of Aluminum Alloys, Vol. 2: Foundry Alloys. 266p. 150.00 (*0-87433-119-6*, NF9000) Am Foundrymen.

Solidification Characteristics of Some Copper Alloys. University of Stockholm Staff. (INCRA Monograph). 129p. 1982. 30.00 (*0-943642-08-6*) Intl Copper.

Solidification Characteristics of Twelve Commercial Copper-Base Alloys. Swedish Institute for Metal Research Staff. 103p. 1973. 15.45 (*0-317-34546-X*, 165) Intl Copper.

Solidification of Metal Matrix Composites: Proceedings of a Conference Jointly Sponsored by TMS Solidification Committee & TMS-ASM Composites Committee at Indianapolis, 1989. Ed. by Pradeep Rohatgi. LC 90-62372. 229p. 1990. reprint ed. pap. 65.30 (*0-608-00779-X*, 2061577) Bks Demand.

Solidification Process. J. F. Jansson. 1996. 73.00 (*3-7985-0911-5*) Spr-Verlag.

Solidification Processes in Polymers. Ed. by U. W. Gedde et al. (Progress in Colloid & Polymer Science Ser.: Vol. 87). 160p. 1992. 76.00 (*0-387-91408-0*) Spr-Verlag.

Solidification Processing. Merton C. Flemings. (Materials Science & Engineering Ser.). (Illus.). (C). 1974. text ed. write for info. (*0-07-021283-X*) McGraw.

Solidification Processing: Proceedings of International Conference, Ranmoor House, Sheffield, 21-24 Sept. 1987. International Conference Staff. 518p. (Orig.). 1988. pap. 94.50 (*0-901462-36-5*, Pub. by Inst Materials UK) Ashgate Pub Co.

Solidification Processing of Eutectic Alloys: Proceedings of a Symposium Sponsored by the TMS Solidification Committee & the Powder Metallurgy Committee Held at the TMS Fall Meeting, October 12-15, 1988, Cincinnati, Ohio. Ed. by D. M. Stefanescu et al. LC 87-43113. 267p. reprint ed. pap. 76.10 (*0-7837-1457-2*, 2052433) Bks Demand.

***Solidification Science & Processing.** Ed. by I. Ohnaka & D. M. Stefanescu. (Illus.). 307p. 1995. 110.00 (*0-87339-338-4*, 3384) Minerals Metals.

Solidly Built. Matt Townsend. (Orig.). 1996. mass mkt. 5.95 (*1-56333-416-X*, Badboy) Masquerade.

Solido Toys. Edward Force. LC 93-85083. (Illus.). 256p. 1993. pap. 16.95 (*0-88740-532-0*) Schiffer.

Solids. Marion Smoothey. LC 92-36220. (Let's Investigate Ser.). (J). (gr. 4 up). 1993. lib. bdg. 17.95 (*1-85435-469-8*) Marshall Cavendish.

Solids & Gas-Solids Flows. Ed. by Nicholas P. Cheremisinoff. LC 85-9742. (Encyclopedia of Fluid Mechanics Ser.: Vol. 4). (Illus.). 1376p. 1986. 195.00 (*0-87201-516-5*, 1516) Gulf Pub.

Solids & Liquids. David Glover. LC 92-40214. (Young Discoverers Ser.). 32p. (J). (gr. 1-4). 1993. 13.90 (*1-85697-845-1*, Kingfisher LKC); pap. 6.95 (*1-85697-934-2*, Kingfisher LKC); lib. bdg. 13.90 (*1-85697-634-3*, Kingfisher LKC) LKC.

Solids & Liquids Conveying Systems. fac. ed. Ed. by Mahesh V. Bhatia. LC 83-186611. (Process Equipment Ser.: No. 4). (Illus.). 260p. pap. 74.10 (*0-7837-7405-2*, 2047199) Bks Demand.

Solids & Surfaces: A Chemist's View of Bonding in Extended Structures. Roald Hoffmann. LC 88-14288. 142p. 1989. 30.00 (*0-89573-709-4*, VCH) Wiley.

Solids Far from Equilibrium. Ed. by C. Godreche. (Collection Alea - Saclay: Monographs & Texts in Statistical Physics: No. 1). (Illus.). 650p. (C). 1992. text ed. 140.00 (*0-521-41170-X*) Cambridge U Pr.

Solids in Cryogenic Liquids. Szczepaniec-Cieciak. (IUPAC Solubility Data Ser.). Date not set. 105.31 (*0-08-040500-2*, Pergamon Pr) Elsevier.

***Solids in Sewers: Selected Proceedings of the IAWQ International Specialized Conference on Sewer Solids - Characteristics, Movement, Effects & Control, Held in Dundee, Scotland, UK, 6-8 September, 1995.** Ed. by R. Ashley. (Water Science & Technology 33 Ser.). 298p. 1996. pap. text ed. 128.00 (*0-08-042901-7*, Pergamon Pr) Elsevier.

Solids, Liquids, & Gases. Jacqueline Barber. Ed. by Lincoln Bergman & Kay Fairwell. (Great Explorations in Math & Science (GEMS) Ser.). (Illus.). 64p. (Orig.). (J). (gr. 3-6). 1992. reprint ed. teacher ed., pap. 16.00 (*0-912511-69-9*) Lawrence Science.

Solids Separation & Mixing. fac. ed. Ed. by Mahesh V. Bhatia & Paul N. Cheremisinoff. LC 79-63114. (Process Equipment Ser.: No. 1). (Illus.). 309p. pap. 88.10 (*0-7837-7402-8*, 2047196) Bks Demand.

Solids under High Pressure Shock Compression: Mechanics, Physics, & Chemistry. R. A. Graham. LC 92-18580. (High Pressure Shock Compression of Condensed Matter Ser.). (Illus.). 240p. 1992. 98.95 (*0-387-97885-2*) Spr-Verlag.

Solids/Liquids Separation. Paul N. Cheremisinoff. LC 95-60053. (Process Engineering Handbook Ser.). (Illus.). 400p. 1995. pap. 49.95 (*1-56676-246-4*, 762464) Technomic.

Soliloquies & Immortality of the Soul. Augustine, Saint. Ed. by Watson. (Classical Texts Ser.). 1980. 49.95 (*0-85668-505-4*, Pub. by Aris & Phillips UK); pap. 24.95 (*0-85668-506-2*, Pub. by Aris & Phillips UK) David Brown.

Soliloquies in England & Later Soliloquies. George Santayana. (BCL1-PS American Literature Ser.). 264p. 1992. reprint ed. lib. bdg. 79.00 (*0-7812-6853-2*) Rprt Serv.

Soliloquies in Hamlet: The Structural Design. Alex Newell. LC 89-46410. (Illus.). 192p. 1991. 36.50 (*0-8386-3404-4*) Fairleigh Dickinson.

Soliloquies of Shakespeare: A Study in Technic. Morris L. Arnold. LC 78-58273. reprint ed. 37.50 (*0-404-00389-3*) AMS Pr.

***Soliloquist: Words Are Weapons.** Rita Haas. 483p. (Orig.). 1996. pap. 25.00 (*0-9654483-0-4*) R Hass.

Soliloquy in Nineteenth-Century Fiction. Carol H. MacKay. 208p. 1987. 48.00 (*0-389-20710-1*, N8268) B&N Imports.

Soliloquy of Prose. Robert F. Dives. (C). 1988. 24.00 (*0-7223-2337-9*, Pub. by A H S Ltd UK) St Mut.

Soliloquy of Satan, & Other Poems. Elliott B. Henderson. LC 72-37597. (Black Heritage Library Collection). 1977. reprint ed. 13.95 (*0-8369-8973-2*) Ayer.

Soliloquy! The Shakespeare Monologues: The Men. Ed. by Michael Earley & Philippa Keil. (Acting Ser.). 192p. (Orig.). 1987. pap. 7.95 (*0-936839-78-3*) Applause Theatre Bk Pubs.

Soliloquy! The Shakespeare Monologues: The Women. Ed. by Michael Earley & Philippa Keil. (Acting Ser.). 192p. (Orig.). 1987. pap. 7.95 (*0-936839-79-1*) Applause Theatre Bk Pubs.

Soliman & Perseda. Thomas Kyd. LC 78-133740. (Tudor Facsimile Texts. Old English Plays Ser.: No. 62). reprint ed. 59.50 (*0-404-53362-0*) AMS Pr.

Solis. A. A. Attanasio. 224p. 1995. mass mkt. 4.50 (*0-06-109092-1*, Harp PBks) HarpC.

Solitaire. Eugene Ionesco. (FRE.). 1976. pap. 10.95 (*0-8288-3695-7*, F106003) Fr & Eur.

Solitaire. Eugene Ionesco. (Folio Ser.: No. 827). 200p. (FRE.). 1973. pap. 9.25 (*2-07-036827-0*) Schoenhof.

***Solitaire & Brahms.** Sarah Dreher. LC 97-19545. 1997. pap. 12.95 (*0-934678-85-5*) New Victoria Pubs.

Solitaire Mystery. Jostein Gaarder. 356p. (YA). 1996. 24.00 (*0-374-26651-4*) FS&G.

***Solitaire Mystery.** Jostein Gaarder. 368p. 1997. reprint ed. mass mkt. 6.99 (*0-425-16047-5*) Berkley Pub.

***Solitaire Mystery: A Novel about Family & Destiny.** Jostein Gaarder. 368p. 1997. reprint ed. pap. 14.00 (*0-425-15999-X*, Berkley Trade) Berkley Pub.

Solitaire/Double Solitaire. Robert Anderson. 1971. pap. 5.25 (*0-8222-1050-9*) Dramatists Play.

Solitary Apprenticeship: James Wright & German Poetry. Saundra R. Maley. LC 96-22211. 718p. 1996. text ed. 139.95 (*0-7734-2257-9*, Mellen Univ Pr) E Mellen.

Solitary Blue. Cynthia Voigt. (Point Romance Ser.). 320p. (J). (gr. 7-9). 1993. pap. 4.99 (*0-590-47157-0*) Scholastic Inc.

Solitary Blue. Cynthia Voigt. LC 83-6007. 204p. (YA). (gr. 7 up). 1983. lib. bdg. 16.00 (*0-689-31008-0*, Atheneum Bks Young) S&S Childrens.

Solitary Blue Guide. 1995. pap. write for info. (*0-590-49632-8*) Scholastic Inc.

Solitary Comrade: Jack London & His Work. Joan D. Hedrick. LC 81-2969. (Illus.). 285p. reprint ed. pap. 81.30 (*0-7837-7077-4*, 2046889) Bks Demand.

Solitary Dance. Robert G. Lane. LC 82-81020. (Illus.). 240p. (Orig.). (C). 1983. 19.00 (*0-943104-82-3*) Serrell & Simons.

Solitary Heart. Amanda Carpenter. (Presents Ser.). 1994. mass mkt. 2.99 (*0-373-11635-7*, 1-11635-9) Harlequin Bks.

Solitary Journey: Cervantes' Voyage to Parnassus. Ellen D. Lokos. LC 90-2224. (Studies on Cervantes & His Times: Vol. 1). 230p. (C). 1991. text ed. 48.95 (*0-8204-1452-2*) P Lang Pubng.

Solitary Pillar: Montreal's Anglican Church & the Quiet Revolution. Joan Marshall. (McGill-Queen's Studies in Ethnic History). 232p. 1994. 39.95 (*0-7735-1224-1*, Pub. by McGill CN) U of Toronto Pr.

Solitary Places. Joan V. Schroeder. 368p. (Orig.). 1996. mass mkt. 6.99 (*0-425-15157-3*) Berkley Pub.

Solitary Places. Joan V. Schroeder. 288p. (Orig.). 1994. 22.95 (*0-399-13987-7*, Putnam) Putnam Pub Group.

Solitary Pleasures: The Historical, Literary & Artistic Discourses of Autoeroticism. Ed. by Paula Bennett & Vernon Rosario, 2nd. LC 95-22216. 288p. (C). (gr. 13). 1995. text ed. 55.00 (*0-415-91173-7*, C0240, Routledge NY) Routledge.

Solitary Pleasures: The Historical, Literary & Artistic Discourses of Autoeroticism. Vernon A. Rosario. LC 95-22216. 300p. (gr. 13). 1995. pap. 18.95 (*0-415-91174-5*, C0243, Routledge NY) Routledge.

Solitary Pussytoes: A Novel. Bonnie J. Dane. LC 94-17138. 144p. 1995. pap. 9.50 (*1-885187-00-9*) Back Alley Pr.

***Solitary Rider.** Diana Summers. LC 96-70688. 1997. 19.95 (*0-9651213-2-1*) Sligo Pr.

Solitary Satanist. Pat Holliday. 60p. 1993. pap. write for info. (*1-884785-00-X*) Miracle OutReach.

Solitary Self: Individuality in the Ancrene Wisse. Linda Georgianna. LC 81-2190. 184p. 1981. 27.50 (*0-674-81751-6*) HUP.

Solitary Self: Jean-Jacques Rousseau in Exile & Adversity. Maurice Cranston. LC 96-12922. (Illus.). 264p. 1997. 29.95 (*0-226-11865-7*) U Ch Pr.

Solitary Slocum: Captain Joshua Slocum. Robert Blondin & Hedley King. 196p. reprint ed. pap. 14.95 (*1-55109-026-0*, Pub. by Nimbus Publishing Ltd CN) Chelsea Green Pub.

Solitary Song: An Autobiography. Pauline Koner. LC 89-1546. (Illus.). xi, 306p. 1989. text ed. 34.95 (*0-8223-0878-9*) Duke.

Solitary Survivor: The First American POW in Southeast Asia. Lawrence R. Bailey & Ron Martz. (Association of the U. S. Army Book Ser.). (Illus.). 240p. 1996. 23.95 (*1-57488-004-7*) Brasseys Inc.

Solitary Traveller. Michele C. 20p. (Orig.). 1990. pap. 3.00 (*0-916397-13-0*) Manic D Pr.

Solitary Twist. Elizabeth Pincus. LC 93-84274. (Neil Fury Ser.). 225p. (Orig.). 1993. pap. 9.95 (*0-933216-93-9*) Spinsters Ink.

An Asterisk (*) at the beginning of an entry indicates that the title is appearing in BIP for the first time.

Solitary Voice: A Collection of Essays on Vardis Fisher. Dorys C. Grover. 1973. 250.00 (*0-87700-198-7*) Revisionist Pr.

Solitary Volcano. Humphrey Carpenter. (J). write for info. (*0-318-59414-5*) HM.

Solitary Waves in Plasmas & in the Atmosphere. Vladimir I. Petviashvili. x, 248p. 1992. text ed. 109.00 (*2-88124-787-3*) Gordon & Breach.

Soliton Equations & Hamiltonian Systems. L. A. Dickey. 320p. (C). 1991. text ed. 44.00 (*981-02-0215-6*) World Scientific Pub.

Soliton Phenomenology. Vladimir G. Makhankov. (Mathematics & Its Applications, Soviet Ser.). 464p. (C). 1990. lib. bdg. 222.50 (*90-277-2830-5*) Kluwer Ac.

Soliton Theory: A Survey of Results. Ed. by A. P. Fordy. (Nonlinear Science: Theory & Applications Ser.). 458p. 1992. text ed. 298.00 (*0-471-93520-4*) Wiley.

Soliton Theory & Its Applications. Ed. by Gu Chaohao. LC 95-34798. 1995. 135.00 (*0-387-57112-4*) Spr-Verlag.

Soliton Theory & Its Applications. Ed. by C. H. Gu. LC 95-34798. (Illus.). 415p. 1995. 125.00 (*3-540-57112-4*) Spr-Verlag.

***Solitons.** Akhmediev. 320p. 1997. text ed. 89.95 (*0-412-75450-9*, Chap & Hall NY) Chapman & Hall.

Solitons. M. Lakshmanan. (Nonlinear Dynamics Ser.). (Illus.). 420p. 1988. 72.95 (*0-387-18588-7*) Spr-Verlag.

Solitons. Ed. by V. L. Pokrovsky et al. (Modern Problems in Condensed Matter Sciences Ser.: Vol. 17). 927p. 1987. 336.25 (*0-444-87002-4*, North Holland) Elsevier.

Solitons: An Introduction. P. G. Drazin & R. S. Johnson. (Cambridge Texts in Applied Mathematics Ser.: No. 3). (Illus.). 230p. 1989. pap. text ed. 30.95 (*0-521-33655-4*) Cambridge U Pr.

Solitons: Mathematical Methods for Physicists. G. Eilenberger. (Solid-State Sciences Ser.: Vol. 19). (Illus.). 192p. 1983. 56.95 (*0-387-10223-X*) Spr-Verlag.

Solitons & Applications. Ed. by Vladimir G. Makhankov et al. 450p. (C). 1990. text ed. 130.00 (*981-02-0130-3*) World Scientific Pub.

Solitons & Chaos. Ed. by I. Antoniou & F. J. Lambert. (Research Reports in Physics). (Illus.). xvi, 333p. 1991. 75.95 (*0-387-54389-9*) Spr-Verlag.

Solitons & Geometry. S. P. Novikov. (Lezione Fermiane Ser.). 55p. (C). 1995. pap. text ed. 20.95 (*0-521-47196-6*) Cambridge U Pr.

Solitons & Instantons: An Introduction to Solitons & Instantons in Quantum Field Theory. R. Rajaraman. (North-Holland Personal Library). 410p. 1987. pap. 79.25 (*0-444-87047-4*, North Holland) Elsevier.

Solitons & Instantons, Operator Quantization. Ed. by V. L. Ginzburg. (Proceedings of the Lebedev Physics Institute Ser.: Vol. 165). 299p. (C). 1987. text ed. 130.00 (*0-941743-00-4*) Nova Sci Pubs.

Solitons & Nonlinear Systems. D. K. Sinha. (C). 1986. 27.00 (*81-7003-067-6*, Pub. by S Asia Pubs II) S Asia.

Solitons & Particles. Ed. by C. Rebbi & G. Soliani. 836p. 1984. text ed. 121.00 (*9971-966-42-5*); pap. text ed. 52.00 (*9971-966-43-3*) World Scientific Pub.

Solitons & Polarons in Conducting Polymers. L. Yu. 772p. 1988. text ed. 99.00 (*9971-5-0053-1*); pap. text ed. 47.00 (*9971-5-0054-X*) World Scientific Pub.

Solitons & Polarons in Solid State Physics. D. Baeriswyl & A. R. Bishop. 300p. (C). 1999. text ed. 79.00 (*9971-5-0407-3*); pap. text ed. 45.00 (*9971-5-0408-1*) World Scientific Pub.

Solitons & the Inverse Scattering Transform. M. J. Ablowitz & H. Segur. LC 81-50600. (Studies in Applied Mathematics: No. 4). x, 425p. 1982. text ed. 76.75 (*0-89871-174-6*) Soc Indus-Appl Math.

***Solitons, Bilinear Transformation & Theta Functions.** LC 96-46747. 1997. write for info. (*0-582-30403-2*) Longman.

Solitons in Liquid Crystals. Ed. by Lui Lam et al. (Partially Ordered Systems Ser.). (Illus.). 368p. 1991. 86.95 (*0-387-96878-4*) Spr-Verlag.

Solitons in Mathematics & Physics. Alan C. Newell. LC 84-71051. (CBMS-NSF Regional Conference Ser.: No. 48). xvi, 244p. (Orig.). 1985. pap. text ed. 42.00 (*0-89871-196-7*) Soc Indus-Appl Math.

Solitons in Molecular Systems. 2nd ed. A. S. Davydov. (Mathematics & Its Applications, Soviet Ser.). 426p. (C). 1990. lib. bdg. 213.50 (*0-7923-1029-2*) Kluwer Ac.

Solitons in Multidimensions: Inverse Spectral Transform Method. Boris G. Konopelchenko. LC 93-16338. 304p. 1993. text ed. 74.00 (*981-02-1348-4*) World Scientific Pub.

Solitons in Nuclear & Elementary Particle Physics: Proceedings of the Lewes Workshop. A. Chodos et al. 324p. 1984. 64.00 (*9971-966-89-1*) World Scientific Pub.

Solitons in Optical Communications. Akira Hasegawa & Yuji Kodama. (Oxford Series on Optical & Imaging Sciences: No. 7). (Illus.). 330p. 1995. 115.00 (*0-19-856507-0*) OUP.

Solitons in Physics, Mathematics, & Nonlinear Optics. Ed. by Peter J. Olver. (IMA Volumes in Mathematics & Its Applications Ser.: Vol. 25). (Illus.). xiii, 215p. 1990. 42.95 (*0-387-97309-5*) Spr-Verlag.

Solitons, Nonlinear Evolution Equations & Inverse Scattering. M. A. Ablowitz & P. A. Clarkson. (London Mathematical Society Lecture Note Ser.: No. 149). 400p. (C). 1992. pap. text ed. 54.95 (*0-521-38730-2*) Cambridge U Pr.

Solitude. Victor Catala, pseud. Tr. by David Rosenthal from CAT. 226p. (Orig.). 1992. 19.95 (*0-930523-91-1*); pap. 11.95 (*0-930523-92-X*) Readers Intl.

Solitude. Henry David Thoreau. 1996. pap. 1.99 (*0-679-77201-4*) Random.

Solitude: A Philosophical Encounter. Philip Koch. LC 94-8836. 389p. 1994. 39.95 (*0-8126-9242-X*); pap. 18.95 (*0-8126-9243-8*) Open Court.

Solitude: A Return to the Self. Anthony Storr. 1989. pap. 11.00 (*0-345-35847-3*, Ballantine Trade) Ballantine.

Solitude: Art & Symbolism in the National Basque Monument. Carmelo Urza. LC 93-2135. (Basque Ser.). (Illus.). 152p. (C). 1993. 34.95 (*0-87417-205-5*) U of Nev Pr.

Solitude & Privacy: A Study of Social Isolation, Its Causes & Therapy. Paul Halmos. LC 77-94608. 181p. 1970. reprint ed. text ed. 35.00 (*0-8371-2455-7*, HASO, Greenwood Pr) Greenwood.

Solitude & Society. Nikolai A. Berdiaev. Tr. by George Reavey from RUS. LC 70-98211. 207p. 1976. reprint ed. text ed. 35.00 (*0-8371-3250-9*, BESS, Greenwood Pr) Greenwood.

Solitude & the Sublime: Romantic Aesthetics of Individuation. Francis Ferguson. 256p. (C). 1992. pap. 16.95 (*0-415-90549-4*, Routledge NY) Routledge.

Solitude de la Pitie. Jean Giono. (FRE.). 1973. pap. 10.95 (*0-7859-2304-7*, 2070033309) Fr & Eur.

Solitude de la Pitie. Jean Giono. (Folio Ser.: No. 330). (FRE.). 1973. pap. 6.95 (*2-07-036330-9*) Schoenhof.

Solitude de la Pitie see Oeuvres Romanesques

Solitude Est Cercueil De Verre. Ray Bradbury. 371p. (FRE.). 1991. pap. 12.95 (*0-7859-2168-0*, 2070383946) Fr & Eur.

Solitude Improved by Divine Meditation. Nathanael Ranew. 341p. 1995. reprint ed. 24.95 (*1-57358-012-0*) Soli Deo Gloria.

Solitude in Society: A Sociological Study in French Literature. Robert F. Sayre. LC 77-16265. 256p. 1978. 26.50 (*0-674-81761-3*) HUP.

Solitude of Collectivism: Romanian Villagers to the Revolution & Beyond. David A. Kideckel. LC 92-31985. (Anthropology of Contemporary Issues Ser.). (Illus.). 280p. 1993. 47.50 (*0-8014-2746-0*); pap. 17.95 (*0-8014-8025-6*) Cornell U Pr.

Solitudes: From Rimbaud to Heidegger. Marc Froment-Meurice. LC 94-49400. (SUNY Series, Intersections). 239p. 1995. text ed. 49.50 (*0-7914-2523-1*); pap. text ed. 16.95 (*0-7914-2524-X*) State U NY Pr.

Solitudes Crowded with Loneliness. Bob Kaufman. LC 65-15673. (Orig.). 1965. pap. 6.95 (*0-8112-0076-0*, NDP199) New Directions.

Solitudes, Galleries, & Other Poems. Antonio Machado y Ruiz. Tr. by Richard L. Predmore from SPA. LC 86-32758. ix, 237p. 1987. text ed. 37.95 (*0-8223-0713-8*) Duke.

***Solitude's Lament & Other Stories.** Dan Siegel. 310p. (Orig.). 1998. mass mkt. 8.99 (*1-889501-69-7*, Appaloosa) Sovereign.

***Solitude's Lawman.** Ray Hogan. 192p. 1997. reprint ed. mass mkt. 3.99 (*0-8439-4317-3*, Leisure Bks) Dorchester Pub Co.

Soll und Haben. unabridged ed. Freytag. (World Classic Literature Ser.). (GER.). pap. 7.95 (*3-89507-007-6*, Pub. by Bookking Intl FR) Distribks Inc.

Sollen und Durfen: Philosophische Grundlagen der Ethischen Rechte und Pflichten. Herbert Spiegelberg. (Primary Sources in Phenomenology Ser.: No. 2). 272p. 1989. lib. bdg. 158.50 (*0-7923-0271-0*, Pub. by Klwr Acad Pubs NE) Kluwer Ac.

Sollicitudo Rei Socialis: On Social Concern. Pope John Paul, II. 104p. 1987. pap. 5.95 (*1-55586-205-5*) US Catholic.

Solnes Engineering Seismology. 1974. lib. bdg. 97.00 (*90-286-0513-4*) Kluwer Ac.

Solnhofen: A Study in Mesozoic Palaeontology. K. Werner Barthel et al. (Illus.). 236p. (C). 1994. pap. text ed. 27.95 (*0-521-45830-7*) Cambridge U Pr.

Solnhofen: A Study in Mesozoic Paleontology. K. W. Barthel et al. (Illus.). 250p. (C). 1990. text ed. 74.95 (*0-521-33344-X*) Cambridge U Pr.

Solo. Paul Geraghty. LC 95-13821. (Illus.). (J). (gr. k-2). 1996. 17.00 (*0-517-70908-2*, Crown); lib. bdg. 18.99 (*0-517-70909-0*, Crown) Crown Pub Group.

Solo. Jack Higgins. 1989. mass mkt. 5.50 (*0-671-67617-2*) PB.

Solo: On Her Own Adventure. Ed. by Susan F. Rogers. LC 96-6947. 288p. (Orig.). 1996. pap. 12.95 (*1-878067-74-5*) Seal Pr WA.

Solo see Life with an Electric Car

***Solo & Ensemble Singer.** John Armstrong. Ed. by Brian Busch. (Illus.). 48p. (Orig.). (C). 1995. teacher ed., pap. text ed. 12.95 (*0-89724-988-7*, SVB9601) Warner Brothers.

***Solo & Ensemble Singer.** John Armstrong. Ed. by Brian Busch. (Illus.). 20p. (Orig.). (C). 1995. student ed., pap. text ed. 3.95 (*0-89724-989-5*, SVB9601S) Warner Brothers.

Solo Canoeing: A Guide to the Fundamentals, Equipment, & Techniques for Running Solo in an Open Canoe. John Foshee. LC 88-2444. (Illus.). 224p. (Orig.). 1988. pap. 12.95 (*0-8117-2281-3*) Stackpole.

Solo Canoeing on Quietwater: Quietwater Paddling for Solo Canoeists. Lou Glaros. (Nuts-n-Bolts Guides Ser.). (Illus.). 32p. (Orig.). 1996. pap. 4.95 (*0-89732-185-5*) Menasha Ridge.

Solo Cello: A Bibliography of the Unaccompanied Violoncello Literature. Dimitry Markevitch. LC 89-23355. (Reference Books in Music: No. 12). viii, 113p. 1989. pap. 14.95 (*0-914913-11-5*) Fallen Leaf.

Solo Diners: The Untapped Mega-Market of the 1990s. Marya C. Alexander. LC 90-49846. 60p. (Orig.). 1990. pap. 30.00 (*0-9623572-3-5*) Rockbridge Pub.

Solo Diving: The Art of Self Sufficiency. Robert Von Maier. 121p. (Orig.). 1991. pap. text ed. 10.95 (*0-922769-13-3*) Watersport Pub.

Solo Dolci: The Italian Dessert Cookbook. Anna B. Benson. LC 96-19362. (Illus.). 208p. 1996. 19.95 (*1-56474-185-0*) Fithian Pr.

Solo Drive. Elaine Erickson. 64p. 1991. pap. 6.95 (*0-932616-38-0*) Brick Hse Bks.

Solo Faces. James Salter. LC 87-82585. 218p. 1988. reprint ed. pap. 12.00 (*0-86547-321-8*, North Pt Pr) FS&G.

Solo Flight. E. Truman Pearce. 16p. (J). (gr. 2 up). 1986. pap. text ed. 3.95 (*0-913277-18-5*) Summy-Birchard.

Solo Flights Through Shard Worlds by Mike Resnick. Mike Resnick. (Illus.). 172p. pap. 8.99 (*1-888993-01-4*) Dark Regions.

Solo Flights Through Shard Worlds by Mike Resnick. limited ed. Mike Resnick. (Illus.). 172p. 19.95 (*1-888993-00-6*) Dark Regions.

Solo for Alto Saxophone & Piano. B. Heiden. 12p. 1986. pap. 7.95 (*0-7935-2484-9*) H Leonard.

Solo Forms of Karate, Tai Chi, Aikido & Kung Fu. Bruce Tegner & Alice McGrath. (Illus.). 112p. 1981. pap. 8.00 (*0-87407-034-1*, T-34) Thor.

Solo Games: Twelve New Exciting Board Games to Be Played by One Person. H. David Jackson. LC 81-17685. (Illus.). 75p. (Orig.). 1982. pap. 12.95 (*0-930256-10-7*) Almar.

***Solo Girl.** Andrea D. Pinkney. (Illus.). 64p. (J). (gr. 2-4). 1997. lib. bdg. 13.89 (*0-7868-2265-1*) Hyprn Child.

***Solo Girl.** Andrea D. Pinkney. (Illus.). 64p. (J). (gr. 2-4). 1997. pap. 3.95 (*0-7868-1216-8*) Hyprn Ppbks.

Solo Guitar Improvisation. David Winters. (Illus.). 100p. (Orig.). 1996. pap. 15.00 (*0-9616283-4-0*) D Winters.

Solo Guitar Playing, Book I. 3rd ed. Frederick M. Noad. 272p. 1994. 18.00 (*0-02-870763-X*) Schirmer Bks.

***Solo Guitar Playing II.** Frederick Noad. 160p. 1997. pap. 16.95 (*0-8256-1307-8*, FN 10008) Music Sales.

Solo Hand. Bill Moody. 304p. 1996. mass mkt. 5.50 (*0-440-22322-9*) Dell.

Solo Hand. Bill Moody. 1994. 19.95 (*0-8027-3248-8*) Walker & Co.

Solo Improvisation Techniques for the Jazz Flute. Fazio & Nunes. 1990. 7.95 (*0-685-32126-6*, O509) Hansen Ed Mus.

Solo in an Instant. Emmanuel Piatos. (Illus.). 24p. (Orig.). (C). pap. 6.95 (*1-56516-033-9*) H Leonard.

Solo in the City: A Sourcebook for Singles in Metropolitan Denver. Daniel Bradford. 128p. (Orig.). 1985. pap. 6.95 (*0-9608012-3-5*) Metrosource Pubns.

Solo in the New Order: Language & Hierarchy in an Indonesian City. James T. Siegel. (Illus.). 346p. 1986. pap. text ed. 19.95 (*0-691-00085-9*) Princeton U Pr.

***Solo Keyboard Works: Franz Seydelmann.** Ed. by Berard Brauchli. (Music Archive Publications Ser.). 1997. text ed. 61.00 (*90-5702-060-2*, Harwood Acad Pubs) Gordon & Breach.

***Solo Keyboard Works: Franz Seydelmann.** Ed. by Bernard Brauchli. (Music Archive Publications Ser.). 1997. pap. text ed. 28.00 (*90-5702-061-0*, Harwood Acad Pubs) Gordon & Breach.

Solo La Voz see Only the Voice

***Solo Librarian's Sourcebook.** Judith A. Siess. LC 97-9949. 246p. 1997. 39.50 (*1-57387-032-3*) Info Today Inc.

Solo Lifestyles: A Single's Survival Guide to Making the Most of Your Mid to Later Years. Judy Salwen. 1995. pap. 12.95 (*0-935016-28-7*) Zinn Communs.

Solo Motets. Ed. by Ernest Warburton. (Johann Christian Bach Ser.: Vol. 18). 260p. 1989. text ed. 85.00 (*0-8240-6067-9*) Garland.

Solo Motets: Rome, No. II. Ed. by Ann Schnoebleen. (Solo Motets from the Seventeenth Century Ser.). 346p. 1989. reprint ed. text ed. 40.00 (*0-8240-0644-5*) Garland.

Solo Motets in Italy, Part 2: Lionardo Simonetti (compiler), Chirlanda Sacra Lib. 1, Op. 2 Venice, 1625, Motetti a Voce Sola da Diversi Ecclentissimi Autori... Lib. 1. Venice, 1645, Federico Vigoni (compiler), Sacre Armonie a Voce Sola di Diversi Celebri Autori, Milan, 1692. Ed. by Anne Schnoebelen. (Solo Motets from the Seventeenth Century Ser.: Vol. 3). 304p. 1987. text ed. 40.00 (*0-8240-0638-0*) Garland.

Solo Muere la Mano Que Te Escribe. Justo J. Padron. (Nueva Austral Ser.: Vol. 98). (SPA.). 1991. pap. text ed. 24.95 (*84-239-1898-X*) Elliots Bks.

Solo of Fortune. William Moss et al. (Cyberpunk Ser.). (Illus.). 80p. 1989. student ed. 10.00 (*0-937279-06-4*, CP 3101) R Talsorian.

Solo of Fortune, Vol. 2. Ross Winn et al. (Cyberpunk Ser.). (Illus.). 96p. (Orig.). 1994. pap. 12.00 (*0-937279-58-7*, CP3361) R Talsorian.

Solo para Muchachos. Frank H. Richardson. 112p. 1986. reprint ed. pap. 4.50 (*0-311-46929-9*) Casa Bautista.

***Solo para Ranas.** (Look-Look Bks.). (Illus.). 24p. (SPA.). (J). (ps-3). 1996. write for info. (*0-614-19549-7*, P12651-10, Golden Books) Western Pub.

***Solo Para Ranas.** (Spanish Golden Look Look Bks.). (J). write for info. (*0-307-72651-7*, P12651-10, Golden Books) Western Pub.

Solo Parenting: Raising Strong & Happy Families. Diane Chambers. 192p. (Orig.). 1997. pap. 12.95 (*1-57749-008-8*) Fairview Press.

Solo Parenting: Your Essential Guide. Kathleen McCoy. 1987. pap. 7.95 (*0-317-56843-4*, Plume) NAL-Dutton.

Solo Partner: Repairing Your Relationship on Your Own. Phil DeLuca. LC 96-14556. (Illus.). 240p. (Orig.). 1996. pap. 14.95 (*0-88179-129-6*) Hartley & Marks.

Solo Pieces for the Intermediate Violinist. Craig Duncan. 1993. 6.95 (*1-56222-801-3*, 94877) Mel Bay.

Solo Publishing. Teddy Milne. LC 90-63045. 100p. 1990. pap. 9.95 (*0-938875-23-X*) Pittenbruach Pr.

***So'lo Quieren la Verdad.** B. Hoskins. p. (SPA.). 1.50 (*0-8297-1455-3*) Life Pubs Intl.

Solo Readings. Marjorie Seligman & Sonya Fogle. 1945. pap. 5.25 (*0-8222-1052-5*) Dramatists Play.

Solo Repertoire & Reading Preliminaries, LV. 2A, Vol. 2. Contrib. by N. Jane Tan. 1995. 5.50 (*0-614-12708-4*) Willis Music Co.

Solo Repertoire & Reading Preliminaries, LV. 2B, Vol. 2. Contrib. by N. Jane Tan. 1995. 5.95 (*0-614-12709-2*) Willis Music Co.

***Solo Safari.** T. Cacek. 1994. 30.00 (*1-57157-058-6*) Safari Pr.

Solo Safari: Hunting Africa on Your Own Without a Professional Hunter. deluxe limited ed. T. Cacek. (Illus.). 240p. 1994. boxed 40.00 (*1-57157-003-9*) Safari Pr.

Solo Scenes from Great Writers. Sydney Thompson. 80p. 1947. 5.00 (*0-573-60075-9*) French.

Solo Sex: The Ultimate Do It Yourself Handbook for Men. Robert Osborne Baron. (Illus.). 150p. write for info. (*0-8290-1917-0*) Irvington.

Solo Sex: Advanced Techniques see Joy of Solo Sex

Solo Spinout: Stories & a Novella. Ann Nietzke. LC 95-47335. 196p. 1996. 22.00 (*1-56947-052-9*) Soho Press.

Solo Tabla Drumming of North India, 2 vols., Set. Robert S. Gottlieb. (C). 1993. 68.00 incl. audio (*81-208-1095-3*, Pub. by Motilal Banarsidass II) S Asia.

Solo Tabla Drumming of North India: Text & Commentary, 2 vols., Vol. 1. Robert S. Gottlieb. (C). 1993. write for info. (*0-318-72198-8*, Pub. by Motilal Banarsidass II) S Asia.

Solo Tabla Drumming of North India: Transcriptions, 2 vols., Vol. 2. Robert S. Gottlieb. (C). 1993. write for info. (*0-318-72199-6*, Pub. by Motilal Banarsidass II) S Asia.

Solo! The Best Monologues of the 80's: Women, Vol. 11. Ed. by Michael Earley & Philippa Keil. (Acting Ser.). 160p. (Orig.). 1987. pap. 7.95 (*0-936839-66-X*) Applause Theatre Bk Pubs.

Solo! The Best Monologues of the 80's: Men, Vol. 1. Michael Earley & Philippa Keil. (Acting Ser.). 160p. (Orig.). 1987. pap. 7.95 (*0-936839-65-1*) Applause Theatre Bk Pubs.

Solo Time U. S. A. Twenty-Three Easy Piano Solos by American Composers. 1948. pap. 4.95 (*0-8258-0224-5*, 04469) Fischer Inc NY.

Solo Trax Easy Disney Favorites: Trombone. 1987. pap. 10.95 incl. audio (*0-7935-2283-8*, 00847155) H Leonard.

Solo Trax Easy Disney Favorites: Viola. 1987. pap. 10.95 incl. audio (*0-7935-2710-4*, 00847157) H Leonard.

Solo Trax Super Hits: Clarinet. 1987. pap. 10.95 incl. audio (*0-7935-2298-6*, 00845542) H Leonard.

Solo Trax Super Hits: Flute. 1987. pap. 10.95 incl. audio (*0-7935-3515-8*, 00845541) H Leonard.

***Solo un Hombre - Just a Man.** Pamela Macaluso. (SPA.). 1997. mass mkt. 3.50 (*0-373-35195-X*, 1-35195-6) Harlequin Bks.

***Solo Verdura: The Complete Cookbook of Tuscan Vegetables.** Anne Bianchi. LC 97-9344. (Illus.). 224p. 1997. 25.00 (*0-88001-543-8*) Ecco Pr.

Sologub Twofold: English Verse Translations with Selected Russian Poems of F. K. Sologub. Fedor Sologub. Ed. by Vassar W. Smith. 40p. (C). (gr. 13). 1991. pap. text ed. 6.45 (*1-880964-00-7*) Zapizdat Pubns.

Sologub's Literary Children: Keys to a Symbolist's Prose. Stanley J. Rabinowitz. (Illus.). 176p. 1980. pap. 18.95 (*0-89357-069-9*) Slavica.

Soloist. Mark Salzman. 1995. pap. 11.00 (*0-679-75926-3*, Vin) Random.

Soloistic English Horn Literature (1736-1984) William W. McMullen. (Juilliard Performance Guides Ser.: No. 4). (Illus.). 1994. 54.00 (*0-918728-78-9*) Pendragon NY.

Soloistic Use of the Trombone in Eighteenth-Century Vienna. C. Robert Wigness. LC 74-8189. (Brass Research Ser.: No.2). 1978. pap. text ed. 6.00 (*0-914282-02-6*) Brass Pr.

Solomita, No. 3. Stephen. 1995. 20.00 (*1-883402-28-X*) S&S Trade.

***Solomon & His Temple.** W. W. Fereday. 1996. pap. 9.99 (*0-946351-36-8*, Pub. by John Ritchie UK) Loizeaux.

Solomon & Rehoboam. Gordon Lindsay. (Old Testament Ser.: Vol. 25). 1966. 1.95 (*0-89985-145-2*) Christ for the Nations.

Solomon & Sheba: Inner Marriage & Individuation. Barbara B. Koltuv. LC 92-44082. (Illus.). 160p. (Orig.). 1993. pap. 10.95 (*0-89254-024-9*) Nicolas-Hays.

Solomon & Solomonic Literature. Moncure D. Conway. LC 72-2032. (Studies in Comparative Literature: No. 35). 1972. reprint ed. lib. bdg. 75.00 (*0-8383-1478-3*) M S G Haskell Hse.

Solomon Bible Study Guide. rev. ed. (Swindoll Bible Study Guide Ser.). 1995. pap. 4.99 (*0-8499-8588-9*) Word Pub.

Solomon Church Baptisms, Seventeen Ninety-Three to Eighteen Fifty, Forestville, Virginia. Tr. by Lois B. Bowman & George M. Smith from GER. (Genealogical Source Bk.: No. 11). (Illus.). 58p. 1989. pap. 9.75 (*0-917968-15-8*) Shenandoah Hist.

Solomon Complex: Reading Wisdom in Old English Poetry. Elaine T. Hansen. (McMaster Old English Studies & Texts: No. 5). 240p. 1988. 40.00 (*0-8020-2618-4*) U of Toronto Pr.

Solomon Crow's Christmas Pockets & Other Tales. Ruth M. Stuart. LC 70-94744. (Short Story Index Reprint Ser.). 1977. 19.95 (*0-8369-3124-6*) Ayer.

Solomon D. Butcher: Photographing the American Dream. John E. Carter. LC 85-5835. (Illus.). x, 142p. 1985. 40.00 (*0-8032-1404-9*) U of Nebr Pr.

Solomon Decision Whose Child Is This? An Adoption Dialogue. Kate Pijanowski. LC 88-71629. 234p. (Orig.). 1989. pap. 9.95 (*0-934896-48-8*) Adopt Aware Pr.

Solomon Goldman Lectures, Vol. I. Ed. by Nathaniel Stampfer. 85p. (C). 1977. pap. 5.95 (*0-935982-03-5*, SGL-01) Spertus Coll.

Solomon Goldman Lectures, Vol. II. Intro. by Nathaniel Stampfer. 90p. (C). 1979. 7.95 (*0-935982-00-0*, SGL-02) Spertus Coll.

S

An Asterisk (*) at the beginning of an entry indicates that the title is appearing in BIP for the first time.

S

Solomon Goldman Lectures, Vol. III. Intro. by Nathaniel Stampfer. 100p. (C). 1982. 7.95 (*0-935982-01-9*, SGL-03) Spertus Coll.

Solomon Goldman Lectures, Vol. IV. Intro. by Nathaniel Stampfer. 149p. (C). 1985. 7.95 (*0-935982-02-7*, SGL-04) Spertus Coll.

Solomon Goldman Lectures, Vol. V. 1988. 7.95 (*0-935982-41-8*, SGL-05) Spertus Coll.

Solomon Goldman Lectures, Vol. VI. 1993. 15.00 (*0-935982-47-7*) Spertus Coll.

Solomon ibn Gabirol: Selected Religious Poems. Solomon Ibn Gabirol. Ed. by Israel Davidson. Tr. by Israel Zangwill. LC 73-2210. (JPS Library of Jewish Classics). 248p. 1974. pap. 9.95 (*0-8276-0060-7*) JPS Phila.

Solomon in All His Glory. Robert S. Lynd. LC 72-86769. (Essay Index Reprint Ser.). 1977. 21.95 (*0-8369-1420-1*) Ayer.

***Solomon Institute in Spirituotherapy.** Theron Messer & Charles Solomon. (Illus.). 230p. 1993. wbk. ed. 25.00 (*0-9622110-5-2*) Grace Minist.

Solomon Islands. Judith Diamond. LC 95-2691. (Enchantment of the World Ser.). 172p. (J). (gr. 5-9). 1995. lib. bdg. 30.00 (*0-516-02637-2*) Childrens.

***Solomon Islands.** 3rd ed. Mark Honan. (Illus.). 272p. 1997. pap. 17.95 (*0-86442-405-1*) Lonely Planet.

***Solomon Islands Campaign, Guadalcanal to Rabaul: Historiography & Annotated Bibliography.** Eugene L. Rasor. LC 96-41333. (Bibliographies of Battles & Leaders Ser.). 176p. 1997. text ed. 65.00 (*0-313-30059-3*) Greenwood.

Solomon Kane. Robert E. Howard. 1995. mass mkt. 5.99 (*0-671-87695-3*) Baen Bks.

Solomon Mangham: His Ancestors & Descendants. Vaughn Ballard. (Illus.). 369p. 1989. 45.00 (*0-685-26973-6*) Family Arlington.

Solomon on Sex. Joseph C. Dillow. LC 77-1049. 1982. pap. 9.99 (*0-8407-5813-8*) Nelson.

Solomon R. Guggenheim Museum. Bruce B. Pfeiffer. (Illus.). 96p. 1996. 24.95 (*0-8109-6889-4*) Abrams.

Solomon R. Guggenheim Museum from A to Z. Diane Waldman et al. (Illus.). 264p. (Orig.). 1992. pap. 19.95 (*0-89207-071-4*) S R Guggenheim.

Solomon Schechter. Norman Bentwich. 1964. 6.00 (*0-8381-3105-0*) USCJE.

Solomon Shilling - Come to Court. Frances D. Parsons. 1991. reprint ed. 12.00 (*0-87012-492-7*) McClain.

Solomon the Rusty Nail. William Steig. (Illus.). 32p. (J). (ps up). 1985. 16.00 (*0-374-37131-8*) FS&G.

Solomon the Rusty Nail. William Steig. (Sunburst Ser.). (Illus.). 32p. (J). (ps up). 1987. pap. 4.95 (*0-374-46903-2*) FS&G.

Solomonic Judgments: Studies in the Limitation of Rationality. Jon Elster. (Illus.). 248p. (C). 1989. text ed. 59.95 (*0-521-37457-X*); pap. text ed. 19.95 (*0-521-37608-4*) Cambridge U Pr.

Solomonic Literature. Moncure D. Conway. (Works of Moncure Daniel Conway Ser.). 1990. reprint ed. lib. bdg. 79.00 (*0-7812-2345-8*) Rprt Serv.

Solomon's Child. Tom Dulack. 1985. pap. 5.25 (*0-8222-1051-7*) Dramatists Play.

Solomon's House Revisited: The Organization & Institutionalization of Science. Ed. by Tore Frangsmyr. LC 90-37426. (Nobel Symposium Seventy-Five Ser.). 320p. 1990. 45.00 (*0-88135-066-4*, Sci Hist) Watson Pub Intl.

Solomon's Instruction of Things Hateful to God. Teacia E. Lucas. LC 95-94287. 50p. (YA). write for info. (*0-9646486-0-1*) TDE Lucas.

Solomons Island & Vicinity: An Illustrated History & Walking Tour. Richard J. Dodds. (Illus.). 80p. 1996. pap. 4.95 (*0-941647-12-9*) Calvert MM Pr.

***Solomon's Legacy: History of Ancient Israel.** Mayfield. 1992. pap. text ed. write for info. (*0-582-87121-2*, Pub. by Longman UK) Longman.

***Solomon's Prayer: Synchrony & Diachrony in the Composition of I Kings 8 16-61.** Eep Talstra. (Contributions to Biblical Exegesis & Theology Ser.: Vol. 3). 306p. 1993. pap. 35.75 (*90-242-3247-3*, Pub. by KOK Pharos NE) Eisenbrauns.

Solomon's Seal. large type ed. Hammond Innes. 556p. 1981. 25.99 (*0-7089-0654-0*) Ulverscroft.

Solomon's Sword: A Practical Guide to Conducting Child Custody Evaluations. Benjamin M. Schutz et al. LC 88-46085. (Social & Behavioral Science Ser.). 224p. text ed. 38.95 (*1-55542-141-5*) Jossey-Bass.

***Solomon's Temple: The European Building Crafts Legacy.** Photos by Laura Volkerding. (Illus.). 132p. 1996. 45.00 (*0-938262-30-0*, 620651) Ctr Creat Photog.

Solomon's Temple, Its History & Its Structure. W. Shaw Caldecott. 358p. 1967. reprint ed. spiral bd. 12.50 (*0-7873-0139-6*) Hlth Research.

Solon & Croesus & Other Greek Essays. Alfred E. Zimmern. LC 67-22130. (Essay Index Reprint Ser.). 1977. 23.95 (*0-8369-1016-8*) Ayer.

Solon Robinson, 2 vols., Set. Herbert A. Keller. 1936. 17.95 (*1-885323-09-3*) IN Hist Bureau.

Solon Robinson, Pioneer & Agriculturalist, 2 Vols, Set. Ed. by Herbert A. Kellar. LC 68-16242. (American Scene Ser.). (Illus.). 1968. reprint ed. lib. bdg. 95.00 (*0-306-71017-X*) Da Capo.

Solon Robinson, Pioneer & Agriculturist. Solon Robinson. Ed. by Herbert A. Kellar. LC 74-145268. (Illus.). 1971. reprint ed. 59.00 (*0-403-01183-3*) Scholarly.

Solon Robinson, Pioneer & Agriculturist Vol. I: 1825-1845. Herbert A. Keller. 582p. 1936. 9.95 (*1-885323-07-7*) IN Hist Bureau.

Solon Robinson, Pioneer & Agriculturist Vol. II: 1846-1851. Herbert A. Keller. 556p. 1937. 9.95 (*1-885323-08-5*) IN Hist Bureau.

Solon the Singer: Politics & Poetics. Emily Anhalt. 160p. (C). 1992. text ed. 54.00 (*0-8476-7782-6*); pap. text ed. 22.00 (*0-8476-7783-4*) Rowman.

Solos. Nubia Kai. LC 88-83010. 121p. (YA). (gr. 9-12). 1988. per. 8.50 (*0-916418-71-5*) Lotus.

Solos, Duets, Trios, & Choruses. Richard Kostelanetz. LC 91-90072. 64p. (Orig.). 1991. pap. 10.00 (*0-87924-030-X*) Archae Edns.

Solos for Classical Guitar. Fred Sokolow. (Carl Fischer's "All Time Favorites" Music Ser.). 148p. (Orig.). 1987. pap. 12.95 (*0-8258-0387-X*, ATF112) Fischer Inc NY.

Solos for English Horn Player with Piano Solos. 1986. pap. 16.95 (*0-7935-0872-X*, 50333080) H Leonard.

Solos for Flute. Donald Peck. (Carl Fischer's "All Time Favorites" Music Ser.). 48p. (Orig.). 1984. pap. 14.95 (*0-8258-0346-2*, ATF104) Fischer Inc NY.

Solos for Horn Player with Piano. 100p. 1986. pap. 15.95 (*0-7935-5400-4*, 50330050) H Leonard.

Solos for Jazz Alto Sax. Contrib. by Stuart Isacoff. (All That Jazz Ser.). 64p. (Orig.). 1985. pap. 8.95 (*0-8258-0382-9*, ATJ303) Fischer Inc NY.

Solos for Jazz Guitar. Contrib. by Fred Sokolow. (All That Jazz Ser.). 56p. (Orig.). 1988. pap. 8.95 (*0-8258-0399-3*, ATJ306) Fischer Inc NY.

Solos for Jazz Piano. Contrib. by John Rodby. (All That Jazz Ser.). 64p. (Orig.). 1988. pap. 9.95 (*0-8258-0398-5*, ATJ305) Fischer Inc NY.

Solos for Jazz Tenor Sax. Contrib. by Stuart Isacoff. (All That Jazz Ser.). 56p. (Orig.). 1985. pap. 9.95 (*0-8258-0381-0*, ATJ302) Fischer Inc NY.

Solos for Kids. pap. 19.95 incl. audio compact disk (*0-7935-4636-2*, 00740021) H Leonard.

Solos for the Alto Saxophone Player with Piano. 80p. 1986. pap. 14.95 (*0-7935-2585-3*, 50330580) H Leonard.

Solos for the Cello Player with Piano - Accompaniment. 60p. 1987. pap. 12.95 (*0-7935-5439-X*, 50329300) H Leonard.

Solos for the Clarinet Player with Piano. 96p. 1986. pap. 12.95 (*0-7935-2604-3*, 50330280) H Leonard.

Solos for the Flute Player with Piano Accompaniment. 76p. 1986. pap. 12.95 (*0-7935-2578-0*, 50329830) H Leonard.

Solos for the Harp Player. 76p. 1987. pap. 12.95 (*0-7935-0505-4*, 50330750) H Leonard.

Solos for the Oboe Player with Piano. 72p. 1986. pap. 14. 95 (*0-7935-5421-7*, 50330190) H Leonard.

Solos for the Percussion Player with Piano. 48p. 1986. pap. 14.95 (*0-7935-5545-0*, 50332090) H Leonard.

Solos for the Student Trombonist: An Annotated Bibliography. Vern Kagarice et al. LC 79-17000. (International Trombone Association Ser.: No. 8). 1979. pap. 5.00 (*0-914282-26-3*) Brass Pr.

Solos for the Tenor Saxophone Player. 76p. 1986. pap. 14. 95 (*0-7935-5407-1*, 50330570) H Leonard.

Solos for the Trombone Player with Piano Accompaniment. 56p. 1986. pap. 14.95 (*0-7935-5414-4*, 50330090) H Leonard.

Solos for the Trumpet Player with Piano. 88p. 1986. pap. 12.95 (*0-7935-5408-X*, 50329980) H Leonard.

Solos for the Tuba Player. Wekselblatt. 56p. 1986. pap. 13. 95 (*0-7935-5429-2*, 50330510) H Leonard.

Solos for the Vibraphone Player. 40p. 1986. pap. 12.95 (*0-7935-3973-0*, 50332660) H Leonard.

Solos for the Violin Player. 60p. 1986. pap. 12.95 (*0-7935-5443-8*, 50329870) H Leonard.

Solos for Viola Player: Piano. 56p. 1986. pap. 14.95 (*0-7935-0664-6*, 50329260) H Leonard.

***Solos for Young Violinists, Vol. 1.** Barbara Barber. 48p. (J). 1997. pap. 12.95 (*0-87487-988-4*, 0988) Summy-Birchard.

***Solos for Young Violinists, Vol. 2.** Barbara Barber. 56p. (J). 1997. pap. 12.95 (*0-87487-989-2*, 0989) Summy-Birchard.

***Solos for Young Violinists, Vol. 3.** Barbara Barber. 48p. (J). 1997. pap. 12.95 (*0-87487-990-6*, 0990) Summy-Birchard.

***Solos for Young Violinists, Vol. 4.** Barbara Barber. 48p. (J). 1997. pap. 12.95 (*0-87487-991-4*, 0991) Summy-Birchard.

***Solos for Young Violinists, Vol. 5.** Barbara Barber. 56p. (J). 1997. pap. 12.95 (*0-87487-992-2*, 0992) Summy-Birchard.

***Solos for Young Violinists, Vol. 6.** Barbara Barber. (J). 1997. pap. 12.95 (*0-87487-993-0*, 0993) Summy-Birchard.

***Solotype Catalog of Typefaces.** Dan X. Solo. pap. 12.95 (*0-486-27169-2*) Dover.

Soloveitchik Heritage: A Daughter's Memoir. Shulamit S. Meiselman. LC 95-17674. 1995. write for info. (*0-88125-525-4*) Ktav.

Soloview, the Character of Old Russia, Vol. 24. Ed. by Alexander V. Muller. 1987. pap. 15.00 (*0-87569-095-5*) Academic Intl.

Solow. Lynn Crawford. (House of Outside Ser.: Vol. 1). 88p. 1995. pap. 10.00 (*0-9638433-3-8*) Hard Pr MA.

Solstice. Grant Sandres. 44p. 1974. pap. 1.50 (*0-915242-05-2*) Pygmalion Pr.

Solstice: A Mystery of the Season. Jan Adkins. (Illus.). 128p. (YA). 1990. 12.95 (*0-8027-6970-5*); lib. bdg. 13.85 (*0-8027-6971-3*) Walker & Co.

Solstice Evergreen: History, Folklore & Origins of the Christmas Tree. Sheryl Karas. LC 90-1168. (Illus.). 188p. (Orig.). 1991. pap. 10.95 (*0-944031-26-9*) Aslan Pub.

***Solstice Evergreen: The History, Folklore & Origins of the Christmas Tree.** 2nd rev. ed. Sheryl A. Karas. (Illus.). 176p. 1997. pap. 14.95 (*0-944031-75-7*) Aslan Pub.

Solstice II. Ed. by Sandra L. Arlinghaus. (Monograph Ser.: No. 15). 1991. pap. 15.95 (*1-877751-53-7*) Inst Math Geo.

Solstice II. Paul J. Payack. Ed. by Merritt Clifton. (Illus.). 1976. pap. 1.00 (*0-686-18735-0*) Chthon Pr.

Solstice III. Ed. by Sandra L. Arlinghaus. (Monograph Ser.: No. 16). 1992. pap. 15.95 (*1-877751-54-5*) Inst Math Geo.

Solstice III. Paul J. Payack. Ed. by Merritt Clifton. (Illus.). 1977. 1.00 (*0-686-19655-4*) Chthon Pr.

Solstice IV. Ed. by Sandra L. Arlinghaus. (Monograph Ser.: No. 17). 1993. pap. 15.95 (*1-877751-55-3*) Inst Math Geo.

Solstice, or Star-Tales. Paul J. Payack. Ed. by Merritt Clifton. (Illus.). 1976. pap. 1.00 (*0-686-16727-9*) Chthon Pr.

Solstice Poems. Charles A. Baar. 40p. (Orig.). 1983. pap. 3.50 (*0-934852-53-7*) Lorien Hse.

Solstice Points. Robert Myers. 1988. pap. write for info. (*0-87500-022-3*) RKM Pub Co.

Solstice SunNet Manager: A Network Management Guide. John R. Graham & James B. Van Treese. LC 96-35381. (Illus.). 324p. 1996. pap. text ed., pap. 45.00 incl. disk (*0-07-912987-0*) McGraw.

Solstice, Vol. 1, No. 1: An Electronic Journal of Geography & Mathematics. Ed. by Sandra L. Arlinghaus. (Illus.). 50p. (Orig.). 1990. pap. 5.00 (*1-877751-51-0*) Inst Math Geo.

Soltane. Bounin. Ed. by Heath. (Exeter French Texts Ser.: Vol. 27). 115p. (FRE.). Date not set. pap. text ed. 19.95 (*0-85989-097-X*, Pub. by Univ Exeter Pr UK) Northwestern U Pr.

Solteria: Regocijate, Invierte, Descansa. Charles R. Swindoll. (Serie Realidades - Realities Ser.). 32p. (SPA.). 1990. pap. 1.79 (*1-56063-028-0*, 498112) Editorial Unilit.

Soltero. Bienvenido M. Noriega, Jr. Tr. by Roland S. Tinio. (Illus.). 159p. (Orig.). (ENG & TAG.). 1985. pap. 15.00 (*971-10-0252-3*, Pub. by New Day Pub PH) Cellar.

Soltero Empedernido: Husband Material. Rita Rainville. (Deseo Ser.). (SPA.). 1996. mass mkt. 3.50 (*0-373-35156-9*, 1-35156-8) Harlequin Bks.

Soltero en Apuros. Elizabeth Bevarly. (Silhouette Deseo Ser.: No. 149). 1996. mass mkt. 3.50 (*0-373-35149-6*, 1-35149-3) Harlequin Bks.

Soltis Variation of the Yugoslav Attack. Steve Mayer. (Studies in Contemporary Opening Theory). 280p. (Orig.). 1994. pap. 22.95 (*1-886040-16-8*) Hypermodern Pr.

Solubilities: Inorganic & Metal-Organic Compounds: A Compilation of Solubility Data from the Periodical Literature, Vol. 1. 4th ed. William F. Linke. LC 65-6490. 1491p. reprint ed. pap. 180.00 (*0-8357-4124-9*, 2052335) Bks Demand.

***Solubilities: Inorganic & Metal-Organic Compounds Vol. 2: A Compilation of Solubility Data from the Periodical Literature.** 4th ed. William F. Linke. LC 65-6490. 1918p. 1965. reprint ed. pap. 180.00 (*0-608-04425-3*, 2052335) Bks Demand.

Solubilities of Inorganic & Organic Compounds, 3 vols., Set. H. Stephen et al. LC 79-40319. 7300p. 1979. 3,254.00 (*0-08-023599-9*, Pub. by Pergamon Repr UK) Franklin.

Solubilities of Inorganic & Organic Compounds, Vol 3. H. Stephen. 1971. 1,489.00 (*0-08-023570-0*, Pub. by Pergamon Repr UK) Franklin.

Solubility & PH Calculations. James N. Butler. LC 64-15563. (Chemistry Ser.). (Orig.). (gr. 9 up). 1964. pap. write for info. (*0-201-00733-9*) Addison-Wesley.

Solubility & Related Properties. James. (Drugs & the Pharmaceutical Sciences Ser.: Vol. 28). 440p. 1986. 160. 00 (*0-8247-7484-1*) Dekker.

Solubility Behavior of Organic Compounds. David J. Grant. 656p. 1990. text ed. 198.00 (*0-471-61314-2*) Wiley.

Solubility Data Series. Incl. Vol. 31. Alkali Metal Orthophosphates. Ed. by J. Eysseltova & T. P. Dirkse. (Illus.). 368p. 1988. 157.00 (*0-08-035937-X*, Pergamon Pr); Sulfites, Selenites & Tellurites. Ed. by M. R. Masson et al. (Illus.). 451p. 1986. 130.00 (*0-08-032518-1*, Pergamon Pr); Sulfites, Selenites & Tellurites. Ed. by M. R. Masson et al. (Illus.). 474p. 1986. 142.00 (*0-08-032517-3*, E125, E120, Pergamon Pr); Vol. 25. Metals in Mercury. Ed. by C. Hirayama et al. 471p. 1986. 142.00 (*0-08-023921-8*, Pergamon Pr); Vol. 24. Propane, Butane & 2-Methylpropane. Ed. by W. Hayduk. 447p. 1986. 130.00 (*0-08-029203-8*, Pub. by PPL UK); Vol. 24. Propane, Butane & 2-Methylpropane. Ed. by W. Hayduk. 470p. 1986. 142.00 (*0-08-029202-X*, Pub. by PPL UK); Tetraphenylborates. Popouych. 260p. 1981. 155.00 (*0-08-023928-5*, Pergamon Pr); Vol. 45 & 46. Gases in Molten Salts. Ed. by R. P. Tomkins & N. P. Bansal. 574p. 1991. 263.75 (*0-08-030735-3*, Pergamon Pr); Vol. 47. Alkali Metal & Ammonium Chlorides in Water & Heavy Water (Binary Systems). Ed. by R. Cohen-Adad & J. W. Lorimer. 564p. 1991. 130.25 (*0-08-023918-8*, Pergamon Pr); Vol. 41. Alkaline Earth Metal Perchlorates. Ed. by Chan Chee-Yan et al. LC 85-641351. 304p. 1989. 111.25 (*0-08-040198-8*, Pergamon Pr); No. 43. Carbon Monoxide. Ed. by R. W. Cargill. (Illus.). 330p. 1990. 111.25 (*0-08-030733-7*, 1901; 1906; 230, Pergamon Pr); Vol. 40. Halides, Oxyhalides & Salts of Halogen Complexes of Titanium, Zirconium, Hafnium, Vanadium, Niobium & Tantalum. Ed. by J. Hala. 364p. 1989. 111.25 (*0-08-036239-7*, 1904; 1907, Pergamon Pr); No. 36. 4-Aminobenzenesulfonamides Pt. III: 6-Membered Heterocyclic Substituents & Miscellaneous Systems. Ed. by A. N. Paruta & R. Piekos. (Illus.). 554p. 1988. 157.00 (*0-08-034710-X*, Pergamon Pr); Molten Alkali Metal Alkanoates. Ed. by P. Franzosini et al. (Illus.). 382p. 1988. 157.00 (*0-08-032522-X*, Pergamon Pr); Vol. 32. Hydrogen Sulfide, Deuterium Sulfide & Hydrogen Selenide. Ed. by P. G. Fogg & C. L. Young. (Illus.). 368p. 1988. 170.00 (*0-08-032481-9*, Pergamon Pr); No. 35. 4-Aminobenzenesulfonamides Pt. II: 5-Membered Heterocyclic Substituents. Ed. by A. N. Paruta & R. Piekos. (Illus.). 372p. 1988. 157.00 (*0-08-034708-8*, Pergamon Pr); No. 34. 4-Aminobenzenesulfonamides Pt. I: Non-Cyclic Substituents. Ed. by A. N. Paruta & R. Piekos. (Illus.). 372p. 1988. 157.00 (*0-08-030742-6*, Pergamon Pr); Methane. Ed. by H. L. Clever & C. L. Young. (Illus.). 801p. 1987. 260.00 (*0-08-029201-1*, Pergamon Pr); Vol. 23. Copper, Silver, Gold & Zinc, Cadmium, Mercury Oxides & Hydroxides. Ed. by T. P. Dirkse. 380p. 1986. 142.00 (*0-08-032497-5*, E125, E120, Pub. by PPL UK); Vol. 19. Cumulative Index: Volumes 1-18. Ed. by C. L. Young. 310p. 1985. 142.00 (*0-08-032495-9*, Pub. by PPL UK); Vol. 16 & 17. Antibiotics I: Beta-Lactams. Ed. by E. Tomlinson & A. Regosz. 812p. 1985. 280.25 (*0-08-029235-6*, Pergamon Pr); Vol. 30. Alkali Metal Halates, Ammonium Iodate & Iodic Acid. A. S. Miyamoto & M. Salamon. (JPN.). 1983. Japanese ed. 130.00 (*0-08-029211-9*, Pergamon Pr); Vol. 30. Alkali Metal Halates, Ammonium Iodate & Iodic Acid. A. S. Miyamoto & M. Salamon. 534p. 1987. 157.00 (*0-08-029210-0*, Pergamon Pr); Vol. 9. Ethane. Ed. by W. Hayduk & Kertes. 286p. 1982. 142.00 (*0-08-026230-9*, Pergamon Pr); Hydrogen Halides in Non-Aqueous Solvents: Gas Solubilities. P. G. Fogg & W. Gerrard. 496p. 1989. 111.25 (*0-08-023925-0*, Pergamon Pr); Alkali- & Alkaline-Earth Metal Oxides & Hydroxides in Water: Solubilities of Solids. Bauman. 389p. 1992. 121.75 (*0-08-023920-X*, Pergamon Pr); write for info. (*0-08-044420-2*, Pergamon Pr) Elsevier.

Solubility Data Series, 5 vols., Set. Incl. Vol. 1. Long Range Mineral Resources & Growth. 1977. 148.00 (*0-08-021445-2*); Vol. 2. Long Range Energetic Resources & Growth. 1977. 86.00 (*0-08-021446-0*); Vol. 3. Biological Balance & Thermal Modification. 1977. 145.00 (*0-08-021447-9*); Vol. 4. Design of Global System Models & Their Limitations. 1977. 120.00 (*0-08-021448-7*); Vol. 5. Conclusions & Perspectives. 1977. 97.00 (*0-08-021449-5*); 1977. 594.00 (*0-08-021850-4*, Pub. by Pergamon Repr UK) Franklin.

Solubility of Gases & Solids: A Literature Source Book, Set, Pts. A & B. J. Wisniak & M. Herskowitz. (Physical Sciences Data Ser.: Vol. 18). 1984. Set. 690.75 (*0-444-42300-1*) Elsevier.

Solubility of Gases in Liquids: A Critical Evaluation of Gas-Liquid Systems in Theory & Practice. P. G. Fogg & W. Gerrard. LC 90-45670. 332p. 1991. text ed. 339.00 (*0-471-92925-5*) Wiley.

Solubility of Magnetite in Water & in Aqueous Solutions of Acid & Alkali. G. Bohnsack. 161p. 1988. 106.00 (*0-89116-831-1*) Hemisp Pub.

***Solubility Test to Confirm the Presence of Sickling Hemoglobins.** (Approved Standard Ser.: Vol. 6). 1995. 75.00 (*1-56238-274-8*, H10-A2) Natl Comm Clin Lab Stds.

***Solubility Testing of Actinides on Breathing-Zone & Area Air Samples.** 1997. lib. bdg. 250.95 (*0-8490-7722-2*) Gordon Pr.

Solubilization in Surfactant Aggregates. John F. Scamehorn. (Surfactant Science Ser.: 55). 568p. 1995. 195.00 (*0-8247-9099-5*) Dekker.

Soluble & Nilpotent Linear Groups. Dimitri A. Suprunenko. LC 63-20676. (Translations of Mathematical Monographs: Vol. 9). 93p. 1963. reprint ed. 34.00 (*0-8218-1559-8*, MMONO/9) Am Math.

Soluble Coffee: Technical & Marketing Opportunities & Constraints for Origin Producers. A. Hone. 1993. pap. 30.00 (*0-85954-339-0*, Pub. by Nat Res Inst UK) St Mut.

An Asterisk (*) at the beginning of an entry indicates that the title is appearing in BIP for the first time.

Soluble Silicates. fac. ed. Ed. by James S. Falcone. LC 82-11514. (ACS Symposium Ser.: No. 194). (Illus.). 375p. 1982. reprint ed. pap. 106.90 (*0-608-00972-5*, 2061826) Bks Demand.

***Solucionando Creativamente los Conflictos de la Ninez, Grade 4.** Fran Schmidt & Alice Friedman. Ed. & Tr. by Yvonne W. Sepulveda. (Illus.). 92p. (Orig.). (ENG & SPA.). Date not set. teacher ed., pap. text ed. 23.95 (*1-878227-30-0*) Peace Educ.

Solucionario del Libro "Elementos de Matematica Comercial" de Ruperto Vazquez Cruz. Lourdes Correa. 251p. 1969. pap. 2.50 (*0-8477-2604-5*) U of PR Pr.

Soluciones A los Problemas De. Billy Graham. 240p. (SPA.). 1991. 1.50 (*0-8297-0392-6*) Life Pubs Intl.

***Soluciones Para los Problemas.** D. Cho. (SPA.). pap. 6.95 (*0-8297-0999-1*) Life Pubs Intl.

Soluna: Collected Earlier Poems. Madison Morrison. 287p. 1989. text ed. 30.00 (*81-207-1035-5*, Pub. by Sterling Pubs II) Apt Bks.

Solute Effects in Very Dilute Ternary Copper Alloys. Stevens Institute of Technology Staff. 22p. 1981. write for info. (*0-318-60408-6*) Intl Copper.

Solute Modelling in Catchment Systems. Ed. by Stephen T. Trudgill. LC 94-49356. 486p. 1995. text ed. 155.00 (*0-471-95717-8*) Wiley.

Solute Processes. Ed. by Stephen T. Trudgill. LC 85-9557. (Landscape Systems Ser.). (Illus.). 528p. reprint ed. pap. 150.50 (*0-7837-4520-6*, 2044299) Bks Demand.

Solute-Solvent Interactions, Vol. 2. Ed. by J. F. Coetzee & Calvin D. Ritchie. LC 69-12718. (Illus.). 473p. reprint ed. pap. 134.90 (*0-7837-4721-7*, 2041263) Bks Demand.

Solute-Solvent Interactions, 1969, Vol. 1. Ed. by J. F. Coetzee & Calvin D. Ritchie. LC 69-12718. (Illus.). 669p. reprint ed. pap. 180.00 (*0-7837-0958-7*, 2041263) Bks Demand.

Solute Transport in Plants. T. J. Flowers & A. Yeo. LC 91-46830. (Tertiary Level Biology Ser.). 200p. 1992. 75.00 (*0-216-93221-1*, A6867, Pub. by Blackie Acad & Prof UK); pap. 37.50 (*0-216-93220-3*, A6871, Pub. by Blackie Acad & Prof UK) Routledge Chapman & Hall.

Solution. 1991. write for info. (*0-9628273-2-0*) Tecstor Corp.

Solution. Ruth Stone. 1989. 25.00 (*0-9621666-3-4*) Haw River Bk.

Solution: Marriage. 1993. mass mkt. 5.50 (*0-373-20096-X*, 1-20096-3) Silhouette.

***Solution: The 6 Causes & 6 Cures of Weight Problems.** Laurel M. Mellin. LC 96-50876. (Illus.). 304p. 1997. 25.00 (*0-06-039186-3*, ReganBooks) HarpC.

Solution Behavior of Surfactants: Theoretical & Applied Aspects, 2 vols., Vol. 1. Ed. by K. L. Mittal et al. LC 82-10120. 770p. 1982. 135.00 (*0-306-41025-7*, Plenum Pr) Plenum.

Solution Behavior of Surfactants: Theoretical & Applied Aspects, 2 vols., Vol. 2. Ed. by K. L. Mittal et al. LC 82-10120. 822p. 1982. 135.00 (*0-306-41026-5*, Plenum Pr) Plenum.

Solution Book: A Guide to Class Discipline. Randall S. Sprick. 1988. Incl. binder, booklets, sheets & charts. ring bd. 68.50 (*0-574-78010-6*, 7-8010) SRA.

Solution Calorimetry Experimental Thermodynamics, IV, IV. K. N. Marsh & P. A. O'Hare. (Illus.). 352p. 1994. 105.00 (*0-86542-852-2*) Blackwell Sci.

Solution Chemistry of Surfactants, 2 vols., Vol. 1. Ed. by K. L. Mittal. LC 79-15067. 542p. 1979. 115.00 (*0-306-40174-6*, Plenum Pr) Plenum.

Solution Chemistry of Surfactants, 2 vols., Vol. 2. Ed. by K. L. Mittal. LC 79-15067. 460p. 1979. 115.00 (*0-306-40175-4*, Plenum Pr) Plenum.

Solution Focused Financial Counseling. 3rd rev. ed. Fred E. Waddell. 244p. 1996. wbk. ed., ring bd. 49.95 (*0-9615923-6-2*) Genesis Finan Srvs.

***Solution-Focused Pastoral Counseling: An Effective Short-Term Approach for Getting People Back on Track.** Charles A. Kollar. LC 96-51062. 256p. 1997. 19.99 (*0-310-21346-0*) Zondervan.

***Solution-Focused Therapy: A Casebook.** 184p. 1996. pap. 9.00 (*1-879771-14-4*) Global Pub NJ.

***Solution-Focused Therapy with Children: Harnessing Family Strengths for Systemic Change.** LC 97-27. 1997. lib. bdg. 27.95 (*1-57230-230-5*, 0230) Guilford Pr.

Solution Group. Bruce Dawson. LC 93-8758. 190p. (Orig.). 1993. pap. 12.00 (*0-944337-16-3*, 163) New View Pubns.

Solution in Asia. Owen Lattimore. LC 72-4439. reprint ed. 31.50 (*0-404-10635-8*) AMS Pr.

Solution Key for Pascal Computer Programming '88. Golden. 1988. teacher ed., pap. 84.00 (*0-15-359112-9*) H Holt & Co.

Solution Machine - So Simple It Works: The Creative Problem Solving Program That Harnesses the Power of Imagery. Kenneth Finn. (Illus.). 26p. (Orig.). 1991. pap. text ed. 150.00 (*0-9628982-0-1*, TX-2-940-660) Gemini Group.

Solution Manual for Structural Dynamics. 6th ed. Mario Paz. 1991. pap. 19.95 (*0-442-00806-6*) Van Nos Reinhold.

Solution Manual to Accompany Horowitz. Anderson. (C). 1995. write for info. (*0-7167-8234-0*, Computer Sci Pr) W H Freeman.

Solution Mining: Leaching & Fluid Recovery of Methods. Robert W. Bartlett. LC 92-4419. 276p. 1992. text ed. 79.00 (*2-88124-546-3*) Gordon & Breach.

Solution Mining Symposium, 1974: Proceedings of a Symposium, 103rd AIME Annual Meeting, Dallas, Texas, Feb. 25-27, 1974. Ed. by F. F. Aplan et al. LC 73-94005. 479p. reprint ed. pap. 136.60 (*0-317-29727-9*, 2017422) Bks Demand.

Solution of a Nondomestic Tame Classification Problem from Integral Representation Theory of Finite Groups (A equals RC3, v(3) equals 4) Dieterich. LC 91-15023. (Memoirs Ser.). 140p. 1991. 24.00 (*0-8218-2521-6*, MEMO/92/450) Am Math.

Solution of Continuous Nonlinear PDEs Through Order Completion. Michael B. Oberguggenberger & Elemer E. Rosinger. LC 94-19266. (Mathematics Studies: Vol. 181). 448p. 1994. 162.50 (*0-444-82035-3*, North Holland) Elsevier.

Solution of Crack Problems: The Distributed Disclocation Technique. D. A. Hills et al. LC 95-47426. (Solid Mechanics & Its Applications Ser.: Vol. 44). 297p. 1996. lib. bdg. 159.00 (*0-7923-3848-0*) Kluwer Ac.

Solution of Doctor Resolutus, His Resolutions for Kneeling. David Calderwood. LC 79-84093. (English Experience Ser.: No. 913). 60p. 1979. reprint ed. lib. bdg. 15.00 (*90-221-0913-5*) Walter J Johnson.

Solution of Initial Value Problems in Classes of Generalized Analytic Functions. W. Tutschke. 210p. 1989. 59.95 (*0-387-50216-5*) Spr-Verlag.

Solution of Large Networks by Matrix Methods. 2nd ed. Homer E. Brown. LC 85-5380. 336p. reprint ed. pap. 95.80 (*0-7837-2835-2*, 2057637) Bks Demand.

Solution of Nutritional Problems: The Contribution of Producers, Distributors & Nutritionists. Ed. by J. C. Somogyi. (Bibliotheca Nutritio et Dieta Ser.: No. 28). (Illus.). 1979. pap. 116.00 (*3-8055-3025-0*) S Karger.

Solution of Ordinary Differential Equations. Ian N. Sneddon. LC 86-2945. (Longman Mathematical Texts Ser.). 244p. reprint ed. pap. 69.60 (*0-7837-4034-4*, 2043863) Bks Demand.

Solution of Partial Differential Equations on Vector & Parallel Computers. James M. Ortega & Robert G. Voigt. LC 85-61387. (Miscellaneous Bks.: No. 13). iii, 96p. 1985. pap. 18.00 (*0-89871-055-3*) Soc Indus-Appl Math.

Solution of Social Problems: Five Perspectives. 2nd ed. Ed. by Martin S. Weinberg et al. 234p. (C). 1981. pap. text ed. 16.95 (*0-19-502787-6*) OUP.

Solution of Superlarge Problems in Computational Mechanics. Ed. by James H. Kane et al. LC 89-22932. (Illus.). 310p. 1989. 95.00 (*0-306-43370-2*, Plenum Pr) Plenum.

***Solution of the Problem of Mind & Matter.** J. H. Greidanus. (Verhandelingen der Koninklijke Nederlandse Akademie van Wetenschappen, Afd. Natuurkunde Ser.: No. 30). 46p. pap. 18.75 (*0-444-85527-0*) Elsevier.

Solution of the Truncated Complex Moment Problem for Flat Data. Raul E. Curto & Lawrence A. Fialkow. LC 95-39135. (Memoirs of the American Mathematical Society Ser.: Vol. 568). 52p. 1996. pap. 32.00 (*0-8218-0485-5*, MEMO/119/568) Am Math.

Solution of the Voynich Manuscript. Leo Levitov. 176p. (Orig.). 1987. pap. 34.80 (*0-89412-148-0*) Aegean Park Pr.

Solution of Variational Inequalities in Mechanics. J. Haslinger et al. (Applied Mathematical Sciences Ser.: Vol. 66). (Illus.). 325p. 1988. 71.95 (*0-387-96597-1*) Spr-Verlag.

Solution-Oriented Brief Therapy for Adjustment Disorders: A Guide for Providers under Managed Care. Daniel L. Araoz & Marie A. Carrese. (Mental Health Practice under Managed Care Ser.: No. 3). 176p. 1996. pap. text ed. 21.95 (*0-87630-790-X*) Brunner-Mazel.

***Solution-Oriented Counseling in Middle & High Schools.** John Murphy. LC 97-5511. 250p. (Orig.). 1997. pap. text ed. 23.95 (*1-55620-170-2*, 72640) Am Coun Assn.

Solution-Oriented Hypnosis: An Ericksonian Approach. William H. O'Hanlon & Michael Martin. LC 92-16410. 180p. (C). 1992. 22.95 (*0-393-70149-2*) Norton.

Solution-Oriented Woman: Creating the Life You Want. Pat Hudson. LC 95-33349. 128p. 1996. 19.95 (*0-393-03825-4*) Norton.

Solution Passage: Poems 1978-1981. Clark Coolidge. 390p. 1986. 18.95 (*0-940650-55-X*); pap. 11.95 (*0-940650-54-1*) Sun & Moon CA.

Solution Passage: Poems 1978-1981. deluxe limited ed. Clark Coolidge. 390p. 1986. 30.00 (*0-940650-59-2*) Sun & Moon CA.

Solution Properties of Polysaccharides. Ed. by David A. Brant. LC 81-236. (ACS Symposium Ser.: No. 150). 1981. 63.95 (*0-8412-0609-0*) Am Chemical.

***Solution Properties of Polysaccharides: Based on a Symposium.** Ed. by David A. Brant. LC 81-236. (ACS Symposium Ser.: Vol. 150). 592p. 1981. reprint ed. pap. 168.80 (*0-608-03036-8*, 2063489) Bks Demand.

Solution Selling: A System for Difficult to Sell Products. 91th ed. Michael Bosworth. 270p. 1994. text ed. 27.50 (*0-7863-0315-8*) Irwin Prof Pubng.

Solution Selling: The Grid Science Approach. Robert R. Blake & Rachel K. McKee. LC 94-1065. 1994. 29.95 (*0-88415-161-1*) Gulf Pub.

***Solution Sets of Diffrential Equations in Abstract Spaces.** Roberto Dragoni. (Pitman Research Notes in Mathematics Ser.). 1996. pap. 35.98 (*0-582-29450-9*) Longman.

Solution Sleuth. Learning Works Staff. (Critical Thinking Ser.). (J). (gr. 4-8). 1989. 8.95 (*0-88160-170-5*, LW 278) Learning Wks.

Solution Strategy: Your Handbook for Solving Life's Problems. Phil McWilliams. Ed. by Diane Parker. LC 91-61309. (Illus.). 1991. pap. 9.95 (*0-88247-875-3*) R & E Pubs.

Solution Talk: Hosting Therapeutic Conversations. Ben Furman & Tapani Ahola. 200p. (C). 1992. 22.95 (*0-393-70135-2*) Norton.

Solution Techniques for Large-Scale CFD Problems. Ed. by Wagdi G. Habashi. (Computational Methods in Applied Sciences Ser.). 454p. 1995. text ed. 155.00 (*0-471-95810-7*) Wiley.

Solution Three. Susan M. Squier. (Orig.). 1995. 29.95 (*1-55861-097-9*); pap. 10.95 (*1-55861-096-0*) Feminist Pr.

Solution to Pollution: One Hundred One Things You Can Do to Clean up Your Environment. Laurence Sombke. 1990. pap. 7.95 (*0-942361-19-9*) MasterMedia Pub.

Solution to Pollution in the Workplace. Larry Sombke et al. 1991. pap. 9.95 (*0-942361-25-3*) MasterMedia Pub.

***Solution to the Ecological Inference Problem: Reconstructing Individual Behavior from Aggregate Data.** Gary King. LC 96-32986. 346p. 1997. text ed. 55.00 (*0-691-01241-5*); pap. text ed. 16.95 (*0-691-01240-7*) Princeton U Pr.

***Solution to the Muslim Crisis.** 2nd ed. Faysad Burhan. 185p. 1996. pap. 6.00 (*0-9653790-0-0*) Inst Arabic & Islamic.

Solution to the World's Debt Problems. 1993. lib. bdg. 250.95 (*0-8490-9015-6*) Gordon Pr.

Solution Training: Overcoming Blocks in Problem Solving. James R. Baugh. LC 79-20717. 256p. 1980. 15.95 (*0-88289-246-0*) Pelican.

Solutions. Ron Marson. (Task Cards Ser.: No. 12). (Illus.). 72p. (YA). (gr. 7-12). 1990. teacher ed. 13.00 (*0-941008-82-7*) Tops Learning.

Solutions. James N. Spencer. (Modular Laboratory Program in Chemistry Ser.). 12p. (C). 1991. pap. text ed. 1.35 (*0-87540-391-3*, PROP 391-3) Chem Educ Res.

Solutions: Access Technologies for People Who Are Blind. Olga Espinola & Diane Croft. 224p. (Orig.). 1992. pap. text ed. 25.45 (*0-939173-21-2*); audio 21.95 (*0-939173-23-9*); disk 21.95 (*0-939173-24-7*) Natl Braille Pr.

Solutions: Practical & Effective Antidotes for Sexual & Relationship Problems. rev. ed. Leslie Cameron-Bandler. LC 85-70138. 259p. (C). 1985. pap. 11.95 (*0-932573-01-0*) FuturePace.

Solutions: The Estate Planning Organizer. Pam Walker & Nancy Roberson. 46p. 1994. student ed. 39.95 (*0-9634180-1-7*) Agape Pubns.

***Solutions, A. P. Calculus Problems, 1982-1996, Pt. II: AB & BC.** Judith Broadwin et al. (Illus.). 162p. (Orig.). 1996. pap. text ed. 12.00 (*1-882144-04-X*) Math Olympiads.

Solutions & Condensed Matter Physics: Proceedings. rev. ed. Ed. by A. R. Bishop & T. Schneider. (Solid-State Sciences Ser.: Vol. 8). (Illus.). 342p. 1981. 57.95 (*0-387-09138-6*) Spr-Verlag.

***Solutions Book for Simulation with Visual SLAM & AweSim.** A. Alan Pritsker & Jean J. O'Reilly. (Illus.). 1997. write for info. (*0-938974-05-X*) Systems Pub.

Solutions for a Dangerous Environment. Concept by L. Ron Hubbard. 32p. 1994. pap. 4.00 (*0-88404-919-1*) Bridge Pubns Inc.

Solutions for a Troubled World. Ed. by Mark Macy. LC 87-8859. (Peace Ser.: Vol. I). (Illus.). 314p. (Orig.). 1987. pap. 8.95 (*0-930705-03-3*) M H Macy & Co.

Solutions for Our Failing Educational System. Lila L. Jones. 77p. (YA). (gr. 7-12). 1993. pap. 6.95 (*1-57515-028-X*) PPI Pubng.

Solutions for Pavement Rehabilitation Problems. Ed. by Sanford P. LaHue, Sr. 304p. 1986. 29.00 (*0-87262-578-8*) Am Soc Civil Eng.

Solutions for Technology-Sharing Networks 1986. Ed. by Public Technology, Inc. Staff. (Annual Ser.). 436p. (Orig.). 1986. pap. 10.00 (*1-55657-001-5*) Pub Tech Inc.

Solutions for Technology-Sharing Networks, 1987. Ed. by Public Technology, Inc. Staff. 400p. (Orig.). 1987. pap. 10.00 (*0-317-60094-X*) Pub Tech Inc.

Solutions for Technology-Sharing Networks, 1988-89. Ed. by Tod Newcombe. 484p. (Orig.). 1988. pap. 25.00 (*1-55657-007-4*) Pub Tech Inc.

Solutions General Chemistry. Joseph Topping. 1995. teacher ed. write for info. (*0-7167-2515-0*) W H Freeman.

Solutions Handbook: For Personal Financial Planning, Business Planning, Employee Benefits & Estate Planning. Dearborn Staff & R&R Newkirk Staff. 500p. 1995. pap. 29.95 (*0-7931-1152-8*, 5606-0201, R & R Newkirk) Dearborn Finan.

Solutions Handbook for PC Programmers. 2nd rev. ed. Julio Sanchez & Maria P. Canton. LC 95-36307. (J. Ranade Workstation Ser.). Orig. Title: Programming Solutions Handbook for IBM Microcomputers. 1996. pap. text ed. 49.95 (*0-07-912249-3*) McGraw.

Solutions in C. Rex Jaeschke. 1986. pap. 17.95 (*0-201-15042-5*) Addison-Wesley.

Solutions in Statistics & Probability. 2nd ed. Edward J. Dudewicz. LC 93-72687. (American Sciences Press Series in Mathematical & Management Sciences: Vol. 3). (Illus.). 318p. (C). 1993. 125.00 (*0-935950-35-4*) Am Sciences Pr.

Solutions Manual: Perturbation Methods in the Computer Age. David C. Wilcox. 163p. (C). 1995. pap. 40.00 (*0-9636051-3-5*) DCW Industries.

Solutions Manual: Turbulence Modeling for CFD. David C. Wilcox. 218p. (C). 1993. pap. 40.00 (*0-9636051-1-9*) DCW Industries.

Solutions Manual & Computer Programs for Physical & Computational Aspects of Convective Heat Transfer by T. Cebeci & P. Bradshaw. T. Cebeci. (Illus.). 130p. 1988. 29.95 (*0-387-96825-3*) Spr-Verlag.

Solutions Manual & Notes for Fluid Dynamics. Z. U. Warsi & Russ Hall. 1992. write for info. (*0-8493-4451-4*, CRC Reprint) Franklin.

Solutions Manual for Automated Spreadsheet - SuperCalc 4. Thomas F. George. 70p. (Orig.). (C). 1990. teacher ed. 12.95 (*0-929683-09-9*) Servs by George.

Solutions Manual for Automated Spreadsheet - the Twin. Thomas F. George. 70p. (Orig.). (C). 1990. teacher ed. 12.95 (*0-929683-08-0*) Servs by George.

Solutions Manual for Basic Hazardous Waste Management. 2nd ed. William C. Blackman, Jr. 1995. write for info. (*1-56670-221-6*) CRC Pr.

Solutions Manual for College Algebra. K. Pothoven. 1988. pap. text ed. 18.50 (*0-931541-09-3*) Mancorp Pub.

Solutions Manual for Continuum Mechanics for Engineers. George E. Mase & G. Thomas Mase. LC 92-42972. 1992. write for info. (*0-8493-8862-7*, CRC Reprint) Franklin.

Solutions Manual for Geometry: A High School Course. S. Lang et al. LC 93-38093. 1994. 32.95 (*0-387-94181-9*) Spr-Verlag.

Solutions Manual for Introduction to Modern Statistical Mechanics. David G. Chandler & David Wu. 96p. (C). 1988. pap. text ed. 12.95 (*0-19-505889-5*) OUP.

***Solutions Manual for Langs Linear Algebra.** R. Shakarchi. 200p. 1996. pap. text ed. 24.95 (*0-387-94760-4*) Spr-Verlag.

Solutions Manual for Lectures on the Electrical Properties of Materials. 5th ed. L. Solymar & L. B. Au. LC 93-30169. (Illus.). 144p. (C). 1994. pap. text ed. 25.00 (*0-19-859943-9*) OUP.

Solutions Manual for Nuclear & Particle Physics. W. S. Williams. (Illus.). 128p. (C). 1994. pap. text ed. 16.95 (*0-19-851763-7*) OUP.

Solutions Manual for Precalculus Algebra & Trigonometry. K. Pothoven. 1988. pap. text ed. 18.50 (*0-931541-08-5*) Mancorp Pub.

***Solutions Manual for Probability, Statistics, & Reliability for Engineers.** Bilal M. Ayyub & Richard H. McCuen. LC 97-22210. 1997. write for info. (*0-8493-2699-0*) CRC Pr.

***Solutions Manual for Quantum Mechanics: Classical Results, Modern Systems, & Visualized Examples.** Robinett et al. 256p. 1997. pap. write for info. (*0-19-511564-3*) OUP.

Solutions Manual for Queueing Systems: Theory, Vol. 1. Leonard Kleinrock & Richard Gail. LC 82-80907. 226p. (Orig.). (C). 1982. pap. text ed. 29.50 (*0-942948-00-9*) Tech Trans Inst.

Solutions Manual for Queueing Systems Vol. II: Computer Applications. Leonard Kleinrock & Richard Gail. LC 82-80907. 250p. (Orig.). (C). 1986. pap. text ed. 29.50 (*0-942948-01-7*) Tech Trans Inst.

Solutions Manual for Queueing Systems Vol. II: Computer Applications, Set, Vols. I & II. Leonard Kleinrock & Richard Gail. LC 82-80907. 250p. (Orig.). (C). 1986. Set, Vol. I & II. 55.00 (*0-685-11461-9*) Tech Trans Inst.

Solutions Manual for Reinforced Concrete Technology. Samuel E. French. 143p. 1994. teacher ed., text ed. 16.95 (*0-8273-5497-5*) Delmar.

Solutions Manual for Signal Detection & Estimation. Mourad Barkat. LC 91-13451. 116p. reprint ed. pap. 33.10 (*0-7837-5848-0*, 2045567) Bks Demand.

Solutions Manual for Statistical Analysis for Business & Economics. 3rd ed. Donald L. Harnett & James L. Murphy. 224p. (C). 1985. teacher ed. write for info. (*0-201-10684-1*) Addison-Wesley.

***Solutions Manual for Structures, Properties & Processing of Materials.** Adams. (C). 1994. pap. text ed. write for info. (*0-06-501216-X*) Addison-Wesley.

***Solutions Manual for Techniques of Problem Solving.** Luis Fernandez et al. 188p. 1997. pap. 29.00 (*0-8218-0628-9*) Am Math.

Solutions Manual for the Chemical Engineering Reference Manual. 5th ed. Randall N. Robinson. LC 96-16477. 64p. 1996. pap. 19.95 (*0-912045-93-0*) Prof Pubns CA.

Solutions Manual for the Civil Engineering Reference Manual. 6th ed. Michael R. Lindeburg. (Engineering Reference Manual Ser.). 168p. 1992. pap. 19.95 (*0-912045-43-4*) Prof Pubns CA.

***Solutions Manual for the Dynamics of Heat.** H. U. Fuchs. (Illus.). 216p. 1996. pap. 19.00 (*0-387-94869-4*) Spr-Verlag.

Solutions Manual for the Electrical Engineering Reference Manual. 5th ed. Raymond B. Yarbrough. (Engineering Reference Manual Ser.). 176p. 1991. pap. 19.95 (*0-912045-28-0*) Prof Pubns CA.

Solutions Manual for the Engineer-in-Training Reference Manual: English Units. 8th ed. Michael R. Lindeburg. (Engineering Reference Manual Ser.). 256p. 1992. pap. 19.95 (*0-912045-39-6*) Prof Pubns CA.

Solutions Manual for the Engineer-in-Training Reference Manual: SI Units. 8th ed. Michael R. Lindeburg. (Engineering Reference Manual Ser.). 256p. 1992. pap. 19.95 (*0-912045-40-X*) Prof Pubns CA.

Solutions Manual for The Keys to Advanced Mathematics: Recurrent Themes in Abstract Reasoning. Daniel Solow. 74p. (Orig.). (C). 1995. pap. text ed. write for info. (*0-9644519-1-3*) Books Unltd.

Solutions Manual for the Land Surveyor Reference Manual. 2nd ed. Andrew L. Harbin. (Illus.). 80p. (C). 1990. pap. text ed. 19.95 (*0-912045-42-6*) Prof Pubns CA.

Solutions Manual for the Mechanical Engineering Reference Manual. 9th rev. ed. Michael R. Lindeburg. (Illus.). 160p. 1995. pap. 19.95 (*0-912045-84-1*, MESL9) Prof Pubns CA.

Solutions Manual to Accompany Auditing. Larry E. Rittenberg & Bradley J. Schwieger. 644p. (C). 1993. 33.25 (*0-03-029918-7*) Dryden Pr.

Solutions Manual to Accompany Auditing. 3rd ed. Dan M. Guy et al. 543p. (C). 1993. teacher ed. 8.50 (*0-03-096535-7*) Dryden Pr.

Solutions Manual to Accompany Boikess-Edelson Chemical Principles. Robert S. Boikess. (Illus.). 211p. (Orig.). (C). reprint ed. pap. text ed. 10.00 (*0-9623459-1-1*) RD Pub Inc.

S

Solutions Manual to Accompany Chemical Principles. 3rd ed. Robert Boikess. 224p. (C). 1994. per. 20.94 (0-8403-7964-1) Kendall-Hunt.

Solutions Manual to Accompany Disc Structures. Judith L. Gersting. (C). 1995. write for info. (0-7167-2095-7) W H Freeman.

Solutions Manual to Accompany Financial Accounting. 7th ed. Ernest I. Hanson et al. 1099p. (C). 1993. teacher ed. 18.75 (0-03-097459-3) Dryden Pr.

Solutions Manual to Accompany Statistical Analysis for Decision Making. 6th ed. Morris Hamburg & Peg Young. 213p. (C). 1994. 26.75 (0-03-097807-6) Dryden Pr.

Solutions Manual to "Foundations of Colloid Science", Vol. I. Robert J. Hunter. (Illus.). 128p. 1992. pap. 32.00 (0-19-855742-6) OUP.

Solutions Manual Turing Omnibus. Dewdney. 1995. student ed., pap. text ed. write for info. (0-7167-8287-1) W H Freeman.

Solutions, Minerals & Equilibria. Robert M. Garrels & Charles L. Christ. 504p. 1990. 50.00 (0-86720-148-7) Jones & Bartlett.

Solutions of Einstein's Equations-Techniques & Results: Proceedings of the International Seminar on Exact Solutions of Einstein's Equations, Held in Retzbach Retzbach Germany, November 14-18, 1983. Ed. by C. Hoenselaers et al. (Lecture Notes in Physics Ser.: Vol. 205). vi, 439p. 1984. 48.95 (0-387-13366-6) Spr-Verlag.

Solutions of Partial Differential Equations. Dean G. Duffy. (Illus.). 448p. 1986. 25.95 (0-8306-0412-X, 2612) McGraw-Hill Prof.

Solutions on Mac - College Physics. 4th ed. Raymond A. Serway. (C). 1994. 246.25 (0-03-003583-X) HB Coll Pubs.

Solutions, Relaxation, or Understanding for Tense, Anxious, Depressive, Hostile (Irritated), & Disgusted States & Problems, Set-ST. Russell E. Mason. 1975. pap. 60.00 incl. audio (0-89533-010-5) F I Comm.

Solutions to Black's Chemistry. 6th ed. Wilson. 1994. pap. text ed. 23.20 (0-13-338690-2) P-H.

Solutions to Boiler & Cooling Water Problems. 2nd ed. C. D. Schroeder. (General Engineering Ser.). 240p. (gr. 13). 1990. reprint ed. text ed. 70.95 (0-442-00501-6) Chapman & Hall.

Solutions to CFD Benchmark Problems in Electronic Packaging. Ed. by D. Agonafer. (HTD Ser.: Vol. 255). 64p. 1993. 30.00 (0-7918-1168-9, G00812) ASME.

Solutions to Cheops' Great Pyramid Mysteries. H. W. Douglas. 1991. pap. 9.95 (1-879384-09-4) Cypress Hse.

***Solutions to Hydrogen Attack in Steels.** P. F. Timmins. 225p. 1997. 143.00 (0-87170-597-4, 6570G) ASM.

***Solutions to Hydrogen Attack in Steels.** P. Timmons. (C). 1997. 143.00 (0-614-20004-0, 6570) ASM.

***Solutions to Office Warehouse.** 4th ed. Walther Solomon. 1993. lab manual ed., pap. write for info. (0-314-02647-9) West Pub.

Solutions to Practice Sets to Accompany Hanson-Hamre-Walgenbach Principles of Accounting, 6-E & Financial Accounting, 7-E. Ronald Burnette et al. 134p. (C). 1993. 7.50 (0-03-097393-7) Dryden Pr.

Solutions to Practice Sets 1-5 to Accompany Hillman, Kochanek, Norgaard "Principles of Accounting," Sixth Edition & Kochanek, Hillman, Norgaard "Financial Accounting," Second Edition. Donald R. Davis et al. 274p. (C). 1993. 8.75 (0-15-500307-0) Dryden Pr.

Solutions to Problems of Race, Class & Gender. Vernon McClean & Lois Lyles. 464p. (C). 1993. per. 32.49 (0-8403-8785-7) Kendall-Hunt.

Solutions to Selected Problems from the Physics of Radiology. 4th ed. Harold E. Johns & John R. Cunningham. (Illus.). 148p. (C). 1991. pap. text ed. 29.95 (0-398-05750-8) C C Thomas.

Solutions to Sexual Problems. 1991. lib. bdg. 79.95 (0-8490-4603-3) Gordon Pr.

***Solutions to Social Problems.** Eitzen & Leedham. 1997. pap. text ed. 24.00 (0-205-15725-4) P-H.

Solutions to Systems Portability in C & C Plus Plus. John L. Bradberry & John E. Swanke. 325p. (Orig.). 1993. pap. 39.95 incl. disk (1-55851-294-2, M&T Books) H Holt & Co.

Solutions to Technical & Analytical Questions Found in Economic Analysis. 6th ed. Maurice S Charles & Owens Phillips. 222p. (C). 1992. 7.50 (0-256-12646-1) Irwin.

Solutions to Tesla's Secrets. (Nikola Tesla Ser.). 1991. lib. bdg. 250.00 (0-8490-4321-2) Gordon Pr.

Solutions to Tesla's Secrets & the Soviet Tesla Weapons with Reference Articles for Solutions to Tesla's Secrets, 2 pts., Set. T. E. Bearden. LC 81-85737. (Illus.). 188p. (Orig.). 1982. pap. 14.00 (0-9603536-3-1) Tesla Bk Co.

Solutions to the Problems in Principles of Physical & Chemical Metallurgy. Giles F. Carter. (Illus.). 49p. reprint ed. pap. 25.00 (0-318-39724-2, 2033082) Bks Demand.

Solv-A-Crime Puzzles. A. C. Gordon. Ed. by Singer Media Corporation Staff & Kurt Singer. LC 94-40593. (Game & Puzzle Activity Bks.). 96p. 1995. pap. text ed. 1.00 (0-486-28552-9) Dover.

Solvability of Nonlinear Equations & Boundry Value Problems. Svatopluk Fucik. (Mathematics & Its Applications Ser.: No. 4). 400p. 1981. lib. bdg. 79.00 (90-277-1077-5) Kluwer Ac.

Solvability, Provability, Definability: The Collected Works of Emil L. Post. Ed. by Martin Davis. LC 93-9347. (Contemporary Mathematicians Ser.). 1993. 109.00 (0-8176-3579-3, Birkhauser) Spr-Verlag.

Solvable Models in Quantum Mechanics. Sergio A. Albeverio et al. (Texts & Monographs in Physics). 480p. 1988. 136.95 (0-387-17841-4) Spr-Verlag.

Solvang: Denmark in the U. S. A. rev. ed. Elaine Kuehl. (Illus.). 48p. 1987. pap. 4.95 (0-9618144-0-3) Trykkeri Pr.

Solvang & the Santa Ynez Valley Address Book. Kirk Irwin. (Illus.). 56p. 1993. ring bd. 12.95 (1-883308-00-3) I & I Images.

***Solvated Electron: A Symposium Sponsored by the Division of Physical Chemistry at the 150th Meeting of the American Chemical Society Held September 15-16, 1965, Atlantic City, NJ. Edwin J. Hart, Symposium Chairman.** LC 65-26801. (Advances in Chemistry Ser.: No. 50). (Illus.). 312p. 1965. reprint ed. pap. 89.00 (0-608-02660-3, 2052555) Bks Demand.

Solvation Dynamics & Charge Transfer Reactions. Ed. by B. Bagchi. 250p. (C). 1991. text ed. 67.00 (981-02-0338-1) World Scientific Pub.

Solvation Thermodynamics. Arieh Ben-Naim. LC 87-21738. (Illus.). 260p. 1987. 75.00 (0-306-42538-6, Plenum Pr) Plenum.

Solvay Conference on Surface Science. Ed. by F. W. De Weitte. (Surface Sciences Ser.: Vol. 14). (Illus.). xii, 501p. 1988. 81.95 (0-387-50450-8) Spr-Verlag.

Solvay Conferences on Physics: Aspects of the Development of Physics Since 1911. Jagdish Mehra. LC 75-28332. 424p. 1975. lib. bdg. 206.00 (90-277-0635-2) Kluwer Ac.

Solve It: Computer-Aided Mathematics for Science & Engineering. Samuel Doughty. LC 95-30439. (Illus.). 164p. 1995. 29.95 (0-88415-266-9, 5266) Gulf Pub.

Solve It! Management Problem Solving with PC Software, Version 2.0. Ken Laudon. (Illus.). 200p. 1988. pap. text ed. 14.00 (0-945991-00-2) Azimuth Corp.

Solve It! Management Problem Solving with PC Software, Version 2.0. Ken Laudon. (Illus.). 250p. 1989. pap. text ed. 14.00 (0-945991-02-9) Azimuth Corp.

Solve It! Management Problem Solving with PC Software, Version 2.0. Ken Laudon. (Illus.). 300p. (C). 1990. pap. text ed. 14.00 (0-945991-03-7) Azimuth Corp.

Solve It! Management Problem Solving with PC Software, Version 2.0. Ken Laudon. (Illus.). 300p. (C). 1991. pap. text ed. 14.00 (0-945991-04-5) Azimuth Corp.

Solve It! Management Problem Solving with PC Software, Version 2.0. Ken Laudon. (Illus.). (C). 1992. pap. text ed. 14.00 (0-945991-05-3) Azimuth Corp.

Solve It! Management Problem Solving with PC Software, Version 2.0. Ken Laudon. (Illus.). (C). 1993. pap. text ed. 14.00 (0-945991-06-1) Azimuth Corp.

Solve It! Management Problem Solving with PC Software, Version 2.0. Ken Laudon. (Illus.). 350p. (C). 1994. pap. text ed. 14.00 (0-945991-08-8) Azimuth Corp.

***Solve It with Salt.** Patty Moosbrugger. 1997. pap. write for info. (0-609-80234-8) Crown Pub Group.

***Solve-It-Yourself Mysteries: Detective Club Puzzlers.** Hy Conrad & Bob Peterson. LC 96-37010. (Illus.). (J). 1997. 14.95 (0-8069-9400-2) Sterling.

***Solve Pronunciation Problem.** Morris. 1984. pap. text ed. write for info. (0-85896-931-9) Addison-Wesley.

***Solve Punctuation Problem.** Longman Publishing Staff. Date not set. pap. text ed. write for info. (0-85896-891-6) Addison-Wesley.

Solve That Problem: Three Steps to Problem-Solving Success. Geof Cox. (Institute of Management Ser.). 300p. 1995. pap. 43.50 (0-273-61182-8, Pub. by Pitman Pub Ltd UK) Trans-Atl Phila.

***Solve the Mystery: 41 Puzzling Cases.** A. C. Gordon et al. LC 96-54008. (Game & Puzzle Activity Bks.). 64p. 1997. reprint ed. pap. text ed. 1.00 (0-486-29662-8) Dover.

Solve Your Children's Math Problems: Quick & Easy Lessons for Parents. Patricia Nordstrom. 352p. 1994. pap. 12.00 (0-671-87026-2, Fireside) S&S Trade.

Solve Your Child's School-Related Problems. Michael Martin & Cynthia W. Greenwood. LC 95-20286. 384p. 1995. pap. 17.00 (0-06-273366-4, Harper Ref) HarpC.

Solve Your Child's Sleep Problems. Richard Ferber. 256p. 1986. pap. 12.00 (0-671-62099-1, Fireside) S&S Trade.

Solve Your Own Business Problems: Staying Sane While Staying Solvent. Wendy M. Greenfield. (Illus.). 1988. 19.95 (0-13-823212-1) P-H.

Solved: The Riddle of Illness. Stephen E. Langer. 206p. (Orig.). 1984. 17.95 (0-87983-370-X); pap. 10.95 (0-87983-357-2) Keats.

Solved: The Riddle of Illness. 2nd expanded rev. ed. Stephen E. Langer & James F. Scheer. LC 95-2608. 240p. 1995. pap. 12.95 (0-87983-667-9) Keats.

***Solved: The Riddle of Osteoporosis.** James Scheer & Stephen E. Langer. LC 97-7975. 96p. 1997. reprint ed. mass mkt. 4.95 (0-87983-785-3) Keats.

Solved - The Riddle of Weight Loss: Restore Healthy Body Chemistry & Lose Weight Naturally. Stephen Langer & James F. Scheer. Orig. Title: How to Win at Weight Loss. 256p. (Orig.). 1989. pap. 12.95 (0-89281-296-6, Heal Arts VT) Inner Tradit.

Solved & Unsolved. 1990. 9.99 (0-517-03755-6) Random Hse Value.

Solved & Unsolved Problems in Number Theory. 4th rev. ed. Daniel Shanks. LC 77-13010. vii, 304p. (C). 1985. text ed. 27.50 (0-8284-1297-9) Chelsea Pub.

Solved by Sunset. Carol Orsborn. 224p. 1996. pap. 14.00 (0-517-88779-7, Harmony) Crown Pub Group.

Solved by Sunset: The Right Brain Way to Resolve Whatever's Bothering You in One Day or Less. Carol Orsborn. 224p. 1995. 21.00 (0-517-70178-2) Random Hse Value.

Solved, The Mystery of Life. Vernon Howard. 294p. (Orig.). 1995. pap. 9.95 (0-911203-37-0) New Life.

Solvent Abuse: A Population-Based Neuropsychological Study. O. Chadwick et al. (Recent Research in Psychology Ser.). xi, 150p. 1991. 57.95 (0-387-97607-8) Spr-Verlag.

Solvent Abuse: The Adolescent Epidemic? Joyce M. Watson. 208p. 1986. pap. 19.95 (0-7099-3684-2, Pub. by Croom Helm UK) Routledge Chapman & Hall.

Solvent Crazing of Polymers. A. L. Volynskii & N. F. Bakeev. LC 95-12077. (Studies in Polymer Science: Vol. 13). 424p. 1995. 278.50 (0-444-81848-0) Elsevier.

Solvent-Dependent Flexibility of Proteins & Principles of Their Function. Alex I. Kaivarainen. 1985. lib. bdg. 157.50 (90-277-1534-3) Kluwer Ac.

Solvent Effects & Chemical Reactivity. Ed. by Orlando Tapia & Juan Bertran. LC 96-10935. (Understanding Chemical Reactivity Ser.: Vol. 17). 392p. (C). 1996. lib. bdg. 196.00 (0-7923-3995-9) Kluwer Ac.

Solvent Extraction: Principles & Applications to Process Metallurgy, Pt. 2. G. M. Ritcey & A. W. Ashbrook. (Process Metallurgy Ser.: Vol. 1, Pt. 2). 738p. 1979. 258.25 (0-444-41771-0) Elsevier.

Solvent Extraction Chemistry: Fundamentals & Applications. Tatsuya Sekine & Yuko Hasegawa. LC 75-32474. 935p. reprint ed. pap. 180.00 (0-685-16291-5, 2027118) Bks Demand.

Solvent Extraction in Biotechnology: Recovery of Primary & Secondary Metabolites. Karl Schugerl. LC 93-51019. 1994. 149.95 (0-387-57694-0) Spr-Verlag.

Solvent Extraction in the Process Industries, 3 Vols., 1. Ed. by D. H. Logsdail & M. J. Slater. LC 93-5518. 1993. write for info. (1-85861-039-7) Elsevier.

Solvent Extraction in the Process Industries, 3 Vols., 2. Ed. by D. H. Logsdail & M. J. Slater. LC 93-5518. 1993. write for info. (1-85861-040-0) Elsevier.

Solvent Extraction in the Process Industries, 3 Vols., 3. Ed. by D. H. Logsdail & M. J. Slater. LC 93-5518. 1993. write for info. (1-85861-041-9) Elsevier.

Solvent Extraction in the Process Industries, 3 Vols., Set. Ed. by D. H. Logsdail & M. J. Slater. LC 93-5518. 1993. write for info. (1-85861-042-7) Elsevier.

Solvent Extraction Plants. National Fire Protection Association Staff. 1993. 20.25 (0-317-63070-9, 36-93) Natl Fire Prot.

Solvent Extraction Research: Proceedings of the 5th International Conference on Solvent Extraction Chemistry, 1968. Ed. by A. S. Kertes & Y. Marcus. LC 75-99274. 459p. reprint ed. pap. 130.90 (0-317-10523-X, 2055150) Bks Demand.

Solvent Extraction Reviews, Vol. 1: 1971. Ed. by Marcus Yizhak. LC 70-172522. 268p. reprint ed. pap. 76.40 (0-7837-0881-5, 2041187) Bks Demand.

***Solvent Extraction 1990, 2 vols.** T. Sekine & S. Kusakabe. (Process Metallurgy Ser.: Vol. 7). lxxviii, 1924p. 1992. 500.00 (0-444-88677-X) Elsevier.

Solvent Neurotoxicity. Peter Arlien-Soborg. 400p. 1991. 192.00 (0-8493-6234-2, RC347) CRC Pr.

Solvent Problems in Industry: Papers from the 3rd & 4th European Solvents Symposia, Manchester, U. K., 1980 & 1983. Ed. by George Kakabadse. (Illus.). 251p. 1984. 79.25 (0-85334-304-7, Pub. by Elsevier Applied Sci UK) Elsevier.

Solvent Properties of Amphiphilic Compounds. Philip A. Winsor. LC 55-2032. 217p. reprint ed. pap. 61.90 (0-317-09038-0, 2051334) Bks Demand.

Solvent Properties of Surfactant Solutions. Ed. by Keozeo Shinoda. LC 68-1233. (Surfactant Science Ser.: Vol. 2). 374p. reprint ed. pap. 106.60 (0-317-28559-9, 2055028) Bks Demand.

Solvent Pulping Symposium, 1992: Marriott Copley Place, Boston, MA, November 5-6, 1992. Technical Association of the Pulp & Paper Industry Staff. (TAPPI Notes Ser.). 102p. reprint ed. pap. 29.10 (0-7837-4053-0, 2043884) Bks Demand.

Solvent Recovery Equipment. Richard K. Miller & Marcia E. Rupnow. LC 90-83881. (Survey on Technology & Markets Ser.: No. 177). 50p. 1991. pap. text ed. 200.00 (1-55865-201-9) Future Tech Surveys.

***Solvent Recovery Handbook.** write for info. (0-340-57467-4, Pub. by E Arnold UK) Routledge Chapman & Hall.

Solvent Recovery Handbook. Ian Smallwood. LC 93-2100. 1993. text ed. 65.50 (0-07-058435-4) McGraw.

Solvent Recycling, Disposal & Substitution. 142p. 1992. 1,950.00 (0-89336-899-7, C-154) BCC.

Solvent Safety Sheets: A Compendium for the Working Chemist. Ed. by H. Henning. 243p. 1994. 73.00 (0-85186-471-6) CRC Pr.

Solvent Spun Rayon, Modified Cellulose Fibers & Derivatives. Ed. by Albin F. Turbak. LC 77-12220. (ACS Symposium Ser.: No. 58). 1977. 29.95 (0-8412-0388-1) Am Chemical.

***Solvent Spun Rayon, Modified Cellulose Fibers & Derivatives.** Ed. by Albin F. Turbak. LC 77-12220. (ACS Symposium Ser.: Vol. 58). 279p. 1977. reprint ed. pap. 79.60 (0-608-03940-3, 2064387) Bks Demand.

Solvent Substitution for Pollution Prevention. U. S. Department of Energy Staff & U. S. Air Force Engineering & Services Center Staff. LC 92-24212. (Pollution Technology Review Ser.: No. 212). (Illus.). 335p. 1993. 48.00 (0-8155-1319-4) Noyes.

Solventless & High Solids Industrial Finishes: Recent Developments. Ed. by M. T. Gillies. LC 80-21553. (Chemical Technology Review Ser.: No. 179). (Illus.). 342p. 1981. 48.00 (0-8155-0828-X) Noyes.

Solvents - New, Used, & Hazardous in Health & Industry: Index of New Information & Research Bible of Current Reviews. Sherrie L. Sinclair. LC 96-3134. 1996. 47.50 (0-7883-0974-9); pap. 44.50 (0-7883-0975-7) ABBE Pubs Assn.

***Solvents & Self-Organization of Polymers: Proceedings, NATO Advanced Study Institute on Solvents & Self-Organization of Polymers, Antalya, Turkey, 1995.** Ed. by Stephen E. Webber et al. (NATO ASI Series E: Vol. 327). 509p. 1996. lib. bdg. 229.00 (0-7923-4222-4, QD382) Kluwer Ac.

Solvents & Solvent Effects in Organic Chemistry. 2nd enl. rev. ed. Christian Reichardt. (Illus.). xxii, 534p. 1988. 130.00 (3-527-26805-7, VCH) Wiley.

Solvents in Common Use: Health Risks to Workers. Royal Society of Chemistry Staff. 1989. 187.00 (0-85186-088-5) CRC Pr.

Solvents Theory & Practice: A Symposium Sponsored by the Division of Organic Coatings & Plastics Chemistry at the 162nd Meeting of the American Chemical Society, Washington, D. C., Sept. 15-16, 1971. Ed. by Roy W. Tess. LC 73-88797. (Advances in Chemistry Ser.: No. 124). (Illus.). 237p. reprint ed. pap. 67.60 (0-8357-7028-1, 2052273) Bks Demand.

Solving Algebra Word Problems. Dale T. Hoffman. (C). 1988. 53.95 (0-534-09595-X) Brooks-Cole.

***Solving America's Sexual Crisis.** Ira L. Reiss. 1997. pap. text ed. 18.95 (1-57392-172-0) Prometheus Bks.

Solving Bible Mysteries: 101 Games, Puzzles, Projects, Crafts, Experiments & More. Joy McKenzie. 112p. (J). 1994. pap. 10.99 (0-310-59761-7) Zondervan.

Solving Bosch Continuous Injection System (CIS) Problems: Theory, Diagnosis, & Repair of the K-Jetronic & the KE-Jetronic Family of Bosch Fuel Injection. James Weber. 113p. 1992. pap. 39.95 (1-885477-08-2) Fut Horizons.

Solving Business Problems on the Electronic Calculator. 2nd ed. Mildred K. Polisky & James R. Meehan. 256p. 1983. text ed. 16.56 (0-07-041281-2) McGraw.

Solving Business Problems on the Electronic Calculator. 3rd ed. Mildred K. Polisky. 256p. 1988. pap. text ed. 13.48 (0-07-041283-9) McGraw.

Solving Business Problems on the Electronic Calculator. 4th ed. Mildred K. Polisky. LC 92-31248. 1993. 16.95 (0-02-800417-5) Glencoe.

Solving Business Problems with MRP II. 2nd ed. Alan D. Luber. 333p. 1995. 41.95 (1-55558-132-3, Digital DEC) Buttrwrth-Heinemann.

Solving Business Problems with Objects. Thom Luce & David M. Kroenke. 1995. pap. text ed. write for info. (0-07-911955-7) McGraw.

***Solving Bycatch: Considerations for Today & Tomorrow.** (Report Ser.: No. 96-03). (Illus.). 326p. (Orig.). 1996. pap. text ed. 25.00 (1-56612-038-1) AK Sea Grant CP.

Solving Child Behavior Problems at Home & at School. Elaine A. Blechman. LC 85-61468. 296p. (Orig.). (C). 1985. pap. 18.95 (0-87822-247-2, 2472) Res Press.

Solving Cipher Problems. Frank W. Lewis. 260p. (Orig.). 1992. pap. 30.80 (0-89412-178-2) Aegean Park Pr.

Solving Combinatorial Optimization Problems in Parallel: Methods & Techniques. Ed. by Alfonso Ferreira & Panos M. Pardalos. LC 96-5677. (Lecture Notes in Computer Science Ser.: Vol. 1054). 274p. 1996. pap. 49.00 (3-540-61043-X) Spr-Verlag.

Solving Control Engineering Problems with MATLAB. Katsuhiko Ogata. LC 93-8443. 320p. (C). 1993. pap. text ed. 52.00 (0-13-045907-0) P-H.

Solving Corrosion Problems in Air Pollution Control Equipment-1981. (Illus.). 193p. 1981. 10.00 (0-915567-49-0) NACE Intl.

Solving Corrosion Problems in Air Pollution Control Equipment, 1992. (Illus.). 470p. 1992. 57.00 (0-614-02630-X) NACE Intl.

Solving Corrosion Problems in Air Pollution Equipment, 1990. (Illus.). 444p. 1990. 48.00 (0-614-02631-8) NACE Intl.

Solving Corrosion Problems in the Air Pollution Control Industry, 1987. LC 87-62856. (Illus.). 180p. 1987. 10.00 (0-915567-31-8) NACE Intl.

Solving Costly Organizational Conflicts: Achieving Intergroup Trust, Cooperation, & Teamwork. Robert R. Blake & Jane S. Mouton. LC 84-47980. (Management Ser.). 311p. text ed. 35.95 (0-87589-612-X) Jossey-Bass.

Solving Credit Problems. Hendon. 1993. pap. 6.95 (0-9640701-0-3) Atlantic.

Solving Crimes: The Investigation of Burglary & Robbery. John E. Eck. LC 83-60846. 349p. (Orig.). (C). 1983. pap. text ed. 16.50 (1-878734-14-8) Police Exec Res.

Solving Cross-Country Problems. Wallace. (Threshold Picture Guide Ser.: No. 31). (Illus.). 24p. (Orig.). 1994. pap. 12.00 (1-872082-61-0) Half Halt Pr.

Solving Discipline Problems: Methods & Models for Today's Teachers. 3rd ed. Charles H. Wolfgang. 1994. text ed. 45.50 (0-205-16569-9) Allyn.

Solving Elliptic Problems Using ELLPACK. J. Rice & R. F. Boisvert. (Computational Mathematics Ser.: Vol. 2). (Illus.). 350p. 1985. 71.95 (0-387-90910-9) Spr-Verlag.

Solving Equilibrium Problems: With Applications to Qualitative Analysis. Steven S. Zumdahl. 200p. (C). 1989. pap. text ed. 25.56 (0-669-16718-5) HM College Div.

Solving Ethical Problems. Murray Friedman. 1.00 (0-914131-58-3, B160) Torah Umesorah.

Solving Flatwork Problems, No. 25: Threshold Picture Guide. Jane Wallace. (Illus.). 24p. (Orig.). (YA). 1993. pap. 12.00 (1-872082-43-2, Pub. by Kenilworth Pr UK) Half Halt Pr.

Solving Frontier Problems of Physics: The Decomposition Method. George Adomian. LC 93-39561. (Fundamental Theories of Physics Ser.: Vol. 60). 368p. (C). 1994. lib. bdg. 163.00 (0-7923-2644-X) Kluwer Ac.

Solving Geometric Constraint Systems: A Case Study in Kinematics. Glenn A. Kramer. (Artificial Intelligence Ser.). (Illus.). 304p. 1992. 45.00 (0-262-11164-0) MIT Pr.

Solving Geometric Originals. Frank C. Touton. LC 76-177698. (Columbia University. Teachers College. Contributions to Education Ser.: No. 146). reprint ed. 37.50 (0-404-55146-7) AMS Pr.

Solving German Codes in World War I. William F. Friedman. 152p. 1979. pap. 20.80 (0-89412-019-0) Aegean Park Pr.

An Asterisk (*) at the beginning of an entry indicates that the title is appearing in BIP for the first time.

Solving Hazardous Waste Problems: Learning from Dioxins. Ed. by Jurgen Exner. LC 87-1389. (Symposium Ser.: No. 338). (Illus.). x, 405p. 1987. 79.95 (*0-8412-1025-X*) Am Chemical.

*__Solving Hazardous Waste Problems: Learning from Dioxins.__ Ed. by Jurgen H. Exner. LC 87-1389. (ACS Symposium Ser.: Vol. 338). 408p. 1987. reprint ed. pap. 116.30 (*0-608-03531-9*, 2064250) Bks Demand.

Solving Heat Radiation Problems Using the Boundary Element Method. R. Bialecki. LC 93-72438. (Topics in Engineering Ser.: Vol. 15). 160p. 1993. 74.00 (*1-56252-178-0*) Computational Mech MA.

Solving Inexact Search Problems. Mikhael M. Botvinnik. Tr. by A. A. Brown. (Symbolic Computation Ser.). (Illus.). 255p. 1983. 65.95 (*0-387-90869-2*) Spr-Verlag.

Solving Inorganic Spectroscopic Problems. Vincent. 1981. wbk. ed. 24.00 incl. audio (*0-85186-368-X*) CRC Pr.

Solving Interference Problems in Electronics. Ralph Morrison. LC 95-12074. 216p. 1995. text ed. 54.95 (*0-471-12796-5*, Wiley-Interscience) Wiley.

Solving International Crime. Katie Roden. (Crimebusters Ser.). (Illus.). 32p. (J). (gr. 4-6). 1996. lib. bdg. 15.40 (*0-7613-0528-9*, Copper Beech Bks) Millbrook Pr.

*__Solving Irregularly Structured Problems in Parallel: 4th International Symposium, Irregular '97, Paderborn, Germany, June 12-13, 1997, Proceedings, Vol. 125.__ G. Bilardi. LC 97-17625. (Lecture Notes in Computer Science). 1997. write for info. (*3-540-63138-0*) Spr-Verlag.

Solving Kepler's Equation over Three Centuries. Peter Colwell. LC 93-6379. 1993. 24.95 (*0-943396-40-9*) Willmann-Bell.

*__Solving Language Problems: From General to Applied Linguistics.__ Ed. by Reinhard R. Hartmann. 304p. 1996. pap. 25.95 (*0-85989-484-3*, Pub. by Univ Exeter Pr UK) Northwestern U Pr.

Solving Large-Scale Problems in Mechanics: Parallel & Distributed Computer Applications. Ed. by Manolis Papadrakakis. Date not set. text ed. 180.00 (*0-471-95696-1*) Wiley.

Solving Large-Scale Problems in Mechanics: The Development & Application of Computational Solution Methods. Ed. by Manolis Papadrakakis. 472p. 1993. text ed. 145.00 (*0-471-93809-2*) Wiley.

Solving Latin American Business Problems. (Research Reports: No. N141). 1994. 295.00 (*0-85058-806-5*) Economist Intell.

Solving Learning & Behavior Problems of Children: A Planning System Integrating Assessment & Treatment. Mark N. Ozer. LC 79-28316. (Jossey-Bass Social & Behavioral Science Ser.). 272p. reprint ed. pap. 77.60 (*0-8357-6882-1*, 2037934) Bks Demand.

Solving Least Squares Problems, Vol. 15. Charles L. Lawson & Richard J. Hanson. LC 95-35178. (Classics in Applied Mathematics Ser.: No. 15). xii, 337p. 1995. pap. 33.00 (*0-89871-356-0*, CL15) Soc Indus-Appl Math.

Solving Life's Problems. David Y. Cho. LC 80-62782. 142p. (Orig.). 1980. pap. 7.95 (*0-88270-450-8*) Bridge-Logos.

Solving Life's Problems. Marilyn Hickey. 49p. (Orig.). pap. 1.00 (*1-56441-165-6*) M Hickey Min.

Solving Linear Systems on Vector & Shared Memory Computers. Jack J. Dongarra et al. LC 90-24045. (Miscellaneous Bks.: No. 23). xii, 256p. 1990. pap. 23.50 (*0-89871-270-X*) Soc Indus-Appl Math.

Solving Marriage Problems: Biblical Solutions for Christian Counselors. Jay E. Adams. (Jay Adams Library). 144p. 1986. pap. 9.99 (*0-310-51081-3*, 12120P) Zondervan.

Solving Math Word Problems Bk. 1: Sums to 99 No Borrowing or Carrying. Linda Donofrio & Andrea Sholl. Ed. by Rnady L. Womack. (Solving Math Word Problems Ser.). Orig. Title: Story Problems Made Easy. (Illus.). 48p. (J). (gr. 1-3). 1996. pap. text ed. 7.95 (*0-614-10695-8*) Gldn Educ.

Solving Math Word Problems Bk. 2: Sums to 500 with Borrowing or Carrying. Linda Donofrio & Andrea Sholl. Ed. by Randy L. Womack. (Solving Math Word Problems Ser.). Orig. Title: Story Problems Made Easy. (Illus.). 48p. (J). 1996. pap. text ed. 7.95 (*0-614-10696-6*) Gldn Educ.

Solving Mathematical Problems: A Personal Perspective. Terence C. Tao. 85p. 1995. pap. 46.00 (*0-7300-1365-0*, ECT469, Pub. by Deakin Univ AT) St Mut.

Solving Mechanical Design Problems with Computer Graphics. Lange. (Mechanical Engineering Ser.: Vol. 48). 416p. 1986. 145.00 (*0-8247-7479-5*) Dekker.

Solving Moral Problems: A Strategy for Practical Inquiry. Ronald McLaren. LC 88-31730. 84p. (C). 1989. pap. text ed. 13.95 (*0-87484-885-7*, 885) Mayfield Pub.

Solving Ode's with Maple V. David Barrow et al. (Brooks/Cole Symbolic Computation Ser.). 264p. (C). 1997. pap. text ed. 21.95 (*0-534-34402-X*) Brooks-Cole.

Solving of Problem-Situations by Preschool Children. Augusta Alpert. LC 74-176514. (Columbia University. Teachers College. Contributions to Education Ser.: No. 323). reprint ed. 37.50 (*0-404-55323-0*) AMS Pr.

Solving Offset Ink Problems. Nelson R. Eldred. LC 86-83038. 96p. 1987. pap. text ed. 45.00 (*0-88362-090-1*, 1310) Graphic Arts Tech Found.

Solving Ordinary Differential Equations I. Ernst Hairer et al. (Computational Mathematics Ser.: Vol. 8). (Illus.). xiv, 480p. 1986. 69.00 (*0-387-17145-2*) Spr-Verlag.

Solving Ordinary Differential Equations I: Nostiff Problems. 2nd rev. ed. Ernst Hairer et al. LC 93-7847. (Computational Mathematics Ser.: Vol. 8). (Illus.). 545p. 1994. 118.95 (*0-387-56670-8*) Spr-Verlag.

Solving Ordinary Differential Equations II. Ernst Hairer & Gerhard Wanner. (Computational Mathematics Ser.: Vol. 14). 464p. 1995. 98.00 (*0-387-53775-9*) Spr-Verlag.

*__Solving Ordinary Differential Equations II: Stiff & Differential Algebraic Problems.__ 2nd expanded rev. ed. E. Hairer & G. Wanner. Ed. by J. Stoer et al. (Springer Series in Computational Mathematics: Vol. 14). (Illus.). xvi, 614p. 1996. 99.50 (*3-540-60452-9*) Spr-Verlag.

Solving Partial Differential Equations on Parallel Computers - An Introduction. Jianping Zhu. 260p. 1994. text ed. 58.00 (*981-02-1578-9*) World Scientific Pub.

Solving Problem Solving: A Potent Force for Effective Managment. Robert L. Flood. 300p. 1996. text ed. 50.00 (*0-471-95590-6*) Wiley.

Solving Problems. (Open Learning for Supervisory Management Ser.). 1989. pap. text ed. 19.50 (*0-08-070138-8*, Pergamon Pr) Elsevier.

Solving Problems. 2nd ed. (Open Learning Super Ser.). 1991. pap. text ed. 26.00 (*0-08-041659-4*, Pergamon Pr) Elsevier.

Solving Problems Creatively. 2nd ed. David A. Whetten & Cameron. (Developing Management Skills Modules Ser.). (C). 1993. 6.00 (*0-06-501793-5*) Addson-Wesley Educ.

Solving Problems in Constitutional & Administrative Law. Andrew Beale. 230p. 1995. pap. 20.00 (*1-85941-001-4*, Pub. by Cavendish UK) Gaunt.

Solving Problems in Couples & Family Therapy: Techniques & Tactics. Robert Sherman et al. LC 91-25757. 352p. 1991. text ed. 41.95 (*0-87630-647-4*) Brunner-Mazel.

Solving Problems in Criminal Law. Roger Geary. 196p. 1995. pap. write for info. (*1-85941-000-6*, Pub. by Cavendish UK) Gaunt.

Solving Problems in Environmental Engineering & Geosciences with Artificial Neural Networks. Farid U. Dowla & Leah L. Rogers. (Illus.). 310p. (C). 1996. 40.00 (*0-262-04148-0*) MIT Pr.

*__Solving Problems in Fluid Dynamics.__ G. J. Sharpe. (C). 1993. pap. text ed. 34.95 (*0-582-03374-8*) Addison-Wesley.

Solving Problems in Fluid Mechanics, Vol. 1. 3rd ed. J. F. Douglas. (C). 1996. pap. text ed. 24.95 (*0-582-23987-7*) Addison-Wesley.

Solving Problems in Scientific Computing Using Maple & Matlab. Walter Gander & Jiri Hrebicek. LC 93-41288. 268p. 1993. 39.00 (*0-387-57329-1*) Spr-Verlag.

Solving Problems in Scientific Computing Using Maple & Matlab. Walter Gander. 1995. pap. text ed. 39.00 (*0-387-58746-2*) Spr-Verlag.

Solving Problems in Scientific Computing Using Maple & MATLAB. 2nd expanded ed. Walter Gander & Jiri Hrebicek. LC 95-4083. (Illus.). 336p. 1995. 39.95 (*3-540-58746-2*) Spr-Verlag.

*__Solving Problems in Scientific Computing Using Maple & Matlab.__ 3rd ed. Walter Gander. LC 97-20204. 1997. pap. text ed. 49.95 (*3-540-61793-0*) Spr-Verlag.

*__Solving Problems in Surveying.__ 2nd ed. A. Bannister. (C). 1994. pap. text ed. 34.95 (*0-582-23644-4*, Pub. by Longman UK) Longman.

Solving Problems in Technical Writing. LynnDianne Beene & Peter White. (Illus.). 256p. (C). 1988. pap. text ed. 18.95 (*0-19-505331-1*) OUP.

Solving Problems Kids Care About: Grades 4-8. Randall J. Souviney. (Illus.). 136p. (Orig.). 1990. pap. 13.95 (*0-673-16534-5*, GoodYrBooks) Addson-Wesley Educ.

*__Solving Problems Through Learning.__ Mike Watts. 208p. 1996. 75.00 (*0-7507-0538-8*, Falmer Pr); pap. 27.00 (*0-7507-0539-6*, Falmer Pr) Taylor & Francis.

Solving Problems Through Technical & Professional Writing. George E. Kennedy & Tracy T. Montgomery. LC 92-26674. 1993. pap. text ed. write for info. (*0-07-034056-0*) McGraw.

Solving Problems with NMR Spectroscopy. Atta-ur-Rahman & Muhammad I. Choudhary. LC 95-15392. (Illus.). 430p. 1995. pap. text ed. 39.95 (*0-12-066320-1*) Acad Pr.

Solving Problems/Making Decisions. Daggett. (CA - Career Development Ser.). 1983. pap. 16.95 (*0-538-07600-3*) S-W Pub.

Solving Production-Management Problems. (Series 1965-1967). 45p. 50.00 (*0-318-19671-9*) Clothing Mfrs.

Solving Rebar Corrosion Problems in Concrete. (Illus.). 147p. 1983. 10.00 (*0-915567-99-7*) NACE Intl.

Solving Riddles & Untying Knots: Biblical, Epigraphic & Semitic Studies in Honor of Jonas C. Greenfield. Ed. by Ziony Zevitn et al. LC 95-16310. xxxiv, 668p. 1995. reprint ed. 49.50 (*0-931464-93-5*) Eisenbrauns.

Solving School Problems: Kindergarten Through Middle School. Elaine K. McEwan. 336p. (Orig.). 1992. pap. 10.99 (*0-87788-640-7*) Shaw Pubs.

Solving Science Mysteries. Bob De Weese. (Science Mini-Unit Intermediate Ser.: Vol. 8). (Illus.). 16p. (J). (gr. 3-6). 1994. pap. text ed. 5.95 (*1-55799-299-1*, ECM839) Evan-Moor Corp.

Solving Sexual Problems in the 1990's. Ben N. Ard, Jr. (American University Studies: Psychology: Ser. VIII, Vol. 15). 225p. (C). 1989. text ed. 44.95 (*0-8204-1061-6*) P Lang Pubng.

Solving Sheetfed Offset Press Problems. 3rd ed. GATF Staff. LC 93-77815. (Illus.). 135p. 1994. text ed. 60.00 (*0-88362-167-3*) Graphic Arts Tech Found.

*__Solving Show Jumping Problems, Vol. 33.__ Jane Wallace. (Threshold Picture Guides Ser.). (Illus.). 24p. (Orig.). (YA). 1995. pap. 12.00 (*1-872082-66-1*, Pub. by Kenilworth Pr UK) Half Halt Pr.

*__Solving Skills Shortages: How to Retain & Recruit Skilled People.__ Patricia Scudamore & Hilton Catt. (Human Resource Management Ser.). 1997. pap. 24.95 (*0-7494-2055-3*) Kogan Page Ltd.

Solving Somebody Else's Blues: A Study of Police Mediation Activities. Paul E. Lawson. LC 81-40881. (Illus.). 246p. (Orig.). 1982. pap. text ed. 23.00 (*0-8191-2174-6*) U Pr of Amer.

Solving Statute of Limitations Problems. Adolph J. Levy. 800p. 1987. suppl. ed. 85.00 (*0-930273-65-6*) MICHIE.

Solving the Anorexia Puzzle: A Scientific Approach. W. F. Epling & W. D. Pierce. LC 90-4426. (Illus.). 256p. 1992. pap. text ed. 34.95 (*0-88937-034-6*) Hogrefe & Huber Pubs.

Solving the Cross-Work Puzzle: Succeeding in the Modern Organization. Robert P. Crosby. (Illus.). 72p. (Orig.). 1994. pap. 12.95 (*0-9643881-0-3*) LIOS Pubng.

*__Solving the Frame Problem: A Mathematical Investigation of the Common Sense Law of Inertia.__ Murray Shanahan. LC 96-27555. (Artifical Intelligence Ser.). (Illus.). 410p. 1997. 45.00 (*0-262-19384-1*) MIT Pr.

*__Solving the Frontline Crisis in Long-Term Care Vol. 1: A Practical Guide to Finding & Keeping Quality Nursing Assistants.__ Karl A. Pillemer. Ed. by Richard Hoffman & Martin Schumacher. 124p. (Orig.). 1996. pap. 39.00 (*0-9653629-0-6*) Frontline Pub.

Solving the Innovation Puzzle. Harvey M. Bernstein & Andrew C. Lemer. 136p. 1996. pap. 22.00 (*0-7844-0023-7*) Am Soc Civil Eng.

Solving the Mysteries of the Dead Sea Scrolls: New Light on the Bible. Edward M. Cook. 192p. 1994. pap. 12.99 (*0-310-38471-0*) Zondervan.

Solving the Mystery of Breast Discharge. Judy C. Kneece. (Illus.). 56p. 1996. pap. 7.95 (*1-886665-07-9*) EduCare Pub.

Solving the Mystery of Breast Pain. Judy C. Kneece. (Illus.). 56p. 1996. pap. 7.95 (*1-886665-06-0*) EduCare Pub.

Solving the Mystery of Daniel's Unnamed Kingdom - Finishing the Puzzle of the Last Days: Daniel's Unnamed Kingdom. Bob Bond. Ed. by Joyce K. Ellis. (Illus.). 148p. (Orig.). 1991. pap. 9.95 (*0-9628613-0-8*) Lrn to Discern.

Solving the Puzzle: Teaching & Learning with Adults. Ellen E. Notar. LC 93-51500. (Illus.). 1994. pap. text ed. 12.95 (*0-944957-20-X*) Rivercross Pub.

Solving the Puzzle of Chronic Fatigue Syndrome. Murray Susser & Michael Rosenbaum. LC 91-53018. (Illus.). 190p. (Orig.). 1992. 29.95 (*0-943685-15-X*); pap. 14.95 (*0-943685-11-7*) Life Sci Pr.

Solving the Puzzle of Dreams. large type ed. Joan Tano. (Illus.). 176p. (Orig.). 1995. pap. 10.95 (*0-913225-02-9*) Tano Tyme Pr.

Solving the Puzzle of Your Hard to Raise Child. William G. Crook & Laura J. Stevens. LC 87-9652. (Illus.). 352p. 1987. 17.95 (*0-394-56054-X*) Random.

*__Solving the Puzzles in Medical Terminology: An Interactive Study Guide to Accompany the Telecourse Medical Terminology with Vikki Wetle.__ Vikki Wetle. 385p. 1997. pap. 26.25 (*0-7637-0214-5*) Jones & Bartlett.

Solving the Riddle of Losing Weight: How to Restore Your Body Chemistry, Overcome Fatigue & Lose Weight, a Practical Program to Fight Allergies, Low Blood Sugar, Candida Albicans & Immune System Deficiency. 1992. lib. bdg. 255.95 (*0-8490-8858-5*) Gordon Pr.

Solving the Riddle of Self: The Search for Self-Discovery. John Powell. (Illus.). 92p. (Orig.). 1995. pap. 9.95 (*0-88347-300-3*) Res Christian Liv.

Solving the Riddle of the Shakespeare Sphinx. Marie B. Hall. 1984. pap. 27.50 (*0-938760-09-2*) Veritat Found.

Solving the Sales Manager/Sales Automation Equation. rev. ed. Ed. by Timothy McMahon. (Illus.). 244p. 1996. 45.00 (*0-85013-252-5*) Dartnell Corp.

*__Solving the Simpson Murder Mystery: The O. J. Book Which Dares to Explain It All.__ Christopher Springer. (Illus.). 736p. (Orig.). 1997. pap. 11.95 (*0-9649649-6-1*) Springer USA.

Solving the U. S. Energy Problem. Ernest J. Oppenheimer. 50p. (Orig.). 1984. pap. 5.00 (*0-9603982-4-4*) Pen & Podium.

Solving the Work-Family Puzzle. Bonnie Michaels & Elizabeth McCarty. 268p. 1992. 25.00 (*1-55623-627-1*) Irwin Prof Pubng.

*__Solving the Year 2000 Problem.__ Jim Keogh & Stephen Ruten. LC 96-40429. (Illus.). 264p. 1997. boxed 27.95 (*0-12-575560-0*, AP Prof) Acad Pr.

*__Solving the Year 2000 Problem.__ Michael Erbschloe. 1997. pap. 34.99 (*0-7645-3101-8*) IDG Bks.

*__Solving the Year 2000 Problem.__ Kappelman. (ITCP-US Computer Science Ser.). (C). 1997. pap. 44.99 (*1-85032-913-3*) ITCP.

Solving Unique Problems: Implementing Strategy Through Projects. Eddie Obeng. (Financial Times Management Ser.). 240p. 1995. 25.00 (*0-273-60265-9*) Pitman Publng.

Solving Urban Location Problems: Human Intuition Versus the Computer. Jerry B. Schneider. (Discussion Paper Ser.: No. 40). 1970. pap. 10.00 (*1-55869-114-6*) Regional Sci Res Inst.

Solving Violence Problems in Your School: Why a Systematic Approach Is Necessary. Carole Remboldt. 52p. 1994. pap. 2.95 (*1-56246-095-1*, P336) Johnsn Inst.

Solving Web Offset Press Problems. GATF Staff. LC 89-81680. (Illus.). 150p. (Orig.). (C). 1990. pap. text ed. 60.00 (*0-88362-144-4*) Graphic Arts Tech Found.

*__Solving Word Problems.__ Stan Vernooy. (Applied Math Ser.). (Illus.). 127p. (Orig.). (YA). (gr. 8 up). 1997. wbk. ed., pap. 6.95 (*0-931993-80-6*, GP-080) Garlic Pr OR.

*__Solving Word Problems (Math)__ Jo E. Moore. (Mathematics Ser.). (Illus.). 32p. (J). (gr. 3-5). 1996. teacher ed., pap. 2.95 (*1-55799-461-7*, 4063) Evan-Moor Corp.

Solving Your Child's Behavior Problems: An Everyday Guide for Parents. Jeffrey A. Kelly. 224p. 1983. pap. 8.95 (*0-316-48695-7*) Little.

Solving Your Child's Reading Problems. Ricki Linksman. pap. write for info. (*0-614-01893-5*, Citadel Pr) Carol Pub Group.

*__Solving Your Financial Problems.__ Ed. by Richard L. Strohm. LC 96-49390. (Layman's Law Guides Ser.). 128p. 1997. lib. bdg. 16.95 (*0-7910-4443-2*) Chelsea Hse.

Solving Your Financial Problems. 2nd ed. Richard L. Strohm. (Layman's Law Guides Ser.). 128p. 1994. pap. 8.95 (*1-56414-088-1*) Career Pr Inc.

*__Solving Your Financial Puzzle: Making Ends Meet Plus More.__ John M. Orth. (Illus.). xvi, 373p. (Orig.). 1996. pap. 24.95 (*0-9655379-0-0*) Fin Sol Ltd.

Solving Your Problems Together: Family Therapy for the Whole Family. Jana Annunziata & Phyllis Jacobson-Kram. LC 94-29708. (Illus.). 37p. 1994. 19.95 (*1-55798-268-6*, 4317460) Am Psychol.

Solzhenitsyn: What a Pity! & Other Short Stories. Ed. by G. Barabtarlo. (Russian Texts Ser.). (RUS.). pap. 16.95 (*1-85399-425-1*, Pub. by Brstl Class Pr UK) Focus Pub-R Pullins.

Solzhenitsyn & the Modern World. Edward E. Ericson, Jr. LC 92-39375. 448p. 1993. 24.00 (*0-89526-501-X*) Regnery Pub.

Solzhenitsyn at Harvard: The Address, Twelve Early Responses, & Six Later Reflections. Ed. by Ronald Berman. LC 79-26033. 160p. 1980. pap. 9.95 (*0-89633-023-0*) Ethics & Public Policy.

Solzhenitsyn Files: Secret Soviet Documents Reveal One Man's Fight Against the Monolith. Ed. by Michael Scammell. Tr. by Catherine A. Fitzpatrick et al. from RUS. LC 95-31827. (Illus.). 472p. 1995. 29.95 (*1-883695-06-6*) Edition Q.

S

Solzhenitsyn in Exile: Critical Essays & Documentary Materials. Ed. by John B. Dunlop et al. LC 85-10821. (Publication Ser.: No. 305). xv, 416p. 1985. lib. bdg. 19.95 (*0-8179-8051-2*) Hoover Inst Pr.

Solzhenitsyn-Sakharov Dialogue: Politics, Society, & the Future. Donald R. Kelley. LC 81-13258. (Contributions in Political Science Ser.: No. 74). xi, 175p. 1982. text ed. 49.95 (*0-313-22940-6*, KSS/, Greenwood Pr) Greenwood.

*__Solzhenitsyn's One Day in the Life of Ivan Denisovitch: A Critical Study.__ R. Porter. (Critical Studies in Russian Literature). 128p. 1997. pap. text ed. 13.95 (*1-85399-470-7*, Pub. by Duckworth UK) Focus Pub-R Pullins.

Solzhenitsyn's Peculiar Vocabulary: Russian-English Glossary. Eugene A. Carpovich & Vera V. Carpovich. LC 76-3932. (ENG & RUS.). 1976. 20.00 (*0-911484-04-3*) Tech Dict.

Solzhenitsyn's Political Thought. James F. Pontuso. 320p. 1990. text ed. 30.00 (*0-8139-1283-0*) U Pr of Va.

*__Solzhenitsyn's Political Thought.__ James F. Pontuso. LC 90-34241. 284p. 1990. reprint ed. pap. 81.00 (*0-608-04239-0*, 2064995) Bks Demand.

Som See & the Magic Elephant. large type ed. Jamie Oliviero. LC 94-1164. (Illus.). 32p. (J). (ps-3). 1995. 14.95 (*0-7868-0025-9*); lib. bdg. 14.89 (*0-7868-2020-9*) Hyprn Child.

*__Som See & the Magic Elephant.__ large type ed. Jamie Oliviero. (Illus.). 32p. (J). (gr. k-4). 1994. 14.95 (*1-895340-04-7*, Pub. by Hyperion Pr Ltd CN) Sterling.

*__Soma: The Divine Hallucinogen.__ David Spess. (Illus.). 224p. 1997. 24.95 (*0-89281-731-3*) Inner Tradit.

*__Soma Blues.__ Robert Sheckley. LC 96-32449. 1997. 20.95 (*0-312-86273-3*) Forge NYC.

Soma in Biblical Theology: With Emphasis on Pauline Anthropology. Robert H. Gundry. LC 75-22975. (Society for New Testament Studies, Monograph: 29). 278p. reprint ed. pap. 79.30 (*0-317-41736-3*, 2025584) Bks Demand.

Somaclonal Variation in Crop Improvement II. Ed. by Y. P. Bajaj. (Biotechnology in Agriculture & Forestry Ser.: Vol. 36). (Illus.). 392p. 1996. 292.00 (*3-540-60549-5*) Spr-Verlag.

Somaclonal Variation in Crop Improvement One. Ed. by Y. P. Bajaj. (Biotechnology in Agriculture & Forestry Ser.: Vol. II). 720p. 1990. 423.95 (*0-387-50785-X*) Spr-Verlag.

Somain Biblical Theology: With Emphasis on Pauline Anthropology. Robert H. Gundry. LC 75-22975. (Society for New Testament Studies: No. 29). reprint ed. pap. 69.50 (*0-317-28002-3*, 2025584) Bks Demand.

Somali Cats: Everything about Purchase, Care, Nutrition, Breeding, Health Care, & Behavior. Karen Davis. LC 95-53672. (Complete Pet Owner's Manual Ser.). (Illus.). 1996. pap. 6.95 (*0-8120-9583-9*) Barron.

Somali Chalenge: From Catastrophe to Renewal? Ed. by Ahmed I. Samatar. LC 93-38661. 298p. 1994. lib. bdg. 42.00 (*1-55587-363-4*) Lynne Rienner.

Somali Conflict: Prospects for Peace:, Oxfam Research Discussion Papers. Mark Bradbury. (Oxfam Research Discussion Papers). 150p. (C). 1994. pap. 15.95 (*0-85598-271-3*, Pub. by Oxfam UK) Humanities.

Somali-English - English-Somali Dictionary. Mohamud Korshel. 445p. 1994. 27.25 (*81-86264-00-0*) IBD Ltd.

Somali-English--English-Somali Dictionary. Mohamud Korshel. 445p. (ENG & SOM.). 1994. 25.95 (*0-7859-8763-0*) Fr & Eur.

Somali-English Dictionary with English Index. 3rd ed. R. David Zorc & Madina M. Osman. LC 92-76091. 625p. 1993. text ed. 79.00 (*0-931745-94-2*) Dunwoody Pr.

Somali Handbook. (Orig.). 1993. audio 19.00 (*0-931745-95-0*) Dunwoody Pr.

Somali Handbook. R. David Zorc & Madina M. Osman. LC 92-84028. 84p. (Orig.). 1993. pap. 5.00 (*0-931745-96-9*) Dunwoody Pr.

Somali Newspaper Reader. 1984. audio 20.00 (*0-931745-13-6*) Dunwoody Pr.

Somali Newspaper Reader. John D. Murphy & Abdullahi A. Issa. LC 84-72438. iii, 186p. 1984. text ed. 44.00 (*0-931745-05-5*) Dunwoody Pr.

Somali Reference Grammar. 2nd rev. ed. John I. Saeed. LC 93-71437. xiv, 336p. (YA). 1993. 64.00 (*0-931745-97-7*) Dunwoody Pr.

An Asterisk (*) at the beginning of an entry indicates that the title is appearing in BIP for the first time.

Somali Republic: An Experiment in Legal Integration. Paolo Contini. 92p. 1969. 30.00 (*0-7146-2395-4*, Pub. by F Cass Pubs UK) Intl Spec Bk.

Somali Textbook. R. David Zorc & Abdullahi A. Issa. LC 88-51592. 681p. 1990. 84.00 (*0-931745-48-9*) Dunwoody Pr.

Somali Woerterbuch: Somali-English-German, German-Somali. 2nd ed. Mohammed A. Farah. 302p. (ENG, GER & SOM.). 1993. 49.95 (*0-7859-8527-1*, 3875480554) Fr & Eur.

Somalia. Mark W. Delancey et al. (World Bibliographical Ser.: No. 92). 250p. 1989. lib. bdg. 43.50 (*1-85109-038-X*) ABC-CLIO.

Somalia. Mary V. Fox. LC 96-2025. (Enchantment of the World Ser.). 128p. (J). 1996. lib. bdg. 30.00 (*0-516-20019-4*) Childrens.

*__Somalia.__ U. S. Government Staff. (Country Studies). 1993. 20.00 (*0-614-30816-X*, USOMAL) Claitors.

Somalia: A Bibliographical Survey. Ed. by Mohamed K. Salad. LC 76-51925. (Special Bibliographic Ser.: No. 4). 468p. 1977. text ed. 89.50 (*0-8371-9480-6*, SSO/, Greenwood Pr) Greenwood.

Somalia: A Crisis of Famine & War. Edward R. Ricciuti. LC 93-15094. (Headliners Ser.). (Illus.). 64p. (J). (gr. 5-8). 1993. pap. 6.95 (*1-56294-751-6*); lib. bdg. 17.40 (*1-56294-376-6*) Millbrook Pr.

Somalia: No Mercy in Mogadishu: The Human Cost of the Conflict & the Struggle for Relief. Physicians for Human Rights Staff & Africa Watch Staff. (Illus.). 30p. 1992. pap. 7.00 (*1-879707-07-1*) Phy Human Rights.

Somalia: State Collapse, Multilateral Intervention, & Strategies for Political Reconstruction. Terrence Lyons. 99p. 1995. pap. 11.95 (*0-8157-5351-9*) Brookings.

Somalia: The Missed Opportunities. Mohamed Sahnoun. LC 94-3624. 1994. pap. text ed. 8.95 (*1-878379-35-6*) US Inst Peace.

Somalia see Cultures of the World - Group 13

Somalia & Operation Restore Hope: Reflections or Peacemaking & Peacekeeping. John Hirsch & Robert Oakley. LC 95-8221. 1995. pap. text ed. 19.95 (*1-878379-41-0*) US Inst Peace.

Somalia Country Studies: Area Handbook. 4th ed. Federal Research Division, Library of Congress Staff. Ed. by Helen C. Metz. LC 93-16246. (Area Handbook Ser.). 1993. 20.00 (*0-8444-0775-5*) Lib Congress.

Somalia Diary: The President of CARE Tells One Country's Story of Hope. Philip Johnston. LC 94-77590. (Illus.). 120p. 1994. pap. 14.95 (*1-56352-188-1*) Longstreet Pr Inc.

Somalia in Word & Image. Ed. by Katheryne S. Loughran et al. LC 85-45470. (Illus.). 176p. 1986. pap. 27.50 (*0-253-20376-7*, MB-376) Ind U Pr.

Somalia Journal. Mark Rausenberger. LC 95-77772. 96p. (Orig.). 1995. pap. 12.95 (*1-878044-26-5*) Mayhaven Pub.

Somaliland. V. A. Peel. 368p. 1986. 265.00 (*1-85077-086-7*, Pub. by Darf Pubs Ltd UK) St Mut.

Somaliland. Angus Hamilton. LC 75-94479. (Illus.). 366p. 1970. reprint ed. text ed. 35.00 (*0-8371-3292-4*, HSO&, Greenwood Pr) Greenwood.

*__Soma's Metamorphoses.__ J. Gonda. (Mededelingen der Koninklijke Nederlandse Akademie van Wetenschappen, Afd. Letterkunde Ser.: No. 46(2)). 1983. pap. text ed. 11.00 (*0-444-85575-0*) Elsevier.

Somatic & Endocrine Studies of Puberal & Adolescent Boys. William W. Greulich. (SRCD Ser.: Vol. 7, No. 3). 1942. pap. 25.00 (*0-527-01524-5*) Periodicals Srv.

*__Somatic Cell Genetics & Molecular Genetics of Trees.__ M. R. Ahuja et al. LC 96-30329. (Forestry Sciences Ser.). 1996. lib. bdg. 130.00 (*0-7923-4179-1*) Kluwer Ac.

Somatic Cell Genetics of Woody Plants. Ed. by M. R. Ahuja. (Forestry Sciences Ser.). (C). 1988. lib. bdg. 99.50 (*90-247-3728-1*) Kluwer Ac.

Somatic Embryogenesis. Jain. 1995. lib. bdg. 205.00 (*0-7923-3035-8*, Pub. by M Nijhoff NE) Kluwer Ac.

Somatic Embryogenesis & Synthetic Seed, 2. Ed. by Y. P. Bajaj. (Biotechnology in Agriculture & Forestry Ser.: Vol. 31). 1995. 398.00 (*3-540-57449-2*) Spr-Verlag.

Somatic Embryogenesis & Synthetic Seed. Y. P. Bajaj. LC 94-28237. (Biotechnology in Agriculture & Forestry Ser.). 1995. 289.00 (*0-387-57449-2*) Spr-Verlag.

Somatic Embryogenesis & Synthetic Seed I. Ed. by Y. P. Bajaj. (Biotechnology in Agriculture & Forestry Ser.: Vol. 30). 494p. 1995. 345.00 (*0-387-57448-4*) Spr-Verlag.

Somatic Embryogenesis in Woody Plants, 1. Ed. by S. Mohan Jain et al. LC 94-18512. (Forestry Sciences Ser.: Vol. 44). 392p. (C). 1995. lib. bdg. 186.00 (*0-7923-2938-4*) Kluwer Ac.

Somatic Embryogenesis in Woody Plants, Set. Ed. by S. Mohan Jain et al. LC 94-18512. (Forestry Sciences Ser.: Vol. 44). 1994. lib. bdg. write for info. (*0-7923-2939-2*) Kluwer Ac.

Somatic Fictions: Imagining Illness in Victorian Culture. Athena Vrettos. 240p. (C). 1995. pap. 14.95 (*0-8047-2533-0*) Stanford U Pr.

Somatic Fictions: Imaginning Illness in Victorian Culture. Athena Vrettos. LC 94-5352. xii ,p. 1995. 39.50 (*0-8047-2424-5*) Stanford U Pr.

Somatic Gene Therapy. Ed. by Patricia L. Chang. LC 94-17728. 320p. 1994. 73.95 (*0-8493-2440-8*) CRC Pr.

Somatic Hybridization in Crop Improvement. Ed. by Y. P. S. Bajaj. LC 94-15685. (Biotechnology in Agriculture & Forestry Ser.: Vol. 27). 1994. 390.95 (*0-387-57445-X*) Spr-Verlag.

Somatic Hypermutation in V-Regions. Steele. 200p. 1991. 142.00 (*0-8493-5348-3*, QR186) CRC Pr.

*__Somatic Psychology: The Body in Psychotherapy.__ Ed. by Don H. Johnson & Ian Grand. LC 97-21280. (IO Ser.: no. 58). 250p. (Orig.). 1997. pap. 16.95 (*1-55643-251-8*) North Atlantic.

Somatic Reality. Stanley Keleman. 128p. 1982. pap. 8.95 (*0-934320-05-5*) Center Pr.

Somatic Selection & Adaptive Evolution: On the Inheritance of Acquired Characters. rev. ed. E. J. Steele. LC 81-11419. (Illus.). 144p. 1981. pap. text ed. 10.00 (*0-226-77163-6*) U Ch Pr.

*__Somatic Technique: A Simplified Method of Releasing Chronically Tight Muscles & Enhancing.__ ACF (Dreaver) Staff. 224p. Date not set. per., pap. text ed. write for info. (*0-7872-3015-4*) Kendall-Hunt.

Somatic Therapies Pt. I: Of the Psychiatric Therapies. Toksoz B. Karasu. LC 84-3048. 924p. 1984. reprint ed. pap. 180.00 (*0-608-02026-5*, 2062682) Bks Demand.

Somatic Therapy: A Neuromuscular Approach to Chronic Pain & Stiffness. Jim Dreaver. 114p. 1991. pap. text ed. 44.95 (*0-9630467-0-5*) Wild Goose.

Somatics: Reawakening the Mind's Control of Movement, Flexibility, & Health. Thomas Hanna. 1988. pap. 15.00 (*0-201-07979-8*) Addison-Wesley.

Somation. John M. Bennett. (Illus.). 1992. pap. 2.00 (*0-935350-38-1*) Luna Bisonte.

Somatisierte Angst und Depressivitaet. Ed. by W. Poeldinger. (Illus.). vi, 136p. 1984. 32.00 (*3-8055-3844-8*) S Karger.

Somatization. C. Bass. 352p. 1990. 95.00 (*0-632-02839-4*) Blackwell Sci.

Somatization & Hypochondriasis. Robert Kellner. LC 85-12343. (Illus.). 426p. 1985. text ed. 105.00 (*0-275-92036-4*, C2036, Praeger Pubs) Greenwood.

Somatization Disorder in the Medical Setting. (Illus.). 98p. (Orig.). (C). 1994. pap. text ed. 25.00 (*0-941375-81-1*) DIANE Pub.

Somatization Disorder in the Medical Setting. G. Richard Smith, Jr. LC 91-6429. 97p. 1991. text ed. 18.50 (*0-88048-374-1*, 8374) Am Psychiatric.

Somatizing Child. E. G. Shapiro & A. A. Rosenfeld. (Contributions to Psychology & Medicine Ser.). (Illus.). 150p. 1987. 87.95 (*0-387-96363-4*) Spr-Verlag.

SomatoEmotional Release & Beyond. John E. Upledger. (Illus.). 266p. 1990. text ed. 40.00 (*0-9627157-0-0*) UI Pub.

Somatostatin: Basic & Clinical Status. Ed. by Seymour Reichlin. (Serono Symposia U. S. A. Ser.). (Illus.). 364p. 1987. 85.00 (*0-306-42573-4*, Plenum Pr) Plenum.

Somatostatin: Recent Advances in Basic Research & Clinical Applications. Ed. by Emilio Del Pozo. (Journal: Hormone Research: Vol. 29, No. 2-3). 88p. (Orig.). 1988. pap. 94.50 (*3-8055-4809-5*) S Karger.

*__Somatostatin Analogues: Basic & Clinical Perspectives Meeting, Sorrento, November, 1995.__ Ed. by R. Arnold. (Journal Digestion Ser.: Vol. 57, Suppl. 1, 1996). (Illus.). vi, 120p. 1996. pap. 50.50 (*3-8055-6337-X*) S Karger.

Somatostatin & Its Receptors: Symposium No. 190. CIBA Foundation Symposium Staff. LC 94-43530. (CIBA Foundation Symposium Ser.: Vol. 190). 274p. 1995. text ed. 84.95 (*0-471-95382-2*) Wiley.

Somatostatin Binding Sites in Functional Systems of the Brain. Brigitte Krisch. (Progress in Histochemistry & Cytochemistry Ser.: No. 28/4). (Illus.). vi, 40p. (Orig.). 1994. pap. 35.00 (*3-437-11538-3*, Pub. by G Fischer Verlag GW) Lubrecht & Cramer.

Somatotrophic Axis & the Reproductive Process in Health & Disease: Proceedings of the Symposium, Held October 28 to 31, 1993. Ed. by Eli Y. Adashi & Michael O. Thorner. LC 94-39174. 1995. 138.00 (*0-387-94419-2*) Spr-Verlag.

Somatotyping - Development & Applications. J. E. Carter & Barbara H. Heath. (Cambridge Studies in Biological Anthropology: No. 5). (Illus.). 500p. (C). 1990. text ed. 150.00 (*0-521-35117-0*) Cambridge U Pr.

Sombra de Galdos: Libra De Lectura, Repaso y Conversacion. Benito Perez Galdos. Ed. by Rudolph Cardona. (C). 1964. Tapes. audio write for info. (*0-393-99114-8*) Norton.

*__Sombra del Arquero.__ Andres Reynaldo. (SPA.). pap. write for info. (*0-89729-821-7*) Ediciones.

*__Sombra del Maestro.__ Juan Farias. (SPA.). 1996. pap. text ed. 8.95 (*84-204-4872-9*) Santillana.

Sombras en la Playa. Carlos Victoria. LC 91-78014. (Coleccion Caniqui). 167p. (Orig.). (SPA.). 1992. pap. 16.00 (*0-89729-633-8*) Ediciones.

Sombras No Se Olvidan. rev. ed. Raul de Cardenas. 57p. (SPA.). 1993. pap. text ed. 3.95 (*1-885901-01-1*) Presbyters Peartree.

Sombrero. Hayden Brown & Roberts Dickins. LC 93-6633. (Voyages Ser.). (Illus.). (J). 1994. write for info. (*0-383-03714-X*) SRA McGraw.

Sombrero de Tres Picos. unabridged ed. Alarcon. (SPA.). pap. 5.95 (*84-410-0043-3*, Pub. by Bookking Intl FR) Distribks Inc.

Sombrero De Tres Picos: El Capitan Veneno. Pedro A. De Alarcon. Tr. by Jesus Rubio-Jimenez. (Nueva Austral Ser.: No. 228). (SPA.). 1991. pap. text ed. 19.95 (*84-239-7228-3*) Elliots Bks.

Sombrero De Tres Picos see Classics of Spanish Literature

Sombrero Del Granjero Volo y Volo. Jane B. Moncure. (Castillo Magico Ser.). (Illus.). 32p. (SPA.). (J). (ps-2). 1987. lib. bdg. 21.36 (*0-89565-909-3*) Childs World.

Sombrero of Luis Lucero. Cecilia Avalos. (J). (gr. k-2). 1993. pap. 8.95 incl. audio (*0-7608-0497-4*); pap. 4.95 (*1-56801-059-1*); pap. 8.95 incl. audio (*0-7608-0498-2*); pap. 4.95 (*1-56801-061-3*) Sundance Pub.

Sombrero of Luis Lucero, Big bk. Cecilia Avalos. (J). (gr. k-2). 1993. pap. 17.95 (*1-56801-058-3*); pap. 17.95 (*1-56801-060-5*) Sundance Pub.

Some Account of the Alien Priories, & of Such Lands As They Are Known to Have Possessed in England & Wales, 2 Vols. in 1. John Nichols. LC 72-173079. reprint ed. 67.50 (*0-404-04689-4*) AMS Pr.

Some Account of the British Army Under the Command of General Howe, & the Battle of Brandywine. Joseph Townsend. LC 70-76565. (Eyewitness Accounts of the American Revolution Ser., No. 1). 1969. reprint ed. 16.95 (*0-405-01185-7*) Ayer.

Some Account of the Capture of the Ship Aurora. Philip Freneau. LC 74-140864. (Eyewitness Accounts of the American Revolution Ser., No. 1). 1971. reprint ed. 12.95 (*0-405-01227-6*) Ayer.

Some Account of the Cone Family in America, Principally of the Descendants of Daniel Cone Who Settled in Haddam, Connecticut, in 1662. W. W. Cone. (Illus.). 547p. 1989. reprint ed. pap. 82.00 (*0-8328-0419-3*); reprint ed. lib. bdg. 90.00 (*0-8328-0418-5*) Higginson Bk Co.

Some Account of the Design of the Trustees for Establishing Colonys in America. James E. Oglethorpe. Ed. by Rodney M. Baine & Phinizy Spalding. LC 89-20639. 60p. (C). 1990. text ed. 30.00 (*0-8203-1237-1*) U of Ga Pr.

Some Account of the Temple Family. 2nd ed. Temple Prime. (Illus.). 111p. 1990. reprint ed. pap. 19.50 (*0-8328-1543-8*); reprint ed. lib. bdg. 27.50 (*0-8328-1542-X*) Higginson Bk Co.

Some Account of the Temple Family. 3rd ed. Temple Prime. (Illus.). 146p. 1990. reprint ed. pap. 22.00 (*0-8328-1545-4*); reprint ed. lib. bdg. 30.00 (*0-8328-1544-6*) Higginson Bk Co.

Some Account of the Temple Family. 4th ed. Temple Prime. (Illus.). 77p. 1990. reprint ed. pap. 16.00 (*0-8328-1547-0*); reprint ed. lib. bdg. 24.00 (*0-8328-1546-2*) Higginson Bk Co.

Some Account of the Temple Family. Temple Prime. (Illus.). 100p. 1990. reprint ed. pap. 18.00 (*0-8328-1541-1*); reprint ed. lib. bdg. 26.00 (*0-8328-1540-3*) Higginson Bk Co.

Some Account of the Travels in Egypt & Nubia. 2nd ed. John L. Burckhardt. 1971. 59.00 (*0-403-03692-5*) Scholarly.

Some Account of the Work of Stephen J. Field As a Legislator, State Judge, & Judge of the Supreme Court of the United States. Ed. by Chauncy F. Black & Samuel B. Smith. (Illus.). 464p. 1986. reprint ed. lib. bdg. 42.50 (*0-8377-1139-8*) Rothman.

Some Accounts of Travels in Egypt & Nubia. Burckhardt. reprint ed. lib. bdg. 79.00 (*0-7812-0741-X*) Rprt Serv.

Some Actual Solutions in the Humanities. Charles Turek. LC 92-44986. 124p. 1993. text ed. 59.95 (*0-7734-9871-0*, Mellen Univ Pr) E Mellen.

Some Adaptations of Marsh-Nesting Blackbirds. Gordon H. Orians. LC 79-84005. (Monographs in Population Biology: No. 14). (Illus.). 312p. 1980. pap. text ed. 22.50 (*0-691-08237-5*) Princeton U Pr.

Some Additional Leguminosae Proceedings of the Third World Orchid Conference, London. D. Prain. (C). 1960. 250.00 (*0-685-22330-2*, Pub. by Scientific UK) St Mut.

Some Additions to the Flora of Burma: Four New Species of the Compositae from Southern India & a New Justicia from Assam. W. W. Smith. 42p. (C). 1977. reprint ed. 35.00 (*0-685-21827-9*, Pub. by Intl Bk Distr II) St Mut.

Some Administrative Problems of the High School Cafeteria. Willard S. Ford. LC 70-176781. (Columbia University. Teachers College. Contributions to Education Ser.: No. 238). reprint ed. 37.50 (*0-404-55238-2*) AMS Pr.

Some Adventures of Captain Simon Suggs. Johnson J. Hooper. LC 73-104487. (Illus.). reprint ed. lib. bdg. 19.50 (*0-8398-0789-9*) Irvington.

Some American Descendants of John Stradley: Plus the Line of Minnie Jackson Stradley & Miscellaneous Stradley Information. June R. Walton. (Illus.). 200p. 1986. pap. 27.00 (*0-9617874-0-6*) J R Walton.

Some American History: Slavery: The Black Man & the Man. Larry Rivers. LC 72-153088. 50p. (Orig.). (YA). 1971. pap. text ed. 8.95 (*0-939594-12-9*) Menil Collect.

Some American Humorists. Napier Wilt. 1973. 59.95 (*0-8490-1074-8*) Gordon Pr.

Some American Ladies. Meade Minnigerode. LC 70-93361. (Essay Index Reprint Ser.). 1977. 23.95 (*0-8369-1362-0*) Ayer.

Some American Story Tellers. F. T. Cooper. 1977. lib. bdg. 59.95 (*0-8490-2623-7*) Gordon Pr.

Some American Story Tellers. Frederic T. Cooper. LC 68-8451. (Essay Index Reprint Ser.). 1977. reprint ed. 23.95 (*0-8369-0336-6*) Ayer.

Some Americans Abroad. Richard Nelson. 99p. 1990. pap. 7.95 (*0-571-14158-7*) Faber & Faber.

Some Ancestors of the Baughman Family in America: Tracing Back Twelve Generations from Switzerland Through Virginia. J. Ross Baughman. LC 89-61454. (Illus.). 171p. 1994. pap. 25.00 (*0-917968-17-4*) Shenandoah Hist.

Some Ancient Novels. Frederick A. Todd. LC 68-29250. (Essay Index Reprint Ser.). 1977. reprint ed. 18.95 (*0-8369-0947-X*) Ayer.

Some Annals of Nahant, Massachusetts. Fred A. Wilson. (Illus.). 412p. 1993. reprint ed. lib. bdg. 45.00 (*0-8328-3220-0*) Higginson Bk Co.

Some Answered Questions. Abdu'l-Baha. Tr. by Laura C. Barney from PER. xviii, 324p. 1981. 11.00 (*0-87743-162-0*) Bahai.

Some Answered Questions. Abdu'l-Baha. Tr. by Laura C. Barney from PER. LC 83-21353. xviii, 324p. 1984. Pocket sized. pap. 3.00 (*0-87743-190-6*) Bahai.

Some Answers from Living. Ed. by Anna E. Keppy. LC 89-51093. 380p. 1992. pap. 10.95 (*1-55523-251-5*) Winston-Derek.

Some Anti-Thyroid & Related Substances, Nitrofurans & Industrial Chemicals. IARC Working Group on the Evaluation of the Carcinogenic Risk of Chemicals to Man (1974: Lyon, France) Staff. (IARC Monographs on the Evaluation of Carcinogenic Risk of Chemicals to Man: No. 7). 328p. reprint ed. pap. 93.50 (*0-8357-6459-1*, 2035830) Bks Demand.

Some Antibiotics: Twelfth Report - Geneva, 1968 see Specifications for the Identity & Purity of Food Additives & Their Toxicological Evaluation

Some Antimicrobials, Antioxidants, Emulsifiers, Stabilizers, Flour-Treatment Agents, Acids & Bases: Ninth Report - Rome, 1965 see Specifications for the Identity & Purity of Food Additives & Their Toxicological Evaluation

*__Some Antineoplastic & Immunosupressive Agents: The Evaluation of Carcinogenic Risks to Humans.__ (IARC Monographs: No. 26). 411p. 1981. text ed. 75.00 (*92-832-1226-6*) World Health.

Some Ants are Farmers. Virginia B. Silverstein et al. LC 93-8753. (J). Date not set. write for info. (*0-688-12529-8*); lib. bdg. write for info. (*0-688-12530-1*) Lothrop.

*__Some Applications of Advanced Instrumentation Techniques to Double Enveloping Worm Gear Testing.__ W. Loveless & R. J. Barlow. (Technical Papers). 1978. pap. text ed. 30.00 (*1-55589-422-4*) AGMA.

Some Applications of Functional Analysis in Mathematical Physics. 3rd ed. Sergei L. Sobolev. LC 91-19869. (Translations of Mathematical Monographs). 286p. 1991. 167.00 (*0-8218-4549-7*, MMONO/90) Am Math.

Some Applications of Modular Forms. Peter Sarnak. (Cambridge Tracts in Mathematics Ser.: No. 99). 128p. (C). 1990. text ed. 34.95 (*0-521-40245-X*) Cambridge U Pr.

Some Applications of Statistics in Occupational Hygiene. P. Dewell. (Technical Handbook Ser.: No. 1). 75p. (C). 1989. 156.00 (*0-905927-18-4*, Pub. by H&H Sci Cnslts UK) St Mut.

Some Appointed Work to Do: Women & Vocation in the Fiction of Elizabeth Gaskell. Robin B. Colby. LC 94-46946. (Contributions in Women's Studies: No. 150). 136p. 1995. text ed. 52.95 (*0-313-29373-2*, Greenwood Pr) Greenwood.

Some Are Drowning. Reginald Shepherd. (Poetry Ser.). 80p. (C). 1994. 22.95 (*0-8229-3867-7*); pap. 10.95 (*0-8229-5547-4*) U of Pittsburgh Pr.

Some Are More Human Than Others. Stevie Smith. LC 89-8309. (Illus.). 96p. 1989. reprint ed. pap. 7.95 (*0-8112-1110-X*, NDP680) New Directions.

*__Some Aromatic Amines & Related Nitro Compounds, Hair Dyes, Colouring Agents & Miscellaneous Industrial Chemicals: The Evaluation of Carcinogenic Risks to Humans.__ (IARC Monographs: No. 16). 400p. 1978. text ed. 60.00 (*92-832-1216-9*) World Health.

*__Some Aromatic Amines, Anthraquinones & Nitroso Compounds, & Inorganic Fluoride Used in Drinking-Water & Dental Preparations: The Evaluation of Carcinogenic Risks to Humans.__ (IARC Monographs: No. 27). 341p. 1982. text ed. 48.00 (*92-832-1227-4*) World Health.

*__Some Aromatic Amines, Hydrazines & Related Substances, N-Nitroso Compounds & Miscellaneous Alkylating Agents.__ (IARC Monographs on the Evaluation of Carcinogenic Risks to Humans: Vol. 4). 286p. 1974. 24.00 (*92-832-1204-5*, 1720004) World Health.

Some Aspect of Ibn Khaldun's Socio-Political Analysis of History. S. M. Imam. 20.50 (*0-933511-56-6*) Kazi Pubns.

Some Aspects of Amino Acid Supplementation. Ed. by William H. Cole. 97p. reprint ed. pap. 27.70 (*0-317-08913-7*, 2050492) Bks Demand.

Some Aspects of Asian History & Culture. Upendra Thakur. 1986. 48.50 (*0-317-61092-9*, Pub. by Abhinav II) S Asia.

Some Aspects of Basic Polymer Science. Blackadder. 1988. 9.00 (*0-85186-939-4*) CRC Pr.

Some Aspects of Bibliography. J. Ferguson. 1976. lib. bdg. 59.95 (*0-8490-2624-5*) Gordon Pr.

Some Aspects of British Trade in India. A. C. Sahu. 1986. 40.00 (*0-8364-1562-0*, Pub. by Ashish II) S Asia.

Some Aspects of Brownian Motion, Pt. 1. LC 92-36583. (Lectures in Mathematics ETH Zurich). xi, 136p. 1992. 34.50 (*0-8176-2807-X*) Birkhauser.

*__Some Aspects of Chabad Chassidism.__ Joseph I. Schneerson. Tr. by Nissan Mindel. 32p. (Orig.). 1945. reprint ed. pap. 2.00 (*0-8266-0425-0*) Machon Ohelei.

Some Aspects of Chinese Music. G. P. Green. 149p. 1991. reprint ed. 69.00 (*0-7812-9315-4*) Rprt Serv.

Some Aspects of Contemporary Greek Orthodox Thought. Frank S. Gavin. LC 73-133818. reprint ed. 55.00 (*0-404-02687-7*) AMS Pr.

Some Aspects of Conventional Military Capability in Soviet Foreign Relations. David D. Finley. (CISA Working Papers: No. 20). 61p. (Orig.). 1980. pap. 15.00 (*0-86682-019-1*) Ctr Intl Relations.

Some Aspects of Gipsy Music. D. C. Parker. 61p. 1991. reprint ed. 59.00 (*0-7812-9317-0*) Rprt Serv.

Some Aspects of Human & Veterinary Nutrition. Ed. by Geoffrey H. Bourne. (World Review of Nutrition & Dietetics Ser.: Vol. 28). 1978. 107.50 (*3-8055-2672-5*) S Karger.

Some Aspects of Human Nutrition. Ed. by H. C. Bourne. (World Review of Nutrition & Dietetics Ser.: Vol. 27). 1977. 91.25 (*3-8055-2393-9*) S Karger.

An Asterisk (*) at the beginning of an entry indicates that the title is appearing in BIP for the first time.

Some Aspects of India's Philosophical & Scientific Heritage. Ed. by Debiprasad Chattopadhyaya & Ravinder Singh. (C). 1995. 12.00 (*81-215-0687-5*, Pub. by Munshiram Manoharial II) S Asia.

Some Aspects of Indonesian Politics under the Japanese Occupation: 1944-1945. Benedict R. Anderson. LC 61-66733. (Cornell University, Modern Indonesian Project, Interim Report Ser.). 136p. reprint ed. pap. 38.80 (*0-317-11172-8*, 2010810) Bks Demand.

Some Aspects of International Library Cooperation. Ernest C. Richardson. 1977. lib. bdg. 75.00 (*0-685-01972-1*) Gordon Pr.

Some Aspects of Iqbal's Thoughts. Asif Iqbal Khan. 100p. 1985. 4.50 (*1-56744-389-3*) Kazi Pubns.

***Some Aspects of Iqbal's Thoughts.** Asif I. Khan. 100p. 1996. 15.95 (*0-614-21407-6*, 1150) Kazi Pubns.

Some Aspects of Irish Emigration from Ireland to the North American Colonies Between 1660-1775. Audrey Lockhart. LC 76-6351. (Irish Americans Ser.). 1976. 23.95 (*0-405-09345-4*) Ayer.

Some Aspects of Islamic Culture. 4.50 (*0-933511-57-4*) Kazi Pubns.

Some Aspects of Italian Immigration to the United States. Antonio Stella. LC 74-17956. (Italian American Experience Ser.). 178p. 1975. reprint ed. 18.95 (*0-405-06425-X*) Ayer.

Some Aspects of Jainism in Eastern India. Pranabananda Jash. (C). 1989. 21.00 (*0-685-30852-9*, Pub. by Munshiram Manoharial II) S Asia.

Some Aspects of Monetary Policy in Nepal. Yuba R. Khatiwada. (C). 1994. 22.00 (*81-7003-188-5*, Pub. by S Asia Pubs II) S Asia.

Some Aspects of Monetary Policy in Nepal. Khatiwada Y. Raj. 1994. pap. 50.00 (*0-7855-0481-8*, Pub. by Ratna Pustak Bhandar) St Mut.

Some Aspects of Mughal Architecture. R. Nath. LC 76-902803. 1976. 38.50 (*0-88386-825-3*) S Asia.

Some Aspects of Musicology see Place of Musicology in American Institutions of Higher Learning

Some Aspects of Orthodox Spirituality. pap. 0.50 (*0-89981-096-9*) Eastern Orthodox.

Some Aspects of Polaron Theory. N. N. Bogolubov, Jr. (Lecture Notes in Physics Ser.: Vol. 4). 132p. 1988. text ed. 37.00 (*9971-978-98-9*); pap. text ed. 21.00 (*9971-978-99-7*) World Scientific Pub.

Some Aspects of Portuguese Colonization & Sea Trade in West Africa in the 15th & 16th Centuries. A. Teixeira Da Mota. (Hans Wolff Memorial Lecture Ser.). 29p. (Orig.). 1978. pap. text ed. 2.50 (*0-941934-22-5*) Indiana Africa.

Some Aspects of Prophet Muhammad's Life. Ed. by M. Tariq Quaraishi. LC 83-71409. 89p. (Orig.). 1985. reprint ed. pap. 4.50 (*0-89259-045-9*) Am Trust Pubns.

***Some Aspects of Selecting & Applying Gears for Rolling Mill Equipment.** E. C. Danne. (Technical Papers). 1950. pap. text ed. 30.00 (*1-55589-388-0*) AGMA.

Some Aspects of Self-Insight As Found in Students of a Two-Year Normal School. Robert W. Shaw. LC 70-178811. (Columbia University. Teachers College. Contributions to Education Ser.: No. 448). reprint ed. 37.50 (*0-404-55448-2*) AMS Pr.

Some Aspects of Socio-Economic & Community Factors in Planning Urban Freeways. Kwame P. Annor. 27p. (Orig.). 1970. pap. 2.50 (*1-55719-047-X*) U NE CPAR.

***Some Aspects of Socio-Economic Changes in South-Western Frontier Bengal since Introduction of Neo-Vaisnavism.** Bishnu Pada Das. 1996. 34.00 (*81-7102-049-6*, Pub. by Firma KLM II) S Asia.

Some Aspects of Strontium Radiobiology. LC 91-25467. (Report Ser.: No. 110). 95p. 1991. pap. text ed. 30.00 (*0-929600-19-3*) NCRP Pubns.

Some Aspects of Technological Economics. Ball. 1989. 8.00 (*0-85186-879-7*) CRC Pr.

Some Aspects of Text Grammars: A Study in Theoretical Linguistics & Poetics. Teun A. Van Dijk. (Janua Linguarum, Ser. Major: No. 63). 375p. 1972. text ed. 78.50 (*90-279-2173-3*) Mouton.

Some Aspects of the Economics of Zakah. AMSS Staff. 229p. 1979. 3.50 (*0-89259-019-X*) Am Trust Pubns.

Some Aspects of the Effect of the Dominant American Culture Upon Children of Italian-Born Parents. Joseph W. Tait. LC 72-81351. (Illus.). ix, 74p. 1972. reprint ed. lib. bdg. 25.00 (*0-678-00919-8*) Kelley.

Some Aspects of the Genius of Giovanni Boccaccio. Edward Hutton. 1977. lib. bdg. 59.95 (*0-8490-2625-3*) Gordon Pr.

Some Aspects of the Islamic Economy. M. N. Siddiqui. pap. 3.95 (*0-933511-58-2*) Kazi Pubns.

Some Aspects of the Multinational Corporation's Exposure to the Exchange Rate Risk. Hassanand T. Jadwani. Ed. by Stuart Bruchey. LC 80-576. (Multinational Corporations Ser.). (Illus.). 1981. lib. bdg. 23.95 (*0-405-13369-3*) Ayer.

Some Aspects of the Optimal Control of Distributed Parameter Systems. J. L. Lions. (CBMS-NSF Regional Conference Ser.: No. 6). vi, 92p. (Orig.). 1972. pap. text ed. 18.00 (*0-89871-004-9*) Soc Indus-Appl Math.

Some Aspects of the Problem of Small Enterprise As Seen in Four Selected Industries. Harold G. Vatter. LC 77-14789. (Dissertations in American Economic History Ser.). 1978. 58.95 (*0-405-11060-X*) Ayer.

Some Aspects of the Ramayana & the Mahabharata. Bibek DebRoy & Dipavali DebRoy. 1989. 35.00 (*81-7169-008-4*) S Asia.

Some Aspects of the Religious Music of the United States Negro. George R. Ricks. Ed. by Richard M. Dorson. LC 77-70621. (International Folklore Ser.). 1979. reprint ed. lib. bdg. 40.95 (*0-405-10123-6*) Ayer.

Some Aspects of the Tariff Question: An Examination of the Development of American Industries under Protection. 3rd enl. ed. Frank W. Taussig. LC 68-58025. (Reprints of Economic Classics Ser.). xiii, 490p. 1972. reprint ed. lib. bdg. 49.50 (*0-678-00734-9*) Kelley.

Some Aspects of the Tariff Question: An Examination of the Development of American Industries Under Protection. Frank W. Taussig. LC 72-137297. reprint ed. 32.50 (*0-404-06348-9*) AMS Pr.

Some Aspects of Vedanta Philosophy. Swami Siddheswarananda. Tr. by Krishna Bhakti & K. Narayana Marar. 318p. (Orig.). 1976. pap. 2.50 (*0-87481-471-5*, Pub. by Ramakrishna Math II) Vedanta Pr.

***Some Assembly Required.** Eugene Stickland. 9.95 (*1-55050-090-2*, Pub. by Coteau CN) Genl Dist Srvs.

Some Asymptotic Problems in the Theory of Partial Differential Equations. Olga Oleinik. (Lezioni Lincee Lectures). 176p. (C). 1996. text ed. 59.95 (*0-521-48083-3*) Cambridge U Pr.

Some Asymptotic Problems in the Theory of Partial Differential Equations. Olga Oleinik. (Lezioni Lincee Lectures). 176p. (C). 1996. pap. text ed. 20.95 (*0-521-48537-1*) Cambridge U Pr.

Some Attic Vases in the Cyprus Museum. rev. ed. John D. Beazley. (Illus.). 46p. 1989. pap. 14.95 (*0-947816-27-5*, Pub. by Oxford Univ Comm Arch UK) David Brown.

Some Australian Poets. Archie J. Coombes. LC 70-107688. (Essay Index Reprint Ser.). 1977. 15.95 (*0-8369-1492-9*) Ayer.

Some Authors. Walter Raleigh. LC 68-55855. (Essay Index Reprint Ser.). 1977. 23.95 (*0-8369-0807-4*) Ayer.

Some Awfully Tame but Kinda Funny Stories about Early Dakota Ladies of the Evening. B. Carlson. (Illus.). 172p. 1992. pap. 9.95 (*1-878488-46-5*) Quixote Pr IA.

Some Awfully Tame, but Kinda Funny Stories about Early Illinois Ladies-of-the-Evening. Bruce Carlson. (Illus.). 152p. (Orig.). 1990. pap. 9.95 (*1-878488-25-2*) Quixote Pr IA.

Some Awfully Tame, but Kinda Funny Stories about Early Iowa Ladies of the Evening. Bruce Carlson. (Illus.). 172p. (Orig.). 1989. pap. 9.95 (*1-878488-18-X*) Quixote Pr IA.

Some Awfully Tame, but Kinda Funny Stories about Early Missouri Ladies-of-the-Evening. Bruce Carlson. (Illus.). 169p. (Orig.). 1990. pap. 9.95 (*1-878488-24-4*) Quixote Pr IA.

Some Baha'is to Remember. O. Z. Whitehead. (Illus.). 304p. 1976. 18.50 (*0-85398-147-7*) G Ronald Pub.

Some Basic Concepts in Mathematics for the Non-Math Major, Pt. II. Norman E. Cromack & Michael A. Iannone. 212p. (C). 1994. spiral bd. 30.39 (*0-8403-8325-8*) Kendall-Hunt.

Some Basic Hypergeometric Orthogonal Polynomials that Generalize Jacobi Polynomials. R. Askey & J. Wilson. LC 84-28117. (Memoirs Ser.: No. 54/319). 55p. 1990. reprint ed. pap. text ed. 17.00 (*0-8218-2321-3*, MEMO/54/319) Am Math.

Some Basic Theory for Statistical Inference. E. J. Pitman. LC 78-11921. (Monographs on Statistics & Applied Probability). 105p. (gr. 13). 1979. text ed. 42.50 (*0-412-21720-1*, 6221) Chapman & Hall.

Some Bastardly People. William H. Waddell. 79p. 1995. pap. 15.00 (*0-87012-534-6*) McClain.

Some Birds Are Black. Josephine S. McDowell. (Orig.). (J). (gr. 1-5). 1996. pap. 7.95 (*0-533-11786-0*) Vantage.

***Some Birds Hang Upside Down: And Other Amazing Facts about Birds.** Claire Llewellyn. LC 97-10033. (I Didn't Know That...Ser.). (J). 1997. 14.90 (*0-7613-0608-0*, Copper Beech Bks); 8.95 (*0-7613-0597-1*, Copper Beech Bks) Millbrook Pr.

Some Birthday! Patricia Polacco. LC 90-10381. (Illus.). 40p. (J). (ps-2). 1991. pap. 15.00 (*0-671-72750-8*, S&S Bks Young Read) S&S Childrens.

Some Birthday. Patricia Polacco. (J). (ps-6). 1993. pap. 5.95 (*0-671-87170-6*, S&S Bks Young Read) S&S Childrens.

Some Black Women: Profiles of Black Women in Canada. Braithwaite. 1993. per. 19.95 (*0-920813-84-4*, Pub. by Sister Vision CN) LPC InBook.

Some Blood: Joint Poems. C. Mehrl Bennett & John M. Bennett. 16p. 1982. pap. 3.00 (*0-935350-07-1*) Luna Bisonte.

Some Blood: Joint Poems. deluxe limited ed. C. Mehrl Bennett & John M. Bennett. 16p. 1982. pap. 8.00 (*0-935350-08-X*) Luna Bisonte.

Some Bodies: The Eucharist & Its Implications. Jonathan Bishop. 240p. 1993. 35.00 (*0-86554-401-8*, MUP/H321) Mercer Univ Pr.

Some Body! A Life-Size Guide. Pete Rowan. LC 94-20402. (Illus.). (J). 1995. 20.00 (*0-679-87043-1*) Knopf.

Some Boone Descendants & Kindred of the St. Charles District. Lilian H. Oliver. LC 84-70107. 442p. 1984. pap. 47.00 (*0-939052-02-4*) Dean Pubns.

***Some Branch Against the Sky: The Practice & Principles of Marginal Gardening.** G. F. Dutton. (Illus.). 160p. 1997. 29.95 (*0-88192-409-1*) Timber.

Some Brief Cases of Inspector Alec Stuart of Scotland Yard. Archibald C. Wagner. (Illus.). 69p. (Orig.). (YA). 1992. pap. 12.95 (*1-880664-01-1*) E M Pr.

Some British Empiricists in the Social Sciences. Richard Stone. LC 96-48242. (Raffaele Mattioli Lectures on the History of Economic Thought). 240p. (C). 1997. text ed. 64.95 (*0-521-57145-6*) Cambridge U Pr.

Some British Pioneers of Social Medicine. Major Greenwood. LC 71-126320. (Biography Index Reprint Ser.). 1977. reprint ed. 17.95 (*0-8369-8026-3*) Ayer.

***Some Bugs Glow in the Dark & Other Amazing Facts about Insects.** Claire Llewellyn. LC 96-43331. (I Didn't Know That Ser.). (Illus.). 32p. (J). (gr. 1-3). 1997. 8.95 (*0-7613-0587-4*, Copper Beech Bks); lib. bdg. 14.90 (*0-7613-0562-9*, Copper Beech Bks) Millbrook Pr.

Some Call It Heresy. Martin Weber. Ed. by Raymond H. Woolsey. 128p. (Orig.). 1985. pap. 7.99 (*0-8280-0248-7*) Review & Herald.

***Some Call It Luck, Some Skill, but Just Maybe Stupidity? (Can We Ever Really Tell)** John A. Walker. 10.00 (*0-9639798-3-3*) J A Walker Pub.

Some Called It "Weaver" Patricia J. Hicks. LC 96-94295. (Illus.). v, 83p. (Orig.). 1996. pap. 7.50 (*0-9626392-5-7*) I Collect Facts.

Some Cambridge Controversies in the Theory of Capital. G. C. Harcourt. (Modern Revivals in Economics Ser.). 272p. 1992. 54.95 (*0-7512-0027-1*, Pub. by Gregg Revivals UK) Ashgate Pub Co.

Some Cambridge Controversies in the Theory of Capital. Geoffrey Harcourt. LC 71-161294. 282p. reprint ed. pap. 80.40 (*0-317-20586-2*, 2024469) Bks Demand.

Some Can Whistle. large type ed. Larry McMurtry. 399p. 1990. lib. bdg. 20.95 (*0-8161-4987-9*, GK Hall) Thorndike Pr.

Some Can Whistle. Larry McMurtry. Ed. by William Grose. 384p. 1990. reprint ed. mass mkt. 5.99 (*0-671-72213-1*) PB.

***Some Carbamates, Thiocarbamates & Carbazides: The Evaluation of Carcinogenic Risks to Humans.** (IARC Monographs: No. 12). 0282p. 1976. text ed. 41.00 (*92-832-1212-6*) World Health.

***Some Carbamates, Thiocarbamates & Carbazides: Views & Expert Opinions of an IARC Working Group on the Evaluation of the Carcinogenic Risk of Chemicals to Man, Which Met in Lyon, 9-15 June 1976.** IARC Working Group on the Evaluation of the Carcinogenic Risk of Chemicals to Man (1976: Lyon, France) Staff. (IARC Monographs on the Evaluation of the Carcinogenic Risk of Chemicals to Humans: No. 12). (Illus.). 286p. pap. 81.60 (*0-608-04969-7*, 2065549) Bks Demand.

Some Case Studies in Latin America. Ed. by Peter J. McEwan. 88p. 1983. pap. 25.00 (*0-08-030843-0*, 27, Pergamon Pr) Elsevier.

Some Catholic Novelists. Patrick Braybrooke. LC 67-22078. (Essay Index Reprint Ser.). 1977. 21.95 (*0-8369-1323-X*) Ayer.

Some Catholic Novelists: Their Art & Outlook. P. Braybrooke. 1972. 59.95 (*0-8490-1075-6*) Gordon Pr.

Some Catholic Prayers. Hubert J. Richards. 48p. (Orig.). 1992. pap. text ed. 3.95 (*0-8146-2196-1*) Liturgical Pr.

Some Catholic Prayers. Hubert J. Richards. (Orig.). (C). 1993. 35.00 (*0-85597-483-4*, Pub. by McCrimmon Pub) St Mut.

***Some Cemetery Inscriptions from Various Massachusetts Towns.** Charles D. Townsend & Edna W. Townsend. 102p. 1996. pap. 25.00 (*1-878545-23-X*) ACETO Bookmen.

***Some Challenges in Contemporary Archaeology.** John C. Barrett. (Oxbow Lectures: No. 2). 12p. 1995. pap. 4.95 (*0-946897-98-0*, Pub. by Oxbow Bks UK) David Brown.

Some Champions: Sketches & Fiction from a Humorist's Career. Ring Lardner, Jr. Ed. by Matthew J. Bruccoli & Richard Layman. LC 92-33699. 205p. 1992. pap. 9.00 (*0-02-022343-9*) Macmillan.

Some Chemicals Used in Plastics & Elastomers. (IARC Monographs on the Evaluation of the Carcinogenic Risk of Chemicals to Humans: Vol. 39). 403p. 1986. pap. text ed. 83.00 (*92-832-1239-8*, 1720039) World Health.

Some Children Under Some Conditions: TV & the High Potential Kid. Robert Abelman. (Illus.). 95p. (Orig.). (C). 1994. pap. text ed. 30.00 (*0-7881-1339-9*) DIANE Pub.

Some Chinese Ghosts. Lafcadio Hearn. 1972. reprint ed. lib. bdg. 29.95 (*0-8422-8074-X*) Irvington.

Some Chinese Ghosts. Lafcadio Hearn. (Notable American Authors Ser.). 1992. reprint ed. lib. bdg. 75.00 (*0-7812-3065-9*) Rprt Serv.

***Some Chose to Stay: Faith & Ethics in a Time of Plague.** Alan C. Mermann. LC 96-52123. (Society/Religion/Religion/Society Ser.). 1997. pap. 17.50 (*0-391-04029-4*); text ed. 55.00 (*0-391-04028-6*) Humanities.

Some Christian & Jewish Perspectives on the Creation. Ed. by Marianne Postiglione. 260p. (Orig.). 1991. pap. 15.95 (*0-9625431-4-4*) ITEST Faith.

Some Christian Convictions: A Practical Restatement in Terms of Present-Day Thinking. Henry S. Coffin. LC 79-167328. (Essay Index Reprint Ser.). 1977. reprint ed. 19.95 (*0-8369-2763-X*) Ayer.

Some Cities. Victor Burgin. LC 95-50336. (Illus.). 217p. (C). 1996. pap. 19.95 (*0-520-20636-3*) U CA Pr.

***Some Civil War Manuscripts: A Finding Tool.** Ed. by Mary Bowman. 1997. per. 13.00 (*0-935057-89-7*) OH Genealogical.

Some Classes of Partial Differential Equations, Vol. 4. A. V. Bitsadze. xii, 504p. 1988. text ed. 145.00 (*2-88124-662-1*) Gordon & Breach.

Some Clinical Experiences of E. E. Case, M.D. Ed. by Jay Yasgur. (C). 1992. pap. text ed. 22.50 (*1-886149-01-1*) Van Hoy Pubs.

Some Clippings from a Writer's Handbook. Gerald N. Lund. 8p. (Orig.). 1995. pap. text ed. 2.50 (*1-57636-003-2*) SunRise Pbl.

Some Code Controls of School Building Construction in American Cities: An Evaluation of Certain Building Code Requirements. John W. Sahlstrom. LC 70-177222. (Columbia University. Teachers College. Contributions to Education Ser.: No. 581). reprint ed. 37.50 (*0-404-55581-0*) AMS Pr.

***Some Common Mosses of British Columbia.** W. B. Schofield. (Illus.). 400p. 1992. pap. 19.95 (*0-7718-9165-2*, Pub. by U BC Pr) U of Wash Pr.

Some Communications of Broad Reference. deluxe limited ed. Laura R. Jackson. 50p. 1983. 75.00 (*0-935716-22-X*) Lord John.

Some Companions of the Prophet, Pt. I. Fazl Ahmad. 115p. (YA). (gr. 4-10). 1985. pap. 3.50 (*1-56744-390-7*) Kazi Pubns.

Some Companions of the Prophet, Pt. II. Fazl Ahmad. 115p. (YA). (gr. 4-10). 1985. pap. 3.50 (*1-56744-391-5*) Kazi Pubns.

Some Companions of the Prophet, Pt. III. Fazl Ahmad. 115p. (YA). (gr. 4-10). 1985. pap. 3.50 (*1-56744-392-3*) Kazi Pubns.

Some Comparative Aspects of Irish Law. Alfred G. Donaldson. LC 57-8815. (Duke University, Commonwealth-Studies Center, Publication Ser.: No. 3). 307p. reprint ed. pap. 87.50 (*0-317-41731-2*, 2023376) Bks Demand.

Some Composers of Opera. Dyneley Hussey. LC 79-167360. (Essay Index Reprint Ser.). 1977. reprint ed. 15.95 (*0-8369-2654-4*) Ayer.

Some Concepts & Consequences of the Theory of Government & Binding. Noam Chomsky. (Linguistic Inquiry Monographs). 96p. 1982. pap. 10.95 (*0-262-53042-2*) MIT Pr.

Some Concepts of Indian Culture. N. A. Nikam. 212p. 1980. 15.95 (*0-318-36979-6*) Asia Bk Corp.

***Some Connections Between Isoperimetric & Sobolev-Type Inequalities.** Serguei G. Bobkov & Christian E. Houdr. LC 97-21758. (Memoirs of the American Mathematical Society Ser.). 1997. write for info. (*0-8218-0642-4*) Am Math.

Some Considerations on the Keeping of Negroes. John Woolman. LC 77-82231. (Anti-Slavery Crusade in America Ser.). 1978. reprint ed. 14.95 (*0-405-00670-5*) Ayer.

Some Contemporary Americans. Percy H. Boynton. LC 66-23516. 1924. 30.00 (*0-8196-0181-0*) Biblo.

Some Contemporary Americans: The Personal Equation in Literature. Percy H. Boynton. (BCL1-PS American Literature Ser.). 289p. 1992. reprint ed. lib. bdg. 79.00 (*0-7812-6619-X*) Rprt Serv.

***Some Contemporary Novelists.** R. Brimley Johnson. 221p. Date not set. 18.95 (*0-8369-1521-6*) Ayer.

Some Contemporary Novelists: Women. Reginald B. Johnson. LC 67-26751. (Essay Index Reprint Ser.). 1977. 19.95 (*0-8369-0575-X*) Ayer.

Some Contemporary Novelists (Men) Reginald B. Johnson. (BCL1-PR English Literature Ser.). 221p. 1992. reprint ed. lib. bdg. 79.00 (*0-7812-7124-X*) Rprt Serv.

Some Contemporary Novelists (Women) Reginald B. Johnson. (BCL1-PR English Literature Ser.). 220p. 1992. reprint ed. lib. bdg. 79.00 (*0-7812-7125-8*) Rprt Serv.

Some Continental European Aberrations of Abraxas Grossulariata Linn. (Lepidoptera) with Notes on the Theoretical Significance of the Variation Observed in the Species. G. Evelyn Hutchinson. (Connecticut Academy of Arts & Sciences Ser., Trans.: Vol. 43). 1969. pap. 39.50 (*0-685-22888-6*) Elliots Bks.

Some Contributions of South India to Indian Culture. S. Krishnaswami Aiyangar. (C). 1995. 34.00 (*81-206-0999-9*, Pub. by Asian Educ Servs II) S Asia.

Some Conversations with an Old Man & Other Poems & Songs. Don Richmond. 67p. 1987. pap. write for info. (*0-943909-02-3*) Gibbs Assocs.

Some Copper Country Names & Places. (Copper Country Local History Ser.: Vol. 5). (Illus.). 54p. 1975. 2.00 (*0-942363-04-3*) C J Monette.

Some Corner of a Foreign Field. James Bentley. 1995. pap. text ed. 18.95 (*0-316-08694-0*) Little.

Some Crawl & Never Walk. Celestine Tate. (Illus.). 128p. 1995. 15.00 (*0-8059-3652-1*) Dorrance.

Some Curious Facts about How We Make Our Living: Why Didn't Somebody Tell Us. John L. Beckley. Ed. by Helen Flint. LC 82-12987. (Illus.). 136p. (Orig.). 1986. 14.95 (*0-910187-00-2*) Economics Pr.

Some Cursory Remarks. James Birket. LC 77-150169. (Select Bibliographies Reprint Ser.). 1977. 15.95 (*0-8369-5682-6*) Ayer.

***Some Customes & Traditions of Menda-Nkwe.** Ndumu L. Taniform. (Illus.). iv, 54p. 1997. pap. 15.00 (*0-9655761-1-6*) Kola Tree Pr.

Some Cypriote "Alexanders" Edward T. Newell. (Illus.). iii, 29p. 1974. pap. 5.00 (*0-916710-14-9*) Obol Intl.

Some-Day Country. large type ed. Luke Short. LC 92-18230. 246p. (Orig.). 1992. reprint ed. lib. bdg. 16.95 (*1-56054-233-0*) Thorndike Pr.

Some Day I'm Going to Fly. Hilary McDowell. 128p. 1995. pap. 6.95 (*0-687-85005-3*, Pub. by Society Promot Chrst Know UK) Abingdon.

Some Day My Prince Will Come: A Guide for Women Whose Dream Has Not Yet Come True. Serena Gray. LC 93-45557. 1994. pap. 10.95 (*0-8065-1510-4*, Citadel Pr) Carol Pub Group.

***Some Day Soon: Profiles of Canadian Songwriters.** Douglas Fetherling. 176p. 1991. pap. 16.95 (*1-55082-000-1*, Pub. by Quarry Pr CN) LPC InBook.

Some Day We'll Laugh: An Autobiography. Esther Ralston. LC 85-2482. (Filmmakers Ser.: No. 11). (Illus.). 244p. 1985. 20.00 (*0-8108-1814-0*) Scarecrow.

Some Day You Will No All about Me: Young Children's Explorations in the World of Letters. Nigel Hall et al. LC 90-49192. 128p. 1991. pap. text ed. 18.50 (*0-435-08549-2*, 08549) Heinemann.

Some Days Are Better Than Others: A Book About Breastfeeding. Diane Reukauf & Mary A. Trause. 1989. pap. text ed. 23.00 (*0-8359-7054-X*, Reston); pap. text ed. 9.95 (*0-686-96872-7*, Reston) P-H.

Some Days, Other Days. P. J. Peterson. LC 93-3871. 32p. (J). 1994. text ed. 14.95 (*0-684-19595-X*) S&S Trade.

Some Days You Get the Bear. Lawrence Block. 304p. 1994. reprint ed. mass mkt. 5.99 (*0-380-71568-6*) Avon.

Some Debris from My Days. 86p. 1984. 25.00 (*0-7212-0644-1*, Pub. by Regency Press UK) St Mut.

Some Deepr Aspects of Masonic Symbolism. Arthur E. Waite. 1993. pap. 9.95 (*1-56459-414-9*) Kessinger Pub.

Some Degree of Power: From Hired Hand to Union Craftsman in the Preindustrial American Printing Trade, 1778-1815. Mark Lause. 224p. 1991. 32.00 (*1-55728-185-8*) U of Ark Pr.

Some Dependent Peoples of the South Pacific. Linden Mander. LC 75-30071. (Institute of Pacific Relations Ser.). reprint ed. 84.50 (*0-404-59544-8*) AMS Pr.

Some Descendants of Nathaniel Woodward Who Came to Boston about 1630. Harold E. Woodward. LC 84-998. 235p. 1984. lib. bdg. 12.50 (*0-88082-007-1*) New Eng Hist.

Some Descendants of Thomas Fuller of Woburn, Vol. IV. 271p. 1919. 15.00 (*0-940748-43-6*) Conn Hist Soc.

Some Desparate Glory: The Diary of a Young Officer, 1917. Edwin C. Vaughan. 232p. 1994. pap. 27.50 (*0-333-38727-9*, Pub. by Papermac UK) Trans-Atl Phila.

Some Dickens Women. E. Charles. 1972. 59.95 (*0-8490-1076-4*) Gordon Pr.

Some Dictyosporous Genera & Species in the Pleosporales in North America. Margaret E. Barr. LC 90-13421. (Memoirs Ser.: No. 62). (Illus.). 92p. 1990. pap. 18.75 (*0-89327-359-7*) NY Botanical.

Some Difficulties in Elementary School History. Adelaide M. Ayer. LC 72-176527. (Columbia University. Teachers College. Contributions to Education Ser.: No. 212). reprint ed. 37.50 (*0-404-55212-9*) AMS Pr.

Some Dilemmas of Naturalism. William R. Dennes. (Select Bibliographies Reprint Ser.). 1977. 18.95 (*0-8369-5551-X*) Ayer.

Some Disassembly Required: Eliminating Chemical Weapons While Protecting the Environment. David A. Koplow. (Flowerree Series on Chemical Weapons Control). (Illus.). 20p. 1994. pap. text ed. 10.00 (*1-884179-02-9*) Lawyers Alliance.

Some Discourses, Sermons & Remains. Joseph Glanvill. Ed. by Bernhard Fabian. (Collected Works: Vol. VIII). 422p. reprint ed. 73.45 (*0-685-66470-8*) G Olms Pubs.

Some Distinguished Americans: Imaginary Portraits. Harvey J. O'Higgins. LC 78-144166. (Short Story Index Reprint Ser.). 1977. reprint ed. 23.95 (*0-8369-3781-3*) Ayer.

Some Diversions of a Man of Letters. Edmund W. Gosse. LC 70-157964. (Essay Index Reprint Ser.). 1977. reprint ed. 23.95 (*0-8369-2225-5*) Ayer.

Some Do Care: Contemporary Lives of Moral Commitment. Anne Colby & William Damon. 1994. pap. 14.95 (*0-02-906356-6*, Free Press) Free Pr.

***Some Dogmas of Religion.** J. M. McTaggart. (Key Texts Ser.). 299p. 1997. reprint ed. pap. 24.99 (*1-85506-519-3*) Thoemmes Pr.

***Some Dogs.** Christopher Middleton. 24p. 9300. pap. 7.95 (*1-870612-93-0*, Pub. by Enitha Pr UK) Dufour.

Some Dreams Die: Utah's Ghost Towns & Lost Treasures. George A. Thompson. (Illus.). 200p. (Orig.). 1997. pap. 19.95 (*0-942688-01-5*) Dream Garden.

Some Early Baha'is of the West. O. Z. Whitehead. (Illus.). 240p. 1976. 11.50 (*0-85398-065-9*) G Ronald Pub.

Some Early Birds: The Memoirs of a Naval Aviation Cadet, 1935-1945. 2nd ed. Joe Hill. (Illus.). 130p. 1988. reprint ed. pap. 15.00 (*0-89745-044-2*) Sunflower U Pr.

Some Early Emigrants to America: And Early Emigrants to America from Liverpool. Gregoe D. Nicholson. 110p. 1989. reprint ed. 12.95 (*0-685-60504-3*, 4110) Clearfield Co.

***Some Early Lloyd (Loyd) Families of New Jersey, Virginia, Tennessee, & Kentucky.** unabridged ed. Illus. by Cover Publishing Co. Staff. LC 97-71574. 165p. (Orig.). 1997. pap. 15.00 (*0-9622972-5-9*) G G Lloyd.

Some Early Massachusetts Broadsides. (Picture Bks.). 32p. 1964. pap. 4.00 (*0-934909-15-6*) Mass Hist Soc.

Some Early Printers & Their Colophons. J. Kennard. 1976. lib. bdg. 59.95 (*0-8490-2626-1*) Gordon Pr.

***Some Early Records of the Lutheran Church, NY Vol. 148: New York Lutheran Church 1704-1772.** Ed. by Holland Society of NY Staff. Orig. Title: Holland Society Yearbook, 1903. 105p. 1997. reprint ed. pap. 20.00 (*1-56012-147-5*) Kinship Rhinebeck.

Some Early Russo-Chinese Relations. Gaston Cahen. 1973. 59.95 (*0-8490-1077-2*) Gordon Pr.

Some Early Sites in the Northern Lake Titicaca Basin. Alfred V. Kidder, 2nd. (Harvard University Peabody Museum of Archaeology & Ethnology Papers). 1974. reprint ed. pap. 25.00 (*0-527-01267-X*) Periodicals Srv.

Some Eclectic Matrix Theory. Kenneth S. Miller. LC 85-18454. 140p. (C). 1987. lib. bdg. 16.00 (*0-89874-895-X*) Krieger.

Some Economic Aspects of Government Ownership & Regulation: Essays From Economia Pubblica. Louis De Alessi. LC 82-84249. (LEC Occasional Paper). 40p. 1983. pap. 3.00 (*0-916770-12-5*) Law & Econ U Miami.

Some Economic Aspects of Railroad Development in Tsarist Russia. Jacob Metzer. Ed. by Stuart Bruchey. LC 77-77180. (Dissertations in European Economic History Ser.). 1978. lib. bdg. 20.95 (*0-405-10793-5*) Ayer.

Some Edible Mushrooms & How to Cook Them. 2nd ed. Nina L. Faubion. LC 62-15309. (Illus.). 200p. 1972. 12.95 (*0-8323-0119-1*) Binford Mort.

Some Educational & Anthropological Aspects of Latin-America. Texas University Institute of Latin-American Studies Staff. LC 69-19005. (Illus.). 85p. 1969. reprint ed. text ed. 49.75 (*0-8371-1032-7*, TLEA, Greenwood Pr) Greenwood.

Some Effects of Incentives: A Study of Individual Differences in Rivalry. Joseph Zubin. LC 70-177605. (Columbia University. Teachers College. Contributions to Education Ser.: No. 532). reprint ed. 37.50 (*0-404-55532-2*) AMS Pr.

Some Effects of Music. D. B. Fry. 11p. 1971. pap. 6.00 (*0-9500029-7-6*, Pub. by Octagon Pr UK) ISHK.

Some Efficient Sequential & Parallel Elliptic Solvers. Marian Vajtersic. LC 92-25136. 1993. lib. bdg. 177.50 (*0-7923-1918-4*) Kluwer Ac.

Some Elementary Gauge Theory Concepts. H. M. Chan & S. T. Tsou. (Lecture Notes in Physics Ser.). 164p. 1993. text ed. 40.00 (*981-02-1080-9*); pap. text ed. 23.00 (*981-02-1081-7*) World Scientific Pub.

Some Elements of the Religious Teaching of Jesus According to the Synoptic Gospels. Claude G. Montefiore. LC 73-2223. (Jewish People; History, Religion, Literature Ser.). 1973. reprint ed. 19.95 (*0-405-05285-5*) Ayer.

Some Emulsifiers & Stabilizers & Certain Other Substances: Tenth Report - Geneva, 1966 see Specifications for the Identity & Purity of Food Additives & Their Toxicological Evaluation

Some Enchanted Eating. Friends of the Symphony Publications Staff. LC 86-82217. 368p. 1986. 21.95 (*0-9617142-0-4*) Friends Symphony Pubns.

Some English Alchemical Books. John Ferguson. 1990. reprint ed. pap. 7.95 (*1-55818-124-5*) Holmes Pub.

Some English Story Tellers. Frederic T. Cooper. LC 68-54341. (Essay Index Reprint Ser.). 1977. 23.95 (*0-8369-0337-4*) Ayer.

Some English Story Tellers: A Book of the Younger Novelists. Frederic T. Cooper. 1977. lib. bdg. 59.95 (*0-8490-2627-X*) Gordon Pr.

Some Ethical Gains Through Legislation. Florence Kelley. LC 75-89742. (American Labor, from Conspiracy to Collective Bargaining Ser., No. 1: No. 1). 341p. 1974. reprint ed. 21.95 (*0-405-02131-3*) Ayer.

Some European Architectural Libraries: Their Methods, Equipment & Administration. Talbot Hamlin. LC 39-2757. reprint ed. 20.00 (*0-404-03092-0*) AMS Pr.

Some Even Volunteered: The Wolfhounds Pacify Vietnam. Alfred S. Bradford. LC 94-8344. 192p. 1994. text ed. 19.95 (*0-275-94785-8*, Praeger Pubs) Greenwood.

Some Experimental Evidence of the Perception of Dot Patterns & Two-Dimensional Shapes. Michael F. Dacey & Gerald J. Karaska. (Discussion Paper Ser.: No. 2). 1963. pap. 10.00 (*1-55869-115-4*) Regional Sci Res Inst.

Some Experiments in Quantitative Measurement of Landscape Quality. Carla B. Rabinowitz & Robert E. Coughlin. (Discussion Paper Ser.: No. 43). 1971. pap. 10.00 (*1-55869-116-2*) Regional Sci Res Inst.

Some Facets of King Lear: Essays in Prismatic Criticism. Ed. by Rosalie L. Colie & F. T. Flahiff. LC 73-81755. 256p. reprint ed. pap. 73.00 (*0-317-27054-0*, 2023616) Bks Demand.

Some Factors Affecting Employee Motivation at the University of South Dakota. Richard L. Bowen. 1982. 1.00 (*1-55614-115-7*) U of SD Gov Res Bur.

Some Factors Affecting Resumption of Interrupted Activities by Preschool Children, Vol. 16. Evelyn Katz. LC 75-12944. (University of Minnesota Institute of Child Welfare Monographs: No. 16). (Illus.). 52p. 1970. reprint ed. text ed. 45.00 (*0-8371-8081-3*, CWKS) Greenwood.

Some Factors Determining the Degree of Retroactive Inhibition see Quantitative Aspects of the Evolution of Concepts

Some Factors in the Undergraduate Careers of Young College Students with Particular Reference to Columbia & Barnard Colleges. Howard A. Gray. LC 77-176819. (Columbia University. Teachers College. Contributions to Education Ser.: No. 437). reprint ed. 37.50 (*0-404-55437-7*) AMS Pr.

Some Factors Influencing Participation in Voluntary School Group Activities: Case Study of One High School. Wayland J. Hayes. LC 73-176850. (Columbia University. Teachers College. Contributions to Education Ser.: No. 419). reprint ed. 37.50 (*0-404-55419-9*) AMS Pr.

Some Factors Influencing the Non-Expert. Elaine Vaughan. LC 90-13855. (Environment: Problems & Solutions Ser.: Vol. 5). 230p. 1990. text ed. 20.00 (*0-8240-0422-1*) Garland.

***Some Factors Influencing the Quality of Ground Gears & Worms.** L. P. Tarasov. (Technical Papers). 1948. pap. text ed. 30.00 (*1-55589-222-1*) AGMA.

Some Facts & More Facts about the Self-Styled "Pastor" C. T. Russell. J. J. Ross. 48p. 1988. reprint ed. pap. 2.95 (*1-883858-40-2*) Witness CA.

***Some Families of Revolutionary War Patriots from Virginia, Maryland, Pennsylvania, South Carolina & Kentucky: Duncan, Miller, Coulter, Fleming, Pomeroy, Junkin, Harned, Galloway, Hartley, Weatherholt, Crawford, Mason, Pate, Moorman, Adams, Lewis, Johnston, Clark, Walker, Martin, Reynolds, Head, Long, Seaton, Kenner, Thompson, Greenwell, Bonum, Philpot...** unabridged ed. Willa M. Coulter. LC 93-73281. 860p. 1993. lib. bdg. 48.00 (*0-9654367-0-5*) W Coulter.

***Some Famous Hamlets, from Burbage to Fechter.** Austin Brereton. 74p. 1972. 12.95 (*0-8369-7276-7*) Ayer.

Some Famous Medical Trials. Leonard A. Parry. LC 74-95631. x, 326p. 1976. reprint ed. 45.00 (*0-678-03754-X*) Kelley.

Some Famous Sea Fights. Fitzhugh Green & Holloway H. Frost. LC 68-58792. (Essay Index Reprint Ser.). 1977. 25.95 (*0-8369-0075-8*) Ayer.

Some Famous Singers of the 19th Century. Francis Rogers. Ed. by Andrew Farkas. LC 76-29963. (Opera Biographies Ser.). (Illus.). 1977. reprint ed. lib. bdg. 18.95 (*0-405-09703-4*) Ayer.

Some Far & Distant Place. Jonathan S. Addleton. LC 96-768. 1997. 29.95 (*0-8203-1858-2*) U of Ga Pr.

Some Fatal Accidents in the Atlantic Baltic, Champion, Trimountain & Winona Copper Mines. (Copper Country Local History Ser.: Vol. 48). (Illus.). 128p. 1994. 3.00 (*0-942363-47-7*) C J Monette.

Some Favorite Trees for Fuel & Fodder. Ram Parkash. 187p. (C). 1986. pap. 125.00 (*81-7089-039-X*, Pub. by Intl Bk Distr II) St Mut.

Some Favourite Books. John Macleod. 128p. 1989. pap. 4.50 (*0-85151-538-X*) Banner of Truth.

Some Fayette County, PA Cemeteries. Kathryn C. Miller. 239p. 1996. pap. text ed. 19.95 (*1-55856-222-2*) Closson Pr.

Some Features of Organization in Nature: A Contribution to Unified Science. 2nd rev. ed. Robert E. Bass. 1991. pap. 14.00 (*0-686-29224-3*) Adamson Print.

***Some Feet Have Noses.** Anna Gustafson. (J). Date not set. pap. write for info. (*0-688-01154-3*) Lothrop.

Some Feudal Coats of Arms from Heraldic Rolls 1298-1418: Illustrated with 830 Zinco Etchings from Effigies, Brasses & Coats of Arms. Joseph Foster. (Illus.). 296p. 1994. reprint ed. pap. 26.00 (*0-685-75104-X*, 9089) Clearfield Co.

Some Fine Dog. Patti Sherlock. LC 91-856. 160p. (J). (gr. 3-7). 1992. 15.95 (*0-8234-0947-3*) Holiday.

Some Fine Grampa! Alan Arkin. LC 92-24436. (Illus.). 32p. (J). (gr. k-3). 1995. 14.95 (*0-06-021533-X*); lib. bdg. 14.89 (*0-06-021534-8*) HarpC Child Bks.

Some Fiscal Aspects of Public Education in American Cities. Edward C. Elliott. LC 77-176748. (Columbia University. Teachers College. Contributions to Education Ser.: No. 6). reprint ed. 37.50 (*0-404-55006-1*) AMS Pr.

Some Flame Retardants & Textile Chemicals, & Exposures in the Textile Manufacturing Industry. (IARC Monographs on the Evaluation of Carcinogenic Risks to Humans: Vol. 48). 345p. 1990. pap. text ed. 72.00 (*92-832-1248-7*, 1720048) World Health.

Some Flavouring Substances & Non-Nutritive Sweetening Agents: Eleventh Report - Geneva, 1967 see Specifications for the Identity & Purity of Food Additives & Their Toxicological Evaluation

Some Folk & Scientific Names for Plants; Vernacular Names for Texas Plants; Gleanings from the Dialect of Grant County, Indiana; A Sample of New Hampshire Dialect; A Word-List from Louisiana; Language Trends in Oil Field Jargon. W. L. McAtee et al. (Publications of the American Dialect Society: No. 15). 95p. 1951. pap. text ed. 9.55 (*0-8173-0615-3*) U of Ala Pr.

***Some Food Additives, Feed Additives, & Naturally Occurring Substances.** IARC Working Group on the Evaluation of the Carcinogenic Risk of Chemicals to Man (1976: Lyon, France) Staff. (IARC Monographs on the Evaluation of the Carcinogenic Risk of Chemicals to Humans: No. 31). (Illus.). 320p. pap. 91.20 (*0-608-04968-9*, 2065548) Bks Demand.

***Some Food Additives, Feed Additives & Naturally Occurring Substances: Evaluation of Carcinogenic Risks to Humans.** (IARC Monographs: No. 31). 314p. 1983. text ed. 66.00 (*92-832-1531-1*) World Health.

***Some Food Additives, Feed Additives Naturally Occurring Substances: The Evaluation of Carcinogenic Risks to Humans.** (IARC Monographs: No. 31). 314p. 1983. text ed. 66.00 (*92-832-1231-2*) World Health.

Some Food Colours, Emulsifiers, Stabilizers, Anti-Caking Agents, & Certain Other Substances: Thirteenth Report - Rome, 1969 see Specifications for the Identity & Purity of Food Additives & Their Toxicological Evaluation

Some Footnotes for the Future. Bob Heman. (Illus.). 24p. (Orig.). 1986. pap. 3.00 (*0-935350-15-2*) Luna Bisonte.

Some Forerunners of Italian Opera. William J. Henderson. LC 70-160976. (Select Bibliographies Reprint Ser.). 1977. reprint ed. 21.95 (*0-8369-5843-8*) Ayer.

Some Foul Play. Anne Quinton. 224p. 1996. 22.00 (*0-7278-4942-5*) Severn Hse.

Some Founders of Physiology: Contributors to the Growth of Functional Biology. Chauncey D. Leake. LC 58-622. 132p. pap. 37.70 (*0-685-15953-1*, 2026395) Bks Demand.

Some Founding Papers of the University of Illinois. Compiled by Richard A. Hatch. LC 66-21365. 145p. reprint ed. 41.40 (*0-8357-9697-3*, 2019018) Bks Demand.

Some French Contemporary Opinions of the Russian Revolution of 1905. Encarnacion Alzona. LC 70-158244. (Columbia University. Studies in the Social Sciences: No. 228). reprint ed. 20.00 (*0-404-51228-3*) AMS Pr.

Some French Writers. Edward Delille. LC 78-37526. (Essay Index Reprint Ser.). 1977. reprint ed. 20.95 (*0-8369-2543-2*) Ayer.

***Some Friend.** (Reading Group Guides Ser.). (J). 1997. pap. write for info. (*0-676-76016-3*) Knopf Bks Yng Read.

Some Friend. Carol Carrick. LC 79-11490. 112p. (J). (gr. 3-6). 1987. pap. 5.95 (*0-89919-525-3*, Clarion Bks) HM.

Some Friend. Warner. (J). 1997. pap. 4.99 (*0-679-87619-7*) Random.

Some Friend. Sally Warner. LC 95-13831. 156p. (J). (gr. 5). 1996. 15.00 (*0-679-87620-0*) Knopf.

***Some Friend.** Sally Warner. (J). (gr. 3-7). 1997. reprint ed. pap. 4.99 (*0-614-28835-5*) Just Us Bks.

Some Friends. Pritish Nandy. 104p. 1983. pap. 6.00 (*0-86578-238-5*) Ind-US Inc.

Some Frog! Eve Bunting. LC 96-24844. (Illus.). (J). 1998. write for info. (*0-15-277082-8*) HarBrace.

Some Fruits of Solitude. William Penn. 96p. 1996. reprint ed. pap. 8.95 (*1-55709-433-0*) Applewood.

Some Fumigants, the Herbicides 2, 4-D & 2, 4, 5-T Chlorinated Dibenzodioxins & Miscellaneous Industrial Chemicals. IARC Working Group on the Evaluation of the Carcinogenic Risk of Chemicals to Man (1976: Lyon, France) Staff. (IARC Monographs on the Evaluation of the Carcinogenic Risk of Chemicals to Humans: No. 15). 354p. reprint ed. pap. 100.90 (*0-7837-4006-9*, 2043836) Bks Demand.

Some Fundamental Approaches in Skin Research. Ed. by J. W. Mali. (Current Problems in Dermatology Ser.: Vol. 9). (Illus.). viii, 152p. 1981. pap. 78.50 (*3-8055-3080-3*) S Karger.

Some Fundamentals of Analytical Chemistry: A Symposium Presented at the Seventy-Sixth Annual Meeting, American Society for Testing & Materials. American Society for Testing & Materials Staff. LC 74-81159. (American Society for Testing & Materials Special Technical Publication Ser.: No. 564). (Illus.). 87p. reprint ed. pap. 25.00 (*0-317-09329-0*, 2015507) Bks Demand.

Some Gangster Pain. Gillian Conoley. LC 86-70209. (Poetry Ser.). 80p. (C). 1987. 20.95 (*0-88748-026-8*); pap. 11.95 (*0-88748-027-6*) Carnegie-Mellon.

Some General Characteristics of Non-Partisan Elections. Charles R. Adrian. (Reprint Series in Social Sciences). (C). 1993. reprint ed. pap. text ed. 1.00 (*0-8290-3424-2*, PS-3) Irvington.

Some Gentle Moving Thing. 2nd ed. James C. Floyd. LC 82-60198. (Illus.). 70p. (J). (gr. 7-9). 1982. 6.95 (*0-938232-11-8*) Winston-Derek.

Some Geographic Factors That Influenced the Ancient Populations of the Chaco Canyon, New Mexico. Reginald G. Fisher. LC 34-27678. 24p. 1982. reprint ed. lib. bdg. 25.00 (*0-89370-734-1*) Borgo Pr.

Some Geometric Beauty Found: Poems, 1920's-1950's. Laurence Hartmus. 58p. 1986. pap. text ed. 8.75 (*0-915868-04-0*) Hartmus Pr.

Some Georgia County Records, Vol. 3. Silas E. Lucas, Jr. 368p. 1990. reprint ed. 40.00 (*0-89308-058-6*, GA 33) Southern Hist Pr.

Some Georgia County Records, Vol. 4. Silas E. Lucas, Jr. 430p. 1990. 40.00 (*0-89308-685-1*, GA 92) Southern Hist Pr.

Some Georgia County Records, Vol. 5. Silas E. Lucas, Jr. 326p. 1990. 40.00 (*0-89308-686-X*, GA 93) Southern Hist Pr.

Some German-American Participants in the American Revolution: The Rattermann Lists. Clifford N. Smith. (German-American Genealogical Research Monographs: No. 27). ii, 47p. (Orig.). 1990. pap. 20.00 (*0-915162-92-X*) Westland Pubns.

Some Ghost Stories. A. M. Burrage. 1981. 8.50 (*0-686-69311-6*) Bookfinger.

Some Girls. Kristin McCloy. 1995. pap. 10.95 (*0-452-27273-4*, Plume) NAL-Dutton.

Some Girls Do. Dahlia Kosinski. (Love Stories Ser.: No. 11). 192p. (YA). (gr. 7 up). 1996. mass mkt. 3.99 (*0-553-56670-9*) BDD Bks Young Read.

Some Glittering Aspects of Islamic Civilization. M. Sibai. 1988. 9.50 (*0-933511-59-0*) Kazi Pubns.

Some Goddesses of the Pen. Patrick Braybrooke. LC 67-22079. (Essay Index Reprint Ser.). 1977. 19.95 (*0-8369-1324-8*) Ayer.

Some Gold Nuggets. Mary R. Swope. 64p. (Orig.). 1996. pap. text ed. 4.00 (*0-9606936-7-X*) Swope Enter.

Some Good Some Bad Some Indifferent. Boyd E. Moffitt. 176p. (Orig.). 1996. pap. 12.95 (*0-9652895-0-8*) Railrd Earth.

Some Great English Novels. Orlo Williams. LC 70-131858. 1971. reprint ed. 9.00 (*0-403-00745-3*) Scholarly.

Some Great English Novels: Studies in the Art of Fiction. Orlo Williams. (BCL1-PR English Literature Ser.). 291p. 1992. reprint ed. lib. bdg. 79.00 (*0-7812-7118-5*) Rprt Serv.

Some Great Leaders in the World Movement. Robert E. Speer. LC 67-26786. (Essay Index Reprint Ser.). 1977. 20.95 (*0-8369-0895-3*) Ayer.

Some Great Men of Queen's. Ed. by Robert C. Wallace. LC 79-86792. (Essay Index Reprint Ser.). 1977. 17.95 (*0-8369-1200-4*) Ayer.

Some Great Political Idealists of the Christian Era. Fossey J. Hearnshaw. LC 78-107711. (Essay Index Reprint Ser.). 1977. 20.95 (*0-8369-1513-5*) Ayer.

Some Habits & Customs of the Working Classes by Journeyman Engineer. Thomas Wright. LC 67-19960. (Reprints of Economic Classics Ser.). x, 276p. 1967. reprint ed. 39.50 (*0-678-00268-1*) Kelley.

Some Half Hidden Aspects of Indian Social Justice. V. R. Iyer. 139p. 1980. 150.00 (*0-317-54656-2*) St Mut.

Some Halogenated Hydrocarbons: Views & Expert Opinions. IARC Working Group on the Evaluation of the Carcinogenic Risk of Chemicals to Man (1976: Lyon, France) Staff. (IARC Monographs on the Evaluation of the Carcinogenic Risk of Chemicals to Humans: No. 20). 615p. reprint ed. pap. 175.30 (*0-8357-6463-X*, 2035834) Bks Demand.

Some Halogenated Hydrocarbons & Pesticide Exposures. (IARC Monographs on the Evaluation of the Carcinogenic Risk of Chemicals to Humans: Vol. 41). 434p. 1987. pap. text ed. 83.00 (*92-832-1241-X*, 1720041) World Health.

Some Hawaiian Oribatoidea. A. P. Jacot. (BMB Ser.). 1974. reprint ed. 20.00 (*0-527-02227-6*) Periodicals Srv.

Some Hellenistic Elements in Primitive Christianity. W. L. Knox. (British Academy, London, Schweich Lectures on Biblical Archaeology Series, 1930). 1974. reprint ed. pap. 25.00 (*0-8115-1284-3*) Periodicals Srv.

Some Heretics of Yesterday. Samuel E. Herrick. LC 83-45614. reprint ed. 37.50 (*0-404-19832-5*) AMS Pr.

Some Hints on the Trial of a Lawsuit. Rolla R. Longenecker. LC 95-77927. xxvii, 314p. 1995. 68.00 (*0-89941-976-3*, 308830) W S Hein.

Some Historical Account of Guinea. A. Benezet. 131p. 1968. reprint ed. 37.50 (*0-7146-1888-8*, Pub. by F Cass Pubs UK) Intl Spec Bk.

Some Holiness Cornerstones. Richard S. Taylor. 1992. pap. 6.99 (*0-88019-293-3*) Schmul Pub Co.

Some Homosexual Men. David Sonenschein. 225p. 1983. pap. 8.95 (*0-915289-07-5*) D Sonenschein.

An Asterisk (*) at the beginning of an entry indicates that the title is appearing in BIP for the first time.

Some Hope. Jonathan Rix. 228p. 1994. pap. 15.95 (*0-233-98834-3*, Pub. by A Deutsch UK) Trafalgar.

Some Huguenot & Other Early Settlers on the Kennebec in the Present Town of Dresden (ME) 31p. 1986. reprint ed. pap. 4.50 (*0-935207-39-2*) Danbury Hse Bks.

Some Hyphomycetes That Prey on Free-Living Terricolous Nematodes. Charles Drechsler. (Mycologia Ser.: No. 29). (Illus.). 103p. 1937. pap. text ed. 20.00 (*0-945345-05-4*) Lubrecht & Cramer.

Some Imaginal Factors Influencing Verbal Expression see Psychology of Clothing

Some Implications of the 1984 Tandem Truck Safety Act for the U. S.-Mexico Border Area. James T. Peach & William F. Hughes. 17p. (Orig.). (C). 1985. pap. text ed. 10.00 (*0-937795-07-0*) Border Res Inst.

Some Impressions of the United States. Edward A. Freeman. LC 76-117875. (Select Bibliographies Reprint Ser.). 1977. 23.95 (*0-8369-5328-2*) Ayer.

Some Indian Saints. Gopinath Talwalker. (Illus.). 64p. (Orig.). (J). (gr. 5 up). 1980. pap. 2.50 (*0-89744-208-3*, Pub. by Natl Bk Trust II) Auromere.

Some Industrial Chemicals. (IARC Monographs on the Evaluation of Carcinogenic Risks to Humans: Vol. 60). 560p. 1994. pap. text ed. 90.00 (*92-832-1260-6*, 1720060) World Health.

***Some Industrial Chemicals & Dyestuffs: The Evaluation of Carcinogenic Risks to Humans.** (IARC Monographs: No. 29). 416p. 1982. text ed. 72.00 (*92-832-1229-0*) World Health.

Some Influences of the Requirements & Examinations of the College Entrance Examination Board on Mathematics in Secondary Schools in the United States. Leslie H. Whitcraft. LC 70-177640. (Columbia University. Teachers College. Contributions to Education Ser.: No. 557). reprint ed. 37.50 (*0-404-55557-8*) AMS Pr.

Some Information Respecting America. Thomas Cooper. LC 67-29498. (Illus.). iv, 240p. 1969. reprint ed. 39.50 (*0-678-00570-2*) Kelley.

Some Inorganic & Organometallic Compounds. IARC Working Group on the Evaluation of the Carcinogenic Risk of Chemicals to Man (1976: Lyon, France) Staff. (IARC Monographs on the Evaluation of Carcinogenic Risk of Chemicals to Man: No. 2). 183p. reprint ed. pap. 52.20 (*0-8357-6455-9*, 2035826) Bks Demand.

Some Instructions to My Wife: Concerning the Upkeep of the House & Marriage & to My Son & Daughter Concerning the Conduct of Their Childhood. Stanley Crawford. LC 85-72645. 176p. 1985. reprint ed. 20.00 (*0-916583-14-7*) Dalkey Arch.

Some Instructions to My Wife: Concerning the Upkeep of the House & Marriage & to My Son & Daughter Concerning the Conduct of Their Childhood. Stanley Crawford. LC 85-72645. 176p. 1996. reprint ed. pap. 11.95 (*0-916583-15-5*) Dalkey Arch.

Some Intellectual Consequences of the English Revolution. Christopher Hill. LC 79-5408. (Curti Lectures). 1980. 19.50 (*0-299-08140-0*); pap. 12.95 (*0-299-08144-3*) U of Wis Pr.

Some Issues Important in Developing Basic Radiation Protection Recommendations: Proceedings of the Twentieth Annual Meeting of the National Council on Radiation Protection & Measurements. LC 84-25504. (Annual Meeting Proceedings Ser.: No. 6). 325p. (Orig.). 1985. pap. 30.00 (*0-913392-75-8*) NCRP Pubns.

Some Issues in Development Administration. Ed. by P. Ramachandran & M. A. Oommen. 223p. (C). 1987. 18.00 (*0-317-89537-0*, Pub. by Oxford IBH II) S Asia.

Some Japanese Portraits. Donald Keene. LC 76-39679. 228p. 1983. pap. 5.95 (*0-87011-575-8*) Kodansha.

***Some Jewels of Maine.** Celia Risen. (Illus.). 184p. 1997. pap. 14.00 (*0-8059-4206-8*) Dorrance.

Some Joe You Don't Know: An American Biographical Guide to 100 British Television Personalities. Anthony Slide. LC 95-19430. 312p. 1996. text ed. 59.95 (*0-313-29550-6*, Greenwood Pr) Greenwood.

Some Just Clap Their Hands: Raising a Handicapped Child. Margaret Mantle. LC 85-15026. 264p. 1985. 16.95 (*0-915361-24-8*, 097331); pap. 12.95 (*0-685-10635-7*) Hemed Bks.

Some Kannada Poems. Ed. by A. K. Ramanujan & M. G. Krishnamurthi. 1975. pap. 8.00 (*0-88253-636-2*) Ind-US Inc.

Some Key Issues for the World. Wionczek. 1981. 55.00 (*0-08-028102-8*, Pergamon Pr) Elsevier.

Some Key-Points of Hindi, Panjabi (Gurmukhi), Panjabi (Persian) or Urdu Grammar. H. J. Dhillon. 85p. (Orig.). (HIN, PAN & URD.). (C). 1990. student ed., pap. text ed. 10.00 (*0-9617188-7-0*); Persian. pap. text ed. write for info. (*0-9617188-9-7*); Gurmukhi. write for info. (*0-9617188-8-9*) H J Dhillon.

Some Kind of Friend. Mary F. Shura. 128p. (J). 1992. pap. 3.50 (*0-380-71181-8*, Camelot) Avon.

***Some Kind of Hero.** Karen Glenn. 1998. pap. 14.99 (*0-670-87337-3*) Viking Penguin.

Some Kind of Hero. Max Layton. 253p. 1995. lib. bdg. 31.00 (*0-8095-4584-5*) Borgo Pr.

Some Kind of Hero. Sandy Steen. 1996. mass mkt. 3.50 (*0-373-25712-0*, 1-25712-0) Harlequin Bks.

Some Kind of Love Story. Arthur Miller. 1983. pap. 3.25 (*0-8222-1053-3*) Dramatists Play.

Some Kind of Madness. Robyn Donald. (Presents Ser.: No. 464). 1992. pap. 2.89 (*0-373-11464-8*, 1-11464-4) Harlequin Bks.

Some Kind of Paradise: The Emergence of American Science Fiction. Thomas D. Clareson. LC 84-29060. (Contributions to the Study of Science Fiction & Fantasy Ser.: No. 16). xiv, 248p. 1985. text ed. 55.00 (*0-313-23167-2*, CSK/, Greenwood Pr) Greenwood.

Some Ksatriya Tribes of Ancient India. Bimala C. Law. LC 78-72468. reprint ed. 42.00 (*0-404-17338-1*) AMS Pr.

Some Last Peoples: A Look at 5 Groups of Peoples That Are Vanishing. (Illus.). 200p. (Orig.). 1998. pap. write for info. (*0-9611632-5-9*) Odier CA.

Some Late Cenozoic Echinoidea from Cabo Blanco, Venezuela, No. 252 see Bulletins of American Paleontology: Vol. 56

Some Late Cenozoic Stony Corals from Northern Venezuela, No. 246 see Bulletins of American Paleontology: Vol. 55

Some Late Pleistocene Diatoms of the Kenai Peninsula, Alaska. R. B. McLaughlin & J. L. Stone. (Nova Hedwigia Beiheft Ser.: No. 82). (Illus.). 150p. 1986. pap. 63.00 (*3-443-51002-7*) Lubrecht & Cramer.

Some Leading Principles of Political Economy Newly Expounded. John E. Cairnes. LC 66-22617. (Reprints of Economic Classics Ser.). 421p. 1967. reprint ed. 49.50 (*0-678-00205-3*) Kelley.

Some Legal Phases of Corporate Financing, Reorganization & Regulation. Francis L. Stetson. LC 87-81957. (Business Enterprises Reprint Ser.). x, 387p. 1987. reprint ed. lib. bdg. 42.00 (*0-89941-582-2*, 305320) W S Hein.

Some Lessons from Our Legal History. William S. Holdsworth. viii, 198p. 1983. reprint ed. lib. bdg. 22.50 (*0-8377-0709-9*) Rothman.

Some Lessons from Our Legal History. William S. Holdsworth. Ed. by Bernard D. Reams, Jr. LC 28-9876. (Historical Reprints in Jurisprudence & Classical Legal Literature Ser.). viii, 198p. 1984. reprint ed. lib. bdg. 42.00 (*0-89941-252-1*, 303220) W S Hein.

Some Letters of William Vaughn Moody. William V. Moody. Ed. by D. G. Mason. LC 76-94471. reprint ed. 31.50 (*0-404-04359-3*) AMS Pr.

Some Letters of William Vaughn Moody. William V. Moody. (American Biography Ser.). 170p. 1991. reprint ed. lib. bdg. 59.00 (*0-7812-8290-X*) Rprt Serv.

Some Letters of William Vaughn Moody. William V. Moody. (BCL1-PS American Literature Ser.). 170p. 1992. reprint ed. lib. bdg. 69.00 (*0-7812-6802-8*) Rprt Serv.

Some Lichens of Tropical Africa IV: Dermatocarpaceae to Pertusariaceae. C. W. Dodge. 1964. pap. 64.00 (*3-7682-5412-7*) Lubrecht & Cramer.

Some Lichens of Tropical Africa V: Lecanoraceae to Physiaceae. C. W. Dodge. 1971. pap. 80.00 (*3-7682-5438-0*) Lubrecht & Cramer.

***Some Lie & Some Die.** Ruth Rendell. lib. bdg. 20.95 (*0-8488-2020-7*) Amereon Ltd.

Some Light: New & Selected Verse. A. L. Lazarus. Ed. by Louise A. Wazbinski. 80p. 1988. 12.50 (*0-934958-05-X*) Bellflower.

Some Light on Christian Education. Ed. by James W. Deuink. (Illus.). 195p. (Orig.). 1984. pap. 5.95 (*0-89084-262-0*, 022848) Bob Jones Univ Pr.

Some Light Remarks. Thomas Dickman. LC 79-92087. 1980. 7.95 (*0-87212-120-8*) Libra.

Some Like It Dark. Kipp Washington. 224p. 1985. mass mkt. 3.50 (*0-87067-344-0*, BH344) Holloway.

Some Like It Hot: The Climate, Culture & Cuisine of South Texas. Junior League of McAllen, Inc. Staff. (Illus.). 288p. 1992. 16.95 (*0-9633359-0-1*) Jr Leag McAllen.

Some Like It Hot Cookbook. Sarah Key & Gail Monaghan. LC 96-2727. (Hollywood Hotplates Ser.). (Illus.). 64p. 1996. 8.95 (*0-7892-0244-1*) Abbeville Pr.

Some Like It Hotter. Roz Denny. 1994. mass mkt. 2.99 (*0-373-03336-2*, 1-03336-4) Harlequin Bks.

***Some Like It Hotter.** Deb Stover. 384p. 1997. mass mkt. 5.50 (*0-7860-0382-0*, Pinncle Kensgtn) Kensgtn Pub Corp.

Some Like It Rough. Clay Caldwell. (Orig.). 1997. mass mkt. 6.50 (*1-56333-476-3*, Badboy) Masquerade.

***Some Like It Rough.** Clay Caldwell. 1998. mass mkt. 6.95 (*1-56333-544-1*, Badboy) Masquerade.

Some Limit Theorems in Statistics. R. R. Bahadur. (CBMS-NSF Regional Conference Ser.: No. 4). vi, 42p. 1971. pap. text ed. 14.00 (*0-89871-175-4*) Soc Indus-Appl Math.

Some Living Masters of the Pulpit: Studies in Religious Personality. Joseph F. Newton. LC 71-152203. (Essay Index Reprint Ser.). 1977. reprint ed. 20.95 (*0-8369-2287-5*) Ayer.

Some Love, Some Pain, Sometime. large type ed. J. California Cooper. 1996. lib. bdg. 24.95 (*0-7862-0639-X*) Thorndike Pr.

Some Love, Some Pain, Sometime: Stories. J. California Cooper. 288p. 1996. pap. 10.00 (*0-385-46788-5*, Anchor NY) Doubleday.

Some Lovely Image. Lawrence J. Quirk. 1989. pap. 9.95 (*0-8216-2007-X*, Univ Books) Carol Pub Group.

Some Loves of the Seraphic Saint. Father Augustine. 162p. 1979. 3.50 (*0-8199-0776-6*, Frncscn Herld) Franciscan Pr.

Some Low Level Walks in Strathspey. Ronald A. Laird. (C). 1986. pap. 29.00 (*0-906664-11-X*, Pub. by Mercat Pr Bks UK) St Mut.

Some Makers of American Literature. William L. Phelps. LC 70-105033. (Essay Index Reprint Ser.). 1977. 20.95 (*0-8369-1477-5*) Ayer.

Some Makers of English Law. William S. Holdsworth. Ed. by Bernard D. Reams, Jr. LC 39-8006. (Historical Reprints in Jurisprudence & Classical Legal Literature Ser.). xi, 308p. 1984. reprint ed. lib. bdg. 75.00 (*0-89941-253-X*, 303240) W S Hein.

Some Makers of the Modern Spirit: A Symposium. Ed. by John Macmurray. LC 68-22926. (Essay Index Reprint Ser.). 1977. reprint ed. 18.95 (*0-8369-0658-6*) Ayer.

Some Marriages in the Burned Record Counties of Virginia. Virginia Genealogical Society Staff. 146p. 1976. reprint ed. pap. 18.50 (*0-89308-266-X*, VA 30) Southern Hist Pr.

Some Masters of Spanish Verse. James Fitzmaurice-Kelly. LC 67-23217. (Essay Index Reprint Ser.). 1977. 18.95 (*0-8369-0443-5*) Ayer.

Some Materials Towards Memoirs of the Reign of King George Second, 3 Vols, Set. John Hervey. Ed. by Romney Sedgwick. LC 79-119102. reprint ed. 225.00 (*0-404-03300-8*) AMS Pr.

***Some Mathematical Problems in Biology.** Ed. by M. Gerstenhaber. (Lectures on Mathematics in the Life Sciences: Vol. 1). 117p. 1969. reprint ed. pap. 31.00 (*0-8218-1151-7*, LLSCI/1) Am Math.

Some Mathematical Questions in Biology. Ed. by Stephen Childress. (Lectures on Mathematics in the Life Sciences: Vol. 14). 214p. 1981. pap. 33.00 (*0-8218-1164-9*, LLSCI/14) Am Math.

Some Mathematical Questions in Biology. Ed. by George F. Oster. (Lectures on Mathematics in the Life Sciences: Vol. 13). 274p. 1980. pap. write for info. (*0-8218-1163-0*, LLSCI/13) Am Math.

Some Mathematical Questions in Biology. Ed. by Simon A. Levin. (Lectures on Mathematics in the Life Sciences: Vol. 12). 218p. 1979. reprint ed. pap. 34.00 (*0-8218-1162-2*, LLSCI/12) Am Math.

Some Mathematical Questions in Biology: DNA Sequence Analysis. Ed. by Robert M. Miura. LC 80-646696. (Lectures in Mathematics in the Life Sciences: Vol. 17). 124p. 1986. reprint ed. pap. text ed. 37.00 (*0-8218-1167-3*, LLSCI/17) Am Math.

Some Mathematical Questions in Biology: Muscle Physiology. Ed. by Robert M. Miura. LC 85-28613. (Lectures in Mathematics in the Life Sciences: Vol. 16). 234p. 1986. pap. text ed. 45.00 (*0-8218-1166-5*, LLSCI/16) Am Math.

Some Mathematical Questions in Biology: Plant Biology. L. Gross & Robert M. Miura. LC 86-71364. (Lectures in Mathematics in the Life Sciences: Vol. 18). 267p. 1986. pap. text ed. 46.00 (*0-8218-1168-1*, LLSCI/18) Am Math.

Some Mathematical Questions in Biology: The Dynamics of Excitable Media. Ed. by Hans G. Othmer. LC 89-17794. (Lectures in Mathematics in the Life Sciences: Vol. 21). 181p. 1989. pap. 37.00 (*0-8218-1171-1*, LLSCI/21) Am Math.

Some Mathematical Questions in Biology - Models in Population Biology. A. Hastings. LC 89-15119. (Lectures in Mathematics in the Life Sciences: Vol. 20). 123p. 1989. 30.00 (*0-8218-1170-3*, LLSCI/20) Am Math.

Some Mathematical Questions in Biology - Neurobiology. Ed. by Robert M. Miura. (Lectures on Mathematics in the Life Sciences: Vol. 15). 122p. 1982. pap. 30.00 (*0-8218-1165-7*, LLSCI/15) Am Math.

Some Mathematical Questions in Biology, Circadian Rhythms. G. Carpenter. LC 86-72815. (Lectures in Mathematics in the Life Sciences: Vol. 19). 265p. 1987. pap. text ed. 46.00 (*0-8218-1169-X*, LLSCI/19) Am Math.

Some Mathematical Questions in Biology, I. Ed. by Murray Gerstenhaber. (Lectures on Mathematics in the Life Sciences: Vol. 2). 156p. 1982. reprint ed. pap. 26.00 (*0-8218-1152-5*, LLSCI/2) Am Math.

Some Mathematical Questions in Biology, II. Ed. by J. D. Cowan. (Lectures on Mathematics in the Life Sciences: Vol. 3). 121p. 1972. 27.00 (*0-8218-1153-3*, LLSCI/3) Am Math.

Some Mathematical Questions in Biology, III. Ed. by J. D. Cowan. (Lectures on Mathematics in the Life Sciences: Vol. 4). 151p. 1972. pap. 31.00 (*0-8218-1154-1*, LLSCI/4) Am Math.

Some Mathematical Questions in Biology, IV. Ed. by J. D. Cowan et al. (Lectures on Mathematics in the Life Sciences: Vol. 5). 150p. 1973. pap. 38.00 (*0-8218-1155-X*, LLSCI/5) Am Math.

Some Mathematical Questions in Biology, IX. Ed. by Simon A. Levin. (Lectures on Mathematics in the Life Sciences: Vol. 10). 244p. 1978. pap. 36.00 (*0-8218-1160-6*, LLSCI/0) Am Math.

Some Mathematical Questions in Biology, V. Ed. by J. D. Cowan. (Lectures on Mathematics in the Life Sciences: Vol. 6). 141p. 1975. pap. 30.00 (*0-8218-1156-8*, LLSCI/6) Am Math.

Some Mathematical Questions in Biology, VI. Ed. by Simon A. Levin. (Lectures on Mathematics in the Life Sciences: Vol. 7). 232p. 1975. pap. 47.00 (*0-8218-9902-3*, LLSCI/7) Am Math.

Some Mathematical Questions in Biology, VII. Ed. by Simon A. Levin. (Lectures on Mathematics in the Life Sciences: Vol. 8). 182p. 1976. pap. 37.00 (*0-8218-1158-4*, LLSCI/8) Am Math.

Some Mathematical Questions in Biology, VIII. Ed. by Simon A. Levin. (Lectures on Mathematics in the Life Sciences: Vol. 9). 186p. 1977. pap. 35.00 (*0-8218-1159-2*, LLSCI/9) Am Math.

Some Mathematical Questions in Biology, X. Ed. by Simon A. Levin. (Lectures on Mathematics in the Life Sciences: Vol. 11). 179p. 1979. pap. 27.00 (*0-8218-1161-4*, LLSCI/11) Am Math.

Some Measures of the Quality of Agricultural Credit. George K. Brinegar & Lyle P. Fettig. (Technical Papers: No. 19). 66p. 1968. reprint ed. 20.00 (*0-87014-493-6*) Natl Bur Econ Res.

Some Memories & Reflections. Emma Eames. Ed. by Andrew Farkas. LC 76-29934. (Opera Biographies Ser.). (Illus.). 1977. reprint ed. lib. bdg. 35.95 (*0-405-09676-3*) Ayer.

Some Memories of a Paleontologist. William B. Scott. Ed. by I. Bernard Cohen. LC 79-7988. (Three Centuries of Science in America Ser.). 1980. reprint ed. lib. bdg. 31.95 (*0-405-12570-4*) Ayer.

Some Memories of Drawings. Georgia O'Keeffe. LC 74-14986. 1974. 250.00 (*0-686-17542-5*, Archway) PB.

Some Men & Women. Marie A. Lowndes. LC 75-150549. (Short Story Index Reprint Ser.). 1977. reprint ed. 23.95 (*0-8369-3846-1*) Ayer.

***Some Men Are Lookers.** Ethan Mordden. LC 96-53928. 1997. 23.95 (*0-312-15660-X*) St Martin.

Some Mental Processes of the Rhesus Monkey see Study of Sensory Control in the Rat

Some Metals & Metallic Compounds: Views & Expert Opinions. IARC Working Group on the Evaluation of the Carcinogenic Risk of Chemicals to Man (1976: Lyon, France) Staff. (IARC Monographs on the Evaluation of the Carcinogenic Risk of Chemicals to Humans: No. 23). 438p. reprint ed. pap. 124.90 (*0-8357-6464-8*, 2035835) Bks Demand.

Some Meteorological Aspects of the D Day Invasion of Europe 6 June 1944: Proceedings of a Symposium 19 May 1984 Fort Ord, California. Roger H. Shaw & William Innes. (Illus.). 170p. (Orig.). 1984. pap. 35.00 (*0-933876-70-X*) Am Meteorological.

Some Methodological Problems of Field Studies. Morris Zelditch, Jr. (Reprint Series in Social Sciences). (C). 1993. reprint ed. pap. text ed. 1.00 (*0-8290-3439-0*, S-545) Irvington.

Some Methods for Microbiological Assay. Ed. by R. G. Board & D. W. Lovelock. 1975. text ed. 144.00 (*0-12-108240-7*) Acad Pr.

Some Methods for the Statistical Analysis of Samples of Benthic Invertebrates. 2nd ed. J. M. Elliott. 1977. 50.00 (*0-900386-29-0*) St Mut.

Some Methods in Mathematical Analysis of Systems & Their Control. J. L. Lions. 1981. text ed. 385.00 (*0-677-60200-6*) Gordon & Breach.

Some Methods of Printing & Reproduction: An Outline Guide (UNESCO) H. R. Verry. (Education Studies & Documents: No. 11). 1974. reprint ed. pap. 25.00 (*0-8115-1335-1*) Periodicals Srv.

Some Methods of Teaching in Six Representative Teachers' Colleges of the United States. P. G. Chandler. LC 77-176634. (Columbia University. Teachers College. Contributions to Education Ser.: No. 425). reprint ed. 37.50 (*0-404-55425-3*) AMS Pr.

Some Mexican Problems. M. Saenz. 1976. lib. bdg. 59.95 (*0-8490-2628-8*) Gordon Pr.

Some Microeconomics of Higher Education: Economics of Scale. James Maynard. LC 76-139371. (Illus.). 202p. reprint ed. pap. 57.60 (*0-8357-3806-X*, 2036534) Bks Demand.

Some Minor Works of Richard Rolle, with the Privity of the Passion by S. Bonaventura. Richard Rolle. (BCL1-PR English Literature Ser.). 225p. 1992. reprint ed. lib. bdg. 79.00 (*0-7812-7191-6*) Rprt Serv.

Some Miracles Take Time: A Love Story, a Tragedy, a Triumph. Art E. Berg. 180p. 1990. pap. 8.95 (*1-883437-00-8*) Invictus Comm.

***Some Miscellaneous Pharmaceutical Substances: The Evaluation of Carcinogenic Risks to Humans.** (IARC Monographs: No. 13). 0255p. 1977. text ed. 36.00 (*92-832-1213-4*) World Health.

Some Mistakes of Moses. Robert G. Ingersoll. 270p. 1986. pap. 19.95 (*0-87975-361-7*) Prometheus Bks.

Some Mistakes of Moses. Robert G. Ingersoll. (Notable American Authors Ser.). 1992. reprint ed. lib. bdg. 75.00 (*0-685-59995-7*) Rprt Serv.

Some Modern American Poets. James G. Southworth. LC 68-8495. (Essay Index Reprint Ser.). 1977. 18.95 (*0-8369-0890-2*) Ayer.

Some Modern Applications of Mathematics. Stephen Barnett. LC 94-48287. 1995. pap. text ed. 48.00 (*0-13-834094-3*) P-H Intl.

Some Modern Authors. Stuart P. Mais. LC 73-128276. (Essay Index Reprint Ser.). 1977. 23.95 (*0-8369-1836-3*) Ayer.

Some Modern Belgian Writers: A Critical Study. Gladys R. Turquet-Milnes. LC 68-16981. (Essay Index Reprint Ser.). 1977. 19.95 (*0-8369-0953-4*) Ayer.

Some Modern Business Problems: A Series of Studies. Ed. by Arnold Plant. LC 67-23260. (Essay Index Reprint Ser.). 1977. 23.95 (*0-8369-0792-2*) Ayer.

Some Modern French Poets. F. S. Flint. Bd. with Younger French Poets. LC 78-64029. LC 78-64029. (Des Imagistes: Literature of the Imagist Movement Ser.). reprint ed. 14.00 (*0-404-17108-7*) AMS Pr.

Some Modern French Writers: A Study in Bergsonism. Gladys R. Turquet-Milnes. LC 68-24858. (Essay Index Reprint Ser.). 1977. reprint ed. 20.95 (*0-8369-0954-2*) Ayer.

Some Modern Mathematics for Physicists & Other Outsiders, Vol. 2: Introduction to Algebra, Topology, & Functional Analysis. Paul M. Roman. LC 75-101. 1975. 151.00 (*0-08-018134-1*, Pub. by Pergamon Repr UK) Franklin.

Some Modern Methods of Organic Synthesis. 3rd ed. W. Carruthers. (Cambridge Texts in Chemistry & Biochemistry Ser.). (Illus.). 580p. 1987. pap. text ed. 38.95 (*0-521-31117-9*) Cambridge U Pr.

Some Modern Novelists: Appreciations & Estimates. Helen T. Follett & Wilson Follett. LC 67-26741. (Essay Index Reprint Ser.). 1977. 23.95 (*0-8369-0449-4*) Ayer.

Some Modern Poets, & Other Critical Essays. Edward L. Davison. LC 68-16926. (Essay Index Reprint Ser.). 1977. reprint ed. 20.95 (*0-8369-0366-8*) Ayer.

Some Modern Sculptors. Stanley Casson. LC 67-28746. (Essay Index Reprint Ser.). 1977. 15.95 (*0-8369-0282-3*) Ayer.

Some Modern Tendencies in the Law. Samuel Williston. 167p. 1986. reprint ed. lib. bdg. 22.50 (*0-8377-2734-0*) Rothman.

S

Some Monomers, Plastics & Synthetic Elastomers, & Acrolein. IARC Working Group on the Evaluation of the Carcinogenic Risk of Chemicals to Humans (1978: Lyon, France) Staff. (IARC Monographs on the Evaluation of the Carcinogenic Risk of Chemicals to Humans: No. 19). 513p. 1979. pap. 146.30 (*0-7837-4007-7*, 2043837) Bks Demand.

Some Moral & Religious Teachings of Al-Ghazzali. Ali Nawab. pap. 5.50 (*0-933511-60-4*) Kazi Pubns.

Some More Horse Tradin' Ben K. Green. (Illus.). 1972. 25.00 (*0-394-46123-1*) Knopf.

Some More Things That Affect School Readiness. James K. Uphoff. 40p. (Orig.). 1992. pap. text ed. 6.00 (*0-935493-83-2*) Programs Educ.

Some More Twigs on the Baldridge Bush. Chester C. Kennedy. (Illus.). 475p. 1993. 52.95 (*1-56869-027-4*) Oldbuck Pr.

Some M(Other) Stories, a Parenthetical Tale. Alison D. Nordstrom & Carol Flax. 32p. 1995. pap. text ed. 15.00 (*1-887040-11-0*) SE Mus Photo.

Some Mothers Don't Come in Pastel. Mary E. Federick. 70p. (Orig.). 1994. pap. 13.95 (*0-911051-65-1*) Plain View.

***Some Mother's Son: The Screenplay.** Terry George. 1997. pap. 11.00 (*0-8021-3509-9*, Grove) Grove-Atltic.

Some Music & a Little War. Peter Finch. 56p. (C). 1988. pap. 25.00 (*0-947612-05-X*, Pub. by Rivelin Grapheme Pr) St Mut.

Some Musical Episodes. Tony Towle. 1992. 18.00 (*0-914610-38-4*); pap. 10.00 (*0-914610-25-2*) Hanging Loose.

Some Musical Recollections of Fifty Years. Richard Hoffman. 168p. 1991. reprint ed. lib. bdg. 69.00 (*0-7812-9349-9*) Rprt Serv.

Some Musical Recollections of Fifty Years. Richard Hoffman. (American Biography Ser.). 168p. 1991. reprint ed. lib. bdg. 59.00 (*0-7812-8186-5*) Rprt Serv.

Some Musicians of Former Days. Romain Rolland. LC 76-177517. 374p. 1972. 26.95 (*0-405-08897-3*, Pub. by Blom Pubns UK) Ayer.

Some Musicians of Former Days. Romain Rolland. LC 68-8490. (Essay Index Reprint Ser.). 1977. 23.95 (*0-8369-0831-7*) Ayer.

Some Must Watch While Some Must Sleep: Exploring the World of Sleep. William C. Dement. (Illus.). 160p. (C). 1978. reprint ed. pap. text ed. 5.95 (*0-393-09001-9*) Norton.

Some Mysteries of Astrology. Mary Elsnau. 49p. 1969. reprint ed. spiral bd. 7.00 (*0-7873-0311-9*) Hlth Research.

Some Mystical Adventures. G. R. Mead. 303p. 1993. pap. 19.95 (*1-56459-359-2*) Kessinger Pub.

Some Mythical Elements in English Literature: Being, the Clark Lectures. E. M. Tilyard. 1988. reprint ed. lib. bdg. 49.00 (*0-7812-0532-8*) Rprt Serv.

Some Mythical Elements in English Literature: Being, the Clark Lectures, 1959-1960. E. M. Tillyard. 1971. reprint ed. 29.00 (*0-403-01302-X*) Scholarly.

***Some N-Nitroso Compounds: The Evaluation of Carcinogenic Risks to Humans.** (IARC Monographs: No. 17). 365p. 1978. text ed. 60.00 (*92-832-1217-7*) World Health.

Some Naturally Occurring & Synthetic Food Components, Furocumoarins & Ultraviolet Radiation. (IARC Monographs on the Evaluation of the Carcinogenic Risk of Chemicals to Humans: Vol. 40). 444p. 1987. pap. text ed. 83.00 (*92-832-1240-1*, 1720040) World Health.

Some Naturally Occurring Substances. IARC Working Group on the Evaluation of the Carcinogenic Risk of Chemicals to Man (1976: Lyon, France) Staff. (IARC Monographs on the Evaluation of Carcinogenic Risk of Chemicals to Man: No. 10). (Illus.). 355p. reprint ed. pap. 101.20 (*0-8357-6460-5*, 2035831) Bks Demand.

Some Naturally Occurring Substances: Food Items & Constituents, Heterocyclic Aromatic Amines & Mycotoxins. (IARC Monographs on the Evaluation of Carcinogenic Risks to Humans: Vol. 56). 599p. 1993. pap. text ed. 95.00 (*92-832-1256-8*, 1720056) World Health.

***Some Nebletts in America.** Dorothy N. Perkins. (Illus.). 787p. 1994. 70.00 (*1-890240-02-8*) Neblett Pr.

***Some Necessary Angels: Essays on Writing & Politics.** Jay Parini. LC 97-25379. 1997. 24.95 (*0-231-11070-7*) Col U Pr.

Some Necessary Questions of the Play: A Stage-Centered Analysis of Shakespeare's Hamlet. Robert E. Wood. LC 94-11462. 1994. 32.50 (*0-8387-5290-X*) Bucknell U Pr.

Some Neglected Aspects of the 'Minorities' Problem. George A. Lundberg. 1994. lib. bdg. 250.00 (*0-8490-5666-7*) Gordon Pr.

Some Neglected Aspects of the Minorities Problems. George A. Lundberg. 1982. lib. bdg. 250.00 (*0-87700-411-0*) Revisionist Pr.

Some New Directions in Linguistics. Roger W. Shuy. LC 73-76752. (Illus.). 152p. reprint ed. pap. 43.40 (*0-7837-6340-9*, 2046052) Bks Demand.

***Some New Directions in Science on Computers.** 250p. 1997. text ed. 40.00 (*981-02-3196-2*) World Scientific Pub.

Some New Letters of Edward FitzGerald. Edward FitzGerald. (BCL1-PR English Literature Ser.). 177p. 1992. reprint ed. lib. bdg. 69.00 (*0-7812-7527-X*) Rprt Serv.

***Some New Materials for Consideration as Gears.** C. M. Schwitter. (Technical Papers). 1950. pap. text ed. 30.00 (*1-55589-345-7*) AGMA.

Some New Methods for Measuring & Describing Economic Inequality. R. L. Basmann et al. LC 93-40398. (Contemporary Studies in Economic & Financial Analysis: Vol. 71). 1993. write for info. (*1-55938-385-2*) Jai Pr.

Some New Trends in Systems Theory. Aron I. Katsenelinboigen. (Systems Inquiry Ser.). 271p. 1984. pap. text ed. 15.95 (*0-914105-25-6*) Intersystems Pubns.

Some Newspapers & Newspapermen. Oswald G. Villard. LC 79-134148. (Essay Index Reprint Ser.). 1977. 23.95 (*0-8369-2206-9*) Ayer.

Some Nigerian Fertility Cults. Percy A. Talbot. (Illus.). 140p. 1967. reprint ed. 45.00 (*0-7146-1019-4*, Pub. by F Cass Pubs UK) Intl Spec Bk.

Some Nineteenth Century Composers. John Horton. LC 72-148221. (Biography Index Reprint Ser.). 1977. 18.95 (*0-8369-8068-9*) Ayer.

***Some Non-Nutritive Sweetening Agents: The Evaluation of Carcinogenic Risks to Humans.** (IARC Monographs: No. 22). 208p. 1980. text ed. 30.00 (*92-832-1222-3*) World Health.

Some Notable Hamlets. Clement W. Scott. LC 78-82845. 1972. reprint ed. 20.95 (*0-405-08940-6*) Ayer.

Some Notes & Observations of the Silver Coinage of William III, 1695-1701. E. Jackson Kent. 1974. 2.00 (*0-685-51505-2*) S J Durst.

Some Notes on 'Flax of Dream' & Other Essays. Henry Williamson. (Aylesford Review Essays Ser.: No. 2). 32p. (C). 1990. reprint ed. pap. 15.00 (*0-946650-10-1*); reprint ed. lib. bdg. 25.00 (*0-8095-6755-5*) Borgo Pr.

Some Notes on the Continental Army. John W. Wright. (New Windsor Cantonment Publication: No. 2). 1975. pap. 8.95 (*0-910746-28-1*, SNO01) Hope Farm.

Some Notes on the Life of Robert Fulton. Randall LeBoeuff, Jr. (Illus.). 1971. 0.50 (*0-913344-11-7*) South St Sea Mus.

Some Notices on the Life & Writings of Fitz Greene Halleck. William C. Bryant. (Works of William Cullen Bryant). 1989. reprint ed. lib. bdg. 79.00 (*0-7812-2141-2*) Rprt Serv.

Some Observations of a Stranger at Zuni in the Latter Part of the Century. Clarence Major. (New American Poetry Ser.: No. 2). 80p. 1990. pap. 9.95 (*1-55713-020-5*) Sun & Moon CA.

Some Observations of Study Design. Samual A. Stouffer. (Reprint Series in Social Sciences). (C). 1993. reprint ed. pap. text ed. 1.00 (*0-8290-2916-8*, S-520) Irvington.

Some Observations on Eighteenth-Century Poetry. 2nd ed. David N. Smith. 83p. reprint ed. pap. 25.00 (*0-8357-4169-9*, 2036943) Bks Demand.

Some Observations on Soviet Industrial Growth. G. Warren Nutter. (Occasional Papers: No. 55). 20p. 1957. reprint ed. 20.00 (*0-87014-369-7*) Natl Bur Econ Res.

Some Observations on the Diseases of Brunus Edwardii. D. K. Blackmore et al. (Illus.). 1983. pap. 5.00 (*0-912184-04-3*) Synergistic Pr.

***Some of Dharma.** Jack Kerouac. LC 97-12870. 1997. pap. 34.95 (*0-670-84877-8*) Viking Penguin.

Some of It Is True. Anne George. 60p. (Orig.). 1993. pap. 8.95 (*0-9632842-1-5*) Curbow Pubns.

Some of It Was Funny. Mary B. Hamlin. 119p. (Orig.). 1982. 10.95 (*0-9610242-1-6*, Poly Two Pr Inc); pap. 7.95 (*0-9610242-0-8*, Poly Two Pr Inc) Murrayhollow.

Some of Me. Isabella Rossellini. 1997. 29.95 (*0-679-45252-4*) Random.

Some of My Best Friends: Essays in Gay History & Biography. A. Nolder Gay. xii, 168p. (Orig.). 1990. pap. 9.95 (*0-9601570-1-8*) Union Park.

Some of My Best Friends Are Angels. Georgianna Lillian. (Illus.). (Orig.). 1994. pap. text ed. 12.95 (*0-931667-06-2*) New Dream Publishing Co.

Some of My Best Friends Are Books: Guiding Gifted Readers from Preschool to High School. enl. rev. ed. Judith W. Halsted. LC 94-32347. 1995. pap. 22.00 (*0-910707-24-3*) Gifted Psych Pr.

Some of My Best Friends Are Crazy: Baseball's Favorite Lunatic Goes in Search of His Peers. Jay Johnstone & Rick Talley. (Illus.). 228p. 1990. text ed. 18.95 (*0-02-559560-1*) Macmillan.

Some of My Best Friends Are Jewish. Gary Fink. (Illus.). 112p. (Orig.). 1996. pap. 14.95 (*1-888016-36-1*) Finkstrom Prods.

Some of My Best Friends Are Monsters. Bruce Coville. (Camp Haunted Hills Ser.). (J). 1989. mass mkt. 3.99 (*0-671-70652-7*, Minstrel Bks) PB.

Some of My Best Friends Are Naked: Interviews with Seven Erotic Dancers. Tim P. Keefe. (Illus.). 378p. (Orig.). 1993. pap. 12.95 (*0-9634466-0-6*) Barbary CA.

Some of My Best Friends Are Smiths. David Campton. 1974. pap. 3.00 (*0-87129-254-8*, S44) Dramatic Pub.

Some of My Favorite Shots. Norm Wangard. (Illus.). 80p. (Orig.). 1995. pap. 18.95 (*0-9645548-0-1*) Classic Boating.

Some of My Life. Irving Younger. 297p. (Orig.). 1991. pap. 17.95 (*0-943380-00-6*) PEG MN.

Some of My Years. P. R. Kaikini. (Writers Workshop Redbird Ser.). 1975. 9.00 (*0-88253-638-9*); pap. text ed. 4.80 (*0-88253-637-0*) Ind-US Inc.

Some of the Ancestors & Descendants of James & George Ashford Jr. of Fairfield County, South Carolina. Charlie R. Ashford, Sr. LC 85-71620. 123p. reprint ed. 60.00 (*0-916497-23-2*); reprint ed. fiche 6.00 (*0-916497-22-4*) Burnett Micro.

Some of the Ancestors & Descendants of Samuel Converse, Jr., Major James Convers, Hon. Heman Allen, Captain Jonathan Bixby, Sr., 2 vols. C. A. Converse. (Illus.). 989p. 1989. reprint ed. pap. 148.00 (*0-8328-0421-5*); reprint ed. lib. bdg. 156.00 (*0-8328-0420-7*) Higginson Bk Co.

Some of the Best from C & H News - Views, Vol. I. (Copper Country Local History Ser.: Vol. 24). (Illus.). 128p. 1985. 5.00 (*0-942363-23-X*) C J Monette.

Some of the Best from C & H News & Views, Vol. II. Clarence J. Monette. (Copper Country Local History Ser.: No. 30). (Illus.). 120p. (Orig.). 1987. pap. 2.50 (*0-942363-29-9*) C J Monette.

Some of the Best from C & H News-Views, Vol. III. (Copper Country Local History Ser.: Vol. 46). (Illus.). 128p. 1993. 3.00 (*0-942363-45-0*) C J Monette.

Some of the Cat Poems. Artie Gold. (Illus.). 1978. pap. 2.00 (*0-916696-08-1*) Cross Country.

Some of the Days of Everett Anderson. Lucille Clifton. 32p. (J). (ps-2). 1987. pap. 5.95 (*0-8050-0289-8*, Bks Young Read) H Holt & Co.

Some of the Earliest Oaths of Allegiance to the United States. Nellie P. Waldenmaier. 99p. 1995. reprint ed. pap. 12.00 (*0-685-69921-8*, 9499) Clearfield Co.

Some of the Essentials of Finance & Investment. Ronald J. Gilson & Bernard S. Black. 253p. 1993. pap. text ed. 15.95 (*1-56662-136-4*) Foundation Pr.

Some of the First Settlers of "The Forks of the Delaware" & Their Decendents. Henry M. Kieffer. (Illus.). 443p. (Orig.). 1995. reprint ed. pap. 30.00 (*0-7884-0313-3*) Heritage Bk.

Some of the First Settlers of "The Forks of the Delaware" & Their Descendants: Being a Translation from the German of the Record Books of the First Reformed Church of Easton, Pena. from 1760 to 1852. Henry M. Kieffer. (Illus.). 404p. reprint ed. pap. 31.50 (*0-614-10013-5*, 3170) Clearfield Co.

Some of the Hardest Glosses in Old English. Herbert D. Meritt. xiv, 130p. 1968. 27.50 (*0-8047-0620-4*) Stanford U Pr.

Some of the Kinder Planets. Tim Wynne-Jones. LC 94-33009. 144p. (J). (gr. 3-7). 1995. 15.95 (*0-531-09451-0*); lib. bdg. 16.99 (*0-531-08751-4*) Orchard Bks Watts.

Some of the Kinder Planets. Tim Wynne-Jones. 144p. (J). 1996. pap. 3.99 (*0-14-038069-8*) Viking Penguin.

Some of the Things I Did Not Do. Stories. Janet B. Shaw. LC 83-18319. (Illinois Short Fiction Ser.). 144p. 1984. 14.95 (*0-252-01109-0*) U of Ill Pr.

Some of the Ways of God in Healing: How to Get Answers & Directiions When You're Suffering. Joy Dawson. 138p. 1991. pap. 7.99 (*0-927545-14-4*) YWAM Pub.

Some of Us: People Who Did Well under Thatcher. Julian Critchley. (Illus.). 176p. 1993. 34.95 (*0-7195-4860-8*, Pub. by John Murray UK) Trafalgar.

Some of Us Survived: The Story of an Armenian Boy. Kerop Bedoukian. LC 79-10601. 186p. (J). (gr. 6 up). 1979. 15.00 (*0-374-37132-6*) FS&G.

Some of Your Blood. Theodore Sturgeon. 144p. 1994. pap. 3.95 (*0-7867-0103-X*) Carroll & Graf.

Some of Your Blood. Theodore Sturgeon. 1993. reprint ed. lib. bdg. 18.95 (*0-89968-441-6*, Lghtyr Pr) Buccaneer Bks.

Some Old Flemish Towns. G. W. Edwards. 1972. 59.95 (*0-8490-1078-0*) Gordon Pr.

Some Old Homes in Frederick County. 346p. 1971. write for info. (*0-318-64330-8*) Winchester-Frederick Cty Hist Soc.

Some Old Portraits. Booth Tarkington. LC 78-93382. (Essay Index Reprint Ser.). 1977. 30.95 (*0-8369-1315-9*) Ayer.

Some Old Testament Characters in a Lighter Vein! J. W. Pope. (Illus.). 100p. (Orig.). 1995. pap. write for info. (*1-885591-91-8*) Morris Pubng.

Some One Myth: Yeat's Autobiographical Prose. Shirley Neuman. (Illus.). 160p. 1982. pap. 19.95 (*0-318-40003-0*, Pub. by Colin Smythe Ltd UK) Dufour.

***Some Organic Solvents, Resin Monomers & Related Compounds, Pigments & Occupational Exposures in Paint Manufacturing: The Evaluation of Carcinogenic Risks to Humans.** (IARC Monographs: No. 47). 535p. 1990. text ed. 94.00 (*92-832-1247-9*) World Health.

Some Organochlorine Pesticides. IARC Working Group on the Evaluation of the Carcinogenic Risk of Chemicals to Man (1976: Lyon, France) Staff. (IARC Monographs on the Evaluation of the Carcinogenic Risk of Chemicals to Man: No. 5). (Illus.). 243p. reprint ed. pap. 69.30 (*0-8357-6457-5*, 2035828) Bks Demand.

Some Other Country: New Zealand's Best Short Stories. Ed. by Marion McLeod & Bill Manhire. 256p. 1985. pap. text ed. 14.95 (*0-86861-633-8*) Routledge Chapman & Hall.

Some Other Country: New Zealand's Best Short Stories. Marion McLeod & Bill Manhire. 296p. 1996. pap. 14.95 (*0-908912-28-5*) Paul & Co Pubs.

Some Other Door. large type ed. Doris Howe. 368p. 1985. 25.99 (*0-7089-1299-0*) Ulverscroft.

Some Other Folks. Sarah P. Greene. LC 74-98570. (Short Story Index Reprint Ser.). 1977. 20.95 (*0-8369-3144-0*) Ayer.

Some Other Frequency: Interviews with Innovative American Authors. Larry McCaffery. (Penn Studies in Contemporary American Fiction). (Illus.). 344p. 1996. pap. 19.95 (*0-8122-1442-0*); text ed. 39.95 (*0-8122-3201-1*) U of Pa Pr.

Some Other Kind of Mission. Lisa Jarnot. LC 96-5349. (Poetry Ser.). (Illus.). 112p. 1996. pap. 11.00 (*1-886224-12-9*) Burning Deck.

Some Other Kind of Mission. limited ed. Lisa Jarnot. LC 96-5349. (Poetry Ser.). (Illus.). 112p. 1996. pap. 20.00 (*1-886224-13-7*) Burning Deck.

Some Other Morning. Jeremy Driscoll. 112p. (Orig.). (C). pap. 10.95 (*0-934257-66-3*) Story Line.

Some Other Place: The Right Place. Donald Harington. 480p. 1989. pap. 10.95 (*0-15-683801-X*) HarBrace.

Some Other Reality: Alice Munro's Something I've Been Meaning to Tell You. Louis K. MacKendrick. (Canadian Fiction Studies: No. 25). 120p. (C). 1993. pap. text ed. 14.95 (*1-55022-129-9*, Pub. by ECW Press CN) Genl Dist Srvs.

Some Other Spring. large type ed. Christine Wilson. 1990. pap. 15.99 (*0-7089-6913-5*, Trailtree Bookshop) Ulverscroft.

Some Other Summer. C. S. Adler. (J). (gr. 3-7). 1988. pap. 2.95 (*0-380-70515-X*, Camelot) Avon.

Some Other Wine & Light. Aleksandar Ristovic. Tr. by Charles Simic. LC 89-60744. 1989. 10.00 (*0-910350-11-6*) Charioteer.

Some Other World to Find: Quest & Negation in the Works of Herman Melville. Bruce L. Grenberg. LC 88-38843. 248p. 1989. text ed. 27.50 (*0-252-01625-4*) U of Ill Pr.

Some Others & Myself: Seven Stories & a Memoir. Ruth Suckow. LC 79-143311. 281p. 1972. reprint ed. text ed. 35.00 (*0-8371-5967-9*, SUSO, Greenwood Pr) Greenwood.

Some Parameters in the Grammar of Basque. Jon O. De Urbina. (Studies in Generative Grammar). xii, 266p. (Orig.). (C). 1989. pap. 90.80 (*90-6765-337-3*) Mouton.

Some Particulars. Thomas A. Clark. 1971. pap. 10.00 (*0-912330-12-0*, Inland Bk) Jargon Soc.

Some Passages of the Life & Death of the Right Honourable John Earl of Rochester. Gilbert Burnet. (Anglistica & Americana Ser.: No. 28). 182p. 1969. reprint ed. 70.00 (*0-685-66439-2*, 05102151) G Olms Pubs.

Some Paths Are Made to Be Taken...I Heard a Call...& I Answered It!, Vol. 1. Rose E. Hlavka-Fluhrer. 198p. (C). 1995. pap. 6.95 (*0-9646859-0-6*) Red Clover Pr.

Some Paths to Sudden Wealth. H. Glenn Carson. 103p. 1992. pap. 9.95 (*0-941620-44-1*) Carson Ent.

Some Pathways in Twentieth-Century History: Essays in Honor of Reginald Charles McGrane. Ed. by Daniel R. Beaver. LC 69-11348. 316p. reprint ed. pap. 90.10 (*0-7837-3791-2*, 2043611) Bks Demand.

***Some People.** Harold Nicolson. 252p. 1996. reprint ed. pap. 27.50 (*0-09-476590-1*, Pub. by Constable Pubs UK) Trans-Atl Phila.

Some People Are Throwing You into Confusion. Pierre Widmer. LC 83-82879. (Mennonite Faith Ser.: Vol. 14). 80p. 1984. pap. 2.99 (*0-8361-3358-7*) Herald Pr.

Some People, Places, & Things That Will Not Appear in My Next Novel. John Cheever. LC 79-116947. (Short Story Index Reprint Ser.). 1977. 18.95 (*0-8369-3449-0*) Ayer.

Some People Think We Don't Learn Anything in This School. Colleen McNally et al. LC 77-71871. (Illus.). 1977. pap. 4.95 (*0-915492-03-2*) Ash Lad Pr.

Some Perpectives of the Major Biochemical Cycles. Ed. by Gene E. Likens. (Scientific Committee on Problems of the Environment Ser.: Report 17). 175p. 1981. text ed. 61.95 (*0-471-27989-7*) Wiley.

Some Persistent Questions on Beginning Reading. Ed. by Robert C. Aukerman. LC 73-190454. 183p. reprint ed. pap. 52.20 (*0-317-55490-5*, 2029595) Bks Demand.

Some Personal Experiences with Popularizing Mathematical Methods in China. L. Hua & F. Wang. (Mathematical Modeling Ser.: No. 2). 250p. 1988. 65.00 (*0-8176-3372-3*) Birkhauser.

Some Personal Letters of Herman Melville & a Bibliography. Meade Minnigerode. LC 78-75511. (Select Bibliographies Reprint Ser.). 1977. 18.95 (*0-8369-5013-5*) Ayer.

Some Personal Papers. JoAllen Bradham. (Southern & Southwestern Novelist Breakthrough Ser.). (Illus.). 148p. (Orig.). 1994. pap. 10.95 (*1-881515-04-4*) TX Review Pr.

Some Perspectives on Fundamental Nuclear & High Energy Research. Carlo Schaerf. 350p. 1983. reprint ed. pap. text ed. 50.00 (*0-911767-10-X*) Hadronic Pr Inc.

***Some Pharmaceutical Drugs.** (IARC Monographs on the Evaluation of Carcinogenic Risks to Humans: Vol. 66). 514p. 1996. pap. 80.00 (*92-832-1266-5*, 1720066) World Health.

***Some Pharmaceutical Drugs: The Evaluation of Carcinogenic Risks to Humans.** (IARC Monographs: No. 24). 335p. 1980. text ed. 48.00 (*92-832-1224-X*) World Health.

***Some Philosophers on Education: Papers Concerning the Doctrines of Augustine, Aristotle, Aquinas & Dewey.** Ed. by Donald A. Gallagher. LC 56-12217. 106p. 1956. reprint ed. pap. 30.30 (*0-608-04199-8*, 2064934) Bks Demand.

Some Physical, Dosimetry & Biomedical Aspects of Californium. (Panel Proceedings Ser.). (Illus.). 278p. 1976. pap. 60.00 (*92-0-111476-1*, ISP418, Pub. by IAEA AU) Bernan Associates.

Some Pictures from My Life: A Diary. Marcia S. Rizzi. LC 72-87034. (Illus.). 64p. (Orig.). 1972. pap. 3.25 (*0-87810-022-9*) Times Change.

Some Pioneer Families of Wisconsin, Vol 2. Ed. by Betty Patterson. 139p. 1988. pap. 8.00 (*0-910255-49-0*) Wisconsin Gen.

***Some Pioneers of Washington County: A Family History.** F. S. Reader. (Illus.). 154p. 1997. reprint ed. pap. 19.00 (*0-8328-6458-7*) Higginson Bk Co.

Some Pitfalls & Problems in Neurosurgery. Ed. by J. C. De Villiers. (Progress in Neurological Surgery Ser.: Vol. 13). (Illus.). xii, 208p. 1990. 172.25 (*3-8055-4989-X*) S Karger.

Some Plant Galls of Illinois. Glen S. Winterringer. (Story of Illinois Ser.: No. 12). (Illus.). 51p. (J). (ps-12). 1961. pap. 1.00 (*0-89792-022-8*) Ill St Museum.

Some Poems - Poets. Samuel B. Charters. 1971. 5.95 (*0-685-04674-5*); pap. 2.95 (*0-685-04675-3*) Oyez.

An Asterisk (*) at the beginning of an entry indicates that the title is appearing in BIP for the first time.

Some Poets & Their Resources the Future Agenda: Lawrence, Emerson, Heaney, Bishop, Muir, Thomas, Melville, Wilbur. Laurence Stapleton. 210p. (C). 1995. pap. text ed. 28.50 (*0-8191-9792-0*); lib. bdg. 48.00 (*0-8191-9791-2*) U Pr of Amer.

***Some Points of Analysis & Their History.** Lars Garding. LC 97-24642. (University Lectures). 1997. write for info. (*0-8218-0757-9*) Am Math.

Some Points to Consider When You Discuss Merit Pay. Luann Van Loozen. 40p. (Orig.). 1983. vhs 195.00 (*0-87652-086-7*, 021-00116) Am Assn Sch Admin.

Some Points to Consider When You Talk about the Summit. American Assoc. of School Administrators Staff. 1983. 2.75 (*0-87652-150-2*, 021-00290) Am Assn Sch Admin.

Some Political Writings of James Otis, 2 vols. in 1. James Otis. LC 75-31099. reprint ed. 34.50 (*0-404-13516-1*) AMS Pr.

***Some Possible Poets.** Walt Hopmans. (Illus.). 76p. (Orig.). 1997. pap. 10.00 (*1-885021-06-2*) Orange Ocean.

Some Post-Independence Bengali Poems. Tr. by Pradeep Banerjee from BEN. 8.00 (*0-89253-606-3*) Ind-US Inc.

Some Practical Suggestions on the Conduct of a Rescue Home: Including Life of Dr. Kate Waller Barrett. Kate W. Barrett. LC 74-3928. (Women in America Ser.). Orig. Title: Fifty Years Work with Girls. 186p. 1974. reprint ed. 23.95 (*0-405-06075-0*) Ayer.

Some Predators Are Male. large type ed. Miles Tripp. 304p. 1987. 25.99 (*0-7089-1618-X*) Ulverscroft.

Some Prefer Nettles. Junichiro Tanizaki. 1995. pap. 11.00 (*0-679-75269-2*) Random.

Some Preliminary Conclusions Regarding Factors which Affect Army Recruiting Success in the Midwestern Regional Recruiting Command. David W. Hinton & Jason Chen. 12p. (Orig.). 1976. pap. 1.00 (*1-55719-068-2*) U NE CPAR.

Some Present Aspects of the Work of Teachers' Voluntary Associations in the United States. Carter Alexander. (Columbia University. Teachers College. Contributions to Education Ser.: No. 36). reprint ed. 37.50 (*0-404-55036-3*) AMS Pr.

Some Presidential Interpretations of the Presidency. Norman J. Small. LC 71-87353. (Politics & Law Ser.). 1970. reprint ed. lib. bdg. 32.50 (*0-306-71663-1*) Da Capo.

Some Presidents: Wilson to Nixon. William A. Williams. 1972. pap. 1.95 (*0-685-04242-1*, 70227) Random.

Some "Prime" Comparisons. Stephen I. Brown. LC 78-12339. (Illus.). 106p. 1978. pap. 8.50 (*0-87353-131-0*) NCTM.

Some Principles of Elizabethan Staging. G. F. Reynolds. LC 78-130233. reprint ed. 22.50 (*0-404-05286-X*) AMS Pr.

Some Principles of Fiction. Robert Liddell. LC 73-433. 162p. 1974. reprint ed. lib. bdg. 9.50 (*0-8371-6764-7*, LIPF, Greenwood Pr) Greenwood.

Some Principles of Maritime Strategy. Julian S. Corbett. LC 76-154122. (BCL Ser. II). reprint ed. 32.50 (*0-404-09227-6*) AMS Pr.

Some Principles of Stratification. Kingsley Davis & Wilbert E. Moore. (Reprint Series in Social Sciences). (C). 1993. reprint ed. pap. text ed. 1.90 (*0-8290-3802-7*, S-68) Irvington.

Some Problems & Alternatives in Developing Federal Block Grants: To States for Public Welfare Purposes. E. A. Lutz. LC 77-74945. (American Federalism-the Urban Dimension Ser.). (Illus.). 1978. lib. bdg. 33.95 (*0-405-10493-6*) Ayer.

***Some Problems in Aegean Prehistory 1450-1380 BC.** H. W. Catling. 7.00 (*0-904920-16-X*) David Brown.

Some Problems in Chemical Kinetics & Reactivity, Vol. 2. Nikolai N. Semenov. Tr. by Michel Boudart. LC 57-10321. (Illus.). reprint ed. pap. 85.80 (*0-317-09946-9*) Bks Demand.

***Some Problems in Manufacturing High Alloy Nickel Carburizing Steel Gears.** N. E. Woldman & R. J. Metzler. (Technical Papers). 1941. pap. text ed. 30.00 (*1-55589-341-4*) AGMA.

Some Problems in Medieval Historiography. G. G. Coulton. 1974. lib. bdg. 59.95 (*0-8490-1079-9*) Gordon Pr.

Some Problems in the Provision of Professional Education for College Teachers. H. M. Byram. LC 79-176621. (Columbia University. Teachers College. Contributions to Education Ser.: No. 576). reprint ed. 37.50 (*0-404-55576-4*) AMS Pr.

Some Problems of Equity. Zechariah Chafee, Jr. LC 51-630. (Michigan Legal Publications). xiv, 441p. 1990. 40.00 (*1-57588-363-5*, 300160) W S Hein.

Some Problems of India's Economic Policy. Ed. by Charan D. Wadhva. 1978. 14.00 (*0-8364-0263-4*) S Asia.

Some Problems of Marx's Theory of History. Ashok Rudra. (R C Dutt Lectures). 76p. (C). 1988. pap. 4.95 (*0-86131-754-8*, Pub. by Orient Longman Ltd II) Apt Bks.

Some Problems of Mathematics & Mechanics. L. V. Ahlfors et al. LC 76-4884. (Translations Ser.: Series 2, Vol. 104). 265p. 1976. 75.00 (*0-8218-3054-6*, TRANS2/104) Am Math.

Some Problems of Philosophy. William James. Ed. by Frederick H. Burkhardt. LC 78-20804. (Works of William James Ser.). 505p. 1979. reprint ed. pap. 144.30 (*0-7837-4157-X*, 2059005) Bks Demand.

Some Problems of Philosophy. William James. (Notable American Authors Ser.). 1992. reprint ed. lib. bdg. 75.00 (*0-7812-3482-4*) Rprt Serv.

Some Problems of Philosophy: A Beginning of an Introduction to Philosophy. William James. LC 95-51056. xviii, 237p. 1996. pap. 12.00 (*0-8032-7587-0*, Bison Books) U of Nebr Pr.

Some Problems of Philosophy: A Beginning of an Introduction to Philosophy. William James. LC 68-19277. 236p. 1968. reprint ed. text ed. 55.00 (*0-8371-4464-7*, JAPP, Greenwood Pr) Greenwood.

Some Problems of Proof Under the Anglo-American System of Litigation. Ed. by Edmund M. Morgan. LC 75-31438. (James S. Carpentier Lectures Ser.: 1955). 207p. 1976. reprint ed. text ed. 35.00 (*0-8371-8517-3*, MOSP, Greenwood Pr) Greenwood.

Some Problems of Rotor Dynamics. Ales Tondl. Ed. by Jan Gonda. Tr. by Pavel Dolan from CZE. LC 66-72920. 434p. reprint ed. pap. 123.70 (*0-317-26203-3*, 2052128) Bks Demand.

Some Problems of Sylow Type in Locally Finite Groups. M. Curzio. 1981. pap. text ed. 95.00 (*0-12-363605-1*) Acad Pr.

Some Problems of Wages & Their Regulation in Great Britain Since 1918. Allan G. Fisher. LC 66-21672. (Reprints of Economic Classics Ser.). xvii, 281p. 1966. reprint ed. 39.50 (*0-678-00183-9*) Kelley.

Some Problems on the Theory of Dynamical Systems in Applied Sciences: Kyoto, Japan, 28-31 January 1991. (Series on Dynamical Systems: Vol. 10). 200p. (C). 1991. text ed. 63.00 (*981-02-0761-1*) World Scientific Pub.

***Some Procedures for Sound Editing on Videotape.** Richard Raskin. (Illus.). 19p. 1996. pap. 4.95 (*87-7288-151-8*, Pub. by Aarhus Univ Pr DK) David Brown.

***Some Progress in the Accurate Evaluation of Tooth Root and Fillet Stresses in Lightweight, Thin-Rimmed Gears.** G. A. Pizzigati & Raymond J. Drago. (Technical Papers). 1980. pap. text ed. 30.00 (*1-55589-288-4*) AGMA.

Some Prominent Virginia Families, 2 vols. in 4, Set. Louise P. du Bellet. (Illus.). 1715p. 1994. pap. 135.00 (*0-614-00898-0*, 1530) Clearfield Co.

Some Properties of Differentiable Varieties & Transformations: With Special Reference to the Analytic & Algebraic Cases. 2nd ed. Beniamino Segre. LC 72-137498. (Ergebnisse der Mathematik und Ihrer Grenzgebiete Ser.: Vol. 13). 1971. 64.95 (*0-387-05085-X*) Spr-Verlag.

Some Properties of the Bank Model. G. P. Dunn et al. (Bank of England. Discussion Papers. Technical Ser.: No. 9). 115p. reprint ed. pap. 32.80 (*0-317-26529-6*, 2023978) Bks Demand.

Some Questions about Language. Mortimer Adler. 203p. (C). 1991. pap. 14.95 (*0-8126-9178-4*) Open Court.

Some Questions in Biology: Predicting Spatial Effects in Ecological Systems. Ed. by Robert H. Gardner. LC 93-28548. (Lectures on Mathematics in the Life Sciences: Vol. 23). 180p. 1993. 33.00 (*0-8218-1174-6*, LLSCI/23) Am Math.

Some Questions in Constructive Functional Analysis: Proceedings. P. Dinh & Phan Dinh Dieu. LC 73-21929. 228p. 1974. pap. 93.00 (*0-8218-3014-7*, STEKLO/114) Am Math.

Some Questions in the Theory of Moments. N. I. Ahiezer & M. G. Krein. Tr. by W. Fleming & D. Prill. LC 63-22077. (Translations of Mathematical Monographs: Vol. 2). 265p. 1962. 42.00 (*0-8218-1552-0*, MMONO/2) Am Math.

Some Questions in the Theory of Oscillations & the Theory of Optimal Control. Ed. by R. V. Gamkrelidze. LC 93-7068. (Proceedings of the Steklov Institute of Mathematics Ser.: Vol. 197). 186p. 1993. pap. 115.00 (*0-8218-3148-8*, STEKLO/197) Am Math.

Some Questions of Differential Geometry in the Large. E. V. Shikin. LC 96-21901. (American Mathematical Society Translations Ser.). 192p. 1996. 89.00 (*0-8218-7506-X*) Am Math.

Some Random Reminiscences: The Autobiography of Harold C. Holmes. limited ed. Harold C. Holmes. (Illus.). 1967. 25.00 (*0-910740-01-1*) Holmes.

Some Random Series of Functions. Jean-Pierre Kahane. (Cambridge Studies in Advanced Mathematics: No. 5). 318p. (C). 1994. pap. text ed. 34.95 (*0-521-45602-9*) Cambridge U Pr.

Some Readings on Historically Black Colleges & Universities. rev. ed. Erskine S. Walther. LC 94-77293. 1994. spiral bd. 25.00 (*1-885327-05-6*) Walther Cnslt.

Some Reasons Why I Am a Freethinker. Robert G. Ingersoll. 39p. 1993. reprint ed. pap. 4.00 (*0-910309-72-8*, 5184) Am Atheist.

Some Recent Advances in Statistics. Ed. by J. Tiago De Oliveira & Benjamin Epstein. 1982. text ed. 143.00 (*0-12-691580-6*) Acad Pr.

Some Recent Attacks: Essays Cultural & Political. James Kelman. (Orig.). 1993. pap. 9.00 (*1-873176-80-5*, AK Pr San Fran) AK Pr Dist.

Some Recent Corrosion Embrittlement Failures of Prestressing Systems in the U. S. (PCI Journal Reprints Ser.). 20p. 1982. pap. 14.00 (*0-686-40158-1*, JR256) P-PCI.

Some Recent Developments in Operator Theory. Carl M. Pearcy. LC 78-8754. (CBMS Regional Conference Series in Mathematics: No. 36). 73p. 1978. reprint ed. pap. 18.00 (*0-8218-1686-1*, CBMS/36) Am Math.

Some Recent Research in Shakespeare's Imagery. U. Ellis-Fermor. LC 75-2255. (Studies in Shakespeare: No. 24). (C). 1970. reprint ed. lib. bdg. 49.95 (*0-8383-0343-9*) M S G Haskell Hse.

***Some Recollections by Emma Hardy.** Emma L. Hardy. (Illus.). 91p. 1972. 17.95 (*0-8369-6913-8*) Ayer.

Some Recollections of Gap Jumping. Derek H. Barton. Ed. by Jeffrey I. Seeman. LC 90-872. (Profiles, Pathways, & Dreams Ser.). (Illus.). 143p. 1991. 34.95 (*0-8412-1770-X*) Am Chemical.

Some Recollections of Our Anti-Slavery Conflict. Samuel J. May. LC 79-83888. (Black Heritage Library Collection). 1977. 17.95 (*0-8369-8630-X*) Ayer.

Some Recollections of Our Anti-Slavery Conflict. Samuel J. May. pap. 15.00 (*1-56675-043-1*, N160P) Mnemosyne.

Some Recollections of Our Anti-Slavery Conflict. Samuel J. May. LC 68-29010. (American Negro: His History & Literature. Series 1). 1968. reprint ed. 17.95 (*0-405-01829-0*) Ayer.

Some Records of Ethiopia Being Extracts from the History of High Ethiopia or Abassia & Bahrey's History of the Ealla. Ed. by Charles F. Beckingham & George W. Huntingford. (Hakluyt Society Second Ser.: Vol. 107). (Illus.). 360p. 1996. 63.00 (*0-85115-988-5*, Pub. by Hakluyt Soc UK) Boydell & Brewer.

Some Records of Sussex County, Delaware. C. H. Turner. (Illus.). 394p. 1989. reprint ed. pap. 25.00 (*1-55613-249-2*) Heritage Bk.

Some Records of the Wingfield Family. Intro. by John M. Wingfield. 263p. 1996. reprint ed. 60.00 (*0-937543-03-9*) Wingfield Family Soc.

Some Reflections about the Use of Case Hardening of Teeth in Large Gear Units. Georges Henriot. (Fall Technical Meeting Papers 88FTM2). (Illus.). 7p. 1988. pap. text ed. 30.00 (*1-55589-507-7*) AGMA.

Some Reflections on Chaucer's "Art Poetical" Dorothy Everett. 24p. (C). 1950. reprint ed. pap. 39.95 (*0-8383-0026-X*) M S G Haskell Hse.

Some Reflections on Jurisprudence. W. W. Buckland. LC 73-13713. viii, 118p. (C). 1974. reprint ed. lib. bdg. 23.50 (*0-208-01407-1*, Archon Bks) Shoe String.

Some Relationships Between Supply & Demand for Newly Trained Teachers: A Survey of the Situation in a Selected Representative State, Missouri. Mary Elliff. LC 76-176745. (Columbia University. Teachers College. Contributions to Education Ser.: No. 654). reprint ed. 37.50 (*0-404-55654-X*) AMS Pr.

Some Relationships Existing in School Expenditure Among Florida Counties. Charles A. Smith. LC 72-177776. (Columbia University. Teachers College. Contributions to Education Ser.: No. 352). reprint ed. 37.50 (*0-404-55352-4*) AMS Pr.

Some Religious Elements in English Literature. Rose MacAulay. (BCL1-PR English Literature Ser.). 160p. 1992. reprint ed. lib. bdg. 69.00 (*0-7812-7027-8*) Rprt Serv.

Some Religious Elements in English Literature. Rose Macaulay. LC 72-158506. 160p. 1972. reprint ed. 13.00 (*0-403-01305-4*) Scholarly.

Some Remarkable Men: Further Memoirs. James Lord. (Illus.). 360p. 1996. 27.50 (*0-374-26655-7*) FS&G.

Some Remarks on the Tragedy of Hamlet, Prince of Denmark. Thomas Hanmer. LC 77-168240. reprint ed. 29.50 (*0-404-03096-3*) AMS Pr.

Some Remembered Words. Oscar Shoenfeld. LC 96-25527. (Illus.). 168p. 1996. 17.00 (*0-89733-439-6*) Academy Chi Pubs.

Some Reminiscences, 2 vols, Set. William M. Rossetti. LC 75-132386. (Illus.). 645p. 1975. reprint ed. 59.50 (*0-404-05440-4*) AMS Pr.

Some Restrictions & Limitations to the Free Interstate Movement of Teachers. William D. Stratford. LC 79-177811. (Columbia University. Teachers College. Contributions to Education Ser.: No. 851). reprint ed. 37.50 (*0-404-55851-8*) AMS Pr.

Some Resues. Michael Carrino. 80p. 1994. 10.00 (*0-932616-48-8*) Brick Hse Bks.

Some River & Creek Systems on Melville & Grant Islands: North & South Creeks on Grant Island see Survey of Tidal River Systems in the Northern Territory & Their Crocodile Populations: Monographs

Some River & Creek Systems on the West Coast of Cape York Peninsula in the Gulf of Carpentaria: Nassau, Staaten & Gilbert Rivers & Duck Creek see Surveys of Tidal River Systems in the Northern Territory & Their Crocodile Populations

Some Rivers & Creeks on the Western Shore of the Gulf of Carpentaria: Rose River, Muntak Creek; Hart, Walker & Koolatong Rivers see Survey of Tidal River Systems in the Northern Territory & Their Crocodile Populations: Monographs

Some Rogues & Vagabonds of Dickens. W. Dexter. 1972. 59.95 (*0-8490-1080-2*) Gordon Pr.

Some Romance Words of Arabic or Germanic Origin. Leslie P. Brown. LC 38-33359. 68p. 1982. reprint ed. lib. bdg. 27.00 (*0-89370-735-X*) Borgo Pr.

Some Rural Quakers. Jack V. Wood. (C). 1989. pap. 25.00 (*1-85072-085-1*, Pub. by W Sessions UK) St Mut.

Some Sanskrit Poems. Tr. by P. Lal from SAN. 16p. 1973. 8.00 (*0-88253-266-9*); 4.00 (*0-89253-520-2*) Ind-US Inc.

***Some Sat in Darkness.** Declan Joyce et al. 172p. (Orig.). 1997. pap. 9.99 (*1-57782-024-X*) Discipleshp.

Some Say Tomato. Ed. by Mariflo Stephens. 70p. (Orig.). 1993. pap. 7.50 (*0-9638892-0-6*) Northwood Pr.

Some Sayings of the Buddha. F. L. Woodeward. 1973. 250.00 (*0-8490-2629-6*) Gordon Pr.

Some Secrets Are For Sharing. Randy Winston-Hiller. (Illus.). 33p. (Orig.). (J). (gr. 4 up). 1986. pap. 5.95 (*0-910223-08-4*) MAC Pub.

Some Seed Fell on Good Ground: The Life of Edwin V. O'Hara. Timothy M. Dolan. LC 91-7315. (Illus.). 300p. 1992. text ed. 29.95 (*0-8132-0748-7*) Cath U Pr.

***Some Semblance of Decay.** Brendan Tripp. 52p. (Orig.). 1996. pap. 5.00 (*1-57353-028-X*) Eschaton Prods.

Some Sex Beliefs & Practices in a Navaho Community. F. L. Bailey. (Harvard University Peabody Museum of Archaeology & Ethnology Papers: Vol. 40, No. 1). 1950. 25.00 (*0-527-01300-5*) Periodicals Srv.

Some Shakespearean Themes & An Approach to "Hamlet" Lionel C. Knights. xii, 260p. 1961. 37.50 (*0-8047-0300-0*) Stanford U Pr.

Some Shenandoah Valley Mennonite Settlers: Where They Came from, Who They Were. Gene P. Hammond. Ed. by Rachael W. Hammond. LC 92-61518. (Illus.). 101p. (C). Date not set. teacher ed., pap. 15.00 (*0-614-10286-3*) G P Hammond Pub.

Some Shenandoah Valley Mennonite Settlers: Where They Came from, Who They Were. Gene P. Hammond. Ed. by Rachael W. Hammond. LC 92-61518. (Illus.). 101p. 1992. per., pap. 15.00 (*1-878014-06-4*) G P Hammond Pub.

Some Shorter Elizabethan Poems. A. H. Bullen. LC 64-16746. (Arber's an English Garner Ser.). 1964. reprint ed. 41.00 (*0-8154-0041-1*) Cooper Sq.

Some Sketches on the Life of Helena Petrovna Blavatsky. Joanne Kyger. 24p. (Orig.). 1996. pap. 5.00 (*1-887289-22-4*) Rodent Pr.

***Some Slaveholders & Their Slaves, Union Parish Louisiana, 1839-1865.** Harry F. Dill & William Simpson. vi, 195p. (Orig.). 1997. pap. 20.00 (*0-7884-0617-5*, D344) Heritage Bk.

Some Sleep Standing Up. Susan Stockdale. LC 95-35924. (J). 1997. 14.00 (*0-671-89831-0*, S&S Bks Young Read) S&S Childrens.

Some Sleep Standing up. Susan Stockdale. LC 95-35924. (Illus.). 32p. (J). (gr. k-1). 1996. 13.00 (*0-689-80509-8*, S&S Bks Young Read) S&S Childrens.

Some Smug Slug. Pamela D. Edwards. LC 94-18682. (Illus.). 32p. (J). (ps-4). 1996. 14.95 (*0-06-024789-4*); lib. bdg. 14.89 (*0-06-024792-4*) HarpC Child Bks.

Some Snakes. Stephen Ray & Kathleen Murdoch. LC 93-113. (J). 1994. pap. write for info. (*0-383-03715-8*) SRA McGraw.

***Some Snakes Spit Poison & Other Amazing Facts about Snakes.** Claire Llewellyn. (I Didn't Know That Ser.). (Illus.). 32p. (J). (gr. 1-3). 1997. 8.95 (*0-7613-0586-6*, Copper Beech Bks); lib. bdg. 14.90 (*0-7613-0561-0*, Copper Beech Bks) Millbrook Pr.

Some Social Aspects of Dentistry. Ed. by W. R. Ayer. 100p. 1981. pap. 18.00 (*0-08-028132-X*, Pergamon Pr) Elsevier.

Some Social Consequences of Achievement Motivation. David C. McClelland. (Reprint Series in Social Sciences). (C). 1993. reprint ed. pap. text ed. 2.30 (*0-8290-2669-X*, S-457) Irvington.

Some Social Requisites of Democracy: Economic Development & Political Legitimacy. Seymour M. Lipset. (Reprint Series in Social Sciences). (C). 1993. reprint ed. pap. text ed. 2.90 (*0-8290-3810-8*, S-175) Irvington.

Some Soldier Poets. Thomas S. Moore. LC 68-16958. (Essay Index Reprint Ser.). 1977. 18.95 (*0-8369-0715-9*) Ayer.

Some Songs & Poems from Rabindranath Tagore. Pratima Bowes. 1986. 11.00 (*0-8364-1870-0*, Pub. by Allied II) S Asia.

***Some Sort of Epic Grandeur: The Life of F. Scott Fitzgerald.** Matthew J. Bruccoli. 16.95 (*0-7867-0907-3*) Carroll & Graf.

Some Sort of Epic Grandeur: The Life of F. Scott Fitzgerald. Matthew J. Bruccoli. (Illus.). 768p. 1993. pap. 16.95 (*0-88184-907-3*) Carroll & Graf.

Some Soul to Keep. J. California Cooper. 224p. 1988. pap. 10.95 (*0-312-02285-9*) St Martin.

Some South Carolina County Records, I. Brent Holcomb & Silas E. Lucas, Jr. 162p. 1976. 20.00 (*0-89308-014-4*) Southern Hist Pr.

Some South Carolina County Records, II. Brent Holcomb & Silas E. Lucas, Jr. 162p. 1976. write for info. (*0-89308-648-7*) Southern Hist Pr.

Some South Carolina Genealogical Records. Janie Revill. 456p. 1985. 35.00 (*0-89308-539-1*) Southern Hist Pr.

Some Southern Balls (& Allied Families) Donna R. Mills. 344p. 1993. lib. bdg. 38.00 (*0-931069-09-2*) Mills Historical.

Some Southern Colonial Families, Vol. 1. David A. Avant, Jr. LC 81-84670. 528p. 1983. 35.00 (*0-914570-04-8*) LAvant Studios.

Some Southern Colonial Families, Vol. 2. David A. Avant, Jr. LC 81-84670. 467p. 1982. 35.00 (*0-914570-06-4*) LAvant Studios.

Some Southern Colonial Families, Vol. 3. David A. Avant, Jr. LC 81-84670. (Illus.). 1260p. 1989. 45.00 (*0-914570-08-0*) LAvant Studios.

Some Southern Colonial Families, Vol. 4. David A. Avant, Jr. LC 81-84670. (Illus.). 860p. 1991. 45.00 (*0-914570-10-2*) LAvant Studios.

Some Southern Colonial Families, Vol. 5. David A. Avant, Jr. 1132p. 1996. 65.00 (*0-914570-11-0*) LAvant Studios.

Some Southern Cotton Mill Workers & Their Villages. Jennings J. Rhyne. Ed. by Leon Stein. LC 77-70527. (Illus.). 1977. reprint ed. lib. bdg. 23.95 (*0-405-10195-3*) Ayer.

Some Southern Documents of the People Called Baptists. H. Rondel Rumburg. 276p. 1995. 24.95 (*0-9639730-1-0*) Soc Bibl & So Stud.

Some Southern Roper "Trees" A Book of Clues. June R. Walton. 400p. 1990. pap. 30.00 (*0-9617874-2-2*) J R Walton.

Some Spanish-American Poets. Tr. by Alice S. Blackwell. LC 68-22694. (ENG & SPA.). 1968. reprint ed. 30.00 (*0-8196-0217-5*) Biblo.

Some Special Aspects of Nutrition. Ed. by Geoffrey H. Bourne. (World Review of Nutrition & Dietetics Ser.: Vol. 33). (Illus.). 1979. 126.50 (*3-8055-2942-2*) S Karger.

***Some Special Problems of Aircraft Gear Manufacture.** J. L. Buehler. (Technical Papers). 1941. pap. text ed. 30.00 (*1-55589-454-2*) AGMA.

Some Special Properties of the Adjunction Theory for 3-Folds in P p5 s. Mauro C. Beltrametti et al. LC 95-15957. (Memoirs Ser.: No. 554). 63p. 1995. pap. 30.00 (*0-8218-0234-8*, MEMO/116/554) Am Math.

S

An Asterisk (*) at the beginning of an entry indicates that the title is appearing in BIP for the first time.

Some Special Times: Selected Poems. Frances Ross. (Illus.). 1976. pap. 3.95 (0-915242-07-9) Pygmalion Pr.

Some Species of Platystrophia from the Trenton of Ontario & Quebec see Palaeontographica Americana: Vol. 3

Some Stanzas from the Puranas. Tr. by Kusakrathadasa from SAN. (Krsna Library: Vol. 190). 65p. (C). 1993. pap. text ed. 6.00 (1-56130-108-6) Krsna Inst.

Some States of Being. State of Being Staff. (Illus.). 22p. (Orig.). (YA). (gr. 7 up). 1988. pap. 2.00 (0-929611-03-9) Plutonium Pr.

Some Statistical Problems in Research Design. Leslie Kish. (Reprint Series in Sociology). (C). 1993. reprint ed. pap. text ed. 1.00 (0-8290-4167-2, S-436) Irvington.

Some Still Want the Moon: A Woman's Guide to Tantra Yoga see Woman's Guide to Tantra Yoga

Some Strange Corners of Our Country. Charles F. Lummis. LC 88-26703. 270p. 1989. reprint ed. pap. 16.95 (0-8165-0852-6) U of Ariz Pr.

Some Strange English Literary Figures of the Eighteenth & Nineteenth Centuries. Lafcadio Hearn. Ed. by R. Tanabe. LC 67-22098. (Essay Index Reprint Ser.). 1977. 19.95 (0-8369-0527-X) Ayer.

Some Studies in Education of Immigrants for Citizenship: Australia, Brazil, Canada, Israel (UNESCO) (Education Studies & Documents: No. 16). 1974. reprint ed. pap. 25.00 (0-8115-1340-8) Periodicals Srv.

Some Studies in Machine Learning Using the Game of Checkers 2 see Annual Review in Automatic Programming

Some Studies in the Modern Novel. Dorothy M. Hoare. LC 72-3668. (Studies in Fiction: No. 34). 1972. reprint ed. lib. bdg. 75.00 (0-8383-1544-5) M S G Haskell Hse.

Some Studies in the Modern Novel. Dorothy M. Hoare. LC 78-58260. (Essay Index in Reprint Ser.). 1979. reprint ed. 20.00 (0-8486-3022-X) Roth Pub Inc.

Some Stuff. Elizabeth Ring. LC 94-26196. (Illus.). 32p. (J). (gr. k-3). 1995. lib. bdg. 15.40 (1-56294-466-5) Millbrook Pr.

Some Successful Marriages. Abby M. Roach. LC 76-152956. (Short Story Index Reprint Ser.). (Illus.). 1977. reprint ed. 21.95 (0-8369-3871-2) Ayer.

Some Suggestions for Using Popular Writing in America: The Interaction of Style & Audience. 5th ed. Ed. by Robert Atwan. LC 92-22724. 784p. (C). 1993. pap. text ed. 27.95 (0-19-507308-8) OUP.

Some Summer! Jean Vandevenne. Ed. by Olivia Tschappler. (Light Line Ser.). (Illus.). 170p. (Orig.). (J). (gr. 4-6). 1987. pap. 6.49 (0-89084-380-5, 031484) Bob Jones Univ Pr.

***Some Sunny Day.** Helen Carey. 380p. 1996. pap. 17.95 (1-85797-617-7, Pub. by Orion Bks UK) Trafalgar.

Some Sunny Day. Eileen Whiteing. 1989. pap. 25.00 (0-907335-07-1, Pub. by Sutton Libs & Arts) St Mut.

Some Sweet Chance. Mary Colquett. 284p. 1997. 20.00 (0-9648890-2-1) Southern Ink.

***Some Sweet Day.** Jennie L. Hansen. LC 97-5632. 1997. write for info. (1-57734-089-2) Covenant Comms.

Some Sweet Day. Bryan Woolley. 1996. 18.00 (0-87404-238-0) Tex Western.

Some Sweet Day. Bryan Woolley. LC 81-84368. 121p. 1981. reprint ed. pap. 12.50 (0-917788-24-9) Gnomon Pr.

Some Swell Pup or: Are You Sure You Want a Dog? Maurice Sendak & Matthew Margolis. (Illus.). 32p. (J). (ps up). 1989. pap. 5.95 (0-374-46963-6) FS&G.

Some Systems of Biological Communication: Journal: Biosciences Communications, Vol. 3, Nos. 5 & 6. Ed. by Stacey B. Day. (Illus.). 1977. 45.75 (3-8055-2817-5) S Karger.

Some Systems of Substitution Correlations in Modern American English: With Implications for the Teaching of English As a Second Language. Ruth Crymes. (Janua Linguarum, Ser. Major: No. 23). 1968. text ed. 64.65 (90-279-0614-9) Mouton.

Some Talk About a Copper Mine: A History of Bagdad, Arizona. Robert C. Bogart & G. Gail Gesell. (Illus.). 230p. 1991. write for info. (0-942078-17-9) R Tanner Assocs Inc.

Some Tastes of Home. Sally L. Newkirk. (Illus.). 480p. 1989. 14.95 (0-9620596-0-9) S L Newkirk.

Some Techniques & Procedures in Equine Surgery. A. Simon Turner. 211p. 1983. text ed. 15.00 (0-935078-26-6) Veterinary Med.

Some Techniques & Procedures in Small Animal Surgery. 3rd ed. Ed. by Robert L. Leighton. 264p. 1982. text ed. 15.00 (0-935078-21-5) Veterinary Med.

Some Tennessee Heroes of the Revolution. Zella Armstrong. 162p. 1989. reprint ed. 18.00 (0-614-16584-9, 170) Clearfield Co.

Some Terms from Liberian Speech. 2nd ed. Warren L. D'Azevedo. 76p. 1970. 5.00 (0-317-93949-1) Arden Assocs.

Some Texas Fusulinidae. M. P. White. (Bulletin Ser.: BULL 3211). (Illus.). 106p. 1932. pap. 0.75 (0-686-29352-5) Bur Econ Geology.

Some Textual Difficulties in Shakespeare. Charles D. Stewart. LC 72-955. reprint ed. 29.50 (0-404-06264-4) AMS Pr.

Some That Smile. Robert Carley. 113p. (C). 1989. 40.00 (0-7223-2298-4, Pub. by A H S Ltd UK) St Mut.

Some Theoretical Problems of Catalysis: Research Reports of the First Soviet-Japanese Seminar on Catalysis. Ed. by Takao Kwan et al. 336p. 1973. reprint ed. pap. 95.80 (0-608-01241-6, 2061929) Bks Demand.

Some Theoretical Problems Suggested by the Movements of Interest Rates, Bond Yields & Stock Prices in the United States Since 1856. Frederick R. Macaulay. Ed. by Stuart Bruchey. LC 80-1161. (Rise of Commercial Banking Ser.). (Illus.). 1981. reprint ed. lib. bdg. 33.95 (0-405-13668-4) Ayer.

Some Theoretical Problems Suggested by the Movements of Interest Rates, Bond Yields & Stock Prices in the United States since 1856. Frederick R. Macaulay. (General Ser.: No. 33). 625p. 1938. reprint ed. 160.00 (0-87014-032-9) Natl Bur Econ Res.

Some Theory of Sampling. William E. Deming. 602p. 1984. reprint ed. pap. 15.95 (0-486-64684-X) Dover.

Some Thing Black. Jacques Roubaud. Tr. by Rosmarie Waldrop from FRE. LC 89-35216. (Illus.). 160p. 1990. 19.95 (0-916583-48-1) Dalkey Arch.

Some Things about Coventry-Benton. William F. Whitcher. (Illus.). 313p. 1996. reprint ed. lib. bdg. 37.00 (0-8328-5055-1) Higginson Bk Co.

Some Things Against the Churches: A Wake-Up Call to the Congregational Churches. unabridged ed. J. Lawrence Miller. 116p. (Orig.). 1996. pap. 7.95 (0-9651142-9-5) Scroll Pubs.

***Some Things Are Not Forgotten: A Pawnee Family Remembers.** Martha R. Blaine. LC 97-2187. (Illus.). 328p. 1997. text ed. 50.00 (0-8032-1275-5) U of Nebr Pr.

Some Things Are Too Good Not to Be True. James W. Moore. LC 93-44091. 144p. (Orig.). 1994. pap. 10.00 (0-687-00237-0) Dimen for Liv.

Some Things Come Back. Robert Morgan. 256p. (Orig.). 1995. mass mkt. 4.99 (0-425-14690-1, Prime Crime) Berkley Pub.

Some Thing's Fishy. Linda Abbott & John R. Smith. (Illus.). 52p. 1993. 11.95 (0-936459-20-4) Stained Glass.

Some Things Harvard Never Taught Me. Clint Nangle. LC 92-97522. 160p. (Orig.). 1993. pap. 14.95 (0-9635615-2-9) Blue Horiz Pr.

Some Things I Did. Roxy L. Gordon. (Illus.). 160p. 1971. 15.00 (0-88426-012-7) Encino Pr.

Some Things I Have Noticed. Sandra P. Lewis. 32p. (Orig.). 1996. pap. 5.00 (1-56167-312-9) Am Literary Pr.

Some Things Last Forever. Lance Wubbels. LC 96-4504. (Gentle Hills Ser.: Vol. 4). 272p. 1996. pap. text ed. 9.99 (1-55661-421-7) Bethany Hse.

Some Things Last Forever. large type ed. Lance Wubbels. LC 96-4504. (Gentle Hills Ser.: Vol. 4). 384p. 1996. pap. text ed. 15.99 (1-55661-824-7) Bethany Hse.

***Some Things Never Change.** Cecile Dahlstrom. 96p. (Orig.). 1996. pap. 10.95 (1-886094-53-5) Chicago Spectrum.

Some Things Never Change: Classic Thoughts That Stand the Test of Time. Jim Moran. 168p. 1995. pap. 5.95 (1-56245-223-1) Great Quotations.

Some Things That Matter. George A. Riddell. LC 74-37793. (Essay Index Reprint Ser). 1977. reprint ed. 20.95 (0-8369-2620-X) Ayer.

Some Things Worth Knowing. Stuart Chase. LC 76-90622. (Essay Index Reprint Ser.). 1977. 23.95 (0-8369-1557-7) Ayer.

Some Things You Just Can't Do by Yourself. (Illus.). (J). (ps-3). 1973. 4.95 (0-938678-00-0) New Seed.

Some Things You Need to Know... Larry Larson & Levi Lee. 1986. pap. 5.25 (0-8222-1056-8) Dramatists Play.

***Some Things You Never Forget: 5 Battle Stars from Tunisia to the Poe Valley.** Clem Miller. 290p. (Orig.). 1996. pap. 15.95 (1-886028-19-2) Savage Pr.

***Some Thoughts about This Thing Called Retirement.** Grampa Gray. (Tree of Life Mini-Books Ser.: Vol. 7). (Illus.). 12p. (Orig.). 1996. pap. 2.50 (1-885631-35-9, 35-9) G F Hutchison.

Some Thoughts Concerning Education. John Locke. Ed. by John W. Yolton & Jean Yolton. (Clarendon Edition of the Works of John Locke Ser.). (Illus.). 352p. 1989. 105.00 (0-19-824582-3) OUP.

***Some Thoughts Concerning Education: 1693 Edition.** John Locke. (Classics in Education Ser.). 276p. 1996. reprint ed. write for info. (1-85506-292-5) Bks Intl VA.

Some Thoughts Concerning Education & of the Conduct of the Understanding. John Locke. Ed. by Ruth W. Grant & Nathan Tarcov. LC 96-23832. (HPC Classics Ser.). 256p. 1996. pap. text ed. 12.95 (0-87220-334-4); lib. bdg. 34.95 (0-87220-335-2) Hackett Pub.

Some Thoughts Concerning the Present Revival of Religion in New England. Jonathan Edwards. (Notable American Authors Ser.). 1992. reprint ed. lib. bdg. 75.00 (0-7812-2767-4) Rprt Serv.

Some Thoughts for My Friends. rev. ed. Mari Stein. (Illus.). 1977. pap. 4.95 (0-918546-02-8) Quarterdeck.

Some Thoughts on Beethoven's Choral Symphony, with Writings on Other Musical Subjects. Ralph Vaughan-Williams. LC 81-2079. (Illus.). 172p. 1981. reprint ed. text ed. 49.75 (0-313-23049-8, VWST, Greenwood Pr) Greenwood.

Some Thoughts on Beethoven's Choral Symphony with Writings on other Musical Subjects. Richard Vaughan Williams. 172p. reprint ed. lib. bdg. 39.00 (0-685-14784-3) Rprt Serv.

Some Thoughts on Byzantine Military Strategy. Walter E. Kaegi, Jr. 18p. 1983. pap. 1.00 (0-916586-95-2) Holy Cross Orthodox.

Some Thoughts on Hemispheric Security & Leadership. Fred F. Woerner. (Chester W. Nimitz Memorial Lectures in National). 56p. (Orig.). 1993. pap. text ed. 6.25 (0-87725-607-1) U of Cal IAS.

Some Thoughts on Hilaire Belloc: Ten Studies. Patrick Braybrooke. LC 68-1140. (Studies in Irish Literature: No. 16). 1969. reprint ed. lib. bdg. 58.95 (0-8383-0649-7) M S G Haskell Hse.

Some Thoughts on Social Responsibility. rev. ed. William D. Eldgidge. 166p. pap. text ed. 21.50 (0-8191-9432-8); lib. bdg. 44.00 (0-8191-9431-X) U Pr of Amer.

Some Thoughts on the Gita. 162p. 1983. reprint ed. pap. 5.95 (0-912181-08-7) East School Pr.

Some Thoughts That Seem Important. Ollie Goldsmith. (Illus.). 1983. 9.90 (0-911843-00-0) Myriad.

Some Thoughts to Live By: Philosophy of Fleet Admiral Chester W. Nimitz of Fredericksburg, Texas. 1985. pap. 2.00 (0-934841-02-0) Adm Nimitz Foun.

Some Time to Grow. Siverman. 1988. pap. text ed. 12.50 (0-201-22164-0) Addison-Wesley.

Some to Mecca Turn to Pray: Islamic Values & the Modern World. Mervyn Hiskett. 300p. 1993. 49.95 (1-870626-48-6, Pub. by Claridge Pr UK) Paul & Co Pubs.

Some Topics in Complex Analysis. Ian N. Sneddon. (International Series of Monographs on Pure & Applied Mathematics: Vol. 86). 69.00 (0-08-011421-0, Pub. by Pergamon Repr UK) Franklin.

Some Topics in Graph Theory. H. Y. Yap. (London Mathematical Society Lecture Note Ser.: No. 108). (Illus.). 230p. 1986. pap. 38.95 (0-521-33944-8) Cambridge U Pr.

Some Topics in Probability & Analysis. R. Gundy. LC 89-303. (CBMS Regional Conference Series in Mathematics: No. 70). 49p. 1989. pap. 18.00 (0-8218-0721-8, CBMS/70) Am Math.

Some Topics on Inverse Problems: Proceedings of the Sixteenth Workshop on Interdisciplinary Study of Inverse Problems, Montpellier, France, Nov. 30-Dec. 4, 1987. Ed. by Pierre C. Sabatier. 432p. 1988. text ed. 108.00 (9971-5-0647-5) World Scientific Pub.

Some Topological & Geometrical Structures in Banach Spaces. N. Ghoussoub et al. LC 87-19556. (Memoirs Ser.: No. 70/378). 116p. 1989. reprint ed. pap. text ed. 21.00 (0-8218-2441-4, MEMO/70/378) Am Math.

Some Touch Is Good, Some Touch Is Bad. James Molnar. (Kid Safe Ser.). (Illus.). 16p. (Orig.). (J). (ps-1). 1994. pap. 5.00 (0-9644142-0-1) Open Book Pubng.

Some Touch Is Good, Some Touch Is Bad - The Coloring Book. James Molnar. (Illus.). 8p. (Orig.). (J). (ps-k). 1995. pap. 1.25 (0-9644142-4-4) Open Book Pubng.

Some Traces of the Pre-Olympian World in Greek Literature & Myth. E. A. Butterworth. LC 85-21959. (Illus.). (C). 1966. 62.35 (3-11-005010-2) De Gruyter.

***Some Trains Run on Water: And Other Amazing Facts about Rail Transport.** Kate Petty. LC 97-8236. (I Didn't Know That...Ser.). (Illus.). 32p. (J). (gr. 1-3). 1997. 8.95 (0-7613-0598-X, Copper Beech Bks) Millbrook Pr.

***Some Trains Run on Water: And Other Amazing Facts about Rail Transport.** Kate Petty. LC 97-8236. (I Didn't Know That...Ser.). (J). 1997. 14.90 (0-7613-0609-9, Copper Beech Bks) Millbrook Pr.

Some Trees. John Ashbery. LC 56-5946. (American Poetry Ser.: No. 14). 1978. pap. 9.95 (0-88001-243-9) Ecco Pr.

Some Tribal Origins, Laws & Customs of the Balkans. Mary E. Durham. LC 76-44710. (Illus.). reprint ed. 44.50 (0-404-15856-0) AMS Pr.

Some Trick of Light: Poems by Jane Glazer. Jane Glazer. Ed. by Thomas L. Ferte. 79p. (Orig.). 1993. pap. 14.95 (0-9629194-2-X) Adrienne Lee.

Some Trouble with Cows: Making Sense of Social Conflict. Beth Roy. LC 93-25761. (C). 1994. 40.00 (0-520-08341-5); pap. 15.00 (0-520-08342-3) U CA Pr.

***Some True Facts about Life: Reflections of Thought from a WWII Survivor.** Henry Sobel. (Illus.). 72p. (Orig.). 1996. pap. 14.50 (0-9654463-0-1) H Sobel.

Some Truer Method: Reflections on the Heritage of Newton. Frank Durham & Robert D. Purrington. 256p. 1990. text ed. 40.00 (0-231-06896-4) Col U Pr.

Some Trust in Chariots. Donald Eidson. 69p. 1984. text ed. 9.95 (0-89390-055-9) Resource Pubns.

Some Turns of Thought in Modern Philosophy: Five Essays. George Santayana. LC 67-23268. (Essay Index Reprint Ser.). 1977. 13.95 (0-8369-0849-X) Ayer.

Some Types of Attention see Report

Some Unknown Person. Sandra Scoppettone. 376p. 1995. mass mkt. 5.95 (0-7867-0285-0) Carroll & Graf.

Some Unpublished Letters of Henry D. & Sophia E. Thoreau: A Chapter in the History of a Still-Born Book. Henry David Thoreau. Ed. by Samuel A. Jones. LC 80-2684. (Thoreau Ser.). (Illus.). 136p. reprint ed. 29.50 (0-404-19078-2) AMS Pr.

Some Unusual Aspects of Communication. Edward Campbell. 12p. 1971. pap. 4.00 (0-9500029-3-3, Pub. by Octagon Pr UK) ISHK.

Some Values Derived from Extensive Reading of General Science. Francis D. Curtis. LC 75-177601. (Columbia University. Teachers College. Contributions to Education Ser.: No. 163). reprint ed. 37.50 (0-404-55163-7) AMS Pr.

Some Verdicts of History Reviewed: Essay Index Reprint Ser. William Stebbing. LC 72-8545. 1977. reprint ed. 26.95 (0-8369-7327-5) Ayer.

Some Verses from the Heartland. Effie R. Larson. (Orig.). 1996. pap. write for info. (1-57553-193-3) Watermrk Pr.

Some Versions of Pastoral. William Empson. LC 52-1182. 1960. pap. 8.95 (0-8112-0038-8, NDP92) New Directions.

Some Very Handsome Work: Scrimshaw at the Cape Cod National Seashore. Kenneth R. Martin. (Illus.). 56p. (Orig.). 1991. pap. 4.95 (0-915992-55-8) Eastern Acorn.

Some Victorian & Georgian Catholics. Patrick Braybrooke. LC 67-22080. (Essay Index Reprint Ser.). 1977. 20.95 (0-8369-1325-6) Ayer.

Some Victorian Portraits & Others. Hilda Martindale. LC 76-126324. (Biography Index Reprint Ser.). 1977. reprint ed. 17.95 (0-8369-8030-1) Ayer.

Some Views from the Campus. Frederick C. Mosher. LC 87-8193. (Papers on Presidential Transitions & Foreign Policy: Vol. IV). 128p. (Orig.). (C). 1987. lib. bdg. 35.50 (0-8191-6331-7, Pub. by White Miller Center) U Pr of Amer.

Some Vistas of Modern Mathematics: Dynamic Programming, Invariant Imbedding, & the Mathematical Biosciences. Richard E. Bellman. LC 68-12974. 151p. reprint ed. pap. 43.10 (0-317-08655-3, 2004315) Bks Demand.

Some Vital Statistics on English Grammar. Joe E. Pierce. 600p. 1991. lib. bdg. 40.00 (0-913244-26-0) Hapi Pr.

Some Voices & Pale Horse. Joe Penhall. (Methuen Modern Plays Ser.). 1996. pap. 15.95 (0-413-70440-8, A0821, Pub. by Methuen UK) Heinemann.

Some Warmer Tone: Alaska Athabaskan Bead Embroidery. Kate C. Duncan. Ed. by Mary B. Smetzer. (Illus.). 64p. (Orig.). 1984. pap. 12.00 (0-931163-00-5) U Alaska Museum.

Some Welch/Welsh/Walsh Families of North Carolina: With the John R. Ashe Material. Ed. by Iris C. Jones & Barbara Mahoney. (Orig.). Date not set. pap. 15.00 (0-9620067-6-9) Links Geneal Pubns.

***Some Went West.** Dorothy M. Johnson. LC 97-1509. (Illus.). xx, 196p. 1997. pap. 10.00 (0-8032-7598-6, Bison Books) U of Nebr Pr.

Some Winded, Wild Beast. Christina V. Pacosz. 1985. pap. 2.50 (0-934868-28-X) Black & Red.

Some Women. Ed. by Laura Antoniou. (Orig.). 1995. mass mkt. 6.95 (1-56333-300-7, Rhinoceros) Masquerade.

Some Women. Robert Mapplethorpe. (Illus.). 120p. 1992. pap. 29.95 (0-8212-1937-5) Bulfinch Pr.

***Some Women.** 2nd ed. Laura Antoniou. 1997. reprint ed. mass mkt. 7.95 (1-56333-573-5, Rhinoceros) Masquerade.

Some Women, Mini ed. Robert Mapplethorpe. (Illus.). 120p. 1995. pap. 10.95 (0-8212-2197-3) Bulfinch Pr.

Some Women of France. Paul B. Watson. LC 73-90691. (Essay Index Reprint Ser.). 1977. 23.95 (0-8369-1433-3) Ayer.

Some Wood Properties of Pinus Patula from Uganda & Techniques Developed. R. A. Plumptre. 1978. 59.00 (0-85074-032-0) St Mut.

Some Words. Ray Boulter. (Orig.). 1996. pap. write for info. (1-57553-268-9) Watermrk Pr.

Some Working-Class Movements of the Nineteenth Century. R. F. Wearmouth. 1977. lib. bdg. 59.95 (0-8490-2630-X) Gordon Pr.

Some Worthy Lives. Garland R. Quarles. LC 88-51619. (Illus.). 280p. (C). 1988. 23.00 (0-923198-00-8) Winchester-Frederick Cty Hist Soc.

Some Worthy Persons of Winchester & Frederick County. 1988. write for info. (0-318-64338-3) Winchester-Frederick Cty Hist Soc.

Some Write to the Future: Essays on Contemporary Latin American Fiction. Ariel Dorfman. Tr. by George Shivers. LC 90-24936. 271p. 1991. text ed. 24.95 (0-8223-1130-5); pap. text ed. 16.95 (0-8223-1269-7) Duke.

Some Yellow Flowers. Mara Smith & Ray Smith. (Orig.). 1978. pap. 2.00 (0-686-02397-8) Kirk Pr.

Some Yorkshire Bridges of Beauty & Romance. Arnold N. Patchett. 135p. (C). 1989. text ed. 65.00 (1-872795-86-2, Pub. by Pentland Pr UK) St Mut.

Some Zines 2: Alternative & Underground Artists' & Eccentric Magazines & Micropresses. Tom Trusky. (Illus.). 60p. 1996. 19.95 (0-916272-64-8) Ahsahta Pr.

Some 19th Century English Woodworking Tools. rev. ed. Kenneth D. Roberts. (Illus.). 500p. 1991. 42.50 (0-913602-68-X) K Roberts.

***Somebody Always Singing You.** Twotrees. LC 96-44080. 1997. write for info. (0-87805-981-4) U Pr of Miss.

Somebody & the Three Blairs. Marilyn Tolhurst. LC 90-7747. (Illus.). 32p. (J). (ps-1). 1991. 15.95 (0-531-05878-6); lib. bdg. 16.99 (0-531-08478-7) Orchard Bks Watts.

Somebody & the Three Blairs. Marilyn Tolhurst. LC 90-7747. (Illus.). 32p. (J). (ps-1). 1994. pap. 5.95 (0-531-07056-5) Orchard Bks Watts.

Somebody Called Me a Retard Today - & My Heart Felt Sad. Ellen O'Shaughnessy. LC 92-10812. (Illus.). 24p. (YA). 1992. 13.95 (0-8027-8196-9); lib. bdg. 14.85 (0-8027-8197-7) Walker & Co.

Somebody Catch My Homework. David Harrison. LC 91-68198. 32p. (J). (gr. 4-7). 1993. 14.95 (1-878093-87-8, Wordsong) Boyds Mills Pr.

Somebody Catch My Homework. David L. Harrison. LC 91-68198. (Illus.). 32p. (J). (gr. 1-5). 1995. pap. text ed. 5.95 (1-56397-520-3, Wordsong) Boyds Mills Pr.

Somebody Come & Play. Clare McNally. 320p. 1987. pap. 4.99 (0-8125-2164-1) Tor Bks.

Somebody Else's Child. Terris Grimes. 272p. 1996. pap. 4.99 (0-451-18672-9, Sig) NAL-Dutton.

***Somebody Else's Child.** Pearl Ketover Prilik. LC 97-24487. 1998. write for info. (0-88048-870-0) Am Psychiatric.

***Somebody Else's Children.** John Hubner. 1998. pap. write for info. (0-609-80170-8) Crown Pub Group.

Somebody Else's Children: The Courts, The Kids, & The Struggle to Save America's Troubled Families. J. Hubner & J. Wolfson. 1997. 25.00 (0-517-59941-4) Random Hse Value.

Somebody Else's Kids. Torey L. Hayden. 336p. 1982. mass mkt. 5.99 (0-380-59949-X) Avon.

Somebody Else's Mama. David Haynes. LC 94-34999. 352p. 1995. 21.95 (1-57131-003-7) Milkweed Ed.

Somebody Else's Mama. David Haynes. 352p. 1996. pap. 13.00 (0-15-600408-9, Harvest Bks) HarBrace.

Somebody Else's Nut Tree & Other Tales from Children. Ruth Krauss. LC 89-28056. (Illus.). 43p. (J). (ps-5). 1990. reprint ed. lib. bdg. 16.00 (0-208-02264-3, Linnet Bks) Shoe String.

Somebody Else's War. Paul Harris. (Illus.). 164p. 1993. pap. 16.95 (0-907590-42-X, Pub. by SPA Bks Ltd UK) Seven Hills Bk.

S

An Asterisk (*) at the beginning of an entry indicates that the title is appearing in BIP for the first time.

Somebody Has to Lose. large type ed. Peter Chambers. (Dales Mystery Ser.). 211p. 1992. pap. 17.99 (*1-85389-307-2*) Ulverscroft.

Somebody Has to Take up the Hurt. Jim Fairbrook. 254p. 1995. pap. 10.95 (*1-881147-14-2*) Lowell Print.

Somebody Help Me. Beverly Hastings. 192p. (Orig.). 1993. pap. 3.99 (*0-425-13906-9*) Berkley Pub.

Somebody Lives Inside: The Holy Spirit. Sharon L. Roberts. (Concept Books for Children). (Illus.). 24p. (Orig.). (J). (gr. k-4). 1986. pap. 3.99 (*0-570-08530-6*, 56-1557) Concordia.

***Somebody Loves You.** Helen S. Rice. LC 97-12527. 1998. 19.99 (*0-8007-1747-3*) Revell.

Somebody Loves You. Charles M. Schulz. LC 96-15819. (Passionate Peanuts Bks.). (Illus.). 32p. 1996. 7.95 (*0-00-225158-2*) Collins SF.

Somebody Loves You. large type ed. Helen Steiner Rice. LC 76-25559. (Illus.). 128p. 1994. 16.99 (*0-8007-1670-1*) Revell.

Somebody Loves You, Mr. Hatch. Eileen Spinelli. LC 90-33016. (Illus.). 32p. (J). (ps-2). 1991. lib. bdg. 15.00 (*0-02-786015-9*, Bradbury S&S) S&S Childrens.

Somebody Loves You, Mr. Hatch. Eileen Spinelli. LC 94-794. 32p. (J). (gr. k-3). 1996. pap. 5.95 (*0-689-71872-1*, Aladdin Paperbacks) S&S Childrens.

Somebody, Please Tell Mama! Rebuilding the African-American Family. R. A. Jackson-Woods. 150p. (Orig.). 1994. pap. 10.25 (*1-883491-03-7*) Mature Minist.

Somebody Real. Compiled by Nicholas Duva. (Illus.). 192p. (Orig.). (J). (gr. 5-12). 1973. 6.95 (*0-912834-01-3*); pap. 3.95 (*0-912834-04-8*) Am Faculty Pr.

Somebody Somewhere. Donna Williams. 288p. 1995. pap. 15.95 (*0-385-25500-4*) Doubleday.

Somebody Somewhere: Breaking Free from the World of Autism. Donna Williams. 1995. pap. 14.00 (*0-8129-2524-6*, Times Bks) Random.

Somebody Somewhere Knows My Name. Linda Lowery. LC 94-49538. (First Person Ser.). (Illus.). 40p. (J). (gr. 3-6). 1995. lib. bdg. 14.21 (*0-87614-946-8*, Carolrhoda) Lerner Group.

Somebody Stole the Pea Out of My Whistle: Referees During the Golden Age of Hoosier Basketball. Max Knight. LC 95-77506. (Illus.). 1995. 21.95 (*1-878208-62-4*); pap. 15.95 (*1-878208-63-2*) Guild Pr IN.

Somebody Talks A Lot. Paul Hoover. LC 82-20217. 1982. pap. 3.50 (*0-916328-17-1*) Yellow Pr.

Somebody Tell Me Who I Am! Reshaping Thoughts on Care & Management of Confused & Memory Impaired Older Adults. R. Cairl. 300p. (Orig.). (C). pap. text ed. 29.95 (*1-887454-00-4*) Caremore Pubns.

Somebody to Love. Chuck Taylor. (Autoficiton Ser.). (Illus.). 116p. (Orig.). (C). 1991. pap. 9.95 (*1-878124-02-1*) Flatland.

SomeBody to Love: A Guide to Loving the Body You Have. Leslea Newman. LC 91-34617. 224p. (Orig.). 1991. pap. 10.95 (*1-879427-03-6*) Third Side Pr.

Somebodyness: Martin Luther King, Jr. & the Theology of Dignity. Garth Baker-Fletcher. LC 93-19847. (Harvard Theological Studies: Vol. 31). 160p. (Orig.). (C). 1993. pap. 12.00 (*0-8006-7087-6*) TPI PA.

Somebody's Baby. Charlotte V. Allen. 304p. 1995. 19.95 (*1-55166-124-1*, Mira Bks) Harlequin Bks.

Somebody's Baby. Charlotte V. Allen. (Mira Bks.). 1996. mass mkt. 5.99 (*0-614-08421-0*, 1-66067-9, Mira Bks) Harlequin Bks.

Somebody's Baby. Jayne Ann Krentz. 1996. mass mkt. 5.99 (*1-55166-067-9*, Mira Bks) Harlequin Bks.

Somebody's Brother: A History of the Salvation Army Men's Social Service Department 1891-1985. E. H. McKinley. LC 86-8604. (Studies in American Religion: Vol. 21). 275p. 1986. lib. bdg. 89.95 (*0-88946-665-3*) E Mellen.

Somebody's Calling My Name. Wyatt T. Walker. LC 79-14155. 1979. pap. 12.50 (*0-8170-0980-9*) Judson.

***Somebody's Child: A Novel.** Dennis A. Williams. LC 97-9173. 1997. write for info. (*0-684-82713-1*) S&S Trade.

Somebody's Darling. Larry McMurtry. Ed. by Bill Grose. 352p. 1991. mass mkt. 5.99 (*0-671-74585-9*) PB.

Somebody's Darling. Larry McMurtry. 352p. 1987. pap. 8.00 (*0-671-63319-8*, Fireside) S&S Trade.

Somebody's Mother. Susan F. Kepner. LC 87-18003. (Illus.). 64p. (Orig.). 1987. pap. 4.95 (*0-89407-088-6*) Strawberry Hill.

Somebody's Neighbors. Rose Cooke. 1972. reprint ed. lib. bdg. 46.00 (*0-8422-8028-6*) Irvington.

Somebody's New Pajamas. Isaac Jackson. LC 93-32213. (Illus.). 32p. (J). (gr. 1-5). 1996. pap. 14.89 (*0-8037-1549-8*) Dial Bks Young.

Somebody's New Pajamas. Isaac Jackson. LC 93-32213. (Illus.). 32p. (J). (ps-3). 1996. pap. 14.99 (*0-8037-1570-6*) Dial Bks Young.

Someday. Anna Hudson. 384p. (gr. k). 1995. mass mkt. 4.99 (*0-8217-0119-3*, Zebra Kensgtn) Kensgtn Pub Corp.

Someday a Tree. Eve Bunting. LC 92-24074. (Illus.). 32p. (J). (gr. k-3). 1993. 15.00 (*0-395-61309-4*, Clarion Bks) HM.

Someday a Tree. Eve Bunting. 32p. (J). 1996. pap. 5.95 (*0-395-76478-5*, Clarion Bks) HM.

Someday Angeline. Louis Sachar. (Illus.). 160p. (Orig.). (J). (gr. 3-7). 1983. pap. 4.50 (*0-380-83444-8*, Camelot) Avon.

Someday Angeline. Louis Sachar. (Louis Sachar GLB Reprints Ser.). 160p. (Orig.). (J). (gr. 2-6). 1990. reprint ed. lib. bdg. 12.99 (*0-679-90412-3*) Knopf Bks Yng Read.

Someday Heaven. Larry R. Libby. 48p. (J). 14.99 (*0-945564-77-5*, Gold & Honey) Multnomah Pubs.

Someday House. Anne Shelby. LC 95-23178. (Illus.). 32p. (J). (ps-1). 1996. lib. bdg. 15.99 (*0-531-08860-X*) Orchard Bks Watts.

Someday House. Anne Shelby. LC 95-23178. (Illus.). 32p. (J). (ps-1). 1996. 14.95 (*0-531-09510-X*) Orchard Bks Watts.

Someday I'll Laugh about This. Linda Crew. 176p. (J). (gr. 5-9). 1992. pap. 3.25 (*0-440-40679-X*, YB BDD) BDD Bks Young Read.

***Someday in a Place Out West.** Jon Sheppard. Ed. by Suzanne Venino & Joe Johnson. (Illus.). 128p. 1997. 39.95 (*0-9658009-0-3*) Stevens Grp Pub.

***Someday Is Here! Thirty Days to Personal Renewal, Spiritual Growth & Enhanced Creativity.** Jeanette Isabella. 160p. 1997. pap. 19.95 (*1-878853-60-0*) Venture Pr FL.

Someday It'll All Be Yours...Or Will It? How to Survive-& Enjoy Succession in a Family Business. Donald J. Jonovic. LC 83-26823. 205p. 1984. 24.95 (*0-915607-00-X*) Jamieson Pr.

Someday It'll All Be...Who's? The Lighter Side of the Family Business. Leon A. Danco. LC 90-49915. 1990. 24.95 (*0-9603614-5-6*) Ctr Family Busn.

Someday Kid: A True Story of Sexual Abuse & Its Relationship to Pornography. Donna Ferguson. LC 93-77693. 230p. (Orig.). 1993. pap. 14.95 (*1-879560-18-6*) Harbor Hse West.

Someday Rider. Ann H. Scott. (Illus.). 32p. (J). (ps-3). 1991. reprint ed. pap. 6.95 (*0-395-58115-X*, Clarion Bks) HM.

Someday Songs. Rochelle Ratner. LC 92-4608. 64p. 1992. 9.50 (*0-933532-89-X*) BkMk.

Someday Soon. Nicole Grey. (Girl Friends Ser.: No. 9). 224p. 1994. mass mkt. 3.50 (*0-8217-4512-3*, Zebra Kensgtn) Kensgtn Pub Corp.

Someday Soon. Debbie Macomber. 352p. 1995. mass mkt. 5.50 (*0-06-108309-7*, Harp PBks) HarpC.

Someday Syndrome. Rod Parsley. 37p. 1986. pap. 2.95 (*0-88144-069-8*) Christian Pub.

Someday the Rabbi Will Leave. Harry Kemelman. 288p. 1986. mass mkt. 5.99 (*0-449-20945-8*, Crest) Fawcett.

Someday There'll Be No Tomorrow. William R. Van Der Zee. Tr. by Gerard M. Verschuuren from DUT. LC 96-29379. 160p. (DUT.). 1997. pap. 16.95 (*1-886670-05-6*) Genesis Publ.

Someday We'll Be Free. Leibel Sanik. LC 94-72051. 300p. (C). write for info. (*1-56062-267-9*) CIS Comm.

Someday We'll Play in Heaven. Shawn Strannigan. (I Can Understand Ser.). (Illus.). 24p. (J). (ps-2). 1995. pap. 2.99 (*0-7847-0290-X*, 03457) Standard Pub.

Someday You'll Write. Elizabeth Yates. Ed. by Debbie Parker. LC 95-4284. (Pennant Ser.). 93p. (YA). (gr. 6-12). 1995. reprint ed. pap. 6.49 (*0-89084-820-3*, 087247) Bob Jones Univ Pr.

Somedays It Feels Like It Wants to Rain. David Zaslow. LC 76-46244. (Illus.). (J). (gr. 2-6). 1976. pap. 3.95 (*0-89411-001-2*) Kids Matter.

Someday...Someday. Wendy Whitten. LC 94-78753. (Adventures of Flumpa (TM) & Friends Ser.: Bk. 1). (Illus.). 44p. (J). (ps-3). 1995. 24.95 incl. audio (*1-886184-00-3*) Ion Imagination.

Somehow a Past: The Autobiography of Marsden Hartley. Marsden Hartley. Ed. & Intro. by Susan E. Ryan. (Illus.). 300p. 1996. 27.50 (*0-262-08251-9*) MIT Pr.

Somehow Tenderness Survives: Stories of Southern Africa. Ed. by Hazel Rochman. LC 88-916. (Charlotte Zolotow Bk.). 160p. (YA). (gr. 7 up). 1988. lib. bdg. 14.89 (*0-06-025023-2*) HarpC Child Bks.

Somehow Tenderness Survives: Stories of Southern Africa. Ed. by Hazel Rochman. LC 88-916. (Charlotte Zolotow Bk.). 208p. (YA). (gr. 7 up). 1990. pap. 3.95 (*0-06-447063-6*, Trophy) HarpC Child Bks.

Somehow These Things are All Connected. Richard Callisch. 1988. pap. 7.95 (*0-941363-03-1*) Lake Shore Pub.

Someone. Robert Pinget. Tr. by Barbara Wright from FRE. LC 83-63101. 253p. (C). 1984. 12.95 (*0-87376-043-3*) Red Dust.

Someone at School Has AIDS: A Guide to Developing Policies for HIV-Infected Students & School Staff. 35p. 1989. 10.50 (*0-317-05336-1*) NASBE.

Someone at the Door. Richie T. Cusick. Ed. by Lisa Clancy. 240p. (Orig.). (YA). (gr. 7 up). 1994. pap. 3.99 (*0-671-88742-4*, Archway) PB.

Someone Awesome. Larry R. Libby. (Illus.). 48p. (J). 1995. 14.99 (*0-88070-632-5*, Gold & Honey) Multnomah Pubs.

***Someone Big Is Drinking the Water.** Lucita Huang. (Illus.). 20p. (Orig.). (J). (gr. 1-3). 1997. pap. 8.99 (*0-614-29758-3*) Partners Pubs Grp.

***Someone Cares.** (Tender Hearts Collection). 32p. 1997. 9.99 (*1-881830-28-4*, DS18410) Garborgs.

***Someone Cares: Encyclopedia of Letter Writing.** 1997. 34.95 (*0-13-861543-8*); pap. text ed. 18.95 (*0-13-861535-7*) P-H.

Someone Cares: Scripture Truths for Those Who Are Ill. large type ed. Edwin D. Roels. (Friendship Ser.). (Illus.). 48p. (Orig.). 1993. reprint ed. pap. 0.55 (*1-882536-04-5*, A100-0050) Bible League.

Someone Cares: Scripture Truths for Those Who Are Ill. Edwin D. Roels. (Friendship Ser.). (Illus.). 48p. (Orig.). 1993. reprint ed. pap. write for info. (*1-882536-03-7*, A100-0018) Bible League.

Someone Cares: The Collected Poems of Helen Steiner Rice. Helen Steiner Rice. LC 75-186538. 128p. 1987. 16.99 (*0-8007-0524-6*) Revell.

Someone Could Win a Polar Bear. John Ciardi. LC 92-61179. (Illus.). 64p. (J). (ps-3). 1993. 13.95 (*1-56397-205-0*, Wordsong) Boyds Mills Pr.

Someone Dies, Someone Lives. Lurlene McDaniel. (One Last Wish Ser.: No. 4). 160p. (YA). 1992. pap. 3.99 (*0-553-29842-9*) Bantam.

***Someone Else with My Fingerprints.** Susan Lang & Hanjo Berressem. (Illus.). 176p. (C). 1997. pap. 30.00 (*3-932189-01-9*) Dist Art Pubs.

Someone Else's Baby. Geraldine Kaye. LC 91-73834. 144p. (YA). (gr. 7 up). 1992. 13.95 (*1-56282-149-0*) Hyprn Child.

Someone Else's Baby. Geraldine Kaye. 1997. mass mkt. 4.50 (*0-449-70457-2*) Fawcett.

Someone Else's Dreams. John Yamrus. LC 80-70611. (Illus.). 60p. (Orig.). 1981. pap. 5.95 (*0-930090-12-8*) Applezaba.

Someone Else's Dreams. deluxe limited ed. John Yamrus. LC 80-70611. (Illus.). 60p. (Orig.). 1981. pap. 10.00 (*0-686-69666-2*) Applezaba.

Someone Else's Ghost. Margaret Buffie. LC 93-48015. 256p. (YA). (gr. 7 up). 1995. 14.95 (*0-590-46922-3*) Scholastic Inc.

***Someone Else's Memoirs.** Ron Charach. 96p. 1994. pap. 14.95 (*1-55082-105-9*, Pub. by Quarry Pr CN) LPC InBook.

Someone Else's Problem? Teacher Development to Meet Special Educational Needs. John Moore & Neil Morrison. 180p. 1988. 55.00 (*1-85000-373-4*, Falmer Pr); pap. 30.00 (*1-85000-374-2*, Falmer Pr) Taylor & Francis.

Someone Else's War. Howard R. Simpson. 200p. 1995. 21.95 (*1-57488-000-4*) Brasseys Inc.

Someone for Sally. large type ed. Marjorie Warby. 1991. 25.99 (*0-7089-2562-6*) Ulverscroft.

Someone Going Home Late. Daryl Jones. 88p. 1990. 16.95 (*0-89672-233-3*); pap. 9.95 (*0-89672-234-1*) Tex Tech Univ Pr.

Someone Had to Live. Kevin Griffith. Ed. by Kathleen Iddings. LC 93-61679. (American Bk.). 66p. (Orig.). 1994. per. 10.00 (*0-931289-14-9*) San Diego Poet Pr.

Someone Has to Take the Fall. large type ed. William Newton. (Linford Mystery Library). 1991. pap. 15.99 (*0-7089-7083-4*) Ulverscroft.

Someone I Know see I Can! Can You?

Someone I Know Has Multiple Personalities: A Book For Significant Others--Friends, Family, & Caring Professionals. Sandra J. Hocking. LC 94-11538. 84p. (Orig.). 1994. pap. 9.95 (*1-877872-08-3*) Launch Pr.

Someone I Love Died. Christine H. Tangvald. LC 87-31474. (Please Help Me God Ser.). 24p. (J). (ps-2). 1988. 8.99 (*1-55513-490-4*, Chariot Bks) Chariot Victor.

Someone I Love Died: A Child's Workbook about Loss & Grieving. Wendy Deaton. 32p. (J). 1994. 17.95 (*0-89793-153-X*); pap. 8.95 (*0-89793-150-5*) Hunter Hse.

Someone I Love Is Gay: How Family & Friends Can Respond. Anita & Bob Davies. LC 96-11252. 215p. (Orig.). 1996. pap. 10.99 (*0-8308-1982-7*, 1982) InterVarsity.

Someone in My Corner. M. Scott Miles. 144p. 1995. pap. 1.30 (*1-56476-409-5*, 6-3409, Victor Bks) Chariot Victor.

Someone in My Family Has Molested Children. Eliana M. Gil & Jeffrey Bodmer-Turner. (Illus.). 28p. (Orig.). (YA). (gr. 5 up). 1994. pap. 5.95 (*1-877872-09-1*) Launch Pr.

Someone in the Dark. August Derleth. 335p. 1980. reprint ed. lib. bdg. 15.50 (*0-89968-213-8*, Lghtyr Pr) Buccaneer Bks.

Someone in the House. Barbara Michaels. 1976. 20.95 (*0-8488-0834-7*) Amereon Ltd.

Someone in the House. Barbara Michaels. 1989. mass mkt. 6.99 (*0-425-11389-2*, Berkley Trade) Berkley Pub.

Someone in the Room. Douglas A. Menville. LC 75-46259. (Supernatural & Occult Fiction Ser.). 1976. reprint ed. lib. bdg. 23.95 (*0-405-08118-9*) Ayer.

Someone Is Buying the Zoo: Balancing Organization & Employee Needs in Mergers & Acquisitions. Charlotte Frampton et al. LC 90-92146. 128p. (Orig.). 1991. pap. text ed. 9.95 (*0-9628090-0-4*) Mollyockett Pr.

Someone Is Following. Ronald Roy. (J). 1996. pap. 3.99 (*0-679-87498-4*) Random.

Someone is Following. Ronald Roy. 1996. lib. bdg. 11.99 (*0-679-97498-9*) Random.

Someone Is Hiding. Dayle Ann Dodds. (J). 1994. lib. bdg. 8.95 (*0-671-75542-0*, Litl Simon S&S) S&S Childrens.

Someone Is Hiding on Alcatraz Island. Eve Bunting. 144p. (YA). 1986. pap. 4.50 (*0-425-10294-7*, Berkley-Pacer) Berkley Pub.

Someone Is Killing Our Scientists. Brett Woods. 1988. 17.95 (*0-931933-77-3*, Univ Books) Carol Pub Group.

Someone Is Killing the Great Chefs of Europe. Nan Lyons & Ivan Lyons. LC 75-45140. 240p. 1990. 19.95 (*0-15-183760-0*) HarBrace.

Someone Just Like Me. Carol A. Marron. (Use Your Imagination Ser.). (J). (ps-3). 1993. pap. 4.95 (*0-8114-8407-6*) Raintree Steck-V.

***Someone Like You.** Elaine Coffman. 1997. mass mkt. 10.00 (*0-449-00007-9*, Columbine) Fawcett.

***Someone Like You.** Elaine Coffman. 1998. mass mkt. write for info. (*0-449-15006-2*, GM) Fawcett.

Someone Like You. Roald Dahl. 1953. 17.95 (*0-394-44615-1*) Knopf.

Someone Like You. Susan Sawyer. (Orig.). 1996. mass mkt. 5.50 (*0-380-78478-5*) Avon.

Someone Lying, Someone Dying. large type ed. Jonathan Burke. 1991. 25.99 (*0-7089-2549-9*) Ulverscroft.

Someone, No One: An Essay on Individuality. Kenelm Burridge. LC 79-83979. 283p. reprint ed. pap. 80.70 (*0-8357-4200-8*, 2036979) Bks Demand.

Someone or Nothing? Vol. 27: Nishitani's Religion & Nothingness As a Foundation for Christian-Buddhist Dialogue. Russell H. Bowers. (Asian Thought & Culture Ser.). 264p. (C). 1995. text ed. 49.95 (*0-8204-2832-9*) P Lang Pubng.

Someone Right for You. Edward A. Dreyfus. 224p. 1992. 17.95 (*0-8306-3969-1*); pap. 9.95 (*0-8306-3087-2*) McGraw-Hill Prof.

Someone Saw a Spider: Spider Facts & Folktales. Shirley Climo. LC 85-45340. (Illus.). 128p. (J). (gr. 4-7). 1985. lib. bdg. 14.89 (*0-690-04436-4*, Crowell Jr Bks) HarpC Child Bks.

***Someone Special.** Lizette Jonker. (With Love to...Ser.). 1997. 6.99 (*0-8007-7163-X*) Revell.

Someone Special - You! Evan Twede. (Illus.). 26p. (J). (gr. k-9). 1991. student ed. 2.50 (*0-944803-76-8*); audio 10.95 (*0-944803-74-1*) Brite Music.

Someone Special Died: Picture Book & Resource Guide, 2 bks., Set. Joan B. Prestine. (Kids Have Feelings, Too Ser.). (J). (ps-3). 16.99 (*1-56417-762-9*, FE0050) Fearon Teach Aids.

Someone Special Died, Picturebook. Joan S. Prestine. (J). (ps-3). 1993. pap. 8.99 (*0-86653-929-8*) Fearon Teach Aids.

Someone Special Died, Resource. Joan S. Prestine. (J). (ps-3). 1993. pap. 8.99 (*0-86653-928-X*) Fearon Teach Aids.

Someone Special Is Very Sick. Jim Boulden & Joan Boulden. Ed. by JoAnn Farness. (Illus.). 16p. (Orig.). (J). (gr. k-2). pap. 5.95 (*1-878076-44-2*) Boulden Pub.

Someone Special, Just Like You. Tricia Brown. LC 83-18377. (Illus.). 64p. (J). (ps-2). 1984. 15.95 (*0-8050-0481-5*, Bks Young Read) H Holt & Co.

Someone Special, Just Like You. Tricia Brown. (Illus.). 64p. (J). (gr. k-4). 1995. pap. 5.95 (*0-8050-4268-7*, Owlet BYR) H Holt & Co.

Someone to Care. large type ed. Audrey Weigh. (Linford Romance Library). 288p. 1993. pap. 15.99 (*0-7089-7404-X*, Linford) Ulverscroft.

Someone to Count On. Patricia Hermes. LC 93-13502. (J). (ps-6). 1993. 15.95 (*0-316-35925-4*) Little.

Someone to Count On. Patricia Hermes. 192p. (J). (gr. 4-7). 1995. pap. 3.50 (*0-590-22275-9*) Scholastic Inc.

Someone to Die For. Richard Posner. Ed. by Patricia MacDonald. 256p. (Orig.). (YA). (gr. 7 up). 1993. pap. 2.99 (*0-671-74940-4*, Archway) PB.

Someone to Hold. Lauren Wilde. 400p. 1995. mass mkt. 4.99 (*0-8217-4931-5*, Pinncle Kensgtn) Kensgtn Pub Corp.

Someone to Love. Barbara Cartland. 176p. (Orig.). 1995. mass mkt. 3.99 (*0-515-11686-6*) Jove Pubns.

Someone to Love. Lori Copeland. 1995. mass mkt. 5.99 (*0-449-14884-X*, GM) Fawcett.

***Someone to Love.** Francess L. Lantz. LC 96-31434. (J). 1997. 14.00 (*0-380-97477-0*) Avon.

***Someone to Love: The Story of Creation.** Marilyn Lashbrook. (Me Too Bks.). (Illus.). 30p. (J). 1996. 7.95 (*0-87973-841-3*) Our Sunday Visitor.

Someone to Love: The Story of Creation. Marilyn Lashbrook. LC 87-60261. (Me Too! Bks.). (Illus.). 32p. (J). (ps). 1987. 5.95 (*0-86606-426-5*, 841) Treasure Pub.

Someone to Love see Alguien a Quien Amar (Creacion)

Someone to Pour the Wine. Miriam Kessler. 52p. (Orig.). 1996. pap. 9.95 (*1-57249-039-X*, Ragged Edge) White Mane Pub.

Someone to Turn To: Experiences of Help Before Divorce. Ann K. Mitchell. 136p. 1981. text ed. 22.00 (*0-08-025741-0*, Pergamon Pr) Elsevier.

Someone to Watch. Jaye Maiman. 288p. 1995. pap. 10.95 (*1-56280-095-7*) Naiad Pr.

***Someone to Watch over Me.** Richard Bausch. 224p. Date not set. 22.00 (*0-06-017333-5*) HarpC.

Someone to Watch over Me. Laura Kenner. (Intrigue Ser.). 1994. mass mkt. 2.99 (*0-373-22263-7*, 1-22263-7) Harlequin Bks.

***Someone to Watch Over Me.** Tricia Sullivan. 1997. mass mkt. 5.99 (*0-553-57702-6*) Bantam.

Someone Waiting. Joan Hohl. (Western Lovers Ser.). 1995. mass mkt. 3.99 (*0-373-88512-1*, 1-88512-8) Harlequin Bks.

Someone Waiting. Emlyn Williams. 1956. pap. 5.25 (*0-8222-1054-1*) Dramatists Play.

Someone Was Watching. David Patneaude. Ed. by Judith Mathews. LC 92-39130. 240p. (J). (gr. 6-9). 1993. lib. bdg. 14.95 (*0-8075-7531-3*) A Whitman.

Someone Was Watching. David Patneaude. (J). (gr. 6-9). 1995. pap. 4.95 (*0-8075-7532-1*) A Whitman.

Someone Who Cares. large type ed. Leslie Lance. 288p. 1995. 25.99 (*0-7089-3432-3*) Ulverscroft.

Someone Who'll Watch over Me. Frank McGuinness. 96p. (Orig.). 1993. pap. 8.95 (*0-571-16804-3*) Faber & Faber.

***Someone Will Go on Owing: Collected Poems, 1966-1996.** Andrew Glaze. LC 97-16915. 224p. 1997. 25.00 (*1-881320-91-X*, Black Belt) Black Belt Comm.

Someone's Been Sleeping in My Bed. Linda Jones. 448p. (Orig.). 1996. mass mkt. 5.99 (*0-505-52094-X*, Love Spell) Dorchester Pub Co.

***Someone's Child.** Alethea A. Wells. 450p. 1997. 25.00 (*0-9645787-3-5*) Unole Pub.

Someone's in the Kitchen with Dennis. Hank Ketcham. (Dennis the Menace Ser.). (Illus.). 1979. pap. 1.50 (*0-449-14253-1*, GM) Fawcett.

***Someone's in the Kitchen with Mommy: 100 Fun & Easy Recipes.** Elaine Moquette-Magee. LC 96-29326. 1997. pap. write for info. (*0-8092-3142-5*) Contemp Bks.

***Someone's Making a Monkey Out of You!** Patrick Marks. Ed. by Jesse Florea. 120p. 1996. pap. 6.95 (*0-89051-210-8*, SOMAMO) Master Bks.

Someone's Mother Is Missing. Harry Mazer. 176p. (YA). 1991. pap. 3.50 (*0-440-21097-6*, YB BDD) BDD Bks Young Read.

Someone's Trying to Cut off My Head. Rob Portlock. LC 92-12483. (Portlock Kids Ser.). (Illus.). 32p. (Orig.). (J). (ps-1). 1992. pap. 4.99 (*0-8308-1902-9*, 1902) InterVarsity.

Someone's Watching. Judith Kelman. 368p. 1991. pap. 5.99 (*0-553-29100-9*) Bantam.

***Someplace Else.** Saul. (J). (gr. k-2). 1997. mass mkt. 5.99 (*0-689-81567-0*) S&S Childrens.

Someplace Else. Carol P. Saul. (J). (gr. 4 up). 1995. pap. 14.00 (*0-671-87283-4*, S&S Bks Young Read) S&S Childrens.

S

S

Someplace Else. Carol P. Saul. (Illus.). 32p. (J). (ps-2). 1995. 15.00 (*0-689-80273-0*, S&S Bks Young Read) S&S Childrens.
Someplace Strange. Ann Nocenti & John Bolton. Ed. by Archie Goodwin. (Limited-Signed Edition Ser.: No. 15). (Illus.). 64p. 1988. 6.95 (*0-936211-13-X*) Marvel Entmnt.
Someplace, Surely: A Quest for Meaning. Bryce W. Yourd. LC 90-91392. 176p. (Orig.). 1990. pap. 9.95 (*0-9627285-0-0*) B W Yourd.
Someplace to Go. Maria Testa. (Illus.). 32p. (J). (gr. 2-4). 1996. lib. bdg. 14.95 (*0-8075-7524-0*) A Whitman.
Somers Tracts: A Collection of Scarce & Valuable Tracts, 13 Vols, Set. Somers. Ed. by Walter Scott. reprint ed. 1, 170.00 (*0-404-06160-5*) AMS Pr.
Somerset, Vol. IV. Ed. by R. W. Dunning. (Victoria History of the Counties of England Ser.). (Illus.). 286p. 1979. 110.00 (*0-19-722747-3*) OUP.
Somerset: An Architectural History. Paul B. Touart. LC 89-622651. 424p. 1990. pap. 25.00 (*1-878399-06-3*) Div Hist Cult Progs.
***Somerset: With Bath & Bristol.** Shirley Toulson. (Pimlico County History Ser.). (Illus.). 208p. 1997. pap. 19.95 (*0-7126-9887-6*, Pub. by Pimlico) Trafalgar.
Somerset & All the Maughams. Robin Maugham. LC 75-22759. (Illus.). 270p. 1977. reprint ed. text ed. 59.75 (*0-8371-8236-0*, MASOM, Greenwood Pr) Greenwood.
Somerset & Avon. Robert Dunning. (Illus.). 192p. 1992. pap. 29.00 (*0-7509-0069-5*, Pub. by Sutton Pubng UK) Bks Intl VA.
Somerset & Dorset Railway. Donald S. Barrie & C. R. Clinker. 52p. (C). 1985. 39.00 (*0-85361-234-X*) St Mut.
Somerset Anthology. Roger Clark. (C). 1988. 37.00 (*0-900657-27-8*, Pub. by W Sessions UK) St Mut.
Somerset County: Three Centuries of Progress. Jessie L. Havens. 1990. 25.95 (*0-89781-364-2*) Am Historical Pr.
Somerset County Historical Quarterly, 2 vols., Set. Ed. by A. Van Doren Honeyman. (Illus.). 668p. 1995. reprint ed. lib. bdg. 75.00 (*0-8328-5069-1*) Higginson Bk Co.
***Somerset Hills, Being a Brief Record of Significant Facts in the Early History of the Hill Country of Somerset County.** Ludwig Schmacher. (Illus.). 133p. 1997. reprint ed. pap. 16.50 (*0-8328-6078-6*) Higginson Bk Co.
Somerset Holmes. Jones et al. (Illus.). 1990. 24.95 (*0-913035-11-4*); pap. 14.95 (*0-913035-10-6*) Eclipse Bks.
Somerset House Wills. (C). 1987. 30.00 (*0-317-89821-3*, Pub. by Birmingham Midland Soc UK) St Mut.
Somerset, MA. James Bradbury. (Images of America Ser.). 128p. 1996. pap. 16.99 (*0-7524-0277-3*, Arcdia) Chalford.
Somerset Medieval Wills. Ed. by F. W. Weaver. 325p. 1987. text ed. 39.95 (*0-312-01219-5*) St Martin.
Somerset of One Hundred Years Ago. Robert Dunning. (One Hundred Years Ago Ser.). (Illus.). 1993. 38.00 (*0-7509-0418-6*, Pub. by Sutton Pubng UK) Bks Intl VA.
Somerset Way. Lawrence Main. (C). 1988. pap. text ed. 29.00 (*0-904110-79-6*, Pub. by Thornhill Pr UK) St Mut.
***Somerset, Wiltshire & the Mednips Walks.** Jarrold Publishing Staff. (Pathfinder Guides Ser.). 80p. 1997. pap. 16.95 (*0-7117-0877-0*, Pub. by Jarrold Pub UK) Seven Hills Bk.
Somervell: Story of a Texas County. William C. Nunn. LC 75-39912. 267p. reprint ed. pap. 76.10 (*0-7837-1240-5*, 2041377) Bks Demand.
Somerville & Ross. John Cronin. LC 78-126031. (Irish Writers Ser.). 111p. 1975. 8.50 (*0-8387-7767-8*); pap. 1.95 (*0-8387-7698-1*) Bucknell U Pr.
Somerville Farce. rev. ed. Michelle Kasey. 224p. 1991. pap. 4.50 (*0-451-16917-4*, Sig) NAL-Dutton.
Somerville for Women: An Oxford College 1879-1993. Pauline Adams. (Illus.). 442p. (C). 1996. 75.00 (*0-19-920179-X*); pap. 30.00 (*0-19-920182-X*) OUP.
***Somerville, MA.** Anthony Sammarco. (Images of America Ser.). 1997. pap. 16.99 (*0-7524-0540-3*, Arcdia) Chalford.
Somerville Papers: Selections from the Private & Official Correspondence of Admiral of the Fleet Sir James Somerville, G. C. B., G. B. E., D. S. O. James Somerville. Ed. by Michael Simpson. LC 95-2621. (Publications of the Navy Records Society). 724p. 1996. 84.95 (*1-85928-207-5*, Pub. by Scolar Pr UK) Ashgate Pub Co.
Somesthesis & the Neurobiology of the Somatosensory Cortex. Ed. by O. Franzen et al. LC 96-6739. 421p. 1996. 113.00 (*0-8176-5322-8*); 113.00 (*3-7643-5322-8*) Birkhauser.
Somesthetic System of the Rat. Raimond Emmers. LC 88-3227. 109p. 1988. reprint ed. pap. 31.10 (*0-608-00307-7*, 2061024) Bks Demand.
Somethin' Michael Talbott. (Illus.). 29p. 1982. 8.95 (*0-317-11165-5*) Joyce Media.
Something. Natalie Babbitt. LC 70-125143. (Illus.). 40p. (J). (ps-3). 1987. 11.00 (*0-374-37137-7*) FS&G.
Something about a Soldier. Mark Harris. LC 84-25652. viii, 175p. 1985. reprint ed. pap. 6.50 (*0-8032-7226-X*, Bison Books) U of Nebr Pr.
Something about Cats, & Other Pieces. H. P. Lovecraft. Ed. by August W. Derleth. LC 79-156681. (Essay Index Reprint Ser.). 1977. reprint ed. 24.95 (*0-8369-2410-X*) Ayer.
Something about O. K. Bouwsma. Ronald E. Hustwit. 110p. (C). 1992. lib. bdg. 37.50 (*0-8191-8652-X*) U Pr of Amer.
Something about Swans. Madeleine Doran. LC 73-2042. 133p. 1973. reprint ed. pap. 38.00 (*0-608-01953-4*, 2062608) Bks Demand.
Something about the Author, Vol. 1. Ed. by Adele Sarkissian. (Autobiography Ser.). 371p. 1985. 96.00 (*0-8103-4450-5*) Gale.
Something about the Author, Vol. 4. Ed. by Adele Sarkissian. (Autobiography Ser.). (Illus.). 403p. 1987. 96.00 (*0-8103-4453-X*) Gale.
Something about the Author, Vol. 5. Ed. by Adele Sarkissian. (Autobiography Ser.). (Illus.). 300p. 1987. 96.00 (*0-8103-4454-8*) Gale.
Something about the Author, Vol. 6. Ed. by Joyce Nakamura. (Autobiography Ser.). 1988. 96.00 (*0-8103-4455-6*) Gale.
Something about the Author, Vol. 7. Ed. by Joyce Nakamura. (Autobiography Ser.). 1988. 96.00 (*0-8103-4456-4*) Gale.
Something about the Author, Vol. 8. Ed. by Joyce Nakamura. (Autobiography Ser.). 1989. 96.00 (*0-8103-4457-2*) Gale.
Something about the Author, Vol. 9. Ed. by Joyce Nakamura. (Autobiography Ser.). 400p. 1989. 96.00 (*0-8103-4458-0*) Gale.
Something about the Author, Vol. 10. Ed. by Joyce Nakamura. LC 86-641293. (Autobiography Ser.). (Illus.). 384p. 1990. 96.00 (*0-8103-4459-9*, 002713) Gale.
Something about the Author, Vol. 11. (Autobiography Ser.). 1990. 96.00 (*0-8103-4460-2*) Gale.
Something about the Author, Vol. 49. Ed. by Anne Commire. (Illus.). 315p. 1987. 96.00 (*0-8103-2259-5*) Gale.
Something about the Author, Vol. 50. Ed. by Anne Commire. (Illus.). 300p. 1987. 96.00 (*0-8103-2260-9*) Gale.
Something about the Author, Vol. 51. Ed. by Anne Commire. LC 72-27107. 300p. 1988. 96.00 (*0-8103-2261-7*) Gale.
Something about the Author, Vol. 54. Ed. by Anne Commire. 1988. 96.00 (*0-8103-2264-1*) Gale.
Something about the Author, Vol. 55. Anne Commire. 1989. 96.00 (*0-8103-2265-X*) Gale.
Something about the Author, Vol. 56. Anne Commire. 1989. 96.00 (*0-8103-2266-8*) Gale.
Something about the Author, Vol. 57. Ed. by Anne Commire. 1989. 96.00 (*0-8103-2267-6*) Gale.
Something about the Author, Vol. 58. Ed. by Anne Commire. 300p. 1989. 96.00 (*0-8103-2268-4*) Gale.
Something about the Author, Vol. 59. Ed. by Anne Commire. 300p. 1990. 96.00 (*0-8103-2269-2*) Gale.
***Something about the Author, Vol. 62.** 1990. 96.00 (*0-8103-2272-2*, 00000066, Gale Res Intl) Gale.
Something about the Author, Vol. 63. Donna Olendorf. 1991. 96.00 (*0-8103-2273-0*) Gale.
Something about the Author, Vol. 64. Donna Olendorf. 1991. 96.00 (*0-8103-2274-9*) Gale.
Something about the Author, Vol. 65. Ed. by Donna Olendorf. 1991. 96.00 (*0-8103-2275-7*) Gale.
Something about the Author, Vol. 66. Ed. by Donna Olendorf. 1991. 96.00 (*0-8103-2276-5*) Gale.
Something about the Author, Vol. 67. Anne Commire. Ed. by Donna Olendorf. 1992. 96.00 (*0-8103-2277-3*) Gale.
Something about the Author, Vol. 68. Anne Commire. Ed. by Donna Olendorf. 1992. 96.00 (*0-8103-2278-1*) Gale.
Something about the Author, Vol. 69. Anne Commire. Ed. by Donna Olendorf. 1992. 96.00 (*0-8103-2279-X*) Gale.
Something about the Author, Vol. 70. Anne Commire. Ed. by Donna Oldendorf & Diane Telgen. 1992. 96.00 (*0-8103-2280-3*) Gale.
Something about the Author, Vol. 71. Ed. by Diane Telgen. 1993. 96.00 (*0-8103-2281-1*) Gale.
Something about the Author, Vol. 72. Ed. by Diane Telgen. 1993. 96.00 (*0-8103-2282-X*) Gale.
Something about the Author, Vol. 73. Ed. by Diane Telgen. 1993. 96.00 (*0-8103-2283-8*) Gale.
Something about the Author, Vol. 74. Ed. by Diane Telgen. 1993. 96.00 (*0-8103-2284-6*) Gale.
Something about the Author, Vol. 75. Ed. by Diane Telgen. 1993. 96.00 (*0-8103-2285-4*) Gale.
Something about the Author, Vol. 76. Ed. by Diane Telgen. 1994. 96.00 (*0-8103-2286-2*) Gale.
Something about the Author, Vol. 77. Ed. by Diane Telgen & Kevin S. Hile. 1994. 96.00 (*0-8103-2287-0*) Gale.
Something about the Author, Vol. 78. Ed. by Kevin S. Hile. 1994. 96.00 (*0-8103-2288-9*) Gale.
Something about the Author, Vol. 79. Ed. by Kevin S. Hile. 324p. 1994. 96.00 (*0-8103-2289-7*) Gale.
Something about the Author, Vol. 80. Ed. by Kevin S. Hile. 1995. 96.00 (*0-8103-2290-0*) Gale.
Something about the Author, Vol. 81. Kevin S. Hile. 1995. 96.00 (*0-8103-2291-9*) Gale.
Something about the Author, Vol. 82. Hile. 275p. 1995. 96.00 (*0-8103-2292-7*, 001711) Gale.
Something about the Author, Vol. 83. Kevin Hile. 320p. 1995. 96.00 (*0-8103-2293-5*, 001712) Gale.
Something about the Author, Vol. 84. Hile. 1995. 96.00 (*0-8103-9370-0*) Gale.
Something about the Author, Vol. 85. Hile. 1996. 96.00 (*0-8103-9371-9*) Gale.
Something about the Author, Vol. 86. Hile. 1996. 96.00 (*0-8103-9372-7*) Gale.
Something about the Author, Vol. 87. Hile. 1996. 96.00 (*0-8103-9373-5*) Gale.
Something about the Author, Vol. 88. Hile. 1996. 96.00 (*0-8103-9945-8*) Gale.
***Something about the Author, Vol. 89.** 1996. 96.00 (*0-8103-9946-6*, 00108496, Gale Res Intl) Gale.
***Something about the Author, Vol. 90.** 1996. 96.00 (*0-8103-9947-4*, 00108497, Gale Res Intl) Gale.
***Something about the Author, Vol. 91.** 1997. 96.00 (*0-8103-9948-2*, 00108498, Gale Res Intl) Gale.
***Something about the Author, Vol. 92.** 1997. 96.00 (*0-8103-9949-0*, 00108499, Gale Res Intl) Gale.
***Something about the Author, Vol. 93.** 1997. 96.00 (*0-7876-1146-8*, 00156250, Gale Res Intl) Gale.
***Something about the Author, Vol. 94.** 1997. 96.00 (*0-7876-1147-6*, 00156251, Gale Res Intl) Gale.
***Something about the Author, Vol. 95.** 1998. 96.00 (*0-7876-1148-4*, 00156252, Gale Res Intl) Gale.
***Something about the Author, Vol. 96.** 1998. 96.00 (*0-7876-1149-2*, 00156253, Gale Res Intl) Gale.
***Something about the Author, Vol. 97.** 1998. 96.00 (*0-7876-1150-6*, 00156254, Gale Res Intl) Gale.
***Something about the Author, Vol. 98.** 1998. 92.00 (*0-7876-1444-0*, 00156617, Gale Res Intl) Gale.
Something about the Author, Vols. 2-3. Incl. Vol. 2. . 300p. 1986. 96.00 (*0-8103-4451-3*); Vol. 3. . 300p. 1986. 96.00 (*0-8103-4452-1*); (Autobiography Ser.). 70.00 (*0-685-73763-2*); 70.00 (*0-685-73764-0*) Gale.
Something about the Author: Facts & Pictures about Contemporary Authors & Illustrators of Books for Young People. Incl. Vol. 1. . Anne Commire. LC 72-27107. 1971. 96.00 (*0-8103-0050-8*); Vol. 2. . Anne Commire. LC 72-27107. 1972. 96.00 (*0-8103-0052-4*); Vol. 3. . Anne Commire. LC 72-27107. 1972. 96.00 (*0-8103-0054-0*); Vol. 4. . Anne Commire. LC 72-27107. 1973. 96.00 (*0-8103-0056-7*); Vol. 5. . Anne Commire. LC 72-27107. 1974. 96.00 (*0-8103-0058-3*); Vol. 6. . Anne Commire. LC 72-27107. 1974. 96.00 (*0-8103-0060-5*); Vol. 7. . Anne Commire. LC 72-27107. 1975. 96.00 (*0-8103-0062-1*); Vol. 8. . Anne Commire. LC 72-27107. 1976. 96.00 (*0-8103-0064-8*); Vol. 9. . Anne Commire. LC 72-27107. 1976. 96.00 (*0-8103-0066-4*); Vol. 10. . Anne Commire. LC 72-27107. 1976. 96.00 (*0-8103-0068-0*); Vol. 11. . Anne Commire. LC 72-27107. 1977. 96.00 (*0-8103-0070-2*); Vol. 12. . Anne Commire. LC 72-27107. 1977. 96.00 (*0-8103-0072-9*); Vol. 13. . Anne Commire. LC 72-27107. 1978. 96.00 (*0-8103-0094-X*); Vol. 14. . Anne Commire. LC 72-27107. 1978. 96.00 (*0-8103-0095-8*); Vol. 15. . Anne Commire. LC 72-27107. 1979. 96.00 (*0-8103-0096-6*); Vol. 16. . Anne Commire. LC 72-27107. 1979. 96.00 (*0-8103-0097-4*); Vol. 17. . Anne Commire. LC 72-27107. 1979. 96.00 (*0-8103-0098-2*); Vol. 18. . Anne Commire. LC 72-27107. 1980. 96.00 (*0-8103-0099-0*); Vol. 19. . Anne Commire. LC 72-27107. 1980. 96.00 (*0-8103-0051-6*); Vol. 20. . Anne Commire. LC 72-27107. 1980. 96.00 (*0-8103-0053-2*); Vol. 21. . Anne Commire. LC 72-27107. 1981. 96.00 (*0-8103-0093-1*); Vol. 22. . Anne Commire. LC 72-27107. 1981. 96.00 (*0-8103-0085-0*); Vol. 23. . Anne Commire. LC 72-27107. 1981. 96.00 (*0-8103-0086-9*); Vol. 24. . Anne Commire. LC 72-27107. 1981. 96.00 (*0-8103-0087-7*); Vol. 25. . Anne Commire. LC 72-27107. 1981. 96.00 (*0-8103-0084-2*); Vol. 26. . Anne Commire. LC 72-27107. 1982. 96.00 (*0-8103-0089-3*); Vol. 27. . Anne Commire. LC 72-27107. 1982. 96.00 (*0-8103-0083-4*); Vol. 28. . Anne Commire. LC 72-27107. 296p. 1982. 96.00 (*0-8103-0082-6*); Vol. 29. . Anne Commire. LC 72-27107. 328p. 1982. 96.00 (*0-8103-0081-8*); Vol. 31. . LC 72-27107. 272p. 1983. 96.00 (*0-8103-0057-5*); Vol. 32. . LC 72-27107. 288p. 1983. 96.00 (*0-8103-0059-1*); Vol. 33. . LC 72-27107. 240p. 1983. 96.00 (*0-8103-0061-3*); Vol. 35. . LC 72-27107. 248p. 1984. 96.00 (*0-8103-0065-6*); Vol. 36. . LC 72-27107. 304p. 1984. 96.00 (*0-8103-0067-2*); Vol. 37. . LC 72-27107. 304p. 1984. 96.00 (*0-8103-0069-9*); Vol. 38. . LC 72-27107. 232p. 1985. 96.00 (*0-8103-0071-0*); Vol. 39. . LC 72-27107. 300p. 1985. 96.00 (*0-8103-0074-5*); LC 72-27107. (Illus.). write for info. (*0-318-59214-2*) Gale.
Something about the Author: Facts & Pictures about Contemporary Authors & Illustrators of Books for Young People. Incl. Vol. 1. . Anne Commire. LC 72-27107. 1971. 96.00 (*0-8103-0050-8*); Vol. 2. . Anne Commire. LC 72-27107. 1972. 96.00 (*0-8103-0052-4*); Vol. 3. . Anne Commire. LC 72-27107. 1972. 96.00 (*0-8103-0054-0*); Vol. 4. . Anne Commire. LC 72-27107. 1973. 96.00 (*0-8103-0056-7*); Vol. 5. . Anne Commire. LC 72-27107. 1974. 96.00 (*0-8103-0058-3*); Vol. 6. . Anne Commire. LC 72-27107. 1974. 96.00 (*0-8103-0060-5*); Vol. 7. . Anne Commire. LC 72-27107. 1975. 96.00 (*0-8103-0062-1*); Vol. 8. . Anne Commire. LC 72-27107. 1976. 96.00 (*0-8103-0064-8*); Vol. 9. . Anne Commire. LC 72-27107. 1976. 96.00 (*0-8103-0066-4*); Vol. 10. . Anne Commire. LC 72-27107. 1976. 96.00 (*0-8103-0068-0*); Vol. 11. . Anne Commire. LC 72-27107. 1977. 96.00 (*0-8103-0070-2*); Vol. 12. . Anne Commire. LC 72-27107. 1977. 96.00 (*0-8103-0072-9*); Vol. 13. . Anne Commire. LC 72-27107. 1978. 96.00 (*0-8103-0094-X*); Vol. 14. . Anne Commire. LC 72-27107. 1978. 96.00 (*0-8103-0095-8*); Vol. 15. . Anne Commire. LC 72-27107. 1979. 96.00 (*0-8103-0096-6*); Vol. 16. . Anne Commire. LC 72-27107. 1979. 96.00 (*0-8103-0097-4*); Vol. 17. . Anne Commire. LC 72-27107. 1979. 96.00 (*0-8103-0098-2*); Vol. 18. . Anne Commire. LC 72-27107. 1980. 96.00 (*0-8103-0099-0*); Vol. 19. . Anne Commire. LC 72-27107. 1980. 96.00 (*0-8103-0051-6*); Vol. 20. . Anne Commire. LC 72-27107. 1980. 96.00 (*0-8103-0053-2*); Vol. 21. . Anne Commire. LC 72-27107. 1981. 96.00 (*0-8103-0093-1*); Vol. 22. . Anne Commire. LC 72-27107. 1981. 96.00 (*0-8103-0085-0*); Vol. 23. . Anne Commire. LC 72-27107. 1981. 96.00 (*0-8103-0086-9*); Vol. 24. . Anne Commire. LC 72-27107. 1981. 96.00 (*0-8103-0087-7*); Vol. 25. . Anne Commire. LC 72-27107. 1981. 96.00 (*0-8103-0084-2*); Vol. 26. . Anne Commire. LC 72-27107. 1982. 96.00 (*0-8103-0089-3*); Vol. 27. . Anne Commire. LC 72-27107. 1982. 96.00 (*0-8103-0083-4*); Vol. 28. . Anne Commire. LC 72-27107. 296p. 1982. 96.00 (*0-8103-0082-6*); Vol. 29. . Anne Commire. LC 72-27107. 328p. 1982. 96.00 (*0-8103-0081-8*); Vol. 31. . LC 72-27107. 272p. 1983. 96.00 (*0-8103-0057-5*); Vol. 32. . LC 72-27107. 288p. 1983. 96.00 (*0-8103-0059-1*); Vol. 33. . LC 72-27107. 240p. 1983. 96.00 (*0-8103-0061-3*); Vol. 35. . LC 72-27107. 248p. 1984. 96.00 (*0-8103-0065-6*); Vol. 36. . LC 72-27107. 304p. 1984. 96.00 (*0-8103-0067-2*); Vol. 37. . LC 72-27107. 304p. 1984. 96.00 (*0-8103-0069-9*); Vol. 38. . LC 72-27107. 232p. 1985. 96.00 (*0-8103-0071-0*); Vol. 39. . LC 72-27107. 300p. 1985. 96.00 (*0-8103-0074-5*); LC 72-27107. (Illus.). (J). (gr. 7-12). write for info. (*0-318-52361-2*) Gale.
Something about the Author: Facts & Pictures about Contemporary Authors & Illustrators of Books for Young People, Vol. 30. Ed. by Anne Commire. (Illus.). 304p. (YA). (gr. 9-12). 1983. 96.00 (*0-8103-0055-9*) Gale.
Something about the Author: Facts & Pictures about Contemporary Authors & Illustrators of Books for Young People, Vol. 34. Ed. by Anne Commire. (Illus.). 224p. (YA). (gr. 9-12). 1984. 96.00 (*0-8103-0063-X*) Gale.
Something about the Author: Facts & Pictures about Contemporary Authors & Illustrators of Books for Young People, Vol. 40. Ed. by Anne Commire. (Illus.). 321p. 1985. 96.00 (*0-8103-2250-1*) Gale.
Something about the Author: Facts & Pictures about Contemporary Authors & Illustrators of Books for Young People, Vol. 41. Ed. by Anne Commire. LC 72-27107. 348p. 1985. 96.00 (*0-8103-2251-X*) Gale.
Something about the Author: Facts & Pictures about Contemporary Authors & Illustrators of Books for Young People, Vol. 42. Ed. by Anne Commire. 299p. 1985. 96.00 (*0-8103-2252-8*) Gale.
Something about the Author: Facts & Pictures about Contemporary Authors & Illustrators of Books for Young People, Vol. 43. Ed. by Anne Commire. (Illus.). 300p. 1986. 96.00 (*0-8103-2253-6*) Gale.
Something about the Author: Facts & Pictures about Contemporary Authors & Illustrators of Books for Young People, Vol. 44. Ed. by Anne Commire. 300p. (J). (gr. 9-12). 1986. 96.00 (*0-8103-2254-4*) Gale.
Something about the Author: Facts & Pictures about Contemporary Authors & Illustrators of Books for Young People, Vol. 45. Ed. by Anne Commire. 304p. 1986. 96.00 (*0-8103-2255-2*) Gale.
Something about the Author: Facts & Pictures about Contemporary Authors & Illustrators of Books for Young People, Vol. 46. Ed. by Anne Commire. 313p. 1986. 96.00 (*0-8103-2256-0*) Gale.
Something About the Author: Facts & Pictures about Contemporary Authors & Illustrators of Books for Young People, Vol. 47. Ed. by Anne Commire. 315p. 1987. 96.00 (*0-8103-2257-9*) Gale.
Something about the Author: Facts & Pictures about Contemporary Authors & Illustrators of Books for Young People, Vol. 48. Ed. by Anne Commire. 323p. 1987. 96.00 (*0-8103-2258-7*) Gale.
Something about the Author Autobiography Series Vol. 20, Vol. 20. Ed. by Joyce Nakamura. 1995. 96.00 (*0-8103-4469-6*) Gale.
Something about the Author, Vol. 53, Vol. 53. Ed. by Anne Commire. 1988. 96.00 (*0-8103-2263-3*) Gale.
Something about the Author, Vol. 60: Facts & Pictures about Authors & Illustrators of Books for Young People, Vol. 60. Ed. by Anne Commire. LC 72-27107. (Illus.). 203p. 1990. 96.00 (*0-8103-2270-6*, 001689) Gale.

An Asterisk (*) at the beginning of an entry indicates that the title is appearing in BIP for the first time.

Something about the Author, Vol. 61: Facts & Pictures about Authors & Illustrators of Books for Young People, Vol. 61. Ed. by Anne Commire. LC 72-27107. (Illus.). 275p. 1990. 96.00 (*0-8103-2271-4*, 001690) Gale.

Something about the Authors, Vol. 52, Vol. 52. Ed. by Anne Commire. 1988. 96.00 (*0-8103-2262-5*) Gale.

Something about the Music, No. 2: Anthology of the Critical Opinions. Thomas P. Lewis. 660p. 1991. 44.50 (*0-912483-66-0*); pap. 29.50 (*0-912483-54-7*) Pro-Am Music.

Something about X-Rays for Everybody. Edward Trevert. (Illus.). 82p. (C). 1988. reprint ed. 16.95 (*0-944838-05-7*) Med Physics Pub.

Something & Nothingness: The Fiction of John Updike & John Fowles. John Neary. LC 90-25137. 288p. (C). 1991. 24.95 (*0-8093-1742-7*) S Ill U Pr.

Something at Last: Dakota Poetry & Sketches. Jerome Freeman & Jean Bailey. (Illus.). (Orig.). 1993. pap. 8.50 (*0-9635858-0-0*) Penstemon Pub.

Something Bad Happened. Debra W. Alexander. 16p. (J). (gr. k-5). 1992. 3.95 (*1-56688-056-4*) Bur For At-Risk.

Something Beautiful. Marilyn Tracy & Jane Toombs. (Shadows Ser.). 1995. mass mkt. 3.50 (*0-373-27051-8*, 1-27051-1) Silhouette.

***Something Beautiful.** Sharon D. Wyeth. LC 96-37872. (Illus.). (J). 1998. write for info. (*0-385-32239-9*) Doubleday.

Something Beautiful Came to Earth: The Angel Bird Story. limited ed. Donald O. Black. LC 90-70072. (Illus.). 64p. 1990. pap. 17.95 (*0-9625753-0-5*) SuperAmerican Bks.

Something Beautiful for God: Mother Teresa of Calcutta. Malcolm Muggeridge. 1986. pap. 11.00 (*0-06-066043-0*) Harper SF.

Something Beautiful for God: Mother Teresa of Calcutta. large type ed. Malcolm Muggeridge. (Large Print Inspirational Ser.). 174p. 1985. pap. 9.95 (*0-8027-2474-4*) Walker & Co.

Something Big Has Been Here. Jack Prelutsky. LC 89-34773. (Illus.). 160p. (J). (gr. k-4). 1990. 17.95 (*0-688-06434-5*) Greenwillow.

Something Blue. Jayne Addison. (Romance Ser.). 1993. pap. 2.75 (*0-373-08944-9*, 5-08944-6) Silhouette.

***Something Blue.** Jean C. Spaugh. LC 96-48782. 1997. 18.95 (*0-89587-167-X*) Blair.

***Something Borrowed.** Davis-Goff. Date not set. write for info. (*0-312-17028-9*) St Martin.

Something Borrowed. Rebecca H. Lee. 288p. (Orig.). 1995. pap. 4.99 (*0-7865-0073-5*) Diamond.

***Something Borrowed.** Alexandra Marshall. LC 96-29516. 1997. 22.00 (*0-395-81665-3*) HM.

Something Borrowed. Linda Varner. (Romance Ser.). 1993. pap. 2.75 (*0-373-08943-0*, 5-08943-8) Silhouette.

***Something Borrowed: 101 Useful Tips for Every Sailor.** Joel Graffley. 1996. pap. text ed. 13.95 (*0-07-011890-6*) McGraw.

Something Borrowed: 101 Useful Tips for Every Sailor. Joel Graffley. (Illus.). 160p. 1995. pap. 13.95 (*0-924486-93-7*) Sheridan.

Something Borrowed, Something Blue. Adrianne Lee. 1994. mass mkt. 2.99 (*0-373-22296-3*, 1-22296-7) Harlequin Bks.

***Something Borrowed, Something Blue.** large type ed. Jillian Karr. (Black Satin Romance Ser.). 512p. 1996. 25.99 (*1-86110-006-X*) Ulverscroft.

Something Borrowed, Something Learned? The Transatlantic Market in Education & Training Reform. Ed. by David Finegold et al. 261p. (C). 1993. 36.95 (*0-8157-2804-2*); pap. 16.95 (*0-8157-2803-4*) Brookings.

Something Breathing. Stanley McNail. LC 87-82454. (Illus.). 58p. (Orig.). reprint ed. pap. 6.00 (*0-940945-01-0*) Embassy Hall Edns.

Something Cloudy, Something Clear. Tennessee Williams. LC 95-35011. 96p. 1995. 19.95 (*0-8112-1310-2*) New Directions.

Something Cloudy, Something Clear. Tennessee Williams. LC 95-35011. 96p. 1996. pap. 9.95 (*0-8112-1311-0*, NDP829) New Directions.

Something Cloudy, Something Clear. Tennessee Williams. 1996. pap. 5.25 (*0-8222-1475-X*) Dramatists Play.

Something Else Press: An Annotated Bibliography. Peter Frank. LC 82-25892. (Illus.). 96p. 1983. 25.00 (*0-914232-40-1*, Documentext) McPherson & Co.

Something Else Yearbook 1974. Ed. by Jan Herman. LC 72-90050. (Illus.). 1973. pap. 25.00 (*0-87110-091-6*) Ultramarine Pub.

Something Evil Lurks in the Woods. Charles E. Price. 126p. (Orig.). 1995. pap. 8.95 (*1-57072-039-8*) Overmountain Pr.

Something Extra. Janet Dailey. 1991. mass mkt. 3.50 (*0-373-83231-1*) Harlequin Bks.

Something Fishy at Macdonald Hall. Gordon Korman. LC 95-2074. 192p. (J). (gr. 3-7). 1995. 14.95 (*0-590-25521-5*, Scholastic Hardcover) Scholastic Inc.

Something Fishy at the Panama Canal. Meldeau Dampfer. (Illus.). 72p. (Orig.). 1986. pap. 10.00 (*0-937953-02-4*) Tiptoe Lit Serv.

Something for Everyone. Susan Whitcher. LC 94-43630. (Illus.). 32p. (J). (gr. 1-3). 1995. 15.00 (*0-374-37138-5*) FS&G.

Something for Everyone: Poetry in Motion. LC 92-81596. 1992. write for info. (*0-9633238-0-6*) H R Dickerson.

Something for James. Shirley Isherwood. LC 95-37383. (Illus.). 32p. (J). (ps-3). 1996. pap. 14.99 (*0-8037-1914-0*) Dial Bks Young.

Something for Joey. Richard Peck. 192p. (J). 1983. mass mkt. 4.50 (*0-553-27199-7*) Bantam.

Something for Mother. Laura Alden. LC 93-37096. (Circle the Year with Holidays Ser.). (Illus.). 32p. (J). (ps-2). 1994. lib. bdg. 17.50 (*0-516-00690-8*) Childrens.

Something for Mother. Laura Alden. (Circle the Year with Holidays Ser.). 1994. pap. 3.95 (*0-516-40690-6*) Childrens.

Something for Peace: A Memoir. Thomas Waring. LC 89-90189. (Illus.). 127p. (Orig.). 1989. pap. 13.95 (*0-9622808-0-1*) S&T Waring.

Something for the Kids: Fifty-two Children's Sermons for Worship. Ted Lazicki. Ed. by Arthur L. Zapel. LC 85-62468. (Illus.). 96p. (Orig.). 1985. pap. 9.95 (*0-916260-34-8*, B192) Meriwether Pub.

Something for 10:30: Involvement Cards for Social Skills. rev. ed. Amy Maid & Tim Timmekmann. LC 77-92392. (Illus.). 158p. (YA). (gr. 7-12). 1987. pap. 29.95 (*0-8290-0353-3*) Irvington.

Something Fresh. P. G. Wodehouse. (Fiction Ser.). 288p. 1986. pap. 8.95 (*0-14-005035-3*, Penguin Bks) Viking Penguin.

Something from Nothing. 32p. (J). 1993. 19.95 (*0-590-72827-X*) Scholastic Inc.

Something from Nothing. Adapted by Phoebe Gilman. LC 92-37587. 32p. (J). 1993. 15.95 (*0-590-47280-1*) Scholastic Inc.

***Something from Nothing.** Phoebe Gilman. (Illus.). (J). pap. 5.99 (*0-590-74557-3*) Scholastic Inc.

Something from the Eaves & Other Poetic Journeys. Riley T. Evans. 40p. 1994. 8.95 (*0-8059-3604-1*) Dorrance.

Something, Furry, Rough, & Wild. (Strategies Program Ser.). (J). (gr. 5). 1991. pap. 23.24 (*0-8123-6911-4*); pap. 7.76 (*0-8123-6912-2*); text ed. 20.12 (*0-8123-6910-6*) McDougal-Littell.

Something Gentle: Quiet Words for Hurried Times. Beryl O. Lumpkin. (Illus.). 60p. (Orig.). 1988. pap. text ed. 3.95 (*0-9622568-0-3*) Earthside Pubns.

Something Good. Robert Munsch. (Illus.). 24p. (J). (ps-2). 1990. pap. 5.95 (*1-55037-100-2*, Pub. by Annick CN); lib. bdg. 15.95 (*1-55037-099-5*, Pub. by Annick CN) Firefly Bks Ltd.

Something Good. Robert Munsch. (Annikin Ser.: No. 14). (Illus.). (J). (ps-2). 1995. pap. 0.99 (*1-55037-390-0*, Pub. by Annick CN) Firefly Bks Ltd.

Something Good for a Change: Essays on Peace Through Living. Wavy Gravy. 288p. 1993. pap. 10.95 (*0-312-09391-8*) St Martin.

Something Grazes Our Hair. S. J. Marks. 80p. (Orig.). 1991. 10.95 (*0-252-06181-0*) U of Ill Pr.

Something Grazes Our Hair: Poems. fac. rev. ed. S. J. Marks. LC 90-44637. 84p. 1991. pap. 25.00 (*0-7837-8078-8*, 2047831) Bks Demand.

Something Happened. Joseph Heller. 544p. 1989. mass mkt. 6.99 (*0-440-20441-0*, LLL BDD) BDD Bks Young Read.

***Something Happened.** Joseph Heller. 1997. pap. 13.00 (*0-684-84121-5*, Scribners PB Fict) S&S Trade.

Something Happened & I'm Scared to Tell: A Book for Young Children Victims of Abuse. Patricia Kehoe. LC 86-62032. (Illus.). 32p. (Orig.). (J). (ps-1). 1987. pap. 5.95 (*0-943990-28-9*); lib. bdg. 15.95 (*0-943990-29-7*) Parenting Pr.

Something Happened in My House: A Journey of Children's Grief. Karen Carpenter & Susie Howard. (Illus.). 36p. (Orig.). (J). (gr. 3-8). 1993. pap. 9.95 (*1-883613-01-9*) Byte Size.

Something Happened to Me. Phyllis Sweet. LC 81-83422. (Illus.). (J). (gr. 2-5). 1985. pap. 5.95 (*0-941300-00-5*) Mother Courage.

Something Happened to Me: Helping a Child to Become a Sexual Abuse Survivor. Sandy McCoy. 18p. (J). (ps-2). 1993. 4.95 (*1-882811-01-1*) Skyline Pubns.

Something Happened Yesterday. B. Bainbridge. pap. 14.95 (*0-7156-2495-4*, Pub. by Duckworth UK) Focus Pub-R Pullins.

Something Happening Here. Robert Lloyd. 320p. 1998. 24.00 (*0-684-80026-8*) S&S Trade.

Something Hidden Behind the Ranges: A Himalayan Quest. Daniel Taylor-Ide. LC 94-38624. (Illus.). 328p. 1995. pap. 14.95 (*1-56279-073-0*) Mercury Hse Inc.

Something I'll Tell You Tuesday & the Loveliest Afternoon of the Year: Two One Act Plays - One Act Acting Edition. John Guare. 1967. pap. 3.25 (*0-8222-0703-6*) Dramatists Play.

Something in Between. Sterling Quinlan. LC 94-16295. 1994. 18.50 (*0-8076-1364-9*) Braziller.

Something in Common: Contemporary Louisiana Stories. Ed. by Ann B. Dobie. LC 90-20232. 302p. 1991. 19.95 (*0-8071-1644-0*) La State U Pr.

***Something in My Eye.** Michael Whelan. 1996. pap. 18.95 (*0-929480-82-1*) Mark Ziesing.

***Something in My Mind Besides the Everyday: Women & Literacy.** Jennifer Horsman. 238p. pap. 13.95 (*0-88961-145-9*, Pub. by Wmns Pr CN) LPC InBook.

***Something in Particular.** John Hughes. 42p. 1986. pap. 11.95 (*1-85235-006-7*) Dufour.

Something in Return. Karen Van der Zee. (Presents Ser.). 1994. mass mkt. 2.99 (*0-373-11630-6*, 1-11630-0) Harlequin Bks.

Something in the Air. Anne Derson. LC 93-74951. 136p. (J). (gr. 4-6). 1994. pap. 6.95 (*0-943864-74-7*) Davenport.

***Something in the Air.** Jenny Randles. 1997. 19.95 (*0-7090-5974-4*, Hale-Parkwest) Parkwest Pubns.

Something in the Air: Corporate Power in the Environment. Andrew Blowers. 372p. (C). 1984. 40.00 (*0-317-93199-7*, Pub. by P Chapman Pub UK) St Mut.

Something in the Blood. Trevor Shearston. 255p. 1979. pap. 10.95 (*0-7022-1336-5*) Intl Spec Bk.

Something in the Blood: The Underground World of Today's Vampires. Jeff Guinn & Andy Grieser. 1996. 19.95 (*1-56530-209-5*) Summit TX.

Something in the Cellar, Ronald Searle's Wonderful World of Wine. 80p. 1987. pap. 11.95 (*0-89815-235-6*) Ten Speed Pr.

***Something in the Software.** Mary A. Devery et al. (Illus.). 40p. (Orig.). (J). (gr. 2-5). 1998. mass mkt. 6.99 (*1-889501-58-1*, Candy Apple) Sovereign.

Something in the Soil. Patricia Limerick. Date not set. write for info. (*0-393-03788-6*) Norton.

Something in the Water. Charlotte MacLeod. 240p. 1995. mass mkt. 5.50 (*0-446-40446-2*, Mysterious Paperbk) Warner Bks.

***Something in This Book Is True.** Bob Frissell. LC 97-15789. (Illus.). 200p. (Orig.). 1997. pap. 14.95 (*1-883319-65-X*) Frog Ltd CA.

Something in Vallarta. Robert Richter. LC 90-53330. 208p. 1991. 22.00 (*1-877946-09-5*) Permanent Pr.

Something Iridescent. Roger Pfingston. LC 85-72587. 98p. (Orig.). 1987. pap. 7.95 (*0-935306-37-4*) Barnwood Pr.

***Something Is about to Happen: Sermons for Advent & Christmas.** Thomas G. Long. LC 96-30408. 1996. 6.25 (*0-7880-0866-8*) CSS OH.

Something Is Coming. Bernice Chardiet. (Illus.). 20p. (J). (ps-1). 1994. pap. 5.99 (*0-14-054996-X*) Puffin Bks.

Something is Growing. Walter L. Krudop. (Illus.). (J). (gr. 2-3). 1995. 15.00 (*0-689-31940-1*, Atheneum Bks Young) S&S Childrens.

Something Is Happening: Poems. Gary Pacernick. LC 91-48235. 60p. 1992. pap. 12.95 (*0-7734-9439-1*, Mellen Poetry Pr) E Mellen.

Something Is Happening Here. Ramon Hernandez. LC 82-61182. 238p. (Orig.). 1983. pap. 15.00 (*0-89295-025-0*) Society Sp & Sp-Am.

Something Is Wrong at My House. Diane Davis. LC 84-62129. (Illus.). 40p. (Orig.). (J). (ps-6). 1985. pap. 5.95 (*0-943990-10-6*); lib. bdg. 15.95 (*0-943990-11-4*) Parenting Pr.

Something I've Been Meaning to Tell You. Alice Munro. 208p. 1983. pap. 2.95 (*0-451-14343-4*, Sig) NAL-Dutton.

Something I've Been Meaning to Tell You: Thirteen Stories. Alice Munro. 256p. 1984. pap. 10.95 (*0-452-26021-3*, Plume) NAL-Dutton.

Something Left to Lose: Personal Relations & Survival among New York's Homeless. Gwendolyn A. Dordick. LC 96-25094. 1997. pap. 17.95 (*1-56639-514-3*) Temple U Pr.

Something Left to Lose: Personal Relations & Survival Among New York's Homeless. Gwendolyn A. Dordick. LC 96-25094. 1997. 59.95 (*1-56639-513-5*) Temple U Pr.

Something Like a Drug: An Unauthorized Oral History of Theatresports. Ed. by Clem Martini & Kathleen Foreman. LC 95-14873. 1995. pap. 16.00 (*0-88734-918-8*) Players Pr.

Something Like a Hero: Stories of Daring & Decision by American Teen Writers. Ed. by R. James Stahl & Kathryn Kulpa. LC 95-10400. (American Teen Writer Ser.). (Illus.). 144p. (Orig.). (YA). (gr. 7-12). 1995. pap. 9.75 (*1-886427-03-8*) Merlyns Pen.

Something Like a Love Affair. Julian Symons. 208p. 1993. 17.95 (*0-89296-495-2*) Mysterious Pr.

Something Like a Poem. Neil Paterson. 32p. 1986. 20.00 (*0-7223-1988-6*, Pub. by A H S Ltd UK) St Mut.

Something Like an Autobiography. Akira Kurosawa. Tr. by Audie E. Bock from JPN. LC 82-48900. 240p. 1983. pap. 15.00 (*0-394-71439-3*, Vin) Random.

Something Like Horace: Studies in the Art & Allusion of Pope's Horatian Satires. John M. Aden. LC 71-83208. 1969. 12.95 (*0-8265-1138-4*) Vanderbilt U Pr.

Something Meaningful for God. Ed. by C. J. Dyck. LC 80-10975. (MCC Story Ser.: Vol. 4). 408p. (Orig.). 1981. pap. 7.99 (*0-8361-1244-X*) Herald Pr.

Something Medieval. J. K. Randall. LC 80-80808. (Illus.). 48p. 1988. 14.50 (*0-939044-24-2*) Lingua Pr.

Something Missing. large type ed. Kate Walker. (Harlequin Ser.). 1993. lib. bdg. 19.95 (*0-263-13541-1*) Thorndike Pr.

Something More. LC 87-83679. (Illus.). 65p. 1987. 10.00 (*0-9620375-1-6*) Faith Unlimited.

Something More. Catherine Marshall. 1976. mass mkt. 4.50 (*0-380-00601-4*) Avon.

Something More. rev. ed. Catherine Marshall. 288p. 1994. pap. 9.00 (*0-380-72203-8*) Avon.

Something More: In Search of a Deeper Faith. Catherine Marshall. LC 96-4174. (Catherine Marshall Library). 336p. (YA). (gr. 10). 1996. pap. 10.99 (*0-8007-9242-4*) Chosen Bks.

Something More: Nurturing Your Child's Spiritual Growth. Jean G. Fitzpatrick. 256p. 1992. reprint ed. pap. 11.00 (*0-14-016951-2*, Penguin Bks) Viking Penguin.

Something More Than Force: Poems for Guatemala, 1971-1982. deluxe limited ed. Zoe Anglesey. 48p. 1982. 25.00 (*0-938566-13-X*) Adastra Pr.

Something More than Force: Poems for Guatemala, 1971-1982. 2nd ed. Zoe Anglesey. 48p. 1984. pap. 3.50 (*0-938566-21-0*) Adastra Pr.

Something More Than Human: Biographies of Leaders in American Methodist Higher Education. Ed. by Charles E. Cole. LC 85-51267. (Illus.). 256p. 1986. 7.95 (*0-938162-04-7*) United Meth Educ.

Something More Than Night: The Case of Raymond Chandler. Peter Wolfe. LC 84-71588. 242p. 1985. 22.95 (*0-87972-293-2*); pap. 11.95 (*0-87972-294-0*) Bowling Green Univ Popular Press.

Something Must Be Wrong with Me: A Boy's Book about Sexual Abuse. Doris Sanford. (Illus.). 24p. (J). (ps-6). 1993. 7.99 (*0-88070-469-1*, Gold & Honey) Multnomah Pubs.

Something Nasty in the Cabbages. Diz Wallis. LC 90-84007. (Illus.). 32p. 1991. 15.95 (*1-878093-10-X*) Boyds Mills Pr.

Something Nasty in the Woodwind. Charles Shaw. 140p. (C). 1989. text ed. 49.00 (*1-872795-16-1*, Pub. by Pentland Pr UK) St Mut.

Something Never Your Own. David Martin. (Amelia Chapbooks Ser.). 90p. (Orig.). 1989. pap. 10.95 (*0-936545-10-0*) Amelia.

Something New. Carla Cassidy. (Romance Ser.). 1993. pap. 2.75 (*0-373-08942-2*, 5-08942-0) Silhouette.

Something New. Anne Pumtree. Ed. by Deborah McLeod. 250p. 1996. pap. 12.95 (*1-55111-079-2*) Broadview Pr.

Something New for a Bear to Do. Shirley Isherwood & Reg Cartwright. (Illus.). 28p. (J). (ps-3). 1996. 19.95 (*0-09-176484-X*, Pub. by Hutchnson UK) Trafalgar.

Something New to Do. Ski Michaels. LC 85-14021. (Illus.). 48p. (Orig.). (J). (gr. 1-3). 1997. pap. 3.50 (*0-8167-0635-2*) Troll Communs.

***Something New under the Sun: Sattelites & the Beginning of the Space Age.** Helen Gavaghan. LC 96-48689. (Copernicus Ser.). (Illus.). 288p. 1997. 26.00 (*0-387-94914-3*) Spr-Verlag.

Something Nice to See. Theodore R. Gardner, II. LC 93-61121. (Illus.). 32p. (J). (gr. k up). 1994. 15.95 (*0-9627297-6-0*) A A Knoll Pubs.

***Something of a Rebel: Thomas Merton, His Life & Works - an Introduction.** William H. Shannon. 1997. pap. write for info. (*0-86716-272-4*, B2724) St Anthony Mess Pr.

Something of a Saint. David M. Owen. pap. 5.95 (*0-687-86239-6*) Abingdon.

Something of Courage. Terese S. Guglielmino. LC 87-72317. 485p. 1987. reprint ed. 18.95 (*0-9619205-0-5*) Courage Pub.

Something of Men I Have Known with Some Papers of a General Nature, Political, Historical & Retrospective. Adlai E. Stevenson. 1977. 34.95 (*0-8369-6992-8*, 7869) Ayer.

Something of Myself & Other Autobiographical Writings. Rudyard Kipling. Ed. by Thomas Pinney. (Illus.). 256p. (C). 1990. text ed. 59.95 (*0-521-35515-X*) Cambridge U Pr.

Something of Myself & Other Autobiographical Writings. Rudyard Kipling. Ed. by Thomas Pinney. (Canto Book Ser.). (Illus.). 330p. (C). 1991. pap. text ed. 11.95 (*0-521-40584-X*) Cambridge U Pr.

Something of Value. large type ed. Nancy Bell. (Linford Romance Library). 272p. 1987. pap. 8.95 (*0-7089-6334-X*, Linford) Ulverscroft.

Something of Value. Robert Ruark. 574p. 1991. reprint ed. lib. bdg. 37.95 (*0-89966-816-X*) Buccaneer Bks.

***Something of Value: Building Business One Transaction at a Time.** Fred A. Gray. (Illus.). 389p. (Orig.). 1997. pap. 14.95 (*0-9655863-0-8*) G & T Enterprises.

Something Old. Toni Collins. (Romance Ser.). 1993. pap. 2.75 (*0-373-08941-4*, 5-08941-2) Silhouette.

***Something Old & Something New: Louisiana Cooking with a Change of Heart.** John D. Folse. LC 96-90706. (Illus.). 484p. (C). 1997. 22.95 (*0-9625152-1-3*) Chef John Folse.

Something Old, Something New. Judy Baer. (Cedar River Daydreams Ser.: Vol. 11). 144p. (Orig.). (J). (gr. 7-9). 1991. mass mkt. 4.99 (*1-55661-183-8*) Bethany Hse.

Something Old, Something New. Catherine Leigh. (Romance Ser.). 1996. mass mkt. 3.25 (*0-373-03426-1*, 1-03426-3) Harlequin Bks.

Something Old, Something New. Donna Sterling. (Temptation Ser.). 1996. mass mkt. 3.50 (*0-373-25686-8*, 1-125686-6) Harlequin Bks.

Something Old Something New. Bailey White. 1995. pap. 25.95 (*0-7871-0345-4*, Dove Bks) Dove Audio.

Something Old, Something New. Carol Yampolsky. 24p. 1994. pap. text ed. 5.95 (*0-87487-684-2*) Summy-Birchard.

Something Old, Something New: College Writing Teachers & Classroom Change. Wendy Bishop. LC 89-27529. (Studies in Writing & Rhetoric). 192p. (C). 1990. pap. text ed. 12.95 (*0-8093-1601-3*) S Ill U Pr.

Something Old, Something New: Ethnic Weddings in America. Pamela B. Nelson et al. LC 87-71305. (Illus.). 35p. (Orig.). 1987. pap. 5.25 (*0-937437-02-6*) Balch Inst Ethnic Studies.

Something Old, Something New: What You Didn't Know about Wedding Ceremonies, Celebrations & Customs. Vera Lee. LC 94-235. 224p. 1994. 14.95 (*1-57071-002-3*) Sourcebks.

***Something Old, Something New: What You Didn't Know about Wedding Ceremonies, Celebrations & Customs.** Vera Lee. 224p. 1997. reprint ed. pap. 9.95 (*1-57071-148-8*, Casablanca) Sourcebks.

Something Olde, Something New, Something Borrowed - Ever True. Judith D. Meade. 48p. (Orig.). 1988. pap. 4.95 (*0-945785-01-1*) LFL Creations.

Something on My Mind. Nikki Grimes. LC 77-86266. (Pied Piper Bks.). (Illus.). 32p. (J). (gr. k up). 1986. pap. 4.95 (*0-8037-0273-6*) Dial Bks Young.

Something Passes This Rambling River. Alan W. Schildroth. 514p. pap. 15.00 (*1-57087-068-3*) Prof Pr NC.

Something Permanent. Cynthia Ryant. LC 93-3861. (Illus.). 64p. (YA). (gr. 9 up). 1994. 17.00 (*0-15-277090-9*) HarBrace.

Something Personal: True & Intimate Tales of Connecticut. Lary Bloom. Ed. by Jan Winburn & Judith H. Hochberg. 128p. (Orig.). 1988. pap. 7.95 (*0-685-22572-0*) NE Press.

Something Queer at the Ball Park. Elizabeth Levy. (Something Queer Ser.). (Illus.). 48p. (J). (gr. 1-4). 1984. pap. 3.50 (*0-440-48116-3*, YB BDD) BDD Bks Young Read.

Something Queer at the Birthday Party. Elizabeth Levy. (Illus.). 48p. (J). (gr. 1-4). 1992. pap. 2.99 (*0-440-40687-0*, YB BDD) BDD Bks Young Read.

S

Something Queer at the Haunted School. Elizabeth Levy. (Something Queer Ser.). (Illus.). 48p. (J). (gr. 1-4). 1983. pap. 3.50 (0-440-48461-8, YB BDD) BDD Bks Young Read.

Something Queer at the Library. Elizabeth Levy. (Something Queer Ser.). (Illus.). 48p. (J). (gr. 1-4). 1989. pap. 3.50 (0-440-48120-1, YB BDD) BDD Bks Young Read.

Something Queer at the Scary Movie. Elizabeth Levy. LC 94-45618. (Something Queer Ser.). (Illus.). 48p. (J). (gr. 2-5). 1995. 14.95 (0-7868-0150-6); pap. 4.95 (0-7868-1056-4) Hyprn Child.

Something Queer in Outer Space. Elizabeth Levy. LC 92-54870. (Something Queer Ser.). (Illus.). 48p. (J). (gr. 2-5). 1993. pap. 4.95 (1-56282-279-9) Hyprn Child.

Something Queer in the Cafeteria. Elizabeth Levy. LC 93-31343. (Illus.). 48p. (J). (gr. 2-5). 1994. pap. 4.95 (0-7868-1000-9) Hyprn Child.

Something Queer in the Cafeteria. Elizabeth Levy. LC 93-31343. (Something Queer Ser.: Bk. 2). (Illus.). 48p. (J). (gr. 2-5). 1994. 13.95 (0-7868-0001-1) Hyprn Child.

Something Queer in the Wild West. Elizabeth Levy. LC 96-2554. (Illus.). (J). 1997. pap. 4.95 (0-7868-1117-X) Hyprn Child.

Something Queer in the Wild West. Elizabeth Levy. LC 96-2554. (Illus.). (J). 1997. 14.95 (0-7868-0258-8) Hyprn Child.

Something Queer Is Going On. Elizabeth Levy. (Something Queer Ser.). (Illus.). 48p. (J). (gr. 1-4). 1982. mass mkt. 3.50 (0-440-47974-6, YB BDD) BDD Bks Young Read.

Something Queer Is Going On. Elizabeth Levy. (J). (gr. 1-3). 1990. 17.50 (0-8446-6257-7) Peter Smith.

Something Rich & Strange: A Treasury of Shakespeare's Verse. Illus. by Emma C. Clark. LC 95-3008. 95p. (YA). (gr. 5 up). 1995. text ed. 16.95 (1-85697-597-5) LKC.

Something Rotten. Marty Engle & Barnes. (Strange Matter Ser.: No. 11). 140p. (J). (gr. 4 up). 1996. pap. 3.50 (1-56714-046-7) Montage Bks.

Something Scary. Particia Hermes. (J). (gr. 4-7). 1996. pap. text ed. 2.99 (0-590-50963-2) Scholastic Inc.

Something Sensitive & Soft. Wanda M. Eck. (Orig.). 1995. pap. write for info. (1-57502-076-9) Morris Pubng.

Something Shady. Sarah Dreher. LC 86-61106. (Stoner McTavish Mystery Ser.). 272p. 1986. pap. 8.95 (0-934678-07-3) New Victoria Pubs.

Something Shady. Pamela Morsi. 336p. (Orig.). 1995. mass mkt. 5.99 (0-515-11628-9) Jove Pubns.

Something Silver, Something Blue. David Drew. LC 92-34256. (Voyages Ser.). (Illus.). (J). 1993. 4.25 (0-383-03654-2) SRA McGraw.

***Something So Right.** Layle Giusto. 288p. 1997. mass mkt. 4.99 (0-7860-0374-X, Pinncle Kensgtn) Kensgtn Pub Corp.

Something Special. Christina Abramowski. (Illus.). 32p. (J). (gr. 2-4). text ed. 9.95 (0-9634927-0-5) Jr Leag Grnd Rapids.

Something Special. Associated Women's Organization, Mars Hill Bible School. Ed. by Peggy Simpson & Linda Stanley. 1977. pap. 6.25 (0-89137-408-6) Quality Pubns.

Something Special. Ullanda Innocent. 1996. pap. text ed. 10.99 (0-8280-0715-2) Review & Herald.

***Something Special.** Ted Lewin. (J). Date not set. write for info. (0-688-14109-9); lib. bdg. write for info. (0-688-14110-2) Lothrop.

Something Special. Nicola Moon. LC 96-24127. (J). 1997. 14.95 (1-56145-137-1) Peachtree Pubs.

Something Special. large type ed. Faith Baldwin. LC 91-8484. 324p. 1991. reprint ed. lib. bdg. 19.95 (1-56054-161-X) Thorndike Pr.

Something Special: Basic Skills Activity Units for Primary Grade Kids Who Need Extra Help in Reading. Cherrie Farnette et al. (Illus.). 200p. (Orig.). (J). (ps-3). 1982. pap. text ed. 14.95 (0-86530-001-1, IP-011) Incentive Pubns.

Something Special for Everyone. Mildred Yeiser. 48p. 1985. pap. text ed. 6.50 (1-56770-158-2) S Scheewe Pubns.

Something Special for Everyone, Vol. 2. Mildred Yeiser. 48p. 1987. pap. text ed. 6.50 (1-56770-178-7) S Scheewe Pubns.

Something Special for Me. Vera B. Williams. LC 82-11884. (Illus.). 32p. (J). (gr. k-3). 1983. 16.00 (0-688-01806-8); lib. bdg. 15.93 (0-688-01807-6) Greenwillow.

Something Special for Me. Vera B. Williams. LC 82-11884. (Illus.). 32p. (J). (ps up). 1986. pap. 4.95 (0-688-06526-0, Mulberry) Morrow.

Something Special for Miss Margery. Janet S. Redhead. LC 93-6632. (Voyages Ser.). (Illus.). (J). 1994. write for info. (0-383-03673-9) SRA McGraw.

Something Special Within. 2nd ed. Betts Richter. (Illus.). 48p. (J). (ps-5). 1982. reprint ed. pap. 7.95 (0-87516-488-9) DeVorss.

Something Spicy. Frances T. Giedt. 1995. 15.00 (0-684-80185-X) S&S Trade.

Something Stirs. Charles L. Grant. 288p. 1993. mass mkt. 4.99 (0-8125-1303-7) Tor Bks.

Something Supernatural. Janet McReynolds. 103p. 1986. pap. 3.95 (0-88144-038-8) Christian Pub.

Something Suspicious. Kathryn O. Galbraith. 128p. (J). (gr. 3 up). 1987. pap. 2.50 (0-380-70253-3, Camelot) Avon.

Something Sweet. Jack Bishop. 1995. 15.00 (0-684-80187-6) S&S Trade.

***Something Tastes Funny.** Sean Donnellan. LC 97-1856. (Illus.). 208p. (Orig.). 1997. pap. 9.99 (0-446-67322-6) Warner Bks.

Something Tells Me It's Your Birthday: A Changing Picture Book. Mary Engelbreit. (Main Street Gift Bks.). (Illus.). 10p. 1996. 6.95 (0-8362-1067-0) Andrews & McMeel.

Something Terrible Happened. Barbara A. Porte. LC 94-6923. 224p. (Orig.). (J). (gr. 6-9). 1994. 16.95 (0-531-06869-2); lib. bdg. 17.99 (0-531-08719-0) Orchard Bks Watts.

Something Terrible Happened. Barbara A. Porte. 224p. (Orig.). (YA). (gr. 5 up). 1996. pap. 4.50 (0-8167-3868-8, Troll Medallion) Troll Communs.

Something That a Cowboy Knows: A Photographic Essay. Photos by L. L. Griffin. (Illus.). 104p. 1996. pap. 23.95 (0-87421-201-4) Utah St U Pr.

Something the Cat Dragged In. Charlotte MacLeod. 208p. (Orig.). 1984. mass mkt. 3.99 (0-380-69096-9) Avon.

Something to Be Desired. Thomas McGuane. (Vintage Contemporaries Ser.). 1985. pap. 10.00 (0-394-73156-5, Vin) Random.

Something to Be Desired. Thomas McGuane. 1994. pap. 10.00 (0-394-25887-8) Random.

Something to Be Remembered: Stories from Seward History. Doug Capra. (Illus.). 80p. 1996. pap. 9.00 (0-9646517-1-8) Yankee-Sourdough Pubns.

***Something to Count On.** Pat Hermes. (J). Date not set. 14.95 (0-399-21767-3) Putnam Pub Group.

Something to Count On. Emily Moore. 1995. 17.75 (0-8446-6799-4) Peter Smith.

Something to Count On. Emily Moore. 112p. (J). (gr. 3-7). 1991. pap. 3.99 (0-14-034791-7, Puffin) Puffin Bks.

Something to Die For. James H. Webb, Jr. 416p. 1992. mass mkt. 5.99 (0-380-71322-5) Avon.

***Something to Do for the Holidays: A Coloring & Activity Book.** Mary Englebreit. (Illus.). 48p. (Orig.). (J). 1997. pap. 9.95 (0-8362-3678-5) Andrews & McMeel.

Something to Do on Monday. Macey Taylor & Laura Perez. (Illus.). (Orig.). 1989. pap. 19.95 (0-940753-00-6) Athelstan Pubns.

Something to Do on Tuesday. Deborah Healey. (Illus.). 1995. pap. 24.95 (0-940753-02-2) Athelstan Pubns.

Something to Do When There's Nothing to Do: A Coloring & Activity Book. Mary Engelbreit. (Illus.). 48p. (J). 1995. 7.95 (0-8362-4634-9) Andrews & McMeel.

Something to Draw On: Activities & Interventions Using an Art Therapy Approach. Carol Ross. 150p. 1996. 24.95 (1-85302-363-9, Pub. by J Kingsley Pubs UK) Taylor & Francis.

Something to Eat. Fred Powledge. 352p. 1997. 25.00 (0-06-016970-2, HarpT) HarpC.

Something to Hide. Rick Chambers. LC 95-16421. (Open Door Books Ser.). 1995. 3.95 (1-56212-103-0) CRC Pubns.

Something to Hide. Carolyn Keene. (Nancy Drew Files Ser.: No. 41). 160p. (YA). 1991. pap. 3.50 (0-671-74659-6, Archway) PB.

Something to Hide: A Novel. Peter Levine. 288p. 1996. 22.95 (0-312-14047-9) St Martin.

Something to Hold on To: Nine Theater Pieces. Dennis Moritz. 1995. pap. 8.00 (0-935992-01-4) United Art Bks.

Something to Kill For. Susan Holtzer. 1995. mass mkt. 5.99 (0-312-95589-8) Tor Bks.

Something to Love: Barbara Pym's Novels. Diana T. Benet. LC 85-20976. (Literary Frontiers Ser.: No. 27). 176p. 1986. pap. 14.95 (0-8262-0493-7) U of Mo Pr.

Something to Quack About, Vol. 1. Sherry Gunter. (Illus.). 32p. (Orig.). 1987. pap. 6.95 (0-941284-46-8) J Shaw Studio.

Something to Read to Someone: Sixteen Drawings. Spencer Holst & Beate Wheeler. 32p. 1980. pap. 3.50 (0-930794-34-6) Station Hill Pr.

Something to Read to Someone: Sixteen Drawings. deluxe limited ed. Spencer Holst & Beate Wheeler. 32p. 1980. 15.00 (0-930794-24-9) Station Hill Pr.

Something to Reckon With: The Logic of Terms. George Englebretsen. 288p. 1996. pap. 27.00 (0-7766-0423-6, Pub. by Univ Ottawa Pr CN) Paul & Co Pubs.

Something to Say. 1990. write for info. (1-879186-00-4) DBH Pub.

Something to Say: Student Essays for Freshman English. Ratner. 1991. 12.00 (0-536-57932-6) Ginn Pr.

Something to Say: William Carlos Williams on Younger Poets. William C. Williams. LC 85-8890. 256p. 1985. 23.95 (0-8112-0955-5) New Directions.

Something to Say to the Children. John R. Gray. Ed. by Sheila Gray. 240p. 1988. pap. 24.95 (0-567-29151-0, Pub. by T & T Clark UK) Bks Intl VA.

Something to Say to the Congregation. John R. Gray. Ed. by Sheila Gray. 192p. 1991. pap. text ed. 24.95 (0-567-29200-2, Pub. by T & T Clark UK) Bks Intl VA.

Something to Talk About. D. Chiel. 1995. mass mkt. 4.99 (0-451-18735-0, Sig) NAL-Dutton.

***Something to Think About.** Margery J. McGreal. (Illus.). 80p. (Orig.). 1997. pap. write for info. (0-9656734-1-3) CHOD.

***Something to Think About.** Symonia Montgomery. (Orig.). 1997. pap. write for info. (1-57553-397-9) Watermrk Pr.

Something to Write Home About. Rachel Ingalls. LC 88-3029. 320p. 1988. 15.95 (0-916782-98-0) Harvard Common Pr.

Something under the Bed Is Drooling: A Calvin & Hobbes Collection. Bill Watterson. (Illus.). 128p. 1988. pap. 9.95 (0-8362-1825-6) Andrews & McMeel.

***Something Untitled.** Mark Sonnenfeld. 28p. Date not set. pap. 3.00 (1-887379-09-6) M Sonnenfeld.

***Something Upstairs.** Avi. 128p. (J). 1997. pap. 4.50 (0-380-79086-6, Camelot) Avon.

Something Upstairs. Avi. 128p. 1990. reprint ed. mass mkt. 4.50 (0-380-70853-1, Flare) Avon.

Something Upstairs: A Tale of Ghosts. Avi. LC 88-60094. 128p. (J). (gr. 5-7). 1988. 15.95 (0-531-05782-8); lib. bdg. 16.99 (0-531-08382-9) Orchard Bks Watts.

Something Ventured, Something Gained: A Business Development Guide for Nonprofit Organizations. Laura Landy. LC 89-15139. 150p. 1989. pap. 19.95 (0-915400-81-2, ACA Bks) Am Council Arts.

Something Ventured Telecourse Small Business: Small Business. 10th ed. Longnecker & Intelecom Staff. (GG - Small Business Management Ser.). 1997. text ed. 25.95 (0-538-85079-5) S-W Pub.

***Something Very Like Murder.** Frank Kuppner. 1994. pap. 18.00 (0-7486-6181-6, Pub. by Polygon UK) Subterranean Co.

Something Very Sorry. Arno Bohlmeijer. LC 95-30208. 176p. (Orig.). (J). (gr. 5-9). 1996. 13.95 (0-395-74679-5) HM.

***Something Very Sorry.** Arno Bohlmeijer. 176p. (Orig.). (J). (gr. 3-7). 1997. pap. 5.95 (0-698-11610-0, Paperstar) Putnam Pub Group.

Something Weird Is Going On. Christie Harris. 144p. (Orig.). (J). (gr. 4-8). 1994. pap. 5.95 (1-55143-022-3) Orca Bk Pubs.

Something Wholesale: My Life & Times in the Rag Trade. large type ed. Eric Newey. 256p. 1991. 19.95 (1-85089-281-4, Pub. by ISIS UK) Transaction Pubs.

Something Wicked. Jo Beverley. 352p. 1997. mass mkt. 5.99 (0-8217-5548-X, Zebra Kensgtn) Kensgtn Pub Corp.

***Something Wicked.** Jo Beverley. 1997. pap. 5.99 (0-451-40780-6, Onyx) NAL-Dutton.

Something Wicked. Carolyn G. Hart. 208p. (Orig.). 1988. mass mkt. 5.99 (0-553-27222-5) Severn Hse.

Something Wicked. Carolyn G. Hart. (Orig.). 1994. 20.00 (0-7278-4656-6) Severn Hse.

Something Wicked This Way Comes. Ray Bradbury. LC 82-48732. 1983. 24.95 (0-394-53041-1) Knopf.

Something Wicked This Way Comes. Ray Bradbury. 224p. 1983. mass mkt. 5.50 (0-553-28032-5, Bantam Classics) Bantam.

Something Wicked This Way Comes. Ray Bradbury. 1994. lib. bdg. 24.95 (1-56849-391-6) Buccaneer Bks.

Something Wild. TSR Hobbies Staff. 1996. 12.95 (0-7869-0377-5) TSR Inc.

***Something Wild, a Sportsmans Journal.** Richard Gauerke. Date not set. write for info. (1-885061-18-8) Adventure Pubns.

Something Wild Cookbook. Richard M. Gauerke. 1992. pap. 11.95 (0-934860-89-0) Adventure Pubns.

Something Wonderful. Martha Gross. 512p. 1995. mass mkt. 4.99 (0-8217-4939-0, Pinncle Kensgtn) Kensgtn Pub Corp.

Something Wonderful. Judith McNaught. Ed. by Linda Marrow. 432p. 1991. pap. 6.50 (0-671-73763-5) PB.

Something Wonderful. Judith McNaught. 1990. reprint ed. 20.00 (0-7278-4017-7) Severn Hse.

Something Wonderful: Artists Outside the Mainstream. 1995. 18.95 (0-8118-1020-8) Chronicle Bks.

***Something Wonderful: Easter.** Carolyn Bergt. 1997. pap. text ed. 22.00 (0-570-05520-2) Concordia.

Something Wonderful Right Away. Jeffrey Sweet. LC 86-27319. (Illus.). 432p. 1987. reprint ed. pap. 20.00 (0-87910-073-7) Limelight Edns.

***Something Worth Doing: The Sub-Arctic Voayge of Aqua Star.** Judith W. Chopra. 1996. text ed. 9.95 (0-07-011879-5) McGraw.

Something You Can Stand For! A Track Finder for New Christians. John Smith & Fuzz Kitto. 56p. 1995. pap. 7.50 (1-86407-059-5, Pub. by JBCE AT) Morehouse Pub.

Something You Do in the Dark. Daniel Curzon. LC 77-150260. 1979. pap. 14.95 (0-87949-138-8) Ashley Bks.

Something's Coming!, Set. Richard Edwards. LC 94-48920. (Illus.). (J). (ps-k). 1995. 9.95 (1-56402-613-2) Candlewick Pr.

Something's Cooking. Joanne Pence. 336p. 1993. mass mkt. 4.50 (0-06-108096-9, Harp PBks) HarpC.

Something's Fishy. Aidel Stein. (Baker's Dozen Ser.: No. 13). 143p. (J). (gr. 6-8). 1994. pap. 7.95 (1-56871-069-0) Targum Pr.

Something's Fishy! Jokes about Sea Creatures. Rick Walton & Ann Walton. (Make Me Laugh! Joke Bks.). (Illus.). 32p. (J). 1987. lib. bdg. 6.95 (0-8225-0993-8, Lerner Publctns) Lerner Group.

Something's Fishy Bk. No. 5. Teresa Reed. (J). 1996. 3.25 (0-689-80821-6) S&S Childrens.

***Something's Fishy at Ash Lake.** Anne Stephenson & Susan Brown. (YA). pap. 3.95 (0-590-74093-8) Scholastic Inc.

Something's Fishy in the Adirondacks. Francis Betters. 1985. 9.95 (0-318-20255-7) Adirondack S P.

Something's in the Woods. Richard Brightfield. (Choose Your Own Nightmare Ser.: No. 12). 96p. (J). 1996. pap. 3.50 (0-553-48331-5) BDD Bks Young Read.

***Something's in the Woods.** Richard Brightfield. LC 96-31016. (Choose Your Own Nightmare Ser.: No. 12). (Illus.). 96p. (J). (gr. 4 up). 1997. lib. bdg. 15.93 (0-8368-1724-9) Gareth Stevens Inc.

Something's Missing in My Life!, 3 pamphlets, Set. Earnie Larsen. 37p. (Orig.). 1987. pap. 3.00 (0-936098-55-4) Intl Marriage.

Something's Not Right: One Family's Struggle with Learning Disabilities. Nancy Lelewer. LC 94-60521. 184p. 1994. 21.95 (0-9641089-0-9); pap. 14.95 (0-9641089-1-7) VanderWyk & Burnham.

***Something's Out There.** Jacqueline Burks-Shiver. 30p. 1996. pap. 5.95 (0-9654212-0-1) Burks-Shiver.

Something's Out There! Chuck D. Charles. 100p. (J). (gr. 2-6). 1996. 16.95 (0-9638639-3-2) Nimrod Hse.

Something's Out There: A Newspaperman's Columns from Days Gone By. Jerry Robinson. 248p. 1992. pap. 16.95 (0-9635444-9-7) Robinson Comm.

Something's Rotten in the State of Maryland. Laura A. Sonnenmark. 176p. (YA). (gr. 7-9). 1993. pap. 2.95 (0-590-42877-2) Scholastic Inc.

Something's Wrong with My Child! A Straightforward Presentation to Help Professionals & Parents to Better Understand Themselves in Dealing with the Emotionally-Charged Subject of Disabled Children. Harriet W. Rose. 210p. 1987. 37.95 (0-398-05325-1); pap. 24.95 (0-398-06407-5) C C Thomas.

Somethin's Cookin' Fifty Easy-to-Do Youth Programs. Ann B. Cannon. LC 93-42361. (Essentials for Christian Youth Ser.). 112p. (Orig.). 1994. pap. 13.95 (0-687-39076-1) Abingdon.

Somethin's Cookin' in the Mountains: A Cookbook Guidebook to Northeast Georgia. rev. ed. Ed. by Jay Bucek & Kathy Bucek. (Illus.). 304p. 1986. 9.95 (0-9608770-3-7); spiral bd. 9.95 (0-9608770-5-3); boxed 9.95 (0-9608770-4-5) Soque.

***Somethng about the Author, Vol. 26.** (Autobiography Ser.). 1998. 96.00 (0-7876-1144-1, 00156248, Gale Res Intl) Gale.

***Somethng about the Author, Vol. 27.** (Autobiography Ser.). 1998. 92.00 (0-7876-1145-X, 00156249, Gale Res Intl) Gale.

***Somethng about the Author Autobiography Series, Vol. 24.** Ed. by Gerard J. Senick. 400p. 1997. 96.00 (0-7876-0117-9, 00108829, Gale Res Intl) Gale.

***Somethng about the Author Autobiography Series, Vol. 24.** Ed. by Gerard J. Senick. 400p. 1997. 96.00 (0-7876-0118-7, 00108830, Gale Res Intl) Gale.

Sometime. Robert Herrick. (Collected Works of Robert Herrick). 1988. reprint ed. lib. bdg. 59.00 (0-7812-1284-7) Rprt Serv.

Sometime see Collected Works of Robert Herrick

Sometime the Cow Kick Your Head: Light Year '88-9. Ed. by Robert Wallace. (Illus.). 235p. 1988. 15.95 (0-933248-11-3) Bits Pr.

Sometimes a Fantasy: Midlife Misadventures with Baseball Heroes. Jeff Guinn. Ed. by Larry Swindell & Mike Towle. LC 93-51043. (Illus.). 349p. 1993. 22.95 (1-56530-042-4) Summit TX.

Sometimes a Great Notion. Ken Kesey. 632p. 1977. pap. 13.95 (0-14-004529-5, Penguin Bks) Viking Penguin.

Sometimes Childhood Stinks. Suzi Thornton. (Illus.). 64p. (Orig.). (J). (gr. k-6). 1994. pap. 15.00 (1-882913-06-X) Thornton LA.

Sometimes Forever. Catherine Palmer. 336p. 1996. mass mkt. 5.99 (0-515-11922-9) Jove Pubns.

Sometimes Giant. Claud C. Crawford. 96p. (Orig.). 1984. pap. 9.95 (0-933697-03-1) Claud Crawford.

***Sometimes Gladness: Collected Poems, 1954-1992.** 4th ed. Dawe. 1993. pap. text ed. write for info. (0-582-90879-5, Pub. by Longman UK) Longman.

Sometimes I Don't Like My Kids. Candace Schap. (Lifeline Ser.). 123p. 1991. pap. 0.97 (0-8163-1037-8) Pacific Pr Pub Assn.

Sometimes I Don't Like School. Paula Z. Hogan. LC 79-24055. (Life & Living from a Child's Point of View Ser.). (Illus.). 32p. (J). (gr. k-6). 1980. lib. bdg. 21.40 (0-8172-1357-0) Raintree Steck-V.

Sometimes I Don't Like School. Paula Z. Hogan. (J). (ps-3). 1993. pap. 4.95 (0-8114-7155-1) Raintree Steck-V.

Sometimes I Drive My Mom Crazy, but I Know She's Crazy about Me: A Self-Esteem Book for ADHD Children. Lawrence E. Shapiro. (Self-Esteem Ser.). (Illus.). 130p. (Orig.). (J). (ps-5). 1993. pap. 14.95 (1-882732-03-0) Ctr Applied Psy.

Sometimes I Feel Awful: Picture Book & Resource Guide, 2 bks., Set. Joan B. Prestine. (Kids Have Feelings, Too Ser.). (J). (ps-3). 16.99 (1-56417-763-7, FE0051) Fearon Teach Aids.

Sometimes I Feel Awful, Picturebook. Joan S. Prestine. (J). (ps-3). 1993. pap. 8.99 (0-86653-927-1) Fearon Teach Aids.

Sometimes I Feel Like a Mouse. Jeanne Modesitt. (J). 1996. pap. 3.95 (0-590-44836-6) Scholastic Inc.

***Sometimes I Feel Like I Don't Have Any Friends.** Tracy Zimmerman & Lawrence E. Shapiro. Ed. by Timothy Parrotte. (Illus.). 47p. (J). (ps-7). 1996. pap. text ed. 14.95 (1-882732-58-8) Ctr Applied Psy.

Sometimes I Feel Like Running Away. Elizabeth C. Newenhuyse. 176p. (Orig.). 1993. pap. 8.99 (1-55661-317-2) Bethany Hse.

Sometimes I Get All Scribbly. Maureen B. Neuville. (Illus.). 120p. (Orig.). 1991. pap. 10.00 (0-941187-64-0) M Abel Assocs.

Sometimes I Get All Scribbly: Living with Attention-Deficit/Hyperactivity Disorder. 2nd ed. Maureen B. Neuville. LC 94-41588. 100p. (C). 1995. pap. text ed. 16.00 (0-89079-667-X, 6976) PRO-ED.

Sometimes I Get So Mad. Paula Z. Hogan. LC 79-24057. (Life & Living from a Child's Point of View Ser.). (Illus.). 32p. (J). (gr. k-6). 1980. lib. bdg. 21.40 (0-8172-1359-7) Raintree Steck-V.

Sometimes I Get So Mad. Paula Z. Hogan. (J). (ps-3). 1993. pap. 4.95 (0-8114-5207-7) Raintree Steck-V.

Sometimes I Hate Myself. Katie Tonn. (Uplook Ser.). 1978. pap. 0.99 (0-8163-0386-X, 19422-5) Pacific Pr Pub Assn.

Sometimes I Like to Cry. Elizabeth Stanton & Henry Stanton. Ed. by Caroline Rubin. LC 77-19131. (Albert Whitman Concept Bks.). (Illus.). 32p. (J). (ps-2). 1978. lib. bdg. 14.95 (0-8075-7537-2) A Whitman.

Sometimes I Like to Fight, but I Don't Do It Much Anymore: A Self-Esteem Book for Children with Difficulty in Controlling Their Anger. Lawrence E. Shapiro. (Self-Esteem Ser.). (Illus.). 64p. (Orig.). (J). (ps-5). 1995. pap. text ed. 14.95 (1-882732-22-7) Ctr Applied Psy.

Sometimes I Prefer to Fuss. Verda Peet. 1984. pap. 4.50 (9971-972-22-0) OMF Bks.

S

An Asterisk (*) at the beginning of an entry indicates that the title is appearing in BIP for the first time.

Sometimes I Really Hate You. Dewey Bertolini. (Straight Talk for Teenagers Ser.). 132p. (YA). 1991. pap. 4.99 (*0-89693-041-6*) SP Pubns.

Sometimes I Really Hate You! see **Secret Wounds & Silent Cries**

Sometimes I Think I Hear My Name. Avi. 160p. (YA). (gr. 5-6). 1995. reprint ed. mass mkt. 3.99 (*0-380-72424-3*, Flare) Avon.

Sometimes I Wake up in the Middle of the Night. Walden Theatre Conservatory Play Writing Program, Walden Theatre Playwrights. 1986. pap. 5.00 (*0-87129-376-5*, S71) Dramatic Pub.

Sometimes I Wish. Gina C. Erickson. (Get Ready...Get Set. ..Read! Ser.). (Illus.). 24p. (J). (ps-2). 1991. pap. 3.50 (*0-8120-4681-1*) Barron.

Sometimes I Wish: A First Book. Kelli C. Foster & Gina C. Erickson. (Get Ready, Get Set, Read! Ser.). (Illus.). 26p. (J). 1995. lib. bdg. 11.95 (*1-56674-112-2*) Forest Hse.

Sometimes I Wish My Mom Was Two People. Marylou M. Kjelle. LC 95-95200. (Illus.). 14p. (J). (ps-4). 1996. pap. text ed. 6.95 (*0-9648855-5-7*) MoranoCo.

Sometimes I Wonder If Poodles Like Noodles. Laura J. Numeroff. LC 96-44988. (J). 1998. 14.00 (*0-689-80563-2*) S&S Childrens.

Sometimes I'm Happy: A Writer's Memoir. Marshall Sprague. (Illus.). 220p. 1995. 24.95 (*0-8040-0986-4*) Swallow.

***Sometimes I'm Silly.** Patricia T. Cousin et al. (Visions: African-American Experiences: No. 21). (Illus.). 8p. (Orig.). (J). (gr. k-1). 1995. pap. text ed. 3.00 (*1-57518-020-0*) Arborlake.

Sometimes in Celebration. Patricia Hammond. 110p. (Orig.). 1995. pap. 12.00 (*0-9639679-1-6*) P Hammond.

***Sometimes in Shadow.** Walton Mendelson. 387p. (Orig.). 1998. mass mkt. 5.99 (*1-55237-369-X*, Pub. by Comnwlth Pub CN) Partners Pubs Grp.

Sometimes in the Wrong, but Never in Doubt: George S. Benson & the Education of the New Religious Right. L. Edward Hicks. LC 94-20275. 224p. (C). 1995. text ed. 32.00 (*0-87049-865-7*) U of Tenn Pr.

Sometimes Invisible Spaceship. Charles Bowles. LC 87-71712. 113p. (Orig.). (J). 1987. pap. 6.00 (*0-916383-25-3*) Aegina Pr.

Sometimes It's Hard to Love God. Dennis Guernsey. LC 89-15306. 171p. 1989. 15.95 (*0-8308-1257-1*, 1257) Hope Pub Hse.

Sometimes It's O. K. to Tell Secrets! Robin Lenett et al. 128p. (Orig.). (J). 1986. pap. 3.95 (*0-8125-9454-1*) Tor Bks.

Sometimes It's OK to Be Afraid of the Dark. Shetal I. Shah. LC 96-60796. 120p. (Orig.). 1997. pap. 7.95 (*1-881636-01-1*) Windsor Hse Pub Grp.

Sometimes It's Too Much. Carolyn Tacey. 42p. 1994. pap. 5.00 (*0-614-04113-9*) Hozomeen Pr.

Sometimes It's Turkey, Sometimes It's Feathers. Lorna Balian. (Illus.). 32p. (J). (ps-3). 1994. lib. bdg. 14.95 (*1-881772-15-2*) Humbug Bks.

Sometimes It's Turkey, Sometimes It's Feathers. Lorna Balian. (Illus.). 32p. (J). (ps-3). 1987. reprint ed. 12.95 (*0-687-37106-6*) Humbug Bks.

Sometimes Laughter, Sometimes Tears. Robert W. Huge. 107p. (Orig.). 1995. pap. 9.95 (*0-9635973-1-0*) Bradbury Bks.

Sometimes Mountains Move. rev. ed. C. Everett Koop & Elizabeth Koop. 96p. 1995. mass mkt., pap. 6.99 (*0-310-48672-6*) Zondervan.

Sometimes Music Rises. Wayne Dodd. LC 85-16533. (Contemporary Poetry Ser.). 72p. 1986. pap. 14.95 (*0-8203-0824-2*) U of Ga Pr.

***Sometimes My Heart Goes Numb: Love & Cargivingin a Time of Aids.** Charles Garfield. LC 97-10993. 1997. pap. text ed. 13.00 (*0-15-600495-X*) HUP.

Sometimes My Heart Goes Numb: Love & Service in a Time of AIDS. Charles A. Garfield et al. (Health Ser.). 340p. 1996. 22.00 (*0-7879-0105-9*) Jossey-Bass.

Sometimes My Mom Drinks Too Much. Kevin Kenny & Helen Krull. LC 80-14515. (Life & Living from a Child's Point of View Ser.). (Illus.). 32p. (J). (gr. k-6). 1980. lib. bdg. 21.40 (*0-8172-1366-X*) Raintree Steck-V.

Sometimes My Mom Drinks Too Much. Kevin Kenny. (J). (ps-3). 1993. pap. 4.95 (*0-8114-7159-4*) Raintree Steck-V.

***Sometimes Mysteriously.** Luis O. Salinas. 64p. (Orig.). 1997. pap. 10.00 (*1-887573-03-8*) Salmon Run.

Sometimes, Seeing Is Believing. Douglas Bond. 1993. spiral bd. 23.35 (*0-88252-164-0*) Paladin Hse.

Sometimes So Easy. Susan S. Deal. Ed. by Michael Duggan. (Illus.). 72p. (Orig.). 1992. pap. 8.00 (*1-878326-03-1*) East Hall Pr.

Sometimes the Books Froze: Wyoming's Economy & its Banks. Lawrence M. Woods. LC 85-70773. (Illus.). 210p. reprint ed. pap. 59.90 (*0-8357-5499-5*, 2035113) Bks Demand.

Sometimes the Distance. Bernice Lever. 74p. 1995. lib. bdg. 25.00 (*0-8095-4585-3*) Borgo Pr.

Sometimes the Dragon Wins. Robert V. Van Trees. (Illus.). 608p. 1994. 20.00 (*0-9616282-2-7*) R Van Trees.

Sometimes the Dragon Wins: Yet More Urban Folklore from the Paperwork Empire. Alan Dundes. LC 95-2880. (Illus.). 15p. 1996. 39.95 (*0-8156-2690-8*); pap. 14.95 (*0-8156-0371-1*) Syracuse U Pr.

Sometimes They Bite. Lawrence Block. 288p. 1992. mass mkt. 4.99 (*0-380-71575-9*) Avon.

Sometimes They Cry: A Study-Action Book. rev. ed. Ed. by Estelle Rountree & Hugh F. Halverstadt. LC 72-129096. (Illus.). 144p. reprint ed. pap. 41.10 (*0-7837-1957-4*, 2042174) Bks Demand.

Sometimes They Sang. Helen Potrebenko. 1994. pap. 6.95 (*0-88974-007-0*, Pub. by Press Gang CN) LPC InBook.

Sometimes Things Change. Patricia Eastman. LC 83-10090. (Rookie Reader Ser.). (Illus.). 32p. (J). (ps-2). 1983. pap. 3.50 (*0-516-42044-5*); lib. bdg. 15.00 (*0-516-02044-7*) Childrens.

Sometimes Things Change Big Book. Patricia Eastman. (Rookie Readers Big Bks.). (Illus.). 32p. (J). (ps-2). 1988. lib. bdg. 32.40 (*0-516-49509-7*) Childrens.

Sometimes We Dance Alone. large type ed. Edith McCall. LC 94-41433. 236p. 1995. 19.95 (*0-7838-1190-X*, GK Hall) Thorndike Pr.

Sometimes We Dance Alone: Your Next Years Can Be Your Best Years. Edith McCall. LC 93-23419. 192p. 1994. 16.95 (*0-9636620-0-7*) Brett Bks.

Sometimes We Flew. Dan Druen. LC 95-61858. 200p. (C). text ed. 14.95 (*0-9638455-3-5*) Warwick Hse.

Sometimes XXX-Rated Humor of the Green Berets. Larry L. Throneburg. 128p. (Orig.). 1990. pap. 15.00 (*0-9625970-4-X*) L L Throneburg.

Sometimes You Gotta Compromise. Dick Hafer. Ed. by Christianson. (Illus.). 80p. 1995. per. 8.95 (*0-89024-564-9*, 12163) Kalmbach.

Sometimes You Just Have to Tell Somebody. Ruth V. Cullen. LC 92-3381. 32p. (C). 1992. pap. 4.95 (*0-8091-6605-4*) Paulist Pr.

Sometimes You Just Want to Feel Like a Human Being: Case Studies of Empowering Psychotherapy with People with Disabilities. Blotzer & Ruth. 288p. 1995. pap. 26.00 (*1-55766-196-0*) P H Brookes.

Somewhat "Compleat" Guide to Walks & Hikes in Idyllwild & Environs. unabridged ed. Bill Havert & Gary Gray. 32p. (Orig.). 1995. pap. 5.95 (*0-9651760-0-2*) Erth Trails.

Somewhat More Independent: The End of Slavery in New York City, 1770-1810. Shane White. LC 90-10843. 278p. 1991. 40.00 (*0-8203-1245-2*) U of Ga Pr.

Somewhat More Independent: The End of Slavery in New York City, 1770-1810. Shane White. LC 90-10843. (C). 1995. pap. text ed. 18.00 (*0-8203-1786-1*) U of Ga Pr.

Somewhat Sea & Partly Land. Webb Young & Jim Young. (Illus.). 34p. (Orig.). 1989. pap. write for info. (*0-318-66626-X*) Pajarito Pr.

Somewhere. Jane Baskwill. (Illus.). (J). 1996. pap. write for info. (*1-57255-130-5*) Mondo Pubng.

Somewhere. Jane Baskwill. (Illus.). (J). (ps-2). 1996. 13.95 (*1-57255-131-3*); spiral bd. 23.95 (*1-57255-132-1*) Mondo Pubng.

Somewhere: From West Side Story for Vocal & Piano. Leonard Bernstein. 6p. 1986. pap. 3.95 (*0-7935-5324-5*, 50288050) H Leonard.

Somewhere: Poems & Drawings. Diana Cohen. 1986. 5.95 (*0-913152-19-6*) Folder Edns.

Somewhere a Child Is Crying. Vincent J. Fontana. 1989. pap. 4.50 (*0-451-62429-7*) NAL-Dutton.

Somewhere a Child Is Crying: Maltreatment--Causes & Prevention. Vincent J. Fontana. 1976. pap. 4.99 (*0-451-62699-0*, ME2196, Ment) NAL-Dutton.

Somewhere along the Way. Elaine Coffman. 440p. (Orig.). 1992. reprint ed. mass mkt. 5.99 (*0-440-20800-9*) Dell.

Somewhere Angels. Larry R. Libby. (Illus.). 42p. (J). (ps up). 1994. 14.99 (*0-88070-651-1*, Gold & Honey) Multnomah Pubs.

***Somewhere Apart: "My Favorite Place in Arkansas": Arkansas Residents Past & Present.** Intro. by Neil Compton. LC 96-45409. 1997. pap. 14.00 (*1-55728-446-6*) U of Ark Pr.

Somewhere Behind the Eyes Vol. 1: Hocus Focus Aha! Richard Burrill. (Illus.). 100p. (YA). (gr. 9-12). 1996. 15.95 (*1-878464-04-3*); pap. 10.95 (*1-878464-05-1*) Anthro Co.

Somewhere Between. Shirley Warren. 36p. 1991. pap. 5.00 (*1-877801-17-8*) Still Waters.

Somewhere Between Life & Death. Lurlene McDaniel. 160p. (J). (gr. 5 up). 1991. pap. 3.99 (*0-553-28349-9*, Starfire BDD) BDD Bks Young Read.

Somewhere Beyond.....The Vile Side. Stephen G. De Lay. (Illus.). 124p. (Orig.). 1988. 6.95 (*0-9621271-0-8*) Wretched Pubns.

Somewhere Dark Guide. (J). 1995. pap. write for info. (*0-590-39252-2*) Scholastic Inc.

Somewhere East of Life. Brian Aldiss. 432p. 1994. 22.95 (*0-7867-0074-2*) Carroll & Graf.

***Somewhere Else.** William Robertson. 96p. 1997. pap. 9.95 (*1-55050-111-9*, Pub. by Coteau CN) Genl Dist Srvs.

Somewhere Else Right Now. Thylias Moss. LC 94-37435. 1996. pap. write for info. (*0-8037-1746-6*); lib. bdg. write for info. (*0-8037-1747-4*) Dial Bks Young.

Somewhere I Have Never Travelled: The Second Self & the Hero's Journey in Ancient Epic. Thomas Van Nortwick. 224p. 1991. 49.95 (*0-19-507149-2*) OUP.

Somewhere I Have Never Travelled: The Second Self & the Hero's Journey in Ancient Epic. Thomas Van Nortwick. 224p. 1996. pap. 14.95 (*0-19-510127-8*) OUP.

Somewhere I'll Find You. Lisa Kleypas. 384p. (Orig.). 1996. mass mkt. 5.99 (*0-380-78143-3*) Avon.

***Somewhere in a Small Town.** T. Stacy Helton. 1997. 9.95 (*1-56352-366-3*) Longstreet Pr Inc.

Somewhere in Advance of Nowhere. Jayne Cortez. (High Risk Bks.). 122p. (Orig.). 1996. pap. 12.99 (*1-85242-422-2*) Serpents Tail.

Somewhere in Africa. Ingrid Mennen & Niki Daly. LC 91-19379. (Illus.). 32p. (J). (gr. 2-7). 1992. pap. 14.99 (*0-525-44848-9*) Dutton Child Bks.

***Somewhere in Africa.** Ingrid Mennen. 1997. pap. 4.99 (*0-14-056242-7*) Viking Penguin.

Somewhere in Africa. Karen E. Young. (Emergent Reader Ser.). 14p. (J). (ps-1). 1991. pap. text ed. 4.25 (*1-56843-078-7*) BGR Pub.

Somewhere in Africa, Big bk. Karen E. Young. (Emergent Reader Ser.). 14p. (J). (ps-1). 1991. pap. text ed. 21.00 (*1-56843-030-2*) BGR Pub.

Somewhere in Between. Anne Frost. (Illus.). 69p. (Orig.). 1987. pap. 9.95 (*0-9614624-3-4*) Frost Pub.

Somewhere in Between. Craig Pospisil. 1996. pap. 5.25 (*0-8222-1522-5*) Dramatists Play.

Somewhere in Between: Quilts & Quilters of Illinois. Rita B. Barber. (Illus.). 77p. 1986. pap. 14.95 (*0-89145-920-0*, 1790) Collector Bks.

Somewhere in Ecclesiastes: Poems. Judson Mitcham. 64p. (Orig.). (C). 1991. text ed. 18.95 (*0-8262-0802-9*) U of Mo Pr.

***Somewhere in France: The Collected Letters of Lewis Windermere Nott.** David Nott. 334p. (Orig.). 1997. pap. 15.00 (*0-7322-5667-4*) HarperColl Wrld.

Somewhere in Loving. Elizabeth Tate. 147p. (C). 1989. pap. 39.00 (*1-872795-27-7*, Pub. by Pentland Pr UK) St Mut.

Somewhere in Southern Indiana: Poems of Midwestern Origins. Norbert Krapf. LC 93-14729. 107p. 1993. 18.95 (*1-877770-89-2*); pap. 12.50 (*1-877770-90-6*); audio 12.95 (*1-877770-91-4*) Time Being Bks.

Somewhere in the Darkness. Walter D. Myers. 176p. (J). (gr. 7-9). 1992. 14.95 (*0-590-42411-4*, Scholastic Hardcover) Scholastic Inc.

Somewhere in the Darkness. Walter D. Myers. 176p. (J). (gr. 7-9). 1993. pap. 3.50 (*0-590-42412-2*) Scholastic Inc.

***Somewhere in the Darkness.** Walter D. Myers. (J). 1997. pap. text ed. 3.99 (*0-590-34186-3*) Scholastic Inc.

Somewhere in the Night. Nicholas Christopher. 1997. 22.95 (*0-02-922915-4*, Free Press); 25.00 (*0-684-82803-0*) Free Pr.

***Somewhere in the Night: Eight Gay Tales of the Supernatural.** Jeffrey N. McMahan. 202p. (Orig.). 1997. pap. 9.95 (*1-55583-432-9*) Alyson Pubns.

***Somewhere in the World Right Now.** Stacey Schuett. (J). 1997. pap. 6.99 (*0-679-88549-8*) Knopf Bks Yng Read.

Somewhere in the World Right Now. Stacey Schuett. LC 94-6223. (Illus.). 40p. (J). 1995. 16.00 (*0-679-86537-3*); lib. bdg. 17.99 (*0-679-96537-8*) Knopf.

Somewhere in Time. Barbara Bretton. 1992. mass mkt. 4.99 (*0-373-83246-X*, 246) Harlequin Bks.

Somewhere in Time. Richard Matheson. 1976. 28.95 (*0-8488-1094-5*) Amereon Ltd.

Somewhere in Time. Bob Timberlake. 1989. 49.95 (*0-942399-09-9*) Lightworks.

Somewhere in Time & What Dreams May Come. rev. ed. Richard Matheson. 512p. 1991. reprint ed. 25.00 (*0-910489-06-8*) Scream Pr.

Somewhere in Time Story: Behind the Scenes of the Making of the Cult Romantic Fantasy Motion Picture. Bill Shepard. LC 94-76732. (Illus.). 116p. (Orig.). 1994. pap. 15.95 (*0-9641698-0-0*) Insite CA.

Somewhere Like This. Arrowsmith. 1995. per. 10.95 (*0-85449-143-0*, Pub. by Gay Mens Pr UK) LPC InBook.

***Somewhere My Love.** Karen Fox. 320p. (Orig.). 1997. mass mkt. 4.99 (*0-505-52210-1*, Love Spell) Dorchester Pub Co.

Somewhere My Love. large type ed. Doris Howe. 1989. 25.99 (*0-7089-2056-X*) Ulverscroft.

Somewhere Other Than the Night. Sandy Steen. (Crystal Creek Ser.). 1994. mass mkt. 3.99 (*0-373-82534-X*, 1-82534-8) Harlequin Bks.

Somewhere Out There. Emilie Richards. (Intimate Moments Ser.). 1993. mass mkt. 3.39 (*0-373-07498-0*, 5-07498-4) Silhouette.

***Somewhere Out There: Showcase.** Connie Bennett. 1997. mass mkt. 3.99 (*0-373-70733-9*, 1-70733-0) Harlequin Bks.

Somewhere Out There, Kokomo, Plus 21 Contemporary Hits. 136p. 1989. otabind 11.95 (*0-7935-3167-5*, 00490063) H Leonard.

Somewhere over the Dan Ryan: Day & Weekend Outings for Chicago-Area Families. rev. ed. Joanne Y. Cleaver. LC 92-44999. (Illus.). 232p. 1993. pap. 11.95 (*1-55652-180-4*) Chicago Review.

Somewhere Over the Rainbow: A Soul's Journey Home. Gloria Chadwick. LC 93-91601. 248p. 1995. pap. 12.95 (*1-883717-33-7*) Myst Mndscapes.

Somewhere South of Suez. Douglas Reed. 9.95 (*0-8159-6816-7*) Devin.

Somewhere to Go on Sunday: A Guide to Natural Treasures in Western New York & Southern Ontario. Margaret Wooster. 116p. 1994. pap. 9.95 (*0-87975-634-9*) Prometheus Bks.

Somewhere Today. Bert Kitchen. LC 91-58754. (Illus.). 32p. (J). (ps up). 1992. 15.95 (*1-56402-074-6*) Candlewick Pr.

Somewhere Today. Bert Kitchen. LC 91-58754. (Illus.). 32p. (J). (ps up). 1994. pap. 5.99 (*1-56402-377-X*) Candlewick Pr.

Somewhere Within: A Journey. Russ Pinto. LC 91-71772. 98p. (Orig.). 1991. pap. 9.95 (*0-9629316-8-3*) A One Pub.

Somites in Developing Embryos. Ed. by Ruth Bellairs et al. LC 86-22543. (NATO ASI Series A, Life Sciences: Vol. 118). 330p. 1986. 75.00 (*0-306-42418-5*, Plenum Pr) Plenum.

***Somme.** Gerald Gliddon. (VCs of the First World War Ser.). (Illus.). 224p. (Orig.). 1997. pap. 22.95 (*0-7509-1599-4*, Pub. by Sutton Pubng UK) Bks Intl VA.

Somme: The Day-By-Day Account. Chris McCarthy. (Illus.). 176p. 1996. pap. 19.95 (*1-85409-330-4*, Pub. by Arms & Armour UK) Sterling.

Sommeil Delivre. Andree Chedid. (FRE.). 1989. pap. 10.95 (*0-7859-3437-5*) Fr & Eur.

Sommeil Provoque et les Etats Anologues. Ambroise-Auguste Liebeault. LC 75-16716. (Classics in Psychiatry Ser.). 1976. reprint ed. 26.95 (*0-405-07444-1*) Ayer.

Sommer: Images - Words, 2 vols., Set. Frederick Sommer. (Illus.). 84p. (Orig.). 1984. pap. 40.00 (*0-938262-09-2*) Ctr Creat Photog.

Sommer-Schoenfeld, Management Dictionary, Deutsch-English (German-English) Fachwoerterbuch Fuer Betriebswirtschaft Wirtschafts-und Steuerrecht und Datenverarbeitung. 4th ed. 290p. (ENG & GER.). (C). 1978. 52.35 (*3-11-004863-9*) De Gruyter.

Sommerfeld's Concepts of Taxation, 1995 Edition. Silvia A. Madeo et al. 683p. (C). 1994. text ed. 49.75 (*0-03-006833-9*) Dryden Pr.

Sommerfeld's Concepts of Taxation, 1995 Edition. 95th ed. Silvia A. Madeo et al. 272p. (C). 1994. student ed., pap. text ed. 33.75 (*0-03-006834-7*) Dryden Pr.

Somnambulism & Cramp. Baron Von Reichenbach. Tr. by John S. Hittell. 253p. 1970. reprint ed. spiral bd. 24.50 (*0-7873-0913-3*) Hlth Research.

Somnambulist. 2nd ed. Ralph Gibson. LC 73-88292. (Illus.). 48p. 1973. 12.95 (*0-912810-09-2*) Lustrum Pr.

Somnium: The Dream, or Posthumous Work on Lunar Astronomy. Johann Kepler. Tr. by Edward Rosen. LC 65-20639. 289p. pap. 82.40 (*0-317-07803-8*, 2004977) Bks Demand.

Somnium et Vigilia in Somnium Scipionis: Commentary on the Dream of Scipio. Juan L. Vives. Ed. & Tr. by Edward V. George from LAT. LC 89-72127. (Library of Rennaissance Humanism: Vol. 2). 392p. 1990. text ed. 85.00 (*0-87921-080-X*) Attic Pr.

Somnolism & Psycheism: Or the Science of the Soul & the Phenomena of Nervation. 2nd ed. Joseph W. Haddock. LC 75-7386. (Perspectives in Psychical Research Ser.). (Illus.). 1975. reprint ed. 23.95 (*0-405-07034-9*) Ayer.

S

Somos - We Are: Five Contemporary Cuban Poets. Victor Casaus et al. Ed. by Anita Whitney. (Illus.). 48p. (Orig.). 1970. pap. 2.50 (*0-87810-000-8*) Times Change.

Somos Como Somos. Andres Rivero. LC 81-70535. (Short Stories in Spanish Ser.). 52p. (Orig.). 1982. pap. 7.95 (*0-933648-04-9*) ARO.

Somos Cuidadores des Zoologico. Cynthia Benjamin. 1995. 6.95 (*0-8120-6415-1*) Barron.

Somos Diferentes: Contextualizacion Cultural. Rogelio Archilla. 92p. (SPA.). 1992. pap. 3.99 (*1-56063-112-0*, 498404) Editorial Unilit.

Somos Pilotos. Cynthia Benjamin. (Illus.). 24p. (J). (ps). 1994. 6.95 (*0-8120-6417-8*) Barron.

S.O.M.O.S. Summer Anthology 1994. (S.O.M.O.S. Summer Writers Ser.). 38p. (Orig.). 1994. pap. text ed. 6.50 (*1-883968-04-6*) Blinking Yellow.

Somos un Arco Iris - We Are a Rainbow. Nancy M. Grande Tabor. Ed. by Elena Dworkin Wright. (Illus.). 32p. (J). (ps-4). 1995. pap. 6.95 (*0-88106-813-6*) Charlesbridge Pub.

Somoza & the Legacy of U. S. Involvement in Central America. Bernard Diederich. 352p. (Orig.). 1989. reprint ed. pap. 12.95 (*0-943862-42-6*) Wiener Pubs Inc.

Somoza Falling: A Case Study of Washington at Work. Anthony Lake. LC 90-34788. 336p. (Orig.). 1990. reprint ed. pap. 17.95 (*0-87023-733-0*) U of Mass Pr.

Somoza's Last Stand: Testimonies from Nicaragua. Larry Towell. LC 89-63825. (Illus.). 210p. (C). 1990. 35.00 (*0-932415-53-9*); pap. 11.95 (*0-932415-54-7*) Red Sea Pr.

***Somthing to Believe In.** Brian P. Brawdy & Patricia M. Novick. viii, 200p. 1997. pap. 19.95 (*0-9658937-4-X*) MindWise.

Son: A Psychopath & His Victims. Jack Olsen. 544p. (Orig.). 1985. mass mkt. 6.99 (*0-440-18148-8*) Dell.

Son & Lover: The Young D. H. Lawrence. Philip Callow. 324p. 1991. reprint ed. pap. text ed. 11.95 (*0-929587-52-9*, Elephant Paperbacks) I R Dee.

Son at the Front. large type ed. Edith Wharton. 412p. 1996. lib. bdg. 22.95 (*0-7838-1651-0*) Thorndike Pr.

Son at the Front. rev. ed. Edith Wharton. LC 95-17536. 280p. (C). 1995. pap. 15.00 (*0-87580-568-X*); lib. bdg. 26.00 (*0-87580-203-6*) N Ill U Pr.

Son Avenger. Sigrid Undset. LC 94-42542. (Master of Hestviken Ser.: Vol. 4). 1995. pap. 10.00 (*0-679-75552-7*, Vin) Random.

Son Excellence Eugene Rougon. Emile Zola. write for info. (*0-318-63600-X*) Fr & Eur.

Son Excellence Eugene Rougon. Emile Zola. 442p. (FRE.). 1990. pap. 10.95 (*0-7859-1430-7*, 2080702645) Fr & Eur.

Son Excellence Eugene Rougon. Emile Zola. (Folio Ser.: No. 1369). (FRE.). pap. 10.95 (*2-07-037369-X*) Schoenhof.

Son from Sleep. Rachel Hadas. LC 86-20. (Wesleyan Poetry Ser.). 58p. 1987. pap. 11.95 (*0-8195-1140-4*, Wesleyan Univ Pr) U Pr of New Eng.

Son I Love You, But... Gwendolyn L. Baines. (Illus.). 32p. (Orig.). (YA). 1994. pap. 4.50 (*0-9614505-2-5*) Nevada Pub.

Son Is Given. Harry Uprichard. 1992. pap. 8.99 (*0-85234-301-9*, Pub. by Evangelical Pr) Presby & Reformed.

Son Ki Channeling. Szuson J. Wong & Roger Davis. (Illus.). 70p. (Orig.). 1988. pap. 14.95 (*0-9620590-0-5*) S J Wong.

***Son Light.** Larry Grogan. (Orig.). 1996. pap. write for info. (*1-57553-456-8*) Watermrk Pr.

Son Master. Peter Seaton. (Roof Bks.). 64p. (Orig.). 1984. pap. text ed. 4.00 (*0-937804-10-X*) Segue NYC.

Son of a Chief. John K. Marah. 1995. 15.95 (*0-533-11324-5*) Vantage.

Son of a Duck is a Floater. Armander & Ashkain Skipwith. (Illus.). 90p. 1995. 15.95 (*0-86685-526-2*, Pub. by Stacey Intl UK) Intl Bk Ctr.

Son of a Fast Gun. Hascal Giles. 224p. 1991. mass mkt. 3.50 (*0-8217-3344-3*, Zebra Kensgtn) Kensgtn Pub Corp.

Son of a Hundred Kings. Thomas B. Costain. 1994. lib. bdg. 24.95 (*1-56849-467-X*) Buccaneer Bks.

Son of a Rail. Thomas V. McDermott. (Illus.). 193p. 1996. pap. 12.95 (*0-9641688-1-2*) Uncommon Buffalo.

*Son of a Smaller Hero. Mordecai Richler. 1996. pap. text ed. 6.95 (0-7710-9970-3) McCland & Stewart.

Son of a Son of a Son of One Hundred & One Aggie Jokes. (One Hundred & One Aggie Jokes Ser.). (Illus.). 50p. (Orig.). 1971. write for info. (0-945430-04-3) Gigem Pr.

Son of a Son of One Hundred & One Aggie Jokes, Vol. 3. Illus. by Bob Taylor. (One Hundred & One Aggie Jokes Ser.). 50p. (Orig.). 1969. write for info. (0-945430-03-5) Gigem Pr.

Son of a Wanted Man. Louis L'Amour. 176p. 1991. mass mkt. 3.99 (0-553-24457-4) Bantam.

Son of a Wanted Man. large type ed. Louis L'Amour. (Special Ser.). 269p. 1993. reprint ed. 18.95 (1-56054-654-9) Thorndike Pr.

Son of Adam. Denis Forman. (Illus.). 240p. 1991. 29.95 (0-233-98593-X, Pub. by A Deutsch UK) Trafalgar.

Son of Adam Wyngate see Devil Enters by a North Window

Son of Alyandabu. Joe McGinness. 1991. pap. 16.95 (0-7022-2335-2, Pub. by Univ Queensland Pr AT) Intl Spec Bk.

S

Son of an Arizona Legend. Stephen Bly. LC 94-360. (Stuart Brannon Western Adventure Ser.). 192p. (Orig.). 1994. pap. 7.99 (0-89107-770-7) Crossway Bks.

Son of an Arizona Legend. large type ed. Stephen A. Bly. LC 96-10458. 242p. 1996. 19.95 (0-7838-1783-5, GK Hall) Thorndike Pr.

Son of an Earl...Sold for a Slave. David B. Weems. LC 92-27917. (Illus.). 112p. (J). (gr. 5 up). 1992. 11.95 (0-88289-921-X) Pelican.

Son of An Engineer. David Greenspan. (American Theater in Literature Ser.). 104p. (Orig.). 1995. pap. 8.95 (1-55713-159-7) Sun & Moon CA.

Son of an Oyster. Robert N. Feinstein. LC 89-8645. (Illus.). 86p. (Orig.). 1989. pap. 10.00 (0-914061-09-7) Orchises Pr.

*Son of Andalusia: The Lyrical Landscapes of Federico Garcia Lorca. C. Brian Morris. (Illus.). 432p. 1997. 39.95 (0-8265-1288-7) Vanderbilt U Pr.

Son of Andy Warhol, Vol. 4: Excerpts from the Anonymous Diary of a New York Youth Taylor Mead. 92p. (Orig.). 1986. pap. 5.95 (0-937815-03-9) Hanuman Bks.

Son of Apollo: Themes of Plato. F. J. Woodbridge. 272p. (J). (gr. 7 up). 1972. reprint ed. 26.00 (0-8196-0278-7) Biblo.

Son of Apollo: Themes of Plato. Frederick J. Woodbridge. LC 88-2965. xii, 272p. 1989. reprint ed. 32.00 (0-918024-62-5); reprint ed. pap. 16.00 (0-918024-61-7) Ox Bow.

Son of Ark's Hacks; More Travesties, 2 bks. in 1. Al Ackerman & Any Salyer. 1990. pap. 5.00 (0-935350-26-8); pap. write for info. (0-935350-27-6) Luna Bisonte.

Son of Arlecchino. Leon Katz. (Commedia in Performance Ser.: Vol. 2). 112p. (Orig.). 1986. pap. 6.95 (0-936839-07-4) Applause Theatre Bk Pubs.

Son of Celluloid. Clive Barker et al. 1991. 6.95 (1-56060-085-3) Eclipse Bks.

*Son of Circumstance. Jim Abdo. 272p. (Orig.). 1997. mass mkt. 4.99 (1-55237-032-1, Pub. by Comnwlth Pub CN) Partners Pubs Grp.

Son of Durango. Laurance L. Priddy. LC 95-34873. 176p. 1996. 26.95 (0-86534-242-3) Sunstone Pr.

Son of Film Flubs: More Memorable Movie Mistakes. Bill Givens. (Illus.). 157p. (Orig.). 1991. pap. 7.95 (0-8065-1279-2, Citadel Pr) Carol Pub Group.

Son of Fletch. Gregory Mcdonald. 272p. (Orig.). 1994. mass mkt. 5.99 (0-515-11470-7) Jove Pubns.

Son of Fletch. Gregory McDonald. Date not set. 4.98 (0-8317-6523-2) Smithmark.

Son of Fletch. large type ed. Gregory Mcdonald. LC 93-33295. 1993. lib. bdg. 22.95 (0-7862-0079-0) Thorndike Pr.

*Son of Frog Pond: Tales of the Not-So-Hot Preacher from the Swamp. Clyde W. Cutrer, Sr. LC 96-71627. 160p. 1996. 12.95 (1-57736-026-5) Providence Hse.

Son of Funnyside. Ed. & Intro. by Carl E. Heffley. (Illus.). 100p. (Orig.). 1994. pap. text ed. 14.95 (1-883331-06-4) Anderie Poetry.

Son of God. J. G. Bellet. pap. 4.25 (0-88172-169-7) Believers Bkshelf.

Son of Golden Turkey Awards. Harry Medved & Michael Medved. 1986. pap. 10.95 (0-394-74341-5, Villard Bks) Random.

Son of Guilty Pleasures of the Horror Film. Ed. by Gary J. Svehla & Susan Svehla. (Illus.). 256p. (Orig.). 1998. pap. 20.00 (1-887664-04-1) Midnght Marquee Pr.

Son of Gun in Cheek. Bill Pronzini. LC 87-7872. 192p. 1988. pap. 9.95 (0-89296-952-0) Mysterious Pr.

*Son of Heaven. Ling Li. Tr. by David Kwan from CHI. 672p. 1995. 16.95 (0-8351-3147-5) China Bks.

Son of Heaven: A Biography of Li Shih-Min, Founder of the T'ang Dynasty. Charles P. Fitzgerald. LC 74-136382. reprint ed. 37.50 (0-404-02404-1) AMS Pr.

Son of His Love. W. J. Hocking. 6.25 (0-88172-088-7) Believers Bkshelf.

Son of Holmes & Rasputin's Revenge: The Early Works of John T. Lescroart. John T. Lescroart. 544p. 1995. pap. 16.95 (1-55611-437-0) D I Fine.

Son of "It Was a Dark & Stormy Night" Compiled by Scott Rice. 160p. 1986. pap. 7.00 (0-14-008839-3, Penguin Bks) Viking Penguin.

Son of Italy. Pascal D'Angelo. LC 74-17925. (Italian American Experience Ser.). 200p. 1975. reprint ed. 17.95 (0-405-06398-9) Ayer.

Son of Joseph: The Parentage of Jesus. Geoffrey Parrinder. 132p. 1992. pap. text ed. 19.95 (0-567-29213-4, Pub. by T & T Clark UK) Bks Intl VA.

Son of Laughter: A Novel. Frederick Buechner. LC 92-53899. 288p. 1994. reprint ed. pap. 12.00 (0-06-250117-8) Harper SF.

Son of Mad Libs, No. 2. Roger Price & Leonard Stern. (Mad Libs Ser.). 48p. (Orig.). (J). (gr. 2 up). 1974. bds., pap. 3.50 (0-8431-0056-7) Price Stern Sloan.

Son of Man. Augusto R. Bastos. (Voices of Resistance Ser.). 288p. (Orig.). 1988. 24.00 (0-85345-767-0); pap. 13.00 (0-85345-733-6) Monthly Rev.

Son of Man. Andrew Klavan. LC 87-62808. 187p. 1988. 22.00 (0-932966-86-1) Permanent Pr.

Son of Man: I Come As a Thief. 106p. 1993. pap. 15.00 (1-57277-000-7) Script Rsch.

Son of Man: Vision & Interpretation. Chrys C. Caragounis. ix, 310p. 1986. lib. bdg. 87.50 (3-16-144963-0, Pub. by J C B Mohr GW) Coronet Bks.

Son of Man in Daniel Seven. Arthur J. Ferch. (Andrews University Seminary Doctoral Dissertation Ser.: Vol. 6). x, 248p. 1983. pap. 19.99 (0-943872-38-3) Andrews Univ Pr.

Son of Man in Mark: A Study of the Background of the Term "Son of Man" & Its Use in St. Mark's Gospel. Morna D. Hooker. LC 67-4912. 240p. reprint ed. pap. 68.40 (0-7837-1031-3, 2023832) Bks Demand.

Son of Man in the Gospel of John. Delbert Burkett. (JSNT Supplement Ser.: No. 56). 188p. (C). 1991. 43.75 (1-85075-292-3, Pub. by Sheffield Acad UK) CUP Services.

Son of Man, Son of God. Eric G. Jay. 124p. reprint ed. pap. 35.40 (0-7837-6926-1, 2046755) Bks Demand.

Son of Man Trilogy, 3 pts., Set. Paula FitzGerald & Edward FitzGerald. 461p. (Orig.). pap. 18.00 (0-935915-03-6) Corinth Pub.

Son of Manitou. Albert R. Booky. LC 86-23169. 144p. 1987. pap. 10.95 (0-86534-097-8) Sunstone Pr.

*Son of Mashpee: Reflections of Chief Flying Eagle, a Wampanoag. unabridged ed. Earl Mills, Sr. & Alicja Mann. (Illus.). 128p. (Orig.). 1996. pap. 24.75 (0-9654360-0-4) Word Studio.

Son of Minos. David M. Cheney. LC 64-25838. (J). (gr. 7). 1970. 21.00 (0-8196-0142-X) Biblo.

Son of Monolith. Michael C. Goodwin. (Illus.). (Orig.). 1991. pap. 4.95 (0-9629432-1-5) Inter Trading.

Son of Monte Cristo. Alexandre Dumas. 1976. 20.95 (0-8488-1294-8) Amereon Ltd.

Son of Monte Cristo. Alexandre Dumas. 190p. 1983. reprint ed. lib. bdg. 19.95 (0-89966-476-8) Buccaneer Bks.

Son of Old Jules: Memoirs of Jules Sandoz, Jr. Caroline S. Pifer & Jules Sandoz, Jr. LC 88-19138. (Illus.). xii, 129p. 1989. reprint ed. pap. 6.50 (0-8032-9190-6, Bison Books); reprint ed. text ed. 30.00 (0-8032-4199-2) U of Nebr Pr.

Son of One Hundred & One Aggie Jokes. Illus. by Bob Taylor. (One Hundred & One Aggie Jokes Ser.: Vol. 2). 50p. (Orig.). 1967. write for info. (0-945430-02-7) Gigem Pr.

*Son of Origins of Marvel Comics. Stan Lee. 1997. pap. text ed. 24.95 (0-7851-0559-X) Marvel Entmnt.

Son of Perdition. James G. Cozzens. LC 83-45738. reprint ed. 29.00 (0-404-20069-9) AMS Pr.

Son of Perfection, No. 1. Hilton Hotema. 78p. 1993. reprint ed. spiral bd. 8.50 (0-7873-0452-2) Hlth Research.

Son of Perfection, No. 2. Hilton Hotema. 100p. 1993. reprint ed. spiral bd. 10.00 (0-7873-0451-4) Hlth Research.

Son of Pew Prompter. Larry Ensco & Annie Ensco. 1996. pap. 9.99 (0-8341-9527-5, MP-774) Nazarene.

Son of Poop. Gerald Locklin. 1973. 5.00 (0-917554-14-0) Maelstrom.

Son of Porthos. Alexandre Dumas. 287p. 1983. reprint ed. lib. bdg. 19.95 (0-89966-316-8) Buccaneer Bks.

Son of Promise. Paula FitzGerald & Edward FitzGerald. (Son of Man Trilogy Ser.: Pt. 1). 122p. (Orig.). 1988. pap. 6.50 (0-935915-00-1) Corinth Pub.

*Son of Rosemary. Ira Levin. LC 97-14803. 1997. pap. 22.95 (0-525-94374-9) NAL-Dutton.

Son of Royal Langbrith. William Dean Howells. (Notable American Authors Ser.). 1992. reprint ed. lib. bdg. 75.00 (0-7812-3257-0) Rprt Serv.

*Son of Sorrow: The Life, Works & Influence of Colonel William C. Falkner 1825-1889. Donald P. Duclos. 256p. 1997. pap. 54.95 (1-57309-179-0, Cath Scholar Pr) Intl Scholars.

*Son of Sorrow: The Life, Works & Influence of Colonel William C. Falkner, 1825-1889. Donald P. Duclos. 364p. 1997. 74.95 (1-57309-180-4) Intl Scholars.

Son of South Mountain & Dust. Thomas W. Wing. Ed. by Carolyn W. Greenlee. 150p. 1996. pap. 14.50 (1-887400-11-7, EVB-1007) Earthen Vessel Prodns.

Son of Spirit: A Novel. David F. Krell. LC 96-31891. (Series in Contemporary Continental Philosophy). 180p. 1997. pap. 12.95 (0-7914-3222-X); text ed. 39.50 (0-7914-3221-1) State U NY Pr.

Son of Stupid Mac Tricks: Eighteen New Insanely Great Tricks for Your Macintosh. Bob Levitus. 1991. pap. 19.95 (0-201-56787-3) Addison-Wesley.

Son of Summer Stars. Meredith A. Pierce. (Firebring Trilogy Ser.: Vol. 3). 256p. (YA). (gr. 7 up). 1996. 17.95 (0-316-70755-4) Little.

Son of Tarzan. 25.95 (1-56723-026-1) Yestermorrow.

Son of Tarzan. Edgar Rice Burroughs. (Tarzan Ser.: No. 4). 222p. 1986. mass mkt. 4.99 (0-345-33556-2, Del Rey) Ballantine.

Son of Tecun Uman: A Maya Indian Tells His Life Story. Ed. by James D. Sexton. 250p. (C). 1990. reprint ed. pap. text ed. 11.50 (0-88133-566-5) Waveland Pr.

Son of the Black Stallion. Walter Farley. (J). Date not set. pap. 2.25 (0-590-30387-2) Scholastic Inc.

Son of the Bowery: The Life Story of an East Side American. Charles Stelzle. LC 74-179540. (Select Bibliographies Reprint Ser.). 1977. reprint ed. 23.95 (0-8369-6669-4) Ayer.

Son of the Carolinas: A Story of the Hurricane Upon the Sea Islands. Elizabeth C. Satterthuait. LC 72-2064. (Black Heritage Library Collection). 1977. reprint ed. 20.95 (0-8369-9062-5) Ayer.

Son of the Cinnamon Tree/The Donkey's Egg. Duance Vorhees & Mark Mueller. (Korean Folk Tales for Children Ser.: Vol. 10). (Illus.). 46p. (J). (gr. 2-5). 1990. lib. bdg. 10.95 (0-930878-93-0) Hollym Intl.

*Son of the Circus. John Irving. 1997. pap. 12.95 (0-345-41799-2) Ballantine.

Son of the Circus. John Irving. 1995. mass mkt. 7.99 (0-345-38996-4) Ballantine.

Son of the Day & the Daughter of the Night. MacDonald. (J). 1998. pap. 7.95 (0-671-75230-8, S&S Bks Young Read) S&S Childrens.

Son of the Duke of Nowhere. Philip Gross. 48p. (Orig.). 1991. pap. 8.95 (0-571-16140-5) Faber & Faber.

*Son of the Forest & Other Writings by William Apess, a Pequot. William Apess. Ed. by Barry O'Connell. 192p. (Orig.). 1997. pap. 12.95 (1-55849-107-4) U of Mass Pr.

Son of the Gamblin' Man: The Youth of an Artist. Mari Sandoz. LC 76-17066. x, 333p. 1976. reprint ed. text ed. 32.00 (0-8032-0895-2) U of Nebr Pr.

Son of the Middle Border. Hamlin Garland. LC 94-28641. 416p. 1995. pap. 11.95 (0-14-018796-0, Penguin Bks) Viking Penguin.

Son of the Middle Border. Hamlin Garland. (Collected Works of Hamlin Garland). 1988. reprint ed. lib. bdg. 59.00 (0-7812-1245-6) Rprt Serv.

Son of the Middle Border see Collected Works of Hamlin Garland

*Son of the Morning. Linda Howard. 1997. mass mkt. 5.99 (0-671-79938-X, Pocket Books) PB.

*Son of the Morning. Linda Howard. LC 97-13852. 1997. write for info. (0-7862-1135-0) Thorndike Pr.

Son of the Morning. Joyce Carol Oates. 1979. pap. 2.75 (0-449-24073-8, Crest) Fawcett.

*Son of the Morning Star: Custer & the Little Bighorn. Evan S. Connell. 1997. pap. text ed. 15.00 (0-86547-510-5, North Pt Pr) FS&G.

Son of the Morning Star: Custer & the Little Bighorn. Evan S. Connell. LC 85-42560. 1991. pap. 10.95 (0-06-097161-4, PL) HarpC.

Son of the Morning Star: Custer & the Little Bighorn. Evan S. Connell. 1993. 14.98 (0-88394-088-4) Promntory Pr.

Son of the Mountain Bike Adventure Guide: Ketchum, Stanley, & Beyond. John Zilly. 60p. 1995. pap. 8.95 (1-881583-01-5) Advent Pr WA.

Son of the People. C. V. Bowman. 1989. pap. 8.95 (0-910452-68-7) Covenant.

Son of the Phoenix. Michael A. Williams. LC 89-92546. 135p. lib. bdg. 24.95 (1-878527-02-9) Black Phoenix Pr.

Son of the Revolution. Llang Heng & Judith Shapiro. 1984. pap. 13.00 (0-394-72274-4, Vin) Random.

Son of the Soil. Wilson Katiyo. (African Classics Ser.). (C). 1976. pap. text ed. 11.95 (0-582-02656-3) Longman.

Son of the Sun: The Life & Philosophy of Akhnaton, King of Egypt. 4th ed. Savitri Devi. LC 80-54808. (Illus.). 323p. 1946. reprint ed. 21.95 (0-912057-17-3, 501740) RO AMORC.

Son of the Wilderness: The Life of John Muir. Linnie M. Wolfe. LC 78-53294. (Illus.). 398p. 1978. reprint ed. 29.50 (0-299-07730-6); reprint ed. pap. 14.95 (0-299-07734-9) U of Wis Pr.

Son of the Wolf. Jack London. 1992. 39.00 (0-403-08613-2) Somerset Pub.

Son of the Wolf. Jack London. reprint ed. lib. bdg. 18.95 (0-89190-654-1, Rivercity Pr) Amereon Ltd.

Son of the Wolf. Jack London. (Illus.). 256p. 1980. reprint ed. pap. 6.95 (0-932458-02-5) Star Rover.

Son of the Wolf. Jack London. 1992. reprint ed. lib. bdg. 18.95 (0-89966-953-0) Buccaneer Bks.

Son of the Wolf: Tales of the Far North. Jack London. Ed. by Charles N. Watson, Jr. LC 95-11746. (World's Classics Ser.). (Illus.). 360p. (C). 1996. pap. 7.95 (0-19-282384-1) OUP.

*Son of the Zubble-Wump. Tish Rabe. 1996. 14.00 (0-679-88419-X) Random Bks Yng Read.

Son-of-Thunder. Stig Holmas. Tr. by Anne Born from NOR. LC 93-4211. (Illus.). 128p. (YA). (gr. 7 up). 15.95 (0-943173-88-4, Harbinger CO); pap. 9.95 (0-943173-87-6, Harbinger CO) R Rinehart.

*Son-of-Thunder. Stig Holmas. Tr. by Anne Born. (Illus.). 48p. (YA). (gr. 7 up). Date not set. teacher ed., pap. 9.95 (1-57140-020-6, Harbinger CO) R Rinehart.

Son of Thunder: Patrick Henry & the American Republic. Henry Mayer. 544p. 1992. reprint ed. pap. text ed. 19.95 (0-8139-1376-4) U Pr of Va.

Son of Two Bloods. Vincent L. Mendoza. LC 95-50326. (North American Indian Prose Award Ser.). ix, 176p. (C). 1996. 25.00 (0-8032-3188-1) U of Nebr Pr.

*Son of Ultrasound Physics for the Fun of It, Animal Applications. Raymond L. Powis & Wendy J. Powis. (Illus.). 70p. (Orig.). 1996. pap. text ed. 27.00 (1-888647-02-7) Ray & Roo Enter.

Son of Wolf. Jack London. reprint ed. lib. bdg. 75.00 (0-7812-0202-7) Rprt Serv.

Son of York. large type ed. Margaret Abbey. LC 94-33761. 248p. 1995. pap. 17.95 (0-8161-7498-9, GK Hall) Thorndike Pr.

Son of Yuppies from Hell, No. 2. Barbara Slate. 48p. 1990. 3.50 (0-87135-737-2) Marvel Entmnt.

Son of Zelman. Oscar Pinkus. 176p. 1982. 19.95 (0-87073-548-9); pap. 14.95 (0-87073-549-7) Schenkman Bks Inc.

Son-Rise: The Miracle Continues. Barry N. Kaufman. 372p. 1995. pap. 12.95 (0-915811-61-8) H J Kramer Inc.

Son-Rise: The Miracle Continues. rev. ed. Barry N. Kaufman. LC 93-38530. (Illus.). 384p. 1994. 20.00 (0-915811-53-7) H J Kramer Inc.

Son Sonnets. Arlene Stone. Ed. by E. Feinberg. 72p. (Orig.). pap. write for info. (0-9640771-0-8) Emmanuel CA.

*Son Thang: An American War Crime. Gary D. Solis. LC 97-18512. (Illus.). 368p. 1997. 29.95 (1-55750-743-0) Naval Inst Pr.

Son Tverdi: (The Dream of Firmament) Victoria Andreyeva. 110p. (RUS.). 1987. pap. 10.00 (0-922792-12-7) Gnosis Pr.

Son-up, Son-down. John Carenen. (Trilogy Ser.: Bk. 3). 1990. pap. 14.95 (0-87868-347-X, 3470) Child Welfare.

Son Who Was Older Than His Father. 2nd deluxe ed. Joseph H. Hughes, Jr. LC 75-36726. 1977. 10.00 (0-89185-034-1) Aaron-Jenkins.

Son Who Was Older Than His Father. 2nd ed. Joseph H. Hughes, Jr. LC 75-36726. 1977. pap. 4.95 (0-89185-035-X) Aaron-Jenkins.

Sonador para un Pueblo. Antonio B. Vallejo. Ed. by Luis I. Feijoo. (Nueva Austral Ser.: No. 75). (SPA.). 1991. pap. text ed. 24.95 (84-239-1875-0) Elliots Bks.

Sonahchi. Pat Carr. LC 88-70067. 80p. (Orig.). 1988. pap. 8.95 (0-938317-06-7) Cinco Puntos.

Sonal Mansingh: Contribution to Odissi Dance. Jiwan Pani. (C). 1992. 5.00 (81-7304-002-8, Pub. by Manohar II) S Asia.

Sonali's Friend. Alaka Shankar. (Illus.). 16p. (Orig.). (J). (gr. k-3). 1980. pap. 2.50 (0-89744-218-0, Pub. by Childrens Bk Trust II) Auromere.

Sonar Bangla. Asif Currimbhoy. 1972. pap. text ed. 4.80 (0-88253-764-4) Ind-US Inc.

Sonar en Cubano: Dreaming in Cuban. Cristina Garcia. 336p. (SPA.). 1994. pap. 11.00 (0-345-39139-X, One World) Ballantine.

Sonar Engineering Handbook. Harrison T. Loeser. LC 92-63044. 216p. 1993. reprint ed. 41.95 (0-932146-59-7) Peninsula CA.

Sonar Images. Harold E. Edgerton. (Illus.). 304p. 1986. text ed. 56.20 (0-13-822651-2); pap. text ed. write for info. (0-13-822644-X) P-H.

Sonar of Dolphins. Whitlow W. Au. LC 92-22696. 344p. 1994. 89.95 (0-387-97835-6) Spr-Verlag.

*Sonar Performance. Crawley. (Illus.). 448p. 1997. text ed. write for info. (0-419-21550-6, E & FN Spon) Routledge Chapman & Hall.

Sonar Signal Processing. Richard O. Nielsen. (Artech House Acoustics Library). 445p. 1991. text ed. write for info. (0-89006-453-9) Artech Hse.

Sonar Signal Processing. Richard O. Nielsen. LC 91-3102. (Artech House Acoustics Library). 380p. 1991. reprint ed. pap. 108.30 (0-608-01418-4, 2062181) Bks Demand.

Sonar y Hacer. Rafael Arrillaga Torrens. LC 76-56437. (Coleccion Mente y Palabra). 176p. 1977. 5.00 (0-8477-0546-3); pap. 4.00 (0-8477-0547-1) U of PR Pr.

Sonata. F. Helena Marks. 1977. text ed. 16.95 (0-8369-8188-X) Ayer.

Sonata de Otono; Sonata de Invierno. Ramon Del Valle-Inclan. Ed. by Leda Schiavo. (Nueva Austral Ser.: Vol. 61). (SPA.). pap. 13.25 (84-239-1861-0) Elliots Bks.

Sonata de Otono; Sonata de Invierno. Ramon Del Valle-Inclan. (SPA.). 9.95 (0-8288-2582-3) Fr & Eur.

Sonata de Primavera. Sonata de Estio. Ramon Del Valle-Inclan. (Nueva Austral Ser.: Vol. 37). (SPA.). pap. 13.25 (84-239-1837-8) Elliots Bks.

*Sonata for a Mountain Man. Michael Mandrake. 244p. (Orig.). 1997. mass mkt. 4.99 (1-55237-041-0, Pub. by Comnwlth Pub CN) Partners Pubs Grp.

Sonata for a Spy. Alan Robbins. (Illus.). 8p. (C). 1991. 19.95 (0-922242-23-2) Bepuzzled.

Sonata for Bassoon & Piano. A. P. Etler. 28p. 1986. pap. 13.50 (0-7935-5239-7) H Leonard.

Sonata for Flute & Piano Opus 14. R. Muczynski. 32p. 1986. pap. 15.95 (0-7935-4437-8, 50336120) H Leonard.

Sonata for Horn & Piano. B. Heiden. 24p. 1986. pap. 15.00 (0-7935-3482-8) H Leonard.

Sonata for Piano, No. 3. Robert Starer. 24p. 1994. pap. 8.95 (0-7935-4202-2, 00120015) H Leonard.

Sonata for Recorder Quartet: For Recorder Quartet. Francis Poulenc. (Contemporary Consort Ser.: No. 11). i, 40p. 1990. pap. text ed. 12.00 (1-56571-013-4) PRB Prods.

Sonata for Sammy. Laura Gutman. (Illus.). 175p. (Orig.). (J). (gr. 6-8). 1996. pap. 12.95 (0-9651845-0-1) IDIM.

Sonata for Trumpet & Piano. Dello Joio. 28p. 1986. pap. 11.95 (0-7935-3720-7) H Leonard.

Sonata for Two Pianists. C. Bolling. 1990. 5.00 (0-685-32229-7, SIL50) Hansen Ed Mus.

Sonata for Two Pianists No. 1: Pianist No. 1 - Classical; Pianist No. 2 - Jazz String Bass, Percussion. C. Bolling. 68p. 1992. pap. 35.00 (0-7935-0054-0, 00490343) H Leonard.

Sonata for Two Pianists No. 2: Pianist No. 2 - Bass, Drums. C. Bolling. 1992. pap. text ed. 35.00 (0-7935-1198-4, 00490534) H Leonard.

Sonata for Viola (or Clarinet) & Piano. Marion Bauer. (Women Composers Ser.: No. 18). 50p. 1986. reprint ed. lib. bdg. 23.50 (0-306-76249-8) Da Capo.

Sonata for Viola (or Violincello) & Piano. Rebecca Clarke. (Women Composers Ser.: No. 20). 65p. 1986. reprint ed. lib. bdg. 32.50 (0-306-76251-X) Da Capo.

Sonata for Violin Cello & Piano 1948. E. Carter. 48p. 1986. pap. 18.00 (0-7935-1743-5) H Leonard.

Sonata Form. William H. Hadow. LC 74-24101. reprint ed. 37.50 (0-404-12943-9) AMS Pr.

Sonata Form: An Introduction. Cecil Hill. 160p. (Orig.). (C). 1987. pap. text ed. 14.95 (0-920490-70-0) Temeron Bks.

Sonata Forms. rev. ed. Charles Rosen. (Illus.). 352p. 1988. reprint ed. pap. 16.95 (0-393-30219-9) Norton.

Sonata in C: For Flute & Piano. 12p. pap. 6.95 (0-7935-5285-0, 50482258) H Leonard.

An Asterisk (*) at the beginning of an entry indicates that the title is appearing in BIP for the first time.

Sonata in C Minor, Opus 13, Piano Solo Sonata Pathetique. Ludwig van Beethoven. 24p. 1986. pap. 3.95 (0-7935-5296-6, 50266370) H Leonard.

Sonata in C Minor, Opus 21 see Three Piano Works

Sonata in D Major OP2 NO5: For Flute. M. Blavet. 24p. 1992. pap. 9.95 (0-7935-1584-X) H Leonard.

Sonata in E Minor: Piano Solo. 11.95 (0-7935-5130-7, 50482491) H Leonard.

Sonata in E Minor Opus 2 No. 3: Flute. M. Blavet. 16p. 1991. pap. 8.95 (0-7935-1206-9, 50488571) H Leonard.

Sonata in the Baroque Era. 4th ed. William S. Newman. (C). 1983. text ed. 18.95 (0-393-95275-4) Norton.

Sonata in the Classic Era. 3rd ed. William S. Newman. (C). 1983. text ed. 22.50 (0-393-95286-X) Norton.

Sonata, Its Form & Meaning as Exemplified in the Piano Sonatas by Mozart: A Descriptive Analysis. F. Helena Marks. 167p. 1990. reprint ed. lib. bdg. 59.00 (0-7812-9170-4) Rprt Serv.

Sonata No. 1 in F Minor, Opus 1: For Piano. S. Prokofiev. 16p. 1985. pap. 4.95 (0-7935-3035-0, 00121203) H Leonard.

Sonata No. 2 in D Minor, Opus 14. S. Prokofiev. 40p. 1985. pap. 5.95 (0-7935-2307-9, 00121204) H Leonard.

Sonata No. 3, Opus 46. D. Kabalevsky. 32p. 1985. pap. 7.95 (0-7935-2461-X, 00122077) H Leonard.

***Sonata No. 7 in B Flat Major, Opus 83.** 6.95 (0-7935-6402-6) H Leonard.

Sonata Number 6 in a Minor: For Flute. M. Blavet. 16p. 1992. pap. 9.95 (0-7935-1585-8) H Leonard.

Sonata of Icarus. Jurgis Gliauda. Tr. by Raphael Sealey. (Illus.). 1968. 5.00 (0-87141-024-9) Manyland.

Sonata Opus 147: Viola & Piano Library of Russian Soviet Music. Shostakovich. 44p. 1986. pap. 13.95 (0-7935-3864-5, 50335600) H Leonard.

Sonata Opus 167: Undine for No Flute & Piano Great Performer's Edition. C. Reinecke. 32p. 1986. otabind 10.95 (0-7935-1562-9, 50336260) H Leonard.

Sonata, Opus 94: For Flute or Violin & Piano. S. Prokofiev. 64p. 1985. pap. 10.95 (0-7935-1343-X, 00121734) H Leonard.

Sonata Per Arpeggione: Flute & Piano Great Performers Edition. Franz Schubert. 32p. 1986. pap. 9.95 (0-7935-5265-6, 50336180) H Leonard.

Sonata since Beethoven: The Third & Final Volume of a History of the Sonata Idea. William S. Newman. LC 76-80924. 880p. reprint ed. pap. 180.00 (0-8357-3860-4, 2036593) Bks Demand.

Sonata Violoncello & Piano. Weins Bolcom. 40p. 1993. pap. 28.00 (0-7935-1238-7, 00009240) H Leonard.

Sonatas: Centennial Edition. R. Schumann. 144p. 1994. 9.95 (0-7935-3068-7) H Leonard.

Sonatas & Sonatinas. Selected by Denes Agay. (Classics to Moderns Ser.: No. MFM67). (Illus.). 208p. pap. 12.95 (0-8256-4067-9, AM48737) Music Sales.

Sonatas for Four & Five Violins or Viols, Opp. 5. Giovanni B. Vitali. Ed. by George Houle. (Viol Consort Ser.: No. 8). ii, 55p. 1991. pap. text ed. 17.00 (1-56571-028-2) PRB Prods.

***Sonatas for Violin & Basso Continuo, Opus 1.** Jean-Marie Leclair. Ed. by Robert E. Preston. (Recent Researches in Music of the Baroque Era Ser.: Vol. RRB76). (Illus.). xxvi, 177p. (Orig.). 1995. pap. 62.40 (0-89579-324-5) A-R Eds.

***Sonatas for Violin & Basso Continuo, Opus 2.** Jean-Marie Leclair. Ed. by Robert E. Preston. (Recent Researches in Music of the Baroque Era Ser.: Vol. RRB58). (Illus.). xxi, 134p. (Orig.). 1988. pap. 48.00 (0-89579-220-6) A-R Eds.

Sonatas of Beethoven, As He Played & Taught Them. Kenneth Drake. LC 80-8608. 220p. reprint ed. pap. 63.60 (0-685-20427-8, 2056420) Bks Demand.

***Sonatas Rondos Fantasies.** Valenzu. 13.95 (0-486-29267-3) Dover.

Sonate: Guitar Solo. E. Denisov. 1987. 35.00 (0-7935-5550-7, 50541010) H Leonard.

Sonate a tre Stromenti: Six Notturnos for String Trio, Op. 7. Giovanni B. Sammartini. LC 80-12339. (Early Musical Masterworks Ser.). 192p. reprint ed. pap. 54.80 (0-8357-3898-1, 2036630) Bks Demand.

Sonate (12) d'Intavolatura per l'Organo e'l'Cemba see Monuments of Music & Music Literature in Facsimile: Series One

Sonatina Album for Piano: Centennial Edition. Ludwig van Beethoven. 64p. 1992. pap. 7.95 (0-7935-2023-1) H Leonard.

Sonatina Album for the Piano: 30 Favorite Sonatinas, Rondos & Pieces. 136p. 1986. per. 8.95 (0-7935-2553-5) H Leonard.

Sonatina No. 1 Opus 13 Piano Solo. D. Kabalevsky. 12p. 1986. pap. 3.95 (0-7935-3496-8, 50292060) H Leonard.

Sonatina, Opus 13, No. 1. D. Kabalevsky. 12p. 1985. pap. 5.95 (0-7935-0437-6, 00121135) H Leonard.

Sonatina 1959 Piano Solo. Aram Khatchaturian. 24p. 1986. pap. 5.95 (0-7935-5008-4, 50292050) H Leonard.

Soncino Books of the Bible, 14 vols., Set. 239.00 (1-871055-70-9) Bloch.

Soncino Chumash. rev. ed. A. Cohen. 1203p. 1993. 27.50 (0-900689-24-2) Soncino Pr.

Sondenos in War: The Story of the Sondeno Family of Turlock, California in World War II. Eric J. Narveson. (Illus.). 110p. (Orig.). 1996. pap. 11.95 (0-9650663-0-4, 1021) BEK Publns.

Sondereinheiten: Special Purpose. Christopher L. Clutter. (Illus.). 168p. (Orig.). 1995. mass mkt. 13.30 (0-9644321-2-9) Camel Dung Writ.

Sonderstab Musik: The Systematic Plundering of the Arts in Nazi-Occupied Europe. Wim De Vries. (Orig.). (C). 1995. pap. 54.50 (90-5356-175-7, Pub. by Amsterdam U Pr NE) U of Mich Pr.

Sondheim & Co. 2nd ed. Craig Zadan. (Illus.). 447p. 1994. pap. 19.95 (0-306-80601-0) Da Capo.

Sondheim's Broadway Musicals. Stephen Banfield. LC 93-12818. (Orig.). (C). 1995. pap. 27.95 (0-472-08083-0) U of Mich Pr.

***Sonet: A Guide to Synchronous Optical Network.** Walter Goralski. LC 97-19683. (Computer Communications Ser.). (Illus.). 500p. 1997. pap. text ed. 60.00 (0-07-024563-0) McGraw.

***SONET: The Third Wave.** 2,995.00 (0-614-26459-6) Info Gatekeepers.

SONET & Broadband Networking. IGIC, Inc. Staff. 200p. 1992. 1,995.00 (0-918435-61-7, IGIC-41) Info Gatekeepers.

SONET Basics. Toni Beninger. (Illus.). 80p. (Orig.). 1991. pap. 29.95 (0-917845-15-3) Intertec IL.

SONET Primer: A Course Workbook. Robert Brown. (Specialized Ser.). (Illus.). 47p. 1993. pap. 14.95 (1-56016-046-2) ABC TeleTraining.

Sonetos 'Al Italico Modo' de Inigo Lopez de Mendoza, Marques de Santillana. Ed. by Maxim P. Kerkhof & Dirk Tuin. (Spanish Ser.: No. 18). vi, 120p. 1985. 11.00 (0-942260-47-3) Hispanic Seminary.

SONET/SDH: An Overview of Synchronous Networking. Ed. by Curtis A. Siller, Jr. & Mansoor Shafi. LC 95-35418. 404p. 1996. 99.95 (0-7803-1168-X, PC4457) Inst Electrical.

Song. Brigit P. Kelly. (American Poets Continuum Ser.: No. 30). 90p. (Orig.). 1995. pap. 12.50 (1-880238-13-6) BOA Edns.

***Song: A Guide to Style & Literature.** Carol Kimball. 514p. 1996. pap. 45.00 (1-877761-68-0) Pst Inc.

Song: A Pigmy Legend. Jyl A. Kelley. (Illus.). 28p. (J). 1995. 35.00 (1-880515-53-9) Schl Mus Fine.

Song among the Ruins. William J. Schull. (Illus.). 336p. 1990. text ed. 32.00 (0-674-82042-8) HUP.

Song & Action: The Victory Odes of Pindar. Kevin Crotty. 176p. 1982. text ed. 30.00 (0-8018-2746-9) Johns Hopkins.

Song & Action: The Victory Odes of Pindar. Kevin Crotty. LC 81-48180. 189p. 1982. reprint ed. pap. 53.90 (0-608-00806-0, 2061594) Bks Demand.

Song & Counter-Song: Sceve's Delie & Petrarch's Rime. JoAnn DellaNeva. LC 83-81597. (French Forum Monographs: No. 49). 128p. (Orig.). 1983. pap. 10.95 (0-917058-49-6) French Forum.

Song & Dance: An Encyclopedia of Musicals. Sheryl Aumack. LC 89-92707. 462p. (C). 1990. spiral bd. 29.95 (0-9625180-1-8) Sea-Maid Pr.

Song & Dance: Poems. Illus. by Cheryl M. Taylor. LC 95-44841. (J). 1997. 16.00 (0-689-80159-9, S&S Bks Young Read) S&S Childrens.

Song & Dance: The Complete Story of Musicals. Kurt Ganzl. 224p. 1995. 19.98 (0-8317-1890-0) Smithmark.

Song & Dance: Vocal Selections. (Illus.). 096p. 1986. 12.95 (0-88188-444-8, 00361100) H Leonard.

Song & Dance Activities for Elementary Children's. Harriet R. Reeves. 1984. 17.95 (0-13-260613-5, Parker Publishing Co) P-H.

Song & Dance Activities for Elementary Children. Harriet R. Reeves. LC 85-12029. 241p. 1985. pap. text ed. 21.95 (0-13-822677-6, Busn) P-H.

Song & Dance Man. Karen Ackerman. LC 87-3200. (Illus.). 32p. (J). (ps-2). 1988. 15.00 (0-394-89330-1); lib. bdg. 15.99 (0-394-99330-6) Knopf Bks Yng Read.

Song & Democratic Culture in Britain. Ian Watson. LC 83-4591. 190p. 1983. text ed. 29.95 (0-312-74473-0) St Martin.

Song & Its Fountains. A. E. Russell. 112p. 1991. reprint ed. pap. 10.95 (0-943914-52-3) Larson Pubns.

Song & Silence: Voicing the Soul. Susan E. Hale. 254p. (Orig.). 1995. pap. 14.00 (0-9631909-3-8) La Alameda Pr.

***Song & Story in Biblical Narrative: The History of a Literary Convention in Ancient Israel.** LC 96-29526. (Indiana Studies in Biblical Literature). 1997. write for info. (0-253-33236-2) Ind U Pr.

***Song & the Silence: The Life of Stoney Indian Chief Frank Kequitts.** Peter Jonker. 224p. 1988. reprint ed. pap. 9.95 (0-919433-54-5) Lone Pine.

Song Anthology One. 3rd rev. ed. Anne L. Leyerle & William D. Leyerle. LC 79-90829. 159p. (J). (gr. 9 up). 1985. spiral bd. 12.95 (0-9602296-3-9) Leyerle Pubns.

Song at the Scaffold. rev. ed. Gertrud F. Von Le Fort. Ed. by Robert Knopp & Martin McMurtrey. (Illus.). (Orig.). 1954. pap. text ed. 4.95 (0-910334-24-2) Neumann Pr.

Song at the Sea: Being a Commentary on a Commentary in Two Parts. Judah Goldin. LC 73-140530. 312p. reprint ed. pap. 89.00 (0-8357-8326-X, 2033733) Bks Demand.

Song at the Sea: Being a Commentary on a Commentary in Two Parts. Judah Goldin. 312p. (C). 1990. reprint ed. pap. text ed. 12.95 (0-8276-0357-6) JPS Phila.

Song Between Two Stars. Gaston Puel. 6.75 (0-89253-770-1); 4.80 (0-89253-771-X) Ind-US Inc.

Song Bird Patterns. William Veasey. LC 82-62972. (Blue Ribbon Pattern Ser.: Bk. IV). (Illus.). 64p. 1983. pap. 14.95 (0-916838-79-X) Schiffer.

Song Birds. John P. Mackenzie. 1990. 24.95 (1-55971-091-8) NorthWord.

***Song by the River.** 2nd ed. Edna Gerstner. 154p. 1996. reprint ed. pap. 14.95 (1-57358-040-6) Soli Deo Gloria.

Song Celestial. Edwin Arnold. 1971. reprint ed. pap. 5.95 (0-8356-0418-7, Quest) Theos Pub Hse.

Song Celestial: Bhagavad-Gita. Tr. by Edwin Arnold from SAN. 176p. 1985. reprint ed. 6.50 (0-87612-210-1) Self Realization.

Song Classics of the Sixties. (Great Songs of the Century Ser.). 160p. (Orig.). 1994. pap. 14.95 (0-89724-231-9, VF2119) Warner Brothers.

Song Contests of Turkish Minstrels: Improvised Poetry Sung to Traditional Music. Yildiray Erdener. LC 94-17173. (Milman Parry Studies in Oral Tradition). (Illus.). 240p. 1994. text ed. 25.00 (0-8153-1239-3) Garland.

Song Crafters Tool Kit: The Basics, Special Gospel Music Edition, Vol. I. Adel Meisenheimer. 1987. Multi-media print/cassette. 39.95 incl. audio (0-944582-00-1) Song Crafters.

Song Crafters Tool Kit, the Basic, Vol. I. Ed. by Adel Meisenheimer. 1987. Multi-media print/cassette. 39.95 incl. audio (0-944582-02-8) Song Crafters.

Song, Dance, & Customs of Peasant Poland. Sula Benet. LC 96-13450. 1996. 24.95 (0-7818-0447-7) Hippocrene Bks.

Song, Dance, & Customs of Peasant Poland. Sula Benet. LC 76-44690. reprint ed. 37.50 (0-404-15906-0) AMS Pr.

***Song Dogs.** McCann. Date not set. pap. write for info. (0-8050-4105-2) St Martin.

Song Dynasty Poems. John Knoepfle & Wang Shouyi. 73p. (CHI & ENG.). 1986. 11.95 (0-933180-85-3); pap. 4.95 (0-933180-82-9) Spoon Riv Poetry.

Song Finder: A Title Index to 32,000 Popular Songs in Collections, 1854-1992. Ed. by Gary L. Ferguson. LC 95-9936. (Music Reference Collection: No. 46). 344p. 1995. text ed. 79.50 (0-313-29470-4, Greenwood Pr) Greenwood.

Song for a Linnet. large type ed. Juliet Gray. 1996. pap. 19.95 (0-7862-0798-1, Thorndike Lrg Prnt) Thorndike Pr.

***Song for a Raggy Boy: A Cork Boyhood.** P. Galvin. 112p. 9100. pap. 10.95 (1-85186-100-9) Dufour.

Song for a Shadow. Bernie Mackinnon. LC 90-39647. 320p. (YA). (gr. 7 up). 1991. 18.00 (0-395-55419-5) HM.

Song for All Seasons. Libby Stopple. Ed. by R. H. Dromgoole & Alison Heinemann. LC 77-89399. (Illus.). 1977. 7.95 (0-913632-15-5); pap. 5.95 (0-913632-13-9) All Things Pr.

Song for All Seasons: Harmony in the Inner Life. Marion K. Rich. 100p. (Orig.). 1992. pap. 6.99 (0-8341-1446-1) Beacon Hill.

Song for Anninho. Gayl Jones. LC 80-85231. 88p. 1981. per. 4.50 (0-916418-26-X) Lotus.

Song for Arbonne. Guy G. Kay. 496p. 1994. pap. 5.99 (0-451-45332-8, ROC) NAL-Dutton.

Song for Ben. 1988. pap. 3.50 (0-19-421902-X) OUP.

***Song for Cecilia Fantini.** Cynthia Astor. LC 96-37539. (Illus.). 32p. (J). (ps-5). 1997. 14.95 (0-915811-75-8, Starseed) H J Kramer Inc.

Song for Children. (Easy Play Ser.: Vol. 155). 1990. pap. 4.95 (0-7935-0166-0) H Leonard.

Song for Grandmother. Dorothy Miller. Ed. by Mary B. Steel. 187p. (Orig.). 1990. pap. 9.95 (1-878993-00-3) Jeremiah Films.

Song for Lena. Hilary H. Hippely. LC 95-44064. (Illus.). (J). 1996. 16.00 (0-689-80763-5) S&S Childrens.

Song for Little Toad. Vivian French. (Illus.). 32p. (YA). (gr. 3 up). 1995. 14.99 (1-56402-614-0) Candlewick Pr.

Song for Mother Earth. Howard Rainer. LC 95-23009. (Illus.). 192p. 1996. pap. 34.95 (0-89802-661-X) Beautiful Am.

Song for Natalie. Heribert Breidenbach. 159p. (Orig.). 1995. pap. 11.95 (1-882792-08-4) Proctor Pubns.

Song for Nobody: A Memory Vision of Thomas Merton. Ron Seitz. (Illus.). 192p. (Orig.). 1995. reprint ed. pap. 10.95 (0-89243-779-0, Triumph Books) Liguori Pubns.

Song for One or Two: Music & the Concept of Art in Early China. Kenneth J. DeWoskin. LC 81-19519. (Michigan Monographs in Chinese Studies: No. 42). (Illus.). 202p. (Orig.). (C). 1982. pap. text ed. 15.00 (0-89264-042-1) Ctr Chinese Studies.

Song for Robbie. Dorothy Dunbar. LC 96-22158. 55p. (Orig.). 1996. pap. 5.00 (0-88734-362-7) Players Pr.

Song for Sarah: A Young Mother's Journey Through Grief & Beyond. Paula D'Arcy. LC 95-10816. 124p. 1995. 12.99 (0-87788-762-4) Shaw Pubs.

***Song for Silas.** Lori Wick. (A Place Called Home Ser.). 204p. 1996. pap. 8.99 (1-56507-589-7) Harvest Hse.

***Song for Summer.** Ibbotson. Date not set. write for info. (0-312-18181-7) St Martin.

Song for the Ancient Forest. Nancy Luenn. LC 91-17187. (Illus.). 32p. (J). (gr. k-3). 1993. lib. bdg. 14.95 (0-689-31719-0, Atheneum Bks Young) S&S Childrens.

***Song for the Asking.** Gannon. 1997. 22.95 (0-553-47791-9) Bantam.

Song for the Asking. Steve Gannon. LC 96-28804. 448p. 1997. 22.95 (0-553-10164-1) Bantam.

***Song for the Nations.** 1988. 1.20 (0-8341-9013-3) Nazarene.

Song for the Navigator. Michael Cowell. 1993. pap. 5.25 (0-87129-185-1, S37) Dramatic Pub.

Song for the Prince. Lisa Latella. (Illus.). 36p. (Orig.). (J). (gr. k up). 1984. pap. write for info. (0-9608592-1-7) Gallery Arts.

Song for the White Rider. Shirley Starke. (Illus.). 28p. (Orig.). (C). 1991. pap. text ed. 10.95 (0-913741-06-X) T B Thomassen.

Song for Three Viols. William Presser. (Contemporary Consort Ser.: No. 20). 7p. 1992. pap. text ed. 6.00 (1-56571-057-6, CC020) PRB Prods.

Song for Three Voices. Curt Johnson. LC 84-11345. 276p. (Orig.). 1984. pap. 12.50 (0-914140-13-2) Carpenter Pr.

Song from the Starting Tree. Adam C. Moore. 48p. 1986. 9.00 (0-7223-2034-5, Pub. by A H S Ltd UK) St Mut.

Song Full of Children. Robert B. Hale. LC 94-11979. (J). Date not set. write for info. (0-688-12218-3); lib. bdg. write for info. (0-688-12219-1) Lothrop.

Song Games from Trinidad & Tobago. J. D. Elder. LC 64-25264. (American Folklore Society Bibliographical & Special Ser.: No. 16). 119p. 1965. pap. 5.95 (0-292-73508-1) U of Tex Pr.

Song Goes On. 1990. 9.95 (0-910452-70-9) Covenant.

Song Heard in a Strange Land: Narcissa Her Story, Bk. 1. Marje Blood. LC 85-81462. 220p. 1985. pap. 9.95 (0-9615233-1-X) Image Imprints.

Song Hits from the Turn of the Century. Paul Charosh & Robert Fremont. LC 74-20444. 296p. 1975. pap. 8.95 (0-486-23158-5) Dover.

Song in a Strange Land. Rosemary Haughton. 180p. 1990. pap. 14.95 (0-87243-188-6) Templegate.

Song in a Strange Land. Gilbert Morris. (Liberty Bell Ser.: Vol. 2). 320p. (Orig.). 1996. pap. 9.99 (1-55661-566-3) Bethany Hse.

Song in a Weary Throat; an American Pilgrimage see Autobiography of a Black Activist, Feminist, Lawyer, Priest, & Poet

Song in My Heart: Selected Creative Works. Jeanne M. Blanchette. LC 88-50616. (Illus.). 70p. (Orig.). 1988. pap. 8.95 (0-9620908-0-8) Kokoro Enter.

Song in the Dark: The Birth of the Musical Film. Richard Barrios. (Illus.). 448p. 1995. pap. 21.95 (0-19-508811-5) OUP.

Song in the Green Thorn Tree: A Novel of the Life & Loves of Robert Burns. James Barke. 512p. 9300. pap. 13.95 (0-85640-484-5, Pub. by Blackstaff Pr IE) Dufour.

Song in the Night: Selections from the Spiritual Canticle of St. John of the Cross. St. John of the Cross. Ed. by St. Patricia of the Resurrection. (Illus.). 120p. 1991. pap. 12.95 (0-940147-15-7) Source Bks CA.

Song in the Silence. Elizabeth K. Bridges. 1996. write for info. (0-615-00548-9) Tor Bks.

***Song in the Silence: The Tale of Lanen Kaelar.** Elizabeth Kerner. LC 96-29345. 1996. 23.95 (0-312-85780-2) Tor Bks.

Song in the South see Saint Francis Solano: Wonder-Worker of the New World & Apostle of Argentina & Peru

Song in the Story: Lyric Insertions in French Narrative Fiction, 1200-1400. Maureen Boulton. LC 93-22097. (Middle Ages Ser.). 352p. (C). 1993. text ed. 41.95 (0-8122-3199-6) U of Pa Pr.

Song Index. Minnie E. Sears & Phyllis Crawford. 650p. 1990. reprint ed. lib. bdg. 109.00 (0-7812-9019-8) Rprt Serv.

Song Irving Berlin, Vol. 330. 176p. 1992. otabind 14.95 (0-7935-0441-4, 00001582) H Leonard.

Song Is a Rainbow: Movement, Music, & Rhythm Instruments in the Nursery School & Kindergarten. Patty Zeitlin. (Illus.). 270p. (Orig.). 1992. pap. 16.95 (0-673-16460-8, GoodYrBooks) Addson-Wesley Educ.

Song Is Ended. large type ed. Margaret Allan. (Dales Romance Ser.). 204p. 1993. pap. 17.99 (1-85389-379-X) Ulverscroft.

Song Is Ended: Songwriters & American Music, 1900-1950. William G. Hyland. (Illus.). 320p. 1995. 25.00 (0-19-508611-2) OUP.

Song Lee & Leech Man. Suzy Kline. LC 94-39231. (Illus.). 53p. (J). (gr. 1-3). 1995. pap. 11.99 (0-670-85848-X, Viking) Viking Penguin.

***Song Lee & Leech Man.** Suzy Kline. (J). (gr. 1-3). 1997. pap. 3.99 (0-14-037255-5) Viking Penguin.

Song Lee & the Hamster Hunt. Suzy Kline. 64p. (J). (gr. 2-5). 1996. pap. 3.50 (0-14-036317-3) Puffin Bks.

Song Lee & the Hamster Hunt. Suzy Kline. (Illus.). 64p. (J). (gr. 2-6). 1994. pap. 12.99 (0-670-84773-9) Viking Child Bks.

Song Lee in Room Two B. Suzy Kline. (Illus.). 64p. (J). (gr. 2-5). 1993. pap. 12.99 (0-670-84772-0) Viking Child Bks.

Song Lee in Room 2B. Suzy Kline. 1995. pap. 2.99 (0-14-036316-5) Puffin Bks.

Song-Lines of a Day. Narendra Sethi. 8.00 (0-89253-737-X); 4.80 (0-89253-738-8) Ind-US Inc.

Song List: A Guide to Contemporary Music from Classical Sources. Ed. by James L. Limbacher. LC 73-78293. 1973. 16.50 (0-87650-041-6) Pierian.

Song Lyrics of Simple Love. 2nd ed. Harry J. Vassilion. 1981. write for info. (0-318-56333-9) Vassilion.

Song Made Out of a Pale Smoke. Bruce Renner. LC 81-15617. 51p. text ed. 9.95 (0-934332-37-1); pap. text ed. 4.95 (0-934332-36-3) LEpervier Pr.

Song No One Liked. Nelson A. Ossorio & Michele B. Salvadeo. (To Be Your Own Ser.). (Illus.). 48p. (J). (gr. 3-5). 1994. pap. 6.95 (1-56721-050-3) Twnty-Fifth Cent Pr.

***Song of a Dark Angel.** large type ed. P. C. Doherty. (Large Print Ser.). 400p. 1996. 25.99 (0-7089-3611-3) Ulverscroft.

Song of a Dark Angel: A Medieval Mystery Featuring Hugh Corbett. P. C. Doherty. 1995. 21.95 (0-312-13605-6) St Martin.

Song of a Fatherless Child. Ginny Knight. 70p. (Orig.). 1994. pap. 10.00 (0-9635690-6-6) TA Pubns.

Song of a Prisoner. Okot P'Bitek. (Illus.). 128p. 1971. 15.95 (0-89388-004-3); pap. 9.95 (0-685-42289-5) Okpaku Communications.

Song of a Simple, Separate Person: A Learning Styles Workbook. Steven L. Berg. (Illus.). (Orig.). (C). 1995. pap. 10.00 (0-9642273-0-4) Back Porch Pr.

Song of a Soldier's Wife. Dang Tran Con & Phan Huy Ich. Tr. by Huynh Sanh Thong. LC 85-73465. (Lac-Viet Ser.: No. 3). (Illus.). 118p. 1986. pap. 10.00 (0-938692-24-0) Yale U SE Asia.

***Song of a Soul.** Lawana Blackwell. LC 96-47577. (Victorian Serenade Ser.: Bk. 4). 1997. pap. 10.99 (0-8423-7965-7) Tyndale.

Song of a Soul. Alban M. Emley. 96p. 1973. pap. 5.95 (0-911336-76-1) Sci of Mind.

Song of a Water Dragon. Norman S. Track. Ed. by Andrew D. Murray. LC 95-61879. (Illus.). 160p. 1996. 15.00 (1-886969-27-2, B024) YMAA Pubn.

Song of Abraham. Ellen G. Traylor. 456p. 1995. pap. 11.99 (0-8423-5975-3) Tyndale.

Song of Africa. Ronald Wheatley. LC 83-22311. 1989. pap. 13.95 (0-87949-239-2) Ashley Bks.

An Asterisk (*) at the beginning of an entry indicates that the title is appearing in BIP for the first time.

Song of Be. Lesley Beake. 112p. (YA). (gr. 7 up). 1993. 14.95 (*0-8050-2905-2*, Bks Young Read) H Holt & Co.
Song of Be. Lesley Beake. LC 94-44587. 1995. pap. 3.99 (*0-14-037498-1*) Puffin Bks.
Song of Bernadette. large type ed. Franz Werfel. 1988. pap. 8.95 (*0-8027-2625-9*) Walker & Co.
Song of Bernadette. Franz Werfel. Tr. by Ludwig Lewisohn. reprint ed. lib. bdg. 32.95 (*0-88411-720-0*) Amereon Ltd.
Song of Bernadette. Franz Werfel. 1990. reprint ed. lib. bdg. 28.95 (*0-89968-558-7*) Buccaneer Bks.
Song of Bernadette. Franz V. Werfel. (Religious Miracles Ser.). 576p. 1989. reprint ed. pap. 13.95 (*0-312-03429-6*) St Martin.
Song of Brotherhood. Eric Doyle. (Pathways Ser.). 205p. 1996. pap. write for info. (*1-57659-003-8*) Franciscan Inst.
Song of Chirimia - La Musica de la Chirimia: A Guatemalan Folktale - Folklore Guatemalteco. Jane A. Volkmer. (Illus.). 40p. (ENG & SPA.). (J). (ps-3). 1990. lib. bdg. 14.96 (*0-87614-423-7*, Carolrhoda) Lerner Group.
*__Song of Colors.__ Judy Hindley. LC 97-6761. (Illus.). (J). 1998. write for info. (*0-7636-0320-1*) Candlewick Pr.
Song of Courage, Song of Freedom: The Story of Mary Campbell. Marilyn Seguin. (Illus.). 120p. (Orig.). (YA). (gr. 4-9). 1993. pap. 12.95 (*0-8283-1952-9*) Branden Pub Co.
Song of Daniel. Philip L. Williams. 320p. 1989. 17.95 (*0-934601-75-5*) Peachtree Pubs.
Song of David. Shelia Allison. (Great Big Bks.). (Illus.). 16p. (J). 1995. pap. 14.95 (*0-687-07065-1*) Abingdon.
Song of David: The Moss Haggadah, 2. David Moss. (Illus.). 340p. (ENG & HEB.). 1987. pap. write for info. (*0-9624473-2-3*) Bet Alpha Editions.
Song of David: The Moss Haggadah, I. David Moss. (Illus.). 340p. (ENG & HEB.). 1987. write for info. (*0-9624473-1-5*) Bet Alpha Editions.
Song of David: The Moss Haggadah, Set, Vols. 1 & 2. deluxe limited ed. David Moss. LC 87-206430. (Illus.). 340p. (ENG & HEB.). 1987. Set. pap. 6,500.00 (*0-9624473-0-7*) Bet Alpha Editions.
Song of Degree. Stephen Kaung. Tr. by Carl Fang from ENG. (CHI.). 1983. pap. write for info. (*0-941598-12-8*) Living Spring Pubns.
Song of el Coqui & Other Tales of Puerto Rico. Nicholasa Mohr. LC 94-43075. (Illus.). (J). 1995. pap. 15.99 (*0-670-85837-4*, Viking) Viking Penguin.
Song of El Coqui & Other Tales of Puerto Rico. Nicholasa Mohr. (Illus.). 1995. pap. 15.99 (*0-670-86296-7*, Viking) Viking Penguin.
Song of Enlightenment. Ch'an Master Yung Chia. Tr. by Buddhist Text Translation Society Staff from CHI. (Illus.). 85p. (Orig.). 1983. pap. 5.00 (*0-88139-100-X*) Buddhist Text.
Song of Erne. Robert Harbinson. 244p. 1988. pap. 9.95 (*0-85640-394-6*, Pub. by Blackstaff Pr IE) Dufour.
Song of Eros: Ancient Greek Love Poems. Tr. by Bradley P. Nystrom. LC 90-35758. (Illus.). 120p. (C). 1990. 15.95 (*0-8093-1640-4*) S Ill U Pr.
*__Song of Eskasoni: More Poems of Rita Joe.__ Rita Joe. 88p. 1989. pap. 9.95 (*0-920304-85-0*, Pub. by Gynergy-Ragweed CN) LPC InBook.
Song of Eve. June Strong. Ed. by Gerald Wheeler. 160p. 1987. 2.50 (*0-8280-0388-2*) Review & Herald.
Song of Everything. 2nd ed. Tracy Leddy. (Illus.). 160p. 1995. pap. 16.00 (*0-9649601-5-X*) Quail Hill.
Song of Faith & Praise: Accompaniment Edition Hymnal. 1030p. 1995. ring bd. 54.99 (*1-878990-45-4*) Howard Pub LA.
Song of Fire. Joseph Bentz. 448p. (Orig.). 1995. pap. 12.99 (*0-7852-7882-6*) Nelson.
Song of Fourteen Songs. M. D. Goulder. pap. 16.95 (*0-905774-87-6*, Pub. by Sheffield Acad UK) CUP Services.
Song of God. Bhagavad-Gita. Tr. by Swami Prabhavananda & Christopher Isherwood. 1954. pap. 5.99 (*0-451-62757-1*, Ment) NAL-Dutton.
Song of God. Eugene E. Whitworth. 101p. 1988. pap. 4.00 (*0-944155-02-2*) Grt Western Univ.
Song of God: A Summary Study of Bhagavad-Gita. Swami Bhaktipada. LC 84-45783. (Illus.). 304p. 1987. 11.95 (*0-932215-09-2*); pap. 7.95 (*0-932215-00-9*) Palace Pub.
Song of God: Bagavad-Gita. Swami Prabhavananda. Tr. by Christopher Isherwood. 1989. pap. 3.50 (*0-451-62671-0*) NAL-Dutton.
Song of Heyoehkah. Hyemeyohsts Storm. 320p. 1983. pap. 16.00 (*0-345-30731-3*, Ballantine Trade) Ballantine.
Song of Hiawatha. Adapted by R. Eugene Jackson. (Illus.). 44p. (Orig.). (J). (gr. 2 up). 1988. pap. 4.50 (*0-88680-302-0*) I E Clark.
Song of Hiawatha. Henry Wadsworth Longfellow. Ed. by Daniel Aaron. 176p. 1993. pap. 2.95 (*0-460-87268-0*, Everyman's Classic Lib) C E Tuttle.
Song of Hiawatha: Piano-Vocal Score. Adapted by R. Eugene Jackson. (Illus.). 44p. (Orig.). (J). (gr. 2 up). 1988. 15.00 (*0-88680-303-9*) I E Clark.
Song of Homana. Jennifer Roberson. (Chronicles of the Cheysuli Ser.: Bk. 2). 352p. 1985. mass mkt. 5.99 (*0-88677-434-9*) DAW Bks.
Song of Hope. Illus. by Flavia. 32p. 1993. 6.95 (*0-8362-4702-7*) Andrews & McMeel.
*__Song of Horse.__ Murray. Date not set. write for info. (*0-312-86123-0*) St Martin.
Song of Igor's Campaign. Tr. by Vladimir Nabokov from RUS. 135p. 1989. reprint ed. pap. 9.95 (*0-87501-061-X*) Ardis Pubs.
Song of India. Intro. by Bruce Carlson. (Illus.). 40p. (Orig.). 1992. pap. 5.00 (*0-912373-06-7*) Schubert.
Song of India. H. Jay Dinshah. (Illus.). 104p. 1973. 4.95 (*0-942401-01-8*); pap. 3.95 (*0-942401-02-6*) Am Vegan Soc.
Song of India. Anees Jung. 255p. (C). 1990. 75.00 (*81-7002-055-7*, Pub. by Himalayan Bks II) St Mut.
Song of Iowa: Iowa - Its Beauty - Bounty - Diversity. Jan Flaming. (Illus.). 400p. (Orig.). 1996. pap. 40.00 (*0-9649668-3-2*) Iowa Legends.
Song of Jacob Zulu. Tug Yourgrau. LC 93-2327. (Illus.). 128p. 1993. 19.95 (*1-55970-237-0*); pap. 10.95 (*1-55970-238-9*) Arcade Pub Inc.
Song of Joy & Echoes of Love, 2 bks. in 1. Elaine L. Schulte. (Romance Reader Ser.: No. 5). 7.95 (*1-55748-143-1*) Barbour & Co.
Song of Joy & Other Poems. Alan Rickard. (Australian Collection). pap. 7.00 (*0-936128-13-5*) De Young Pr.
Song of Joy & Other Poems. Byron H. Reece. LC 85-22355. 128p. 1985. reprint ed. 15.95 (*0-87797-105-6*) Cherokee.
Song of Kali. Dan Simmons. 1991. mass mkt. 4.99 (*0-8125-1592-7*) Tor Bks.
*__Song of Karmapa.__ Chokyi N. Rinpoche. 128p. 1996. pap. 12.95 (*962-7341-14-2*, Pub. by Rang Jung Yshe HK) Bookpeople.
Song of Krsna. Ed. by Deben Bhattacharya. LC 77-9240. (Illus.). 195p. 1978. pap. 5.95 (*0-87728-422-9*) Weiser.
Song of Lake Trahlyta. Sylvia D. Turnage. 9p. (Orig.). 1995. pap. text ed. 3.75 (*1-880726-06-8*) Turnage Pub.
Song of Lawino & Song of Ocol. Okot P'Bitek. (African Writers Ser.: No. 266). (Illus.). 151p. (C). 1984. reprint ed. pap. 9.95 (*0-435-90266-0*, 90266) Heinemann.
*__Song of Life.__ deluxe ed. Sushil K. Gupta. (Illus.). Date not set. lib. bdg. 50.00 (*0-614-24296-7*) Sverge-Haus.
Song of Life. Charles Johnston. 69p. 1983. reprint ed. pap. 3.95 (*0-912181-00-1*) East School Pr.
Song of Longing: An Ethiopian Journey. Kay K. Shelemay. 208p. 1992. text ed. 29.95 (*0-252-01798-6*) U of Ill Pr.
Song of Longing: An Ethiopian Journey. Kay K. Shelemay. 208p. (C). 1994. pap. text ed. 12.95 (*0-252-06432-1*) U of Ill Pr.
Song of Louise in the Morning. Patricia Joudry. 1961. pap. 3.25 (*0-8222-1057-6*) Dramatists Play.
Song of Love. Tr. by George Keyt. Orig. Title: Gita Govinda. 123p. 1969. pap. 2.00 (*0-88253-048-8*) Ind-US Inc.
Song of Love & Death: The Meaning of Opera. Peter Conrad. LC 96-75707. (Graywolf Rediscovery Ser.). 384p. 1996. reprint ed. pap. 16.00 (*1-55597-241-1*) Graywolf.
Song of Madness & Other Poems. Ed. by Yvette E. Miller. Tr. by Frances R. Aparicio. LC 85-11. 160p. (ENG & SPA.). 1985. pap. 12.95 (*0-935480-18-8*) Lat Am Lit Rev Pr.
Song of Mary & David: A Romance. Charles Wolcott. LC 94-76240. 254p. 1994. 18.50 (*0-9640881-4-2*); pap. 10.50 (*0-9640881-3-4*) Luna Press.
Song of Miriam: And Other Stories, Vol. 1. Marie Corelli. LC 71-37263. (Short Story Index Reprint Ser.). 1977. reprint ed. 18.95 (*0-8369-4074-1*) Ayer.
Song of Miriam & Other Stories. Marie Corelli. 234p. 1996. pap. 18.95 (*1-56459-760-1*) Kessinger Pub.
Song of Miriam & Other Stories. Marie Corelli. 234p. 1971. reprint ed. spiral bd. 10.00 (*0-7873-0215-5*) Hlth Research.
Song of Moses: A Theological Quarry. George A. Knight. 176p. 1995. pap. text ed. 13.00 (*0-8028-0599-X*) Eerdmans.
Song of Motley: Being the Reminiscences of a Hungry Tenor. Leo Slezak. Ed. by Andrew Farkas. LC 76-29968. (Opera Biographies Ser.). (Illus.). 1977. reprint ed. lib. bdg. 26.95 (*0-405-09707-7*) Ayer.
Song of Mu Lan. Jeanne M. Lee. LC 95-9594. (Illus.). 40p. (J). (gr. k-5). Date not set. 15.95 (*1-886910-00-6*, Front Street) Front Str.
Song of Muhammad. M. R. Muhaiyaddeen. 300p. 1996. pap. 17.00 (*0-914390-50-3*); text ed. 23.00 (*0-914390-49-X*) Fellowship Pr PA.
Song of My Life: A Journey to the Feet of Sathya Sai Baba. Jeannette Caruth. 128p. (Orig.). 1996. pap. 9.00 (*0-9629835-8-6*) Leela Pr.
Song of Myself. Walt Whitman. Ed. by Stephen Mitchell. LC 93-20168. (Pocket Classics Ser.). 140p. (Orig.). 1993. pap. 6.00 (*0-87773-950-1*) Shambhala Pubns.
Song of Napalm. Bruce Weigl. LC 88-6161. 70p. 1991. pap. 10.95 (*0-87113-471-3*, Atlntc Mnthly) Grove-Atltic.
Song of Nightingale: An Anthology of Modern Soviet Short Stories. Margrita A. Belai et al. Tr. by Y. C. Bhatnagar. 214p. (C). 1987. 17.50 (*81-202-0189-2*, Pub. by Ajanta II) S Asia.
Song of Norway. (Vocal Score Ser.). 232p. 1981. pap. 40.00 (*0-88188-211-9*, 00312387) H Leonard.
Song of Norway - Motion Picture Only: Vocal Selections. 1983. 7.95 (*0-88188-112-0*, 00447068) H Leonard.
Song of Orpheus. Barbara Hambly. (Beauty & the Beast Ser.). 1990. pap. 3.95 (*0-380-75798-2*) Avon.
Song of Our Syrian Guest. William A. Knight. LC 72-4580. 48p. 1972. 7.95 (*0-8298-0834-5*) Pilgrim OH.
Song of Percival Peacock. Russell Edson. LC 92-22804. 144p. (Orig.). 1992. pap. 11.95 (*1-56689-002-0*) Coffee Hse.
Song of Power & the Power of Song: Essays on the Book of Deuteronomy. Ed. by Duane L. Christensen. LC 93-6413. (Sources for Biblical & Theological Study Ser.: No. 3). xiv, 418p. 1993. 37.95 (*0-931464-74-9*) Eisenbrauns.
Song of Rising Consciousness: Poem of Animal Rights. Chuck Taylor. 24p. 1989. pap. 3.00 (*0-941720-76-4*) Slough Pr TX.
Song of Rita Joe: Autobiography of a Mi'Kmaq Poet. Rita Joe. (American Indian Lives Ser.). (Illus.). 199p. 1996. pap. 16.00 (*0-8032-7594-3*, Bison Books) U of Nebr Pr.
*__Song of Rita Joe: Autobiography of a Mi'kmaq Poet.__ Rita Joe. (Illus.). 208p. 1996. pap. 16.95 (*0-921556-59-4*, Pub. by Gynergy-Ragweed CN) LPC InBook.
Song of Roland. Tr. & Intro. by Glyn S. Burgess. (Classics Ser.). 224p. 1990. pap. 8.95 (*0-14-044532-3*, Penguin Classics) Viking Penguin.
Song of Roland. Tr. by Frederick Goldin. (C). 1978. pap. text ed. 6.95 (*0-393-09008-6*) Norton.
Song of Roland. Tr. by Robert Harrison. 1970. pap. 5.99 (*0-451-62822-5*, Ment) NAL-Dutton.
Song of Roland. Tr. by D. D. Owen from FRE. (Illus.). 166p. (C). 1990. 28.00 (*0-85115-537-5*) Boydell & Brewer.
Song of Roland. Tr. by Dorothy L. Sayers. (Classics Ser.). 208p. (Orig.). (YA). (gr. 9 up). 1957. pap. 11.95 (*0-14-044075-5*, Penguin Classics) Viking Penguin.
Song of Roland. 2nd ed. Patricia Terry. (Library of Liberal Arts). (Illus.). 176p. (C). 1992. pap. text ed. 13.00 (*0-02-419835-8*, Macmillan Coll) P-H.
Song of Roland: An Analytical Edition - Introduction & Commentary, 2 vols., 1. Ed. by Gerard J. Brault. Tr. by Gerard Brault. (Illus.). (C). 1978. 35.00 (*0-271-00516-5*) Pa St U Pr.
Song of Roland: An Analytical Edition - Oxford Text & English Translation, 2 vols., 2. Ed. by Gerard J. Brault. Tr. by Gerard Brault. (Illus.). (C). 1978. 25.00 (*0-271-00204-2*) Pa St U Pr.
Song of Roland: Formulaic Style & Poetic Craft. Joseph J. Duggan. LC 75-186101. (Center for Medieval & Renaissance Studies, UCLA: Contribution: No. 6). 1973. 42.00 (*0-520-02201-7*) U CA Pr.
Song of Sacajawea. Rabbit. 1997. pap. 19.95 (*0-689-80233-1*) Macmillan.
Song of Salvation: The Magnificat. Isidro Goma-Civit. (C). 1988. 39.00 (*0-85439-260-2*, Pub. by St Paul Pubns UK) St Mut.
Song of Scotland. (Illus.). 80p. 1972. pap. 8.95 (*0-86001-195-X*, AM11446) Music Sales.
Song of Sedna. Illus. by Daniel San Souci. 32p. (J). (gr. 5-9). 1994. 15.95 (*0-385-15866-1*) Doubleday.
Song of Sedna. Robert D. San Souci & Daniel San Souci. (Illus.). 32p. (J). (gr. 1-4). 1989. pap. 5.99 (*0-440-40948-9*) Dell.
Song of Sirius. Dorothy McManus. Ed. by M. Myhre. 155p. (Orig.). (YA). 1990. pap. 8.00 (*0-929686-01-2*) Temple Golden Pubns.
Song of Sixpence. A. J. Cronin. 1992. reprint ed. lib. bdg. 18.95 (*0-89966-965-4*) Buccaneer Bks.
Song of Solomon. Henry A. Ironside. (Ironside Commentaries Ser.). Date not set. pap. 9.99 (*0-87213-405-9*) Loizeaux.
Song of Solomon. Toni Morrison. 1977. 18.95 (*0-394-49784-8*) Knopf.
Song of Solomon. Toni Morrison. 352p. 1978. pap. 4.50 (*0-451-12933-4*, AE2933, Sig) NAL-Dutton.
Song of Solomon. Toni Morrison. LC 87-5809. 320p. 1987. pap. 11.95 (*0-452-26011-6*, Plume) NAL-Dutton.
Song of Solomon. Toni Morrison. 1989. pap. 4.50 (*0-451-15261-1*) NAL-Dutton.
Song of Solomon. Toni Morrison. 1995. 20.00 (*0-679-44504-8*) Knopf.
Song of Solomon. Toni Morrison. 1993. pap. 5.99 (*0-451-18237-5*, Sig) NAL-Dutton.
Song of Solomon. O. Talmadge Spence. 272p. 1996. 19.95 (*1-882542-14-2*) Fndtns NC.
Song of Solomon. Donald J. Wiseman. LC 83-22651. (Tyndale Old Testament Commentary Ser.). 175p. (C). 1984. pap. 11.99 (*0-87784-268-X*, 268) InterVarsity.
Song of Solomon. Ed. by Donald J. Wiseman & G. Lloyd Carr. LC 83-22651. (Tyndale Old Testament Commentary Ser.). 175p. (C). 1984. 18.99 (*0-87784-918-8*, 918) InterVarsity.
Song of Solomon. James Durham. (Geneva Commentaries Ser.). 460p. 1982. reprint ed. 21.99 (*0-85151-352-2*) Banner of Truth.
Song of Solomon. Toni Morrison. 1995. reprint ed. lib. bdg. 24.95 (*1-56849-632-X*) Buccaneer Bks.
Song of Songs. Sholom Aleichem. LC 96-22670. (Illus.). 112p. 1996. 22.00 (*0-684-81486-2*) S&S Trade.
Song of Songs. John F. Brug. LC 94-74992. 96p. 1995. 16.99 (*0-8100-0542-5*, 15N2003) Northwest Pub.
*__Song of Songs.__ Jeanne Guyon. 221p. (Orig.). 1997. mass mkt. 4.99 (*0-88368-404-7*) Whitaker Hse.
Song of Songs. Beverley Hughesdon. 1990. 19.95 (*0-446-51543-4*) Warner Bks.
Song of Songs. Beverley Hughesdon. 1991. mass mkt. 5.95 (*0-446-36098-8*) Warner Bks.
*__Song of Songs.__ Peter Jay & David Goldstein. 64p. 1997. pap. 14.95 (*0-85646-286-1*, Pub. by Anvil Press UK) Dufour.
Song of Songs. Roland E. Murphy. LC 89-16891. (Hermeneia: A Critical & Historical Commentary on the Bible Ser.). 176p. 1990. 29.00 (*0-8006-6024-2*, 1-6024) Augsburg Fortress.
Song of Songs. Watchman Nee. 1992. pap. 6.95 (*0-87508-442-7*) Chr Lit.
Song Of Songs. Watchman Nee. 129p. per. 5.00 (*0-87083-872-5*, 07048001) Living Stream Ministry.
Song of Songs. Intro. by Marvin H. Pope. LC 72-79417. (Anchor Bible Ser.: Vol. 7C). (Illus.). 768p. 1977. 44.95 (*0-385-00569-5*, Anchor NY) Doubleday.
Song of Songs. Marcia Falk. LC 90-80329. (Illus.). 160p. 1990. reprint ed. 22.00 (*0-06-062339-X*) Harper SF.
Song of Songs: A Continental Commentary. Othmar Keel. Tr. by Frederick J. Gaiser from GER. LC 93-11518. 1994. 36.00 (*0-8006-9507-0*, Fortress Pr) Augsburg Fortress.
Song of Songs: A Mystical Exposition. Juan G. Arintero. Tr. by James Valender & Jose L. Morales. 571p. 1992. reprint ed. pap. 20.00 (*0-89555-382-1*) TAN Bks Pubs.
Song of Songs: A New Translation & Interpretation. Marcia Falk. LC 90-80329. (Illus.). 1993. reprint ed. pap. 12.00 (*0-06-250306-5*) Harper SF.
Song of Songs: A New Translation with an Introduction & Commentary. Ariel Bloch & Chana Bloch. LC 93-33249. 1995. 27.50 (*0-679-40962-9*) Random.
Song of Songs: Tracing the Story of the Church. Theodore E. Wade, Jr. LC 92-90660. 64p. (Orig.). 1992. pap. 5.95 (*0-930192-27-3*) Gazelle Pubns.
Song of Songs & Enlightenment: A Metaphysical Interpretation. Dorothy Elder. LC 88-72028. 119p. (Orig.). 1989. pap. 9.95 (*0-87516-611-3*) DeVorss.
Song of Songs & Jonah. George A. Knight & Friedemann W. Golka. (International Theological Commentary Ser.). 136p. 1988. pap. 11.00 (*0-8028-0336-9*) Eerdmans.
Song of Songs & Lamentations: A Commentary & Translation. Robert Gordis. 1974. 25.00 (*0-87068-256-3*) Ktav.
Song of Songs & the Ancient Egyptian Love Songs. Michael V. Fox. LC 84-40494. 482p. 1985. reprint ed. pap. 137.40 (*0-608-01914-3*, 2062566) Bks Demand.
Song of Songs in the Middle Ages. Ann W. Astell. LC 89-70831. 208p. 1990. 35.00 (*0-8014-2347-3*) Cornell U Pr.
Song of Songs in the Middle Ages. Ann W. Astell. LC 89-70831. 208p. 1995. pap. 12.95 (*0-8014-8267-4*) Cornell U Pr.
Song of Songs in the Targumic Tradition: Vocalized Aramaic Text with Facing English Translation & Ladino Versions, Aramaic Concordance, Aramaic-English & Ladino-English Glossaries. Tr. & Intro. by Isaac Jerusalmi. LC 93-78088. (Ladino Bks.: No. 4). xlv, 506p. (ARC, ENG & LAD.). (C). 1993. text ed. 27.00 (*1-878191-03-9*) Ladino Bks.
*__Song of Songs Rabbah: An Analytical Translation, Vol. I.__ Jacob Neusner. 278p. 1990. 56.95 (*1-55540-418-9*, 140197) Scholars Pr GA.
*__Song of Songs Rabbah: An Analytical Translation, Vol. II.__ Jacob Neusner. 280p. 1989. 57.95 (*1-55540-419-7*, 140198) Scholars Pr GA.
Song of Songs, Ruth, Lamentations, Ecclesiastes, Esther. James A. Fischer. (Collegeville Bible Commentary - Old Testament Ser.). 112p. 1986. pap. 3.95 (*0-8146-1481-7*) Liturgical Pr.
Song of Songs/Lamentations. David A. Hubbard. (Biblical Commentary Ser.: VOL. 23b). 1998. 29.99 (*0-8499-0825-6*) Word Pub.
Song of Sonora. Griffing Bancroft. LC 93-80573. (Illus.). 65p. (Orig.). 1993. pap. 8.95 (*1-882803-05-1*) Jerseydale Ranch.
Song of Sorrow: Massacre at Sand Creek. Patrick Mendoza. LC 93-93930. 43p. 1993. teacher ed. 2.75 (*0-9636362-1-9*); pap. 10.95 (*0-9636362-0-0*) Willow Wind.
Song of Stars. Tom Birdseye. LC 89-20066. (Illus.). 32p. (J). (gr. 4-8). 1990. lib. bdg. 14.95 (*0-8234-0790-X*) Holiday.
Song of Suffering: Meditations from Job. C. Michael Lister, II. 120p. (Orig.). 1995. pap. write for info. (*1-57502-021-1*) Morris Pub.
Song of Survival: Women Interned. Helen Colijn. 224p. 1995. 22.95 (*1-883991-10-2*) Whte Cloud Pr.
*__Song of Survival: Women Interned.__ Helen Colijn. (Illus.). 224p. 1997. pap. 13.95 (*1-883991-14-5*) Whte Cloud Pr.
Song of the Andoumboulou: 18-20. Nathaniel Mackey. (Illus.). 24p. (Orig.). 1994. pap. 66.00 (*0-939952-16-5*) Moving Parts.
Song of the Bird. Anthony DeMello. LC 84-10105. (Illus.). 192p. 1984. pap. 10.95 (*0-385-19615-6*, Image Bks) Doubleday.
Song of the Blood. Jared Smith. 48p. 1983. pap. 6.00 (*0-912292-73-3*) Smith.
Song of the Bride. Jeanne Guyon. 123p. (Orig.). 1990. pap. 9.95 (*0-940232-38-3*) Seedsowers.
Song of the Broken String: After the Xam Bushmen : Poems from a Lost Oral Tradition. Stephen Watson. LC 95-1567. 1995. pap. 12.95 (*1-878818-43-0*) Sheep Meadow.
Song of the Buffalo Boy. Sherry Garland. 192p. (YA). (gr. 5 up). 1992. 16.00 (*0-15-277107-7*, HB Juv Bks) HarBrace.
Song of the Buffalo Boy. Sherry Garland. LC 91-31872. 192p. (YA). (gr. 5 up). 1994. pap. 4.00 (*0-15-200098-4*, HB Juv Bks) HarBrace.
*__Song of the Camels: A Christmas Poem.__ Elizabeth Coatsworth. LC 97-20944. (Illus.). (J). 1997. 15.95 (*1-55858-811-6*) North-South Bks NYC.
*__Song of the Camels: A Christmas Poem.__ Elizabeth J. Coatsworth. LC 97-20944. (Illus.). 32p. (J). (gr. k-3). 1997. lib. bdg. 15.88 (*1-55858-812-4*) North-South Bks NYC.
Song of the Cardinal. Gene S. Porter. 1990. reprint ed. lib. bdg. 21.95 (*0-89968-545-5*) Buccaneer Bks.
Song of the Cardinal. Gene Stratton-Porter. reprint ed. lib. bdg. 19.95 (*0-89190-945-1*, Rivercity Pr) Amereon Ltd.
Song of the Cathar Wars: A History of the Albigensian Crusade. Tr. by Janet Shirley. (Illus.). 220p. 1996. 59.95 (*1-85928-331-4*, Pub. by Scolar Pr UK) Ashgate Pub Co.
Song of the Cheyenne. Jory Sherman. 192p. 1993. mass mkt. 3.99 (*0-8125-3095-0*) Tor Bks.
Song of the Chirimia - La Musica de la Chirimia: A Guatemalan Folktale - Folklore Guatemalteco. Jane A. Volkmer. (ENG & SPA.). (J). (ps-3). 1992. pap. 6.95 (*0-87614-592-6*, First Ave Edns) Lerner Group.
Song of the Christmas Mouse. Shirley R. Murphy. LC 89-19744. (Illus.). 96p. (J). (gr. 2-5). 1990. 13.95 (*0-06-024357-0*) HarpC Child Bks.
Song of the Cosmos. Devarakunda B. Tilak. 8.00 (*0-89253-613-6*); 4.80 (*0-89253-614-4*) Ind-US Inc.
Song of the Coyote: Freeing the Imagination Through the Arts. Phyllis L. Sawyers & Frances L. Henry. (Illus.). 302p. (Orig.). 1980. pap. text ed. 19.95 (*0-89641-036-6*) American Pr.
*__Song of the Dodo.__ David Quammen. 1997. pap. 17.00 (*0-684-82712-3*, Touchstone Bks) S&S Trade.

An Asterisk (*) at the beginning of an entry indicates that the title is appearing in BIP for the first time.

***Song of the Dodo.** David Quammen. Date not set. write for info. (0-688-10744-3) Morrow.

Song of the Dodo: Island Biogeography in an Age of Extinctions. David Quammen. (Illus.). 704p. 1996. 32.50 (0-684-80083-7) S&S Trade.

***Song of the Dodo Reading Group Guide.** David Quammen. 1997. pap. write for info. (0-684-00447-X, Touchstone Bks) S&S Trade.

***Song of the Dolphins: A South Seas Mystical Adventure.** unabridged ed. Derek Ryan. LC 97-65700. (Illus.). ii, 170p. (Orig.). 1997. pap. 14.00 (0-9657262-0-7) Soular Pub.

Song of the Earth: Heidegger & the Grounds of the History of Being. Michel Haar. Tr. by Reginald Lilly. LC 92-21043. (Studies in Continental Thought). 212p. (C). 1993. 31.50 (0-253-32694-X) Ind U Pr.

Song of the Earth & Other Poems. M. G. Adiga. Tr. by A. K. Ramanujan from KAN. (Writers Workshop Redbird Ser.). 1975. 8.00 (0-88253-640-0); pap. text ed. 4.00 (0-88253-639-7) Ind-US Inc.

Song of the Evening. Nandini Satpathi. Tr. by J. B. Mohanty from ORI. 110p. (Orig.). 1975. pap. 1.50 (0-88253-770-9) Ind-US Inc.

Song of the Free Self: The Song of Who I Am. Tisziji Munoz. 43p. (Orig.). (C). 1981. pap. text ed. 10.00 (0-945174-03-9) Illum Soc Pubns.

Song of the Gargoyle. Zilpha K. Snyder. 240p. (J). (gr. 4-7). 1994. pap. 3.99 (0-440-40898-9) Dell.

Song of the Gargoyle. 93th ed. 1993. pap. text ed. 14.75 (0-15-300378-2, HB Juv Bks) HarBrace.

Song of the Gypsy & Other Verse: I Give You Verse. Madeline C. Fish. (Illus.). 9p. 1988. write for info. (0-9621176-0-9) M C Fish.

Song of the Hawk: The Life & Recordings of Coleman Hawkins. John Chilton. (American Music Ser.). (Illus.). 456p. 1993. pap. 26.95 (0-472-08201-9) U of Mich Pr.

Song of the Heart. Sylvie F. Sommerfield. 448p. 1995. mass mkt. 4.99 (0-8217-0141-X, Zebra Kensgtn) Kensgtn Pub Corp.

Song of the Heart: Selected Poems. Ramon L. Velarde. Tr. by Margaret S. Peden from SPA. (Texas Pan American Ser.). (Illus.). 120p. (Orig.). 1995. text ed. 19.95 (0-292-74685-7) U of Tex Pr.

Song of the Heart: Selected Poems by Ramon Lopez Velarde. Ramon L. Velarde. Tr. by Margaret S. Peden from SPA. (Texas Pan American Ser.). (Illus.). 120p. (Orig.). 1995. pap. 9.95 (0-292-74686-5) U of Tex Pr.

Song of the Hermit Thrush: An Iroquois Legend. Gloria Dominic. LC 96-5113. (Native American Lore & Legends Ser.). (J). 1996. write for info. (0-86593-428-2) Rourke Corp.

***Song of the Highlands.** Sharon Gillenwater. LC 96-50930. 432p. 1997. pap. 11.99 (0-88070-946-4, Palisades OR) Multnomah Pubs.

Song of the Hummingbird. Graciela Limon. LC 95-37666. 217p. 1996. pap. 11.95 (1-55885-091-0) Arte Publico.

***Song of the Kalahari: Why the Giraffe is Silent.** B. J. Ernst. LC 96-34568. (J). 1997. write for info. (1-56763-283-1) Ozark Pub.

***Song of the Kalahari: Why the Giraffe Is Silent.** B. J. Ernst. LC 96-34568. (J). 1997. pap. write for info. (1-56763-284-X) Ozark Pub.

Song of the King. Max Lucado. LC 95-12970. (Illus.). 32p. (J). (gr. 2-6). 1995. 12.99 (0-89107-827-4) Crossway Bks.

***Song of the King: Read-Along Sing-Along Audio Cassette.** Max Lucado. (J). 1995. 9.99 incl. audio (0-89107-894-0, Crossway Audio) Crossway Bks.

Song of the Lark. Willa Cather. 1983. pap. 9.95 (0-395-34530-8) HM.

Song of the Lark. large type ed. Willa Cather. 667p. 1991. reprint ed. lib. bdg. 21.95 (1-56054-281-0) Thorndike Pr.

Song of the Lark. Willa Cather. 1990. reprint ed. lib. bdg. 31.95 (0-89968-493-9) Buccaneer Bks.

Song of the Lark: The Sleeper-McCann House. Willa Cather. 432p. 1991. pap. 5.95 (0-451-52533-7, Sig Classics) NAL-Dutton.

Song of the Last Miguel. Carol P. Saul. (Illus.). 32p. (J). 1995. 14.95 (1-879085-90-9) Whsprng Coyote Pr.

Song of the Loom: New Traditions in Navajo Weaving. Frederick J. Dockstader. LC 86-27610. (Illus.). 132p. 1987. 39.95 (0-933920-87-3) Hudson Hills.

Song of the Lord. David K. Blomgren. 78p. 1986. pap. 6.95 (0-914936-31-X) BT Pub.

Song of the Lord: Bhagavadgita. Tr. by Edward J. Thomas & D. Litt. (C). 1995. 8.50 (0-8364-2907-9, Pub. by Rupa II) S Asia.

Song of the Magdalene. Donna J. Napoli. LC 96-7066. 256p. (YA). (gr. 7 up). 1996. 15.95 (0-590-93705-7) Scholastic Inc.

Song of the Moon. Judith Harris. LC 83-82014. 16p. (Orig.). 1983. pap. 3.50 (0-914061-00-3) Orchises Pr.

Song of the Mourning Dove. Lee Magner. (Intimate Moments Ser.: No. 420). 1992. mass mkt. 3.29 (0-373-07420-4, 5-07420-8) Harlequin Bks.

Song of the Nibelungs: A Verse Translation from the Middle High German Nibelungenlied. Tr. by Frank G. Ryder. LC 82-17432. 436p. 1963. pap. text ed. 16.95 (0-8143-1192-X, WB15) Wayne St U Pr.

Song of the Night, No. 3. Fiona McHugh. (Road to Avonlea Ser.). 128p. (J). (gr. 3-7). 1992. pap. 3.99 (0-553-48029-4, Skylark BDD) BDD Bks Young Read.

Song of the Nightingale. Constance O'Banyon. 336p. (J). 1992. pap. 8.99 (0-06-104122-X, Harp PBks) HarpC.

Song of the Nightingale. Constance O'Banyon. 352p. 1993. mass mkt. 5.99 (0-06-108003-9, Harp PBks) HarpC.

Song of the Outer Banks: A Poem in Twelve Cantos. Ed. by Finley P. Dunn, Jr. (Illus.). 105p. (Orig.). 1989. pap. write for info. (0-318-64790-7) Gresham Pubns.

***Song of the Paddle: An Illustrated Guide to Wilderness Camping.** Bill Mason. (Illus.). 208p. 1997. pap. 19.95 (1-55209-089-2) Firefly Bks Ltd.

Song of the Paddle: An Illustrated Guide to Wilderness Camping. Bill Mason. (Illus.). 208p. 1988. 29.95 (0-942802-83-7); pap. 19.95 (0-942802-84-5) NorthWord.

***Song of the Phoenix: Voices of Comfort & Healing from the Afterlife.** Lily Fairchilde. LC 96-48914. 1997. 18.95 (0-312-15212-4) St Martin.

Song of the Pines. large type ed. Christina Green. 1990. 25.99 (0-7089-2329-1) Ulverscroft.

Song of the Prairie. Esther L. Vogt. 182p. 1995. pap. 8.99 (0-88965-109-4, Pub. by Horizon Books CN) Chr Pubns.

Song of the Profound View. Geshe Rabten. 96p. 1989. pap. 10.95 (0-86171-086-X) Wisdom MA.

Song of the Purple: Poems & Photographs. Stacy Smith. Ed. by Don Williams. 64p. (Orig.). 1996. pap. 7.95 (1-888338-02-4) New Messenger Bks.

Song of the Rainbird. large type ed. Barbara Whitnell. 560p. 1985. 27.99 (0-7089-8244-1) Ulverscroft.

***Song of the Raven.** Patricia A. Wilson. LC 96-68631. (Illus.). 32p. (Orig.). (J). (gr. 3-6). 1997. pap. 12.95 (1-888125-06-3) Publ Consult.

Song of the Reich. Richard S. Hoehler. (Illus.). 850p. 1990. text ed. 20.00 (0-930590-03-1) R Hoehler Pub.

Song of the Righteous. Darwin Wolford. 355p. 1995. 14.95 (1-55517-193-1) CFI Dist.

Song of the River. rev. ed. Billy C. Clark. Ed. by James M. Gifford et al. LC 92-31483. (Illus.). 144p. (YA). 1994. pap. 10.00 (0-945084-46-3) J Stuart Found.

Song of the Rock. Don Coldsmith. (Spanish Bit Saga Ser.: Bk. 15). 224p. (J). 1991. mass mkt. 4.99 (0-553-29123-8) Bantam.

Song of the Sea. Jean Ferris. (American Dreams Ser.). 192p. (Orig.). 1996. pap. 3.99 (0-380-78199-9, Flare) Avon.

Song of the Sea; Ex 15: 1-21. Martin L. Brenner. (Beiheft zur Zeitschrift fuer die Alttestamentliche Wissenschaft Ser.: Vol. 195). viii, 193p. 1991. lib. bdg. 67.70 (3-11-012340-1) De Gruyter.

Song of the Sea Otter. Edith T. Hurd. (Illus.). 40p. (J). (gr. 2-5). 1989. pap. 5.95 (0-316-38323-6) Little.

Song of the Seed: A Monastic Way of Tending the Soul. Macrina Wiederkehr. LC 95-9271. 1997. pap. 12.00 (0-06-069554-4) Harper SF.

Song of the Self: Biblical Spirituality & Human Holiness. Carol Ochs. LC 94-4924. 112p. (Orig.). (C). 1994. pap. 11.00 (1-56338-096-X) TPI PA.

Song of the Servant. Bernard Haring. (C). 1988. 39.00 (0-85439-143-6, Pub. by St Paul Pubns UK) St Mut.

Song of the Seven Herbs. Walking Nightbear Staff. LC 87-10234. (Illus.). 60p. (Orig.). (J). (gr. 4 up). 1987. reprint ed. pap. 11.95 (0-913990-56-6) Book Pub Co.

Song of the Shepherd Boy. Janet Z. Rowzee & James A. Watson. 20p. (J). (gr. 4-8). 1993. pap. 6.95 (0-9638941-0-2) Eagles Three.

Song of the Silent Harp. B. J. Hoff. (Emerald Ballad Ser.). 416p. (Orig.). 1991. pap. 10.99 (1-55661-110-2) Bethany Hse.

Song of the Silent Snow. Hubert Selby, Jr. LC 85-14940. 244p. 1986. 16.95 (0-7145-2840-4) M Boyars Pubs.

Song of the Silent Snow & Other Stories. Hubert Selby, Jr. LC 87-7388. 224p. (ENG & SPA.). 1987. pap. 10.95 (0-8021-3008-9, Grove) Grove-Atltic.

Song of the Simple Truth: The Complete Poems of Julia de Burgos, Obra Completa Poetica. Julia De Burgos. Tr. by Jack Agueros from SPA. LC 94-39149. 524p. (Orig.). (SPA.). 1997. pap. 21.95 (1-880684-24-1) Curbstone.

Song of the Siren. large type ed. Philippa Carr. 1981. 12.00 (0-7089-0651-6) Ulverscroft.

Song of the Siren: Tales of Rhythm & Revolution. Dana Bryant. 128p. (Orig.). 1995. pap. 8.00 (1-57297-004-9) Blvd Books.

Song of the Sirens & Other Essays. Pietro Pucci. 208p. (C). 1997. pap. text ed. 21.95 (0-8226-3059-1); lib. bdg. 52.50 (0-8226-3058-3) Rowman.

Song of the Sky: Versions of Native American Song-Poems. rev. ed. Brian Swann. LC 93-5152. 168p. (Orig.). 1993. pap. 16.95 (0-87023-872-8) U of Mass Pr.

Song of the Skylark One: Foundations of Experiential Religion. Gabriel Gomes. 428p. (C). 1991. pap. text ed. 34.00 (0-8191-8223-0); lib. bdg. 53.00 (0-8191-8222-2) U Pr of Amer.

Song of the Skylark Two: Meditation - Teachings & Practices. 308p. (C). 1991. pap. text ed. 28.00 (0-8191-8225-7); lib. bdg. 45.00 (0-8191-8224-9) U Pr of Amer.

Song of the Soul: An Introduction to the Namokar Mantra & the Science of Sound. Acharya S. Kumar. 104p. (Orig.). 1987. 5.00 (0-943207-00-2) Siddhachalam.

Song of the Soul: In Celebration of Korea. Lenore Beechman. LC 83-15536. (Illus.). 38p. (Orig.). 1984. pap. 4.95 (0-377-00137-6) Friendship Pr.

Song of the Soul: In Celebration of Korea. Lenore Beecham. LC 83-16526. (Illus.). 44p. 1984. reprint ed. pap. 25.00 (0-608-00234-8, 2060736) Bks Demand.

***Song of the Sparrow.** Dorothy M. Birdwell. 113p. (Orig.). 1997. mass mkt. 5.99 (1-55237-109-3, Pub. by Comnwlth Pub CN) Partners Pubs Grp.

Song of the Sparrow: Meditations & Poems to Pray by. Murray Bodo. (Illus.). 178p. (Orig.). 1976. pap. 4.95 (0-912228-26-1) St Anthony Mess Pr.

Song of the Spirit. Herbert L. Beierle. (C). 1978. 20.00 (0-940480-01-8) UNI Press.

Song of the Spirit & the Bride: Finding Jesus in the Song of Songs. Stephen Long. 76p. (Orig.). 1991. pap. 4.95 (0-9629550-0-0) Word in Action.

Song of the Stars. Credo Mutwa. Ed. by Stephen Larsen. LC 95-12499. 1995. pap. 14.95 (1-886449-01-5) Barrytown Ltd.

***Song of the Stranger.** Angela Tung. LC 97-11751. (J). 1997. write for info. (1-56565-774-8) Lowell Hse.

***Song of the Swallows.** Politi. (SPA.). 1996. pap. 4.99 (0-689-80880-1) S&S Childrens.

Song of the Swallows. Leo Politi. LC 49-8215. (Illus.). 32p. (J). (gr. 1-4). 1987. lib. bdg. 15.00 (0-684-18831-7, C Scribner Sons Young) S&S Childrens.

Song of the Swallows. Leo Politi. (Illus.). 32p. (J). (gr. k-3). 1987. reprint ed. pap. 4.95 (0-689-71140-9, Aladdin Paperbacks) S&S Childrens.

Song of the Swallows Literature Mini-Unit. Janet Lovelady. (Illus.). 32p. (J). (gr. 2-4). 1989. student ed. 4.95 (1-56096-007-8) Mari.

Song of the Swan: Lucretius & the Influence of Callimachus. Harold Donohue. LC 93-13876. 170p. (C). 1993. lib. bdg. 39.50 (0-8191-9187-6) U Pr of Amer.

Song of the Toad. Earle J. Stone. (Toad Ser.). (Illus.). 144p. (Orig.). 1988. 18.95 (0-938699-02-4); pap. 12.95 (0-938699-04-0) Paige Pubns.

***Song of the Trees.** Mildred Taylor. 64p. (J). 1996. pap. 3.50 (0-440-41396-6); mass mkt. 3.50 (0-440-22699-6) BDD Bks Young Read.

Song of the Trees. Mildred D. Taylor. LC 74-18598. (Illus.). 56p. (J). (gr. 2-5). 1975. pap. 15.99 (0-8037-5452-3); lib. bdg. 11.89 (0-8037-5453-1) Dial Bks Young.

Song of the Turtle: American Indian Literature, 1974-1994. Ed. by Paula G. Allen. 1996. 25.00 (0-614-96849-6, One World) Ballantine.

Song of the Turtle: American Indian Literature, 1974-1994, Vol. 2. Ed. by Paula G. Allen. 352p. 1996. 25.00 (0-345-37525-4, One World) Ballantine.

Song of the Uncharted Heart: Essential Poetry. Jon Schruber. (Illus.). 110p. (Orig.). 1993. pap. 14.95 (0-9623581-5-0) CA Health Pubns.

Song of the Undersea. Ronald Kirkbride. 1967. 10.95 (0-8392-1163-5) Astor-Honor.

Song of the Vampire. Carmen Adams. 160p. (Orig.). (J). 1996. pap. 3.99 (0-380-78031-3, Flare) Avon.

Song of the Virgin. Spiros Zodhiates. LC 82-71643. 142p. 1974. pap. 3.99 (0-89957-510-2) AMG Pubs.

Song of the Warrior. Georgina Gentry. 432p. 1995. mass mkt. 4.99 (0-8217-4962-5, Pinncle Kensgtn) Kensgtn Pub Corp.

Song of the Wave & Other Poems. George C. Lodge. LC 70-104517. 135p. reprint ed. lib. bdg. 19.00 (0-8398-1168-3) Irvington.

Song of the Wave & Other Poems. George C. Lodge. 135p. (C). 1986. reprint ed. pap. text ed. 5.95 (0-8290-2030-6) Irvington.

Song of the Whango-Whee. John F. Smith. (Illus.). 24p. (J). (ps-5). 1993. 14.95 (1-884375-00-6) Chinky-Po Tree.

Song of the Whip. Max Brand. 261p. 1975. reprint ed. lib. bdg. 20.95 (0-89190-210-4, Rivercity Pr) Amereon Ltd.

Song of the Whip. Max Brand. 1990. reprint ed. lib. bdg. 16.95 (0-89968-486-6) Buccaneer Bks.

Song of the Wild Violets. Peggy Thompson. LC 93-641. (Illus.). 36p. (J). (gr. 2 up). 1993. pap. 5.95 (0-913990-37-X) Book Pub Co.

Song of the Willow. Charlotte McPherren. 368p. (Orig.). 1993. mass mkt., pap. text ed. 4.50 (0-8439-3483-2) Dorchester Pub Co.

Song of the Wizard. B. James Hanlin. 1994. pap. 11.95 (1-883405-03-3) Grey Pilgrim.

Song of the Wolf. F. Rosanne Bittner. 496p. 1992. mass mkt. 5.99 (0-553-29014-2) Bantam.

***Song of the Zubble-Wump.** Dr. Seuss. (J). 1996. lib. bdg. 15.99 (0-679-98419-4) Random Bks Yng Read.

Song of Time. Teri McLaren. (Gathering Ser.). 304p. 1996. mass mkt. 5.50 (0-06-105622-7, HarperPrism) HarpC.

Song of Troilus: Lyric Authority in the Medieval Book. Thomas C. Stillinger. LC 92-28021. (Middle Ages Ser.). 304p. (C). 1992. text ed. 34.95 (0-8122-3144-9) U of Pa Pr.

Song of Truth & Semblance. A Novel. Cees Nooteboom. Tr. by Adrienne Dixon from DUT. LC 84-848. Orig. Title: Een Liedvan schijn en wezen. 83p. 1984. 12.95 (0-8071-1176-7) La State U Pr.

Song of Wovoka. Earl P. Murray. 416p. (Orig.). 1992. pap. 10.99 (0-8125-2091-2) Tor Bks.

Song of Wovoka. Earl P. Murray. 416p. (Orig.). 1993. mass mkt. 4.99 (0-8125-1318-5) Tor Bks.

Song of Years. Bess S. Aldrich. 1985. pap. 2.95 (0-451-13925-9, Sig Vista) NAL-Dutton.

Song of Years. large type ed. Bess S. Aldrich. LC 91-30615. 735p. 1992. lib. bdg. 20.95 (1-56054-275-6) Thorndike Pr.

Song of Years. Bess S. Aldrich. LC 91-17881. 405p. 1991. reprint ed. pap. 12.95 (0-8032-5918-2, Bison Books) U of Nebr Pr.

Song of Yvonne. Cecilia M. Brainard. 183p. (Orig.). 1991. pap. 12.50 (971-10-0449-6, Pub. by New Day Pub PH) Cellar.

Song on Record, Vol. 2. Ed. by Alan Blyth. 300p. 1988. text ed. 49.95 (0-521-33155-2) Cambridge U Pr.

Song Out of Harlem. Antar S. Mberi. LC 80-12500. (Vox Humana Ser.). 96p. 1980. 9.95 (0-89603-018-0); pap. 4.95 (0-89603-021-0) Humana.

Song Pleases the King. Cheryl L. Foster. 32p. (J). 1994. pap. 7.95 (0-9639270-4-3) Light Rain Commun.

Song-Poems from Xanadu. James I. Crump. LC 92-39788. (Michigan Monographs in Chinese Studies: No. 64). 1993. pap. text ed. 15.00 (0-89264-095-2) Ctr Chinese Studies.

Song Prophet. Gregory D. Brown. 210p. (Orig.). (YA). 1996. pap. 10.99 (1-57502-160-9, PO758) Morris Pubng.

Song Send Greetings to Duplicate & Use. Lamp Light Press Staff. (Illus.). 52p. 1993. ring bd. 29.95 (0-917593-31-6, Lamp Light Pr) Prosperity & Profits.

Song Session Community Songbook. Ed. by Carol Cuellar. 128p. (Orig.). 1994. pap. 8.95 (0-89724-419-2, VF0248) Warner Brothers.

Song She Guards. Irene K. Howe. LC 95-79149. 96p. (Orig.). 1995. pap. 8.00 (1-879418-18-5) Biddle Pub.

Song Spectrum, Vol. 1. (Ultimate Ser.). 304p. 1984. pap. 17.95 (0-88188-276-3, 00361413) H Leonard.

Song Spinner. Pauline Le Bel. (Illus.). 112p. (YA). 1994. pap. 7.95 (0-88995-120-9, Pub. by Red Deer CN) Orca Bk Pubs.

***Song Stars, Vol. 2.** Richard Grudens. 1997. pap. text ed. 15.95 (1-57579-045-9) Pine Hill Pr.

Song to Tame the Storm. Daniel Durham. 7.95 (0-941720-83-7) Slough Pr TX.

Song to the Creator: Traditional Arts of Native American Women of the Plateau. Ed. by Lillian A. Ackerman. LC 96-32388. (Illus.). 132p. 1996. 29.95 (0-8061-2876-3, 2876); pap. 18.95 (0-8061-2877-1, 2877) U of Okla Pr.

***Song to the Prodigal Bride.** Geraldine Harris. 224p. (Orig.). 1997. pap. 9.99 (1-884369-47-2, EBED Pubns) McDougal Pubng.

Song to the Rising Sun. Paulette Jiles. 168p. (Orig.). 1989. pap. 10.95 (0-919591-45-0, Pub. by Polestar Bk Pubs CN) Orca Bk Pubs.

Song to the Sun. large type ed. Elizabeth Clare. 1990. 25.99 (0-7089-2214-7) Ulverscroft.

Song Wise, Three: Battle Hymn of the Republic. Woody Young. (Illus.). 24p. (Orig.). (J). 1986. pap. text ed. 2.95 (0-939513-13-7) Joy Pub SJC.

Song Wise, Vol. Four: America. Woody Young. (Illus.). 24p. (Orig.). (J). 1986. pap. text ed. 2.95 (0-939513-14-5) Joy Pub SJC.

Song Wise, Vol. One: The Star Spangled Banner. Woody Young. (Illus.). 24p. (Orig.). (J). 1986. pap. text ed. 2.95 (0-939513-11-0) Joy Pub SJC.

Song Wise, Vol. Two: America the Beautiful. Woody Young. (Illus.). 24p. (Orig.). (J). 1986. pap. text ed. 2.95 (0-939513-12-9) Joy Pub SJC.

***Song Within.** Meagan Davidson. 1998. mass mkt. 5.50 (0-7860-0402-9) Kensgtn Pub Corp.

***Song Within.** Megan Davidson. 384p. 1998. mass mkt. 4.99 (0-8217-5824-1, Zebra Kensgtn) Kensgtn Pub Corp.

Song Writer's Manuscript Book. 2.50 (1-56222-147-7, 94568) Mel Bay.

Songbird Carving, Vol. I. Roslyn L. Daisey & Sina P. Kurman. LC 85-52376. (Illus.). 256p. 1986. 45.00 (0-88740-057-4) Schiffer.

Songbird Carving, Vol. II. Roslyn L. Daisey & Sina P. Kurman. LC 85-52376. (Illus.). 1988. 45.00 (0-88740-119-8) Schiffer.

Songbird Carving with Ernest Muehlmatt: World-Class Ribbon Winner Teaches You How to Carve & Paint 10 Favorite Songbirds. Roger Schroeder & Ernest Muehlmatt. LC 86-14580. (Illus.). 288p. 1987. pap. 29.95 (0-8117-2573-1) Stackpole.

Songbirds. Alice K. Flanagan. LC 95-25803. (New True Bks.). (Illus.). 48p. (J). (gr. 2-3). 1996. lib. bdg. 19.00 (0-516-01095-6) Childrens.

Songbirds. Alice K. Flanagan. (New True Bks.). (J). 1996. pap. 5.50 (0-516-20077-1) Childrens.

***Songbirds.** John P. Mackenzie. (Birds of the World Ser.). (Illus.). 144p. (Orig.). 1997. pap. 19.95 (1-55013-801-4, Pub. by Key Porter Bks CN) Firefly Bks Ltd.

***Songbirds.** Ronald Orenstein. LC 97-9668. 1997. 35.00 (0-87156-947-7) Sierra.

Songbirds in Singapore: The Growth of a Pastime. Lesley Layton. (Images of Asia Ser.). (Illus.). 120p. 1991. 21.00 (0-19-588999-1) OUP.

Songbirds in Your Garden. John K. Terres. LC 94-2277. 256p. 1994. pap. 14.95 (1-56512-044-2) Algonquin Bks.

Songbirds, Truffles & Wolves: An American Naturalist in Italy. Gary P. Nabhan. 256p. 1994. reprint ed. pap. 10.95 (0-14-023972-3, Penguin Bks) Viking Penguin.

***Songbook: Selected Poems of Umberto Saba.** Umberto Saba. Tr. by Stephen Sartarelli from ITA. Orig. Title: Il Canzoniere. Date not set. pap. 12.95 (1-878818-52-X) Sheep Meadow.

Songbook for Living Waters, Vol. I. (J). 1993. pap. text ed. 24.95 (0-7829-0384-3, 88090) Tabor Pub.

Songbook for Living Waters, Vol. II. (J). 1993. pap. text ed. 24.95 (0-7829-0385-1, 88091) Tabor Pub.

Songbook of Absences. Miguel Hernandez. Tr. by Tom Jones. LC 72-91778. 1980. 7.50 (0-910350-06-X) Charioteer.

Songbook of the American Revolution. Carolyn Rabson. 1974. pap. 4.00 (0-911014-18-7) Neo Pr.

Songcite: An Index to Popular Songs. William D. Goodfellow. LC 94-44768. (Reference Library of the Humanities: Vol. 1918). 448p. 1995. text ed. 65.00 (0-8153-2059-0) Garland.

Songdog Diary: 66 Stories from the Road. Michael Wallis & Suzanne F. Wallis. (Illus.). 214p. 1996. 19.95 (1-57178-018-1) Coun Oak Bks.

Songdogs. Colum Mccann. LC 96-19572. 224p. 1996. pap. 12.00 (0-312-14741-4, Picador USA) St Martin.

Songdogs: A Novel. Colum McCann. 224p. 1995. 22.50 (0-8050-4104-4) H Holt & Co.

Songe. Henry De Montherlant. (Folio Ser.: No. 1458). (FRE.). pap. 10.95 (2-07-037458-0) Schoenhof.

Songe. Henry De Montherlant. (FRE.). 1982. pap. 13.95 (0-8288-3756-2, F115510) Fr & Eur.

Songhay, 14 vols. Tuude Adeleke. Ed. by George Bond. LC 95-1272. (Heritage Library of African Peoples: Set 2). (Illus.). 64p. (YA). (gr. 7-12). 1996. lib. bdg. 15.95 (0-8239-1986-2) Rosen Group.

Songhay: The Empire Builders. Philip Koslow. LC 94-31095. (Kingdoms of Africa Ser.). (Illus.). (YA). (gr. 3 up). 1995. pap. 8.95 (0-7910-2943-3); lib. bdg. 17.95 (0-7910-3128-4) Chelsea Hse.

An Asterisk (*) at the beginning of an entry indicates that the title is appearing in BIP for the first time.

S

Songket: Malaysia's Woven Treasure. Grace I. Selvanayagam. (Illus.). 228p. 1991. 55.00 (0-19-588928-2) OUP.

Songlines. Bruce Chatwin. 1987. 10.95 (0-224-02452-3) Random.

Songlines. Bruce Chatwin. 304p. 1988. pap. 12.95 (0-14-009429-6, Penguin Bks) Viking Penguin.

Songlines: Hymns, Songs, Rounds, Refrains for Prayer & Praise. Miriam T. Winter. 192p. 1996. pap. text ed. 14.95 (0-8245-1563-3) Crossroad NY.

Songlines & Dreamings: Contemporary Australian Aboriginal Art. Patrick C. Stourton. (Illus.). 192p. 1996. 55.00 (0-85331-691-0, Pub. by Lund Humphries UK) Antique Collect.

Songmaster. Orson Scott Card. 1992. mass mkt. 4.99 (0-8125-3322-4) Tor Bks.

Songmaster. Orson Scott Card. 1993. mass mkt. 6.99 (0-8125-2486-1) Tor Bks.

Songmaster. Orson Scott Card. 1994. reprint ed. lib. bdg. 22.00 (0-7278-4654-X) Severn Hse.

Songprints: The Musical Experience of Five Shoshone Women. Judith Vander. LC 87-24488. (Music in American Life Ser.). 376p. 1988. 34.95 (0-252-01492-8); 40.50 incl. audio (0-252-01532-0); digital audio 9.95 (0-252-01531-2) U of Ill Pr.

Songprints: The Musical Experience of Five Shoshone Women. Judith Vander. 376p. 1996. pap. text ed. 19.95 (0-252-06545-X) U of Ill Pr.

***Songprints: The Musical Experience of Five Shoshone Women.** Judith Vander. (Illus.). 376p. 1997. pap. 26.95 incl. audio, digital audio (0-252-02256-4) U of Ill Pr.

Songs. Charley J. Greasybear. Ed. by Tom Trusky & Judson Crews. LC 78-58484. (Ahsahta Press Modern & Contemporary Poets of the West Ser.). 48p. (Orig.). 1979. pap. 6.95 (0-916272-10-9) Ahsahta Pr.

Songs. Christopher Logue. 1960. 10.95 (0-8392-1106-6) Astor-Honor.

Songs. Louise Reichardt. LC 80-22799. (Women Composers Ser.). 1980. 27.50 (0-306-79552-3) Da Capo.

Songs. Henry C. Work. LC 73-5099. (Earlier American Music Ser.). 1974. 32.50 (0-306-70586-9) Da Capo.

Songs: Bulat Okudzhava, Vol. II. Bulat Okudzhava. Ed. by Vladimir Frumkin. Tr. by Tanya Wolfson et al. 117p. (ENG & RUS.). 1986. pap. text ed. 11.95 (0-87501-022-9) Ardis Pubs.

Songs - Read-Premium. Raffi. 1995. 39.92 (0-517-88300-7) Random.

***Songs about God & His Son.** David L. Pitts. 85p. 1995. 3.95 (0-9649138-0-1) Passwrd Pubng.

Songs about the Sky. rev. ed. Hannah Russell. (Illus.). 18p. (J). 1988. reprint ed. pap. 4.50 (0-9614089-2-8) Avitar Bks.

Songs about Work: Essays in Occupational Culture. Ed. by Archie Green. LC 93-34120. (Special Publications: No. 3). (Illus.). 360p. (C). 1993. text ed. 39.95 (1-879407-05-1); pap. text ed. 17.50 (1-879407-04-3) IN Univ Folk Inst.

Songs along the Mahantonga: Pennsylvania Dutch Folksongs. Walter E. Boyer et al. 232p. 1970. reprint ed. 35.00 (0-8103-5002-5) Gale.

Songs & Activities for Best, Best Friends: A Complete Music Curriculum for Early Childhood. Bob Messano. 256p. 1991. student ed. 24.95 incl. audio (0-87628-796-8, 710117) Ctr Appl Res.

Songs & Ballads. Federico Garcia Lorca. (Essential Poets Ser.: No. 53). 66p. 1993. pap. 10.00 (0-920717-65-9) Guernica Editions.

Songs & Ballads from Nova Scotia. Helen Creighton. 1993. pap. 9.95 (0-486-21703-5) Dover.

Songs & Ballads from over the Sea. Ed. by E. A. Helps. LC 78-168783. (Granger Index Reprint Ser.). 1977. reprint ed. 23.95 (0-8369-6303-2) Ayer.

Songs & Ballads of Greater Britain. Ed. by E. A. Helps. LC 70-37016. (Granger Index Reprint Ser.). 1977. reprint ed. 23.95 (0-8369-6315-6) Ayer.

***Songs & Ballads of Ireland.** Ed. & Selected by John Loesberg. 56p. 1997. pap. 7.95 (0-946005-53-2, OS 00076) Music Sales.

Songs & Ballads of the American Revolution. Ed. by Frank Moore & Peter Decker. LC 79-76562. (Eyewitness Accounts of the American Revolution Ser., No. 1). (Illus.). 1976. reprint ed. 25.95 (0-405-01164-4) Ayer.

Songs & Ballads of the American Revolution. Frank Moore. (BCL1 - U. S. History Ser.). 288p. 1991. reprint ed. lib. bdg. 79.00 (0-7812-6106-6) Rprt Serv.

Songs & Carols. Random House Staff. 1995. 7.99 (0-517-12439-4) Random.

Songs & Dances. Philip M. Royster. LC 80-85233. 61p. (YA). (gr. 9-12). 1981. per. 3.50 (0-916418-28-6) Lotus.

Songs & Dances of England. Liz Thomson. (Illus.). 80p. 1982. pap. 10.95 (0-7119-0101-5, AM31428) Music Sales.

Songs & Dances of Ireland. Peter Lavender. (Illus.). 80p. 1982. pap. 10.95 (0-7119-0099-X, AM31402) Music Sales.

Songs & Dances of Scotland. Liz Thomson. (Illus.). 80p. 1982. pap. 10.95 (0-7119-0100-7, AM31410) Music Sales.

Songs & Folklore of Puerto Rico. Monserrate Deliz. (Puerto Rico Ser.). 1979. lib. bdg. 59.95 (0-8490-3007-2) Gordon Pr.

***Songs & Games for Babies.** Ed. by Susan Hodges. (Learn with Piggyback Songs Ser.). (Illus.). 48p. (Orig.). (J). (ps). 1997. pap. 3.95 (1-57029-163-2, 3301, Totline Bks) Warren Pub Hse.

***Songs & Games for Fours.** Ed. by Gayle Bittinger. (Learn with Piggyback Songs Ser.). (Illus.). 48p. (Orig.). (J). (ps). 1997. pap. 3.95 (1-57029-166-7, 3304, Totline Bks) Warren Pub Hse.

***Songs & Games for Threes.** Ed. by Elizabeth McKinnon. (Learn with Piggyback Songs Ser.). (Illus.). 48p. (Orig.). (J). (ps). 1997. pap. 3.95 (1-57029-165-9, 3303, Totline Bks) Warren Pub Hse.

***Songs & Games for Toddlers.** Ed. by Carol Gnojewski. (Learn with Piggyback Songs Ser.). (Illus.). 48p. (Orig.). (J). (ps). 1997. pap. 3.95 (1-57029-164-0, 3302, Totline Bks) Warren Pub Hse.

Songs & Heroes. Robinson Jeffers. 34p. (C). 1988. 165.00 (0-923980-07-5) Arundel Pr.

Songs & Heroes. deluxe limited ed. Robinson Jeffers. 34p. (C). 1988. 300.00 (0-923980-06-7) Arundel Pr.

Songs & Lyrics. Ed. by Boas. LC 77-14508. 1978. reprint ed. text ed. 65.00 (0-8371-9842-9, BOMO, Greenwood Pr) Greenwood.

Songs & Lyrics from the English Masques & Light Operas. Ed. by Frederick S. Boas. 175p. 1949. reprint ed. 15.00 (0-403-03693-3) Scholarly.

Songs & Lyrics from the English Playbooks. Ed. by Frederick S. Boas. reprint ed. 15.00 (0-403-04290-9) Somerset Pub.

Songs & Lyrics from the Plays of Beaumont & Fletcher. Francis Beaumont & John Fletcher. Ed. by E. H. Fellows. LC 79-180038. 1972. reprint ed. 26.95 (0-405-08249-5, Pub. by Blom Pubns UK) Ayer.

Songs & Missing Pieces. Timothy J. Sheehan. LC 88-70922. 28p. (Orig.). 1988. pap. 8.00 (0-938041-03-7) Arc Pr AR.

Songs & Musicians in Fifteenth Century Europe. David Fallows. LC 95-45521. (Collected Studies: Vol. CS519). 336p. 1996. 89.95 (0-86078-561-0, Pub. by Variorum UK) Ashgate Pub Co.

Songs & Poems: About Love, Life, & Dance. Shelegh Krainer. 89p. 1995. write for info. (0-9643330-0-7) S Krainer.

Songs & Poems of Robert Burns. Ed. by Ralph Knight. 1959. 29.95 (0-8084-0384-2) NCUP.

Songs & Prayers for Children. (Illus.). 32p. (J). (ps). 1993. 3.98 (0-8317-5184-3) Smithmark.

Songs & Prayers of Victory. Basilea Schlink. 1978. pap. 1.50 (3-87209-652-4) Evang Sisterhood Mary.

Songs & Profiles. Mark Dunster. 31p. (Orig.). (YA). (gr. 9-12). 1996. pap. 5.00 (0-89642-299-2) Linden Pubs.

Songs & Rhymes for a Rainy Day Big Book. Illus. by Melissa Saylor. (J). (ps-2). 1988. pap. text ed. 15.00 (0-922053-07-3) N Edge Res.

Songs & Rhymes for Wiggle Worms. Mary Hollingsworth. (Illus.). 36p. (J). 1995. bds. 6.99 (0-88070-772-0, Gold & Honey) Multnomah Pubs.

Songs & Sayings of Walther Von der Vogelweide. Ed. by Frank Betts. 1973. 250.00 (0-8490-2631-8) Gordon Pr.

Songs & Sayings of Walther von der Vogelweide, Minnesanger. Walther von der Vogelweide. Tr. by Frank Betts. LC 75-41287. reprint ed. 32.50 (0-404-14752-6) AMS Pr.

Songs & Seeds: A Journal with John Muir. John Muir. 150p. 1996. pap. 12.00 (0-945519-17-6) Mountn Meadw Pr.

***Songs & Sermons.** John Wesley. 1997. pap. text ed. 7.00 (0-00-628012-9) Harper SF.

Songs & Solos for Uke. Ken Eidson & Ross Cherednik. 1993. 5.95 (1-56222-142-6, 93938) Mel Bay.

Songs & Song Writers. Henry T. Finck. 1977. 17.95 (0-8369-7135-3, 7968) Ayer.

Songs & Song Writers. Henry T. Finck. 1972. 59.95 (0-8490-1083-7) Gordon Pr.

***Songs & Sonnets.** Peter Washington. 1997. 12.50 (0-679-45465-9, Everymans Lib) Knopf.

***Songs & Sonnets of Love Still Innocent: A Representative Anthology of the Poetry of Gerardo Diego.** Carl W. Cobb. (Romance Monographs: Vol. 51). 323p. (Orig.). 1997. pap. 40.00 (1-889441-01-5) Romance.

Songs & Sounds of My Heart. Amadeo M. Abaya. 1995. 10.00 (0-533-11398-9) Vantage.

Songs & Stories from Tennessee. John T. Moore. LC 70-94739. (Short Story Index Reprint Ser.). 1977. 23.95 (0-8369-3119-X) Ayer.

Songs & Stories from the American Revolution. Jerry Silverman. (Illus.). 72p. (J). (gr. 3-6). 1994. lib. bdg. 19.90 (1-56294-429-0) Millbrook Pr.

Songs & Stories from Uganda. W. Moses Serwadda. Ed. by Hewitt Pantaleoni. LC 87-18904. (Illus.). 96p. 1987. reprint ed. pap. 12.95 (0-937203-15-7) World Music Pr.

***Songs & Stories from Uganda.** W. Moses Serwadda. Ed. by Hewitt Pantaleoni. LC 87-18904. (Illus.). 1987. reprint ed. pap. 17.95 incl. audio compact disk (0-937203-85-8) World Music Pr.

Songs & Stories from Uganda, Set. W. Moses Serwadda. Ed. by Hewitt Pantaleoni. LC 87-18904. (Illus.). 96p. 1987. reprint ed. pap. 17.95 incl. audio (0-937203-17-3) World Music Pr.

Songs & Stories, Selected & Annotated. Edwin Markham. 1977. 31.95 (0-8369-4268-X, 6066) Ayer.

Songs Are Thoughts: Poems of the Inuit. Ed. by Neil Philip. LC 94-27866. 32p. (J). (gr. 1 up). 1995. 15.95 (0-531-06893-5) Orchard Bks Watts.

Songs Around the Campfire. Ron Middlebrook. (Illus.). 168p. 1994. pap. 24.95 (0-931759-86-2) Centerstream Pub.

***Songs at the River's Edge.** Katy Gardner. 1997. pap. text ed. 13.95 (0-7453-1094-X, Pub. by Pluto Pr UK) LPC InBook.

***Songs at the River's Edge: Stories from a Bangladesh Village.** LC 96-49025. 1997. write for info. (0-7453-1095-8, Pub. by Pluto Pr UK) LPC InBook.

Songs, Ballads & Instrumental Pieces Composed by King Henry the VIII. Henry VIII. LC 74-26054. reprint ed. 32.50 (0-404-12962-5) AMS Pr.

Songs, Ballads, & Stories. William Allingham. LC 75-148743. reprint ed. 41.50 (0-404-00347-8) AMS Pr.

Songs by Charles Gounod (1818-1893), Songs by Leo Delibes (1836-1891), Six Poesies d'Armand Silvestre by Alexis de Castillon (1838-1873) fac. ed. Ed. by David Tunley. LC 94-21136. (Romantic French Song 1830-1870 Ser.: Vol. 5). (Illus.). 320p. 1995. text ed. 100.00 (0-8153-1357-8) Garland.

Songs by Felicien David (1810-1876) fac. ed. Ed. by David Tunley. LC 94-46135. (Romantic French Song 1830-1870 Ser.: Vol. 2). 272p. 1995. text ed. 100.00 (0-8153-1359-4) Garland.

Songs by Henri Reber (1807-1880), Six Romances Populaires (1849), Six Melodies de Victor Hugo (1855), & Five Other Songs by Edouard Lalo (1823-1892) Ed. by David Tunley. LC 94-21136. (Romantic French Song 1830-1870 Ser.: Vol. 3). 224p. 1995. text ed. 100.00 (0-8153-1356-X) Garland.

Songs by Jules Massenet (1842-1912) Louis Lacombe (1818-1884) & Auguste Vaucorbeil (1821-1884) fac. ed. Ed. by David Tunley. LC 94-21136. (Romantic French Song 1830-1870 Ser.: Vol. 6). 240p. 1995. text ed. 100.00 (0-8153-1361-6) Garland.

Songs by the Ettrick Shepherd. James Hogg. LC 90-118426. 328p. 1989. reprint ed. 48.00 (1-85477-023-3, Pub. by Woodstock Bks UK) Cassell.

Songs by Thirty Americans for High Voice. Ed. by Rupert Hughes. LC 77-1942. (Music Reprint Ser.). 1976. reprint ed. lib. bdg. 32.50 (0-306-70824-8) Da Capo.

Songs by Victor Masse (1822-1884), Including Chants Bretons (1853), & Songs by Georges Bizet (1838-1875), Including Feuilles D'Album (1867) Ed. by David Tunley. LC 94-21136. (Romantic French Song 1830-1870 Ser.: Vol. 4). 320p. 1995. text ed. 100.00 (0-8153-1358-6) Garland.

Songs by 22 Americans: Low Voice Piano. 152p. 1986. per. 16.95 (0-7935-4004-6, 50329410) H Leonard.

Songs, Carols & Other Miscellaneous Poems, from the Balliol Ms. Richard Hill. Ed. by Roman Dyboski. (EETS, ES Ser.: No. 101). 1974. reprint ed. 45.00 (0-527-00305-0) Periodicals Srv.

Songs Divine. Swami Abhedananda. Tr. by P. S. Aiyer from SAN. 69p. 1985. pap. 5.95 (0-87481-653-X, Pub. by Ramakrishna Math II) Vedanta Pr.

Songs, Eighteen Eighty to Nineteen Hundred & Four. Claude Debussy. Ed. by Rita Benson. (Orig.). 1981. pap. 8.95 (0-486-24131-9) Dover.

Songs Every User of Music Should Know. 176p. 1994. per. write for info. (0-7935-3467-4, 00657721) H Leonard.

Songs for a New World. O. R. Dathorne. 1988. 15.00 (0-916057-01-1) Assn Carib Stud.

Songs for All Seasons. 1984. 4.95 (0-88188-464-2, 00008637) H Leonard.

Songs for Annie: Flute & Piano. 44p. 1986. pap. 12.95 (0-7935-4397-5, 50335060) H Leonard.

Songs for Awakening. Heng Yin et al. (Illus.). 112p. (Orig.). 1979. pap. 8.00 (0-917512-63-4) Buddhist Text.

Songs for Bass Voice: An Annotated Guide to Works for Bass Voice. Alan J. Ord. 228p. 1994. 32.50 (0-8108-2897-9) Scarecrow.

Songs for Camps & Reunions. Jack Ergo. 1986. pap. 5.00 (0-8309-0453-0) Herald Hse.

***Songs for Cats (& the People Who Love Them)** Anne Bryant & Ellen Bernfeld. (Songs for...Ser.: Vol. 2). (Illus.). 48p. (Orig.). 1997. boxed, mass mkt. 18.95 incl. cd-rom (0-9648762-1-3, Cats/CD) Gloryvision.

***Songs for Cats (& the People Who Love Them), Vol. 2.** Anne Bryant & Ellen Bernfeld. (Songs for...Ser.: Vol. 2). (Illus.). 48p. (Orig.). 1997. boxed, mass mkt. 16.95 incl. audio (0-9648762-0-5, Cats/Cass) Gloryvision.

Songs for Children, EFS5. (Illus.). 192p. 1962. pap. 12.95 (0-8256-2005-8, AM40049) Music Sales.

Songs for Computing & Marching: Adapted from Turkish Melodies. Turkan K. Gardenier. LC 89-90942. (Gardenier Math-Stat Ser.). (Illus.). (YA). (gr. 7-12). 1989. 20.00 (0-685-67706-0, 0007) Teka Trends.

***Songs for Discharming: Poems by Denise Sweet.** Denise Sweet. LC 97-70245. 64p. 1997. pap. 12.95 (0-912678-95-X) Greenfld Rev Lit.

Songs for Dogs (& the People Who Love Them) Ellen Bernfeld & Anne Bryant. (Illus.). 48p. (Orig.). 1995. pap. write for info. (0-9648762-2-1) Gloryvision.

Songs for Dogs (& the People Who Love Them) abr. ed. Ellen Bernfeld & Anne Bryant. (Illus.). 28p. (Orig.). 1995. pap. write for info. (0-9648762-4-8) Gloryvision.

***Songs for Dogs (& the People Who Love Them), Vol. 3.** 2nd rev. ed. Anne Bryant & Ellen Bernfeld. (Songs for... Ser.). (Illus.). 48p. (Orig.). 1995. boxed, mass mkt. 18.95 incl. cd-rom (0-9648762-8-0, Dogs/CD) Gloryvision.

***Songs for Earthlings.** Julie F. Middleton. 1997. pap. text ed. 25.00 (1-885349-06-8) Astarte Shell Pr.

***Songs for Earthlings.** Ed. & Compiled by Julie J. Middleton. 1997. pap. 21.95 (0-614-27452-4) Astarte Shell Pr.

Songs for Easy Piano: One Hundred Irish Ballads. 112p. (YA). 1981. pap. 16.95 incl. audio (0-7119-1868-6, S11245) Audio-Forum.

Songs for Easy Piano: Popular Irish Songs. 48p. (YA). 1989. pap. 16.95 incl. audio (0-7119-1866-X, S11260) Audio-Forum.

Songs for Every Season. Susan A. Muto et al. LC 88-63860. (Illus.). 55p. 1989. pap. 5.95 (0-932506-70-4) St Bedes Pubns.

Songs for Harmony. Stephen Gill. 80p. (Orig.). 1992. pap. 9.95 (0-934536-49-X) Rose Shell Pr.

Songs for Isadora. Linda W. Wagner. (Dialogues on Dance Ser.: No.1). 32p. 1981. pap. 6.00 (0-317-06435-5) Ommation Pr.

Songs for Jadina. Alan C. Lau. LC 80-66984. 94p. (Orig.). 1981. pap. 4.95 (0-912678-46-1, Greenfld Rev Pr) Greenfld Rev Lit.

Songs for Kids. (Xylotone Fun! Ser.). (Illus.). 16p. (J). 1992. 14.95 (0-7935-1770-2, 00824019) H Leonard.

Songs for Kids. (Recorder Fun! Ser.). (Illus.). 24p. (J). 1993. spiral bd. 9.95 (0-7935-2328-1, 00710393) H Leonard.

Songs for Kids. (Harmonica Fun Ser.). (Illus.). 00024p. (J). 1993. spiral bd. 9.95 (0-7935-2299-4, 00821016) H Leonard.

Songs for Kids. 12.95 (0-7935-4888-8, 00310070) H Leonard.

Songs for Life. (J). 1995. teacher ed. 42.50 (1-56212-114-6) CRC Pubns.

Songs for LIFE. CRC Publications Staff. LC 94-40068. 1994. spiral bd. 9.25 (1-56212-070-0) CRC Pubns.

Songs for Little Ones - Canciones Para Pequenos: Teacher's Guide - Guia de Maestros. Silvia Leon. (Illus.). 61p. (Orig.). 1995. pap. text ed. 8.95 (0-9643490-0-0) Smarty Kat.

***Songs for Mom & Me: Songs to Sing, Things to Do, for Mom & Me & Teacher Too.** Tonja E. Weimer. (Orig.). (J). (ps-3). 1997. audio 9.95 (0-936823-16-X) Pearce Evetts.

***Songs for Mom & Me: Songs to Sing, Things to Do, for Mom & Me & Teacher Too.** Tonja E. Weimer. (Illus.). 120p. (Orig.). (J). (ps-3). 1997. pap. 14.95 incl. audio (0-936823-15-1) Pearce Evetts.

Songs for My Sisters. Abba Elethea & James W. Thompson. 118p. (Orig.). 1993. pap. 12.95 (0-912607-02-5) Fire Pr.

Songs for My Sisters. Catharine S. Jones. 61p. 1992. pap. 10.00 (0-9633778-4-1) C S Jones.

Songs for Our Voices: Winning Poems in the Sixth Annual Anna Davidson Rosenberg Award for Poems on the Jewish Experience. Elaine Terranova et al. 80p. (Orig.). 1993. pap. 8.95 (0-943376-60-2) Magnes Mus.

Songs for Renewal. Janet L. Janzen. 1995. pap. 13.00 (0-06-066742-7) Harper SF.

***Songs for Scratching Mosquito Bites & Petting the Cat.** Shelley Kaplan. (Illus.). 32p. (J). (ps-8). 1998. 16.00 (0-9631833-1-1) Kaplan IL.

Songs for Seers. Pol Ndu. LC 73-91413. 35p. 1974. pap. 2.95 (0-88357-036-X) NOK Pubs.

Songs for Senior Centers. large type ed. Ed. by San Francisco Council of Churches Staff. ring bd. 10.00 (0-685-28626-6) NAVH.

Songs for Sheep School, Vol. I. Carol S. Wimmer. Ed. by Linda Rice. (Illus.). (Orig.). (J). (gr. k-4). 1996. digital audio 4.99 (1-888877-02-2) Sheep Schl.

Songs for Sheep School, Vol. I. Carol S. Wimmer. Ed. by Linda Rice. (Illus.). 42p. (Orig.). (J). (ps-4). 1996. teacher ed. 7.95 (1-888877-01-4); pap. 2.50 (1-888877-00-6) Sheep Schl.

Songs for Solo Voice & Piano. Ludwig van Beethoven. 1986. pap. 9.95 (0-486-25125-X) Dover.

Songs for Spiritual Warfare. M. Basilea Schlink. 48p. 1990. pap. 1.25 (3-87209-635-4) Evang Sisterhood Mary.

***Songs for Sugarloaf.** Robert G. Deamer. LC 97-17839. (J). 1997. pap. write for info. (0-7734-2818-6) E Mellen.

Songs for Survival: Songs & Chants from Tribal Peoples Around the World. Illus. by Bernard Lodge. LC 95-35649. 80p. (J). (gr. 3-12). 1996. pap. 18.99 (0-525-45564-7) Dutton Child Bks.

Songs for Thankful Hearts: A Music Resource from the Central States Synod. Compiled by Steven B. Eulberg. 44p. 1992. pap. text ed. 3.00 (0-9639663-2-4) Owl Mtn Music.

Songs for the Italian Class - Songbook. R. De Cesare. (C). 1984. 40.00 (0-8442-8063-1, Pub. by S Thornes Pubs UK); 110.00 incl. audio (0-8442-8062-3, Pub. by S Thornes Pubs UK) St Mut.

Songs for the Journey. Mary Christopher. (Illus.). 158p. (Orig.). 1988. pap. 7.98 (0-943699-00-2) Entheo Bks.

Songs for the Joy of Living. Illus. by Children at Sunrise Ranch. 50p. (J). (gr. 1-10). 1985. ring bd. 11.95 (0-932869-01-7) Emissaries.

Songs for the People: Teachings on the Natural Way. Arthur Solomon. 192p. 1990. pap. 14.95 (1-55021-058-0, Pub. by NC Press CN) U of Toronto Pr.

Songs for the Phoenix: Selected Poems 1982-1992. Michael Fitzgerald. 234p. (Orig.). 1995. pap. 19.95 (0-85398-393-3) G Ronald Pub.

***Songs for the Poor: Singers' Edition.** rev. ed. S. T. Kimbrough, Jr. Ed. by Timothy E. Kimbrough et al. 32p. 1997. pap. 3.00 (1-890569-00-3) Gnl Brd Glbl Minis.

Songs for the Queen of the Animals: A Book of Animal Poems. Scott Bates. (Illus.). 96p. (Orig.). (ENG & FRE.). 1993. pap. 7.00 (0-9627687-5-8) Proctors Hall Pr.

Songs for the Revolution. Hunce Voelcker. (Illus.). 3.00 (0-917996-03-8) Panjandrum.

Songs for the Russian Class - Songbook. R. De Cesare. (C). 1984. text ed. 40.00 (0-8442-4272-1, Pub. by S Thornes Pubs UK) St Mut.

Songs for the Russian Class - Songbook & Cassette. R. De Cesare. (C). 1984. text ed. 125.00 (0-8442-4271-3, Pub. by S Thornes Pubs UK) St Mut.

Songs for the Seasons. Jamake Highwater. LC 93-8094. (Illus.). (J). 1995. lib. bdg. 14.93 (0-688-10659-5) Lothrop.

Songs for the Seasons. Jamake Highwater. LC 93-8094. (Illus.). 32p. (J). (gr. k up). 1995. 15.00 (0-688-10658-7) Lothrop.

Songs for the Soul: Selections from Psalms. Jimmy Kessler. 32p. (Orig.). 1995. pap. 1.99 (0-9627775-5-2) Ledero Pr.

Songs for Worship: Toward a Quaker Hymnody. Carroll S. Feagins. (Illus.). 51p. (Orig.). 1995. pap. 10.00 (0-942727-27-4) NC Yrly Pubns Bd.

Songs from a Colonial Tavern. Tayler Vrooman. LC 64-8087. (Illus.). 48p. (Orig.). 1964. pap. 9.95 (0-910412-46-4) Colonial Williamsburg.

***Songs from a Mother's Heart: Meditations on the Psalms.** Pamela J. Kennedy. LC 96-44101. 192p. 1996. 12.99 (0-570-04891-5, 12-3308) Concordia.

An Asterisk (*) at the beginning of an entry indicates that the title is appearing in BIP for the first time.

Songs from Around the World. Ed. by Tony Esposito. 136p. 1995. pap. text ed. 12.95 (*0-89724-576-8*, MF9505) Warner Brothers.

Songs from Exile. Fritz-Meyer Sannon. (Orig.). 1996. pap. write for info. (*1-57553-110-0*) Watermrk Pr.

Songs from My Father's Pockets. Llewellyn I. Giles. (Illus.). 64p. (C). 1983. per. 4.50 (*0-937724-01-7*) Shadow Pr.

Songs from Sad to Glad Alleluias. William Kenefick. 120p. (Orig.). 1992. pap. text ed. 10.00 (*0-9620092-9-6*) Pine Isl Pr.

***Songs from Seasons on the Plains.** Elizabeth B. Lewis. 37p. 1990. pap. 3.50 (*0-614-24770-5*) Tesseract SD.

Songs from Spirit. Ed. by Larry G. Wayne & Grace P. Johnston. 179p. 1990. 16.95 (*1-55059-017-0*) Temeron Bks.

Songs from the American Revolutions. Kate Van Winkle Keller. (Illus.). 52p. (Orig.). 1992. pap. 5.95 (*1-877984-17-5*) Hendricksn Group.

Songs from the Center of the Well. rev. ed. Swami Chetanananda. 76p. 1985. pap. 7.95 (*0-915801-03-5*) Rudra Pr.

Songs from the Ghetto. Morris Rosenfeld. LC 76-104556. 123p. reprint ed. lib. bdg. 19.00 (*0-8398-1766-5*) Irvington.

Songs from the Hills. (*0-8317-5384-6*) Smithmark.

Songs from the House of Pilgrimage. Stephen Isaac. LC 77-169595. 213p. 1971. 16.00 (*0-8283-1334-2*) Christward.

Songs from the Land of Dawn. Tr. by Lois J. Erickson. LC 68-58828. (Granger Index Reprint Ser.). 1977. 17.95 (*0-8369-6014-9*) Ayer.

Songs from the Loom: A Navajo Girl Learns to Weave. Monty Roessel. LC 94-48765. (We Are Still Here Ser.). (Illus.). (J). (gr. 4-6). 1995. lib. bdg. 19.95 (*0-8225-2657-3*, Lerner Publctns) Lerner Group.

Songs from the Loom: A Navajo Girl Learns to Weave. Monty Roessel. (J). 1995. pap. 6.95 (*0-8225-9712-8*) Lerner Group.

Songs from the Native Lands. Victoria L. Manyarrows. LC 95-67634. 96p. 1995. pap. 9.95 (*0-9645234-1-8*) Nopal Pr.

Songs from the Pursuit of a No Strings Vision. Gloria George. LC 87-70420. 69p. 1987. 12.95 (*0-942275-00-4*) Cedar Pr.

***Songs from the Rainbow Worm: Poems, Drawings, Ceremonial Masks & Photographs.** Al Beck. (Illus.). 112p. (Orig.). 1997. pap. 9.00 (*0-934852-65-0*) Lorien Hse.

Songs from the Restoration Theatre. Willard Thorp. LC 76-102003. (Music Reprint Ser.). 1970. reprint ed. lib. bdg. 25.00 (*0-306-71867-7*) Da Capo.

Songs from the Sea. Samuel Salerno. 72p. (Orig.). (C). 1993. pap. 5.95 (*0-9638322-7-1*) S Salerno.

***Songs from the Sermon on the Mount.** 43p. 1994. 4.99 (*1-882854-03-9*) Lillenas.

Songs from This Earth on Turtle's Back: An Anthology of Poetry by American Indian Writers. Intro. by Joseph Bruchac. LC 82-82420. 300p. (Orig.). 1983. pap. 10.95 (*0-912678-58-5*, Greenfld Rev Pr) Greenfld Rev Lit.

Songs from Unsung Worlds: Science in Poetry. Ed. by Bonnie B. Gordon. LC 84-23677. (Illus.). 256p. reprint ed. pap. 73.00 (*0-7837-6743-9*, 2046371) Bks Demand.

Songs from Vagabondia. Bliss Carman & Richard Hovey. 1972. 59.95 (*0-87968-314-7*) Gordon Pr.

Songs from Vagabondia. Bliss Carman & Richard Hovey. LC 68-57593. 1970. reprint ed. text ed. 65.00 (*0-8371-1800-X*, CASO, Greenwood Pr) Greenwood.

Songs from Vagabondia. Bliss Carman. (BCL1-PR English Literature Ser.). 54p. 1992. reprint ed. lib. bdg. 59.00 (*0-7812-7495-8*) Rprt Serv.

Songs from Xanadu: Studies in Mongol-Dynasty Song-Poetry (San-Ch'u) James I. Crump. LC 83-7809. (Michigan Monographs in Chinese Studies: No. 47). (Illus.). xi, 232p. (Orig.). (C). 1983. pap. text ed. 15.00 (*0-89264-047-2*) Ctr Chinese Studies.

Songs I Can Play: Easy-to-Learn Numeral Notation Method for 8-Bar Xylophone, Resonator Bells, Piano. 5th ed. Peg Hoenack et al. (Melody Bells Ser.). (Illus.). 40p. (J). (ps-2). 1983. reprint ed. Big Book - Classrom Size. 49.95 (*0-913500-17-8*, S-3C); reprint ed. Little Book - Child's Size. spiral bd. 4.50 (*0-913500-21-6*, S-1) Peg Hoenack MusicWorks.

Songs I Can Play Teacher's Book: Easy-to-Learn Number Notation Method for 8-Bar Xylophone, Bells, Piano. 3rd ed. Peg Hoenack et al. (Melody Bells Ser.). (Illus.). 80p. 1974. spiral bd. 21.95 (*0-913500-01-1*, S-2TE) Peg Hoenack MusicWorks.

Songs in Action. Dale Griffee. 173p. 1992. pap. 13.95 (*0-13-824988-1*) P-H.

Songs in Action. 2nd ed. R. Phyllis Gelineau. 304p. (Orig.). 1988. pap. 26.95 (*0-318-35309-1*, Parker Publishing Co) P-H.

Songs in Many Keys. Oliver W. Holmes. (Notable American Authors Ser.). 1992. reprint ed. lib. bdg. 75.00 (*0-7812-3162-0*) Rprt Serv.

Songs in Ordinary Time. Mary McGarry Morris. 752p. 1996. pap. 12.95 (*0-14-024482-4*, Penguin Bks) Viking Penguin.

Songs in Sign. S. Harold Collins. (Beginning Sign Language Ser.). (Illus.). 16p. (J). 1995. pap. 2.95 (*0-931993-71-7*, GP-071) Garlic Pr OR.

Songs in Signed English. Harry Bornstein et al. (Signed English Ser.). (Illus.). 44p. (J). (ps-2). 1984. pap. 9.00 (*0-913580-12-0*, Pub. by K Green Pubns) Gallaudet Univ Pr.

Songs in the Night. Judy Miller. 500p. 1995. 12.95 (*0-942341-10-4*) Dawn Pubns TX.

Songs in the Night. Tracy L. Moore. 44p. (Orig.). 1995. pap. 8.00 (*0-9646927-0-8*) T L Moore.

Songs in the Night: How to Have Peace under Pressure. Donald A. Miller. 1992. pap. 1.49 (*0-87509-489-9*) Chr Pubns.

Songs in the Night: Inspiring Stories Behind 100 Hymns Born in Trial & Suffering. Henry Gariepy. 272p. (Orig.). 1996. 20.00 (*0-8028-3802-2*) Eerdmans.

Songs in the Plays of Lope de Vega: A Study of Their Dramatic Function. Gustavo Umpierre. (Monagrafias A Ser.: Vol. XLVI). 110p. (Orig.). (C). 1975. pap. 35.00 (*0-900411-97-X*, Pub. by Tamesis Bks Ltd UK) Boydell & Brewer.

***Songs in the Rough.** Bishop. Date not set. pap. 19.95 (*0-312-17029-7*) St Martin.

Songs in the Rough. Stephen Bishop. LC 95-45128. 160p. 1996. 27.95 (*0-312-14048-7*) St Martin.

Songs in 3/4 Time. 1988. per. 12.95 (*0-7935-0743-X*, 00361129) H Leonard.

Songs Kids Love. (Big Note Ser.). (J). 8.95 (*0-7935-5073-4*, 00310090) H Leonard.

***Songs My Father Never Sang.** J. C. Leissring. LC 96-94306. (Illus.). 476p. (Orig.). 1995. pap. 25.00 (*0-9630085-1-X*) J C Leissring.

Songs My Mother Sang to Me: An Oral History of Mexican American Women. Patricia P. Martin. LC 92-6745. (Illus.). 224p. (Orig.). 1992. 39.95 (*0-8165-1279-5*); pap. 17.95 (*0-8165-1329-5*) U of Ariz Pr.

Songs My Mother Taught Me. Audrey Thomas. 208p. 1993. pap. 14.95 (*0-88922-329-7*) Genl Dist Srvs.

Songs My Mother Taught Me: Stories, Plays, & Memoir. Wakako Yamauchi. 350p. 1994. 35.00 (*1-55861-085-5*); pap. 14.95 (*1-55861-086-3*) Feminist Pr.

***Songs My Paddle Sings: Native American Legends.** James Riordan. (Illus.). 128p. (J). (gr. 3-5). 1997. pap. 16.95 (*1-86205-076-7*, Pub. by Pavilion UK) Trafalgar.

Songs, Odes, Glees, & Ballads: A Bibliography of American Presidential Campaign Songsters. William Miles. LC 90-44938. (Music Reference Collection: No. 27). 256p. 1990. text ed. 59.95 (*0-313-27697-8*, MGI, Greenwood Pr) Greenwood.

Songs of a Bridge Builder. D. B. Steinman. 12.00 (*0-88253-762-8*); 4.80 (*0-88253-761-X*) Ind-US Inc.

***Songs of a Dead Dreamer.** Thomas Ligotti. 4.50 (*0-7867-0721-6*) Carroll & Graf.

Songs of a Dead Dreamer. Thomas Ligotti. 288p. 1991. pap. 4.50 (*0-88184-721-6*) Carroll & Graf.

Songs of a Far Walking Woman. Maggie Smith. (Illus.). 96p. (Orig.). 1996. pap. 9.50 (*0-9642979-1-4*) New Energy Pr.

Songs of a Friend: Love Lyrics of Medieval Portugal. Barbara H. Fowler & Cantigas De Amigo. LC 95-38532. (Illus.). 144p. (C). 1996. pap. 13.95 (*0-8078-4574-4*) U of NC Pr.

Songs of a Friend: Love Lyrics of Medieval Portugal. Barbara H. Fowler. LC 95-38532. (Illus.). 144p. (C). 1996. lib. bdg. 29.95 (*0-8078-2271-X*) U of NC Pr.

***Songs of a Happy Heart.** Grace McKee. 70p. (Orig.). 1996. pap. write for info. (*1-57502-353-9*, P01152) Morris Pubng.

Songs of a Mountain Plowman. Jesse H. Stuart. 162p. 1986. pap. 10.95 (*0-945084-00-5*) J Stuart Found.

Songs of a Returning Soul. Elizabeth Libbey. LC 81-71587. 1982. pap. 11.95 (*0-915604-67-1*) Carnegie-Mellon.

Songs of Aliscans. Michael A. Newth. LC 91-43662. (Library of Medieval Literature: Vol. 85B). 288p. 1992. text ed. 10.00 (*0-8153-0488-9*, GLML 85B) Garland.

Songs of America: A Cavalcade of Popular Songs with Commentaries. Ed. by David Ewen. LC 77-26155. (Illus.). 246p. 1978. reprint ed. text ed. 35.00 (*0-313-20166-8*, EWSA, Greenwood Pr) Greenwood.

Songs of America: A Cavalcade of Popular Songs, with Commentaries: Music Book Index. David Ewen. 246p. 1993. reprint ed. lib. bdg. 79.00 (*0-7812-9650-1*) Rprt Serv.

Songs of America: Big Note. 48p. 1986. pap. 4.95 (*0-7935-2703-1*, 00240881) H Leonard.

Songs of American Experience: The Vision of O'Neill & Melville. Marc Maufort. LC 90-41225. (American University Studies: American Literature: Ser. XXIV, Vol. 24). 226p. (C). 1991. text ed. 35.00 (*0-8204-1407-7*) P Lang Pubng.

Songs of American Folks. Ed. by Satis N. Coleman & Adolph Bregman. LC 68-57060. (Granger Index Reprint Ser.). 1977. 16.95 (*0-8369-6011-4*) Ayer.

Songs of American Labor, Industrialization & the Urban Work Experience: A Discography. Richard A. Reuss. Ed. by Yvonne Lockwood. (Program on Workers Culture Ser.). (Illus.). 109p. 1983. pap. 4.75 (*0-87736-344-7*) U of Mich Inst Labor.

Songs of Aristophanes. L. P. Parker. 608p. (C). 1997. 140.00 (*0-19-814944-1*) OUP.

Songs of Ascent. Jerry Hochbaum. 48p. (Orig.). 1993. pap. 5.95 (*1-57087-031-4*) Prof Pr NC.

Songs of Ascents (Psalms 120-134) Their Place in Israelite History & Religion. Loren D. Crow. LC 95-52852. (Society of Biblical Literature Dissertation Ser.). 240p. (C). 1996. 29.95 (*0-7885-0218-2*, 062148); pap. 19.95 (*0-7885-0219-0*, 062148) Scholars Pr GA.

Songs of Autumn: Bilingual Edition. Sigitas Geda. Tr. by Jonas Zdanys from LIT. LC 78-26139. 1979. pap. 3.00 (*0-918366-11-9*) Slow Loris.

Songs of Babyface. 80p. 1995. otabind 14.95 (*0-7935-4032-1*, 00313004) H Leonard.

***Songs of Belfast.** pap. 6.95 (*0-85342-776-3*, Pub. by Mercier Pr IE) Music Sales.

Songs of Berry Gordy: The Music, the Magic, the Memories of Motown. Ed. by Jeannette Delisa. 236p. (Orig.). 1995. pap. 29.95 (*0-89724-721-3*, PF9510) Warner Brothers.

Songs of Bilitis. Pierre Louys. (Illus.). 192p. 1988. reprint ed. pap. 5.95 (*0-486-25670-7*) Dover.

Songs of Bleeding. Spider. (Illus.). 232p. 1992. 15.00 (*0-9628181-3-5*) Black Thistle Pr.

Songs of Bloody Harlan. Lee Pennington. 1975. pap. 10.00 (*0-87423-017-9*) Westburg.

Songs of Bob Dylan, Nineteen Sixty-Six to Nineteen Seveny-Five. Bob Dylan. Ed. by R. Ball & M. Okun. 1978. pap. 29.95 (*0-394-73523-4*) Knopf.

Songs of Burton Lane. (Composer Ser., Piano, Vocal, Guitar). (Illus.). 176p. 1991. pap. 16.95 (*0-7935-0085-0*, 00490474) H Leonard.

Songs of C. Griffes, Vol. 3: Medium Voice. C. Griffes. Date not set. pap. 16.95 (*0-7935-5197-8*) H Leonard.

Songs of Cat Stevens. (Illus.). 80p. 1983. pap. 14.95 (*0-7119-0289-5*, AM32954) Music Sales.

Songs of Cathay. Tr. by T. Z. Koo. 1984. reprint ed. pap. text ed. 15.00 (*0-87556-384-8*) Saifer.

Songs of Celtic Christianity. Dennis Doyle & Paula Doyle. (Illus.). 64p. (Orig.). 1994. write for info. (*1-886314-00-4*) Incarnat Music.

Songs of Chanukah. Jeanne Modesitt. (J). (ps-3). 1992. 15.95 (*0-316-57739-1*) Little.

Songs of Childhood. Reginald De Koven. 1972. 59.95 (*0-8490-1084-5*) Gordon Pr.

Songs of Childhood. Walter J. De La Mare. 106p. (J). (gr. 3 up). pap. 4.50 (*0-486-21972-0*) Dover.

Songs of Childhood. Walter J. De La Mare. (Granger Poetry Library). 184p. 1985. reprint ed. 25.00 (*0-89609-257-7*) Roth Pub Inc.

Songs of Christmas, No. 5. 64p. 1979. pap. 6.95 (*0-7935-0936-X*, 00106950) H Leonard.

Songs of Christmas: Upper Intermediate Piano Solos. (Upper Intermediate Piano Solos Ser.). 80p. 1988. pap. 9.95 (*0-7935-1886-5*, 00361111) H Leonard.

Songs of Christmas for Autoharp. Meg Peterson & Dan Fox. 1993. 5.95 (*0-87166-618-9*, 93696) Mel Bay.

Songs of Cities. Georgette Preston. 30p. (Orig.). (C). 1992. pap. text ed. 5.00 (*1-878173-27-8*) Birnham Wood.

Songs of Claude Debussy Vol. 1: High Voice. Claude Debussy. 168p. 1993. otabind 18.95 (*0-7935-2987-5*, 00660164) H Leonard.

Songs of Claude Debussy Vol. 2: Medium Voice. Claude Debussy. 184p. 1993. otabind 18.95 (*0-7935-2962-X*, 00660283) H Leonard.

Songs of Cornell. rev. ed. Ed. by Thomas A. Sokol. LC 88-47654. (Illus.). 128p. (C). 1988. 20.00 (*0-9620103-0-8*) Cornell U Glee Club.

Songs of Cornwall. Kenneth Pelmear. (C). 1989. 30.00 (*1-85022-010-7*, Pub. by Dyllansow Truran UK) St Mut.

Songs of Craig Carnelia. (Piano-Vocal-Guitar Ser.). (Illus.). 96p. (Orig.). 1993. pap. 12.95 (*0-7935-2816-X*, HL00312487) H Leonard.

Songs of Death: Performance, Interpretation & the Text of Richard III. Rudolph C. Hassel. LC 86-14659. 206p. 1987. reprint ed. pap. 58.80 (*0-608-02133-4*, 2062802) Bks Demand.

Songs of Degrees. Stephen Kaung. Ed. by Herbert L. Fader. 235p. 1970. 6.00 (*0-935008-32-2*); pap. 4.00 (*0-935008-33-0*) Christian Fellow Pubs.

Songs of Degrees: Essays on Contemporary Poetry & Poetics. John Taggart. LC 93-41326. 272p. (Orig.). 1994. pap. text ed. 29.95 (*0-8173-0713-3*) U of Ala Pr.

Songs of Deliverance. Flower A. Newhouse. LC 72-94582. 250p. 1972. 14.00 (*0-910378-08-8*) Christward.

Songs of Deliverance, Vol. 1. Bill Banks. (Power for Deliverance Ser.). (Orig.). 1987. pap. 5.95 (*0-89228-031-X*) Impact Christian.

Songs of Distant Earth. Arthur C. Clarke. 336p. 1987. mass mkt. 5.95 (*0-345-32240-1*, Del Rey) Ballantine.

Songs of Divinity: Songs of the Bards of Karnatak. Ed. by Keshav M. Mutalik. (C). 1995. 80.00 (*81-7154-788-5*, Pub. by Popular Prakashan II) S Asia.

Songs of Doc Watson. Doc Watson. (Illus.). 128p. pap. 17.95 (*0-8256-0120-7*, AM62489) Music Sales.

Songs of Don McLean. (Piano-Vocal-Guitar Personality Folio Ser.). (Illus.). 88p. (Orig.). 1991. pap. 14.95 (*0-7935-0070-2*, 00490401) H Leonard.

Songs of Don Williams. 120p. 1984. per. 14.95 (*0-88188-285-2*, 00358578) H Leonard.

Songs of Earth & Power. Greg Bear. 560p. 1994. 24.95 (*0-312-85669-5*) Tor Bks.

***Songs of Earth & Power.** Greg Bear. 1996. mass mkt. 6.99 (*0-8125-3603-7*) Tor Bks.

Songs of Eastern Birds. Donald J. Borror. 64p. 1984. pap. 8.95 incl. audio (*0-486-99912-2*); pap. 7.95 incl. lp (*0-486-22378-7*) Dover.

Songs of Ecstasy. Carolyn M. Kleefeld. (Illus.). 20p. (Orig.). 1990. pap. 5.95 (*0-9629133-0-8*) Atoms Mirror.

Songs of Edvard Grieg. Beryl Foster. (Illus.). 376p. 1990. text ed. 76.95 (*0-85967-791-5*, Pub. by Scolar Pr UK) Ashgate Pub Co.

Songs of England. Jerry Silverman. 12.95 (*1-56222-109-4*, 94408); audio 9.98 (*1-56222-110-8*, 94408C) Mel Bay.

***Songs of England.** Jerry Silverman. 19.95 incl. audio (*1-56222-512-X*, 94408P) Mel Bay.

Songs of England, Ireland, & Scotland: A Bonnie Bunch of Roses. Dan Milner & Paul Kaplan. 1983. pap. 17.95 (*0-8256-0256-4*, Oak) Music Sales.

Songs of Eternal Faith: Artistic Piano Arrangements of Best-Loved Hymns. Lynn S. Lund. LC 81-80954. 56p. (Orig.). 1982. pap. 9.98 (*0-88290-184-2*, 2901) Horizon Utah.

Songs of Everlasting Joy: Artistic Piano Arrangements of Best-Loved Hymns. Lynn S. Lund. 1980. 9.98 (*0-88290-155-9*) Horizon Utah.

Songs of Exile. Brian Daldorph. Ed. by Robert A. Manaster. (Chapbook Ser.: No. 17). 56p. 1990. pap. 4.95 (*0-932884-17-2*) Red Herring.

Songs of Experience. R. Clements. 10.99 (*1-85792-019-8*, Pub. by Christian Focus UK) Spring Arbor Dist.

Songs of Experience. William Blake. (Fine Art Ser.). 48p. 1984. reprint ed. pap. 3.95 (*0-486-24636-1*) Dover.

Songs of Experience: An Anthology of Literature on Growing Old. Margaret Fowler. 384p. 1991. pap. 12.50 (*0-345-36057-5*, Ballantine Trade) Ballantine.

Songs of Experience: Making Your Feelings an Ally of Your Faith. Roy Clements. LC 95-4939. 176p. (gr. 10). 1995. reprint ed. pap. 12.99 (*0-8010-5271-8*) Baker Bks.

Songs of Experience: The Poetics of Tamil Devotion. Norman Cutler. LC 86-45051. (Religion in Asia & Africa Ser.). (Illus.). 224p. 1987. 31.50 (*0-253-35334-3*) Ind U Pr.

Songs of Faith & Praise: Conventional Note Hymnal. Alton H. Howard. 1068p. 1994. text ed. 9.99 (*1-878990-32-2*) Howard Pub LA.

Songs of Faith & Praise: Shaped Hymnal. Alton H. Howard. 1068p. 1994. text ed. 9.99 (*1-878990-34-9*) Howard Pub LA.

Songs of Faith & Praise - Leaders Worship Planner Hymnal. 1030p. 1994. teacher ed., ring bd. 54.99 (*1-878990-35-7*) Howard Pub LA.

***Songs of Faith for Young People: 26 Songs to Play & Sing.** Ed. by Tony Esposito. 56p. (Orig.). (J). 1997. pap. text ed. 10.95 (*1-57623-969-1*, AF9737) Warner Brothers.

Songs of Flying Dragons. Peter H. Lee. LC 73-92866. (Harvard-Yenching Institute Monographs: No. 22). 352p. 1975. 22.50 (*0-674-82075-4*) HUP.

Songs of France. Jerry Silverman. 9.95 (*0-7866-0093-4*, 95230) Mel Bay.

Songs of Freedom. 24.95 (*0-7935-3669-3*, 00694945) H Leonard.

Songs of Fun & Faith by "Fish & Chip" Kenneth L. Pike & Stephen B. Pike. LC 79-115755. (Edward Sapir Monograph Ser. in Language, Culture & Cognition: No. 1). (Illus.). viii, 48p. (Orig.). 1977. pap. 10.00 (*0-933104-00-6*) Jupiter Pr.

Songs of Fun & Foolishness. Jerry Silverman. 12.95 (*1-56222-266-X*, 94553) Mel Bay.

Songs of Glory: Read & Play Elementary Piano Solos. 24p. 1993. pap. 7.95 (*0-7935-1930-6*, 00290396) H Leonard.

Songs of Glory: Stories of 300 Great Hymns & Gospel Songs. William J. Reynolds. 352p. (YA). (gr. 10). 1996. reprint ed. pap. 14.99 (*0-8010-5527-X*) Baker Bks.

Songs of God. Joseph Murphy. LC 79-52353. (Orig.). 1979. pap. 8.00 (*0-87516-379-3*) DeVorss.

Songs of God & Me. (J). 1979. 6.99 (*0-8341-9099-0*, MB-483) Lillenas.

Songs of God & Me, 1. (J). 1981. audio 12.99 (*0-685-68226-9*, TA-9026C) Lillenas.

Songs of God & Me, 2. (J). 1980. audio 12.99 (*0-685-68227-7*, TA-9027C) Lillenas.

Songs of God's Grace. M. R. Bawa Muhaiyaddeen. LC 73-91016. (Illus.). 154p. 1974. pap. 7.00 (*0-914390-02-3*) Fellowship Pr PA.

Songs of Gods, Songs of Humans: The Epic Tradition of the Ainu. Tr. by Donald L. Philippi. 432p. 1995. 55.00 (*0-86008-235-0*, Pub. by U of Tokyo JA) Col U Pr.

Songs of Gods, Songs of Humans: The Epic Tradition of the Ainu. Donald L. Philippi. LC 78-18002. (Illus.). 426p. reprint ed. pap. 121.50 (*0-8357-3704-7*, 2036429) Bks Demand.

Songs of Gold Mountain: Cantonese Rhymes from San Francisco Chinatown. Marion K. Hom. 1992. pap. 14.00 (*0-520-08104-8*) U CA Pr.

Songs of Henri Duparc: Music Book Index. Sydney Northcote. 122p. 1993. reprint ed. lib. bdg. 69.00 (*0-7812-9595-5*) Rprt Serv.

Songs of Hispanic Americans. Ruth DeCesare. Ed. by John O'Reilly & Patrick Wilson. 64p. (J). (gr. 4-12). 1991. teacher ed. 12.95 (*0-88284-486-5*, 3569); student ed. 5.50 (*0-88284-487-3*, 3568); teacher ed. 19.95 incl. audio (*0-88284-488-1*, 3570) Alfred Pub.

Songs of Homer. G. S. Kirk. 438p. 1962. text ed. 90.00 (*0-521-05890-2*) Cambridge U Pr.

Songs of Homer, Il see Homer & the Epic

Songs of Hope. Ed. by Holland Boring. 1979. pap. 2.75 (*0-88027-059-4*) Firm Foun Pub.

Songs of Hope. David Werdyger. LC 93-72595. 300p. 1993. 18.95 (*1-56062-226-1*) CIS Comm.

Songs of Hugo Wolf. Eric Sams. LC 92-28981. 416p. 1993. 39.95 (*0-253-35064-6*) Ind U Pr.

Songs of Hugo Wolf. Eric Sams. LC 92-28981. 416p. 1993. pap. 19.95 (*0-253-20790-8*, MB-790) Ind U Pr.

Songs of Idaho. Ed. by Glen Lockery. 94p. 1988. 25.00 (*0-9619700-0-6*); pap. 8.00 (*0-9619700-1-4*) Univ ID Alumni Assn.

Songs of Innocence. William Blake. LC 70-165396. 1971. reprint ed. pap. 4.95 (*0-486-22764-2*) Dover.

Songs of Innocence & Experience. Christopher Devinck. 1999. pap. 9.95 (*0-14-023296-6*) Viking Penguin.

Songs of Innocence & Experience, 2 bks., Set. William Blake. 112p. 1986. pap. 7.00 (*0-486-25264-7*) Dover.

Songs of Innocence & of Experience. William Blake. (Illus.). 156p. (Orig.). 1977. pap. 14.95 (*0-19-281089-8*) OUP.

Songs of Innocence & of Experience. William Blake et al. Ed. by Morton D. Paley & Andrew Lincoln. (Blake's Illuminated Bks.: Vol. 2). (Illus.). 212p. (Orig.). 1991. 75.00 (*0-691-06936-0*) Princeton U Pr.

Songs of Innocence & Songs of Experience. William Blake. (Thrift Editions Ser.). 64p. 1992. reprint ed. pap. 1.00 (*0-486-27051-3*) Dover.

Songs of Inspiration. (Easy Play Ser.: Vol. 267). 48p. 1990. pap. 5.95 (*0-7935-0112-1*, 00001265) H Leonard.

Songs of Inspiration, Vol. 307. 1990. pap. 4.95 (*0-7935-0168-7*, 00001376) H Leonard.

Songs of Inspiration: Artistic Piano Arrangements of New Latter-Day Saint Hymns. Lynn S. Lund. 40p. 1986. pap. text ed. 9.98 (*0-88290-276-8*) Horizon Utah.

Songs of Ireland. Jerry Silverman. 12.95 (*1-56222-113-2*, 94395); audio 9.98 (*1-56222-114-0*, 94395C) Mel Bay.

***Songs of Ireland.** Jerry Silverman. 19.95 incl. audio (*1-56222-513-8*, 94395P) Mel Bay.

S

Songs of Irish Rebellion: Political Street Ballads & Rebel Songs, 1780-1900. Georges D. Zimmermann. LC 67-21410. 344p. 1970. 35.00 (0-8103-5025-4) Gale.

Songs of Italy. Aleister Crowley. 1993. reprint ed. pap. 5.95 (1-55818-252-7) Holmes Pub.

***Songs of Jerry Livingston: The Twelfth of Never & Other Great Standards.** Ed. by Sy Feldman. 120p. (Orig.). (C). 1996. pap. text ed. 18.95 (1-57623-566-1, PF9637) Warner Brothers.

Songs of Jim Reeves. Jim Reeves. (Piano-Vocal-Guitar Personality Folio Ser.). (Illus.). 80p. 1985. pap. 12.95 (0-88188-340-9, 00358033) H Leonard.

Songs of John Jacob Niles: For High Voice & Piano. John J. Niles. 104p. 1990. otabind 12.95 (0-7935-2584-5, 50481076) H Leonard.

Songs of Joseph Marx: High Voice. Joseph Marx. 1993. pap. 18.95 incl. audio compact disk (0-7935-1945-4, 00747027) H Leonard.

Songs of Joseph Marx: Medium Voice. Joseph Marx. 1993. pap. 18.95 incl. audio compact disk (0-7935-1944-6, 00747026) H Leonard.

***Songs of Joy: New Meditations on the Psalms for Every Day of the Year.** Joan Chittister. LC 97-1676. 144p. (Orig.). 1997. pap. 12.95 (0-8245-1661-3) Crossroad NY.

Songs of Joyful Praise. Ed. by Frank Roberts. 1975. pap. 2.00 (0-88027-060-8) Firm Foun Pub.

Songs of Jubilee: New & Selected Poems. Sam Cornish. 150p. (Orig.). 1986. 20.00 (0-87775-195-1); pap. 10.95 (0-87775-196-X) Unicorn Pr.

Songs of Kabir. Tr. by Rabindranath Tagore. LC 74-82318. 187p. 1974. pap. 7.95 (0-87728-695-7) Weiser.

Songs of Kabir. Kabir. Tr. by Rabindranath Tagore & Norma B. Szekely. 96p. 1989. reprint ed. 7.50 (0-89564-080-5) IBS Intl.

Songs of Kabir from the Adi Granth. Nirmal Dass. LC 90-34852. 359p. 1991. text ed. 54.50 (0-7914-0560-5); pap. text ed. 21.95 (0-7914-0561-3) State U NY Pr.

Songs of Latin America. Jerry Silverman. 9.95 (0-7866-0094-2, 95231) Mel Bay.

Songs of Leonard Cohen. (Illus.). 96p. 1969. pap. 15.95 (0-8256-2654-4, AM23813) Music Sales.

Songs of Life. George R. Margetson. LC 76-39095. (Black Heritage Library Collection). 1977. reprint ed. 15.95 (0-8369-9033-1) Ayer.

Songs of Life: The Meaning of Country Music. Jennifer Lawler. LC 96-69695. (Illus.). 160p. (Orig.). 1996. pap. 15.95 (1-880654-09-1) Pogo Pr.

Songs of Living. Eithne Strong. LC 62-41413. 69p. reprint ed. pap. 25.00 (0-317-26740-X, 2024356) Bks Demand.

Songs of Livingston & Evans. (Piano-Vocal-Guitar Personality Folio Ser.). (Illus.). 048p. (Orig.). 1993. pap. 8.95 (0-7935-2403-2, 00312485) H Leonard.

Songs of Love. Jan Renfrow. (Illus.). 32p. (Orig.). 1987. pap. 10.00 (0-9613072-2-6) Jan Renfrow.

Songs of Love, Vol. 132. 56p. 1980. pap. 5.95 (0-7935-4438-6, 00101944) H Leonard.

Songs of Love: The Heights of Ecstasy, the Depths of Despair. Kenneth F. Wainner. (Orig.). 1996. pap. write for info. (1-57553-295-6) Watermrk Pr.

Songs of Love & Death: The Classical American Horror Film of the 1930s. Michael Sevastakis. LC 92-32226. (Contributions to the Study of Popular Culture Ser.: No. 37). 232p. 1993. text ed. 52.95 (0-313-27949-7, SKT, Greenwood Pr) Greenwood.

Songs of Love & Grief: A Bilingual Anthology in the Verse Forms of the Originals. Heinrich Heine. Tr. by Walter W. Arndt. LC 95-36589. (European Poetry Classics Ser.). 146p. (C). 1995. pap. 14.95 (0-8101-1324-4) Northwestern U Pr.

Songs of Love & Grief: A Bilingual Anthology in the Verse Forms of the Originals. Heinrich Heine. Tr. by Walter W. Arndt. LC 95-36589. (European Poetry Classics Ser.). 150p. 1995. text ed. 49.95 (0-8101-1323-6) Northwestern U Pr.

Songs of Love & Wind. Luis H. Duran. Tr. by Diana Russell-Pineda from ENG. LC 92-72431. (Illus.). 224p. (Orig.). 1992. pap. 10.00 (0-9623552-9-1) Ed Arcas.

Songs of Madness. Eve Rabel. 1994. 12.95 (0-533-10476-9) Vantage.

Songs of Many Seasons. Oliver W. Holmes. (Notable American Authors Ser.). 1992. reprint ed. lib. bdg. 75.00 (0-7812-3163-9) Rprt Serv.

Songs of Mary Chapin Carpenter. Mary C. Carpenter. 112p. 1991. per. 14.95 (0-7935-0341-8, 00490542) H Leonard.

Songs of Meera: Lyrics in Ecstasy. Tr. by Baldoon Dhingra. 136p. 1977. pap. 2.50 (0-86578-093-5) Ind-US Inc.

Songs of Mexico. Jerry Silverman. 9.95 (0-7866-0147-7, 95065) Mel Bay.

Songs of Miriam: A Women's Book of Devotions. Ed. by Mary L. Mild. LC 93-45872. 1994. pap. 7.00 (0-8170-1207-9) Judson.

Songs of Mortals, Dialogues of the Gods: Music & Theatre in Seventeenth-Century Spain. Louise K. Stein. LC 92-38274. (Oxford Monographs on Music). (Illus.). 592p. 1993. 95.00 (0-19-816273-1, Old Oregon Bk Store) OUP.

Songs of My Heart. Sandy Ray. Ed. by Cheryle Sytsma. (Illus.). 160p. (Orig.). 1991. pap. 7.98 (1-879068-07-9) Ray-Ma Natsal.

Songs of My Hunter Heart: A Western Kinship. Robert F. Gish. LC 91-20947. (Illus.). 164p. 1992. 21.95 (0-8138-0703-4) Iowa St U Pr.

Songs of My Hunter Heart: A Western Kinship. Robert F. Gish. LC 93-41728. 168p. 1994. pap. 8.95 (0-8263-1524-0) U of NM Pr.

***Songs of My People.** Charles B. Johnson. Date not set. write for info. (0-88143-149-4) Ayer.

Songs of My People. Charles B. Johnson. LC 76-161263. (Black Heritage Library Collection). reprint ed. 11.25 (0-8369-8822-1) Ayer.

Songs of My People: African Americans; A Self-Portrait. Ed. by Eric Easter. LC 91-18933. (Illus.). 209p. 1992. 39.95 (0-316-10966-5) Little.

Songs of My Pilgrimage. Leona Choy. 84p. (Orig.). 1994. pap. 5.95 (1-882324-07-2) Ambssdrs Christ.

Songs of My Soul: Daily Devotions from the Writings of Phillip Keller. W. Phillip Keller. 256p. 1993. pap. 11.99 (0-8254-2995-1) Kregel.

Songs of Nature. Ed. by John Burroughs. LC 79-98077. (Granger Index Reprint Ser.). 1977. 21.95 (0-8369-6070-X) Ayer.

Songs of Nature. Anne M. Rogel. (Illus.). 109p. (Orig.). 1995. pap. 10.00 (0-9645205-0-8) Dandelion Drms.

Songs of Nepal: An Anthropology of Newar Folksongs & Hymns. Siegfried Lienhard. 1992. 50.00 (0-7855-0287-4, Pub. by Ratna Pustak Bhandar) St Mut.

Songs of Nepal - An Anthropology of Newar Folk Songs & Hymns. Siegfried Lienhard. (C). 1991. text ed. 30.00 (0-7855-0155-X, Pub. by Ratna Pustak Bhandar) St Mut.

Songs of Oberlin. Ed. by Carolyn Rabson. LC 83-8152. (Illus.). 120p. 1983. reprint ed. 8.50 (0-9611434-0-1); reprint ed. pap. 5.00 (0-9611434-1-X) Oberlin Con Lib.

Songs of Our Ancestors: Poems about Native Americans. Mark Turcotte. LC 94-38380. (Many Voices, One Song Ser.). (Illus.). 48p. (J). (gr. 3 up). 1995. lib. bdg. 22.10 (0-516-05154-7) Childrens.

Songs of Our Ancestors: Poems about Native Americans. Mark Turcotte. (Many Voices, One Song Ser.). (Illus.). (J). (gr. 4-6). 1995. pap. 7.95 (0-516-45154-5) Childrens.

Songs of Our Faith. Nancy Tipton et al. (Illus.). 51p. 1990. reprint ed. pap. 8.95 (0-89084-532-8, 048520) Bob Jones Univ Pr.

Songs of Our Heritage. Nancy Tipton & Joan J. Pinkston. (Sound Forth Ser.). (Illus.). 80p. (Orig.). (YA). 1991. pap. 8.95 (0-89084-608-1, 053900) Bob Jones Univ Pr.

Songs of Ourselves. Rose B. Green. LC 81-67779. 64p. 1983. 9.95 (0-8453-4737-3, Cornwall Bks) Assoc Univ Prs.

Songs of Papa's Island. Barbara Kerley. LC 94-24581. (Illus.). 64p. (J). (gr. 2-5). 1995. 14.95 (0-395-71548-2) HM.

Songs of Passion. Leonard A. Temme. Ed. by Ronald B. Cannon. 51p. (Orig.). 1990. pap. 7.95 (0-944206-02-6) W FL Lit Fed.

Songs of Paul Francis Webster: The Greatest Standards. Ed. by Ronny S. Schiff. (Piano-Vocal-Guitar Ser.). 152p. (Orig.). 1992. pap. 14.95 (0-7935-0665-4, 00311508) H Leonard.

Songs of Paul McCartney, Vol. 118. 64p. 1979. pap. 6.95 (0-7935-2649-3, 00101946) H Leonard.

Songs of Paul Simon for Easy Piano. (Illus.). 88p. pap. 14.95 (0-8256-3306-0, PS11097) Music Sales.

Songs of Peace & Friendship. Jerry Silverman. 7.95 (1-56222-299-6, 94625) Mel Bay.

***Songs of Percy French.** James N. Healy. 80p. 9300. pap. 12.95 (1-900428-25-3, Pub. by Ossian IE) Dufour.

Songs of Power. Jean Starr. Ed. by Ana Takseena. 24p. (Orig.). 1987. pap. text ed. 3.00 (0-944667-00-7) Little Sister Pubns.

Songs of Praise. Kathleen Krull. LC 87-751091. (Illus.). 32p. (J). 1993. pap. 6.00 (0-15-277109-3) HarBrace.

Songs of Praise. Ed. by Percy Dearmer et al. Incl. Music Ed. enl. rev. ed. 932p. 1931. 49.95 (0-19-231207-3); write for info. (0-318-54893-3) OUP.

Songs of Praise: Late Elementary Piano Solos. 24p. 1993. pap. 7.95 (0-7935-2355-9, 00290423) H Leonard.

Songs of Praise Leatherflex. George Martin. 1982. pap. text ed. 10.99 (0-89283-172-3) Servant.

***Songs of Praises: Welsh-Rooted Churches Beyond Britain.** unabridged ed. Jay G. Williams, III. (Illus.). 334p. (Orig.). 1997. pap. 25.00 (0-9629662-3-1) G Santes.

Songs of Protest & Civil Rights. Compiled by Jerry Silverman. (Traditional Black Music Ser.). (Illus.). 80p. (YA). (gr. 5 up). 1992. lib. bdg. 18.95 (0-7910-1827-X) Chelsea Hse.

Songs of Psyche. Prem Kirpal. 104p. (C). 1989. 60.00 (81-209-0058-8, Pub. by Pitambar Pub II); pap. 25.00 (81-209-0052-9, Pub. by Pitambar Pub II) St Mut.

***Songs of Rechelesnesse: Langland & the Franciscans.** Lawrence M. Clopper. LC 97-23685. (C). 1997. 52.50 (0-472-10744-5) U of Mich Pr.

Songs of Rejoicing: Hymns for Worship, Meditation, & Praise. Ed. by John Worst & David P. Schaap. LC 89-90970. 320p. 1989. 12.00 (0-9622553-0-0); pap. 8.75 (0-9622553-1-9) Selah Pub Co.

Songs of Richard Faith. Richard Faith & High Voice. 99p. (C). 1993. pap. 17.50 (1-878617-04-4) Leyerle Pubns.

***Songs of Richard Faith - Low Voice.** Richard Faith. 99p. (C). 1995. pap. 17.50 (1-878617-16-8) Leyerle Pubns.

Songs of Richard Strauss: High Voice. 184p. 18.95 (0-7935-2935-2, 00747062) H Leonard.

Songs of Richard Strauss: Low Voice. 176p. 18.95 (0-7935-2936-0, 00747063) H Leonard.

Songs of Robert Burns. Ed. by Donald Low. LC 91-33768. (Illus.). 800p. (C). (gr. 13 up). 1993. text ed. 225.00 (0-415-03414-0, Routledge NY) Routledge.

Songs of Robert Burns. Robert Burns. Ed. by James C. Dick. LC 79-144552. reprint ed. 67.50 (0-404-08511-3) AMS Pr.

Songs of Robert Schumann. Eric Sams. 304p. 1993. pap. 15.95 (0-253-20809-2, MB-809) Ind U Pr.

Songs of Rod McKuen. Rod McKuen. 1960. 5.95 (0-318-00972-2) Cheval Bks.

Songs of Romance - Easy Piano. (Easy Piano Ser.). 144p. (Orig.). 1990. pap. 12.95 (0-7935-0050-8, 00490369) H Leonard.

Songs of Sacramento. Poets of Little Sister Publications Staff. Ed. by Ana Takseena. (Illus.). 43p. (Orig.). 1987. pap. text ed. 4.00 (0-944667-01-5) Little Sister Pubns.

Songs of Saint Francis. Wyn Aveyard. 1994. 12.50 (0-533-10701-6) Vantage.

Songs of Salanda: And Other Stories of Sulu. H. Arlo Nimmo. LC 93-42674. 248p. 1994. 22.50 (0-295-97334-X); pap. write for info. (0-295-97335-8) U of Wash Pr.

Songs of Sara. Elaine S. Brown. 1997. 19.95 (1-878647-30-X) Duncan & Duncan.

Songs of Scandinavia. G. Borrow. 1972. 59.95 (0-8490-1085-3) Gordon Pr.

Songs of Scotland. Wilma Paterson & Alasdair Gray. (Illus.). 208p. 1996. 50.00 (1-85158-722-5, Pub. by Mnstream UK) Trafalgar.

Songs of Scotland. Jerry Silverman. 12.95 (1-56222-111-6, 94391); audio 9.98 (1-56222-112-4, 94391C) Mel Bay.

***Songs of Scotland.** Jerry Silverman. 19.95 incl. audio (1-56222-514-6, 94391P) Mel Bay.

Songs of Scotland, Ancient & Modern, 4 vols, Set. Allan Cunningham. LC 75-144551. reprint ed. 295.00 (0-404-08640-3) AMS Pr.

Songs of Scotland Prior to Burns. Ed. by Robert Chambers. LC 73-144548. reprint ed. 57.50 (0-404-08627-6) AMS Pr.

Songs of Self-Esteem. Minnie O'Leary et al. (Illus.). 23p. 1981. pap. 4.95 (0-9603656-2-1); pap. 10.95 incl. audio (0-686-79640-3); audio 6.95 (0-686-79639-X) Whitenwife Pubns.

Songs of Sesame Street. (Easy ABC Music Ser.: No. 352). (Illus.). 64p. (J). 1990. pap. 4.95 (0-7935-0186-5, 00001408) H Leonard.

Songs of Sesame Street. 1990. pap. 5.95 (0-7935-0136-9, 00001298) H Leonard.

Songs of Seventy Six: A Folksinger's History of the Revolution. Oscar Brand. LC 72-83733. (Illus.). 176p. (YA). 1972. 16.95 (0-87131-092-9) M Evans.

Songs of Seventy Six: A Folksinger's History of the Revolution. Oscar Brand. LC 72-83733. (Illus.). 176p. (YA). 1975. pap. 8.95 (0-87131-170-4) M Evans.

Songs of Seydou Camara, Vol. 1: Kambili. Charles Bird et al. (Occasional Papers in Mande Studies). 120p. (Orig.). 1974. pap. text ed. 7.00 (0-941934-12-8) Indiana Africa.

Songs of Simon. Lonnie A. Simon. (Illus.). 64p. 6.95 (0-936369-94-9) Son-Rise Pubns.

Songs of Solitude, No. I. Michael Wrenn. (Songs Ser.). (Illus.). 64p. 1984. 12.50 (0-9612012-0-7) M Wrenn Pubns.

Songs of Something Else: Selected Poems of Gunnar Ekelof. Tr. by Leonard Nathan & James Larson from SWE. LC 81-47915. (Lockert Library of Poetry in Translation). 344p. 1982. pap. 12.95 (0-691-01389-6); text ed. 29.95 (0-691-06511-X) Princeton U Pr.

Songs of Sorrow Songs of Praise. Sandy Ray. Ed. by Cheryle Sytsma. LC 90-91937. (Illus.). 160p. (Orig.). 1990. pap. 7.98 (1-879068-00-1) Ray-Ma Natsal.

Songs of South Street--Street of Ships. Eric P. Russell & Mark Lovewell. (Illus.). 1978. pap. text ed. 4.00 (0-9601250-0-0) Chanteyman.

Songs of Steel. Andrew Ekwuru. (Kenya People Ser.). 160p. 1991. pap. 4.95 (0-237-49007-2, Pub. by Evans Bros Ltd UK) Trafalgar.

Songs of Sunrise: Seeds of Prayer. Wayne Simsic. LC 94-60154. 152p. (Orig.). 1991. pap. 9.95 (0-89622-600-X) Twenty-Third.

Songs of Surrender: Poems. Thomas Claire. LC 92-18520. 80p. (Orig.). 1991. pap. 8.95 (0-931832-94-2) Fithian Pr.

Songs of the American People. Jerry Silverman. 19.95 (1-56222-284-8, 94694) Mel Bay.

Songs of the Ancestors: A Comparative Study of Bashic Folklore. Dezxo Benedek. (Illus.). 642p. 1991. 55.00 (957-638-057-X, ANE008, Pub. by SMC Pub CC) Oriental Bk Store.

Songs of the Arcturians BK 1: Arcturian Star Chronicles. Patricia L. Pereira. (Arcturian Star Chronicles Ser.). 200p. (Orig.). 1996. pap. 12.95 (1-885223-43-9) Beyond Words Pub.

Songs of the British Isles. Jerry Silverman. 12.95 (1-56222-426-3, 94706) Mel Bay.

Songs of the British Music Hall. Peter Davison. (Illus.). 224p. 1971. pap. 19.95 (0-8256-0063-4, OK64007, Oak) Music Sales.

***Songs of the British Music Hall.** Peter Davison. 224p. 1997. pap. 19.95 (0-8256-0099-5, OK 64007) Music Sales.

Songs of the Church Hymnal. Ed. by Alton H. Howard. 735p. 1977. pap. 7.50 (1-878990-13-6) Howard Pub LA.

Songs of the Church, 21st Century Edition Hymnal. Alton H. Howard. 748p. 1990. pap. 7.99 (1-878990-14-4) Howard Pub LA.

Songs of the Civil War. Ed. & Compiled by Irwin Silber. 400p. Date not set. pap. 14.95 (0-486-28438-7) Dover.

Songs of the Cowboy. Ron Middlebrook. 96p. (Orig.). 1990. pap. 12.95 (0-931759-46-3) Centerstream Pub.

Songs of the Cowboy. N. Howard Thorp. 50p. 1989. pap. 7.95 (1-55709-122-6) Applewood.

***Songs of the Cowboys.** Compiled by Nathan H. Thorp & Guy Logsdon. LC 84-11872. 206p. 1984. reprint ed. pap. 58.80 (0-608-03993-4, 2064725) Bks Demand.

Songs of the Dancing Gods. Jack L. Chalker. 1990. mass mkt. 4.95 (0-345-34799-4, Del Rey) Ballantine.

Songs of the Doomed: More Notes on the Death of the American Dream, Vol. 3. Hunter S. Thompson. 320p. 1991. reprint ed. pap. 14.00 (0-671-74326-0) PB.

Songs of the Dove & the Nightingale: Sacred & Secular Music c.900-c.1600. Ed. by Greta M. Hair & Robyn E. Smith. (Book Ser.: Vol. 17). 304p. 1995. pap. text ed. 40.00 (2-88449-141-4, ECU33) Gordon & Breach.

Songs of the Dybbuk: New & Selected Poems. Adrienne Wolfert. 1990. pap. 10.00 (0-931642-25-6) Lintel.

Songs of the Earth: A Tribute to Nature, in Word & Image. (Miniature Editions Ser.). (Illus.). 128p. 1995. 4.95 (1-56138-523-9, Running Pr Mini Edtns) Running Pr.

Songs of the Fluteplayer: Seasons of Life in the Southwest. Sharman A. Russell. 1991. 18.95 (0-201-57093-9) Addison-Wesley.

Songs of the Fluteplayer: Seasons of Life in the Southwest. Sharman A. Russell. (Illus.). 176p. 1992. pap. 10.00 (0-201-60821-9) Addison-Wesley.

Songs of the Free. Compiled by Maria W. Chapman. LC 71-170693. (Black Heritage Library Collection). 1977. reprint ed. 20.95 (0-8369-8883-3) Ayer.

Songs of the Garden. HSA-UWC Staff. 211p. 9.95 (0-910621-55-1) HSA Pubns.

Songs of the Gay Nineties, EFS55. (Illus.). 160p. pap. 8.95 (0-8256-2055-4, AS10015) Music Sales.

Songs of the Good Earth. Margaret Phillips. LC 79-10731. 62p. 1980. pap. 5.95 (0-88289-221-5) Pelican.

Songs of the Great American West. unabridged ed. Ed. by Irwin Silber. 352p. 1995. reprint ed. pap. text ed. 14.95 (0-486-28704-1) Dover.

Songs of the Great Outdoors. Jerry Silverman. 15.00 (1-56222-236-8, 94570) Mel Bay.

Songs of the Harp: Twenty Songs about Harps & Harpers. Sylvia Woods. 48p. 1983. pap. 5.95 (0-9602990-1-7) Woods Mus Bks.

Songs of the Harp: 20 Songs about Harps & Harpers. 1987. pap. 9.95 (0-9602990-7-6, 00722140) H Leonard.

Songs of the Harp: 20 Songs about Harps & Harpers. 2nd ed. Sylvia Woods. 48p. 1993. pap. write for info. (0-936661-14-3) Woods Mus Bks.

Songs of the Harsh Devotee: The Tevaram of Cuntaramurttinayanar. Tr. & Intro. by David D. Shulman. LC 90-33158. (Studies on South Asia: No. 6). lxiv, 633p. 1990. 25.00 (0-936115-07-6) U Penn South Asia.

Songs of the Heart. Dorothy G. De Hart. 60p. (Orig.). 1995. pap. write for info. (1-57553-019-8) Watermrk Pr.

Songs of the Heart. large type ed. Date not set. 5.99 (1-871676-60-6, Pub. by Christian Focus UK) Spring Arbor Dist.

***Songs of the Heart: A Celebration of Kindred Spirits.** Flavia Weedn. (Flavia Main Street Gift Bks.). 1997. 6.95 (0-8362-5102-4) Andrews & McMeel.

Songs of the Hearth. Rose U. Mezu. 64p. (Orig.). 1994. 35.00 (0-87831-065-7); pap. 20.00 (0-87831-066-5) Blck Acad Pr.

Songs of the Holy Spirit. 1992. 2.45 (0-685-74849-9, AC-2001) Lillenas.

Songs of the Human Earth. Robert N. Erman. Ed. by Edy L. Benjamin. LC 93-80775. 48p. (Orig.). 1993. pap. 4.95 (1-883821-02-9) Mother Bird.

Songs of the Humpback Whale: A Novel in Five Voices. Jodi Picoult. 1992. 22.95 (0-571-12927-7) Faber & Faber.

Songs of the Immortals: An Anthology of Classical Chinese Poetry. Tr. by Yuan Z. Xu. 256p. 1994. pap. 10.95 (0-14-058685-7, Penguin Bks) Viking Penguin.

Songs of the Incarnation. 1987. 20.00 (0-9501351-8-6, Pub. by Wild Goose Pubns UK) St Mut.

Songs of the Irish. Ed. by Donal O'Sullivan. 199p. 8100. pap. 16.95 (0-85342-653-8) Dufour.

***Songs of the Irish.** Donal O'Sullivan. 200p. write for info. (1-900428-15-6, OS 00113, Pub. by Ossian Publns IE) Music Sales.

***Songs of the Kingdom.** Ed. by Sherwin MacIntosh. 256p. 1996. spiral bd. 6.99 (1-57782-008-8) Discipleshp.

Songs of the Kingdom. 4th ed. Ed. by Sherwin Macintosh. 184p. 1994. ring bd. 4.00 (1-884553-46-X) Discipleshp.

Songs of the Kingdom - Update. Ed. by Sherwin Mackintosh. 24p. 1994. ring bd. 0.75 (1-884553-47-8) Discipleshp.

***Songs of the Kisaeng.** Tr. by Constantine Contogenis & Wolhee Choe. (New American Translations Ser.: Vol. 10). (Illus.). 80p. (Orig.). 1997. pap. 11.50 (1-880238-53-5) BOA Edns.

Songs of the Maggodee. Keith D. Holmes. (Illus.). 95p. (Orig.). (J). 1982. pap. text ed. 5.00 (0-9608250-0-2) Educ Serv Pub.

Songs of the Martyrs: Hassidic Melodies of Maramures. Max Eisikovits. LC 79-67624. 1980. pap. 7.95 (0-87203-089-X) Hermon.

Songs of the Master's Love: Artistic Pinao-Vocal Arrangements. Jeff Bradford. 36p. (Orig.). 1991. pap. 9.98 (0-88290-369-1) Horizon Utah.

Songs of the Michigan Lumberjacks. Earl C. Beck. (University of Michigan Studies & Publications). 316p. reprint ed. pap. 90.10 (0-317-29151-3, 2055620) Bks Demand.

Songs of the Miller's Maid. Ginny Dustin. (Illus.). 50p. 1991. 30.00 (1-880551-00-4) Silver Hill.

***Songs of the Morning: Meditations for Healing & Self-Knowledge.** Michael Roden. LC 96-79639. 112p. (Orig.). 1997. pap. 11.95 (0-9652996-1-9) Infinite Passion.

Songs of the Nightingale: Poetry of the Heart. John C. Drake. LC 93-83991. (Illus.). 132p. (Orig.). 1993. 17.95 (0-9636472-5-3); pap. 13.99 (0-9636472-9-6) Nghtngale Pub.

Songs of the North. Sigurd F. Olson. 288p. 1987. pap. 11.95 (0-14-025218-5, Penguin Bks) Viking Penguin.

Songs of the Russian People: As Illustrative of Slavonic Mythology & Russian Social Life. W. R. Ralston. LC 77-132444. (Studies in Music: No. 42). 1970. reprint ed. lib. bdg. 75.00 (0-8383-1224-1) M S G Haskell Hse.

Songs of the Sabbath Sacrifice: Edition, Translation, & Commentary. Carol Newsom. (Harvard Semitic Studies). 476p. (C). 1985. 39.95 (0-89130-918-7, 04-04-27) Scholars Pr GA.

S

An Asterisk (*) at the beginning of an entry indicates that the title is appearing in BIP for the first time.

***Songs of the Sage: Original Songs of Range Doug.** Doug Green. (Illus.). 72p. (Orig.). 1997. pap. 14.95 (*1-57424-038-2*) Centerstream Pub.

Songs of the Sailor & Lumberman. 2nd ed. William M. Doerflinger. LC 72-81076. (Illus.). 397p. 1992. reprint ed. pap. 19.95 (*0-916638-40-5*) Meyerbooks.

Songs of the Saints of India. John S. Hawley & Mark Juergensmeyer. (Illus.). 256p. (C). 1988. pap. text ed. 16.95 (*0-19-505221-8*) OUP.

Songs of the Savior: Artistic Piano - Vocal Arrangements. Jeff Bradford. 30p. 1989. pap. 9.98 (*0-88290-341-1*) Horizon Utah.

Songs of the Sea. Jerry Silverman. 19.95 (*1-56222-283-X*, 94693) Mel Bay.

Songs of the Sea & Sailor's Chanteys. Ed. by Robert Frothingham. LC 70-99029. (Granger Index Reprint Ser.). 1977. 20.95 (*0-8369-6103-X*) Ayer.

Songs of the Season. Mark Parker et al. (Sound Forth Ser.). (Illus.). 80p. (Orig.). (YA). 1991. pap. 8.95 (*0-89084-555-7*, 051532) Bob Jones Univ Pr.

Songs of the Seasons. Colleen J. Houghtaling. (Illus.). 36p. (Orig.). 1988. pap. 4.50 (*0-317-91221-6*) H & H Pr.

Songs of the Seder: A Music Book to Accompany the Passover Haggadah - Twenty-Three Songs, Prayers, & Chants - Traditional & Contemporary - Transliteration & English - Keys That Are Easy to Sing & Play - Chords for Piano & Guitar. Ed. by Howard S. Rubenstein. 70p. (Orig.). (J). 1994. pap. 9.95 (*0-9638886-1-7*) Granite Hills Pr.

***Songs of the Serbian People: From the Collection of Vuk Karadzic.** Ed. by Milne Holton & Vasa D. Mihailovich. Tr. by Vasa D. Mihailovich. LC 97-4561. (Russian & East European Studies). 350p. 1997. 50.00 (*0-8229-3952-5*); pap. 19.95 (*0-8229-5609-8*) U of Pittsburgh Pr.

Songs of the Shaman: The Ritual Chants of the Korean Mudang. Boudewijn Walraven. 220p. 1994. 56.50 (*0-7103-0403-X*, A6841) Routledge Chapman & Hall.

Songs of the Shore. Robert L. Malone. (Illus.). 72p. 1981. 8.95 (*0-9606234-0-X*) Ark & Arbor.

Songs of the Sierras. Joaquin Miller. LC 71-104528. 309p. reprint ed. lib. bdg. 36.50 (*0-8398-1260-4*) Irvington.

Songs of the Slave: Vocal Score. K. Mechem. 64p. 1994. pap. 7.95 (*0-7935-3859-9*, 50482274) H Leonard.

Songs of the Soil. Fenton Johnson. LC 73-18583. reprint ed. 27.50 (*0-404-11394-X*) AMS Pr.

***Songs of the Soul.** Anne C. Decker. 138p. (Orig.). 1996. pap. 14.95 (*0-9652504-0-7*) Veritas Pr Ltd.

Songs of the Soul. Paramahansa Yogananda. LC 83-60701. (Illus.). 200p. 1983. 10.50 (*0-87612-251-9*) Self Realization.

Songs of the Soul. Paramahansa Yogananda. LC 80-69786. 112p. 1980. reprint ed. pap. 13.95 (*0-937134-02-3*) Amrita Found.

Songs of the South: An Anthology of Ancient Chinese Poems by Qu Yuan & Other Poets. Qu Yuan et al. Tr. & Intro. by David Hawks. (Classics Ser.). 352p. 1986. pap. 11.95 (*0-14-044375-4*, Penguin Classics) Viking Penguin.

Songs of the Spirit. Aleister Crowley. 1973. lib. bdg. 250.00 (*0-87968-220-5*) Krishna Pr.

Songs of the Spirit. Doug Hyde. (Illus.). 24p. 1985. pap. 4.95 (*0-685-33264-0*) Southwest Mus.

Songs of the Spirit. Ed. by Karl Bach et al. (Illus.). 160p. (Orig.). 1992. reprint ed. pap. text ed. 9.00 (*0-9620912-5-1*) Friends Genl Conf.

Songs of the Spirit. Aleister Crowley. 1992. reprint ed. pap. 27.50 (*1-872736-18-1*, Pub. by Mandrake Pr UK) Holmes Pub.

***Songs of the Starspinner.** Paula Van Meter. Ed. by R. C. Van Meter. LC 96-90730. 360p. (Orig.). 1996. pap. 18.95 (*0-9653899-1-X*) Digi Print.

***Songs of the Teton Sioux.** Harry W. Paige. lib. bdg. 20.95 (*0-8488-1902-0*) Amereon Ltd.

Songs of the Tewa. Ed. & Tr. by Herbert J. Spinden. LC 74-9023. (ENG.). reprint ed. 32.50 (*0-404-11901-8*) AMS Pr.

Songs of the Tewa: American Indian Home Songs, Sacred Chants, Ceremonial Songs, Magic Songs & Prayers. 3rd ed. Herbert J. Spinden. LC 92-33989. 125p. 1993. pap. 12.95 (*0-86534-193-1*) Sunstone Pr.

Songs of the Theater: A Definitive Index to the Songs of the Musical Stage. Richard Lewine & Alfred Simon. LC 84-13068. 916p. 1984. 82.00 (*0-8242-0706-8*) Wilson.

Songs of the Trail. Ron Middlebrook. (Illus.). 112p. (Orig.). 1992. pap. 14.95 (*0-931759-67-6*, 00000152) Centerstream Pub.

Songs of the Western Frontier. Jerry Silverman. 12.95 (*1-56222-310-0*, 94555) Mel Bay.

Songs of the Wild West. Comment by Alan Axelrod. (Illus.). 128p. (YA). 1991. pap. 19.95 (*0-671-74775-4*, S&S Bks Young Read) S&S Childrens.

Songs of the Wild West. Buffalo. (J). 1998. 20.00 incl. audio (*0-671-87175-7*, S&S Bks Young Read) S&S Childrens.

Songs of the Women Troubadors. Ed. by Matilda T. Bruckner et al. LC 95-2961. (Library of Medieval Literature: Vol. 97A). 194p. 1995. text ed. 46.00 (*0-8153-0817-5*) Garland.

Songs of the 1890s, No. 263. 160p. 1994. otabind 10.95 (*0-7935-3177-2*, 00102299) H Leonard.

Songs of the 1900s, No. 264. 160p. 1994. otabind 10.95 (*0-7935-3178-0*, 00102300) H Leonard.

Songs of the 1910s, No. 265. 168p. 1994. otabind 10.95 (*0-7935-3179-9*, 00102301) H Leonard.

Songs of the 20s. (Easy Piano Decade Ser.). 192p. 1993. otabind 14.95 (*0-7935-2672-8*, 00110023) H Leonard.

Songs of the '20s, No. 136. (Decade Ser.). 128p. 1988. per. 10.95 (*0-7935-1984-5*, 00243697) H Leonard.

Songs of the 20s, Vol. 228. (Decade Ser.). 136p. 1988. per. 12.95 (*0-7935-3685-5*, 00101931) H Leonard.

Songs of the 30s. (Easy Piano Decade Ser.). 208p. 1993. otabind 14.95 (*0-7935-2667-1*, 00110022) H Leonard.

Songs of the 30s, Vol. 229. (Decade Ser.). 136p. 1988. otabind 12.95 (*0-7935-4622-2*, 00101932) H Leonard.

Songs of the '60s, No. 35. (Decade Ser.). 64p. 1985. pap. 5.95 (*0-7935-0814-2*, 00243706) H Leonard.

Songs of the '60s, No. 140. (Decade Ser.). 160p. 1988. per. 11.95 (*0-7935-4568-4*, 00243701) H Leonard.

Songs of Three Centuries. enl. fac. rev. ed. Ed. by John Greenleaf Whittier. LC 72-38606. (Granger Index Reprint Ser.). 1977. 23.95 (*0-8369-6338-5*) Ayer.

Songs of Tradition. JTG of Nashville Staff. (J). (ps-3). 1996. 18.95 (*1-884832-77-6*) JTG Nashville.

***Songs of Troubadour & Trouveres.** Gerard Le Vot & Margaret Switten. Ed. by Samuel N. Rosenberg. Date not set. write for info. (*0-8153-1341-1*) Garland.

Songs of Urea & Futuna. E. G. Burrows. (BMB Ser.). 1974. reprint ed. 25.00 (*0-527-02291-8*) Periodicals Srv.

Songs of Vagabondia (with Bliss Carman) Richard Hovey. (Notable American Authors Ser.). 1992. reprint ed. lib. bdg. 75.00 (*0-7812-3191-4*) Rprt Serv.

Songs of Vittorio Giannini on Poems by Karl Flaster. Jeffrey W. Price. 112p. 1994. per. 16.95 (*0-8403-9398-9*) Kendall-Hunt.

Songs of Wade Hemsworth. Wade Hemsworth. 1989. pap. 19.95 (*0-921254-10-5*, Pub. by Penumbra Pr CN) U of Toronto Pr.

Songs of War. large type ed. Kate Alexander. 1988. 19.95 (*0-7089-8457-6*, Charnwood) Ulverscroft.

Songs of Western Birds. Donald J. Borror. 64p. 1984. pap. 8.95 incl. audio (*0-486-99913-0*) Dover.

***Songs of Western Frontiers for Fingerstyle Guitar.** pap. 12.95 (*0-7935-6570-7*) H Leonard.

Songs of Winnie-the-Pooh. A. A. Milne. (Illus.). 10p. (J). (gr. 4-7). 1994. pap. 5.99 (*0-525-45206-0*) Dutton Child Bks.

Songs of Wisdom & Circles of Dance: Hymns by the Satpanth Isma'ili Muslim Saint, Pir Shams. Tazim R. Kassam. LC 94-36269. (McGill Studies in the History of Religions). 424p. (C). 1995. text ed. 49.50 (*0-7914-2591-6*); pap. text ed. 16.95 (*0-7914-2592-4*) State U NY Pr.

Songs of Work & Protest. Edith Fowke & Joe Glazer. 290p. 1973. reprint ed. 9.95 (*0-486-22899-1*) Dover.

Songs of Zion. Michael Bushell. 240p. 1993. pap. 11.00 (*1-884527-04-3*) Crown & Covenant.

Songs of Zion. Silas L. Monk. 416p. 1997. write for info. (*1-887399-03-8*) Daystar Hse.

Songs of Zion: Accompanist's Edition. Ed. by Verolga Nix & Jefferson Cleveland. LC 81-8039. 352p. (Orig.). 1981. spiral bd. 11.95 (*0-687-39121-0*) Abingdon.

Songs of Zion: Songbook. Ed. by Verolga Nix & Jefferson Cleveland. LC 81-8039. 352p. (Orig.). 1981. pap. 9.95 (*0-687-39120-2*) Abingdon.

Songs of Zion: The African Methodist Episcopal Church in the United States & South Africa. James T. Campbell. (Illus.). 432p. 1995. 55.00 (*0-19-507892-6*) OUP.

Songs on the Death of Children. Ronit Lentin. 220p. 1996. pap. 13.95 (*1-85371-625-1*, Pub. by Poolbeg Pr IE) Dufour.

Songs on the Wind. Ed. by Cynthia Stevens & Nicole Walstrum. 1995. 69.95 (*1-56167-265-3*) Nat Lib Poetry.

Songs (Op. 40, 47, 56, 58, 60) Edward MacDowell. LC 73-170392. (Earlier American Music Ser.). 1972. 23.50 (*0-685-45908-X*) Da Capo.

Songs Remembered in Exile: Traditional Gaelic Songs from Nova Scotia Recorded in Cape Breton & Antigonish County Mostly in 1937. John L. Campbell. (Illus.). 260p. 1990. text ed. 60.00 (*0-08-037977-X*, Pub. by Aberdeen U Pr) Macmillan.

***Songs Running Deep: Notes from a Birder's Paradise.** Sheryl DeVore. LC 97-64. (Illus.). 176p. 1997. 21.95 (*1-883755-12-3*, 5123) Lost Riv Pr.

Songs Sacred & Serious: For Two-Part Choir. 65p. pap. 4.50 (*0-318-13638-4*) Board Jewish Educ.

Songs That Every Child Should Know. M. Bacon. (J). (ps-6). 1972. 59.95 (*0-8490-1086-1*) Gordon Pr.

Songs That Made History. Jerry Silverman. 12.95 (*1-56222-585-5*, 94626) Mel Bay.

Songs That Made Nashville Music City U. S. A. 224p. otabind 16.95 (*0-7935-4450-5*, 00310039) H Leonard.

Songs the Angels Sing. Kenneth Hayes. 24p. 1994. 16.95 (*1-885514-01-8*) Elizabeth Lee.

Songs Through the Centuries-High Voice. Bernard Taylor. (Carl Fischer's "All Time Favorites" Music Ser.). 176p. (Orig.). 1987. pap. 14.95 (*0-8258-0388-8*, ATF110) Fischer Inc NY.

Songs Through the Centuries-Low Voice. Bernard Taylor. (Carl Fischer's "All Time Favorites" Music Ser.). 176p. (Orig.). 1987. pap. 14.95 (*0-8258-0389-6*, ATF111) Fischer Inc NY.

***Songs to an African Sunset: A Zimbabwean Story.** Sekai Nzenza-Shand. (Illus.). 270p. 1997. pap. 10.95 (*0-86442-472-8*) Lonely Planet.

Songs to Birds. Jake Page. (Illus.). 144p. 1993. 18.95 (*0-87923-957-3*) Godine.

Songs to Birds. Jake Page. (Nonpareil Bks.). (Illus.). 144p. 1995. pap. 12.95 (*1-56792-042-X*) Godine.

Songs to Brighten Your Day: For Teachers of Young Children - Grades Ps-2. Dee Gibson & Joe Scruggs. (Illus.). (Orig.). 1984. pap. 9.95 incl. audio (*0-916123-00-6*) Ed Graphics Pr.

***Songs to Grow On.** 86p. 1979. 6.99 (*0-8341-9300-0*) Lillenas.

Songs to Krishna. Subramania Bharati. Tr. by David Bunce from TAM. (Writers Workshop Saffronbird Ser.). 1975. 14.00 (*0-88253-642-7*) Ind-US Inc.

Songs to Live By. Rick Cua. 1994. 9.99 (*1-56292-041-3*) Honor Bks OK.

Songs to Make the Dust Dance: The Ryojin Hisho of Twelfth-Century Japan. Yung-Hee Kim. LC 93-10237. 1993. 40.00 (*0-520-08066-1*) U CA Pr.

Songs to Poems by Arlo Bates. George W. Chadwick. LC 79-18584. (Earlier American Music Ser.). 1980. 29.50 (*0-306-77316-3*) Da Capo.

Songs to Remember, First Half of the 20th Century: Vol. 1. large type ed. Compiled by Robert W. Haacker. (Illus.). 140p. 1991. pap. 11.95 (*0-929442-07-5*) Publicare Pr.

Songs to Remember, First Half of the 20th Century: Vol. 2. large type ed. Compiled by Robert W. Haacker. (Illus.). 158p. 1991. pap. 11.95 (*0-929442-08-3*) Publicare Pr.

Songs to Seven Strings: Russian Guitar Poetry & Soviet "Mass Song" Gerald S. Smith. LC 83-49453. (Soviet History, Politics, Society & Thought Ser.). (Illus.). 288p. 1985. 27.50 (*0-253-35391-2*) Ind U Pr.

Songs to Share. Rose B. Goldstein. (Illus.). 64p. (ENG & HEB.). (J). (ps-5). 2.95 (*0-8381-0720-6*, 10-720) USCJE.

Songs to Sing & Picture: Grades PreK-2. Lillian L. Dudley & Harriet R. Kinghorn. 115p. (J). (ps-2). 1996. pap. text ed. 17.50 (*1-56308-367-1*) Teacher Ideas Pr.

Songs to Sing with Babies: Songs & Games to Develop Skills in Young Children 0-6 Yrs. Jackie Weissman. 64p. 1983. pap. 9.95 (*0-939514-05-2*) Miss Jackie.

***Songs Unsung.** Elizabeth Long. LC 96-27223. 1996. pap. 16.95 (*1-880090-37-6*) Galde Pr.

Songs Visions Traditions of Northwest Indian Tribes. Paul Martin. 4.00 (*0-686-15297-2*) Great Raven Pr.

Songs We Sing. Harry Coopersmith. (Illus.). 1950. 22.50 (*0-8381-0723-0*) USCJE.

Songs We Sing Around the Clock. (Sing-Along Bks.). (J). 1990. 3.50 (*0-685-31996-2*, H480) Hansen Ed Mus.

Songs We Sing on the Bus. (Sing-Along Bks.). (J). 1990. 3.50 (*0-685-31995-4*, G011) Hansen Ed Mus.

Songs Without Words for Piano. Mendelssohn. 152p. 1986. per. 8.95 (*0-7935-2596-9*) H Leonard.

***Songs 1895-1914.** Maurice Ravel. pap. 9.95 (*0-486-26354-1*) Dover.

Songsmith. Andre Norton & A. C. Crispin. 304p. 1992. 19.95 (*0-312-85123-5*) Tor Bks.

Songsmith. Andre Norton & A. C. Crispin. 304p. 1993. mass mkt. 4.99 (*0-8125-1107-7*) Tor Bks.

Songsters & Saints: Vocal Traditions on Race Records. Paul Oliver. (Illus.). 339p. 1984. pap. text ed. 19.95 (*0-521-26942-3*) Cambridge U Pr.

Songworks Vol. I: Singing in the Education of Children. Peggy D. Bennett & Douglas R. Bartholomew. (Music Ser.). (C). 1997. pap. text ed. 44.95 (*0-534-51327-1*) Wadsworth Pub.

Songwriter-Publisher Contract. Robert A. Livingston. 1985. pap. 20.00 (*0-932303-04-8*) GLGLC Music.

***Songwriters & Lyricists Handbook.** R. B. Makinson. 50p. (Orig.). 1996. spiral bd., pap. 15.00 (*0-9654228-2-8*) R Makinson.

Songwriter's Companion. Amy Appleby & Peter Pickow. (Illus.). 48p. 1992. pap. 4.95 (*0-8256-1347-7*, AM90164) Music Sales.

Songwriter's Demo Manual & Success Guide. 2nd rev. ed. George J. Williams, III. Ed. by Bill Dalton. LC 82-50166. (Illus.). 240p. 1997. lib. bdg. 29.95 (*0-935174-33-8*, Mus Bus Bks) Tree by River.

Songwriter's Guide to Chords & Progressions. Joseph R. Lilore. 48p. 1982. pap. 15.95 incl. audio (*0-9646596-0-3*) Lionhead Pubng.

Songwriter's Guide to Collaboration. Walter Carter. 198p. (Orig.). 1988. pap. 12.95 (*0-89879-322-X*, Wrtrs Digest Bks) F & W Pubns Inc.

Songwriter's Guide to Melodies. Joseph R. Lilore. 80p. 1989. pap. 11.95 (*0-9646596-1-1*) Lionhead Pubng.

Songwriter's Handbook. rev. ed. Tom T. Hall. LC 87-9468. (Illus.). 160p. 1987. reprint ed. 14.95 (*0-934395-40-3*) Rutledge Hill Pr.

Songwriter's Idea Book. Sheila Davis. 240p. 1992. 18.99 (*0-89879-519-2*, Wrtrs Digest Bks) F & W Pubns Inc.

Songwriter's Market Guide to Song & Demo Submission Formats. Ed. by Songwriter's Market Staff. 160p. 1994. 19.99 (*0-89879-544-3*, Wrtrs Digest Bks) F & W Pubns Inc.

***Songwriter's Market 1997.** 538p. 1997. 22.99 (*0-614-29478-9*, Wrtrs Digest Bks) F & W Pubns Inc.

***Songwriter's Market, 1998: 2500 Places to Sell Your Songs.** Cindy Laufenburg. 1997. pap. text ed. 22.99 (*0-89879-795-0*, Wrtrs Digest Bks) F & W Pubns Inc.

***Songwriters on Songwriting: The Expanded Version.** expanded ed. Paul Zollo. LC 97-2764. (Illus.). 650p. 1997. pap. 18.95 (*0-306-80777-7*) Da Capo.

Songwriters Playground, Vol. 1: Innovative Exercises in Creative Songwriting. Barbara L. Jordan. LC 93-72243. (Illus.). 110p. (Orig.). 1993. pap. 19.95 (*0-9637466-0-X*) Creat Music.

Songwriters' Rhyming Dictionary. Jane Whitfield. 1974. pap. 10.00 (*0-87980-293-6*) Wilshire.

Songwriters' Success Manual. Lee Pincus. LC 77-352498. (Illus.). 1976. pap. 9.95 (*0-918318-01-7*) Music Pr.

Songwriters' Success Manual. 2nd ed. Lee Pinus. LC 78-60263. 1978. pap. 9.95 (*0-918318-02-5*) Music Pr.

Songwriter's Workshop. Ed. by Harvey Rachlin. 86p. 1991. pap. 24.95 incl. audio (*0-89879-452-8*, Wrtrs Digest Bks) F & W Pubns Inc.

Songwriting: A Complete Guide to the Craft. Stephen Citron. LC 89-49700. (Illus.). 352p. 1990. reprint ed. pap. 15.95 (*0-87910-137-7*) Limelight Edns.

Songwriting: A Structured Approach. Robert A. Berger. LC 83-70101. (Illus.). 108p. (Orig.). 1983. pap. 8.95 (*0-911999-00-0*) Beer Flat.

Songwriting & the Creative Process. 1995. pap. 14.95 (*0-7935-5219-2*, 00330172) H Leonard.

Songwriting & the Creative Process: Suggestions & Starting Points for Songwriters. Steve Gillette. Ed. by Mark Moss. LC 94-17026. (Illus.). 128p. (Orig.). 1995. pap. 16.95 (*1-881322-03-3*) Sing Out.

Sonia. Timothy Cooper. LC 91-73764. 304p. (J). 1991. 19.95 (*0-9619914-1-0*) Americus Pr.

Sonia: Survival in War & Peace. Sonia Milner. LC 83-50758. 1983. pap. 8.95 (*0-88400-102-4*) Shengold.

Sonia & Barnie & the Noise in the Night. Rachel Pank. (J). 1991. pap. 13.95 (*0-590-44657-6*) Scholastic Inc.

Sonia & Kaye Marvins Portrait Collection. rev. ed. Anne W. Tucker et al. (Illus.). 48p. 1996. pap. 14.95 (*0-89090-068-X*) Tex A&M Univ Pr.

Sonia Balassanian. Donald Kuspit. (Illus.). 10p. (Orig.). 1989. pap. 10.00 (*0-913263-27-3*) Exit Art.

Sonia Begonia. Joanne Rocklin. 112p. (J). (gr. 3-7). 1987. pap. 2.50 (*0-380-70307-6*, Camelot) Avon.

Sonia Delaunay: A Retrospective. Ed. by Robert T. Buck et al. LC 79-57450. (Illus.). 236p. 1980. pap. 27.50 (*0-914782-32-0*) Buffalo Fine-Albrght-Knox.

Sonia Delaunay: Art into Fashion. Sonia Delaunay. 104p. 1986. pap. 17.95 (*0-8076-1166-2*) Braziller.

***Sonia Delaunay: Fashion & Fabrics.** Jacques Damase. LC 96-61494. (Illus.). 176p. 1997. pap. 34.95 (*0-500-27947-0*) Thames Hudson.

Sonia Delaunay: The Life of an Artist. Stanley Baron & Jacques Damase. LC 94-35072. (Illus.). 208p. 1995. 39.95 (*0-8109-3222-9*) Abrams.

Sonia Delaunay Patterns & Designs in Full Color. Sonia Delaunay. (Illus.). 64p. 1989. pap. 11.95 (*0-486-25975-7*) Dover.

Sonia's Daughters: Prostitutes & Their Regulation in Imperial Russia. Laurie A. Bernstein. LC 94-41271. 357p. 1995. 45.00 (*0-520-08916-2*) U CA Pr.

Sonic: Friend or Foe. Michael Teitelbaum. (J). 1995. pap. 2.50 (*0-8167-3672-3*) Troll Communs.

Sonic & Hedgehog: Golden Mini Play Lights. (J). (ps-3). 1993. 14.95 (*0-307-75401-4*) Western Pub.

Sonic & Knuckles. Michael Teitelbaum. (J). 1995. pap. 2.95 (*0-8167-3781-9*) Troll Communs.

Sonic Design: Practice & Problems. 2nd ed. Robert Cogan & Pozzi Escot. (Illus.). 191p. (C). 1992. reprint ed. Practice & Problems, 191p. student ed., pap. text ed. 25.00 (*0-9634500-1-8*) Pubn Contact Intl.

Sonic Design: The Nature of Sound & Music. 4th ed. Robert Cogan & Pozzi Escot. (Illus.). 350p. (C). Date not set. reprint ed. The Nature of Sound & Music, 425p. pap. 35.00 (*0-9634500-0-X*) Pubn Contact Intl.

Sonic Temple: The Cult. 1991. 18.95 (*0-7935-0300-0*, 00660055) H Leonard.

Sonic the Hedgehog. (J). 1995. write for info. (*0-7853-0849-0*) Pubns Intl Ltd.

Sonic the Hedgehog. (J). 1995. pap. 1.00 (*0-8167-3782-7*) Troll Communs.

Sonic the Hedgehog. Ken Penders & Mike Kanterovich. (Look & Find Ser.). (Illus.). 24p. (J). (ps-6). 1996. lib. bdg. 13.95 (*1-56674-125-4*, HTS Bks) Forest Hse.

Sonic the Hedgehog. Michael Teitelbaum. LC 93-14029. (Illus.). (J). (gr. 2-4). 1993. pap. 2.50 (*0-8167-3199-3*) Troll Communs.

Sonic the Hedgehog: Double Trouble. Parker Smith. (Big Golden Bks.). (Illus.). (J). (ps-3). 1996. 3.99 (*0-614-15643-2*, Golden Books) Western Pub.

Sonic the Hedgehog: Fortress of Fear. Michael Teitelbaum. LC 94-5271. (Illus.). 64p. (J). (gr. k-3). 1995. pap. 2.50 (*0-8167-3582-4*) Troll Communs.

Sonic the Hedgehog: Robotnik's Revenge. Michael Teitelbaum. LC 93-48920. (Illus.). 64p. (J). (gr. 2-4). 1996. pap. 2.50 (*0-8167-3438-0*) Troll Communs.

Sonic the Hedgehog: Up Against the Wall. John Michlig. (Look-Look Bks.). (J). (ps-3). 1996. pap. text ed. 3.95 (*0-307-12921-7*, Golden Pr) Western Pub.

Sonic the Hedgehog Activity Book. Michael Teitelbaum. LC 93-14029. (J). 1995. pap. 2.95 (*0-8167-3787-8*) Troll Communs.

Sonic Theology: Hinduism & Sacred Sound. Guy L. Beck. LC 92-42734. (Studies in Comparative Religion). 306p. (C). 1993. text ed. 39.95 (*0-87249-855-7*) U of SC Pr.

Sonic Transports: New Frontiers in Our Music. Cole Gagne. 1990. pap. 15.95 (*0-9625145-0-0*) De Falco Bks.

Sonic Transports: New Frontiers in Our Music. Cole Gagne. (Illus.). 256p. 1990. write for info. (*0-614-14151-6*) De Falco Bks.

Sonic 3 Official Play Guide. Eddie McKendrick. 1994. pap. 12.95 (*1-55958-536-6*) Prima Pub.

***Sonic 3D Blast Survival Guide.** Paz Derham. 1996. pap. 12.95 (*1-884364-46-2*) Sandwich Islands.

Sonidos a Mi Alrededor. Paul Showers. Tr. by Aida E. Marcuse from SPA. LC 95-10709. (Illus.). 32p. (SPA.). (J). (ps-2). 1996. 16.95 (*0-06-026228-1*, HpArco Iris); pap. 5.95 (*0-06-443418-4*, HpArco Iris) HarpC Child Bks.

Sonidos de la Noche. Lois G. Grambling. (Illus.). 40p. (SPA.). (J). (ps-6). 1996. pap. text ed. 6.95 (*1-877810-82-7*) Rayve Prodns.

Sonidos para Empezar: Beginning Sounds. Barbara Gregorich. Ed. by Joan Hoffman. Tr. by Shepherd-Bartram from ENG. (Illus.). 32p. (Orig.). (SPA.). (J). (ps). 1987. student ed. 1.99 (*0-938256-77-7*, 02077) Sch Zone Pub Co.

Soninke, 14 vols. C. O. Nwanunibu. Ed. by George Bond. LC 94-45813. (Heritage Library of African Peoples: Set 2). (Illus.). 64p. (YA). (gr. 7-12). 1996. lib. bdg. 15.95 (*0-8239-1978-1*) Rosen Group.

Sonja. Marian Lokvam et al. Ed. by Emily Lovas & Rhoda-Gale Pollack. LC 81-82156. (Illus.). 100p. 1981. 12.95 (*0-940316-00-5*) E J Hill & Co Inc.

Sonjo of Tanganyika. Robert F. Gray. LC 73-13319. (Illus.). 181p. 1974. reprint ed. text ed. 49.75 (*0-8371-7119-9*, GRST, Greenwood Pr) Greenwood.

Sonlu Elemanlarla Hesabin Esaslari. Tr. by N. Gokhan Sarigul & Nesrin Sarigul-Klijn from ENG. (TUR.). (C). 1994. 49.95 (*0-9643757-0-2*) N Sarigul-Klijn.

Sonnenergie: Herausforderung Fur Forschung, Entwicklung und Internationale Zusammenarbeit. Ed. by Academy of Sciences & Technology in Berlin Staff. (Akademie der Wissenschaften zu Berlin, Forschungsbericht Ser.: Bd. 1). (Illus.). xx, 281p. (GER.). (C). 1991. pap. 52.35 (*3-11-012954-X*) De Gruyter.

Sonnentempel. Herge. (Illus.). 62p. (GER.). (J). pap. 19.95 (*0-8288-5076-3*) Fr & Eur.

Sonnet: Its Origin, Structure & Place in Poetry. C. Tomlinson. 1972. 59.95 (*0-8490-1087-X*) Gordon Pr.

*__Sonnet: One Woman's Voyage from Maryland to Greece.__ Lydia Bird. LC 96-50352. 1997. pap. write for info. (*0-86547-507-5*, North Pt Pr) FS&G.

Sonnet Adoration of the Avatar: The Splendor of the Sathya Sai. Benito F. Reyes. (Illus.). 300p. 1985. reprint ed. pap. 20.00 (*0-939375-06-0*) World Univ Amer.

Sonnet in England & America: A Bibliography of Criticism. Compiled by Herbert S. Donow. LC 82-929. xxii, 477p. 1982. text ed. 59.95 (*0-313-21336-4*, DSE/, Greenwood Pr) Greenwood.

Sonnet-No Me Mueve, Mi Dios-Its Theme in Spanish Tradition. M. Cyria Huff. LC 73-94177. (Catholic University of America. Studies in Romance Languages & Literatures: No. 33). reprint ed. 37.50 (*0-404-50333-0*) AMS Pr.

Sonnet over Time: A Study in the Sonnets of Petrarch, Shakespeare, & Baudelaire. Sandra L. Bermann. LC 87-87220. (Studies in Comparative Literature: No. 63). ix, 174p. (C). 1988. 32.50 (*0-8078-7063-3*) U of NC Pr.

*__Sonnet Sequence: A Study of Its Strategies.__ LC 96-40461. (Studies in Literary Themes & Genres). 1997. write for info. (*0-8057-0970-3*, Twayne) Scribnrs Ref.

Sonnets. Donald Franklin. 84p. (Orig.). 1973. pap. 3.95 (*0-914714-00-7*) Donald Franklin.

Sonnets. Paul Jacob. 8.00 (*0-89253-553-9*); 4.00 (*0-89253-554-7*) Ind-US Inc.

Sonnets. Richard Jones. 1990. 25.00 (*0-938566-47-4*); pap. 6.00 (*0-938566-48-2*) Adastra Pr.

Sonnets. Mary Y. Sampson. Ed. by Mary Bertschmann. 64p. (Orig.). 1991. pap. 10.00 (*0-935505-07-5*) Bank St Pr.

Sonnets. William Shakespeare. Ed. by Hyder E. Rollins. (Crofts Classics Ser.). 96p. 1951. pap. text ed. write for info. (*0-88295-082-7*) Harlan Davidson.

Sonnets. William Shakespeare. Ed. by William Burto. pap. 2.95 (*0-451-51795-4*, CE1795, Sig Classics) NAL-Dutton.

*__Sonnets.__ William Shakespeare. 1997. 5.99 (*0-517-18725-6*) Random Hse Value.

Sonnets. William Shakespeare. Ed. by Levi Fox. (Shakespeare Collection). 160p. 1993. 4.95 (*0-85306-093-2*, Pub. by Jarrold Pub UK); 5.95 (*0-85306-533-0*, Pub. by Jarrold Pub UK) Seven Hills Bk.

Sonnets. William Shakespeare. Ed. by Douglas Bush & Alfred Harbage. (Pelican Shakespeare Ser.). 192p. (YA). (gr. 9 up). 1963. pap. 4.95 (*0-14-071423-5*, Pelican Bks) Viking Penguin.

*__Sonnets.__ William Shakespeare. (English Ser.). (C). 1998. pap. 9.95 (*0-17-443473-1*) Wadsworth Pub.

Sonnets. William Shakespeare. Ed. by G. Blakemore Evans. (The New Cambridge Shakespeare Ser.). (Illus.). 500p. (C). 1996. pap. text ed. 10.95 (*0-521-29403-7*) Cambridge U Pr.

Sonnets. William Shakespeare. Ed. by G. Blakemore Evans. (New Cambridge Shakespeare Ser.). (Illus.). 500p. (C). 1996. text ed. 39.95 (*0-521-22225-7*) Cambridge U Pr.

*__Sonnets.__ William Shakespeare. Ed. by Rex Gibson. (School Shakespeare Ser.). 208p. (C). 1997. pap. text ed. 7.95 (*0-521-55947-2*) Cambridge U Pr.

Sonnets. William Shakespeare. Ed. by Martin Dodsworth. 196p. 1993. pap. 2.95 (*0-460-87329-6*, Everyman's Classic Lib) C E Tuttle.

Sonnets. William Shakespeare. 160p. 1980. 9.95 (*0-312-74499-4*) St Martin.

Sonnets. William Shakespeare. Date not set. write for info. (*0-517-15124-3*) Random Hse Value.

*__Sonnets.__ William Shakespeare. Tr. by Ostap Tarnawsky. LC 97-93165. (Illus.). 321p. (ENG & UKR.). 1997. 25.00 (*0-9656983-0-0*) Mosty.

Sonnets. large type ed. William Shakespeare. 1992. pap. 24.95 (*0-7089-4516-3*, Trail West Pubs) Ulverscroft.

Sonnets. limited ed. Hayden Carruth. (Illus.). 48p. 1989. pap. 150.00 (*0-916375-10-2*) Press Alley.

Sonnets. rev. ed. William Shakespeare. 1964. pap. 4.95 (*0-451-52262-1*, Sig Classics) NAL-Dutton.

*__Sonnets.__ 3rd ed. William Shakespeare. (English Ser.). (C). 1998. text ed. 45.00 (*0-17-443474-X*) Wadsworth Pub.

Sonnets. William Shakespeare. Ed. by Arthur Quiller-Couch et al. (New Shakespeare Ser.). (C). 1969. reprint ed. pap. 9.95 (*0-521-09498-4*) Cambridge U Pr.

Sonnets & a Dream. William R. Huntington. LC 72-4965. (Romantic Tradition in American Literature Ser.). 64p. 1972. reprint ed. 18.95 (*0-405-04636-7*) Ayer.

Sonnets & a Lover's Complaint. William Shakespeare. (New Penguin Shakespeare Ser.). 448p. 1987. pap. 10.95 (*0-14-070732-8*, Penguin Classics) Viking Penguin.

Sonnets & a Lover's Complaint. rev. ed. William Shakespeare. Ed. by Martin Dodsworth. (Everyman Paperback Classics Ser.). 144p. (C). 1995. pap. 4.95 (*0-460-87516-7*, Everyman's Classic Lib) C E Tuttle.

Sonnets & Canzonets. A. Bronson Alcott. (Illus.). 1969. reprint ed. 15.00 (*0-87556-008-3*) Saifer.

Sonnets & Canzonets. Amos B. Alcott. LC 72-86166. reprint ed. 27.50 (*0-404-00305-2*) AMS Pr.

Sonnets & Canzonets. Amos B. Alcott. (Works of Amos Bronson Alcott). 1989. reprint ed. lib. bdg. 79.00 (*0-685-27406-3*) Rprt Serv.

Sonnets & Canzonets. Amos B. Alcott. (BCL1-PS American Literature Ser.). 149p. 1992. reprint ed. lib. bdg. 69.00 (*0-7812-6666-1*) Rprt Serv.

Sonnets & Lyrics. Helen H. Jackson. (Notable American Authors Ser.). 1992. reprint ed. lib. bdg. 75.00 (*0-7812-3360-7*) Rprt Serv.

Sonnets & Metrical Tales. Mary Bryan. LC 94-44532. (Revolution & Romanticism, 1789-1834 Ser.). 1995. 48.00 (*1-85477-178-7*, Pub. by Woodstock Bks UK) Cassell.

Sonnets & Narrative Poems: The Complete Non-Dramatic Poetry. rev. ed. William Shakespeare. Ed. by William Burto. 1986. pap. 5.95 (*0-451-52314-8*, Sig Classics) NAL-Dutton.

Sonnets & Other Dead Forms. Murphre Roos. 1980. pap. 3.50 (*0-916696-15-4*) Cross Country.

Sonnets & Other Poems. William L. Garrison. LC 78-104464. 96p. reprint ed. lib. bdg. 17.00 (*0-8398-0658-2*) Irvington.

Sonnets & Poems of Anthero De Quental. Anthero De Quental. 1972. 59.95 (*0-8490-1088-8*) Gordon Pr.

Sonnets & Songs. Francesco Petrarca. Tr. by Anna M. Armi. LC 75-41212. reprint ed. 67.50 (*0-404-14695-3*) AMS Pr.

Sonnets for a Christian Year. David R. Wones. (Illus.). 94p. (Orig.). 1987. pap. 5.95 (*0-936015-06-3*) Pocahontas Pr.

Sonnets for a Second Summer. Margaret Menamin. 60p. 1996. 15.95 (*1-882935-23-3*) Westphalia.

Sonnets for Ethiopians. J. Baxter & L. Harvey. LC 74-38009. (Black Heritage Library Collection). 1977. reprint ed. 21.95 (*0-8369-8977-5*) Ayer.

*__Sonnets for Lovers.__ unabridged ed. Thompson Lennox. 74p. (Orig.). 1997. pap. 12.00 (*1-890283-03-7*, 9702) L Thompson NY.

Sonnets for Mamie & Other Poems. Martha N. Kemp. LC 91-67747. 128p. 1993. pap. 8.00 (*1-56002-148-9*, Univ Edtns) Aegina Pr.

Sonnets from Later Life, 1981-1993. Kenneth E. Boulding. LC 94-30016. 1995. pap. 12.00 (*0-87574-920-8*) Pendle Hill.

Sonnets from the Portuguese. Elizabeth Barrett Browning. 112p. 1990. 14.95 (*0-385-41618-0*) Doubleday.

*__Sonnets from the Portuguese.__ Random House Value Publishing Staff. 1997. 4.99 (*0-517-18721-3*) Random Hse Value.

Sonnets from the Portuguese: A Celebration of Love. Elizabeth Barrett Browning. 64p. 1986. 8.95 (*0-312-74501-X*) St Martin.

*__Sonnets from the Portuguese: Illuminated by the Brownings' Love Letters.__ Elizabeth Barrett Browning. Ed. by William S. Peterson & Julia Markus. 128p. 1998. pap. 14.00 (*0-88001-510-1*) Ecco Pr.

Sonnets from the Portuguese: Illuminated by the Love Letters. Elizabeth-Barrett Browning. Ed. by Julia Markus & William S. Peterson. LC 95-43253. (Illus.). 128p. 1996. 22.00 (*0-88001-451-2*) Ecco Pr.

Sonnets from the Portuguese & Other Poems. Elizabeth Barrett Browning. (Thrift Editions Ser.). 64p. (Orig.). 1992. pap. 1.00 (*0-486-27052-1*) Dover.

Sonnets from the Puerto Rican. Jack Agueros. 1996. 20.00 (*1-882413-23-7*); pap. 12.00 (*1-882413-22-9*) Hanging Loose.

Sonnets from the Studio. Rose M. Walch. LC 85-51413. 54p. 1986. 3.95 (*0-938232-86-X*, Baker & Taylor) Winston-Derek.

Sonnets in the Name of Love: In the Names of Love. Nelson G. Alston. Ed. by Barbara P. Avent. (Illus.). 64p. (Orig.). (YA). 1993. pap. 10.95 (*0-9632202-2-5*) Alpha Bk Pr.

Sonnets of Andreas Gryphius: Use of the Poetic Word in the Seventeenth Century. Marvin S. Schindler. LC 79-630254. 187p. reprint ed. pap. 53.30 (*0-7837-4906-6*, 2044571) Bks Demand.

Sonnets of G. S. O. Marie B. Hall. LC 79-7102. 104p. 1979. 10.98 (*0-938760-06-8*) Veritat Found.

Sonnets of Giuseppe Belli. Giuseppe Belli. Tr. by Miller Williams from ITA. LC 80-24331. (Illus.). xx, 164p. 1981. text ed. 22.50 (*0-8071-0762-X*) La State U Pr.

Sonnets of Heart & Soul. Dana L. Andrews. (Illus.). 50p. (Orig.). 1996. pap. 6.95 (*1-888530-01-4*) Starchild Rdrs.

Sonnets of Jocelyn Hollis. Jocelyn Hollis. LC 81-90002. 59p. 1991. reprint ed. pap. text ed. 9.95 (*0-933486-21-9*) Am Poetry & Lit.

*__Sonnets of Robert Frost: A Critical Examination of the 28 Poems.__ H. A. Maxson. 192p. 1997. lib. bdg. 32.50 (*0-7864-0389-6*) McFarland & Co.

Sonnets of Shakespeare Solved. Henry Brown. LC 70-39545. reprint ed. 41.50 (*0-404-01135-7*) AMS Pr.

Sonnets of the English Renaissance. Ed. by J. W. Lever. LC 75-305102. (Renaissance Library). 186p. (C). 1974. pap. 22.00 (*0-485-12604-4*, Pub. by Athlone Pr UK) Humanities.

Sonnets of Thomas Edwards. Thomas Edwards. LC 92-23995. (Augustan Reprints Ser.: No. 164). 1974. reprint ed. 14.50 (*0-404-70164-7*, PR3431) AMS Pr.

Sonnets of William Shakespeare. Illus. by Frederick Marns. 168p. 25.00 (*0-85683-013-5*, Pub. by Shepheard-Walwyn Pubs UK) Paul & Co Pubs.

Sonnets of William Shakespeare. William Shakespeare. (Illus.). 1987. 3.99 (*0-517-63750-2*) Random Hse Value.

Sonnets of William Shakespeare: The Royal Shakespeare Theatre Edition. William Shakespeare. (Illus.). 176p. 1982. 19.95 (*0-685-06080-2*) Dufour.

Sonnets on Life. 2nd ed. Jerry R. Jax. LC 93-117604. 90p. 1993. Perfect bdg. pap. 9.95 (*0-9635472-0-8*) J R Jax.

Sonnets on Love & Death. Jean De Sponde. Tr. by Robert Nugent. LC 78-12395. 77p. 1979. reprint ed. text ed. 45.00 (*0-313-21126-4*, SPSL, Greenwood Pr) Greenwood.

Sonnets pour Helene. Pierre D. Ronsard. (Illus.). 228p. (FRE.). 1970. pap. 29.95 (*0-7859-5474-0*) Fr & Eur.

Sonnets pour une Fin de Siecle. Alain Bosquet. (FRE.). 1982. pap. 11.95 (*0-7859-2785-9*) Fr & Eur.

*__Sonnets to an Imaginary Madonna.__ Vardis Fisher. 84p. Date not set. 24.95 (*0-614-22024-6*) Idaho Ctr Bk.

*__Sonnets to Human Beings & Other Selected Works.__ 2nd ed. Tafolla. 1996. pap. text ed. write for info. (*0-07-063300-2*) McGraw.

Sonnets to My Psychiatrist. Jim Jordan. 1974. 4.00 (*0-685-67929-2*) Windless Orchard.

Sonnets to Orpheus. Tr. by Leslie Norris & Alan F. Keele. LC 88-63602. (Studies in German Literature, Linguistics & Culture: Vol. 42). (Illus.). 88p. (Orig.). (GER.). 1989. pap. 12.95 (*0-938100-66-1*) Camden Hse.

Sonnets to Orpheus. Rainer M. Rilke. Tr. & Intro. by David Young. LC 87-6146. (Wesleyan Poetry in Translation Ser.). 134p. (ENG & GER.). 1987. pap. 13.95 (*0-8195-6165-7*, Wesleyan Univ Pr) U Pr of New Eng.

Sonnets to Orpheus. Rainer M. Rilke. Tr. by C. F. MacIntyre. (C). 1960. pap. 10.95 (*0-520-01069-8*) U CA Pr.

Sonnets to Orpheus. Rainer M. Rilke. Tr. by Paul Wadden. 77p. (Orig.). 1989. pap. 8.00 (*0-933704-78-X*) Dawn Pr.

Sonnets to Orpheus. Rainer M. Rilke. Tr. by Kenneth Pitchford from GER. LC 81-84492. (Illus.). 68p. (Orig.). 1983. pap. 10.00 (*0-938266-01-2*) Purchase Pr.

Sonnets to Orpheus. Rainer M. Rilke. Tr. by Leslie Norris & Alan F. Keele. LC 88-63602. (GERM Ser.: Vol. 42). (Illus.). xix, 60p. (Orig.). (GER.). 1989. 29.95 (*0-938100-65-3*) Camden Hse.

Sonnets to Orpheus. Rainer M. Rilke. (Orig.). 1985. 13.70 (*0-671-55708-4*, Touchstone Bks) S&S Trade.

Sonnets to Orpheus. Rainer M. Rilke. Tr. & Intro. by Stephen Mitchell. LC 92-50444. (Pocket Classics Ser.). 128p. (Orig.). 1993. reprint ed. pap. 6.00 (*0-87773-874-2*) Shambhala Pubns.

Sonnets to Orpheus: Score Book One for Soprano & Chamber Ensemble. R. Danielpour. 168p. 1995. per. 50.00 (*0-7935-4998-1*, 50482477) H Leonard.

Sonnets to P. L. A. Harry Smith. 16p. (Orig.). 1979. pap. 5.00 (*0-933292-00-7*) Arts End.

Sonny Bloch's Cover Your Assets. Sonny Bloch & Jerome L. Hollingsworth. LC 92-10939. 160p. (Orig.). 1992. pap. 9.95 (*0-399-51778-2*, Perigee Bks) Berkley Pub.

Sonny Bubba's Southern Fried, Semi-Low Calorie Cookbook. Sonny B. Ferguson. LC 89-10839. (Illus.). 192p. (Orig.). 1989. pap. 8.95 (*1-55853-034-7*) Rutledge Hill Pr.

Sonny Jim of Sandy Point. S. B. Jones-Hendrickson. LC 88-81954. 297p. (Orig.). 1991. pap. 12.95 (*0-932831-07-9*) Eastern Caribbean Inst.

Sonny Rollins for Saxophone, MFM200. Charlie Gerard. (Illus.). 72p. 1987. pap. 12.95 (*0-8256-4200-0*, AM42201) Music Sales.

Sonny Stitt's Greatest Transcribed Solos. Gary Keller. Ed. by Scott Houston. (Illus.). 42p. (Orig.). (C). reprint ed. pap. 7.95 (*1-56516-013-4*) H Leonard.

Sonny Terry Licks for Blues Harmonica. Tom Ball. (Illus.). 48p. 1995. pap. text ed. 19.95 incl. audio compact disk (*1-57424-018-8*) Centerstream Pub.

Sonny Terry's Country Blues Harmonica. Sonny Terry et al. LC 74-23037. (Illus.). 96p. (Orig.). 1975. pap. 15.95 (*0-8256-0166-5*, OK63685, Oak) Music Sales.

*__Sonny the Trick Horse.__ Eddie Bowman. (J). 1997. write for info. (*1-56763-322-6*); pap. write for info. (*1-56763-323-4*) Ozark Pub.

*__Sonny's Beloved Bootsies.__ Lisa Stubbs. (J). 1997. pap. text ed. 5.95 (*0-7641-0166-8*) Barron.

Sonny's Secret. Judy Delton. 96p. (J). (ps-3). 1991. mass mkt. 3.99 (*0-440-40429-0*) Dell.

Sonochemistry: The Uses of Ultrasound in Chemistry. Mason. 1990. 109.00 (*0-85186-293-4*) CRC Pr.

Sonochemistry & Cavitation. Ed. by Milia A. Margulis. Tr. by Garson Leib. 544p. 1995. text ed. 220.00 (*2-88124-849-7*) Gordon & Breach.

*__Sonographic Review of the Abdomen.__ Janice Hickey. 200p. 1997. text ed. 42.95 (*0-397-51691-6*) Lppncott-Raven.

Sonographie des Knochens: Experimentelle und Klinische Ergebnisse Zur Verlaufskontrolle Nach Frakturen und Spongiosatransplantationen. H. B. Reith. (Illus.). vi, 58p. 1994. pap. 28.00 (*3-8055-5965-8*) S Karger.

Sonography of the Abdomen. Brooke Jeffrey & Philip W. Ralls. LC 93-36007. 432p. 1994. text ed. 155.00 (*0-7817-0130-9*) Lppncott-Raven.

Sonography of the Infant Hip: An Atlas. Reinhard Graf & Peter Schuler. Tr. by Terry Telger. LC 86-13178. 276p. 1986. 170.00 (*0-89573-451-6*, VCH) Wiley.

Sonography of the Infant Hip & Its Therapeutic Implications. Reinhard Graf et al. LC 95-25117. 127p. 1995. 64.95 (*3-8261-0041-7*, Chap & Hall NY) Chapman & Hall.

Sonoma: The Ultimate Winery Guide. Heidi Cusick. LC 94-34732. (Illus.). 120p. 1994. pap. 18.95 (*0-8118-0773-8*) Chronicle Bks.

Sonoma Coast: The Untameable Coast. 1995. 4.95 (*0-916310-05-1*) North of San Francisco.

Sonoma County Bike Trails. 2nd ed. Phyllis L. Neumann. (Illus.). 128p. (Orig.). 1996. pap. 111.95 (*0-9621694-1-2*) Penngrove Pubns.

Sonoma County Breeding Bird Atlas: Detailed Maps & Accounts for Our Nesting Birds. Ed. by Betty Burridge. LC 95-77779. 216p. 1995. pap. 15.00 (*0-9647516-3-1*) Madrone Audubon.

Sonoma County Guide 1996-1997: Your Most Complete Guide to the Sonoma County Wine Country. 13th ed. Mary B. Carey. (Illus.). 96p. 1996. pap. 5.95 (*0-931973-30-9*) Vintage Pubns.

Sonoma County Street Guide & Directory: 1995 Edition. Thomas Bros. Maps Staff. (Illus.). 156p. 1994. pap. 11.95 (*0-88130-738-6*) Thomas Bros Maps.

*__Sonoma County...Its Bounty: Chefs, Wineries & Food Producers.__ Ed. by Ellen D. Moorehead et al. (Illus.). 224p. 1997. 19.95 (*0-9658701-0-3*) E D Moorehead.

Sonoma-Mendocino Wine Tour. Vintage Image Staff et al. 144p. 1996. pap. 8.95 (*0-932664-32-6*) Wine Appreciation.

Sonoma Poets Collection. Ed. & Intro. by Kathleen Hill. 128p. (Orig.). 1986. pap. 6.95 (*0-912133-07-4*) Hilltop Pub Co.

Sonoma Poets Collection II. Sam Keen et al. 163p. (Orig.). 1996. pap. 9.95 (*0-912133-09-0*) Hilltop Pub Co.

Sonoma Valley: The Secret Wine Country. Kathleen T. Hill & Gerald N. Hill. Ed. by Mary E. Arnold. (Hill Guides: No. 1). (Illus.). 306p. (Orig.). 1996. pap. 12.95 (*0-912133-10-4*) Hilltop Pub Co.

*__Sonoma Valley Story: Pages Through the Ages.__ Robert M. Lynch. LC 97-91567. (Illus.). xviii, 312p. 1997. 29.95 (*0-9653857-0-1*) Sonoma Index-Tribune.

Sonomammography: An Atlas of Comparative Breast Ultrasound. P. B. Guyer & Keith C. Dewbury. 205p. 1987. text ed. 320.00 (*0-471-91342-1*, A R Liss) Wiley.

*__Sonora.__ Howard E. Hunt. 1998. pap. write for info. (*1-55611-535-0*) D I Fine.

Sonora: A Description of the Province. Ignaz Pfefferkorn. LC 89-5245. (Southwest Center Ser.). 329p. 1990. reprint ed. pap. 15.95 (*0-8165-1144-6*) U of Ariz Pr.

Sonora: An Intimate Geography. David Yetman. LC 95-32463. (University of Arizona Southwest Center Ser.). 272p. 1996. 45.00 (*0-8263-1701-4*) U of NM Pr.

Sonora: Its Geographical Personality. Robert C. West. LC 92-12490. (Illus.). 207p. (C). 1993. text ed. 24.95 (*0-292-76538-X*) U of Tex Pr.

Sonora - 2010. Robert C. Haywood & Richard L. Bolin. 100p. (Orig.). (C). 1989. pap. text ed. 40.00 (*0-945951-03-5*) Flagstaff Inst.

*__Sonoran Desert.__ Photos by Jack W. Dykinga. 167p. 1997. pap. 24.95 (*0-8109-2669-5*) Abrams.

Sonoran Desert: The Story Behind the Scenery. Christopher L. Helms. LC 80-82918. (Illus.). 48p. (Orig.). 1980. pap. 7.95 (*0-916122-71-9*) KC Pubns.

Sonoran Desert Handbook. Kathleen Paul. 1987. 3.95 (*0-9605656-4-7*) Desert Botanical.

Sonoran Desert Plants: An Ecological Atlas. rev. ed. Raymond M. Turner et al. LC 94-18723. (Illus.). 501p. 1995. 72.50 (*0-8165-1532-8*) U of Ariz Pr.

Sonoran Desert Spring. John Alcock. LC 93-41190. (Illus.). 180p. 1994. reprint ed. pap. 17.95 (*0-8165-1399-6*) U of Ariz Pr.

Sonoran Desert Summer. John Alcock. LC 89-20235. 187p. 1990. 32.95 (*0-8165-1150-0*) U of Ariz Pr.

Sonoran Desert Summer. John Alcock. LC 89-20235. (Illus.). 187p. 1994. reprint ed. pap. 16.95 (*0-8165-1438-0*) U of Ariz Pr.

Sonoran Seasons: A Year in the Desert. Gisela Jernigan. LC 93-38709. (Illus.). 32p. (Orig.). (J). (ps-5). 1994. pap. 10.95 (*0-943173-91-4*, Harbinger CO) R Rinehart.

Sonoran Strongman: Ignacio Pesqueira & His Times. Rodolfo Acuna. LC 73-76304. 191p. reprint ed. pap. 54.50 (*0-317-58223-2*, 2056379) Bks Demand.

Sonota Complex & Associated Sites on the Northern Great Plains. Robert W. Neuman. (Publications in Anthropology: No. 6). 216p. 1975. pap. 2.00 (*0-933307-11-X*) Nebraska Hist.

Sonovagun Stew: A Folklore Miscellany. Ed. by Francis E. Abernethy. LC 85-14290. (Texas Folklore Society Publications: No. 46). (Illus.). 184p. 1985. 21.95 (*0-87074-211-6*) UNTX Pr.

Sonrie - Dice el Crocodilo Tranquilo. Jane B. Moncure. LC 87-13833. (Castillo Magico Ser.). (Illus.). 32p. (SPA.). (J). (ps-2). 1987. lib. bdg. 21.36 (*0-89565-932-8*) Childs World.

Sonrie Otra Vez: Experimenta el Gozo Rebosante. Charles R. Swindoll. 198p. (SPA.). 1991. pap. 7.99 (*1-56063-288-7*, 490276) Editorial Unilit.

Sonriete y Muerete!/Say Cheese & Die. R. L. Stine. (Escalofrios - Goosebumps Ser.: No. 4). (J). (gr. 3 up). 1996. pap. text ed. 3.99 (*0-590-58292-5*) Scholastic Inc.

Sonrisa Etrusca. Jose L. Sampedro. 1995. pap. 14.95 (*0-679-76338-4*, Vin) Random.

Sons. Pearl S. Buck. LC 92-14988. 314p. 1992. pap. 8.95 (*1-55921-039-7*) Moyer Bell.

*__Sons...__ Ed. by Helen Exley. (Miniature Square Bks.). (Illus.). 64p. 1996. 6.00 (*1-85015-792-8*) Exley Giftbooks.

Sons. Franz Kafka. Ed. by Mark Anderson. LC 88-43243. (Kafka Library). 1989. pap. 10.00 (*0-8052-0886-0*) Schocken.

Sons. deluxe ed. Thomas McGuane. 1993. 75.00 (*0-935716-58-0*) Lord John.

Sons: A Mother's Manual. Elise Z. Karlin & Muriel Warren. 240p. 1994. pap. 10.00 (*0-380-76997-2*) Avon.

Sons & Adversaries: Women in William Blake & D. H. Lawrence. Margaret Storch. LC 90-31101. 256p. 1990. text ed. 30.00 (*0-87049-656-5*) U of Tenn Pr.

Sons & Daughters of America. Augustus Graham. (Orig.). 1993. pap. write for info. (*0-9636740-9-9*) Eldorado Pr.

Sons & Daughters of God. Joseph F. McConkie. 1994. 14.95 (*0-88494-936-2*) Bookcraft Inc.

Sons & Daughters of Labor: Class & Clerical Work in Turn-of-the-Century Pittsburgh. Ileen A. Devault. LC 90-55134. (Illus.). 208p. 1990. 30.50 (*0-8014-2026-1*) Cornell U Pr.

Sons & Daughters of Labor: Class & Clerical Work in Turn-of-the-Century Pittsburgh. Ileen A. DeVault. (Illus.). 208p. 1995. pap. 12.95 (*0-8014-8307-7*) Cornell U Pr.

*__Sons & Daughters of the Light: A National Pastoral Plan for Ministry with Young Adults.__ United States Catholic Conference Staff. 68p. (Orig.). 1997. pap. 9.95 (*1-57455-127-2*) US Catholic.

*__Sons & Fathers.__ Christopher Hallowell. Date not set. write for info. (*0-688-06958-4*) Morrow.

An Asterisk (*) at the beginning of an entry indicates that the title is appearing in BIP for the first time.

Sons & Lovers. (Book Notes Ser.). 1985. pap. 2.50 (0-8120-3540-2) Barron.

***Sons & Lovers.** Lawrence. Date not set. pap. text ed. write for info. (0-17-556631-3) Addison-Wesley.

Sons & Lovers. D. H. Lawrence. (Longman Simplified English Ser.). 124p. pap. text ed. 5.95 (0-582-52634-5) Addison-Wesley.

Sons & Lovers. D. H. Lawrence. 432p. 1991. 17.00 (0-679-40572-0, Everymans Lib) Knopf.

Sons & Lovers. D. H. Lawrence. 1976. 23.95 (0-8488-0561-5) Amereon Ltd.

Sons & Lovers. D. H. Lawrence. (Classics Ser.). 432p. 1985. 4.95 (0-553-21192-7) Bantam.

Sons & Lovers. D. H. Lawrence. Ed. by Helen Baron & Carl Baron. (Cambridge Edition of the Works of D. H. Lawrence). 760p. (C). 1992. 34.95 (0-521-43221-9); text ed. 120.00 (0-521-24276-2) Cambridge U Pr.

Sons & Lovers. D. H. Lawrence. (Study Texts Ser.). 1988. pap. text ed. 5.95 (0-582-33166-8, 72062) Longman.

Sons & Lovers. D. H. Lawrence. 1985. pap. 5.95 (0-451-51882-9, Sig Classics) NAL-Dutton.

Sons & Lovers. D. H. Lawrence. LC 63-1407. 1978. 8.95 (0-394-60452-0, Modern Lib) Random.

***Sons & Lovers.** D. H. Lawrence. LC 96-37891. 1997. 18.50 (0-679-60268-2, Modern Lib) Random.

Sons & Lovers. D. H. Lawrence. 1982. mass mkt. 4.95 (0-14-043154-3, Penguin Bks) Viking Penguin.

Sons & Lovers. D. H. Lawrence. 1989. pap. 8.95 (0-14-018215-2, 462, Penguin Classics) Viking Penguin.

Sons & Lovers. D. H. Lawrence. Ed. by Helen Baron & Carl Baron. 544p. 1995. pap. 10.95 (0-14-018832-0, Penguin Classics) Viking Penguin.

Sons & Lovers. D. H. Lawrence. (Critical Edition Ser.). (C). Date not set. pap. text ed. write for info. (0-393-95758-6, Norton Paperbks) Norton.

Sons & Lovers. D. H. Lawrence. 1976. pap. 6.95 (0-14-004217-2, Viking) Viking Penguin.

Sons & Lovers. Ed. by Rick Rylance. (New Casebooks Ser.). 224p. 1996. text ed. 39.95 (0-312-15958-7) St Martin.

Sons & Lovers. Ed. by David Trotter. LC 94-11777. (World's Classics Ser.). 528p. 1995. pap. 7.95 (0-19-283107-0) OUP.

Sons & Lovers. large type ed. D. H. Lawrence. (Classics Ser.). 1988. 16.95 (0-7089-8008-2, Charnwood) Ulverscroft.

***Sons & Lovers.** large type ed. D. H. Lawrence. 642p. 1997. reprint ed. lib. bdg. 25.00 (0-939495-13-9) North Bks.

Sons & Lovers. D. H. Lawrence. 1982. reprint ed. lib. bdg. 28.95 (0-89966-400-8) Buccaneer Bks.

Sons & Lovers: Text & Criticism. D. H. Lawrence. Ed. by Julian Moynahan. (Critical Studies: No. 4). 624p. 1977. pap. 14.95 (0-14-015504-X, Viking) Viking Penguin.

Sons & Lovers: Trevor Griffith's Screenplay of the Novel by D. H. Lawrence. Trevor Griffith. (Illus.). 317p. 1982. pap. 18.95 (0-85124-334-7, Pub. by Spokesman Bks UK) Coronet Bks.

Sons & Lovers Notes. Rita G. Shaw. 1965. pap. 4.25 (0-8220-1210-3) Cliffs.

***Sons & Mothers: Letters of Luminaries in the Arts.** Karen E. Gordon & Holly Johnson. LC 97-14494. 1997. write for info. (1-56512-121-X) Algonquin Bks.

Sons for the Return Home. Albert Wendt. (Talanoa Ser.). 218p. 1996. pap. 12.95 (0-8248-1796-6) UH Pr.

Sons from Afar. Cynthia Voigt. 3.95p. 1988. mass mkt. 4.50 (0-449-70293-6, Juniper) Fawcett.

Sons from Afar. Cynthia Voigt. LC 87-1857. 224p. (YA). (gr. 7 up). 1987. lib. bdg. 15.95 (0-689-31349-7, Atheneum Bks Young) S&S Childrens.

Sons from Afar. Cynthia Voigt. 1996. 4.99 (0-689-80889-5, S&S Bks Young Read) S&S Childrens.

***Sons, Lovers & Fathers: Understanding Male Sexuality.** Didier Dumas et al. Tr. by Anne Trager from FRE. LC 96-31300. 200p. 1997. 29.95 (0-7657-0033-6) Aronson.

Sons of Africa. Georgina A. Gollock. LC 75-89001. 247p. 1969. reprint ed. text ed. 52.50 (0-8371-1746-1, GSA&, Greenwood Pr) Greenwood.

Sons of an Ancient Glory. B. J. Hoff. LC 93-16176. (Emerald Ballad Ser.: Vol. 4). 400p. (Orig.). 1993. pap. 10.99 (1-55661-113-7) Bethany Hse.

Sons of Babylon: One Financial Step for Man One Monetary Leap for Mankind. Phillip J. Maltese. (Illus.). 120p. 1996. write for info. (0-9649478-0-3) B J Mud.

Sons of Babylon: One Financial Step for Man One Monetary Leap for Mankind. Phillip J. Maltese. (Illus.). 120p. 1996. pap. write for info. (0-9649478-1-1) B J Mud.

Sons of Batt Coltrain. large type ed. Amy Sadler. (Linford Western Large Print Ser.). 1994. pap. 15.99 (0-7089-7643-3) Ulverscroft.

Sons of Ben: Jonsonian Comedy in Caroline England. Joe L. Davis. LC 67-11271. 252p. reprint ed. 71.90 (0-685-16234-6, 2027602) Bks Demand.

Sons of Darkness: Tales of Men, Blood & Immortality. Ed. by Michael Rowe & Thomas Roche. 180p. (Orig.). 1996. pap. 12.95 (1-57344-059-0) Cleis Pr.

Sons of Darkness, Sons of Light. Mary LaCroix. 537p. (Orig.). 1987. pap. 9.95 (0-87604-202-7, 334) ARE Pr.

Sons of Eli. David I. Naglee. (Illus.). 400p. 1993. pap. 14.95 (0-938991-82-5) Colonial Pr AL.

Sons of God. R. Swinburne Clymer. 1925. 15.00 (0-686-00829-4) Philos Pub.

Sons of God. Christine Mercie. 1954. pap. 6.95 (0-87516-059-X) DeVorss.

Sons of God, Sons of Men. Catherine Young. 100p. 1984. 29.00 (0-317-43637-6, Pub. by Regency Press UK) St Mut.

Sons of Grady Rourke. Douglas Savage. LC 95-9453. 210p. 1995. 19.95 (0-87131-785-0) M Evans.

Sons of Grady Rourke. large type ed. Douglas Savage. (Western Ser.). 424p. 1996. 19.95 (0-7862-0820-1, Thorndike Lrg Prnt) Thorndike Pr.

***Sons of Grady Rourke.** Douglas Savage. 320p. 1996. reprint ed. mass mkt. 4.99 (0-8439-4120-0) Dorchester Pub Co.

Sons of Heaven. large type ed. Terence Strong. 1991. 27.99 (0-7089-8592-0, Trail West Pubs) Ulverscroft.

Son's of Inu: Secret of the Hidden Valley. Gary Flint. 115p. (J). (gr. 4-9). 1994. pap. 10.00 (1-885631-05-7) G F Hutchison.

Sons of Ishmael: A Study of the Egyptian Bedouin. George W. Murray. LC 74-15071. reprint ed. 49.50 (0-404-12115-2) AMS Pr.

***Sons of Jacob: Thomas Mann, Freud, & Joseph & His Brothers.** William E. McDonald. 1998. 54.95 (1-57113-258-9) Camden Hse.

***Sons of Liberty.** Adele Griffin. 160p. (J). (gr. 3-7). 1997. pap. 13.95 (0-7868-0351-7); lib. bdg. 13.89 (0-7868-2292-9) Hyprn Child.

Sons of Liberty. large type ed. Adam Rutledge. (General Ser.). 318p. 1992. pap. 16.95 (0-8161-5495-3, GK Hall) Thorndike Pr.

Sons of Liberty: The Masculine Mind in Nineteenth Century America. David G. Pugh. LC 83-10755. (Contributions in American Studies: No. 68). xxii, 186p. 1983. text ed. 45.00 (0-313-23934-7, PSL/, Greenwood Pr) Greenwood.

Sons of Liberty in New York. Henry B. Dawson. LC 71-90172. (Mass Violence in America Ser.). 1975. reprint ed. 13.95 (0-405-01306-X) Ayer.

Sons of Martha: Civil Engineering Readings in Modern Literature. Ed. by Augustine J. Fredrich. 610p. 1989. text ed. 35.00 (0-87262-720-9) Am Soc Civil Eng.

Sons of Samurai: Japanese Males. John R. Terry. 176p. 1988. pap. 9.95 (0-933704-70-4) Dawn Pr.

Sons of Science: The Story of the Smithsonian Institution & Its Leaders. Paul H. Oehser. LC 69-10144. (Illus.). 220p. 1969. reprint ed. text ed. 59.75 (0-8371-0185-9, OESI, Greenwood Pr) Greenwood.

Sons of Sergei: Khrushchev & Gorbachev as Reformers. Ed. by Donald R. Kelly & Shannon G. Davis. LC 91-46993. 264p. 1992. text ed. 55.00 (0-275-94011-X, C4011, Praeger Pubs) Greenwood.

Sons of Sheba's Race: African-Americans & the Italo-Ethiopian War, 1935-1941. William R. Scott. LC 92-7900. (Blacks in the Diaspora Ser.). (Illus.). 384p. 1993. 42.50 (0-253-35126-X) Ind U Pr.

Sons of Texas: Rogues & Ranchers. Annette Broadrick. 1996. mass mkt. 4.99 (0-373-48336-8) Harlequin Bks.

Sons of the American Revolution, 1962-1982: An Historical Anthology. Harry L. Walen, Jr. et al. (Illus.). xvi, 304p. 1985. 20.00 (0-9607188-0-X) Nat Soc of Sons.

Sons of the Eagle. George Creel. LC 79-117778. (Essay Index Reprint Ser.). 1977. 23.95 (0-8369-1797-9) Ayer.

Sons of the Empire: The Frontier & the Boy Scout Movement 1890-1918. Robert H. MacDonald. LC 93-93285. 258p. 1993. 35.00 (0-8020-2843-8) U of Toronto Pr.

Sons of the Father. Gordon Dalbey. LC 96-26298. 1996. pap. 10.99 (0-8423-6156-1) Tyndale.

Sons of the Gods, Children of Earth: Ideology & Literary Form in Ancient Greece. Peter W. Rose. LC 91-31562. 432p. 1992. 49.95 (0-8014-2425-9); pap. 17.95 (0-8014-9983-6) Cornell U Pr.

Sons of the Machine: Case Studies of Social Change in the Workplace. Charles H. Savage, Jr. & George Lombard. (Organization Studies). (Illus.). 389p. 1986. 30.00 (0-262-19243-8) MIT Pr.

Sons of the Morning. Lenora Boneck. LC 88-92285. 112p. 1989. pap. 8.95 (0-940415-08-9) B & K Pub Hse.

Sons of the Old Country. Waldemar Ager. Tr. by Trygve M. Ager from NOR. LC 82-17484. Orig. Title: Gamlelandets Sonner. xvi, 255p. 1983. pap. 8.95 (0-8032-5905-0, Bison Books) U of Nebr Pr.

Sons of the Prophets Vol. 1: Nine Inspirational Stories about African Men & Boys in the Land of Captivity. Mamadou Chinyelu. LC 95-90985. 80p. (Orig.). 1996. pap. 9.95 (0-9652664-1-9) Mstrd Seed.

Sons of the Revolution: Radical Democrats in France, 1860-1914. Judith F. Stone. LC 95-32092. (Illus.). 448p. (C). 1996. text ed. 55.00 (0-8071-2020-0) La State U Pr.

Sons of the Revolution in the State of Alabama: Centennial Register. Frwd. by Centennial Committee Sons of the Revolution in the State of Alabama Staff & Norman Woodall. LC 93-74916. (Illus.). 214p. (C). 1994. 25.00 (0-9640149-0-4) Sons Revolution AL.

Sons of the Sea Goddess: Economic Practice & Discursive Conflict in Brazil. Antonius C. Robben. 360p. 1989. text ed. 39.50 (0-231-06842-5) Col U Pr.

Sons of the Shaking Earth. Eric R. Wolf. LC 59-12290. (Illus.). 314p. 1962. pap. text ed. 13.95 (0-226-90500-4, P90) U Ch Pr.

Sons of the Sheik. E. M. Hull. 1976. reprint ed. lib. bdg. 26.95 (0-89190-735-1, Rivercity Pr) Amereon Ltd.

Sons of the Sheik. E. M. Hull. 1990. reprint ed. lib. bdg. 23.95 (0-89968-530-7) Buccaneer Bks.

Sons of the Soil: Migration & Ethnic Conflict in India. Myron Weiner. LC 78-51202. (Illus.). 403p. reprint ed. pap. 114.90 (0-8357-7897-5, 2036316) Bks Demand.

Sons of the South. Clayton Rand. LC 61-8069. (Illus.). 212p. 1961. 13.95 (0-911116-76-1) Pelican.

Sons of the Wild Jackass. Ray T. Tucker & Frederick R. Barkley. LC 70-99727. (Essay Index Reprint Ser.). 1977. 29.95 (0-8369-1385-X) Ayer.

Sons of the Wilderness. Charles Thompson. LC 88-70987. 1988. reprint ed. 12.95 (0-9617367-6-3) Guild Pr IN.

Sons of the Wind: The Sacred Stories of the Lakota. Ed. by D. M. Dooling. LC 91-58396. 160p. (Orig.). 1992. pap. 11.00 (0-06-250234-4) Harper SF.

Sons of the Wind: The Search for Identity in Spanish American Indian Literature. Braulio Munoz. LC 81-15403. 335p. (Orig.). reprint ed. pap. 95.50 (0-7837-5678-X, 2059106) Bks Demand.

Sons of the Wolf. Barbara Michaels. 1989. mass mkt. 6.50 (0-425-11687-5, Berkley Trade) Berkley Pub.

Sons of the Wolf. Barbara Michaels. 1994. reprint ed. lib. bdg. 20.00 (0-7278-4665-5) Severn Hse.

Sons of the Yellow Emperor: A History of the Chinese Diaspora. Lynn Pan. Ed. by Paul De Angelis. (Illus.). 432p. 1994. pap. 16.00 (1-56836-032-0) Kodansha.

Sons of Thunder. Barbara F. Vroman. LC 81-81756. 395p. 1981. 16.95 (0-9606240-1-5) Pearl-Win.

Sons of Thunder: A Search for Identity. Bonnie S. Speer. LC 92-8061. (Illus.). 200p. (Orig.). (YA). (gr. 6-12). 1992. pap. 10.95 (0-9619639-8-0) Reliance Pr.

Sons of Toil. Margaret Sunley. 304p. 1992. 24.95 (0-7126-4691-4, Pub. by Century UK) Trafalgar.

Sons of Toil. large type ed. Margaret Sunley. (Ulverscroft). 592p. 1994. 25.99 (0-7089-3052-2) Ulverscroft.

Sons of Ulster. Richard Doherty. (Illus.). 144p. (Orig.). 1992. pap. 15.95 (0-86281-342-5, Pub. by Appletree Pr IE) Irish Bks Media.

Sons of Usna. Thomas H. Chivers. (Works of Thomas Holley Chivers Ser.). 1990. reprint ed. lib. bdg. 79.00 (0-7812-2291-5) Rprt Serv.

Sons of Zebulon: Jewish Maritime History. George T. Radan. LC 78-54621. 85p. (Orig.). (C). 1978. pap. 9.95 (0-935982-24-8, GTR-01) Spertus Coll.

Son's Return: Selected Essays. Sterling A. Brown. Ed. & Intro. by Mark A. Sanders. LC 96-1192. (Northeastern Library of Black Literature). 304p. 1996. text ed. 45.00 (1-55553-274-8); pap. text ed. 15.95 (1-55553-275-6) NE U Pr.

Sons, Slaves, & Freedmen in Roman Commerce. Aaron Kirschenbaum. LC 87-1506. (Illus.). 243p. 1987. reprint ed. pap. 69.30 (0-7837-9115-1, 2049916) Bks Demand.

Sonya & Jack: A Novel. David Homel. 368p. 1996. pap. 14.00 (0-00-224374-1) Harper SF.

Soo Bahk Do. Hwang Kee. Ed. & Tr. by H. C. Hwang. (Illus.). 424p. (KOR.). 1992. pap. text ed. write for info. (0-9631358-1-3) H Kee.

***Soo Line 1975-1992 Photo Archive.** Ed. by Frank W. Jordan. LC 96-78345. (Photo Archive Ser.). (Illus.). 128p. (Orig.). 1997. pap. 29.95 (1-882256-68-9) Iconografix.

Soo Ling: The Story of the Silkworm. Billie M. Miller. Tr. by Rose Mary Luna. (Illus.). 12p. (ENG & SPA.). (J). 1991. 12.00 (1-878742-01-9); pap. 6.00 (1-878742-02-7) Kidship Assoc.

Soo-Scenes in & about Sault Ste. Marie Michigan in 1887. Chase Osborn. (Illus.). 46p. 1983. pap. 5.50 (0-912382-30-9) Black Letter.

Sooch! Joe Soucheray. LC 81-11322. (Illus.). 270p. 1984. 8.95 (0-932272-07-X) Minneapolis Tribune.

Soochow University Political Science Series see Shaping of British Policy During the Nationalist Revolution in China

Soodlum's Irish Ballad Book. (Illus.). pap. 14.95 (0-7119-0208-9, OK64626, Oak) Music Sales.

Soohrab, a Poem see Suhrab & Rustam: A Poem from the Shah Namah of Firdausi

Sook America: An Arabic Guide to the American Market. Ed. by Joseph R. Haiek. (Illus.). 320p. (ARA.). 1998. pap. 29.95 (0-915652-18-8) News Circle.

Soon, Annala. Riki Levinson. LC 92-44588. (Illus.). 32p. (J). (ps-2). 1993. 15.95 (0-531-05494-2); lib. bdg. 16.99 (0-531-08644-5) Orchard Bks Watts.

Soon Found, Soon Lost. Elizabeth Ferber. LC 94-4280. 1994. 18.95 (1-882611-02-0); pap. 11.95 (1-882611-03-9) Yardbird Bks.

Soon-Hee in America. Schi-Zhin Rhie. LC 77-81780. (Illus.). 36p. (J). (gr. k-3). 1977. 8.50 (0-930878-00-0) Hollym Intl.

Soon Jack November. Sharon Thie. (Illus.). 44p. (Orig.). 1984. pap. 4.00 (0-88680-215-6) I E Clark.

***Soon She Will Be Gone.** John Farris. LC 96-53281. 1997. 24.95 (0-312-85375-0) St Martin.

Soon to Be a Major Motion Picture. Abbie Hoffman. 1994. reprint ed. lib. bdg. 35.95 (1-56849-291-X) Buccaneer Bks.

Soon Will Come the Light: A View from Inside the Autism Puzzle. Thomas A. McKean. Ed. by R. Wayne Gilpin. (Illus.). 172p. (C). 1994. pap. 19.95 (1-885477-11-2) Fut Horizons.

Sooner. Calvert. 1998. 15.00 (0-689-81114-4) S&S Childrens.

Sooner Century: 100 Glorious Years of Oklahoma Football. J. Brent Clark. Ed. by Susan Smith. (Illus.). 256p. 1995. 39.50 (1-885758-04-9) Quality Sports.

Sooner or Later. Bruce Hart. 1978. pap. 2.95 (0-380-42978-0, Flare) Avon.

Sooner or Later. Millie R. Hynes. (Illus.). 106p. (Orig.). 1982. pap. 4.95 (0-939688-07-7) Directed Media.

Sooner or Later. Debbie Macomber. 368p. 1996. mass mkt. 5.99 (0-06-108345-3, Harp PBks) HarpC.

Sooner or Later: Tales of a Western Pioneer Family. Virginia Stumbough. LC 92-41761. (Illus.). 200p. (Orig.). 1993. pap. 14.95 (0-940666-25-1) Clear Light.

***Sooner Spy.** Jim Lehrer. LC 97-3972. (One-Eyed Mack Mystery Ser.). 222p. 1997. pap. 12.95 (1-57178-041-6) Coun Oak Bks.

Sooner Spy. large type ed. Jim Lehrer. LC 90-45972. 290p. 1990. reprint ed. lib. bdg. 19.95 (1-56054-067-2) Thorndike Pr.

Sooner than You Think: Mapping a Course for a Comfortable Retirement. Gordon K. Williamson. 275p. 1993. text ed. 25.00 (1-55623-541-0) Irwin Prof Pubng.

Sooners: A Story of Oklahoma Football. enl. rev. ed. Jim Weeks. LC 74-84330. (College Sports Bks.). Orig. Title: Oklahoma Football. 1982. 10.95 (0-87397-238-4, Strode Pubs) Circle Bk Service.

***Sooners Handbook: Stories, Stats & Stuff about Oklahoma University Football.** Jim Weeks. (Illus.). 160p. (Orig.). 1996. pap. 9.95 (1-880652-78-1) Wichita Eagle.

Soong Dynasty. Sterling Seagrave. 540p. 1991. reprint ed. lib. bdg. 41.00 (0-8095-9087-5) Borgo Pr.

Soong Dynasty. Sterling Seagrave. LC 83-48802. (Illus.). 544p. 1986. reprint ed. pap. 16.00 (0-06-091318-5, PL 1318, PL) HarpC.

Sooo Big! Teddy Slater. (Baby's First Bks.). (Illus.). 12p. (J). (ps). 1994. bds. 2.25 (0-307-06034-9, Golden Books) Western Pub.

Sooper Dooper Mad Libs, No. 3. Roger Price & Leonard Stern. (Mad Libs Ser.). 48p. (Orig.). (J). (gr. 2 up). 1974. bds., pap. 3.50 (0-8431-0057-5) Price Stern Sloan.

Sooretama: The Atlantic Forest of Brazil. F. D. Por. (Illus.). x, 130p. 1992. pap. 35.00 (90-5103-077-0, Pub. by SPB Acad Pub NE) Balogh.

Soot Formation in Combustion: Mechanisms & Models. Ed. by Henning Bockhorn. LC 94-40218. (Chemical Physics Ser.: Vol. 59). 1994. 108.95 (3-540-58398-X) Spr-Verlag.

Sootblowers, Lances, & Rods. Center for Occupational Research & Development Staff. (EUTEC Power Plant Operator Curriculum Ser.). (Illus.). 32p. (C). 1985. pap. text ed. write for info. (1-55502-215-4) CORD Commns.

Sootface: An Ojibwa Cinderella Story. Illus. by Daniel San Souci. LC 93-10553. 32p. (J). 1994. 16.95 (0-385-31202-4) Doubleday.

***Sootface: An Ojibwa Cinderella Story.** Robert D. San Souci. 1997. pap. 5.99 (0-440-41363-X) Dell.

***Soothing Soaps: For Healthy Skin.** Sandy Maine. 1997. pap. text ed. 9.95 (1-883010-36-5) Interweave.

Soothing the Establishment: The Impact of Foreign-Born Scientists & Engineers on America. David S. North. LC 95-3988. 192p. (C). 1995. lib. bdg. 34.00 (0-8191-9887-0) U Pr of Amer.

Soothsayer. Rene De Goscinny & M. Uderzo. (Illus.). (J). 1990. 19.95 (0-8288-4905-6) Fr & Eur.

Soothsayers, the Omens see Florentine Codex, General History of the Things of New Spain

Soothsayings of Bakis: Goethe's Tragi-Comic Observations on Life, Time, & History. Johann Wolfgang Von Goethe. Ed. by Harold S. Jantz. LC 66-25527. 96p. reprint ed. pap. 27.40 (0-317-08237-X, 2003864) Bks Demand.

***Soothslayer.** D. J. Conway. LC 97-3558. (Illus.). 400p. (Orig.). 1997. pap. write for info. (1-56718-162-7) Llewellyn Pubns.

Sooty Little Mouse. Illus. by Peter Lawson. 16p. (J). (ps). 1994. 10.98 (1-881445-30-5) Sandvik Pub.

Sopa de Galleta. (Illus.). 24p. (SPA.). (J). (ps-3). 1993. pap. 3.50 (0-307-52114-1, Golden Pr) Western Pub.

Sopa de Piedras. Marcia Brown. Tr. by Teresa Mlawer from ENG. (Illus.). (J). (gr. 5-7). 1991. lib. bdg. 12.95 (0-9625162-1-X) Lectorum Pubns.

Sopa De Piedras. Marcia Brown. Tr. by Teresa Mlawer. (Illus.). (J). (gr. 5-7). 1994. pap. 5.95 (0-9625162-4-4) Lectorum Pubns.

Sopa De Piedras. Marcia Brown. (Illus.). (SPA.). (J). (gr. k-3). 1992. 22.95 incl. audio (0-87499-279-6); pap. 15.95 incl. audio (0-87499-278-8) Live Oak Media.

Sopa De Piedras, 4 bks., Set. Marcia Brown. (Illus.). (J). (gr. k-3). 1992. pap. 33.95 incl. audio (0-87499-280-X) Live Oak Media.

Sopa de Pollo para el Alma: Relatos que Conmerven el Corazon y Ponen Fuego en el Espiritu. Jack Canfield & Mark V. Hansen. (Chicken Soup for the Soul Ser.). 305p. (SPA.). 1995. pap. 12.95 (1-55874-353-7) Health Comm.

Sopa Marciana. Lynn Salem & Josie Stewart. Tr. by Mariana Robles. (Illus.). 8p. (J). (gr. k-1). 1993. pap. 3.50 (1-880612-17-8) Seedling Pubns.

Sopena Dictionary of Difficulties & Ambiguities of the Language: Diccionario Sopena de Dudas y Dificultades del Idioma. Sopena Staff. 621p. (SPA.). 1981. pap. 16.95 (0-8288-2018-X, S5190) Fr & Eur.

Sopena Robertson English-Spanish, Spanish-English Dictionary: Robertson Diccionario Ingles-Espanol-Ingles. Robertson. 900p. (ENG & SPA.). 1984. 35.00 (0-8288-2327-8, S50396) Fr & Eur.

Soper's Scrap Book Recitation, First Series. LC 72-84354. (Granger Index Reprint Ser.). 1977. 17.95 (0-8369-6063-7) Ayer.

Soper's Scrap Book Recitation, Fourth Series. LC 72-84354. (Granger Index Reprint Ser.). 1977. 17.95 (0-8369-6091-2) Ayer.

Soper's Scrap Book Recitation, Sixth Series. LC 72-84354. (Granger Index Reprint Ser.). 1977. 17.95 (0-8369-6131-5) Ayer.

Soper's Scrap Book Recitation, Third Series. LC 72-84354. (Granger Index Reprint Ser.). 1977. 17.95 (0-8369-6090-4) Ayer.

***SOPHE Heritage Collection of Health Education Monographs, 3 vols.** Society for Public Health Education Staff. LC 81-51486. 1000p. 1982. text ed. 40.00 (0-89914-013-0) Third Party Pub.

SOPHE Heritage Collection of Health Education Monographs, 3 vols., Set. Society for Public Health Education Staff. LC 81-51486. 1000p. 1982. text ed. 60.00 (0-89914-008-4) Third Party Pub.

Sopher Mahir: Northwest Semitic Studies Presented to Stanislav Segert. Ed. by Edward M. Cook. LC 90-2924. 384p. 1990. text ed. 37.50 (0-931464-56-0) Eisenbrauns.

***Sophia: Aspects of the Divine Feminine, Past & Present.** Susanne Schaup. LC 97-9189. (Illus.). 288p. (Orig.). 1997. pap. 16.95 (0-89254-036-2) Nicolas-Hays.

S

An Asterisk (*) at the beginning of an entry indicates that the title is appearing in BIP for the first time.

Sophia: The Science Aristotle Sought. Chung-Hwan Chen. (Studien und Materialien Zur Geschichte der Philosophie Ser.: Vol. 2). xiv, 827p. 1976. 160.00 (*3-487-05834-0*) G Olms Pubs.
Sophia - Goddess of Wisdom: The Divine Feminine from Black Goddess to World Soul. Caitlin Matthews. (Illus.). 1993. reprint ed. pap. 17.00 (*1-85538-275-X*, Pub. by Mandala UK) Thorsons SF.
Sophia - Goddess of Wisdom: The Divine Wisdom from Black Goddess to World Soul. Caitlin Matthews. (Illus.). 224p. 1991. 27.95 (*0-04-440590-1*, Pub. by Mandala UK) Thorsons SF.
Sophia - The Wisdom of God: An Outline of Sophiology. rev. ed. Sergei Bulgakov. (Esalen Institute - Library of Russian Philosophy). 224p. 1993. reprint ed. pap. 17.95 (*0-940262-60-6*) Lindisfarne Bks.
Sophia & Praxis: The Boundaries of Politics. Ed. by J. M. Porter. LC 84-12154. 160p. (Orig.). reprint ed. pap. 45.60 (*0-7837-2599-X*, 2042763) Bks Demand.
Sophia & the Johannine Jesus. Martin Scott. (JSNT Supplement Ser.: No. 71). (C). 1992. 57.50 (*1-85075-349-0*, Pub. by Sheffield Acad UK) CUP Services.
Sophia Jex-Blake: A Woman Pioneer in Nineteenth Century Medical Reform. Shirley Roberts. LC 93-14890. (Wellcome Institute Series in the History of Medicine). (Illus.). 192p. (C). 1993. text ed. 79.95 (*0-415-08753-8*, B0865) Routledge.
***Sophia Loren: A Biography.** Warren G. Harris. 1997. 25.00 (*0-684-80273-2*, S&S) S&S Trade.
***Sophia-Maria: A Holistic Vision of Creation.** Thomas Schipflinger. LC 97-23006. (Illus.). 384p. (Orig.). 1997. pap. 19.95 (*1-57863-022-3*) Weiser.
***Sophia Mystery in Our Time: The Birth of Imagination.** Mario Betti. Tr. by Pauline Wehrle. (Illus.). 96p. 1994. pap. write for info. (*0-904693-65-1*, Pub. by Temple Ldge Pub UK) Anthroposophic.
Sophia of the Bible: The Spirit of Wisdom. Aurora Terrenus. 89p. (Orig.). (C). 1988. pap. 4.95 (*0-945717-89-X*) Celestial Comns.
Sophia Parnok: The Life & Work of Russia's Sappho. Diana L. Burgin. LC 94-1266. (Cutting Edge: Lesbian Life & Literature Ser.). (C). 1994. 50.00 (*0-8147-1190-1*); pap. 18.50 (*0-8147-1221-5*) NYU Pr.
Sophia, Regent of Russia, Sixteen Fifty-Seven to Seventeen Hundred Four. Lindsey A. Hughes. (Illus.). 352p. 1991. 40.00 (*0-300-04790-8*) Yale U Pr.
Sophia (The Sophisticated Essence of the Flow of Creative Reality) Sadia (The Substantial Absolute, Downright, Activity of Reality), Vol. 1. Kalki Kumar. (Illus.). 140p. (C). 1994. pap. text ed. 25.00 (*0-9640434-0-8*) Lovers Reality.
Sophia und Kosmos. Burkhard Gladigow. 156p. (GER.). 1965. write for info. (*0-318-70609-1*) G Olms Pubs.
Sophia Vari-Papers on Canvas, 1992-1995. Pascal Bouafoux. (Illus.). 88p. 1995. 20.00 (*1-886125-02-3*) N Haime Gallery.
Sophia Vari Small Format. Nohra Haime. (Illus.). 110p. 1994. 25.00 (*1-886125-00-7*) N Haime Gallery.
Sophia's Unfaithful Lovers: How Philosophers Have Seduced the Church. Charles E. Brewster. (Illus.). 288p. (Orig.). 1996. pap. 10.99 (*1-57502-189-7*, P0813) Morris Pubng.
Sophic Hydrolith. Johann A. Siebmacher. Tr. by A. E. Waite from LAT. 1987. pap. 8.95 (*0-916411-59-1*) Holmes Pub.
***Sophie.** Fox. 1997. pap. write for info. (*0-15-201598-1*) HarBrace.
Sophie. Mem Fox. LC 94-1976. (Illus.). 32p. (J). (ps-3). 1994. 14.00 (*0-15-277160-3*) HarBrace.
Sophie: A Very Precious Angel. Joanne E. De Jonge. LC 95-47611. 128p. (J). 1996. text ed. 14.99 (*0-8010-4135-X*) Baker Bks.
***Sophie: Signed Copy.** Fox. 1994. 13.95 (*0-15-201756-9*) HarBrace.
***Sophie & Her Uncle: A Program about Abuse in the Family.** Bonnie R. McGowan. (Illus.). 30p. (Orig.). (J). (gr. k-6). 1993. pap. 6.95 (*1-884063-54-3*) Mar Co Prods.
Sophie & Lou. Petra Mathers. LC 90-37562. (Illus.). 32p. (J). (ps-3). 1991. lib. bdg. 14.89 (*0-06-024072-5*) HarpC Child Bks.
Sophie & Lou. Petra Mathers. LC 90-37562. (Illus.). 32p. (J). (ps-3). 1991. 15.00 (*0-06-024071-7*) HarpC Child Bks.
Sophie & Sammy's Library Sleepover. Judith Caseley. LC 91-48160. (Illus.). 32p. (J). (ps up). 1993. 16.00 (*0-688-10615-3*); lib. bdg. 15.93 (*0-688-10616-1*) Greenwillow.
Sophie & the Incas. Dagmar Plenk. LC 90-71979. 72p. (Orig.). (J). (gr. 3-7). 1991. pap. 9.00 (*1-56002-039-3*) Aegina Pr.
Sophie Calle: A Survey. Deborah Imis. Tr. by Winter Horton from FRE. (Illus.). 30p. 1989. pap. 20.00 (*0-317-93497-X*) F Hoffman Gallery.
Sophie Calle: Absence. Sophie Calle et al. (Illus.). 72p. (FRE.). 1995. pap. 25.00 (*90-6918-131-2*) Dist Art Pubs.
Sophie Calle: Proofs. Kathleen Merrill & Lawrence Rinder. LC 93-39485. 1993. pap. 4.95 (*0-944722-16-4*) Hood Mus Art.
Sophie Canetang: The Tale Jemima Puddle-Duck: French Edition. Beatrix Potter. 58p. (FRE.). 1990. 9.95 (*0-7859-3622-X*, 2070569678) Fr & Eur.
***Sophie Est En Danger.** Louise Leblanc. (Novels in the Premier Roman Ser.). 64p. (FRE.). (J). (gr. 2-5). 1996. pap. 7.95 (*2-89021-212-2*, Pub. by Les Editions CN) Firefly Bks Ltd.
***Sophie Fait Des Foilies.** Louise Lablanc. (Novels in the Premier Roman Ser.). 64p. (FRE.). (J). (gr. 2-5). 1996. pap. 7.95 (*2-89021-244-0*, Pub. by Les Editions CN) Firefly Bks Ltd.
Sophie Hits Six. Dick King-Smith. LC 92-54692. (Illus.). 128p. (J). (gr. k-4). 1993. 14.95 (*1-56402-216-1*) Candlewick Pr.
Sophie Hits Six. Dick King-Smith. LC 92-54692. (J). (ps-3). 1995. pap. 4.99 (*1-56402-462-8*) Candlewick Pr.
Sophie Horowitz Story. Sarah Schulman. 176p. (Orig.). 1984. pap. 7.95 (*0-930044-54-1*) Naiad Pr.
Sophie in Love. large type ed. Carol Marsh. 198p. 1995. 25.99 (*0-7505-0791-8*, Pub. by Magna Print Bks UK) Ulverscroft.
Sophie in the Saddle. Dick King-Smith. LC 93-26723. (J). (gr. k-4). 1996. pap. 3.99 (*1-56402-607-8*) Candlewick Pr.
Sophie Is Gone. large type ed. Anne Fleming. 320p. 1996. 25.99 (*0-7089-3538-9*) Ulverscroft.
Sophie Is Seven. Dick King-Smith. LC 94-14830. (J). (gr. k-4). 1995. 14.95 (*1-56402-542-X*) Candlewick Pr.
***Sophie Lance et Compte.** Louise Leblanc. (Novels in the Premier Roman Ser.). 64p. (FRE.). (J). (gr. 2-5). 1996. pap. 7.95 (*2-89021-158-4*, Pub. by Les Editions CN) Firefly Bks Ltd.
Sophie ou les Galanteries Exemplaires. Hubert Monteilhet. (FRE.). 1978. pap. 10.95 (*0-7859-4097-9*) Fr & Eur.
***Sophie Part En Voyage.** Louise Leblanc. (Novels in the Premier Roman Ser.). 64p. (FRE.). (J). (gr. 2-5). 1996. pap. 7.95 (*2-89021-195-9*, Pub. by Les Editions CN) Firefly Bks Ltd.
Sophie the Rag Picker. Tilde Michels. (Illus.). (J). (gr. k-1). 1962. 10.95 (*0-8392-3036-2*) Astor-Honor.
***Sophie the Snowflake.** Eddie Bowman. LC 96-54300. (Illus.). (J). 1997. write for info. (*1-56763-320-X*); pap. write for info. (*1-56763-321-8*) Ozark Pub.
***Sophie Treadwell: A Research & Production Sourcebook.** Jerry Dickey. LC 96-43986. (Modern Dramatists Research & Production Sourcebooks: Vol. 12). 304p. 1997. text ed. 79.50 (*0-313-29388-0*, Greenwood Pr) Greenwood.
Sophie Willard Dana Ripley: Co-Founder of Brook Farm. Helen D. Raymond. (Illus.). 124p. (Orig.). 1995. 15.00 (*0-914339-51-6*) P E Randall Pub.
Sophie's Attic. large type ed. Robin Elliott. (Silhouette Romance Ser.). 1995. lib. bdg. 18.95 (*0-373-59420-8*) Thorndike Pr.
Sophie's Bucket. Catherine Stock. LC 93-20987. (Illus.). 40p. (J). (ps-1). 1994. pap. 5.00 (*0-15-277162-X*) HarBrace.
Sophie's Choice. William Styron. 1979. 29.95 (*0-394-46109-6*) Random.
Sophie's Choice. William Styron. 1992. pap. 13.00 (*0-679-73637-9*, Publishers Media) Random.
Sophie's Choice Chili or How to Cure Your Frigidity. Compiled by Madeleine S. Gary. 96p. (Orig.). 1985. pap. 4.50 (*0-913459-02-X*) New Writers Guild.
Sophie's Dance Class: A Pull-the Tab Book. Ruth Tilden. LC 95-76706. (Illus.). 10p. (J). (ps-2). 1996. 9.95 (*0-7868-0239-1*) Hyprn Child.
Sophie's Heart. Lori Wick. LC 95-13823. (Orig.). 1995. pap. 10.99 (*1-56507-311-8*) Harvest Hse.
***Sophie's Kiss: The True Love Story of Prince Edward & Sophie Rhys-Jones.** Sean Smith & Garth Gibbs. (Illus.). 300p. 1997. 25.95 (*1-85782-175-0*, Pub. by Blake Publng UK) Seven Hills Bk.
Sophie's Legacy. Dareion Morgan. LC 94-90744. 176p. (Orig.). 1996. pap. 9.95 (*1-56002-536-0*, Univ Edtns) Aegina Pr.
Sophie's Lucky. Dick King-Smith. LC 95-33670. (Illus.). 108p. (J). 1996. 14.99 (*1-56402-869-0*) Candlewick Pr.
Sophie's Masterpiece. Eileen Spinelli. LC 95-44063. (Illus.). (J). Date not set. 16.00 (*0-689-80112-2*, S&S Bks Young Read) S&S Childrens.
Sophie's Name. Phyllis A. Grode. LC 90-4833. (Illus.). 32p. (J). (gr. k-3). 1990. 12.95 (*0-929371-18-6*); pap. 4.95 (*0-929371-19-4*) Kar-Ben.
***Sophie's Secret.** large type ed. Anne Weale. (Mills & Boon Large Print Ser.). 288p. 1997. 22.50 (*0-263-15071-2*, Pub. by M & B UK) Ulverscroft.
Sophie's Surprise. 2nd ed. Lee Richardson. (Illus.). 28p. (J). (gr. 3-8). 1984. 16.95 (*0-9613476-0-0*) Shirlee.
Sophie's Tom. Dick King-Smith. LC 91-58756. (Illus.). 112p. (J). (gr. k-4). 1992. 14.95 (*1-56402-107-6*) Candlewick Pr.
Sophie's Tom. Dick King-Smith. LC 91-58756. (Illus.). 112p. (J). (gr. k-4). 1994. pap. 3.99 (*1-56402-373-7*) Candlewick Pr.
Sophie's World: A Novel about the History of Philosophy. Jostein Gaarder. Tr. by Paulette Miller. LC 94-12467. 1994. 19.00 (*0-374-26642-5*) FS&G.
***Sophie's World: A Novel About the History of Philosophy.** Joestein Gaarder. 416p. 1997. reprint ed. pap. 14.00 (*0-425-15684-2*, Berkley Trade) Berkley Pub.
Sophie's World: A Novel about the History of Philosophy. Jostein Gaarder. Tr. by Paulette Moller. 672p. 1996. reprint ed. mass mkt. 6.99 (*0-425-15225-1*) Berkley Pub.
Sophismata of Richard Kilvington. Richard Kilvington. Ed. by Norman Kretzmann & Barbara E. Kretzmann. Tr. by Barbara E. Kretzmann. (Illus.). 304p. (C). 1990. 80.00 (*0-521-35419-6*) Cambridge U Pr.
Sophisms in Medieval Logic & Grammar: Acts of the Ninth European Symposium on Medieval Logic & Semantics, Held at St, Andrews, June 1990. Nineth European Symposium on Medieval Logic & Semantics Staff. Ed. by Stephen Read. LC 93-16500. (Nijhoff International Philosophy Ser.: Vol. 48). 440p. (C). 1993. Alk. paper. lib. bdg. 200.00 (*0-7923-2196-0*, Pub. by Klwr Acad Pubs NE) Kluwer Ac.
Sophist. Charles Bernstein. 180p. 1987. 16.95 (*0-940650-78-9*); pap. 11.95 (*0-940650-79-7*) Sun & Moon CA.
Sophist. Plato. Tr. & Intro. by Nicholas White. (Hackett Classics Ser.). 128p. (Orig.). (C). 1993. pap. text ed. 9.95 (*0-87220-202-X*); lib. bdg. 28.95 (*0-87220-203-8*) Hackett Pub.
Sophist. deluxe ed. Charles Bernstein. 180p. 1987. 30.00 (*0-940650-80-0*) Sun & Moon CA.
Sophistes & Politicus of Plato. Plato. LC 72-9286. (Philosophy of Plato & Aristotle Ser.). 1977. reprint ed. 35.95 (*0-405-04836-X*) Ayer.
Sophistic Movement. George B. Kerferd. LC 80-41934. 200p. 1981. pap. text ed. 19.95 (*0-521-28357-4*) Cambridge U Pr.
Sophistical Rhetoric in Classical Greece. John Poulakos. (Studies in Rhetoric-Communication). 236p. 1994. text ed. 39.95 (*0-87249-899-9*) U of SC Pr.
Sophisticated Alligators. Noel Miller. LC 95-247. (Illus.). 1995. pap. 15.00 (*0-679-44321-5*, Villard Bks) Random.
Sophisticated Cat: An Anthology. Ed. by Joyce Carol Oates & Daniel Halpern. LC 93-803. 416p. 1993. reprint ed. pap. 12.00 (*0-452-27045-6*, Dutton-W Abrahams Bk) NAL-Dutton.
Sophisticated Leisure: Nineteen Eighty-Seven Travel Directory. Bruce Coville et al. (Illus.). 348p. 1986. pap. 8.95 (*0-9614965-5-X*) Schueler Comm.
Sophisticated Leisure Travel Directory, 1986. Bruce Coville et al. (Illus.). 348p. 1986. pap. 8.95 (*0-9614965-4-1*) Schueler Comm.
Sophisticated Rebels: The Political Culture of European Dissent, 1968-1987. H. Stuart Hughes. LC 88-527. (Studies in Cultural History: No 4). 192p. 1988. 29.00 (*0-674-82130-0*) HUP.
Sophisticated Rebels: The Political Culture of European Dissent, 1968-1987. H. Stuart Hughes. (Studies in Cultural History: Vol. 4). 192p. 1990. pap. text ed. 9.95 (*0-674-82131-9*) HUP.
Sophisticated Silhouettes: The Shape of Fashion, 1910-1960. Beverly Birks. (Illus.). 24p. 1986. 8.00 (*0-915171-06-6*) Katonah Gal.
Sophisticated Traveler's Pocket Guide to Airport Facilities & Ground Services, 1987. G. H. Gizinski. LC 86-63679. (Illus.). 116p. 1986. pap. 14.95 (*0-941521-00-1*) Mkt Dynam Consults.
Sophisticated Traveler's Pocket Guide to Airport Facilities & Ground Services, 1988. G. H. Gizinski. (Illus.). 150p. 1987. pap. 14.95 (*0-941521-01-X*) Mkt Dynam Consults.
Sophistication: Rhetoric & the Rise of Self-Consciousness. Mark Backman. LC 91-31004. 1992. 24.95 (*0-918024-91-9*) Ox Bow.
Sophistry. Jonathan M. Sherman. 1995. pap. 5.25 (*0-8222-1347-8*) Dramatists Play.
Sophists: Rhetoric, Democracy, & Plato's Idea of Sophistry. Harold Barrett. LC 87-21051. 96p. (Orig.). (C). 1987. pap. text ed. 7.95 (*0-88316-557-0*) Chandler & Sharp.
Sophoclean Chorus: A Study of Character & Function. Cynthia P. Gardiner. LC 86-16008. 216p. (C). 1986. text ed. 28.95 (*0-87745-155-9*) U of Iowa Pr.
Sophocles. Ed. by Don Nardo. LC 96-18327. (Literary Companion Ser.). (YA). (gr. 9-12). 1996. pap. 12.96 (*1-56510-581-8*); lib. bdg. 20.96 (*1-56510-582-6*) Greenhaven.
Sophocles: A Study of Heroic Humanism. Cedric H. Whitman. LC 51-10794. 302p. reprint ed. pap. 86.10 (*0-7837-4200-2*, 2059050) Bks Demand.
Sophocles: Ajax. W. Bedell Stanford. (Bristol Greek Texts Ser.). 384p. (GRE.). 1981. reprint ed. 29.95 (*0-86292-009-4*, Pub. by Brstl Class Pr UK) Focus Pub-R Pullins.
Sophocles' Antigone. Mary W. Blundell. (Classical Library). Date not set. pap. 6.95 (*0-941051-25-0*) Focus Pub-R Pullins.
Sophocles: Antigone & Oedipus the King. Ed. by J. Wilkins & M. Macleod. (Classics Companions Ser.). 111p. (GRE.). 1987. 14.95 (*0-86292-240-2*, Pub. by Brstl Class Pr UK) Focus Pub-R Pullins.
Sophocles: Dramatist & Philosopher. Humphrey D. Kitto. LC 80-22360. 64p. 1981. reprint ed. text ed. 35.00 (*0-313-22625-3*, KISD, Greenwood Pr) Greenwood.
Sophocles: Fragments, vol. III. Hugh Lloyd-Jones. 440p. Date not set. 18.95 (*0-674-99532-5*) HUP.
Sophocles: Oedipus Tyrannus. Ed. by Richard C. Jebb. (Bristol Greek Texts Ser.). 208p. (GRE.). 1981. reprint ed. 19.95 (*0-86292-002-7*, Pub. by Brstl Class Pr UK) Focus Pub-R Pullins.
Sophocles: Plays Two. Sophocles. Tr. by Kenneth McLeigh et al. from GRE. (Methuen World Dramatists Ser.). 227p. (C). 1990. pap. 7.95 (*0-413-62880-9*, A0459, Pub. by Methuen UK) Heinemann.
Sophocles: The Classical Heritage. Roger D. Dawe. Ed. by Ward Briggs. LC 95-53958. (Classical Heritage Ser.: Vol. 04). 344p. 1996. reprint ed. text ed. 50.00 (*0-8153-0334-3*, H1455) Garland.
Sophocles: The Dramatist. Arthur J. Waldock. 244p. reprint ed. pap. 69.60 (*0-317-26367-6*, 2024565) Bks Demand.
Sophocles: The Theban Plays. Tr. & Intro. by Don Taylor. 320p. 1986. pap. 5.50 (*0-413-42460-X*, 9997) Routledge.
Sophocles see Modern Critical Views Series
Sophocles' Antigone. Nicolas P. Gross. (Greek Commentaries Ser.). 111p. (Orig.). (C). 1988. pap. text ed. 7.00 (*0-929524-33-0*) Bryn Mawr Commentaries.
Sophocle's Antigone: A New Version. Ed. by Brendan Kennelly. 80p. 1996. 29.95 (*1-85224-363-5*, Pub. by Bloodaxe Bks UK); pap. 14.95 (*1-85224-364-3*, Pub. by Bloodaxe Bks UK) Dufour.
Sophocles I, 2 vols., 1. Sophocles. Ed. by Hugh Lloyd-Jones. (Loeb Classical Library: No. 20-21). 492p. 1994. 18.95 (*0-674-99023-4*) HUP.
Sophocles II, 2 vols., 2. Ed. by Hugh Lloyd-Jones. LC 92-19295. (Loeb Classical Library: Nos. 20-21). 528p. 1994. 18.95 (*0-674-99557-0*) HUP.
Sophocles' Oedipus: Evidence & Self-Conviction. Frederick Ahl. LC 90-55733. 366p. 1991. 47.50 (*0-8014-2558-1*); pap. 17.95 (*0-8014-9929-1*) Cornell U Pr.
Sophocles Oedipus at Colonus. Gilbert P. Rose. (Greek Commentaries Ser.). 132p. (Orig.). (C). 1988. pap. text ed. 7.00 (*0-929524-34-9*) Bryn Mawr Commentaries.
Sophocles' Oedipus at Colonus: Translated with Notes, Introduction & Essay. Sophocles. Tr. by Mary W. Blundell from GRE. (Classical Library). 90p. (C). 1990. pap. 6.95 (*0-941051-09-9*) Focus Pub-R Pullins.
Sophocles' Oedipus Trilogy see Bloom's Notes
Sophocles, Oedipus Tyrannus. Intro. by John A. Symonds. 132p. 1970. pap. 8.50 (*0-87291-009-1*) Coronado Pr.
Sophocles Oidipous Tyrannos. Jeffrey Rusten. (Bryn Mawr Greek Commentaries Ser.). 146p. (Orig.). (C). 1990. pap. text ed. 8.00 (*0-929524-67-5*) Bryn Mawr Commentaries.
Sophocles One. Incl. Oedipus the King. Tr. by David Grene. 1969. (*0-318-56075-5*); Oedipus at Colonus. Tr. by Robert Fitzgerald. 1969. (*0-318-56076-3*); Antigone. Tr. by Elizabeth Wycoff. 1969. (*0-318-56077-1*); (Complete Greek Tragedies Ser.). 55p. 1969. pap. text ed. 6.95 (*0-226-30785-9*, P313) U Ch Pr.
Sophocles, the Plays & Fragments, 1892-1900, 7 vols., Set. Richard C. Jebb. 1995. 475.00 (*0-403-00289-3*) Scholarly.
Sophocles' Tragic World: Divinity, Nature, Society. Charles Segal. LC 95-15249. 288p. (C). 1995. 39.95 (*0-674-82100-9*) HUP.
Sophocles Two. Incl. Ajax. John Moore. LC 54-10731. 1969. (*0-318-56078-X*); Women of Trachis. Michael Jameson. LC 54-10731. 1969. (*0-318-56079-8*); Electra. David Grene. LC 54-10731. 1969. (*0-318-56080-1*); Philoctetes. David Grene. LC 54-10731. 1969. (*0-318-56081-X*); LC 54-10731. (Complete Greek Tragedies Ser.: No. 4). 70p. 1969. pap. text ed. 8.95 (*0-226-30786-7*, P314) U Ch Pr.
Sophocles's Oedipus Rex see Modern Critical Interpretations
Sophomore Slumps: Disasterous Second Movies, Albums, Songs, Books, & Seasons. Chris Golden. LC 94-20517. 1994. 9.95 (*0-8065-1584-8*, Citadel Pr) Carol Pub Group.
Sophomores: Tales of Reality, Conflict & the Road. Ed. by R. James Stahl. (American Teen Writer Ser.). 128p. (Orig.). (YA). (gr. 7 up). 1996. pap. text ed. 9.75 (*1-886427-10-0*) Merlyns Pen.
***Sophon of Carthage: Heroine of a Holocaust.** Richard Hardy. (Illus.). 244p. (Orig.). 1997. pap. 9.00 (*0-9656945-1-8*) LHA Bks.
Sophrosynics: The Book of Life: A Field Guide to Living the Good Life. Good Morning Group Staff. 992p. 1994. pap. 35.45 (*0-9641781-0-9*) Good Morning.
Sophus K. Winther. Barbara H. Meldrum. LC 82-74094. (Western Writers Ser.: No. 60). (Illus.). 52p. (Orig.). 1983. pap. 4.95 (*0-88430-034-X*) Boise St U W Writ Ser.
Sophus Lie Memorial Conference: Oslo 1992-Proceedings. Ed. by Olav A. Laudal & Bjorn Jahren. 381p. 1994. 58.00 (*82-00-21646-2*) Scandnvan Univ Pr.
Sophus Lie's Eighteen Eighty Transformation Group Paper. M. Ackerman & Robert Hermann. LC 75-17416. (Lie Groups:: No. 1). 1975. 60.00 (*0-915692-10-4*) Math Sci Pr.
Sophus Lie's 1884 Differential Invariants Paper. Robert Hermann & M. Ackerman. LC 75-43189. (Lie Groups; History, Frontiers & Applications Ser.: No. 3). 273p. 1975. 50.00 (*0-915692-13-9*, 991600053) Math Sci Pr.
Sophy. large type ed. Dilys Gater. (Linford Romance Library). 320p. 1993. pap. 15.99 (*0-7089-7338-8*, Linford) Ulverscroft.
Sophy. large type ed. Dilys A. Gater. (Linford Romance Library). 272p. 1993. pap. 15.99 (*0-7089-7336-1*, Linford) Ulverscroft.
Sophy & Auntie Pearl. Jeanne Titherington. LC 94-22620. (Illus.). 24p. (J). (ps up). 1995. 15.00 (*0-688-07835-4*); lib. bdg. 14.93 (*0-688-07836-2*) Greenwillow.
Sopplimenti Musicali. Gioseffo Zarlino. (Monuments of Music & Music Literature in Facsimile, II Ser.: No. 15). (Illus.). 1979. reprint ed. lib. bdg. 75.00 (*0-8450-2215-6*) Broude.
Soprano & Tenor see Voice Placing & Training Exercise
Soprano on Her Head: Right-side-up Reflections on Life-& Other Performances. Eloise Ristad. LC 81-23369. 201p. (Orig.). 1982. 14.00 (*0-911226-20-6*); pap. 10.50 (*0-911226-21-4*) Real People.
Soprano Recorder Songbook for Children. Rhoda B. Weber & Bob Margolis. (Illus.). (Orig.). 1984. pap. 3.50 (*0-931329-00-0*, SRS-1) Manhattan Beach.
Soprano Recorder Songbook for Children. Rhoda B. Weber & Bob Margolis. (Illus.). (Orig.). 1985. teacher ed., pap. 20.00 (*0-931329-01-9*, TMSRS-1) Manhattan Beach.
***Soprano Sorceress.** Lee E. Modesitt. 1997. 25.95 (*0-312-86022-6*) Tor Bks.
***Soprano Sorceress.** Lee E. Modesitt, Jr. 1997. 24.95 (*0-614-20658-8*) Tor Bks.
***Sopranos, Mezzos, Tenors & Bassos.** S. Chapin & J. Radiches. Date not set. 17.99 (*0-517-18015-4*) Random Hse Value.
Sopranos, Mezzos, Tenors, Bassos & Other Friends. Schuyler Chapin. LC 94-32068. 272p. 1995. 50.00 (*0-517-58864-1*, Crown) Crown Pub Group.
Sopresas: Antologia de Cuentos Hispanicos. Elena Olazagasti-Segovia. 242p. (SPA.). 1993. pap. text ed. write for info. (*0-03-054823-3*) HB Coll Pubs.
Sor Juana: A Trailblazing Thinker. Elizabeth C. Martinez. (Hispanic Heritage Ser.). (Illus.). 32p. (J). (gr. 2-4). 1994. lib. bdg. 14.90 (*1-56294-406-1*) Millbrook Pr.
Sor Juana: Or, the Traps of Faith. Octavio Paz. Tr. by Margaret S. Peden from SPA. LC 88-3002. (Illus.). 560p. 1988. 42.50 (*0-674-82105-X*) HUP.

Sor Juana: Or, the Traps of Faith. Octavio Paz. Tr. by Margaret S. Peden. 560p. 1990. pap. text ed. 16.95 (*0-674-82106-8*) HUP.

Sor Juana & Other Plays. Estela P. Trambley. LC 82-73752. ii, 195p. 1983. pap. 15.00 (*0-916950-33-6*) Biling Rev-Pr.

Sor Juana Anthology. Tr. by Alan S. Trueblood. LC 87-27693. 264p. 1988. 42.50 (*0-674-82120-3*) HUP.

Sor Juana Anthology. Tr. by Alan S. Trueblood. 264p. 1990. pap. text ed. 14.95 (*0-674-82121-1*) HUP.

Sor Juana Ines de la Cruz. Gerard Flynn. LC 75-120482. (Twayne's World Authors Ser.). 1971. lib. bdg. 17.95 (*0-8057-2256-4*) Irvington.

Sor Juana Ines De La Cruz. Kathleen Thompson. Ed. & Intro. by Frank De Varona. (Hispanic Stories Ser.). 32p. (ENG & SPA.). (J). (gr. 2-6). 1990. pap. 4.95 (*0-8114-6752-X*) Raintree Steck-V.

Sor Juana Ines De La Cruz. Kathleen Thompson. (Hispanic Stories Ser.). (Illus.). 32p. (ENG & SPA.). (J). (gr. 2-6). 1990. lib. bdg. 21.40 (*0-8172-3377-6*) Raintree Steck-V.

Sor Juana Ines de la Cruz: Amor, Poesia, Soledumbre. Victoria Urbano. 1990. 43.50 (*0-916379-82-5*) Scripta.

Sor Juana Ines de la Cruz: Poems. Tr. & Intro. by Margaret S. Peden. LC 85-71537. 144p. (ENG & SPA.). 1985. pap. text ed. 13.00 (*0-916950-60-3*) Biling Rev-Pr.

***Sor Juana Ines de la Cruz, Fenix de America.** Andres D. Puello. (Cuadernos Panamericanos: Vol. 2). 1997. spiral bd. write for info. (*0-9631210-3-0*) DPA Intl.

Sor Juana's Dream. Luis Harss. (Orig.). 1987. pap. 9.95 (*0-930829-07-7*) Lumen Inc.

***Sor Juana's Love Poems.** Tr. by Joan Larkin & Jaime Manrique. LC 97-23522. (ENG & SPA.). 1997. pap. 10.00 (*0-9651558-6-2*) Painted Leaf.

S.O.R. Losers. Avi. LC 84-11022. 112p. (J). (gr. 5-7). 1984. text ed. 15.00 (*0-02-793410-1*, Bradbury S&S) S&S Childrens.

S.O.R. Losers. 93th ed. 1993. pap. text ed. 12.50 (*0-15-300351-0*, HB Juv Bks) HarBrace.

Sorabji: A Critical Celebration. Paul Rapoport. 250p. 1992. 69.95 (*0-85967-923-3*, Pub. by Scolar Pr UK) Ashgate Pub Co.

Soranus' Gynecology. Tr. by Owsei Temkin et al. from GRE. LC 91-20791. (Softshell Bks.). (Illus.). 258p. 1991. reprint ed. pap. text ed. 19.95 (*0-8018-4320-0*) Johns Hopkins.

***Sorayama Call in Beauties.** Haijime Sorayama. (Illus.). 32p. 1997. 15.95 (*4-568-50189-X*, Pub. by Bijutsu Shuppan-Sha JA) Bks Nippan.

Sorayama, Hyer Illustrations, Pt. 2. Hajime Sorayama. (Illus.). 104p. 1992. pap. 29.95 (*4-568-50146-6*, Pub. by Bijutsu Shuppan-Sha JA) Bks Nippan.

Sorayama, Hyper Illustrations. Hajime Sorayama. pap. 29.95 (*4-568-50102-4*, Pub. by Bijutsu Shuppan-Sha JA) Bks Nippan.

Sorayama Hyper Illustrations, Pt. 2. Hajime Sorayama. 1993. pap. 29.95 (*4-568-50129-6*, Pub. by Bijutsu Shuppan-Sha JA) Bks Nippan.

Sorbate Food Preservatives. John N. Sofos. 240p. 1989. 153.00 (*0-8493-6786-7*, TP371) CRC Pr.

Sorbent Extraction Technology: Handbook. 2nd ed. Ed. by Nigel Simpson. (Illus.). (C). 1993. pap. text ed. 26.00 (*0-9616096-0-5*) Varian Sample Preparation Products.

Sorbent Materials: Technical Review. 214p. 1992. 1,000.00 (*0-89336-907-1*, C-132B) BCC.

Sorbent Materials for Spills & Other Liquid Pickups, No. C-133. Business Communications Co., Inc. Staff. 270p. 1991. 2,850.00 (*0-89336-803-2*) BCC.

Sorbents. Richard K. Miller & Marcia E. Rupnow. LC 90-83873. (Survey on Technology & Markets Ser.: No. 168). 50p. 1991. pap. text ed. 200.00 (*1-55865-193-4*) Future Tech Surveys.

***Sorbents.** Richard K. Miller & Christy H. Gunter. (Market Research Survey Ser.: No. 309). 50p. 1996. 200.00 (*1-55865-333-3*) Future Tech Surveys.

Sorbents for Liquid Hazardous Substance Cleanup & Control. Robert W. Melvold et al. LC 87-31550. (Pollution Technology Review Ser.: No. 150). (Illus.). 154p. 1988. 36.00 (*0-8155-1159-0*) Noyes.

Sorbents Materials for Non-Spill Applications, No. C-132A. Business Communications Co., Inc. Staff. 1992. 2,850.00 (*0-89336-802-4*) BCC.

***Sorbets & Granitas.** Joy S. Hamburger & Mimi S. Taft. LC 96-39423. (Illus.). 96p. (Orig.). 1997. pap. 12.95 (*0-89815-902-4*) Ten Speed Pr.

Sorbets & Ice Creams: And Other Frozen Confections. Lou S. Pappas. LC 96-28040. 1997. 14.95 (*0-8118-1573-0*) Chronicle Bks.

Sorbos de Luz - Sips of Light. Juana R. Pita. Tr. by Mario De Salvatierra. (Eboli Poetry Ser.). (Illus.). 64p. (Orig.). (ENG & SPA.). 1990. pap. write for info. (*0-932367-09-7*) Ed El Gato Tuerto.

Sorby Centennial Symposium on the History of Metallurgy, Cleveland, Ohio, October 22-23, 1963. Ed. by Cyril S. Smith. LC 65-17635. (Metallurgical Society Conference Ser.: Vol. 27). 580p. reprint ed. pap. 165.30 (*0-317-10418-7*, 2001515) Bks Demand.

Sorby on Geology, Vol. III. Ed. by Charles H. Summerson. (Geological Milestones Ser.). (Illus.). 241p. 1978. 10.00 (*0-932981-28-3*) Univ Miami CSL.

Sorby on Sedimentology, Vol. I. Ed. by Charles H. Summerson. (Geological Milestones Ser.). (Illus.). 226p. 1976. 10.00 (*0-932981-27-5*) Univ Miami CSL.

Sorcellerie et Justice Criminelle: Le Parlement de Paris (16e-18e Siecles) Alfred Soman. (Collected Studies: Vol. CS368). 346p. 1992. 98.95 (*0-86078-320-0*, Pub. by Variorum UK) Ashgate Pub Co.

Sorcerer. Anne E. Crompton. LC 82-61042. 176p. 1982. reprint ed. 22.00 (*0-933256-36-1*) Second Chance.

Sorcerer & a Gentleman. Elizabeth Willey. 416p. 1995. 23.95 (*0-312-85783-7*) Tor Bks.

Sorcerer & a Gentleman, Vol. 1. Elizabeth Willey. 1996. mass mkt. 5.99 (*0-8125-5047-1*) Tor Bks.

Sorcerer & Witch in Melanesia. Ed. by Michele Stephen. 208p. (C). 1987. text ed. 40.00 (*0-8135-1227-1*) Rutgers U Pr.

Sorcerer As Apprentice: Stalin As Commissar of Nationalities, 1917-1924. Stephen Blank. LC 93-18148. (Contributions in Military Studies: No. 145). 312p. 1994. text ed. 65.00 (*0-313-28683-3*, BVK/) Greenwood.

Sorcerer of Kings: The Case of Daniel Dunglas Home & William Crookes. Gordon Stein. 140p. 1994. 25.95 (*0-87975-863-5*) Prometheus Bks.

Sorcerers. Jacob Needleman. LC 86-8733. 235p. 1986. 16.95 (*0-916515-10-9*) Mercury Hse Inc.

Sorcerers & Healing Spirits. Reid. (Australian National University Press Ser.). 1983. pap. text ed. 32.00 (*0-08-032902-0*, Pergamon Pr) Elsevier.

Sorcerer's Apprentice. David Bronstein. 1995. pap. 19.95 (*1-85744-151-6*) S&S Trade.

Sorcerer's Apprentice. Christopher Bulis. (Dr. Who Missing Adventures Ser.). 1995. mass mkt. 5.95 (*0-426-20447-6*, Pub. by Virgin Pub UK) London Brdge.

***Sorcerer's Apprentice.** Ted Dewan. LC 97-12073. (J). 1998. write for info. (*0-385-32537-1*, DD Bks Yng Read) BDD Bks Young Read.

Sorcerer's Apprentice. David Eastman. LC 87-13767. (Illus.). 32p. (J). (gr. k-4). 1988. pap. 3.95 (*0-8167-1068-6*); lib. bdg. 11.89 (*0-8167-1067-8*) Troll Communs.

Sorcerer's Apprentice. Walt Disney Staff. (Penguin-Disney Ser.). (J). (ps-3). 1992. 5.98 (*0-453-03025-4*) Viking Penguin.

Sorcerer's Apprentice. Nancy Willard. Ed. by Leo D. Dillon et al. LC 93-19912. (Illus.). 32p. (J). (ps-6). 1993. 15.95 (*0-590-47329-8*) Scholastic Inc.

Sorcerer's Apprentice. Michael Williams. 288p. (Orig.). 1990. mass mkt. 4.50 (*0-445-21054-0*) Warner Bks.

Sorcerer's Apprentice: For the Piano. P. Dukas. 28p. 1992. pap. 5.95 (*0-7935-1745-1*) H Leonard.

Sorcerer's Apprentice: Tales & Conjurations. Charles Johnson. 192p. 1994. pap. 9.95 (*0-452-27237-8*, Plume) NAL-Dutton.

Sorcerer's Apprentice: Tales & Conjurations. Charles Johnson. 180p. 1987. pap. 8.95 (*0-14-009865-8*, Penguin Bks) Viking Penguin.

Sorcerer's Apprentice: Tales of the Modern Hospital. Sallie Tisdale. 1988. pap. 9.95 (*0-8050-0578-1*, Owl) H Holt & Co.

Sorcerer's Apprentice: The French Scientist's Image of German Science, 1840-1919. Harry W. Paul. LC 77-178986. (University of Florida Monographs: Social Sciences: No. 44). 96p. reprint ed. pap. 27.40 (*0-7837-5086-2*, 2044784) Bks Demand.

Sorcerer's Apprentice: The Life of Franz von Papen. Richard W. Rolfs. (Illus.). 484p. (Orig.). (C). 1994. pap. text ed. 42.00 (*0-7618-0163-4*); lib. bdg. 58.00 (*0-7618-0162-6*) U Pr of Amer.

Sorcerer's Apprentice (Playscript) Mary H. Surface. (Orig.). (J). 1994. pap. 5.00 (*0-87602-323-5*) Anchorage.

Sorcerer's Apprentice Storybook & Magic Tricks. Bob Friedhoffer. LC 91-73813. (Illus.). 64p. (J). (gr. 1-7). 1993. 12.95 (*1-56282-144-X*) Disney Pr.

***Sorcerer's Crib Sheet.** (Bloodshadows Ser.). 15.00 (*0-87431-386-4*, 33012) West End Games.

Sorcerers' Crossing: A Woman's Journey. Taisha Abelar. 266p. 1993. reprint ed. pap. 12.95 (*0-14-019366-9*, Arkana) Viking Penguin.

Sorcerer's Guide to Good Health. Peggy Cochrane. LC 92-36262. 208p. 1993. pap. 14.99 (*0-942637-86-0*) Barricade Bks.

Sorcerer's Handbook. Wade Baskin. (Illus.). 640p. 1974. reprint ed. pap. 4.95 (*0-8065-0399-8*, Citadel Pr) Carol Pub Group.

***Sorcerer's Legacy.** Janny Wurts. mass mkt. write for info. (*0-06-105745-2*, HarperPrism) HarpC.

Sorcerers of Dobu: The Social Anthropology of the Dobu Islanders of the Western Pacific. R. F. Fortune. (Illus.). 326p. (C). 1989. reprint ed. pap. text ed. 13.95 (*0-88133-452-9*) Waveland Pr.

Sorcerers of Majipoor. Robert Silverberg. LC 96-35027. 480p. 1997. 23.00 (*0-06-105254-X*) HarpC.

***Sorcerers of Majipoor.** Robert Silverberg. 1997. mass mkt. write for info. (*0-06-105780-0*, HarperPrism) HarpC.

Sorcerers of Pan Tang. Mark Morrison et al. (Stormbringer Roleplaying Game System Ser.). (Illus.). 128p. (Orig.). 1991. pap. 18.95 (*0-933635-79-6*, 2112) Chaosium.

Sorcerer's Samplecase: Selected Poems in a Jugular Vein. Ed. by Stanley McNail. (Illus.). 26p. (Orig.). (YA). (gr. 7 up). 1986. pap. 3.00 (*0-940945-00-2*) Embassy Hall Edns.

Sorcerer's Shadow. David C. Smith. 1982. mass mkt. 2.50 (*0-686-97453-0*, Zebra Kensgtn) Kensgtn Pub Corp.

Sorceress. Claire Delacroix. (Historical Ser.). 1994. mass mkt. 3.99 (*0-373-28835-2*, 1-28835-6) Harlequin Bks.

Sorceress of Ambermere. J. Calvin Pierce. 256p. (Orig.). 1993. mass mkt. 4.99 (*0-441-33741-4*) Ace Bks.

Sorceress of Attu. Dan De Quille. Ed. by Lawrence I. Berkove. (Illus.). 60p. (Orig.). 1994. pap. 20.00 (*0-933691-06-8*) U Mich-Dearborn.

Sorceress of Darshiva. David Eddings. (Malloreon Ser.: Vol. 4). 384p. 1990. mass mkt. 6.99 (*0-345-36935-1*, Del Rey) Ballantine.

***Sorceress of Darshiva.** David Eddings. 1997. pap. 12.95 (*0-345-41921-9*, Del Rey) Ballantine.

Sorceress of Darshiva: Book Four of the Malloreon. David Eddings. LC 89-6705. 448p. 1989. 19.95 (*0-345-33005-6*, Del Rey) Ballantine.

Sorceress or Witch: The Image of Gender in Medieval Iceland & Northern Europe. Katherine Morris. 262p. (C). 1991. pap. text ed. 32.50 (*0-8191-8257-5*); lib. bdg. 57.50 (*0-8191-8256-7*) U Pr of Amer.

Sorcery - Witchcraft Course: Teachings of Magick 11 Lessons, 11 lessons, Set. Thorguard Templar. 65p. (Orig.). 1994. 165.00 (*1-883147-83-2*) Intern Guild ASRS.

Sorcery & Shamanism: Curanderos & Clients in Northern Peru. Donald Joralemon & Douglas Sharon. (Illus.). 336p. 1993. 35.00 (*0-87480-423-X*) U of Utah Pr.

***Sorcery & the UFO Experience: Magic & UFOs.** 2nd unabridged ed. V. Macer-Story. 345p. 1997. spiral bd. 18.00 (*1-57179-068-3*) Intern Guild ASRS.

Sorcery Club. Douglas A. Menville. LC 75-46295. (Supernatural & Occult Fiction Ser.). (Illus.). 1976. reprint ed. lib. bdg. 29.95 (*0-405-08156-1*) Ayer.

Sorcery Four: The Crown of Kings. Steve Jackson. (Fiction Ser.). 240p. (Orig.). 1985. pap. 4.95 (*0-14-007209-8*, Penguin Bks) Viking Penguin.

Sorcery Trial of Alice Kyteler (1324) Tr. by L. S. Davidson & John O. Ward. (Medieval & Renaissance Texts & Studies). 104p. 1993. pap. 7.95 (*0-86698-171-3*, P21) Pegasus Pr.

Sorciere au Village. Robert Muchembled. (FRE.). 1991. pap. 15.95 (*0-7859-3979-2*) Fr & Eur.

***Sorciere dans la Soupe.** Marie-Francine Hebert. (Novels in the Premier Roman Ser.). 64p. (FRE.). (J). (gr. 2-5). 1996. pap. 7.95 (*2-89021-129-0*, Pub. by Les Editions CN) Firefly Bks Ltd.

Sorciere de la Rue Mouffetard et Autre Contes de la Rue Broca. Pierre Gripari. (Folio - Junior Ser.: No. 440). (Illus.). 153p. (FRE.). (J). (gr. 5-10). 1987. pap. 8.95 (*2-07-033440-6*) Schoenhof.

Sordariaceous Ascomycetes Without Ascospore Ejaculation. J. A. Von Arx et al. (Beihefte zur Nova Hedwigia Ser.: Heft 94). (Illus.). 104p. 1988. pap. 53.20 (*3-443-51016-7*) Lubrecht & Cramer.

Sordid Images: The Poetry of Masculine Desire. Steve H. Clark. LC 93-43826. 296p. (C). (gr. 13). 1994. text ed. 85.00 (*0-415-06801-0*, B3940, Routledge NY) Routledge.

***Soreceror's Apprentice.** Jerry Pinkney. (J). Date not set. write for info. (*0-688-14318-0*, Morrow Junior); lib. bdg. write for info. (*0-688-14319-9*, Morrow Junior) Morrow.

Sorediose, Corticole Krustenflaechen Im Ostalpenraum. I. Die Flechtenstoffe und die Gesicherte Verbreitung der Besser Bekannten Arten. Edith Schreiner & J. Hafellner. (Bibliotheca Lichenologica Ser.: Vol. 45). 291p. (GER.). 1992. pap. text ed. 77.00 (*3-443-58024-6*, Pub. by Cramer-Borntraeger GW) Lubrecht & Cramer.

Sorel Etrog: Human Traces: Paintings, Drawings, & Sculpture. Sorel Etrog. (Illus.). 144p. 1995. lib. bdg. 53.00 (*0-8095-4894-1*) Borgo Pr.

Sorel Etrog Human Traces: Paintings, Drawings & Sculpture by Sorel Etrog. Text by David Moos. (Illus.). 144p. 1995. pap. 24.95 (*0-88962-587-5*) Mosaic.

Sorel in Love. Barbara Sorel. LC 89-82353. 192p. (Orig.). 1990. pap. 8.95 (*0-9625422-0-2*) Fifth St Pr.

Soren Kierkegaard: Modern Philosopher & Existentialist. Alan L. Paley. LC 72-81903. (Outstanding Personalities Ser.: No. 40). 32p. 1972. lib. bdg. 7.25 (*0-87157-550-7*) SamHar Pr.

Soren Kierkegaard: The Mystique of Prayer & Pray-er. George K. Bowers. LC 94-29859. 144p. (Orig.). 1995. pap. 11.95 (*0-7880-0301-1*) CSS OH.

Soren Kierkegaard & His Critics: An International Bibliography of Criticism. Compiled by Francois H. Lapointe. LC 80-783. viii, 430p. 1980. text ed. 79.50 (*0-313-22333-5*, LKI/, Greenwood Pr) Greenwood.

Soren Kierkegaard's Christian Psychology: Insight for Counseling & Pastoral Care. C. Stephen Evans. 135p. 1995. reprint ed. spiral bd., pap. 14.95 (*1-57383-038-0*) Regent College.

Soren Kierkegaard's Journals & Papers, 7 vols. Incl. Vol. 2. F-K. 640p. 1970. 59.95 (*0-253-18241-7*); Vol. 3. L-R. 944p. 1976. 69.95 (*0-253-18242-5*); Vol. 4. S-Z. Soren Kierkegaard. Ed. by Howard V. Hong & Edna H. Hong. 800p. 1976. 75.00 (*0-253-18243-3*); Vol. 5. Autobiographical, Part One, 1829-1848. Soren Kierkegaard. Ed. by Howard V. Hong & Edna H. Hong. 576p. 1978. 59.95 (*0-253-18244-1*); Vol. 6. Autobiographical, Part Two, 1848-1855. Soren Kierkegaard. Ed. by Howard V. Hong & Edna H. Hong. 648p. 1978. 64.95 (*0-253-18245-X*); Vol. 7. Index & Composite Collation. Soren Kierkegaard. Ed. by Howard V. Hong & Edna H. Hong. 160p. 1978. 44.95 (*0-253-18246-8*); Vol. 1. A-E. 572p. 1967. 57.50 (*0-253-18240-9*); write for info. (*0-318-53524-6*) Ind U Pr.

Sorensen & Luckmann's Basic Nursing: A Psychophysiologic Approach. 3rd ed. Verolyn B. Bolander. 379p. 1994. write for info. (*0-7216-5237-9*) Saunders.

Sorensen & Luckmann's Basic Nursing: A Psychophysiologic Approach. 3rd ed. Ed. by Verolyn R. Bolander. LC 93-21589. (Illus.). 1664p. 1994. text ed. 57.95 (*0-7216-4013-3*) Saunders.

***Sorensen & Luckmann's Basic Nursing: A Psychophysiologic Approach, Study Guide/Checklist Package.** 3rd ed. Ed. by Verolyn B. Bolander. (Illus.). 1994. student ed. write for info. (*0-7216-5218-2*) Saunders.

Sorghum & Millets: Chemistry & Technology. Ed. by David A. Dendy. LC 94-72775. (Monograph Ser.). (Illus.). 415p. 1995. 145.00 (*0-913250-84-8*, BEF 6265) Am Assn Cereal Chem.

Sorghum & Millets in Human Nutrition. F. A. O. Staff. (Food and Nutrition Series: Vol. 27). 190p. 1995. pap. 30.00 (*92-5-103381-1*) Food & Agriculture Organization of.

Sorghum Makin' Time in Choestoe. Sylvia D. Turnage. 6p. (Orig.). 1994. pap. text ed. 3.75 (*1-880726-03-3*) Turnage Pub.

Sorghum Science. 2nd rev. ed. R. K. Maiti. (Illus.). 300p. 1996. lib. bdg. 69.00 (*1-886106-68-1*) Science Pubs.

Sorin of Notre Dame: A Centennial Celebration in Poetry on the Anniversary of the Death of Edward Sorin, C. S. C. 1814-1893. Ed. by M. A. Myers. LC 91-75432. 211p. (Orig.). 1991. pap. text ed. 14.95 (*1-879183-07-2*) Bristol Banner.

Sorley Maclean Poems 1932-82. Sorley MacLean et al. Ed. by Daniel Gillis. Tr. by Sorley MacLean from GAE. LC 87-2755. (Columban Celtic Ser.: Vol. 2). 180p. (Orig.). 1986. 12.95 (*0-941638-01-4*); pap. 8.95 (*0-941638-02-2*) Iona Phila.

Soroban (Abacus) to Silicon Chip. Floyd T. Waterman. 49p. (Orig.). 1984. pap. 3.50 (*1-55719-061-5*) U NE CPAR.

Sorokin & Civilization: A Centennial Assessment. Roger W. Wescott. 320p. (C). 1995. text ed. 49.95 (*1-56000-247-6*) Transaction Pubs.

Sorolla: A Selection from His Paintings in HSA. (Illus.). 15p. 1989. 15.00 (*0-87535-144-1*) Hispanic Soc.

Sorority of Survival: Memoirs of a Multiple. Katherine A. Newman. (Illus.). 179p. (Orig.). 1996. pap. 23.95 (*1-56072-346-7*) Nova Sci Pubs.

Sorority Scandal. Francine Pascal. (Sweet Valley University Ser.: No. 9). 240p. (YA). (gr. 9-12). 1995. 3.99 (*0-553-56654-7*) Bantam.

Sorority Sister. Diane Hoh. (Nightmare Hall Ser.: No. 10). 176p. (YA). (gr. 7-9). 1994. pap. 3.50 (*0-590-47689-0*) Scholastic Inc.

Sororophobia: Differences among Women in Literature & Culture. Helena Michie. (Illus.). 256p. 1992. 42.00 (*0-19-507387-8*) OUP.

Soros: The Life, Times & Trading Secrets of the World's Greatest Investor. Robert Slater. 260p. 1995. text ed. 25.00 (*0-7863-0361-1*) Irwin Prof Pubng.

***Soros: The Unauthorized Biography: The Life, Times & Trading Secrets of the World's Greatest Investor.** Robert Slater. 1997. pap. text ed. 14.95 (*0-7863-1247-5*) McGraw.

Soros on Soros: Staying Ahead of the Curve. George Soros. LC 95-12861. 326p. 1995. text ed. 45.00 (*0-471-12014-6*); pap. text ed. 19.95 (*0-471-11977-6*) Wiley.

Sorotchintzy Fair. Nikolai Gogol. (Illus.). 1991. 16.95 (*0-87923-879-8*) Godine.

***Sorprendido por el Poder del Espiritu Santo.** Deere. 338p. (SPA.). pap. write for info. (*1-56063-753-6*) Editorial Unilit.

Sorpresa de Navidad para Chabilita. Argentina Palacios. (Illus.). 32p. (J). (gr. k-4). 1996. pap. 14.95 (*0-8167-3545-X*) BrdgeWater.

Sorpresa de Navidad para Chabilita. Argentina Palacios. (Illus.). 32p. (J). (gr. k-4). 1996. pap. 3.95 (*0-8167-3541-7*, Troll Medallion) Troll Communs.

Sorpresa Dominical: Cristobal Raton de Iglesia. Barbara Davoll. (Cristobal Raton de Iglesia Ser.). 23p. (SPA.). 1990. 6.99 (*1-56063-299-2*, 490377) Editorial Unilit.

***Sorpresa Para Josefina: Un Cuento de Navidad.** Valerie Tripp. Tr. by Jose Moreno. (American Girls Collection: Vol. 3). (Illus.). (Orig.). (SPA.). (J). (gr. 2-5). 1997. pap. 5.95 (*1-56247-498-7*, Amer Girl Library) Pleasant Co.

Sorpresas. 2nd ed. Elena Olazagasti-Segovia. 240p. (C). 1996. pap. text ed. write for info. (*0-03-017524-0*) HR&W Schl Div.

Sorpresivamente. Andres Rivero. LC 01-67366. (Short Stories in Spanish Ser.). 80p. 1981. pap. 9.95 (*0-933648-03-0*) ARO.

Sorption & Degradation of Pesticides & Organic Chemicals in Soil: Proceedings of a Symposium Sponsored by Divisions S-3, S-1, S-2, and A5 of the Soil Science Society of America & American Society of Agronomy in Denver, Colorado, October 20, 1991. Soil Science Society of America, Division S-3 Staff. Ed. by D. M. Linn et al. LC 93-25573. (Special Publications: No. 32). 1993. pap. 30.00 (*0-89118-803-7*) Soil Sci Soc Am.

Sorrat: A History of the Neihardt Psychokinesis Experiments, 1961-1981. John T. Richards. LC 81-18312. 356p. 1982. 27.50 (*0-8108-1491-9*) Scarecrow.

Sorrel. Rita M. Cleary. LC 92-43522. 288p. (Orig.). 1993. pap. 12.95 (*0-86534-191-5*) Sunstone Pr.

***Sorrow, Vol. 5.** Upper Room Books Staff. (In Your Time of Ser.). 1997. pap. text ed. 19.75 (*0-8358-0751-7*) Upper Room Bks.

Sorrow & Consolation in Italian Humanism. George W. McClure. 309p. (C). 1990. text ed. 52.50 (*0-691-05598-X*) Princeton U Pr.

Sorrow Built a Bridge: Friendship & AIDS. Daniel Berrigan. 231p. (Orig.). 1989. pap. 14.95 (*1-879175-04-5*) Fortkamp.

Sorrow Child. Shara Herington. 1983. pap. 15.00 (*0-318-04448-X*) Pudding Hse Pubns.

***Sorrow Floats.** Tim Sandlin. LC 96-46253. 416p. 1997. pap. 12.00 (*1-57322-604-1*, Riverhd Trade) Berkley Pub.

***Sorrow Floats.** Tim Sandlin. 352p. 4.98 (*0-8317-7748-6*) Smithmark.

Sorrow, Grief & God. Salvatore Cipparone. 4.95 (*0-686-20577-4*) Ivory Scroll.

Sorrow in Christian, No. 28. pap. 0.15 (*0-87377-153-2*) GAM Pubns.

Sorrow in Our Heart: The Life of Tecumseh. Allan W. Eckert. 1088p. 1993. mass mkt. 7.50 (*0-553-56174-X*) Bantam.

Sorrow Is the Only Faithful One: The Life of Owen Dodson. James V. Hatch. LC 92-18612. (Illus.). 328p. (C). 1993. text ed. 34.95 (*0-252-01977-6*) U of Ill Pr.

Sorrow Is the Only Faithful One: The Life of Owen Dodson. James V. Hatch. 392p. 1995. 14.95 (*0-252-06477-1*) U of Ill Pr.

Sorrow Not! Winning over Grief & Sorrow. Kenneth Copeland. 18p. 1992. pap. 1.00 (*0-88114-813-X*) K Copeland Pubns.

S

Sorrow of Architecture. Liam Rector. LC 83-20685. 75p. 1984. 14.00 (*0-937872-16-4*); pap. 6.00 (*0-937872-17-2*) Dragon Gate.

Sorrow of Belgium. Kate Chopin. Tr. by Arnold J. Pomerans. 608p. 1994. pap. 11.95 (*0-14-018801-0*, Penguin Classics) Viking Penguin.

Sorrow of Belgium. Hugo Claus. 1990. 24.95 (*0-394-56263-1*) Pantheon.

Sorrow of the Lonely & the Burning of the Dancers. Edward L. Schieffelin. LC 75-10999. (Illus.). 256p. (C). 1976. pap. text ed. 13.00 (*0-312-74550-8*) St Martin.

Sorrow of the Snows. Upendranath Askh. Tr. by Jai Ratan from HIN. 9.00 (*0-89253-639-X*); 6.75 (*0-89253-640-3*) Ind-US Inc.

Sorrow of War: A Novel of North Vietnam. Bao Ninh. Tr. by Phan T. Hao from VIE. 240p. 1996. pap. 12.00 (*1-57322-543-6*, Riverhd Trade) Berkley Pub.

Sorrow, the Sacrifice & the Triumph. Thomas W. Petrisko. 1995. pap. 12.00 (*0-684-80388-7*, Touchstone Bks) S&S Trade.

Sorrowful & Immaculate Heart of Mary. Duffner. 47p. 1.25 (*0-911988-24-6*, 37702) AMI Pr.

***Sorrowful City.** Harry Morris. LC 65-29103. 63p. reprint ed. pap. 25.00 (*0-608-04491-1*, 2065236) Bks Demand.

Sorrowful Mysteries & Other Stories. Normandi Ellis. 1991. 19.95 (*0-934847-13-4*); pap. 9.95 (*0-934847-14-2*) Arrowood Bks.

Sorrows below Apollyon, Vol. 1. Kevin Redlake. Ed. by Jacob Stohlmberg. (Illus.). 120p. 1995. pap. 4.00 (*0-9639186-0-5*) Stohlmberg Horror.

Sorrow's End. Hilda Vest. LC 93-73756. 72p. (YA). (gr. 12 up). 1993. pap. 8.00 (*0-940713-09-8*) Broadside Pr.

Sorrow's Kitchen: The Life & Folklore of Zora Neale Hurston. Mary E. Lyons. LC 92-30600. (Great Achievers Ser.). (Illus.). 160p. (YA). (gr. 7 up). 1993. pap. 6.95 (*0-02-044445-1*) Macmillan.

Sorrow's Kitchen: The Life & Folklore of Zora Neale Hurston. Mary E. Lyons. LC 90-8058. (Illus.). 160p. (YA). (gr. 7 up). 1990. lib. bdg. 15.00 (*0-684-19198-9*, C Scribner Sons Young) S&S Childrens.

Sorrows of an Exile: Tristia. Ovid. Tr. by A. D. Melville. LC 92-5682. (Illus.). 206p. (ENG & LAT.). 1992. 65.00 (*0-19-814792-9*, Old Oregon Bk Store) OUP.

Sorrows of an Exile (Tristia) Ovid. Tr. by A. D. Melville. (The World's Classics Ser.). (Illus.). 208p. 1995. pap. 10.95 (*0-19-282452-X*) OUP.

Sorrows of Cold Stone: Poems, 1940-1950. John M. Brinnin. LC 73-110817. 109p. 1971. reprint ed. text ed. 35.00 (*0-8371-3220-7*, BRSO, Greenwood Pr) Greenwood.

Sorrows of Fat City: A Selection of Literary Essays & Reviews. George P. Garrett. LC 91-30494. 340p. (Orig.). 1992. pap. 9.95 (*0-87249-789-5*) U of SC Pr.

Sorrows of Frederick. Romulus Linney. 1976. pap. 5.25 (*0-8222-1058-4*) Dramatists Play.

Sorrows of Priapus: The Poetic Truths of Mind & Body in Myth & Experience. Edward Dahlberg. (Illus.). 120p. 1988. reprint ed. pap. 10.95 (*0-7145-0670-2*) M Boyars Pubs.

Sorrows of Satan. Marie Corelli. (Oxford Popular Fiction Ser.). 416p. 1996. pap. 10.95 (*0-19-283220-4*) OUP.

Sorrows of the Ancient Romans: The Gladiator & the Monster. Carlin A. Barton. 224p. (C). 1992. pap. text ed. 15.95 (*0-691-01091-9*) Princeton U Pr.

Sorrows of the Quaker Jesus: James Nayler & the Puritan Crackdown on the Free Spirit. Leo Damrosch. (Illus.). 384p. 1996. 39.95 (*0-674-82143-2*) HUP.

Sorrows of Werter. Johann W. Von Goethe. LC 91-16916. 242p. 1991. reprint ed. 48.00 (*1-85477-069-1*, Pub. by Woodstock Bks UK) Cassell.

Sorrows of Young Werther. Johann Wolfgang Von Goethe. LC 89-40604. 1990. pap. 11.00 (*0-679-72951-8*, Vin) Random.

Sorrows of Young Werther. Johann Wolfgang Von Goethe. Tr. by W. H. Auden. 224p. 1993. 14.50 (*0-679-60064-7*, Modern Lib) Random.

Sorrows of Young Werther. Johann Wolfgang Von Goethe. Tr. & Intro. by Michael Hulse. 144p. 1989. pap. 9.95 (*0-14-044503-X*, Penguin Classics) Viking Penguin.

Sorrows of Young Werther & Novella. Johann Wolfgang Von Goethe. Tr. by Elizabeth Mayer et al. LC 84-4592. 201p. 1984. 7.95 (*0-394-60509-8*, Modern Lib) Random.

Sorrows of Young Werther & Selected Writings. Johann W. Von Goethe. Tr. by Catherine Hutter. (Orig.). 1962. pap. 5.95 (*0-451-52303-2*, Sig Classics) NAL-Dutton.

Sorrows of Young Werther, Elective Affinities, Novella, Vol. 11. Johann W. Von Goethe. Ed. by David E. Wellbery. Tr. by Victor Lange & Judith Ryan. LC 95-36759. (Princeton Paperbacks Ser.). 304p. (C). 1995. pap. 13.95 (*0-691-04346-9*) Princeton U Pr.

Sorrows of Young Werther, the New Melusina, Novelle. Lange. 177p. (C). 1949. pap. text ed. 22.50 (*0-03-008900-X*) HB Coll Pubs.

Sorry. Chariot Books Staff. LC 50-6524. (Talking with God Ser.). 22p. (J). (ps). 1993. bds. 3.29 (*0-7814-0105-4*, Chariot Bks) Chariot Victor.

Sorry: What Does It Mean? Sue Riley. LC 77-16811. (What Does It Mean? Ser.). (Illus.). 32p. (J). (ps-2). 1978. lib. bdg. 18.50 (*0-89565-013-4*) Childs World.

Sorry about That. Ruth Steinberg. (Baker's Dozen Ser.: No. 15). 142p. (J). (gr. 6-8). 1995. pap. 7.95 (*1-56871-089-5*) Targum Pr.

Sorry about the Explosion: A Humorous Guide to Computers. David D. Busch. (Personal Computing Ser.). (Illus.). 128p. (C). 1985. pap. 8.50 (*0-13-822834-5*) P-H.

Sorry I Asked: Intimate Interviews with Gay Porn's Rank & File. Dave Kinnick. (Orig.). 1993. mass mkt. 4.95 (*1-56333-090-3*, Badboy) Masquerade.

Sorry, Miss Folio! Jo Furtado. (Illus.). (J). (ps-3). 1992. reprint ed. pap. 6.95 (*0-916291-41-3*) Kane-Miller Bk.

Sorry, No Can Do! National Notary Association Editors. 12p. 1993. pap. 15.95 (*0-685-72113-2*) Natl Notary.

***Sorry, No Can Do, No. 2.** National Notary Association Editors. 12p. 1995. pap. 15.95 (*0-614-24073-5*) Natl Notary.

Sorry, No Can Do!, No. 2. R. Roelandts. No. 21. 131p. 1990. pap. 32.50 (*0-614-10470-X*, Pub. by Leuven Univ BE) Coronet Bks.

Sorry! No Hard Feelings? David Hayes. (Irish Play Ser.). 1978. pap. 2.50 (*0-912262-44-3*) Proscenium.

Sorry, No Turkeys This Year: The Bizarre Behavior of Management in Corporate America. Brian Eden. (Illus.). 150p. 1996. pap. 14.95 (*0-930753-19-4*) Spect Ln Pr.

Sorry Now? Mark R. Zubro. (Stonewall Inn Mysteries Ser.). 192p. 1992. pap. 8.95 (*0-312-08299-1*) St Martin.

Sorry Tale. Patience Worth. 640p. 1976. reprint ed. spiral bd. 35.00 (*0-7873-0981-8*) Hlth Research.

Sorry, the Bride Has Escaped. Raye Morgan. 1994. mass mkt. 2.99 (*0-373-05892-6*, 1-05892-4) Harlequin Bks.

Sorry, the Bride Has Escaped. large type ed. Raye Morgan. (Romance Ser.). 1996. 19.95 (*0-373-59668-5*) Silhouette.

Sorry, We're Open: A Geech Collection. Jerry Bittle. (Illus.). 128p. (Orig.). 1993. pap. 7.95 (*1-880652-19-6*) Wichita Eagle.

Sorry, Wrong Number. Patricia Ellis. (Romance Ser.). 1993. pap. 2.69 (*0-373-08931-7*, 5-08931-3) Silhouette.

Sorry, Wrong Number - The Hitch-Hiker. Lucille Fletcher. 1952. pap. 5.25 (*0-8222-1059-2*) Dramatists Play.

***Sorry Wrong Suspect.** Anthony Evans. 1997. mass mkt. 4.99 (*1-55197-162-3*, Pub. by Comnwlth Pub CN) Partners Pubs Grp.

***Sort It Out.** Andy Cooke. (Bear's Playschool Kits Ser.). (J). 1997. pap. text ed. 8.95 (*0-8120-8479-9*) Barron.

Sort of Diver. Richard Collins & Patricia Collins. (Illus.). 70p. (Orig.). 1995. pap. 9.95 (*1-878348-11-6*) New World FL.

***Sort of Forever.** Sally Warner. 1998. lib. bdg. 17.99 (*0-679-98648-0*) Knopf Bks Yng Read.

***Sort of Forever.** Sally Warner. (J). 1998. 16.00 (*0-679-88648-6*) Knopf Bks Yng Read.

***Sort of Forever.** Sally Warner. 1998. pap. write for info. (*0-679-88649-4*, Bullseye Bks) Random Bks Yng Read.

Sort of Utopia: Scarsdale, 1891-1981. Carol A. O'Connor. LC 82-5855. (Illus.). 283p. 1983. text ed. 64.50 (*0-87395-659-1*); pap. text ed. 21.95 (*0-87395-660-5*) State U NY Pr.

Sort Tragedy. large type ed. Philip Lauben. (Linford Mystery Large Print Ser.). 1994. pap. 15.99 (*0-7089-7639-5*) Ulverscroft.

Sorta Silly, Smart-Aleck Study Tips Even Teens Will Like. Carole Marsh. (Quantum Leap Ser.). (YA). (gr. 7-12). 1994. pap. 19.95 (*0-7933-7353-0*); lib. bdg. 29.95 (*0-7933-7352-2*); disk 29.95 (*0-7933-7354-9*) Gallopade Pub Group.

Sortie: A Bibliography of Combat Aviation Unit Histories of World War II. John W. Lambert. 48p. (C). 1993. pap. 10.95 (*0-9625860-6-4*) Phalanx Pub.

Sorties. James Dickey. LC 83-24421. 227p. 1984. reprint ed. pap. 11.95 (*0-8071-1140-6*) La State U Pr.

Sortileges. Alphonse Daudet. (Illus.). 125p. (FRE.). 1991. 24.95 (*0-7859-1204-5*, 2878580184) Fr & Eur.

Sortilegios. Maria R. Jaen. 82p. (SPA.). 1984. pap. 10.00 (*84-398-1485-2*) Society Sp & Sp-Am.

Sortiments-und Verlagskunde: Band 2. Klaus-Wilhelm Bramann et al. (Grundwissen Buchhandel-Verlage). 396p. 1995. 45.00 (*3-598-20065-X*) K G Saur.

Sorting. (Look & Learn Ser.). (Illus.). 24p. (J). 1993. 7.98 (*1-56173-906-5*) Pubns Intl Ltd.

Sorting. (Sticker Activity Ser.). (J). (ps-1). 1993. pap. 6.95 (*1-56458-246-9*) DK Pub Inc.

Sorting. (Stickers (Concepts) Ser.). (Illus.). 12p. (J). 1996. pap. 3.95 (*0-7894-1140-7*) DK Pub Inc.

Sorting. David Kirkby. LC 95-38708. (Mini Math Ser.). (Illus.). (J). 1996. write for info. (*1-57572-006-X*) Rigby Interact Libr.

Sorting. Photos by Stephen Oliver. LC 90-8575. (My First Look At Ser.). (Illus.). 24p. (J). (ps). 1991. 7.00 (*0-679-81162-1*) Random Bks Yng Read.

Sorting. Henry Pluckrose. (Math Counts Ser.). 32p. (J). 1995. lib. bdg. 17.80 (*0-516-05458-9*) Childrens.

Sorting. Henry Pluckrose. (Math Counts Ser.). (J). 1995. pap. 4.95 (*0-516-45458-7*) Childrens.

Sorting. Shereen G. Rutman. (Toddler Time Ser.). (Illus.). 16p. (J). (ps). 1992. student ed. pap. 2.95 (*1-56293-186-5*) McClanahan Bk.

Sorting. Istar Schwager. (Look & Learn Ser.). (Illus.). 24p. (J). (ps-3). 1993. lib. bdg. 12.95 (*1-56674-069-X*, HTS Bks) Forest Hse.

Sorting. Snapshot. 16p. (J). 1996. pap. 4.95 (*0-7894-0648-9*) DK Pub Inc.

***Sorting & Classifying.** Ed. by Janet Bruno. (Child-Centered Math Ser.: Vol. 4). (Illus.). 80p. (Orig.). 1997. pap. 4.98 (*1-57471-237-3*, 2654) Creat Teach Pr.

Sorting & Sets. Sally Hewitt. (Take Off With Ser.). (J). 1996. lib. bdg. 21.40 (*0-8172-4112-4*) Raintree Steck-V.

Sorting & Sort Systems. Harold Lorin. (Illus.). 480p. 1975. write for info. (*0-201-14453-0*) Addison-Wesley.

Sorting It Out. Anne S. Perlman. LC 82-70744. 1982. pap. 11.95 (*0-915604-73-6*) Carnegie-Mellon.

Sorting Life Out. Carolyn B. Purgraski. 36p. 1978. student ed. write for info. (*0-318-51257-2*); 24.00 (*0-930004-00-0*) C E M Comp.

Sorting Metaphors. Ricardo Pau-Llosa. 1983. pap. 8.00 (*0-938078-15-1*) Anhinga Pr.

Sorting Out Darkness. Ayres. 1992. pap. 10.95 (*0-944870-05-8*) Pacific Writers Pr.

***Sorting Out Ethics.** R. M. Hare. LC 97-8001. 184p. 1997. 25.00 (*0-19-823727-8*) OUP.

Sorting Out Money Values & Student Packet of Ready-to-Be-Duplicated Worksheets. rev. ed. Carolyn B. Purgraski et al. LC 59-4503. (Sorting Life Out Ser.). 292p. (C). 1981. teacher ed. 25.00 (*0-930004-02-7*); P. 68. student ed. write for info. (*0-318-51258-0*) C E M Comp.

Sorting Out OPNQRYF: The Desktop Guide to Open Query File. Mike Manto & Mike Dawson. (Illus.). 182p. (Orig.). 1994. pap. 69.00 (*1-884322-20-4*) Duke Commns Intl.

***Sorting Out Spelling.** unabridged ed. Clifford Russell. (Illus.). 68p. (Orig.). (C). 1997. teacher ed., ring bd., pap. 48.00 (*0-9657270-2-5*) Germane Pubs.

Sorting the Pieces: Relative Connections, Vol. IV. Gyeorgos C. Hatonn. (The Phoenix Journals). 240p. 1993. pap. 6.00 (*1-56935-021-3*) Phoenix Source.

Sorts & Types in Artificial Intelligence. Ed. by K. H. Blasius et al. (Lecture Notes in Artificial Intelligence Ser.: Vol. 418). viii, 307p. 1990. 36.00 (*0-387-52337-5*) Spr-Verlag.

Sorts, Ontology, & Metaphor: The Semantics of Sortal Structure. Shalom Lappin. (Foundations of Communication & Cognition Ser.). 173p. 1981. 65.40 (*3-11-008309-4*) De Gruyter.

S.O.S. Frank J. Lombardo. 320p. (Orig.). 1991. pap. write for info. (*0-945702-02-7*) Vertizon Bks.

SOS: Save Our Schools. Brian Simon & Clyde Chitty. 176p. (C). 1993. pap. 19.95 (*0-85315-782-0*, Pub. by Lawrence & Wishart UK) NYU Pr.

SOS: Sustain Our Schools. Patricia A. Graham. 1993. pap. 12.00 (*0-8090-1557-9*) Hill & Wang.

SOS at Midnight. Tompkins. 1985. pap. 5.00 (*0-87259-500-5*) Am Radio.

SOS English: Workbook. Jan Kaluza & Blazej Kruppik. Ed. by Polish Book Fair, Inc. Staff. (Illus.). 144p. (C). 1995. pap. 12.00 (*1-885889-23-2*) Home Tutor.

SOS for DOS. Katherine Murray. 256p. 1993. pap. 12.95 (*1-56884-043-8*) IDG Bks.

SOS for Windows. Katherine Murray. 256p. 1993. pap. 12.95 (*1-56884-045-4*) IDG Bks.

SOS for WordPerfect. Katherine Murray. 256p. 1994. pap. 12.95 (*1-56884-053-5*) IDG Bks.

SOS Guide to Effective Networking: The Best Way to Get the Job You Want. Susan O. Saidman. (Career Management Tools Ser.). 28p. 1993. pap. 6.00 (*0-9640171-0-5*) SOS Assocs.

***SOS Help for Emotions: Managing Anxiety, Anger, & Depression.** Lynn Clark. (Illus.). (Orig.). 1997. pap. write for info. (*0-935111-50-6*) Parents Pr KY.

SOS Help for Parents. rev. ed. Lynn F. Clark. LC 95-47640. (Illus.). 242p. 1996. pap. 12.00 (*0-935111-20-4*) Parents Pr KY.

SOS Pressure Defense. 3rd ed. Seattle Supersonics Staff & Bob Kloppenburg. 154p. (Orig.). 1996. pap. 19.95 (*1-56404-051-8*) Championship Bks & Vid Prodns.

SOS: Save Our Spines: A Backschool for Kids. rev. ed. Cindy O. Zech. (Illus.). 95p. (J). (gr. 3-6). student ed. 6.95 (*0-9638765-1-1*); teacher ed., spiral bd. 18.95 (*0-9638765-0-3*) Prevent Educ.

S.O.S. (Ships Operational Safety) Manual. Lorne & MacLean Marine & Offshore Publications Staff. (C). 1987. 300.00 (*0-685-33854-1*, Pub. by Lorne & MacLean Marine) St Mut.

S.O.S. Sobriety: The Proven Alternative to 12-Step Programs. James Christopher. 240p. (C). 1992. pap. 16.95 (*0-87975-726-4*) Prometheus Bks.

S.O.S.-Someone Special Facilitator Manual. Vickie Kaczmarek. 29p. 1989. pap. text ed. 14.95 (*1-882472-00-4*) Comm Grief Ctr.

S.O.S.-Someone Special Teen Manual. Vickie Kaczmarek. 17p. 1989. student ed. 8.95 (*1-882472-01-2*) Comm Grief Ctr.

SOS Titanic. Eve Bunting. LC 95-10712. 256p. (YA). (gr. 7 up). 1996. 12.00 (*0-15-200271-5*); pap. 6.00 (*0-15-201305-9*) HarBrace.

SOS Video, No. 2. (Exploring Transcription Practices Ser.). 10p. 1995. student ed. 200.00 (*0-935229-25-6*) Am Assoc Med.

So's Your Old Man: A Curmudgeon's Words to His Son. Peter Cross. LC 96-26177. (Orig.). 1997. write for info. (*1-877946-83-4*) Permanent Pr.

***Sosegaro el Alma: La Respuesta Para Su Salud Fisica y Espiritual.** Bruce Goldberg. 288p. (Orig.). (SPA.). 1997. 9.95 (*1-56718-486-3*) Llewellyn Pubns.

Soshu School of Swordsmiths. Kizu. 1991. pap. 4.95 (*0-910704-13-9*) Hawley.

Soslasno li c Evangelijem Dejstvoval i uchil Ljuter? N. I. Florinsky. 166p. 1975. reprint ed. pap. text ed. 6.00 (*0-317-30257-4*) Holy Trinity.

Sot-Weed Factor. John Barth. LC 87-1399. 768p. 1987. reprint ed. pap. 18.95 (*0-385-24088-0*, Anchor NY) Doubleday.

***Sotades: Symbols of Immortality on Greek Vases.** Herbert Hoffman. LC 96-36932. (Illus.). 240p. 1997. 120.00 (*0-19-815061-X*, Clarendon Pr) OUP.

Sotah, 1 vol. (ENG & HEB.). 15.00 (*0-910218-70-6*) Bennet Pub.

Sotah. Naomi Ragen. 496p. 1993. mass mkt. 5.99 (*0-06-100707-2*, Harp PBks) HarpC.

Sotai: Balance & Health Through Natural Movement. Keizo Hashimoto & Yoshizaki Kawakami. (Illus.). 240p. 1983. pap. 18.00 (*0-87040-534-9*) Japan Pubns USA.

Sotana de Juan Ruiz-Elementos Eclesiasticos en el Libro de Buen Amor. Julian A. Bueno. LC 81-84295. 166p. 1983. 17.00 (*0-938972-02-2*) Spanish Lit Pubns.

***Sotheby's.** Peter Watson. 1997. 25.00 (*0-679-41403-7*) Random.

***Sotheby's, Vol. 1.** Lacey. 1997. 25.95 (*0-316-51139-0*) Little.

Sotheby's Art & Auction: The Art Market Review 1994-95. (Illus.). 312p. 1995. 65.00 (*1-85029-707-X*, Pub. by Conran Octop Ltd UK) Antique Collect.

Sotheby's Art at Auction: The Art Market Review, 1993-4. (Illus.). 312p. 1995. 65.00 (*1-85029-646-4*, Pub. by Conran Octop Ltd UK) Antique Collect.

Sotheby's Art at Auction: The Art Market Review 1994-1995. John D. Block et al. (Illus.). 312p. 1996. 65.00 (*1-85029-718-5*) Antique Collect.

***Sotheby's Art at Auction: The Year in Review 1995-96.** (Illus.). 256p. 1997. 85.00 (*1-85029-787-8*, Pub. by Conran Octop Ltd UK) Antique Collect.

Sotheby's Caring for Antiques: A Guide to Handling, Cleaning, Display & Restoration. Michael Huntley & Mette T. Simpson. (Illus.). 192p. 1996. pap. 24.95 (*1-85029-867-X*, Pub. by Conran Octop Ltd UK) Antique Collect.

Sotheby's Collectors Guide: Animation Art. Sotheby's Staff. 1997. pap. 18.95 (*0-8050-4854-5*) H Holt & Co.

Sotheby's Collectors Guide: Art Deco/Art Nouveau. Sotheby's Staff. 1996. pap. 18.95 (*0-8050-4853-7*) H Holt & Co.

Sotheby's Collectors Guide: Photographs. Sotheby's Staff. 1996. pap. 18.95 (*0-8050-4855-3*) H Holt & Co.

Sotheby's Collectors Guide: Pocket Watches & Waist Watches. Sotheby's Staff. 1996. pap. 19.95 (*0-8050-4856-1*) H Holt & Co.

Sotheby's Collectors Guide: Prints. Sotheby's Staff. 1996. pap. 19.95 (*0-8050-4858-8*) H Holt & Co.

Sotheby's Collectors Guide: Silver. Sotheby's Staff. 1996. pap. 19.95 (*0-8050-4857-X*) H Holt & Co.

Sotheby's Concise Encyclopedia of Furniture. Ed. by Christopher Payne. (Illus.). 208p. 1995. pap. 24.95 (*1-85029-649-9*, Pub. by Conran Octop Ltd UK) Antique Collect.

Sotheby's Concise Encyclopedia of Glass. David Battie & Simon Cottle. (Illus.). 208p. 1995. pap. 24.95 (*1-85029-654-5*, Pub. by Conran Octop Ltd UK) Antique Collect.

Sotheby's Concise Encyclopedia of Porcelain. Ed. by David Battie. (Illus.). 208p. 1995. pap. 24.95 (*1-85029-648-0*, Pub. by Conran Octop Ltd UK) Antique Collect.

Sotheby's Concise Encyclopedia of Silver. Ed. by Charles Truman. 208p. 1996. pap. 24.95 (*1-85029-759-2*, Pub. by Conran Octop Ltd UK) Antique Collect.

Sotheby's Field Guide to American Decorative & Fold Arts. 1994. pap. 16.00 (*0-02-037449-6*) Macmillan.

Sotheby's Guide to American Folk Art. Jacquelyn Oak. (Illus.). 256p. 1994. pap. 16.00 (*0-671-89950-3*, Fireside) S&S Trade.

Sotheby's Guide to American Furniture. Patricia P. Petraglia. LC 95-321. (Illus.). 1995. pap. 18.00 (*0-684-80681-9*, Fireside) S&S Trade.

Sotheby's the Country House Guide. George Plumptre. (Illus.). 288p. 1996. pap. 19.95 (*0-7063-7519-X*, Pub. by Ward Lock UK) Sterling.

***Sotheby's Wine Encyclopedia.** Tom Stevenson. LC 97-16170. 552p. 1997. pap. 50.00 (*0-7894-2079-1*) DK Pub Inc.

Sotho English English Sotho Dictionary. T. J. Kriel. (Hippocrene African Language Dictionaries Ser.). 335p. 1995. pap. 14.95 (*0-7818-0392-6*) Hippocrene Bks.

Sotileza. Jose M. De Pereda. Ed. by German Gullon. (Nueva Austral Ser.: Vol. 117). (SPA.). 1991. pap. text ed. 19.95 (*84-239-1917-X*) Elliots Bks.

Sotira: A Neolithie Settlement in Cyprus. Porphyrios Dikaois et al. (University Museum Monographs: No. 23). (Illus.). xiii, 252p. 1961. pap. 30.00 (*0-934718-15-6*) U PA Mus Pubns.

Soto Zen in Medieval Japan. William M. Bodiford. LC 92-37843. (Studies in East Asian Buddhism: No. 8). 400p. (C). 1993. text ed. 36.00 (*0-8248-1482-7*) UH Pr.

***Sotos Syndrome: A Handbook for Families.** Rebecca R. Anderson & Bruce A. Buehler. (Illus.). 55p. (Orig.). 1992. spiral bd. 11.00 (*1-889843-01-6*) Meyer Rehab Inst.

Sots Art. Margarita Tupitsyn & John E. Bowlt. LC 85-72523. (Illus.). 60p. (Orig.). (C). 1986. pap. 4.00 (*0-915557-53-3*) New Mus Contemp Art.

Sots Art: Soviet Artists of the 1970s & 1980s. Yekaterina Andreeva. 120p. 1995. text ed. 39.95 (*976-8097-85-X*) Gordon & Breach.

***Sottie Lou.** Grace C. Johnson. Ed. by Rowena Carter. 95p. (Orig.). (C). 1996. pap. 13.50 (*0-614-21742-3*) Enrobialc.

Sotto Voce Massacres. Hale Chatfield. (Orig.). 1990. pap. 8.00 (*0-9628478-0-1*) North Star Assocs.

Soudan Francais: Contes Soudanaises. Charles Monteil. (B. E. Ser.: No. 119). (FRE.). 1905. 25.00 (*0-8115-3048-5*) Periodicals Srv.

Souffle see Comedies et Actes Divers

Souffle Cookbook. Myra Waldo. 1990. pap. 5.95 (*0-486-26416-5*) Dover.

Souffles: Forty Recipes from Savory to Sweet. Ann Amernick & Richard Chirol. (Illus.). 128p. 1989. 9.95 (*0-517-56978-7*, C P Pubs) Crown Pub Group.

Souffrances de Jeune Werther. Johann Wolfgang Von Goethe. 192p. (FRE.). 1973. pap. 10.95 (*0-7859-2326-8*, 2070364968) Fr & Eur.

Souffrances et Bonheur du Chretien. Francois Mauriac. pap. 9.50 (*0-685-34305-7*) Fr & Eur.

Soul. Friedman-Fairfax & Sony Music Staff. (Life, Times & Music Book/CD Ser.). 1995. pap. 16.98 incl. audio compact disk (*1-56799-183-1*, Friedman-Fairfax) M Friedman Pub Grp Inc.

***Soul.** Erikka Haa. 1997. 13.50 incl. audio compact disk (*1-56799-544-6*, Friedman-Fairfax) M Friedman Pub Grp Inc.

Soul. Adrian Kuzminski. LC 93-8720. (Revisioning Philosophy Ser.: Vol. 15). 157p. (C). 1994. text ed. 43.95 (*0-8204-2279-7*) P Lang Pubng.

An Asterisk (*) at the beginning of an entry indicates that the title is appearing in BIP for the first time.

Soul: An Owner's Manual: The Life of Fullness in the Post-Religious Era. George Jaidar. LC 94-31789. 160p. 1995. pap. 18.95 (*1-55778-710-7*) Paragon Hse.

Soul: Archaeology of the Spirit--Readings from Socrates to Ray Charles. Ed. by Phil Cousineau. LC 93-30040. 288p. 1995. 13.00 (*0-06-250243-3*) Harper SF.

Soul: Black Power, Politics, & Pleasure. Ed. by Monique Guillory & Richard C. Green. (Illus.). 320p. (C). 1997. 45.00 (*0-8147-3084-1*); pap. 18.95 (*0-8147-3085-X*) NYU Pr.

***Soul Aerobics: How to Build & Use Your Body-Mind-Soul Connection.** Jesse Weeks. 286p. (Orig.). 1997. pap. 14.95 (*0-9653593-0-1*) Sovrgnty Pubng.

Soul after Death. Johan L. Heiberg. 74p. 1991. pap. 6.95 (*1-880755-02-5*) Mermaid Pr.

Soul after Death: Contemporary "After-Death" Experiences in the Light of the Orthodox Teaching on the Afterlife. 3rd ed. Seraphim Rose. LC 93-85175. 105p. 1993. pap. 8.95 (*0-938635-14-X*) St Herman Pr.

Soul among Lions: The Cougar As Peaceful Adversary. Harley Shaw. LC 89-92196. 150p. 1989. pap. 11.95 (*1-55566-053-3*) Johnson Bks.

Soul & Body. C. A. Meier. Ed. by Julia Butterfield et al. LC 85-50669. 351p. (C). 1986. 29.95 (*0-932499-00-7*); pap. 15.95 (*0-932499-01-5*) Lapis Pr.

Soul & Body in Husserlian Phenomenology. Anna-Teresa Tymieniecka. 400p. 1983. lib. bdg. 158.50 (*90-277-1518-1*, D Reidel) Kluwer Ac.

Soul & Body of an Army. Ian Hamilton. (Modern Revivals in Military History Ser.). 310p. 1992. 61.95 (*0-7512-0032-8*, Pub. by Gregg Revivals UK) Ashgate Pub Co.

Soul & Everyday Life. Thomas Moore. 121p. 1995. 19.95 (*1-879323-16-8*) Sound Horizons AV.

Soul & Intellect: Studies in Plotinus & Later Neoplatonism. H. J. Blumenthal. (Collected Studies: No. CS 426). 352p. 1993. 94.95 (*0-86078-392-8*, Pub. by Variorum UK) Ashgate Pub Co.

Soul & Its Instrument. Lucille Cedercrans. 200p. 1994. disk 24.95 (*1-883493-19-6*) Wisdom Impress.

Soul & Its Instrument. Lucille Cedercrans. (Path of Initiation Ser.). 250p. 1995. text ed. 24.95 (*1-883493-20-X*); pap. text ed. 18.95 (*1-883493-21-8*) Wisdom Impress.

Soul & Its Mechanism. Alice A. Bailey. LC 31-995. 1973. pap. 10.00 (*0-85330-115-8*) Lucis.

Soul & Its Powers. The Mother. LC 92-70605. 147p. (Orig.). 1992. pap. 9.95 (*0-941524-67-1*) Lotus Light.

Soul & Its Vestures. C. W. Leadbeater. 24p. 1983. pap. 1.50 (*0-918980-12-7*) St Alban Pr.

Soul & Life after Death. Francis Harber. LC 77-84782. 144p. reprint ed. pap. 7.95 (*0-912444-36-3*) DARE Bks.

***Soul & Silicon: Spirits in a High-Tech World.** Carl A. Goldman. 280p. 1997. 24.00 (*0-933670-01-X*) Rising Star.

Soul & Spice: African Cooking in the Americas. Heidi H. Cusick. (Illus.). 320p. 1995. pap. 16.95 (*0-8118-0419-4*) Chronicle Bks.

Soul & Spirit. Jessie Penn-Lewis. 1993. pap. 4.95 (*0-87508-953-4*) Chr Lit.

Soul & the Ethic. Ann R. Colton. LC 67-31989. 262p. 1965. 7.95 (*0-917187-07-5*) A R Colton Fnd.

Soul Approach to Depression: Our Normal Transitional Emotions. Kathy Oddenino. (Illus.). 348p. (Orig.). 1995. pap. 24.95 (*0-923081-05-4*) Joy Pubns MD.

Soul As Virgin Wife Vol. 1: Mechthild of Magdeburg, Marguerite Porete, & Meister Eckhart. Amy Hollywood. LC 94-40479. (Studies in Spirituality & Theology: Vol. 1). (C). 1996. text ed. 32.95 (*0-268-01753-0*) U of Notre Dame Pr.

Soul Asylum: Let Your Dim Light Shine. Ed. by Aaron Stang. (Illus.). 136p. (Orig.). 1995. pap. text ed. 21.95 (*0-89724-794-9*, PG9541) Warner Brothers.

Soul Asylum - Grave Dancers Union: Grave Dancers Union. Ed. by Carol Cuellar. (Illus.). 72p. (Orig.). (C). 1993. pap. text ed. 19.95 (*0-89724-092-8*, VF1985) Warner Brothers.

Soul Asylum-Grave Dancers Union. (Guitar Super Tab Ser.). 56p. (Orig.). 1994. pap. 16.95 (*0-89724-129-0*, GF0635) Warner Brothers.

Soul Asylum-Grave Dancers Union. (Authentic Guitar-Tab Ser.). 132p. (Orig.). 1994. pap. 26.95 (*0-89724-399-4*, GF0641) Warner Brothers.

Soul at Rest: Journey into Contemplative Prayer. Tricia M. Rhodes. 224p. 1996. 13.99 (*1-55661-809-3*) Bethany Hse.

***Soul at Work: Reflections on a Spirituality of Working.** Barbara Smith-Moran. Ed. by Carl Koch. (Illus.). 112p. (Orig.). 1997. pap. 7.95 (*0-88489-396-0*) St Marys.

***Soul Bearer.** Jonathan Cross. 1997. mass mkt. 6.95 (*1-56315-081-6*) Sterling Hse.

***Soul-Biz: Merging Spiritual & Material Values for Profit & Sanity.** Jesse Weeks. 224p. (Orig.). 1997. pap. 12.95 (*0-9653593-2-8*) Sovrgnty Pubng.

***Soul Blade: Unauthorized Game Secrets.** Anthony Lynch. 112p. 1997. per. 12.99 (*0-7615-1062-1*) Prima Pub.

Soul Bodies. Chris Griscom. LC 96-16027. (Orig.). 1996. pap. 15.00 (*0-9623696-3-2*) Light Inst Fndtn.

Soul Brothers & Sister Lou. Kristin Hunter. 249p. (J). 1997. pap. 9.95 (*0-7043-4900-0*, Pub. by Womens Press UK) Trafalgar.

Soul Brothers & Sisters. Date not set. pap. 1.95 (*0-590-08021-0*) Scholastic Inc.

Soul Call. Brenda B. Aaron. 70p. (Orig.). 1996. pap. write for info. (*1-57502-130-7*) Morris Pubng.

Soul Care. Peter Lord. 264p. 1990. pap. 12.99 (*0-8010-5661-6*) Baker Bks.

***Soul Care: Deliverance & Renewal through the Christian Life.** 208p. 1995. pap. 14.99 (*0-8010-5747-7*, Bridgept Bks) Baker Bks.

Soul Catalysts & How to Use Them. Brown Landone. 62p. 1971. reprint ed. spiral bd. 4.50 (*0-7873-1044-1*) Hlth Research.

Soul Catcher. Colin Kersey. 272p. 1995. 22.95 (*0-312-13606-4*) St Martin.

Soul Catcher. Katia Spiegelman. 1990. 19.95 (*0-7145-2908-7*) M Boyars Pubs.

Soul-Centered Astrology: A Key to Your Expanding Self. Alan Oken. (Illus.). 248p. 1996. pap. 18.95 (*0-89594-811-7*) Crossing Pr.

Soul Claiming. Jody Aliesan & Julie King. LC 75-23822. (Haystack Bks.). (Illus.). 76p. 1975. 6.00 (*0-913142-16-6*); pap. 3.50 (*0-913142-15-8*) Mulch Pr.

Soul Clap Hands & Sing. Paule Marshall. (Howard University Press Library of Contemporary Literature). 208p. 1988. pap. 12.95 (*0-88258-155-4*) Howard U Pr.

Soul Clap Its Hands & Sing. Natalie Petesch. LC 81-51386. 206p. 1981. pap. 6.50 (*0-89608-119-2*) South End Pr.

Soul Concepts of the Navaho. Berard Haile. 1964. reprint ed. pap. 6.50 (*0-686-32654-7*) St Michaels.

Soul Consciousness. R. Swinburne Clymer. 1955. 10.95 (*0-686-00830-8*) Philos Pub.

Soul Daddy. J. Roy. 224p. (YA). (gr. 7 up). 1992. 17.00 (*0-15-277193-X*, Gulliver Bks) HarBrace.

***Soul Deep.** Monique Guilmore. 256p. 1997. mass mkt. 4.99 (*0-7860-0395-2*, Pinncle Kensgtn) Kensgtn Pub Corp.

Soul Development. (Library: Vol. 21). 435p. 1986. lib. bdg. 19.95 (*0-87604-173-X*, 1121) ARE Pr.

Soul Development in the Divine Love of the Father. F.C. D.T. Trustees Staff. 1989. pap. write for info. (*1-887621-19-9*) Found Ch Divine Truth.

Soul Echoes. Eloise C. Williams. 68p. (Orig.). 1994. pap. text ed. write for info. (*0-915515-04-0*) Way Pub.

***Soul Empowerment: A Guidebook for Healing Yourself & Others.** Michael Bradford & Rosalie D. Heart. 200p. (Orig.). 1997. pap. 15.95 (*0-9651576-1-X*) Heart Link.

Soul Enchantments: Mystical Stories to Charm Remembrance. Jacqueline Snyder. Ed. by Scott E. Miners. (Illus.). 96p. (Orig.). (C). 1992. pap. 7.95 (*0-9625812-2-4*) Windsor WA.

Soul Feast: An Invitation to the Christian Spiritual Life. Marjorie Thompson. 180p. (Orig.). 1995. pap. 13.00 (*0-664-25548-5*) Westminster John Knox.

Soul Fire. Stanley E. Sayers. 1991. pap. 7.95 (*0-89137-126-5*) Quality Pubns.

Soul Fish No. I: An Eskimo Tale. J. Grubbs. Ed. by Abell. (Eskimo Tales Ser.). 50p. 1995. text ed. 32.00 (*1-56611-522-1*); pap. text ed. 28.00 (*1-56611-523-X*) Jones.

Soul Flight. Emily Powell. LC 86-62447. 72p. (J). 1986. pap. 3.95 (*0-938875-02-7*) Pittenbruach Pr.

***Soul Food.** Lajoyce Brookshire. 1997. mass mkt. 6.50 (*0-06-101298-X*) HarpC.

Soul Food. Ilene Dunn. 10p. 1995. write for info. (*1-887975-02-0*) Romance & Miracles.

Soul Food, No. II. J. Grubbs Wu. Ed. by Abell. (Eskimo Tales Ser.). 50p. Date not set. pap. text ed. 28.00 (*0-614-08593-4*); lib. bdg. 32.00 (*0-614-08592-6*) Jones.

Soul Food: Classic Cuisine from the Deep South. Sheila Ferguson. LC 89-9028. 208p. 1993. pap. 12.95 (*0-8021-3283-9*, Grove) Grove-Atltic.

***Soul Food: Recipes & Reflections from African-American Churches.** Joyce White. 288p. Date not set. 30.00 (*0-06-018716-6*) HarpC.

Soul Food: Spiritual Staples for the Journey of Life. Maureen Bass. Ed. by Jennifer Garrett & Linda Altman. (Illus.). 134p. (Orig.). (C). 1990. pap. text ed. 9.95 (*0-9645510-0-4*) Valhalla Press.

Soul Food: Stories to Nourish the Spirit & the Heart. rev. ed. Ed. by Jack Kornfield & Christina Feldman. LC 96-11418. Orig. Title: Stories of the Spirit, Stories of the Heart. 1996. pap. 14.00 (*0-06-251442-3*) Harper SF.

Soul Food III: Eskimo Stories. J. Grubbs Wu. Ed. by Abell. (Eskimo Tales Ser.). 50p. 1995. pap. text ed. 28.00 (*0-614-08591-8*); lib. bdg. 32.00 (*0-614-08590-X*) Jones.

Soul Force: The Psycho-Spiritual Development of Black Folks. John L. Bolling. (Illus.). 250p. (Orig.). 1989. pap. text ed. 19.95 (*0-317-93367-1*) Mandala Rising Pr.

***Soul Forge.** 1998. 23.99 (*0-7869-0645-6*) TSR Inc.

Soul Friend: An Invitation to Spiritual Direction. Kenneth Leech. LC 91-58136. 272p. 1992. reprint ed. pap. 14.00 (*0-06-065214-4*) Harper SF.

Soul Gallery. Albert Huffstickler. Ed. by Richard A. Spiegel. (Illus.). 38p. (Orig.). 1987. pap. 3.50 (*0-934776-06-7*) Bard Pr.

Soul Gifts. Nancy Hyle. LC 94-70818. (Illus.). 108p. 1994. lib. bdg. 10.00 (*1-878149-24-5*) Counterpoint Pub.

Soul Graft. Brad Hill. 1988. pap. 6.95 (*0-910452-66-0*) Covenant.

***Soul Healing.** Bruce Goldberg. LC 96-35824. (Whole Life Ser.). 288p. (Orig.). 1997. pap. 14.95 (*1-56718-317-4*) Llewellyn Pubns.

***Soul Healing: A Spiritual Orientation in Counseling & Therapy.** Dorothy S. Becvar. 256p. 1997. 35.00 (*0-465-09552-6*) Basic.

Soul Hits of the Seventies: Over 40 Songs. (Piano-Vocal-Guitar Ser.). 208p. (Orig.). 1992. pap. 14.95 (*0-7935-1239-5*, 00311556) H Leonard.

Soul Improvement. Mike Taylor. (Illus.). 96p. (Orig.). 1996. pap. 9.95 (*1-57312-044-8*, Peake Road) Smyth & Helwys.

Soul in Bondage: Stories from Tibet. Tashi Dawa. 234p. (Orig.). 1992. pap. 8.95 (*0-8351-2096-1*) China Bks.

***Soul in Cyberspace.** Douglas Groothuis. 192p. (Orig.). 1997. pap. 9.99 (*0-8010-5760-4*, Hour Glass) Baker Bks.

***Soul in Distress: What Every Pastoral Counselor Should Know about Emotional & Mental Illness.** Richard W. Roukema. LC 96-48818. 274p. 1997. 49.95 (*0-7890-0168-3*, Haworth Pastrl) Haworth Pr.

***Soul in Distress: What Every Pastoral Counselor Should Know about Emotional & Mental Illness.** Richard W. Roukema. LC 96-48818. 274p. 1997. pap. 19.95 (*0-7890-0198-5*, Haworth Pastrl) Haworth Pr.

Soul in Exile: Lives of a Palestinian Revolutionary. Fawaz Turki. 288p. 1987. pap. 12.00 (*0-85345-747-6*) Monthly Rev.

Soul in Management: How African-American Managers Can Succeed in a White Business Environment. Richard F. America & Bernard E. Anderson. LC 95-50092. 256p. 1996. 19.95 (*1-55972-353-X*, Birch Ln Pr) Carol Pub Group.

***Soul in Management: How African-American Managers Thrive in the Competitive Corporate Environment.** Richard F. America. 1997. pap. text ed. 13.95 (*0-8065-1946-0*, Citadel Pr) Carol Pub Group.

Soul in Paraphrase. 2nd ed. Don E. Saliers. 144p. 1991. pap. 14.95 (*1-878009-08-7*, OSL Pubns) Order St Luke Pubns.

Soul in Place: Reclaiming Home As Sacred Space. Carol Bridges. (Illus.). 256p. (Orig.). 1996. 15.00 (*0-945111-11-8*) Earth Nation.

Soul in Progress: A Divorced Mother's Spiritual Adventure. Dorian Caruso. 243p. (Orig.). 1995. pap. 14.95 (*0-87604-336-8*, 409) ARE Pr.

Soul in Society: The Making & Renewal of Social Christianity. Gary Dorrien. LC 95-4023. 1995. pap. 24.00 (*0-8006-2891-8*, 1-2891, Fortress Pr) Augsburg Fortress.

Soul in Suspense: Hitchcock's Fright & Delight. Neil P. Hurley. LC 92-43921. (Illus.). 404p. 1993. 47.50 (*0-8108-2526-0*) Scarecrow.

Soul in the Opera House. W. Calvin McCain. LC 82-229693. 80p. 1982. pap. 5.00 (*0-931680-02-6*) Dunbar Pub.

Soul Is a Traveller in Time. Irwyn Greif. 1995. 15.95 (*0-533-11228-1*) Vantage.

***Soul Is Here for Its Own Joy.** Bly. 1997. 7.98 (*1-56731-158-X*) Fine Comms.

Soul Is Here for Its Own Joy: Sacred Poems from Many Cultures. Ed. by Robert Bly. LC 95-16868. 1995. 20.00 (*0-88001-355-9*) Ecco Pr.

Soul Is Here for Its Own Joy: Sacred Poems from Many Cultures. Robert Bly. 288p. 1997. reprint ed. pap. 15.00 (*0-88001-475-X*) Ecco Pr.

Soul Journey: A Jungian Analyst Looks at Reincarnation. John A. Sanford. 180p. 1991. pap. 11.95 (*0-8245-1370-3*) Crossroad NY.

***Soul Kiss.** Shay Youngblood. LC 96-51142. 224p. 1997. 21.00 (*1-57322-063-9*, Riverhead Books) Putnam Pub Group.

Soul-Kissed. Ann T. Linhorst. 180p. 1996. pap. 15.95 (*0-8245-1492-0*) Crossroad NY.

Soul-Kissed: The Experience of Bliss in Everyday Life. Ann T. Linthorst. 1995. pap. 15.95 (*0-8245-1574-9*) Crossroad NY.

Soul Level Healing -- Techniques to Peel Away the Layers (PAL) Smith. 1996. 16.95 (*0-938650-76-9*) Thinkers Pr.

Soul Liberty: The Baptists' Struggle in New England, 1630-1833. William G. McLoughlin. LC 90-43369. 357p. 1991. text ed. 40.00 (*0-87451-532-7*) U Pr of New Eng.

***Soul Love: Awakening Your Heart Centers.** Sanaya Roman. LC 97-19845. (Soul Life Ser.: Bk. 1). 276p. (Orig.). 1997. pap. 12.95 (*0-915811-77-4*) H J Kramer Inc.

Soul Magic: Understanding Your Journey. Katherine Torres. LC 95-74969. (Illus.). 160p. (Orig.). 1995. pap. 12.95 (*1-56184-077-7*) New Falcon Pubns.

Soul Make a Path Through Shouting. Cyrus Cassells. LC 94-9847. 1994. pap. 12.00 (*1-55659-065-2*) Copper Canyon.

Soul Make a Path Through Shouting. Cyrus Cassells. LC 94-9842. 1994. 22.00 (*1-55659-066-0*) Copper Canyon.

Soul Making. Alan Jones. LC 84-48222. 1989. pap. 16.00 (*0-06-064179-7*) Harper SF.

Soul-Making: The Telling of a Spiritual Journey. Edward Sellner. LC 90-71376. 208p. (Orig.). 1991. pap. 9.95 (*0-89622-457-0*) Twenty-Third.

Soul Management: Maximizing Your Spiritual Assets in a Bottom-Line World. Wayne Schmidt. 176p. 1996. 15.99 (*0-310-20102-0*) Zondervan.

***Soul Mate Practices: A Guidebook for Developing a Soul Mate Relationship.** Ernie Stech. 49p. 1995. spiral bd. 7.95 (*0-9645661-2-5*) Chief Mtn Pub.

***Soul Mates.** Bridget Anderson. 288p. 1997. mass mkt. 4.99 (*0-7860-0386-3*, Pinncle Kensgtn) Kensgtn Pub Corp.

Soul Mates. Darlene P. Hopson. 1992. pap. 19.56 (*0-13-824871-0*) P-H.

Soul Mates. Ruby Williams. Ed. by Barbara Meeker. 185p. (Orig.). 1995. pap. 15.95 (*0-938041-25-8*) Arc Pr AR.

Soul Mates. Ruby Williams. LC 94-73538. 184p. (Orig.). 1995. pap. 15.95 (*0-938041-52-5*) Arc Pr AR.

Soul Mates. large type ed. Thomas Moore. LC 94-19123. 1994. 26.95 (*1-56895-110-8*) Wheeler Pub.

Soul Mates, No. 2. 2nd ed. Ruby Williams. 350p. 1996. pap. 23.00 (*0-614-13936-8*) Arc Pr AR.

Soul Mates: Honoring the Mysteries of Love & Relationship. Thomas Moore. 320p. 1994. 25.00 (*0-06-016928-1*, HarpT) HarpC.

Soul Mates: Honoring the Mysteries of Love & Relationship. Thomas Moore. 288p. 1994. pap. 13.00 (*0-06-092575-2*, HarpT) HarpC.

***Soul-Mates: How to Find Them, Keep Them.** Enid Vien. (Illus.). 150p. (Orig.). 1997. pap. text ed. 12.95 (*0-9648330-5-0*) Dynamism Pubns.

Soul Medicine: Medical Challenges on Life's Uncertain Journey. John E. Postley. 288p. (Orig.). 1995. pap. 14.95 (*0-944634-33-8*, Love & Logic Pr) Cline-Fay Inst.

***Soul Moments: Marvelous Stories of Synchroncidy - Meaning Coincidences from a Seemingly Random World.** Phil Cousineau. LC 97-1301. 224p. (Orig.). 1997. pap. 11.95 (*1-57324-079-6*) Conari Press.

Soul Murder & Slavery. unabridged ed. Nell I. Painter. LC 95-78744. (Charles Edmondson Historical Lectures: Vol. 15). 38p. (Orig.). (C). 1995. pap. 5.95 (*0-918954-62-2*) Baylor Univ Pr.

Soul Murder Effects of Childhood. Leonard Shengold. 1991. pap. 12.00 (*0-449-90549-7*) Fawcett.

Soul Music. Terry Pratchett. 1995. mass mkt. 6.99 (*0-552-14029-5*) Bantam.

Soul Music. Terry Pratchett. 384p. 1995. mass mkt. 5.50 (*0-06-105489-5*) HarpC.

Soul Music: A Novel of Discworld. Terry Pratchett. LC 94-29450. 1995. 20.00 (*0-06-105203-5*) P-H.

Soul Music: The Birth of a Sound in Black America. Michael Haralambos. (Quality Paperbacks Ser.). (Illus.). 188p. 1985. reprint ed. pap. 12.95 (*0-306-80246-5*) Da Capo.

Soul Music: Who's Who: The Complete Encyclopedia of Soul! Ralph Tee. 320p. (Orig.). 1992. pap. 16.95 (*1-55958-228-6*) Prima Pub.

Soul Music A-Z. rev. ed. Hugh Gregory. (Illus.). 384p. 1995. pap. 17.95 (*0-306-80643-6*) Da Capo.

Soul Never Sleeps: Advanced Perceptions to a More Loving, Purposeful & Joyous Life. 2nd ed. Marian Massie. Ed. by Phyllis Mueller. 244p. (Orig.). 1992. pap. 11.95 (*0-9633140-2-5*) Advanced Percept.

Soul of a Business: Managing for Profit & the Common Good. Tom Chappell. 240p. 1994. pap. 11.95 (*0-553-37415-X*) Bantam.

Soul of a Child. Edwin Bjorkman. LC 79-144883. (Literature Ser.). 322p. 1972. reprint ed. 39.00 (*0-403-00869-7*) Scholarly.

Soul of a Cop. Paul Ragonese. 1992. mass mkt. 4.99 (*0-312-92816-5*) St Martin.

Soul of a Marriage. Patrick J. McDonald & Claudette M. McDonald. LC 94-44929. 160p. (Orig.). 1995. pap. 9.95 (*0-8091-3555-8*) Paulist Pr.

Soul of a New Machine. Tracy Kidder. 304p. 1982. mass mkt. 4.95 (*0-380-59931-7*) Avon.

Soul of a New Machine. Tracy Kidder. 304p. 1990. pap. 12.50 (*0-380-71115-X*) Avon.

***Soul of a New Machine.** Tracy Kidder. LC 96-51975. 1997. 16.50 (*0-679-60261-5*, Modern Lib) Random.

Soul of a Patriot: or Various Epistles to Ferfichkin. Evgeny Popov. Tr. by Robert Porter from RUS. LC 94-18887. (Writings from an Unbound Europe). 194p. 1994. reprint ed. 49.95 (*0-8101-1203-5*); reprint ed. pap. 14.95 (*0-8101-1193-4*) Northwestern U Pr.

Soul of a Tree: A Master Woodworker's Reflections. George Nakashima. LC 81-80655. 224p. 1988. pap. 45.00 (*0-87011-903-6*) Kodansha.

***Soul of a Woman.** Harriet E. Wilson et al. 1997. pap. 9.95 (*1-874509-39-5*, Pub. by X Pr UK) LPC InBook.

Soul of a Writer: Intimate Interviews with Successful Songwriters. Susan Tucker & Linda L. Strother. 300p. (Orig.). 1996. pap. 21.95 (*0-9651705-2-7*) Jrny Publng.

Soul of Adulthood: Opening the Doors... John C. Friel & Linda Friel. 248p. (Orig.). 1995. pap. 9.95 (*1-55874-341-3*, 3413) Health Comm.

Soul of Ambiguity: The Tiger in Southeast Asia. Robert Wessing. (Special Reports: No. 24). vi, 148p. (Orig.). (C). 1986. pap. 10.00 (*1-877979-74-0*) SE Asia.

Soul of America: Documenting Our Past, Vol. I: 1492-1870. Ed. by Robert C. Baron. LC 93-21115. 305p. (C). 1994. pap. text ed. 14.95 (*1-55591-921-9*) Fulcrum Pub.

Soul of America: Documenting Our Past, Vol. I: 1492-1870, 2 vols., Set. Ed. by Robert C. Baron. (C). 1994. pap. text ed. 26.95 (*1-55591-924-3*) Fulcrum Pub.

Soul of America: Documenting Our Past, Vol. II: 1858-1993. Ed. by Robert C. Baron. LC 93-21115. 212p. (C). 1994. pap. text ed. 14.95 (*1-55591-922-7*) Fulcrum Pub.

Soul of an Immigrant. Constantine M. Panunzio. LC 69-18787. (American Immigration Collection. Series 1). 1969. reprint ed. 16.95 (*0-405-00535-0*) Ayer.

Soul of an Indian: And Other Writings from Ohiyesa (Charles Alexander Eastman) Ed. by Kent Nerburn. LC 93-24678. (Classic Wisdom Collection). 128p. 1993. 12.95 (*1-880032-23-6*) New Wrld Lib.

Soul of Ancient Mexico. Edmond B. Szekely. (Illus.). 136p. 1968. pap. 7.50 (*0-89564-027-9*) IBS Intl.

Soul of Beauty: A Psychological Investigation of Appearance. Ronald Schenk. LC 91-55125. 176p. 1992. 34.50 (*0-8387-5214-4*) Bucknell U Pr.

***Soul of Business.** Ed. by Michael Toms. 200p. (Orig.). 1997. pap. 12.95 (*1-56170-377-X*, 819) Hay House.

***Soul of California: Music of African Americans.** Jacqueline C. Djedje & Eddie S. Meadows. LC 96-49288. Date not set. pap. write for info. (*0-520-20628-2*) U CA Pr.

***Soul of California: Music of African Americans.** Jacqueline C. Djedje & Eddie S. Meadows. LC 96-49288. 1998. write for info. (*0-520-20627-4*) U CA Pr.

Soul of Cambria. rev. ed. E. J. Macaulay. LC 88-71795. (Illus.). 128p. 1989. reprint ed. pap. 6.00 (*0-934666-28-8*) Artisan Sales.

Soul of China. Amaury De Riencourt. 326p. (C). 1990. 90.00 (*0-907855-08-3*, Pub. by Honeyglen Pub Ltd UK) St Mut.

***Soul of Cyberspace.** Jeff Zaleski. LC 97-12611. 272p. 1997. 22.00 (*0-06-251451-2*) Harper SF.

***Soul of Cyberspace.** Jeff Zaleski. pap. 14.00 (*0-06-251452-0*) HarpC.

Soul of Darkness: Introduction to African Metaphysics, Philosophy & Religion. David Carney. LC 91-72774. (Illus.). 146p. (Orig.). 1991. pap. 10.00 (*1-879320-01-0*) Adastra.

S

An Asterisk (*) at the beginning of an entry indicates that the title is appearing in BIP for the first time.

Soul of Denmark. S. Desmond. 1977. lib. bdg. 59.95 (0-8490-2632-6) Gordon Pr.

***Soul of Development: Biblical Christianity & Economic Transformation in Guatemala.** Amy L. Sherman. (Religion in America Ser.). 232p. 1997. 45.00 (0-19-510671-7) OUP.

Soul of Dickens. Walter Crotch. LC 73-21705. (Studies in Dickens: No. 52). 1974. lib. bdg. 75.00 (0-8383-1763-4) M S G Haskell Hse.

Soul of Economies: Spiritual Evolution Goes to the Marketplace. Denise Breton & Christopher Largent. LC 90-81854. (Illus.). 375p. 1991. pap. 14.95 (0-9626238-2-2); lib. bdg. 24.95 (0-9626238-1-4) Idea Hse Pub.

Soul of Elizabeth Seton: A Spiritual Portrait. Joseph I. Dirvin. LC 89-83260. (Illus.). 232p. (Orig.). 1990. pap. 11.95 (0-89870-269-0) Ignatius Pr.

***Soul of Golf.** William Hallberg. 1997. 25.00 (0-449-91124-1) Fawcett.

Soul of Healing: An Autobiography. Graciela Damewood. (Orig.). 1996. pap. 14.00 (0-9650642-0-4) Openway.

Soul of India. Amaury De Riencourt. 432p. (C). 1990. 80.00 (0-907855-03-2, Pub. by Honeyglen Pub Ltd UK) St Mut.

Soul of Indonesia: A Cultural Journey. fac. ed. Umar Kayam. LC 84-82424. (Illus.). 153p. 1985. reprint ed. pap. 43.70 (0-7837-7741-8, 2047497) Bks Demand.

Soul of Japan. Elie Faure. 1972. lib. bdg. 59.95 (0-8490-1089-6) Gordon Pr.

Soul of John Brown. Stephen Graham. LC 70-109915. reprint ed. 41.50 (0-404-00162-9) AMS Pr.

Soul of Liberty: The Universal Ethic of Freedom & Human Rights. Fred E. Foldvary. LC 79-56782. (Illus.). 330p. (C). 1980. pap. 6.75 (0-9603872-1-8) Gutenberg.

Soul of Lilith. Marie Corelli. 446p. 1996. pap. 29.95 (1-56459-681-8) Kessinger Pub.

Soul of Lilith. Marie Corelli. 431p. 1972. reprint ed. spiral bd. 16.50 (0-7873-0211-2) Hlth Research.

Soul of London. Ford Madox Ford. Ed. by A. G. Hill. 288p. (Orig.). 1995. pap. 7.95 (0-460-87621-X, Everyman's Classic Lib) C E Tuttle.

Soul of London. Ford Madox Ford. LC 72-91. (English Literature Ser.: No. 33). 1972. reprint ed. lib. bdg. 75.00 (0-8383-1407-4) M S G Haskell Hse.

Soul of Man. Paul Carus. 1972. 250.00 (0-8490-1090-X) Gordon Pr.

Soul of Man & Prison Writings. Oscar Wilde. Ed. by Isobel M. Murray. (World's Classics Ser.). 256p. 1990. pap. 6.95 (0-19-281797-3) OUP.

Soul of Man under Socialism. Oscar Wilde. 1995. pap. 10.00 (1-85172-020-0, Pub. by Pluto Pr UK) LPC InBook.

Soul of Man under Socialism. Oscar Wilde. (C). 1988. pap. text ed. 10.00 (0-8157-2020-3) Westview.

Soul of Man under Socialism. Oscar Wilde. (Illus.). 64p. reprint ed. pap. 10.00 (0-88286-056-9) C H Kerr.

Soul of Mbira: Music & Traditions of the Shona People of Zimbabwe. Paul F. Berliner. LC 92-41356. (Illus.). xxii, 334p. (C). 1993. pap. 16.95 (0-226-04379-7) U Ch Pr.

Soul of Mbira: Music & Traditions of the Shona People of Zimbabwe. Paul Berliner. LC 76-24578. (Perspectives on Southern Africa Ser.: No. 26). (Illus.). 332p. reprint ed. pap. 94.70 (0-7837-4761-6, 2044508) Bks Demand.

***Soul of Ministry.** Ray S. Anderson. LC 97-11496. 1997. write for info. (0-664-25744-5) Westminster John Knox.

Soul of Nature: Visions of a Living Earth. Ed. by Michael Tobias & Georgianne Cowan. 304p. 1996. pap. 11.95 (0-452-27573-3, Plume) NAL-Dutton.

Soul of Nigeria. Isaac O. Delano. (B. E. Ser.: No. 140). 1937. 35.00 (0-8115-3063-9) Periodicals Srv.

Soul of Nigeria. Isaac O. Delano. LC 74-15026. (Illus.). reprint ed. 45.00 (0-404-12024-5) AMS Pr.

Soul of Osiris. Aleister Crowley. 1973. lib. bdg. 250.00 (0-87968-177-2) Krishna Pr.

Soul of Osiris. Aleister Crowley. 1992. reprint ed. pap. 27.50 (1-872736-20-3, Pub. by Mandrake Pr UK) Holmes Pub.

Soul of Politics: A Practical & Prophetic Vision for Change. Jim Wallis. 320p. 1994. 19.95 (1-56584-204-9) New Press NY.

Soul of Politics: Beyond Religious Right & Secular Left. Jim Wallis. LC 95-18526. (Harvest Bks.). 1995. pap. 12.00 (0-15-600328-7, Harvest Bks) HarBrace.

***Soul of Popular Culture: Looking at Contemporary Heroes, Myths, & Monsters.** Ed. by Mary L. Kittelson. 256p. (Orig.). (C). 1997. pap. 17.95 (0-8126-9363-9) Open Court.

Soul of Prayer. P. T. Forsythe. 1986. pap. 4.99 (0-88019-206-2) Schmul Pub Co.

Soul of Prayer. P. T. Forsyth. 92p. (C). 1993. reprint ed. pap. 7.95 (1-57383-040-2) Regent College.

Soul of Science: Christian Faith & Natural Philosophy. Nancy Pearcey & Charles Thaxton. LC 93-42580. (Turning Point Christian Worldview Ser.). 224p. (Orig.). 1994. pap. 12.99 (0-89107-766-9) Crossway Bks.

Soul of Selling: How to Focus Your Energy to Achieve a Successful & Happy Sales Career. Billy L. Skinner. LC 94-27598. 144p. (Orig.). 1994. pap. 16.95 (0-8144-7874-3) AMACOM.

***Soul of Sex: Deepening Our Imaginaton of the Sexual Life.** Thomas Moore. 320p. Date not set. 25.00 (0-06-018697-6) HarpC.

Soul of Shamanism: Western Fantasies, Imaginal Realities. Daniel C. Noel. LC 96-32504. 176p. 1997. 24.50 (0-8264-0932-6) Continuum.

Soul of Soil: A Guide to Ecological Soil Management. 3rd ed. Grace Gershuny & Joseph Smillie. LC 95-76375. (Illus.). 174p. (Orig.). 1996. pap. 12.00 (0-932857-16-7) Ag Access.

***Soul of Sound.** Lynn T. Olson. (Illus.). 160p. (Orig.). 1996. pap. 29.95 (0-9653367-0-0) Nutshell High Fidlty.

Soul of Southern Cooking. Kathy Starr. LC 89-36245. 192p. 1989. lib. bdg. 35.00 (0-87805-421-9) U Pr of Miss.

Soul of Spain. Havelock Ellis. LC 75-22642. (Illus.). 420p. 1976. reprint ed. text ed. 65.00 (0-8371-8373-1, ELSS, Greenwood Pr) Greenwood.

Soul of Sponsorship: The Friendship of Fr. Ed Dowling & Bill Wilson in Letters. Robert Fitzgerald. LC 95-9773. 1995. 9.95 (1-56838-084-4) Hazelden.

***Soul of Surfing.** Ed M. Warshaw. 128p. 1997. pap. 20.00 (0-00-649179-0) HarperColl Wrld.

Soul of the Age: Selected Letters of Hermann Hesse, 1891-1962. Theodore J. Ziolkowski. 1992. pap. 14.00 (0-374-52363-0, Noonday) FS&G.

Soul of the Age: The Selected Letters of Hermann Hesse, 1891-1962. Theodore J. Ziolkowski. (Illus.). 422p. 1991. 25.00 (0-374-12612-7) FS&G.

Soul of the American University: From Protestant Establishment to Established Non-Belief. George M. Marsden. (Illus.). 448p. 1994. 35.00 (0-19-507046-1) OUP.

Soul of the American University: From Protestant Establishment to Established Nonbelief. George M. Marsden. 480p. 1996. pap. 17.95 (0-19-510650-4) OUP.

Soul of the Apostolate. Jean-Baptiste Chautard. 1977. reprint ed. pap. 10.00 (0-89555-031-8) TAN Bks Pubs.

Soul of the Condor: A Forgotten Holocaust. Carlos J. Sanchez. (Illus.). 304p. (Orig.). 1996. pap. 15.95 (0-9652499-0-5) C J Sanchez.
This testimonial narrative sets out to portray the feelings of most Indian descendants & mestizos. The author, a South American of Inca descent, tries to come to the essence of the oppression of ancient & present-day Native Americans: South, Central, & North American Indians. His is the journey of a humble immigrant who comes to North America in adolescence & through tenacity & perseverance becomes a doctor of medicine. But although grateful for the bounty of his adopted country, he cannot shake his past. Having witnessed the hopelessness of his people throughout his life, with the renewed spirit of an American he courageously testifies to the holocaust of the original American inhabitants & exposes their present predicament in all the Americas, to raise public awareness of these bypassed cultures. The author hopes to make the world aware of the injustices of the Indians' past & to seek remedies for the injustices of the present. The answer lies partly in the Indians themselves, for history has shown that the oppressed must break their own chains, because the weight of them is on their souls. Only they can shatter the links & free their spirits. Please address all inquiries to the publisher: CARLOS J. SANCHEZ M.D., INC., 1635 Third Ave., Suite J, Chula Vista, CA 91911, telephone: (619) 426-8121, FAX: (619) 426-5950, e-mail: condorsoul@aol.com. *Publisher Provided Annotation.*

Soul of the Enterprise: Creating a Dynamic Vision for American Manufacturing. Robert Hall. LC 93-61777. 382p. 1994. pap. 18.00 (0-939246-56-2) Wiley.

Soul of the Enterprise: Creating a Dynamic Vision for American Manufacturing. Robert Hall. 380p. 1995. pap. text ed. 19.95 (0-471-13192-X) Wiley.

Soul of the Firm. C. William Pollard. 176p. 1996. 18.00 (0-310-20103-9) Zondervan.

***Soul of the Game: Images & Voices from the Street.** John Huet. LC 97-24966. 1997. 30.00 (0-7611-1028-3) Workman Pub.

Soul of the Ghost Moth: Paths of a Naturalist. Philip S. Callahan. (Illus.). 1980. 12.00 (0-8159-6840-X) Devin.

***Soul of the Hunter: A Half Century of Big Game Hunting.** John H. Brandt. LC 96-80505. (Illus.). xii, 308p. (Orig.). 1997. 55.00 (0-9621314-0-7) Jungle Tracks.

Soul of the Indian: An Interpretation. Charles A. Eastman. LC 79-26355. (Illus.). xvi, 170p. 1980. reprint ed. pap. 6.95 (0-8032-6701-0, Bison Books) U of Nebr Pr.

Soul of the Internet: Net Gods, Netizens & the Wiring of the World. Neil Randall. (Illus.). 320p. 1996. pap. 24.95 (1-85032-191-4) ITCP.

Soul of the Law: A Psychology of Law & Lawyers. Benjamin Sells. 1994. pap. 22.95 (1-85230-482-0) Element MA.

Soul of the Law: Understanding the Psychology of Lawyers & the Law. Benjamin Sells. 1996. pap. 14.95 (1-85230-796-X) Element MA.

Soul of the Lion: A Biography of General Joshua L. Chamberlain. Willard M. Wallace. (Illus.). 357p. 1989. reprint ed. 25.00 (1-879664-00-3); reprint ed. pap. 12.95 (1-879664-01-1) Stan Clark Military.
Chamberlain was a born soldier but he planned to be a missionary. A graduate of Bangor Theological Seminary, he was an instructor at Bowdoin College when the Civil War broke out & he discovered his true vocation. His military career was one of exceptional gallantry. He was an officer always in the thick of battle. Fourteen horses were shot under him, & finally he was terribly wounded, yet recovered to fight in the closing campaign of the war. He was designated to receive the surrender of the Confederate infantry after the Appomattox meeting of Grant & Lee, & he played the role with magnanimity. Chamberlain's peacetime career was no less notable. Four times he was elected Governor of the State of Maine, & later became president of Bowdoin College. In 1880 Chamberlain, unarmed & alone, faced down a mob that threatened to kill him. With magnificent courage, he said: "I am here to see that the laws of this state are put into effect...If anybody wants to kill me for it, here I am." Willard Wallace has told with sympathy, insight & understanding, the life story of Joshua Lawrence Chamberlain. Stan Clark Military Books, 915 Fairview Avenue, Gettysburg, PA 17325, (717) 337-1728. *Publisher Provided Annotation.*

Soul of the Macintosh. Waite Group Staff. write for info. (0-318-59644-X) S&S Trade.

Soul of the Matter: A Jewish-Kabbalistic Perspective on the Human Soul Before, During, & After "Life" Gershon Winkler. LC 92-15678. 96p. 1992. 6.95 (0-910818-49-5) Judaica Pr.

Soul of the Night: An Astronomical Pilgrimage. Chet Raymo. (Illus.). 209p. 1996. pap. 15.00 (1-886913-11-0) Hungry Mind.

Soul of the Salesman: The Moral Ethos of Personal Sales. Guy Oakes. LC 90-31350. 128p. (C). 1990. pap. 12.50 (0-391-03683-1); text ed. 35.00 (0-391-03682-3) Humanities.

Soul of the Shepherd. Lloyd E. Miller, Jr. 175p. (Orig.). 1995. pap. 4.95 (0-9639322-2-5) Literary Prods.

Soul of the Silver Dog. Lynn Hall. 132p. (J). (gr. 5-9). reprint ed. pap. 3.50 (0-685-71034-3) Random Bks Yng Read.

Soul of the Tiger: Searching for Nature's Answers in Southeast Asia. Paul S. Sochaczewski. LC 94-45557. (Illus.). 432p. 1995. pap. 18.95 (0-8248-1669-2, Kolowalu Bk) UH Pr.

Soul of the Wobblies: The I.W.W., Religion, & American Culture in the Progressive Era, 1905-1917. Donald E. Winters. LC 84-27973. (Contributions in American Studies: No. 81). (Illus.). xi, 159p. 1985. text ed. 45.00 (0-313-24472-3, WFW/) Greenwood.

Soul of the Wolf: A Meditation on Wolves & Man. Michael W. Fox. 144p. 1992. pap. 16.95 (1-55821-150-0) Lyons & Burford.

Soul of the World: A Modern Book of Hours. Ed. by Phil Cousineau. LC 92-53902. (Illus.). 1993. pap. 15.00 (0-06-251004-5) Harper SF.

Soul of the World: Notes on the Future of Public Catholicism. George Weigel. 216p. (Orig.). 1996. pap. 18.00 (0-8028-4207-0) Eerdmans.

Soul of Wit: Joke Theory from Grimm to Freud. Carl Hill. LC 93-447. (Modern German Culture & Literature Ser.). vi, 248p. 1993. text ed. 40.00 (0-8032-2369-2) U of Nebr Pr.

Soul of Woman. Paul Jordan-Smith. 1972. 59.95 (0-8490-1091-8) Gordon Pr.

Soul of Yamato: A History & Anthology of Japanese Poetry, 2 vols., Set. Robert W. Clack. 1975. lib. bdg. 600.00 (0-87968-446-1) Gordon Pr.

Soul on CD: The Essential Guide. Lloyd Bradley. 352p. 1995. pap. 22.95 (1-85626-162-X) Trafalgar.

Soul on Ice. Eldridge Cleaver. 208p. 1970. mass mkt. 6.50 (0-440-21128-X) Dell.

Soul on Rice: African Influences on American Cooking. Patricia B. Mitchell. 1993. pap. 4.00 (0-925117-69-2) Mitchells.

Soul on the Couch: Spirituality, Religion, & Morality in Contemporary Psychoanalysis. Ed. by Charles Spezzano & Gerald J. Gargiulo. (RPBS Ser.). 312p. 1997. 45.00 (0-88163-181-7) Analytic Pr.

Soul Provider. Tim Elmore. (Orig.). 1992. pap. 8.99 (0-8407-4287-8) Nelson.

Soul Psychology. Joshua D. Stone. 282p. 1995. pap. 14.95 (0-929385-56-X) Light Tech Comns Servs.

Soul Psychology: How to Understand Your Soul in Light of the Mental Health Movement. Jeffrey H. Boyd. 464p. 1994. pap. 14.95 (0-9636990-6-7) Soul Res Inst.

***Soul-Purpose, Vol. 1.** Thurston. 1997. mass mkt. write for info. (0-312-96327-0) St Martin.

Soul Quest. Denese Shervington & Billie J. Pace. 80p. 1996. 28.50 (0-517-70383-1); pap. 16.00 (0-517-88632-4) Crown Pub Group.

Soul, R&B & Funk Guitar. 12.95 (0-7935-5166-8, 00695036) H Leonard.

Soul Re-Creation: Developing Your Cosmic Potential. Robert E. Detzler. LC 94-92009. (Illus.). 240p. 1994. pap. 15.95 (0-9640041-1-9) S R C Pubng.

***Soul Re-Creation: Developing Your Cosmic Potential.** 2nd rev. ed. Robert E. Detzler. Ed. by Kathryn Hamilton & Elizabeth Grobes. (Illus.). 240p. 1997. pap. 15.95 (0-9640041-4-3) S R C Pubng.

Soul Rebels: The Rastafari. William F. Lewis. (Illus.). 139p. (Orig.). (C). 1993. pap. text ed. 9.95 (0-88133-739-0) Waveland Pr.

Soul Recovery & Extraction. Ai G. Waya. 74p. (Orig.). 1993. pap. 9.95 (0-9634662-0-8) Blue Turtle.

***Soul Reflections/Heart Expressions: The Art & Poetry of Fred R. Wilson.** Fred R. Wilson. (Illus.). 80p. (Orig.). 1996. pap. 19.95 (0-9654742-0-8) Turtle Cove.

Soul Remembers. Carlos Warter. 210p. (Orig.). 1992. pap. 12.00 (0-929385-36-5) Light Tech Comns Servs.

Soul Remembers Hiroshima. Dolores Cannon. LC 92-83932. 167p. 1993. pap. 13.00 (0-9632776-6-9) Ozark Mountn.

Soul Rescue - Ascenceur Pour la Lumiere: Help on the Way Home to Spirit. Carole Sanborn-Langlois. 288p. 1993. pap. 12.95 (0-9637744-2-5) Thats The Spirit.

Soul Retrieval: Mending the Fragmented Self Through Shamanic Practice. Sandra Ingerman. LC 90-56447. (Illus.). 224p. (Orig.). 1991. pap. 14.00 (0-06-250406-1) Harper SF.

Soul Retriever. Thomas B. Sipes. 32p. 1995. pap. 7.00 (0-8059-3685-8) Dorrance.

***Soul Sanctified: Catholic Wisdom on the Way of Salvation.** 287p. pap. 9.00 (0-89555-538-7) TAN Bks Pubs.

Soul-Saving Preaching. Thomas Cook. 1993. reprint ed. pap. 5.99 (0-88019-304-2) Schmul Pub Co.

***Soul Saving Stories.** John Powers. LC 97-14703. 1997. write for info. (0-8091-3730-5) Paulist Pr.

Soul Says: On Recent Poetry. Helen H. Vendler. (Illus.). 280p. 1996. pap. 14.00 (0-674-82147-5) Belknap Pr.

Soul Says: Recent Poetry. Helen H. Vendler. LC 94-42913. (Illus.). 256p. 1995. 24.95 (0-674-82146-7) Belknap Pr.

Soul School: Confessions of a Passenger on Planet Earth. Guy Murchie. (Illus.). 672p. 1994. pap. 14.95 (1-56474-105-2) Fithian Pr.

***Soul Seachers: The First Mission.** Davey G. Roberson. (Illus.). (Orig.). 1997. pap. 10.99 (0-9656344-0-X) Destiny Pubg.

***Soul Search.** David Darling. Date not set. 5.99 (0-517-17819-2) Random Hse Value.

Soul Search: The Healing Possibilities of Past Lives. Edward Klein. Ed. by Kenneth M. Skidmore. LC 95-23277. 209p. (Orig.). 1995. pap. 14.95 (0-87604-341-4, 453) ARE Pr.

***Soul Searchers: Battle of Darkness.** Davey G. Roberson. (Illus.). 100p. (Orig.). 1997. pap. 9.95 (0-9656344-1-8) Destiny Pubg.

Soul-Searcher's Guide to the Galaxy: Figuring Out Life's Challenges from Housework to Sex to Global Warming. Douglas Todd. (Lifestyles Ser.). 168p. 1994. pap. 9.95 (0-88908-770-9) Self-Counsel Pr.

Soul Searching. 384p. 1995. pap. 9.99 (0-7852-7718-8, J Thoma Bks) Nelson.

***Soul Searching.** Darlene H. Powell. Date not set. write for info. (0-688-15110-8) Morrow.

Soul Searching: Why Psychotherapy Must Promote Moral Responsibility. William J. Doherty. 224p. 1996. pap. 12.00 (0-465-00945-X) Basic.

***Soul Shadows.** Victor Klein. 144p. 1996. pap. 9.95 (1-57087-248-1) Prof Pr NC.

***Soul Side: Big Mama Remembers.** Nancy W. Williams. (Illus.). 50p. (Orig.). Date not set. pap. 10.00 (0-9635690-9-0) TA Pubns.

***Soul Signs: How Your Sun Signs Reveals Your Personal Path to Fulfillment, Growth & Happiness.** Diane Eichenbaum. 1998. pap. 12.00 (0-684-82366-7, Fireside) S&S Trade.

Soul Snatcher. Camarin Grae. 224p. (Orig.). 1986. reprint ed. pap. 8.95 (0-941483-23-1) Naiad Pr.

Soul Song. Bonnie C. Goochey. LC 95-69310. 60p. (Orig.). (C). 1995. pap. 9.95 (1-886225-02-8) Dageforde Pub.

Soul Songs: A Woman's Journey to Self. Nancy G. Souza. (Illus.). 64p. (Orig.). (C). 1992. pap. text ed. 8.95 (0-9632477-0-0) Priestess Pr.

Soul Sounds: Mourning the Tears of Truth. Mary S. Rain. 472p. 1992. pap. 12.95 (1-878901-33-8) Hampton Roads Pub Co.

Soul Sounds: Reflections on the Higher Self. Henry C. Blount, Jr. Ed. by Marlen Waters. (Illus.). 107p. (Orig.). 1988. pap. 6.95 (0-9614047-1-X) McArthur Pub.

Soul, Spirit, & Mountain: Preoccupations of Contemporary Indonesian Painters. Astri Wright. (Illus.). 320p. 1994. 110.00 (967-65-3042-5) OUP.

Soul Stirring Sermons: Evangelistic Voices from the Past & Present. Ken Lynch. 295p. (Orig.). 1996. pap. 12.00 (1-57502-221-4, PO875) Morris Pubng.

Soul Stories: African American Christian Education. Anne S. Wimberly. LC 94-7422. (Afro-American Sunday Schools Ser.). 160p. (Orig.). 1994. pap. 14.95 (0-687-00932-4) Abingdon.

Soul Stories & Steps. Trudy Ettelson. LC 94-8696. (Illus.). 144p. (Orig.). (C). 1994. pap. 6.95 (1-881283-07-0) Alef Design.

***Soul Surfing: Use Your Imagination, Intuition, & Emotions to Reclaim Your Spiritual Destiny.** Dawnea Adams. 240p. 1998. 21.95 (0-385-31933-9) Delacorte.

Soul Surgery: The Ultimate Self-Healing. Richard Jafolla. LC 81-71018. 176p. (Orig.). 1982. pap. 8.95 (0-87516-473-0) DeVorss.

***Soul Survival: Poetic Inspirations about Love, Life & Family Values.** Joyce Rawls. LC 96-92625. 71p. (Orig.). 1997. pap. 10.00 (0-9652317-0-4) J R Prods.

***Soul Survivor: A Metaphysical Suspense Novel.** Stephen H. Martin. 240p. 1996. 18.95 (0-9646601-8-0) Oaklea Pr.

Soul Survivors. Hanoch Teller. (Soul Ser.). 286p. 1985. 13.95 (0-9614772-0-2) NYC Pub Co.

***Soul Survivors: An African American Spirituality.** Carlyle F. Stewart, III. LC 97-1729. 160p. (Orig.). 1997. pap. 15.00 (0-664-25606-6) Westminster John Knox.

Soul, Sweat & Survival on the Pacific Crest Trail. Bob Holtel. LC 93-74046. (Illus.). 196p. (Orig.). 1994. pap. 14.95 (0-931255-07-4) Bittersweet Pub.

***Soul, Sweat & Survival on the Pacific Crest Trail.** Bob Holtel. 194p. 1994. 14.95 (0-915297-23-X) Cedarwinds.

Soul Sword: The Way & Mind of a Warrior. Vernon K. Turner. 128p. (Orig.). 1996. pap. 9.95 (1-57174-039-2) Hampton Roads Pub Co.

***Soul Talk: Poetry & Thoughts That Help Us See the Sacredness of All Life.** Jim Jacobson. 60p. (Orig.). 1996. pap. write for info. (0-7880-0689-4) CSS OH.

Soul Talk: Positive Mind Treatments to Turn Your Life Around. Hubert Pryor. LC 95-30102. 168p. 1995. pap. 12.95 (0-8245-1523-4) Crossroad NY.

An Asterisk (*) at the beginning of an entry indicates that the title is appearing in BIP for the first time.

Soul Talk: Thoughts That Keep on Thinking. Jerry De Shazo. Ed. by Cynthia J. Porter. 150p. (Orig.). 1993. pap. 10.95 (*0-9637611-6-1*) Pure Light.

Soul Tapestry. Rundu Staggers. 80p. 1996. 35.00 (*0-517-70354-8*) Random Hse Value.

***Soul That Kissed the Body.** Pearse Hutchinson. 112p. 1990. pap. 14.95 (*1-85235-060-1*) Dufour.

Soul That Sinneth--It Shall Die. Helen N. Hussey. Ed. by Franklin Loehr. (Illus.). 192p. (Orig.). 1981. pap. 2.75 (*0-915151-08-1*) Religious Res Pr.

Soul That Sinneth--It Shall Die see Destiny of the Soul

Soul, the Body & Death. 2nd ed. Lazar Puhalo. 1989. pap. 8.00 (*0-911523-03-0*) Synaxis Pr.

Soul! The Soul World! Paschal B. Randolph. Ed. by R. Swinburne Clymer. 246p. 1932. 10.95 (*0-932785-45-X*) Philos Pub.

Soul Theology: The Heart of American Black Culture. Henry H. Mitchell & Nicholas C. Lewter. 176p. 1991. reprint ed. pap. 14.95 (*0-687-39125-3*) Abingdon.

***Soul Therapy.** Joy Manne. LC 97-15002. 178p. (Orig.). 1997. pap. 13.95 (*1-55643-255-0*) North Atlantic.

Soul Ties. large type ed. Karen Van Der Zee. 320p. 1996. 25.99 (*0-7505-0776-4*, Pub. by Magna Print Bks UK) Ulverscroft.

***Soul to Comfort.** Kitturah B. Westenhouser. Ed. by Geoffrey A. Westenhouser. 200p. 1997. pap. 9.95 (*1-57502-511-6*, PO1517) Morris Pubng.

Soul to Soul: A Black Russian Jewish Woman's Search for Her Roots. Yelena Khanga. 1994. pap. 10.95 (*0-393-31155-4*) Norton.

Soul to Soul: A Daring Adventure. John Ballard. (MacBurnie King Soul to Soul Adventure Ser.: Bk. 1). (Illus.). pap. 14.95 (*0-932279-10-4*) World Citizens.

Soul to Soul: A Vegetarian Soul Food Cook Book. 2nd ed. Mary McKinney. 181p. 1992. reprint ed. pap. 19.95 (*0-9635395-0-7*) Soul to Soul.

Soul to Soul: The Story of a Black Russian American Family, 1865-1992. Yelena Khanga & Susan Jacoby. (Illus.). 416p. 1992. 22.95 (*0-393-03404-6*) Norton.

Soul to Take. C. N. Bean. 1996. pap. 5.50 (*0-451-40664-8*, Onyx) NAL-Dutton.

Soul Traditional Southern Food Practices, Customs, & Holidays. Cathryn B. Burke & Susan P. Raia. LC 95-17614. (Ethnic & Regional Food Practices - A Ser.). 1995. 10.00 (*0-88091-144-1*) Am Dietetic Assn.

***Soul Train.** Allison Joseph. 80p. 1997. pap. 11.95 (*0-88748-247-3*) Carnegie-Mellon.

Soul Traveler: A Guide to Out of Body Experiences & the Wonders Beyond. Albert Taylor. (Illus.). 147p. 1996. 16.95 (*0-9647534-6-4*) Verity Press.

Soul Trek: Meeting Our Children on the Way to Birth. Elisabeth Hallett. LC 95-94300. 328p. (Orig.). 1995. pap. 14.95 (*0-9646097-0-3*) Light Hearts Pub.

Soul Unearthed: Celebrating Wildness & Personal Renewal Through Nature. Ed. by Cass Adams. (New Consciousness Reader Ser.). 288p. (Orig.). 1996. pap. 14.95 (*0-87477-838-7*, Tarcher Putnam) Putnam Pub Group.

Soul up for Sale. Dwight A. Osborne. pap. 5.95 (*0-9632817-8-X*) Osborne Bks.

Soul Vibrations: Astrology for African Americans. Gilda Matthews. 1996. pap. 10.00 (*0-688-14601-5*, Quill) Morrow.

Soul Weavings: A Gathering of Women's Prayers. Lyn Klug. 160p. 1996. 13.99 (*0-8066-2849-9*, 9-2849) Augsburg Fortress.

Soul Wence & Whither. Hazrat I. Khan. 240p. 1984. 19.95 (*0-85692-134-3*, Pub. by East-West NE) Omega Pubns NY.

Soul Winner. (Spurgeon Collection). 1995. 9.99 (*1-871676-95-9*, Pub. by Christian Focus UK) Spring Arbor Dist.

Soul-Winner. Charles H. Spurgeon. (Orig.). 1963. pap. 15.00 (*0-8028-8081-9*) Eerdmans.

Soul Winner. Charles H. Spurgeon. 304p. 1995. mass mkt. 5.99 (*0-88368-340-7*) Whitaker Hse.

Soul Winner. Charles H. Spurgeon. 1978. reprint ed. mass mkt. 5.00 (*1-56186-330-0*) Pilgrim Pubns.

Soul Winner's Secret. Samuel L. Brengle. pap. 5.99 (*0-88019-155-4*) Schmul Pub Co.

Soul Winner's Secret. Samuel L. Brengle. 1978. reprint ed. pap. 4.95 (*0-86544-007-7*) Salv Army Suppl South.

***Soul Winning.** 2nd ed. T. L. Osborn. (Illus.). (Orig.). (RUS.). 1995. mass mkt. write for info. (*1-890863-09-2*) Wrld Wide Print.

Soul-Winning: A Problem & Its Solution. Phidelia Carroll. LC 92-62567. 108p. 1993. reprint ed. 10.95 (*0-9605642-5-X*) Messengers Hope.

Soul-Winning Classics. deluxe ed. Charles H. Spurgeon et al. (Fifty Greatest Christian Classics Ser.). 1990. 24.95 (*1-878442-53-8*) Sovereign Grace Trust Fund.

Soul-Winning Made Easy. C. S. Lovett. 1978. pap. 6.25 (*0-938148-10-9*) Prsnl Christianity.

Soul Work: A Workbook for Couples. Patrick J. McDonald & Claudette M. McDonald. 88p. (Orig.). 1995. pap. 10.95 (*0-8091-3558-2*) Paulist Pr.

Soul World: The Home of the Dead. Paschal B. Randolph. reprint ed. spiral bd. 12.00 (*0-7873-0699-1*) Hlth Research.

***Soul Worm.** Edward Willett. (YA). (gr. 9 up). 1997. pap. 7.99 (*0-88092-411-X*) Royal Fireworks.

Soul Would Have No Rainbow If the Eyes Had No Tears: And Other Native American Proverbs. Guy A. Zona. 144p. 1994. pap. 9.00 (*0-671-79730-1*, Touchstone Bks) S&S Trade.

Soulages. Bernard Geysson. (CAL Art Ser.). (Illus.). 96p. 1984. 14.95 (*0-517-54105-X*, Crown) Crown Pub Group.

Soulages: Etchings & Lithographs, 1952-1973. Yves Riviere. 146p. (FRE.). 1974. 175.00 (*1-55660-152-2*) A Wofsy Fine Arts.

SoulCards: To Inspire Your Inner Wisdom & Creativity. Deborah Koff-Chapin. (Illus.). 96p. (Orig.). 1995. pap. 22.95 (*0-9645623-0-8*) Ctr Touch Drawing.

Soulcycle. Jean Houston. (Mythos Bks.). (Illus.). 160p. 1988. 18.95 (*0-916349-62-4*); pap. 9.95 (*0-916349-61-6*) Amity Hse Inc.

Souldiery Spiritualized: Seven Sermons Preached Before the Artillery Companies of New England, 1674-1774. LC 79-9727. 1979. 60.00 (*0-8201-1325-5*) Schol Facsimiles.

Souled. Mark Dunster. 18p. (Orig.). (YA). (gr. 9-12). 1996. pap. 5.00 (*0-89642-309-3*) Linden Pubs.

Souled! Hanoch Teller. (Soul Ser.). 384p. 1986. 14.95 (*0-9614772-1-0*) NYC Pub Co.

Soule's New Science & Practice of Accounts. 7th ed. George Soule. LC 75-18485. (History of Accounting Ser.). (Illus.). 1979. reprint ed. 59.95 (*0-405-07567-7*) Ayer.

Soulfire. Lorri Hewett. 231p. (YA). (gr. 7 up). 1996. pap. 15.99 (*0-525-45559-0*) Dutton Child Bks.

***Soulfire: Love Poems in Black & Gold.** Alla R. Bozarth. LC 97-11755. 155p. (Orig.). 1997. pap. 13.00 (*0-936663-18-9*) Yes Intl.

Soulfire: The Patterns of Chaos #4. Charles Ingrid. 352p. 1995. pap. 5.50 (*0-88677-676-7*) DAW Bks.

Soulfires: Young Black Men on Love & Violence. Ed. by Daniel J. Wideman & Rohan Preston. LC 95-31585. Orig. Title: Dispatches from the Front. 406p. 1996. pap. 13.95 (*0-14-024215-5*, Penguin Bks) Viking Penguin.

***Soulful Sex.** Victoria Lee. 1997. 8.98 (*1-56731-198-9*, MJF Bks) Fine Comms.

Soulful Sex: Opening Your Heart, Body, & Spirit to Lifelong Passion. Victoria Lee. 350p. (Orig.). 1996. 37.00 (*0-8095-6055-0*) Borgo Pr.

Soulful Sex: Opening Your Heart, Body, & Spirit to Lifelong Passion. Victoria Lee. (Illus.). 350p. (Orig.). 1996. pap. 14.95 (*1-57324-006-0*) Conari Press.

Soulful Travel. Noble Press Staff. 1997. pap. text ed. 15.95 (*1-879360-42-X*) Noble Pr.

Soulier de Satin. Paul Claudel. (FRE.). 1963. pap. 10.95 (*0-8288-9116-8*, F94551) Fr & Eur.

Soulier de Satin. Paul Claudel. (Folio Ser.: No. 774). (FRE.). 1963. pap. 11.95 (*2-07-036774-6*) Schoenhof.

Soulier de Satin Ou le Pire. Paul Claudel. (FRE.). 1972. pap. 13.95 (*0-8288-3632-9*, FC1197) Fr & Eur.

Soulmaker: True Stories from the Far Side of the Psyche. Michael Grosso. 160p. 1992. pap. 9.95 (*1-878901-21-4*) Hampton Roads Pub Co.

***Soulmaking: Uncommon Paths to Self-Understanding.** Michael Grosso. 118p. (Orig.). 1997. pap. 11.95 (*1-57174-078-3*) Hampton Roads Pub Co.

***Soulmapping: A Spiritual Exercise.** John Cunyus. (Illus.). 48p. 1997. pap. 10.00 (*0-9644609-3-9*, 2) Srchlight Pr.

Soulmate. Carly Bishop. (Intrigue Ser.). 1996. mass mkt. 3.75 (*0-373-22370-6*, 1-22370-0) Harlequin Bks.

***Soulmate.** Helen O. Bradley. (Orig.). Date not set. pap. write for info. (*0-9658140-2-5*) Bradleys Pub.

***Soulmate.** L. J. Smith. (J). 1997. mass mkt. 3.99 (*0-671-55138-8*, Archway) PB.

Soulmate Process. Bob Lancer. 128p. (Orig.). (C). 1992. pap. 9.98 (*0-87554-501-7*, B928) Valley Sun.

SoulMates. Thomas Moore. 1996. pap. 13.50 (*0-614-17408-2*) HarpC.

Soulmates. Jess Stearn. 240p. 1985. mass mkt. 5.99 (*0-553-25150-3*) Bantam.

Soulmates No. 3: Kissed by an Angel. Elizabeth Chandler. (YA). (gr. 7 up). 1995. mass mkt. 3.99 (*0-671-89147-2*) PB.

Soulprints. Rusty Berkus. (Illus.). 64p. (Orig.). 1988. pap. 19.95 (*0-9609888-3-1*) Red Rose Pr.

Souls. Katina Alexis. Ed. by Sally Peters. 304p. (Orig.). 1992. mass mkt. 4.99 (*0-671-67626-1*) PB.

Souls--Illusions or Realities. Francis W. Bessler. Ed. by Jamie Teasley. LC 89-51427. 86p. 1990. 6.95 (*1-55523-272-8*) Winston-Derek.

Soul's Address to the Body: The Worcester Fragments. Ed. by Douglas Moffat. LC 86-72187. (Medieval Texts & Studies: No. 1). 133p. 1987. 29.95 (*0-937191-01-9*) Colleagues Pr Inc.

Souls Aflame. Patricia Hagan. 416p. 1980. pap. 3.50 (*0-380-75507-6*) Avon.

Souls Aflame. Patricia Hagan. 496p. 1996. mass mkt. 3.99 (*0-06-108219-8*, Harp PBks) HarpC.

Souls & Bodies. David Lodge. 256p. 1990. pap. 11.95 (*0-14-013018-7*, Penguin Bks) Viking Penguin.

Souls & Cells Remember: A Love Story. Harry Willson. LC 87-71108. 188p. (Orig.). 1987. pap. 8.00 (*0-938513-03-6*) Amador Pubs.

Souls & Secrets: Hasidic Stories. Joseph Patai. Tr. by Raphael Patai. LC 94-45339. (Illus.). 272p. 1995. 30.00 (*1-56821-355-7*) Aronson.

Souls Are Made of Endurance: Surviving Mental Illness in the Family. Stewart D. Govig. LC 94-8688. 112p. (Orig.). 1994. pap. 13.00 (*0-664-25289-3*) Westminster John Knox.

***Soul's Awakening: A Drama of the Soul & Spirit.** Rudolf Steiner. Tr. by Michael H. Burton & Adrian Locher. 144p. 1994. pap. write for info. (*0-904693-66-X*, Pub. by Temple Ldge Pub UK) Anthroposophic.

Souls Bizarre. Joseph Green. 208p. (Orig.). 1991. mass mkt. 3.50 (*0-87067-334-3*) Holloway.

Soul's Code: In Search of Character & Calling. James Hillman. LC 95-26855. 352p. 1996. 23.00 (*0-679-44522-6*) Random.

***Soul's Code: In Search of Character & Calling.** James Hillman. LC 97-8702. 352p. 1997. pap. 12.99 (*0-446-67371-4*) Warner Bks.

Soul's Companion: Connecting with the Soul Through Daily Meditations. Tian Dayton. 392p. (Orig.). 1995. pap. 8.95 (*1-55874-358-8*, 3588) Health Comm.

Souls, Evolution & the Father. Arthur Fanning. (Orig.). 1995. pap. 12.95 (*0-929385-33-0*) Light Tech Comns Servs.

Souls Exist. Richard Schain. LC 88-82801. 104p. (Orig.). 1989. pap. 5.00 (*0-9609922-8-6*) Garric Pr.

***Souls II.** 2nd rev. ed. Sara Thacke & Earl Taft. 161p. 1996. pap. 10.00 (*0-9648074-1-6*) ARC-Taurs R&D.

Souls in Action: The Crucible of the New Life. Harold Begbie. LC 95-75902. 308p. 1995. 14.95 (*1-886787-00-X*) Messengers Hope.

Souls in Jeopardy. Walter E. Adams. 80p. (Orig.). 1987. pap. 3.95 (*0-937408-40-9*) GMI Pubns Inc.

Soul's Journey. Peter Richelieu. Orig. Title: From the Turret. (Illus.). 208p. 1989. pap. 14.00 (*0-7225-3291-1*, Pub. by Aquarian Pr UK) Thorsons SF.

Soul's Journey: Empowering the Present Through Past Life Regression. Jeanne Avery. Ed. by Nann Gatewood. LC 96-85199. 175p. (Orig.). 1996. pap. 13.95 (*1-887161-12-0*) Boru Pubng.

Soul's Journey: Exploring the Three Passages of the Spiritual Life with Dante as a Guide. Alan Jones. LC 95-1345. 224p. 1995. 18.00 (*0-06-064253-X*); pap. 10.00 (*0-06-064254-8*) Harper SF.

***Soul's Journey: Whispers from the Light.** Patricia Idol. 160p. 1997. pap. 12.95 (*1-56184-098-X*) New Falcon Pubns.

***Soul's Journey after Death.** Tr. by Layla Mabrouk. 40p. 1996. pap. 3.95 (*0-614-21347-9*, 1407) Kazi Pubns.

Soul's Journey to Its Destiny. Swani Ashokananda. 312p. (Orig.). 1994. pap. 5.95 (*0-87481-243-7*, Pub. by Advaita Ashrama II) Vedanta Pr.

***Soul's Jubilee.** John T. Ferrier. 24p. Date not set. pap. text ed. 5.00 (*0-900235-65-9*) Order Of The Cross.

Souls Made Great Through Love & Adversity: The Film Work of Frank Borzage. Frederick Lamster. LC 80-28441. 242p. 1981. 22.50 (*0-8108-1404-8*) Scarecrow.

Souls of Animals. Gary Kowalski. 128p. 1991. pap. 8.95 (*0-913299-84-7*) Stillpoint.

Souls of Black Folk. Blight. 1997. pap. text ed. 7.50 (*0-312-09114-1*) St Martin.

Souls of Black Folk. Blight. 1997. pap. 12.95 (*0-312-14996-4*) St Martin.

Souls of Black Folk. W. E. B. Du Bois. 224p. 1989. mass mkt. 4.95 (*0-553-21336-9*) Bantam.

Souls of Black Folk. W. E. B. Du Bois. (Classic Ser.). 1969. pap. 4.95 (*0-451-52397-0*, Sig Classics) NAL-Dutton.

Souls of Black Folk. W. E. B. Du Bois. 228p. 1990. pap. 11.50 (*0-679-72519-9*, Vin) Random.

Souls of Black Folk. W. E. B. Du Bois. 224p. 1989. pap. 9.95 (*0-14-039074-X*, Penguin Classics) Viking Penguin.

Souls of Black Folk. W. E. B. Du Bois. 322p. 1996. 14.50 (*0-679-60187-2*, Modern Lib) Random.

Souls of Black Folk. W. E. B. Dubois. 288p. 1996. pap. 9.95 (*0-14-018998-X*, Viking) Viking Penguin.

Souls of Black Folk. W. E. B. Du Bois. 280p. 1986. reprint ed. lib. bdg. 22.95 (*0-89966-535-7*) Buccaneer Bks.

Souls of Black Folk. W. E. B. Du Bois. (Thrift Editions Ser.). 176p. 1994. reprint ed. pap. 2.00 (*0-486-28041-1*) Dover.

Souls of Black Folk see Three Negro Classics

***Souls of Black Folks.** 1997. text ed. 35.00 (*0-312-12806-1*) St Martin.

Souls of Black Folks. W. E. B. Du Bois. LC 93-1859. 1993. 15.00 (*0-679-42802-X*, Everymans Lib) Knopf.

Souls of Black Folks. W. E. B. Du Bois. 1976. 22.95 (*0-8488-0995-5*) Amereon Ltd.

Souls of Black Folks. W. E. B. Du Bois. 288p. 1995. mass mkt. 4.95 (*0-451-52603-1*, Sig) NAL-Dutton.

Souls of Black Testament: With Notes & Tablature. 112p. 1991. otabind 18.95 (*0-7935-0418-X*, 00694765) H Leonard.

Souls of Light: A Beginners Guide to Spiritual Transformation. Ronald D. Bissell. (Orig.). pap. 10.95 (*0-9639446-0-6*) Inn Voice Prods.

Souls of My Feet. Elsie F. Gerald. 81p. 1987. 10.00 (*0-9610096-1-6*) E F Gerald.

***Souls of Our Children: Lessons of Love & Guidance.** LC 96-37300. 1997. write for info. (*0-06-251391-5*) Harper SF.

***Souls of Our Children: Lessons of Love & Guidance.** LC 96-37300. 1997. pap. write for info. (*0-06-251392-3*) Harper SF.

Souls of Summer. D. Pryzbyla. LC 91-66857. 429p. 1992. pap. 9.95 (*1-55523-476-3*) Winston-Derek.

Souls of the Skyscraper: Female Clerical Workers in Chicago, 1870-1930. Lisa M. Fine. (Illus.). 264p. 1990. 34.95 (*0-87722-674-1*) Temple U Pr.

Souls on Board: Responses to the United 232 Tragedy. Emily Dee. LC 90-34136. (Illus.). 173p. (Orig.). 1990. pap. 9.95 (*0-9626818-1-4*) Loess Hills Pr.

Souls on Fire. Elie Wiesel. 368p. (Orig.). 1982. pap. 13.00 (*0-671-44171-X*) S&S Trade.

Souls on Fire: Portraits & Legends of Hasidic Masters. Elie Wiesel. LC 92-28680. 258p. 1993. 30.00 (*0-87668-255-7*) Aronson.

Souls or the Social Order: The Two-Party System in American Protestantism. Jean M. Schmidt. LC 91-26848. (Chicago Studies in the History of American Religion Ser.: Vol. 18). 285p. 1991. 50.00 (*0-926019-54-6*) Carlson Pub.

Soul's Passion for God: Selected Writings of Teresa of Avila see Upper Room Spiritual Classics: Series 1

Soul's Preparation for Christ: or A Treatise of Contrition. Thomas Hooker. 225p. 1994. 21.95 (*0-9641803-2-4*) Internat Outreach.

Soul's Quest for God. R. C. Sproul. 254p. 1994. pap. 10.99 (*0-8423-6088-3*) Tyndale.

Souls Raised from the Dead: A Novel. Doris Betts. 352p. 1995. pap. 12.00 (*0-684-80104-3*) S&S Trade.

Soul's Secret. Hilton Hotema. 79p. 1958. reprint ed. spiral bd. 8.50 (*0-7873-0448-4*) Hlth Research.

Soul's Sincere Desire. Glenn Clark. 1988. pap. 9.95 (*0-910924-93-7*) Macalester.

Soul's Sincere Desire. Glenn Clark. 128p. 1996. pap. 7.95 (*1-886158-09-6*) Macalester.

***Souls to Soles: A Self-Help Exploration of Reflexology.** Paul Rude. (Illus.). 160p. (Orig.). 1997. pap. 12.95 (*0-914955-51-9*) Lotus Light.

Souls II. Sara Thacker & Earl Taft. 153p. 1995. pap. 5.00 (*0-9648074-0-8*) ARC-Taurs R&D.

***Souls with Wings.** David Kaufmann & Susan M. Zakar. 1998. pap. write for info. (*0-7657-9984-7*) Aronson.

Soulsearchers & Company Vol. 1: On the Case. Peter David & Richard Howell. (Illus.). 152p. (Orig.). 1996. pap. 12.95 (*0-9653109-1-4*, Claypool Comics) Boffin Bks.

Soulshaping: Taking Care of Your Spiritual Life Through Godly Disciplines. Douglas J. Rumford. LC 96-20351. 1996. pap. 10.99 (*0-8423-3593-5*) Tyndale.

Soulside: Inquiries into Ghetto Culture & Community. Ulf Hannerz. LC 78-96865. 236p. 1971. pap. text ed. 17.00 (*0-231-08651-2*) Col U Pr.

Soulskin. Marilyn Krysl. 120p. (Orig.). 1996. pap. 12.95 (*0-88737-684-3*) Natl League Nurse.

Soulsmith. Tom Deitz. 464p. (Orig.). 1991. mass mkt. 4.99 (*0-380-76289-7*) Avon.

Soulstealers: The Chinese Sorcery Scare of 1768. Philip A. Kuhn. LC 90-32807. (Illus.). 299p. 1990. 39.95 (*0-674-82151-3*) HUP.

Soulstealers: The Chinese Sorcery Scare of 1768. Philip A. Kuhn. (Illus.). 320p. 1992. pap. 15.00 (*0-674-82152-1*) HUP.

Soulstorm: Stories. Clarice Lispector. Tr. by Alexis Levitin from POR. LC 89-2938. 160p. 1989. 19.95 (*0-8112-1090-1*); pap. 10.95 (*0-8112-1091-X*, NDP671) New Directions.

***Soultown.** Mercedes Lambert. 1997. pap. 5.95 (*0-14-025492-7*) Penguin.

Soultown: A Whitney Logan Mystery. Mercedes Lambert. 242p. 1996. pap. 21.95 (*0-670-86684-9*, Viking) Viking Penguin.

Soulways: The Developing Soul-Life Phases, Thresholds & Biography. Rudolf Treichler. 320p. 1990. 26.95 (*1-869890-13-2*, 1293, Pub. by Hawthorn Press UK) Anthroposophic.

***Soulwinning.** T. L. Osborn & Daisy Osborn. Date not set. pap. 10.99 (*0-89274-186-4*) Harrison Hse.

SoulWork: Clearing the Mind, Opening the Heart, Replenishing the Spirit. Betty C. Moffat. 200p. (Orig.). 1994. pap. 10.95 (*1-885171-01-3*) Wldcat Canyon.

Soulworker's Companion: A Year of Spiritual Discovery. BettyClare Moffatt. 240p. (Orig.). 1996. pap. 12.95 (*1-885171-11-0*) Wldcat Canyon.

Soumchi. Amos Oz. Tr. by Penelope Farmer from HEB. LC 94-45033. (Illus.). 96p. (J). (gr. 4 up). 1995. pap. 10.00 (*0-15-600193-4*, Harvest Bks) HarBrace.

Soun Tetoken: Nez Perce Boy Tames a Stallion. 2nd ed. Kenneth Thomasma. LC 89-14877. (American Indian Children Ser.). (Illus.). 264p. (J). (gr. 6). 1984. reprint ed. pap. 7.99 (*0-8010-8873-9*) Baker Bks.

Soun Tetoken: Nez Perce Boy Tames a Stallion. 2nd ed. Kenneth Thomasma. LC 89-14877. (American Indian Children Ser.). (Illus.). 264p. (YA). (gr. 6 up). 1984. reprint ed. 12.99 (*0-8010-8874-7*) Baker Bks.

***Sound.** Wendy Baker et al. (Make It Work! Ser.). (Illus.). (J). 15.95 (*0-590-74522-0*) Scholastic Inc.

***Sound.** Wendy Baker et al. (Make It Work! (Eureka!) Ser.). (Illus.). (FRE.). (J). pap. 9.99 (*0-590-24631-3*) Scholastic Inc.

Sound. Ed Catherall. LC 89-38614. (Exploring Science Ser.). (Illus.). 48p. (J). (gr. 4-8). 1990. lib. bdg. 24.26 (*0-8114-2592-4*) Raintree Steck-V.

Sound. Jason Cooper. LC 92-8809. (Science Secrets Ser.). (J). 1992. 12.67 (*0-86593-167-4*); 9.50 (*0-685-59296-0*) Rourke Corp.

Sound. Robert Friedhoffer. LC 92-16961. (Scientific Magic Ser.: Bk. 4). (Illus.). 112p. (J). (gr. 7-9). 1992. lib. bdg. 22.70 (*0-531-11083-4*) Watts.

***Sound.** Andrew Haslam et al. (Make It Work! Ser.). (Illus.). (J). pap. 7.99 (*0-590-24615-1*) Scholastic Inc.

Sound. Ron Marson. (Task Cards Ser.: No. 18). (Illus.). 56p. (YA). (gr. 7-12). 1990. teacher ed. 9.50 (*0-941008-88-6*) Tops Learning.

***Sound.** Steve Parker. LC 97-11525. (Science Works! Ser.). (J). 1997. lib. bdg. write for info. (*0-8368-1965-9*) Gareth Stevens Inc.

***Sound.** Simon D. Pinna. LC 97-5989. (Science Projects Ser.). (J). 1998. write for info. (*0-8172-4944-3*) Raintree Steck-V.

Sound. Bonita Searle-Barnes. LC 50-87. (Wonder of God's World Ser.). (Illus.). 32p. (J). (gr. k-3). 1993. 6.99 (*0-7459-2692-4*) Lion USA.

***Sound.** Snape & Rowlands. (Science at Work Ser.). 1992. pap. text ed. write for info. (*0-582-07425-8*, Pub. by Longman UK) Longman.

Sound. Daniel J. Spero. (Science Mini-Unit Intermediate Ser.: Vol. 4). (Illus.). 16p. (J). (gr. 3-6). 1994. pap. text ed. 5.95 (*1-55799-295-9*, EMC835) Evan-Moor Corp.

Sound. Alan Ward. (Experimenting With Ser.). (Illus.). 48p. (J). (gr. 3-8). 1991. lib. bdg. 15.95 (*0-7910-1511-4*) Chelsea Hse.

Sound. 3rd rev. ed. John Tyndall. LC 70-89021. 448p. 1970. reprint ed. text ed. 38.50 (*0-8371-2255-4*, TYS, Greenwood Pr) Greenwood.

Sound: A Creative Hands-on Approach to Science. Wendy Baker & Andrew Haslam. LC 92-30104. (Make It Work! Ser.). (Illus.). 48p. (J). (gr. 2-5). 1993. 12.95 (*0-689-71665-6*, Aladdin Paperbacks) S&S Childrens.

***Sound: Big Book.** Ed. by Don Curry. (Ranger Rick Science Spectacular Ser.). 16p. (J). (gr. 2-5). 1997. pap. 14.95 (*1-56784-453-7*) Newbridge Comms.

S

An Asterisk (*) at the beginning of an entry indicates that the title is appearing in BIP for the first time.

***Sound: Big Book.** Lisa Trumbauer. Ed. by Susan Evento. (Early Science Ser.). 16p. (J). (ps-2). 1997. pap. 14.95 (*1-56784-317-4*) Newbridge Comms.

Sound: Hands on Elementary School Science. Linda Poore. 29p. 1994. teacher ed. 35.00 (*1-883410-19-3*) L Poore.

***Sound: Mini Book.** Ed. by Don Curry. (Ranger Rick Science Spectacular Ser.). 16p. (J). (gr. 2-5). 1997. pap. text ed. 19.95 (*1-56784-478-2*) Newbridge Comms.

***Sound: Mini Book.** Lisa Trumbauer. Ed. by Susan Evento. (Early Science Ser.). 16p. (J). (ps-2). 1997. pap. 16.95 (*1-56784-342-5*) Newbridge Comms.

Sound: Space. Bernhard Leitner. LC 77-93954. (Illus.). 109p. (C). 1978. pap. text ed. 20.00 (*0-8147-4983-6*) NYU Pr.

***Sound-A-Likes Vol. 1: One-Won!** Alan Fowler. (Illus.). 32p. (J). (gr. 2-4). pap. 6.95 (*1-56674-703-1*) Forest Hse.

***Sound-A-Likes Vol. 2: Two-To-Too!** Alan Fowler. (Illus.). 32p. (J). (gr. 2-4). pap. 5.95 (*1-56674-704-X*) Forest Hse.

Sound-a-Likes One: One, Won. Allan Fowler. LC 94-7613. (Illus.). 32p. (J). (gr. k-2). 1996. lib. bdg. 10.95 (*1-878363-97-2*) Forest Hse.

Sound-a-Likes Two: Two, To, Too. Allan Fowler. LC 94-24150. (Illus.). 32p. (J). (gr. 2-4). 1996. lib. bdg. 10.95 (*1-878363-98-0*) Forest Hse.

Sound Advantage: A Pronunciation Book. Stacy Hagen & Pat Grogan. 192p. (C). 1991. pap. text ed. 16.95 (*0-13-816190-9*) P-H.

Sound Advice: A Basis for Listening. Stacy Hagen. (Illus.). 208p. (C). 1988. pap. text ed. write for info. (*0-13-823162-1*) P-H.

***Sound Advice: A Basis for Listening.** Stacy A. Hagen. 1988. pap. text ed. 8.00 (*0-13-823154-0*) P-H.

Sound Advice: CD Set. Wayne Wadhams. 1990. 32.00 (*0-02-872693-6*) Schirmer Bks.

Sound Advice: The Musician's Guide to the Record Industry. Wayne Wadhams. 545p. 1990. 30.00 (*0-02-872692-8*) Schirmer Bks.

Sound Advice: The Musician's Guide to the Recording Studio. Wayne Wadhams. 357p. 1990. 38.00 (*0-02-872694-4*) Schirmer Bks.

***Sound Affects.** Fred Hale. (Illus.). 190p. (Orig.). 1997. pap. 7.99 (*1-57502-486-1*) Morris Pubng.

Sound All Around. Fay Robinson. LC 93-38592. (Rookie Read-about Science Ser.). (Illus.). 32p. (J). (ps-2). 1994. lib. bdg. 17.30 (*0-516-06024-4*) Childrens.

Sound All Around. Fay Robinson. LC 93-38592. (J). (ps-2). 1994. pap. 3.95 (*0-516-46024-2*) Childrens.

Sound All Around. Ed. by Phyllis B. Susen. (Illus.). 40p. (Orig.). (J). (ps-4). 1992. pap. 8.50 (*0-9635667-0-9*) Phila Orchestra.

Sound Alternative. John J. Thompson. 32p. (YA). 1995. pap. 4.99 (*0-7814-0204-2*) Chariot Victor.

***Sound Analysis & Noise Control.** J. Foreman. (Illus.). 461p. 1990. text ed. 79.95 (*0-442-31949-5*, Osprey Bks) Chapman & Hall.

Sound Anatomiz'd, in a Philosophical Essay on Musick. fac. ed. William Turner. (Monuments of Music & Music Literature in Facsimile, II Ser.: No. 127). (Illus.). 1974. lib. bdg. 35.00 (*0-8450-2327-6*) Broude.

Sound & Action Stories. Jerry J. Mallett & Timothy Ervin. 48p. (Orig.). (J). (ps-3). 1992. pap. text ed. 6.95 (*0-913853-23-2*, 32534, Alleyside) Highsmith Pr.

Sound & Articulation Activities for Children with Speech-Language Problems. Elisabeth Krepelin. 352p. 1996. pap. 32.95 (*0-87628-128-5*) P-H.

Sound & Articulation Game. Genevieve Arnold. 1973. text ed. 3.00 (*0-686-09406-9*) Expression.

Sound & Feel of Blues Guitar. John Tapella. 64p. (Orig.). 1995. pap. 17.95 incl. cd-rom (*0-931759-93-5*) Centerstream Pub.

Sound & Form in Modern Poetry. 2nd ed. Harvey Gross & Robert McDowell. LC 95-52355. (C). 1996. 44.50 (*0-472-09517-X*); pap. 17.95 (*0-472-06517-3*) U of Mich Pr.

Sound & Fury: The Science & Politics of Global Warming. Patrick J. Michaels. 196p. 1992. 21.95 (*0-932790-90-9*) Cato Inst.

Sound & Fury: The Science & Politics of Global Warming. Patrick J. Michaels. LC 92-36264. 1992. 11.95 (*0-932790-89-5*) Cato Inst.

Sound & Glory: The Incredible Story of Bill Haley, the Father of Rock 'n' Roll & the Music That Shook the World. John W. Haley & John Von Hoelle. LC 90-82945. (Illus.). 250p. (Orig.). 1990. 29.95 (*1-878970-00-3*); pap. 14.95 (*1-878970-01-1*) Dyne-American.

Sound & Hearing. R. Duncan Luce. 344p. 1993. pap. 32.50 (*0-8058-1389-6*); text ed. 69.95 (*0-8058-1251-2*); cd-rom 49.95 (*0-8058-1450-7*); cd-rom 19.95 (*1-56321-116-5*) L Erlbaum Assocs.

Sound & Light. Karen Bryant-Mole. LC 97-12313. (Science All Around Me Ser.). 1996. write for info. (*1-57572-136-8*) Rigby Interact Libr.

Sound & Light. David Glover. LC 92-40213. (Young Discoverers Ser.). 32p. (J). (gr. 1-4). 1993. 13.90 (*1-85697-839-7*, Kingfisher LKC); pap. 6.95 (*1-85697-935-0*, Kingfisher LKC) LKC.

Sound & Light. David Glover. (Young Discoverers Ser.). (J). (gr. 1-4). lib. bdg. 13.90 (*1-85697-632-7*, Kingfisher LKC) LKC.

Sound & Light. Ed. by Carol Spelius. 128p. (Orig.). 1987. pap. 8.95 (*0-941363-00-7*) Lake Shore Pub.

***Sound & Light: La Monte Young Marian Zazeela.** Ed. by William Duckworth & Richard Fleming. LC 55-58217. (Bucknell Review Ser.: Vol. 40, No. 1). (Illus.). 232p. 1997. 24.00 (*0-8387-5346-9*) Bucknell U Pr.

Sound & Light in Synthesis: Synthesis of Enantiomerically Pure Compounds with C, C Bond Formation. Rolf Scheffold. (Modern Synthetic Methods Ser.: Vol. 4). 370p. 1986. 75.95 (*0-387-16526-6*) Spr-Verlag.

Sound & Motion Stories. Joanna H. Kraus. 38p. 1980. 4.95 (*0-932720-68-4*) New Plays Inc.

Sound & Music. Kay Davies & Wendy Oldfield. LC 91-23475. (Starting Science Ser.). (Illus.). 32p. (J). (gr. 2-5). 1991. pap. 4.95 (*0-8114-1534-1*); lib. bdg. 19.97 (*0-8114-3003-0*) Raintree Steck-V.

Sound & Music. Alan Ward. LC 92-370. (Project Science Ser.). 32p. (J). 1993. lib. bdg. 20.00 (*0-531-14237-X*) Watts.

Sound & Music for the Theatre: The Art & Technique of Design. Deena Kaye & James LeBrecht. 256p. (Orig.). 1992. pap. 18.95 (*0-8230-7664-4*, Back Stage Bks) Watsn-Guptill.

Sound & Music Studio. Jeff Essex. 352p. 1996. pap. 45.00 (*0-679-76191-8*) Random.

Sound & Music Workshop. Richard Grace. 372p. 1996. pap. 29.99 incl. cd-rom (*0-7821-1801-1*) Sybex.

Sound & Number: The Law of Destiny & Design. Mabel L. Ahmad. 130p. 1996. pap. 16.95 (*1-56459-928-0*) Kessinger Pub.

Sound & Number: The Law of Destiny & Design. Mabel L. Ahmad. 128p. 1970. reprint ed. spiral bd. 7.00 (*0-7873-1275-4*) Hlth Research.

Sound & Poetry see English Institute Essays

Sound & Recording: An Introduction. 2nd ed. Francis Rumsey & Tim McCormick. 356p. 1994. pap. 39.95 (*0-240-51383-5*, Focal) Buttrwrth-Heinemann.

***Sound & Recording: An Introduction.** 3rd ed. Francis Rumsey. 1997. pap. text ed. 37.95 (*0-240-51487-4*) Buttrwrth-Heinemann.

Sound & Semblance: Reflections on Musical Representation. Peter Kivy. LC 91-55159. 264p. 1991. reprint ed. pap. 14.95 (*0-8014-9946-1*) Cornell U Pr.

Sound & Sense. 8th ed. Laurence Perrine. (C). 1992. teacher ed., pap. text ed. 32.00 (*0-15-582611-5*) HB Coll Pubs.

Sound & Sense: An Introduction to Poetry. 3rd ed. Laurence Perrine & Thomas R. Arp. 350p. (C). 1992. pap. text ed. 4.00 (*0-15-565732-1*) HB Coll Pubs.

Sound & Sense: An Introduction to Poetry. 9th ed. Laurence Perrine. (C). 1996. teacher ed., pap. text ed. 28.00 (*0-15-503743-9*) HB Coll Pubs.

Sound & Sense: Linguistic Essays on Phonosemic Subjects. Roger W. Wescott. LC 81-12415. (Edward Sapir Monograph Ser. in Language, Culture & Cognition: No. 8). xiv, 405p. (Orig.). (C). 1980. pap. 44.00 (*0-933104-12-X*) Jupiter Pr.

Sound & Sense: Musical Allusion & Imagery in the Novels of Iris Murdoch. Darlene D. Mettler. LC 90-22130. (American University Studies: English Language & Literature: Ser. IV, Vol. 127). 169p. (C). 1991. text ed. 34.95 (*0-8204-1462-X*) P Lang Pubng.

Sound & Sentiment: Birds, Weeping, Poetics & Song in Kaluli Expression. 2nd ed. Steven Feld. LC 89-36978. (Conduct & Communication Ser.). (Illus.). 312p. (C). 1990. pap. text ed. 19.95 (*0-8122-1299-1*) U of Pa Pr.

Sound & Shape of Language. Roman Jakobson & Linda R. Waugh. xvi, 335p. 1987. 36.95 (*0-89925-335-0*) Mouton.

Sound & Sources of Sound. Ann Dowling & John E. Williams. LC 82-15687. 321p. 1983. text ed. 84.95 (*0-470-27370-4*) P-H.

Sound & Structural Vibration: Radiation, Transmission & Response. Frank J. Fahy. 309p. 1987. text ed. 53.00 (*0-12-247671-9*) Acad Pr.

Sound & Structure. John Paynter. (Resources of Music Ser.). (Illus.). 224p. (C). 1992. text ed. 74.95 (*0-521-35581-8*); pap. text ed. 34.95 (*0-521-35676-8*); digital audio 38.95 (*0-521-35677-6*) Cambridge U Pr.

Sound & Symbol in Chinese. Bernhard Kalgren. 106p. (C). 1990. pap. text ed. 24.00 (*962-209-257-8*, Pub. by Hong Kong U Pr HK) St Mut.

Sound & the Fury. (Book Notes Ser.). 1985. pap. 2.95 (*0-8120-3541-0*) Barron.

Sound & the Fury. William Faulkner. (Modern Library College Editions). (C). 1967. pap. text ed. write for info. (*0-07-553666-8*, T94) McGraw.

Sound & the Fury. William Faulkner. 1966. 14.00 (*0-394-44640-2*) Random.

Sound & the Fury. William Faulkner. 1984. 25.00 (*0-394-53241-4*) Random.

Sound & the Fury. William Faulkner. LC 90-50274. (Vintage International Ser.). 448p. 1991. pap. 10.00 (*0-679-73224-1*, Vin) Random.

Sound & the Fury. William Faulkner. LC 92-50217. 364p. 1992. 15.50 (*0-679-60017-5*, Modern Lib) Random.

Sound & the Fury. 2nd ed. William Faulkner. Ed. by David Minter. (Critical Editions Ser.). (C). 1993. pap. text ed. 8.95 (*0-393-96481-7*) Norton.

Sound & the Fury: Carbon Typescript. William Faulkner. Ed. by Noel Polk. (William Faulkner Manuscripts). 464p. 1987. text ed. 55.00 (*0-8240-6806-8*) Garland.

Sound & the Fury Notes. James L. Roberts. 1992. pap. 3.95 (*0-8220-1219-7*) Cliffs.

Sound & the Story: NPR & the Art of Radio. Thomas Looker. (Richard Todd Book). 256p. 1995. 24.95 (*0-395-67439-5*) HM.

Sound & Vibration Damping with Polymers. Leslie H. Sperling. (ACS Symposium Ser.: No. 424). (Illus.). 480p. 1990. 99.95 (*0-8412-1778-5*) Am Chemical.

Sound & Vibration Engineered Environments - Manufacturers & Fabricators of Architectural, Building & Mechanical System Products. James R. Ramsey. vi, 246p. 1988. pap. 28.00 (*0-940737-03-5*) RT Books.

Sound & Vision. Jenny Bryan. LC 93-37306. (Body Talk Ser.). (Illus.). 48p. (J). (gr. 5). 1994. lib. bdg. 13.95 (*0-87518-591-6*, Dillon Silver Burdett) Silver Burdett Pr.

Sound & Vision: The Music Video Reader. Ed. by Simon Frith et al. LC 92-25419. 1993. write for info. (*0-04-445605-0*, Routledge NY); pap. write for info. (*0-04-445606-9*, Routledge NY) Routledge.

Sound & Vision: The Music Video Reader. Ed. by Lawrence Grossberg et al. LC 92-25419. 240p. (C). (gr. 13). 1993. pap. 16.95 (*0-415-09431-3*, B0274); text ed. 62.95 (*0-415-09430-5*, B0270) Routledge.

Sound Approach to Teaching Instrumentalists. 2nd ed. June Schleuter. LC 96-42540. 1996. 31.00 (*0-02-864716-5*) Mac Lib Ref.

Sound As Thought: Poems 1982-1984. Clark Coolidge. (New American Poetry Ser.: No. 5). 192p. 1990. pap. 11.95 (*1-55713-065-5*) Sun & Moon CA.

Sound Assistance. Michael Talbot-Smith. (Illus.). 160p. 1996. pap. 29.95 (*0-240-51439-4*, Focal) Buttrwrth-Heinemann.

Sound Barrier: The Story of High-Speed Flight. Neville Duke & Edward Lanchbery. Ed. by James B. Gilbert. LC 79-7248. (Flight: Its First Seventy-Five Years Ser.). (Illus.). 1980. reprint ed. lib. bdg. 17.95 (*0-405-12160-1*) Ayer.

Sound Bites for Healthy, Wealthy, Living. Marilyn August. 64p. 1996. pap. 7.50 (*1-888834-07-2*, ITD696, Stonehill Bks) Idyllwild Typeset.

Sound Blaster: Making WAVES with Multimedia. Valda Hilley. 1995. pap. text ed. 19.95 (*0-7615-0095-2*) Prima Pub.

Sound Business Bites: A Common Sense Approach to Customer Service & Management. Margery Miller. 100p. (Orig.). 1994. pap. 10.00 (*1-884363-04-0*) Odenwald Pr.

Sound Cards. Barbara A. Wilson. (Wilson Reading System Ser.). 1988. 10.00 (*1-56778-006-7*) Wilson Lang Trning.

Sound Catering for Hard Times: How to Economize on Food Without Starving the Body. V. H. Mottram & E. C. Mottram. 1974. lib. bdg. 69.95 (*0-685-51375-0*) Revisionist Pr.

Sound Change in Progress: A Study of Phonological Change & Lexical Diffusion. Sullivan. 128p. 1992. pap. text ed. 25.00 (*0-85989-374-X*, Pub. by Univ Exeter Pr UK) Northwestern U Pr.

Sound Check: The Basics of Sound & Sound Systems. (Illus.). 104p. (Orig.). 1994. pap. 14.95 (*0-7935-3559-X*, HL00330118) H Leonard.

Sound Choices: Guiding Your Child's Musical Experiences. Machover & Uszler. (Illus.). 400p. 1996. 35.00 (*0-19-509207-4*) OUP.

Sound Choices: Guiding Your Child's Musical Experiences. Wilma Machover & Uszler. (Illus.). 400p. 1996. pap. 19.95 (*0-19-509208-2*) OUP.

Sound Church Growth & Christian Development. J. C. Cagle. 85p. (Orig.). 1989. pap. 3.95 (*0-685-34665-X*, 5556) White Wing Pub.

Sound Conditioning Manual. R. Chanaud. 1992. text ed. write for info. (*0-442-00631-4*) Van Nos Reinhold.

Sound Connections. Jane C. Webb & Barbara Duckett. (Illus.). 248p. 1996. pap. text ed. 39.95 (*0-937857-62-9*, 1487) Speech Bin.

Sound Construction. Jean G. DeGaetano. 85p. 1988. pap. text ed. 29.95 (*1-886143-25-0*) Grt Ideas Tching.

Sound Designs: A Handbook of Musical Instrument Building. rev. ed. John Scoville & Reinhold Banek. 224p. 1995. pap. 11.95 (*0-89815-775-7*) Ten Speed Pr.

Sound Doctrine, Vol. 1. C. R. Nichol. 1984. pap. 6.95 (*0-915547-57-0*) Abilene Christ U.

Sound Doctrine, Vol. 2. C. R. Nichol. 1984. pap. 6.95 (*0-915547-58-9*) Abilene Christ U.

Sound Doctrine, Vol. 3. C. R. Nichol. 1984. pap. 6.95 (*0-915547-59-7*) Abilene Christ U.

Sound Doctrine, Vol. 4. C. R. Nichol. 1984. pap. 6.95 (*0-915547-60-0*) Abilene Christ U.

Sound Doctrine, Vol. 5. C. R. Nichol. 1984. pap. 6.95 (*0-915547-61-9*) Abilene Christ U.

Sound Economic Basis for Schools of Nursing. Adelaide M. Nutting. LC 83-49131. (History of American Nursing Ser.). 372p. 1984. reprint ed. text ed. 15.00 (*0-8240-6519-0*) Garland.

Sound Effects: Radio, TV & Film. Robert L. Mott. 222p. 1990. 42.95 (*0-240-80029-X*, Focal) Buttrwrth-Heinemann.

Sound Effects: Youth, Leisure, & the Politics of Rock 'n' Roll. Simon Frith. 1982. pap. 10.36 (*0-394-74811-5*) Pantheon.

Sound Energy. Frank Schaffer Publications, Inc. Staff. (Science Notes Ser.). (Illus.). 8p. 1996. 2.49 (*0-86734-894-1*, FS-62031) Schaffer Pubns.

Sound Engineer's Pocket Book. 6th ed. Michael Talbot-Smith. LC 95-23310. 192p. 1995. 22.95 (*0-240-51406-8*, Focal) Buttrwrth-Heinemann.

Sound Eternal, 2 vols., 1. Richard J. Pugsley & Betty C. Pugsley. LC 87-61191. 64p. (Orig.). 1987. pap. 9.95 (*0-941478-50-5*) Paraclete MA.

Sound Eternal, 2 vols., 2. Richard J. Pugsley & Betty C. Pugsley. LC 87-61191. 92p. (Orig.). 1987. pap. 9.95 (*0-941478-91-2*) Paraclete MA.

Sound Eternal, 2 vols., Set. Richard J. Pugsley & Betty C. Pugsley. LC 87-61191. (Orig.). 1987. pap. 18.95 (*0-941478-92-0*) Paraclete MA.

Sound Experiments. Ray Broekel. LC 82-17869. (New True Bks.). (Illus.). 48p. (J). (gr. k-4). 1983. pap. 5.50 (*0-516-41686-3*); lib. bdg. 19.00 (*0-516-01686-5*) Childrens.

Sound-Field FM Amplification: Theory & Practical Applications. Carl C. Crandell et al. (Illus.). 256p. (C). 1995. pap. text ed. 42.50 (*1-56593-450-4*, 1066) Singular Publishing.

Sound Films, 1927-1939: A United States Filmography. Alan G. Fetrow. LC 91-52635. 966p. 1992. lib. bdg. 82.00 (*0-89950-546-5*) McFarland & Co.

***Sound for Enclosed Helical, Herringbone & Spiral Bevel Gear Drives.** 3rd rev. ed. AGMA Technical Committee Staff. (ANSI/AGMA Standard Ser.). 1990. pap. text ed. 60.00 (*1-55589-552-2*) AGMA.

***Sound for Film & Television.** Tomlinson Holman. LC 96-48404. 1997. pap. write for info. (*0-240-80291-8*, Focal) Buttrwrth-Heinemann.

Sound for Picture: An Insider's Look at Audio Production in Film & Television. Mix Editors. 144p. 1993. pap. 17.95 (*0-7935-2002-9*, 00183014) H Leonard.

Sound for the Theatre. Graham Walne. LC 90-36479. 176p. (gr. 13). 1990. pap. 22.95 (*0-87830-119-4*, A4962, Thtre Arts Bks) Routledge.

Sound Foundation - Computer Applications. 2nd ed. Gerver & Sgroi. (MA - Academic Math Ser.). 1995. pap. 12.95 (*0-538-63381-6*) S-W Pub.

Sound Foundations. Gerver. (MA - Academic Math Ser.). 1987. pap. 26.95 (*0-538-13121-7*) S-W Pub.

Sound Foundations. 2nd ed. Gerver. (MA - Academic Math Ser.). 1995. wbk. ed., pap. 20.95 (*0-538-63379-4*) S-W Pub.

Sound Foundations. 2nd ed. Gerver. (Ma - Academic Math Ser.). 1995. teacher ed. 78.95 (*0-538-63380-8*) S-W Pub.

Sound Foundations, Teacher's Supplies. Gerver. (MA - Academic Math Ser.). 1987. 37.95 (*0-538-13122-5*) S-W Pub.

Sound Friendships: The Story of Willa & Her Hearing Dog. Elizabeth Yates. Ed. by Christine Leaman. (Pennant Ser.). (Illus.). 113p. (Orig.). (YA). (gr. 7-12). 1992. reprint ed. pap. 6.49 (*0-89084-650-2*, 063321) Bob Jones Univ Pr.

***Sound Fundamentals.** Robert W. Wood. (Funtastic Science Activities for Kids Ser.). (Illus.). 150p. (YA). (gr. 3 up). 1997. text ed. 22.50 (*0-7910-4840-3*) Chelsea Hse.

***Sound FUNdamentals: FUNtastic Science Activities for Kids.** Robert W. Wood. LC 97-19423. (Illus.). 192p. (J). 1997. teacher ed., text ed. 22.95 (*0-07-071810-5*); teacher ed., pap. text ed. 14.95 (*0-07-071811-3*) McGraw.

Sound Hearing: Or...Hearing What You Miss. S. Harold Collins. 12p. 1988. 7.95 incl. reel tape (*0-931993-26-1*, GP-026) Garlic Pr OR.

Sound Ideas. Fragiadakis. (College ESL Ser.). 1995. pap. 22.95 (*0-8384-4700-7*) Heinle & Heinle.

Sound Ideas. Fragiadakis. (College ESL Ser.). 1996. teacher ed., pap. 9.95 (*0-8384-4701-5*) Heinle & Heinle.

Sound In-Between. Paul Carter. (C). 1992. pap. 32.95 (*0-86840-109-9*, Pub. by New South Wales Univ Pr AT) Intl Spec Bk.

Sound in the Theatre. rev. ed. Harold Burris-Meyer et al. LC 78-66064. 1979. 16.95 (*0-87830-157-7*, Thtre Arts Bks) Routledge.

Sound in the Visual Arts. Jean-Yves Bosseur. (Illus.). 160p. (Orig.). 1992. pap. 24.95 (*2-906571-26-1*, Pub. by Editions Dis Voir FR) Dist Art Pubs.

Sound Intensity. 2nd ed. Fahy. 1995. pap. 51.50 (*0-419-19810-5*, E & FN Spon) Routledge Chapman & Hall.

Sound Investment. Sonia Sanchez. LC 74-75591. (Illus.). 1993. 18.95 (*0-88378-070-4*) Third World.

Sound Is My Number: Handbook for the Outreach Writing Program at Naropa. Ed. & Intro. by Jack Collom. 85p. (C). 1995. pap. text ed. 10.00 (*1-887997-03-2*) Baksun Bks.

Sound Jubilee. Sandra Forrester. 1997. pap. 4.99 (*0-14-037930-4*) Viking Penguin.

Sound Judgment. J. P. Swain. (Illus.). 1987. pap. 10.00 (*0-911302-60-3*) San Francisco Pr.

Sound Ladder Game. Genevieve Arnold. 1973. text ed. 3.00 (*0-686-09404-2*) Expression.

Sound Language & Awareness Psychology. Joseph M. Jones. LC 85-90320. (Illus.). 236p. (Orig.). 1985. pap. 12.50 (*0-9615111-1-7*) Sandbird Pub.

Sound-Learning in the First Two Years see Speech Development of a Bilingual Child

Sound, Light, & Music: Projects for the LM3909. Delton T. Horn. LC 92-11640. (Illus.). 256p. 1992. 27.95 (*0-8306-3802-4*, 4110); pap. 17.95 (*0-8306-3801-6*, 4110) McGraw-Hill Prof.

Sound Linkage: An Integrated Programme for Overcoming Reading Difficulties. Peter J. Hatcher. 1994. pap. text ed. 76.99 (*1-56593-389-3*, 0761) Singular Publishing.

Sound, Man & Building. L. H. Schaudinischky. (Illus.). xv, 413p. 1991. 112.00 (*0-85334-655-0*, Pub. by Elsevier Applied Sci UK) Elsevier.

Sound Medicine: Healing with Music, Voice & Song. Laeh M. Garfield. LC 87-13223. 192p. 1995. pap. 9.95 (*0-89087-483-2*) Celestial Arts.

Sound Military Decision. Naval War College Staff. Ed. by John B. Hatendorf & Wayne P. Hughes, Jr. LC 91-45244. (Classics of Sea Power Ser.). (Illus.). 243p. 1992. 39.95 (*1-55750-752-X*) Naval Inst Pr.

Sound Mind in a Sound Body. Armando B. Rico. 23p. (Orig.). (YA). 1990. pap. 16.00 (*1-879219-03-4*) Veracruz Pubs.

Sound Mind Investing: A Step-by-Step Guide to Financial Stability & Growth As We Move Toward the Year 2000. Austin Pryor. 1996. pap. 23.99 (*0-8024-7947-2*) Moody.

Sound Mind, Sound Body. Kenneth R. Pelletier. 320p. 1994. 23.00 (*0-671-77000-4*) S&S Trade.

Sound Mind, Sound Body: A New Model for Lifelong Health. Kenneth R. Pelletier. 1995. pap. 13.00 (*0-684-80251-1*, Fireside) S&S Trade.

Sound, Music, & Signal Processing on a Next Computer Concepts. Next Computer Inc. Staff. 1991. pap. 19.95 (*0-201-58137-X*) Addison-Wesley.

Sound, Noise & Vibration Control. 2nd ed. Lyle F. Yerges. LC 83-11303. 272p. 1983. reprint ed. text ed. 33.50 (*0-89874-654-X*) Krieger.

Sound Not Silence. Nicola Baxter. LC 94-44721. (Toppers Ser.). (Illus.). 24p. (J). (ps-3). 1995. lib. bdg. 15.00 (*0-516-09269-3*) Childrens.

Sound of a Cry. D. Peck. pap. 6.99 (*1-85792-134-8*, Pub. by Christian Focus UK) Spring Arbor Dist.

An Asterisk (*) at the beginning of an entry indicates that the title is appearing in BIP for the first time.

Sound of a Miracle. Annabel Stehli. 256p. 1992. mass mkt. 4.99 (*0-380-71739-5*) Avon.

***Sound of a Miracle: A Child's Triumph over Autism.** Annabel Stehli. 226p. 1999. pap. 14.95 (*0-614-28311-6*) Georgiana Orgn.

***Sound of a Miracle: A Child's Triumph over Autism.** 2nd ed. Annabel Stehli. 226p. 1997. reprint ed. pap. 14.95 (*0-9644838-1-5*) Georgiana Orgn.

Sound of a Voice. David H. Hwang. 1984. pap. 3.25 (*0-8222-1060-6*) Dramatists Play.

Sound of Bells: The Episcopal Church in South Florida, 1892-1969. Joseph D. Cushman, Jr. LC 75-30946. (Illus.). 1976. 24.95 (*0-8130-0518-3*) U Press Fla.

***Sound of Bells: The Episcopal Church in South Florida, 1892-1969.** Joseph D. Cushman. LC 75-30946. (Illus.). 412p. reprint ed. pap. 117.50 (*0-608-04474-1*, 2065219) Bks Demand.

Sound of Broadway, No. 11. 64p. 1984. pap. 5.95 (*0-7935-3694-4*, 00243721) H Leonard.

Sound of Chariots. Mollie Hunter. LC 72-76523. (Trophy Bk.). 256p. (J). (gr. 5-9). 1972. pap. 3.95 (*0-06-440235-5*, Trophy) HarpC Child Bks.

Sound of Chariots. Mollie Hunter. LC 72-76523. 256p. (J). (gr. 7 up). 1972. lib. bdg. 12.89 (*0-06-022669-2*) HarpC Child Bks.

Sound of Chariots. Mollie Hunter. 1995. 18.50 (*0-8446-6815-X*) Peter Smith.

Sound of Christmastime & Other Yuletide Yarns. Gerald D. Sullivan. LC 92-80174. (Illus.). 100p. (Orig.). 1992. pap. 9.95 (*0-9644573-5-0*) Shamrock Sky Bks.

Sound of Coming Darkness. Bill Fountain. (Illus.). 42p. (Orig.). 1994. pap. 6.95 (*1-883611-07-5*) Blckbird Comics.

Sound of Death, Vol. 1. Fred Hale. 186p. (Orig.). 1996. pap. 6.99 (*1-57502-166-8*, PO771) Morris Pubng.

Sound of Detection: Ellery Queen's Adventures in Radio. Francis M. Nevins, Jr. & Ray Stanich. LC 85-25462. viii, 109p. 1985. reprint ed. pap. 17.00 (*0-941028-01-1*, Brownstone Bks); reprint ed. lib. bdg. 27.00 (*0-89370-556-X*, Brownstone Bks) Borgo Pr.

***Sound of Fish Dreaming.** Benjamin Green. 70p. (Orig.). 1996. pap. 11.00 (*0-944920-23-3*) Bellowing Ark Pr.

Sound of Gunfire. large type ed. Frank Bonham. LC 94-42788. (Nightingale Ser.). 232p. 1995. pap. 16.95 (*0-7838-1150-0*, GK Hall) Thorndike Pr.

Sound of Healing: Create Your Own Music Program for Better Health. Judith Pinkerton. 1996. pap. 16.00 (*1-887110-00-3*) Allian Pubng.

Sound of His Name. Bernard J. Honeysett. 132p. (Orig.). 1995. pap. 9.50 (*0-85151-677-7*) Banner of Truth.

Sound of His Voice. Kim Clement. 180p. 1993. pap. 8.99 (*0-88419-339-X*) Creation House.

***Sound of History: Songs & Social Comment.** Roy Palmer. (Illus.). 384p. 1997. pap. 27.50 (*0-7126-7316-4*, Pub. by Pimlico) Trafalgar.

Sound of Horns. David Lyon. LC 82-24968. 63p. 1984. pap. 4.95 (*0-934332-38-X*) LEpervier Pr.

Sound of Leadership: Presidential Communication in the Modern Age. Roderick P. Hart. LC 87-5863. (Illus.). 300p. (C). 1987. pap. text ed. 18.00 (*0-226-31813-3*) U Ch Pr.

Sound of Leaves. Lenore Blegvad. LC 94-46961. (Illus.). 64p. (J). (gr. 3-6). 1996. 15.00 (*0-689-80038-X*, McElderry) S&S Childrens.

Sound of Light: A History of Gospel Music. Don Cusic. LC 90-82744. 256p. (C). 1990. 19.95 (*0-87972-497-8*); pap. 40.95 (*0-87972-498-6*) Bowling Green Univ Popular Press.

Sound of Light: Experiencing the Transcendental. deluxe ed. Irina Starr. 272p. 1991. reprint ed. 12.95 (*0-930596-12-9*) Pilgrims Path.

Sound of Maroons: The Story of Life-Saving Services on the Kent & Sussex Coasts. Howard Biggs. 176p. 1994. 30.00 (*0-900963-83-2*, Pub. by T Dalton UK) St Mut.

Sound of Money: A Musical Adventure about Economics & the Building of Community. Tobin J. Mueller. (Illus.). (J). (ps-8). Audio tape incl. 14.95 incl. audio (*1-56213-031-5*) Ctr Stage Prodns.

Sound of Murder. Patricia Matthews. 1994. 20.00 (*0-7278-4594-2*) Severn Hse.

Sound of Murder. large type ed. Patricia Mattews & Clayton Matthews. LC 94-33231. 1995. 23.95 (*1-56054-335-3*) Thorndike Pr.

Sound of Music. (Big Note Ser.). 1985. 3.95 (*0-7935-0949-1*, 00301931) H Leonard.

Sound of Music. 1993. pap. 6.95 incl. audio (*0-7935-2383-4*, 00823028) H Leonard.

Sound of Music. Richard Rodgers & Oscar Hammserstein. 48p. 1982. pap. 7.95 (*0-7935-0758-8*, 00312715) H Leonard.

Sound of Music: Alto Saxophone. 16p. 1992. pap. 5.95 (*0-7935-1319-7*, 00850198) H Leonard.

Sound of Music: Big Note Piano. Richard Rodgers & Oscar Hammerstein. 32p. 1982. pap. 5.95 (*0-7935-1150-X*, 00302211) H Leonard.

Sound of Music: Piano Selection. Richard Rodgers & Oscar Hammerstein. 20p. 1981. pap. 5.95 (*0-7935-2562-4*, 00312713) H Leonard.

Sound of Music: Souvenir Folio. Richard Rodgers & Oscar Hammerstein. 76p. 1981. otabind 9.95 (*0-88188-218-6*, 00312394) H Leonard.

Sound of Music: The Making of America's Movie. Julia A. Hirsch. 240p. 1993. pap. 19.95 (*0-8092-3837-3*) Contemp Bks.

Sound of Music: Trumpet. 16p. 1992. pap. 5.95 (*0-7935-1320-0*, 00850199) H Leonard.

Sound of Music: Upper Intermediate for One Piano, Four Hands. Richard Rodgers & Oscar Hammerstein. 24p. 1981. pap. 5.95 (*0-7935-1152-6*, 00312714) H Leonard.

Sound of Music: Violin. 16p. 1992. pap. 5.95 (*0-7935-1388-X*, 00850208) H Leonard.

Sound of Music Piano Duets. 80p. 1993. pap. 9.95 (*0-7935-1865-2*, 00290389) H Leonard.

Sound of Music Piano Solo. 56p. 1995. pap. 9.95 (*0-7935-3144-6*, 00292052) H Leonard.

Sound of Music Selections: Beginners. Richard Rodgers & Oscar Hammerstein. 16p. 1981. pap. 5.95 (*0-7935-0967-X*, 00301933) H Leonard.

Sound of My Waves: Selected Poems by Ko Un. Tr. by Brother Anthony of Taize & Young-moo Kim from KOR. (Cornell East Asia Ser.: No. 68). 124p. (C). 1993. 18.00 (*0-939657-87-2*); pap. 12.00 (*0-939657-68-6*) Cornell East Asia Pgm.

Sound of One Hand Clapping. Louise O. Neaderland. (Illus.). 1995. pap. 25.00 (*0-942561-23-6*) Bone Hollow.

Sound of One Mind Thinking. Eugene M. Schwartz. LC 80-27128. (Illus.). 160p. (Orig.). 1981. pap. 6.95 (*0-89407-040-1*) Strawberry Hill.

Sound of Rattles & Clappers: A Collection of New California Indian Writing. Ed. by Greg Sarris. (Sun Tracks Ser.: Vol. 26). 161p. (Orig.). 1994. pap. 16.95 (*0-8165-1434-8*); lib. bdg. 32.95 (*0-8165-1280-9*) U of Ariz Pr.

Sound of Rock: Acoustic Six-String, Twelve-String, & Arched-Top Guitars. Mike Doyle. (Illus.). 68p. 1993. reprint ed. pap. 14.95 (*0-933224-19-2*, T/40) Bold Strummer Ltd.

Sound of Silence: Moving with T'ai Chi. Carol R. Murphy. LC 75-41548. (Orig.). 1976. pap. 3.00 (*0-87574-205-X*) Pendle Hill.

Sound of Sleigh Bells: A Christmas Story for all Seasons. Paul E. Pross & Jack H. Yungclas. 70p. 1991. 13.95 (*0-9630307-0-1*) Vertex Pr.

Sound of Sleigh Bells: A Christmas Story for All Seasons. rev. ed. Paul E. Pross & Jack H. Yungclas. 70p. 1993. 13.95 (*0-9630307-2-8*) Vertex Pr.

Sound of Strangers: Musical Culture, Acculturation, & the Post-Civil War Ethnic American. Nicholas E. Tawa. LC 81-21235. 318p. 1982. 29.50 (*0-8108-1504-4*) Scarecrow.

Sound of Strings: Sequel to Komantcia. Harold Keith. LC 91-62777. 175p. (Orig.). (J). (gr. 5 up). 1992. 17.00 (*0-927562-10-3*) Levite Apache.

Sound of Success: Musical Motivation. Michael Maxfield & Myrica Maxfield. 32p. (YA). 1992. 19.95 (*0-9634682-1-9*, 232822) Myrichael Way.

Sound of Surprise. Whitney Balliett. LC 77-17852. (Roots of Jazz Ser.). 1978. reprint ed. lib. bdg. 29.50 (*0-306-77543-3*) Da Capo.

Sound of the City: The Rise of Rock & Roll. 2nd expanded rev. ed. Charlie Gillett. (Illus.). 604p. 1996. pap. 16.95 (*0-306-80683-5*) Da Capo.

***Sound of the Dolphin's Psalm.** Libby Layne, pseud. Ed. by Molly R. Jenkins. LC 97-60211. (Illus.). 255p. (Orig.). 1997. pap. 12.00 (*1-890306-01-0*) Warwick Hse.

Sound of the Dove: Singing in Appalachian Primitive Baptist Churches. Beverly B. Patterson. LC 94-1697. (Music in American Life Ser.). 264p. 1995. text ed. 37.50 (*0-252-02123-1*) U of Ill Pr.

Sound of the Dove: Singing in Appalachian Primitive Baptist Churches. Beverly B. Patterson. 1995. 45.00 incl. audio, digital audio (*0-252-02174-6*) U of Ill Pr.

Sound of the Earth: A Man's Midlife Passage & Spiritual Awakening. 2nd rev. ed. Hart Sprager. Ed. by Joy Parker. LC 95-67505. 312p. (Orig.). 1996. pap. 16.00 (*1-880823-13-6*) N Star Pubns.

Sound of the Flute: The Cuban Impact. Raoul J. Fajardo. (Illus.). 216p. (Orig.). 1981. pap. 5.00 (*0-940774-00-3*) Pulsante Assn News.

Sound of the Fortepiano: A Discography of Music on Early Pianos. Ann P. Basart. LC 85-1660. (Reference Books in Music: No. 2). xiv, 472p. (Orig.). 1986. pap. 9.95 (*0-914913-01-8*) Fallen Leaf.

Sound of the Harp: Reflections. Genevieve S. Whitford. (Illus.). 52p. 1989. 12.95 (*0-9610456-1-2*) Harp Pr.

Sound of the Mountain. Yasunari Kawabata. 1996. pap. 12.00 (*0-679-76264-7*) Random.

***Sound of the Mountain.** Wallace Stegner. 1997. pap. 12.95 (*0-14-026674-7*) Viking Penguin.

***Sound of the Seventh Trumpet.** Jesus Christ et al. 112p. (Orig.). 1996. pap. 19.95 (*0-9654861-1-7*) Svnth Trumpet CA.

Sound of the Silver Horn: Reclaiming the Heroism in Women's Lives. Kathleen Noble. LC 93-14264. 240p. 1994. 20.00 (*0-449-90588-8*, Columbine) Fawcett.

Sound of the Soul: Discovering the Power of Your Voice. Arthur S. Joseph. 200p. (Orig.). 1996. pap. 10.95 (*1-55874-407-X*, 407X) Health Comm.

Sound of the Trumpet. Rob Lindsted. 50p. (Orig.). 1994. pap. 2.50 (*1-879366-57-6*) Hearthstone OK.

Sound of the Trumpet. large type ed. Grace L. Hill. LC 92-14131. (General Ser.). 400p. 1992. lib. bdg. 19.95 (*0-8161-4909-7*, GK Hall) Thorndike Pr.

Sound of the Trumpet, No. 90. Grace L. Hill. (Grace Livingston Hill Ser.: Vol. 90). 266p. 1990. pap. 4.99 (*0-8423-6107-3*) Tyndale.

Sound of the Trumpet: An Evan Horne Mystery. Bill Moody. LC 96-42149. (Evan Horne Mystery Ser.). 240p. 1997. 21.95 (*0-8027-3291-7*) Walker & Co.

Sound of the Week. Sally Barrett. 144p. (J). (gr. k-4). 1980. 13.99 (*0-916456-63-3*, GA 184) Good Apple.

Sound of the Whistle: Railroads & the State in Meiji, Japan. Steven Ericson. (Harvard East Asian Monographs: No. 168). (Illus.). 450p. Date not set. pap. 42.00 (*0-674-82167-X*) HUP.

Sound of the Wind: The Life & Works of Uno Chiyo. Rebecca L. Copeland. LC 91-48130. (Illus.). 256p. 1992. text ed. 29.00 (*0-8248-1409-6*) UH Pr.

Sound of Thunder. Wilbur Smith. 1992. mass mkt. 5.99 (*0-449-14819-X*, GM) Fawcett.

Sound of Virtue: Philip Sidney's Arcadia & Elizabethan Politics. Blair Worden. LC 96-18713. 1996. write for info. (*0-300-06693-7*) Yale U Pr.

Sound of Voices. large type ed. Elisabeth Hargreaves. 352p. 1982. 25.99 (*0-7089-0847-0*) Ulverscroft.

Sound of War. Peter Stursberg. (Illus.). 180p. 1993. 35.00 (*0-8020-2992-2*) U of Toronto Pr.

Sound of Waves. Yukio Mishima. 1994. pap. 10.00 (*0-679-75268-4*) Random.

Sound of Wings: The Life of Amelia Earhart. Mary S. Lovell. (Illus.). 448p. 1991. pap. 12.95 (*0-312-05160-3*) St Martin.

Sound-On-Film: Interviews with Creators of Film Sound. Vincent Lobrutto. LC 93-50686. 320p. 1994. text ed. 69.50 (*0-275-94442-5*, Praeger Pubs); pap. text ed. 19.95 (*0-275-94443-3*, Praeger Pubs) Greenwood.

Sound on Sound. Christopher Sorrentino. LC 94-37596. 200p. 1995. 19.95 (*1-56478-073-2*) Dalkey Arch.

Sound Out! Ready-to-Use Phonics Activities for Special Children. Rosella Bernstein. LC 93-17470. (Illus.). 1993. spiral bd. 28.95 (*0-87628-867-0*) Ctr Appl Res.

Sound Pattern of English. Noam Chomsky & Morris Halle. 487p. 1991. pap. 22.00 (*0-262-53097-X*) MIT Pr.

Sound Pattern of Russian: A Linguistic & Acoustical Investigation. Morris Halle. (D A C S R Ser.: No. 1). 1971. reprint ed. text ed. 44.65 (*90-279-1561-X*) Mouton.

Sound Patterns for Primary Children. Debby Miller et al. (Illus.). 98p. 1988. teacher ed., spiral bd. 8.95 (*1-886131-29-5*, SP) Math Lrning.

Sound Patterns in Second Language Acquisition. Ed. by A. James & J. Leather. (Studies on Language Acquisition). iv, 250p. 1987. pap. 53.85 (*90-6765-307-1*) Mouton.

***Sound Programming.** Tim Kientzle. (C). 1997. pap. text ed. write for info. (*0-201-41972-6*) Addison-Wesley.

Sound Propagation in Stratified Fluids. C. H. Wilcox. (Applied Mathematical Sciences Ser.: Vol. 50). ix, 198p. 1984. 57.95 (*0-387-90986-9*) Spr-Verlag.

Sound Propagation in the Sea. Robert J. Urick. LC 82-81923. 272p. 1982. 38.95 (*0-932146-08-2*) Peninsula CA.

Sound Recall: One Typical Midwestern Town Remembers the Events of World War II. Bob D. Fahey. Ed. by Steve Meyer. LC 95-75320. (Illus.). 192p. (Orig.). 1995. pap. 18.95 (*0-9630284-4-8*) Meyer Pub.

Sound Recording & Reproduction. 3rd ed. Glyn Alkin. LC 96-6731. (Media Manual Ser.). 1996. pap. write for info. (*0-240-51467-X*, Focal) Buttrwrth-Heinemann.

Sound Recording Practice. 4th ed. John Borwick. (Illus.). 624p. 1996. pap. 35.00 (*0-19-816608-7*) OUP.

Sound Recordings & the Library. Sharon G. Almquist. (Occasional Papers: No. 179). 1987. pap. 2.50 (*0-685-34542-4*) U of Ill Grad Sch.

***Sound Reinforcement Engineering.** Ahnert. 400p. 1997. text ed. write for info. (*0-419-21810-6*, E & FN Spon) Routledge Chapman & Hall.

Sound Reinforcement Handbook. 2nd ed. Gary Davis & Ralph Jones. (Illus.). 418p. (Orig.). 1988. pap. 34.95 (*0-88188-900-8*, 00500964) H Leonard.

Sound Reporting: National Public Radio's Guide to Radio Journalism & Production. NPR Staff. 352p. 1993. pap. text ed. 38.95 (*0-8403-7202-7*) Kendall-Hunt.

Sound Science. Etta Kaner. 96p. 1991. pap. 9.95 (*0-201-56758-X*) Addison-Wesley.

Sound Scriptural Outlines, No. 3. Wade H. Horton. 1977. 9.99 (*0-87148-781-0*) Pathway Pr.

Sound Scriptural Sermon Outlines, No. 4. Wade H. Horton. 1979. 9.99 (*0-87148-783-7*); pap. 7.99 (*0-87148-784-5*) Pathway Pr.

Sound Search: A Speech & Language Drillbook. Jerry Griffith & Lynn E. Miner. LC 85-23224. 319p. reprint ed. pap. 91.00 (*0-8357-3541-9*, 2034433) Bks Demand.

Sound, Self, & Song: Essays on the Teaching of Singing. Earl W. Jones. LC 89-6419. 231p. 1989. 22.50 (*0-8108-2221-0*) Scarecrow.

Sound Sentiment: An Essay on the Musical Emotions. Peter Kivy. (Arts & Their Philosophies Ser.). 304p. (C). 1989. pap. 22.95 (*0-87722-677-6*) Temple U Pr.

Sound Sex & the Aging Heart: Sex in the Mid & Later Years with Special Reference to Cardiac Problems. Lee Scheingold & Nathaniel N. Wagner. LC 74-662. (Illus.). 168p. 1974. 32.95 (*0-87705-155-0*) Human Sci Pr.

Sound-Shadows of the New World. Ved Mehta. LC 85-5045. 1987. pap. 8.95 (*0-393-30437-X*) Norton.

Sound Shape of Language. Linda R. Waugh. LC 78-19552. 320p. reprint ed. pap. 91.20 (*0-317-27826-6*, 2056041) Bks Demand.

Sound, Sign & Meaning: Quinquagenary of the Prague Linguistic Circle. Ed. by Ladislav Matejka. (Michigan Slavic Contributions Ser.: No. 6). 1978. 25.00 (*0-930042-26-3*) Mich Slavic Pubns.

Sound Skill Builder: Use with Sure Steps to Reading & Spelling, 3 bks. Incl. Bk. 1. pap. text ed. (*0-916720-04-7*); Bk. 2. pap. text ed. (*0-916720-05-5*); Bk. 3. pap. text ed. (*0-916720-06-3*); (J). (gr. 1-7). pap. write for info. (*0-318-56397-5*) Weiss Pub.

Sound, Speech, & Music. David Burrows. LC 89-4947. 152p. 1990. 22.50 (*0-87023-685-7*) U of Mass Pr.

***Sound Start: Teaching Phonological Awareness in the Classroom.** Orna Lenchner & Blanche Podhajski. (Illus.). 111p. 1997. teacher ed., spiral bd. 95.00 (*0-9657567-0-X*) Stern Ctr.

***Sound States: Innovative Poetics & Acoustical Technologies.** Adalaide K. Morris. LC 97-9884. 360p. (C). (gr. 13). 1998. pap. text ed. 24.95 (*0-8078-4670-8*); lib. bdg. 55.00 (*0-8078-2364-3*) U of NC Pr.

Sound Strategist. Rita Samuelson. 86p. (YA). (gr. k-12). 1989. spiral bd., pap. 35.00 (*0-930599-50-0*) Thinking Pubns.

Sound Structures: Studies for Antonie Cohen. Wim Zonneveld. (Publications in Language Sciences). xxvi, 318p. 1983. 98.50 (*90-70176-18-1*); pap. 73.10 (*3-11-013346-6*) Mouton.

Sound Structures & Their Interaction. 2nd ed. Miguel C. Junger & David Feit. (Illus.). 451p. (C). 1993. reprint ed. 26.00 (*0-262-10034-7*) Acoustical Soc Am.

Sound Studio. 6th rev. ed. Alec Nisbett. LC 94-24609. (Illus.). 400p. 1995. pap. 49.95 (*0-240-51395-9*, Focal) Buttrwrth-Heinemann.

Sound Studio Construction on a Budget. F. Alton Everest. (Illus.). 352p. 1996. pap. text ed. 29.95 (*0-07-021382-8*) McGraw.

Sound Studio Production Techniques. Dennis N. Nardantonio. (Illus.). 288p. 1989. 28.95 (*0-8306-9250-9*); pap. 19.95 (*0-8306-3250-6*) McGraw-Hill Prof.

Sound Symbolism. Ed. by Leanne Hinton et al. LC 93-34988. (Illus.). 349p. (C). 1995. text ed. 65.00 (*0-521-45219-8*) Cambridge U Pr.

Sound Synthesis: Analog & Digital Techniques. Terence Thomas. 1990. pap. text ed. 14.95 (*0-07-157515-4*) McGraw.

Sound Synthesis: Analog & Digital Techniques. Terence Thomas. (Illus.). 160p. 1989. 22.95 (*0-8306-9276-2*); pap. 14.95 (*0-8306-3276-X*) McGraw-Hill Prof.

Sound Synthesis & Sampling. Martin Russ. (Illus.). 224p. 1996. pap. 32.95 (*0-240-51429-7*, Focal) Buttrwrth-Heinemann.

***Sound System Engineering.** 2nd ed. Don Davis. 1986. pap. text ed. 49.95 (*0-240-80305-1*) Buttrwrth-Heinemann.

Sound System Engineering. 2nd ed. Don Davis et al. 688p. 1986. 49.95 (*0-672-21857-7*) Buttrwrth-Heinemann.

Sound System of French. fac. ed. Jean Casagrande. LC 83-20594. 256p. 1984. reprint ed. pap. 73.00 (*0-7837-7801-5*, 2047557) Bks Demand.

Sound Systems for Your Automobile: The How-To Guide for Audio System Selection & Installation. rev. ed. Alvis J. Evans & Eric J. Evans. (Illus.). 124p. (C). 1993. reprint ed. pap. 16.95 (*0-7906-1046-9*) Prompt Publns.

Sound Techniques for Video & TV. 2nd ed. Glyn Alkin. 240p. 1989. pap. 26.95 (*0-240-51277-4*, Focal) Buttrwrth-Heinemann.

***Sound Testing - Noises in Gears Due to the Design, Material, & Manufacture (Not Wear)** R. S. Drummond. (Technical Papers). 1938. pap. text ed. 30.00 (*1-55589-377-5*) AGMA.

Sound the Charge. Richard Weingardt. LC 78-59321. (Illus.). 184p. (J). (gr. 6-12). 9.95 (*0-932446-00-0*); pap. 4.95 (*0-932446-01-9*) Jacqueline Enter.

Sound the Deep Waters: Women's Romantic Poetry in the Victorian Age. Ed. by Pamela Norris. (Illus.). 120p. 1992. 18.95 (*0-8212-1895-6*) Bulfinch Pr.

Sound, the Fury, & the Significance, Vol. I-95-2. unabridged ed. John C. LeGates. 19p. (Orig.). 1995. pap. text ed. write for info. (*1-879716-22-4*) Ctr Info Policy.

Sound the Great Shofar. Menachem M. Schneerson. Tr. by Uri Kaploun & Eliyahn Touger. 176p. 17.00 (*0-8266-0482-X*) Kehot Pubn Soc.

Sound the Jubilee. Sandra Forrester. 183p. (J). (gr. 5-9). 1995. pap. 15.99 (*0-525-67486-1*, Lodestar Bks) Dutton Child Bks.

Sound the Retreat. Simon Raven. 224p. 1986. 14.95 (*0-8253-0343-5*) Beaufort Bks NY.

Sound the Trumpet. Gilbert Morris. (Liberty Bell Ser.: Bk. 1). 320p. 1995. pap. 9.99 (*1-55661-565-5*) Bethany Hse.

Sound the Trumpet: Reflections on the Paschal Mystery. Michele T. Gallagher. LC 92-40309. 144p. 1993. pap. 6.95 (*0-8189-0665-0*) Alba.

Sound Theory - Sound Practice. Rick Altman. 256p. (C). 1992. pap. 17.95 (*0-415-90457-9*, Routledge NY) Routledge.

***Sound to Jubilee.** Sandra Forrester. (J). (gr. 5-9). 1997. pap. 4.99 (*0-614-28898-3*, Puffin) Puffin Bks.

Sound Toys. Voyager Company Staff. Date not set. write for info. (*1-55940-704-2*) Voyager NY.

Sound Track to Reading. 3rd ed. Monica Foltzer. (Professor Phonics System Ser.). (Illus.). 80p. (YA). (gr. 3 up). 1985. pap. text ed. 9.00 (*0-9607918-4-1*, 764921) St Ursula.

Sound Track to Reading. 4th ed. Monica Foltzer. 52p. (J). (gr. 3 up). 1985. pap. text ed. 6.50 (*0-9607918-5-X*, 764921) St Ursula.

***Sound Tracks: Pattern Music.** 26p. 1978. pap. text ed. 9.95 (*0-521-20581-6*) Cambridge U Pr.

***Sound Tracks: Rites & Ceremonies.** 30p. 1978. pap. text ed. 9.95 (*0-521-20579-4*) Cambridge U Pr.

Sound Transmission Through Buildings: Using Statistical Energy Analysis. Robert J. Craik. (Illus.). 280p. 1996. 94.95 (*0-566-07572-5*, Pub. by Gower UK) Ashgate Pub Co.

Sound Underwater Images: A Guide to the Generation & Interpretation of Side Scan Sonar Data. John P. Fish & H. Arnold Carr. LC 90-63112. (Illus.). 195p. 1990. pap. text ed. 125.00 (*0-936972-14-9*) Lower Cape.

***Sound Way.** Love & Reilly. 1994. pap. text ed. write for info. (*0-582-80414-0*, Pub. by Longman UK) Longman.

Sound Ways of Knowing: Enhancing the Curriculum Through Music. Janet R. Barrett et al. LC 97-19813. 375p. (C). 1997. 35.00 (*0-02-864530-8*) Schirmer Bks.

Sound Xpressions. John J. Thompson. 32p. (YA). 1995. pap. 4.99 (*0-7814-0205-0*) Chariot Victor.

***Soundbites & Spin Doctors: How Politicians Manipulate the Media & Vice Versa.** Nicholas Jones. (Illus.). 264p. 1996. pap. 19.95 (*0-575-40052-8*, Pub. by V Gollancz UK) Trafalgar.

Sounder. William H. Armstrong. LC 70-85030. (Illus.). 128p. (YA). (gr. 6 up). 1969. 14.95 (*0-06-020143-6*); lib. bdg. 14.89 (*0-06-020144-4*) HarpC Child Bks.

Sounder. William H. Armstrong. LC 70-85030. (Trophy Bk.). (Illus.). 128p. (YA). (gr. 7 up). 1972. reprint ed. pap. 4.50 (*0-06-440020-4*, Trophy) HarpC Child Bks.

Sounder. William H. Armstrong. LC 88-45956. 136p. 1989. reprint ed. pap. 6.00 (*0-06-080975-2*, P 975, PL) HarpC.

Sounder: L-I-T Guide. Charlotte Jaffe & Barbara Roberts. (L-I-T Guides: Literature in Teaching Ser.). Grades 4 up. teacher ed. 8.95 (*0-910857-86-5*) Educ Impress.

Sounder: Literature Unit. Mari L. Robbins. Ed. by Janet Cain. (Illus.). 48p. (Orig.). 1994. student ed., pap. 7.95 (*1-55734-530-9*) Tchr Create Mat.

Sounder - Study Guide. Marcia Tretler. Ed. by Joyce Friedland & Rikki Kessler. (Novel-Ties Ser.). (YA). (gr. 6-9). 1993. pap. text ed. 15.95 (*0-88122-130-9*) Lrn Links.

Soundex Reference Guide. Precision Indexing Staff. Ed. by Bradley W. Stueart. 253p. 1990. pap. 19.96 (*1-877677-09-4*); lib. bdg. 29.95 (*1-877677-12-4*) Precision Indexing.

Soundgarden. Jon Ewing. (CD Bks.). (Illus.). 120p. (Orig.). 1996. pap. 7.99 (*1-886894-36-1*) Mus Bk Servs.

Soundgarden: New Metal Crown. Chris Nickson. 1995. pap. 10.95 (*0-312-13607-2*) St Martin.

Soundgarden - Badmotorfinger: Play-It-Like-It-Is-Bass. pap. 16.95 (*0-89524-762-3*) Cherry Lane.

Soundgarden - Badmotorfinger: Play-It-Like-It-Is-Guitar. pap. 19.95 (*0-89524-708-9*) Cherry Lane.

***Soundgarden - Down on the Upside Guitar/Vocal.** 109p. (YA). pap. 21.95 (*1-57560-012-9*) Cherry Lane.

Soundgarden - Louder Than Love: Play-It-Like-It-Is-Guitar. pap. 19.95 (*0-89524-605-8*) Cherry Lane.

***Soundgarden-down on the Upside: Bass/Vocal.** Ed. by Steve Gorenberg. 93p. (YA). Date not set. pap. 19.95 (*1-57560-029-3*) Cherry Lane.

Soundies Distributing Corporation of America: A History & Filmography of Their "Jukebox" Musical Films of the 1940s. Maurice Terenzio et al. LC 90-53527. (Illus.). 232p. 1991. lib. bdg. 38.50 (*0-89950-578-3*) McFarland & Co.

Sounding. Hank Searls. 288p. 1985. mass mkt. 5.99 (*0-345-32526-5*) Ballantine.

Sounding Boards: Oral Testimony & the Local Historian. David Marcombe. 90p. 1994. pap. 10.00 (*1-85041-075-5*, Pub. by U Nottingham UK) Paul & Co Pubs.

Sounding Differences: Conversations with Seventeen Canadian Women Writers. Janice Williamson. 370p. 1993. 50.00 (*0-8020-2762-8*) U of Toronto Pr.

Sounding Forms: African Musical Instruments. Arthur P. Bourgeois et al. (Illus.). 208p. (Orig.). 1989. pap. 35.00 (*0-917418-89-1*) Am Fed Arts.

***Sounding Forth the Trumpet.** Peter Marshall & David Manuel. 512p. Date not set. 19.99 (*0-8007-1746-5*) Revell.

Sounding of the Trumpet. Frances J. Roberts. 1966. pap. 3.25 (*0-932814-24-7*) Kings Farspan.

***Sounding of Women: Autobiographies from Unexpected Places.** Martha C. Ward. LC 97-4169. 1997. 28.00 (*0-205-27015-8*) Allyn.

Sounding Off! Music As Subversion/Resistance/Revolution. Ed. by Ron Sakolsky & Fred W. Ho. 1995. pap. 20.00 incl. cd-rom (*1-57027-026-0*, Semiotexte) Autonomedia.

Sounding Off! Music As Subversion/Resistance/Revolution. Ho F. Wei-Han. 352p. Date not set. 20.00 incl. cd-rom (*0-614-14962-2*); 14.00 (*1-57027-058-9*) Autonomedia.

Sounding Stillness. Kenneth Von Gunden. 1993. mass mkt. 4.99 (*0-441-77598-5*) Ace Bks.

***Sounding Symbol: Music Education in Action.** George Odam. 144p. (Orig.). 1995. pap. 42.50 (*0-7487-2323-4*, Pub. by Stanley Thornes UK) Trans-Atl Phila.

***Sounding the Classics: From Sophocles to Thomas Mann.** Rudolph Binion. LC 97-1693. 176p. 1997. text ed. 18.95 (*0-275-95965-1*, Praeger Pubs) Greenwood.

***Sounding the Classics: From Sophocles to Thomas Mann.** Rudolph Binion. LC 97-1693. (Contributions to the Study of World Literature: Vol. 83). 1997. text ed. 55.00 (*0-313-30458-0*, Greenwood Pr) Greenwood.

Sounding the Depths: One Hundred Fifty Years of American Seascape. Intro. by Harold B. Nelson. (Illus.). 112p. (C). 1989. pap. 18.95 (*0-87701-598-8*) Am Fed Arts.

Sounding the Full Circle: Concerning Music Improvisation & Other Related Matters. Malcolm Goldstein. LC 88-91387. (Illus.). 96p. (Orig.). 1988. pap. 15.00 (*0-9621508-0-0*) M Goldstein.

Sounding the Iceberg: An Essay on Canadian Historical Novels. Dennis Duffy. 100p. (C). 1986. pap. text ed. 14.00 (*0-920763-14-6*, Pub. by ECW Press CN) Genl Dist Srvs.

***Sounding the Inner Landscape: Music as Medicine.** Kay Gardner. LC 96-41500. 1997. pap. 16.95 (*1-85230-973-3*) Element MA.

Sounding the Inner Landscape: Music as Medicine. Kay L. Gardner. LC 90-83112. (Illus.). 250p. (Orig.). 1990. pap. 13.95 (*0-9627200-3-8*) Caduceus Pubns.

Sounding the Silence: Why People Sing in the Shower. Sue Parker & Rebekah Nix. (Illus.). 172p. (Orig.). 1994. pap. 12.99 (*0-9641407-0-5*) RNIX.

***Sounding the Silence: or Why People Sing in the Shower Workbook.** Sue Parker. 76p. 1995. wbk. ed. 12.95 (*0-9641407-1-3*) RNIX.

Sounding the Soul: The Art of Listening. Mary L. Kittelson. 210p. 1996. pap. text ed. 18.00 (*3-85630-554-8*, Pub. by Daimon Pubs SZ) Continuum.

Sounding the Waters. James Glickman. LC 95-34132. 288p. 1996. 23.00 (*0-517-70040-9*) Crown Pub Group.

***Sounding the Waters.** large type ed. James Glickman. (Niagara Large Print Ser.). 433p. 1997. 29.50 (*0-7089-5859-1*, Linford) Ulverscroft.

Sounding the Whale: Moby-Dick As Epic Novel. Christopher Sten. LC 96-17392. 112p. (Orig.). (C). 1996. pap. text ed. 9.50 (*0-87338-560-8*) Kent St U Pr.

Soundings. Allan Chawner & Paul Kavanagh. (C). 1990. 60.00 (*0-7316-4447-6*, Pub. by Pascoe Pub AT) St Mut.

Soundings. Liam Davison. (Orig.). 1993. pap. 14.95 (*0-7022-2462-6*, Pub. by Univ Queensland Pr AT) Intl Spec Bk.

Soundings. Sally Gibbs. LC 92-91114. 104p. 1993. pap. 9.00 (*1-56002-267-1*, Univ Edtns) Aegina Pr.

Soundings. Ed. by Carol Spelius. 240p. 1985. pap. 7.95 (*0-317-60866-5*) Lake Shore Pub.

Soundings. Quincy Troupe. 1988. 14.95 (*0-86316-002-6*); pap. 8.95 (*0-86316-102-2*) Writers & Readers.

Soundings: Cross Channel Photographic Mission. Ed. by Jane Alison. (Illus.). 108p. (C). 1994. pap. 29.95 (*0-9517427-5-2*, Pub. by Lund Humphries UK) Antique Collect.

Soundings: Music in the Twentieth Century. Glenn Watkins. (Illus.). 728p. 1987. 40.00 (*0-02-873290-1*) Schirmer Bks.

Soundings: On Shakespeare, Modern Poetry, Plato & Other Subjects. Albert Cook. LC 90-22103. 254p. 1991. text ed. 34.95 (*0-8143-2331-6*) Wayne St U Pr.

Soundings at Tell Fakhariyah. Calvin W. McEwan et al. LC 57-11216. (Oriental Institute Publications: No. 79). (Illus.). 104p. 1958. lib. bdg. 48.00 (*0-226-62180-4*, OIP79) U Ch Pr.

***Soundings Book.** Bell. Date not set. pap. text ed. write for info. (*0-582-79539-7*, Drumbeat) Longman.

Soundings in Critical Theory. Dominick LaCapra. LC 89-30080. 248p. 1989. 36.50 (*0-8014-2322-8*); pap. 13.95 (*0-8014-9572-5*) Cornell U Pr.

Soundings in St. Augustine's Imagination. Robert J. O'Connell. LC 93-11257. 309p. 1995. 40.00 (*0-8232-1347-1*); pap. 19.95 (*0-8232-1348-X*) Fordham.

Soundings in Tibetan Civilization. Barbara N. Aziz & Matthew Kapstein. 1986. 32.00 (*0-8364-1587-6*, Pub. by Manohar II) S Asia.

Soundings, NAPA Bulletin No. 10: Rapid & Reliable Research Methods for Practicing Anthropologists. Ed. by John Van Willigen & Timothy L. Finan. 1991. 7.50 (*0-913167-43-6*) Am Anthro Assn.

Soundings of Things Done: Essays in Early Modern Literature in Honor of S. K. Heninger Jr. Ed. by Peter E. Medine & Joseph Wittreich. LC 96-1363. (Illus.). 344p. 1997. 48.50 (*0-87413-606-7*) U Delaware Pr.

Soundings 1. Ed. by Stuart Hall & Doreen Massey. (C). 1995. pap. 19.95 (*0-85315-817-7*) Humanities.

Soundness in the Horse. Peter Gray. 245p. 1990. 95.00 (*0-85131-563-1*, Pub. by J A Allen & Co UK) St Mut.

Soundpieces Two: Interviews with American Composers. Cole Gagne. LC 93-34663. (Illus.). 568p. 1993. 52.50 (*0-8108-2710-7*) Scarecrow.

Sounds. Illus. by Tedd Arnold. (Nursery Rhyme Concept Bks.). 16p. (J). (ps). 1992. pap. 3.95 (*0-671-77826-9*, Litl Simon S&S) S&S Childrens.

Sounds. Wassily Kandinsky. LC 80-6211. (Illus.). 136p. 1981. 42.50 (*0-300-02510-6*); pap. 17.00 (*0-300-02664-1*) Yale U Pr.

Sounds a Little Fishy to Me. D. Amorosia. 56p. 1992. teacher ed., pap. 19.95 (*0-7935-2891-7*) H Leonard.

Sounds Abound, 2 Vols. Carter. (C). 1993. teacher ed., pap. 2.76 (*0-395-52931-X*) HM.

Sounds Abound: Listening, Rhyming & Reading. Hugh Catts & Tina Vartiainen. 1993. student ed., spiral bd. 34.95 (*1-55999-394-4*) LinguiSystems.

Sounds All Around: Initial & Final Consonants. Marilyn M. Toomey. (Illus.). 384p. 1989. pap. 19.95 (*0-923573-11-9*) Circuit Pubns.

Sounds & Colors of Power: The Sacred Metallurgical Technology of Ancient West Mexico. Dorothy Hosler. (Illus.). 416p. 1995. 50.00 (*0-262-08230-6*) MIT Pr.

Sounds & Images of the Fabulous Fifties: History of the Tahoe Truckee Unified School District: 1949-1956. Everett V. O'Rourke. (Illus.). (Orig.). 1990. pap. text ed. 10.00 (*0-9621369-1-3*) E ORourke.

Sounds & Inflections of the Greek Dialects, Vol. 1: Ionic. Herbert W. Smyth. xxvii, 668p. 1974. reprint ed. 115.70 (*3-487-05317-9*) G Olms Pubs.

Sounds & Letters see Reading Readiness Program

***Sounds & Letters for Readers & Spellers: Phoneme Awareness Drills for Teachers & Speech-Language Pathologists.** Jane F. Greene. (Language!). 82p. (Orig.). 1997. pap. text ed. 9.95 (*1-57035-126-0*, C 74 Sounds) Sopris.

Sounds & Light of Bethlehem. Betty L. Schwab. 1992. pap. 2.75 (*1-55673-454-9*, 9250) CSS OH.

Sounds & Music. Robin Kerrod. LC 90-25543. (Secrets of Science Ser.: Group 2). (Illus.). 32p. (J). (gr. 3-8). 1991. lib. bdg. 10.95 (*1-85435-270-9*) Marshall Cavendish.

Sounds & Phonemes of Wulfila's Gothic. James W. Marchand. (Janua Linguarum, Series Practica: No. 25). 1973. pap. text ed. 49.25 (*90-279-2432-5*) Mouton.

Sounds & Rhythm: A Pronunciation Course. 2nd ed. Williard Sheeler. 1991. pap. text ed. 17.50 (*0-13-834003-X*, 640203) P-H.

Sounds & Scores. Henry Mancini. 1995. pap. text ed. 29.95 incl. audio (*0-89898-666-4*, P0732SMXAT) Warner Brothers.

Sounds & Scores. Henry Mancini. 1995. pap. text ed. 32.95 incl. cd-rom (*0-89898-667-2*, P0732SMXCD) Warner Brothers.

***Sounds & Society.** Martin. 1997. text ed. 24.95 (*0-7190-3224-5*) St Martin.

Sounds & Spelling Patterns of English: Phonics for Teachers & Parents. Phyllis E. Fischer. 141p. (Orig.). 1993. pap. 17.95 (*1-881929-01-9*) Oxton Hse Pubs.

Sounds & Symbols in American English: Keys to Phonics & Spelling Patterns. Bea Schramm. 70p. 1994. spiral bd. 12.50 (*0-9640725-0-5*) B Schramm.

Sounds Around Us. Seth H. Wittner. (Illus.). 32p. (Orig.). (J). (ps). 1988. Incl. audio-cassette. 11.95 incl. audio (*0-9619269-8-8*) Sound World Record.

Sounds Around Us. Seth H. Wittner. (Illus.). 32p. (Orig.). (J). (ps up). 1988. pap. write for info. incl. audio (*0-614-04796-X*) Sound World Record.

Sounds Easy! Sharron Bassano. (Sounds Easy Ser.). (Illus.). 57p. 1980. pap. text ed. 5.50 (*0-13-829821-1*); audio 10.95 (*0-88084-041-2*) Alemany Pr.

Sounds, Feelings, Thoughts: Seventy Poems by Wislawa Szymborska. Wislawa Szymborska. Tr. by Magnus J. Krynski & Robert A. Maguire from POL. LC 80-8579. (Lockert Library of Poetry in Translation). 261p. (C). 1981. reprint ed. pap. 12.95 (*0-691-01380-2*) Princeton U Pr.

Sounds for Little Folks. Clara B. Stoddard. 1973. text ed. 6.00 (*0-686-09395-X*) Expression.

Sounds for Sax Vol. 2: Alto - Tenor. Richard Pepper. pap. 8.95 (*0-7119-2056-7*, CH55658) Shawnee Pr.

Sounds from the Bell Jar: Ten Psychotic Authors. Gordon Claridge et al. LC 89-70354. 290p. 1990. text ed. 45.00 (*0-312-04632-4*) St Martin.

Sounds from the Heart: Learning to Listen to Girls. Maureen Barbieri. LC 94-45705. 249p. 1995. pap. text ed. 20.00 (*0-435-08843-2*, 08843) Heinemann.

Sounds Great. Beverly Beisbier. LC 93-41029. 1994. pap. 21.95 (*0-8384-3964-0*) Heinle & Heinle.

Sounds Great. Beverly Beisbier. (College ESL Ser.: Bk. 1). 1994. teacher ed., pap. 7.95 (*0-8384-4272-2*) Heinle & Heinle.

Sounds Great. Beverly Beisbier. (College ESL Ser.). (C). 1994. pap. 21.95 (*0-8384-4273-0*) Heinle & Heinle.

Sounds Great. Beverly Beisbier. (College ESL Ser.: Bk. 2). 1994. teacher ed., pap. 7.95 (*0-8384-4275-7*) Heinle & Heinle.

Sounds Great. Beverly Beisbier. (College ESL Ser.: Bk. 2). 1994. suppl. ed. 36.95 incl. audio (*0-8384-4274-9*) Heinle & Heinle.

Sounds in Stories - Long Vowel Sounds. Carole Osterink & Beth Spencer. Ed. by J. Friedland & R. Kessler. (Novel-Ties Ser.). 1993. student ed., pap. text ed. 20.95 (*1-56982-031-7*) Lrn Links.

Sounds in Stories - Short Vowel Sounds. Carole Osterink & Beth Spencer. Ed. by J. Friedland & R. Kessler. (Novel-Ties Ser.). 1993. student ed., pap. text ed. 20.95 (*1-56982-033-3*) Lrn Links.

Sounds Interesting: The Science of Acoustics. David Darling. LC 91-4002. (Experiment! Ser.). (Illus.). 60p. (J). (gr. 4-6). 1991. lib. bdg. 13.95 (*0-87518-477-4*, Dillon Silver Burdett) Silver Burdett Pr.

Sounds Intriguing: Resource Material for Teachers. Alan Maley & Alan Duff. 73p. 1979. pap. text ed. 12.95 (*0-521-22138-2*); digital audio 17.95 (*0-521-22135-8*) Cambridge U Pr.

Sounds Like - Looks Like Wordbook, No. 4. Jeannette A. Fidell. 1992. pap. write for info. (*1-881124-03-7*) Ctr Creat Endeavors.

Sounds Like Business: Improving English Pronunciation Skills in the Business World, Set 6. Sheri Miller & Berry Garber. 77p. (C). 1994. audio write for info. (*0-9640809-0-7*) S Miller.

Sounds Like Life: Sound-Symbolic Grammar, Performance, & Cognition in Pastaza Quechua. Janis B. Nuckolls. (Oxford Studies in Anthropological Linguistics). (Illus.). 312p. 1996. 65.00 (*0-19-508985-5*) OUP.

***Sounds Like That!** Thomas-Cochran. (What a Wonderful World Intro Ser.). 1993. pap. text ed. write for info. (*0-582-91076-5*, Pub. by Longman UK) Longman.

Sounds Like Wordbook, No. 1. Jeannette A. Fidell. 69p. 1992. pap. write for info. (*1-881124-00-2*) Ctr Creat Endeavors.

Sounds Like Wordbook: Words Often Confused & Misspelled, No. 2. Jeannette A. Fidell. 69p. 1992. pap. write for info. (*1-881124-01-0*) Ctr Creat Endeavors.

Sounds of a Cowhide Drum. Oswald J. Mtshali & Nadine Gordimer. LC 73-183198. 96p. 1972. 15.95 (*0-89388-034-5*); pap. 9.95 (*0-89388-035-3*) Okpaku Communications.

Sounds of American English: A Handbook for English as a Foreign Language, English-Vietnamese Edition. Virginia F. Allen & Cao Quan. 49p. 1986. teacher ed. 8.95 (*0-940723-04-2*) SIIS.

Sounds of American English: A Handbook for English As a Second Language. Virginia F. Allen. 33p. 1989. teacher ed. 5.00 (*0-940723-06-9*) SIIS.

***Sounds of Christmas.** Ed. by Carol Cuellar. 128p. (Orig.). (YA). 1996. pap. text ed. 9.95 (*1-57623-589-0*, AF9680) Warner Brothers.

Sounds of Creation: Genesis in Song Sounds of Freedom: Exodus in Song: A Contemporary Anthology Featuring a Song for Every Torah Portion in the Books of Genesis & Exodus. Ed. & Tr. by Randee Friedman. 1988. audio 10.95 (*1-890161-00-4*) Sounds Write.

***Sounds of Creation: Genesis in Song Sounds of Freedom: Exodus in Song: A Contemporary Anthology Featuring a Song for Every Torah Portion in the Books of Genesis & Exodus.** Ed. & Tr. by Randee Friedman. 1991. audio 10.95 (*1-890161-01-2*) Sounds Write.

Sounds of Creation: Genesis in Song Sounds of Freedom: Exodus in Song: A Contemporary Anthology Featuring a Song for Every Torah Portion in the Books of Genesis & Exodus. Ed. & Tr. by Randee Friedman. 1992. audio compact disk 17.95 (*1-890161-02-0*) Sounds Write.

Sounds of Creation: Genesis in Song Sounds of Freedom: Exodus in Song: A Contemporary Anthology Featuring a Song for Every Torah Portion in the Books of Genesis & Exodus. Ed. & Tr. by Randee Friedman. 92p. (ENG & HEB.). 1992. per. 19.95 (*0-9626286-2-X*) Sounds Write.

Sounds of Cyberspace: Rock, Pop, & Alternative Music on the Internet. Victoria Bell. (Go! Guides Ser.). (Illus.). 64p. (Orig.). 1996. pap. 10.95 (*1-57712-013-2*) Motion Works.

Sounds of Disaster. 2nd ed. Wes Oleszewski. LC 92-75915. (Illus.). 144p. 1993. pap. 11.95 (*0-932212-76-X*) Avery Color.

Sounds of English. Keith D. Holmes. Set. teacher ed. 25.00 (*0-9608250-4-5*); disk 25.00 (*0-9608250-3-7*) Educ Serv Pub.

Sounds of English & Italian. Frederick B. Agard & Robert J. DiPietro. LC 65-25118. (Midway Reprint, Contrastive Structure Ser.). (Illus.). 83p. reprint ed. pap. 25.00 (*0-685-23840-7*, 2056621) Bks Demand.

Sounds of French: An Introduction. Bernard Tranel. (Illus.). 256p. 1987. text ed. 59.95 (*0-521-30443-1*); pap. text ed. 19.95 (*0-521-31510-7*) Cambridge U Pr.

Sounds of French: An Introduction. Bernard Tranel. (Illus.). 256p. 1988. digital audio 19.95 (*0-521-35002-6*) Cambridge U Pr.

Sounds of Jazz, Bk. 1. Tony Caramia. 16p. 1983. pap. text ed. 3.50 (*0-913277-01-0*) Summy-Birchard.

Sounds of Jazz, Bk. 2. Tony Caramia. 16p. 1983. pap. text ed. 3.50 (*0-913277-02-9*) Summy-Birchard.

Sounds of Language: An Inquiry into the Role of Genetic Factors in the Development of Sound Systems. Leonard F. Brosnahan. LC 82-975. 250p. 1982. reprint ed. text ed. 55.00 (*0-313-23353-5*, BRSOL, Greenwood Pr) Greenwood.

Sounds of Latin. Roland G. Kent. (Language Monographs: Vol. 12). 1932. 25.00 (*0-527-00816-8*) Periodicals Srv.

Sounds of Life. Dolores Conley. LC 92-60291. 50p. 1993. 6.95 (*1-55523-526-3*) Winston-Derek.

Sounds of Movies: Interviews with Creators of Feature Sound Tracks. Nicholas Pasquariello. 240p. (Orig.). 1996. pap. 19.95 (*0-9653114-7-3*) Port Bridge.

***Sounds of Music: Perception & Notation.** Gerald Eskelin. (Illus.). 250p. (Orig.). 1997. pap. write for info. incl. audio compact disk (*0-614-29769-9*) Stage Three.

***Sounds of Music: Perception & Notation.** Gerald R. Eskelin. (Illus.). 250p. 1997. 32.50 (*1-886209-13-8*) Stage Three.

Sounds of Orchestra, 2 Vols. Hopkins. 1995. pap. 10.00 (*0-19-521150-2*) OUP.

Sounds of People & Places: Readings in the Geography of American Folk & Popular Music. Ed. by George O. Carney. LC 87-10481. (Illus.). 362p. (Orig.). (C). 1987. pap. text ed. 26.00 (*0-8191-6414-3*) U Pr of Amer.

Sounds of People & Places: Readings in the Geography of American Folk & Popular Music. 2nd ed. Ed. by George O. Carney. 320p. (Orig.). (C). 1993. lib. bdg. 62.50 (*0-8476-7787-7*) Rowman.

Sounds of People & Places: Readings in the Geography of American Folk & Popular Music. 2nd ed. Ed. by George O. Carney. 356p. (Orig.). (C). 1994. pap. text ed. 27.95 (*0-8476-7788-5*) Rowman.

Sounds of Poetry Vol. 1, Bk. 1: The Simple Sad Collection. Randel Horton. Ed. by Melanie Hampton. 90p. 1996. pap. 6.95 (*0-9650836-0-8*) Sounds of Poetry.

Sounds of Rescue, the Signs of Hope. Robert Flynn. LC 89-4809. (Texas Tradition Ser.: No. 12). 278p. 1989. reprint ed. pap. 11.95 (*0-87565-039-2*) Tex Christian.

Sounds of Science. Barbara S. Dreher. LC 89-52116. (Illus.). 44p. (J). (gr. k-3). 1990. 5.95 (*1-55523-310-4*) Winston-Derek.

Sounds of Silence. Marlyn Levy. Date not set. pap. 1.50 (*0-590-03166-X*) Scholastic Inc.

Sounds of Silence: Japanese Women. John R. Terry. 176p. 1988. pap. 9.95 (*0-933704-69-0*) Dawn Pr.

Sounds of Silence, Sounds of Fury. Domini Torrevillas-Suarez. 114p. (Orig.). (C). 1989. pap. 10.75 (*971-10-0368-6*, Pub. by New Day Pub PH) Cellar.

Sounds of Summer. David Updike. (Illus.). 40p. (J). (gr. 2-5). 1993. 15.95 (*0-945912-20-X*) Pippin Pr.

Sounds of the Diseased Heart. Aldo A. Luisada. LC 74-176171. (Illus.). 416p. 1973. text ed. 27.60 (*0-87527-113-8*) Green.

Sounds of the Farm: Big Book. Kari J. Gold. Ed. by Janet Reed. (Early Learning Program Ser.). (Illus.). 16p. (J). (ps-1). 1996. pap. 14.95 (*1-56784-304-2*) Newbridge Comms.

Sounds of the Farm: Mini Book. Kari J. Gold. Ed. by Janet Reed. (Early Learning Program Ser.). (Illus.). 16p. (J). (ps-1). 1996. pap. 2.95 (*1-56784-329-8*) Newbridge Comms.

Sounds of the Girgenti Dialect, & Their Development. Luigi Pirandello. Tr. & Intro. by Giovanni R. Bussino. LC 92-21618. (American University Studies: Linguistics: Ser. XIII, Vol. 18). 228p. (C). 1992. text ed. 45.95 (*0-8204-1457-3*) P Lang Pubng.

Sounds of the Morning Sun. Diane V. Cirincione. LC 93-33200. 192p. 1993. 15.00 (*1-56170-073-8*, 113) Hay House.

Sounds of the Normal Heart. Aldo A. Luisada. LC 78-176172. (Illus.). 280p. 1972. 27.60 (*0-87527-051-4*) Green.

Sounds of the Orchestra. Anthony Hopkins. (Illus.). 176p. (C). pap. write for info. (*0-19-816517-X*) OUP.

Sounds of the Orchestra. Anthony Hopkins. (Illus.). 176p. (C). 1993. pap. 7.95 (*0-19-521027-1*, 7782) OUP.

Sounds of the River Naranjana. Armand Schwerner. LC 82-16910. 128p. 1983. 15.95 (*0-930794-59-1*); pap. 6.95 (*0-930794-60-5*) Station Hill Pr.

Sounds of the River Naranjana. deluxe limited ed. Armand Schwerner. LC 82-16910. 128p. 1983. 30.00 (*0-88268-032-3*) Station Hill Pr.

Sounds of the Sacred: Chants of Love & Prayer. Ed. by JoAnn Levitt & Todd Norian. LC 90-62313. (Illus.). 158p. (Orig.). pap. 14.95 (*0-940258-23-4*) Kripalu Pubns.

Sounds of the Season, Vol. 1. Maggie Sansone. 7.95 (*1-56222-865-X*, 95021); audio 10.98 (*1-56222-866-8*, 95021C); cd-rom 15.98 (*1-56222-867-6*, 95021CD) Mel Bay.

S

An Asterisk (*) at the beginning of an entry indicates that the title is appearing in BIP for the first time.

***Sounds of the Season, Vol. 1.** Maggie Sansone. 22.95 incl. audio compact disk (0-7866-1177-4, 95021CDP); 17.95 incl. audio (0-7866-1178-2, 95021P) Mel Bay.

***Sounds of the Season, Vol. 2.** Maggie Sansone. 7.95 (0-7866-2579-1, 95566); 22.95 incl. audio compact disk (0-7866-2598-8, 95566CDP); 17.95 incl. audio (0-7866-2599-6, 95566P); audio 10.98 (0-7866-0625-8, 95566C); audio compact disk 15.98 (0-7866-0626-6, 95566CD) Mel Bay.

Sounds of the South. Ed. by Daniel W. Patterson. LC 91-30427. (Illus.). 219p. 1991. pap. text ed. 15.95 (0-8223-1343-X) Duke.

Sounds of the World's Languages. Peter Ladefoged & Ian Maddieson. (Phonological Theory Ser.). (Illus.). 400p. (C). 1995. pap. 31.95 (0-631-19815-6) Blackwell Pubs.

Sounds of the 60's. 10.95 (0-7935-4910-8, 00310079) H Leonard.

Sounds of the 70's. (Big Note Ser.). 10.95 (0-7935-4911-6, 00310080) H Leonard.

Sounds of Valley Streams: Enlightenment in Dogen's Zen: Translation of Nine Essays from Shobogenzo. Francis H. Cook. LC 88-12180. (SUNY Series in Buddhist Studies). 164p. 1988. text ed. 59.50 (0-88706-922-3); pap. text ed. 19.95 (0-88706-924-X) State U NY Pr.

Sounds of Yourself. Theta Burke. LC 76-48010. 1977. pap. 5.95 (0-916872-02-5) Delafield Pr.

Sounds So Good to Me: The Bluesman's Story. Barry L. Pearson. LC 83-14764. (Illus.). 186p. 1984. pap. 19.95 (0-8122-1171-5) U of Pa Pr.

Sounds Speech Communication. 2nd ed. Pickett. 1996. text ed. write for info. (0-205-19887-2) Allyn.

Sounds That Arouse Me: Selected Writings. Bern Porter. LC 91-67868. 128p. (Orig.). 1992. pap. 9.95 (0-88448-101-8) Tilbury Hse.

Soundscape: Our Sonic Environment & the Tuning of the World. R. Murray Schafer. 320p. 1993. pap. 14.95 (0-89281-455-1) Inner Tradit.

Soundscape with Humans. Tony Perez. (Orig.). 1974. pap. 1.50 (0-915242-02-8) Pygmalion Pr.

***Soundtrack Selections from "The Mambo Kings"** Ed. by Carol Cuellar. 28p. (Orig.). (C). 1992. pap. text ed. 10.95 (0-7692-0699-9, VF1834) Warner Brothers.

***Soundtracks.** Harmer. Date not set. pap. text ed. write for info. (0-582-01853-6, Pub. by Longman UK) Longman.

Soundtracks: A Study of Auditory Perception, Memory, & Valuation. Jean G. Harrell. 117p. 28.95 (0-87975-334-X) Prometheus Bks.

Soup. Robert N. Peck. LC 73-15117. (Illus.). 104p. (J). (gr. 3 up). 1974. lib. bdg. 14.99 (0-394-92700-1) Knopf Bks Yng Read.

Soup. Robert N. Peck. 112p. (J). (gr. 3 up). 1979. pap. 3.50 (0-440-48186-4, YB BDD) BDD Bks Young Read.

Soup. 2nd ed. Coralie Castle. LC 92-30791. (One Hundred One Productions Ser.). (Illus.). 192p. 1993. reprint ed. pap. 11.95 (1-56426-552-8, One Hund One Prods) Cole Group.

Soup Ahoy. Robert N. Peck. LC 93-14097. (Illus.). 144p. (J). (gr. 2-6). 1994. lib. bdg. 15.99 (0-679-94978-X) Knopf Bks Yng Read.

Soup Ahoy. Robert N. Peck. 1995. pap. 4.50 (0-679-87617-0) Random.

Soup Alive! Eleanor S. Rosenast. LC 93-6656. (Illus.). 196p. (Orig.). 1993. pap. 9.95 (0-88007-198-2) Woodbridge Pr.

Soup & Stew Sampler. Jan Siegrist. (Illus.). 48p. (Orig.). 1993. pap. 3.95 (1-881535-06-1) New Eng Pr VT.

Soup Bible. David P. Larousse. LC 96-25881. 260p. 1997. text ed. 49.95 (0-471-13562-3) Wiley.

Soup Bone. Tony Johnston. (Illus.). 32p. (J). (ps-3). 1990. 13.00 (0-15-277255-3) HarBrace.

Soup Bone. Tony Johnston. (Illus.). 32p. (J). (ps-3). 1992. pap. 5.00 (0-15-277256-1, HB Juv Bks) HarBrace.

Soup Book. Louis P. De Gouy. LC 73-88332. 428p. 1974. reprint ed. pap. 7.95 (0-486-22998-X) Dover.

Soup Collection. Ed. by Elaine M. Myers. 1995. write for info. (0-944943-55-1, 25272-8) Current Inc.

Soup Diet. Rudolf E. Noble. 80p. 1993. pap. 9.95 (1-885078-04-8) Noble Enter.

Soup Du Jour: Healthy Homemade Soups for All Seasons. Wendy Esko. (Basic Macrobiotic Cooking Ser.: Vol. 2). (Illus.). 96p. (Orig.). 1996. pap. 8.95 (1-882984-19-6) One Peaceful World.

Soup for President. Robert N. Peck. LC 77-3548. (Illus.). (J). (gr. 6 up). 1978. lib. bdg. 10.99 (0-394-93675-2) Knopf Bks Yng Read.

Soup for President. Robert N. Peck. 112p. (J). (gr. 3-6). 1986. reprint ed. pap. 3.99 (0-440-48188-0, YB BDD) BDD Bks Young Read.

***Soup from a Can.** Jackie Gannaway. 32p. 1997. pap. 3.95 (1-885597-20-7) Cookbook Cup.

Soup in Love. Robert N. Peck. 128p. (J). (gr. 4-7). 1993. pap. 3.50 (0-440-40755-9) Dell.

Soup in the Saddle. Robert N. Peck. LC 82-14010. (Illus.). 96p. (J). (gr. 3-6). 1983. lib. bdg. 11.99 (0-394-95294-4) Knopf Bks Yng Read.

Soup on Ice. Robert N. Peck. LC 85-218. (Illus.). 128p. (J). (gr. 3-7). 1985. lib. bdg. 13.99 (0-394-97613-4) Knopf Bks Yng Read.

Soup Pot: Stories for All Seasons for Children of All Ages. Ethel Pochocki. (Illus.). 112p. (Orig.). 1996. pap. 8.95 (1-878718-33-9) Resurrection.

***Soup 'R Sandwich Sampler.** Date not set. write for info. (0-9637312-8-9) Jac-Lynn Ent.

Soup 'R Sandwich Sampler. Ferne C. Chapman. 64p. (Orig.). 1990. pap. 7.50 (1-880222-02-7) Red Apple Pub.

Soup Should Be Seen, Not Heard: The Kids' Etiquette Book. Beth Brainard & Sheila Behr. 160p. 1990. pap. 12.95 (0-440-50333-7, Dell Trade Pbks) Dell.

Soup Suppers: Over One Hundred Soup Recipes & Forty Accompaniments. Arthur Schwartz. LC 93-29399. 288p. (Orig.). 1994. pap. 15.00 (0-06-096948-2, PL) HarpC.

Soup 1776. Robert N. Peck. 160p. (J). 1995. lib. bdg. 17.99 (0-679-97320-6) Knopf.

Soup 1776. Robert N. Peck. LC 94-23879. (Illus.). 160p. (J). 1995. 16.00 (0-679-87320-1) Knopf.

Soupault: Collected Poems, Vol. 1. Philippe Soupault. Tr. by Alex Gordon from FRE. 201p. (Orig.). 1998. pap. 19.95 (0-7145-4190-7) Riverrun NY.

Soupe au Choux. Rene Fallet. 288p. (FRE.). 1983. pap. 10.95 (0-7859-2475-2, 2070374793) Fr & Eur.

Souper Skinny Soups. Yolanda Fintor & Carla L. Henry. LC 93-3597. (Illus.). 288p. 1993. pap. 14.95 (0-88289-954-6) Pelican.

Soupes Fantastique De Monique: From the Artist Palette Cafe. Monique Fisher. 80p. 1994. pap. 7.00 (0-9640198-1-7) Strawbry Press.

***Souping the Stock Engine.** Roger Huntington. (Illus.). 192p. 1997. pap. 14.95 (1-55561-137-0) Fisher Bks.

Souping up Your Sound Card. Gurewich. 1994. pap. text ed. 27.95 (0-07-911881-X) McGraw.

***Soupline Cookbook.** Elliott & James Publishing Staff. 1997. pap. text ed. 12.95 (0-9637899-4-5) Elliott & James Pubs.

Soups. (Popular Brands Cookbooks Ser.). (Illus.). 24p. 1995. pap. write for info. (1-56144-675-0) Modern Pub NYC.

***Soups.** LC 97-14911. 72p. 1997. pap. 6.95 (0-7894-1980-7) DK Pub Inc.

Soups. Janice W. Braeder. 36p. (Orig.). 1983. pap. 3.25 (0-940844-17-6) Wellspring.

Soups. Norman Kolpas. Ed. by Laurie Wertz. LC 93-16086. (Williams-Sonoma Kitchen Library). (Illus.). 108p. 1993. 17.95 (0-7835-0250-8); lib. bdg. write for info. (0-7835-0251-6) Time-Life.

Soups. Jeannette Seaver. 214p. 1983. 13.95 (0-86579-031-0) Seaver Bks.

***Soups.** Smithmark Staff. (Little Cookbook Ser.). 1996. 6.98 (0-7651-9821-5) Smithmark.

Soups. Louise Stoltzfus. (Best of Favorite Recipes from Quilters Ser.). 1994. 7.95 (1-56148-112-2) Good Bks PA.

Soups: Cook Books from Amish Kitchens. Phyllis P. Good & Rachel T. Pellman. (From Amish Kitchens Ser.). 32p. 1996. mass mkt. 2.95 (1-56148-194-7) Good Bks PA.

Soups: Souper Starters. Ed. by G & R Publishing Staff. (Uni-Bks.). 160p. (Orig.). 1994. pap. text ed. 3.00 (1-56383-022-1, 2600) G & R Pub.

Soups: The International Market. Euromonitor Staff. 120p. (C). 1988. 2,925.00 (0-685-30330-6, Pub. by Euromonitor Pubns UK) Gale.

Soups see Great Cook's Guide to Appetizers

Soups & Appetizers. Carolyn Garner. 64p. 1995. write for info. (1-57215-021-1) World Pubns.

***Soups & Broths.** Smithmark Staff. (Cooking for Today Ser.). 1996. 4.98 (0-7651-9856-8) Smithmark.

Soups & Muffins: Nutritious & Delicious. 2nd rev. ed. Sue Gregg & Emilie Barnes. (Eating Better Cookbooks: Basic Set: Vol. 3). (Illus.). 102p. 1994. spiral bd. 7.00 (1-878272-04-7) Eating Better.

Soups & Salads: Traditional American Recipes. Frances T. Geidt. LC 96-7241. (Heartland Cooking Ser.). (Illus.). 1996. write for info. (0-89577-877-7) RD Assn.

Soups & Salads...with Love. Jeannine B. Browning. 1994. pap. write for info. (0-9627729-4-1) J B Browning.

Soups & Starters. Creative Cooking Library Staff. (Creative Cooking Library). 1995. 10.98 (0-8317-5343-9) Smithmark.

Soups & Stews. (Deluxe Color Cookbook Ser.). (Illus.). 64p. Date not set. text ed. write for info. (1-56987-140-X) Landoll.

Soups & Stews. Corinne T. Netzer. (Corinne T. Netzer Good Eating Gourmet Ser.: Bk. 5). 1997. mass mkt. 5.99 (0-440-22340-7) Dell.

Soups & Stews: Stocks to One Pot Meals. 2nd ed. Cynthia Sheer. 128p. 1995. reprint ed. pap. 11.95 (1-56426-066-6) Cole Group.

Soups & Stews Collection. Date not set. 25.95 (0-916103-25-0) Am Express Food.

Soups & Stews Cookbook. Barbara Grunes. (Illus.). 64p. (Orig.). 1988. pap. 3.95 (0-8249-3043-6) Ideals.

***Soups & Stones from the Realm of Queen Arnold.** Penrod Waterman & Richard Elms. Date not set. pap. write for info. (0-7880-0662-2) CSS OH.

Soups & Vegetables - les Potages et Legumes. Illus. by Nadine Wickenden. LC 94-14137. (Marie-Pierre Moine's French Kitchen Ser.). (ENG & FRE.). 1994. 14.00 (0-671-89660-1) S&S Trade.

Soups, Chowders & Gumbos. Carter. 1991. pap. 11.00 (1-55788-014-X, HP Books) Berkley Pub.

Soups from A - Z 1994. Frances Levine. 59p. 1994. spiral bd. 14.95 (0-938911-08-2) Indiv Educ Syst.

Soups from Around the World. Kay S. Nelson. 1993. pap. 14.95 (0-8128-8552-X, Scrbrough Hse) Madison Bks UPA.

Soup's Hoop. Robert N. Peck. 144p. (J). (gr. 4-7). 1992. pap. 3.50 (0-440-40589-0, YB BDD) BDD Bks Young Read.

***Soups of the People.** Lois A. Rothert. Date not set. write for info. (0-688-11819-4) Morrow.

***Soup's On! Hot Recipes from Cool Chefs.** Gail Hobbs & Bob Carter. LC 96-94804. 192p. (Orig.). 1997. pap. 12.95 (0-9642012-1-6) Gold Coast Pr.

***Soups On! Vegetarian Soups, Muffins & Accompaniments.** Barb Bloomfield. LC 97-25156. 1997. write for info. (1-57067-047-1) Book Pub Co.

***Soups, Salads, Memories of Milo, Vol. 1.** Kathryn R. Vaclav. (Illus.). 148p. 1997. pap. 9.95 (0-9656522-0-3) Milo Indust.

***Soups, Stews & Chowders.** Sheila Kaufman. 1997. pap. text ed. 9.95 (1-883283-15-9) Brick Tower.

***Soups, Stews, & Quick Breads: Hearty Homestyle Recipes.** Janet Thompson. 175p. (Orig.). 1997. pap. 14.95 (1-57416-002-8) Clear Light.

Soups, Stews Etc. Cy DeCosse Incorporated Staff. LC 95-48229. (Meals for Life Ser.). (Illus.). 112p. 1996. spiral bd. 14.95 (0-86573-985-4) Cowles Creative.

Soupsongs & Webster's Ark. Roy Blount, Jr. 1988. 12.95 (0-317-67391-2) HM.

Sour Dough & the Navajos. Ione B. Jones. (Illus.). 40p. 1990. 6.95 (0-943480-70-1) Friis-Pioneer Pr.

Sour Grapes: Studies in the Subversion of Rationality. Jon Elster. LC 82-22034. 220p. 1983. text ed. 80.00 (0-521-25230-X) Cambridge U Pr.

Sour Grapes: Studies in the Subversion of Rationality. Jon Elster. 220p. 1985. pap. text ed. 23.95 (0-521-31368-6) Cambridge U Pr.

Sour Land. William H. Armstrong. LC 70-135783. 128p. (J). (gr. 6 up). 1991. lib. bdg. 14.89 (0-06-020142-8) HarpC Child Bks.

Sour Land. William H. Armstrong. LC 70-135783. (Trophy Bk.). 128p. (YA). (gr. 7 up). 1992. reprint ed. pap. 3.95 (0-06-440074-3, Trophy) HarpC Child Bks.

Sour Prince. Ed Flesch. 24p. 1972. pap. 3.25 (0-88680-180-X); Piano-Vocal Score. pap. 5.00 (0-88680-181-8) I E Clark.

Source. James A. Michener. 1088p. 1986. mass mkt. 6.99 (0-449-21147-9, Crest) Fawcett.

Source. James A. Michener. 1965. 45.00 (0-394-44630-5) Random.

Source. James A. Michener. 1995. reprint ed. lib. bdg. 39.95 (1-56849-611-7) Buccaneer Bks.

Source, Vol. 1. Steve Barta. 96p. 1987. pap. 12.95 (0-937589-00-4, 00240885) H Leonard.

***Source: A Guidebook of American Genealogy.** rev. ed. Loretto D. Szucs et al. LC 96-41402. 846p. 1996. 49.95 (0-916489-67-1) Ancestry.

Source: A Reference Guide to Information & Resources. 3rd ed. Randall L. Voight & Ronald Olson. LC 78-51744. (Illus.). 1986. 12.00 (0-930318-03-X); pap. 7.95 (0-930318-04-8) Intl Res Eval.

Source: A Resource Guide for Using Creative Arts in Church Services. Scott Dyer & Nancy Beach. 352p. 1996. pap. 49.99 (0-310-50021-4) Zondervan.

Source: Necroscope III. Brian Lumley. 1989. mass mkt. 4.95 (0-8125-2127-7) Tor Bks.

Source see History of Roman Private Law

Source Adventure. Janet McClure. Ed. by Lillian Harben. 157p. (Orig.). 1988. pap. 11.95 (0-929385-06-3) Light Tech Comns Servs.

Source & Migration Processes & Evaluation Techniques. Ed. by Robert K. Merrill. (Treatise of Petroleum Geology, Handbook of Petroleum Geology Ser.). (Illus.). 213p. 1991. 10.00 (0-89181-600-3, 436) AAPG.

Source & Sediment: A Case Study of Provenance & Mass Balance at an Active Plate Margin, Calabria, Southern Italy. Ed. by H. Ibbeken & R. Schleyer. (Illus.). x, 286p. 1991. 185.95 (0-387-53282-X) Spr-Verlag.

Source & Temple Doors Editions 1980-1992: Doctrine of Sacred Inner Mysteries, 3 bks., Set. Maia C. Shamayyim. (Source/Temple Doors - Back Issues Ser.). (Illus.). 797p. 1992. spiral bd. 98.00 (1-888420-20-0) Johannine Grove.

Source Book: A Presentation of Demographic & Social Data for Nashville/Davidson County. Center for Social Research Staff. 69p. 1995. spiral bd. 29.95 (1-888334-02-9) Coun Commun Serv.

Source Book for African Anthropology, Set, Pts. 1-2. W. D. Hambly. (Field Museum of Natural History Ser.: Vol. 26). (Illus.). 1937. Set. 68.00 (0-527-01886-4) Periodicals Srv.

Source Book for Creative Problem Solving: A Fifty Year Digest of Proven Innovation Processes. Ed. by Sidney J. Parnes. (Orig.). 1992. pap. 37.95 (0-930222-92-X) Creat Educ Found.

Source Book for Electrophotography. Technical Association of the Pulp & Paper Industry Staff. LC 72-190595. (Technical Association of the Pulp & Paper Car Ser.: No. 42). 84p. reprint ed. pap. 25.00 (0-317-29315-X, 2022364) Bks Demand.

Source Book for Energy Auditors, 2 vols., Set. Ed. by M. D. Lyberg. 694p. (Orig.). 1987. pap. 170.00 (91-540-4763-3) Coronet Bks.

***Source Book for Graphic Arts Industry Information 1994.** 151p. 150.00 (0-614-25547-3, 00BT54007) Print Indus Am.

Source Book for Linguistics. William Cowan & Jeromira Rakusan. LC 85-26862. (Paperbacks Ser.: No. 5). xxvi, 338p. 1985. pap. 19.95 (0-915027-82-8) Benjamins North Am.

Source Book for Linkage in Man. Bronya J. Keats et al. LC 78-21207. 1979. 65.00 (0-8018-2188-6) Johns Hopkins.

Source Book for Medieval Economic History. Roy C. Cave & Herbert H. Coulson. LC 64-25840. 1936. 30.00 (0-8196-0145-4) Biblo.

Source Book for Medieval History. Oliver J. Thatcher & E. H. McNeal. LC 70-149676. reprint ed. 55.00 (0-404-06363-2) AMS Pr.

***Source Book for Modern Catechetics, Vol. 2.** Michael Warren. Ed. by Robert Stamschror. (Illus.). 496p. (Orig.). 1997. pap. 29.95 (0-88489-392-8) St Marys.

Source Book for Russian History from Early Times to 1917, 3 vols. Incl. Vol. 1. Early Times to Late 17th Century. George Vernadsky. Ed. by Ralph T. Fisher et al. LC 70-115369. 66.70 (0-685-07771-3); Vol. 3. Alexander Second to the February Revolution. George Vernadsky. Ed. by Ralph T. Fisher et al. LC 70-115369. 65.00 (0-685-07772-1); LC 70-115369. reprint ed. write for info. (0-318-57565-5, 2016776) Bks Demand.

Source Book for Teaching English As a Second Language. Michael Lewis & Jimmie Hill. 136p. 1993. pap. text ed. 22.00 (0-435-24060-9, 24060) Heinemann.

***Source Book for the Inland Fishery Resources of Africa Vol. 1: Angola, Botswana, Burundi, Central African Rep., Comoros, Congo, Kenya, Lesotho, Madagascar, Malawi, Mauritius, Mozambique, Namibia, Reunion, Rwanda, Seychelles, Swaziland, Tanzania, Uganda, Zaire, Zambia, Zimbabwe.** 424p. 1990. 50.00 (92-5-102983-0, Pub. by FAO IT) Bernan Associates.

Source Book for the Inland Fishery Resources of Africa, No. 18. J. P. Bossche & G. M. Bernacsek. (Commission for Inland Fisheries of Africa Technical Papers: No. 3). 252p. 1991. pap. 30.00 (92-5-103073-1, F0731, Pub. by FAO IT) Bernan Associates.

Source Book for the Study of Thomas Harriot. John W. Shirley. Ed. by I. Bernard Cohen. LC 80-2111. (Development of Science Ser.). (Illus.). 1981. lib. bdg. 55.95 (0-405-13831-8) Ayer.

Source Book Health Insurance. 35th ed. America Insurance Assoc. Staff. 1996. pap. text ed. 26.50 (1-879143-31-3) Health Ins Assn Am.

Source Book in Animal Biology. Thomas S. Hall. LC 74-120317. (Source Books in the History of the Sciences). 732p. 1951. 57.50 (0-674-82141-6) HUP.

Source Book in APL: Papers by Adin D. Falkoff & Kenneth E. Iverson. Ed. by Eugene E. McDonnell. 144p. (Orig.). 1981. pap. 15.00 (0-917326-10-5) APL Pr.

Source Book in Astronomy & Astrophysics, 1900-1975. Ed. by Kenneth R. Lang & Owen Gingerich. LC 78-9463. (Source Books in the History of the Sciences). 942p. 1979. 90.00 (0-674-82200-5) HUP.

Source Book in Chemistry, Nineteen Hundred to Nineteen Fifty. Henry M. Leicester. (Source Books in the History of the Sciences). 432p. 1968. 32.00 (0-674-82231-5) HUP.

Source Book in Chinese Philosophy. W. Chan. 874p. 1963. pap. text ed. 19.95 (0-691-01964-9) Princeton U Pr.

Source Book in Classical Analysis. Uta C. Merzbach. LC 72-85144. (Source Books in the History of the Sciences). 484p. reprint ed. pap. 138.00 (0-7837-4448-X, 2057978) Bks Demand.

Source Book in Failure Analysis: A Discriminative Selection of Outstanding Articles & Case Histories from the Periodical Literature. American Society for Metals Staff. LC 74-22347. (ASM Engineering Bookshelf Ser.). (Illus.). 414p. reprint ed. pap. 118.00 (0-317-09642-7, 2019492) Bks Demand.

Source Book in Geography. Ed. by George Kish. LC 77-25972. (Source Bks. in the History of the Sciences). (Illus.). 469p. reprint ed. pap. 133.70 (0-7837-6075-2, 2059121) Bks Demand.

Source Book in Geology, 1400-1900. Kirtley F. Mather & Shirley L. Mason. LC 67-12100. (Source Books in the History of the Sciences). (Illus.). 726p. reprint ed. pap. 180.00 (0-7837-3850-1, 2043672) Bks Demand.

Source Book in Greek Science. Morris R. Cohen & I. E. Drabkin. LC 58-12979. (Source Books in the History of the Sciences). (Illus.). 602p. reprint ed. pap. 171.60 (0-7837-4457-9, 2057987) Bks Demand.

Source Book in Mathematics. David E. Smith. 701p. 1984. reprint ed. pap. 13.95 (0-486-64690-4) Dover.

Source Book in Mathematics, 1200-1800. Dirk J. Struik. 448p. 1986. pap. text ed. 27.50 (0-691-02397-2) Princeton U Pr.

Source Book in Mathematics, 1200-1800. Dirk J. Struik. LC 68-21986. (Source Books in the History of the Sciences). 443p. reprint ed. pap. 126.30 (0-317-09449-1, 2017753) Bks Demand.

Source Book in Medieval Science. Ed. by Edward Grant. LC 70-183977. (Source Books in the History of the Sciences). (Illus.). 882p. reprint ed. pap. 180.00 (0-7837-4152-9, 2059000) Bks Demand.

Source Book in Physics. William F. Magie. LC 63-21307. (Source Books in the History of the Sciences). (Illus.). 634p. reprint ed. pap. 180.00 (0-7837-4118-9, 2057941) Bks Demand.

Source Book in the History of Psychology. Ed. by Richard J. Herrnstein & Edwin G. Boring. LC 65-11595. (Illus.). 653p. reprint ed. pap. 180.00 (0-7837-3957-5, 2043786) Bks Demand.

Source Book in Theatrical History. Alois M. Nagler. Orig. Title: Sources of Theatrical History. (Illus.). 1952. pap. 9.95 (0-486-20515-0) Dover.

Source Book of Advaita Vedanta. Eliot Deutsch & J. A. Van Buitenen. LC 75-148944. 345p. reprint ed. pap. 98.40 (0-317-12996-1, 2017216) Bks Demand.

Source Book of Agricultural Chemistry. Charles A. Browne. Ed. by Frank N. Egerton, 3rd. LC 77-74205. (History of Ecology Ser.). 1978. reprint ed. lib. bdg. 25.95 (0-405-10375-1) Ayer.

Source Book of American Architecture: 500 Notable Buildings from the 10th Century to the Present. Kidder Smith. (Illus.). 700p. 1996. 50.00 (1-56898-024-8); pap. 34.95 (1-56898-025-6) Princeton Arch.

Source Book of American State Legislation, 1985-1986. American Legislative Exchange Council Staff & James Butcher. LC 82-642083. 1985. 10.00 (0-317-37050-2) Am Legislative.

Source Book of Ancient Indian Psychology. B. Kuppuswamy. (C). 1993. 35.00 (81-220-0312-5, Pub. by Konark Pubs Pvt Ltd II) Advent Bks Div.

Source Book of Australian Legal History. J. M. Bennett & Alex C. Castles. x, 299p. 1979. pap. 47.50 (0-455-19954-X, Pub. by Law Bk Co AT) Gaunt.

Source Book of Automatic Identification & Data Collection. Russ Adams. 1990. text ed. 69.95 (0-442-31850-2) Van Nos Reinhold.

Source-Book of Biological Names & Terms. 3rd ed. Edmund C. Jaeger. (Illus.). 360p. 1977. 55.95 (0-398-00916-3); pap. 38.95 (0-398-06179-3) C C Thomas.

Source Book of Discipline: A Synthesis of Moralia in Job by Gregory the Great: A Translation of Peter Waltham's Remediarium Conversorum. Tr. by Joseph Gildea. LC 91-17221. (American University Studies: Theology & Religion: Ser. VII, Vol. 117). 371p. (C). 1992. text ed. 54.95 (*0-8204-1650-9*) P Lang Pubng.

Source Book of Educational Materials for Medical Radiographers. 1986. lib. bdg. 79.95 (*0-8490-3806-5*) Gordon Pr.

Source Book of European Community Environmental Law. Richard Macrory & Steve Hollins. 90p. 1995. 45.00 (*0-19-825937-9*) OUP.

Source Book of Flavors. Henry B. Heath. (Illus.). 1981. text ed. 135.00 (*0-87055-370-4*) AVI.

Source Book of Franchise Opportunities, 1993. 6th ed. Robert E. Bond. 560p. 1992. pap. 35.00 (*1-55623-899-1*) Irwin Prof Pubng.

Source Book of Franchise Opportunities 1994. 7th ed. Robert E. Bond & Jeffery M. Bond. 560p. 1993. pap. 35.00 (*0-7863-0153-8*) Irwin Prof Pubng.

Source Book of Franchise Opportunities 1995 Edition. Robert E. Bond & Jefferey Bond. 1995. pap. 35.00 (*0-7863-0394-8*) Irwin Prof Pubng.

Source Book of Free & Low-Cost Software. Nelson Ford. (Orig.). (C). 1989. pap. 19.95 (*0-685-26327-4*) PSL Comput Prods.

***Source Book of Gestalt Psychology.** Willis D. Ellis. 403p. 1997. reprint ed. pap. 45.00 (*0-939266-30-X*) Gestalt Journal.

Source Book of Health Insurance Data, 1993. 33th ed. 200p. 1994. pap. 12.00 (*1-879143-24-0*) Health Ins Assn Am.

Source Book of Indian Archaeology. Ed. by F. R. Allchin & D. K. Chakrabarti. (Illus.). 366p. 1979. text ed. 30.00 (*0-685-13822-4*) Coronet Bks.

Source Book of Indian Medicine: An Anthology. K. H. Krishnamurthy. (C). 1991. 46.00 (*81-7018-612-9*, Pub. by BR Pub II) S Asia.

Source Book of Medical History. Logan Clendening. (C). 1942. pap. 14.95 (*0-486-20621-1*) Dover.

Source-Book of Modern Hinduism. Glyn Richards. 228p. (Orig.). (C). 1996. pap. text ed. 20.00 (*0-7007-0317-9*, Pub. by Curzon Press UK) UH Pr.

Source Book of Ophthalmology. D. M. Albert. (Illus.). 416p. 1995. 99.95 (*0-86542-240-0*) Blackwell Sci.

Source Book of Practical Experiments in Physiology Requiring Minimal Equipment. International Union of Physiological Sciences Congress Staff. 204p. (C). 1991. text ed. 44.00 (*981-02-0570-8*); pap. text ed. 18.00 (*981-02-0571-6*) World Scientific Pub.

Source Book of Proposed Music Notation Reforms. Gardner Read. LC 86-14315. (Music Reference Collection: No. 11). 489p. 1987. text ed. 69.50 (*0-313-25446-X*, RHN/, Greenwood Pr) Greenwood.

Source Book of Royal Commissions & Other Major Governmental Inquiries in Canadian Education, 1787-1978. Cary F. Goulson. LC 82-105166. 428p. reprint ed. pap. 122.00 (*0-8357-6399-4*, 2035756) Bks Demand.

Source Book of Statistics Relating to Construction. Robert E. Lipsey & Doris Preston. (General Ser.: No. 82). 319p. 1966. reprint ed. 83.00 (*0-87014-082-5*) Natl Bur Econ Res.

Source Book of Substance Abuse & Addiction. Lawrence Friedman et al. 348p. 1995. pap. 32.95 (*0-683-03364-6*) Williams & Wilkins.

Source Book of the Genus Phytophtora. O. K. Ribeiro. (Illus.). 1978. lib. bdg. 45.00 (*3-7682-1200-9*) Lubrecht & Cramer.

Source Book of Worship Resources. Larry J. Peacock et al. Ed. by Stan Purdum. 232p. 1994. pap. 39.95 (*0-930921-05-4*) Comm Res OH.

Source Book on Applications of the Laser in Metalworking: A Comprehensive Collection of Outstanding Articles from the Periodical & Reference Literature. American Society for Metals Staff. Ed. by Edward A. Metzbower. LC 81-52317. (ASM Engineering Bookshelf Ser.). (Illus.). 399p. reprint ed. pap. 113.80 (*0-8357-3542-7*, 2034315) Bks Demand.

Source Book on Astronomy & Astrophysics. Ed. by Kenneth R. Lang & Owen Gingerich. 922p. 1980. 41.95 (*0-318-13544-2*, B0163) HUP.

Source Book on Brazing & Brazing Technology: A Comprehensive Collection of Outstanding Articles from the Periodical & Reference Literature. American Society for Metals Staff. LC 80-17457. 440p. reprint ed. pap. 125.40 (*0-685-15735-0*, 2027050) Bks Demand.

Source Book on Brazing & Brazing Technology (SBB) 428p. 1980. 48.00 (*0-685-06028-4*, SBB) Am Welding.

Source Book on Cold Forming: A Discriminative Selection of Outstanding Articles from the Periodical Literature. American Society for Metals Staff. LC 75-6855. (American Society for Metals. Engineering Bookshelf Ser.). (Illus.). 375p. reprint ed. pap. 106.90 (*0-317-11151-5*, 2019501) Bks Demand.

***Source Book on Collective Bargaining: Wages, Benefits, & Other Contract Issues.** 1,997th ed. 279p. 1997. 70.00 (*1-55871-353-0*, XCMP 43) BNA Plus.

Source Book on Copper & Copper Alloys: A Comprehensive Collection of Outstanding Articles from the Periodical & Reference Literature. American Society for Metals Staff. LC 79-21667. 424p. reprint ed. pap. 120.90 (*0-685-15678-8*, 2027045) Bks Demand.

Source Book on Ductile Iron: A Discriminative Selection of Outstanding Articles from the Periodical & Reference Literature. American Society for Metals Staff. Ed. by A. H. Rauch. LC 77-9278. (ASM Engineering Bookshelf Ser.). 400p. reprint ed. pap. 114.00 (*0-317-27679-4*, 2019500) Bks Demand.

Source Book on Electron Beam & Laser Welding: A Comprehensive Collection of Outstanding Articles from the Periodical & Reference Literature. American Society for Metals Staff. Ed. by Melvin M. Schwartz. LC 81-109899. (ASM Engineering Bookshelf Ser.). (Illus.). 408p. reprint ed. pap. 116.30 (*0-8357-3543-5*, 2034316) Bks Demand.

Source Book on Environmental & Safety Considerations for Planning & Design of LNG Marine Terminals. 46p. 1976. pap. 8.00 (*0-87262-158-8*) Am Soc Civil Eng.

Source Book on Forming of Steel Sheet: A Discriminative Selection of Outstanding Articles from the Periodical & Reference Literature. Ed. by John R. Newby. LC 76-28176. (American Society for Metals. Engineering Bookshelf Ser.). (Illus.). 399p. reprint ed. pap. 113.80 (*0-317-11148-5*, 2019498) Bks Demand.

Source Book on Gear Design, Technology & Performance: A Comprehensive Collection of Outstanding Articles from the Periodical & Reference Literature. American Society for Metals Staff. LC 79-27246. 429p. reprint ed. pap. 122.30 (*0-685-23453-3*, 2032715) Bks Demand.

Source Book on Heat Treating: A Discriminative Selection of Outstanding Articles from the Literature Periodicals. American Society for Metals Staff. LC 75-25598. (ASM Engineering Bookshelf Ser.: Vol. 1: Materials & Processes). (Illus.). 398p. reprint ed. pap. 113.50 (*0-317-09661-3*, 2051904) Bks Demand.

Source Book on Industrial Alloy & Engineering Data: A Comprehensive Collection of Alloy & Engineering Data in Tabular & Graphical Form. American Society for Metals Staff. LC 77-28985. 483p. reprint ed. pap. 137.70 (*0-317-26761-2*, 2024347) Bks Demand.

Source Book on Innovative Welding Processes: A Comprehensive Collection of Outstanding Articles from the Periodical & Reference Literature. American Society for Metals Staff. Ed. by Melvin M. Schwartz. LC 81-3535. (ASM Engineering Bookshelf Ser.). (Illus.). 384p. reprint ed. pap. 109.50 (*0-8357-3544-3*, 2034314) Bks Demand.

Source Book on Maraging Steels: A Comprehensive Collection of Outstanding Articles from the Periodical & Reference Literature. American Society for Metals Staff. LC 79-13743. (AMS Engineering Bookself Ser.). (Illus.). 400p. reprint ed. pap. 114.00 (*0-317-09610-9*, 2019493) Bks Demand.

Source Book on Materials Selection: A Discriminative Selection of Outstanding Articles from the Periodical & Reference Literature. American Society for Metals Staff. Ed. by Russell B. Gunie. LC 77-1347. 487p. reprint ed. pap. 138.80 (*0-685-15690-7*, 2027047) Bks Demand.

Source Book on Nitriding: A Discriminative Selection of Outstanding Articles from the Periodical & Reference Literature. American Society for Metals Staff. LC 77-23934. 328p. reprint ed. pap. 93.50 (*0-685-15704-0*, 2027048) Bks Demand.

Source Book on Powder Metallurgy: A Comprehensive Collection of Outstanding Articles from the Periodical & Reference Literature. American Society for Metals Staff. Ed. by Samuel Bradbury. LC 78-24466. 439p. reprint ed. pap. 125.20 (*0-317-26758-2*, 2024348) Bks Demand.

Source Book on Selection & Fabrication of Aluminum Alloys: A Comprehensive Collection of Outstanding Articles from the Industrial & Reference Literature. American Society for Metals Staff. LC 78-18869. 480p. reprint ed. pap. 136.80 (*0-685-15669-9*, 2027044) Bks Demand.

Source Book on Stainless Steels: A Discriminative Selection of Outstanding Articles from the Periodical & Reference Literature. Compiled by American Society for Metals Staff, Periodical Publication Department Staff. LC 76-867. (ASM Engineering Bookshelf Ser.). (Illus.). 416p. reprint ed. pap. 118.60 (*0-317-09622-2*, 2019497) Bks Demand.

Source Book on Wear Control Technology: A Comprehensive Collection of Outstanding Articles from the Periodical & Reference Literature. American Society for Metals Staff. Ed. by David A. Rigney & W. A. Glaeser. LC 78-12162. (ASM Engineering Bookshelf Ser.). 464p. reprint ed. pap. 132.30 (*0-317-26756-6*, 2024349) Bks Demand.

Source Book Relative to the History of the University of Texas. H. Y. Benedict. 1993. reprint ed. lib. bdg. 75.00 (*0-7812-5864-2*) Rprt Serv.

Source Book 1995-96: Social & Health Services in the Greater New York Area. United Way of New York City Staff. 1200p. 1995. pap. 55.00 (*0-89774-999-5*) Oryx Pr.

Source Check: A Research Checklist for United States Genealogical Research. Toni I. Benson. 25p. 1995. pap. 7.00 (*0-9620998-5-6*) F-Ami-Lee.

Source Coding Theory. Robert M. Gray. (International Series in Engineering & Computer Science, VLSI, Computer Architecture, & Digital Screen Processing). 208p. (C). 1989. lib. bdg. 78.00 (*0-7923-9048-2*) Kluwer Ac.

Source Collection, Vols. 1-5. Dorothy L. Williams. 57p. 1990. pap. 8.00 (*1-57482-309-4*) Search Inst.

Source Directory of Camera Restoration Materials. 1989. 4.95 (*0-89816-041-3*) Embee Pr.

Source Documents in American Lutheran Hymnody. annot. ed. Ed. & Tr. by Carl F. Schalk. LC 96-10541. 1996. 12.95 (*0-570-01352-6*, 99-1620) Concordia.

Source Edition, Vol 1. Maia C. Shamayyim. (Illus.). 162p. 1984. spiral bd. 25.00 (*1-888420-08-1*) Johannine Grove.

Source Edition, Vol. 2. Maia C. Shamayyim. (Illus.). 285p. 1989. spiral bd. 38.00 (*1-888420-09-X*) Johannine Grove.

Source for Local Prices: Southern Africa. Jim Heck & Keith Bates. (Illus.). 250p. (Orig.). 1992. pap. 17.95 (*1-882776-00-3*) Via Direct Trvl.

Source for North American Racing & Breeding, 1994-95. Ed. by Raymond S. Paulick & Dan Mearns. Orig. Title: The List, The Blood-Horse Directory of North American Racing & Breeding. 470p. (Orig.). 1994. pap. 19.95 (*0-939049-59-7*) Blood-Horse.

Source for North American Racing & Breeding, 1995-96: Annual Supplement to the Blood-Horse. Ed. by Raymond S. Paulick & Dan Mearns. (Blood-Horse Supplement Ser.). 515p. (Orig.). 1995. pap. 19.95 (*0-939049-67-8*) Blood-Horse.

Source for North American Racing & Breeding, 1996-97. Ed. by Raymond S. Paulick & Dan Mearns. (Illus.). 500p. (Orig.). 1996. pap. 19.95 (*0-939049-73-2*) Blood-Horse.

***Source for North American Racing & Breeding, 1997-98.** Ed. by Raymond S. Paulick & Dan Mearns. (Illus.). 500p. (Orig.). 1997. pap. 19.95 (*0-939049-84-8*) Blood-Horse.

Source for Oral & Facial Exercises. Debra Gangale. 1993. student ed., spiral bd. 37.95 (*1-55999-265-4*) LinguiSystems.

Source for Professional Skip Tracers - Collectors, Attorneys, Investigators Insurance Subrogation Departments. 750p. (Orig.). 1989. 125.00 (*0-9622995-0-2*) Tolo Pub.

Source for Professional Skip Tracers & Collectors, Investigators, Attorneys, Insurance Subrogation Departments. Intro. by Arnold R. Todd, III & Neal Loper. 725p. 1989. write for info. (*0-318-65029-0*) Tolo Pub.

***Source Guide for Performance Improvement: Working with Individuals & Organizations.** Ed. by Roger Kaufman et al. 640p. 1996. 49.95 (*0-7879-0353-1*) Jossey-Bass.

Source Guide to the Music of Percy Grainger. Ed. by Thomas Lewis. (Illus.). 352p. 1991. pap. 35.00 (*0-912483-56-3*) Pro-Am Music.

***Source-Matched Mobile Communications.** W. C. Wong. 268p. 1995. 79.95 (*0-7803-1163-9*, PC5635) Inst Electrical.

Source Material for the Social & Ceremonial Life of the Choctaw Indians. John R. Swanton. (Bureau of American Ethnology Bulletins Ser.). 282p. 1995. lib. bdg. 89.00 (*0-7812-4103-0*) Rprt Serv.

Source Material for the Social & Ceremonial Life of the Choctaw Indians. John R. Swanton. (Illus.). 295p. 1993. reprint ed. pap. text ed. 25.00 (*0-942301-21-8*) Birm Pub Lib.

Source Material on the History & Ethnology of the Caddo Indians. Ed. by John R. Swanton. (Bureau of American Ethnology Bulletins Ser.). 332p. 1995. lib. bdg. 99.00 (*0-7812-4132-4*) Rprt Serv.

Source Material on the History & Ethnology of the Caddo Indians. John R. Swanton & Helen H. Tanner. LC 96-18016. (Illus.). 376p. 1996. pap. 15.95 (*0-8061-2856-9*) U of Okla Pr.

Source Materials on the Government & Politics of Germany. James K. Pollock. 1964. pap. 15.00 (*0-911586-26-1*) Wahr.

Source Mechanism & Seismotectonics. Ed. by A. Udias & E. Buforn. Orig. Title: Pure & Applied Geophysics. 216p. 1992. reprint ed. 27.50 (*0-8176-2709-X*) Spr-Verlag.

Source Methodology in Islamic Jurisprudence: (Usul al Fiqh al Islami) 2nd rev. ed. Taha J. Alwani. Tr. by Yusuf G. DeLorenzo & A. S. Al Shaikh-Ali from ARA. LC 90-26084. (Research Monographs: No. 1). 112p. (Orig.). 1993. pap. 5.00 (*0-685-70283-9*) IIIT VA.

Source Music in Motion Pictures. Irene K. Atkins. LC 81-65338. (Illus.). 192p. 1983. 32.50 (*0-8386-3076-6*) Fairleigh Dickinson.

Source of All Evil: African Proverbs & Sayings on Women. Mineke Schipper. 128p. 1991. text ed. 15.95 (*0-929587-73-1*) I R Dee.

***Source of All Our Strength: More Sayings of White Eagle.** White Eagle. 118p. 1996. 11.95 (*0-85487-097-0*, Pub. by White Eagle UK) DeVorss.

Source of Human Good. Henry N. Wieman. 345p. 1995. pap. 24.95 (*0-7885-0144-5*, 01 02 08) Scholars Pr GA.

***Source of Life: The Holy Spirit & the Theology of Life.** Jurgen Moltmann. LC 97-25134. 1997. pap. text ed. 14.00 (*0-8006-3099-8*, Fortress Pr) Augsburg Fortress.

Source of Light. Reynolds Price. 1995. pap. 12.00 (*0-684-81338-6*) S&S Trade.

Source of Magic. Piers Anthony. 336p. 1987. mass mkt. 5.95 (*0-345-35058-8*, Del Rey) Ballantine.

***Source of Magic.** Piers Anthony. 1997. pap. 11.00 (*0-345-41850-6*, Del Rey) Ballantine.

Source of My Strength. Charles Stanley. LC 93-48445. 256p. 1994. 18.99 (*0-7852-8273-4*) Nelson.

Source of My Strength. large type ed. Charles Stanley. LC 93-48445. 320p. 1995. pap. 12.95 (*0-8027-2688-7*) Walker & Co.

Source of Precious Life. Leonard J. Cirino. 64p. (Orig.). 1988. write for info. (*0-944550-03-7*) Pygmy Forest Pr.

Source of Supply: 1995 Edition. Carla J. Hook. 705p. 1995. per. 139.00 (*1-57053-015-7*) Global Eng Doc.

***Source of the Dream: My Way to Sathya Sai Baba.** Robert Priddy. (Illus.). 320p. (Orig.). 1997. pap. 16.95 (*1-57863-028-2*) Weiser.

Source of the Light: A Witness & Testimony of Jesus Christ, the Savior & Redeemer of All. Maurine J. Proctor & Scot F. Proctor. LC 92-27973. (Illus.). 208p. 1992. 39.95 (*0-87579-648-6*) Deseret Bk.

Source of the River Po: Winning, Losing & High Living in Drug Research. Gerhard Zbinden. 308p. (Orig.). 1994. pap. text ed. 50.00 (*3-89228-908-5*) Am Overseas Bk Co.

Source of Trouble. Debra Monroe. 176p. 1995. pap. 10.00 (*0-671-89716-0*) S&S Trade.

Source of Trouble. Debra Monroe. LC 90-31189. (Flannery O'Connor Award for Short Fiction Ser.). 184p. 1990. 19.95 (*0-8203-1246-0*) U of Ga Pr.

Source. Poems. Fred Chappell. LC 85-13315. 57p. 1985. pap. 11.95 (*0-8071-1277-1*) La State U Pr.

Source Readings: Greek Views. rev. ed. Thomas Mathiesen. (C). Date not set. pap. text ed. write for info. (*0-393-96694-1*) Norton.

Source Readings Vol. 2: Early Christ. rev. ed. James McKinnon. (C). Date not set. pap. text ed. write for info. (*0-393-96695-X*) Norton.

Source Readings Vol. 3: Renaissance. rev. ed. Gary Tomlinson. (C). Date not set. pap. text ed. write for info. (*0-393-96696-8*) Norton.

Source Readings Vol. 4: Baroque Era. rev. ed. Lawrence Dreyfus. (C). Date not set. pap. text ed. write for info. (*0-393-96697-6*) Norton.

Source Readings Vol. 5: Late 18th Century. rev. ed. Wye Allanbrook. (C). Date not set. pap. text ed. write for info. (*0-393-96698-4*) Norton.

Source Readings Vol. 6: 19th Century. rev. ed. Ruth A. Solie. (C). Date not set. pap. text ed. write for info. (*0-393-96699-2*) Norton.

Source Readings Vol. 7: 20th Century. rev. ed. Robert Morgan. (C). Date not set. pap. text ed. write for info. (*0-393-96700-X*) Norton.

Source Readings for American Government. Bennett. (C). 1995. pap. text ed. 8.75 (*0-15-502976-2*) HB Coll Pubs.

Source Readings in Music Education History. rev. ed. Michael L. Mark. 270p. 1986. pap. 19.95 (*1-57171-002-7*) Lincoln-Rembrandt.

Source Readings in Music History. rev. ed. Ed. by Oliver Strunk & Leo Treitler. LC 94-34569. 1000p. 1996. 45.00 (*0-393-03752-5*) Norton.

Source Readings in Music History, 5 vols. Ed. by Oliver Strunk. Incl. Vol. 1. Antiquity & the Middle Ages. (C). 1966. pap. text ed. 9.95 (*0-393-09680-7*); Vol. 2. Renaissance Era. (C). 1966. pap. text ed. 8.95 (*0-393-09681-5*); Vol. 3. Baroque Era. (C). 1966. pap. text ed. 11.95 (*0-393-09682-3*); Vol. 4. Classic Era. (C). 1966. pap. text ed. 7.95 (*0-393-09683-1*); Vol. 5. Romantic Era. (C). 1966. pap. text ed. 8.95 (*0-393-09684-X*); (Illus.). (C). 1950. reprint ed. Set text ed. 24.95 (*0-393-09742-0*) Norton.

Source Region of the Solar Wind. Ed. by W. K. Schmidt & H. Grunwaldt. 1982. lib. bdg. 135.00 (*90-277-1537-8*) Kluwer Ac.

Source Rocks in a Sequence Stratigraphic Framework. Ed. by Barry J. Katz & Lisa M. Pratt. (Studies in Geology: No. 37). (Illus.). vi, 247p. (Orig.). 1993. pap. 44.00 (*0-89181-045-5*, 582) AAPG.

Source Selection: A Seller's Perspective: How the Federal Government Selects Contractors. LC 89-85398. (Illus.). 300p. 1990. pap. 65.00 (*0-685-28058-6*) Edmunds Co.

Source Studies in American Colonial Education. Robert F. Seybolt. LC 71-165731. (American Education, Ser, No. 2). 1977. reprint ed. 18.95 (*0-405-03720-1*) Ayer.

Source, Transport & Deposition of Metals: Proceedings of the 25 Years SGA Anniversary Meeting, Nancy, 30 August-3 September 1991. Ed. by Maurice Pagel & Jacques L. Leroy. (Illus.). 850p. 1991. text ed. 140.00 (*90-5410-020-6*, Pub. by A A Balkema NE) Ashgate Pub Co.

Source 1 - WordPerfect 6.0. Don Cassel. 1994. pap. text ed. 5.00 (*0-685-70619-2*) P-H.

Source 1-Computing Essentials DBase IV 1.5. Cassel. pap. text ed. 5.00 (*0-685-70923-X*) P-H.

Source 1-Computing Essentials Lotus 1-2-3-2.3. Cassel. pap. text ed. 5.00 (*0-13-106535-1*) P-H.

Source 1-Lotus 3.1. Don Cassel. 1994. pap. text ed. 5.00 (*0-13-101494-3*) P-H.

Source 1-Paradox 4.0. Don Cassel. 1994. pap. text ed. 5.00 (*0-13-101502-8*) P-H.

Source 1 Quattro Pro 5.0. Don Cassel. 1994. pap. text ed. 5.00 (*0-13-101528-1*) P-H.

Source 1-Word for Windows. Don Cassel. 1994. pap. text ed. 5.00 (*0-13-101536-2*) P-H.

***Source 1996/97: The Greater Boston Theatre Resource Guide.** 4th rev. ed. Ed. by Peggy Roberts. 424p. (Orig.). 1996. pap. 19.95 (*0-9624740-3-7*) StageSource.

Sourcebook: A Guide for Volunteer Community Caregiving. 33p. 1995. pap. text ed. 14.50 (*0-9647918-1-1*) Lend a Hand.

Sourcebook: Activities for Infants & Young Children. 2nd ed. George W. Maxim. 336p. (C). 1990. pap. text ed. 36.00 (*0-675-21055-0*, Merrill Coll) P-H.

Sourcebook: Annotated Resources for Family Based Service Practice. 4th rev. ed. 91p. 1993. lib. bdg. 5.00 (*0-614-14690-9*) U of Iowa Sch Soc Wk.

Sourcebook Vol. 1: Hard Copy Version. Ed. by Mary V. Orna et al. (Illus.). (Orig.). (C). 1994. pap. text ed. write for info. (*0-9637747-2-7*) Chemsource.

Sourcebook Vol. 2: Hard Copy Version. Ed. by Mary V. Orna et al. (Illus.). (Orig.). (C). 1994. pap. text ed. write for info. (*0-9637747-3-5*) Chemsource.

Sourcebook Vol. 3: Hard Copy Version. Ed. by Mary V. Orna et al. (Illus.). (Orig.). (C). 1994. pap. text ed. write for info. (*0-9637747-4-3*) Chemsource.

Sourcebook Vol. 4: Hard Copy Version. Ed. by Mary V. Orna et al. (Illus.). (Orig.). (C). 1994. pap. text ed. write for info. (*0-9637747-5-1*) Chemsource.

Sourcebook Vols. 1-4: Hardcopy Version Overall Bound Volumes, 4 Vols., Set. Ed. by Mary V. Orna et al. (Illus.). 2100p. (Orig.). (C). 1994. pap. text ed. 70.00 (*0-9637747-1-9*) Chemsource.

Sourcebook about Christian Death. Ed. by Virginia Sloyan. (Seasonal Sourcebook Ser.). 160p. (Orig.). 1990. pap. 15.00 (*0-929650-09-3*, DEATH) Liturgy Tr Pubns.

An Asterisk (*) at the beginning of an entry indicates that the title is appearing in BIP for the first time.

Sourcebook about Liturgy. Ed. by Gabe Huck. LC 94-3514. (Illus.). 189p. 1994. pap. 15.00 (*1-56854-029-9*, LITSB) Liturgy Tr Pubns.

Sourcebook about Music. Ed. by Alan Hommerding. 200p. (Orig.). 1997. pap. 15.00 (*1-56854-153-8*, MUSISB) Liturgy Tr Pubns.

***Sourcebook America: County & Zip Code.** 9th ed. 1996. 995.00 (*0-918417-67-8*, 00155482, Gale Res Intl) Gale.

Sourcebook for Alternative Energy. 1991. lib. bdg. 250.00 (*0-8490-4738-2*) Gordon Pr.

Sourcebook for Baptist Heritage. H. Leon McBeth. LC 89-33091. 544p. 1990. 29.99 (*0-8054-6589-8*, 4265-89) Broadman.

Sourcebook for Basic Writing Teachers. Theresa Enos. 676p. (C). 1987. text ed. write for info. (*0-07-554935-2*) McGraw.

Sourcebook for Bibliographic Instruction. Bibliographic Instruction Section, Editorial Board Staff. 96p. 1993. pap. 18.95 (*0-8389-7673-5*) Assn Coll & Res Libs.

Sourcebook for College Mathematics Teaching. Ed. by Alan H. Schoenfeld. (MAA Notes Ser.). 80p. (Orig.). 1990. pap. 8.00 (*0-88385-068-0*, SRCE) Math Assn.

Sourcebook for Earth's Community of Religions. rev. ed. Joel D. Beversluis. 376p. 1995. pap. 19.95 (*0-9637897-1-6*) CoNexus Pr.

Sourcebook for Elementary Science. 2nd ed. Elizabeth B. Hone et al. Ed. by Paul F. Brandwein. (C). 1971. text ed. 41.25 (*0-15-582855-X*) HB Coll Pubs.

Sourcebook for Environmental Education: A Practical Review Based on the Belgrade Charter. Ed. by Walter L. Filho et al. (Illus.). 230p. (Orig.). 1996. pap. 34.00 (*1-85070-768-5*) Prthnon Pub.

Sourcebook for Fire Company Training Evolutions. Ed. by Michael A. Wieder et al. (Illus.). 240p. (Orig.). pap. text ed. 25.00 (*0-87939-116-2*) IFSTA.

Sourcebook for Helping People with Spiritual Problems. 2nd rev. ed. Emma Bragdon. (Illus.). 320p. (C). 1994. reprint ed. pap. 14.95 (*0-9620960-1-6*) Lightening Up Pr.

Sourcebook for Hispanic Literature & Language: A Selected Annotated Guide to Spanish, Spanish-American, & United States Hispanic Bibliography, Literature, Linguistics, Journals, & Other Source Materials. 3rd ed. Donald W. Bleznick. LC 94-47011. 322p. 1995. 57.00 (*0-8108-2981-9*) Scarecrow.

Sourcebook for Investigation & Valuation of Fish Kills. Southwick Associates Staff. LC 93-70792. (Supplement to Special Publication Ser.: No. 24). 151p. 1993. pap. 40.00 (*0-913235-84-9*) Am Fisheries Soc.

***Sourcebook, for Jewish Genealogies & Family Histories.** David S. Zubatsky & Irwin M. Berent. LC 96-9712. 480p. 1996. 69.50 (*1-886223-03-3*) Avotaynu.

Sourcebook for Law Library Governing Boards & Committees. American Association of Law Libraries Staff et al. LC 93-26593. (AALL Publications: No. 45). 438p. 1994. ring bd. 70.00 (*0-8377-9291-6*) Rothman.

Sourcebook for Medical Speech Pathology. Lee A. Golper. LC 92-20427. (Clinical Competence Ser.). (Illus.). 433p. (C). 1992. pap. text ed. 49.95 (*1-879105-80-2*, 0343) Singular Publishing.

***Sourcebook for Medical Speech Pathology.** 2nd ed. Lee A. Golper. LC 97-24423. (Clinical Competence Ser.). 1997. write for info. (*1-56593-861-5*) Singular Publishing.

Sourcebook for Modern Catechetics. Ed. by Michael Warren. LC 83-50246. 493p. (Orig.). (C). 1983. pap. 24.95 (*0-88489-152-6*) St Marys.

***Sourcebook for Modern Japanese Philosophy: Selected Documents.** Agustin J. Zavala. Ed. by David A. Dilworth et al. LC 97-12763. (Resources in Asian Philosophy & Religion). 1997. text ed. write for info. (*0-313-27433-9*, Greenwood Pr) Greenwood.

Sourcebook for Parents of Intellectually Gifted Preschool-Elementary School Children see Identifying & Cultivating Talent in Preschool & Elementary School Children

Sourcebook for Petroleum Geology: Semicentennial Commemorative Volume. Robert Henry Dott & Merrill J. Reynolds. LC 73-91979. (American Association of Petroleum Geologists. Memoir Ser.: No. 5). (Illus.). 481p. reprint ed. pap. 137.10 (*0-685-23713-3*, 2032234) Bks Demand.

Sourcebook for Research in Music. Phillip D. Crabtree & Donald H. Foster. LC 92-32038. 260p. (C). 1993. 25.00 (*0-253-31476-3*) Ind U Pr.

Sourcebook for Rio Grande-Rio Bravo Water Management. Contrib. by David Eaton. (Policy Research Project Report: No. 57). 66p. 1983. pap. 7.50 (*0-89940-659-9*) LBJ Sch Pub Aff.

Sourcebook for Science, Mathematics & Technology Education 1992. Ed. by Mary B. Lennon & Barbara Walthall. 218p. 1991. 12.95 (*0-87168-429-2*, 91-38S) AAAS.

Sourcebook for Science Supervisors. 4th ed. Ed. by Gerry M. Madrazo, Jr. 134p. 1993. pap. text ed. 17.95 (*0-87355-114-1*) Natl Sci Tchrs.

Sourcebook for Smart Managers: One-Page Management Tool. Laddie F. Hutar. 16p. 1995. pap. 15.00 (*0-614-06668-9*, 90005) Hutar.

Sourcebook for Speech, Language & Cognition: Stimulus Materials for Rehabilitation, Bk. 1. Susan H. Brubaker. LC 92-13721. (William Beaumont Hospital Speech & Language Pathology Ser.: Bks. 1-2). 200p. 1992. 45.00 (*0-8143-2411-8*) Wayne St U Pr.

Sourcebook for Speech, Language & Cognition: Stimulus Materials for Rehabilitation, Bk. 2. Susan H. Brubaker. LC 92-13721. (William Beaumont Hospital Speech & Language Pathology Ser.: Bks. 1-2). 194p. 1992. 45.00 (*0-8143-2412-6*) Wayne St U Pr.

Sourcebook for Speech, Language & Cognition, Bk. 3: Stimulus Materials for Rehabilitation. Susan H. Brubaker. LC 92-13721. 208p. 1994. text ed. 45.00 (*0-8143-2501-7*) Wayne St U Pr.

Sourcebook for Substitutes...& Other Teachers. Miriam Freedman & Teri Perl. (gr. k-8). 1974. pap. text ed. 16.50 (*0-201-05786-7*) Addison-Wesley.

Sourcebook for Sundays & Seasons 1997. Peter Scagnelli. (Illus.). 228p. (Orig.). 1996. pap. 12.00 (*1-56854-122-8*, SSS97) Liturgy Tr Pubns.

***Sourcebook for Sundays & Seasons 1998.** Peter Scagnelli. (Illus.). 228p. (Orig.). 1997. pap. 15.00 (*1-56854-194-5*, SSS98) Liturgy Tr Pubns.

***Sourcebook for Teachers on Writing.** 13th ed. Roberts. (C). 1997. pap. text ed. write for info. (*0-15-508158-6*) HB Coll Pubs.

Sourcebook for Teaching Problem Solving. Stephen Krulik & Jesse A. Rudnik. 416p. 1984. pap. 39.95 (*0-205-08106-1*, H81060) Allyn.

Sourcebook for the Academically Able Adolescent see Educational Resources for Academically Talented Adolescents

Sourcebook for the Biological Sciences. 3rd ed. Evelyn Morholt & Paul F. Brandwein. 813p. (C). 1986. text ed. 41.25 (*0-15-582852-5*) HB Coll Pubs.

Sourcebook for the Performing Arts: A Directory of Collections, Resources, Scholars, & Critics in Theatre, Film, & Television. Ed. by Patricia K. Hanson & Stephen L. Hanson. LC 87-23630. 235p. 1988. text ed. 55.00 (*0-313-24872-9*, SDR/, Greenwood Pr) Greenwood.

***Sourcebook for Watershed Education.** Sally Cole-Misch et al. 216p. 1996. per., pap. text ed. 29.95 (*0-7872-2372-7*) Kendall-Hunt.

Sourcebook for Working with Battered Women: A Comprehensive Manual. Nancy Kilgore. LC 93-18367. (Family Violence Prevention Ser.). 120p. 1993. pap. 17.95 (*0-912078-97-9*) Volcano Pr.

Sourcebook Health Insurance. Health Insurance Association Staff. 1995. pap. text ed. 25.25 (*1-879143-25-9*) Health Ins Assn Am.

Sourcebook in Asian Philosophy. John M. Koller. 608p. (C). 1991. pap. text ed. 44.00 (*0-02-365811-8*, Macmillan Coll) P-H.

Sourcebook in Indian Philosophy. Ed. by Sarvepalli Radhakrishnan & Charles A. Moore. 720p. 1957. pap. text ed. 22.95 (*0-691-01958-4*) Princeton U Pr.

***Sourcebook Intermediate.** Shepherd. 1993. student ed., pap. text ed. write for info. (*0-582-00952-9*, Pub. by Longman UK) Longman.

***Sourcebook Intermediate.** Shepherd. 1993. wbk. ed., pap. text ed. write for info. (*0-582-00953-7*, Pub. by Longman UK) Longman.

Sourcebook of Adult Assessment Strategies. Nicola S. Schutte & John M. Malouff. LC 95-9524. (Applied Clinical Psychology Ser.). 471p. (C). 1995. 65.00 (*0-306-45029-1*, Plenum Pr) Plenum.

Sourcebook of Advanced Organic Laboratory Preparations. Stanley R. Sandler & Wolf Karo. (Illus.). 352p. 1992. pap. 45.00 (*0-12-618506-9*) Acad Pr.

Sourcebook of African Customary Law for Southern Africa. T. W. Bennett. 462p. 1991. pap. 44.00 (*0-7021-2546-6*, Pub. by Juta SA) Gaunt.

Sourcebook of Alaskan Shipwrecks, 1786-1932. Dale Stirling. (Heritage North Publication in History: No. 1). 57p. 1984. spiral bd. 5.00 (*0-913905-01-1*) Heritage N Pr.

Sourcebook of American Literary Journalism: Representative Writers in an Emerging Genre. Ed. by Thomas B. Connery. LC 91-17127. 424p. 1992. text ed. 72.50 (*0-313-26594-1*, CYJ, Greenwood Pr) Greenwood.

Sourcebook of Ancient Church History. Joseph C. Ayer. LC 70-113536. reprint ed. lib. bdg. 64.50 (*0-404-00436-9*) AMS Pr.

Sourcebook of Apraxia Remediation Activities. Kenneth G. Shipley et al. 160p. 1990. pap. text ed. 32.00 (*0-930951-47-6*) Acad Comm.

***Sourcebook of Artists.** Kraus Sikes Inc. Staff. 1995. 34.95 (*0-688-14592-2*) Morrow.

Sourcebook of Bacterial Protein Toxins. Ed. by J. E. Alouf & J. H. Freer. (Illus.). 518p. 1991. text ed. 99.00 (*0-12-053078-3*) Acad Pr.

Sourcebook of Biotechnology Activities. 1990. 35.00 (*0-941212-09-2*) Natl Assn Bio Tchrs.

***Sourcebook of Buying Power.** 88th ed. 1988. 295.00 (*0-8103-6863-3*, 00009804, Gale Res Intl) Gale.

Sourcebook of Buying Power County U. S., 1992. 1995. 595.00 (*0-8103-9671-8*, 072115) Gale.

Sourcebook of Buying Power Zip Code U. S., 1992. 1992. 345.00 (*0-8103-9970-9*) Gale.

Sourcebook of College & University Records: A National Guide to Student Attendance, Degree, & Transcript Records. Michael Sankey. (Public Record Research Library). 464p. (Orig.). 1995. 15.00 (*1-879792-24-9*) BRB Pubns.

Sourcebook of Contemporary North American Architecture. Sylvia H. Wright. (Illus.). 256p. 1989. text ed. 26.95 (*0-442-29190-6*) Van Nos Reinhold.

***Sourcebook of Control Systems Engineering.** Westphal. (Illus.). 960p. 1995. text ed. 119.00 (*0-412-48460-9*, Chap & Hall NY) Chapman & Hall.

Sourcebook of County Asset/Lien Records. Ed. by Michael Sankey & Carl Ernst. (Public Record Research Library). 464p. (Orig.). 1995. 15.00 (*1-879792-17-6*) BRB Pubns.

***Sourcebook of County Court Records: A National Guide to Civil, Criminal, & Probate Records at the County & Municipal Levels Within the State Court Systems.** 3rd rev. ed. Ed. by Carl R. Ernst & Michael Sankey. (Public Record Research Library). 480p. 1997. 35.00 (*1-879792-33-8*) BRB Pubns.

Sourcebook of County Demographics. 5th ed. 500p. 1990. 209.00 (*0-918417-00-7*) CACI Mktg Systs.

Sourcebook of County Demographics. 6th ed. CACI Marketing Systems Staff. 600p. 1993. 245.00 (*0-918417-04-X*) CACI Mktg Systs.

Sourcebook of County Demographics. 7th ed. CACI Marketing Systems Staff. 500p. 1994. 295.00 (*0-918417-51-1*) CACI Mktg Systs.

Sourcebook of County Demographics. 9th ed. 1996. 395.00 (*0-918417-66-X*) CACI Mktg Systs.

Sourcebook of County Demographics: Census Edition, 2 vols., 1. CACI Marketing Systems Staff. 500p. 1992. 195.00 (*0-918417-09-0*, 072119) CACI Mktg Systs.

Sourcebook of County Demographics: Census Edition, 2 vols., 2. CACI Marketing Systems Staff. 500p. 1992. 195.00 (*0-918417-10-4*, 072123) CACI Mktg Systs.

Sourcebook of County Demographics: Census Edition, 2 vols., Set. CACI Marketing Systems Staff. 500p. 1992. 390.00 (*0-918417-11-2*) CACI Mktg Systs.

Sourcebook of Craft Artists. 120p. 1994. pap. 19.95 (*1-56496-131-1*) Rockport Pubs.

Sourcebook of Craft Artists: Gallery Edition. 2nd ed. Intro. by Toni F. Sikes. (Illus.). 144p. 1995. pap. text ed. 24.95 (*1-880140-14-4*) Guild.

Sourcebook of Craft Artists: Gallery Edition. 2nd ed. Toni F. Sikes. (Illus.). 144p. 1995. text ed. 24.95 (*1-880140-13-6*) Guild.

Sourcebook of Criminal Justice Statistics, 2 vols. (Orig.). 1991. Set. lib. bdg. 995.00 (*0-8490-4480-4*) Gordon Pr.

***Sourcebook of Criminal Justice Statistics, 2 vols.** 1997. lib. bdg. 600.95 (*0-8490-8221-8*) Gordon Pr.

Sourcebook of Criminal Justice Statistics (1993) Ed. by Kathleen Maguire & Ann L. Pastore. (Illus.). 785p. (Orig.). (C). 1995. pap. text ed. 50.00 (*0-7881-2208-8*) DIANE Pub.

***Sourcebook of Criminal Justice Statistics (1995)** 23th ed. Ed. by Kathleen Maguire & Ann L. Pastore. (Illus.). 710p. 1996. pap. 50.00 (*0-7881-3277-6*) DIANE Pub.

***Sourcebook of Criminal Justice Statistics, 1995.** 23th ed. Kathleen Maguire. 746p. 1996. per., pap. 58.00 (*0-16-053335-X*, 027-000-01370-8) USGPO.

***Sourcebook of Criminal Justice Statistics 1995.** 23th ed. Ed. by Kathleen Maguire & Ann L. Pastore. (Illus.). xxiii, 725p. pap. text ed. 70.00 (*1-57979-051-8*) BPI Info Servs.

Sourcebook of Demographics & Buying Power for Every Zip Code in the U. S. A., 1989. 6th ed. 1750p. 1990. text ed. 195.00 (*0-918417-23-6*) CACI Mktg Systs.

Sourcebook of Elegant Historic Ornament. Emile Leconte & Charles E. Clerget. LC 95-32794. (Pictorial Archive Ser.). 1995. pap. write for info. (*0-486-28709-2*) Dover.

Sourcebook of Family Theories & Methods: A Contextual Approach. Ed. by P. Boss et al. (Illus.). 754p. (C). 1993. 95.00 (*0-306-44264-7*, Plenum Pr) Plenum.

Sourcebook of Federal Courts - U. S. District & Bankruptcy. 2nd rev. ed. Ed. by Michael Sankey & Carl Ernst. (Public Record Research Library). 448p. 1996. 36.00 (*1-879792-25-7*) BRB Pubns.

Sourcebook of Flavors. 2nd ed. Gary A. Reineccius. 928p. (C). (gr. 13). 1993. text ed. 194.00 (*0-442-00376-5*) Chapman & Hall.

Sourcebook of Franchise Opportunities. Robert E. Bond & Jeffrey M. Bond. 48p. 1994. per. 10.00 (*0-7863-0338-7*) Irwin Prof Pubng.

Sourcebook of Global Statistics. George T. Kurian. 420p. 1986. 95.00 (*0-87196-063-X*) Facts on File.

***Sourcebook of Global Statistics.** George T. Kurian. LC 83-14035. 413p. 1985. reprint ed. pap. 117.80 (*0-608-02835-5*, 2063902) Bks Demand.

Sourcebook of Korean Civilization, 2. Ed. by Peter H. Lee et al. (Introduction to Asian Civilizations Ser.). 1996. 85.00 (*0-231-10444-8*) Col U Pr.

Sourcebook of Korean Civilization: From Early Times to the Sixteenth Century. Ed. by Peter H. Lee et al. (Introduction to Asian Civilizations Ser.: Vol. 1). 576p. 1993. text ed. 49.50 (*0-231-07912-5*) Col U Pr.

Sourcebook of Korean Civilization: From the Seventeenth Century to the Modern Period, Vol. 2. Ed. by Peter H. Lee et al. (Introduction to Asian Civilizations Ser.: Vol. 2). 576p. 1996. 49.50 (*0-231-07914-1*) Col U Pr.

***Sourcebook of Local Court & County Record Retrievers.** rev. ed. Ed. by Carl R. Ernst & Michael Sankey. (Public Record Research Library). 560p. 1997. per., pap. 45.00 (*1-879792-37-0*) BRB Pubns.

Sourcebook of Management Simulations. Ken Jones. 128p. 1989. pap. 24.95 (*0-89397-345-9*) Nichols Pub.

Sourcebook of Marriage & Family Evaluation. Luciano L'Abate & Dennis A. Bagarozzi. LC 92-22541. 336p. 1993. text ed. 41.95 (*0-87630-676-8*) Brunner-Mazel.

Sourcebook of Medical Illustration. Ed. by P. Cull. (Illus.). 480p. 1989. 85.00 (*1-85070-255-1*) Prthnon Pub.

Sourcebook of Modern Furniture. 2nd ed. Jerryll Habegger & Joseph H. Osman. (Illus.). 608p. 1996. 75.00 (*0-393-73010-7*) Norton.

***Sourcebook of Nineteenth-Century American Sacred Music for Brass Instruments.** Mark J. Anderson. LC 97-8763. (Music Reference Collection: Vol. 59). 160p. 1997. text ed. 65.00 (*0-313-30380-0*, Greenwood Pr) Greenwood.

Sourcebook of Online Public Record Experts. Ed. by Carl R. Ernst & Michael Sankey. (Public Record Research Library). 368p. (Orig.). 1996. pap. text ed. 29.00 (*1-879792-31-1*) BRB Pubns.

Sourcebook of Oral Histories of Trade Union & Working in the United States. M. Brady Mikusko. (Program on Workers Culture Ser.). 94p. 1982. pap. 6.50 (*0-87736-348-X*) U of Mich Inst Labor.

Sourcebook of Pediatric Psychology. Ed. by Roberta A. Olson et al. 438p. 1994. text ed. 69.95 (*0-205-15182-5*, Longwood Div) Allyn.

Sourcebook of Poetry. Compiled by Al Bryant. LC 92-16102. 768p. 1992. reprint ed. pap. 24.99 (*0-8254-2192-6*) Kregel.

Sourcebook of Psychological Treatment Manuals for Adult Disorders. Ed. by Vincent B. Van Hasselt & Michel Hersen. (Illus.). 720p. (C). 1995. 100.00 (*0-306-45144-1*, Plenum Pr) Plenum.

Sourcebook of Pyroelectricity, Vol. 2. Sidney B. Lang. (Ferroelectricity & Related Phenomena Ser.). 562p. 1974. text ed. 403.00 (*0-677-01580-1*) Gordon & Breach.

***Sourcebook of Reference Methods, Materials & Related Information for the Clinical Laboratory: Proposed Guideline (1994)** Contrib. by Harry S. Hertz. 1994. 75.00 (*1-56238-222-5*, NRSC12-P) Natl Comm Clin Lab Stds.

Sourcebook of Singapore & Malaysian Company Law. Philip N. Pillai. 1386p. 1986. 277.00 (*0-409-99511-8*) MICHIE.

***Sourcebook of Social Support & Personality.** LC 97-17811. (Volume in the Plenum Series in Social/Clinical Psychology Ser.). (Illus.). 444p. (C). 1997. write for info. (*0-306-45535-8*, Plenum Pr) Plenum.

***Sourcebook of State Public Records: The Definitive Guide to Searching for Public Record Information at the State Level.** 3rd rev. ed. Ed. by Carl R. Ernst & Michael Sankey. (Public Record Research Library). 352p. 1997. 35.00 (*1-879792-32-X*) BRB Pubns.

Sourcebook of the Buying Power County U. S. 91. 1991. 309.00 (*0-8103-8341-1*) Gale.

Sourcebook of Titanium Alloy Superconductivity. E. W. Collings. 550p. 1983. 125.00 (*0-306-41344-2*, Plenum Pr) Plenum.

Sourcebook of U. S. Postal Relations in the Western Hemisphere. Intro. by Robert D. Harris. (Illus.). 1990. pap. 50.00 (*0-941480-09-7*) Subway Stamp.

***Sourcebook of Wit & Wisdom.** Joe T. Ford. Ed. by Stan Purdum. 260p. 1996. pap. 39.95 (*0-930921-06-2*) Comm Res OH.

Sourcebook of Woodwaste Recovery & Recycling in the Southeast. C. T. Donovan Associates Staff. 235p. (Orig.). (C). 1995. pap. text ed. 50.00 (*0-7881-1908-7*) DIANE Pub.

***Sourcebook of Worship Resources, Vol. 2.** John Bodo et al. Ed. by Stan Purdum. 243p. 1996. 39.00 (*0-930921-08-9*, SBWR2) Comm Res OH.

Sourcebook of Zip Code Demographics. 7th ed. 1990. 245.00 (*0-918417-01-5*) CACI Mktg Systs.

Sourcebook of Zip Code Demographics. 8th ed. 1993. 295.00 (*0-918417-03-1*) CACI Mktg Systs.

Sourcebook of Zip Code Demographics. 9th ed. CACI Marketing Systems Staff. 1750p. 1994. 295.00 (*0-918417-50-3*) CACI Mktg Systs.

Sourcebook of Zip Code Demographics. 11th ed. 1996. 495.00 (*0-918417-65-1*) CACI Mktg Systs.

Sourcebook of Zip Code Demographics: And User's Guide. 10th ed. 690p. 1995. 495.00 (*0-918417-56-2*) CACI Mktg Systs.

Sourcebook of ZIP Code Demographics: Census Edition, 2 vols., 1. CACI Marketing Systems Staff. 1600p. 1992. 195.00 (*0-918417-06-6*) CACI Mktg Systs.

Sourcebook of ZIP Code Demographics: Census Edition, 2 vols., 2. CACI Marketing Systems Staff. 1600p. 1992. 195.00 (*0-918417-07-4*, 072117) CACI Mktg Systs.

Sourcebook of ZIP Code Demographics: Census Edition, 2 vols., Set. CACI Marketing Systems Staff. 1600p. 1992. 390.00 (*0-918417-08-2*, 072116) CACI Mktg Systs.

Sourcebook on Accounting Principles & Auditing Procedures: 1917 - 1953, 2 vols., Set. Ed. by Stephen A. Zeff & Maurice Moonitz. LC 83-49448. (Accounting History & the Development of a Profession Ser.). 1018p. 1989. text ed. 20.00 (*0-8240-6315-5*) Garland.

Sourcebook on Artificial Intelligence. Stephen J. Andriole & Gerald W. Hopple. 500p. 1988. 49.95 (*0-89433-274-0*, 8263, TAB Bks) Petrocelli.

Sourcebook on Asbestos Diseases. George A. Peters. 3500p. 1989. boxed 500.00 (*0-614-05965-8*) MICHIE.

Sourcebook on Asbestos Diseases: Asbestos Control & Medical Treatment, Vol. 7. George A. Peters & Barbara J. Peters. 1993. 95.00 (*0-88063-797-8*) MICHIE.

Sourcebook on Asbestos Diseases: Asbestos Medical Research, Vol. 4. George A. Peters & Barbara J. Peters. 1989. boxed 75.00 (*0-88063-759-5*) MICHIE.

Sourcebook on Asbestos Diseases: International Asbestos Medical Research, Vol. 6. Ed. by George A. Peters & Barbara J. Peters. 600p. 1991. boxed 95.00 (*0-88063-796-X*) MICHIE.

Sourcebook on Asbestos Diseases Vol. Medical, Legal & Engineering Aspects, Vol. 1. George A. Peters & Barbara J. Peters. 1980. boxed 75.00 (*0-88063-756-0*) MICHIE.

Sourcebook on Asbestos Diseases Vol. Medical, Legal & Engineering Aspects, Vol. 2. George A. Peters & Barbara J. Peters. 1986. boxed 75.00 (*0-88063-757-9*) MICHIE.

Sourcebook on Asbestos Diseases Vol. Medical, Legal & Engineering Aspects, Vol. 3. George A. Peters & Barbara J. Peters. 1988. boxed 75.00 (*0-88063-758-7*) MICHIE.

Sourcebook on Asbestos Diseases Vol. 9: Medical, Legal & Engineering Aspects. George A. Peters & Barbara J. Peters. 1994. boxed 95.00 (*0-614-03169-9*) MICHIE.

Sourcebook on Asbestos Diseases Case Law Quarterly. Quarterly Journal Staff. 1989. 85.00 (*0-8240-7348-7*) MICHIE.

Sourcebook on Asbestos Diseases, Vol. 5: Asbestos Abatement, Vol. 5. George A. Peters & Barbara J. Peters. 800p. 1991. boxed 85.00 (*0-88063-792-7*) MICHIE.

S

Sourcebook on Asbestos Diseases, 1980-1993: Medical, Legal & Engineering Aspects, 8 vols., Set. George A. Peters & Barbara J. Peters. 7100p. 1993. boxed 500.00 (*0-8240-7175-1*) MICHIE.

Sourcebook on Atomic Energy. 3rd ed. Samuel Glasstone. LC 79-1206. 892p. 1979. reprint ed. lib. bdg. 103.50 (*0-88275-898-5*) Krieger.

Sourcebook on Central American Refugee Policy: A Bibliography with Subject & Country Index. Ed. by Milton Jamail & Chandler Stolp. (Special Project Report). 69p. 1985. pap. 7.50 (*0-89940-851-6*) LBJ Sch Pub Aff.

Sourcebook on Child Sexual Abuse. David Finkelhor. (Illus.). 200p. 1986. text ed. 48.00 (*0-8039-2748-7*); pap. text ed. 23.50 (*0-8039-2749-5*) Sage.

Sourcebook on Children & Television. Nancy Signorielli. LC 90-47502. 216p. 1991. text ed. 47.95 (*0-313-26642-5*, SQC/, Greenwood Pr) Greenwood.

Sourcebook on Civil Liberties. Helen Fenwick. (Sourcebook Ser.). 800p. 1996. pap. 33.00 (*1-85941-181-9*, Pub. by Cavendish UK) Gaunt.

Sourcebook on Contract Law. Martin Davis & David W. Oughton. (Sourcebook Ser.). 700p. 1996. pap. 40.00 (*1-85941-048-0*, Pub. by Cavendish UK) Gaunt.

Sourcebook on Criminal Law. Peter Hungerford-Welch & Alan Taylor. (Sourcebook Ser.). 800p. 1997. pap. write for info. (*1-85941-100-2*, Pub. by Cavendish UK) Gaunt.

Sourcebook on Criminal Litigation & Sentencing. Colin Bobb-Semple. (Sourcebook Ser.). 800p. 1996. pap. write for info. (*1-85941-101-0*, Pub. by Cavendish UK) Gaunt.

***Sourcebook on Domestic & International Terrorism: An Analysis of Issues, Organizations, Tactics & Responses.** 2nd ed. Wayman C. Mullins. LC 96-30404. (Illus.). 610p. 1997. text ed. 129.95 (*0-398-06722-8*); pap. text ed. 99.95 (*0-398-06723-6*) C C Thomas.

Sourcebook on Employment Law. Steven Silvester & Tracy Reeves. (Sourcebook Ser.). 750p. 1996. pap. write for info. (*1-85941-184-3*, Pub. by Cavendish UK) Gaunt.

Sourcebook on English Legal System. Gary Slapper. (Sourcebook Ser.). 800p. 1997. pap. 48.00 (*1-85941-106-1*, Pub. by Cavendish UK) Gaunt.

Sourcebook on Environmental Law. James J. Busuttil et al. Ed. by Maurice Sunkin. (Sourcebook Ser.). 750p. 1996. pap. 32.00 (*1-85941-109-6*, Pub. by Cavendish UK) Gaunt.

Sourcebook on Evidence. Christopher Allen. (Sourcebook Ser.). 750p. 1996. pap. 44.00 (*1-85941-110-X*, Pub. by Cavendish UK) Gaunt.

Sourcebook on Feminist Jurisprudence. Hilaire Barnett. (Sourcebook Ser.). 639p. 1997. pap. 98.00 (*1-85941-113-4*, Pub. by Cavendish UK) Gaunt.

Sourcebook on Feminist Theatre & Performance: On & Beyond the Stage. Ed. by Carol Martin. LC 96-17794. (Worlds of Performance Ser.). 336p. (C). 1996. pap. 19.95 (*0-415-10645-1*); text ed. 65.00 (*0-415-10644-3*) Routledge.

Sourcebook on French Law. David Pollard. (Sourcebook Ser.). 340p. 1996. pap. 44.00 (*1-85941-183-5*, Pub. by Cavendish UK) Gaunt.

Sourcebook on German Law. Raymond Youngs. (Sourcebook Ser.). 727p. 1995. pap. 44.00 (*1-85941-108-8*, Pub. by Cavendish UK) Gaunt.

Sourcebook on Intellectual Property Law. Peter J. Groves. (Sourcebook Ser.). 800p. 1997. pap. write for info. (*1-85941-107-X*, Pub. by Cavendish UK) Gaunt.

Sourcebook on Land Law. S. H. Goo. (Sourcebook Ser.). 1134p. 1995. pap. write for info. (*1-85941-105-3*, Pub. by Cavendish UK) Gaunt.

Sourcebook on Law of Trusts. M. Ramjohn. (Sourcebook Ser.). 838p. 1995. pap. write for info. (*1-85941-102-9*, Pub. by Cavendish UK) Gaunt.

Sourcebook on Lead-Acid Batteries. LC 93-23737. 1993. write for info. (*1-55937-365-2*) IEEE Standards.

***Sourcebook on Lead-Acid Batteries & Standards Battery Standards Collection, 2 vols.** 437p. 1993. per. 140.00 (*1-55937-369-5*, SH16744) IEEE Standards.

Sourcebook on New Immigration, Vol. II. Ed. by Roy S. Bryce-Laporte. 302p. 1980. pap. text ed. 29.95 (*0-87855-796-2*) Transaction Pubs.

Sourcebook on Obligations & Legal Remedies. Geoffrey Samuel. (Sourcebook Ser.). 485p. 1995. pap. 36.00 (*1-85941-180-0*, Pub. by Cavendish UK) Gaunt.

Sourcebook on Parenting & Child Care. Ed. by Kathryn H. Carpenter. LC 94-39012. 288p. 1994. pap. 35.00 (*0-89774-780-1*) Oryx Pr.

Sourcebook on Population Nineteen Seventy to Nineteen Seventy-Six. Ed. by Tine Bussink et al. LC 76-27595. 72p. (C). 1976. pap. text ed. 3.95 (*0-917136-01-2*) Population Ref.

Sourcebook on Postretirement Health Care Benefits. Ed. by Robert D. Paul & Diane M. Disney. LC 88-15194. 603p. 1988. 89.00 (*0-916592-76-6*) Panel Pubs.

Sourcebook on Public International Law. Tim Hillier. (Sourcebook Ser.). 800p. 1996. pap. write for info. (*1-85941-050-2*, Pub. by Cavendish UK) Gaunt.

Sourcebook on Public Law. Helen Fenwick & Gavin Phillipson. (Sourcebook Ser.). 1056p. 1997. pap. 50.00 (*1-85941-182-7*, Pub. by Cavendish UK) Gaunt.

Sourcebook on Serious, Violent, & Chronic Juvenile Offenders. Ed. by James C. Howell et al. LC 95-19875. 296p. 1995. 29.95 (*0-8039-7432-9*) Sage.

Sourcebook on Socialist International Organizations. Ed. by William E. Butler. 1168p. 1979. lib. bdg. 280.00 (*90-286-0798-6*) Kluwer Ac.

Sourcebook on Standards Information: Education, Access & Development. Ed. by Steven M. Spivak & Keith A. Winsell. (Professional Librarian Ser.). 425p. (C). 1991. 30.00 (*0-8161-1949-X*, Hall Reference) Macmillan.

Sourcebook on Standards Information: Education, Access & Development. Ed. by Steven M. Spivak & Keith A. Winsell. (Professional Librarian Ser.). 425p. (C). 1991. 45.00 (*0-8161-1948-1*, Hall Reference) Macmillan.

Sourcebook on Succession, Wills & Probate. Ian Jones. (Sourcebook Ser.). 800p. 1997. pap. write for info. (*1-85941-104-5*, Pub. by Cavendish UK) Gaunt.

Sourcebook on the Environment: A Guide to the Literature. Kenneth A. Hammond et al. LC 77-17407. 592p. 1978. lib. bdg. 33.00 (*0-226-31522-3*) U Ch Pr.

Sourcebook on the Teaching of Black Psychology: Instructional Material, Vol. II. Ed. by Reginald L. Jones. 320p. 27.50 (*0-318-13407-1*) Assn Black Psych.

Sourcebook on the Teaching of Black Psychology: Perspectives & Course Outlines, Vol. I. Ed. by Reginald L. Jones. 640p. 35.00 (*0-318-13409-8*) Assn Black Psych.

Sourcebook on Torts. Graham Stephenson. (Sourcebook Ser.). 750p. 1996. pap. write for info. (*1-85941-049-9*, Pub. by Cavendish UK) Gaunt.

Sourcery. Terry Pratchett. 240p. 1989. mass mkt. 6.99 (*0-552-13107-5*) Bantam.

Sourcery for Books One & Two of B. P. Nichol's The Martyrology. Irene Niechoda. 214p. (C). 1992. pap. text ed. 25.00 (*1-55022-102-7*, Pub. by ECW Press CN) Genl Dist Srvs.

Sources. deluxe ed. Adrienne Rich. LC 83-81462. (Illus.). 48p. (Orig.). 1983. 225.00 (*0-940592-15-0*); pap. 19.00 (*0-940592-16-9*) Heyeck Pr.

Sources: An Annotated Bibliography of Women's Issues. Ed. by Rita I. McCullough. 320p. (Orig.). 1991. pap. 24.95 (*1-879198-28-2*) Knwldg Ideas & Trnds.

Sources: Multicultural Influences on Contemporary African American Sculptors. Intro. by Stephanie E. Pogue. 20p. (Orig.). (C). 1994. pap. 4.00 (*0-937123-30-7*) Art Gal U MD.

Sources: Notable Selections in Early Childhood Education. Karen M. Paciorek & Joyce H. Munro. 400p. (C). 1995. per. write for info. (*1-56134-321-8*) Dushkin Pub.

Sources: Notable Selections in Education. Ed. by Fred Schultz. LC 94-48861. 400p. (C). 1995. per. 14.95 (*1-56134-332-3*) Dushkin Pub.

***Sources: Notable Selections in Environmental Studies.** Theodore D. Goldfarb. 368p. (C). 1996. per. write for info. (*0-697-32894-5*) Wm C Brown Pubs.

***Sources: Notable Selections in Human Development.** Diessner. 1997. text ed. 12.70 (*0-697-31051-5*) McGraw.

***Sources: Notable Selections in Psychology.** 2nd ed. Terry F. Pettijohn. 384p. (C). 1996. per. write for info. (*0-697-34331-6*) Wm C Brown Pubs.

Sources: Notable Selections in Race & Ethnicity. Ed. by Adalberto Aguirre, Jr. & David V. Baker. LC 95-122. 416p. (C). 1995. per. 14.95 (*1-56134-319-6*) Dushkin Pub.

Sources: Notable Selections in Social Psychology. Ed. by Terry F. Pettijohn. (Illus.). 336p. (Orig.). (C). 1995. per. 14.95 (*1-56134-314-5*) Dushkin Pub.

Sources: Notable Selections in Sociology. 2nd ed. Kurt Finsterbusch & Janet S. Schwartz. 432p. (C). 1995. per. write for info. (*1-56134-448-6*) Brown & Benchmark.

Sources: One. Ed. by Ernest Warburton. LC 92-33289. (Librettos of Mozart's Operas Ser.: Vol. 6). (Illus.). 312p. 1993. text ed. 70.00 (*0-8153-0113-8*) Garland.

Sources & Analogues of a Midsummer Night's Dream. Frank Sidgwick. LC 78-176018. reprint ed. 27.50 (*0-404-05994-5*) AMS Pr.

Sources & Analogues of Old English Poetry: The Major Latin Texts in Translation. Tr. by Daniel G. Calder & Michael J. Allen. LC 75-2240. 253p. 1970. 59.00 (*0-85991-013-X*) Boydell & Brewer.

Sources & Documents Illustrating the American Revolution, 1764-1788, & the Formation of the Federal Constitution. 2nd ed. Ed. by Samuel E. Morison. 424p. (YA). (gr. 9 up). 1965. pap. 18.95 (*0-19-500262-8*) OUP.

Sources & Documents of U. S. Constitutions, 5 vols. Ed. by William F. Swindler & Donald J. Musch. LC 82-2284. (Second Series, 1942-1900: National Documents). 1982. Incl. bibliography. lib. bdg. 250.00 (*0-379-16187-7*) Oceana.

Sources & Documents of U. S. Constitutions: State Documents, 12 vols. Ed. by William F. Swindler & Bernard D. Reams, Jr. LC 73-170979. 1973. Set. lib. bdg. 555.00 (*0-379-16175-3*) Oceana.

Sources & Effects on Ionizing Radiation: UNSCEAR 1994 Report to the General Assembly. 272p. 1994. 45.00 (*92-1-142211-6*) UN.

***Sources & Effects on Ionizing Radiation: UNSCEAR 1994 Report to the General Assembly.** United Nations Scientific Committee on the Effects of Atomic Radiation. 86p. 1996. pap. 25.00 (*92-1-142219-1*) UN.

Sources & Evidences of International Law. Clive M. Parry. LC 65-17525. (Melland Schill Lectures). 130p. reprint ed. pap. 37.10 (*0-317-30008-3*, 2051868) Bks Demand.

Sources & Fates of Aquatic Pollutants. Ed. by Ronald A. Hites & S. J. Eisenreich. LC 87-1290. (Advances in Chemistry Ser.: No. 216). xiii, 576p. 1987. 99.95 (*0-8412-0983-9*) Am Chemical.

***Sources & Fates of Aquatic Pollutants.** Ed. by Ronald A. Hites & S. J. Eisenreich. LC 87-1290. (Advances in Chemistry Ser.: Vol. 216). 576p. 1987. reprint ed. pap. 164.20 (*0-608-03895-4*, 2064342) Bks Demand.

Sources & Literature of Scottish Church History. Malcolm B. MacGregor. LC 76-1125. 260p. 1977. reprint ed. lib. bdg. 20.00 (*0-915172-10-0*) Richwood Pub.

Sources & Magnitude of Occupational & Public Exposures from Nuclear Medicine Procedures: Recommendations of the National Council on Radiation Protection & Measurements. Intro. by Charles B. Meinhold. LC 96-690. (NCRP Reports: Vol. 124). 77p. (Orig.). 1996. pap. 25.00 (*0-929600-51-7*) NCRP Pubns.

Sources & Methods for Family & Community Historians: A Handbook. Ed. by Ruth Finnegan et al. (Studying Family & Community History Ser.: No. 4). 288p. (C). 1994. text ed. 59.95 (*0-521-46004-2*) Cambridge U Pr.

Sources & Methods for Family & Community Historians: A Handbook. Ed. by Ruth Finnegan et al. (Studying Family & Community History Ser.: No. 4). 288p. (C). 1994. pap. text ed. 19.95 (*0-521-46580-X*) Cambridge U Pr.

Sources & Methods of Historical Demography. Dennis J. Willigan & K. Lynch. (Studies in Social Discontinuity). 1982. pap. text ed. 47.00 (*0-12-757022-5*) Acad Pr.

Sources & Problems in British History Since 1688, 2 Vols. 2nd ed. Ed. & Intro. by Walter L. Arnstein. (Past Speaks Ser.: Vol. II). 427p. (C). 1993. pap. text ed. 23.96 (*0-669-24602-6*) HM College Div.

Sources & Problems in English History to 1688, 2 Vols. 2nd ed. Ed. by Jean R. Smith. (Past Speaks Ser.: Vol. I). 418p. (C). 1993. pap. text ed. 23.96 (*0-669-24601-8*) HM College Div.

Sources & Resources for the Small Business Owner: A Practical & Bibliographic Guide for Profitable Ideas & Solutions. 1992. lib. bdg. 255.75 (*0-8490-8883-6*) Gordon Pr.

***Sources & Resources of Feminist Theologies: Sources et Resources des Theologies Feministes Quellen Feministischer Theologien.** Ed. by Elisabeth Hartlieb & Charlotte Methuen. (Yearbook of the European Society of Women in Theological Research Ser.: Vol. 5). 192p. 1997. pap. 21.00 (*90-390-0215-0*, Pub. by KOK Pharos NE) Eisenbrauns.

Sources & Structure of Flaubert's Salammbo. A. Coleman. (Elliott Monographs: Vol. 2). 1914. pap. 25.00 (*0-527-02606-9*) Periodicals Srv.

Sources & Structures of James Joyce's "Oxen" Robert Janusko. LC 83-6984. (Studies in Modern Literature: No. 15). 180p. reprint ed. pap. 51.30 (*0-8357-1424-1*, 2070482) Bks Demand.

***Sources & Studies on the Ottoman Black Sea: The Customs Register of Caffa, 1487-1490.** Halil Inalcik. (Illus.). 216p. 1997. pap. 39.95 (*0-916458-82-2*) Harvard Ukrainian.

Sources & Text of Richard Wagner's Opera "Die Meistersinger Von Nuernberg" Anne M. Bowen. LC 74-24047. reprint ed. 29.50 (*0-404-12870-X*) AMS Pr.

Sources & Traditions: Types of Compositions in the Talmud of Babylonia. Jacob Neusner. (USF Studies in the History of Judaism). 212p. (C). 1992. 59.95 (*1-55540-675-0*, 240036) Scholars Pr GA.

Sources & Traditions of Classification in Psychiatry. Norman Sartorius. LC 89-24610. 254p. 1990. text ed. 49.00 (*0-920887-74-0*) Hogrefe & Huber Pubs.

***Sources & Trajectories: Eight Early Articles by Jacques Ellul That Set the Stage.** Tr. by Marva J. Dawn from FRE. 224p. (Orig.). 1997. pap. 30.00 (*0-8028-4268-2*) Eerdmans.

Sources, Chemistry, Fate & Effects of Chromium in Aquatic Environments. Ecological Analysts. LC 82-71261. (Orig.). 1982. pap. 20.00 (*0-89364-046-8*, 847-89600) Am Petroleum.

Sources Cited & Artifacts Illustrated see Handbook of Middle American Indians

Sources de la Morale Chretienne see Sources of Christian Ethics

Sources de l'Histoire du Montanisme. Pierre C. Labriolle. LC 80-13175. (Heresies of the Early Christian & Medieval Era Ser.: Second Ser.). reprint ed. 57.50 (*0-404-16184-7*) AMS Pr.

Sources de l'Histoire du Proche-Orient et de l'Afrique dans les Archives et Bibliotheques Francaises, Pt. 2: Bibliotheque Nationale, Pt. 2, Bibliotheque Nationale see Guide to the Sources for the History of Nations

Sources du Travail Bibliographique, 3 tomes. Malcles. Incl. Tome I. Bibliographies Generales. 22.50 (*0-685-35977-8*); Set. Bibliographies Specialisees: Sciences Humaines. , 2 pts. 46.50 (*0-685-35978-6*); Tome III. Bibliographies Specialisees: Sciences Exactes et Techniques. 22.50 (*0-685-35979-4*); write for info. (*0-318-52266-7*) Fr & Eur.

Sources du Vent: Avec: La Balle au Bond. Pierre Reverdy. 256p. (FRE.). 1971. pap. 10.95 (*0-7859-1355-6*, 2070317919) Fr & Eur.

Sources du Vent - Balle au Bond. Pierre Reverdy. (FRE.). 1971. pap. 10.95 (*0-8288-3872-0*, F121020) Fr & Eur.

Sources du Vent. La Balle au Bond. Pierre Reverdy. (Poesie Ser.). 256p. (FRE.). 1971. pap. 9.95 (*2-07-031791-9*) Schoenhof.

Sources, Effects & Risks of Ionizing Radiation, 1988 Report. 647p. 1989. 90.00 (*92-1-142143-8*, E.88.IX.7) UN.

Sources for Alexander the Great: An Analysis of Plutarch's Life & Arrian's Anabasis Alexandrou. Nicholas G. Hammond. LC 92-12772. (Cambridge Classical Studies). 345p. (C). 1993. text ed. 65.00 (*0-521-43264-2*) Cambridge U Pr.

Sources for American Studies. Ed. by Jefferson B. Kellogg & Robert H. Walker. LC 82-11701. (Contributions in American Studies: No. 64). (Illus.). xviii, 766p. 1983. text ed. 85.00 (*0-313-22555-9*, WTO/, Greenwood Pr) Greenwood.

Sources for Colonial Studies in the Public Record Office: British Documents on the End of Empire. Anne Thurston. (Series C: Vol. 1). (Illus.). 479p. 1995. pap. 125.00 (*0-11-440246-9*, HM02469, Pub. by Stationery Ofc UK) Bernan Associates.

Sources for Early Babi Doctrine & History: A Survey. Denis MacEoin. LC 91-43294. ix, 274p. 1992. 89.00 (*90-04-09462-8*) E J Brill.

Sources for History of Quantum Physics: An Inventory & Report. John L. Heilbron & Thomas S. Kuhn. LC 66-26634. (American Philosophical Society, Memoirs Ser.: Vol. 68). 190p. reprint ed. pap. 54.20 (*0-317-08066-0*, 2019709) Bks Demand.

Sources for Jones-Winslow Genealogy: Ancestors of Merrill Elaine Jones & Their Descendants. Richard M. Jones & Merrill E. Jones. x, 270p. 1988. text ed. write for info. (*0-9619805-0-8*) Michael Jones.

Sources for Mass Communications, Film & Theater Research: A Guide. Wisconsin Mass Communications Center Staff. LC 81-12569. 176p. pap. 15.00 (*0-87020-211-1*) State Hist Soc Wis.

Sources for Reinterpretation: The Use of Nineteenth-Century Literary Documents. Ed. by David Farmer. 1975. pap. 10.00 (*0-87959-130-7*) U of Tex H Ransom Ctr.

Sources for Researching Ukrainian Family History No. 6: Research Report. John-Paul Himka & Frances A. Swyripa. 37p. pap. 6.00 (*0-614-14387-X*) Ukrainian Acad.

Sources for the Early History of Ireland: Ecclesiastical. James F. Kenney. 836p. 1994. reprint ed. text ed. 85.00 (*1-85182-115-5*, Pub. by Four Cts Pr IE) Intl Spec Bk.

Sources for the History of Cyprus. Ed. by Paul W. Wallace & Andreas G. Orphanides. pap. write for info. (*0-9651704-0-3*) Greece & Cyprus Res.

Sources for the History of Greek Athletics. Rachel Robinson. 289p. 1980. pap. 20.00 (*0-89005-297-2*) Ares.

Sources for the History of Irish Civilization Articles in Irish Periodicals. 1989. 1,200.00 (*0-8161-1750-0*, Hall Library) G K Hall.

Sources for the History of Medicine in Medieval England. Tr. & Intro. by Carole Rawcliffe. LC 94-45554. (Documents of Practice Ser.). 1996. pap. 6.00 (*1-879288-54-0*) Medieval Inst.

Sources for the Study of Gender in American History. Ellen Skinner. 192p. reprint ed. pap. 7.95 (*1-886746-17-6*, 93366) Talman.

Sources for the Study of Greek Religion. David G. Rice & John E. Stambaugh. LC 79-18389. (Society of Biblical Literature Resources for Biblical Study: No. 14). 277p. 1979. pap. 14.95 (*0-89130-347-2*, 060314) Scholars Pr GA.

Sources for the Study of Puerto Rican Migration, 1879-1930. History Task Force Centro de Estudios Staff. (Illus.). 224p. 1982. pap. 10.00 (*1-878483-10-2*) Hunter Coll CEP.

Sources for the Study of the Administration of Criminal Justice, 1938 - 1948: A Selected Bibliography. Dorothy C. Tompkins. LC 73-108218. (Criminology, Law Enforcement, & Social Problems Ser.: No. 101). 1970. reprint ed. 30.00 (*0-87585-101-0*) Patterson Smith.

Sources for U. S. History: Nineteenth-Century Communities. W. B. Stephens. (Sources of History Ser.). 576p. (C). 1991. text ed. 29.95 (*0-521-35315-7*) Cambridge U Pr.

Sources for Vital Records Before Nineteen Hundred. Arlene H. Eakle. 83p. 1974. pap. 18.00 (*0-940764-09-1*) Genealog Inst.

***Sources in American Constitutional History.** Ed. by Michael Les Benedict. 330p. (C). 1996. pap. text ed. 22.76 (*0-669-39471-8*) HM College Div.

Sources in British Political History, 1900-1950, Consolidated Vol. 6. Christopher Cook. LC 75-4012. 256p. 1985. text ed. 39.95 (*0-312-74659-8*) St Martin.

Sources in British Political History, 1900-1951: A Guide to the Papers of Selected Public Servants, 1. Christopher Cook. LC 75-15220. 320p. 1975. text ed. 32.50 (*0-312-74620-2*) St Martin.

Sources in British Political History, 1900-1951: A Guide to the Papers of Selected Public Servants, 2. Christopher Cook. LC 75-15220. 320p. 1975. text ed. 32.50 (*0-312-74655-5*) St Martin.

Sources in Educational Research: A Selected & Annotated Bibliography, Vol. 1. Theodore Manheim et al. LC 68-64690. 319p. reprint ed. 91.00 (*0-685-16227-3*, 2027601) Bks Demand.

Sources in Electrical History 3: An International Guide to Corporate Records & Archives of Companies in the Electrical, Electronics, & Computer Industries. John Riddle et al. ix, 77p. (Orig.). 1995. pap. 15.00 (*0-7803-9997-8*) Inst Electrical.

Sources in European Political History, Vol. 1: The European Left. Chris Cook & Geoff Pugh. 256p. 1987. 40.00 (*0-8160-1016-1*) Facts on File.

Sources in European Political History, Vol. 2: Diplomacy & International Affairs. Chris Cook et al. 288p. 1989. 40.00 (*0-8160-1756-5*) Facts on File.

Sources in European Political History, Vol. 3: War & Resistance. Ed. by Chris Cook. 260p. 1992. lib. bdg. 35.00 (*0-8160-1757-3*) Facts on File.

***Sources in Iconography at the Blackader-Lauterman Library of Architecture & Art, McGill University: An Annotated Biography.** Irena Z. Murray. (Illus.). 230p. 1997. 45.00 (*0-7735-1452-X*, Pub. by McGill CN) U of Toronto Pr.

Sources in the History of American Pharmacology. John Parascandola & Elizabeth Keeney. 1983. pap. 5.60 (*0-931292-12-3*) Am Inst Hist Pharm.

Sources, Musical, Prior to 1450: In His Harvard Dictionary of Music. Willi Apel. 1993. reprint ed. lib. bdg. 89.00 (*0-7812-9696-X*) Rprt Serv.

Sources, Occurrence, & Control of Chlorine Dioxide By-Product Residuals in Drinking Water. (Illus.). 208p. 1994. pap. 90.00 (*0-89867-769-6*, 90656) Am Water Wks Assn.

Sources of African & Middle-Eastern Economic Information, 2 vols. Ed. by Euan Blauvelt & Jennifer Durlacher. LC 81-4125. 1982. text ed. 250.00 (*0-313-23058-7*, BAF/) Greenwood.

An Asterisk (*) at the beginning of an entry indicates that the title is appearing in BIP for the first time.

Sources of African & Middle-Eastern Economic Information, 2 vols., 1. Ed. by Euan Blauvelt & Jennifer Durlacher. LC 81-4125. 1982. text ed. 250.00 (*0-313-23059-5*, BAF/01) Greenwood.

Sources of African & Middle-Eastern Economic Information, 2 vols., Vol. 2. Ed. by Euan Blauvelt & Jennifer Durlacher. LC 81-4125. 1982. text ed. 250.00 (*0-313-23060-9*, BAF/02) Greenwood.

Sources of Ancient & Primitive Law. Albert Kocourek & John H. Wigmore. LC 93-78307. (Evolution of Law Ser.). iv, 720p. 1994. reprint ed. 75.00 (*0-89941-860-0*, 308060) W S Hein.

Sources of Anglo-Saxon Culture. Ed. by Paul E. Szarmach & Virginia Oggins. (Studies in Medieval Culture: No. 20). 1986. pap. 17.95 (*0-918720-68-0*); boxed 37.95 (*0-918720-67-2*) Medieval Inst.

Sources of Anglo-Saxon Literary Culture: A Trial Version. Ed. by Frederick M. Biggs et al. (Medieval & Renaissance Texts & Studies: Vol. 74). 300p. 1990. pap. 20.00 (*0-86698-084-9*, MR74) MRTS.

Sources of Architectural Form: A Critical History of the Western Design Theory. Mark Gelernter. LC 94-12283. 1995. text ed. 79.95 (*0-7190-4128-7*, Pub. by Manchester Univ Pr UK); text ed. 29.95 (*0-7190-4129-5*, Pub. by Manchester Univ Pr UK) St Martin.

Sources of Art Nouveau. Stephan T. Madsen. LC 75-26819. (Quality Paperbacks Ser.). (Illus.). 1976. pap. 10.95 (*0-306-80024-1*) Da Capo.

Sources of Art Noveau. Stephan T. Madsen. Tr. by Ragnar Christopherson. LC 74-34464. (Architecture & Decorative Art Ser.). (Illus.). 488p. 1975. reprint ed. lib. bdg. 59.50 (*0-306-70733-0*) Da Capo.

Sources of Asian Pacific Economic Information, 2 vols., 1. Ed. by Euan Blauvelt & Jennifer Durlacher. LC 80-28645. 1981. text ed. 250.00 (*0-313-22964-3*, BLS/1) Greenwood.

Sources of Asian Pacific Economic Information, 2 vols., Set. Ed. by Euan Blauvelt & Jennifer Durlacher. LC 80-28645. 1981. text ed. 250.00 (*0-313-22963-5*, BLS/) Greenwood.

Sources of Asian Pacific Economic Information, 2 vols., Vol. 2. Ed. by Euan Blauvelt & Jennifer Durlacher. LC 80-28645. 1981. text ed. 250.00 (*0-313-22965-1*, BLS/2) Greenwood.

Sources of British Chronicle History in Spenser's Faerie Queene. Carrie A. Harper. LC 65-15868. (Studies in Spenser: No. 26). 1969. reprint ed. lib. bdg. 75.00 (*0-8383-0565-2*) M S G Haskell Hse.

Sources of British Feminism. Ed. by Marie M. Roberts. 2017p. (C). 1993. text ed. 615.00 (*0-415-10164-6*, Routledge NY) Routledge.

***Sources of Cadmium in the Environment.** OECD Staff. 484p. (Orig.). 1996. pap. 67.00 (*92-64-15343-8*, 97-96-13-1, Pub. by Org for Econ FR) OECD.

Sources of Capital for Community Economic Development. Leonard E. Smollen et al. 261p. 1976. pap. text ed. 18.95 (*0-87855-776-8*, Pergamon Pr) Elsevier.

Sources of Charlotte Bronte's Novels: Persons & Places. Herbert E. Wroot. LC 68-1923. 1970. reprint ed. 75.00 (*0-8383-0688-8*) M S G Haskell Hse.

Sources of Chinese Tradition, 2 Vols, Vol. 1. Ed. by William T. Debary. LC 60-9911. (Records of Civilization: Sources & Studies). 578p. 1964. pap. text ed. 19.50 (*0-231-08602-4*) Col U Pr.

Sources of Chinese Tradition, 2 Vols, Vol. 2. Ed. by William T. Debary. LC 60-9911. (Records of Civilization: Sources & Studies). 322p. 1964. pap. text ed. 17.00 (*0-231-08603-2*) Col U Pr.

***Sources of Christian Ethics.** Servais Pinckaers. Tr. by Mary T. Moble. LC 94-28663. 489p. 1995. 44.95 (*0-8132-0834-3*) Cath U Pr.

Sources of Christian Ethics. 3rd ed. Servais Pinckaers. Tr. by Mary T. Noble from FRE. LC 94-28663. Orig. Title: Sources de la Morale Chretienne. 489p. 1995. pap. 24.95 (*0-8132-0818-1*) Cath U Pr.

Sources of Classicism: Five Centuries of Architectural Books from the Collections of the Humanities Research Center. Drury B. Alexander. (Illus.). 1978. pap. 8.00 (*0-87959-084-X*) U of Tex H Ransom Ctr.

Sources of Coherence in Reading. Ed. by Robert F. Lorch & Edward J. O'Brien. 416p. 1995. pap. 39.95 (*0-8058-1637-2*); text ed. 89.95 (*0-8058-1339-X*) L Erlbaum Assocs.

Sources of Compiled Legislative Histories: Bibliography of Government Documents, Periodical Articles & Books, 1st Congress - 99th Congress. Nancy P. Johnson. (American Association of Law Libraries Publications Ser.: No. 14). 1988. ring bd., vinyl bd. 35.00 (*0-8377-0112-0*) Rothman.

Sources of Confirmation from the Fathers Through the Reformers. Paul Turner. 96p. (Orig.). 1993. pap. 6.95 (*0-8146-2006-X*) Liturgical Pr.

***Sources of Consciousness: The Biophysical & Computational Basis of Thought.** 400p. 1997. 38.00 (*981-02-2921-6*) World Scientific Pub.

Sources of Contemporary Philosophical Realism in America. Herbert W. Schneider. LC 62-16954. 1964. reprint ed. pap. text ed. 6.95 (*0-672-60282-2*) Irvington.

Sources of Dark Matter in the Universe. David B. Cline. 332p. 1995. text ed. 86.00 (*981-02-2131-2*) World Scientific Pub.

Sources of Dramatic Theory: Plato to Congreve, Vol. 1. Ed. by Michael J. Sidnell. 325p. (C). 1991. text ed. 69.95 (*0-521-32694-X*) Cambridge U Pr.

Sources of Dramatic Theory Vol. 2: Voltaire to Hugo. Michael J. Sidnell. 292p. (C). 1995. text ed. 69.95 (*0-521-32695-8*) Cambridge U Pr.

Sources of Economic Growth. Richard R. Nelson. LC 96-16498. (Illus.). 288p. 1996. 39.95 (*0-674-82145-9*) HUP.

Sources of English Constitutional History, Vol. 1: A Selection of Documents from A. D. 600 to the Interregnum. rev. ed. Ed. by Carl Stephenson & Frederick G. Marcham. LC 72-84325. 548p. reprint ed. pap. 156.20 (*0-7837-4508-7*, 2044285) Bks Demand.

Sources of English Legal History: Private Law to 1750. J. H. Baker. 698p. 1986. pap. 39.50 (*0-614-05966-6*) MICHIE.

Sources of English Legal History, 1750-1950. A. H. Manchester. 1984. 102.00 (*0-406-51659-6*, U.K.) MICHIE.

Sources of European Economic & Business Information. 6th ed. Ed. by British Library Business Information Research Service Staff. LC 94-11836. 352p. 1995. 199.95 (*0-566-07487-7*, Pub. by Gower UK) Ashgate Pub Co.

Sources of Four Plays Ascribed to Shakespeare. G. Harold Metz. LC 88-4793. (Illus.). 528p. 1989. text ed. 48.00 (*0-8262-0690-5*) U of Mo Pr.

Sources of Gravitational Radiation. Larry Smarr. LC 79-50177. (Illus.). 1979. 39.50 (*0-521-22778-X*) Cambridge U Pr.

Sources of Growth: A Study of Seven Latin American Economies. Elias. 300p. 1992. pap. 14.95 (*1-55815-143-5*); 5.00 (*1-55815-189-3*) ICS Pr.

Sources of Hamlet: With Essays on the Legend. Israel Gollance. (BCL1-PR English Literature Ser.). 321p. 1992. reprint ed. lib. bdg. 89.00 (*0-7812-7270-X*) Rprt Serv.

Sources of Hermeneutics. Jean Grondin. LC 94-22339. (SUNY Series in Contemporary Continental Philosophy). 193p. (C). 1995. text ed. 39.50 (*0-7914-2465-0*); pap. text ed. 12.95 (*0-7914-2466-9*) State U NY Pr.

Sources of Hong Kong Law. Peter Wesley-Smith. 356p. 1994. pap. 52.50 (*962-209-363-9*, Pub. by Hong Kong Univ Pr HK) Coronet Bks.

Sources of Hope. Fitzgerald. 1979. text ed. 28.00 (*0-08-023105-5*, Pergamon Pr); pap. text ed. 17.50 (*0-08-023104-7*, Pergamon Pr) Elsevier.

Sources of Hyperbolic Geometry. John C. Stillwell. LC 96-3894. (History of Mathematics Ser.: Vol. 10). 1996. 39.00 (*0-8218-0529-0*, HMATH/10) Am Math.

Sources of Ignition: Flammability Characteristics of Chemical & Products. John Bond. 200p. 1991. 49.95 (*0-7506-1180-4*) Buttrwrth-Heinemann.

Sources of Income Inequality: A Case Study of Delhi. Harbhajan Sighn. (C). 1990. 24.00 (*81-7050-126-1*, Pub. by Patriot II) S Asia.

Sources of Income Inequality & Poverty in Rural Pakistan. Richard H. Adams, Jr. & Jane J. He. (Research Report Ser.: No. 102). 1995. write for info. (*0-89629-105-7*) Intl Food Policy.

Sources of Indian Tradition, 2 vols., I. 2nd ed. Ed. by Ainslie T. Embree. (Introduction to Oriental Civilizations Ser.). 1988. pap. text ed. 19.50 (*0-231-06651-1*) Col U Pr.

Sources of Indian Tradition, 2 vols., II. 2nd ed. Ed. by Ainslie T. Embree. (Introduction to Oriental Civilizations Ser.). 1988. pap. text ed. 19.50 (*0-231-06415-2*) Col U Pr.

Sources of Indian Tradition, 2 vols., Vol. II. 2nd ed. Ed. by Ainslie T. Embree. (Introduction to Oriental Civilizations Ser.). 464p. 1988. text ed. 65.00 (*0-231-06414-4*) Col U Pr.

Sources of Indoor Air Contaminants: Characterizing Emissions & Health Impacts. Ed. by W. G. Tucker et al. LC 92-9221. (Annals Ser.: Vol. 641). 329p. 1992. pap. 65.00 (*0-89766-716-6*, RA566) NY Acad Sci.

Sources of Information for Historical Research. Thomas P. Slavens. LC 94-8119. 577p. 1994. 45.00 (*1-55570-093-4*) Neal-Schuman.

Sources of Information for Independent & Overland Travellers. Shane Winser. (C). 1993. 20.00 (*0-907649-59-9*) St Mut.

Sources of Information for the Offshore Industry: Papers Presented at the Joint Conference Between the Information for Energy Group & the Association of British Offshore Industries on 12th June, 1986. Institute of Petroleum, London Staff. Ed. by J. J. Etherton. LC 87-134526. (Illus.). 74p. reprint ed. pap. 25.00 (*0-7837-6847-8*, 2046676) Bks Demand.

Sources of Information in Librarianship & Information Science. 2nd ed. Raymond J. Prytherch. 190p. 1987. text ed. 49.95 (*0-566-05509-0*, Pub. by Gower UK) Ashgate Pub Co.

Sources of Information in the Social Sciences: A Guide to the Literature. 2nd ed. Carl M. White. LC 73-9825. 720p. reprint ed. pap. 180.00 (*0-7837-5910-X*, 2045708) Bks Demand.

Sources of Innovation. Eric A. Von Hippel. (Illus.). 232p. (C). 1994. reprint ed. pap. text ed. 19.95 (*0-19-509422-0*) OUP.

Sources of Innovation: An Economic Analysis. Ira R. Bikar. 1992. 22.50 (*81-7040-275-1*, Pub. by Himalaya II) Apt Bks.

Sources of Inspiration: Fifteen Modern Religious Leaders. Ed. by Gene I. Maeroff. LC 92-27494. 308p. (Orig.). 1992. 29.95 (*1-55612-602-6*); pap. 19.95 (*1-55612-556-9*, LL1556) Sheed & Ward MO.

Sources of Inter-State Conflict. Robert Litwak. LC 80-28448. (Security in the Persian Gulf Ser.: Vol. 2). 100p. 1981. pap. text ed. 19.50 (*0-86598-045-4*) Rowman.

***Sources of International Law.** Date not set. text ed. 295.00 (*90-411-0421-6*) Kluwer Law Tax Pubs.

***Sources of Irish Traditional Music c. 1600-1855: An Annotated Catalogue of Prints & Manuscripts, 1583-1855, 2 vols.** Ed. by Aloys Fleischmann et al. LC 97-21886. 1428p. 1997. 250.00 (*0-8240-6948-X*) Garland.

Sources of Islamic Law. John Burton. 272p. 1990. 65.00 (*0-7486-0108-2*, Pub. by Edinburgh U Pr UK) Col U Pr.

Sources of Japanese Industrial Success: The Case of the Television Receiver Industry. Vincent A. LaFrance. LC 96-535. (Contributions in Economics & Economic History Ser.: No. 179). 1997. text ed. write for info. (*0-313-26070-2*, Greenwood Pr) Greenwood.

Sources of Japanese Tradition, 2 Vols, 1. Ed. by William T. Debary. LC 58-7167. (Records of Civilization: Sources & Studies). 1964. pap. text ed. 19.00 (*0-231-08604-0*) Col U Pr.

Sources of Japanese Tradition, 2 Vols, 2. Ed. by William T. Debary. LC 58-7167. (Records of Civilization: Sources & Studies). 1964. pap. text ed. 18.00 (*0-231-08605-9*) Col U Pr.

Sources of John Dryden's Comedies. Ned B. Allen. LC 67-21718. 316p. 1967. reprint ed. 60.00 (*0-87752-002-X*) Gordian.

Sources of Keyboard Music in England. Charles V. Borren. Tr. by James E. Matthew. LC 78-106714. 378p. 1970. reprint ed. text ed. 65.00 (*0-8371-3444-7*, BOKM, Greenwood Pr) Greenwood.

Sources of Keyboard Music in England. Charles Van Den Borren. 378p. 1990. reprint ed. lib. bdg. 79.00 (*0-7812-9111-9*) Rprt Serv.

Sources of Keyboard Music in England. Charles Van Den Borren. 378p. 1991. reprint ed. lib. bdg. 89.00 (*0-7812-9351-0*) Rprt Serv.

Sources of Korean Tradition: From Early Times Through the 16th Century. Ed. by Peter H. Lee & W. Theodore De Bary. LC 96-17701. 480p. 1996. pap. 22.50 (*0-231-10567-3*) Col U Pr.

Sources of Law: A Comparative Empirical Study - National Systems of Sources of Law. Heinz Schaffer et al. 375p. (C). 1982. 84.00 (*963-05-0000-0*) St Mut.

Sources of Law, Legal Change & Ambiguity. Alan Watson. LC 83-21783. 164p. 1984. 38.95 (*0-8122-7919-0*) U of Pa Pr.

Sources of Light: Contemporary American Luminism. Harvey West & Chris Bruce. (Illus.). 84p. (Orig.). 1985. pap. 22.50 (*0-935558-13-6*) Henry Art.

Sources of London English: Medieval Thames Vocabulary. Laura Wright. (Illus.). 256p. 1996. 60.00 (*0-19-823909-2*) OUP.

Sources of Masonic Symbolism. Alex Horne. (Illus.). xii, 83p. 1982. reprint ed. text ed. 12.50 (*0-88053-074-X*, M-064) Macoy Pub.

Sources of Meaning in Motion Pictures & Television. Calvin Pryluck. Ed. by Garth S. Lowett. LC 75-21434. (Dissertations on Film Ser.). 1976. lib. bdg. 23.95 (*0-405-07535-9*) Ayer.

Sources of Medical Technology: Universities & Industry, Vol. 5. Institute of Medicine Staff. Ed. by Annetine C. Gelijns & Nathan Rosenberg. (Medical Innovation at the Crossroads Ser.). 280p. (Orig.). (C). 1995. pap. text ed. 32.00 (*0-309-05189-4*) Natl Acad Pr.

Sources of Metropolitan Growth. Ed. by Edwin S. Mills & John F. McDonald. LC 91-8650. 331p. (C). 1992. 29.95 (*0-88285-135-7*) Ctr Urban Pol Res.

Sources of Military Doctrine: France, Britain & Germany Between the World Wars. Barry R. Posen. LC 84-7610. (Cornell Studies in Security Affairs). 288p. 1984. 39.95 (*0-8014-1633-7*); pap. 15.95 (*0-8014-9427-3*) Cornell U Pr.

Sources of Modern Architecture & Design. Nikolaus Pevsner. (World of Art Ser.). (Illus.). 216p. 1985. pap. 14.95 (*0-500-20072-6*) Thames Hudson.

Sources of Modern Eclecticism. Demetri Porphyrios. (Academy Architecture Ser.). (Illus.). 128p. 1982. 19.95 (*0-312-74673-3*) St Martin.

Sources of Modern Eclecticism. Demetri Porphyrios. (Academy Architecture Ser.). (Illus.). 128p. 1982. pap. 19.95 (*0-312-74674-1*) St Martin.

Sources of Modern Painting. Ed. by James S. Plaut. LC 79-91372. (Contemporary Art Ser.). 1970. reprint ed. 19.95 (*0-405-00734-5*) Ayer.

Sources of Modern Photography Series, 51 bks., Vol. 26. Ed. by Peter C. Bunnell & Robert A. Sobieszek. (Illus.). 1979. Vols. 26-51. lib. bdg. 1,393.00 (*0-405-18980-X*) Ayer.

Sources of Modern Photography Series, 51 bks., Vols. 1-25. Ed. by Peter C. Bunnell & Robert A Sobieszek. (Illus.). 1979. lib. bdg. 1,393.00 (*0-405-09597-X*) Ayer.

Sources of Montaigne's Thought. Ed. by Dikka Berven. LC 94-41683. (Montaigne Ser.: Vol. 2). 376p. 1995. text ed. 70.00 (*0-8153-1840-5*) Garland.

Sources of Moral Agency: Essays in Moral Psychology & Freudian Theory. John Deigh. 304p. (C). 1996. text ed. 59.95 (*0-521-55418-7*); pap. text ed. 18.95 (*0-521-55622-8*) Cambridge U Pr.

Sources of Mortality Changes in Italy Since Unification. Elizabeth Hoffman. Ed. by Stuart Bruchey. LC 80-2811. (Dissertations in European Economic History Ser.). (Illus.). 1981. lib. bdg. 30.95 (*0-405-13995-0*) Ayer.

Sources of Much Ado about Nothing. Charles T. Prouty. LC 76-128893. (Select Bibliographies Reprint Ser.). 1977. reprint ed. 19.95 (*0-8369-5513-7*) Ayer.

Sources of Normativity. Christine M. Korsgaard. 295p. (C). 1996. pap. text ed. 17.95 (*0-521-55960-X*) Cambridge U Pr.

Sources of Normativity. Christine M. Korsgaard. 295p. (C). 1996. text ed. 49.95 (*0-521-55059-9*) Cambridge U Pr.

Sources of Our Liberties. Ed. by Richard L. Perry. LC 78-67316. 466p. 1994. reprint ed. 47.50 (*0-89941-752-3*, 305030) W S Hein.

***Sources of Power: How People Make Decisions.** Gary Klein. 1997. 40.00 (*0-262-11227-2*) MIT Pr.

Sources of Power of the Apostolic Witness. Robert Shank. 125p. 1982. pap. 3.95 (*0-911620-05-2*) Westcott.

Sources of Productivity Growth. Ed. by David G. Mayes. (National Institute of Economic & Social Research Occasional Papers: No. 49). (Illus.). 407p. (C). 1996. text ed. 59.95 (*0-521-55437-3*) Cambridge U Pr.

Sources of Products for Blind & Visually Impaired Persons. American Foundation for the Blind Staff. LC 92-159159. 59p. reprint ed. pap. 25.00 (*0-7837-5188-5*, 2044922) Bks Demand.

Sources of Published & Unpublished Administrative Opinions in New York State. Robert A. Carter. 12p. 1985. 5.00 (*0-318-22976-5*) NYS Library.

Sources of Quantum Mechanics. Ed. by B. L. Van Der Waerden. pap. text ed. 8.95 (*0-486-61881-1*) Dover.

Sources of Roman Law: Problems & Methods for Ancient Historians. O. F. Robinson. (Approaching the Ancient World Ser.). 168p. (C). 1996. pap. write for info. (*0-415-08995-6*); text ed. write for info. (*0-415-08994-8*) Routledge.

Sources of Russian Foreign Policy After the Cold War. Ed. by Celeste A. Wallander. (John M. Olin Critical Issues Ser.). (C). 1996. pap. text ed. 22.95 (*0-8133-2833-0*) Westview.

Sources of Secession. Gerrit J. Ten Zythoff. (Historical Series of the Reformed Church in America: Vol. 17). 216p. (Orig.). 1987. pap. 13.00 (*0-8028-0328-8*) Eerdmans.

Sources of Self Evaluation: A Formal Theory of Significant Others & Social Influence. Murray Webster, Jr. & Barbara Sobieszek. LC 74-5066. 213p. reprint ed. pap. 60.80 (*0-8357-9981-6*, 2016473) Bks Demand.

S

Sources of Semiotic: Readings with Commentary from Antiquity to the Present. D. S. Clarke, Jr. LC 89-26105. 240p. (C). 1990. 29.95 (*0-8093-1613-7*); pap. 15.95 (*0-8093-1614-5*) S Ill U Pr.

Sources of Shang History: The Oracle-Bone Inscriptions of Bronze Age China. David N. Keightley. LC 74-29806. 1979. pap. 35.00 (*0-520-05455-5*) U CA Pr.

Sources of Social Power, Vol. 1: A History of Power from the Beginning to AD 1760. Michael Mann. (Illus.). 608p. 1986. text ed. 95.00 (*0-521-30851-8*); pap. text ed. 32.95 (*0-521-31349-X*) Cambridge U Pr.

Sources of Social Power, Vol. 2: The Rise of Classes & Nation States, 1760-1914. Michael Mann. (Illus.). 816p. (C). 1993. text ed. 80.00 (*0-521-44015-7*); pap. text ed. 31.95 (*0-521-44585-X*) Cambridge U Pr.

Sources of Soviet Perestroika. John Lenczowski. (Essay Ser.: No. 2). 60p. (Orig.). (C). 1990. pap. text ed. 3.00 (*1-878802-01-1*) J M Ashbrook Ctr Pub Affairs.

Sources of Spenser's Classical Mythology. Alice E. Randall. 1972. 35.00 (*0-8490-1092-6*) Gordon Pr.

Sources of Spenser's Classical Mythology. Alice E. Randall. LC 72-115364. reprint ed. 21.50 (*0-404-05223-1*) AMS Pr.

Sources of Spiritual Strength. John M. Drescher. 1975. pap. 1.99 (*0-8361-1772-7*) Herald Pr.

Sources of Stones Used in Prehistoric Mesoamerican Sites. Ed. by Robert F. Heizer et al. (Illus.). 103p. 1976. reprint ed. pap. 7.95 (*0-87919-060-4*) Ballena Pr.

***Sources of Strength.** large type ed. Jimmy Carter. (Large Print Ser.). 1997. pap. 22.00 (*0-679-77453-X*) Random.

***Sources of Strength: Meditations on Scripture for Daily Living.** Jimmy Carter. 1997. 22.00 (*0-8129-2944-6*, Times Bks) Random.

Sources of Swiss Anabaptism: The Grebel Letters & Related Documents. Ed. by Leland Harder. LC 85-5520. (Classics of the Radical Reformation Ser.: Vol. 4). (Illus.). 821p. 1985. reprint ed. pap. 180.00 (*0-608-01764-7*, 2062422) Bks Demand.

Sources of the African-American Past. Roy Finkenbine. 192p. reprint ed. pap. 6.95 (*1-886746-16-8*, 93388) Talman.

Sources of the African Past. David Robinson & Douglas Smith. LC 79-5399. 203p. 1979. 47.95 (*0-8419-0337-9*, Africana) Holmes & Meier.

Sources of the Biography of Aldhelm. Albert S. Cook. (Connecticut Academy of Arts & Sciences Ser., Trans.: Vol. 28). 1927. pap. 39.50 (*0-685-22809-6*) Elliots Bks.

Sources of the Constitution of the United States Considered in Relation to Colonial & English History. 2nd enl. rev. ed. C. Ellis Stevens. xviii, 313p. 1987. reprint ed. lib. bdg. 30.00 (*0-8377-2616-6*) Rothman.

Sources of the Faust Tradition. Philip M. Palmer & Robert P. More. LC 65-29231. (Studies in Comparative Literature: No. 35). 1969. reprint ed. lib. bdg. 75.00 (*0-8383-0608-X*) M S G Haskell Hse.

***Sources of the Grail.** John Matthews. 1997. 45.00 (*0-940262-86-X*) Lindisfarne Bks.

***Sources of the Grail.** Ed. & Intro. by John Matthews. 576p. 1997. pap. 19.95 (*0-940262-87-8*, 2026) Lindisfarne Bks.

Sources of the History of Africa, Asia, Australia & Oceania in Hungary. Ed. by International Council on Archives Staff & National Archives of Hungary Staff. (Guide to the Sources of the History of Nations Ser.). 520p. 1991. lib. bdg. 82.00 (*3-598-21485-5*) K G Saur.

Sources of the History of Asia & Oceania in the Netherlands, Pt. 1, Up to 1796 see Guide to the Sources for the History of Nations

Sources of the History of Asia & Oceania in the Netherlands, Pt. 2, Sources 1796-1940 see Guide to the Sources for the History of Nations

Sources of the Increases in Poverty, Work Effort, & Income Distribution Data. 1994. lib. bdg. 255.95 (*0-8490-5698-5*) Gordon Pr.

Sources of the Parson's Tale. Kate O. Petersen. LC 72-954. reprint ed. 27.50 (*0-404-04997-4*) AMS Pr.

Sources of the Pentateuch: Texts, Introductions, Annotations. Anthony F. Campbell & Mark A. O'Brien. LC 92-20894. 286p. 1992. 29.00 (*0-8006-2701-6*, 1-2701) Augsburg Fortress.

An Asterisk (*) at the beginning of an entry indicates that the title is appearing in BIP for the first time.

Sources of the Polish Tradition, 3 vols., Set. Raymond Cwieka. Bd. with Vol. 1. Great Polish Walking Dance: Polonaise.; Vol. 2. Elegant Running-Sliding Dance: Mazur, Mazurka.; Vol. 3. Dance Figures: Historical Contemporary (A Choreographer's Handbook). Complete 3 vols. set. Set pap. 35.00 (*0-317-13907-X*) R Cwieka.

Sources of the Polish Tradition, 3 vols., Set, Vols. II & II. Raymond Cwieka. Bd. with Vol. 1. Great Polish Walking Dance: Polonaise.; Vol. 2. Elegant Running-Sliding Dance: Mazur, Mazurka.; Vol. 3. Dance Figures: Historical Contemporary (A Choreographer's Handbook). Vols. II & III Bound as a Set. Set pap. 25.00 (*0-915277-01-8*) R Cwieka.

Sources of the Quaker Peace Testimony. Howard H. Brinton. (C). 1944. pap. 3.00 (*0-87574-027-8*) Pendle Hill.

Sources of the Quaran. Hamza M. Njozi. 96p. 1991. pap. write for info. (*1-882837-29-0*) W A M Y Intl.

Sources of the Religious Element in Flaubert's Salammbo. A. Hamilton. (Elliott Monographs: Vol. 4). 1917. 25.00 (*0-527-02608-5*) Periodicals Srv.

Sources of the River: Tracking David Thompson Across Western North America. Jack Nisbet. LC 94-6478. 288p. 1995. pap. 14.95 (*1-57061-006-1*) Sasquatch Bks.

Sources of the Self: The Making of the Modern Identity. Charles Taylor. 624p. (C). 1992. pap. 19.95 (*0-674-82426-1*) HUP.

Sources of the Transformation of Judaism: From Philosophy to Religion in the Classics of Judaism: A Reader. Jacob Neusner. LC 92-42836. (USF Studies in the History of Judaism: Vol. 68). 307p. 1993. 74.95 (*1-55540-813-3*, 240068) Scholars Pr GA.

Sources of the West, Vol. I. Mark A. Kishlansky. (C). 1991. pap. text ed. 30.50 (*0-673-38473-X*) Addson-Wesley Educ.

Sources of the West, Vol. II. Mark A. Kishlansky. (C). 1991. pap. text ed. 33.95 (*0-673-38474-8*) Addson-Wesley Educ.

Sources of the West: Readings for Western Civilization, 2 vols., 1. 2nd ed. Mark A. Kishlansky. LC 94-33127. (C). 1995. text ed. 32.50 (*0-673-99290-X*) Addson-Wesley Educ.

Sources of the West: Readings for Western Civilization, 2 vols., 2. 2nd ed. Mark A. Kishlansky. LC 94-33127. (C). 1995. pap. text ed. 32.50 (*0-673-99291-8*) Addson-Wesley Educ.

***Sources of the Western Tradition, 3 Vols.** 3rd ed. Marvin Perry et al. (C). 1995. teacher ed., text ed. 11.96 (*0-395-68975-9*) HM.

***Sources of the Western Tradition, 3 Vols., Vol. I.** 3rd ed. Marvin Perry et al. 464p. (C). 1994. pap. text ed. 27.96 (*0-395-68973-2*) HM.

Sources of the Western Tradition, Vol. 2. Marvin Perry et al. LC 86-81593. (C). 1987. pap. text ed. 19.16 (*0-685-17245-7*) HM.

***Sources of the Western Tradition, 3 Vols., Vol. II.** 3rd ed. Marvin Perry et al. 464p. (C). 1994. pap. text ed. 27.96 (*0-395-68974-0*) HM.

Sources of the White Devil. Gunnar Boklund. (Essays & Studies on English Language & Literature: Vol. 17). 1974. reprint ed. pap. 25.00 (*0-8115-0215-5*) Periodicals Srv.

Sources of the White Devil, John Webster. Gunnar Boklund. LC 68-1396. (Studies in Comparative Literature: No. 35). 1969. reprint ed. lib. bdg. 75.00 (*0-8383-0648-9*) M S G Haskell Hse.

Sources of Theatrical History see Source Book in Theatrical History

Sources of Thermodynamic Data on Mesogens: A Special Issue of the Journal of Molecular Crystals & Liquid Crystals. A. Beguin et al. 340p. 1984. pap. text ed. 287.00 (*0-677-16575-7*) Gordon & Breach.

Sources of Tritium & Its Behavior upon Release to the Environment. D. G. Jacobs. LC 68-67209. (AEC Critical Review Ser.). 90p. 1968. 10.25 (*0-87079-345-4*, TID-24635); fiche 9.00 (*0-87079-346-2*, TID-24635) DOE.

Sources of Unofficial U. K. Statistics. 2nd ed. Univ. of Warwick Business Information Service Staff. 496p. 1990. text ed. 89.95 (*0-566-02795-X*, Pub. by Gower UK) Ashgate Pub Co.

***Sources of Unofficial U. K. Statistics.** 3rd ed. David Mort. LC 96-51905. 480p. 1997. text ed. 95.95 (*0-566-07672-1*, Pub. by Gower UK) Ashgate Pub Co.

Sources of Vijayanagar History. Ed. by S. Krishnaswamy Ayyangar. 414p. 1986. 22.00 (*81-212-0038-5*, Pub. by Gian Pubing Hse II) S Asia.

Sources of Vitality in American Church Life. Ed. by Robert L. Moore. LC 78-71065. (Studies in Ministry & Parish Life). 1978. text ed. 14.95 (*0-913552-14-3*) Exploration Pr.

Sources of Wealth & the Causes of Poverty. Intro. by Paul C. Goelz. LC 90-63055. (Illus.). 136p. 1990. 18.95 (*0-945632-02-9*) St Marys Univ Pr.

***Sources of Western Civilization, Vol. 1.** 3rd ed. Ed. by Kishlansky. (C). 1998. text ed. write for info. (*0-321-01135-X*) Addson-Wesley Educ.

***Sources of Western Civilization, Vol. 2.** 3rd ed. Ed. by Kishlansky. (C). 1998. text ed. write for info. (*0-321-01136-8*) Addson-Wesley Educ.

Sources of Western Literacy: The Middle Eastern Civilizations. Felix Reichmann. LC 79-8292. (Contributions in Librarianship & Information Science Ser.: No. 29). 274p. 1980. text ed. 55.00 (*0-313-20948-0*, RWL/, Greenwood Pr) Greenwood.

Sources of Western Morality: From Primitive Society Through the Beginning of Christianity. Georgia E. Harkness. LC 72-10723. reprint ed. pap. 29.50 (*0-404-10643-9*) AMS Pr.

Sources of Western Zhou History: Inscribed Bronze Vessels. Edward L. Shaughnessy. LC 90-49891. (Illus.). 312p. 1991. 58.00 (*0-520-07028-3*, SHASOU) U CA Pr.

Sources of World Civilization. Ed. by Oliver A. Johnson. LC 93-11660. 444p. 1994. pap. text ed. 31.40 (*0-13-962457-0*) P-H.

Sources of World Civilization Vol. II: Since 1500. Oliver A. Johnson. (Illus.). 444p. 1993. pap. text ed. 31.40 (*0-13-095829-8*) P-H.

Sources of World History, 2 vols., I. Mark A. Kishlansky. (C). 1995. text ed. 29.50 (*0-06-501034-5*) Addson-Wesley Educ.

Sources of World History, 2 vols., II. Mark A. Kishlansky. (C). 1995. text ed. 29.50 (*0-06-501035-3*) Addson-Wesley Educ.

Sources of World History Vol. 1: Beginnings-1500, Vol. I. Mark A. Kishlansky. 352p. reprint ed. pap. 28.00 (*1-886746-12-5*, 93370) Talman.

Sources of World History Vol. 2: 1500-Present, Vol. II. Mark A. Kishlansky. 402p. reprint ed. pap. 28.00 (*1-886746-13-3*, 93371) Talman.

Sources on National Movement, Vol. 1: January 1919-Septemer 1920, Protest, Disturbance & Defiance. Ed. by V. N. Datta & S. C. Mittal. 1985. 24.00 (*0-8364-1499-3*, Pub. by Allied II) S Asia.

Sources on the History of Women's Magazines, 1792-1960: An Annotated Bibliography. Compiled by Mary E. Zuckerman. LC 91-12151. (Bibliographies & Indexes in Women's Studies: No. 12). 352p. 1991. text ed. 59.95 (*0-313-26378-7*, WSZ, Greenwood Pr) Greenwood.

Sources, Processes & Methods in Coleridge's Biographia Literaria. Kathleen M. Wheeler. LC 79-41683. 240p. 1980. 74.95 (*0-521-22690-2*) Cambridge U Pr.

Sources, Structures & Synthesis Vol. 1: Proceedings of the Groningen 1983 Achaemenid History Workshop. Ed. by Heleen Sancisi-Weerdenburg. (Achaemenid History Ser.: Vol. 1). xiv, 196p. 1987. pap. text ed. 59.50 (*90-6258-401-2*, Pub. by Netherlands Inst NE) Eisenbrauns.

***Sources to Teach Any Phase of Baseball.** Bud Zeiger. (Illus.). vi, 122p. (Orig.). 1996. pap. 14.95 (*0-9653623-0-2*) BJKSZ.

Sources 2. Ed. by Ernst Warburton. LC 92-33289. (Librettos of Mozart's Operas Ser.: Vol. 7). 328p. 1993. text ed. 70.00 (*0-8153-0897-3*) Garland.

Sourciere. Marie Cardinal. (FRE.). 1978. pap. 10.95 (*0-7859-3208-9*, 2266006495) Fr & Eur.

Sourcing Prehistoric Ceramics at Chodistaas Pueblo, Arizona: The Circulation of People & Pots in the Grasshopper Region. Maria N. Zedeno. (Anthropological Papers: No. 58). (Illus.). 150p. (Orig.). 1994. 13.95 (*0-8165-1455-0*) U of Ariz Pr.

Sourcing the Moment. (Illus.). (Orig.). pap. write for info. (*1-884068-06-5*) Amethyst Pub.

Sourdough Baking: Fabulous Recipes for Bread Machines & Traditional Methods. Susan Draudt. LC 94-34432. (Illus.). 144p. 1994. pap. 10.95 (*1-55561-067-6*) Fisher Bks.

Sourdough Breads & Coffee Cakes from Lane Farm: Worth 104 Recipes. Ada L. Roberts. (Cookery, Wine, Nutrition Ser.). 192p. 1983. reprint ed. pap. 4.95 (*0-486-24529-2*) Dover.

Sourdough Cookin'. Dean Tucker. 1976. 3.95 (*0-89036-071-5*) Hawkes Pub Inc.

Sourdough Jim Pitcher: The Autobiography of a Pioneer Alaskan. James S. Pitcher. LC 85-22857. (Northern History Library). (Illus.). 64p. (Orig.). 1985. pap. 6.95 (*0-88240-308-7*) Alaska Northwest.

***Sourdough Sagas.** Ed. by Herbert L. Heller. 256p. 1997. pap. 7.95 (*0-89174-062-7*) Comstock Edns.

Sourdough Schoolmarm: An Alaskan Adventure. C. Donald Chrysler. LC 92-90425. 178p. 1992. pap. 7.95 (*0-9633908-1-3*) Chrysler Bks.

Sourdough Wars. Julie Smith. 1992. mass mkt. 5.99 (*0-8041-0929-X*) Ivy Books.

Sourire de la Joconde et Autre Tres Courts Romans. Aldous Huxley. 320p. (FRE.). 1981. pap. 11.95 (*0-7859-2643-7*, 207037291X) Fr & Eur.

Sourires Pinces see Oeuvres

Sourwood. Venelda H. Leonard. 430p. 1995. 24.95 (*0-9647919-0-0*) Leonard Publ.

Sous Benefice d'Inventaire. Marguerite Yourcenar. 312p. (FRE.). 1988. 13.95 (*0-7859-0460-3*, 2070324974) Fr & Eur.

Sous Benefice d'Inventaire. Marguerite Yourcenar. (Folio Essais Ser.: No. 110). (FRE.). pap. 11.95 (*2-07-032497-4*) Schoenhof.

Sous la Lumiere Froide. Pierre Mac Orlan. 224p. (FRE.). 1979. pap. 10.95 (*0-7859-4124-X*, 2070371530) Fr & Eur.

Sous la Revolution, le Consulat, l'Empire see Histoire de la Presse Francaise

Sous le Filet. Iris Murdoch. (FRE.). 1985. pap. 15.95 (*0-7859-4221-1*) Fr & Eur.

Sous le Signe du Dragon. Paul Claudel. 232p. (FRE.). 1958. 10.95 (*0-7859-1127-8*, 2070215318) Fr & Eur.

Sous le Soleil de Satan. Georges Bernanos. 1957. 11.95 (*0-7859-0610-X*, F87820) Fr & Eur.

Sous les Rois Tres Chretiens (Du XIIIe au XVIIIe Siecle) see Histoire du Catholicisme en France

Sousa Band: A Discography. 1992. lib. bdg. 76.00 (*0-8490-8768-6*) Gordon Pr.

Sousa's Great Marches in Piano Transcription. John P. Sousa. LC 74-93543. 111p. (Orig.). 1975. pap. 5.95 (*0-486-23132-1*) Dover.

Souslinoid & Analytic Sets in a General Setting. Arthur Kruse. LC 52-42839. (Memoirs Ser.: No. 1/86). 127p. 1969. pap. 16.00 (*0-8218-1286-6*, MEMO/1/86) Am Math.

Souterrains. Jack Kerouac. 177p. (FRE.). 1985. pap. 10.95 (*0-7859-2510-4*, 2070376907) Fr & Eur.

South. Ariel Books Staff. (Illus.). 80p. 1995. 4.95 (*0-8362-3131-7*) Andrews & McMeel.

South. David Clark. (Battlefield Walks Ser.). (Illus.). 192p. 1996. pap. 17.95 (*0-7509-0260-4*, Pub. by Sutton Pubng UK) Bks Intl VA.

South. Tom Egerton. LC 87-81210. (Illus.). 128p. (Orig.). 1987. 39.95 (*0-932575-32-3*) Gr Arts Ctr Pub.

South. B. C. Hall & C. T. Wood. 432p. 1995. 28.00 (*0-02-547450-2*) S&S Trade.

South. B. C. Hall. 352p. 1996. pap. 13.00 (*0-684-81893-0*, Touchstone Bks) S&S Trade.

South. Tony Horwitz. 1997. write for info. (*0-679-43978-1*) Pantheon.

South. Darcy Richardson. (Bertinetti Ser.). 1992. 14.98 (*0-8317-7939-X*) Smithmark.

***South.** Woodalls Publishing Staff. (Woodall's Camping Guide Ser.). 1997. pap. text ed. 5.99 (*0-7627-0151-X*) Globe Pequot.

South. Colm Toibin. 240p. 1992. reprint ed. pap. 11.95 (*0-14-014986-4*, Penguin Bks) Viking Penguin.

South: A Central Theme. Ed. by Monroe L. Billington. LC 76-23223. (American Problem Studies). 122p. 1976. reprint ed. pap. text ed. 10.50 (*0-88275-410-6*) Krieger.

South: A Play. Julian Green. 128p. (Orig.). 1992. pap. 14.95 (*0-7145-2936-2*) M Boyars Pubs.

South: A Tour of Its Battle Fields & Ruined Cities. John T. Trowbridge. LC 69-18549. (American Negro: His History & Literature. Series 2). 1969. reprint ed. 25.95 (*0-405-01898-3*) Ayer.

South: A Treasury of Art & Literature. Lisa N. Howorth. (Illus.). 384p. 1993. 75.00 (*0-88363-593-3*) H L Levin.

South: Modern Southern Literature. Louis D. Rubin, Jr. & Robert D. Jacobs. LC 73-16744. 434p. 1974. reprint ed. text ed. 65.00 (*0-8371-7224-1*, RUS, Greenwood Pr) Greenwood.

South see Crime & Justice in American History

South Africa. (World Focus Ser.). (Illus.). (J). (gr. 3-7). pap. 3.99 (*0-431-07268-X*, Pub. by Oxfam UK) Humanities.

South Africa. John Barraclough. LC 95-25035. (World Forum Ser.). (J). 1996. write for info. (*1-57572-025-6*) Rigby Interact Libr.

South Africa. Berlitz Editors. (Pocket Guides Ser.). (Illus.). 144p. 1994. pap. 7.95 (*2-8315-1583-1*) Berlitz.

South Africa. Don Brothers. (Let's Visit Places & Peoples of the World Ser.). (Illus.). 120p. (YA). (gr. 5 up). 1989. lib. bdg. 16.95 (*1-55546-790-3*) Chelsea Hse.

South Africa. David J. Cranmer & Valerie A. Woolston. (Pelham Guides Ser.). 33p. (C). Date not set. 22.00 (*0-929851-86-2*) Am Assn Coll Registrars.

South Africa. Zo E. Dawson. LC 95-16714. (Postcards From Ser.). 32p. (J). (gr. k-3). 1995. lib. bdg. 21.40 (*0-8172-4015-2*) Raintree Steck-V.

***South Africa.** Zoe Dawson. (Postcards From Ser.). (J). 1996. pap. text ed. 4.95 (*0-8172-4236-8*) Raintree Steck-V.

South Africa. Paul Duncan. (Thomas Cook Illustrated Guides Ser.). (Illus.). 192p. (Orig.). 1996. pap. 12.95 (*0-8442-9124-2*, Passport Bks) NTC Pub Grp.

***South Africa.** Ann Heinrichs. LC 96-31634. (True Bk.). (J). 1997. lib. bdg. 19.00 (*0-516-20340-1*) Childrens.

South Africa. Peter Joyce. (Regional Guides of Africa Ser.). 1995. pap. text ed. 19.95 (*0-8442-8959-0*, Passport Bks) NTC Pub Grp.

***South Africa.** Peter Joyce. (Globetrotter Travel Guide Ser.). 1995. pap. 9.95 (*1-85368-365-5*) St Mut.

South Africa. Peter Lowis. LC 95-12096. (Topics in the News Ser.). (J). 1996. lib. bdg. 22.83 (*0-8172-4175-2*) Raintree Steck-V.

***South Africa.** Gary Mead. 328p. 1997. pap. 17.95 (*0-8442-4851-7*) NTC Pub Grp.

South Africa. Nelles/Verlag Staff. (Nelles Guides Ser.). 1996. pap. text ed. 14.95 (*3-88618-411-0*, Pub. by Nelles Verlag GW) Seven Hills Bk.

South Africa. Charles K. Robertson. 128p. 1986. pap. 3.95 (*0-88144-072-8*) Christian Pub.

***South Africa.** Patrick M. Ryan. LC 96-30664. (Country Bks.). 32p. (J). (gr. 2-6). 1997. lib. bdg. 22.79 (*1-56766-373-7*) Childs World.

***South Africa.** Anthony Trollope. Ed. by J. H. Davidson. (South African Biographical & Historical Studies: No. 14). 614p. 1973. 60.00 (*0-86961-029-5*, Pub. by A A Balkema NE) Ashgate Pub Co.

South Africa. rev. ed. Geoffrey V. Davis. 463p. 1994. lib. bdg. 99.00 (*1-85109-203-X*) ABC-CLIO.

South Africa. A. J. Christopher. LC 81-8254. (World's Landscapes Ser.). (Illus.). 255p. (Orig.). reprint ed. pap. 72.70 (*0-8357-3545-1*, 2034494) Bks Demand.

South Africa, Pt. 1. Anthony Trollope. 1987. pap. 5.00 (*0-86299-319-9*, Pub. by Sutton Pubng UK) Bks Intl VA.

South Africa: A Glance at Current Conditions. John H. Browne. LC 70-76494. 238p. 1969. reprint ed. text ed. 35.00 (*0-8371-1091-2*, BRS&, Greenwood Pr) Greenwood.

South Africa: A Modern History. 3rd rev. ed. T. R. Davenport. LC 85-223940. 716p. reprint ed. pap. 180.00 (*0-7837-1230-8*, 2041367) Bks Demand.

South Africa: A Modern History. 4th ed. T. H. Davenport. 658p. 1991. 60.00 (*0-8020-5940-6*); pap. 27.50 (*0-8020-6880-4*) U of Toronto Pr.

South Africa: A Modern History. T. R. Davenport. LC 77-375725. 447p. reprint ed. pap. 127.40 (*0-685-16081-5*, 2056136) Bks Demand.

South Africa: A Study in Conflict. Pierre L. Van den Berghe. 1967. pap. 16.00 (*0-520-01294-1*) U CA Pr.

South Africa: A Study in Conflict. Pierre L. Van Den Berghe. LC 79-27899. (Illus.). x, 371p. 1980. reprint ed. text ed. 65.00 (*0-313-22349-1*, VASA, Greenwood Pr) Greenwood.

South Africa: An Annotated Bibliography with Analytical Introductions. Newell M. Stultz. LC 88-39540. (Resources on Contemporary Issues Ser.: No. 3). 191p. 1989. pap. 40.00 (*0-87650-254-0*) Pierian.

South Africa: Blue Portraits. Reiner Leist. (Illus.). 176p. 1996. pap. 35.00 (*3-923922-42-6*, Pub. by Nazraeli Pr GW) Dist Art Pubs.

South Africa: Blue Portraits. Reiner Leist. (Illus.). 1996. 50.00 (*3-923922-23-X*, Pub. by Nazraeli Pr GW) Dist Art Pubs.

South Africa: Briefing - Extensive Violations of Human Rights. (Illus.). 1986. 4.00 (*0-939994-16-X*) Amnesty Intl USA.

South Africa: Colonialism, Apartheid & African Dispossession. Alfred T. Moleah. 550p. (Orig.). 1993. 45.00 (*0-913255-02-5*); pap. 35.00 (*0-913255-03-3*); text ed. 45.00 (*0-685-67439-8*); pap. text ed. 35.00 (*0-685-67441-X*); lib. bdg. 45.00 (*0-685-67438-X*) Disa Press Inc.

South Africa: Coming of Age under Apartheid. Jason Laure & Ettagale Laure. LC 79-23109. (Illus.). 192p. 1980. 15.95 (*0-374-37146-6*) FS&G.

South Africa: Crossing the Rubicon. Guy Arnold. LC 91-25584. 190p. 1992. text ed. 65.00 (*0-312-06812-3*) St Martin.

***South Africa: Designing New Political Institutions.** Ed. by Murray Faure & Jan-Erik Lane. 288p. 1996. 75.00 (*0-7619-5302-7*); pap. 22.95 (*0-7619-5303-5*) Sage.

South Africa: Diary of Troubled Times. Nomavenda Mathiane. Ed. by James Finn. LC 88-33590. (Focus on Issues Ser.: No. 7). (Illus.). 189p. 1989. 23.95 (*0-932088-38-4*); pap. 12.95 (*0-932088-37-6*) Freedom Hse.

South Africa: Economic & Political Aspects. Hector M. Robertson. LC 57-8817. (Duke University, Commonwealth-Studies Center, Publication Ser.: No. 2). 204p. reprint ed. pap. 58.20 (*0-317-20422-X*, 2023442) Bks Demand.

South Africa: Foreign Investment & Apartheid. Lawrence Litvak et al. 100p. 1978. write for info. (*0-318-59935-X*); pap. 3.95 (*0-685-43367-6*) Inst Policy Stud.

South Africa: From Apartheid to Natural Unity, 1981-1994. Ed. by William Gutteridge. (Research Institute for the Study of Conflict & Terrorism Ser.). 250p. 1995. text ed. 59.95 (*1-85521-632-9*, Pub. by Dartmth Pub UK) Ashgate Pub Co.

South Africa: Human Rights & the Rule of Law. International Commission of Jurists. Ed. by Geoffrey Bindman. 250p. 1988. pap. 16.50 (*0-86187-779-9*); text ed. 55.00 (*0-86187-979-1*) St Martin.

***South Africa: In the Midst of Change.** Peter Kizilos. LC 97-6774. (World in Conflict Ser.). (J). 1998. lib. bdg. write for info. (*0-8225-3558-0*, Lerner Publctns) Lerner Group.

South Africa: In Transition to What? Ed. by Helen Kitchen. LC 87-35918. (Washington Papers: No. 132). 206p. 1988. pap. text ed. 12.95 (*0-275-92974-4*, B2974, Praeger Pubs) Greenwood.

South Africa: In Transition to What? Ed. by Helen Kitchen. LC 87-35918. (Washington Papers: No. 132). 206p. 1988. text ed. 45.00 (*0-275-92975-2*, C2975, Praeger Pubs) Greenwood.

South Africa: Land of Hope. 2nd ed. Taffy G. McCallum. 1990. 21.95 (*0-620-14195-6*) Fielden Bks.

South Africa: Myths & Realities of Divestiture. Ed. by Linda Griffin & Amy Meharg. (International Economics Seminar Ser.). (Illus.). 36p. (Orig.). (C). 1985. pap. 5.95 (*0-87641-250-9*) Carnegie Ethics & Intl Affairs.

South Africa: No Easy Path to Peace. Graham Leach. (Illus.). 312p. 1987. pap. 8.95 (*0-413-15330-4*, A0168) Routledge.

South Africa: Prison Conditions in South Africa. Africa Watch Staff & Human Rights Watch Prison Project Staff. 136p. (Orig.). 1994. pap. 10.00 (*1-56432-126-6*) Hum Rts Watch.

South Africa: Prospects for Successful Transition. Ed. by Bob Tucker & Bruce R. Scott. 314p. 1992. pap. 20.00 (*0-7021-2920-8*, Pub. by Juta SA) Gaunt.

South Africa: Pt. 1 - Human Rights & Genocide; Pt. 2 - Biography as Interpretation. Leo Kuper & Hilda Kuper. (Hans Wolff Memorial Lecture Ser.). 1981. pap. text ed. 5.00 (*0-941934-33-0*) Indiana Africa.

South Africa: Race & Residence. Joyce E. Kirk. (C). 1997. text ed. 65.00 (*0-8133-2769-5*) Westview.

***South Africa: Regional Guide of Africa.** Peter Joyce. 1997. pap. 19.95 (*0-8442-8958-2*) NTC Pub Grp.

South Africa: Swaziland & Lesotho. Rupert Isaacson. (Cadogan Country Guides Ser.). (Illus.). 576p. 1995. pap. 21.95 (*0-947754-71-7*) Globe Pequot.

***South Africa: The Battle over the Constitution.** Siri Gloppen. LC 97-24962. (Law, Social Change & Development Ser.). (Illus.). 320p. 1997. text ed. 63.95 (*1-85521-922-0*, KTL2070.G59, Pub. by Dartmth Pub UK) Ashgate Pub Co.

South Africa: The Making of U. S. Policy, 1962-1989, Guide & Index, 2 vols., Set. National Security Archive Staff & Chadwyck-Healey Staff. Ed. by Kenneth Mokoena. (Making of U. S. Policy Ser.). (Illus.). 1992. 900.00 (*0-89887-073-9*) Chadwyck-Healey.

South Africa: The New Beginning. (C). 1990. 295.00 (*1-85564-084-8*) St Mut.

South Africa: The Peasant's Revolt. Govan Mbeki. 1990. 14.50 (*0-8446-0791-6*) Peter Smith.

South Africa: The Poltical Economy of Transformation. Ed. by Stephen J. Stedman. LC 93-33330. (SAIS African Studies Library). 215p. 1994. lib. bdg. 42.00 (*1-55587-421-5*) Lynne Rienner.

South Africa: The Press & the Politics of Liberation. Chenhamo C. Chimutengwende. 208p. (C). 1978. pap. 75.00 (*0-905507-05-3*, Pub. by Barbican Bks UK) St Mut.

An Asterisk (*) at the beginning of an entry indicates that the title is appearing in BIP for the first time.

South Africa: The Process of Political Transformation. Robert M. Price. (Illus.). 336p. (C). 1991. pap. 20.95 (0-19-506750-9) OUP.

South Africa: The Prospects of Peaceful Change. Theodor Hanf et al. LC 81-47583. (Prospect of Peaceful Change). 512p. 1981. 35.00 (0-253-35394-7) Ind U Pr.

South Africa: The Sanctions Report. Ed. by Joseph Hanlon. 342p. (C). 1990. pap. 25.00 (0-435-08049-0, 08049) Heinemann.

South Africa: The Struggle for a New Order. Marina Ottaway. 1993. 36.95 (0-8157-6716-1); pap. 16.95 (0-8157-6715-3) Brookings.

South Africa: Time of Agony, Time of Destiny. Martin Murray. 496p. (C). (gr. 13). 1994. text ed. 64.95 (0-86091-365-1, Pub. by Verso UK) Routledge Chapman & Hall.

South Africa: Time of Agony, Time of Destiny. Martin Murray. 496p. (C). 1994. pap. text ed. 19.00 (0-86091-577-8, Pub. by Vrso UK) Norton.

South Africa: Time Running Out. Commission on U. S. Policy Toward Southern Africa Study Staff. LC 81-2742. (Perspectives on Southern Africa Ser.: No. 29). (Illus.). 1981. pap. 16.00 (0-520-04547-5) U CA Pr.

South Africa: To the Sources of Apartheid. Steven Debroey. LC 88-37221. 626p. (Orig.). (C). 1989. pap. text ed. 44.00 (0-8191-7319-3) U Pr of Amer.

***South Africa: Traveler's Survival Kit.** (Illus.). 1997. pap. 17.95 (1-85458-175-9, Pub. by Vacation-Work UK) Petersons.

South Africa: Troubled Land. rev. ed. Elaine Pascoe. LC 92-13608. (Illus.). 144p. (YA). (gr. 9-12). 1992. lib. bdg. 22.70 (0-531-11139-3) Watts.

South Africa: Twelve Perspectives on the Transition, Vol. 2. Ed. by Helen Kitchen & J. Coleman Kitchen. LC 94-35607. (Washington Papers: Vol. 165). 203p. 1994. text ed. 55.00 (0-275-95086-7, Praeger Pubs); pap. text ed. 18.95 (0-275-95087-5, Praeger Pubs) Greenwood.

South Africa: Walking the Last Mile. S. C. Saxena. xi, 508p. 1992. 42.00 (81-85163-30-8, Pub. by Kalinga Pubns) Nataraj Bks.

South Africa: Walking the Last Mile. S. C. Saxena. (C). 1992. text ed. 48.00 (0-685-67751-6, Pub. by Asian Educ Servs II) S Asia.

South Africa see Women in Society - Group 1

South Africa see Cultures of the World - Group 6

***South Africa: A Botched Civilization? Racial Conflict & Identity in Selected South African Novels.** Jane Davis. LC 96-36986. 216p. 1997. 52.50 (0-7618-0604-0); pap. 29.50 (0-7618-0605-9) U Pr of Amer.

South Africa a Century Ago. Anne L. Barnard. Ed. by W. H. Wilkins. LC 71-116271. x, 316p. 1972. reprint ed. 29.00 (0-403-00461-6) Scholarly.

South Africa: A Tapestry of Peoples & Traditions see Exploring Cultures of the World

***South Africa After Apartheid.** Henry F. Jackson. Date not set. write for info. (0-688-07689-0) Morrow.

South Africa & Africa: Within or Apart? Ed. by Adebayo Adedeji. 256p. 1996. 59.95 (1-85649-403-9, Pub. by Zed Bks Ltd UK); pap. 25.00 (1-85649-404-7, Pub. by Zed Bks Ltd UK) Humanities.

South Africa & Bantustans. Abnash Kaur. (Illus.). iv, 169p. 1995. 23.00 (81-85163-62-6, Pub. by Kalinga Pubns) Nataraj Bks.

South Africa & Nuclear Proliferation. J. D. Moore. 260p. 1988. text ed. 39.95 (0-312-74698-9) St Martin.

South Africa & the Anthropologist. Adam Kuper. 256p. 1987. text ed. 59.95 (0-7102-0982-7, 09872, RKP) Routledge.

South Africa & the Marxist Movement: A Study in Double Standards. Panos D. Bardis. LC 89-12643. (African Studies: Vol. 13). 250p. 1989. lib. bdg. 89.95 (0-88946-174-0) E Mellen.

South Africa & the United States: The Declassified History. Ed. by Kenneth Mokoena. 344p. 1994. 35.00 (1-56584-081-X) New Press NY.

South Africa & the United States: The Erosion of an Influence Relationship. Richard E. Bissell. LC 81-22663. (Studies of Influence in International Relations). 172p. 1982. text ed. 55.00 (0-275-90764-3, C0764, Praeger Pubs) Greenwood.

South Africa & the World: The Foreign Policy of Apartheid. Amry Vandenbosch. LC 76-111516. 311p. reprint ed. pap. 88.70 (0-8357-8597-1, 2034972) Bks Demand.

South Africa & the World Economy in the 1990's. Pauline H. Baker. 1993. pap. 16.95 (0-8157-0775-4) Brookings.

South Africa As Apartheid Ends: An Annotated Bibliography with Analytical Introductions. Newell M. Stultz. 240p. 1994. pap. 40.00 (0-87650-330-X) Pierian.

***South Africa at a New Crossroads: Planning Scenarios, Sectoral Prospects & Corporate Strategies to 2001.** 1996. 545.00 (0-85058-930-4, P518) Economist Intell.

South Africa at the Crossroads. Jacqueline D. Meisel. LC 94-8350. (Headliners Ser.). (Illus.). 64p. (J). (gr. 5-8). 1994. lib. bdg. 17.40 (1-56294-511-4) Millbrook Pr.

South Africa at War: White Power & the Crisis in Southern Africa. Richard Leonard & Lawrence Hill. 280p. (Orig.). 1983. 8.95 (0-317-36642-4) Africa Fund.

South Africa Atlas. Globe Pequot Press Staff. 1996. pap. text ed. 12.95 (1-85368-393-0) Globe Pequot.

South Africa Belongs to Us: A History of the ANC. Francis Meli. LC 88-39946. (Illus.). 290p. 1989. pap. 15.95 (0-253-28591-7) Ind U Pr.

South Africa Contemporary Analysis. Ed. by Glenn Moss & Ingrid Obery. 650p. 1990. lib. bdg. 82.00 (0-905450-42-6, Pub. by H Zell Pubs UK) Bowker-Saur.

South Africa: From Soweto to Uitenhage: The Political Economy of the South African Revolution. Bernard M. Magubane. LC 86-73223. 225p. (C). 1989. 35.00 (0-86543-050-0); pap. 11.95 (0-86543-051-9) Africa World.

South Africa in Crisis. Ed. by Jesmond Blumenfeld. 312p. 1987. lib. bdg. 45.00 (0-7099-4252-4, A0408, Pub. by Croom Helm UK) Routledge Chapman & Hall.

South Africa in Focus. Ed. by Willem Drechsel et al. Tr. by Jacky Meyer from DUT. LC 92-40867. (In Focus Ser.). (Illus.). 158p. 1993. 39.95 (0-7103-0462-5, B2339) Routledge Chapman & Hall.

South Africa in Pictures. Department of Geography, Lerner Publications. (Visual Geography Ser.). (Illus.). 64p. (YA). (gr. 5 up). 1988. lib. bdg. 19.95 (0-8225-1835-X, Lerner Publctns) Lerner Group.

South Africa in Southern Africa: The Intensifying Vortex of Violence. Ed. by Thomas M. Callaghy. 432p. 1983. text ed. 75.00 (0-275-90956-5, C0956, Praeger Pubs) Greenwood.

South Africa in the 21st Century. Ettagale Blauer. 1998. pap. 17.99 (0-525-45637-6) Viking Penguin.

***South Africa, Lesotho & Swaziland.** 3rd ed. Jon Murray et al. (Illus.). 672p. 1997. pap. 21.95 (0-86442-508-2) Lonely Planet.

South Africa, Lesotho & Swaziland: Travel Survival Kit. 2nd ed. Richard Everist et al. (Illus.). 656p. 1996. pap. 17.95 (0-86442-323-3) Lonely Planet.

South Africa Nuclear-Tipped Ballistic Missile Capability. (Study Ser.: No. 23). 57p. 1991. 20.00 (92-1-142178-0, 91.IX.15) UN.

South Africa Plays: New South African Drama. Ed. by Stephen Gray. 256p. 1993. pap. 19.95 (1-85459-148-7, Pub. by N Hern Bks UK) Theatre Comm.

***South Africa Since 1945.** Shillington. 1995. pap. text ed. write for info. (0-582-05524-5, Pub. by Longman UK) Longman.

South Africa, the Colonial Powers & "African Defence" The Rise & Fall of the White Entente, 1948-60. Geoff R. Berridge. LC 92-18426. 1993. text ed. 59.95 (0-312-08592-3) St Martin.

***South Africa Travel Atlas.** Jon Murray. (Illus.). 80p. 1997. pap. 14.95 (0-86442-443-4) Lonely Planet.

South Africa under Apartheid: A Select & Annotated Bibliography. Jacqueline A. Kalley. LC 89-31983. 554p. 1989. text ed. 95.00 (0-313-28088-6, KSG/, Greenwood Pr) Greenwood.

South Africa under the Curse of Apartheid. Steven Debroey. LC 89-22619. 660p. (C). 1990. lib. bdg. 57.50 (0-8191-7546-3) U Pr of Amer.

South Africa Without Apartheid: Dismantling Racial Domination. Heribert Adam & Kogila A. Moodley. (Perspectives on Southern Africa Ser.: No. 39). 300p. 1986. 38.00 (0-520-05769-4); pap. 16.00 (0-520-05770-8) U CA Pr.

South African Banking Legislation. F. R. Malan & A. N. Oelofse. 400p. 1991. ring bd. write for info. (0-7021-2572-5, Pub. by Juta SA) Gaunt.

South African Bibliography: A Survey of Bibliographies & Bibliographical Work. 3rd ed. Reuben Musiker. 160p. (C). 1996. text ed. 70.00 (0-7201-2225-2, Mansell Pub) Cassell.

South African Campaign, 1879. J. P. Mackinnon & S. H. Shadbolt. (Illus.). 384p. 1995. 50.00 (1-85367-203-3, Pub. by Greenhill Bks UK) Stackpole.

South African Churches in a Revolutionary Situation. Marjorie Hope & James Young. LC 81-9584. 282p. reprint ed. pap. 80.40 (0-8357-2677-0, 2040213) Bks Demand.

South African Company Law Through the Cases. 5th ed. H. R. Hahlo et al. 820p. 1991. write for info. (0-7021-2548-2, Pub. by Juta SA); pap. 70.00 (0-685-70147-6, Pub. by Juta SA) Gaunt.

South African Constitutional Law. Dion Basson & H. Viljoen. 450p. 1988. pap. 40.00 (0-7021-2015-4, Pub. by Juta SA) Gaunt.

***South African Criminal Law & Procedure: General Principles of Criminal Law.** 3rd ed. Jonathan M. Burchell. 430p. 1997. 129.00 (0-7021-3855-X, Pub. by Juta SA) Gaunt.

South African Criminal Law & Procedure, Vol. I: General Principles of Criminal Law. 2nd ed. E. M. Burchell et al. 576p. 1982. write for info. (0-7021-1345-X, Pub. by Juta SA); pap. write for info. (0-7021-1346-8, Pub. by Juta SA) Gaunt.

South African Criminal Law & Procedure, Vol. II: Common Law Crimes. 2nd rev. ed. J. R. Milton. 965p. 1990. write for info. (0-7021-2378-1, Pub. by Juta SA) Gaunt.

South African Criminal Law & Procedure, Vol. III: Statutory Offences. 2nd ed. J. R. Milton & M. Cowling. 1988. ring bd. write for info. (0-7021-2036-7, Pub. by Juta SA) Gaunt.

South African Criminal Law & Procedure, Vol. V: Criminal Procedure & Evidence. A. V. Lansdown & J. Campbell. 1192p. 1982. write for info. (0-7021-1257-7, Pub. by Juta SA) Gaunt.

South African Criminal Law Reports, 1990-1992, 3 vols. 525.00 (0-685-71055-6, Pub. by Juta SA) Gaunt.

***South African Diaries of Sir Garnet Wolseley 1875.** Garnet Wolseley. Ed. by Adrian Preston. (South African Biographical & Historical Studies: No. 12). 307p. 1971. 60.00 (0-86961-009-0, Pub. by A A Balkema NE) Ashgate Pub Co.

South African Disease: Apartheid Health & Health Services. Cedric De Beer. LC 86-70877. 240p. 1986. 19.95 (0-86543-038-1); pap. 7.95 (0-86543-039-X) Africa World.

South African Economy: Macroeconomic Prospects for the Medium Term. Finn Tarp & Peter Brixen. (Studies in Development Economics: No. 7). 240p. (C). 1996. text ed. 65.00 (0-415-14260-1) Routledge.

South African Economy, 1910-90. Stuart Jones & Andre Muller. LC 91-33633. 380p. 1992. text ed. 49.95 (0-312-07507-3) St Martin.

South African Feminisms: Writing, Theory & Criticism, 1990-1994. Margaret Daymond. Ed. by Barbara Bowen. (Gender & Genre in Literature Ser.: Vol. 5). 402p. 1996. text ed. 60.00 (0-8153-1626-7) Garland.

South African Folk-Tales. James A. Honeij. LC 78-67717. (Folktale Ser.). reprint ed. 29.50 (0-404-16094-8) AMS Pr.

South African Food & Agriculture in World War II. J. M. Tinley. (Illus.). ix, 138p. 1954. 27.50 (0-8047-0457-0) Stanford U Pr.

South African Fossil Ape-Man: The "Australopithecinae" Robert Broom & G. W. Schepers. LC 76-44698. reprint ed. 67.50 (0-404-15910-9) AMS Pr.

South African Freedom Reader. 4th ed. Ed. by South African Scholars Center Staff. (Illus.). 1997. 40.00 (0-939074-14-1) Harvest Pubns.

South African Geology. Ernest H. Schwarz. 1977. 24.95 (0-8369-9194-X, 9063) Ayer.

South African Geotechnical Conference, 1980: A Supplement to the Proceedings of the Regional Conference for Africa on Soil Mechanics & Foundation Engineering Held in Accra, 7th, in June 1980. Ed. by A. A. Williams. 120p. (C). 1985. text ed. 90.00 (90-6191-592-9, Pub. by A A Balkema NE) Ashgate Pub Co.

South African Human Rights Yearbook, 1993. Ed. by Neil Boister. 1993. pap. 25.00 (1-86840-106-5, Pub. by Univ Natal Pr SA) Intl Spec Bk.

***South African Journal of Sir Garnet Solseley 1879-1880.** Garnet Wolseley. Ed. by Adrian Preston. (South African Biographical & Historical Studies: No. 12). 367p. 1973. 43.50 (0-86961-040-6, Pub. by A A Balkema NE) Ashgate Pub Co.

South African Journal on Human Rights Vols. 1-11: 1985-1995. 1995. lib. bdg. 990.00 (0-614-07689-7, Pub. by Juta SA) Gaunt.

South African Kingdom: The Pursuit of Security in Nineteenth Century Lesotho. Elizabeth A. Eldridge. LC 92-31675. (African Studies: No. 78). (Illus.). 288p. (C). 1993. text ed. 74.95 (0-521-44067-X) Cambridge U Pr.

***South African Labour Glossary.** Frans Barker & Maggie Holtzhausen. 208p. (AFR & ENG.). 1996. pap. 38.00 (0-7021-3631-X, Pub. by Juta SA) Gaunt.

South African Law of Estate Succession. I. Isaacs. 203p. 1979. pap. 98.00 (0-409-03410-X, SA) MICHIE.

South African Law of Evidence. 4th ed. D. T. Zeffertt. 753p. 1989. pap. 104.00 (0-409-03325-1, SA); boxed 151.00 (0-409-03324-3, SA) MICHIE.

South African Law of Husband & Wife. 5th ed. H. R. Hahlo. 600p. 1985. write for info. (0-7021-1568-1, Pub. by Juta SA); pap. 50.00 (0-7021-1572-X, Pub. by Juta SA) Gaunt.

South African Law of Insurance. 4th ed. D. M. Davis. 626p. 1993. 110.00 (0-685-70611-7, Pub. by Juta SA); pap. 83.00 (0-685-70612-5, Pub. by Juta SA) Gaunt.

South African Law of Landlord & Tenant. W. E. Cooper. 570p. 1973. write for info. (0-7021-0407-8, Pub. by Juta SA) Gaunt.

South African Law of Partnership. J. J. Henning. (Lawsa Student Text Ser.). 370p. 1984. pap. text ed. 52.00 (0-409-04022-3, SA) MICHIE.

South African Law of Persons & Family Law. D. S. Cronje. 419p. 1990. pap. 92.00 (0-409-04622-1, SA) MICHIE.

South African Law of Succession. H. J. Erasmus. (Lawsa Student Text Ser.). 197p. 1989. pap. 52.00 (0-409-02742-1, SA) MICHIE.

South African Law of Trade Marks. 3rd ed. G. C. Webster. 1986. boxed 223.00 (0-409-06329-0, SA) MICHIE.

South African Law of Trusts. 4th ed. A. M. Honore & E. Cameron. 700p. 1992. 135.00 (0-7021-2641-1, Pub. by Juta SA) Gaunt.

South African Law of Unfair Dismissal. Pak Le Roux & Andre Van Niekerk. 380p. 1994. pap. 52.00 (0-7021-3162-8, Pub. by Juta SA) Gaunt.

South African Legal System & Its Background. H. R. Hahlo & E. Kahn. 602p. 1968. pap. 28.00 (0-7021-0309-8, Pub. by Juta SA) Gaunt.

South African Literature & Culture: Rediscovery of the Ordinary. Njabulo S. Ndebele. LC 93-47154. 1994. text ed. 59.95 (0-7190-4051-5, Pub. by Manchester Univ Pr UK); text ed. 24.95 (0-7190-4052-3, Pub. by Manchester Univ Pr UK) St Martin.

South African Managed Trade Policy: The Wasting of a Mineral Endowment. Graham A. Davis. LC 93-40568. 168p. 1994. text ed. 55.00 (0-275-94814-5, Praeger Pubs) Greenwood.

South African Mercantile & Company Law. 6th ed. J. T. Gibson & R. G. Comrie. 732p. 1988. write for info. (0-7021-1970-9, Pub. by Juta SA); pap. 45.00 (0-7021-1971-7, Pub. by Juta SA) Gaunt.

***South African Merchant Ships.** Brian D. Ingpen. 159p. 1979. 105.00 (0-86961-115-1, Pub. by A A Balkema NE) Ashgate Pub Co.

South African Mosaic: A Sociological Analysis of Post-Apartheid Conflict. Nomazengele A. Mangaliso. 144p. (Orig.). 1994. pap. text ed. 29.50 (0-8191-9506-5); lib. bdg. 46.00 (0-8191-9505-7) U Pr of Amer.

South African Mounted Irregular Forces 1899-1902: A Multinational Force in the Boer War. Roberts Staff. (C). 1993. 90.00 (1-873058-65-9, Pub. by Roberts UK) St Mut.

South African Night. Rachel Isadora. LC 97-11203. (Illus.). 24p. (YA). (gr. 8 up). 1997. lib. bdg. 14.96 (0-688-11390-7) Greenwillow.

South African Night. Rachel Isadora. LC 97-11203. (Illus.). 24p. (J). (ps up). 1997. 15.00 (0-688-11389-3) Greenwillow.

South African Novel in English: Essays in Criticism & Society. Ed. by Kenneth Parker. LC 78-18343. 202p. 1979. 39.50 (0-8419-0425-1, Africana) Holmes & Meier.

South African Passage: Diaries of the Wilderness Leadership School. Ian Player. LC 86-25752. (Illus.). 195p. 1987. 13.95 (1-55591-009-2) Fulcrum Pub.

South African Patent Law & Practice. 2nd ed. T. D. Burrell. 699p. 1985. boxed 223.00 (0-409-01355-2, SA) MICHIE.

South African Perspective on the New Testament: Essays by South African New Testament Scholars Presented to Bruce Manning Metzger During His Vist to South Africa in 1985. J. H. Petzer & P. J. Hartin. (Illus.). xii, 274p. 1986. 66.00 (90-04-07720-0) E J Brill.

South African Recipients of the France & Germany Star or Clasp. Don Forsyth. (C). 1989. 70.00 (1-873058-61-6, Pub. by Roberts UK) St Mut.

South African Review, No. 6: From "Red Friday" to Codesa. Ed. by Glenn Moss & Ingrid Obery. xxi, 508p. (C). 1993. pap. text ed. 24.95 (0-86975-418-1, Pub. by Ravan Pr ZA) Ohio U Pr.

South African Society: Realities & Future Prospects. Human Sciences Research Council Staff. LC 86-27107. (Contributions in Ethnic Studies: No. 21). (Illus.). 232p. 1987. text ed. 55.00 (0-313-25724-8, MSB/, Greenwood Pr) Greenwood.

South African Special Forces. Robert Pitta & Jeff Fannell. (Elite Ser.: No. 47). (Illus.). 64p. pap. 12.95 (1-85532-295-1, Pub. by Osprey UK) Stackpole.

South African Sugar Art. Margie Smuts. Ed. by Jackie Athey. LC 79-52244. (Continental's Creative Cake Ser.). (Illus.). 64p. (Orig.). 1979. pap. 4.95 (0-916096-21-1) Books Bakers.

South African Symposium on Communications & Signal Processing, 1993. IEEE, South African Section Staff. Ed. by Institute of Electrical & Electronics Engineers, Inc. Staff. LC 93-77780. 300p. 1993. pap. write for info. (0-7803-1292-9, 93TH0546-2); fiche write for info. (0-7803-1293-7, 93TH0546-2) Inst Electrical.

South African Tax Cases, Vol. 55. Ed. by J. Silke & M. M. Corbett. 1993. ring bd. write for info. (0-318-72247-X, Pub. by Juta SA) Gaunt.

South African Testament: From Personal Encounter to Theological Challenge. H. Paul Santmire. LC 87-436. 104p. (Orig.). reprint ed. pap. 29.70 (0-8357-8563-7, 2034926) Bks Demand.

South African Voices. Ed. by Bernth Lindfors. 36p. 1975. pap. 10.00 (0-87959-125-0) U of Tex H Ransom Ctr.

South African War Casualty Rolls: Natal Field Force, 20th October, 1899-26th October, 1900. Ed. by Picton Publishing Staff. 237p. (C). 1987. 133.00 (0-317-90430-2, Pub. by Picton UK) St Mut.

South African War Medal 1877-89 the Medal Roll. Roberts Staff. (C). 1989. 90.00 (1-873058-20-9, Pub. by Roberts UK) St Mut.

South African Wine Guide 1996. John Platter. 315p. 13.95 (1-85732-815-9, Pub. by Reed Illust Books UK) Antique Collect.

***South African Wining & Dining.** Myrna Rosen & Lesley Loon. (Illus.). 256p. 1997. pap. 28.00 (0-8059-4187-8) Dorrance.

***South African Women's Health Book.** Women's Health Project Staff. 516p. 1996. pap. 16.95 (0-19-571254-4) OUP.

South Africans: A Set of Portrait Poems. Chris Mann. 80p. 1996. pap. 17.00 (0-86980-922-9, Pub. by Univ Natal Pr SA) Intl Spec Bk.

South Africa's Alternative Press: Voices of Protest & Resistance, 1873-1963. Ed. by Les Switzer. LC 95-44814. (Studies in the History of Mass Communications). (Illus.). 300p. (C). 1997. text ed. 80.00 (0-521-55351-2) Cambridge U Pr.

South Africa's City of Diamonds. William H. Worger. LC 86-26675. 330p. 1987. text ed. 42.50 (0-300-03716-3) Yale U Pr.

South Africa's Crisis of Constitutional Democracy: Can the U. S. Constitution Help? Bertus De Villiers & Robert A. Licht. Ed. by David Van Wyk & Lawrence Schlemmer. LC 93-43191. 200p. 1994. pap. 20.00 (0-8447-3834-4, AEI Pr) Am Enterprise.

South Africa's Crisis of Constitutional Democracy: Can the U. S. Constitution Help? Robert A. Licht & Bertus De Villiers. Ed. by David Van Wyk et al. LC 93-43191. 200p. 1994. 39.75 (0-8447-3835-2, AEI Pr) Am Enterprise.

South Africa's Crisis of Constitutional Democracy Vol. 1: Can the U.S. Constitution Help? Ed. by R. Licht & B. De Villiers. 261p. 1994. pap. text ed. 20.00 (0-7021-3143-1, Pub. by Juta SA) Gaunt.

South Africa's Defence & Security into the 21st Century. Ed. by William Gutteridge. (RISCT (Research Institute for the Study of Conflict & Terrorism) Ser.). (Illus.). 200p. 1996. text ed. 59.95 (1-85521-711-2, Pub. by Dartmth Pub UK) Ashgate Pub Co.

***South Africa's Destabilization of Zimbabwe, 1980-89.** John Dzimba. LC 97-19534. 1997. write for info. (0-312-17669-4) St Martin.

South Africa's Economic Crisis. Ed. by Stephen Gelb. 308p. (C). 1991. pap. 22.50 (1-85649-023-8, Pub. by Zed Bks Ltd UK); text ed. 55.00 (1-85649-022-X, Pub. by Zed Bks Ltd UK) Humanities.

South Africa's Foreign Policy: The Search for Status & Security 1945-1988. James Barber & John Barratt. (Cambridge Studies in International Relations: No. 11). (Illus.). 384p. (C). 1990. pap. 24.95 (0-521-38876-7) Cambridge U Pr.

South Africa's Freedom Struggle: Statements, Speeches & Articles Including Correspondence with Mahatma Gandhi. Yusuf M. Dadoo. Ed. by E. S. Reddy. 352p. 1990. text ed. 50.00 (81-207-1289-7, Pub. by Sterling Pubs II) Apt Bks.

S

An Asterisk (*) at the beginning of an entry indicates that the title is appearing in BIP for the first time.

South Africa's Impact on Britain's Return to Gold, 1925. Bruce R. Dalgaard. Ed. by Stuart Bruchey. LC 80-2801. (Dissertations in European Economic History Ser.). (Illus.). 1981. lib. bdg. 23.95 (*0-405-13985-3*) Ayer.

South Africa's Interim Constitution: Text & Notes. Dion Basson. 369p. 1994. pap. 40.00 (*0-7021-3286-1*, Pub. by Juta SA) Gaunt.

South Africa's Military Capabilities. W. F. Gutteridge. (Illus.). 200p. 1988. 20.01 (*0-08-031173-3*, Pergamon Pr); pap. text ed. 11.01 (*0-08-031174-1*, Pergamon Pr) Elsevier.

South Africa's Moment of Truth. Edgar Lockwood. 196p. 1988. pap. 5.95 (*0-377-00180-5*) Friendship Pr.

South Africa's Outward Strategy: A Foreign Policy Dilemma for the United States. Larry W. Bowman. LC 72-183388. (Papers in International Studies: Africa Ser.: No. 13). 39p. reprint ed. pap. 25.00 (*0-317-11331-3*, 2007421) Bks Demand.

South Africa's Road to Change, 1987-1990: A Select & Annotated Bibliography. Jacqueline A. Kalley. LC 91-18078. (African Special Bibliographic Ser.: No. 15). 456p. 1991. text ed. 69.50 (*0-313-28117-3*, KST, Greenwood Pr) Greenwood.

South Africa's Roll of Honour 1914-1918. Roberts Staff. (C). 1989. 95.00 (*1-873058-75-6*, Pub. by Roberts UK) St Mut.

South Africa's Security Dilemmas. Christopher Coker. LC 87-2437. (Washington Papers: No. 126). 125p. 1987. text ed. 45.00 (*0-275-92771-7*, C2771, Praeger Pubs); pap. text ed. 11.95 (*0-275-92772-5*, B2772, Praeger Pubs) Greenwood.

South Africa's Transkei, the Politics of Domestic Colonialism. Gwendolyn Carter et al. LC 67-15937. 214p. reprint ed. pap. 61.00 (*0-317-27594-1*, 2014773) Bks Demand.

South Africa's War Against Capitalism. Walter E. Williams. LC 88-34028. 160p. 1989. text ed. 49.95 (*0-275-93179-X*, C3179, Praeger Pubs) Greenwood.

South After Gettysburg: Letters of Cornelia Hancock from the Army of the Potomac, 1863-1865. Cornelia Hancock. Ed. by Henrietta S. Jaquette. LC 77-160975. (Select Bibliographies Reprint Ser.). 1977. reprint ed. 23.95 (*0-8369-5845-4*) Ayer.

South After Gettysburg: Letters of Cornelia Hancock, 1863-1868. Cornelia Hancock. (American Biography Ser.). 288p. 1991. reprint ed. lib. bdg. 69.00 (*0-7812-8165-2*) Rprt Serv.

South America. 288p. (Orig.). 1989. 200.00 (*0-86338-125-1*, Pub. by Euromonitor Pubns UK) Gale.

South America. Cesar Caviedes & Gregory W. Knapp. 1995. write for info. (*0-615-00113-0*) P-H.

South America. Cesar Caviedes. 468p. 1994. pap. text ed. 67.00 (*0-13-825118-5*) P-H.

South America. D. V. Georges. LC 86-9584. (New True Bks.). (Illus.). 48p. (J). (gr. k-4). 1986. pap. 5.50 (*0-516-41296-5*); lib. bdg. 19.00 (*0-516-01296-7*) Childrens.

***South America.** Ewan Mcleish. LC 96-41311. (Continents Ser.). (J). 1997. lib. bdg. 24.26 (*0-8172-4777-7*) Raintree Steck-V.

South America. J. Rosenstein. (Rifts World Bks.). (Illus.). 168p. (Orig.). (YA). (gr. 8 up). 1994. pap. 15.95 (*0-916211-71-1*, 814) Palladium Bks.

***South America.** 3rd ed. Fodors Travel Staff. 1997. pap. 19.50 (*0-679-03537-0*) Fodors Travel.

***South America.** 3rd ed. Insight Guides Staff. (Insight Guides Ser.). 1997. pap. 23.95 (*0-395-85059-2*) HM.

South America. 3rd ed. Arthur S. Morris. (Illus.). 285p. 1991. pap. text ed. 36.00 (*0-340-40607-0*, Pub. by Hodder & Stoughton Ltd UK) Lubrecht & Cramer.

South America. 6th ed. James Lyon et al. (Illus.). 1176p. 1997. pap. 29.95 (*0-86442-401-9*) Lonely Planet.

South America: A Letter to the Present State of That Country to James Monroe. Henry M. Brachenridge. (Works of Henry Marie Brackenridge). 1989. reprint ed. lib. bdg. 79.00 (*0-7812-2029-7*) Rprt Serv.

South America: An Economic & Regional Geography. Edward W. Shanahan. 1976. lib. bdg. 59.95 (*0-8490-2633-4*) Gordon Pr.

South America: Geography Mini Unit. Jo E. Moore. (Illus.). 16p. (J). (gr. 3-6). 1993. pap. 5.95 (*1-55799-242-8*, EMC 264) Evan-Moor Corp.

South America: Observations & Impressions. James Bryce. (Latin America in the 20th Century Ser.). 1977. reprint ed. lib. bdg. 69.50 (*0-306-70835-3*) Da Capo.

South America see Encyclopedia of World Geography

***South America, Central America, & the Caribbean, Vol. 2.** Ed. by Dale A. Olsen & Daniel E. Sheehy. (Encyclopedia of World Music Ser.: Vol. 2). (Illus.). 816p. 1997. 125.00 (*0-8240-4947-0*) Garland.

South America, Central America & the Caribbean, 1993. 4th ed. 582p. 1992. 295.00 (*0-946653-86-0*, EUR3860, Pub. by Europ Com UK) Bernan Associates.

***South America, Central America & the Caribbean 1997.** 6th ed. 700p. 1996. 325.00 (*1-85743-026-3*, Pub. by Eurpa Publns UK) Taylor & Francis.

South America Country Studies. Randy L. Womack. (Illus.). 96p. (J). (gr. 4 up). 1996. student ed. 10.95 (*1-56500-023-4*) Gldn Educ.

South America Looks at the United States. Clarence H. Haring. LC 72-111716. (American Imperialism: Viewpoints of United States Foreign Policy, 1898-1941 Ser.). 1970. reprint ed. 19.95 (*0-405-02025-2*) Ayer.

South America Mi Hija. Sharon Doubiago. LC 90-20875. (Poetry Ser.). 312p. (C). 1992. 29.95 (*0-8229-3671-2*); pap. 15.95 (*0-8229-5450-8*) U of Pittsburgh Pr.

South America Ski Guide. Chris I. Lizza. (Bradt Hiking Guides Ser.). (Illus.). 312p. 1994. pap. 16.95 (*1-56440-559-1*, Pub. by Bradt Pubns UK) Globe Pequot.

South America Travel Digest. 27th ed. Charles Jacobs & Babette Jacobs. (Illus.). 160p. 1996. pap. 12.95 (*0-912640-52-9*) P Richmond.

South America Travel Digest. 27th ed. Charles Jacobs & Babette Jacobs. (Illus.). 168p. 1996. pap. 12.95 (*0-912640-56-1*) Travel Digests.

***South America Travellers Survival Kit.** Emily Hatchwell & Simon Calder. (Travellers Survival Kit Guides Ser.). 768p. (Orig.). 1997. pap. 21.95 (*1-85458-069-8*, Pub. by Vac Wrk Pubns UK) Seven Hills Bk.

***South America TSK.** 2nd ed. Emily Hatchwell & Simon Calder. (Travellers Survival Kit Ser.). 768p. 1997. pap. 24.95 (*1-85458-178-3*, Pub. by Vac Wrk Pubns UK) Seven Hills Bk.

South American. 71th ed. (Handbooks of the World Ser.). 1994. 39.95 (*0-8442-8979-5*, Passport Bks) NTC Pub Grp.

South American Birds: A Photographic Aid to Identification. John S. Dunning. LC 88-6299. (Illus.). 352p. 1989. 47.50 (*0-915180-25-1*); pap. 35.00 (*0-915180-26-X*) Harrowood Bks.

South American Camelids: An Action Plan for Their Conservation. Ed. by Herman Torres. 40p. (SPA.). 1992. pap. 16.00 (*2-8317-0058-2*, Pub. by IUCN SZ) Island Pr.

South American Cinema: A Critical Filmography, 1915-1994. Ed. by Timothy Barnard & Peter Rist. LC 95-48076. (Illus.). 432p. 1996. text ed. 64.00 (*0-8240-4574-2*, H1077) Garland.

South American Cinema: A Dictionary of Film Makers. Luis T. Plazaola. 236p. 1989. pap. 10.95 (*0-8477-2011-X*) U of PR Pr.

South American Cook Book: Including Central America, Mexico & the West Indies. Bob Brown et al. LC 72-166427. 1971. reprint ed. pap. 7.95 (*0-486-20190-2*) Dover.

South American Cooking: Foods & Feast from the New World. Barbara Karoff. 1990. pap. 12.45 (*0-201-55094-6*) Addison-Wesley.

South American Development. 2nd ed. Rosemary D. Bromley & Ray Bromley. (Cambridge Topics in Geography Ser.). 128p. (C). 1988. pap. 15.50 (*0-521-36727-1*) Cambridge U Pr.

South American Handbook. 1988. pap. 28.95 (*0-671-88271-6*) PB.

South American Handbook. Ed. by Ben Box. (Handbooks of the World Ser.). 1995. pap. 39.95 (*0-614-15524-X*) NTC Pub Grp.

South American Handbook. 72th ed. Ed. by Ben Box. 1552p. 1995. 39.95 (*0-8442-8881-0*, Passport Bks) NTC Pub Grp.

South American Handbook, 1988. 64th ed. 1370p. 1987. write for info. (*0-900751-26-6*) Taylor & Francis.

South American Handbook, 1994. 70th ed. Ben Box. 1424p. 1994. pap. 39.95 (*0-8442-9979-0*, Passport Bks) NTC Pub Grp.

South American Indian Languages: Retrospect & Prospect. Ed. by Harriet E. Klein & Louisa R. Stark. (Texas Linguistics Ser.). 869p. 1985. text ed. 40.00 (*0-292-77592-X*) U of Tex Pr.

South American Indians: A Case Study in Evolution. Francisco M. Salzano & Sidia M. Callegari-Jacques. (Research Monographs on Human Population Biology). 272p. 1988. 79.00 (*0-19-857635-8*) OUP.

South American Kinship: Eight Kinship Systems from Brazil & Colombia. Ed. by William R. Merrifield. LC 85-80410. (International Museum of Cultures Publications: No. 18). (Illus.). 132p. (Orig.). 1985. fiche 8.00 (*0-88312-255-3*) Summer Instit Ling.

South American Monkeys. Amanda Harman. LC 95-44806. (Endangered! Ser.). 32p. (J). (gr. 3-5). 1996. lib. bdg. 14.95 (*0-7614-0218-7*, Benchmark NY) Marshall Cavendish.

South American Packets 1808-1880. J. Howat. (C). 1988. 132.00 (*0-900657-95-2*, Pub. by W Sessions UK) St Mut.

South American Population Censuses since Independence: An Annotated Bibliography of Secondary Sources. Karin Simoneau. (Bibliography & Reference Ser.: No. 26). 75p. (Orig.). 1990. pap. 22.00 (*0-917617-26-6*) SALALM.

South American Portraits. Dorothy Hobbler & Thomas Hobbler. LC 93-38361. (J). 1994. lib. bdg. 27.11 (*0-8114-6383-4*) Raintree Steck-V.

South American Sociologists, A Directory. Gunter W. Remmling. (Guides & Bibliographies Ser.). 57p. reprint ed. pap. 25.00 (*0-685-15616-8*, 2027326) Bks Demand.

South American Trilogy: Osman Lins, Felisberto Hernandez & Luis Fernando Vidal. Ed. by Luis A. Ramos-Garcia. (ENG, POR & SPA.). 1982. 5.95 (*0-934840-04-0*) Studia Hispanica.

South Americans. Alan Cullison. (Peoples of North America Ser.). (Illus.). 112p. (J). (gr. 5 up). 1991. lib. bdg. 19.95 (*0-87754-863-3*) Chelsea Hse.

South America's Economic Development & Emerging Markets: A Bibliography. Ed. by Mary E. Lassanyi. 57p. (Orig.). (C). 1994. pap. text ed. 30.00 (*0-7881-1541-3*) DIANE Pub.

South America's National Parks: A Visitor's Guide. William Leitch. LC 90-35389. (Illus.). 336p. (Orig.). 1990. 25.00 (*0-89886-259-0*); pap. 16.95 (*0-89886-248-5*) Mountaineers.

South & Central America: Including Mexico. Ed. by Jason Wilson. (Traveller's Literary Companion Ser.). 472p. 1995. pap. 17.95 (*0-8442-8973-6*, Passport Bks) NTC Pub Grp.

South & Meso-American Native Spirituality: From the Cult of the Feathered Serpent to the Theology of Liberation. Ed. by Gary H. Gossen & Miguel Leon-Portilla. (Illus.). 500p. 1993. 49.50 (*0-8245-1224-3*) Crossroad NY.

***South & Meso-American Native Spirituality: From the Cult of the Feathered Serpent to the Theology of Liberation.** Ed. by Gary H. Gossen. (World Spirituality Ser.: Vol. 4). 576p. 1997. pap. 29.95 (*0-8245-1662-1*, Crossrd Herd) Crossroad NY.

South & North, East & West: The Oxfam Book of Children's Stories. Ed. by Michael Rosen. LC 91-58749. (Illus.). 96p. (J). (ps up). 1992. 19.95 (*1-56402-117-3*) Candlewick Pr.

South & North, East & West: The Oxfam Book of Children's Stories. Ed. by Michael Rosen. (Illus.). 96p. 1992. 12.99 (*0-7445-2193-9*, Pub. by Oxfam UK) Humanities.

South & North, East & West: The Oxfam Book of Children's Stories. Ed. by Michael Rosen. (Illus.). 96p. 1995. pap. 7.95 (*0-7445-4366-5*, Pub. by Oxfam UK) Humanities.

South & North, East & West: The Oxfam Book of Children's Stories. Ed. by Michael Rosen. LC 91-58749. (Illus.). 96p. (J). (ps-6). 1994. pap. 12.99 (*1-56402-396-6*) Candlewick Pr.

South & Southeast Asia. Ed. by John A. Harrison. LC 72-83465. (Thirtieth Anniversary Commemorative Ser.: No. 3). 256p. 1972. reprint ed. pap. 73.00 (*0-608-02357-4*, 2062998) Bks Demand.

South & Southeast Asia in the 1990s: Indian & American Perspectives. Ed. by V. Suryanarayan. 225p. (C). 1992. text ed. 25.00 (*81-220-0271-4*, Pub. by Konark Pubs Pvt Ltd II) Advent Bks Div.

South & Southeast Asia Studies, 55 titles in 57 vols., Set. (AMS Press Reprint Ser.). reprint ed. write for info. (*0-404-54800-8*) AMS Pr.

South & the Middle West. Thomas D. Clark. (BCL1 - U. S. History Ser.). 350p. 1991. reprint ed. lib. bdg. 89.00 (*0-7812-6001-9*) Rprt Serv.

South & the Nation. E. P. Lawton. LC 63-16251. 1963. pap. 6.95 (*0-87208-003-X*) Shoeless Pub.

South & the New Deal. Roger Biles. LC 93-20816. 216p. (C). 1994. 23.00 (*0-8131-1836-0*) U Pr of Ky.

South & the Politics of Slavery, 1828-1856. William J. Cooper, Jr. LC 78-751. 456p. 1978. pap. text ed. 16.95 (*0-8071-0775-1*) La State U Pr.

South & the Presidency: From Reconstruction to Carter. Henry Paolucci. 1978. pap. 3.00 (*0-918680-07-7*) Bagehot Council.

South & the Sectional Conflict. David M. Potter. LC 68-8941. 335p. 1968. pap. 95.50 (*0-7837-8531-3*, 2049340) Bks Demand.

South & the Southerner. Ralph McGill. LC 92-6038. (Brown Thrasher Bks.). 328p. 1992. reprint ed. pap. 15.95 (*0-8203-1443-9*) U of Ga Pr.

South & West Coasts of Ireland Sailing Directions. Irish Cruising Club Staff. (C). 1990. text ed. 330.00 (*0-9501717-3-5*, Pub. by Imray Laurie Norie & Wilson UK) St Mut.

South as a Conscious Minority, 1789-1861: A Study in Political Thought. Jesse T. Carpenter. (BCL1 - United States Local History Ser.). 315p. 1991. reprint ed. text ed. 89.00 (*0-7812-6286-0*) Rprt Serv.

South As an American Problem. Ed. by Larry J. Griffin & Don H. Doyle. LC 94-23969. 1995. 30.00 (*0-8203-1729-2*) U of Ga Pr.

***South As an American Problem.** Ed. by Larry J. Griffin & Don H. Doyle. LC 94-23969. 1995. pap. 18.95 (*0-8203-1752-7*) U of Ga Pr.

South As It Is, 1865-1866. John R. Dennett. Ed. by Henry M. Christman. 370p. 1995. pap. 15.95 (*0-8071-1998-9*) La State U Pr.

South Asia. (Insight Guides Ser.). 1993. pap. 21.95 (*0-395-66316-4*) HM.

South Asia. Ed. by Hamza Alavi & John Harriss. (Sociology of "Developing Societies" Ser.). 288p. (C). 1989. 28.00 (*0-85345-779-4*); pap. 16.00 (*0-85345-778-6*) Monthly Rev.

South Asia. Ed. by K. I. Koppedrayer. LC 92-39880. (Contacts Between Cultures Ser.: Vol. 2). 444p. 1993. text ed. 109.95 (*0-7734-9202-X*) E Mellen.

South Asia. Angus Maude. LC 66-18564. 6600. 18.95 (*0-8023-1076-1*) Dufour.

South Asia: A Short History. rev. ed. Hugh Tinker. LC 89-5099. (Illus.). 310p. 1990. pap. text ed. 18.00 (*0-8248-1287-5*) UH Pr.

South Asia: A Short History of the Subcontinent. 2nd ed. Milton W. Meyer. (Quality Paperback Ser.: No. 34). 268p. (Orig.). 1976. pap. 10.00 (*0-8226-0034-X*) Littlefield.

South Asia: The Challenges & Opportunities of the Nineteen Nineties. William R. Thomson. LC 92-27481. 21p. 1992. pap. 6.95 (*1-55815-226-1*) ICS Pr.

***South Asia & the United States after the Cold War.** Satu Limaye. (Illus.). xxii, 86p. (Orig.). 1994. pap. 5.00 (*0-614-27187-8*, X88904) Asia Soc.

South Asia in a Changing International Order. Gowher Rizvi. LC 92-40699. 180p. 1993. 28.95 (*0-8039-9467-2*) Sage.

South Asia in International Politics. P. K. Mishra. 498p. 1986. 24.95 (*81-85044-01-5*) Asia Bk Corp.

South Asia in the World Today. Henry Brodie et al. Ed. by Phillips Talbot. LC 78-161774. (BCL Ser. I). reprint ed. 22.50 (*0-404-09042-7*) AMS Pr.

South Asia in Transition: Conflicts & Tensions. Ed. by Kalim Bahadur. 1988. 35.00 (*81-7050-023-0*) Nataraj Bks.

South Asia Media Handbook. Sadhan Mukherjee. (C). 1990. 19.50 (*81-7023-305-4*, Pub. by Allied II) S Asia.

South Asia-Pacific Region: Emerging Trends. Kashi P. Misra & V. D. Chopra. 1988. 27.00 (*0-685-21059-6*, Pub. by Patriot II) S Asia.

***South Asian Americans.** Karen I. Leonard. LC 97-2219. (New Americans Ser.). 1997. text ed. write for info. (*0-313-29788-6*, Greenwood Pr) Greenwood.

South Asian Archaeology Studies. Ed. by Gregory L. Possehl. (C). 1992. text ed. 45.00 (*81-204-0734-2*, Pub. by Oxford IBH II) S Asia.

South Asian Archaeology 1985: A Richly Illustrated Survey. Ed. by Karen Frifelt & Per Sorenson. (Scandinavian Institute of Asian Studies Monograph: No. 4). (Illus.). 520p. (C). 1989. text ed. 75.00 (*0-913215-50-3*, Pub. by Curzon Press UK) UH Pr.

South Asian Archaeology 1985: A Richly Illustrated Survey. Ed. by Karen Frifelt & Per Sorenson. (Illus.). 520p. (C). 1989. text ed. 75.00 (*0-7007-0200-8*, Pub. by Curzon Press UK) UH Pr.

South Asian Civilizations: A Bibliographic Synthesis. Maureen L. Patterson. LC 81-52518. (Illus.). 893p. 1981. lib. bdg. 84.00 (*0-226-64910-5*) U Ch Pr.

***South Asian Cultural Studies: A Bibliography.** Vinay Lal. (C). 1996. 34.00 (*81-7304-134-2*, Pub. by Manohar II) S Asia.

***South Asian Dance: The British Experience.** Ed. by Alessandra Iyer. 1997. pap. text ed. 23.00 (*90-5702-043-2*, Harwood Acad Pubs) Gordon & Breach.

***South Asian Drama: Travails of Misgovernance.** Sundeep Waslekar. 1996. 34.11 (*81-220-0416-4*, Pub. by Konark Pubs II) S Asia.

South Asian English: Structure, Use, & Users. Ed. by Robert J. Baumgardner. LC 95-8057. (English in the Global Context Ser.). 312p. 1995. text ed. 44.95 (*0-252-02196-7*); pap. text ed. 16.95 (*0-252-06493-3*) U of Ill Pr.

South Asian Handbook, 1994. Robert Bradnock. 1456p. 1994. pap. 39.95 (*0-8442-9980-4*, Passport Bks) NTC Pub Grp.

South Asian History, 1750-1950: A Guide to Periodicals, Dissertations, & Newspapers. Margaret H. Case. LC 67-21019. 575p. reprint ed. pap. 163.90 (*0-8357-7029-X*, 2033406) Bks Demand.

South Asian Intellectuals & Social Change. Yogendra Malik. 1982. 24.00 (*0-8364-0825-X*); 15.00 (*0-686-81181-X*) S Asia.

South Asian Languages: A Handbook. Christopher Shackle. 1986. pap. 9.00 (*0-8364-1629-5*) S Asia.

South Asian Languages: Structure, Convergence & Diglossia. B. Krishnamurti et al. 1986. 38.00 (*81-208-0033-8*, Pub. by Motilal Banarsidass II) S Asia.

South Asian Music Teaching in Change. Gerry Farrell. (Advanced Studies in Music Education). 80p. 1994. pap. 18.95 (*1-85346-330-2*, Pub. by D Fulton UK) Taylor & Francis.

South Asian Perspectives: Seven Nations in Conflict & Co-Operation. Bhabani S. Gupta. (C). 1988. 29.00 (*81-7018-467-3*, Pub. by BR Pub II) S Asia.

South Asian Petty Bourgeoisie in Britain. Shaila Srinivasan. (Ethnic Relations Ser.). 256p. 1995. 63.95 (*1-85628-972-9*, Pub. by Avebury Pub UK) Ashgate Pub Co.

South Asian Religion & Society. Ed. by Asko Parpola & Bent S. Hansen. (Studies on Asian Topics (Scandinavian Institute of Asian Studies): No. 11). 262p. (C). 1986. pap. 25.00 (*0-913215-16-3*) Riverdale Co.

South Asian Religions in the Americas: An Annotated Bibliography of Immigrant Religious Traditions. John Y. Fenton. LC 94-39769. (Bibliographies & Indexes in Religious Studies: Vol. 34). 256p. 1995. text ed. 79.50 (*0-313-27835-0*, Greenwood Pr) Greenwood.

South Asian Responses to Chinua Achebe. Ed. by Bernth Lindfors & Bala Kothandaraman. 200p. (C). 1993. text ed. 27.50 (*81-85218-66-8*, Pub. by Prestige II) Advent Bks Div.

South Asian Security: Problems & Prospects. B. M. Jain. 201p. 1985. 24.95 (*0-318-37270-3*) Asia Bk Corp.

South Asian Strategic Issues: Sri Lankan Perspectives. Ed. by Shelton U. Kodikara. (Illus.). 208p. (C). 1990. 24.00 (*0-8039-9622-5*) Sage.

***South Asian Studies, Vol. 2.** annuals Ed. by Bridget Allchin. (Illus.). 86p. 1986. pap. 36.00 (*0-614-21887-X*) David Brown.

***South Asian Studies, Vol. 3.** annuals Ed. by Bridget Allchin. (Illus.). 94p. 1987. pap. 36.00 (*0-614-21886-1*) David Brown.

***South Asian Studies, Vol. 4.** annuals Ed. by Bridget Allchin. (Illus.). 147p. 1988. pap. 36.00 (*0-614-21885-3*) David Brown.

***South Asian Studies, Vol. 5.** annuals Ed. by Bridget Allchin. (Illus.). 168p. 1989. pap. 36.00 (*0-614-21884-5*) David Brown.

***South Asian Studies, Vol. 6.** annuals Ed. by Bridget Allchin. (Illus.). 265p. 1990. pap. 45.00 (*0-614-21883-7*) David Brown.

***South Asian Studies, Vol. 7.** annuals Ed. by Bridget Allchin. (Illus.). 183p. 1991. pap. 45.00 (*0-614-21882-9*) David Brown.

***South Asian Studies, Vol. 8.** annuals Bridget Allchin. (Illus.). 183p. 1992. pap. 45.00 (*0-614-21881-0*) David Brown.

***South Asian Studies, Vol. 9.** annuals Ed. by Bridget Allchin. (Illus.). 179p. 1993. pap. 45.00 (*0-614-21880-2*) David Brown.

***South Asian Studies, Vol. 10.** annuals Ed. by Bridget Allchin. (Illus.). 204p. 1994. pap. 45.00 (*0-614-21879-9*) David Brown.

***South Asian Studies, Vol. 11.** annuals Ed. by Bridget Allchin. (Illus.). 187p. 1995. pap. 54.00 (*0-614-21878-0*) David Brown.

South Asian Studies Dissertations & Theses: Completed at the University of Hawaii at Manoa 1947-1989. Linda Wiig. (South Asia Occasional Papers: No. 2). 63p. (C). 1990. pap. text ed. write for info. (*1-879153-01-7*) U HI South Asian.

An Asterisk (*) at the beginning of an entry indicates that the title is appearing in BIP for the first time.

South Asians in North America: An Annotated & Selected Bibliography. Ed. by Jane Singh et al. LC 87-73457. (Occasional Papers: No. 14). 200p. (Orig.). (C). 1988. pap. 14.00 (*0-944613-03-9*) UC Berkeley Ctrs SE Asia.

***South Asia's Security: Primacy of Internal Dimension.** Ed. by Iftekharuzzaman. (C). 1995. 38.00 (*0-7069-8751-9*, Pub. by Vikas II) S Asia.

South at the End of the Twentieth Century: Rethinking the Political Economy of Foreign Policy in Africa, Asia, the Caribbean, & Latin America. Ed. by Larry A. Swatuk & Timothy M. Shaw. LC 93-44271. (International Political Economy Ser.). 1994. text ed. 65.00 (*0-312-12128-8*) St Martin.

***South Atlantic Vol. X: Present & Past Circulation.** Gerold E. Wefer. LC 96-50016. (Illus.). 644p. 1997. 133.00 (*3-540-62079-6*) Spr-Verlag.

South Atlantic Studies for Sturgis E. Leavitt. South Atlantic Modern Language Association Staff. Ed. by Thomas B. Stroup & Sterling A. Stoudemire. LC 77-37941. (Essay Index Reprint Ser.). 1977. reprint ed. 21.95 (*0-8369-2628-5*) Ayer.

South Atlantic War. Edward Kettler. (Harpoon Ser.). 136p. (Orig.). (YA). 1991. pap. 12.00 (*1-55878-064-5*) Game Designers.

South Australia. Denis O'Byrne. (Illus.). 336p. 1996. pap. 14.95 (*0-86442-383-7*) Lonely Planet.

South Australia's Heritage. Environment & Planning Staff. 240p. (C). 1989. text ed. 80.00 (*0-89771-028-2*) St Mut.

South Australia's Opal. Dept. of Mines & Energy Staff. (C). 1989. pap. text ed. 60.00 (*0-89771-036-3*, Pub. by Bob Mossel AT) St Mut.

South Bay: Bay Trail Alternatives & Implementation Procedures. 1991. 7.00 (*0-317-05697-2*, P92003TRL) Assn Bay Area.

South Bay Bike Trails: Road & Mountain Bicycle Rides Through Santa Clara & Santa Cruz Counties. Conrad J. Boisvert. (Bay Area Bike Trails Ser.). (Illus.). 128p. (Orig.). 1994. pap. 11.95 (*0-9621694-2-0*) Penngrove Pubns.

***South Bay Monogatari Vol. 5: Tales of the South Bay Nikkei Community.** Donald H. Estes. Ed. by Carol Bowers. (Chula Vista - The Early Years Ser.: Vol. 5). (Illus.). 206p. (Orig.). 1996. pap. 12.50 (*0-938711-39-3*) Tecolote Pubns.

South Bay Trails: Outdoor Adventures Around the Santa Clara Valley. Frances Spangle & Jean Rusmore. LC 90-21511. (Illus.). 224p. (Orig.). 1991. pap. 14.95 (*0-89997-118-0*) Wilderness Pr.

South Beach: America's Riviera, Miami Beach, Florida. Bill Wisser. (Illus.). 128p. (Orig.). 1995. pap. 21.95 (*1-55970-268-0*) Arcade Pub Inc.

South Bend Saturdays: A Recipe Guide to Notre Dame Tailgating. Lucy Littleton. 1995. pap. 8.95 (*1-885623-06-2*) Owl Bay Pubs.

South Biscay Pilot. 4th ed. Robin Brandon. (Illus.). 240p. 1995. 90.00 (*0-7136-3698-X*) Sheridan.

South Biscay Pilot: The Gironde Estuary to la Coruna. 3rd rev. ed. Robin Brandon. (Illus.). 388p. (C). 1989. 185.00 (*0-229-11680-9*, Pub. by Imray Laurie Norie & Wilson UK) St Mut.

South Boston, MA. Anthony Sammarco. (Images of America Ser.). 128p. 1996. pap. 16.99 (*0-7524-0258-7*, Arcdia) Chalford.

South Boston, My Home Town: The History of an Ethnic Neighborhood. Thomas H. O'Connor. LC 93-43535. 272p. (C). 1994. reprint ed. pap. text ed. 14.95 (*1-55553-188-1*) NE U Pr.

South Britain, Connecticut: Sketches & Records. W. C. Sharpe. (Illus.). 162p. 1988. reprint ed. lib. bdg. 23.00 (*0-8328-0012-0*, CT0009) Higginson Bk Co.

South Bronx & the Founding of America: An Activity Book for Teachers & Students. Lisa Garrison. (Illus.). 38p. (Orig.). 1987. pap. text ed. 10.00 (*0-941980-20-0*) Bronx County.

***South Brooklyn Casket Company.** Klaus Kertess. LC 96-70954. (High Risk Ser.). 125p. (Orig.). 1997. pap. 12.99 (*1-85242-448-6*, High Risk Bks) Serpents Tail.

***South by Its Photographers.** Susan S. Elliot. (Illus.). 1997. pap. 20.00 (*0-614-27476-1*) U Pr of Miss.

***South by Its Photographers.** Susan S. Elliott. LC 96-38440. 1996. write for info. (*0-87805-954-7*) Birmingham Mus.

South by Java Head. Alistair MacLean. 1976. 23.95 (*0-89190-173-6*) Amereon Ltd.

South by Southwest: 24 Stories from Modern Texas. Ed. by Don Graham. 300p. (Orig.). (C). 1986. 22.50 (*0-292-77600-4*) U of Tex Pr.

South by West: A Galaxy of Southwestern & Western Scenes & Portraits. Everett A. Gillis. 48p. (Orig.). 1981. pap. 5.00 (*0-938328-00-X*) Pisces Pr TX.

***South Caribbean Pocket Guide.** Berlitz Editors. 192p. 1997. pap. 8.95 (*2-8315-6322-4*) Berlitz.

***South Carolina.** Capstone Press Staff. LC 96-35114. (One Nation Ser.). (J). 1997. write for info. (*1-56065-502-X*) Capstone Pr.

South Carolina. Dennis B. Fradin. LC 91-32921. (From Sea to Shining Sea Ser.). (Illus.). 64p. (J). (gr. 3-5). 1992. pap. 5.95 (*0-516-43840-9*); lib. bdg. 24.00 (*0-516-03840-0*) Childrens.

South Carolina. Charles Fredeen. (Hello U. S. A. Ser.). (Illus.). 72p. (J). (gr. 3-6). 1991. lib. bdg. 18.95 (*0-8225-2712-X*, Lerner Publctns) Lerner Group.

***South Carolina.** Paul Joseph. LC 97-21418. (The United States Ser.). 1998. write for info. (*1-56239-876-8*) Abdo & Dghtrs.

South Carolina. Henry Leifermann. (Compass American Guides Ser.). 1995. pap. 18.95 (*1-878867-66-0*, Compass Amrcn) Fodors Travel.

South Carolina. Kathleen Thompson. (Portrait of America Library). 48p. (J). (gr. 3 up). 1996. lib. bdg. 22.83 (*0-8114-7386-4*) Raintree Steck-V.

South Carolina. Kathleen Thompson. (Portrait of America Library). 48p. (J). (gr. 3 up). 1996. pap. 5.95 (*0-8114-7467-4*) Raintree Steck-V.

***South Carolina.** Charlotte Wilcox. (One Nation Ser.). (Illus.). (J). 1997. 18.40 (*0-516-20532-3*) Childrens.

South Carolina. rev. ed. Deborah Kent. LC 89-858. (America the Beautiful Ser.). (Illus.). 144p. (J). (gr. 4 up). 1992. lib. bdg. 28.30 (*0-516-00486-7*) Childrens.

South Carolina: A Day at a Time. Caroline Todd & Sidney Wait. (Illus.). 374p. (Orig.). 1997. pap. 18.75 (*0-87844-126-3*) Sandlapper Pub Co.

South Carolina: A Guide to the Palmetto State. Federal Writers' Project Staff & Writers Program-WPA Staff. (American Guide Ser.). 1989. reprint ed. lib. bdg. 79.00 (*0-7812-1039-9*, 1039) Rprt Serv.

South Carolina: A Guide to the Palmetto State. Federal Writers' Project Staff. (American Guidebook Ser.). 514p. 1941. reprint ed. 89.00 (*0-403-02189-8*) Somerset Pub.

South Carolina: A Journalist & His State. Eugene B. Sloan. LC 74-20533. (Illus.). (C). 1974. text ed. 39.95 (*0-915114-01-1*) Lewis-Sloan.

South Carolina: A Synoptic History for Laymen. 3rd rev. ed. Lewis P. Jones. LC 72-143040. (Illus.). 300p. (Orig.). 1971. pap. 11.95 (*0-87844-004-6*) Sandlapper Pub Co.

South Carolina: A Timeless Journey. Photos by Robert C. Clark. LC 93-32324. (Illus.). 115p. (YA). (gr. 9). 1994. 39.95 (*0-87249-975-8*) U of SC Pr.

South Carolina: An Illustrated History of the Palmetto State. Ernest M. Lander, Jr. (Illus.). 208p. (YA). (gr. 7 up). 1988. 32.95 (*0-89781-262-X*) Am Historical Pr.

South Carolina: Economic & Social Conditions in 1944. W. H. Callcott. LC 74-34437. 248p. 1975. reprint ed. 18.50 (*0-87152-189-X*) Reprint.

South Carolina: From the Highlands to the Lowlands. 32p. (J). (ps-12). 2.50 (*0-936672-66-8*) Aerial Photo.

South Carolina: Off the Beaten Path: A Guide to Unique Places. William P. Fox. LC 95-43697. (Off the Beaten Path Ser.). (Illus.). 176p. 1996. pap. 10.95 (*1-56440-747-0*) Globe Pequot.

South Carolina: Resources & Population, Institutions & Industries. LC 78-187375. (Illus.). 768p. 1972. reprint ed. 30.00 (*0-87152-103-2*) Reprint.

South Carolina: The Making of a Landscape. Charles F. Kovacik & John J. Winberry. 253p. 1989. reprint ed. pap. 12.95 (*0-87249-684-8*) U of SC Pr.

South Carolina: The Natural Heritage. Robert C. Clark et al. (Illus.). 96p. 1989. 24.95 (*0-87249-665-1*) U of SC Pr.

South Carolina: The State & Its Educational System. Harold L. Hodgkinson. 10p. 1990. 7.00 (*0-937846-61-9*) Inst Educ Lead.

South Carolina: The WPA Guide to the Palmetto State. Federal Works Agency, Work Projects Administration, Federal Writers' Project Staff. (American Guide Ser.). (Illus.). 558p. 1988. reprint ed. pap. 19.95 (*0-87249-603-1*) U of SC Pr.

South Carolina: 1790 Census. 150p. 1990. pap. 22.00 (*0-935931-53-8*) Borgo Pr.

South Carolina: 1790 Census. 150p. (C). 1990. reprint ed. lib. bdg. 52.00 (*0-8095-8162-0*) Borgo Pr.

South Carolina see Official Precancel Catalog, State Sections

South Carolina see Atlas of Historical County Boundaries

South Carolina - Collected Works of Federal Writers Project, Vol. 1. Federal Writers' Project Staff. 1991. reprint ed. lib. bdg. 98.00 (*0-7812-5732-8*) Rprt Serv.

South Carolina - Collected Works of Federal Writers Project, Vol. 2. Federal Writers' Project Staff. 1991. reprint ed. lib. bdg. 98.00 (*0-7812-5737-9*) Rprt Serv.

South Carolina Album, 1936-1948: Documentary Photography in the Palmetto State. Ed. by Constance B. Schulz. LC 91-20241. (Illus.). 152p. 1992. pap. 14.95 (*0-87249-816-6*) U of SC Pr.

South Carolina & Other State Greats (Biographies) Carole Marsh. (Carole Marsh South Carolina Bks.). (Illus.). (J). 1994. pap. 19.95 (*0-7933-2007-0*); lib. bdg. 29.95 (*0-7933-2006-2*); disk 29.95 (*0-7933-2008-9*) Gallopade Pub Group.

South Carolina Architects, 1885-1935: A Biographical Dictionary. John E. Wells & Robert E. Dalton. xv, 262p. (C). 1992. 34.95 (*1-882595-00-9*) New So Archit.

South Carolina As a Royal Province, Seventeen Nineteen to Seventeen Seventy-Six. William R. Smith. LC 75-114897. (Select Bibliographies Reprint Ser.). 1977. 30.95 (*0-8369-5301-0*) Ayer.

South Carolina Automotive Directory. Ed. by T. L. Spelman. 1985. 24.95 (*1-55527-029-8*) Auto Contact Inc.

South Carolina Ballads. Ed. by Reed Smith. LC 74-38025. (Black Heritage Library Collection). 1977. reprint ed. 18.95 (*0-8369-8991-0*) Ayer.

South Carolina Bandits, Bushwackers, Outlaws, Crooks, Devils, Ghosts, Desperadoes & Other Assorted & Sundry Characters! Carole Marsh. (Carole Marsh South Carolina Bks.). (Illus.). (J). 1994. pap. 19.95 (*0-7933-1009-1*); lib. bdg. 29.95 (*0-7933-1010-5*); disk 29.95 (*0-7933-1011-3*) Gallopade Pub Group.

South Carolina Becomes a State. Terry W. Lipscomb. (Illus.). 56p. 1976. pap. 5.00 (*1-880067-00-5*) SC Dept of Arch & Hist.

South Carolina Begins: The Records of a Proprietary Colony, 1663-1721. Charles H. Lesser. 540p. 1995. pap. 50.00 (*1-880067-31-5*) SC Dept of Arch & Hist.

South Carolina Bench Book for Magistrates & Municipal Court Judges. 3rd ed. Office of South Carolina Court Administration Staff. 1997. ring bd. 100.00 (*0-943856-02-7*, 410) SC Bar CLE.

South Carolina Biographical Dictionary: People of All Times & Places Who Have Been Important to the History & Life of the State. LC 94-25945. 1994. 79.00 (*0-403-09933-1*) Somerset Pub.

South Carolina Bookstore Book: A Surprising Guide to Our State's Bookstores & Their Specialties for Students, Teachers, Writers & Publishers. Carole Marsh. (South Carolina Bks.). (Illus.). 1994. pap. 19.95 (*0-7933-2976-0*); lib. bdg. 29.95 (*0-7933-2975-2*); disk 29.95 (*0-7933-2977-9*) Gallopade Pub Group.

***South Carolina Business Directory 1997.** rev. ed. American Business Directories Staff. 1520p. 1997. boxed 375.00 (*1-56105-922-6*) Am Busn Direct.

South Carolina Census Index, 1790. Ronald V. Jackson. (Illus.). lib. bdg. 35.00 (*0-317-17067-8*) Accelerated Index.

South Carolina Census Index 1850 Mortality Schedule. (Illus.). 1989. lib. bdg. 63.00 (*0-89593-479-5*) Accelerated Index.

South Carolina Census Index 1850 Slave Schedule. (Illus.). lib. bdg. 86.00 (*0-89593-480-9*) Accelerated Index.

South Carolina Census Index 1860 Slave Schedule. (Illus.). 1988. lib. bdg. 89.00 (*0-89593-482-5*) Accelerated Index.

South Carolina Census Index, 1870, 2 vols., Set. Precision Indexing Staff. Ed. by Bradley W. Steuart. 1983p. 1989. lib. bdg. 195.00 (*1-877677-10-8*) Precision Indexing.

South Carolina Census Index, 1880. (Illus.). lib. bdg. write for info. (*0-89593-484-1*) Accelerated Index.

South Carolina Census Index, 1890: Union Veterans. Ronald V. Jackson. (Illus.). lib. bdg. 45.00 (*0-89593-774-3*) Accelerated Index.

***South Carolina Christmas.** Jan Kiefer. (Illus.). 120p. 1997. 39.95 (*1-56579-237-8*) Westcliffe Pubs.

South Carolina Chronology, 1497-1992. 2nd ed. George C. Rogers, Jr. & C. James Taylor. LC 93-27306. 188p. (C). 1993. pap. 12.95 (*0-87249-971-5*) U of SC Pr.

***South Carolina Civil Procedure.** 2nd ed. James F. Flanagan. 1996. 119.95 (*0-943856-41-8*, 725) SC Bar CLE.

South Carolina Classic Christmas Trivia: Stories, Recipes, Activities, Legends, Lore & More! Carole Marsh. (Carole Marsh South Carolina Bks.). (Illus.). (J). 1994. pap. 19.95 (*0-7933-1012-1*); lib. bdg. 29.95 (*0-7933-1013-X*); disk 29.95 (*0-7933-1014-8*) Gallopade Pub Group.

South Carolina Coastales. Carole Marsh. (Carole Marsh South Carolina Bks.). (Illus.). (J). 1994. pap. 19.95 (*1-55609-115-X*); lib. bdg. 29.95 (*0-7933-2001-1*); disk 29.95 (*0-7933-2002-X*) Gallopade Pub Group.

South Carolina Coastales! Carole Marsh. (South Carolina Bks.). (J). 1994. lib. bdg. 29.95 (*0-7933-7305-0*) Gallopade Pub Group.

South Carolina Colony. Dennis B. Fradin. LC 91-32330. (Thirteen Colonies Ser.). (Illus.). 190p. (J). (gr. 4 up). 1992. lib. bdg. 28.00 (*0-516-00397-6*) Childrens.

South Carolina Community Legal Education Materials. 74p. 1988. pap. 10.00 (*0-317-03742-0*, 44,310) NCLS Inc.

***South Carolina Consumer Protection Code: 1982 Text with Comments.** 3rd ed. Kathleen G. Smith & Harry J. Haynsworth. 1996. pap. 80.00 (*0-943856-49-3*) SC Bar CLE.

South Carolina Cookbook. Charles Jordan & Joann Jordan. 2.85 (*0-936672-28-5*) Aerial Photo.

South Carolina Corporate Practice Manual, 2 vols., I. Sherwood M. Cleveland et al. 1989. write for info. (*0-943856-10-8*) SC Bar CLE.

South Carolina Corporate Practice Manual, 2 vols., II. Sherwood M. Cleveland et al. 1989. write for info. (*0-318-67279-0*) SC Bar CLE.

South Carolina Corporate Practice Manual, 2 vols., Set. Sherwood M. Cleveland et al. 1989. ring bd. 225.00 (*0-943856-09-4*, 419) SC Bar CLE.

South Carolina County Maps. rev. ed. Ed. by C. J. Puetz. (Illus.). 128p. 1995. pap. 14.85 (*0-916514-14-5*) Cnty Maps.

South Carolina Court Records: An Introduction for Genealogists. Alexia J. Helsley & Michael E. Stauffer. Ed. by Judith M. Brimelow. 32p. 1993. pap. 3.00 (*1-880067-18-8*) SC Dept of Arch & Hist.

South Carolina Crime Perspective 1996. Ed. by Kathleen O. Morgan et al. 24p. 1996. pap. 19.00 (*1-56692-539-8*) Morgan Quitno Corp.

***South Carolina Crime Perspective 1997.** Ed. by Kathleen O. Morgan & Scott E. Morgan. 24p. 1997. pap. 19.00 (*1-56692-789-7*) Morgan Quitno Corp.

South Carolina Criminal Defense. 3rd ed. Jon P. Thames & Suzanne H. Bauknight. 1996. pap. 65.00 (*0-943856-07-8*, 740) SC Bar CLE.

South Carolina Criminal Law & Motor Vehicle Handbook: Annual Edition. Gould Editors. 1060p. (C). 1996. pap. 24.95 (*1-882476-05-0*) G Pubns FL.

South Carolina "Crinkum-Crankum" A Funny Word Book about Our State. Carole Marsh. (South Carolina Bks.). (Illus.). (J). (gr. 3-12). 1994. 29.95 (*0-7933-4928-1*); pap. 19.95 (*0-7933-4929-X*); disk 29.95 (*0-7933-4930-3*) Gallopade Pub Group.

***South Carolina Damages Awards: 1996 Edition.** rev. ed. Ed. by Timothy M. Hall. LC 94-76228. 600p. 1996. pap. text ed. write for info. (*0-7620-0087-2*) Lawyers Cooperative.

South Carolina Deed Abstracts, 1719-1772. Clara B. Langley. Incl. Vol. 1. 1719-1740, Books A-T. 392p. 1983. 37.50 (*0-89308-271-6*); Vol. 2. 1740-1755, Books V-PP. 370p. 1983. 37.50 (*0-89308-272-4*); Vol. 3. 1755-1768, Books QQ-HHH. 386p. 1983. 37.50 (*0-89308-273-2*); Vol. 4. 1768-1772, Books III-ZZZ. 400p. 1983. 37.50 (*0-89308-317-8*); 1983. 37.50 (*0-685-73578-8*) Southern Hist Pr.

South Carolina Deed Abstracts 1773-1778: Books F-4 Through X-4. Brent H. Holcomb. 1993. lib. bdg. 35.00 (*0-913363-14-6*) SCMAR.

South Carolina Deed Abstracts 1776-1783: Books Y-4 Through H-5. Brent H. Holcomb. 1994. 35.00 (*0-913363-18-9*) SCMAR.

South Carolina Deed Abstracts 1783-1788: Books I-5 Through Z-5. Brent H. Holcomb. 560p. 1996. 50.00 (*0-913363-22-7*) SCMAR.

South Carolina Dingbats! Bk. 1: A Fun Book of Games, Stories, Activities & More about Our State That's All in Code! for You to Decipher. Carole Marsh. (South Carolina Bks.). (Illus.). (J). (gr. 3-12). 1994. pap. 19.95 (*0-7933-3894-8*); lib. bdg. 29.95 (*0-7933-3893-X*); disk 29.95 (*0-7933-3895-6*) Gallopade Pub Group.

***South Carolina Dispensary: A Bottle Collector's Atlas & History of the System.** Phillip K. Huggins. LC 75-177908. 216p. 1997. reprint ed. write for info. (*0-87844-006-2*); reprint ed. pap. write for info. (*0-87844-136-0*) Sandlapper Pub Co.

South Carolina Early Census, Vol. 1. Ronald V. Jackson. (Illus.). 1980. lib. bdg. 47.00 (*0-89593-744-1*) Accelerated Index.

South Carolina Early Census, Vol. 2. Ronald V. Jackson. (Illus.). 1976. lib. bdg. 48.00 (*0-89593-745-X*) Accelerated Index.

***South Carolina Elder Law.** Franchelle C. Millender. 415p. 1995. ring bd. 89.95 (*0-943856-68-X*, 540) SC Bar CLE.

South Carolina Environmental Law Handbook. McNair Law Firm Staff. 224p. (Orig.). 1992. pap. text ed. 79.00 (*0-86587-294-5*) Gov Insts.

***South Carolina Evidence.** Danny R. Collins. 1995. pap. 34.95 (*0-943856-53-1*, 570) SC Bar CLE.

***South Carolina Evidence Handbook.** Justin S. Kahn. 298p. (Orig.). 1995. pap. 40.00 (*0-943856-52-3*, 595) SC Bar CLE.

South Carolina Facts & Factivities. Carole Marsh. (Carole Marsh State Bks.). (Illus.). 1996. 29.95 (*0-614-11550-7*, C Marsh) Gallopade Pub Group.

South Carolina Facts & Factivities. Carole Marsh. (Carole Marsh State Bks.). (Illus.). (J). 1996. teacher ed., pap. 19.95 (*0-7933-7927-X*, C Marsh) Gallopade Pub Group.

***South Carolina Family Court Handbook.** James T. Melaren. 619p. (Orig.). 1996. pap. 50.00 (*0-943856-67-1*) SC Bar CLE.

South Carolina Farm Bureau - Fifty Years of Service & Leadership. R. Lawrence Smith. (Illus.). 214p. (Orig.). 1994. pap. text ed. 5.00 (*0-9641041-0-5*) SC Farm Bureau.

South Carolina Federal Census Index, 1800. Ronald V. Jackson. (Illus.). 1973. lib. bdg. 50.00 (*0-89593-773-5*) Accelerated Index.

South Carolina Federal Census Index, 1810. Ronald V. Jackson & Gary R. Teeples. LC 77-86086. (Illus.). 1976. lib. bdg. 54.00 (*0-89593-128-1*) Accelerated Index.

South Carolina Federal Census Index, 1820. Ronald V. Jackson. LC 77-86087. (Illus.). 1976. lib. bdg. 58.00 (*0-89593-129-X*) Accelerated Index.

South Carolina Federal Census Index, 1830. Ronald V. Jackson. LC 77-86088. (Illus.). 1976. lib. bdg. 63.00 (*0-89593-130-3*) Accelerated Index.

South Carolina Federal Census Index, 1840. Ronald V. Jackson. LC 77-86078. (Illus.). 1977. lib. bdg. 68.00 (*0-89593-131-1*) Accelerated Index.

South Carolina Federal Census Index, 1850. Ronald V. Jackson & Gary R. Teeples. LC 77-86079. (Illus.). 1978. lib. bdg. 104.00 (*0-89593-132-X*) Accelerated Index.

South Carolina Federal Census Index, 1860. (Illus.). 1988. lib. bdg. 225.00 (*0-89593-481-7*) Accelerated Index.

South Carolina Federal Census Index, 1870. (Illus.). lib. bdg. 290.00 (*0-89593-483-3*) Accelerated Index.

South Carolina Festival Fun for Kids! Carole Marsh. (South Carolina Bks.). (Illus.). (YA). (gr. 3-12). 1994. pap. 19.95 (*0-7933-4047-0*); lib. bdg. 29.95 (*0-7933-4046-2*); disk 29.95 (*0-7933-4048-9*) Gallopade Pub Group.

South Carolina Fishing Digest. Ed. by Joel Terwilliger. (Illus.). 104p. 1992. pap. 6.95 (*1-881279-01-4*) Pisces Pr GA.

South Carolina Folktales. Writers Program, South Carolina Staff. LC 73-3651. (American Guide Ser.). reprint ed. write for info. (*0-404-57951-5*) AMS Pr.

***South Carolina Gardener's Guide: The What, Where, When, How & Why of Gardening in South Carolina.** Jim Wilson. (Illus.). 408p. (Orig.). 1997. pap. 18.95 (*1-888608-10-2*) Cool Springs Pr.

South Carolina Genealogical Research. 170p. 1993. pap. 15.00 (*0-913857-08-4*) Genealog Sources.

South Carolina Genealogies: Articles from the South Carolina Historical & Geneological Magazine, Set, Vols. I-V. LC 82-20497. 1983. Set. 125.00 (*0-87152-368-X*) Reprint.

South Carolina Genealogies: Articles from the South Carolina Historical & Geneological Magazine, Vol. I. LC 82-20497. 456p. 1983. 25.00 (*0-87152-369-8*) Reprint.

South Carolina Genealogies: Articles from the South Carolina Historical & Geneological Magazine, Vol. IV. LC 82-20497. 464p. 1983. 25.00 (*0-87152-372-8*) Reprint.

South Carolina Genealogies: Articles from the South Carolina Historical & Geneological Magazine, Vol. V. LC 82-20497. 208p. 1983. 25.00 (*0-87152-373-6*) Reprint.

South Carolina Ghost Tales. Nell S. Graydon. 16.95 (*0-910206-06-6*) Beaufort SC.

South Carolina Ghosts: From the Coast to the Mountains. Nancy Roberts. (Illus.). 152p. 1984. 16.95 (*0-87249-428-4*); pap. 9.95 (*0-87249-429-2*) U of SC Pr.

***South Carolina Government! The Cornerstone of Everyday Life in Our State!** Carole Marsh. (Carole Marsh South Carolina Bks.). (Illus.). (J). (gr. 3-12). 1996. pap. 19.95 (*0-7933-6302-0*); lib. bdg. 29.95 (*0-7933-6301-2*); disk 29.95 (*0-7933-6303-9*) Gallopade Pub Group.

South Carolina Health Care Perspective 1996. Ed. by Kathleen O. Morgan et al. 24p. 1996. pap. 19.00 (*1-56692-639-4*) Morgan Quitno Corp.

S

An Asterisk (*) at the beginning of an entry indicates that the title is appearing in BIP for the first time.

S

South Carolina Health Care Perspective 1997. Ed. by Kathleen O. Morgan & Scott E. Morgan. 24p. 1997. pap. 19.00 (*1-56692-739-0*) Morgan Quitno Corp.

South Carolina Highway Historical Marker Guide. South Carolina Department of Archives & History Staff. Ed. by Judith M. Brimelow. 244p. 1992. pap. text ed. 12.00 (*1-880067-14-5*) SC Dept of Arch & Hist.

South Carolina Historical & Biographical Index, Vol. 1. Ronald V. Jackson. LC 78-53716. (Illus.). 1984. lib. bdg. 30.00 (*0-89593-199-0*) Accelerated Index.

South Carolina Historical Magazine Index 71-81, 1970-1980, with Additions & Corrections 1-53, 1900-1952. rev. ed. Ed. by Harlan Greene & Frank Q. O'Neill. LC 05-32201. 384p. 1981. pap. 25.00 (*0-87152-356-6*) Reprint.

South Carolina History! Surprising Secrets about Our State's Founding Mothers, Fathers & Kids! Carole Marsh. (Carole Marsh South Carolina Bks.). (Illus.). (J). (gr. 3-12). 1996. pap. 19.95 (*0-7933-6149-4*); lib. bdg. 29.95 (*0-7933-6148-6*); disk 29.95 (*0-7933-6150-8*) Gallopade Pub Group.

South Carolina Hot Air Balloon Mystery. Carole Marsh. (Carole Marsh South Carolina Bks.). (Illus.). (J). (gr. 2-9). 1994. 29.95 (*0-7933-2678-8*); pap. 19.95 (*0-7933-2679-6*); disk 29.95 (*0-7933-2680-X*) Gallopade Pub Group.

South Carolina in Perspective 1996. Ed. by Kathleen O. Morgan et al. 26p. 1996. pap. 19.00 (*1-56692-589-4*) Morgan Quitno Corp.

South Carolina in Perspective 1997. Ed. by Kathleen O. Morgan & Scott E. Morgan. 26p. 1997. pap. 19.00 (*1-56692-689-0*) Morgan Quitno Corp.

South Carolina in Postcards. W. Howard. (Images of America Ser.). 1997. pap. 16.99 (*0-7524-0510-1*, Arcdia) Chalford.

South Carolina in Postcards, Vol. II. W. Howard. (Images of America Ser.). 1997. pap. 16.99 (*0-7524-0511-X*, Arcdia) Chalford.

South Carolina in the Confederation. Charles G. Singer. LC 76-49490. (Perspectives in American History Ser.: No. 39). (Illus.). viii, 183p. 1976. reprint ed. lib. bdg. 35.00 (*0-87991-363-0*) Porcupine Pr.

South Carolina in the Mexican War: A History of the Palmetto Regiment of Volunteers 1846-1917. Jack A. Meyer. (Illus.). 316p. 1996. 35.00 (*1-880067-35-8*) SC Dept of Arch & Hist.

South Carolina in the Modern Age. Walter B. Edgar. LC 92-9357. (Illus.). 181p. 1992. pap. 14.95 (*0-87249-831-X*); text ed. 39.95 (*0-87249-830-1*) U of SC Pr.

South Carolina in the 1880s: A Gazetteer. John H. Moore. LC 89-6377. 342p. 1989. 19.95 (*0-87844-069-0*) Sandlapper Pub Co.

South Carolina in 1791: George Washington Tours the State. Terry W. Lipscomb. Ed. by Judith M. Andrews. 112p. 1993. pap. 9.00 (*1-880067-21-8*) SC Dept of Arch & Hist.

South Carolina Indian Dictionary for Kids! Carole Marsh. (Carole Marsh State Bks.). (J). (gr. 2-9). 1996. 29.95 (*0-7933-7764-1*, C Marsh); pap. 19.95 (*0-7933-7765-X*, C Marsh) Gallopade Pub Group.

South Carolina Indians, Indian Traders, & Other Ethnic Connections: Beginning in 1670. Theresa M. Hicks & Wes Taukchiray. LC 97-14446. 1997. write for info. (*0-87152-508-9*) Reprint.

South Carolina Jeopardy! Answers & Questions about Our State! Carole Marsh. (South Carolina Bks.). (Illus.). (J). (gr. 3-12). 1994. pap. 19.95 (*0-7933-4200-7*); lib. bdg. 29.95 (*0-7933-4199-X*); disk 29.95 (*0-7933-4201-5*) Gallopade Pub Group.

South Carolina Jography: A Fun Run Through the Palmetto State. Carole Marsh. (Statemeant Ser.). (Illus.). 50p. (Orig.). (J). (gr. 3-9). 1994. pap. 19.95 (*0-935326-96-0*) Gallopade Pub Group.

South Carolina "Jography" A Fun Run Thru Our State! Carole Marsh. (Carole Marsh South Carolina Bks.). (Illus.). (J). 1994. pap. 19.95 (*1-55609-049-8*); lib. bdg. 29.95 (*0-7933-1985-4*); disk 29.95 (*0-7933-1986-2*) Gallopade Pub Group.

South Carolina Kid's Cookbook: Recipes, How-to, History, Lore & More! Carole Marsh. (Carole Marsh South Carolina Bks.). (Illus.). (J). 1994. pap. 19.95 (*0-7933-1021-0*); lib. bdg. 29.95 (*0-7933-1022-9*); disk 29.95 (*0-7933-1023-7*) Gallopade Pub Group.

South Carolina Land Grants Index, 1794-1800. Ronald V. Jackson. LC 77-86082. (Illus.). lib. bdg. 55.00 (*0-89593-134-6*) Accelerated Index.

South Carolina Legal Ethics. Robert M. Wilcox. 497p. 1996. ring bd. 89.95 (*0-943856-40-X*, 620) SC Bar CLE.

South Carolina Legal Research Handbook. Robin K. Mills & Jon S. Schultz. LC 75-21933. vi, 115p. 1976. lib. bdg. 32.00 (*0-930342-16-X*, 301040) W S Hein.

South Carolina Legislative Handbook Vol. 2: Reference Information, Vol. 2. Ed. by Susan S. Hendricks. 135p. Date not set. pap. text ed. 30.00 (*1-886629-04-8*) Hendricks & Co.

South Carolina Library Book: A Surprising Guide to the Unusual Special Collections in Libraries Across Our State for Students, Teachers, Writers & Publishers - Includes Reproducible Mailing Labels Plus Activities for Young People! Carole Marsh. (South Carolina Bks.). (Illus.). 1994. pap. 19.95 (*0-7933-3126-9*); lib. bdg. 29.95 (*0-7933-3125-0*); disk 29.95 (*0-7933-3127-7*) Gallopade Pub Group.

South Carolina Limited Liability Companies & Limited Liability Partnerships. 2nd ed. James R. Burkhard et al. 812p. 1997. ring bd. 100.00 (*0-943856-75-2*, 685) SC Bar CLE.

South Carolina Living: History, Geography, Government, Today (3rd grade Social Studies text) Kathleen L. Sloan. 1987. pap. 25.00 (*0-915114-05-4*) Lewis-Sloan.

South Carolina Lizard Man. Nancy Rhyne. LC 92-17289. (Illus.). 128p. (J). (gr. 5-9). 1992. pap. 8.95 (*0-88289-907-4*) Pelican.

South Carolina Marriages, 1688-1779. Brent H. Holcomb. 349p. 1995. reprint ed. 25.00 (*0-614-10545-5*, 2774) Genealog Pub.

South Carolina Marriages, 1800-1820. Brent H. Holcomb. 171p. 1995. reprint ed. 20.00 (*0-614-10546-3*, 2775) Genealog Pub.

South Carolina Media Book: A Surprising Guide to the Amazing Print, Broadcast & Online Media of Our State for Students, Teachers, Writers & Publishers - Includes Reproducible Mailing Labels Plus Activities for Young People! Carole Marsh. (South Carolina Bks.). (Illus.). 1994. pap. 19.95 (*0-7933-3282-6*); lib. bdg. 29.95 (*0-7933-3281-8*); disk 29.95 (*0-7933-3283-4*) Gallopade Pub Group.

South Carolina Military Men in Revolutionary War. 1989. 30.00 (*0-89593-639-9*) Accelerated Index.

South Carolina Mortality Schedule, 1860. Ronald V. Jackson. 1992. 60.00 (*0-89593-856-1*) Accelerated Index.

South Carolina Mystery Van Takes Off! Book 1: Handicapped South Carolina Kids Sneak Off on a Big Adventure. Carole Marsh. (South Carolina Bks.). (Illus.). (J). (gr. 3-12). 1994. 29.95 (*0-7933-5081-6*); pap. 19.95 (*0-7933-5082-4*); disk 29.95 (*0-7933-5083-2*) Gallopade Pub Group.

South Carolina Negro Legislators: A Glorious Success. Lawrence C. Bryant. 1974. 15.00 (*0-686-05553-5*); pap. 10.00 (*0-686-05554-3*) L C Bryant.

South Carolina Politics: The More Things Change, the More They Stay the Same. 40p. 1994. pap. 4.00 (*1-880067-26-9*) SC Dept of Arch & Hist.

South Carolina Politics & Government. Cole B. Graham, Jr. & William V. Moore. LC 94-8616. (Politics & Governments of the American States Ser.). (Illus.). xxxi, 283p. 1994. pap. text ed. 20.00 (*0-8032-7043-7*, Bison Books) U of Nebr Pr.

South Carolina Politics & Government. Cole B. Graham, Jr. & William V. Moore. LC 94-8616. (Politics & Governments of the American States Ser.). (Illus.). xxxi, 283p. 1994. text ed. 42.95 (*0-8032-2136-3*) U of Nebr Pr.

South Carolina Probate Practice Manual. Moses. 1990. 125.00 (*0-685-46188-2*, NO. 421) SC Bar CLE.

South Carolina Probate Practice Manual. Albert L. Moses. 1990. ring bd. 125.00 (*0-943856-33-7*, 421) SC Bar CLE.

South Carolina Public Sector Employer's Legal Reference Manual. rev. ed. Ed. by Thomas L. Stephenson & Susan B. McWilliams. 98p. 1995. ring bd. 20.00 (*0-917069-09-9*) Univ SC Inst Pub Affairs.

South Carolina Quiz Bowl Crash Course! Carole Marsh. (Carole Marsh South Carolina Bks.). (Illus.). (J). 1994. pap. 19.95 (*0-7933-1999-4*); lib. bdg. 29.95 (*0-7933-1998-6*); disk 29.95 (*0-7933-2000-3*) Gallopade Pub Group.

South Carolina Rollercoasters! Carole Marsh. (South Carolina Bks.). (Illus.). (YA). (gr. 3-12). 1994. pap. 19.95 (*0-7933-5345-9*); lib. bdg. 29.95 (*0-7933-5344-0*); disk 29.95 (*0-7933-5346-7*) Gallopade Pub Group.

South Carolina Rules of Procedure Annotated - 1997. rev. ed. Justin S. Kahn. 433p. 1997. pap. 45.00 (*0-943856-74-4*, 553) SC Bar CLE.

South Carolina School Trivia: An Amazing & Fascinating Look at Our State's Teachers, Schools & Students! Carole Marsh. (Carole Marsh South Carolina Bks.). (Illus.). (J). 1994. pap. 19.95 (*0-7933-1018-0*); lib. bdg. 29.95 (*0-7933-1019-9*); disk 29.95 (*0-7933-1020-2*) Gallopade Pub Group.

South Carolina Silly Basketball Sportsmysteries, Vol. 1. Carole Marsh. (Carole Marsh South Carolina Bks.). (Illus.). (J). 1994. pap. 19.95 (*0-7933-1015-6*); lib. bdg. 29.95 (*0-7933-1016-4*); disk 29.95 (*0-7933-1017-2*) Gallopade Pub Group.

South Carolina Silly Basketball Sportsmysteries, Vol. 2. Carole Marsh. (Carole Marsh South Carolina Bks.). (Illus.). (J). 1994. pap. 19.95 (*0-7933-2010-0*); lib. bdg. 29.95 (*0-7933-2009-7*); disk 29.95 (*0-7933-2011-9*) Gallopade Pub Group.

South Carolina Silly Football Sportsmysteries, Vol. 1. Carole Marsh. (Carole Marsh South Carolina Bks.). (Illus.). (J). 1994. pap. 19.95 (*0-7933-1990-0*); lib. bdg. 29.95 (*0-7933-1989-7*); disk 29.95 (*0-7933-1991-9*) Gallopade Pub Group.

South Carolina Silly Football Sportsmysteries, Vol. 2. Carole Marsh. (Carole Marsh South Carolina Bks.). (Illus.). (J). 1994. pap. 19.95 (*0-7933-1993-5*); lib. bdg. 29.95 (*0-7933-1992-7*); disk 29.95 (*0-7933-1994-3*) Gallopade Pub Group.

South Carolina Silly Trivia! Carole Marsh. (Carole Marsh South Carolina Bks.). (Illus.). (J). 1994. lib. bdg. 29.95 (*0-7933-1983-8*); disk 29.95 (*0-7933-1984-6*) Gallopade Pub Group.

South Carolina Statutes at Large of South Carolina, 12 vols., Set. LC 74-19726. reprint ed. 648.00 (*0-404-12500-X*) AMS Pr.

South Carolina Story. Anne R. Osborne. LC 87-37628. (Illus.). 168p. 1988. 12.95 (*0-87844-083-6*) Sandlapper Pub Co.

South Carolina Survival. Betty L. Hall & Hunter Draper. 160p. (Orig.). (gr. 10-12). 1979. pap. text ed. 5.84 (*0-03-055521-3*) Westwood Pr.

South Carolina Timeline: A Chronology of South Carolina History, Mystery, Trivia, Legend, Lore & More. Carole Marsh. (South Carolina Bks.). (Illus.). (J). (gr. 3-12). 1994. pap. 19.95 (*0-7933-5996-1*); lib. bdg. 29.95 (*0-7933-5995-3*); disk 29.95 (*0-7933-5997-X*) Gallopade Pub Group.

South Carolina Tokens. Tony Chibbaro. Ed. by David E. Schenkman. LC 90-71295. (Illus.). 262p. 1991. text ed. 49.95 (*0-918492-09-2*) TAMS.

South Carolina Trivia. Al Menendez & Shirley Menendez. LC 96-4020. 191p. 1996. pap. text ed. 6.95 (*1-55853-391-5*) Rutledge Hill Pr.

South Carolina Upcountry, Fifteen Forty to Nineteen Eighty: Historical & Biographical Sketches, Vol. II. E. D. Herd, Jr. 294p. (Orig.). 1982. pap. 9.95 (*0-87921-067-2*) Attic Pr.

South Carolina Water Ways. Ronald V. Jackson. LC 77-86081. (Illus.). lib. bdg. 35.00 (*0-89593-775-1*) Accelerated Index.

South Carolina Women. rev. ed. Idella F. Bodie. Ed. by Louise Pettus & Linda Benefield. LC 90-48424. Orig. Title: South Carolina Women: They Dared to Lead. (Illus.). 1990. 22.95 (*0-87844-079-8*); pap. 12.95 (*0-87844-102-6*) Sandlapper Pub Co.

South Carolina Women: A Timeline. Benjamin F. Hornsby, Jr. 16p. 1995. pap. 2.00 (*1-880067-32-3*) SC Dept of Arch & Hist.

South Carolina Women: They Dared to Lead see South Carolina Women

South Carolina's Expansion into Colonial Georgia, 1720-1765. David R. Chestnutt. (Outstanding Studies in Early American History). 251p. 1989. reprint ed. 15.00 (*0-8240-6175-6*) Garland.

South Carolina's Historic Restaurants & Their Recipes. rev. ed. Dawn O'Brien & Karen S. Mulford. (Illus.). 204p. 1992. 14.95 (*0-89587-097-5*) Blair.

South Carolina's Low Country: A Past Preserved. Catherine C. Messmer & C. Andrew Halcomb. LC 87-4312. (Illus.). 143p. 1988. 19.95 (*0-87844-070-4*) Sandlapper Pub Co.

South Carolina's (Most Devastating!) Disasters & (Most Calamitous!) Catastrophies! Carole Marsh. (Carole Marsh South Carolina Bks.). (Illus.). (J). 1994. pap. 19.95 (*0-7933-1006-7*); lib. bdg. 29.95 (*0-7933-1007-5*); disk 29.95 (*0-7933-1008-3*) Gallopade Pub Group.

South Carolina's Mountain Wilderness. Tommy Wyche & Tom Blagden, Jr. (Illus.). 128p. 1994. 35.00 (*1-56579-056-1*) Westcliffe Pubs.

South Carolina's Unsolved Mysteries (& Their "Solutions") Includes Scientific Information & Other Activities for Students. Carole Marsh. (South Carolina Bks.). (Illus.). (J). (gr. 3-12). 1994. pap. 19.95 (*0-7933-5843-4*); lib. bdg. 29.95 (*0-7933-5842-6*); disk 29.95 (*0-7933-5844-2*) Gallopade Pub Group.

South Carolina's Wetland Wilderness: The Ace Basin. Tom Blagden, Jr. (Illus.). 112p. 1992. 29.95 (*0-929969-71-5*) Westcliffe Pubs.

South Cascades Arc Volcanism, California & Southern Oregon. Ed. by Muffler. (IGC Field Trip Guidebooks Ser.). 64p. 1989. 21.00 (*0-87590-563-3*, T312) Am Geophysical.

South Cemeteries of Lisht, Vol. One: The Pyramid of Senwosret I. Dieter Arnold. (Metropolitan Museum of Art Egyptian Expedition Publications: No. 22). (Illus.). 156p. 1988. 75.00 (*0-87099-506-5*) Metro Mus Art.

South Cemeteries of Lisht, Vol. Two: The Control Notes & Team Marks. Felix Arnold. (Metropolitan Museum of Art Egyptian Expedition Publications: No. 23). (Illus.). 204p. 1991. 75.00 (*0-87099-551-0*) Metro Mus Art.

South Central Frontiers: A History of the South Central Mennonite Conference. Paul Erb. LC 74-12108. (Studies in Anabaptist & Mennonite History: No. 17). 520p. reprint ed. pap. 148.20 (*0-8357-2662-2*, 2040198) Bks Demand.

South-Central Section Field Guide. Ed. by O. T. Hayward. (DNAG Centennial Field Guides Ser.: No. 4). (Illus.). 475p. 1988. 43.50 (*0-8137-5404-6*) Geol Soc.

South China: State, Culture & Social Change During the 20th Century. Ed. by L. M. Douw & P. Post. 272p. 1996. pap. 47.00 (*0-444-85811-3*) Elsevier.

South China Caves. Ed. by Rondal R. Bridgemon & Karen B. Lindsley. (Illus.). 62p. (Orig.). 1991. pap. 7.95 (*0-939748-27-4*) Cave Bks MO.

South China Silk District: Local Historical Transformation & World System Theory. Alvin Y. So. LC 86-14575. 206p. (C). 1986. text ed. 64.50 (*0-88706-321-7*); pap. text ed. 21.95 (*0-88706-322-5*) State U NY Pr.

South Clyde Estuary: An Illustrated Architectural Guide. Frank A. Walker. (Illus.). 152p. (C). 1986. pap. 35.00 (*1-873190-27-1*, Pub. by Rutland Pr UK) St Mut.

South Coast New Guinea Cultures: History, Comparison, Dialectic. Bruce M. Knauft. LC 92-12472. (Cambridge Studies in Social & Cultural Anthropology: No. 89). (Illus.). 220p. (C). 1993. text ed. 59.95 (*0-521-41882-8*); pap. text ed. 20.95 (*0-521-42931-5*) Cambridge U Pr.

South Coast of Puerto Rico. Wilson Ltd. Staff & Imray L. Norie. (C). 1984. 65.00 (*0-685-40410-2*, Pub. by Imray Laurie Norie & Wilson UK) St Mut.

South Coast Way. Laurence Main. (C). 1988. pap. 29.00 (*0-904110-86-9*, Pub. by Thornhill Pr UK) St Mut.

South Corner of Time: Hopi, Navajo, Papago, Yaqui Tribal Literature. Ed. by Larry Evers et al. LC 76-617570. (Illus.). 250p. reprint ed. pap. 71.30 (*0-7837-5046-3*, 2044724) Bks Demand.

South Country. Edward Thomas. Ed. by George Thomas. 304p. 1993. pap. 6.95 (*0-460-87291-5*, Everyman's Classic Lib) C E Tuttle.

South County Studies: Of Some Eighteenth Century Persons, Places & Conditions. in That Portion of Rhode Island Called Narragansett. Esther B. Carpenter & Caroline Hazard. LC 75-160961. (Select Bibliographies Reprint Ser.). 1977. reprint ed. 23.95 (*0-8369-5829-2*) Ayer.

South Dakata History! Surprising Secrets about Our State's Founding Mothers, Fathers & Kids! Carole Marsh. (Carole Marsh South Dakata Bks.). (Illus.). (J). (gr. 3-12). 1996. pap. 19.95 (*0-7933-6152-4*); lib. bdg. 29.95 (*0-7933-6151-6*); disk 29.95 (*0-7933-6153-2*) Gallopade Pub Group.

South Dakota. Childrens Press Staff. (From Sea to Shining Sea Ser.). (J). 1995. pap. 5.95 (*0-516-43841-7*) Childrens.

South Dakota. Dennis B. Fradin. LC 94-43043. (From Sea to Shining Sea Ser.). (Illus.). 64p. (J). (gr. 3-5). 1995. lib. bdg. 24.00 (*0-516-03841-9*) Childrens.

South Dakota. Tom Griffith. LC 93-43502. (Compass American Guides Ser.). (Illus.). 1994. pap. 16.95 (*1-878867-26-1*, Compass Amrcn) Fodors Travel.

South Dakota. Melissa McDaniel. LC 96-49272. (Celebrate the States Ser.: Group 3). (Illus.). 144p. (J). (gr. 4 up). 1997. lib. bdg. 22.95 (*0-7614-0419-8*, Benchmark NY) Marshall Cavendish.

South Dakota. Karen Sirvaitis. LC 94-5451. (Hello U. S. A. Ser.). (Illus.). 72p. (J). (gr. 3-6). 1994. 18.95 (*0-8225-2747-2*, Lerner Publctns) Lerner Group.

South Dakota. Kathleen Thompson. LC 95-25722. (Portrait of America Library). 48p. (J). (gr. 3 up). 1996. lib. bdg. 22.83 (*0-8114-7387-2*) Raintree Steck-V.

South Dakota. Kathleen Thompson. LC 95-25722. (Portrait of America Library). 48p. (J). (gr. 3 up). 1996. pap. text ed. 5.95 (*0-8114-7468-2*) Raintree Steck-V.

South Dakota. rev. ed. Emilie U. Lepthien. LC 90-21137. (America the Beautiful Ser.). (Illus.). 144p. (J). (gr. 4 up). 1992. lib. bdg. 28.30 (*0-516-00487-5*) Childrens.

South Dakota: A Guide to the State. Federal Writers' Project Staff & Writers Program-WPA Staff. (American Guide Ser.). 1989. reprint ed. lib. bdg. 79.00 (*0-7812-1040-2*, 1040) Rprt Serv.

South Dakota: A Guide to the State. Federal Writers' Project Staff. (American Guidebook Ser.). 421p. 1938. reprint ed. 89.00 (*0-403-02190-1*) Somerset Pub.

South Dakota: A History. John R. Milton. 1989. pap. 9.95 (*0-393-30571-6*) Norton.

South Dakota: Land of Shining Gold. Francie M. Berg. LC 81-67726. (Old West Region Ser.: Vol. 2). (Illus.). 176p. 1982. 21.95 (*0-918532-07-8*) Flying Diamond Bks.

South Dakota see Atlas of Historical County Boundaries

South Dakota - Collected Works of Federal Writers Project. Federal Writers' Project Staff. 1991. reprint ed. lib. bdg. 98.00 (*0-7812-5742-5*) Rprt Serv.

South Dakota & Other State Greats (Biographies) Carole Marsh. (Carole Marsh South Dakota Bks.). (Illus.). (J). 1994. pap. 19.95 (*0-7933-2039-9*); lib. bdg. 29.95 (*0-7933-2038-0*); disk 29.95 (*0-7933-2040-2*) Gallopade Pub Group.

South Dakota Bandits, Bushwackers, Outlaws, Crooks, Devils, Ghosts, Desperadoes & Other Assorted & Sundry Characters! Carole Marsh. (Carole Marsh South Dakota Bks.). (Illus.). (J). 1994. pap. 19.95 (*0-7933-1033-4*); lib. bdg. 29.95 (*0-7933-1034-2*); disk 29.95 (*0-7933-1035-0*) Gallopade Pub Group.

South Dakota Bookstore Book: A Surprising Guide to Our State's Bookstores & Their Specialties for Students, Teachers, Writers & Publishers. Carole Marsh. (South Dakota Bks.). (Illus.). 1994. pap. 19.95 (*0-7933-2979-5*); lib. bdg. 29.95 (*0-7933-2978-7*); disk 29.95 (*0-7933-2980-9*) Gallopade Pub Group.

South Dakota Budgetary Developments: Process & Trends, 1967-1983. Loren M. Carlson. 1984. 1.00 (*1-55614-116-5*) U of SD Gov Res Bur.

South Dakota Business Directory 1997. rev. ed. American Business Directories Staff. 480p. 1997. boxed 295.00 (*1-56105-923-4*) Am Busn Direct.

South Dakota Census Index 1860 Mortality Schedule. (Illus.). lib. bdg. 28.00 (*0-89593-486-8*) Accelerated Index.

South Dakota Census Index 1870 Mortality Schedule. (Illus.). lib. bdg. 28.00 (*0-89593-487-6*) Accelerated Index.

South Dakota Census Index 1880 Mortality Shedule. (Illus.). lib. bdg. 29.00 (*0-89593-488-4*) Accelerated Index.

South Dakota Census Index 1885 Mortality Schedule. (Illus.). 1984. lib. bdg. 34.00 (*0-89593-489-2*) Accelerated Index.

South Dakota Census Index, 1890: Union Veterans. Ronald V. Jackson. (Illus.). lib. bdg. 49.00 (*0-89593-777-8*) Accelerated Index.

South Dakota Classic Christmas Trivia: Stories, Recipes, Activities, Legends, Lore & More! Carole Marsh. (Carole Marsh South Dakota Bks.). (Illus.). (J). 1994. pap. 19.95 (*0-7933-1036-9*); lib. bdg. 29.95 (*0-7933-1037-7*); disk 29.95 (*0-7933-1038-5*) Gallopade Pub Group.

South Dakota Coastales. Carole Marsh. (Carole Marsh South Dakota Bks.). (Illus.). (J). 1994. pap. 19.95 (*0-7933-2033-X*); lib. bdg. 29.95 (*0-7933-2032-1*); disk 29.95 (*0-7933-2034-8*) Gallopade Pub Group.

South Dakota Coastales! Carole Marsh. (South Dakota Bks.). (J). 1994. lib. bdg. 29.95 (*0-7933-7306-9*) Gallopade Pub Group.

South Dakota Codified Laws. 1978. write for info. (*0-87473-037-6*) MICHIE.

South Dakota Codified Laws. write for info. (*0-614-05967-4*) MICHIE.

South Dakota Court Rules, 1994 Edition. Michie Butterworth Editorial Staff. pap. 50.00 (*1-55834-144-7*) MICHIE.

South Dakota Crime Perspective 1996. Ed. by Kathleen O. Morgan et al. 24p. 1996. pap. 19.00 (*1-56692-540-1*) Morgan Quitno Corp.

South Dakota Crime Perspective 1997. Ed. by Kathleen O. Morgan & Scott E. Morgan. 24p. 1997. pap. 19.00 (*1-56692-790-0*) Morgan Quitno Corp.

An Asterisk (*) at the beginning of an entry indicates that the title is appearing in BIP for the first time.

South Dakota Criminal & Traffic Law Manual, 1993 Edition. 25.00 (*0-614-05968-2*) MICHIE.

South Dakota "Crinkum-Crankum" A Funny Word Book about Our State. Carole Marsh. (South Dakota Bks.). (Illus.). (J). (gr. 3-12). 1994. 29.95 (*0-7933-4931-1*); pap. 19.95 (*0-7933-4932-X*); disk 29.95 (*0-7933-4933-8*) Gallopade Pub Group.

South Dakota Dingbats! Bk. 1: A Fun Book of Games, Stories, Activities & More about Our State That's All in Code! for You to Decipher. Carole Marsh. (South Dakota Bks.). (Illus.). (J). (gr. 3-12). 1994. pap. 19.95 (*0-7933-3897-2*); lib. bdg. 29.95 (*0-7933-3896-4*); disk 29.95 (*0-7933-3898-0*) Gallopade Pub Group.

South Dakota Evidence. John W. Larson. 960p. 1991. 95.00 (*0-87473-748-6*) MICHIE.

South Dakota Facts & Factivities. Carole Marsh. (Carole Marsh State Bks.). (Illus.). 1996. 29.95 (*0-614-11551-5*, C Marsh) Gallopade Pub Group.

South Dakota Facts & Factivities. Carole Marsh. (Carole Marsh State Bks.). (Illus.). (J). 1996. teacher ed., pap. 19.95 (*0-7933-7929-6*, C Marsh) Gallopade Pub Group.

South Dakota Federal Census Index, 1885. Ronald V. Jackson. (Illus.). 1981. lib. bdg. 85.00 (*0-89593-776-X*) Accelerated Index.

South Dakota Festival Fun for Kids! Carole Marsh. (South Dakota Bks.). (Illus.). (YA). (gr. 3-12). 1994. pap. 19.95 (*0-7933-4050-0*); lib. bdg. 29.95 (*0-7933-4049-7*); disk 29.95 (*0-7933-4051-9*) Gallopade Pub Group.

***South Dakota Government! The Cornerstone of Everyday Life in Our State!** Carole Marsh. (Carole Marsh South Dakota Bks.). (Illus.). (J). (gr. 3-12). 1996. pap. 19.95 (*0-7933-6305-5*); lib. bdg. 29.95 (*0-7933-6304-7*); disk 29.95 (*0-7933-6306-3*) Gallopade Pub Group.

South Dakota Governments Performance Standards, 1990. Ed. by Greg Michels. (Governments Performance Standards Ser.). (Illus.). 150p. 1990. text ed. 125.00 (*1-55507-500-2*) Municipal Analysis.

South Dakota Health Care Perspective 1996. Ed. by Kathleen O. Morgan et al. 24p. 1996. pap. 19.00 (*1-56692-640-8*) Morgan Quitno Corp.

***South Dakota Health Care Perspective 1997.** Ed. by Kathleen O. Morgan & Scott E. Morgan. 24p. 1997. pap. 19.00 (*1-56692-740-4*) Morgan Quitno Corp.

South Dakota History: An Annotated Bibliography. Ed. by Karen P. Zimmerman & Christopher J. Hoover. LC 93-14048. (Bibliographies of the States of the United States Ser.: No. 2). 552p. 1993. text ed. 79.50 (*0-313-28263-3*, AMSTSD, Greenwood Pr) Greenwood.

South Dakota Hot Air Balloon Mystery. Carole Marsh. (Carole Marsh South Dakota Bks.). (Illus.). (J). (gr. 2-9). 1994. 29.95 (*0-7933-2687-7*); pap. 19.95 (*0-7933-2688-5*); disk 29.95 (*0-7933-2689-3*) Gallopade Pub Group.

South Dakota in Perspective 1996. Ed. by Kathleen O. Morgan et al. 26p. 1996. pap. 19.00 (*1-56692-590-8*) Morgan Quitno Corp.

***South Dakota in Perspective 1997.** Ed. by Kathleen O. Morgan & Scott E. Morgan. 26p. 1997. pap. 19.00 (*1-56692-690-4*) Morgan Quitno Corp.

South Dakota in Washington: Profile of a Congressional Delegation. Charles O. Jones. 1966. 1.00 (*1-55614-117-3*) U of SD Gov Res Bur.

South Dakota Indian Dictionary for Kids! Carole Marsh. (Carole Marsh South Dakota Bks.). (J). (gr. 2-9). 1996. 29.95 (*0-7933-7767-6*, C Marsh); pap. 19.95 (*0-7933-7768-4*, C Marsh) Gallopade Pub Group.

South Dakota Jails: Current Conditions & Proposed Directions. Donald C. Dahlin. 1971. 5.00 (*1-55614-000-2*) U of SD Gov Res Bur.

South Dakota Jeopardy! Answers & Questions about Our State! Carole Marsh. (South Dakota Bks.). (Illus.). (J). (gr. 3-12). 1994. pap. 19.95 (*0-7933-4203-1*); lib. bdg. 29.95 (*0-7933-4202-3*); disk 29.95 (*0-7933-4204-X*) Gallopade Pub Group.

South Dakota "Jography" A Fun Run Thru Our State! Carole Marsh. (Carole Marsh South Dakota Bks.). (Illus.). (J). 1994. pap. 19.95 (*0-7933-2016-X*); lib. bdg. 29.95 (*0-7933-2015-1*); disk 29.95 (*0-7933-2017-8*) Gallopade Pub Group.

***South Dakota Justice: The Judges & the System.** Ross H. Oviatt. 67p. 1989. per. 7.95 (*0-614-24800-0*) Tesseract SD.

South Dakota Kid's Cookbook: Recipes, How-to, History, Lore & More! Carole Marsh. (Carole Marsh South Dakota Bks.). (Illus.). (J). 1994. pap. 19.95 (*0-7933-1045-8*); lib. bdg. 29.95 (*0-7933-1046-6*); disk 29.95 (*0-7933-1047-4*) Gallopade Pub Group.

South Dakota Legal Research Guide. Delores A. Jorgensen. LC 88-4757. vi, 198p. 1988. ring bd. 35.00 (*0-89941-633-0*, 305550) W S Hein.

South Dakota Library Book: A Surprising Guide to the Unusual Special Collections in Libraries Across Our State for Students, Teachers, Writers & Publishers - Includes Reproducible Mailing Labels Plus Activities for Young People! Carole Marsh. (South Dakota Bks.). (Illus.). 1994. pap. 19.95 (*0-7933-3129-3*); lib. bdg. 29.95 (*0-7933-3128-5*); disk 29.95 (*0-7933-3130-7*) Gallopade Pub Group.

South Dakota Media Book: A Surprising Guide to the Amazing Print, Broadcast & Online Media of Our State for Students, Teachers, Writers & Publishers - Includes Reproducible Mailing Labels Plus Activities for Young People! Carole Marsh. (South Dakota Bks.). (Illus.). 1994. pap. 19.95 (*0-7933-3285-0*); lib. bdg. 29.95 (*0-7933-3284-2*); disk 29.95 (*0-7933-3286-9*) Gallopade Pub Group.

South Dakota Mystery Van Takes Off! Book 1: Handicapped South Dakota Kids Sneak Off on a Big Adventure. Carole Marsh. (South Dakota Bks.). (Illus.). (J). (gr. 3-12). 1994. 29.95 (*0-7933-5084-0*); pap. 19.95 (*0-7933-5085-9*); disk 29.95 (*0-7933-5086-7*) Gallopade Pub Group.

South Dakota, Pembina District Census Index, 1850 (Same As Dakota Territory 1850) Ronald V. Jackson. 1991. 40.00 (*0-89593-818-9*) Accelerated Index.

South Dakota Pioneer Daughters Collection, 6 vols., Set. (Illus.). pap. write for info. (*1-880589-00-1*) Sky Carrier Pr.

South Dakota Poll: A Critical Analysis. Kenneth A. Bode. 1970. 1.00 (*1-55614-001-0*) U of SD Gov Res Bur.

South Dakota Presidential Trivia. Gregory J. Nedved. 57p. 1995. pap. write for info. (*0-9651949-0-6*) G J Nedved.

***South Dakota Presidential Trivia.** Gregory J. Nedved. 57p. 1995. pap. 6.00 (*0-614-24798-5*) Tesseract SD.

South Dakota Quiz Bowl Crash Course! Carole Marsh. (Carole Marsh South Dakota Bks.). (Illus.). (J). 1994. pap. 19.95 (*0-7933-2030-5*); lib. bdg. 29.95 (*0-7933-2029-1*); disk 29.95 (*0-7933-2031-3*) Gallopade Pub Group.

South Dakota Recreation Guide. Lynn D. Soli & Barbara McCaig. LC 85-51898. (Illus.). 82p. (Orig.). 1985. pap. 9.95 (*0-9610130-3-6*) Melius Pub.

South Dakota Rollercoasters! Carole Marsh. (South Dakota Bks.). (Illus.). (YA). (gr. 3-12). 1994. pap. 19.95 (*0-7933-5348-3*); lib. bdg. 29.95 (*0-7933-5347-5*); disk 29.95 (*0-7933-5349-1*) Gallopade Pub Group.

South Dakota School Trivia: An Amazing & Fascinating Look at Our State's Teachers, Schools & Students! Carole Marsh. (Carole Marsh South Dakota Bks.). (Illus.). (J). 1994. pap. 19.95 (*0-7933-1042-3*); lib. bdg. 29.95 (*0-7933-1043-1*); disk 29.95 (*0-7933-1044-X*) Gallopade Pub Group.

South Dakota Silly Basketball Sportsmysteries, Vol. 1. Carole Marsh. (Carole Marsh South Dakota Bks.). (Illus.). (J). 1994. pap. 19.95 (*0-7933-1039-3*); lib. bdg. 29.95 (*0-7933-1040-7*); disk 29.95 (*0-7933-1041-5*) Gallopade Pub Group.

South Dakota Silly Basketball Sportsmysteries, Vol. 2. Carole Marsh. (Carole Marsh South Dakota Bks.). (Illus.). (J). 1994. lib. bdg. 29.95 (*0-7933-2041-0*); disk 29.95 (*0-7933-2043-7*) Gallopade Pub Group.

South Dakota Silly Basketball Sportsmysteries, Vol. 2. Carole Marsh. (Carole Marsh South Dakota Bks.). (Illus.). (J). 1997. pap. 19.95 (*0-7933-2042-9*) Gallopade Pub Group.

South Dakota Silly Football Sportsmysteries, Vol. 1. Carole Marsh. (Carole Marsh South Dakota Bks.). (Illus.). (J). 1994. pap. 19.95 (*0-7933-2021-6*); lib. bdg. 29.95 (*0-7933-2020-8*); disk 29.95 (*0-7933-2022-4*) Gallopade Pub Group.

South Dakota Silly Football Sportsmysteries, Vol. 2. Carole Marsh. (Carole Marsh South Dakota Bks.). (Illus.). (J). 1994. lib. bdg. 29.95 (*0-7933-2023-2*); disk 29.95 (*0-7933-2025-9*) Gallopade Pub Group.

South Dakota Silly Trvia! Carole Marsh. (Carole Marsh South Dakota Bks.). (Illus.). (J). 1994. pap. 19.95 (*0-7933-2013-5*); lib. bdg. 29.95 (*0-7933-2012-7*); disk 29.95 (*0-7933-2014-3*) Gallopade Pub Group.

South Dakota State Finance. 1951. 5.00 (*1-55614-002-9*) U of SD Gov Res Bur.

South Dakota Timeline: A Chronology of South Dakota History, Mystery, Trivia, Legend, Lore & More. Carole Marsh. (South Dakota Bks.). (Illus.). (J). (gr. 3-12). 1994. pap. 19.95 (*0-7933-5999-6*); lib. bdg. 29.95 (*0-7933-5998-8*); disk 29.95 (*0-7933-6000-5*) Gallopade Pub Group.

South Dakota's American Mother: The Life Story of Christina K. Lacey - South Dakota State Mother - 1946. Christina K. Lacey et al. LC 89-8452. (Illus.). 160p. (Orig.). 1989. 12.95 (*0-9622491-0-6*); pap. 9.95 (*0-9622491-1-4*) Pheasant Pr.

South Dakota's Congressional Staffs. Alan L. Clem. 1981. 1.00 (*1-55614-003-7*) U of SD Gov Res Bur.

South Dakota's (Most Devastating!) Disasters & (Most Calamitous!) Catastrophies! Carole Marsh. (Carole Marsh South Dakota Bks.). (Illus.). (J). 1994. pap. 19.95 (*0-7933-1030-X*); lib. bdg. 29.95 (*0-7933-1031-8*); disk 29.95 (*0-7933-1032-6*) Gallopade Pub Group.

South Dakota's Nineteen Sixty-Five Legislative Session. George M. Platt. 1965. 1.00 (*1-55614-004-5*) U of SD Gov Res Bur.

South Dakota's Roadkill Cookbook: A Collection of Spurious Recipes Using Ventre Montant (French for Belly-Up) Animals One Finds on South Dakota Highways. Bruce Carlson. (Illus.). 104p. (Orig.). 1990. pap. 7.95 (*1-878488-19-8*) Quixote Pr IA.

South Dakota's Unsolved Mysteries (& Their "Solutions") Includes Scientific Information & Other Activities for Students. Carole Marsh. (South Dakota Bks.). (Illus.). (J). (gr. 3-12). 1994. pap. 19.95 (*0-7933-5846-9*); lib. bdg. 29.95 (*0-7933-5845-0*); disk 29.95 (*0-7933-5847-7*) Gallopade Pub Group.

South Denver Saga. Phil Goodstein. vi, 250p. 1991. 14.95 (*0-685-40821-3*) New Social.

South Devon & Dartmoor. (Ordnance Survey Landranger Guides Ser.). (Illus.). 144p. 1993. pap. 15.95 (*0-7117-0542-9*) Seven Hills Bk.

South Devon & Dartmoor Car Tours. Ed. by Jarrold Publishing Staff. (Ordnance Survey Travelmaster Guides Ser.). (Illus.). 96p. (Orig.). 1995. pap. 15.95 (*0-7117-0824-X*, Pub. by Jarrold Pub UK) Seven Hills Bk.

South Devon & Dartmoor Walks. Ordnance Survey Pathfinder Guild Staff. 1996. pap. text ed. 16.95 (*0-7117-0851-7*, Pub. by Jarrold Pub UK) Seven Hills Bk.

South Down. Becky Ingram. LC 95-90850. 1996. 14.95 (*0-533-11731-3*) Vantage.

***South Downs.** Insight Guides Staff. (Insight Compact Guides Ser.). 1997. pap. 7.95 (*0-395-82937-2*) HM.

South Downs: Travels Through White Cliff Country. Michael George. (Classic Country Companions Ser.). (Illus.). 144p. 1992. 34.95 (*1-85145-734-8*, Pub. by Pavilion UK) Trafalgar.

South Downs: Travels Through White Cliff Country. Michael George. (Classic Country Companions Ser.). (Illus.). 144p. 1993. pap. 17.95 (*1-85145-863-8*, Pub. by Pavilion UK) Trafalgar.

South Downs Way. Paul Millmore. (National Travel Guide Ser.). (Illus.). 168p. 1995. pap. 19.95 (*1-85410-099-8*, Pub. by Aurum Pr UK) London Bridge.

South During Reconstruction, 1865-1877. E. Merton Coulter. LC 48-5161. (History of the South Ser.: Vol. 8). (Illus.). 426p. 1947. text ed. 45.00 (*0-8071-0008-0*) La State U Pr.

South-East Asia. 2nd ed. Charles Fisher. 1966. 75.00 (*0-416-42480-5*, NO.2200) Routledge Chapman & Hall.

South-East Asia: A Guide to Reference Material. Ed. by Andrew Dalby. (Regional Reference Guides Ser.: No. 2). 320p. 1993. 100.00 (*1-873836-00-7*, Pub. by H Zell Pubs UK) Bowker-Saur.

South-East Asia: Languages & Literatures: A Select Guide. Ed. by Patricia Herbert & Anthony Milner. (Illus.). 192p. 1989. pap. text ed. 20.00 (*0-8248-1267-0*) UH Pr.

***South-East Asia: On a Shoestring.** 9th ed. Peter Turner et al. (Illus.). 1024p. 1997. pap. 21.95 (*0-86442-412-4*) Lonely Planet.

South East Asia: Phrasebook. David Bradley et al. (Illus.). 380p. 1997. pap. 6.95 (*0-86442-435-3*) Lonely Planet.

South East Asia: Unity in Diversity. Gennadi Chifrin & I. Mozheiko. 1989. 23.00 (*81-7023-261-9*, Pub. by Allied II) S Asia.

South East Asia Atlas. Oilfield Publications Limited Staff. (C). 1993. 1,490.00 (*1-870945-36-0*, Pub. by Oilfield Pubns UK) St Mut.

South East Asia Golf Guide. Neil French-Blake & Alan Clarke. (Illus.). 144p. 1996. pap. 19.95 (*1-56554-209-6*) Pelican.

South-East Asia in Indian Foreign Policy. Asis K. Majumdar. 1983. 22.50 (*0-8364-0932-9*, Pub. by Naya Prokash IA) S Asia.

South East Asia Wildlife. (Insight Guides Ser.). 1993. pap. 21.95 (*0-395-66201-X*) HM.

South-East Asia Wildlife. (Insight Guides Ser.). 1993. pap. 21.95 (*0-395-66283-4*) HM.

South East Asia, 1930-1970: The Legacy of Colonialism & Nationalism. Fred R. Von Der Mehden, pseud. (Library of World Civilization). (Illus.). 144p. (C). 1974. text ed. 9.95 (*0-393-05513-2*) Norton.

South-East Asia 1943-1945. Louis Mountbatten. 280p. 1987. 125.00 (*0-614-08405-9*, Pub. by Himalayan Bks II) St Mut.

South-East Asian Ceramics: Thai, Khmer, & Vietnamese from the Collection of the Art Gallery of South Australia, Adelaide. Dick Richards. (Asia Collection). (Illus.). 150p. 1995. 95.00 (*967-65-3075-1*) OUP.

South-East Asian Oil, Gas, Coal & Mineral Deposits. Charles S. Hutchison. (Oxford Monographs on Geology & Geophysics). (Illus.). 336p. (C). 1996. 105.00 (*0-19-854295-X*) OUP.

South-East Asian Transport: Issues in Development. Thomas R. Leinbach & Chai Lin Sien. (South-East Asian Social Science Mongographs). (Illus.). 286p. 1989. 39.95 (*0-19-588895-2*) OUP.

South-East Asia's Environmental Future: The Search for Sustainability. Ed. by Harold Brookfield & Yvonne Byron. LC 93-10193. 1993. 58.00 (*0-685-65144-4*) OUP.

South East Berkshire. Paul Felix. 48p. 1993. pap. 6.00 (*0-7509-0310-4*, Pub. by Sutton Pubng UK) Bks Intl VA.

***South East from 1000 A.D.** Brandon. 1990. pap. text ed. write for info. (*0-582-49245-9*, Pub. by Longman UK) Longman.

South-Eastern Europe: A Political & Economic Survey. Royal Institute of International Affairs Staff. LC 81-7168. xvi, 203p. 1982. reprint ed. text ed. 35.00 (*0-313-23195-8*, ROSU, Greenwood Pr) Greenwood.

South-Eastern Museums: Ancient British, Anglo-Saxon, & Later Coins to 1279. A. J. Gunstone et al. (Sylloge of Coins of the British Isles Ser.: No. 42). (Illus.). 224p. 1993. 150.00 (*0-19-726115-9*) OUP.

***South East/Midlands/East Anglia Map.** 1996. 8.95 (*2-06-700404-2*, 404) Michelin.

South England Pilot. Robin Brandon. (C). 1983. text ed. 135.00 (*0-85288-080-4*, Pub. by Imray Laurie Norie & Wilson UK) St Mut.

South England Pilot, Vol. I: North Foreland to Selsey Bill. Robin Brandon. 1984. 60.00 (*0-317-14446-4*, Pub. by Imray Laurie Norie & Wilson UK) St Mut.

South England Pilot, Vol. II: Selsey Bill to Hengistbury Head & the Isle of Wight. Robin Brandon. 1984. 60.00 (*0-317-14448-0*, Pub. by Imray Laurie Norie & Wilson UK) St Mut.

South England Pilot, Vol. IV: Start Point to Land's End. Robin Brandon. 160p. 1979. 60.00 (*0-85288-067-7*, Pub. by Imray Laurie Norie & Wilson UK) St Mut.

South English Legendary. Ed. by C. Horstmann. (EETS, OS Ser.: No. 87). 1974. reprint ed. 75.00 (*0-527-00084-1*) Periodicals Srv.

South English Legendary: Corpus Christi College Cambridge, MS 145 & British Museum MS Harley 2277 with Variants, Vol. I. Ed. by C. D'Evelyn & Anna J. Mill. (EETS Original Ser.: Vol. 235). 1967. reprint ed. 30.00 (*0-19-722235-8*, Pub. by EETS UK) Boydell & Brewer.

South English Legendary Vol. II: Text. Ed. by C. D'Evelyn & Anna J. Mill. (EETS Original Ser.: Vol. 236). 1967. reprint ed. 30.00 (*0-19-722236-6*, Pub. by EETS UK) Boydell & Brewer.

South English Legendary Vol. III: Introduction & Glossary, Vol. III, Intro. & Glossary. Ed. by C. D'Evelyn. (EETS Original Ser.: Vol. 244). 1963. reprint ed. 30.00 (*0-19-722244-7*, Pub. by EETS UK) Boydell & Brewer.

***South Florida & the Keys Travel Smart Trip Planner.** Marylyn Springer. (Travel Smart Trip Planner Ser.). 224p. (Orig.). 1997. pap. 14.95 (*1-56261-376-6*) John Muir.

South Florida Bay & Coastal Fishing. Mike Fuery. LC 76-360969. (Illus.). (Orig.). 1987. pap. 6.95 (*0-944295-00-2*) Sanibel Sanddollar Pubns.

South Florida Benthic Marine Algae. W. J. Woekerling. (Sedimenta Ser.: Vol. V). (Illus.). 150p. (C). 1976. pap. 10.00 (*0-932981-04-6*) Univ Miami CSL.

South Florida Folklife. Tina Bucuvalas et al. LC 93-29928. (Folklife in the South Ser.). (Illus.). 224p. 1994. pap. 16.95 (*0-87805-660-2*); text ed. 37.50 (*0-87805-659-9*) U Pr of Miss.

South Florida Outdoor Guide, 1994. Ed. by Ken Millman. 300p. 1993. pap. 10.95 (*0-9634818-1-9*) Keynoter Pub.

South Florida Rehab & Healthcare Directory, 1991. Ed. by Kester J. Nedd. 490p. 1991. 39.00 (*1-879657-00-7*, Nedmar Graphics) HealthNet Pages.

***South Florida Retirement & Relocation Guide.** Kristen Bergman. (Illus.). 350p. (Orig.). 1997. pap. 19.95 (*1-56559-104-6*) HGI Mrktng.

***South Florida's Peacock Bass.** Carlos Hidalgo. (Illus.). 176p. (Orig.). 1997. mass mkt. 12.95 (*0-9657109-0-4*) Catfish Bks.

South Florida's Vanished People: Travels in the Homeland of Ancient Calusa. Byron D. Voegelin. LC 72-94649. (Illus.). 1977. pap. 6.95 (*0-87208-038-2*) Shoeless Pub.

South for New Southerners. Ed. by Paul D. Escott & David R. Goldfield. LC 90-50015. (Illus.). xi, 168p. (C). 1991. 27.50 (*0-8078-1932-8*); pap. 12.95 (*0-8078-4293-1*) U of NC Pr.

South Fork. Everett Rattray. 1989. pap. 15.00 (*0-916366-41-3*) Pushcart Pr.

South Fork of the American River: From Chili Bar Dam to Salmon Falls Road. Keith Robinson & Fred Lehman. (Whitewater Ser.). (Illus.). 1982. pap. 3.95 (*0-941838-00-5*) Lore Unlim.

South France Pilot: Corsica. Robin Brandon. (Illus.). 232p. (C). 1991. 57.95 (*0-85288-145-2*) Bluewater Bks.

South France Pilot: The Riviera. Robin Brandon. (Illus.). 130p. 1989. pap. 34.95 (*0-85288-130-4*) Bluewater Bks.

South France Pilot, Chapter I: Introduction & Information. Robin Brandon. 640p. 1983. 50.00 (*0-85288-088-X*, Pub. by Imray Laurie Norie & Wilson UK) St Mut.

South France Pilot, Chapter II: Languedoc-Roussillon. Robin Brandon. 640p. 1984. 50.00 (*0-317-14450-2*, Pub. by Imray Laurie Norie & Wilson UK) St Mut.

South France Pilot, Chapter III: West Cote d'Azur. Robin Brandon. 640p. 1984. 50.00 (*0-317-14451-0*, Pub. by Imray Laurie Norie & Wilson UK) St Mut.

South France Pilot, Chapter V: The Riviera. Robin Brandon. 640p. 1982. 90.00 (*0-85288-078-2*, Pub. by Imray Laurie Norie & Wilson UK) St Mut.

South from Hell-fer-Sartin: Kentucky Mountain Folk Tales. Leonard W. Roberts. LC 87-30039. 296p. 1988. 28.00 (*0-8131-1637-6*) U Pr of Ky.

South from Hell-fer-Sartin: Kentucky Mountain Folk Tales. Leonard W. Roberts. LC 87-30039. 296p. 1988. pap. 14.95 (*0-8131-0175-1*) U Pr of Ky.

South Group Ball Court: Structures R-11-a & R-11-b, with a Preliminary Note on the West Group Ball Court (Structures K-6-a & K-6-b) Linton Satterthwaite. (Piedras Negras Preliminary Papers: No. 2). 35p. reprint ed. pap. 25.00 (*0-317-26208-4*, 2052123) Bks Demand.

South in American Literature, 1607-1900. Jay B. Hubbell. LC 54-9434. 1002p. reprint ed. pap. 180.00 (*0-317-26775-2*, 2023404) Bks Demand.

South in History & Literature. Mildred L. Rutherford. 1972. 59.95 (*0-8490-1093-4*) Gordon Pr.

South in Northern Eyes. Howard R. Floan. LC 72-6774. (American History & Americana Ser.: No. 47). 1972. reprint ed. lib. bdg. 75.00 (*0-8383-1647-6*) M S G Haskell Hse.

South in the New Nation, 1789-1819. Thomas P. Abernathy. LC 61-15488. (History of the South Ser.: Vol. 4). (Illus.). xvi, 530p. 1961. text ed. 45.00 (*0-8071-0004-8*) La State U Pr.

South in the New Nation, 1789-1819. Thomas P. Abernathy. LC 61-15488. (History of the South Ser.: Vol. 4). (Illus.). xvi, 530p. 1961. pap. text ed. 16.95 (*0-8071-0014-5*) La State U Pr.

South in the Revolution, 1763-1789. John R. Alden. LC 57-12096. (History of the South Ser.: Vol. 3). (Illus.). xvi, 442p. 1957. text ed. 45.00 (*0-8071-0003-X*); pap. text ed. 16.95 (*0-8071-0013-7*) La State U Pr.

South India. (Insight Guides Ser.). 1993. pap. 22.95 (*0-395-66249-4*) HM.

South India. Frank Kusy & Rupert Isaacson. (Cadogan Guides Ser.). (Illus.). 416p. (Orig.). 1995. pap. 19.95 (*1-86011-070-3*) Globe Pequot.

South India: Tamil Nadu, Kerala, Goa - A Travel Guide. Philip Ward. (Travel Bks.: Vol. 18). (Illus.). 251p. (Orig.). 1991. pap. 19.95 (*0-900891-31-9*) Oleander Pr.

South Indian Agaricales, Preliminary Study of Some Dark Spored Species. K. Natarajan & N. Raman. (Bibliotheca Mycologica Ser.: No. 89). (Illus.). 204p. 1983. text ed. 80.00 (*3-7682-1344-7*) Lubrecht & Cramer.

S

South Indian Buddhist Antiquities: Including the Stups of Bhattiprolu, Gudivada, & Ghanta Sala & Other Ancient Sites in the Krishna District Madras Presidency; with Notes on Dome Construction; Andhra Numismatics & Marble Sculpture. Alexander Rea. (C). 1989. reprint ed. 18.00 (81-206-0512-8, Pub. by Asian Educ Servs II) S Asia.

South Indian Coins. Sri T. Desikachari. (Illus.). 210p. 1986. 18.00 (0-8364-1724-0, Pub. by Chanakya II) S Asia.

South Indian Cookery. Mary L. Skelton & G. Gopal Rao. 115p. 1975. pap. 3.00 (0-89253-030-8) Ind-US Inc.

South Indian Customs. P. V. Ayyar. 182p. 1986. reprint ed. 18.00 (0-8364-1723-2, Pub. by Usha II) S Asia.

South Indian Economy: Agrarian Change, Industrial Structure, & State Policy, 1914-1947. Ed. by Sachchidananda Bhattacharya et al. 320p. 1992. 27.00 (0-19-562642-7) OUP.

South Indian Festivities. P. V. Ayyar. (Illus.). 212p. 1986. 32.00 (0-8364-1722-4, Pub. by Usha II) S Asia.

South Indian Images of Gods & Goddesses. H. Krishna Sastri. 308p. 1986. reprint ed. 37.50 (0-8364-1710-0, Pub. by Chanakya II) S Asia.

South Indian Inscriptions, 3 vols., 1. E. Hultzsch. (C). 1988. reprint ed. 42.50 (81-7013-009-3, Pub. by Navrang) S Asia.

South Indian Inscriptions, 3 vols., Vol. II, Pts. 1-2. E. Hultzsch. (C). 1988. reprint ed. Vol II, Pts. 1-2. 64.00 (0-8364-2284-8, Pub. by Navrang) S Asia.

South Indian Inscriptions, 3 vols., Vol. II, Pts. 3-5. E. Hultzsch. (C). 1988. reprint ed. Vol. II, Pts 3-5. 70.00 (0-8364-2285-6, Pub. by Navrang) S Asia.

South Indian Shrines. P. V. Ayyar. 648p. 1986. reprint ed. 14.00 (0-8364-1721-6, Pub. by Usha II) S Asia.

South Indian Subcaste: Social Organization & Religion of the Pramalai Kallar. Louis Dumont. Ed. & Tr. by Michael Moffatt. Tr. by L. Morton et al. (French Studies on South Asia). (Illus.). 524p. 1986. 38.00 (0-19-561785-1) OUP.

South Indians on the Plantation Frontier in Malaya. Ravindra K. Jain. LC 71-81420. (Yale Southeast Asia Studies: No. 5). 487p. reprint ed. pap. 138.80 (0-8357-8327-8, 2033769) Bks Demand.

South Is Another Land: Essays on the Twentieth-Century South. Ed. by Bruce L. Clayton & John A. Salmond. LC 86-29625. (Contributions in American History Ser.: No. 124). 230p. 1987. text ed. 55.00 (0-313-25556-3, CMR/, Greenwood Pr) Greenwood.

South Italian Greek Vases from the Collection of George Walter Vincent Smith & Belle Townsley Smith. Wendy Watson. (Illus.). 124p. 1986. 10.00 (0-916746-51-8) Springfield Lib & Mus.

South, Its Economic-Geographic Development. Almon E. Parkins. LC 70-98865. 528p. 1970. reprint ed. text ed. 85.00 (0-8371-2904-4, PATS, Greenwood Pr) Greenwood.

South Jersey Dining Guide. Ed Hitzel. (South Jersey Dining Ser.: IV). (Illus.). (Orig.). 1986. pap. 4.95 (0-9612852-2-2) S Jersey Pub.

South Jersey Dining Guide. 1,987th ed. 1986. 4.95 (0-9612852-3-0) S Jersey Pub.

South Jersey Dining Guide. 2nd ed. Ed Hitzel. Ed. by Charles Wray. 100p. 1987. 9.95 (0-9612852-4-9) S Jersey Pub.

South Jersey Dining Guide III. 3rd ed. Edward Hitzel. (Illus.). 1984. pap. 3.95 (0-9612852-0-6) S Jersey Pub.

South Jersey Dining Guide III: 1986 Edition. Edward Hitzel. 1985. pap. 4.95 (0-9612852-1-4) S Jersey Pub.

South Jersey Dining Guide, 1992-93. (Orig.). 1992. pap. write for info. (0-9612852-7-3) S Jersey Pub.

South Jersey Towns: History & Legend. William McMahon. LC 78-163961. (Illus.). 384p. 1973. reprint ed. pap. 14.95 (0-8135-0718-9) Rutgers U Pr.

***South Korea.** Sung-Hoon Jung. LC 96-17969. (Economically Developing Countries Ser.). (J). 1997. lib. bdg. 24.26 (0-8172-4530-8) Raintree Steck-V.

***South Korea.** U. S. Government Staff. (Country Studies). 1996. 22.00 (1-57980-054-8, USKORE) Claitors.

***South Korea.** U. S. Government Staff. (Country Studies). 1996. 22.00 (0-614-30836-4, USKORE) Claitors.

South Korea. Charles R. Frank, Jr. et al. LC 74-82375. (Foreign Trade Regimes & Economic Development Ser.: No. 7). 288p. reprint ed. pap. 82.10 (0-8357-7580-1, 2056901) Bks Demand.

South Korea. Charles R. Frank, Jr. & Kwang S. Kim. (Special Conference Series on Foreign Trade Regimes & Economic Development: No. 7). 288p. 1975. reprint ed. 74.90 (0-87014-507-X) Natl Bur Econ Res.

South Korea: Dissent Within the Economic Miracle. George B. Ogle. LC 90-21221. 192p. (C). 1990. pap. 19.95 (1-85649-003-3, Pub. by Zed Bks Ltd UK); text ed. 49.95 (1-85649-002-5, Pub. by Zed Bks Ltd UK) Humanities.

South Korea: Education, Culture & Economy. Georgie D. Hyde. LC 87-34908. 320p. 1988. text ed. 55.00 (0-312-01666-2) St Martin.

South Korea & the Socialist Countries: The Politics of Trade. Dan C. Sanford. LC 89-29415. 175p. 1990. text ed. 45.00 (0-312-04229-9) St Martin.

South Korea, Compilation Document: Long-term Political Prisoners, 1989; Return to "Repressive Force & Torture" 57p. 1990. 5.00 (0-685-50864-1, ASA 25-42 - 43-89) Amnesty Intl USA.

South Korea Environmental Report: A Resource for Business. Lee S. Bom. LC 95-49406. (International Environemental Report Ser.). 284p. 1995. 495.00 (0-86587-508-1) Gov Insts.

***South Korea Handbook.** 2nd ed. Robert Nilsen. (Illus.). 770p. (Orig.). 1997. pap. 18.95 (1-56691-074-9) Moon Trvl Hdbks.

South Korea in Pictures. Ed. by Lerner Publications, Department of Geography Staff. (Visual Geography Ser.). (Illus.). 64p. (YA). (gr. 5 up). 1989. lib. bdg. 19.95 (0-8225-1868-6, Lerner Publctns) Lerner Group.

South Korean Poets of Resistance. Tr. by Won Ko. LC 79-90037. (Cross-Cultural Review Chapbook Ser.: No. 4). (Illus.). (ENG & KOR.). 1980. 15.00 (0-89304-606-X, CCC124); pap. 5.00 (0-89304-607-8) Cross-Cultrl NY.

South Korean Solid Wood Products Market: Profile & Outlook. 1994. lib. bdg. 250.00 (0-8490-5708-6) Gordon Pr.

South Korea's Minjung Movement: The Culture & Politics of Dissidence. Ed. by Kenneth M. Wells. LC 95-17225. (Illus.). 272p. 1995. text ed. 35.00 (0-8248-1700-1) UH Pr.

***South Korea's Motor Industry.** 1996. 775.00 (0-85058-870-7, R333) Economist Intell.

South Lebanon. Ed. by Elaine Hagopian & Samih Farsoun. (Special Reports: No. 2). 38p. (Orig.). (C). 1978. pap. 3.50 (0-937694-09-6) Assn Arab-Amer U Grads.

South Light. large type ed. Michael Parfit. 400p. 1992. 27.99 (0-7089-8627-7, Trail West Pubs) Ulverscroft.

South Line. Carroll Arnett. 1979. 12.00 (0-686-26666-8, Elizabeth Pr); pap. 5.00 (0-686-26667-6, Elizabeth Pr) Elizabeth Pr.

South Melbourne: A History. Susan Priestley. 448p. 1995. pap. 59.95 (0-522-84649-1, Pub. by Melbourne Univ Pr AT) Paul & Co Pubs.

South Midatlantic States see Encyclopedia of Associations: Regional

South New Berlin, Chenango Co., New York: Records & Recollections of Leona Bagg. Leona Bagg. Ed. & Intro. by Shirley B. Goerlich. (Illus.). 112p. 1994. 38.00 (0-9614858-7-6) RSG Pub.

South of Aswan: Narratives of the Nile Basin. Robert O. Collins. 320p. Date not set. text ed. 36.95 (1-55876-113-6); pap. text ed. 16.95 (1-55876-114-4) Wiener Pubs Inc.

***South of France.** Thomas Cook. (On the Road Around... Ser.). (Illus.). Date not set. pap. 15.95 (0-8442-4954-8) NTC Pub Grp.

South of France. Laura Raison. (Illus.). 256p. 1986. 19.95 (0-8253-0334-6) Beaufort Bks NY.

South of France. 3rd ed. Dana Facaros & Michael Pauls. LC 94-3021. (Cadogan Country Guides Ser.). (Illus.). 528p. 1994. pap. 18.95 (1-56440-466-8) Globe Pequot.

***South of France.** 3rd ed. Dana Facaros. (Cadogan Guide Ser.). 1997. pap. text ed. 19.95 (1-86011-008-8, Pub. by Cadogan Bks UK) Globe Pequot.

South of France in Your Pocket Guide: Riviera. Michelin Travel Publications, Staff. (In Your Pocket Guides Ser.). (Orig.). 1996. per. 9.95 (2-06-630301-1, 6303) Michelin.

***South of Freedom.** Carl T. Rowan. LC 97-7075. 288p. 1997. pap. 14.95 (0-8071-2170-3) La State U Pr.

South of Haunted Dreams. Eddy L. Harris. LC 93-6558. 256p. 1994. pap. 11.00 (0-671-89437-4, Fireside) S&S Trade.

***South of Haunted Dreams: A Ride Through Slavery's Old Backyard.** Eddy L. Harris. 1997. pap. text ed. 11.95 (0-8050-5574-6) H Holt & Co.

South of Heaven. Jim Thompson. 1994. pap. 9.00 (0-679-74017-1, Vin) Random.

South of Heaven: Welcome to High School at the End of the Twentieth Century. Thomas French. Ed. by Julie Rubenstein. 384p. 1996. reprint ed. pap. 12.00 (0-671-89801-9, PB Trade Paper) PB.

South of Mandraki. large type ed. Anne Hampson. 282p. 1993. 25.99 (0-7505-0558-3) Ulverscroft.

South of My Village. Zack L. Toll. 192p. (Orig.). (C). 1996. pap. 12.00 (1-880222-24-8) Red Apple Pub.

South of No North. Charles Bukowski. LC 73-19672. 192p. 1997. reprint ed. 25.00 (0-87685-190-1); reprint ed. pap. 13.00 (0-87685-189-8) Black Sparrow.

South of Sanity. Gregory E. Stearns. 256p. (Orig.). 1994. pap. 12.95 (0-9626780-1-5) Medium Prodns.

South of the Big Four. Donald Kurtz. 384p. 1996. pap. 12.00 (0-380-72765-X) Avon.

South of the Big Four. Donald Kurtz. 288p. 1995. 19.95 (0-8118-0908-0) Chronicle Bks.

South of the Border. Richard Brightfield. (Chronicles of Young Indiana Jones Ser.: No. 2). 128p. (J). (gr. 4-7). 1992. pap. 3.25 (0-553-29757-0, Starfire BDD) BDD Bks Young Read.

South of the Border: Mexico in the American Imagination, 1914-1947. James Oles. LC 92-41507. (Illus.). 354p. 1993. pap. 29.95 (1-56098-295-0); text ed. 75.00 (1-56098-294-2) Smithsonian.

South of the Border: U. S. Trucking in Mexico. 1995. pap. text ed. 25.00 (0-88711-291-9) Am Trucking Assns.

South of the Clouds: Tales of Yunnan. Ed. & Tr. by Lucien Miller. Tr. by Guo Xu et al. LC 93-36563. (McLellan Bks.). 342p. (C). 1994. 40.00 (0-295-97293-9); pap. 19.95 (0-295-97348-X) U of Wash Pr.

South of the Line. Catherine Ennis. 224p. 1989. pap. 8.95 (0-941483-29-0) Naiad Pr.

South of the Main Offensive. Grigory Baklanov. Tr. by R. Ainsztein from RUS. LC 64-25464. 192p. 6300. 16.95 (0-8023-1006-0) Dufour.

South of the West: Postcolonialism & the Narrative Construction of Australia. Ross Gibson. LC 91-20394. (Arts & Politics of the Everyday Ser.). (Illus.). 272p. 1992. text ed. 35.00 (0-253-32581-1); pap. text ed. 6.95 (0-253-32582-X) Ind U Pr.

South of Wall Street: Pioneer Investing in the Booming Markets of South America. William J. Schmick. 250p. 1995. 29.95 (1-55738-870-9) Irwin Prof Pubng.

South of Yosemite: Selected Writings of John Muir. John Muir. Ed. by Frederic Gunsky. LC 88-40000. (Illus.). 144p. 1988. pap. 15.95 (0-89997-095-8) Wilderness Pr.

South on Paper: Line, Color & Light. James C. Kelly. (Illus.). 155p. (Orig.). 1985. pap. text ed. 20.00 (0-9632836-3-4) R M Hicklin.

South Pacific. (Vocal Score Ser.). 176p. 1981. pap. 40.00 (0-88188-835-4, 00312401) H Leonard.

South Pacific. Bill Manhire. 239p. 1995. 27.95 (1-85754-046-8, Pub. by Carcanet Pr UK) Paul & Co Pubs.

South Pacific. James A. Michener. (Performing Arts Ser.). (Illus.). 40p. (J). 1992. 17.00 (0-15-200618-4, Gulliver Bks) HarBrace.

South Pacific. Bille Yenne. (Great Rails Ser.). 128p. 1994. 14.98 (0-8317-3788-3) Smithmark.

South Pacific Agriculture Challenges & Opportunities for ACIAR & Its Research Partners. P. Ferrar & Gabrielle J. Persley. 87p. (C). 1987. text ed. 72.00 (0-949511-45-5, Pub. by ACIAR) St Mut.

***South Pacific Anchorages.** Warwick Clay. (Illus.). (C). 1996. pap. 59.95 (0-85288-362-5) Bluewater Bks.

South Pacific at Cost. 2nd ed. Joan Beard. (At Cost Travel Guide Ser.). (Illus.). 256p. 1996. pap. 16.95 (1-86315-103-6) Pelican.

South Pacific Birds. John E. DuPont. 230p. 1976. 45.00 (0-913176-04-4, Tycooly Pub) Weidner & Sons.

South Pacific Diary, 1942-1943. Mack Morriss. Ed. by Ronnie Day. LC 95-44095. (Illus.). 256p. 1996. text ed. 24.95 (0-8131-1969-3) U Pr of Ky.

South Pacific Foreign Affairs Handbook. Steve Hoadley. (Illus.). 272p. (Orig.). 1992. pap. text ed. 19.95 (1-86373-176-8, Pub. by Allen Unwin AT) Paul & Co Pubs.

South Pacific Handbook. 6th rev. ed. David Stanley. (Moon Travel Handbooks Ser.). (Illus.). 900p. (Orig.). 1996. pap. 22.95 (1-56691-040-4) Moon Trvl Hdbks.

South Pacific Islanders. Patricia H. Vilsoni. (Original People Ser.). (Illus.). 48p. (J). (gr. 4-8). 1987. 12.50 (0-685-67606-4); lib. bdg. 16.67 (0-86625-259-2) Rourke Corp.

South Pacific Islands Legal Systems. Ed. by Michael A. Ntumy. LC 92-41464. 720p. (C). 1993. text ed. 100.00 (0-8248-1438-X) UH Pr.

South Pacific Oral Traditions. Ed. by Ruth H. Finnegan & Margaret Orbell. (Voices in Performance & Text Ser.). 264p. 1995. pap. 12.95 (0-253-20958-7) Ind U Pr.

South Pacific Oral Traditions. Ed. by Ruth H. Finnegan & Margaret Orbell. (Voices in Performance & Text Ser.). 264p. 1995. text ed. 29.95 (0-253-32868-3) Ind U Pr.

South Pacific Sedimentary Basins. Ed. by P. F. Ballance. (Sedimentary Basins of the World Ser.: Vol. 2). 434p. 1993. 228.00 (0-444-88287-1) Elsevier.

South Pacific Selections: Piano. Richard Rodgers & Oscar Hammerstein. 16p. 1981. pap. 5.95 (0-7935-5185-4, 00301934) H Leonard.

South Pacific Travel Digest. 14th rev. ed. Charles Jacobs & Babette Jacobs. 1996. pap. 12.95 (0-912640-55-3) Travel Digests.

South Pass, & Its Tales. 3rd ed. James L. Sherlock. (Illus.). 160p. 1988. reprint ed. pap. 9.95 (0-941875-04-0) Wolverine Distrib.

South Pass, 1868: James Chisholm's Journal of the Wyoming Gold Rush. James Chisholm. Ed. & Intro. by Lola M. Homsher. LC 60-12692. (Illus.). vi, 246p. 1996. pap. 12.00 (0-8032-5824-0, Bison Books) U of Nebr Pr.

***South Pennines Walks.** Ordnance Survey Staff. (Ordnance Survey Pathfinder Guides Ser.). (Illus.). 80p. 1996. pap. 16.95 (0-7117-0849-5, Pub. by Jarrold Pub UK) Seven Hills Bk.

South Philadelphia: Mummers, Memories, & the Melrose Diner. Murray Dubin. (Illus.). 220p. (C). 1996. 29.95 (1-56639-429-5) Temple U Pr.

***South Platte.** Peter Hubbel. (Classic Rock Climbs Ser.: Vol. 9). (Illus.). (Orig.). 1997. pap. 10.95 (1-57540-034-0) Chockstone Pr.

***South Platte Rock: A Guide to Every Route Worth Climbing.** Ken Trout. (Illus.). 96p. (Orig.). 1997. pap. 12.95 (0-9657079-0-3) Sharp End.

South Portland, ME. C. Scott. (Images of America Ser.). 1995. pap. 16.99 (0-7524-0090-8, Arcdia) Chalford.

South Puget Sound, Afoot & Afloat. 3rd ed. Marge Mueller & Ted Mueller. LC 95-46945. 1996. pap. 14.95 (0-89886-465-8) Mountaineers.

South Reports the Civil War. J. Cutler Andrews. LC 84-25610. (Illus.). 632p. 1985. reprint ed. pap. 24.95 (0-8229-5902-X) U of Pittsburgh Pr.

South Returns to Congress: Men, Economic Measures, & Intersectional Relationships, 1868-1879. Terry L. Seip. LC 82-4654. xii, 322p. 1983. text ed. 40.00 (0-8071-1052-3) La State U Pr.

South Revisited: Forty Years of Change. Sam B. Hilliard. LC 92-9987. (Touring North America Ser.). (Illus.). 150p. 1992. 25.00 (0-8135-1874-1); pap. 9.95 (0-8135-1875-X) Rutgers U Pr.

South Salem Past: Illustrated Historical Essays. David Duniway. LC 87-12396. (Illus.). 56p. (Orig.). 1987. pap. 9.95 (0-943297-00-1) Marion Coun Hist Soc.

***South San Juan Wilderness - Del Norte - CO.** (Illus.). 1997. 8.99 (1-56695-042-2) Trails Illustrated.

***South Sandwich Islands Vol. IV: Botany.** R. E. Longton. (British Antarctic Survey Report Ser.: No. 94). 56p. 1979. 25.00 (0-85665-048-X, Pub. by Brit Antarctic Surv UK) Balogh.

South Sea Bubble. Gerald R. Reading. LC 73-109972. (Illus.). 176p. 1978. reprint ed. text ed. 49.75 (0-8371-4480-9, RESO, Greenwood Pr) Greenwood.

South Sea Company. John G. Sperling. (Kress Library of Business & Economics Publication: No. 17). (Illus.). xii, 92p. 1962. pap. 12.95 (0-678-09911-1, Kress Lib Business) Kelley.

South Sea Supercargo. Louis Becke. Ed. by A. Grove Day. 200p. reprint ed. pap. 57.00 (0-8357-8530-0, 2034832) Bks Demand.

***South Sea Tales.** Jack London. lib. bdg. 24.95 (0-8488-2001-0) Amereon Ltd.

***South Sea Tales.** Robert Louis Stevenson. Ed. & Intro. by Roslyn Jolly. (The World's Classics Ser.). (Illus.). 336p. 1996. pap. 9.95 (0-19-282439-2) OUP.

***South Sea Tales.** Robert Louis Stevenson. lib. bdg. 23.95 (0-8488-1884-9) Amereon Ltd.

South Sea Tales. Jack London. 324p. 1985. reprint ed. mass mkt. 5.95 (0-935180-14-1) Mutual Pub HI.

South Sea Whaler: An Annotated Bibliography of Published Historical, Literary & Art Material Relating to Whaling in the Pacific Ocean in the Nineteenth Century. Honore Forster. LC 85-50792. xvi, 157p. 1986. 30.00 (0-9617194-4-3) E J Lefkowicz.

South Sea Whaler: An Annotated Bibliography of Published Historical, Literary & Art Material Relating to Whaling in the Pacific Ocean in the Nineteenth Century. Honore Forster. LC 85-50792. 1985. 30.00 (0-937854-22-0) Kendall Whaling.

South Seas Fiction of Robert Louis Stevenson. Robert I. Hillier. (American University Studies: English Language & Literature: Ser. IV, Vol. 91). 239p. (C). 1989. text ed. 36.95 (0-8204-0889-1) P Lang Pubng.

South Seas in Transition: A Study of Post-War Rehabilitation & Reconstruction in Three British Pacific Dependencies. W. E. Stanner. LC 75-30084. (Institute of Pacific Relations Ser.). reprint ed. 57.50 (0-404-59562-6) AMS Pr.

South Seas in Transition: A Study of Post-War Rehabilitation & Reconstruction in Three British Pacific Dependencies. W. E. Stanner. LC 82-15534. xiv, 448p. 1982. reprint ed. text ed. 75.00 (0-313-23661-5, STSOS, Greenwood Pr) Greenwood.

South Seas Sailor (John Williams) Cecil Northcott. 1979. 3.95 (0-87508-622-5) Chr Lit.

***South Side High School - The First Seventy-Five Years.** G. Stanley Hood. (Illus.). 152p. (Orig.). 1996. pap. 20.00 (0-9655144-0-4) South Side HS.

South Side of Boston. Bill Peach. LC 95-77743. 128p. (Orig.). 1995. pap. 9.95 (1-881576-42-6, Hillsboro Pr) Providence Hse.

South Side Stories. Ed. by Steve Bosak. LC 93-70954. (Chicago Voices Ser.). 172p. 1994. reprint ed. pap. 9.95 (0-929968-40-9) Another Chicago Pr.

South Side Stories: A Multicultural Anthology of Contemporary Short Stories. Ed. by Steve Bosak. (Orig.). 1993. pap. 9.95 (0-9627425-2-X) City Stoop Pr.

South-Side View of Slavery. Nehemiah Adams. LC 74-83939. (Black Heritage Library Collection). 1977. 17.95 (0-8369-8501-X) Ayer.

South Since Eighteen Sixty-Five. 2nd ed. John S. Ezell. LC 74-15132. 1978. 24.95 (0-8061-1480-0) U of Okla Pr.

South Since the War. Sidney Andrews. LC 69-18546. (American Negro: His History & Literature, Ser. No. 2). 1969. reprint ed. 32.95 (0-405-01847-9) Ayer.

South Slav Conflict: History, Religion, Ethnicity, & Nationalism. Ed. by Raju G. Thomas & H. Richard Friman. LC 95-45055. (Contemporary Issues in European Politics Ser.: Vol. 01). (Illus.). 436p. 1996. text ed. 75.00 (0-8153-2117-1, SS1059) Garland.

South Slav Nationalisms: Textbooks & Yugoslav Union Before 1914. Charles Jelavich. (Illus.). 360p. 1990. 52.50 (0-8142-0500-3) Ohio St U Pr.

South Slav Settlement in Western Washington: Perception & Choice. Roger H. Green, Jr. LC 74-83372. 1974. 10.00 (0-88247-286-0) Ragusan Pr.

South Slavic Dances in California: A Compendium for the Years 1924-1977. Elsie I. Dunin. LC 79-63063. 1979. 10.00 (0-918660-11-4) Ragusan Pr.

South Slavic Folk Culture: A Bibliography of Literature in English, German, & French. Klaus Roth & Gabriele Wolf. 553p. (ENG, FRE & GER.). 1994. 29.95 (0-89357-244-6) Slavica.

***South Slavic Writers Since World War II.** Vasa D. Mihailovich. LC 97-15112. (Dictionary of Literary Biography Ser.). 1997. 140.00 (0-7876-1070-4) Gale.

South Sound Places. Nancy Patterson. (Illus.). 64p. (Orig.). 1993. pap. 11.95 (0-9627201-2-7) Patcha Pubng.

South-South Aid: How Developing Countries Help Each Other. Donald Bobiash. LC 91-24060. 260p. 1992. text ed. 69.95 (0-312-06839-5) St Martin.

South-South & South-North Cooperation in Sciences: Proceedings of the Conference Organised by the Third World Academy of Sciences, Trieste, Italy July 5-10, 1985. Ed. by A. Hamende et al. 350p. 1986. text ed. 68.00 (9971-5-0106-6) World Scientific Pub.

South-South Economic Cooperation: Problems & Prospects. Govind R. Agrawal et al. (Research & Information System for Nonaligned & Other Developing Countries Ser.). xii, 263p. 1987. text ed. 27.50 (81-7027-102-9, Pub. by Radiant Pubs II) S Asia.

South-South Trade: Trends, Issues, & Obstacles to Its Growth. Ed. by Vivianne Ventura-Dias. LC 88-25155. 360p. 1989. text ed. 65.00 (0-275-92920-5, C2920, Praeger Pubs) Greenwood.

South-South Trade & Development: Industrialization in the Late Twentieth Century. Steen Folke et al. (International Political Economy Ser.). 225p. (C). 1993. text ed. 69.50 (0-312-08372-6) St Martin.

South-South Trade in Global Development. Elizabeth Parsan. 193p. 1993. 59.95 (1-85628-432-8, Pub. by Avebury Technical UK) Ashgate Pub Co.

South-South Trade Options & Development. Elizabeth Parsan. 1991. text ed. 59.00 (0-86187-163-4) St Martin.

South-South Trade Preferences: The GSTP & Trade in Manufactures. Hans Linnemann. (Illus.). 236p. (C). 1992. text ed. 29.95 (0-8039-9421-4) Sage.

South Speaks. Compiled by Jill E. Grossman. (Petites Ser.). (Illus.). 80p. 1993. 4.95 (0-88088-765-6) Peter Pauper.

An Asterisk (*) at the beginning of an entry indicates that the title is appearing in BIP for the first time.

South Stoa & Its Roman Successors. Oscar Broneer. LC 75-25700. (Corinth Ser.: Vol. 1, Pt. 4). (Illus.). xix, 167p. 1971. reprint ed. 35.00 (*0-87661-014-9*) Am Sch Athens.

South Street. Richard C. McKay. LC 76-160128. (American History & Americana Ser.: No. 47). 1971. lib. bdg. 75.00 (*0-8383-1280-2*) M S G Haskell Hse.

South Street: A Photographic Guide to New York City's Historic Seaport. Ellen F. Rosebrock. 1977. pap. 5.95 (*0-486-23396-0*) Dover.

South Street Around 1900. Peter Stanford. (Illus.). 334p. 1970. pap. 1.50 (*0-913344-12-5*) South St Sea Mus.

South Texas Garden Book. Bob Webster. (Illus.). 135p. (Orig.). 1980. pap. 12.95 (*0-931722-03-9*) Corona Pub.

South Texas Mexican Cookbook. Lucy M. Garza. (Illus.). 96p. 1982. 14.95 (*0-89015-344-2*) Sunbelt Media.

South Texas Uranium Province, Geologic Perspective. W. E. Galloway et al. (Guidebook Ser.: GB 18). (Illus.). 81p. 1979. pap. 3.00 (*0-686-29323-1*) Bur Econ Geology.

South Texas Uranium Seminar, Corpus Christi, Texas, September 10-13, 1978. South Texas Uranium Seminar Staff. LC 78-73975. (Illus.). 139p. reprint ed. pap. 39.70 (*0-7837-1219-7*, 2041750) Bks Demand.

South the Beautiful Cookbook: Authentic Recipes from the American South. Photos by Philip Salaverry & Randy Olson. (Illus.). 240p. 1996. 50.00 (*0-00-225196-5*) Collins SF.

South Through Time: A History of An America Region. John B. Boles. LC 94-3343. 640p. 1994. text ed. 42.00 (*0-13-825050-2*) P-H.

South Through Time: A History of an American Region, Vol. 2. John B. Boles. (Illus.). 272p. (C). 1994. pap. text ed. 30.00 (*0-13-157314-4*) P-H.

South Through Time Vol. 1: A History of an American Region. John B. Boles. 400p. 1994. pap. text ed. 28.40 (*0-13-157306-3*) P-H.

South Tibetan Detachment System, Himalayan Orogen: Extension Contemporaneous with & Parallel to Shortening in a Collisional Mountain Belt. Ed. by B. C. Burchfiel et al. (Special Papers: No. 269). (Illus.). 1992. pap. 9.38 (*0-8137-2269-1*) Geol Soc.

South to a Very Old Place. Albert Murray. 1992. 20.50 (*0-8446-6630-0*) Peter Smith.

South to a Very Old Place. Albert Murray. LC 91-50214. 240p. 1991. pap. 11.00 (*0-679-73695-6*, Vin) Random.

South to a Very Old Place. Albert Murray. LC 94-32198. 294p. 1995. 13.50 (*0-679-60147-3*, Modern Lib) Random.

South to Antarctica. 2nd ed. Sharon R. Chester & James L. Oetzel. (Illus.). 108p. (Orig.). 1995. pap. text ed. 12.00 (*0-9638511-4-4*) Wander Albatross.

South to Bataan, North to Mukden: The Prison Diary of Brigadier General W. E. Brougher. William E. Brougher. Ed. by D. Clayton James. LC 77-135182. 247p. reprint ed. pap. 70.40 (*0-318-34882-9*, 2031181) Bks Demand.

South to Java. William P. Mack & William P. Mack, Jr. LC 87-24768. (Destroyer Ser.). 460p. 1987. 22.95 (*0-933852-70-3*) Nautical & Aviation.

South to Louisiana: The Music of the Cajun Bayous. John Broven. LC 82-11247. (Illus.). 416p. 1983. pap. 14.95 (*0-88289-608-3*) Pelican.

South to Posterity. rev. ed. Douglas S. Freeman. (Illus.). xxix, 235p. 1983. reprint ed. 30.00 (*0-916107-05-1*) Broadfoot.

***South to Sillytown.** Bill Marks. 1997. pap. 14.95 (*1-86368-175-2*, Pub. by Fremantle Arts AT) Intl Spec Bk.

South Today. John M. Moore. LC 75-152996. (Select Bibliographies Reprint Ser.). 1977. reprint ed. 25.95 (*0-8369-5748-2*) Ayer.

South Town. Lorenz Graham. LC 94-41577. (J). (gr. 1 up). 1995. pap. 4.95 (*0-382-24854-6*); lib. bdg. 13.95 (*0-382-24853-8*) Silver Burdett Pr.

South Vietnam: Nation Under Stress. Robert Scigliano. LC 78-16521. 237p. 1978. reprint ed. text ed. 52.50 (*0-313-20595-7*, SCSV, Greenwood Pr) Greenwood.

South Vietnam: Trial & Experience. Nguyen Anh Tuan. LC 86-23532. (Monographs in International Studies, Southeast Asia Ser.: No. 80). 186p. 1986. pap. text ed. 18.00 (*0-89680-141-1*, Ohio U Ctr Intl) Ohio U Pr.

South Vietnam on Trial: The Test of Vietnamization, 1970-1973. Ed. by Robert Manning. (Vietnam Experience Ser.). (Illus.). 192p. 1984. 16.30 (*0-201-11264-7*) Addison-Wesley.

South Vietnamese Society. Nguyen Duy Hinh & Tran Dinh Tho. 175p. 1989. reprint ed. pap. 18.50 (*0-923135-14-6*) Dalley Bk Service.

South Wales & the Rising of 1839. Ivor Wilks. 270p. (C). 1989. pap. 21.00 (*0-86383-605-4*, Pub. by Gomer Pr UK) St Mut.

***South Wales Car Tours.** Jarrold Publishing Staff. 1996. pap. text ed. 15.95 (*0-7117-0846-0*, Pub. by Jarrold Pub UK) Seven Hills Bk.

South Wales Railways at the Grouping. Brian J. Miller. 96p. (C). 1989. 75.00 (*0-905928-55-5*, Pub. by D Brown & Sons Ltd UK) St Mut.

South-Watching: Selected Essays. Gerald W. Johnson. Ed. & Intro. by Fred Hobson. LC 82-2620. (Fred W. Morrison Series in Southern Studies). 239p. 1983. reprint ed. pap. 68.20 (*0-7837-9888-1*, 2060614) Bks Demand.

South Wessex Way. Laurence Main. (C). 1988. pap. 29.00 (*0-904110-81-8*, Pub. by Thornhill Pr UK) St Mut.

South West Africa. Ruth First. 1990. 14.50 (*0-8446-2061-0*) Peter Smith.

South West Africa & the United Nations. Faye Carroll. LC 75-3984. 123p. 1975. reprint ed. text ed. 45.00 (*0-8371-7441-4*, CASWA, Greenwood Pr) Greenwood.

South West Africa & the United Nations: An International Mandate in Dispute. Solomon Slonim. LC 72-4020. 432p. reprint ed. pap. 123.20 (*0-317-42346-0*, 2025873) Bks Demand.

South West Africa Namibia Dispute: Documents & Scholarly Writings on the Controversy Between South Africa & the United Nations. Ed. by John Dugard. LC 76-142052. (Perspectives on Southern Africa Ser.: No. 9). 1973. pap. 40.00 (*0-520-02614-4*) U CA Pr.

South West Climbs: A Selection of Rock Climbs from Cornwall, Devon, Somerset, Dorset & Jersey. Pat Littlejohn. (Illus.). 300p. 1992. 34.95 (*0-906371-82-1*, Pub. by H & S UK) Trafalgar.

South West Coast Path: Exmouth to Poole. Roland Tarr. (National Travel Guides Ser.). (Illus.). 1995. pap. 19.95 (*1-85410-020-3*, Pub. by Aurum Pr UK) London Brdge.

South West Coast Path: Falmouth to Exmouth. Brian Le Messurier. (National Trail Guides Ser.). (Illus.). 168p. 1995. pap. 19.95 (*1-85410-096-3*, Pub. by Aurum Pr UK) London Brdge.

South West Coast Path: Minehead to Padstow. Roland Tarr. (National Trail Guides Ser.). (Illus.). 168p. 1995. pap. 19.95 (*1-85410-330-X*, Pub. by Aurum Pr UK) London Brdge.

South West Coast Path: Padstow to Falmouth. John Macadam. (National Trail Guides Ser.). (Illus.). 168p. 1995. pap. 19.95 (*1-85410-098-X*, Pub. by Aurum Pr UK) London Brdge.

South West France. Andrew Sanger. 1994. pap. 16.95 (*0-8442-9944-8*, Passport Bks) NTC Pub Grp.

South West France: Aquitaine, Gascony, the Pyrenees. 2nd ed. Andrew Sanger. 224p. 1994. pap. 16.95 (*0-8442-9085-8*, Passport Bks) NTC Pub Grp.

South West Scotland: A Guidebook to the Best Of: Kyle, Carrick, Galloway, Dumfries-Shire, Kircudbright-Shire, Wigtownshire. Tom Atkinson. 180p. 1989. pap. 35.00 (*0-946487-04-9*, Pub. by Luath Pr UK) St Mut.

South West to AD One Thousand. Malcolm Todd. (Regional History of England Ser.). 400p. 1987. text ed. 42.95 (*0-582-49273-4*) Longman.

South-Western College Keyboarding. 13th ed. Charles H. Duncan et al. LC 93-27530. 1994. text ed. 39.95 (*0-538-71041-1*) S-W Pub.

South-Western College Keyboarding: Complete Course. 13th ed. Charles H. Duncan et al. LC 93-7728. 1994. text ed. 56.95 (*0-538-70804-2*) S-W Pub.

South-Western College Keyboarding: Complete Course with WordPerfect 5.1. 13th ed. Charles H. Duncan & Susie H. VanHuss. LC 93-33854. 1994. text ed. 56.95 (*0-538-71258-9*) S-W Pub.

South-Western Geometry. Gerver & Sgroi. (MA - Academic Math Ser.). 1998. student ed., pap. 45.95 (*0-538-67399-0*) S-W Pub.

South-Western Pre-GED Interpreting Literature & the Arts. South-Western Educational Publishing Staff. LC 95-16116. 1996. pap. 10.95 (*0-538-63991-1*) S-W Pub.

South-Western Pre-GED Mathematics. LC 95-15982. 1996. pap. 10.95 (*0-538-63992-X*) S-W Pub.

South-Western Pre-GED Science. LC 95-15981. 1996. pap. 10.95 (*0-538-63990-3*) S-W Pub.

South-Western Pre-GED Social Studies. South-Western Educational Publishing Staff. LC 95-15764. 1996. pap. 10.95 (*0-538-63989-X*) S-W Pub.

South-Western Pre-GED Writing Skills. South-Western Educational Publishing Staff. LC 95-16115. 1996. pap. 10.95 (*0-538-63988-1*) S-W Pub.

South Wind. Norman Douglas. 1976. 26.95 (*0-8488-0987-4*) Amereon Ltd.

South Wind. Melvin Kenne. LC 85-61617. (Illus.). 80p. 1985. lib. bdg. 10.95 (*0-941720-26-8*) Slough Pr TX.

South Wind. Norman Douglas. 416p. 1982. reprint ed. pap. 6.95 (*0-486-24361-3*) Dover.

South Wind Blow Softly. Ruth L. Hill. 255p. 1975. reprint ed. lib. bdg. 22.95 (*0-89190-253-8*, Rivercity Pr) Amereon Ltd.

South Wind Changing. Jade N. Huynh. 305p. 1994. 20.00 (*1-55597-198-9*) Graywolf.

South 97: With Plantations, Civil War Sites, & a Midnight in the Garden Tour. Fodor's Staff. (Illus.). 1996. pap. 18.00 (*0-679-03284-3*) Fodors Travel.

***South '98.** Fodors Travel Staff. 1997. pap. 18.50 (*0-679-03535-4*) Fodors Travel.

Southall: April Twenty-Third, 1979. NCCL Staff. (C). 1988. 21.00 (*0-901108-85-5*) St Mut.

Southampton at War, 1939-45. Anthony Kemp. (C). 1989. 39.00 (*1-85455-033-0*, Pub. by Ensign Pubns & Print UK) St Mut.

Southampton Blitz. Anthony Brode. 96p. 1987. 50.00 (*0-905392-15-9*) St Mut.

Southampton County: Virginia Publick Claims. Janice L. Abercrombie & Richard Slatten. (Virginia Publick Claims Ser.). ix, 25p. 1991. pap. 5.00 (*0-8095-8693-2*) Borgo Pr.

Southampton County: Virginia Publick Claims. Janice L. Abercrombie & Richard Slatten. (Virginia Publick Claims Ser.). ix, 25p. (C). 1991. reprint ed. lib. bdg. 25.00 (*0-8095-8361-5*) Borgo Pr.

Southampton County Marriages, Seventeen Fifty to Eighteen Ten. Catherine L. Knorr. 152p. 1955. 18.50 (*0-89308-255-4*, VA 18) Southern Hist Pr.

Southampton Finds Vol. 2: The Gold, Silver & Other Non-Ferrous Alloy Objects from Hamwic. D. A. Hinton. (Illus.). 128p. 1996. pap. 35.95 (*0-7509-1167-0*, Pub. by Sutton Pubng UK) Bks Intl VA.

Southampton Finds, Vol. 1: Coins & Pottery from Hamwic. Ed. by P. Andrews. (Illus.). 142p. 1993. pap. text ed. 33.00 (*0-901723-12-6*, Pub. by Sutton Pubng UK) Bks Intl VA.

Southampton, NY. M. Cummings. (Images of America Ser.). 1996. pap. 16.99 (*0-7524-0459-8*, Arcdia) Chalford.

Southampton Past & Present. John E. Mann. 96p. 1987. 30.00 (*0-905392-53-1*) St Mut.

Southampton People Eminent Sotonians & Assorted Characters. John E. Mann. (C). 1989. 39.00 (*1-85455-021-7*, Pub. by Ensign Pubns & Print UK) St Mut.

Southampton Through the Ages. P. Kilby. 150p. 1996. text ed. 38.00 (*1-85312-392-7*, 3927) Computational Mech MA.

Southbound: Advice for Northerners Moving South. large type ed. Heath Coleman & Susan Coleman. LC 96-9614. (Illus.). 96p. 1996. mass mkt. 6.95 (*0-9652350-0-9*) Doberdor Pub.

Southbridge, Massachusetts Vital Records to 1850. Jay M. Holbrook. LC 80-83873. 316p. 1981. lib. bdg. 35.00 (*0-931248-09-4*) Holbrook Res.

***Southcentral Alaska: A Comprehensive Guide to the Hiking & Canoeing Trails & Public Use Cabins.** Alan Jubenville. (Illus.). 198p. (Orig.). 1997. pap. 12.95 (*1-55650-781-X*) Hunter NJ.

Southcentral Alaska: Including Anchorage, Matanuska-Susitna Valleys, Kenai Peninsula, & Prince William Sound. Scott McMurren. (Umbrella Guides Ser.). (Illus.). 160p. (Orig.). 1995. pap. 12.95 (*0-945397-40-2*, Umbrella Bks) Epicenter Pr.

Southcon '96. IEEE Staff. 662p. 1996. pap. text ed. 136.00 (*0-7803-3268-7*, 96CH35925); lib. bdg. 136.00 (*0-7803-3269-5*, 96CB35925); fiche 136.00 (*0-7803-3270-9*, 96CM35925) Inst Electrical.

Southeast: Georgia, Kentucky, Tennessee. Thomas G. Aylesworth & Virginia L. Aylesworth. LC 94-42017. (J). 1995. pap. 8.95 (*0-7910-3429-1*); lib. bdg. 18.95 (*0-7910-3411-9*) Chelsea Hse.

Southeast Alaska. Alaska Geographic Society Staff. Ed. by Penny Rennick. LC 72-92087. (Alaska Geographic Ser.: Vol. 20-2). (Illus.). 128p. (Orig.). 1993. pap. 19.95 (*1-56661-010-9*) Alaska Geog Soc.

Southeast Alaska Current Atlas. Randel Washburne. Ed. by Robert Hale. 144p. (Orig.). 1989. pap. 19.95 (*0-935727-05-1*) Weatherly Pr.

Southeast & Gulf States. Jill C. Wheeler. (America, This is Your Land Ser.). (J). (gr. 3-4). 1994. lib. bdg. 15.98 (*1-56239-296-4*) Abdo & Dghtrs.

***Southeast Asia.** Christie. Date not set. text ed. 59.50 (*1-86064-063-X*, Pub. by I B Tauris UK); text ed. 19.95 (*1-86064-075-3*, Pub. by I B Tauris UK) St Martin.

Southeast Asia. Ed. by Alastair Dingwall. (Traveller's Literary Companion Ser.). 472p. (Orig.). 1995. pap. 22.95 (*0-8442-8974-4*, Passport Bks) NTC Pub Grp.

Southeast Asia. Anita Ganeri. LC 95-11407. (Places & People Ser.). (Illus.). 32p. (J). (gr. 5-8). 1995. lib. bdg. 20.00 (*0-531-14367-8*) Watts.

Southeast Asia. Anita Ganeri. (Places & People Ser.). 1996. pap. 6.95 (*0-531-15289-8*) Watts.

Southeast Asia. Antony Mason. LC 91-24807. (World in View Ser.). (Illus.). 96p. (J). (gr. 6-12). 1992. lib. bdg. 25.68 (*0-8114-2447-2*) Raintree Steck-V.

Southeast Asia. Drew Middleton & Gene Brown. (Great Contemporary Issues Ser.). 27.95 (*0-405-13399-5*) Ayer.

Southeast Asia. Jonathan Rigg. LC 94-20444. (Country Fact Files Ser.). (J). 1995. lib. bdg. 24.26 (*0-8114-2788-9*) Raintree Steck-V.

***Southeast Asia.** St. Martin's Press Staff. (Let's Go Ser.). 1997. pap. 19.99 (*0-312-16902-7*) St Martin.

Southeast Asia. Z. Michael Szaz. (JSPES Monograph: No. 12). 1984. pap. 15.00 (*0-930690-15-X*) Coun Soc Econ.

Southeast Asia: A Critical Bibliography. Kennedy G. Tregonning. LC 68-9845. 115p. reprint ed. pap. 32.80 (*0-318-34750-4*, 2031486) Bks Demand.

Southeast Asia: A Cultural Study Through Celebration. Phil Scanlon, Jr. (Special Reports: No. 23). xvii, 185p. (Orig.). (C). 1985. pap. 15.00 (*1-877979-73-2*) SE Asia.

Southeast Asia: A History. Lea E. Williams. LC 75-32358. (Illus.). 316p. 1976. pap. 18.95 (*0-19-502000-6*) OUP.

Southeast Asia: A Past Regained. Time-Life Books Editors. Ed. by Dale M. Brown. LC 95-34501. (Lost Civilizations Ser.). (Illus.). 168p. 1995. 19.95 (*0-8094-9112-5*) Time-Life.

***Southeast Asia: A Ten Nation Region.** Ed. by Ashok K. Dutt. LC 96-26424. (GeoJournal Library). 352p. (C). 1996. lib. bdg. 169.00 (*0-7923-4171-6*) Kluwer Ac.

Southeast Asia: An Illustrated Introductory History. 4th ed. Milton E. Osborne. (Illus.). 264p. 1989. pap. text ed. 15.95 (*0-04-352238-6*) Routledge Chapman & Hall.

Southeast Asia: An Illustrated Introductory History. 5th ed. Milton E. Osborne. (Illus.). 228p. 1994. pap. 19.95 (*0-04-442215-6*, Pub. by Allen Unwin AT) Broad St Bks.

Southeast Asia: An Illustrated Introductory History. 6th ed. Milton Osborne. (Illus.). 272p. pap. 22.95 (*1-86373-823-1*, Pub. by Allen Unwin AT) Paul & Co Pubs.

***Southeast Asia: Architectural Markets & Practice.** pap. 40.00 (*1-879304-75-9*, W162) AIA DC.

***Southeast Asia: Human Landscape of Modernization & Development.** Jonathan Rigg. 352p. (C). 1997. pap. 22.95 (*0-415-13921-X*, Routledge NY); text ed. 69.95 (*0-415-13920-1*, Routledge NY) Routledge.

Southeast Asia: Illusion & Reality in Politics & Economics. Lennox A. Mills. LC 64-17805. 373p. reprint ed. pap. 106.40 (*0-8357-7030-3*, 2033271) Bks Demand.

Southeast Asia: Indonesia, Malaysia, Brunei, the Philippines, Singapore, Vietnam & Thailand. 20th ed. Fodor's Travel Staff. 1997. pap. 19.50 (*0-679-03286-X*) Fodors Travel.

***Southeast Asia: Past & Present.** 4th ed. D. R. Sardesai. LC 96-37295. (C). 1997. pap. text ed. 25.00 (*0-8133-3301-6*) Westview.

Southeast Asia: Region in Transition. Jonathan Rigg. (Illus.). 304p. (C). 1989. text ed. 69.95 (*0-04-445377-9*) Routledge Chapman & Hall.

Southeast Asia: South Africa's Transkei - What Happened to It? John Taylor & Andrew Turton. (Sociology of "Developing Societies" Ser.). 288p. (C). 1989. pap. 16.00 (*0-85345-764-6*) Monthly Rev.

Southeast Asia: Tradition & Modernity in the Contemporary World. 2nd ed. Donald G. McCloud. LC 95-5014. 360p. (C). 1995. pap. text ed. 24.00 (*0-8133-1896-3*) Westview.

Southeast Asia: Women, Changing Social Structure & Cultural Continuity, Selected Proceedings, Ninth Annual Conference, Canadian Council for Southeast Asian Studies at the Institute of Asian Research, U. B. C. Vancouver, November 1979. Ed. by Geoffrey B. Hainsworth et al. LC 82-205933. 234p. 1981. reprint ed. pap. 66.70 (*0-608-02205-5*, 2062875) Bks Demand.

Southeast Asia see Encyclopedia of World Geography

***Southeast Asia & Papua New Guinea Cruising Guide Vol. 1: South China Sea, Philippines, Gulf of Thailand, Singapore.** (Illus.). (C). 1997. pap. write for info. (*0-85288-296-3*) Bluewater Bks.

***Southeast Asia & Papua New Guinea Cruising Guide Vol. 2: Papua New Guinea, Indonesia, Malacca Strait, & West Coast of Thailand.** (Illus.). (C). 1997. pap. write for info. (*0-85288-378-1*) Bluewater Bks.

Southeast Asia Between Autocracy & Democracy: Identity & Political Processes. Ed. by Mikael Gravers et al. (Nordic Association for Southeast Asian Studies). 264p. (Orig.). (C). 1989. pap. 23.00 (*87-7288-217-4*, Pub. by Aarhus Univ Pr DK) David Brown.

S

Southeast Asia Catalog. Cornell University Libraries Staff. 1981. 750.00 (*0-8161-1329-7*) G K Hall.

Southeast Asia Cookbook. Ruth Law. (Illus.). 1990. pap. 28.00 (*1-55611-214-9*) D I Fine.

Southeast Asia Cookbook. Ruth Law. (Illus.). 464p. 1995. pap. 17.95 (*1-55611-469-9*, Primus) D I Fine.

Southeast Asia Emerges. rev. ed. LC 73-93982. (Asia Emerges Ser.). (Illus.). 104p. 1987. reprint ed. teacher ed., pap. 9.95 (*0-87297-059-0*) Diablo.

Southeast Asia Emerges. rev. ed. Steven Warshaw. LC 73-93982. (Asia Emerges Ser.). (Illus.). 356p. (Orig.). 1987. reprint ed. teacher ed., pap. 19.95 (*0-87297-021-3*) Diablo.

Southeast Asia Emerges. rev. ed. Steven Warshaw et al. LC 73-93982. (Asia Emerges Ser.). (Illus.). 356p. (Orig.). 1987. reprint ed. pap. 19.95 (*0-87297-020-5*) Diablo.

Southeast Asia Handbook. 2nd ed. Carl Parkes. LC 93-30740. (Illus.). 1103p. (Orig.). 1994. pap. 21.95 (*1-56691-002-1*) Moon Trvl Hdbks.

Southeast Asia in International Politics, 1941-1956. Evelyn Colbert. LC 76-28008. 384p. 1977. 49.95 (*0-8014-0971-3*) Cornell U Pr.

Southeast Asia in the Age of Commerce, 1450-1680 Vol. 2: Expansion & Crisis. Anthony Reid. (C). 1995. pap. text ed. 17.00 (*0-300-06516-7*) Yale U Pr.

Southeast Asia in the Age of Commerce, 1450-1680, Vol. 1: The Lands Below the Winds. Anthony Reid. 291p. (C). 1990. reprint ed. pap. 17.00 (*0-300-04750-9*) Yale U Pr.

Southeast Asia in the Age of Commerce, 1450-1680, Vol. 2: Expansion & Crisis. Anthony Reid. (Illus.). 392p. 1993. 40.00 (*0-300-05412-2*) Yale U Pr.

Southeast Asia in the Coming World. Ed. by Philip W. Thayer. LC 70-167426. (Essay Index Reprint Strait,). 1977. reprint ed. 23.95 (*0-8369-2444-4*) Ayer.

Southeast Asia in the Early Modern Era: Trade, Power, & Belief. Ed. by Anthony Reid. LC 92-54969. (Asia East by South Ser.). (Illus.). 286p. 1993. 45.00 (*0-8014-2848-3*); pap. 16.95 (*0-8014-8093-0*) Cornell U Pr.

Southeast Asia in the New International Era. 2nd ed. Clark D. Neher. (Politics in Asia & the Pacific Ser.). 242p. (C). 1994. pap. text ed. 19.95 (*0-8133-1989-7*) Westview.

Southeast Asia in the New World Order. Ed. by David Wurfel & Bruce Burton. LC 95-14919. (International Political Economy Ser.). 300p. 1996. text ed. 49.95 (*0-312-12834-7*); text ed. 17.95 (*0-312-12835-5*) St Martin.

Southeast Asia in the 1990s: Authoritarianism, Democracy & Capitalism. Richard Robison et al. 240p. pap. 22.95 (*1-86373-230-6*, Pub. by Allen Unwin AT) Paul & Co Pubs.

Southeast Asia in 1980's. Robinson & Hewison. 1989. pap. text ed. 14.95 (*0-04-176012-3*, Pub. by Allen Unwin AT) Paul & Co Pubs.

Southeast Asia Rainforests: A Resource Guide & Directory. Ed. by Martha Belcher & Angela Gennino. (Illus.). 100p. (Orig.). 1993. pap. 8.50 (*0-9628033-2-4*) Rainforest Act.

Southeast Asia Subject Catalog. Library Staff. 1979. 720.00 (*0-8161-1234-7*, Hall Library) G K Hall.

Southeast Asia-The Information Age: 1995 State-of-the-Art-Institute Proceedings. Ed. by Special Libraries Association Staff. 151p. 1996. 16.00 (*0-87111-456-9*) SLA.

***Southeast Asia Tomorrow: Problems & Prospects for U. S. Policy.** Melvin Gurtov. LC 79-101457. 126p. 1970. reprint ed. pap. 36.00 (*0-608-04022-3*, 2064758) Bks Demand.

Southeast Asia Tropical Fish Guide. Rudie H. Kuiter. 1996. 29.95 (*1-56465-170-3*) Tetra Pr.

Southeast Asia Under Japanese Occupation: Transition & Transformation. Ed. by Alfred W. McCoy. LC 80-610. (Monograph Ser.: No. 22). (Illus.). 250p. 1980. pap. 14.00 (*0-938692-08-9*) Yale U SE Asia.

***Southeast Asia/Escape from Socialist Burma & Capitalist Thailand.** Aung Chin Win Aung. 220p. (Orig.). 1997. pap. 30.00 (*0-9652612-7-1*) Yoma Pubng.

Southeast Asian American Women, Dual Identities, Multiple Roles. Falk. 1996. 22.95 (*0-8057-4593-9*, Twayne); 14.95 (*0-8057-4594-7*, Twayne) Scribnrs Ref.

Southeast Asian Archipelagic States: Concept, Evolution & Current Practice. Phiphat Tangsubkul. LC 83-25487. (East-West Environment & Policy Institute Research Report Ser.: No. 15). vi, 90p. 1984. pap. text ed. 3.00 (*0-685-08516-3*) EW Ctr HI.

***Southeast Asian Art Today.** Ed. by Joyce Van Fenema. (Illus.). 256p. 1995. text ed. 75.00 (*976-641-087-9*, Harwood Acad Pubs) Gordon & Breach.

Southeast Asian Art Today. Ed. by Joyce Van Fenema. 256p. 1996. 45.00 (*0-295-97538-5*) U of Wash Pr.

Southeast Asian Birth Customs: Three Studies in Human Reproduction. Donn V. Hart et al. LC 65-18348. (Monographs). 315p. 1965. pap. 15.00 (*0-87536-318-0*) HRAFP.

Southeast Asian Book of the Dead. Bill Shields. Ed. by Rollins Staff. (Illus.). 96p. (Orig.). 1993. pap. 9.00 (*1-880985-13-6*) Two Thirteen Sixty-one.

Southeast Asian Boom. Gerrit W. Gong & Keith W. Eirinberg. (Global Business White Paper Ser.). 1994. 20.00 (*0-614-13866-3*) CSI Studies.

Southeast Asian Capitalists. Ed. by Ruth T. McVey. (Studies on Southeast Asia: No. 9). 220p. (Orig.). (C). 1992. pap. text ed. 16.00 (*0-87727-708-7*) Cornell SE Asia.

Southeast Asian Ceramics. Robert J. Moes. (Illus.). 16p. 1975. pap. 1.00 (*0-87273-051-4*) Bklyn Mus.

Southeast Asian Ceramics: Ninth Through Seventeenth Centuries. Dean F. Frasche. LC 76-20204. (Illus.). 144p. 1976. 25.00 (*0-87848-047-1*) Asia Soc.

Southeast Asian Ceramics from the Collection of Margot & Hans Ries. Virginia Dofflemyer. (Illus.). 100p. (C). 1989. pap. text ed. write for info. (*0-318-65502-0*) Pacific Asia.

***Southeast Asian Chinese: The Socio-Cultural Dimension.** Ed. by Leo Suryadinata. 336p. 1995. boxed 29.50 (*981-210-067-9*, Pub. by Times Academic SI) Intl Spec Bk.

***Southeast Asian Chinese & China: The Politico-Economic Dimension.** Ed. by Leo Suryadinata. 272p. 1995. boxed write for info. (*981-210-066-0*, Pub. by Times Academic SI) Intl Spec Bk.

Southeast Asian Cooking: Menus & Recipes from Thailand, Singapore, Vietnam, Brunei, Malaysia, Indonesia & the Philippines. Barbara Hansen. LC 92-29049. (Illus.). 144p. (Orig.). 1992. pap. 9.95 (*1-55561-050-1*) Fisher Bks.

Southeast Asian Economic Miracle. Ed. by Young C. Kim. 200p. (C). 1995. 34.95 (*1-56000-196-8*) Transaction Pubs.

Southeast Asian Ephemeris: Solar & Planetary Positions, A. D. 638-2000. J. D. Eade. (Studies on Southeast Asia: No. 5). (Illus.). 175p. (Orig.). (C). 1989. pap. text ed. 16.00 (*0-87727-704-4*) Cornell SE Asia.

Southeast Asian Languages & Literatures: A Bibliographic Guide to Burmese, Cambodian, Indonesian, Javanese, Malay, Manangkaku, Thai & Vietnamese. Ed. by E. Ulrich Kratz. 256p. 1996. text ed. 95.00 (*1-86064-114-8*) St Martin.

Southeast Asian Management: Cases & Concepts. Stanley Richardson. 302p. 1991. 42.50 (*9971-69-160-4*, Pub. by Sgapore Univ SI) Coronet Bks.

Southeast Asian Refugee English Proficiency & Education in Texas. Eric H. Taylor & Lisa S. Barton. (Illus.). 53p. (Orig.). (C). 1995. pap. text ed. 20.00 (*0-7881-2173-1*) DIANE Pub.

Southeast Asian Security in the New Millennium. Ed. by Richard J. Ellings & Sheldon W. Simon. LC 96-12786. (Study of the National Bureau of Asian Research Ser.). (Illus.). 340p. (C). (gr. 13). 1996. pap. text ed. 24.95 (*1-56324-659-7*) M E Sharpe.

Southeast Asian Security in the New Millennium. Ed. by Richard J. Ellings & Sheldon W. Simon. LC 96-12786. (Study of the National Bureau of Asian Research Ser.). (Illus.). 216p. (C). (gr. 13). 1996. text ed. 62.95 (*1-56324-658-9*) M E Sharpe.

Southeast Asian Studies: Options for the Future. Report of a Conference at the Wilson Center March 1984. Ed. by Ronald A. Morse. 192p. (Orig.). 1985. pap. text ed. 23.00 (*0-8191-4318-9*, Woodrow Wilson Schl); lib. bdg. 55.50 (*0-8191-4317-0*, Woodrow Wilson Schl) U Pr of Amer.

Southeast Asian Studies & International Business. Ed. by Ronald Provencher. (Crossroads Ser.: Ser. 1.3). 123p. (Orig.). 1983. pap. 6.00 (*1-877979-82-1*) SE Asia.

Southeast Asian Studies in the Balance: Reflections from America. Ed. by Charles Hirschman et al. LC 92-53041. (Occasional Papers). 146p. (Orig.). 1992. pap. 9.00 (*0-924304-09-X*) Assn Asian Studies.

Southeast Asian Textile Designs. Caren Caraway. (International Design Library). (Illus.). 48p. (Orig.). 1983. pap. 5.95 (*0-88045-034-7*) Stemmer Hse.

Southeast Asian Transitions: Approaches Through Social History. Ed. by Ruth T. McVey & Adrienne Suddard. LC 78-4171. (Yale Southeast Asia Studies: No. 8). 252p. reprint ed. pap. 71.90 (*0-7837-2989-8*, 2043194) Bks Demand.

Southeast Asian Tribal Groups & Ethnic Minorities: Prospects for the Eighties & Beyond. Ed. by Ruth Taswell & R. O'G. Anderson. (Cultural Survival Reports: No. 22). 171p. 1989. 19.95 (*0-939521-39-3*); pap. 10.00 (*0-939521-33-4*) Cultural Survival.

Southeast Asian World. John F. Cady. LC 76-53353. (World of Asia Ser.). (Illus.). 1977. pap. text ed. 6.95 (*0-88273-502-0*) Forum Pr IL.

Southeast Asians in Rhode Island: The New Americans. Louise Lind. (Rhode Island Ethnic Heritage Pamphlet Ser.). (Illus.). (Orig.). 1989. pap. 4.75 (*0-917012-86-0*) RI Pubns Soc.

***Southeast Asia's Misunderstood.** K. S. Jomo. (C). 1997. text ed. 48.00 (*0-8133-9020-6*) Westview.

Southeast Bank Collects: A Corporation Views Contemporary Art. Lisa Liebmann. Ed. by Esther Perez. 70p. (Orig.). 1990. write for info. (*0-943411-21-1*) Norton Gal Art.

Southeast Building, the Twin Basilicas, the Mosaic House. Saul S. Weinberg. LC 75-25699. (Corinth Ser.: Vol. 1, Pt. 5). (Illus.). xviii, 128p. 1971. reprint ed. 35.00 (*0-87661-015-7*) Am Sch Athens.

Southeast Classic Maya Zone: Symposium at Dumbarton Oaks. Ed. by Elizabeth H. Boone et al. LC 87-22290. (Illus.). 420p. 1988. 40.00 (*0-88402-170-X*) Dumbarton Oaks.

Southeast Coast: Photos of Art Carter. Photos by Art Carter. LC 85-71193. (Illus.). 160p. 1985. 29.50 (*0-912856-95-5*) Gr Arts Ctr Pub.

Southeast Coast of Ireland: Tuskar Rock to Old Head of Kinsale. Imray, Laurie, Norie & Wilson Ltd. Staff. (Illus.). (C). 1990. text ed. 60.00 (*0-685-40192-8*, Pub. by Imray Laurie Norie & Wilson UK) St Mut.

Southeast Coast of Puerto Rico. Wilson Ltd. Staff & Imray L. Norie. (C). 1990. 65.00 (*0-685-40409-9*, Pub. by Imray Laurie Norie & Wilson UK) St Mut.

Southeast Connecticut, CT. (Streetfinder Ser.). (Illus.). 1994. pap. 14.95 (*0-528-91318-2*) Rand McNally.

Southeast-East Asian Publications in Print, 1987-89. 350p. 1986. 165.00 (*4-900178-06-3*) Taylor & Francis.

Southeast England. (Insight Pocket Guides Ser.). (Illus.). 97p. 1993. pap. 9.95 (*0-395-66906-5*) HM.

Southeast Europe Axis: Army Order of Battle. 172p. 1993. 14.00 (*0-941052-61-3*) Valor Pub.

Southeast Europe Axis Handbook. 172p. 1993. 14.00 (*0-941052-62-1*); pap. 14.00 (*0-941052-10-9*) Valor Pub.

Southeast Exporting: Profiles, Typology, & the Role of Technology in Selected U. S. Firms. Delwin A. Roy et al. (Research Monograph: No. 90). 175p. 1981. spiral bd. 25.00 (*0-88406-146-9*) GA St U Busn Pr.

Southeast, Forgotten Memories: An Angel Trilogy. Blair Cunnyngham. LC 94-67745. 489p. (Orig.). (YA). (gr. 11-12). 1995. pap. 13.95 (*0-9628603-2-8*) Still Meadow Pubs.

Southeast Frontier of New Spain. rev. ed. Peter Gerhard. LC 92-41923. 1993. 29.95 (*0-8061-2543-8*) U of Okla Pr.

Southeast Frontier of New Spain. Peter Gerhard. LC 78-70295. 227p. 1979. reprint ed. pap. 64.70 (*0-7837-8167-9*, 2047872) Bks Demand.

***Southeast Germany Map.** 1996. 8.95 (*2-06-700420-4*, 420) Michelin.

***Southeast Great Trips.** Linda L. Burton. LC 96-70440. 256p. (Orig.). 1996. pap. 11.95 (*0-9644760-1-0*) Phase II Publ.

Southeast Guide to Saltwater Fishing & Boating. Outdoor Action Communications Staff. 1993. pap. text ed. 24.95 (*0-07-047979-8*) McGraw.

Southeast Guide to Saltwater Fishing & Boating. 2nd ed. Vin T. Sparano. (Illus.). 320p. 1996. pap. text ed. 24.95 (*0-07-059892-4*) McGraw.

Southeast Guide to Saltwater Fishing & Boating. 2nd ed. Vin T. Spoarano & Outdoor Action, Inc. Staff. (Illus.). 448p. 1995. pap. 24.95 (*0-87742-322-9*, 60299) Intl Marine.

Southeast Indians: An Educational Coloring Book. Spizzirri Publishing Co. Staff. Ed. by Linda Spizzirri. (Illus.). 32p. (J). (gr. k-5). 1985. pap. 1.99 (*0-86545-065-X*) Spizzirri.

Southeast Maya Periphery. Ed. by Patricia A. Urban & Edward M. Schortman. (Illus.). 407p. 1986. text ed. 40.00 (*0-292-77589-X*) U of Tex Pr.

Southeast of Fourteen. Dorothy Williams. Ed. by Margaret Ames. (Illus.). 206p. 1988. 10.95 (*0-9621458-0-7*); pap. 8.95 (*0-685-44371-X*) Sundown Pub.

***Southeast Scotland Car Tours.** Jarrold Publishing Staff. 1996. pap. text ed. 15.95 (*0-7117-0848-7*, Pub. by Jarrold Pub UK) Seven Hills Bk.

Southeast Transaction Guide, 20 vols. Bender's Editorial Staff & Byron L. Sparber. 1976. Updates available. ring bd. write for info. (*0-8205-1632-5*) Bender.

Southeastcon '95. IEEE (Region 3) Staff. Ed. by IEEE (Institute of Electrical & Electronics Engineers, Inc.) Staff. LC 84-643372. 300p. 1995. pap. text ed. write for info. (*0-7803-2642-3*, 95CH35793); lib. bdg. write for info. (*0-7803-2643-1*, 95CH35793); mic. film write for info. (*0-7803-2644-X*, 95CH35793) Inst Electrical.

Southeastern Arkansas Death Record Index, 1914-1923: Arkansas, Ashley, Bradley, Chicot, Cleveland, Desha, Drew, Jefferson, & Lincoln Counties. Ed. by Desmond W. Allen. 54p. (Orig.). 1996. pap. 15.00 (*1-56546-083-9*) Arkansas Res.

Southeastern Arkansas Death Record Index, 1934-1940: Arkansas, Ashley, Bradley, Chicot, Cleveland, Desha, Drew, Jefferson, & Lincoln Counties. Ed. by Desmond W. Allen. 52p. (Orig.). 1996. pap. 15.00 (*1-56546-091-X*) Arkansas Res.

Southeastern Broadsides Before 1877: A Bibliography. Ed. by Ray O. Hummel, Jr. LC 71-634933. (Publication Ser.: No. 33). xii, 501p. 1971. 19.95 (*0-88490-064-9*) Library of VA.

Southeastern Broadsides Before 1877: A Bibliography. Ed. by Ray O. Hummel, Jr. LC 71-634933. (Virginia State Library Publicatons: No. 33). 515p. reprint ed. pap. 146.80 (*0-317-29836-4*, 2017496) Bks Demand.

Southeastern Caribbean. James Henderson. (Cadogan Island Guides Ser.). (Illus.). 276p. 1994. pap. 12.95 (*0-947754-77-6*) Globe Pequot.

Southeastern Ceremonial Complex: Artifacts & Analysis. Ed. by Patricia Galloway. LC 88-12223. (Indians of the Southeast Ser.). (Illus.). xviii, 389p. 1989. text ed. 62.50 (*0-8032-2131-2*) U of Nebr Pr.

Southeastern Check Stamped Pottery Tradition: A View from Louisiana. Ian W. Brown. LC 82-10101. (MCJA Special Paper Ser.: No. 4). (Illus.). 100p. reprint ed. pap. 28.50 (*0-7837-0502-6*, 2040826) Bks Demand.

Southeastern Europe Under Ottoman Rule, 1354-1804. Peter F. Sugar. LC 76-7799. (History of East Central Europe Ser.: Vol. 5). 384p. 1977. pap. 27.50 (*0-295-96033-7*) U of Wash Pr.

Southeastern European Maritime Commerce & Naval Policies from the Mid-18th Centuries to 1914. Apostolos E. Vacalopoulos et al. 410p. 1989. text ed. 91.50 (*0-88033-163-1*) East Eur Monographs.

Southeastern Indians. Mira Bartok & Christine Ronan. (Ancient & Living Cultures Ser.). 32p. (Orig.). (J). (gr. 3 up). 1995. pap. 9.95 (*0-673-36305-8*, GoodYrBooks) Addson-Wesley Educ.

Southeastern Indians. Charles Hudson. LC 75-30729. (Illus.). 592p. 1976. 40.00 (*0-87049-187-3*); pap. 18.95 (*0-87049-248-9*) U of Tenn Pr.

Southeastern Indians: Life Portraits. Ed. by Emma L. Fundaburk. (Illus.). 136p. 1991. reprint ed. 14.00 (*0-685-60184-6*) Am Bicent Mus.

Southeastern Journal of Music Education, Vol. 1, 1989. Ed. by James A. Braswell. (Orig.). 1990. pap. text ed. write for info. (*0-9619031-3-9*) U GA GA Ctr Cnt Educ.

Southeastern Journal of Music Education, 1990, Vol. 2. Ed. by James A. Braswell. (Orig.). 1991. pap. text ed. write for info. (*0-9619031-4-7*) U GA GA Ctr Cnt Educ.

Southeastern Michigan Pioneer Families: Especially Lenawee County & New York Origins. Ed. by Helen F. Lewis. 426p. 1994. lib. bdg. 73.95 (*1-56012-130-0*, 128) Kinship Rhinebeck.

Southeastern Michigan Pioneer Families: Especially Livingston County & New York Origins. Helen F. Lewis. 302p. 1995. lib. bdg. 51.95 (*1-56012-138-6*, 136) Kinship Rhinebeck.

Southeastern Nigeria in the Nineteenth Century. C. C. Ifemesia. LC 78-95186. 1978. 12.95 (*0-88357-066-1*); pap. 4.95 (*0-88357-091-2*) NOK Pubs.

Southeastern Pomo Ceremonials: The Kuksu Cult & Its Successors. Abraham M. Halpern. (UC Publications in Anthropological Records: Vol. 29). (Orig.). 1988. pap. 30.00 (*0-520-09731-9*) U CA Pr.

Southeastern Prehistory. Kathleen Lynch. (Early Alaskan Peoples Ser.: Vol. 4). (Illus.). 34p. (Orig.). 1982. reprint ed. pap. 8.95 (*1-878051-31-8*, CP073) Circumpolar Pr.

***Southeastern Region from Puerto Rico to the Panama Canal.** 2nd ed. Kay Showker. LC 97-22104. (Caribbean Ports of Call Ser.). 1997. pap. text ed. 14.95 (*1-56440-981-3*) Globe Pequot.

Southeastern Section Field Guide. Ed. by T. L. Neathery. (DNAG Centennial Field Guides Ser.: No. 6). (Illus.). 477p. 1986. 40.50 (*0-8137-5406-2*) Geol Soc.

Southeastern States see Mobil Travel Guide

Southeastern Stories. Kathleen Lynch. (Illus.). 26p. (Orig.). 1978. reprint ed. pap. 7.95 (*0-614-16022-7*, CP062) Circumpolar Pr.

Southeastern Studies: Toward A.D. 2000. Ed. by John I. Durham. LC 77-80400. (Emerging Directions in Christian Ministry Ser.: Vol. 1). viii, 146p. 1981. 8.95 (*0-86554-026-8*, MUP-H004) Mercer Univ Pr.

Southeastern Symposium on System Theory, 26th. LC 74-642491. 696p. 1994. pap. text ed. 100.00 (*0-8186-5320-5*, 5320) IEEE Comp Soc.

Southeastern Symposium on System Theory 27th, 1995: Starkville, Mississippi. LC 74-64291. 552p. 1995. pap. 110.00 (*0-8186-6985-3*, PR06985) IEEE Comp Soc.

Southeastern Symposium on System Theory, 28th (SSST '96) LC 74-642491. 552p. 1996. pap. 150.00 (*0-8186-7352-4*, PRO7352) IEEE Comp Soc.

***Southeastern Symposium on System Theory, 29th (SSST '97)** LC 96-80046. 700p. 1997. pap. 100.00 (*0-8186-7873-9*, PR07873) IEEE Comp Soc.

Southeastern United States: Third Annual Midyear Meeting, 1986, Raleigh, North Carolina. Society of Economic Paleontologists & Mineralogists Staff. (SEPM Field Guidebks.: No. 1986). 419p. reprint ed. pap. 119.50 (*0-7837-2416-0*, 2042553) Bks Demand.

Southeastern Whitewater: Fifty of the Best River Trips from Alabama to West Virginia. Monte Smith. 467p. (Orig.). 1995. pap. 22.00 (*1-886694-00-1*) Pahsimeroi Pr.

Southeastern Wildlife Cookbook. South Carolina Wildlife Magazine Staff. 224p. 1989. spiral bd. 14.95 (*0-87249-659-7*) U of SC Pr.

Southeastern Woodland Indian Designs. Caren Caraway. (International Design Library). (Illus.). 48p. (Orig.). 1985. pap. 5.95 (*0-88045-072-X*) Stemmer Hse.

Southeastern Yavapai. fac. ed. E. W. Gifford. (University of California Publications in American Archaeology & Ethnology: Vol. 29: 3). 82p. (C). 1932. reprint ed. pap. text ed. 7.50 (*1-55567-280-9*) Coyote Press.

Southeastern Zip Code Directory. 8th rev. ed. Kelly King. 288p. reprint ed. pap. 10.95 (*0-943983-04-5*) Natl Direct.

Southend Pier Railway. K. A. Frost & D. J. Carson. (Illus.). 44p. (Orig.). 1991. pap. 9.00 (*0-86025-431-3*, Pub. by Ian Henry Pubns UK) Empire Pub Srvs.

Southerland: Notes on the Southerland, Latham & Allied Families, Register of the Ancestors of Imogen Southerland Voorhees. E. K. Voorhees. (Illus.). 137p. 1992. reprint ed. pap. 21.00 (*0-8328-2733-9*); reprint ed. lib. bdg. 31.00 (*0-8328-2732-0*) Higginson Bk Co.

Southern: A Motive Power Pictorial 1968-1982. Paul K. Withers & Tom L. Sink. LC 87-90068. 238p. 1987. 32.95 (*0-9618503-0-2*) Withers Pub.

Southern, a Narrow Gauge Odyessey. 2nd ed. Richard L. Dorman. (Illus.). 156p. 1988. 29.95 (*0-9616656-3-7*) RD Pubns.

Southern Accent: Award Winning Southern Recipes. Junior League of Pine Bluff AR Staff. 1994. 16.95 (*0-87483-376-0*) August Hse.

***Southern Accent Cookbook.** Frances Wood. (Illus.). 128p. 1997. pap. 14.95 (*0-9697079-7-5*, Pub. by Moulin Pub CN) Genl Dist Srvs.

Southern Accents Vol. 39: The Fiction of Peter Taylor. Catherine C. Graham. LC 92-27582. (American University Studies: No. XXIV). 167p. (C). 1994. text ed. 43.95 (*0-8204-1884-6*) P Lang Pubng.

Southern Accents Historic Houses of the South. Southern Accents Magazine Editors. 208p. 1984. 35.00 (*0-685-08721-2*) S&S Trade.

Southern Africa. Nick Middleton. LC 94-18330. (Country Fact Files Ser.). 47p. (J). (gr. 6-9). 1995. lib. bdg. 24.26 (*0-8114-2785-4*) Raintree Steck-V.

Southern Africa. Francis Fleming. 1981. reprint ed. lib. bdg. 59.00 (*0-403-00408-X*) Scholarly.

Southern Africa: A Study of the Educational Systems of Botswana, Lesotho, South Africa, Southwest Africa - Namibia, & Swaziland with an Addendum on Zimbabwe-Rhodesia: A Guide to the Academic Placement of Students in Educational Institutions of the United States. David J. Cranmer & Valerie A. Woolston. LC 80-14066. (World Education Ser.). 264p. reprint ed. pap. 75.30 (*0-8357-7533-X*, 2036246) Bks Demand.

Southern Africa: An American Enigma. R. Ali. LC 85-31254. 239p. 1987. text ed. 55.00 (*0-275-92380-0*, C2380, Praeger Pubs) Greenwood.

Southern Africa: Civilizations in Turmoil. Richard Hull. 240p. (C). 1981. pap. text ed. 14.00 (*0-8147-3411-1*) NYU Pr.

***Southern Africa: Landmines in Southern Africa, Still Killing.** 206p. (Orig.). 1997. pap. 15.00 (*1-56432-206-8*) Hum Rts Watch.

Southern Africa: Regional Security Problems & Prospects. Ed. by Robert S. Jaster. LC 85-2031. (Adelphi Library). 170p. 1985. text ed. 32.50 (*0-312-74684-9*) St Martin.

Southern Africa: The Continuing Crisis. 2nd ed. Ed. by Gwendolen M. Carter & Patrick O'Meara. LC 81-48324. 416p. reprint ed. pap. 118.60 (*0-685-23878-4*, 2056696) Bks Demand.

Southern Africa: Toward Economic Liberation. Ed. by Amon J. Nskela. 274p. 1981. 35.00 (*0-86036-154-3*) St Mut.

Southern Africa see Encyclopedia of World Geography

Southern Africa - Prospects for Peace & Security: International Conference of Peace & Security in Southern, 2nd, Dar es Salaam, March 2-6, 1986. (Report Ser.: No. 25). 186p. 1900. pap. text ed. write for info. (*0-89838-921-6*) Kluwer Ac.

***Southern Africa & Eastern Asia: Experiences & Opportunities in Development.** Ed. by Jan Isaksen et al. LC 97-18550. (Illus.). xi, 235p. (Orig.). (C). 1997. pap. 14.95 (*0-9656930-2-3*) Intl Ctr Economic.

Southern Africa & Western Security. Robert J. Hanks. LC 83-48628. (Foreign Policy Reports). 71p. 1984. 11.95 (*0-89549-055-2*) Inst Foreign Policy Anal.

Southern Africa Bibliography. Reuben Musiker & Naomi Musiker. LC 96-7264. (Area Bibliographies Ser.: No. 11). 1996. 52.00 (*0-8108-3175-9*) Scarecrow.

Southern Africa in Conflict: Implications for U. S. Policies in the 1980's. Robert S. Jaster. LC 81-86522. (AEI Special Analyses Ser.: No. 81-10). 56p. reprint ed. pap. 25.00 (*0-8357-4535-X*, 2037416) Bks Demand.

Southern Africa in Crisis. Ed. by Gwendolyn M. Carter & Patrick O'Meara. LC 76-48534. 279p. reprint ed. pap. 79.60 (*0-317-27939-4*, 2056027) Bks Demand.

Southern Africa in Crisis: Regional & International Responses. No. 28. 1988. write for info. (*0-318-62250-5*) Intl Peace.

Southern Africa in Crisis: Regional & International Responses. International Peace Academy Staff. 272p. 1988. lib. bdg. 77.50 (*0-89838-929-1*) Kluwer Ac.

Southern Africa in the World: Autonomy or Interdependence? Richard E. Bissell. LC 78-102899. (Foreign Policy Research Institute. Monograph Ser.: No. 23). 74p. reprint ed. pap. 25.00 (*0-7837-1776-8*, 2041974) Bks Demand.

Southern Africa in the 1980s. Ed. by Olajide Aluko & Timothy M. Shaw. 320p. 1985. text ed. 60.00 (*0-04-320169-5*) Routledge Chapman & Hall.

***Southern Africa on the Wild Side.** Rupert Isaacson. 1998. pap. text ed. 21.95 (*1-86011-042-8*, Pub. by Cadogan Books UK) Macmillan.

Southern Africa since 1800. 2nd ed. Donald Denoon & Balam Nyeko. 246p. (C). 1984. pap. text ed. 27.50 (*0-582-72707-3*, 74744) Longman.

Southern African Annual Review, 1987-88, 2 vols., Set. Barry Munslow. 1100p. 1989. 170.00 (*0-905450-02-7*, Pub. by H Zell Pubs UK) Bowker-Saur.

Southern African Annual Review, 1987-88, 2 vols., Vol. 1, Country Reviews. Barry Munslow. 550p. 1990. 85.00 (*0-905450-03-5*, Pub. by H Zell Pubs UK) Bowker-Saur.

Southern African Annual Review, 1987-88, 2 vols., Vol. 2, Regional Review. Barry Munslow. 550p. 1990. 85.00 (*0-905450-04-3*, Pub. by H Zell Pubs UK) Bowker-Saur.

Southern African Birds: A Photographic Guide. Ian Sinclair. (Illus.). 144p. 1994. pap. 14.95 (*0-88359-030-1*) R Curtis Pubng.

Southern African Environment: Environmental Profiles of the SADC Countries. Sam Moyo et al. 416p. (Orig.). 1992. 55.00 (*1-85383-171-9*, Pub. by Erthscan Pubns UK) Island Pr.

Southern African Literatures. Michael Chapman. (Literature in English Ser.). 560p. (C). 1996. text ed. 79.50 (*0-582-05306-4*, Pub. by Longman UK) Longman.

Southern African Prehistory & Paleoenvironments. Ed. by Richard G. Klein. 416p. (C). 1984. text ed. 105.00 (*90-6191-097-8*, Pub. by A A Balkema NE) Ashgate Pub Co.

Southern African Snakes & Other Reptiles: A Photographic Guide. Bill Branch. (Illus.). 144p. 1993. pap. 15.95 (*0-88359-027-1*) R Curtis Pubng.

An Asterisk (*) at the beginning of an entry indicates that the title is appearing in BIP for the first time.

S

Southern Agrarians. Paul K. Conkin. LC 87-22496. (Illus.). 210p. 1988. 26.00 (*0-87049-560-7*); pap. 14.00 (*0-87049-561-5*) U of Tenn Pr.

Southern Agriculture During the Civil War Era, 1860-1880. John S. Otto. LC 93-32981. (Contributions in American History Ser.: No. 153). 184p. 1994. text ed. 52.95 (*0-313-26714-6*, Greenwood Pr) Greenwood.

***Southern Angler's Guide.** (Illus.). 130p. (Orig.). Date not set. mass mkt. 4.95 (*1-890280-06-2*) B A S S.

Southern Anglicanism: The Church of England in Colonial South Carolina. Charles S. Bolton. LC 81-6669. (Contributions to the Study of Religion Ser.: No. 5). (Illus.). 248p. 1982. text ed. 49.95 (*0-313-23090-0*, BOS/, Greenwood Pr) Greenwood.

Southern Animal Tales. Nancy Van Laan. (J). 1998. 20.00 (*0-689-81061-X*) S&S Childrens.

Southern Appalachia, 1885-1915: Oral Histories from the State Corner Area of North Carolina, Tennessee, & Virginia. Roy E. Thomas. LC 91-52598. 286p. 1991. lib. bdg. 35.00 (*0-89950-620-8*) McFarland & Co.

Southern Appalachian Reader. Cratis D. Williams et al. LC 87-19589. (Illus.). 500p. (YA). (gr. 10-12). 1988. pap. text ed. 14.95 (*0-913239-50-X*) Appalach Consortium.

Southern Appalachian Windows: Comparison of Styles, Scales, Geometry, & Detachment Levels of Thrust Faults in the Foreland & Internides of a Thrust-Dominated Orogen. Ed. by Hatcher. (IGC Field Trip Guidebooks Ser.). 104p. 1989. 21.00 (*0-87590-616-8*, T167) Am Geophysical.

Southern Appalachians. David Emblidge. (Appalachian Trail Companions Ser.). (Illus.). 368p. 1998. pap. 19.95 (*0-8117-2668-1*) Stackpole.

***Southern Argus: Obituaries, Death Notices & Implied Deaths 1869-1874.** Michael Kelsey et al. 410p. (Orig.). 1996. pap. 32.00 (*0-7884-0513-6*, K150) Heritage Bk.

Southern Arizona Folk Arts. James S. Griffith. LC 88-17471. 234p. (Orig.). 1988. 35.95 (*0-8165-1001-6*); pap. 11.95 (*0-8165-1084-9*) U of Ariz Pr.

Southern Arizona Nature Almanac: A Seasonal Guide to Pima County & Beyond. Roseann B. Hanson & Jonathan M. Hanson. LC 96-44764. (Illus.). 288p. (Orig.). 1996. pap. 19.95 (*0-87108-869-X*) Pruett.

Southern Arizona the Last Twelve Thousand Years: A Cultural-Historic Overview for the Western Army National Guard Aviation Training Site. Stephanie M. Whittlesey et al. (Statistical Research Technical Ser.: No. 48). (Illus.). 441p. (Orig.). (C). 1994. spiral bd. 25.00 (*1-879442-10-8*) Stats Res.

Southern Asia - Afghanistan, Bhutan, Burma, Cambodia, Ceylon, India, Laos, Malaya, Nepal, Pakistan, Sikkiin, Singapore, Thailand, Vietnam: Classified, Alphabetical, & Chronological Listings. Harvard University Library Staff. LC 68-15927. (Widener Library Shelflist: No. 19). 551p. 1968. text ed. 25.00 (*0-674-82500-4*) HUP.

Southern Asia Accessions List 1952-1960, 9 Vols., Set. Cecil Hobbs et al. LC 71-151056. (Library of Congress Publications in Reprint). 1971. reprint ed. 217.95 (*0-405-03423-7*) Ayer.

Southern Asia Accessions List 1952-1960, 9 Vols., Vol. 1. Cecil Hobbs et al. LC 71-151056. (Library of Congress Publications in Reprint). 1971. reprint ed. 36.95 (*0-405-03437-7*) Ayer.

Southern Asia Accessions List 1952-1960, 9 Vols., Vol. 2. Cecil Hobbs et al. LC 71-151056. (Library of Congress Publications in Reprint). 1971. reprint ed. 35.95 (*0-405-03438-5*) Ayer.

Southern Asia Accessions List 1952-1960, 9 Vols., Vol. 3. Cecil Hobbs et al. LC 71-151056. (Library of Congress Publications in Reprint). 1971. reprint ed. 35.95 (*0-405-03439-3*) Ayer.

Southern Asia Accessions List 1952-1960, 9 Vols., Vol. 4. Cecil Hobbs et al. LC 71-151056. (Library of Congress Publications in Reprint). 1971. reprint ed. 35.95 (*0-405-03440-7*) Ayer.

Southern Asia Accessions List 1952-1960, 9 Vols., Vol. 5. Cecil Hobbs et al. LC 71-151056. (Library of Congress Publications in Reprint). 1971. reprint ed. 40.95 (*0-405-03441-5*) Ayer.

Southern Asia Accessions List 1952-1960, 9 Vols., Vol. 6. Cecil Hobbs et al. LC 71-151056. (Library of Congress Publications in Reprint). 1971. reprint ed. 35.95 (*0-405-03442-3*) Ayer.

Southern Athapaskan Migration: A. D. 200-1750. LC 85-60644. 128p. 1987. 10.50 (*0-912586-60-5*) Navajo Coll Pr.

Southern Atlantic Coast Job Seekers Sourcebook. 2nd ed. Donald D. Walker & Valerie A. Shipe. LC 92-46337. (Illus.). 416p. (Orig.). 1994. pap. 14.95 (*1-882499-22-0*) Net Research.

Southern Aurora. large type ed. Angela Devine. (Linford Romance Library). 320p. 1992. pap. 15.99 (*0-7089-7192-X*, Linford) Ulverscroft.

Southern Baptist Convention: A Sesquicentennial History. Jesse C. Fletcher. LC 94-8576. 448p. 1994. 29.99 (*0-8054-1167-4*, 4211-67) Broadman.

Southern Baptist Convention & the Judgement of History: The Taint of an Original Sin. E. Luther Copeland. LC 95-12894. 198p. (Orig.). 1995. lib. bdg. 47.50 (*0-8191-9934-6*) U Pr of Amer.

Southern Baptist Convention & the Judgement of History: The Taint of an Original Sin. E. Luther Copeland. 198p. (Orig.). (C). 1995. pap. text ed. 28.00 (*0-8191-9935-4*) U Pr of Amer.

Southern Baptist Mission in Japan, 1889-1989. F. Calvin Parker. (Illus.). 362p. (Orig.). (C). 1991. pap. text ed. 34.50 (*0-8191-8108-0*); lib. bdg. 54.50 (*0-8191-8107-2*) U Pr of Amer.

***Southern Baptist Periodical Index.** Ed. by Eldonna DeWeese. LC 72-625602. 1997. lib. bdg. 95.00 (*0-925359-10-6*) SBU Library.

Southern Baptist Periodical Index, 1985-86. Ed. by Eldonna DeWeese. LC 72-625602. xx, 727p. 1994. lib. bdg. 150.00 (*0-925359-00-9*) SBU Library.

Southern Baptist Periodical Index, 1987. Ed. by Eldonna DeWeese. LC 72-625602. xv, 490p. (C). 1988. lib. bdg. 50.00 (*0-925359-01-7*) SBU Library.

Southern Baptist Periodical Index, 1988. Ed. by Eldonna DeWeese. LC 72-625602. xvii, 563p. 1989. lib. bdg. 50.00 (*0-925359-02-5*) SBU Library.

Southern Baptist Periodical Index, 1989. Ed. by Eldonna DeWeese. LC 72-625602. xix, 575p. 1990. lib. bdg. 50.00 (*0-925359-03-3*) SBU Library.

Southern Baptist Periodical Index, 1990. Ed. by Eldonna DeWeese. LC 72-625602. xxii, 349p. 1991. lib. bdg. 95.00 (*0-925359-04-1*) SBU Library.

Southern Baptist Periodical Index, 1991. Ed. by Eldonna DeWeese. LC 72-625602. xxii, 364p. 1992. lib. bdg. 95.00 (*0-925359-05-X*) SBU Library.

Southern Baptist Periodical Index, 1992. Ed. by Eldonna DeWeese. LC 72-625602. xxii, 397p. 1993. lib. bdg. 95.00 (*0-925359-06-8*) SBU Library.

Southern Baptist Periodical Index, 1993. Ed. by Eldonna DeWeese. LC 72-625602. xxii, 409p. 1995. lib. bdg. 95.00 (*0-925359-07-6*) SBU Library.

Southern Baptist Periodical Index, 1994. Ed. by Eldonna DeWeese & Betty Heifner. LC 72-625602. (C). 1996. lib. bdg. 95.00 (*0-925359-08-4*) SBU Library.

Southern Baptist Periodical Index, 1995. Ed. by Eldonna Deweese & Betty Heifner. LC 72-625602. 1997. lib. bdg. 95.00 (*0-925359-09-2*) SBU Library.

Southern Baptist Politics: Authority & Power in the Restructuring of an American Denomination. Arthur E. Farnsley, II. LC 93-6039. 176p. (C). 1994. 29.95 (*0-271-01001-0*) Pa St U Pr.

Southern Baptists: A Subculture in Transition. Ellen M. Rosenberg. LC 88-31610. 256p. 1989. 28.00 (*0-87049-598-4*) U of Tenn Pr.

Southern Baptists & American Evangelicals. David Dockery. 240p. (Orig.). 1993. pap. 16.99 (*0-8054-6041-1*, 4260-41) Broadman.

Southern Baptists Observed: Multiple Perspectives on a Changing Denomination. Ed. by Nancy T. Ammerman. LC 92-18725. 376p. (Orig.). (C). 1993. pap. 21.00 (*0-87049-770-7*); lib. bdg. 40.00 (*0-87049-769-3*) U of Tenn Pr.

Southern Baroque Art: A Study of Painting, Architecture & Music in Italy & Spain of the 17th & 18th Centuries. Sacheverell Sitwell. LC 70-179539. (Select Bibliographies Reprint Ser.). 1980. reprint ed. 20.95 (*0-8369-6668-6*) Ayer.

Southern Beeches. A. L. Poole. 1987. 27.50 (*0-477-02510-2*, Pub. by Manaaki Whenua NZ) Balogh.

Southern Belle in the American Novel. Kathryn L. Seidel. LC 85-8519. 220p. 1985. 29.95 (*0-8130-0811-5*); pap. 17.95 (*0-8130-0835-2*) U Press Fla.

Southern Belle Primer: or Why Princess Margaret Will Never Be a Kappa Kappa Gamma. 144p. 1991. pap. 10.00 (*0-385-41667-9*) Doubleday.

***Southern Belles Paper Dolls.** Tom Tierney. (Illus.). pap. 4.95 (*0-486-27534-5*) Dover.

Southern Biomedical Engineering Conference, 12th, 1993. IEEE (Engineering in Medicine & Biology Society) Staff. Ed. by IEEE (Institute of Electrical & Electronics Engineers, Inc.) Staff. LC 93-77069. 400p. 1993. pap. write for info. (*0-7803-0976-6*, 93TH0525-6); fiche write for info. (*0-7803-0977-4*) Inst Electrical.

Southern Bivouac, 6 bks., Set. Intro. by Gary W. Gallagher. (Illus.). 1993. reprint ed. 300.00 (*1-56837-000-8*) Broadfoot.

Southern Black: Slave & Free. Compiled by Lawrence Thompson. LC 74-97478. 576p. 1970. 15.00 (*0-87875-004-5*) Whitston Pub.

***Southern Black Belt: Dependence, Quality of Life, & Policy.** Ronald C. Wimberley & Libby V. Morris. (Illus.). 64p. (Orig.). (C). 1997. pap. text ed. 9.95 (*0-9649746-2-2*) Ctr Rural Studies.

Southern Black Creative Writers, 1829-1953: Biobibliographies. Compiled by M. Marie Foster. LC 88-5595. (Bibliographies & Indexes in Afro-American & African Studies: No. 22). 130p. 1988. text ed. 39.95 (*0-313-26207-1*, FSW/, Greenwood Pr) Greenwood.

Southern Black Leaders of the Reconstruction Era. Ed. by Howard N. Rabinowitz. LC 81-11372. (Blacks in the New World Ser.). (Illus.). 448p. 1982. pap. text ed. 16.95 (*0-252-00972-X*) U of Ill Pr.

Southern Black Utterances Today. Ed. by Toni Cade Bambara & Leah Wise. (Southern Exposure Ser.). (Illus.). 120p. (Orig.). (C). 1975. pap. 4.50 (*0-943810-04-3*) Inst Southern Studies.

***Southern Blood: Vampire Stories from the American South.** Ed. by Lawrence Schimel & Martin H. Greenberg. LC 97-15897. (American Vampire Ser.). 240p. (Orig.). 1997. pap. 12.95 (*1-888952-49-0*) Cumberland Hse.

***Southern Born & Bread.** Junior Service League of LaGrange Staff. Ed. by Miriam W. Lukken. (Illus.). 416p. 1996. 15.95 (*0-9637193-0-0*) Jr Svce LaGrange.

Southern Born & Bread. 4th ed. Patricia B. Mitchell. 1992. pap. 4.00 (*0-925117-54-4*) Mitchells.

Southern Boy in Blue: The Memoir of Marcus Woodcock, 9th Kentucky Infantry (U. S. A.) Ed. by Kenneth W. Noe. LC 95-32485. (Voices of the Civil War Ser.). (Illus.). 376p. 1996. 32.95 (*0-87049-921-1*) U of Tenn Pr.

Southern Bread Winners. Linda G. Hatcher. 190p. 1992. pap. 9.95 (*0-941162-12-5*) D Gibson.

Southern Bronze: Capt. Garden's (S.C.) Artillery Co. During the War Between the States. Glenn Dedmondt. (Illus.). 255p. 1993. 30.00 (*0-9623065-4-1*) Palmetto Bookworks.

Southern Business: The Decades Ahead. David A. Shannon. (ITT Key Issues Lecture Ser.). 123p. 1981. pap. text ed. 6.50 (*0-672-97877-6*, Bobbs) Macmillan.

Southern Businessmen & Desegregation. Ed. by Elizabeth Jacoway & David R. Colburn. LC 81-19362. xii, 332p. (C). 1982. text ed. 40.00 (*0-8071-0893-6*) La State U Pr.

Southern But Lite. Jen B. Avis & Kathy F. Ward. (Illus.). 278p. 1989. 15.95 (*0-9628683-0-2*) Avis & Ward.

Southern by the Grace of God. Michael Grissom. LC 89-25568. 1989. 22.95 (*0-88289-761-6*) Pelican.

Southern by the Grace of God: Lewis Grizzard on the South. Lewis Grizzard. 1996. pap. 9.95 (*1-56352-279-9*) Longstreet Pr Inc.

Southern CA Harley-Davidson Dealers' Motorcycle Touring in So Cal. Jan Williams & Judith Uthus. 96p. (Orig.). 1996. pap. 9.95 (*0-9639927-1-6*) Black Ball.

Southern California: An Island on the Land. Carey McWilliams. LC 73-77787. 415p. 1973. pap. 12.95 (*0-87905-007-1*, Peregrine Smith) Gibbs Smith Pub.

Southern California: Family Adventure Guide: Great Things to See & Do for the Entire Family. Laura Kath & Pamela Lechtman. (Family Adventure Guide Ser.). (Illus.). 160p. 1995. pap. 9.95 (*1-56440-744-6*) Globe Pequot.

Southern California: Off the Beaten Path: A Guide to Unique Places. 2nd ed. Kathy Strong. LC 95-23874. (Off the Beaten Path Ser.). (Illus.). 224p. 1995. pap. 10.95 (*1-56440-761-6*) Globe Pequot.

Southern California: The State & Its Educational System. Harold L. Hodgkinson. 17p. 1989. 7.00 (*0-937846-64-3*) Inst Educ Lead.

Southern California - One Hundred Years Go, 1. Compiled by Skip Whitson. (Historical Ser.). (Illus.). (Orig.). 1976. pap. 3.50 (*0-89540-033-2*, SB-033) Sun Pub.

Southern California - One Hundred Years Go, 2. Compiled by Skip Whitson. (Historical Ser.). (Illus.). (Orig.). 1976. pap. 3.50 (*0-89540-034-0*, SB-034) Sun Pub.

Southern California Anthology, Vol. V. Ed. by Andrew Ragan & Cherilyn Cummings. 144p. (Orig.). 1987. pap. 5.95 (*0-9615108-2-X*) Scanthology.

***Southern California Anthology, Vol. XIII.** X. J. Kennedy et al. 143p. (Orig.). 1996. pap. 9.95 (*1-889217-00-X*) Scanthology.

Southern California Atlas & Gazetteer. 2nd ed. DeLorme Mapping Staff. (Atlas & Gazetteer Ser.). (Illus.). 12p. (Orig.). 1994. pap. 16.95 (*0-89933-205-6*, 2206) DeLorme Map.

Southern California Beach Recipe: Recipes from Favorite Coastal Restaurants - Malibu to Laguna Beach. Joan Stromquist & Carl Stromquist. (Illus.). 352p. (Orig.). 1990. 17.95 (*0-9622807-3-9*) Tierra Pubns.

Southern California Bouldering Guide. 2nd ed. Craig Fry. (Illus.). 232p. 1995. pap. 20.00 (*0-934641-57-9*) Chockstone Pr.

***Southern California Business Directory & Buyers Guide, 1997.** 34th ed. 1808p. 1997. 169.00 (*1-57541-031-1*) Database Pub Co.

Southern California Business Directory 1997-1998 see California Business Directory 1997-1998

Southern California Business Directory, 1997-98. rev. ed. American Business Directories Staff. 5632p. 1996. boxed 795.00 (*1-56105-844-0*) Am Busn Direct.

Southern California Country: An Island on the Land. Carey McWilliams. LC 76-111847. (Essay Index Reprint Ser.). 1977. 29.95 (*0-8369-1674-3*) Ayer.

Southern California Creative Journal, Vol. 1, No. 1. 26p. 1987. 6.50 (*0-934487-16-2*) R M Greene.

Southern California Dog Owners Guide: The Starter Book. rev. ed. Bob Christiansen & Laura Christiansen. LC 93-90942. 240p. 1994. pap. 9.95 (*1-884421-88-1*) Canine Lrning.

Southern California Dog Owners Guide: Your Complete Resource for Successful Dog Ownership. Bob Christiansen & Laura Christiansen. 192p. (Orig.). pap. 9.95 (*1-884421-93-8*) Canine Lrning.

Southern California Extended: Las Vegas to San Diego & Los Angeles. Larry Ford & Ernie Griffin. LC 92-10530. (Touring North America Ser.). (Illus.). 126p. 1992. 25.00 (*0-8135-1884-9*); pap. 9.95 (*0-8135-1885-7*) Rutgers U Pr.

Southern California for Kids. Kay Sanger. 1990. pap. 12.95 (*0-517-57347-4*, C P Pubs) Crown Pub Group.

Southern California Gardens: An Illustrated History. Victoria Padilla. LC 94-77674. (Illus.). 376p. 1994. 39.95 (*0-9627297-1-X*) A A Knoll Pubs.

***Southern California Handbook.** Kim Weir. 1997. pap. text ed. 19.95 (*1-56691-102-8*) Moon Trvl Hdbks.

***Southern California Harley-Davidson Dealers' Motorcycle Touring in Southern California.** 2nd ed. Jan Williams & Judith Uthus. Ed. by Mark Blocker. (Illus.). 96p. 1994. reprint ed. pap. 9.95 (*0-614-30128-9*) Black Ball.

Southern California Local History: A Gathering of the Writings of W. W. Robinson. Ed. by Doyce B. Nunis, Jr. LC 93-78012. (Illus.). 520p. 1993. 45.00 (*0-914421-10-7*) Hist Soc So CA.

Southern California Ordinal Scales of Development, Set. Ashurst Doanld et al. (Series in Six). 638p. 1985. 130.00 (*0-943292-16-6*, Flaming Sparrow) Foreworks.

Southern California Performing Arts Venues. Fringe Festival-Los Angeles Staff & Community Arts Resources, Inc. Staff. Ed. by Aaron Paley & Cathy Carpenter. 198p. (Orig.). 1993. pap. 12.95 (*0-9635872-1-8*) Fringe Fest LA.

Southern California Retirement Living: A Guide to the Best Residences. Sally Ravel & Lee A. Wolfe. (Illus.). 300p. (Orig.). 1992. reprint ed. lib. bdg. 39.00 (*0-8095-5862-9*) Borgo Pr.

Southern California Sport Climbing: The Guide. Troy Mayr & Anthony Sweeney. 216p. 1995. pap. 24.00 (*0-9647462-0-4*) Mobius Pubns.

Southern California Tennis Champions Centennial 1887-1987. Patricia H. Yeomans. LC 87-61603. (Illus.). 320p. 1987. 10.00 (*0-685-19219-9*) S CA Committee.

***Southern California Travel-Smart Trip Planner.** Gary Gordon. 1997. pap. 14.95 (*1-56261-253-0*) John Muir.

Southern California Wedding & Reception Site Directory. Alan Ibarra. (Angeles-Orange County Ser.). (Illus.). 152p. 1990. pap. text ed. 4.95 (*0-685-29430-7*) Amer Ind Mktg.

Southern California's Best Ghost Towns: A Practical Guide. Philip Varney. LC 89-22742. (Illus.). 152p. 1994. pap. 12.95 (*0-8061-2608-6*) U of Okla Pr.

Southern California's Spanish Heritage: An Anthology. Ed. by Doyce B. Nunis, Jr. LC 92-74172. (Illus.). 550p. 1992. 90.00 (*0-914421-08-5*) Hist Soc So CA.

Southern Campaigns of the American Revolution. Dan Morrill. 300p. 1993. 29.95 (*1-877853-21-6*) Nautical & Aviation.

Southern Capitalism: The Political Economy of North Carolina, 1880-1980. Phillip Wood. LC 86-11469. (Illus.). xiii, 273p. 1986. pap. text ed. 18.95 (*0-8223-0746-4*) Duke.

Southern Capitalism: The Political Economy of North Carolina, 1880-1980. Phillip Wood. LC 86-11469. (Illus.). xiii, 273p. 1986. text ed. 46.95 (*0-8223-0673-5*) Duke.

Southern Capitalists: The Ideological Leadership of an Elite, 1832-1885. Laurence Shore. LC 86-1395. (Fred W. Morrison Series in Southern Studies). xii, 282p. (C). 1986. text ed. 34.95 (*0-8078-1702-3*) U of NC Pr.

S

Southern Caribbean. Berlitz Editors. (Pocket Guides Ser.). (Illus.). 1993. pap. 7.95 (*2-8315-2248-X*) Berlitz.

Southern Cemetery of Matrica. Judit Topal. 106p. (C). 1981. 108.00 (*963-05-2540-2*, Pub. by Akad Kiado HU) St Mut.

Southern, Central & East African Mammals: A Photographic Guide. Chris Stuart & Tilde Stuart. (Illus.). 144p. 1994. pap. 15.95 (*0-88359-028-X*) R Curtis Pubng.

Southern Cheyenne Women's Songs. Virginia Giglio. LC 93-23221. (Illus.). 272p. 1994. 29.95 (*0-8061-2605-1*); 35.00 incl. audio (*0-8061-2648-5*); audio 9.95 (*0-8061-2644-2*) U of Okla Pr.

Southern Cheyennes. Donald J. Berthrong. LC 63-8990. (Civilization of the American Indian Ser.: No. 66). (Illus.). 456p. 1975. pap. 17.95 (*0-8061-1199-2*) U of Okla Pr.

Southern China, Hong Kong & Taiwan: The Evolution of a Subregional Economy. Ed. by Jane Khanna. LC 95-2896. (Significant Issues Ser.: Vol. 17, No. 7). 110p. (C). 1995. pap. text ed. 14.95 (*0-89206-321-1*) CSI Studies.

Southern Chivalry. LC 71-178482. (Black Heritage Library Collection). 1977. reprint ed. 18.95 (*0-8369-8931-7*) Ayer.

***Southern Christmas Book: The Full Story from Earliest Times to Present - People, Customs, Conviviality, Carols, Cooking.** Harnett T. Kane. 337p. 1997. reprint ed. lib. bdg. 40.00 (*0-7808-0272-1*) Omnigraphics Inc.

***Southern Circle.** Drumbeat Publishing Staff. Date not set. pap. text ed. write for info. (*0-582-78520-0*, Drumbeat) Longman.

Southern Cities, Southern Schools: Public Education in the Urban South. Ed. by David N. Plank & Rick Ginsberg. LC 89-49230. (Contributions to the Study of Education Ser.: No. 38). 296p. 1990. text ed. 55.00 (*0-313-26297-7*, GIB/, Greenwood Pr) Greenwood.

Southern City: National Ambition The Growth of Early Washington, D. C., 1800-1860. Ed. by Howard Gillette. (Illus.). 120p. (Orig.). 1995. 17.95 (*1-888028-00-9*) GWU Ctr WAS.

Southern Collection. Estill C. Pennington. LC 92-23560. (Illus.). 1992. 34.95 (*0-9618270-5-X*); pap. 19.95 (*0-9618270-6-8*) Morris Mus Art.

Southern Collection: A Publication of the Morris Museum of Art. Estill C. Pennington. LC 92-23560. 248p. (C). 1992. 39.95 (*0-8203-1534-6*); pap. 24.95 (*0-8203-1535-4*) U of Ga Pr.

Southern Collection - Then & Now. Junior League of Columbus, Georgia, Inc. Staff. Ed. by Susan Mitchell. 286p. 1994. 17.95 (*0-9606300-1-5*) JL Columbus GA.

Southern Colonies: Williamsburg, Jamestown, St. Mary's City. Ed. by Jeanne M. Bracken. (Perspectives on History Ser.: Vol. 31). (Illus.). 64p. (Orig.). 1997. pap. 5.95 (*1-878668-74-9*) Disc Enter Ltd.

Southern Colonies in the Seventeenth Century, 1607-1689. Wesley F. Craven. LC 49-3595. (History of the South Ser.: Vol. 1). (Illus.). xvi, 452p. 1949. text ed. 45.00 (*0-8071-0001-3*) La State U Pr.

Southern Colonies in the Seventeenth Century, 1607-1689. Wesley F. Craven. LC 49-3595. (History of the South Ser.: Vol. 1). (Illus.). xvi, 452p. 1949. pap. text ed. 14.95 (*0-8071-0011-0*) La State U Pr.

Southern Columbia County, New York Families, a Genealogy. Ed. by Arthur C. Kelly. (Illus.). 227p. 1996. lib. bdg. 46.00 (*1-56012-143-2*, 141) Kinship Rhinebeck.

Southern Comfort. Ed. by David Laurents. (Orig.). 1996. mass mkt. 6.50 (*1-56333-466-6*, Badboy) Masquerade.

Southern Comforts. Joann Ross. 1996. mass mkt. 5.99 (*1-55166-167-5*, Mira Bks) Harlequin Bks.

Southern Common People: Studies in Nineteenth-Century Social History. Edward Magdol & Jon L. Wakelyn. LC 79-7724. (Contributions in American History Ser.: No. 86). (Illus.). xii, 386p. (C). 1980. text ed. 65.00 (*0-313-21403-4*, MLL/, Greenwood Pr) Greenwood.

Southern Community in Crisis: Harrison County, Texas, 1850-1880. limited ed. Randolph B. Campbell. LC 83-50844. 460p. 1983. boxed 65.00 (*0-87611-059-6*) Tex St Hist Assn.

An Asterisk (*) at the beginning of an entry indicates that the title is appearing in BIP for the first time.

Southern Cone: Realities of the Authoritarian State in South America. Cesar Caviedes. LC 83-17842. 222p. (C). 1984. text ed. 59.00 (0-86598-109-4, R3907) Rowman.
Southern Cone Nations. William F. Sater. LC 84-5920. (World of Latin America Ser.). (Illus.). 112p. (C). 1984. pap. text ed. 6.95 (0-88273-606-X) Forum Pr IL.
Southern Congregational Churches. Richard H. Taylor. LC 94-90333. 270p. (C). 1994. text ed. 30.00 (0-9622486-2-2) Richard H Taylor.
Southern Connection. Robert B. Heilman. LC 90-40452. 296p. 1991. text ed. 37.50 (0-8071-1631-9) La State U Pr.
***Southern Cooking.** Art Ginsburg. (Mr. Food Ser.). Date not set. write for info. (0-688-14580-9) Morrow.
Southern Cooking. Marjie Lambert. 1994. 17.98 (0-7858-0025-5) Bk Sales Inc.
Southern Cooking. Jillian Stewart. LC 93-85547. (Illus.). 96p. 1994. 12.98 (1-56138-372-4) Courage Bks.
Southern Cooking. Henrietta Dull. LC 88-19299. (Illus.). 352p. 1989. reprint ed. 18.95 (0-87797-151-X) Cherokee.
Southern Cooking from Mary Mac's Tea Room. Margaret Lupo. LC 93-38488. 320p. 1993. reprint ed. pap. 14.95 (0-87797-257-5) Cherokee.
Southern Cooking Plus One Cup History. Lorine O. Hendricks. (Illus.). 288p. 1991. 15.95 (0-9629256-0-8) Southern Cooking.
Southern Cooking to Remember. Kathryn T. Windham. (Muscadine Bk.). 1994. reprint ed. pap. 15.95 (0-87805-746-3) U Pr of Miss.
Southern Country Cooking. 160p. 1993. spiral bd. 5.95 (0-941016-90-0) Penfield.
Southern Country Editor. T. D. Clark. 1992. 14.50 (0-8446-1115-8) Peter Smith.
Southern Country Editor. John G. Sproat. LC 91-10189. (Southern Classics Ser.). 382p. 1991. reprint ed. text ed. 29.95 (0-87249-766-6); reprint ed. pap. text ed. 14.95 (0-87249-767-4) U of SC Pr.
Southern Cross. Jon Klein. 1991. pap. 5.25 (0-8222-1061-4) Dramatists Play.
Southern Cross. Jack McKinney. (Robotech Ser.: No. 7). 224p. (Orig.). 1987. mass mkt. 4.95 (0-345-34140-6, Del Rey) Ballantine.
Southern Cross. Kevin Siembieda. Ed. by Alex Marciniszyn. (Robotech RPG Ser.: Bk. 4). (Illus.). 112p. (Orig.). (YA). (gr. 8 up). 1987. pap. 11.95 (0-916211-27-4, 553) Palladium Bks.
***Southern Cross.** Ed. by Reinhard Zimmermann & Daniel Visser. 900p. 1996. 120.00 (0-7021-3861-4, Pub. by Juta SA) Gaunt.
Southern Cross: Civil Law & Common Law in South Africa. Ed. by Reinhard Zimmermann & Daniel Visser. 500p. 1997. 125.00 (0-19-826087-3) OUP.
Southern Cross: The Beginnings of the Bible Belt. Christine Leigh Heyrman. LC 97-6354. 1997. 27.50 (0-679-44638-9) Random.
Southern Cross Saints: The Mormons in Australia. Marjorie Newton. LC 91-8229. (Mormons in the Pacific Ser.). (Illus.). 312p. (Orig.). 1991. pap. 12.95 (0-939154-49-8) Inst Polynesian.
Southern Daughter: The Life of Margaret Mitchell. Darden A. Pyron. (Illus.). 576p. 1991. 30.00 (0-19-505276-5) OUP.
Southern Decoys of Virginia & the Carolinas. Henry A. Fleckenstein, Jr. LC 83-61650. (Illus.). 232p. 1983. 39.50 (0-916838-86-2) Schiffer.
Southern Deer & Deer Hunting. Larry Weishuhn. LC 95-77306. (Illus.). 256p. 1995. pap. text ed. 14.95 (0-87341-335-0, SDD01) Krause Pubns.
Southern Delights. Williamson County Chamber of Commerce Staff. LC 92-33339. 1992. 13.50 (0-87197-357-X) Favorite Recipes.
Southern Democrats. Nicol C. Rae. LC 93-32876. 224p. 1994. pap. 16.95 (0-19-508709-7) OUP.
Southern Derringers of the Mississippi Valley. Turner Kirkland. 1972. 4.00 (0-913150-00-2) Pioneer Pr.
Southern Diegueno Customs. fac. ed. Leslie Spier. (University of California Publications in American Archaeology & Ethnology: Vol. 20: 16). 83p. (C). 1923. reprint ed. pap. text ed. 7.50 (1-55567-252-3) Coyote Press.
Southern Discomfort. Rita Mae Brown. 320p. 1983. mass mkt. 6.50 (0-553-27446-5, Bantam Classics) Bantam.
Southern Discomfort. Margaret Maron. 224p. 1994. mass mkt. 5.50 (0-446-40080-7, Mysterious Paperbk) Warner Bks.
Southern Discomfort, Bk. II. Margaret Maron. 256p. 1993. 17.95 (0-89296-446-4) Mysterious Pr.
Southern Echoes. Louise Pike. LC 72-1519. (Black Heritage Library Collection). 1977. reprint ed. 15.95 (0-8369-9046-3) Ayer.
Southern Economic Journal: Cumulative Index, Vols. 1-49. Ed. by Vincent J. Tarascio. LC 84-27781. 240p. 1985. 143.75 (0-89232-455-4) Jai Pr.
Southern Elegance: A Collection of the Best of Carolina Cuisine. Junior League Staff. 1987. 15.95 (0-9621734-0-1) JL Gaston.
***Southern Elephant Seal.** Jason Cooper. LC 96-52193. (Giants among Us Ser.). (J). 1997. write for info. (1-55916-188-4) Rourke Bk Co.
Southern Employer's Guide: A Handbook of Employment Laws & Regulations. Ed. by Charles Lewis. LC 93-11897. 618p. 1996. ring bd. 92.50 (1-56759-008-X) Summers Pr.
Southern Enchantment. Sierra Leone. 256p. (Orig.). 1995. pap. text ed. 3.95 (1-877606-02-2) R Romance.
Southern Encounters: Southerners of Note in Ralph McGill's South. Ralph McGill. Ed. by Calvin M. Logue. LC 83-953. 344p. 1982. 23.50 (0-86554-050-0, MUP-H048) Mercer Univ Pr.
Southern Enigma: Essays on Race, Class, & Folk Culture. Ed. by Walter J. Fraser, Jr. & Winfred B. Moore, Jr. LC 82-20966. (Contributions in American History Ser.: No. 105). (Illus.). x, 240p. 1983. text ed. 55.00 (0-313-23640-2, FSE/) Greenwood.
Southern Enterprize: The Work of National Evangelical Societies in the Antebellum South. John W. Kuykendall. LC 81-23723. (Contributions to the Study of Religion Ser.: No. 7). xv, 188p. 1982. text ed. 49.95 (0-313-23212-1, KSE/, Greenwood Pr) Greenwood.
Southern Entertaining Cookbook with a New Twist. Lucy Cooper. 1988. pap. 12.95 (0-942084-90-X) SeaSide Pub.
Southern Essays of Richard M. Weaver. Richard M. Weaver. Ed. by James J. Thompson, Jr. LC 87-2624. xxii, 288p. 1987. 12.00 (0-86597-057-2); pap. 5.50 (0-86597-058-0) Liberty Fund.
Southern Europe: A Systematic Geographical Study. Monica Beckinsale & Robert P. Beckinsale. LC 74-14940. (Illus.). 352p. 1975. 55.00 (0-8419-0178-3) Holmes & Meier.
Southern Europe see International Dictionary of Historic Places
Southern Europe since 1945: Tradition & Modernity in Portugal, Spain, Italy, Greece & Turkey. Guilio Sapelli. 320p. (C). 1996. pap. text ed. 29.50 (0-582-07065-1, 76978, Pub. by Longman UK) Longman.
Southern Europe since 1945: Tradition & Modernity in Portugal, Spain, Italy, Greece & Turkey. Guilio Sapelli. Tr. by Ann Fuller. LC 95-8640. 320p. (C). 1996. text ed. 58.95 (0-582-07064-3, 76979) Longman.
Southern Europe Transformed: Political & Economic Change in Greece, Italy, Portugal & Spain. Ed. by Allan M. Williams. 320p. (C). 1984. 36.00 (0-317-93196-2, Pub. by P Chapman Pub UK) St Mut.
Southern European Security in the 1990s. Ed. by Roberto Aliboni. LC 92-10508. 1992. text ed. 59.00 (1-85567-023-2) St Martin.
Southern European Studies Guide: Critical Guide to the Academic Literature. Ed. by Sean Loughlin. 256p. 1994. lib. bdg. 70.00 (0-86291-786-7) Bowker-Saur.
***Southern European Welfare States: Between Crisis & Reform.** Martin Rhodes. LC 97-10305. 296p. 1997. 39.50 (0-7146-4788-8, Pub. by F Cass Pubs UK); pap. 19.50 (0-7146-4344-0, Pub. by F Cass Pubs UK) Intl Spec Bk.
Southern Evangelicals & the Social Order, 1800-1860. Anne C. Loveland. LC 80-11200. xiv, 354p. 1980. pap. text ed. 17.95 (0-8071-0783-2) La State U Pr.
Southern Exposure. Alice Adams. 1996. mass mkt. write for info. (0-449-14949-8) Fawcett.
Southern Exposure. Alice Adams. 320p. 1996. pap. 12.00 (0-449-91113-6) Fawcett.
Southern Exposure. Stetson Kennedy. 384p. (C). 1991. pap. 17.95 (0-8130-1078-0) U Press Fla.
***Southern Exposure.** Marvin Woods. 1998. write for info. (0-517-70850-7, C P Pubs) Crown Pub Group.
Southern Exposure. large type ed. Alice Adams. LC 96-10296. 1996. pap. 22.95 (1-56895-324-0) Wheeler Pub.
Southern Exposure: A Novel. Alice Adams. LC 95-16109. 304p. 1995. 23.00 (0-679-44452-1) Knopf.
Southern Exposure: Canadian Promoters in Latin America & the Caribbean, 1896-1930. Christopher Armstrong & H. V. Nelles. (Illus.). 391p. (C). 1988. 40.00 (0-8020-2660-5) U of Toronto Pr.
Southern Exposure: Manuscript Edition. Owen Crump. 1957. pap. 13.00 (0-8222-1310-9) Dramatists Play.
Southern Exposure: Not a Regional Exhibition. Alternative Museum Staff. LC 85-71155. (Illus.). 56p. (Orig.). (C). 1985. pap. text ed. 8.00 (0-932075-02-9) Alternative Mus.
Southern Exposure Turns Twenty: A Special Anniversary Edition. Ed. by Eric R. Bates. (Southern Exposure Ser.). (Illus.). 127p. (Orig.). (C). 1993. pap. 8.95 (0-943810-56-6) Inst Southern Studies.
Southern Expressions: A Sense of Self. (Illus.). 48p. 1988. pap. 2.00 (0-939802-48-1) High Mus Art.
Southern Expressions: Points of View. (Illus.). 47p. 1989. pap. 7.50 (0-939802-56-2) High Mus Art.
Southern Expressions: Tales Untold. Susan Krane & Carrie Pryzbilla. (Illus.). 48p. 1991. pap. 12.95 (0-939802-70-8) High Mus Art.
Southern Fairfield County. CCS Inc. Staff. (Street Directions Without a Map Ser.). 180p. 1992. pap. 14.95 (1-881638-02-2) CCS Inc.
Southern Family. Gail Godwin. 604p. 1988. mass mkt. 6.99 (0-380-70313-0) Avon.
***Southern Family.** Gail Godwin. 544p. 1997. reprint ed. pap. 13.00 (0-380-72987-3) Avon.
Southern Family Favorites. Carla Capalbo. (Illus.). 64p. 1995. 5.98 (0-8317-7459-2) Smithmark.
Southern Fictions. Ed. by Monroe K. Spears. (Illus.). 80p. 1983. pap. 12.50 (0-936080-11-6) Cont Arts Museum.
Southern Fire: Naval Exploits of the Confederacy. R. Thomas Campbell. LC 96-29725. 250p. 1997. 24.95 (1-57249-046-2) White Mane Pub.
Southern Fires. Mary L. Baxter. 368p. (Orig.). 1996. pap. 5.99 (0-446-60204-3) Warner Bks.
Southern Fish & Seafood Cookbook. 3rd ed. Jon Wongrey. LC 80-50790. (Illus.). 141p. 1975. pap. 9.95 (0-87844-026-7) Sandlapper Pub Co.
Southern Florida: Eastern North America as Seen by a Botanist: Pictorial. III. Supplement. In-Cho Chung. (Illus.). 64p. (Orig.). 1992. pap. 27.50 (0-9622951-4-0) IC Chung.
Southern Flower Gardening. fac. ed. William D. Adams. LC 79-29715. (Illus.). 94p. pap. 26.80 (0-7837-7407-9, 2047201) Bks Demand.
Southern Folk Ballads, Vol. I. W. K. McNeil. LC 87-751904. (American Folklore Ser.). 220p. 1987. 24.95 (0-87483-038-9); pap. 11.95 (0-87483-039-7) August Hse.
Southern Folk Ballads, Vol. II. W. K. McNeil. (American Folklore Ser.). 1988. pap. 11.95 (0-87483-046-X) August Hse.
Southern Folk, Plain & Fancy: Native White Social Types. John S. Reed. LC 86-1479. (Brown Thrasher Bks.). (Illus.). 136p. 1988. pap. 12.95 (0-8203-1023-9) U of Ga Pr.
Southern Folly. large type ed. Paula Allardyce. 382p. 1982. 25.99 (0-7089-0831-4) Ulverscroft.
Southern Food: At Home, on the Road, in History. John Egerton. LC 92-50828. (Chapel Hill Bks.). 416p. 1993. pap. 18.95 (0-8078-4417-9) U of NC Pr.
Southern Forages. 2nd ed. Donald M. Ball et al. (Illus.). 264p. (C). 1996. pap. text ed. write for info. (0-9629598-2-0) PPI.
Southern Forest: A Chronicle. Laurence C. Walker. (Illus.). 336p. 1991. 32.95 (0-292-77648-9) U of Tex Pr.
***Southern France.** (Charming Small Hotels Ser.). (Illus.). 192p. (Orig.). 1997. pap. 14.95 (1-55650-796-8) Hunter NJ.
Southern France: Off the Beaten Track. LC 93-47309. (Illus.). 320p. 1994. pap. 14.95 (1-56440-458-7, Pub. by Moorland Pubng UK) Globe Pequot.
***Southern France Map.** 1997. 6.95 (2-06-700919-2, 919) Michelin.
Southern Fried. William P. Fox, Jr. LC 83-46019. (Classics of Modern American Humor Ser.). reprint ed. 24.00 (0-404-19931-3) AMS Pr.
Southern Fried Cracker Tales (Playscript) Judith Kase-Polisini. (J). 1994. 5.00 (0-87602-329-4) Anchorage.
***Southern Fried Murder: A Dinner Theater Comedy/Murder Mystery.** Billy St. John. 104p. (Orig.). 1997. pap. 5.00 (0-87440-036-8) Bakers Plays.
Southern Fried Plus Six. William P. Fox. LC 91-32588. 255p. 1991. 13.95 (0-87844-106-9) Sandlapper Pub Co.
Southern Fried Rat & Other Gruesome Tales. Daniel Cohen. 128p. (J). (gr. 5). 1989. pap. 3.50 (0-380-70655-5, Flare) Avon.
Southern Fried Rock. Friedman-Fairfax & Sony Music Staff. (Life, Times & Music Book/CD Ser.). 1995. pap. 16.98 incl. audio compact disk (1-56799-232-3, Friedman-Fairfax) M Friedman Pub Grp Inc.
Southern Front. Alejandro Murguia. LC 89-7336. 128p. 1990. pap. 11.00 (0-916950-97-2) Biling Rev-Pr.
Southern Front: History & Politics in the Cultural War. Eugene D. Genovese. 336p. (C). 1995. text ed. 29.95 (0-8262-1001-5) U of Mo Pr.
Southern Frontiers, 1607-1860: The Agricultural Frontiers of the Colonial & Antebellum South. John S. Otto. LC 88-32793. (Contributions in American History Ser.: No. 133). 190p. 1989. text ed. 49.95 (0-313-26092-3, OSF, Greenwood Pr) Greenwood.
***Southern Furniture 1680-1830: The Colonial Williamsburg Collection.** Ronald L. Hurst et al. LC 97-11154. (Williamsburg Decorative Arts Ser.). 1997. write for info. (0-87935-200-0) Colonial Williamsburg.
***Southern Furniture 1680-1830: The Colonial Williamsburg Collection.** Ronald L. Hurst et al. LC 97-11154. (Williamsburg Decorative Arts Ser.). 1997. write for info. (0-8109-4175-9) Abrams.
Southern Galaxy Catalogue: A Catalogue of 5481 Galaxies South of Declination-17 Degress Found on 1.2m U. K. Schmidt IIIa-J Plates. Harold G. Corwin et al. LC 85-50556. (Monographs in Astronomy: No. 4). 342p. (Orig.). 1985. pap. write for info. (0-9603796-3-0) U of Tex Dept Astron.
Southern Garden: Fiftieth Anniversary Edition. rev. ed. Elizabeth Lawrence. LC 90-44658. (Illus.). xxxvi, 252p. (C). 1991. reprint ed. pap. 16.95 (0-8078-4355-5) U of NC Pr.
Southern Garden: Fiftieth Anniversary Edition. 4th rev. ed. Elizabeth Lawrence. LC 90-44658. (Illus.). xxxvi, 252p. (C). 1991. reprint ed. 24.95 (0-8078-1962-X) U of NC Pr.
Southern Gardener's Book of Lists: The Best Plants for All Your Needs, Wants, & Whims. Lois T. Chaplin. LC 93-44529. (Illus.). 192p. 1994. pap. 17.95 (0-87833-844-6) Taylor Pub.
Southern Gardening: A Complete Handbook. Charles J. Hudson, Jr. (Illus.). 464p. 1996. reprint ed. pap. 15.95 (0-89176-088-1) R Bemis Pub.
Southern Gardens, Southern Gardening. William L. Hunt. LC 81-69425. (Illus.). 208p. 1992. 19.95 (0-8223-0463-5); pap. text ed. 15.95 (0-8223-1223-9) Duke.
Southern Gates of Arabia: A Journey in the Hadhramaut. Freya Stark. 365p. 1994. 24.95 (1-85695-210-X, Pub. by ISIS UK) Transaction Pubs.
Southern Germany. Hunter. (Visitor's Guides Ser.). (Illus.). 256p. (Orig.). 1991. pap. 14.95 (1-55650-475-6) Hunter NJ.
Southern Ghost. Carolyn G. Hart. (Annie Darling Ser.). 320p. 1993. mass mkt. 5.99 (0-553-56275-4) Bantam.
Southern Ghosts. Nancy Roberts. LC 86-21955. (Illus.). 72p. (J). (gr. 4 up). 1987. reprint ed. pap. 7.95 (0-87844-075-5) Sandlapper Pub Co.
Southern Girls. Sheri Bailey & Dura Temple. 64p. 1996. pap. 5.25 (0-87129-659-4, SB2) Dramatic Pub.
Southern Gold. James A. Vitti. LC 95-2256. 1995. 12.99 (0-7852-7781-1) Nelson.
Southern Gothic: Of Remembering & Releasing. J. Michael Clark. 1991. pap. 10.00 (0-938659-04-9) Scholars Bks.
Southern Gourmet: Upscale Southern Dining for the Down-Home Kitchen. Virginia C. Robbins. 1995. 13.95 (0-9649067-0-8) Precision Foods.
Southern Governors & Civil Rights: Racial Segregation As a Campaign Issue in the Second Reconstruction. Earl Black. 446p. 1976. 42.50 (0-674-82510-1) HUP.
Southern Harmony & Musical Companion. William Walker. Ed. by Glenn C. Wilcox. LC 93-14113. 360p. (C). 1993. 29.95 incl. cd-rom (0-8131-1859-X) U Pr of Ky.
***Southern Harvest.** Clare Leighton. LC 97-16773. (Illus.). 176p. 1997. reprint ed. 24.95 (0-8203-1948-1) U of Ga Pr.
Southern Harvest: A Collection of Stories. Renato E. Madrid. viii, 187p. (Orig.). 1987. pap. 15.00 (971-10-0297-3, Pub. by New Day Pub PH) Cellar.
Southern Heirloom Garden: A Celebration of Grandmother's Garden. William C. Welch & Greg Grant. LC 94-49724. 208p. 1995. 29.95 (0-87833-877-2) Taylor Pub.
Southern Hemisphere Upper Atmosphere & Ionosphere. Ed. by G. Hernandez & R. W. Smith. (Advances in Space Research (RJ) Ser.: Vol. 16). 164p. 1995. pap. 97.75 (0-08-042625-5, Pergamon Pr) Elsevier.
Southern Herb Growing. Madalene Hill & Gwen Barclay. Ed. by Jean Hardy. (Illus.). 288p. 1987. 29.95 (0-940672-41-3) Shearer Pub.
***Southern Herb Growing.** Madalene Hill & Gwen Barclay. Ed. by Jean Hardy. (Illus.). 288p. 1997. pap. 24.95 (0-940672-66-9) Shearer Pub.
Southern Historian & His Critics. John D. Smith et al. LC 89-26040. (Studies in Historiography: No. 1). 296p. 1990. text ed. 55.00 (0-313-26814-2, SUI/, Greenwood Pr) Greenwood.
Southern Historical Society Papers, 55 vols., Set. Ed. by Lee A. Wallace et al. (Illus.). 1992. reprint ed. 1,700.00 (0-916107-98-1) Broadfoot.
Southern Historical Society Papers, Vol. XVII. Ed. by R. A. Brock. 438p. 1991. reprint ed. 40.00 (1-56837-120-9) Broadfoot.
Southern Historical Society Papers, Vol. XVIII. Ed. by R. A. Brock. 435p. 1991. reprint ed. 40.00 (1-56837-121-7) Broadfoot.
Southern Historical Society Papers, Vol. XIX. Ed. by R. A. Brock. (Illus.). 417p. 1991. reprint ed. 40.00 (1-56837-122-5) Broadfoot.
Southern Historical Society Papers, Vol. XX. Ed. by R. A. Brock. 401p. 1991. reprint ed. 40.00 (1-56837-123-3) Broadfoot.
Southern Historical Society Papers, Vol. XXI. Ed. by R. A. Brock. (Illus.). 383p. 1991. reprint ed. 40.00 (1-56837-124-1) Broadfoot.
Southern Historical Society Papers, Vol. XXII. Ed. by R. A. Brock. 389p. 1991. reprint ed. 40.00 (1-56837-125-X) Broadfoot.
Southern Historical Society Papers, Vol. XXIII. Ed. by R. A. Brock. (Illus.). 383p. 1991. reprint ed. 40.00 (1-56837-126-8) Broadfoot.
Southern Historical Society Papers, Vol. XXIV. Ed. by R. A. Brock. 380p. 1991. reprint ed. 40.00 (1-56837-127-6) Broadfoot.
Southern Historical Society Papers, Vol. XXV. Ed. by R. A. Brock. 384p. 1991. reprint ed. 40.00 (1-56837-128-4) Broadfoot.
Southern Historical Society Papers, Vol. XXVI. Ed. by R. A. Brock. 380p. 1991. reprint ed. 40.00 (1-56837-129-2) Broadfoot.
Southern Historical Society Papers, Vol. XXVII. Ed. by R. A. Brock. 384p. 1991. reprint ed. 40.00 (1-56837-130-6) Broadfoot.
Southern Historical Society Papers, Vol. XXVIII. Ed. by R. A. Brock. 384p. 1991. reprint ed. 40.00 (1-56837-131-4) Broadfoot.
Southern Historical Society Papers, Vol. XXIX. Ed. by R. A. Brock. (Illus.). 372p. 1991. reprint ed. 40.00 (1-56837-132-2) Broadfoot.
Southern Historical Society Papers, Vol. XXX. Ed. by R. A. Brock. 372p. 1991. reprint ed. 40.00 (1-56837-133-0) Broadfoot.
Southern Historical Society Papers, Vol. XXXI. Ed. by R. A. Brock. 372p. 1991. reprint ed. 40.00 (1-56837-134-9) Broadfoot.
Southern Historical Society Papers, Vol. XXXII. Ed. by R. A. Brock. 372p. 1991. reprint ed. 40.00 (1-56837-135-7) Broadfoot.
Southern Historical Society Papers, Vol. XXXIII. Ed. by R. A. Brock. 376p. 1991. reprint ed. 40.00 (1-56837-136-5) Broadfoot.
Southern Historical Society Papers, Vol. XXXIV. Ed. by R. A. Brock. 372p. 1991. reprint ed. 40.00 (1-56837-137-3) Broadfoot.
Southern Historical Society Papers, Vol. XXXV. Ed. by R. A. Brock. 372p. 1991. reprint ed. 40.00 (1-56837-138-1) Broadfoot.
Southern Historical Society Papers, Vol. XXXVI. Ed. by R. A. Brock. (Illus.). 372p. 1991. reprint ed. 40.00 (1-56837-139-X) Broadfoot.
Southern Historical Society Papers, Vol. XXXVII. Ed. by R. A. Brock. (Illus.). 372p. 1991. reprint ed. 40.00 (1-56837-140-3) Broadfoot.
Southern Historical Society Papers, Vol. XXXVIII. Ed. by R. A. Brock. 384p. 1991. reprint ed. 40.00 (1-56837-141-1) Broadfoot.
Southern Historical Society Papers Index, 3 vols., Set. Ed. by Lee A. Wallace et al. 1768p. 1992. 150.00 (0-916107-99-X) Broadfoot.
Southern History of the War. Edward A. Pollard. 1990. 14.99 (0-517-22899-8) Random Hse Value.
Southern History of the War, 2 vols. Edward A. Pollard. LC 79-95075. (Select Bibliographies Reprint Ser.). 1977. reprint ed. 72.95 (0-8369-5075-5) Ayer.
Southern Homes: Over Two Hundred Home Plans for the South & Southeast. Home Planners, Inc. Staff. 1994. pap. 8.95 (1-881955-18-4) Home Planners.
Southern Honor: Ethics & Behavior in the Old South. Bertram Wyatt-Brown. 597p. 1983. pap. 17.95 (0-19-503310-8) OUP.
Southern Horizons. Williams Haynes. LC 78-152174. (Essay Index Reprint Ser.). 1977. reprint ed. 24.95 (0-8369-2366-9) Ayer.

S

An Asterisk (*) at the beginning of an entry indicates that the title is appearing in BIP for the first time.

Southern Horrors. Royster. 1997. pap. 12.95 (0-312-14994-8) St Martin.

Southern Horrors & Other Writings: The Anti-Lynching Campaign of Ida B. Wells, 1892-1900. Ida B. Wells. Ed. & Intro. by J. Jones Royster. (Bedford Series in History & Culture). 176p. 1996. text ed. 35.00 (0-312-12812-6) St Martin.

***Southern Hospitality.** Natalie Dupree. Date not set. write for info. (0-688-09768-5) Morrow.

Southern Hospitality. Marion B. Sullivan. 36p. (Orig.). 1991. pap. 3.25 (0-940844-43-5) Wellspring.

Southern Hospitality Cookbook: Menus & Recipes for Entertaining Simply & Graciously. Sara Pitzer. 1993. pap. 11.95 (0-87483-348-5) August Hse.

Southern Humor. Harry L. Watson. (Special Issue of Southern Cultures Ser.: Vol. 1, No. 4). 110p. 1995. pap. 8.00 (0-8223-6427-1) Duke.

***Southern Hunter's Guide.** B. A. S. S. Inc. Staff. (Illus.). 130p. (Orig.). 1994. pap. 4.95 (1-890280-01-1) B A S S.

Southern Hunting in Black & White: Nature, History & Ritual in a Carolina Community. Stuart A. Marks. (Illus.). 345p. 1991. pap. 19.95 (0-691-02851-6); text ed. 49.50 (0-691-09452-7) Princeton U Pr.

Southern Idaho Ghost Towns. Wayne Sparling. LC 73-156484. (Illus.). (Orig.). 1974. pap. 12.95 (0-87004-229-7) Caxton.

Southern Illinois: A Photographer's Love for the Countryside & Its Beauty. Ned Trovillion & Lonnie Russell. (Illus.). 121p. 1995. 34.95 (0-9627422-5-2); pap. 24.95 (0-9627422-6-0) Cache River Pr.

Southern Illinois Album: Farm Security Administration Photographs, 1936-1943. Herbert K. Russell. LC 89-6241. (Illus.). 160p. (C). 1990. pap. text ed. 17.95 (0-8093-1589-0) S Ill U Pr.

Southern Illinois Birds: An Annotated List & Sight Guide. W. Douglas Robinson. LC 95-14767. (Illus.). 480p. (C). 1996. 39.95 (0-8093-2032-0) S Ill U Pr.

Southern Illinois Coal: A Portfolio. C. William Horrell. Ed. by Herbert K. Russell. LC 94-13871. (Shawnee Books Ser.). (Illus.). 128p. (C). 1994. 39.95 (0-8093-1341-3) S Ill U Pr.

Southern Illinois University: A Pictorial History. Betty Mitchell. (Illinois Pictorial History Ser.). (Illus.). 1993. write for info. (0-943963-32-X) G Bradley.

Southern Illinois University Law Journal: 1976-1994/95, 19 vols., Set. 877.50 (0-8377-9142-1) Rothman.

***Southern India.** George Michell. Date not set. pap. 25.95 (0-393-31748-X) Norton.

Southern India Land, People & Culture. F. E. Penny. (C). 1992. 75.00 (81-7305-029-5, Pub. by Aryan Bks Intl II) S Asia.

Southern Indian Boy. Caroline Dormon. (Illus.). (J). 1967. 8.95 (0-87511-027-4) Claitors.

Southern Indian Myths & Legends. Ed. by Virginia P. Brown & Laurella Owens. (Illus.). 160p. (J). (gr. 6-9). 1994. reprint ed. pap. 12.95 (0-912221-05-4) Beechwood.

***Southern Indiana Review.** Ed. by Teresa J. Kramer et al. (Illus.). (Orig.). 1997. pap. text ed. 10.00 (0-9640288-4-0) Univ So IN.

Southern Indiana Review - 1996. Ed. by Martha W. Chapin et al. (Illus.). 145p. 1996. pap. 10.00 (0-9640288-2-4) Univ So IN.

Southern Indians: The Story of the Civilized Tribes Before Removal. R. S. Cotterill. LC 54-5931. (Civilization of the American Indian Ser.: Vol. 38). 259p. 1954. pap. 12.95 (0-8061-1171-2) U of Okla Pr.

Southern Indians & Benjamin Hawkins, 1796-1816. Florette Henri. LC 85-40945. (Illus.). 392p. 1986. 28.95 (0-8061-1968-3) U of Okla Pr.

Southern Indians in the American Revolution. James H. O'Donnell. LC 76-146662. 185p. reprint ed. pap. 52.80 (0-317-28845-8, 2020630) Bks Demand.

Southern Institutes: Or, an Inquiry into the Origin & Early Prevalence of Slavery & the Slave Trade. George S. Sawyer. LC 78-83877. (Black Heritage Library Collection). 1977. 27.95 (0-8369-8648-2) Ayer.

Southern Is... Norton Kratt. 1995. pap. 6.95 (1-56145-113-4) Peachtree Pubs.

***Southern Italy.** Burton Holmes. Ed. by Fred L. Israel & Arthur M. Schlesinger, Jr. (World 100 Years Ago Ser.). (Illus.). 130p. 1997. lib. bdg. 29.95 (0-7910-4672-9) Chelsea Hse.

***Southern Italy.** Burton Holmes. Ed. by Fred L. Israel & Arthur M. Schlesinger, Jr. (World 100 Years Ago Ser.). (Illus.). 130p. 1997. pap. 17.95 (0-7910-4673-7) Chelsea Hse.

Southern Italy. Hunter. (Visitor's Guides Ser.). (Illus.). 224p. (Orig.). 1993. pap. 14.95 (1-55650-578-7) Hunter NJ.

Southern Italy. 8th ed. Paul Blanchard. (Blue Guides Ser.). (Illus.). 416p. 1996. pap. 24.95 (0-393-31418-9, Norton Paperbks) Norton.

***Southern Italy Map.** 1997. 8.95 (2-06-700431-X, 431) Michelin.

Southern Journalism Awards. Ed. & Intro. by Pat Arnow. (Southern Exposure Ser.). (Illus.). 64p. (Orig.). (C). 1996. pap. 5.00 (0-943810-67-1) Inst Southern Studies.

Southern Journey: My Return to the Civil Rights Movement. Tom Dent. LC 96-28395. 320p. 1997. 25.00 (0-688-14099-8) Morrow.

Southern Junction: A History of the American South, 1877-1906. Edward L. Ayers. LC 94-9755. (Illus.). 336p. 1995. pap. 13.95 (0-19-508689-9) OUP.

Southern Junior League Cookbook. Ed. by Ann Seranne. (Illus.). 1977. 12.95 (0-679-50769-8) McKay.

***Southern Justice.** Nathaniel E. Dozier. 147p. (Orig.). reprint ed. pap. 10.00 (1-56411-134-2) Untd Bros & Sis.

Southern Kensington: Brompton. Ed. by Francis H. Sheppard. (Survey of London Ser.: Vol. XLI). (C). 1983. text ed. 110.00 (0-485-48241-X, Pub. by Athlone Pr UK) Humanities.

Southern Kensington: Kensington Square to Earl's Court. Hermione Hobhouse. (Survey of London Ser.: Vol. XLII). (Illus.). 475p. (C). 1986. text ed. 120.00 (0-485-48242-8, Pub. by Athlone Pr UK) Humanities.

Southern Labor & Black Civil Rights: Organizing Memphis Workers, 1929-55. Michael K. Honey. LC 92-28735. (Working Class in American History Ser.). (Illus.). 400p. (C). 1993. text ed. 49.95 (0-252-02000-6); pap. text ed. 17.95 (0-252-06305-8) U of Ill Pr.

***Southern Labor in Transition, 1940-1995.** Robert H. Zieger. LC 97-21057. 1997. write for info. (0-87049-990-4) U of Tenn Pr.

***Southern Lacrimosa: The Mexican War Journal of Dr. Thomas Neely Love, Surgeon, Second Regiment Mississippi Volunteer Infantry, U. S. A.** LC 95-69091. (Illus.). 329p. write for info. (0-614-28355-8) Chickasaw Bayou.

Southern Ladies & Gentlemen. Florence King. 256p. 1993. pap. 10.95 (0-312-09915-0) St Martin.

Southern Lady: From Pedestal to Politics, 1830-1930. Anne F. Scott. (C). 1995. pap. 12.95 (0-8139-1644-5) U Pr of Va.

Southern Land, Known. Gabriel De Foigny. Ed. & Tr. by David Fausett from FRE. (Utopianism & Communitarianism Ser.). 260p. 1992. text ed. 34.95 (0-8156-2571-5) Syracuse U Pr.

Southern Lau, Fiji: An Ethnography. L. Thompson. (BMB Ser.). 1974. reprint ed. 35.00 (0-527-02270-5) Periodicals Srv.

Southern Lawyer: Fifty Years at the Bar. Aubrey L. Brooks. LC 50-10879. 224p. reprint ed. pap. 63.90 (0-7837-5240-7, 2044974) Bks Demand.

Southern League: Baseball in Dixie, 1885-1994. Bill O'Neal. LC 93-47554. 1994. 17.95 (0-89015-952-1) Sunbelt Media.

Southern Legislative Dictionary. Richard Allin. (Illus.). 36p. 1983. pap. 3.95 (0-914546-50-3) Rose Pub.

Southern Lesser Antilles Platform: Pre-Late Miocene Stratigraphy, Structure, & Tectonic Evolution. Ed. by R. C. Speed et al. (Special Papers: No. 277). 1993. pap. 17.50 (0-8137-2277-2) Geol Soc.

Southern Letters. Noble L. Prentis. 1977. text ed. 16.95 (0-8369-9232-6, 9086) Ayer.

Southern Liberal Journalists & the Issue of Race, 1920-1944. John T. Kneebone. LC 85-1104. (Fred W. Morrison Series in Southern Studies). xx, 312p. 1985. 37.50 (0-8078-1660-4) U of NC Pr.

Southern Life, Vol. 1. James A. Lewis. (Illus.). 68p. 1987. pap. 10.00 (0-9617322-4-5) Flat Surface.

Southern Life: Letters of Paul Green, 1916-1981. Ed. by Laurence G. Avery. LC 93-24738. (Fred W. Morrison Series in Southern Studies). (Illus.). 737p. (C). 1994. 49.95 (0-8078-2105-5) U of NC Pr.

Southern Light Cooking: Easy, Healthy, Low-Calorie Recipes from BBQ to Bourbon Peach Shortcake. Charles Pierce. 192p. 1993. pap. 15.95 (0-399-51808-8, Perigee Bks) Berkley Pub.

Southern Lighthouses: Chesapeake Bay to the Gulf of Mexico. 2nd ed. Ray Jones & Bruce Roberts. LC 94-46908. (Lighthouse Ser.). (Illus.). 128p. 1995. pap. 19.95 (1-56440-644-X) Globe Pequot.

Southern Lights & Shadows. Ed. by William Dean Howells & Henry M. Alden. LC 75-83907. (Black Heritage Library Collection). 1977. 17.95 (0-8369-8606-7) Ayer.

Southern Literary Journal & Monthly Magazine, Set. Incl. Vol. 1-3. Old Series. reprint ed. (0-318-57238-9); Set. New Series., 3 vols. reprint ed. 215.00 (0-685-67490-8); 215.00 (0-404-19555-5) AMS Pr.

Southern Literary Messenger, Set. reprint ed. lib. bdg. 2,745.00 (0-404-19556-3) AMS Pr.

Southern Literary Study: Problems & Possibilities. Ed. by Louis D. Rubin, Jr. & C. Hugh Holman. LC 75-11553. 250p. reprint ed. pap. 71.30 (0-8357-3874-4, 2036606) Bks Demand.

Southern Literature & Literary Theory. Jefferson Humphries. LC 89-20282. 400p. 1992. pap. 25.00 (0-8203-1486-2) U of Ga Pr.

Southern Living: All Time Favorite Low Fat Recipes. LC 95-74599. 1996. pap. 14.95 (0-8487-2223-X) Oxmoor Hse.

Southern Living: All Time Favorite Pasta Recipes. LC 96-67712. 1996. pap. 14.95 (0-8487-2224-8) Oxmoor Hse.

Southern Living: Our Best Christmas Recipes. Oxmoor House Staff. 1994. 24.95 (0-8487-1183-1) Oxmoor Hse.

Southern Living All-Time Favorite Chicken Recipes. 144p. 1995. pap. 14.95 (0-8487-2220-5) Oxmoor Hse.

Southern Living All-Time Favorite Cookie Recipes. 144p. 1995. pap. 14.95 (0-8487-2222-1) Oxmoor Hse.

Southern Living All Time Favorite Dessert Recipes. Oxmoor House Staff. 1996. pap. text ed. 14.95 (0-8487-2226-4) Leisure AR.

***Southern Living All-Time Favorite Dessert Recipes.** Souther Living Staff. LC 96-67714. 144p. 1996. pap. 14.95 (0-8487-2228-0, 104056) Oxmoor Hse.

***Southern Living All Time Favorite Light Meals.** Oxmoor House Staff. LC 96-68033. 1996. pap. 14.95 (0-8487-2229-9) Oxmoor Hse.

Southern Living All-Time Favorite Thirty-Minute Meals. 144p. 1995. pap. 14.95 (0-8487-2221-3) Oxmoor Hse.

Southern Living Annual Recipes - 94. Southern Living Staff. 1994. 29.95 (0-8487-1403-2) Oxmoor Hse.

Southern Living Annual Recipes, 1980. Southern Living Staff. LC 79-88364. (Illus.). 352p. 1981. 17.95 (0-8487-0516-5) Oxmoor Hse.

Southern Living Annual Recipes, 1986. Southern Living Staff. (Illus.). 384p. 1986. 19.95 (0-8487-0686-2) Oxmoor Hse.

Southern Living Annual Recipes, 1987. Southern Living Staff. (Illus.). 384p. 1987. 19.95 (0-8487-0717-6) Oxmoor Hse.

Southern Living Annual Recipes, 1988. Southern Living Staff. (Illus.). 1988. 19.95 (0-8487-0733-8) Oxmoor Hse.

Southern Living Annual Recipes, 1990. Southern Living Staff. 1990. 24.95 (0-8487-1032-0) Oxmoor Hse.

Southern Living Annual Recipes, 1992. Southern Living Staff. 352p. 1992. 24.99 (0-8487-1102-5) Oxmoor Hse.

***Southern Living Annual Recipes 1996.** Oxmoor House Staff. 368p. 1996. 29.95 (0-8487-1523-3, 102572) Oxmoor Hse.

***Southern Living Best Recipes Made Lighter.** LC 96-69579. 1997. 29.95 (0-8487-1548-9) Oxmoor Hse.

Southern Living Big Book of Christmas Baking. 160p. 1996. 29.95 (0-8487-1541-1) Oxmoor Hse.

Southern Living Complete Do-Ahead Cookbook. LC 91-60996. 240p. 1993. pap. 14.99 (0-8487-1165-3) Oxmoor Hse.

Southern Living Cookbook. rev. ed. 520p. 1995. 29.95 (0-8487-1471-7) Oxmoor Hse.

Southern Living Courtyards to Country Gardens. Southern Living Staff. 192p. 1992. 40.00 (0-8487-1015-0) Oxmoor Hse.

***Southern Living Garden Guide: Container Gardening.** LC 96-71090. 1998. pap. 12.95 (0-8487-2249-3) Oxmoor Hse.

***Southern Living Garden Guide: Garden Projects.** LC 96-71087. 1998. pap. 12.95 (0-8487-2250-7) Oxmoor Hse.

***Southern Living Garden Guide: Landscaping.** LC 96-71089. 1998. pap. 12.95 (0-8487-2251-5) Oxmoor Hse.

***Southern Living Garden Guide: Lawns & Groundcovers.** LC 96-71088. 1997. pap. 12.95 (0-8487-2248-5) Oxmoor Hse.

Southern Living Garden Guide Annuals. Oxmoor House Staff. LC 95-74602. 1996. pap. 12.95 (0-8487-2240-X) Oxmoor Hse.

***Southern Living Garden Guide Herbs.** LC 96-67709. 1997. pap. 12.95 (0-8487-2247-7) Oxmoor Hse.

Southern Living Garden Guide Perennials. Oxmoor House Staff. LC 95-74603. 1996. pap. 12.95 (0-8487-2241-8) Oxmoor Hse.

Southern Living Garden Guide Shrubs. Oxmoor House Staff. LC 95-74605. 1996. pap. 12.95 (0-8487-2243-4) Oxmoor Hse.

Southern Living Garden Guide to Houseplants. Oxmoor House Staff. LC 96-67716. 128p. 1996. pap. 12.95 (0-8487-2244-2) Oxmoor Hse.

Southern Living Garden Guide Trees. Oxmoor House Staff. LC 95-74604. 1996. pap. 12.95 (0-8487-2242-6) Oxmoor Hse.

***Southern Living Garden Guide Vegetables.** LC 96-67715. 128p. 1996. pap. 12.95 (0-8487-2245-0) Oxmoor Hse.

Southern Living Garden Low Maintenance Gardening. Oxmoor House Staff. LC 96-67717. 1997. 12.95 (0-8487-2246-9) Oxmoor Hse.

Southern Living Holidays & Celebrations. Southern Living Staff. 1994. 24.95 (0-8487-1100-9) Oxmoor Hse.

Southern Living Microwave Cookbook. Margaret C. Agnew. (Illus.). 1988. 19.95 (0-8487-0725-7) Oxmoor Hse.

***Southern Living Our Best Easy Weeknights Favorites.** 1998. 29.95 (0-8487-1631-0) Oxmoor Hse.

***Southern Living Our Best Five-Star Recipes.** LC 96-71641. 1997. 29.95 (0-8487-1567-5) Oxmoor Hse.

***Southern Living Our Best Low-Fat, Low-Calorie Recipes.** 1997. 29.95 (0-8487-1546-2) Oxmoor Hse.

Southern Living Our Best One-Dish Meals. 240p. 1995. 24.95 (0-8487-1438-5) Oxmoor Hse.

***Southern Living Our Best Quick & Easy Recipes.** Southern Living Staff. 240p. 1996. 29.95 (0-8487-1502-0, 102571) Oxmoor Hse.

Southern Living Quick Decorating. LC 93-87429. 160p. 1994. pap. 19.95 (0-8487-1416-4) Oxmoor Hse.

Southern Living 1993 Annual Recipes. Southern Living Staff. LC 79-88364. 365p. 1993. 29.99 (0-8487-1142-4) Oxmoor Hse.

Southern Living 1995 Annual Recipes. Southern Living Staff. 368p. 1995. 29.95 (0-8487-1453-9) Oxmoor Hse.

Southern Living 1995 Garden Annual. annuals 208p. 1995. pap. 14.95 (0-8487-1409-1) Oxmoor Hse.

Southern Love for Christmas. Robert Bernardini. (Illus.). 32p. (J). (gr. k-3). 1993. reprint ed. 14.95 (0-88289-974-0) Pelican.

Southern Loyalists in the Civil War: A Composite Directory of Case Files Created by the U. S. Commissioner of Claims, 1871-1880, Including Those Appealed to the War Claims Committee of the U. S. House of Representatives & the U. S. Court of Claims. Gary B. Mills. 684p. 1994. 45.00 (0-614-03819-7, 3847) Genealog Pub.

Southern Mail. Antoine de Saint-Exupery. Tr. by Curtis Cate. LC 79-182749. 120p. 1972. reprint ed. pap. 7.00 (0-15-683901-6, Harvest Bks) HarBrace.

Southern Massachusetts Cemetery Collection, Vol. 1. Susan Salisbury. 566p. (Orig.). 1995. pap. 38.00 (0-7884-0353-2, S043) Heritage Bk.

***Southern Massachusetts Cemetery Collection, Vol. 2.** Susan Salisbury. x, 467p. (Orig.). 1996. pap. 25.00 (0-7884-0570-5, S042) Heritage Bk.

Southern Mexico & Yucatan Guide. Eric Hamovitch. Ed. by J. Stein. LC 94-66041. 384p. (Orig.). 1995. pap. 14.95 (1-883323-11-8) Open Rd Pub.

Southern Minnesota Fishing Map Guide. James F. Billig. 1996. spiral bd. 16.95 (1-885010-13-3) Sptsmans Connect.

Southern Mountain Folksongs: Traditional Folksongs for Worshiping, for Wooing, for Socializing, for Cradeling, for Working, & Comic Relief. W. K. McNeil. (American Folklore Ser.). 240p. 1992. 24.95 (0-87483-284-5); pap. 12.95 (0-87483-285-3) August Hse.

Southern Mountain Speech. Cratis D. Williams. (Illus.). 151p. (Orig.). (C). 1992. pap. 8.95 (0-938211-07-2) Berea College Pr.

Southern Mountaineers in Silent Films: Plot Synopses of Movies about Moonshining, Feuding, & Other Mountain Topics, 1904-1929. Jerry W. Williamson. LC 93-38738. 328p. 1994. lib. bdg. 52.50 (0-89950-809-X) McFarland & Co.

Southern National Forests. Sharyn Kane & Richard Keeton. LC 93-9514. (National Forests of America Ser.). (Illus.). 160p. (Orig.). 1993. pap. 14.95 (1-56044-131-3) Falcon Pr MT.

Southern Negro Agricultural Worker: 1850-1870. Charles E. Seagrave. LC 75-2596. (Dissertations in American Economic History Ser.). (Illus.). 1978. 19.95 (0-405-07217-1) Ayer.

Southern Nevada Birds: A Seekers Guide. Carolyn K. Titus. 65p. pap. write for info. (0-9635550-0-6) Red Rock Audubon.

***Southern Nevada Retirement & Relocation Guide.** Robert Talley. (Illus.). 350p. (Orig.). 1997. pap. 19.95 (1-56559-102-X) HGI Mrktng.

Southern New England. David Emblidge. (Appalachian Trail Companions Ser.). (Illus.). 240p. 1998. pap. 19.95 (0-8117-2669-X) Stackpole.

***Southern New England.** Henry Wiencek & Paul Rocheleau. (Smithsonian Guide to Historic America Ser.). 1998. write for info. (1-55670-633-2) Stewart Tabori & Chang.

Southern New England: Connecticut, Massachusetts, Rhode Island. Thomas G. Aylesworth & Virginia L. Aylesworth. LC 94-45825. (Discovering America Ser.). (J). 1995. pap. 8.95 (0-7910-3416-X); lib. bdg. 19.95 (0-7910-3398-8) Chelsea Hse.

Southern New England: Massachusetts, Connecticut, Rhode Island. Henry Wiencek. Ed. by Roger G. Kennedy. LC 88-15704. (Smithsonian Guide to Historic America Ser.). (Illus.). 416p. (Orig.). 1989. 24.95 (1-55670-059-8); pap. 18.95 (1-55670-051-2) Stewart Tabori & Chang.

***Southern New England/Hudson Valley Map (U. S. A.)** 1997. 4.95 (2-06-700473-5, 473) Michelin.

Southern New Haven County. CCS Inc. Staff. (Street Directions Without a Map Ser.). 143p. 1992. pap. 14.95 (1-881638-06-5) CCS Inc.

Southern New Hebrides: An Ethnological Record. Clarence B. Humphreys. LC 75-35123. reprint ed. 42.50 (0-404-14139-0) AMS Pr.

Southern New Mexico Empire: First National Bank of Dona Ana Country. Leon C. Metz. LC 90-61912. 1990. 21.00 (0-930208-28-5) Mangan Books TX.

Southern Nights. Margot Dalton. 1994. mass mkt. 3.99 (0-373-82528-5, 1-82528-0) Harlequin Bks.

Southern Nights. Susan Weldon. 352p. 1995. mass mkt. 4.99 (0-8217-5072-0, Zebra Kensgtn) Kensgtn Pub Corp.

Southern Nilotic History: Linguistic Approaches to the Study of the Past. Christopher Ehret. LC 70-116611. 214p. reprint ed. 61.00 (0-8357-9472-5, 2015430) Bks Demand.

Southern Ocean Atlas. A. L. Gordon et al. 291p. (C). 1986. text ed. 285.00 (90-6191-630-5, Pub. by A A Balkema NE) Ashgate Pub Co.

Southern Ocean Ecology: The Biomass Perspective. Ed. by Sayed Z. El-Sayed. LC 92-40608. (Illus.). 400p. (C). 1994. text ed. 69.95 (0-521-44332-6) Cambridge U Pr.

***Southern Odyssey: Selected Writings by Sherwood Anderson.** Sherwood Anderson. Ed. by Welford D. Taylor & Charles E. Modlin. LC 96-30789. 1997. 29.95 (0-8203-1899-X) U of Ga Pr.

Southern Odyssey - Travelers in the Antebellum North. John Hope Franklin. LC 74-27190. (Walter Lynwood Fleming Lectures). (Illus.). 320p. 1976. pap. text ed. 14.95 (0-8071-0351-9) La State U Pr.

Southern of the Western States see Report on the Social Statistics of Cities

Southern Omnibus: Contemporary Southern Short Fiction & Poetry, 2 vols. Ed. by Donald Hays & Leon Stokesbury. 1991. pap. 28.00 (1-55728-163-7) U of Ark Pr.

Southern Ontario: Cross-Country Ski Guide. Terry Burt-Garrans. (Illus.). 176p. pap. 14.95 (1-55046-126-5, Pub. by Boston Mills Pr CN) Genl Dist Srvs.

Southern Oregon: Short Trips into History. Marjorie L. O'Harra. (Illus.). 200p. 1985. pap. 11.95 (0-943388-06-6) South Oregon.

Southern Oregon Cross Country Ski Trails. John W. Lund. (Illus.). 222p. (Orig.). 1987. pap. 9.95 (0-9619389-1-9) J W Lund.

Southern Oregon Restaurants: A Guide to Pleasant Dining in & Around Ashland & Medford. Hadley Nesbitt. LC 96-84998. 144p. (Orig.). 1996. pap. 10.95 (0-9652271-5-4) Bell Rose.

Southern Oregon Wilderness Areas. Donna Aitkenhead. (Illus.). 112p. (Orig.). 1994. pap. 12.95 (0-911518-78-9) F Amato Pubns.

Southern Outcasts: Green, Nolan, & Wood. Coppie Green et al. Ed. by Fred Lauter & Barbara Brennan. 64p. (Orig.). 1990. pap. 8.00 (0-685-63235-0) Moonlight Pubns.

***Southern Outdoors Guide to Deer Hunting: A How-To Treasury - The Best of 25 Years.** B. A. S. S. Inc. Staff. (Illus.). 304p. (Orig.). 1991. pap. 19.95 (1-890280-05-4) B A S S.

Southern Pacific Dieselization. John B. Garmany. Ed. by Pacific Fast Mail Staff. 400p. 1985. 42.50 (0-915713-12-8) Pac Fast Mail.

S

Southern Pacific In Color. David R. Sweetland. (Illus.). 128p. 1992. 49.95 (*1-878887-23-8*) Morning NJ.

Southern Pacific in Oregon. 2nd ed. Ed Austin & Tom Dill. Ed. by Pacific Fast Mail Staff et al. (Illus.). 320p. 1994. 54.50 (*0-915713-14-4*) Pac Fast Mail.

Southern Pacific in the Bay Area: The San Francisco-Sacramento-Stockton Triangle. George H. Drury. (Golden Years of Railroading Ser.: No. 3). (Illus.). 128p. 1996. pap. 18.95 (*0-89024-274-7*, 01070) Kalmbach.

***Southern Pacific in the West, Pt. 2.** Wesley Fox. (Illus.). 160p. 1996. 47.50 (*1-884831-03-6*) Fox Pubns.

Southern Pacific into the 90's. Joseph W. Shine. 200p. (Orig.). 1991. 45.95 (*0-9616874-4-4*); pap. 35.95 (*0-685-75210-0*) Four Ways.

Southern Pacific Passenger Trains Night Trains of the Coast Route. Joseph W. Shine & Dennis Ryan. 190p. (Orig.). 1986. 44.50 (*0-9616874-1-X*) Four Ways.

Southern Pacific Steam Switchers of the Pacific Lines. Gene Deimling. 98p. 1987. pap. 17.95 (*0-9615467-1-9*) Benchmark Ltd.

Southern Pacific, 1901-1985. Don L. Hofsommer. LC 85-40745. (Illus.). 394p. 1989. 49.95 (*0-89096-246-4*) Tex A&M Univ Pr.

Southern Pacific's Blue Streak Merchandise. Fred W. Frailey. 1992. 39.95 (*0-89024-130-9*, 01048) Kalmbach.

Southern Pacific's Coast Line. John R. Signor. LC 95-67525. (Illus.). 314p. 1995. 65.00 (*0-9633791-3-5*) Signature CA.

Southern Pacifics of Mexico & the West Coast Route. John R. Signor. (Illus.). 168p. 1993. 39.95 (*0-87095-099-1*) Gldn West Bks.

Southern Paiute. Edward Sapir. Bd. with Texts of the Kaibab Paiutes & Uintah Utes. LC 76-44081.; Southern Paiute Dictionary. LC 76-44081. LC 76-44081. (Proceedings of the American Academy of Arts & Sciences Ser.: Vol. 65). reprint ed. 87.50 (*0-404-15788-2*) AMS Pr.

Southern Paiute Dictionary see Southern Paiute

Southern Paiute Ethnohistory. Robert C. Euler. (Glen Canyon Ser.: No. 28). reprint ed. 24.00 (*0-404-60678-4*) AMS Pr.

Southern Paiute Ethnology. Isabel T. Kelly. (Glen Canyon Ser.: No. 21). reprint ed. 17.50 (*0-404-60669-5*) AMS Pr.

Southern Paiutes: Legends Lore Language & Lineage. LaVan Martineau. LC 92-74128. (Illus.). 336p. 1992. 24.95 (*0-88714-070-X*) KC Pubns.

Southern Palate Cookbook, Chinese, Jamaican, Cajun, Creole & Southern Recipes. rev. ed. S. L. Foster. LC 91-93136. (Illus.). 130p. (Orig.). 1991. 20.00 (*0-9634263-2-X*); pap. 13.00 (*0-9634263-1-1*); lib. bdg. 15.00 (*0-9634263-3-8*) Abrak-Happy Girl.

Southern Pamphlets on Secession, November 1860-April 1861. Ed. by Jon L. Wakelyn. LC 95-49492. (Civil War America Ser.). 448p. (C). 1996. pap. text ed. 45.00 (*0-8078-2278-7*) U of NC Pr.

***Southern Parties & Elections: Studies in Regional Political Change.** Ed. by Robert P. Steed et al. LC 96-35563. 240p. 1997. pap. text ed. 34.95 (*0-8173-0862-8*) U of Ala Pr.

Southern Passage: Soundings Overland: Tijuana to Tierra del Fuego. Sandy S. McMath. (Illus.). 543p. (C). 1993. 34.95 (*0-9622515-2-6*) Columbus & Co.

Southern Passion Edited from Pepysian Ms. (EETS, OS Ser.: No. 169). 1974. reprint ed. 45.00 (*0-527-00166-X*) Periodicals Srv.

Southern Passions. large type ed. Sara Wood. (Harlequin Ser.). 1993. lib. bdg. 19.95 (*0-263-13543-8*) Thorndike Pr.

Southern Photographs. William Christenberry. (Illus.). 138p. 1983. 40.00 (*0-89381-110-6*) Aperture.

Southern Photographs. deluxe limited ed. William Christenberry. (Illus.). 138p. 1983. 750.00 (*0-89381-130-0*) Aperture.

Southern Pine Beetle: Annotated Bibliography, 1868-1982. David L. Kulhavy & Paul C. Johnson. (Illus.). 95p. 1983. pap. text ed. 8.00 (*0-938361-01-5*) Austin Univ Forestry.

Southern Pioneers in Social Interpretation. Ed. by Howard W. Odum. LC 67-23254. (Essay Index Reprint Ser.). 1977. 19.95 (*0-8369-0750-7*) Ayer.

Southern Plantation: A Study in the Development & the Accuracy of a Tradition. F. P. Gaines. 1990. 14.50 (*0-8446-1193-X*) Peter Smith.

Southern Plantation Cookbook. Corinne C. Geer. 1976. 9.95 (*0-9601508-1-1*) C C Geer.

Southern Plantation Overseer As Revealed in His Letters. John S. Bassett. (History - United States Ser.). 280p. 1992. reprint ed. lib. bdg. 79.00 (*0-7812-6152-X*) Rprt Serv.

Southern Plantation Stories & Sketches. George E. Wiley. LC 78-161277. (Black Heritage Library Collection). (Illus.). 1977. reprint ed. 18.95 (*0-8369-8836-1*) Ayer.

Southern Poets. Edd W. Parks. LC 74-93251. 567p. (C). 1970. reprint ed. 75.00 (*0-87753-032-7*) Phaeton.

Southern Pointe Shamanism. fac. ed. Isabel J. Kelly. Ed. by Robert H. Lowie et al. (University of California Publications: No. 2:4). 21p. (C). 1939. reprint ed. pap. 2.15 (*1-55567-123-3*) Coyote Press.

***Southern Political Reader: Change & Continuity in Southern Politics.** Ed. by Charles S. Bullock, III & Mark J. Rozell. 250p. 1997. 63.00 (*0-8476-8612-4*) Rowman.

***Southern Political Reader: Change & Continuity in Southern Politics.** Ed. by Charles S. Bullock, III & Mark J. Rozell. 250p. (Orig.). 1997. pap. 19.95 (*0-8476-8613-2*) Rowman.

Southern Politics in State & Nation. V. O. Key. LC 84-3665. 752p. 1984. text ed. 40.00 (*0-87049-434-1*); pap. text ed. 18.00 (*0-87049-435-X*) U of Tenn Pr.

Southern Politics Since the Civil War. Monroe L. Billington. LC 83-23885. 208p. 1984. pap. 11.50 (*0-89874-673-6*) Krieger.

Southern Primaries & Elections 1920-1949. Alexander Heard & Donald S. Strong. LC 70-130551. (Select Bibliographies Reprint Ser.). 1977. 27.95 (*0-8369-5524-2*) Ayer.

Southern Progressive Periodicals Directory. Craig T. Canan. LC 80-644934. 1983. 8.00 (*0-935396-01-2*) Prog Educ.

Southern Progressivism: The Reconciliation of Progress & Tradition. Dewey W. Grantham. LC 82-25918. (Twentieth-Century America Ser.). (Illus.). 490p. (C). 1983. text ed. 45.00 (*0-87049-389-2*); pap. text ed. 22.50 (*0-87049-390-6*) U of Tenn Pr.

Southern Prose Writers. Ed. by Gregory L. Paine. LC 79-101832. (Biography Index Reprint Ser.). 1977. 39.95 (*0-8369-8006-9*) Ayer.

Southern Prose Writers: Representative Selections. Gregory L. Paine. (BCL1-PS American Literature Ser.). 392p. 1993. reprint ed. lib. bdg. 89.00 (*0-7812-6930-X*) Rprt Serv.

Southern Prospect Development. David W. Felder. 48p. 1996. pap. text ed. 8.95 (*0-910959-73-0*, B&G 14D) Wellington Pr.

Southern Quarterly Review, Set. reprint ed. lib. bdg. 2,295.00 (*0-404-19557-1*) AMS Pr.

Southern Question. Antonio Gramsci. Tr. & Intro. by Pasquale Verdicchio. (VIA Folios Ser.). xvi, 45p. (C). 1995. pap. 5.00 (*1-884419-04-6*) Bordighera.

Southern Quilts: A New View. Bets Ramsey & Gail Trechsel. LC 91-425. (Illus.). 96p. (Orig.). 1991. pap. 12.50 (*0-939009-52-8*) EPM Pubns.

Southern Railroad Man: Conductor N. J. Bell's Recollections of the Civil War Era. Nimrod J. Bell. Ed. by James A. Ward. LC 93-34199. (Illus.). 232p. (C). 1994. 25.00 (*0-87580-184-6*) N Ill U Pr.

Southern Railway: From Stevenson to Memphis: A History of the Southern Railroad in Memphis. Jack Daniel. LC 96-76332. (Illus.). 384p. (Orig.). 1996. pap. 24.95 (*1-884289-17-7*) Grandmother Erth.

Southern Railway: Road of the Innovators. Burke Davis. LC 84-15343. 317p. reprint ed. pap. 90.40 (*0-7837-0288-4*, 2040609) Bks Demand.

Southern Railway Vol. 7: Steam-Locomotives & Trains 1935 to 1937. Robert K. Durham. (Illus.). 52p. (Orig.). 1996. pap. 14.95 (*0-9644480-6-8*) R K Durham.

Southern Railway Color Guide to Freight & Passenger Equipment. James Kinkaid. (Illus.). 128p. 1996. 49.95 (*1-878887-60-2*) Morning NJ.

Southern Railway Depots: North Carolina, Vol. 1. Ralph Ward. LC 91-92877. (Illus.). 72p. (Orig.). 1991. pap. 19.95 (*0-9622999-1-X*) R Ward.

Southern Railway Depots Vol. 2. Ralph Ward. LC 91-92877. (Illus.). 64p. (Orig.). 1994. pap. 19.95 (*0-9622999-3-6*) R Ward.

Southern Railway In Color. Fred D. Cheney & David R. Sweetland. LC 92-63038. (Illus.). 128p. 1993. 49.95 (*1-878887-14-9*) Morning NJ.

Southern Railway Varnish, 1964-1979: An All-Color Pictorial. rev. ed. Ralph Ward. LC 86-91666. (Illus.). 88p. (Orig.). 1993. pap. 18.95 (*0-9622999-2-8*) R Ward.

Southern Railway 1923-47: Steam on the Portsmouth Direct Line. E. J. Rose. (Illus.). 144p. 1996. 30.95 (*0-7509-1195-6*, Pub. by Sutton Pubng UK) Bks Intl VA.

Southern Rapture. Jennifer Blake. 1987. pap. 8.95 (*0-449-90177-7*) Fawcett.

Southern Rapture. Jennifer Blake. 1991. mass mkt. 5.95 (*0-449-14729-0*, GM) Fawcett.

Southern Reason, Western Rhyme. Sharon Brondos. 1992. mass mkt. 3.39 (*0-373-70527-1*, 1-70527-6) Harlequin Bks.

Southern Rebel: The Life & Times of Aubrey Willis Williams 1890-1965. John A. Salmond. LC 81-23087. (Fred W. Morrison Series in Southern Studies). 349p. reprint ed. pap. 99.50 (*0-7837-2462-4*, 2042615) Bks Demand.

Southern Recipes, Vol. 1. Johanna S. Siebert. (Bookshoppe Cookbook Ser.). 250p. 1991. 7.95 (*0-9631563-0-6*) Steeplechase.

Southern Recipes & Legends. Nancy Rhyne. Ed. by Barbara Stone. 350p. (Orig.). 1996. pap. 14.95 (*0-87844-134-4*) Sandlapper Pub Co.

Southern Recipes & Legends. Nancy Rhyne. Ed. by Barbara Stone. 350p. (Orig.). 1996. 19.95 (*0-87844-133-6*) Sandlapper Pub Co.

Southern Redneck: A Phenomenological Class Study. Julian B. Roebuck & Mark L. Hickson, III. LC 82-9831. 222p. 1982. text ed. 38.50 (*0-275-90886-0*, C0886, Praeger Pubs) Greenwood.

Southern Redwood Co., Set. 5th ed. Herbert O'Keefe. 56p. (C). 1991. Manual practice set. student ed., per. 20.95 (*0-256-09254-0*, 36-1345-05) Irwin.

Southern Renascence Man: Views of Robert Penn Warren. fac. ed. Thomas L. Connelly et al. Ed. by Walter B. Edgar. LC 83-14922. (Southern Literary Studies). 132p. 1984. reprint ed. pap. 37.70 (*0-7837-7769-8*, 2047525) Bks Demand.

Southern Reporter: Stories. fac. ed. John W. Corrington. LC 80-26204. 200p. 1981. reprint ed. pap. 57.00 (*0-7837-7728-0*, 2047484) Bks Demand.

Southern Revenge: The Confederate Burning of Chambersburg, Pennsylvania. Chambersburg Chamber of Commerce Staff. LC 89-22608. (Illus.). 200p. 1989. 29.95 (*0-942597-14-1*) White Mane Pub.

Southern Review, Set. reprint ed. lib. bdg. 1,912.50 (*0-404-19558-X*) AMS Pr.

Southern Review & Modern Literature, 1935-1985. Ed. by Lewis P. Simpson et al. LC 87-21384. (Southern Literary Studies). 264p. 1988. text ed. 35.00 (*0-8071-1424-3*) La State U Pr.

Southern Rhythms. Robert T. Jones, Jr. (Illus.). 24p. 1986. pap. 3.00 (*0-938896-46-6*) Mississippi Archives.

***Southern Rose.** Bruce Horaz. 56p. 1997. pap. 8.00 (*0-8059-4042-1*) Dorrance.

***Southern Rules: The Advanced Course for Women Who Are Serious about Taming the Male Beast.** LC 96-50489. 1997. mass mkt. 5.99 (*1-889372-18-8*) Sweetwtr Pr AL.

Southern Sayin' Aerial Photography Services, Inc. Staff. 2.95 (*0-936672-30-7*) Aerial Photo.

Southern Schools: An Evaluation of the Emergency School Assistance Program (EASP) & of School Desegregation, Set. Robert L. Crain. (Report Ser.: Nos. 124A-124B). 1973. 10.00 (*0-932132-21-9*) Natl Opinion Res.

Southern Sea Fare. Marion B. Sullivan. 36p. (Orig.). 1995. pap. 3.25 (*1-886367-04-3*) Wellspring.

Southern Seas. Manuel V. Montalban. Tr. by Patrick Camiller from SPA. 224p. (Orig.). 1990. pap. 9.95 (*1-85242-132-0*) Serpents Tail.

Southern Seasons: Month-by-Month Gardening in the Piedmont Plateau. Frances Worthington. (Illus.). 96p. (Orig.). 1993. pap. 10.95 (*0-9620923-1-2*) GNP Pub.

Southern Secrets. Reginald Martin. (Illus.). 80p. 1996. 18.95 (*0-9624889-5-X*) Seymour-Smith.

***Southern Selves.** Ed. by Jim Watkins. 1997. pap. write for info. (*0-679-78103-X*, Vin) Random.

Southern Sensibilities. 1993. write for info. (*0-9615622-7-7*) McElyea Pubns.

***Southern Settings.** 264p. 1996. 24.95 (*0-9654734-0-6*) Decatur Genl Hosp.

Southern Settings: Creating Delightful Masterpieces. Moultrie Service League Staff. (Illus.). 1996. 17.95 (*0-9651477-0-3*) Moultrie Srv.

Southern Side, or Andersonville Prison. R. Randolph Stevenson. 504p. 1996. reprint ed. 30.00 (*1-888433-00-0*) J M Bracken.

Southern Sides. Marian B. Sullivan. 36p. (Orig.). 1994. pap. 3.25 (*1-886367-05-1*) Wellspring.

Southern Skies Cry... Valerie Lawrence. LC 88-61291. 60p. 1988. pap. 8.95 (*0-929917-03-0*) Magnolia PA.

Southern Sky. Wallace & David Reidy. 1988. pap. text ed. 29.95 (*0-04-300094-0*, Pub. by Allen Unwin AT) Paul & Co Pubs.

Southern Sky Guide. David Ellyard & Wil Tirion. (Illus.). 80p. (C). 1993. pap. text ed. 20.95 (*0-521-42839-4*) Cambridge U Pr.

Southern Sky Guide. David Ellyard & Wil Tirion. LC 92-39556. 1995. pap. write for info. (*0-521-42829-7*) Cambridge U Pr.

Southern Slavery & the Law, 1619-1860. Thomas D. Morris. LC 95-6565. (Studies in Legal History). 608p. (C). 1996. text ed. 49.95 (*0-8078-2238-8*) U of NC Pr.

Southern Slavery at the State & Local Level. Ed. by Paul Finkelman. (Articles on American Slavery Ser.). 350p. 1990. reprint ed. text ed. 30.00 (*0-8240-6787-8*) Garland.

Southern Slaves in Free State Courts: The Pamphlet Literature, 3 vols. Ed. by Paul Finkelman. LC 87-35970. (Slavery, Race & the American Legal System, 1700-1872 Ser.). 1696p. 1990. text ed. 188.00 (*0-8240-6718-5*) Garland.

Southern Soldiers of American Revolution. Harry Knill. (J). (gr. 1-9). 1997. pap. 3.95 (*0-88388-164-0*) Bellerophon Bks.

Southern South. Albert B. Hart. LC 74-96438. (American Scene Ser.). 1969. reprint ed. lib. bdg. 55.00 (*0-306-71826-X*) Da Capo.

Southern Spain. (Insight Guides Ser.). 1993. pap. 22.95 (*0-395-66247-8*) HM.

Southern Spain. 2nd ed. Dana Facaros & Michael Pauls. LC 93-48980. (Cadogan Guides Ser.). 1994. write for info. (*0-947754-60-1*, Pub. by Cadogan Books UK) Macmillan.

Southern Spain Andalucia & Gilbralter. 3rd rev. ed. Dana Facaros & Michael Pauls. (Country Guides Ser.). (Illus.). 204p. (Orig.). 1996. pap. 14.95 (*1-86011-016-9*, Pub. by Cadogan Bks UK) Globe Pequot.

Southern Spain in Your Pocket Guide. Michelin Travel Publications, Staff. (In Your Pocket Guides Ser.). (Orig.). 1996. per. 9.95 (*2-06-650701-6*, 6507) Michelin.

***Southern Spain Map.** 1997. 8.95 (*2-06-700446-8*, 446) Michelin.

Southern Specialty Vegetables. Patricia B. Mitchell. 1992. pap. 4.00 (*0-925117-61-7*) Mitchells.

Southern Spice a la Microwave. Margie Brignac. LC 81-19241. (Illus.). 240p. (Orig.). 1982. spiral bd. 13.95 (*0-88289-318-1*) Pelican.

Southern Star for Maryland: Maryland & the Secession Crisis, 1860-1861. Lawrence M. Denton. LC 95-74770. 256p. 1995. 23.95 (*0-9635159-3-4*) Pub Concepts.

***Southern Star Mystery.** Jules Verne. lib. bdg. 22.95 (*0-8488-2074-6*) Amereon Ltd.

Southern State Party Organizations & Activists. Ed. by Charles D. Hadley & Lewis Bowman. LC 94-32915. 272p. 1995. text ed. 59.95 (*0-275-94766-1*, Praeger Pubs) Greenwood.

Southern States since the War Eighteen Seventy to Eighteen Seventy-One. Robert Somers. 1977. text ed. 27.95 (*0-8369-9253-9*, 9106) Ayer.

Southern States Since the War, 1870-71. Robert Somers. LC 72-11347. (American South Ser.). 1973. reprint ed. 27.95 (*0-405-05063-1*) Ayer.

Southern Stories: Slaveholders in Peace & War. Drew G. Faust. (Illus.). 264p. 1992. text ed. 32.50 (*0-8262-0865-7*); pap. text ed. 16.95 (*0-8262-0975-0*) U of Mo Pr.

Southern Storms. Marcia Martin. 1992. mass mkt. 4.99 (*0-515-10870-7*) Jove Pubns.

***Southern Strategies: Southern Women & the Woman Suffrage Question.** Elna C. Green. LC 96-36992. (Illus.). 304p. (C). 1997. 45.00 (*0-8078-2332-5*); pap. 16.95 (*0-8078-4641-4*) U of NC Pr.

Southern Strategy Revisited: Republican Top-Down Advancement in the South. Joseph A. Aistrip. LC 94-41601. (Illus.). 288p. 1996. 39.95 (*0-8131-1904-9*) U Pr of Ky.

Southern Stuff. Mildred J. Brooks. 224p. (Orig.). 1992. pap. 9.00 (*0-380-76491-1*) Avon.

Southern-Style Diabetic Cooking. Martha Chitwood. LC 96-47060. 116p. 1996. pap. 11.95 (*0-945448-69-4*) Am Diabetes.

Southern Subculture of Drinking & Driving: A Generalized Deviance Model for the Southern White Male. Julian B. Roebuck & Komanduri S. Murty. Ed. by Marilyn D. McShane & Frank P. Williams, III. LC 95-53726. (Current Issues in Criminal Justice Ser.: Vol. 17). (Illus.). 248p. 1996. text ed. 36.00 (*0-8153-2376-X*, SS1107) Garland.

Southern Sudan: The Problem of National Integration. Dunstan M. Wai. (Illus.). 252p. 1973. 39.50 (*0-7146-2985-5*, Pub. by F Cass Pubs UK) Intl Spec Bk.

Southern Survey. Ed. by Brian Denton. 48p. (C). 1987. pap. 30.00 (*0-317-90463-9*, Pub. by Picton UK) St Mut.

***Southern Tables.** 230p. 1996. write for info. (*0-9654358-0-6*) Pinewood Christian Acad.

Southern Tagalog Voting, 1946-1963: Political Behavior in a Philippine Region. Carl H. Lande et al. (Special Reports: No. 7). (Illus.). 159p. (Orig.). (C). 1973. pap. 7.00 (*1-877979-57-0*) SE Asia.

Southern Tailgating: Game Day Recipes & Traditions. Michael D. Looney & Kim Looney. LC 94-23210. (Illus.). 168p. (Orig.). 1994. pap. 12.95 (*0-9630700-9-6*, 641.5'78...dc20) Vision AL.

Southern Tales. Webb Garrison. 1996. 11.98 (*0-88365-963-8*) Galahad Bks.

Southern Talk: A Disappearing Language. rev. ed. Ray Cunningham. LC 93-30379. 192p. 1994. pap. 8.95 (*0-914875-22-1*) Bright Mtn Bks.

***Southern Textile Basketball Tournament: A History, 1921-1996.** Mac C. Kirkpatrick & Thomas K. Perry. 360p. 1997. boxed 38.50 (*0-7864-0398-5*) McFarland & Co.

Southern Thanksgiving: Recipes & Musings for a Manageable Feast. Robb Forman Dew. LC 92-11561. (Illus.). 80p. 1992. 10.00 (*0-201-63215-2*) Addison-Wesley.

Southern Thunder: A Story of the Civil War 1861-1865. Ronald E. Morgan. LC 95-71272. 288p. (Orig.). 1996. pap. 12.00 (*1-884570-42-9*) Research Triangle.

Southern Thunder: Exploits of the Confederate States Navy. R. Thomas Campbell. LC 96-37062. (Illus.). 168p. 1997. 19.95 (*1-57249-029-2*, Burd St Pr) White Mane Pub.

Southern Tier Lines: Transportation Documentary. Todd E. Humphrey & John W. Humphrey. (Illus.). 96p. 1992. per. 29.95 (*0-9635319-0-5*) Rainy Day Bks.

Southern Time Christmas. Robert Bernardini. LC 91-12467. (Illus.). 32p. (J). 1991. reprint ed. 14.95 (*0-88289-828-0*) Pelican.

Southern Tradition. Ed. by Lisa C. Mullins. (Architectural Treasures of Early America Ser.). (Illus.). 224p. 1988. 19.95 (*0-918678-34-X*) Natl Hist Soc.

Southern Tradition: The Achievement & Limitations of an American Conservatism. Eugene D. Genovese. LC 94-4586. (William E. Massey Sr. Lectures in the History of American Civilization). 154p. 1994. 22.50 (*0-674-82527-6*, GENSOU) HUP.

Southern Tradition: The Achievement & Limitations of an American Conservatism. Eugene D. Genovese. (William E. Massey Sr. Lectures in the History of American Civilization). 160p. 1996. pap. 12.95 (*0-674-82528-4*) HUP.

Southern Tradition at Bay: A History of Postbellum Thought. Richard Weaver. LC 88-39616. 422p. 1989. reprint ed. 21.95 (*0-89526-760-8*); reprint ed. pap. 11.95 (*0-89526-758-6*) Regnery Pub.

Southern Tradition in Theology & Social Criticism, 1830-1930. Ralph Luker. LC 84-8954. (Studies in American Religion: Vol. 11). 468p. 1984. lib. bdg. 109.95 (*0-88946-655-6*) E Mellen.

Southern Travels: Journal of John H. B. Latrobe, 1834. Ed. by Samuel Wilson, Jr. LC 85-81188. (Illus.). xxii, 122p. 1986. 14.95 (*0-917860-21-7*) Historic New Orleans.

Southern Turkey, the Levant & Cyprus: A Sea-Guide to the Coasts & Islands. H. M. Denham. (Illus.). 1976. 19.95 (*0-393-03198-5*) Norton.

Southern United States. Ed. by Christine J. Dillon. (My First Report Ser.). (Illus.). 47p. (J). (gr. 1-3). 1994. pap. 5.95 (*0-913717-48-7*, 1997) Hewitt Res Fnd.

***Southern Utah University: A Heritage History.** Anne O. Leavitt. LC 97-66545. 480p. 1997. 30.00 (*0-935615-10-5*) S Utah U Pr.

Southern Ute Indians of Early Colorado. Verner Z. Reed. Ed. by William R. Jones. (Illus.). 1980. reprint ed. pap. 2.95 (*0-89646-067-3*) Vistabooks.

Southern Vampires: 13 Deep-Fried Bloodcurdling Tales. Karyn K. Zweifel. 132p. (Orig.). (J). 1995. pap. 12.95 (*1-881548-14-7*) Crane Hill AL.

Southern Vanguard. Ed. by Allen Tate. LC 76-107740. (Essay Index Reprint Ser.). 1977. 23.95 (*0-8369-1726-X*) Ayer.

Southern Vanguard. Allen Tate. (BCL1-PS American Literature Ser.). 331p. 1993. reprint ed. lib. bdg. 89.00 (*0-7812-6931-8*) Rprt Serv.

Southern Vegetable Cooking. 2nd ed. Jon Wongrey. LC 80-50790. (Illus.). 162p. 1981. spiral bd. 9.95 (*0-87844-045-3*) Sandlapper Pub Co.

Southern Vignettes. Sarah Hudson-Pierce. (Illus.). 128p. (Orig.). 1995. pap. 11.95 (*0-9645451-3-6*) F Swann Pubns.

Southern Vision of Andrew Lytle. Mark Lucas. LC 86-21076. (Southern Literary Studies). 192p. 1987. text ed. 29.95 (*0-8071-1338-7*) La State U Pr.

Southern Voices: Profiles & Other Stories. Frye Gaillard. Ed. by Nancy Gaillard & Jerry Bledsoe. 227p. 1991. 19.95 (*1-878086-06-5*) Down Home NC.

***Southern Voices in Every Direction.** LC 94-37391. 1996. write for info. (*1-882845-01-3*) Bell Buckle.

Southern Voices in Every Direction. LC 94-37391. 1994. write for info. (*0-916078-37-X*) Iris Pr.

Southern Weave of Women: Fiction of the Contemporary South. Linda Tate. LC 93-33744. 256p. 1996. pap. 16.95 (*0-8203-1850-7*) U of Ga Pr.

Southern White Protestantism in the Twentieth Century. Kenneth K. Bailey. 1990. 16.00 (*0-8446-1035-6*) Peter Smith.

Southern Wildflowers. Laura C. Martin. (Illus.). 272p. 1991. 12.99 (*0-517-05548-1*) Random Hse Value.

Southern Woman's Story. Phoebe Y. Pember. Ed. by Bell I. Wiley. 242p. 1987. pap. 3.95 (*0-89176-024-5*, 6024, Mckingbird) R Bemis Pub.

Southern Women. Lois Battle. 432p. 1985. pap. 3.95 (*0-312-90328-6*) St Martin.

Southern Women. Lois Battle. 1994. mass mkt. 5.99 (*0-312-95267-8*) St Martin.

Southern Women. Caroline M. Dillman. 226p. 1988. 63.95 (*0-89116-668-8*); pap. 29.95 (*0-89116-838-9*) Hemisp Pub.

Southern Women: Black & White in the Old South. Sally G. McMillen. Ed. by John H. Franklin & A. S. Eisenstadt. (American History Ser.). 140p. 1992. pap. text ed. write for info. (*0-88295-881-X*) Harlan Davidson.

Southern Women: Histories & Identities. Ed. by Virginia Bernhard et al. 240p. 1993. text ed. 34.95 (*0-8262-0868-1*) U of Mo Pr.

Southern Women Artists: From the Collection of the Columbia Museum of Art. Lisa Ray. 38p. (Orig.). 1990. pap. 3.00 (*0-9627858-0-6*) Columbia Mus Art.

Southern Women in the Recent Educational Movement in the South. fac. ed. Amory D. Mayo. Ed. by Dan T. Carter & Amy Friedlander. LC 78-1554. (Library of Southern Civilization). 333p. 1978. reprint ed. pap. 95.00 (*0-7837-7807-4*, 2047563) Bks Demand.

Southern Women Writers: The New Generation. Ed. by Tonette B. Inge. LC 89-33863. 408p. 1990. pap. 29.95 (*0-8173-0470-3*) U of Ala Pr.

Southern Women's Writing: Colonial to Contemporary. Ed. by Mary L. Weaks & Carolyn Perry. 420p. 1995. 49.95 (*0-8130-1410-7*); pap. 24.95 (*0-8130-1411-5*) U Press Fla.

Southern Workers & Their Unions, Eighteen Eighty to Nineteen Seventy-Five: Selected Papers, the Second Southern Labor History Conference, 1q78. Ed. by Merl E. Reed et al. LC 80-24724. (Contributions in Economics & Economic History Ser.: No. 39). (Illus.). 256p. 1981. text ed. 59.95 (*0-313-22701-2*, RSW/) Greenwood.

Southern World. (Trade & Travel Routes Ser.). (Illus.). 128p. (YA). 1990. 17.95 (*0-8160-1881-2*) Facts on File.

Southern Writer in the Postmodern World. Fred Hobson. LC 90-11031. (Mercer University Lamar Memorial Lectures: No. 33). 120p. 1991. 22.00 (*0-8203-1275-4*) U of Ga Pr.

Southern Writers. Ed. by Rinaldo C. Simonini. LC 69-17588. (Essay Index Reprint Ser.). 1977. 23.95 (*0-8369-0054-5*) Ayer.

***Southern Writers.** Photos by David G. Spielman. LC 97-4914. (Illus.). 160p. 1997. 24.95 (*1-57003-224-6*) U of SC Pr.

Southern Writers: A Biographical Dictionary. Ed. by Robert Bain et al. LC 78-25899. 1979. pap. text ed. 19.95 (*0-8071-0390-X*) La State U Pr.

Southern Writers & the Machine: Faulkner to Percy. Jeffrey J. Folks. LC 92-12061. (Worcester Polytechnic Institute Studies in Science, Technology, & Culture: Vol. 11). 186p. (C). 1993. text ed. 45.95 (*0-8204-1856-0*) P Lang Pubng.

Southern Writers & Their Worlds. Ed. by Christopher Morris & Steven G. Reinhardt. LC 95-39356. (Walter Prescott Webb Memorial Lectures: No. 29). 176p. 1996. 24.95 (*0-89096-692-3*) Tex A&M Univ Pr.

***Southern Writers at Century's End.** Ed. by Jeffrey J. Folks & James A. Perkins. LC 97-14744. (Illus.). 304p. (C). 1997. 29.95 (*0-8131-2032-2*) U Pr of Ky.

Southern Writing. Ed. by Martin Tucker. (Confrontation Special Anthology Issue Ser.). 352p. 1987. pap. 8.00 (*0-913057-14-2*) L I U Press.

Southern Yarn. R. W. Richards. Ed. by Jeffrey Bogart. LC 89-92811. (Illus.). (Orig.). (YA). 1990. pap. 12.95 (*0-9625502-0-5*) RoKarn Pubns.

Southerner Discovers the South. Intro. by Jonathan Daniels. LC 68-16228. (American Scene Ser.). 1970. reprint ed. lib. bdg. 42.50 (*0-306-71011-0*) Da Capo.

Southerners All: Revised Edition. rev. ed. F. N. Boney. LC 90-5619. 1990. pap. 12.95 (*0-86554-375-5*, MUP/P087) Mercer Univ Pr.

Southerners & Europeans: Essays in a Time of Disorder. Andrew Lytle. LC 87-24169. (Library of Southern Civilization). xix, 308p. 1988. text ed. 37.50 (*0-8071-1420-0*) La State U Pr.

Southerner's Book of Lists. Jim Erskine. LC 96-13703. (Illus.). 128p. (Orig.). 1996. pap. 5.95 (*1-56554-149-9*) Pelican.

Southerner's Instruction Book. Jim Erskine & Susan Erskine. 96p. 1994. pap. 4.95 (*1-56554-042-5*) Pelican.

Southernmost & Other Stories. Michael Brodsky. LC 96-1449. 384p. 1996. 25.00 (*1-56858-064-9*); pap. 14.95 (*1-56858-065-7*) FWEW.

Southernmost Cat. John Cech. LC 93-40671. (Illus.). (J). 1995. text ed. 14.00 (*0-02-717885-4*, S&S Bks Young Read) S&S Childrens.

Southernmost Cat. John Cech. LC 93-40671. (Illus.). 40p. (J). (ps-3). 1996. 16.00 (*0-689-80510-1*, S&S Bks Young Read) S&S Childrens.

Southey. Edward Dowden. Ed. by John Morley. LC 68-58377. (English Men of Letters Ser.). reprint ed. lib. bdg. 26.50 (*0-404-51709-9*) AMS Pr.

Southey. Edward Dowden. (BCL1-PR English Literature Ser.). 205p. 1992. reprint ed. lib. bdg. 79.00 (*0-7812-7662-4*) Rprt Serv.

Southey's Life of Nelson. Robert Southey. Ed. by G. Callender. LC 71-153357. reprint ed. 49.50 (*0-404-07828-1*) AMS Pr.

Southfield Township Cemeteries, Oakland County, Michigan. Intro. by Joan Pate. 135p. (Orig.). 1989. pap. 10.00 (*1-879766-12-4*) OCG Society.

Southfield United Presbyterian Church, Early Records. Ed. by Joan Pate. 101p. (Orig.). 1985. pap. 10.00 (*1-879766-02-7*) OCG Society.

Southie Won't Go: A Teacher's Diary of the Desegregation of South Boston High School. Ione Malloy. LC 86-16563. (Illus.). 304p. 1986. text ed. 29.95 (*0-252-01276-3*) U of Ill Pr.

Southland: Poems of the South. Harold A. Lawrence. (Illus.). 256p. (Orig.). 1992. pap. 14.95 (*0-87797-251-6*) Cherokee.

Southland Firestorms: October, 1993 Fires. Linda S. Athey. Ed. by Ronda Guyette. 150p. (Orig.). 1994. pap. write for info. (*1-885612-00-1*) Significant Events.

Southlands of Siva: Some Reminiscences of Life in Southern India. A. Butterworth. 1990. reprint ed. 20.00 (*81-206-0337-0*, Pub. by Asian Educ Servs II) S Asia.

Southpaw. Mark Harris. 1976. 17.95 (*0-8488-1356-1*) Amereon Ltd.

Southpaw. Mark Harris. 1982. lib. bdg. 25.95 (*0-89966-394-X*) Buccaneer Bks.

Southpaw. Mark Harris. LC 83-19821. 350p. 1984. reprint ed. pap. 12.95 (*0-8032-7220-0*, Bison Books) U of Nebr Pr.

***Southport.** Edward P. Norvell. 224p. (Orig.). 1997. pap. 12.95 (*1-884570-68-2*) Research Triangle.

***Southport: The War Years: An Island Remembers.** unabridged ed. Sarah S. Brewer. (Illus.). ix, 389p. 1996. 33.00 (*0-9655925-0-2*) Cozy Harbor.

South's Bed & Breakfasts: Delightful Place to Stay & Great Things to do When You Get There. 3rd ed. Fodor's Travel Staff. (Bed & Breakfasts & Country Inn Ser.). 1997. pap. 17.00 (*0-679-03285-1*) Fodors Travel.

South's Finest: The First Missouri Confederate Brigade from Pea Ridge to Vicksburg. Phillip T. Tucker. LC 93-8732. (Illus.). 271p. (C). 1993. 27.95 (*0-942597-31-1*) White Mane Pub.

South's Last Boys in Gray. Jay S. Hoar. LC 86-70851. 605p. 1986. 40.95 (*0-87972-358-0*) Bowling Green Univ Popular Press.

***South's Legendary Frances Virginia Tea Room Cookbook.** 2nd ed. Mildred H. Coleman. Orig. Title: The Frances Virginia Tea Room Cookbook. (Illus.). 190p. 1996. reprint ed. spiral bd. 14.95 (*0-9653416-0-7*) M H Coleman.

South's New Politics: Realignment & Dealignment. Robert H. Swansbrough & David M. Brodsky. 330p. 1988. text ed. 24.95 (*0-87249-566-3*) U of SC Pr.

South's Part in Mongrelizing the Nation. E. S. Cox. 1982. lib. bdg. 59.95 (*0-87700-379-3*) Revisionist Pr.

Southshore: The Awakeners Two. Sheri S. Tepper. 256p. 1988. pap. 3.95 (*0-8125-5619-4*) Tor Bks.

Southside: Twenty-One Poems by Children from Tucson's South Side. Ed. by Rolly Kent. (Illus.). 28p. 1982. pap. 5.00 (*0-9608370-1-9*) Friends Tucson.

Southside Rudy Yid. Morry Frank. LC 97-66863. 246p. (Orig.). 1997. pap. 9.00 (*0-9640912-0-8*) Silverback Bks.

Southside Virginia Families, Vol. 1. John B. Boddie. (Illus.). 390p. 1996. pap. 31.50 (*0-614-16566-0*, 531) Clearfield Co.

Southside Virginia Families, Vol. II. John B. Boddie. (Illus.). 298p. 1996. pap. 29.50 (*0-614-16567-9*, 532) Clearfield Co.

Southtrap. large type ed. Geoffrey Jenkins. 482p. 1981. 25.99 (*0-7089-0611-7*) Ulverscroft.

Southward. Greg Delanty. LC 91-27438. 64p. 1992. pap. 7.95 (*0-8071-1734-X*); text ed. 14.95 (*0-8071-1733-1*) La State U Pr.

Southward Ho: A Spell of Sunshine. W. Gilmore Simms. LC 75-116012. reprint ed. 29.50 (*0-404-06036-6*) AMS Pr.

Southward Ho! - Other Essays. Holbrook Jackson. LC 68-29219. (Essay Index Reprint Ser.). 1977. reprint ed. 19.95 (*0-8369-0564-4*) Ayer.

Southwell Minster after the Civil Wars. A. Rogers. (C). 1974. text ed. 40.00 (*0-685-22172-5*, Pub. by Univ Nottingham UK) St Mut.

Southwell-Sibthorpe Commonplace Book: Folger MS V. b. 198. Ed. by Jean Klene. LC 95-21783. (Medieval & Renaissance Texts & Studies: Vol. 147). (Illus.). 250p. 1997. 30.00 (*0-86698-187-X*, MR147) MRTS.

Southwest. Compass American Guides Staff. (Compass American Guides Ser.). (Illus.). 1996. pap. 18.95 (*1-878867-79-2*, Compass Amrcn) Fodors Travel.

Southwest. David H. Hundley. LC 94-9099. (American Food Library). (J). 1994. write for info. (*0-86625-512-5*) Rourke Pubns.

Southwest. David Lavender. LC 83-19740. 362p. 1984. pap. 16.95 (*0-8263-0736-1*) U of NM Pr.

Southwest. Ed. by Alfonso Ortiz. LC 77-17162. (Handbook of North American Indians Ser.: Vol. 9). (Illus.). 702p. 1980. 49.00 (*0-87474-189-0*, ORV9) Smithsonian.

Southwest, Vol. 10. Ed. by Alfonso Ortiz. LC 77-17162. (Handbook of North American Indians Ser.). (Illus.). 868p. 1983. 52.00 (*0-87474-190-4*) Smithsonian.

Southwest: A Family Adventure. Tish Minear & Janet Limon. (U. S. A. Guides Ser.). (Illus.). 440p. (Orig.). 1990. pap. 16.95 (*0-87052-640-5*) Hippocrene Bks.

Southwest: A Lonely Planet Travel Survival Kit. Rob Rachowiecki. (Illus.). 944p. 1995. pap. 19.95 (*0-86442-255-5*) Lonely Planet.

***Southwest: A Pictorial History of the Land & Its People.** Walker. (Illus.). 80p. 1996. pap. 9.95 (*1-879924-09-9*) Camelback Design.

Southwest: A Postcard Folio Book. Ansel Adams. 1996. pap. text ed. 9.95 (*0-8212-2344-5*) Little.

Southwest: Colorado, New Mexico, Texas. Thomas G. Aylesworth & Virginia L. Aylesworth. LC 94-45786. (Discovering America Ser.). 1995. pap. 8.95 (*0-7910-3430-5*) Chelsea Hse.

Southwest: Colorado, New Mexico, Texas. Thomas G. Aylesworth & Virginia L. Aylesworth. LC 94-45786. (Discovering America Ser.). (J). 1995. lib. bdg. 19.95 (*0-7910-3412-7*) Chelsea Hse.

Southwest: New Mexico & Arizona. Photos by George H. Huey. LC 94-33281. (The Smithsonian Guides to Natural America). 1995. pap. write for info. (*0-89599-045-8*) Smithsonian Bks.

Southwest: Photographic Journey. Bill Harris. (Illus.). 1991. 15.99 (*0-517-06029-9*) Random Hse Value.

Southwest: Three Peoples in Geographical Change, 1600-1970. Donald W. Meinig. (Historical Geography of North America Ser.). 164p. (Orig.). (C). 1971. pap. text ed. 18.95 (*0-19-501289-5*) OUP.

Southwest Adventures: The Complete Road Guide. Fraser Bridges. LC 95-10894. 1995. pap. 16.95 (*0-7615-0134-7*) Prima Pub.

Southwest Adventures: The Driver's Guide. Fraser Bridges. (Illus.). 1992. pap. 14.95 (*0-9694136-6-1*) Amer Traveler.

Southwest Alluvial Basins of Arizona: Papers Presented at 21st Annual AWRA Conference & Symposium, August 11-16, 1985, Tucson, AZ. American Water Resources Association Staff. Ed. by T. W. Anderson & A. Ivan Johnson. (AWRA Monograph Series Regional Aquifer Systems of the United States: No. 7). (Illus.). 120p. 1986. reprint ed. pap. 34.20 (*0-7837-9596-3*, 2060353) Bks Demand.

Southwest American Indian Designs. Caren Caraway. (International Design Library). (Illus.). 48p. (Orig.). 1983. pap. 5.95 (*0-88045-035-5*) Stemmer Hse.

Southwest & South Central see Mobil Travel Guide

Southwest Art Review. Karen Kodner. (Illus.). 224p. 1983. 19.95 (*0-913765-00-7*); pap. 14.95 (*0-913765-02-3*) Krantz Co.

Southwest Camping: The Complete Guide to More Than 35,000 Campsites in Arizona & New Mexico. 2nd ed. Dennis Lewon et al. (Illus.). 544p. 1995. pap. 17.95 (*0-935701-88-5*) Foghorn Pr.

Southwest Ceramic Art. Jean Kristofer. LC 91-61120. 52p. 1991. pap. text ed. 9.95 (*0-916809-50-1*) Scott Pubns MI.

Southwest China off the Beaten Track. 1992. pap. 12.95 (*0-8442-9804-2*, Passport Bks) NTC Pub Grp.

Southwest Classics: The Creative Literature of the Arid Lands: Essays on the Books & Their Writers. Lawrence C. Powell. LC 82-20314. 378p. reprint ed. pap. 107.80 (*0-7837-5053-6*, 2044731) Bks Demand.

Southwest Coast of Ireland: Cork Harbour to Dingle Bay. Imray, Laurie, Norie & Wilson Ltd. Staff. (Illus.). (C). 1986. text ed. 75.00 (*0-685-40193-6*, Pub. by Imray Laurie Norie & Wilson UK) St Mut.

Southwest Coasts of Wales. Wilson Ltd. Staff & Imray L. Norie. (C). 1989. 60.00 (*0-685-40431-5*, Pub. by Imray Laurie Norie & Wilson UK) St Mut.

Southwest Conference Baseball's Greatest Hits. Neal Farmer. LC 96-1636. (Illus.). 150p. 1996. 24.95 (*1-57168-083-7*, Eakin Pr); pap. 16.95 (*1-57168-084-5*, Eakin Pr) Sunbelt Media.

Southwest Cooking. Consumer Guide Editors. 1990. 6.99 (*0-517-68757-7*) Random Hse Value.

***Southwest Cooking.** Northland Publishing Staff. 1997. pap. text ed. 13.95 (*0-87358-704-9*) Northland AZ.

Southwest Cooking. June Towers. (Illus.). 96p. 1991. 9.95 (*0-89015-801-0*) Sunbelt Media.

Southwest Corner. John C. Holm. 1955. pap. 5.25 (*0-8222-1062-2*) Dramatists Play.

Southwest Corner. Mildred Walker. LC 94-40444. (Illus.). vi, 144p. 1995. pap. 7.95 (*0-8032-9768-8*, Bison Books) U of Nebr Pr.

Southwest Corner Stories: Seventy-Five Years of Memories. Floyd McCracken. LC 98-85273. (Illus.). 176p. (Orig.). 1993. pap. 8.95 (*0-9637445-7-7*) Shasta Valley.

Southwest Creative Sourcebook 1996. Ed. by Joey D. Petelle. (Illus.). 1996. spiral bd., pap. 50.00 (*1-886295-01-8*) Everest Pubng.

***Southwest Creative Sourcebook 1997.** 300p. 1997. 50.00 (*1-886295-11-5*) Everest Pubng.

Southwest Drifter. large type ed. Gordon D. Shirreffs. (Linford Western Library). 384p. 1986. pap. 15.99 (*0-7089-6208-4*, Linford) Ulverscroft.

***Southwest Drifter.** Gordon D. Shirreffs. 192p. 1997. reprint ed. mass mkt. 3.99 (*0-8439-4207-X*) Dorchester Pub Co.

Southwest Economy in the Nineteen Nineties: A Different Decade. Ed. by Gerald P. O'Driscoll, Jr. & Stephen P. Brown. 224p. 1990. lib. bdg. 64.50 (*0-7923-9092-X*) Kluwer Ac.

Southwest Energy Complex: A Policy Evaluation. Malcolm F. Baldwin. LC 73-79429. 79p. reprint ed. pap. 25.00 (*0-317-11229-5*, 2015787) Bks Demand.

Southwest Expedition of Jedediah Smith: His Personal Account of the Journey to California, 1826-1827. Jedediah S. Smith. Ed. & Intro. by George R. Brooks. LC 89-4939. (Illus.). 259p. 1989. pap. 8.95 (*0-8032-9197-3*, Bison Books) U of Nebr Pr.

Southwest Expressions. Publications International, Ltd. Editors et al. (Illus.). 256p. 1992. 29.95 (*1-56173-585-X*) Pubns Intl Ltd.

Southwest Florida's Wetland Wilderness: Big Cypress Swamp & the Ten Thousand Islands. Jeff Ripple. (Florida Sand Dollar Bk.). (Illus.). 112p. 1996. pap. 16.95 (*0-8130-1454-9*) U Press Fla.

***Southwest for Free.** 2nd rev. ed. Greg Edwards & Mary J. Edwards. LC 96-49223. (Illus.). 160p. (Orig.). 1997. pap. 9.95 (*0-914457-83-7*) Mustang Pub.

Southwest France: Dordogne, Lot & Bordeaux. Dana Facaros & Michael Pauls. LC 94-3018. (Cadogan Country Guides Ser.). (Illus.). 448p. 1994. pap. 17.95 (*1-56440-467-6*) Globe Pequot.

Southwest France: Gascony & the Pyrenees. Dana Facaros & Michael Pauls. (Cadogan Guides Ser.). (Illus.). 384p. (Orig.). 1995. pap. 17.95 (*1-86011-020-7*, Pub. by Cadogan Bks UK) Globe Pequot.

Southwest France Blue Guide. Frank Woodman. (Blue Guides Ser.). 1994. pap. 17.95 (*0-393-31188-0*) Norton.

Southwest Gardening. rev. ed. Rosalie Doolittle & Harriet Tiedebohl. LC 52-11535. (Illus.). 237p. 1968. reprint ed. pap. 12.95 (*0-8263-0027-8*) U of NM Pr.

***Southwest Germany Map.** 1996. 8.95 (*2-06-700419-0*, 419) Michelin.

Southwest Graduate Symposium of Spanish & Portuguese, Literature & Language at the University of Texas. Ed. by Luis A. Ramos-Garcia. 1980. 5.00 (*0-934840-03-2*) Studia Hispanica.

Southwest Heritage: Literary History with Bibliography. Mabel Major. (BCL1-PS American Literature Ser.). 199p. 1993. reprint ed. lib. bdg. 69.00 (*0-7812-6581-9*) Rprt Serv.

***Southwest Home Plans: 138 Sun-Loving Designs for Building Anywhere!** (Illus.). 144p. 1997. pap. 10.95 (*1-881955-35-4*) Home Planners.

Southwest Impressions. Jean Kristopher. LC 89-60298. 52p. (Orig.). 1989. pap. 8.95 (*0-916809-29-3*) Scott Pubns MI.

Southwest in the American Imagination: The Writings of Sylvester Baxter, 1881-1889. Ed. by Curtis M. Hinsley & David R. Wilcox. LC 95-41783. (Southwest Center Ser.). (Illus.). 266p. (C). 1996. pap. 16.95 (*0-8165-1618-9*) U of Ariz Pr.

Southwest in the American Imagination: The Writings of Sylvester Baxter, 1881-1889, Vol. 1. Ed. by Curtis M. Hinsley & David R. Wilcox. LC 95-41783. (Southwest Center Ser.). (Illus.). 266p. 1996. 40.00 (*0-8165-1533-6*) U of Ariz Pr.

Southwest Indian Cookbook: Authentic Pueblo & Navajo Recipes. Marcia Keegan. LC 77-84927. (Illus.). 120p. 1988. pap. 12.95 (*0-940666-03-0*) Clear Light.

Southwest Indian Craft Arts. Clara L. Tanner. LC 66-24299. (Illus.). 216p. reprint ed. pap. 61.60 (*0-7837-1913-2*, 2042117) Bks Demand.

Southwest Indian Designs: With Some Explanations. Mark Bahti. (Illus.). 32p. (Orig.). 1995. pap. 4.95 (*0-918080-51-7*) Treas Chest Bks.

Southwest Indian Silver from the Doneghy Collection. Ed. by Louise Lincoln. (Illus.). 189p. 1982. text ed. 29.95 (*0-292-72440-3*) U of Tex Pr.

Southwest Indians: An Educational Coloring Book. Spizzirri Publishing Co. Staff. Ed. by Linda Spizzirri. (Illus.). 32p. (J). (gr. 1-8). 1986. pap. 1.99 (*0-86545-075-7*) Spizzirri.

Southwest Indians, Bk. 1: (Navajo, Pima, Apache), Bk. 1. Caroline Olin & Bertha P. Dutton. (Illus.). (J). (gr. 5). 1978. pap. 4.95 (*0-88388-049-0*) Bellerophon Bks.

Southwest Indians, Bk. 2: Hopi, Acoma, Tewa, Zuni. Bertha P. Dutton. (J). (gr. 1-9). 1992. pap. 4.95 (*0-88388-062-8*) Bellerophon Bks.

Southwest Ireland: Counties Cork, Kerry, Limerick. Catharina Day. (Cadogan Country Guides Ser.). (Illus.). 320p. (Orig.). 1995. pap. 16.95 (*0-947754-96-2*, Pub. by Cadogan Bks UK) Globe Pequot.

Southwest Louisiana: Biographical & Historical. William H. Perrin. 1971. 35.00 (*0-87511-094-0*) Claitors.

Southwest Louisiana Veterans Remember Vol. I: A 50th Anniversary Remembrance of World War I. Nola M. Ross. (Illus.). 157p. 1993. 18.00 (*1-887144-00-5*) N M Ross.

Southwest Louisiana Veterans Remember Vol. II: A 50th Anniversary Remembrance of World War II. Nola M. Ross. (Illus.). 1995. 18.00 (*1-887144-07-2*) N M Ross.

Southwest Montana Auto Adventures: Day Trips & Destinations, Vol. 1. Judy Kinnaman & Wayne Scherr. (Illus.). 68p. 1995. 5.95 (*1-885122-00-4*) Canyon Pubns.

Southwest Necropolis of Satricum (Le Ferriere) Excavations, 1981-1986. M. Gnade et al. (Scrinium (Monographs on History, Archaeology & Art History. Published under the Auspices of the Netherlands Institute & the Foundation of Friends of the Dutch Institute in Rome) Ser.: Vol. 2). (Illus.). 600p. 1992. 177.00 (*90-5170-158-6*, Pub. by Thesis Pubs NE) IBD Ltd.

Southwest New Mexico Ghost Towns Sites. H. Glenn Carson. 40p. 1991. pap. 7.95 (*0-941620-41-7*) Carson Ent.

Southwest of England. Martyn F. Wakelin. LC 86-8315. (Varieties of English Around the World General Ser.: Series T5). xii, 231p. (Orig.). 1986. pap. 53.00 (*90-272-4713-7*) Benjamins North Am.

S

An Asterisk (*) at the beginning of an entry indicates that the title is appearing in BIP for the first time.

Southwest Pac & War. California University Committee on International Relations. LC 74-3750. 168p. 1974. reprint ed. text ed. 65.00 (*0-8371-7473-2*, CUSP, Greenwood Pr) Greenwood.

Southwest Pacific Campaign, 1941-1945: Historiography & Annotated Bibliography. Eugene L. Rasor. LC 96-5845. (Bibliographies of Battles & Leaders Ser.: No. 19). 304p. 1996. text ed. 75.00 (*0-313-28874-7*, Greenwood Pr) Greenwood.

Southwest Publishing Marketplace: A Comprehensive Directory of Markets, Opportunities, & Resources for Writers. Ed. by Marjorie Gersh. 1990. pap. 14.95 (*0-9622592-2-5*) Writers Connection.

Southwest Rock Climbing: SoCal Select. Randy Vogel. (Southwest Rock Climbing Ser.). (Illus.). 212p. (Orig.). 1993. pap. 18.00 (*0-934641-62-5*) Chockstone Pr.

Southwest Scroll Saw Patterns. Patrick Spielman & Dan Kihl. LC 94-20413. (Illus.). 168p. 1994. pap. 14.95 (*0-8069-0679-0*) Sterling.

Southwest Seasons Cookbook. Ed. by Kathryn B. Godfrey. 285p. 1991. 14.95 (*0-9630530-0-0*) C A Aux.

Southwest Seminar on Energy & Economic Development. Frank Anderson. 117p. (Orig.). 1989. pap. 10.00 (*0-936440-79-1*) U TX SUPA.

Southwest Symposium on Image Analysis & Interpretation, 1994. LC 94-75271. 176p. 1994. pap. text ed. 40.00 (*0-8186-6250-6*, 6250) IEEE Comp Soc.

Southwest Tastes. 4th ed. Ellen Brown. LC 87-14865. (Illus.). 212p. 1990. reprint ed. pap. 24.95 (*0-929714-24-5*) Great Chefs TV.

Southwest Tastes. 6th ed. Ellen Brown. LC 87-14865. (Illus.). 212p. 1987. reprint ed. 29.95 (*0-929714-04-0*) Great Chefs TV.

Southwest the Beautiful Cookbook. Barbara P. Fenzl. 1994. 45.00 (*0-00-255348-1*) Collins SF.

Southwest Traveler: A Travelers Guide to: Southwest Indian Arts & Crafts. Charlotte S. Neyland. (American Traveler Ser.). (Illus.). 48p. (Orig.). 1992. pap. 5.95 (*1-55838-129-5*) R H Pub.

Southwest Traveler: Parks & Monuments of New Mexico, Colorado & Utah. Deborahann Smith. (Illus.). 48p. 1993. pap. 4.95 (*1-55838-146-5*) R H Pub.

Southwest Traveler: The Anasazi: A Guide to Ancient Southwest Indians. Eleanor H. Ayer. (American Traveler Ser.). (Illus.). 48p. (Orig.). 1991. pap. 4.95 (*1-55838-126-0*) R H Pub.

Southwest under Stress: National Resource Development Issues in a Regional Setting. Allen V. Kneese & F. Lee Brown. LC 81-47618. 268p. 1981. pap. 14.95 (*0-8018-2708-6*) Resources Future.

Southwest Virginia in the Civil War: The Battles for Saltville. William Maravel. (Virginia Civil War Battles & Leaders Ser.). (Illus.). 192p. 1992. 19.95 (*1-56190-026-5*) H E Howard.

Southwest Virginia's Railroad: Modernization & the Sectional Crisis. Kenneth W. Noe. LC 93-5632. (Illus.). 232p. 1994. text ed. 27.95 (*0-252-02070-7*) U of Ill Pr.

Southwest Visions Address Book. Helen Hardin. (Illus.). 110p. 1993. 12.95 (*0-87358-550-X*) Northland AZ.

***Southwestern Agriculture: Pre-Columbian to Modern.** Ed. by Henry C. Dethloff & Irvin M. May, Jr. LC 81-48381. 320p. 1982. 39.95 (*0-89096-121-2*) Tex A&M Univ Pr.

Southwestern Algebra I: An Integrated Approach. Gerver et al. (MA - Academic Math Ser.). 1997. student ed., pap. 56.95 (*0-538-64417-6*) S-W Pub.

Southwestern Algebra I: An Integrated Approach. Gerver et al. (MA - Academic Math Ser.). 1997. teacher ed., pap. 65.95 (*0-538-64418-4*) S-W Pub.

Southwestern Algebra I: An Integrated Approach. Gerver et al. (MA - Academic Math Ser.). 1997. teacher ed., pap. 93.95 (*0-538-64419-2*) S-W Pub.

Southwestern Algebra II: An Integrated Approach. Gerver et al. (MA - Academic Math Ser.). 1997. student ed., pap. 60.95 (*0-538-64421-4*) S-W Pub.

Southwestern Algebra II: An Integrated Approach. Gerver et al. (MA - Academic Math Ser.). 1997. teacher ed., pap. 93.95 (*0-538-64422-2*) S-W Pub.

Southwestern Algebra 1, Lesson Plans: An Integrated Approach. Gerver et al. (MA - Academic Math Ser.). 1997. pap. 17.95 (*0-538-66469-X*) S-W Pub.

Southwestern Algebra 1, Math Handbook: An Integrated Appraoch. Gerver et al. (MA - Academic Math Ser.). (SPA.). 1997. pap. 17.95 (*0-538-66463-0*) S-W Pub.

Southwestern Algebra 1, Math Handbook: An Integrated Approach. Gerver et al. (MA - Academic Math Ser.). 1997. pap. 17.95 (*0-538-66462-2*) S-W Pub.

Southwestern Algebra 1, Multicultural Connections: An Integrated Approach. Gerver et al. (MA - Academic Math Ser.). 1997. pap. 17.95 (*0-538-66466-5*) S-W Pub.

Southwestern Algebra 1, Pass-Test-Assessment: An Integrated Approach. Gerver et al. (MA - Academic Math Ser.). 1997. pap. 72.95 (*0-538-66473-8*) S-W Pub.

Southwestern Algebra 1, Resource Book Chapter 1: An Integrated Appraoch. Gerver et al. (MA - Academic Math Ser.). 1997. pap. 7.95 (*0-538-66444-4*) S-W Pub.

Southwestern Algebra 1, Resource Book Chapter 10: An Integrated Approach. Gerver et al. (MA - Academic Math Ser.). 1997. pap. 7.95 (*0-538-66457-6*) S-W Pub.

Southwestern Algebra 1, Resource Book Chapter 11: An Integrated Approach. Gerver et al. (MA - Academic Math Ser.). 1997. pap. 7.95 (*0-538-66458-4*) S-W Pub.

Southwestern Algebra 1, Resource Book Chapter 13: An Integrated Approach. Gerver et al. (MA - Academic Math Ser.). 1997. pap. 7.95 (*0-538-66460-6*) S-W Pub.

Southwestern Algebra 1, Resource Book Chapter 14: An Integrated Approach. Gerver et al. (MA - Academic Math Ser.). 1997. pap. 7.95 (*0-538-66461-4*) S-W Pub.

Southwestern Algebra 1, Resource Book Chapter 2: An Integrated Approach. Gerver et al. (MA - Academic Math Ser.). 1997. pap. 7.95 (*0-538-66445-2*) S-W Pub.

Southwestern Algebra 1, Resource Book Chapter 3: An Integrated Approach. Gerver et al. (MA - Academic Math Ser.). 1997. pap. 7.95 (*0-538-66446-0*) S-W Pub.

Southwestern Algebra 1, Resource Book Chapter 4: An Integrated Approach. Gerver et al. (MA - Academic Math Ser.). 1997. pap. 7.95 (*0-538-66447-9*) S-W Pub.

Southwestern Algebra 1, Resource Book Chapter 5: An Integrated Approach. Gerver et al. (MA - Academic Math Ser.). 1997. pap. 7.95 (*0-538-66448-7*) S-W Pub.

Southwestern Algebra 1, Resource Book Chapter 6: An Integrated Approach. Gerver et al. (MA - Academic Math Ser.). 1997. pap. 7.95 (*0-538-66449-5*) S-W Pub.

Southwestern Algebra 1, Resource Book, Chapter 7. Gerver et al. (MA - Academic Math Ser.). 1997. pap. 1.99 (*0-538-66376-6*) S-W Pub.

Southwestern Algebra 1, Resource Book Chapter 8: An Integrated Approach. Gerver et al. (MA - Academic Math Ser.). 1997. pap. 7.95 (*0-538-66450-9*) S-W Pub.

Southwestern Algebra 1, Resource Book Chapter 9: An Integrated Approach. Gerver et al. (MA - Academic Math Ser.). 1997. pap. 7.95 (*0-538-66456-8*) S-W Pub.

Southwestern Algebra 1, Solutions Manual: An Integrated Approach. Gerver et al. (MA - Academic Math Ser.). 1997. pap. 45.95 (*0-538-66464-9*) S-W Pub.

Southwestern Algebra 1, Study Skills & Activities: An Integrated Approach. Gerver et al. (MA - Academic Math Ser.). 1997. pap. 10.95 (*0-538-66468-1*) S-W Pub.

Southwestern Algebra 1, Teacher's Edition Sampler Chapter 7. Gerver et al. (MA - Academic Math Ser.). 1997. pap. 2.95 (*0-538-66375-8*) S-W Pub.

Southwestern Algebra 1, Technology Activities: An Integrated Approach. Gerver et al. (MA - Academic Math Ser.). 1997. pap. 17.95 (*0-538-66467-3*) S-W Pub.

Southwestern Algebra 2, Lesson Plans: An Integrated Approach. Gerver et al. (MA - Academic Math Ser.). 1997. pap. 17.95 (*0-538-66525-4*) S-W Pub.

Southwestern Algebra 2, Math Handbook: An Integrated Approach. Gerver et al. (MA - Academic Math Ser.). 1997. pap. 17.95 (*0-538-66516-5*) S-W Pub.

Southwestern Algebra 2, Math Handbook: An Integrated Approach. Gerver et al. (MA - Academic Math Ser.). (SPA.). 1997. pap. 17.95 (*0-538-66517-3*) S-W Pub.

Southwestern Algebra 2, Multicultural Connections: An Integrated Approach. Gerver et al. (MA - Academic Math Ser.). 1997. pap. 17.95 (*0-538-66522-X*) S-W Pub.

Southwestern Algebra 2, Pass-Tests-Assessment: An Integrated Approach. Sgroi et al. (MA - Academic Math Ser.). 1997. pap. 72.95 (*0-538-66529-7*) S-W Pub.

Southwestern Algebra 2, Resource Book Chapter 1: An Integrated Approach. Gerver et al. (MA - Academic Math Ser.). 1997. pap. 7.95 (*0-538-66502-5*) S-W Pub.

Southwestern Algebra 2, Resource Book Chapter 10: An Integrated Approach. Gerver et al. (MA - Academic Math Ser.). 1997. pap. 7.95 (*0-538-66511-4*) S-W Pub.

Southwestern Algebra 2, Resource Book Chapter 11: An Integrated Approach. Gerver et al. (MA - Academic Math Ser.). 1997. pap. 7.95 (*0-538-66512-2*) S-W Pub.

Southwestern Algebra 2, Resource Book Chapter 12: An Integrated Approach. Gerver et al. (MA - Academic Math Ser.). 1997. pap. 7.95 (*0-538-66513-0*) S-W Pub.

Southwestern Algebra 2, Resource Book Chapter 13: An Integrated Approach. Gerver et al. (MA - Academic Math Ser.). 1997. pap. 7.95 (*0-538-66514-9*) S-W Pub.

Southwestern Algebra 2, Resource Book Chapter 15: An Integrated Approach. Gerver et al. (MA - Academic Math Ser.). 1997. pap. 7.95 (*0-538-66518-1*) S-W Pub.

Southwestern Algebra 2, Resource Book Chapter 16: An Integrated Approach. Gerver et al. (MA - Academic Math Ser.). 1997. pap. 7.95 (*0-538-66519-X*) S-W Pub.

Southwestern Algebra 2, Resource Book Chapter 2: An Integrated Approach. Gerver et al. (MA - Academic Math Ser.). 1997. pap. 7.95 (*0-538-66503-3*) S-W Pub.

Southwestern Algebra 2, Resource Book Chapter 3: An Integrated Approach. Gerver et al. (MA - Academic Math Ser.). 1997. pap. 7.95 (*0-538-66504-1*) S-W Pub.

Southwestern Algebra 2, Resource Book Chapter 4: An Integrated Approach. Gerver et al. (MA - Academic Math Ser.). 1997. pap. 7.95 (*0-538-66505-X*) S-W Pub.

Southwestern Algebra 2, Resource Book Chapter 5: An Integrated Approach. Gerver et al. (MA - Academic Math Ser.). 1997. pap. 7.95 (*0-538-66506-8*) S-W Pub.

Southwestern Algebra 2, Resource Book Chapter 6: An Integrated Approach. Gerver et al. (MA - Academic Math Ser.). 1997. pap. 7.95 (*0-538-66507-6*) S-W Pub.

Southwestern Algebra 2, Resource Book Chapter 7: An Integrated Approach. Gerver et al. (MA - Academic Math Ser.). 1997. pap. 7.95 (*0-538-66508-4*) S-W Pub.

Southwestern Algebra 2, Resource Book Chapter 8: An Integrated Approach. Gerver et al. (MA - Academic Math Ser.). 1997. pap. 7.95 (*0-538-66509-2*) S-W Pub.

Southwestern Algebra 2, Resource Book Chapter 9: An Integrated Approach. Gerver et al. (MA - Academic Math Ser.). 1997. pap. 7.95 (*0-538-66510-6*) S-W Pub.

Southwestern Algebra 2, Solutions Manual: An Integrated Approach. Gerver et al. (MA - Academic Math Ser.). 1997. pap. 45.95 (*0-538-66520-3*) S-W Pub.

Southwestern Algebra 2, Study Skills & Activities: An Integrated Approach. Gerver et al. (MA - Academic Math Ser.). 1997. pap. 10.95 (*0-538-66524-6*) S-W Pub.

Southwestern Algebra 2, Technology Activities: An Integrated Approach. Gerver et al. (MA - Academic Math Ser.). 1997. pap. 17.95 (*0-538-66523-8*) S-W Pub.

Southwestern Archaeology. 2nd ed. John C. McGregor. LC 65-10079. (Illus.). 518p. 1982. pap. text ed. 19.95 (*0-252-00989-4*) U of Ill Pr.

Southwestern Arkansas Death Record Index, 1914-1923: Calhoun, Clark, Columbia, Dallas, Hempstead, Howard, Lafayette, Little River, Miller, Nevada, Ouachita, Pike, Sevier, & Union Counties. Ed. by Desmond W. Allen. 72p. (Orig.). 1996. pap. 16.00 (*1-56546-084-7*) Arkansas Res.

Southwestern Arkansas Death Record Index, 1934-1940: Calhoun, Clark, Columbia, Dallas, Hempstead, Howard, Lafayette, Little River, Miller, Nevada, Ouachita, Pike, Sevier, & Union Counties. Ed. by Desmond W. Allen. 61p. (Orig.). 1996. pap. 15.00 (*1-56546-092-8*) Arkansas Res.

Southwestern Arts & Crafts Projects. rev. ed. Patricia Byrnes & Nancy Krenz. LC 77-18988. (Illus.). (J). (gr. 1-8). 1979. pap. 9.95 (*0-913270-62-8*) Sunstone Pr.

Southwestern College Key-Boarding for Windows Introductory Course with Microsoft Word 6.0 & WordPerfect 6.0. 13th ed. Charles H. Duncan et al. 1996. text ed. 39.95 (*0-538-70866-2*) S-W Pub.

Southwestern College Keyboarding for Windows Document Processing with Microsoft Word 6.0 & WordPerfect 6.0. 13th ed. Charles H. Duncan et al. 1996. text ed. 39.95 (*0-538-71042-X*) S-W Pub.

Southwestern Cookery: Indian & Spanish Influences. Franklin H. Giddings & John B Clark. 1973. 17.95 (*0-405-05054-2*) Ayer.

Southwestern Country Classics: Early American Woodworking Projects. Gloria Saberin. (Illus.). 160p. 1992. pap. 14.95 (*0-8306-4195-5*, 4259) McGraw-Hill Prof.

Southwestern Cuisine. Jim Martin. (Illus.). 64p. (Orig.). 1993. pap. 7.95 (*0-9624640-3-1*) Crow Canyon Archaeol.

***Southwestern Desert Life.** James Kavanagh. (Illus.). 1997. 7.95 (*1-889903-04-3*) Waterford WA.

Southwestern Expedition of Zebulon M. Pike. Ed. by Milo M. Quaife. LC 70-124252. (Select Bibliographies Reprint Ser.). 1977. 18.95 (*0-8369-5440-8*) Ayer.

Southwestern Expedition of Zebulon M. Pike. Aebulon M. Pike. (American Biography Ser.). 239p. 1991. reprint ed. lib. bdg. 69.00 (*0-7812-8316-7*) Rprt Serv.

***Southwestern Grilling: Light & Simple Cooking Year-Round.** Jane Stacey. LC 96-53568. 112p. 1998. pap. 13.00 (*0-553-06166-6*) Broadway BDD.

Southwestern Heritage Cookbook: A Legacy of Good Food. Marian W. Clark. (Illus.). 1989. pap. 9.95 (*0-9622437-0-1*) M Clark.

Southwestern Historical Quarterly, 42 vols., Set. Texas State Historical Association Staff. 1993. reprint ed. lib. bdg. 3,150.00 (*0-7812-5907-X*) Rprt Serv.

***Southwestern Indian Arts & Crafts.** 3rd rev. ed. Tom Bahti & Mark Bahti. LC 97-70255. (Illus.). 64p. 1997. pap. 7.95 (*0-88714-095-5*) KC Pubns.

Southwestern Indian Baskets: Their History & Their Makers. Andrew H. Whiteford. (Illus.). 219p. 1988. pap. 18.95 (*0-933452-24-1*) Schol Am Res.

Southwestern Indian Baskets: Their History & Their Makers. Andrew H. Whiteford. LC 88-3255. (Illus.). 236p. 1988. pap. 18.95 (*0-295-96686-6*) U of Wash Pr.

***Southwestern Indian Ceremonials.** 3rd rev. ed. Tom Bahti & Mark Bahti. LC 97-70256. (Illus.). 64p. 1997. pap. 7.95 (*0-88714-096-3*) KC Pubns.

Southwestern Indian Designs. Madeleine Orban-Szontagh. 1992. pap. 3.95 (*0-486-26985-X*) Dover.

Southwestern Indian Detours. Diane Thomas. LC 77-94331. (Illus.). 328p. 1978. 8.95 (*0-918126-12-6*) Hunter Ariz.

Southwestern Indian Jewelry. Dexter Cirillo. (Illus.). 240p. 1992. 49.95 (*1-55859-282-2*) Abbeville Pr.

Southwestern Indian Recipe Book. Zora G. Hesse. (Wild & Woolly West Ser.: No. 23). (Illus.). 60p. (Orig.). 1973. pap. 4.00 (*0-910584-89-3*) Filter.

***Southwestern Indian Tribes.** 2nd rev. ed. Tom Bahti & Mark Bahti. LC 97-70257. (Illus.). 80p. 1997. pap. 7.95 (*0-88714-097-1*) KC Pubns.

Southwestern Journal of Adolph F. Bandelier, 1883-1884. Adolph F. Bandelier. Ed. by Charles H. Lange & Carroll L. Riley. LC 65-17862. 562p. reprint ed. pap. 160.20 (*0-317-26629-2*, 2025431) Bks Demand.

Southwestern Journals of Adolf F. Bandelier, 1880-1882. Adolph F. Bandelier. Ed. by Charles H. Lange & Carroll L. Riley. LC 65-17862. 502p. reprint ed. pap. 143.10 (*0-317-26625-X*, 2025430) Bks Demand.

Southwestern Journals of Adolph F. Bandelier, 1885-1888. Adolph F. Bandelier. Ed. by Charles H. Lange & Carroll L. Riley. LC 65-17862. 720p. reprint ed. pap. 180.00 (*0-317-26630-6*, 2025432) Bks Demand.

Southwestern Landscaping with Native Plants. Judith Phillips. (Illus.). 160p. 1987. pap. 24.95 (*0-89013-166-X*) Museum NM Pr.

Southwestern Lore. Ed. by J. Frank Dobie. LC 33-1134. (Texas Folklore Society Publications: No. 9). (Illus.). 208p. 1965. reprint ed. 12.95 (*0-87074-042-3*) UNTX Pr.

Southwestern Medical Dictionary: Spanish-English & English-Spanish. Margarita A. Kay. LC 76-54591. 217p. (ENG & SPA.). 1977. pap. 12.50 (*0-8165-0529-2*) U of Ariz Pr.

***Southwestern Minnesota Archaeology: 12,000 Years in the Prairie Lake Region.** Scott F. Anfinson. LC 97-518. (Minnesota Prehistoric Archaeology Ser.: Vol. 14). (Illus.). 156p. (Orig.). 1997. pap. 18.00 (*0-87351-355-X*) Minn Hist.

***Southwestern Night Sky: Easy Field Guide to the Southwestern Night Sky.** Dan Heim. (Illus.). 32p. (Orig.). 1997. pap. 1.25 (*0-935810-62-5*) Primer Pubs.

Southwestern Ornamentation & Design: The Architecture of John Gaw Meem. Anne Taylor. LC 85-2785. (Illus.). 105p. 1989. pap. 16.95 (*0-86534-069-2*) Sunstone Pr.

Southwestern Pennsylvania Painters, 1800-1945: Collection of Westmoreland Museum of Art. Paul A. Chew. LC 89-50233. (Illus.). 136p. (Orig.). 1989. pap. 14.95 (*0-931241-21-9*) Westmoreland.

***Southwestern Pizza Cookbook.** Dennis Rohde. LC 97-17037. (Illus.). 160p. 1997. spiral bd. 14.95 (*0-87358-677-8*) Northland AZ.

Southwestern Pottery: An Annotated Bibliography & List of Types & Wares. Norman T. Oppelt. LC 88-6424. (Illus.). 333p. 1988. 45.00 (*0-8108-2119-2*) Scarecrow.

Southwestern Pottery: Anasazi to Zuni. Allan Hayes. LC 96-16957. (Illus.). 200p. 1996. 40.00 (*0-87358-663-8*); pap. 21.95 (*0-87358-656-5*) Northland AZ.

Southwestern United States Under Mexico: Rare Imprints Concerning California, Arizona, New Mexico & Texas, 1821-1846. Ed. & Intro. by David J. Weber. LC 76-7344. (Chicano Heritage Ser.). (Illus.). 1977. 39.95 (*0-405-09543-0*) Ayer.

Southwestern University Law Review: Los Angeles, 1916-1994/95, 22 vols. mic. film write for info. (*0-318-57460-8*) Rothman.

Southwestern University Law Review: Los Angeles, 1916-1994/95, 24 vols., Set. Bound set. 1,040.00 (*0-8377-9143-X*) Rothman.

***Southwestern Women: New Voices.** Ed. by Caitlin L. Gannon. LC 96-78474. 184p. (Orig.). 1997. pap. 12.95 (*0-9654418-3-0*) Javelina Press.

Southwest's Best Bed & Breakfasts: Delightful Places to Stay & Great Things to Do When You Get There. 2nd ed. Berkeley Travel Staff. (Fodor's Bed & Breakfast & Country Inns Ser.). 1995. pap. 15.00 (*0-679-02977-X*) Fodors Travel.

Southwick: The D-Day Village That Went to War. Geoffrey O'Connell. 1995. 8.95 (*1-85253-299-8*) Cimino Pub Grp.

Southwold Diary of James Maggs Vol. II: 1848-1876. Ed. by Alan F. Bottomley. (Suffolk Records Society Ser.: No. XXVI). (Illus.). 192p. 1985. 24.00 (*0-85115-411-5*) Boydell & Brewer.

Soutien De Famille. Alphonse Daudet. 460p. (FRE.). 1898. 14.95 (*0-8288-9191-5*, F59870) Fr & Eur.

Soutine. Raymond Cogniat. (CAL Art Ser.). (Illus.). 96p. 1984. 14.95 (*0-517-51136-3*, Crown) Crown Pub Group.

Soutine. Monroe Wheeler. LC 66-26125. (Museum of Modern Art Publications in Reprint). 1967. reprint ed. 17.95 (*0-405-01523-2*) Ayer.

***Soutine I & II.** Maurice Tuchman. 1994. 79.90 (*3-8228-9504-0*) Taschen Amer.

***Souto de Moura.** Oscar R. Ojeda. (Ten Houses Ser.). (Illus.). 108p. (Orig.). 1997. pap. 19.99 (*1-56496-394-2*) Rockport Pubs.

Souvenir. Patricia Carlon. LC 95-18477. 183p. 1996. 20.00 (*1-56947-048-0*) Soho Press.

Souvenir. Patricia Carlon. LC 95-18477. (Soho Crime Ser.). 183p. 1996. pap. 12.00 (*1-56947-065-0*) Soho Press.

Souvenir Book of the Ephrata Cloister: Complete History from Its Settlement in 1728 to the Present Time. Samuel G. Zerfass. LC 72-2960. reprint ed. 36.00 (*0-404-10724-9*) AMS Pr.

Souvenir Buildings & Miniature Monuments: From the Collection of Ace Architects. Margaret Majua & David Weingarten. LC 96-10852. (Illus.). 128p. 1996. 19.95 (*0-8109-4470-7*) Abrams.

Souvenir D'Amour: Erotic Memoirs of Paris in the 1920s. Anne-Marie Villefranche. 224p. 1992. pap. 4.50 (*0-88184-827-1*) Carroll & Graf.

Souvenir de Deux Existences. Jean Giraudoux. (FRE.). 1975. 6.95 (*0-7859-0101-9*, M3513) Fr & Eur.

Souvenir Flute Viola Harp. W. Piston. 8p. 1991. pap. 6.95 (*0-7935-0954-8*) H Leonard.

***Souvenir Lives Forever.** Margarette R. Peck. (Orig.). 1997. pap. write for info. (*1-57553-452-5*) Watermrk Pr.

Souvenir Pillows from Mars. unabridged ed. James Magorian. LC 94-79911. 118p. 1996. 25.00 (*0-930674-42-1*) Black Oak.

Souvenir Portraits. Jean Cocteau. (Illus.). 173p. 1994. 17.95 (*1-56924-961-X*) Marlowe & Co.

Souvenir Program Book, 1993. 112p. 1993. write for info. (*0-9636080-0-2*) Shenand Apple.

Souvenir Programs of Five Great World Series - 1914, 1917, 1919, 1926, 1934. Ed. by Bert R. Sugar. 1990. 17.00 (*0-8446-5822-7*) Peter Smith.

Souvenir View Book of Washington. Illus. by White House Historical Association Staff et al. 96p. (ENG, FRE, GER & SPA.). reprint ed. pap. 7.50 (*1-879295-02-4*) L B Prince.

Souvenirs. Alexis De Tocqueville. (FRE.). 1978. pap. 13.95 (*0-7859-2891-X*, 2070369919) Fr & Eur.

***Souvenirs.** Photos by Benjamin Katz. (Illus.). 340p. 1997. 50.00 (*3-89508-256-2*) Knckerbocker.

Souvenirs. Charles Peguy. pap. 1.95 (*0-685-37041-0*) Fr & Eur.

Souvenirs. Melissa Snyder. 192p. (Orig.). (YA). (gr. 6 up). 1995. pap. 3.50 (*0-380-77805-X*, Flare) Avon.

Souvenirs: A Feast of Local Color & Home Cooking. Gini Ogle & Karen Noice. 205p. 1993. 18.95 (*0-9640623-0-5*) Echo Designs.

Souvenirs: Gifts from the Gardens. Kathryn Klienman. 1995. pap. 15.00 (*0-00-649223-1*) Collins SF.

Souvenirs: Les Casques, La Mort d'Ivan Illitch, Maitre et Serviteur, etc. Leo Tolstoy. 1620p. 41.50 (*0-686-56587-8*) Fr & Eur.

Souvenirs Acadiens. Benjamin Stevens. 60p. (Orig.). 1995. pap. write for info. (*1-57553-041-4*) Watermrk Pr.

Souvenirs Ballet Suite Opus 28: One Piano, Four Hands Original. S. Barber. 68p. 1986. pap. 19.95 (*0-7935-4991-4*, 50286370) H Leonard.

***Souvenirs d'Amour.** Danielle Steel. 520p. (FRE.). 1997. pap. 25.99 (*2-84011-201-9*) Ulverscroft.

Souvenirs De Guerre **see Memoirs of War, 1914-15**

Souvenirs de la Cour d'Assises. Andre Gide. 120p. (FRE.). 1914. 12.95 (*0-8288-9781-6*, F102840) Fr & Eur.

Souvenirs de la Maison des Morts. Fyodor Dostoyevsky. 446p. (FRE.). 1977. pap. 11.95 (*0-7859-1851-5*, 2070369250) Fr & Eur.

Souvenirs de la Vie du Paradis. Georges Duhamel. 204p. 9.95 (*0-686-55196-6*) Fr & Eur.

An Asterisk (*) at the beginning of an entry indicates that the title is appearing in BIP for the first time.

Souvenirs de l'Enfance de Leonardo da Vinci. Sigmund Freud. 151p. (FRE.). 1977. pap. 10.95 (0-7859-2626-7, 207035377X) Fr & Eur.

Souvenirs d'Egotisme. Stendhal. (Folio Ser.: No. 1430). (FRE.). pap. 9.95 (2-07-037430-0) Schoenhof.

Souvenirs d'Enfance, 3 tomes. Marcel Pagnol. Incl. Tome I. Gloire de Mon Pere. 14.95 (0-685-37010-0); Tome II. Chateau de Ma Mere. 15.50 (0-685-37011-9); Tome III. Temps des Secrets. 15.95 (0-685-37012-7); write for info. (0-318-52267-5) Fr & Eur.

Souvenirs d'Enfance: Le Temps des Amours, Vol. 4. Marcel Pagnol. 290p. (FRE.). 1979. 21.95 (0-7859-4730-2) Fr & Eur.

Souvenirs d'Enfance et de Jeunesse. Ernest Renan. (FRE.). 1992. pap. 8.95 (0-7859-3173-2, 2253061751) Fr & Eur.

Souvenirs du Triangle d'Or. Alain Robbe-Grillet. (FRE.). 1985. pap. 16.95 (0-7859-2700-X, 2020086123) Fr & Eur.

Souvenirs due triangle d'or see Recollections of the Golden Triangle

Souvenirs, Eighteen Ninety-Five to Nineteen Eighteen: My Life with Maeterlinck. Georgette Leblanc. Tr. by Janet Flanner from FRE. LC 76-22154. (Music Reprint Ser.). 352p. 1976. reprint ed. lib. bdg. 39.50 (0-306-70841-8) Da Capo.

Souvenirs, Eighteen Seventy-Eight to Eighteen Ninety-Three. Charles L. De Freycinet. LC 73-258. (Europe 1815-1945 Ser.). 524p. 1973. reprint ed. lib. bdg. 65.00 (0-306-70560-5) Da Capo.

Souvenirs et Recits. Leo Tolstoy. (FRE.). 1978. lib. bdg. 95.00 (0-8288-3577-2, M5198) Fr & Eur.

Souvenirs from a Boarding School. 208p. (Orig.). 1996. pap. 7.95 (1-56201-084-0, North Star Line) Blue Moon Bks.

Souvenirs from a Boarding School. 1995. mass mkt. 7.95 (1-56201-092-1) Blue Moon Bks.

Souvenirs, Notes et Pensees Intimes. Gustave Flaubert. 109p. (FRE.). 1965. pap. 24.95 (0-7859-5526-7) Fr & Eur.

Souvenirs of Tuscany. Helen D. Whiting. 288p. 1990. 21.95 (0-9627035-0-8) H D Whiting.

Souvenirs Personnels, 1848-1851. Victor Hugo. 328p. (FRE.). 1952. 7.95 (0-7859-0002-0, F64090) Fr & Eur.

Souvenirs Pieux. Marguerite Yourcenar. (Folio Ser.: No. 1165). (FRE.). pap. 9.95 (2-07-037165-4) Schoenhof.

Souvenirs Pieux, le Labyrinthe du Monde, Vol. 2. Margurite Yourcenar. (FRE.). 1980. pap. 11.95 (0-8288-3809-7, M11970) Fr & Eur.

Souvenirs Poetiques. Paul Valery. pap. 3.95 (0-685-36626-X) Fr & Eur.

Souverain. Therese De Saint Phalle. (FRE.). 1976. pap. 10.95 (0-7859-4060-X, 2070367975) Fr & Eur.

Sou'west in Wanderer 4. Eric C. Hiscock. (Illus.). 236p. 1973. 25.00 (0-19-217528-9) OUP.

Sovereign All-Creating Mind-The Motherly Buddha: A Translation of the Kun Byed Rgyal Po'i Mdo. E. K. Neumaier-Dargyay. LC 91-2500. (SUNY Series in Buddhist Studies). 246p. 1992. text ed. 59.50 (0-7914-0895-7); pap. text ed. 19.95 (0-7914-0896-5) State U NY Pr.

Sovereign Council of New France: A Study in Canadian Constitutional History. Raymond D. Cahall. LC 15-13350. (Columbia University. Studies in the Social Sciences: No. 156). reprint ed. 36.50 (0-404-51156-2) AMS Pr.

Sovereign Creations: Pan-Arabism & Political Order in Syria & Iraq. Malik Mufti. 288p. 1996. 35.00 (0-8014-3168-9) Cornell U Pr.

Sovereign Entrepreneur: Oil Policies in Advanced & Less Developed Capitalist Countries. Merrie G. Klapp. LC 86-19909. (Cornell Studies in Political Economy). 256p. 1987. 42.50 (0-8014-1997-2) Cornell U Pr.

Sovereign Ghost: Studies in Imagination. Denis Donoghue. LC 75-27923. 239p. reprint ed. pap. 68.20 (0-685-44500-3, 2031532) Bks Demand.

Sovereign God - Chinese Edition. James M. Boice. Tr. by John Liu. 208p. (CHI.). 1988. pap. 7.00 (1-56582-095-9) Christ Renew Min.

Sovereign Idea: Essays on Canada As a Democratic Community. Reg Whitaker. 1991. 55.00 (0-7735-0841-4, Pub. by McGill CN); pap. 22.95 (0-7735-0878-3, Pub. by McGill CN) U of Toronto Pr.

Sovereign Individual: How to Survive & Thrive During the Collapse of the Welfare State. James D. Davidson & Rees Mogg. LC 96-48244. 400p. 1997. 24.50 (0-684-81007-7, S&S) S&S Trade.

Sovereign Individuals of Capitalism. Nicholas Abercrombie et al. 224p. (C). 1986. 55.00 (0-04-301230-2); pap. text ed. 17.95 (0-04-301231-0) Routledge Chapman & Hall.

Sovereign Lady: Essays on Women in Middle English Literature. Ed. by Muriel A. Whitaker. LC 94-30711. (Medieval Casebooks Ser.: Vol. 11). (Illus.). 240p. 1995. text ed. 40.00 (0-8153-1888-X, H1876) Garland.

Sovereign Nations or Reservations? An Economic History of American Indians. Terry L. Anderson. 180p. 19.95 (0-936488-81-6) PRIPP.

Sovereign of the Sea. Howarth. 1986. 14.95 (0-689-10517-7, Atheneum S&S) S&S Trade.

Sovereign Prerogative: The Supreme Court & the Quest for Law. Eugene V. Rostow. LC 73-17923. 318p. 1974. reprint ed. text ed. 35.00 (0-8371-7276-4, RSOP, Greenwood Pr) Greenwood.

Sovereign Rescheduling: Risk & Portfolio Management. Ronald L. Solberg. (Illus.). 220p. 1988. text ed. 55.00 (0-04-332122-4) Routledge Chapman & Hall.

Sovereign Risk Analysis. Shelagh A. Heffernan. 200p. (C). 1986. text ed. 49.95 (0-04-332119-4); pap. text ed. 24.95 (0-04-445150-4) Routledge Chapman & Hall.

Sovereign Seven. Chris Claremont. Ed. by Bob Kahan & Dwayne Turner. (Illus.). 208p. 1996. pap. 12.95 (1-56389-269-3) DC Comics.

***Sovereign State & Its Competitors: An Analysis of Systems Change.** Hendrik Spruyt. 302p. 1994. pap. text ed. 16.95 (0-691-02910-5) Princeton U Pr.

Sovereign State of Boogedy Boogedy & Other Plays. Lonnie Carter. LC 86-18503. (Illus.). 205p. (Orig.). 1986. pap. text ed. 7.50 (0-933951-04-3) Locust Hill Pr.

Sovereign Statehood: The Basis of International Society. Alan James. LC 85-26707. (Key Concepts in International Relations Ser.: No. 2). 1986. text ed. 55.00 (0-04-320190-3); pap. text ed. 19.95 (0-04-320191-1) Routledge Chapman & Hall.

Sovereign States in an Age of Uncertainty. Ed. by Ronald Hoffman & Peter J. Albert. LC 81-19660. (U. S. Capitol Historical Society, Perspectives on the American Revolution Ser.). 261p. 1982. text ed. 35.00 (0-8139-0926-0) U Pr of Va.

Sovereign Sun: Selected Poems. Odysseus Elytis. 208p. 9000. pap. 18.95 (1-85224-120-9, Pub. by Bloodaxe Bks UK) Dufour.

Sovereign Virtue: Aristotle on the Relation Between Happiness & Prosperity. Stephen A. White. LC 91-26348. (Series in Philosophy). 360p. (C). 1992. 42.50 (0-8047-1694-3) Stanford U Pr.

Sovereignes & the Admiral. Jon Bauman. (Illus.). 1992. 24.95 (1-878096-23-0, Epigram Pr) Best E TX Pubs.

***Sovereigns - Peacefully - Take Charge: An Agenda for Liberty & Justice.** Allan Matthews. LC 96-92954. (Illus.). x, 149p. (Orig.). 1997. pap. 8.00 (0-9655953-0-7) Sovereign People Press.

Sovereigns, Quasi Sovereigns, & Africans: Race & Self-Determination in International Law. Siba N. Grovogui. LC 95-24824. (Borderlines Ser.: Vol. 3). 1996. text ed. 54.95 (0-8166-2666-9); pap. text ed. 21.95 (0-8166-2667-7) U of Minn Pr.

Sovereignty. 2nd ed. Francis H. Hinsley. 272p. 1986. pap. 18.95 (0-521-33988-X) Cambridge U Pr.

Sovereignty & Coinage in Classical Greece. Thomas R. Martin. LC 84-26292. (Illus.). 300p. 1985. text ed. 55.00 (0-691-03580-6) Princeton U Pr.

***Sovereignty & Coinage in Classical Greece.** Thomas R. Martin. LC 84-26292. reprint ed. pap. 98.70 (0-608-04643-4, 2065330) Bks Demand.

Sovereignty & Intelligence: Spying & Court Culture in the English Renaissance. John M. Archer. LC 92-30593. 216p. 1993. 37.50 (0-8047-2079-7) Stanford U Pr.

Sovereignty & Liberty: Constitutional Discourse in American Culture. Michael G. Kammen. LC 88-40200. 256p. (C). 1989. text ed. 15.95 (0-299-11730-8) U of Wis Pr.

Sovereignty & Protection: A Study of British Jurisdictional Imperialism in the Late Nineteenth Century. W. Ross Johnston. LC 72-96681. (Duke University, Commonwealth-Studies Center, Publication Ser.: No. 41). 368p. reprint ed. pap. 104.90 (0-317-26778-7, 2023407) Bks Demand.

Sovereignty & Rebellion: The White Hmong of Northern Thailand. Nicholas C. Tapp. (South-East Asian Social Science Monographs). 284p. 1990. 39.95 (0-19-588912-6) OUP.

***Sovereignty & the Sword: Harrington, Hobbes, & Mixed Government in the English Civil Wars.** Arihiro Fukuda. (Oxford Historical Monographs). 192p. 1997. 75.00 (0-19-820683-6) OUP.

Sovereignty As Responsibility: Conflict Management in Africa. Francis M. Deng et al. 275p. 1996. 42.95 (0-8157-1828-4); pap. 18.95 (0-8157-1827-6) Brookings.

Sovereignty Association. Adalbert G. Lallier. 86p. 1991. pap. 10.95 (0-88962-477-1) Mosaic.

Sovereignty Association: Economic Realism or Utopia? Adalbert G. Lallier. 87p. 1995. lib. bdg. 31.00 (0-8095-4864-X) Borgo Pr.

Sovereignty at the Crossroads? Morality & International Politics in the Post-Cold War Era. Ed. by Luis E. Lugo. 208p. (C). 1996. pap. text ed. 22.95 (0-8476-8215-3); lib. bdg. 57.50 (0-8476-8214-5) Rowman.

Sovereignty Dispute over the Falkland (Malvinas) Islands. Lowell S. Gustafson. 288p. 1988. 49.95 (0-19-504184-4) OUP.

Sovereignty of God. Arthur W. Pink. 272p. (gr. 10). 1984. pap. 12.99 (0-8010-7088-0) Baker Bks.

Sovereignty of God. Arthur W. Pink. 1976. pap. 6.50 (0-85151-133-3) Banner of Truth.

Sovereignty of God, No. 50. pap. 0.15 (0-87377-160-5) GAM Pubns.

Sovereignty of God in Providence. John G. Reisinger. 40p. (Orig.). 1989. reprint ed. pap. write for info. (0-925703-06-0) Crown MA.

Sovereignty of Grace. Arthur C. Custance. 398p. 1989. reprint ed. 24.95 (0-919857-03-5, Pub. by Doorway Pubns CN) Doorway USA.

Sovereignty of Reason: The Defense of Rationality in the Early English Enlightenment. Frederick C. Beiser. LC 96-14461. 328p. 1997. text ed. 39.50 (0-691-03395-1) Princeton U Pr.

***Sovereignty of the Father & Son.** Roger E. Dickson. (Biblical Research Library: No. 1). 125p. (Orig.). 1996. pap. 7.95 (1-56794-114-1, C-2434) Star Bible.

Sovereignty of the Individual. Stephen P. Andrews. 1972. 250.00 (0-8490-1094-2) Gordon Pr.

Sovereignty of the Law: Selections from Blackstone's Commentaries on the Laws of England. William Blackstone. LC 72-94916. 312p. reprint ed. pap. 89.00 (0-8357-4720-4, 2037636) Bks Demand.

***Sovereignty over Natural Resources: Balancing Rights & Duties.** Nico Schrijver. (Studies in International & Comparative Law). 490p. (C). 1997. text ed. 90.00 (0-521-56269-4) Cambridge U Pr.

***Sovereignty Through Interdependence.** Harry G. Gelber. LC 96-39075. 1997. write for info. (90-411-0946-3) Kluwer Law Tax Pubs.

Soverign Shame: A Study of King Lear. William F. Zak. LC 82-74489. 208p. 1984. 32.50 (0-8387-5056-7) Bucknell U Pr.

Sovetsko-Kitaiskie Otnosheniia, Nineteen Seventeen to Nineteen Fifty-Seven: Sbornik Dokumentov. Akademiia Nauk SSSR Staff. Ed. by I. F. Kurdiukov et al. LC 70-38048. (China, Classic & Contemporary Works in Reprint Ser.). reprint ed. 57.50 (0-404-56902-1) AMS Pr.

Sovetskoe Literaturovedenie I Kritika, 1917-1925, Bibliograficheskii Ukazetel' Literatury Na Russkom Iazyke - Soviet Studies in Literature & Literary Criticism, 1917-1925 Vols. 1-3, 3 vols., Set. (RUS.). 1994. lib. bdg. 300.00 (0-88354-382-6) N Ross.

Sovetskoe Literaturovedenie I Kritika, 1917-1925, Bibliograficheskii Ukazetel' Literatury Na Russkom Iazyke - Soviet Studies in Literature & Literary Criticism, 1917-1925 Vols. 1-3, Vol. 1. Ed. by Iurii D. Ryskin. xii, 266p. (RUS.). 1994. lib. bdg. write for info. (0-88354-367-2) N Ross.

Sovetskoe Literaturovedenie I Kritika, 1917-1925, Bibliograficheskii Ukazetel' Literatury Na Russkom Iazyke - Soviet Studies in Literature & Literary Criticism, 1917-1925 Vols. 1-3, Vol. 2. 389p. (RUS.). 1994. lib. bdg. write for info. (0-88354-368-0) N Ross.

Sovetskoe Literaturovedenie I Kritika, 1917-1925, Bibliograficheskii Ukazetel' Literatury Na Russkom Iazyke - Soviet Studies in Literature & Literary Criticism, 1917-1925 Vols. 1-3, Vol. 3. 265p. (RUS.). 1994. lib. bdg. write for info. (0-88354-369-9) N Ross.

Soviet Academy of Sciences & the Communist Party, 1927-1932. Loren R. Graham. LC 67-12346. (Studies of the Russian Institute, Columbia University & Harvard Series in Ukrainian Studies). 275p. reprint ed. pap. 78.40 (0-8357-2785-8, 2039911) Bks Demand.

***Soviet Aces of World War 2.** Hugh Morgan. (Aircraft of the Aces Ser.: No. 15). (Illus.). 96p. 1996. pap. 15.95 (1-85532-632-9, Pub. by Osprey Pubng Ltd UK) Motorbooks Intl.

Soviet Administrative Elite. Kenneth C. Farmer. LC 91-33599. 320p. 1992. text ed. 59.95 (0-275-94139-6, C4139, Praeger Pubs) Greenwood.

Soviet Administrative Law: Theory & Policy. Ed. by George Ginsburgs & William B. Simons. (C). 1989. lib. bdg. 210.00 (0-7923-0288-5) Kluwer Ac.

Soviet Administrative Legality: The Role of the Attorney General's Office. Glenn G. Morgan. x, 281p. 1962. 42.50 (0-8047-0143-1) Stanford U Pr.

Soviet Advances in Applied Geophysics. 130p. (C). 1990. text ed. 70.00 (90-6191-139-7, Pub. by A A Balkema NE) Ashgate Pub Co.

Soviet Afghan Relations. Satish Ganjoo. 1990. 23.50 (81-7158-100-5, Pub. by Anmol II) S Asia.

Soviet Agricultural & Peasant Affairs. Conference on Soviet Agricultural & Peasant Affairs. LC 81-20287. (Slavic Studies: No. 1). xi, 335p. 1982. reprint ed. text ed. 55.00 (0-313-23450-7, COSO, Greenwood Pr) Greenwood.

Soviet Agricultural Trade Unions, 1917-70. Peter J. Potichnvj. LC 70-163810. 288p. reprint ed. pap. 82.10 (0-317-09701-6, 2014344) Bks Demand.

Soviet Agriculture: Comparative Perspectives. Ed. by Kenneth R. Gray. LC 89-15401. (Special Study of the Kennan Institute for Advanced Russian Studies, Woodrow Wilson International Center for Scholars). (Illus.). 298p. 1990. reprint ed. pap. 85.00 (0-608-00100-7, 2060865) Bks Demand.

Soviet Agriculture: Development & Issues. R. G. Gidadhubli. (C). 1988. 16.00 (81-7050-074-5, Pub. by Patriot II) S Asia.

Soviet Agro-Industrial Complex: Structure & Performance: From Research to Production. Valentin Litvin. Ed. by Patra McSharry. (Illus.). 158p. (Orig.). 1985. pap. text ed. 75.00 (1-55831-027-4) Delphic Associates.

Soviet Aims in Central America: The Case of Nicaragua. G. W. Sand. LC 89-33959. 138p. 1989. text ed. 45.00 (0-275-93050-5, C3050, Praeger Pubs) Greenwood.

Soviet Air & Rocket Forces. Ed. by Asher Lee. LC 75-27682. (Illus.). 311p. 1976. reprint ed. text ed. 65.00 (0-8371-8456-8, LESAR, Greenwood Pr) Greenwood.

Soviet Air Force. Baker. LC 88-12121. (Soviet Military Power Ser.). (Illus.). 48p. (J). (gr. 3-8). 1987. lib. bdg. 18.60 (0-86625-331-9); lib. bdg. 13.95 (0-685-58301-5) Rourke Corp.

Soviet Air Power in Transition. Robert P. Berman. LC 77-86493. (Studies in Defense Policy). 82p. 1978. pap. 7.95 (0-8157-0923-4) Brookings.

Soviet Aircraft & Aviation, 1917-1941. Lennart Andersson. (Illus.). 352p. 1995. 59.95 (1-55750-770-8) Naval Inst Pr.

Soviet Airwomen in Combat in World War Two. Tr. by K. J. Cottam. 141p. 1983. pap. 30.95 (0-89126-118-4) MA-AH Pub.

Soviet Aluminum Industry: Methods & Materials. Sergei Solntsev. 128p. (Orig.). 1983. pap. text ed. 75.00 (1-55831-045-2) Delphic Associates.

Soviet-American Conflict Resolution in the Third World: Opportunities & Obstacles. Ed. by Mark N. Katz. LC 90-41049. 1991. pap. text ed. 19.95 (1-878379-07-0) US Inst Peace.

Soviet-American Confrontation: Postwar Reconstruction & the Origins of the Cold War. Thomas G. Paterson. LC 73-8120. 302p. reprint ed. pap. 86.10 (0-7837-5387-X, 2045151) Bks Demand.

Soviet-American Dance Medicine: Proceedings of the 1990 Glasnost Dance Medicine Conference & Workshops. Lyle J. Micheli. (Illus.). 113p. (Orig.). 1991. pap. text ed. 12.00 (0-88314-512-X) AAHPERD.

Soviet-American Dialogue in the Social Sciences: Research Workshops on Interdependence among Nations. National Research Council Staff. 84p. (C). 1990. pap. text ed. 15.00 (0-309-04289-5) Natl Acad Pr.

Soviet-American Dialogue on the New Deal. Ed. by Otis L. Graham, Jr. LC 88-27559. (Soviet-American Dialogues on U. S. History Ser.). 312p. 1989. text ed. 42.50 (0-8262-0612-3) U of Mo Pr.

Soviet-American Relations: Understanding Differences, Avoiding Conflicts. Ed. by Daniel N. Nelson & Roger B. Anderson. LC 88-19726. 211p. (C). 1988. 40.00 (0-8420-2300-3); pap. text ed. 15.95 (0-8420-2326-7) Scholarly Res Inc.

Soviet-American Relations after the Cold War. Ed. by Robert Jervis & Seweryn Bialer. LC 90-42413. 380p. (C). 1991. text ed. 49.95 (0-8223-1080-5); pap. text ed. 23.95 (0-8223-1098-8) Duke.

Soviet-American Relations in Asia, 1945-1954. Russell D. Buhite. LC 81-40285. (Illus.). 256p. 1989. 29.95 (0-8061-1729-X); pap. 14.95 (0-8061-2173-4) U of Okla Pr.

Soviet-American Relations in the 1980's: Super-Power Politics & East-West Trade. Lawrence Caldwell & William Diebold, Jr. (Illus.). 1980. pap. text ed. 24.75 (0-07-009616-3) McGraw.

Soviet-American Relations with Pakistan, Iran & Afghanistan. Hafeez Malik. 480p. 1987. text ed. 45.00 (0-312-00240-8) St Martin.

Soviet-American Relations, 1917-1920. George F. Kennan. 557p. 1989. pap. text ed. 18.95 (0-691-00841-8); pap. text ed. 18.95 (0-691-00842-6) Princeton U Pr.

Soviet-American Relations, 1917-1920, Set. George F. Kennan. 108p. 1989. pap. text ed. 29.95 (0-691-00847-7) Princeton U Pr.

Soviet-American Trade Negotiations. John W. De Pauw. LC 78-25883. (Praeger Special Studies). 200p. 1979. text ed. 59.95 (0-275-90346-X, C0346, Praeger Pubs) Greenwood.

***Soviet & American Psychology During World War II.** Albert R. Gilgen et al. LC 97-8773. (Contributions in Psychology: Vol. 34). 1997. text ed. write for info. (0-313-28794-5, Greenwood Pr) Greenwood.

Soviet & Chinese Aid to African Nations. Ed. by Warren Weinstein & Thomas H. Henriksen. LC 79-21128. (Praeger Special Studies). 202p. 1980. text ed. 49.95 (0-275-90565-9, C0565, Praeger Pubs) Greenwood.

Soviet & East European Linguistics see Current Trends in Linguistics

Soviet & East European Transport Problems. Ed. by John S. Ambler et al. LC 85-11917. 288p. 1985. text ed. 39.95 (0-312-74757-8) St Martin.

Soviet & Eastern European Studies: A Guide to Western Institutions. Ed. by Peter J. Potichnyj et al. 90p. 1995. lib. bdg. 35.00 (0-8095-4944-1) Borgo Pr.

Soviet & Eastern European Studies: A Guide to Western Institutions. Ed. by Peter J. Potichnyj et al. 90p. pap. 12.95 (0-88962-260-4) Mosaic.

Soviet & Post-Soviet Economic Structure & Performance. 5th ed. Paul R. Gregory & Robert C. Stuart. 392p. (C). 1994. text ed. 57.95 (0-673-46971-9) Addson-Wesley Educ.

Soviet & Post-Soviet Russia in a World of Change. Ed. by Allen C. Lynch & Kenneth W. Thompson. LC 93-35876. (Miller Center Series on a World in Change: Vol. 5). 238p. (Orig.). 1994. pap. text ed. 23.50 (0-8191-8706-2, Pub. by White Miller Center); lib. bdg. 52.00 (0-8191-8705-4, Pub. by White Miller Center) U Pr of Amer.

Soviet & Post-Soviet Telecommunications: An Industry under Reform. Robert W. Campbell. 256p. (C). 1995. text ed. 75.00 (0-8133-2547-1) Westview.

Soviet Antireligious Campaigns & Persecutions: A History of Soviet Atheism in Theory & Practice, & the Believer, Vol. 2. Dimitry V. Pospielovsky. LC 87-4826. 256p. 1988. pap. 14.95 (0-312-00905-4); text ed. 39.95 (0-312-00904-6) St Martin.

Soviet Applied Research in Microelectronics: The Institute of Semiconductor Physics, Siberian Department, USSR Academy of Sciences. Felix Edelman. Ed. by Andrew Michta. (Illus.). 135p. (Orig.). 1989. pap. text ed. 75.00 (1-55831-105-X) Delphic Associates.

Soviet Approach. Mark M. Boguslavski. Tr. by David Winter & William B. Simons. (C). 1988. lib. bdg. 127.50 (90-247-3629-3) Kluwer Ac.

Soviet Architecture. Ed. by Catherine Cooke & Alexander Kudriavtsev. (Architectural Design Profiles Ser.). (Illus.). 80p. 1987. pap. 21.95 (0-312-01281-0) St Martin.

Soviet Architecture, Nineteen Seventeen to Nineteen Sixty-Two: A Bibliographical Guide to Source Material. Anatole Senkevitch. LC 73-75335. 320p. reprint ed. pap. 91.20 (0-317-10311-3, 2020272) Bks Demand.

Soviet Arctic. Pier Horensma. 304p. (C). (gr. 13). 1991. text ed. 99.95 (0-415-05537-7, A5737) Routledge.

Soviet Arctic Shipping (From Design to Operation) Arthur Tertyshny. Ed. by Andreas Tamberg. 81p. (Orig.). 1987. pap. text ed. 75.00 (1-55831-069-X) Delphic Associates.

Soviet Armed Forces Review Annual, 1977-1988, Vols. 1-4 & 7-11. Ed. by David R. Jones. (SAFRA Ser.). Non-subscription. 95.00 (0-685-24293-5) Academic Intl.

Soviet Armed Forces, 1918-1992: A Research Guide to Soviet Sources. Compiled by John Erickson & Ljubica Erickson. LC 95-41983. (Research Guides in Military Studies: Vol. 8). 224p. 1996. text ed. 75.00 (0-313-29071-7, Greenwood Pr) Greenwood.

Soviet Arms Transfer Policy in South Asia, 1955-1981. N. S. Achuthan. (C). 1988. 32.00 (81-7062-037-6, Pub. by Lancer II) S Asia.

Soviet Army. Wood. (Soviet Military Power Ser.). (Illus.). 48p. (J). (gr. 3-8). 1987. lib. bdg. 18.60 (0-86625-334-3); lib. bdg. 13.95 (0-685-58298-1) Rourke Corp.

S

S

Soviet Army in Search of a New Identity. Catherine Bacarrere-Becane. Tr. by Robert P. Grant from FRE. (European Viewpoint Ser.). 51p. (Orig.). 1991. pap. 9.00 (*0-9629930-1-8*) US Crest.

Soviet Army Insignia 1917-1985: A Collectors Guide. M. Furlan. 72p. 1990. pap. 12.00 (*0-929757-25-4*, Pub. by Militaria Hse CN) Regt QM.

Soviet Army Order of Battle (Gehlen Red Book), 1941-1945. LC 83-81813. 200p. 1993. 14.00 (*0-941052-66-4*) Valor Pub.

Soviet Army Today. Steven J. Zaloga. (Elite Ser.: No. 12). (Illus.). 64p. pap. 12.95 (*0-85045-741-6*, 9411, Pub. by Osprey UK) Stackpole.

***Soviet Art: The Origins & Development.** Misha Jelisavcic. Ed. by Natalia Alexeyeva. (Illus.). 397p. 1996. lib. bdg. 39.00 (*1-57751-143-3*) Russ Info & Busn Ctr.

Soviet Art of Brainwashing. Kenneth Goff. 64p. 1979. pap. 3.50 (*0-911038-27-2*, Noontide Pr) Legion Survival.

Soviet Art, 1920's-1930's. O. Leniashin. (C). 1990. 170.00 (*0-685-34343-X*, Pub. by Collets) St Mut.

Soviet Art, 1928-1945: Glavbe Hoffnung-Anpassung. Margarita Tupitsyn. (Illus.). 192p. 1996. 70.00 (*3-9802395-9-4*, 610702, Pub. by Plitt Druck-und GW) Dist Art Pubs.

Soviet Artificial Intelligence Research: The Tallinn Institute of Cybernetics. Gabriel Jakobson. Ed. by Regina Gross. (Illus.). 102p. (Orig.). 1985. pap. text ed. 75.00 (*1-55831-019-3*) Delphic Associates.

Soviet Asian Ethnic Frontiers. Ed. by William O. McCagg, Jr. & Brian D. Silver. LC 77-11796. (Policy Studies). (Illus.). 1979. 96.00 (*0-08-024637-0*, Pergamon Pr) Elsevier.

Soviet Assignment. Peter N. Bankoff. LC 88-18563. 192p. 1988. 14.75 (*0-930950-19-4*); pap. 8.75 (*0-930950-20-8*) Nopoly Pr.

Soviet Attitudes Toward American Writing. Deming Brown. LC 62-11954. 350p. reprint ed. pap. 99.80 (*0-685-15203-0*, 2014640) Bks Demand.

Soviet Attitudes Toward Authority: An Interdisciplinary Approach to Problems of Soviet Character. Margaret Mead. LC 78-10846. 148p. 1979. reprint ed. text ed. 49.75 (*0-313-21081-0*, MESO, Greenwood Pr) Greenwood.

Soviet Automated Information Retrieval Systems. Valery Frants. Ed. by John William. (Illus.). 122p. (Orig.). 1986. pap. text ed. 75.00 (*1-55831-011-8*) Delphic Associates.

Soviet Automation: Perspectives & Prospects. Jack Baranson et al. LC 86-83289. 1986. 49.50 (*0-912338-61-X*); fiche 29.50 (*0-317-55060-8*) Lomond.

Soviet Ballet. Juri Slonimsky. LC 77-107873. (Music Ser.). (Illus.). 1970. reprint ed. lib. bdg. 39.50 (*0-306-71897-9*) Da Capo.

Soviet Ballistic Missile Defense & the Western Alliance. David S. Yost. LC 88-2674. (Illus.). 352p. 1988. 45.00 (*0-674-82610-8*) HUP.

Soviet Banking & Finance. Kathleen J. Woody. 1991. 34.95 (*0-13-818774-6*) P-H.

Soviet Believers: The Religious Sector of the Population. William C. Fletcher. LC 80-25495. x, 262p. 1981. 29.95 (*0-7006-0211-9*) U Pr of KS.

Soviet Biochemical Threat to NATO. John Hemsley. LC 87-26415. 200p. 1988. text ed. 49.95 (*0-312-01589-5*) St Martin.

Soviet Biographical Service, Vol. 12. J. L. Scherer. 1996. ring bd. 100.00 (*0-685-67188-7*) J L Scherer.

Soviet Blitzkrieg Theory. P. H. Vigor. LC 82-10421. 200p. 1984. pap. 12.95 (*0-312-74756-X*) St Martin.

Soviet Bloc: Unity & Conflict. enl. rev. ed. Zbigniew K. Brzezinski. LC 67-12531. (Center for International Affairs Ser.: No. 37). 599p. 1976. pap. 19.95 (*0-674-82548-9*) HUP.

Soviet Bloc Elite Forces. Steven J. Zaloga & James Loop. (Elite Ser.: No. 5). (Illus.). 64p. pap. 12.95 (*0-85045-631-2*, 9404, Pub. by Osprey Pubng Ltd UK) Stackpole.

Soviet Book Publishing Policy. Gregory Walker. LC 77-12543. (Soviet & East European Studies). 180p. reprint ed. pap. 51.30 (*0-685-20577-0*, 2030627) Bks Demand.

Soviet Breakup & U. S. Foreign Policy. Allen C. Lynch. Ed. by Nancy L. Hoepli. LC 92-71574. (Headline Ser.: No. 297). (Illus.). 72p. (Orig.). 1992. pap. 5.95 (*0-87124-146-3*) Foreign Policy.

Soviet Brigade in Cuba: A Study in Political Diplomacy. David D. Newson. LC 86-45943. 142p. 1987. pap. 4.95 (*0-253-20429-1*, MB-429) Ind U Pr.

Soviet Brigade in Cuba: A Study in Political Diplomacy. David D. Newsom. LC 86-45943. 138p. 1987. reprint ed. pap. 39.40 (*0-608-01068-5*, 2059376) Bks Demand.

Soviet-British Relations Since the 1970s. Ed. by Alex Pravda & Peter J. Duncan. (Illus.). 228p. (C). 1990. text ed. 69.95 (*0-521-37494-4*) Cambridge U Pr.

Soviet Business Law: Institutions, Principles & Processes. Christopher Osakwe. 1992. suppl. ed., ring bd. 90.00 (*1-56257-194-X*) MICHIE.

Soviet Business Law: Institutions, Principles & Processes, 2 vols., Set. Christopher Osakwe. 700p. 1992. ring bd. 180.00 (*0-88063-338-7*) MICHIE.

Soviet Camp Speech. Compiled by Meyer Galler. 1994. 24.00 (*965-223-865-1*) Soviet Studies.

Soviet Capital Stock, Nineteen Twenty-Eight to Nineteen Sixty-Two. Richard H. Moorsteen & Raymond P. Powell. LC 65-27841. (Economic Growth Center, Yale University Publication Ser.). 695p. reprint ed. pap. 180.00 (*0-8357-8328-6*, 2033833) Bks Demand.

***Soviet Casualties & Combat Losses in the Twentieth Century.** G. F. Krivosheev. LC 97-19004. 1997. write for info. (*1-85367-280-7*, Pub. by Greenhill Bks UK) Stackpole.

Soviet Central Asia: A Tragic Experiment. Boris Rumer. 240p. (C). 1990. pap. 19.95 (*0-04-445896-7*) Routledge Chapman & Hall.

Soviet Central Asia, a Bibliography: 1558-1966, 3 pts. Richard A. Pierce. 1966. pap. 15.00 (*0-919642-94-2*) Limestone Pr.

Soviet Central Asia in Ferment. Ann Sheehy. 1988. write for info. (*0-318-63176-8*, Praeger Pubs) Greenwood.

Soviet Challenge in the Gorbachev Era: Western Perceptions & Policy Recommendations. Aspen Strategy Group Staff & European Strategy Group Staff. LC 89-5537. 170p. (Orig.). (C). 1989. pap. text ed. 19.50 (*0-8191-7400-9*, Aspen Strategy Group); lib. bdg. 38.00 (*0-8191-7399-1*, Aspen Strategy Group) U Pr of Amer.

Soviet Challenge in the Nineteen Nineties. Ed. by Stephen J. Cimbala & John Starron, Jr. LC 89-16128. 325p. 1989. text ed. 59.95 (*0-275-92788-1*, C2788, Praeger Pubs) Greenwood.

***Soviet Championships.** Cafferty & Taimanov. 1997. pap. 29.95 (*1-85744-201-6*) S&S Trade.

Soviet Chess School. A. Kotov & M. Yudovich. 192p. 1983. 7.95 (*0-8285-2901-9*) Firebird NY.

Soviet-Chinese Relations, Nineteen Forty-Five to Nineteen Hundred Seventy. Oleg B. Borisov & B. T. Koloskov. Ed. by Vladimir Petrov. LC 74-31443. 382p. reprint ed. pap. 108.90 (*0-685-16408-X*, 2056219) Bks Demand.

Soviet Choreographers in the 1920s. Elizabeth Souritz. Ed. & Tr. by Sally Banes from RUS. Tr. by Lynn Visson from RUS. LC 89-16877. (Illus.). 384p. (C). 1990. text ed. 32.95 (*0-8223-0952-1*) Duke.

Soviet Cinema. Thorold Dickinson & Catherine De La Roche. Ed. by Roger Manvell. LC 77-169327. (National Cinema Ser.). (Illus.). 140p. 1974. reprint ed. 20.95 (*0-405-03891-7*) Ayer.

Soviet Cinema in the Silent Era, 1918-1935. Denise J. Youngblood. (Film Studies). (Illus.). 352p. 1991. pap. 14.95 (*0-292-77645-4*) U of Tex Pr.

Soviet Cinematography, 1918-1991: Ideological Conflict & Social Reality. Dmitry Shlapentokh & Vladimir Shlapentokh. LC 93-12309. (Communication & Social Order Ser.). 293p. 1993. pap. text ed. 24.95 (*0-202-30462-0*); lib. bdg. 42.95 (*0-202-30461-2*) Aldine de Gruyter.

Soviet Civil Law. Olimpiad S. Ioffe. (C). 1988. lib. bdg. 159.50 (*90-247-3676-5*) Kluwer Ac.

Soviet Civil Law. Ed. by O. N. Sadikov. LC 87-4518. 544p. (gr. 13). 1988. text ed. 183.95 (*0-87332-429-3*) M E Sharpe.

Soviet Civil Law, 2 vols., Set. Vladimir Gsovski. LC 49-767. (Michigan Legal Publications). 1990. 90.00 (*1-57588-364-3*, 300480) W S Hein.

Soviet Codes of Law. William B. Simons. (Law in Eastern Europe Ser.: No. 23). 1288p. 1980. lib. bdg. 503.00 (*90-286-0810-9*) Kluwer Ac.

Soviet Collapse & the Post-Communist World: A Critical Reassessment. Ed. by Michael Cox. 256p. (C). 1997. 39.95 (*1-85567-321-5*, Pub. by Pntr Pubs UK); pap. 15.95 (*1-85567-322-3*, Pub. by Pntr Pubs UK) Bks Intl VA.

Soviet Collective Farm: 1929-1930. Richard W. Davies. LC 79-15273. (Industrialization of Soviet Russia Ser.: Vol. 2). 226p. 1980. 29.00 (*0-674-82600-0*) HUP.

Soviet Colossus: A History of the U. S. S. R. Michael G. Kort. 352p. (C). 1990. pap. text ed. 19.95 (*0-04-445762-6*) Routledge Chapman & Hall.

Soviet Colossus: History & Aftermath. 4th ed. Michael G. Kort. LC 95-38318. (Illus.). 384p. (C). (gr. 13). 1996. text ed. 65.95 (*1-56324-662-7*); pap. text ed. 24.95 (*1-56324-663-5*) M E Sharpe.

Soviet Colossus: The Rise & Fall of the U. S. S. R. 3rd ed. Michael G. Kort. LC 92-28618. 388p. (C). (gr. 13). 1992. text ed. 63.95 (*0-87332-675-X*); pap. text ed. 25.95 (*0-87332-676-8*) M E Sharpe.

Soviet Combat Vehicle Handbook. Loren K. Wiseman. (Twilight: Two Thousand Ser.). (Illus.). 104p. (Orig.). (YA). (gr. 9-12). 1990. pap. 12.00 (*1-55878-067-X*) Game Designers.

Soviet Comes of Age. LC 68-20337. (Essay Index Reprint Ser.). 1977. 23.95 (*0-8369-0892-9*) Ayer.

Soviet Commercial Design of the Twenties. A. Anikst. (C). 1990. 280.00 (*0-685-34342-1*, Pub. by Collets) St Mut.

Soviet Commercial Design of the Twenties. Ed. by Mikhail Anikst. (Illus.). 144p. 1991. pap. 30.00 (*1-55859-152-4*) Abbeville Pr.

Soviet Communism: Programme & Rules. Stephen White. 160p. 1989. 58.00 (*0-415-03479-5*, A3799) Routledge.

Soviet Communism: The Socialist Vision. Ed. by Julius Jacobson. LC 73-164981. (New Politics Ser.). 372p. 1972. 32.95 (*0-87855-005-4*); pap. text ed. 19.95 (*0-87855-505-6*) Transaction Pubs.

Soviet Communism from Reform to Collapse. Robert V. Daniels. (Problems in European Civilization Ser.). 387p. (C). 1995. pap. text ed. 21.16 (*0-669-33144-9*) HM College Div.

Soviet Communist Party. 3rd ed. Ed. by Ronald J. Hill & Peter Frank. 172p. (C). 1986. pap. text ed. 17.95 (*0-04-497024-2*) Routledge Chapman & Hall.

Soviet Communist Party Officials: A Study in Organizational Roles & Change. Bohdan Harasymiw. LC 96-25173. 298p. (C). 1996. lib. bdg. 79.00 (*1-56072-309-2*) Nova Sci Pubs.

***Soviet Communists & Communism: Seventy-Four Years of Oppression.** Nicholas V. Feodoroff. 137p. (C). 1996. lib. bdg. 49.00 (*1-56072-407-2*) Nova Sci Pubs.

Soviet Communists in Power: A Study Moscow During the Civil War 1918-21. Richard Sakwa. LC 87-24167. 324p. 1988. text ed. 59.95 (*0-312-01582-8*) St Martin.

Soviet Concept of Security. 1985. 6.00 (*92-9045-009-6*, E GV.85.0.2) UN.

Soviet Concepts of Peace, Peaceful Coexistence & Detente. Ronald R. Nelson & Peter Schweizer. LC 87-34520. 198p. (Orig.). (C). 1988. pap. text ed. 22.50 (*0-8191-6833-5*, Natl Forum Found); lib. bdg. 47.00 (*0-8191-6832-7*, Natl Forum Found) U Pr of Amer.

Soviet Conduct. Compiled by Alexander Dallin. LC 75-31359. 318p. 1975. reprint ed. text ed. 65.00 (*0-8371-8511-4*, DASCW, Greenwood Pr) Greenwood.

Soviet Conduct of Tactical Maneuver: Spearhead of the Offensive. David M. Glantz. (Cass Series on Military Theory & Practice). 263p. 1991. text ed. 47.50 (*0-7146-3373-9*, Pub. by F Cass Pubs UK); pap. text ed. 24.50 (*0-7146-4079-4*, Pub. by F Cass Pubs UK) Intl Spec Bk.

Soviet Connection: State Sponsorship of Terrorism. Jillian Becker. (C). 1981. pap. 29.00 (*0-907967-69-8*) St Mut.

Soviet Connection: State Sponsorship of Terrorism. Jillian Becker. (C). 1990. 40.00 (*0-907967-60-4*, Pub. by Inst Euro Def & Strat UK) St Mut.

Soviet Constitutional Crisis: From De-Stalinization to Disintegration. Robert Sharlet. LC 92-5285. (Contemporary Soviet - Post-Soviet Politics Ser.). 204p. (gr. 13). 1992. text ed. 65.95 (*1-56324-063-7*); pap. text ed. 24.95 (*1-56324-064-5*) M E Sharpe.

Soviet Construction Materials Industry. Genrikh Bukhsbaum. Ed. by Andreas Tamberg. 102p. (Orig.). 1987. pap. text ed. 75.00 (*1-55831-004-5*) Delphic Associates.

Soviet Contributions to the Sociology of Language. P. Luelsdorff. 1977. pap. text ed. 60.80 (*90-279-7613-9*) Mouton.

Soviet Conventional Arms Transfers to the Third World: Main Missile & Artillery Directorate (1966-1990) Moysey Rabinovich. (Foreign Technology Assessment Ser.). ix, 49p. (Orig.). 1994. pap. 45.00 (*1-881874-09-5*) Global Cnslts.

Soviet Conversion 1991: Report & Recommendations of an International Working Group on Economic Demilitarization & Adjustment. John T. Martin & Paul Grenier. 95p. 1991. 8.00 (*0-614-16164-9*) CEP.

Soviet Cost-Accounting in the Machine-Building & Metal-Working Sector (Theory & Practice) Selected Papers with Analysis. Ehiel Ash et al. Ed. by Erika D. Nobel. Tr. by Vladimir Talmy from RUS. (Illus.). 200p. (Orig.). 1988. Transcript. pap. text ed. 100.00 (*1-55831-071-1*) Delphic Associates.

Soviet Court: Guide to the Constitutional Principles of the Administration of Justice in the U. S. S. R. Vladimir Terebilov. 182p. (C). 1973. 19.95 (*0-8464-0866-X*) Beekman Pubs.

Soviet Court & Human Rights. 21p. 1975. pap. 3.00 (*0-685-42905-9*, 700-0013) Amer Bar Assn.

Soviet Criminal Justice under Stalin. Peter H. Solomon, Jr. (Cambridge Russian, Soviet & Post-Soviet Studies: No. 100). (Illus.). 325p. (C). 1996. pap. text ed. 29.95 (*0-521-56451-4*) Cambridge U Pr.

Soviet Criminal Justice under Stalin. Peter H. Solomon, Jr. (Russian, Soviet & Post-Soviet Studies: No. 100). (Illus.). 325p. (C). 1996. text ed. 80.00 (*0-521-40089-9*) Cambridge U Pr.

Soviet Criminal Law & Procedure, the RSFSR Codes. 2nd ed. Tr. by Harold J. Berman. LC 72-81269. (Russian Research Center Studies: No. 50). 408p. 1965. 38.00 (*0-674-82636-1*) HUP.

Soviet Criminologists & Criminal Policy. Peter H. Solomon, Jr. LC 77-3357. (Studies of the Russian Institute). 1978. text ed. 49.50 (*0-231-04316-3*) Col U Pr.

Soviet Criminology Update. 179p. 1990. 29.00 (*92-9078-012-6*, 90.III.N.4) UN.

Soviet-Cuban Alliance, 1959-1991. 2nd ed. Yuri Pavlov. LC 95-50925. 320p. (C). 1996. pap. 22.95 (*1-57454-004-1*) U Miami N-S Ctr.

Soviet Cultural Offensive. Frederick C. Barghoorn. LC 75-18397. 353p. 1976. reprint ed. text ed. 69.50 (*0-8371-8334-0*, BASCO, Greenwood Pr) Greenwood.

Soviet Cultural Offensive: The Role of Cultural Diplomacy in Soviet Foreign Policy. Frederick C. Barghoorn. LC 60-12227. 361p. reprint ed. pap. 102.90 (*0-317-09488-2*, 2000893) Bks Demand.

Soviet Cybernetic Technology: A Timeline Researcher's Data Base & Guide to Professional Literature from Early First Generation Through Third Generation, Volume II, 2 vols., I. Ed. by George M. Weinberger. 342p. (Orig.). 1985. pap. text ed. 28.00 (*0-8191-4822-9*); lib. bdg. 55.50 (*0-8191-4821-0*) U Pr of Amer.

Soviet C3. Ed. by Stephen J. Cimbala. LC 87-26967. (AFCEA Signal Magazine C3I Ser.: Vol. VII). (Illus.). 472p. 1987. text ed. 39.95 (*0-916159-15-9*) AFCEA Intl Pr.

Soviet Decipherment of the Indus Valley Script: Translation & Critique. Kamil V. Zvelebil. 1976. pap. text ed. 88.50 (*90-279-3104-6*) Mouton.

Soviet Decision Making for National Security. Ed. by Jiri Valenta & W. C. Potter. 400p. (C). 1984. pap. text ed. 21.95 (*0-04-351065-5*) Routledge Chapman & Hall.

Soviet Decision Making in Practice: The U. S. S. R. & Israel, 1947-1954. Yaacov Ro'i. LC 79-64857. 540p. 1980. 44.95 (*0-87855-267-7*) Transaction Pubs.

Soviet Defectors: The KGB Wanted List. Vladislav Krasnov. LC 85-17661. (Publication Ser.: No. 323). 264p. 1987. pap. 3.98 (*0-8179-8232-9*) Hoover Inst Pr.

Soviet Defense Decision-Making: An Integrated View, Vol. I. Erika D. Nobel et al. (Illus.). 200p. (Orig.). 1989. pap. text ed. 125.00 (*1-55831-101-7*) Delphic Associates.

Soviet Defense Decision-Making: An Integrated View, Vol. II. Edward Melikov et al. (Illus.). 331p. (Orig.). 1989. pap. text ed. 125.00 (*1-55831-100-9*) Delphic Associates.

Soviet Defense Decision-Making: An Integrated View, Vol. III. William F. Scott & Harriet F. Scott. (Illus.). 258p. (Orig.). 1989. pap. text ed. 125.00 (*1-55831-108-4*) Delphic Associates.

Soviet Defense Decisionmaking: What Do We Know & What Do We Understand? Stephen M. Meyer. (CISA Working Papers: No. 33). 72p. (Orig.). 1982. pap. 15.00 (*0-86682-041-8*) Ctr Intl Relations.

Soviet Developmental Psychology: An Anthology. Michael Cole. LC 77-85709. 644p. reprint ed. pap. 180.00 (*0-317-08144-6*, 2021854) Bks Demand.

Soviet Diary 1927 & Other Writings. Sergei Prokofiev. Ed. by Oleg Prokofiev & Christopher Palmer. 290p. 1992. text ed. 42.50 (*1-55553-120-2*) NE U Pr.

Soviet Diplomacy & Negotiating Behavior, 4 vols., Set. Ed. by Congressional Research Center Library of Congress Staff. LC 89-82366. 1604p. 1993. lib. bdg. 200.00 (*0-89941-732-9*, 201950) W S Hein.

Soviet Dissident Artists: Interviews after Perestroika. Renee Baigell & Matthew Baigell. LC 95-12435. (Illus.). 375p. (C). 1995. text ed. 39.95 (*0-8135-2223-4*) Rutgers U Pr.

Soviet Disunion: A History of the Nationalities Problem in the USSR. Bohdan Nahaylo & Victor Swoboda. 448p. 1990. 35.00 (*0-02-922401-2*, Free Press) Free Pr.

Soviet Doctrine of "Limited Sovereignty" from Lenin to Gorbachev. Robert A. Jones. LC 88-39264. 330p. 1990. text ed. 49.95 (*0-312-02816-4*) St Martin.

Soviet Documents on the Use of War Experience, Vol. 1: The Initial Period of War 1941. Tr. by Harold S. Orenstein. 83p. 1991. text ed. 35.00 (*0-7146-3392-5*, Pub. by F Cass Pubs UK) Intl Spec Bk.

Soviet Documents on the Use of War Experience, Vol. 2: The Winter Campaign 1941-1942. Tr. by Harold S. Orenstein. 255p. 1991. text ed. 37.50 (*0-7146-3393-3*, Pub. by F Cass Pubs UK) Intl Spec Bk.

Soviet Documents on the Use of War Experiences, Vol. 3: Military Operations, 1941-1942. Harold S. Orenstein. LC 91-11452. 224p. 1993. 39.50 (*0-7146-3402-6*, Pub. by F Cass Pubs UK) Intl Spec Bk.

Soviet-East European Relations: Consolidation & Conflict, 1968-1980. Robert L. Hutchings. LC 83-47761. 336p. 1988. pap. 12.50 (*0-299-09314-X*) U of Wis Pr.

Soviet-East European Relations As a Problem for Western Policy. Richard D. Vine. 272p. 1987. lib. bdg. 65.00 (*0-7099-5113-2*, Pub. by Croom Helm UK) Routledge Chapman & Hall.

Soviet-East European Survey, 1983-1984: Selected Research & Analysis from Radio Free Europe - Radio Liberty. Ed. by Vojtech Mastny. LC 85-10281. (Duke Press Policy Studies). xvi, 436p. (C). 1985. 52.50 (*0-8223-0643-3*); pap. 26.95 (*0-8223-0650-6*) Duke.

Soviet-East European Survey, 1984-1985: Selected Research & Analysis from Radio Free Europe-Radio Liberty. Ed. by Vojtech Mastny. LC 85-10281. xii, 400p. (Orig.). 1986. text ed. 62.50 (*0-8223-0656-5*); pap. text ed. 26.95 (*0-8223-0699-9*) Duke.

Soviet-East European Survey, 1985-1986: Selected Research & Analysis from Radio Free Europe-Radio Liberty. Ed. by Vojtech Mastny. LC 85-10281. x, 451p. (C). 1987. 55.50 (*0-8223-0721-9*) Duke.

Soviet-East German Military Alliance. Douglas A. Macgregor. (Illus.). 192p. (C). 1989. text ed. 54.95 (*0-521-36562-7*) Cambridge U Pr.

Soviet Economic Conversion: Perceptions, Problems, & Prospects. Francis M. Jeffries. 1990. pap. 50.00 (*1-878974-00-9*) Jeffries & Assocs.

Soviet Economic Development. 2nd ed. Raymond Hutchings. 368p. (C). 1982. pap. text ed. 13.20 (*0-8147-3420-0*) NYU Pr.

Soviet Economic Experiment. James R. Millar. 352p. 1990. pap. text ed. 14.95 (*0-252-06088-1*) U of Ill Pr.

Soviet Economic Growth: A Comparison with the United States. U. S. Library of Congress, Legislative Reference Service Staff. LC 69-10165. 149p. 1968. reprint ed. text ed. 52.50 (*0-8371-0722-9*, ULSE, Greenwood Pr) Greenwood.

Soviet Economic Planning: Theory & Practice. Andrew A. Michta. (Orig.). 1986. pap. text ed. 75.00 (*1-55831-050-9*) Delphic Associates.

Soviet Economic Reform: Progress & Problems. A. M. Rumyantsev et al. 247p. 1975. 22.95 (*0-8464-0867-8*) Beekman Pubs.

Soviet Economic System. 3rd ed. Alec Nove. 420p. (C). 1986. pap. text ed. 25.00 (*0-04-497025-0*) Routledge Chapman & Hall.

Soviet Economy: A Collection of Western & Soviet Views. 2nd ed. Ed. by Harry G. Shaffer. LC 69-16223. (Illus.). (Orig.). 1969. pap. text ed. 16.95 (*0-89197-420-2*) Irvington.

Soviet Economy: New Economic Strategy. Vinod Mehta. 210p. 1987. text ed. 27.50 (*81-207-0670-6*, Pub. by Sterling Pubs II) Apt Bks.

Soviet Economy & Society. David Lane. 384p. (C). 1985. text ed. 40.00 (*0-8147-5015-X*); pap. text ed. 20.00 (*0-8147-5016-8*) NYU Pr.

Soviet Economy & the Red Army, 1930-1945. Walter S. Dunn. LC 95-7016. 272p. 1995. text ed. 59.95 (*0-275-94893-5*, Praeger Pubs) Greenwood.

Soviet Economy Forges Ahead: A Look at the Five-Year Plan Ending 1975. F. I. Kotov et al. 235p. 1975. 18.95 (*0-8464-0868-6*) Beekman Pubs.

Soviet Economy Today: With Guidelines for the Economic & Social Development of the U. S. S. R. for 1981 to 1985 & for the Period Ending in 1990. LC 81-1121. (Contributions in Economics & Economic History Ser.: No. 41). 220p. 1981. text ed. 75.00 (*0-313-21414-X*, NSE/) Greenwood.

Soviet Economy Towards the Year 2000. Ed. by Abram Bergson & Herbert S. Levine. 496p. (Orig.). (C). 1985. text ed. 55.00 (*0-04-335045-3*); pap. text ed. 24.95 (*0-04-335053-4*) Routledge Chapman & Hall.

Soviet Education: An Annotated Bibliography & Readers' Guide to Works in English, 1893-1978. Compiled by Yushin Yoo. LC 79-54058. xvi, 408p. 1980. text ed. 105.00 (*0-313-22085-9*, YSE/, Greenwood Pr) Greenwood.

An Asterisk (*) at the beginning of an entry indicates that the title is appearing in BIP for the first time.

Soviet Education: Anton Makarenko & the Years of Experiment. James Bowen. LC 62-15991. 244p. 1962. reprint ed. pap. 69.60 (*0-608-01941-0*, 2062596) Bks Demand.
Soviet Education: The Gifted & the Handicapped. Ed. by James Riordan. 240p. (C). 1988. lib. bdg. 55.00 (*0-415-00574-4*) Routledge.
Soviet Education for Science & Technology. Alexander G. Korol. LC 73-9212. 513p. 1974. reprint ed. text ed. 89.50 (*0-8371-6978-X*, KOSE, Greenwood Pr) Greenwood.
Soviet Education under Perestroika. Ed. by John Dunstan. LC 91-31163. 240p. (C). (gr. 13). 1992. text ed. 69.95 (*0-415-06947-5*, A7075) Routledge.
Soviet Emigre Artists. Marilyn Reuschemeyer et al. LC 84-23558. 184p. (gr. 13). 1985. text ed. 58.95 (*0-87332-296-7*); pap. text ed. 30.95 (*0-87332-810-8*) M E Sharpe.
Soviet Empire: Its Nations Speak Out. Ed. by O. Glebov. (Soviet Studies). xxx, 190p. 1989. pap. text ed. 32.00 (*3-7186-5017-7*, Harwood Acad Pubs) Gordon & Breach.
Soviet Empire: Its Nations Speak Out. Ed. by O. Glebov & J. Crowfoot. (Soviet Studies: Vol. A). xxx, 190p. 1989. text ed. 65.00 (*3-7186-5000-2*) Gordon & Breach.
Soviet Empire & the Challenge of National & Democratic Movements. Ed. by Uri Ra'anan. 272p. 1990. pap. 24.95 (*0-669-24676-X*) Free Pr.
Soviet Encyclopaedic Dictionary. A. Prokhorov. 1600p. (RUS.). (C). 1981. 160.00 (*0-685-46852-6*, Pub. by Collets) St Mut.
Soviet Energy Technologies: Planning, Policy, Research, & Development. Robert W. Campbell. LC 80-7562. 278p. reprint ed. pap. 79.30 (*0-8357-3958-9*, 2057054) Bks Demand.
Soviet Environment: Problems, Policies & Politics. Ed. by John Massey-Stewart. (International Council for Soviet & East European Studies). 280p. (C). 1992. text ed. 69.95 (*0-521-41418-0*) Cambridge U Pr.
Soviet Environmental Policies & Practices: The Most Critical Investments. Mimi Turnbull. 255p. 1991. text ed. 64.95 (*1-85521-181-5*, Pub. by Dartmth Pub UK) Ashgate Pub Co.
Soviet Era: From Lenin to Yeltsin. Geoffrey Ponton. LC 93-14804. 320p. 1994. 61.95 (*0-631-18775-8*); pap. 28.95 (*0-631-18776-6*) Blackwell Pubs.
Soviet Estimate: U. S. Intelligence Analysis & Soviet Strategic Forces. John Prados. LC 85-43379. 384p. 1986. pap. text ed. 17.95 (*0-691-02235-6*) Princeton U Pr.
Soviet Ethnology & Anthropology Today. Ed. by Yu Bromley. (Studies in Anthropology: No. 1). 401p. 1974. pap. text ed. 84.65 (*90-279-2725-1*) Mouton.
Soviet Evangelicals Since World War II. Walter Sawatsky. LC 81-94121. 560p. 1981. 19.99 (*0-8361-1238-5*) Herald Pr.
Soviet Expansion in the Third World: Afghanistan, A Case Study. Nasir Shansab. LC 86-51372. (Illus.). 214p. 1987. 15.95 (*0-910155-07-0*) Bartleby Pr.
Soviet Family Law. Yuri I. Luryi. LC 80-83797. vi, 93p. 1980. lib. bdg. 34.00 (*0-89941-062-6*, 300890) W S Hein.
Soviet Far East: Geographical Perspectives on Development. Ed. by Allan Rodgers. (Illus.). 336p. (C). (gr. 13). 1990. text ed. 74.95 (*0-415-02406-4*, A4721) Routledge.
Soviet Far East & Central Asia. William Mandel. LC 75-30111. (Institute of Pacific Relations Ser.). reprint ed. 32.50 (*0-404-59545-6*) AMS Pr.
Soviet Far East Military Buildup: Nuclear Dilemma & Asian Security. Ed. by Richard A. Solomon & Masataka Kosaka. LC 85-30664. 250p. 1986. text ed. 55.00 (*0-86569-140-1*, Auburn Hse) Greenwood.
Soviet Far Eastern Policy, 1931-1945. Harriet L. Moore. 40.00 (*0-86527-187-9*) Fertig.
Soviet Federalism: Nationalism & Economic Decentralisation. Ed. by Alastair McAuley. LC 91-28124. 210p. 1991. text ed. 55.00 (*0-312-07191-4*) St Martin.
Soviet Fiction since Stalin: Science, Politics & Literature. Rosalind J. Marsh. LC 85-30610. 352p. 1986. 56.00 (*0-389-20609-1*, N8172) B&N Imports.
Soviet Film Posters of the Silent Cinema: Colour Poster of Alexander Ilyich Naumov's "Bella Donna" Museum of Modern Art Oxford Staff. (Illus.). 1987. pap. 20.00 (*0-905836-59-6*, Pub. by Museum Modern Art UK) St Mut.
Soviet First Strike Threat: The U. S. Perspective. Jack H. Nunn. LC 82-344. 304p. 1982. text ed. 55.00 (*0-275-90871-2*, C0871, Praeger Pubs) Greenwood.
Soviet Forces in Space. Baker. LC 88-14050. (Soviet Military Power Ser.). (Illus.). 48p. (J). (gr. 3-8). 1987. lib. bdg. 18.60 (*0-86625-335-1*); lib. bdg. 13.95 (*0-685-58299-X*) Rourke Corp.
Soviet Foreign Economic Policy & International Security. Ed. by Eric Stubbs. LC 91-7458. 200p. (C). (gr. 13). 1991. text ed. 56.95 (*0-87332-666-0*) M E Sharpe.
Soviet Foreign Policy. (Proceedings of the Academy of Political Science Ser.: Vol. 36, No. 4). 1987. pap. 12.95 (*0-614-04168-6*) Acad Poli Sci.
Soviet Foreign Policy. 4th ed. Joseph L. Nogee. 1992. pap. text ed. 36.00 (*0-02-387665-4*, Macmillan Coll) P-H.
Soviet Foreign Policy: A Guide to Research & Research Materials. Ed. by Robert H. Johnston. LC 90-23883. (European Diplomatic History Ser.). 236p. 1991. 50.00 (*0-8420-2312-7*) Scholarly Res Inc.
Soviet Foreign Policy: Classic & Contemporary Issues. Ed. by Frederic J. Fleron, Jr. et al. 868p. 1991. pap. text ed. 44.95 (*0-202-24171-8*); lib. bdg. 76.95 (*0-202-24170-X*) Aldine de Gruyter.
Soviet Foreign Policy: New Dynamics, New Themes. Ed. by Carl G. Jacobsen. LC 89-10571. 208p. 1989. text ed. 49.95 (*0-312-03607-8*) St Martin.
Soviet Foreign Policy: Nineteen Seventeen to Nineteen Forty-One. George F. Kennan. LC 78-11494. (Anvil Ser.). 192p. 1979. reprint ed. pap. text ed. 11.50 (*0-88275-749-0*) Krieger.
Soviet Foreign Policy: Nineteen Seventeen to Nineteen Ninety. Zafar Imam. 1990. text ed. 27.95 (*81-207-1215-3*, Pub. by Sterling Pubs II) Apt Bks.
Soviet Foreign Policy after Stalin. David J. Dallin. LC 75-14596. (Illus.). 543p. 1975. reprint ed. text ed. 85.00 (*0-8371-8223-9*, DASF, Greenwood Pr) Greenwood.
Soviet Foreign Policy & East-West Relations. Ed. by Roger E. Kanet. LC 82-3649. (Policy Studies on International Politics). 212p. 1982. 64.00 (*0-08-029366-2*, K125, Pergamon Pr) Elsevier.
Soviet Foreign Policy Documents, 1978. Ed. by Darshan Singh. 328p. (C). 1984. text ed. 35.00 (*0-86590-173-2*, Pub. by Sterling Pubs II) Apt Bks.
Soviet Foreign Policy Documents, 1979. Ed. by Darshan Singh. 220p. (C). 1984. text ed. 25.00 (*0-86590-174-0*, Pub. by Sterling Pubs II) Apt Bks.
Soviet Foreign Policy Documents, 1980. Ed. by Darshan Singh. 144p. (C). 1984. text ed. 17.95 (*0-86590-175-9*, Pub. by Sterling Pubs II) Apt Bks.
Soviet Foreign Policy Documents, 1981. Ed. by Darshan Singh. 176p. (C). 1984. text ed. 20.00 (*0-86590-176-7*, Pub. by Sterling Pubs II) Apt Bks.
Soviet Foreign Policy Documents 1982. Ed. by Darshan Singh. xxxi, 214p. 1984. text ed. 30.00 (*0-86590-227-5*, Pub. by Sterling Pubs II) Apt Bks.
Soviet Foreign Policy Documents, 1983. Ed. by Darshan Singh. 271p. 1984. text ed. 32.50 (*0-86590-533-9*, Pub. by Sterling Pubs II) Apt Bks.
Soviet Foreign Policy Documents, 1984. Ed. by Darshan Singh. 231p. (C). 1986. text ed. 35.00 (*81-207-0273-5*, Pub. by Sterling Pubs II) Apt Bks.
Soviet Foreign Policy Documents, 1985. Darshan Singh. 486p. 1987. text ed. 50.00 (*81-207-0550-5*, Pub. by Sterling Pubs II) Apt Bks.
Soviet Foreign Policy Documents, 1986. Ed. by Darshan Singh. 504p. 1988. text ed. 50.00 (*81-207-0823-7*, Pub. by Sterling Pubs II) Apt Bks.
Soviet Foreign Policy Documents, 1987. Darshan Singh. xli, 609p. 1989. text ed. 65.00 (*81-207-0871-7*, Pub. by Sterling Pubs II) Apt Bks.
Soviet Foreign Policy Documents, 1988. 1990. 60.00 (*81-207-1043-6*, Pub. by Sterling Pubs II) Apt Bks.
Soviet Foreign Policy Documents, 1989. Darshan Singh. 676p. 1990. text ed. 75.00 (*81-207-1233-1*, Pub. by Sterling Pubs II) Apt Bks.
Soviet Foreign Policy in a Changing World. Ed. by Robbin F. Laird & Erik P. Hoffmann. LC 85-18712. 993p. (Orig.). 1986. pap. text ed. 36.95 (*0-202-24167-X*); lib. bdg. 69.95 (*0-202-24166-1*) Aldine de Gruyter.
Soviet Foreign Policy in Transition. Ed. by Roger E. Kanet et al. (International Council for Soviet & East European Studies). 320p. (C). 1992. text ed. 69.95 (*0-521-41365-6*) Cambridge U Pr.
Soviet Foreign Policy, Nineteen Seventenn to Nineteen Forty-One. George F. Kennan. LC 78-1568. 192p. 1978. reprint ed. lib. bdg. 49.75 (*0-313-20355-5*, KESF, Greenwood Pr) Greenwood.
Soviet Foreign Policy since World War II. Joseph L. Nogee & Robert H. Donaldson. (Policy Studies on International Politics). 300p. 1981. text ed. 43.00 (*0-08-025997-9*, Pergamon Pr); pap. text ed. 12.00 (*0-08-025996-0*, Pergamon Pr) Elsevier.
Soviet Foreign Policy since World War II. 2nd ed. Joseph L. Nogee & Robert H. Donaldson. 400p. 1984. text ed. 47.00 (*0-08-030152-5*, Pergamon Pr); pap. text ed. 13.95 (*0-08-030151-7*, Pergamon Pr) Elsevier.
Soviet Foreign Policy Since World War II. 3rd ed. Joseph L. Nogee & Robert H. Donaldson. 350p. 1988. pap. write for info. (*0-08-035886-1*, Pergamon Pr); text ed. write for info. (*0-08-035885-3*, Pergamon Pr) Elsevier.
Soviet Foreign Policy since World War II. 4th ed. Alvin Z. Rubinstein. (C). 1992. text ed. 32.50 (*0-673-52163-X*) Addson-Wesley Educ.
Soviet Foreign Policy, the League of Nations & Europe, 1917-1939. R. H. Haigh et al. 224p. 1986. 50.50 (*0-389-20611-3*, N8170) B&N Imports.
***Soviet Foreign Policy Today: Gorbachev & the New Political Thinking.** Robert F. Miller. 203p. (C). 1991. text ed. 49.95 (*0-04-445997-1*) Routledge Chapman & Hall.
Soviet Foreign Policy Today, 1983-1986. 2nd ed. Ed. by Gordon Livermore. 200p. (Orig.). (C). 1986. 10.00 (*0-913601-61-6*) Current Digest.
Soviet Foreign Policy Today, 1986-1989. 3rd ed. Gordon Livermore. Tr. by Current Digest of the Soviet Press Staff from RUS. 192p. (Orig.). (C). 1989. pap. 10.00 (*0-913601-62-4*) Current Digest.
Soviet Foreign Policy Today, 1989-1990. 4th ed. Gordon Livermore. Tr. by Current Digest of the Soviet Press Staff. 220p. (Orig.). 1990. pap. 10.00 (*0-913601-63-2*) Current Digest.
Soviet Foreign Policy Towards Egypt. Karen Dawisha. LC 78-10539. 276p. 1979. text ed. 39.95 (*0-312-74837-X*) St Martin.
Soviet Foreign Policy under Gorbachev: New Political Thinking & Its Impact. Gerhard Wettig. (C). 1990. 50.00 (*0-907967-95-7*, Pub. by Inst Euro Def & Strat UK) St Mut.
Soviet Foreign Policy, 1917-1990. Ed. by Alexander Dallin. LC 91-44951. (Articles on Russian & Soviet History, 1500-1991 Ser.: Vol. 13). 544p. 1992. text ed. 30.00 (*0-8153-0570-2*) Garland.
Soviet Foreign Policy, 1917-1991: A Retrospective. Ed. by Gabriel Gorodetsky. LC 93-30555. (Cummings Center Ser.). 240p. 1994. 40.00 (*0-7146-4506-0*, Pub. by F Cass Pubs UK); pap. 20.00 (*0-7146-4112-X*, Pub. by F Cass Pubs UK) Intl Spec Bk.
Soviet Foreign Propaganda. Frederick C. Barghoorn. LC 63-12667. 341p. reprint ed. pap. 97.20 (*0-685-23414-2*, 2032639) Bks Demand.
Soviet Foreign Trade: The Decision Process. H. Stephen Gardner. 1982. lib. bdg. 64.50 (*0-89838-111-8*) Kluwer Ac.
Soviet Gas Campaign: Politics & Policy in Soviet Decisionmaking. Thane Gustafson. LC 83-13942. 118p. 1983. pap. 10.00 (*0-8330-0513-8*, R-3036-AF) Rand Corp.
Soviet Generals Recall World War II. Ed. by Igor Vitqkhin. Tr. by Anatol Kagan from RUS. (Illus.). 429p. 1981. 35.00 (*0-943071-08-9*) Sphinx Pr.
Soviet Genocide in Lithuania. Joseph Pajaujis-Javis. 1980. 10.95 (*0-87141-060-5*) Manyland.
Soviet Geographical Explorations & Discoveries: In the U. S. S. R., Antarctica & World Oceans. N. A. Gvozdetsky. (Illus.). 343p. 1975. 27.95 (*0-8464-0871-6*) Beekman Pubs.
Soviet-German Nationalism. Alfred A. Curran. LC 86-71860. 135p. (Orig.). 1986. pap. 8.50 (*0-9617186-0-9*) A A Curran.
Soviet Glass. N. Voronov. 348p. (C). 1981. 385.00 (*0-685-34469-X*, Pub. by Collets) St Mut.
Soviet Grassroots: Citizen Participation in Local Soviet Government. Jeffrey W. Hahn. 304p. 1988. text ed. 49.50 (*0-691-07767-3*) Princeton U Pr.
Soviet Grotesque. Ed. by Natasha Perova & Arch Tait. (Glas Ser.: No. 2). 224p. pap. 14.95 (*0-939010-47-X*) I R Dee.
Soviet Heretic. Yevgeny Zamyatin. Ed. & Tr. by Mirra Ginsburg from RUS. (Illus.). 322p. 1992. reprint ed. pap. 15.95 (*0-8101-1091-1*) Northwestern U Pr.
Soviet Hieroglyphics: Visual Culture in Late Twentieth-Century Russia. Ed. by Nancy Condee. LC 94-22839. (Illus.). 208p. 1995. 29.95 (*0-253-31402-X*); pap. 12.95 (*0-253-20945-5*) Ind U Pr.
Soviet Historians & Perestroika: The First Phase. Ed. by Donald J. Raleigh. LC 89-10724. 300p. (gr. 13). 1990. text ed. 55.95 (*0-87332-554-0*) M E Sharpe.
Soviet Historians in Crisis, 1928-1932. John Barber. LC 80-13798. 194p. 1981. 39.50 (*0-8419-0614-9*) Holmes & Meier.
Soviet History in the Gorbachev Revolution. Richard W. Davies. LC 89-7589. 240p. 1989. 18.95 (*0-253-31604-9*); pap. 6.95 (*0-253-20552-2*, MB-552) Ind U Pr.
***Soviet History in the Yeltsin Era.** Davies. LC 96-29714. 1997. text ed. 69.95 (*0-312-17372-5*) St Martin.
Soviet History of World War II: Myths, Memories & Realities. Matthew P. Gallagher. LC 75-32458. 205p. 1976. reprint ed. text ed. 55.00 (*0-8371-8551-3*, GASH, Greenwood Pr) Greenwood.
Soviet History, 1917-1953: Essays in Honour of R. W. Davies. Ed. by Julian Cooper et al. LC 94-49543. 1995. text ed. 69.95 (*0-312-12615-8*) St Martin.
Soviet Home Front 1941-1945. John Barber & Mark Harrison. (Illus.). 264p. (C). 1991. text ed. 70.50 (*0-582-00964-2*, 78912); pap. text ed. 31.95 (*0-582-00965-0*, 78913) Longman.
Soviet Household under the Old Regime: Economic Conditions & Behaviour in the 1970s. Gur Ofer & Aaron Vinokur. (Illus.). 450p. (C). 1992. text ed. 80.00 (*0-521-38398-6*) Cambridge U Pr.
Soviet Human Rights Movement: A Memoir. Valery Chalidze. LC 84-72146. xii, 50p. 1984. pap. 2.50 (*0-87495-064-3*) Am Jewish Comm.
Soviet Hypocrisy & Western Gullibility. Sidney Hook et al. LC 87-3545. 74p. (Orig.). (C). 1987. pap. text ed. 13.50 (*0-89633-113-X*) Ethics & Public Policy.
Soviet Ideologies in the Period of Glasnost: Responses to Brezhnev's Stagnation. Vladimir Shlapentokh & Dmitry Shlapentokh. LC 88-5878. 224p. 1988. text ed. 55.00 (*0-275-92671-0*, C2671, Praeger Pubs) Greenwood.
Soviet Image of Utopia. Jerome M. Gilison. LC 74-24388. 200p. reprint ed. pap. 57.00 (*0-317-41641-3*, 2025838) Bks Demand.
Soviet Images of Dissidents & Nonconformists. Walter Parchomenko. LC 86-3178. 266p. 1986. text ed. 49.95 (*0-275-92021-6*, C2021, Praeger Pubs) Greenwood.
Soviet Impact on Commodity Markets. M. M. Kostecki. LC 81-9223. 271p. 1984. text ed. 45.00 (*0-312-74839-6*) St Martin.
Soviet Impact on World Grain Trade. D. Gale Johnson. LC 77-78146. (British-North American Committee Ser.). 72p. 1977. 3.00 (*0-902594-30-3*) Natl Planning.
Soviet Imperialism. Ed. by Waldemar Gurian. LC 75-1099. (International Studies of the Comm. on International Relations, U. of Notre Dame). 166p. 1975. reprint ed. text ed. 49.75 (*0-8371-7993-9*, GUSI, Greenwood Pr) Greenwood.
Soviet Imperialism: Its Origins & Tactics. Ed. by Waldemar Gurian. LC 53-7350. (Notre Dame University, Committee on International Relations, International Studies). 171p. reprint ed. pap. 48.80 (*0-317-42110-7*, 2025946) Bks Demand.
Soviet Indian Phenomenon. G. Ivashentsov & N. Koltsov. 1989. 23.00 (*0-8364-2594-4*, Pub. by Allied II) S Asia.
Soviet-Indian Relations: Issues & Influence. Robert C. Horn. LC 81-15678. 254p. 1982. text ed. 55.00 (*0-275-90820-8*, C0820, Praeger Pubs) Greenwood.
Soviet Industrial Communications Systems. Froim Shraer. Ed. by Andreas Tamberg. 118p. (Orig.). 1987. pap. text ed. 75.00 (*1-55831-044-4*) Delphic Associates.
Soviet Industrial Enterprise: Theory & Practice. Andrew F. Freris. LC 83-40626. 192p. 1984. text ed. 45.00 (*0-312-74840-X*) St Martin.
Soviet Industrial Terminology: Terminologie Industrielle Sovietique: Lexique Russe-Francais d'Organization. 2nd ed. Pierre Cavoleau. 72p. (FRE & RUS.). 1983. pap. 19.95 (*0-8288-2131-3*, F53070) Fr & Eur.
Soviet Industrial Theory. Voytek Zubek. LC 83-49221. (American University Studies: Political Science: Ser. X, Vol. 3). 319p. (Orig.). (C). 1984. pap. text ed. 30.00 (*0-8204-0085-8*) P Lang Pubng.
Soviet Industrial Worker: Social Class, Education & Control. David Lane & Felicity O'Dell. LC 78-60509. 180p. 1978. text ed. 35.00 (*0-312-74841-8*) St Martin.
Soviet Industry from Stalin to Gorbachev: Essays on Management & Innovation. Joseph S. Berliner. LC 87-47839. (Cornell Studies in Soviet History & Science). 288p. 1988. 45.00 (*0-8014-2170-5*) Cornell U Pr.
Soviet Influence in Eastern Europe: Political Autonomy & the Warsaw Pact. Christopher D. Jones. LC 81-5848. 336p. 1981. text ed. 55.00 (*0-275-90657-4*, C0657, Praeger Pubs); pap. text ed. 18.95 (*0-275-91512-3*, B1512, Praeger Pubs) Greenwood.
Soviet Intellectuals & Political Power: The Post-Stalin Era. Vladimir Shlapentokh. 321p. (C). 1990. text ed. 49.50 (*0-691-09459-4*) Princeton U Pr.
***Soviet Intellectuals & Political Power: The Post-Stalin Era.** Vladimir Shlapentokh. LC 90-36648. reprint ed. pap. 99.20 (*0-608-04574-8*, 2065343) Bks Demand.
Soviet Interests in the Third World. Ed. by Robert Cassen. LC 85-61574. 341p. reprint ed. pap. 97.20 (*0-8357-4773-5*, 2037710) Bks Demand.
Soviet International Law & the World Economic Order. Kazimierz Grzybowski. LC 87-8979. (Illus.). xii, 226p. (C). 1987. text ed. 52.95 (*0-8223-0734-0*) Duke.
Soviet Intervention in Afghanistan. M. P. Srivastava. 128p. 1980. 12.95 (*0-318-37265-7*) Asia Bk Corp.
Soviet Intervention in Afghanistan. Alfred L. Monks. LC 81-2003. (Studies in Defense Policy: Vol. 314). 64p. reprint ed. 25.00 (*0-685-15977-9*, 2027554) Bks Demand.
Soviet Intervention in Afghanistan: Causes, Consequences & India's Response. Arundhati Roy. 140p. 1987. text ed. 22.50 (*81-7045-006-3*, Pub. by Associated Pub Hse II) Advent Bks Div.
Soviet Intervention in Czechoslovakia, 1968: Anatomy of a Decision. rev. ed. Jiri Valenta. LC 91-24536. 240p. 1991. pap. text ed. 14.95 (*0-8018-4117-8*) Johns Hopkins.
Soviet Intervention in Czechoslovakia, 1968: Anatomy of a Decision. 2nd rev. ed. Jiri Valenta. LC 91-24536. 240p. 1991. text ed. 45.00 (*0-8018-4297-2*) Johns Hopkins.
Soviet Intervention in Czechoslovakia, 1968: Anatomy of a Decision. Jiri Valenta. LC 78-20522. 222p. reprint ed. pap. 63.30 (*0-8357-6750-7*, 2035406) Bks Demand.
Soviet Invasion of Afghanistan: Three Perspectives. Vernon V. Aspaturian et al. (CISA Working Papers: No. 27). 71p. (Orig.). 1980. pap. 15.00 (*0-86682-026-4*) Ctr Intl Relations.
***Soviet Invasion of Finland, 1939-1940.** Carl Van Dyke. LC 97-22032. (Cass Series on Soviet Military Experience). 1997. write for info. (*0-7146-4753-5*, Pub. by F Cass Pubs UK); pap. write for info. (*0-7146-4314-9*, Pub. by F Cass Pubs UK) Intl Spec Bk.
Soviet Investment for Planned Industrialisation, 1929-1937, Policy & Practice: Selected Papers from the Second World Congress for Soviet & East European Studies. Ed. by R. W. Davies. (Orig.). 1985. pap. 12.00 (*0-933884-32-X*) Berkeley Slavic.
Soviet-Iraqi Relations, 1968-1988: In the Shadow of the Iran-Iraq Conflict. Haim Shemesh. LC 91-30996. 286p. 1992. lib. bdg. 45.00 (*1-55587-293-X*) Lynne Rienner.
Soviet Iron & Steel Industry. Craig ZumBrunnen & Jeffrey P. Osleeb. (Illus.). 256p. (C). 1986. 59.00 (*0-86598-158-2*, R3967) Rowman.
Soviet Jewish Aliyah, 1989 to 1992: Impact & Implications for Israel & the Middle East. Ed. by Clive Jones. LC 95-17863. 256p. (C). 1996. text ed. 39.50 (*0-7146-4625-3*, Pub. by F Cass Pubs UK) Intl Spec Bk.
Soviet-Jewish Emigration & Soviet Nationality Policy. Victor Zaslavsky & Robert J. Brym. LC 83-3160. 172p. 1983. text ed. 35.00 (*0-312-74844-2*) St Martin.
Soviet Jewish History, 1917-1991: An Annotated Bibliography. Yelena Luckert. LC 92-1682. 296p. 1992. text ed. 49.00 (*0-8240-2583-0*, SS611) Garland.
Soviet Jewry & Soviet Policy. Alfred D. Low. (East European Monographs). 272p. 1990. text ed. 44.00 (*0-88033-178-X*) Col U Pr.
Soviet Jewry in the Decisive Decade, 1971-1980. Ed. by Robert O. Freedman. LC 83-20592. (Duke Press Policy Studies). xvi, 167p. (C). 1984. text ed. 44.95 (*0-8223-0544-5*) Duke.
Soviet Jewry in the Nineteen Eighties: The Politics of Anti-Semitism & Emigration & the Dynamics of Resettlement. Ed. by Robert O. Freedman. LC 89-1074. xix, 261p. (C). 1989. text ed. 44.95 (*0-8223-0906-8*) Duke.
Soviet Jewry since the Second World War: Population & Social Structure. Mordechai Altshuler. LC 86-12139. (Studies in Population & Urban Demography: No. 5). (Illus.). 296p. 1987. text ed. 55.00 (*0-313-24494-4*, ASO/, Greenwood Pr) Greenwood.
Soviet Journey. Louis Fischer. LC 72-136529. (Illus.). 308p. 1973. reprint ed. text ed. 69.50 (*0-8371-5450-2*, FISJ, Greenwood Pr) Greenwood.
Soviet Laughter, Soviet Tears: An American Couple's Six-Month Adventure in a Ukrainian Village. Ralph Dull & Christine Dull. Ed. by Rebecca Atkinson. (Illus.). 384p. 1991. 23.50 (*0-9628038-6-3*) Stillmore Pr.
Soviet Law. Olimpiad S. Ioffe. 120p. 1987. pap. 16.00 (*0-685-45840-7*) U CT Law Sch Found.
Soviet Law & Economy. Laee & A. D. Ioffe. 1986. lib. bdg. 132.00 (*90-247-3265-4*, Pub. by M Nijhoff NE) Kluwer Ac.
Soviet Law & Soviet Reality. Olimpiad S. Ioffe. 1985. lib. bdg. 120.00 (*90-247-3106-2*) Kluwer Ac.

S

An Asterisk (*) at the beginning of an entry indicates that the title is appearing in BIP for the first time.

Soviet Law in English: Research Guide & Bibliography. Igor I. Kavass. LC 87-83674. viii, 653p. 1988. lib. bdg. 60.00 (*0-89941-631-4*, 305540) W S Hein.

Soviet Law of Property. George M. Armstrong, Jr. 1984. lib. bdg. 73.00 (*90-247-2864-9*) Kluwer Ac.

Soviet Lawyer & His System: A Historical & Bibliographic Study. George D. Cameron. LC 78-9652. (Michigan International Business Studies: No. 14). 210p. reprint ed. pap. 59.90 (*0-317-55653-3*, 2056359) Bks Demand.

Soviet Leaders: From the Cult of Personality to Collective Rule. Olga A. Narkiewicz. LC 86-75516. 320p. 1986. text ed. 45.00 (*0-312-74857-4*) St Martin.

Soviet Leaders from Lenin to Gorbachev. Thomas Streissguth. LC 92-19903. (Profiles Ser.). (Illus.). 160p. (YA). (gr. 5-12). 1992. lib. bdg. 16.95 (*1-881508-02-1*) Oliver Pr MN.

Soviet Leadership in Transition. Jerry F. Hough. LC 80-67873. 175p. 1980. 26.95 (*0-8157-3742-4*); pap. 9.95 (*0-8157-3741-6*) Brookings.

Soviet Legacy. Roy D. Laird. LC 92-41617. 240p. 1993. text ed. 55.00 (*0-275-94558-8*, C4558, Praeger Pubs) Greenwood.

Soviet Legal Bibliography: A Classified & Annotated Listing of Books & Serials Published in the Soviet Union Since 1917 as Represented in the Collection of the Harvard Law School Library as of January 1, 1965. Harvard University, Law School Library Staff. xii, 300p. 1968. 22.50 (*0-674-82745-7*) HUP.

Soviet Legal Institutions: Doctrines & Social Functions. Kazimierz Grzybowski. LC 62-12163. (Michigan Legal Publications). xiv, 285p. 1982. reprint ed. lib. bdg. 42.00 (*0-89941-172-X*, 302200) W S Hein.

Soviet Legal System & Arms Inspection: A Case Study in Policy Implementation. Zigurds L. Zile et al. LC 71-151963. (Special Studies in International Politics & Government). 1972. 28.75 (*0-275-28211-2*) Irvington.

Soviet Literary Culture in the 1970s: The Politics of Irony. Anatoly Vishevsky. Tr. by Michael Biggins. LC 93-12529. (Illus.). 336p. (C). 1993. pap. text ed. 19.95 (*0-8130-1226-0*); lib. bdg. 49.95 (*0-8130-1225-2*) U Press Fla.

Soviet Literary Structuralism: Background Debate Issues. Peter Seyffert. 378p. (Orig.). 1985. pap. 23.95 (*0-89357-140-7*) Slavica.

Soviet Literary Theory & Practice During the First Five-Year Plan, 1928-1932. Harriet Borland. LC 69-13833. 256p. 1969. reprint ed. text ed. 59.75 (*0-8371-1075-0*, BOSL, Greenwood Pr) Greenwood.

Soviet Literature & Glasnost, Vol. 1: A Study in Povests. Y. C. Bhatnagar. 1990. 16.00 (*81-202-0268-6*, Pub. by Ajanta II) S Asia.

Soviet Literature in the Nineteen Seventies: Artistic Diversity & Ideological Conformity. N. N. Shneidman. LC 79-14942. 142p. reprint ed. pap. 40.50 (*0-8357-8329-4*, 2034069) Bks Demand.

Soviet Literature in the 1980s: Decade of Transition. N. N. Shneidman. 45.00 (*0-8020-5812-4*) U of Toronto Pr.

Soviet Machine-Tool Industry: An Assessment. Naum Bogoras. Ed. by Jonathan Gullant. Tr. by Peter Saigent from RUS. (Illus.). 121p. (Orig.). 1989. pap. text ed. 75.00 (*1-55831-098-3*) Delphic Associates.

Soviet Man & His World. Klaus Mehnert. Tr. by Maurice Rosenbaum. LC 76-14778. 310p. 1976. reprint ed. text ed. 59.75 (*0-8371-8567-X*, MESOM, Greenwood Pr) Greenwood.

Soviet Man in an Open Society. Ed. by Tamar R. Horowitz. LC 89-16681. 380p. 1989. 65.00 (*0-8191-7573-0*); pap. 31.00 (*0-8191-7574-9*) U Pr of Amer.

Soviet Management & Labor Relations. Bruno Grancelli. 272p. 1987. text ed. 47.95 (*0-04-497040-4*) Routledge Chapman & Hall.

Soviet Maritime Radioteletype Dictionary. Fred J. Osterman & Gary Gorka. (Illus.). 102p. (Orig.). 1988. pap. 11.95 (*1-882123-20-4*) Universal Radio Rsch.

***Soviet Market Economy: Challenges & Reality.** B. Z. Milner & Dmitri S. Lvov. viii, 316p. 1991. 127.00 (*0-444-88979-5*, North Holland) Elsevier.

Soviet Marriage Market: Mate Selection in Russia & the U. S. S. R. Wesley A. Fisher. LC 78-19737. 320p. 1980. text ed. 55.00 (*0-275-90483-0*, C0483, Praeger Pubs) Greenwood.

Soviet Marxism: A Critical Analysis. Herbert Marcuse. LC 57-10943. 271p. 1985. pap. text ed. 18.00 (*0-231-08379-3*) Col U Pr.

Soviet Marxism & Nuclear War: An International Debate. Ed. by John Somerville. LC 80-25820. (Contributions in Philosophy Ser.: No. 18). 176p. 1981. text ed. 59.95 (*0-313-22531-1*, SSM/, Greenwood Pr) Greenwood.

Soviet Marxism-Leninism: The Decline of an Ideology. Alfred B. Evans. LC 93-19089. 256p. 1993. text ed. 65.00 (*0-275-94549-9*, C4549, Praeger Pubs); pap. text ed. 20.95 (*0-275-94763-7*, Praeger Pubs) Greenwood.

Soviet Media in Transition: Structural & Economic Alternatives. Eleana Androunas. LC 93-2862. 184p. 1993. text ed. 49.95 (*0-275-94147-7*, C4147, Praeger Pubs) Greenwood.

Soviet Medical Reviews Section F Oncology Reviews, Vol. 1. N. N. Blokhin & Trapeznikov. 222, xiip. 1987. text ed. 321.00 (*3-7186-0313-6*) Gordon & Breach.

Soviet Medical Reviews Section F Oncology Reviews, Vol. 2. N. N. Blokhin & Trapeznikov. 130, ixp. 1987. text ed. 195.00 (*3-7186-0436-1*) Gordon & Breach.

Soviet Men of Science. John Turkevich. Ed. by J. Blanshei et al. LC 75-19267. 441p. 1975. reprint ed. text ed. 75.00 (*0-8371-8246-8*, TUSM, Greenwood Pr) Greenwood.

Soviet Metal-Fabricating & Economic Development: Practice vs. Policy. David Granick. LC 67-12005. 381p. reprint ed. pap. 108.60 (*0-7837-7023-5*, 2046838) Bks Demand.

Soviet Military: Political Education, Training & Morale. E. S. Williams. LC 86-6556. 256p. 1986. text ed. 45.00 (*0-312-74835-3*) St Martin.

Soviet Military: 1980-1982, 3 vols., Set. Myron J. Smith, Jr. 29.95 (*0-87436-408-6*) Regina Bks.

Soviet Military & Arms Control. Douglas Garthoff. (CISA Working Papers: No. 10). 29p. (Orig.). 1978. pap. 15.00 (*0-86682-009-4*) Ctr Intl Relations.

Soviet Military & the Future. Ed. by Stephen J. Blank & Jacob W. Kipp. LC 92-14617. (Contributions in Military Studies: No. 130). 328p. 1992. text ed. 55.00 (*0-313-27506-8*, KSM, Greenwood Pr) Greenwood.

Soviet Military Art in a Time of Change: Command & Control of the Future Battlefield. Robert Hall. LC 90-9049. 224p. 1990. text ed. write for info. (*0-312-05592-7*) St Martin.

Soviet Military Buildup & U. S. Defense Spending. Barry M. Blechman et al. LC 77-86492. (Brookings Institution Studies in Defense Policy). 69p. reprint ed. pap. 25.00 (*0-317-30181-0*, 2025363) Bks Demand.

***Soviet Military Deception in the Second World War.** Glantz. Date not set. pap. 24.50 (*0-7146-4063-8*, Pub. by F Cass Pubs UK) Intl Spec Bk.

Soviet Military Deception in the Second World War. David M. Glantz. (Cass Series on Soviet Military Theory & Practice). (Illus.). 688p. 1989. text ed. 55.00 (*0-7146-3347-X*, Pub. by F Cass Pubs UK) Intl Spec Bk.

Soviet Military Doctrine & Western Security Policy. Gregory Flynn. 320p. 1989. 45.00 (*0-415-00488-8*) Routledge.

Soviet Military Doctrine, 1915-1991. Ed. by Willard C. Frank, Jr. & Philip S. Gillette. LC 91-37134. (Contributions in Military Studies: No. 125). 448p. 1992. text ed. 65.00 (*0-313-27713-3*, FSV/, Greenwood Pr) Greenwood.

Soviet Military Encyclopedia, Set, Vols. 1-3. abr. ed. Ed. & Tr. by William C. Green. Tr. by W. Robert Reeves. LC 92-32531. 1437p. (C). 1993. Set. 375.00 (*0-8133-1432-1*) Westview.

Soviet Military Intelligence in War. David Glantz. 440p. 1990. pap. 24.50 (*0-7146-4076-X*, Pub. by F Cass Pubs UK); text ed. 55.00 (*0-7146-3374-7*, Pub. by F Cass Pubs UK) Intl Spec Bk.

Soviet Military Interventions since Nineteen Forty-Five. Alex P. Schmid. 200p. (C). 1985. 39.95 (*0-88738-063-8*) Transaction Pubs.

Soviet Military Medicine: Research Subject Index with Bibliography. Russell Manedov. LC 88-47621. 150p. 1988. 44.50 (*0-88164-722-5*); pap. 39.50 (*0-88164-723-3*) ABBE Pubs Assn.

Soviet Military Operational Art: In Pursuit of Deep Battle. David M. Glantz. 300p. 1991. text ed. 47.50 (*0-7146-3362-3*, Pub. by F Cass Pubs UK); pap. text ed. 24.50 (*0-7146-4077-8*, Pub. by F Cass Pubs UK) Intl Spec Bk.

Soviet Military Policy: An International Security Reader. Ed. by Sean M. Lynn-Jones et al. 350p. (Orig.). 1989. pap. 14.95 (*0-262-62066-9*) MIT Pr.

Soviet-Military Power. Tom Gervasi. 176p. 1988. 14.95 (*0-394-75715-7*, Vin) Random.

Soviet Military Power. U. S. Department of the Army, Army Library Staff. LC 78-90731. 186p. 1969. reprint ed. text ed. 35.00 (*0-8371-2502-2*, SOMP, Greenwood Pr) Greenwood.

Soviet Military Power & Performance. John Erickson & E. J. Feuchtwanger. LC 78-26158. ix, 219p. (C). 1979. 32.50 (*0-208-01779-8*, Archon Bks) Shoe String.

Soviet Military Psychiatry: The Theory & Practice of Coping with Battle Stress. Richard A. Gabriel. LC 85-24795. (Contributions in Military Studies: No. 53). (Illus.). 186p. 1986. text ed. 49.95 (*0-313-25225-4*, GSM/, Greenwood Pr) Greenwood.

Soviet Military Reform in the Twentieth Century: Three Case Studies. Raymond J. Swider, Jr. LC 92-14351. (Contributions in Military Studies: No. 129). 192p. 1992. text ed. 49.95 (*0-313-28525-X*, SQW, Greenwood Pr) Greenwood.

Soviet Military Strategy in Western Europe in the Nineteen Seventies. Stuart K. Schwartzman. 191p. (Orig.). 1979. pap. text ed. 32.95 (*0-89126-078-1*) MA-AH Pub.

Soviet Military System. Jacques Sapir. Tr. by David Macey from FRE. 300p. (C). 1991. 55.95 (*0-7456-0671-7*) Blackwell Pubs.

Soviet Military Thinking. Ed. by Derek Leebaert. 304p. (C). 1981. pap. text ed. 16.95 (*0-04-355016-9*) Routledge Chapman & Hall.

Soviet Military Trends: Implications for U. S. Security. William R. Kintner & Robert L. Pfaltzgraff, Jr. LC 71-170291. (American Enterprise Institute for Public Policy Research. High School Debate Ser.: No. 6). 56p. reprint ed. pap. 25.00 (*0-317-29840-2*, 2017445) Bks Demand.

Soviet Multinational State: Readings & Documents. Ed. by Martha B. Olcott et al. LC 88-36747. (USSR in Transition: Readings & Documents Ser.). 616p. (gr. 13). 1990. text ed. 75.95 (*0-87332-389-0*) M E Sharpe.

Soviet National Income & Product in 1937. Abram Bergson. LC 75-104222. 156p. 1970. reprint ed. text ed. 52.50 (*0-8371-3332-7*, BESO, Greenwood Pr) Greenwood.

Soviet National Income, Nineteen Fifty-Eight to Nineteen Sixty-Four: National Accounts of the U. S. S. R. in the Seven Year Plan Period. Abraham S. Becker. LC 70-77483. 626p. reprint ed. pap. 178.50 (*0-685-20496-0*, 2029944) Bks Demand.

Soviet National Security Policy under Perestroika. Ed. by George E. Hudson. (Mershon Center Series on International Security & Foreign Policy: Vol. IV). 352p. 1989. 55.00 (*0-04-445532-1*); pap. 21.95 (*0-04-445535-6*) Routledge Chapman & Hall.

Soviet Nationality Policies: Ruling Ethnic Groups in the U. S. S. R. Ed. by Henry R. Huttenbach. LC 89-29070. 320p. 1990. text ed. 100.00 (*0-7201-2055-1*, Mansell Pub) Cassell.

Soviet Nationality Policies & Practices. Ed. by Jeremy R. Azrael. LC 77-83478. 408p. 1978. text ed. 75.00 (*0-275-90283-8*, C0283, Praeger Pubs) Greenwood.

Soviet Nationality Policy, Urban Growth, & Identity Change in the Ukrainian SSR, 1923-1934. George O. Liber. (Cambridge Russian, Soviet & Post-Soviet Studies: No. 84). (Illus.). 280p. (C). 1992. text ed. 69.95 (*0-521-41391-5*) Cambridge U Pr.

Soviet Nationality Problems. Ed. by Edward Allworth. LC 77-166211. (Illus.). 296p. 1971. text ed. 55.00 (*0-231-03493-8*) Col U Pr.

Soviet Natural Resources in the World Economy. Ed. by Robert G. Jensen et al. LC 82-17317. 720p. 1983. lib. bdg. 120.00 (*0-226-39831-5*) U Ch Pr.

Soviet Naval Architecture Theory & Application of Hydrodynamics. Ephraim Suhir. Ed. by Rebecca Krafft. 128p. (Orig.). 1986. pap. text ed. 75.00 (*1-55831-047-9*) Delphic Associates.

Soviet Naval Developments. United States Navy, Office of Information Staff & Norman Polmar. 18.95 (*0-405-13276-X*) Ayer.

Soviet Naval Influence: Domestic & Foreign Dimensions. Ed. by Michael McGwire & John McDonnell. LC 75-23982. (Special Studies). 698p. 1977. text ed. 95.00 (*0-275-90271-4*, C0271, Praeger Pubs) Greenwood.

Soviet Naval Tactics. Milan Vego. LC 91-42467. (Illus.). 480p. 1992. 65.00 (*0-87021-675-9*) Naval Inst Pr.

Soviet Naval Theory & Policy: Gorshkov's Inheritance. Robert W. Herrick. 352p. 1989. 29.95 (*0-87021-677-5*) Naval Inst Pr.

Soviet Navy. Miller. LC 88-11327. (Soviet Military Power Ser.). (Illus.). 48p. (J). (gr. 3-8). 1988. lib. bdg. 18.60 (*0-86625-336-X*); lib. bdg. 13.95 (*0-685-58300-7*) Rourke Corp.

Soviet Non-Capitalist Development: The Case of Nasser's Egypt. Esmail Hosseinzadeh. LC 88-27511. 222p. 1989. text ed. 55.00 (*0-275-93135-8*, C3135, Praeger Pubs) Greenwood.

Soviet Nonferrous Metals Industry: Strategic Metals. Yuri Yelenshy et al. Ed. by Anne H. Johnson. (Illus.). 138p. (Orig.). 1989. pap. 100.00 (*1-55831-099-1*) Delphic Associates.

Soviet Nuclear Policy under Gorbachev: A Policy of Disarmament. Daniel Calingaert. LC 90-23452. 192p. 1991. text ed. 45.00 (*0-275-93737-2*, C3737, Praeger Pubs) Greenwood.

Soviet Nuclear Power Plants: Reactor Types, Water, & Chemical Control Systems, Turbines. David Katsman. Ed. by Walter Guntharp. Tr. by Vladimir Talmy from RUS. 201p. (Orig.). 1986. pap. text ed. 75.00 (*1-55831-020-7*) Delphic Associates.

Soviet Nuclear Weapon Legacy. Marco De Andreis & Francesco Calogero. (SIPRI Research Reports: No. 10). 100p. 1995. 45.00 (*0-19-829192-2*); pap. 19.95 (*0-19-829197-3*) OUP.

Soviet of Justice: Figures & Policy. P. Van den Berg. 1985. lib. bdg. 181.50 (*90-247-3086-4*) Kluwer Ac.

Soviet Oil & Gas Exports to the West: Commercial Transaction or Security Threat? Jonathan Stern. (Energy Policy Studies). 250p. 1987. text ed. 49.95 (*0-566-05124-9*, Pub. by Dartmth Pub UK) Ashgate Pub Co.

Soviet Oil & Gas to 1990. David Wilson & Geoffrey Drayton. (Economist Intelligence Unit Ser.). (Illus.). 250p. 1982. text ed. 30.00 (*0-89011-581-8*) Abt Bks.

Soviet Oil & Natural Gas Industries: Problems of Reserve Estimation. Alexei Mahmoudov. Ed. by John Williams. 95p. (Orig.). 1986. pap. text ed. 75.00 (*1-55831-029-0*) Delphic Associates.

Soviet Oil & Security Interests in the Barents Sea. Helge O. Bergesen et al. LC 86-29773. 159p. 1987. text ed. 45.00 (*0-312-00491-5*) St Martin.

Soviet Operations in the Initial Period of War, 22 June-August 1941: Proceedings of the Fourth Art of War Symposium, Garmisch, FRG, October 1987. Ed. by David M. Glantz. LC 92-28672. (Cass Series on Soviet Military Experience: Vol. 2). 1997. reprint ed. 55.00 (*0-7146-3375-5*, Pub. by F Cass Pubs UK) Intl Spec Bk.

Soviet Painting in the Tretyakov Gallery. A. Lebedev. 136p. 1976. 50.00 (*0-569-08318-4*) St Mut.

Soviet Paradox: External Expansion & Internal Decline. Seweryn Bialer. 1986. 24.95 (*0-394-54095-6*) Knopf.

Soviet Partisan Movement, Nineteen Forty-One to Nineteen Forty-Four. (Illus.). 227p. reprint ed. per. 16.00 (*0-16-001995-8*, 008-029-00193-4) USGPO.

Soviet Partisan Movement 1941-1944. Edgar M. Howell. (World War II Historical Society Monograph Ser.). 134p. 1995. pap. 10.00 (*1-57638-014-9*) Merriam Pr.

Soviet Party-State: Aspects of Ideocratic Despotism. Carl A. Linden. LC 83-13984. 144p. 1983. text ed. 45.00 (*0-275-91037-7*, C1037, Praeger Pubs) Greenwood.

Soviet Passage: Sixty-One Days across the Soviet Union. Jon H. Gates. Ed. by Beverly Hanly. (Illus.). 176p. (Orig.). 1989. pap. 9.95 (*0-923000-00-3*) Summer Run Pub.

Soviet Peasants, or: The Peasants' Art of Starving. Lev Timofeev. Tr. by Jean Alexander & Alexander Zaslavsky from RUS. 160p. 1985. 25.00 (*0-914386-12-3*) Telos Pr.

Soviet Penal Policy. Ivo Lapenna. LC 80-15755. (Background Bk.). 148p. 1980. reprint ed. text ed. 49.75 (*0-313-22570-2*, LASP, Greenwood Pr) Greenwood.

Soviet Penetration of Afghanistan: 1950-1979. Patrick J. Garrity. (Occasional Paper of the Study of Statesmanship & Political Philosophy: No. 4). 34p. (Orig.). (C). 1982. pap. text ed. 2.00 (*0-930783-10-7*) Claremont Inst.

Soviet Perceptions of the United States. Morton Schwartz. LC 76-7767. 1978. pap. 12.00 (*0-520-04094-5*) U CA Pr.

Soviet Perestroika, 1985-1993: Russia's Road to Democracy. Ed. by John F. Bradley. 220p. 1996. 31.00 (*0-88033-332-4*) Col U Pr.

Soviet Perspectives on African Socialism. Arthur J. Klinghoffer. LC 68-26304. 276p. 1975. 24.50 (*0-8386-6907-7*) Fairleigh Dickinson.

Soviet Philosophy Revisited. Adelmann. (Boston College Studies in Philosophy: No. 5). 104p. 1977. pap. text ed. 78.00 (*90-247-1977-1*, Pub. by M Nijhoff NE) Kluwer Ac.

Soviet Photograph, 1924-1937. Margarita Tupitsyn. LC 95-49373. (Illus.). 228p. 1996. 40.00 (*0-300-06450-0*) Yale U Pr.

Soviet Planned Economic Order. William H. Chamberlin. LC 70-107342. (BCL Ser.: No. I). 1970. reprint ed. 27.50 (*0-404-00595-0*) AMS Pr.

Soviet Planned Economic Order. William H. Chamberlin. LC 77-95088. 1970. reprint ed. text ed. 69.50 (*0-8371-2544-8*, CHSE, Greenwood Pr) Greenwood.

Soviet Planning: Evolution in 1965-1980. Fyodor I. Kushnirsky. 196p. (Orig.). 1981. pap. text ed. 75.00 (*1-55831-000-2*) Delphic Associates.

Soviet Planning & Spatial Efficiency: The Prewar Cement Industry. Alan Abouchar. LC 70-126203. (Indiana University Russian & East European Ser.: Vol. 39). (Illus.). 144p. reprint ed. pap. 41.10 (*0-317-08589-1*, 2015812) Bks Demand.

Soviet Planning in Peace & War, 1938-1945. Mark Harrison. (Cambridge Russian, Soviet & Post-Soviet Studies: No. 45). 320p. 1985. text ed. 69.95 (*0-521-30371-0*) Cambridge U Pr.

Soviet Poets & Poetry. Alexander S. Kaun. LC 68-14906. (Essay Index Reprint Ser.). 1977. 16.95 (*0-8369-0586-5*) Ayer.

Soviet Policies in China, 1917-1924. Allen S. Whiting. viii, 350p. 1954. 47.50 (*0-8047-0612-3*); pap. 16.95 (*0-8047-0613-1*) Stanford U Pr.

Soviet Policies in the Eighties. Rakesh Gupta. 1988. 20.00 (*81-7050-060-5*, Pub. by Patriot II) S Asia.

Soviet Policies in the Middle East: From World War II to Gorbachev. Galia Golan. (Soviet Paperbacks Ser.: No. 2). (Illus.). 344p. (C). 1990. text ed. 59.95 (*0-521-35332-7*); pap. text ed. 19.95 (*0-521-35859-0*) Cambridge U Pr.

Soviet Policies Toward the Nordic Countries. Orjan Berner. LC 86-9087. 206p. (Orig.). 1986. pap. 22.50 (*0-8191-5382-6*); lib. bdg. 44.50 (*0-8191-5381-8*) U Pr of Amer.

Soviet Policy & the Chinese Communists, 1931-1946. Charles B. McLane. LC 73-37861. (Select Bibliographies Reprint Ser.). 1977. reprint ed. 18.95 (*0-8369-9964-9*) Ayer.

Soviet Policy in Eastern Europe. Ed. by Sarah M. Terry. LC 83-21889. (Council on Foreign Relations Bks.). 376p. 1984. 17.00 (*0-300-03131-9*) Yale U Pr.

Soviet Policy in the Arc of Crisis. Fred Halliday. (Illus.). 143p. (Orig.). (C). 1981. pap. 4.95 (*0-89758-028-1*) Inst Policy Stud.

Soviet Policy in the Far East, 1944-1951. Max Beloff. LC 75-146852. (Select Bibliographies Reprint Ser.). 1977. reprint ed. 23.95 (*0-8369-5619-2*) Ayer.

Soviet Policy in West Africa. Robert H. Legvold. LC 79-115477. 386p. 1970. 34.50 (*0-674-82775-9*) HUP.

Soviet Policy Toward East Germany Reconsidered: The Postwar Decade. Ann L. Phillips. LC 85-17729. (Contributions in Political Science Ser.: No. 142). (Illus.). 274p. 1986. text ed. 55.00 (*0-313-24671-8*, PSP/, Greenwood Pr) Greenwood.

Soviet Policy Toward India: Ideology & Strategy. Robert H. Donaldson. LC 73-89708. (Russian Research Center Studies: No. 74). 355p. reprint ed. pap. 101.20 (*0-317-09565-X*, 2021769) Bks Demand.

Soviet Policy Toward Israel under Gorbachev. Robert O. Freedman. LC 90-25867. (Washington Papers: No. 150). 160p. 1991. pap. text ed. 13.95 (*0-275-93994-4*, B3994, Praeger Pubs) Greenwood.

Soviet Policy Toward Israel under Gorbachev. Robert O. Freedman. LC 90-25867. (Washington Papers: No. 150). 160p. 1991. text ed. 45.00 (*0-275-93993-6*, C3993, Praeger Pubs) Greenwood.

Soviet Policy Toward the Middle East since 1970. 3rd ed. R. Freedman. LC 82-9014. 485p. 1982. text ed. 69.50 (*0-275-90796-1*, C0796, Praeger Pubs) Greenwood.

Soviet Policy Toward Turkey, Iran & Afghanistan: The Dynamics of Influence. Alvin Z. Rubinstein. LC 82-7513. 218p. 1982. text ed. 35.00 (*0-275-90891-7*, C0891, Praeger Pubs) Greenwood.

Soviet Policy Toward Western Europe: Implications for the Atlantic Alliance. Ed. by Herbert J. Ellison. LC 83-47977. 312p. 1984. pap. 17.50 (*0-295-96036-1*) U of Wash Pr.

Soviet Policy Towards South Africa. Kurt M. Campbell. LC 86-10092. 272p. 1987. text ed. 39.95 (*0-312-74853-1*) St Martin.

Soviet Policy Towards South Asia since 1970. Linda Racioppi. (Cambridge Russian, Soviet & Post-Soviet Studies: No. 91). (Illus.). 256p. (C). 1994. text ed. 69.95 (*0-521-41457-1*) Cambridge U Pr.

Soviet-Polish Relations, 1917-1921. Piotr S. Wandycz. LC 69-18047. (Russian Research Center Studies: No. 59). 420p. reprint ed. pap. 119.70 (*0-7837-3837-4*, 2043659) Bks Demand.

Soviet Political Economy in Transition: From Lenin to Gorbachev. Abu F. Dowlah. LC 91-28147. (Contributions in Economics & Economic History Ser.: No. 130). 296p. 1992. text ed. 55.00 (*0-313-27944-6*, DPF, Greenwood Pr) Greenwood.

Soviet Political Elites: The Case of Tiraspol. Ronald J. Hill. 1977. text ed. 29.95 (*0-312-74846-9*) St Martin.

An Asterisk (*) at the beginning of an entry indicates that the title is appearing in BIP for the first time.

Soviet Political, Military & Economic Involvement in Sinkaing, 1928-1949. Arthur C. Hasiotis. (Modern European History Ser.). 272p. 1987. text ed. 15.00 (*0-8240-8055-6*) Garland.

Soviet Political Mind. Robert C. Tucker. 320p. 1972. reprint ed. pap. 9.95 (*0-393-00582-8*) Norton.

Soviet Political Poster, 1917-1980. M. Hahl-Koch. (C). 1990. pap. 120.00 (*0-685-34344-8*, Pub. by Collets) St Mut.

Soviet Political Scientists & American Politics. Neil Malcolm. LC 83-16122. 256p. 1984. text ed. 39.95 (*0-312-74855-8*) St Martin.

Soviet Political Society. 3rd ed. Leon P. Baradat. LC 91-18143. 461p. (C). 1991. pap. text ed. 33.40 (*0-13-824962-8*) P-H.

Soviet Political System: Transformation or Degeneration. Zbigniew Brzezinski. (Reprint Series in Political Science). (C). 1993. reprint ed. pap. text ed. 1.00 (*0-8290-3572-9*, PS-438) Irvington.

Soviet Political Thought: An Anthology. Ed. & Tr. by Michael Jaworskyj. LC 67-23573. 596p. 1968. 68.00 (*0-8018-0316-0*) Johns Hopkins.

Soviet Politics: An Introduction. Richard Sakwa. (Illus.). 380p. 1989. 45.00 (*0-415-00505-1*); pap. 14.95 (*0-415-00506-X*) Routledge.

Soviet Politics: Continuity & Contradiction. Gordon B. Smith. LC 87-4610. 1987. text ed. 39.95 (*0-312-00795-7*) St Martin.

Soviet Politics: Russia after Brezhnev. Ed. by Joseph L. Nogee. LC 84-26289. 254p. 1985. text ed. 55.00 (*0-275-90148-3*, C0148, Praeger Pubs) Greenwood.

Soviet Politics: Struggling with Change. 2nd ed. Gordon B. Smith. 1991. text ed. 49.95 (*0-312-06614-7*) St Martin.

Soviet Politics: Struggling with Change. 2nd ed. Gordon B. Smith. LC 91-31130. 432p. (C). 1991. pap. text ed. 24.50 (*0-312-03655-8*) St Martin.

Soviet Politics - The Dilemma of Power: The Role of Ideas in Social Change. Barrington Moore, Jr. LC 76-19137. 518p. (gr. 13). 1976. reprint ed. pap. text ed. 48.95 (*0-87332-088-3*) M E Sharpe.

Soviet Politics & Education. Frank M. Sorrentino & Frances R. Curcio. (Orig.). 426p. (Orig.). (C). 1986. pap. text ed. 34.50 (*0-8191-5124-6*); lib. bdg. 62.00 (*0-8191-5123-8*) U Pr of Amer.

Soviet Politics & Political Science. Archie Brown. LC 75-29858. 128p. 1976. text ed. 35.00 (*0-312-74865-5*) St Martin.

Soviet Politics from Brezhnev to Gorbachev. Donald R. Kelley. LC 87-11677. 242p. 1987. pap. text ed. 19.95 (*0-275-92732-6*, B2732, Praeger Pubs) Greenwood.

Soviet Politics from Brezhnev to Gorbachev. Donald R. Kelley. LC 87-11677. 242p. 1987. text ed. 55.00 (*0-275-92522-6*, C2522, Praeger Pubs) Greenwood.

Soviet Politics in the Brezhnev Era. Ed. by Donald R. Kelley. LC 79-24741. (Praeger Special Studies). 282p. 1980. text ed. 55.00 (*0-275-90502-0*, C0502, Praeger Pubs) Greenwood.

Soviet Politics in Transition. Joan DeBardeleben. 188p. (C). 1992. pap. text ed. 32.36 (*0-669-28676-1*) HM College Div.

Soviet Politics, Nineteen Forty-Five to Nineteen Fifty-Three. Timothy Dunmore. LC 83-40702. 176p. 1984. text ed. 35.00 (*0-312-74869-8*) St Martin.

Soviet Politics, Nineteen Seventeen to Nineteen Ninety-One. Mary McAuley. LC 92-7517. 160p. (C). 1992. 25.00 (*0-19-878066-4*); pap. 11.95 (*0-19-878067-2*) OUP.

Soviet Politics, Political Science, & Reform. Ronald J. Hill. LC 79-55751. 233p. 1980. reprint ed. pap. 66.50 (*0-7837-9982-9*, 2060709) Bks Demand.

Soviet Polity: Government & Politics in the U. S. S. R. 3rd ed. John S. Reshetar, Jr. 416p. (C). 1988. pap. text ed. 32.50 (*0-06-045398-2*) Addson-Wesley Educ.

Soviet Polity in the Modern Era. Ed. by Erik P. Hoffmann & Robbin F. Laird. LC 84-3078. 958p. (C). 1984. pap. text ed. 36.95 (*0-202-24165-3*); lib. bdg. 59.95 (*0-202-24164-5*) Aldine de Gruyter.

Soviet Postmortem: Philosophical Roots of the 'Grand Failure' Sigmund Krancberg. 184p. 1994. pap. text ed. 22.95 (*0-8476-7928-4*); lib. bdg. 54.50 (*0-8476-7927-6*) Rowman.

Soviet Potentials: A Geographic Appraisal. George B. Cressey. LC 62-8478. (Illus.). (C). 1962. pap. 12.95 (*0-8156-2034-9*) Syracuse U Pr.

Soviet Power. Jordan A. Hodgkins. LC 75-31801. 190p. 1975. reprint ed. text ed. 49.75 (*0-8371-8491-6*, HOSP, Greenwood Pr) Greenwood.

Soviet Power: The Continuing Challenge. James G. Sherr. 260p. 1987. text ed. 39.95 (*0-312-74873-6*) St Martin.

Soviet Power: The Continuing Challenge. 2nd ed. James G. Sherr. LC 90-35161. (Military Studies). 320p. 1991. text ed. 59.95 (*0-312-04817-3*) St Martin.

Soviet Power & the Third World. Rajan Menon. 1986. 37.50 (*0-300-03500-4*) Yale U Pr.

Soviet Power & the Third World. Rajan Menon. LC 85-40988. 272p. (C). 1989. reprint ed. pap. 18.00 (*0-300-04489-5*) Yale U Pr.

Soviet Prefects: The Local Party Organs in Industrial Decision-Making. Jerry F. Hough. LC 69-18033. (Russian Research Center Studies: No. 58). 432p. reprint ed. pap. 123.20 (*0-7837-3866-8*, 2043688) Bks Demand.

Soviet Prison Camp Speech: A Survivor's Glossary. Ed. by Meyer Galler & Harlan E. Marquess. LC 75-176411. 216p. 1972. 30.00 (*0-299-06080-2*) U of Wis Pr.

Soviet Prison Camp Speech: Supplement. Meyer Galler. LC 77-89596. (RUS.). 1977. 18.00 (*0-930232-01-1*) Soviet Studies.

Soviet Procuracy Protests: 1937-1973. Ed. by L. Boim & G. G. Morgan. (Law in Eastern Europe Ser.: No. 21). 324p. 1978. lib. bdg. 223.50 (*90-286-0138-4*) Kluwer Ac.

Soviet Product Quality. Malcolm R. Hill & Richard McKay. LC 87-4669. 256p. 1988. text ed. 49.95 (*0-312-00764-7*) St Martin.

Soviet Propaganda. Baruch A. Hazan. 293p. 1976. 34.95 (*0-87855-192-1*) Transaction Pubs.

Soviet Propaganda As a Foreign Policy Tool. Marian Leighton. 198p. (C). 1991. 19.95 (*0-932088-51-1*) Freedom Hse.

Soviet Psycholinguistics. Jan Prucha. (Janua Linguarum, Ser. Minor: No. 143). 117p. (Orig.). 1972. pap. text ed. 53.10 (*90-279-2317-5*) Mouton.

Soviet Psychology: Philosophical, Theoretical & Experimental Issues. Levy Rahmani. LC 72-182041. 560p. 1973. 55.00 (*0-8236-6110-5*) Intl Univs Pr.

Soviet Psychotherapy. Tr. by E. Salisbury & Ann Lauterbach. (Illus.). 255p. 1984. 117.00 (*0-08-024291-X*, Pub. by Pergamon Repr UK) Franklin.

Soviet Public Opinion & Ideology: Mythology & Pragmatism in Interaction. Vladimir Shlapentokh. LC 86-15161. 256p. 1986. text ed. 49.95 (*0-275-92561-7*, C2561, Praeger Pubs) Greenwood.

Soviet Publications on Judaism, Zionism, & the State of Israel, 1984-1988: An Annotated Bibliography. Boris Korsch. LC 89-35483. 168p. 1990. text ed. 33.00 (*0-8240-4108-9*, SS482) Garland.

Soviet Quantitative History. Ed. by Don K. Rowney. LC 83-19196. (New Approaches to Social Science History Ser.: No. 4). (Illus.). 216p. reprint ed. pap. 61.60 (*0-8357-8506-8*, 2034793) Bks Demand.

Soviet Quest for Economic Efficiency: Issues, Controversies & Reforms. George R. Feiwel. LC 72-145952. (Special Studies in International Economics & Development). 1972. 39.50 (*0-89197-944-1*) Irvington.

Soviet Question in British Politics: From October Revolution to Cold War. Charles G. Bolte. LC 86-50037. 288p. (C). 1989. pap. text ed. 19.95 (*0-932269-79-6*) Wyndham Hall.

Soviet Radio Frequency Discharge Research. Valery Godyak. Ed. by Andreas Tamberg. 166p. (Orig.). 1986. pap. text ed. 75.00 (*1-55831-012-6*) Delphic Associates.

Soviet Realities: Culture & Politics from Stalin to Gorbachev. Walter Laqueur. 305p. 1989. 44.95 (*0-88738-302-5*) Transaction Pubs.

Soviet Reforms & Beyond. Leo Cooper. LC 91-9977. 215p. 1991. text ed. 69.95 (*0-312-06504-3*) St Martin.

Soviet Regime: Communism in Practice. Wadysaw W. Kulski. LC 63-21982. 458p. reprint ed. pap. 130.60 (*0-317-52017-2*, 2027411) Bks Demand.

Soviet Regime in Czechoslovakia. Zdenek Krystufek. (East European Monographs: No. 81). 340p. 1981. text ed. 63.00 (*0-914710-75-3*) East Eur Monographs.

Soviet Regional Dilemma: Planning, People & Natural Resources. Jan A. Dellenbrant. Tr. by Michel Vale from SWE. LC 86-13049. 230p. (gr. 13). 1986. text ed. 72.95 (*0-87332-384-X*) M E Sharpe.

Soviet Regional Economic Autonomy Baltics vs. Moscow. Misha V. Belkindas. Ed. by Suzanne R. Possehl. Tr. by Peter Sargent from RUS. (Illus.). x, 103p. (Orig.). 1989. pap. 75.00 (*1-55831-109-2*) Delphic Associates.

Soviet Regional Economic Policy: The East-West Debate over Pacific Siberian Development. Jonathan R. Schiffer. LC 88-28195. 384p. 1989. text ed. 55.00 (*0-312-02515-7*) St Martin.

Soviet Regional Elite Mobility from Brezhnev to Gorbachev. William A. Clark. LC 88-36973. 217p. 1989. text ed. 55.00 (*0-275-93124-2*, C3124, Praeger Pubs) Greenwood.

Soviet Relations in South East Asia. R. A. Longmire. 280p. 1989. 65.00 (*0-7103-0343-2*, A3918) Routledge Chapman & Hall.

Soviet Relations with ASEAN, 1967-1988. Bilveer Singh. 240p. (Orig.). 1989. 49.50 (*9971-69-133-7*, Pub. by Sgapore Univ SI) Coronet Bks.

Soviet Relations with India & Vietnam. Ramesh Thakur & Carlyle A. Thayer. LC 91-30213. 256p. 1992. text ed. 69.95 (*0-312-07207-4*) St Martin.

Soviet Relations with Latin America, 1959-1987. Nicola Miller. (Cambridge Soviet Paperbacks Ser.: No. 1). (Illus.). 264p. (C). 1990. pap. text ed. 17.95 (*0-521-35979-1*) Cambridge U Pr.

Soviet Research in New Semiconductor Materials. Ed. by Dmitrii N. Nasledov & N. A. Goryunova. Tr. by A. Tybulewicz. LC 65-11956. 126p. reprint ed. pap. 36.00 (*0-317-09195-6*, 2020668) Bks Demand.

Soviet Research Institutes & the Formulation of Foreign Policy: The Institute of World Economy & International Relations (IMEMO) Andrew A. Michta. 120p. (Orig.). 1987. pap. text ed. 75.00 (*1-55831-036-3*) Delphic Associates.

Soviet Revolution. Ed. by Bloomfield. (C). 1989. pap. 19.95 (*0-85315-713-8*, Pub. by Lawrence & Wishart UK) NYU Pr.

Soviet Risk Taking & Crisis Behavior: A Theoretical & Empirical Analysis. Hannes Adomeit. 450p. (C). 1984. text ed. 37.50 (*0-04-335043-7*); pap. text ed. 15.95 (*0-04-335051-8*) Routledge Chapman & Hall.

Soviet Rocket Forces. Miller. LC 88-11367. (Soviet Military Power Ser.). (Illus.). 48p. (J). (gr. 3-8). 1988. lib. bdg. 18.60 (*0-86625-333-5*); lib. bdg. 13.95 (*0-685-58297-3*) Rourke Corp.

Soviet RPG-18 Antitank Rocket Launcher. Ed. by Bruce A. Hanesalo. Tr. by Cyril Koob from GER. (Antiarmor Ser.). (Illus.). 47p. 1994. vinyl bd. 10.00 (*1-886848-11-4*) Mil-Info.

Soviet Russia & Indian Communism. David N. Druhe. 1959. 19.95 (*0-8084-0385-0*) NCUP.

Soviet Russia & the East, 1920-1927: A Documentary Survey. Xenia J. Eudin & Robert C. North. xviii, 478p. 1957. 59.50 (*0-8047-0477-5*) Stanford U Pr.

Soviet Russia & the Middle East. Aaron Klieman. (School of Advanced International Studies: No. 14). 107p. 1970. 12.50 (*0-8018-1223-2*) Johns Hopkins.

Soviet Russia & the Middle East. Aaron Klieman. LC 71-128822. (Washington Center of Foreign Policy Research. Studies in International Affairs: No. 14). 117p. reprint ed. pap. 33.40 (*0-317-08403-8*, 2003227) Bks Demand.

Soviet Russia & the West, 1920-1927: A Documentary Survey. Xenia J. Eudin et al. xxxvii, 450p. 1957. 59.50 (*0-8047-0478-3*) Stanford U Pr.

Soviet Russia in the Second Decade. American Trade Union Delegation to the Soviet Union Staff. Ed. by Stuart Chase et al. LC 72-8432. (Select Bibliographies Reprint Ser.). 1977. reprint ed. 20.95 (*0-8369-6961-8*) Ayer.

Soviet Russia Since the War. Hewlett Johnson. LC 78-21070. 1979. reprint ed. text ed. 69.50 (*0-313-20865-4*, JOSR, Greenwood Pr) Greenwood.

Soviet Russia, 1917-Present see Readings in Russian Civilization

Soviet Russian Literature Since Stalin. Deming Brown. LC 77-73275. 1978. 69.95 (*0-521-21694-X*) Cambridge U Pr.

Soviet Russian Tokarev "TT" Pistols & Cartridges 1929-1953. Fred A. Datig. LC 90-71931. 168p. 1991. 29.95 (*1-882824-15-6*) Graphic Pubs.

Soviet Satire of the Twenties. Richard L. Chapple. LC 79-23575. (University of Florida Humanities Monographs: No. 47). 186p. (Orig.). reprint ed. pap. 53.10 (*0-7837-5093-5*, 2044792) Bks Demand.

Soviet Scene: A Geographical Perspective. James H. Bater. (Illus.). 256p. 1989. 49.50 (*0-7131-6613-4*, Pub. by E Arnold UK); pap. 16.95 (*0-7131-6420-4*, Pub. by E Arnold UK) Routledge Chapman & Hall.

***Soviet Scene: Six Plays of Russian Life.** Alexander Bakshy. 348p. 1970. 22.95 (*0-8369-8200-2*) Ayer.

Soviet Scene, Nineteen Eighty-Eight: A Selection of Articles & Interviews from the Soviet Press. Ed. by V. Mezhenkov & E. Skelley. (C). 1987. pap. 45.00 (*0-569-09093-8*, Pub. by Collets) St Mut.

Soviet Scholar-Bureaucrat: M. N. Pokrovskii & the Society of Marxist Historians. George M. Enteen. LC 78-50002. 1978. 35.00 (*0-271-00548-3*) Pa St U Pr.

Soviet Scholarship under Gorbachev. Ed. by Alexander Dallin & Bertrand Patenaude. 100p. (Orig.). 1988. pap. write for info. (*0-318-64415-0*) Stanford U CFREES.

***Soviet Schooling in the Second World War.** John Dunstan. LC 96-43240. 1997. text ed. 65.00 (*0-312-16601-X*) St Martin.

Soviet Science, Technology, Design: Interaction & Convergence. Raymond Hutchings. (Royal Institute of International Affairs Ser.). (Illus.). 1976. 34.95 (*0-19-218318-4*) OUP.

***Soviet Science under Control.** Roberg. Date not set. text ed. 65.00 (*0-312-17736-4*) St Martin.

Soviet Scientists & the State: An Examination of the Social & Political Aspects of Science in the U. S. S. R. Peter Kneen. LC 83-26931. 138p. 1985. text ed. 59.50 (*0-87395-895-0*); pap. text ed. 19.95 (*0-87395-896-9*) State U NY Pr.

Soviet Sea Power. Ed. by John Skogan et al. (Studies in Contemporary Maritime Policy & Strategy). 224p. 1990. text ed. 49.95 (*0-312-04179-9*) St Martin.

Soviet Secondary School. Dora Shturman. 320p. (C). 1989. lib. bdg. 67.50 (*0-415-00575-2*) Routledge.

Soviet Secrecy & Non-Secrecy. Ed. by Raymond Hutchings. 240p. 1987. 53.00 (*0-389-20754-3*, N8313) B&N Imports.

Soviet Secret Police. Ed. by Simon Wolin & Robert M. Slusser. LC 74-20280. 408p. 1974. reprint ed. text ed. 75.00 (*0-8371-7852-5*, WOSS, Greenwood Pr) Greenwood.

Soviet Secret Services. Otto Heilbrunn. LC 80-27994. 216p. 1981. reprint ed. text ed. 45.00 (*0-313-22892-2*, HESSE, Greenwood Pr) Greenwood.

Soviet Security & Intelligence Organizations 1917-1990: A Biographical Dictionary & Review of Literature in English. Michael Parrish. LC 91-34996. 704p. 1992. text ed. 79.50 (*0-313-28305-2*, PSV/, Greenwood Pr) Greenwood.

Soviet Security Policy Towards South Asia, 1971-1983. Nisha Sahai-Achuthan. 1988. 48.50 (*81-7062-038-4*, Pub. by Lancer II) S Asia.

Soviet Seizure of the Kuriles. David Rees. LC 84-18373. 204p. 1985. text ed. 55.00 (*0-275-90154-8*, C0154, Praeger Pubs) Greenwood.

Soviet Semiotics: An Anthology. Ed. by Daniel P. Lucid. LC 77-4543. (Illus.). 1978. text ed. 35.00 (*0-8018-1980-6*) Johns Hopkins.

Soviet Semiotics: An Anthology. Ed. by Daniel P. Lucid. LC 77-4543. 272p. 1988. reprint ed. pap. text ed. 14.95 (*0-8018-3656-5*) Johns Hopkins.

Soviet Sobranie of Laws: Problems of Codification & Non-Publication. Ed. by Richard M. Buxbaum & Kathryn Hendley. LC 91-6393. (Research Ser.: No. 78). (Illus.). xii, 226p. (Orig.). (C). 1991. pap. text ed. 16.95 (*0-87725-178-9*) U of Cal IAS.

Soviet Social Contract & Why It Failed: Welfare Policy & Workers' Politics from Brezhnev to Yeltsin. Linda J. Cook. LC 93-19068. (Russian Research Center Studies: No. 86). 288p. 1994. text ed. 47.50 (*0-674-82800-3*) HUP.

Soviet Social Reality in the Mirror of Glasnost. Ed. by James Riordan. LC 91-44871. 188p. 1992. text ed. 65.00 (*0-312-07901-X*) St Martin.

Soviet Socialism: Utopian or Scientific? Sam Marcy. 1992. pap. 2.50 (*0-89567-107-7*) World View Forum.

Soviet Socialist Realist Painting 1930s-1960s. Contrib. by David Elliott et al. (Illus.). 1995. pap. 60.00 (*0-614-03382-9*, Pub. by Museum Modern Art UK) St Mut.

Soviet Socialist Republic of Iran, 1920-21: Birth of the Trauma. Cosroe Chaqueri. (Russian & East European Studies Ser.). (Illus.). 624p. (C). 1994. 75.00 (*0-8229-3792-1*) U of Pittsburgh Pr.

Soviet Society & the Communist Party. Ed. by Karl W. Ryavec. LC 78-53179. 240p. (C). 1978. 30.00 (*0-87023-258-4*) U of Mass Pr.

Soviet Society Today. Michael Rywkin. LC 89-4192. 256p. (gr. 13). 1989. text ed. 72.95 (*0-87332-444-7*); pap. text ed. 30.95 (*0-87332-445-5*) M E Sharpe.

Soviet Society under Gorbachev: Current Trends & the Prospects for Change. Ed. by Maurice Friedberg & Heyward Isham. LC 87-16572. 288p. (gr. 13). 1987. text ed. 63.95 (*0-87332-442-0*); pap. text ed. 30.95 (*0-87332-443-9*) M E Sharpe.

Soviet Society under Perestroika. David Lane. 256p. 1990. text ed. 75.00 (*0-04-445166-0*); pap. text ed. 22.95 (*0-04-445167-9*) Routledge Chapman & Hall.

Soviet Society under Perestroika. David Lane. 300p. 1992. pap. 14.95 (*0-00-302060-6*, A8325) Routledge Chapman & Hall.

Soviet Society under Perestroika. David Lane. 416p. (Orig.). (C). 1992. pap. 22.95 (*0-415-07600-5*, Routledge NY) Routledge.

Soviet Sources of Military Doctrine & Strategy. William F. Scott. LC 75-18537. (Strategy Papers: No. 26). 72p. 1975. 12.00 (*0-8448-0709-5*, Crane Russak) Taylor & Francis.

Soviet Space. Jay Miller. LC 91-65880. (Orig.). 1991. 35.00 (*0-9629867-0-4*); pap. 15.00 (*0-9629867-3-9*) Ft Worth Mus Sci Hist.

Soviet Space Programme. Ronald Humble. (Illus.). 160p. 1989. 59.95 (*0-415-02109-X*) Routledge.

Soviet State & Society Between Revolutions, 1918- 1929. Lewis H. Siegelbaum. (Soviet Paperbacks Ser.: No. 8). 320p. (C). 1992. pap. text ed. 19.95 (*0-521-36987-8*) Cambridge U Pr.

Soviet Statistics. B. P. Pockney. 350p. 1992. text ed. 59.95 (*0-312-04003-2*) St Martin.

Soviet Statistics of Physical Output of Industrial Commodities: Their Compilation & Quality. Gregory Grossman. LC 85-8016. (National Bureau of Economic Research: No. 69). xvi, 151p. 1985. reprint ed. text ed. 52.50 (*0-313-24623-8*, GSOS) Greenwood.

Soviet Steam Generator Technology (Fossil Fuel & Nuclear Power Plants) Joseph Rosengaus. Ed. by Andreas Tamberg. (Illus.). (Orig.). 1987. pap. text ed. 75.00 (*1-55831-042-8*) Delphic Associates.

Soviet Steel: The Challenge of Industrial Modernization in the U. S. S. R. Boris Z. Rumer. LC 88-47745. (Cornell Studies in Soviet History & Science). (Illus.). 264p. 1989. 39.95 (*0-8014-2077-6*) Cornell U Pr.

Soviet Strategic Arms Policy Before SALT. Christoph Bluth. (Cambridge Russian, Soviet & Post-Soviet Studies: No. 83). (Illus.). 336p. (C). 1992. text ed. 69.95 (*0-521-40372-3*) Cambridge U Pr.

Soviet Strategic Forces: Requirements & Responses. Robert P. Berman & John C. Baker. LC 82-70889. (Studies in Defense Policy). 171p. 1982. 26.95 (*0-8157-0926-9*); pap. 9.95 (*0-8157-0925-0*) Brookings.

Soviet Strategic Initiatives: Challenge & Response. C. J. Jacobsen. LC 79-89850. 183p. 1979. text ed. 45.00 (*0-275-90369-9*, C0369, Praeger Pubs) Greenwood.

Soviet Strategy & Islam. Ed. by Alexandre A. Benningsen et al. 200p. 1989. text ed. 49.95 (*0-312-02481-9*) St Martin.

Soviet Strategy & the New Military Thinking. Ed. by Derek Leebaert & Timothy Dickinson. 320p. (C). 1992. pap. text ed. 19.95 (*0-521-40769-9*) Cambridge U Pr.

Soviet Strategy & the New Military Thinking. Ed. by Derek Leebaert & Timothy Dickinson. 320p. (C). 1992. text ed. 59.95 (*0-521-40429-0*) Cambridge U Pr.

Soviet Strategy in Southern Africa: Gorbachev's Pragmatic Approach. Peter Vanneman. 142p. (C). 1990. pap. text ed. 15.95 (*0-8179-8902-1*, P390) Hoover Inst Pr.

Soviet Strategy in the Middle East. George W. Breslauer. 352p. (C). (gr. 13). 1989. text ed. 62.95 (*0-04-445232-2*) Routledge Chapman & Hall.

Soviet Strategy in the Nuclear Age. Raymond L. Garthoff. LC 74-10015. 283p. 1975. reprint ed. text ed. 85.00 (*0-8371-7658-1*, GASS, Greenwood Pr) Greenwood.

Soviet Strategy Interests in the North. Kirsten Amundsen. 256p. 1990. text ed. 49.95 (*0-312-04189-6*) St Martin.

Soviet Strategy Toward African National Liberation Movements. Daniel R. Kempton. LC 88-30278. 261p. 1989. text ed. 59.95 (*0-275-93118-8*, C3118, Praeger Pubs) Greenwood.

Soviet Strategy Toward Western Europe. Ed. by Edwina Moreton & Gerald Segal. 304p. (C). 1984. pap. text ed. 19.95 (*0-04-330346-3*) Routledge Chapman & Hall.

Soviet Structural Folkloristics: Texts by Meletinsky, Nekludov, Novik, & Segal, with Tests of the Approach by Jilek & Jilek-Aall, Reid, & Layton, Vol. 1. Ed. by Pierre Maranda. LC 73-79892. (Approaches to Semiotics Ser.: No. 42). 194p. 1974. 47.70 (*90-279-2683-2*) Mouton.

Soviet Studies Guide: Critical Reference to the Political, Economic & Social Sciences Literature. Ed. by Tania Konn. 258p. 1992. lib. bdg. 75.00 (*0-86291-790-5*) Bowker-Saur.

Soviet Studies of Premodern China: Assessments of Recent Scholarship. Ed. by Gilbert Rozman. (Michigan Monographs in Chinese Studies: No. 50). 247p. (C). 1984. text ed. 35.00 (*0-89264-052-9*); pap. text ed. 20.00 (*0-89264-053-7*) Ctr Chinese Studies.

Soviet Studies on the Church & the Believer's Response to Atheism. Dimitry V. Pospielovsky. 1988. text ed. 49.95 (*0-312-01291-8*) St Martin.

Soviet Study of International Relations. Allen C. Lynch. (Soviet & East European Studies). 224p. (C). 1989. pap. text ed. 19.95 (*0-521-36763-8*) Cambridge U Pr.

S

Soviet Submarine Operations in Swedish Waters 1980-1986. Milton Leitenberg. LC 87-13216. (Washington Papers: No. 128). 208p. 1987. text ed. 45.00 (*0-275-92841-1*, C2841, Praeger Pubs); pap. text ed. 13.95 (*0-275-92842-X*, B2842, Praeger Pubs) Greenwood.

Soviet Submarines. Miller. (Soviet Military Power Ser.). (Illus.). 48p. (J). (gr. 3-8). 1987. lib. bdg. 18.60 (*0-86625-332-7*); lib. bdg. 13.95 (*0-685-58296-5*) Rourke Corp.

Soviet Succession Struggles: Kremlinology & the Russian Question from Lenin to Gorbachev. Anthony D'Agostino. 274p. 1989. pap. 19.95 (*0-685-28246-5*) Routledge Chapman & Hall.

Soviet System: From Crisis to Collapse. 2nd rev. ed. Ed. by Alexander Dallin & Gail W. Lapidus. LC 94-37941. (C). 1994. pap. text ed. 29.95 (*0-8133-1876-9*) Westview.

Soviet System in Theory & Practice. Ed. by Harry G. Shaffer. write for info. (*0-318-61399-9*, Pergamon Pr) Elsevier.

Soviet System of Education. Erika Popovych & Brian Levin-Stankevich. 123p. (C). 1992. pap. text ed. 40.00 (*0-910054-97-5*) Am Assn Coll Registrars.

Soviet Telecommunications Systems Reliability Theory. Eugene Litvak. Ed. by Suzanne R. Possehl. (Illus.). 102p. (Orig.). 1989. pap. 75.00 (*1-55831-111-4*) Delphic Associates.

Soviet Theory of Development: India & the Third World in Marxist-Leninist Scholarship. Stephen Clarkson. LC 78-1771. 336p. reprint ed. pap. 95.80 (*0-685-16282-6*, 2026430) Bks Demand.

Soviet Theory of International Relations. Margot Light. 384p. 1988. pap. 15.95 (*0-312-01891-6*) St Martin.

Soviet Theory of International Relations. Margot Light. LC 87-34021. 1988. text ed. 45.00 (*0-312-01889-4*) St Martin.

Soviet Thin Film Technology: From Research to Production. Aleksey Lusnikov. Ed. by Erika D. Nobel. (Illus.). 130p. (Orig.). 1987. pap. text ed. 75.00 (*1-55831-002-9*) Delphic Associates.

Soviet-Third World Relations: Vol. 2: Soviet-Asian Relations. Charles B. McLane. 1974. text ed. 49.50 (*0-903424-07-X*) Col U Pr.

Soviet-Third World Relations in a Capitalist World. Ellen Brun & Jacques Hersh. LC 89-70054. 340p. 1990. text ed. 59.95 (*0-312-04070-9*) St Martin.

Soviet-Third World Relations, Vol. 3: Soviet-African Relations. Charles B. McLane. 190p. 1975. pap. text ed. 39.50 (*0-903424-08-8*) Col U Pr.

Soviet Threat in NATO's Northern Flank. Marian Leighton. 95p. 1979. pap. 17.95 (*0-87855-803-9*) Transaction Pubs.

Soviet Trade Unions & Labor Relations. Emily C. Brown. LC 66-21332. 406p. reprint ed. pap. 115.80 (*0-317-29769-4*, 2017260) Bks Demand.

Soviet Tragedy. Martin E. Malia. 1996. pap. 18.00 (*0-02-874120-X*) Free Pr.

Soviet Tragedy: A History of Socialism in Russia 1917-1991. Martin E. Malia. 500p. 1994. 24.95 (*0-02-919795-3*, Free Press) Free Pr.

Soviet Tragedy: A History of Socialism in Russia 1917-1991. Martin E. Malia. 576p. 1995. pap. 18.00 (*0-684-82313-6*) Free Pr.

Soviet Transition: From Gorbachev to Yeltsin. Ed. by Stephen White et al. LC 93-14683. 241p. 1993. text ed. 35.00 (*0-7146-4528-1*, Pub. by F Cass Pubs UK) Intl Spec Bk.

Soviet Turmoil. Jeffrey B. Symynkywicz. LC 95-35511. (Fall of Communism Ser.). (J). 1996. pap. 7.95 (*0-382-39301-5*, Dillon Silver Burdett); lib. bdg. 14.95 (*0-87518-633-5*, Dillon Silver Burdett) Silver Burdett Pr.

Soviet-Type Economic Systems: A Guide to Information Sources. Z. Edward O'Relley. LC 73-17583. (Economics Information Guide Ser.: Vol. 12). 240p. 1978. 68.00 (*0-8103-1306-5*) Gale.

Soviet U. S. Relations: The Selected Speeches & Writings of Chernenko. Ed. by Victor Pribytkov. LC 84-23789. 218p. 1984. text ed. 45.00 (*0-275-91243-4*, C1243, Praeger Pubs) Greenwood.

Soviet Ukraine. Ed. by Collet's Holdings, Ltd. Staff. 1984. 45.00 (*0-317-42832-2*) St Mut.

Soviet Union. Barbara Bardes. Date not set. pap. text ed. 5.75 (*0-314-01673-2*) West Pub.

Soviet Union. Cecilia Fannon. (World Partners Ser.). (Illus.). 64p. (YA). (gr. 7 up). 1990. lib. bdg. 17.27 (*0-86593-092-9*); lib. bdg. 12.95 (*0-685-36367-8*) Rourke Corp.

Soviet Union. 2nd ed. Ed. by Richard W. Davies. 240p. (C). 1989. pap. text ed. 18.95 (*0-04-445215-2*) Routledge Chapman & Hall.

Soviet Union. 2nd ed. Ed. by Richard W. Davies. 240p. (C). (gr. 13). 1989. text ed. 59.95 (*0-04-445205-5*) Routledge Chapman & Hall.

Soviet Union. 4th rev. ed. Vadim Medish. 432p. (C). 1990. pap. text ed. 48.00 (*0-13-818196-9*) P-H.

Soviet Union: A Biographical Dictionary. Archie Brown. 512p. 1991. 70.00 (*0-02-897071-3*) Macmillan.

Soviet Union: A New Regional Geography? Michael J. Bradshaw. 250p. 1991. pap. text ed. 39.95 (*0-470-21815-0*) Halsted Pr.

Soviet Union: A Systematic Geography. 2nd ed. Ed. by Leslie Symons. 280p. (C). 1992. pap. text ed. 54.50 (*0-389-20984-8*) B&N Imports.

Soviet Union: A Systematic Geography. 2nd ed. Leslie Symons. (Illus.). 304p. (C). 1990. pap. 29.95 (*0-415-90358-0*, A4812, Routledge NY) Routledge.

Soviet Union: Domestic Policy, the Economy & Foreign Policy, 1978-1979, Vol. 1. Wolfgang Berner et al. LC 74-22285. 200p. 1975. 39.50 (*0-8419-0188-0*) Holmes & Meier.

Soviet Union: Domestic Policy, the Economy & Foreign Policy, 1978-1979, Vol. 2. Wolfgang Berner et al. LC 74-22285. 288p. 1976. 39.50 (*0-8419-0216-X*) Holmes & Meier.

Soviet Union: Domestic Policy, the Economy & Foreign Policy, 1978-1979, Vol. 3. Wolfgang Berner et al. LC 74-22285. 308p. 1978. 39.50 (*0-8419-0316-6*) Holmes & Meier.

Soviet Union: Domestic Policy, the Economy & Foreign Policy, 1978-1979, Vol. 4. Wolfgang Berner et al. Tr. by Hannes Adomeit from GER. LC 74-22285. (Illus.). 270p. 1979. 39.50 (*0-8419-0450-2*) Holmes & Meier.

Soviet Union: Domestic Policy, the Economy & Foreign Policy, 1978-1979, Vol. 5. Wolfgang Berner. 340p. 1981. 39.50 (*0-8419-0632-7*) Holmes & Meier.

Soviet Union: Domestic Policy, the Economy & Foreign Policy, 1978-1979, Vol. 6. Wolfgang Berner. 348p. 1983. 39.50 (*0-8419-0866-4*) Holmes & Meier.

Soviet Union: Domestic Policy, the Economy & Foreign Policy, 1982-1985, Vol. 7. 250p. 1985. 39.50 (*0-8419-0992-X*) Holmes & Meier.

Soviet Union: Empire Nation & System. Aron I. Katsenelinboigen. 260p. (C). 1990. 49.95 (*0-88738-332-7*) Transaction Pubs.

Soviet Union: Party & Society. Ed. by Peter J. Potichnyj. (Illus.). 264p. 1988. text ed. 59.95 (*0-521-34460-3*) Cambridge U Pr.

Soviet Union: Politics. Hill. 1992. 49.00 (*0-86187-446-3*); pap. 19.50 (*0-86187-447-1*) St Martin.

Soviet Union: Politics, Economics & Society from Lenin to Gorbachev. 2nd ed. Hill. (Marxist Regimes Ser.). 264p. 1989. text ed. 49.00 (*0-86187-800-0*); pap. text ed. 17.50 (*0-86187-801-9*) St Martin.

Soviet Union: Security Policies & Constraints. Ed. by Jonathan Alford. LC 85-2011. (Adelphi Library). 180p. 1985. text ed. 32.50 (*0-312-74901-5*) St Martin.

Soviet Union: Socialist or Social-Imperialist? Pt. II: The Question Is Joined. Raymond Lotta & Albert Szymanski. LC 83-17746. 90p. (Orig.). 1983. pap. 4.95 (*0-89851-067-8*) RCP Pubns.

Soviet Union: The Challenge of Change. 1989. 25.00 (*1-55862-029-X*) St James Pr.

Soviet Union: The Incomplete Superpower. 2nd ed. Paul Dibb. 320p. (Orig.). 1988. pap. text ed. 12.95 (*0-252-06017-2*) U of Ill Pr.

Soviet Union: 1917-1991. 2nd ed. Martin McCauley. LC 92-25942. (Longman History of Russia Ser.). 440p. (C). 1994. pap. text ed. 33.95 (*0-582-01323-2*, 79637) Longman.

Soviet Union: 1979-1990. Richard E. Ericson. 62p. 1990. pap. 5.00 (*1-55815-103-6*) ICS Pr.

Soviet Union see International Directory of Cinematographers, Set & Costume Designers in Film

Soviet Union see Passport to Russia

***Soviet Union, a Half-Century of Communism: International Conference on World Politics, 6th, Berlin, 1967.** Ed. by Kurt London. LC 68-28874. 509p. 1968. reprint ed. pap. 145.10 (*0-608-04041-X*, 2064777) Bks Demand.

Soviet Union after Brezhnev. Ed. by Martin McCauley. LC 83-12956. (Illus.). 160p. (C). 1983. 19.95 (*0-8419-0918-0*); pap. 13.95 (*0-8419-0919-9*) Holmes & Meier.

Soviet Union & Arab Nationalism. Seyyed H. Nasr. 320p. 1987. text ed. 65.00 (*0-7103-0213-4*) Routledge Chapman & Hall.

Soviet Union & Arms Control: Negotiating Strategy & Tactics. Paul R. Bennett. LC 89-8627. 201p. 1989. text ed. 55.00 (*0-275-93168-4*, C3168, Praeger Pubs) Greenwood.

Soviet Union & Black Africa. Christopher Stevens. LC 75-38653. 276p. 1976. 37.95 (*0-8419-0251-8*) Holmes & Meier.

Soviet Union & Cuba: Interests & Influences. W. Raymond Duncan. Ed. by Alvin Z. Rubinstein. LC 84-26296. 240p. 1985. pap. 15.95 (*0-275-91662-6*, B1662, Praeger Pubs); text ed. 55.00 (*0-275-90088-6*, C0088, Praeger Pubs) Greenwood.

Soviet Union & Eastern Europe: State of the Environment, a Source Guide. 1991. lib. bdg. 79.75 (*0-8490-4811-7*) Gordon Pr.

Soviet Union & Eastern Europe in the Global Economy. Ed. by Marie Lavigne. (International Council for Soviet & East European Studies). 224p. (C). 1992. text ed. 69.95 (*0-521-41417-2*) Cambridge U Pr.

Soviet Union & Egypt, 1945-1955. Rami Ginat. LC 93-18150. 1993. 45.00 (*0-7146-3486-7*, Pub. by F Cass Pubs UK) Intl Spec Bk.

Soviet Union & Europe in the Cold War, 1943-53. Francesco Gori & Pons Silvio. LC 96-24517. 1996. text ed. 75.00 (*0-312-16343-6*) St Martin.

Soviet Union & European Security. L. C. Kumar. LC 86-73079. 1987. text ed. 25.00 (*0-89891-011-0*) Advent Bks Div.

Soviet Union & European Security. Y. Nalin & A. Nikolayev. 141p. 1975. 19.95 (*0-8464-0875-9*) Beekman Pubs.

Soviet Union & Finland, 1940-1945 see British Documents on Foreign Affairs: Series A: Russia/The Soviet Union

Soviet Union & International Cooperation in Legal Matters. George Ginsburgs. (C). 1988. lib. bdg. 105.50 (*90-247-3677-3*) Kluwer Ac.

Soviet Union & International Cooperation in Legal Matters, Part 2: Civil Law. George Ginsburgs. 393p. (C). 1991. lib. bdg. 171.00 (*0-7923-1332-1*) Kluwer Ac.

Soviet Union & Its Southern Neighbors: Iran & Afghanistan, 1917-1933. Mikhail I. Volodarsky. LC 93-22806. (Illus.). 300p. 1994. 37.50 (*0-7146-3485-9*, Pub. by F Cass Pubs UK) Intl Spec Bk.

Soviet Union & National Liberation Movements in the Third World. Galia Golin. 368p. (C). (gr. 13). 1988. text ed. 85.00 (*0-04-445111-3*) Routledge Chapman & Hall.

Soviet Union & Northeast Asia. Herbert J. Ellison. LC 88-31337. (Asian Agenda Reports: No. 13). 74p. (Orig.). (C). 1989. pap. text ed. 12.00 (*0-8191-7259-6*) U Pr of Amer.

Soviet Union & Northern Waters. Ed. by Clive Archer. 288p. 1988. lib. bdg. 52.50 (*0-415-00489-6*) Routledge.

***Soviet Union & Palestine Resistance.** Dannreuther. Date not set. text ed. 59.95 (*0-312-17223-0*) St Martin.

Soviet Union & Republics of the Former U. S. S. R. (Microform) Special Studies, 1992-1994: Supplement. LC 95-26364. (Special Studies). 1995. write for info. (*1-55655-533-4*) U Pubns Amer.

Soviet Union & Revolutionary Warfare: Principles, Practices, & Regional Comparisons. Richard H. Shultz, Jr. (Publication Ser.: No. 371). 283p. 1988. text ed. 25.95 (*0-8179-8711-8*); pap. text ed. 16.95 (*0-8179-8712-6*) Hoover Inst Pr.

Soviet Union & Social Science Theory. Jerry F. Hough. LC 77-1545. (Russian Research Center Studies: No. 77). 297p. reprint ed. pap. 84.70 (*0-7837-4155-3*, 2059003) Bks Demand.

Soviet Union & the Arab East under Khrushchev. Oles M. Smolansky. LC 73-2890. 326p. 1974. 27.50 (*0-8387-1338-6*) Bucknell U Pr.

Soviet Union & the Arabian Peninsula: Soviet Policy Towards the Persian Gulf & Arabia. Aryeh Y. Yodfat. LC 82-42717. 208p. 1983. text ed. 29.95 (*0-312-74907-4*) St Martin.

Soviet Union & the Arms Race. 2nd ed. David Holloway. LC 84-40205. 237p. reprint ed. pap. 67.60 (*0-7837-5300-4*, 2080269) Bks Demand.

Soviet Union & the Arms Race. 2nd ed. David Holloway. LC 84-40205. 214p. 1984. pap. 13.00 (*0-300-03281-1*) Yale U Pr.

Soviet Union & the Arms Race. David Holloway. LC 82-20050. 221p. reprint ed. pap. 63.00 (*0-8357-8330-8*, 2033758) Bks Demand.

Soviet Union & the Asia-Pacific Region: New Prospects. Ed. by Pushpa Thambipillai & Daniel Matuszewski. LC 88-27506. 226p. 1989. text ed. 55.00 (*0-275-93212-5*, C3212, Praeger Pubs) Greenwood.

Soviet Union & the Challenge of the Future, 4 vols., Vol. I: The Soviet System: Stasis & Change. Ed. by Alexander Shtromas & Morton A. Kaplan. LC 87-6904. 555p. 1988. 34.95 (*0-943852-29-3*) Prof World Peace.

Soviet Union & the Challenge of the Future, 4 vols., Vol. II: Economics & Society. Ed. by Alexander Shtromas & Morton A. Kaplan. LC 87-6904. 764p. 1989. 39.95 (*0-943852-33-1*) Prof World Peace.

Soviet Union & the Challenge of the Future, 4 vols., Vol. III: Idealogy, Culture & Nationality. Ed. by Alexander Shtromas & Morton A. Kaplan. LC 87-6904. 776p. 1989. 39.95 (*0-943852-35-8*) Prof World Peace.

Soviet Union & the Challenge of the Future, 4 vols., Vol. IV: Russia & the World. Ed. by Alexander Shtromas & Morton A. Kaplan. LC 87-6904. 384p. 1989. 34.95 (*0-943852-37-4*) Prof World Peace.

Soviet Union & the Czechoslovak Army, 1948-1983: Uncertain Allegiance. Condoleezza Rice. LC 84-42566. 318p. 1984. reprint ed. pap. 90.70 (*0-7837-9432-0*, 2060174) Bks Demand.

Soviet Union & the Developing Nations. Ed. by Roger E. Kanet. LC 73-15530. (Illus.). 314p. 1974. pap. 15.95 (*0-8018-1758-7*) Johns Hopkins.

Soviet Union & the Failure of Collective Security, 1934-1938. Jiri Hochman. LC 84-45149. (Cornell Studies in Security Affairs). 253p. 1984. 42.50 (*0-8014-1655-8*) Cornell U Pr.

Soviet Union & the Iran-Iraq War. Alvin Z. Rubinstein. (Pew Case Studies in International Affairs). 50p. (C). 1991. pap. text ed. 3.50 (*1-56927-352-9*) Geo U Inst Dplmcy.

Soviet Union & the Nordic Nuclear-Weapons-Free-Zone Proposal. Ingemar B. Lindahl. LC 87-13133. 200p. 1988. text ed. 55.00 (*0-312-01187-3*) St Martin.

Soviet Union & the Origins of Second World War: Russo-German Relations & the Road to War. Geoffrey Roberts. LC 94-46862. (Making of the Twentieth Century Ser.). 1995. text ed. 45.00 (*0-312-12603-4*) St Martin.

Soviet Union & the Pacific. Gerald Segal. 272p. (C). 1990. pap. text ed. 19.95 (*0-04-445814-2*) Routledge Chapman & Hall.

Soviet Union & the Politics of Nuclear Weapons in Europe, 1969-1987. Jonathan Haslam. LC 89-7273. (Cornell Studies in Security Affairs). 256p. 1990. pap. 17.95 (*0-8014-9616-0*) Cornell U Pr.

Soviet Union & the Second World War. Roberts. 1995. pap. text ed. 18.00 (*0-312-13259-X*) St Martin.

Soviet Union & the Strategy of Non-Alignment in the Third World. Roy Allison. 304p. (C). 1989. text ed. 59.95 (*0-521-35511-7*) Cambridge U Pr.

Soviet Union & the Third World: An Economic Bind. Elizabeth K. Valkenier. LC 83-6304. 208p. 1983. text ed. 49.95 (*0-275-91097-0*, C1097, Praeger Pubs) Greenwood.

Soviet Union & the Third World: The Last Three Decades. Ed. by Andrzej Korbonski & Francis Fukuyama. 352p. 1987. pap. 18.95 (*0-8014-9454-0*) Cornell U Pr.

Soviet Union & the Threat from the East, 1933-41: Moscow, Tokyo & the Prelude to the Pacific War. Jonathan Haslam. LC 91-50756. (Series in Russian & East European Studies). 200p. 1992. 49.95 (*0-8229-1167-1*) U of Pittsburgh Pr.

Soviet Union & the Vietnam War. Ilya V. Gaiduk. 320p. 1996. 28.50 (*1-56663-103-3*) I R Dee.

Soviet Union & the Yemens. Stephen Page. LC 84-512. 254p. 1985. text ed. 55.00 (*0-275-90153-X*, C0153, Praeger Pubs) Greenwood.

Soviet Union at the United Nations: An Inquiry into Soviet Motives & Objectives. Alexander Dallin. LC 75-27679. (Illus.). 244p. 1976. reprint ed. text ed. 65.00 (*0-8371-8454-1*, DASU, Greenwood Pr) Greenwood.

Soviet Union at War, 4 vols., Set. Elena Skrjabina. boxed 79.95 (*0-87855-497-1*) Transaction Pubs.

Soviet Union, Eastern Europe & the Third World. Ed. by Roger E. Kanet. 288p. 1988. text ed. 59.95 (*0-521-34459-X*) Cambridge U Pr.

Soviet Union in Arctic Waters. Willy Ostreng. (Law of the Sea Occasional Papers: No. 36). 87p. (Orig.). 1987. pap. 10.00 (*0-911189-15-7*) Law Sea Inst.

Soviet Union in Literature for Children & Young Adults: An Annotated Bibliography of English-Language Books. Compiled by Frances F. Povsic. LC 91-25095. (Bibliographies & Indexes in World Literature Ser.: No. 31). 320p. 1991. text ed. 55.00 (*0-313-25175-4*, PSU/, Greenwood Pr) Greenwood.

Soviet Union in Pictures. Ed. by Lerner Publications, Department of Geography Staff. (Visual Geography Ser.). (Illus.). 64p. (YA). (gr. 5 up). 1989. lib. bdg. 19.95 (*0-8225-1864-3*, Lerner Publctns) Lerner Group.

Soviet Union in the Horn of Africa: The Diplomacy of Intervention & Disengagement. Robert Patman. (Cambridge Russian, Soviet & Post-Soviet Studies: No. 71). (Illus.). 250p. (C). 1990. text ed. 74.95 (*0-521-36022-6*) Cambridge U Pr.

Soviet Union in the 1980s. (Proceedings of the Academy of Political Science Ser.: Vol. 35, No. 3). 1984. pap. 12.95 (*0-614-04174-0*) Acad Poli Sci.

Soviet Union in World Affairs: A Documented Analysis, 1964-1972. Wadysaw W. Kulski. LC 72-3845. 542p. reprint ed. pap. 154.50 (*0-317-52018-0*, 2027412) Bks Demand.

Soviet Union, Nineteen Eighty-Eight: Essays from the Harriman Institute Forum. Ed. by Paul Learner. 128p. (C). 1989. pap. text ed. 44.00 (*0-8448-1611-6*, Crane Russak) Taylor & Francis.

Soviet Union, Pt. II, 1859-1914 see British Documents on Foreign Affairs: Series A: Russia/The Soviet Union

Soviet Union since Stalin. Ed. by Stephen F. Cohen et al. LC 79-3092. 352p. 1980. 27.50 (*0-253-32272-3*) Ind U Pr.

Soviet Union since Stalin. Ed. by Stephen F. Cohen et al. LC 79-3092. 350p. 1980. reprint ed. pap. 99.80 (*0-608-01055-3*, 2059363) Bks Demand.

Soviet Union Socialist or Social-Imperialist: Essays Toward the Debate on the Nature of Soviet Society. Santosh K. Mehrotra et al. LC 83-559. 210p. (Orig.). 1983. pap. 6.95 (*0-89851-062-7*) RCP Pubns.

Soviet Union, the Communist Movement, & the World Prelude to the Cold War. Alan J. Levine. LC 89-16335. 189p. 1990. text ed. 45.00 (*0-275-93443-8*, C3443, Greenwood Pr) Greenwood.

Soviet Union, the West & the Nuclear Arms Race. Robbin F. Laird. LC 86-2559. 256p. (C). 1986. text ed. 40.00 (*0-8147-5024-9*) NYU Pr.

Soviet Union Through French Eyes, 1945-85. Robert Desjardins. LC 88-4544. 208p. 1988. text ed. 49.95 (*0-312-02068-6*) St Martin.

Soviet Union Through Its Laws. Ed. by Leo Hecht. LC 83-16079. 280p. 1983. text ed. 49.95 (*0-275-91001-6*, C1001, Praeger Pubs) Greenwood.

***Soviet Union to Commonwealth Transformation & Challenges.** Kalipada Deb. 315p. 1996. pap. 250.00 (*81-85880-95-6*, Pub. by Print Hse II) St Mut.

Soviet Union Today. (Illus.). 272p. 1990. vhs 24.95 (*0-87044-816-1*) Natl Geog.

Soviet Union Today: An Interpretive Guide. 2nd ed. Ed. by James Cracraft. (Illus.). 396p. 1987. pap. text ed. 14.95 (*0-226-11663-8*) U Ch Pr.

Soviet Union Two Thousand: Reform or Revolution? Walter Laqueur. 224p. 1991. pap. 10.95 (*0-312-06471-3*) St Martin.

Soviet Union under Gorbachev. LC 87-7002. 176p. 1987. text ed. 49.95 (*0-275-92701-6*, Greenwood Pr) Greenwood.

Soviet Union under Gorbachev. Ed. by Martin McCauley. LC 87-9537. 259p. 1987. text ed. 14.95 (*0-312-00903-8*) St Martin.

Soviet Union under Gorbachev: Prospects for Reform. Ed. by David A. Dyker. LC 87-15432. 240p. 1987. lib. bdg. 37.50 (*0-7099-4519-1*, Pub. by Croom Helm UK) Routledge Chapman & Hall.

Soviet Union under Gorbachev Assessing the First Year. Ed. by Arthur B. Gunlicks & John D. Treadway. LC 87-7002. 173p. 1987. pap. text ed. 14.95 (*0-275-92702-4*, B2702, Praeger Pubs) Greenwood.

Soviet Union, 1917-1967: An Annotated Bibliography of Soviet Semicentennial Publications in the Collection of the University of Miami at Coral Gables, Florida. Compiled by Jan Czarnecki. LC 74-14893. 1974. 9.95 (*0-87024-273-3*) U of Miami Pr.

Soviet Union, 1917-1967: An Annotated Bibliography of Soviet Semicentennial Publications in the Collection of the University of Miami at Coral Gables, Florida. Compiled by Jan Czarnecki. LC 74-14893. 1974. 11.95 (*0-87024-330-6*) U of Miami Pr.

Soviet Union's Hard-Currency Balance of Payments & Creditworthiness in 1985. Gregory Grossman & Ronald L. Sulberg. LC 83-12640. xiii, 90p. 1983. pap. 7.50 (*0-8330-0485-9*, R-2956-USDP) Rand Corp.

Soviet Urban & Regional Planning: A Bibliography with Abstracts. 1980. text ed. 45.00 (*0-312-74912-0*) St Martin.

An Asterisk (*) at the beginning of an entry indicates that the title is appearing in BIP for the first time.

Soviet Urban Management: With Comparisons to the United States. Carol Lewis & Stephen Sternheimer. LC 78-19748. (Praeger Special Studies). 255p. 1979. text ed. 59.95 (0-275-90381-8, C0381, Praeger Pubs) Greenwood.

Soviet View of Disarmament. P. H. Vigor. LC 85-10771. 224p. 1986. text ed. 39.95 (0-312-74916-3) St Martin.

Soviet View of the Indonesian Revolution, No. 7. Ruth T. McVey. 1969. reprint ed. pap. 2.50 (0-87763-018-6) Cornell Mod Indo.

Soviet View of U. S. Strategic Doctrine: Implications for Decisionmaking. Jonathan S. Lockwood. LC 82-14191. (Illus.). 202p. 1983. 39.95 (0-87855-467-X) Transaction Pubs.

Soviet Violations of Arms Control Agreements: A Legal Perspective. Phillip R. Trimble. (CISA Working Papers: No. 53). 36p. (Orig.). 1985. pap. 15.00 (0-86682-067-1) Ctr Intl Relations.

Soviet Volunteers: Modernization & Bureaucracy in a Public Mass Organization. William E. Odom. LC 72-6517. 376p. 1973. reprint ed. pap. 107.20 (0-7837-9406-1, 2060151) Bks Demand.

Soviet War at Sea, Vol. 1: Submarine Warfare. Ed. by James F. Gebhardt. LC 94-19237. Date not set. write for info. (1-879944-35-9) East View Pubns.

Soviet War in Afghanistan: Patterns of Russian Imperialism. Milan Hauner. 168p. (C). 1991. pap. text ed. 22.50 (0-8191-8201-X); lib. bdg. 49.50 (0-8191-8200-1) U Pr of Amer.

Soviet Warships: The Soviet Surface Fleet, 1960-1983. John Jordan. LC 83-80385. (Illus.). 128p. 1983. 39.95 (0-87021-878-6) Naval Inst Pr.

Soviet Way of Crime: Beating the System in the Soviet Union & the U. S. A. Lydia S. Rosner. LC 86-6095. 160p. 1986. text ed. 55.00 (0-89789-098-1, Bergin & Garvey) Greenwood.

Soviet Withdrawal from Afghanistan. Ed. by Amin Saikal & William Maley. 192p. (C). 1989. text ed. 54.95 (0-521-37577-0); pap. text ed. 17.95 (0-521-37588-6) Cambridge U Pr.

Soviet Withdrawal from Afghanistan: Analysis & Chronology. Tom Rogers. LC 92-24260. 256p. 1992. text ed. 59.95 (0-313-27907-1, RSE, Greenwood Pr) Greenwood.

Soviet Women Writing: Fifteen Short Stories. Intro. by I. Grekova. (Illus.). 336p. 1990. 26.95 (0-89659-882-9) Abbeville Pr.

Soviet Work Attitudes: the Issue of Participation in Management. Ed. by Murray Yanowitch. Tr. by Michael Vale. LC 79-4871. 147p. reprint ed. pap. 41.90 (0-317-41975-7, 2026128) Bks Demand.

Soviet Workers & the Collapse of Perestroika: The Soviet Labour Process & Gorbachev's Reforms, 1985-1991. Donald Filtzer. (Cambridge Russian, Soviet & Post-Soviet Studies: No. 93). 328p. (C). 1994. text ed. 69.95 (0-521-45292-9) Cambridge U Pr.

Soviet Workers of the Modern System of Soviet Production Relations, 1953-1964. Donald Filtzer. (Cambridge Russian, Soviet & Post-Soviet Studies: No. 87). (Illus.). 280p. (C). 1992. text ed. 69.95 (0-521-41899-2) Cambridge U Pr.

***Soviet World of American Communism.** Harvey Klehr et al. LC 97-18123. (Annals of Communism). 1998. write for info. (0-300-07150-7) Yale U Pr.

Soviet Writings on Earth Satellites & Space Travel. LC 78-117846. (Essay Index Reprint Ser.). 1977. 21.95 (0-8369-1719-7) Ayer.

Soviet Youth Culture. Ed. by James Riordan. LC 88-13487. (Illus.). 158p. 1989. 31.50 (0-253-35423-4) Ind U Pr.

Soviet Zion: The Quest for a Russian Jewish Homeland. Allan Kagedan. 320p. 1994. text ed. 49.95 (0-312-09095-1) St Martin.

Sovietization of Ukraine, 1917-1923: The Communist Doctrine & Practice of Self-Determination. Jurij Borys. xxii, 488p. 19.95 (0-920862-01-2); pap. 12.95 (0-920862-03-9) Ukrainian Acad.

Sovietology, Rationality, Nationality: Coming to Grips with Nationalism in the U. S. S. R. Alexander J. Motyl. 1990. text ed. 39.50 (0-231-07326-7) Col U Pr.

Sovietrek: A Journey by Bicycle across Russia. Dan Buettner. LC 94-5449. (Illus.). 104p. (YA). (gr. 5 up). 1994. 22.95 (0-8225-2950-5, Lerner Publctns) Lerner Group.

Soviets & Afghanistan. Cyriac Maprayil. 129p. 1986. 19.95 (81-85047-07-3) Asia Bk Corp.

Soviets & the Pacific Challenge. Ed. by Peter Drysdale & Martin O'Hare. LC 91-8373. 182p. (gr. 13). 1992. text ed. 63.95 (0-87332-866-3); pap. text ed. 30.95 (0-87332-867-1) M E Sharpe.

Soviets in Central Asia. William P. Coates & Zelda Coates. LC 73-88983. 288p. 1969. reprint ed. text ed. 59.75 (0-8371-2091-8, COSA, Greenwood Pr) Greenwood.

Soviets in International Organizations: Changing Policy Toward Developing Countries, 1953-1963. Alvin Z. Rubinstein. LC 64-12184. 400p. 1964. reprint ed. pap. 114.00 (0-7837-9437-1, 2060179) Bks Demand.

Soviets in the Pacific in the 1990s. Ross Babbage. 130p. 1989. 33.95 (0-08-037159-0, Pergamon Pr) Elsevier.

Soviets Procuracy & the Supervision of Administration. Gordon B. Smith. 166p. 1978. lib. bdg. 67.50 (90-286-0358-1) Kluwer Ac.

Soviets, Their Successors & the Middle East: Turning Point. Ed. by Rosemary Hollis. LC 93-17298. 1993. text ed. 59.95 (0-312-09995-9) St Martin.

Soviets Want Peace: Chernenko, Gromyko, Gorbachev, Tikhonov, Ustinov, Ponomarev. Konstantin U. Chernenko. LC 85-5219. 143p. reprint ed. pap. 40.80 (0-685-20780-3, 2030039) Bks Demand.

Sovremennost' v svjetje Slova Bozhija - Slove i Rechi Arkiepiskopa Averkija, 4 vols. Ed. by Archimandrite Anthony Yamshcikov. 2100p. 1976. 89.00 (0-317-29057-6); pap. 69.00 (0-317-29058-4) Holy Trinity.

Sow in Tears, Reap in Joy: A Study Guide to Central America: People of a Prophetic Church. Elice Higginbotham & David Kalke. 1990. pap. 5.95 (0-377-00205-4) Friendship Pr.

Sow-Litter Production-Health Records & Binder. 1995. 12.95 (0-944079-16-4) Lessiter Pubns.

Sow the Golden Seed. John I. Kolehmainen. Ed. by Franklyn D. Scott. LC 78-15192. (Scandinavians in America Ser.). (Illus.). 1979. reprint ed. lib. bdg. 19.95 (0-405-11645-4) Ayer.

***Sow the Seeds of Love.** Gertrude Hyde. (Special Keepsakes Ser.). (Illus.). 56p. 1997. 7.99 (0-88088-894-6) Peter Pauper.

Sow the Wind. Antonia Chambers. LC 93-18512. 48p. 1993. pap. 12.95 (0-7734-0025-7, Mellen Poetry Pr) E Mellen.

Sowa Family History: Six Generations of Polish-Texans. Janet D. Ebrom & Richard A. Sowa. LC 80-70502. (Illus.). 220p. 1981. 29.95 (0-9605638-0-6); pap. 15.95 (0-9605638-1-4) Sowa Bks.

Sowa's Ark: An Enchanted Bestiary. Michael Sowa. LC 96-6904. (Illus.). 72p. 1996. 19.95 (0-8118-1415-7) Chronicle Bks.

Sowbelly & Sourdough: Original Recipes from the Trail Drives & Cow Camps of the 1800s. Scott Gregory. LC 95-39895. (Illus.). 167p. 1996. pap. 12.95 (0-87004-369-2) Caxton.

Sower & His Seed: Essays on Chretien de Troyes. Ed. by Rupert T. Pickens. LC 82-84402. (French Forum Monographs: No. 44). 164p. (Orig.). 1983. pap. 12.95 (0-917058-43-7) French Forum.

***Sower & the Seed.** Elaine M. Ward. 56p. 1995. pap. 7.95 (1-877871-84-2, 3340) Ed Ministries.

Sower Went Forth. Martha S. Palmer. 1978. 7.75 (0-686-24055-3) Rod & Staff.

Sowerby's Shells. G. B. Sowerby. 1990. 14.99 (0-517-02199-4) Random Hse Value.

Sower's Book: A Workbook & Planning Guide for Homilists & Preachers, Cycle A. Jay Cormier. 260p. (Orig.). (C). 1989. pap. 19.95 (1-55612-254-3) Sheed & Ward MO.

Sowers of Myth. Intro. by Gregory G. Knight & Lanny Silverman. (Illus.). 32p. (Orig.). 1991. pap. 12.00 (0-938903-13-6) Cty of Chicago.

Sower's Seeds: One Hundred Inspiring Stories for Preaching, Teaching, & Public Speaking. Brian Cavanaugh. 112p. 1990. pap. 6.95 (0-8091-3138-2) Paulist Pr.

Sower's Seeds Aplenty: Fourth Planting. Brian Cavanaugh. 99p. 1996. pap. 6.95 (0-8091-3629-5, 3629-5) Paulist Pr.

***Sower's Seeds of Virtue: Stories of Faith, Hope & Love.** Brian Cavanaugh. LC 96-6812. (Spiritual Samplers Ser.). 96p. (Orig.). 1997. pap. 1.95 (0-8091-3722-4) Paulist Pr.

***Sower's Seeds Pack.** Brian Cavanaugh. 1996. pap. 24.95 (0-8091-3688-0) Paulist Pr.

Sowers Series, 26 Vols. (Orig.). (J). (gr. 5-8). 1994. write for info. (0-88062-162-1) Mott Media.

Soweto: Portrait of a City. Peter Magubane. (Illus.). 156p. 1992. 24.95 (1-56757-007-0) Appleton Comms.

Soweto: Portrait of a City. Stan Motzwadi. 144p. (C). 1989. 130.00 (0-685-32441-9, Pub. by New Holland Pubs UK) St Mut.

Soweto: The Fruit of Fear: A School Children's Revolt That Ignited a Nation. Peter Magubane. LC 86-71992. 125p. (C). 1987. 29.95 (0-86543-041-1); pap. 14.95 (0-86543-040-3) Africa World.

Soweto's Children: The Development of Attitudes. Beryl Geber & Stanton Newman. (European Monographs in Social Psychology: No. 20). 1980. text ed. 124.00 (0-12-278750-1) Acad Pr.

So...What Are You Doing After College? Real-Life Advice from People Who've Been There. Ed. by Sven Newman. LC 95-19934. (Illus.). 256p. 1995. pap. 12.95 (0-8050-3467-6, Owl) H Holt & Co.

Sowieso, Arbeitsbuch 1. Funk et al. 111p. 1994. 13.95 (3-468-47651-5) Langenscheidt.

Sowieso, Glossary English 1. Funk et al. 64p. 1995. 8.95 (3-468-47660-4) Langenscheidt.

Sowieso, Kursbuch 1. Funk et al. 120p. 1994. 16.50 (3-468-47650-7) Langenscheidt.

Sowieso, Lehrerhandbuch 1. Funk et al. 192p. 1994. teacher ed. 24.50 (3-468-47652-3) Langenscheidt.

Sowieso, No. 1. Funk. 29p. 1995. trans. 112.65 (3-468-47656-6) Langenscheidt.

Sowieso, No. 1A. Funk et al. 1994. audio 20.00 (3-468-47653-1) Langenscheidt.

Sowieso, No. 1B. Funk et al. 1994. audio 14.95 (3-468-47654-X) Langenscheidt.

Sowieso, Textbk. 1. Funk et al. 128p. 1995. text ed. 19.95 (3-468-96813-2) Langenscheidt.

Sowieso, Textbk. 2. Funk et al. 128p. 1996. student ed. 21.50 (3-468-96814-0) Langenscheidt.

Sowieso: Deutsch Als Fremdsprache Fur Jugendliche. Funk et al. (GER.). 1995. wbk. ed. 14.95 incl. audio (3-468-47674-4) Langenscheidt.

Sowieso: Deutsch Als Fremdsprache Fur Jugendliche, Arbeitsbuch 2. Funk et al. 111p. (GER.). 1995. 15.95 (3-468-47671-X) Langenscheidt.

Sowieso: Deutsch Als Fremdsprache Fur Jugendliche, Glossaire Francaise. Funk et al. (FRE & GER.). 1996. 7.95 (3-468-47681-7) Langenscheidt.

Sowieso: Deutsch Als Fremdsprache Fur Jugendliche, Glossary English 2. Funk et al. 1996. 8.95 (3-468-47680-9) Langenscheidt.

Sowieso: Deutsch Als Fremdsprache Fur Jugendliche, Kursbuch 1. Funk et al. 128p. (GER.). 1995. 17.50 (3-468-47670-1) Langenscheidt.

Sowieso: Deutsch Als Fremdsprache Fur Jugendliche, Lehrerhandbuch 2. Funk et al. (GER.). 1995. teacher ed. 30.95 (3-468-47672-8) Langenscheidt.

Sowieso: Deutsch Als Fremdsprache Fur Jugendliche, No. 2A. Funk et al. (GER.). 1996. audio 33.50 (3-468-47673-6) Langenscheidt.

Sowieso: Deutsch Als Fremdsprache Fur Jugendliche (U. S. /Canada Edition), No. 2. Funk et al. 128p. (GER.). 1996. wbk. ed. 12.50 (3-468-96820-5) Langenscheidt.

Sowieso Glossary French 1: Deutsch Als Fremdsprache Fur Jugendliche. Hermann Funk et al. (FRE.). (YA). 1996. 8.95 (3-468-47661-2) Langenscheidt.

Sowieso Level 1, Workbook 1: Deutsch Als Fremdsprache Fur Jegendliche. Hermann Funk et al. 128p. (GER.). (YA). 1996. wbk. ed. 12.50 (3-468-96811-6) Langenscheidt.

Sowing: An Autobiography of the Years 1880 to 1904, Vol. I. Leonard Woolf. LC 75-12870. (Illus.). 206p. 1989. pap. 8.95 (0-15-683945-8, HB319, Harvest Bks) HarBrace.

Sowing & Growing: The Parable of the Sower & the Soils. Marilyn Lashbrook. LC 93-86767. (Me Too! Bks.). (Illus.). 32p. (J). (ps). 1995. 5.95 (0-86606-450-8, 878) Treasure Pub.

Sowing & Reaping. Lilian Hance. 1981. 25.00 (0-7223-1418-3, Pub. by A H S Ltd UK) St Mut.

Sowing & Reaping. Booker T. Washington. LC 70-161275. (Black Heritage Library Collection). 1977. reprint ed. 13.95 (0-8369-8834-5) Ayer.

Sowing & the Reaping. George Stewart. LC 71-109540. 1971. pap. 2.50 (0-87004-200-9) Caxton.

Sowing Fear: The Uses of Torture & Psychological Abuse in Chile. 116p. 1988. pap. 7.00 (0-614-14415-9) Phy Human Rights.

Sowing Good Seeds: The Northwest Suffrage Campaigns of Susan B. Anthony. G. Thomas Edwards. LC 89-8824. (Illus.). 416p. 1990. 22.50 (0-87595-192-9) Oregon Hist.

***Sowing Modernity: America's First Agricultural Revolution.** Peter D. McClelland. LC 97-9030. (Illus.). 384p. 1996. 45.00 (0-8014-3326-6) Cornell U Pr.

Sowing New Seed: Directions for Evangelization Today. Frank De Siano. LC 94-10551. 176p. 1994. pap. 9.95 (0-8091-3479-9) Paulist Pr.

Sowing the Body: Psychoanalysis & Ancient Representations of Women. Page DuBois. (Women in Culture & Society Ser.). (Illus.). 244p. 1991. pap. text ed. 16.95 (0-226-16758-5) U Ch Pr.

Sowing the Dragon's Teeth: Byzantine Warfare in the Tenth Century. Eric McGeer. LC 94-29133. 405p. 1996. 40.00 (0-88402-224-2, Dumbarton Rsch Lib) Dumbarton Oaks.

***Sowing the Dragon's Teeth: Land Mines & the Global Legacy of War.** Philip C. Winslow. LC 97-2721. 160p. 1997. 21.00 (0-8070-5004-0) Beacon Pr.

Sowing the Gospel: Mark's World in Literary-Historical Perspective. Mary A. Tolbert. 352p. 1996. pap. 24.00 (0-8006-2974-4, 1-2974, Fortress Pr) Augsburg Fortress.

Sowing the Seeds of Change: Chinese Students, Japanese Teachers, 1895-1905. Paula Harrell. LC 91-39189. 350p. (C). 1992. 42.50 (0-8047-1985-3) Stanford U Pr.

Sowing the Seeds of Democracy in China: Political Reform in the Deng Xiaoping Era. Merle R. Goldman. LC 93-26965. 444p. 1994. 42.50 (0-674-83007-5) HUP.

Sowing the Seeds of Democracy in China: Political Reform in the Deng Xiaoping Era. Merle R. Goldman. 444p. 1995. pap. text ed. 15.95 (0-674-83008-3, GOLSOX) HUP.

Sowing the Seeds of Time: A History of the Jefferson Family in the Parishes of Lythe & Hinderwell in the North Riding of Yorkshire, 1631-1994. Barbara J. Christie. LC 94-76674. (Illus.). 200p. 1994. 29.95 (0-9641758-0-0); pap. 17.95 (0-9641758-1-9) Jefferson WA.

Sowing the Spring. James G. Southworth. LC 68-54372. (Essay Index Reprint Ser.). 1977. 19.95 (0-8369-0891-0) Ayer.

Sowing the Wind & Other Stories. Timothy S. Arthur. LC 77-137721. (American Fiction Reprint Ser.). 1977. reprint ed. 19.95 (0-8369-7020-9) Ayer.

Sowing Ti Leaves: Writings by Multicultural Women. Ed. by Mitsuye Yamada & Sarie S. Hylkema. 1991. write for info. (0-9630978-0-6) Multi Cult W W.

Sowing Weapons of War: A Pastoral Reflection on the Arms Trade & Landmines. National Conference of Catholic Bishops. 9p. (Orig.). 1995. pap. text ed. 1.50 (1-57455-028-4) US Catholic.

Sowing 1880-1904. Leonard Woolf. 1992. 20.25 (0-8446-6513-4) Peter Smith.

Sowkins. Denise Dee. Ed. by Cole Palme. (Illus.). 112p. (Orig.). 1993. pap. 8.00 (0-944388-02-7) TBS Pubns.

Sow's Head & Other Poems. Robert Peters. LC 68-24447. 91p. reprint ed. 26.00 (0-685-16224-9, 2027600) Bks Demand.

Sox: A Fantasy. Jib Ellis et al. 101p. 1993. pap. 14.95 (1-883353-00-9) New Shoes Prods.

Soy Boricua Porque Soy: Decimas de Salvador Tio. Salvador Tio. (Illus.). 104p. (SPA.). 1995. pap. 10.00 (1-56328-067-1) Edit Plaza Mayor.

Soy Fiber & Dietary Fiber - Bibliography & Sourcebook, A.D. 1445-1995: Detailed Information on 633 Published Documents. Compiled by William Shurtleff & Akiko Aoyagi. (Bibliographies & Sourcebooks on Soya Ser.). 315p. (Orig.). 1996. pap. 79.00 (0-933332-96-3) Soyfoods Center.

Soy Ice Cream - Bibliography & Sourcebook, 1918 to 1994: Detailed Information on 725 Published Documents (Extensively Annotated Bibliography), 230 Commercial Soy Ice Cream Products, 210 Original Interviews (Many Full Text) & Overviews, 91 Unpublished Archival Documents. Ed. by Akiko Aoyagi. (Bibliographies & Sourcebooks on Soya Ser.). 349p. (Orig.). 1994. spiral bd. 88.00 (0-933332-90-4) Soyfoods Center.

Soy Joven! Soy Importante! - That Very Special Person - Me! La Autoestima En la Adolescencia - Self-Esteem for Teens. Margaret Houk. Tr. by Edgar O. Morales from ENG. 144p. (SPA.). (YA). (gr. 8 up). 1993. pap. 7.99 (0-311-46134-4) Casa Bautista.

Soy Mujer, Soy Especial. Joyce Cope de Wyatt. 112p. (Orig.). (SPA.). 1988. pap. 8.50 (0-311-12100-4) Casa Bautista.

Soy of Cooking: Easy to Make Vegetarian, Low-Fat, Fat-Free, & Antioxidant-Rich Gourmet Recipes. Marie Oser. 1996. pap. text ed. 15.95 (1-56561-086-5) Chronimed.

***Soy Sauce Cookbook.** J. Stacey. 1996. 12.98 (0-7858-0659-8) Bk Sales Inc.

***Soy Solution: 75 Delicious & Healthful Soy Protein Recipes.** Robin Robertson. 1998. pap. 10.95 (0-452-27922-4) NAL-Dutton.

S

Soy Source. Downes. 1988. pap. 8.95 (1-85327-001-6, Pub. by Prism Pr UK) Assoc Pubs Grp.

Soy Source: The Practical Guide to Cooking with Soy Foods. John Downes. 128p. pap. 8.95 (0-89529-417-6) Avery Pub.

Soy Yogurt - Bibliography & Sourcebook, 1910 to 1994: Detailed Information on 312 Published Documents (Extensively Annotated Bibliography), 90 Commercial Soy Yogurt Products, 104 Original Interviews (Many Full Text) & Overviews, 44 Unpublished Archival Documents. Ed. by Akiko Aoyagi. (Bibliographies & Sourcebooks on Soya Ser.). 201p. (Orig.). 1994. spiral bd., pap. 59.95 (0-933332-89-0) Soyfoods Center.

Soya Bean: Its Value in Dietetics, Cultivation & Uses. F. S. Kale. 479p. 1985. pap. 175.00 (0-7855-0392-7, Pub. by Intl Bks & Periodicals II) St Mut.

Soya Bean Pests in India & Their Management. G. G. Kunda. 90p. 1991. 30.00 (1-55528-264-4, Messers Today & Tomorrow) Scholarly Pubns.

Soya in Canada - Bibliography & Sourcebook 1855 to 1993: Detailed Information on 780 Published Documents (Extensively Annotated Bibliography), 221 Commercial Soy Products, 115 Original Interviews (Many Full Text) & Overviews, 93 Unpublished & Archival Documents. Ed. by Akiko Aoyagi. (Bibliographies & Sourcebooks on Soya Ser.). 305p. (Orig.). 1993. spiral bd. 92.00 (0-933332-79-3) Soyfoods Center.

***Soyabean in Asia.** FAO Staff. (Illus.). 220p. (C). 1995. 39.00 (1-886106-51-7) Science Pubs.

Soybean. Snyder. 360p. (gr. 13). 1987. text ed. 85.95 (0-442-28216-8) Chapman & Hall.

Soybean: Genetics, Molecular Biology & Biotechnology. Ed. by Desh P. Verma & Shoemaker. (Biotechnology in Agriculture Ser.: No. 14). 280p. 1996. 95.00 (0-85198-984-5, Pub. by CAB Intntl UK) OUP.

Soybean Cookery. Virg Lemley & Jo Lemley. 1975. pap. 5.99 (0-931798-04-3) Wilderness Hse.

Soybean Diseases: A Reference Source for Seed Technologists. D. C. McGee. 1993. 28.00 (0-89054-141-8) Am Phytopathol Soc.

Soybean Diseases of the North Central Region. Ed. by T. D. Wyllie & D. H. Scott. LC 88-70266. (Illus.). 149p. 1988. 22.00 (0-89054-087-X) Am Phytopathol Soc.

Soybean Granule Recipes. Alan K. Briscoe. 24p. 1974. pap. 3.98 (0-88290-040-4) Horizon Utah.

Soybean Pests in India & Their Management. G. G. Kundu & K. P. Srivastava. 137p. 1992. text ed. 30.00 (81-7019-411-3, Pub. by Today Tomorrow II) Lubrecht & Cramer.

Soybean Rust. Ed. by K. R. Bromfield. (APS Monographs). 65p. 1984. 15.00 (0-89054-062-4) Am Phytopathol Soc.

Soybean Trading & Hedging. William Grandmill. 1988. pap. 34.95 (0-930233-26-3) Windsor.

Soybean Utilization. Harry E. Snyder & T. W. Kwon. 1987. 42.95 (0-317-58961-X) AVI.

***Soybeans: Chemistry, Technology, & Utilization.** Keshun Liu. LC 96-44547. 1997. write for info. (0-412-08121-0) Chapman & Hall.

Soybeans: Improvement, Production & Uses. 2nd ed. Ed. by J. R. Wilcox. (Illus.). 926p. 1987. 44.00 (0-89118-090-7) Am Soc Agron.

Soybeans & Their Products: Markets, Models, & Policy. James P. Houck et al. LC 72-79099. 290p. reprint ed. pap. 82.70 (0-7837-2946-4, 2057508) Bks Demand.

Soybeans & Their Uses with Recipe Ingredient Replacements. Compiled by Center for Self-Sufficiency, Research Division Staff. LC 83-90709. 50p. 1985. ring bd. 19.95 (0-910811-03-2) Ctr Self Suff.

Soybeans, Cooperatives & AG Processing, Inc. Margaret Finnerty. 176p. (C). 1992. write for info. (0-929690-14-1) Herit Pubs AZ.

Soybeans for the Tropics: Research, Production, & Utilization. Ed. by S. R. Singh et al. LC 87-16137. 250p. reprint ed. pap. 71.30 (0-7837-0197-7, 2040493) Bks Demand.

Soybeans in Family Meals. 1986. lib. bdg. 69.95 (0-8490-3792-1) Gordon Pr.

Soyem, Sanskar. Ram Challa. 12p. 1991. 1.50 (0-317-03095-7) Samisdat.

Soyfoods Cookery: Your Road to Better Health. Louise Hagler. LC 95-52962. 160p. (Orig.). 1996. pap. text ed. 9.95 (1-57067-022-6) Book Pub Co.

Soyfoods Industry & Market: Directory & Databook 1985. William Shurtleff & Akiko Aoyagi. (Soyfoods Market Studies). (Illus.). 222p. (Orig.). 1985. spiral bd. 135.00 (0-933332-20-3) Soyfoods Center.

Soyfoods Industry & Market - Bibliography & Sourcebook, 1985-1993. Ed. by Akiko Aoyagi. (Soyfoods Market Studies). 359p. (Orig.). 1994. spiral bd. 250.00 (0-933332-87-4) Soyfoods Center.

Soymilk & Soymilk Products - Bibliography & Sourcebook, 1500 to 1993: Detailed Information on 3,120 Published Documents, (Extensively Annotated Bibliography), 968 Commercial Soymilk Products, 506 Original Interviews (Many Full Text) & Overviews, 462 Unpublished Archival Documents. Compiled by William Shurtleff & Akiko Aoyagi. LC 93-45575. (Bibliographies & Sourcebooks on Soya Ser.). 1106p. (Orig.). 1994. pap. 275.00 (0-933332-85-8) Soyfoods Center.

Soymilk Industry & Market: Worldwide & Country-by-Country Analysis. 2nd ed. William Shurtleff & Akiko Aoyagi. (Soyfoods Market Studies). 220p. 1987. spiral bd. 350.00 (0-933332-27-0) Soyfoods Center.

So...You Want to Be an Innkeeper. 2nd ed. Mary E. Davies et al. LC 90-1946. 224p. 1990. pap. 12.95 (0-87701-721-2) Chronicle Bks.

So...You Want to See Jesus. Ira A. Kellman. 210p. (Orig.). 1993. pap. 7.95 (1-56043-773-1) Destiny Image.

Sozaboy. Ken Saro-Wiwa. (Longman African Writers Ser.). (C). 1994. pap. text ed. 11.95 (0-582-23699-1) Addison-Wesley.

Sozialarbeit fur und mit Alten Menschen. Ernst Von Kardorff & Hubert Oppl. (Soziokulturelle Herausforderungen-Sozialpolitische Aufgaben: Aspekte Moderner Sozialarbeit Ser.). 134p. 1989. lib. bdg. 17.00 (3-597-10682-X) K G Saur.

Soziale Beschlftigungsformen: Zur Zukunft der Arbeit. Ed. by Dietmar Radke & Hubert Oppl. (Soziokulturelle Herausforderungen-Sozialpolitische Aufgaben: Aspekte Moderner Sozialarbeit Ser.: Vol. 3). 240p. (GER.). 1991. pap. 28.00 (3-597-10684-6) K G Saur.

Soziale Institutionen. Wolfgang Balzer. (Philosophie und Wissenschaft - Transdisziplinaere Studien Ser.: No. 4). x, 306p. (Orig.). (GER.). 1993. pap. 36.95 (3-11-013850-6) De Gruyter.

***Soziale Mietwohnungsbau Vol. XIV: Mangel und Alternativen.** Kerstin Keil. (Finanzwissenschaftliche Schriften Ser.: Bd. 78). (Illus.). 275p. (GER.). 1996. pap. 54.95 (3-631-30345-9) P Lang Pubng.

Soziale Phobie: Eine Anleitung Zur Durchfuehrung Einer Exposition in Vivo. Z. Wlazlo. xii, 128p. 1995. pap. 35.00 (3-8055-5918-6) S Karger.

Soziales Europa 1993: Noch eine Illusion. Winfried Bottcher. 234p. (GER.). 1990. pap. 44.00 (3-7890-1971-2, Pub. by Nomos Verlags GW) Intl Bk Import.

Sozialismus in Theorie & Praxis: Festschrift Fuer Richard Loewenthal Zum 70. Geburtstag Am 15. April 1978. Ed. by Horn et al. (C). 1978. 126.95 (3-11-007221-1) De Gruyter.

Sozialistisches Zivilrecht. Valentin Petev. (Sammlung Goeschen Ser.: No. 2851). 246p. (C). 1975. 15.25 (3-11-004697-0) De Gruyter.

Sozialstrategien der Deutschen Arbeitsfront (Social Strategies of the German Labor Front) Yearbooks of the Institute of Labor Science, 6 vols., Set, Pt. A. Ed. by Foundation for 20th-Century Social History. 5250p. (GER.). 1987. Set. lib. bdg. 1,100.00 (3-598-31572-4) K G Saur.

Sozialverhalten von Prostituierten: Eine Emprische Untersuchung Auch zur Vergleichbarkeit der Lebenslaufe von Weiblichen Prostituierten und Mannlichen Straftatern. Hans Friedrichsmeier. Ed. by Hans Goppinger. (Beitraege zur Empirischen Kriminologie Ser.). 152p. (GER.). 1991. lib. bdg. 22.00 (3-597-10694-3) K G Saur.

Soziologie der Angestellten: Sociology of the White Collar. Fritz Croner. LC 74-25744. (European Sociology Ser.). 312p. 1975. reprint ed. 25.95 (0-405-06499-3) Ayer.

Soziologie des Krieges: Sociology of War. 2nd ed. Sebald R. Steinmetz. LC 74-25789. 720p. 1975. reprint ed. 58.95 (0-405-06541-8) Ayer.

Soziologie des Risikos. Niklas Luhmann. 252p. 1993. pap. 37.70 (3-11-012939-6) De Gruyter.

Soziologie-Lexikon. 2nd ed. Gerd Reinhold. 677p. (GER.). 1992. 85.00 (0-614-00539-6, 3486223402) Fr & Eur.

Soziologischer Almanach. Elke Ballerstedt & Wolfgang Glatzer. 616p. (GER.). (C). 1982. text ed. 34.50 (3-593-32419-9) Irvington.

Sozo, Survival Guide for a Remnant Church. Ellis H. Skolfield. 244p. (Orig.). 1995. pap. 12.95 (0-9628139-3-1) Fish Hse.

Sozo, Survival Guide for a Remnant Church. Ellis H. Skolfield. (Illus.). 72p. (Orig.). 1995. student ed., teacher ed. 30.00 (0-9628139-4-X) Fish Hse.

Sozo What It Means to Be Saved. David Pacetti. 62p. 1985. pap. 2.95 (0-88144-041-8) Christian Pub.

SO2, NO, & NO2 Oxidation Mechanisms: Atmospheric Considerations. Ed. by Jack G. Calvert & John I. Teasley. (Acid Precipitation Ser.: Vol. 3). 326p. 1984. 69.95 (0-250-40568-7) Buttrwrth-Heinemann.

Sp-Big Golden Books. (J). 4.19 (0-307-52349-7) Western Pub.

***SP-Como Mejorar la Salud Con la Reflexologia.** Mildred Carter. (SPA.). 1997. pap. text ed. 12.95 (0-13-848730-8) P-H.

SP in the West Pt. 1: The Hard Road to Promontory. Wesley Fox. (Illus.). 80p. 1994. 34.95 (0-9604122-9-8) Fox Pubns.

***Sp-la Bella y La Bestia: Beauty & the Beast.** Walt Disney. Orig. Title: Sp-la Bella y la Bestia. (J). 1996. 7.98 (1-57082-372-3) Mouse Works.

Sp-la Bella y la Bestia see Sp-la Bella y La Bestia: Beauty & the Beast

***SP-LA Enciclopedia Heinerman de Jugos Que Curan.** John Heinerman. LC 97-12276. (SPA.). 1997. pap. text ed. 12.95 (0-13-847880-5) P-H.

Spa. Edward Chodorov. 1951. pap. 5.25 (0-8222-1063-0) Dramatists Play.

spa see Inciensos, Aceites e Infusiones, Recetario Magico: Incenses, Oils & Brews, Magic Recipes

***Spa at Home.** Kalia Doner & Margaret Doner. 224p. 1997. pap. 12.00 (0-425-15769-5, Berkley Trade) Berkley Pub.

Spa Finder. (Illus.). 100p. (Orig.). 1987. pap. text ed. 4.00 (0-9619967-0-6) Spa Finders Travel.

Spa Finder. (Illus.). 132p. (Orig.). 1989. pap. text ed. 4.95 (0-9619967-1-4) Spa Finders Travel.

Spa-Finders Guide to Spa Vacations at Home & Abroad. Jeffrey Joseph. 286p. 1990. pap. text ed. 14.95 (0-471-51555-8) Wiley.

Spa Food: Menus & Recipes from the Sonoma Mission Inn. Edward J. Safdie & Judy Knipe. (Illus.). 174p. 1985. 27.50 (0-517-55654-5, C P Pubs) Crown Pub Group.

***Spa Life.** Diane Tugmeyer. 1997. pap. 21.95 (1-56352-372-8) Longstreet Pr Inc.

***Spa Life at Home.** Margaret Pierpont & Diane Tegmeyer. 1997. pap. 22.95 (0-614-27359-5) Longstreet Pr Inc.

Spa Plumbing: Be Your Own Consultant. Sharon R. Hines. (Hot Tub & Spa Workbook Ser.: No. 3). (Illus.). 36p. (Orig.). 1982. pap. 4.95 (0-941904-09-1) Hot Water Pubs.

Space. (Ultimate Sticker Ser.). (Illus.). 20p. (J). (gr. 1-6). 1993. pap. 6.95 (1-56458-402-X) DK Pub Inc.

Space. (Quizmasters Ser.). (Illus.). 96p. (J). (ps-4). 1994. write for info. (1-56458-796-7) DK Pub Inc.

Space. (Learners Ser.). 48p. (J). 3.50 (0-7214-1702-7, Ladybrd) Penguin.

Space. (What If...Ser.). (Illus.). 32p. (J). (gr. 4-6). 1995. pap. 5.95 (1-56294-947-0, Copper Beech Bks) Millbrook Pr.

***Space.** (Illus.). (J). pap. 8.99 (0-590-24424-8) Scholastic Inc.

Space. Donna Bailey. (J). (gr. 4-7). 1993. pap. 4.95 (0-8114-6628-0) Raintree Steck-V.

Space. Donna Bailey. LC 89-21762. (Facts about...Ser.). (Illus.). 48p. (J). (gr. 2-6). 1994. lib. bdg. 24.26 (0-8114-2504-5) Raintree Steck-V.

Space. Pam Beasant. LC 92-53103. (One-Thousand Facts about...Ser.). (Illus.). 48p. (Orig.). (J). (gr. 3-8). 1992. pap. 6.95 (1-85697-811-7, Kingfisher LKC) LKC.

***Space.** Sue Becklake. LC 97-12168. (Picture Reference Ser.). (J). 1997. write for info. (0-7166-9900-1); pap. write for info. (0-7166-9901-X) World Bk.

***Space.** Amanda Bennett. (Unit Study Adventures Ser.). 164p. Date not set. pap. text ed. 13.99 (1-888306-09-2, Home School Pr) GCB.

Space. Berry-Anne Billingsley. (Fact Finders Ser.). (Illus.). 48p. (Orig.). (J). (gr. 4 up). 1992. pap. 7.95 (0-563-34789-9, BBC-Parkwest) Parkwest Pubns.

Space. Moira Butterfield. LC 94-18480. (Look Inside Cross-Sections Ser.). (Illus.). 32p. (J). (gr. 1-4). 1994. pap. 5.95 (1-56458-682-0) DK Pub Inc.

Space. Mary K. Carson. 1996. pap. text ed. 12.95 (0-590-60344-2) Scholastic Inc.

Space. Robert Gardner. (Yesterday's Science, Today's Technology Ser.). (Illus.). 96p. (J). (gr. 5-8). 1994. lib. bdg. 16.98 (0-8050-2851-X) TFC Bks NY.

Space. Roy Gibson. (Science, Technology, & Society Ser.: No. 7). (Illus.). 150p. 1992. 40.00 (0-19-858343-5) OUP.

***Space.** Nicholas Harris. (Big Book of Mobiles). (Illus.). 24p. (J). (gr. 1 up). 1997. write for info. (0-7835-4887-7) Time-Life.

***Space.** Andrew Haslam et al. (Make It Work! Ser.). (Illus.). (J). pap. 7.99 (0-590-24690-9) Scholastic Inc.

***Space.** Bobbie Kalman & Niki Walker. LC 97-3640. (Crabapple Ser.). (Illus.). 32p. (J). (gr. k-7). 1997. lib. bdg. 16.95 (0-86505-638-2) Crabtree Pub Co.

***Space.** Bobbie Kalman & Niki Walker. LC 97-3640. (Crabapple Ser.). (Illus.). 32p. (J). (gr. k-7). 1997. pap. 5.95 (0-86505-738-9) Crabtree Pub Co.

Space. Larsen. pap. 10.00 (0-06-250979-9, PL) HarpC.

Space. James A. Michener. 864p. 1983. mass mkt. 6.99 (0-449-20379-4, Crest) Fawcett.

Space. James A. Michener. 1982. 17.95 (0-394-50555-7) Random.

Space. Ting Morris & Neil Morris. LC 93-24435. (Sticky Fingers Ser.). (Illus.). 32p. (J). (gr. 2-4). 1994. lib. bdg. 20.00 (0-531-14282-5) Watts.

Space. Judy Nayer. (At Your Fingertips Ser.). (Illus.). 12p. (J). (ps-3). 1993. bds. 6.95 (1-56293-338-8) McClanahan Bk.

Space. Ann Packard & Shirley Stafford. (Learning Experiences for Young Children Ser.). 58p. (J). (ps-3). 1981. write for info. (0-9607580-2-X) S Stafford.

Space. Steve Parker. LC 95-23980. (What If...Ser.). (Illus.). 32p. (J). (gr. 4-6). 1995. lib. bdg. 14.90 (1-56294-912-8, Copper Beech Bks) Millbrook Pr.

Space. Carole Scott. (Worldwise Ser.). 48p. (J). (gr. 4-6). 1994. lib. bdg. 22.70 (0-531-14335-X) Watts.

Space. Carole Scott. (Worldwise Ser.). (Illus.). 48p. (J). (gr. 4-6). 1995. pap. 7.00 (0-531-15269-3) Watts.

Space. Robert Snedden. LC 94-41166. (Science Horizons Ser.). 48p. (J). 1995. lib. bdg. 16.95 (0-7910-3029-6) Chelsea Hse.

Space. Sterling Staff. (BipQuiz Ser.). (J). (gr. 4-7). 1995. pap. 2.95 (0-8069-0935-8) Sterling.

Space. Peter Telep. 272p. 1995. mass mkt. 5.50 (0-06-105650-2) HarpC.

Space. rev. ed. (Understanding Computers Ser.). (Illus.). 128p. 1991. 19.93 (0-8094-7590-1); lib. bdg. 25.93 (0-8094-7591-X) Time-Life.

Space: A Developing Role for Europe, 18th European Space Symposium. Ed. by L. J. Carter & Peter M. Bainum. (Science & Technology Ser.: Vol. 46). (Illus.). 278p. 1984. suppl. ed. 15.00 incl. fiche (0-87703-195-9) Univelt Inc.

Space: A Developing Role for Europe, 18th European Space Symposium. Ed. by L. J. Carter & Peter M. Bainum. (Science & Technology Ser.: Vol. 56). (Illus.). 278p. 1984. pap. text ed. 35.00 (0-87703-194-0); lib. bdg. 45.00 (0-87703-193-2) Univelt Inc.

***Space: A Memoir.** Jesse L. Kercheval. LC 97-22537. 1998. 18.95 (1-56512-146-5) Algonquin Bks.

Space: A Vital Stimulus to Out National Well-Being, 31st Goddard Memorial Symposium, & World Space Programs & Fiscal Reality, 30th Goddard Memorial Symposium. Saunders B. Kramer & Gayle L. May. (Science & Technology Ser.: 83). (Illus.). 334p. 1994. lib. bdg. 70.00 (0-87703-389-7) Univelt Inc.

Space: And Other Poems. Eliot Katz. LC 90-80747. 160p. 1990. text ed. 9.95 (1-880811-01-4) North Lights.

***Space: Black Holes.** Childrens Press Staff. (New True Books Ser.). 1997. pap. 6.95 (0-516-26162-2) Childrens.

***Space: Comets & Meteor Showers.** Childrens Press Staff. (New True Books Ser.). 1997. pap. 6.95 (0-516-26166-5) Childrens.

***Space: Constellations.** Childrens Press Staff. (New True Books Ser.). 1997. pap. 6.95 (0-516-26167-3) Childrens.

Space: Countdown to the Future: A Report on Third National Space. Ed. by Steven D. Mitchell. 314p. 1987. 50.00 (0-9616962-1-4) US Space Found.

Space: Discovery & Exploration. Ed. by Martin P. Collins & Sylvia K. Kraemer. (Illus.). 320p. 1994. 75.00 (0-88363-893-2) H L Levin.

***Space: Emerging Options for National Power.** Dana J. Johnson et al. LC 97-12219. (Illus.). 84p. 1997. pap. 15.00 (0-8330-2493-0, MR-517-JS) Rand Corp.

***Space: Galaxies.** Childrens Press Staff. (New True Books Ser.). 1997. pap. 6.95 (0-516-26169-X) Childrens.

Space: Great Big Themes. Jean Warren. Ed. by Gayle Bittinger. LC 90-71741. (ABC Ser.). (Illus.). 48p. (Orig.). (J). (ps). 1991. pap. 6.95 (0-911019-39-1, WPH 1401) Warren Pub Hse.

Space: Hands on Elementary School Science. Linda Poore. 58p. 1994. teacher ed. 35.00 (1-883410-09-6) L Poore.

Space: Its Impact on Man & Society. Ed. by Lillian Levy. LC 72-13181. (Essay Index Reprint Ser.). 1977. reprint ed. 19.95 (0-8369-8164-2) Ayer.

Space: Mankind's Fourth Environment, Vol. II. Luigi G. Napolitano. 1983. pap. 75.00 (0-08-029986-5, Pergamon Pr) Elsevier.

Space: New Frontiers. Ed. by Mark Siegel et al. (Compact Reference Ser.). (Illus.). 60p. (J). (gr. 6-9). 1995. pap. text ed. 11.95 (1-57302-010-9) Info Plus TX.

Space: New Opportunities for International Ventures. Ed. by William C. Hayes, Jr. (Science & Technology Ser.: Vol. 49). 300p. 1980. pap. text ed. 25.00 (0-87703-125-8); lib. bdg. 35.00 (0-87703-124-X) Univelt Inc.

Space: Readiness Activities for Preschool & Kindergarten. Gloria Harbin & Kenn Goin. (Topics for Preschool Ser.). (Illus.). 64p. 1987. pap. text ed. 8.95 (0-943129-01-X) Chatterbox Pr.

SPACE: Specifications for Publication Agency Communications Exchange. Ed. by William C. Strub & Peter Brehm. 78p. 1991. 72.00 (0-933505-20-5) Graph Comm Assn.

***Space: Stars.** Childrens Press Staff. (True Books Ser.). 1997. pap. 6.95 (0-516-26177-0) Childrens.

Space: The High Frontier in Perspective. Daniel Dudney. LC 82-50920. (Worldwatch Papers). 1982. pap. 5.00 (0-916468-49-6) Worldwatch Inst.

Space: The Official Planetarium Book. Sue Becklake. 128p. 1994. pap. 14.95 (1-55958-583-8) Prima Pub.

***Space: The Solar System.** Childrens Press Staff. (New True Books Ser.). 1997. pap. 6.95 (0-516-26175-4) Childrens.

Space - A Call for Action: Proceedings of the 10th Annual International Space Development Conference. Ed. by Robert C. Blackledge et al. 404p. 1991. pap. 27.50 (0-912183-05-5) Univelt Inc.

Space - A New Community of Opportunity. Ed. by William G. Straight & Henry N. Bowes. LC 57-43769. (Advances in the Astronautical Sciences Ser.: Vol. 67). (Illus.). 472p. 1989. pap. text ed. 55.00 (0-87703-298-X); lib. bdg. 70.00 (0-87703-297-1) Univelt Inc.

Space - Gagarin & After. K. P. Prakasan. 1987. text ed. 25.00 (81-207-0584-X, Pub. by Sterling Pubs II) Apt Bks.

Space - The Next Renaissance: Proceedings of the 7th Annual International Space Development Conference. Ed. by Jill S. Mayer. 518p. 1991. pap. 30.00 (0-912183-06-3) Univelt Inc.

Space, a New Era: Fifth National Space Symposium Proceedings Report. Ed. by Allison P. Kinsley et al. 292p. 1989. pap. 50.00 (0-9616962-3-0) US Space Found.

Space Activities of the United Nations & International Organizations. 271p. 1986. 27.00 (92-1-100287-7, E.86.I.2) UN.

Space Activities of the United Nations & International Organizations. 318p. Date not set. 35.00 (92-1-100500-0, E.92.I.30) UN.

Space Activity Book. 1993. write for info. (0-201-52357-4) Addison-Wesley.

Space Adrift: Landmark Preservation & the Marketplace. fac. ed. John J. Costonis. LC 73-5405. (Illus.). 227p. 1974. pap. 64.70 (0-7837-7617-9, 2047369) Bks Demand.

Space Adventure. pap. 35.00 (1-56997-094-7) Knowldge Adv.

Space Affair. 1988. pap. 3.50 (0-19-421913-5) OUP.

Space Age Crystals: The Art & Science of Crystal Growing - On Earth & in Space. Heinz J. Teige. (Illus.). 64p. (Orig.). 1992. pap. text ed. 2.00 (0-9633525-0-4) Kristal Corp.

Space Age Facilities: Papers, Specialty Conference, Cocoa Beach, Fl., November 17-19, 1965. American Society of Civil Engineers, Aero-Space Transport Division Staff. LC 68-23. 398p. reprint ed. pap. 113.50 (0-317-10983-9, 2004908) Bks Demand.

Space Age Facilities Conference: Second Aero Space Transport Division Specialty Conference, Los Angeles, California, April 24-26, 1968. Space Age Facilities Conference Staff. LC 74-15643. 461p. reprint ed. pap. 131.40 (0-317-10926-X, 2007869) Bks Demand.

Space Age in Fiscal Year 2001: Proceedings of the Goddard Memorial Symposium, Washington, D.C., 1961. Ed. by Eugene B. Konecci et al. (Science & Technology Ser.: Vol. 10). 1967. 35.00 (0-87703-038-3) Univelt Inc.

Space Age Laws of Success. George S. Lewis. LC 87-6009. (Orig.). 1987. text ed. 15.95 (0-937771-14-7); pap. text ed. 10.95 (0-937771-15-5) Spencers Intl.

Space Age Marriage Techniques. George S. Lewis. LC 87-60010. (Orig.). 1987. text ed. 15.95 (0-937771-13-9); pap. text ed. 12.95 (0-937771-12-0) Spencers Intl.

Space Age Mazes. Elvira Gamiello. (Illus.). (Orig.). (J). (gr. 4-6). 1989. pap. 1.95 (0-942025-94-6) Kidsbks.

Space Age Mazes. Dave Phillips. (J). (gr. 2 up). 1988. pap. 2.95 (0-486-25659-6) Dover.

Space Age Predictions. George S. Lewis. LC 86-90555. 71p. 1986. pap. text ed. 10.95 (0-937771-02-3); lib. bdg. 10.95 (0-937771-00-7) Spencers Intl.

Space Age Science. 2nd ed. Edward F. Hills. (Illus.). 50p. 1979. pap. 1.50 (0-915923-02-5) Christian Res Pr.

Space-Age Solar System. Joseph F. Baugher. LC 87-6255. 464p. 1987. Net. pap. text ed. 43.50 (0-471-85034-9) Wiley.

Space Aliens from the Pentagon: Flying Saucers Are Man-Made Electrical Machines. 2nd expanded rev. ed. William R. Lyne. (Illus.). 264p. 1995. pap. 17.95 (0-9637467-1-5) Creatopia Prods.

Space Allowances for Building Services Distribution Systems. 1992. 120.00 (0-86022-350-7, Pub. by Build Servs Info Assn UK) St Mut.

Space Almanac. 2nd ed. Ed. by Anthony R. Curtis. 760p. 1992. 36.95 (0-88415-039-9); pap. 24.95 (0-88415-030-5) Gulf Pub.

Space Analysis for Management. Richard M. Greene, Jr. (Building Space Analysis Ser.). (Illus.). 1988. pap. 39.95 (0-934487-50-2) R M Greene.

Space Analysis for Management. Richard M. Greene, Jr. (Illus.). 136p. 1986. reprint ed. 20.00 (0-934487-04-9) R M Greene.

Space & Aircraft. Nigel Hawkes. (New Technology Ser.). (Illus.). 32p. (J). (gr. 5-8). 1994. lib. bdg. 13.98 (0-8050-3416-1) TFC Bks NY.

Space & Alien Jokes That Are Out of This World. Dianne Woo. 128p. (Orig.). 1994. mass mkt. 3.99 (0-8125-2051-3) Tor Bks.

Space & Astronomy: Forty-Nine Science Fair Projects. Robert L. Bonnet & G. Daniel Keen. 1992. pap. text ed. 10.95 (0-07-157873-0) McGraw.

Space & Astronomy: Forty-Nine Science Fair Projects. Robert L. Bonnet & G. Daniel Keen. 144p. (J). 1991. 16.95 (0-8306-3939-X); pap. 9.95 (0-8306-3938-1) McGraw-Hill Prof.

Space & Back. 95th ed. HB Staff. (J). (gr. 5). 1995. text ed., lib. bdg., pap. text ed. 13.00 (0-15-305228-7) HB Coll Pubs.

Space & Beyond. Raymond A. Montgomery. (Choose Your Own Adventure Ser.: No. 4). 128p. (J). (ps-7). 1982. pap. 3.50 (0-553-27453-8) Bantam.

Space & Beyond. large type ed. Raymond A. Montgomery. (Choose Your Own Adventure Ser.). 117p. (J). (gr. 3-7). 1987. reprint ed. 8.95 (0-942545-11-7); reprint ed. lib. bdg. 9.95 (0-942545-16-8) Grey Castle.

Space & Development: Proceedings of Vikram Sarabhi Symposium of the Twenty-Second Plenary Meeting of the Committee on Space Research, Bangalore, India, 29 May -9 June 1979. Ed. by Yash Pal. LC 79-41358. (Illus.). 100p. 1980. 25.00 (0-08-024441-6, Pergamon Pr) Elsevier.

***Space & Earth.** Nancy J. Hopper. (Orig.). 1996. pap. write for info. (1-57553-304-9) Watermrk Pr.

Space & Environment: An Annotated Bibliography, No. 954. David R. Unruh. 5.00 (0-686-20382-8, Sage Prdcls Pr) Sage.

Space & Equipment Guidelines for Student Publications. Campbell & Kennedy. 2.00 (0-318-19223-3) Quill & Scroll.

Space & National Security. Paul B. Stares. LC 87-14694. 219p. 1987. 34.95 (0-8157-8110-5); pap. 14.95 (0-8157-8109-1) Brookings.

Space & Nuclear Weaponry in the 1990s. Ed. by Carlo Schaerf et al. (Studies in Disarmament & Conflict Ser.). 204p. (C). 1992. text ed. 75.00 (0-333-56778-1) St Martin.

Space & Place: A Centennial Appreciation of His Life & Work: Four Hundred Years of Western & Chinese Cartography. Cordell D. Yee. (Illus.). 80p. (Orig.). 1996. pap. 27.50 (0-9603690-0-7) SJC Annapolis.

Space & Place: The Perspective of Experience. Yi-Fu Tuan. LC 77-72910. (Illus.). 1979. pap. text ed. 15.95 (0-8166-0884-9) U of Minn Pr.

Space & Place: Theories of Identity & Location. Ed. by Erica Carter et al. 256p. (C). 1993. pap. 21.50 (0-85315-775-8, Pub. by Lawrence & Wishart UK) NYU Pr.

Space & Planets. Time-Life Books Editors. (Understanding Science & Nature Ser.). 176p. (J). 1991. 17.95 (0-8094-9650-X); lib. bdg. write for info. (0-8094-9651-8) Time-Life.

S

An Asterisk (*) at the beginning of an entry indicates that the title is appearing in BIP for the first time.

Space & Revolution: Projects for Monuments, Squares, & Public Buildings in France, 1789-1799. James A. Leith. (Illus.). 1991. 70.00 (*0-7735-0757-4*, Pub. by McGill CN) U of Toronto Pr.

Space & Safety Rescue 1988-1989. Ed. by Gloria W. Heath. LC 57-43769. (Science & Technology Ser.: Vol. 77). (Illus.). 500p. 1990. pap. text ed. 55.00 (*0-87703-328-5*); lib. bdg. 70.00 (*0-87703-327-7*) Univelt Inc.

Space & Social Theory: Interpreting Modernity & Postmodernity. Georges Benko & Ulf Strohmayer. (Institute of British Geographers Special Publications Ser.). (Illus.). 384p. (Orig.). (C). 1997. text ed. 69.95 (*0-631-19466-5*) Blackwell Pubs.

Space & Social Theory: Interpreting Modernity & Postmodernity. Georges Benko & Ulf Strohmayer. LC 96-25628. (Special Publications Ser. (Institute Of British Geographers) ;). (Illus.). 384p. (Orig.). (C). 1997. pap. text ed. 24.95 (*0-631-19467-3*) Blackwell Pubs.

Space & Society: Challenges & Choices. Ed. by Paul Anaejionu et al. (Science & Technology Ser.: Vol. 59). (Illus.). 442p. (Orig.). 1984. pap. text ed. 35.00 (*0-87703-205-X*); lib. bdg. 55.00 (*0-87703-204-1*) Univelt Inc.

Space & Storage. (Home Repair & Improvement Ser.). (Illus.). 136p. 1976. 14.60 (*0-8094-2350-2*); lib. bdg. 20.60 (*0-8094-2351-0*) Time-Life.

***Space & the American Imagination.** Howard E. McCurdy. (Smithsonian History of Aviation Ser.). (Illus.). 416p. 1997. 29.95 (*1-56098-764-2*) Smithsonian.

Space & the Doctrine of Maya. G. De Purucker. (Esoteric Teachings Ser.: Vol. III). 118p. 1987. pap. 9.95 (*0-913004-54-5*) Point Loma Pub.

Space & the Eighteenth-Century English Novel. Simon Varey. (Studies in Eighteenth-Century English Literature & Thought: No. 7). (Illus.). 250p. (C). 1990. text ed. 59.95 (*0-521-37483-9*) Cambridge U Pr.

Space & the Hydrogen Age. 1991. write for info. (*1-879605-05-8*) U Sci & Philos.

Space & Time. Keshavamurti. 100p. (C). 1991. text ed. 15.95 (*81-207-1383-4*, Pub. by Sterling Pubs II) Apt Bks.

Space & Time in Homer. rev. ed. Geoffrey C. Horrocks. Ed. by W. R. Connor. LC 80-2655. (Monographs in Classical Studies). 1981. lib. bdg. 38.95 (*0-405-14042-8*) Ayer.

Space & Time In Landscape Architectural History. William Mann. 290p. 1981. 15.00 (*0-318-17832-X*, Landscape Architecture) Am Landscape Arch.

Space & Time in Special Relativity. N. David Mermin. (Illus.). 240p. (C). 1989. reprint ed. pap. text ed. 19.95 (*0-88133-420-0*) Waveland Pr.

Space & Time, Matter & Mind. W. Schommers. (Foundations of Natural Science & Technology Ser.). 160p. 1994. text ed. 32.00 (*981-02-1851-6*) World Scientific Pub.

Space & Time Scale Variability & Interdependencies in Hydrological Processes. Ed. by Reinder A. Feddes. (International Hydrology Ser.). (Illus.). 420p. (C). 1995. text ed. 85.00 (*0-521-49508-3*) Cambridge U Pr.

Space & Transatmospheric Propulsion Technology. Ed. by Charles L. Merkle. (JTEC Panel Reports). xviii, 211p. 1990. pap. write for info. (*1-883712-22-X*, JTEC) Intl Tech Res.

***Space & Transport in the World-System.** Ed. by Paul S. Ciccantell & Stephen G. Bunker. LC 97-16715. (Contributions in Economics & Economic History: Vol. 191). 1998. text ed. write for info. (*0-313-30502-1*, Greenwood Pr) Greenwood.

Space & Weather & Seasons Pack. Sterling Staff. (BipQuiz Ser.). (J). (gr. 4-7). 1995. pap. 10.95 (*0-8069-0940-4*) Sterling.

Space & Weight Allowances for Building Services Plant - Inception Stage Design. M. Hejab. 1992. 175.00 (*0-86022-345-0*, Pub. by Build Servs Info Assn UK) St Mut.

Space Apple Story: The Children's Tribute to the Seven Challenger Astronauts. Arthur E. Coords. (Illus.). 32p. (J). (gr. 2-6). 1992. lib. bdg. 7.70 (*0-9631106-0-8*) A E Coords.
Just before the first space teacher, Christa McAuliffe, climbed aboard Space Shuttle Challenger, a NASA technician handed her a bright red apple. That apple never made it into space. Children who witnessed the tragic explosion of the Challenger on that cold morning of January 28, 1986, which killed everyone on board, expressed their loss by making a special, wooden memorial apple. Those children convinced NASA to fly their "SPACE APPLE" on the next shuttle flight, STS-26, Space Shuttle Discovery. Photographs & words tell this true story. A GREAT children's book! Available through Baker & Taylor wholesalers. ***Publisher Provided Annotation.***

Space Applications of the Crossroads. Ed. by John H. McElroy & Larry E. Heacock. (Science & Technology Ser.: Vol. 55). (Illus.). 308p. 1983. 35.00 (*0-87703-187-8*); lib. bdg. 45.00 (*0-87703-186-X*) Univelt Inc.

Space Architecture: Lunar Base Scenarios. Anthony J. Schnarsky et al. (Publications in Architecture & Urban Planning: No. R88-1). (Illus.). vi, 80p. 1988. 10.00 (*0-938744-59-3*) U of Wis Ctr Arch-Urban.

Space Astronomy. Ed. by J. Trumper et al. (Advances in Space Research Ser.: Vol. 13). 758p. 1993. pap. 190.25 (*0-08-042353-1*, Pergamon Pr) Elsevier.

Space Astronomy, ser. vol. 6. Gry. (Advances in Space Research Ser.). 1988. pap. 56.00 (*0-08-036637-6*, Pergamon Pr) Elsevier.

Space Atlas: A Pictorial Guide to Our Universe. H. Couper & Nigel Henbest. (Illus.). 64p. (J). (gr. 3-7). 1992. 17.00 (*0-15-200598-6*, Gulliver Bks) HarBrace.

Space Baltic. Anselm Hollo. (Doubles Ser.). 224p. 1993. pap. 14.95 (*0-938075-38-1*) Ocean View Bks.

Space Baltic. deluxe limited ed. Anselm Hollo. (Doubles Ser.). 224p. 1993. boxed 50.00 (*0-938075-13-6*) Ocean View Bks.

***Space Bar Official Strategy Guide.** BradyGames Staff. 1996. pap. text ed. 19.99 (*1-56686-647-2*) Brady Pub.

Space-Based Radar Handbook. Leopold J. Cantafio. (Radar Library). 686p. 1989. text ed. 65.00 (*0-89006-281-1*) Artech Hse.

***Space Before A.** Barbara Drake. 26p. 1996. 5.00 (*0-614-30121-1*) Skydog OR.

Space Between: Literary Epiphany in the Work of Annie Dillard. Sandra H. Johnson. LC 91-11437. 224p. 1992. 28.00 (*0-87338-446-6*) Kent St U Pr.

Space Between: Poets from Notre Dame, 1950-1990. Ed. by James H. Walton. LC 91-50578. 1991. text ed. 23.00 (*0-268-01743-3*) U of Notre Dame Pr.

Space Between Her Bed & Clock. Edward Foster. Ed. by Edward Mycue. (Took Modern Poetry in English Ser.: No. 37). 60p. (Orig.). 1993. pap. 6.00 (*1-879457-42-3*) Norton Coker Pr.

Space Between: or All about Anna. Hartwig Kopp. 220p. 1990. pap. 35.00 (*0-9515685-1-5*, Pub. by Montag Pubns UK) St Mut.

Space Between the Notes. Richard A. Wing. 72p. (Orig.). 1994. pap. text ed. 9.95 (*0-940882-20-5*) HB Pubns.

Space Between the Notes: Rock & the Counter-Culture. Sheila Whiteley. (Illus.). 176p. (C). 1992. pap. 16.95 (*0-415-06816-9*, A6716) Routledge.

Space Between the Stars. Anna Kirby. (Lewiston Poetry Ser.: Vol. 4). 56p. 1987. lib. bdg. 24.95 (*0-88946-044-2*) E Mellen.

Space Between Us: Exploring the Dimensions of Human Relationships. Ruthellen Josselson. LC 91-39213. (Social & Behavioral Sciences Ser.). 316p. 31.95 (*1-55542-410-4*) Jossey-Bass.

Space Between Us: Exploring the Dimensions of Human Relationships. Ruthellen Josselson. 312p. 1995. pap. 19.50 (*0-7619-0126-4*) Sage.

***Space Between Words: The Origins of Silent Reading.** Paul H. Saenger. LC 96-35088. (Figurae Ser.). 1997. write for info. (*0-8047-2653-1*) Stanford U Pr.

Space Bingo. Tony Abbott. (Time Surfers Ser.: No. 1). 80p. (J). 1996. mass mkt. 3.50 (*0-553-48303-X*) Bantam.

Space Biospheres. John Allen & Mark Nelson. LC 86-33226. 96p. (C). 1987. reprint ed. lib. bdg. 12.95 (*0-89464-011-9*) Krieger.

Space Boat. (Series 9011-3: No. 3). (Illus.). (J). (ps-2). 1990. Series 9011-3, No. 3. student ed. 2.95 (*0-7214-3222-0*, Ladybrd) Penguin.

Space Boat. (Read with Me Key Words to Reading Ser.: No. 9010-3). (Illus.). (J). (ps-2). 1990. 3.50 (*0-7214-1316-1*, Ladybrd); teacher ed. 3.95 (*0-317-04027-8*, Ladybrd) Penguin.

Space-Born. Manly P. Hall. pap. 6.95 (*0-89314-399-5*) Philos Res.

Space Brat. Bruce Coville. Ed. by Patricia MacDonald. (Illus.). 80p. (Orig.). (J). (gr. 2-4). 1992. mass mkt. 3.99 (*0-671-74567-0*, Minstrel Bks) PB.

Space Brat. Bruce Coville. Ed. by Patricia MacDonald. (Illus.). (Orig.). (J). (gr. 2-4). 1993. 12.00 (*0-671-87059-9*, Minstrel Bks) PB.

Space Brat 3: The Wrath of Squat. Bruce Coville. LC 93-50602. (Illus.). (J). 1994. pap. 3.50 (*0-671-86844-6*, Minstrel Bks) PB.

Space Brat Two: Blork's Evil Twin. Bruce Coville. (Illus.). 80p. (Orig.). (J). (gr. 2-4). 1993. 12.00 (*0-671-87038-6*, Minstrel Bks); pap. 3.50 (*0-671-77713-0*, Minstrel Bks) PB.

Space Business Indicators. (Illus.). 54p. (Orig.). (C). 1993. pap. text ed. 20.00 (*1-56806-366-0*) DIANE Pub.

Space Business Opportunities. Ed. by Wayne J. Esser & Don K. Tomajan. LC 57-43769. (Advances in the Astronautical Sciences Ser.: Vol. 80). (Illus.). 380p. 1992. pap. text ed. 70.00 (*0-87703-361-7*); lib. bdg. 90.00 (*0-87703-360-9*) Univelt Inc.

Space Business Opportunities, Vol. 66. Ed. by Robert H. Jacobs. LC 57-43769. (Advances in the Astronautical Sciences Ser.). 1992. fiche 60.00 (*0-87703-362-5*) Univelt Inc.

Space Cadet. Robert A. Heinlein. 201p. 1987. mass mkt. 5.99 (*0-345-35311-0*, Del Rey) Ballantine.

Space Cadet & the Marionette. Hoagy Carmichael. Ed. by Helen M. Sterns. (Singing Stories: Vol. 1). (Illus.). 36p. (J). 1986. audio 19.95 (*0-685-73739-X*, 1477-A, Cricketfld Pr) Picton Pr.

Space Cadet & the Marionette. Helen M. Stearns. (Singing Stories: Vol. 1). (Illus.). 36p. (J). 1986. 8.95 (*0-9614281-2-0*, 1474, Cricketfld Pr) Picton Pr.

***Space Cadets' Treasury of Football Nostalgia 2097.** Derek Hammond & Jez Prins. (Illus.). 120p. 1997. 22.95 (*1-85158-854-X*, Pub. by Mnstream UK) Trafalgar.

***Space Camp.** Ted Pedersen. (J). (gr. 3-6). 1997. mass mkt. 3.99 (*0-671-00730-0*, Archway) PB.

Space Camp: The Great Adventure for NASA Hopefuls. Anne Baird. LC 91-21587. (Illus.). 48p. (J). (gr. 3 up). 1995. pap. 6.95 (*0-688-14423-3*) Morrow.

Space Camp: The Great Adventures for NASA Hopefuls. Anne Baird. LC 91-21587. (Illus.). 48p. (J). (gr. 3 up). 1992. 14.00 (*0-688-10227-1*, Morrow Junior); lib. bdg. 13.93 (*0-688-10228-X*, Morrow Junior) Morrow.

Space Careers. Charles Sheffield & Carol Rosin. LC 84-60203. 267p. 1984. pap. 7.95 (*0-688-03256-7*, Quill) Morrow.

Space Case. Edward Marshall. LC 80-13369. (Illus.). 32p. (J). (ps-3). 1980. pap. 14.99 (*0-8037-8005-2*); lib. bdg. 12.89 (*0-8037-8007-9*) Dial Bks Young.

Space Case. Edward Marshall. (Pied Piper Bks.). (Illus.). 40p. (J). (gr. k-3). 1982. pap. 4.99 (*0-8037-8431-7*) Dial Bks Young.

Space Case. James Marshall. (J). 1992. pap. 4.99 (*0-14-054704-5*, Puff Pied Piper) Puffin Bks.

***Space Cases 2.** Pocket Books, Staff. (J). 1997. mass mkt. 3.99 (*0-671-00809-9*) PB.

Space Cat. Ruthven Todd. 1992. 22.50 (*0-8446-6561-4*) Peter Smith.

Space Centers. Edward Hymoff. (American Traveler Ser.). 1992. 7.98 (*0-8317-0507-8*) Smithmark.

Space Challenge '88: Fourth National Space Symposium Proceedings Report. Ed. by Allison P. Kinsley et al. 346p. 1988. pap. 50.00 (*0-9616962-2-2*) US Space Found.

***Space Challenger.** HarBrace Staff. 1995. pap. 11.00 (*0-15-305607-X*) HarBrace.

Space Challenger. Houghton Mifflin Company Staff. (Literature Experience 1993 Ser.). (J). (gr. 5). 1992. pap. 9.16 (*0-395-61820-7*) HM.

Space Challenger. 93th ed. 1993. pap. text ed. 11.00 (*0-15-300353-7*, HB Juv Bks) HarBrace.

Space Challenger: The Story of Guion Bluford. Kathleen Benson & James Haskins. LC 84-4251. (Trailblazers Ser.). (Illus.). 64p. (J). (gr. 4-7). 1984. lib. bdg. 16.13 (*0-87614-259-5*, Carolrhoda) Lerner Group.

Space Challengers. Houghton Mifflin Company Staff. (Literature Experience 1991 Ser.). (J). (gr. 5). 1990. pap. 9.16 (*0-395-55166-8*) HM.

***Space Chase on Planet Zog.** Karen L. King. LC 96-49500. (J). 1997. write for info. (*0-7636-0273-6*) Candlewick Pr.

Space Clinical Medicine: A Prospective Look at Medical Problems from Hazards of Space Operations. D. E. Busby. 276p. 1968. lib. bdg. 88.00 (*90-277-0110-5*) Kluwer Ac.

Space Colonies. Isaac Asimov. LC 95-7229. (New Library of the Universe). (J). (gr. 3 up). 1995. lib. bdg. 18.60 (*0-8368-1225-5*) Gareth Stevens Inc.

Space Colonization: Technology & the Liberal Arts. C. H. Holbrow et al. LC 86-71675. (Conference Proceeding Ser.: No. 148). 176p. 1986. 55.00 (*0-88318-347-1*) Am Inst Physics.

***Space Colony.** Peter Seymour. (J). Date not set. pap. 9.95 (*0-448-18993-3*) Putnam Pub Group.

Space Commerce. John L. McLucas. LC 90-43957. (Frontiers of Space Ser.: No. 3). (Illus.). 241p. 1991. 32.00 (*0-674-83020-2*, MCLSPA) HUP.

Space Commerce: The Second International Conference & Exhibition on the Commercial & Industrial Uses of Outer Space, Montreux, Switzerland, February 1988. K. Gossweiler. x, 483p. 1988. 250.00 (*0-685-74291-1*) Gordon & Breach.

Space Commerce 1992: Proceedings of the 4th International Conference for Space Technology, Development & Business, Montreux, Switzerland, 23-26 March 1992. Ed. by Peter Kleber. LC 92-40050. 562p. 1993. text ed. 308.00 (*2-88124-903-5*) Gordon & Breach.

Space Commerce '90. John J. Egan. 494p. 1990. text ed. 350.00 (*2-88124-757-1*) Gordon & Breach.

Space Communication & Nuclear Scintillation. Nirode C. Mohanty. 1991. text ed. 84.95 (*0-442-23696-4*) Van Nos Reinhold.

Space Cops: High Moon. Diane Duane & Peter Morwood. 256p. (Orig.). 1992. mass mkt. 3.99 (*0-380-75855-5*, AvoNova) Avon.

Space Cops: Kill Station. Diane Duane & Peter Morwood. 256p. (Orig.). 1992. mass mkt. 3.99 (*0-380-75854-7*, AvoNova) Avon.

Space Cops: Mindblast. Diane Duane & Peter Morwood. 256p. (Orig.). 1991. pap. 3.95 (*0-380-75852-0*) Avon.

Space Craft: An Educational Coloring Book. Spizzirri Publishing Co. Staff. Ed. by Linda Spizzirri. (Illus.). 32p. (J). (gr. 1-8). 1981. pap. 1.99 (*0-86545-036-6*) Spizzirri.

Space Crescent. Edwin R. Ling, Sr. 1984. 19.95 (*0-87397-264-3*, Strode Pubs) Circle Bk Service.

***Space, Culture & Power: Identity Struggles in Globalizing Cities.** Ed. by Petra Weyland & Ayse Oncu. LC 96-39525. 256p. 1997. 62.50 (*1-85649-503-5*, Pub. by Zed Bks Ltd UK); pap. 25.00 (*1-85649-504-3*, Pub. by Zed Bks Ltd UK) Humanities.

Space Curves. Ed. by F. Ghione et al. (Lecture Notes in Mathematics Ser.: Vol. 1266). vi, 272p. 1987. 43.95 (*0-387-18020-6*) Spr-Verlag.

Space Daze: The History & Mystery of Electronic Ambient Space Rock. Dave Thompson. (Illus.). 132p. (Orig.). 1994. pap. 11.99 (*0-614-13014-X*) Cleopatra.

Space Debris. Flury. (Advances in Space Research Ser.). 182p. 1995. pap. 97.75 (*0-08-042636-0*, Pergamon Pr) Elsevier.

Space Debris. Ed. by W. Flury. (Advances in Space Research Ser.: Vol. 13). 320p. 1993. pap. 190.25 (*0-08-042336-1*, Pergamon Pr) Elsevier.

Space Debris, Asteroids & Satellite Orbits: Proceedings of Workshop IV & XIII & of the COSPAR Interdisciplinary Scientific Commission P (Meeting PI) of the COSPAR Twenty-fifth Plenary Meeting Held in Graf, Austria, 25 June-7 July, 1984. Ed. by D. J. Kessler. LC 83-645550. (Illus.). 236p. 1985. pap. 54.00 (*0-08-033189-0*, Pub. by PPL UK) Elsevier.

Space Defenders Do. Maria Aschwanden. Ed. by Richard J. Aschwanden et al. 126p. (Orig.). 1987. pap. 4.95 (*0-913071-04-8*) Rama Pub Co.

Space Demons. Gillian Rubenstein. Ed. by Patricia MacDonald. (YA). (gr. 6-9). 1989. pap. 2.95 (*0-671-67912-0*, Archway) PB.

Space Developments for the Future of Mankind II: Proceedings of the Thirtieth International Astronautical Congress, Munich, FRG. September 16-23 1979. Ed. by Luigi G. Napolitano. 228p. 1980. pap. 58.00 (*0-08-026159-0*, Pergamon Pr) Elsevier.

Space Diary. Kenneth Gatland. (Fact Finders Ser.). (Illus.). 64p. 1989. 7.99 (*0-517-66778-9*) Random Hse Value.

Space Distribution of Quasars. Ed. by D. Crampton. (ASP Conference Series Proceedings: Vol. 21). 401p. 1991. 28.00 (*0-937707-40-6*) Astron Soc Pacific.

Space Dog & Roy. Natalie Standiford. 80p. (J). 1990. pap. 2.95 (*0-380-75953-5*, Camelot) Avon.

***Space Dog & Roy.** Natalie Standiford. LC 97-15560. (Illus.). (J). 1998. pap. 3.99 (*0-679-88903-5*); lib. bdg. 11.99 (*0-679-98903-X*) Random.

Space Dog & the Pet Show. Natalie Standiford. 80p. (J). 1990. pap. 2.95 (*0-380-75954-3*, Camelot) Avon.

Space Dog in Trouble. Natalie Standiford. 1991. pap. 2.95 (*0-380-75955-1*, Camelot) Avon.

Space Dog the Hero. Natalie Standiford. 80p. 1991. pap. 2.95 (*0-380-75956-X*, Camelot) Avon.

Space Dots. Tim Furniss. 1990. pap. 0.99 (*0-517-02778-X*) Random Hse Value.

Space Dreams. Elizabeth D. Leary. LC 84-80867. 168p. (Orig.). 1984. pap. 7.95 (*0-937884-08-1*, Bennington Bks) Hystry Mystry.

***Space Dust & Debris.** D. J. Kessler et al. (Advances in Space Research (RJ) Ser.: Vol. 11). 208p. 1991. 147.00 (*0-08-041842-2*, Pergamon Pr) Elsevier.

Space Dynamics & Celestial Mechanics. Ed. by K. B. Bhatnagar. 1986. lib. bdg. 188.00 (*90-277-2311-7*) Kluwer Ac.

Space, Earth & Communication. Edward W. Ploman. LC 84-12969. ix, 237p. 1984. text ed. 49.95 (*0-89930-094-4*, PSE/, Quorum Bks) Greenwood.

Space, Eighteen Eighty-Nine. Frank Chadwick. (Illus.). 216p. 1988. 30.00 (*0-943580-80-3*) Game Designers.

Space Electronics Symposium: Proceedings of the Symposium, Los Angeles, 1965. Space Electronics Symposium Staff. Ed. by C. M. Wong. (Science & Technology Ser.: Vol. 6). 1965. 30.00 (*0-87703-034-0*) Univelt Inc.

Space Encounters. Louis A. Iozzi. (Preparing for Tomorrow's World (PFTW) Ser.). (YA). 1991. teacher ed., pap. text ed. 45.00 (*0-944584-30-6*, SEMOD) Sopris.

***Space Engineering Symposium, 10th National, 1996.** Chris Graham. (National Conference Proceedings Ser.: Vol. 96/02). 151p. 1996. pap. 60.00 (*0-85825-646-0*, Pub. by Inst Engrs Aust-EA Bks AT) Accents Pubns.

Space-Enhancing Technological Leadership. Ed. by Lawrence P. Greene. LC 57-43769. (Advances in the Astronautical Sciences Ser.: Vol. 44). (Illus.). 630p. 1981. pap. text ed. 50.00 (*0-87703-148-7*); lib. bdg. 65.00 (*0-87703-147-9*) Univelt Inc.

Space-Enhancing Technological Leadership. Ed. by Robert H. Jacobs. LC 57-43769. (Advances in the Astronautical Sciences Ser.: Vol. 35). 1981. suppl. ed. 10.00 incl. fiche (*0-87703-164-9*) Univelt Inc.

Space Enterprise: Beyond NASA. David P. Gump. LC 89-31463. 220p. 1989. text ed. 29.95 (*0-275-93314-8*, C3314, Praeger Pubs) Greenwood.

Space Environment: Implications for Spacecraft Design. Alan C. Tribble. LC 94-46481. 224p. 1995. text ed. 49.50 (*0-691-03454-0*) Princeton U Pr.

Space Environmental Hazards: A Guide to Building Better Spacecraft. Thomas F. Tascione. LC 90-32076. (C). 1991. lib. bdg. write for info. (*0-89464-037-2*) Krieger.

Space Expectation , Second National Space Symposium Report, 1986. Victor Wegenhoft et al. 264p. 1986. 35.00 (*0-317-65297-4*) US Space Found.

Space Expectations: Second National Space Symposium Report. Ed. by Victor Wegenhoft et al. 264p. 1986. pap. 35.00 (*0-9616962-0-6*) US Space Found.

Space Exploitation & Utilization Symposium. Ed. by Gayle L. May et al. LC 57-43769. (Advances in the Astronautical Sciences Ser.: Vol. 60). (Illus.). 740p. 1986. pap. text ed. 55.00 (*0-87703-255-6*); lib. bdg. 70.00 (*0-87703-254-8*); suppl. ed. 10.00 incl. fiche (*0-87703-256-4*) Univelt Inc.

Space Exploration. (Illus.). 64p. (J). (gr. 6-12). 1983. pap. 2.40 (*0-8395-3354-3*, 33354) BSA.

Space Exploration. Mrinal Bali. LC 90-19204. (Contemporary World Issues Ser.). 240p. 1990. lib. bdg. 39.50 (*0-87436-578-3*) ABC-CLIO.

Space Exploration. John Davies. (Compact Reference Ser.). (Illus.). 256p. (Orig.). 1992. pap. 9.95 (*0-550-17013-8*, Chambers LKC) LKC.

Space Exploration. Michael George. (Images Ser.). (J). (gr. 5 up). 1993. lib. bdg. 16.95 (*0-88682-481-8*) Creative Ed.

Space Exploration. Anita L. McCormick. LC 93-1830. (Overview Ser.). 100p. (J). (gr. 4 up). 1994. lib. bdg. 17.96 (*1-56006-149-9*) Lucent Bks.

Space Exploration: Opposing Viewpoints. Ed. by Charles P. Cozic. LC 92-8149. (Illus.). 192p. (YA). (gr. 10 up). 1992. pap. text ed. 12.96 (*0-89908-172-X*); lib. bdg. 20.96 (*0-89908-197-5*) Greenhaven.

Space Exploration & Travel. Louis Sabin. LC 84-2698. (Illus.). 32p. (J). (gr. 3-6). 1985. pap. text ed. 3.50 (*0-8167-0259-4*) Troll Communs.

Space Exploration Mission Engineering. Gordon R. Woodcock. 1999. write for info. (*0-89464-025-9*) Krieger.

Space Exploration Science & Technologies Research. Ed. by W. J. Craft & D. M. Achgill. (AD Ser.: Vol. 31). 160p. 1993. 45.00 (*0-7918-1106-9*, G00750) ASME.

Space Explorer. Dale McCreedy. (National Science Partnership for Girl Scouts & Science Museums Ser.). (Illus.). 56p. (Orig.). 1995. pap. 8.00 (*0-9625622-5-4*) Franklin PA.

S

Space Explorers. Isaac Asimov. LC 95-7232. (New Library of the Universe). Orig. Title: Piloted Space Flights. (J). (gr. 3 up). 1995. lib. bdg. 18.60 (*0-8368-1226-3*) Gareth Stevens Inc.

Space Explorers: An Educational Coloring Book. Spizzirri Publishing Co. Staff. Ed. by Linda Spizzirri. (Illus.). 32p. (J). (gr. 1-8). 1981. pap. 1.99 (*0-86545-037-4*) Spizzirri.

***Space Eyewitness Books.** LC 97-9546. 1997. 19.00 (*0-679-88563-3*) Knopf.

***Space Eyewitness Books.** Eyewitness Books Staff. LC 97-9546. 1997. lib. bdg. 20.99 (*0-679-98563-8*) Knopf.

***Space Factfinders.** Smithmark Staff. 1997. 4.98 (*0-7651-9319-1*) Smithmark.

Space Facts. S. Reid. (Facts & Lists Ser.). (Illus.). 48p. (J). (gr. 3-7). 1987. pap. 5.95 (*0-7460-0024-3*); lib. bdg. 13.95 (*0-88110-240-7*) EDC.

Space Facts. Ed. by Carole Stott. LC 94-24740. (DK Pockets Ser.). (Illus.). 160p. (YA). (gr. 7 up). 1995. pap. 6.95 (*1-56458-892-0*) DK Pub Inc.

***Space Family Robinson: The True Story.** Edward B. Shifres. 1996. 19.95 (*1-881636-04-6*) Windsor Hse Pub Grp.

Space Fido Frontier Vol. 1. Leah Rewolinski. (Star Wreck Ser.: No. 07). 1994. mass mkt. 4.50 (*0-312-95362-3*) St Martin.

S

Space Filled with Moving. Maggie Anderson. LC 91-50759. (Poetry Ser.). 80p. 1992. 19.95 (*0-8229-3704-2*); pap. 10.95 (*0-8229-5467-2*) U of Pittsburgh Pr.

Space-Filling Curves. Hans Sagan. LC 94-246. (Universitext Ser.). (Illus.). 200p. 1994. 36.95 (*0-387-94265-3*) Spr-Verlag.

Space Flight: Index of Modern Authors & Subjects with Guide for Rapid Research. rev. ed. Vasnil S. Sokov. LC 94-31237. 157p. 1994. pap. 44.50 (*0-7883-0403-8*); text ed. 49.50 (*0-7883-0402-X*) ABBE Pubs Assn.

Space Flight: The First Thirty Years. (Illus.). 36p. (Orig.). (C). 1993. pap. text ed. 25.00 (*1-56806-289-3*) DIANE Pub.

Space Flight Mechanics Symposium. Ed. by M. L. Anthony. (Science & Technology Ser.: Vol. 11). 1966. suppl. ed. 15.00 incl. fiche (*0-87703-221-1*) Univelt Inc.

Space for Freedom. Ismail Serageldin. (Aga Khan Awards for Architecture Ser.: Vol. 3). (Illus.). 207p. 1989. 57.95 (*0-408-50049-2*) Buttrwrth-Heinemann.

Space for God: Study & Practice of Spirituality & Prayer. Donald H. Postema. LC 83-15504. 180p. 1983. pap. 15.90 (*0-933140-46-0*) CRC Pubns.

Space for God: The Study & Practice of Prayer & Spirituality. Donald H. Postema. 120p. 1983. teacher ed., pap. 7.35 (*0-933140-47-9*) CRC Pubns.

Space for Hire. William F. Nolan. 200p. 1985. reprint ed. pap. 4.95 (*0-930330-19-6*) Intl Polygonics.

Space for Science: The Development of the Scientific Community in Brazil. Simon Schwartzman. 272p. 1992. 35.00 (*0-271-00740-0*) Pa St U Pr.

***Space for Small Enterprise: Reflections on Urban Livelihood & Urban Planning in the Sudan.** Johan Post. 223p. 1996. pap. 26.50 (*90-5170-384-8*, Pub. by Thesis Pubs NE) IBD Ltd.

Space for the Continuous Present in the Residential Architecture of Bart Prince. Christopher Mead. (Illus.). 49p. (Orig.). 1989. pap. 9.95 (*0-944282-03-2*) UNM Art Mus.

Space Fun Stickers. Robbie Stillerman. (Illus.). (J). (gr. k-3). 1994. pap. 1.00 (*0-486-28111-6*) Dover.

Space Gate: The Veil Removed. Gyeorgos C. Hatonn. (The Phoenix Journals). 175p. 1993. pap. 6.00 (*1-56935-015-9*) Phoenix Source.

Space, Geography, & Politics in the Early Roman Empire. Claude Nicolet. (Illus.). 276p. 1990. text ed. 42.50 (*0-472-10096-3*) U of Mich Pr.

Space Gods Sourcebook: Torg. (Torg Ser.). 18.00 (*0-87431-324-4*, 20511) West End Games.

***Space Governance: A Blueprint for Future Activities.** George S. Robinson & Declan O'Donnell. LC 96-51977. (Wiley-Praxis Series in Space Science & Technology). 1997. write for info. (*0-471-97259-2*) Wiley.

Space Groups for Solid State Scientists. 2nd ed. Ed. by Gerald Burns & A. M. Glazer. 343p. 1990. text ed. 61.00 (*0-12-145761-3*) Acad Pr.

Space Handbook, 2 vols., Set. 1996. lib. bdg. 602.99 (*0-8490-5990-9*) Gordon Pr.

Space Handbook: A Reference Source on the Physical Laws & Principles of the Outer Space Environment & the Evolution of Space Policy & Doctrine. 1991. lib. bdg. 75.95 (*0-8490-5073-1*) Gordon Pr.

Space Handbook: A War Fighter's Guide to Space. (Illus.). 182p. (Orig.). (C). 1994. pap. text ed. 40.00 (*0-7881-1297-X*) DIANE Pub.

Space Handbook: A War Fighter's Guide to Space. 1995. lib. bdg. 256.75 (*0-8490-7416-9*) Gordon Pr.

Space Harmony. rev. ed. Cecily Dell et al. 24p. (C). 1972. reprint ed. pap. text ed. 6.95 (*0-932582-12-5*, Pub. by Dance Bks UK) Princeton Bk Co.

Space Heating Efficiency & Low Carbon Comfort, Pt. 5: Space Heating Efficiency & Low Carbon Comfort. Florentin Krause et al. (Energy Policy in the Greenhouse: Vol. 2). 140p. (Orig.). 1993. pap. 35.00 (*1-883774-08-X*) IPSEP.

Space Heating Efficiency Improvement Program Status Report, 1977-78. Space Heating Efficiency Improvement Program Staff. 160p. pap. 3.00 (*0-318-12702-4*, S60078) Am Gas Assn.

Space Imagery & News Gathering for the 1990's: So What? 121p. 1991. 15.00 (*0-944426-46-8*) ASP & RS.

Space Images. NASA, Jet Propulsion Lab Staff. LC 81-84668. (Illus.). 100p. 1982. 27.95 (*0-912810-37-8*); pap. 15.95 (*0-912810-36-X*) Lustrum Pr.

Space in Danish Sign Language: The Semantics & Morphosyntax of the Use of Space in a Visual Language. Elisabeth Engberg-Pedersen. 406p. 1993. text ed. 45.00 (*3-927731-45-5*, Pub. by Signum-Verlag GW) Gallaudet Univ Pr.

Space in Japanese Architecture. Mitsuo Inoue. Tr. by Hiroshi Watanabe from JPN. (Illus.). 214p. 1985. pap. 25.00 (*0-8348-0193-0*) Weatherhill.

Space in Medieval Painting & the Forerunners of Perspective. Miriam S. Bunim. (BCL Ser. I). (Illus.). reprint ed. 32.50 (*0-404-01229-9*) AMS Pr.

Space in Mind: East-West Psychology & Contemporary Buddhism. John Crook. 1993. pap. 17.95 (*1-85230-154-6*) Element MA.

Space in Motion. Juan Goytisolo. Tr. by Helen R. Lane from SPA. 96p. (Orig.). 1988. pap. 9.95 (*0-930829-03-4*) Lumen Inc.

Space in Persian Painting. Leo Bronstein. (Illus.). 142p. (C). 1994. 59.95 (*1-56000-197-6*) Transaction Pubs.

Space in the Nineteen Eighties, & Beyond, the Seventeenth European Space Symposium. Ed. by Peter M. Bainum. (Science & Technology Ser.: Vol. 53). (Illus.). 302p. 1981. pap. text ed. 30.00 (*0-87703-155-X*); lib. bdg. 40.00 (*0-87703-154-1*) Univelt Inc.

Space in the Twenty-First Century. Richard S. Lewis. (Illus.). 240p. 1990. 34.00 (*0-231-06304-0*) Col U Pr.

Space Industrialization, Vol. I. Ed. by Brian O'Leary. 176p. 1982. 105.00 (*0-8493-5890-6*, TL797, CRC Reprint) Franklin.

Space Industrialization, Vol. II. Ed. by Brian O'Leary. 240p. 1982. 136.00 (*0-8493-5891-4*, CRC Reprint) Franklin.

Space Industrialization Opportunities. Ed. by Camille M. Jernigan & Elizabeth Pentecost. LC 85-14477. (Illus.). 601p. 1986. 54.00 (*0-8155-1045-4*) Noyes.

Space Industry Internat. 93th ed. 1994. 522.00 incl. fiche (*0-8103-9913-X*, 071054, Pub. by Longman Grp UK) Gale.

Space Industry International. Ed. by Geoffrey K. Pardoe. 353p. 1987. 155.00 (*0-582-00314-8*, 071053-99584) Longman.

Space Inside the Night: A Collection of Poetry. Sherril Willis. 80p. (Orig.). 1994. pap. 7.50 (*1-884540-04-X*) Haleys.

Space is the Machine: A Configurational Theory of Architecture. Bill Hillier. 288p. (C). 1996. text ed. 80.00 (*0-521-56039-X*) Cambridge U Pr.

***Space Is the Place.** John F. Szwed. LC 96-40414. 320p. 1997. 26.00 (*0-679-43589-1*) Pantheon.

***Space Jam.** (Look & Find Ser.). (Illus.). 24p. (J). 1996. lib. bdg. 13.95 (*1-56674-209-9*) Forest Hse.

***Space Jam.** Leondardo Batic et al. Ed. by Katie Main. (Illus.). 48p. 1996. pap. 5.95 (*1-56389-288-X*) DC Comics.

***Space Jam.** Ed. by Jeannette DeLisa. 60p. (Orig.). (YA). 1996. pap. text ed. 16.95 (*1-57623-695-1*, PF9657) Warner Brothers.

***Space Jam.** Scholastic Staff. (J). 1996. pap. text ed. 2.95 (*0-590-94554-8*) Scholastic Inc.

***Space Jam: Easy Piano Edition.** Ed. by Jeannette DeLisa. 36p. (Orig.). (J). 1996. pap. text ed. 12.95 (*1-57623-728-1*, AF96101) Warner Brothers.

***Space Jam: Hello Reader!** Scholastic Staff. (J). 1996. pap. text ed. 3.99 (*0-590-98481-0*) Scholastic Inc.

Space Jam Digest. Gail Herman. (J). 1996. pap. 3.50 (*0-590-94555-6*) Scholastic Inc.

***Space Jam Look & Find.** (J). 1996. 6.95 (*0-7853-1873-9*) Pubns Intl Ltd.

***Space Jam Pull-Out Poster Book.** (J). 1996. 4.99 (*0-590-94557-2*) Pubns Intl Ltd.

Space Jam Storybook. Nancy E. Krulik. (J). 1996. pap. 7.99 (*0-590-94556-4*) Scholastic Inc.

***Space Jam 1-Button Board Book.** (J). 1996. bds. 12.95 (*0-7853-1966-2*) Pubns Intl Ltd.

***Space Jam 10-Button.** (J). 1996. 12.95 (*0-7853-1872-0*) Pubns Intl Ltd.

Space Jammin' The Courtship of Michael & Bugs. Ed. by Gina Misiroglu & Charles Carney. 176p. 1996. 19.95 (*1-55853-426-1*) Rutledge Hill Pr.

Space Jokes. Viki Woodworth. (Funny Side up Ser.). (Illus.). 32p. (J). (gr. 1-4). 1991. lib. bdg. 19.93 (*0-89565-730-9*) Childs World.

Space Jokes & Riddles. Nelsen. 1988. pap. 1.95 (*0-02-689071-2*) Macmillan.

Space Kid. Roberta Edwards. (Picture Readers Ser.). (Illus.). 32p. (Orig.). (J). (ps-1). 1997. pap. 3.95 (*0-448-41566-6*, G&D) Putnam Pub Group.

Space Kinematics & Lie Groups. A. Karger & J. Novak. xvi, 422p. 1985. text ed. 226.00 (*2-88124-023-2*) Gordon & Breach.

Space Law: Basic Legal Documents - Basic Works. Ed. by Karl-Heinz Bockstiegel & Marietta Benko. (C). 1990. pap. text ed. 317.00 (*0-7923-0091-2*) Kluwer Ac.

Space Law: Basic Legal Documents - First Supplement. Karl-Heinz Bockstiegel & Marietta Benko. (C). 1990. pap. text ed. 165.00 (*0-7923-0554-X*) Kluwer Ac.

Space Law: Basic Legal Documents - Installment 5. Karl-Heinz Bockstiegel. 416p. (C). 1993. lib. bdg. 205.00 (*0-7923-2060-3*) Kluwer Ac.

Space Law: Basic Legal Documents - Second Supplement. Ed. by Karl-Heinz Bockstiegel & Marietta Benko. (C). 1990. pap. text ed. 324.00 (*0-7923-0555-8*) Kluwer Ac.

Space Law: Basic Legal Documents - Third Supplement. Ed. by Karl-Heinz Bockstiegel. (C). 1991. lib. bdg. 210.00 (*0-7923-0556-6*) Kluwer Ac.

Space Law: Changes & Expectations at the Turn to Commercial Space Activities. Karl-Heinz Bockstiegel. (Forum Internationale Ser.: No. 8). 1987. 24.00 (*90-6544-256-1*) Kluwer Law Tax Pubs.

Space Law: Development & Scope. Nandasiri Jasentuliyana. LC 92-10136. 312p. 1992. text ed. 59.95 (*0-275-94036-5*, C4036, Praeger Pubs) Greenwood.

Space Law: Past, Present & Future. Carl Q. Christol. 280p. 1991. pap. 103.00 (*90-6544-475-0*) Kluwer Law Tax Pubs.

Space Law: Views of the Future. Ed. by Tanja L. Zwann. 204p. 1988. 95.00 (*90-6544-374-6*) Kluwer Law Tax Pubs.

Space Law - A Case Study for the Practitioner: Implementing a Telecommunications Satellite Business Concept. P. L. Meredith. 408p. (C). 1992. lib. bdg. 169.50 (*0-7923-1786-6*) Kluwer Ac.

Space Law Perspectives: Commentaries Based on Volumes 1-15 (1957-1972) of the Colloquia on the Law of Outer Space. Ed. by Mortimer D. Schwartz. ix, 302p. 1976. text ed. 25.00 (*0-8377-1106-1*) Rothman.

Space Law (1990) 199p. 1990. pap. text ed. 15.00 (*1-56986-171-4*) Federal Bar.

Space-Like Time: Consequences of, Alternatives to, & Arguments Regarding the Theory That Time Is Like Space. F. M. Christensen. 384p. 1993. 60.00 (*0-8020-2816-0*) U of Toronto Pr.

Space Logistics. Robert J. Dellacamera. 1999. write for info. (*0-89464-052-6*) Krieger.

Space Machines. Susan Abernathy. (Illus.). (J). (ps-3). 1991. 8.50 (*0-307-17872-2*, Golden Books) Western Pub.

Space Machines. Norman Barrett. LC 93-33237. (Visual Guides Ser.). (Illus.). 48p. (J). (gr. 5-7). 1994. lib. bdg. 22.00 (*0-531-14300-7*) Watts.

Space Mall. Susan Schade. LC 96-25564. (J). 1997. pap. 3.99 (*0-679-87919-6*) Random Bks Yng Read.

Space Mall. Susan Schade. LC 96-25564. (J). 1997. lib. bdg. 11.99 (*0-679-97919-0*) Random Bks Yng Read.

Space Manager. Jack Rudman. (Career Examination Ser.: C-1055). 1994. pap. 34.95 (*0-8373-1055-5*) Nat Learn.

Space Manufacturing 1983. Ed. by James D. Burke & April S. Whitt. (Advances in the Astronautical Sciences Ser.: Vol. 53). (Illus.). 496p. 1983. fiche 50.00 (*0-87703-188-6*) Univelt Inc.

Space Mappings with Bounded Distortion. Y. Reshtenyak. Tr. by H. H. McFaden. LC 89-72. (Translations of Mathematical Monographs: Vol. 73). 362p. 1989. 150.00 (*0-8218-4526-8*, MMONO/73) Am Math.

***Space Master Combat.** 1988. 6.00 (*1-55806-009-X*) Iron Crown Ent Inc.

Space Master Companion, No. I. Thomas Arnold. Ed. by Kevin Barrett. (Space Master Ser.). (Illus.). 96p. (Orig.). (C). 1990. pap. 13.00 (*1-55806-135-5*, 9002) Iron Crown Ent Inc.

***Space Mathematics.** American Mathematical Society Staff. Ed. by J. B. Rosser. (Lectures in Applied Mathematics: Vol. 5). 296p. 1966. reprint ed. pap. 57.00 (*0-8218-1105-3*, LAM-5) Am Math.

Space Mathematics, Pt. 1. (Lectures in Applied Mathematics: Vol. 6). 258p. 1966. reprint ed. 45.00 (*0-8218-1106-1*, LAM-6) Am Math.

Space Mathematics, Pt. 2. American Mathematical Society Staff. Ed. by J. B. Rosser. (Lectures in Applied Mathematics: Vol. 7). 315p. 1966. 49.00 (*0-8218-1107-X*, LAM-7) Am Math.

Space Mathematics see Gottsched, Johann Christoph: Ausgewaehlte Werke

***Space Mazes.** Roger Moreau. Date not set. write for info. (*0-8069-9863-6*) Sterling.

***Space Mazes.** Roger Moreau. 1997. pap. text ed. 59.50 (*0-8069-1309-6*) Sterling.

***Space Mazes-Mountain Mazes.** Roger Moreau. 1997. pap. text ed. 95.20 (*0-8069-1311-8*) Sterling.

Space Medicine. Paul Rambaut. Ed. by J. J. Head. LC 84-45837. (Carolina Biology Readers Ser.: No. 166). (Illus.). 16p. (Orig.). (YA). (gr. 10 up). 1985. pap. text ed. 2.75 (*0-89278-366-4*, 45-9766) Carolina Biological.

Space Medium: The Key to Unified Physics. Thomas G. Barnes. (Illus.). 170p. 1986. reprint ed. pap. text ed. 12.95 (*0-940384-14-0*) Creation Research.

Space Merchants. Frederik Pohl & C. M. Kornbluth. 1987. pap. 3.50 (*0-312-90655-2*) St Martin.

Space Merchants. Pohl & Cyril Kornbluth. 1993. reprint ed. lib. bdg. 18.95 (*0-89968-359-2*, Lghtyr Pr) Buccaneer Bks.

Space Microgravity. R. G. Hathaway. 200p. 1992. text ed. write for info. (*0-318-68769-0*) P-H.

Space Microgravity. R. G. Hathaway. 250p. 1993. text ed. write for info. (*0-318-69555-3*) P-H.

Space Mission Analysis & Design. Ed. by James R. Wertz & Wiley J. Larson. (C). 1991. lib. bdg. 157.50 (*0-7923-0970-7*) Kluwer Ac.

Space Mission Analysis & Design. 2nd ed. Ed. by Wiley J. Larson & James R. Wertz. LC 92-64312. (Space Technology Library). 1992. lib. bdg. 177.00 (*0-7923-1998-2*) Kluwer Ac.

Space Mission Analysis & Design. 2nd ed. Ed. by Wiley J. Larson & James R. Wertz. LC 92-64312. (Space Technology Library). (Illus.). 904p. (C). 1992. pap. text ed. 44.75 (*1-881883-01-9*) Microcosm.

***Space Mission Analysis & Design Workbook.** Ed. by Wiley J. Larson & James R. Wertz. (Space Technology Library). 202p. (C). 1993. wbk. ed., pap. text ed. 16.95 (*1-881883-02-7*) Microcosm.

Space Models. Mat Irvine. (Illus.). 336p. 1997. 45.00 (*1-883685-07-9*) Pincushion Pr.

***Space Monitoring of Global Change: Proceedings of the La Jolla Conference, October 8-10, 1992.** Paul F. Uhlir et al. 56p. (Orig.). 1992. pap. 3.50 (*0-934637-15-6*) U of CA Inst Global.

Space Movies: Classics of Science Fiction. Stephen King et al. 256p. 1995. 20.00 (*0-7278-4790-2*) Severn Hse.

Space Movies II. Peter Haining. 256p. 1996. 22.00 (*0-7278-4897-6*) Severn Hse.

Space Needle: Journey to Mars. 2nd ed. Idore. (Space Needle Adventure Bks.). (Illus.). 37p. (Orig.). (J). (ps-3). 1991. reprint ed. pap. 4.95 (*0-926060-08-2*) Anschell Pub Co.

Space Needle Journey to Mars. Idore. (Space Needle Adventure Bks.). (Illus.). 38p. (J). (gr. k-3). 1991. pap. 4.95 (*0-926060-07-4*) Anschell Pub Co.

***Space News Directory of Worldwide Space/1997.** Ed. by Diane Murphy. 200p. (Orig.). 1997. pap. 95.00 (*0-9654543-0-4*) Army Times Pubng.

Space Nuclear Power. Joseph A. Angelo, Jr. & David Buden. LC 84-16701. 304p. 1985. 69.50 (*0-89464-000-3*) Krieger.

Space Nuclear Power & Propulsion. Ed. by Mohamed S. El-Genk & Mark D. Hoover. (AIP Conference Proceedings Ser.: No. 301). 1700p. 1994. text ed. 285.00 (*1-56396-305-1*) Am Inst Physics.

Space Nuclear Power & Propulsion, 2 vols., Set. Ed. by Mohamed S. El-Genk. LC 94-73603. (AIP Conference Proceedings Ser.). 1149p. 1995. 225.00 (*1-56396-427-9*) Am Inst Physics.

Space Nuclear Power Systems. Ed. by M. S. El-Genk. (Conference Proceeding Ser.: No. 246). 352p. 1992. 95.00 (*1-56396-007-9*) Am Inst Physics.

Space Nuclear Power Systems, 11 vols., Set. Ed. by Mohamed S. El-Genk & Mark D. Hoover. 3380p. 1993. 500.00 (*0-89464-045-3*) Krieger.

Space Observations for Climate Studies: Proceedings of Symposium 4 of the COSPAR Twenty-Fifth Plenary Meeting Held in Graz Austria, 25 June-7 July 1984. Ed. by G. Ohring & H. J. Bolle. (Illus.). 404p. 1985. pap. 54.00 (*0-08-033195-5*, Pub. by PPL UK) Elsevier.

Space Observations of Aerosols & Ozone: Proceedings of the Topical Meeting of the COSPAR Interdisciplinary Scientific Commission A (Meetings A1 & A2) of the COSPAR 24th Plenary Meeting held in Ottawa, Canada, 16 May-2 June, 1982, Vol. 2/5. Ed. by Patrick M. McCormick & J. E. Lovill. (Illus.). 120p. 1983. pap. 50.00 (*0-08-030427-3*, Pergamon Pr) Elsevier.

Space Observatories. J. Pecker. 1970. lib. bdg. 73.00 (*90-277-0168-7*) Kluwer Ac.

Space Oceanography - An Intensive Course. Arthur P. Cracknell. 550p. 1992. pap. 41.00 (*981-02-0507-4*); text ed. 151.00 (*981-02-0506-6*) World Scientific Pub.

Space Odysseys of Arthur C. Clarke. George E. Slusser. LC 77-24438. (Milford Series: Popular Writers of Today: Popular Writers of Today: Vol. 8). 64p. 1977. pap. 13.00 (*0-89370-212-9*); lib. bdg. 23.00 (*0-89370-112-2*) Borgo Pr.

Space Of. David Jaffin. 1978. 20.00 (*0-686-26668-4*); pap. 8.00 (*0-686-26669-2*) Elizabeth Pr.

Space of Appearance. George Baird. (Illus.). 512p. 1995. 47.50 (*0-262-02378-4*) MIT Pr.

Space of Death: A Study of Funerary Architecture, Decoration, & Urbanism. Michel Ragon. Tr. by Alan Sheridan. LC 83-5958. (Illus.). 336p. reprint ed. pap. 95.80 (*0-8357-3129-4*, 2039391) Bks Demand.

Space of Dynamical Systems with the C POS-Topology. Sergei Y. Pilyugin. LC 94-887. (Lecture Notes in Mathematics Ser.: Vol. 1571). (Illus.). x, 188p. 1994. 34.95 (*0-387-57702-5*) Spr-Verlag.

Space of Half an Hour. Keith Waldrop. (Poetry Ser.). 80p. 1983. pap. 4.00 (*0-930901-20-7*) Burning Deck.

Space of Literature: A Translation of "L'Espace Litteraire" Maurice Blanchot. Tr. by Ann Smock. LC 82-2062. viii, 279p. 1982. pap. text ed. 12.00 (*0-8032-6092-X*, Bison Books) U of Nebr Pr.

Space of Mathematics: Philosophical, Epistemological, & Historical Explorations. Ed. by Javier Echeverria et al. LC 92-26535. (Foundations of Communication & Cognition Ser.). xvi, 422p. (C). 1992. lib. bdg. 175.40 (*3-11-013249-4*) De Gruyter.

***Space of Service to Humanity: Preserving Earth & Improving Life: Symposium Proceedings: International Symposium, 5-7 February 1996, Strasbourg, France.** G. Haskell & Michael J. Rycroft. LC 97-8160. (Space Studies). 1997. pap. text ed. 149.00 (*0-7923-4344-1*) Kluwer Ac.

Space of Time. Sandra Antelo-Suarez. 1994. pap. 17.50 (*1-879128-07-1*) Americas Soc.

***Space of Yiddish in the German & German-Jewish Discourse.** Jeffrey Grossman. Date not set. 52.95 (*1-57113-183-3*) Camden Hse.

Space on Earth. Joel Rosenblatt. 1996. 17.50 (*0-533-11676-7*) Vantage.

Space on My Hands. Fredric Brown. 1993. reprint ed. lib. bdg. 18.95 (*0-89968-332-0*, Lghtyr Pr) Buccaneer Bks.

Space on the Side of the Road: Cultural Poetics in an "Other" America. Kathleen Stewart. LC 95-24365. 264p. 1996. pap. text ed. 15.95 (*0-691-01103-6*) Princeton U Pr.

Space on the Side of the Road: Cultural Poetics in an "Other" America. Kathleen Stewart. LC 95-24365. 264p. (C). 1996. text ed. 49.50 (*0-691-01104-4*) Princeton U Pr.

Space Opera. Anne Mccaffrey. 1996. pap. 5.99 (*0-88677-714-3*) DAW Bks.

Space Optics for Astrophysics & Earth & Planetary Remote Sensing. LC 88-60868. (Technical Digest Series, 1988: Vol. 10). 159p. (Orig.). 1988. pap. 75.00 (*1-55752-049-6*) Optical Soc.

Space Optics for the Astrophysics. LC 90-66974. (Technical Digest Series, 1991: Vol. 19). 200p. (Orig.). 1991. lib. bdg. 66.00 (*1-55752-209-X*) Optical Soc.

Space Out: Jokes about Outer Space. Peter Roop et al. LC 84-5650. (Make Me Laugh! Joke Bks.). (Illus.). 32p. (J). 1984. lib. bdg. 6.95 (*0-8225-0984-9*, Lerner Publctns) Lerner Group.

Space Outside. Guy Russell. LC 75-35693. 1975. pap. 15.00 (*0-916348-07-5*) Sigga Pr.

Space Partition Within Aquatic Ecosystems: Proceedings of the Second International Congress of Limnology & Oceanography, Held in Evian, May 25-28, 1993. Ed. by Gerard Balvay & International Congress of Limnology & Oceanography Staff. LC 94-43528. (Developments in Hydrobiology Ser.: Vol. 104). 1995. lib. bdg. 313.50 (*0-7923-3293-8*) Kluwer Ac.

Space Patrol Comics. Frances Linke. (Space Patrol Ser.: No. 2). 70p. (Orig.). 1977. pap. 15.00 (*0-933276-05-2*) Nin-Ra Ent.

Space Patrol III. Frances Linke. Ed. by Ray Linke. (Space Patrol Ser.: No. 3). (Illus.). 205p. 1980. 30.00 (*0-933276-06-0*); lib. bdg. 40.00 (*0-933276-07-9*) Nin-Ra Ent.

Space Patrol Memories, by Tonga. Frances Linke, pseud. Ed. by Ted Wahle. (Space Patrol Ser.: No. 1). (Illus.). 173p. (Orig.). 1976. 35.00 (*0-933276-00-1*); pap. 30.00 (*0-933276-03-6*); lib. bdg. 40.00 (*0-933276-01-X*) Nin-Ra Ent.

Space People. Eve Bunting. (Author's Signature Collection). (Illus.). 64p. (J). (gr. 3-8). 1992. lib. bdg. 12.79 (*0-89565-765-1*) Childs World.

Space People from A to Z. Ray Spangenburg & Diane K. Moser. (Space Exploration Ser.). 136p. (YA). 1990. 22.95 (*0-8160-1851-0*) Facts on File.

***Space, People, Place.** Camm. 1981. pap. text ed. write for info. (*0-582-68214-2*, Pub. by Longman UK) Longman.

Space-Perception & the Philosophy of Science. Patrick A. Heelan. LC 82-4842. (Illus.). 300p. 1982. pap. 16.00 (*0-520-05739-2*) U CA Pr.

Space Physics. 2nd ed. Edwin F. Taylor. LC 92-722. (C). 1995. pap. text ed. write for info. (*0-7167-2327-1*) W H Freeman.

Space Physics & Space Astronomy. Michael D. Papagiannis. LC 72-179021. (Illus.). 294p. (C). 1972. text ed. 180.00 (*0-677-04000-8*) Gordon & Breach.

Space Physics Paradox: Why Has Increased Funding Been Accompanied by Decreased Effectiveness in the Conduct of Space Physics Research? National Research Council, Solar-Terrestrial Research Committee. 112p. (Orig.). (C). 1994. pap. text ed. 29.00 (*0-309-05177-0*) Natl Acad Pr.

Space Physiology & Medicine. 1994. lib. bdg. 260.95 (*0-8490-6402-3*) Gordon Pr.

Space Physiology & Medicine. 3rd ed. Arnauld E. Nicogossian et al. (Illus.). 400p. 1993. text ed. 95.00 (*0-8121-1595-3*) Williams & Wilkins.

Space Pirates. Laurence Swinburne. 64p. 1984. text ed. 2.99 (*0-07-025752-3*) McGraw.

Space Place. Barry Asmus. Ed. by Helen Graves. LC 87-42903. 140p. 1987. 9.95 (*1-55523-115-2*) Winston-Derek.

Space, Place, & Environmental Ethics: Philosophy & Geography I. Ed. by Andrew Light & Jonathan M. Smith. LC 96-23667. (Philosophy & Geography Ser.: No. 98). 256p. 1996. 57.50 (*0-8476-8220-X*); pap. 22.95 (*0-8476-8221-8*) Rowman.

Space, Place, & Gender. Doreen Massey. 290p. 1994. pap. 19.95 (*0-8166-2617-0*); text ed. 44.95 (*0-8166-2616-2*) U of Minn Pr.

Space Planning Basics. Mark Karlen. LC 92-14425. 1993. pap. 29.95 (*0-442-00970-4*) Van Nos Reinhold.

Space Planning for the Art Library. Ed. by Beryl K. Smith. (Occasional Papers: No. 9). (Illus.). v, 32p. (Orig.). 1991. pap. 15.00 (*0-942740-09-2*) Art Libs Soc.

Space Planning in the Special Library. Caryl Masyr & Roberta Freifeld. 1991. 16.00 (*0-87111-356-2*) SLA.

Space Plasma Physics. Ed. by P. A. Bernhardt et al. 350p. 1993. pap. 197.75 (*0-08-042342-6*, Pergamon Pr) Elsevier.

Space Plasma Simulations. Ed. by Maha Ashour-Abdalla & Daryl A. Dutton. 1985. reprint ed. lib. bdg. 197.00 (*90-277-2108-4*) Kluwer Ac.

Space Plasma, Vol. 1: Theory & Main Properties. Ya. L. Al'pert. (Illus.). 322p. (C). 1990. pap. text ed. 42.95 (*0-521-38971-2*) Cambridge U Pr.

Space Plasma, Vol. 2: Flow, Waves & Oscillations. Ya. L. Al'pert. (Illus.). 298p. (C). 1990. pap. text ed. 42.95 (*0-521-38972-0*) Cambridge U Pr.

Space Plasmas: Coupling Between Small & Medium Scale Processes. Ed. by Maha Ashour-Abdalla et al. LC 95-3752. (Geophysical Monograph: Vol. 86). 390p. 1995. 80.00 (*0-87590-043-7*) Am Geophysical.

Space Policy: An Introduction. Nathan C. Goldman. LC 91-30936. (Illus.). 332p. 1992. text ed. 39.95 (*0-8138-1024-8*) Iowa St U Pr.

Space Power Interests. Ed. by Peter Hayes. 237p. (C). 1996. text ed. 59.00 (*0-8133-8879-1*) Westview.

Space Precinct: Alien Island. David Bischoff. 272p. 1996. mass mkt. 4.99 (*0-06-105626-X*) HarpC.

Space Probes to the Planets. Fay Robinson. Ed. by Christy Grant. LC 92-10792. (Illus.). 32p. (J). (gr. k-3). 1993. lib. bdg. 14.95 (*0-8075-7548-8*) A Whitman.

***Space Propulsion Analysis & Design.** Ronald W. Humble et al. (Space Technology Ser.). (Illus.). 768p. 1996. text ed. write for info. (*0-07-031329-6*); pap. text ed. write for info. (*0-07-031320-2*) McGraw.

***Space Race.** Kirk Sneddon. 154p. (Orig.). 1997. mass mkt. 4.99 (*1-55237-042-9*, Pub. by Comnwlth Pub CN) Partners Pubs Grp.

***Space Race.** Judith B. Stamper & Wiley Blevins. LC 97-23395. (Hello Reader Ser.). (Illus.). (J). 1998. write for info. (*0-590-76267-2*) Scholastic Inc.

Space Radiation Effects. American Society for Testing & Materials Staff. LC 64-14650. (American Society for Testing & Materials Special Technical Publication Ser.: Special Technical Publication, No. 363). 165p. reprint ed. pap. 47.10 (*0-317-11242-2*, 2000753) Bks Demand.

Space Radiation Effects on Materials. Radioisotopes & Radiation Effects Committee E-10. LC 62-20905. (American Society for Testing & Materials: No. 330). 71p. reprint ed. pap. 25.00 (*0-317-09203-0*, 2000123) Bks Demand.

Space Relativity: Selected Papers Presented at the 4th, 5th & 6th International Symposia on Space Relativity. Ed. by W. Wrigley. 80p. 1983. pap. 40.00 (*0-08-029339-5*, A140, Pergamon Pr) Elsevier.

Space Remote Sensing System: An Introduction. H. S. Chen. 1985. text ed. 126.00 (*0-12-170880-2*) Acad Pr.

Space Rendezvous, Rescue, Recovery, 2 Vols, Pt. 1. Ed. by N. V. Petersen. (Advances in the Astronautical Sciences Ser.: Vol. 16). 1963. 45.00 (*0-87703-017-0*) Univelt Inc.

Space Rendezvous, Rescue, Recovery, 2 Vols, Pt. 2. Ed. by N. V. Petersen. (Advances in the Astronautical Sciences Ser.: Vol. 16). 1963. 30.00 (*0-87703-018-9*) Univelt Inc.

Space Rescue & Safety, 1975. Ed. by Philip H. Bolger & C. Stark Draper. (Science & Technology Ser.: Vol. 41). (Illus.). 1976. lib. bdg. 25.00 (*0-87703-077-4*) Univelt Inc.

Space Research, Vol. 13. Ed. by Michael J. Rycroft. 1977. 115.00 (*0-08-021787-7*, Ed Skills Dallas) Elsevier.

Space Research, Vol. 14. Ed. by Michael J. Rycroft. 1977. 140.00 (*0-08-021788-5*) Elsevier.

Space Research, Vol. 15. Ed. by Michael J. Rycroft. 1977. 115.00 (*0-08-021789-3*) Elsevier.

Space Research, Vol. 17. Ed. by Michael J. Rycroft. 1977. 115.00 (*0-08-021636-6*) Elsevier.

Space Research, Vol. 18. Ed. by Michael J. Rycroft. 1978. 140.00 (*0-08-022021-5*) Elsevier.

Space Research, Vol. 19. Ed. by Michael J. Rycroft. 642p. 1979. 145.00 (*0-08-023417-8*, Pergamon Pr) Elsevier.

Space Research Vol.20: Proceedings of the Open Meetings of the Working Groups on Physical Sciences of the Twenty-Second Plenary Meeting of the Committee on Space Research, Bangalore, India, 29 May- 9 June 1979. Michael J. Rycroft. LC 79-41359. (Illus.). 294p. 1980. 70.00 (*0-08-024437-8*, Pergamon Pr) Elsevier.

Space Resources, 5 vols., Set. 1994. lib. bdg. 2,755.95 (*0-8490-6403-1*) Gordon Pr.

Space Resources: Breaking the Bonds of the Earth. John S. Lewis & Ruth A. Lewis. LC 86-32677. (Illus.). 384p. 1987. text ed. 59.00 (*0-231-06498-5*) Col U Pr.

Space Robotics: Dynamics & Control. Ed. by Yangesheng Xu & Takeo Kanade. 1992. lib. bdg. 122.50 (*0-7923-9265-5*) Kluwer Ac.

Space Robotics in Japan. Ed. by William L. Whittaker & Takeo Kanade. (JTEC Panel Reports). xii, 241p. 1991. pap. write for info. (*1-883712-20-3*, JTEC) Intl Tech Res.

Space Rock. Ed. by Susan Schade. LC 87-12762. (Step into Reading Bks.). (Illus.). 48p. (Orig.). (J). (gr. 2-3). 1988. pap. 3.99 (*0-394-89384-0*) Random Bks Yng Read.

Space Safety & Rescue: 1979-1981, Vol. 39. Ed. by H. Jacobs. (Science & Technology Ser.). (Illus.). 456p. 1983. fiche write for info. (*0-87703-222-X*) Univelt Inc.

Space Safety & Rescue: 1979-1981, Vol. 40. Ed. by H. Jacobs. (Science & Technology Ser.). (Illus.). 456p. 1983. fiche write for info. (*0-87703-223-8*) Univelt Inc.

Space Safety & Rescue: 1979-1981, Vol. 41. Ed. by H. Jacobs. (Science & Technology Ser.). (Illus.). 456p. 1983. fiche write for info. (*0-87703-224-6*) Univelt Inc.

Space Safety & Rescue: 1979-1981, Vol. 54. Jeri W. Brown. (Science & Technology Ser.). (Illus.). 456p. 1983. pap. text ed. 35.00 (*0-87703-178-9*); lib. bdg. 45.00 (*0-87703-177-0*) Univelt Inc.

Space Safety & Rescue, Nineteen Eighty-Six to Nineteen Eighty-Seven. Ed. by Gloria W. Heath. (Science & Technology Ser.: Vol. 70). (Illus.). 360p. 1988. pap. text ed. 45.00 (*0-87703-292-0*); lib. bdg. 55.00 (*0-87703-291-2*) Am Astronaut.

Space Safety & Rescue Nineteen Eighty-Two to Nineteen Eighty-Three. Ed. by Gloria W. Heath. (Science & Technology Ser.: Vol. 58). (Illus.). 378p. (Orig.). 1984. pap. text ed. 40.00 (*0-87703-203-3*); lib. bdg. 50.00 (*0-87703-202-5*) Univelt Inc.

***Space Safety & Rescue 1984-1985: Proceedings of the International Academy of Astronautics Held in Conjunction with the 35th & 36th International Astronautical Congresses, Lausanne, Switzerland, Oct. 7-13, 1984, & Stockholm, Sweden, Oct. 7-12, 1985.** Ed. by Gloria W. Heath. (Science & Technology Ser.: Vol. 64). 400p. 1986. 55.00 (*0-87703-248-3*) Am Astronaut.

***Space Safety & Rescue 1984-1985: Proceedings of the International Academy of Astronautics Held in Conjunction with the 35th & 36th International Astronautical Congresses, Lausanne, Switzerland, Oct. 7-13, 1984, & Stockholm, Sweden, Oct. 7-12, 1985.** Ed. by Gloria W. Heath. (Science & Technology Ser.: Vol. 64). 400p. 1986. pap. 45.00 (*0-87703-249-1*) Am Astronaut.

Space Safety & Rescue, 1990: Proceedings of the International Academy of Astronautics Held in Conjunction with the 41st International Astronautical Congress, Dresden, Germany, Oct. 6-12, 1990. Ed. by Gloria W. Heath. LC 57-43769. (Science & Technology Ser.: Vol. 79). (Illus.). 232p. 1991. pap. 50.00 (*0-87703-342-0*); lib. bdg. 65.00 (*0-87703-341-2*) Univelt Inc.

Space Safety & Rescue 1991. Ed. by Gloria W. Heath. LC 57-43769. (Science & Technology Ser.: Vol. 82). (Illus.). 270p. 1993. pap. text ed. 50.00 (*0-87703-373-0*); lib. bdg. 65.00 (*0-87703-372-2*) Univelt Inc.

Space Safety & Rescue 1992. Gloria W. Heath. LC 57-43769. (Science & Technology Ser.: 84). (Illus.). 372p. 1994. pap. text ed. 55.00 (*0-87703-392-7*); lib. bdg. 70.00 (*0-87703-391-9*) Univelt Inc.

***Space Safety & Rescue 1993: Proceedings of the International Academy of Astronautics Held in Conjunction with the 44th International Astronautical Congress, Graz, Austria, Oct. 16-22, 1993.** Ed. by Gloria W. Heath. (Science & Technology Ser.: Vol. 87). (Illus.). 344p. 1996. 70.00 (*0-87703-410-9*) Am Astronaut.

***Space Safety & Rescue, 1993: Proceedings Symposium of the International Academy of Astronautics, International Astronautical Federation Congress, 44th, Graz, Austria.** (Science & Technology Ser.: Vol. 87). 332p. 1996. pap. 50.00 (*0-87703-411-7*, 70144) Am Astronaut.

***Space Safety & Rescue 1994: Conference Proceedings.** Ed. by Gloria W. Heath. (Science & Technology Ser.: Vol. 88). (Illus.). 326p. 1996. 70.00 (*0-87703-416-8*); pap. 50.00 (*0-87703-417-6*) Am Astronaut.

Space Sailing. D. M. Souza. LC 92-45176. (Space & Aviation Ser.). (Illus.). (YA). (gr. 5 up). 1994. lib. bdg. 21.50 (*0-8225-2850-9*, Lerner Publctns) Lerner Group.

Space Sailing. Jerome Wright. LC 91-38093. 258p. 1992. pap. text ed. 29.00 (*2-88124-842-X*, TL783) Gordon & Breach.

Space Sailing. Jerome L. Wright. 258p. 1992. text ed. 83.00 (*2-88124-803-9*) Gordon & Breach.

Space Satellite Handbook. 3rd ed. Anthony R. Curtis. LC 93-37563. 346p. 1994. 39.00 (*0-88415-192-1*, 5642) Gulf Pub.

Space Science. Ian Graham. LC 92-18319. (Facing the Future Ser.). 48p. (J). (gr. 5). 1992. lib. bdg. 22.80 (*0-8114-2806-0*) Raintree Steck-V.

Space Science Comes of Age: Perspectives in the History of the Space Sciences. Ed. by Paul A. Hanle & Von Del Chamberlain. LC 80-28966. (Illus.). 194p. 1981. text ed. 37.00 (*0-87474-508-X*, HASS); pap. text ed. 19.95 (*0-87474-507-1*, HASSP) Smithsonian.

***Space Science in China.** Ed. by Wen-Rui Hu. (Earth Space Institute Book Series on Public & Private Sector Interest in Space: No. 1). 416p. 1997. text ed. 155.00 (*90-5699-023-3*) Gordon & Breach.

Space Science in the Planetarium. David Hurd. 1995. pap. 10.60 (*0-910042-69-1*) Allegheny.

Space Science Projects: A Source Guide. 1991. lib. bdg. 75.00 (*0-8490-4817-6*) Gordon Pr.

Space Science Projects for Young Scientists. David W. McKay & Bruce G. Smith. LC 86-7745. (Projects for Young Scientists Ser.). (Illus.). 128p. (YA). (gr. 7-12). 1986. lib. bdg. 22.00 (*0-531-10244-0*) Watts.

Space Science Projects for Young Scientists. David W. McKay. (J). 1989. pap. 6.95 (*0-531-15134-4*) Watts.

***Space Sciences Dictionary Vol. 2: Motion/Space Flight/Data.** Josip Kleczek & H. Kleczkova. 808p. 1993. 243.25 (*0-444-98818-1*) Elsevier.

***Space Sciences Dictionary Vol. 4: Earth Sciences/Solar System/Deep Space.** Josip Kleczek & H. Kleczkova. 894p. 1992. 227.25 (*0-444-98816-5*) Elsevier.

Space Sciences Dictionary, Vol. 1: Radiation & Matter - in English, French, German, Spanish, Portuguese & Russian. Josip Kleczek & H. Kleczkova. 664p. (ENG, FRE, GER, POR, RUS & SPA.). 1990. 225.50 (*0-444-98872-6*) Elsevier.

Space Sex: A Novel. Keith Kirts. 1995. pap. 12.95 (*1-882639-04-9*) Synapse Cent.

***Space Ships.** Amanda Davis. LC 96-54498. (Exploring Space Ser.). (J). 1997. lib. bdg. 11.95 (*0-8239-5063-8*, PowerKids) Rosen Group.

***Space Shuttle.** Bobbie Kalman. (Eye on the Universe Ser.). (Illus.). 32p. (J). 1997. lib. bdg. 18.64 (*0-86505-678-1*) Crabtree Pub Co.

***Space Shuttle.** Bobbie Kalman. (Eye on the Universe Ser.). (Illus.). 32p. (J). 1997. pap. 5.95 (*0-86505-688-9*) Crabtree Pub Co.

Space Shuttle. rev. ed. Bill Yenne. (Illus.). 128p. 1992. reprint ed. 14.98 (*0-8317-7989-6*) Smithmark.

Space Shuttle: Dawn of an Era. Ed. by William F. Rector, III & Paul A. Penzo. (Advances in the Astronautical Sciences Ser.: Vol. 41). 1980. pap. 35.00 (*0-87703-112-6*); pap. 40.00 (*0-87703-114-2*); suppl. ed. 10.00 incl. fiche (*0-87703-136-3*) Univelt Inc.

Space Shuttle: Dawn of an Era, Pt. 1. Ed. by William F. Rector, III & Paul A. Penzo. (Advances in the Astronautical Sciences Ser.: Vol. 41). 452p. 1980. Part 1, 452pp. lib. bdg. 45.00 (*0-87703-111-8*) Univelt Inc.

Space Shuttle: Dawn of an Era, Pt. 2. Ed. by William F. Rector, III & Paul A. Penzo. (Advances in the Astronautical Sciences Ser.: Vol. 41). 528p. 1980. Part 2, 528pp. lib. bdg. 55.00 (*0-87703-113-4*) Univelt Inc.

Space Shuttle: NASA Must Continue to Reduce Costs to Operate Within Future Projected Funds. (Illus.). 42p. (Orig.). (C). 1996. pap. text ed. 20.00 (*0-7881-2860-4*) DIANE Pub.

Space Shuttle: Need to Sustain Launch Risk Assessment Process Improvements. (Illus.). 64p. (Orig.). (C). 1996. pap. text ed. 25.00 (*0-7881-2864-7*) DIANE Pub.

Space Shuttle: The History of Developing the National Space Transportation System. 2nd ed. Dennis Jenkins. (Illus.). 352p. 1996. 29.95 (*0-9633974-4-3*) D Jenkins Pub.

Space Shuttle & Spacelab Utilization: Near-Term & Long-Term Benefits for Mankind, Pt. I, Vol. 37. Ed. by George W. Morgenthaler & M. Hollstein. (Advances in the Astronautical Sciences Ser.). 400p. 1978. Pt. I, 400p. lib. bdg. 40.00 (*0-87703-096-0*) Univelt Inc.

Space Shuttle & Spacelab Utilization: Near-Term & Long-Term Benefits for Mankind, Pt. II, Vol. 37. Ed. by George W. Morgenthaler & M. Hollstein. (Advances in the Astronautical Sciences Ser.). 465p. 1978. Pt. II, 465p. lib. bdg. 45.00 (*0-87703-097-9*) Univelt Inc.

Space Shuttle Challenger Explosion. Sue Hamilton. Ed. by John Hamilton. LC 88-71720. (Day of Disaster Ser.). (Illus.). 32p. (J). (gr. 4). 1989. lib. bdg. 12.98 (*0-939179-40-7*) Abdo & Dghtrs.

Space Shuttle Environment. Ed. by Thomas D. Wilkerson et al. LC 85-81606. 460p. 1985. 50.00 (*0-939204-28-2*, 84-20) Eng Found.

Space Shuttle Missions of the 80's. Ed. by W. J. Bursnall et al. LC 57-43769. (Advances in the Astronautical Sciences Ser.: Vol. 32, Pts. 1 & 2). (Illus.). 1977. suppl. ed. 65.00 incl. fiche (*0-87703-133-9*) Univelt Inc.

Space Shuttle Missions of the 80's, Pt. 1. Ed. by W. J. Bursnall et al. LC 57-43769. (Advances in the Astronautical Sciences Ser.: Vol. 32, Pts. 1 & 2). (Illus.). 1977. lib. bdg. 40.00 (*0-87703-078-2*) Univelt Inc.

Space Shuttle Missions of the 80's, Pt. 2. Ed. by W. J. Bursnall et al. LC 57-43769. (Advances in the Astronautical Sciences Ser.: Vol. 32, Pts. 1 & 2). (Illus.). 1977. lib. bdg. 55.00 (*0-87703-087-1*) Univelt Inc.

Space Shuttle Operators' Manual. Kerry M. Joels & David Larkin. (Illus.). 145p. (Orig.). 1985. pap. 17.95 (*0-345-33103-6*) Ballantine.

Space Shuttle Operator's Manual. rev. ed. Kerry M. Joels et al. 160p. (Orig.). 1988. pap. 17.50 (*0-345-34181-3*, Ballantine Trade) Ballantine.

Space Shuttle Payloads. Ed. by George W. Morgenthaler et al. (Science & Technology Ser.: Vol. 30). 530p. 1973. lib. bdg. 40.00 (*0-87703-063-4*) Univelt Inc.

Space Shuttles. Stuart A. Kallen. (Giant Leaps Ser.). (J). 1996. lib. bdg. 14.98 (*1-56239-569-6*) Abdo & Dghtrs.

Space Shuttles & Interplanetary Missions: Proceedings of the Annual Meeting, 16th, Anaheim, California, 1970. Ed. by Lewis Larmore & Robert L. Gervais. (Advances in the Astronautical Sciences Ser.: Vol. 28). 1970. 35.00 (*0-87703-055-3*) Univelt Inc.

Space Simulation, Aerospace & Aircraft, High Modulus Fibers & Composites see 1997 Annual Book of ASTM Standards: General Products, Chemical Specialties, & End Use Products, Section 15

Space Simulation Conference, 3rd, 1968: Proceedings. 226p. 45.00 (*0-317-36285-2*) Inst Environ Sci.

Space Songs. Myra C. Livingston. LC 87-19628. (Illus.). 32p. (J). (ps-3). 1988. lib. bdg. 15.95 (*0-8234-0675-X*) Holiday.

Space Songs. Ed. by Seymour Simon. LC 94-16643. (Illus.). 32p. (J). 1995. lib. bdg. 14.93 (*0-688-11888-7*, Morrow Junior) Morrow.

Space Songs. Cohn Livingston. (Illus.). (J). (ps-3). 1993. reprint ed. pap. 5.95 (*0-8234-1029-3*) Holiday.

Space Songs for Children: Fun Songs & Activities about Outer Space. Tonja E. Weimer. (Orig.). (J). (ps-3). 1993. audio 9.95 (*0-936823-12-7*) Pearce Evetts.

Space Songs for Children: Fun Songs & Activities about Outer Space. Tonja E. Weimer. (Illus.). 100p. (Orig.). (J). (ps-3). 1993. pap. 14.95 incl. audio (*0-936823-11-9*) Pearce Evetts.

Space Stamps. 88p. 1985. 11.00 (*0-318-13310-5*) Am Topical Assn.

Space, Stars, Planets & Spacecraft. Sue Becklake. LC 91-60144. (See & Explore Library). (Illus.). 64p. (J). (gr. 3 up). 1991. 12.95 (*1-879431-14-9*) DK Pub Inc.

Space Station: A Personal Journey. Hans Mark. LC 86-32892. (Illus.). viii, 264p. 1987. text ed. 29.95 (*0-8223-0727-8*) Duke.

***Space Station: Cost Control Difficulties Continue.** (Illus.). 38p. (Orig.). (C). 1996. pap. 25.00 (*0-7881-3462-0*) DIANE Pub.

Space Station: The Troubled History of Developing American Manned Orbital Platforms. Dennis R. Jenkins. (Illus.). 352p. Date not set. 29.95 (*0-9633974-3-5*) D Jenkins Pub.

Space Station Beyond IOC. Ed. by M. Jack Friedenthal. (Advances in the Astronautical Sciences Ser.: Vol. 59). (Illus.). 1986. pap. text ed. 30.00 (*0-87703-253-X*); lib. bdg. 40.00 (*0-87703-252-1*) Univelt Inc.

Space Station Decision: Incremental Politics & Technological Choice. Howard E. McCurdy. LC 90-30831. (New Series in NASA History). (Illus.). 320p. 1990. text ed. 45.00 (*0-8018-4004-X*) Johns Hopkins.

Space Station Ice-3, No. 3. Bruce Coville. (YA). (gr. 6 up). 1996. mass mkt. 3.99 (*0-671-53641-9*) PB.

Space Station Program: Description, Applications & Opportunities. National Aeronautics & Space Administration, Lyndon B. Johnson Space Center Staff. LC 85-4963. (Illus.). 754p. 1985. 67.00 (*0-8155-1024-1*) Noyes.

Space Station Seventh Grade. Jerry Spinelli. (J). (gr. 3-7). 1991. write for info. (*0-318-68733-X*); mass mkt. 5.95 (*0-316-80804-0*) Little.

Space Stations. Stuart A. Kallen. (Giant Leaps Ser.). (J). 1996. lib. bdg. 14.98 (*1-56239-568-8*) Abdo & Dghtrs.

***Space Stations.** Diane M. Sipiera & Paul P. Sipiera. LC 97-3662. (True Book Ser.). (J). 1997. write for info. (*0-516-20450-5*) Childrens.

***Space Stations: Living & Working in Space.** Amanda Davis. LC 96-54497. (Exploring Space Ser.). 1997. write for info. (*0-8239-5062-X*) Rosen Group.

Space Stations: Proceedings of the Annual Meeting, 16th, Anaheim, California, 1970. Ed. by Lewis Larmore & Robert L. Gervais. (Advances in the Astronautical Sciences Ser.: Vol. 27). 1970. 45.00 (*0-87703-054-5*) Univelt Inc.

Space Stations & Platforms. Gordon R. Woodcock. LC 84-25442. 232p. 1986. text ed. 56.50 (*0-89464-001-1*) Krieger.

Space Sticker Book. Robin Kerrod. (Illus.). (J). 1988. pap. 5.99 (*0-517-64549-1*) Random Hse Value.

Space Strategy for Texas for the 1990s. Kenneth W. Tolo & Dean Kastel. (Policy Research Project Report: No. 102). 122p. 1993. pap. 11.50 (*0-89940-710-2*) LBJ Sch Pub Aff.

S

*Space, Structure & Form. Rochelle Newman & Donna M. Fowler. 1996. pap. text ed. 31.40 (0-697-33058-3) Pythagorean Pr.

Space Structures: Their Harmony & Counterpoint. Arthur L. Loeb. 192p. 1976. pap. text ed. 35.50 (0-201-04651-2) Addison-Wesley.

Space Structures: Their Harmony & Counterpoint. 5th rev. ed. Arthur L. Loeb. (Design Science Collections). xviii, 169p. 1991. 29.50 (0-8176-3588-2) Birkhauser.

Space Systems. Ed. by Vincent L. Pisacane & Robert C. Moore. LC 92-9490. (Johns Hopkins Applied Physics Laboratory Series in Science & Engineering). 784p. 1994. 85.00 (0-19-507497-1) OUP.

Space Systems & Thermal Technology for the 70s: Proceedings of the Space Technology & Heat Transfer Conference, Los Angeles, 1970, Pt. 1. Space Technology & Heat Transfer Conference Staff. LC 72-17650. 493p. reprint ed. pap. 140.60 (0-317-10961-8, 2005682) Bks Demand.

Space Systems & Thermal Technology for the 70s: Proceedings of the Space Technology & Heat Transfer Conference, Los Angeles, 1970, Pt. 2. Space Technology & Heat Transfer Conference Staff. LC 72-17650. 406p. reprint ed. pap. 115.80 (0-317-10230-3, 2013322) Bks Demand.

Space Systems Economics. Koell. 1995. pap. 45.00 (0-08-031656-5, Pergamon Pr) Elsevier.

Space Systems Economics: Cost Reductions in Space Operations. Ed. by Dietrich E. Koelle. 60p. 1985. pap. 45.00 (0-08-032800-8, Pergamon Pr) Elsevier.

Space Tech Conference Proceedings, September 23-25, 1985, Anaheim, CA. Space Tech (1st: 1985: Anaheim, CA) Staff. LC 85-61971. (Illus.). 420p. reprint ed. pap. 119.70 (0-8357-6478-8, 2035849) Bks Demand.

Space Technologies & Applications International Forum, Pt. 1. Mohamed S. El-Genk. (AIP Press Conference Proceedings Ser.: No. 361). (Illus.). 1996. write for info. (1-56396-568-2, AIP); pap. write for info. (1-56396-571-2, AIP) Am Inst Physics.

Space Technologies & Applications International Forum, Pt. 2. Mohamed S. El-Genk. (AIP Press Conference Proceedings Ser.: No. 361). (Illus.). 1996. write for info. (1-56396-569-0, AIP); pap. write for info. (1-56396-572-0, AIP) Am Inst Physics.

Space Technologies & Applications International Forum, Pt. 3. Mohamed S. El-Genk. (AIP Press Conference Proceedings Ser.: No. 361). (Illus.). 1996. write for info. (1-56396-570-4, AIP); pap. write for info. (1-56396-573-9, AIP) Am Inst Physics.

Space Technologies & Applications International Forum, 3 vols., Set. Mohamed S. El-Genk. (AIP Press Conference Proceedings Ser.: No. 361). (Illus.). 1601p. 1996. 275.00 (1-56396-562-3, CP 361, AIP); pap. 275.00 (1-56396-574-7, CP 361, AIP) Am Inst Physics.

Space Technology. (Young Scientist Ser.). 64p. (J). (gr. 4-6). 1995. 9.95 (0-7166-6309-0) World Bk.

Space Technology & Applications for Sustainable Development: Proceedings of the Symposium, Beijing, China, 19-21 September 1994. 500p. 1995. 45.00 (92-1-119689-2) UN.

*Space Technology & Applications International Forum 1997. Ed. by Mohamed S. El-Genk. (AIP Conference Proceedings Ser.: No. 387). (Illus.). 1600p. 1997. 295.00 (1-56396-679-4, AIP) Am Inst Physics.

Space Technology & Earth Problems. Ed. by C. Quentin Ford. (Science & Technology Ser.: Vol. 23). (Illus.). 1970. lib. bdg. 35.00 (0-87703-051-0); suppl. ed. 20.00 incl. fiche (0-87703-134-7) Univelt Inc.

Space Technology & Planetary Astronomy. Joseph N. Tatarewicz. LC 89-45469. (Science, Technology, & Society Ser.). (Illus.). 208p. 1990. 12.95 (0-253-35655-5) Ind U Pr.

Space Technology Transfer to Community & Industry. Ed. by John K. Stotz, Jr. et al. (Science & Technology Ser.: Vol. 29). 1972. 20.00 (0-87703-062-6); fiche 15.00 (0-685-00197-0) Univelt Inc.

Space Telescope: A Study of NASA, Science, Technology, & Politics. Robert W. Smith et al. (Illus.). 496p. (C). 1989. text ed. 26.95 (0-521-26634-3) Cambridge U Pr.

Space Telescope: A Study of NASA, Science, Technology, & Politics. Robert W. Smith et al. (Illus.). 528p. (C). 1993. pap. 25.95 (0-521-45768-8) Cambridge U Pr.

Space, Text & Gender: An Anthropological Study of the Marakwet of Kenya. Henrietta Moore. (Illus.). 220p. 1986. 79.95 (0-521-30333-8) Cambridge U Pr.

Space, Text & Gender: An Anthropological Study of the Marakwet of Kenya. Henrietta L. Moore. LC 95-46816. (Mappings: Society-Theory-Space Ser.). (Illus.). 234p. 1995. pap. text ed. 17.95 (0-89862-825-3, 2825) Guilford Pr.

*Space, the Dormant Frontier: Changing the Paradigm for the 21st Century. Joan Johnson-Freese & Roger Handberg. LC 96-53546. 288p. 1997. text ed. 59.95 (0-275-95887-6, Praeger Pubs) Greenwood.

Space, the Next Ten Years, Symposium Report, 1985. Ted W. Jensen et al. 176p. 25.00 (0-317-65298-2) US Space Found.

Space-Time: Fabric of the Universe. James C. LoPresto. LC 94-78959. (Illus.). 258p. 1995. pap. 29.95 (0-910042-72-1) Allegheny.

Space-Time Algebra. David Hestenes. (Documents on Modern Physics Ser.). viii, 94p. (Orig.). (C). 1966. text ed. 106.00 (0-677-01390-6) Gordon & Breach.

Space, Time, & Archeological Landscapes. Ed. by J. Rossignol & L. Wandsnider. (Interdisciplinary Contributions to Archaeology Ser.). (Illus.). 275p. 1992. 49.50 (0-306-44161-6, Plenum Pr) Plenum.

Space, Time & Architecture: The Growth of a New Tradition. 5th enl. rev. ed. Sigfried Giedion. LC 67-17310. (Charles Eliot Norton Lectures). (Illus.). 953p. 1967. text ed. 45.00 (0-674-83040-7) HUP.

Space, Time & Causality. Richard Swinburne. 228p. 1982. lib. bdg. 104.50 (90-277-1437-1, D Reidel) Kluwer Ac.

Space, Time & Crisis: The Theatre of Rene Marques. Bonnie H. Reynolds. LC 87-61514. 181p. 1988. 20.00 (0-938972-13-8) Spanish Lit Pubns.

Space, Time, & Freedom. Major L. Wilson. LC 74-287. 309p. 1974. text ed. 59.95 (0-8371-7373-6, WIT/, Greenwood Pr) Greenwood.

Space, Time & Geometry. Patrick C. Suppes. LC 73-86097. (Synthese Library: No. 56). 435p. 1973. lib. bdg. 135.00 (90-277-0386-8, D Reidel) Kluwer Ac.

Space, Time & Gravitation: An Outline of the General Theory. Arthur S. Eddington. (Cambridge Science Classics Ser.). 240p. 1987. pap. text ed. 22.95 (0-521-33709-7) Cambridge U Pr.

Space, Time & Gravity: The Theory of the Big Bang & Black Holes. Robert M. Wald. LC 77-4038. (Illus.). 144p. 1981. pap. text ed. 9.95 (0-226-87031-6) U Ch Pr.

Space, Time, & Gravity: The Theory of the Big Bang & Black Holes. Robert M. Wald. LC 91-28034. (Illus.). 164p. 1992. pap. 13.95 (0-226-87029-4) U Ch Pr.

Space, Time, & Gravity: The Theory of the Big Bang & Black Holes. 2nd ed. Robert M. Wald. LC 91-28034. (Illus.). 164p. 1992. lib. bdg. 29.00 (0-226-87028-6) U Ch Pr.

Space, Time & Man: A Prehistorian's View. Grahame Clark. (Canto Book Ser.). (Illus.). 179p. (C). 1994. pap. text ed. 9.95 (0-521-46762-4) Cambridge U Pr.

Space, Time, & Mechanics. D. Mayr & G. Sussmann. 260p. 1982. lib. bdg. 93.00 (90-277-1525-4, D Reidel) Kluwer Ac.

Space, Time & Medicine. Larry Dossey. 1982. pap. 18.00 (0-394-71091-6) Shambhala Pubns.

Space, Time & Motion: A Philosophical Introduction. 2nd rev. ed. Wesley C. Salmon. LC 80-18423. (Illus.). 171p. reprint ed. pap. 48.80 (0-318-39664-5, 2033233) Bks Demand.

Space, Time, & Organized Crime. 2nd ed. Alan A. Block. 264p. (C). 1993. text ed. 44.95 (1-56000-104-6) Transaction Pubs.

Space, Time & Perversion: Essays on the Politics of Bodies. Elizabeth Grosz. LC 95-8699. 250p. (C). 1995. pap. 17.95 (0-415-91137-0) Routledge.

Space, Time, & Perversion: Essays on the Politics of Bodies. Elizabeth Grosz. LC 95-8699. 288p. (C). (gr. 13). 1996. text ed. 59.95 (0-415-91136-2) Routledge.

Space, Time, & Spacetime. Lawrence Sklar. 1974. pap. 15.00 (0-520-03174-1) U CA Pr.

Space, Time & Synthesis in Art: Essays on Art, Literature & Philosophy. Ernst Niezvestny. Ed. by Albert Leong. (Illus.). 240p. 24.95 (0-88962-436-4); pap. 14.95 (0-88962-437-2) Mosaic.

Space, Time, & Thought in Kant. Arthur Melnick. 576p. (C). 1989. lib. bdg. 171.50 (0-7923-0135-8, Pub. by Klwr Acad Pubs NE) Kluwer Ac.

Space Time Information Processing. Alan A. Winder & Charles J. Loda. LC 80-83559. (Illus.). 200p. 1980. reprint ed. 33.95 (0-932146-04-X) Peninsula CA.

Space, Time, Matter. Hermann Weyl. 1922. pap. text ed. 7.95 (0-486-60267-2) Dover.

Space-Time of the Bororo of Brazil. Stephen M. Fabian. (Illus.). 272p. (C). 1992. lib. bdg. 49.95 (0-8130-1104-3) U Press Fla.

Space, Time, Quantum Physics. Robert Mills. (C). 1995. pap. text ed. write for info. (0-7167-2436-7) W H Freeman.

Space-Time Structure. Erwin Schrodinger. (Cambridge Science Classics Ser.). (Illus.). 119p. 1985. pap. text ed. 20.95 (0-521-31520-4) Cambridge U Pr.

Space-Time Transients & Unusual Events. Michael A. Persinger & Gyslaine F. Lafreniere. LC 76-12634. 224p. 1977. 32.95 (0-88229-334-6) Nelson-Hall.

Space to Act: The Theater of J. M. R. Lenz. Ed. by Alan C. Leidner & Helga S. Madland. LC 93-4998. (GERM Ser.). xvii, 194p. 1993. 59.50 (1-879751-62-3) Camden Hse.

Space to Seabed. J. Rawlinson. (Great Adventure Ser.). (Illus.). 32p. (J). (gr. 4 up). 1988. 12.95 (0-685-58292-2); lib. bdg. 17.27 (0-86592-872-X) Rourke Corp.

Space Tour. Dan Mackie. (Hayes Technology Ser.). (Illus.). 32p. (J). (gr. 5-9). 1985. pap. 5.95 (0-88625-103-6) Durkin Hayes Pub.

Space Transport Liability: National & International Aspects, Vol. 15. R. Bender. LC 95-23649. (Utrecht Studies in Air & Space Law). 1995. lib. bdg. 175.00 (90-411-0106-3, Pub. by M Nijhoff NE) Kluwer Ac.

Space Travel. Steven Blackman. LC 93-13310. (Technology Craft Topics Ser.). (Illus.). 32p. (J). (gr. 5-7). 1993. lib. bdg. 20.00 (0-531-14275-2) Watts.

*Space Travel. Ben Bova & Anthony R. Lewis. LC 96-36003. (Science Fiction Writing Ser.). (Illus.). 288p. 1997. pap. 16.99 (0-89879-747-0, Wrtrs Digest Bks) F & W Pubns Inc.

Space Travel. Philip Steele. LC 90-20735. (Pocket Facts Ser.). (Illus.). 32p. (J). (gr. 5-6). 1991. lib. bdg. 11.95 (0-89686-585-1, Crstwood Hse) Silver Burdett Pr.

Space Travel: Blast-Off Day. Janet McDonnell. LC 89-23999. (Discovery World Ser.). (Illus.). 32p. (J). (ps-2). 1990. lib. bdg. 21.36 (0-89565-556-X) Childs World.

Space Travel for the Beginner. Patrick Moore. (Illus.). 48p. (C). 1992. text ed. 13.95 (0-521-41835-6) Cambridge U Pr.

Space Trials: The Hubble Space Telescope Story. Eric J. Chaisson. 512p. 28.00 (0-393-03604-9) Norton.

Space Trilogy. C. S. Lewis. 1996. boxed, pap. 20.85 (0-684-83118-X, S&S) S&S Trade.

Space Trilogy, 3 vols., Set. 2nd ed. C. S. Lewis. 1986. pap. 16.95 (0-02-022360-9) Macmillan.

Space Trip see Phonics Is My Way Series

Space Twin. Natalie L. Davis. 112p. (J). (gr. 4-8). 1987. 7.95 (1-55523-037-7) Winston-Derek.

Space Two Thousand: Meeting the Challenge of a New Era. Harry L. Shipman. LC 87-2401. 442p. 1987. 21.95 (0-306-42534-3, Plenum Pr) Plenum.

Space Two Thousand-Activities to Be Performed for the Next Decade: Selected Papers from the 33rd IAF Congress, Paris, France, 27 September - 2 October 1982. Ed. by Luigi G. Napolitano. 150p. 1983. pap. 91.00 (0-08-031106-7, Pergamon Pr) Elsevier.

Space Utilization & Application in the Pacific. Ed. by Peter M. Bainum et al. LC 57-43769. (Advances in the Astronautical Sciences Ser.: Vol. 73). (Illus.). 764p. 1990. pap. text ed. 80.00 (0-87703-326-9); lib. bdg. 95.00 (0-87703-325-0) Univelt Inc.

*Space Vehicle Mechanisms: Elements of Successful Design. Peter Conley. LC 97-13993. 760p. 1997. 99.00 (0-471-12141-X) Wiley.

Space Vehicles. Anne Rockwell & David Brion. LC 93-43594. (Illus.). 24p. (J). (ps-1). 1994. pap. 13.99 (0-525-45270-2) Dutton Child Bks.

Space Wars. Poul Anderson. Ed. by Martin H. Greenberg & Charles Waugh. 384p. 1988. pap. 3.95 (0-8125-3046-2) Tor Bks.

Space Weapons: Deterrence or Delusion. Rip Bulkeley & Graham Spinardi. LC 86-10880. (Illus.). 352p. 1986. 59.50 (0-389-20640-7, N8197); pap. 23.00 (0-389-20641-5, N8198) B&N Imports.

Space Weapons: The Arms Control Dilemma. Ed. by Bhupendra Jasani. (Peace Studies). 300p. 1984. 63.00 (0-8002-3874-5) Taylor & Francis.

Space Where Anything Can Happen: Creative Drama in a Middle School. rev. ed. Rosilyn Wilder. LC 77-82855. (Illus.). 184p. (C). 1977. pap. text ed. 11.95 (0-932720-70-6) New Plays Inc.

Space Winners. Gordon R. Dickson. 256p. 1986. pap. 2.95 (0-8125-3558-8) Tor Bks.

Space Work. Barry Oshry. (Notes on Power Ser.). (Orig.). 1994. pap. text ed. 13.95 (0-910411-12-3) Power & Sys.

Spacebear Lands on Earth. Dorathye B. Wallace. (Illus.). 16p. (Orig.). (J). (ps up). 1988. pap. 2.95 (0-614-02537-0) Univ Class.

Spaceborne Synthetic Aperture Radar for Oceanography. Ed. by Robert C. Beal et al. LC 81-5966. (Johns Hopkins Oceanographic Studies: No. 7). 216p. 1981. text ed. 40.00 (0-8018-2668-3) Johns Hopkins.

Spaceborne Weather Radar. Robert Meneghini & Toshiaka Kozu. (Radar Library). 208p. 1990. text ed. 39.00 (0-89006-382-6) Artech Hse.

Spacebridges: Television & U. S. -Soviet Dialogue. Ed. by Michael Brainerd. LC 89-5528. 120p. (Orig.). (C). 1989. pap. text ed. 18.00 (0-8191-7433-5); lib. bdg. 35.00 (0-8191-7432-7) U Pr of Amer.

Spaceburger: A Kevin Spoon & Mason Mintz Story. Daniel Pinkwater. LC 93-6658. (Illus.). 32p. (J). (gr. k-3). 1993. lib. bdg. 13.95 (0-02-774643-7, Mac Bks Young Read) S&S Childrens.

Spacebusters. Campbell Morris. 40p. (gr. 4-6). 1995. pap. 2.99 (0-590-22284-8) Scholastic Inc.

Spacecast 2020: Surveillance & Reconnaissance...The U. S. Air Force's Future in Space. Comment by Michael P. Carns. 64p. (Orig.). (C). 1995. pap. text ed. 20.00 (0-7881-2539-7) DIANE Pub.

Spacecraft. LC 92-52832. (What's Inside? Ser.). (Illus.). 24p. (J). (ps-3). 1993. 8.95 (1-56458-136-5) DK Pub Inc.

Spacecraft. Ian Graham. LC 94-2875. (Pointers Ser.). (Illus.). (J). 1994. lib. bdg. 22.83 (0-8114-6193-9) Raintree Steck-V.

Spacecraft. Ian Graham. (J). 1996. pap. text ed. 4.95 (0-8114-9363-6) Raintree Steck-V.

Spacecraft Attitude Determination & Control. Ed. by James R. Werz. (Astrophysics & Space Science Library: No. 73). 858p. 1978. lib. bdg. 182.50 (90-277-0959-9) Kluwer Ac.

Spacecraft Attitude Dynamics & Control. Vladimir A. Chobotov. (Orbit Ser.). 150p. 1991. 79.50 (0-89464-031-3) Krieger.

Spacecraft Design - Thermal & Radiation. Frank L. Bouquet. (Illus.). 225p. (Orig.). (C). 1991. 89.00 (1-56216-011-7); pap. 60.00 (1-56216-012-5) Systems Co.

Spacecraft Design - Thermal & Radiation. 2nd ed. Frank L. Bouquet. (Illus.). 230p. (Orig.). 1993. 95.00 (1-56216-124-5); pap. 65.00 (1-56216-150-4) Systems Co.

*Spacecraft Dynamics & Control: A Practical Engineering Approach. Marcel J. Sidi. (Cambridge Aerospace Ser.: No. 7). (Illus.). 450p. (C). 1997. text ed. 85.00 (0-521-55072-6) Cambridge U Pr.

Spacecraft Environment Interactions. Daniel Hastings & Henry Garrett. (Cambridge Atmosphere & Space Science Ser.). (Illus.). 304p. (C). 1996. text ed. 84.95 (0-521-47128-1) Cambridge U Pr.

Spacecraft Maximum Allowable Concentrations for Selected Airborne Contaminants, Vol. 2. National Research Council Staff. 408p. (Orig.). 1996. pap. text ed. 35.00 (0-309-05478-8) Natl Acad Pr.

*Spacecraft Maximum Allowable Concentrations for Selected Airborne Contaminants, Vol. 3. National Research Council Staff. 362p. (Orig.). (C). 1997. pap. text ed. 45.00 (0-309-05629-2, Joseph Henry Pr) Natl Acad Pr.

Spacecraft Propulsion for Systems Engineers. Gorin. 1998. write for info. (0-89464-059-3) Krieger.

Spacecraft Structures & Mechanisms: From Concept to Launch. Thomas P. Sarafin. Ed. by Wiley J. Larson. (Space Technology Ser.). (Illus.). 850p. (Orig.). (C). 1995. pap. text ed. 49.90 (1-881883-03-5) Microcosm.

Spacecraft Structures & Mechanisms from Concept to Launch. Ed. by Thomas P. Sarafin & Wiley J. Larson. LC 95-12381. (Space Technology Library: Vol. 4). 1995. lib. bdg. 139.50 (0-7923-3476-0) Kluwer Ac.

Spacecraft Systems Engineering. 2nd ed. Ed. by Peter Fortescue & John Stark. LC 94-42861. 581p. 1995. pap. text ed. 60.00 (0-471-95220-6) Wiley.

Spacecraft Tables, 1957-1990. Jos Heyman. (Illus.). 300p. 1991. pap. 30.00 (0-912183-07-1) Univelt Inc.

Spacedog's Best Friend. Toni Sweeney. (Illus.). (Orig.). (J). (gr. 5-12). 1989. pap. 6.95 (0-933025-13-0) Blue Bird Pub.

Spacefacts. Susan Goodman. 144p. (J). Date not set. pap. write for info. (0-19-910277-5) OUP.

Spacefarers. (Voyage Through the Universe Ser.). (Illus.). 144p. 1990. 17.27 (0-8094-6891-3); lib. bdg. 25.93 (0-8094-6892-1) Time-Life.

Spacefarers of the Eighties & Nineties: The Next Thousand People in Space. Alcestis R. Oberg. (Illus.). 320p. 1985. text ed. 40.50 (0-231-05906-X) Col U Pr.

Spacefaring Nation: Perspectives on American Space History & Policy. Ed. by Martin J. Collins & Sylvia D. Fries. LC 90-9762. 224p. (C). 1991. text ed. 39.00 (0-87474-907-7) Smithsonian.

SpaceFlight. Valerie Neal et al. (Illus.). 256p. 1995. 24.95 (0-02-860007-X); 18.00 (0-02-860040-1) Macmillan.

Spaceflight & Rocketry: A Chronology. David Baker. (Illus.). 576p. 1996. 65.00 (0-8160-1853-7) Facts on File.

*Spaceflight & the Myth of Presidential Leadership. Roger D. Launius & Goward E. McCurdy. LC 96-51213. 1997. text ed. 36.95 (0-252-02336-6) U of Ill Pr.

*Spaceflight & the Myth of Presidential Leadership. Roger D. Launius & Howard E. McCurdy. LC 96-51213. 1997. pap. text ed. 19.95 (0-252-06632-4) U of Ill Pr.

Spaceflight Dynamics. William E. Wiesel. (Aeronautical & Aerospace Engineering Ser.). 352p. 1989. text ed. write for info. (0-07-070106-7) McGraw.

Spaceflight Dynamics. 2nd ed. William E. Wiesel. (Series in Aeronautical & Aerospace Engineering). (Illus.). 368p. 1996. text ed. 53.00 (0-07-070110-5) McGraw.

Spaceflight Dynamics, 1993. Ed. by Jerome Teles & Mina V. Samii. LC 57-43769. (Advances in the Astronautical Sciences Ser.: Vol. 84 I & II). (Illus.). 4p. 1993. lib. bdg. 240.00 (0-87703-378-1) Univelt Inc.

Spaceflight Dynamics, 1993, Vol. 69. Ed. by Robert H. Jacobs. LC 57-43769. (Advances in the Astronautical Sciences Ser.: Vol. 69). (Illus.). 1450p. 1993. suppl. ed. 10.00 incl. fiche (0-87703-379-X) Univelt Inc.

Spaceflight in the Era of Aero-Space Planes. Russell J. Hannigan. LC 92-37687. 320p. (C). 1994. lib. bdg. 74.50 (0-89464-046-1) Krieger.

Spaceflight Life Support & Biospheres. Peter Eckart. 1996. lib. bdg. 159.00 (0-7923-3889-8) Kluwer Ac.

Spaceflight Life Support & Biospherics. Peter Eckart. (Space Technology Library). 444p. (Orig.). (C). 1996. pap. text ed. 35.50 (1-881883-04-3) Microcosm.

Spaceflight Mechanics, 1991. Ed. by Robert H. Jacobs. (Advances in the Astronautical Sciences Ser.: Vol. 62). 1991. suppl. ed. 50.00 incl. fiche (0-87703-340-4) Univelt Inc.

Spaceflight Mechanics, 1991. Ed. by John K. Soldner et al. (Advances in the Astronautical Sciences Ser.: Vol. 75, Pts. I & II). (Illus.). 1354p. 1991. pap. text ed. 190.00 (0-87703-339-0); lib. bdg. 220.00 (0-87703-338-2) Univelt Inc.

Spaceflight Mechanics 1994. Ed. by John E. Cochran, Jr. et al. LC 57-43769. (Advances in the Astronautical Sciences Ser.: 87, I & II). (Illus.). 1272p. 1994. lib. bdg. 240.00 (0-87703-386-2) Univelt Inc.

*Spaceflight Mechanics 1995. Ed. by Ronald J. Proulx et al. (Advances in the Astronautical Sciences Microfiche Ser.: Vol. 71). 1995. suppl. ed. 15.00 incl. fiche (0-87703-402-8) Am Astronaut.

Spaceflight Mechanics 1995. Ed. by Ronald J. Proulx et al. LC 57-43769. (Advances in the Astronautical Sciences Ser.: Vol. 89, Nos. I & II). (Illus.). 1774p. 1995. lib. bdg. 280.00 (0-87703-401-X) Am Astronaut.

*Spaceflight Revolution, 2 vols. 1997. lib. bdg. 600.95 (0-8490-6157-1) Gordon Pr.

Spaceflight Revolution: A Sociological Study. William S. Bainbridge. LC 82-21725. 304p. 1983. reprint ed. 24.50 (0-89874-501-2) Krieger.

Spaceflight Revolution: NASA Langley Research Center from Sputnik to Apollo. James R. Hansen. (NASA History & NASA SP Ser.). 1995. write for info. (0-615-00262-5) NASA Info.

Spacelab: An International Success Story, 2 vols., Set. 1994. lib. bdg. 600.75 (0-8490-6401-5) Gordon Pr.

Spacelab: Research in Earth Orbit. David Shapland & Michael J. Rycroft. LC 84-17456. (Illus.). 192p. 1984. 39.95 (0-521-26077-9) Cambridge U Pr.

Spacelab, Space Platforms & the Future. Ed. by Peter M. Bainum & Dietrich E. Koelle. LC 57-43769. (Advances in the Astronautical Sciences Ser.: Vol. 49). (Illus.). 502p. (Orig.). 1982. pap. text ed. 45.00 (0-87703-175-4); lib. bdg. 55.00 (0-87703-174-6); suppl. ed. 15.00 incl. fiche (0-87703-181-9) Univelt Inc.

Spacelab to Space Station. Napolit. (Earth Oriented Applications of Space Technology). 1985. pap. 73.00 (0-08-032539-4, Pergamon Pr) Elsevier.

Spacelab 2 Mission. G. Fazio. 96p. 1990. pap. text ed. 119.00 (2-88124-328-2) Gordon & Breach.

Spaceman. Jane Cutler. LC 96-46224. 1997. pap. 14.99 (0-525-45636-8) NAL-Dutton.

Spaceman. Jane Cutler. Date not set. pap. write for info. (0-14-038150-3) Viking Penguin.

*Spacemind. Dana M. Taylor, Jr. 327p. (Orig.). 1997. mass mkt. 4.99 (1-55197-955-1, Pub. by Comnwlth Pub CN) Partners Pubs Grp.

Spacepaw. Gordon R. Dickson. 224p. 1988. pap. 3.50 (0-8125-3542-1) Tor Bks.

SpacePlaceGuide: An Introduction to Spatial Directions & Their Symbology. Ed. & Illus. by G. W. Gorchoff. (YA). 1995. pap. text ed. 65.00 incl. mac hd (1-878084-06-2) Danscores.

An Asterisk (*) at the beginning of an entry indicates that the title is appearing in BIP for the first time.

SpacePlaceGuide, Version 2.0: Notation Man's Unique Introduction to Labenotation. rev. ed. G. W. Gorchoff. (Illus.). 12p. 1996. pap. text ed. 75.00 incl. mac hd (*1-878084-07-0*) Danscores.

Spacer Dreams. Larry Segriff. 256p. 1995. mass mkt. 5.99 (*0-671-87696-1*, Baen Books) Baen Bks.

***Spaces.** Karla Margaret, pseud. (Illus.). 80p. 1972. pap. write for info. (*0-935430-04-0*) In Between.

Spaces. Peter Parnall. LC 92-1712. (Illus.). 32p. (J). (gr. k-3). 1993. lib. bdg. 16.40 (*1-56294-336-7*) Millbrook Pr.

***Spaces: Solving Problems of Access to Careers in Engineering & Science.** Rudolf Steiner. LC 16-95. (J). (gr. 4-10). 1997. pap. text ed. 10.00 (*0-86651-147-4*) Seymour Pubns.

Spaces - Hallwalls: An Artists' Exchange. Catherine Howe & Susan R. Channing. (Illus.). 32p. (Orig.). 1987. pap. write for info. (*0-936739-08-8*) Hallwalls Inc.

Spaces & Significations. Ed. by Roberta Kevelson. (Critic of Institutions Ser.: Vol. 10). 248p. (C). 1996. text ed. 55.95 (*0-8204-3017-X*) P Lang Pubng.

Spaces Between Birds: Mother - Daughter Poems, 1967-1995. Sandra McPherson. LC 95-39746. (Wesleyan Poetry Ser.). 75p. 1996. pap. 11.95 (*0-8195-2228-7*, Wesleyan Univ Pr) U Pr of New Eng.

Spaces for Children: Learning-Play Structures for Home & School. Peter A. Bergson. (Illus.). 55p. (Orig.). 1984. pap. 8.00 (*0-9606434-1-9*) Open Connections.

Spaces for Children: The Built Environment & Child Development. Ed. by Thomas G. David & Carol S. Weinstein. 318p. 1987. 54.50 (*0-306-42423-1*, Plenum Pr) Plenum.

Spaces in Her Day: Australian Women's Diaries, 1920s & 1930s. Katie Holmes. 216p. 1996. pap. 24.95 (*1-86373-731-6*, Pub. by Allen & Unwin Aust Pty AT) Paul & Co Pubs.

Spaces in the Light Said to Be Where One Comes From. Stephen Ratcliffe. 88p. (Orig.). 1993. pap. 9.50 (*0-937013-42-0*) Potes Poets.

***Spaces Like Stairs.** Gail Scott. 144p. pap. 9.95 (*0-88961-131-9*, Pub. by Wmns Pr CN) LPC InBook.

***Spaces of a Life.** Ricardo Bofill & Jean Andre. 192p. 1998. pap. 14.95 (*0-06-430213-X*, Icon Edns) HarpC.

Spaces of Approximating Functions with Haar-Like Conditions. Kazuaki Kitahara. LC 94-16024. (Lecture Notes in Mathematics Ser.: No. 1576). 1994. 29.95 (*0-387-57974-5*) Spr-Verlag.

Spaces of Constant Curvature. 5th ed. Joseph A. Wolf. LC 83-6351. 412p. 1984. text ed. 50.00 (*0-914098-07-1*) Publish or Perish.

***Spaces of Homotopy Self-Equivalences: A Survey, Vol. 166.** John W. Rutter. LC 97-24992. (Lecture Notes in Mathematics Ser.). 1997. write for info. (*3-540-63103-8*) Spr-Verlag.

Spaces of Identity: Global Media, Electronic Landscapes & Cultural Boundaries. David Morley & Kevin Robins. LC 94-42068. (International Library of Sociology). 264p. (C). 1995. pap. 17.95 (*0-415-09597-2*); text ed. 59.95 (*0-415-09596-4*) Routledge.

Spaces of Measures. Corneliu Constantinescu. LC 84-5815. (Studies in Mathematics: Vol. 4). 444p. 1984. 99.95 (*3-11-008784-7*) De Gruyter.

***Spaces of Orderings & Abstract Real Spectra, Vol. 163.** Murry Marshall. LC 96-35288. (Lecture Notes in Mathematics Ser.). 1996. pap. 35.00 (*3-540-61729-9*) Spr-Verlag.

Spaces of the Living & the Dead. Ed. by Catherine E. Karkov et al. (American Early Medieval Studies: No. 3). (Illus.). (Orig.). 1997. pap. 27.00 (*1-879836-01-7*) Am Erly Medieval.

Spaces of Vector-Valued Continuous Functions. J. Schmets. (Lecture Notes in Mathematics Ser.: Vol. 1003). 117p. 1983. 29.95 (*0-387-12327-X*) Spr-Verlag.

Spaces Wild & Tame. Richard Grossinger. (Illus.). 144p. (Orig.). 6.00 (*0-685-22801-0*); pap. 3.50 (*0-685-22802-9*) Mudra.

Spaces Wild & Tame. deluxe ed. Richard Grossinger. (Illus.). 144p. (Orig.). boxed 15.00 (*0-685-22800-2*) Mudra.

Spaces with Distinguished Geodiscs. Busemann & Bhalchandra. (Pure & Applied Mathematics Ser.: Vol. 108). 176p. 1987. 115.00 (*0-8247-7545-7*) Dekker.

Spaces with Non-Symmetric Distance. E. M. Zaustinsky. LC 52-42839. (Memoirs Ser.: No. 1/34). 91p. 1990. reprint ed. pap. 16.00 (*0-8218-1234-3*, MEMO/1/34) Am Math.

Spaces, Worlds, & Grammar. Gilles Fauconnier & Eve Sweetser. LC 96-12878. (Cognitive Theory of Language & Culture Ser.). (Illus.). 320p. 1996. pap. text ed. 24.95 (*0-226-23924-1*) U Ch Pr.

Spaces, Worlds, & Grammar. Ed. by Gilles Fauconnier & Eve Sweetser. (Cognitive Theory of Language & Culture Ser.). (Illus.). 320p. 1996. lib. bdg. 65.00 (*0-226-23923-3*) U Ch Pr.

***Spaceship.** (Illus.). 60p. (J). (ps-2). 1997. pap. 4.95 (*0-9656811-1-4*) Four Seasons.

***Spaceship Earth.** Adam Ford. (J). Date not set. write for info. (*0-688-00734-1*) Lothrop.

Spaceship Earth. Barbara Ward. LC 66-18062. (George B. Pegram Lectures). 156p. 1968. pap. text ed. 17.50 (*0-231-08586-9*) Col U Pr.

Spaceship Neutrino. Christine Sutton. (Illus.). 270p. (C). 1992. text ed. 85.00 (*0-521-36404-3*); pap. text ed. 30.95 (*0-521-36703-4*) Cambridge U Pr.

Spaceships in Pre-History. Peter Kolosimo. (Illus.). 380p. 1982. pap. text ed. 7.95 (*0-8065-0731-4*, Citadel Pr) Carol Pub Group.

Spaceships of the Pleiades: The Billy Meier Story. Kal K. Korff. LC 94-46992. (Illus.). 550p. 1995. 25.95 (*0-87975-959-3*) Prometheus Bks.

Space...the Final Exam. Terry Moss. (Final Exam Ser.). (Illus.). 68p. (Orig.). 1997. pap. 5.49 (*1-885962-60-6*) Lincoln Lrning.

Spacetime. Jeremy Butterfield et al. (International Research Library of Philosophy). (Illus.). 500p. 1996. text ed. 127.95 (*1-85521-640-X*, Pub. by Dartmth Pub UK) Ashgate Pub Co.

SpaceTime: Science-Fiction Roleplaying in a Future That's Too Close for Comfort. Greg Porter. (Illus.). 128p. (Orig.). 1988. pap. 14.95 (*0-943891-03-5*) Blacksburg Tactical.

Spacetime & Electromagnetism. John R. Lucas & P. E. Hodgson. 328p. 1990. pap. 35.00 (*0-19-852038-7*) OUP.

Spacetime & Singularities: An Introduction. Gregory L. Naber. (London Mathematical Society Student Texts Ser.: No. 10). (Illus.). 176p. 1989. pap. text ed. 23.95 (*0-521-33612-0*) Cambridge U Pr.

Spacetime Without Reference Frames. Tamas Matolcsi. (Illus.). 411p. (C). 1993. text ed. 50.00 (*963-05-6433-5*, Pub. by A K HU) Intl Spec Bk.

Spaceward Ho! A Game of Stellar Conquest: Official Secrets & Solutions. John Withers. 1995. pap. text ed. 12.95 (*0-7615-0222-X*) Prima Pub.

Spacey Riddles. Katy Hall & Lisa Eisenberg. LC 90-42508. (Illus.). 48p. (J). (ps-3). 1992. pap. 10.89 (*0-8037-0815-7*) Dial Bks Young.

Spacey Riddles. Katy Hall et al. (Easy-to-Read Ser.: Level 3, Yellow). (Illus.). (J). (gr. 1-4). 1995. pap. 3.50 (*0-14-037385-3*) Puffin Bks.

***Spach. Descendants of Adam Spach: Autobiography & Memoirs of Adam Spach & His Wife.** A. L. Fries. 202p. 1996. reprint ed. pap. 37.00 (*0-8328-5238-4*); reprint ed. lib. bdg. 47.00 (*0-8328-5237-6*) Higginson Bk Co.

Spacialist. Michael Blitz. 50p. 1986. 12.50 (*0-916258-15-7*); pap. 7.50 (*0-916258-16-5*) Woodbine Pr.

Spacing of Planets: The Solution to a 400-Year Mystery - The New Fourth Law of Planetary Motion. limited ed. Alexander A. Scarborough. (Energy Crisis Ser.). (Illus.). 128p. (Orig.). 1996. pap. 19.95 (*0-930258-03-7*) Ander Pubns.

Spacings--of Reason & Imagination in Texts of Kant, Fichte, Hegel. John Sallis. LC 86-11417. 192p. (C). 1987. pap. text ed. 21.00 (*0-226-73441-2*) U Ch Pr.

Spacion. Evan Adar. LC 85-51325. 226p. 1986. 18.95 (*0-912159-03-0*) Center Pr CA.

Spacious Body: Explorations in Somatic Ontology. Jeffrey Maitland. LC 95-8725. 1995. pap. write for info. (*1-55643-188-0*) North Atlantic.

***Spacious Days.** Michael F. Twist. (Illus.). 192p. 1992. pap. 12.95 (*0-85236-241-2*, Pub. by Farming Pr UK) Diamond Farm Bk.

Spacious Dreams: The First Wave of Asian Immigration. Ronald Takaki. (Asian American Experience Ser.). (Illus.). (YA). (gr. 5 up). 1994. lib. bdg. 19.95 (*0-7910-2176-9*) Chelsea Hse.

***Spacious Heart: Essays on Identity & Belonging.** Judith M. Gundry-Volf & Miroslav Volf. LC 97-12709. (Christian Mission & Modern Culture Ser.). 80p. (Orig.). 1997. pap. 8.00 (*1-56338-201-6*) TPI PA.

Spacks Street: New & Selected Poems. Barry Spacks. LC 82-15377. (Johns Hopkins Poetry & Fiction Ser.). 128p. 1982. pap. 9.95 (*0-8018-2892-9*); text ed. 14.95 (*0-8018-2890-2*) Johns Hopkins.

Spadacrene Anglica: Or, the English Spaw-Fountaine in Yorkshire. Edmund Deane. LC 74-80172. (English Experience Ser.: No. 651). 32p. 1974. reprint ed. 15.00 (*90-221-0651-9*) Walter J Johnson.

Spadafore Diagnostic Reading Test Manual. Gerald J. Spadafore. 80p. 1983. pap. 15.00 (*0-87879-342-9*); teacher ed. 15.00 (*0-87879-344-5*); 22.00 (*0-87879-343-7*) Acad Therapy.

Spade Fresh with Mud. Nicholas Hagger. 1995. pap. 40.00 (*1-85230-637-8*) Element MA.

Spade Series: Introduction to Duplicate Bridge. Audrey Grant. 1994. pap. 11.95 (*0-943855-09-8*) Amer Contrct Brdg Lge.

Spadework: A Collection of "Nameless Detective" Stories. Bill Pronzini. 248p. (Orig.). 1996. pap. 16.00 (*1-885941-07-2*) Crippen & Landru.

Spadework: A Collection of "Nameless Detective" Stories. deluxe limited ed. Bill Pronzini. 248p. (Orig.). 1996. 40.00 (*1-885941-06-4*) Crippen & Landru.

Spaetantike Bildschmuck des Konstantinsbogen: Text Vol. & Vol. with Plates. Hans P. L'Orange & Arnim Von Gerkan. (Studien zur Spaetantiken Kunstgeschichte: Vol. 10). (Illus.). 238p. (C). 1978. reprint ed. 542.35 (*3-11-002249-4*) De Gruyter.

Spaetantike Kaiserportraits. Richard Delbrueck. (Studien zur Spaetantiken Kunstgeschichte: Vol. 8). (Illus.). xx, 252p. (C). 1978. reprint ed. 365.40 (*3-11-005700-X*) De Gruyter.

Spaetarchaische Tempel der Aphaia auf Aegina. Hansgeorg Bankel. (Denkmaeler Antiker Architektur Ser.: Bd 19). (Illus.). xi, 180p. (GER.). (C). 1993. lib. bdg. 229.25 (*3-11-012808-X*) De Gruyter.

Spaetbronzezeitliche Seevoelkersturm: Ein Forschungsueberblick mit Folgerungen zur biblischen Exodusthematik. August Strobel. (Beiheft 145 zur Zeitschrift fuer die Alttestamentliche Wissenschaft Ser.). (C). 1976. 123.10 (*3-11-006761-7*) De Gruyter.

Spaete 18, Jahrhundert - das Zeitalter der Romantik see Geschichte der Literaturkritik 1750-1950

Spaete 19, Jahrhundert see Geschichte der Literaturkritik 1750-1950

Spaffords 1824 Guide for New York Travelers. G. Martin Sleeman. 104p. 1991. pap. 9.95 (*0-932052-62-2*) North Country.

SPAG: Standard Products Application Guide. 1984. 50.00 (*0-318-01729-6*) Milford Null.

Spaghetti, Again? Jean W. Bodman. 1988. audio 17.95 (*0-8384-3344-8*) Heinle & Heinle.

***Spaghetti & Meatballs.** Marilyn Burns. LC 96-36082. (Illus.). (J). 1997. 15.95 (*0-590-94459-2*) Scholastic Inc.

Spaghetti Breath. Page McBrier. (Treehouse Times Ser.: No. 3). 128p. (J). (gr. 4). 1989. pap. 2.50 (*0-380-75782-6*, Camelot) Avon.

Spaghetti Forever. Jean W. Bodman. 1988. pap. 18.95 (*0-8384-3351-0*) Heinle & Heinle.

Spaghetti Nightmares: Italian Fantasy-Horror As Seen Through the Eyes of Their Protagonists. Luca Palmerini & Gaetano Mistretta. Ed. by Margot Winick. LC 95-61740. (Illus.). 194p. 1996. pap. 25.95 (*0-9634982-7-4*) Fantasma Bks.

Spaghetti Party. Doris Orgel. LC 94-9788. (Bank Street Ready-to-Read Ser.). (J). 1995. 12.95 (*0-553-09052-6*); pap. 3.99 (*0-553-37571-7*) Bantam.

Spaghetti Westerns - the Good, the Bad & the Violent: A Comprehensive, Illustrated Filmography of 558 Eurowesterns & Their Personnel, 1961-1977. Thomas Weisser. LC 92-50002. (Illus.). 498p. 1992. lib. bdg. 49.95 (*0-89950-688-7*) McFarland & Co.

Spagnolo Senza Sforzo. Albert O. Cherel. 24.95 (*0-685-11571-2*); Three cassettes. audio 125.00 (*0-685-01765-6*) Fr & Eur.

Spago Desserts. Judith Gethers. 1994. 29.95 (*0-679-42248-X*) Random.

Spain. (Panorama Bks.). (Illus.). (FRE.). 3.95 (*0-685-11572-0*) Fr & Eur.

Spain. (Illus.). 64p. pap. 6.95 (*0-8442-7636-7*, Natl Textbk) NTC Pub Grp.

Spain. (Getting to Know Ser.). 48p. (J). 1994. 8.95 (*0-8442-7627-8*, Natl Textbk) NTC Pub Grp.

Spain. 1988. 5.95 (*0-671-84878-X*) PB.

Spain. (Eyewitness Travel Guides Ser.). 672p. 1996. pap. 29.95 (*0-7894-1068-0*) DK Pub Inc.

Spain. 1996. pap. 15.00 (*0-614-12783-1*) Fodors Travel.

Spain. Helen Arnold. LC 95-10300. (Postcards from Ser.). (J). 1995. lib. bdg. 21.40 (*0-8172-4009-8*) Raintree Steck-V.

Spain. Donna Bailey. LC 91-23716. (Where We Live Ser.). (Illus.). 32p. (J). (gr. 1-4). 1992. pap. 3.95 (*0-8114-7186-1*); lib. bdg. 21.40 (*0-8114-2569-X*) Raintree Steck-V.

Spain. Berlitz Editors. (Berlitz Pocket Guide Ser.). (Illus.). 192p. 1996. pap. (*2-8315-5104-8*) Berlitz.

***Spain.** Clare Boast. LC 97-16744. (Next Stop! Ser.). (J). 1997. write for info. (*1-57572-570-3*) Rigby Interact Libr.

Spain. Fabio Bourbon. (Illus.). 128p. 1992. 12.98 (*0-8317-7962-4*) Smithmark.

Spain. Ed. by Tom Burns. (Everything under the Sun Ser.). 496p. 1995. pap. 12.95 (*0-8442-9210-9*, Passport Bks) NTC Pub Grp.

Spain. Daphne Butler. LC 92-17032. (On the Map Ser.). (Illus.). 32p. (J). (gr. 3-4). 1992. lib. bdg. 22.83 (*0-8114-3678-0*) Raintree Steck-V.

Spain. Catherine Chambers & Rachel Wright. LC 92-27137. (Country Topics Ser.). 32p. (J). 1993. lib. bdg. 18.60 (*0-531-14257-4*) Watts.

Spain. Catherine Chambers & Rachel Wright. (Country Topics for Craft Projects Ser.). (Illus.). 32p. (J). (gr. 5-8). 1995. pap. 5.95 (*0-531-15279-0*) Watts.

Spain. Wilbur Cross & Esther Cross. LC 85-16588. (Enchantment of the World Ser.). 128p. (J). (gr. 5-9). 1985. lib. bdg. 30.00 (*0-516-02786-7*) Childrens.

Spain. G. W. Edwards. 1972. 59.95 (*0-8490-1095-0*) Gordon Pr.

Spain. J. Harrison. 1976. lib. bdg. 59.95 (*0-8490-2635-0*) Gordon Pr.

Spain. Philippa Leahy. LC 93-2663. (Discovering Our Universe Ser.). (Illus.). 32p. (J). (gr. 5). 1993. lib. bdg. 13.95 (*0-89686-772-2*, Crstwood Hse) Silver Burdett Pr.

Spain. Romulus Linney. 1994. pap. 5.25 (*0-8222-1376-1*) Dramatists Play.

Spain. Arthur Miller. (Places & Peoples of the World Ser.). (Illus.). 112p. (J). (gr. 5 up). 1989. lib. bdg. 16.95 (*1-55546-795-4*) Chelsea Hse.

***Spain.** John Noble et al. (Illus.). 800p. 1997. pap. 19.95 (*0-86442-474-4*) Lonely Planet.

Spain. Anna Selby. LC 93-28438. (Country Fact Files Ser.). (J). 1993. lib. bdg. 24.26 (*0-8114-1848-0*) Raintree Steck-V.

Spain. R. Tyler. 1976. lib. bdg. 134.95 (*0-8490-2636-9*) Gordon Pr.

Spain. David Wright & Jill Wright. (Focus On Ser.). (Illus.). 32p. (J). (gr. 4-6). 1991. 19.95 (*0-237-51659-4*, Pub. by Evans Bros Ltd UK) Trafalgar.

Spain. 2nd ed. William Chislett. (Illus.). 209p. 1995. 170.00 (*1-85564-174-7*, Pub. by Euromoney UK) Am Educ Systs.

Spain. 2nd ed. Compiled by Graham J. Shields. (World Bibliographical Ser.: Vol. 60). 448p. 1994. lib. bdg. 97.00 (*1-85109-220-X*) ABC-CLIO.

Spain. 4th ed. Dana Facaros. (Cadogan Country Guides Ser.). 1996. pap. text ed. 24.95 (*1-86011-036-3*, Pub. by Cadogan Bks UK) Globe Pequot.

Spain. 16th ed. Frommer Staff. (Frommer's Travel Guides Ser.). 1994. 16.95 (*0-02-860053-3*) Macmillan.

Spain, 2 vols., Set. A. Calvert. 1976. lib. bdg. 500.00 (*0-8490-2634-2*) Gordon Pr.

Spain: A Companion to Spanish Studies. Ed. by P. E. Russell. (Illus.). 608p. 1983. pap. 25.00 (*0-416-84110-4*, NO. 3908) Routledge Chapman & Hall.

Spain: A Hugo Phrase Book. (Hugo's Language Courses Ser.: No. 567). 96p. 1970. pap. 4.00 (*0-8226-0567-8*) Littlefield.

Spain: A Land Blighted by Religion. Joseph Lewis. (Illus.). 96p. (C). reprint ed. write for info. (*0-318-70299-1*) Hakims Pubs.

Spain: A Land Blighted by Religion. Joseph Lewis. (Illus.). 96p. (C). 1993. reprint ed. pap. 5.95 (*0-317-05574-7*) Hakims Pubs.

Spain: A Literary Companion. Jimmy Burns. (Illus.). 256p. 1995. 34.95 (*0-7195-5098-X*); pap. 24.95 (*0-7195-5216-8*) Trafalgar.

Spain: An Interpretation. Angel Ganivet. LC 75-41109. 1976. reprint ed. 31.50 (*0-404-14755-0*) AMS Pr.

Spain: Converging with the European Community. Michel Galy et al. (Occasional Paper Ser.: No. 101). 58p. 1993. 15.00 (*1-55775-319-9*) Intl Monetary.

Spain: Costa Brava. (Visitor's Guides Ser.). (Illus.). 256p. (Orig.). 1991. pap. 13.95 (*1-55650-470-5*) Hunter NJ.

Spain: Democracy Regained. 2nd ed. Ramon E. Arango. (Nations of the Modern World Ser.). (C). 1996. pap. text ed. 24.00 (*0-8133-2915-9*) Westview.

Spain: Dictatorship to Democracy. 2nd ed. Raymond Carr & Juan P. Fusi. 304p. (C). 1981. pap. text ed. 16.95 (*0-04-946014-5*) Routledge Chapman & Hall.

Spain: Directory & Sourcebook. 1993. 390.00 (*0-86338-437-4*, 073011, Pub. by Euromonitor Pubns UK) Gale.

Spain: Eighteen Hundred Eight to Nineteen Seventy-Five. 2nd ed. Raymond Carr. (Oxford History of Modern Europe Ser.). 886p. 1982. pap. 35.00 (*0-19-822128-2*) OUP.

S

Spain: European Market for the 1990s. Euromonitor Staff. 175p. 1987. 675.00 (*0-86338-224-X*, Pub. by Euromonitor Pubns UK) Gale.

Spain: Explorers & Conquerors. Richard Sanchez. LC 94-17409. (Hispanic Heritage Ser.: Vol. 2). (J). (gr. 4-8). 1994. lib. bdg. 15.98 (*1-56239-332-4*) Abdo & Dghtrs.

***Spain: Gateway to Europe.** 2nd ed. Geraldine Woods. LC 96-36996. (Discovering Our Heritage Ser.). 1998. lib. bdg. write for info. (*0-382-39767-3*, Dillon Silver Burdett) Silver Burdett Pr.

Spain: Off the Beaten Track. Barbara Mandell & Roger Penn. LC 93-10704. (Illus.). 315p. (Orig.). 1993. pap. 14.95 (*1-56440-296-7*, Pub. by Moorland Pubng UK) Globe Pequot.

***Spain: Recent Economic Developments.** Jeffrey R. Franks. (IMF Staff Country Report Ser.: Vol. 96/56). 80p. pap. 25.00 (*0-608-04871-2*, 2065530) Bks Demand.

***Spain: Selected Issues: Labor Market Policies & Unemployment Dynamics.** Jeffrey R. Franks. (IMF Staff Country Report Ser.: Vol. 96/57). 46p. pap. 25.00 (*0-608-04872-0*, 2065531) Bks Demand.

Spain: Studies in Political Security. Ed. by Joyce Lasky Schub & Raymond Carr. LC 85-16948. (Washington Papers: No. 117). 125p. 1985. text ed. 49.95 (*0-275-90192-0*, C0192, Praeger Pubs) Greenwood.

Spain: The Root & the Flower: An Interpretation of Spain, the Spanish People. John A. Crow. LC 84-8652. 1985. pap. 14.95 (*0-520-05133-5*) U CA Pr.

Spain: The Root & the Flower: An Interpretation of Spain, the Spanish People. 3rd ed. John A. Crow. LC 84-8652. 1985. 55.00 (*0-520-05123-8*) U CA Pr.

Spain: Tragedy & Truth. Rudolf Rocker. 1972. 250.00 (*0-8490-1098-5*) Gordon Pr.

Spain: World in View. Nicholas Caistor. (J). 1992. lib. bdg. 25.68 (*0-8114-2450-2*) Raintree Steck-V.

Spain see Cultures of the World - Group 4

Spain after Franco. Juan Kattan-Ibarra & Tim Connell. 192p. (C). 1988. 70.00 (*0-85950-152-3*, Pub. by S Thornes Pubs UK) St Mut.

Spain after Franco: The Making of a Competitive Party System. Richard Gunther et al. LC 84-16172. 416p. 1985. pap. 18.00 (*0-520-06336-8*) U CA Pr.

Spain Again. Alvah Bessie. LC 74-28742. (Illus.). 242p. 1975. pap. 5.95 (*0-88316-516-3*) Chandler & Sharp.

Spain & Africa. Archer M. Huntington. 1943. 6.00 (*0-87535-054-2*) Hispanic Soc.

Spain & Central America: Democracy & Foreign Policy. Robin L. Rosenberg. LC 91-824. (Contributions in Political Science Ser.: No. 288). 280p. 1992. text ed. 55.00 (*0-313-27885-7*, RSJ, Greenwood Pr) Greenwood.

Spain & EC Membership Evaluated. Ed. by Maria A. Barbado. LC 93-21485. (EC Membership Evaluated Ser.). 1993. text ed. 55.00 (*0-312-10367-0*) St Martin.

Spain & Her People. J. Zimmerman. 1976. lib. bdg. 75.00 (*0-8490-2637-7*) Gordon Pr.

Spain & Her Rivals on the Gulf Coast. (Gulf Coast History & Humanities Conference Publications Ser.). 1971. 15.00 (*0-940836-02-5*); pap. 10.00 (*0-940836-03-3*) U of W Fla.

Spain & Its World: Selected Essays. J. H. Elliott. 316p. (C). 1990. reprint ed. 17.00 (*0-300-04863-7*) Yale U Pr.

Spain & Portugal. Graeme M. Adam. 1976. lib. bdg. 59.95 (*0-8490-2638-5*) Gordon Pr.

***Spain & Portugal.** St. Martin's Press Staff. (Let's Go Ser.). 1997. pap. 18.99 (*0-312-15749-5*) St Martin.

Spain & Portugal, 2 vols., Set. Graeme M. Adam. 1980. lib. bdg. 199.00 (*0-8490-3183-4*) Gordon Pr.

Spain & Portugal see Encyclopedia of World Geography

Spain & Portugal Atlas. Michelin Staff. 1993. spiral bd. 39.95 (*0-7859-9148-4*) Fr & Eur.

Spain & Portugal by Rail. Norman P. Renouf. (Bradt Rail Guides Ser.). (Illus.). 208p. 1994. pap. 15.95 (*1-56440-553-2*, Pub. by Bradt Pubns UK) Globe Pequot.

Spain & Portugal in the New World, 1492-1700. Lyle N. McAlister. LC 83-21745. (Europe & the World in the Age of Expansion Ser.: Vol. 3). (Illus.). 612p. 1984. pap. text ed. 19.95 (*0-8166-1218-8*) U of Minn Pr.

***Spain & Portugal Map.** 1997. 10.95 (*2-06-700990-7*, 990) Michelin.

Spain & Portugal Road Atlas. Michelin Staff. (FRE.). spiral bd., pap. 9.95 (*0-7859-7258-7*) Fr & Eur.

Spain & the Early Stuarts, 1585-1655. Albert J. Loomie. (Variorum Collected Studies: Vol. CS522). 304p. 1996. 84.95 (*0-86078-576-9*, Pub. by Variorum UK) Ashgate Pub Co.

Spain & the Great Powers, Nineteen Thirty-Six to Nineteen Forty-One. Dante A. Puzzo. LC 72-3101. (Select Bibliographies Reprint Ser.). 1980. reprint ed. 23.95 (*0-8369-6868-9*) Ayer.

Spain & the Loss of America. Timothy E. Anna. LC 82-11118. 367p. reprint ed. pap. 104.60 (*0-8357-2918-4*, 2039158) Bks Demand.

Spain & the Mediterranean. Ed. by Benjamin F. Taggie et al. (Mediterranean Studies). 153p. 1992. 35.00 (*0-943549-14-0*) TJU Pr.

Spain & the Plains: Myths & Realities of Spanish Exploration & Settlement on the Great Plains. Ed. by Ralph H. Vigil et al. (Illus.). 192p. 1994. 29.95 (*0-87081-352-8*) Univ Pr Colo.

Spain & the Roanoke Voyages. Paul E. Hoffman. (America's 400th Anniversary Ser.). (Illus.). xiii, 74p. (Orig.). 1987. pap. 5.00 (*0-86526-209-8*) NC Archives.

Spain & the Spaniards, 2 vols. Edmondo De Amicis. 1976. lib. bdg. 250.00 (*0-8490-2639-3*) Gordon Pr.

Spain & the Spanish. Wardell Villiers. 1976. lib. bdg. 59.95 (*0-8490-2640-7*) Gordon Pr.

Spain & the Tragic Week in May. A. Souchy. 1972. 250.00 (*0-8490-1096-9*) Gordon Pr.

Spain & the United States: Since World War II. Richard R. Rubottom & J. C. Murphy. LC 83-19247. 176p. 1984. text ed. 45.00 (*0-275-91259-0*, C1259, Praeger Pubs) Greenwood.

Spain & the Western Tradition: The Castilian Mind in Literature from "El Cid" to Calderon, Vol. 1. Otis H. Green. 1969. pap. 9.95 (*0-299-02954-9*) U of Wis Pr.

Spain & the Western Tradition: The Castilian Mind in Literature from El Cid to Calderon, 2 vols., Vol. 2. Otis H. Green. LC 63-13745. 373p. pap. 97.00 (*0-8357-6773-6*, 2035450) Bks Demand.

Spain & the Western Tradition: The Castilian Mind in Literature from "El Cid" to Calderon, Vol. 3. Otis H. Green. 1969. pap. 9.95 (*0-299-03794-0*) U of Wis Pr.

Spain & the Western Tradition: The Castilian Mind in Literature from El Cid to Calderon, 2 vols., Vol. 4. Otis H. Green. LC 63-13745. 357p. pap. 101.80 (*0-8357-6774-4*) Bks Demand.

Spain & the Western Tradition: The Castilian Mind in Literature from "El Cid" to Calderon, Vols. 1-4. Otis H. Green. write for info. (*0-318-56178-6*) U of Wis Pr.

Spain at Its Best. Robert S. Kane. (World at Its Best Travel Ser.). 352p. 1994. pap. 12.95 (*0-8442-9577-9*, Passport Bks) NTC Pub Grp.

Spain at Its Best. 3rd ed. Robert S. Kane. 348p. 1995. pap. 12.95 (*0-8442-9570-1*, Passport Bks) NTC Pub Grp.

Spain at the Dawn of History: Iberians, Phoenicians, & Greeks. Richard J. Harrison. LC 88-51688. (Ancient Peoples & Places Ser.). (Illus.). 176p. 1988. 27.50 (*0-500-02111-2*) Thames Hudson.

Spain at the Polls, Nineteen Seventy-Seven, Nineteen Seventy-Nine & Nineteen Eighty-Two: A Study of the National Elections. Ed. by Howard R. Penniman & Eusebio M. Mujal-Leon. LC 85-20523. (Illus.). 392p. reprint ed. pap. 111.80 (*0-8357-4536-8*, 2037417) Bks Demand.

Spain at the Polls, 1977, 1979, & 1982: A Study of the National Elections. Ed. by Howard R. Penniman & Eusebio M. Mujal-Leon. LC 85-20523. (At the Polls Ser.). xviii, 372p. 1985. text ed. 52.95 (*0-8223-0663-8*) Duke.

Spain at the Polls, 1977, 1979, & 1982: A Study of the National Elections. Ed. by Howard R. Penniman & Eusebio M. Mujal-Leon. LC 85-20523. (At the Polls Ser.). xviii, 372p. 1985. pap. text ed. 21.95 (*0-8223-0695-6*) Duke.

Spain at War: The Spanish Civil War in Historical Perspective. George Esenwein & Adrian Schubert. LC 94-22117. 296p. (C). 1995. pap. text ed. 25.50 (*0-582-55272-9*) Longman.

Spain: Bridge Between Continents see Exploring Cultures of the World: Group 4

Spain Discover Guide. Berlitz Editors. (Discover Guides Ser.). (Illus.). 352p. 1994. pap. 18.95 (*2-8315-0681-6*) Berlitz.

Spain, EEC & NATO. Paul Preston. 1985. pap. 10.95 (*0-7100-9559-7*, RKP) Routledge.

Spain, Espagne, Spanien: Foreign Artists Discover Spain 1800-1900. Suzanne L. Stratton. (Illus.). 144p. 1994. pap. 30.00 (*0-295-97354-4*) U of Wash Pr.

Spain, Europe & the Atlantic World: Essays in Honour of John H. Elliott. Ed. by Richard L. Kagan & Geoffrey Parker. (Illus.). 300p. (C). 1995. text ed. 49.95 (*0-521-47045-5*) Cambridge U Pr.

Spain, Europe, & the "Spanish Miracle", 1700-1900. David R. Ringrose. (Illus.). 455p. (C). 1996. text ed. 64.95 (*0-521-43486-6*) Cambridge U Pr.

Spain, Fourteen Sixty-Nine to Seventeen Fourteen: A Society of Conflict. 2nd ed. Henry Kamen. 320p. (C). 1991. pap. text ed. 27.50 (*0-582-06723-5*, 78826) Longman.

Spain from the South. John B. Trend. 1976. lib. bdg. 34.95 (*0-8490-2641-5*) Gordon Pr.

Spain from the South. John B. Trend. 304p. (C). 1988. 200.00 (*0-685-67675-7*, Pub. by Darf Pubs Ltd UK) St Mut.

Spain from the South. John B. Trend. (C). 1990. text ed. 110.00 (*0-685-65764-7*, Pub. by Darf Pubs Ltd UK) St Mut.

Spain Green Guide. Michelin Staff. 1993. pap. 19.95 (*0-7859-9149-2*) Fr & Eur.

Spain Green Guide. Ed. by Michelin Travel Publications, Staff. (JPN.). 1996. per. 36.00 (*4-408-01310-2*, 9526) Michelin.

Spain Green Guide. 2nd ed. Ed. by Michelin Travel Publications, Staff. 1996. per. 20.00 (*2-06-152302-1*, 1523) Michelin.

Spain Green Guide English Edition. Michelin Staff. pap. 17.95 (*0-7859-7193-9*, 2061523013) Fr & Eur.

Spain Guide. Ron Charles. Ed. by J. Stein. LC 95-70242. (Illus.). 592p. (Orig.). 1996. pap. 16.95 (*1-883323-22-3*) Open Rd Pub.

Spain (Hotel & Restaurant Guide) 1996. Michelin Staff. 1996. 24.95 (*0-7859-9904-3*) Fr & Eur.

Spain in America. Charles Gibson. (New American Nation Ser.). 1967. pap. text ed. 13.00 (*0-06-133077-9*, TB3077, Torch) HarpC.

Spain in America. Edward G. Bourne. (Works of Edward Gaylord Bourne). 1989. reprint ed. lib. bdg. 79.00 (*0-7812-2012-2*) Rprt Serv.

Spain in Pictures. Ed. by Lerner Geography Department Staff. (Visual Geography Ser.). (Illus.). 64p. (YA). (gr. 5 up). 1995. lib. bdg. 19.95 (*0-8225-1887-2*, Lerner Publctns) Lerner Group.

Spain in Revolt. H. Gannes. 1972. 59.95 (*0-8490-1097-7*) Gordon Pr.

Spain in Revolt, 1814-1931. Joseph McCabe. 1976. lib. bdg. 59.95 (*0-8490-2642-3*) Gordon Pr.

***Spain in the Age of Exploration.** Heather Millar. LC 97-2090. (Cultures of the Past Ser.). 1999. lib. bdg. write for info. (*0-7614-0303-5*, Benchmark NY) Marshall Cavendish.

***Spain in the Heart.** Pablo Neruda. 1997. pap. text ed. 12.95 (*1-885214-14-6*) Azul Edits.

Spain in the Heart: Hymn to the Glories of the People at War. Pablo Neruda. Tr. by Richard Schaaf from SPA. LC 92-71332. 150p. (Orig.). 1993. pap. 12.95 (*0-9632363-1-8*) Azul Edits.

Spain in the Name of Allah. Ashley Egarton. (Illus.). 224p. 1993. 15.95 (*0-8059-3355-7*) Dorrance.

Spain in the Nineteenth-Century World: Essays on Spanish Diplomacy, 1789-1898. Ed. by James W. Cortada. LC 93-2232. (Contributions to the Study of World History Ser.: No. 41). 192p. 1994. text ed. 52.95 (*0-313-27655-2*, CSW/, Greenwood Pr) Greenwood.

Spain in the Seventeenth Century. Graham Darby. LC 94-1990. (Seminar Studies in History). (C). 1995. pap. text ed. 13.50 (*0-582-07234-4*, Pub. by Longman UK) Longman.

Spain in the Twentieth-Century World: Essays on Spanish Diplomacy, 1898-1978. Ed. by James W. Cortada. LC 78-75257. (Contributions in Political Science Ser.: No. 30). 294p. 1980. text ed. 59.95 (*0-313-21326-7*, CST/, Greenwood Pr) Greenwood.

Spain in the 19th Century. E. Latimer. 1976. lib. bdg. 59.95 (*0-8490-2643-1*) Gordon Pr.

Spain Is Different. Helen W. Ames. LC 92-28959. (InterAct Ser.). 130p. (Orig.). 1992. pap. text ed. 13.95 (*1-877864-11-0*, 1409) Intercult Pr.

Spain, Let This Cup Pass from Me. Cesar Vallejo. Tr. by Alvaro Cardona-Hine from SPA. LC 72-85850. 1978. pap. 4.00 (*0-88031-049-9*) Invisible-Red Hill.

Spain on Backroads. Duncan Peterson. (Illus.). 256p. (Orig.). 1994. pap. 14.95 (*1-55650-637-6*) Hunter NJ.

Spain-Portugal Road Atlas. 3rd ed. Michelin Staff. 1996. spiral bd., pap. 20.00 (*2-06-146003-8*, 1460) Michelin.

Spain, South. Nelles/Verlag Staff. (Nelles Guides Ser.). 1996. pap. text ed. 14.95 (*3-88618-399-8*, Pub. by Nelles Verlag GW) Seven Hills Bk.

Spain, Take This Cup from Me. Cesar Vallejo. Tr. by Mary Sarko from SPA. 144p. 1995. pap. 12.95 (*1-885214-03-0*) Azul Edits.

Spain, the Monarchy & the Atlantic Community. David C. Jordan. LC 79-65887. (Foreign Policy Reports). 55p. 1979. 11.95 (*0-89549-010-2*) Inst Foreign Policy Anal.

Spain, the Unfinished Revolution. Arthur H. Landis. LC 75-21091. 463p. reprint ed. pap. 132.00 (*0-7837-0583-2*, 2040927) Bks Demand.

***Spain to 2005.** 1996. 515.00 (*0-85058-902-9*, M226) Economist Intell.

Spain under the Habsburgs, 2 vols. rev. ed. John Lynch. (C). 1984. reprint ed. Vol. 1, Empire & Absolutism, 1516-1598, 400p. pap. text ed. 12.00 (*0-8147-5009-5*) NYU Pr.

Spain, 1469-1714: A Society of Conflict. Henry Kamen. (Illus.). 305p. (C). 1983. pap. text ed. 17.95 (*0-582-49226-2*, 73536) Longman.

Spain 1516-1598: From Nation State to World Empire. John Lynch. (History of Spain Ser.). (Illus.). 432p. (C). 1991. text ed. 69.95 (*0-631-17696-9*) Blackwell Pubs.

Spain 1516-1598: From Nation State to World Empire. John Lynch. 1994. pap. 29.95 (*0-631-19398-7*) Blackwell Pubs.

Spain, 1936-39: Social Revolution & Counter-Revolution. Ed. by Vernon Richards. (Centenary Ser.: Vol. 2). 270p. (Orig.). 1990. pap. 10.00 (*0-900384-54-9*) Left Bank.

Spain, 1985. Pat Brooks & Lester Brooks. Ed. by Robert C. Fisher. (Fisher Annotated Travel Guides Ser.). 384p. 1984. 12.95 (*0-8116-0063-7*) NAL-Dutton.

Spain 1995-1996. (OECD Economic Surveys Ser.). 150p. 1996. pap. 26.00 (*92-64-14773-X*) OECD.

***Spain '98.** Fodors Travel Staff. 1997. pap. 19.50 (*0-679-03538-9*) Fodors Travel.

***Spain's Cause Was Mine: A Memoir of an American Medic in the Spanish Civil War.** Hank Rubin. LC 97-15733. 1997. write for info. (*0-8093-2159-9*) Southern Ill U.

Spains' Civil War. (C). 1983. 13.50 (*0-582-35313-0*) Addison-Wesley.

Spain's Civil War. 2nd ed. Harry Browne. LC 96-16745. (Seminar Studies in History). (C). 1996. pap. text ed. 11.50 (*0-582-28988-2*, Pub. by Longman UK) Longman.

Spain's Colonial Outpost. John A. Schutz. Ed. by Norris Hundley, Jr. (Golden State Ser.). (Illus.). 138p. 1985. pap. 10.00 (*0-87835-150-7*) MTL.

Spain's Empire in the New World: The Role of Ideas in Institutional & Social Change. Colin M. MacLachlan. 215p. 1991. pap. 15.00 (*0-520-07410-6*) U CA Pr.

Spain's Entry into NATO: Conflicting Political & Strategic Perspectives. Ed. by Federico G. Gil & Joseph S. Tulchin. LC 88-4973. 180p. 1988. lib. bdg. 28.00 (*1-55587-117-8*) Lynne Rienner.

Spain's First Democracy: The Second Republic, 1931-1936. Stanley G. Payne. LC 92-56925. (Illus.). 494p. (Orig.). (C). 1993. pap. 19.95 (*0-299-13674-4*); lib. bdg. 60.00 (*0-299-13670-1*) U of Wis Pr.

Spain's Forgotten Novelist: Armando Palacio Valdes, 1853-1938. Brian J. Dendle. LC 94-28808. 1995. 34.50 (*0-8387-5294-2*) Bucknell U Pr.

***Spain's Golden Fleece: Wool Production & the Wool Trade from the Middle Ages to the Nineteenth Century.** Carla R. Phillips & William D. Phillips. LC 96-47945. 1997. write for info. (*0-8018-5518-7*) Johns Hopkins.

Spain's New Social Economy: Workers' Self-Management in Catalonia. Mark Holmstrom. 224p. 1993. text ed. 29.95 (*0-85496-821-0*) Berg Pubs.

Spain's Struggle for Europe, 1598-1668. R. A. Stradling. LC 94-27305. 1994. 60.00 (*1-85285-089-2*) Hambledon Press.

Spalding Book of Rules. rev. ed. Bing Broido. (Illus.). 352p. 1993. pap. 14.95 (*0-940279-82-7*) Masters Pr IN.

Spalding Memorial: A Genealogical History of Edward Spalding of Virginia & Massachusetts Bay, & His Descendants. enl. rev. ed. C. W. Spalding. Ed. by S. J. Spalding. (Illus.). 1276p. 1989. reprint ed. pap. 191.00 (*0-8328-1095-9*); reprint ed. lib. bdg. 199.00 (*0-8328-1094-0*) Higginson Bk Co.

Spalding Memorial & Personal Reminiscences & the Life & Selected Poems of Caroline A. Spalding. G. B. Spalding & P. Spaulding. (Illus.). 324p. 1989. reprint ed. pap. 48.00 (*0-8328-1093-2*); reprint ed. lib. bdg. 56.00 (*0-8328-1092-4*) Higginson Bk Co.

***Spalding Super Book of Rules.** 3rd rev. ed. Bing Broido. 424p. 1997. pap. 14.95 (*1-57028-149-1*) Masters Pr IN.

Spall Spirula. limited unabridged ed. Marilyn R. Rosenberg. (Illus.). 37p. (Orig.). 1994. pap. 12.00 (*0-614-13815-9*) Marilyn R Rosenberg.

Spallation Nuclear Reactions & Their Applications. Ed. by Benjamin S. Shen & Milton Merker. (Astrophysics & Space Science Library: No. 59). 1976. lib. bdg. 104.50 (*90-277-0746-4*) Kluwer Ac.

Spalliera Paintings of Renaissance Tuscany: Fables of Poets for Patrician Homes. Anne B. Barriault. LC 92-19920. (Illus.). 240p. (C). 1994. 57.50 (*0-271-00897-0*) Pa St U Pr.

Spalona Rzeka: Burned River. Leszek Zielinski. Ed. by Milada Zapolnik & Joseph Conrad. LC 84-90253. (Illus.). 60p. (Orig.). (POL.). 1984. pap. 6.00 (*0-930401-00-X*) Artex Pub.

Spalpeens & Tatie Hokers: History & Folklore of the Irish Migratory Agricultural Worker in Ireland & Britain. Anne O'Dowd. (Illus.). 456p. 1990. 45.00 (*0-7165-2450-3*, Pub. by Irish Acad Pr IE) Intl Spec Bk.

Spam: A Biography. Wyman. 1997. pap. write for info. (*0-15-600477-1*) HarBrace.

Span. John M. Bennett. 39p. (Orig.). 1990. pap. 3.00 (*0-926935-44-5*) Runaway Spoon.

Span of Wings: An Autobiography. Archibald Russell. 202p. 1993. 19.00 (*1-56091-401-7*, R-132) Soc Auto Engineers.

***Span System of Measuring Involute Gear Tooth Size.** J. E. Van Acker. (Technical Papers). 1954. pap. text ed. 30.00 (*1-55589-298-1*) AGMA.

***SPAN 1997 Resource Directory of Independent Publishers & Publishing Industry Vendors.** Ed. by Marilyn Ross. 120p. (Orig.). 1997. pap. 25.00 (*0-918880-39-4*) Comm Creat.

Spanda-Karikas: The Divine Creative Pulsation. Tr. by Jaideva Singh. (C). 1995. reprint ed. 11.00 (*81-208-0816-9*, Pub. by Motilal Banarsidass II) S Asia.

Spanda-Karikas: The Divine Creative Pulsation. Tr. by Jaideva Singh. (C). 1995. reprint ed. pap. 11.00 (*81-208-0821-5*, Pub. by Motilal Banarsidass II) S Asia.

Spandau: The Secret Diaries. Albert Speer. 1981. pap. 3.95 (*0-671-42447-5*) PB.

Spandau Phoenix. Greg Iles. 704p. 1994. 5.99 (*0-451-17980-3*, Sig) NAL-Dutton.

Spandrel Beam Behavior & Design. (PCI Journal Reprints Ser.). 70p. 1984. pap. 28.00 (*0-318-19816-9*, JR304) P-PCI.

Spanende Werkzeugmaschinen, Deutsch-Englische Begriffserlauterungen und Kommentare. Henry G. Freeman. 617p. (ENG & GER.). 1973. Machine Tools, German-English Explanations & Comments. 150.00 (*0-8288-6330-X*, M-7624) Fr & Eur.

Spanende Werkzeugmaschinen und Werkzeuge. Helmut Gross. 272p. (GER & RUS.). 1987. 95.00 (*0-8288-2138-0*, F49180) Fr & Eur.

Spangled Unicorn. Noel Coward. LC 82-83582. (Illus.). 101p. 1982. reprint ed. 12.50 (*0-911638-00-4*) Frisch H.

Spanglers & Tingles (the Rival Belles) John B. Jones. (Notable American Authors Ser.). 1992. reprint ed. lib. bdg. 75.00 (*0-7812-3516-2*) Rprt Serv.

Spaniard in Elizabethan England: The Correspondence of Antonio Perez's Exile Volume I. Gustav Ungerer. (Monagrafias A Ser.: Vol. XXVII). 550p. (Orig.). (C). 1974. pap. 70.00 (*0-900411-84-8*, Pub. by Tamesis Bks Ltd UK) Boydell & Brewer.

Spaniard in Elizabethan England: The Correspondence of Antonio Perez's Exile Volume I. Gustav Ungerer. (Monagrafias A Ser.: Vol. XXVII). 450p. (Orig.). (C). 1976. pap. 63.00 (*0-7293-0021-8*, Pub. by Tamesis Bks Ltd UK) Boydell & Brewer.

Spaniard in the Portuguese Indies: The Narrative of Martin Fernandez De Figueroa. Martin Fernandez De Figueroa. Ed. by James B. McKenna. LC 67-27089. (Studies in Romance Languages: No. 31). 296p. 1967. 17.50 (*0-674-83085-7*) HUP.

Spaniard in the Works. John Lennon. 1994. reprint ed. lib. bdg. 27.95 (*1-56849-299-5*) Buccaneer Bks.

Spaniard in the Works: John Lennon. John Lennon. 1987. pap. text ed. 4.95 (*0-06-097122-3*) HarpC.

Spaniards: An Introduction to Their History. Americo Castro. Tr. by Willard F. King & Selma Margaretten from SPA. LC 67-14000. 638p. 1985. reprint ed. 60.00 (*0-520-05469-5*) U CA Pr.

Spaniards & Indians in Southeastern Mesoamerica: Essays on the History of Ethnic Relations. Ed. by Murdo J. MacLeod & Robert Wasserstrom. LC 82-23725. (Latin American Studies). xviii, 291p. 1983. text ed. 30.00 (*0-8032-3082-6*) U of Nebr Pr.

***Spaniels.** Andrews & McMeel Staff. 1997. pap. 8.95 (*0-8362-2881-2*) Andrews & McMeel.

Spaniels. H. J. Ullman & Edward L. Ullmann. (Complete Pet Owner's Manuals Ser.). (Illus.). (J). (gr. k-12). 1982. pap. 6.95 (*0-8120-2424-9*) Barron.

Spanisch fur Kaufleute: Spanish Business Correspondence guide. 10th ed. Francisco Lopez-Casero Olmedo & Otto Hierneis. 455p. (GER & SPA.). 1981. reprint ed. 49.95 (*0-7859-5673-5*, 3468403402) Fr & Eur.

Spanisch In der Praxis: Intermediate Spanish for German Speakers. Assimil Staff. (GER & SPA.). 28.95 (*0-8288-4494-1*) Fr & Eur.

Spanisch In der Praxis: Intermediate Spanish for German Speakers, Set 4. Assimil Staff. (GER & SPA.). audio 125.00 (*0-685-53072-8*) Fr & Eur.

Spanisch-Islamische Systeme Sich Kreuzender Boegen. Christian Ewert. (Madrider Forschungen Ser: Vol. 12, Pt. 1). (C). 1978. 346.15 (*3-11-006967-9*) De Gruyter.

***Spanisch Ohne Muhe Heute.** (Illus.). (Orig.). (GER & SPA.). 1997. pap. 75.00 incl. audio (*2-7005-1002-X*, Pub. by ASSIMIL FR) Distribks Inc.

Spanisch Ohne Muhe Heute: Spanish for German Speakers. Assimil Staff. (GER & SPA.). 28.95 (*0-8288-4318-X*, M9910); cd-rom, digital audio 125.00 (*0-685-52991-6*) Fr & Eur.

Spanisches Liederbuch. Paul Heyse & Emmanuel Geibel. 295p. reprint ed. write for info. (*0-318-71635-6*) G Olms Pubs.

Spanisches Supplement Zu Medizinisches Woerterbuch. E. Veillon & Albert Nobel. (GER.). 1971. 48.00 (*0-7859-0834-X*, M-7623) Fr & Eur.

Spanish. (College Board SAT II Subject Test Ser.). 1997. pap. 23.95 (*0-8373-6314-4*, SATII-14) Nat Learn.

Spanish. (Express Track CDs Ser.). 1992. 39.95 incl. disk (*0-8120-7898-5*) Barron.

***Spanish.** (Business Cassette Pack Ser.). (ENG & SPA.). 1997. pap. 19.95 incl. audio (*2-8315-5158-7*) Berlitz.

***Spanish.** (CD Pack Ser.). (ENG & SPA.). 1997. pap. 18.95 incl. audio compact disk (*2-8315-1094-5*) Berlitz.

***Spanish.** (LinguaFun Travel Ser.). (ENG & SPA.). 1997. pap. 12.95 incl. audio (*1-56015-602-3*) Penton Overseas.

***Spanish.** (Traveler's Language Course Ser.). (ENG & SPA.). 1997. pap. 19.95 incl. audio (*0-8050-3468-4*) H Holt & Co.

Spanish. Globe Pequot Press Staff. (Essentials Ser.). 1996. pap. text ed. 10.95 (*2-8315-5718-6*) Berlitz.

Spanish. Harrap's Books Limited Staff. (Indispensable Ser.). 128p. 1992. pap. 13.00 incl. digital audio (*0-13-391111-X*, Harraps IN) Macmillan Gen Ref.

Spanish. Jack Rudman. (National Teacher Examination Ser.: NT-14). 1994. pap. 23.95 (*0-8373-8424-9*) Nat Learn.

Spanish. Jack Rudman. (Graduate Record Examination (GRE) Ser.: Vol. GRE-19). 1994. pap. 23.95 (*0-8373-5219-3*) Nat Learn.

Spanish. Jack Rudman. (Undergraduate Program Field Tests (UPFT) Ser.: Vol. UPFT-24). 1994. pap. 23.95 (*0-8373-6024-2*) Nat Learn.

***Spanish.** Jack Rudman. (Advanced Placement Test (AP) Ser.: Vol. AP-20). 1997. pap. 23.95 (*0-8373-6220-2*) Nat Learn.

Spanish. Kim M. Thompson & Karen M. Hilderbrand. (Listen & Learn a Language Ser.). (Illus.). 64p. (J). (ps-6). 1995. wbk. ed. 14.99 incl. audio (*1-882331-38-9*, Twin 309) Twin Sisters.

Spanish. Kim M. Thompson & Karen M. Hilderbrand. (Listen & Learn a Language Ser.). (Illus.). 24p. (J). (ps-6). 1994. pap. 9.98 incl. audio (*1-882331-25-7*, TWIN 409) Twin Sisters.

Spanish. rev. ed. Frank Hill. (LanguageCard Pac Ser.). 1993. Incl. 4 language cards. 4.00 (*0-88699-003-3*) Travel Sci.

Spanish, Vol. I. Brad Caudle & Richard Caudle. (Rock 'N Learn Ser.). (Illus.). 28p. (J). (gr. 1-12). 1993. pap. 9.95 incl. audio (*1-878489-19-4*, RL919) Rock n Learn.

Spanish, Vol. II. Melissa Caudle & Trey Herbert. (Rock 'N Learn Ser.). (Illus.). 32p. (J). (gr. 1-12). 1995. pap. 9.95 incl. audio (*1-878489-34-8*, RL934) Rock n Learn.

Spanish: A Modular Approach, Bk. 2. 2nd ed. Katherine J. Hampares & Nelly E. Santos. LC 80-23538. 414p. reprint ed. 118.00 (*0-685-16287-7*, 2027612) Bks Demand.

Spanish: A Short Course. 4th ed. DaSilva. 1991. pap. 55.95 (*0-8384-3505-X*); student ed., pap. 34.95 (*0-8384-3509-2*) Heinle & Heinle.

Spanish: A Short Course. 4th ed. Dasilva. (College Spanish Ser.). (SPA.). 1991. teacher ed., pap. 6.95 (*0-8384-5128-4*) Heinle & Heinle.

Spanish: Concise Grammar. 190p. (SPA.). 1992. pap. text ed. 23.95 incl. audio (*0-88432-455-9*, SSP350) Audio-Forum.

An Asterisk (*) at the beginning of an entry indicates that the title is appearing in BIP for the first time.

***Spanish: Language Survival Kit.** Izaskun Arretxe & Allison Jones. (Illus.). 256p. 1997. pap. 5.95 (*0-86442-475-2*) Lonely Planet.

***Spanish: Level 1.** (Learning Curve Ser.). (ENG & SPA.). 1997. pap. 9.98 incl. audio (*0-88676-121-2*) Metacom Inc.

***Spanish: Level 1.** Medley. (Secondary Spanish Ser.). Date not set. text ed. 62.95 (*0-8384-7889-1*) Heinle & Heinle.

***Spanish: Level 13.** Medley. (Secondary Spanish Ser.). Date not set. wbk. ed., text ed. 15.95 (*0-8384-7882-4*) Heinle & Heinle.

***Spanish: Level 2.** (Learning Curve Ser.). (ENG & SPA.). 1997. pap. 9.98 incl. audio (*0-88676-122-0*) Metacom Inc.

***Spanish: Level 2.** Medley. (Global ESL/ELT Ser.). Date not set. wbk. ed., pap. 15.95 (*0-8384-7890-5*) Heinle & Heinle.

***Spanish: Level 3.** (Learning Curve Ser.). (ENG & SPA.). 1997. pap. 9.99 incl. audio (*0-88676-123-9*) Metacom Inc.

***Spanish: Levels 1, 2, 3.** (Learning Curve Ser.). (ENG & SPA.). 1997. pap. 19.99 incl. audio (*0-88676-144-1*) Metacom Inc.

Spanish: Serving Safe Food. Education Foundation of N. R. A. Staff. 208p. 1995. per., pap. 4.75 (*0-7872-1664-X*) Kendall-Hunt.

Spanish: Short Course. Dasilva. (College Spanish Ser.). 1991. suppl. ed., pap. 32.95 (*0-8384-3784-2*) Heinle & Heinle.

Spanish: Short Course. 4th ed. Dasilva. (College Spanish Ser.). 1991. teacher ed., pap. 56.95 (*0-8384-3758-3*) Heinle & Heinle.

Spanish: Short Course. 4th ed. Dasilva. (College Spanish Ser.). 1991. suppl. ed., pap. 6.95 (*0-8384-3517-3*) Heinle & Heinle.

Spanish - Analysis for Advanced Students. Quilter. 1993. pap. text ed. write for info. (*0-07-051389-9*) McGraw.

Spanish - Arabic Dictionary of Verbs, Grammar, & Conversation Terms (Diccionario Espanol-Arabe de Verbos, Gramatica y Temas de Conversacion. 2nd ed. Mufid Al-Guindi Abd Al-Monem. 368p. (ARA & SPA.). 1974. 24.95 (*0-8288-4016-4*, S50423) Fr & Eur.

Spanish - English Handbook for Medical Professionals: Compendio en Ingles y Espanol Para Profesionales de la Medicine. 4th ed. Jesus Perez-Sabido. Ed. by Gregg Rogers. LC 93-37022. 400p. (ENG & SPA.). 1993. 29. 95 (*1-878487-61-2*) Practice Mgmt Info.

***Spanish - English Mini-Books Set with Audio, 11 bks.** Claudia Schwalm. (Illus.). (Orig.). (ENG & SPA.). (J). (gr. k-6). 1997. pap. 21.95 incl. audio (*0-614-24736-5*) Cultural Cnnect.

Spanish - English Patient Education Collection: Women & Infants. Aspen Reference Group Staff & Sara N. Di Lima. Ed. by Sandra J. Painter. LC 95-12765. 672p. (ENG & SPA.). 1995. 49.00 (*0-8342-0717-6*) Aspen Pub.

Spanish - English Picture Dictionary. Claudia Schwalm. (Illus.). 89p. (J). (gr. k-6). 1995. 22.95 incl. audio (*1-57371-004-0*) Cultural Cnnect.

Spanish - English Tarot. Stuart R. Kaplan. 108p. 1975. pap. 15.00 (*0-913866-57-1*) US Games Syst.

Spanish - Italian, Italian - Spanish Commercial Dictionary: Concise Edition. A. M. Gallina. 1992. 95.00 (*0-8288-8440-4*) Fr & Eur.

Spanish - Italian, Italian - Spanish Dictionary. A. M. Gallina. 1991. 35.00 (*0-8288-8442-0*) Fr & Eur.

Spanish a la Cartoon. Albert H. Small. 120p. (SPA.). pap. 6.95 (*0-8442-7326-0*, Natl Textbk) NTC Pub Grp.

Spanish Advanced, Set. Foreign Service Institute Staff. 614p. 1980. pap. text ed. 185.00 incl. audio (*0-88432-057-X*, AFS153) Audio-Forum.

Spanish Advanced Course, Set 12. Foreign Service Institute Staff. 472p. (C). 1980. pap. text ed. 185.00 incl. audio (*0-88432-058-8*, AFS170) Audio-Forum.

Spanish Advanced Think & Talk. Berlitz Editors. (Think & Talk Language Courses Ser.). (Illus.). (SPA.). 1991. pap. 185.00 incl. audio (*2-8315-1116-X*) Berlitz.

Spanish Agriculture: The Long Siesta, 1765-1965. James Simpson. (Studies in Modern Economic History: No. 2). 336p. (C). 1996. text ed. 59.95 (*0-521-49630-6*) Cambridge U Pr.

Spanish Alcoholic Drinks. Euromonitor Staff. 60p. (C). 1988. 975.00 (*0-86338-278-9*, Pub. by Euromonitor Pubns UK) Gale.

Spanish Alive!, Level I. Lonnie G. Daizovi & Ed Saxon. (Spanish Alive! Spanish for Young Children Ser.). (Illus.). 177p. (Orig.). (SPA.). (J). (ps-3). 1990. reprint ed. teacher ed. 18.95 (*0-935301-59-3*); reprint ed. audio 11.95 (*0-935301-50-X*) Vibrante Pr.

Spanish Alphabet Coloring Book. Nina Barbaresi. (Illus.). (J). (gr. k-3). 1992. pap. 2.50 (*0-486-27249-4*) Dover.

Spanish Alta California. Alberta J. Denis. 1992. reprint ed. lib. bdg. 75.00 (*0-7812-5024-2*) Rprt Serv.

Spanish America after Independence, c. 1820-c 1870. Ed. by Leslie Bethell. 448p. 1987. 64.95 (*0-521-34128-0*); pap. 19.95 (*0-521-34926-5*) Cambridge U Pr.

Spanish America in Song & Story. H. A. Holmes. 1972. 59. 95 (*0-8490-1099-3*) Gordon Pr.

Spanish American Authors: The Twentieth Century. Angel Flores. 915p. 1992. 100.00 (*0-8242-0806-4*) Wilson.

Spanish-American Blanketry: Its Relationship to Aboriginal Weaving in the Southwest. H. P. Mera. LC 87-12715. (Illus.). 81p. (Orig.). 1987. pap. 14.95 (*0-933452-22-5*) Schol Am Res.

Spanish American Cookbook. L. Mendoza. 1974. lib. bdg. 69.95 (*0-685-51363-7*) Revisionist Pr.

Spanish-American Diplomatic Relations Preceding the War of 1898. Horace E. Flack. LC 78-63912. (Johns Hopkins University. Studies in the Social Sciences. Thirtieth Ser. 1912: 1-2). reprint ed. 32.50 (*0-404-61164-8*) AMS Pr.

Spanish-American Folktales. Teresa Pijoan de Van Etten. (Illus.). 128p. (Orig.). 1990. pap. 14.95 (*0-87483-155-5*) August Hse.

Spanish-American Homeland: Four Centuries in New Mexico's Rio Arriba. Alvar W. Carlson. LC 90-4345. (Creating the North American Landscape Ser.). (Illus.). 312p. 1991. text ed. 42.50 (*0-8018-3990-4*) Johns Hopkins.

Spanish American Literature: A History, Vol. 2, 1910-1963. 2nd enl. rev. ed. Enrique Anderson-Imbert. LC 70-75087. (Waynebooks Ser.: Vol. 29). 370p. 1969. pap. 24. 95 (*0-8143-1388-4*) Wayne St U Pr.

Spanish American Modernism: A Selected Bibliography. Robert Anderson. LC 73-82616. 191p. reprint ed. pap. 54.50 (*0-317-26809-0*, 2024315) Bks Demand.

Spanish-American Modernista Poets: A Critical Anthology. 2nd ed. Ed. by G. Brotherston. (Bristol Spanish Texts Ser.). (SPA.). 1995. pap. 16.95 (*1-85399-463-4*, Pub. by Brstl Class Pr UK) Focus Pub-R Pullins.

Spanish-American Poetry: A Dual-Language Anthology. rev. ed. Seymour Resnick. LC 96-7769. 64p. 1996. reprint ed. pap. text ed. 4.95 (*0-486-29380-7*) Dover.

Spanish American Regional Novel: Modernity & Autochthony. Carlos J. Alonso. (Cambridge Studies in Latin American & Iberian Literature: No. 2). 240p. (C). 1990. text ed. 69.95 (*0-521-37210-0*) Cambridge U Pr.

Spanish-American Revolutions 1808-1826. John Lynch. (C). 1986. pap. text ed. 13.95 (*0-393-95537-0*) Norton.

Spanish American Roots of William Carlos Williams. Julio Marzan. LC 93-38636. 280p. (C). 1994. text ed. 30.00 (*0-292-75160-5*) U of Tex Pr.

Spanish American Short Story: A Critical Anthology. Seymour Menton. LC 76-7765. (Latin American Studies Center, UCLA: No. 49). 1980. pap. 17.00 (*0-520-04641-2*) U CA Pr.

Spanish-American Song & Game Book. Writers Program, New Mexico Staff. LC 73-3642. (American Guide Ser.). reprint ed. 42.50 (*0-404-57941-8*) AMS Pr.

Spanish-American War. R. A. Alger. 1976. lib. bdg. 59.95 (*0-8490-2644-X*) Gordon Pr.

Spanish-American War. Deborah Bachrach. LC 91-16730. (America's Wars Ser.). (Illus.). 112p. (J). (gr. 5-8). 1991. lib. bdg. 20.96 (*1-56006-405-6*) Lucent Bks.

***Spanish-American War.** Mary Collins. LC 97-10964. (Cornerstones of Freedom Ser.). (J). 1998. write for info. (*0-516-20759-8*) Childrens.

Spanish-American War. Kathlyn Gay & Martin Gay. (Voices from the Past Ser.). (Illus.). 64p. (J). (gr. 5-8). 1996. lib. bdg. 15.98 (*0-8050-2847-1*) TFC Bks NY.

Spanish-American War. Michael Golay. LC 94-39157. (American at War Ser.). (Illus.). 112p. (J). (gr. 6-10). 1995. 17.95 (*0-8160-3174-6*) Facts on File.

Spanish-American War. Albert Marrin. LC 90-935. (Illus.). 192p. (YA). (gr. 5 up). 1991. lib. bdg. 15.95 (*0-689-31663-1*, Atheneum Bks Young) S&S Childrens.

Spanish-American War. Russell A. Alger. LC 78-146850. (Select Bibliographies Reprint Ser.). 1977. reprint ed. 36. 95 (*0-8369-5617-6*) Ayer.

***Spanish-American War: April-August 1898 - A Pictorial History.** Stan Cohen. 1997. pap. text ed. 29.95 (*1-57510-031-2*) Pictorial Hist.

Spanish-American War: Conflict in the Caribbean & the Pacific, 1895-1902. Joseph Smith. LC 93-44809. (Modern Wars in Perspective Ser.). (C). 1994. text ed. 62.50 (*0-582-04300-X*, Pub. by Longman UK) Longman.

Spanish-American War: Conflict in the Caribbean & the Pacific, 1895-1902. Joseph Smith. LC 93-44809. (Modern Wars in Perspective Ser.). (C). 1995. pap. text ed. 24.50 (*0-582-04340-9*, Pub. by Longman UK) Longman.

Spanish-American War: Imperial Ambitions. Alden R. Carter. LC 91-14753. (First Bks.). (Illus.). 64p. (J). (gr. 5-8). 1992. lib. bdg. 21.00 (*0-531-20078-7*) Watts.

Spanish-American War: Imperial Ambitions. Alden R. Carter. (First Bks.). (Illus.). 64p. (J). (gr. 5-8). 1993. pap. 6.95 (*0-531-15657-5*) Watts.

Spanish-American War: The Story & Photographs. Donald M. Goldstein et al. (Illus.). 192p. 1997. 31.95 (*1-57488-076-4*) Brasseys Inc.

Spanish American War: 1898. Albert A. Nofi. (Great Campaigns Ser.). (Illus.). 256p. Date not set. 24.95 (*0-938289-57-8*, Combined Bks) Combined Pub.

Spanish-American War & President McKinley. Lewis L. Gould. LC 82-13672. (Illus.). x, 166p. 1982. pap. 7.95 (*0-7006-0227-5*) U Pr of KS.

Spanish-American War at Sea: Naval Action in the Atlantic. A. B. Feuer. LC 95-17948. 280p. 1995. text ed. 57.95 (*0-275-95106-5*, Praeger Pubs) Greenwood.

Spanish-American War Volunteer. 2nd enl. rev. ed. William H. Coston. LC 75-164384. (Black Heritage Library Collection). 1977. reprint ed. 29.95 (*0-8369-8843-4*) Ayer.

Spanish American Women Writers: A Bio-Bibliographical Source Book. Ed. by Diane E. Marting. LC 89-27283. 672p. 1990. text ed. 89.50 (*0-313-25194-0*, MSA/, Greenwood Pr) Greenwood.

Spanish-Americans As a Political Factor in New Mexico, 1912-1950. Ernest B. Fincher. LC 73-14202. (Mexican American Ser.). 332p. 1975. 25.95 (*0-405-05676-1*) Ayer.

***Spanish Anarchists: The Heroic Years 1868-1936.** Murray Bookchin. (Illus.). 384p. 1996. pap. 19.95 (*1-873176-04-X*, AK Pr San Fran) AK Pr Dist.

***Spanish & British Land Grants in Mississippi Territory, 1750-1784.** unabridged ed. Clifford N. Smith. (Selections from the American State Papers: Vol. 6). 48p. (Orig.). 1996. pap. 20.00 (*0-915162-58-X*, ASP6) Westland Pubns.

***Spanish & British Land Grants in Mississippi Territory, 1750-1784.** unabridged ed. Ed. by Clifford N. Smith. (Selections from the American State Papers: Vol. 5). 47p. (Orig.). 1996. pap. 20.00 (*0-915162-68-7*, ASP5) Westland Pubns.

***Spanish & British Land Grants in Mississippi Territory, 1750-1784.** unabridged ed. Ed. by Clifford N. Smith. (Selections from the American State Papers: Vol. 7). 42p. (Orig.). 1996. pap. 20.00 (*0-915162-59-8*, ASP7) Westland Pubns.

Spanish & Dutch Dictionary of Electronics & Waveguides. Hans Schnellman. 120p. (DUT & SPA.). 1990. 95.00 (*0-8288-0936-4*, M373) Fr & Eur.

Spanish & English Computer Dictionary: Diccionario de Informatica. Pablo T. Dietrich. 783p. (ENG & SPA.). 1985. 59.95 (*0-8288-0258-0*, F14700) Fr & Eur.

***Spanish & English Dictionary, Vol. 1.** 2nd ed. Onyria H. McElroy. 560p. 1996. pap. text ed. 29.95 (*0-316-55448-0*) Lppncott-Raven.

Spanish & English Dictionary of Chemical Processes & Products. Hans Schnellman. 120p. (ENG & SPA.). 1986. pap. 95.00 (*0-8288-0176-2*, M 8381) Fr & Eur.

Spanish & English Dictionary of Technical & Scientific Terminology: Diccionario de Terminos Cientificos y Tecnicos, 5 vols., Set. D. N. Lapedes. 2952p. (ENG & SPA.). 1981. 895.00 (*0-8288-0668-3*, S38580) Fr & Eur.

Spanish & English, English & Spanish Dictionary - Self Pronouncing. rev. ed. Ed. by Velazquez et al. LC 72-94281. (ENG & SPA.). 1973. 28.95 (*0-13-615534-0*) P-H.

Spanish & English Literature of the 16th & 17th Centuries: Studies in Discretion, Illusion, & Mutability. Edward M. Wison. Ed. by D. W. Cruickshank. LC 79-41612. 301p. reprint ed. pap. 85.80 (*0-685-16137-4*, 2027255) Bks Demand.

Spanish & English of United States Hispanos: A Critical, Annotated, Linguistic Bibliography. Ed. by Richard V. Teschner et al. LC 75-21564. 382p. reprint ed. pap. 108. 90 (*0-8357-3339-4*, 2039567) Bks Demand.

Spanish & French Rivalry in the Gulf Region of the U. S., 1678-1702: The Beginnings of Texas & Pensacola. William E. Dunn. (Select Bibliographies Reprint Ser.). 1977. reprint ed. 20.95 (*0-8369-5792-X*) Ayer.

Spanish & Hispanic Etymological Dictionary. Vicente Garcia de Diego. 1100p. (SPA.). 1985. 195.00 (*0-8288-7323-2*, S60226) Fr & Eur.

Spanish & Hispanic Etymological Dictionary: Diccionario Etimologico Espanol E Hispanico. 2nd ed. Vicente Garcia de Diego. 1091p. (SPA.). 1985. 195.00 (*0-8288-2047-3*, S60226) Fr & Eur.

Spanish & Hispanic Presence in Florida from the Discovery to the Bicentennial. Jose A. Cubenas. 1979. pap. 4.00 (*84-499-2888-5*) Edit Mensaje.

Spanish & Indian Place Names of California: Their Meaning & Their Romance. Nellie V. Sanchez. Ed. by Carlos E. Cortes. LC 76-1573. (Chicano Heritage Ser.). (Illus.). 1977. reprint ed. 25.95 (*0-405-09523-6*) Ayer.

Spanish & Indian Place Names of California, Their Meaning & Their Romance. Nellie V. Sanchez. 1992. reprint ed. lib. bdg. 75.00 (*0-7812-5084-6*) Rprt Serv.

***Spanish & Italian Songbooks.** Wolf. (ITA & SPA.). pap. 13.95 (*0-486-26156-5*) Dover.

Spanish & Mexican Card Readings: Modern English Version. (Illus.). 146p. (Orig.). 1995. pap. 9.95 (*0-9644720-0-7*) L Angel.

Spanish & Mexican Land Grants. Ed. by Carlos E. Cortes. LC 73-14216. (Mexican American Ser.). (Illus.). 1975. reprint ed. 33.95 (*0-405-05690-7*) Ayer.

Spanish & Mexican Land Grants & the Law. Ed. by Malcolm Ebright. (Illus.). 126p. 1989. pap. 15.00 (*0-89745-120-1*) Sunflower U Pr.

Spanish & Mexican Land Grants in California. Rose H. Avina. Ed. by Carlos E. Cortes. LC 76-1231. (Chicano Heritage Ser.). (Illus.). 1977. 18.95 (*0-405-09483-3*) Ayer.

Spanish & Mexican Land Grants in New Mexico & Colorado. Ed. by John R. Van Ness & Christine M. Van Ness. (Illus.). 119p. 1980. pap. text ed. 15.00 (*0-89745-012-4*) Sunflower U Pr.

Spanish & Mexican Records of the American Southwest: A Bibliographical Guide to Archive & Manuscript Sources. fac. ed. Henry P. Beers. LC 79-4313. 507p. reprint ed. pap. 144.50 (*0-7837-6956-3*, 2046906) Bks Demand.

Spanish & Portugese Languages in the United States: An Original Anthology. Ed. by Carlos E. Cortes. LC 79-6234. (Hispanics in the United States Ser.). 1981. lib. bdg. 36.95 (*0-405-13181-X*) Ayer.

Spanish & Portuguese Gardens. R. Nichols. 1976. 59.95 (*0-8490-2646-6*) Gordon Pr.

Spanish & Portuguese in Social Context. Ed. by John J. Bergen & Garland D. Bills. LC 83-9076. 124p. (Orig.). reprint ed. pap. 35.40 (*0-7837-6306-9*, 2046021) Bks Demand.

Spanish & Portuguese Jewry: A Classified Bibliography. Compiled by Robert Singerman. LC 92-34760. (Bibliographies & Indexes in World History Ser.: No. 30). 740p. 1993. text ed. 105.00 (*0-313-25752-3*, SJY, Greenwood Pr) Greenwood.

Spanish & Portuguese Jewry Before & after 1492. David F. Altabe. 168p. (Orig.). 1993. pap. 11.95 (*0-87203-139-X*) Hermon.

Spanish & Portuguese Monastic History, 600-1300. Charles J. Bishko. (Collected Studies: No. CS188). 336p. (C). 1984. reprint ed. lib. bdg. 64.95 (*0-86078-136-4*, Pub. by Variorum UK) Ashgate Pub Co.

Spanish & Portuguese South America, 2 vols., Set. Robert G. Watson. LC 76-177856. reprint ed. 60.00 (*0-404-06874-X*) AMS Pr.

Spanish & Portuguese South America During the Colonial Period, 2 vols. Robert G. Watson. 1972. 200.00 (*0-8490-1100-0*) Gordon Pr.

Spanish Anthology: A Collection of Lyrics from the Thirteenth Century to the Present Time. Ed. by J. D. Ford. 1977. lib. bdg. 59.95 (*0-685-01973-X*) Gordon Pr.

Spanish Approach to Pensacola 1689-1693. Ed. by Irving A. Leonard. LC 67-24720. (Quivira Society Publications: Vol. 9). 1967. reprint ed. 19.95 (*0-405-00083-9*) Ayer.

Spanish Arcadia. Nellie V. Sanchez. Ed. by Carlos E. Cortes. LC 76-1579. (Chicano Heritage Ser.). (Illus.). 1977. reprint ed. 29.95 (*0-405-09524-4*) Ayer.

Spanish Archives of New Mexico, 2 Vols., Set. Ralph E. Twitchell. Ed. by Carlos E. Cortes. LC 76-1607. (Chicano Heritage Ser.). (Illus.). 1977. reprint ed. 89.95 (*0-405-09529-5*) Ayer.

Spanish Archives of New Mexico, 2 Vols., Vol. 1. Ralph E. Twitchell. Ed. by Carlos E. Cortes. LC 76-1607. (Chicano Heritage Ser.). (Illus.). 1977. reprint ed. 41.95 (*0-405-09544-9*) Ayer.

Spanish Archives of New Mexico, 2 Vols., Vol. 2. Ralph E. Twitchell. Ed. by Carlos E. Cortes. LC 76-1607. (Chicano Heritage Ser.). (Illus.). 1977. reprint ed. 48.95 (*0-405-09549-X*) Ayer.

Spanish Armada. James A. Froude. 76p. 1972. pap. 5.00 (*0-87291-036-9*) Coronado Pr.

Spanish Armada. Colin Martin & Geoffrey Parker. 288p. 1992. pap. 11.95 (*0-393-30926-6*) Norton.

Spanish Armada: The Experience of War in 1588. Felipe Fernandez-Armesto. (Illus.). 318p. 1988. reprint ed. 35. 00 (*0-19-822926-7*) OUP.

Spanish Armada of Fifteen Eighty-Eight: Historiography & Annotated Bibliography. Eugene L. Rasor. LC 92-31759. (Bibliographies of Battles & Leaders Ser.: No. 10). 295p. 1992. text ed. 65.00 (*0-313-28303-6*, RXS, Greenwood Pr) Greenwood.

Spanish Armada Prisoners: The Story of the Nuestra Senors del Rosario & Her Crew & of Other Prisoners. Martin. 126p. 1984. text ed. 29.00 (*0-85989-305-7*, Pub. by Univ Exeter Pr UK) Northwestern U Pr.

***Spanish Art Song in the Seventeenth Century.** Jose Marin et al. Ed. by John H. Baron. (Recent Researches in Music of the Baroque Era Ser.: Vol. RRB49). (Illus.). xxxviii, 89p. 1985. pap. 43.20 (*0-89579-203-6*) A-R Eds.

***Spanish Artist Dictionary, 4.** Frick Art Gallery Staff. 1996. 140.00 (*0-7838-8037-5*) Mac Lib Ref.

Spanish Artists from Fourth to Twentieth Century: Critic Dictionary, Vol. 2 G-M. Frick Art Staff. 1996. 140.00 (*0-8161-0656-8*, Hall Reference) Macmillan.

Spanish Artists from Fourth to Twentieth Century Vol. 1: A Critical Dictionary. 1994. 140.00 (*0-8161-0655-X*) G K Hall.

Spanish Artists from the Fourth to the Twentieth Century: A Critical Dictionary, 3 vols., Set. Frick Art Reference Library Staff. 2700p. 1996. 420.00 (*0-8161-0614-2*, Hall Reference) Macmillan.

Spanish Artists from the Fourth to the Twentieth Century: A Critical Dictionary, Vol. 3, N-Z. Frick Art Staff. 1996. 140.00 (*0-8161-0657-6*, GK Hall) Thorndike Pr.

Spanish at a Glance. 2nd ed. Heywood Wald. 1992. pap. 6.95 (*0-8120-1398-0*) Barron.

Spanish at the Wheel. (Hugo's Language Courses Ser.). 1990. pap. 29.95 (*0-85285-149-9*) Hunter NJ.

Spanish at Work. I. Kattan-Ibarra Connell. Ed. by J. Kattan-Ibarra. (C). 1989. student ed. 70.00 (*0-85950-931-1*, Pub. by S Thornes Pubs UK); teacher ed. 55.00 (*0-7487-0146-X*, Pub. by S Thornes Pubs UK); audio 200.00 (*0-7487-0142-7*, Pub. by S Thornes Pubs UK) St Mut.

Spanish Avantgarde. Ed. by Derek Harris. LC 94-5409. 1995. text ed. 45.00 (*0-7190-4341-7*, Pub. by Manchester Univ Pr UK); text ed. 19.95 (*0-7190-4342-5*, Pub. by Manchester Univ Pr UK) St Martin.

Spanish Award Certificates, No. 1472. (Illus.). 48p. (SPA.). 1993. 7.95 (*1-878259-17-2*) Neibauer Pr.

Spanish Ballads. Ed. by S. Griswold Morley. 1977. lib. bdg. 59.95 (*0-8490-2647-4*) Gordon Pr.

Spanish Ballads. C. Smith. 224p. (SPA.). 1996. pap. 16.95 (*1-85399-445-6*, Pub. by Brstl Class Pr UK) Focus Pub-R Pullins.

Spanish Ballads. Ed. by Sylvanus G. Morley. LC 78-137068. 226p. 1977. reprint ed. text ed. 55.00 (*0-8371-5531-2*, MOSB, Greenwood Pr) Greenwood.

Spanish Ballads with English Verse Translations. Ed. by Wright. (Hispanic Classics Ser.). 1987. 49.95 (*0-85668-339-6*, Pub. by Aris & Phillips UK); pap. 22.00 (*0-85668-340-X*, Pub. by Aris & Phillips UK) David Brown.

Spanish Baroque Art. Sacheverell Sitwell. LC 71-175874. (Illus.). 1972. reprint ed. 21.95 (*0-405-08979-1*) Ayer.

Spanish, Basic, Programmatic. Foreign Service Institute Staff. 614p. pap. text ed. 165.00 incl. audio (*0-88432-016-2*, AFS121); wbk. ed., pap. text ed. 14.95 (*0-88432-697-7*, AFS995) Audio-Forum.

Spanish Bayonet. Stephen Vincent Benet. LC 73-131621. 1926. reprint ed. 29.00 (*0-685-27275-3*) Scholarly.

Spanish Best: The Fine Shotguns of Spain. Terry Wieland. (Illus.). 256p. 1994. 49.00 (*0-924357-44-4*, 21320-A) Countrysport Pr.

Spanish Best: The Fine Shotguns of Spain. deluxe limited ed. Terry Wieland. (Illus.). 256p. 1994. lthr. 95.00 (*0-924357-45-2*, 21320-B) Countrysport Pr.

Spanish Bilingual Dictionary: A Beginner. Gladys C. Lipton. (SPA.). 1985. pap. 11.95 (*0-8120-0468-X*) Barron.

Spanish Bit No. 24: Bearer of the Pipe. Don Coldsmith. 256p. 1996. reprint ed. mass mkt. 4.99 (*0-553-29470-9*) Bantam.

Spanish Blood, Vol. 1. Mike Blakely. 1996. mass mkt. 4.99 (*0-8125-4831-0*) Forge NYC.

S

Spanish Borderlands. Herbert E. Bolton. 1993. reprint ed. lib. bdg. 75.00 (*0-7812-5918-5*) Rprt Serv.

Spanish Borderlands: A Chronicle of Old Florida & the Southwest. Herbert E. Bolton. LC 95-24340. (Historians of the Frontier & American West Ser.). (Illus.). 368p. (C). 1996. pap. 22.50 (*0-8263-1681-6*) U of NM Pr.

Spanish Borderlands Frontier, 1513-1821. John F. Bannon. LC 74-110887. (Histories of the American Frontier Ser.). (Illus.). 320p. 1974. reprint ed. pap. 17.95 (*0-8263-0309-9*) U of NM Pr.

Spanish Business Correspondence. Michael Gorman & Maria-Luisa Henson. LC 96-20559. (Languages for Business Ser.). 176p. 1997. pap. 9.95 (*0-415-13713-6*) Routledge.

Spanish Business Situations: A Spoken Language Guide. Michael Gorman & Maria-Luisa Henson. LC 95-35515. 128p. (C). 1995. pap. 8.95 (*0-415-12848-X*) Routledge.

Spanish Business Situations: A Spoken Language Guide. Michael Gorman & Maria-Luisa Henson. LC 95-35515. (C). (gr. 13). 1995. audio 18.95 (*0-415-12853-6*) Routledge.

Spanish Business Situations: A Spoken Language Guide. Michael Gorman & Maria-Luisa Henson. LC 95-35515. (C). 1995. pap. 24.95 incl. audio (*0-415-12849-8*) Routledge.

Spanish Businessmate. 192p. 1995. pap. 5.95 (*0-8442-9650-3*, Natl Textbk) NTC Pub Grp.

Spanish by Association. Michael M. Gruneberg. 264p. 1995. pap. 7.95 (*0-8442-9447-0*, Natl Textbk) NTC Pub Grp.

***Spanish Cape Mystery.** Ellery Queen. lib. bdg. 25.95 (*0-8488-1868-7*) Amereon Ltd.

Spanish Captives in North Africa in the Early Modern Age. Ellen G. Friedman. LC 83-47759. 246p. 1983. text ed. 29.50 (*0-299-09380-8*) U of Wis Pr.

Spanish Car Talk for English Speakers: Over 500 Things to Ask or Say about Your Car to a Spanish Speaking Mechanic Without Knowing Any Spanish. Charles E. Hugenberger. LC 92-93528. 76p. (ENG & SPA.). 1992. pap. 9.95 (*1-885057-00-8*) C E Hugenberger.

Spanish Caribbean: Trade & Plunder, 1530-1630. Kenneth R. Andrews. LC 77-90944. 279p. reprint ed. pap. 79.60 (*0-8357-8764-8*, 2033662) Bks Demand.

Spanish Cassette Pack. Berlitz Editors. (Cassette Pack Ser.). (SPA.). 1993. pap. 15.95 incl. audio (*2-8315-1104-6*) Berlitz.

Spanish, Catalan, & Galician Literary Authors of the Eighteenth & Nineteenth Centuries: An Annotated Guide to Bibliographies. David S. Zubatsky. LC 94-32155. 166p. 1995. 25.00 (*0-8108-2947-9*) Scarecrow.

Spanish, Catalan, & Galician Literary Authors of the Twentieth Century: An Annotated Guide to Bibliographies. David S. Zubatsky. LC 92-4041. 192p. 1992. 27.50 (*0-8108-2518-X*) Scarecrow.

Spanish, Catalan & Spanish-American Poetry from "Modernismo" to the Spanish Civil War: The Hispanic Connection. Stephen M. Hart. LC 90-24276. (Hispanic Literature Ser.: Vol. 11). 216p. 1991. lib. bdg. 89.95 (*0-88946-697-1*) E Mellen.

Spanish Cathedral Music in the Golden Age. Robert Stevenson. LC 76-1013. (Illus.). 523p. 1976. reprint ed. text ed. 45.50 (*0-8371-8744-3*, STSP, Greenwood Pr) Greenwood.

Spanish Catholicism: An Historical Overview. Stanley G. Payne. LC 83-25946. 280p. 1984. text ed. 27.50 (*0-299-09800-1*) U of Wis Pr.

Spanish Ceramic Designs. Anita Benarde. (International Design Library). (Illus.). 48p. (Orig.). 1984. pap. 5.95 (*0-88045-059-2*) Stemmer Hse.

Spanish Character & Other Essays: With a Bibliography of His Publications & an Index to His Collected Works. Irving Babbitt. Ed. by Frederick Manchester et al. LC 83-45695. reprint ed. 34.50 (*0-404-20013-3*) AMS Pr.

Spanish Christian Cabala: The Works of Luis de Leon, Santa Teresa de Jesus, & San Juan de la Cruz. Catherine Swietlicki. LC 86-7018. (Illus.). 240p. 1987. text ed. 29.95 (*0-8262-0608-5*) U of Mo Pr.

Spanish Chronicles of Infamy: Short Stories. Tomas M. Segundo. 85p. (Orig.). 1995. pap. 7.50 (*0-9635358-1-1*) ARS Historica.

Spanish Church Year One, No. 1471. (Illus.). 48p. 1993. 7.95 (*1-878259-16-4*) Neibauer Pr.

Spanish Civil War. Sheelagh M. Ellwood. (Historical Association Studies). (Illus.). 112p. (C). 1991. pap. text ed. 13.95 (*0-631-16617-3*) Blackwell Pubs.

***Spanish Civil War.** Abel Paz. (Pocket Archives Ser.). 1997. pap. text ed. 12.95 (*2-85025-532-7*) Emile Hazan Editeur.

Spanish Civil War. Hugh Thomas. 1134p. 1994. pap. 20.00 (*0-671-75876-4*, Touchstone Bks) S&S Trade.

Spanish Civil War. Patrick Turnbull. (Men-at-Arms Ser.: No. 74). (Illus.). 48p. pap. 11.95 (*0-85045-282-1*, 9202, Pub. by Osprey UK) Stackpole.

Spanish Civil War: A Cultural & Historical Reader. Ed. by Alun Kenwood. LC 92-10649. 288p. 1992. 38.95 (*0-85496-318-9*); pap. 19.95 (*0-85496-338-3*) Berg Pubs.

Spanish Civil War: A History in Pictures. Ed. by Raymond Carr. 1989. pap. 19.95 (*0-393-30499-X*) Norton.

Spanish Civil War: An Exhibit. Compiled by Paul P. Rogers. (Illus.). 1978. pap. 8.00 (*0-87959-083-1*) U of Tex H Ransom Ctr.

Spanish Civil War: Guide to the Microfilm Collection. (Illus.). 686p. (C). 1988. text ed. 190.00 (*0-89235-128-4*) Primary Srce Media.

Spanish Civil War: Revolution & Counterrevolution. Burnett Bolloten. LC 89-77911. xxxiii, 1074p. (C). 1991. 70.00 (*0-8078-1906-9*) U of NC Pr.

Spanish Civil War & the British Labour Movement. Tom Buchanan. 272p. (C). 1991. text ed. 59.95 (*0-521-39333-7*) Cambridge U Pr.

Spanish Civil War & the Visual Arts. Ed. by Kathleen M. Vernon. (Western Societies Papers). 100p. 1989. pap. 11.95 (*0-8014-9647-0*) Cornell U Pr.

Spanish Civil War in American & European Films. Marjorie A. Valleau. LC 82-1944. (Studies in Cinema: No. 18). (Illus.). 221p. reprint ed. pap. 63.00 (*0-685-20879-6*, 2070211) Bks Demand.

Spanish Civil War in Literature. Ed. by Janet Perez & Wendell M. Aycock. LC 90-10999. (Studies in Comparative Literature: No. 21). 1990. 24.95 (*0-89672-196-5*) Tex Tech Univ Pr.

Spanish Civil War in Literature, Film & Art: An International Bibliography of Secondary Literature. Peter Monteath. LC 94-16070. (Bibliographies & Indexes in World Literature Ser.: No. 43). 160p. 1994. text ed. 55.00 (*0-313-29262-0*, Greenwood Pr) Greenwood.

Spanish Civil War, 1936-39: American Hemispheric Perspectives. Ed. by Mark Falcoff & Frederick B. Pike. LC 81-14644. 381p. reprint ed. pap. 108.60 (*0-7837-6881-8*, 2046711) Bks Demand.

Spanish Classics for GT Tablature Albeni. Contrib. by Albeniz. 1994. 24.95 (*0-7119-3411-8*, AM91080) Omnibus NY.

Spanish Colonial Administration, 1782-1810: The Intendant System in the Viceroyalty of the Rio De la Plata. John Lynch. LC 69-13979. 335p. 1969. reprint ed. text ed. 65.00 (*0-8371-0546-3*, LYSC, Greenwood Pr) Greenwood.

Spanish Colonial Adobe Architecture of California, 1800-1850. Donald R. Hannaford & Revel Edwards. (Illus.). 128p. 1990. reprint ed. pap. 22.50 (*0-942655-01-X*) Archit CT.

Spanish-Colonial Architecture in the United States. Rexford Newcomb. 1990. pap. 12.95 (*0-486-26263-4*) Dover.

Spanish Colonial Frontier Research. Ed. by Henry F. Dobyns. (Spanish Borderlands Research Ser.: No. 1). 1980. 20.00 (*0-932752-05-5*) Ctr Anthrop Studies.

Spanish Colonial or Adobe Architecture of California, 1800-1850. Donald R. Hannaford. 1992. reprint ed. lib. bdg. 75.00 (*0-7812-5046-3*) Rprt Serv.

Spanish Colonial Tucson: A Demographic History. Henry F. Dobyns. LC 75-10344. (Illus.). 256p. reprint ed. pap. 73.00 (*0-7837-5043-9*, 2044720) Bks Demand.

Spanish Colonie, or Briefe Chronicle or the Acts & Gestes of the Spaniardes in the West Indies. Bartholome De Las Casas. LC 77-6866. (English Experience Ser.: No. 859). 1977. reprint ed. lib. bdg. 27.50 (*90-221-0859-7*) Walter J Johnson.

Spanish Colonization in the Southwest. Frank W. Blackmar. 1976. lib. bdg. 59.95 (*0-8490-2648-2*) Gordon Pr.

Spanish Colonization in the Southwest. Frank W. Blackmar. LC 78-63794. (Johns Hopkins University. Studies in the Social Sciences. Thirtieth Ser. 1912: 4). reprint ed. 27.50 (*0-404-61059-5*) AMS Pr.

***Spanish Coloring Book.** Anne-Francoise Pattis. (Let's Learn Ser.). 64p. (J). pap. 9.95 incl. audio (*0-8442-9172-2*) NTC Pub Grp.

Spanish Comedy & Contexts in the 1620s. William R. Blue. 1996. 42.50 (*0-271-01546-2*) Pa St U Pr.

***Spanish Communication Made Easy.** Lolita L. Grabb & Onyria H. McElroy. 200p. 1997. spiral bd. write for info. (*0-316-15844-5*) Lppncott-Raven.

Spanish, Complete, 2 bks., 8 cassettes, Set. (Hugo's Language Ser.). 224p. (Orig.). 1996. pap. 54.95 incl. audio (*0-85285-286-X*) Hunter NJ.

Spanish Composition through Literature. 3rd ed. Ayllon & Smith. 1994. text ed. 78.00 (*0-13-186594-3*) P-H.

Spanish Composition through Literature. 3rd ed. Candido Ayllon & Smith. 1995. text ed. 51.00 (*0-13-186586-2*) P-H.

Spanish Connection. Kay Thorpe. (Presents Ser.). 1994. mass mkt. 2.99 (*0-373-11667-5*, 1-11667-2) Harlequin Bks.

Spanish Connection. large type ed. Thorpe. 1995. 25.99 (*0-7505-0825-6*, Pub. by Magna Print Bks UK) Ulverscroft.

Spanish Conquest. Thomas Campanella. 1972. 59.95 (*0-8490-1101-9*) Gordon Pr.

Spanish Conquest in America & Its Relation to the History of Slavery & to the Government of Colonies, 4 Vols. Arthur Helps. Ed. by M. Oppenheim. LC 72-15297. reprint ed. 300.00 (*0-404-03270-2*) AMS Pr.

Spanish Conspiracy: A Review of Early Spanish Movements in the South-West. Thomas M. Green. 1990. reprint ed. 14.50 (*0-8446-1207-3*) Peter Smith.

Spanish Contact Vernaculars in the Philippine Islands. Keith Whinnom. LC 57-18812. 144p. reprint ed. pap. 41.10 (*0-317-28809-1*, 2020772) Bks Demand.

Spanish Conversation & Composition. Thomas O. Bente. (C). 1976. text ed. write for info. (*0-07-004808-8*) McGraw.

Spanish Cooking. Judith Ferguson. 64p. 1995. write for info. (*1-57215-012-2*) World Pubns.

Spanish Cooking. Manuel Rebarto. 1993. 12.98 (*1-55521-928-4*) Bk Sales Inc.

Spanish Corporation's Law & Limited Liability Companies Law. Santiago C. Minguela & Herbert F. Riband. LC 95-48139. (Series of Legislation in Translation: No. 9). 1996. write for info. (*90-411-0191-8*) Kluwer Law Tax Pubs.

Spanish Costume: Extremadura. Ruth M. Anderson. (Illus.). 1951. 15.00 (*0-87535-067-4*) Hispanic Soc.

Spanish Cross in Georgia. David Arias. 242p. (C). 1994. lib. bdg. 45.00 (*0-8191-9700-9*) U Pr of Amer.

***Spanish Crossing.** Lemay. 1998. 20.00 (*0-7862-1158-X*) Thorndike Pr.

Spanish Crossword Puzzles for Beginners: Crucigramas Para Principiantes. Elizabeth Reid. (Illus.). 32p. (Orig.). (SPA.). 1995. student ed. 1.95 (*1-881791-04-1*) In One EAR.

Spanish Crown & the Defense of the Caribbean, 1535-1585: Precedent, Patrimonialism & Royal Parsimony. Paul E. Hoffman. LC 79-16864. (Illus.). 332p. 1980. reprint ed. pap. 94.70 (*0-608-00866-4*, 2061658) Bks Demand.

Spanish-Cuban-American War & the Birth of American Imperialism, 1895-1902, 2 vols., 2. Philip S. Foner. LC 79-187595. 385p. reprint ed. pap. 109.80 (*0-8357-3547-8*, 2034341) Bks Demand.

Spanish-Cuban-American War & the Birth of American Imperialism, 1895-1902, 2 vols., Vol. 1, 1895-1898. Philip S. Foner. LC 79-187595. 372p. reprint ed. pap. 106.10 (*0-8357-3546-X*, 2034341) Bks Demand.

Spanish Cuisine: The Gourmet's Companion. Matt A. Casado. LC 96-15478. 224p. 1997. pap. text ed. 16.95 (*0-471-13722-7*) Wiley.

Spanish Cultural Studies: An Introduction: The Struggle for Modernity. Ed. by Helen Graham & Jo Labanyi. (Illus.). 480p. 1996. 68.00 (*0-19-815195-0*); pap. 18.95 (*0-19-815199-3*) OUP.

Spanish Dancing. Lalagia. Ed. by Ana Ivanova. (Illus.). 168p. 1995. pap. 19.95 (*0-903102-88-9*, Pub. by Dance Bks UK) Princeton Bk Co.

Spanish Dancing. Harrold Wingrave. (Ballroom Dance Ser.). 1986. lib. bdg. 79.95 (*0-8490-3301-2*) Gordon Pr.

Spanish Dancing. Harrold Wingrave. (Ballroom Dance Ser.). 1985. lib. bdg. 79.95 (*0-87700-861-2*) Revisionist Pr.

Spanish Demand for Household Furniture. FIRA Consultancy Services Staff. LC 93-40546. (Illus.). 46p. (Orig.). 1993. pap. 330.00 (*0-921577-38-9*) AKTRIN.

Spanish Dial-a-Verb 5000. (SPA.). 1986. pap. text ed. 15.95 (*0-9616884-1-6*) ProLogo.

Spanish Dial-a-Verb 8000. (SPA.). 1986. pap. text ed. 15.95 (*0-9616884-2-4*) ProLogo.

Spanish Diction Manual for Singers. Darhon Rees-Rohrbacher. 100p. (C). pap. text ed. 10.00 (*1-882712-01-3*) Dragonflower.

Spanish Dictionary. (Hugo Pocket Dictionaries Ser.). 620p. (Orig.). 1986. pap. 5.95 (*0-85285-077-8*) Hunter NJ.

Spanish Dictionary. G. H. Calvert. (Routledge Pocket Dictionaries Ser.). 560p. 1980. pap. 9.95 (*0-415-05913-5*, 0558X) Routledge.

Spanish Dictionary. rev. ed. James R. Jump. 1152p. 1995. pap. 12.95 (*0-14-051298-5*) Viking Penguin.

***Spanish Dictionary.** rev. ed. James R. Jump. 1999. pap. write for info. (*0-14-051299-3*) Viking Penguin.

Spanish Dictionary of Antonyms & Synonyms: Diccionario Espanol de Sinonimos y Antonimos. 24th ed. Federico C. De Robles Correa. 1152p. (SPA.). 1991. 135.00 (*0-7859-4958-5*) Fr & Eur.

***Spanish Dictionary of Business, Commerce & Finance: Spanish-English/English-Spanish.** 800p. (C). 1997. 89.00 (*0-415-09393-7*, D1367) Routledge.

Spanish Dictionary of Law & Political & Social Science. 21th rev. ed. Manuel Ossorio. 1030p. 1994. 69.50 (*950-885-005-1*) IBD Ltd.

Spanish Dictionary of Marketing: Diccionario Del Marketing. J. B. Gonzalez. 273p. 1992. pap. 35.00 (*0-7859-8921-8*) Fr & Eur.

Spanish Dictionary of Marketing - Diccionario Del Marketing. J. B. Gonzalez & J. A. Sanchez. 273p. 1992. pap. 36.75 (*84-283-1989-8*, Pub. by Paraninfo) IBD Ltd.

Spanish Dictionary of Practical Examples: El Diccionario Castellano de Ejemplos Practicos. Kenneth A. Hornak. 900p. (SPA.). (C). 1994. 249.50 (*0-9643569-0-2*) Edit Castilla.

Spanish Dictionary of Synonyms, Equivalences & Related Ideas: Diccionario Espanol de Sinonimos, Equivalencias e Ideas Afines. 9th ed. M. F. Andres. 443p. (SPA.). 1982. 19.95 (*0-8288-2014-7*, S12233) Fr & Eur.

Spanish Dictionary of the Hotel Trade. J. F. Gallego. 488p. (SPA.). 1993. pap. 38.00 (*0-7859-8828-9*) Fr & Eur.

Spanish Dictionary of the Hotel Trade - Diccionario de Hosteleria. J. F. Gallego & R. P. Melendo. 488p. 1993. pap. 40.00 (*84-283-2015-2*) IBD Ltd.

Spanish Dictionary of Uncommon Words: Diccionario de Palabras Olvidadas. E. Munoz. 409p. (SPA.). 1992. pap. 30.00 (*0-7859-8922-6*) Fr & Eur.

Spanish Dictionary of Uncommon Words - Diccionario de Palabras Olvidadas. E. Munoz. 409p. (SPA.). 1992. pap. 31.50 (*84-283-1986-3*, Pub. by Paraninfo) IBD Ltd.

Spanish Dishes from the Old Clay Pot. rev. ed. Elinor Burt. (Cookery Ser.). (Illus.). 280p. 1979. reprint ed. pap. 9.95 (*0-89496-001-6*) Ross Bks.

Spanish Doctor. Matt Cohen. LC 84-6426. 352p. 1985. 16.95 (*0-8253-0227-7*) Beaufort Bks NY.

Spanish Dollars & Silver Tokens: Of England. E. M. Kelly. 1977. 30.00 (*0-685-51517-6*) S J Durst.

Spanish Drama: Lope De Vaga & Calderon. George H. Lewes. 1980. lib. bdg. 59.95 (*0-8490-3201-6*) Gordon Pr.

Spanish Drama of Pathos, 1750-1808, Vol. 2. Ivy L. McClelland. LC 70-504666. 300p. reprint ed. pap. 85.50 (*0-8357-3767-5*, 2036496) Bks Demand.

Spanish Drama of Pathos, 1750-1808, Vol. 1: High Tragedy. Ivy L. McClelland. LC 70-504666. 360p. reprint ed. pap. 102.60 (*0-7837-0039-3*, 2036496) Bks Demand.

Spanish Drama of the Golden Age. Ed. by Raymond R. MacCurdy. (SPA.). 1985. reprint ed. 49.50 (*0-89197-985-9*); reprint ed. pap. text ed. 24.95 (*0-89197-986-7*) Irvington.

Spanish Drama of the Golden Age, Vols. 1-2. Regueiro & Riechenberger. 85.00 (*0-87535-137-9*) Hispanic Soc.

Spanish Drama of the Golden Age: A Catalogue of the Comedia Collection in the University of Pennsylvania Libraries. Jose M. Regeiro. LC 75-172289. 106p. 1971. 75.00 (*0-89235-009-1*) Primary Srce Media.

***Spanish Dramatists of the Golden Age: A Bio-Bibliographical Sourcebook.** Ed. by Mary Parker. LC 97-21976. 1998. text ed. write for info. (*0-313-28893-3*, Greenwood Pr) Greenwood.

Spanish-Dutch Concise Dictionary. Van Dale. (DUT & SPA.). 1992. 125.00 (*0-8288-7370-4*) Fr & Eur.

Spanish Economy: From the Civil War to the European Community. Joseph Harrison. (New Studies in Economic & Social History: No. 22). 88p. (C). 1995. text ed. 34.95 (*0-521-55281-8*); pap. text ed. 10.95 (*0-521-55772-0*) Cambridge U Pr.

Spanish Elizabethans: The English Exiles at the Court of Philip II. Albert J. Loomie. LC 63-14407. 293p. reprint ed. pap. 83.60 (*0-7837-0453-4*, 2040776) Bks Demand.

Spanish Empire in America. C. H. Haring. 1990. 14.50 (*0-8446-4021-2*) Peter Smith.

Spanish Empire in America. Clarence H. Haring. LC 47-1142. 1963. pap. 7.95 (*0-15-684701-9*, Harvest Bks) HarBrace.

Spanish-English - English-Spanish. 5th ed. E. MacCrach. 758p. 1990. 26.25 (*84-261-0079-1*) IBD Ltd.

Spanish-English - English-Spanish: Diccionario Conciso Modismos. 3rd ed. Benedito F. Sanchez. 437p. 1988. pap. 36.00 (*84-205-1387-3*); pap. 35.00 (*84-205-2452-2*) IBD Ltd.

Spanish-English - English-Spanish Banking Dictionary. 3rd enl. rev. ed. Rafael G. Esteban. 457p. 1991. pap. 31.50 (*84-283-1848-4*) IBD Ltd.

Spanish-English - English-Spanish Commercial Dictionary. Cuevas Mesa. 255p. 1993. 49.95 (*968-842-422-6*) IBD Ltd.

Spanish-English - English-Spanish Dictionary of Business. P. H. Collin et al. 700p. (ENG & SPA.). 1993. 39.95 (*0-948549-30-0*, Pub. by Peter Collin UK) IBD Ltd.

Spanish-English - English-Spanish Dictionary of Economics & Business. 3rd rev. ed. J. Lozano Irueste. 901p. 1993. 121.50 (*84-368-0757-X*) IBD Ltd.

Spanish-English - English-Spanish Dictionary of Fashion, Garment & Industrial Textiles. L. Zeldis. 251p. 1988. pap. 30.50 (*84-283-1561-2*) IBD Ltd.

Spanish-English - English-Spanish Dictionary of Legal Terms. E. Muniz Castro. 613p. (ENG & SPA.). 1992. 105.00 (*84-7695-108-6*, Pub. by La Ley SP) IBD Ltd.

Spanish-English - English-Spanish Dictionary of Law, Economics & Politics. 4th ed. R. Lacasa Navarro & I. Diaz De Bustamante. 761p. 1991. 138.00 (*84-7130-306-X*, Pub. by Edit De Derecho) IBD Ltd.

Spanish-English - English-Spanish Dictionary of Misleading Terms: False Friends. M. Cuenca. 215p. 1989. pap. 35.75 (*84-205-1548-5*) IBD Ltd.

Spanish-English - English-Spanish Glossary of Audiovisual Communication. Aguadero. 199p. (ENG & SPA.). 1991. pap. 22.25 (*84-283-1879-4*) IBD Ltd.

Spanish-English - English-Spanish Glossary of Psychiatric Terminology. F. P. Gallardo. 316p. (ENG & SPA.). 1989. pap. 42.50 (*84-87189-14-8*) IBD Ltd.

***Spanish-English - English-Spanish Glossary of Psychiatric Terminology.** F. P. Gallardo. 316p. (ENG & SPA.). 1996. pap. 48.00 (*84-7978-234-X*) IBD Ltd.

Spanish-English - English-Spanish Glossary of Science with Spanish Definitions. Hartman. (ENG & SPA.). 1991. 71.00 (*0-7859-8947-1*) Fr & Eur.

Spanish-English - English-Spanish Glossary of Science with Spanish Definitions. Hartman. (Illus.). 604p. 1991. 74.75 (*84-283-1849-2*) IBD Ltd.

Spanish-English - English-Spanish Glossary of Selected Terms Used in International Organizations. 3rd ed. Marina Orellana. 645p. 1993. pap. 36.00 (*0-88431-149-X*) IBD Ltd.

Spanish-English - English-Spanish Law Dictionary. Gerardo Solis & Raul Gasteazoro. 747p. (ENG & SPA.). (C). 1992. pap. text ed. write for info. (*0-314-00846-2*) West Pub.

Spanish-English - English-Spanish Legal Dictionary. E. Alcaraz Varo. Ed. by B. Hughes. 576p. 1993. 60.00 (*84-344-1579-8*) IBD Ltd.

***Spanish-English - English-Spanish Legal Dictionary.** E. Alcaraz Varo & B. Hughes. 576p. 1995. 60.00 (*84-344-0506-7*) IBD Ltd.

Spanish-English - English-Spanish Maritime Dictionary. M. R. Barrientos. 230p. 1986. pap. 28.50 (*84-283-1514-0*) IBD Ltd.

Spanish-English - English-Spanish Thematic Dictionary. J. Merino. 597p. 1977. pap. 15.00 (*84-283-0918-3*); pap. 23.75 (*84-283-1765-8*) IBD Ltd.

Spanish-English--English-Spanish Dictionary of Economics & Business. 3rd ed. J. Lozano Irueste. 901p. (ENG & SPA.). 1993. 110.00 (*0-7859-8829-7*) Fr & Eur.

Spanish-English--English-Spanish Legal Dictionary. E. Alcaraz Varo. 576p. (ENG & SPA.). 1993. 83.00 (*0-7859-8830-0*) Fr & Eur.

Spanish-English & English-Spanish Army-Air Force Terms. Franco F. Ibeas. 121p. (ENG & SPA.). 1983. 49.95 (*0-8288-1911-4*, S60507) Fr & Eur.

Spanish, English & French Computers Dictionaries: Diccionario de Informatica. Georges A. Nania. 783p. (ENG, FRE & SPA.). 1985. 95.00 (*0-8288-0271-8*, S16405) Fr & Eur.

Spanish-English Chemical Dictionary, Hawley's: With English-Spanish Glossary. rev. ed. I. Sax & R. Lewis. 1176p. (ENG & SPA.). 1993. 221.00 (*84-282-0891-3*) IBD Ltd.

Spanish-English Comparative Dictionary of Cognates: Diccionario Comparativo de Cognados en Espanol e Ingles. Elizabeth R. Donn. Ed. by Isabel Camacho De Rodas & Jean K. Lyle. LC 85-90321. (Illus.). 212p. (Orig.). (ENG & SPA.). 1985. pap. 12.95 (*0-932058-02-7*) RoDonn Pub.

S

An Asterisk (*) at the beginning of an entry indicates that the title is appearing in BIP for the first time.

Spanish-English Contrasts: An Introduction to Spanish Linguistics. M. Stanley Whitley. LC 86-22917. 400p. (ENG & SPA.). (C). 1986. 29.95 (*0-87840-095-8*) Georgetown U Pr.

Spanish-English Dictionary. Berlitz Editors. LC 78-78079. (Bilingual Pocket Dictionaries Ser.). 360p. 1994. pap. 7.95 (*2-8315-0989-0*) Berlitz.

Spanish-English Dictionary. Ed. by R. F. Brown. (ENG & SPA.). 35.00 (*0-87559-033-0*) Shalom.

Spanish-English Dictionary. R. F. Brown. 35.00 (*0-87557-076-3*) Saphrograph.

Spanish-English Dictionary. Andrew Morehead. 1996. pap. 4.50 (*0-451-18874-8*, Sig) NAL-Dutton.

Spanish-English Dictionary. rev. ed. Salvatore Ramondino. 1996. pap. 5.99 (*0-451-18168-9*, Sig) NAL-Dutton.

Spanish-English Dictionary. 4th ed. Carlos Castillo. pap. 4.99 (*0-671-74348-1*) PB.

Spanish-English Dictionary of Architecture & Construction: With English Vocabulary. R. E. Putnam. (Illus.). 535p. 1988. pap. 68.25 (*84-283-1560-4*) IBD Ltd.

Spanish-English Dictionary of Common Expressions. Jose Merino & Ana Merino. 187p. 1991. pap. 26.25 (*84-86623-39-1*) IBD Ltd.

Spanish-English Dictionary of Electronics. S. W. Amos. 456p. (ENG & SPA.). 1988. 95.00 (*0-8288-4020-2*, S30010) Fr & Eur.

Spanish-English Dictionary of Electronics with an English-Spanish Vocabulary. 2nd ed. S. W. Amos. (Illus.). 456p. 1988. 56.75 (*84-283-1605-8*) IBD Ltd.

Spanish English Dictionary of Human & Physical Geography. Steven L. Driever. LC 93-29895. 736p. 1993. text ed. 105.00 (*0-313-27920-9*, Greenwood Pr) Greenwood.

Spanish-English Dictionary of Microelectronics. M. Plant. 227p. (ENG & SPA.). 1987. 49.95 (*0-8288-7252-X*, S30009) Fr & Eur.

Spanish-English Dictionary of Microelectronics with an English-Spanish Vocabulary. M. Plant. 227p. 1987. pap. 30.50 (*84-283-1559-0*) IBD Ltd.

Spanish-English, English-Spanish Commercial Dictionary. C. R. Orozco. 208p. (ENG & SPA.). 1969. pap. 35.25 (*0-08-006380-2*, Pergamon Pr) Elsevier.

Spanish-English, English-Spanish Commercial Dictionary: "The Secretary" 4th ed. A. Frias-Sucre Giraud. 298p. (ENG & SPA.). 1990. 20.00 (*84-261-1223-4*) IBD Ltd.

Spanish English, English Spanish Concise Dictionary: Latin American. Ila Warner. 500p. (Orig.). (ENG & SPA.). 1994. pap. 11.95 (*0-7818-0261-X*) Hippocrene Bks.

Spanish-English, English-Spanish Crossword Puzzle Book. Lily Powell-Froissard. (ENG & SPA.). 1979. pap. 2.95 (*0-8065-0676-8*, Citadel Pr) Carol Pub Group.

Spanish-English, English-Spanish Dictionary. Lib. Sanchez Staff. 1704p. 1991. 55.00 (*0-7859-6246-8*, 8476300980) Fr & Eur.

Spanish-English, English-Spanish Dictionary of Banking & Stock Exchange, 2 Vols. Bellisco Hernandez. 163p. Span.-Eng., 163 pp. pap. 45.25 (*84-85198-05-0*); Eng.-Span., 135 pp. pap. 45.25 (*84-85198-02-6*) IBD Ltd.

Spanish-English English-Spanish Dictionary of Computer Terms. Alfred U. Chiri. 120p. 1993. 16.95 (*0-7818-0148-6*) Hippocrene Bks.

Spanish-English, English-Spanish Dictionary of False Friends. M. Cuenca. 215p. (ENG & SPA.). 1989. pap. 34.95 (*0-7859-7483-0*, 8420515485) Fr & Eur.

Spanish-English, English-Spanish Dictionary of Legal Terms: Diccionario de Terminos Legales Espanol-Ingles-Espanol. 12th ed. Louis A. Robb. 228p. (ENG & SPA.). 1982. pap. 49.95 (*0-8288-0405-2*, S28548) Fr & Eur.

Spanish-English, English-Spanish Dictionary of the Fashion, Garment & Textile Industries. L. Zeldis. 251p. (ENG & SPA.). 1988. pap. 49.95 (*0-8288-7395-X*, S30007) Fr & Eur.

***Spanish-English English-Spanish Medical Dictionary.** Onyria H. McElroy & Lola L. Grabb. (ENG & SPA.). pap. 27.50 (*0-614-19693-0*, OP931094WE) AMA.

Spanish-English, English-Spanish Naval Dictionary. 3rd enl. rev. ed. Luis Leal. 232p. 1987. pap. 24.25 (*84-283-1089-0*) IBD Ltd.

Spanish-English, English-Spanish Political, Legal & Economics Dictionary: Diccionario de Derecho, Economia y Politica Espanol-Ingles-Espanol. 4th ed. R. Lacasa & I. D. Bustamante. 763p. (ENG & SPA.). 1991. 125.00 (*0-8288-0404-4*, S39842) Fr & Eur.

Spanish-English, English-Spanish Practical Dictionary. enl. rev. ed. (Practical Dictionaries Ser.). 338p. 1993. pap. 9.95 (*0-7818-0179-6*) Hippocrene Bks.

Spanish-English Grammar Flipper. 49p. (ENG & SPA.). (YA). (gr. 5 up). 1992. 6.75 (*1-878383-24-8*) C Lee Pubns.

Spanish-English Handbook. 3rd ed. Jesus Perez-Sabido. 224p. 1988. pap. 29.95 (*0-87489-478-6*) Med Econ.

Spanish-English Horticultural Dictionary. D. O. Bourke et al. 148p. 1987. pap. 95.00 (*0-8288-0064-2*, F46900); pap. text ed. 35.00 (*0-85198-572-6*) CAB Intl.

Spanish-English Housekeeping. Ruth M. Dietz. (Illus.). 156p. (ENG & SPA.). 1983. pap. 14.95 (*0-89015-379-5*) Sunbelt Media.

Spanish-English Illustrated Medical Dictionary, 2 Vols. 27th ed. Dorlands. (Illus.). (ENG & SPA.). 1992. 250.00 (*0-7859-8835-1*) Fr & Eur.

Spanish English Pocket Dictionary. Houghton Mifflin Company Staff. 1993. pap. 3.95 (*0-395-67769-6*) HM.

Spanish-English-Spanish Encyclopedic Dictionary of Technical Terms, 3 vols. J. L. Collazo. 2300p. (ENG & SPA.). 1981. 195.00 (*0-8288-0665-9*, S32369) Fr & Eur.

Spanish-English-Spanish Lexicon of Entomological & Related Terms. Margaret Greiff. 262p. (ENG & SPA.). 1985. pap. 85.00 (*0-8288-0750-7*, M1541) Fr & Eur.

Spanish-English Technical Dictionary. R. L. Guinle. 37.50 (*0-87559-187-6*) Shalom.

Spanish-English Technical Dictionary. 4th ed. Guy Malgorn. Tr. by M. R. Rodriguez & P. Armisen. 570p. (ENG & SPA.). 1990. 41.00 (*84-283-1354-7*) IBD Ltd.

Spanish-English Technical Dictionary. 4th ed. Guy Malgorn. (ENG & SPA.). 1990. 39.00 (*0-7859-8966-8*) Fr & Eur.

Spanish-English/English-Spanish Dictionary. Philip Lief. 320p. (ENG & SPA.). 1996. mass mkt. 5.99 (*0-440-22087-4*) Dell.

Spanish Englishwoman: The Glass Graduate & the Power of Blood. Cervantes. Ed. by Price. (Complete Exemplary Novels Ser.: Vol. 2). 1992. 49.95 (*0-85668-493-7*, Pub. by Aris & Phillips UK); pap. 22.00 (*0-85668-494-5*, Pub. by Aris & Phillips UK) David Brown.

Spanish, European Fast-Track. 304p. pap. text ed. 125.00 incl. audio (*0-88432-786-8*, FTSP10) Audio-Forum.

Spanish Exchange! Ron Henley & Paul Hodges. (ChessBase University Power Play! Ser.). (Illus.). 64p. (Orig.). 1994. pap. 12.95 (*1-883358-08-6*) R&D Pub NJ.

Spanish Expeditions into Texas, 1689-1768. William C. Foster. LC 94-37235. 1995. 45.00 (*0-292-72488-8*); pap. 19.95 (*0-292-72489-6*) U of Tex Pr.

Spanish Exploration in the Southwest, 1542-1706. Herbert E. Bolton. (BCL1 - United States Local History Ser.). 487p. 1991. reprint ed. lib. bdg. 99.00 (*0-7812-6333-6*) Rprt Serv.

Spanish Exploration in the Southwest, 1542-1706. Herbert E. Bolton. 1992. reprint ed. lib. bdg. 75.00 (*0-7812-5009-9*) Rprt Serv.

Spanish Explorations in the Southwest, 1542-1706. Herbert E. Bolton. 1993. reprint ed. lib. bdg. 75.00 (*0-7812-5867-7*) Rprt Serv.

Spanish Explorations in the Strait of Juan De Fuca. Henry R. Wagner. LC 70-137275. reprint ed. 49.50 (*0-404-06801-4*) AMS Pr.

Spanish Explorers in the Southern United States, 1528-1543. LC 84-80799. (Illus.). 411p. 1990. reprint ed. 24.95 (*0-87611-066-9*) Tex St Hist Assn.

Spanish Explorers in the Southern United States, 1528-1543, 3 pts., Set. 1993. reprint ed. lib. bdg. 75.00 (*0-7812-5905-3*) Rprt Serv.

***Spanish Family Cookbook.** 2nd rev. ed. Juan Serano & Susan Serano. (Original Cookbook Ser.). 270p. 1997. pap. 11.95 (*0-7818-0546-5*) Hippocrene Bks.

Spanish Fighters: An Oral History of War & Exile. Neil MacMaster. 260p. 1991. text ed. 49.95 (*0-312-04738-X*) St Martin.

Spanish Film under Franco. Virginia Higginbotham. LC 87-15649. (Illus.). 176p. 1987. pap. 11.95 (*0-292-77603-9*); text ed. 20.00 (*0-292-77591-1*) U of Tex Pr.

***Spanish Fly.** Tobalina. (Illus.). 48p. (Orig.). 1997. pap. 8.95 (*1-56163-179-5*, Eurotica) NBM.

***Spanish Fly.** Tobalina. (Illus.). 64p. 1997. pap. 12.95 (*1-56163-195-7*, Eurotica) NBM.

Spanish Fly, Vol. 1. Tobalina. 64p. (Orig.). 1994. pap. 9.95 (*1-56163-115-9*, Eurotica) NBM.

Spanish Fly, Vol. 2. Tobalina. (Illus.). 64p. (Orig.). 1996. pap. 9.95 (*1-56163-154-X*, Eurotica) NBM.

Spanish for Americans. Yara Marrase. 88p. 1983. pap. 2.95 (*1-884249-02-7*, TX 139-381) Pub Especiales.

Spanish for Beginners. Charles Duff. (Orig.). 1971. pap. 12.00 (*0-06-463271-7*, EH 271) HarpC.

Spanish for Beginners. Angela Wilkes. (Beginners Ser.). 50p. (J). (ps-1). 1994. 8.95 (*0-8442-7628-6*, Natl Textbk) NTC Pub Grp.

Spanish for Bus-Finance. 3rd ed. Ana C. Jarvis. LC 87-81232. (C). 1988. pap. text ed. 27.56 (*0-669-12247-5*); audio 31.16 (*0-669-12248-3*) HM College Div.

Spanish for Business. (Hugo Ser.). 220p. (Orig.). 1994. pap. 9.95 (*0-85285-207-X*); pap. 39.95 incl. audio (*0-85285-208-8*) Hunter NJ.

Spanish for Business. Ralph Kite. 1993. pap. text ed. write for info. (*0-07-911379-6*) McGraw.

Spanish for Business: Intermediate Level. Albert C. Eyde & Beatriz P. Zeller. 162p. (Orig.). 1984. pap. text ed. 185.00 incl. audio (*0-88432-129-0*, S24300) Audio-Forum.

Spanish for Business & Finance. 4th ed. Ana C. Jarvis & Raquel Lebredo. (Basic Spanish Grammar Ser.). 300p. (ENG & SPA.). (C). 1992. pap. text ed. 27.56 (*0-669-24298-5*); Cassettes. audio 31.16 (*0-669-24300-0*) HM College Div.

***Spanish for Business & Finance.** 5th ed. Jarvis & Raquel Lebredo. 369p. (C). 1996. pap. text ed. 26.76 (*0-669-35463-5*) HM College Div.

Spanish for Children: For Young Learners. Catherine Bruzzone. 80p. (SPA.). (J). 1995. pap. 15.95 (*0-8442-9166-8*, Natl Textbk) NTC Pub Grp.

Spanish for Children: For Young Learners. Catherine Bruzzone. 80p. (SPA.). (J). 1995. pap. 29.95 incl. audio (*0-8442-9165-X*, Natl Textbk) NTC Pub Grp.

Spanish for Communication. William E. Bull. 1972. 35.96 (*0-685-39915-X*) HM.

Spanish for Communication. 3rd ed. Ana C. Jarvis. LC 87-81232. (C). 1988. student ed., pap. text ed. 27.56 (*0-669-12245-9*); audio 31.16 (*0-669-12246-7*) HM College Div.

Spanish for Communication. 4th ed. Ana C. Jarvis & Raquel Lebredo. (Basic Spanish Grammar Ser.). 346p. (ENG & SPA.). (C). 1992. pap. text ed. 27.56 (*0-669-24292-6*); Cassettes. audio 31.16 (*0-669-24293-4*) HM College Div.

Spanish for Communication, Level 1. William E. Bull et al. (C). 1975. write for info. (*0-318-53418-5*) HM.

Spanish for Communication, Level 2. William E. Bull. (C). 1976. student ed. 6.60 (*0-685-02312-5*); text ed. 20.40 (*0-685-02311-7*); teacher ed. 26.76 (*0-685-02313-3*) HM.

Spanish for Gringos. William C. Harvey. 160p. 1990. pap. 9.95 (*0-8120-4434-7*) Barron.

Spanish for Gringos, Set 2. William C. Harvey. 1992. 21.95 incl. audio (*0-8120-7889-6*) Barron.

***Spanish for Gringos Level 2.** William Harvey. 1997. pap. text ed. 10.95 (*0-8120-9743-2*) Barron.

Spanish for Health Care Professionals. William C. Harvey. 1994. pap. 11.95 (*0-8120-1730-7*) Barron.

***Spanish for Health Care Workers: A Cassette Study Course for Beginning to Intermediate Spanish Speakers.** Sarah Ison. (Illus.). 90p. 1997. wbk. ed., pap. text ed. 44.95 incl. audio (*0-9655168-4-9*) Around Wrld Pub.

***Spanish for Health Professionals: Ingles para Profesionistas de la Salud.** Dario Sanchez. (Significant Learning Ser.: Vol. 1). (Illus.). 242p. 1997. pap. text ed. 39.95 incl. cd-rom (*0-9658803-1-1*) Comp Res Assocs.

***Spanish for Human Resources Managers.** William C. Harvey. 1997. pap. text ed. 11.95 (*0-8120-9887-0*) Barron.

Spanish for Kids. Pamela Rand. (Illus.). 31p. (Orig.). (J). (ps-6). 1990. pap. 19.95 incl. digital audio (*1-878245-01-5*) OptimaLearning.

***Spanish for Las Enforcement.** (Living Language Ser.). 1997. pap. write for info. (*0-609-60088-5*) Crown Pub Group.

Spanish for Law & Law Enforcement. Ralph Kite. (SPA.). 1993. pap. text ed. write for info. (*0-07-911382-6*) McGraw.

Spanish for Law Enforcement. 3rd ed. Ana C. Jarvis et al. LC 87-81232. (ENG & SPA.). (C). 1988. audio 31.16 (*0-669-12253-X*) HM College Div.

Spanish for Law Enforcement. 4th ed. Ana C. Jarvis & Oliver. (Basic Spanish Grammar Ser.). 255p. (ENG & SPA.). (C). 1992. pap. text ed. 27.56 (*0-669-24301-9*); Cassettes. audio 31.16 (*0-669-24302-7*) HM College Div.

***Spanish for Law Enforcement.** 5th ed. Oliver et al. 284p. (C). 1996. pap. text ed. 26.76 (*0-669-35461-9*) HM College Div.

Spanish for Law Enforcement Officers. Tr. by Roberto I. Berger. 16p. (Orig.). 1993. pap. 2.00 (*1-884493-02-5*) Pocket Pr.

Spanish for Law Enforcement Officers, 2 vols. Mariano Garcia. 1990. teacher ed. 6.60 (*0-8325-9625-6*, Natl Textbk) NTC Pub Grp.

Spanish for Law Enforcement Officers, 2 vols., 1. Mariano Garcia. 1994. pap. text ed. 18.60 (*0-8325-9626-4*, Natl Textbk) NTC Pub Grp.

Spanish for Law Enforcement Officers, 2 vols., 2. Mariano Garcia. 1995. pap. text ed. 10.60 (*0-8325-9628-0*, Natl Textbk) NTC Pub Grp.

Spanish for Law Enforcement Officers, 2 vols., No. 1. 85th ed. Mariano Garcia. 1993. student ed. 9.25 (*0-8325-9627-2*, Natl Textbk) NTC Pub Grp.

Spanish for Law Enforcement Officers, 2 vols., No. 2. 72th ed. Mariano Garcia. 1990. student ed. 9.25 (*0-8325-9629-9*, Natl Textbk) NTC Pub Grp.

Spanish for Law Enforcement Personnel. William C. Harvey. 165p. 1996. pap. 10.95 (*0-8120-9367-4*) Barron.

***Spanish for Law Enforecement.** Crown Publishing Group Staff. 1997. pap. 18.00 (*0-609-80137-6*, Living Language) Crown Pub Group.

Spanish for Librarians. 25p. 1992. pap. 24.95 incl. audio (*1-879090-13-9*, SSP370) Audio-Forum.

Spanish For Med-Personnel. 3rd ed. Ana C. Jarvis. LC 87-81232. (C). 1988. student ed., pap. text ed. 27.56 (*0-669-12249-1*); audio 31.16 (*0-669-12250-5*) HM College Div.

Spanish for Medical Personnel. Janet E. Meizel. 1993. pap. 21.95 (*1-56930-001-1*) Skidmore Roth Pub.

Spanish for Medical Personnel. 4th ed. Ana C. Jarvis & Raquel Lebredo. (Basic Spanish Grammar Ser.). 243p. (ENG & SPA.). (C). 1992. pap. text ed. 27.56 (*0-669-24296-9*); Cassettes. audio 31.16 (*0-669-24297-7*) HM College Div.

***Spanish for Medical Personnel.** 5th ed. Jarvis & Raquel Lebredo. (C). 1996. pap. text ed. 26.76 (*0-669-35459-7*) HM College Div.

Spanish for Oral & Writing. 5th ed. Iglesias. (C). 1994. lab manual ed., wbk. ed., pap. text ed. 29.50 (*0-15-501094-8*) HB Coll Pubs.

Spanish for Oral & Written Review. 4th ed. Mario Iglesias & Walter Meiden. 464p. (C). 1991. pap. text ed. 25.50 (*0-03-030448-2*) HB Coll Pubs.

Spanish for Oral & Written Review. 5th ed. Mario Iglesias & Walter Meiden. 580p. (C). 1994. pap. text ed. write for info. (*0-15-501093-X*) HB Coll Pubs.

Spanish for Police & Firefighters, Set. Jose Cerrudo. 55p. 1995. pap. 59.50 incl. audio (*0-88432-072-3*, SSP450) Audio-Forum.

***Spanish for Public Safety Personnel.** 2nd rev. ed. Arthur M. McCarthy & James A. Nocito. (Illus.). 149p. 1996. pap. text ed. 24.99 (*1-890431-00-1*) Anticipatory Lang Lrning.

***Spanish for Public Safety Personnel Laminated Booklet.** 2nd rev. ed. Arthur M. McCarthy & James A. Nocito. 60p. 1996. ring bd. 39.95 (*1-890431-02-8*) Anticipatory Lang Lrning.

Spanish for Social Sciences. Denis L. Heck. (SPA.). 1993. pap. text ed. write for info. (*0-07-911384-2*) McGraw.

Spanish for Social Services. 3rd ed. Ana C. Jarvis. LC 87-81232. (C). 1988. student ed., pap. text ed. 27.56 (*0-669-12254-8*); audio 31.16 (*0-669-12255-6*) HM College Div.

Spanish for Social Services. 4th ed. Ana C. Jarvis & Raquel Lebredo. (Basic Spanish Grammar Ser.). 234p. (ENG & SPA.). (C). 1992. pap. text ed. 27.56 (*0-669-24303-5*); Cassettes. audio 31.16 (*0-669-24304-3*) HM College Div.

***Spanish for Social Services.** 5th ed. Jarvis & Raquel Lebredo. 274p. (C). 1996. pap. text ed. 26.76 (*0-669-35465-1*) HM College Div.

Spanish for Teachers. 2nd ed. Ana C. Jarvis et al. LC 87-81232. (ENG & SPA.). (C). 1988. pap. text ed. 27.56 (*0-669-12256-4*) HM College Div.

Spanish for Teachers. 3rd ed. Ana C. Jarvis & Raquel Lebredo. LC 87-81232. (Basic Spanish Grammar Ser.). 201p. (ENG & SPA.). (C). 1992. pap. text ed. 27.56 (*0-669-24305-1*); Cassettes. audio 31.16 (*0-669-24306-X*) HM College Div.

***Spanish for Teachers.** 4th ed. Jarvis & Raquel Lebredo. 263p. (C). 1996. pap. text ed. 26.76 (*0-669-35467-8*) HM College Div.

Spanish for the Business Traveler. T. Bruce Fryer & Hugo J. Faria. LC 93-23414. (Foreign Language Business Dictionaries Ser.). 600p. 1994. pap. 9.95 (*0-8120-1773-0*) Barron.

***Spanish for the Business Traveler Cassette Package.** Morrison & Conaway. (ENG & SPA.). 1996. 21.95 incl. audio (*0-8120-8399-7*) Barron.

Spanish for the Health Professional, Set 4. Jose Cerrudo. 40p. 1993. pap. 49.50 incl. audio (*0-88432-650-0*, SSP300) Audio-Forum.

Spanish for the Housewife. Rex R. Kelly & George W. Kelly. 163p. (Orig.). 1973. reprint ed. pap. 8.50 (*0-9623796-1-1*) Kelly Brothers.

Spanish for the Medical Professions. Ralph Kite. 1992. pap. text ed. write for info. (*0-07-911383-4*) McGraw.

Spanish for the School Nurse's Office: English-Spanish. Barbara Thuro. LC 85-70256. (Orig.). (J). (ps-12). 1991. pap. 17.95 (*0-932825-02-8*) Ammie Enter.

Spanish, French, & English Relations with Native Americans: Native Populations of the Americas. George E. Ellis & Justin Winsor. 250p. 1997. pap. 25.00 (*0-918680-53-0*) Bagehot Council.

Spanish-French, French-Spanish Diccionario Cuyas. (FRE & SPA.). 1990. 15.00 (*84-7183-047-7*) Colton Bk.

Spanish from Within Transcript. Petit. (College Spanish Ser.). 1989. pap. 19.95 (*0-8384-1582-2*) Wadsworth Pub.

Spanish Frontier in North America. David J. Weber. (Illus.). 592p. (C). 1992. 40.00 (*0-300-05198-0*) Yale U Pr.

Spanish Frontier in North America. David J. Weber. (Illus.). 599p. 1994. pap. 16.00 (*0-300-05917-5*) Yale U Pr.

Spanish Frontier in the Enlightened Age: Franciscan Beginnings in Sonora & Arizona, 1767-1770. Kieran McCarthy. (Monograph Ser.). 1981. 30.00 (*0-88383-063-9*) AAFH.

Spanish Fun: Games & Puzzles, Cutting, Sticking & Colouring. Catherine Bruzzone. (Illus.). 16p. 1995. pap. 5.95 (*0-8442-7644-8*, Passport Bks) NTC Pub Grp.

Spanish Fun Books. (Illus.). (SPA.). (J). 1995. boxed, pap. 7.00 (*0-486-28661-4*) Dover.

Spanish Gardens & Patios. M. Byne. 1976. lib. bdg. 75.00 (*0-8490-2649-0*) Gordon Pr.

Spanish Genre Painting in the Seventeenth Century. Mariana Haraszti-Takacs. 284p. 1983. 182.00 (*0-685-18072-7*) St Mut.

Spanish Genre Painting in the 17th Century. M. Haraszti-Takacs. 283p. (C). 1983. pap. 135.00 (*963-05-2818-5*, Pub. by Akad Kiado HU) St Mut.

Spanish-German Business Dictionary: Wirtschaftssprache Spanisch-Deutsch. 3rd ed. Gunther Haensch. 484p. (GER & SPA.). 1982. 85.00 (*0-8288-0823-6*, M7684) Fr & Eur.

Spanish-German, German-Spanish Diccionario Cuyas. (GER & SPA.). 1990. 15.00 (*84-7183-002-7*) Colton Bk.

Spanish Gipsy Paso Doble Flamenco Style. (Ballroom Dance Ser.). 1986. lib. bdg. 79.95 (*0-8490-3422-1*) Gordon Pr.

Spanish Girl & Boy Paper Dolls. Kathy Allert. (Illus.). (J). (gr. k-3). 1993. pap. 2.95 (*0-486-27499-3*) Dover.

***Spanish Glossary for Lial Mathematics Books.** Distravalo. (C). 1998. pap. text ed. write for info. (*0-321-01647-5*) Addson-Wesley Educ.

Spanish Glossary of Insurance Terms. 2nd ed. Merritt Company Staff. 209p. 1994. pap. 9.95 (*0-930868-83-8*) Merritt Pub.

Spanish Golden Age Autobiography in Its Context Vol. 203. Rainer H. Goetz. LC 93-13112. (American University Studies: No. II). 208p. (C). 1994. text ed. 42.95 (*0-8204-2053-0*) P Lang Pubng.

Spanish Golden Age in Poetry & Drama. Ed. by Edgar A. Peers. LC 74-5001. 220p. 1974. reprint ed. 50.00 (*0-87753-060-2*) Phaeton.

Spanish Golden Age Poetry & Drama. Edgar A. Peers. LC 76-28691. reprint ed. 32.50 (*0-404-15032-2*) AMS Pr.

***Spanish Government in New Mexico.** 2nd ed. Marc Simmons. LC 89-70757. (Illus.). 256p. 1990. reprint ed. pap. 73.00 (*0-608-04142-4*, 2064875) Bks Demand.

Spanish Grammar. Bridget Aldaraca & Edward Baker. LC 85-14162. (College Outline Ser.). 250p. (C). 1986. pap. text ed. 10.25 (*0-15-601689-3*) HB Coll Pubs.

***Spanish Grammar.** Berlitz Editors. 262p. 1998. pap. 10.95 (*2-8315-6396-8*) Berlitz.

Spanish Grammar. Ed. by John Butt. 352p. 1997. pap. 6.95 (*0-19-860043-7*) OUP.

***Spanish Grammar.** Christopher Kendris. (Grammar Card Guides Ser.). (ENG & SPA.). 1966. pap. 3.95 (*0-8120-5081-9*) Barron.

Spanish Grammar. Christopher Kendris. (Grammar Ser.). 256p. 1990. pap. 6.95 (*0-8120-4295-6*) Barron.

Spanish Grammar. Juan Mendez. LC 90-56014. (College Outline Ser.). 336p. (Orig.). 1991. pap. 14.00 (*0-06-467129-1*, Harper Ref) HarpC.

Spanish Grammar. Hippocrene Staff. 224p. 1997. reprint ed. pap. 12.95 (*0-87052-893-9*) Hippocrene Bks.

Spanish Grammar & Culture Through Proverbs. Richard D. Woods. xvi, 108p. 1990. 35.00 (*0-916379-53-1*) Scripta.

***Spanish Grammar & Exercises.** Harraps. 1997. 6.95 (*0-02-861724-X*) Macmillan.

Spanish Grammar Flipper 1. Sherry Kiracofe. 39p. (YA). (gr. 5 up). 1992. 6.75 (*1-878383-19-1*) C Lee Pubns.

S

S

Spanish Grammar Flipper 2: A Guide to Correct Spanish Usage. James M. Hendrickson. 49p. (YA). (gr. 8 up). 1988. 6.75 (1-878383-11-6) C Lee Pubns.

Spanish Grammar for Independent Learners: SGIL. Avagail Azoulay & Arie Vicenete. (Illus.). 380p. (ENG & SPA.). 1996. pap. text ed. write for info. (1-888762-00-4) VIC Lang.

***Spanish Grammar for Public Safety Personnel.** 2nd rev. ed. Arthur M. McCarthy & James A. Nocito. (Illus.). 36p. 1996. pap. text ed. 8.95 (1-890431-01-X) Anticipatory Lang Lrning.

Spanish Grammar for Reading. Francis A. Giuliano. (C). 1976. text ed. write for info. (0-13-087776-X) P-H.

Spanish Grammar Handbook. Berlitz Editors. (Handbook Ser.). 262p. 1993. pap. 8.95 (2-8315-1355-3) Berlitz.

Spanish Grammar in Review. Kenneth Chastain. 352p. 1994. pap. 16.95 (0-8442-7670-7, Natl Textbk) NTC Pub Grp.

Spanish Grammar in Review. 2nd ed. Holton et al. (Illus.). 336p. (C). 1994. pap. text ed. 45.00 (0-13-181660-8) P-H.

***Spanish Grammar Notebook.** unabridged ed. Mila Vujovich-LaBarre. 299p. (YA). (gr. 5-12). 1994. pap. text ed. 22.50 (1-890753-00-9) Ganas Co.

Spanish Guitar. Laurence Libin et al. (Illus.). 210p. (ENG & SPA.). (C). reprint ed. pap. 65.00 (0-933224-79-6, Pub. by Opera Tres SP) Bold Strummer Ltd.

Spanish Guitar Music. 32p. 1986. pap. 4.95 (0-7935-3583-2, 50336960) H Leonard.

Spanish Gypsy Paso Doble Flamenco Style. (Ballroom Dance Ser.). 1985. lib. bdg. 75.00 (0-87700-814-0) Revisionist Pr.

Spanish Handy Dictionary. (ENG & SPA.). 1992. pap. 8.95 (0-7818-0012-9) Hippocrene Bks.

Spanish Harlem. Joseph Rodriguez. LC 94-35015. (American Scene Ser.: Vol. 3). (Illus.). 1994. pap. 27.50 (1-881616-24-X) Dist Art Pubs.

Spanish Hebrew Literature & the Arab Literary Tradition: Arabic Themes in Hebrew Andalusian Poetry. Arie Schippers. LC 93-44404. (Medieval Iberian Peninsula, Texts & Studies: Vol. 7). 1993. 122.50 (90-04-09869-0) E J Brill.

Spanish Heritage in the United States. Dario Fernandez-Florez. Ed. by Carlos E. Cortes. LC 79-6204. (Hispanics in the United States Ser.). (Illus.). 1981. reprint ed. lib. bdg. 37.95 (0-405-13155-0) Ayer.

Spanish Historical Novel Eighteen Seventy to Nineteen Seventy: A Study of Ten Spanish Novelists, & Their Treatment of the "Episodio Nacional" Madeleine D. Fletcher. (Monagrafias A Ser.: Vol. XXXII). 174p. (Orig.). (C). 1973. pap. 36.00 (0-900411-69-4, Pub. by Tamesis Bks Ltd UK) Boydell & Brewer.

Spanish Historical Writing about the New World, 1493-1700. Susan L. Newbury & Angel Delgado-Gomez. (Illus.). xiv, 130p. (Orig.). 1994. 50.00 (0-916617-40-8) J C Brown.

Spanish History: Selected Texts from the Fall of Granada in 1492 to Modern Times. Ed. by Salvador Ortiz-Carboneres. LC 89-31905. 221p. 1989. 19.95 (0-85496-095-3) Berg Pubs.

Spanish History & Literature: Classification Schedule, Author & Title Listing, Chronological Listing. Harvard University Library Staff. LC 72-75827. (Widener Library Shelflist: No. 41). 783p. 1972. text ed. 60.00 (0-674-83095-4) HUP.

Spanish Holiday. Lizbeth Dusseau. (Orig.). 1993. mass mkt. 4.95 (1-56333-185-3) Masquerade.

Spanish Holiday Activity Workbook. Patricia Snyder. (Illus.). 100p. (Orig.). (YA). (gr. 9-12). 1986. 19.95 (0-9617764-0-4) PS Enterprises.

***Spanish Holiday Book.** Leslie C. Stockham. (Illus.). 48p. (J). (ps-2). 1986. pap. 5.98 (0-9624096-5-0) Bilingual Lang Mat.

***Spanish House.** large type ed. Nancy John. (Linford Romance Large Print Ser.). 384p. 1997. pap. 16.99 (0-7089-5016-7, Linford) Ulverscroft.

Spanish-Hungarian Concise Dictionary. Gy. Dorogman. 876p. 1992. 45.00 (963-05-5987-0, Pub. by Akad Kiado HU) St Mut.

Spanish-Hungarian Dictionary: Diccionario Manual Espano-Hungaro. 3rd ed. Laszlo Galdi. 800p. (HUN & SPA.). 1981. 14.95 (0-8288-1672-7, S7423) Fr & Eur.

Spanish-Hungarian Dictionary: Spanyol-Magyar Szotar: Diccionario Espanol-Hungaro. Laszlo Galdi. 800p. (HUN & SPA.). 1981. 39.95 (0-8288-1673-5, S12399) Fr & Eur.

Spanish-Hungarian Pocket Dictionary. Laszlo Galdi. 800p. 1992. 21.00 (963-205-282-X, Pub. by Akad Kiado HU) St Mut.

Spanish Idioms. 2nd ed. Eugene Saviano & Lynn W. Winget. 350p. 1996. pap., vinyl bd. 6.95 (0-8120-9027-6) Barron.

Spanish Imperialism & the Political Imagination. Anthony Pagden. LC 89-22644. 196p. (C). 1990. text ed. 30.00 (0-300-04676-6) Yale U Pr.

Spanish in a Taco Shell. Yolanda P. Garcia. (Illus.). (Orig.). (ENG & SPA.). (J). (gr. 4-9). pap. 10.95 (0-935303-04-9) Victory Pub.

***Spanish in Contact: Issues in Bilingualism.** Ed. by Ana Roca & John Jensen. LC 96-44936. 1996. pap. 23.95 (1-57473-008-8) Cascadilla Pr.

Spanish in Four Continents: Studies in Language Contact & Bilingualism. Ed. by Carmen Silva-Corvalan. LC 94-23284. 316p. (ENG & SPA.). 1995. 49.95 (0-87840-247-0) Georgetown U Pr.

***Spanish in Four Continents: Studies in Language Contact & Bilingualism.** Ed. by Carmen Silva-Corvalan & Hector Campos. LC 94-23284. (Studies in Romance Linguistics). 316p. 1997. pap. 23.95 (0-87840-649-2) Georgetown U Pr.

Spanish in Review. J. B. Dalbor. 184p. 1992. pap. text ed. 19.50 (0-471-54569-4) Wiley.

Spanish in Review. 2nd ed. John B. Dalbor & H. Tracy Sturcken. 352p. (C). 1992. pap. text ed. 27.50 (0-471-60093-8) Wiley.

Spanish in the Americas, Set. Eleanor G. Cotton & John M. Sharp. LC 87-12005. 399p. (Orig.). (C). 1988. 39.95 incl. audio (0-87840-094-X) Georgetown U Pr.

Spanish in the Field: Practical Spanish for Ranchers, Farmers, Vintners, Set 4. Carmen P. Clough. LC 83-62192. 256p. 1983. Set. 59.95 incl. audio (0-932857-02-7) Ag Access.

Spanish in the Field Dictionary: English-Spanish - Spanish-English for Farm & Agribusiness. Carmen P. Clough et al. 160p. (C). 1990. reprint ed. pap. 7.95 (0-932857-01-9, 83062192) Ag Access.

Spanish in the United States: Linguistic Contact & Diversity. Ed. by Ana Roca & John M. Lipski. LC 93-14956. (Studies in Anthropological Linguistics: No. 6). viii, 212p. (C). 1993. lib. bdg. 106.15 (3-11-013204-4) Mouton.

***Spanish in the United States: Sociolinguistic Issues.** Ed. by John J. Bergen. LC 90-32166. (Illus.). 179p. 1990. reprint ed. pap. 51.10 (0-608-04092-4, 2064824) Bks Demand.

Spanish in the United States: Sociological Issues. Ed. by John J. Bergen. LC 90-32166. 175p. (Orig.). 1990. pap. 11.95 (0-87840-232-2) Georgetown U Pr.

Spanish in Three Months. (Hugo's Language Bks.). 192p. (Orig.). 1987. pap. 9.95 (0-85285-065-4) Hunter NJ.

Spanish in Three Months. (Hugo's Language Bks.). 192p. (Orig.). 1987. 39.95 incl. audio (0-85285-070-0) Hunter NJ.

***Spanish in 10 Minutes a Day.** Kris Kerchul. 1997. pap. text ed. 19.95 (0-944502-59-8) Bilingual Bk Pr.

Spanish in 32 Lessons. Adrienne. 224p. 1995. pap. 11.00 (0-393-31305-0, Norton Paperbks) Norton.

Spanish in 7 Days. Shirley Baldwin et al. (Language in 7 Days Ser.). 96p. (SPA.). 1995. pap. 12.95 incl. audio (0-8442-9130-7, Natl Textbk) NTC Pub Grp.

Spanish-Indian Relations in Florida: A Study of Two Visitas, 1657-1678. Fred L. Pearson, Jr. LC 90-14048. (Evolution of North American Indians Ser.: Vol. 15). 336p. 1990. reprint ed. text ed. 20.00 (0-8240-2510-5) Garland.

Spanish Influences on English Literature. Martin Hume. LC 65-15903. (Studies in Comparative Literature: No. 35). 1969. reprint ed. lib. bdg. 75.00 (0-8383-0573-3) M S G Haskell Hse.

Spanish Inquisition. Cecil Roth. Date not set. reprint ed. pap. write for info. (0-393-31549-5) Norton.

Spanish Inquisition & the Inquisitional Mind. Ed. by Angel Alcala. (Atlantic Studies: No. 49). 1987. text ed. 84.00 (0-88033-952-7, SC49) Brooklyn Coll Pr.

Spanish Inquisition I: Zaitsev Variation. Ed. by Eric Schiller. 106p. (Orig.). 1990. pap. 6.50 (0-931462-89-4) Chess Ent.

Spanish Institutions of the Southwest. Frank W. Blackmar. LC 78-64254. (Johns Hopkins University. Studies in the Social Sciences. Thirtieth Ser. 1912: 10). reprint ed. 47.50 (0-404-61358-6) AMS Pr.

Spanish Interpreter. Michele Melaragno. 150p. 1996. pap. text ed. 11.95 (1-889421-05-7) Minerva Archit.

Spanish Ironwork. M. Byne. 1976. lib. bdg. 75.00 (0-8490-2650-4) Gordon Pr.

Spanish-Italian, Italian-Spanish Diccionario Cuyas: Spanish-Italian, Italian-Spanish. (ITA & SPA.). 1990. 15.00 (84-7183-045-0) Colton Bk.

Spanish-Italian, Italian-Spanish Dictionary: Diccionario Italiano-Espanol-Italiano, Vol. 2. E. M. Amador. 1550p. 1983. 150.00 (0-8288-0377-3, S12383) Fr & Eur.

Spanish-Japanese Dictionary: Diccionario Espanol-Japones. L. S. Martinez & M. M. Kato. 1103p. (JPN & SPA.). 1982. 150.00 (0-8288-1021-4, S40503) Fr & Eur.

Spanish Jesuit Churches in Mexico's Tarahumara. Paul M. Roca. LC 78-14467. 394p. 1979. reprint ed. pap. 112.30 (0-608-02360-4, 2063002) Bks Demand.

Spanish, Jr. H. S. Jack Rudman. (Teachers License Examination Ser.: T-56). 1994. pap. 27.95 (0-8373-8056-1) Nat Learn.

Spanish, Just Enough Book. (Hugo's Language Courses Ser.). 128p. (Orig.). 1995. pap. 5.95 (0-85285-224-X) Hunter NJ.

Spanish, Just Enough Cassette Course. (Hugo's Language Courses Ser.). 128p. 1995. pap. 15.95 incl. audio (0-85285-225-8) Hunter NJ.

Spanish Key Words: The Basic Two Thousand Word Vocabulary Arranged by Frequency in a Hundred Units with Comprehensive Italian & English Indexes. Pedro Casal. (Language & Literature Ser.: Vol. 14). 144p. (Orig.). 1992. pap. 13.50 (0-906672-26-0) Oleander Pr.

Spanish Kidnapping Disaster. Mary D. Hahn. 144p. (J). 1993. pap. 3.99 (0-380-71712-3, Camelot) Avon.

Spanish Kidnapping Disaster. Mary D. Hahn. Ed. by James C. Giblin. 144p. (J). (gr. 4-7). 1991. 14.95 (0-395-55696-1, Clarion Bks) HM.

Spanish Labyrinth: An Account of the Social & Political Background of the Spanish Civil War. Gerald Brenan. (Canto Book Ser.). 404p. 1950. text ed. 89.95 (0-521-04314-X) Cambridge U Pr.

Spanish Labyrinth: An Account of the Social & Political Background of the Spanish Civil War. Gerald Brenan. (Canto Book Ser.). 416p. (C). 1990. pap. text ed. 11.95 (0-521-39827-4) Cambridge U Pr.

Spanish Language Assessment Procedures: A Communication Skills Inventory. Larry j. Mattes. (Illus.). 1985. pap. text ed. 38.00 (0-930951-03-4) Acad Comm.

Spanish Language Books, Set 1: Animales de Granja (Farm Animals), 6 bks. L. Stone. (J). 1991. 53.70 (0-86592-948-3) Rourke Enter.

Spanish Language Books, Set 2: Animales Norteamericanos (North American Animals), 6 bks. L. Stone. (J). 1991. 53.70 (0-86592-786-3) Rourke Enter.

Spanish Language Books, Set 3: Los Jardines de la Tierra (The Earth's Garden), 6 bks. J. Cooper. (J). 1991. 53.70 (0-86592-496-1) Rourke Enter.

Spanish Language Books, Set 4: Mamifero Marino (Sea Mammals), 6 bks. Sarah Palmer. (J). 1991. 53.70 (0-86592-835-5) Rourke Enter.

Spanish Language Books, Set 5: Maquinas de Viaje (Traveling Machines), 6 bks. J. Cooper. (J). 1991. 53.70 (0-86592-473-2) Rourke Enter.

Spanish Language Fundamentals: Expanded Foreign Language Card Guides. 1992. pap. 5.95 (0-8120-6310-4) Barron.

Spanish Language Glossary - Cosmetology. Milady Publishing Company Staff. (Cosmetology Ser.). (SPA.). 1985. pap. 13.95 (0-87350-414-3) Milady Pub.

Spanish-Language Radio in the Southwestern United States. Felix F. Gutierrez & Jorge R. Schement. (Mexican American Monographs: No. 5). (Illus.). 144p. 1979. pap. text ed. 9.95 (0-292-77550-4, Ctr Mex Am Stud) U of Tex Pr.

Spanish Language, Together with Portuguese, Catalan & Basque. W. J. Entwistle. 1975. lib. bdg. 69.95 (0-8490-1102-7) Gordon Pr.

Spanish Language Trail. 1996. 9.99 (0-517-16011-0) Random Hse Value.

Spanish Language Use & Public Life in the U. S. A. Olivarez Elias et al. 232p. 1985. pap. 23.10 (0-89925-227-3); text ed. 75.40 (0-89925-054-8) Mouton.

Spanish (Latin American)-English, English-Spanish Compact Dictionary. 310p. (Orig.). (ENG & SPA.). 1996. pap. 8.95 (0-7818-0497-3) Hippocrene Bks.

Spanish Left: Resurgence after Four Decades of Franco. Richard S. Fischer. (Western Societies Papers). 119p. 1979. 11.95 (0-8014-9633-0) Cornell U Pr.

Spanish Liberalism in Crisis: A Study of the Liberal Party During Spain's Parliamentary Collapse, 1913-1923. Thomas G. Trice. LC 91-2975. (Modern European History Outstanding Studies & Dissertations). 350p. 1991. text ed. 20.00 (0-8240-2543-1) Garland.

Spanish Lingo for the Savvy Gringo: A Do-it-Yourself Guide to Learning the Language. 2nd expanded rev. ed. Elizabeth Reid. LC 89-85923. (Illus.). 186p. 1994. per. 12.95 (0-9627080-2-X) In One EAR.

***Spanish Lingo for the Savvy Gringo: A Do-It-Yourself Guide to Learning the Language.** 3rd expanded rev. ed. Elizabeth Reid. (Illus.). 216p. (Orig.). 1997. per. 14.95 (1-881791-08-4) In One EAR.

Spanish Literature: A Handbook. Henry B. Clarke. 1980. lib. bdg. 64.50 (0-8490-3194-X) Gordon Pr.

Spanish Literature: A Handbook with Index. H. B. Clarke. 1977. lib. bdg. 59.95 (0-8490-2651-2) Gordon Pr.

Spanish Literature: 1700-1900. Ed. by Beatrice Patt & Martin Nozick. 463p. (C). 1989. reprint ed. pap. text ed. 18.95 (0-88133-454-5) Waveland Pr.

Spanish Literature in English Translation: A Bibliographical Syllabus. Angel Flores. 1972. 59.95 (0-8490-1103-5) Gordon Pr.

Spanish Literature in Mexican Languages As a Source for the Study of Spanish Pronunciation. De Los Lincoln Canfield. 257p. 3.00 (0-318-14306-2) Hispanic Inst.

Spanish Literature in the England of the Tudors. John G. Underhill. 1972. 59.95 (0-8490-1104-3) Gordon Pr.

Spanish Literature in the England of the Tudors. John G. Underhill. LC 70-131496. reprint ed. 49.50 (0-404-06702-6) AMS Pr.

Spanish Literature, 1500-1700: A Bibliography of Golden Age Studies in Spanish & English, 1925-1980. Compiled by William W. Moseley et al. LC 84-8965. (Bibliographies & Indexes in World Literature Ser.: No. 3). lxiii, 765p. 1984. text ed. 115.00 (0-313-21491-3, MSL/) Greenwood.

Spanish Loanwords in the English Language: A Tendency Towards Hegemony Reversal. Ed. by Felix R. Gonzales. (Topics in English Language Ser.: No. 18). xii, 301p. (C). 1996. lib. bdg. 124.45 (3-11-014845-5) Mouton.

Spanish Lover. Joanna Trollope. 384p. 1994. pap. 12.95 (0-552-99549-5) Bantam.

Spanish Lover. Joanna Trollope. LC 96-24846. 336p. 1997. 23.00 (0-679-42586-1) Random.

Spanish Made Easy, Custom Pub. Page. 1992. pap. text ed. write for info. (0-07-048135-0) McGraw.

***Spanish Made Fun & Easy: For Ages 10 to Adult.** large type ed. Kathleen Fisher. 125p. (Orig.). (ENG & SPA.). 1995. pap. text ed. 14.95 (0-614-20953-6, 09-3) Fisher Hill.

Spanish Made Simple. rev. ed. Eugene Jackson & Antonio Rubio. LC 83-2036. (Made Simple Ser.). 192p. 1984. pap. 12.00 (0-385-18818-8) Doubleday.

Spanish Main: Focus of Envy, 1492-1700. Philip A. Means. LC 65-24994. (Illus.). 278p. 1965. reprint ed. 75.00 (0-87752-074-7) Gordian.

Spanish Majolica in the New World: Types of the Sixteenth to Eighteenth Centuries. John M. Goggin. LC 68-24636. (Publications in Anthropology: No. 72). 1968. pap. 12.00 (0-913516-05-8) Yale U Anthro.

Spanish Manuscript Letter on the Lacandones, in the Archives of the Indies at Seville. Antonio Marjil de Jesus et al. Ed. & Tr. by Alfred M. Tozzer. LC 83-83343. (Illus.). 1984. pap. 10.00 (0-911437-03-7) Labyrinthos.

Spanish Marxism vs. Soviet Communism: A History of the P.O.U.M. Victor Alba & Stephen Schwartz. 448p. 1988. 49.95 (0-88738-198-7) Transaction Pubs.

Spanish, Medical: A Conversational Approach. Maria DiLorenzo-Kearon. 256p. 1982. pap. text ed. 195.00 incl. audio (0-88432-079-0, AFMS20) Audio-Forum.

Spanish Memory Book: A New Approach to Vocabulary Building. William F. Harrison & Dorothy W. Welker. 110p. 1991. pap. 8.95 (0-292-77641-1); text ed. 17.95 (0-292-77640-3) U of Tex Pr.

Spanish Memory Book, Junior Edition: A New Approach to Vocabulary Building. William F. Harrison & Dorothy W. Welker. LC 93-12717. (Illus.). 96p. (YA). (gr. 7-12). 1993. pap. 8.95 (0-292-73081-0); text ed. 22.50 (0-292-73079-9) U of Tex Pr.

Spanish Mercantilism: Geronimo de Uztariz-Economist. Andres V. Castillo. LC 79-20392. ix, 193p. 1980. reprint ed. lib. bdg. 35.00 (0-87991-858-6) Porcupine Pr.

Spanish Mexican Families of Early California, Vol. I: 1769-1850. 2nd ed. Marie E. Northrop. (Illus.). 421p. 1987. 30.00 (0-9617773-0-3) S CA Geneal Soc.

Spanish Michelin Espana Green Guide. Michelin Staff. 1995. pap. 19.95 (0-7859-9103-4) Fr & Eur.

Spanish Mission Churches of New Mexico. L. Bradford Prince. LC 77-1749. (Beautiful Rio Grande Classics Ser.). (Illus.). 535p. 1983. reprint ed. lib. bdg. 50.00 (0-87380-126-1) Rio Grande.

Spanish Missions. Bobbie Kalman & Greg Nickles. LC 96-26738. (Historic Communities Ser.). 32p. 1996. pap. 7.95 (0-86505-466-5); lib. bdg. 19.16 (0-86505-436-3) Crabtree Pub Co.

Spanish Missions of Baja California. Robert H. Jackson. LC 90-22358. (Spanish Borderlands Sourcebooks Ser.: Vol. 16). 408p. 1991. reprint ed. text ed. 25.00 (0-8240-2094-4) Garland.

Spanish Missions of Florida. Compiled by WPA Florida Writers' Project 1940 Staff. LC 93-1270. 88p. (C). 1993. reprint ed. pap. 8.95 (1-877633-16-X) Luthers.

Spanish Missions of la Florida. Ed. by Bonnie G. McEwan. LC 93-7937. (Illus.). 488p. 1993. pap. text ed. 24.95 (0-8130-1232-5); lib. bdg. 49.95 (0-8130-1231-7) U Press Fla.

Spanish Missions of New Mexico, after 1860. Ed. by John L. Kessell & Rick Hendricks. LC 90-22757. (Spanish Borderlands Sourcebooks Ser.: Vol. 18). 536p. 1991. reprint ed. text ed. 30.00 (0-8240-2349-8) Garland.

Spanish Missions of New Mexico, Vol. I: Before 1860. Ed. by John L. Kessell & Rick Hendricks. LC 90-22757. (Spanish Borderlands Sourcebooks Ser.: Vol. 17). 488p. 1992. text ed. 25.00 (0-8240-2095-2) Garland.

Spanish Missions of the Old Southwest. Cleve Hellenback. 1993. reprint ed. lib. bdg. 75.00 (0-7812-5935-5) Rprt Serv.

Spanish Monarchy & Irish Mercenaries, 1618-68. R. A. Stradling. (Illus.). 208p. 1994. 39.50 (0-7165-2509-7, Pub. by Irish Acad Pr IE) Intl Spec Bk.

Spanish Monuments & Trailmarkers to Treasure in the United States. Charles A. Kenworthy. (Illus.). 80p. (Orig.). 1993. pap. 13.95 (0-9632156-1-2) Quest Pubns.

Spanish Music for Piano. Compiled by Joseph Castle. 1993. 5.95 (1-56222-580-4, 94771) Mel Bay.

Spanish Music in the Twentieth Century. Tomas Marco. Tr. by Cola Franzen. LC 92-14270. 269p. (C). 1993. 42.50 (0-674-83102-0) HUP.

Spanish Mustang: From the Plains of Andalusia to the Prairies of Texas. Don Worcester. 1986. 12.00 (0-87404-095-7) Tex Western.

Spanish Mystic in Quito: Sor Mariana de Jesus Torres. Luis F. Cadena y Almeida. Ed. & Tr. by Foundation for a Christian Civilization Staff from SPA. Tr. by Jose L. De Zayas from SPA. LC 90-82119. (Illus.). 159p. (Orig.). 1990. pap. 13.95 (1-877905-18-6) Am Soc Defense TFP.

***Spanish Naval Power, 1589-1665: Reconstruction & Defeat.** David Goodman. (Cambridge Studies in Early Modern History). (Illus.). 320p. (C). 1997. 59.95 (0-521-58063-3) Cambridge U Pr.

Spanish New Mexico, 2 vols., Set. Donna Pierce & Marta Weigle. (Spanish New Mexico Ser.). (Illus.). 320p. (Orig.). 1996. pap. 60.00 (0-89013-311-5) Museum NM Pr.

Spanish North America: Three Hundred Thirty-Eight Years of Spanish Colonization. Ernesto Vega Pagan. 280p. 1992. pap. 21.95 (0-9629908-1-7) Mini-Series Pubns.

Spanish North Carolina: 1526-1600. C. D. Huneycutt. (Illus.). 180p. (Orig.). pap. 9.95 (0-915153-05-X) Gold Star Pr.

Spanish Now! Christopher Kendris. 1996. pap. 16.95 (0-8120-9324-0) Barron.

Spanish Now! A Level I Worktext. 5th ed. Ruth J. Silverstein et al. 544p. 1990. pap. 16.95 (0-8120-4431-2) Barron.

Spanish Now! Level 2. 2nd ed. Christopher Kendris. 1996. pap. 3.95 (0-8120-9322-4) Barron.

Spanish Now! Level 1. 5th ed. 1991. teacher ed., pap. 4.95 (0-8120-4833-4) Barron.

***Spanish Now, Level 1: El Espanol Actual - Prima Program.** 6th rev. ed. Ruth J. Silverstein et al. 526p. 1997. pap. text ed. 16.95 (0-8120-9653-3) Barron.

Spanish Observers & the American Revolution, 1775- 1783. Light T. Cummins. LC 91-13795. 280p. 1991. text ed. 35.00 (0-8071-1690-4) La State U Pr.

Spanish of Argentina & Uruguay: An Annotated Bibliography for 1940-1978. Jack E. Davis. (Janua Linguarum, Series Major: No. 105). 360p. 1982. text ed. 98.50 (90-279-3339-1) Mouton.

Spanish Ohne Muhe Heure. Albert O. Cherel. 24.95 (0-685-11573-9); Four cassettes. audio 125.00 (0-685-01766-4) Fr & Eur.

Spanish Oil Industry: Structural Change & Modernization. Aad Correlje. (Tinbergen Institute Research Ser.: No. 84). 349p. 1994. pap. 30.00 (90-5170-309-0, Pub. by Thesis Pubs NE) IBD Ltd.

Spanish on Location. LC 91-39646. (Languages on Location Ser.). 1992. pap. 10.95 incl. audio (0-8120-7901-9) Barron.

An Asterisk (*) at the beginning of an entry indicates that the title is appearing in BIP for the first time.

Spanish on the Go. (Languages on the Go Ser.). 1992. pap. 12.95 incl. audio (0-8120-7829-2) Barron.

Spanish on the Job: Quick, Easy Word Guide. Sharon S. Prosser. 107p. (Orig.). 1990. pap. 6.95 (0-923176-09-8) SW Pr.

***Spanish on the Road, Level 2.** Lawton. (Languages on the Road Ser.). (ENG & SPA.). 1992. pap. 11.95 incl. audio (0-8120-7934-5) Barron.

Spanish Oral Drill Book. K. L. Mason & J. C. Sager. 1969. pap. text ed. 7.80 (0-08-013362-2, Pergamon Pr) Elsevier.

Spanish Paintings of the Fifteenth through Nineteenth Centuries. Jonathan Brown & Richard G. Mann. (Collections of the National Gallery of Art Systematic Catalogue). (Illus.). 165p. (C). 1991. 95.00 (0-521-40107-0) Natl Gallery Art.

Spanish Paintings of the Fifteenth Through Nineteenth Centuries. Jonathan Brown & Richard Mann. LC 90-5640. (Collections of the National Gallery of Art Systematic Catalogue: Vol. 7). (Illus.). 166p. (Orig.). 1990. 25.00 (0-89468-149-4); pap. 19.95 (0-685-58664-2) Natl Gallery Art.

Spanish Papers. Washington Irving. Ed. by Pierre Irving. LC 78-74516. (Children's Literature Reprint Ser.). (YA). (gr. 7 up). 1979. reprint ed. 50.00 (0-8486-0219-6) Roth Pub Inc.

Spanish Part 1: Short Course. 4th ed. Dasilva. (College Spanish Ser.). 1991. suppl. ed. 17.95 incl. audio (0-8384-3507-6) Heinle & Heinle.

Spanish Part 2: Short Course. 4th ed. Dasilva. (College Spanish Ser.). 1991. suppl. ed. 17.95 incl. audio (0-8384-3506-8) Heinle & Heinle.

Spanish Pastoral, 2 bks., Set. Romuald Zantua & Karen Eberle-McCarthy. 1993. student ed., pap. text ed. 199.00 (0-88432-689-6, SSP320) Audio-Forum.

Spanish Pastoral Romances. Hugo A. Rennert. LC 67-29552. 1968. reprint ed. 28.00 (0-8196-0214-0) Biblo.

Spanish Pathways in Florida. Ed. by Ann L. Henderson & Gary R. Mormino. Tr. by Carlos J. Cano. LC 91-20036. (Illus.). 368p. (ENG & SPA.). 1991. 24.95 (1-56164-003-4); pap. 18.95 (1-56164-004-2) Pineapple Pr.

Spanish People. M. Hume. 1976. lib. bdg. 59.95 (0-8490-2652-0) Gordon Pr.

Spanish Peru, 1532-1560: A Colonial Society. James Lockhart. LC 68-14032. (Illus.). 298p. 1974. pap. 14.95 (0-299-04664-8) U of Wis Pr.

Spanish Peru, 1532-1560: A Social History. 2nd ed. James Lockhart. LC 93-23338. 342p. 1994. 50.00 (0-299-14160-8); pap. 14.95 (0-299-14164-0) U of Wis Pr.

Spanish Phonology & Morphology: A Generative View. William W. Cressey. LC 78-23327. 184p. 1978. reprint ed. pap. 11.00 (0-87840-045-1) Georgetown U Pr.

Spanish Phrase-a-Day for Young Children, Set 2. Foreign Language for Young Children Staff & Judith White. 98p. 1989. 24.95 incl. audio (0-88432-283-1, SSP850) Audio-Forum.

Spanish Phrase Book. pap. 19.50 (0-87557-133-6) Saphrograph.

Spanish Phrase Book. Maria V. Alvarez. 1968. mass mkt. 4.95 (0-14-002708-4, Penguin Bks) Viking Penguin.

Spanish Phrase Book. Berlitz Editors. (Phrase Book). 192p. (SPA.). 1992. pap. 6.95 (2-8315-0888-6) Berlitz.

Spanish Picaresque Fiction: A New Literary History. Peter N. Dunn. LC 92-36854. 352p. 1993. 37.00 (0-8014-2800-9) Cornell U Pr.

Spanish Picture Dictionary. Ed. by Passport Books Staff. (Let's Learn...Picture Dictionary Ser.). (Illus.). 70p. (SPA.). (J). 10.95 (0-8442-7558-1, Natl Textbk) NTC Pub Grp.

Spanish Picture Dictionary. Ed. by Angela Wilkes. (Illus.). 94p. (J). (gr. 1 up). 10.95 (0-8442-7630-8, Natl Textbk) NTC Pub Grp.

Spanish Picture Word Book: Learn over Five Hundred Commonly Used Spanish Words Through Pictures. Hayward Cirker & Barbara Steadman. (Illus.). 32p. (Orig.). (ENG & SPA.). (J). 1993. pap. text ed. 2.95 (0-486-27779-8) Dover.

Spanish Piggyback Songs. Sonya Kranwinkel. Ed. by Kathleen Cubley. LC 94-78420. (Piggyback Songs Ser.). (Illus.). 64p. (J). (ps-1). 1995. 7.95 (1-57029-044-X, WPH 0210, Totline Bks) Warren Pub Hse.

Spanish Pilgrimage. large type ed. Robin Hanbury-Tenison. (Non-Fiction Ser.). 320p. 1992. 27.99 (0-7089-8637-4) Ulverscroft.

Spanish Pioneers of the Southwest. Joan Anderson. 1989. pap. 16.99 (0-525-67546-9) NAL-Dutton.

Spanish Plays of Neoclassical England. John C. Loftis. LC 87-8685. 280p. 1987. reprint ed. text ed. 67.50 (0-313-25133-9, LSPA, Greenwood Pr) Greenwood.

Spanish Plot. E. N. Dzelepy. 1972. 59.95 (0-8490-1105-1) Gordon Pr.

Spanish Pocket Dictionary. Donald F. Sola & Frederick B. Agard. (SPA.). 1974. 5.00 (0-394-40064-X) Random.

Spanish Poetry of the Golden Age. Ed. by Bruce W. Wardropper. LC 78-132806. (Illus.). (SPA.). 1977. reprint ed. 39.50 (0-89197-981-6); reprint ed. pap. text ed. 19.95 (0-89197-982-4) Irvington.

Spanish Poetry of the Twentieth Century: Modernity & Beyond. Andrew P. Debicki. 272p. (Orig.). 1994. pap. 14.95 (0-8131-0835-7) U Pr of Ky.

Spanish Poetry of the Twentieth Century: Modernity & Beyond. Andrew P. Debicki. LC 93-36928. (Studies in Romance Languages: No. 37). 272p. (Orig.). (C). 1994. lib. bdg. 29.95 (0-8131-1869-7) U Pr of Ky.

Spanish Poetry Since 1939. Charles D. Ley. LC 62-52819. 289p. reprint ed. pap. 82.40 (0-685-17851-X, 2029511) Bks Demand.

Spanish Policy in Colonial Chile: The Struggle for Social Justice, 1535-1700. Eugene H. Korth. LC 68-26779. xi, 320p. 1968. 45.00 (0-8047-0666-2) Stanford U Pr.

Spanish-Polish Technical Dictionary: Diccionario Tecnico Espanol-Polaco. Ed. by T. Weroniecki. 545p. (POL & SPA.). 1981. 75.00 (0-8288-4436-4, S37602) Fr & Eur.

Spanish Polychrome Sculpture 1500-1800 in U. S. Collections: In United Collections. Suzanne L. Stratton. LC 93-86726. (Spanish Institute Ser.). (Illus.). 192p. 1994. pap. 45.00 (0-295-97390-0) U of Wash Pr.

Spanish-Portuguese Dictionary: Diccionario Espanol-Portugues. 4th ed. J. C. Fernandez. 1016p. (POR & SPA.). 1980. 24.95 (0-8288-1043-5, S50428) Fr & Eur.

***Spanish Presence in Louisiana, 1763-1803.** Ed. by Gilbert C. Din & Glenn R. Conrad. LC 96-84494. (Louisiana Purchase Bicentennial: Vol. II). 579p. 1996. 40.00 (1-887366-03-2) U of SW LA Ctr LA Studies.

Spanish Prisoner. large type ed. Frank Gruber. (Linford Mystery Library). 368p. 1992. pap. 15.99 (0-7089-7266-7, Trailtree Bookshop) Ulverscroft.

***Spanish Program: Level 1.** Medley. (Secondary Spanish Ser.). Date not set. 49.95 (0-8384-7880-8) Heinle & Heinle.

Spanish Programmatic Vol. 1. Foreign Service Institute Staff. 128p. 1992. wbk. ed., pap. 7.95 (0-88432-696-9, AFS990) Audio-Forum.

Spanish Programmatic Vol. 1, Set. Foreign Service Institute Staff. 464p. (SPA.). 1978. Vol. I, 464p. pap. 185.00 incl. audio (0-88432-015-4, AFS101) Audio-Forum.

Spanish Programmatic Course, 2 vols., 1. C. Cleland Harris. LC 75-5674. (Spoken Language Ser.). (SPA.). 1975. student ed., pap. 110.00 incl. audio (0-87950-359-9); audio 90.00 (0-87950-358-0) Spoken Lang Serv.

Spanish Programmatic Course, 2 vols., 2. C. Cleland Harris. LC 75-5674. (Spoken Language Ser.). (SPA.). 1975. student ed., pap. 90.00 incl. audio (0-87950-361-0); audio 70.00 (0-87950-360-2) Spoken Lang Serv.

Spanish Programmatic Course, 2 vols., Vol. 1. C. Cleland Harris. LC 75-5674. (Spoken Language Ser.). xii, 464p. (SPA.). 1975. pap. 20.00 (0-87950-354-8) Spoken Lang Serv.

Spanish Programmatic Course, 2 vols., Vol. 1 & 2. C. Cleland Harris. LC 75-5674. (Spoken Language Ser.). (SPA.). 1975. audio 200.00 (0-87950-362-9) Spoken Lang Serv.

Spanish Programmatic Course, 2 vols., Vol. 2. C. Cleland Harris. LC 75-5674. (Spoken Language Ser.). 614p. (SPA.). 1975. pap. 20.00 (0-87950-356-4) Spoken Lang Serv.

Spanish Pronunciation: Theory & Practice. 2nd ed. John B. Dalbor. 352p. (ENG & SPA.). (C). 1989. text ed. 36.75 (0-03-049056-1) HB Coll Pubs.

Spanish Pronunciation: Theory & Practice. 3rd ed. John B. Dalbor. 418p. (C). 1996. text ed. write for info. (0-03-018077-5) HR&W Schl Div.

Spanish Pronunciation in the Americas. D. Lincoln Canfield. LC 80-23664. 128p. 1981. pap. 9.95 (0-226-09263-1) U Ch Pr.

Spanish Prose - Poetry, Old - New. Ida Farnell. LC 70-165630. (Select Bibliographies Reprint Ser.). 1977. reprint ed. 19.95 (0-8369-5937-X) Ayer.

Spanish Rare Books of the Golden Ages, 1472-1700: Guide to the Microfilm Collection. 259p. (C). 1988. text ed. 155.00 (0-89235-103-9) Primary Srce Media.

Spanish Reactions to the Anglo-Irish Literary Revival in the Early Twentieth Century: The Stone by the Elixir. Jean Andrews. LC 91-32592. (Studies in Comparative Literature: Vol. 17). 228p. 1991. lib. bdg. 89.95 (0-7734-9698-X) E Mellen.

Spanish Readiness Skills, Vol. 1. Eliseo R. Martinez & Irma C. Martinez. (Illus.). 78p. (J). (ps-3). 1986. student ed. 8.75 (1-878300-01-6) Childrens Work.

Spanish Regime in Missouri: A Collection of Papers & Documents Relating to Upper Louisiana Principally Within the Present Limits of Missouri During the Dominion of Spain, from the Archives of the Indies at Seville, 2 Vols. Louis Houck. LC 70-146403. (First American Frontier Ser.). (Illus.). 1971. reprint ed. 62.95 (0-405-02860-1) Ayer.

Spanish Religious Folktheatre in the Southwest, Second Series. Arthur L. Campa. LC 34-27430. 157p. 1982. reprint ed. lib. bdg. 35.00 (0-89370-736-8) Borgo Pr.

Spanish Renaissance Songbook. Ed. by Charles Jacobs. LC 85-43568. 188p. 1988. 32.50 (0-271-00435-5) Pa St U Pr.

Spanish Republic & the Civil War, 1931-1939. Gabriel Jackson. (Illus.). 600p. 1965. pap. text ed. 26.95 (0-691-00757-8) Princeton U Pr.

Spanish Revolution, 1931-39. Leon Trotsky. Ed. by George Breitman & Naomi Allen. LC 78-156382. (Illus.). 446p. 1973. reprint ed. pap. 27.95 (0-87348-273-5); reprint ed. lib. bdg. 70.00 (0-87348-274-3) Pathfinder NY.

Spanish Riddles & Colcha Designs. rev. ed. Ed. by Reynalda Ortiz y Pino de Dinkel & Dora Gonzales de Martinez. LC 94-17455. (ENG & SPA.). 1994. 10.95 (0-86534-226-1) Sunstone Pr.

Spanish Romances of the Sixteenth Century. Thomas Binkley & Margit Frenk. LC 94-44095. 192p. 1995. pap. text ed. 20.00 (0-253-20964-1) Ind U Pr.

Spanish Romantic Literary Theory & Criticism. Derek Flitter. (Cambridge Studies in Latin American & Iberian Literature: No. 5). 220p. (C). 1992. text ed. 69.95 (0-521-39068-0) Cambridge U Pr.

Spanish Roots of America. David Arias. LC 91-66665. (Illus.). 352p. (Orig.). 1992. pap. 7.95 (0-87973-476-0, 476) Our Sunday Visitor.

Spanish Rose. Shirlee Busbee. 460p. 1986. mass mkt. 5.50 (0-380-89833-0) Avon.

Spanish Rose. Shirlee Busbee. 496p. 1992. reprint ed. 22.00 (0-7278-4313-3) Severn Hse.

Spanish Rule of Trade to the West-Indies. Linaje J. De Veitia. Tr. by John Stevens. LC 72-177863. reprint ed. 49.50 (0-404-06759-X) AMS Pr.

Spanish-Russian Dictionary: Diccionario Espanol-Ruso. L. Martinez Calvo. 1916p. (RUS & SPA.). 1982. 125.00 (0-8288-0797-3, S50411) Fr & Eur.

SPANISH Say Hello. 2nd rev. ed. Louis Aarons. 181p. (SPA.). 1996. student ed., wbk. ed., spiral bd. 39.95 incl. audio (1-887447-00-8) WordMate.

Spanish School. rev. ed. Neil MacLaren. (National Gallery Publications). (Illus.). 1989. text ed. 25.00 (0-300-06143-9) Yale U Pr.

Spanish Scientists in the New World: The Eighteenth-Century Expeditions. Iris H. Engstrand. LC 80-50863. (Illus.). 234p. 1981. 30.00 (0-295-95764-6) U of Wash Pr.

Spanish Sculpture. Marjorie Trusted. (Illus.). 256p. 1996. 95.00 (1-85177-177-8, Pub. by V&A Ent UK) Antique Collect.

Spanish Seaborne Empire. J. H. Parry. 417p. 1990. pap. 14.00 (0-520-07140-9) U CA Pr.

Spanish Serenade. Jennifer Blake. 1994. mass mkt. 5.99 (0-449-14603-0) Fawcett.

Spanish Serenade. large type ed. Jennifer Blake. (Niagara Large Print Ser.). 525p. 1996. 27.99 (0-7089-5831-1) Ulverscroft.

Spanish Short Stories. Ed. by Jean Franco. 208p. (YA). (gr. 9 up). 1966. pap. 10.95 (0-14-002500-6, Penguin Bks) Viking Penguin.

Spanish Short Stories & Poems. Fernando Rubio-Boitel. 1979. pap. 1.50 (0-686-23892-3) Rubio-Boitel.

Spanish Short Stories Two. Ed. by Gudie Lawaetz. 216p. 1993. pap. 10.95 (0-14-003378-5, Penguin Bks) Viking Penguin.

***Spanish Slaughter.** David Thompson. (Wilderness Ser.). 320p. (Orig.). 1997. mass mkt. 4.99 (0-8439-4307-6, Leisure Bks) Dorchester Pub Co.

Spanish Sleuth: The Detective in Spanish Fiction. Patricia Hart. LC 85-45932. 256p. 1987. 35.00 (0-8386-3278-5) Fairleigh Dickinson.

Spanish Smile. Scott O'Dell. 160p. 1984. mass mkt. 4.50 (0-449-70094-1, Juniper) Fawcett.

Spanish Socialist Party: A History of Factionalism. Richard Gillespie. (Illus.). 554p. 1989. 95.00 (0-19-822798-1) OUP.

Spanish Song Companion. Ed. by Richard Stokes. Tr. by Jacqueline Cockburn & Richard Stokes. 224p. 1993. 65.00 (0-575-04674-0, Pub. by V Gollancz UK) Trafalgar.

Spanish Southwest Fifteen Forty-Two to Seventeen Ninety-Four, 2 Vols, Set. Henry R. Wagner. LC 66-30073. (Quivira Society Publications, Vol. 7, 2 Pts). 1967. reprint ed. 65.95 (0-405-00079-0) Ayer.

Spanish Speakers. HRW Staff. 1997. student ed., pap. text ed. 8.00 (0-03-095654-4) HarBrace.

Spanish-Speaking Cultures Coloring Book. Anne-Francoise Pattis. (Illus.). 45p. (SPA.). (J). 1996. wbk. ed. 4.95 (0-8442-7538-7, Natl Textbk) NTC Pub Grp.

Spanish-Speaking People in the United States: American Ethnological Society Proceedings, 1968. Ed. by June Helm. LC 84-45504. 1988. reprint ed. pap. 65.00 (0-404-62662-9) AMS Pr.

Spanish Speaking Radio & TV: Emisoras De Radio y Television En Espanol. Charles E. Hugenberger. 8p. (ENG & SPA.). 1994. pap. 1.95 (1-885057-06-7) C E Hugenberger.

***Spanish-Speaking World: A Practical Introduction to Sociolinguistic Issues.** Clare Mar-Molinero. LC 96-43952. (Routledge Language in Society Ser.). 166p. (C). 1997. pap. write for info. (0-415-12983-4); text ed. write for info. (0-415-12982-6) Routledge.

Spanish-Speaking World: An Anthology of Cross-Cultural Perspectives. Louise F. Luce. 400p. 1994. pap. 21.95 (0-8442-7161-6, Natl Textbk) NTC Pub Grp.

Spanish Splendor. Universe Staff. 1995. pap. 40.00 (0-7893-0013-3) Universe.

Spanish Splendor: Palaces, Castles, & Country Houses. Photos by Roberto Schezen. LC 92-8643. (Illus.). 420p. 1992. 125.00 (0-8478-1497-1) Rizzoli Intl.

Spanish, Sr. H. S. Jack Rudman. (Teachers License Examination Ser.: T-57). 1994. pap. 27.95 (0-8373-8057-X) Nat Learn.

Spanish St. Augustine: The Archaeology of a Colonial Creole Community (Monographs) Ed. by Kathleen Deagan. (Studies in Historical Archaeology). 1983. text ed. 73.00 (0-12-207880-2) Acad Pr.

Spanish Starter Pack. Veronica Hyks. LC 93-29199. (ENG & SPA.). 1994. pap. 27.00 (0-671-88347-X, Harraps IN) Macmillan Gen Ref.

Spanish Step-by-Step. Charles Berlitz. LC 89-25106. 348p. (YA). (gr. 10). 1990. pap. 11.99 (0-922066-28-0) Wynwood.

Spanish Still Life in the Golden Age: 1600-1650. William B. Jordan & Sarah Schroth. LC 85-50356. (Illus.). 250p. 1985. 45.00 (0-912804-19-X) Kimbell Art.

Spanish Stories - Cuentos Espanoles: A Dual-Language Book. Ed. by Angel Flores. 352p. (ENG & SPA.). 1987. reprint ed. pap. 8.95 (0-486-25399-6) Dover.

Spanish Story: Franco & the Nations at War. Herbert Feis. LC 86-25772. 298p. 1987. reprint ed. text ed. 69.50 (0-313-25208-4, FESS, Greenwood Pr) Greenwood.

Spanish Story of the Armada & Other Essays. James A. Froude. LC 71-144613. reprint ed. 47.50 (0-404-02628-1) AMS Pr.

Spanish Storybook Set: Mathematics Connection, 28 bks., Set. (Illus.). (Orig.). (SPA.). (J). (ps-2). 1991. teacher ed., pap. 210.00 (1-56334-110-7) Hampton-Brown.

Spanish Storybook Set: Science Connection, 28 bks., Set. (Illus.). (Orig.). (SPA.). (J). (gr. 1-3). 1991. teacher ed., pap. 210.00 (1-56334-109-3) Hampton-Brown.

Spanish Storybook Set: Social Studies Connection, 28 bks., Set. (Illus.). (Orig.). (SPA.). (J). (gr. 1-3). 1991. teacher ed., pap. 210.00 (1-56334-108-5) Hampton-Brown.

Spanish Storybook Sets: Combo Pack, 84 bks., Set. (Illus.). (Orig.). (SPA.). (J). (gr. 1-3). 1991. teacher ed., pap. 595.00 (1-56334-111-5) Hampton-Brown.

Spanish StoryBridges Activity Workbook. (Illus.). 48p. (YA). 1992. pap. 8.95 (0-88432-490-7, BSP125) Audio-Forum.

Spanish Studies in the Philosophy of Science. Ed. by Gonzalo Munevar. LC 96-26716. (Boston Studies in the Philosophy of Science: Vol. 186). 376p. (C). 1996. lib. bdg. 143.00 (0-7923-4147-3) Kluwer Ac.

Spanish Study. Joyce Lopez-Solar. Ed. by Elizabeth Burchard. (Exambusters Ser.). 384p. (YA). (gr. 7 up). 1996. pap. 9.95 (1-881374-97-1, Exambusters) Ace Acad.

Spanish Study Aid. Gerard R. Wolfe. (J). 1978. pap. 2.75 (0-87738-033-3) Youth Ed.

***Spanish Style.** Cliff Slesin & Brittain Cliff. Date not set. 17.99 (0-517-19280-2) Random Hse Value.

Spanish Style. Suzanne Slesin et al. (Illus.). 1990. 45.00 (0-517-57438-1, C P Pubs) Crown Pub Group.

Spanish Summer. large type ed. Mary Howard. 432p. 1980. 25.99 (0-7089-0524-2) Ulverscroft.

Spanish Sunshine. E. Elsner. 1976. lib. bdg. 59.95 (0-8490-2653-9) Gordon Pr.

Spanish-Swedish-Spanish Dictionary. 340p. (SPA & SWE.). 1968. pap. 14.95 (0-8288-6661-9, S-37811) Fr & Eur.

Spanish Synonyms & Antonyms. Date not set. 25.00 (0-671-84868-2) PB.

Spanish Teacher's Book of Instant Word Games. Josephine Carreno. LC 96-20549. 1996. write for info. (0-87628-757-7); pap. write for info. (0-87628-892-1) Ctr Appl Res.

***Spanish Technical Dictionary, Vol. 1.** 830p. (C). 1997. 140.00 (0-415-11272-9) Routledge.

Spanish Terror: Spanish Imperialism in the Sixteenth Century. Maurice Rowdon. LC 74-196578. 343p. reprint ed. pap. 97.80 (0-317-28441-X, 2051265) Bks Demand.

Spanish Texas, Fifteen Nineteen to Eighteen Ten. David M. Vigness. (Texas History Ser.). (Illus.). 52p. 1983. pap. text ed. 8.95 (0-89641-128-1) American Pr.

Spanish Texas Pilgrimage. Marion A. Habig. 304p. 1990. 10.95 (0-8199-0883-5, Frncscn Herld) Franciscan Pr.

Spanish Texas, 1519-1821. Donald E. Chipman. LC 92-6116. (Illus.). 359p. (Orig.). (C). 1992. pap. 14.95 (0-292-77659-4); text ed. 30.00 (0-292-77656-X) U of Tex Pr.

Spanish the Easy Way. 3rd ed. Ruth J. Silverstein. 1996. pap. 12.95 (0-8120-9412-3) Barron.

***Spanish, the Savvy Traveler: Business, 2 cass.** Ed. by Janis M. Yates. (Savvy Traveler Ser.). 36p. (SPA.). 1996. 19.95 incl. audio (0-88432-914-3, SSP575) Audio-Forum.

***Spanish, the Savvy Traveler: Food & Dining, 2 cass.** Ed. by Janis M. Yates. (Savvy Traveler Ser.). 36p. (SPA.). 1996. 19.95 incl. audio (0-88432-915-1, SSP580) Audio-Forum.

***Spanish, the Savvy Traveler: Shopping.** Ed. by Janis M. Yates. (Savvy Traveler Ser.). 36p. (SPA.). 1996. 12.95 incl. audio (0-88432-916-X, SSP585) Audio-Forum.

***Spanish, the Savvy Traveler: Travel.** Ed. by Janis M. Yates. (Savvy Traveler Ser.). 36p. (SPA.). 1996. 12.95 incl. audio (0-88432-917-8, SSP590) Audio-Forum.

***Spanish Theatre, 1920-1995: Strategies in Protest & Imagination 1.** Ed. by Maria Delgado. 1997. pap. text ed. 21.00 (90-5702-099-8, Harwood Acad Pubs) Gordon & Breach.

***Spanish Theatre 1920-1995: Strategies in Protest & Imagination 2.** Ed. by Maria Delgado. 1997. pap. text ed. 21.00 (90-5702-115-3, Harwood Acad Pubs) Gordon & Breach.

***Spanish Theatre 1920-1995: Strategies in Protest & Imagination 3.** Ed. by Maria Delgado. 1997. pap. text ed. 21.00 (90-5702-116-1, Harwood Acad Pubs) Gordon & Breach.

Spanish Thesaurus for Children. Joan Greisman. (J). 1996. pap. text ed. 6.95 (0-8120-9595-2) Barron.

Spanish Think & Talk. Berlitz Editors. (Think & Talk Language Courses Ser.). (Illus.). (SPA.). 1986. pap. 185.00 incl. audio (2-8315-1196-8) Berlitz.

Spanish Thread on Indian Looms: Mexican Folk Costumes. Frances F. Berdan & Russell J. Barber. Tr. by Rafael E. Correa. (Illus.). 112p. (ENG & SPA.). 1988. per. 17.00 (0-945486-04-9) CSU SBRVFAM.

Spanish to Brazilian Portuguese. Foreign Service Institute Staff. 91p. (POR & SPA.). 1980. pap. text ed. 45.00 incl. audio (0-88432-059-6, AFSP50) Audio-Forum.

Spanish Tradition in Louisiana. Samuel Armistead. Ed. by Thomas Lathrop et al. 274p. 1991. 22.00 (0-936388-51-X); pap. 15.00 (0-936388-48-X) Juan de la Cuesta.

Spanish Traditional Ballads from Aragon. Michele S. De Cruz-Saenz. LC 95-9256. (Illus.). 264p. 1995. 36.50 (0-8387-5304-3) Bucknell U Pr.

Spanish Tragedy. Thomas Kyd. Ed. by Charles T. Prouty. (Crofts Classics Ser.). 112p. 1951. pap. text ed. write for info. (0-88295-051-7) Harlan Davidson.

Spanish Tragedy. Thomas Kyd. Ed. by David Bevington. LC 95-21694. (Revels Student Editions Ser.). 1995. text ed. write for info. (0-7190-4343-3, Pub. by Manchester Univ Pr UK) St Martin.

Spanish Tragedy. Thomas Kyd. Ed. by David Bevington. LC 95-21694. (Revels Student Editions Ser.). 160p. 1996. text ed. 12.95 (0-7190-4344-1, Pub. by Manchester Univ Pr UK) St Martin.

***Spanish Tragedy.** Thomas Kyd. (Nick Hern Books, Drama Classics). 1997. pap. text ed. 6.95 (1-85459-377-3, Pub. by N Hern Bks UK) Theatre Comm.

Spanish Tragedy. 2nd ed. Thomas Kyd. Ed. by J. R. Mulryne. (New Mermaid Ser.). (C). 1989. pap. text ed. 5.95 (*0-393-90057-6*) Norton.

Spanish Tragedy. Thomas Kyd. Ed. by Philip Edwards. (Revels Plays Ser.). 153p. 1988. reprint ed. text ed. 24.95 (*0-7190-1609-6*, Pub. by Manchester Univ Pr UK) St Martin.

Spanish Tragedy, Nineteen Thirty to Nineteen Thirty-Six. Edgar A. Peers. LC 75-8724. 247p. 1975. reprint ed. text ed. 35.00 (*0-8371-8048-1*, PEST, Greenwood Pr) Greenwood.

Spanish Translations. Tr. & Intro. by John H. Hann. (Florida Archaeology Ser.: No. 2). (Illus.). 225p. 1986. pap. 10.00 (*0-923308-02-4*) FL Bur Archaeol.

Spanish Travel Pack. Hugo. 748p. 1986. 14.95 incl. audio (*0-85285-201-0*) Hunter NJ.

Spanish Travelmate. (Travelmate Ser.). (Illus.). 128p. (Orig.). 1991. pap. 3.95 (*0-87701-869-3*) Chronicle Bks.

Spanish Treasure Fleets. Timothy R. Walton. LC 93-46419. (Illus.). 224p. 1994. 24.95 (*1-56164-049-2*) Pineapple Pr.

Spanish TV: February 1996. UMBC Staff. (College Spanish Ser.). 1997. teacher ed., pap. 13.95 (*0-8384-6811-X*) Heinle & Heinle.

Spanish TV - April 96. Crapotta & UMBC Staff. (College Spanish Ser.). 1997. teacher ed., pap. 13.95 (*0-8384-6814-4*) Heinle & Heinle.

Spanish TV - January 96. Crapotta & UMBC Staff. (College Spanish Ser.). 1996. teacher ed., pap. 13.95 (*0-8384-6809-8*) Heinle & Heinle.

Spanish Tv- December 95 Teachers Guide. Umbc & Crapotta. (College Spanish Ser.). 1996. pap. 13.95 (*0-8384-6813-6*) Heinle & Heinle.

Spanish Unemployment: Is There a Solution? Javier Andres et al. 146p. (C). 1995. pap. 21.95 (*1-898128-18-9*, Pub. by Centre Econ Policy Res UK) Brookings.

Spanish Verb. Tim Connell. Ed. by Elizabeth Van Heusden. 96p. (C). 1980. 85.00 (*0-85950-452-2*, Pub. by S Thornes Pubs UK) St Mut.

Spanish Verb Conjugations for Language Proficiency: A Complete & Systematic Guide to the Conjugation of 15,000 Spanish Verbs. Stephen J. Thompson. LC 96-83512. 182p. (Orig.). 1996. pap. 11.95 (*0-9651418-0-2*) Ctr For Innovat.

Spanish Verb Drills. 2nd ed. Pauline Baker. 176p. 1995. pap. 6.95 (*0-8442-7034-2*, Natl Textbk) NTC Pub Grp.

Spanish Verb Handbook. Berlitz Editors. (Handbook Ser.). 231p. 1993. pap. 8.95 (*2-8315-1352-9*) Berlitz.

Spanish Verbs. (Hugo's Verbs Simplified Ser.). 96p. 1988. pap. 6.95 (*0-85285-100-6*) Hunter NJ.

***Spanish Verbs.** Berlitz Editors. 240p. 1997. pap. 10.95 (*2-8315-6397-6*) Berlitz.

Spanish Verbs. Ed. by John Butt. 256p. 1997. pap. 6.95 (*0-19-860037-2*) OUP.

Spanish Verbs. Christopher Kendris. (Verbs Ser.). 350p. 1990. pap. 5.95 (*0-8120-4283-2*) Barron.

Spanish Verbs: Future & Conditional. Steven Guemann. (Pocket Review Ser.). 172p. (C). 1994. spiral bd., pap. 6.24 (*0-8403-9713-5*) Kendall-Hunt.

Spanish Verbs: Perfect Tense. Steven Guemann. (Pocket Review Ser.). 160p. (C). 1994. spiral bd. 6.24 (*0-8403-9714-3*) Kendall-Hunt.

Spanish Verbs: Present Subjunctive. Steven Guemann. (Pocket Review Ser.). 160p. (C). 1994. spiral bd., pap. 6.24 (*0-8403-9712-7*) Kendall-Hunt.

Spanish Verbs: Present Tense. Steven Guemann. (Pocket Review Ser.). 160p. (C). 1994. spiral bd., pap. 6.24 (*0-8403-9710-0*) Kendall-Hunt.

Spanish Verbs: Preterite Tense. Steven Guemann. (Pocket Review Ser.). 164p. (C). 1994. spiral bd., pap. 6.24 (*0-8403-9711-9*) Kendall-Hunt.

Spanish Verbs & Essentials of Grammar. Ed. by Ina W. Ramboz. 136p. (C). 1988. 55.00 (*0-8442-7214-0*, Pub. by S Thornes Pubs UK) St Mut.

Spanish Verbs, Ser & Estar: The Key to Mastering the Language. 225p. (ENG & SPA.). 1996. pap. 9.95 (*0-7818-0024-2*) Hippocrene Bks.

Spanish Verse of the Sixteenth Age. Ed. by P. D. Tettenborn. 1977. lib. bdg. 59.95 (*0-8490-2654-7*) Gordon Pr.

***Spanish Vocabulary.** Berlitz Editors. 256p. 1998. pap. 10.95 (*2-8315-6398-4*) Berlitz.

Spanish Vocabulary. Julianne Dueber. 256p. 1990. pap. 5.95 (*0-8120-4498-3*) Barron.

***Spanish Vocabulary & Verbs.** Harraps. 1997. 6.95 (*0-02-861722-3*) Macmillan.

Spanish Vocabulary Handbook. Berlitz Editors. (Handbook Ser.). (Illus.). 256p. 1994. pap. 8.95 (*2-8315-1358-8*) Berlitz.

Spanish Vocabulary of Four Native Spanish-Speaking Pre-First-Grade Children. Loyd S. Tireman. LC 48-45159. 64p. 1982. reprint ed. lib. bdg. 27.00 (*0-89370-737-6*) Borgo Pr.

Spanish Voyage to Vancouver & the North-West Coast of America. Jose Espinosa y Tello. Tr. by Cecil Jane. LC-70-136389. (Illus.). reprint ed. 27.50 (*0-404-02356-8*) AMS Pr.

Spanish Voyage to Vancouver & the North-West Coast of America. Jose Espinosa Y Tello. (BCL1 - United States Local History Ser.). 142p. 1991. reprint ed. lib. bdg. 69.00 (*0-7812-6335-2*) Rprt Serv.

Spanish War: An American Epic, 1898. G. J. O'Toole. (Illus.). 448p. 1986. reprint ed. pap. 15.95 (*0-393-30304-7*) Norton.

***Spanish Way with Legumes.** Perla Meyers. Date not set. write for info. (*0-688-11008-8*) Morrow.

Spanish Whole Language Big Book, 16 Book Set. (Illus.). (J). (ps-2). 1994. pap. write for info. (*1-56784-089-2*) Newbridge Comms.

Spanish with Ease, 4 CDs. (ENG & SPA.). pap. 69.95 incl. audio compact disk (*2-7005-1070-4*, Pub. by ASSIMIL FR) Distribks Inc.

Spanish with Ease, 4 cass. (ENG & SPA.). pap. 59.95 incl. audio (*2-7005-1310-X*, Pub. by ASSIMIL FR) Distribks Inc.

Spanish with Ease. J. Anton. Tr. by John Smellie from FRE. (With Ease Ser.). 479p. 1987. 24.95 (*2-7005-0131-4*, Pub. by ASSIMIL FR) Distribks Inc.

Spanish with Ease: Spanish for English Speakers. Assimil Staff. (ENG & SPA.). 28.95 (*0-8288-4319-8*, F70420); cd-rom, digital audio 125.00 (*0-685-52992-4*) Fr & Eur.

Spanish WithCase. Albert O. Cherel. 24.95 (*0-685-11574-7*); Four cassettes. audio 125.00 (*0-685-01767-2*) Fr & Eur.

Spanish Women in the Golden Age: Images & Realities. Ed. by Magdalena S. Sanchez & Alain Sainte-Saens. LC 95-36432. (Contributions in Women's Studies: No. 155). 248p. 1996. text ed. 57.95 (*0-313-29481-X*, Greenwood Pr) Greenwood.

Spanish Women Writers: A Bio-Bibliographical Source Book. Ed. by Linda G. Levine et al. LC 92-42432. 632p. 1993. text ed. 99.50 (*0-313-26823-1*, LSB, Greenwood Pr) Greenwood.

Spanish Word Formation: Productive Derivational Morphology in the Modern Lexis. M. F. Lang. (Romance Linguistics Ser.). 304p. (C). (gr. 13). 1990. text ed. 74.95 (*0-415-04143-0*, A4105) Routledge.

Spanish Word Games for Beginners: Early Intermediate to Advanced. Marcia Seidletz. 80p. (SPA.). (YA). 1993. pap. 17.25 (*0-8442-7191-8*, Natl Textbk) NTC Pub Grp.

Spanish Workbook. Berlitz Editors. (Workbook Ser.). (Illus.). 128p. 1995. pap. 11.95 (*2-8315-1322-7*) Berlitz.

Spanish Worksheets: Hands on Elementary School Science. Linda Poore. 94p. 1994. teacher ed. 75.00 (*1-883410-27-4*) L Poore.

Spanish Worksheets - Earth Science: Hands on Elementary School Science. Linda Poore. 38p. 1994. teacher ed. 25.00 (*1-883410-30-4*) L Poore.

Spanish Worksheets - Life Science: Hands on Elementary School Science. Linda Poore. 38p. 1994. teacher ed. 25.00 (*1-883410-29-0*) L Poore.

Spanish Worksheets - Physical Science: Hands on Elementary School Science. Linda Poore. 30p. 1993. teacher ed. 25.00 (*1-883410-28-2*) L Poore.

Spanish Writers of Nineteen Thirty-Six: Crisis & Commitment in the Poetry of the Thirties & Forties. An Anthology of Literary Studies & Essays. Ed. by Jaime Ferran & Daniel P. Testa. (Monagrafias A Ser.: Vol. XXXI). 141p. (Orig.). (C). 1973. pap. 36.00 (*0-900411-71-6*, Pub. by Tamesis Bks Ltd UK) Boydell & Brewer.

Spanish Yearbook of International Law, 1991, Vol. I. Ed. by Asociaion Espanola de Professores de Derecho International Publico Staff. 404p. (C). 1994. lib. bdg. 160.00 (*0-7923-2017-4*) Kluwer Ac.

Spanish 2 All the Way. Daniel Holodyk. 1995. 85.00 incl. cd-rom (*0-517-70217-7*, Living Language) Crown Pub Group.

***Spanish/English.** (Lyric Language Series 1). (ENG & SPA.). (J). 1997. pap. 19.95 incl. audio, vhs (*1-56015-418-1*) Penton Overseas.

***Spanish/English Business Glossary.** Michael Gorman & Maria-Luisa Henson. (Language Manuals for Business Ser.). 160p. (C). 1997. pap. 9.95 (*0-415-16043-X*) Routledge.

***Spanish/English Dictionary.** Berlitz Editors. 368p. 1997. pap. 7.95 (*2-8315-6384-4*) Berlitz.

***Spanish/English Dictionary of Medical Sciences: Spanish - English, 2 vols.** 25th ed. Stedman. 1530p. (ENG & SPA.). 1993. 295.00 (*0-7859-9305-3*) Fr & Eur.

Spanish/English Reference Guide for the Professional: A Dictionary of Financial & Legal Terminology. Hermelinda G. Dunagan. 432p. (ENG & SPA.). 1995. 79.00 (*1-880047-36-5*) Creative Des.

Spanking: Why? When? How? Roy Lessin. LC 79-54028. 96p. 1989. mass mkt. 4.99 (*0-87123-494-7*) Bethany Hse.

Spanking the Maid. Robert Coover. LC 81-48546. 96p. 1982. pap. 4.95 (*0-394-17971-4*, Grove) Grove-Atltic.

Spanking the Maid. deluxe limited ed. Robert Coover. 1981. 125.00 (*0-89723-024-8*) Bruccoli.

Spanking the Maid. limited ed. Robert Coover. 1981. 75.00 (*0-89723-023-X*) Bruccoli.

Spanning a Century: A Greek American Odyssey. Ann Sederocanellis. 1995. 19.95 (*0-533-11397-0*) Vantage.

Spanning Berkshire Waterways: A Personal Excursion into the History of Metal Truss Highway Bridge Construction in Western New England 1865-1905. Bernard A. Drew. (Illus.). 32p. (Orig.). 1990. pap. 5.00 (*0-941583-18-X*) Attic Rev Pr.

Spanning Boundaries: Rethinking Community, Competitiveness & Cooperation. Carol L. James. (Illus.). (Orig.). 1995. write for info. (*0-910440-05-0*) NCBA.

Spanning the Gate: Building the Golden Gate Bridge. rev. ed. Stephen Cassady. (Illus.). 144p. 1987. pap. 18.95 (*0-916290-36-0*) Squarebooks.

Spanning the Years. Juanita Torrence-Thompson. LC 96-90360. 80p. 1996. per. 9.00 (*0-9652892-0-6*) Torderwarz.

Spanning Time. Elizabeth Yates. (YA). (gr. 3 up). 1996. reprint ed. pap. 17.50 (*0-614-15575-4*) Cobblestone Bks.

Spanning Time: A Diary Keeper Becomes a Writer. Elizabeth Yates. LC 96-14192. (J). 1996. write for info. (*0-942389-13-1*) Cobblestone Pub.

***Spanning Time: Vermont's Covered Bridges.** Joseph C. Nelson. LC 97-23083. (Illus.). 288p. 1997. 60.00 (*1-881535-25-8*) New Eng Pr VT.

Spanos: Eine Byzantinische Satire als Parodie, Einleitung, Kritischer Text, Kommentar und Glossar. Ed. by Hans Eideneier. (C). 1977. 211.55 (*3-11-006606-8*) De Gruyter.

Spansk-Norsk Ordbok: Spanish-Norwegian Dictionary. 2nd ed. S. Loenneoken. 411p. (NOR & SPA.). 1980. 39.95 (*0-8288-1033-8*, S37620) Fr & Eur.

SPAR Membership Directory. (Orig.). pap. 35.00 (*0-318-11806-8*) SPAR.

SPARC Architecture Assembly Language Programming & C. Richard P. Paul. LC 93-10038. 448p. (C). 1993. text ed. 63.00 (*0-13-876889-7*) P-H Gen Ref & Trav.

SPARC Architecture Manual: Version Eight. SPARC International, Inc. Staff. 352p. 1991. pap. text ed. 47.00 (*0-13-825001-4*) P-H.

SPARC Architecture Manual Version 9. Sparc International, Inc. Staff. 384p. (C). 1993. pap. text ed. 42.00 (*0-13-099227-5*) P-H.

SPARC Artic Scenes: Scene Pictures for Articulation Remediation & Carryover. Susan R. Simms. (J). (ps-5). 1993. student ed., spiral bd. 41.95 (*1-55999-401-0*) LinguiSystems.

SPARC Picture Scenes: Scene Pictures for Assessment Remediation & Carryover. M. Sherry Smith & Karen Hanson. Tr. by Laura Morales. 1992. student ed., spiral bd. 41.95 (*1-55999-226-3*) LinguiSystems.

SPARC Technical Papers. Ed. by B. J. Catanzaro. (Sun Technical Reference Library). (Illus.). 416p. 1991. 52.95 (*0-387-97634-5*) Spr-Verlag.

Sparda by the Bitter Sea: Imperial Interaction in Western Anatolia. Jack Balcer. (Brown Judaic Studies: No. 52). 616p. (C). 1985. 41.95 (*0-89130-657-9*, 14 00 52); pap. 31.95 (*0-89130-818-0*) Scholars Pr GA.

***Spare Change.** Kevin Pilkington. Ed. by Kathleen Iddings. LC 97-72360. (National Poetry Book Ser.: Vol. 2). (Illus.). 80p. (Orig.). 1997. per. 10.00 (*0-931721-14-8*) La Jolla Poets.

***Spare Change or When.** Love Letters Incorporated, Staff. Date not set. pap. write for info. (*0-688-15742-4*, Beech Tree Bks) Morrow.

Spare No Exertions: One Hundred Seventy-Five Years of the Reformed Presbyterian Theological Seminary. Robert M. Copeland. LC 86-60501. (Illus.). 144p. 1986. 5.00 (*0-9616417-0-3*) Ref Presby Theo.

***Spare-Not the Rod & Save the Child.** 2nd large type ed. Earlene Jackson. 143p. (Orig.). (C). 1995. pap. 10.00 (*0-9653371-1-1*) Elliott & James Pubs.

Spare Parts. Rick Hanson. 288p. 1994. 20.00 (*0-8217-4738-X*, Zebra Kensgtn) Kensgtn Pub Corp.

Spare Parts. Rick Hanson. 256p. 1995. mass mkt. 4.99 (*0-8217-0156-8*, Zebra Kensgtn) Kensgtn Pub Corp.

Spare Parts. Rick Hanson. 256p. 1995. mass mkt. 4.99 (*0-7860-0156-9*, Pinncle Kensgtn) Kensgtn Pub Corp.

Spare Parts: Organ Replacement in American Society. Renee C. Fox & Judith P. Swazey. 320p. 1992. 33.50 (*0-19-507650-8*) OUP.

Spare Parts for People. Margery Facklam & Howard Facklam. (Illus.). 128p. (YA). (gr. 7 up). 1987. 16.00 (*0-15-277410-6*, HB Juv Bks) HarBrace.

Spare the Child: The Religious Roots of Punishment & the Psychological Impact of Physical Abuse. Philip Greven. 1992. pap. 11.00 (*0-679-73338-8*, Vin) Random.

***Spare the Rod, Spoil the Child? Classroom Discipline.** Ginger Hanson. 90p. (Orig.). (YA). (gr. 7-12). 1996. pap. 6.95 (*1-57515-099-9*) PPI Pubng.

Spare Time at Sea. 2nd ed. Ronald Hope. (Illus.). 231p. 1974. 19.95 (*0-8464-0878-3*) Beekman Pubs.

Spare Time Cash: Every Student's Guide to Making Money on the Side. Mick Sullivan. Ed. by Mary Moe. 114p. (Orig.). (YA). (gr. 10 up). 1989. pap. 12.95 (*1-878330-00-4*) Sullivan MT.

Spare-Time Profits for Women. Rhoda T. Holmes. 16p. 1995. pap. 6.00 (*0-915665-33-6*) Premier Publishers.

Spare Your People! Richard A. Swanson. LC 85-73213. 230p. 1986. pap. 4.95 (*0-88270-596-2*) Bridge-Logos.

***Spared Angola: Memories from a Cuban-American Childhood.** Virgil Suarez. LC 96-39825. 1997. pap. 11.95 (*1-55885-197-6*) Arte Publico.

Spares. Caroline Gray. 384p. 1993. lib. bdg. 22.00 (*0-7278-4473-3*) Severn Hse.

Spares. Michael M. Smith. 336p. 1997. 22.95 (*0-553-10604-X*) Bantam.

***Spares.** aut. ed. Michael M. Smith. (C). 1997. boxed 200.00 (*0-9633397-7-X*) Overlook Connect.

***Spares.** limited ed. Michael M. Smith. (C). 1997. boxed 75.00 (*0-9633397-5-3*) Overlook Connect.

***Spares.** limited ed. Michael M. Smith. (C). 1997. 40.00 (*0-9633397-6-1*) Overlook Connect.

Spares Management: An Introduction. Douglas K. Orsburn. (Illus.). 250p. 1991. 49.95 (*0-8306-7626-0*, 3626) TAB Bks.

Spares Management Handbook. Douglas K. Orsburn. 1991. text ed. 49.95 (*0-07-157637-1*) McGraw.

Sparhawk's Angel. Miranda Jarrett. (Historical Ser.). 1996. mass mkt. 4.99 (*0-373-28915-4*, 1-28915-6) Harlequin Bks.

Sparhawk's Lady. Miranda Jarrett. (Historical Ser.). 1995. mass mkt. 4.50 (*0-373-28871-9*, 1-28871-1) Harlequin Bks.

Sparhwak Bride. Miranda Jarrett. 1995. mass mkt. 4.50 (*0-373-28892-1*) Harlequin Bks.

Sparing to Spend. Timothy S. Arthur. (Works of Timothy Shay Arthur). 1989. reprint ed. lib. bdg. 79.00 (*0-7812-1801-2*) Rprt Serv.

Sparire, 2 vols., Set. Enzo Cucchi. Tr. by Meg Shore & Catherine Schelbert. (Illus.). 30p. (Orig.). (ENG, GER & ITA.). 1987. bds. 22.50 (*0-935875-05-0*) P Blum Edit.

Spark. John G. Hughes. 300p. 1997. pap. 15.00 (*1-881320-81-2*, Black Belt) Black Belt Comm.

Spark & Other Stories. Elspeth Davie. 288p. (Orig.). 1983. pap. 11.95 (*0-7145-0538-2*) Riverrun NY.

***Spark Discharge.** Eduard M. Bazellan & I. U. Raizer. LC 97-14858. 1997. write for info. (*0-8493-2868-3*) CRC Pr.

Spark from Heaven: The Mystery of the Madonna of Medjugorje. Mary Craig. LC 88-71358. 232p. (Orig.). 1988. pap. 7.95 (*0-87793-386-3*) Ave Maria.

***Spark-Ignition Engine Combustion & Emissions.** 1997. 44.00 (*1-56091-979-5*) Soc Auto Engineers.

Spark in the Dark. Richard Tichnor & Jenny Smith. (Illus.). 32p. (J). (ps-5). 1994. 14.95 (*1-883220-25-4*); pap. 6.95 (*1-883220-26-2*) Dawn CA.

***Spark in the Dark.** Richard Tichnor & Jenny Smith. (Illus.). 32p. (J). (ps-5). 1997. 21.95 (*1-883220-62-9*) Dawn CA.

***Spark in the Dark, Incl. Mobile.** Richard Tichnor & Jenny Smith. 32p. (J). (ps-5). 1997. pap. 13.95 (*1-883220-63-7*, SPK-MP) Dawn CA.

Spark in the Stone: Skills & Projects from the Native American Tradition. Peter Goodchild. LC 90-27324. (Illus.). 144p. (Orig.). (J). (gr. 5 up). 1991. pap. 14.95 (*1-55652-102-2*) Chicago Review.

Spark of Enterprise: A History of Dixie Foundry - Magic Chef, Inc. John C. Longwith. LC 87-91291. (Illus.). 192p. 1988. 16.95 (*0-944897-00-2*) Magic Chef.

Spark of Enterprise: A History of Dixie Foundry - Magic Chef, Inc. deluxe ed. John C. Longwith. LC 87-91291. (Illus.). 192p. 1988. ring bd. 29.95 (*0-944897-01-0*) Magic Chef.

***Spark of Life.** Eric M. Remarque. 1998. pap. 12.00 (*0-449-91251-5*) Fawcett.

***Spark Tests for Steel.** S. P. Rockwell. (Technical Papers). 1923. pap. text ed. 30.00 (*1-55589-322-8*) AGMA.

Spark Your Social Science. teacher ed., pap. 4.95 (*0-686-19379-2*) E V Salitore.

Sparke: The Compulsory Competitive Tendering Guide. Andrew Sparke. 275p. 1993. pap. 75.00 (*0-406-00908-2*, U.K.) MICHIE.

Sparke Towards the Kindling of Sorrow for Zion. Thomas Gataker. LC 76-57382. (English Experience Ser.: No. 800). 1977. reprint ed. lib. bdg. 15.00 (*90-221-0800-7*) Walter J Johnson.

***Sparking Brilliance: Nurturing Creativity in the Classroom.** Lifetouch Natl. School Studios Staff. (Illus.). 60p. 1997. teacher ed. 8.95 (*0-943535-18-2*) Primarius Ltd.

***Sparking the Thinking of Students, Ages 10-14: Strategies for Teachers.** Glenda W. Beamon. LC 97-4796. 168p. 1997. 45.95 (*0-8039-6582-6*); pap. 19.95 (*0-8039-6583-4*) Sage.

Sparkle. Sadie T. Pitts. 1989. pap. 5.95 (*0-913543-12-8*) African Am Imag.

Sparkle: PR for Library Staff. Virginia Baeckler. LC 80-50566. (Illus.). 80p. (Orig.). 1980. pap. 5.00 (*0-9603232-1-X*) Sources.

Sparkle Fairy. Dan Witkowski. 1996. pap. 4.99 (*0-679-87992-7*) Random.

Sparklefeet's Quest. Hattie Perdue. 24p. (J). (gr. k-3). 1996. pap. 7.00 (*0-8059-3935-0*) Dorrance.

Sparkles in the Sand. Ed. by Rich Schaub. 1996. 69.95 (*1-56167-272-6*) Nat Lib Poetry.

Sparkles of Life. 1992. pap. 13.95 (*0-87949-325-9*) Ashley Bks.

Sparkle's Tidbits of Advice for Cats (& Their Owners) Charlotte Dalton. LC 95-68992. (Illus.). 68p. (Orig.). 1995. pap. 7.95 (*0-9646162-0-3*) C Dalton.

Sparkley, the Tooth Fairy: The Story of Susie & Scotty in Toothdom. Mary Casey. Ed. by M. E. Pettigrew. LC 95-94501. (Illus.). 32p. (J). (ps up). 1996. 14.95 (*0-9647073-0-6*) MECK & Co.

Sparkling Christmas Ornaments. Sallie Baldwin. (J). 1996. pap. 6.95 (*0-8167-3564-6*) Troll Communs.

Sparkling Cyanide. Agatha Christie. 240p. 1992. mass mkt. 4.99 (*0-06-100379-4*, Harp PBks) HarpC.

Sparkling Fountain. Fred T. Corum et al. Ed. by Corum & Associates, Inc. Staff. LC 89-60777. 308p. (Orig.). (C). 1989. pap. text ed. 5.95 (*0-924758-02-3*) Corum & Assocs.

Sparkling Lavender Dust of Lust. Tee A. Corinne. 144p. (Orig.). 1991. pap. 8.95 (*0-934411-49-2*, Banned Bks) Edward-William Austin.

Sparkling Object Sermons for Children. C. W. Bess. (Object Lessons Ser.). 112p. (Orig.). (gr. 10). 1993. pap. 6.99 (*0-8010-0824-7*) Baker Bks.

Sparkling Plug Collectors Guide, Vol. 1. Cornelius Bergbower. (Illus.). 96p. (Orig.). 1986. pap. 9.95 (*0-9616653-0-0*) C Bergbower.

Sparkling River. (Shimmer Book). 24p. (J). (ps-3). 1995. 8.98 (*1-57082-245-X*) Mouse Works.

Sparkling, Silent Snow. Madelyn W. Carlisle. LC 92-16832. (Let's Investigate Ser.). (Illus.). 32p. (J). (gr. 2-6). 1996. lib. bdg. 13.95 (*1-56674-149-1*) Forest Hse.

Sparkling Words. Ruth K. Carlson. 1979. 29.35 (*0-88252-009-1*) Paladin Hse.

***Sparkman in the Sky: And Other Stories.** Brian Griffin. LC 96-39817. 192p. 1997. 21.95 (*1-889330-05-1*) Sarabande Bks.

***Sparkman in the Sky: And Other Stories.** Brian Griffin. LC 96-39817. 192p. 1997. pap. 13.95 (*1-889330-06-X*) Sarabande Bks.

Sparks. Carole Buck. (Desire Ser.). 1993. mass mkt. 2.99 (*0-373-05808-X*, 5-05808-6) Silhouette.

Sparks. Meg Wolitzer. 294p. 1985. 15.95 (*0-685-10190-8*) HM.

Sparks. Chayym Zeldis. 152p. (Orig.). 1995. pap. 14.95 (*965-229-142-0*, Pub. by Gefen Pub Hse IS) Gefen Bks.

***Sparks Amidst the Ashes: The Spiritual Legacy of Polish Jewry.** Byron L. Sherwin. 192p. 1997. 29.95 (*0-19-510685-7*) OUP.

Sparks Beneath the Surface: A Spiritual Commentary on the Torah. Lawrence S. Kushner & Kerry M. Olitzky. LC 93-26265. 296p. 1994. 30.00 (*1-56821-016-7*) Aronson.

An Asterisk (*) at the beginning of an entry indicates that the title is appearing in BIP for the first time.

Sparks Beneath the Surface: A Spiritual Commentary on the Torah. Lawrence S. Kushner & Kerry M. Olitzky. LC 93-26265. 296p. 1996. pap. 27.50 (*1-56821-743-9*) Aronson.

***Sparks Fly.** Eric Norton, pseud. (Orig.). 1997. mass mkt. 6.95 (*1-56333-551-4*, Badboy) Masquerade.

Sparks Fly Upward. Glen Haley. (Illus.). 264p. (Orig.). 1988. pap. 9.95 (*0-9608764-8-0*) Wayfinder Pr.

Sparks Fly Upward. Jerome Lawrence & Robert E. Lee. 1967. pap. 5.25 (*0-8222-1064-9*) Dramatists Play.

Sparks from His Heart. Frank Parrish. 110p. 1992. pap. text ed. 9.00 (*1-881068-00-5*) Oaktree Bks.

Sparks from Synergy's Fire. 2nd ed. Mary K. Cox. LC 83-50644. (Illus.). 80p. 1983. pap. 1.95 (*0-910217-02-5*) Synergetics WV.

Sparks from the Anvil of Oppression: Philadelphia's African Methodists & Southern Migrants, 1890-1940. Robert Gregg. LC 92-34589. 288p. 1993. 49.95 (*1-56639-063-X*) Temple U Pr.

Sparks from the Apostles: Orthodox Homilies on the Sunday Apostolic Readings. Augoustinos N. Kantiotes. Tr. by Asterios Gerostergios. LC 91-76723. 220p. 1992. 17.50 (*0-914744-92-5*) Inst Byzantine.

***Sparks from the Camp Fire: Tales of the Old Veterans.** unabridged ed. Ed. by Joseph W. Morton, Jr. LC 96-44046. (Illus.). xiii, 648p. (C). 1996. reprint ed. 44.95 (*1-889881-06-6*) Old Bks Pub.

Sparks in the Night. Beth Batlle. LC 87-5563. 158p. 1987. 13.75 (*0-930950-11-9*); pap. 8.75 (*0-930950-12-7*) Nopoly Pr.

Sparks Might Fly. Cris Newport. LC 94-15387. 250p. (Orig.). 1994. pap. 9.95 (*0-934678-61-8*) Pride OH.

Sparks of Fire: William Blake in a New Age. Ed. by James Bogan & Fred Goss. (Io Ser.: No. 29). (Illus.). 484p. (Orig.). 1982. 35.00 (*0-913028-89-4*); pap. 12.95 (*0-913028-90-8*) North Atlantic.

Sparks of Genius: Portraits of Electrical Engineering Excellence. R. Nebeker. LC 93-15916. (Illus.). 280p. 1993. text ed. 39.95 (*0-7803-1033-0*, PC03822) Inst Electrical.

Sparks of Glory: Inspiring Episodes of Jewish Spiritual Resistance. Moshe Prager. (ArtScroll History Ser.). (Illus.). 208p. 1985. 17.99 (*0-89906-456-6*) Mesorah Pubns.

Sparks of Innovation in Human-Computer Interaction. Ed. by Ben Shneiderman. LC 93-17704. 400p. 1993. pap. 42.50 (*1-56750-078-1*); text ed. 82.50 (*1-56750-079-X*) Ablex Pub.

Sparks of Life. Shlomo Wolpo. 268p. 1994. 14.95 (*1-56871-038-0*) Targum Pr.

Sparks of Spirit: A Handbook for Personal Happiness. Rolf Gompertz. LC 83-50870. 124p. 1983. pap. 12.95 (*0-918248-04-3*) Word Doctor.

Sparks of the Truth: From the Dissertations of Meher Baba. Meher Baba. Ed. by C. D. Deshmukh. (Illus.). 96p. (Orig.). 1971. pap. 5.95 (*0-913078-02-6*) Sheriar Pr.

Sparks Out of the Plowed Ground. Bob Doll. LC 95-67243. (Illus.). 322p. 1996. pap. 19.99 (*1-886745-05-6*) Streamlne Pr.

Sparks That Leap. Ed. by Matthew C. Morrison. LC 91-73112. 1991. pap. 10.95 (*0-89112-225-7*) Abilene Christ U.

Sparks That Lit the Recent Islamic Movement: June 5, 1963. Ayatullah R. Khomeini. Tr. by Laleh Bakhtiar. 96p. 1989. pap. text ed. 6.70 (*1-871031-25-7*) Abjad Bk.

***Sparky & Eddie: The First Day of School.** Tony Johnston. LC 96-38192. (Illus.). (J). 1997. 13.95 (*0-590-47978-4*); pap. 3.99 (*0-590-47979-2*) Scholastic Inc.

***Sparky & Eddie: The Rodeo.** Tony Johnston. LC 96-38188. (Illus.). (J). 1997. write for info. (*0-590-47984-9*); pap. write for info. (*0-590-47985-7*) Scholastic Inc.

***Sparky's Builders Kit.** Michele Borba. Ed. by Marie Conte. (Esteem Builder's Complete Program Ser.). (Illus.). (J). (ps-2). 1997. pap. text ed. write for info. (*1-880396-28-9*, JP9628-9) Jalmar Pr.

Sparky's Rainbow Repair. Max Haynes. LC 91-1687. (Illus.). (J). (ps-3). 1992. 15.00 (*0-688-11193-9*) Lothrop.

Sparo: The Wild & Crazy Pretty Dog. 2nd ed. Frank Nwabugwu. 26p. (J). (gr. 2-8). 1993. write for info. (*1-881687-08-2*) F Nwabugwu.

Sparring With Charlie: Motorbiking Down the Ho Chi Minh Trail. Christopher Hunt. LC 95-36322. 304p. (Orig.). 1996. pap. 12.95 (*0-385-48128-4*, Anchor NY) Doubleday.

Sparring with Hemingway: And Other Legends of the Fight Game. Budd Schulberg. LC 94-49153. 256p. 1995. 25.00 (*1-56663-080-0*) I R Dee.

***Sparrow.** Mary D. Russell. 1997. pap. 12.00 (*0-449-91255-8*) Fawcett.

Sparrow. Mary D. Russell. 416p. 1996. 23.00 (*0-679-45150-1*) Random.

Sparrow. Giovanni Verga. Tr. by Lucy Gordan & Frances Frenaye from ITA. LC 96-45542. 128p. (Orig.). 1997. pap. 12.00 (*0-934977-42-9*) Italica Pr.

***Sparrow.** Giovanni Verga. 177p. pap. 11.95 (*1-873982-46-1*, Pub. by Dedalus Bks UK) Hippocrene Bks.

Sparrow. 4th ed. Jane T. Clement. Ed. by Hutterian Brethren Staff. LC 68-21133. (Illus.). 212p. (J). (gr. 4 up). 1992. reprint ed. pap. 5.00 (*0-87486-009-1*) Plough.

***Sparrow: New & Selected Poems.** Reginald Gibbons. 1997. 22.95 (*0-614-29427-4*) La State U Pr.

***Sparrow: New & Selected Poems.** Reginald Gibbons. 1997. pap. 15.95 (*0-614-29428-2*) La State U Pr.

***Sparrow: New & Selected Poems.** Reginald Gibbons. (Southern Messenger Poets Ser.). 152p. 1997. text ed. 22.95 (*0-8071-2232-7*) La State U Pr.

***Sparrow: New & Selected Poems.** Reginald Gibbons. (Southern Messenger Poets Ser.). 152p. 1997. pap. 15.95 (*0-8071-2233-5*) La State U Pr.

Sparrow & the Hawk: Costa Rica & the United States During the Rise of Jose Figueres. Kyle Longley. LC 96-19042. 1997. pap. text ed. 29.95 (*0-8173-0831-8*) U of Ala Pr.

Sparrow Falls. Wilbur Smith. 608p. 1991. reprint ed. lib. bdg. 38.95 (*0-89966-779-1*) Buccaneer Bks.

Sparrow Hawk. H. H. Holly. 1969. 2.95 (*0-940628-39-2*) Pilgrim Soc.

Sparrow Hawk. Meridel Le Sueur. LC 87-80573. (Illus.). 176p. (YA). (gr. 7 up). 1987. reprint ed. 13.95 (*0-930100-22-0*) Holy Cow.

Sparrow Hawk Red. Ben Mikaelsen. LC 92-53458. 224p. (J). (gr. 5-9). 1993. 14.95 (*1-56282-387-6*) Hyprn Child.

Sparrow Hawk Red. Ben Mikaelsen. LC 92-53458. 224p. (J). (gr. 5-9). 1994. pap. 4.50 (*0-7868-1002-5*) Hyprn Child.

Sparrow Songs: An Anthology of Father-Daughter Verse. Rene Bozarth & Alla Bozarth-Campbell. LC 81-84948. 98p. (Orig.). 1981. 15.00 (*0-932560-02-4*); pap. 12.00 (*0-932560-03-2*) Wisdom House.

Sparrowgrass Papers. Frederic S. Cozzens. LC 72-76922. (American Fiction Reprint Ser.). 1977. 18.95 (*0-8369-7001-2*) Ayer.

***Sparrowhook Curse.** Robin Moore. 424p. (Orig.). 1996. pap. 12.95 (*0-924771-70-4*, Covered Brdge Pr) D C Press.

Sparrows. J. Denis Summers-Smith. (Illus.). 160p. 1990. text ed. 37.00 (*0-85661-048-8*, 784648, Pub. by Poyser UK) Acad Pr.

Sparrows & Buntings. Clive Byers et al. LC 95-4862. (Illus.). 256p. 1995. 40.00 (*0-395-73873-3*) HM.

Sparrows Don't Sing in the Philippines. Paulino Lim, Jr. 133p. (Orig.). 1994. pap. 10.75 (*971-10-0527-1*, Pub. by New Day Pub PH) Cellar.

***Sparrows in the Scullery.** Wallace. (J). Date not set. mass mkt. 4.95 (*0-689-81718-5*) S&S Childrens.

***Sparrows in the Scullery.** Barbara B. Wallace. 1997. 15.00 (*0-689-81585-9*, Atheneum S&S) S&S Trade.

Sparrow's Inn. Ralph F. McCarthy. (Children's Classics Ser.). (Illus.). 48p. (J). 1994. 14.95 (*4-7700-1849-5*) Kodansha.

Sparrow's Song. Ralph H. Allen, Jr. LC 87-63404. 115p. 1990. reprint ed. pap. 4.95 (*0-945277-00-8*) New Creation Bks.

Sparrow's Song. Irma Stoll & Catherine Brandt. 134p. (Orig.). 1991. reprint ed. pap. 2.50 (*0-937779-19-9*) Greenlawn Pr.

Sparrow's Yard. large type ed. Audrey Curling. 320p. 1987. 25.99 (*0-7089-1683-X*) Ulverscroft.

Sparse Distributed Memory. Pentti Kanerva. 176p. 1988. 30.00 (*0-262-11132-2*, Bradford Bks) MIT Pr.

Sparta: To Kryton tes Politeias ton Lakedaimonoin. Humphrey Michell. LC 85-12537. x, 348p. 1985. reprint ed. text ed. 59.75 (*0-313-24955-5*, MISP, Greenwood Pr) Greenwood.

Sparta Between Empire & Revolution: 404-243 B.C. rev. ed. Ephraim David. Ed. by W. R. Connor. LC 80-2646. (Monographs in Classical Studies). 1981. lib. bdg. 30.00 (*0-405-14033-9*) Ayer.

***Sparta Between Empire & Revolution 404-243 B. C.** David Ephraim. Date not set. write for info. (*0-88143-029-3*) Ayer.

Sparta Gold, Vol. 1. Glenn Densley. (Illus.). Date not set. pap. write for info. (*0-9623748-1-4*) Snake Riv Secrets.

Sparta with a Hoe. Gina V. Kaiper. 246p. (Orig.). 1997. pap. 14.50 (*0-9645206-4-8*) Days & Years Pr.

Spartacus. Howard Fast. LC 96-15113. 320p. (C). (gr. 13). 1996. pap. 13.50 (*1-56324-599-X*, N Castle) M E Sharpe.

Spartacus. T. L. Mancour. Ed. by Dave Stern. (Star Trek: The Next Generation Ser.: No. 20). 288p. (Orig.). 1992. mass mkt. 5.50 (*0-671-76051-3*) PB.

Spartacus. Howard Fast. 1982. reprint ed. lib. bdg. 17.95 (*0-89966-433-4*) Buccaneer Bks.

***Spartacus' Uprising & Soviet Historical Writing.** W. Z. Rubinsohn. 56p. 1987. pap. 4.95 (*0-9511243-1-5*, Pub. by Oxbow Bks UK) David Brown.

Spartakusbund & the German Working Class Movement, 1914-1919. William A. Pelz. LC 87-5637. (Studies in German Thought & History: Vol. 1). (Illus.). 423p. 1987. lib. bdg. 109.95 (*0-88946-355-7*) E Mellen.

Spartan. Don Harrison. 175p. 1992. reprint ed. pap. 7.95 (*0-932870-20-1*) Alyson Pubns.

Spartan Education. Albert D. Werder. 1979. 19.95 (*0-8464-0040-5*) Beekman Pubs.

Spartan Football: 100 Seasons of Gridiron Glory. Ken Hoffman. (Illus.). 300p. 1996. 34.95 (*1-57167-040-8*) Sagamore Pub.

Spartan Rhetra. Intro. by John E. Longhurst. 76p. 1970. pap. 7.50 (*0-87291-008-3*) Coronado Pr.

Spartan Run - Madman Run. David Robbins. (Endworld Double Edition Ser.). 384p. 1993. mass mkt., pap. text ed. 4.50 (*0-8439-3484-0*) Dorchester Pub Co.

Spartan Seasons: The Triumphs & Turmoil of Michigan State Sports. Lynn Henning. (Illus.). 314p. 1987. 17.95 (*0-9618726-0-8*) Momentum Bks.

Spartan Tradition in European Thought. Elizabeth Rawson. (Illus.). 408p. 1991. pap. 39.95 (*0-19-814733-3*) OUP.

***Spartan Tutorial.** Warren J. Hehre et al. (Illus.). 125p. 1997. pap. text ed. 25.00 (*1-890661-00-7*) Wavefunction.

Spartan Twilight. Linda J. Piper. (Illus.). xx, 244p. 1986. lib. bdg. 60.00 (*0-89241-378-6*) Caratzas.

SPARTAN User's Guide. Warren J. Hehre. 270p. (Orig.). 1995. pap. 35.00 (*0-9643495-3-1*) Wavefunction.

***Spartan User's Guide, Version 5.0.** Warren J. Hehre. (Illus.). 270p. 1997. pap. text ed. 35.00 (*1-890661-02-3*) Wavefunction.

Spartanburg County - District, South Carolina, Deed Abstracts, Book A-T, 1785-1827. Albert B. Pruitt. 872p. 1988. 55.00 (*0-89308-553-7*, SC 86) Southern Hist Pr.

Spartanburg County, South Carolina Will Abstracts 1787-1840. Brent H. Holcomb. (Illus.). 179p. 1983. 25.00 (*0-913363-01-4*) SCMAR.

Spartans: Michigan State Football. rev. ed. Fred W. Stabley. LC 75-12206. (College Sports Bks.). 1988. 16.95 (*0-87397-308-9*, Strode Pubs) Circle Bk Service.

Spartina. John Casey. 384p. 1990. pap. 12.00 (*0-380-71104-4*) Avon.

Spas: Planning, Selecting & Installing. Ed Scott. Ed. by Alan Ahlstrand. LC 90-86166. (Illus.). 112p. (Orig.). 1992. pap. 9.95 (*0-89721-238-X*) Meredith Bks.

Spas: The International Spa Guide, 1995-1996 Edition. 4th ed. Eli Dror. Ed. by Joseph H. Bain. (Illus.). 400p. 1995. pap. 25.00 (*0-9618612-7-4*) Bain Dror.

***Spas & Hot Springs of Mexico: Over 30 Restful Places from World-Class Spas to Simple Hot Springs.** 2nd ed. Mike Nelson. 124p. 1997. pap. 16.95 (*1-889489-01-8*) Rds Scholar.

Spas & Hot Tubs, Saunas & Home Gyms. Tom Cowan & Jack Maguire. Ed. by Roundtable Press Staff. LC 88-20216. (Illus.). 160p. (Orig.). 1988. pap. 9.95 (*0-932944-85-X*) Creative Homeowner.

Spasio Sam Ustastvo. Ivo Omrcanin. 104p. (CRO.). 1994. pap. 10.00 (*1-878716-17-4*) Ivor Pr.

Spasm: Virtual Reality, Android Music & Electric Flesh. Arthur Kroker. LC 93-20262. (Culture Texts Ser.). 196p. 1993. Includes compact disc. 19.95 incl. cd-rom (*0-312-09681-X*) St Martin.

Spasmodic Career of Sydney Dobell. Martha Westwater. 180p. (C). 1992. lib. bdg. 39.00 (*0-8191-8579-5*) U Pr of Amer.

Spasticity: Mechanisms & Management. Ed. by A. F. Thilmann et al. LC 93-34850. 1994. 103.00 (*0-387-56981-2*) Spr-Verlag.

Spasticity: The Current Status of Research & Treatment. Ed. by M. Emre & R. Benecke. (New Trends in Clinical Neurology Ser.). (Illus.). 200p. 1989. 55.00 (*1-85070-274-8*) Prthnon Pub.

Spatgotische Tafelmalerei in Sachsen. I. Sandner. 460p. (GER.). 1992. text ed. 148.00 (*3-364-00271-1*) Gordon & Breach.

Spatial Analysis: Modelling in a GIS Environemt. Ed. by Paul Longley & Michael Batty. Date not set. text ed. write for info. (*0-470-23615-9*) Halsted Pr.

Spatial Analysis & GIS: Applications in GIS. Ed. by A. Stewart Fotheringham & Peter Rogerson. LC 93-33031. 375p. 1994. 85.00 (*0-7484-0103-2*, Pub. by Tay Francis Ltd UK); pap. 39.50 (*0-7484-0104-0*, Pub. by Tay Francis Ltd UK) Taylor & Francis.

Spatial Analysis & Planning Under Imprecision. Y. C. Leung. (Studies in Regional Science & Urban Economics: Vol. 17). 376p. 1988. 145.25 (*0-444-70390-X*, North Holland) Elsevier.

Spatial Analysis & Spatial Policy Using Geographic Information Systems. Ed. by Les Worrall. (Illus.). 248p. 1992. text ed. 69.00 (*1-85293-141-8*) St Martin.

Spatial Analysis & Spatial Policy Using Geographic Information Systems. Les Worrall. LC 91-33579. (Illus.). 248p. 1991. reprint ed. pap. 70.70 (*0-608-00191-0*, 2060974) Bks Demand.

Spatial Analysis in Archaeology. Ian Hodder & Clive Orton. LC 75-44582. (New Studies in Archaeology). (Illus.). 260p. 1980. pap. 34.95 (*0-521-29738-9*) Cambridge U Pr.

***Spatial Analysis in Soil Dynamics & Earthquake Engineering: Proceedings of Sessions Held in Conjunction with Geo-Logan '97: Sponsored by the Geo-Institute of the American Society of Civil Engineers: Utah State University, Logan, Utah, July 16-19, 1997.** J. David Frost & American Society of Civil Engineers Staff. LC 97-20894. (Geotechnical Special Publication Ser.). 1997. write for info. (*0-7844-0258-2*) Am Soc Civil Eng.

Spatial Analysis of Interacting Economies. David F. Batten. 1982. lib. bdg. 52.50 (*0-89838-109-6*) Kluwer Ac.

Spatial Analysis of Urban Community Development Policy in India. Derek R. Hall. LC 80-40952. (Geography & Public Policy Research Studies: No. 1). (Illus.). 190p. reprint ed. pap. 54.20 (*0-8357-7031-1*, 2033335) Bks Demand.

Spatial Analysis of Urban-Industrial Development in Ethiopia. Mulatu Wubneh. LC 82-9968. (Foreign & Comparative Studies Program, African Ser.: No. 39). (Illus.). (Orig.). 1982. pap. text ed. 8.00 (*0-915984-62-8*) Syracuse U Foreign Comp.

Spatial & Contextual Models in Political Research. Ed. by Munroe Eagles. 352p. 1995. 69.50 (*0-7484-0210-1*, Pub. by Tay Francis Ltd UK) Taylor & Francis.

Spatial & Temporal Analysis in Ecology. Ed. by R. M. Cormack & J. Keith Ord. (Statistical Ecology Ser.: Vol. 8). 1979. 45.00 (*0-89974-005-7*) Intl Co-Op.

***Spatial & Temporal Reasoning in Geographic Information Systems.** Ed. by Max J. Egenhofer & Reginald G. Golledge. (Spatial Information Systems Ser.). (Illus.). 320p. 1997. 60.00 (*0-19-510342-4*) OUP.

Spatial Aspects of Aging. Robert Wiseman. Ed. by Salvatore J. Natoli. LC 78-59103. (Resource Papers for College Geography). (Illus.). 1979. pap. text ed. 15.00 (*0-89291-133-6*) Assn Am Geographers.

Spatial Aspects of Development. Ed. by B. S. Hoyle. LC 73-2785. 388p. reprint ed. pap. 110.60 (*0-317-30316-3*, 2024800) Bks Demand.

Spatial Autocorrelation: A Primer. Daniel A. Griffith. (Resource Publications in Geography). (Orig.). 1987. pap. 15.00 (*0-89291-197-2*) Assn Am Geographers.

Spatial Behavior of Hospital Patients: A Behavioral Approach to Spatial Interaction in Metropolitan Chicago. Robert Earickson. LC 79-104877. (University of Chicago, Department of Geography, Research Paper Ser.: No. 124). (Illus.). 153p. reprint ed. pap. 43.70 (*0-7837-0401-1*, 2040722) Bks Demand.

Spatial Boundaries & Social Dynamics: Case Studies from Food-Producing Societies. Ed. by Augustin Holl & Thomas E. Levy. LC 93-21778. (Ethnoarchaeological Ser.: No. 2). (Illus.). vi, 133p. (Orig.). 1993. pap. 19.50 (*1-879621-04-5*); lib. bdg. 38.00 (*1-879621-05-3*) Intl Mono Prehstry.

Spatial Child. John P. Dixon. (Illus.). 248p. 1983. pap. 31.95 (*0-398-06096-7*) C C Thomas.

Spatial Child. John P. Dixon. (Illus.). 248p. (C). 1983. 44.95 (*0-398-04821-5*) C C Thomas.

Spatial Choices & Processes. Ed. by M. M. Fischer et al. (Regional Science & Urban Economics Ser.: No. 21). 372p. 1990. 131.50 (*0-444-88195-6*, North Holland) Elsevier.

Spatial Cognition: Brain Bases & Development. Ed. by J. Stiles-Davis et al. 488p. 1988. 99.95 (*0-8058-0046-8*); pap. 49.95 (*0-8058-0078-6*) L Erlbaum Assocs.

***Spatial Cognition: Of Geographic Environments.** Robert Lloyd. LC 96-52349. (GeoJournal Library). 316p. (C). 1997. lib. bdg. 145.00 (*0-7923-4375-1*) Kluwer Ac.

Spatial Cognition: The Structure & Development of Mental Representations of Spatial Relations. David R. Olson & Ellen Bialystok. 296p. 1983. text ed. 69.95 (*0-89859-252-6*) L Erlbaum Assocs.

Spatial Components of Manufacturing Change, 1950-1960. Yehoshua S. Cohen & Brian J. Berry. LC 75-33654. (University of Chicago, Department of Geography, Research Paper Ser.: No. 172). 272p. 1975. reprint ed. pap. 77.60 (*0-608-02273-X*, 2062914) Bks Demand.

***Spatial Computing: Issues in Vision, Multimedia & Visualization Technologies.** 250p. 1997. 52.00 (*981-02-2924-0*) World Scientific Pub.

Spatial Context of Technological Development. Riccardo Cappellin & Peter Nujkamp. (Illus.). 513p. 1990. text ed. 93.95 (*0-566-07149-5*, Pub. by Avebury Pub UK) Ashgate Pub Co.

Spatial Data Analysis by Example: Categorical & Directional Data, Vol. 2. Graham J. Upton & Bernard Fingleton. LC 84-11806. 416p. 1989. text ed. 336.00 (*0-471-92086-X*) Wiley.

Spatial Data Analysis by Example: Point Pattern & Quantitative Data, Vol. 1. Graham J. Upton & Bernard Fingleton. LC 84-11806. (Probability & Mathematical Statistics Ser.). 410p. 1985. text ed. 354.00 (*0-471-90542-9*) Wiley.

Spatial Data Analysis in the Social & Environmental Sciences. Robert P. Haining. (Illus.). 250p. (C). 1990. text ed. 90.00 (*0-521-38416-8*) Cambridge U Pr.

Spatial Data Analysis in the Social & Environmental Sciences. Robert P. Haining. (Illus.). 431p. (C). 1993. pap. text ed. 31.95 (*0-521-44866-2*) Cambridge U Pr.

Spatial Data Structures: Hierarchical Methods for Representing Points, Lines & Figures. Hanan Samet. (Computer Science Ser.). (Illus.). 496p. (C). 1990. text ed. 44.25 (*0-201-50255-0*) Addison-Wesley.

Spatial Database Transfer Standards: Current International Status. Ed. by H. Moellering. 248p. 1991. 107.50 (*1-85166-677-X*) Elsevier.

Spatial Database Transfer Standards 2: Characteristitcs for Assessing Standards & Full Descriptions of the National & International Standards in the World. H. Moellering. LC 96-42334. (International Cartographic Association Ser.). 350p. 1997. 182.00 (*0-08-042433-3*, Pergamon Pr) Elsevier.

Spatial Demand Theory & Monopoly Price Policy. Benjamin H. Stevens & C. Peter Rydell. (Discussion Paper Ser.: No. 5). 1964. pap. 10.00 (*1-55869-117-0*) Regional Sci Res Inst.

Spatial Development & Religious Orientation in Kenya. Robert Wortham. LC 91-6518. (Distinguished Dissertations Ser.: Vol. 9). 376p. 1991. lib. bdg. 99.95 (*0-7734-9954-7*) E Mellen.

Spatial Development in Indonesia: Review & Prospects. T. John Kim et al. 250p. 1992. 76.95 (*1-85628-309-7*, Pub. by Avebury Pub UK) Ashgate Pub Co.

***Spatial Diffusion.** Richard Morrill et al. LC 87-62683. (Scientific Geography Ser.: No. 10). (Illus.). 86p. 1988. reprint ed. pap. 25.00 (*0-608-04319-2*, 2065098) Bks Demand.

Spatial Diffusion: An Historical Geography of Epidemics in an Island Community. A. D. Cliff et al. (Cambridge Geographical Studies: No. 14). (Illus.). 244p. 1981. text ed. 59.95 (*0-521-22840-9*) Cambridge U Pr.

Spatial Dimensions of Development Administration: American Society for Public Administration. American Society for Public Administration Staff. LC 75-161358. (Comparative Administration Group Ser.). 288p. reprint ed. pap. 82.10 (*0-317-42184-0*, 2026201) Bks Demand.

Spatial Dimensions of Scheduled Castes in India. R. C. Chandna. (C). 1989. 22.50 (*81-7076-020-8*, Pub. by Intellectual Pub Hse II) S Asia.

Spatial Dimensions of Urban Government. I. M. Barlow. LC 80-41972. (Geographical Research Studies: No. 3). (Illus.). 209p. reprint ed. pap. 59.60 (*0-8357-7032-X*, 2033328) Bks Demand.

Spatial Discounting & the Gravity Hypothesis. Tony E. Smith. (Discussion Paper Ser.: No. 82). 1975. pap. 10.00 (*1-55869-118-9*) Regional Sci Res Inst.

Spatial Discounting Theory of Travel Preferences. Tony E. Smith. (Discussion Paper Ser.: No. 75). 1974. pap. 10.00 (*1-55869-119-7*) Regional Sci Res Inst.

Spatial Divisions of Labour: Social Structures & the Geography of Production. 2nd ed. Doreen Massey. LC 94-44809. 432p. (C). 1995. pap. 22.95 (*0-415-91296-2*, B7279, Routledge NY) Routledge.

S

An Asterisk (*) at the beginning of an entry indicates that the title is appearing in BIP for the first time.

Spatial Divisions of Labour: Social Structures & the Geography of Production. 2nd ed. Doreen Massey. LC 94-44809. 432p. (C). (gr. 13). 1995. text ed. 69.95 (0-415-91295-4, B7275, Routledge NY) Routledge.

Spatial Dynamics of Business Growth in the Witwatersrand. Gillian P. Cook. LC 73-92654. (University of Chicago, Department of Geography, Research Paper Ser.: No. 157). 156p. 1975. reprint ed. pap. 44.50 (0-608-02253-5, 2062894) Bks Demand.

Spatial Dynamics of Crime. Gerald F. Pyle et al. LC 74-80718. (University of Chicago, Department of Geography, Research Paper Ser.: No. 159). (Illus.). 234p. reprint ed. pap. 66.70 (0-8357-3722-5, 2036444) Bks Demand.

***Spatial Ecology: The Role of Space in Population Dynamics & Interspecific Interactions.** David Tilman & Peter M. Kareiva. LC 97-8460. (Monographs in Population Biology). 1997. write for info. (0-691-01653-4); pap. write for info. (0-691-01652-6) Princeton U Pr.

Spatial Econometrics of Services. Jean H. Paelinck et al. 109p. 1992. 72.95 (1-85628-297-X, Pub. by Avebury Pub UK) Ashgate Pub Co.

Spatial Economic Analysis of Telecommunications Network Externalities. Robert Capello. LC 94-19836. 322p. 1994. 72.95 (1-85628-942-7, Pub. by Avebury Pub UK) Ashgate Pub Co.

Spatial Economics: Density, Potential & Flow. Martin J. Beckmann & Tonu Puu. (Studies in Regional Science & Urban Economics: Vol. 14). 276p. 1985. 120.75 (0-444-87771-1, North Holland) Elsevier.

Spatial Electric Load Forecasting. H. Lee Willis. (Electrical Engineering & Electronics Ser.: Vol. 98). 480p. 1996. 150.00 (0-8247-9425-7) Dekker.

Spatial Energy Analysis: Models for Strategic Decisions in an Urban & Regional Context. L. Lundquist et al. 398p. 1989. text ed. 69.95 (0-566-05580-5, Pub. by Avebury Pub UK) Ashgate Pub Co.

Spatial Formations. Nigel Thrift. (Theory, Culture & Society Ser.). 1996. pap. 28.95 (0-8039-8546-0) Sage.

Spatial Formations. Nigel Thrift. (Theory, Culture & Society Ser.). 300p. (C). 1996. 79.95 (0-8039-8545-2) Sage.

Spatial Geometries. Karen Wirth. 24p. 1991. pap. 20.00 (0-89822-071-8) Visual Studies.

Spatial Hearing: The Psychophysics of Human Sound Localization. rev. ed. Jens Blauert. Tr. by John S. Allen from GER. LC 96-12637. (Illus.). 480p. (C). 1996. 35.00 (0-262-02413-6) MIT Pr.

Spatial Impact of Economic Changes in Europe. Ed. by William Lever & Antione Bailly. (ESF Ser.). 384p. (C). 1996. 76.95 (1-85628-611-8, Pub. by Avebury Pub UK) Ashgate Pub Co.

Spatial Impact of Technological Change. Ed. by John Brotchie et al. 336p. 1987. lib. bdg. 55.00 (0-7099-5006-3, Pub. by Croom Helm UK) Routledge Chapman & Hall.

Spatial Impacts of Federal Expenditure & Tax Policy. George Tolley et al. (Studies in Urban & Resource Economics). (Illus.). x, 82p. 1986. 35.00 (0-943893-01-1); pap. 15.00 (0-943893-00-3) Blackstone.

Spatial Infinite at Greenwich in Works by Christopher Wren, James Thornhill, & James Thomson: The Newton Connection. Ann S. Balakier & James J. Balakier. LC 94-38758. (Illus.). 172p. 1995. text ed. 79.95 (0-7734-9057-4) E Mellen.

Spatial Information Theory: A Theoretical Basis for GIS. Ed. by Andrew U. Frank & Irene Campari. LC 93-30185. (Lecture Notes in Computer Science Ser.: Vol. 716). 1993. 65.95 (0-387-57207-4) Spr-Verlag.

Spatial Information Theory: A Theoretical Basis for GIS: International Conference, COSIT '95, Semmering, Austria, September 21-23, 1995, Proceedings. Ed. by Andrew U. Frank & Werner Kuhn. LC 95-39594. (Lecture Notes in Computer Science Ser.: No. 988). 571p. 1995. 87.00 (3-540-60392-1) Spr-Verlag.

Spatial Inhomogeneities & Transient Behavior in Chemical Kinetics. Ed. by P. Gray et al. (Proceedings in Nonlinear Science Ser.). 776p. 1992. text ed. 289.00 (0-471-93497-6) Wiley.

Spatial, Lattice & Tension Structures: Proceedings of the IASS-ASCE International Sympsoium 1994, Held in Conjunction with the ASCE Structures Congress XII, April 24-29, 1994, Georgia World Congress, Atlanta, Georgia, U. S. A. International Association for Shell & Spatial Structures Staff & Committee on Special Structures Staff, Structural Division, American Society of Civil Engineers. Ed. by John F. Abel et al. LC 94-7103. 1994. 85.00 (0-87262-953-8) Am Soc Civil Eng.

Spatial Light Modulator Technology: Materials, Devices & Applications. Ed. by Uzi Efron. (Optical Engineering Ser.: No. 47). 688p. 1994. 180.00 (0-8247-9108-8) Dekker.

Spatial Light Modulators. LC 95-67803. (1995 Technical Digest Ser.: Vol. 9). 189p. (Orig.). 1995. pap. 75.00 (1-55752-388-6) Optical Soc.

Spatial Light Modulators. Richard K. Miller & Terri C. Walker. LC 88-80482. (Survey on Technology & Markets Ser.: No. 13). 50p. 1989. pap. text ed. 200.00 (1-55865-012-1) Future Tech Surveys.

Spatial Light Modulators & Applications: Postconference Edition. LC 89-64052. (Technical Digest Series, 1990: Vol. 14). 350p. (Orig.). 1990. lib. bdg. 75.00 (1-55752-142-5) Optical Soc.

Spatial Light Modulators & Applications: Postconference Edition. LC 92-62845. (Technical Digest Series, 1993: Vol. 6). 350p. (Orig.). 1993. pap. 75.00 (1-55752-288-X) Optical Soc.

Spatial Light Modulators & Applications: Postconference Edition. LC 89-64052. (Technical Digest Series, 1988: Vol. 8). 175p. (Orig.). 1988. lib. bdg. 75.00 (1-55752-051-8) Opticians Assn Amer.

Spatial Microeconomics: Theoretical Underpinnings & Applications. Melvin L. Greenhut. LC 95-7198. (Economists of the Twentieth Century Ser.). 608p. 1995. 100.00 (1-85898-137-9) E Elgar.

Spatial Models of Party Competition. Donald E. Stokes. (Reprint Series in Political Science). (C). 1993. reprint ed. pap. text ed. 1.00 (0-8290-2740-8, PS-564) Irvington.

Spatial Neglect Vol. 4, No. 2, 1994: Position Papers on Theory & Practice: A Special Issue of "Neuropsychological Rehabilitation" Halligan & Marshall. 144p. 1995. 36.00 (0-86377-928-X) L Erlbaum Assocs.

Spatial Nosing: New & Selected Poems. Eithne Strong. 152p. 9300. pap. 13.95 (1-897648-04-9, Pub. by Salmon Poetry IE) Dufour.

Spatial Objective Analysis. T. J. Thiebaux. 300p. 1987. text ed. 128.00 (0-12-686930-8) Acad Pr.

***Spatial Optimization for Managed Ecosystems.** John G. Hof & Michael Bevers. LC 97-25439. (Complexity in Ecological Systems Ser.). 1998. write for info. (0-231-10636-X) Col U Pr.

Spatial Organization & Exchange: Archaeological Survey on Northern Black Mesa. Ed. by Stephen Plog. LC 84-23646. (Illus.). 400p. 1985. text ed. 29.95 (0-8093-1214-X) S Ill U Pr.

Spatial Organization in Eukaryotic Microbes. Ed. by R. K. Poole & A. P. Trinci. (Society for General Microbiology Special Publications: Vol. 23). 152p. (C). 1987. 69.00 (1-85221-053-2, IRL Pr); pap. text ed. 45.00 (1-85221-052-4, IRL Pr) OUP.

Spatial Organization of Multinational Corporations. Ian M. Clarke. LC 85-2265. 288p. 1985. text ed. 39.95 (0-312-75028-5) St Martin.

Spatial Orientation. Hermann Schone. Tr. by Camilla Strausfeld. LC 84-42561. (Neurobiology & Behavior Ser.). (Illus.). 368p. 1984. pap. text ed. 27.50 (0-691-08364-9) Princeton U Pr.

Spatial Orientation: Theory, Research, & Application. Ed. by Herbert L. Pick & Linda P. Acredolo. 398p. 1983. 85.00 (0-306-41255-1, Plenum Pr) Plenum.

Spatial Patterning in Historical Archaeology: Selected Studies of Settlement. Ed. by Donald W. Linebaugh & Gary C. Robinson. (Occasional Papers in Archaeology: No. 2). (Illus.). 144p. (Orig.). (C). 1994. pap. 17.00 (0-9615670-6-6, King & Queen Pr) Soc Alu Wm.

Spatial Perspectives on Industrial Organization & Decision Making. Ed. by F. E. Hamilton. LC 73-14379. 557p. reprint ed. pap. 158.80 (0-318-34685-0, 2031757) Bks Demand.

Spatial Perspectives on School Desegregation & Busing. J. Dennis Lord. Ed. by Salvatore J. Natoli. LC 76-57034. (Resource Papers for College Geography). (Illus.). 1977. pap. text ed. 15.00 (0-89291-124-7) Assn Am Geographers.

Spatial Planning for Recreation & Tourism in the Countries of the ECE Region. 22p. 1988. 9.00 (92-1-116424-9, E. 88.II.E.20) UN.

Spatial Planning of Health Services, Vol. 33: Case Studies in Warsaw, Poland. Jacek Malczewski. (Progress in Planning Ser.: No. 2). (Illus.). 63p. 1990. pap. 41.50 (0-08-040171-6, Pergamon Pr) Elsevier.

Spatial Point Processes. Antonio Possolo. 1990. 32.50 (0-412-01221-9, 9750, Chap & Hall NY) Chapman & Hall.

Spatial Policy in a Divided Nation. Ed. by Richard T. Harrison. 220p. 1993. 60.00 (1-85302-103-2) Taylor & Francis.

Spatial Practices: Critical Explorations in Social - Spatial Theory. Helen Liggett & David C. Perry. 264p. 1995. text ed. 49.95 (0-8039-5114-0); pap. text ed. 23.50 (0-8039-5115-9) Sage.

Spatial Prepositions: A Case Study from French. Claude Vandeloise. Tr. by Anna R. Bosch. (Illus.). 276p. 1991. pap. text ed. 29.95 (0-226-84728-4) U Ch Pr.

Spatial Prepositions: A Case Study from French. Claude Vandeloise. Tr. by Anna R. Bosch. (Illus.). 276p. 1991. lib. bdg. 66.00 (0-226-84727-6) U Ch Pr.

Spatial Price Equilibrium: Advances in Theory, Computation & Application. P. T. Harker. (Lecture Notes in Economics & Mathematical Systems Ser.: Vol. 249). (Illus.). vii, 277p. 1985. 38.50 (0-387-15681-X) Spr-Verlag.

Spatial Price Theory of Imperfect Competition. Hiroshi Ohta. LC 87-22333. (Economics Ser.: No. 8). (Illus.). 254p. 1988. lib. bdg. 39.95 (0-89096-372-X) Tex A&M Univ Pr.

Spatial Problem Solving. Davidson. 1992. pap. 9.50 (0-201-48027-1) Addison-Wesley.

Spatial Problem Solving: With Cuisenaire Rods. Robert E. Willcutt. 64p. (J). (gr. 4-9). 1984. pap. text ed. 9.50 (0-914040-99-5) Cuisenaire.

Spatial Problem Solving with Paper Folding & Cutting. Patricia S. Davidson & Robert E. Willcutt. 64p. (J). (gr. 4-12). 1984. pap. text ed. 9.50 (0-914040-36-7) Cuisenaire.

Spatial Processes in Plant Communities: Proceedings of the Workshop Held in Liblice, 18-22 September 1989. Ed. by F. Krahulec et al. (Illus.). x, 259p. 1990. 60.00 (90-5103-041-X, Pub. by SPB Acad Pub NE) Balogh.

Spatial Reasoning & Multi-Sensor Fusion: Proceedings of the 1987 Workshop. Ed. by Avinash C. Kak & Chen. 441p. 1987. pap. 29.95 (0-934613-59-1) Morgan Kaufmann.

Spatial Reasoning for Effective GIS. Joseph K. Berry. (Illus.). 224p. (Orig.). 1995. pap. text ed. 32.95 (1-882610-14-8) GIS World Bks.

Spatial Reasoning for Effective Gis. Joseph K. Berry. 1996. pap. text ed. 29.95 (0-470-23633-7) Halsted Pr.

Spatial Reasoning with Soma Cube Activities. Charlotte W. Mack & Constance C. Feldt. 79p. (J). (gr. 5-8). 1993. pap. 19.95 (0-939765-61-6, G157) Janson Pubns.

Spatial Regression Analysis on the PC. Daniel A. Griffith. (Illus.). 84p. (Orig.). 1989. pap. 12.95 (1-877751-24-3) Inst Math Geo.

Spatial Regression Analysis on the PC: Spatial Statistics Using SAS. Daniel A. Griffith. Ed. by Ellen Cromley & Richard Cromley. (Resource Publications in Geography). (Orig.). (C). 1993. pap. 15.00 (0-89291-213-8) Assn Am Geographers.

Spatial Relationships. Fred Justus. (Early Education Ser.). 24p. (gr. k-1). 1981. student ed. 5.00 (0-8209-0221-7, K-23) ESP.

Spatial Representation & Motion Planning. Ed. by Angel P. Pobil & Miguel A. Serna. LC 95-46103. (Lecture Notes in Computer Science Ser.: Vol. 1014). 242p. 1995. 49.00 (3-540-60620-3) Spr-Verlag.

Spatial Representation & Spatial Interaction. Ian Masser & P. J. B. Brown. (Studies in Applied Regional Science: Vol. 10). 1978. pap. text ed. 60.00 (90-207-0717-5) Kluwer Ac.

Spatial Search: Applications to Planning Problems in the Public Sector. Bryan H. Massam. (Urban & Regional Planning Ser.: Vol. 23). 1983. text ed. 140.00 (0-08-024286-3, Pub. by Pergamon Repr UK) Franklin.

Spatial Search Structure, Complexity, & Implications. G. Maier. Ed. by D. Bos et al. (Studies in Contemporary Economics). (Illus.). viii, 254p. 1995. pap. 71.00 (3-7908-0874-1) Spr-Verlag.

Spatial Sector Programming Models in Agriculture. Ed. by Earl O. Heady & Uma K. Srivastava. LC 74-20873. (Illus.). 504p. 1975. reprint ed. pap. 143.70 (0-608-00184-8, 2060966) Bks Demand.

Spatial Specials: Perceptual Skills Development: Grades K-2. Avaril Wedemeyer & Joyce Cejka. 1988. pap. 5.95 (0-89108-191-7, 8818) Love Pub Co.

Spatial Statistics. Brian D. Ripley. LC 80-26104. (Probability & Mathematical Statistics Ser.). 252p. 1981. text ed. 106.00 (0-471-08367-4) Wiley.

Spatial Statistics: Past, Present, & Future. Daniel A. Griffith et al. (Institute of Mathematical Geography, Monograph Ser.: No. 12). (Illus.). 418p. (Orig.). (C). 1990. pap. 39.95 (1-877751-42-1); pap. text ed. 39.95 (1-877751-43-X) Inst Math Geo.

Spatial Statistics & Digital Image Analysis. National Research Council (U.S.) Panel on Spatial Statistics & Image Processing Staff. LC 90-63215. 245p. 1991. reprint ed. pap. 69.90 (0-608-02340-X, 2062981) Bks Demand.

Spatial Statistics & Imaging. Ed. by Antonio Possolo. LC 91-77910. (IMS Lecture Notes - Monograph Ser.: Vol. 20). vii, 426p. 1991. pap. 35.00 (0-940600-27-7) Inst Math.

Spatial Stochastic Processes: A Festschrift in Honor of Ted Harris on His 70th Birthday. Ed. by K. L. Alexander & J. C. Watkins. (Progress in Probability Ser.: No. 19). xii, 256p. 1991. 103.50 (0-8176-3477-0) Birkhauser.

Spatial Strategies in Retailing. Risto Laulajainen. (C). 1987. lib. bdg. 134.00 (90-277-2595-0) Kluwer Ac.

Spatial Structure of the Medical Care Process. Jerry B. Schneider. (Discussion Paper Ser.: No. 14). 1967. pap. 10.00 (1-55869-120-0) Regional Sci Res Inst.

Spatial Structures. Martin J. Beckmann & Tonu Puu. (Advances in Spatial & Network Economics Ser.). (Illus.). 144p. 1990. 55.95 (0-387-51957-2) Spr-Verlag.

Spatial Tessellations: Concepts & Applications of Voroni Diagrams. Atsuyuki Okabe et al. LC 91-47687. (Series in Probability & Mathematics). 532p. 1992. text ed. 130.00 (0-471-93430-5) Wiley.

Spatial Theory of Voting: An Introduction. James M. Enelow & Melvin J. Hinich. LC 83-7758. 334p. 1984. pap. 22.95 (0-521-27515-6); text ed. 69.95 (0-521-25507-4) Cambridge U Pr.

***Spatial Transportation Modeling.** Christian Werner. LC 85-62289. (Scientific Geography Ser.: Vol. 5). 95p. 1985. reprint ed. pap. 27.10 (0-608-02792-8, 2063859) Bks Demand.

Spatial Variation. 2nd ed. B. Matern. (Lecture Notes in Statistics Ser.: Vol. 36). (Illus.). 155p. 1986. 42.95 (0-387-96365-0) Spr-Verlag.

Spatial Variation of Black Urban Households. David R. Meyer. LC 72-129455. (University of Chicago, Department of Geography, Research Paper Ser.: No. 129). 144p. reprint ed. pap. 41.10 (0-7837-0404-6, 2040725) Bks Demand.

Spatial Vision. Cronly-Dillon. 1991. 137.00 (0-8493-7510-X, QP474) CRC Pr.

Spatial Vision. Russell L. De Valois & Karen K. De Valois. (Oxford Psychology Ser.: No. 14). (Illus.). 402p. 1990. reprint ed. pap. 50.00 (0-19-506657-X) OUP.

Spatial Vision in Humans & Robots. Ed. by L. Harris & M. Jenkin. 400p. (C). 1994. text ed. 69.95 (0-521-43071-2) Cambridge U Pr.

Spatial Visualization: Middle Grades Mathematics Project. Glenda Lappan. 1986. text ed. 18.95 (0-201-21477-6) Addison-Wesley.

Spatiality of the Novel. Joseph A. Kestner. LC 78-14377. 204p. reprint ed. pap. 58.20 (0-318-39787-0, 2033189) Bks Demand.

Spatially Oriented Behavior. Ed. by A. Hein & M. Jeanherod. (Illus.). 365p. 1983. 97.95 (0-387-90789-0) Spr-Verlag.

Spatially Reinforced Composites. Yu. M. Tarnopol'skii et al. LC 91-66743. 350p. 1991. text ed. 89.95 (0-87762-679-0) Technomic.

***Spatio-Pattern Formation in Nonlinear Geophysical Systems Induced by Sedimentary Convection.** Marc Leu. (Bonner Geowissen Schaftliche Schriften Ser.: Band 23). 80p. 1997. pap. 35.00 (3-931251-14-4, Pub. by Martina Galunder GW) Balogh.

Spatio-Temporal Image Processing: Theory & Scientific Applications. Bernd Jahne. LC 93-34944. (Lecture Notes in Computer Science Ser.: Vol. 751). 1993. 39.00 (0-387-57418-2) Spr-Verlag.

***Spatio-Temporal Pattern Formation: With Examples from Physics, Chemistry & Materials Science.** D. Walgraef. LC 96-33167. (Partially Ordered Systems Ser.). (Illus.). 352p. 1996. 69.00 (0-387-94857-0) Spr-Verlag.

Spatio-Temporal Patterns in Nonequilibrium Complex Systems - NATO Advanced Research Workshop: Proceedings of the NATO Advanced Research Workshop on Spatio-Temporal Patterns in Nonequilibrium Complex Systems, Held April 13-17, 1993, in Santa Fe, NM. P. E. Cladis. LC 94-43003. (Santa Fe Institute Studies in the Sciences of Complexity: Vol. 21). (C). 1995. pap. 31.95 (0-201-40987-9) Addison-Wesley.

Spatio-Temporal Patterns in Nonequilibrium Complex Systems - NATO Advanced Research Workshop: Proceedings of the NATO Advanced Research Workshop on Spatio-Temporal Patterns in Nonequilibrium Complex Systems, Held April 13-17, 1993, in Santa Fe, NM. Ed. by P. E. Cladis & P. Palffy-Muhoray. LC 94-43003. (Santa Fe Institute Studies in the Sciences of Complexity: Vol. 21). 679p. (C). 1995. 55.95 (0-201-40984-4) Addison-Wesley.

Spatiotemporal Characteristics of Laser Emission. M. V. Pyatakhin & A. F. Suchkov. (Proceedings of the Lebedev Physics Institute Ser.: Vol. 199). (Illus.). 249p. (C). 1994. lib. bdg. 115.00 (1-56072-163-4) Nova Sci Pubs.

***Spatiotemporal Models in Biological & Artifical Systems.** Ed. by Silva. (Frontiers in Artificial Intelligence & Applications: No. 37). 1996. 89.00 (90-5199-304-8) IOS Press.

Spaulding's Official Baseball Guide 1894. Spaulding. 21.95 (0-8488-1539-4) Amereon Ltd.

***Spawn.** Todd McFarlane. 1997. 16.00 (0-679-88626-5) Random Bks Yng Read.

***Spawn.** 2nd ed. Todd McFarlane et al. Ed. by Tom Orzechowski. (Illus.). (YA). 1996. reprint ed. pap. 9.95 (1-887279-38-5) Image Comics.

Spawn, Vol. I. Todd McFarlane. (Illus.). 116p. (YA). 1995. pap. 9.95 (1-887279-01-6) Image Comics.

***Spawn, Vol. 1.** 5th rev. ed. Todd McFarlane. (Illus.). 120p. Date not set. pap. 9.95 (1-887279-50-4) Image Comics.

***Spawn, Vol. 2.** 3rd rev. ed. Todd McFarlane et al. (Illus.). 128p. Date not set. pap. 9.95 (1-887279-53-9) Image Comics.

***Spawn, Vol. III.** Todd McFarlane. Ed. by Tom Orzechowski. (Illus.). 96p. (YA). pap. 9.95 (1-887279-35-0) Image Comics.

***Spawn, Vol. 3.** 2nd rev. ed. Todd McFarlane. Ed. by Tom Orzechowski. (Illus.). 100p. Date not set. pap. 9.95 (1-887279-54-7) Image Comics.

***Spawn, Vol. 4.** Grant Morrison et al. (Illus.). 128p. 1997. pap. 9.95 (1-887279-52-0) Image Comics.

***Spawn: Born in Darkness, Sworn to Justice.** Rob MacGregor. 1997. pap. text ed. 4.99 (0-380-79443-8); mass mkt. 5.99 (0-380-79441-1) Avon.

Spawn of Dykes to Watch Out For: Cartoons. Alison Bechdel. LC 93-37734. (Illus.). 136p. (Orig.). 1993. pap. 10.95 (1-56341-039-7); lib. bdg. 22.95 (1-56341-040-0) Firebrand Bks.

Spawn of Loki. Jason Henderson. 1994. pap. 5.99 (0-671-87635-X) S&S Trade.

Spawn of the Devil. Carolyn Gray. 320p. 1994. 22.00 (0-7278-4549-7) Severn Hse.

Spawn of the Winds. deluxe ed. Brian Lumley. LC 95-77334. (Illus.). 1995. boxed 42.50 (0-932445-60-8) Ganley Pub.

Spawn of the Winds. Brian Lumley. LC 95-77334. (Illus.). 1995. reprint ed. 26.50 (0-932445-59-4) Ganley Pub.

Spawn TPB, No. II. Todd McFarlane et al. Ed. by Tom Orzechowski. (Illus.). 128p. (Orig.). (YA). pap. text ed. 9.95 (1-887279-18-0) Image Comics.

Spawning of Protons. Amy Stafford et al. (Cyborg Proton Anthologies Ser.). 48p. 1994. pap. text ed. 3.00 (1-879665-17-4) Cyborg Prods.

Spaziergang - ein Literarisches Lesebuch. (Illus.). 368p. (GER.). 1992. 40.00 (3-487-08333-7) G Olms Pubs.

Spaziergange durch Cambridge. Frank A. Reeve. (Cambridge Town, Gown & County Ser.: Vol. 27). (Illus.). (GER.). 1978. pap. 4.95 (0-900891-44-0) Oleander Pr.

SPC at the Esquire Club. Donald J. Wheeler. Ed. by David Wheeler. Tr. by Kaz Koike. (Illus.). 80p. 1992. pap. 15.00 (0-945320-30-2) SPC Pr.

SPC Digital Telephone Exchanges. rev. ed. F. J. Redmill & A. R. Valdar. (Telecommunications Ser.: No. 21). 537p. 1994. pap. 45.00 (0-86341-298-X, TE021Z, Pub. by Peregrinus UK); boxed 115.00 (0-86341-301-3, TE021, Pub. by Peregrinus UK) Inst Elect Eng.

***SPC Essentials & Productivity Improvement: A Manufacturing Approach.** William A. Levinson & Frank Tumbelty. 215p. (Orig.). 1996. pap. 35.00 (0-87389-372-7, H0937) ASQC Qual Pr.

SPC for Practitioners: Special Cases & Continuous Processes. Gary Fellers. (Illus.). 197p. 1991. 12.98 (0-87389-102-3, H0623) ASQC Qual Pr.

SPC for the Rest of Us: A Personal Path to Statistical Process Control. Hy Pitt. LC 93-8311. (C). 1994. text ed. 41.95 (0-201-56366-5) Addison-Wesley.

***SPC Methods for Quality Improvement.** Charles P. Quesenberry. LC 96-44726. text ed. 79.95 (0-471-13087-7) Wiley.

An Asterisk (*) at the beginning of an entry indicates that the title is appearing in BIP for the first time.

SPC Primer: Programmed Introduction to Statistical Process Control Techniques. Thomas Pyzdek. Orig. Title: Applied Industrial Statistics. 55p. (Orig.). 1984. pap. 19.95 (*0-930011-00-7*, H0657) ASQC Qual Pr.

***SPC Simplified.** Amsden et al. 1997. write for info. (*0-614-23476-X*) Qual Resc.

SPC Simplified: Practical Steps to Quality. Robert T. Amsden et al. (Illus.). 300p. 1986. pap. text ed. 21.00 (*0-527-91617-X*, 91617X) Qual Resc.

SPC Simplified for Services: Practical Tools for Continuous Quality Improvement. Davida M. Amsden et al. 317p. 1991. pap. text ed. 25.00 (*0-527-91639-0*, 916390) Qual Resc.

SPC Simplified Workbook: Practical Steps to Quality. Robert T. Amsden et al. 368p. 1990. spiral bd. 21.00 (*0-527-91638-2*, 916382) Qual Resc.

SPC-Statistical Process Control in Extrusion. Chris J. Rauwendaal. 224p. (C). 1992. text ed. 54.50 (*1-56990-086-8*) Hanser-Gardner.

SPC Tools for Everyone. John T. Burr. LC 93-9436. (Illus.). 77p. 1993. pap. 21.00 (*0-87389-244-5*, H0797) ASQC Qual Pr.

SPC Using Lotus 1-2-3. Steven M. Zimmerman & Robert N. Zimmerman. 350p. 1992. pap. text ed. 49.00 (*0-527-91656-0*, 916560) Qual Resc.

***SPC Workout Workbook: The Official Companion Guide to the SPC Workout.** Resource Engineering, Inc. Staff. (Illus.). 58p. (C). 1996. 7.95 (*1-882307-23-2*) Res Engineering.

SPD's Best Magazine Design, No. 28. (Illus.). 240p. 1994. 49.99 (*1-56496-054-4*, 30545) Rockport Pubs.

SPE: Society of Petroleum Engineers Technical Papers: Cumulative Index to the Microfiche Collection, 1980-1984 Supplements. (Society of Petroleum Engineers Technical Papers). 749p. 1986. 100.00 (*0-8357-0710-5*) Univ Microfilms.

Speak! Children's Book Illustrators Brag about Their Favorite Dogs. Ed. by Michael J. Rosen. LC 92-30325. (Illus.). 48p. (J). (ps up). 1993. 17.00 (*0-15-277848-9*) HarBrace.

Speak & Get Results: The Complete Guide to Speeches & Presentations That Work in Any Business Situation. Sandy Linver. 288p. 1994. pap. 11.00 (*0-671-89316-5*, Fireside) S&S Trade.

Speak & Get Results: The Complete Guide to Speeches & Presentations That Work in Any Business Situation. rev. ed. Sandy Linver & Jim Mengert. LC 93-46040. 1994. 22.00 (*0-671-88996-6*) S&S Trade.

Speak & Grow Rich. Dottie Walters & Lillett Walters. 276p. 1989. pap. text ed. 15.95 (*0-13-825803-1*) P-H.

Speak & Grow Rich. 2nd ed. Walters. LC 97-21559. 1997. pap. text ed. 14.95 (*0-13-490400-1*) P-H.

Speak & Grow Rich. 2nd ed. Walters. 1996. text ed. 27.95 (*0-13-490418-4*) P-H.

Speak & Write: Language Activities for Intermediate & Advanced ESL Students. Paul J. Hamel. (Illus.). 43p. (Orig.). 1989. pap. text ed. 11.50 (*0-937354-48-1*) Delta Systems.

***Speak Art! The Best of Bomb Magazine's Interviews with Artists.** Besty Sussler. 130p. 1997. pap. 22.50 (*90-5701-341-X*) Dist Art Pubs.

Speak, Bird, Speak Again: Palestinian Arab Folktales. Ibrahim Muhawi & Sharif Kanaana. 512p. 1988. pap. 17.95 (*0-520-06292-2*) U CA Pr.

***Speak Bird, Speak Again: Palestinian Arab Folktales.** Ibrahim Muhawi. 420p. 1996. pap. 18.50 (*0-614-21654-0*, 1156) Kazi Pubns.

Speak Cantonese, Bk. 1. rev. ed. Po-fei Huang & Gerard P. Kok. 1960. 19.95 (*0-88710-094-5*); audio 170.95 (*0-88710-095-3*) Yale Far Eastern Pubns.

Speak Cantonese, Bk. 2. Po-fei Huang. 1982. 19.95 (*0-88710-096-1*); audio 63.95 (*0-88710-097-X*) Yale Far Eastern Pubns.

Speak Cantonese, Bk. 3. rev. ed. Po-Fei Huang. 1967. 17.95 (*0-88710-098-8*); audio 81.95 (*0-88710-099-6*) Yale Far Eastern Pubns.

Speak Chinese (MTC Version) rev. ed. (Mandarin Training Center Ser.). 572p. (CHI.). 1991. pap. text ed. 19.95 (*0-88710-170-4*) Yale Far Eastern Pubns.

Speak Chinese (MTC Version) Stroke Order Exercise Book. (Mandarin Training Center Ser.). 100p. (Orig.). (CHI.). 1991. pap. text ed. 8.95 (*0-88710-169-0*) Yale Far Eastern Pubns.

Speak Chinese Today: A Basic Course in the Modern Language. Beverly Hong. LC 91-65063. (Illus.). 324p. (Orig.). 1991. pap. 12.95 (*0-8048-1715-4*); pap. 24.95 incl. audio (*0-8048-1701-4*) C E Tuttle.

Speak Daggers to Her. Rosemary Edghill. 224p. mass mkt. 5.99 (*0-8125-3438-7*) Tor Bks.

Speak Easy. Sarah K. Silverson et al. (Video Course Through Mime Sketches Ser.). 1984. teacher ed. 7.95 (*0-582-79891-4*, 75130); pap. text ed. 12.50 (*0-582-79857-4*, 75103); audio 55.00 (*0-582-79837-X*, 75112) Longman.

Speak Easy. Sarah K. Silverson et al. (Video Course Through Mime Sketches Ser.). 1984. vhs 283.09 (*0-582-79836-1*, 75083) Longman.

Speak Easy, Set. 32p. teacher ed., pap. 195.00 incl. vhs (*0-88432-882-1*, V71111) Audio-Forum.

Speak Easy: A Guide to Successful Performances, Presentations, Speeches, & Lectures. Carol Roan. 96p. (Orig.). 1995. pap. 8.95 (*1-57359-000-2*, Starhill Pr) Black Belt Comm.

Speak Easy - Read Write. Lee S. Peel. (Illus.). 128p. (Orig.). 1988. pap. 7.95 (*0-9626618-0-5*); pap. 5.95 (*0-685-41319-5*) L S Peel.

Speak Easy Phrase Guide. Carolyn M. Heard. pap. 4.95 (*0-686-45241-0*) S&S Trade.

Speak English, Text 1. Joseph M. Coyle & Mary A. Corley. (Illus.). 80p. (Orig.). 1992. pap. text ed. 7.95 (*0-8325-0501-3*, Natl Textbk) NTC Pub Grp.

Speak English!, Text 2. Mary Ann Corley & Betty Smallwood. (Illus.). 96p. (Orig.). 1992. pap. 7.95 (*0-8325-0506-4*, Natl Textbk) NTC Pub Grp.

Speak English!, Text 3. Mary Ann Corley & Charles Hancock. (Illus.). 96p. (Orig.). 1992. pap. text ed. 7.95 (*0-8325-0510-2*, Natl Textbk) NTC Pub Grp.

Speak English!, Text 4. Barbara Izzo & Marie Keefe. (Illus.). 46p. (Orig.). (C). 1988. pap. text ed. 7.95 (*0-8325-0514-5*, Natl Textbk) NTC Pub Grp.

Speak English!, Wkbk. 1. Barbara Weitz. (Illus.). 72p. (Orig.). 1987. student ed. 7.95 (*0-8325-0502-1*, Natl Textbk) NTC Pub Grp.

Speak English!, Wkbk. 2. Mary Ann Corley & Betty Smallwood. (Illus.). 72p. (Orig.). 1994. pap. 7.95 (*0-8325-0507-2*, Natl Textbk) NTC Pub Grp.

Speak English!, Wkbk. 3. Charles Hancock. (Illus.). 64p. (Orig.). 1988. pap. text ed. 7.95 (*0-8325-0511-0*, Natl Textbk) NTC Pub Grp.

Speak English!, Workbook 4. Lowry L. Taylor. (Illus.). 72p. (Orig.). (C). 1992. pap. text ed. 7.95 (*0-8325-0515-3*, Natl Textbk) NTC Pub Grp.

Speak English from the Heart. John R. Terry. (Special Advanced Course Ser.). 200p. 1982. pap. 7.50 (*0-933704-03-8*) Dawn Pr.

Speak English from the Heart. 2nd ed. John R. Terry. (Intermediate Course Ser.). 220p. 1979. pap. 7.50 (*0-933704-13-5*) Dawn Pr.

Speak English from the Heart. 4th ed. John R. Terry. (Intermediate Course Ser.). 220p. 1987. pap. 7.50 (*0-933704-62-3*) Dawn Pr.

Speak English from the Heart. 8th ed. John R. Terry. (Elementary Course Ser.). 216p. 1984. pap. 7.50 (*0-933704-49-6*) Dawn Pr.

Speak English from the Heart, Vol. 3: Advanced Course. 5th ed. John R. Terry. 250p. 1991. pap. 7.50 (*0-933704-79-8*) Dawn Pr.

Speak English Well: A Handbook of Spoken English for Foreign - Overseas Students. Domino Books Ltd Staff. 250p. (C). 1988. 130.00 (*1-85122-030-5*, Pub. by Domino Bks Ltd UK); pap. 90.00 (*1-85122-011-9*, Pub. by Domino Bks Ltd UK) St Mut.

Speak English Well: The Sounds of English. Alan Dury. (C). 1988. text ed. 80.00 (*1-85122-062-3*, Pub. by Domino Bks Ltd UK) St Mut.

***Speak for Yourself.** Richard Denny. (Personal Development Ser.). 1994. 24.95 (*0-7494-0963-0*); pap. 15.95 (*0-7494-0964-9*) Kogan Page Ltd.

Speak for Yourself. Robert Montgomery. (Smart Tapes Ser.). 36p. 1994. pap. text ed. 19.95 incl. audio (*1-55678-052-4*) Learn Inc.

Speak for Yourself. rev. ed. Jessica S. Driver. LC 55-11267. (Essentials of Speaking & Reading Aloud Ser.: No. 193-96). (Illus.). 245p. 1984. reprint ed. pap. 15.95 (*0-9614864-0-6*) Speak Yourself.

Speak for Yourself: A Practical Guide to Giving Successful Presentations, Speeches & Talks. John Campbell. 144p. 1992. pap. 9.95 (*0-563-21511-9*, BBC-Parkwest) Parkwest Pubns.

Speak for Yourself: An Integrated Method of Voice & Speech Training. Julia Cummings-Wing. LC 83-26862. (Illus.). 272p. 1984. pap. text ed. 24.95 (*0-88229-827-5*); lib. bdg. 38.95 (*0-8304-1024-4*) Nelson-Hall.

Speak for Yourself: An Introduction to Public Speaking. 3rd ed. James H. Byrns. LC 93-26863. 1994. pap. text ed. write for info. (*0-07-009513-2*) McGraw.

Speak for Yourself: An Introduction to Public Speaking. 4th ed. James H. Byrns. LC 96-19071. 1996. pap. text ed. write for info. (*0-07-009632-5*) McGraw.

Speak French. (Just Listen 'n Learn Ser.). (FRE.). 1995. 59.95 incl. audio (*0-8442-1616-X*, Natl Textbk) NTC Pub Grp.

Speak French in Fifteen Minutes. Bill Beer. 108p. (Orig.). 1993. pap. 3.50 (*0-9634055-1-9*) Fifteen Minute Pr.

Speak French to Your Children: Easy French Phrases to Teach Your Children. Therese S. Pirz. (Bilingual Children Ser.: Vol. 1). (Illus.). 152p. (FRE.). 1981. 12.95 (*0-929724-07-0*, 07-0); pap. 12.95 (*0-929724-06-2*, 06-2) Command Performance.

Speak French to Your Children: Easy French Phrases to Teach Your Children. Therese S. Pirz. (Bilingual Children Ser.: Vol. 1). (Illus.). 152p. (FRE.). 1981. 24.95 incl. audio (*0-929724-12-7*, 12-7); pap. 24.95 incl. audio (*0-929724-11-9*, 11-9); audio 12.95 (*0-929724-09-7*, 09-7) Command Performance.

Speak German, Set 6. Ed. by Brian Hill. (Just Listen 'n Learn Ser.). 1995. 59.95 incl. audio (*0-8442-2524-X*, Natl Textbk) NTC Pub Grp.

Speak Ill of the Dead. large type ed. Peter Chambers. (Linford Mystery Library). 368p. 1993. pap. 15.99 (*0-7089-7385-X*, Linford) Ulverscroft.

***Speak Indirect/Speak Around: Skills for Mastering Resistance.** L. Michael Hall. 36p. (Orig.). 1990. pap. 3.00 (*1-890001-04-X*) Empowerment Tech.

Speak Japanese Today: A Self-Study Program for Learning Everyday Japanese. Taeko Kamiya. 184p. 1989. pap. 12.95 (*0-8048-1563-1*) C E Tuttle.

Speak Like a Pro. Maggie M. Bedrosian. 1994. 25.00 (*1-884798-25-X*) B C I Press.

Speak Like Rain. Frances Ottesen. 50p. (Orig.). 1986. pap. 6.00 (*0-9605220-1-8*) Otafra.

Speak Lord! Reflections on the Ordination Rite for Deacons. Steve Landregan. 52p. (Orig.). 1987. pap. 2.95 (*1-55586-150-4*) US Catholic.

Speak Lord: Your Servants Are Listening. Dolores Gordon. 144p. (Orig.). 1983. pap. 5.95 (*0-9621477-3-7*) Cachners Pub.

Speak Lord, Your Servant Is Listening. large type ed. David E. Rosage. (Large Print Inspirational Ser.). 1987. pap. 9.95 (*0-8027-2568-6*) Walker & Co.

Speak, Lord, Your Servant Is Listening. rev. ed. David E. Rosage. 131p. 1987. pap. 6.99 (*0-89283-371-8*) Servant.

Speak Low (When You Speak Love) The Letters of Kurt Weill & Lotte Lenya. Ed. by Lys Symonette & Kim H. Kowalke. Tr. by Kim H. Kowalke from GER. LC 95-40544. (Illus.). 554p. (C). 1996. 39.95 (*0-520-07853-5*) U CA Pr.

***Speak Low (When You Speak Love) The Letters of Kurt Weill & Lotte Lenya.** Kurt Weill. 1997. pap. text ed. 24.95 (*0-520-21240-1*) U CA Pr.

Speak Mandarin. Henry C. Fenn & M. Gardner Tewksbury. (Yale Linguistic Ser.). 1967. student ed. 20.00 (*0-300-00085-5*); text ed. 30.00 (*0-300-00084-7*) Yale U Pr.

Speak Memory. Vladimir Nabokov. pap. 17.00 (*0-679-43318-X*) Random.

Speak, Memory: An Autobiography Revisited. Vladimir Nabokov. (International Ser.). 1989. pap. 13.00 (*0-679-72339-0*, Publishers Media) Random.

Speak My Name: Black Men on Masculinity & the American Dream. Ed. & Intro. by Don Belton. LC 94-36887. 288p. (C). 1996. 24.00 (*0-8070-0936-9*) Beacon Pr.

***Speak My Name: Black Men on Masculinity & the American Dream.** Don Belton. 1997. pap. 16.00 (*0-8070-0937-7*) Beacon Pr.

***Speak My Soul.** Francyl Gawryn. (Illus.). 61p. (Orig.). 1996. pap. 15.00 (*0-938380-03-6*, SMS01) Highreach WA.

Speak My Soul. Anil Horn. 144p. 1985. reprint ed. 7.95 (*0-87516-549-4*) DeVorss.

***Speak My Words unto Them: A History of Unevangelized Fields Mission (UFM International)** Homer E. Dowdy. Ed. by James H. Nesbitt. 317p. (Orig.). 1997. pap. 10.00 (*0-9656830-0-1*) UFM Intl.

Speak No Evil. Rochelle M. Krich. 416p. 1996. 21.95 (*0-89296-584-3*) Mysterious Pr.

Speak No Evil. Rochelle M. Krich. 384p. 1997. mass mkt. 6.50 (*0-446-40505-1*, Mysterious Paperbk) Warner Bks.

Speak No Evil: The Promotional Heritage of Nuclear Risk Communication. Louis Gwin. LC 90-32299. (Political Communication Ser.). 200p. 1990. text ed. 49.95 (*0-275-93445-4*, C3445, Praeger Pubs) Greenwood.

Speak Now Against the Day: The Generation Before the Civil Rights Movement in the South. John Egerton. LC 93-47491. 1994. 35.00 (*0-679-40808-8*) Knopf.

Speak Now Against the Day: The Generation Before the Civil Rights Movement in the South. John Egerton. LC 95-16179. (Chapel Hill Bks.). (Illus.). 768p. (C). 1995. reprint ed. pap. 19.95 (*0-8078-4557-4*) U of NC Pr.

Speak Now or Forever Fall to Pieces: The Art of Public Speaking. Tom Mira. (Princeton Review Ser.). 1995. pap. 12.00 (*0-679-76468-2*, Villard Bks) Random.

Speak of Me As I Am: The Life & Work of Masud Khan. Judy Cooper. 176p. 1994. pap. text ed. 27.50 (*1-85575-044-9*, Pub. by Karnac Bks UK) Brunner-Mazel.

Speak of the Devil. George Sewell. LC 95-4210. 55p. 1995. pap. 6.00 (*0-88734-237-X*) Players Pr.

Speak of the Ghost: In the Name of Emotion Literacy. Pamela Sackett. LC 94-22099. 240p. (Orig.). 1994. pap. 15.95 (*0-929904-03-6*) Emotion Lit Adv.

***Speak of the Mearns.** Grassic L. Gibbon. 1994. pap. 18.00 (*0-7486-6167-0*, Pub. by Polygon UK) Subterranean Co.

Speak Out! Donald R. Thomas-Blocher. 140p. (C). 1996. per., pap. text ed. 26.25 (*0-8403-7647-2*) Kendall-Hunt.

Speak Out! Authentic Communication Activities for the Intermediate & Advanced ESL Student. Ellen Measday & Lisa F. Knight. 160p. (C). 1994. per. 17.79 (*0-8403-9536-1*) Kendall-Hunt.

Speak Out for Age. Grace Goldin. 1976. pap. 8.95 (*0-8488-0878-9*) Amereon Ltd.

Speak Russian! Marisa Fushille et al. (Illus.). 200p. (C). 1990. pap. 19.95 (*0-292-71120-4*); audio 12.95 (*0-292-71127-1*) U of Tex Pr.

Speak Silence: Rhetoric & Culture in Blake's "Poetical Sketches" Ed. by Mark L. Greenberg. LC 95-39561. 222p. 1996. 39.95 (*0-8143-1985-8*) Wayne St U Pr.

***Speak Smart.** Thomas Mira. 1997. pap. 12.00 (*0-679-77868-3*) Random.

Speak So I Shall Know Thee: Interviews with Southern Writers. William J. Walsh. LC 89-43689. 328p. 1990. lib. bdg. 38.50 (*0-89950-521-X*) McFarland & Co.

Speak So I Shall Know Thee: Interviews with Southern Writers. William J. Walsh. LC 93-71407. 316p. 1993. reprint ed. pap. 14.95 (*1-878086-21-9*) Down Home NC.

Speak Softly, & Carry a Beagle. Charles M. Schulz. 192p. 1990. pap. 7.95 (*0-8050-1484-5*, Owl) H Holt & Co.

Speak Softly & Carry Your Own Gym Key: A Female High School Principal's Guide to Survival. Anna T. Hicks. LC 95-40561. 88p. 1996. 37.00 (*0-8039-6383-1*); pap. 17.00 (*0-8039-6384-X*) Corwin Pr.

Speak Spanish, Set 6. Ed. by Brian Hill. (Just Listen 'n Learn Ser.). 1995. 59.95 incl. audio (*0-8442-7528-X*, Natl Textbk) NTC Pub Grp.

Speak Spanish in Fifteen Minutes. Bill Beer. 104p. (Orig.). 1992. pap. 3.50 (*0-9634055-0-0*) Fifteen Minute Pr.

Speak Spanish to Your Children: Easy Spanish Phrases to Teach Your Children. Therese S. Pirz. (Bilingual Children Ser.: Vol. 2). (Illus.). 160p. (Orig.). (SPA.). 1985. pap. 12.95 (*0-929724-08-9*, 08-9); pap. 24.95 incl. audio (*0-929724-13-5*, 13-5); audio 12.95 (*0-929724-10-0*, 10-0) Command Performance.

***Speak Standard Indonesian.** 285p. 1994. pap. 11.95 (*0-7818-0186-9*) Hippocrene Bks.

Speak Standard, Too: Add Mainstream American English to Your Talking Style. Mary I. Berger. 150p. 1991. audio 35.00 (*0-9630778-1-3*) Orchrd Bks IL.

Speak Standard, Too: Add Mainstream American English to Your Talking Style. Mary I. Berger. 150p. 1993. pap. 20.00 (*0-9630778-0-5*) Orchrd Bks IL.

Speak Standard, Too: Add Mainstream American English to Your Talking Style, Set. Mary I. Berger. 150p. 1991. 50.00 incl. audio (*0-9630778-2-1*) Orchrd Bks IL.

Speak Sunlight. Alan Jolis. 1996. 20.95 (*0-312-14049-5*) St Martin.

***Speak Sunlight: A Memoir.** Alan Jolis. 256p. 1997. mass mkt. 6.99 (*0-425-15799-7*) Berkley Pub.

Speak That We May Know: A Spirituality for Uttering the Inner You. Justus Lawler. LC 88-42726. 96p. (Orig.). 1988. 7.95 (*0-940989-41-7*) Meyer Stone Bks.

Speak the Speech: The Shakespeare Quotation Book. Ed. by Louis Marder. 496p. 1995. pap. 15.00 (*0-06-272063-5*, PL) HarpC.

Speak the Thought: How to Read & Speak in Public, with Bible-Lesson Applications. 2nd exp. ed. Muriel F. Reid. 64p. 1984. 7.00 (*0-915878-05-4*) Joseph Pub Co.

Speak the Truth in Love. Rowena M. Pope. 71p. (Orig.). 1988. pap. 4.00 (*0-9608182-2-7*) Bold Blue Jay Pubns.

Speak the Word. Marilyn Hickey. 19p. (Orig.). pap. 1.00 (*1-56441-166-4*) M Hickey Min.

Speak the Word with Boldness: Homilies for Risen Christians. Walter J. Burghardt. LC 94-4905. 400p. (Orig.). 1994. pap. 14.95 (*0-8091-3470-5*) Paulist Pr.

Speak! Thy Servant Heareth: Understanding & Discerning the Voice of God. John Tetsola. 112p. (Orig.). 1997. pap. 8.99 (*0-9634306-9-6*) End-Time Wave.

Speak to Me. 2nd rev. ed. Marcia Calhoun Forecki. LC 84-28740. 160p. 1985. pap. 12.95 (*0-930323-68-8*) Gallaudet Univ Pr.

Speak to Me: Swedish-language Women Poets. Ed. by Lennart Bruce & Sonja Bruce. Tr. by Sonja Bruce. LC 88-15874. (Contemporary Anthology Ser.: No. 7). (Illus.). 224p. (ENG & SWE.). 1989. per., pap. 8.75 (*0-930370-36-8*) Spirit That Moves.

Speak to Me: Swedish-language Women Poets. Ed. by Lennart Bruce & Sonja Bruce. Tr. by Sonja Bruce. LC 88-15874. (Contemporary Anthology & Ethnic Diversity Ser.: No. 7, Vol. 4). (Illus.). 224p. (ENG & SWE.). 1989. 14.75 (*0-930370-35-X*) Spirit That Moves.

Speak to Me: Swedish-language Women Poets. limited ed. Ed. by Lennart Bruce & Sonja Bruce. Tr. by Sonja Bruce. LC 88-15874. (Contemporary Anthology Ser.: No. 7). (Illus.). 224p. (ENG & SWE.). 1989. 30.00 (*0-930370-37-6*) Spirit That Moves.

Speak to Me from Dreams. Barbara B. Curiel. LC 88-39775. 96p. (Orig.). (C). 1989. pap. 8.95 (*0-943219-03-5*) Third Woman.

Speak to the Earth. William Bell. 160p. 1994. pap. 11.95 (*0-385-25487-3*) Doubleday.

Speak to the Earth. William Bell. 208p. 1996. mass mkt. 4.99 (*0-7704-2724-3*) Bantam.

Speak to the Earth: Creation Studies in Geoscience. 2nd rev. ed. Ed. by George F. Howe. LC 75-15446. (Illus.). 463p. 1990. reprint ed. pap. text ed. 13.95 (*0-940384-07-8*) Creation Research.

Speak to the Hills: An Anthology of Twentieth Century British & Irish Mountain Poetry. Ed. by H. Brown & M. Berry. (Illus.). 550p. 1985. text ed. 29.00 (*0-08-030406-0*, Pub. by Aberdeen U Pr) Macmillan.

Speak to the Winds. Ruth Moore. 1987. pap. 9.95 (*0-942396-54-5*) Blackberry ME.

Speak to Us of Mary: Biblical Homilies As Aids to Prayer with the Blessed Virgin. Jean Laurenceau. 181p. (Orig.). 1987. pap. 3.95 (*0-8199-0802-9*, Frncscn Herld) Franciscan Pr.

Speak To Your Mountain. Kenneth Hagin. 224p. 1993. pap. 5.95 (*0-89276-728-6*) Hagin Ministries.

Speak Truth to Power: Black Professional Class in United States History. Darlene C. Hine. LC 95-47307. 222p. 1996. 40.00 (*0-926019-91-0*) Carlson Pub.

Speak Up. Phyllis Childs. 78p. (J). (ps). 1985. student ed. 6.50 (*0-931749-00-X*) PJC Lrng Mtrls.

Speak Up. Nancy N. Dill. 1990. 10.95 (*0-533-08612-4*) Vantage.

***Speak Up.** Bev Kusuya. 1994. student ed., pap. text ed. 14.67 (*0-582-22805-0*, Pub. by Longman UK) Longman.

Speak Up! Kathy M. Littlefield & Robert S. Littlefield. (Illus.). 32p. (Orig.). (J). (gr. 3-6). 1989. pap. text ed. 8.95 (*1-879340-00-3*, K0101) Kidspeak.

Speak Up, Set 4. Cheryl Pavlik. 1982. audio 50.00 (*0-8384-2960-2*, Newbury) Heinle & Heinle.

Speak Up: A Step-by-Step Guide to Presenting Powerful Public Speeches. 2nd rev. ed. Don A. Aslett. Ed. by Carol Cartaino. LC 89-5764. Orig. Title: Is There a Speech Inside You?. (Illus.). 160p. (Orig.). 1996. pap. 12.99 (*0-937750-15-8*) Marsh Creek Pr.

Speak Up: Book 2. 2nd ed. Pavlik. (College ESL Ser.: Bk. 2). 1995. pap. 20.95 (*0-8384-4998-0*) Heinle & Heinle.

Speak Up: Books 1 & 2. Pavlik. (College ESL Ser.). 1995. suppl. ed., pap. 8.95 (*0-8384-5018-0*) Heinle & Heinle.

Speak Up Bk. 1. 2nd ed. Cheryl Pavlik & Anna Stumpfhauser De Hernandez. LC 94-25204. 112p. 1995. pap. 20.95 (*0-8384-4996-4*) Heinle & Heinle.

Speak up, Chelsea Martin! Becky T. Lindberg. Ed. by Kathleen Tucker. LC 91-313. (Illus.). 128p. (J). (gr. 2-4). 1991. lib. bdg. 12.95 (*0-8075-7552-6*) A Whitman.

Speak up for Just War or Pacifism: A Critique of the United Methodist Bishop's Pastoral Letter "In Defense of Creation" Paul Ramsey. LC 87-21295. 256p. 1988. pap. 14.95 (*0-271-00639-0*); lib. bdg. 30.00 (*0-271-00619-6*) Pa St U Pr.

***Speak up for Yourself.** Beddows. 1989. pap. text ed. write for info. (*0-273-03025-6*) Addison-Wesley.

***Speak up Patch.** (J). 1997. 6.98 (*1-57082-669-2*) Mouse Works.

Speak up, Say No! 3rd ed. Elaine Krause. (Illus.). 40p. (J). (ps-3). 1989. reprint ed. pap. text ed. 3.95 (*0-930359-01-1*) Krause Hse.

Speak up to Move Up: Public Speaking for the Union Representative. Duane Beeler. 101p. (Orig.). 1979. pap. 3.95 (*0-317-12254-1*) Union Rep.

S

***Speak up with Confidence: A Step-By-Step Guide for Speakers & Leaders.** Carol Kent. LC 96-47523. 1996. pap. 14.00 (*0-89109-991-3*) NavPress.

Speak up with Confidence: A Step-by-Step Guide to Successful Public Speaking. Carol Kent. 1993. pap. 9.99 (*0-7852-8340-4*) Nelson.

***Speak Up/Speak Clear/Speak Kind: Assertive Communication Skills.** L. Michael Hall. (Illus.). 100p. (Orig.). 1987. pap. 5.00 (*1-890001-02-3*) Empowerment Tech.

Speak with a Purpose. Carole Urzua. Ed. by Curtis W. Hayes & Carolyn Kessler. LC 81-81672. (Teacher Idea Ser.). 72p. (Orig.). 1993. pap. text ed. 13.25 (*0-8325-9291-9*, Natl Textbk) NTC Pub Grp.

Speak with Comfort. 2nd ed. John E. Hilbert. 224p. 1996. per. 29.61 (*0-8403-8287-1*) Kendall-Hunt.

Speak with Confidence: A Practical Guide. 6th ed. Albert J. Vasile & Harold K. Mintz. LC 92-22638. (C). 1992. 21.25 (*0-673-46786-4*, HarpT) HarpC.

Speak with Distinction. rev. ed. Edith Skinner. Ed. by Timothy Monich & Lilene Mansell. (Acting Ser.). (Illus.). 352p. (C). 1990. text ed. 49.95 incl. audio (*1-55783-053-3*); audio 18.95 (*1-55783-052-5*) Applause Theatre Bk Pubs.

Speak with Distinction. 2nd rev. ed. Edith Skinner. Ed. by Timothy Monich & Lilene Mansell. (Acting Ser.). (Illus.). 416p. (C). 1990. text ed. 36.95 (*1-55783-047-9*) Applause Theatre Bk Pubs.

***Speak with Power & Grace: A Woman's Guide to Public Speaking.** Linda D. Swink. 1997. pap. text ed. 12.95 (*0-8065-1913-4*, Citadel Pr) Carol Pub Group.

***Speak with Power & Grace: A Woman's Guide to Public Speaking.** Linda O. Swink. LC 95-92406. 214p. (Orig.). 1996. pap. write for info. (*0-7880-0629-0*) CSS OH.

Speak Your Mind: A Public Speaking Program for Middle School Students. Barbara Baldwin. Ed. by Stanley C. Coy. 44p. (C). 1992. teacher ed. 6.50 (*1-881459-03-9*) Eagle Pr SC.

Speakable & Unspeakable in Quantum Mechanics: Collected Papers in Quantum Mechanics. John S. Bell. (Illus.). 180p. 1988. pap. text ed. 22.95 (*0-521-36869-3*) Cambridge U Pr.

Speaker, 1. Ed. by Paul M. Pearson. LC 72-5498. (Granger Index Reprint Ser.). 1977. reprint ed. 26.95 (*0-8369-6374-1*) Ayer.

Speaker, Vol. 3. Ed. by Paul M. Pearson. LC 72-5498. (Granger Index Reprint Ser.). 1977. reprint ed. 26.95 (*0-8369-6375-X*) Ayer.

Speaker, Vol. 6. Ed. by Paul M. Pearson. LC 72-5498. (Granger Index Reprint Ser.). 1977. reprint ed. Vol 6. 29.95 (*0-8369-6376-8*) Ayer.

Speaker, Vol. 8. Ed. by Paul M. Pearson. LC 72-5498. (Granger Index Reprint Ser.). 1977. reprint ed. 34.95 (*0-8369-6377-6*) Ayer.

Speaker: A Collection of the Best Orations, Poems, Stories, Debates & One Net Plays for Public Speaking & Voice training, 4 Vols. Paul M. Pearson. text ed. 166.95 (*0-8369-9361-6*, 19732) Ayer.

Speaker & the Budget: Leadership in the Post-Reform House of Representatives. Daniel J. Palazzolo. LC 92-11903. (Series in Policy & Institutional Studies). 272p. (C). 1992. text ed. 49.95 (*0-8229-3715-8*) U of Pittsburgh Pr.

Speaker for the Dead. Orson Scott Card. (Ender Ser.: No. 1). 304p. 1992. pap. 11.95 (*0-312-85325-4*) Tor Bks.

Speaker for the Dead. Orson Scott Card. (Ender Ser.: No. 2). 1994. pap. 5.99 (*0-8125-5075-7*) Tor Bks.

Speaker of Mandarin. Ruth Rendell. (Chief Inspector Wexford Ser.). 224p. 1984. mass mkt. 5.99 (*0-345-30274-5*) Ballantine.

***Speaker of Mandarin.** Ruth Rendell. lib. bdg. 21.95 (*0-8488-2016-9*) Amereon Ltd.

Speaker of the House: The Political Career & Times of John L. O'Brien. Daniel J. Chasan. (Illus.). 208p. 1989. 19.95 (*0-295-96848-6*) U of Wash Pr.

Speaker of the House of Representatives Since 1896. Chang-Wei Ch'iu. LC 68-58558. (Columbia University. Studies in the Social Sciences: No. 297). reprint ed. 32.50 (*0-404-51297-6*) AMS Pr.

Speaker, the Listener, & the Child: Festschrift on the Occasion of Bjorn Lindblom's 60th Birthday. Ed. by O. Engstrand & K. J. Kohler. (Journal: Reprint of Phonetica Ser.: Vol. 51, Nos. 1-3, 1994). (Illus.). 194p. 1994. 62.75 (*3-8055-6021-4*) S Karger.

Speakers: The Role of Listeners. Ed. by Carl F. Graumann. 128p. 1989. 59.00 (*1-85359-059-2*, Pub. by Multilingual Matters UK) Taylor & Francis.

Speakers & Clerks of the Virginia House of Burgesses. Jon Kukla. LC 81-5051. x, 163p. 1981. pap. text ed. 7.95 (*0-88490-076-2*) Library of VA.

Speakers & Lecturers: How to Find Them, 2 vols. 2nd ed. Ed. by Paul Wasserman. 1392p. 1981. Set. 180.00 (*0-8103-0393-0*) Gale.

Speaker's & Toastmaster's Handbook. Herbert V. Prochnow. 368p. 1992. pap. 14.95 (*1-55958-146-8*) Prima Pub.

Speaker's Book of Quotations. Henry O. Dormann. (Orig.). 1987. pap. 7.50 (*0-449-90221-8*, Columbine) Fawcett.

Speaker's Dictionary of Quotoons. O. A. Battista. LC 77-80327. 1977. 14.95 (*0-915074-08-7*) Knowledge Bk Pubs.

Speakers Digest: Business Quotations. Ed. by Rolf White. 271p. (Orig.). 1987. pap. 22.50 (*0-572-01415-5*, Pub. by W Foulsham UK) Trans-Atl Phila.

Speaker's Electoral Connection: Willie Brown & the California Assembly. Richard A. Clucas. LC 94-23863. 173p. (Orig.). (C). 1995. pap. 12.95 (*0-87772-361-3*) UCB IGS.

Speakers for Your Home & Automobile: How to Build & Enjoy a Quality Audio System. rev. ed. Gordon McComb et al. (Illus.). 164p. (C). 1992. reprint ed. pap. 14.95 (*0-7906-1025-6*) Prompt Publns.

Speaker's Handbook. 2nd ed. Jo Sprague & Douglas Stuart. 416p. (C). 1988. pap. text ed. 21.50 (*0-15-583177-1*) HB Coll Pubs.

Speaker's Handbook. 3rd ed. Jo Sprague & Douglas Stuart. 400p. (C). 1992. text ed. 24.00 (*0-15-583173-9*) HB Coll Pubs.

Speaker's Handbook. 4th ed. Sprague. (C). 1996. teacher ed., pap. text ed. 28.00 (*0-15-502501-5*) HB Coll Pubs.

Speaker's Handbook. 4th ed. Sprague. (C). 1995. text ed. 28.00 (*0-15-501614-8*) HB Coll Pubs.

***Speaker's Handbook.** 5th ed. Sprague. (C). 1998. text ed. write for info. (*0-15-508137-3*) HB Coll Pubs.

***Speaker's Handbook.** 5th ed. Sprague. (C). 1998. teacher ed., pap. text ed. 26.75 (*0-15-508170-5*) HB Coll Pubs.

Speaker's Handbook of Successful Openers & Closers. Winston K. Pendleton. 261p. 1984. pap. 7.95 (*0-13-824517-7*, Busn) P-H.

Speaker's Illustrations for Special Days. Charles L. Wallis. LC 56-5373. (Charles L. Wallis Library). (Illus.). 240p. 1991. reprint ed. pap. 7.99 (*0-8010-9555-7*) Baker Bks.

Speaker's Library of Business Stories, Anecdotes & Humor. Joe Griffith. 640p. 1990. 34.95 (*0-13-826975-0*); pap. text ed. 17.95 (*0-13-826983-1*) P-H.

Speaker's Lifetime Library. Leonard Spinrad & Thelma Spinrad. 1979. 39.95 (*0-13-824557-6*, Parker Publishing Co) P-H.

***Speaker's Lifetime Library.** expanded rev. ed. Leonard Spinrad. LC 97-474. 1997. 45.00 (*0-13-496530-2*) P-H.

***Speakers, Listeners & Communication: Exploration in Discourse Analysis.** Gillian Brown. 265p. 1996. pap. text ed. 19.95 (*0-521-58705-0*) Cambridge U Pr.

Speakers, Listeners & Communication: Explorations in Discourse Analysis. Gillian Brown. 256p. (C). 1995. text ed. 57.95 (*0-521-48157-0*) Cambridge U Pr.

Speaker's Meaning. Owen Barfield. LC 67-24113. 125p. 1984. pap. 12.95 (*0-8195-6113-4*, Wesleyan Univ Pr) U Pr of New Eng.

Speakers of the House. Judith Bentley. LC 94-15073. (Democracy in Action Ser.). (Illus.). 128p. (YA). (gr. 9-12). 1994. lib. bdg. 22.70 (*0-531-11156-3*) Watts.

Speakers of the House. Hubert B. Fuller. LC 73-19147. (Politics & People Ser.). (Illus.). 322p. 1974. reprint ed. 25.95 (*0-405-05871-3*) Ayer.

Speakers of the House of Representatives of the United States. William H. Smith. LC 70-137291. reprint ed. 32.50 (*0-404-06128-1*) AMS Pr.

Speakers of the U. S. House of Representatives: A Bibliography, Seventeen Eighty-Nine to Nineteen Eighty-Four. Ed. by Donald R. Kennon. LC 85-45047. (Studies in Historical & Political Science: No. 1). 360p. 1986. text ed. 50.00 (*0-8018-2786-8*) Johns Hopkins.

Speaker's Perspective in Grammar & Lexicon: The Case of Russian, Vol. 5. Valentina A. Zaitseva. LC 94-17828. (History & Language Ser.: Vol. 5). 208p. (C). 1995. text ed. 43.95 (*0-8204-2307-6*) P Lang Pubng.

Speaker's Portable Answer Book. Stephen R. Maloney. LC 93-8251. 1993. 29.95 (*0-13-501016-0*) P-H.

Speaker's Primer: A Professional's Guide to Successful Presentations. Ronne T. Jacobs. Ed. by Tina Chovanec. (Illus.). 85p. 1984. pap. 14.95 (*0-9614051-0-4*) Jacobs Assocs.

***Speaker's Quotebook: Over 4,000 Illustrations & Quotations for All Occasions.** Roy B. Zuck. LC 96-33123. (Illus.). 432p. 1997. pap. 16.99 (*0-8254-4098-X*) Kregel.

Speaker's Quotebook: Stories, Illustrations & Anecdotes. Benjamin R. De Jong. 310p. (C). 1995. reprint ed. pap. 11.99 (*0-8010-3030-7*) Baker Bks.

Speaker's Sourcebook, No. II. Glenn Van Ekeren. 375p. 34.95 (*0-13-825217-3*) P-H.

Speaker's Sourcebook, No. II. 2nd ed. Glenn Van Ekeren. 375p. pap. 15.95 (*0-13-825225-4*) P-H.

Speakers Sourcebook of New Illustrations: 500 Stories & Anecdotes for Preachers, Teachers. V. Hurley. 1995. pap. 19.99 (*0-8499-3675-6*) Word Pub.

Speakers, Tours & Films, 1984-85. Ed. by Dion Shea. 176p. (Orig.). 1984. pap. 10.00 (*0-88318-269-6*) Am Inst Physics.

Speakers Treasury of Political Stories, Anecdotes & Humor. Gerald Tomlinson. 450p. 1990. pap. text ed. 12.95 (*0-13-829722-3*) P-H.

Speaker's Treasury of Political Stories, Anecdotes, & Humor. Gerald Tomlinson. 1996. 8.98 (*1-56731-110-5*, MJF Bks) Fine Comms.

Speaker's Treasury of Sports Anecdotes, Stories & Humor. Gerald Tomlinson. 1996. 8.98 (*1-56731-109-1*, MJF Bks) Fine Comms.

Speaker's Treasury of Stories for All Occasions. Herbert V. Prochnow. 344p. 1982. 16.95 (*0-685-05562-0*) P-H.

Speakin' O' Christmas & Other Christmas & Special Poems. Paul L. Dunbar. LC 73-18574. (Illus.). reprint ed. 19.50 (*0-404-11385-0*) AMS Pr.

Speakin' Southern. 2.00 (*0-936672-57-9*) Aerial Photo.

Speakin' Vegan: Favorite Recipes from Picniques' Take-Out. Grace Semple. (Illus.). 39p. (Orig.). 1992. pap. 4.50 (*0-9635207-0-9*) G Semple.

Speaking. 1987. 14.50 (*0-19-437134-0*) OUP.

Speaking. Georges Gusdorf. Tr. by Paul T. Brockelman. (Studies in Phenomenology & Existential Philosophy). 132p. 1965. pap. 16.95 (*0-8101-0531-4*) Northwestern U Pr.

Speaking: From Intention to Articulation. William J. M. Levelt. (ACL-MIT Series in Natural Language Processing). (Illus.). 584p. 1993. pap. 25.00 (*0-262-62089-8*, Bradford Bks) MIT Pr.

Speaking about Custer, a Collection of Lectures. Ed. by Sandy Barnard. (Illus.). 104p. (Orig.). 1991. pap. 15.00 (*0-9618087-2-1*) AST Pr.

Speaking about Writing: Reflections on Research Methodology. Ed. by Peter Smagorinsky. (Written Communication Annual Ser.: Vol. 8). 304p. (C). 1994. pap. text ed. 24.95 (*0-8039-5232-5*) Sage.

Speaking Aids Through the Grades. Ruth K. Carlson. LC 74-14719. 93p. reprint ed. pap. 26.60 (*0-8357-3459-5*, 2039721) Bks Demand.

Speaking American English. Jean H. Miculka. (PS - Communication/English Ser.). 1992. pap. 24.95 (*0-538-70328-8*) S-W Pub.

Speaking & Listening: A Contemporary Approach. 2nd ed. Wayne A. Shrope. 305p. (C). 1979. pap. text ed. 20.00 (*0-15-583182-8*) HB Coll Pubs.

Speaking & Listening in Multilingual Classrooms. 1995. student ed. 179.00 (*0-7049-0773-9*, Pub. by Multilingual Matters UK); student ed., pap. 12.95 (*0-7049-0780-1*, Pub. by Multilingual Matters UK) Taylor & Francis.

Speaking & Presentation Skills Skillbook. Educational Foundation of the National Restaurant Association Staff. (Management Skills Program Ser.). 52p. (Orig.). 1992. pap. 10.95 (*0-915452-45-6*) Educ Found.

Speaking & Semiology: Maurice Merleau-Ponty's Phenomenological Theory of Existential Communication. 2nd ed. Richard L. Lanigan. LC 91-30860. (Approaches to Semiotics Ser.: No. 22). vi, 257p. 1991. lib. bdg. 106.15 (*3-11-012864-0*) Mouton.

Speaking & Writing Communication Guide. Webb et al. 1991. 25.00 (*0-536-58100-2*) Ginn Pr.

Speaking & Writing Skills for Educators. American Association of School Administrators Staff. LC 92-74902. (Orig.). 1993. pap. 2.50 (*0-87652-182-0*, 21-00240) Am Assn Sch Admin.

Speaking As a Friend. Dean Freiday. 116p. 1995. pap. 12.00 (*0-913342-78-5*) Barclay Pr.

Speaking As a Woman. Alison Laing. 40p. 1989. pap. 10.00 (*1-880715-03-1*) Creat Des Srvs.

Speaking As a Writer. Illus. by David Ross-Rovertson. 76p. 1979. 7.75 (*0-9602342-1-7*); pap. 5.95 (*0-9602342-0-9*) Westwind Pr.

***Speaking As One: A Look at the Ecumenical Creeds.** Scott Hoezee. LC 97-3424. 1997. write for info. (*1-56212-247-9*) CRC Pubns.

Speaking As One Friend to Another. John R. Yungblut. LC 82-63177. (Orig.). (C). 1983. pap. 3.00 (*0-87574-249-1*) Pendle Hill.

***Speaking Beyond the Podium: A Public Speaking Handbook.** Anne Harrell. 218p. (C). 1996. spiral bd. 22.95 (*0-7872-3244-0*) Kendall-Hunt.

Speaking Chinese about China, No. 1. Du Rong et al. (Chinese Language Library). (Illus.). 490p. (Orig.). (C). 1985. pap. 18.95 (*0-8351-1583-6*) China Bks.

Speaking Chinese about China, No. 2. Ed. by Du Rong et al. (Chinese Language Library). (Illus.). 602p. (Orig.). (C). 1987. pap. 18.95 (*0-8351-1905-X*) China Bks.

Speaking Chinese in China. Hsu Ying & J. Marvin Brown. LC 82-48904. (C). 1983. text ed. 50.00 (*0-300-02955-1*); pap. text ed. 20.00 (*0-300-03032-0*) Yale U Pr.

Speaking Christ For The Building Up Of The Body Of Christ. Witness Lee. 143p. per. 5.50 (*0-87083-422-3*, 12019001) Living Stream Ministry.

Speaking Clearly: Improving Voice & Diction. 3rd ed. Jeffrey C. Hahner et al. 400p. (C). 1990. pap. text ed. write for info. (*0-07-557316-4*) McGraw.

Speaking Clearly: Improving Voice & Diction. 4th ed. Jeffrey C. Hahner et al. LC 92-11033. 1993. pap. text ed. write for info. (*0-07-025825-2*) McGraw.

Speaking Clearly: Improving Voice & Diction. 5th ed. Jeffrey C. Hahner et al. LC 96-22891. 1996. pap. text ed. write for info. (*0-07-025919-4*) McGraw.

Speaking Clearly: The Basics of Voice & Articulation. 3rd rev. ed. Noah F. Modisett & James G. Luter, Jr. (Illus.). 304p. 1988. pap. text ed. write for info. (*0-8087-3295-1*) Burgess MN Intl.

Speaking Culturally: Explorations in Social Communication. Gerry Philipsen. LC 91-33107. (SUNY Series, Human Communication Processes). 154p. 1992. text ed. 57.50 (*0-7914-1163-X*); pap. text ed. 18.95 (*0-7914-1164-8*) State U NY Pr.

***Speaking Dreams.** Severna Park. 1997. mass mkt. 5.99 (*0-380-72924-5*) Avon.

***Speaking Dreams.** Severna Park. 1997. mass mkt. 5.99 (*0-614-27711-6*, AvoNova) Avon.

Speaking Effectively. Janet L. Kayfetz & Smith. 1992. pap. 26.95 (*0-8384-2276-4*) Heinle & Heinle.

Speaking Effectively - A Guide for Air Force Speakers. John A. Kline. LC 89-78063. (Illus.). 86p. 1990. per. 5.00 (*0-16-019036-3*, S/N 008-070-006) USGPO.

Speaking Effectively in Public Settings: A Modern Rhetoric with a Traditional Base. Ray E. Nadeau et al. 296p. (Orig.). (C). 1993. pap. text ed. 27.50 (*0-8191-9122-1*) U Pr of Amer.

***Speaking Emotions: Beauty of Thought & Inspiration.** Norman Barnhart. (Illus.). 94p. 1997. pap. 7.95 (*1-57502-530-2*, PO1566) Morris Pubng.

Speaking English for Mom. Houghton Mifflin Company Staff. (Literature Experience 1993 Ser.). (J). (gr. 2). 1992. pap. 8.48 (*0-395-61776-6*) HM.

Speaking English Through Video. James Steinman. 112p. 1985. pap. 10.95 (*0-933704-54-2*) Dawn Pr.

Speaking Fire at Stones. William Carpenter. LC 92-50420. (Illus.). 128p. 1992. 22.00 (*0-88448-104-2*); pap. 15.00 (*0-88448-105-0*) Tilbury Hse.

Speaking Flame: Re-creations of Rumi. Andrew Harvey. 120p. (Orig.). 1989. pap. 8.95 (*0-9622973-1-3*) Meeramma Pubns.

Speaking for Clio. Richard Sullivan. 230p. (C). 1991. lib. bdg. 48.50 (*0-943549-07-8*) TJU Pr.

Speaking for Effect: The Strategy of Successful Speaking. Michael B. Young & Thomas M. Lovil. Ed. by Gary Hofer & Phyllis Ortman. LC 89-92282. (Illus.). 120p. (Orig.). 1990. pap. 8.95 (*0-9624503-0-8*) Speaking Effect.

Speaking for Nature. Paul Brooks. LC 82-16997. (Paperback Library). (Illus.). 320p. 1983. reprint ed. pap. 8.95 (*0-87156-332-0*) Sierra.

Speaking for Ourselves: Women & Distance Education in India. Ed. by Asha S. Kanwar & Neela Jagannathan. (C). 1995. 30.00 (*81-7304-112-1*, Pub. by Manohar II) S Asia.

Speaking for Ourselves: Women's Wit & Wisdom. Andrews & McMeel Staff. (Illus.). 40p. 1994. 6.95 (*0-8362-4721-3*) Andrews & McMeel.

Speaking for Ourselves, Too: More Autobiographical Sketches by Notable Authors of Books for Young Adults. Intro. by Donald R. Gallo. 235p. (Orig.). (YA). (gr. 7-12). 1992. pap. 14.95 (*0-8141-4623-6*) NCTE.

***Speaking for Sex: Sexual Communication in Intimate Relationships.** Wells & Jacobson. 64p. (C). 1997. per. 15.95 (*0-7872-3886-4*) Kendall-Hunt.

Speaking for the Chief: Okyeame & the Politics of Akan Royal Oratory. Kwesi Yankah. LC 94-27094. 256p. 1995. 35.00 (*0-253-36801-4*); pap. 15.95 (*0-253-20946-3*) Ind U Pr.

***Speaking for the Generations: Native Writers on Writing.** Simon J. Ortiz. LC 97-21107. (Sun Tracks Ser.). 1998. write for info. (*0-8165-1849-1*); pap. write for info. (*0-8165-1850-5*) U of Ariz Pr.

Speaking for the Negative. John Loengard. LC 94-14301. (Illus.). 96p. 1994. lib. bdg. 29.95 (*1-55970-282-6*) Arcade Pub Inc.

***Speaking for the Polis: Isocrates' Rhetorical Education.** Takis Poulakos. LC 97-4865. (Studies in Rhetoric/Communication). 139p. 1997. 24.95 (*1-57003-177-0*) U of SC Pr.

Speaking for Themselves: Ethnographic Interviews with Adults with Learning Disabilities. Paul J. Gerber & Henry B. Reiff. (International Academy for Research in Learning Disabilities Monograph Ser.). 176p. 1991. text ed. 36.50 (*0-472-10246-X*) U of Mich Pr.

Speaking for Themselves: Neomexicano Cultural Identity & the Spanish-Language Press, 1880-1920. Doris Meyer. LC 96-4526. 304p. 1996. 29.95 (*0-8263-1749-9*) U of NM Pr.

Speaking for Vice: Homosexuality in the Art of Charles Demuth, Marsden Hartley. Jonathan E. Weinberg. 1995. pap. text ed. 22.50 (*0-300-06254-0*) Yale U Pr.

Speaking for Vice: Homosexuality in the Art of Charles Demuth, Marsden Hartley, & the First American Avante-Garde. Jonathan E. Weinberg. LC 93-18547. (Publications in the History of Art). (Illus.). 304p. (C). 1993. 45.00 (*0-300-05361-4*) Yale U Pr.

Speaking For You: The Vision of Ralph Ellison. Kimberly W. Benston. 438p. 1988. 29.95 (*0-88258-169-4*) Howard U Pr.

Speaking for You-PA: The Vision of Ralph Ellison. 2nd ed. Ed. by Kimberly W. Benston. LC 87-17019. 448p. (C). 1990. reprint ed. pap. 17.95 (*0-88258-005-1*) Howard U Pr.

Speaking Frankly. James F. Byrnes. LC 74-4657. (Illus.). 324p. 1974. reprint ed. text ed. 35.00 (*0-8371-7480-5*, BYSF, Greenwood Pr) Greenwood.

***Speaking Freely.** Nat Hentoff. LC 97-6353. 1997. 25.00 (*0-679-43647-2*) Knopf.

***Speaking Freely: Stuart Berg Flexner's Guided Tour of American English from Plymouth Rock to Sillicon Valley.** Ed. by Anne H. Soukhanov & Stuart B. Flexner. LC 97-15369. (Illus.). 448p. 1997. 39.95 (*0-19-510692-X*) OUP.

Speaking Freely: The Case Against Speech Codes. Ed. by Henry M. Holzer. 277p. 1994. 24.95 (*1-886442-04-5*, Sec Thght Bks); pap. 17.95 (*1-886442-00-2*, Sec Thght Bks) Ctr Study Popular.

Speaking Freely: Unlearning the Lies of the Fathers' Tongues. Julia Penelope. (Athene Ser.). 370p. 1990. text ed. 37.50 (*0-08-036556-6*, Pub. by PPI UK); pap. text ed. 16.95 (*0-08-036555-8*, Pub. by PPI UK) Elsevier.

Speaking Freely: Unlearning the Lies of the Fathers' Tongues. Julia Penelope. (Athene Ser.). 328p. (C). 1990. text ed. 37.50 (*0-8077-6245-8*); pap. text ed. 19.95 (*0-8077-6244-X*) Tchrs Coll.

Speaking Freely: Your Right of Free Speach & Its Legal Limitations. Harold Van Winkle. 602p. 1995. 39.50 (*0-931541-20-4*) Mancorp Pub.

Speaking Freely Vol. 1: The Public Interest in Unfettered Speech. John Corry et al. LC 95-79861. 135p. (Orig.). (C). 1995. pap. 14.95 (*0-937790-51-6*, 4460) Media Institute.

Speaking French in Kansas & Other Stories. Robert Day. 112p. (Orig.). 1989. per. 8.95 (*0-685-30040-4*) Cottonwood KS.

Speaking from Experience: Illustrated Solutions to the Business Problems You Face Every Day. L. Ron Hubbard. Ed. by Bill Kilpatrick & Stephanie Deyette. (Illus.). 235p. 1996. 24.95 (*0-9648491-0-0*) Concept Tech.

Speaking from the Depths: Alfred North Whitehead's Hermeneutical Metaphysics of Propositions, Experience, Symbolism, Language, & Religion. Stephen T. Franklin. LC 89-1204. 424p. reprint ed. pap. 120.90 (*0-7837-5557-0*, 2045332) Bks Demand.

Speaking from the Heart. Mertis John. 1995. 12.95 (*0-533-11558-2*) Vantage.

Speaking from the Heart: A Feminist Perspective on Ethics. Rita C. Manning. 224p. (C). 1992. text ed. 49.00 (*0-8476-7733-8*) Rowman.

An Asterisk (*) at the beginning of an entry indicates that the title is appearing in BIP for the first time.

Speaking from the Heart: An Anthology of Writing by New Writers. Ed. by Literacy Volunteers of New York City Staff. (New Writers' Voices Ser.). 64p. (Orig.). 1990. pap. text ed. 3.50 (*0-929631-16-1*, Signal Hill) New Readers.

Speaking from the Heart: Preaching with Passion. Richard F. Ward. (Preacher's Library). 144p. (Orig.). 1992. pap. 12.95 (*0-687-39166-0*) Abingdon.

Speaking Globally: English in an International Context. Grohe & Root. 1995. pap. text ed. 12.60 (*0-205-15600-2*) Allyn.

***Speaking Globally: How to Make Effective Presentations Across International Boundaries.** Elizabeth Urech. 1997. pap. text ed. 15.95 (*0-7494-2221-1*) Kogan Page Ltd.

Speaking Heart to Heart: Metaphors & Parables As a Communication Form. E. Gene Rooney. 102p. (Orig.). 1993. student ed. 20.00 (*1-881596-01-X*) L E A D Cnslts.

Speaking His Mind. Stephen J. Trachtenberg. 160p. 1994. 19.95 (*0-89774-885-9*) Oryx Pr.

Speaking in America. Harold Barrett. (Illus.). 420p. (Orig.). (C). 1993. pap. text ed. 25.50 (*0-03-076117-4*) HB Coll Pubs.

Speaking in America. 7th ed. Barrett. (C). 1993. teacher ed., pap. text ed. 9.75 (*0-03-094052-4*) HB Coll Pubs.

Speaking in Other Tongues: A Scholarly Defense. Donald L. Barnett & Jeffrey P. McGregor. 840p. 1986. 25.00 (*0-934287-23-6*) Comm Chapel Pubns.

Speaking in Our Tongues: Proceedings of a Colloquium on Medieval Dialectology & Related Disciplines. Ed. by Margaret Laing & Keith Williamson. LC 93-38900. (Illus.). 243p. (C). 1994. 53.00 (*0-85991-403-8*, DS Brewer) Boydell & Brewer.

***Speaking in Public.** Date not set. pap. 12.95 (*0-8464-4421-6*) Beekman Pubs.

Speaking in Public. Richard F. Whitman & Ted J. Foster. 575p. (C). 1987. pap. write for info. (*0-02-427350-3*, Macmillan Coll) P-H.

Speaking in Public & Private. Gerald M. Phillips et al. 384p. (Orig.). (C). 1985. teacher ed. write for info. (*0-672-61613-0*); pap. text ed. write for info. (*0-672-61612-2*); student ed. write for info. (*0-672-61622-X*) Macmillan.

Speaking in Public & Private. Gerald M. Phillips et al. 384p. (Orig.). (C). 1985. pap. text ed. 51.00 (*0-02-395740-9*, Macmillan Coll) P-H.

Speaking in Stories: Resources for Christian Storytellers. William R. White. LC 82-70954. 128p. (Orig.). 1982. pap. 11.99 (*0-8066-1929-5*, 10-5886, Augsburg) Augsburg Fortress.

Speaking in Tongues. Larry Christenson. LC 97-5595. 144p. 1987. pap. 7.99 (*0-87123-996-5*) Bethany Hse.

Speaking in Tongues. Jeffrey Deaver. Date not set. pap. 21.95 (*0-670-86073-5*, Viking) Viking Penguin.

***Speaking in Tongues.** Dirk Hanson. Date not set. write for info. (*0-688-08888-0*) Morrow.

Speaking in Tongues. Fisher Humphreys & Malcolm D. Tolbert. LC 73-86749. 94p. (Orig.). 1973. pap. 4.00 (*0-914520-05-9*) Insight Pr.

Speaking in Tongues. Philip Mauro. 1978. pap. 0.79 (*0-87377-059-5*) GAM Pubns.

Speaking in Tongues: New & Selected Poems 1974-1994. Charles Ghigna. LC 94-75464. (Illus.). 133p. (Orig.). 1994. 23.95 (*0-942979-19-2*); pap. 11.95 (*0-942979-20-6*) Livingston U Pr.

Speaking in Tongues: Poetry by Linguists. Ed. by Bradley R. Strahan. (International Visions Ser.: Vol. 1). (Illus.). 80p. (Orig.). pap. 7.95 (*0-938872-19-2*) Black Buzzard.

***Speaking in Tongues: Understanding the Uses & Abuses of This Supernatural Phenomenon.** 4th ed. Harold McDougal. (Master Keys Ser.). 140p. 1997. reprint ed. pap. 6.99 (*1-884369-07-3*) McDougal Pubng.

Speaking in Whispers: African-American Lesbian Erotica. Kathleen E. Morris. LC 96-22395. 160p. (Orig.). 1996. pap. 11.95 (*1-879427-28-1*) Third Side Pr.

Speaking into Space (Textual Spaces) Aboriginality & Cultural Studies. Stephen Muecke. 1992. pap. 32.95 (*0-86840-101-3*, Pub. by New South Wales Univ Pr AT) Intl Spec Bk.

Speaking Kapampangan. Leatrice T. Mirikitani. Ed. by Howard P. McKaughan. LC 70-152468. (PALI Language Texts Philippines). 1011p. (C). reprint ed. 180.00 (*0-8357-9827-5*, 2017219) Bks Demand.

Speaking Korean, Bk. I. rev. ed. Francis Y. Park. LC 84-80023. (ENG & KOR.). 1994. audio 125.00 (*0-930878-77-9*) Hollym Intl.

Speaking Korean, Bk. 1. rev. ed. Francis Y. Park. LC 84-80023. 484p. (ENG & KOR.). 1994. pap. text ed. 38.50 (*1-56591-101-6*) Hollym Intl.

Speaking Korean, Bk. 2. rev. ed. Francis Y. Park. LC 84-80023. 493p. (KOR.). 1994. pap. text ed. 38.50 (*1-56591-103-2*) Hollym Intl.

Speaking Korean: A Guide to Chinese Characters, Bk. III. Francis Y. Park. LC 89-83652. 401p. 1989. 44.50 (*0-930878-81-7*) Hollym Intl.

Speaking Land: Myth & Story in Aboriginal Australia. Ronald M. Berndt & Catherine H. Berndt. LC 94-15525. 468p. 1994. pap. 16.95 (*0-89281-518-3*) Inner Tradit.

Speaking Life: The Legacy of John Keble. Charles R. Henery. (Illus.). 150p. (Orig.). 1995. pap. 15.95 (*0-85244-263-7*, Pub. by Gracewing UK) Morehouse Pub.

Speaking Likeness. large type ed. Sheila Bishop. 1990. 25.99 (*0-7089-2197-3*) Ulverscroft.

Speaking, Listening, Understanding: The Art of Conscious Conversation for Insight & Decision Making. Heinz Zimmerman. Tr. by J. H. Hindes from GER. 112p. (Orig.). 1996. pap. 12.95 (*0-940262-75-4*) Lindisfarne Bks.

Speaking Magic. Carolyn Dickson & Paula DePasquale. 204p. 1994. pap. 12.95 (*0-9619590-8-8*) Oak Hill Pr OH.

Speaking Magic. Carolyn Dickson. 208p. 1992. 22.95 (*0-915677-62-8*) Roundtable Pub.

Speaking Mathematically: Communications in Mathematics Classrooms. David Pimm. 240p. 1989. 44.95 (*0-7102-1133-3*, 11333, RKP) Routledge.

Speaking Mexicano: The Dynamics of Syncretic Language in Central Mexico. Jane H. Hill & Kenneth C. Hill. LC 86-1370. 493p. 1986. 56.00 (*0-8165-0898-4*) U of Ariz Pr.

Speaking Minds: Cognitive Science Past, Present & Future. Ed. by Peter Baumgartner & Sabine Payr. LC 94-24797. 376p. 1995. text ed. 39.50 (*0-691-03678-0*) Princeton U Pr.

***Speaking Minds: Interviews with Twenty Eminent Cognitive Scientists.** Peter Baumgartner. 350p. 1995. pap. text ed. 17.95 (*0-691-02901-6*) Princeton U Pr.

***Speaking My Mind.** Rhodes Boyson. 256p. 9500. 45.00 (*0-7206-0901-1*, Pub. by P Owen Ltd UK) Dufour.

Speaking My Mind: An Autobiography. Rhodes Boyson. 254p. 9600. pap. 21.00 (*0-7206-0983-6*, Pub. by P Owen Ltd UK) Dufour.

Speaking Naturally: Communication Skills in American English. Ed. by Bruce Tillitt & Mary N. Bruder. (Illus.). 115p. 1985. pap. text ed. 14.95 (*0-521-27130-4*); digital audio 18.95 (*0-521-25007-2*) Cambridge U Pr.

Speaking of: Asthma. Dietrich Nolte. (Sterling Health & Cure Ser.). 96p. 1989. text ed. 15.95 (*81-207-0840-7*, Pub. by Sterling Pubs II) Apt Bks.

Speaking Of: Ayurvedic Remedies for Common Diseases. T. L. Devaraj. 145p. 1985. 17.95 (*0-318-36357-7*) Asia Bk Corp.

Speaking Of: Child Care: Everything You Wanted To Know. Suraj Gupte. 232p. 1991. text ed. 30.00 (*81-207-1297-8*, Pub. by Sterling Pubs II) Apt Bks.

Speaking Of: Diabetics & Diet. Deepak Mehta. 128p. 1991. text ed. 18.95 (*81-207-1047-9*, Pub. by Sterling Pubs II) Apt Bks.

Speaking Of: Homoeopathy. H. L. Chitkara. 72p. 1987. text ed. 17.95 (*81-207-0606-4*, Pub. by Sterling Pubs II) Apt Bks.

Speaking Of: Nature Cure. K. Lakshmana Sarma & S. Swaminathan. 230p. 1987. text ed. 27.95 (*81-207-0614-5*, Pub. by Sterling Pubs II) Apt Bks.

Speaking Of: Skin Care: Look Younger Be More Beautiful. Parvesh Handa. (Health & Cure Ser.). 1985. text ed. 15.95 (*0-86590-614-9*, Pub. by Sterling Pubs II) Apt Bks.

Speaking Of: Yoga: A Practical Guide to Better Living. Pandit S. Nath. 192p. 1989. text ed. 22.50 (*81-207-0684-6*, Pub. by Sterling Pubs II) Apt Bks.

Speaking Of: Yoga & Nature Cure. K. S. Joshi. 160p. 1991. text ed. 25.00 (*81-207-1053-3*, Pub. by Sterling Pubs II) Apt Bks.

Speaking of: Yoga & Nature-Cure Therapy. K. S. Joshi. (C). 1993. 7.00 (*81-207-1360-5*, Pub. by Sterling Plns Pvt II) S Asia.

Speaking of, a Book of Drill for the Older Student. Marilyn M. Toomey. 239p. 1985. pap. 19.95 (*0-685-24082-7*) Circuit Pubns.

Speaking of a Personal God. Vincent Brummer. 176p. (C). 1992. text ed. 54.95 (*0-521-43052-6*); pap. text ed. 17.95 (*0-521-43632-X*) Cambridge U Pr.

Speaking of Alternative Medicine: Accupuncture, the Needle That Heals All Ailments. Nilesh Baxi & C. H. Asrani. (Health & Cure Ser.). 1985. text ed. 15.95 (*0-86590-612-2*, Pub. by Sterling Pubs II) Apt Bks.

Speaking of Animals: A Dictionary of Animal Metaphors. Robert A. Palmatier. LC 94-29273. 496p. 1995. text ed. 69.50 (*0-313-29490-9*, Greenwood Pr) Greenwood.

Speaking of Art. Peter Kivy. 144p. 1973. pap. text ed. 47.00 (*90-247-1491-5*, Pub. by M Nijhoff NE) Kluwer Ac.

Speaking of Arts: A Giriama Impression. David Parkin. LC 82-70267. (First Annual Alan P. Merriam Lecture). 1982. pap. text ed. 5.00 (*0-941934-37-3*) Indiana Africa.

Speaking of Ayurvedic Remedies for Common Diseases: Simple Remedies Based on Herbal Medicines. T. L. Devaraj. (Health & Cure Ser.). 1985. text ed. 15.95 (*0-317-19697-9*, Pub. by Sterling Pubs II) Apt Bks.

Speaking of Business. England. (College ESL Ser.). 1995. teacher ed., pap. 19.95 (*0-8384-4258-7*) Heinle & Heinle.

Speaking of Business: Advanced Business-Tapestry. Lizabeth England & Christine Uber Grosse. (College ESL Ser.). 244p. 1995. pap. 26.95 (*0-8384-3962-4*) Heinle & Heinle.

Speaking of Cardinals. Thomas B. Morgan. LC 70-134119. (Essay Index Reprint Ser.). 1977. 20.95 (*0-8369-2002-3*) Ayer.

Speaking of Change: A Selection of Speeches & Articles. Edward A. Filene. LC 76-156640. (Essay Index Reprint Ser.). 1977. reprint ed. 24.95 (*0-8369-2355-3*) Ayer.

***Speaking of Chaucer.** E. Talbot Donaldson. 192p. (C). 1995. pap. 10.99 (*0-8010-2033-6*, Labyrinth) Baker Bks.

Speaking of Chaucer. E. Talbot Donaldson. LC 83-11973. 192p. (C). 1983. reprint ed. pap. 8.95 (*0-939464-15-2*, Labyrinth) Baker Bks.

Speaking of Chinese. Raymond Chang & Margaret S. Chang. (Illus.). 1983. pap. 11.00 (*0-393-30061-7*) Norton.

Speaking of Christ: A Lesbian Feminist Voice. Carter Heyward. LC 89-35064. 96p. (Orig.). 1989. pap. 9.95 (*0-8298-0829-9*) Pilgrim OH.

Speaking of Diversity: Language & Ethnicity in Twentieth-Century America. Philip Gleason. 320p. 1992. text ed. 45.00 (*0-8018-4295-6*) Johns Hopkins.

Speaking of Ethnography. Michael H. Agar. (Qualitative Research Methods Ser.: Vol. 2). 96p. (Orig.). 1985. 22.95 (*0-8039-2561-1*); pap. text ed. 9.95 (*0-8039-2492-5*) Sage.

Speaking of Florida. Ed. by John Ames. (Illus.). 224p. 1991. 24.95 (*0-8130-1048-9*); pap. 17.95 (*0-8130-1090-X*) U Press Fla.

Speaking of Frank Waters, Premier Volume. 45p. 1992. write for info. (*1-878277-09-X*) Frank Waters Soc.

Speaking of Friendship: Middle-Class Women & Their Friends. Helen Gouldner. LC 86-29407. (Contributions in Women's Studies: No. 80). 196p. 1987. text ed. 49.95 (*0-313-25068-5*, GSF/, Greenwood Pr) Greenwood.

Speaking of Gender. Ed. by Elaine Showalter. 256p. 1988. 39.50 (*0-415-90026-3*, Routledge NY) Routledge.

Speaking of Gender. Ed. by Elaine Showalter. 256p. (C). 1989. pap. 13.95 (*0-415-90027-1*, Routledge NY) Routledge.

***Speaking of God... A User's Guide to Our Contemporary Testimony.** Robert DeMoor. 103p. (Orig.). 1996. pap. 5.40 (*1-56212-221-5*, 1344-2075) CRC Pubns.

Speaking of God: Evangelism As Initial Spiritual Guidance. Ben C. Johnson. 192p. (Orig.). 1991. pap. 14.00 (*0-664-25200-1*) Westminster John Knox.

Speaking of God: Reading & Preaching the Word of God. Jerry Camery-Hoggatt. 260p. (C). 1995. pap. 16.95 (*1-56563-172-2*) Hendrickson MA.

***Speaking of History: Conversations with Historians, 1990-1995.** Ed. by Roger Adelson. LC 96-53683. (Illus.). 230p. (Orig.). 1997. pap. 18.95 (*0-87013-464-7*) Mich St U Pr.

Speaking of Home. Lillian W. Tryon. LC 77-86789. (Essay Index Reprint Ser.). 1977. 17.95 (*0-8369-1198-9*) Ayer.

Speaking of Horror: Interviews with Writers of the Supernatural. Darrell Schweitzer. LC 84-357. (Milford Series: Popular Writers of Today: Vol. 48). 136p. (Orig.). 1994. pap. 19.00 (*0-89370-277-3*); lib. bdg. 29.00 (*0-89370-177-7*) Borgo Pr.

Speaking of Indians: With an Accent on the Southwest. Bernice E. Johnston. LC 72-134776. 112p. reprint ed. pap. 32.00 (*0-317-28049-X*, 2025554) Bks Demand.

Speaking of Jesus: Reaching Your World with the Good News of Christ. J. Mack Stiles. LC 95-16640. 192p. (Orig.). 1995. pap. 9.99 (*0-8308-1645-3*, 1645) InterVarsity.

Speaking of Journalism: 12 Writers & Editors Talk about Their Work. William K. Zinsser. 192p. 1995. pap. 13.00 (*0-06-272064-3*, PL) HarpC.

Speaking of Language: An International Guide to Language Service Organizations. Paula Conru et al. 1993. pap. write for info. (*0-13-827023-6*) P-H.

Speaking of Language: An International Guide to Language Service Organizations. Paula Conru et al. (Language in Education Ser.). (Illus.). 191p. (Orig.). 1993. pap. text ed. 16.50 (*0-937354-80-5*) Delta Systems.

Speaking of Life: Horizons of Meaning for Nursing Home Residents. Jaber F. Gubrium. LC 93-28591. (Communication & Social Order Ser.). 213p. 1993. pap. text ed. 25.95 (*0-202-30482-5*); lib. bdg. 47.95 (*0-202-30481-7*) Aldine de Gruyter.

Speaking of Love. Carol B. Gerrond. 192p. 1994. 17.95 (*0-8034-9041-0*) Bouregy.

Speaking of Love. Fred Kendall et al. 1995. 18.99 (*0-7852-8154-1*) Nelson.

Speaking of Man. Abraham Myerson. Ed. by Gerald N. Grob. LC 78-22577. (Historical Issues in Mental Health Ser.). 1980. reprint ed. lib. bdg. 23.95 (*0-405-11929-1*) Ayer.

Speaking of Marriage: Irreverent Reflections on Matrimony. Ed. by Tina Reed & Robert Reed. LC 94-39474. 1995. pap. 10.00 (*0-399-51941-6*, Perigee Bks) Berkley Pub.

Speaking of Monks: Religious Biography in India & China. Ed. by Phyllis Granoff & Koichi Shinohara. 232p. 1995. lib. bdg. 47.00 (*0-8095-4834-8*) Borgo Pr.

Speaking of Monks: Religious Biography in India & China. Ed. by Phyllis Granoff & Koichi Shinohara. 232p. pap. 18.95 (*0-88962-544-1*) Mosaic.

***Speaking of Montana: A Guide to the Oral History Collection at the Montana Historical Society.** Ed. by Jodie Foley & Dave Walter. LC 97-19548. 250p. (Orig.). 1996. pap. 24.95 (*0-917298-53-5*) MT Hist Soc.

Speaking of My Life. Far West Editions Staff. 149p. 1979. pap. 7.00 (*0-06-250643-9*) Far West Edns.

Speaking of Nature Cure: Regain, Retain & Improve Health the Drugless Way. K. Lakshmana Sarma & S. Swaminathan. (C). 1993. 6.50 (*81-207-0632-3*, Pub. by Sterling Plns Pvt II) S Asia.

Speaking of Networks: A Glossary for Network Users. Apple Computer, Inc. Staff. 224p. 1989. pap. 14.95 (*0-201-51761-2*) Addison-Wesley.

Speaking of New England: The Place & Her People: 72 Poems by 56 of Her Poets, Past & Present. Ed. by Richard Aldridge. LC 93-15597. 112p. 1993. pap. 12.95 (*0-945980-41-8*) Nrth Country Pr.

Speaking of Nuclear Energy: Highlights of Proceedings from IAEA Public Information Regional Seminars. Ed. by Valerie A. Gillen. 103p. (Orig.). (C). 1994. pap. text ed. 30.00 (*0-7881-1577-4*) DIANE Pub.

Speaking of Numbers: Skillbuilding in English & Arithmetic Worktext 1. Daniel Rusthoi. (Illus.). (gr. 9-12). 1994. pap. text ed. 11.95 (*0-8325-0468-8*, Natl Textbk) NTC Pub Grp.

Speaking of Numbers: Skillbuilding in English & Arithmetic Worktext 1, Answer Keys. Daniel Rusthoi. (Illus.). (YA). (gr. 9-12). 1990. teacher ed. 2.65 (*0-8325-0469-6*, Natl Textbk) NTC Pub Grp.

Speaking of Operations. Irvin S. Cobb. LC 71-92422. 65p. 1928. reprint ed. 39.00 (*0-403-00556-6*) Scholarly.

Speaking of Our Past: A Narrative History of Owings Mills, Maryland, 1640-1988. Marie Forbes. (Illus.). xiv, 390p. (Orig.). 1988. pap. 20.00 (*1-55613-142-9*) Heritage Bk.

Speaking of Pianists. 3rd ed. Abram Chasins. (Quality Paperbacks Ser.). x, 330p. 1982. reprint ed. pap. 13.95 (*0-306-80168-X*) Da Capo.

Speaking of Poets: Interviews with Poets Who Write for Children & Young Adults. Jeffrey S. Copeland. 128p. 1993. pap. 12.95 (*0-8141-4622-8*) NCTE.

Speaking of Poets 2: More Interviews with Poets Who Write for Children & Young Adults. Jeffrey S. Copeland et al. LC 94-47005. 204p. 1995. pap. 15.95 (*0-8141-4620-1*) NCTE.

Speaking of Principle. Byrns. 1995. pap. text ed. write for info. (*0-07-009624-4*) McGraw.

Speaking of Race, Speaking of Sex: Hate Speech, Civil Rights, & Civil Liberties. Henry Louis Gates, Jr. et al. 299p. (C). 1995. 40.00 (*0-8147-3070-1*) NYU Pr.

Speaking of Race, Speaking of Sex: Hate Speech, Civil Rights, & Civil Liberties. Henry Louis Gates, Jr. et al. 299p. (C). 1996. pap. 18.95 (*0-8147-3090-6*) NYU Pr.

Speaking of Reading. Rosenthal. LC 95-5102. 232p. 1997. pap. write for info. (*0-435-08118-7*, 08118) Heinemann.

Speaking of Reading. Compiled by Nadine Rosenthal. LC 95-5102. 213p. 1995. 23.95 (*0-435-08119-5*, 08119) Heinemann.

Speaking of Sadness: Depression, Disconnection & the Meanings of Illness. David A. Karp. 240p. 1996. 30.00 (*0-19-509486-7*) OUP.

***Speaking of Sadness: Depression, Disconnection, & the Meanings of Illness.** David A. Karp. 256p. 1997. reprint ed. pap. text ed. 12.95 (*0-19-511386-1*) OUP.

Speaking of Science: Proceedings of the Royal Institution, Vol. 51. 176p. 1979. pap. 34.00 (*0-85066-186-2*) Taylor & Francis.

Speaking of Sex. Antony Grey. 320p. 1993. pap. text ed. 13.95 (*0-304-32698-4*, LPC InBook) Cassell.

***Speaking of Sex: The Denial of Gender Inequality.** LC 96-49905. 1997. write for info. (*0-674-83177-2*) HUP.

Speaking of Silence: Christians & Buddhists on the Contemplative Way. Ed. by Susan Walker. 336p. 1987. pap. 12.95 (*0-8091-2880-2*) Paulist Pr.

Speaking of Silents: First Ladies of the Screen. William M. Drew. LC 89-9025. (Illus.). 312p. 1989. 39.95 (*0-911572-81-3*); pap. 24.95 (*0-911572-74-0*) Madison Bks UPA.

Speaking of Siva. Thomas Wyatt. Tr. & Intro. by A. K. Ramanujian. (Classics Ser.). 208p. 1973. pap. 11.95 (*0-14-044270-7*, Penguin Classics) Viking Penguin.

Speaking of Soap Operas. Robert C. Allen. LC 84-21894. x, 245p. (C). 1985. 39.95 (*0-8078-1643-4*); pap. 14.95 (*0-8078-4129-3*) U of NC Pr.

Speaking of Speaking: Marking Direct Discourse in the Hebrew Bible. Samuel A. Meier. LC 92-16149. (Supplements to Vetus Testamentum Ser.: Vol. 46). xvi, 383p. 1992. 126.00 (*90-04-09602-7*) E J Brill.

Speaking of Summit: An Oral History Handbook. Stephen H. Paschen. 55p. (Orig.). 1989. pap. 2.95 (*0-9621895-2-9*) Summit Cty Hist Soc.

Speaking of Survival. Daniel B. Freeman. (Illus.). 1982. pap. 10.50 (*0-19-503110-5*) OUP.

Speaking of Survival. Daniel B. Freeman. (Illus.). 1983. audio 17.50 (*0-19-434105-4*) OUP.

Speaking of Survival. Daniel B. Freeman. (Illus.). 1993. 9.95 (*0-88336-157-4*); audio 17.50 (*0-88336-197-3*) OUP.

***Speaking of the Middle Ages - Parlez du Moyen Age.** Paul Zumthor. LC 85-16545. (Regents Studies in Medieval Culture). 114p. 1986. reprint ed. pap. 32.50 (*0-608-03479-7*, 2064191) Bks Demand.

***Speaking of the Short Story: Interviews with Contemporary Writers.** Farhat Iftekharuddin & Mary Rohrberger. LC 96-54886. 1997. write for info. (*0-87805-970-9*); pap. write for info. (*0-87805-971-7*) U Pr of Miss.

Speaking of the University: Two Decades at Vanderbilt. Alexander Heard. LC 94-48422. 400p. (Orig.). 1995. 29.95 (*0-8265-1264-X*); pap. 15.95 (*0-8265-1265-8*) Vanderbilt U Pr.

Speaking of Washington: Facts, Firsts, Folklore. John L. Moore. 288p. 1993. 36.95 (*0-87187-762-7*); pap. 17.95 (*0-87187-741-4*) Congr Quarterly.

Speaking of Words: A Language Reader. 3rd ed. James MacKillop & Donna Woolfolk. LC 81-6734. 324p. (C). 1986. pap. text ed. 20.75 (*0-03-003953-3*) HB Coll Pubs.

Speaking of Writing. (J). 1993. pap. 7.95 (*0-590-73437-7*) Scholastic Inc.

Speaking of Writing: Selected Hopwood Lectures. Ed. by Nicholas Delbanco. 352p. (C). 1990. reprint ed. pap. text ed. 15.95 (*0-472-06422-3*) U of Mich Pr.

Speaking of Your Money: Great Financial Advice from Harry S. Gross. Harry Gross. (Illus.). 144p. (Orig.). 1996. pap. 9.95 (*0-8362-7034-7*) Andrews & McMeel.

Speaking on Issues. Ellen W. Echeverria. 240p. (C). 1987. pap. text ed. 19.00 (*0-03-003433-7*) HB Coll Pubs.

Speaking on Stage: Interviews with Contemporary American Playwrights. Ed. by Philip C. Kolin & Colby H. Kullman. LC 95-21171. (Illus.). 440p. (Orig.). 1996. pap. text ed. 29.95 (*0-8173-0796-6*) U of Ala Pr.

Speaking Out. 74p. 1995. write for info. (*1-888258-01-2*) Evangel Concern Wstrn.

Speaking Out. Ken Hanes. 1997. pap. write for info. (*0-517-88791-6*) Random Hse Value.

Speaking Out. Susan Kuklin. 192p. 1993. pap. 8.95 (*0-399-22532-3*, Putnam) Putnam Pub Group.

Speaking Out: Early Childhood Advocacy. Stacie G. Goffin & Joan Lombardi. LC 88-62479. 122p. 1988. pap. 6.00 (*0-935989-19-6*, NAEYC #270) Natl Assn Child Ed.

Speaking Out: Jewish Voices from United Germany. Ed. by Susan Stern. LC 95-15752. (Illus.). 271p. 1995. 19.95 (*1-883695-08-2*) Edition Q.

Speaking Out: Partners in Advocacy - Family Action Guide. Epilepsy Foundation of America Staff. 50p. 1992. pap. 9.95 (*0-916570-07-X*) Epilepsy Foundation of America.

S

An Asterisk (*) at the beginning of an entry indicates that the title is appearing in BIP for the first time.

Speaking Out: Partners in Advocacy - Tools & Resources. Epilepsy Foundation of America Staff. 89p. 1992. pap. 10.95 (0-916570-08-8) Epilepsy Foundation of America.

Speaking Out: Partners in Advocacy - Understanding the Process. Epilepsy Foundation of America Staff. 20p. 1992. pap. 5.95 (0-916570-09-6) Epilepsy Foundation of America.

***Speaking Out: Sex, Law, Politics & Society 1954-95.** Antony Grey. (Lesbian & Gay Studies). 224p. 1997. 79.50 (0-304-33340-9) Cassell.

***Speaking Out: Sex, Law, Politics & Society 1954-95.** Antony Grey. (Lesbian & Gay Studies). 224p. 1997. pap. 27.50 (0-304-33344-1) Cassell.

Speaking Out: The Reagan Presidency from Inside the White House. Larry Speakes & Robert Pack. 416p. 1989. mass mkt. 4.95 (0-380-70726-8) Avon.

***Speaking Out: Women's Economic Empowerment in South Asia.** Ed. by Marilyn Carr et al. 252p. (Orig.). 1996. pap. 18.95 (1-85339-382-7) Women Ink.

Speaking Out for Psychiatry: A Handbook for Involvement with the Mass Media. Group for the Advancement of Psychiatry Staff. LC 87-24229. (Group for the Advancement of Psychiatry, Symposium Ser.: No. 124). 124p. reprint ed. pap. 35.40 (0-7837-2095-5, 2042371) Bks Demand.

Speaking Out on Health: An Anthology. Ed. by Literacy Volunteers of New York City Staff. (New Writers' Voices Ser.). 64p. (Orig.). 1989. pap. text ed. 3.50 (0-929631-05-6, Signal Hill) New Readers.

Speaking Out on Home & Family: An Anthology of Writing by New Writers. Ed. by Literacy Volunteers of New York City Staff. (New Writers' Voices Ser.). (Illus.). 64p. (Orig.). 1990. pap. text ed. 3.50 (0-929631-08-0, Signal Hill) New Readers.

Speaking-out on Sod-House Times! Pauline N. Diede. Ed. by John H. Gengler. Tr. by Abbey Press Printing Staff. (Pioneer Life Bks.: Vol. III). (Illus.). 112p. (Orig.). 1985. pap. text ed. 6.95 (0-685-26961-2) P Neher Diede.

Speaking out on Work: An Anthology of Writing by New Writers. Ed. by Literacy Volunteers of New York City Staff. (New Writers' Voices Ser.). (Illus.). 64p. (Orig.). 1991. pap. text ed. 3.15 (0-929631-35-8, Signal Hill) New Readers.

Speaking Personally: Quizzes & Questionnaires for Fluency Practice. Gillian P. Ladousse. 113p. 1983. pap. text ed. 13.95 (0-521-28869-X) Cambridge U Pr.

Speaking Pictures: English Emblem Books & Renaissance Culture. Michael Bath. LC 93-10073. (Medieval & Renaissance Library). 1993. write for info. (0-582-06197-0) Longman.

Speaking Pictures: English Emblem Books & Renaissance Culture. Michael Bath. LC 93-10073. (Medieval & Renaissance Library). 1994. pap. text ed. write for info. (0-582-06196-2) Longman.

Speaking, Relating, & Learning: A Study of Hawaiian Children at Home & at School. Stephen T. Boggs. LC 85-7388. 216p. (C). 1986. text ed. 73.25 (0-89391-330-8) Ablex Pub.

***Speaking Respect.** Abel. 1997. pap. 17.95 (0-226-00057-5) U Ch Pr.

***Speaking Respect.** Abel. 1997. 29.95 (0-226-00056-7) U Ch Pr.

Speaking Secrets of the Masters: The Personal Techniques Used by 22 of the Worlds' Top Professional Speakers. Speakers Roundtable Staff. (Illus.). 274p. 1995. 21.95 (0-937539-14-7) Executive Bks.

Speaking Silences: Stillness & Voice in Modern Thought & Jewish Tradition. Andrew V. Ettin. LC 94-9178. 256p. (C). 1994. text ed. 35.00 (0-8139-1509-0) U Pr of Va.

Speaking Skills. (Open Learning for Supervisory Management Ser.). 1986. pap. text ed. 19.50 (0-08-034032-6, Pergamon Pr) Elsevier.

Speaking Skills. (Open Learning for Supervisory Management Ser.). 1986. pap. text ed. 19.50 (0-08-070070-5, Pergamon Pr) Elsevier.

Speaking Skills. Masters. (YA - Adult Education Ser.). 1993. pap. 5.95 (0-538-70778-X) S-W Pub.

Speaking Skills. 2nd ed. (Open Learning Super Ser.). 1991. pap. text ed. 26.00 (0-08-041570-9, Pergamon Pr) Elsevier.

Speaking Skills for Bankers. Lyle Sussman & Samuel D. Deep. (Illus.). 1992. student ed. 49.00 (0-685-62687-3) Am Bankers.

Speaking Skills for Prospective Teachers. 2nd ed. Donald W. Klopf & Ronald E. Cambra. 432p. (C). 1991. pap. 25.95 (0-89582-219-9) Morton Pub.

Speaking Solutions: Interaction, Presentation, Listening, & Pronunciation. Candace Matthews & Phillip Edmondson. 240p. 1994. pap. text ed. 18.75 (0-13-701229-2) P-H.

Speaking Statistics. Cecily K. Bodnar. pap. write for info. (0-13-030180-9) P-H.

Speaking Stones: Communiques from the Intifada Underground. Shaul Mishal. (Contemporary Issues in the Middle East Ser.). 272p. 1994. text ed. 45.00 (0-8156-2606-1); pap. text ed. 19.95 (0-8156-2607-X) Syracuse U Pr.

***Speaking Technically: A Handbook for Scientists, Engineers & Physicians.** 115p. 1996. pap. 8.00 (1-86094-034-X) World Scientific Pub.

Speaking Terms. Mary Wesley. 128p. (J). (gr. 7 up). 1994. 14.95 (0-87951-524-4) Overlook Pr.

Speaking the Christian God: The Holy Trinity & the Challenge of Feminism. Ed. by Alvin F. Kimel, Jr. LC 92-17173. viii, 336p. (Orig.). 1992. pap. 22.00 (0-8028-0612-0) Eerdmans.

Speaking the Gospel Today: A Theology for Evangelism. Robert Kolb. 1995. 15.99 (0-570-04258-5, 53-1018) Concordia.

Speaking the Language of Desire: The Films of Carl Dreyer. Raymond Carney. (Illus.). 250p. (C). 1989. 64.95 (0-521-37163-5); pap. text ed. 21.95 (0-521-37807-9) Cambridge U Pr.

Speaking the Language of Power: Communication, Collaboration, & Advocacy--Translating Ethnography into Action. Ed. by David M. Fetterman. LC 93-729. (Social Research & Educational Studies: No. 11). 192p. 1993. 75.00 (0-7507-0202-8, Falmer Pr); pap. 26.00 (0-7507-0203-6, Falmer Pr) Taylor & Francis.

Speaking the Language of Respiratory Care. California College for Health Sciences Staff. LC 85-4141. 48p. (C). 1991. pap. 22.95 incl. audio (0-933195-00-1) CA College Health Sci.

***Speaking the Other Self: American Women Writers.** Jeanne C. Reesman. LC 96-48850. 1997. 50.00 (0-8203-1903-1); pap. 24.95 (0-8203-1909-0) U of Ga Pr.

Speaking the Speech. 2nd ed. Edwin Cohen. (C). 1983. pap. text ed. 26.75 (0-03-062006-6) HB Coll Pubs.

Speaking the Truth in Love. Kenneth C. Haugk & Ruth Koch. 1992. pap. 10.95 (0-9633831-1-6) Stephen Minist.

Speaking the Truth in Love: The Purposes of Christian Educational Services. Mark H. Graeser et al. 61p. 1992. pap. 4.00 (0-9628971-1-6) Chris Ed Ser.

Speaking the Truth in Love to Mormons. Mark Cares. LC 93-83034. 300p. (Orig.). 1993. pap. 11.99 (0-8100-0487-9, 15N0545) Northwest Pub.

Speaking the Unspeakable: A Poetics of Obscenity. Peter Michelson. LC 91-46954. (SUNY Series, The Margins of Literature). 312p. 1992. pap. text ed. 24.95 (0-7914-1224-5) State U NY Pr.

Speaking the Unspeakable: A Poetics of Obscenity. Peter Michelson. LC 91-46954. (SUNY Series, The Margins of Literature). 312p. 1992. text ed. 74.50 (0-7914-1223-7) State U NY Pr.

Speaking the Word to Modern Man. David Mendez. 72p. (Orig.). 1983. pap. 9.00 (1-56428-001-2) Logos Intl Pub.

Speaking the Words Anthology. Ed. by Bertha Rogers. 48p. 1994. pap. 5.00 (0-9646844-0-3) Bright Hill.

***Speaking Their Language Using Astrology: Communicating Clearly Using Astrology.** Patricia G. Finlayson. (Illus.). 1997. write for info. (1-878535-25-0) De Seta-Finlayson.

***Speaking Through My Skin.** Bruce A. Jacobs. 1997. pap. 10.95 (0-87013-455-8) Mich St U Pr.

Speaking to a Group Mastering the Skill of Public Speaking. Marian K. Woodall. LC 89-27258. (Illus.). 224p. (Orig.). 1989. pap. 16.95 (0-941159-02-7) Prof Busn Comns.

Speaking to an Audience. J. Jerome Zolten. (C). 1985. pap. write for info. (0-02-432020-X, Macmillan Coll) P-H.

Speaking to God: Prayers for Moments of Joy & Times of Need. Nancy Benvenga. LC 92-97150. 144p. (Orig.). 1993. pap. 5.95 (0-87793-502-5) Ave Maria.

Speaking to Groups: Eyeball to Eyeball. James B. Anderson. (Illus.). 368p. (Orig.). 1989. 29.95 (0-922749-05-1); pap. 19.95 (0-922749-06-X) Wyndmoor Pr.

Speaking to One Another: An Anthology by New Writers. Reader's Digest Editors. (New Writers' Voices Ser.). 64p. 1993. pap. text ed. 3.15 (1-56853-007-2, Signal Hill) New Readers.

Speaking to Persuade. Breaden. (C). 1995. pap. text ed. 27.75 (0-15-502132-X) HB Coll Pubs.

Speaking to Power: Gender Politics in the Western Pacific. Lynn B. Wilson. LC 94-17760. 256p. (C). 1995. pap. 18.95 (0-415-90924-4, B3849) Routledge.

Speaking to Power: Gender Politics in the Western Pacific. Lynn B. Wilson. LC 94-17760. 256p. (C). (gr. 13). 1995. text ed. 49.95 (0-415-90923-6, B3845) Routledge.

Speaking to Strangers. J. Day Mason. (Illus.). 105p. 1987. 40.00 (0-933858-22-1) Kennebec River.

***Speaking to the Heart.** McCarty. 1997. pap. 12.00 (0-205-26894-3) P-H.

Speaking to Think/Thinking to Speak: The Importance of Talk in the Learning Process. Virginia O'Keefe. LC 94-45175. 183p. 1995. pap. text ed. 25.00 (0-86709-358-7, 0358) Boynton Cook Pubs.

Speaking to You of Grief. Martha O. Williams. 1988. pap. 3.25 (0-89137-446-9) Quality Pubns.

Speaking Tree: A Study of Indian Culture & Society. Richard Lannoy. LC 74-158205. (Illus.). 494p. 1974. pap. 14.95 (0-19-519754-2) OUP.

***Speaking Truth to Power.** Anita Hill. LC 97-1316. 1997. write for info. (0-385-47625-6) Doubleday.

Speaking Truth to Power. Robert J. Myers. (Eleventh Morgenthau Memorial Lectures). 23p. 1991. pap. 4.00 (0-87641-116-2) Carnegie Ethics & Intl Affairs.

Speaking Truth to Power. Aaron Wildavsky. 464p. 1987. pap. 24.95 (0-88738-697-0) Transaction Pubs.

Speaking Truth to Power: An Essay. Manning Marable. 268p. 1996. text ed. 24.50 (0-8133-8827-9) Westview.

***Speaking Truth to Power: Essays on Race, Resistance & Radicalism.** Manning Marable. 288p. 1996. pap. 14.95 (0-8133-8828-7) Westview.

Speaking Two Languages. Bethanie L. Boswell. LC 95-2016. (Growing up Latino Ser.). (J). (gr. 2-6). 1995. write for info. (0-86625-543-5) Rourke Pubns.

Speaking Two Languages: Traditional Disciplines & Contemporary Theory in Medieval Studies. Ed. by Allen J. Frantzen. LC 90-9638. (SUNY Series in Medieval Studies). 313p. (C). 1991. text ed. 64.50 (0-7914-0505-2); pap. text ed. 21.95 (0-7914-0506-0) State U NY Pr.

Speaking Up: A Book for Every Woman Who Talks. Janet Stone & Jane Bachner. (Illus.). 216p. pap. 12.95 (0-7867-0116-1) Carroll & Graf.

Speaking Up: What to Say to Your Boss & Everyone Else Who Gets on Your Case. Mark Ruskin. 180p. 1993. pap. 7.95 (1-55850-258-0) Adams Media.

Speaking up at Work. 1993. 9.95 (0-88336-193-0); teacher ed. 5.95 (0-88336-194-9) OUP.

Speaking up at Work. Catherine Robinson & Jenise Rowekamp. (Illus.). 180p. 1985. pap. 10.50 (0-19-434196-8) OUP.

Speaking up at Work. Catherine Robinson & Jenise Rowekamp. (Illus.). 180p. 1985. teacher ed. 6.95 (0-19-434197-6) OUP.

Speaking up, Speaking Out: A Kid's Guide to Making Speeches, Oral Reports, & Conversation. Steven Otfinoski. LC 96-509. (Illus.). 80p. (J). (gr. 5-8). 1996. lib. bdg. 17.90 (1-56294-345-6) Millbrook Pr.

***Speaking up, Speaking Out: A Kid's Guide to Making Speeches, Oral Reports, & Conversation.** Steven Otfinoski. (Illus.). 80p. (J). (gr. 4-8). 1997. pap. 8.95 (0-7613-0138-0) Millbrook Pr.

Speaking with a Purpose. 3rd ed. Arthur L. Koch. LC 94-20556. 1994. pap. text ed. 19.00 (0-13-110710-0) Allyn.

***Speaking with a Purpose.** 4th ed. Koch. LC 97-11119. 1997. pap. text ed. 18.00 (0-205-27301-7) P-H.

Speaking with a Thesis. Jimmy E. Cato. 256p. (C). 1993. per. 27.24 (0-8403-8618-4) Kendall-Hunt.

Speaking with Beads: Zulu Arts from Southern Africa. Eleanor Preston-Whyte. LC 94-60280. (Illus.). 96p. (Orig.). 1994. pap. 19.95 (0-500-27757-5) Thames Hudson.

Speaking with Confidence: A Guidebook for Public Speakers. Wanda Vassallo. 176p. (Orig.). 1990. pap. 9.95 (1-55870-147-8, Betrwy Bks) F & W Pubns Inc.

Speaking with Confidence: A Practical Guide. 7th ed. McKiernan. LC 95-12310. (C). 1995. write for info. (0-673-97118-X) Addson-Wesley Educ.

Speaking with Confidence: A Practical Guide. 7th ed. Albert J. Vasile & Harold K. Mintz. LC 95-12310. (Illus.). 432p. (C). 1996. pap. text ed. 32.95 (0-673-99718-9) Addson-Wesley Educ.

Speaking with Deaf-Blind Children. Judy Katz-Levine. (Illus.). 20p. (Orig.). (C). 1983. pap. 4.25 (0-930707-00-1) Free Begin Pr.

Speaking with Impact. Thomas Rizzo. 144p. 1994. per., pap. text ed. 19.95 (0-7872-0261-4) Kendall-Hunt.

Speaking with Magic: How to Grab An Audience's Attention & Hold It! Michael Jeffreys. (Illus.). 277p. (Orig.). 1989. pap. 24.95 (1-878407-01-5) Powerful Magic Pub.

Speaking with Signs: Children's Object Lessons for Lent & Easter. 2nd ed. Wesley T. Runk. (Illus.). 24p. (Orig.). 1995. pap. 4.25 (0-7880-0371-2) CSS OH.

Speaking with Style: The Socio-Linguistic Skills of Children. Elaine S. Andersen. 176p. 1989. 45.00 (0-415-02256-8) Routledge.

Speaking with Style: The Sociolinguistic Skills of Children. Elaine S. Andersen. LC 91-30980. 212p. (C). 1992. pap. text ed. 17.95 (0-415-07502-5, A6736) Routledge.

Speaking with the Dead: Development of Afro-Latin Religion among Puerto Ricans in the United States. Andres I. Perez y Mena. LC 91-8469. (Immigrant Communities & Ethnic Minorities in the U. S. & Canada Ser.: No. 75). 1991. 55.00 (0-404-19485-0) AMS Pr.

***Speaking with the Devil.** Carl Goldberg. 1997. pap. 13.95 (0-14-023739-9) Viking Penguin.

Speaking with the Devil: A Dialogue with Evil. Carl Goldberg. LC 95-34239. 336p. 1996. pap. 27.95 (0-670-85557-X, Viking) Viking Penguin.

Speaking with the Sun. Ed. by Stephanie Dowrick & Jane Parkin. 228p. 1991. pap. 12.95 (0-04-442296-2, Pub. by Allen & Unwin Aust Pty AT) Paul & Co Pubs.

Speaking with Tongues: Historically & Psychologically Considered. George B. Cutten. 1927. 59.50 (0-685-69805-X) Elliots Bks.

Speaking Without Fear. rev. ed. Dale L. Minnick. 194p. 1995. pap. 14.95 (0-9633476-8-3) Desert Rain.

Speaking, Writing & Reading: Teaching Children to Read & Write Naturally. Jack Friedland. 128p. (Orig.). 1996. spiral bd. 16.95 (0-9642390-2-7) New Gateway Pr.

Speaking Your Best: The Beginners Guide to Public Speaking. Kevin Boland. Ed. by Computype, Inc. Staff & Karen Hansell. 144p. (Orig.). 1996. pap. 12.95 (0-9645364-0-4) Great Bks.

Speaking Your Mind: Public Speaking. Frank Dance & Carol C. Zak-Dance. 384p. (C). 1995. per., pap. text ed. 36.69 (0-7872-1694-1) Kendall-Hunt.

Speaking Your Mind in One Hundered-One Different Situations. Don Gabor. 224p. 1994. pap. 11.00 (0-671-79505-8, Fireside) S&S Trade.

***Speaking/Writing of God: Jewish Philosophical Reflections on the Life with Others.** Michael D. Oppenheim. LC 96-41186. (SUNY Series in Jewish Philosophy). 201p. (C). 1997. text ed. 59.50 (0-7914-3457-5); pap. text ed. 19.95 (0-7914-3458-3) State U NY Pr.

SpeakUp! Spanish Accent Elimination: Learn to Speak Standard American English. Sam Chwat. LC 93-22954. (ENG & SPA.). 1994. 22.00 (0-517-59233-9, Crown) Crown Pub Group.

SpeakUp! American Regional Accent Elimination: Learn to Speak Standard American English. Sam Chwat. LC 93-22956. 1994. 22.00 (0-517-59231-2, Crown) Crown Pub Group.

Speakup! Asian Accent Elimination: Learn to Speak Standard American English. Sam Chwat. LC 93-25235. 1994. 22.00 (0-517-59232-0, Crown) Crown Pub Group.

Spear. James Herbert. 1990. pap. 4.50 (0-451-16666-3) NAL-Dutton.

Spear & the Spindle: Ancestors of Sir Francis Bryan, 1550. T. A. Fuller. 146p. (Orig.). 1993. pap. 23.50 (1-55613-842-3) Heritage Bk.

***Spear Fishing & Underwater Hunting Handbook: Beginner Through Advanced.** B. Allen Patrick. (Illus.). 128p. (Orig.). 1996. pap. 17.95 (1-890079-11-1) Active Advent.

Spear-it Land. Mary Preston. (Illus.). 152p. (Orig.). pap. 12.95 (0-9636819-0-7) Kairos Books.

Spear-Nosed Bat. Pamela J. Gerholdt. (J). (gr. k-3). 1995. lib. bdg. 13.98 (1-56239-502-5) Abdo & Dghtrs.

Spear of Destiny. Trevor Ravenscroft. LC 82-60165. 400p. 1982. pap. 12.95 (0-87728-547-0) Weiser.

***Spear of Golgotha.** Richard D. Greenwald. (Orig.). 1997. pap. 6.99 (0-9586627-0-3, Pub. by Montrose AT) Baker & Taylor.

Spear of Heaven. Judith Tarr. 352p. 1995. 5.99 (0-8125-3034-9) Tor Bks.

Speare Family, from 1642: Genealogical Records of Certain Branches. C. L. Speare. (Illus.). 294p. 1992. reprint ed. pap. 46.00 (0-8328-2735-5); reprint ed. lib. bdg. 56.00 (0-8328-2734-7) Higginson Bk Co.

***Spearfishing for Skin & Scuba Divers.** Steven M. Barsky. LC 97-71104. (Illus.). 224p. (Orig.). 1997. pap. 14.95 (0-941332-59-4, D927) Best Pub Co.

***Spearhead.** Richard Murff. 300p. (Orig.). Date not set. mass mkt. 7.99 (1-889501-83-2, Appaloosa) Sovereign.

Spearhead: A Novel. Peter Driscoll. 304p. 1989. 17.95 (0-316-19341-0) Little.

Spearhead: The World War History of the 5th Marine Division. 11th ed. Howard M. Conner. (Elite Unit Ser.). 325p. 1987. reprint ed. 39.95 (0-89839-103-2) Battery Pr.

Spearhead for Blitzkrieg: Luftwaffe Operations in Support of the Army, 1939-1945. Paul Deichmann. Ed. & Intro. by Alfred Price. 160p. 1996. 29.95 (1-85367-241-6, Pub. by Greenhill Bks UK) Stackpole.

Spearhead Governatore: Remembrances of the Campaign in Italy. William A. Lessa. LC 85-50821. (Illus.). 272p. 1985. 31.25 (0-89003-163-0) Undena Pubns.

Spearhead in the West: The Third Armored Division, 1941-1945. (Divisional Ser.: No. 12). (Illus.). 260p. 1980. reprint ed. 39.95 (0-89839-030-3) Battery Pr.

Spearheaders: A Personal History of Darby's Rangers. James Altieri. LC 79-18951. 1979. reprint ed. 25.95 (0-89201-061-4) Zenger Pub.

Spearheads for Reform: The Social Settlements & the Progressive Movement, 1890 to 1914. Allen F. Davis. 340p. (C). 1985. reprint ed. pap. 17.00 (0-8135-1073-2) Rutgers U Pr.

Spearless Leader: Senator Borah & the Progressive Movement in the 1920s. Leroy Ashby. LC 74-170963. 336p. 95.80 (0-8357-9698-1, 2011733) Bks Demand.

Spearplay. David Huey. LC 85-52271. 180p. (Orig.). 1986. pap. 7.95 (0-86568-073-6, 220) Unique Pubns.

Spears of Twilight: Life & Death in the Amazon Jungle. Philippe Descola. Tr. by Janet Lloyd. (Illus.). 400p. Date not set. 25.00 (1-56584-228-6) New Press NY.

***Spec-Lit: Speculative Fiction.** Ed. by Phyllis Eisenstein. (Illus.). 176p. (Orig.). 1997. pap. 6.95 (0-932026-45-1) Columbia College Chi.

***Spec Ops: Case Studies in Special Operations Warfare, Theory & Practice.** William H. Mcraven. LC 94-46452. 1996. pap. text ed. 17.95 (0-89141-600-5) Presidio Pr.

Spec Writers' Handbook: A Textbook & Reference Book for Writing Architectural Specifications. John A. Weyl. 220p. (Orig.). 1989. pap. 39.95 (0-9623293-0-4); 3.5 hd 39.95 (0-9623293-1-2) Pacific Odyssey.

Spec Writers' Handbook: A Textbook & Reference Book for Writing Architectural Specifications. 2nd ed. John A. Weyl. 222p. (Orig.). (C). 1993. pap. text ed. 39.95 (0-9623293-7-1); disk 39.95 (0-9623293-8-X) Pacific Odyssey.

Specht Journal: A Military Journal of the Burgoyne Campaign. Ed. by Mary C. Lynn. Tr. by Helga Doblin et al. LC 94-23828. (Contributions in Military Studies: Vol. 158). 224p. 1995. text ed. 57.95 (0-313-29446-1, Greenwood Pr) Greenwood.

Special Access Required: A Practitioner's Guide to Law Enforcement Intelligence Literature. Henry W. Prunckun, Jr. LC 90-46292. (Illus.). 212p. 1990. 27.50 (0-8108-2371-3) Scarecrow.

Special Agent. 8th ed. E. P. Steinberg. 272p. 1996. 19.95 (0-02-861057-1) Macmillan.

Special Agent DEA. (Career Examination Ser.: C-3748). 1994. pap. 29.95 (0-8373-3748-8) Nat Learn.

Special Agent (Department of Justice) Jack Rudman. (Career Examination Ser.: C-3287). 1994. pap. 29.95 (0-8373-3287-7) Nat Learn.

Special Agent (FBI) Jack Rudman. (Career Examination Ser.: C-1060). 1994. pap. 29.95 (0-8373-1060-1) Nat Learn.

Special Agent in the Pacific, WW II: Counter-Intelligence-Military, Politcal & Economic. William B. Simpson. LC 94-41772. (Illus.). 230p. 1995. 18.95 (0-944957-77-3) Rivercross Pub.

Special Agent (INS) Jack Rudman. (Career Examination Ser.: C-3490). 1994. Cloth bdg. avail. pap. 29.95 (0-8373-3490-X) Nat Learn.

***Special Agent Scully: The Gillian Anderson Files.** Malcolm Butt. (Illus.). 112p. 1997. pap. 15.95 (0-85965-254-8, Pub. by Plexus UK) Publishers Group.

Special Agent, U. S. Treasury Department: Treasury Enforcement Agent Test. 6th ed. Eve P. Steinberg. 272p. 1989. pap. 16.00 (0-13-930561-0, Arco) Macmillan Gen Ref.

Special Agent (Wildlife) Jack Rudman. (Career Examination Ser.: C-2221). 1994. pap. 29.95 (0-8373-2221-9) Nat Learn.

Special Aging Populations & Systems Linkages. Ed. by M. Joanna Mellor. LC 96-7980. (Journal of Gerontological Social Work: Vol. 25, Nos. 1/2). 155p. 1996. 39.95 (1-56024-831-9) Haworth Pr.

Special Air Service. James Shortt. (Men-at-Arms Ser.: No. 116). (Illus.). 48p. pap. 11.95 (0-85045-396-8, 9049, Pub. by Osprey UK) Stackpole.

Special Analysis of City & County Taxes. 1992. 10.45 (0-685-61057-8) U VA Ctr Pub Serv.

An Asterisk (*) at the beginning of an entry indicates that the title is appearing in BIP for the first time.

***Special & Compensatory Programs: The Administrator's Role.** Floyd Boschee et al. LC 97-60882. 285p. 1997. text ed. 49.95 (*1-56676-537-4*) Technomic.

Special & Spurious Solutions of X(T) equals -aF(X(T-1)), Vol. 310. Roger Nussbaum & Heinz-Otto Peitgen. LC 84-14568. (Memoirs of the American Mathematical Society Ser.: No. 51/310). 129p. 1984. pap. 21.00 (*0-8218-2311-6*, MEMO/51/310) Am Math.

Special Angel. Lighten-Up Staff. (Small Wonders Ser.). 120p. 1994. spiral bd. 4.99 (*1-879127-50-4*) Lighten Up Enter.

Special Anniversary Issue: Highlights from the Past. (Special Issues of the Anthropology & Education Quarterly Ser.: Vol. 15, No. 1). 1984. 7.50 (*0-317-66343-7*) Am Anthro Assn.

Special Applications & Advanced Techniques for Crack Size Determination: Symposium on Special Applications & Advanced Techniques for Crack Size Determination (1993: Atlanta, GA), STP 1251. Ed. by John J. Ruschau et al. LC 94-49349. (Special Technical Publication Ser.: No. 1251). (Illus.). 163p. 1995. pap. 62.00 (*0-8031-2003-6*, 04-012510-30) ASTM.

***Special Applications of REBT: A Therapist's Casebook.** Joseph Yankura & Windy Dryden. LC 97-23193. 1997. write for info. (*0-8261-9801-5*) Springer Pub.

Special Artist in American Culture: A Biography of Frank Hamilton Taylor (1846-1927) Nancy L. Gustke. LC 93-41678. (American University Studies, Series XX: Vol. 21). 231p. (C). 1995. text ed. 51.95 (*0-8204-2348-3*) P Lang Pubng.

Special Artist's Handbook: Art Activities & Adaptive Aids for Handicapped Children. Susan Rodriguez. LC 84-4704. (Illus.). 288p. (Orig.). 1984. pap. 17.95 (*0-13-826355-8*) P-H.

***Special Artist's Handbook: Art Activities & Adaptive Aids for Handicapped Students.** Susan Rodriguez. (Illus.). 278p. (J). 1988. teacher ed., pap. 21.50 (*0-86651-476-7*, 11907) Seymour Pubns.

Special Aspects of the Therapy for Gastric Carcinoma. Ed. by R. Kirchner & K. Maruyama. (Journal Ser.: Vol. 11, No. 2, 1994). (Illus.). 82p. 1995. pap. 68.00 (*3-8055-6134-2*) S Karger.

Special Assessment Procedures for Cities & Villages. Michigan Municipal League Staff. (Ordinance Analysis Ser.: No. 11). 1987. pap. 12.50 (*0-317-00871-4*) MI Municipal.

Special Assessments: A Study in Municipal Finance. Victor Rosewater. LC 68-56686. (Columbia University. Studies in the Social Sciences: No. 7). reprint ed. 29.50 (*0-404-51007-8*) AMS Pr.

Special Beginnings: For Parents of NICU Babies. Joy Johnson & Marv Johnson. (Illus.). 24p. 1982. pap. 3.25 (*1-56123-027-8*) Centering Corp.

***Special Bites.** Janet A. McIlhenny. (Illus.). vi, 112p. (Orig.). 1996. pap. write for info. (*0-9657631-0-2*, 6126) J A McIlhenny.

Special Branch: The Spy Novel from 1890 to 1980. Leroy L. Panek. LC 81-80214. 288p. 22.95 (*0-87972-178-2*) Bowling Green Univ Popular Press.

Special Capacity. Michael Friedman. 88p. (Orig.). 1993. pap. 8.95 (*0-9624653-1-3*) Intermezzo Editions.

Special Care: Improving the Police Response to the Mentally Disabled. Gerard Murphy. LC 85-62557. (Illus.). 292p. (Orig.). (C). 1986. pap. text ed. 16.50 (*1-878734-16-4*) Police Exec Res.

Special Care: Medical Decisions at the Beginning of Life. Fred M. Frohock. LC 85-31806. xiv, 280p. (C). 1986. 23.95 (*0-226-26581-1*) U Ch Pr.

Special Care Babies & Their Developing Relationships. Anne McFadyen. LC 94-8491. 208p. (C). 1994. pap. 17.95 (*0-415-10614-1*, B4309); text ed. 62.95 (*0-415-10613-3*, B4305) Routledge.

Special Care Programs for People with Dementia. Ed. by Stephanie B. Hoffman & Mary Kaplan. LC 96-14721. (Illus.). 256p. (Orig.). 1996. pap. text ed. 28.95 (*1-878812-33-5*) Hlth Prof Pr.

***Special Cases: Natural Anomalies & Historical Monsters.** Rosamond W. Purcell. 1998. 24.95 (*0-8118-1568-4*) Chronicle Bks.

Special Challenges in Career Management: The Counselor's Perspective. Alan J. Pickman. LC 96-18079. 264p. 1996. 49.95 (*0-8058-1856-1*); pap. 21.00 (*0-8058-1857-X*) L Erlbaum Assocs.

Special Chapters in the Theory of Analytic Functions of Several Complex Variables. Boris A. Fuks. LC 65-26324. (Translations of Mathematical Monographs: Vol. 14). 357p. 1965. reprint ed. 55.00 (*0-8218-1564-4*, MMONO/14) Am Math.

Special Child: A Source Book for Parents of Children with Developmental Disabilities. 2nd ed. Siegfried M. Pueschel et al. LC 94-1018. 464p. (Orig.). 1994. pap. 26.00 (*1-55766-167-7*) P H Brookes.

Special Child in the Library. Ed. by Barbara H. Baskin & Karen H. Harris. LC 76-21268. 207p. reprint ed. pap. 59.00 (*0-317-26574-1*, 2023955) Bks Demand.

***Special Child of God.** Sue Isbell. (Great Big Bks.). (Illus.). 16p. (J). (ps). 1996. pap. 14.95 (*0-687-06669-7*) Abingdon.

Special Children: An Integrative Approach. 2nd ed. Bernard G. Suran & Joseph V. Rizzo. LC 82-23039. 603p. reprint ed. pap. 171.90 (*0-7837-3955-9*, 2043784) Bks Demand.

Special Children: Meeting the Challenge in the Primary School. Jane Leadbetter & Peter Leadbetter. Ed. by Jonathan Solity. LC 92-38452. (Introduction to Education Ser.). 160p. 1993. 75.00 (*0-304-32522-8*); pap. 25.00 (*0-304-32524-4*) Weidner & Sons.

Special Children Handbook. Ed. by Paul Widlake. 224p. (C). 1989. 60.00 (*0-7478-0393-5*, Pub. by S Thornes Pubs UK) St Mut.

Special Children Handbook. Paul Widlake. (C). 1989. 130.00 (*0-09-175774-6*, Pub. by S Thornes Pubs UK); teacher ed. 70.00 (*0-7487-0393-4*, Pub. by S Thornes Pubs UK) St Mut.

Special Children, Special Risks: The Maltreatment of Children with Disabilities. James Garbarino et al. (Modern Applications of Social Work Ser.). 320p. (C). 1987. pap. text ed. 30.95 (*0-202-36046-6*); lib. bdg. 49.95 (*0-202-36045-8*) Aldine de Gruyter.

Special Christmas. Francine Pascal. (Sweet Valley High Ser.: No. 2). 240p. (Orig.). (YA). 1985. 3.50 (*0-553-25377-8*) Bantam.

***Special Christmas Gift.** Aquilla Walton. (Illus.). 12p. (Orig.). (J). (gr. 1-2). 1997. pap. 8.99 (*1-55237-190-5*, Pub. by Comnwlth Pub CN) Partners Pubs Grp.

Special Circumstances. Marc Berrenson. 272p. (Orig.). 1991. pap. 3.50 (*0-380-76077-0*) Avon.

Special Class (Playscript) Brian Kral. (Orig.). 1981. 5.00 (*0-87602-235-2*) Anchorage.

***Special Class Projects.** Peter Lerangis. Ed. by Anne Buckingham. (Thinking Skills Library). (Illus.). 108p. (Orig.). (J). (gr. 2-5). 1997. teacher ed., pap. 9.95 (*1-56784-710-2*) Newbridge Comms.

Special Classes of Linear Operators & Other Topics. Ed. by Grigore Arsene & F. H. Vasilescu. (Operator Theory Ser.: No. 28). 322p. 1988. 129.00 (*0-8176-1970-4*) Birkhauser.

Special Collection, in Praise of Mothers. Helen Exley. (Square Giftbooks Ser.). (Illus.). 96p. 1995. 9.99 (*1-85015-533-X*) Exley Giftbooks.

Special Collections: The Photographic Order from Pop to Now. Charles A. Stainback. (Illus.). 72p. 1992. 29.95 (*0-933642-20-2*); pap. 19.95 (*0-933642-19-9*) Intl Ctr Photo.

Special Collections: What They Mean to Librarians, Professors, & Collectors. N. Orwin Rush et al. LC 72-93783. 1972. 5.00 (*0-9607778-4-9*) Friends Fla St.

Special Collections in Children's Literature: An International Directory. 3rd ed. Ed. by Dolores B. Jones. LC 95-10998. 235p. pap. 40.00 (*0-8389-3454-4*, 3454-4-2045) ALA.

Special Collections in College & University Libraries. Ed. by Modoc Press Editors. 650p. 1989. 110.00 (*0-02-921651-6*, Free Press) Free Pr.

Special Collections in German Libraries. Walter Gebhardt. 1977. 126.95 (*3-11-005839-1*) De Gruyter.

Special Collections Policies, Procedures & Guidelines: A Model Plan for the Management of Special Legal Collections. Christopher T. Anglim. LC 92-37234. 556p. 1993. 68.50 (*0-89941-814-7*, 307570) W S Hein.

Special Commando. W. Wood. (C). 1986. text ed. 115.00 (*0-685-38784-4*, Pub. by Maritime Bks UK) St Mut.

Special Computer Architectures for Pattern Processing. Ed. by K. S. Fu & T. Ichikawa. 272p. 1982. 156.00 (*0-8493-6100-1*, TK7882, CRC Reprint) Franklin.

***Special Concretes Workability & Mixing.** Ed. by Bartos. (Rilem Proceedings Ser.). (Illus.). 288p. 1994. text ed. 104.95 (*0-419-18870-3*, E & FN Spon) Routledge Chapman & Hall.

Special Conference: San Francisco Bay Area Economy 1993 & 1994. 100p. 1993. 15.00 (*0-317-05665-4*, P93004PRO) Assn Bay Area.

Special Constable: A Study of the Police Reserve. M. L. Gill & R. I. Mawby. 180p. 1990. text ed. 55.95 (*1-85628-025-X*, Pub. by Avebury Pub UK) Ashgate Pub Co.

Special Corps of Austria & Czechoslovakia 1918-1945. Marcel Roubicek. (Military History Monograph). 32p. 1995. pap. 3.50 (*1-57638-038-6*) Merriam Pr.

***Special Courses for National Staff with Higher Administrative Responsibilities in the Health Services.** (Technical Report Ser.: No. 311). 31p. 1965. pap. text ed. 3.00 (*92-4-120311-0*) World Health.

Special Creation vs. Evolution. Edward F. Blick. 38p. (Orig.). 1994. pap. 2.50 (*1-879366-65-7*) Hearthstone OK.

Special Curricula Needs. Ed. by Keith Bovair et al. 160p. 1992. pap. 32.50 (*1-85346-216-0*, Pub. by D Fulton UK) Taylor & Francis.

***Special CVT for a New Power Train Concept.** Bernd-Robert Hohn & B. Pinnekamp. (1994 Fall Technical Meeting). 1994. pap. text ed. 30.00 (*1-55589-639-1*) AGMA.

Special Day. Dubravka Kolanovic. Ed. by Nancy R. Thatch. LC 93-13419. (Books for Students by Students). (Illus.). 29p. (J). (gr. k-2). 1993. lib. bdg. 14.95 (*0-933849-45-1*) Landmark Edns.

Special Day Celebrations: Seasonal Mini Celebrations to Enjoy with Young Children. Elizabeth S. McKinnon. Ed. by Gayle Bittinger. LC 89-50765. (Celebration Ser.). (Illus.). 128p. (Orig.). (J). (ps-1). 1989. pap. 14.95 (*0-911019-24-3*, WPH 0702) Warren Pub Hse.

Special Day Exercises. Ed. by Amos M. Kellogg. LC 70-139766. (Granger Index Reprint Ser.). 1977. 19.95 (*0-8369-6220-6*) Ayer.

***Special-Day Sermon Outlines.** Stephen F. Olford. 64p. 1997. pap. 5.99 (*0-8010-9046-6*) Baker Bks.

Special Days: The Book of Anniversaries & Holidays. Ruth W. Gregory. 1978. pap. 5.95 (*0-8065-0659-8*, Citadel Pr) Carol Pub Group.

Special Days & Occasions. Billy Apostolon. (Sermon Outline Ser.). 64p. (gr. 13). 1959. pap. 3.99 (*0-8010-0007-6*) Baker Bks.

Special Days & Weeks for Planning the School Calendar, 1988-89. 104p. 1987. 14.00 (*0-318-37609-1*) Ed Research.

Special Days Throughout the Year: Fifty Ready-to-Use Activities, Unit 6. Audrey J. Adair. (Music Curriculum Activities Library). 112p. (J). (gr. 3-9). 1987. pap. 12.95 (*0-13-826421-X*, Parker Publishing Co) P-H.

Special Days to Remember. 14p. 1994. 7.98 (*0-8317-2159-6*) Smithmark.

Special Deception. large type ed. Alexander Fullerton. 547p. 1989. 27.99 (*0-7089-8501-7*, Charnwood) Ulverscroft.

Special Deliverance. large type ed. Alexander Fullerton. 432p. 1987. 27.99 (*0-7089-8387-1*, Charnwood) Ulverscroft.

Special Deliveries: New & Selected Poems. James Broughton. Ed. by Mark Thompson. LC 89-81100. 272p. (Orig.). 1990. pap. 19.95 (*0-913089-09-5*) Broken Moon.

Special Deliveries: Selecting the Gender of Your Baby Before Conception, Boy or Girl? Theresa Hebert. (Illus.). 69p. (Orig.). 1995. pap. 19.95 (*0-9648777-0-8*) Spec Deliv MA.

***Special Deliveries: 1941 Miracles Delivered Free!** Edwin H. Riedell. LC 97-11656. 144p. (Orig.). 1998. pap. 12.95 (*1-56474-233-4*) Fithian Pr.

Special Delivery. Rahima Baldwin. LC 78-61611. 192p. 1995. pap. 17.95 (*0-89087-934-6*) Celestial Arts.

***Special Delivery.** Elaine R. Chase. LC 97-22551. 1997. lib. bdg. write for info. (*0-7862-1212-8*) Thorndike Pr.

***Special Delivery.** Danielle Steel. LC 97-5349. 1997. 16.95 (*0-385-31691-7*) Delacorte.

Special Delivery. large type ed. Becki Dilley & Keith Dilley. (Niagara Large Print Ser.). 217p. 1996. 27.99 (*0-7089-5835-4*) Ulverscroft.

Special Delivery: A Cartoonist's View of Expected Parenthood & Bouncing Babies. Val C. Bagley. (Illus.). 96p. (Orig.). 1980. pap. 6.98 (*0-88290-154-0*, 2041) Horizon Utah.

Special Delivery: Epistolary Modes in Modern Fiction. Linda S. Kauffman. LC 91-23819. (Women in Culture & Society Ser.). (Illus.). 310p. 1991. pap. text ed. 18.95 (*0-226-42681-5*) U Ch Pr.

Special Delivery: Epistolary Modes in Modern Fiction. Linda S. Kauffman. LC 91-23819. (Women in Culture & Society Ser.). (Illus.). 310p. 1992. lib. bdg. 52.00 (*0-226-42680-7*) U Ch Pr.

Special Delivery: How We Are Raising America's Only Sextuplets...& Loving It. Keith Dilley & Becki Dilley. 1995. 21.00 (*0-679-43706-1*) Random.

Special Delivery: The Letters of C. L. R. James to Constance Webb, 1939-1948. C. L. James. Ed. by Anna Grimshaw. 400p. (C). Date not set. 29.95 (*1-55786-627-9*) Blackwell Pubs.

Special Delivery Mess. Effin Older. (Silver Blades Figure Eight Ser.: Vol. 5). 80p. (J). 1997. pap. 3.50 (*0-553-48502-4*) Bantam.

Special Delivery Symphony. Stephanie Hill. (Looney Tunes Discover Music Ser.). 24p. (J). 1993. pap. 7.98 incl. audio (*0-943351-58-8*, XL1001) Astor Bks.

***Special Detail.** Brian T. Yates. 373p. (Orig.). 1998. mass mkt. 5.99 (*1-55237-387-8*, Pub. by Comnwlth Pub CN) Partners Pubs Grp.

***Special Diet Solutions: Healthy Cooking Without Wheat, Gluten, Dairy, Eggs, Yeast or Refined Sugar.** Carol Fenster. 200p. 1997. pap. 15.95 (*1-889374-00-8*) Savory Palate.

Special District Governments in the United States. John C. Bollens. LC 77-26250. 280p. 1978. reprint ed. text ed. 59.75 (*0-313-20065-3*, BOSD, Greenwood Pr) Greenwood.

Special Districts: A Useful Technique for Financing Infrastructure. 2nd ed. Douglas R. Porter. LC 92-85303. 90p. 1992. pap. text ed. 37.95 (*0-87420-736-3*, S38) Urban Land.

Special Districts: The Ultimate in Neighborhood Zoning. Richard F. Babcock & Wendy U. Larsen. 187p. 1990. pap. 15.00 (*1-55844-112-3*) Lincoln Inst Land.

Special Districts in Cook County: Toward a Geography of Local Government. Donald F. Stetzer. LC 75-14240. (University of Chicago, Department of Geography, Research Paper Ser.: No. 169). 192p. 1975. reprint ed. pap. 54.80 (*0-608-02280-2*, 2062921) Bks Demand.

Special Drilling Operations. (Drilling Technology Ser.: Segment III). (Illus.). 230p. 1984. 40.00 (*0-88698-145-X*, 2.01310) PETEX.

Special Duty. large type ed. Peter N. Walker. 336p. 1992. pap. 15.99 (*0-7089-7160-1*, Trailtree Bookshop) Ulverscroft.

Special Dynamic. large type ed. Alexander Fullerton. 480p. 1987. 27.99 (*0-7089-8445-2*, Charnwood) Ulverscroft.

Special Economic Zones of China & Their Impact on Its Economic Development. Jung-Dong Park. LC 96-26875. 240p. 1997. text ed. 65.00 (*0-275-95613-X*, Praeger Pubs) Greenwood.

Special Edition: A Guide to Network Television Documentary Series & Special News Reports, 1980-1989. Daniel Einstein. LC 96-17904. 1997. 110.00 (*0-8108-3220-8*) Scarecrow.

Special Edition, Guide to Network Television Documentary Series & Special News Reports, 1955-1979. Daniel Einstein. LC 86-6599. 1069p. 1987. 87.50 (*0-8108-1898-1*) Scarecrow.

***Special Edition Using Access 97.** Roger Jennings et al. 1344p. 1996. 49.99 (*0-7897-0916-3*) Mac Comp Pub.

Special Edition Using America Online. Gene Steinberg. (Illus.). 800p. 1995. 29.99 (*0-7897-0278-9*) Que.

Special Edition Using America Online. 2nd ed. Gene Steinberg. 1056p. 1996. 39.99 (*0-7897-0879-5*) Mac Comp Pub.

Special Edition Using Ami Pro for Windows 3.11. Elaine Marmel et al. (Illus.). 1100p. (Orig.). 1995. 34.99 (*0-7897-0363-7*) Que.

Special Edition Using Asymetrix Multimedia ToolBook. Wayne Brooks et al. (Illus.). 672p. (Orig.). 1995. 49.99 (*0-7897-0291-6*) Que.

***Special Edition Using BackOffice Vol. 1: Back Office.** 2nd ed. G. A. Sullivan. (Special Edition Ser.). 912p. 1997. 75.00 (*0-7897-1142-7*) Mac Comp Pub.

Special Edition Using Borland C Plus Plus, New Edition. Edward B. Toupin. (Illus.). 912p. (Orig.). 1996. 49.99 (*0-7897-0284-3*) Que.

***Special Edition Using CGI.** 2nd ed. Jeffry Dwight & Robert Niles. 864p. 1997. 49.99 (*0-7897-1139-7*) Mac Comp Pub.

Special Edition Using Collabra Share: Special Edition. Alastair Dallas. (Illus.). 550p. (Orig.). 1995. 34.99 (*0-7897-0410-2*) Que.

Special Edition Using CompuServe. Que Development Group Staff. (Illus.). 1000p. (Orig.). 1995. pap. 39.99 (*0-614-07263-8*) Que.

Special Edition Using CorelDRAW! 2nd ed. Que Development Group Staff. (Illus.). 709p. (Orig.). 1995. 39.99 (*0-7897-0295-9*) Que.

Special Edition Using Delphi: Special Edition. 2nd ed. Jonathan Matcho. (Illus.). 900p. (Orig.). 1996. 49.99 (*0-7897-0591-5*) Que.

***Special Edition Using Delphi 3.** David Powell & Todd Miller. 1080p. 1997. 49.99 (*0-7897-1118-4*) Mac Comp Pub.

Special Edition Using Desktop PC Video. Roger Jennings. (Illus.). 900p. (Orig.). 1996. 45.00 (*0-7897-0265-7*) Que.

***Special Edition Using Dynamic HTML.** Ramesh Chandak. 600p. 39.99 (*0-7897-1154-0*) Mac Comp Pub.

Special Edition Using Excel for Windows 95. Ron Person. (Illus.). 1211p. (Orig.). 1995. 34.99 (*0-7897-0112-X*) Que.

Special Edition Using FileMaker Pro. Chris Moyer. (Illus.). 600p. (Orig.). 1996. 34.99 (*0-7897-0662-8*) Que.

***Special Edition Using HTML 3.2: Version X.** 3rd ed. Mark Brown & Jerry Honeycutt. 1000p. 1997. 49.99 (*0-7897-1097-8*) Mac Comp Pub.

Special Edition Using Internet Chameleon. Todd Stauffer. (Illus.). 600p. (Orig.). 1995. 27.99 (*0-7897-0287-8*) Que.

***Special Edition Using IntranetWare.** Craig Zacker & Roger Kresge. 872p. 1997. 49.99 (*0-7897-1156-7*) Mac Comp Pub.

Special Edition Using ISAPI. Steve Genusa. 608p. 1996. 49.99 (*0-7897-0913-9*) Mac Comp Pub.

Special Edition Using ISDN. 2nd ed. James Y. Bryce. 700p. 1996. 39.99 (*0-7897-0843-4*) Mac Comp Pub.

Special Edition Using ISDN: Special Edition. deluxe ed. James Bryce. (Illus.). 500p. (Orig.). 1995. 29.99 (*0-7897-0405-6*) Que.

Special Edition Using Jakarta. Que Development Group Staff. 704p. 1996. pap. text ed. 49.99 incl. cd-rom (*0-7897-0884-1*) Que.

***Special Edition Using Java.** 2nd ed. Joseph Weber et al. 1176p. 1996. 59.99 (*0-7897-0936-8*) Mac Comp Pub.

Special Edition Using Java: Special Edition. Edward B. Toupin. (Illus.). 869p. (Orig.). 1996. 49.99 (*0-7897-0604-0*) Que.

***Special Edition Using JavaScript.** 2nd ed. Mark C. Reynolds & Andrew Wooldridge. 888p. 1997. 49.99 (*0-7897-1138-9*) Mac Comp Pub.

***Special Edition Using JScript.** Mark Reynolds. 700p. 1996. 49.99 (*0-7897-1079-X*) Mac Comp Pub.

Special Edition Using LINUX. Jack Tackett et al. (Illus.). 800p. (Orig.). 1995. 49.99 (*0-7897-0100-6*) Que.

***Special Edition Using Linux.** 3rd ed. Jack Tackett, Jr. & David Gunter. 816p. 1997. 59.99 (*0-7897-1132-X*) Mac Comp Pub.

Special Edition Using Lotus Approach for Windows 95: Special Edition. Dave Plotkin. (Illus.). 1024p. (Orig.). 1996. 39.99 (*0-7897-0208-8*) Que.

Special Edition Using Lotus Notes, New Edition. Que Development Group Staff. (Illus.). 1008p. (Orig.). 1996. 49.99 (*0-7897-0368-8*) Que.

Special Edition Using Lotus SmartSuite for Windows 95: Special Edition. Que Development Group Staff & Gastieger. (Illus.). 1024p. (Orig.). 1995. pap. 34.99 (*0-7897-0187-1*) Que.

Special Edition Using MFC & ATL. Clay Walnum. 888p. 1997. 59.99 (*0-7897-0751-9*) Mac Comp Pub.

Special Edition Using Microsoft Backoffice. 1120p. 1996. 59.99 (*0-7897-0688-1*) Que.

***Special Edition Using Microsoft Commercial Internet System.** Judy Petersen et al. 696p. 1997. 59.99 (*0-7897-1016-1*) Mac Comp Pub.

***Special Edition Using Microsoft Exchange Server 5.** Software Spectrum Staff. 864p. 1997. 59.99 (*0-7897-1116-8*) Mac Comp Pub.

***Special Edition Using Microsoft FrontPage 97.** Neil Randall & Dennis Jones. 1040p. 1996. 49.99 (*0-7897-1036-6*) Mac Comp Pub.

Special Edition Using Microsoft Internet Explorer 3. Jim O'Donnell. 864p. 1996. pap. text ed. 49.99 incl. cd-rom (*0-7897-0878-7*) Que.

***Special Edition Using Microsoft Internet Explorer 4.** Eric Ladd & Jim O'Donnell. 750p. 1997. 39.99 (*0-7897-1046-3*) Mac Comp Pub.

Special Edition Using Microsoft Internet Information Server 2. Victor Wolters. 624p. 1996. 49.99 (*0-7897-0850-7*) Mac Comp Pub.

Special Edition Using Microsoft Office Professional Resource Center. Ron Person et al. 1996. 125.00 (*0-7897-0873-6*) Mac Comp Pub.

***Special Edition Using Microsoft Project.** Tim Pyron. 850p. 1997. 39.99 (*0-7897-1252-0*) Que.

Special Edition Using Microsoft Project: Special Edition. Tim Pyron. (Illus.). 742p. (Orig.). 1995. 34.99 (*0-7897-0540-0*) Que.

Special Edition Using Microsoft SQL Server 6.5. Bob Branchek et al. (Illus.). 672p. (Orig.). 1996. 59.99 (*0-7897-0097-2*) Mac Comp Pub.

***Special Edition Using Microsoft SQL Server 6.5.** 2nd ed. Stephen Wynkoop et al. 912p. 1997. 59.99 (*0-7897-1117-6*) Mac Comp Pub.

S

Special Edition Using Microsoft Works for Windows 95: Special Edition. Debbie Walkowski et al. (Illus.). 682p. (Orig.). 1995. 29.99 (0-7897-0462-5) Que.

Special Edition Using MS Network. 1996. 39.99 (0-7897-0739-X) Que.

Special Edition Using NaviServer & NaviPress: Special Edition. deluxe ed. Que Development Group Staff. (Illus.). 768p. (Orig.). 1995. 39.99 (0-7897-0407-2) Que.

***Special Edition Using Netscape Communicator.** Mark Brown et al. 800p. 1997. 39.99 (0-7897-0980-5) Mac Comp Pub.

***Special Edition Using Netscape LiveConnect.** Lori Leonardo. 400p. 1997. 34.99 (0-7897-1171-0) Que.

Special Edition Using NetWare 4.X. Bill Lawrence et al. (Illus.). 1275p. (Orig.). 1995. 39.99 (1-56529-894-2) Que.

Special Edition Using Oracle. John Boring & David Kreins. (Illus.). 1024p. (Orig.). 1996. 49.99 (0-7897-0101-4) Que.

***Special Edition Using Oracle Web Application Server 3.** Rick Greenwald. 500p. 1997. 39.99 (0-7897-0822-1) Mac Comp Pub.

***Special Edition Using Outlook 97.** 1997. pap. 34.99 (0-614-28480-5) Que.

Special Edition Using PageMaker for Windows 95: Special Edition. Rick Wallace. (Illus.). 916p. (Orig.). 1996. 39. 99 (0-7897-0610-5) Que.

Special Edition Using Paradox for Windows 95: Special Edition. Que Development Group Staff. (Illus.). 1200p. (Orig.). 1996. 39.99 (0-7897-0205-3) Que.

Special Edition Using Perl. Monte Mitzelfelt. (Illus.). 672p. (Orig.). 1996. pap. 49.99 incl. cd-rom (0-7897-0659-8) Que.

Special Edition Using PowerPoint for Windows 95: Special Edition. deluxe ed. Que Development Group Staff. (Illus.). 813p. (Orig.). 1995. 34.99 (0-7897-0464-1) Que.

Special Edition Using Progress. George Kassabgi. (Illus.). 750p. (Orig.). 1995. 59.99 (0-7897-0493-5) Que.

Special Edition Using Quarterdeck Normandy. Que Development Group Staff. (Illus.). 600p. (Orig.). 1998. 34.99 (0-7897-0360-2) Que.

Special Edition Using SGML: Special Edition. deluxe ed. Que Development Group Staff. (Illus.). 600p. (Orig.). 1996. 49.99 (0-7897-0414-5) Que.

Special Edition Using Sybase. Que Development Group Staff. (Illus.). 792p. (Orig.). 1996. 59.99 (0-7897-0087-5) Que.

***Special Edition Using TCP/IP & HTTP.** David Baker & CBT Systems Staff. 800p. 1997. 59.99 (0-7897-1169-9) Mac Comp Pub.

Special Edition Using the Internet. 3rd ed. Mary A. Pike et al. 1232p. 1996. 49.99 (0-7897-0846-9) Mac Comp Pub.

Special Edition Using the Internet with Windows 95. Mary A. Pike. (Illus.). 1300p. (Orig.). 1996. 49.99 (0-7897-0646-6) Que.

Special Edition Using the Internet with Your Mac. Que Development Group Staff. (Illus.). 927p. (Orig.). 1995. 39.99 (0-7897-0212-6) Que.

Special Edition Using the Microsoft Network. 1996. 39.99 (0-7897-0397-1) Que.

Special Edition Using Turbo C Plus Plus for Windows. David Medinets et al. (Illus.). 800p. (Orig.). 1995. pap. 39.99 (0-614-07261-1) Que.

Special Edition Using V R M L: Special Edition. Que Development Group Staff. (Illus.). 700p. (Orig.). 1996. 49.99 (0-7897-0494-3) Que.

***Special Edition Using Visual Basic for Applications.** Paul Sanna. 816p. 1997. 49.99 (0-7897-0959-7) Mac Comp Pub.

Special Edition Using Visual Basic for Applications. 2nd ed. Jeff Webb. (Illus.). 868p. (Orig.). 1995. 39.99 (0-7897-0269-X) Que.

Special Edition Using VisuaL Basic 5. Mike McKelvy et al. 1000p. 1997. 39.99 (0-7897-0922-8) Mac Comp Pub.

Special Edition Using Visual Basic 95, New Edition. Webb et al. (Illus.). 1120p. (Orig.). 1995. 39.99 (1-56529-998-1) Que.

Special Edition Using Visual C Plus Plus: Special Edition. Chane Cullené et al. (Illus.). 1000p. (Orig.). 1995. 49.99 (0-7897-0401-3) Que.

Special Edition Using Windows NT Workstation 4.0. Funk et al. 1248p. 1996. 49.99 (0-7897-0673-3) Que.

Special Edition Using Windows NT 4.0. Que Development Group Staff. (Illus.). 1100p. (Orig.). 1997. 49.99 (0-7897-0251-7) Que.

***Special Edition Using Windows NT 4.0 & 95 Registry.** Jerry Honeycutt. 1200p. 1997. 49.99 (0-7897-1272-5) Que.

Special Edition Using Word Pro for Windows 95: Special Edition. deluxe ed. Sue Plumley & Robert Weberg. (Illus.). 646p. (Orig.). 1995. 34.99 (0-7897-0149-9) Que.

Special Edition Using WordPerfect for Windows 95. Gordon McComb & Laura Acklen. (Illus.). 1264p. (Orig.). 1996. 34.99 (0-7897-0140-5) Que.

Special Edition Using 1-2-3 for Windows 95. Joce Nielson. (Illus.). 984p. (Orig.). 1997. 39.99 (0-7897-0143-X) Que.

Special Edition Using Vi6sual FoxPro. Michael P. Antonovich. 960p. 1996. 59.99 (0-7897-0885-X) Mac Comp Pub.

***Special Editon Using Microsoft Office 97 Professional.** Rick Winter & Patty Winter. 1280p. 1996. 39.99 (0-7897-0896-5) Mac Comp Pub.

***Special Education.** Adams. 1986. pap. text ed. write for info. (0-900313-37-4) Addison-Wesley.

Special Education. Morris. (C). 1986. 65.95 (0-205-14423-3, H4423) Allyn.

Special Education. Jack Rudman. (National Teacher Examination Ser.: NT-41). 1994. pap. 23.95 (0-8373-8451-6) Nat Learn.

Special Education. Jonathan Solity. Ed. by C. E. Wragg. LC 92-17101. (Education Matters Ser.). 128p. 1993. text ed. 60.00 (0-304-32407-8); pap. text ed. 18.95 (0-304-32427-2) Cassell.

Special Education: A Biblical Approach. John J. McCormick & John C. Vaughn. Ed. & Pref. by Joe P. Sutton. LC 92-74588. (Illus.). 408p. (Orig.). (C). 1993. pap. text ed. 14.95 (0-9634315-0-1) Hidden Treas.

Special Education: As You Liked It. Edward G. Scagliotta. 230p. (C). 1993. text ed. 25.00 (1-57092-000-1) Midland Pubns.

***Special Education: Common Questions - Common-Sense Answers.** Thomas C. Lovitt. 46p. (Orig.). 1997. pap. 6.95 (1-57035-106-6, C97SPEC) Sopris.

Special Education: Good Intentions Gone Awry. Edward Moscovitch. (Pioneer Paper Ser.: No. 8). 165p. 1993. pap. 10.00 (0-929930-10-X) Pioneer Inst.

***Special Education: Music Therapy.** Manorma Sharma. viii, 204p. 1996. 22.00 (81-7024-745-4, Pub. by Assoc Pub Hse II) Nataraj Bks.

Special Education: Past, Present, Future. Evans & Varma. 1990. 75.00 (1-85000-464-1, Falmer Pr); pap. 33.00 (1-85000-465-X, Falmer Pr) Taylor & Francis.

Special Education: Research & Practice:Synthesis of Findings. Ed. by Margaret C. Wang et al. 836p. 1990. pap. 47.95 (0-08-040237-2, Prgamon Press) Buttrwrth-Heinemann.

Special Education: The Challenge of the Future. Ed. by Karen A. Woldron et al. LC 92-20928. 248p. 1992. pap. 29.95 (0-7734-1936-5) E Mellen.

Special Education: The Way Ahead. John Fish. 144p. 1985. 80.00 (0-335-15038-1, Open Univ Pr); pap. 27.00 (0-335-15037-3, Open Univ Pr) Taylor & Francis.

Special Education & Student Disability: Traditional, Emerging, & Alternative Perspectives. 4th ed. Ed. by Edward L. Meyen & Thomas M. Skrtic. LC 92-74811. Orig. Title: Exceptional Children & Youth. (Illus.). 700p. 1995. text ed. 54.00 (0-89108-231-X) Love Pub Co.

Special Education at the Century's End: Evolution of Theory & Practice since 1970. Ed. by Thomas Hehir & Thomas Latus. LC 92-70561. (Reprint Ser.: No. 23). (Illus.). 464p. (Orig.). 1992. pap. 22.95 (0-916690-25-3) Harvard Educ Rev.

***Special Education Audit Handbook.** Donald F. Weinstein. LC 96-61123. 145p. 1996. pap. text ed. 39.95 (1-56676-463-7) Technomic.

Special Education Coordinator. (Career Examination Ser.: C-3678). pap. 34.95 (0-8373-3678-3) Nat Learn.

***Special Education Desk Reference.** Mary Buchanan. Ed. by Carol Weller & Michelle Buchanan. LC 96-32706. (Illus.). 850p. (Orig.). 1997. pap. 55.00 (1-56593-800-3, 1556) Singular Publishing.

***Special Education Dictionary.** LRP Publications (Firm) Staff. LC 97-10261. 1997. write for info. (1-57834-002-0) LRP Pubns.

***Special Education for All Teachers.** Colaruss & O'Rourke. 350p. (C). 1997. per. 37.95 (0-7872-3863-5) Kendall-Hunt.

Special Education for the Early Childhood Years. Janet W. Lerner et al. 416p. 1981. text ed. write for info. (0-13-826461-9) P-H.

Special Education for the 21st Century. Sands & Kozleski. (Special Education Ser.). Date not set. text ed. 57.95 (0-534-23820-3) Brooks-Cole.

Special Education Handbook, 3 vols., Vol. 1. Wang et al. (Advances in Education Ser.). 1987. 50.00 (0-08-033386-9, Pergamon Pr) Elsevier.

Special Education Handbook, 3 vols., Vol. 2. Wang et al. (Advances in Education Ser.). 1988. 50.00 (0-08-033387-7, Pergamon Pr) Elsevier.

Special Education Handbook, 3 vols., Vol. 3. Wang et al. (Advances in Education Ser.). 1988. 50.00 (0-08-033388-5, Pergamon Pr) Elsevier.

Special Education Handbook: A Comprehensive Guide for Parents & Educators. Kenneth Shore. 224p. 1986. pap. text ed. 17.95 (0-8077-2806-3) Tchrs Coll.

Special Education Handbook: An Introductory Reference. Phillip Williams. 320p. 1990. 150.00 (0-335-09314-0, Open Univ Pr) Taylor & Francis.

Special Education in a Diverse Society. Herbert Grossman. LC 94-980. 1994. pap. text ed. 50.00 (0-205-15516-2) Allyn.

Special Education in America's Cities: A Descriptive Study. Council of the Great City Schools Staff. 121p. 1988. pap. 21.95 (1-56602-022-0) Research Better.

Special Education in Britain after Warnock. Ed. by John Visser & Graham Upton. 176p. 1993. pap. 29.00 (1-85346-250-0, Pub. by D Fulton UK) Taylor & Francis.

Special Education in Context: An Ethnographic Study in Persons with Developmental Disabilities. John J. Gleason. (Illus.). 200p. (C). 1989. text ed. 39.95 (0-521-35187-1) Cambridge U Pr.

Special Education in Latin America: Experiences & Issues. Ed. by Alfredo J. Artiles & Daniel P. Hallahan. LC 95-14429. 312p. 1995. text ed. 65.00 (0-275-94667-3, Praeger Pubs) Greenwood.

Special Education in Minority Communities. Ed. by Phillip Williams. 128p. 1984. pap. 23.00 (0-335-10416-9, Open Univ Pr) Taylor & Francis.

Special Education in the Criminal Justice System. C. Michael Nelson et al. 352p. (C). 1987. pap. write for info. (0-675-20477-1, Merrill Coll) P-H.

Special Education Integration in Europe. Christine O'Hanlon. 192p. 1993. pap. 32.00 (1-85346-236-5, Pub. by D Fulton UK) Taylor & Francis.

***Special Education Issues.** Susan Benner. (C). 1997. pap. text ed. 32.95 (0-534-25230-3) Wadsworth Pub.

Special Education Law. Thomas Guernsey & Klare Kathe. LC 92-76162. 320p. 1993. lib. bdg. 55.00 (0-89089-530-9) Carolina Acad Pr.

Special Education Law. Laura F. Rothstein. 464p. (Orig.). (C). 1990. pap. text ed. 34.95 (0-8013-0209-9, 75868) Longman.

Special Education Law. 2nd ed. Laura F. Rothstein. (Orig.). (C). 1995. teacher ed. write for info. (0-8013-1249-3, 79880); pap. text ed. 43.95 (0-8013-1234-5) Longman.

Special Education Law: A Guide for Parents, Advocates, & Educators. Steven S. Goldberg. (Critical Topics in Law & Society Ser.). 244p. 1982. 45.00 (0-306-40848-1, Plenum Pr) Plenum.

Special Education Law: Case Summaries & Federal Regulations. Stephen B. Thomas & Carol Denzinger. (Case Citation Ser.). 153p. (Orig.). 1993. pap. text ed. 35.00 (1-56534-080-9) Ed Law Assn.

Special Education Law: Issues & Implications for the 90's, 2 vols., Set. Stephen B. Thomas & Charles J. Russo. 238p. 1995. 34.95 (1-56534-088-4) Ed Law Assn.

Special Education Law & Litigation Treatise Includes Supplement for November 1994. Mark C. Weber. LC 92-35378. 1000p. 1992. ring bd. 140.00 (0-934753-64-4) LRP Pubns.

***Special Education Law & Practice: A Manual for the Special Education Practitioner.** LC 96-39406. 1996. write for info. (1-57834-000-4) LRP Pubns.

***Special Education Law in America.** Reed Martin. 119p. (Orig.). (C). 1997. pap. 19.95 (1-885477-34-1) Fut Horizons.

Special Education Lesson Plan Booklet. Ella D. Davis. 10p. (C). 1992. pap. text ed. 19.95 (1-888185-52-X) Davis Pubng LA.

Special Education Needs Policy in the 1990s: Warnock in the Market Place. Ed. by Sheila Riddell & Sally Brown. LC 94-8490. 240p. (C). 1994. pap. text ed. 25.00 (0-415-09759-2, B3598) Routledge.

Special Education Needs Review, Vol. 2. Neville Jones. 1989. write for info. (0-318-65443-1, Falmer Pr) Taylor & Francis.

Special Education Practice: Applying the Knowledge, Affirming the Values... James L. Paul et al. LC 96-39238. (Special Education Ser.). 384p. 1997. text ed. 49. 95 (0-534-34201-9) Brooks-Cole.

Special Education Program Level A. Addison-Wesley Staff. (ESOL Elementary Supplement Ser.). (Illus.). 16p. 1988. 27.25 (0-201-19767-7) Addison-Wesley.

Special Education Program Level A, Set. Addison-Wesley Staff. (ESOL Elementary Supplement Ser.). (Illus.). 16p. 1988. pap. 190.75 (0-201-19766-9) Addison-Wesley.

Special Education Program Level B. Addison-Wesley Staff. (ESOL Elementary Supplement Ser.). (Illus.). 16p. 1989. teacher ed. 27.25 (0-201-19357-4); pap. text ed. 192.83 (0-201-19356-6) Addison-Wesley.

Special Education Programs: A Guide to Evaluation. Ada L. Vallecorsa et al. (Essential Tools for Educators Ser.). 128p. 1992. pap. 24.95 (0-8039-6034-4) Corwin Pr.

Special Education Sourcebook. Michael S. Rosenberg & Irene Edmond-Rosenberg. LC 94-21554. 325p. (Orig.). 1994. pap. 21.95 (0-933149-52-2) Woodbine House.

Special Education Students Write. Ray Marik. (Writing Teachers at Work Ser.). 145p. (C). 1982. pap. text ed. 7.00 (1-883920-04-3) Nat Writing Proj.

Special Education Teacher's Book of Lists. Roger Pierangelo. LC 95-36912. 320p. 1995. spiral bd. 29.95 (0-87628-876-X) Ctr Appl Res.

***Special Education Teacher's Book of Lists.** Roger Pierangelo. 1997. pap. text ed. 29.50 (0-87628-578-7) Ctr Appl Res.

Special Education Team. Stuart M. Losen & Joyce G. Losen. 242p. 1984. text ed. 36.95 (0-205-08203-3, H82035) Allyn.

Special Education Technology: Practical Applications. Rena B. Lewis. LC 92-35860. 552p. 1993. pap. 40.95 (0-534-20286-1) Brooks-Cole.

Special Educational Needs. 2nd ed. Ed. by Ronald Gulliford & Graham Upton. LC 92-9348. 192p. (C). (gr. 13). 1992. text ed. 85.00 (0-415-07124-0, A7709) Routledge.

Special Educational Needs & Human Resource Management. Ed. by Tony Bowers. 192p. 1987. pap. text ed. 19.95 (0-7099-5014-4, Pub. by Croom Helm UK) Routledge Chapman & Hall.

Special Educational Needs in Schools. Sally Beveridge. LC 92-40455. (Education in Society Ser.). 144p. (C). (gr. 13). 1993. text ed. 69.95 (0-415-07550-5, B0646, Routledge NY) Routledge.

Special Educational Needs in Schools. Sally Beveridge. LC 92-40455. (Education in Society Ser.). 144p. 1993. pap. write for info. (0-415-07551-3, Routledge NY) Routledge.

Special Educational Needs in the Primary School: A Practical Guide. Jean Gross. LC 93-16194. 1993. pap. 21.00 (0-335-19035-9, Open Univ Pr) Taylor & Francis.

Special Educational Needs in the Primary School: A Practical Guide. 2nd ed. Jean Gross. LC 96-10724. 244p. 1996. pap. 21.00 (0-335-19656-X, Open Univ Pr) Taylor & Francis.

Special Educational Needs Review, Vol. 1. Ed. by Neville Jones. (Education & Alienation Ser.). 250p. 1989. 70.00 (1-85000-488-9, Falmer Pr); pap. 35.00 (1-85000-489-7, Falmer Pr) Taylor & Francis.

Special Educational Needs Review, Vol. 2. Ed. by Neville Jones. (Education & Alienation Ser.). 250p. 1989. 70.00 (1-85000-490-0, Falmer Pr); pap. 35.00 (1-85000-491-9, Falmer Pr) Taylor & Francis.

Special Educational Needs Review, Vol. 3. Neville Jones. (Education & Alienation Ser.). 240p. 1990. 70.00 (1-85000-670-9, Falmer Pr); pap. 33.00 (1-85000-671-7, Falmer Pr) Taylor & Francis.

Special Educator Desk Book, 1996. Patrick W. McKee & Richard H. Barbe. 350p. 1992. pap. 55.00 (0-934753-73-3) LRP Pubns.

Special Educator's Almanac: Ready-to-Use Activities for a Resource Room or a Self-Contained Classroom. Natalie M. Elman. (Illus.). 420p. 1984. pap. 29.95 (0-87628-769-0) Ctr Appl Res.

Special Educator's Consultation Handbook. 2nd ed. Lorna Idol. LC 92-11521. 357p. 1992. text ed. 39.00 (0-89079-539-8, 5193) PRO-ED.

Special Educator's Handbook. Westling & Koorland. (Orig.). (C). 1988. pap. text ed. 36.95 (0-205-11137-8, H11372) Allyn.

Special Educator's Perspective on Interfacing Special & General Education: A Review for Administrators. David E. Greenburg. 20p. 1987. pap. text ed. 7.30 (0-86586-167-6, R315) Coun Exc Child.

Special Educator's Survival Guide: Practical Techniques & Materials for Supervision & Instruction. David Barnes & Cheryle Barnes. 272p. 1989. text ed. 32.95 (0-87628-784-4) Ctr Appl Res.

Special Effects. David P. Gollub. (Orig.). 1992. pap. 3.00 (0-929730-41-0) Zeitgeist Pr.

Special Effects, No. 5. David Hutchison. 1996. pap. write for info. (0-934551-12-X) Starlog Pr.

Special Effects: Pro-Lighting. Rotovision S. A. Staff. (Pro-Lighting Ser.). (Illus.). 160p. 1995. pap. 29.95 (0-8230-6467-0, Amphoto) Watsn-Guptill.

Special Effects: Wire, Tape & Rubber Band Style. L. B. Abbott. Tr. by George E. Turner. LC 83-73058. 275p. 1984. 29.95 (0-935578-06-4) ASC Holding.

Special Effects & Stunts Guide. 2nd ed. Ed. by Tassilo Baur. 240p. 1993. pap. 39.95 (0-943728-54-1) Lone Eagle Pub.

***Special Effects & Stunts Guide.** 3rd ed. Tassilo Baur. 1997. pap. 45.00 (0-943728-81-9) Lone Eagle Pub.

Special Effects & Topical Alphabets. Dan X. Solo. 1978. pap. 5.95 (0-486-23657-9) Dover.

Special Effects in Motion Pictures. Frank P. Clark. (Illus.). 238p. 1982. reprint ed. pap. text ed. 20.00 (0-940690-00-4) Soc Motion Pic & TV Engrs.

Special Effects in Television. 3rd ed. Bernard Wilkie. (Illus.). 264p. 1995. pap. 49.95 (0-240-51435-1, Focal) Buttrwrth-Heinemann.

Special Effects in Watercolors. Kolan Peterson. (How to Draw & Paint Ser.). (Illus.). 32p. (Orig.). 1989. pap. 6.95 (0-929261-49-6, HT207) W Foster Pub.

***Special Effects Photography Handbook: A Complete, Fully Illustrated Guide.** Elinor Stecker-Orel. (Illus.). 1997. pap. text ed. 29.95 (0-936262-56-7) Amherst Media.

Special Effects Sourcebook. Robert E. McCarthy. 96p. 1992. 46.95 (0-240-80147-4, Focal) Buttrwrth-Heinemann.

Special Electrical License. Jack Rudman. (Career Examination Ser.: C-1492). 1994. pap. 34.95 (0-8373-1492-5) Nat Learn.

Special Emphasis Program Managers Handbook. rev. ed. Carrolle A. Rushford. (Illus.). 300p. (Orig.). (C). 1990. ring bd. 89.95 (1-877645-00-1) Rushford & Assocs.

Special English for Tourism, 2 bks., Bk. 2. rev. ed. Vivien Worsdall. 1984. pap. write for info. (0-318-61566-5) Macmillan.

Special Enrollment Examination (IRS) Jack Rudman. (Career Examination Ser.: C-747). 1994. pap. 49.95 (0-8373-0747-3) Nat Learn.

Special Events: Inside & Out. Robert Jackson & Steven W. Schmader. LC 90-61609. 108p. 1990. pap. 21.95 (0-915611-27-9) Sagamore Pub.

Special Events: Planning for Success. April L. Harris. 75p. 1988. 32.00 (0-89964-262-4) Coun Adv & Supp Ed.

Special Events: The Art & Science of Modern Event Management. 2nd ed. Joe J. Goldblatt. LC 96-48572. (Hospitality, Travel & Tourism Ser.). (Illus.). 352p. 1997. text ed. 59.95 (0-442-02207-7) Van Nos Reinhold.

Special Events: The Art of Science Celebration. Joe Goldblatt. 1990. text ed. 49.95 (0-442-22681-0) Van Nos Reinhold.

Special Events Assistant. (Career Examination Ser.: C-3749). 1994. pap. 23.95 (0-8373-3749-6) Nat Learn.

Special Events from A to Z: The Complete Educator's Handbook. Gayle Jasso. LC 95-50164. (1-Off Ser.). (Illus.). 136p. 1996. 40.00 (0-8039-6387-4); pap. 18.00 (0-8039-6388-2) Corwin Pr.

Special Events in the Church. 1961. 5.50 (0-8341-9186-5, MP-601) Lillenas.

Special Events in the Church Program Builder, No. 2. Compiled by Paul M. Miller. 1982. 5.50 (0-8341-9111-3, MP-612) Lillenas.

Special Events Programs in School Library Media Centers: A Guide to Making Them Work. Marcia Trotta. LC 96-22009. (Professional Guides in School Librarianship Ser.). 128p. 1997. text ed. 35.00 (0-313-29190-X, Greenwood Pr) Greenwood.

Special Events Security Screening. Charles Garrett. LC 92-84320. (Illus.). 142p. (Orig.). 1993. pap. 5.95 (0-915920-83-2) Ram Pub.

Special Exhibition of Paintings of Children at Play. (Collections of the National Palace Museum, Taipei). (Illus.). 97p. (CHI & ENG.). 1994. pap. 29.95 (957-562-022-4) Heian Intl.

Special Exhibition of Winter Landscapes. (Landscape Exhibition of the Four Seasons Ser.). (Illus.). 74p. (Orig.). (CHI & ENG.). 1991. pap. 24.50 (0-89346-802-9) Heian Intl.

***Special Father.** Contrib. by Lizette Jonker. (With Love to.. .Ser.). (Illus.). 44p. 1997. 6.99 (0-8007-7160-5) Revell.

***Special Fiction Issue.** Ed. by John O'Brien. (Review of Contemporary Fiction Ser.: Vol. 6. No. 1). 228p. 1986. pap. 8.00 (1-56478-106-2) Dalkey Arch.

Special Financial Report Financial & Economic Data of the Men's & Boys Clothing Industry. 25p. 1976. 7.00 (0-318-19683-2) Clothing Mfrs.

Special Forces. Book Sales, Inc. Staff. 1990. 12.98 (1-55521-575-0) Bk Sales Inc.

An Asterisk (*) at the beginning of an entry indicates that the title is appearing in BIP for the first time.

Special Forces: A History of the World's Elite Fighting Units. Peter MacDonald. 1988. 12.98 (*1-55521-112-7*) Bk Sales Inc.

Special Forces Air Operations: TC 31-24. (Illus.). 112p. 1989. pap. 15.00 (*0-87364-536-7*) Paladin Pr.

Special Forces & Missions. Time-Life Books Editors. (New Face of War Ser.). (Illus.). 176p. 1991. write for info. (*0-8094-8600-8*); lib. bdg. write for info. (*0-8094-8601-6*) Time-Life.

***Special Forces Bibliography: An Indexed Guide to References about the U. S. Army Special Forces.** Dan C. Godbee. LC 96-71709. (Special Forces Reference Resources). 124p. 1996. pap. 15.00 (*0-9624009-6-3*) Radix Pr.

Special Forces Foreign Weapons Handbook. F. Moyer. 1986. lib. bdg. 79.95 (*0-8490-3663-1*) Gordon Pr.

Special Forces Foreign Weapons Handbook. Frank A. Moyer. 1987. pap. 14.95 (*0-8065-1044-7*, Citadel Pr) Carol Pub Group.

***Special Forces Guerrilla Warfare Manual.** Scott Wimberley. (Illus.). 248p. 1997. pap. 25.00 (*0-87364-921-4*) Paladin Pr.

Special Forces Handbook. U. S. Government Staff. (Illus.). 216p. 1965. pap. 10.00 (*0-87364-109-4*) Paladin Pr.

***Special Forces Handbook: For Business Management & Marketing.** Ed. by Thomas J. Rundquist. (Illus.). 100p. (Orig.). 1996. pap. 19.95 (*1-884239-14-5*) Nova Media.

Special Forces Operational Techniques, Dept. of the Army Field Manual 31-20. (Illus.). 536p. 1965. reprint ed. pap. 25.00 (*0-87364-047-0*) Paladin Pr.

Special Forces Soldier's Manual of Common Tasks for SQI's, 2 vols., Set. 1995. lib. bdg. 658.95 (*0-8490-6610-7*) Gordon Pr.

Special Forces Waterborne Operations. (Illus.). 104p. 1989. pap. 15.00 (*0-87364-493-X*) Paladin Pr.

Special Format Serials & Issues: Annual Review of... Advances in...Symposia on...Methods in... Ed. by Tony Stankus. LC 96-1022. (Serials Librarian Ser.: Vol. 27, Nos. 2 & 3). 262p. 1996. 39.95 (*1-56024-799-1*) Haworth Pr.

***Special Friend.** (With Love to...Ser.). (Illus.). 44p. 1997. 6.99 (*0-8007-7166-4*) Revell.

Special Friends. Peter Enns. (Stories that Live Ser.: No. II, Bk. 2). (Illus.). 24p. (J). (ps-5). 4.95 (*0-936215-22-4*); audio (*0-318-60369-1*) STL Intl.

Special Friends Postcard Book. Laura Kelly. (Little Lamb Mini Activity Bks.). (Illus.). 6p. (J). 1994. pap. 1.49 (*0-7847-0193-8*, 01543) Standard Pub.

Special Functions. Z. X. Wang & D. R. Guo. 720p. 1989. text ed. 95.00 (*9971-5-0659-9*); pap. text ed. 40.00 (*9971-5-0667-X*) World Scientific Pub.

Special Functions. Earl D. Rainville. LC 70-172380. (Illus.). xii, 365p. 1972. reprint ed. text ed. 27.50 (*0-8284-0258-2*) Chelsea Pub.

Special Functions: An Introduction to the Classical Functions of Mathematical Physics. Nico M. Temme. LC 95-42939. 259p. 1996. text ed. 54.95 (*0-471-11313-1*, Wiley-Interscience) Wiley.

Special Functions: Group Theoretical Aspects & Applications. Ed. by R. A. Askey et al. 1984. lib. bdg. 137.50 (*90-277-1822-9*) Kluwer Ac.

Special Functions & Linear Representations of Lie Groups. Jean Dieudonne. LC 79-22180. (CBMS Regional Conference Series in Mathematics: Vol. 42). 59p. 1980. reprint ed. pap. 14.00 (*0-8218-1692-6*, CBMS/42) Am Math.

Special Functions & the Theory of Group Representations. rev. ed. N. J. Vilenkin. Tr. by V. N. Singh. LC 68-19438. (Translations of Mathematical Monographs: Vol. 22). 613p. 1968. reprint ed. 73.00 (*0-8218-1572-5*, MMONO/22) Am Math.

Special Functions & Their Applications. rev. ed. N. N. Lebedev. Tr. by Richard A. Silverman from RUS. LC 72-86228. 320p. 1972. reprint ed. pap. 7.95 (*0-486-60624-4*) Dover.

Special Functions of Mathematical Physics. A. Nikiforov & V. Uvarov. 500p. 1988. 180.50 (*0-8176-3183-6*) Birkhauser.

***Special Functions of Mathematics for Engineers.** Larry C. Andrews. LC 97-13896. 1997. write for info. (*0-8194-2616-4*) SPIE.

***Special Functions, Q-Series, & Related Topics.** Mourad E. Ismail et al. LC 96-37968. (Fields Institute Communications Ser.: Vol. 14). 1997. 82.00 (*0-8218-0524-X*, FIC/14) Am Math.

Special Gift. Steve McKinstry. (Illus.). 32p. 1981. 6.95 (*0-910079-01-3*) Lucy & Co.

Special Gift For Santa. Clay Howard & Jim Brown. 320p. 1993. pap. write for info. (*0-9638902-0-4*) Howard-Brown.

Special Gift to God. Theodore Iakovina. (Illus.). 38p. (J). (gr. k-4). 1986. lib. bdg. write for info. (*0-9623721-1-0*) Amnos Pubns.

Special Guest. Lee Allen & Donna Allen. 96p. 1996. 12.95 (*1-57566-120-9*, Knsington); 8.95 (*1-57566-117-9*, Knsington) Kensgtn Pub Corp.

Special Guest: A Christmas Story. Lee Allen. (Illus.). 112p. 1995. text ed. 6.95 (*1-884369-24-3*) McDougal Pubng.

Special Guest Cookbook: Elegant Menus & Recipes for Those Who Are Allergic to Certain Foods, Bland Dieters, Calorie Counters, Cholesterol Conscious, Diabetic, Hypoglycemic, Kosher, Milk Sensitive, Pritikin Porselytes, Salt-Avoiding, Strictly Vegetarian. Arlene Eisenberg et al. LC 81-17106. 400p. 1982. 19.95 (*0-8253-0090-8*) Beaufort Bks NY.

Special Guitar Method. D. Bennett. 48p. 1992. pap. 4.95 (*0-7935-5527-2*) H Leonard.

Special Guitar Method. D. Bennett. 48p. 1992. pap. 4.95 (*0-7935-5517-5*) H Leonard.

Special Guitar Method. D. Bennett. 40p. 1993. pap. 5.95 (*0-7935-5556-6*) H Leonard.

Special Handling. Mark Pawlak. LC 93-160. 1993. Casebound. 18.00 (*0-914610-99-6*); pap. 10.00 (*0-914610-57-0*) Hanging Loose.

Special Happenings, Level 12. 83th ed. E. Evertts. (J). 1983. wbk. ed., pap. text ed. 15.75 (*0-03-061437-6*) HR&W Schl Div.

Special Happenings: Level 12. Evertts. 1983. 40.00 (*0-03-061394-9*) HB Schl Dept.

Special Happenings: Level 12. Evertts. 1986. 34.25 (*0-03-002369-6*) HB Schl Dept.

Special Health Care in the School. Terry H. Caldwell et al. (Exceptional Children at Risk Ser.). 56p. 1991. pap. text ed. 9.75 (*0-86586-209-5*, P352) Coun Exc Child.

***Special Honeymoon Hotels.** Cadogan Books Staff. 1998. pap. text ed. 9.95 (*1-86011-004-5*, Pub. by Cadogan Books UK) Macmillan.

Special Horoscope Dimensions. Noel Tyl. LC 73-19924. (Principles & Practice of Astrology Ser.: Vol. 9). (Illus.). 206p. (Orig.). 1975. pap. 3.95 (*0-87542-808-8*) Llewellyn Pubns.

Special Ichthyology: Israel Program for Scientific Translation. G. V. Nikol'skii. Tr. by J. I. Lengy & Z. Krauthamer. (Illus.). 538p. (RUS.). 1989. reprint ed. 55.00 (*1-55528-162-1*, Pub. by Today & Tomorrows P & P II) Scholarly Pubns.

Special Illumination: The Sufi Use of Humour. Idries Shah. 64p. 1977. 17.00 (*0-900860-57-X*, Pub. by Octagon Pr UK) ISHK.

Special Improvement Districts: Business Self-Help. Mary McClean. Ed. by Jenny Murphy. 52p. (Orig.). 1988. pap. 18.00 (*0-317-04850-3*) Natl Coun Econ Dev.

Special Infant: An Interdisciplinary Approach to the Optimal Development of Infants. Ed. by Jack M. Sack. LC 81-4478. 351p. 1982. 45.95 (*0-89885-028-2*) Human Sci Pr.

Special Inheritance. Margaret James. 1994. lib. bdg. 20.00 (*0-7278-4702-3*) Severn Hse.

Special Institute Index 1970-1994. 250p. 1994. ring bd. 30.00 (*0-929047-53-2*, SII) Rocky Mtn Mineral Law Found.

Special Interest Groups in American Politics. Stephen Miller. LC 83-4691. 160p. 1983. 34.95 (*0-87855-485-8*) Transaction Pubs.

***Special Interest Tourism.** B. Weiler & Colin M. Hall. LC 91-40465. 1992. write for info. (*1-85293-072-1*, Belhaven) Halsted Pr.

Special-Interest Tourism. Betty Weiler & C. Michael Hall. LC 00-91. 225p. 1992. text ed. 64.95 (*0-470-21843-6*) Halsted Pr.

Special Interest Tourism. Ed. by Betty Weiler & Colin M. Hall. LC 91-40465. 214p. 1993. text ed. 95.00 (*0-471-94786-5*) Wiley.

***Special Interests: How Lobbyists Influence Our Legislation.** Jules Archer. LC 96-27076. 144p. (YA). (gr. 7 up). 1997. lib. bdg. 16.90 (*0-7613-0060-0*) Millbrook Pr.

Special Interests & Policymaking: Agricultural Policies & Politics in Britain & The United States of America, 1956-70. Graham K. Wilson. LC 77-684. 214p. reprint ed. pap. 61.00 (*0-317-09612-5*, 2022407) Bks Demand.

Special Interests, the State & the Anglo-American Alliance, 1939-1945. Inderjeet Parmar. LC 95-14432. 200p. (C). 1995. 39.50 (*0-7146-4569-9*, Pub. by F Cass Pubs UK); pap. 22.50 (*0-7146-4226-6*, Pub. by F Cass Pubs UK) Intl Spec Bk.

Special Investigations Inspector. Jack Rudman. (Career Examination Ser.: C-748). 1994. pap. 29.95 (*0-8373-0748-1*) Nat Learn.

Special Investigator. Jack Rudman. (Career Examination Ser.: C-1588). 1994. pap. 29.95 (*0-8373-1588-3*) Nat Learn.

***Special Issue: Poems & Narrative Verse.** Frank Stefanile. (Orig.). 1996. pap. write for info. (*1-57553-324-3*) Watermrk Pr.

Special Issue on Incommensurate Phase Transitions. Ed. by A. R. Bishop et al. (Journal Ferroelectrics). 412p. 1986. text ed. 499.00 (*2-88124-121-2*) Gordon & Breach.

***Special Issue on Novel Aspects of Membrane-Mediated Cellular Responses: The Roles of Reactive Oxygens, NO, CO II.** Ed. by M. P. Blaustein et al. (Reviews of Physiology, Biochemistry & Pharmacology Ser.: Vol. 131). (Illus.). xiv, 115p. 1997. 89.00 (*3-540-61992-5*) Spr-Verlag.

Special Issue on Signal Transduction III. Ed. by M. P. Blaustein et al. (Reviews of Physiology, Biochemistry & Pharmacology Ser.: Vol. 124). 140p. 1994. 113.00 (*0-387-57587-1*) Spr-Verlag.

***Special Issue on Technology, Productivity, & Employment.** (STI Review Ser.: No. 18). 170p. 1996. 32.00 (*92-64-14719-5*, 90-96-18-1, Pub. by Org for Econ FR) OECD.

Special Issue on the Centenary Perspective. 80p. 1977. pap. 2.00 (*0-916694-48-8*) Central Conf.

Special Issue on Universalism - Particularism. 1977. pap. text ed. 2.75 (*0-916694-51-8*) Central Conf.

Special Issues in Child Care: A Comprehensive NVQ-Linked Textbook. Maureen O'Hagan & Maureen Smith. (Illus.). 252p. 1993. pap. 29.50 (*0-7020-1604-7*, Pub. by W B Saunders UK) Saunders.

Special Issues in Nutrition. Ed. by Lucille S. Hurley. 96p. (Orig.). 1987. reprint ed. pap. 17.50 (*0-943029-00-7*) Am Inst Nutrition.

Special Issues Index: Specialized Contents of Business, Industrial, & Consumer Journals. Compiled by Robert Sicignano & Doris Prichard. LC 82-11725. ix, 309p. 1982. text ed. 39.95 (*0-313-23278-4*, SII/, Greenwood Pr) Greenwood.

Special Kids' Stuff: High-Interest/Low Vocabulary Reading & Language Skills Activities. rev. ed. Sally D. Sharpe et al. LC 76-505. (Illus.). 240p. 1989. pap. text ed. 16.95 (*0-86530-088-7*, IP 20-X) Incentive Pubns.

Special Kind of Doctor: A History of Veterinary Medicine in Texas. Henry C. Dethloff & Donald H. Dyal. LC 91-456. (Illus.). 232p. 1991. 29.50 (*0-89096-483-1*) Tex A&M Univ Pr.

Special Kind of Freedom. Fay D. Lindsay. (Illus.). 99p. (Orig.). 1982. pap. 7.00 (*0-943980-01-1*) AIGA Pubns.

Special Kind of Leadership. Ron Short. 61p. (Orig.). 1991. pap. text ed. 16.95 (*1-887259-00-7*) TLG Pubns.

Special Kind of Love. Judy Baer. (Cedar River Daydreams Ser.). (YA). (gr. 7-10). 1993. mass mkt. 4.99 (*1-55661-367-9*) Bethany Hse.

Special Kind of Love. Stephen M. King. LC 95-21828. (Illus.). 32p. (J). 1996. 15.95 (*0-590-67681-4*) Scholastic Inc.

Special Kind of Parenting: Meeting the Needs of Handicapped Children. Julia P. Good & Joyce G. Reis. LC 85-80903. (Illus.). 172p. 1985. pap. 5.95 (*0-912500-27-1*) La Leche.

Special Language: From Human Thinking to Thinking Machines. Ed. by Christer Lauren & Marianne Nordman. 490p. 1989. 99.00 (*1-85359-034-7*, Pub. by Multilingual Matters UK); pap. 39.95 (*1-85359-033-9*, Pub. by Multilingual Matters UK) Taylor & Francis.

Special Leave. Phil Long & Margaret Hill. 84p. (C). 1988. 90.00 (*0-85292-400-3*, Pub. by IPM Hse UK) St Mut.

***Special Leave to Appeal: The Law & Practice of Special Leave to Appeal to the High Court of Australia.** David O'Brien. 200p. 1996. pap. 75.00 (*0-455-21421-2*, Pub. by Law Bk Co AT) Gaunt.

Special Lectures: Proceedings of the International Congress of Phonetic Sciences, 9th, Copenhagen, 1979. Ed. by Fischer-Jorgensen. (Journal: Phonetica: Vol. 37, No. 1-2). (Illus.). 108p. 1980. pap. 26.50 (*3-8055-1414-X*) S Karger.

Special Librarianship: A New Reader. Ed. by Eugene B. Jackson. LC 80-11530. 775p. reprint ed. pap. 180.00 (*0-317-52031-8*, 2027493) Bks Demand.

Special Librarianship As a Career: An SLA Information Kit. 105p. 1995. pap. 20.00 (*0-87111-440-2*) SLA.

Special Libraries: A Cataloging Guide. Sheila S. Intner & Jean Weihs. 225p. 1997. lib. bdg. 35.00 (*0-87287-955-0*) Libs Unl.

Special Libraries: A Cumulative Index, 1971-1980. Compiled by Ron Coplen. 94p. 1982. pap. 6.00 (*0-87111-314-7*) SLA.

Special Libraries: A Cumulative Index, 1981-1986. Compiled by Joyce A. Post. 40p. 1987. pap. 6.00 (*0-87111-327-9*) SLA.

Special Libraries: A Cumulative Index, 1987-1991. 32p. 1992. 6.00 (*0-87111-393-7*) SLA.

Special Libraries: A Guide for Management. 2nd ed. Janet L. Ahrensfeld et al. (Illus.). 85p. reprint ed. pap. 25.00 (*0-7837-1184-0*, 2041713) Bks Demand.

Special Libraries: A Guide for Management. 3rd ed. Elin B. Christianson et al. LC 91-33524. 98p. 1991. reprint ed. pap. 28.00 (*0-608-02392-2*, 2063033) Bks Demand.

***Special Libraries: A Guide for Management.** 4th ed. Cathy A. Porter & Elin B. Christianson. LC 97-8193. 1997. write for info. (*0-87111-466-6*) SLA.

Special Libraries: Increasing the Information Edge. Jose-Marie Griffiths & Donald W. King. 194p. 1993. 37.50 (*0-87111-414-3*) SLA.

Special Libraries & Information Centers: An Introductory Text. 3rd ed. Ellis Mount. LC 95-10605. 272p. 1995. pap. 37.50 (*0-87111-437-2*) SLA.

Special Libraries & Information Centers: An Introductory Text. Ellis Mount. LC 83-571. (Illus.). 200p. 1983. reprint ed. pap. 57.00 (*0-8357-6428-1*, 2035796) Bks Demand.

Special Libraries at Work. Elizabeth Ferguson & Emily R. Mobley. LC 83-25533. ix, 206p. (C). 1984. lib. bdg. 31.00 (*0-208-01939-1*, Lib Prof Pubns) Shoe String.

Special Libraries in Action: Cases & Crises. Esther G. Bierbaum. LC 92-43530. (Illus.). x, 114p. 1993. pap. text ed. 25.00 (*0-87287-983-6*) Libs Unl.

Special Library Role in Networks: A Conference Held at the General Motors Research Laboratories, Warren, Michigan, May 5-6, 1980. Special Libraries Association Staff. Ed. by Robert W. Gibson, Jr. LC 81-140531. 306p. reprint ed. pap. 87.30 (*0-317-30408-9*, 2024959) Bks Demand.

Special License. Elliott. 256p. 1995. mass mkt. 3.99 (*0-06-108335-6*, Harp PBks) HarpC.

Special Lines. Patricia R. Herring. 37p. (Orig.). 1986. pap. 5.95 (*0-9616484-0-6*) Santos-Santos Pubns.

Special Living Lessons for Relief Society Sisters by Sister Fonda AlaMode. Laurie M. Johnson. LC 96-43317. (Illus.). 60p. (Orig.). 1996. pap. 10.95 (*1-56085-090-6*) Signature Bks.

Special Love - Special Sex: An Oneida Community Diary. Ed. by Robert S. Fogarty. (Utopianism & Communitarianism Ser.). (Illus.). 1994. 28.95 (*0-8156-0286-3*) Syracuse U Pr.

Special Make-up Effects. Vincent J. Kehoe. 144p. 1991. pap. 38.95 (*0-240-80099-0*, Focal) Buttrwrth-Heinemann.

Special Management Needs of Alpine Ecosystems. Ed. by D. Johnson. 100p. 4.50 (*0-9603692-0-1*) Soc Range Mgmt.

Special Markets Chicken Book. 13.95 (*0-06-007917-7*, HarpT) HarpC.

Special Marriage Act. Mantha R. Murty. (C). 1990. 138.00 (*0-89771-142-4*) St Mut.

Special Meditations for Health, Wealth, Love. Joseph Murphy. 1952. pap. 2.50 (*0-87516-336-X*) DeVorss.

Special Melting & Processing Technologies. Ed. by G. K. Bhat. LC 89-9337. (Illus.). 987p. 1989. 98.00 (*0-8155-1202-3*) Noyes.

Special Men: A LRP's Recollections. Dennis Foley. (Orig.). 1994. mass mkt. 5.99 (*0-8041-0915-X*) Ivy Books.

Special Men & Special Missions: Inside American Special Operations Forces, 1945 to the Present. Joel Nadel & J. R. Wright. LC 93-41727. (Illus.). 256p. 1994. 29.95 (*1-85367-159-2*, 5593) Stackpole.

Special Men, Special War: Portraits of the SAS & Dhofar. Bruce M. Niven. (Illus.). 76p. 1992. 21.95 (*0-911977-10-4*, Imago Prod) Seven Hills Bk.

Special Methods in Light Microscopy, Vol. 17. Robert B. McLaughlin. LC 77-86749. (Illus.). 1977. 35.00 (*0-904962-06-7*) Microscope Pubns.

Special Minister of the Eucharist, Vol. 1: First Steps in Ministry. Liturgical Commission Publishings Diocese of Lansing Staff. Ed. by Mary J. Gilliland. 25p. (Orig.). (C). 1995. pap. text ed. 3.00 (*1-878268-04-X*) Lit Comm Pubs.

Special Ministers of the Eucharist. William J. Belford. 64p. 1992. pap. 2.95 (*0-8146-6039-8*, Pueblo Bks) Liturgical Pr.

Special Moments: Daily Activities to Share with Children. Diana Finley. 384p. 1993. pap. 9.95 (*1-882626-24-9*) Impress Ink.

Special Moments: Daily Activities to Share with Children. Diana Finley. 384p. 1993. pap. 9.95 (*1-882626-12-5*) Impress Ink.

***Special Mother.** (With Love to...Ser.). (Illus.). 44p. 1997. 6.99 (*0-8007-7162-1*) Revell.

Special National Procedures Concerning Non-Discrimination in Employment with Particular Reference to the Private Sector: A Practical Guide. 2nd ed. 65p. 1981. 12.00 (*92-2-100199-7*) Intl Labour Office.

Special Needs: Bridging the Curriculum Gap. Jonathan Solity & Shirley Bull. 272p. 1987. 85.00 (*0-335-10282-4*, Open Univ Pr); pap. 29.00 (*0-335-10281-6*, Open Univ Pr) Taylor & Francis.

Special Needs: Caring for Infants & Toddlers with Special Needs. Staisey Hodge. (Bright Ideas Ser.). (Illus.). 30p. (Orig.). (C). 1995. pap. 4.00 (*0-942388-16-X*) So Early Chldhood Assn.

Special Needs: One School's Whole School Approach. Anton Florek & Bob Spalding. 1989. write for info. (*1-85000-468-4*, Falmer Pr); pap. write for info. (*1-85000-469-2*, Falmer Pr) Taylor & Francis.

Special Needs: Special Answers. Lillie Pope et al. (Illus.). (J). (gr. k-6). 1979. pap. 19.95 (*0-87594-181-8*) Book-Lab.

Special-Needs Adoption: A Study of Intact Families. James A. Rosenthal & Victor K. Groze. LC 91-30278. 264p. 1992. text ed. 49.95 (*0-275-93790-9*, C3790, Praeger Pubs) Greenwood.

Special Needs Dementia Units: Design, Development & Operations. Nancy R. Peppard. LC 91-12278. 152p. 1991. 25.95 (*0-8261-5950-8*) Springer Pub.

Special Needs in Ordinary Classroom: From Staff Support to Staff Development. 3rd ed. Gerda Hanko. 176p. 1995. pap. 24.95 (*1-85346-391-4*, Pub. by D Fulton UK) Taylor & Francis.

Special Needs in the Classroom: A Teacher Education Guide. Mel Aibscow. 232p. 1994. pap. 35.00 (*92-3-102939-8*, U2934, Pub. by UNESCO FR) Bernan Associates.

***Special Needs Provision: Assessment, Concern & Action.** Geoff Sewell. (Special Needs in Ordinary Schools Ser.). 160p. 1996. pap. 22.00 (*0-304-33640-8*); text ed. 70.00 (*0-304-33635-1*) Cassell.

Special-Needs Reading List: An Annotated Guide to the Best Publications for Parents &... Wilma K. Sweeney. 1997. pap. text ed. 18.95 (*0-933149-74-3*) Woodbine House.

Special Needs Resource Guide: For Home Schooling & Or Supplementing Education. Patty Rendoff. 100p. 1994. 20.95 (*0-9644479-0-8*) Diggies Do It All.

Special Needs Software & Resources: A Guide & Directory. 4th ed. Joseph C. Clancy. (For the Apple II Series Computers). 445p. 1991. pap. text ed. 49.95 (*0-9627249-0-4*) SW & Resources.

Special Needs Student in Vocational Education: Selected Readings. Ed. by Stanley J. Urban. 1974. text ed. 9.50 (*0-8422-5155-3*); pap. text ed. 7.50 (*0-8422-0378-8*) Irvington.

Special Neuroendocrine Systems: Journal: Neuroendocrinology, Vol. 53, Suppl. 1, 1991. Ed. by S. F. Pang & F. Tang. (Illus.). iv, 84p. 1991. pap. 54.00 (*3-8055-5357-9*) S Karger.

Special No More: Anglo-American Relations: Rhetoric & Reality. John Dickie. 320p. 1994. 50.00 (*0-297-81486-9*) Trafalgar.

Special Nurse. large type ed. Quenna Tilbury. (Linford Romance Library). 313p. 1984. pap. 15.99 (*0-7089-6048-0*) Ulverscroft.

Special Object Lessons for Young Children. Greg Squyres. (Object Lessons Ser.). 112p. (Orig.). (YA). (gr. 10). 1995. pap. 5.99 (*0-8010-5012-X*) Baker Bks.

Special Occasion Letters: Recognizing Important Times in Your Members' Lives. CGI Staff. Ed. by Cindy G. Spear & Christine B. Norton. 66p. 1995. ring bd. 44.95 incl. disk (*1-57052-033-X*) Chrch Grwth VA.

Special Occasion Patterns for Cake Decorating. Roland A. Winbeckler. (Illus.). 24p. (Orig.). 1987. pap. 4.95 (*0-930113-12-8*) Winbeckler.

Special Occasions. Teresa Nelson. (Illus.). 28p. 1985. pap. 5.95 (*0-933491-02-6*) Hot off Pr.

Special Occasions: Holiday Entertaining All Year Round. John Hadamuscin. 1988. 29.00 (*0-517-57005-X*, Harmony) Crown Pub Group.

S

Special Occasions: The Best of Martha Stewart Living. Martha Stewart. LC 94-40128. 1995. pap. 20.00 (*0-517-88402-X*, C P Pubs) Crown Pub Group.

Special Occasions in Lace. Ed. by Bridget M. Cook. (Illus.). 48p. 1996. pap. 19.95 (*0-7134-7791-1*, Pub. by Batsford UK) Trafalgar.

Special Occasions in the Black Church. Benjamin S. Baker. LC 88-35601. 254p. (Orig.). 1989. 15.99 (*0-8054-2320-6*, 4223-20) Broadman.

Special Officer. Jack Rudman. (Career Examination Ser.: C-749). 1994. pap. 23.95 (*0-8373-0749-X*) Nat Learn.

Special Olympics. Fern G. Brown. Ed. by Mary P. Rich. LC 91-31661. (First Bks.). (Illus.). 64p. (J). (gr. 3-5). 1992. lib. bdg. 21.00 (*0-531-20062-0*) Watts.

Special Olympics. Nancy Gilbert. (Great Moments in Sports Ser.). 32p. (J). (gr. 4). 1990. lib. bdg. 14.95 (*0-88682-311-0*) Creative Ed.

Special Olympics: The First Twenty-Five Years. California Special Olympics Staff. 232p. 1994. 19.95 (*0-935701-85-0*) Foghorn Pr.

S

Special One: The Story of a Police Dog. Trish Keating. (Illus.). 32p. (J). (gr. 1-6). 1995. 14.95 (*1-886991-00-6*) Shamrck Pub.

Special Operations. Craig Sheeley. Ed. by Loren K. Wiseman. (Twilight: Two Thousand Ser.). 104p. (Orig.). (YA). 1992. pap. 12.00 (*1-55878-108-0*) Game Designers.

Special Operations: AAF Aid to European Resistance Movements 1943-45. Harris G. Warren. (USAF Historical Studies: No. 121). 269p. 1947. pap. text ed. 40.00 (*0-89126-020-X*) MA-AH Pub.

Special Operations & Elite Units, 1939-1988: A Research Guide. Roger A. Beaumont. LC 88-25083. (Research Guides in Military Studies: No. 2). 258p. 1988. text ed. 59.95 (*0-313-26001-X*, BUP/, Greenwood Pr) Greenwood.

Special Operations Forces. (Military Science Ser.). 1995. lib. bdg. 252.95 (*0-8490-6698-0*) Gordon Pr.

Special Operations Forces: An Assessment. John M. Collins. (Illus.). 189p. (Orig.). (C). 1994. pap. text ed. 30.00 (*0-7881-1361-5*) DIANE Pub.

Special Operations Forces: Force Structure & Readiness Issues. (Illus.). 53p. (Orig.). 1994. pap. text ed. 30.00 (*0-7881-0787-9*) DIANE Pub.

***Special Operations Forces: Force Structure & Readiness Issues.** (Illus.). 54p. 1994. pap. text ed. 40.00 (*1-57979-127-1*) BPI Info Servs.

Special Parent, Special Child: Parents of Children with Disabilites Share Their Trials, Triumphs & Hard-Won Wisdom. Tom Sullivan. 256p. 1996. pap. 13.95 (*0-87477-830-1*, Tarcher Putnam) Putnam Pub Group.

Special Parents: Birth & Early Years. Barbara Furneaux. (Children with Special Needs Ser.). 1988. 80.00 (*0-335-15123-X*, Open Univ Pr); pap. 27.00 (*0-335-15122-1*, Open Univ Pr) Taylor & Francis.

Special Parents, Special Children. Joanne E. Bernstein & Bryna Fireside. Ed. by Judith Mathews. LC 90-42442. (Illus.). 64p. (J). (gr. 3-7). 1991. 12.95 (*0-8075-7559-3*) A Whitman.

Special Partnership - A Practical Guide for Named Persons & Parents of Children. Linda Kerr et al. 64p. 1994. pap. 9.00 (*0-11-495237-X*, HM5237X, Pub. by Stationery Ofc UK) Bernan Associates.

Special People. Rachael Letch. LC 90-48944. (Who Cares Ser.). (J). (gr. 4 up). 1990. 7.99 (*0-85953-360-3*); pap. 3.99 (*0-85953-350-6*) Childs Play.

***Special People.** Rachael Letch. (Who Cares Ser.). (ITA.). (J). 1990. pap. 3.99 (*0-85953-580-0*) Childs Play.

Special People. Tom Mahon. LC 93-60738. 144p. 1994. 9.95 (*1-55523-635-9*) Winston-Derek.

Special People. Julie N. Eisenhower. (Illus.). 208p. (YA). 1990. reprint ed. pap. text ed. 6.95 (*0-939631-24-5*) Thomas Publications.

***Special People: Who Cares about Them.** Child's Play Staff. (J). 1996. lib. bdg. 11.95 (*0-85953-884-2*) Childs Play.

Special People... Getting to Know Them: Resources in Mental Retardation. 1.00 (*0-686-70272-7*) Boston Public Lib.

Special Physical Education. 2nd rev. ed. Paul Jansma & Ronald W. French. LC 93-10842. 1994. pap. text ed. 66.00 (*0-13-827056-2*) P-H Gen Ref & Trav.

***Special Physical Education.** 7th adapted ed. John M. Dunn. 656p. (C). 1996. text ed. write for info. (*0-697-38187-0*) Brown & Benchmark.

Special Physical Education. 7th ed. John M. Dunn & Hollis F. Fait. 608p. (C). 1996. per. write for info. (*0-697-12623-4*) Brown & Benchmark.

Special Physical Education: Adapted, Individualized, Developmental. 6th ed. John M. Dunn & Hollis F. Fait. 608p. (C). 1989. text ed. write for info. (*0-697-08624-0*) Brown & Benchmark.

Special Picture Cookbook. Freida R. Steed. 108p. 1977. pap. 18.00 (*0-89079-010-8*, 1056) PRO-ED.

Special Piece of Hell: The Untold Story of Peleliu - the Pacific War's Forgotten Battle. Bill D. Ross. 1993. mass mkt. 6.99 (*0-312-95004-7*) St Martin.

***Special Place.** Lemieux. (Fairy Lair Ser.: No. 1). 1997. mass mkt. 3.99 (*0-689-81725-8*) S&S Childrens.

Special Place: A Child's Story about Entering Counseling for Children Ages 4 Through 6. Diana L. McCoy. (Illus.). 32p. (Orig.). (J). (gr. 2-5). 1988. pap. text ed. 5.50 (*0-9619250-3-5*) Magic Lantrn.

Special Place: A Child's Story about Entering Counseling for Children Ages 4 Through 6. Diana L. McCoy. (Illus.). 24p. (Orig.). (J). (ps-1). 1988. pap. 5.50 (*0-9619250-2-7*) Magic Lantrn.

***Special Place for Charlee: A Child's Companion Through Pet Loss.** Debby Morehead. LC 96-92552. (Illus.). 36p. (Orig.). (J). (gr. 2-6). 1996. pap. 6.95 (*0-9654049-0-0*) Partners In Pub.

Special Place for Santa: A Legend for Our Time. Jeanne Pieper. (Illus.). 1991. write for info. (*0-9616286-1-8*) Kneeling Santa.

Special Places: For the Discerning Traveler. 6th ed. Fred Nystom & Mardi M. Nystrom. Ed. by Brandy K. Demisco. 312p. 1994. pap. 16.95 (*0-936777-03-6*) Special Pl.

***Special Places: For the Discerning Traveler.** 7th rev. ed. Fred Mystrom & Mardi Mystrom. Ed. by Alex Jones. (Illus.). 208p. (Orig.). 1997. pap. 18.95 (*0-936777-04-4*) Special Pl.

***Special Places to Stay in Spain & Portugal.** 2nd ed. Alastair Sawday. 1997. pap. 19.95 (*0-9521954-6-1*) St Martin.

Special Planet: Understanding People & Their Environment. Sabine Helling. (Orig.). 1995. pap. text ed. 15.95 (*0-472-08375-9*); teacher ed., pap. text ed. 13.95 (*0-472-08381-3*) U of Mich Pr.

Special Plays for Holidays. Helen L. Miller. LC 86-9332. (Orig.). (J). (gr. 1-6). 1986. pap. 12.95 (*0-8238-0275-2*) Plays.

Special Plays for Special Days: 30 Minute Holiday & Seasonal Plays. Judy T. Mecca. (Illus.). 96p. (Orig.). 1991. pap. text ed. 9.95 (*0-86530-203-0*, IP 194-4) Incentive Pubns.

***Special Polymers for Electronics & Optoelectronics.** Ed. by J. Chilton & Goosey. (Illus.). 384p. 1995. text ed. 99.95 (*0-412-58400-X*, Chap & Hall NY) Chapman & Hall.

Special Populations of Gifted Learners. Richert & Feldhusen. Ed. by Reva C. Jenkins-Friedman et al. 1991. pap. 10.00 (*0-89824-528-1*) Trillium Pr.

Special Princess. Sophie A. Luth. (Illus.). 36p. (J). 1990. 3.95 (*0-9626153-0-7*) Luth & Assocs.

Special Privileges. Donald Charroux. LC 90-70902. 181p. 1991. pap. 6.95 (*1-55523-356-2*) Winston-Derek.

Special Problems in Child & Adolescent Behavior. fac. ed. Ed. by Larry E. Beutler & Richard Greene. LC 78-56115. 416p. pap. 118.60 (*0-7837-7400-1*, 2047194) Bks Demand.

Special Problems in Counseling the Chemically Dependent Adolescent. Eileen S. Sweet. LC 91-20804. (Journal of Adolescent Chemical Dependency). (Illus.). 170p. 1991. pap. 29.95 (*1-56024-162-4*); lib. bdg. 12.95 (*1-56024-163-2*) Haworth Pr.

Special Problems in Gear Tooth Couplings. Georges Henriot. (Fall Technical Meeting Papers 88FTM10). (Illus.). 12p. 1988. pap. text ed. 30.00 (*1-55589-515-8*) AGMA.

Special Problems in Managing Eating Disorders. Ed. by Joel Yager et al. LC 91-4580. (Clinical Practice Ser.: No. 20). 245p. 1991. text ed. 32.50 (*0-88048-457-8*, 8457) Am Psychiatric.

Special Problems of Negro Education. Doxey A. Wilkerson. LC 76-82097. (Illus.). 171p. 1970. reprint ed. text ed. 45.00 (*0-8371-3210-X*, WIN&, Negro U Pr) Greenwood.

Special Problems on Non-Compliance among Elderly Women of Color. Ed. by Barbara L. Kail. LC 92-16194. 148p. 1992. lib. bdg. 69.95 (*0-7734-9531-2*) E Mellen.

Special Procedures for Testing Soil & Rock for Engineering Purposes. 5th ed. American Society for Testing & Materials Staff. LC 70-114701. (ASTM Special Technical Publication Ser.: No. 479). 641p. reprint ed. pap. 180.00 (*0-317-55525-1*, 2056329) Bks Demand.

Special Programme of Research, Development, & Research Training in Human Reproduction: Annual Technical Report 1992. 293p. 1993. pap. text ed. 22.50 (*0-614-08037-1*, 1930041) World Health.

Special Projects Coordinator. Jack Rudman. (Career Examination Ser.: C-2933). 1994. pap. 34.95 (*0-8373-2933-7*) Nat Learn.

Special Publication Copy Unit 2. Bragger. (Secondary French Ser.). (C). 1988. text ed. write for info. (*0-8384-1734-5*) Heinle & Heinle.

Special Purpose Rooms. rev. ed. Time-Life Books Editors. (Home Repair & Improvement Ser.). (Illus.). 136p. 1989. reprint ed. 14.60 (*0-8094-7358-5*); reprint ed. pap. write for info. (*0-8094-7361-5*); reprint ed. text ed. write for info. (*0-8094-7360-7*); reprint ed. lib. bdg. 20.60 (*0-8094-7359-3*) Time-Life.

Special-Purpose Steam Turbines for Refinery Services. 3rd ed. 1987. 50.00 (*0-685-24466-0*, 822-61200) Am Petroleum.

Special Raccoon. Kim Carlisle. LC 94-66764. 1994. pap. 9.95 (*0-88282-096-6*) New Horizon NJ.

Special Reaction Teams: Selecting, Training & Equipping Elite Counterterrorist Units. 74p. 1990. pap. 12.00 (*0-87364-561-8*) Paladin Pr.

Special Reading Problems: Some Helps Training Module-Trainer's Guide. rev. ed. Susanne Miller. 32p. 1983. audio 132.00 (*0-930713-47-8*) Lit Vol Am.

Special Reading Problems Some Helps Tutor Notes. Susanne Miller. 9p. 1983. 2.00 (*0-930713-25-7*) Lit Vol Am.

Special Recreation. 2nd ed. Dan Kennedy et al. 384p. (C). 1995. per. write for info. (*0-697-28930-3*) Brown & Benchmark.

Special Recreation: Opportunities for Persons with Disabilities. 2nd ed. Dan Kennedy et al. 384p. (C). 1991. boxed write for info. (*0-697-10965-8*) Brown & Benchmark.

Special Recreation: Opportunities for Persons with Disabilities. 3rd ed. Ralph Smith et al. 384p. (C). 1995. text ed. write for info. (*0-697-15246-4*) Brown & Benchmark.

Special Recreational Services: Therapeutic & Adapted. Jay S. Shivers & Hollis F. Fait. LC 84-14329. 369p. reprint ed. pap. 105.20 (*0-7837-2845-X*, 2057627) Bks Demand.

Special Relationship. Eleanor Eley. (You & Your Baby Ser.). 36p. 1994. 2.65 (*0-9642374-1-5*) Corner Hlth.

***Special Relationship.** Robyn Sisman. 1996. mass mkt. 5.99 (*0-614-20515-8*, Onyx) NAL-Dutton.

Special Relationship. Robyn Sisman. 432p. 1996. pap. 6.50 (*0-451-18201-4*, Sig) NAL-Dutton.

Special Relationship: A Political History of Anglo-American Relations since 1945. C. J. Bartlett. (Post War World Ser.). 196p. (C). 1992. pap. text ed. 27.50 (*0-582-02395-5*, 79340) Longman.

Special Relationship: A Political History of Anglo-American Relations Since 1945. Christopher A. Bartlett. (C). 1992. text ed. 55.95 (*0-582-02396-3*) Addison-Wesley.

Special Relationship? American Influences on Public Law in the UK. Ed. by Ian Loveland. 336p. 1996. 75.00 (*0-19-826014-8*) OUP.

Special Relationship: Anglo-American Relations since 1945. Ed. by William R. Louis & Hedley Bull. 432p. 1987. reprint ed. 75.00 (*0-19-822925-9*) OUP.

Special Relationship: Anglo-American Relations since 1945. Ed. by William R. Louis & Hedley Bull. 432p. 1989. reprint ed. pap. 29.95 (*0-19-820183-4*) OUP.

Special Relationship: Our Teachers & How We Learn. John C. Board. 1991. 28.95 (*0-916366-68-5*) Pushcart Pr.

Special Relationship: The United States & Military Government in Thailand, 1947-1958. Daniel M. Fineman. 344p. 1997. text ed. 39.00 (*0-8248-1818-0*) UH Pr.

Special Relationship Between W. Germany & Israel. Lily G. Feldman. 352p. 1984. text ed. 44.95 (*0-04-327068-9*) Routledge Chapman & Hall.

***Special Relativity.** French. (MIT Introductory Physics Ser.). (Illus.). 296p. (Orig.). (C). (gr. 13 up). 1989. pap. text ed. 48.95 (*0-412-34320-7*) Chapman & Hall.

Special Relativity. Anthony P. French. (M.I.T. Introductory Physics Ser.). (C). 1968. pap. text ed. 17.95 (*0-393-09793-5*) Norton.

Special Relativity. V. E. Schroder. (Lecture Notes in Physics Ser.: Vol. 33). 228p. 1990. text ed. 48.00 (*981-02-0068-4*); pap. text ed. 23.00 (*981-02-0132-X*) World Scientific Pub.

***Special Relativity.** Albert Shadowitz. pap. 6.95 (*0-486-65743-4*) Dover.

Special Relativity. N. M. Woodhouse. Ed. by W. Beiglbock et al. (Lecture Notes in Physics, New Series, Monographs: Vol. M6). viii, 86p. (C). 1992. 48.95 (*0-387-55049-6*) Spr-Verlag.

Special Relativity: Applications to Particle Physics & the Classical Theory of Fields. Mohammad Saleem & Muhammad Rafique. LC 92-21707. (Ellis Horwood Series in Physics & Its Applications). 1992. 71.95 (*0-13-827106-2*, Pub. by Tavistock-E Horwood UK) Routledge Chapman & Hall.

***Special Relativity & Its Experimental Foundations.** (Advanced Series on Theoretical Physical Science). 250p. 1997. lib. bdg. 31.00 (*981-02-2749-3*) World Scientific Pub.

Special Relativity & Quantum Theory: A Collection of Papers on the Poincare Group. Ed. by Marilyn E. Noz & Y. S. Kim. (C). 1988. lib. bdg. 197.00 (*90-277-2799-6*) Kluwer Ac.

Special Relativity for Physicists. G. Stephenson & C. W. Kilmister. (Illus.). 108p. 1987. reprint ed. pap. text ed. 4.95 (*0-486-65519-9*) Dover.

Special Report: A Doctor's Proven New Way to Conquer Back Pain. John E. Eichenlaub. LC 92-28322. 1992. 24.95 (*0-13-827049-X*, Parker Publishing Co) P-H.

Special Report: Guide to Overseas Correspondence Clubs & Services. Richard H. Rongstad. 108p. 1994. pap. text ed. 25.00 (*1-887897-01-1*) Vikng-Phoenix.

Special Report: Interstate Banking & Community Development Acts. Murray A. Indick & Thomas J. Delaney. 400p. 1995. pap. 95.00 (*0-7913-2245-9*) Warren Gorham & Lamont.

Special Report: Osteoporosis: How to Stop It, How to Prevent It, How to Reverse It. Elizabeth Vierck. LC 93-5849. 1993. 24.95 (*0-13-559782-X*, Parker Publishing Co) P-H.

Special Report Financial & Economic Data of the Men's & Boys' Clothing Industry. 25p. 1975. 7.00 (*0-318-19682-4*) Clothing Mfrs.

Special Report on Financial & Economic Data of the Men's & Boys' Clothing Industry. 18p. 1980. 7.00 (*0-318-19696-4*) Clothing Mfrs.

Special Report on Medical Records. Meridith B. Cox. (Risk Management Ser.). Date not set. pap. 50.00 (*0-912665-29-7*) Cox Pubns.

Special Report on Spouse Abuse in Texas. James S. Stachura & Raymond H. Teske, Jr. 18p. 1979. 2.00 (*0-318-02508-6*) S Houston Employ.

Special Report on Surnames in Ireland: Together with Varieties & Synonymes of Surnames & Christian Names in Ireland, 2 vols. in 1. Robert E. Matheson. LC 68-54684. 172p. 1994. reprint ed. 18.50 (*0-8063-0187-2*, 3830) Genealog Pub.

Special Report on the Pollution of River Waters. James P. Kirkwood. LC 75-125750. (American Environmental Studies). (Illus.). 1971. reprint ed. 26.95 (*0-405-02676-5*) Ayer.

Special Report: State Lotteries - How to Get in It & Win see Lottery Master Guide

Special Reports on American Broadcasting, 1932-1947. Ed. by Christopher H. Sterling. LC 74-7682. (Telecommunications Ser.). 1974. reprint ed. 57.95 (*0-405-06059-9*) Ayer.

Special Request. Judith Duncan. (To Mother with Love Ser.). 1993. pap. 4.99 (*0-685-61546-4*) Silhouette.

Special Research Methods for Gerontology. Ed. by M. P. Lawton & A. R. Herzog. (Society & Aging Ser.: Vol. 2). 257p. 1989. text ed. 37.95 (*0-89503-061-6*); pap. text ed. 28.46 (*0-89503-053-5*) Baywood Pub.

Special Revenue Sources for Parks & Recreation: A Survey of the States. Kenneth Hunter. 52p. reprint ed. pap. 25.00 (*0-7837-1540-4*, 2041824) Bks Demand.

Special Rigger. Jack Rudman. (Career Examination Ser.: C-750). 1994. pap. 27.95 (*0-8373-0750-3*) Nat Learn.

Special Salute to the U. S. Airforce, 1990. Photos by Randy Jolly. (Illus.). 1989. 10.00 (*0-685-29814-0*) Aero Graphics.

Special Scar: The Experiences of People Bereaved by Suicide. Allison Wertheimer. 256p. (C). 1991. pap. text ed. 17.95 (*0-415-01763-7*, A5415) Routledge.

Special Schools: Students, Parents, Teachers. Ed. by Ken Dovey & Joe Graffam. 250p. 1995. pap. 80.00 (*0-909184-36-4*, Pub. by Deakin Univ AT) St Mut.

Special Seating. Jean A. Zollars. (Illus.). 95p. (Orig.). 1993. pap. 20.00 (*1-882632-01-X*); pap. 10.00 (*1-882632-05-2*) PAX Pr.

Special Sections & Promotions. Arnold A. DeLuca. (Illus.). 48p. 1981. pap. 5.00 (*1-878666-08-8*) Dynamo Inc.

Special Senses. Braem. 1994. pap. text ed. 19.95 (*1-878576-29-1*) Flash Anatomy Inc.

Special Sermons for Special Days. Roger Ellsworth. LC 96-24007. 128p. (Orig.). 1996. pap. 7.99 (*0-87213-150-5*) Loizeaux.

Special Services for Adult Learners, Options: Expanding Educational Sources for Adults. National Center for Research in Vocational Education Staff. 1987. 29.50 (*0-317-04616-0*, SP500F) Ctr Educ Trng Employ.

Special Services Manager. Jack Rudman. (Career Examination Ser.: C-2147). 1994. reprint ed. pap. 39.95 (*0-8373-2147-6*) Nat Learn.

Special Sessions Convened in February 1892 (for 1893) & Convened in June 1893 see Laws of the Choctaw Nation, Passed at the Regular Session of the General Council Convened at Tushka Humma, Oct. 6, 1890, Adjourned Nov. 14, 1890

Special Sign Hanger. Jack Rudman. (Career Examination Ser.: C-751). 1994. pap. 27.95 (*0-8373-0751-1*) Nat Learn.

Special Sisters: Woman in the European Middle Ages. 4th ed. Arthur F. Ide. LC 82-23352. (Woman in History Ser.: Vol. 12b). (Illus.). 115p. 1983. lib. bdg. 35.00 (*0-86663-097-X*) Ide Hse.

***Special Skills of Children & Adolescents: Conceptualization, Assessment, Treatment.** Kenneth W. Merrell & Gretchen A. Gimpel. LC 97-11805. 250p. 1997. write for info. (*0-8058-2655-6*) L Erlbaum Assocs.

***Special Skills of Children & Adolescents: Conceptualization, Assessment, Treatment.** Kenneth W. Merrell & Gretchen A. Gimpel. LC 97-11805. 250p. 1997. pap. write for info. (*0-8058-2656-4*) L Erlbaum Assocs.

Special Sorrows: The Diasporic Imagination of Irish, Polish, & Jewish Immigrants in the United States. Matthew F. Jacobson. LC 94-31496. 335p. 1995. text ed. 45.00 (*0-674-83185-3*, JACSPE) HUP.

Special Sort of Man. Natalie Fox. 1994. 2.99 (*0-373-11653-5*) Harlequin Bks.

Special Special. Bessie Ashworth. 53p. (Orig.). 1995. pap. 12.95 (*0-922510-11-3*) Lucky Bks.

Special Species: An Anthology Written by & for the Children of San Diego County. San Diego County School Children Staff. Ed. by Barbara Moran. (Illus.). 40p. (Orig.). (J). (gr. 1-12). 1992. pap. 3.95 (*0-9634474-0-8*) Ms B Bks.

Special Species by California Kids. 4th ed. Intro. by Barbara Moran. (Anthology Ser.: No. 4). (Illus.). 90p. (J). (gr. k-12). 1994. pap. 14.95 (*0-9634474-2-4*) Ms B Bks.

Special Statistical Report on Profit, Sales & Production Trends for the Men's & Boys' Tailored Clothing Industry. 12p. 1982. 15.00 (*0-318-19697-2*) Clothing Mfrs.

Special Statistical Report on Profit, Sales, Production & Marketing Trends for the Men's & Boys' Tailored Clothing Industry. 15p. 1983. 15.00 (*0-318-19698-0*) Clothing Mfrs.

Special Status of Cornals: Internal & External Evidence. Ed. by Carole Paradis & Jean-Francois Prunet. (Phonetics & Phonology Ser.: Vol. 2). 231p. 1991. pap. text ed. 53.00 (*0-12-544967-4*) Acad Pr.

***Special Stocking.** (J). (ps up). 1996. pap. 4.99 (*0-318-68392-X*) RD Assn.

Special Stocking. Stewart Cowley. (Fluffy Tale Ser.). (Illus.). 10p. (J). (ps up). 1996. bds. 4.99 (*0-88705-963-5*) Rdrs Dgst Yng Fam.

Special Street. Renate Kozikowski. (Illus.). (ps-3). 1994. 12.95 (*0-307-17604-5*, Golden Books) Western Pub.

Special Studies of the First Five Years of the Panel Study of Income Dynamics see Five Thousand American Families: Patterns of Economic Progress

Special Study of Securities Markets: Report, 4 bks., Set. U. S. Securities & Exchange Commission. LC 63-61766. 1982. reprint ed. lib. bdg. 195.00 (*0-89941-227-0*, 201590) W S Hein.

Special Study of the Incidence of Retardation. L. B. Blan. LC 79-176569. (Columbia University. Teachers College. Contributions to Education Ser.: No. 40). reprint ed. 37.50 (*0-404-55040-1*) AMS Pr.

Special Tasks. Pavel Sudoplatov et al. 1995. pap. 14.95 (*0-316-82115-2*) Little.

Special Taste of Florida: An Authorized Collection of 400 Outstanding Recipes From the Kitchens of Florida's Premier Restaurants, Resorts & Luxury Hotels. G. Dean Foster. LC 94-74944. (Illus.). 346p. 1995. 24.95 (*0-9644572-7-X*) Seagate Pub.

***Special-Teas.** M. Dalton King. 1996. 14.98 (*0-7651-9744-8*) Smithmark.

Special Techniques for the Enzymologist see Methods in Enzymology

An Asterisk (*) at the beginning of an entry indicates that the title is appearing in BIP for the first time.

Special Techniques in Internal Fixation. C. F. Brunner & B. G. Waber. (Illus.). 198p. 1981. 155.00 (*0-387-11056-9*) Spr-Verlag.

***Special Tests for Orthopedic Examination.** Jeff Konin et al. LC 97-21469. (Illus.). 200p. (Orig.). 1997. pap. 28.00 (*1-55642-351-9*) SLACK Inc.

Special Tests of Visual Function. Ed. by E. Zrenner. (Developments in Ophthalmology Ser.: Vol. 9). (Illus.). xii, 240p. 1984. 119.25 (*3-8055-3885-5*) S Karger.

Special Themes for Moving & Learning. Rae Pica. LC 90-27862. (Illus.). 168p. (Orig.). 1991. pap. text ed. 18.00 (*0-87322-319-5*, BPIC0319) Human Kinetics.

***Special Theory of Relativity.** David Bohm. LC 96-27226. 256p. (C). 1996. text ed. 59.95 (*0-415-14808-1*) Routledge.

***Special Theory of Relativity.** David Bohm. LC 96-27226. 256p. 1996. pap. 18.95 (*0-415-14809-X*) Routledge.

Special Theory of Relativity: A Mathematical Approach. Anadijiban Das. LC 93-10256. 1996. 39.95 (*0-387-94042-1*) Spr-Verlag.

Special Theory of Relativity: A Mathematical Exposition. Anadijiban Das. (Illus.). 220p. 1993. write for info. (*3-540-94042-1*) Spr-Verlag.

Special Theory of Relativity: Its Origin, Meanings, & Implications. David Bohm. 1979. text ed. write for info. (*0-8053-1001-0*, Adv Bk Prog) Addison-Wesley.

Special Theory of Relativity for Mathematics Students. P. Lorimer. 112p. 1990. text ed. 28.00 (*981-02-0254-7*) World Scientific Pub.

Special Theory of Relativity for Mathematics Students. P. Lorimer. 112p. (C). 1990. pap. text ed. 21.00 (*981-02-0255-5*) World Scientific Pub.

Special Time for Special People. John Wetherwax. 1990. pap. 8.95 (*1-877871-02-8*) Ed Ministries.

Special Times: Honoring Our Jewish & Christian Heritages for Grades 1 & 2. Betty J. Middleton. 208p. 1994. pap. 30.00 (*1-55896-281-6*) Unitarian Univ.

Special Times: 365 Low-Cost Activities for Children. Ed. & Intro. by Gloria Beverage. (Illus.). 384p. (J). 1995. pap. 10.00 (*0-9635089-0-3*) PWC Pub.

Special Times with God. David Shibley & Naomi Shibley. LC 93-87428. (Illus.). 160p. 1994. reprint ed. pap. 7.95 (*0-89221-253-5*) New Leaf.

Special to the Daily: The First One Hundred Years of Editorial Freedom at the Michigan Daily. Ed. by Susan Holtzer. 282p. 1990. pap. text ed. 24.95 (*0-9625945-2-0*) Caddo Gap Pr.

Special Topics & Master Index for Books 1-9. Richard Braden. (Hands-on Windows Programming Ser.: Bk. 9). 160p. 1995. pap. 15.95 (*1-55622-480-X*) Wordware Pub.

Special Topics in Fluid Dynamics. K. O. Friedrichs. (Notes on Mathematics & Its Applications Ser.). 190p. (C). 1966. 147.00 (*0-685-01961-6*); pap. text ed. 106.00 (*0-677-01005-2*) Gordon & Breach.

Special Topics in Foundations. Ed. by Braja M. Das. (Sessions Proceedings Ser.). 136p. 1988. 17.00 (*0-87262-645-8*) Am Soc Civil Eng.

Special Topics in Justice & Peace: Nine Articles for Student Handouts. Julia Ahlers. Ed. by Barbara Allaire. 32p. (Orig.). (YA). (gr. 11-12). 1990. pap. text ed. 8.95 (*0-88489-244-1*) St Marys.

Special Topics in Policing. Harry W. More. LC 91-70608. 268p. (C). 1991. pap. text ed. 25.95 (*0-87084-574-8*) Anderson Pub Co.

***Special Topics in Survival Analysis.** 1995. text ed. 54.95 (*0-412-98711-2*, Chap & Hall NY) Chapman & Hall.

Special Topics in the Afro-Diasporan Political Experience. Getachew Metaferia et al. 1990. pap. 5.00 (*1-879893-05-3*) IAAS Pubs.

Special Topics of Elementary Mathematics see History of Mathematics

Special Touches. Sharon Brondos. (Men Made in America Ser.). 1995. mass mkt. 3.99 (*0-373-45200-4*, 1-45200-2) Harlequin Bks.

***Special Trade.** Sally Wittman. (Illus.). (J). (ps-3). 1978. 7.79 (*0-06-026553-1*, 959175) HarpC.

Special Trade. Sally Wittman. LC 77-25673. (Trophy Picture Bk.). (Illus.). 32p. (J). (ps-2). 1985. reprint ed. pap. 5.95 (*0-06-443071-5*, Trophy) HarpC Child Bks.

Special Treatment: The Untold Story of the Survival of Thousands of Jews in Hitler's Third Reich. Alan Abrams. (Illus.). 261p. 1985. 14.95 (*0-8184-0364-0*) Carol Pub Group.

Special Trends in Thermal Analysis. Ferenc Paulik. 1995. text ed. 125.00 (*0-471-95769-0*) Wiley.

Special Trigonometric Series in K Dimensions. Stephen Wainger. LC 52-42839. (Memoirs Ser.: No. 1/59). 102p. 1965. pap. 16.00 (*0-8218-1259-9*, MEMO/1/59) Am Math.

Special Trust & Confidence: The Making of an Officer. Cathy Downes. 270p. 1991. text ed. 37.50 (*0-7146-3354-2*, Pub. by F Cass Pubs UK) Intl Spec Bk.

Special Twentieth Anniversary Issue of the ASME Biomechanics Symposium. 160p. 1993. 20.00 (*0-7918-0695-2*, I00358) ASME.

Special Urgency of Mercy: Why Sister Faustina? George W. Kosicki. 101p. 1990. pap. 4.95 (*0-940535-36-X*, UP136) Franciscan U Pr.

***Special Valor.** Richard Wheeler. 1996. 11.98 (*0-7858-0751-9*) Bk Sales Inc.

Special Values of Dirichlet Series, Monodromy, & the Periods of Automorphic Forms. Peter Stiller. LC 84-3060. (Memoirs of the American Mathematical Society Ser.: No. 49/299). 116p. 1984. pap. 18.00 (*0-8218-2300-0*, MEMO/49/299) Am Math.

Special Victims. Nick Gaitano. 1994. 21.00 (*0-671-87014-9*) S&S Trade.

Special Visions: Profiles of Fifteen Women Artists from the Renaissance to the Present Day. Olga S. Opfell. LC 90-53603. (Illus.). 231p. 1991. lib. bdg. 32.50 (*0-89950-603-8*) McFarland & Co.

Special Voices: Teaching Children with Special Needs in the Regular Classroom. Cora L. Five. LC 91-24709. 193p. 1991. pap. text ed. 22.00 (*0-435-08594-8*, 08594) Heinemann.

Special Way to Care: A Guide for Neighbors, Friends, & Community in their Efforts to Provide Financial & Emotional Support for Terminally & Catastrophically Ill Children. Sheila Petersen. 180p. (Orig.). 1988. pap. write for info. (*0-9619785-0-3*) Friends Karen.

Special Ways with Ordinary Days. Sharon Meisenheimer. (J). (gr. k-3). 1988. pap. 12.99 (*0-8224-6347-4*) Fearon Teach Aids.

***Special Welcomes.** Corrine Miller. 76p. 1993. pap. 9.50 (*1-56770-287-2*) S Scheewe Pubns.

***Special Welcomes, No. 2.** Corrine Miller. 94p. 1994. pap. 9.50 (*1-56770-298-8*) S Scheewe Pubns.

***Special Welcomes: All Wrapped Up, Vol. 5.** Corinne Miller. 63p. 1995. pap. 9.50 (*1-56770-333-X*) S Scheewe Pubns.

***Special Welcomes No. 3: Crazy about Crafting.** Corrine Miller. 72p. 1994. pap. 9.50 (*1-56770-309-7*) S Scheewe Pubns.

***Special Welcomes Crop Keepers, Vol. 6.** Corinne Miller. 83p. 1996. pap. 9.50 (*1-56770-347-X*) S Scheewe Pubns.

Special Women? The Experience of Women in the Special Hospital System. Ed. by Catherine Hemingway. 172p. 1996. 55.95 (*1-85628-868-4*, Pub. by Avebury Pub UK) Ashgate Pub Co.

Special Women: The Role of the Professional Labor Assistant. Paulina Perez & Cheryl Snedeker. (Illus.). 157p. (Orig.). 1990. pap. 8.95 (*0-937604-10-0*, Pennypr) Intl Childbirth.

Special Women: The Role of the Professional Labor Assistant. 2nd ed. Paulina Perez & Cheryl Snedeker. LC 94-94211. (Illus.). 157p. (Orig.). 1994. pap. 9.95 (*0-9641159-9-9*) Cutting Edge.

***Special Words.** Joyce L. Heatherley. (Hallmark Ser.). Date not set. write for info. (*0-345-41106-4*) Ballantine.

Special Words: Notes for When You Don't Know What to Say. Joyce L. Heatherley. 256p. 1996. 19.99 (*0-345-40301-0*, Moorings) Ballantine.

Special Worship Resources. Compiled by Paul M. Miller. 1982. 5.50 (*0-685-68737-6*, MP-613) Lillenas.

Specialisation & Choice in Urban Education: The City Technology College Experiment. Geoff Whitty et al. LC 93-9649. 240p. (C). (gr. 13). 1993. text ed. 74.95 (*0-415-08527-6*, B2546, Routledge NY) Routledge.

Specialist. Dale J. Smith. LC 90-93096. 1991. 18.95 (*0-87212-239-5*) Libra.

Specialist. Chic Sale. LC 29-5733. 1929. reprint ed. 6.00 (*0-911416-00-5*, 911416) Specialist.

Specialist: His Philosophy, His Disease, His Cure. Archie J. Bahm. LC 77-81834. 126p. 1977. 8.00 (*0-911714-08-1*, World Bks) Bahm.

Specialist, Aging Services. Jack Rudman. (Career Examination Ser.: C-3565). 1994. pap. 29.95 (*0-8373-3565-5*) Nat Learn.

Specialist Care of the Competition Horse. British Horse Society Staff. (British Horse Society Manual of Stable Management Ser.: Bk. 5). (Illus.). 160p. 1988. pap. 10.95 (*0-939481-13-8*) Half Halt Pr.

Specialist Food Retailing in the UK 1980-1990. Euromonitor Staff. 80p. (C). 1988. 825.00 (*0-86338-313-0*, Pub. by Euromonitor Pubns UK) Gale.

Specialist Foster Family Care: A Normalizing Experience. Ed. by Joe Hudson. LC 89-15648. (Child & Youth Services Ser.: Vol. 12, Nos. 1 & 2). (Illus.). 273p. 1989. text ed. 49.95 (*0-86656-939-1*) Haworth Pr.

Specialist in Adult Services. Jack Rudman. (Career Examination Ser.: C-3548). 1994. pap. 29.95 (*0-8373-3548-5*) Nat Learn.

Specialist in Education. Jack Rudman. (Career Examination Ser.: C-752). 1994. pap. 34.95 (*0-8373-0752-X*) Nat Learn.

Specialist Mathematics: Core. Ed. by Barry McCrae et al. 192p. (C). 1993. pap. 24.95 (*0-522-84578-9*, Pub. by Melbourne Univ Pr AT) Paul & Co Pubs.

Specialist Mathematics: Core: Solutions Manual. John Burrow. 240p. 1993. pap. 35.00 (*0-522-84564-9*, Pub. by Melbourne Univ Pr AT) Paul & Co Pubs.

Specialist Mathematics: Mechanics. Ed. by Barry McCrae et al. 176p. 1994. pap. 14.95 (*0-522-84590-8*, Pub. by Melbourne Univ Pr AT) Paul & Co Pubs.

Specialist Mathematics: Mechanics: Solutions Manual. Margaret Thom. 240p. 1994. pap. 20.00 (*0-522-84661-0*, Pub. by Melbourne Univ Pr AT) Paul & Co Pubs.

***Specialist Surfactants.** Ed. by Robb. (Illus.). 288p. 1996. text ed. 109.00 (*0-7514-0340-7*, Pub. by Blackie Acad & Prof UK) Routledge Chapman & Hall.

Specialists. Lawrence Block. 160p. 1993. 3.95 (*0-7867-0046-7*) Carroll & Graf.

***Specialists.** Lawrence Block. Ed. by James Cahill. (Illus.). 160p. Date not set. 25.00 (*0-9640454-3-5*) J Cahill Pubng.

***Specialists.** deluxe limited ed. Lawrence Block. Ed. by James Cahill. (Illus.). 160p. Date not set. text ed. 75.00 (*0-9640454-4-3*) J Cahill Pubng.

Specialist's Guide to Bureau Print Precancels. 3rd ed. (Illus.). 1980. 30.00 (*0-686-74110-2*) G W Noble.

Speciality Care Products for Your Home Entertainment Center. Thomas J. Zarecki. (Illus.). 100p. 2.00 (*0-936503-02-5*) TJ Enter IL.

Speciality, Generality, And Practicality Of The Church Life, The. Witness Lee. 70p. per. 2.75 (*0-87083-121-6*, 08025001) Living Stream Ministry.

Speciality Polymers - Polymers Physics. (Advances in Polymer Science Ser.: Vol. 88). (Illus.). 210p. 1989. 90.00 (*0-387-50472-9*) Spr-Verlag.

Speciality Polymers & Polymer Processing. Ed. by Geoffrey Allen & J. C. Bevington. (Comprehensive Polymer Science Ser.: Vol. 7). (Illus.). 685p. 1990. 440.00 (*0-08-036211-7*, Pergamon Pr) Elsevier.

Speciality Shop Retailing: How to Run Your Own Store. Carol L. Schroeder. LC 96-41395. (National Retail Federation Ser.). 304p. 1997. text ed. 29.95 (*0-471-14721-4*) Wiley.

Specialization & Economic Organization: A New Classical Microeconomic Framework. Xiaokai Yang & Yew-Kwang Ng. LC 92-47418. (Contributions to Economic Analysis Ser.: Vol. 215). 508p. 1993. 98.50 (*0-444-88698-2*, North Holland) Elsevier.

Specialization, Exchange & Complex Societies. Ed. by Elizabeth M. Brumfiel & Timothy K. Earle. (New Directions in Archaeology Ser.). (Illus.). 160p. 1987. text ed. 74.95 (*0-521-32118-2*) Cambridge U Pr.

Specialization in Landscape Architectural Education: Proceedings NCILA, 1975, Texas A & M, July 10-12. National Council of Instructors in Landscape Architecture Staff. 98p. pap. 28.00 (*0-8357-3042-5*, 2039297) Bks Demand.

Specialization of Medicine with Particular Reference to Ophthalmology. George Rosen. LC 79-180586. (Medicine & Society in America Ser.). 106p. 1972. reprint ed. 13.95 (*0-405-03966-2*) Ayer.

Specialization of Verbal Facility at the College Entrance Level. Warren G. Findley. LC 70-176770. (Columbia University. Teachers College. Contributions to Education Ser.: No. 567). reprint ed. 37.50 (*0-404-55567-5*) AMS Pr.

Specialize Legal Research, Set. Chanin. 1987. 145.00 (*0-316-13633-6*) Little.

Specialized Cleaning, Finishing & Coating Processes: Proceedings of a Conference Held February 5-6, 1980, Los Angeles, California. American Society for Metals Staff. LC 81-2755. (Materials-Metalworking Technology Ser.). 424p. reprint ed. pap. 120.90 (*0-317-26754-X*, 2024350) Bks Demand.

Specialized Computer Architectures for Robotics & Automation. Ed. by James H. Graham. 250p. 1987. text ed. 141.00 (*2-88124-154-9*) Gordon & Breach.

Specialized Course Outlines for Gerontology Social Work Education. 1984. 12.05 (*0-87293-010-6*) Coun Soc Wk Ed.

Specialized Courts Dealing with Sex Delinquency, a Study of the Procedure in Chicago, Boston, Philadelphia, & New York. George E. Worthington & Ruth Topping. LC 69-14954. (Criminology, Law Enforcement, & Social Problems Ser.: No. 50). 1969. reprint ed. 26.00 (*0-87585-050-2*) Patterson Smith.

Specialized Curing Methods for Coatings & Plastics-Recent Advances. M. William Ranney. LC 77-71928. (Chemical Technology Review Ser.: No. 88). (Illus.). 1977. 39.00 (*0-8155-0660-0*) Noyes.

Specialized Dementia Care Units. Ed. by Dorothy H. Coons. LC 90-4743. (Series in Contemporary Medicine & Public Health). (Illus.). 288p. 1990. text ed. 48.50 (*0-8018-4076-7*) Johns Hopkins.

Specialized Dictionary of Beverages: English, French, German. Ann-Marie Rouquite. 400p. (ENG, FRE & GER.). 1986. 275.00 (*0-7859-9966-3*) Fr & Eur.

Specialized Drug Delivery Systems: Manufacturing & Production Technology. Tyle. (Drugs & the Pharmaceutical Sciences Ser.: Vol. 41). 496p. 1989. 165.00 (*0-8247-8190-2*) Dekker.

Specialized Information Service: Amphetamines. rev. ed. 1997. pap. 5.95 (*0-89230-195-3*) Do It Now.

Specialized Information Service: Anabolic Steroids. rev. ed. 1997. 5.95 (*0-89230-239-9*) Do It Now.

Specialized Information Service: Designer Drugs. rev. ed. 1997. pap. 5.95 (*0-89230-194-5*) Do It Now.

Specialized Information Service: Drugs & Sexuality. rev. ed. 1997. 5.95 (*0-89230-240-2*) Do It Now.

Specialized Information Service: Drugs & Violence. rev. ed. 1997. pap. 5.95 (*0-89230-251-8*) Do It Now.

Specialized Information Service: Legal Stimulants. rev. ed. 1997. pap. 5.95 (*0-89230-205-4*) Do It Now.

Specialized Information Service: Marijuana. rev. ed. 1997. pap. 5.95 (*0-89230-203-8*) Do It Now.

Specialized Information Service: Minor Tranquilizers. rev. ed. 1997. 5.95 (*0-89230-238-0*) Do It Now.

Specialized Information Service: PCP. rev. ed. 1997. pap. 5.95 (*0-89230-186-4*) Do It Now.

Specialized Justice: Courts, Administrative Tribunals, & a Cross-National Theory of Specialization. Stephen H. Legomsky. 144p. 1990. 55.00 (*0-19-825429-6*) OUP.

Specialized Legal Research. Ed. by Leah F. Chanin. LC 86-80068. 432p. 1987. 145.00 (*0-316-13625-5*) Little.

***Specialized Medical Education in the European Region.** J. Parkhouse & J. Menu. (Euro Reports & Studies Ser.: No. 112). 266p. 1989. pap. text ed. 18.00 (*92-890-1278-1*) World Health.

Specialized Pharmaceuticals Dictionary: Diccionario de Especialidades Farmaceuticas. 28th ed. Emilio S. Rosenstein. 1350p. (SPA.). 1982. 49.95 (*0-8288-1877-0*, S39848) Fr & Eur.

Specialized Processors for Real-Time Image Analysis: Workshop Proceedings. Ed. by E. Montseny & J. Frau. (ESPRIT Basic Research Ser.). xi, 220p. 1994. 63.95 (*0-387-57016-0*) Spr-Verlag.

***Specialized Society: The Plight of the Individual in an Age of Individualism.** Fathali M. Moghaddam. LC 96-33186. 200p. 1997. text ed. 55.00 (*0-275-95670-9*, Praeger Pubs) Greenwood.

Specialized Studies in Polynesian Anthropology. K. Luomala et al. (BMB Ser.). 1974. reprint ed. 25.00 (*0-527-02301-9*) Periodicals Srv.

Specialized Techniques for Specific Clinical Problems in Psychotherapy. Ed. by Toksoz B. Karasu & Leopold Bellak. LC 93-74195. 520p. 1994. pap. 35.00 (*1-56821-189-9*) Aronson.

Specially for Christmas. Pauline Smith. (C). 1990. pap. 21.00 (*0-908175-82-5*, Pub. by Boolarong Pubns AT) St Mut.

Specially Selected. Edward V. Lucas. LC 77-117891. (Essay Index Reprint Ser.). 1977. 19.95 (*0-8369-1673-5*) Ayer.

Specialties of the House. 1992. 16.95 (*0-9631216-1-8*) Kenmore Assn.

Specialties of the House: A Cookbook to Benefit the Ronald McDonald House of Rochester, New York. (Illus.). 288p. 1995. 18.95 (*0-9647955-0-7*) R McDonald Hse.

Specialties of the House: A Country Inn & Bed & Breakfast Cookbook. Julia M. Pitkin. LC 96-18008. (Illus.). 600p. 1996. 27.95 (*1-888952-00-8*, Cumberland Hearthside) Cumberland Hse.

***Specialties of the House: Restaurants & Their Recipes - Cincinnati, Ohio.** Martha Johnston & Ralph Johnston. (Illus.). 176p. (Orig.). 1996. pap. 14.95 (*0-913383-45-7*) McClanahan Pub.

Specialty Adhesives: Where To. Contrib. by George Innes. 131p. 1996. 2,750.00 (*1-56965-354-2*, C-176B) BCC.

Specialty Ag Chems: Update. Business Communications Co., Inc. Staff. 140p. 1987. pap. 1,950.00 (*0-89336-543-2*, GA-035N) BCC.

Specialty & Minor Crops Handbook. Ed. by Cynthia Myers. (Illus.). 144p. 1991. ring bd. 30.00 (*1-879906-00-7*, 3346) ANR Pubns CA.

Specialty Board Review: Anesthesiology (MEPC) 9th ed. DeKornfeld. (C). 1994. pap. text ed. 39.95 (*0-8385-0256-3*, A0256-6) Appleton & Lange.

Specialty Board Review: Neurology. 4th ed. Barbara S. Giesser. 1995. pap. text ed. 39.95 (*0-8385-8650-3*) Appleton & Lange.

Specialty Board Review: Otolaryngology (MEPC) Willet. (C). 1994. pap. text ed. 39.95 (*0-8385-7580-3*, A7580-2) Appleton & Lange.

***Specialty Breads in Your Bread Machine.** Norman Garrett. Date not set. write for info. (*0-8069-9511-4*) Sterling.

Specialty Bugler: An Eclectic Survey of Diverse American Bugling Traditions Co-Ordinated with Recordings. Mark Johnson. (The Complete Bugler Series (Basic, Harmony, & Specialty Buglers)). 28p. (Orig.). (J). (gr. 4-12). 1995. pap. 2.99 (*1-883988-17-9*); pap. 8.99 incl. audio (*1-883988-18-7*); audio compact disk 13.99 (*1-883988-19-5*) RSV Prods.

Specialty Cements with Advanced Properties: Symposium Held November 27-29, 1989, Boston, Massachusetts, U. S. A. Materials Research Society Staff et al. Ed. by Barry E. Scheetz. LC 90-41629. (Materials Research Society Symposium Proceedings Ser.: No. 179). (Illus.). 317p. reprint ed. pap. 90.40 (*0-7837-6804-4*, 2046636) Bks Demand.

***Specialty Chemicals Source Book, 2 vols., Vols. 1 & 2.** LC 97-66347. 2500p. 1997. write for info. (*1-890595-00-4*) Synapse Info.

Specialty Contact Lenses: A Fitter's Guide. Carol A. Schwartz. LC 95-17561. (Illus.). 288p. 1995. pap. text ed. 59.00 (*0-7216-4747-2*) Saunders.

Specialty Cookbooks: A Bibliography. Harriet Ostroff & Tom Nichols. LC 91-37398. 672p. 1992. text ed. 95.00 (*0-8240-6947-1*, H1297) Garland.

Specialty Corn. Arnel R. Hallauer. 416p. 1993. 188.95 (*0-8493-4612-6*, SB191) CRC Pr.

Specialty Cut Flowers: The Production of Annuals, Perennials, Bulbs, & Woody Plants for Fresh & Dried Cut Flowers. Allan M. Armitage. LC 92-34463. (Illus.). 392p. 1993. 39.95 (*0-88192-225-0*) Timber.

Specialty Directory Publishing: Market Analysis & Forecast. Victor Rubell et al. Ed. by Mike Hayes. (Illus.). 282p. 1996. 1,595.00 (*0-88709-102-4*) Simba Info Inc.

Specialty Enzymes & Advanced Enzyme Tchnologies. BCC Staff. 268p. 1989. 2,650.00 (*0-89336-633-1*, C105) BCC.

Specialty Food Processors Handbook: A Guide to Getting Started. 51p. (Orig.). (C). 1992. pap. text ed. 20.00 (*1-56806-054-8*) DIANE Pub.

Specialty Gas Analysis: A Practical Guidebook. Jeremiah D. Hogan. LC 96-24426. 300p. 1996. 95.00 (*1-56081-671-6*, VCH) Wiley.

***Specialty Gas Analysis: A Practical Guidebook.** Ed. by Jeremiah D. Hogan. 1996. text ed. 95.01 (*0-471-18598-1*) Wiley.

***Specialty Hotels.** PBC International Staff. Date not set. write for info. (*0-688-12232-9*) Morrow.

Specialty Ingredients & Related Technologies for Lowfat & Fat-Free Applications, No. GA-082. Dorothy Kroll. 118p. 1994. 2,450.00 (*1-56965-101-9*) BCC.

Specialty Inorganic Chemicals, No. 40. Royal Society of Chemistry Staff. 1989. 50.00 (*0-85186-835-5*) CRC Pr.

Specialty Items Used Today (Sheet Metal) Including Methods of Design & Fabrication & Important Trade Topics. 4th ed. Richard S. Budzik. LC 74-79537. (Illus.). (C). 1987. 64.95 (*0-912914-30-0*) Practical Pubns.

Specialty Medicine Series I, Newton. Paul D. Chan. (Current Clinical Strategies Ser.). 1080p. (C). 1995. 79.95 incl. disk (*1-57443-009-2*) Educ Res Lab.

Specialty Needles Market. (Market Research Reports: No. 185). (Illus.). 91p. 1990. 295.00 (*0-317-05011-7*) Theta Corp.

Specialty Occupational Outlook. J. Jakubiak. 1995. 49.95 (*0-8103-9645-9*) Gale.

***Specialty Occupational Outlook: Professional.** 2nd ed. 1997. 49.95 (*0-7876-0096-2*, 00108787, Gale Res Intl) Gale.

S

An Asterisk (*) at the beginning of an entry indicates that the title is appearing in BIP for the first time.

S

Specialty Occupational Outlook: Professions. Joyce Jakubiak. (Career Information Guide Ser.). 254p. 1994. 49.95 (*0-8103-9644-0*) Gale.

***Specialty Occupational Outlook: Vocation.** 2nd ed. 1997. 49.95 (*0-7876-0095-4*, 00108786, Gale Res Intl) Gale.

***Specialty Performance Customizing Product Aftermarket.** Frost & Sullivan. 284p. 1996. write for info. (*0-7889-0605-4*, 5299) Frost & Sullivan.

Specialty Plastics In New Military Applications. Business Communications Co., Inc. Staff. 275p. 1986. pap. 2,250.00 (*0-89336-540-8*, P-093) BCC.

Specialty Polymers. Ed. by H. J. Cantow et al. (Advances in Polymer Science Ser.: Vol. 41). (Illus.). 186p. 1981. 67.00 (*0-387-10554-9*) Spr-Verlag.

Specialty Retailing: Markets & Strategies for the 1990s. Ed. by Peter Allen. 250p. 1987. 995.00 (*0-941285-15-4*) FIND-SVP.

Specialty Water Treatment Chemicals. 212p. 1995. 2,750.00 (*0-614-03473-6*, C002U) BCC.

Speciation & the Recognition Concept: Theory & Application. Ed. by David M. Lambert & Hamish G. Spencer. (Illus.). 528p. 1994. text ed. 65.00 (*0-8018-4740-0*); pap. text ed. 35.00 (*0-8018-4741-9*) Johns Hopkins.

Speciation in Ancient Lakes. Ed. by Ken Martens. (Advances in Limnology Ser.: No. 44). (Illus.). 508p. 1994. pap. 145.00 (*3-510-47045-1*, Pub. by Schweizerbartsche GW) Lubrecht & Cramer.

***Species: Human Race.** Phillip Amara. 1997. pap. text ed. 11.95 (*1-56971-219-0*) Dark Horse Comics.

Species Algarum. F. T. Kuetzing. 1970. reprint ed. 79.00 (*90-6123-084-5*) Lubrecht & Cramer.

Species Algarum Rite Cognitae Cum Symonymus, Differentis Specificis et Descriptionibus Succinctis, 2 vols., Set. C. A. Agardh. 1970. reprint ed. 69.30 (*90-6123-001-2*) Lubrecht & Cramer.

Species & Specificity: An Interpretation of the History of Immunology. Pauline M. Mazumdar. LC 93-31219. (Illus.). 530p. (C). 1995. text ed. 69.95 (*0-521-43172-7*) Cambridge U Pr.

Species & Varieties, Their Origin by Mutation: Lectures Delivered at the University of California. Hugo DeVries. LC 88-11715. (Genes Cells & Organisms Ser.). 872p. 1988. text ed. 15.00 (*0-8240-1387-5*) Garland.

Species at Risk: Research in Australia. Ed. by R. H. Groves & W. D. Ride. 250p. 1983. 63.95 (*0-387-11416-5*) Spr-Verlag.

Species Concept in Hymenomycetes: Proceedings of a Herbett Symposium at Lausanne, Switzerland, Aug. 16-20, 1976. Ed. by H. Clemencon. (Bibliotheca Mycologica Ser.: No. 61). (Illus.). 516p. 1978. pap. text ed. 72.00 (*3-7682-1173-8*) Lubrecht & Cramer.

Species Design. H. R. Giger. (Illus.). 84p. 1995. pap. text ed. 29.50 (*1-883398-12-6*) Morpheus Intl.

***Species Design.** H. R. Giger. (Illus.). 86p. 1997. 150.00 (*1-883398-19-3*) Morpheus Intl.

Species Diagnostics Protocols: PCR & Other Nucleic Acid Methods. Ed. by Justin P. Clapp. LC 95-24805. (Methods in Molecular Biology Ser.: No. 50). (Illus.). 440p. 1995. spiral bd. 69.50 (*0-89603-323-6*) Humana.

Species Dispersal in Agricultural Habitats. Ed. by R. G. Bunce & D. C. Howard. (Illus.). 296p. 1992. text ed. 55.00 (*1-85293-076-4*) St Martin.

Species Diversity in Ecological Communities: Historical & Geographical Perspectives. Ed. by Robert E. Ricklefs & Dolph Schluter. LC 93-16747. (Illus.). 432p. 1993. Acid-free paper. pap. text ed. 33.50 (*0-226-71823-9*); Acid-free paper. lib. bdg. 98.00 (*0-226-71822-0*) U Ch Pr.

Species Diversity in Space & Time. Michael L. Rosenzweig. (Illus.). 458p. (C). 1995. text ed. 80.00 (*0-521-49618-7*); pap. text ed. 29.95 (*0-521-49952-6*) Cambridge U Pr.

Species Evolution: The Role of Chromosome Change. Max King. 358p. 1995. pap. text ed. 31.95 (*0-521-48454-5*) Cambridge U Pr.

Species Filicum, 5 vols. W. J. Hooker. 1970. reprint ed. 350.00 (*3-7682-0690-4*) Lubrecht & Cramer.

Species Graminum Iconibus et Descriptionbus Illustravit, 3 vols. in 1. K. B. Trinius. (Illus.). 1970. reprint ed. 210.00 (*3-7682-0669-6*) Lubrecht & Cramer.

***Species-Group Taxa of the False Coral Snake Genus Pliocercus.** Smith & Chiszar. 10.00 (*0-614-30003-7*) Serpents Tale.

Species-Index to Schmidt-Hustedt: Atlas Zur Diatomaceen Kunde. G. Dallas Hanna. (Illus.). 1969. pap. 27.00 (*3-7682-0611-4*) Lubrecht & Cramer.

Species of Abandoned Light. Jake Berry. 80p. (Orig.). 1995. pap. 8.95 (*1-880766-09-4*) Pantograph Pr.

Species of Aphytis of the World (Hymenoptera: Aphelinidae) Rosen. (Entomologica Ser.: No. 17). 1979. lib. bdg. 353.00 (*90-6193-127-4*) Kluwer Ac.

Species of Artocarpus Indigenous to the British India: And the Indo-Malayan Species of Quercus & Castnopsis, 2 pts., Vol. II. Royal Botanic Garden, Calcutta Staff & George King. (Illus.). 107p. 1979. reprint ed. 80.00 (*0-88065-010-9*, Messers Today & Tomorrow) Scholarly Pubns.

Species of Asellotes (Isopoda: Paraselloidea) from Anvers Island, Antarctica: Paper 1 in Antarctic Biology of the Antarctic Seas VI. George A. Schultz. Ed. by David L. Pawson. (Antarctic Research Ser.: Vol. 26). 36p. 1976. pap. 14.95 (*0-87590-129-8*) Am Geophysical.

Species of Dalbargia of South Eastern Asia. Royal Botanic Garden, Calcutta Staff & D. Prain. (Annals of Royal Botanic Garden, Calcutta Ser.: Vol. X, Pt. 1). (Illus.). 114p. 1979. reprint ed. 100.00 (*0-88065-013-3*, Messers Today & Tomorrow) Scholarly Pubns.

Species of Dalbergia of South-Eastern Asia: Annals of the Royal Botanic Garden, Calcutta, Vol. 10, Pt. 1. D. Prain. 114p. (C). 1983. 170.00 (*0-685-22301-9*, Pub. by Scientific UK) St Mut.

Species of Ficus of the Indo-Malayan & Chinese Countries. G. King. (Illus.). 1969. reprint ed. 400.00 (*3-7682-0609-2*) Lubrecht & Cramer.

Species of Intoxication. Michael Gizzi. (Burning Deck Poetry Ser.). 68p. 1983. pap. 4.00 (*0-930901-11-8*) Burning Deck.

***Species of Mind: The Philosophy & Biology of Cognitive Ethology.** Colin Allen & Marc Bekoff. LC 97-3263. 1997. write for info. (*0-262-01163-8*) MIT Pr.

Species of Selenophoma on North American Grasses. Roderick Sprague & A. G. Johnson. LC 50-62673. (Oregon State Monographs, Studies in Botany: No. 10). 49p. reprint ed. pap. 25.00 (*0-7837-0158-6*, 2040455) Bks Demand.

Species of Special Concern in Pennsylvania. Ed. by Hugh H. Genoways & Fred J. Brenner. LC 84-73248. (Special Publications: No. 11). (Illus.). 436p. (Orig.). 1985. 33.00 (*0-935868-11-9*) Carnegie Mus.

Species of the Genus Schwagerina & Their Stratigraphic Significance. J. W. Beede & H. T. Kniker. (Bulletin Ser.: BULL 2433). (Illus.). 96p. 1924. pap. 1.00 (*0-686-29344-4*) Bur Econ Geology.

Species of the Genus Spirogyra from Kerala India (Chlorophyceae) Zygnemataceae. K. Usha Devi & M. V. Panikkar. (Bibliotheca Phycologica Ser.: Vol. 97). (Illus.). 124p. 1994. teacher ed., pap. 64.00 (*3-443-60024-7*, Pub. by E Schweizerbartsche GW) Lubrecht & Cramer.

Species Problem. Ed. by Ernst W. Mayr. LC 73-17831. (Natural Sciences in America Ser.). (Illus.). 410p. 1974. reprint ed. 28.95 (*0-405-05749-0*) Ayer.

Species Relationships in the Avian Genus Aimophila. Larry L. Wolf. 220p. 1977. 12.00 (*0-943610-23-0*) Am Ornithologists.

Species, Species Concepts, & Primate Evolution. Ed. by William H. Kimbel & Lawrence B. Martin. LC 93-6920. (Advances in Primatology Ser.). (Illus.). 565p. (C). 1993. 120.00 (*0-306-44297-3*, Plenum Pr) Plenum.

***Species Survival in Fragmented Landscapes.** Ed. by J. Settele. (GeoJournal Library). 400p. (C). 1996. lib. bdg. 189.00 (*0-7923-4239-9*) Kluwer Ac.

Species Survival Plans: Strategies for Wildlife Conservation. Robert J. Wiese & Michael Hutchins. 64p. 1994. pap. text ed. 15.95 (*1-885491-00-X*) Am Zoo & Aquar.

Species Taxa of North American Birds: A Contribution to Comparative Systematics. Ernst W. Mayr & Lester L. Short. (Publications of the Nuttall Ornithological Club: No. 9). (Illus.). 127p. 1970. 7.00 (*1-877973-19-X*, 9) Nuttall Ornith.

***Specific Articles, Vol. 2.** Wallace Johnson. 609p. 1997. text ed. 79.50 (*0-691-02579-7*) Princeton U Pr.

Specific Characteristics of Adolescent Suicide Attempters. E. J. De Wilde. (Tinbergen Institute Ser.). 136p. 1993. pap. 25.00 (*90-5170-184-5*, Pub. by Thesis Pubs NE) IBD Ltd.

Specific Distinctness & Adaptive Differences in Southwestern Meadowlarks. Sievert Rohwer. (Occasional Papers: No. 44). 14p. 1976. pap. 1.00 (*0-317-04634-9*) U KS Nat Hist Mus.

Specific Immunotherapy of Cancer with Vaccines. Ed. by Jean-Claude Bystryn et al. LC 93-20752. (Annals Ser.: Vol. 690). 411p. 1993. write for info. (*0-89766-825-1*); pap. 110.00 (*0-89766-826-X*) NY Acad Sci.

Specific Interactions & Biological Recognition Processes. Simon & Schuster Staff. 352p. 1993. 207.00 (*0-8493-5398-X*, QP517) CRC Pr.

Specific Interactions & the Miscibility of Polymer Blends. Michael M. Coleman et al. LC 91-65261. 520p. 1991. disk 399.95 (*0-685-40902-3*, 628238-A) Technomic.

Specific Interactions & the Miscibility of Polymer Blends. Michael M. Coleman et al. LC 91-65261. 520p. 1991. 99.95 (*0-87762-823-8*) Technomic.

Specific Language Impairments in Children. Ed. by Ruth V. Watkins & Mabel L. Rice. LC 93-39230. (Communication & Language Intervention Ser.: Vol. 4). 224p. 1994. 36.00 (*1-55766-139-1*) P H Brookes.

Specific Learning Difficulties (Dyslexia) Challenges & Responses. Ed. by Peter D. Pumfrey & Rea Reason. 336p. (C). 1992. pap. text ed. 35.00 (*0-415-06470-8*, Routledge NY) Routledge.

Specific Malformations see Congenital Malformations of the Heart

Specific Mysteries. Holly Prado. 55p. 1990. pap. 8.00 (*0-9649240-1-3*) Cahuenga Pr.

Specific Pathogen Free Swine: Development, Application, Consequences. Norman R. Underdahl. LC 73-77749. (Illus.). 171p. 1973. reprint ed. pap. 48.80 (*0-8357-8680-3*, 2056837) Bks Demand.

Specific Performance. Gareth Jones & William Goodhart. 1986. 110.00 (*0-406-25809-0*, U.K.) MICHIE.

Specific Performance. 2nd ed. Gareth Jones & William Goodhart. 1996. 143.00 (*0-406-06561-6*) MICHIE.

Specific Reading Disability. Dirk J. Bakker. Ed. by Paul Satz. (Modern Approaches to the Diagnosis & Instruction of Multi-Handicapped Children Ser.: Vol. 3). xii, 166p. 1970. 25.00 (*90-237-4103-X*) Taylor & Francis.

Specific Receptors of Antibodies, Antigens & Cells: Proceedings of the International Convocation on Immunology, 3rd, Buffalo, 1972. International Convocation on Immunology Staff. Ed. by N. R. Rose. 300p. 1973. 123.25 (*3-8055-1372-0*) S Karger.

Specific Relief Act. S. Sarkar. (C). 1990. 110.00 (*0-89771-285-4*) St Mut.

Specific Situations in Effective Oral Communication. Don M. Morlan & George E. Tuttle, Jr. (gr. 12). 1977. teacher ed. 3.33 (*0-672-61411-1*, Bobbs); pap. 9.50 (*0-672-61410-3*, Bobbs) Macmillan.

Specific Skill Development Through the Use of Newspapers & Magazines: A Manual for Resource Teachers. Lynn E. Johnson. (Illus.). 100p. 1991. 25.00 (*1-878276-40-9*) Educ Systs Assocs Inc.

Specific Speech & Language Disorders in Children. Ed. by Paul Fletcher et al. LC 92-19316. (Orig.). 1992. 49.95 (*1-879105-59-4*, 0238) Singular Publishing.

Specific Techniques for the Psychotherapy of Schizophrenic Patients. Andrew Lotterman. 172p. 1996. 35.00 (*0-8236-6130-X*) Intl Univs Pr.

Specification: Fittings. Ed. by Engineering Equipment & Materials Users Assoc. Staff. 1988. 175.00 (*0-317-90367-5*, Pub. by EEMUA UK) St Mut.

Specification: Flanges - Composite & Solid. Engineering Equipment & Materials Users Assoc. Staff. 1988. 175.00 (*0-317-90366-7*, Pub. by EEMUA UK) St Mut.

Specification: Tubes - Seamless & Welded. Engineering Equipment & Materials Users Association Staff. 1988. 150.00 (*0-317-90365-9*, Pub. by EEMUA UK) St Mut.

Specification & Analysis of Concurrent Systems: The COSY Approach. R. Janicki & P. E. Lauer. Ed. by W. Brauer et al. (EATCS Monographs on Theoretical Computer Science: Vol. 26). 485p. 1992. 107.95 (*0-387-55204-9*) Spr-Verlag.

Specification & Compositional Verification of Real-Time Systems. J. Hooman. (Lecture Notes in Computer Science Ser.: Vol. 558). viii, 235p. 1991. 39.00 (*0-387-54947-1*) Spr-Verlag.

Specification & Design of Concurrent Systems. Percy Mett et al. LC 93-44210. (McGraw-Hill International Series in Software Engineering). 1994. write for info. (*0-07-707966-3*) McGraw.

Specification & Design of Embedded Systems. Daniel D. Gajski et al. LC 94-11529. 468p. 1994. text ed. 66.00 (*0-13-150731-1*) P-H.

Specification & Proof in Real Time CSP. Jim Davies. (Distinguished Dissertations in Computer Science Ser.: No. 6). (Illus.). 200p. (C). 1993. text ed. 52.95 (*0-521-45055-1*) Cambridge U Pr.

Specification & Transformation of Programs: A Formal Approach to Software Development. Ed. by David Gries. (Texts & Monographs in Computer Science). (Illus.). 512p. 1990. 59.95 (*0-387-52356-1*) Spr-Verlag.

Specification & Transformation of Programs: A Formal Approach to Software Development. Ed. by David Gries. (Texts & Monographs in Computer Science). (Illus.). 512p. 1990. 42.95 (*0-387-52589-0*) Spr-Verlag.

Specification & Uses of Econometric Models. T. Merritt Brown. LC 70-88172. (C). 1970. text ed. 32.50 (*0-312-75110-9*) St Martin.

Specification & Validation Methods. Ed. by Egon Borger. (International Schools for Computer Scientists Ser.). 480p. 1995. 115.00 (*0-19-853854-5*) OUP.

Specification & Verification of Concurrent Systems. Ed. by C. Rattray & C. J. Van Rijsbergen. (Workshops in Computing Ser.). 624p. 1990. 59.00 (*0-387-19581-5*) Spr-Verlag.

Specification EMLOOP: Electronic Documents to Close the Paper Control Loop. 2nd ed. EDI User Requirements Task Force Staff. Ed. by Timothy Babilon et al. 115p. pap. text ed. 95.00 (*0-933505-14-0*) Graph Comm Assn.

Specification, Estimation, & Analysis of Macroeconomic Models. Ray C. Fair. (Illus.). 496p. 1984. 47.00 (*0-674-83180-2*) HUP.

Specification for Allowable Stress Design of Single-Angle Members. 15p. 1989. 10.00 (*1-56424-010-X*, S336) Am Inst Steel Construct.

Specification for Aluminum & Aluminum Alloy Electrodes for Shielded Metal Arc Welding (A5.3-91) (Illus.). 19p. 1991. pap. 21.00 (*0-87171-363-2*) Am Welding.

Specification for Automotive Frame Weld Quality Arc Welding (D8.8-89) (Illus.). 16p. 1989. pap. 21.00 (*0-87171-306-3*) Am Welding.

Specification for Bare Aluminum & Aluminum Alloy Welding Electrodes & Rods (A5.10-92) (Illus.). 24p. 1992. pap. 21.00 (*0-87171-374-8*) Am Welding.

Specification for Bare Stainless Steel Welding Electrodes & Rods (A5.9-93) (Illus.). 24p. 1993. pap. 27.00 (*0-87171-406-X*) Am Welding.

Specification for Carbon & Low Alloy Steel Electrodes & Fluxes for Electroslag Welding (A5.25-91) (Illus.). 19p. 1991. pap. 21.00 (*0-87171-362-4*) Am Welding.

Specification for Carbon & Low Alloy Steel Electrodes for Electrogas Welding (A5.26-91) (Illus.). 20p. 1991. pap. 21.00 (*0-87171-364-0*) Am Welding.

Specification for Carbon & Low Alloy Steel Rods for Oxyfuel Gas Welding (A5.2-92) (Illus.). 9p. 1992. pap. 21.00 (*0-87171-372-1*) Am Welding.

Specification for Carbon Steel Electrodes & Fluxes for Submerged Arc Welding (A5.17-89) (Illus.). 64p. 1989. pap. 21.00 (*0-87171-311-X*) Am Welding.

Specification for Carbon Steel Electrodes for Flux Cored Arc Welding (A5.20-95) (Illus.). 32p. 1995. pap. write for info. (*0-87171-451-5*) Am Welding.

Specification for Carbon Steel Electrodes for Shielded Metal Arc Welding (A5.1-91) (Illus.). 46p. 1991. pap. 21.00 (*0-87171-349-7*) Am Welding.

Specification for Carbon Steel Filler Metals for Gas Shielded Arc Welding (A5.18-93) (Illus.). 30p. 1993. pap. 27.00 (*0-87171-416-7*) Am Welding.

Specification for Composite Surfacing Welding Rods & Electrodes (A5.21-80) 16p. 1980. pap. 21.00 (*0-87171-198-2*) Am Welding.

Specification for Consumable Inserts (A5.30-79) 6p. 1979. pap. 21.00 (*0-87171-179-6*) Am Welding.

Specification for Copper & Copper Alloy Bare Welding Rods & Electrodes (A5.7-84) 11p. 1984. pap. 21.00 (*0-87171-242-3*) Am Welding.

Specification for Copper & Copper Alloy Rods for Oxyfuel Gas Welding (A5.27-85) 7p. 1985. pap. 21.00 (*0-87171-253-9*) Am Welding.

Specification for Covered Copper & Copper Alloy Arc Welding Electrodes (A5.6-84) (Illus.). 18p. 1984. pap. 21.00 (*0-87171-241-5*) Am Welding.

Specification for Covered Corrosion-Resisting Chromium & Chromium-Nickel Steel Welding Electrodes (A5.4-92) (Illus.). 31p. 1992. pap. 21.00 (*0-87171-385-3*) Am Welding.

Specification for Exchange of Product Analysis Data. Ed. by D. Thomas et al. (Research Reports ESPRIT, Project 322: Vol. 2). xvi, 146p. 1989. pap. 29.00 (*0-387-51579-8*) Spr-Verlag.

Specification for Filler Metals for Brazing & Braze Welding (A5.8-92) (Illus.). 25p. 1992. pap. 27.00 (*0-87171-394-2*) Am Welding.

Specification for Flux Cored Corrosion-Resisting Chromium & Chromium Nickel Stell Electrodes (A5.22-95) (Illus.). 20p. 1995. pap. 27.00 (*0-87171-456-6*) Am Welding.

Specification for Fluxes for Brazing & Braze Welding (AS. 31-92) (Illus.). 11p. 1992. pap. 27.00 (*0-87171-384-5*) Am Welding.

Specification for Furnace Brazing (C3.6-90) 7p. 1990. pap. 27.00 (*0-87171-330-6*) Am Welding.

Specification for Ground Investigation. (Site Investigation in Construction Ser.: No. 3). 112p. 1993. text ed. 58.00 (*0-7277-1984-X*) Am Soc Civil Eng.

Specification for Ground Investigation with Bills of Quantities & Notes for Guidance. Institution of Civil Engineers Staff. 64p. 1989. pap. text ed. 31.50 (*0-7277-1343-4*, 1343) Am Soc Civil Eng.

Specification for Ground Treatment, 2 vols. 64p. 1987. 20.00 (*0-7277-0389-7*) Am Soc Civil Eng.

Specification for High Frequency Electric Welded Line Pipe. EEMUA Staff. 1994. 130.00 (*0-85931-144-9*, Pub. by EEMUA UK) St Mut.

***Specification for High Speed Helical Gear Units.** 7th rev. ed. AGMA Technical Committee Staff. (ANSI/AGMA Standard Ser.). 1992. pap. text ed. 50.00 (*1-55589-575-1*) AGMA.

Specification for Induction Brazing (C3.5-90) 7p. 1990. pap. 21.00 (*0-87171-331-4*) Am Welding.

Specification for Line Pipe for Offshore. EEMUA Staff. 1991. 130.00 (*0-85931-124-4*, Pub. by EEMUA UK) St Mut.

Specification for Low-Alloy Steel Covered Arc Welding Electrodes (A5.5-96) (Illus.). 29p. 1981. pap. 21.00 (*0-87171-280-6*) Am Welding.

Specification for Low Alloy Steel Electrodes & Fluxes for Submerged Arc Welding (A5.23-90) (Illus.). 20p. 1990. pap. 21.00 (*0-87171-326-8*) Am Welding.

Specification for Low Alloy Steel Electrodes for Flux Gored Arc Welding (A5.29-80) (Illus.). 20p. 1980. pap. 21.00 (*0-87171-208-3*) Am Welding.

Specification for Low Alloy Steel Filler Metals for Gas Shielded Arc Welding (A5.28-79) (Illus.). 21p. 1979. pap. 21.00 (*0-87171-172-9*) Am Welding.

Specification for Magnesium Alloy Welding Electrodes & Rods (A5.19-92) (Illus.). 17p. 1992. pap. 27.00 (*0-87171-399-3*) Am Welding.

Specification for Mapping at Scales Between 1:1,000 & 1:10,000. RICS Staff. (C). 1988. text ed. 90.00 (*0-85406-375-7*, Pub. by Surveyors Pubns) St Mut.

***Specification for Measurement of Linear Vibration on Gear Units.** 2nd rev. ed. AGMA Technical Committee Staff. (ANSI/AGMA Standard Ser.). 1994. pap. text ed. 60.00 (*1-55589-666-9*) AGMA.

Specification for Metal Cutting Machine Tool Weldments (D14.2-86) (Illus.). 40p. 1986. pap. 27.00 (*0-87171-256-3*) Am Welding.

Specification for Nickel & Nickel Alloy Bare Welding Electrodes & Rods (A5.14-89) (Illus.). 14p. 1989. pap. 21.00 (*0-87171-304-7*) Am Welding.

Specification for Nickel & Nickel Alloy Welding Electrodes for Shielded Metal Arc Welding (A5.11-90) (Illus.). 26p. 1991. pap. 21.00 (*0-87171-348-9*) Am Welding.

Specification for Piling & Contract Documentation & Measurement, 2 vols. 128p. 1988. 43.00 (*0-7277-1303-5*) Am Soc Civil Eng.

Specification for Qualification of Welding Procedures & Welders for Piping & Tubing (D10.9-80) (Illus.). 60p. 1980. pap. 32.00 (*0-87171-210-5*) Am Welding.

Specification for Rotating Elements of Equipment (D14.6-96) (Illus.). 101p. 1996. pap. 27.00 (*0-87171-449-3*) Am Welding.

Specification for Solid Surfacing Welding Rods & Electrodes (A5.13-80) (Illus.). 22p. 1980. pap. 21.00 (*0-87171-196-6*) Am Welding.

Specification for Structural Steel Buildings - Allowable Stress Design, Plastic Design. 220p. 1989. 20.00 (*1-56424-011-8*, S335) Am Inst Steel Construct.

Specification for Surveys of Land, Buildings & Utility Services at Scales of L:500 & Larger. Ed. by RICS Staff. (C). 1986. text ed. 49.00 (*0-85406-297-1*, Pub. by Surveyors Pubns) St Mut.

Specification for the Design, Fabrication & Erection of Steel Safety-Related Structures for Nuclear Facilities: ANSI-AISC N690-1994. 288p. 1994. 20.00 (*1-56424-017-7*, S327) Am Inst Steel Construct.

Specification for the Design of Cold-Formed Stainless Steel Structural Members: Updated & Revised Version of the 1974 AISI Standard, An ASCE Standard 8-90. rev. ed. LC 91-22952. 114p. 1991. pap. text ed. 52.00 (*0-87262-794-2*) Am Soc Civil Eng.

Specification for Three Phase Cage Industion Motors. EEMUA Staff. 1988. 150.00 (*0-685-22640-9*, Pub. by EEMUA UK) St Mut.

Specification for Titanium & Titanium Alloy Welding Electrodes & Rods (A5.16-90) (Illus.). 24p. 1990. pap. 21.00 (*0-87171-322-5*) Am Welding.

Specification for Torch Brazing (C3.4-90) 7p. 1990. 21.00 (*0-87171-321-7*) Am Welding.

Specification for Tungsten & Tungsten Alloy Electrodes for Arc Welding & Cutting (A5.12-92) (Illus.). 8p. 1992. pap. 21.00 (*0-87171-382-9*) Am Welding.

Specification for Underground Armoured Cable Protected Against Solvent Penetration & Corrosive Attack. EEMUA Staff. 1988. 100.00 (*0-685-22641-7*, Pub. by EEMUA UK) St Mut.

Specification for Underwater Welding (D3.6-93) (Illus.). 109p. 1993. pap. 48.00 (*0-87171-389-6*) Am Welding.

Specification for Vertical Air Photography. Surveyors Publications Staff. (C). 1989. text ed. 65.00 (*0-85406-388-9*, Pub. by Surveyors Pubns) St Mut.

Specification for Welding Earthmoving & Construction Equipment (D14.3-93) (Illus.). 47p. 1993. pap. 57.00 (*0-87171-417-5*) Am Welding.

Specification for Welding Electrodes & Rods for Cast Iron (A5.15-90) (Illus.). 10p. 1990. pap. 21.00 (*0-87171-328-4*) Am Welding.

Specification for Welding Industrial & Mill Crane & Other Material Handling Equipment (D14.1-85) (Illus.). 121p. 1985. pap. 39.00 (*0-87171-255-5*) Am Welding.

Specification for Welding of Presses & Press Components (D14.5-80) (Illus.). 83p. 1980. pap. 27.00 (*0-87171-187-7*) Am Welding.

Specification for Zirconium & Zirconium Alloy Welding Electrodes & Rods (A5.24-90) (Illus.). 24p. 1990. pap. 16.00 (*0-87171-323-3*) Am Welding.

Specification Forms for Process Measurement & Control Instruments, Primary Elements & Control Valves: ISA Standard S20. 72p. 1981. pap. text ed. 70.00 (*0-87664-347-0*, I347-0) ISA.

***Specification in B: An Introduction Using the B Toolkit.** 252p. 1996. 33.00 (*1-86094-008-0*); pap. 17.00 (*1-86094-018-8*) World Scientific Pub.

Specification, Installation, & Calibration of Turbine Flowmeters. 1977. pap. 30.00 (*0-87664-371-3*, RP31.1) ISA.

Specification of a CAD One: Neutral File of CAD Geometry. 2nd rev. ed. Ed. by E. G. Schlechtendahl. (Research Reports ESPRIT, Project 322, CAD Interfaces: Vol. 1). xv, 255p. 1988. pap. 27.10 (*0-387-18397-3*) Spr-Verlag.

***Specification of Abstract Data Types.** Jacques Loeckx et al. LC 96-32367. 1996. text ed. 60.00 (*0-471-95067-X*) Wiley.

Specification of Complex Systems. B. Cohen et al. 160p. (C). 1986. text ed. write for info. (*0-201-14400-X*) Addison-Wesley.

Specification of Computer Programs. Wladyslaw M. Turski & Thomas S. Maibum. 300p. (C). 1987. text ed. 30.25 (*0-201-14226-0*) Addison-Wesley.

Specification of Gamma - Ray Brachytherapy Sources. LC 73-94306. (Report Ser.: No. 41). 24p. 1974. pap. text ed. 20.00 (*0-913392-23-5*) NCRP Pubns.

Specification of High Activity Gamma-Ray Sources, No. 18. International Commission on Radiation Units & Measurements. LC 72-131967. 1970. 25.00 (*0-913394-36-X*) Intl Comm Rad Meas.

Specification of Indoor Environmental Performance of Buildings. P. J. Jackman. (C). 1987. 105.00 (*0-86022-139-3*, Pub. by Build Servs Info Assn UK) St Mut.

Specification of Parallel Algorithms: DIMACS Workshop, May 9-11, 1994. Ed. by Giy E. Blelloch et al. LC 94-30810. (DIMACS Series in Discrete Mathematics & Theoretical Computer Science: 18). 1994. 79.00 (*0-8218-0253-4*, DIMACS/18) Am Math.

Specification of Real-Time Distributed Systems. Leo Motus & Michael G. Rodd. 350p. 1993. pap. text ed. 36.00 (*0-13-834060-9*) P-H.

***Specification of Time Series Models.** 320p. 1998. 38.00 (*981-02-2539-3*) World Scientific Pub.

Specification Searches: Ad Hoc Inference with Nonexperimental Data. Edward E. Leamer. LC 77-26855. 383p. reprint ed. pap. 109.20 (*0-7837-2816-6*, 2057656) Bks Demand.

Specification Tested Products Guide. 64p. 10.00 (*0-318-18037-5*); 5.00 (*0-317-01172-3*) Factory Mutual.

Specification Writing: For Architects & Surveyors. 10th ed. C. J. Willis & J. A. Willis. (Illus.). 136p. 1991. pap. 44.95 (*0-632-03202-2*) Blackwell Sci.

Specification Writing & Management. McRobb. (Quality & Reliability Ser.: Vol. 20). 200p. 1989. 99.75 (*0-8247-8082-5*) Dekker.

***Specification Writing for Architects & Surveyors.** 11th ed. Christopher J. Willis et al. LC 97-14889. 1997. write for info. (*0-632-04206-0*) Blackwell Sci.

Specifications & Standards. Thomas P. Cassidy. 128p. (Orig.). 1984. pap. 14.95 (*0-940343-15-0*, A12A) Natl Contract Mgmt.

Specifications & Standards for Plastics & Composites. 224p. 1990. 81.00 (*0-87170-395-5*, 6152) ASM.

***Specifications & Standards for Plastics & Composites.** Frank T. Traceski. LC 90-82161. (Illus.). 211p. 1990. reprint ed. pap. 60.20 (*0-608-02643-3*, 2063302) Bks Demand.

Specifications & Tests for Piezoelectric Pressure & Sound-Pressure Transducers. 1982. reprint ed. pap. 40.00 (*0-87664-382-9*, S37.10) ISA.

Specifications & Tests for Potentiometric Displacement Transducers. 1982. reprint ed. pap. 40.00 (*0-87664-359-4*, S37.12) ISA.

Specifications & Tests for Strain Gage Force Transducers. 1982. reprint ed. pap. 40.00 (*0-87664-381-0*, S37.08) ISA.

Specifications & Tests for Strain Gage Linear Acceleration Transducers. 1982. reprint ed. pap. 40.00 (*0-87664-379-9*, S37.5) ISA.

Specifications & Tests for Strain Gage Pressure Transducers. 1982. reprint ed. pap. 40.00 (*0-87664-378-0*, S37.3) ISA.

Specifications & Tests of Potentiometric Pressure Transducers. 1982. reprint ed. pap. 40.00 (*0-87664-380-2*, S37.6) ISA.

Specifications for a Quality Assurance-Risk Management (QA-RM) Information Management System. 300p. 1988. 1,800.00 (*0-86688-162-X*) Joint Comm Hlthcare.

Specifications for Carbon & Alloy-Steel Plates for Pressure Vessels. American Society for Testing & Materials Staff. 186p. reprint ed. pap. 53.10 (*0-317-28482-7*, 2019125) Bks Demand.

Specifications for Commercial Interiors. rev. ed. S. C. Reznikoff. (Illus.). 352p. 1989. 49.95 (*0-8230-4893-4*, Whitney Lib) Watsn-Guptill.

Specifications for Electric Overhead Traveling Cranes, No. 70. rev. ed. 84p. 1988. 10.00 (*0-318-17123-6*, III-11) Material Handling.

***Specifications for Electric Overhead Traveling Cranes for Steel Mill Service.** AISE Staff. (Technical Papers). 1949. pap. text ed. 30.00 (*1-55589-457-7*) AGMA.

***Specifications for Immunological Testing for Infectious Diseases: Approved Guideline (1994)** Contrib. by A. Myron Johnson. 1994. 75.00 (*1-56238-251-9*, I/LA18-A) Natl Comm Clin Lab Stds.

Specifications for Masonry Structures (ACI 530.1- 92 - ASCE 6-92 - TMS 602-92), Detroit, Mich. American Concrete Institute Staff & American Society of Civil Engineers Staff. LC 92-33527. 16p. 1992. 18.95 (*0-87262-929-5*) Am Soc Civil Eng.

Specifications for Pesticides Used in Public Health: Insecticides - Molluscicides - Repellents - Methods. 6th ed. 384p. (ENG, FRE & SPA.). 1985. pap. text ed. 48.00 (*92-4-156084-3*, 1150259) World Health.

Specifications for Selecting a Vocabulary & Teaching Method for Beginning Braille Readers. Hilda Caton et al. 84p. 1979. pap. text ed. 15.95 (*0-89128-971-2*) Am Foun Blind.

Specifications for Selecting a Vocabulary & Teaching Method for Beginning Braille Readers. Hilda Caton. (AFB Research Report Ser.). 84p. reprint ed. pap. 25.00 (*0-7837-3076-4*, 2043150) Bks Demand.

Specifications for Speed in the Racehorse: The Airflow Factors. W. Robert Cook. (Illus.). 253p. (Orig.). (C). 1989. pap. 25.00 (*0-929346-05-X*) R Meerdink Co Ltd.

Specifications for Steel Welding Consumables. Ralph B. Yeo. 72p. 1988. pap. 79.95 (*0-85300-227-4*, Pub. by Woodhead Pubng UK) Am Educ Systs.

Specifications for Structural Concrete for Buildings. 34p. 1989. 48.50 (*0-685-62963-5*, 301-89) ACI.

Specifications for the Application & Finishing of Gypsum Board. (Illus.). 16p. 1996. reprint ed. pap. 5.95 (*1-56532-002-6*, GA-216-96) Gypsum Assn.

Specifications for the Chemical & Process Industries: A Manual for Development & Use. ASQC Chemical & Process Industries Division, Chemical Interest Committee. LC 95-45500. 183p. 1996. pap. 26.00 (*0-87389-351-4*, H0908) ASQC Qual Pr.

Specifications for the Identity & Purity of Food Additives & Their Toxicological Evaluation. FAO-WHO Joint Committee on Food Additives. Incl. Some Antimicrobials, Antioxidants, Emulsifiers, Stabilizers, Flour-Treatment Agents, Acids & Bases: Ninth Report - Rome, 1965. 24p. 1966. pap. 1.20 (*92-4-120339-0*); Some Emulsifiers & Stabilizers & Certain Other Substances: Tenth Report - Geneva, 1966. 47p. 1967. pap. 2.00 (*92-4-120373-0*); Some Flavouring Substances & Non-Nutritive Sweetening Agents: Eleventh Report - Geneva, 1967. 18p. 1968. pap. 1.20 (*92-4-120383-8*); Some Antibiotics: Twelfth Report - Geneva, 1968. 49p. 1969. pap. 5.00 (*92-4-120430-3*); Some Food Colours, Emulsifiers, Stabilizers, Anti-Caking Agents, & Certain Other Substances: Thirteenth Report - Rome, 1969. 36p. 1970. pap. 5.00 (*92-4-120445-1*); Set pap. write for info. (*0-318-56498-X*) World Health.

Specifications for the Identity & Purity of Some Food Colours, Flavour Enhancers, Thickening Agents & Certain Other Food Additives. (Food Additive Ser.: No. 7). 1976. pap. text ed. 22.00 (*92-4-166007-4*, 1270007) World Health.

Specifications for Tune-up & Service of Farm Tractors. 85p. 1983. 11.00 (*0-89606-039-X*, 101) Am Assn Voc Materials.

Specifications for 16 & 35mm Roll Microfilm: ANSI-AIIM MS14-1988. Association for Information & Image Management Staff. (Standards & Recommended Practices Ser.). 1988. 33.00 (*0-89258-130-1*, MS14) Assn Inform & Image Mgmt.

Specifications of Database Systems: First International Workshop on Specifications of Database Systems, Glasgow, 3-5 July, 1991 Proceedings. Ed. by D. J. Harper et al. (Workshops in Computing Ser.). (Illus.). 336p. 1992. 59.00 (*0-387-19732-X*) Spr-Verlag.

Specifications of Organs see **Art of Organ Building**

Specifications, Tolerances, & Other Technical Requirements for Weighing & Measuring Devices. Ed. by Henry V. Opperman & Tina G. Butcher. (Illus.). 300p. (Orig.). (C). 1995. pap. text ed. 50.00 (*0-7881-2464-1*) DIANE Pub.

Specificity in Biological Interactions. Ed. by Bernard Pullman. 1984. lib. bdg. 224.00 (*90-277-1813-X*) Kluwer Ac.

Specificity of Proteolysis. B. Keil. (Illus.). ix, 336p. 1992. 225.95 (*0-387-53118-1*) Spr-Verlag.

***Specificity of Serological Reactions.** Landsteiner. pap. 8.95 (*0-486-66203-9*) Dover.

Specifying: Black Women Writing the American Experience. Susan Willis. LC 86-20202. 200p. 1989. pap. 12.95 (*0-299-10894-5*) U of Wis Pr.

Specifying Air Pollution Control Equipment. fac. ed. Ed. by Richard A. Young & Frank L. Cross, Jr. LC 82-1548. (Pollution Engineering & Technology Ser.: No. 20). 293p. 1982. reprint ed. pap. 83.60 (*0-7837-8333-7*, 2049120) Bks Demand.

***Specifying & Diagnostically Testing Econometric Models.** 2nd ed. Houston H. Stokes. LC 96-46718. 464p. 1997. text ed. 75.00 (*1-56720-069-9*, Quorum Bks) Greenwood.

Specifying Interiors: A Guide to Construction & FF&E for Commercial Interiors Projects. Maryrose McGowan. LC 95-24631. (Illus.). 368p. 1996. text ed. 49.95 (*0-471-10619-4*) Wiley.

Specifying Message Passing & Time-Critical Systems with Temporal Logic. Ron Koymans. LC 92-41122. (Lecture Notes in Computer Science Ser.: Vol. 651). 1992. 39.00 (*0-387-56283-4*) Spr-Verlag.

Specifying Performance for BEMS. 1992. 75.00 (*0-86022-375-2*, Pub. by Build Servs Info Assn UK) St Mut.

Specifying Statistical Models, from Parametric to Non-Parametric, Using Bayesian or Non-Bayesian Approaches: Proceedings, Louvain-la-Neuve, Belgium, 1981. Ed. by J. P. Florens et al. (Lecture Notes in Statistics Ser.: Vol. 16). (Illus.). 204p. 1983. 47.95 (*0-387-90809-9*) Spr-Verlag.

***Specifying Syntactic Structures.** Ed. by Patrick Blackburn & Maarten De Rijke. LC 96-52733. (Studies in Logic, Language & Information). 312p. (C). 1997. 59.95 (*1-57586-085-6*) CSLI.

***Specifying Syntactic Structures.** Ed. by Patrick Blackburn & Maarten De Rijke. LC 96-52733. (Studies in Logic, Language & Information). 312p. (C). 1997. pap. text ed. 22.95 (*1-57586-084-8*) Cambridge U Pr.

Specifying the Noun Phrase. P. Coppen. 384p. 1991. pap. 30.00 (*90-5170-105-5*, Pub. by Thesis Pubs NE) IBD Ltd.

Specimen. Edward E. Burrows. 144p. (Orig.). 1991. pap. 12.95 (*0-9629618-0-9*) Willowby Bks.

Specimen Angling by Design. Martin Hooper. (Illus.). 176p. 39.95 (*1-85223-734-1*, Pub. by Crowood Pr UK) Trafalgar.

Specimen Banking: Environmental Monitoring & Modern Analytical Approaches. Ed. by M. Rossbach et al. LC 92-12244. (Illus.). x, 242p. 1992. 153.95 (*0-387-55001-1*) Spr-Verlag.

***Specimen Collection & Transport for Microbiological Investigation.** K. Engbaek & M. El-Nageh. (WHO Regional Publications, Eastern Mediterranean Ser.: No. 8). 1995. pap. text ed. 12.00 (*92-9021-196-2*) World Health.

Specimen Days & Collect: And Collect. Walt Whitman. LC 95-6123. (Illus.). 374p. 1995. pap. text ed. 9.95 (*0-486-28641-X*) Dover.

Specimen Dissection & Photography: For the Pathologist, Anatomist & Biologist. M. Donald McGavin & Samuel W. Thompson. (Illus.). 300p. (C). 1988. text ed. 68.95 (*0-398-05451-7*) C C Thomas.

Specimen Handling & Use of Rubella Serology Tests in the Clinical Laboratory: Proposed Guideline, Vol. 4. National Committee for Clinical Laboratory Standards. 1984. 75.00 (*1-56238-070-2*, I/LA7-P) Natl Comm Clin Lab Stds.

Specimen Preparation for Transmission Electron Microscopy of Materials. Ed. by J. C. Bravman et al. (Symposium Proceedings Ser.: Vol. 115). 1988. text ed. 40.00 (*0-931837-83-9*) Materials Res.

Specimen Preparation for Transmission Electron Microscopy of Materials. Peter J. Goodhew. (Royal Microscopical Society Microscopy Handbooks Ser.). (Illus.). 48p. 1984. pap. 12.95 (*0-19-856403-1*) OUP.

Specimen Preparation for Transmission Electron Microscopy of Materials III. Ed. by R. Anderson et al. (Symposium Proceedings Ser.: Vol. 254). 287p. 1992. text ed. 62.00 (*1-55899-148-4*) Materials Res.

***Specimen Preparation for Transmission Electron Microscopy of Materials IV: Materials Research Society Symposium Proceedings, Vol. 480.** Ed. by R. M. Anderson & S. D. Walck. 1997. text ed. 62.00 (*1-55899-384-3*) Materials Res.

Specimen Seventy-Three: A Catalog of Poets for the Season 1973-1974. Ed. by Paul Vangelisti. 1973. pap. 4.00 (*0-88031-012-X*) Invisible-Red Hill.

Specimen Song. Peter Bowen. LC 94-45770. 1995. 18.95 (*0-312-11896-1*) St Martin.

Specimen Song. Peter Bowen. 1996. mass mkt. 5.50 (*0-312-95763-7*) Tor Bks.

Specimen Tank. Buzz Callaway. 256p. (Orig.). 1993. pap. 10.95 (*0-916397-20-3*) Manic D Pr.

Specimens Filed in the New York Botanical Garden Vascular Plant Type Herbarium Index. 587p. 1985. 370.00 (*0-930466-86-1*) Chadwyck-Healey.

Specimens Filed in the United States National Herbarium, Smithsonian Institution Vascular Plant Type Collection: Index & Guide to the Microfiche Edition. Ed. by Christian Tuccinardi. 856p. 1988. 370.00 (*0-89887-058-5*) Chadwyck-Healey.

Specimens of American Poetry, with Critical & Biographical Notices, 3 vols., Set. Ed. by Samuel Kettell. LC 67-12457. 1972. reprint ed. 108.95 (*0-405-08697-0*, Pub. by Blom Pubns UK) Ayer.

Specimens of American Poetry, with Critical & Biographical Notices, 3 vols., Vol. 1. Ed. by Samuel Kettell. LC 67-12457. 1972. reprint ed. 36.95 (*0-405-08698-9*, Pub. by Blom Pubns UK) Ayer.

Specimens of American Poetry, with Critical & Biographical Notices, 3 vols., Vol. 2. Ed. by Samuel Kettell. LC 67-12457. 1972. reprint ed. 36.95 (*0-405-08699-7*, Pub. by Blom Pubns UK) Ayer.

Specimens of American Poetry, with Critical & Biographical Notices, 3 vols., Vol. 3. Ed. by Samuel Kettell. LC 67-12457. 1972. reprint ed. 36.95 (*0-405-08700-4*, Pub. by Blom Pubns UK) Ayer.

Specimens of Bantu Folk-Lore from Northern Rhodesia. J. Torrend. LC 72-78777. (Illus.). 187p. 1969. reprint ed. text ed. 49.75 (*0-8371-1398-9*, TOB&, Negro U Pr) Greenwood.

Specimens of Bantu Folklore from Northern Rhodesia. J. Torrend. 1976. lib. bdg. 69.95 (*0-8490-2655-5*) Gordon Pr.

Specimens of Bushman Folklore. Whilhelm H. Bleek & Lucy C. Lloyd. LC 78-67687. (Folktale Ser.). (Illus.). reprint ed. 49.50 (*0-404-16056-5*) AMS Pr.

Specimens of Early English Metrical Romances. George Ellis. Ed. by James O. Halliwell. LC 68-55549. (Bohn's Antiquarian Library). reprint ed. 57.00 (*0-404-50007-2*) AMS Pr.

Specimens of English Dramatic Criticism: 17th-20th Centuries. Alfred C. Ward. LC 73-138605. 355p. (C). 1971. reprint ed. text ed. 62.50 (*0-8371-5545-2*, WASE, Greenwood Pr) Greenwood.

Specimens of Irish Eloquence. Charles L. Phillips. 1977. text ed. 22.95 (*0-8369-8171-5*, 8311) Ayer.

Specimens of Middle Scots. George G. Smith. LC 70-144582. reprint ed. 57.50 (*0-404-08692-6*) AMS Pr.

Specimens of Newspaper Literature, 2 vols, Set. Joseph T. Buckingham. LC 79-146853. (Select Bibliographies Reprint Ser.). 1977. reprint ed. 48.95 (*0-8369-5620-6*) Ayer.

Specimens of Pre-Shakespearean Drama. John M. Manly. (BCL1-PR English Literature Ser.). 1992. reprint ed. lib. bdg. 75.00 (*0-7812-7152-5*) Rprt Serv.

Specimens of Show Printing: Early American Theatrical Posters. LC 86-33442. 519p. 1986. reprint ed. lib. bdg. 45.00 (*0-8095-6105-0*) Borgo Pr.

Specimens of the American Poets. LC 72-1864. 320p. 1972. reprint ed. 50.00 (*0-8201-1100-7*) Schol Facsimiles.

Specimens of the British Critics. John Wilson. LC 78-12061. 1979. 50.00 (*0-8201-1326-3*) Schol Facsimiles.

Specimens of the Pre-Shakespearean Drama, 2 Vols, Set. John M. Manly. LC 67-18432. 1997. 50.00 (*0-8196-0200-0*) Biblo.

Specimens of the Short Story. Ed. by George H. Nettleton. LC 75-94740. (Short Story Index Reprint Ser.). 1977. 19.95 (*0-8369-3120-3*) Ayer.

Specious Origins of Liberalism. A. M. Ludovici. 1972. 59.95 (*0-8490-1106-X*) Gordon Pr.

***Speck in the Universe: The Bible on Self-Esteem & Peer Pressure.** Steve Ropp. (Generation Why: Vol. 2:4). 40p. (YA). (gr. 9-12). 1996. pap. 14.95 (*0-87303-268-3*) Faith & Life.

Speckle Metrology. Ed. by Rajpal S. Sirohi. LC 93-734. (Optical Engineering Ser.: Vol. 38). 576p. 1993. 210.00 (*0-8247-8932-6*) Dekker.

Speckle-Wave Interactions in Application to Holography & Nonlinear Optics. Boris Y. Zel'dovick. 272p. 1994. 75.95 (*0-8493-4479-4*, 4479) CRC Pr.

Speckled Band: The Adventures of Sherlock Holmes. Jeremy Paul. (Illus.). 48p. (Orig.). 1991. pap. 11.00 (*0-86025-436-4*, Pub. by Ian Henry Pubns UK) Empire Pub Srvs.

Speckled Rose of Oz. Donald Abbott. (Illus.). 95p. (J). (gr. 2 up). 1995. 34.95 (*0-929605-42-X*, Emerald Cty Pr); pap. 9.95 (*0-929605-43-8*) Books Wonder.

SPECS: Specification & Programming Environment for Communication Software. M. F. Michel. 364p. 1993. 156.25 (*0-444-89923-5*, North Holland) Elsevier.

Specs: The Comprehensive Foodservice Purchasing & Specification Manual. 2nd ed. Lewis Reed. LC 92-12414. 712p. 1993. text ed. 108.95 (*0-442-00705-1*) Van Nos Reinhold.

Specs: The True Story of Baseball Player George Toporcer. Mitchell Motomora. (Ready-Set-Read Ser.). (Illus.). 24p. (J). (ps-2). 1990. lib. bdg. 21.40 (*0-8172-3585-X*) Raintree Steck-V.

Specs: The True Story of Baseball Player George Toporcer. Mitchell Motomora. (J). 1995. pap. text ed. 4.95 (*0-8114-6746-5*) Raintree Steck-V.

SPECT: A Primer: Single-Photon Emission Computed Tomography: A Primer. 3rd ed. Robert J. English. Ed. by John Childs. LC 95-40807. 223p. 1995. pap. text ed. 40.00 (*0-932004-43-1*) Soc Nuclear Med.

***SPECT Imaging of the Brain.** Ed. by R. Duncan. LC 96-28961. (Developments in Nuclear Medicine Ser.). 260p. (C). 1997. lib. bdg. 169.00 (*0-7923-4186-4*) Kluwer Ac.

Spect Properties/Inorganic & Organometallic Compounds, Vol. 10. Davidson. 1990. 153.00 (*0-85186-093-1*) CRC Pr.

Spect Properties/Inorganic & Organometallic Compounds, Vol. 12. Davidson. 1991. 175.00 (*0-85186-920-3*) CRC Pr.

Spect Properties/Inorganic & Organometallic Compounds, Vol. 14. Davidson. 1989. 274.00 (*0-85186-123-7*) CRC Pr.

Spect Properties/Inorganic & Organometallic Compounds, Vol. 15. Davidson. 1989. 274.00 (*0-85186-133-4*) CRC Pr.

Spect Properties/Inorganic & Organometallic Compounds, Vol. 16. Davidson. 1989. 263.00 (*0-85186-143-1*) CRC Pr.

Spect Properties/Inorganic & Organometallic Compounds, Vol. 17. Davidson & Ebswor. 1988. 286.00 (*0-85186-153-9*) CRC Pr.

Spect Properties/Inorganic & Organometallic Compounds, Vol. 18. Davidson & Ebswor. 1988. 286.00 (*0-85186-163-6*) CRC Pr.

S

Spect Properties/Inorganic & Organometallic Compounds, Vol. 19. Davidson & Ebswor. 1988. 286.00 (0-85186-173-3) CRC Pr.

Spect Properties/Inorganic & Organometallic Compounds, Vol. 21. Davidson & Ebswor. 1989. 330.00 (0-85186-193-8) CRC Pr.

Spect Properties/Inorganic & Organometallic Compounds, Vol. 22. Davidson & Ebswor. 1989. 362.00 (0-85186-203-9) CRC Pr.

Spect Properties/Inorganic & Organometallic Compounds, Vol. 23. Davidson & Ebswor. 1990. 362.00 (0-85186-213-6) CRC Pr.

Spectacle. Jacques Prevert. (FRE.). 1972. pap. 11.95 (0-7859-1628-8, 2070361047) Fr & Eur.

Spectacle. Jacques Prevert. (Folio Ser.: No. 104). (FRE.). 1972. pap. 10.50 (2-07-036104-7) Schoenhof.

***Spectacle: Media & the Making of the O. J. Simpson Story.** Paul Thaler. LC 97-5593. 1997. text ed. write for info. (0-275-95319-X, Praeger Pubs); pap. text ed. 22.95 (0-275-95320-3, Praeger Pubs) Greenwood.

Spectacle: Operation Desert Storm & the Triumph of Illusion. Mark C. Miller. 320p. 1993. 22.00 (0-671-78504-4) S&S Trade.

Spectacle & Image in Renaissance Europe: Selected Papers of the 32nd Conference at the Centre d'Etudes Superieures de la Renaissance de Tours 29 June-8 July 1989. Ed. by Andre Lascombes. LC 92-44780. (Symbola et Emblemata, Studies in Renaissance & Baroque Symbolism: No. 4). (Illus.). viii, 367p. (FRE.). 1993. 114.00 (90-04-09774-0) E J Brill.

Spectacle at the Tower. Gert Hofmann. Tr. by Christopher Middleton from GER. LC 83-27472. 234p. 1989. pap. 8.95 (0-88064-114-2) Fromm Intl Pub.

Spectacle Frame Dispensing. George Clayton. (C). 1989. 110.00 (0-900099-04-6, Pub. by Assn Brit Dispen Opticians UK) St Mut.

Spectacle Frame Dispensing. Henri Obstfeld. 1996. text ed. write for info. (0-7020-1928-3) HarBrace.

Spectacle Frames & Their Dispensing. Henri Obstfeld. 1995. write for info. (0-7506-2061-7) Buttrwrth-Heinemann.

Spectacle of Death. K. M. Islam. pap. 16.50 (0-933511-11-6) Kazi Pubns.

Spectacle of Democracy: Spanish Television, Nationalism, & Political Transition. Richard Maxwell. 256p. 1994. pap. 17.95 (0-8166-2358-9) U of Minn Pr.

Spectacle of History: Speech, Text, & Memory at the Iran-Contra Hearings. Michael Lynch et al. LC 95-35529. (Post-Contemporary Interventions Ser.). 352p. 1996. text ed. 49.95 (0-8223-1729-X); pap. text ed. 18.95 (0-8223-1738-9) Duke.

Spectacle of Nature: Landscape & Bourgeois Culture in Nineteenth-Century France. Nicholas Green. LC 89-12647. 224p. 1990. 59.95 (0-7190-2843-4, Pub. by Manchester Univ Pr UK) St Martin.

Spectacle of Nature: Landscape & Bourgeois Culture in Nineteenth-Century France. Nicholas Green. (Illus.). 256p. (C). 1993. text ed. 29.95 (0-7190-3909-6, Pub. by Manchester Univ Pr UK) St Martin.

Spectacle of the Body: Stories. Noy Holland. LC 93-34640. 1994. 20.00 (0-679-40481-3) Knopf.

Spectacle of Women: Imagery of the Suffrage Campaign, 1907-14. Lisa Tickner. (Illus.). 346p. 1988. 45.00 (0-226-80245-0) U Ch Pr.

Spectacle, Pageantry, & Early Tudor Policy. 2nd ed. Sydney Anglo. (Oxford-Warburg Studies). (Illus.). 416p. (C). 1997. 85.00 (0-19-920603-1) OUP.

Spectacle, Silence & Subversion: Women's Performance Language & Strategies, Vol. 2, Part 1. Ed. by Margaret Llewellyn-Jones. 118p. 1994. pap. text ed. 23.00 (3-7186-5515-2, Harwood Acad Pubs) Gordon & Breach.

Spectacle unto God: The Life & Death of Christopher Love. Don Kistler. (Illus.). 193p. 1995. 23.95 (1-877611-98-0) Soli Deo Gloria.

Spectacled Angel. Eleanora D. Dodds. LC 95-90928. (Orig.). 1996. pap. 10.95 (0-533-11762-3) Vantage.

Spectacles. Samuele Mazza. (Illus.). 192p. 1996. pap. 16.95 (0-8118-1367-3) Chronicle Bks.

Spectacles. 2nd ed. Ellen Raskin. LC 88-10363. (Illus.). 48p. (J). (gr. k-4). 1988. pap. 4.95 (0-689-71271-5, Aladdin Paperbacks) S&S Childrens.

Spectacles & Other Vision Aids: A History & Guide to Collecting. J. William Rosenthal. LC 95-16408. 550p. 1996. 148.00 (0-930405-71-4, NP31395) Norman SF.

Spectacles & Predicaments: Essays in Social Theory. Ernest Gellner. LC 78-67304. 1980. 74.95 (0-521-22486-1) Cambridge U Pr.

Spectacles & Predicaments: Essays in Social Theory. Ernest Gellner. 392p. (C). 1991. pap. 25.95 (0-521-42434-8) Cambridge U Pr.

Spectacles, Lorgnettes & Monocles. D. C. Davidson. (Shire Album Ser.: No. 227). (Illus.). 32p. 1989. pap. text ed. 5.50 (0-85263-975-9, Pub. by Shire Pubns UK) Lubrecht & Cramer.

Spectacles, Lorgnettes & Monocles. D. C. Davidson. 1989. pap. 25.00 (0-85263-957-0, Pub. by Shire UK) St Mut.

Spectacles of Realism: Gender, Body, Genre. Margaret Cohen & Christopher Prendergast. (Cultural Politics Ser.: Vol. 10). 1995. pap. text ed. 21.95 (0-8166-2521-2) U of Minn Pr.

Spectacles of Realism: Gender, Body, Genre. Margaret Cohen & Christopher Prendergast. (Cultural Politics Ser.: Vol. 10). 1995. text ed. 54.95 (0-8166-2520-4) U of Minn Pr.

Spectacles of Strangeness: Imperialism, Alienation, & Marlowe. Emily C. Bartels. LC 92-45865. 240p. (C). 1993. text ed. 31.50 (0-8122-3193-7) U of Pa Pr.

Spectacular America. Letitia B. O'Connor. (Illus.). 132p. 1994. 75.00 (0-88363-394-9) H L Levin.

Spectacular Bodies: Gender, Genre, & the Action Cinema. Yvonne Tasker. LC 92-44020. (Comedia Bk.). (Illus.). 240p. (C). (gr. 13). 1993. pap. 16.95 (0-415-09224-8, B2398); text ed. 62.95 (0-415-09223-X, B2394) Routledge.

Spectacular Body: Science, Method, & Meaning in the Work of Degas. Anthea Callen. LC 94-30122. 1995. 50.00 (0-300-05443-2) Yale U Pr.

Spectacular California: A Pictorial Guide. 32p. (Orig.). 1990. pap. 2.50 (1-878395-14-9) Smith-Western.

***Spectacular China.** 1997. 75.00 (0-88363-157-1) H L Levin.

Spectacular Color Floral Designs of E.A. Seguy. E. A. Seguy. (Illus.). 48p. (Orig.). 1983. pap. 7.95 (0-486-24488-1) Dover.

***Spectacular Confessions.** Green. LC 97-21441. 1997. text ed. write for info. (0-312-17267-2) St Martin.

Spectacular Gift & Other Tales from Tell Me a Story. Illus. by Jillian H. Gilliland. LC 95-41105. 144p. (J). 1995. 14.95 (0-8362-0746-7) Andrews & McMeel.

***Spectacular Hanging Baskets.** John Feltwell. 1997. 24.95 (0-304-34614-4, Pub. by Cassell UK) Sterling.

***Spectacular Healing Foods.** Dubin. 1997. 24.95 (0-13-621269-7); pap. 13.95 (0-13-621251-4) P-H.

Spectacular Improvements of the Chess Masters: Better Moves in the Cream of World Chess. Bradford L. Drake. 142p. 1993. pap. text ed. 4.00 (0-9636260-8-6) AAA Pony Pub.

Spectacular Mazes. Ulrich Koch. LC 92-33877. (Illus.). 48p. (Orig.). 1993. pap. text ed. 2.95 (0-486-27387-3) Dover.

Spectacular Narratives: Representations of Class & War in Stephen Crane & the American 1890s. Giorgio Mariani. LC 91-47738. (American University Studies: American Literature: Ser. XXIV, Vol. 37). 184p. 1993. 36.95 (0-8204-1875-7) P Lang Pubng.

***Spectacular Nature: Corporate Culture & the Sea World Experience.** Susan G. Davis. LC 96-44902. 1997. write for info. (0-520-20031-4); pap. write for info. (0-520-20981-8) U CA Pr.

***Spectacular Politics: Louis-Napoleon Bonaparte & the Fete Imperial, 1849-1870.** Matthew N. Truesdell. (Illus.). 256p. 1997. text ed. 45.00 (0-19-510689-X) OUP.

Spectacular Politics: Theatrical Power & Mass Culture in Early Modern England. Paula R. Backscheider. LC 92-40746. (Illus.). 296p. (C). 1993. text ed. 42.50 (0-8018-4568-8) Johns Hopkins.

Spectacular Railroad Photography: A Full Color Guide to Weather & Lighting Conditions. Intro. by Roger M. Ingbretsen. 128p. 1988. 32.50 (0-945434-00-6) Hundman Pub.

***Spectacular Realities: Early Mass Culture in Fin-de-Siecle, Paris.** Vanessa R. Schwartz. LC 97-2201. 1998. write for info. (0-520-20959-1) U CA Pr.

***Spectacular Sharks & Other Marine Creatures.** Jinny Johnson. (J). 1996. pap. 8.95 (0-614-18982-9) Scholastic Inc.

***Spectacular Space.** Annalisa Suid. (Super-Duper Science Ser.). (Illus.). 80p. (Orig.). (J). (gr. 1-3). 1996. pap. 9.95 (1-878279-90-4, MM2019) Monday Morning Bks.

Spectacular Sports. Stuart A. Kallen. Ed. by Rosemary Wallner. LC 91-73056. (World Record Library). (J). 1991. lib. bdg. 12.94 (1-56239-045-7) Abdo & Dghtrs.

Spectacular Stink Rolling Magazine. Pip Wilson. 1992. pap. 15.99 (0-551-02117-9) Zondervan.

Spectacular Stone Soup. Patricia R. Giff. (New Kids at the Polk Street School Ser.: No. 5). 80p. (Orig.). (J). (gr. k-6). 1989. mass mkt. 3.50 (0-440-40134-8, YB BDD) BDD Bks Young Read.

Spectacular Sunsets: The Golden Rules for Enjoying Your Golden Years. Murray Fisher. (Life's Golden Rules Ser.). 160p. 1994. 5.99 (1-881649-15-6) Genl Pub Grp.

Spectacular Teamwork: How to Develop the Leadership Skills for Team Success. Robert Blake et al. LC 86-28123. 219p. 1987. text ed. 29.95 (0-471-85311-9) Wiley.

Spectacular Vernacular: The Adobe Tradition. Jean-Louis Bourgeois & Basil Davidson. (Illus.). 192p. 1996. pap. 39.95 (0-89381-672-8) Aperture.

Spectacular Vernaculars: Hip-Hop & the Politics of Postmodernism. Russell A. Potter. LC 94-24990. (SUNY Series in Postmodern Culture). 197p. 1995. pap. text ed. 16.95 (0-7914-2626-2) State U NY Pr.

Spectacular Vernaculars: Hip-Hop & the Politics of Postmodernism. Russell A. Potter. LC 94-24990. (SUNY Series in Postmodern Culture). 197p. 1995. text ed. 44.50 (0-7914-2625-4) State U NY Pr.

Spectacular Vision: The George & Susan Proskauer Collection. William T. Henning & Eason Eige. Ed. & Intro. by Harriet W. Fowler. LC 94-61131. (Illus.). 136p. (Orig.). (C). 1994. pap. 20.00 (1-882007-07-7) Univ KY Art Mus.

Spectator, 5 vols., Vol. 3. Ed. by Donald F. Bond. (Illus.). 608p. 1987. 140.00 (0-19-818612-6) OUP.

Spectator, 5 vols., Vol. 4. Ed. by Donald F. Bond. (Illus.). 608p. 1987. 140.00 (0-19-818613-4) OUP.

Spectator, 5 vols., Vol. 5. Ed. by Donald F. Bond. (Illus.). 512p. 1987. 140.00 (0-19-818614-2) OUP.

Spectator: A Novel. Rachel Salazar. LC 86-4477. 128p. 1986. 15.95 (0-932511-04-X); pap. 6.95 (0-932511-05-8) Fiction Coll.

Spectator & the City in Nineteenth Century American Literature. Dana Brand. 200p. (C). 1991. text ed. 54.95 (0-521-36207-5) Cambridge U Pr.

Spectator & the Landscape in the Art Criticism of Diderot & His Contemporaries. Ian Lochhead. LC 82-4770. (Studies in the Fine Arts: Criticism: No. 14). 133p. reprint ed. pap. 38.00 (0-685-20813-3, 2070027) Bks Demand.

Spectator Bird. Wallace Stegner. 1992. 21.75 (0-8446-6607-6) Peter Smith.

Spectator Bird. Wallace Stegner. 224p. 1990. reprint ed. pap. 11.95 (0-14-013940-0, Penguin Bks) Viking Penguin.

Spectator Harvest. Spectator Magazine Staff. LC 79-105038. (Essay Index Reprint Ser.). 1935. 23.95 (0-8369-1481-3) Ayer.

Spectator Reader. Ed. & Intro. by Michael McFee. LC 85-61379. (Illus.). 224p. (Orig.). 1985. pap. 7.95 (0-9614785-1-9) Spectator Publ.

Spectator Society: The Philippines under Martial Rule. Benjamin N. Muego. LC 88-25304. (Monographs in International Studies, Southeast Asia Ser.: No. 77). 201p. 1986. pap. text ed. 17.00 (0-89680-138-1, Ohio U Ctr Intl) Ohio U Pr.

Spectators on the Paris Stage in the Seventeenth & Eighteenth Centuries. Barbara G. Mittman. LC 84-16339. (Theater & Dramatic Studies: No. 25). (Illus.). 170p. reprint ed. pap. 48.50 (0-8357-1610-4, 2070484) Bks Demand.

Specter. Joan L. Nixon. 192p. (YA). 1993. mass mkt. 3.99 (0-440-97740-1) Dell.

Specter Is Haunting Europe: A Sociohistorical Approach to the Fantastic. Jose B. Monleon. 199p. (C). 1990. text ed. 32.50 (0-691-06862-3) Princeton U Pr.

Specter Is Haunting Texas. Fritz Leiber. 256p. 1992. pap. 9.00 (0-02-022347-1) Macmillan.

Specter of Capitalism & the Promise of a Classless Society. Donald H. Weiss. LC 91-45221. 184p. (C). 1992. text ed. 49.95 (0-391-03752-8) Humanities.

Specter of Communism: The United States & the Origins of the Cold War, 1917-1953. Melvyn P. Leffler. Ed. by Eric Foner. LC 94-13419. 144p. 1994. pap. 7.95 (0-8090-1574-9) Hill & Wang.

Specter of Communism in Hawaii. T. Michael Holmes. LC 93-45841. 1994. 19.95 (0-8248-1550-5) UH Pr.

Specter of Dido: Spenser & Virgilian Epic. John Watkins. LC 94-33643. 1995. 20.00 (0-300-05883-7) Yale U Pr.

Specter of Mass Death. Ed. by Kabasele Lumbala & David N. Power. (Concilium Ser.). 1993. 15.00 (0-88344-871-8) Orbis Bks.

Specter of Neutralism: The United States & the Emergence of the Third World. H. W. Brands, Jr. (Columbia Studies in Contemporary American History). 372p. 1990. text ed. 49.50 (0-231-07168-X) Col U Pr.

Specter of Relativism: Truth, Dialogue & Phronesis in Philosophical Hermeneutics. Ed. by Lawrence Schmidt. LC 95-16129. (Studies in Phenomenology & Existential Philosophy). 316p. 1995. text ed. 49.95 (0-8101-1256-6) Northwestern U Pr.

Specter of the Absurd: The Sources & Criticism of Modern Nihilism. Donald A. Crosby. LC 87-20917. (SUNY Series in Philosophy). 456p. 1988. text ed. 67.50 (0-88706-719-0); pap. text ed. 24.95 (0-88706-720-4) State U NY Pr.

***Specter of the Past.** Timothy Zahn. (Star Wars Ser.). 256p. 1997. 23.95 (0-553-09542-0) Bantam.

***Specters of Liberation: Great Refusals in the New World Order.** Martin J. Matustik. LC 97-17277. (SUNY Series in Radical Social & Political Theory). 320p. 1998. text ed. 71.50 (0-7914-3691-8); pap. text ed. 23.95 (0-7914-3692-6) State U NY Pr.

Specters of Marx: The State of the Debt, the Work of Mourning, & the New International. Jacques Derrida. Tr. by Peggy Kamuf from FRE. LC 94-20564. 256p. (gr. 13). 1994. pap. 17.95 (0-415-91045-5, B4396, Routledge NY) Routledge.

Specters of Marx: The State of the Debt, the Work of Mourning, & the New International. Jacques Derrida. Tr. by Peggy Kamuf from FRE. LC 94-20564. 256p. (C). (gr. 13). 1994. text ed. 69.95 (0-415-91044-7, B4392, Routledge NY) Routledge.

Specters of the Dawn. S. Andrew Swann. 288p. (Orig.). 1994. mass mkt. 4.50 (0-88677-613-9) DAW Bks.

Specterworld. Isidore Haiblum. 224p. (Orig.). 1991. pap. 3.95 (0-380-75858-X) Avon.

Spectgroscopic Properties of Inorganic & Organometallic Compounds, Vol. 27. G. Davidson. 474p. 1994. 341.00 (0-85186-981-5, R6981) CRC Pr.

Spector Group: Partnership in Corporate Architecture. 192p. 1994. 39.99 (1-56496-117-6) Rockport Pubs.

Spector of Relativism: Truth, Dialogue, & Phronesis in Philosophical Hermeneutics. Ed. by Lawrence Schmidt. LC 95-16129. (Studies in Phenomenology & Existential Philosophy). 316p. 1995. pap. text ed. 18.95 (0-8101-1257-4) Northwestern U Pr.

Spectoscopy in Environmental Science, 24. Ed. by R. J. Clark & R. E. Hester. LC 94-23082. (Advances in Spectroscopy Ser.). 462p. 1995. text ed. 265.00 (0-471-95370-9) Wiley.

Spectra & Energy Levels of Rare Earth Ions in Crystals. Gerhard H. Dieke. Ed. by H. M. Crosswhite & Hannah Crosswhite. LC 67-29453. 413p. reprint ed. pap. 117.80 (0-317-09061-5, 2011960) Bks Demand.

Spectra & Structures of Simple Free Radicals: An Introduction to Molecular Spectroscopy. Gerhard Herzberg. 240p. 1988. pap. 7.95 (0-486-65821-X) Dover.

Spectra for the Identification of Monomers in Food Packaging. Jane Bush. LC 93-25450. 448p. (C). 1993. lib. bdg. 236.50 (0-7923-2400-5) Kluwer Ac.

Spectra of Atoms & Molecules. Peter F. Bernath. (Illus.). 384p. (C). 1995. text ed. 58.00 (0-19-507598-6) OUP.

***Spectra of Common Rock Forming Minerals.** Severin. (Illus.). 352p. 1997. text ed. write for info. (0-412-73090-1, Chap & Hall NY) Chapman & Hall.

Spectra of Graphs: Theory & Applications. Ed. by Dragos Cvetlovic et al. LC 79-50490. (Pure & Applied Mathematics Ser.). 1980. text ed. 135.00 (0-12-195150-2) Acad Pr.

Spectra of Random & Almost Periodic Operators. A. Figotin. Ed. by M. Berger et al. (Grundlehren der Mathematischen Wissenschaften Ser.: Vol. 297). viii, 587p. 1991. 158.95 (0-387-50622-5) Spr-Verlag.

Spectral Analysis: Methods & Techniques. Ed. by James A. Blackburn. LC 70-107752. (Illus.). 303p. reprint ed. pap. 86.40 (0-7837-0955-2, 2041260) Bks Demand.

Spectral Analysis & Its Applications. Gwilym M. Jenkins & Donald G. Watts. LC 67-13840. (C). 1968. 52.95 (0-8162-4464-2) Holden-Day.

Spectral Analysis & the Time Series, 2 Vols. in 1, Vol. 1 & Vol.2. Ed. by M. B. Priestley. (Probability & Mathematical Statistics Ser.). 1983. pap. text ed. 53.00 (0-12-564922-3) Acad Pr.

Spectral Analysis for Physical Applications: Multitaper & Conventional Univariate Techniques. Donald B. Percival & Andrew T. Walden. (Illus.). 580p. (C). 1993. text ed. 100.00 (0-521-35532-X); pap. text ed. 45.95 (0-521-43541-2) Cambridge U Pr.

***Spectral Analysis in Engineering.** write for info. (0-340-63171-6, Pub. by E Arnold UK) Routledge Chapman & Hall.

Spectral Analysis in Engineering: Concepts & Cases. Grant E. Hearn & Andrew V. Metcalfe. 350p. 1995. text ed. 84.95 (0-470-23562-4) Halsted Pr.

***Spectral Analysis of Economic Time Series.** C. W. Granger. LC 63-9991. (Princeton Studies in Mathematical Economics: Vol. 1). 1964. reprint ed. pap. 90.40 (0-608-02875-4, 2063939) Bks Demand.

Spectral Analysis of Physical Oceanomgraphic Data. K. V. Konyaev. Tr. by Y. V. Kathavate from RUS. (Russian Translation Ser.: No. 80). (Illus.). 217p. (C). 1990. text ed. 85.00 (90-6191-936-3, Pub. by A A Balkema NE) Ashgate Pub Co.

Spectral Analysis of Time Series. Lambert H. Koopmans. (Probability & Mathematical Statistics Ser.: Vol. 22). (Illus.). 366p. 1995. pap. text ed. 39.95 (0-12-419251-5) Acad Pr.

Spectral Analysis of Time Series. I. G. Zurbenko. (North-Holland Series in Statistics & Probability: No. 2). 248p. 1986. 160.00 (0-444-87607-3, North Holland) Elsevier.

Spectral & Chemical Characterization of Organic Compounds: A Laboratory Handbook. 2nd ed. W. J. Criddle & G. P. Ellis. LC 80-40497. (Illus.). 127p. reprint ed. pap. 36.20 (0-8357-5563-0, 2035192) Bks Demand.

Spectral & Chemical Characterization of Organic Compounds: A Laboratory Handbook. 3rd ed. W. J. Criddle & G. P. Ellis. LC 89-21467. 119p. 1990. text ed. 72.95 (0-471-92715-5) Wiley.

Spectral & High Order Methods for Partial Differential Equations: Proceedings of the International Conference, Como, Italy, 26-29 June, 1989. Ed. by C. Canuto & A. Quarteroni. 514p. 1990. 286.25 (0-444-88475-0, North Holland) Elsevier.

Spectral & Scattering Theory. Ed. by Mitsuru Ikawa. LC 94-18955. (Lecture Notes in Pure & Applied Mathematics Ser.: Vol. 161). 352p. 1994. pap. 135.00 (0-8247-9251-3) Dekker.

Spectral & Scattering Theory for Wave Propagation in Perturbed Stratified Media. R. Weder. Ed. by F. John et al. (Applied Mathematical Sciences Ser.: Vol. 87). (Illus.). 216p. 1990. 58.95 (0-387-97357-5) Spr-Verlag.

Spectral Approximation of Linear Operators. Francoise Chatelin. (Computer Science & Applied Mathematics Ser.). 1983. text ed. 118.00 (0-12-170620-6) Acad Pr.

Spectral Atlas of Polycyclic Aromatic Compounds: Including Data on Occurrence & Biological Activity. Ed. by Walter Karcher et al. 1985. lib. bdg. 284.50 (90-277-1652-8) Kluwer Ac.

Spectral Atlas of Polycyclic Aromatic Compounds Vol. 3: Including Information on Aquatic Toxicity, Occurrence & Biological Activity. Ed. by Walter Karcher et al. 1168p. 1991. lib. bdg. 355.00 (0-7923-1464-6) Kluwer Ac.

Spectral Decomposition & Eisenstein Series: A Paraphrase of the Scriptures. C. Moeglin & J. L. Waldspurger. (Cambridge Tracts in Mathematics Ser.: No. 113). (Illus.). 350p. (C). 1995. text ed. 85.00 (0-521-41893-3) Cambridge U Pr.

Spectral Domain Method for Microwave Integrated Circuits. D. Mirshekar-Syahkal. LC 89-21499. 243p. 1990. text ed. 189.00 (0-471-92684-1) Wiley.

Spectral Domain Method in Electromagnetics. Craig R. Scott. (Microwave Library). 120p. 1992. text ed. 40.00 (0-89006-349-4) Artech Hse.

***Spectral Domain Method in Electromagnetics.** Craig Scott. LC 88-32750. (Artech House Microwave Library). (Illus.). 149p. 1989. reprint ed. pap. 42.50 (0-608-02499-6, 2063143) Bks Demand.

***Spectral Elements for Transport-Dominated Equations.** Daniele Funaro. LC 97-6500. (Lecture Notes in Computational Science & Engineering Ser.). 1997. write for info. (3-540-62649-2) Spr-Verlag.

***Spectral Evidence.** Johnston. LC 97-9026. 1997. 25.00 (0-395-71822-8) HM.

Spectral Evolution of Galaxies. Ed. by Cesare Chiosi & Alvio Renzini. (Astrophysics & Space Science Library). 1986. lib. bdg. 184.00 (90-277-2187-4) Kluwer Ac.

Spectral Geometry. Peter B. Gilkey. 1995. write for info. (0-8493-7871-0) CRC Pr.

Spectral Geometry: Direct & Inverse Problems. P. H. Berard. (Lecture Notes in Mathematics Ser.: Vol. 1207). xiv, 272p. 1986. pap. 33.80 (0-387-16788-9) Spr-Verlag.

***Spectral Graph Theory.** Fan R. Chung. LC 96-45112. (Regional Conference Series in Mathematics Ser.: No. 92). 207p. 1996. pap. 25.00 (0-8218-0315-8) Am Math.

Spectral Hole-Burning & Related Spectroscopies. LC 94-65371. (Nineteen Ninety-Four Technical Digest Ser.: Vol. 15). 300p. (Orig.). 1994. pap. 75.00 (1-55752-359-2) Optical Soc.

An Asterisk (*) at the beginning of an entry indicates that the title is appearing in BIP for the first time.

Spectral Line Shapes. Ed. by Burkhard Wende. 1981. 184. 65 (*3-11-008150-4*) De Gruyter.

Spectral Line Shapes, Vol. 4. Ed. by Reginald J. Exton. LC 81-1328. (Illus.). 646p. 1987. 70.00 (*0-937194-09-3*) A Deepak Pub.

Spectral Line Shapes, Vol. 7. Ed. by R. Stamm & B. Talin. (Illus.). 538p. 1993. lib. bdg. 165.00 (*1-56072-130-8*) Nova Sci Pubs.

***Spectral Line Shapes, Vol. 9.** Ed. by Marco Zoppi & Lorenzo Ulivi. 592p. 1997. 125.00 (*1-56396-656-5*, AIP) Am Inst Physics.

Spectral Line Shapes: Proceedings, Seventh International Congress Aussois, France, June 11-15, 1984. Ed. by Francois Rostas. (Illus.). xx, 769p. 1985. 273.10 (*3-11-010119-X*) De Gruyter.

Spectral Line Shapes: Proceedings, 6th International Conference, Boulder, CO, July, 1982, Vol. 2. Ed. by Keith Burnett. 1057p. 1983. 300.00 (*3-11-008846-0*) De Gruyter.

Spectral Line Shapes: Tenth ICSLS, Austin TX 1990, XVol. 6. Ed. by Lothar Frommhold & John W. Keto. LC 90-85194. (AIP Conference Proceedings Ser.: No. 216). (Illus.). 648p. 1990. 99.00 (*0-88318-791-4*) Am Inst Physics.

Spectral Line Shapes: 12th ICSLS. Eugene A. Oks. (Conference Proceedings Ser.: No. 328). (Illus.). 448p. (C). 1995. text ed. 140.00 (*1-56396-326-4*, AIP) Am Inst Physics.

Spectral Localization & Analytic Sheaves. J. Eschmeier & M. Putinar. (London Mathematical Society Monographs: No. 10). 376p. 1996. 115.00 (*0-19-853667-4*) OUP.

Spectral Methods in Econometrics. George S. Fishman. LC 72-78517. (Illus.). 224p. reprint ed. pap. 63.90 (*0-7837-3860-9*, 2043682) Bks Demand.

Spectral Methods in Fluid Dynamics. C. Canuto, Jr. et al. (Computational Physics Ser.). (Illus.). 600p. 1987. 90.50 (*0-387-17371-4*) Spr-Verlag.

Spectral Methods in Fluid Dynamics. 3rd ed. C. Canuto et al. (Computational Physics Ser.). (Illus.). xv, 567p. 1996. pap. 59.95 (*3-540-52205-0*) Spr-Verlag.

Spectral Methods in Fluid Dynamics. C. Canuto, Jr. et al. Ed. by R. Glowinski et al. (Computational Physics Ser.). (Illus.). 591p. 1993. reprint ed. 53.95 (*0-387-52205-0*) Spr-Verlag.

Spectral Methods in Infinite-Dimensional Analysis, 2 vols. Y. M. Berezansky & Y. G. Kondratiev. (Mathematical Physics & Applied Mathematics Ser.: Vol. 12). 572p. 1995. lib. bdg. 495.00 (*0-7923-2849-3*) Kluwer Ac.

Spectral Methods in Linear Transport Theory. Ed. by Hans G. Kaper et al. (Operator Theory, Advances & Applications Ser.: Vol. 5). 360p. 1982. 65.00 (*0-8176-1372-2*) Birkhauser.

Spectral Methods in Soliton Equations. I. Iliev et al. 1994. write for info. (*0-318-72598-3*) Longman.

Spectral Mother: Freud, Feminism, & Psychoanalysis. Madelon Sprengnether. LC 89-39688. 280p. 1992. pap. 14.95 (*0-8014-9611-X*) Cornell U Pr.

Spectral of Partial Differential Operators. Martin Schechter. (North-Holland Series in Applied Mathematics & Mechanics: No. 14). 310p. 1986. 153.25 (*0-444-87822-X*, North Holland) Elsevier.

Spectral Properties of Disordered Chains & Lattices. J. Hori. 1968. 113.00 (*0-08-012359-7*, Pub. by Pergamon Repr UK) Franklin.

Spectral Sequence Constructors in Algebra & Topology. D. Barnes. LC 84-24622. (Memoirs Ser.: No. 53/317). 174p. 1987. reprint ed. pap. text ed. 26.00 (*0-8218-2319-1*, MEMO/53/317) Am Math.

***Spectral Snow: The Dark Fantasies of Jack Snow.** Jack Snow. Ed. by David Maxine. (Illus.). 100p. (Orig.). 1996. pap. 9.95 (*0-9644988-3-9*) Hungry Tiger.

Spectral Techniques in Digital Logic. Stanley L. Hurst et al. (Microelectronics & Signal Processing Ser.). 1985. text ed. 149.00 (*0-12-362680-3*) Acad Pr.

Spectral Theorem. H. Helson. (Lecture Notes in Mathematics Ser.: Vol. 1227). vi, 104p. 1986. 35.95 (*0-387-17197-5*) Spr-Verlag.

Spectral Theory. Ed. by M. Birman. LC 78-93768. (Topics in Mathematical Physics Ser.: Vol. 3). 99p. reprint ed. pap. 28.30 (*0-317-12984-8*, 2020693) Bks Demand.

Spectral Theory. Edgar R. Lorch. LC 62-9824. (University Texts in the Mathematical Sciences). 170p. reprint ed. pap. 48.50 (*0-317-08657-X*, 2051947) Bks Demand.

Spectral Theory & Analytic Geometry over Non-Archimedean Fields. V. Berkovich. (Mathematical Surveys & Monographs: Vol. 33). 169p. 1990. 55.00 (*0-8218-1534-2*, SURV/33) Am Math.

***Spectral Theory & Computational Methods of Sturm-Liouville Problems.** Don Hinton & P. W. Schaefer. LC 97-2838. (Lecture Notes in Pure & Applied Mathematics Ser.). 1997. pap. write for info. (*0-8247-0030-9*) Dekker.

Spectral Theory & Differential Operators. E. B. Davies. (Cambridge Studies in Advanced Mathematics: No. 42). 250p. (C). 1995. 49.95 (*0-521-47250-4*) Cambridge U Pr.

***Spectral Theory & Differntial Operators.** E. B. Davies. (Cambridge Studies in Advanced Mathematics: No. 42). 196p. 1996. pap. 24.95 (*0-521-58710-7*) Cambridge U Pr.

Spectral Theory of Approximation Methods for Convolution Equations. Roland Hagen et al. (Operator Theory, Advances & Applications Ser.: Vol. 74). xii, 373p. 1994. 124.00 (*3-7643-5112-8*); 146.50 (*0-8176-5112-8*) Birkhauser.

Spectral Theory of Automorphic Functions: Proceedings of the Steklov Institute of Mathematics, No. 153. Alexei B. Venkov. LC 83-2694. 163p. 1983. pap. 92.00 (*0-8218-3078-3*, STEKLO/153) Am Math.

Spectral Theory of Automorphic Functions & Its Applications. Alexei B. Venkov. (C). 1990. lib. bdg. 137.50 (*0-7923-0487-X*) Kluwer Ac.

Spectral Theory of Banach Space Operators. S. Kantorovitz. (Lecture Notes in Mathematics Ser.: Vol. 1012). 179p. 1983. 32.95 (*0-387-12673-2*) Spr-Verlag.

Spectral Theory of Differential Operators: Self-Adjoint Differential Operators. V. A. Il'in. LC 95-36856. 390p. (C). 1995. 115.00 (*0-306-11037-7*, Plenum Pr) Plenum.

Spectral Theory of Families of Self-Adjoint Operators. Y. S. Samoilenko. 312p. (C). 1991. lib. bdg. 178.50 (*0-7923-0703-8*) Kluwer Ac.

Spectral Theory of Functions & Operators. Ed. by N. K. Nikol'skii. LC 80-1102. (Proceedings of the Steklov Institute of Mathematics Ser.: No. 130). 233p. 1980. pap. 70.00 (*0-8218-3030-9*, STEKLO/130) Am Math.

Spectral Theory of Functions & Operators, II: 1983. Ed. by N. K. Nikol'skii. LC 80-11102. (Proceedings of the Steklov Institute of Mathematics Ser.: Vol. 155). 176p. 1983. pap. text ed. 75.00 (*0-8218-3072-4*, STEKLOV/155) Am Math.

Spectral Theory of Geometrically Periodic Hyperbolic 3-Manifolds. Charles L. Epstein. LC 85-21443. (Memoirs of the AMS Ser.: No. 58/335). 161p. 1985. pap. 23.00 (*0-8218-2336-1*, MEMO/58/335) Am Math.

***Spectral Theory of Guided Waves.** A. S. Silbergleit & Yu I. Kopilevich. LC 96-31116. (Illus.). 332p. 1996. 200.00 (*0-7503-0381-6*) IOP Pub.

Spectral Theory of Hyponormal Operators. Daoxing Xia. (Operator Theory, Advances & Applications Ser.: Vol. 10). 256p. (C). 1983. text ed. 46.95 (*3-7643-1541-5*) Birkhauser.

***Spectral Theory of Indefinite Krein-Feller Differential Operators.** Andreas Fleige. 1996. pap. text ed. 78.00 (*3-05-501742-0*) Wiley.

Spectral Theory of Linear Operators & Related Topics. H. Helson et al. (Operator Theory Series: Advances & Applications: No. 14). 308p. 1985. 83.00 (*0-8176-1642-X*) Birkhauser.

Spectral Theory of Operators: Proceedings of the 14th School on Operators in Functional Spaces. S. Gindikin. LC 91-41699. (Translations Ser.: Series 2, Vol. 150). 176p. 1992. 112.00 (*0-8218-7500-0*, TRANS2/150) Am Math.

Spectral Theory of Ordinary Differential Operators. J. Weidmann. (Lecture Notes in Mathematics Ser.: Vol. 1258). vi, 303p. 1987. 47.95 (*0-387-17902-X*) Spr-Verlag.

Spectral Theory of Random Fields. Mikhail I. Yadrenko. Ed. by A. V. Balakrishnan. LC 82-60934. (Translations Series in Mathematics & Engineering). 267p. 1983. pap. text ed. 52.00 (*0-911575-00-6*) Optimization Soft.

Spectral Theory of Random Fields. Mikhail I. Yadrenko. Ed. by A. V. Balakrishnan. (Translation Series in Mathematics & Engineering). 272p. 1983. 64.95 (*0-387-90823-4*) Spr-Verlag.

Spectral Theory of Random Schrodinger Operators. Rene Carmona & Jean LaCroix. (Probability & Its Applications Ser.). 587p. 1990. 72.50 (*0-8176-3486-X*) Birkhauser.

Spectral Theory of Self-Adjoint Operators in Hilbert Space. M. S. Birman & M. Z. Solomjak. 1987. lib. bdg. 175.00 (*90-277-2179-3*) Kluwer Ac.

***Spectral Theory of the Riemann Zeta-Function.** Y. Motohashi. (Cambridge Tracts in Mathematics Ser.: No. 127). 250p. (C). 1997. text ed. 44.95 (*0-521-44520-5*) Cambridge U Pr.

Spectral Visions in Blake's Poetry. Steven Vine. LC 92-2799. 176p. 1993. text ed. 45.00 (*0-312-07970-2*) St Martin.

Spectrally Selective Surfaces for Heating & Cooling Applications. Claes G. Granqvist. (Tutorial Texts in Optical Engineering Ser.: Vol. TT 1). 119p. 1989. pap. 15.00 (*0-8194-0228-1*) SPIE.

Spectre. Knox Gordon. (Hatchet Ser.: No. 205). 1992. mass mkt. 3.50 (*0-373-63205-3*, 1-63205-8) Harlequin Bks.

Spectre. Robert Tyler. 100p. (Orig.). (YA). 1987. pap. 4.95 (*0-943449-03-0*) Excel Pub.

Spectre: Crimes & Punishments. deluxe ed. John Ostrander. Ed. by Bob Kahan. (Illus.). 104p. (J). 1993. pap. 9.95 (*1-56389-127-1*) DC Comics.

Spectre Bridegroom & Other Horrors: Original Anthology. Douglas A. Menville. LC 75-46305. (Supernatural & Occult Fiction Ser.). (Illus.). 1976. lib. bdg. 25.95 (*0-405-08165-0*) Ayer.

***Spectre of Babeuf.** Birchall. LC 96-52824. 1997. text ed. 65.00 (*0-312-17365-2*) St Martin.

***Spectre of Comparison.** Benedict Anderson. Date not set. pap. 19.00 (*1-85984-184-8*, Pub. by Verso UK) Routledge Chapman & Hall.

***Spectre of Comparison.** Benedict Anderson. (C). Date not set. text ed. 60.00 (*1-85984-813-3*, Pub. by Verso UK) Routledge Chapman & Hall.

Spectre of Democracy: The Rise of Modern Democracy As Seen by Its Opponents. Michael Levin. 272p. (C). 1992. 50.00 (*0-8147-5060-5*) NYU Pr.

***Spectre of Hegel.** Louis Althusser. 1997. 60.00 (*1-85984-964-4*, Pub. by Verso UK); pap. 19.00 (*1-85984-099-X*, Pub. by Verso UK) Routledge Chapman & Hall.

Spectre of Samos Island. John Satsmadjis. 1990. 13.95 (*0-533-08468-7*) Vantage.

Spectres De Vibration et Symetrie des Cristaux. H. Poulet & J. P. Mathieu. 438p. (FRE.). 1970. text ed. 347.00 (*0-677-50180-3*) Gordon & Breach.

Spectro Biology. Maryla De Chrapowicki. 62p. 1965. reprint ed. spiral bd. 5.50 (*0-7873-0262-7*) Hlth Research.

Spectro-Biology: Radio-Activity, Light Rays & Rays of Solar Spectrum. M. DeChrapowicki. (Alternative Energy & Medicine Ser.). 1991. lib. bdg. 79.75 (*0-8490-4268-2*) Gordon Pr.

***Spectro-Chrome Guide.** Darius Dinshah. (Illus.). 104p. 1997. 9.00 (*0-933917-15-5*) Dinshah Hlth Soc.

***Spectro-Chrome Magazines.** abr. ed. Dinshah P. Ghadiali. Ed. by Darius Dinshah. (Illus.). 496p. 1996. pap. 11.00 (*0-933917-14-7*) Dinshah Hlth Soc.

Spectro-Chrome Metry Encyclopedia. 3rd ed. Dinshah P. Chadiali. (Illus.). 240p. 1992. 14.00 (*0-933917-08-2*) Dinshah Hlth Soc.

Spectrochemical Analysis. James D. Ingle, Jr. & Stanley R. Crouch. (Illus.). 608p. (C). 1988. text ed. 93.33 (*0-13-826876-2*) P-H.

Spectrochemical Analysis by Atomic Absorption. William J. Price. 404p. reprint ed. pap. 105.10 (*0-8357-7033-8*, 2033347) Bks Demand.

Spectrochemical Analysis in the U. S. S. R. Ed. by S. L. Mandelstam. 112p. 1982. pap. 19.25 (*0-08-028747-6*, Pergamon Pr) Elsevier.

Spectrochemical Trace Analysis for Metals & Metalloids. R. Lobinski & Z. Marczenko. LC 96-5734. (Comprehensive Analytical Chemistry Ser.: No. 30). 838p. 1996. text ed. 293.25 (*0-444-82368-9*) Elsevier.

Spectrochemical Trace Analysis for Metals & Metalloids. Ryszard Lobinski & Zygmunt Marczenko. (Ellis Horwood Series in Analytical Chemistry). 1995. write for info. (*0-13-122755-6*) P-H.

Spectrocopies of Semiconductors & Insulators, Highlights On: Proceedings of International School. Ed. by A. Balzarotti et al. 532p. (C). 1989. text ed. 141.00 (*9971-5-0959-8*) World Scientific Pub.

Spectroelectrochemistry: Theory & Practice. Ed. by Robert J. Gale. LC 88-15431. (Illus.). 466p. 1988. 105.00 (*0-306-42855-5*, Plenum Pr) Plenum.

Spectrometric Identification of Organic Compounds. 5th ed. R. M. Silverstein et al. LC 90-15514. 419p. 1991. Net. text ed. 51.00 (*0-471-63404-2*) Wiley.

***Spectrometric Identification of Organic Compounds.** 6th ed. Robert M. Silevrstein & Francis X. Webster. LC 97-21336. 448p. 1997. text ed. write for info. (*0-471-13457-0*) Wiley.

Spectrometric Titrations: Analysis of Chemical Equilibria. Ed. by J. Polster & H. Lachmann. LC 89-5544. 433p. 1989. 170.00 (*3-527-26436-1*, VCH) Wiley.

Spectrophotometric Analysis of Food Dye Solutions. Robert P. Pinnell. Ed. by H. Anthony Neidig. (Modular Laboratory Program in Chemistry Ser.). 16p. (C). 1989. pap. text ed. 1.35 (*0-87540-361-1*, ANAL 361-1) Chem Educ Res.

Spectrophotometric Analysis of Permanganate Ion Solutions. Donald F. Clemens & Warren A. McAllister. Ed. by H. Anthony Neidig. (Modular Laboratory Program in Chemistry Ser.). 12p. (C). 1989. pap. text ed. 1.35 (*0-87540-359-X*, ANAL 359-X) Chem Educ Res.

Spectrophotometric Determination of Copper in Brass. E. J. Billingham. Ed. by H. Anthony Neidig. (Modular Laboratory Program in Chemistry Ser.). 8p. (C). 1989. pap. text ed. 1.35 (*0-87540-357-3*, ANAL 357-3) Chem Educ Res.

Spectrophotometric Reactions. Ed. by Nemcova et al. (Practical Spectroscopy Ser.: Vol. 22). 264p. 1996. 135.00 (*0-8247-9451-6*) Dekker.

Spectrophotometry, Luminescence & Colour: Science & Compliance: Papers Presented at the Second Joint Meeting of the UV Spectrometry Group of the U. K. & the Council for Optical Radiation Measurements of the U. S. A., Rindge, New Hampshire, U. S. A., June 20-23, 1994. Ed. by C. Burgess & D. G. Jones. LC 95-12166. (Analytical Spectroscopy Library: Vol. 6). 448p. 1995. 278.50 (*0-444-81718-2*) Elsevier.

Spectroradiometric Measurements. (Lighting Measurements Ser.). (Illus.). 4p. 1994. pap. 16.00 (*0-87995-042-0*, LM-58-94) Illum Eng.

Spectroscopic Analysis of Heterogenous Catalysts, Part A: Methods of Surface Analysis, Part B: Chemisorption of Probe Molecules, 2 pts., Pt. A. Ed. by J. L. Fierro. (Studies in Surface Science & Catalysis: No. 57A-57B). 382p. 1990. 190.00 (*0-444-88242-1*) Elsevier.

Spectroscopic Analysis of Heterogenous Catalysts, Part A: Methods of Surface Analysis, Part B: Chemisorption of Probe Molecules, 2 pts., Pt. B. Ed. by J. L. Fierro. (Studies in Surface Science & Catalysis: No. 57A-57B). 394p. 1990. 212.75 (*0-444-88243-X*) Elsevier.

Spectroscopic Analysis of Heterogenous Catalysts, Part A: Methods of Surface Analysis, Part B: Chemisorption of Probe Molecules, 2 pts., Set. Ed. by J. L. Fierro. (Studies in Surface Science & Catalysis: No. 57A-57B). 776p. 1990. 362.00 (*0-444-88812-8*) Elsevier.

Spectroscopic & Computational Studies of Supramolecular Systems. Ed. by J. Eric Davies. LC 92-26743. (Topics in Inclusion Science Ser.: Vol. 4). 320p. 1992. lib. bdg. 153.00 (*0-7923-1958-3*) Kluwer Ac.

Spectroscopic & Diffraction Techniques in Interfacial Electrochemistry. C. A. Melendres. (NATO Advanced Science Institutes Series C: Mathematical & Physical Sciences). 504p. 1990. lib. bdg. 206.00 (*0-7923-0974-X*) Kluwer Ac.

Spectroscopic & Photometric Classification of Population II Stars. Ed. by A. G. Davis Philip. 114p. 1986. 27.00 (*0-933485-05-0*); pap. 17.00 (*0-933485-04-2*) L Davis Pr.

Spectroscopic Characterization of Minerals & their Surfaces. Ed. by Lelia M. Coyne et al. (ACS Symposium Ser.: No. 415). (Illus.). 492p. 1989. 94.95 (*0-8412-1716-5*) Am Chemical.

Spectroscopic Constants of Atoms & Ions: Spectra of. V. A. Boyko. 1993. write for info. (*0-318-72372-7*, 889938) CRC Pr.

Spectroscopic Constants of Atoms & Ions: Spectra of Atoms with One or Two Electrons. V. A. Boyko. LC 93-39797. 240p. 1993. 180.95 (*0-8493-9938-6*) CRC Pr.

Spectroscopic Membrane Probes. Ed. by Leslie M. Loew. 1988. write for info. (*0-318-62936-4*, QH601) CRC Pr.

Spectroscopic Membrane Probes, Vol. I. Ed. by Leslie M. Loew. 240p. 1988. 137.00 (*0-8493-4535-9*, CRC Reprint) Franklin.

Spectroscopic Membrane Probes, Vol. II. Ed. by Leslie M. Loew. 208p. 1988. 126.00 (*0-8493-4536-7*, CRC Reprint) Franklin.

Spectroscopic Membrane Probes, Vol. III. Ed. by Leslie M. Loew. 240p. 1988. 137.00 (*0-8493-4537-5*, CRC Reprint) Franklin.

Spectroscopic Methods. Thomas J. Bruno. 250p. 1993. boxed 44.67 (*0-13-827007-4*) P-H.

Spectroscopic Methods & Analyses: NMR, Mass Spectrometry, & Metalloprotein Techniques. Ed. by Christopher Jones et al. LC 92-48555. (Methods in Molecular Biology Ser.: Vol. 17). (Illus.). 416p. 1993. spiral bd. 69.50 (*0-89603-215-9*) Humana.

Spectroscopic Methods for Determining Protein Structure in Solution. Ed. by Henry A. Havel. LC 95-45549. (Illus.). 250p. 1995. 89.95 (*1-56081-091-2*, VCH) Wiley.

***Spectroscopic Methods for Determining Protein Structure in Solution.** Ed. by Henry A. Havel. 1995. text ed. 89.95 (*0-471-18559-0*) Wiley.

Spectroscopic Methods in Mineralogy & Geology. Ed. by F. C. Hawthorne. (Reviews in Mineralogy Ser.: Vol. 18). 698p. 1988. per. 25.00 (*0-939950-22-7*) Mineralogical Soc.

***Spectroscopic Methods in Organic Chemistry.** Manfred Hesse et al. LC 96-35773. (Thieme Foundations of Organic Chemistry Ser.). 1996. pap. 54.00 (*0-86577-667-9*) Thieme Med Pubs.

***Spectroscopic Methods in Organic Chemistry.** Manfred Hesse et al. LC 96-35773. (Thieme Foundations Of Organic Chemistry Ser.). 1996. 115.00 (*0-86577-668-7*) Thieme Med Pubs.

Spectroscopic Methods in Organic Chemistry. 4th rev. ed. D. Williams & I. Fleming. 1989. pap. text ed. write for info. (*0-07-707212-X*) McGraw.

Spectroscopic Methods in Organic Chemistry. 5th ed. Dudley H. William & Ian Fleming. LC 95-14474. 1996. pap. text ed. write for info. (*0-07-709147-7*) McGraw.

Spectroscopic Properties of Inorganic & Organometallic Compounds, Vol. 13. 428p. 1980. 131.00 (*0-85186-113-X*) Am Chemical.

Spectroscopic Properties of Inorganic & Organometallic Compounds, Vols. 1-11. Incl. 1967 Literature. LC 76-6662. 1968. 32.00 (*0-85186-003-6*); 1968 Literature. LC 76-6662. 1969. 36.00 (*0-85186-013-3*); 1969 Literature. LC 79-67610. 1970. 37.00 (*0-85186-023-0*); 1970 Literature. LC 72-23822. 1971. 41.00 (*0-85186-033-8*); 1971 Literature. LC 72-83459. 1972. 43.00 (*0-85186-043-5*); 1972 Literature. LC 72-83459. 1973. 47.00 (*0-85186-053-2*); 1973 Literature. LC 72-83459. 1974. 61.00 (*0-85186-063-X*); 1974 Literature. LC 72-83459. 1975. 65.00 (*0-85186-073-7*); 1975 Literature. Ed. by E. A. Ebsworth. LC 72-83459. 1976. 72.00 (*0-85186-083-4*); 1976 Literature. LC 72-83459. 1977. 82.00 (*0-685-55715-4*); 1977 Literature. Ed. by E. A. Ebsworth. LC 76-6662. 1978. 82.00 (*0-85186-103-2*); LC 76-6662. write for info. (*0-318-50485-5*) Am Chemical.

Spectroscopic Properties of Inorganic/Organometall Compounds, Vol. 26. Davidson. 1993. 341.00 (*0-85186-474-0*) CRC Pr.

Spectroscopic Properties of Inorganic/Organometric Materials, Vol. 24. Davidson. 1991. 331.00 (*0-85186-223-3*) CRC Pr.

Spectroscopic Techniques for Food Analysis. Ed. by Reginald H. Wilson. LC 94-4188. 1994. 95.00 (*1-56081-037-8*, VCH) Wiley.

Spectroscopy. 2nd ed. Donald L. Pavia. (C). 1995. teacher ed., pap. text ed. 26.75 (*0-03-058428-0*) HB Coll Pubs.

Spectroscopy: NMR, Fluorescence, FT-IR. C. W. Frank et al. (Advances in Polymer Science Ser.: Vol. 54). (Illus.). 170p. 1983. 68.00 (*0-387-12591-4*) Spr-Verlag.

Spectroscopy & Collisions of Few-Electron Ions: Proc. of Study Conference. Ed. by M. Ivascu et al. 572p. (C). 1989. text ed. 130.00 (*9971-5-0947-4*) World Scientific Pub.

***Spectroscopy & Dynamics of Collective Excitations in Solids: Proceedings of a NATO ASI & an International School of Atomic & Molecular Spectroscopy Workshop on Spectroscopy & Dynamics of Collective Excitation in Solids Held in Erice, Italy, June 1-July 1, 1995.** North Atlantic Treaty Organization Staff. Ed. by Baldassare Di Bartolo. LC 96-47008. (NATO ASI Series B: Vol. 356). 516p. 1997. 135.00 (*0-306-45390-8*) Plenum.

Spectroscopy & Kinetics. Ed. by James S. Mattson et al. LC 72-91433. (Computers in Chemistry & Instrumentation Ser.: Vol. 3). 346p. 1973. reprint ed. pap. 98.70 (*0-608-00733-1*, 2061509) Bks Demand.

Spectroscopy & Optoelectronics in Semiconductors & Related Materials. Z. P. Wang et al. 440p. 1990. text ed. 118.00 (*981-02-0419-1*) World Scientific Pub.

***Spectroscopy & Relaxation of Molecular Liquids.** D. Steele & J. Yarwood. (Studies in Physical & Theoretical Chemistry: Vol. 74). xviii, 544p. 1991. 291.25 (*0-444-89136-6*) Elsevier.

Spectroscopy & Structure of Molecules & Nuclei: Proceedings. N. R. Johnson et al. 408p. 1992. text ed. 121.00 (*981-02-1103-1*) World Scientific Pub.

Spectroscopy & the Dynamics of Molecular Biological Systems. Peter M. Bayley & Robert E. Dale. 1985. text ed. 135.00 (*0-12-083240-2*) Acad Pr.

Spectroscopy & the Fourier Transform: An Interactive Tutorial. Ron Williams. LC 95-4562. (Illus.). x, 102p. 1995. 69.95 incl. 3.5 hd (*1-56081-576-0*, VCH) Wiley.

Spectroscopy in Biochemistry, 2 vols., Vol. 1. Ed. by J. Ellis Bell. 336p. 1981. 129.00 (*0-8493-5551-6*, QP519) CRC Pr.

Spectroscopy in Biochemistry, 2 vols., Vol. 2. Ed. by J. Ellis Bell. 336p. 1981. 185.00 (*0-8493-5552-4*, QP519) CRC Pr.

Spectroscopy in Catalysis: An Introduction. J. W. Niemantsverdriet. LC 93-15537. 1993. 95.00 (*3-527-28593-8*, VCH) Wiley.

Spectroscopy in Catalysis: An Introduction. J. W. Niemantsverdriet. LC 93-15537. 288p. 1995. pap. 45.00 (*3-527-28726-4*, VCH) Wiley.

Spectroscopy in Environmental & Occupational Health Applications. Richard K. Miller & Marcia E. Rupnow. LC 90-83875. (Survey on Technology & Markets Ser.: No. 170). 50p. 1991. pap. text ed. 200.00 (*1-55865-195-0*) Future Tech Surveys.

Spectroscopy in the Biomedical Science. Ed. by R. Michael Gendreau. 240p. 1986. 123.00 (*0-8493-5740-3*, QP519, CRC Reprint) Franklin.

Spectroscopy of Advanced Materials, Vol. 19. Ed. by R. J. Clark & R. E. Hester. LC 91-14672. (Advances in Spectroscopy Ser.). 405p. 1991. text ed. 464.00 (*0-471-92981-6*) Wiley.

Spectroscopy of Astrophysical Plasmas. Ed. by A. Dalgarno & David Layzer. (Illus.). 320p. 1987. 79.95 (*0-521-26315-8*); pap. text ed. 36.95 (*0-521-26927-X*) Cambridge U Pr.

Spectroscopy of Biological Molecules, No. 94. Hester. 1991. 132.00 (*0-85186-437-6*) CRC Pr.

***Spectroscopy of Biological Molecules: Modern Trends.** P. Carmona et al. LC 97-23871. 1997. write for info. (*0-7923-4685-8*) Kluwer Ac.

Spectroscopy of Biological Molecules: New Advances. Ed. by E. D. Schmid et al. 509p. 1988. text ed. 195.00 (*0-471-91934-9*) Wiley.

***Spectroscopy of Biological Molecules: Proceedings of the First European Conference on the Spectroscopy of Biological Molecules, Reims, France, 1985.** European Conference on the Spectroscopy of Biological Molecules Staff. Ed. by Alain J. Alex et al. LC 85-17771. (Illus.). 489p. reprint ed. pap. 139.40 (*0-608-05291-4*, 2065829) Bks Demand.

Spectroscopy of Biological Molecules: 6th European Conference on the Spectroscopy of Biological Molecules 3 - 8 September 1995 - Villeneuve d'Ascq - France. Ed. by Jean C. Merlin et al. LC 95-30330. 656p. (C). 1995. lib. bdg. 274.00 (*0-7923-3628-3*) Kluwer Ac.

Spectroscopy of Biological Molecules, Theory & Applications: Chemistry, Physics, Biology & Medicine. Ed. by Camille Sandorfy & Theophile M. Theophanides. (NATO Advanced Science Institutes Series C: Mathematical & Physical Sciences). 1984. lib. bdg. 245.00 (*90-277-1849-0*) Kluwer Ac.

Spectroscopy of Defects in Organic Crystals. N. I. Ostapenko et al. Tr. by Alexander I. Onipko from RUS. LC 93-3224. 272p. (C). 1993. Acid-free paper. lib. bdg. 148.00 (*0-7923-2230-4*) Kluwer Ac.

Spectroscopy of Inorganic-Based Materials. Ed. by R. J. Clark & R. E. Hester. LC 86-32563. (Advances in Laser Spectroscopy Ser.). 472p. 1987. text ed. 654.00 (*0-471-91483-5*) Wiley.

Spectroscopy of Inorganic Bioactivators. Ed. by Theophile M. Theophanides. (C). 1989. lib. bdg. 194.50 (*0-7923-0301-6*) Kluwer Ac.

Spectroscopy of Light & Heavy Quarks. Ed. by U. Gastaldi et al. (Ettore Majorana International Science Series, Life Sciences: Vol. 37). (Illus.). 452p. 1989. 120.00 (*0-306-43098-3*, Plenum Pr) Plenum.

Spectroscopy of Molecular Excitons. V. L. Broude et al. (Chemical Physics Ser.: Vol. 16). (Illus.). 290p. 1985. 117.95 (*0-387-12409-8*) Spr-Verlag.

***Spectroscopy of Molecular Ions.** 220p. 1989. text ed. 105.00 (*0-521-37107-4*) Cambridge U Pr.

Spectroscopy of Molecular Rotation in Gases & Liquids. A. I. Brushtein & S. I. Temkin. (Illus.). 330p. (C). 1994. text ed. 69.95 (*0-521-45465-4*) Cambridge U Pr.

Spectroscopy of Mott Insulators & Correlated Metals: Proceedings of the 17th Taniguchi Symposium, Kashikojima, Japan, October 24-28, 1994. A. Fujimori & Y. Tokura. LC 95-32243. (Springer Series in Solid-State Sciences: Vol. 119). 1995. 89.95 (*3-540-58971-6*) Spr-Verlag.

Spectroscopy of New Materials, Vol. 22. Ed. by R. J. Clark & R. E. Hester. LC 92-43292. (Advances in Spectroscopy Ser.). 339p. 1993. text ed. 255.00 (*0-471-93911-0*) Wiley.

Spectroscopy of Nonequilibrium Solids. C. V. Shank & B. P. Zakharchenya. LC 92-34984. (Modern Problems in Condensed Matter Sciences Ser.: No. 35). 498p. 1992. 307.00 (*0-444-89637-6*, North Holland) Elsevier.

Spectroscopy of Organic Compounds. 2nd ed. P. S. Kalsi. 1995. write for info. (*81-224-0719-6*, Pub. by Wiley Estrn II) Franklin.

Spectroscopy of Polymers. Jack L. Koenig. LC 91-13352. (Illus.). 328p. 1991. 99.95 (*0-8412-1904-4*); pap. 49.95 (*0-8412-1924-9*) Am Chemical.

Spectroscopy of Semiconductor Microstructures. Ed. by G. Fasol et al. LC 89-23015. (NATO ASI Ser.: Series B, Physics: Vol. 206). (Illus.). 681p. 1989. 155.00 (*0-306-43378-8*, Plenum Pr) Plenum.

Spectroscopy of Shallow Centers in Semiconductors: Selected Proceedings of the International Conference, 1st, Berkeley, CA, Aug. 2-3, 1984. Ed. by K. K. Bajaj et al. 120p. 1985. pap. 28.00 (*0-08-032569-6*, Pub. by PPL UK) Elsevier.

Spectroscopy of Solid-State Laser-Type Materials. Ed. by Baldassare Di Bartolo. LC 87-15271. (Ettore Majorana International Science Series, Life Sciences: Vol. 30). (Illus.). 618p. 1987. 135.00 (*0-306-42617-X*, Plenum Pr) Plenum.

Spectroscopy of Solids Containing Rare Earth Ions. A. A. Kaplyanski & R. M. Macfarlene. (Modern Problems in Condensed Matter Sciences Ser.: Vol. 21). 1988. 332.50 (*0-444-87051-2*) Elsevier.

Spectroscopy of Surfaces. Ed. by R. J. Clark & R. E. Hester. LC 87-35741. (Advances in Spectroscopy Ser.). 488p. 1988. text ed. 624.00 (*0-471-91895-4*) Wiley.

Spectroscopy One see Encyclopedia of Physics

Spectroscopy Two see Encyclopedia of Physics

Spectroscopy with Polarized Light: Solute Alignment by Photoselection, in Liquid Crystals, Polymers, & Membranes. expanded rev. ed. Josef Michl & Erik W. Thulstrup. LC 86-19122. (Illus.). xvi, 576p. 1995. pap. 65.00 (*1-56081-910-3*, VCH) Wiley.

***Spectroscopy with Polarized Light: Solute Alignment by Photoselection, Liquid Crystal, Polymers & Membranes - Corrected Software Edition.** J. Michl & Erik W. Thulstrup. 1995. pap. text ed. 59.95 (*0-471-18624-4*) Wiley.

Spectrovision Inc. Ackley & Greer. 1989. pap. text ed. 23.00 (*0-13-004656-6*) P-H.

Spectrum. S. M. Dobson. 32p. 1986. 20.00 (*0-7223-2010-8*, Pub. by A H S Ltd UK) St Mut.

Spectrum: A Guide to the Independent Press & Informative Organizations, 1996. 25th ed. Laird M. Wilcox. (Orig.). 1996. pap. text ed. 24.95 (*0-933592-85-X*) L Wilcox.

Spectrum: A Reader. Hans A. Ostrom et al. 552p. (C). 1987. teacher ed. write for info. (*0-15-583187-9*); pap. text ed. 18.75 (*0-15-583186-0*) HB Coll Pubs.

Spectrum: A Science Fiction Anthology. Ed. by Kingsley Amis & Robert Conquest. 20.95 (*0-8488-0105-9*) Amereon Ltd.

Spectrum No. 3: The Best in Contemporary Fantastic Art. Ed. by Arnie Fenner & Cathy Burnett. (Illus.). 144p. 1996. 34.95 (*1-887424-10-5*); pap. 24.95 (*1-887424-09-1*) Underwood Bks.

Spectrum Achievement Tests Five & Six. Donald R. Byrd. write for info. (*0-13-830290-1*) P-H.

Spectrum Achievement Tests One & Two. Donald R. Byrd. write for info. (*0-13-830274-X*) P-H.

Spectrum Achievement Tests Three & Four. Donald R. Byrd. write for info. (*0-13-830282-0*) P-H.

Spectrum Analyzer Theory & Applications. Morris Engelson & Fred Telewski. LC 73-81244. (Modern Frontiers in Applied Science Ser.). 286p. reprint ed. pap. 81.60 (*0-317-30035-0*, 2025050) Bks Demand.

Spectrum & Network Measurements. Robert A. Witte. LC 92-34112. 1992. pap. text ed. 45.00 (*0-13-030800-5*) P-H.

Spectrum Anthology of Short Classics, 2 Vols. Ed. by Charles Bangs. LC 86-60606. (Orig.). Set. pap. write for info. (*0-938555-02-2*) Spectrum Music.

Spectrum Anthology of Short Classics, 2 Vols., Vol. 1. Ed. by Charles Bangs. LC 86-60606. 226p. (Orig.). write for info. (*0-938555-00-6*) Spectrum Music.

Spectrum Anthology of Short Classics, 2 Vols., Vol. 2. Ed. by Charles Bangs. LC 86-60606. 219p. (Orig.). write for info. (*0-938555-01-4*) Spectrum Music.

***Spectrum Dancer.** Spike Ostmann. LC 97-91928. 210p. 1997. pap. 11.95 (*0-9658711-0-X*, 001) Qumoy Pub.

Spectrum Five New Edition. Donald R. Byrd. 144p. 1994. pap. text ed. 9.50 (*0-13-830191-3*) P-H.

Spectrum Four. 1987. pap. text ed. 7.25 (*0-13-826660-3*) Prentice ESL.

Spectrum Four New Edition. Donald R. Byrd. 176p. 1994. pap. text ed. 9.50 (*0-13-830159-X*) P-H.

***Spectrum Guide to India.** Ed. & Compiled by Camerapix Staff. (Spectrum Guides Ser.). (Illus.). 364p. 1997. pap. 19.95 (*1-56656-268-6*) Interlink Pub.

Spectrum Guide to Kenya. Mohamed Amin. 1992. pap. 19.95 (*0-86190-458-3*) Hunter NJ.

***Spectrum Guide to Mauritius.** Ed. & Compiled by Camerapix Staff. (Spectrum Guides Ser.). (Illus.). 364p. 1997. pap. 19.95 (*1-56656-271-6*) Interlink Pub.

***Spectrum Guide to Nepal.** Ed. & Compiled by Camerapix Staff. (Spectrum Guides Ser.). (Illus.). 364p. 1997. pap. 19.95 (*1-56656-269-4*) Interlink Pub.

***Spectrum Guide to the United Arab Emirates.** Ed. & Compiled by Camerapix Staff. (Spectrum Guides Ser.). (Illus.). 364p. 1997. pap. 19.95 (*1-56656-272-4*) Interlink Pub.

***Spectrum Guide to Uganda.** Ed. & Compiled by Camerapix Staff. (Spectrum Guides Ser.). (Illus.). 364p. 1997. pap. 19.95 (*1-56656-270-8*) Interlink Pub.

Spectrum of Atomic Hydrogen: Advances. G. Series. 536p. 1988. pap. 43.00 (*9971-5-0287-9*); text ed. 114.00 (*9971-5-0261-5*) World Scientific Pub.

Spectrum of Child Abuse: Assessment, Treatment, & Prevention. R. Kim Oates. (Basic Principles into Practice Ser.: Vol. 8). 208p. 1996. pap. text ed. 22.95 (*0-87630-807-8*) Brunner-Mazel.

Spectrum of Consciousness. rev. ed. Ken Wilber. LC 93-2154. (Illus.). 367p. 1993. pap. 14.00 (*0-8356-0695-3*, Quest) Theos Pub Hse.

Spectrum of Factitious Disorders. Ed. by Marc D. Feldman & Stuart J. Eisendrath. (Clinical Practice Ser.: No. 40). 304p. 1996. text ed. 36.00 (*0-88048-909-X*, 8909) Am Psychiatric.

Spectrum of Lexicography: Papers from AILA Brussels 1984. Ed. by Robert Ilson. LC 87-18414. ix, 158p. 1987. 43.00 (*1-55619-033-6*) Benjamins North Am.

Spectrum of Psychoanalysis: Essays in Honor of Martin S. Bergmann. Arnold D. Richards. 378p. 1994. 60.00 (*0-8236-4505-3*) Intl Univs Pr.

Spectrum of Reflections: An Anthology of Young Poets. Ed. by Annie Yount. LC 94-60762. 52p. (Orig.). (YA). (gr. 6-12). 1994. pap. 5.95 (*1-880964-08-2*) Zapizdat Pubns.

Spectrum of Responsibility. Peter A. French. LC 89-63895. 256p. (Orig.). (C). 1991. pap. text ed. 17.00 (*0-312-03496-2*) St Martin.

Spectrum of Rhetoric. Dorothy Guinn & Daniel Marder. (C). 1987. pap. text ed. write for info. (*0-316-33132-5*) Little.

Spectrum of the Fantastic: Selected Essays from the Sixth International Conference on the Fantastic in the Arts. Ed. by Donald Palumbo. LC 87-25216. (Contributions to the Study of Science Fiction & Fantasy Ser.: No. 31). (Illus.). 288p. 1988. text ed. 59.95 (*0-313-25502-4*, PPF/) Greenwood.

Spectrum of UFO Research: The Proceedings of the Second CUFOS Conference, Held September 25-27, 1981, in Chicago, Illinois. Ed. by Mimi Hynek. (Illus.). 226p. (C). 1988. pap. text ed. 11.00 (*0-929343-56-5*) J A Hynek Ctr UFO.

Spectrum One. Byrd. 1993. pap. text ed. 6.25 (*0-13-829946-3*) P-H.

Spectrum One. Donald R. Byrd. 176p. (C). 1992. pap. text ed. 9.50 (*0-13-829862-9*) P-H.

Spectrum One: Textbook. Diane Warshawsky. (Spectrum Ser.). (Illus.). 136p. (gr. 7-12). 1987. pap. text ed. 7.25 (*0-13-826637-9*, 20088) Prentice ESL.

Spectrum One: Workbook. Peter D. Abrams et al. (Spectrum Ser.). (Illus.). 92p. (YA). (gr. 7-12). 1987. pap. text ed. 4.75 (*0-13-826694-8*, 20090) Prentice ESL.

Spectrum Placement Test. Donald R. Byrd. write for info. (*0-13-830308-8*) P-H.

Spectrum Six New Edition. Donald R. Byrd. 144p. 1994. pap. text ed. 9.50 (*0-13-830233-2*) P-H.

Spectrum Student Placement & Evaluation Package. Don Byrd. 1994. pap. 12.00 (*0-13-102443-4*) P-H.

Spectrum Three New Edition. Donald R. Byrd. 88p. 1993. pap. text ed. 9.50 (*0-13-830068-2*) P-H.

Spectrum Two. Donald R. Byrd. 96p. 1993. pap. text ed. 9.50 (*0-13-829979-X*) P-H.

Spectrum Two: Teacher's Edition. Dye & Frankfort. (Spectrum Ser.). 1987. pap. text ed. 14.00 (*0-13-826769-3*, 20266) Prentice ESL.

Spectrum 1A. Donald R. Byrd. 96p. (C). 1991. pap. text ed. 5.95 (*0-13-829870-X*) P-H.

Spectrum 1B. Donald R. Byrd. 96p. (C). 1992. pap. text ed. 5.25 (*0-13-829888-2*) P-H.

Spectrum 2A. Donald R. Byrd. 1993. pap. text ed. 5.25 (*0-13-829987-0*) P-H.

***Spectrum 2B.** Byrd. 1993. pap. text ed. 5.95 (*0-13-830027-5*) P-H.

***Spectrum 4: The Fourth Annual Collection of the Best in Contemporary Art.** Ed. by Arnie Fenner & Cathy Burnett. (Illus.). 144p. 1997. pap. 24.95 (*1-887424-28-8*) Underwood Bks.

***Spectrum 4: The Fourth Annual Collection of the Best in Contemporary Art.** Ed. by Arnie Fenner & Cathy Burnett. (Illus.). 144p. 1997. 34.95 (*1-887424-29-6*) Underwood Bks.

Spectrum 4b. Donald R. Byrd. 1994. pap. text ed. 5.25 (*0-13-832791-2*) P-H.

Spectrum 6 New Edition. Donald R. Byrd. 1994. wbk. ed., pap. text ed. 6.25 (*0-13-830258-8*) P-H.

Spectrum '88: International Topical Meeting on Nuclear & Hazardous Waste Management, Pasco, WA. 640p. 1988. 75.00 (*0-89448-143-6*, 700135) Am Nuclear Soc.

Spectrum '92, Proceedings, Boise, ID, Aug. 23-27, 1992, 2 vols., Set. 1647p. 185.00 (*0-89448-175-4*, 700179) Am Nuclear Soc.

***SpectrumGuide: Radio Frequency Allocations in the United States, 30 MHz-300 GHz.** 3rd ed. Bennett Z. Kobb. 376p. (Orig.). 1996. pap. 30.00 (*0-9641546-1-7*) New Signals.

Specula: Selected Uncollected Poems, 1968-1993. Bruce Boston. 64p. (Orig.). 1993. pap. 6.95 (*0-9626708-5-5*) Talisman IN.

Specular Microscopy of Intraocular Lenses: Atlas & Textbook for Slit-Lamp & Specular Microscopic Examinations. Martin Wenzel. LC 92-48361. (Illus.). 128p. 1993. text ed. 59.00 (*0-86577-458-7*) Thieme Med Pubs.

Specular Moment: Goethe's Early Lyric & the Beginnings of Romanticism. David E. Wellbery. LC 95-36711. (Meridian: Crossing Aesthetics Ser.). 492p. 1996. 55.00 (*0-8047-2618-3*) Stanford U Pr.

Specular Moment: Goethe's Early Lyric and the Beginnings of Romanticism. David E. Wellbery. LC 95-36711. 492p. (Orig.). 1996. pap. 18.95 (*0-8047-2694-9*) Stanford U Pr.

Specular Shards: Poems 1993. David H. Stone. 76p. 1995. pap. 10.00 (*1-884185-03-7*) O Zone.

Speculation: How to Make It a Profitable Profession. William D. Gann. Ed. by William F. Eng. 210p. 1995. pap. text ed. 19.95 (*1-886375-00-3*) J W Martin.

Speculation: Its Sound Principles & Rules for Its Practice. Thomas T. Hoyne. LC 88-81704. 279p. 1988. reprint ed. pap. 19.00 (*0-87034-085-9*) Fraser Pub Co.

Speculation & Monopoly in Urban Development: Analytical Foundations with Evidence for Toronto. David T. Scheffman. LC 80-490583. (Ontario Economic Council Research Studies: No.10). (Illus.). 173p. reprint ed. pap. 49.40 (*0-685-46307-9*, 2036697) Bks Demand.

Speculation As a Fine Art & Thoughts on Life. Dickson G. Watts. 1979. reprint ed. pap. 8.00 (*0-87034-056-5*) Fraser Pub Co.

Speculation in Commodity Contracts & Options. 2nd ed. L. Dee Belveal. 250p. 1985. text ed. 40.00 (*0-87094-672-2*) Irwin Prof Pubng.

Speculation in Gold & Silver, Vol. 14. Kenneth E. Carpenter. LC 74-367. 1974. 16.95 (*0-405-05928-0*) Ayer.

Speculation on the New York Stock Exchange, September, 1904-March, 1907. Algernon A. Osborne. (Columbia University. Studies in the Social Sciences: No. 137). reprint ed. 37.50 (*0-404-51137-6*) AMS Pr.

Speculation on the Stock & Produce Exchanges of the United States. Henry C. Emery. LC 70-76663. (Columbia University. Studies in the Social Sciences: No. 18). reprint ed. 27.50 (*0-404-51018-3*) AMS Pr.

Speculations, 1 Vol. J. H. Hacsi. 205p. (Orig.). 1983. pap. text ed. 9.95 (*0-9612146-0-0*) Champagne Pr.

Speculations. 2nd ed. Charles I. Schuster & Vanpelt. 640p. (C). 1996. pap. text ed. 30.00 (*0-13-442294-5*) P-H.

Speculations. Thomas E. Hulme. LC 78-64034. (Des Imagistes: Literature of the Imagist Movement Ser.). reprint ed. 24.00 (*0-404-17115-X*) AMS Pr.

Speculations after Freud: Psychoanalysis, Philosophy, & Culture. Ed. by Sonu Shamdasani & Michael Munchow. LC 93-26967. 208p. (C). 1994. text ed. 59.95 (*0-415-07655-2*, Routledge NY) Routledge.

Speculations after Freud: Psychoanalysis, Philosophy, & Culture. Ed. by Sonu Shamdasani & Michael Munchow. LC 93-26967. 208p. (C). (gr. 13). 1994. pap. 16.95 (*0-415-07656-0*, Routledge NY) Routledge.

Speculative Aphorisms. Keith N. Ferreira. LC 96-90152. 1996. 12.50 (*0-533-11920-0*) Vantage.

Speculative Art of Alchemy. A. S. Raleigh. 191p. 1992. reprint ed. pap. 16.95 (*1-56459-006-2*) Kessinger Pub.

Speculative Bubbles, Speculative Attacks & Policy Switching. Robert P. Flood & Peter M. Garber. (Illus.). 440p. 1994. 55.00 (*0-262-06169-4*) MIT Pr.

Speculative Dialogues. Lascelles Abercrombie. 1988. reprint ed. lib. bdg. 49.00 (*0-7812-0108-X*) Rprt Serv.

Speculative Dialogues. Lascelles Abercrombie. 1971. reprint ed. 39.00 (*0-403-00799-2*) Scholarly.

Speculative Free Masonry. John Yarker. 21p. 1995. reprint ed. pap. 6.00 (*1-887560-32-7*) M Poll Pub.

Speculative Freemasonary. John Yarker. 1987. pap. 3.95 (*0-916411-66-4*, Sure Fire) Holmes Pub.

Speculative Freemasony & the Enlightenment: A Study of the Craft in London, Paris, Prague, & Vienna. R. William Weisberger. 243p. 1993. 47.50 (*0-88033-264-6*, 367) East Eur Monographs.

Speculative Grammar, Universal Grammar, Philosophical Analysis: Papers in the Philosophy of Language. Ed. by Dino Buzzetti & Maurizio Ferriani. LC 87-8081. (Studies in the History of the Language Sciences: No. 42). x, 268p. (C). 1987. 59.00 (*90-272-4525-8*) Benjamins North Am.

Speculative High-Rise Dilemma: Fully Sprinklered or Hydraulic Fire Alarm. David R. Baker. 1984. 4.35 (*0-318-03823-4*, TR84-6) Society Fire Protect.

Speculative Investor's Guide to the Electric Vehicle Industry. Steve McCrea. (Illus.). 40p. 1995. pap. text ed. 13.00 (*1-57074-263-4*) Greyden Pr.

Speculative Markets. Strong. (C). 1994. text ed. 70.95 (*0-06-501249-6*) Addson-Wesley Educ.

Speculative Masonry Its Mission, Its Evolution & Its Landmarks. A. S. Macbride. 254p. 1986. reprint ed. pap. text ed. 7.50 (*0-88053-040-5*, M-89) Macoy Pub.

Speculative Notes & Notes on Speculation: Ideal & Real. D. Morier Evans. LC 73-85788. (Library of Money & Banking History). x, 340p. 1969. reprint ed. 45.00 (*0-678-00560-5*) Kelley.

Speculative Pragmatism. Sandra B. Rosenthal. 213p. 1990. pap. 19.95 (*0-8126-9109-1*) Open Court.

Speculative Pragmatism. Sandra B. Rosenthal. LC 85-31813. 224p. 1986. lib. bdg. 30.00 (*0-87023-526-5*) U of Mass Pr.

Speculative Strategist: High Return from Controlled Risk Strategies in Stock & Futures Markets. Will Slatyer. (Illus.). 288p. 1996. text ed. 34.95 (*0-07-058143-6*) McGraw.

Speculator. Andrew MacAllan. 608p. 1994. pap. 13.95 (*0-7472-4181-3*, Pub. by Headline UK) Trafalgar.

Speculator: Bernard M. Baruch in Washington, 1917-1965. Jordan A. Schwarz. LC 80-17386. (Illus.). xvii, 679p. 1981. text ed. 45.00 (*0-8078-1396-6*) U of NC Pr.

Speculators & Patriots: Essays in Business Biography. Ed. by R. P. Davenport-Hines. 224p. 1986. 32.00 (*0-7146-3301-1*, Pub. by F Cass Pubs UK) Intl Spec Bk.

Speculators & Slaves: Masters, Traders & Slaves in the Old South. Michael Tadman. LC 89-40269. (Illus.). 356p. (C). 1989. text ed. 27.75 (*0-299-11850-9*) U of Wis Pr.

Speculators & Slaves: Masters, Traders & Slaves in the Old South. Michael Tadman. LC 89-40269. (Illus.). 356p. 1996. pap. 17.95 (*0-299-11854-1*) U of Wis Pr.

Speculator's Edge: Strategies for Profit in the Futures Market. Albert P. Pacelli. LC 88-37862. 304p. 1989. text ed. 29.95 (*0-471-50360-6*) Wiley.

Speculi Britanniae Pars. John Norden. Ed. by Henry Ellis. (Camden Society, London. Publications, First Ser.: No. 9). reprint ed. 30.00 (*0-404-50109-5*) AMS Pr.

Speculi Britanniae; the Description of Hartfordshire. John Norden. LC 74-171778. (English Experience Ser.: No. 403). 38p. 1971. reprint ed. 20.00 (*90-221-0403-6*) Walter J Johnson.

Speculum Amantis: Love Poems from Rare Song-Books & Miscellanies of the Seventeenth Century see Collections of Lyrics & Poems: Sixteenth & Seventeenth Centuries

Speculum Astronomiae & Its Engima: Astrology, Theology & Science in Albertus Magnus & His Contemporaries. Paola Zambelli. (Boston Studies in the Philosophy of Science: No. 135). 384p. 1992. lib. bdg. 153.00 (*0-7923-1380-1*) Kluwer Ac.

Speculum Britanniae: Regional Study, Antiquarianism, & Science in Britain to 1700. Stanley A. Mendyk. (Illus.). 432p. 1989. 45.00 (*0-8020-5744-6*) U of Toronto Pr.

Speculum Britanniae: The First Parte, a Description of Middlesex. John Norden. LC 70-171777. (English Experience Ser.: No. 402). 58p. 1971. reprint ed. 20.00 (*90-221-0402-8*) Walter J Johnson.

Speculum Christiani: A Middle English Religious Treatise of the 14th Century. (EETS, OS Ser.: No. 182). 1974. reprint ed. 75.00 (*0-527-00179-1*) Periodicals Srv.

Speculum Ecclesiae see Giraldi Cambrensis Opera

Speculum Guidonis de Warewyke. Ed. by Georgiana L. Morrill. (EETS, ES Ser.: No. 75). 1974. reprint ed. 54.00 (*0-527-00277-1*) Periodicals Srv.

Speculum Mentis: The Map of Knowledge. Robin G. Collingwood. LC 82-15552. 327p. 1982. reprint ed. text ed. 41.50 (*0-313-23701-8*, COSM, Greenwood Pr) Greenwood.

Speculum Musicae, Jacobi Leodiensis I. F. Joseph Smith. (Wissenschaftliche Abhandlungen-Musicological Studies: Vol. 13). 72p. 1967. lib. bdg. 16.00 (*0-912024-83-6*) Inst Mediaeval Mus.

An Asterisk (*) at the beginning of an entry indicates that the title is appearing in BIP for the first time.

Speculum Musicae, Jacobi Leodiensis II. F. Joseph Smith. (Wissenschaftliche Abhandlungen-Musicological Studies: Vol. 22). 160p. 1971. lib. bdg. 67.00 (*0-912024-95-X*) Inst Mediaeval Mus.

Speculum Musicae, Jacobi Leodiensis, III. F. Joseph Smith. (Wissenschaftliche Abhandlungen-Musicological Studies: Vol. 43). 140p. 1983. lib. bdg. 54.00 (*0-931902-37-1*) Inst Mediaeval Mus.

Speculum Nauticum: A Looking Glasse, for Sea-Men. John Aspley. LC 77-6849. (English Experience Ser.: No. 844). 1977. reprint ed. lib. bdg. 20.00 (*90-221-0844-9*) Walter J Johnson.

Speculum of Archbishop Thomas Secker. Ed. by Jeremy Gregory. (Church of England Record Society Ser.: Vol. 2). (Illus.). 420p. (C). 1996. 63.00 (*0-85115-569-3*) Boydell & Brewer.

Speculum of the Other Woman. Luce Irigaray. Tr. by Gillian C. Gill from FRE. LC 84-45151. 416p. (C). 1985. 48.95 (*0-8014-1663-9*); pap. 17.95 (*0-8014-9330-7*) Cornell U Pr.

Speculum Philosophiae Medii Aevi: Die Handschriftensammlung des Dominike Aners Georg Schwartz (Nach 1484) Maarten J. Hoenen. LC 94-11951. (Bochumer Studien zur Philosophie Ser.: No. 22). xii, 169p. 1994. lib. bdg. 42.00 (*90-6032-340-8*, Pub. by Gruner NE) Benjamins North Am.

Speculum Romanum. Gregory A. Staley. (Illus.). 159p. (Orig.). (LAT.). 1991. spiral bd. 13.55 (*0-939507-17-X*, B25) Amer Classical.

Speculum Sacerdotale. (EETS, OS Ser.: No. 200). 1974. reprint ed. 55.00 (*0-527-00200-3*) Periodicals Srv.

Speculum Topographicum: Or, the Topographicall Glasse. Arthur Hopton. LC 74-80189. (English Experience Ser.: No. 669). (Illus.). 203p. 1974. reprint ed. 45.00 (*90-221-0669-1*) Walter J Johnson.

***Speech.** Alvin Silverstein. (J). Date not set. lib. bdg. write for info. (*0-688-06535-X*, Morrow Junior) Morrow.

Speech. Rudolph F. Verderber. 1994. teacher ed., text ed. 80.50 (*0-03-094649-2*) H Holt & Co.

Speech. Roy Wilkinson. write for info. (*0-614-09714-2*, Pub. by Hawthorn Press UK) Anthroposophic.

Speech: A Guide to Effective Speaking. John R. Greene. 112p. (C). 1993. per. 18.84 (*0-8403-8633-8*) Kendall-Hunt.

Speech: A Special Code. Alvin M. Liberman. (Learning, Development, & Conceptual Change Ser.). (Illus.). 504p. 1996. 55.00 (*0-262-12192-1*, Bradford Bks) MIT Pr.

Speech: Code, Meaning, & Communication. John W. Black & Wilbur E. Moore. LC 72-6686. (Illus.). 430p. 1973. reprint ed. text ed. 65.00 (*0-8371-6493-1*, BLSC, Greenwood Pr) Greenwood.

Speech: Dynamic Communication. 3rd ed. Milton Dickens. 400p. (C). 1974. pap. text ed. 22.75 (*0-15-583193-3*) HB Coll Pubs.

Speech: Exploring Communication. 3rd ed. O'Connor. 20. 28 (*0-13-827296-4*) P-H.

Speech: Index of New Information with Authors & Subjects. rev. ed. Holly F. Holliday. LC 94-31092. 147p. 1994. 47.50 (*0-7883-0274-4*); pap. 44.50 (*0-7883-0275-2*) ABBE Pubs Assn.

Speech: Science-Art. Elwood Murray et al. LC 79-77823. (C). 1969. text ed. write for info. (*0-672-60863-4*, Bobbs) Macmillan.

Speech Acoustics & Perception. Philip Lieberman. LC 70-183114. (Studies in Communicative Disorders). (C). 1972. write for info. (*0-672-61293-3*, Bobbs) Macmillan.

Speech Act & Sachverhalt: Reinach & the Foundation of Realist Phenomenology. Ed. by Kevin Mulligan. (Primary Sources in Phenomenology Ser.: Vol. 1). 356p. 1987. lib. bdg. 180.50 (*90-247-3427-4*, Pub. by M Nijhoff NE) Kluwer Ac.

Speech Act Theory & Pragmatics. Ed. by John R. Searle et al. (Synthese Language Library: No. 10). 329p. 1980. lib. bdg. 96.00 (*90-277-1043-0*, D Reidel) Kluwer Ac.

Speech Acts. John R. Searle. LC 68-24484. 212p. 1970. pap. text ed. 19.95 (*0-521-09626-X*) Cambridge U Pr.

Speech Acts Across Cultures: Challenges to Communication in a Second Language. Ed. by Susan M. Gass & Joyce Neu. LC 95-40820. (Studies on Language Acquisition: No. 11). vi, 350p. (C). 1995. lib. bdg. 136.95 (*3-11-014082-9*) Mouton.

Speech Acts & Conversational Interaction. Michael L. Geis. 236p. (C). 1996. text ed. 57.95 (*0-521-46499-4*) Cambridge U Pr.

Speech Acts & Happenings. Robert Vas Dias. LC 71-173226. 1972. pap. 2.45 (*0-672-51690-X*, Bobbs) Macmillan.

Speech Acts & the First Amendment. Franklyn S. Haiman. LC 92-21157. 128p. (YA). (gr. 6 up). 1993. 18.95 (*0-8093-1882-2*) S Ill U Pr.

Speech Acts in Argumentative Discussions: A Theoretical Model for the Analysis of Discussions Directed Towards Solving Conflicts of Opinion. F. H. Van Eemeren & R. Grootendorst. (PDA Ser.). vi, 215p. 1984. 67.70 (*90-6765-018-8*) Mouton.

Speech Acts, Meaning & Intentions: Critical Approaches to the Philosophy of J. R. Searle. Ed. by Armin Burkhardt. (Foundations of Communication & Cognition Ser.). v, 428p. (C). 1990. lib. bdg. 136.95 (*3-11-011300-7*) De Gruyter.

Speech Acts Taxonomy As a Tool for Ethnographic Description: An Analysis Based on Videotapes of Continuous Behavior in Two New York Households. Nira Reiss. LC 86-8207. (Pragmatics & Beyond Ser.: VI-7). x, 153p. (Orig.). 1985. pap. 53.00 (*0-915027-93-3*) Benjamins North Am.

Speech After Laryngectomy. Louis M. DiCarlo et al. (Special Education & Rehabilitation Monograph Ser.: No. 1). (Illus.). 1955. 24.95 (*0-8156-2016-0*) Syracuse U Pr.

Speech After Stroke: A Manual for the Speech-Language Pathologist & the Family Member. 2nd ed. S. Stryker. (Illus.). 442p. 1981. spiral bd., pap. 42.95 (*0-398-04122-9*) C C Thomas.

Speech & Audio Coding for Wireless & Network Applications. Ed. by Bishnu S. Atal et al. LC 93-13233. (International Series in Engineering & Computer Science, VLSI, Computer Architecture, & Digital Screen Processing). 296p. (C). 1993. lib. bdg. 117.00 (*0-7923-9345-7*) Kluwer Ac.

***Speech & Brain-Mechanisms.** Wilder Penfield & Lamar Roberts. LC 59-5602. 300p. 1959. reprint ed. pap. 85.50 (*0-608-02929-7*, 2063995) Bks Demand.

Speech & Communication Disorder in Psychiatry. Rosemary Gravell & Jenny France. (Therapy in Practice Ser.: No. 22). pap. 29.95 (*0-412-34700-8*) Chapman & Hall.

Speech & Communication Problems in Psychiatry. Ed. by Rosemary Gravell & Jenny France. (Illus.). 364p. (Orig.). (C). 1991. pap. text ed. 51.50 (*1-879105-58-6*, 0254) Singular Publishing.

Speech & Deafness: A Text for Learning & Teaching. rev. ed. Donald R. Calvert & S. Richard Silverman. LC 83-71360. 300p. 1983. reprint ed. pap. 85.50 (*0-7837-9095-3*, 2049845) Bks Demand.

Speech & Drama. 2nd ed. Rudolf Steiner. 417p. 1985. pap. 18.95 (*0-88010-142-3*) Anthroposophic.

Speech & Equality: Do We Really Have to Choose? Ed. by Gara Lamarche. 150p. (C). 1996. 40.00 (*0-8147-5091-5*); pap. 16.50 (*0-8147-5105-9*) NYU Pr.

Speech & Hearing. Billy Alstetter. (Encyclopedia of Health). (Illus.). 112p. (YA). (gr. 7 up). 1991. lib. bdg. 19.95 (*0-7910-0029-X*) Chelsea Hse.

Speech & Hearing Clinical Manual. Pat Summers. (C). 1995. 23.20 (*1-56870-166-7*) RonJon Pub.

Speech & Hearing in Communication. Harvey Fletcher. Ed. by J. B. Allen. LC 94-47509. 1995. 49.00 (*1-56396-393-0*) Acoustical Soc Am.

Speech & Hearing Science: Anatomy & Physiology. 2nd ed. W. R. Zemlin. (Illus.). 704p. 1981. text ed. 42.00 (*0-13-827378-2*) P-H.

***Speech & Hearing Science: Anatomy & Physiology.** 4th ed. LC 96-53899. 1997. 71.33 (*0-13-827437-1*) P-H.

Speech & Hearing Science: Selected Readings. Ed. by Norman J. Lass. 382p. 1974. text ed. 49.50 (*0-8422-5154-5*); pap. text ed. 14.50 (*0-8422-0377-X*) Irvington.

Speech & Hearing Therapist. Jack Rudman. (Career Examination Ser.: C-754). 1994. pap. 27.95 (*0-8373-0754-6*) Nat Learn.

Speech & Language. 1981. 2.50 (*0-939418-39-8*) Ferguson-Florissant.

Speech & Language. Doreen Kimura. (Readings from the Encyclopedia of Neuroscience Ser.). 110p. 1988. 38.00 (*0-8176-3400-2*) Birkhauser.

Speech & Language. Wheddon. (C). 1990. text ed. 114.50 (*0-412-37800-0*) Chapman & Hall.

Speech & Language: Principles & Processes of Behavior Change. C. Woodruff Starweather. (Illus.). 448p. 1983. text ed. write for info. (*0-13-832501-4*) P-H.

Speech & Language Classroom Intervention Manual. Jacquelin S. Hagan et al. 208p. (Orig.). 1990. pap. 22.00 (*1-878372-02-5*, 1120) Hawthorne Educ Servs.

Speech & Language Difficulties in the Classroom. Deirdre Martin & Carol Miller. 160p. 1996. pap. 23.95 (*1-85346-302-7*, Pub. by D Fulton UK) Taylor & Francis.

Speech & Language Evaluation in Neurology. Darby. 1989. text ed. 109.95 (*0-205-10084-8*) Allyn.

Speech & Language in Psychoanalysis. Jacques Lacan. Tr. by Anthony Wilden from FRE. LC 68-15446. 368p. (C). 1981. pap. 14.95 (*0-8018-2617-9*) Johns Hopkins.

Speech & Language Pathology. Jack Rudman. (National Teacher Examination Ser.: NT-33). 1994. pap. 23.95 (*0-8373-8443-5*) Nat Learn.

***Speech & Law in a Free Society.** Franklyn S. Haiman. LC 81-7546. 509p. reprint ed. pap. 145.10 (*0-608-04452-0*, AU00484) Bks Demand.

Speech & Music. Ed. by Herbert Eimert & Karlheinz Stockhausen. Tr. by Margaret Shenfield & Ruth Koenig from GER. (Reihe Ser.: No. 6). 1964. pap. 14.95 (*0-900938-14-5*, UE26106E) Eur-Am Music.

Speech & Natural Language Workshop: Spring 1989 Proceedings. Ed. by DARPA Staff. 295p. 1989. pap. 19.95 (*1-55860-073-6*) Morgan Kaufmann.

Speech & Phenomena: And Other Essays on Husserl's Theory of Signs. Jacques Derrida. Tr. by David B. Allison from FRE. LC 72-80565. (Studies in Phenomenology & Existential Philosophy). 166p. (C). 1973. 24.95 (*0-8101-0397-4*); pap. 16.95 (*0-8101-0590-X*) Northwestern U Pr.

***Speech & Political Practice: Recovering the Place of Human Responsibility.** Murray Jardine. LC 97-19490. (Philosophy of the Social Sciences Ser.). 288p. (C). 1998. text ed. 65.50 (*0-7914-3685-3*) State U NY Pr.

***Speech & Political Practice: Recovering the Place of Human Responsibility.** Murray Jardine. LC 97-19490. (Philosophy of the Social Sciences Ser.). 288p. (C). 1998. pap. text ed. 21.95 (*0-7914-3686-1*) State U NY Pr.

Speech & Power: The African-American Essay & Its Cultural Content from Polemics to Pulpit, Vol. 2. Gerald Early. 1993. 17.00 (*0-88001-333-8*) Ecco Pr.

Speech & Power: The Afro-American Essay, Vol. 1. Intro. by Gerald Early. 320p. (Orig.). 1993. pap. 16.95 (*0-88001-264-1*) Ecco Pr.

Speech & Reality. Eugen Rosenstock-Huessy. LC 72-103629. 1970. 9.50 (*0-912148-01-2*); pap. 15.00 (*0-912148-02-0*) Argo Bks.

Speech & Reasoning in Everyday Life. Uli Windisch. (European Monographs in Social Psychology). (Illus.). 232p. (C). 1990. text ed. 69.95 (*0-521-35438-2*) Cambridge U Pr.

Speech & Response: A Rhetorical Analysis of the Introductions of Speeches of the Book of Job, Chapters 4-24. John E. Course. LC 94-26566. (Catholic Biblical Quarterly Monographs: Vol. 25). 1994. 8.50 (*0-915170-24-8*) Catholic Bibl Assn.

Speech & Reticence: Sounds & Silence. Carl Johnson. LC 73-83225. (C). 1973. pap. 4.95 (*0-88310-001-0*) Publishers Consult.

***Speech & Rhetoric in Statius' Thebaid.** William J. Dominik. (Altertumswissenschaftliche Texte und Studien: Bd. 27). xii, 378p. (GER.). 1994. write for info. (*3-487-09814-8*) G Olms Pubs.

Speech & Situation. 1983. 51.95 (*0-387-12768-2*) Spr-Verlag.

Speech & Sociability at French Urban Marketplaces. Jacqueline Lindenfeld. LC 90-31713. (Pragmatics & Beyond Ser.: Vol. 7). viii, 173p. 1990. 47.00 (*1-55619-109-X*) Benjamins North Am.

Speech & Society: The Christian Linguistic Social Philsophy of Eugen Rosenstock-Huessy. George A. Morgan. 192p. 1987. 39.95 (*0-8130-0852-2*) U Press Fla.

Speech & Speaker Recognition. Ed. by Manfred R. Schroeder. (Bibliotheca Phonetica Ser.: No. 12). (Illus.). viii, 204p. 1985. 111.25 (*3-8055-4012-4*) S Karger.

Speech & Speech Disorders in Western Thought Before 1600. Ynez V. O'Neill. LC 79-7361. (Contributions in Medical History Ser.: No. 3). 246p. 1980. text ed. 55.00 (*0-313-21058-6*, OSD, Greenwood Pr) Greenwood.

Speech & System. Peter Bornedal. 533p. 1996. 92.00 (*87-7289-352-4*, Pub. by Mus Tusculanum DK) Paul & Co Pubs.

Speech & the Hearing Impaired Child: Theory & Practice. Daniel Ling. LC 76-21920. (Illus.). 1976. text ed. 25.95 (*0-88200-074-8*, A0669) Alexander Graham.

Speech & Voice Characteristics of the Deaf. Joanne D. Subtelny et al. (C). 1981. student ed., teacher ed. 50.00 incl. audio (*0-88200-142-6*, A0235) Alexander Graham.

Speech & Ways of Speaking in a Bilingual Puerto Rican Community. Celia Alvarez et al. 232p. (Orig.). 1988. pap. 10.00 (*1-878483-12-9*) Hunter Coll CEP.

Speech Art Classification. T. T. Ballmer & W. Brennenstuhl. (Language & Communication Ser.: Vol. 8). (Illus.). 274p. 1980. 46.95 (*0-387-10294-9*) Spr-Verlag.

Speech As Instruction. Hanley C. Shands. 1977. 91.55 (*90-279-7725-9*) Mouton.

Speech Assessment & Speech Improvement for the Hearing Impaired. Ed. by Joanne D. Subtelny. LC 80-6786. 440p. reprint ed. pap. 125.40 (*0-7837-1251-0*, 2041388) Bks Demand.

Speech Audiologist. Jack Rudman. (Career Examination Ser.: C-753). 1994. pap. 27.95 (*0-8373-0753-8*) Nat Learn.

Speech Audiometry. Ed. by Michael Martin. 300p. 1987. 64.50 (*0-85066-641-4*, 0047) Singular Publishing.

Speech Audiometry. 2nd ed. Ed. by Michael Martin. LC 97-8329. (Illus.). 360p. 1997. pap. text ed. 49.95 (*1-56593-516-0*, 1190) Singular Publishing.

Speech Chain: The Physics & Biology of Spoken Language. 2nd ed. Peter B. Denes. LC 92-35642. (C). 1995. text ed. 26.95 (*0-7167-2256-9*) W H Freeman.

Speech Chain: The Physics & Biology of Spoken Language. 2nd ed. Peter B. Denes. LC 92-35642. (C). 1995. pap. text ed. 16.95 (*0-7167-2344-1*) W H Freeman.

Speech Choir. Marjorie Gullan. LC 71-116405. (Granger Index Reprint Ser.). 1977. 21.95 (*0-8369-6146-3*) Ayer.

Speech Coding: A Computer Laboratory Textbook. Thomas P. Barnwell et al. LC 95-31853. (Georgia Tech Digital Signal Processing Laboratory Ser.). 184p. 1995. pap. text ed., pap. 26.00 incl. disk (*0-471-51692-9*) Wiley.

Speech Coding & Synthesis. Ed. by W. B. Kleijn & K. K. Paliwal. 774p. 1995. text ed. 207.50 (*0-444-82169-4*) Elsevier.

Speech-Communication. Kathleen M. Galvin & Cassandra Book. 1995. pap. text ed. 11.95 (*0-8442-5127-5*, Natl Textbk) NTC Pub Grp.

***Speech Communication.** Ross. 1997. pap. text ed. 31.00 (*0-205-27304-1*) P-H.

Speech Communication. Jack Rudman. (National Teacher Examination Ser.: NT-35). 1994. pap. 23.95 (*0-8373-8445-1*) Nat Learn.

Speech Communication. 2nd ed. Robert C. Jeffrey & Owen Peterson. (Speech Ser.). (Illus.). 410p. (C). 1995. pap. text ed. 29.95 (*0-89641-234-2*) American Pr.

Speech Communication. 3rd ed. Zimmerman. Date not set. teacher ed., pap. text ed. write for info. (*0-314-97529-2*) West Pub.

Speech Communication. 7th ed. William D. Brooks & Robert W. Heath. 400p. (C). 1992. per. write for info. (*0-697-12915-2*) Brown & Benchmark.

Speech Communication: A Contemporary Introduction. 3rd ed. Gordon I. Zimmerman et al. (Illus.). 288p. (C). 1986. pap. text ed. 43.25 (*0-314-93529-0*) West Pub.

Speech Communication: Essays to Commemorate the 75th Anniversary of the Speech Communication Association. Ed. by Gerald M. Phillips & Julia T. Wood. LC 89-5875. 256p. (C). 1989. text ed. 29.95 (*0-8093-1520-3*) S Ill U Pr.

***Speech Communication: The Speechmaking Process.** 10th ed. Ross. (C). Date not set. pap. text ed. 33.00 (*0-205-18953-9*) Allyn.

Speech Communication for International Students. Paulette Dale & James C. Wolf. (Illus.). 160p. 1988. pap. text ed. 17.25 (*0-13-827312-X*) P-H.

Speech Communications. Douglas O'Shaughnessy. (Electrical & Computer Engineering Ser.). (Illus.). 600p. (C). 1987. text ed. 64.95 (*0-201-16520-1*) Addison-Wesley.

Speech Communications 101. Mary Forrest. 147p. (C). 1994. 11.06 (*1-56870-135-7*) RonJon Pub.

Speech Correction: An Introduction to Speech Pathology & Audiology. 9th ed. Charles Van Ripper & Robert L. Erickson. LC 95-41718. 1995. text ed. 58.00 (*0-13-825142-8*) P-H.

Speech Correction Through Story-Telling Units. Elizabeth M. Nemoy. 1973. text ed. 6.00 (*0-686-09399-2*) Expression.

Speech, Crime, & the Uses of Language. Kent Greenawalt. 368p. 1992. pap. 24.00 (*0-19-507711-3*) OUP.

Speech Delivered in the Starr-Chamber, at the Censure of J. Bastwick. William Laud. LC 79-171771. (English Experience Ser.: No. 396). 92p. 1971. reprint ed. 20.00 (*90-221-0396-X*) Walter J Johnson.

Speech Development of a Bilingual Child, 4 vols, Set. Werner F. Leopold. Incl. Vol. 6. Vocabulary Growth in the First Two Years. reprint ed. 38.75 (*0-404-50706-9*); Vol. 11. Sound-Learning in the First Two Years. reprint ed. 38.75 (*0-404-50711-5*); Vol. 18. Grammar & General Problems in the First Two Years. reprint ed. 38.75 (*0-404-50718-2*); Vol. 19. Diary from Age Two. reprint ed. 38.75 (*0-404-50719-0*); (Northwestern University. Humanities Ser.). 155.00 (*0-404-50749-2*) AMS Pr.

Speech Disorders: Aphasia, Apraxia & Agnosia. Walter R. Brain. LC 63-5076. (Illus.). 200p. reprint ed. pap. 57.00 (*0-317-41727-4*, 2025730) Bks Demand.

Speech Disorders: Clinical Evaluation & Diagnosis. Ed. by E. Jeffrey Metter. LC 84-23794. (Neurologic Illness: Diagnosis & Treatment Ser.). 256p. 1985. text ed. 40.00 (*0-89335-223-3*); audio 12.95 (*0-685-10331-5*) PMA Pub Corp.

Speech Disorders: Clinical Evaluation & Diagnosis, Set. Ed. by E. Jeffrey Metter. LC 84-23794. (Neurologic Illness: Diagnosis & Treatment Ser.). 256p. 1985. 49.95 (*0-685-10332-3*) PMA Pub Corp.

Speech Distinct & Pleasing. Frank Philip. 162p. 1991. reprint ed. 69.00 (*0-7812-9302-2*) Rprt Serv.

Speech Drills for Children in Form of Play. Barrows & Case. 1973. text ed. 2.00 (*0-686-09392-5*) Expression.

***Speech, Equality, & Harm: New Legal Paradigms.** Ed. by Laura J. Lederer. 1998. text ed. 55.00 (*0-8133-2928-0*) Westview.

***Speech, Equality, & Harm: New Legal Paradigms.** Ed. by Laura J. Lederer. (C). 1998. pap. text ed. 21.95 (*0-8133-2929-9*) Westview.

Speech Errors As Linguistic Evidence. Ed. by Victoria A. Fromkin. LC 73-78443. (Janua Linguarum, Ser. Major: No. 77). (Illus.). 269p. 1973. text ed. 56.70 (*90-279-2668-9*) Mouton.

***Speech Evaluation of the Patient with a Tracheostomy Tube.** Nancy Conway. Ed. by Cindy Drolet. (Illus.). 124p. (Orig.). 1997. 43.95 (*1-883315-23-9*, 7097) Imaginart Pr.

Speech for Effective Communication. 1994. teacher ed., text ed. 80.50 (*0-03-097526-3*) H Holt & Co.

Speech for Effective Communication. Rudolph F. Verderber. 1994. student ed., text ed. 53.00 (*0-03-097525-5*) H Holt & Co.

Speech For Effective Communication 1988. Rudolph F. Verderber. 1988. 53.00 (*0-15-319581-9*) HB Schl Dept.

Speech for Foreign Students. Morris M. Womack & Elinor Bernstein. (Illus.). 190p. 1990. pap. 26.95 (*0-398-06504-7*) C C Thomas.

Speech for Foreign Students. Morris M. Womack & Elinor Bernstein. (Illus.). 190p. (C). 1990. text ed. 39.95 (*0-398-05699-4*) C C Thomas.

Speech for the Hearing-Impaired Child. George Leshin. 151p. 1975. pap. 17.95 (*0-8165-0540-3*) U of Ariz Pr.

Speech for the Speaker. John Miles-Brown. LC 89-81770. 128p. 8900. pap. 18.95 (*0-7206-0726-4*, Pub. by P Owen Ltd UK) Dufour.

Speech for the Stage. Evangeline Machlin. LC 80-51639. 1980. 17.95 (*0-87830-120-8*, Thtre Arts Bks) Routledge.

Speech for the Stage. 2nd ed. Evangeline Machlin. 248p. (C). (gr. 13). 1992. pap. 17.95 (*0-87830-015-5*, Thtre Arts Bks) Routledge.

Speech Fright: The Key to Successful Speaking. Alice Frantz. LC 92-97509. (Illus.). 253p. (Orig.). (C). 1992. pap. text ed. 20.00 (*1-882735-00-5*) Huron Univ.

Speech Fundamentals: A Contemporary Approach. Sue Andersen & Burt Pryor. 1992. 21.00 (*0-536-58230-0*) Ginn Pr.

Speech Genres & Other Late Essays. M. M. Bakhtin. Ed. by Caryl Emerson & Michael Holquist. Tr. by Vern W. McGee from RUS. (Slavic Ser.: No. 8). 203p. (C). 1986. text ed. 25.00 (*0-292-72046-7*); pap. text ed. 10.95 (*0-292-77560-1*) U of Tex Pr.

Speech Hearing & Neural Networks Models. S. Amari. LC 94-77518. 200p. (gr. 12). 1995. 74.00 (*90-5199-178-9*) IOS Press.

Speech Hearing Science. 3rd ed. W. R. Zemlin. 1988. text ed. 78.00 (*0-13-827429-0*) P-H.

Speech, Image, & Video Data Compression Markets: Chips, Board, & Software Transcend Data Cram Barriers. Market Intelligence Staff. 208p. (Orig.). 1992. 1,895.00 (*1-56753-075-3*) Frost & Sullivan.

Speech Improvement. Jack Rudman. (Teachers License Examination Ser.: T-59). 1994. pap. 27.95 (*0-8373-8059-6*) Nat Learn.

Speech Improvement: Do-It-Yourself. Phyllis R. Weiss. (Illus.). (Orig.). 1981. pap. text ed. 39.50 incl. audio (*0-88432-075-8*, S23720) Audio-Forum.

Speech Improvement: Tapescripts for Business English Three-Zero-One. 2nd ed. Margaret Z. Mergal. 112p. 1979. pap. 3.50 (*0-8477-2611-8*) U of PR Pr.

Speech Improvement Work & Practice Book. Grace A. McCullough. text ed. 3.50 (*0-686-00149-4*) Expression.

S

***Speech in Speech: Studies in Incorporated Oratio Recta in Attic Drama & Oratory.** Victor Bers. LC 96-48908. (Greek Studies). 256p. 1997. 62.50 (*0-8476-8449-0*); pap. 23.95 (*0-8476-8450-4*) Rowman.

Speech in the English Novel. rev. ed. Norman Page. LC 87-19718. 208p. (C). 1988. pap. 17.50 (*0-391-03563-0*) Humanities.

Speech Index. 4th ed. Roberta B. Sutton. LC 66-13749. 1966. 72.50 (*0-8108-0138-8*) Scarecrow.

Speech Index: An Index to Collections of World Famous Orations & Speeches for Various Occasions-Supplement, 1966-1980. 4th ed. Charity Mitchell. LC 81-23282. 484p. 1982. 65.00 (*0-8108-1518-4*) Scarecrow.

Speech, Language, & Communication. 2nd ed. Ed. by Joanne L. Miller & Peter D. Eimas. (Handbook of Perception & Cognition Ser.). (Illus.). 415p. 1995. text ed. 59.95 (*0-12-497770-7*) Acad Pr.

Speech, Language & Hearing: Normal Processes & Disorders. Paul H. Skinner & Ralph L. Shelton. LC 77-73956. (Speech Pathology & Audiology Ser.). 1978. teacher ed. write for info. (*0-201-07462-1*); text ed. write for info. (*0-201-07461-3*) Addison-Wesley.

Speech, Language, & Hearing Disorders. 2nd ed. Franklin H. Silverman. LC 94-9654. 1994. text ed. 55.00 (*0-13-827445-2*) P-H.

Speech, Language, & Hearing Disorders: A Guide for the Teacher. 2nd ed. Herbert J. Oyer et al. LC 93-22943. 256p. 1993. pap. text ed. 38.50 (*0-205-14908-1*) Allyn.

***Speech, Language & Hearing Problems in School.** O'Connell. 1996. 42.00 (*0-614-22121-8*) Aspen Pub.

***Speech Language & Learning.** Vankeulen & Weddington. 1997. text ed. 39.33 (*0-205-15268-6*) P-H.

Speech-Language Delights. Janet M. Shaw. (Illus.). 128p. (J). (gr. k-8). 1993. teacher ed. 25.00 (*0-937857-42-4*, 1541) Speech Bin.

Speech-Language In-Services for Colleagues in Education (SLICE) Denise A. Mantione. 112p. 1992. 24.95 (*0-937857-33-5*, 1510) Speech Bin.

***Speech Language Pathology.** Rebecca Johnson. 164p. 1996. spiral bd. 95.00 (*1-879575-74-4*) Acad Med Sys.

Speech Language Pathology & Audio. McLaughlin. 1989. text ed. 64.50 (*0-205-10146-1*) Allyn.

Speech Language Pathology & Related Professions in the Schools. Robert J. Lowe. 250p. (C). 1992. text ed. 59.00 (*0-205-13499-8*, H34994) Allyn.

***Speech-Language Pathology Desk Reference.** Ross J. Roeser et al. LC 97-22115. 1998. write for info. (*3-13-110541-0*) Thieme Med Pubs.

Speech-Language Pathology Services in the Schools. 2nd ed. Joyce S. Taylor. 304p. (C). 1991. text ed. 66.00 (*0-205-13262-6*) Allyn.

Speech Motor Control & Stuttering: Proc. of the 2nd Internat. Conf., Held in Nijmegen, The Netherlands, June 13-16, 1990. Ed. by H. F. Peters et al. (International Congress Ser.: No. 950). 582p. 1991. 273.50 (*0-444-81408-6*, Excerpta Medica) Elsevier.

Speech Motor Dynamics in Stuttering. Ed. by H. F. Peters & W. Hulstijn. (Illus.). xv, 420p. 1987. 87.95 (*0-387-81971-1*) Spr-Verlag.

Speech-O, a Phonetic Game. Genevieve Arnold. 1973. text ed. 4.25 (*0-686-09407-7*) Expression.

Speech of Demosthenes Against the Law of Leptines. Demosthenes. Ed. by John E. Sandys. LC 78-18605. (Greek Texts & Commentaries Ser.). (Illus.). 1979. reprint ed. lib. bdg. 22.95 (*0-405-11445-1*) Ayer.

Speech of General George S. Patton to His Third Army. George S. Patton. 1982. pap. 2.50 (*0-910746-03-6*, SOG01) Hope Farm.

Speech of Gold: Reason & Enlightenment in the Tibetan Buddhism. Robert A. Thurman. 1989. 32.00 (*81-208-0451-1*, Pub. by Motilal Banarsidass II) S Asia.

Speech of Hon. Israel Washburn, Jun. Delivered in the House of Representatives, May 19, 1860 see Dred Scott Case

Speech of Honorable Isaac I. Stevens Delegate from Washington Territory on the Washington & Oregon War Claims, May 31, 1858. Isaac I. Stevens. 16p. 1970. pap. 1.00 (*0-87770-074-5*) Ye Galleon.

Speech of John Quincy Adams of Massachusetts, Upon the Right of the People, Men & Women, to Petition. John Q. Adams. LC 78-82163. (Anti-Slavery Crusade in America Ser.). 1978. reprint ed. 22.95 (*0-405-00602-0*) Ayer.

Speech of Mr. Benton on the Oregon Question. Thomas H. Benton. 99p. write for info. (*0-87770-458-9*) Ye Galleon.

Speech of Primates. Philip Lieberman. (Janua Linguarum, Ser. Minor: No. 148). (Illus.). 133p. (Orig.). 1972. pap. text ed. 46.95 (*90-279-2321-3*) Mouton.

Speech of Reality. Laszlo. 1994. 21.00 (*0-226-46925-5*) U Ch Pr.

Speech of the Central Coast of North Carolina: The Carteret County Version of the Banks "Brogue" Hilda Jaffe. Ed. by Virginia McDavid. (Publications of the American Dialect Society: No. 60). 83p. (Orig.). 1973. pap. text ed. 10.45 (*0-8173-0660-9*) U of Ala Pr.

Speech of the Grail: A Journey Toward Speaking That Heals & Transforms. Linda Sussman. 288p. (Orig.). 1995. pap. 18.95 (*0-940262-69-X*) Lindisfarne Bks.

Speech of the Negros Congos of Panama. John M. Lipski. LC 88-7617. (Creole Language Library: Vol. 4). vii, 159p. (C). 1989. 59.00 (*1-55619-049-2*) Benjamins North Am.

Speech Pathologist. Jack Rudman. (Career Examination Ser.: C-755). 1994. pap. 27.95 (*0-8373-0755-4*) Nat Learn.

Speech Pathology: A Dynamic Neurological Treatment of Normal Speech & Speech Deviations. Lee E. Travis. LC 78-72851. (Brainedness, Handedness, & Mental Abilities Ser.). reprint ed. 42.50 (*0-404-60895-7*) AMS Pr.

Speech Pathology: An Introduction, 2 Vols. 2nd ed. Oliver Bloodstein. LC 83-82315. 464p. (C). 1983. text ed. 60.76 (*0-395-34100-0*) HM.

Speech Pathology & Audiology. Jack Rudman. (Undergraduate Program Field Tests Ser.: UPFT-25). 1994. pap. 23.95 (*0-8373-6025-0*) Nat Learn.

***Speech Pathology Desk Reference.** Ed. by Ross J. Roeser et al. LC 97-22115. (Illus.). 448p. 1997. pap. 45.00 (*0-86577-696-2*) Thieme Med Pubs.

Speech Perception & Linguistic Experience: Issues in Cross-Language Research, Vol. IV. Ed. by Winifred Strange. (Illus.). 502p. (C). 1995. text ed. 59.00 (*0-912752-36-X*) York Pr.

Speech Perception & Production: Studies in Selective Adaptation. William E. Cooper. LC 79-17281. (Language & Being Ser.). 208p. 1979. text ed. 73.25 (*0-89391-027-9*) Ablex Pub.

Speech Perception by Ear & Eye: A Paradigm for Psychological Inquiry. Dominic W. Massaro. 336p. 1987. text ed. 59.95 (*0-8058-0061-1*); pap. text ed. 39.95 (*0-8058-0062-X*) L Erlbaum Assocs.

Speech Perception, Production & Linguistic Structure. Ed. by Yoh'ichi Tohkura et al. LC 92-52687. 350p. (gr. 12). 1992. 115.00 (*90-5199-084-7*, Pub. by IOS Pr NE) IOS Press.

Speech Physiology, Speech Perception, & Acoustic Phonetics. Philip Lieberman & Shelia E. Blumstein. (Cambridge Studies in Speech Science & Communication). (Illus.). 260p. 1988. text ed. 64.95 (*0-521-30866-6*); pap. text ed. 21.95 (*0-521-31357-0*) Cambridge U Pr.

Speech, Place, & Action: Studies in Deixis & Related Topics. Ed. by Robert J. Jarvella & Wolfgang Klein. LC 81-14659. (Illus.). 401p. reprint ed. pap. 114.30 (*0-8357-8516-5*, 2034813) Bks Demand.

Speech Plus! Supplement & Study Guide to Power Talk: Standard American English - Your Ladder to Success. Bettye P. Zoller & John A. Watleins. Ed. & Intro. by John A. Watleins. 65p. 1995. student ed., teacher ed., lib. bdg. 24.95 (*1-884643-11-6*, SPP95) ZWL Pubng.

Speech Power. Preston Miles. Ed. by Mario A. Pei. 59p. 1983. pap. text ed. 99.95 (*1-55678-024-9*) Learn Inc.

Speech Practice Manual. Thomas Keith. 248p. (gr. 13). 1988. pap. text ed. 23.95 (*1-55664-134-6*) Mosby Yr Bk.

Speech Processing. C. Rowden. 288p. 1992. text ed. 60.00i (*0-07-707324-X*) McGraw.

***Speech Production: Motor Control, Brain Research, & Fluency Disorders: Proceedings of the Third International Conference on Speech Motor Production & Fluency Disorders, June 5-8, 1996, Nijmegen, The Netherlands.** W. L. Hulstijn et al. LC 97-24975. (International Congress Ser.). 1997. write for info. (*0-444-82460-X*) Elsevier.

Speech Production & Speech Modelling. William J. Hardcastel & Alain Marchal. (C). 1990. lib. bdg. 188.00 (*0-7923-0746-1*) Kluwer Ac.

Speech Recognition. Peter Foster. 1993. 34.95 (*0-936648-39-2*) Flatiron Pubng.

***Speech Recognition: The Future Now.** Michael Koerner. 1996. pap. 45.95 incl. cd-rom (*0-13-618190-2*) P-H.

Speech Recognition & Coding: New Advances & Trends, Vol. XI. Ed. by Antonio J. Ayuso & Juan M. Soler. (NATO ASI Series F: Computer & Systems Science: Vol. 147). 505p. 1995. 150.00 (*3-540-60098-1*) Spr-Verlag.

Speech Recognition & Understanding: Recent Advances, Trends & Applications. Ed. by P. Laface & Renato De Mori. (NATO ASI Series F: Computer & Systems Sciences, Special Programme AET: Vol. 75). 576p. 1992. 144.00 (*0-387-54032-6*) Spr-Verlag.

Speech Recognition Reference Manual & Buyer's Guide. 4th ed. Marc Robins. 305p. 1996. pap. 85.00 (*0-9624360-5-4*) Robins Pr.

Speech Resources: Exercises & Activities. 2nd ed. Ellen A. Hay. LC 91-6157. (Illus.). 165p. (C). 1992. pap. text ed. write for info. (*0-935732-34-9*) Roxbury Pub Co.

Speech Reticence: Sounds & Silence. Carl Johnson. LC 73-83225. (C). 1973. 8.95 (*0-88310-015-0*) Publishers Consult.

***Speech Sampler: Speeches & Analyses.** Joe Ayres. (Illus.). 111p. (Orig.). (C). 1997. pap. text ed. 22.00 (*0-9651646-2-4*) Commun Vntures.

Speech Science & Technology. Ed. by Shuzo Saito. 400p. (gr. 12). 1992. 95.00 (*90-5199-048-0*, Pub. by IOS Pr NE) IOS Press.

Speech Science Primer: Physiology, Acoustics, & Perception of Speech. 3rd ed. Gloria J. Borden et al. LC 93-7592. (Illus.). 384p. 1993. 43.00 (*0-683-00944-3*) Williams & Wilkins.

***Speech Sciences.** Raymond D. Kent. LC 97-9480. (Illus.). 550p. (Orig.). 1997. pap. text ed. 45.00 (*1-56593-689-2*, 1364) Singular Publishing.

***Speech Sound Sourcebook.** C. Gilles-Brown. Ed. by Cindy Drolet. 230p. (Orig.). (J). 1996. pap. text ed. 34.95 (*1-883315-18-2*, 7171) Imaginart Pr.

Speech Sounds. Ashby. 120p. (C). 1995. pap. 12.95 (*0-415-08571-3*) Routledge.

Speech Sports: Games for Speech & Language Fun. Janet M. Shaw. (Illus.). 98p. (J). (gr. k-8). 1991. 24.95 (*0-937857-23-8*, 1590) Speech Bin.

Speech, Sr. H. S. Jack Rudman. (Teachers License Examination Ser.: T-58). 1994. pap. 27.95 (*0-8373-8058-8*) Nat Learn.

Speech Stations: The One-Stop Speech Book. Janet S. DeVaney. (Illus.). 205p. (J). (ps-5). 1987. 27.50 (*0-937857-03-3*, 1552) Speech Bin.

Speech Surrogates: Drum & Whistle Systems, 2 vols., 1. Ed. by Thomas A. Sebeok & Donna J. Umiker. (Approaches to Semiotics Ser.: No. 23 1-2). (Illus.). 1456p. 1976. text ed. 404.65 (*90-279-3424-X*) Mouton.

Speech Surrogates: Drum & Whistle Systems, 2 vols., Set. Ed. by Thomas A. Sebeok & Donna J. Umiker. (Approaches to Semiotics Ser.: No. 23 1-2). (Illus.). 1456p. 1976. text ed. 350.70 (*90-279-3423-1*) Mouton.

Speech Synthesis. Ed. by Jan P. Van Santen et al. LC 96-10596. (Illus.). 608p. 1996. 129.00 incl. cd-rom (*0-387-94701-9*) Spr-Verlag.

Speech Synthesis & Recognition. Holmes. (C). 1987. pap. text ed. 56.95 (*0-412-53430-4*) Chapman & Hall.

Speech Takes Off. Cathy Boudreau. (Illus.). 176p. (J). (gr. k-6). 1991. 24.95 (*0-937857-30-0*, 1595) Speech Bin.

Speech Teacher: A Random Narrative. Loren Reid. LC 90-63139. (Illus.). 109p. (C). 1990. pap. 7.00 (*0-944811-05-1*) Speech Commun Assn.

Speech Technician. Jack Rudman. (Career Examination Ser.: C-1034). 1994. pap. 27.95 (*0-8373-1034-2*) Nat Learn.

Speech Technology. Jack Hollingum & G. Cassford. (Illus.). 120p. 1989. 54.95 (*0-387-16356-5*) Spr-Verlag.

Speech Technology: A Survey. Ed. by Mervyn Jack & John Laver. (Edinburgh Information Technology Ser.: No. 4). 228p. 1988. 55.00 (*0-85224-568-8*, Pub. by Edinburgh U Pr UK) Col U Pr.

***Speech Technology for Telecommunications.** F. Westall. (BT Telecommunications Ser.). 600p. 1997. 99.95 (*0-412-79080-7*) Chapman & Hall.

Speech Through Pictures. McCausland et al. 1973. text ed. 2.50 (*0-686-09390-9*) Expression.

Speech-to-Speech Translation: A Massively Parallel Memory-Based Approach. Hiroaki Kitano. (International Series in Engineering & Computer Science, VLSI, Computer Architecture, & Digital Screen Processing). 216p. (C). 1993. lib. bdg. 105.00 (*0-7923-9425-9*) Kluwer Ac.

Speech Workbook for Public Speaking. 3rd ed. Steven A. Beebe. 1996. wbk. ed., pap. text ed. write for info. (*0-205-26163-9*) Allyn.

Speech, Writing, & Sign: A Functional View of Linguistic Representation. Naomi S. Baron. LC 79-3626. (Advances in Semiotics Ser.). (Illus.). 319p. 1980. reprint ed. pap. 91.00 (*0-7837-3690-8*, 2057868) Bks Demand.

Speech 1000: Introduction to Speech Communication. Chapman. 1993. wbk. ed., pap. text ed. write for info. (*0-07-011083-2*) McGraw.

Speechcraft: An Introduction to Public Speaking. Brent C. Oberg & Theodore O. Zapel. LC 94-21529. 168p. (Orig.). 1994. pap. 12.95 (*1-56608-006-1*, B149) Meriwether Pub.

Speechcrafts. Marcia Gilmore. (Illus.). 96p. (J). (ps-5). 1996. pap. text ed. 19.95 (*0-937857-65-3*, 1490) Speech Bin.

Speeches. Aeschines. (Loeb Classical Library: No. 106). 552p. 1919. 18.95 (*0-674-99118-4*) HUP.

Speeches. Richard M. Nixon. 1997. 25.00 (*0-679-44111-5*) Random.

Speeches. (Works of Henry Clay). 1990. reprint ed. lib. bdg. 79.00 (*0-7812-2303-2*) Rprt Serv.

Speeches. Edmund E. Burke. Ed. by F. G. Selby. LC 73-9127. 328p. 1974. reprint ed. text ed. 65.00 (*0-8371-6984-4*, BUSP, Greenwood Pr) Greenwood.

Speeches & Articles by Henry George, 11 pts. 188p. 1995. reprint ed. Avail. in SPA. pap. 3.00 (*0-911312-20-X*) Schalkenbach.

Speeches & Letters. Abraham Lincoln. 316p. 1993. pap. 6.95 (*0-460-87146-3*, Everyman's Classic Lib) C E Tuttle.

Speeches & New Letters. Henrik Ibsen. LC 71-184646. (Studies in European Literature: No. 56). 222p. 1972. reprint ed. lib. bdg. 75.00 (*0-8383-1377-9*) M S G Haskell Hse.

Speeches & Presentations - Discours & Exposes: In French & English - En Anglais Comme en Francais. Pamela Sheppard & Benedicte Lapeyre. (Business Across Borders Ser.). 111p. (Orig.). 1993. pap. 15.95 (*1-85788-048-X*) Nicholas Brealey.

Speeches & Table Talk of the Prophet Muhammad. Stanley Lane-Poole. 189p. 1990. 8.95 (*0-318-36781-5*) Asia Bk Corp.

Speeches & Toasts for All Occasions. Foulsham Editors. 154p. (Orig.). 1995. pap. 7.95 (*0-572-00003-0*, Pub. by Foulsham UK) Assoc Pubs Grp.

Speeches & Writings. Andropov. 1983. 20.00 (*0-08-028177-X*, Pergamon Pr) Elsevier.

Speeches & Writings. Y. V. Andropov. 1983. pap. 11.50 (*0-08-028182-6*, Pergamon Pr) Elsevier.

Speeches & Writings. Deng Xiaoping. (Leaders of the World Ser.). (Illus.). 115p. 1984. 19.25 (*0-08-028165-6*, Pergamon Pr); pap. 9.75 (*0-08-028166-4*, Pergamon Pr) Elsevier.

Speeches & Writings. Deng Xiaoping. (Leaders of the World Ser.). (Illus.). 120p. 1987. 44.00 (*0-08-034872-6*, Pergamon Pr) Elsevier.

Speeches & Writings: Presidential Messages & Proclamations, 1859-1865, Vol. 2. Abraham Lincoln. 1990. write for info. (*0-318-66783-5*, Penguin Bks) Viking Penguin.

Speeches & Writings: The Lincoln-Douglas Debates, 1832-1858, Vol. 1. Abraham Lincoln. 1990. write for info. (*0-318-66782-7*, Penguin Bks) Viking Penguin.

Speeches & Writings Vol. I: 1832-1858. Abraham Lincoln. Ed. by Don E. Fehrenbacher. 889p. 1989. Vol. I, 1832-1858, 889p., 89-2362. 35.00 (*0-940450-43-7*) Library of America.

Speeches & Writings Vol. II: 1859-1865. Abraham Lincoln. Ed. by Don E. Fehrenbacher. 788p. 1989. Vol. II, 1859-1865, 788 p., 89-45349. 35.00 (*0-940450-63-1*) Library of America.

Speeches & Writings of Mother Jones. Ed. by Edward M. Steel. LC 87-25192. (Social & Labor History Ser.). (Illus.). 349p. (C). 1988. 49.95 (*0-8229-3575-9*) U of Pittsburgh Pr.

Speeches & Writings of Mr. Jinnah. Jamil ud-Din Ahmad. 608p. (Orig.). 1985. pap. 12.50 (*1-56744-393-1*) Kazi Pubns.

Speeches at Full Length in the Cause of the People Against Harry Croswell. William P. Van Ness. LC 78-125716. (American Journalists Ser.). 1977. reprint ed. 15.95 (*0-405-01697-2*) Ayer.

Speeches at Home & Abroad (18 Speeches) Charles H. Spurgeon. 1974. pap. 6.00 (*1-56186-203-7*) Pilgrim Pubns.

Speeches by Lord Macaulay, with His Minute on Indian Education. Thomas B. Macaulay. Ed. by G. M. Young. LC 76-29441. 1935. 55.00 (*0-404-15348-8*) AMS Pr.

Speeches, Debates, & Interviews, 1881-1895. Frederick Douglass. Ed. by John W. Blassingame & John R. McKivigan. (Frederick Douglass Papers: Series One, Vol. 5). 832p. (C). 1992. text ed. 90.00 (*0-300-04877-7*) Yale U Pr.

Speeches for Every Occasion: All the Words You Need. David Belson. 192p. 1995. pap. 8.95 (*0-8065-1679-8*, Citadel Pr) Carol Pub Group.

Speeches for Socialism. James P. Cannon. Ed. by George L. Weissman. LC 72-92843. 462p. 1971. pap. 22.95 (*0-87348-198-4*); lib. bdg. 60.00 (*0-87348-196-8*) Pathfinder NY.

Speeches from the Heart. Kay R. Jones. 41p. 1995. pap. 5.95 (*0-9646856-0-4*) EKH Ch Sup.

Speeches in Acts: Their Content, Context, & Concerns. Marion L. Soards. LC 93-40127. 256p. (Orig.). 1994. pap. 23.00 (*0-664-25221-4*) Westminster John Knox.

Speeches in Thucydides: A Collection of Original Studies with a Bibliography. Ed. by Philip A. Stadter. LC 73-7816. 184p. reprint ed. pap. 52.50 (*0-8357-3870-1*, 2036602) Bks Demand.

Speeches, Lectures & Letters: Second Series. Wendell Phillips. LC 79-82210. (Anti-Slavery Crusade in America Ser.). 1970. reprint ed. 41.95 (*0-405-00649-7*) Ayer.

Speeches National Press Club, Vol. 1. NPC (Randell) National Press Club Staff. 232p. 1995. 34.95 (*0-7872-1005-6*) Kendall-Hunt.

Speeches of Adolf Hitler, 4 vols., Set. Adolf Hitler. 1975. lib. bdg. 800.00 (*0-8490-1107-8*) Gordon Pr.

Speeches of Isaeus. Isaeus. Ed. by W. R. Connor. LC 78-18614. (Greek Texts & Commentaries Ser.). (Illus.). 1979. reprint ed. lib. bdg. 63.95 (*0-405-11453-2*) Ayer.

Speeches of Isaeus. Wilhelm Wyse. 735p. reprint ed. lib. bdg. 128.70 (*0-685-13885-2*, 05101580) G Olms Pubs.

Speeches of Isaeus. William Wyse. lxiv, 735p. 1967. reprint ed. write for info. (*0-318-71064-1*) G Olms Pubs.

Speeches of Juan Domingo Peron. Juan D. Peron. 698p. 1973. 300.00 (*0-8490-1108-6*) Gordon Pr.

Speeches of Lord Erskine, While at the Bar, 4 vols., Set. Ed. by James L. High. 1993. reprint ed. 210.00 (*0-8377-2176-8*) Rothman.

Speeches of Micah. C. S. Shaw. 49.50 (*1-85075-362-8*, Pub. by Sheffield Acad UK) CUP Services.

Speeches of Oliver Cromwell. Oliver Cromwell. 275p. 1989. pap. 8.95 (*0-460-01254-1*, Everyman's Classic Lib) C E Tuttle.

Speeches of the American Presidents. Ed. by Steven Anzovin. 820p. 1988. 65.00 (*0-8242-0761-0*) Wilson.

Speeches of Thucydides. H. F. Harding. 1973. pap. 15.00 (*0-87291-060-1*) Coronado Pr.

Speeches on Foreign Policy, 1934-1939. Edward F. Halifax. Ed. by H. H. Craster. LC 72-156658. (Essay Index Reprint Ser.). 1977. reprint ed. 23.95 (*0-8369-2401-0*) Ayer.

Speeches on the American War & Letters to the Sheriffs of Bristol. Edmund E. Burke. LC 72-8666. (American Revolutionary Ser.). 272p. reprint ed. lib. bdg. 34.50 (*0-8398-0191-2*) Irvington.

Speeches to the Party. James P. Cannon. LC 73-86189. 431p. 1973. reprint ed. pap. 21.95 (*0-87348-321-9*); reprint ed. lib. bdg. 60.00 (*0-87348-320-0*) Pathfinder NY.

***Speeches (1910)** Mark Twain. Ed. by Shelley F. Fishkin. (Oxford Mark Twain Ser.). 528p. 1997. lib. bdg. 25.00 (*0-19-511428-0*) OUP.

Speechless: Facilitating Communication for People Without Voices. Rosemary Crossley. LC 96-49707. 1997. pap. 24.95 (*0-525-94156-8*) NAL-Dutton.

Speechless: My Recovery from Stroke. Jennifer Gordon. 176p. pap. 16.95 (*1-875560-33-5*, Pub. by Univ of West Aust Pr AT) Intl Spec Bk.

Speechmaking: An Introduction to Rhetorical Competence. D. Michael Sproule. 512p. (C). 1990. text ed. write for info. (*0-697-07639-3*) Brown & Benchmark.

Speechmaking: An Introduction to Rhetorical Competence. 2nd ed. D. Michael Sproule. 512p. (C). 1996. per. write for info. (*0-697-20160-0*) Wm C Brown Pubs.

***Speechmaking: Rhetorical Competence in a Postmodern World.** 2nd ed. Michael J. Sproule. 448p. (C). 1996. per. write for info. (*0-07-114699-7*) McGraw.

Speechphone Spoken Word List, Set 3. Hazel Brown. (Speechphone Ser.). 125p. 1980. pap. text ed. 39.50 incl. audio (*0-88432-064-2*, S23713) Audio-Forum.

Speechreading: A Way to Improve Understanding. 2nd ed. Harriet Kaplan et al. LC 87-7599. (Illus.). 162p. 1985. pap. text ed. 14.95 (*0-930323-32-7*, Clerc Bks) Gallaudet Univ Pr.

Speechreading by Man & Machine: Models, Systems, & Applications. Ed. by David G. Stork & Marcus E. Hennecke. LC 96-23719. (NATO ASI Series F: Computer & Systems Science). 685p. 1996. 189.50 (*3-540-61264-5*) Spr-Verlag.

Speechreading (Lipreading) Janet Jeffers & Margaret Barley. (Illus.). 408p. 1980. 59.95 (*0-398-02185-6*); pap. 39.95 (*0-398-06182-3*) C C Thomas.

An Asterisk (*) at the beginning of an entry indicates that the title is appearing in BIP for the first time.

***Speechway: How to Grip & Hold Attention in Public Speaking.** Robert E. Bryant. LC 96-90232. (Orig.). 1996. pap. 12.95 (0-533-11965-0) Vantage.

Speechwriting: A Professional Step-by-Step Guide for Executives. Edward H. McCarthy. LC 89-83450. 121p. 1989. pap. 19.95 (0-930255-01-1) Exec Speaker Co.

Speed. pap. 22.00 (1-56997-096-3) Knowldge Adv.

Speed. Brenda Walpole. LC 95-21853. (Measure up with Science Ser.). (J). 1995. lib. bdg. 18.60 (0-8368-1362-6) Gareth Stevens Inc.

Speed. large type ed. Mark Harris. (General Ser.). 431p. 1991. lib. bdg. 21.95 (0-8161-5208-X, GK Hall) Thorndike Pr.

Speed: The Biography of Charles W. Holman. 2nd ed. Noel E. Allard. LC 76-44068. (Illus.). 94p. 1986. reprint ed. pap. 13.95 (0-911139-01-X) Flying Bks.

Speed & Accuracy at Your Keyboard: Incentive Learning Systems. 41p. 1994. 34.50 incl. digital audio (0-88432-751-5, S17085) Audio-Forum.

Speed & Kentucky Ham: Two Novels. William S. Burroughs, Jr. 384p. 1993. pap. 14.95 (0-87951-505-8) Overlook Pr.

***Speed & Luxury: The World's Greatest Cars 1910-1948.** Dennis Adler. LC 97-20671. (Illus.). 160p. 1997. 19.98 (0-7603-0362-2) Motorbooks Intl.

***Speed & Luxury the Great Cars: The Great Cars.** Dennis Adler. LC 97-20671. (Illus.). 160p. 1997. 29.95 (0-7603-0486-6) Motorbooks Intl.

Speed & Politics. Paul Virilio. 1986. pap. 7.00 (0-936756-24-1) Autonomedia.

Speed & Power. rev. ed. Time-Life Books Editors. (Understanding Computers Ser.). (Illus.). 128p. 1990. write for info. (0-8094-7586-3); lib. bdg. write for info. (0-8094-7587-1) Time-Life.

Speed & the Quarter Horse: A Payload of Sprinters. Nelson C. Nye. LC 73-140120. 374p. 1973. reprint ed. pap. 106.60 (0-7837-7136-3, 2059163) Bks Demand.

Speed & Thrash Metal Drum Method. Bush & T. Stetina. 1992. pap. 17.95 incl. audio compact disk (0-7935-1854-7, 06621762) H Leonard.

Speed & Thrash Metal Drum Method. Bush & T. Stetina. 1992. pap. 14.95 incl. audio (0-7935-1855-5, 06621761) H Leonard.

Speed & Thrash Metal Guitar Method. Burt & T. Stetina. 1991. per. 14.95 incl. audio (0-7935-0254-3, 00660171) H Leonard.

Speed & Thrash Metal Guitar Method. Stettina & Burt. 1991. pap. 17.95 incl. audio compact disk (0-7935-0916-5, 00697218) H Leonard.

Speed Bag Bible: The Ultimate Speed Bag Training Program. Alan H. Kahn. LC 94-92116. (Illus.). 200p. (Orig.). 1995. pap. 29.95 (0-9641827-6-9) Rehab & Sports.

Speed Cleaning. rev. ed. Jeff Campbell & Clean Team Staff. 208p. (Orig.). 1997. pap. 8.99 (0-440-50374-4) Dell.

Speed Culture: Amphetamine Use & Abuse in America. Lester Grinspoon & Peter Hedblom. LC 74-27257. 368p. 1975. 34.50 (0-674-83192-6) HUP.

Speed Culture: Amphetamine Use & Abuse in America. Lester Grinspoon & Peter Hedblom. LC 74-27257. 368p. 1976. pap. text ed. 9.95 (0-674-83194-2) HUP.

Speed-Cut Quilts. Donna Poster. LC 88-43312. (Illus.). 232p. 1989. pap. 18.95 (0-8019-7889-0) Chilton.

Speed Dictation with Previews in Gregg Shorthand. Charles E. Zoubek. (Diamond Jubilee Ser.). 1963. text ed. 30.95 (0-07-073041-5) McGraw.

Speed English. 2nd rev. ed. Louis Aarons. 200p. (JPN.). (YA). 1996. student ed. 59.95 incl. audio (1-887447-02-4) WordMate.

***Speed Increasing Gears & Their Technical Differences From Reducing Gears.** P. C. Day & W. P. Schmitter. (Technical Papers). 1935. pap. text ed. 30.00 (1-55589-404-6) AGMA.

Speed King, Rudy Kling: Triumph & Tragedy in Air Racing's "Golden Age" Ron Britzke. LC 94-37920. 1995. pap. 20.00 (0-912526-74-2) Lib Res.

Speed Laws & Motorcycle Laws. Amoco Pathfinder Staff. 1992. pap. 2.25 (0-671-84032-0) S&S Trade.

***Speed Learning.** rev. ed. Ed. by Margaret M. Bynum & Debra Giffen. (Illus.). 275p. (YA). (gr. 10 up). 1997. pap. 129.00 incl. audio (1-55678-059-1, 4000) Learn Inc.

***Speed Learning: High Efficiency Reading, Bk. 1.** rev. ed. Ed. by Margaret M. Bynum & Debra Giffen. (Illus.). 88p. (YA). (gr. 10 up). 1997. wbk. ed., pap. 25.00 (1-55678-060-5, 3276) Learn Inc.

***Speed Learning: High Efficiency Reading, Bk. 2.** rev. ed. Ed. by Margaret M. Bynum & Debra Giffen. (Illus.). 115p. (YA). (gr. 10 up). 1997. wbk. ed., pap. 25.00 (1-55678-061-3, 3277) Learn Inc.

***Speed Learning: High Efficiency Reading, Bk. 3.** rev. ed. Ed. by Margaret M. Bynum & Debra Giffen. (Illus.). 72p. (YA). (gr. 10 up). 1997. wbk. ed., pap. 25.00 (1-55678-062-1, 3278) Learn Inc.

Speed Learning; Science-Engineering Edition. Learn Inc. Staff. 39p. 1990. student ed. 25.00 (1-55678-035-4) Learn Inc.

Speed Learning Trainer's Guide. Margaret M. Bynum & Debra Giffen. 1989. teacher ed. 75.00 (1-55678-033-8) Learn Inc.

Speed, Light, & Song: Poems. Linda P. Williams. LC 93-2657. 64p. 1993. pap. 12.95 (0-7734-2782-1, Mellen Poetry Pr) E Mellen.

Speed Limits & Zones: A Guide to Establishing Speed Zones. (Illus.). 40p. (Orig.). (C). 1995. pap. text ed. 25.00 (0-7881-2390-4) DIANE Pub.

Speed Mathematics Simplified. Edward Stoddard. x, 271p. 1994. reprint ed. pap. text ed. 6.95 (0-486-27887-5) Dover.

Speed Measurement in Traffic Law Enforcement from Radar to Laser. Kevin M. Morrison. (Illus.). 107p. (C). 1994. pap. text ed. 24.95 (1-884566-17-0) Inst Police Tech.

Speed Mechanics for Lead Guitar. T. Stetina. 1990. pap. 14.95 incl. audio (0-7935-0023-0, 00715172) H Leonard.

Speed Mechanics for Lead Guitar. T. Stetina. 1992. pap. 17.95 incl. audio compact disk (0-7935-0962-9, 00699323) H Leonard.

Speed Metal. Dave Celentano. 48p. 1989. pap. text ed. 16.95 (0-931759-34-X) Centerstream Pub.

***Speed Moderation.** ECMT Staff. (Road Safety Ser.). 88p. (Orig.). 1996. pap. 24.00 (92-821-1215-2, 75-96-05-1) OECD.

Speed Mushing Manual: How to Train Racing Sled Dogs. Jim Welch. LC 89-91976. (Illus.). 128p. (Orig.). 1989. pap. 12.95 (0-9623643-0-4) Sirius Pub AK.

Speed of Dark. Julia Vinograd. (Illus.). 56p. 1996. pap. text ed. 4.95 (0-929730-58-5) Zeitgeist Pr.

Speed of Darkness. Rodney Morales. LC 88-24246. (Bamboo Ridge Ser.: Nos. 39-40). 177p. (Orig.). 1988. pap. 8.00 (0-910043-16-7) Bamboo Ridge Pr.

***Speed of Flight.** Paul Leonard. (Dr. Who Missing Adventures Ser.). 280p. 1996. mass mkt. 5.95 (0-426-20487-5, Pub. by Virgin Pub UK) London Brdge.

Speed of Information Processing & Intelligence. Ed. by Philip A. Vernon. LC 87-14532. 416p. 1988. text ed. 78.50 (0-89391-427-4) Ablex Pub.

Speed of Light. Susan Pashman. LC 96-3048. 1997. write for info. (1-877946-86-9) Permanent Pr.

Speed of Love: An Exploration of Christian Faithfulness in a Technological World. David P. Young. 150p. (Orig.). 1986. pap. 6.95 (0-377-00159-7) Friendship Pr.

Speed of Sound. Scott Eyman. LC 96-45941. (Illus.). 413p. 1997. 30.00 (0-684-81162-6) S&S Trade.

Speed of Sound Data & Related Models for Mixtures of Natural Gas Constituents. 1994. lib. bdg. 250.00 (0-8490-5718-3) Gordon Pr.

Speed of Sound Data & Related Models for Mixtures of Natural Gas Constituents. (Illus.). 120p. (Orig.). (C). 1994. pap. text ed. 40.00 (0-7881-1120-5) DIANE Pub.

Speed of the Bishop Image. David J. Donovan, II. (Illus.). 5p. 1989. 60.00 (0-685-26796-2) dG Printers.

***Speed of the Wheel Is up to the Potter.** Sandy Shreve. 80p. 1990. pap. 12.95 (0-919627-79-X, Pub. by Quarry Pr CN) LPC InBook.

Speed of Violence. Blacky Hix. (Illus.). 30p. (Orig.). 1989. pap. 5.00 (1-885466-04-8) Smoke The Soul.

Speed on the Ship: A Centennial History of the Society of Naval Architects & Marine Engineers: 1893-1993. William D. Thomas. (Illus.). 205p. 1993. pap. 30.00 (0-939773-13-9, SOS) Soc Naval Arch.

Speed Picking Chart. 1990. 4.95 (0-931759-39-0) Centerstream Pub.

Speed Queen. Stewart O'Nan. LC 96-9647. 256p. 1997. 22.95 (0-385-48701-0) Doubleday.

Speed Quilting: Projects Using Rotary Cutting & Other Shortcuts. Cheryl Fall. LC 95-22914. 128p. 1996. 27.95 (0-8069-1328-2) Sterling.

***Speed Quilting: Projects Using Rotary Cutting & Other Shortcuts.** Cheryl Fall. 128p. 1997. pap. 14.95 (0-8069-1329-0) Sterling.

***Speed Racer: The Official 30th Anniversary Guide.** Elizabeth Moran. LC 97-3161. (Illus.). 160p. 1997. pap. 11.95 (0-7868-8246-8); pap. text ed. 95.60 (0-7868-9941-7) Hyperion.

Speed Reading. Luther Misenheimer, III. (Language Arts Ser.). 24p. (gr. 6-10). 1979. student ed. 5.00 (0-8209-0324-8, LA-10) ESP.

Speed Reading. Steve Moidel. (Business Success Ser.). (Orig.). 1994. pap. 4.95 (0-8120-1845-1) Barron.

Speed Reading. Robert L. Zorn. LC 79-2744. 176p. (Orig.). 1996. mass mkt. 4.99 (0-06-109301-7, Harp PBks) HarpC.

Speed Reading. rev. ed. Tony Buzan. (Illus.). 1991. pap. 11.95 (0-452-26604-1, Plume) NAL-Dutton.

Speed Reading. 3rd ed. Tony Buzan. (Illus.). 1991. 19.95 (0-525-24982-6, Dutton) NAL-Dutton.

Speed Reading: The Computer Course, Apple IIC. Bureau of Business Practice Staff. write for info. (0-318-58237-6) P-H.

***Speed Reading for Dummies.** Warner Books Staff. 1986. 3.50 (0-446-73396-2) Warner Bks.

Speed Reading for Progressive Adults. Donna Litherland. (Illus.). 128p. (Orig.). 1993. pap. 14.95 (1-56474-075-7) Fithian Pr.

Speed Reading for Progressive Adults. Donna Litherland. (Illus.). 134p. (C). 1993. pap. text ed. 14.95 (0-9607888-3-2) Barney Pr.

Speed Reading for Progressive Adults. rev. ed. Donna Litherland. (Illus.). 128p. (Orig.). (C). 1993. lib. bdg. 14.95 (1-56474-657-7) Fithian Pr.

Speed Reading Naturally. 2nd ed. Lillian P. Wenick. 300p. (C). 1990. pap. text ed. 37.20 (0-13-833955-4) P-H.

***Speed Skating.** Larry D. Brimner. LC 97-2920. (True Book Ser.). (J). 1997. write for info. (0-516-20451-3) Childrens.

Speed Strength Training for Football. E. J. Kreis. Ed. by J. P. Montgomery. (Illus.). 144p. (Orig.). 1992. pap. 16.95 (0-9632677-0-1) E J Doc Kreis.

***Speed-Strength Training for Martial Artists: Mind-Body Link.** unabridged ed. Donald E. Maib, Jr. & James A. Tindall. (Illus.). (Orig.). 1997. pap. 49.95 incl. vdisk (1-890540-00-5) Taylor Sports.

***Speed Surf.** Michael Coleman. (Internet Detectives Ser.: No. 3). (YA). 1997. mass mkt. 3.99 (0-553-48622-5) BDD Bks Young Read.

Speed Tailoring. Mary A. Roehr. (Illus.). 45p. (C). 1992. reprint ed. pap. 14.95 (0-9619229-3-1) M Roehr Bks & Vid.

Speed-the-Plow. David Mamet. LC 87-37252. 82p. 1988. pap. 8.95 (0-8021-3046-1) Grove) Grove-Atltic.

Speed-the-Plow. David Mamet. 1995. reprint ed. lib. bdg. 21.95 (1-56849-630-3) Buccaneer Bks.

Speed Train Your Own Bird Dog. Larry Mueller. LC 89-39933. (Illus.). 256p. (Orig.). 1990. pap. 19.95 (0-8117-2304-6) Stackpole.

Speed Train Your Own Retriever: The Quick, Efficient, Proven System for Training a Finished Dog. Larry Mueller. LC 86-23109. (Illus.). 192p. (Orig.). 1987. pap. 19.95 (0-8117-2201-5) Stackpole.

Speed Training: How to Develop Your Maximum Speed for Martial Arts. Loren Christensen. (Illus.). 256p. 1996. pap. 24.00 (0-87364-859-5) Paladin Pr.

Speed Tribes: Days & Nights with Japan's Next Generation. Karl T. Greenfeld. 304p. 1995. pap. 14.00 (0-06-092665-1, PL) HarpC.

***Speed 2: Cruise Control.** Cathy E. Dubowski. 1997. pap. text ed. 4.50 (0-06-107469-1) HarpC.

***Speed 2: Cruise Control.** George Ryan. 1997. mass mkt. 6.99 (0-06-101257-2) HarpC.

Speedball. D. A. Hodgman. (Code Zero Ser.: No. 404). 1992. mass mkt. 3.50 (0-373-63404-8, 1-63404-7) Harlequin Bks.

Speedball Textbook. 22th ed. J. C. Fink et al. 96p. 1991. pap. text ed. 7.95 (0-9631532-0-X) Hunt Manufact.

Speedboat. Don W. Fostle. (Illus.). 218p. 1988. 69.95 (0-939510-07-3) Mystic Sea Mus.

Speedboat. James Marshall. (J). (ps-3). 1994. pap. 5.95 (0-395-68977-5) HM.

Speedboat Kings. J. Lee Barrett. (Michigan Heritage Library: Vol. 4). 145p. 1986. reprint ed. 15.00 (0-915056-21-6, Historical Soc MI) Hardscrabble Bks.

Speedbuilding for Court Reporting, Vol. 1. Dot Mathias & Sally Floyd. Ed. by Beverly L. Ritter. (Realtime Machine Shorthand Ser.). 252p. (C). 1990. reprint ed. pap. text ed. 40.00 (0-938643-02-7) Stenotype Educ.

Speedbuilding for Court Reporting, Vol. 2. Sally Floyd & Dot Mathias. Ed. by Beverly L. Ritter. (Realtime Machine Shorthand Ser.). 254p. (C). 1991. reprint ed. pap. text ed. 40.00 (0-938643-04-3) Stenotype Educ.

Speeder's Guide to Avoiding Tickets. James M. Eagan. 1991. mass mkt. 5.99 (0-380-71733-6) Avon.

Speeder's Guide to Avoiding Tickets: Every Driver Speeds Sometimes. James M. Eagan. (Illus.). 160p. (Orig.). 1991. pap. 12.95 (0-9628337-0-3) Caretaker.

Speeding Bullet. Neal Shusterman. 208p. (YA). (gr. 7-9). 1992. 3.25 (0-590-45424-2, Point) Scholastic Inc.

Speeding into Lost Landscapes. Jeannette G. Maino. (Orig.). 1982. pap. 5.50 (0-941885-00-3) Dry Creeks Bks.

Speeding up Shakespeare. William J. Lawrence. LC 68-20235. 1972. reprint ed. 20.95 (0-405-08739-X) Ayer.

Speeding up to Normal: Metabolic Solutions to Fibromyalgia. John C. Lowe. Ed. by Jackie G. Yellin. (Illus.). 400p. 1997. 29.95 (0-914609-03-3) McDowell Pub Co.

Speedsters Series. (Illus.). (J). (gr. 2-5). write for info. (0-525-44950-7) Dutton Child Bks.

***Speedsters Todays Air Racers in Action.** Philip Handleman. LC 97-652. (Illus.). 112p. 1997. pap. 21.95 (0-7603-0374-6) Motorbooks Intl.

Speedway. Ruth L. Schechter. LC 83-7408. (Orig.). 1983. pap. 5.95 (0-941608-03-4) Chantry Pr.

Speedwell. Ann Turnbull. LC 91-58757. 128p. (J). (gr. 5-9). 1992. 14.95 (1-56402-112-2) Candlewick Pr.

Speedwell. Ann Turnbull. LC 91-58757. 128p. (J). (gr. 5-9). 1994. pap. 3.99 (1-56402-281-1) Candlewick Pr.

Speedwriting. 2nd ed. 1986. pap. 8.76 (0-02-679660-0) Macmillan.

Speedwriting Dictation & Transcription: College Edition. LC 76-41046. 1977. teacher ed. write for info. (0-672-98052-5); pap. text ed. write for info. (0-672-98051-7) Macmillan.

Speedwriting Dictionary: College Edition. LC 76-41047. (Landmark Ser.). 1977. text ed. write for info. (0-672-98095-9) Macmillan.

Speedwriting for Notetaking & Study Skills. Joe M. Pullis. 1990. 18.70 (0-02-685155-5) Macmillan.

Speedwriting for the Legal Secretary. Craft. 1984. pap. 18.80 (0-02-679670-8) Macmillan.

Speedwriting for the Legal Secretary. Berniece R. Craft et al. LC 78-10833. 1979. pap. write for info. (0-672-97013-9) Macmillan.

Speedwriting Legal Dictionary. 1986. pap. 7.00 (0-02-679680-5) Macmillan.

Speedwriting Legal Dictionary. Berniece R. Craft. 170p. 1972. pap. write for info. (0-672-96142-3) Macmillan.

Speedwriting Medical Dictation Course. Goodwin W. Gilson & David Werheimer. 266p. 1960. teacher ed. write for info. (0-672-96154-7); text ed. write for info. (0-672-96153-9); audio 232.92 (0-672-97884-9) Macmillan.

Speedwriting Principles Regen. Cheryl Pullis. 1984. pap. 19.96 (0-02-679810-7) Macmillan.

Speedwriting Regency SW PP 98503. Cheryl Pullis. 1984. pap. 9.92 (0-02-679430-6) Macmillan.

Speedwriting Shorthand Abridged Dictionary: Regency Edition. Joe M. Pullis & Cheryl Pullis. (Speedwriting Shorthand Ser.). 192p. (gr. 10-12). 1984. text ed. write for info. (0-672-98504-7) Macmillan.

Speedwriting Shorthand Dictation & Transcription: Regency Edition. Joe M. Pullis et al. (Speedwriting Shorthand Ser.). 352p. (gr. 10-12). 1984. teacher ed. write for info. (0-317-00348-8); text ed. write for info. (0-672-98506-3) Macmillan.

Speedwriting Shorthand Training System. 1982. student ed., teacher ed. write for info. incl. audio (0-672-90022-X) Macmillan.

Speedy. Max Brand. 1993. 15.00 (0-86025-234-5, Pub. by Ian Henry Pubns UK) Empire Pub Srvs.

Speedy. large type ed. Max Brand. LC 90-34621. 398p. 1990. lib. bdg. 16.95 (1-56054-001-X) Thorndike Pr.

Speedy. Max Brand. 224p. 1995. reprint ed. mass mkt., pap. text ed. 4.50 (0-8439-3890-0) Dorchester Pub Co.

Speedy Disposition: Monetary Incentives & Policy Reform in Criminal Courts. Ed. by Thomas W. Church & Milton Heumann. LC 91-34691. 171p. (C). 1992. text ed. 64.50 (0-7914-1185-0); pap. text ed. 21.95 (0-7914-1186-9) State U NY Pr.

Speedy Extinction of Evil & Misery: Selected Prose of James Thomson (B. V.) James Thomson. Ed. by William D. Schaefer. LC 67-11799. 359p. reprint ed. pap. 102.40 (0-685-20505-3, 2029961) Bks Demand.

Speedy French: To Get You There & Back. Babe Hart. (Speedy Ser.). 24p. (Orig.). (FRE.). pap. 4.95 (0-9602838-1-1) Baja Bks.

Speedy German: To Get You There & Back. Babe Hart. (Speedy Ser.). (Illus.). 24p. (ITA.). (C). pap. 4.95 (0-9602838-3-8) Baja Bks.

Speedy Greek. Babe Hart. (Speedy Ser.). (Illus.). 24p. (Orig.). (C). pap. 4.95 (0-9602838-8-9) Baja Bks.

Speedy Ingles. Babe Hart & T. L. Hart. (Speedy Ser.). 24p. pap. 4.95 (1-882196-00-7) Baja Bks.

Speedy Italian: To Get You There & Back. Babe Hart. (Speedy Ser.). (Illus.). 24p. (C). pap. 4.95 (0-9602838-2-X) Baja Bks.

Speedy Japanese: To Get You There & Back. Babe Hart. (Speedy Ser.). (Illus.). 24p. (Orig.). (JPN.). (C). pap. 4.95 (0-9602838-4-6) Baja Bks.

S

Speedy Justice: The Tragic Last Voyage of His Majesty's Vessel Speedy. Brendan O'Brien. (Publications of the Osgoode Society). (Illus.). 200p. 1992. 35.00 (0-8020-2910-8) U of Toronto Pr.

***Speedy Machines.** Snapshot Staff. (My First Board Bks.). (Illus.). 22p. (J). 1997. bds. 2.95 (0-7894-1538-0) DK Pub Inc.

***Speedy Medical/Nursing in Spanish.** Terry Hart. (ENG & SPA.). 1997. pap. 16.95 (0-9615829-9-5) Baja Bks.

Speedy O'Hare's Sun Valley Race. Gene Kay. (Illus.). 36p. (J). (ps-7). 1987. pap. 8.95 (0-945222-24-6) Gazelle Prodns.

Speedy Russian: To Get You There & Back. Babe Hart. (Speedy Ser.). 24p. (Orig.). (RUS.). pap. 4.95 (0-9602838-5-4) Baja Bks.

Speedy Spanish: To Get You There & Back. Babe Hart. (Speedy Ser.). 24p. (Orig.). (SPA.). pap. 4.95 (0-9602838-0-3) Baja Bks.

Speedy Spanish for Employers. Babe Hart & T. L. Hart. 1993. pap. 4.95 (0-9615829-1-X) Baja Bks.

Speedy Spanish for Medical Personnel. T. L. Hart. Ed. & Tr. by Babe Hart. (Speedy Language Ser.). (Illus.). 24p. (Orig.). (SPA.). (C). 1980. pap. 4.95 (0-9602838-6-2) Baja Bks.

Speedy Spanish for Nursing Personnel. T. L. Hart. (Orig.). (ENG & SPA.). 1988. pap. 4.95 (0-9615829-4-4) Baja Bks.

Speedy Spanish for Physical Therapists. T. L. Hart. (Speedy Language Ser.). 24p. (Orig.). (ENG & SPA.). 1987. pap. 4.95 (0-9615829-3-6) Baja Bks.

Speedy Spanish for Police Personnel. T. L. Hart. (Speedy Language Ser.). 24p. 1991. 4.95 (0-9615829-8-7) Baja Bks.

Speedy Spares. R. A. Hill. 120p. 1985. pap. 16.00 (0-409-49085-7, NZ) MICHIE.

Speedy Sparrow. J. Jay Tamburina. 1989. 13.95 (0-9620915-0-2) Cobra Pub.

***Speegle Family Newsletter (8 Years) 1986-1994.** 298p. 1997. pap. write for info. (0-614-30159-9) Ima Boyd.

Speere: Ten Generations of George Speer, 1642-1942: Three Centuries of American Life. R. C. Speer. 205p. 1993. reprint ed. pap. 33.50 (0-8328-3409-2); reprint ed. lib. bdg. 43.50 (0-8328-3408-4) Higginson Bk Co.

Spehlmann's EEG Primer. enl. rev. ed. Ed. by B. J. Fisch. 650p. 1991. pap. 97.75 (0-444-81420-5) Elsevier.

Spehlmann's EEG Primer. 2nd enl. rev. ed. Ed. by B. J. Fisch. 634p. 1991. 267.50 (0-444-81242-3) Elsevier.

Spehlmann's Evoked Potential Primer: Visual, Auditory, & Somatosensory Evoked Potentials in Clinical Diagnosis. 2nd rev. ed. R. Spehlmann. LC 94-6178. 243p. 1994. pap. text ed. 50.00 (0-7506-9512-9) Buttrwrth-Heinemann.

Speical Guitar Method. D. Bennett. 40p. 1993. pap. 5.95 (0-7935-5564-7) H Leonard.

Speisekarten-Fuer sie Uebersetzt: Menu Reader. 15th ed. E. Pauli. 86p. (ENG, FRE & GER.). 1983. 19.95 (0-8288-1302-7, M15238) Fr & Eur.

Spektrum: Grammatik Im Kontext. Helga Bister et al. 416p. (C). 1992. text ed. 51.00 (0-13-517293-4) P-H.

Spekulative und Positive Theologie Des Islam Nach Razi (Gest. 1209) und Ihre Kritik Durch Tusi (Gest. 1273) Max Horten. vi, 383p. 1967. reprint ed. write for info. (0-318-71519-8) G Olms Pubs.

SPEL Data for EU Agriculture 1985-1994. European Commission Staff. 305p. 1995. pap. 25.00 (92-827-4200-8, CA-88-95-5733AC, Pub. by Europ Com UK) Bernan Associates.

***Spel-Data for European Agriculture 1985-1996.** European Commission. 305p. 1997. pap. 35.00 (92-827-9624-8, CA-99-96-5283AC, Pub. by Europ Com UK) Bernan Associates.

Spel Is a Four-Letter Word. J. Richard Gentry. LC 86-33526. 56p. (Orig.). 1989. pap. 8.00 (0-435-08440-2, 08440) Heinemann.

SPEL LEP: A Phonetic Approach to Spelling. Art Freifeld. (Illus.). 10p. (Orig.). 1986. teacher ed. 1.45 (0-685-50630-4); student ed., pap. 7.95 (0-916177-03-3) Am Eng Pubns.

SPEL System: Methodological Documentation. European Communities Staff. 330p. 1992. pap. 30.00 (92-826-4497-9, CA-75-92-356ENC, Pub. by Europ Com UK) Bernan Associates.

SPEL System Methodological Documentation Basics BS - SFSS, Vol. 1. European Communities Staff. 330p. 1995. pap. 35.00 (*92-826-9773-8*, CA-41-94-001ENC, Pub. by Europ Com UK) Bernan Associates.

SPEL System Methodological Documentation (Rev. 1) MFSS, Vol. 2. European Communities Staff. 330p. 1995. pap. 20.00 (*92-826-9774-6*, CA-41-94-002ENC, Pub. by Europ Com UK) Bernan Associates.

SPEL System Technical Documentation Basics, Vol. 1. European Communities Staff. 330p. 1995. pap. 20.00 (*92-826-9770-3*, CA-40-94-001ENC, Pub. by Europ Com UK) Bernan Associates.

SPEL System Technical Documentation (Rev. 1) BS, SFSS, MFSS, Vol. 2. European Communities Staff. 330p. 1995. pap. 20.00 (*92-826-9771-1*, CA-40-94-002ENC, Pub. by Europ Com UK) Bernan Associates.

Speleology: Caves & the Cave Environment. 3rd ed. George W. Moore & Nicholas Sullivan. LC 77-18176. (Illus.). 1997. 21.95 (*0-939748-46-0*) Cave Bks MO.

Speleology: Caves & the Cave Environment. 3rd ed. George W. Moore & Nicholas Sullivan. LC 77-18176. (Illus.). xiii, 176p. 1997. reprint ed. pap. text ed. 15.95 (*0-939748-45-2*) Cave Bks MO.

Speleology: The Study of Caves. George W. Moore & Nicholas Sullivan. LC 77-18176. (Illus.). xiii, 150p. 1981. reprint ed. pap. text ed. 6.95 (*0-939748-00-2*) Cave Bks MO.

Spell. Lynn Beach. Ed. by Patricia MacDonald. (Phantom Valley Ser.: No. 5). 128p. (Orig.). (YA). 1992. pap. 2.99 (*0-671-75923-X*, Minstrel Bks) PB.

Spell. Becky Daniel. (Preschool Basic Skills Ser.). (Illus.). 64p. 1992. 7.99 (*0-86653-673-6*, GA1403) Good Apple.

Spell: It's Time for Revenge, Vol. 3. Bill Myers. (Forbidden Doors Ser.: Vol. 3). 1995. pap. 5.99 (*0-8423-5927-3*) Tyndale.

***Spell Bound.** Saranne Dawson. 368p. (Orig.). 1996. mass mkt. 5.50 (*0-505-52152-0*) Dorchester Pub Co.

Spell by Writing. Wendy Bean & Christine Bouffler. LC 90-27028. 92p. (Orig.). (C). 1991. pap. text ed. 16.50 (*0-435-08577-8*, 08577) Heinemann.

Spell Check: A Spelling Guide to More Than 40,000 Words. 384p. 1996. 5.95 (*0-395-75691-X*) HM.

Spell Crafts: Creating Magical Objects. Scott Cunningham & David Harrington. LC 93-24190. (Practical Magick Ser.). (Illus.). 224p. 1993. pap. 10.00 (*0-87542-185-7*) Llewellyn Pubns.

Spell for Chameleon. Piers Anthony. LC 77-1666. (The Wizards of Fantasy Promotion). 352p. 1987. mass mkt. 5.95 (*0-345-34753-6*, Del Rey) Ballantine.

***Spell for Chameleon.** Piers Anthony. 1997. pap. 11.00 (*0-345-41849-2*, Del Rey) Ballantine.

Spell for Old Bones. Eric Linklater. Ed. by R. Reginald & Douglas Melville. LC 77-84250. (Lost Race & Adult Fantasy Ser.). 1978. reprint ed. lib. bdg. 23.95 (*0-405-10996-2*) Ayer.

Spell for the Fulfillment of Desire. Don Webb. 147p. (Orig.). 1996. pap. 7.95 (*1-57366-012-4*) Fiction Coll.

Spell Is Cast. Eleanor Cameron. 1992. 23.25 (*0-8446-6560-6*) Peter Smith.

Spell It M-U-R-D-E-R. Ivy Ruckman. 160p. (J). (gr. 4-7). 1994. pap. 3.50 (*0-553-48175-4*) Bantam.

Spell It Right! Harry Shaw. 224p. 1996. mass mkt. 4.99 (*0-06-100814-1*) HarpC.

Spell It Right!, Set 4. 40p. 1992. 39.50 incl. audio (*0-88432-454-0*) Audio-Forum.

***Spell of a Bird.** Shinji Watanabe. LC 96-90872. (Orig.). 1997. pap. 8.95 (*0-533-12190-6*) Vantage.

Spell of Algeria & Tunisia. F. Miltoun. 554p. 1985. 300.00 (*1-85077-060-3*, Pub. by Darf Pubs Ltd UK) St Mut.

Spell of Amon Ptah. Ed. by Lloyd A. Eshbach. pap. write for info. (*0-345-37595-5*, Del Rey) Ballantine.

Spell of Apocalypse. Mayer A. Brenner. (Dance of Gods Ser.: No. 4). 320p. (Orig.). 1994. mass mkt. 4.99 (*0-88677-602-3*) DAW Bks.

Spell of Fate. Mayer A. Brenner. (Dance of Gods Ser.: No. 3). 432p. (Orig.). 1992. mass mkt. 4.99 (*0-88677-508-6*) DAW Bks.

Spell of Hawaii. Ed. by A. Grove Day & Carl Stroven. LC 69-11908. 338p. 1985. reprint ed. mass mkt. 4.95 (*0-935180-13-3*) Mutual Pub HI.

Spell of Intrigue. Mayer A. Brenner. (Dance of Gods Ser.: No. 2). 336p. 1990. mass mkt. 4.50 (*0-88677-453-5*) DAW Bks.

Spell of Making. Blackson. 208p. (C). 1996. pap. 12.50 (*1-57353-109-X*, Eschaton Bks) Eschaton Prods.

Spell of Music: An Attempt to Analyse the Enjoyment of Music. John A. Fuller-Maitland. LC 76-102239. (Select Bibliographies Reprint Ser.). 1977. 18.95 (*0-8369-5124-7*) Ayer.

Spell of New Mexico. Ed. by Tony Hillerman. LC 76-21523. 113p. 1984. pap. 9.95 (*0-8263-0776-0*) U of NM Pr.

Spell of Plato see Open Society & Its Enemies

***Spell of Power: A History of Balinese Politics, 1650-1940.** Henk S. Nordholt. (Verhandelingen Ser.: Vol. 170). (Illus.). 389p. 1997. pap. 37.00 (*90-6718-090-4*, Pub. by KITLV Pr NE) Cellar.

Spell of Sorcerer's Skull. John Bellairs. 176p. (J). 1985. 3.99 (*0-553-15726-4*) Bantam.

Spell of the Black Stone. E. L. Flood. LC 94-22760. (Welcome Inn Ser.: No. 4). (J). (gr. 4-7). 1995. pap. 2.95 (*0-8167-3579-4*) Troll Communs.

Spell of the Blue Bulb. Stephen O. Walcutt. 213p. (Orig.). 1996. mass mkt. 4.99 (*1-55197-205-0*, Pub. by Comnwlth Pub CN) Partners Pubs Grp.

Spell of the Misty Forest. Francois Bourgeon. Ed. by Bernd Metz. Tr. by Elizabeth Bell from FRE. (Companions of the Dusk Ser.). (Illus.). 49p. (Orig.). 1991. pap. 9.95 (*0-87416-126-6*) Catalan Communs.

***Spell of the Rockies.** Enos A. Mills. LC 89-33076. (Illus.). 436p. pap. 124.30 (*0-608-04824-0*, 2065481) Bks Demand.

Spell of the Sensuous: Perception & Language in a More-Than-Human World. David Abram. 336p. 1996. 25.00 (*0-679-43819-X*) Pantheon.

Spell of the Sensuous: Perception & Language in a More-Than-Human World. David Abram. 1997. pap. 14.00 (*0-679-77639-7*) Random.

Spell of the Sorcerer's Skull. John Bellairs. 1997. pap. 3.99 (*0-14-038044-2*) Viking Penguin.

Spell of the Tiger: Man-Eaters of the Sundarbans. Sy Montgomery. (Peter Davidson Bk.). 256p. 1995. 22.95 (*0-395-64169-1*) HM.

Spell of the Tiger: The Man-Eaters of Sundarbans. Sy Montgomery. 256p. 1996. pap. 12.95 (*0-395-79150-2*) HM.

Spell of the Yukon. Robert W. Service. (Robert Service Ser.). 1989. 11.95 (*0-399-15011-0*, Putnam) Putnam Pub Group.

Spell of Words. Lina Eckenstein. 1972. 59.95 (*0-8490-1109-4*) Gordon Pr.

Spell Sword. Marion Zimmer Bradley. (Darkover Ser.). 1974. mass mkt. 3.99 (*0-88677-237-0*) DAW Bks.

***Spell Users Companion.** 1992. 16.00 (*1-55806-149-5*) Iron Crown Ent Inc.

Spell Well. Bobbe D'Ambrosio et al. (Makemaster Bk.). (J). (gr. 1-6). 1980. pap. 12.99 (*0-8224-6455-1*) Fearon Teach Aids.

Spella-Ho. large type ed. H. E. Bates. 1991. 25.99 (*0-7089-2474-3*) Ulverscroft.

Spellbinder. Bethany Campbell. (Romance Ser.: No. 187). 1992. pap. 2.89 (*0-373-03187-4*, 1-03187-1) Harlequin Bks.

Spellbinder. Harold Robbins. 1993. mass mkt. 5.99 (*0-671-87495-0*) PB.

Spellbinder. large type ed. Una Power. 1995. 25.99 (*0-7089-3296-7*) Ulverscroft.

Spellbinder: Nightworld. L. J. Smith. (YA). (gr. 7 up). 1996. mass mkt. 3.99 (*0-671-55135-3*) PB.

Spellbinders. Margaret C. Banning. 1976. lib. bdg. 14.35 (*0-89968-008-9*, Lghtyr Pr) Buccaneer Bks.

Spellbinders: Charismatic Political Leadership. Ann R. Willner. LC 83-5914. 232p. 1984. 35.00 (*0-300-02809-1*) Yale U Pr.

Spellbinders: Charismatic Political Leadership. Ann R. Willner. LC 83-5914. 232p. 1985. reprint ed. pap. 13.00 (*0-300-03405-9*, Y-528) Yale U Pr.

***Spellbinder's Gift.** Og Madino. 1996. pap. 10.00 (*0-449-91224-8*) Fawcett.

Spellbinding. Charlotte Lamb. (Presents Ser.: No. 1393). 1991. pap. 2.79 (*0-373-11393-5*) Harlequin Bks.

Spellbinding. large type ed. Charlotte Lamb. 1990. lib. bdg. 18.95 (*0-263-12418-5*, Pub. by Mills & Boon UK) Thorndike Pr.

Spellbound. Allison Hayes. 400p. (Orig.). 1990. pap. 3.95 (*0-380-76214-5*) Avon.

Spellbound. Christopher Pike. (Orig.). (YA). (gr. 8 up). 1990. pap. 3.99 (*0-671-73681-7*, Archway) PB.

Spellbound. Hilary Norman. 464p. 1994. reprint ed. pap. 5.99 (*0-451-40458-0*, Onyx) NAL-Dutton.

***Spellbound: Art & Film in Britain.** Ed. by Ian Christie & Philip Dodd. (Distributed for the British Film Institute Ser.). (Illus.). 180p. 1996. pap. 39.95 (*0-85170-610-X*, Pub. by British Film Inst UK) Ind U Pr.

Spellbound: Growing up in God's Country. David W. McKain. LC 92-37590. 272p. 1993. reprint ed. pap. 14.95 (*0-8229-5507-5*) U of Pittsburgh Pr.

Spellbound: Growing up in God's Country. David W. McKain. LC 88-4721. 271p. 1988. reprint ed. pap. 77.30 (*0-7837-9756-7*, 2060484) Bks Demand.

Spellbound: Spells, Blessings & Ceremony. Helen Glisic. 96p. 1995. 12.00 (*0-207-18641-3*) HarpC.

Spellbound: Thay, Rashemen & Aglarond. TSR Inc. Staff. (TSR Forgotten Realms Game World Ser.). 1995. 25.00 (*0-7869-0139-X*) TSR Inc.

Spellbound Concerto: Intermediate Piano. M. Rozsa. 20p. 1981. pap. 3.95 (*0-7935-2281-1*, 00312718) H Leonard.

***Spellbound Hearts.** Ferguson et al. 288p. 1997. mass mkt. 4.99 (*0-8217-5769-5*, Zebra Kensgtn) Kensgtn Pub Corp.

Spellbound Kisses. Ed. by John Scognamiglio. 352p. 1993. mass mkt. 4.50 (*0-8217-4335-X*, Zebra Kensgtn) Kensgtn Pub Corp.

Spellcasting Two Hundred-One: The Official Hint Book from Legend Entertainment Company. 82p. 1993. pap. 9.95 (*1-880520-04-4*) Legend Enter.

Spellcoats. Diana W. Jones. LC 94-1507. (Dalemark Quartet Ser.). (Illus.). 288p. (YA). (gr. 7 up). 1995. pap. 4.95 (*0-688-13401-7*) Greenwillow.

Spellcoats. Diana W. Jones. LC 94-1507. (Dalemark Quartet Ser.: Bk. III). (Illus.). 288p. (YA). (gr. 7 up). 1995. 15.00 (*0-688-13362-2*) Greenwillow.

***Spellcraft.** Robin Skelton. (Illus.). 206p. 1997. reprint ed. pap. 9.95 (*0-919345-21-2*) Phoenix WA.

Spellcraft: Old English Heroic Legends. Kathleen Herbert. 292p. (Orig.). pap. 14.95 (*0-9516209-9-1*, Pub. by Anglo-Saxon Bks UK) Paul & Co Pubs.

Spellcraft, Hexcraft & Witchcraft. Anna Riva. (Illus.). 64p. 1977. pap. 4.50 (*0-943832-00-4*) Intl Imports.

***Speller's Law Relating to Hospitals.** 7th ed. Finch. (Illus.). 968p. (C). (gr. 13 up). 1994. text ed. 195.00 (*0-412-41000-1*, Chap & Hall NY) Chapman & Hall.

Spellfire. Ed Greenwood. LC 88-50056. (Forgotten Realms Novel Ser.). 392p. (Orig.). 1988. pap. 5.99 (*0-88038-587-1*) TSR Inc.

***Spellfire: Master the Magic Card Game.** 3rd ed. Brown et al. (Collector's Cards (Tsr)). 1994. 8.95 (*0-7869-0229-9*) TSR Inc.

Spellfire Reference Guide, 2. Lester Smith. 1996. 19.95 (*0-7869-0613-8*) TSR Inc.

Spelling. Ann Arbor. (C). Date not set. pap. text ed. write for info. (*0-393-95837-X*) Norton.

Spelling. Madden. 1983. wbk. ed., pap. 12.25 (*0-15-328550-8*) HB Schl Dept.

Spelling: A Mnemonics Approach. 3rd ed. Alvin R. Brown. LC 92-34000. 1994. pap. 21.95 (*0-538-70536-1*) S-W Pub.

Spelling: Basic Skills for Effective Communication. Ed. by Walter B. Barbe et al. 1982. 14.95 (*0-88309-118-6*) Zaner-Bloser.

Spelling: Development, Disabilities & Instruction. Louisa C. Moats. LC 95-44438. (Orig.). 1995. pap. 21.00 (*0-912752-40-8*) York Pr.

***Spelling: Grade 2.** Frank Schaffer Publications Staff. 1997. pap. text ed. 3.95 (*0-7647-0235-1*) Schaffer Pubns.

Spelling: Grade 4. Madden. 1983. 26.00 (*0-15-328560-5*) HB Schl Dept.

Spelling: Patterns of Sound. Odette P. Sims. 128p. (C). 1974. pap. text ed. write for info. (*0-07-057500-2*) McGraw.

***Spelling: Remedial Strategies.** Diane Montgomery. (Special Needs in Ordinary Schools Ser.). (Illus.). 160p. 1996. pap. 15.95 (*0-304-32974-6*); text ed. 60.00 (*0-304-32972-X*) Cassell.

Spelling: Syllabus. 2nd ed. Delpha Hurlburt. (gr. 7-12). 1980. pap. text ed. 9.95 (*0-89420-053-4*, 187898); audio 134.10 (*0-89420-185-9*, 187900) Natl Book.

***Spelling & Grammar.** Martha A. Lane. (Passport to the World of English Ser.: Bk. 2). (Illus.). 248p. 1996. teacher ed., ring bd. 23.00 incl. audio (*1-877596-25-6*); student ed., ring bd. 20.00 incl. audio (*1-877596-26-4*) Literacy & Evangelism.

Spelling & Reading Word List. 8th ed. Monica Foltzer. 16p. (J). 1984. pap. text ed. 1.50 (*0-9607918-2-5*, 801878) St Ursula.

Spelling & Usage Vocabulary Builder. large type ed. Ed. by Myrna T. McCulloch & Sharon Madsen. (Illus.). 478p. (J). (gr. k-2). 1993. reprint ed. 26.50 (*0-924277-04-1*) K & M Pub.

Spelling & Writing Grade 1. Carson & Dellosa. (Home Workbooks Ser.). (Illus.). 64p. (Orig.). (J). (gr. 1). 1995. wbk. ed., pap. 2.49 (*0-88724-334-7*, CD6831) Carson-Dellos.

Spelling & Writing Grade 2. Carson & Dellosa. (Home Workbooks Ser.). (Illus.). 64p. (Orig.). (J). (gr. 2). 1995. wbk. ed., pap. 2.49 (*0-88724-335-5*, CD6832) Carson-Dellos.

Spelling & Writing Grade 3. Carson & Dellosa. (Home Workbooks Ser.). (Illus.). 64p. (Orig.). (J). (gr. 3). 1995. wbk. ed., pap. 2.49 (*0-88724-336-3*, CD6833) Carson-Dellos.

Spelling As a Secondary Learning: The Extension of Spelling Vocabularies with Different Methods of Organizing & Teaching the Social Studies. I. Keith Tyler. LC 79-177688. (Columbia University. Teachers College. Contributions to Education Ser.: No. 781). reprint ed. 37.50 (*0-404-55781-3*) AMS Pr.

Spelling Basics. Christine Maxwell & O. B. Gregory. 128p. (C). 1993. pap. text ed. 13.95 (*1-56118-091-2*) Paradigm MN.

Spelling Basics. Christine Maxwell & O. B. Gregory. 128p. (C). 1993. teacher ed., pap. text ed. 8.00 (*1-56118-092-0*) Paradigm MN.

***Spelling Bee.** Brent Davis. 304p. 1996. 23.00 (*1-881320-66-9*, Black Belt) Black Belt Comm.

Spelling Bee. Sharon Gordon. LC 81-4648. (Illus.). 32p. (J). (gr. k-2). 1981. lib. bdg. 12.95 (*0-89375-535-4*) Troll Communs.

Spelling Bee. Sharon Gordon. LC 81-4648. (Illus.). 32p. (J). (gr. k-2). 1997. pap. 3.95 (*0-89375-536-2*) Troll Communs.

Spelling Book: Words Most Needed Plus Phonics, Level 1-2. Edward Fry. (Illus.). 48p. (Orig.). 1995. student ed., pap. 4.95 (*0-87673-028-4*) Laguna Bch Ed.

Spelling Book: Words Most Needed Plus Phonics, Level 2-3. Edward Fry. (Illus.). 48p. (Orig.). 1995. student ed., pap. 4.95 (*0-87673-029-2*) Laguna Bch Ed.

Spelling Book: Words Most Needed Plus Phonics, Level 3-4. Edward Fry. (Illus.). 48p. (Orig.). 1995. student ed., pap. 4.95 (*0-87673-030-6*) Laguna Bch Ed.

Spelling Book: Words Most Needed Plus Phonics, Level 4-5. Edward Fry. (Illus.). 48p. (Orig.). 1995. student ed., pap. 4.95 (*0-87673-031-4*) Laguna Bch Ed.

Spelling Book: Words Most Needed Plus Phonics, Level 5-6. Edward Fry. (Illus.). 48p. (Orig.). 1995. student ed., pap. 4.95 (*0-87673-032-2*) Laguna Bch Ed.

Spelling Book: Words Most Needed Plus Phonics, Level 6+ Edward Fry. (Illus.). 48p. (Orig.). 1995. student ed., pap. 4.95 (*0-87673-033-0*) Laguna Bch Ed.

Spelling Book: Words Most Needed, Plus Phonics, for Grades One to Six. 2nd ed. Edward Fry. 1993. pap. 29.95 (*0-87673-021-7*) Laguna Bch Ed.

Spelling Boosters. Wanda K. Sanseri. 50p. 1993. pap. 12.95 (*1-880045-07-9*) Back Home Indust.

Spelling by Sound & Structure. Rachel Siegrist. (J). (gr. 2-7). 1979. write for info. (*0-686-25261-6*); teacher ed. write for info. (*0-686-25262-4*) Rod & Staff.

Spelling DoodleLoops. Sandy Baker. (DoodleLoops Ser.). 96p. 1996. teacher ed. 11.99 (*1-56417-843-9*, GA1550) Good Apple.

Spelling Drills & Exercises: Programmed for the Typewriter. 3rd ed. LeRoy A. Brendel & Doris Near. (Illus.). 1979. text ed. 13.24 (*0-07-007491-7*) McGraw.

Spelling Fifteen Hundred. 3rd ed. J. N. Hook. 294p. (C). 1986. pap. text ed. 20.00 (*0-15-583212-3*) HB Coll Pubs.

Spelling Fitness: One Thousand One of the Most Frequently Misspelled Words. Tiffany Downey. Ed. by Cynthia Downey. 102p. (Orig.). (YA). (gr. 7-12). 1988. 29.95 (*0-685-22519-4*) Infini Educ.

Spelling for Job & Personal Use. Wood. (YA - Adult Education Ser.). 1992. pap. 9.95 (*0-538-70447-0*) S-W Pub.

Spelling for Writing. Houghton Mifflin Company Staff. (Literature Experience 1993 Ser.). (J). (gr. 2). 1992. pap. 5.52 (*0-395-62370-7*) HM.

Spelling for Writing. Houghton Mifflin Company Staff. (Literature Experience 1993 Ser.). (J). (gr. k). 1992. teacher ed., pap. 4.20 (*0-395-62378-2*) HM.

Spelling for Writing. Houghton Mifflin Company Staff. (Literature Experience 1993 Ser.). (J). (gr. 1). 1992. teacher ed., pap. 4.20 (*0-395-62380-4*) HM.

Spelling for Writing. Houghton Mifflin Company Staff. (Literature Experience 1993 Ser.). (J). (gr. 2). 1992. teacher ed., pap. 5.76 (*0-395-62382-0*) HM.

Spelling for Writing. Houghton Mifflin Company Staff. (Literature Experience 1993 Ser.). (J). (gr. 3). 1992. teacher ed., pap. 5.76 (*0-395-62384-7*) HM.

Spelling for Writing. Houghton Mifflin Company Staff. (Literature Experience 1993 Ser.). (J). (gr. 4). 1992. teacher ed., pap. 9.56 (*0-395-62385-5*) HM.

Spelling for Writing. Houghton Mifflin Company Staff. (Literature Experience 1993 Ser.). (J). (gr. 5). 1992. teacher ed., pap. 9.56 (*0-395-62386-3*) HM.

Spelling for Writing. Houghton Mifflin Company Staff. (Literature Experience 1993 Ser.). (J). (gr. 6). 1992. teacher ed., pap. 10.08 (*0-395-62387-1*) HM.

Spelling for Writing. Houghton Mifflin Company Staff. (Literature Experience 1993 Ser.). (J). (gr. 6). 1992. pap. 9.36 (*0-395-62375-8*) HM.

Spelling for Writing. Houghton Mifflin Company Staff. (Literature Experience 1993 Ser.). (J). (gr. 5). 1992. pap. 9.36 (*0-395-62374-X*) HM.

Spelling for Writing. Houghton Mifflin Company Staff. (Literature Experience 1993 Ser.). (J). (gr. 4). 1992. pap. 9.36 (*0-395-62373-1*) HM.

Spelling for Writing. Houghton Mifflin Company Staff. (Literature Experience 1993 Ser.). (J). (gr. 3). 1992. pap. 5.52 (*0-395-62371-5*) HM.

Spelling for Writing. Houghton Mifflin Company Staff. (Literature Experience 1993 Ser.). (J). (gr. 2). 1992. pap. 5.52 (*0-395-62369-3*) HM.

Spelling for Writing. Houghton Mifflin Company Staff. (Literature Experience 1993 Ser.). (J). (gr. 1). 1992. pap. 3.92 (*0-395-62367-7*) HM.

Spelling for Writing. Houghton Mifflin Company Staff. (Literature Experience 1993 Ser.). (J). (gr. k). 1992. pap. 3.92 (*0-395-62366-9*) HM.

Spelling for Writing. alternate ed. Houghton Mifflin Company Staff. (Literature Experience 1993 Ser.). (J). (gr. 1). 1992. teacher ed., pap. 4.20 (*0-395-62379-0*) HM.

Spelling for Writing. alternate ed. Houghton Mifflin Company Staff. (Literature Experience 1993 Ser.). (J). (gr. 2). 1992. teacher ed., pap. 5.76 (*0-395-62381-2*) HM.

Spelling for Writing. alternate ed. Houghton Mifflin Company Staff. (Literature Experience 1993 Ser.). (J). (gr. 3). 1992. teacher ed., pap. 5.76 (*0-395-62383-9*) HM.

Spelling for Writing. alternate ed. Houghton Mifflin Company Staff. (Literature Experience 1993 Ser.). (J). (gr. 3). 1992. pap. 5.52 (*0-395-62372-3*) HM.

Spelling for Writing. alternate ed. Houghton Mifflin Company Staff. (Literature Experience 1993 Ser.). (J). (gr. 1). 1992. pap. 3.92 (*0-395-62368-5*) HM.

Spelling Games & Puzzles for Junior High. Robert D. Miller. (Makemaster Bk.). (J). (gr. 6-8). 1976. pap. 9.99 (*0-8224-6460-8*) Fearon Teach Aids.

Spelling Improvement. 5th ed. Patricia M. Fergus. 1991. pap. text ed. write for info. (*0-07-020487-X*) McGraw.

Spelling Improvement: A Program for Self-Instruction. 4th ed. Patricia M. Gergus. 1983. pap. text ed. write for info. (*0-07-020477-2*) McGraw.

***Spelling in Use: Looking Closely at Spelling in Whole Language Classrooms.** Lester L. Laminack & Katie Wood. LC 96-28685. (Illus.). 128p. (Orig.). (J). (gr. k-6). 1996. teacher ed., pap. 11.95 (*0-8141-4663-5*) NCTE.

***Spelling Is Not a Health Hazard.** Traill. 1994. pap. text ed. write for info. (*0-582-80379-9*, Pub. by Longman UK) Longman.

Spelling It Out. Rhiannedd Pratley. 128p. 1988. pap. 7.95 (*0-563-21437-6*, Pub. by BBC UK) Parkwest Pubns.

Spelling Keys to Five Hundred One Words from 12 Old-Middle English Roots. Raymond E. Laurita. 63p. (Orig.). (YA). (gr. 9-12). 1992. pap. text ed. 9.50 (*0-914051-31-8*) Leonardo Pr.

Spelling Keys to One Thousand One Words from Ten Greek Based Roots. Raymond E. Laurita. 80p. (Orig.). (YA). (gr. 9-12). 1991. pap. text ed. 11.50 (*0-914051-26-1*) Leonardo Pr.

Spelling Keys to One Thousand Words from 10 Latin Based Roots. Raymond E. Laurita. 64p. (Orig.). (YA). (gr. 9-12). 1991. pap. text ed. 9.50 (*0-914051-24-5*) Leonardo Pr.

Spelling Keys to Two Thousand One Words from 10 Indo-European Roots. Raymond E. Laurita. 140p. (Orig.). (YA). (gr. 9-12). 1992. pap. text ed. 11.50 (*0-914051-30-X*) Leonardo Pr.

Spelling Made Easy. Lester D. Basch & Milton Finkelstein. 1974. pap. 3.00 (*0-87980-288-X*) Wilshire.

Spelling Made Easy. Visual Education Corporation Staff. (Illus.). 168p. (gr. 9 up). 1984. student ed. 9.36 (*0-07-039661-2*) McGraw.

Spelling Made Simple. Sheila Henderson. 192p. 1990. pap. 12.00 (*0-385-26642-1*) Doubleday.

Spelling Made Simple. Hayden Mead. 1996. mass mkt. 5.99 (*0-425-15524-2*) Berkley Pub.

***Spelling Matters Bk. 1.** Woods. 1994. pap. text ed. write for info. (*0-582-80141-9*, Pub. by Longman UK) Longman.

An Asterisk (*) at the beginning of an entry indicates that the title is appearing in BIP for the first time.

***Spelling Matters Bk. 2.** Woods. Date not set. pap. text ed. write for info. (0-582-80142-7, Pub. by Longman UK) Longman.

***Spelling of Low German & Plautdietsch.** Reuben Epp. 176p. 1996. pap. 12.95 (0-9638494-1-7) Readers Pr KS.

Spelling Plus: Spelling for Success in Kindergarten - 6th Grade. Susan C. Anthony. LC 94-78302. 170p. (Orig.). (J). (gr. k-6). 1995. teacher ed., spiral bd. 19.95 (1-879478-04-8, 048) Instr Res Co.

***Spelling Power.** 3rd rev. ed. Beverly L. Adams-Gordon. (Illus.). 368p. (Orig.). 1997. teacher ed., pap. 49.95 (1-888827-19-X) Castlemoyle Bks.

Spelling Power: A Spelling Workbook with Comprehension Drills. Burton Goodman. 224p. (Orig.). 1987. pap. text ed. 9.24 (0-89061-449-0) Jamestown Pubs.

Spelling Practice. Frank Schaffer Publications, Inc. Staff. (Back-to-Basics Ser.). 32p. (J). (gr. 1). 1996. wbk. ed. 3.95 (0-86734-985-9, FS-30060) Schaffer Pubns.

Spelling Practice. Frank Schaffer Publications, Inc. Staff. (Back-to-Basics Ser.). 32p. (J). (gr. 2). 1996. wbk. ed. 3.95 (0-86734-986-7, FS-30061) Schaffer Pubns.

Spelling Practice. Frank Schaffer Publications, Inc. Staff. (Back-to-Basics Ser.). 32p. (J). (gr. 3). 1996. wbk. ed. 3.95 (0-86734-987-5, FS-30062) Schaffer Pubns.

Spelling Practice. Frank Schaffer Publications, Inc. Staff. (Back-to-Basics Ser.). 32p. (J). (gr. 4). 1996. wbk. ed. 3.95 (0-86734-988-3, FS-30063) Schaffer Pubns.

Spelling Practice. Frank Schaffer Publications, Inc. Staff. (Back-to-Basics Ser.). 32p. (J). (gr. 5). 1996. wbk. ed. 3.95 (0-86734-989-1, FS-30064) Schaffer Pubns.

Spelling Practice. Frank Schaffer Publications, Inc. Staff. (Back-to-Basics Ser.). 32p. (J). (gr. 6). 1996. wbk. ed. 3.95 (0-86734-990-5, FS-30065) Schaffer Pubns.

Spelling Practice. Frank Schaffer Publications, Inc. Staff. (Back-to-Basics Ser.). 32p. (J). (gr. 7). 1996. wbk. ed. 3.95 (0-86734-991-3, FS-30066) Schaffer Pubns.

Spelling Practice. Frank Schaffer Publications, Inc. Staff. (Back-to-Basics Ser.). 32p. (J). (gr. 8). 1996. wbk. ed. 3.95 (0-86734-992-1, FS-30067) Schaffer Pubns.

Spelling Puzzles. J. Tyler & R. Gee. (English Skills Ser.). (Illus.). 32p. (J). (gr. 2-5). 1992. pap. 4.95 (0-7460-1053-2) EDC.

Spelling Puzzles: Grade 1. Jean Syswerda. Ed. by Joan Hoffman. (I Know It! Bks.). (Illus.). 32p. (J). (gr. 1). 1980. student ed. 1.99 (0-938256-16-5) Sch Zone Pub Co.

Spelling Puzzles: Grade 2. Jean Syswerda. Ed. by Joan Hoffman. (I Know It! Bks.). (Illus.). 32p. (J). (gr. 2). 1979. student ed. 1.99 (0-938256-17-3) Sch Zone Pub Co.

Spelling Puzzles: Grade 3. Jean Syswerda. Ed. by Joan Hoffman. (I Know It! Bks.). (Illus.). 32p. (J). (gr. 3). 1979. student ed. 1.99 (0-938256-18-1) Sch Zone Pub Co.

Spelling Scores for Five Thousand Five Hundred Six Words: Grade & Age Scores for Common English Words see Why Americans Read or Spell Poorly: Problem, Cause, & Correction of 80 Years of Educational Decline

Spelling Simplified. Judi Kesselman-Turkel & Franklynn Peterson. 176p. (Orig.). 1983. pap. 8.86 (0-8092-5510-3) Contemp Bks.

Spelling Skillbuilder. 2nd ed. Aiken. (PS - Communication/English Ser.). 1992. pap. 21.95 (0-538-70382-2) S-W Pub.

Spelling Smart! A Ready-to-Use Activities Program for Students with Spelling Difficulties. Cynthia Stowe. 416p. 1995. spiral bd. 28.95 (0-87628-880-8) Ctr Appl Res.

***Spelling Strategies.** 1997. pap. 10.95 (0-590-96575-1) Scholastic Inc.

Spelling Success. R. Kent Smith. 200p. (C). 1989. pap. text ed. 17.50 (0-03-023333-X) HB Coll Pubs.

Spelling Success. 4th ed. Smith & Merken. (C). 1988. teacher ed., pap. text ed. 34.00 (0-03-023334-8) HB Coll Pubs.

Spelling Tests: Grade 3. Incl. Grade 4. student ed. 5.00 (0-8209-0169-5, ST-4); Grade 5. student ed. 5.00 (0-8209-0170-9, ST-5); Grade 6. student ed. 5.00 (0-8209-0171-7, ST-6); (Spelling Ser.). 24p. 1979. Set student ed. 5.00 (0-8209-0168-7, ST-3) ESP.

Spelling the Easy Way. 3rd ed. Joseph E. Mersand et al. 352p. 1996. pap. 11.95 (0-8120-9143-4) Barron.

Spelling the Written Word, Bk. C. Mildred Middleton & Eddie Tsang. (Administrator's Guide SD100). 64p. 1984. per. 24.90 (0-8403-3192-4) Kendall-Hunt.

Spelling the Written Word, Bk. B. Mildred Middleton & Eddie Tsang. (Administrator's Guide SD100). 64p. 1984. per. 24.90 (0-8403-3191-6) Kendall-Hunt.

Spelling the Written Word: Administration Guide, Bk. A. 2nd ed. Mildred Middleton. 264p. 1994. per. 24.90 (0-8403-3190-8) Kendall-Hunt.

Spelling the Written Word, SD100, Bk. D. Mildred Middleton & Eddie Tsang. 200p. (YA). (gr. 10). 1984. per. 8.90 (0-8403-3198-3) Kendall-Hunt.

Spelling the Written Word, SD100: Administrators Guide, Bk. D. Mildred Middleton & Eddie Tsang. 64p. 1984. per. 24.90 (0-8403-3193-2) Kendall-Hunt.

Spelling the 100 Most Used Words. Wood. (YA - Adult Education Ser.). 1993. pap. 5.95 (0-538-70781-X) S-W Pub.

Spelling Thinker Sheets. Becky Daniel. 64p. (J). (gr. 4-8). 1988. student ed. 8.99 (0-86653-423-7, GA1035) Good Apple.

Spelling Through Phonics. 2nd rev. ed. Marlene J. McCracken & Robert A. McCracken. (Illus.). 175p. (J). (gr. 1-3). 1996. teacher ed., pap. 18.00 (1-895411-86-6) Peguis Pubs Ltd.

Spelling Trends, Contest, & Methods. Ruel A. Allred. (What Research Says to the Teacher Ser.). 1987. pap. 3.95 (0-8106-1062-0) NEA.

Spelling Window. Dawn L. Watkins. LC 92-47049. (Pennant Ser.). (Illus.). 32p. (J). 1993. pap. 5.49 (0-89084-677-4, 069005) Bob Jones Univ Pr.

Spelling Workbook: English As a Second Language, 3 cass., Set. 96p. teacher ed. 55.00 incl. audio (1-57970-017-9, SEN120) Audio-Forum.

Spelling Works. L. Schwartz. (Spelling Activities Ser.). 48p. (J). (gr. 3-8). 1993. 6.95 (0-88160-257-4, LW288) Learning Wks.

Spelling 1. (Illus.). (J). (ps-3). 1993. pap. 3.50 (0-307-03668-5, Golden Books) Western Pub.

Spelling 101. Claudia Sorsby. 1996. mass mkt. 4.99 (0-312-95974-5) St Martin.

Spelling 1983: Grade 3. Madden. 1983. 26.00 (0-15-328558-3) HB Schl Dept.

Spelling 1987. Madden. 1983. 26.00 (0-15-328559-1) HB Schl Dept.

Spelling 2. (Step Ahead Workbooks Ser.). (Illus.). 32p. (J). (gr. 2-3). 1995. pap. 2.19 (0-307-23575-0, Golden Pr) Western Pub.

Spelling 83: Grade 1. Madden. (Illus.). 1983. 56.25 (0-15-328565-6) HB Schl Dept.

Spelling 83: Grade 2. Madden. 1983. 67.25 (0-15-328567-2) HB Schl Dept.

Spelling 83: Grade 3. Madden. 1983. 67.25 (0-15-328568-0) HB Schl Dept.

Spelling 83: Grade 5. Madden. 1983. 67.25 (0-15-328569-9) HB Schl Dept.

Spelling 83: Grade 6. Madden. 1983. 26.75 (0-15-328562-1) HB Schl Dept.

Spelling 83: Grade 6. Madden. 1989. 67.25 (0-15-328570-2) HB Schl Dept.

Spelling 83: Grade 7. Madden. 1983. 73.00 (0-15-328571-0) HB Schl Dept.

Spelling 83: Grade 7. Madden. 1983. 28.00 (0-15-328563-X) HB Schl Dept.

Spelling 83: Grade 8. Madden. 1983. 28.25 (0-15-328564-8) HB Schl Dept.

Spelling 85: Grade 5. Madden. (Illus.). 1983. 26.75 (0-15-328561-3) HB Schl Dept.

Spellkey Trilogy. Ann Downer. 640p. 1995. mass mkt. 5.99 (0-671-87644-9) Baen Bks.

Spellright: A Medical Word Book. Jane Rice. 772p. (C). 1990. pap. text ed. 21.95 (0-8385-6290-6, A6290-9) Appleton & Lange.

Spells, & How They Work. Janet Farrar & Stewart Farrar. 192p. 1991. pap. 9.95 (0-919345-63-8) Phoenix WA.

Spells for Everything. IGOOS Staff. Ed. by Thorguard Templar. 105p. 1994. 12.00 (1-57179-028-4) Intern Guild ASRS.

***Spells for Not Dying Again: Poems.** Diana O'Hehir. LC 96-32793. 80p. 1997. 26.00 (0-910055-30-0); pap. 14.00 (0-910055-31-9) East Wash Univ.

Spells of a Voodoo Doll. Assoto Saint. 400p. (Orig.). 1996. pap. 12.95 (1-56333-393-7, R Kasak Bks) Masquerade.

Spells of Enchantment: The Wondrous Fairy Tales of Western Culture. Ed. by Jack D. Zipes. (Illus.). 848p. 1992. pap. 17.95 (0-14-012783-6, Penguin Bks) Viking Penguin.

Spells of Fury: Building Games in Windows 95. Michael J. Norton. 700p. (Orig.). 1996. pap. 49.99 incl. cd-rom (1-57169-067-0, Waite Grp Pr) Sams.

Spells of Mortal Weaving. Esther M. Friesner. (Twelve Kingdom Ser.). 224p. 1986. pap. 2.95 (0-380-75001-5) Avon.

Spells, Splits, & Survival in a Russian Canadian Community: A Study of Russian Organizations in the Greater Vancouver Area. Koozma J. Tarasoff. LC 88-84007. (Immigrant Communities & Ethnic Minorities in the U. S. & Canada Ser.: No. 60). 1989. 64.50 (0-404-19470-2) AMS Pr.

Spellsinger II: The Hour of the Gate. Alan Dean Foster. 304p. 1988. mass mkt. 5.50 (0-446-35650-6) Warner Bks.

Spelt Cookbook: Cooking with Nature's Grain for Life. Helga Hughes. (Illus.). 208p. Date not set. pap. 14.95 (0-89529-696-9) Avery Pub.

Spelunking. Van K. Brock. 1978. 1.50 (0-936814-04-7) New Collage.

Spence & Lila. Bobbie Ann Mason. LC 87-46155. (Illus.). 176p. 1989. reprint ed. pap. 9.00 (0-06-091559-5, PL 1559, PL) HarpC.

Spence & the Mean Old Bear. Christa Chevalier. Ed. by Abby Levine. LC 86-1570. (Spence Bks.). (Illus.). 32p. (J). (ps-1). 1986. 12.95 (0-8075-7572-0) A Whitman.

Spence in Petal Park. large type ed. Michael Allen. 345p. 1980. 25.99 (0-7089-0533-1) Ulverscroft.

Spence Is Small. Christa Chevalier. Ed. by Abby Levine. LC 87-2054. (Illus.). (J). (ps-1). 1987. lib. bdg. 12.95 (0-8075-7567-4) A Whitman.

Spence Isn't Spence Anymore. Christa Chevalier. Ed. by Abby Levine. LC 84-29195. (Illus.). 32p. (J). (ps-1). 1985. 12.95 (0-8075-7565-8) A Whitman.

Spencer: Genealogical Sketch of Descendants of Samuel Spencer of Pennsylvania. H. M. Jenkins. 253p. 1991. reprint ed. pap. 39.00 (0-8328-1942-5); reprint ed. lib. bdg. 49.00 (0-8328-1941-7) Higginson Bk Co.

Spencer: Property Tax Planning. 3rd ed. Philip Spencer. 1994. pap. write for info. (0-406-03486-9) MICHIE.

Spencer Baird of the Smithsonian. E. M. Youssef & Edward F. Rivinus. LC 92-6897. (Illus.). 232p. (C). 1992. text ed. 29.95 (1-56098-155-5) Smithsonian.

Spencer Brade M. D. large type ed. Frank G. Slaughter. 528p. 1983. 25.99 (0-7089-0937-X) Ulverscroft.

Spencer Brade, M.D. Frank Slaughter. 375p. 1975. reprint ed. lib. bdg. 26.95 (0-89190-287-2, Rivercity Pr) Amereon Ltd.

Spencer Brewer: Solos for New Age Piano. (Piano Solos Ser.). 80p. (Orig.). 1992. pap. 12.95 (0-7935-1217-4, 00308125) H Leonard.

Spencer Butte Pioneers: One Hundred Years on the Sunny Side of the Butte 1850-1950. Lois Barton. Ed. by Northwest Matrix Staff & Charlotte Mills. LC 82-61837. (Illus.). 144p. 1982. pap. 11.95 (0-9609420-0-9) S Butte Pr.

Spencer Christian's Geography Book. Spencer Christian. LC 95-3761. 1995. pap. 12.95 (0-312-13183-6, Thomas Dunne Bks) St Martin.

Spencer Collection of American Art. (Illus.). 64p. 1990. pap. 25.00 (0-945936-08-7) Spanierman Gallery.

Spencer Fullerton Baird & the U. S. Fish Commission: A Study in the History of American Science. Dean C. Allard, Jr. Ed. by Keir B. Sterling. LC 77-81138. (Biologists & Their World Ser.). 1978. lib. bdg. 36.95 (0-405-10738-2) Ayer.

Spencer Haywood: The Rise, the Fall, the Recovery. Spencer Haywood & Scott Ostler. (Illus.). 272p. 1992. 24.95 (1-56743-001-5) Amistad Pr.

Spencer Haywood: The Rise, the Fall, the Recovery. Spencer Haywood & Scott Ostler. LC 92-24388. (Illus.). 284p. 1994. reprint ed. pap. 10.95 (1-56743-042-2) Amistad Pr.

Spencer House: Chronicle of a Great London Mansion. Joe Friedman. 1993. 65.00 (0-302-00617-6, Pub. by Zwemmer Bks UK) Sothebys Pubns.

Spencer, New York History: Tales of Trails & Crossroads Days Before Yesterday. Edison Signor & Emogene Signor. 248p. (Orig.). 1985. text ed. 37.50 (0-943240-21-2); pap. text ed. 30.00 (0-685-43311-0) UHLs Pub.

Spencer Optical Manufacturing Catalog, No. 8. 95p. 1874. pap. 35.00 (0-87556-176-4) Saifer.

Spencer Repeating Firearms. Roy M. Marcot. (Illus.). 317p. 1995. 60.00 (1-884849-14-8) R&R Bks.

Spencer Repeating Firearms. 2nd rev. ed. Roy M. Marcot. LC 89-92524. (Illus.). 316p. 1989. reprint ed. 59.95 (0-9611494-3-4) Northwood Heritage Pr.

***Spencer Road: A Short Story Sequence.** Morris Smith. LC 97-21056. 1997. write for info. (0-87049-995-5) U of Tenn Pr.

Spencer Tracy: A Bio-Bibliography, 5. James Fisher. LC 94-22462. (Bio-Bibliographies in the Performing Arts Ser.: Vol. 59). 360p. 1994. text ed. 59.95 (0-313-28727-9, Greenwood Pr) Greenwood.

Spencer Tracy, Tragic Idol. Bill Davidson. 1989. mass mkt. 5.99 (0-8217-3738-4, Zebra Kensgtn) Kensgtn Pub Corp.

Spencer W. Kimball: Resolute Disciple, Prophet of God. Francis M. Gibbons. LC 95-21428. xv, 320p. 1995. 24.95 (0-87579-994-9) Deseret Bk.

Spencerian Copybook, No. 1. P. R. Spencer. 1985. pap. 2.99 (0-88062-083-8) Mott Media.

Spencerian Copybook, No. 2. P. R. Spencer. 1985. pap. 2.99 (0-88062-084-6) Mott Media.

Spencerian Copybook, No. 3. P. R. Spencer. 1985. pap. 2.99 (0-88062-085-4) Mott Media.

Spencerian Copybook, No. 4. P. R. Spencer. 1985. pap. 2.99 (0-88062-086-2) Mott Media.

Spencerian Copybook, No. 5. P. R. Spencer. 1985. pap. 2.99 (0-88062-087-0) Mott Media.

Spencerian Script & Ornamental Penmanship: Early American Handwriting, 2 vols., Set. Michael R. Sull. Ed. by Wendy E. Cook et al. LC 88-82719. (Illus.). 630p. (Orig.). (C). 1990. pap. text ed. 44.95 (0-9621025-0-4) LDG Pub.

Spencerian Theory Book, Set. P. R. Spencer. 1985. pap. 15.99 (0-88062-096-X) Mott Media.

Spencer's Bride. Laura Gordon. 1996. mass mkt. 3.75 (0-373-22396-X, 1-22396-5) Harlequin Bks.

Spencer's Hospital. large type ed. Alex Stuart. 400p. 1988. 25.99 (0-7089-1921-9) Ulverscroft.

Spencer's Illustrated Computer Dictionary. Donald D. Spencer. LC 94-33107. (Illus.). 238p. (Orig.). 1995. pap. 24.95 (0-89218-220-2) Camelot Pub.

Spencer's Last Journey, Being the Journal of an Expedition to Tierra Del Fuego. Baldwin Spencer. LC 76-44790. reprint ed. 57.50 (0-404-15972-9) AMS Pr.

Spencer's Mountain. Earl Hamner, Jr. 1993. reprint ed. lib. bdg. 27.95 (1-56849-022-4) Buccaneer Bks.

Spencers of Amberson Avenue: A Turn-of-the-Century Memoir. Ethel Spencer. LC 83-47827. (Illus.). 169p. 1983. pap. 12.95 (0-8229-5356-0) U of Pittsburgh Pr.

Spencer's Pathology of the Lung. 5th ed. Ed. by Philip S. Hasleton. LC 95-19711. (Illus.). 1888p. 1996. text ed. 179.00 (0-07-105448-0) McGraw-Hill HPD.

Spencer's Revenge. large type ed. Jim Miller. (Linford Western Library). 237p. 1989. pap. 15.99 (0-7089-6671-3, Linford) Ulverscroft.

Spencer's Scientific Correspondence with Sir J. G. Frazer & Others. Baldwin Spencer. Ed. by Robert R. Marett & T. K. Penniman. LC 76-44792. reprint ed. 19.50 (0-404-15973-7) AMS Pr.

Spencer's Shadow. Laura Gordon. (Intrigue Ser.). 1996. mass mkt. 3.75 (0-373-22387-0, 1-22387-4) Harlequin Bks.

Spencertown: Recent Paintings by Ellsworth Kelly. Intro. by Yve-Alain Bois. 102p. 1995. 35.00 (0-947564-57-8) Dist Art Pubs.

Spencerville. Nelson DeMille. 576p. 1995. mass mkt. 6.99 (0-446-60245-0) Warner Bks.

Spencerville. large type ed. Nelson DeMille. LC 94-31286. 1995. 25.95 (0-7862-0340-4) Thorndike Pr.

Spencerville. large type ed. Nelson DeMille. LC 94-31286. 755p. 1995. pap. 20.95 (0-7862-0341-2) Thorndike Pr.

Spend Game. Jonathan Gash. (Crime Monthly Ser.). 204p. 1982. pap. 5.95 (0-14-006190-8, Penguin Bks) Viking Penguin.

Spend Game. large type ed. Jonathan Gash. 1981. 12.00 (0-7089-0673-7) Ulverscroft.

Spend It or Save It? Pension Lump-Sum Distributions & Tax Reform. G. Lawrence Atkins. LC 86-6413. 85p. 1986. pap. 14.95 (0-86643-046-6) Empl Benefit Res Inst.

Spend Less, Sell More: Thirteen Simple Steps You Can Take Right Now to Grow Your Business. David J. Rosenweig. 1994. per. 21.95 (1-55738-819-9) Irwin Prof Pubng.

Spend on Your Future: Investing & Money Management Made Easy. Tim Collins & Jane Lehr. (Illus.). 187p. (Orig.). 1994. pap. 13.95 (0-9639889-3-X) Orca Bks.

Spend Sad Sundays Singing Songs to Sassy Sisters. Chester Fuller. 1974. pap. 1.50 (0-88378-037-2) Third World.

***Spend the Days in Ancient Greece! Projects & Activities That Bring the Past to Life.** Linda Honan & Ellen Kosmer. (Spend the Days Ser.). 128p. (YA). (gr. 9). 1998. pap. 12.95 (0-471-15454-7) Wiley.

Spender: Poetry. Stephen Spender. 1997. pap. 9.95 (0-14-086396-6) Viking Penguin.

Spending in Congressional Elections: A Never-Ending Spiral. Herb K. Shultz. 68p. (Orig.). (C). 1988. pap. text ed. 10.50 (0-939715-10-4) Ctr Politics.

Spending, Taxes, & Deficits: International-Intertemporal Approach. Jacob A. Frenkel & Assaf Razin. LC 88-39091. (Studies in International Finance: No. 63). 48p. 1988. pap. text ed. 11.00 (0-88165-235-0) Princeton U Int Finan Econ.

Spending the Light. Janice M. Reash. (Illus.). (Orig.). Date not set. pap. text ed. 7.95 (0-9616908-1-X) Piedmont Pr OH.

Spending Time Alone with God, Bk. 2. Barry St. Clair. (Moving Toward Maturity Ser.). 132p. (YA). 1991. pap. 6.50 (0-89693-292-3, 6-1292) SP Pubns.

Spending Time Together: An Anthology by New Writers. (New Writers' Voices Ser.). 64p. 1993. pap. text ed. 3.15 (1-56853-008-0, Signal Hill) New Readers.

Spending Time with God: A Teen's Guide to Devotions. Mark Gilroy. 72p. (Orig.). (YA). 1987. pap. 5.99 (0-8341-1197-7) Beacon Hill.

Spending Time with the Lord. Bill Freeman. LC 90-92301. 87p. (Orig.). 1990. pap. 4.00 (0-914271-10-5) Mnstry Wrd.

Spengler: The Annals of the Families of Caspar, Henry, Baltzer & George Spengler, Who Settled in York Co. (Pa.) Respectively in 1729, 1732, & 1751, with Biographical & Historical Sketches. E. W. Spangler. (Illus.). 604p. 1992. reprint ed. pap. 91.00 (0-8328-2292-2); reprint ed. lib. bdg. 101.00 (0-8328-2291-4) Higginson Bk Co.

Spengler im Dritten Reich see Hour of Decision

Spengler's Future. John J. Reilly. 198p. 1993. pap. 14.95 (0-9639606-0-1) Millennium.

Spenser. Richard W. Church. Ed. by John Morley. LC 68-58372. (English Men of Letters Ser.). reprint ed. lib. bdg. 41.50 (0-404-51703-X) AMS Pr.

Spenser. Richard W. Church. (BCL1-PR English Literature Ser.). 188p. 1992. reprint ed. lib. bdg. 69.00 (0-7812-7226-2) Rprt Serv.

Spenser: Selected Writings. Ed. by Elizabeth P. Watson. LC 91-28662. (English Texts Ser.). 320p. (C). 1992. pap. 17.95 (0-415-01636-3, A6750) Routledge.

Spenser: Selections, with Essays by Hazlitt, Coleridge & Leigh Hunt. Edmund Spenser. LC 76-29399. 1977. reprint ed. 37.50 (0-404-15358-5) AMS Pr.

Spenser: The Faerie Queene. Ed. by A. C. Hamilton. LC 77-2738. (Longman Annotated English Poets Ser.). 1977. text ed. 32.95 (0-685-42243-7, 73632) Longman.

Spenser: The Faerie Queene. Ed. by A. C. Hamilton. LC 77-2738. (Longman Annotated English Poets Ser.). (C). 1977. pap. text ed. 47.95 (0-582-49705-1) Longman.

Spenser & His Poetry, 3 vols. in 1. rev. ed. George L. Craik. LC 74-99247. reprint ed. 76.50 (0-404-01826-2) AMS Pr.

Spenser & His Poetry. Samuel E. Winbolt. LC 70-120978. (Poetry & Life Ser.). reprint ed. 27.50 (0-404-52534-2) AMS Pr.

***Spenser & Literary Pictorialism.** John B. Bender. LC 71-166361. 232p. 1972. reprint ed. pap. 66.20 (0-608-02889-4, 2063953) Bks Demand.

***Spenser & the Discourses of Reformation England.** Richard Mallette. LC 95-52793. 304p. 1997. text ed. 42.50 (0-8032-3195-4) U of Nebr Pr.

Spenser & the Poetics of Pastoral: A Study of the World of Colin Clout. David R. Shore. 1985. 49.95 (0-7735-0577-6, Pub. by McGill CN) U of Toronto Pr.

Spenser & the System of Courtly Love. Earle B. Fowler. LC 67-30903. 91p. 1967. reprint ed. 35.00 (0-87753-016-5) Phaeton.

Spenser & the Table Round: A Study in the Contemporaneous Background for Spenser's Use of the Arthurian Legend. Charles B. Milligan. 1977. lib. bdg. 59.95 (0-8490-2656-3) Gordon Pr.

Spenser As a Fabulist. Louis S. Friedland. (Studies in Spenser: No. 26). 1970. reprint ed. pap. 39.95 (0-8383-0031-6) M S G Haskell Hse.

Spenser Chronology. Willy Maley. LC 93-2455. 164p. (C). 1994. lib. bdg. 44.00 (0-389-21010-2) B&N Imports.

Spenser Encyclopedia. Ed. by A. C. Hamilton et al. 864p. 1990. 250.00 (0-8020-2676-1) U of Toronto Pr.

***Spenser Encyclopedia.** A. C. Hamilton. 1997. pap. text ed. 50.00 (0-8020-7923-7) U of Toronto Pr.

Spenser in Ireland. Pauline Henley. (BCL1-PR English Literature Ser.). 231p. 1992. reprint ed. lib. bdg. 79.00 (0-7812-7227-0) Rprt Serv.

Spenser in Ireland. Pauline Henley. LC 70-131741. 1970. reprint ed. 7.00 (0-403-00628-7) Scholarly.

Spenser, Marvell, & Renaissance Pastoral. Patrick Cullen. LC 76-123566. 224p. reprint ed. pap. 63.90 (0-685-15242-1, 2014653) Bks Demand.

Spenser, Milton, & Renaissance Pastoral. Richard Mallette. LC 78-73154. 224p. 1980. 32.50 (0-8387-2412-4) Bucknell U Pr.

S

S

Spenser Studies: A Renaissance Poetry Annual, 1980-1993, 11 vols. Ed. by Patrick Cullen & Thomas P. Roche, Jr. 1980. write for info. (*0-404-19200-9*) AMS Pr.

Spenserian Poetics: Idolatry, Iconoclasm & Magic. Kenneth Gross. LC 85-47701. 256p. (C). 1985. 39.95 (*0-8014-1805-4*) Cornell U Pr.

Spenser's Allegory: The Anatomy of Imagination. Isabel G. MacCaffrey. LC 75-30197. 457p. reprint ed. pap. 130.30 (*0-8357-3548-6*, 2034296) Bks Demand.

Spenser's Allegory of Love: Social Vision in Books III, IV & V of The Faerie Queene. James W. Broaddus. LC 95-1119. 192p. 1996. 33.50 (*0-8386-3632-2*) Fairleigh Dickinson.

Spenser's Amoretti: A Critical Study. Donna Gibbs. (Illus.). 200p. 1990. text ed. 49.95 (*0-85967-777-X*, Pub. by Scolar Pr UK) Ashgate Pub Co.

Spenser's Amoretti: Analogies of Love. William C. Johnson. LC 88-43409. 280p. 1990. 43.50 (*0-8387-5164-4*) Bucknell U Pr.

Spenser's Art: A Companion to Book One of "The Faerie Queene" Mark Rose. LC 74-21229. 160p. (C). 1975. 19.00 (*0-674-83193-4*) HUP.

***Spenser's Arthur: The British Arthurian Tradition & "The Faerie Queene"** David A. Summers. LC 96-51557. 286p. 1997. text ed. 47.50 (*0-7618-0659-8*) U Pr of Amer.

Spenser's Boston. Robert B. Parker. 208p. 1994. 22.50 (*1-883402-50-6*) S&S Trade.

Spenser's Cosmic Philosophy of Religion. E. M. Albright. LC 72-100730. 1970. reprint ed. pap. 50.00 (*0-8383-0001-4*) M S G Haskell Hse.

Spenser's Defense of Lord Grey. Harry S. Jones. LC 73-170822. reprint ed. 20.00 (*0-404-03599-X*) AMS Pr.

Spenser's English Rivers. Charles G. Osgood. (Connecticut Academy of Arts & Sciences Ser., Trans.: Vol. 23). 1920. pap. 49.50 (*0-685-22835-5*) Elliots Bks.

Spenser's Famous Flight: A Renaissance Idea of a Literary Career. Patrick Cheney. 352p. 1993. 60.00 (*0-8020-2934-5*) U of Toronto Pr.

Spenser's 'Fierce Warres & Faithful Loves' Martial & Chivalric Symbolism in 'The Faerie Queene' Michael Leslie. (Illus.). 223p. 1984. 79.00 (*0-85991-150-0*) Boydell & Brewer.

Spenser's Images of Life. C. S. Lewis. Ed. by Alastair Fowler. 1978. pap. 19.95 (*0-521-29284-0*) Cambridge U Pr.

***Spenser's Irish Experience: Wilde Fruit & Savage Soyl.** Andrew Hadfield. 240p. 1997. 65.00 (*0-19-818345-3*) OUP.

Spenser's Life & the Subject of Biography. Ed. by Judith H. Anderson et al. LC 96-19287. (Massachusetts Studies in Early Modern Culture). 232p. (C). 1996. 37.50 (*1-55849-050-7*) U of Mass Pr.

Spenser's Moral Allegory. Sean Kane. 250p. 1989. 40.00 (*0-8020-2621-4*) U of Toronto Pr.

Spenser's Pastorals: The Shepheardes Calender & Colin Clout. Nancy J. Hoffman. LC 77-4540. 165p. reprint ed. pap. 47.10 (*0-8357-6614-4*, 2035259) Bks Demand.

Spenser's Poetry & the Reformation Tradition. John N. King. (Illus.). 270p. (C). 1990. text ed. 45.00 (*0-691-06800-3*) Princeton U Pr.

Spenser's Proverb Lore: With Special Reference to His Use of the Sententiae of Leonard Culman & Publilius Syrus. Charles G. Smith. LC 78-85078. 379p. reprint ed. pap. 108.10 (*0-8357-3724-1*, 2036446) Bks Demand.

Spenser's Secret Career. Richard Rambuss. LC 92-8539. (Studies in Renaissance Literature & Culture: No. 3). (Illus.). 200p. (C). 1993. text ed. 54.95 (*0-521-41663-9*) Cambridge U Pr.

Spenser's Theory of Friendship. Charles G. Smith. reprint ed. 27.50 (*0-404-06119-2*) AMS Pr.

Spent Arrow. Inez Evans. Ed. by Robley Evans & Bob Evans. 306p. (YA). (gr. 7-12). 1987. 15.95 (*0-934188-24-6*) Evans Pubns.

Spent Cartridges of Revolution: An Anthropological History of Namiquipa, Chihuahua. Daniel Nugent. LC 93-15997. (Illus.). 242p. 1993. pap. text ed. 15.95 (*0-226-60742-9*) U Ch Pr.

Spent Cartridges of Revolution: An Anthropological History of Namiquipa, Chihuahua. Daniel Nugent. LC 93-15997. (Illus.). 244p. 1993. lib. bdg. 39.95 (*0-226-60741-0*) U Ch Pr.

Spent Matches. Shelly Reuben. 240p. 1996. 21.00 (*0-684-80107-8*) S&S Trade.

Spent Nuclear Fuel Discharges from U. S. Reactors (1993) (Illus.). 240p. (Orig.). (C). 1995. pap. text ed. 4.00 (*0-7881-2070-0*) DIANE Pub.

Spent Nuclear Fuel Heat Transfer: Fuel Casks & Transfer Operations: Proceedings of ASME, Annual Winter Meeting, December 1971. ASME Staff. Ed. by D. J. Groetch & Neil E. Todreas. LC 79-180673. (American Society of Mechanical Engineers Handbook: Vol. 2). 50p. reprint ed. pap. 25.00 (*0-317-09924-8*, 2016901) Bks Demand.

Speranza: A Biography of Lady Wilde. Horace Wyndham. LC 79-8088. reprint ed. 34.50 (*0-404-18396-4*) AMS Pr.

Sperling. Jane T. Clement. 154p. (GER.). 1986. pap. 6.00 (*3-922819-36-2*) Plough.

Sperm Action: Proceedings of the International Seminar on Reproductive Physiology & Sexual Endocrinology, 5th, Brussels, May, 1975. International Seminar on Reproductive Physiology & Sexual Endocrinology Staff. Ed. by P. O. Hubinont. 1976. 78.50 (*3-8055-2244-4*) S Karger.

***Sperm Biology: Index of New Information for Research & Clinical Medicine.** Yoon S. Kim. 150p. 1997. 47.50 (*0-7883-1386-X*); pap. 44.50 (*0-7883-1387-8*) ABBE Pubs Assn.

Sperm Causing Diseases: A Major Medical Breakthrough. Donald E. Tyler. LC 90-84852. 95p. 1990. pap. 25.00 (*1-884981-04-6*) Discov Bks.

Sperm Cell. Ed. by Jean Andre. 1982. lib. bdg. 194.00 (*90-247-2784-7*) Kluwer Ac.

Sperm Competition in Birds: Evolutionary Causes & Consequences. Tim R. Birkhead & A. P. Moller. (Illus.). 282p. 1991. text ed. 94.00 (*0-12-100540-2*); pap. text ed. 49.95 (*0-12-100541-0*) Acad Pr.

***Sperm Donor's Daughter & Other Tales of Modern Families.** Kathryn Trueblood. LC 97-21534. 1998. write for info. (*1-57962-006-X*) Permanent Pr.

***Sperm Wars: The Evolutionary Logic of Love & Lust.** Robin Baker. 1997. pap. 14.00 (*0-465-08180-0*) Basic.

Sperm Wars: The Science of Sex. Robin Baker. 352p. 1996. 25.00 (*0-465-08179-7*) Basic.

Sperm Whale. 54p. 7.50 (*0-318-13866-2*) Ctr Action Endangered.

Sperm Whale. Robert L. Buyer. LC 94-26514. (Illus.). 1995. pap. 12.95 (*0-8117-2521-9*) Stackpole.

Sperm Whale. John F. Prevost. LC 95-12364. (Whales Ser.). (J). (gr. k-3). 1995. lib. bdg. 13.98 (*1-56239-478-9*) Abdo & Dghtrs.

Spermatogenesis - Fertilization Contraception: Molecular, Cellular, & Endocrine Events in Male Reproduction. Ed. by E. Nieschlag et al. LC 92-2300. (Schering Foundation Workshop Ser.: Vol. 4). (Illus.). 528p. 1992. 59.00 (*0-387-55436-X*); write for info. (*3-540-55436-X*) Spr-Verlag.

Spermatogenesis, Genetic Aspects. W. Hennig. (Results & Problems in Cell Differentiation Ser.: Vol. 15). (Illus.). 200p. 1987. 79.95 (*0-387-17959-3*) Spr-Verlag.

Spermatophores: Development, Structure, Biochemical Attributes & Role in the Transfer of Spermatozoa. T. Mann. (Zoophysiology Ser.: Vol. 15). (Illus.). 240p. 1984. 114.95 (*0-387-13583-9*) Spr-Verlag.

Spermatozoa: The Probable Etiology of Gonorrhea, Nonspecific Urethritis & Other Diseases. Donald E. Tyler. LC 90-80362. 90p. 1990. pap. 25.00 (*1-884981-03-8*) Discov Bks.

Spermotoxicos. Alexey Gorbatov. 52p. (Orig.). (RUS.). 1993. pap. 5.99 (*0-9643971-0-2*) Isometry.

Sperner Theory. Konrad Engel. (Encyclopedia of Mathematics & Its Applications Ser.: No. 65). (Illus.). 350p. (C). 1997. text ed. 69.95 (*0-521-45206-6*) Cambridge U Pr.

Spero Learns of Palm Sunday & Jesus' Love. Jane Sarlas-Fontana. (Adventures of Spero the Orthodox Church Mouse Ser.). 28p. (J). (ps-4). 1993. pap. 5.95 (*0-9638336-0-X*) Spero & Me.

Spero's First Orthodox Alphabet Book: The Adventures of Spero...the Orthodox Church Mouse. Jane S. Fontana. (Illus.). 36p. (Orig.). (J). (ps-4). 1998. pap. 7.95 (*0-9638336-1-8*) Spero & Me.

Spertus College of Judaica Yemenite Manuscripts: An Illustrated Catalogue. Norman Golb. LC 72-89585. (Illus.). 116p. (C). 1972. 19.95 (*0-935982-29-9*, NG-01) Spertus Coll.

SPES: Atlas Chronologico de Historia. SPES Staff. 303p. (SPA.). 1980. 19.95 (*0-8288-1495-3*, S2562) Fr & Eur.

Spes--Diccionario Abreviado Latino-Espanol, Espanol-Latino. 9th ed. SPES Staff. 316p. (LAT & SPA.). 1979. 17.95 (*0-8288-5272-3*, S12409) Fr & Eur.

Spes--Diccionario Ilustrado Latino-Espanol, Espanol-Latino. 12th ed. SPES Staff. 800p. (LAT & SPA.). 1979. 24.95 (*0-8288-4836-X*, S17540) Fr & Eur.

Spetsnaz Threat: Can Britain Be Defended? Michael Hickey. (C). 1990. 35.00 (*0-907967-81-7*, Pub. by Inst Euro Def & Strat UK) St Mut.

Speusippi Academici Scriptis. Paul Lang. 89p. 1965. reprint ed. write for info. (*0-318-70952-X*) G Olms Pubs.

***Spew.** Bax. LC 96-90202. 1996. 17.95 (*0-533-11950-2*) Vantage.

Spex Success: Full Length Practice Test. Stanley Zaslau. 156p. (C). 1995. pap. text ed. 34.00 (*1-886468-08-7*) FMSG.

Speycasting: A New Technique. Hugh Falkus. (Illus.). 256p. 1995. 45.00 (*1-85487-331-8*) Lyons & Burford.

Speyside Railways: Exploring the Remains of the Great North of Scotland Railway & Its Environs. R. Burgess & Robert Kinghorn. (Illus.). 128p. 1988. pap. 17.80 (*0-08-036411-X*, Pub. by Aberdeen U Pr) Macmillan.

Spezialwoerterbuch Maschinenwesen. Henry G. Freeman. 207p. (ENG & GER.). 1971. Dictionary of Mechanical Engineering. 95.00 (*0-8288-6481-0*, M-7625) Fr & Eur.

Spezielle Chirurgie der Gallenwege: Aus Chirurgischer Sicht. Ed. by C. E. Zoeckler et al. (Illus.). vi, 328p. 1993. 127.00 (*3-8055-5614-4*) S Karger.

Spezielle Plastische Chirurgie see Handbuch der Plastischen Chirurgie

Sphaera. Franz Boll. xiv, 564p. 1967. reprint ed. 135.00 (*0-318-70880-9*) G Olms Pubs.

Sphagnopsida - Sphagnaceae. H. A. Crum. LC 84-4705. (North American Flora Ser.: No. 2, Pt. 2). (Illus.). 180p. 1984. pap. 18.75 (*0-89327-252-3*) NY Botanical.

Sphecidae (Hymenoptera) of Fennoscandia & Denmark. O. Lomboldt. (Fauna Entomologica Scandinavica Ser.: No. 4). (Illus.). 452p. 1984. text ed. 67.50 (*87-87491-06-0*) Lubrecht & Cramer.

***Sphecidae (Insecta: Hymenoptera)** A. C. Harris. (Fauna of New Zealand Ser.: Vol. 32). (Illus.). 112p. 1994. pap. 33.50 (*0-478-04534-4*, Pub. by Manaaki Whenua NZ) Balogh.

Sphere. Michael Crichton. LC 86-46321. 1987. 27.50 (*0-394-56110-4*) Knopf.

Sphere. Michael Crichton. 1988. mass mkt. 6.99 (*0-345-35314-5*, Del Rey) Ballantine.

***Sphere.** Michael Crichton. 1997. pap. 12.00 (*0-345-41897-2*) Ballantine.

Sphere. large type ed. Michael Crichton. 638p. 1989. 17.95 (*0-7089-1941-3*) Ulverscroft.

Sphere. Michael Crichton. 1993. reprint ed. lib. bdg. 29.95 (*1-56849-127-1*) Buccaneer Bks.

***Sphere.** Michael Crichton. 1996. reprint ed. mass mkt. 6.99 (*0-345-91067-2*) Ballantine.

Sphere: The Form of a Motion. A. R. Ammons. 80p. 1995. pap. 8.95 (*0-393-31310-7*) Norton.

Sphere & Duties of Government. Wilhelm Von Humboldt. Tr. by Joseph Coulthard from GER. (Key Texts Ser.). 218p. 1996. pap. 19.95 (*1-85506-430-8*) Bks Intl VA.

Sphere & the Labyrinth: Avant-Gardes & Architecture from Piranesi to the 1970's. Manfredo Tafuri. Tr. by Pellegrino D'Acierno & Robert Connolly. (Illus.). 400p. 1987. 52.50 (*0-262-20061-9*) MIT Pr.

Sphere & the Labyrinth: Avant-Garde & Architecture from Piranesi to the 1970s. Manfredo Tafuri. Tr. by Pellegrino D'Acierno & Robert Connolly. (Illus.). 394p. 1990. reprint ed. pap. 27.50 (*0-262-70039-5*) MIT Pr.

Sphere of Application of the Vienna Sales Convention. Franco Ferrari. LC 95-20684. 1995. write for info. (*90-411-0957-9*) Kluwer Law Tax Pubs.

Sphere of Glass. Marianne Gruber. Tr. & Afterword by Alexandra Strelka. LC 92-12457. (Studies in Austrian Literature, Culture, & Thought. Translation Ser.). 1993. pap. 14.95 (*0-929497-56-2*) Ariadne CA.

Sphere of Infinity. Dale Henson. 12.95 (*1-56076-865-7*) Random.

***Sphere of Silence Broken: 40 Selected Poems.** Lana E. Wolkonsky. 1996. 19.95 (*0-9653306-1-3*) L E Wolkonsky.

***Sphere of the Cartographer: Descriptive Exhibit Catalog.** Compiled by Scott R. McEathron & Sharon Hill. (American Geographical Society Collection Special Publication: No. 5). (Illus.). vi, 30p. (Orig.). 1996. pap. 3.00 (*1-879281-18-X*) G Meir Lib.

Sphere Packings, Lattices, & Groups. J. C. Conway & N. J. Sloane. (Grundlehren der Mathematischen Wissenschaften Ser.: Vol. 290). (Illus.). 550p. 1987. 89.90 (*0-387-96617-X*) Spr-Verlag.

Sphere Packings, Lattices & Groups. 2nd ed. J. H. Conway & N. J. Sloane. Ed. by M. Berger et al. (Grundlehren der Mathematischen Wissenschaften Ser.: Vol. 290). (Illus.). xliv, 679p. 1992. 90.95 (*0-387-97912-3*) Spr-Verlag.

Sphereland. Dionys Burger. Tr. by Cornelie J. Rheinboldt from FRE. (Illus.). 224p. 1983. pap. 12.00 (*0-06-463574-0*, EH 574) HarpC.

Spheres & Satellites. William B. Martin. (Hi Map Ser.: No. 12). (Illus.). 60p. pap. text ed. 11.99 (*0-614-05314-5*, HM 5612) COMAP Inc.

Spheres of Influence. Corneliu Bogdan & Eugen Preda. (Social Science Monograph Ser.). 179p. 1988. text ed. 60.00 (*0-88033-961-6*) East Eur Monographs.

Spheres of Influence. Sydney Morrell. LC 70-142672. (Essay Index Reprint Ser.). 1977. 23.95 (*0-8369-2197-6*) Ayer.

Spheres of Influence: The Great Powers Partition Europe, from Munich to Yalta. Lloyd C. Gardner. 320p. 1993. text ed. 28.50 (*1-56663-011-8*) I R Dee.

Spheres of Influence: The Great Powers Partition Europe, from Munich to Yalta. Lloyd C. Gardner. 320p. 1994. pap. 14.95 (*1-56663-058-4*, Elephant Paperbacks) I R Dee.

Spheres of Justice: A Defense of Pluralism & Equality. Michael Walzer. LC 82-72409. 368p. 1984. pap. 19.00 (*0-465-08189-4*) Basic.

Spheres of Liberty: Changing Perceptions of Liberty in American Culture. Michael G. Kammen. LC 89-42934. (Illus.). 208p. 1989. pap. 13.95 (*0-8014-9682-9*) Cornell U Pr.

Spheres of Liberty: Changing Perceptions of Liberty in American Culture. Michael G. Kammen. LC 86-40052. 208p. 1986. 13.95 (*0-299-10840-6*) U of Wis Pr.

Spheres of Love: Toward a New Ethics of the Family. Stephen G. Post. LC 94-7166. 208p. 1994. pap. 12.95 (*0-87074-371-6*); text ed. 25.95 (*0-87074-370-8*) SMU Press.

Spherical & Ellipsoidal Harmonics. Ernest W. Hobson. LC 55-233. xi, 500p. 1955. 29.50 (*0-8284-0104-7*) Chelsea Pub.

Spherical Astronomy for Astrologers. George Noonan. 64p. 1974. 5.00 (*0-86690-134-5*, N1357-014) Am Fed Astrologers.

Spherical Harmonics & Tensors for Classical Field Theory. M. N. Jones. (Applied & Engineering Mathematical Ser.). 230p. 1985. text ed. 145.00 (*0-471-90766-9*) Wiley.

***Spherical Means for PDEs.** K. K. Sabelfeld & I. A. Shalimova. (Illus.). 196p. 1996. 144.00 (*90-6764-211-8*, Pub. by VSP NE) Coronet Bks.

Spherical Models. Magnus J. Wenninger. LC 78-58806. 1979. pap. 25.95 (*0-521-29432-0*) Cambridge U Pr.

Spherical Near-Field Antenna Measurements: Theory & Practice. J. E. Hansen et al. Ed. by James R. Wait et al. (Electromagnetic Waves Ser.). 1988. 124.00 (*0-86341-110-X*, EW026) Inst Elect Eng.

Spherical Tensor Operators: Tables of Matrix Elements & Symmetries. J. A. Tuszynski. 332p. (C). 1990. text ed. 48.00 (*981-02-0283-0*) World Scientific Pub.

Sphericity. Mei-Mei Berssenbrugge & Richard Tuttle. Ed. by Patricia Dienstfrey & Rena Rosenwasser. LC 92-37586. (Illus.). 48p. (Orig.). (C). 1993. pap. 14.00 (*0-932716-30-X*) Kelsey St Pr.

Sphericity. deluxe ed. Mei-Mei Berssenbrugge & Richard Tuttle. Ed. by Patricia Dienstfrey & Rena Rosenwasser. LC 92-37586. (Illus.). 48p. (Orig.). (C). 1993. 350.00 (*0-932716-31-8*) Kelsey St Pr.

Sphericles: The Business Oracle. Joanne Black & Christine Roess. Ed. by Judith Yellen. 100p. (Orig.). 1995. pap. 29.95 (*0-9643680-0-5*) Sphericles.

Spheroid Culture in Cancer Research. Bjerkvig. 1991. 99.95 (*0-685-59982-5*, RC267) CRC Pr.

Sphincter of Oddi: Proceedings of the Gastroenterological Symposium, 3rd. Gastroenterological Symposium Staff. Ed. by J. Delmont. (Illus.). 1977. 49.75 (*3-8055-2623-7*) S Karger.

Sphincters: Normal Function - Changes in Diseases. Daniel. 464p. 1992. 184.00 (*0-8493-6748-4*, QP322) CRC Pr.

Sphingolipid Biochemistry. Julian N. Kanfer & Sen-itiroh Hakomori. (Handbook of Lipid Research Ser.: Vol. 3). 500p. 1983. 110.00 (*0-306-41092-3*, Plenum Pr) Plenum.

***Sphingolipid-Mediated Signal Transduction.** Yusuf A. Hannun. (Molecular Biology Intelligence Unit Ser.). 236p. 1997. 89.95 (*1-57059-436-8*) R G Landes.

Sphinx. Robin Cook. 1994. lib. bdg. 21.95 (*1-56849-490-4*) Buccaneer Bks.

Sphinx. Robin Cook. 4.50 (*0-451-14871-1*) NAL-Dutton.

Sphinx. Robin Cook. 320p. 1983. pap. 6.99 (*0-451-15949-7*, Sig) NAL-Dutton.

Sphinx & Mars Face Identified: Crop Circle Analysis Leads to New Findings. Steve Canada. (Inanna Book Ser.: No. 3). 76p. 1994. pap. 7.95 (*1-883424-26-7*) S Canada.

Sphinx & the Lotus: The Egyptian Movement in American Decorative Arts, 1865-1935. Bernadette M. Sigler. LC 89-71727. (Illus.). 55p. (Orig.). 1990. 10.00 (*0-943651-21-2*) Hudson Riv.

Sphinx des Glaces. Jules Verne. 8.95 (*0-686-55951-7*) Fr & Eur.

Sphinx in the City: Urban Life, the Control of Disorder, & Women. Elizabeth Wilson. LC 91-31209. 191p. 1992. 40.00 (*0-520-07850-0*); pap. 15.95 (*0-520-07864-0*) U CA Pr.

Sphota Theory of Language. Harold G. Coward. 1981. 12.00 (*0-8364-0692-3*) S Asia.

Sphota Theory of Language: A Philosophical Analysis. Harold G. Coward. xx, 158p. 1986. 14.00 (*81-208-0181-4*, Pub. by Motilal Banarsidass II) S Asia.

Sphynx des Glaces. Jules Verne. (FRE.). 1988. pap. 16.95 (*0-7859-3142-2*, 2253045721) Fr & Eur.

SPI-SPE Plastics Show & Conference - East: Conference Proceedings, Philadelphia Civic Center, Philadelphia, PA, June 21-23, 1984. The SPI-SPE Connection- An Industry First. Society of Plastics Engineers Staff. 344p. reprint ed. pap. 98.10 (*0-317-30376-7*, 2024725) Bks Demand.

***Spice.** Smithmark Staff. (Little Cookbook Ser.). 1996. 6.98 (*0-7651-9819-3*) Smithmark.

SPICE. 2nd ed. Adel S. Sedra & Gordon W. Roberts. LC 96-33744. (Oxford Series in Electrical & Computer Engineering). (Illus.). 464p. (C). 1996. pap. text ed. 27.00 (*0-19-510842-6*) OUP.

Spice: A Guide to Circuit Simulation & Analysis Using PSPICE. 2nd ed. Paul W. Tuinenga. 224p. 1992. pap. text ed. 30.20 incl. disk (*0-13-735010-4*) P-H.

SPICE: A Guide to Circuit Simulation & Analysis Using PSpice. 3rd ed. Paul W. Tuinenga. LC 94-42313. (C). 1995. pap. text ed. 36.20 (*0-13-158775-7*) P-H.

SPICE: A Guide to Circuit Simulation & Analysis Using PSpice: IBM-PC 3.5" Disk. 3rd ed. Paul W. Tuinenga. LC 94-42393. 1995. pap. text ed. 49.00 incl. disk (*0-13-436049-4*) P-H.

SPICE: A Guide to Circuit Simulation & Analysis Using SPICE. Paul W. Tuinenga. 1988. 8.25 incl. disk (*0-13-834649-6*) P-H.

***Spice: Poems from Hollywood.** 16p. (Orig.). 1997. pap. 5.00 (*0-89642-385-9*) Linden Pubs.

***Spice: The Theory & Practicve of Software Process Improvement & Capability Determination.** Ed. by Khaled El Emam et al. 450p. 1997. 58.00 (*0-8186-7798-8*, BP07798) IEEE Comp Soc.

***S.P.I.C.E. - The Essential Ingredients for Effective Living.** Duffy Spencer. 40p. (Orig.). 1997. pap. 14.95 (*0-9647619-3-9*) BDCI.

Spice Alphabet Book: Herbs, Spices, & Other Natural Flavors. Jerry Pallotta. LC 94-5178. (Jerry Pallotta Alphabet Bks.). (Illus.). 32p. (Orig.). (J). (ps-4). 1994. 14.95 (*0-88106-898-5*); pap. 6.95 (*0-88106-897-7*); lib. bdg. 15.88 (*0-88106-899-3*) Charlesbridge Pub.

Spice & Diet Cookbooklet. 13p. pap. 1.50 (*0-318-19109-1*) Am Spice Trade.

Spice & Spirit: The Complete Kosher Cookbook. Ed. by Esther Blau. LC 89-8053. (Illus.). 1996. reprint ed. 33.00 (*0-8266-0238-X*, Neshei Chabad) Kehot Pubn Soc.

Spice & Spirit of Kosher-Jewish Cooking. Lubavitch Women's Organization Staff. Ed. by Esther Blau. LC 77-72116. (Illus.). 1977. 16.95 (*0-930178-01-7*) Lubavitch Women.

Spice & Spirit of Kosher-Passover Cooking. Ed. by Esther Blau & Cyrel Deitsch. LC 77-72116. (Lubavitch Women's Organization Ser.). 1981. 7.95 (*0-317-14690-4*) Lubavitch Women.

Spice Applications Handbook, Vol. 1. L. G. Meares & C. E. Hymowitz. (Illus.). 200p. (Orig.). (C). 1990. pap. 29.95 (*0-923345-01-9*) INTUSOFT.

***Spice Book.** Arabella Boxer. LC 97-24253. 1997. write for info. (*1-57145-094-7*) Thunder Bay Pr.

Spice Box, Vol. 38. Grace L. Hill. (Grace Livingston Hill Ser.: Vol. 38). 1996. pap. 4.99 (*0-8423-5939-7*) Tyndale.

Spice Box: A Vegetarian Indian Cookbook. Manju S. Singh. LC 81-3179. (Illus.). 221p. 1981. pap. 12.95 (*0-89594-053-1*) Crossing Pr.

***Spice Companion: The Culinary, Cosmetic & Medicinal Uses of Spices.** Richard Craze & People's Medical Society Staff. LC 97-8032. 1997. write for info. (*1-882606-35-3*) Peoples Med Soc.

SPICE for Circuits & Electronics Using PSpice. 2nd ed. Muhammad H. Rashid. LC 94-17481. 1994. pap. text ed. 36.20 (*0-13-124652-6*) P-H Gen Ref & Trav.

SPICE for Electronics. Clifford D. Ferris. (West - Engineering Ser.). 1995. text ed. 30.95 (*0-534-94595-3*) PWS Pubs.

SPICE for Power Electronics. Muhammed H. Rashid. 464p. 1993. pap. text ed. 34.60 (*0-13-030420-4*) P-H.

***Spice Girls.** Anna L. Golden. 1997. pap. 10.95 (*0-345-41965-0*) Ballantine.

***Spice Girls: Giving You Everything.** Rebecca Aplin. (Illus.). 64p. (Orig.). pap. 12.95 (*1-873884-95-8*, VX06000, Pub. by UFO Books UK) Music Sales.

***Spice Ingredients Cookbook: A Definitive Guide to Spices, Spice Blends & Aromatic Seeds & How to Use Them in the Kitchen - with 100 Classic & Contemporary Recipes.** Sallie Morris & Lesley Mackley. (Illus.). 256p. 1997. 32.50 (*1-85967-372-4*, Lorenz Bks) Anness Pub.

Spice Islands. 2nd ed. Kal Muller. (Regional Guides of Indonesia Ser.). (Illus.). 288p. 1994. pap. 15.95 (*0-8442-9899-9*, Passport Bks) NTC Pub Grp.

Spice Islands: Exotic Eastern Indonesia. Kal Muller. 1992. pap. 12.95 (*0-8442-9902-2*, Passport Bks) NTC Pub Grp.

Spice Islands: The Moluccas. Kal Muller. Ed. by David Pickell. (Indonesia Travel Guides Ser.). (Illus.). 200p. 1993. pap. 19.95 (*0-945971-07-9*) Periplus.

Spice Islands Mystery. Alice Poynor. 1989. pap. 3.95 (*9971-972-82-4*) OMF Bks.

Spice It Up! The Art of Making Condiments. Jeffree Itrick. (Illus.). 327p. (Orig.). 1993. pap. 12.95 (*0-9623865-6-1*) Out West Pub.

Spice of Life. Louise F. Underhill. 36p. (Orig.). 1995. pap. 12.50 (*0-614-95921-7*) Underhill Ent.

Spice of Life. Geraldine J. Vernon. Ed. by Ruth Anthony. (Illus.). 49p. (Orig.). 1990. pap. 5.50 (*1-879433-02-8*) First Jewel Pr.

Spice of Life: A Beginner's Guide to the World of Ethnic Vegetarianism. Robyn Fisher. 40p. (Orig.). 1995. reprint ed. pap. text ed., spiral bd. 15.00 (*0-934172-43-9*) WIM Pubns.

***Spice of Life: Biodiversity & the Extinction Crisis.** Chris Howes. 1997. 27.95 (*0-7137-2390-4*, Pub. by Blandford Pr UK) Sterling.

***Spice of Life Cookbook.** Treva Davis. (Illus.). vii, 159p. (Orig.). 1995. spiral bd., pap. 14.95 (*0-9654972-0-8*) Spice of Life Inc.

Spice of Torah. Gutman G. Locks. 318p. 1985. 14.95 (*0-910818-58-4*) Judaica Pr.

Spice of Vegetarian Cooking. Martha R. Shulman. 1990. pap. 10.95 (*0-89281-399-7*) Inner Tradit.

SPICE Practical Device Modeling. R. Kielkowski. 1995. text ed. 55.00 incl. disk (*0-07-911524-1*) McGraw.

Spice Trade: A Bibliographic Guide to Sources of Historical & Economic Information. Jeanie M. Welch. LC 94-22863. (Bibliographies & Indexes in World History Ser.: Vol. 37). 200p. 1994. text ed. 65.00 (*0-313-29117-9*, Greenwood Pr) Greenwood.

Spice Trail: One Hundred Hot Dishes from India to Indonesia. Sandeep Chatterjee. LC 95-12649. 144p. (Orig.). 1995. pap. 15.95 (*0-89815-781-1*) Ten Speed Pr.

Spice up Your Life with Joy. Sandy Petro. (Women's Inductive Bible Study Ser.). 96p. 1990. pap. text ed. 6.50 (*0-89693-817-4*, 6-1817, Victor Bks) Chariot Victor.

***Spicecrafts: Inspirations for Practical Gifts, Crafts & Displays.** Tessa Evelegh. (Illus.). 128p. 1997. 19.95 (*1-85967-494-1*, Lorenz Bks) Anness Pub.

Spiced Laughter: A Collection of Humorous Short Stories. Dalip Singh. (Orig.). (C). 1994. pap. 6.00 (*0-614-01848-X*, Pub. by Sterling Plns Pvt II) S Asia.

***Spiced to Death.** Peter King. 352p. 1997. 23.95 (*0-312-15661-8*) St Martin.

***Spiced with Spirit's Light.** Robert B. Walker. (Orig.). 1997. mass mkt. 5.99 (*1-55197-872-5*, Pub. by Comnwlth Pub CN) Partners Pubs Grp.

Spiced with Wit: Will Rogers' Tomfoolery More Aunt Susan Recipes. Ed. by Patty V. MacDonald. (Illus.). 220p. 1992. 15.95 (*0-9624490-1-6*) P V MacDonald.

Spiceland Quaker Training Centre Nineteen Forty to Nineteen Forty-Six. Stanley Smith. (C). 1989. pap. 50.00 (*1-85072-064-9*, Pub. by W Sessions UK) St Mut.

Spicer & Pegler's Book-Keeping & Accounts. 23th ed. Paul Gee. 608p. 1996. pap. 41.00 (*0-406-99088-3*) MICHIE.

Spicer & Pegler's Executorship Law & Accounts. 24th ed. K. S. Carmichael. boxed write for info. (*0-406-03598-9*, U.K.) MICHIE.

Spicers Peak Road: A New Way to the Downs. J. C. Gill. 80p. (C). 1990. pap. 33.00 (*0-7242-1493-3*, Pub. by Boolarong Pubns AT) St Mut.

Spicer's Practical Auditing. 18th ed. Amyas Mascarenhas & Stuart Turley. 1990. U.K. pap. 34.00 (*0-406-12300-4*, U.K.) MICHIE.

Spices. Jane Wilsher. Ed. by Rebecca Stefoff. (Threads Ser.). (Illus.). 28p. (J). (gr. 2-4). 1995. lib. bdg. 15.93 (*1-56074-062-0*) Garrett Ed Corp.

***Spices, Vol. 1.** John W. Parry. (Story of Spices Ser.). (Illus.). 235p. 1969. pap. text ed. 35.00 (*0-8206-0350-3*) Chem Pub.

Spices: Book on Medicinal Plants. Henry N. Ridley. 449p. (C). 1983. reprint ed. pap. 325.00 (*81-7089-015-2*, Pub. by Intl Bk Distr II) St Mut.

***Spices: Delectables for All Seasons.** Maryjo Koch. LC 96-43799. 96p. 1997. 15.95 (*0-00-225068-3*) Collins SF.

***Spices: Flavor Chemistry & Antioxidant Properties, Vol. 660.** American Chemical Society Staff. Ed. by Sara J. Risch & Chi-Tang Ho. LC 96-52322. (Symposium Ser.: No. 660). (Illus.). 264p. 1997. 99.95 (*0-8412-3495-7*) Am Chemical.

Spices: Their Botanical Origin, Their Chemical Composition, Their Commercial Use Including Seeds, Herbs & Leaves. Joseph K. Jank. 1980. lib. bdg. 49.95 (*0-8490-3111-7*) Gordon Pr.

Spices & Civilizations. Duncan Townson. Ed. by Malcolm Yapp et al. (World History Program Ser.). (Illus.). (YA). (gr. 6-11). 1980. reprint ed. pap. text ed. 4.72 (*0-89908-004-9*) Greenhaven.

Spices & Herbs: Raw, Processed & Prepared. 1991. lib. bdg. 69.95 (*0-8490-4333-6*) Gordon Pr.

Spices & Herbs: Their Lore & Use. Elizabeth S. Hayes. (Illus.). 256p. 1980. reprint ed. pap. 5.95 (*0-486-24026-6*) Dover.

Spices & Seasonings: A Food Technology Handbook. Donna R. Tainter & Anthony T. Grenis. LC 93-7798. (Food Science & Technology Ser.). 226p. 1993. 95.00 (*1-56081-572-8*, VCH) Wiley.

Spices, Condiments & Seasonings. K. Farrell. (Illus.). 496p. 1990. text ed. 94.00 (*0-442-00464-8*) Chapman & Hall.

***Spices, Condiments & Seasonings.** 2nd ed. Farrell. 1991. 99.95 (*0-412-12281-2*) Chapman & Hall.

Spices, Herbs & Edible Fungi. George Charalambous. LC 93-40928. (Developments in Food Science Ser.: Vol. 34). 780p. 1994. 324.25 (*0-444-81761-1*) Elsevier.

Spices in the Indian Ocean World. Ed. by M. N. Pearson. LC 96-238. (Expanding World Ser.: Vol. 11). 400p. 1996. 115.95 (*0-86078-510-6*, Pub. by Variorum UK) Ashgate Pub Co.

***Spices of Life.** Troth Wells. 1997. pap. 17.95 (*0-929005-02-3*, Pub. by Second Story Pr CN) LPC InBook.

Spices of Life: The Well Being Handbook for Older Americans. Ruth Fort. 160p. (Orig.). 1990. pap. 8.00 (*0-936758-27-9*) Ctr Responsive Law.

Spices to the Rescue. Hanna Kroeger. 64p. (Orig.). 1995. pap. 6.00 (*1-883713-12-9*) Hanna Kroeger.

Spicey Circuits: Elements of Computer-Aided Circuit Analysis. Rahul Chattergy. 200p. 1992. 46.95 (*0-8493-7173-2*, QA) CRC Pr.

Spicy Camp Cookbook. Tim O'Keefe. LC 96-48481. (Illus.). 128p. (Orig.). 1996. pap. 12.95 (*0-89732-188-X*) Menasha Ridge.

Spicy Detective Stories. 2nd ed. Jerome Barreaux et al. (Illus.). 96p. 1990. pap. 7.95 (*0-944735-11-8*) Malibu Comics Ent.

Spicy Fat Free Cooking Secrets: Over 125 Flavorful Recipes to Help. Sangita Chandra. LC 96-51111. 304p. 1997. pap. 15.00 (*0-7615-0547-4*) Prima Pub.

***Spicy, Fresh, & Stir-Fried.** Beverly Leblanc. 1996. 15.98 (*0-7858-0557-5*) Bk Sales Inc.

Spicy Horror Stories. Ed. by Tom Mason. 105p. 1990. pap. 9.95 (*0-944735-66-5*) Malibu Comics Ent.

Spicy Mystery Stories: Classic Uncensored Tales of Mysteries & Horror. Ed. by Tom Mason. (Illus.). 112p. 1990. pap. 9.95 (*0-944735-23-1*) Malibu Comics Ent.

Spicy Postcard Book: Naughty 30's Pulp Covers. Ed. by Dave Schreiner. 24p. 1993. pap. 10.95 (*0-87816-171-6*) Kitchen Sink.

Spicy Singles, Vol. I. Crystal K. Pearson. (Illus.). 130p. (Orig.). 1992. pap. text ed. 9.50 (*0-9631853-0-6*) Spicy Singles.

Spicy Tales. Intro. by Tom Mason & John Wooley. (Illus.). 128p. 1991. pap. 9.95 (*0-944735-32-0*) Malibu Comics Ent.

Spicy Western Stories: Uncensored Tales of the Wild West. Ed. by Tom Mason. (Illus.). 107p. 1990. pap. 9.95 (*0-944735-53-3*) Malibu Comics Ent.

Spider. Michael Chinery. LC 90-10941. (Life Story Ser.). (Illus.). 32p. (J). (gr. 4-6). 1991. pap. 4.95 (*0-8167-2109-2*); lib. bdg. 12.95 (*0-8167-2108-4*) Troll Communs.

***Spider.** Sabrina Crewe. LC 96-40493. (Life Cycles Bks.). (J). 1998. write for info. (*0-8172-4380-1*) Raintree Steck-V.

Spider. Margaret Lane. LC 82-71354. (Illus.). 32p. (J). (ps-4). 1983. pap. 13.99 (*0-8037-8303-5*, 0339-110) Dial Bks Young.

Spider. Margaret Lane. (Illus.). 32p. (J). (gr. k-4). 1994. pap. 4.99 (*0-14-055277-4*, Puff Pied Piper) Puffin Bks.

Spider. Patrick McGrath. LC 91-50095. (Vintage Contemporaries Ser.). 224p. 1991. pap. 13.00 (*0-679-73630-1*, Vin) Random.

***Spider.** Jacky Robb & Berny Stringle. (Bang on the Door Ser.). (Illus.). 30p. (J). (ps up). 1997. 4.95 (*0-8431-7929-5*) Price Stern Sloan.

Spider. Robert Sampson. LC 87-71412. 250p. 1987. 32.95 (*0-87972-397-1*); pap. 16.95 (*0-87972-398-X*) Bowling Green Univ Popular Press.

***Spider.** Nancy Shaw. (Illus.). 32p. (J). (gr. 1-4). 1998. lib. bdg. write for info. (*0-88682-968-2*) Creative Ed.

***Spider.** Rebecca Stefoff. LC 97-9131. (Living Things Ser.: No. 3). (Illus.). 32p. (J). (gr. 1 up). 1998. lib. bdg. 14.95 (*0-7614-0442-2*, Benchmark NY) Marshall Cavendish.

Spider. Hans H. Ewers. Tr. by Walter F. Kohn from GER. (Illus.). 54p. 1989. reprint ed. 30.00 (*0-9618918-3-1*); reprint ed. pap. 8.00 (*0-9618918-4-X*) Jwindz Pub.

Spider, Bk. 1. Timothy Truman et al. (Illus.). 1991. 4.95 (*1-56060-099-3*) Eclipse Bks.

Spider, Bk. 2. Timothy Truman et al. (Illus.). 1991. 4.95 (*1-56060-100-0*) Eclipse Bks.

Spider, Bk. 3. Timothy Truman et al. (Illus.). 1991. 4.95 (*1-56060-101-9*) Eclipse Bks.

Spider & a Pig. Carol Morley. LC 92-53215. (J). 1993. 14.95 (*0-316-58405-3*) Little.

Spider & Scorpion. Rod Theodorou & Carole Telford. LC 96-7236. (Discover the Difference Ser.). (Illus.). (J). 1996. write for info. (*1-57572-102-3*) Rigby Interact Libr.

Spider & the Bee: The Artistry of Spenser's Faerie Queene. Judith Dundas. LC 83-18253. (Illus.). 248p. 1986. text ed. 24.95 (*0-252-01118-X*) U of Ill Pr.

***Spider & the Fly: Are You Caught in an Abusive Relationship?** Ruth M. Raffaeli. 1997. pap. 10.95 (*0-440-50733-2*) Dell.

Spider & the Sky God: An Akan Legend. Deborah M. Chocolate. LC 92-13277. (Legends of the World Ser.). (Illus.). 32p. (J). (gr. 2-5). 1992. lib. bdg. 13.95 (*0-8167-2811-9*) Troll Communs.

Spider & the Sky God: An Akan Legend. Deborah M. Chocolate. LC 92-13277. (Legends of the World Ser.). (Illus.). 32p. (J). (gr. 2-5). 1997. pap. 4.95 (*0-8167-2812-7*) Troll Communs.

***Spider Boy.** Ralph J. Fletcher. LC 96-31464. (J). 1997. 14.95 (*0-395-77606-6*, Clarion Bks) HM.

Spider Boy. Gloria Skurzynski. (J). Date not set. 16.00 (*0-02-782923-5*) S&S Trade.

***Spider Communication: Mechanisms & Ecological Significance.** Ed. by Peter N. Witt & Jerome S. Rovner. LC 81-47164. 451p. 1982. reprint ed. pap. 128.60 (*0-608-02926-2*, 2063991) Bks Demand.

***Spider Dan.** Norman Foote. 1997. 10.95 (*1-56352-439-2*) Longstreet Pr Inc.

***Spider Eaters.** Rae Yang. LC 96-31622. (Illus.). 1997. pap. 27.50 (*0-520-20480-8*) U CA Pr.

Spider for Loco Shoat. Douglas C. Jones. 1997. 25.00 (*0-8050-4849-9*) H Holt & Co.

***Spider for Loco Shoat: A Novel.** large type ed. Douglas C. Jones. LC 97-25503. 1997. write for info. (*0-7862-1202-0*) Thorndike Pr.

Spider Garden. Michael Manning. 96p. 1995. pap. 11.95 (*1-56163-117-5*, Amerotica) NBM.

Spider Hider: And Other Creepy Crawly Games to Play. Joe Boddy. (Illus.). 8p. (J). (ps-3). 1994. pap. 2.95 (*0-590-48404-4*, Cartwheel) Scholastic Inc.

Spider in My Sink: On Politics, Love & Children. rev. ed. A. Marie Bangs. (Illus.). 162p. reprint ed. pap. 11.95 (*0-9641427-0-8*) TSInc.

Spider in the Cup: Yoknapatawpha County's Fall into the Unknowable. Barbara Fried. (LeBaron Russell Briggs Prize Honors Essays in English). 64p. 1978. pap. 3.75 (*0-674-83205-1*) HUP.

***Spider in the Sink.** Celestine Sibley. (A Kate Mulcay Mystery Ser.). 1997. 22.50 (*0-06-017515-X*) HarpC.

Spider Is Special. Illus. by Milda Vizbar. (Squeaky Bug Bk.). 20p. (J). 1995. bds. 3.99 (*1-57584-000-6*) Rdrs Dgst Yng Fam.

***Spider Legs.** Anthony. Date not set. write for info. (*0-312-86465-5*) St Martin.

Spider Magic. Illus. by Ruth Young & Mitchell Rose. LC 89-61632. (Rhyme-Fingerplay-Puppet Bk.). 12p. (J). (ps-1). 1990. bds. 5.95 (*1-877779-03-2*) Schneider Educational.

Spider-Man. Funworks Staff. (J). 1996. pap. text ed. 5.98 (*1-57082-337-5*) Mouse Works.

Spider-Man. Stan Lee & Steve Ditko. (Marvel Masterworks Ser.: Vol. 5). 232p. 1988. 34.95 (*0-87135-480-2*) Marvel Entmnt.

Spider-Man. Stan Lee. (Masterworks Ser.). 1994. 34.95 (*0-7851-0051-2*) Marvel Entmnt.

***Spider-Man.** Michael Stewart. (My Favorite Sound Story Bks.). (Illus.). 32p. (J). 1996. write for info. (*0-307-71142-0*, 61142, Golden Books) Western Pub.

Spider-Man: Carnage. David Michelinie. (Illus.). 80p. 1993. pap. 6.95 (*0-87135-971-5*) Marvel Entmnt.

Spider-Man: Carnage in New York. David Michelinie & Dean W. Smith. (Orig.). 1995. mass mkt. 5.99 (*1-57297-019-7*) Blvd Books.

***Spider-Man: Caught in the Web.** Mike Teitelbaum. (Look-Look Bks.). (Illus.). (J). (ps-3). 1997. pap. 2.99 (*0-614-28795-2*, Golden Books) Western Pub.

Spider-Man: Cosmic Adventures. David Michelinie et al. (Illus.). 1993. pap. 19.95 (*0-87135-963-4*) Marvel Entmnt.

Spider Man: Eye of the Storm. Martin Delrio. 1996. mass mkt. 4.99 (*0-671-56851-5*, PB Trade Paper) PB.

Spider-Man: Fear Itself. Gerry Conway et al. 64p. 1992. 12.95 (*0-87135-752-6*) Marvel Entmnt.

Spider-Man: Fearful Symmetry: Kraven's Last Hunt. Mike Zeck et al. 160p. 1989. 19.95 (*0-685-59754-7*) Marvel Entmnt.

Spider-Man: Hooky. Susan Putney & Berni Wrightson. 64p. 1986. 6.95 (*0-87135-154-4*) Marvel Entmnt.

***Spider-Man: Lights, Camera, Danger! with Sound Stix.** Xyz Distributors Staff. (Spider Man Ser.). 1996. pap. text ed. 9.25 (*1-879332-45-0*) XYZ Group.

Spider Man: Magic Eye. (Illus.). 32p. 1996. 14.95 (*0-8362-1332-7*) Andrews & McMeel.

Spider-Man: Maximum Carnage. 336p. 1994. 24.95 (*0-7851-0038-5*) Marvel Entmnt.

Spider-Man: Night of the Lizard. (Favorite Sound Story Bks.). (Illus.). 24p. (J). (ps-3). 1995. 9.95 (*0-307-70925-6*, Golden Books) Western Pub.

Spider-Man: Nothing Stops the Juggernaut. John S. Romita et al. 48p. 1989. 4.95 (*0-87135-572-8*) Marvel Entmnt.

Spider-Man: Origin of Hobgoblin. 160p. 1992. pap. 14.95 (*0-87135-917-0*) Marvel Entmnt.

Spider-Man: Parallel Lives. Gerry Conway. (Illus.). 64p. 1990. 9.95 (*0-87135-573-6*) Marvel Entmnt.

***Spider-Man: Revelations.** Todd Dezago. 1997. pap. text ed. 14.95 (*0-7851-0560-3*) Marvel Entmnt.

Spider-Man: Revenge of Sinister Six. Eric Larsen. (Spider-Man Ser.). 128p. 1994. pap. 15.95 (*0-7851-0047-4*) Marvel Entmnt.

Spider-Man: Round Robin. Al Milgrom. 144p. 1994. pap. 15.95 (*0-7851-0027-X*) Marvel Entmnt.

Spider-Man: Saga of the Alien Costume. DeFalco et al. (Illus.). 192p. 1988. pap. 9.95 (*0-87135-396-2*) Marvel Entmnt.

Spider-Man: Soul of the Hunter. J. M. DeMatteis et al. 48p. 1992. 5.95 (*0-87135-942-1*) Marvel Entmnt.

***Spider-Man: The Annotated Death of Gwen Stacy.** Gerry Conway. 1997. pap. text ed. 7.95 (*0-7851-0260-4*) Marvel Entmnt.

Spider-Man: The Assassin Nation Plot. David Michelinie et al. (Illus.). 144p. 1992. pap. 14.95 (*0-87135-889-1*) Marvel Entmnt.

Spider-Man: The Death of Jean DeWolff. Peter David et al. (Illus.). 96p. 1990. pap. 10.95 (*0-87135-704-6*) Marvel Entmnt.

Spider-Man: The First Adventure. Michael Teitelbaum. (Look-Look Bks.). (J). (ps-3). 1996. pap. text ed. 3.95 (*0-307-12905-5*, Golden Pr) Western Pub.

Spider-Man: The Lost Years. J. M. Dematteis. 1996. pap. text ed. 9.95 (*0-7851-0202-7*) Marvel Entmnt.

Spider-Man: The Octopus Agenda. Diane Duane. LC 96-32951. (Illus.). 352p. 1996. 21.95 (*0-399-14211-8*, Putnam) Putnam Pub Group.

***Spider-Man: The Octopus Agenda.** Diane Duane. 272p. 1997. mass mkt. 6.50 (*1-57297-279-3*) Blvd Books.

Spider-Man: The Postcard Book. Running Press Staff. 64p. 1995. pap. 8.95 (*1-56138-648-0*) Running Pr.

Spider-Man: The Return of Sinister Six. David Michelinie. (Spider-Man Ser.). 144p. 1994. pap. 15.95 (*0-7851-0043-1*) Marvel Entmnt.

Spider-Man: The Return of Venom. David Michelinie. (Illus.). 1993. pap. 12.95 (*0-87135-966-9*) Marvel Entmnt.

***Spider-Man: Valley of the Lizard.** John Vornholt. 1998. mass mkt. write for info. (*1-57297-333-1*) Blvd Books.

Spider-Man - Punisher - Sabretooth: Designer Genes. 64p. 8.95 (*0-87135-977-4*) Marvel Entmnt.

***Spider-Man & the Fantastic Four: Wreckage.** Eric Fein & Pierce Askergren. (Doom's Day Bk.: No. 3). 1997. mass mkt. write for info. (*1-57297-311-0*) Blvd Books.

Spider-Man Clone Genesis. Gerry Conway. (Illus.). 192p. 1995. pap. 16.95 (*0-7851-0134-9*) Marvel Entmnt.

Spider-Man Masterworks. Stan Lee & Steve Ditko. 144p. 1992. pap. 12.95 (*0-87135-902-2*) Marvel Entmnt.

Spider-Man, Sensational. 80p. 1988. 6.95 (*0-87135-514-0*) Marvel Entmnt.

***Spider-Man Unmasked.** Steve Ditko et al. (Illus.). 64p. 1997. pap. 5.95 (*0-7851-0288-4*) Marvel Entmnt.

***Spider-Man Versus the Incredible Hulk, Vol. 2.** Richie Chevat. (J). 1997. mass mkt. 4.99 (*0-671-00797-1*, Archway) PB.

Spider-Man vs. Doctor Doom. David Michelinie. (Illus.). 64p. 1995. pap. 5.95 (*0-7851-0110-1*) Marvel Entmnt.

Spider-Man vs. Greatest Super Villians. Stan Lee. (Illus.). 176p. 1995. pap. 15.95 (*0-7851-0136-5*) Marvel Entmnt.

Spider-Man vs. Green Goblin. John S. Romita. (Illus.). 176p. 1995. pap. 15.95 (*0-7851-0139-X*) Marvel Entmnt.

Spider-Man vs. Venom. David Michelinie & Todd McFarlane. 112p. 1992. pap. 12.95 (*0-87135-616-3*) Marvel Entmnt.

Spider-Man Wedding. Stan Lee. 144p. 1991. pap. 12.95 (*0-87135-770-4*) Marvel Entmnt.

Spider-Man X-Men Team-Ups. Roy Thomas. 1996. pap. 16.95 (*0-7851-0200-0*) Marvel Entmnt.

Spider-Man's Greatest Team-Ups. Stan Lee. 1996. pap. text ed. 16.95 (*0-7851-0203-5*) Marvel Entmnt.

***Spider-Man's Strangest Adventures.** Stan Lee. 1996. pap. text ed. 16.95 (*0-7851-0221-3*) Marvel Entmnt.

Spider Mites: Their Biology, Natural Enemies & Control, 1A. W. Helle & M. W. Sabelis. (World Crop Pests Ser.). 406p. 1986. 260.50 (*0-444-42372-9*) Elsevier.

Spider on the Floor. Raffi. LC 92-33442. (Raffi Songs to Read Ser.). (Illus.). 32p. (J). (ps-3). 1993. 13.00 (*0-517-59381-5*) Crown Bks Yng Read.

Spider on the Floor. Raffi. (J). (ps-3). 1996. pap. 5.99 (*0-517-88553-0*) Crown Bks Yng Read.

Spider Orchid. Celia Fremlin. 192p. 1986. reprint ed. pap. 5.95 (*0-89733-196-6*) Academy Chi Pubs.

Spider Principle: Improving Local Marketing Performance. Ian Linton. (Financial Times Management Ser.). 224p. 1993. 77.50 (*0-273-60328-0*, Pub. by Pitman Pub Ltd UK) Trans-Atl Phila.

Spider Sapphire Mystery. Carolyn Keene. (Nancy Drew Ser.: Vol. 45). (Illus.). 180p. (J). (gr. 4-7). 1967. 5.95 (*0-448-09545-9*, G&D) Putnam Pub Group.

Spider School. Francesca Simon. LC 95-38293. (Illus.). 32p. (J). (ps-3). 1996. pap. 14.99 (*0-8037-1975-2*) Dial Bks Young.

Spider Sisters: We'll Always Have Each Other. John Trent. (Illus.). 32p. (J). 1996. 12.99 (*0-8499-1211-3*) Word Pub.

Spider, Spider. Kate Banks. LC 96-11653. (Illus.). 32p. (J). 1996. 14.00 (*0-374-37151-2*) FS&G.

Spider Spin Me a Web: A Handbook for Fiction Writers. Lawrence Block. 1996. pap. 12.00 (*0-688-14690-2*, Quill) Morrow.

***Spider Spins a Story.** Jill Max. LC 97-18970. (Illus.). 48p. (J). (gr. k up). 1997. lib. bdg. 16.95 (*0-87358-611-5*, Rising Moon Bks) Northland AZ.

***Spider Storch's Carpool Catastrophe.** Gina Willner-Pardo. LC 97-6126. (Illus.). 56p. (J). (gr. 3-5). 1997. lib. bdg. 11.95 (*0-8075-7575-5*) A Whitman.

***Spider Storch's Carpool Catastrophe.** Gina Willner-Pardo. LC 97-6126. (Illus.). 56p. (J). (gr. 3-5). 1997. pap. 3.95 (*0-8075-7576-3*) A Whitman.

***Spider Storch's Teacher Torture.** Gina Willner-Pardo. 56p. (J). (gr. 3-5). 1997. lib. bdg. 11.95 (*0-8075-7577-1*) A Whitman.

***Spider Storch's Teacher Torture.** Gina Willner-Pardo. LC 97-6125. (Illus.). 56p. (J). (gr. 3-5). 1997. pap. 3.95 (*0-8075-7578-X*) A Whitman.

Spider Watching. Vivian French. LC 94-10447. (Read & Wonder Bks.). (Illus.). 32p. (J). (ps up). 1996. reprint ed. pap. 5.99 (*0-7636-0058-X*) Candlewick Pr.

Spider Web. Bernice L. Webb. LC 91-92735. xi, 52p. 1993. pap. 10.00 (*0-9631384-1-3*) Spider Pr.

"Spider Web" Congress & Lobbying in the Age of Grant. Margaret S. Thompson. LC 85-47706. (Illus.). 288p. (C). 1985. 39.95 (*0-8014-1815-1*) Cornell U Pr.

Spider Webs. Margaret Millar. 324p. 1988. pap. 5.95 (*0-930330-76-5*) Intl Polygonics.

S

Spider Who Created the World. Amy MacDonald. LC 95-23181. (Illus.). 32p. (J). (ps-3). 1996. 15.95 (*0-531-09505-3*); lib. bdg. 16.99 (*0-531-08855-3*) Orchard Bks Watts.

Spider Woman: A Story of Navajo Weavers & Chanters. Gladys A. Reichard. (Illus.). 344p. 1968. pap. 12.00 (*0-87380-160-1*) Rio Grande.

***Spider Woman: A Story of Navajo Weavers & Chanters.** Gladys A. Reichard. LC 96-43353. 1997. pap. 16.95 (*0-8263-1793-6*) U of NM Pr.

Spider Woman Stories. G. M. Mullett. LC 78-11556. 142p. 1979. pap. 11.95 (*0-8165-0621-3*) U of Ariz Pr.

Spider Woman's Granddaughters: Traditional Tales & Contemporary Writing by Native American Women. Ed. by Paula G. Allen. 256p. 1990. pap. 12.50 (*0-449-90508-X*, Columbine) Fawcett.

***Spider Worlds, No. 1.** Duncan Long. 112p. (J). (gr. 3-7). 1997. mass mkt. 3.99 (*0-06-106458-0*, Harp PBks) HarpC.

***Spider Worlds, No. 2.** Duncan Long. 112p. (J). (gr. 3-7). 1997. mass mkt. 3.99 (*0-06-106459-9*, Harp PBks) HarpC.

***Spider Worlds, No. 3.** Duncan Long. 112p. (J). (gr. 3-7). 1997. mass mkt. 3.99 (*0-06-106460-2*, Harp PBks) HarpC.

S

Spiderman: Dangerous Dr. Octopus. Michael Teitelbaum. (Look-Look Bks.). (Illus.). 24p. (J). (ps-3). 1995. pap. 2.25 (*0-307-12909-8*, Golden Books) Western Pub.

SpiderMan: The Venom Factor. Diane Duane. 352p. (Orig.). 1995. mass mkt. 5.99 (*1-57297-038-3*) Blvd Books.

Spiderman - Hide, Seek & Destroy. (Open Door Mystery Ser.). 16p. (J). (ps-3). 1995. 7.98 (*1-57082-229-8*) Mouse Works.

Spiderman - Lizard's Deadly Trap. (Pop Up Ser.). 12p. (J). (ps-3). 1995. 6.98 (*1-57082-227-1*) Mouse Works.

Spiderman Cartoon Maker. Knowledge Adventure Staff. 1995. 16.00 (*1-56997-144-7*) Knowldge Adv.

Spiderman Monster Mayhem Book & Rubber Stamp Set. (Stamp Box Book Ser.). 24p. (J). (ps-2). 1995. 6.98 (*1-57082-237-9*) Mouse Works.

Spiders. (Zoobooks Ser.). (J). 1991. lib. bdg. 14.95 (*0-88682-410-9*) Creative Ed.

***Spiders.** (Portrait of the Animal World Ser.). 1996. 10.98 (*0-7651-9968-8*) Smithmark.

***Spiders.** (Eyes on Nature Ser.). (Illus.). 32p. (J). (gr. 1 up). write for info. (*1-56156-462-1*) Kidsbks.

Spiders. Donna Bailey. LC 90-22113. (Animal World Ser.). (Illus.). 32p. (J). (gr. 1-4). 1992. pap. 4.95 (*0-8114-4623-9*); lib. bdg. 21.40 (*0-8114-2648-3*) Raintree Steck-V.

Spiders. Micheal Chinery. (Illus.). 128p. text ed. 19.95 (*1-873580-09-6*, Pub. by Whittet Bks UK) Diamond Farm Bk.

Spiders. Jane Dallinger & Satoshi Kuribayashi. LC 80-27548. (Natural Science Bks.). (Illus.). 48p. (J). (gr. 4 up). 1981. pap. 5.95 (*0-8225-9534-6*, First Ave Edns) Lerner Group.

Spiders. Jane Dallinger. LC 80-27548. (Lerner Natural Science Bks.). (Illus.). 48p. (J). (gr. 4 up). 1981. lib. bdg. 21.50 (*0-8225-1456-7*, Lerner Publctns) Lerner Group.

Spiders. Enid Fisher. (New Creepy Crawly Collection). (Illus.). (J). 1996. lib. bdg. 18.60 (*0-8368-1582-3*) Gareth Stevens Inc.

Spiders. Gail Gibbons. LC 92-54414. (Illus.). 32p. (J). (ps-3). 1993. lib. bdg. 15.95 (*0-8234-1006-4*) Holiday.

Spiders. Gail Gibbons. (Illus.). (J). 1994. pap. 6.95 (*0-8234-1081-1*) Holiday.

***Spiders.** Kevin J. Holmes. LC 97-11966. (Animals Ser.). 1998. write for info. (*1-56065-605-0*) Capstone Pr.

Spiders. Terry Jennings. LC 88-83614. (Junior Science Ser.). (Illus.). 24p. (J). (gr. 1-3). 1989. lib. bdg. 10.40 (*0-531-17176-0*) Denison.

Spiders. Jones. (Easy Theme Reader Ser.). (Illus.). 16p. (J). (ps-1). 1996. pap. 2.49 (*1-55734-926-6*) Tchr Create Mat.

Spiders. Maria A. Julivert. (Fascinating World Of Ser.). (Illus.). 32p. (J). (gr. 3-7). 1996. lib. bdg. 14.95 (*1-56674-166-1*) Forest Hse.

***Spiders.** Maria A. Julivert. (Fascinating World Of...Ser.). (Illus.). 32p. (J). (gr. 2-6). lib. bdg. 14.95 (*1-56674-202-1*) Forest Hse.

***Spiders.** Art L'Hommedieu. LC 97-883. (Information Ser.). (J). 1997. pap. 6.99 (*0-85953-957-1*) Childs Play.

Spiders. Peter Murray. (Nature Bks.). 32p. (J). (gr. 2-6). 1992. lib. bdg. 22.79 (*0-89565-847-X*) Childs World.

Spiders. Illa Podendorf. LC 81-38444. (New True Bks.). (Illus.). 48p. (J). (gr. k-4). 1982. pap. 5.50 (*0-516-41653-7*); lib. bdg. 19.00 (*0-516-01653-9*) Childrens.

Spiders. Jenny E. Tesar. LC 93-10446. (Our Living World Ser.). (Illus.). 64p. (J). (gr. 4-8). 1993. lib. bdg. 18.95 (*1-56711-043-6*) Blackbirch.

Spiders. Wildlife Education, Ltd. Staff. (Illus.). 20p. (Orig.). (YA). (gr. 5 up). 1985. pap. 2.75 (*0-937934-39-9*) Wildlife Educ.

Spiders. Wildlife Education, Ltd. Staff. (Zoobooks Ser.). (Illus.). 24p. (Orig.). (J). 1992. 13.95 (*0-937934-88-7*) Wildlife Educ.

Spiders. 3rd ed. B. J. Kaston et al. (Pictured Key Nature Ser.). 288p. (C). 1978. spiral bd. write for info. (*0-697-04898-5*) Wm C Brown Pubs.

***Spiders: The Great Spinners.** Andreu Llamas & Gabriel Casadevall. LC 97-8486. (Secrets of the Animal World Ser.). (Illus.). (J). 1997. lib. bdg. write for info. (*0-8368-1397-9*) Gareth Stevens Inc.

Spiders: Thematic Unit. Gosnell. (Illus.). 80p. (J). (gr. 3-5). 1995. wbk. ed., pap. text ed. 9.95 (*1-55734-591-0*) Tchr Create Mat.

Spiders: Webs, Behavior, & Evolution. Ed. by William A. Shear. LC 83-42833. (Illus.). 512p. 1986. 69.50 (*0-8047-1203-4*) Stanford U Pr.

Spiders see Books for Young Explorers

Spiders & Flies. Scott Adlerberg. (Orig.). 1997. pap. text ed. 10.95 (*1-57532-068-1*) Press-Tige Pub.

Spiders & Flies: Help for Parents & Teachers of Sexually Abused Children. Donald Hillman & Janice Solex-Tefft. 198p. 12.95 (*0-669-17983-3*, Lexington) Jossey-Bass.

Spiders & Scorpions. Paul Hillyard. (Illus.). 16p. (J). 1995. 10.99 (*0-89577-800-9*) RD Assn.

Spiders & Spinsters: Women & Mythology. Marta Weigle. LC 82-13611. 352p. 1982. pap. 12.95 (*0-8263-0644-6*) U of NM Pr.

***Spiders & Spirits of Petunia Manor.** Yvette A. Schnoeker-Shorb & Terril L. Shorb. LC 96-292728. 64p. (Orig.). 1996. pap. 6.95 (*0-9653849-1-8*) Native West Pr.

Spiders & Switchel. Mary Barile. (Illus.). 62p. 1992. pap. 6.95 (*0-9622903-3-5*) DCHA.

Spiders & Their Kin. rev. ed. Herbert W. Levi & Lorna R. Levi. Ed. by Herbert S. Zim & George S. Fichter. (Golden Guide Ser.). (Illus.). 160p. (J). (ps-3). 1969. pap. 5.50 (*0-307-24021-5*, Golden Books) Western Pub.

Spiders & Webs. Carolyn Lunn. LC 89-34665. (Rookie Readers Ser.). (Illus.). 32p. (J). (ps-2). 1989. pap. 3.50 (*0-516-42093-3*); lib. bdg. 15.00 (*0-516-02093-5*) Childrens.

Spiders Are Not Insects. Allan Fowler. LC 95-39673. (Rookie Read-About Science Ser.). (Illus.). 32p. (J). (ps-2). 1996. lib. bdg. 17.30 (*0-516-06054-6*) Childrens.

Spiders Are Not Insects. Allan Fowler. (Rookie Read-About Science Ser.). (J). 1996. pap. 3.95 (*0-516-20219-7*) Childrens.

***Spiders Are Unique.** Arthur Morton. (Illus.). (J). (gr. k-3). 1992. write for info. (*1-57842-084-9*) Delmas Creat.

***Spiders Are Unique.** Tr. by Manny Phantha. (LAO.). (J). (gr. k-3). 1995. write for info. (*1-57842-087-3*) Delmas Creat.

***Spiders Are Unique.** Tr. by Suon Thach. (CAM.). (J). (gr. k-3). 1994. write for info. (*1-57842-088-1*) Delmas Creat.

***Spiders Everywhere.** Betty L. Baker. (Books for Young Learners). (Illus.). 8p. (Orig.). (J). (gr. k-2). 1997. pap. 5.00 (*1-57274-081-7*) R Owen Pubs.

Spiders from the Virgin Islands. Alexander Petrunkevitch. (Connecticut Academy of Arts & Sciences Ser., Trans.). 1926. pap. 49.50 (*0-685-44361-2*) Elliots Bks.

***Spiders, Giant.** large type ed. Art L'Hommedieu. (Information Ser.). (J). 1997. pap. 13.99 (*0-85953-960-1*) Childs Play.

***Spiders Have Fangs.** Claire Llewellyn. LC 97-1256. (I Didn't Know That Ser.). (Illus.). 32p. (J). (gr. 1-3). 1997. 8.95 (*0-7613-0599-8*, Copper Beech Bks) Millbrook Pr.

***Spiders Have Fangs: And Other Amazing Facts about Arachnids.** Claire Llewellyn. (I Didn't Know That... Ser.). (J). 1997. 14.90 (*0-7613-0610-2*, Copper Beech Bks) Millbrook Pr.

Spider's House. rev. ed. Paul Bowles. LC 82-4195. 410p. (C). 1994. reprint ed. 25.00 (*0-87685-546-X*); reprint ed. pap. 15.00 (*0-87685-545-1*) Black Sparrow.

Spiders in Ecological Webs. David H. Wise. (Cambridge Studies in Ecology). (Illus.). 300p. (C). 1993. text ed. 80.00 (*0-521-32547-1*) Cambridge U Pr.

Spiders in Ecological Webs. David H. Wise. (Studies in Ecology). (Illus.). 341p. (C). 1995. pap. text ed. 28.95 (*0-521-31061-X*) Cambridge U Pr.

Spiders in the House & Workers in the Field. Ernesto Galarza. LC 77-105730. 320p. 1970. reprint ed. pap. 91.20 (*0-608-00885-0*, 2061679) Bks Demand.

Spider's Lunch. Joanna Cole. LC 94-22490. (All Aboard Reading Ser.). (Illus.). 32p. (J). (ps-1). 1995. pap. 3.95 (*0-448-40223-8*, G&D) Putnam Pub Group.

***Spider's Nest.** Kate Scarborough. LC 96-36500. (Watch It Grow Ser.). (Illus.). 24p. (J). (ps-4). 1997. write for info. (*0-7835-4878-8*) Time-Life.

Spiders of Galveston Island (Texas) William F. Rapp. (Novitates Arthropodae Ser.). 10p. 1984. pap. 3.00 (*0-916170-23-3*) J-B Pub.

Spiders of Great Britain & Ireland, 3 vols., Set. Michael J. Roberts. (Illus.). 1985. 400.00 (*90-04-07658-1*) Lubrecht & Cramer.

Spiders of Great Britain & Ireland, 3 vols., Vol. I. Michael J. Roberts. (Illus.). 229p. 1985. write for info. (*0-318-64516-5*) Lubrecht & Cramer.

Spiders of Great Britain & Ireland, 3 vols., Vol. II. Michael J. Roberts. (Illus.). 204p. 1985. write for info. (*0-318-64517-3*) Lubrecht & Cramer.

Spiders of Great Britain & Ireland, 3 vols., Vol. III. Michael J. Roberts. (Illus.). 1985. write for info. (*0-318-64518-1*) Lubrecht & Cramer.

Spiders of Panama. W. Nentwig. (Flora & Fauna Handbook Ser.: No. 12). (Illus.). 274p. (Orig.). 1993. pap. 49.95 (*1-877743-18-6*) Sandhill Crane.

Spiders of Porto Rico. Alexander Petrunkevitch. (Connecticut Academy of Arts & Sciences Ser., Trans.: Vol. 30, Pt. 1). 1929. pap. 75.00 (*0-685-22805-3*) Elliots Bks.

Spiders of Porto Rico. Alexander Petrunkevitch. (Connecticut Academy of Arts & Sciences Ser., Trans.: Vol. 30, Pt. 2). 1930. pap. 75.00 (*0-685-22804-5*) Elliots Bks.

Spiders of Porto Rico. Alexander Petrunkevitch. (Connecticut Academy of Arts & Sciences Ser., Trans.: Vol. 31, Pt. 3). 1930. pap. 75.00 (*0-685-44359-0*) Elliots Bks.

Spiders of the World. Rod Preston-Mafham & Ken Preston-Mafham. 191p. 1984. 25.95 (*0-87196-996-3*) Facts on File.

Spiders, Spiders Everywhere! Rozanne L. Williams. (Emergent Reader Bks.). (Illus.). 16p. (Orig.). (J). (gr. k-2). 1995. pap. 2.49 (*0-916119-95-5*) Creat Teach Pr.

Spiders, Spiders Everywhere! Rozanne L. Williams. (Emergent Reader Big Bks.). (Illus.). 16p. (Orig.). (J). (gr. k-2). 1996. pap. 11.98 (*1-57471-113-X*) Creat Teach Pr.

Spider's Test. Dixie L. McKeone. 1996. pap. 5.99 (*0-7869-0512-3*) TSR Inc.

Spider's Web. Christine Back & Barrie Watts. LC 86-10017. (Stopwatch Ser.). (Illus.). 25p. (J). (gr. k-4). 1986. pap. 3.95 (*0-382-24020-0*, Silver Pr NJ) Silver Burdett Pr.

Spider's Web & Other Stories. J. P. Das. 1990. text ed. 15.95 (*0-7069-4958-7*, Pub. by Vikas II) S Asia.

Spider's Web & Zipper & His Father. Joseph Roth. Tr. by John Hoare from GER. 224p. (ENG.). 1990. 22.95 (*0-87951-345-4*) Overlook Pr.

Spider's Web & Zipper & His Father. Joseph Roth. 224p. 1991. reprint ed. pap. 11.95 (*0-87951-361-6*) Overlook Pr.

Spidertown. Abraham Rodriguez, Jr. 336p. 1994. reprint ed. pap. 11.95 (*0-14-023838-7*, Penguin Bks) Viking Penguin.

Spidertown: A Novel. Abraham Rodriguez, Jr. LC 92-34088. 336p. 1993. 19.95 (*1-56282-845-2*) Hyperion.

***Spiderweb.** Susan Berman. 1997. mass mkt. 5.99 (*0-380-78180-8*) Avon.

***Spiderweb for Two: A Melendy Mystery.** Elizabeth Enright. LC 97-13629. 1997. pap. 4.99 (*0-14-038396-4*) Viking Penguin.

Spiderweb Trail. Bob Terrell. Ed. by Lorna Bolkey et al. LC 95-16879. (Illus.). 160p. (Orig.). 1995. pap. 9.95 (*1-57090-022-1*) Alexander Bks.

Spiderwebs to Skyscrapers: The Science of Structure. David Darling. LC 91-4001. (Experiment! Ser.). (Illus.). 60p. (J). (gr. 4-6). 1991. lib. bdg. 13.95 (*0-87518-478-2*, Dillon Silver Burdett) Silver Burdett Pr.

Spiderwoman's Dream. Alicia Otis. LC 87-1944. 64p. (Orig.). 1987. pap. 7.95 (*0-86534-099-4*) Sunstone Pr.

Spiderwoman's Third Avenue Rhapsody. Mary O'Donnell. 90p. 9300. pap. 11.95 (*1-897648-00-6*, Pub. by Salmon Poetry IE) Dufour.

Spiderwort. Damon R. Galeassi. LC 93-41116. 250p. 1994. 15.95 (*0-944957-43-9*) Rivercross Pub.

Spides Mites: Their Biology & Control, Pt. B. W. Helle & M. W. Sabelis. (World Crop Pests Ser.: Vol. 1B). 458p. 1986. 273.00 (*0-444-42374-5*) Elsevier.

Spiegel. Helene Zimmer-Loew & Anne Moss. 168p. (GER.). 1995. pap. 39.95 incl. audio (*0-8442-2281-X*) NTC Pub Grp.

Spiegel: Aktuelle Themen in der Bundesrepublik Deutschland: Advanced. Helene Zimmer-Loew & Anne Moss. (GER.). (YA). 1993. teacher ed. 7.95 (*0-8442-2282-8*, Natl Textbk) NTC Pub Grp.

Spiegel: Aktuelle Themen in der Bundesrepublik Deutschland: Advanced. Helene Zimmer-Loew & Anne Moss. (GER.). (YA). 1994. pap. text ed. 23.95 (*0-8442-2280-1*, Natl Textbk) NTC Pub Grp.

Spiegel: Aktuelle Themen in der Bundesrepublik Deutschland: Advanced. Helene Zimmer-Loew & Anne Moss. (GER.). (YA). 1995. 46.60 incl. audio (*0-8325-2283-X*, Natl Textbk) NTC Pub Grp.

Spiegel Story. Leo B. Brawand. (Illus.). 80p. (GER.). 33.50 (*0-08-037257-0*, Pergamon Pr) Elsevier.

Spiegelschrift: Zur Lage der Kunst in Berlin. M. Flugge et al. 140p. 1994. pap. text ed. 8.00 (*3-364-00267-3*) Gordon & Breach.

Spiegelungen. Ernst Renk. 291p. (GER.). 1985. text ed. 29.50 (*0-930329-40-6*) Kabel Pubs.

Spiegelungen der Seele: Projektion und Innere Sammlung see Projection & Re-Collection in Jungian Psychology: Reflections of the Soul

Spiel im Morgengrauen. Arthur Schnitzler. 164p. (GER.). 1996. pap. 11.75 (*3-596-29101-1*, Pub. by Fischer Taschbch Verlag GW) Intl Bk Import.

Spiel Mit Albert! (Illus.). (GER.). (J). 1996. pap. 10.95 (*88-8148-060-3*, Pub. by European Lang IT) Distribks Inc.

Spiel und Konversation im Barock: Untersuchungen zu Harsdoerffers Gespraechspielen. Rosmarie Zeller. LC 73-75496. (Quellen und Forschungen zur Sprach und Kulturgeschichte der Germanischen Voelker Ser.: NF 58). 198p. (C). 1974. 96.95 (*3-11-004245-2*) De Gruyter.

Spiel und Sprache. Ed. by Armin Wishard & Edward Diller. (Illus.). (Orig.). (C). 1971. pap. text ed. 17.95 (*0-393-09545-2*) Norton.

Spiel vor der Menge. Donna C. Van Handle. (American University Studies: Germanic Languages & Literature: Ser. I, Vol. 44). 172p. (GER.). 1986. text ed. 24.50 (*0-8204-0260-5*) P Lang Pubng.

Spielanleitung fuer die Maultrommel. Josef Klima. (Illus.). 16p. (GER.). pap. 4.50 (*0-317-28713-3*, Virtuoso Jawharp Pubns) Intl Fanorona.

Spielberg: The Man, the Movies, the Mythology. Frank Sanello. LC 95-39329. 256p. 1996. 22.95 (*0-87833-911-6*) Taylor Pub.

***Spielberg's Holocaust: Critical Perspectives on Schindler's List.** Yosefa Loshitzky. LC 96-35930. 1997. write for info. (*0-253-33232-X*); pap. write for info. (*0-253-21098-4*) Ind U Pr.

Spiele Gute Eroffnungszuge! Edmar Mednis. (Praxis Schach Ser.: Bd. 6). 120p. (GER.). 1992. write for info. (*3-283-00250-9*) G Olms Pubs.

Spielend Deutsch Lernen: Interaktive Arbeitsblatter fur Anfanger Bis Fortgeschrittene. J. Sanchez Benito et al. 96p. (SPA.). 1996. 29.95 (*3-468-45558-5*); 29.95 (*3-468-49988-4*) Langenscheidt.

Spielman's Original Scroll Saw Patterns. Patrick Spielman & Patricia Spielman. LC 89-49314. (Illus.). 224p. (Orig.). 1990. pap. 14.95 (*0-8069-7214-9*) Sterling.

Spieltexte der Wanderbuehne, 4 vols. Ed. by Martin Brauneck. Incl. Vol. 1. Englische Comedue und Tragedean. (C). 1970. 469.25 (*3-11-002695-3*); Vol. 2. Liebeskampf. (C). 1975. 450.00 (*3-11-005716-6*); Vol. 3. Schau-Buehne Englischen und Frantzosischer Comoedianten, 1670. (C). 1970. 411.55 (*3-11-004685-7*); 4. Schau-Buehne Englischen und Frantzosischer Comoedianten, 1670. 1972. 423.10 (*3-11-004001-8*); (Ausgaben Deutscher Literatur des XV bis XVIII Jahrhunderts Ser.). (C). write for info. (*0-318-51649-7*) De Gruyter.

Spies: A Narrative Encyclopedia of Dirty Deeds & Double Dealing from Biblical Times to Today. Jay R. Nash. (Illus.). 640p. (Orig.). 1996. pap. 27.50 (*0-87131-790-7*) M Evans.

Spies: The Secret Agents Who Changed the Course of History. Ernest Volkman. 288p. 1994. text ed. 24.95 (*0-471-55714-5*) Wiley.

***Spies: The Secret Agents Who Changed the Course of History.** Ernest Volkman. 1997. mass mkt. 5.99 (*0-471-19361-5*) Wiley.

Spies: The Secret Agents Who Changed the Course of History. Ernest Volkman. LC 93-13786. 304p. 1996. pap. text ed. 16.95 (*0-471-15403-2*) Wiley.

Spies & Detectives: Cut & Color Activity Book. (J). 1989. pap. 3.99 (*0-517-68795-X*) Random Hse Value.

Spies & Lies. Carolyn Keene. Ed. by Anne Greenberg. (Nancy Drew & Hardy Boys Supermystery Ser.). 224p. (YA). 1992. mass mkt. 3.99 (*0-671-73125-4*, Archway) PB.

Spies & Provocateurs: A Worldwide Encyclopedia of Persons Conducting Espionage & Covert Action, 1946-1991. Wendell L. Minnick. LC 92-50312. 320p. 1992. lib. bdg. 57.50 (*0-89950-746-8*) McFarland & Co.

Spies & Sleuths. CineBooks Staff. LC 88-71573. (CineBooks Home Library Ser.: No. 1). 224p. (Orig.). 1997. pap. 8.95 (*0-933997-18-3*) CineBks.

Spies & Spymasters of the Civil War. Donald E. Markle. 244p. 1995. pap. 11.95 (*0-7818-0428-0*) Hippocrene Bks.

***Spies, Black Ties & Mango Pies: Stories & Recipes from CIA Families All over the World.** Ed. by F. Clifton Berry, Jr. et al. LC 97-21347. 208p. 1997. 19.95 (*1-885352-80-8*) Community Comm.

Spies in the Blue Smoke: Stories. G. W. Hawkes. 152p. (C). 1992. 22.50 (*0-8262-0823-1*) U of Mo Pr.

Spies, Incorporated. Debra Hess. LC 93-34116. (Spy from Outer Space Ser.: Vol. 4). (Illus.). 128p. (J). (gr. 3-6). 1994. pap. 3.50 (*1-56282-683-2*) Hyprn Child.

Spies Like Us. Hugh Lunn. 1995. pap. 16.95 (*0-7022-2757-9*, Pub. by Univ Queensland Pr AT) Intl Spec Bk.

***Spies of the Confederacy.** John E. Bakeless. LC 97-23084. 1997. pap. write for info. (*0-486-29865-5*) Dover.

***Spies of the Kaiser: Plotting the Downfall of England.** 2nd ed. William Le Queux. (Classics in Espionage Ser.). (Illus.). 256p. 1996. 35.00 (*0-7146-4728-4*); pap. 16.95 (*0-7146-4278-9*) Intl Spec Bk.

Spies on the Devils Belt. Betsy Haynes. (J). pap. 1.75 (*0-590-04006-5*) Scholastic Inc.

Spies on Wheels. Ann Gerfin. 1995. 14.00 (*0-922242-89-5*) Bepuzzled.

Spies, Scouts & Raiders. (Civil War Ser.). (Illus.). 176p. 1985. 18.95 (*0-8094-4712-6*); lib. bdg. 25.93 (*0-8094-4713-4*) Time-Life.

Spies, Thumbsuckers, Etc. deluxe ed. Ross Thomas. 50p. 1989. 50.00 (*0-935716-50-5*) Lord John.

Spies Without Cloaks: The KGB's Successors. Amy Knight. (Illus.). 328p. 1996. 24.95 (*0-691-02577-0*) Princeton U Pr.

***Spies Without Cloaks: The KGB's Successors.** Amy Knight. 1998. pap. text ed. 14.95 (*0-691-01718-2*) Princeton U Pr.

Spiesser-Spiegel. George Grosz. LC 68-9232. (Contemporary Art Ser.). (Illus.). 1968. reprint ed. 18.95 (*0-405-00720-5*) Ayer.

***Spike.** Paulette Bogan. (J). Date not set. 15.95 (*0-399-23163-3*) Putnam Pub Group.

Spike. Loretta Castellarin & Ken Roberts. (Degrassi Book Ser.). (J). (gr. 7-9). 1995. pap. 4.95 (*1-55028-113-5*) Formac Dist Ltd.

Spike. Loretta Castellarin & Ken Roberts. (Degrassi Book Ser.). (J). (gr. 7-9). 1995. bds. 16.95 (*1-55028-115-1*) Formac Dist Ltd.

Spike. Mark Dunster. (Rin Ser.: Pt. 42 - Nightpeople Pt. 2). 37p. (Orig.). 1986. pap. 5.00 (*0-89642-141-4*) Linden Pubs.

Spike. Katherine Potter. LC 93-11476. (J). 1994. 15.00 (*0-671-86733-4*, S&S Bks Young Read) S&S Childrens.

Spike. Dave Sargent. 199p. (YA). 1992. write for info. (*0-318-69581-2*) Ozark Pub.

Spike. Gordon Spurlock. (Illus.). 120p. (Orig.). 1994. pap. 12.95 (*0-9642478-0-1*) Minotaur Comics.

Spike & Chain. C. V. Gruzanski. 9.95 (*0-685-38452-7*) Wehman.

Spike & Chain see Ninja Weapons: Chain & Shuriken

Spike & Mike & the Treasure Hunt. Mary Packard. LC 92-50295. (Pictureback Ser.). (J). 1993. write for info. (*0-679-93936-9*) Random Bks Yng Read.

Spike & the Cowboy Band. John Patience. (Tales from Fern Hollow Ser.). (Illus.). (J). (ps-3). Date not set. 4.95 (*1-56987-113-2*) Landoll.

Spike & the Professor. Tony Hickey. LC 89-51005. (Illus.). 160p. (Orig.). (J). (gr. 4-7). 1989. pap. 6.95 (*1-85371-039-3*, Pub. by Poolbeg Pr IE) Dufour.

Spike & Zola: Patterns Designed for Laughter, & Applique, Painting, or Stenciling. Donna F. Collins. LC 93-34458. 1993. 9.95 (*0-89145-828-X*) Collector Bks.

Spike Jones & His City Slickers: An Illustrated Biography. Jordan R. Young. LC 84-12051. (Illus.). 192p. (Orig.). 1984. 49.95 (*0-940410-73-7*, Disharmony Bks) Past Times.

An Asterisk (*) at the beginning of an entry indicates that the title is appearing in BIP for the first time.

Spike Jones off the Record: The Man Who Murdered Music. rev. ed. Jordan R. Young. (Vintage Comedy Ser.). (Illus.). 416p. 1994. pap. 17.95 (*0-940410-27-3*, Moonstone Pr) Past Times.

Spike Lee. Kathleen F. Chapman. LC 93-49821. (Ovations Ser.). (Illus.). 32p. (YA). (gr. 4 up). 1998. lib. bdg. 14.95 (*0-88682-697-7*) Creative Ed.

Spike Lee. Alex Patterson. 248p. (Orig.). 1992. mass mkt. 4.99 (*0-380-76994-8*) Avon.

***Spike Lee: By Any Means Necessary.** Jim Haskins. LC 96-41774. (Illus.). 160p. (YA). (gr. 7 up). 1997. 15.95 (*0-8027-8494-1*); lib. bdg. 16.85 (*0-8027-8496-8*) Walker & Co.

Spike Lee: Filmmaker. James E. Hardy. Ed. by Nathan I. Huggins. (Black Americans of Achievement Ser.). (Illus.). 127p. (YA). (gr. 5 up). 1994. lib. bdg. 19.95 (*0-7910-1875-X*) Chelsea Hse.

***Spike Lee: Filmmaker.** James E. Hardy. Ed. by Nathan I. Huggins. (Black Americans of Achievement Ser.). (Illus.). 144p. (YA). (gr. 5 up). 1995. pap. 8.95 (*0-7910-1904-7*) Chelsea Hse.

Spike Lee & the African American Filmmakers: A Choice of Colors. K. Maurice Jones. LC 96-4851. (Illus.). 144p. (YA). (gr. 7 up). 1996. lib. bdg. 17.90 (*1-56294-518-1*) Millbrook Pr.

***Spike Lee's "Do the Right Thing"** Ed. by Mark A. Reid. (Film Handbooks Ser.). (Illus.). 208p. (C). 1997. 49.95 (*0-521-55076-9*) Cambridge U Pr.

***Spike Lee's "Do the Right Thing"** Ed. by Mark A. Reid. (Film Handbooks Ser.). (Illus.). 208p. (C). 1997. pap. 13.95 (*0-521-55954-5*) Cambridge U Pr.

Spike Magazine: The Air of Hell Does Not Permit Hymns. Federico Garcia Lorca et al. Ed. by Darin Daniel. Tr. by Walt Curtis from SPA. (Spike Ser.: No. 4). (Illus.). 96p. (Orig.). 1994. pap. 8.00 (*1-885089-00-7*) Cityful Pr.

Spike, Mike, Slackers & Dykes: A Guided Tour Across a Decade of American Independent Cinema. John Pierson & Kevin Smith. (Illus.). 352p. 1996. 22.95 (*0-7868-6189-4*) Hyperion.

Spike, Mike, Slackers & Dykes: A Guided Tour Across a Decade of American Independent Cinema. John Pierson. (Illus.). 384p. 1997. pap. 12.95 (*0-7868-8222-0*) Hyperion.

Spike Milligan: A Celebration. Roger Sawyer. (Illus.). 160p. 1996. 14.95 (*1-85227-561-8*, Pub. by Virgin Pub UK) London Brdge.

Spike Mosquito & the Flying Ants. Jack Wilkinson & Orrin Tubbs. Ed. by Debbie Haigis. (Spike Mosquito Adventure Ser.). (Illus.). (Orig.). (J). (gr. 1-6). 1991. pap. write for info. (*0-9629543-0-6*) Maine Heritage.

***Spike of Swift River.** unabridged ed. Jack O'Brien. 200p. 1997. reprint ed. pap. 14.95 (*1-57002-043-4*) Univ Publng Hse.

Spike Tailed Dinosaur Stegosar. Michael Berenstain. (Golden Look-Look Bks.). (Illus.). (J). (ps-3). 1989. pap. write for info. (*0-307-11978-5*, Golden Books) Western Pub.

Spike, the Black Wolf. Dave Sargent. (Illus.). 191p. (J). 1996. 18.95 (*1-56763-098-7*); pap. 4.95 (*1-56763-028-6*) Ozark Pub.

Spiked: The Short Life & Death of the National News Council - A Twentieth Century Fund Paper. Patrick Brogan. 129p. 1985. pap. text ed. 8.00 (*0-87078-162-6*) TCFP-PPP.

Spikes: Exploring the Neural Code. Fred Rieke et al. LC 95-46161. (Computational Neuroscience Ser.). (Illus.). 395p. 1996. 45.00 (*0-262-18174-6*, Bradford Bks) MIT Pr.

Spike's Christmas. Drescher. (J). 1997. write for info. (*0-15-200213-8*) HarBrace.

Spiks. Pedro J. Soto. Tr. & Intro. by Victoria Ortiz. LC 73-8057. 96p. 1974. pap. 8.00 (*0-85345-331-4*, PB3314) Monthly Rev.

Spill. Les Standiford. 352p. 1993. mass mkt. 4.99 (*0-06-100669-6*, Harp PBks) HarpC.

Spill! The Story of the Exxon Valdez. Terry Carr. LC 90-13104. (Illus.). 64p. (YA). (gr. 5-8). 1991. lib. bdg. 28.80 (*0-531-10998-4*) Watts.

***Spill-Movie Tie-In.** Les Standiford. mass mkt. 4.99 (*0-06-101103-7*, Harp PBks) HarpC.

Spill Prevention, 4 vols., Vol. 4, Module 4. Multimedia Development Services Staff. (Safety, Health & Environmental Fundamentals Ser.). (Illus.). (Orig.). (C). 1996. teacher ed., text ed. 65.00 (*1-57431-124-7*); pap. text ed. 30.00 (*1-57431-123-9*) Tech Trng Systs.

Spill Prevention & Fail-Safe Engineering for Petroleum & Related Products. J. L. Goodier et al. LC 83-2204. (Pollution Technology Review Ser.: No. 100). (Illus.). 329p. (Orig.). 1983. 36.00 (*0-8155-0944-8*) Noyes.

Spill Prevention, Control & Countermeasure. 1995. lib. bdg. 256.95 (*0-8490-7535-1*) Gordon Pr.

***Spill Reporting Procedures Guide: 1997 Edition.** Ed. by Jeffrey J. Kimmel. 408p. Date not set. ring bd. 215.00 (*1-57018-051-2*, 9051) BNA Books.

***Spillage of Mercury.** Neil Rollinson. 64p. 1997. pap. 14.95 (*0-224-04008-1*, Pub. by Jonathan Cape UK) Trafalgar.

Spilled Milk, Vol. 1. Intro. by Charlotte Weisman. LC 85-8860. (Special Collection from the Journal of Commercial Bank Lending). 76p. (Orig.). 1985. pap. 16.75 (*0-936742-22-4*) Robt Morris Assocs.

Spilled Milk: A Special Collection, Vol. 2. Journal of Commercial Bank Lending Staff. LC 85-8860. 72p. 1987. pap. 16.75 (*0-936742-44-5*) Robt Morris Assocs.

Spilled Nightmares, Revelations & Reflections. Studio Museum in Harlem Staff & Susan Fleminger. (Illus.). 24p. (Orig.). 1987. pap. 10.00 (*0-942949-00-5*) Studio Mus Harlem.

Spillikins. James O. Hannay. LC 72-107707. (Essay Index Reprint Ser.). 1977. 19.95 (*0-8369-1509-7*) Ayer.

Spillin' the Beans: Behind the Scenes at L. L. Bean. 2nd ed. Carlene Griffin. LC 93-90057. 144p. 1993. pap. 12.95 (*0-9635996-3-1*) C Griffin.

Spilling the Beans: Loteria Chicana. Jose A. Burciaga. 1994. pap. 12.95 (*1-877741-11-6*) J Odell Editions.

Spillville: A Collaboration. Patricia Hampl. LC 86-60749. (Seeing Double Collaborative Book). (Illus.). 112p. (Orig.). 1987. 25.00 (*0-915943-18-2*); pap. 14.95 (*0-915943-17-4*) Milkweed Ed.

Spin. Donald E. Axinn. 1991. 19.95 (*0-88268-125-7*) Station Hill Pr.

Spin. Tim Geary. 416p. 1996. 10.95 (*0-340-61369-6*, Pub. by H & S UK) Trafalgar.

Spin. Donald E. Axinn. 328p. 1994. reprint ed. pap. 11.95 (*1-55970-250-8*) Arcade Pub Inc.

Spin a Soft Black Song. rev. ed. Nikki Giovanni. (Illus.). (J). (gr. k up). 1987. pap. 3.95 (*0-374-46469-3*, Sunburst Bks) FS&G.

Spin-a-Story, the Haunted Banana & Other Wacky Mysteries. Jennifer Daniel. (Spin-a-Story Ser.). (Illus.). 24p. (Orig.). (J). (gr. 4-7). 1990. pap. 2.95 (*1-878890-02-6*) Palisades Prodns.

Spin-a-Story, Twenty Thousand French Fries under the Sea & Other Crazy Classics. Jennifer Daniel. (Spin-a-Story Ser.). (Illus.). 24p. (J). (gr. 4-7). 1990. pap. 2.95 (*1-878890-01-8*) Palisades Prodns.

SPIN Alternative Record Guide. Ed. by Eric Weisbard & Craig Marks. LC 95-15753. 460p. 1995. pap. 20.00 (*0-679-75574-8*, Vin) Random.

Spin & Isospin in Nuclear Interactions. Ed. by S. W. Wissink et al. (Illus.). 536p. 1992. 135.00 (*0-306-44111-X*, Plenum Pr) Plenum.

Spin & Polarization Dynamics in Nuclear & Particle Physics. Ed. by Asim O. Barut et al. 372p. (C). 1990. text ed. 141.00 (*981-02-0018-8*) World Scientific Pub.

Spin & Symmetry in the Standard Model. B. A. Campbell et al. 600p. 1992. text ed. 121.00 (*981-02-1034-5*) World Scientific Pub.

Spin & Torsion in Gravitation. Venzo De Sabbata & C. Sivaram. 328p. 1994. text ed. 74.00 (*981-02-1766-8*) World Scientific Pub.

***Spin Choreography: Basic Steps in High Resolution NMR.** Ray Freeman. LC 96-44630. (Illus.). 432p. (Orig.). (C). 1996. text ed. 58.50 (*0-935702-95-4*, Pub. by Spektrum Acad UK) Univ Sci Bks.

Spin Control: The White House Office of Communications & the Management of Presidential News. 2nd rev. ed. John A. Maltese. LC 93-29368. (Illus.). xii, 323p. (C). 1994. pap. 16.95 (*0-8078-4452-7*) U of NC Pr.

Spin Doctors: Turn It Upside down with Notes & Tablature. 96p. 1994. otabind 19.95 (*0-7935-3735-5*, 00694962) H Leonard.

Spin Doctors: Up for Grabs. 88p. 1995. otabind 14.95 (*0-7935-3286-8*, 00694917) H Leonard.

Spin Dry. Greg Hollingshead. (Fiction Ser.). 210p. 1992. 19.95 (*0-88962-518-2*) Mosaic.

Spin Eigenfunctions: Construction & Use. Ed. by Ruben Pauncz. LC 78-27632. (Illus.). 386p. 1979. 95.00 (*0-306-40141-X*, Plenum Pr) Plenum.

Spin Fluctuations in Itinerant Electron Magnetism. T. Moriya. (Solid-State Sciences Ser.: Vol. 56). (Illus.). 260p. 1985. 88.95 (*0-387-15422-1*) Spr-Verlag.

Spin Geometry. H. Blaine Lawson, Jr. & Marie-Louise Michelsohn. 450p. 1990. text ed. 69.50 (*0-691-08542-0*) Princeton U Pr.

Spin Glass Theory & Beyond. M. Mezard et al. (Lecture Notes in Physics Ser.: Vol. 9). 476p. 1987. text ed. 99.00 (*9971-5-0115-5*); pap. text ed. 55.00 (*9971-5-0116-3*) World Scientific Pub.

Spin Glasses. K. H. Fischer & J. A. Hertz. (Cambridge Studies in Magnetism: No. 1). (Illus.). 450p. (C). 1991. 94.95 (*0-521-34296-1*) Cambridge U Pr.

Spin Glasses. K. H. Fischer & J. A. Hertz. (Cambridge Studies in Magnetism: No. 1). (Illus.). 418p. (C). 1993. pap. text ed. 38.95 (*0-521-44777-1*) Cambridge U Pr.

Spin Glasses: An Experimental Introduction. John A. Mydosh. 280p. 1993. 85.00 (*0-7484-0038-9*) Taylor & Francis.

Spin Glasses & Biology. Ed. by D. Stein. (Series on Directions in Condensed Matter Physics: Vol. 6). 550p. 1992. text ed. 71.00 (*9971-5-0537-1*); pap. text ed. 36.00 (*9971-5-0538-X*) World Scientific Pub.

Spin Glasses & Other Frustrated Systems. D. Chowdhury. 200p. 1986. text ed. 40.00 (*9971-5-0029-9*) World Scientific Pub.

Spin Glasses & Other Frustrated Systems. Debashish Chowdhury. LC 86-28923. (Princeton Series in Physics). (Illus.). 399p. 1986. reprint ed. pap. 113.80 (*0-7837-9496-7*, 2060240) Bks Demand.

***Spin Glasses & Random Fields.** P. Young. 400p. 1997. 86.00 (*981-02-3183-0*) World Scientific Pub.

Spin Labeling Methods in Molecular Biology. Gerktis Likhtenshtefin. LC 76-15500. 271p. reprint ed. pap. 77.30 (*0-317-28454-1*, 2055151) Bks Demand.

Spin Management & Recovery. Michael C. Love. (Illus.). 224p. 1996. text ed. 36.95 (*0-07-038809-1*); pap. text ed. 24.95 (*0-07-038810-5*) McGraw.

Spin Observables of Nuclear Probes. Ed. by C. J. Horowitz et al. (Illus.). 472p. 1988. 110.00 (*0-306-43110-6*, Plenum Pr) Plenum.

Spin Off. Catharine T. Herford. 60p. 1984. 15.00 (*0-7212-0690-5*, Pub. by Regency Press UK) St Mut.

Spin-Off, Dual-Use & Conversion: Fashion or Reality? Jakob Lorentzi & Magnus Nilsson. 51p. (Orig.). (C). 1994. pap. text ed. 25.00 (*0-7881-1381-X*) DIANE Pub.

Spin-Off Technologies Developed Through Nuclear Activities. OECD Staff. 114p. (Orig.). 1993. pap. 20.00 (*92-64-13965-6*) OECD.

Spin-Orbit-Influenced Spectroscopies of Magnetic Solids: Proceedings of an International Workshop Held at Herrsching, Germany, April 20-23, 1995. Ed. by Hubert Ebert & Gisela Schutz. LC 96-3904. (Lecture Notes in Physics Ser.: Vol. 466). viii, 288p. 1996. 73.00 (*3-540-60843-5*) Spr-Verlag.

Spin Phenomena in Particle Interactions. S. M. Troshin & N. E. Tyurin. 220p. 1994. text ed. 61.00 (*981-02-1692-0*) World Scientific Pub.

Spin Polarized Quantum Systems. Ed. by S. Stringari. 440p. (C). 1989. text ed. 125.00 (*9971-5-0878-8*) World Scientific Pub.

***Spin Roulette Gold: Secrets of Beating the Wheel.** Frank Scoblete. LC 97-11215. 250p. 1997. pap. 14.95 (*1-56625-074-9*) Bonus Books.

S.P.I.N. Selling. Neil Rackham. 224p. 1988. text ed. 24.95 (*0-07-051113-6*) McGraw.

Spin Selling Fieldbook. Neil Rackham. (Illus.). 192p. 1996. pap. text ed. 17.95 (*0-07-052235-9*) McGraw.

Spin Span Spun: Fact & Folklore for Spinners. B. Hochberg. LC 79-89003. (Illus.). (Orig.). 1979. pap. 6.95 (*0-9600990-3-4*) B Hochberg.

***Spin Structure of the Nucleon.** 132p. 1996. lib. bdg. 24.00 (*981-02-2788-4*) World Scientific Pub.

Spin Systems. W. J. Caspers. 232p. (C). 1989. text ed. 40.00 (*9971-5-0788-9*) World Scientific Pub.

Spin the Spin. S. Tomonaga. 300p. 1990. text ed. 64.00 (*9971-5-0330-1*) World Scientific Pub.

Spin WA Meguru. Tomonaga. LC 97-12189. 1996. lib. bdg. 50.00 (*0-226-80793-2*) U Ch Pr.

Spin WA Meguru. Tomonaga. LC 97-12189. 1996. pap. text ed. 22.00 (*0-226-80794-0*) U Ch Pr.

Spin Wave Amplification: Electron Mechanisms. Ed. by Victor D. Lakhno. 148p. (C). 1992. text ed. 125.00 (*1-56072-067-0*) Nova Sci Pubs.

Spin Waves & Magnetic Excitations, Pt. 1. Ed. by A. S. Borovik-Romanov & S. K. Sinha. (Modern Problems in Condensed Matter Sciences Ser.: Vol. 22). 502p. 1988. Part 1. 211.25 (*0-444-87068-7*) Elsevier.

Spin Waves & Magnetic Excitations, Pt. 2. Ed. by A. S. Borovik-Romanov & S. K. Sinha. (Modern Problems in Condensed Matter Sciences Ser.: Vol. 22). 502p. 1988. Part 2. 211.25 (*0-444-87078-4*) Elsevier.

Spin-1 NMR. Ed. by P. Diehl et al. (NMR-Basic Principles & Progress Ser.: Vol. 34). (Illus.). 160p. 1996. 157.00 (*3-540-60581-9*) Spr-Verlag.

***Spina Bifida: A Comprehensive Guide for Parents & Professionals.** LC 96-47697. 296p. (C). (gr. 13). 1997. pap. text ed. 19.95 (*0-8078-4657-0*) U of NC Pr.

***Spina Bifida: A Comprehensive Guide for Parents & Professionals.** Adrian Sandler. LC 96-47697. 296p. (C). (gr. 13). 1997. text ed. 45.00 (*0-8078-2352-X*) U of NC Pr.

Spina Bifida: A Multidisciplinary Approach. Ed. by Robert L. McLaurin et al. LC 86-8184. 509p. 1986. text ed. 95.00 (*0-275-92100-X*, C2100, Praeger Pubs) Greenwood.

Spina Bifida-Neural Tube Defects: Basic Research, Interdisciplinary Diagnostics & Treatment, Results & Prognosis. Ed. by P. Glees et al. (Illus.). xi, 320p. 1986. 119.25 (*3-11-010768-6*) De Gruyter.

Spinabilities: A Young Person's Guide to Spina Bifida. Marlene Lutkenhoff. (YA). 1996. pap. text ed. 16.95 (*0-933149-86-7*) Woodbine House.

Spinach & Zwieback: Writings of Newell Martin. Compiled by Cynthia Parsons. LC 93-73174. (Illus.). 512p. 1993. 29.95 (*0-9635190-1-8*) Grinnell & Lawton.

***Spinach with Chocolate Sauce.** Francess Lantz. (J). 1997. pap. 3.95 (*0-8167-4286-3*) Troll Communs.

Spinal Adjustment Technic. Alva Gregory. 100p. 1993. reprint ed. spiral bd. 12.50 (*0-7873-0356-9*) Hlth Research.

Spinal Afferent Processing. Ed. by Tony L. Yaksh. 540p. 1986. 115.00 (*0-306-42046-5*, Plenum Pr) Plenum.

Spinal Anatomy. Cramer & Darby. 300p. (gr. 13). 1995. text ed. 99.95 (*0-8016-6467-5*) Mosby Yr Bk.

Spinal & Supraspinal Mechanisms of Voluntary Motor Control & Locomotion. Ed. by J. E. Desmedt. (Progress in Clinical Neurophysiology Ser.: Vol. 8). (Illus.). x, 374p. 1980. 110.50 (*3-8055-0022-X*) S Karger.

Spinal Center. David W. Felder. 44p. 1996. pap. text ed. 8.95 (*0-910959-69-2*, B&G 13E) Wellington Pr.

Spinal Cord & Deuterencephalon see Central Nervous System of Vertebrates: A General Survey of Its Comparative Anatomy with an Introduction to Pertinent Fundamental Biologic & Logical Concepts

Spinal Cord & Its Reaction to Traumatic Injury: Anatomy, Physiology, Pharmacology, Therapeutics. Ed. by William F. Windle. LC 80-19592. (Modern Pharmacology-Toxicology Ser.: No. 18). (Illus.). 400p. reprint ed. pap. 114.00 (*0-7837-0825-4*, 2041139) Bks Demand.

Spinal Cord Compression: Diagnosis & Principles of Management. Thomas N. Byrne & Stephen G. Waxman. (Contemporary Neurology Ser.: No. 33). (Illus.). 278p. (C). 1990. text ed. 72.00 (*0-8036-1465-9*) Davis Co.

Spinal Cord Disease: Basic Science, Diagnosis & Management, Vol. XIV. 2nd ed. Ed. by E. M. Critchley & Andrew A. Eisen. LC 96-24791. (Illus.). 610p. 1996. 169.00 (*3-540-19935-7*) Spr-Verlag.

Spinal Cord Dysfunction: Assessment. L. S. Illis. (Illus.). 320p. 1988. 85.00 (*0-19-261624-2*) OUP.

Spinal Cord Dysfunction: Functional Stimulation, Vol. III. Ed. by L. S. Illis. (Illus.). 320p. 1992. 115.00 (*0-19-261919-5*) OUP.

Spinal Cord Dysfunction, Vol. 2: Intervention & Treatment. Ed. by L. S. Illis. (Illus.). 228p. 1992. 78.00 (*0-19-261787-7*) OUP.

Spinal Cord Injured Patient: Comprehensive Management. Lee et al. (Illus.). 400p. 1991. text ed. 95.00 (*0-7216-5699-4*) Saunders.

Spinal Cord Injuries. Ed. by John Alderson & E. A. Frost. (Illus.). 256p. 1990. 175.00 (*0-407-01148-X*) Buttrwrth-Heinemann.

Spinal Cord Injury. Ed. by N. E. Naftchi. LC 81-8573. (Illus.). 306p. 1982. text ed. 45.00 (*0-88331-202-6*) Luce.

Spinal Cord Injury. Martha Somers. (Illus.). (C). 1991. text ed. 65.00 (*0-8385-8649-X*, A8649-4) Appleton & Lange.

Spinal Cord Injury. Ed. by Hazel V. Adkins. LC 85-4143. (Clinics in Physical Therapy Ser.: No. 6). (Illus.). 302p. reprint ed. pap. 86.10 (*0-8357-4653-4*, 2037584) Bks Demand.

Spinal Cord Injury: A Guide for Patient & Family. Lynn Phillips et al. 320p. 1987. text ed. 18.00 (*0-88167-274-2*); pap. text ed. 18.00 (*0-88167-275-0*) Lppncott-Raven.

Spinal Cord Injury: A Guide to Functional Outcomes in Occupational Therapy. Ed. by Judy P. Hill. LC 84-25852. 264p. (C). 1986. 67.00 (*0-87189-604-4*) Aspen Pub.

Spinal Cord Injury: A Guide to Functional Outcomes in Physical Therapy Management. A Rehabilitation Institute of Chicago Procedure Manual. LC 84-18474. (Illus.). 251p. (C). 1985. 63.00 (*0-89443-552-3*) Aspen Pub.

Spinal Cord Injury: An Illustrated Guide for Health Care Professionals. 2nd ed. Marcia Hanak & Anne Scott. 188p. 1993. pap. text ed. 29.95 (*0-8261-4172-2*) Springer Pub.

Spinal Cord Injury: Clinical Outcomes from the Model Systems. Samuel L. Stover et al. 376p. 1995. 70.00 (*0-8342-0697-8*) Aspen Pub.

Spinal Cord Injury: Medical Management & Rehabilitation. Ed. by Gary M. Yarkony. LC 94-14208. (Rehabilitation Institute of Chicago Procedure Manual Ser.). 252p. 1994. 66.00 (*0-8342-0553-X*, 20553) Aspen Pub.

Spinal Cord Injury Patient Education Resource Manual. Ed. by Sara N. Di Lima et al. LC 96-11459. 1996. 169.00 (*0-8342-0772-9*) Aspen Pub.

Spinal Cord Injury Rehabilitation. Ed. by K. Whalley-Hammell. (Illus.). 368p. 1994. pap. text ed. 39.95 (*1-56593-195-5*, 0510) Singular Publishing.

Spinal Cord Reconstruction. Ed. by Carl C. Kao et al. (Illus.). 510p. 1983. text ed. 173.50 (*0-89004-538-0*) Lppncott-Raven.

Spinal Cord (Spinal Medulla) Primatologia, Vol. 2, Pt. 2. C. R. Noback & J. K. Harting. Ed. by H. Hofer et al. (Illus.). 1971. pap. 36.00 (*3-8055-1205-8*) S Karger.

***Spinal Cord Stimulation.** Horsch. 1995. text ed. 71.95 (*3-540-00967-1*) Spr-Verlag.

***Spinal Cord Stimulation.** Richard North et al. (Illus.). 280p. 1997. text ed. 110.00 (*0-7817-0270-4*) Lppncott-Raven.

Spinal Cord Stimulation: An Innovative Method for Critical Limb Ischemia. Ed. by S. Horsch & L. Claeys. 1994. 59.95 (*0-387-91463-3*) Spr-Verlag.

Spinal Cord Stimulation II: An Innovative Method in the Treatment of PVD. Ed. by S. Horsch & L. Claeys. 240p. 1996. 79.00 (*3-7985-1028-8*) Spr-Verlag.

Spinal Cord Trauma: Handbook of Clinical Neurology, Vol. 61. Ed. by Pierre J. Vinken et al. LC 92-48797. 586p. 1993. 293.25 (*0-444-81280-6*, Pub. by Elsevier Applied Sci UK) Elsevier.

Spinal Degenerative Disease. R. S. Maurice-Williams. (Illus.). 356p. 1981. 48.00 (*0-685-24837-2*, Yr Bk Med Pubs) Mosby Yr Bk.

***Spinal Discord: One Man's Wrenching Tale of Woe in Twenty-Four (Vertebral) Segments.** Tilman Spengler. 1997. 17.95 (*0-8050-5552-5*) H Holt & Co.

Spinal Disorders: Diagnosis & Treatment. Ed. by Daniel Ruge & Leon L. Wiltse. LC 77-1875. (Illus.). 458p. reprint ed. pap. 130.60 (*0-8357-7655-7*, 2056981) Bks Demand.

Spinal Disorders in Growth & Aging. Ed. by H. E. Takahashi. (Illus.). 338p. 1995. 158.00 (*0-387-70141-9*) Spr-Verlag.

Spinal Fitness Class. Raymond K. Woltz. Ed. by T. Bruce Henderson. (Illus.). 92p. 1983. pap. 14.95 (*0-9613447-0-9*) R K Woltz.

Spinal Fusion: Science & Technique. J. M. Cotler & H. B. Cotler. (Illus.). xvi, 407p. 1990. 298.00 (*0-387-97054-1*) Spr-Verlag.

Spinal Injuries Handbook. 2nd ed. Hugh Dickson et al. 1992. pap. text ed. 25.00 (*0-07-470001-4*) McGraw-Hill HPD.

Spinal Instability. Ed. by Robert N. Holtzman et al. LC 92-48680. (Contemporary Perspectives in Neurosurgery Ser.). 1993. 152.00 (*0-387-97941-7*); write for info. (*3-540-97941-7*) Spr-Verlag.

Spinal Instrumentation. Howard S. An & Jerome M. Cotter. (Illus.). 496p. 1992. 165.00 (*0-683-00127-2*) Williams & Wilkins.

Spinal Instrumentation. Ed. by Edward Benzel. (Neurosurgical Topics Ser.). (Illus.). 256p. 1994. 95.00 (*1-879284-14-6*) Am Assn Neuro.

Spinal Manipulation. enl. ed. J. F. Bourdillon et al. (Illus.). 352p. 1992. vhs 280.00 (*0-7506-9425-4*) Buttrwrth-Heinemann.

Spinal Manipulation. 5th ed. J. F. Bourdillon et al. (Illus.). 381p. 1992. pap. 55.00 (*0-7506-0576-6*) Buttrwrth-Heinemann.

***Spinal Meningiomas.** A. Pansini & P. Conti. LC 96-37039. (Illus.). 260p. 1996. 279.00 (*3-540-75030-4*) Spr-Verlag.

Spinal MRI: A Teaching File Approach. John H. Bisese. (Illus.). 305p. 1991. text ed. 45.00 (*0-07-005406-1*) McGraw-Hill HPD.

Spinal Narcotics. Ed. by Narinder Rawal & Dennis W. Coombs. (Current Management of Pain Ser.). (C). 1989. lib. bdg. 108.50 (*0-7923-0374-1*) Kluwer Ac.

S

Spinal Opiate Analgesia: Experimental & Clinical Studies. Ed. by Tony L. Yaksh & H. Mueller. (Anaesthesiology & Intensive Care Medicine Ser.: Vol. 144). (Illus.). 164p. 1982. 51.00 (*0-387-11036-4*) Spr-Verlag.

Spinal Stenosis. Nixon. 1991. 150.00 (*0-7131-4525-0*) Routledge.

Spinal Surgery: Science & Practice. Robert A. Dickson. (Illus.). 560p. 1990. 225.00 (*0-407-01791-7*) Buttrwrth-Heinemann.

Spinal Trauma - Current Evaluation & Management. Ed. by Gary L. Rea & C. Arden Miller. (Neurosurgical Topics Ser.). (Illus.). 237p. 1993. 90.00 (*1-879284-19-7*) Am Assn Neuro.

***Spinal Tumors in Children & Adolescents.** Ignacio P. Castroviejo. LC 89-10646. (International Review of Child Neurology Ser.). 314p. 1990. reprint ed. pap. 89.50 (*0-608-03437-1*, 2064138) Bks Demand.

Spindle Stage: Principles & Practice. Donald F. Bloss. LC 80-21488. (Illus.). 416p. 1981. text ed. 95.00 (*0-521-23292-9*) Cambridge U Pr.

Spindle Stories: World History Units for the Middle Grades, Bk. 2. Lyn Reese. Ed. by Mary A. Dougherty & Jean B. Wilkinson. (Illus.). 90p. (J). (gr. 5-9). 1991. pap. 15.00 (*0-9625880-0-8*) Women World CRP.

Spindle Stories: World History Units for the Middle Grades, Bk. 2. Lyn Reese. Ed. by Mary Dougherty & Jean Wilkinson. 1991. write for info. (*0-318-67277-4*) Women World CRP.

Spindle Stories Bk. 3: Three Units on Women's World History. Lyn Reese. Ed. by Jean Wilkinson & Mary A. Doughtery. (Spindle Stories Ser.). (Illus.). 125p. (Orig.). (YA). (gr. 6 up). 1994. pap. text ed. 15.00 (*0-9625880-2-4*) Women World CRP.

Spindle Stories, Bk. Two: Three Units on Women's World History. Lyn Reese. Ed. by Mary A. Dougherty & Jean B. Wilkinson. (Illus.). 118p. (J). (gr. 6-10). 1991. pap. text ed. 15.00 (*0-9625880-1-6*) Women World CRP.

Spindle Turning. Woodturning Magazine Staff. (Illus.). 128p. 1996. pap. 14.95 (*1-86108-016-6*, Pub. by Guild Mstr Craftsman UK) Sterling.

***Spindle Whorl: A Northwest Coast Indian Art Activity Book.** Nan McNutt. (Illus.). 44p. (Orig.). (J). 1997. pap. 10.95 (*1-57061-115-7*) Sasquatch Bks.

***Spindles: Comprehensive Guide to Making Light Milling or Grinding Spindles with a Small Lathe.** Harprit S. Sandhu. (Workshop Practice Ser.: Vol. 27). (Illus.). 144p. (Orig.). 1997. pap. 19.95 (*1-85486-149-2*, Pub. by Nexus Special Interests UK) Trans-Atl Phila.

Spindle's Picnic. (Tales of Oaktree Wood Ser.). (J). 1989. 2.99 (*0-517-69123-X*) Random Hse Value.

Spindletop Gusher: The Story of the Texas Oil Boom. Carmen Bredeson. LC 95-31485. (Spotlight on American History Ser.). (Illus.). 64p. (J). (gr. 4-6). 1996. lib. bdg. 16.40 (*1-56294-916-0*) Millbrook Pr.

***Spindletop Unwound.** Roger L. Shaffer. LC 97-12739. 278p. 1997. pap. 16.95 (*1-55622-550-4*, Rep of TX Pr) Wordware Pub.

Spindoc. Steve Perry. 272p. (Orig.). 1994. mass mkt. 5.50 (*0-441-00008-8*) Ace Bks.

Spindrift. Miranda Jarrett. (Historical Ser.). 1993. mass mkt. 3.99 (*0-373-28774-7*, 1-28774-7) Harlequin Bks.

***Spindrift.** Pete Sarsfield. 1997. pap. text ed. 14.95 (*0-88801-215-2*, Pub. by Turnstone CN) LPC InBook.

Spindrift Ridge. R. C. House. Ed. by Doug Grad. 256p. (Orig.). 1993. mass mkt. 3.99 (*0-671-76044-0*) PB.

Spine. Karen Hanson. LC 73-161968. 69p. 1971. 2.95 (*0-87886-009-6*, Greenfld Rev Pr) Greenfld Rev Lit.

Spine. Michael W. Spence. LC 87-2452. (Illus.). 76p. (Orig.). 1987. pap. 5.75 (*0-911198-89-X*) Purdue U Pr.

***Spine, 2 vols.** 3rd ed. Contrib. by Richard H. Rothman & Frederick A. Simeone. (Illus.). 2172p. 1992. write for info. (*0-7216-3203-3*) Saunders.

Spine: Basic Evaluation & Mobilization Techniques. 3rd ed. Freddy M. Kaltenborn. (Illus.). 289p. 1993. pap. text ed. 39.95 (*82-7054-052-8*) Orthopedic Phys.

Spine: Diagnosis, Treatment & Rehabilitation. A. White. 3300p. (C). (gr. 13). 1995. text ed. 305.00 (*0-8016-6328-8*) Mosby Yr Bk.

Spine Care: Diagnosis & Conservative Treatment, Vol. 1. White. 848p. (C). (gr. 13). 1995. text ed. 160.00 (*0-8151-9664-4*) Mosby Yr Bk.

Spine Care: Operative Treatment, Vol. 2. White. 1072p. (C). (gr. 13). 1995. text ed. 175.00 (*0-8151-9665-2*) Mosby Yr Bk.

***Spine-Chilling.** (Activity Fun Packs Ser.). (Illus.). (YA). (gr. 6 up). 1996. pap. 5.95 (*0-7894-1161-X*) DK Pub Inc.

Spine in Sports. Intro. by Stephen H. Hochschuler. LC 90-82772. (Illus.). 340p. 1990. text ed. 57.00 (*1-56053-005-7*) Hanley & Belfus.

Spine in Sports. Watkins. 352p. (C). (gr. 13). 1995. text ed. 105.00 (*0-8016-7502-2*) Mosby Yr Bk.

Spine of Software: Designing Provably Correct Software-Theory & Practice. Robert L. Baber. 316p. 1988. text ed. 84.95 (*0-471-91474-6*) Wiley.

***Spine of Software: Designing Provably Correct Software: Theory & Practice, Or a Mathematical Introduction to the Semantics of Computer Programs.** Robert L. Baber. LC 86-32483. (Illus.). 329p. pap. 93.80 (*0-608-05254-X*, 2065792) Bks Demand.

Spine Tinglers, 90 titles, Set. Ed. by Christina Krayer. (Illus.). (J). (gr. 3-8). 1993. pap. 299.00 (*1-882869-03-6*) Varsity Read Servs.

***Spine Tinglers - More Tales to Make You Shiver.** Bruce Coville. (Coville Anthologies Ser.: No. 11). (J). 1997. mass mkt. 3.99 (*0-590-85296-5*, Apple Paperbacks) Scholastic Inc.

***Spine Tingling Tales.** World Book Editors. LC 96-60470. (Info-Adventure Ser.). 32p. 1996. pap. text ed. 4.95 (*0-7166-1740-4*) World Bk.

Spine Tumors. Ed. by AANS Publications Committee & Gary L. Rea. (Neurosurgical Clinical Presentations Ser.). (Illus.). 109p. (Orig.). 1994. pap. 35.00 (*1-879284-18-9*) Am Assn Neuro.

Spineless Creatures. Robert De Weese. (Science Primary Mini-Unit Ser.: Vol. 3). (Illus.). 16p. (J). (gr. 1-3). 1994. pap. text ed. 5.95 (*1-55799-291-6*, EMC831) Evan-Moor Corp.

***Spineless Wonders.** Richard Conniff. 1997. pap. 12.95 (*0-8050-5531-2*) H Holt & Co.

Spineless Wonders: Strange Tales from the Invertabrate World. Richard Conniff. LC 96-11748. (Illus.). 256p. 1996. 25.00 (*0-8050-4218-0*) H Holt & Co.

***Spinetingler Vol. 24: Your Turn - to Scream, Vol. 24.** M. T. Coffin. (Spinetinglers Ser.). 128p. (Orig.). (J). 1997. mass mkt. 3.99 (*0-380-78927-2*, Camelot) Avon.

Spingold Challenge. Allan Falk. 154p. (Orig.). 1988. pap. 11.95 (*0-940257-02-5*) Granovetter Bks.

Spinifex Book of Women's Answers. Susan Hawthorne. 1993. pap. 9.95 (*1-875559-03-5*, Pub. by SpiniFex Pr AT) LPC InBook.

Spinifex Quiz Book: A Book of Women's Answers. Hawthorne. 113p. 1993. pap. 10.95 (*1-875559-15-9*, Pub. by SpiniFex Pr AT) LPC InBook.

Spinks Catalog of British Commemorative Medals (1558 to Present) D. Fearon. (Illus.). 1984. lib. bdg. 30.00 (*0-86350-029-3*) S J Durst.

Spink's Catalogue of British Colonial & Commonwealth Coins. Andre P. DeClermont & John Wheeler. Ed. by Colin R. Bruce, II. LC 85-50753. (Illus.). 704p. 1986. 40.00 (*0-87341-076-9*, BT01) Krause Pubns.

Spinky Sulks. William Steig. LC 88-81292. (Illus.). 32p. (J). (ps up). 1988. 15.00 (*0-374-38321-9*) FS&G.

Spinky Sulks. William Steig. (J). (gr. 4-8). 1991. pap. 4.95 (*0-374-46990-3*) FS&G.

Spinnaker Handling. 2nd ed. Bent Aarre. Tr. by Christopher Croft & Anne Firth from DAN. (Illus.). 112p. (ENG.). 1993. pap. 14.95 (*0-924486-51-1*) Sheridan.

Spinner: People & Culture in Southeastern Massachusetts, Vol. 4. Joseph D. Thomas. (Orig.). 1988. pap. 17.95 (*0-932027-09-1*) Spinner Pubns.

Spinner: People & Culture in Southeastern Massachusetts, Vol. V. Marsha McCabe. Ed. by Joseph D. Thomas. (Illus.). 192p. (Orig.). 1996. pap. 19.95 (*0-932027-30-X*) Spinner Pubns.

Spinner: People & Culture in Southeastern Massachusetts, Vol. V. Marsha McCabe. Ed. by Joseph D. Thomas. (Illus.). 192p. (Orig.). 1996. 39.95 (*0-932027-31-8*) Spinner Pubns.

Spinner Dolphins. John F. Prevost. LC 95-12368. (Dolphins Ser.). (J). 1995. lib. bdg. 13.98 (*1-56239-497-5*) Abdo & Dghtrs.

Spinner Fishing for Steelhead, Salmon & Trout. Jed Davis. LC 88-31377. (Illus.). 97p. 1985. 24.95 (*0-936608-41-2*) F Amato Pubns.

Spinner Fishing for Steelhead, Salmon & Trout. 3rd ed. Jed Davis. LC 88-31377. (Illus.). 97p. 1995. pap. 19.95 (*0-936608-40-4*) F Amato Pubns.

Spinner in the Sun. Myrtle Reed. 1976. lib. bdg. 17.25 (*0-89968-111-5*, Lghtyr Pr) Buccaneer Bks.

***Spinnerbait Bassin' 100 Tips for Using Spinner Baits.** 2nd ed. B. A. S. S. Inc. Staff. (Illus.). 160p. 1994. pap. 4.95 (*1-890280-04-6*) B A S S.

Spinners & Weavers of Auffay: Rural Industry & the Sexual Division of Labor in a French Village, 1750-1850. Gay L. Gullickson. (Illus.). 288p. 1986. text ed. 69.95 (*0-521-32280-4*) Cambridge U Pr.

Spinner's Daughter. Amy Littlesugar. (Illus.). 40p. (J). (gr. 1-4). 1994. lib. bdg. 14.95 (*0-945912-22-6*) Pippin Pr.

Spinnin' How to Score a Hit As a Mobile DJ for Fun & Profit. Robert A. Lindquist. Ed. by David Warner & Clare Dygert. (Illus.). 110p. 1987. pap. 15.00 (*0-943047-00-5*) TNT Prodns.

***Spinnin' 2000: The Ultimate Guide to Fun & Profit As a Mobile Disc Jockey.** rev. ed. Robert Lindquist. (Illus.). 160p. (Orig.). Date not set. pap. text ed. 24.95 (*0-943047-01-3*) TNT Prodns.

Spinning. 1987. 50.00 (*0-85083-009-5*) St Mut.

Spinning: A Guide to the World of Cycling. Paul McCallum. (Illus.). 192p. (Orig.). 1993. pap. 14.95 (*1-55870-286-5*, Betrwy Bks) F & W Pubns Inc.

Spinning a Web. Lisa Trumbauer. (Early Science Ser.). 16p. (Orig.). (J). (ps-2). 1996. pap. 14.95 (*1-56784-312-3*) Newbridge Comms.

Spinning a Web: Mini Book. Lisa Trumbauer. (Early Science Mini Bks.). 16p. (Orig.). (J). (ps-2). 1996. pap. 2.95 (*1-56784-337-9*) Newbridge Comms.

***Spinning a Web Theme Pack.** (Early Science Ser.). (Illus.). (Orig.). (J). (ps-2). 1996. pap. 46.85 (*1-56784-362-X*) Newbridge Comms.

Spinning & Spinning Wheels. Eliza Leadbeater. 1989. pap. 25.00 (*0-85263-469-2*, Pub. by Shire UK) St Mut.

Spinning & Weaving. Enid Gauldie. (Illus.). 88p. 1995. pap. 6.95 (*0-948636-68-8*, 3668, Pub. by Natl Mus Scotland UK) A Schwartz & Co.

Spinning & Weaving: A Practical Guide. Eileen Hobden. (Illus.). 114p. 1987. 15.95 (*0-900873-68-X*, Pub. by Bishopsgte Pr UK); pap. 11.95 (*0-900873-72-8*, Pub. by Bishopsgte Pr UK) Intl Spec Bk.

Spinning & Weaving with Wool. rev. ed. Paula Simmons. Ed. by Betsy R. Fulwiler. (Illus.). 224p. 1991. reprint ed. pap. 16.95 (*0-9625586-1-3*) Unicorn Bks & Crafts.

Spinning Blackboard & Other Dynamic Experiments on Force & Motion. Exploratorium Teacher Institute Staff et al. LC 95-10878. (Exploratorium Science Snackbook Ser.). (Illus.). 128p. (J). 1996. pap. text ed. 10.95 (*0-471-11514-2*) Wiley.

Spinning Designer Yarns. Diane Varney. LC 87-82121. (Illus.). 96p. (Orig.). 1987. pap. 12.00 (*0-934026-29-7*) Interweave.

***Spinning Fantasies: Rabbis, Gender & History.** Miriam Peskowitz. LC 96-43149. (Contraversions Ser.). 1997. write for info. (*0-520-20831-5*); pap. write for info. (*0-520-20967-2*) U CA Pr.

Spinning Inward: Using Guided Imagery with Children. enl. rev. ed. Maureen Murdock. LC 87-9740. (Illus.). 158p. 1987. pap. 22.50 (*0-87773-422-4*) Shambhala Pubns.

Spinning Jenny No. 1: Fall 1995-Winter 1996. 56p. 1995. pap. 4.00 (*1-887672-00-1*) Black Dress.

Spinning Jenny No. 2: Fall 1996-Winter 1997. 56p. 1997. pap. 4.00 (*1-887672-01-X*) Black Dress.

Spinning Lives. Luciana A. Bittencourt. (Illus.). 242p. 1995. lib. bdg. 42.50 (*0-7618-0121-9*) U Pr of Amer.

Spinning Metal Made Easy. Fred D. Crawshaw. (Illus.). 72p. 1991. reprint ed. pap. 6.00 (*1-877767-36-0*) Univ Publng Hse.

Spinning Off Bukowski. Steve Richmond. (Illus.). 144p. (Orig.). 1996. pap. 12.95 (*0-941543-10-2*) Sun Dog Pr.

Spinning Off Bukowski. limited ed. Steve Richmond. (Illus.). 144p. (Orig.). 1996. pap. 20.95 (*0-941543-11-0*) Sun Dog Pr.

***Spinning Our Stories: A Media Guide for Lesbian, Gay, Bisexual & Transgender Activists.** Robert Bray. 1997. pap. text ed. 10.00 (*0-9652779-2-5*) Natl Gay & Lesbian.

Spinning Shoes. Charles Ludwig. 1989. pap. 2.99 (*0-87162-582-2*, D7225) Warner Pr.

Spinning Spells, Weaving Wonders: Modern Magic for Everyday Life. Patricia Telesco. 192p. (Orig.). 1996. pap. 14.95 (*0-89594-803-6*) Crossing Pr.

Spinning Straw into Gold. Valerie M. Bailey. (Poetry Palette Ser.: Vol. 2). 96p. (Orig.). 1990. pap. 5.00 (*0-945641-03-6*) Castle Hills.

Spinning Straw into Gold. C. C. Cribb. LC 79-84880. (If God Has It I Want It! Ser.). pap. 2.95 (*0-932046-15-0*) Manhattan Ltd NC.

Spinning Straw into Gold: Your Emotional Recovery from Breast Cancer. Ronnie Kaye. 224p. (Orig.). 1991. pap. 9.95 (*0-671-70164-9*, Fireside) S&S Trade.

Spinning Sun, Grinning Moon. Max Evans. (Illus.). zp. 1995. 19.95 (*1-878610-52-X*) Red Crane Bks.

***Spinning Tales.** Shirley Shapiro. 100p. (Orig.). 1996. pap. 11.00 (*0-9647280-5-2*) Perry Pubng.

***Spinning Tales.** Shirley Shapiro. 124p. (Orig.). 1996. pap. 11.00 (*0-9643728-5-1*) Perry Pubng.

Spinning Tales, Weaving Hope: Stories, Storytelling & Activities for Peace, Justice, & the Environment. Ed. by Ed Brody et al. (Illus.). 288p. (Orig.). (J). 1992. pap. 22.95 (*0-86571-229-8*) New Soc Pubs.

Spinning Tales, Weaving Hope: Stories, Storytelling & Activities for Peace, Justice, & the Environment. Ed. by Ed Brody et al. (Illus.). 288p. (Orig.). (J). 1992. lib. bdg. 49.95 (*0-86571-228-X*) New Soc Pubs.

Spinning the Symbolic Web: Human Communication As Symbolic Interaction. Julia T. Wood. Ed. by Brenda Dervin. (Communication & Information Science Ser.). 317p. (C). 1992. pap. 39.50 (*0-89391-838-5*); text ed. 73.25 (*0-89391-799-0*) Ablex Pub.

Spinning the Web: A Guide to Serving Information on the World Wide Web. Yuval Fisher. 536p. 1996. text ed. 27.95 (*0-387-94539-3*) Spr-Verlag.

Spinning the Web: How to Provide Information on the Internet. Andrew Ford. (B & F - Computer Science Ser.). 250p. 1995. pap. 29.95 (*0-442-01996-3*) Van Nos Reinhold.

Spinning the Web: How to Provide Information on the Internet. 2nd ed. Andrew Ford & Tim Dixon. 288p. 1996. pap. 39.95 (*1-85032-141-8*) ITCP.

Spinning the Web: How to Provide Information on the Internet. 2nd ed. Andrew Ford. (ITCP-UK Computer Science Ser.). (Illus.). 288p. 1996. pap. 39.95 incl. cd-rom (*1-85032-290-2*) Van Nos Reinhold.

Spinning Tops: A Course on Integrable Systems. Michele Audin. LC 96-11648. (Studies in Advanced Mathematics: No. 51). (Illus.). 160p. (C). 1996. text ed. 34.95 (*0-521-56129-9*) Cambridge U Pr.

Spinning Wheel: The Art of Mythmaking. Gwendolyn Endicott. 200p. 1994. pap. 14.00 (*0-9641187-0-X*) Attic Pr OR.

Spinning Wheel Primer. 2nd rev. ed. Alden Amos. (Illus.). 60p. 1990. reprint ed. pap. 6.00 (*0-934026-55-6*) Interweave.

Spinning Wheel Stories. Louisa May Alcott. (Works of Louisa May Alcott). 1989. reprint ed. lib. bdg. 79.00 (*0-7812-1640-0*) Rprt Serv.

Spinning Wheels, Spinners & Spinning. Patricia Baines. 1987. reprint ed. pap. 12.95 (*0-923150-48-X*) Robin & Russ.

Spinning with Gold: Poems for Young & Old. Dorothy C. Raemsch. (Illus.). 32p. 1991. pap. 6.00 (*0-9605398-2-4*) D C Raemsch.

***Spinning Worlds.** Michael Carroll. 32p. (J). (gr. 1-5). 1996. 12.99 (*1-56476-571-7*, 6-3571, Victor Bks) Chariot Victor.

***Spinoff to Payoff: An Analytical Guide to Investing in Corporate Divestitures.** Joseph W. Cornell. LC 97-13945. 1997. 50.00 (*0-7863-1204-1*) Irwin Prof Pubng.

***Spinoff 1995: NASA & Technology & U. S. Competitiveness in Global Markets & at Home.** 1997. lib. bdg. 250.95 (*0-8490-6158-X*) Gordon Pr.

***Spinoff 1996.** James J. Haggerty. (Illus.). 135p. 1996. per., pap. 13.00 (*0-16-048742-0*, 033-000-01170-9) USGPO.

Spinor Construction of Vertex Operator Algebras, Triality, & E (sub 8)(1) A. Feingold et al. LC 91-24409. (Contemporary Mathematics Ser.: Vol. 121). 146p. 1991. pap. 34.00 (*0-8218-5128-4*, CONM/121) Am Math.

Spinorial Chessboard. P. Budinich & Andrzej Trautman. (Trieste Notes in Physics Ser.). 130p. 1988. 34.95 (*0-387-19078-3*) Spr-Verlag.

Spinors & Calibrations. F. Reese Harvey. (Perspectives in Mathematics Ser.: Vol. 8). 323p. 1990. text ed. 69.00 (*0-12-329650-1*) Acad Pr.

Spinors & Space-Time, Vol. 1: Two-Spinor Calculus & Relativistic Fields. Roger Penrose & Wolfgang Rindler. (Monographs on Mathematical Physics). 450p. 1987. pap. text ed. 52.95 (*0-521-33707-0*) Cambridge U Pr.

Spinors & Space-Time, Vol. 2: Spinor & Twistor Methods in Space-Time Geometry. Roger Penrose & Wolfgang Rindler. (Monographs on Mathematical Physics). (Illus.). 500p. 1986. text ed. 140.00 (*0-521-25267-9*) Cambridge U Pr.

Spinors & Space-Time, Vol. 2: Spinor & Twistor Methods in Space-Time Geometry. Roger Penrose & Wolfgang Rindler. (Monographs on Mathematical Physics). (Illus.). 512p. 1988. pap. text ed. 52.95 (*0-521-34786-6*) Cambridge U Pr.

Spinors, Clifford, & Cayley Algebras. Robert Hermann. (Interdisciplinary Mathematics Ser.: No. 7). 276p. 1974. 35.00 (*0-915692-06-6*, 991600215) Math Sci Pr.

Spinors in Hilbert Space. Roger Plymen & Paul Robinson. (Tracts in Mathematics Ser.: No. 114). 150p. (C). 1995. text ed. 47.95 (*0-521-45022-5*) Cambridge U Pr.

Spinors in Physics & Geometry: Trieste, 11-13 Sept. 1986. Ed. by Andrzej Trautman & G. Furlan. 368p. 1988. text ed. 90.00 (*9971-5-0763-3*) World Scientific Pub.

Spinors, Twistors & Clifford Algebras: Proceedings of the Second Max Born Syposium Held Near Wroclaw, Poland, September, 1992. Ed. by Andrzej Borowiec. (Fundamental Theories of Physics Ser.). 472p. (C). 1993. lib. bdg. 218.50 (*0-7923-2251-7*) Kluwer Ac.

Spinosaurus. D. White. (Dinosaur Library). (Illus.). 24p. (J). (gr. 3 up). 1989. lib. bdg. 14.60 (*0-86592-517-8*); lib. bdg. 10.95 (*0-685-58287-6*) Rourke Corp.

Spinoza. R. J. Delahunty. (Arguments of the Philosophers Ser.). 352p. 1985. 49.95 (*0-7102-0375-6*, RKP) Routledge.

Spinoza. Alan Donagan. LC 88-27896. xviii, 238p. 1989. 41.95 (*0-226-15569-2*) U Ch Pr.

Spinoza. Stuart Hampshire. (Orig.). 1952. mass mkt. 4.95 (*0-14-020253-6*, Penguin Bks) Viking Penguin.

Spinoza. Stuart Hampshire. 192p. (Orig.). 1988. mass mkt. 5.95 (*0-14-022778-4*, Penguin Bks) Viking Penguin.

Spinoza. Frederick Pollock. 1972. 59.95 (*0-8490-1110-8*) Gordon Pr.

Spinoza. Roger Scruton. 140p. 1986. pap. 8.95 (*0-19-287630-9*) OUP.

Spinoza. John Caird. LC 75-164593. (Select Bibliographies Reprint Ser.). 1977. reprint ed. 23.95 (*0-8369-5877-2*) Ayer.

Spinoza: His Life & Philosophy. Frederick Pollock. (Reprints in Philosophy Ser.). (Illus.). reprint ed. lib. bdg. 47.00 (*0-697-00055-9*) Irvington.

Spinoza: His Life, Correspondence & Ethics. R. Willis. 1977. lib. bdg. 76.95 (*0-8490-2657-1*) Gordon Pr.

Spinoza: Issues & Directions, the Proceedings of the Chicago Spinoza Conference. Ed. by Edwin Curley & Pierre-Francois Moreau. LC 90-49020. (Brill's Studies in Intellectual History: Vol. 14). xiv, 404p. (ENG & FRE.). 1990. 128.50 (*90-04-09334-6*) E J Brill.

Spinoza: Practical Philosophy. Gilles Deleuze. Tr. by Robert Hurley from FRE. 160p. (Orig.). 1988. pap. 10.95 (*0-87286-218-6*) City Lights.

Spinoza: The Enduring Questions. Ed. by Graeme Hunter. (Studies in Philosophy). 208p. 1994. 70.00 (*0-8020-2876-4*) U of Toronto Pr.

Spinoza: The Way to Wisdom. Herman De Dijn. LC 95-46211. (Series in the History of Philosophy). 300p. 1996. 30.00 (*1-55753-081-5*); pap. 16.95 (*1-55753-082-3*) Purdue U Pr.

Spinoza & Moral Freedom. S. Paul Kashap. LC 86-30210. (SUNY Series in Philosophy). 198p. 1987. text ed. 59.50 (*0-88706-529-5*); pap. text ed. 19.95 (*0-88706-530-9*) State U NY Pr.

Spinoza & Other Heretics. Yirmiyahu Yovel. 264p. 1989. Marrano of Reason. text ed. 45.00 (*0-691-07344-9*) Princeton U Pr.

Spinoza & Other Heretics: The Adventures of Immanence. Yirmiyahu Yovel. 248p. 1989. pap. text ed. 15.95 (*0-691-02079-5*) Princeton U Pr.

Spinoza & Other Heretics: The Marrano of Reason. Yirmiyahu Yovel. 264p. 1989. pap. text ed. 16.95 (*0-691-02078-7*) Princeton U Pr.

***Spinoza & Politics.** Etienne Balibar. Date not set. 60.00 (*1-85984-801-X*, Pub. by Verso UK) Routledge Chapman & Hall.

***Spinoza & Politics.** Etienne Balibar. Date not set. pap. 20.00 (*1-85984-102-3*) Norton.

Spinoza & the Rise of Liberalism. Lewis S. Feuer. 344p. 1987. pap. 24.95 (*0-88738-701-2*) Transaction Pubs.

Spinoza & the Rise of Liberalism. Lewis S. Feuer. LC 83-18508. x, 323p. 1984. reprint ed. text ed. 52.50 (*0-313-24250-X*, FESR, Greenwood Pr) Greenwood.

Spinoza & the Sciences. Ed. by Nails Grene. 352p. 1986. lib. bdg. 134.00 (*90-277-1976-4*, D Reidel) Kluwer Ac.

Spinoza As Educator. William L. Rabenort. LC 70-177175. (Columbia University. Teachers College. Contributions to Education Ser.: No. 38). reprint ed. 37.50 (*0-404-55038-X*) AMS Pr.

Spinoza Bibliography. 1970. 150.00 (*0-8161-1539-7*, Hall Library) G K Hall.

Spinoza Conversations Between Lessing & Jacobi: Text with Excerpts from the Ensuing Controversy. Gerard Vallee. LC 88-21091. 182p. (Orig.). (C). 1988. lib. bdg. 45.00 (*0-8191-7015-1*, Pub. by McMaster Colloquium) U Pr of Amer.

Spinoza in English: A Bibliography from the Seventeenth Century to the Present. Wayne I. Boucher. LC 91-24542. (BSIH Ser.: No. 28). ix, 226p. 1991. 86.00 (*90-04-09499-7*) E J Brill.

S

An Asterisk (*) at the beginning of an entry indicates that the title is appearing in BIP for the first time.

***Spinoza, Liberalism & the Question of Jewish Identity.** Steven B. Smith. LC 96-34870. 1997. write for info. (*0-300-06680-5*) Yale U Pr.

Spinoza on Knowledge & the Human Mind: Papers Presented at the Second Jerusalem Conference (Ethica II) Ed. by Yirmiyahu Yovel & Gideon Segal. LC 93-38035. xii, 244p. 1993. 87.50 (*90-04-09981-6*) E J Brill.

Spinoza Reader: The Ethics & Other Works. Benedict De Spinoza. Ed. & Tr. by Edwin Curley. LC 93-1628. (Illus.). 352p. (ENG & LAT.). 1994. text ed. 55.00 (*0-691-03363-3*); pap. text ed. 15.95 (*0-691-00067-0*) Princeton U Pr.

***Spinozan Power in a Naturalistic Perspective: And Other Essays.** Tom Rubens. 265p. 1997. pap. 18.95 (*1-85756-218-6*, Pub. by Janus Pubng UK) Paul & Co Pubs.

Spinoza's Critique of Religion. Leo Strauss. LC 96-3464. vi, 328p. 1996. pap. text ed. 15.95 (*0-226-77688-3*) U Ch Pr.

Spinoza's Ethics. Lewis Schipper. LC 92-37622. (American University Studies: Philosophy: Ser. V, Vol. 147). 205p. (C). 1993. text ed. 47.95 (*0-8204-2071-9*) P Lang Pubng.

Spinoza's Metaphysics: An Essay in Interpretation. Edwin M. Curley. LC 70-85073. 190p. 1969. reprint ed. pap. 51.30 (*0-7837-4102-2*, 2057925) Bks Demand.

***Spinoza's Mouse.** George Young. LC 96-61280. 1997. pap. 10.00 (*0-915380-35-8*) Word Works.

Spinoza's Philosophy: An Outline. Errol E. Harris. LC 91-35694. 128p. (C). 1992. pap. 15.00 (*0-391-03737-4*) Humanities.

Spinoza's Philosophy of Law. Gail Belaief. LC 78-118275. (Studies in Philosophy: No. 24). (Illus.). 151p. (Orig.). 1971. pap. text ed. 33.85 (*90-279-1851-1*) Mouton.

Spinoza's Political & Ethical Philosophy. Robert A. Duff. LC 71-108858. xii, 516p. 1970. reprint ed. lib. bdg. 49.50 (*0-678-00615-6*) Kelley.

Spinoza's Theory of Knowledge. George H. Parkinson. (Modern Revivals in Philosophy Ser.). 208p. 1993. 59.95 (*0-7512-0159-6*, Pub. by Gregg Pub UK) Ashgate Pub Co.

Spinoza's Theory of Truth. Thomas C. Mark. LC 72-3721. 151p. reprint ed. pap. 43.10 (*0-317-09237-5*, 2006117) Bks Demand.

Spin's Really Wild Africa Tour. Jonathan Grupper. LC 96-14700. (Illus.). 32p. (J). 1996. pap. 7.95 (*0-7922-3501-0*) Natl Geog.

Spin's Really Wild U. S. A. Tour. Barbara Brownell. LC 95-44643. (Illus.). 32p. (J). (gr. k-4). 1996. pap. 7.95 (*0-7922-3422-7*) Natl Geog.

***Spin's Underground U. S. A.** Spin Magazine Staff. 1997. pap. 14.00 (*0-679-75575-6*, Vin) Random.

***Spinster of the Parish.** Ann Purser. 288p. 1996. 24.95 (*1-85797-655-X*, Pub. by Orion Bks UK); pap. 8.95 (*0-7528-0279-8*, Pub. by Orion Bks UK) Trafalgar.

Spinster of This Parish. large type ed. Ann Purser. 445p. 1996. pap. 20.95 (*0-7862-0667-5*, Thorndike Lrg Prnt) Thorndike Pr.

Spinsters. Pagan Kennedy. 160p. (Orig.). 1995. pap. 11.99 (*1-85242-405-2*, High Risk Bks) Serpents Tail.

Spinsters & Lesbians: Independent Womanhood in the United States. Trisha Franzen. (The Cutting Edge: Lesbian Life & Literature Ser.). 264p. (C). 1995. pap. 16.95 (*0-8147-2642-9*) NYU Pr.

Spinsters & Lesbians: Independent Womanhood in the United States. Trisha Franzen. (The Cutting Edge: Lesbian Life & Literature Ser.). 264p. (C). 1996. 45.00 (*0-8147-2641-0*) NYU Pr.

Spinster's Tour Through North Wales. Agusta Pearson. (C). 1988. text ed. 34.00 (*0-86383-412-4*, Pub. by Gomer Pr UK) St Mut.

Spiny. Jurgen Lassig. LC 94-40893. (Illus.). 64p. (J). (gr. 1-3). 1995. lib. bdg. 13.88 (*1-55858-402-1*) North-South Bks NYC.

Spiny. Jurgen Lassig. 64p. (J). (gr. 2-4). 1996. pap. 5.95 (*1-55858-552-4*) North-South Bks NYC.

Spionidae: Invertebrates of the San Francisco Bay Estuary System, Vol. 1. William J. Light. Ed. by Welton L. Lee. (Illus.). 1978. text ed. 12.50 (*0-910286-58-2*) Boxwood.

SPIR Treatment Strategies for Negative Acting out Behavior. Douglas K. Isaackson et al. 346p. (Orig.). 1987. teacher ed. 55.00 (*1-878276-00-X*) Educ Systs Assocs Inc.

Spiral. David L. Lindsey. (Orig.). 1990. pap. 5.99 (*0-671-73337-0*) S&S Trade.

Spiral Calendar & Its Effect on Financial Markets & Human Events. Christopher L. Carolan. (Illus.). 159p. 1992. 49.00 (*0-932750-21-4*) New Classics Lib.

***Spiral CT: A Teaching File.** Elliot K. Fishman & R. Brooke Jeffrey. LC 96-30754. 336p. 1996. text ed. 145.00 (*0-397-51668-1*) Lppncott-Raven.

Spiral CT: Principles, Techniques, & Clinical Applications. R. Brooke Jeffery, Jr. Ed. by Elliot K. Fishman. LC 94-13678. 240p. 1994. text ed. 139.95 (*0-7817-0218-6*) Lppncott-Raven.

***Spiral CT of the Chest: Medical Radiology, Diagnostic Imaging & Radiation Oncology.** M. Remy-Jardin & H. Remy. (Illus.). 352p. 1996. 198.00 (*3-540-59185-0*) Spr-Verlag.

Spiral Dance. Starhawk. LC 89-45400. 298p. 1989. pap. 16.00 (*0-06-250814-8*) HarpC.

Spiral Dance. R. Garcia y Robertson. 256p. 1993. reprint ed. mass mkt. 4.99 (*0-380-76518-7*, AvoNova) Avon.

Spiral Dynamics. Don Beck & Chris Cowan. (Illus.). 400p. (Orig.). 1995. 34.95 (*1-55786-940-5*) Blackwell Pubs.

Spiral Flame: A Study in the Meaning of D. H. Lawrence. David Boadella. Ed. by Arthur Efron & Dennis Hoerner. (Illus.). 1977. reprint ed. pap. 6.00 (*0-9602478-2-3*) Paunch.

Spiral Galaxies in the Near-IR: Proceedings of the ESO Workshop Held at Garching, Germany, 7-9 June 1995. Ed. by D. Minniti & H. W. Rix. LC 96-15599. (ESO Astrophysics Symposia Ser.). 350p. 1996. 39.95 (*3-540-60937-7*) Spr-Verlag.

Spiral Grain & Wave Phenomena in Wood Formation. J. M. Harris. (Wood Science Ser.). (Illus.). 225p. 1988. 158.95 (*0-387-19382-0*) Spr-Verlag.

***Spiral Grain of the Universe: In Search of the Archimedes File.** Vladimir B. Ginzlurg. LC 96-90198. (Orig.). 1997. pap. 9.95 (*1-56002-665-0*, Univ Edtns) Aegina Pr.

Spiral Guide to Research Writing. Martin Maner. LC 95-34860. 425p. (Orig.). 1995. spiral bd. 18.95 (*1-55934-492-X*, 1492) Mayfield Pub.

Spiral-Horn Dreams. Terry Wieland. LC 95-61363. (Illus.). 344p. 1995. 85.00 (*1-882458-08-7*) Trophy Rm Bks.

Spiral of Artificiality. Paul Laster & Renee Riccardo. Ed. by Deborah Bershad. (Illus.). 24p. (Orig.). 1987. pap. write for info. (*0-936739-09-6*) Hallwalls Inc.

***Spiral of Cynicism: The Press & the Public Good.** Kathleen H. Jamieson & Joseph N. Cappella. LC 96-24735. 288p. 1997. 45.00 (*0-19-509063-2*); pap. 15.95 (*0-19-509064-0*) OUP.

Spiral of Fire: Book III of The Mages of Garillon. Deborah T. Harris. 1989. pap. 3.95 (*0-8125-3954-0*) Tor Bks.

Spiral of Life. Mona Rolfe. 176p. (Orig.). pap. 12.50 (*0-8464-4291-4*) Beekman Pubs.

Spiral of Life. Mona Rolfe. 189p. 1992. pap. 12.50 (*0-85435-432-8*, Pub. by C W Daniel UK) Natl Bk Netwk.

Spiral of Memory: Interviews. Joy Harjo. Ed. by Laura Coltelli. LC 95-40043. (Poets on Poetry Ser.). (C). 1995. 39.50 (*0-472-09581-1*); pap. 13.95 (*0-472-06581-5*) U of Mich Pr.

Spiral of Silence: Public Opinion, Our Social Skin. 2nd ed. Elisabeth Noelle-Neumann. LC 93-15484. 304p. (ENG & GER.). 1993. pap. text ed. 14.95 (*0-226-58936-6*); lib. bdg. 44.00 (*0-226-58935-8*) U Ch Pr.

***Spiral Path: Explorations in Women's Spirituality.** 2nd ed. Theresa King. LC 92-20291. 315p. 1996. pap. 15.95 (*0-936663-13-8*) Yes Intl.

Spiral Road. Jan De Hartog. 1977. reprint ed. lib. bdg. 28.95 (*0-89244-092-9*) Queens Hse-Focus Serv.

Spiral Road: Change in a Chinese Village Through the Eyes of a Communist Party Leader. Huang Shu-min. 222p. (C). 1989. pap. text ed. 21.50 (*0-8133-0938-7*) Westview.

Spiral Staircase. adapted ed. Mel Dinelli. 1962. pap. 5.25 (*0-8222-1065-7*) Dramatists Play.

Spiral Structure in Galaxies: A Density Wave Theory. G. Bertin & C. C. Lin. LC 95-11635. (Illus.). 280p. (C). 1996. 40.00 (*0-262-02396-2*) MIT Pr.

Spiral Structure of Our Galaxy: Proceedings of the I.A.U. Symposium, No. 38, Basel, Swetzerland, 1969. International Astronomical Union Staff. Ed. by W. Becker & G. Contopoulos. LC 75-115886. (I.A.U. Symposia Ser.). 478p. 1970. lib. bdg. 117.50 (*90-277-0109-1*) Kluwer Ac.

Spiral Symmetry. Ed. by Istvan Hargittai & Clifford A. Pickover. 650p. (C). 1993. text ed. 61.00 (*981-02-0615-1*) World Scientific Pub.

Spiral to Economic Disaster. Gyeorgos C. Hatonn. 137p. (Orig.). 1995. pap. 6.00 (*1-56935-092-2*) Phoenix Source.

Spiral Vector Theory of AC Circuits & Machines. Sakae Yamamura. (Monographs in Electrical & Electronic Engineering: No. 26). (Illus.). 140p. 1992. 75.00 (*0-19-859379-1*) OUP.

***Spiral Waves in Active Media.** 300p. 1998. 31.00 (*981-02-2524-5*) World Scientific Pub.

Spiral Way. Aldo Carotenuto. 1995. pap. 16.00 (*0-919123-24-4*, Pub. by Inner City CN) BookWorld Dist.

Spiralen. Fink & Berka. 1994. pap. 40.95 (*0-8384-4508-X*) Heinle & Heinle.

Spiralen. Fink & Berka. 1994. pap. 46.95 (*0-8384-4510-1*) Heinle & Heinle.

Spiralen. Fink. (College German Ser.). (GER.). 1994. suppl. ed., pap. 36.95 (*0-8384-4516-0*) Heinle & Heinle.

Spiralen. Fink. (College German Ser.). (GER.). 1994. suppl. ed. 12.95 incl. audio (*0-8384-4512-8*) Heinle & Heinle.

Spiralen. annot. ed. Fink. (College German Ser.). (GER.). 1994. teacher ed., pap. 40.95 (*0-8384-4509-8*) Heinle & Heinle.

Spiraling: Selected Poems. Sallie Nixon. (Persephone Press Poetry Ser.: No. 4). (Illus.). 40p. 1990. per., pap. 10.00 (*1-879009-00-5*) S P-Persephone Pr.

Spirals. Lydia Goings. (Orig.). 1995. pap. write for info. (*1-57553-058-9*) Watermrk Pr.

Spirals. Douglas MacDonald. (Offset Offshoot Ser.: No.4). 34p. 1979. pap. 10.00 (*0-317-06440-1*) Ommation Pr.

Spirals: From Theodorus to Chaos. Philip J. Davis. LC 92-14062. 248p. (C). 1993. 34.00 (*1-56881-010-5*) AK Peters.

Spirals & Circles: A Key to Thematic Patterns in Classisism & Realism, 2 vols. Horst S. Daemmrich & Ingrid G. Daemmrich. LC 93-27275. (Studies on Themes & Motifs in Literature: Vols. 7 & 8). 452p. 1994. 39.95 (*0-8204-2338-6*); text ed. 39.95 (*0-8204-2337-8*) P Lang Pubng.

Spirals & Circles: A Key to Thematic Patterns in Classisism & Realism, 2 vols., Set. Horst S. Daemmrich & Ingrid G. Daemmrich. LC 93-27275. (Studies on Themes & Motifs in Literature: Vols. 7 & 8). 1994. write for info. (*0-8204-2404-8*) P Lang Pubng.

Spirals, Curves, Fanshapes, & Lines. Tana Hoban. LC 91-30159. (Illus.). 32p. (J). (ps-4). 1992. 14.00 (*0-688-11228-5*); lib. bdg. 13.93 (*0-688-11229-3*) Greenwillow.

Spirals Plays Evaluation Pack, 9 titles, No. 2. Stanley Thornes. (C). 1990. 144.00 (*0-685-37719-9*, Pub. by Stanley Thornes UK) Trans-Atl Phila.

Spirals Special Value Pack, 8 copies of new title. Stanley Thornes. (C). 1990. 120.00 (*0-7487-0465-5*, Pub. by Stanley Thornes UK) Trans-Atl Phila.

Spirals Special Value Pack, 1 each of 23 titles, Set. Stanley Thornes. (C). 1990. 372.00 (*0-7487-0469-8*, Pub. by Stanley Thornes UK) Trans-Atl Phila.

Spirals Special Value Pack of New Titles, 8 copies. Stanley Thornes. (C). 1990. 120.00 (*0-7487-0470-1*, Pub. by Stanley Thornes UK) Trans-Atl Phila.

Spirals Stories Evaluation, 7 titles, Set. Ed. by Stanley Thornes. (C). 1990. 110.00 (*0-7487-0468-X*, Pub. by Stanley Thornes UK) Trans-Atl Phila.

Spirals Stories Evaluation Pack, 8 titles, No. 1. Stanley Thornes. (C). 1990. 116.00 (*0-7487-0466-3*, Pub. by Stanley Thornes UK) Trans-Atl Phila.

Spirals Stories Evaluation Pack, 8 titles, Set. Ed. by Stanley Thornes. (C). 1990. 116.00 (*0-7487-0467-1*, Pub. by Stanley Thornes UK) Trans-Atl Phila.

Spirals Value Pack, Set. Stanley Thornes. (C). 1990. 278.00 (*0-7487-0464-7*, Pub. by Stanley Thornes UK) Trans-Atl Phila.

Spire. William Golding. 1991. lib. bdg. 27.95 (*1-56849-062-3*) Buccaneer Bks.

Spire. William Golding. LC 63-15314. 1965. pap. 10.00 (*0-15-684741-8*, Harvest Bks) HarBrace.

Spires & Poplars. Alfred R. Bellinger. LC 72-144711. (Yale Younger Poets Ser.: No. 4). reprint ed. 18.00 (*0-404-53804-5*) AMS Pr.

Spires of Form: A Study of Emerson's Aesthetic Theory. Vivian C. Hopkins. LC 80-2537. reprint ed. 33.50 (*0-404-19263-7*) AMS Pr.

***Spires of Spirit.** Gael Baudino. 1997. pap. 5.99 (*0-451-45568-1*, ROC) NAL-Dutton.

Spiridon. George Sand, pseud. 270p. (FRE.). 1976. pap. 45.00 (*0-7859-5396-5*) Fr & Eur.

Spiridonova, Revolutionary Terrorist. Isaac Steinberg. LC 72-150201. (Select Bibliographies Reprint Ser.). 1977. 26.95 (*0-8369-5714-8*) Ayer.

Spirit. (Slim Goodbody Ser.). (Illus.). (J). 1996. 14.95 (*1-57749-016-9*) Fairview Press.

***Spirit!** Heidi Bratton. LC 97-7464. (Walking with God Ser.). (J). 1997. write for info. (*0-8091-6640-2*) Paulist Pr.

Spirit. Witness Lee. 122p. per. 4.75 (*0-87083-553-X*, 07027001) Living Stream Ministry.

Spirit: Mind, Body & the Will to Existence. Arthur Kornhaber. 1990. pap. 9.95 (*0-446-39127-1*) Warner Bks.

Spirit: The Last Two Hundred Forty-Five Dailies. Will Eisner. (U. S. Classics Ser.). (Illus.). 72p. 1980. pap. 6.95 (*0-912277-18-1*) K Pierce Inc.

Spirit: Two Hundred Dailies. Will Eisner. (U. S. Classics Ser.). (Illus.). 64p. 1978. pap. 5.95 (*0-912277-16-5*) K Pierce Inc.

Spirit: Two Hundred More Dailies. Will Eisner. (U. S. Classics Ser.). (Illus.). 64p. 1980. pap. 5.95 (*0-912277-17-3*) K Pierce Inc.

Spirit - Symbols: In Native American Art. Leone L. Kasner. (Illus.). 234p. (Orig.). 1992. pap. 15.95 (*0-9633225-0-8*) Ayers Mtn Pr.

Spirit - Transformation & Development in Organizations. Harrison Owen. LC 87-70469. 248p. (Orig.). 1987. pap. text ed. 20.00 (*0-9618205-0-0*) Abbott Pub.

Spirit & Ancestor. Bill Holm. 1987. pap. 24.95 (*0-02-959510-X*, Free Press) Free Pr.

Spirit & Beauty: An Introduction to Theological Aesthetics. Patrick Sherry. 208p. 1992. 55.00 (*0-19-826743-6*) OUP.

Spirit & Community Vol. 1: Essays on Soul & Society. George A. Kendall. 189p. (Orig.). 1996. pap. 11.95 (*0-9651080-5-8*) St George MI.

Spirit & Existence: A Philosophical Inquiry. Michael Gelven. LC 89-40754. (Library of Religious Philosophy: Vol. 4). 288p. (C). 1990. text ed. 34.50 (*0-268-01736-0*) U of Notre Dame Pr.

***Spirit & Flame: An Anthology of African American Poetry.** Ed. by Keith Gilyard. LC 96-35253. 325p. 1997. 49.95 (*0-8156-2730-0*); pap. 24.95 (*0-8156-2731-9*) Syracuse U Pr.

Spirit & Flight Vol. 1: A Photographic Salute to the United States Air Force Academy. Ed. & Photos by Elizabeth G. Lui. LC 96-84751. (Illus.). xxv, 135p. 1996. 60.00 (*0-9652585-0-5*) Assoc Graduate USAF Academy.

Spirit & Influence of Chivalry. Joseph Clair Batty. 1976. lib. bdg. 59.95 (*0-8490-2658-X*) Gordon Pr.

Spirit & Intellect: Thomas Upham's Holiness Theology. Darius L. Salter. LC 86-10048. (Studies in Evangelicalism: No. 7). 283p. 1986. 29.50 (*0-8108-1899-X*) Scarecrow.

***Spirit & Intent of Treaty 7.** (McGill-Queen's Native & Northern Ser.). (Illus.). 272p. 1996. 44.95 (*0-7735-1521-6*, Pub. by McGill CN) U of Toronto Pr.

Spirit & Its Letter: Traces of Rhetoric in Hegel's Philosophy of "Bildung" John H. Smith. LC 87-47960. 320p. 1988. 42.50 (*0-8014-2048-2*) Cornell U Pr.

Spirit & Joy. Joan Albarella. 12p. 1993. write for info. (*0-914620-04-5*) Alpha Pr.

Spirit & Letter in Paul. Arthur J. Dewey. (Studies in the Bible & Early Christianity: Vol. 33). 256p. 1996. 89.95 (*0-7734-9703-X*) E Mellen.

Spirit & Life, Book of the Sun. Ed. by Daniel H. Shubin. Tr. by John W. Volkov from RUS. 768p. 1984. 40.00 (*0-318-20027-9*) D H Shubin.

Spirit & Matter: New Horizons for Medicine. Jose Lacerda de Azevedo. LC 95-74972. (Illus.). 320p. (Orig.). pap. 16.95 (*1-56184-083-1*) New Falcon Pubns.

Spirit & Me. large type ed. write for info. (*0-318-68658-9*, 7265) LBW.

Spirit (& Mind) of Christ: Are You Really a Christian? Maralene Wesner & Miles Wesner. 106p. (Orig.). 1989. pap. 4.95 (*0-936715-36-7*) Diversity Okla.

Spirit & Nature. Richard A. Bowen. (Illus.). 78p. (Orig.). 1995. pap. 9.95 (*0-9649343-1-0*) Ariadne Pubs.

Spirit & Nature: Visions of Interdependence. Steven C. Rockefeller & John C. Elder. (Illus.). 94p. (Orig.). 1990. pap. 15.00 (*0-9625262-1-5*) Middlebury Coll Mus.

Spirit & Nature: Why the Environment Is a Religious Issue - an Interfaith Dialogue. Ed. by Steven C. Rockefeller & John C. Elder. LC 91-37116. (Illus.). 240p. 1992. pap. 16.00 (*0-8070-7709-7*) Beacon Pr.

Spirit & Nature see Papers from Eranos Yearbooks

Spirit & Renewal: Essays in Honor of J. Rodman Williams. Mark W. Wilson. (Journal of Pentecostal Theology Supplement Ser.: No. 5). 271p. pap. 19.95 (*1-85075-471-3*, Pub. by Sheffield Acad UK) CUP Services.

Spirit & Soul: Essays in Philosophical Psychology. Edward S. Casey. LC 91-13223. xii, 309p. (Orig.). 1991. pap. 18.00 (*0-88214-346-8*) Spring Pubns.

Spirit & Structure of German Fascism. Robert A. Brady. LC 68-9629. 1970. reprint ed. 47.50 (*0-86527-189-5*) Fertig.

Spirit & Symbol: The Japanese New Year. Reiko M. Brandon & Barbara B. Stephan. LC 93-41794. 1994. 34.00 (*0-937426-24-5*); pap. 20.00 (*0-937426-25-3*) Honolu Arts.

Spirit & Symbol: The Japanese New Year. Ed. by Reiko M. Brandon & Barbara B. Stephan. (Illus.). 144p. (C). 1994. text ed. 34.00 (*0-8248-1626-9*); pap. text ed. 19.95 (*0-8248-1627-7*) UH Pr.

Spirit & Symbol: The Japanese New Year (Postcard Book) (Illus.). 30p. (Orig.). 1994. pap. 9.95 (*0-937426-26-1*) Honolu Arts.

Spirit & Technology. Adnan Sarhan. 70p. 1988. pap. 5.00 (*1-884328-08-3*) Sufi Fnd Amer.

Spirit & the Body. Witness Lee. 230p. per. 8.75 (*0-87083-459-2*, 07017001) Living Stream Ministry.

Spirit & the Bride Say, "Come!" Mary's Role in the New Pentecost. George W. Kosicki & Gerald J. Farrell. 112p. 1981. pap. 2.95 (*0-911988-41-6*, 38450) AMI Pr.

Spirit & the Drum: A Memoir of Africa. Edith Turner. LC 86-30825. 165p. 1987. 11.95 (*0-8165-1009-1*) U of Ariz Pr.

Spirit & the Flesh: Sexual Diversity in American Indian Culture. Walter L. Williams. (Illus.). 368p. 1992. pap. 16.00 (*0-8070-4615-9*) Beacon Pr.

Spirit & the Form. A. Rogers. 159p. (C). 1976. text ed. 60.00 (*0-685-22165-2*, Pub. by Univ Nottingham UK) St Mut.

Spirit & the Form Essays in Adult Education in Honour of Professor Harold Wiltshire. A. Rogers. (C). 1976. 39.00 (*0-902031-38-4*, Pub. by Univ Nottingham UK) St Mut.

Spirit & the Forms of Love. Daniel D. Williams. LC 81-40368. 316p. 1981. reprint ed. pap. text ed. 24.50 (*0-8191-1692-0*) U Pr of Amer.

***Spirit & the Glory: An Overview of Ezekiel.** Jack Hayford et al. (Bible Book-a-Month Ser.: Vol. 6). 70p. 1997. pap. 3.95 (*0-916847-23-3*) Living Way.

Spirit & the Mind. Samuel H. Sandweiss. 1985. pap. 9.00 (*0-9600958-9-6*) Birth Day.

Spirit & the New Age. Ed. by R. Larry Shelton & Alex R. Deasley. (Wesleyan Theological Perspectives Ser.: Vol. 5). 1989. 9.95 (*0-87162-412-5*, D4854) Warner Pr.

Spirit & the Vision: The Influence of Christian Romanticism on the Development of 19th-Century American Art. Diane Apostolos-Cappadona. LC 94-7797. (Academy Ser.). 246p. (C). 1995. 39.95 (*1-55540-974-1*, 010184); pap. 24.95 (*1-55540-975-X*, 010184) Scholars Pr GA.

***Spirit & Tradition: An Essay on Change.** Stephen Platten & George Pattison. 176p. (Orig.). 1996. pap. 23.95 (*1-85311-130-9*, Pub. by Canterbury Press Norwich UK) Morehouse Pub.

Spirit & Vision of Notre Dame: The First 150 Years. Keith Kaczorek. Ed. by Harriett Harrow. (Illus.). 96p. (J). 1992. 28.00 (*0-9623171-4-4*); pap. 18.50 (*0-9623171-5-2*); pap. text ed. 8.50 (*0-9623171-6-0*) LBCo Pub.

Spirit As Lord. Philip Rosato. 240p. 1981. 39.95 (*0-567-09305-0*, Pub. by T & T Clark UK) Bks Intl VA.

Spirit Ascendant: The Art & Life of Patrocino Barela. David L. Witt & Edward Gonzales. (Illus.). 232p. 1996. 49.95 (*1-878610-46-5*) Red Crane Bks.

Spirit at Work: A Journey of Healing. Lois M. Grant. LC 96-84870. (Illus.). 280p. (Orig.). 1997. pap. 15.00 (*0-942531-35-3*) Emerald Wave.

Spirit at Work: Discovering the Spirituality in Leadership. Jay A. Conger. (Business-Management Ser.). 264p. text ed. 25.95 (*1-55542-639-5*) Jossey-Bass.

Spirit Baptism: A Biblical Investigation. Howard M. Ervin. 208p. 1987. pap. 9.95 (*0-913573-79-5*) Hendrickson MA.

Spirit Bear: Encounters with the White Bear of the Western Rainforest. Charles Russell. (Illus.). 144p. (Orig.). 1994. pap. 22.95 (*1-55013-649-6*, Pub. by Key Porter Bks CN) Firefly Bks Ltd.

Spirit, Being & Self. P. T. Raju. (Studies in Indian & Western Philosophy). 285p. 1982. 29.95 (*0-940500-98-1*, Pub. by S Asian Pubs II) Asia Bk Corp.

Spirit, Being & Self: Studies in Indian & Western Philosophy. P. T. Raju. 284p. 1986. 20.00 (*0-8364-1853-0*, Pub. by S Asia Pubs II) S Asia.

Spirit, Being, & Self: Studies in Indian & Western Philosophy. P. T. Raju. 285p. 1982. 29.95 (*0-318-37031-X*) Asia Bk Corp.

Spirit Bodies: Poems by David McKain. David McKain. LC 90-83510. (Ithaca House Poetry Ser.). 64p. (Orig.). (C). 1990. pap. 9.95 (*0-87886-133-5*) Greenfld Rev Lit.

An Asterisk (*) at the beginning of an entry indicates that the title is appearing in BIP for the first time.

Spirit Bone. Gino Sky. (Illus.). 40p. (Orig.). 1991. pap. 12.00 (*0-931659-12-4*) Limberlost Pr.

Spirit Born Creativity. Mark Virkler & Patti Virkler. 238p. (Orig.). 1990. pap. 9.99 (*1-56043-004-4*) Destiny Image.

Spirit Boy & the Insatiable Soul. Robert Bly. LC 93-41009. 128p. 1994. pap. 11.00 (*0-06-095063-3*, PL) HarpC.

Spirit Brides. Kahlil Gibran. Tr. & Intro. by Juan R. Cole. (Illus.). 92p. 1993. 16.00 (*1-883991-00-5*) Whte Cloud Pr.

Spirit Broods over the World. George A. Maloney. LC 92-40239. 210p. 1993. pap. 9.95 (*0-8189-0633-2*) Alba.

Spirit Builder. Clinton White. 214p. 1985. pap. 7.00 (*0-934109-02-8*) Banquet Hse.

***Spirit by Barbara-Marie Green.** Barbara-Marie Green. 100p. (Orig.). 1997. pap. 12.00 (*1-883414-06-7*) Bar JaMae.

***Spirit Called My Name: A Journey of Deepening into Soul.** unabridged ed. Sally M. O'Neil. 140p. 1997. pap. 11.95 (*0-9658844-0-6*) Soar Eagle.

Spirit Caller. Jean Hager. 272p. 1997. 22.00 (*0-89296-640-8*) Mysterious Pr.

***Spirit Caller.** Jean Hager. 1998. mass mkt. write for info. (*0-446-40488-8*, Mysterious Paperbk) Warner Bks.

***Spirit Caller.** large type ed. Jean Hager. LC 97-11759. 1997. 24.95 (*0-7862-1124-5*) Thorndike Pr.

Spirit Calls...Rejoice! A Collection of Songs for Worship. Handt Hanson & Paul Murakami. 219p. 1991. pap. 19.95 (*0-933173-38-5*) Chging Church Forum.

Spirit Capable: The Story of Commonwealth Edison. John Hogan. LC 86-61287. (Illus.). 464p. 1986. 24.95 (*0-916371-04-2*) Mobium Pr.

Spirit Casebook. Will Eisner. Ed. by Dave Schreiner. (Illus.). 158p. 1990. 29.95 (*0-87816-093-0*); pap. 12.95 (*0-87816-094-9*) Kitchen Sink.

Spirit Catcher: The Life & Art of John Coltrane. John Fraim. LC 95-75444. 216p. Date not set. pap. 14.95 (*0-9645561-0-3*) Greathse Co.

***Spirit Catches You & You Fall Down: A Hmong Child, Her Doctors, & an American Tragedy.** Anne Fadiman. LC 97-5175. 1997. 23.00 (*0-374-26781-2*) FS&G.

Spirit-Centered Wholeness: Beyond the Psychology of Self. Ed. by H. Newton Malony. LC 87-23028. (Studies in the Psychology of Religion: Vol. 2). 256p. 1987. lib. bdg. 89.95 (*0-88946-246-1*) E Mellen.

Spirit Channeling & the American Religious Imagination. Brown. Date not set. 24.00 (*0-02-904831-1*, Free Press) Free Pr.

Spirit Controlled Life. Bob Yandian. 272p. 1995. mass mkt. 4.99 (*0-88368-356-3*) Whitaker Hse.

Spirit-Controlled Temperament. large type ed. Tim LaHaye. 1986. 13.95 (*0-8027-2563-5*) Walker & Co.

Spirit-Controlled Woman. rev. ed. Beverly LaHaye. LC 94-29312. 1995. pap. 9.99 (*1-56507-223-5*) Harvest Hse.

Spirit Dogs: Heroes in Heaven. Susan L. Metzger. (Illus.). 20p. (Orig.). 1996. pap. 7.95 (*0-9650495-0-7*) Owl of Athene.

Spirit Drive. Cottman. Date not set. write for info. (*0-517-70328-9*) Random Hse Value.

Spirit Faces: Contemporary Native American Masks from the Northwest. Intro. by Gary Wyatt. 136p. 1995. pap. 17.95 (*0-8118-0825-4*) Chronicle Bks.

Spirit-Filled: Anointed by Christ the King. Jack W. Hayford. LC 84-80747. (Orig.). 1984. pap. 3.95 (*0-916847-04-7*) Living Way.

Spirit Filled Believer's Daily Devotional. Dick Mills. Orig. Title: Word Daily Devotional. 384p. (Orig.). 1996. pap. 9.99 (*0-89274-844-3*, HH-844) Harrison Hse.

Spirit-Filled Believer's Handbook Bible: Foundations for Christian Living from the. Derek Prince. 1993. 19.99 (*0-88419-329-2*) Creation House.

Spirit-Filled Christian. rev. ed. Navigators Staff. (Design for Discipleship Ser.: Bk. 2). (Illus.). 48p. 1980. pap. 4.00 (*0-89109-037-1*) NavPress.

Spirit-Filled Church in Action. Albert B. Simpson. 1996. pap. 9.99 (*0-87509-654-9*) Chr Pubns.

Spirit-Filled Family. expanded rev. ed. Tim LaHaye & Beverly LaHaye. 1995. pap. 9.99 (*1-56507-332-0*) Harvest Hse.

Spirit-Filled Family: Holy Wisdom to Build Happy Homes. 160p. 1994. pap. text ed. 6.99 (*0-8407-2085-8*) Nelson.

***Spirit-Filled Family/La Familia Iena del Espirity.** Jack Hayford. 1995. pap. 5.99 (*0-89922-517-9*) Edit Betania.

Spirit-Filled Father's Guide to Total Victory. Harrison House, Inc., Editors. 208p. 1994. 12.99 (*0-89274-775-7*, HH-775) Harrison Hse.

Spirit Filled Life. Charles Stanley. 1994. 7.99 (*0-7852-8137-1*) Nelson.

***Spirit-Filled Life Bible Discovery Guides: James, 1 & 2 Peter, 1-3 John, Jude Passing Faith's Tests with Love & Joy.** Ed. by Jack Hayford. 160p. 1997. 6.99 (*0-7852-1205-1*) Nelson.

Spirit-Filled Life Booklet. Bill Bright. 1990. 5.99 (*0-86605-066-3*) Nelson.

Spirit-Filled Living, No. 4. Charles Stanley. 24p. 1995. pap. 2.50 (*1-56476-435-4*, 6-3435, Victor Bks) Chariot Victor.

Spirit-Filled Man. Harrison House, Inc., Editors. 160p. (Orig.). 1996. mass mkt. 5.99 (*0-89274-789-7*, HH-789) Harrison Hse.

Spirit Filled Mother's Guide to Total Victory. Harrison House, Inc., Editors. 208p. 1994. 12.99 (*0-89274-908-3*, HH-908) Harrison Hse.

Spirit-Filled Pocket Bible on Faith. Harrison House, Inc., Editors. (Spirit-Filled Pocket Bible Ser.). 128p. (Orig.). 1995. mass mkt. 4.99 (*0-89274-833-8*, HH-833) Harrison Hse.

Spirit-Filled Pocket Bible on Finances. Harrison House, Inc., Editors. (Spirit-Filled Pocket Bible Ser.). 128p. (Orig.). 1995. mass mkt. 4.99 (*0-89274-835-4*, HH-835) Harrison Hse.

Spirit-Filled Pocket Bible on Healing. Harrison House, Inc., Editors. (Spirit-Filled Pocket Bible Ser.). 128p. (Orig.). 1995. mass mkt. 4.99 (*0-89274-832-X*, HH-832) Harrison Hse.

Spirit-Filled Pocket Bible on Protection. Harrison House, Inc., Editors. (Spirit-Filled Pocket Bible Ser.). 128p. (Orig.). 1995. mass mkt. 4.99 (*0-89274-834-6*, HH-834) Harrison Hse.

***Spirit-Filled Woman: 365 Daily Devotions.** J. M. Martin. 1997. 14.99 (*0-88419-483-3*) Creation House.

Spirit-Filled Women. Harrison House, Inc., Editors. 160p. (Orig.). 1996. mass mkt. 5.99 (*0-89274-790-0*, HH-790) Harrison Hse.

Spirit Flyer Series, 8 bks., Set. John Bibee. (Illus.). 1993. pap. 53.13 (*0-8308-1200-8*, 1200) InterVarsity.

Spirit Flyer Series, Set, Bks. 5-8. John Bibee. (Illus.). (J). 1993. Set. boxed 24.99 (*0-8308-1289-X*, 1289) InterVarsity.

Spirit Flyers Series, Set, Bks. 1-4. John Bibee. (Illus.). (Orig.). (J). 1992. Boxed Set. boxed 24.99 (*0-8308-1208-3*, 1208) InterVarsity.

Spirit Fruit: A Gentle Utopia. H. Roger Grant. (Illus.). 217p. 1988. 25.00 (*0-87580-137-4*) N Ill U Pr.

Spirit Fruit & Voice. 2nd ed. Jacob Beilhart. (Illus.). 176p. 1986. reprint ed. pap. 6.95 (*0-918588-08-1*, 507-100) Barksdale Foun.

Spirit Gate. Maya K. Bohnhoff. 352p. 1996. mass mkt. 5.99 (*0-671-87712-7*) Baen Bks.

Spirit Gifts: Participant's Workbook. Patricia D. Brown. 96p. (Orig.). 1996. pap. 5.95 (*0-687-00858-1*) Abingdon.

Spirit, Giver of Life & Love. Pope John Paul, II. 300p. 1996. pap. 16.95 (*0-8198-6987-2*) Pauline Bks.

Spirit Guide. Christian Harfouche. 58p. (Orig.). 1993. pap. text ed. 6.00 (*0-9634451-4-6*) Power House Pub.

***Spirit Guides.** Norma Kalina. 1997. pap. 5.99 (*0-451-19087-4*, Sig) NAL-Dutton.

Spirit Guides: We Are Not Alone. Iris Belhayes & Enid. 200p. (Orig.). 1996. pap. 12.95 (*0-917086-80-5*) ACS Pubns.

Spirit Guides Book: Communicating with Your Unseen Friends. Victoria Young. 150p. (Orig.). 1989. pap. 9.95 (*0-929684-00-1*); pap. 18.95 incl. audio (*0-929684-01-X*) Silver Forest Pub.

Spirit Has Come. Earl H. Andrews. 1991. pap. 14.00 (*0-85234-162-8*) Pilgrim Pubns.

Spirit Healing: Native American Magic & Medicine. Mary D. Atwood. LC 91-21220. (Illus.). 160p. 1991. pap. 12.95 (*0-8069-8266-7*) Sterling.

Spirit Helps Us Pray: A Biblical Theology of Prayer. Robert J. Brandt & Zenas J. Bicket. 464p. 1994. 24.95 (*0-88243-678-3*) Gospel Pub.

Spirit Himself. rev. ed. Ralph M. Riggs. 224p. 1977. pap. 6.95 (*0-88243-590-6*, 02-0590) Gospel Pub.

Spirit! Historic Ketchikan, Alaska. Ed. by June Allen & Patricia Charles. 148p. (Orig.). pap. 12.95 (*0-9634438-0-1*) Hist Ketchikan.

***Spirit Horse.** Ned Ackerman. LC 97-8547. (J). 1998. write for info. (*0-590-39650-1*) Scholastic Inc.

***Spirit Horses.** Jaime Jackson & D. Marisa Huntinghorse. (Illus.). 144p. 1997. pap. 17.95 (*0-87358-633-6*) Northland AZ.

Spirit House. William Sleator. LC 93-7485. 144p. (J). (gr. 7 up). 1993. pap. 3.99 (*0-14-036483-8*, Puffin) Puffin Bks.

Spirit, Hurry: Poems by Rolly Kent. Rolly Kent. LC 85-70799. 64p. 1985. 14.95 (*0-917652-51-7*); pap. 7.95 (*0-917652-50-9*) Confluence Pr.

Spirit in Ashes: Hegel, Heidegger & Man-Made Mass Death. Edith Wyschogrod. LC 84-26932. 248p. 1985. 30.00 (*0-300-03322-2*) Yale U Pr.

Spirit in Ashes: Hegel, Heidegger, & Man-Made Mass Death. Edith Wyschogrod. 263p. (C). 1990. reprint ed. pap. 17.00 (*0-300-04622-7*) Yale U Pr.

Spirit in Exile: Peter Porter & His Poetry. Bruce Bennett. (Illus.). 350p. 1992. 55.00 (*0-19-554970-8*) OUP.

Spirit in Galatia: Paul's Interpretation of Pneuma As Divine Power. David J. Lull. LC 79-26094. (Society of Biblical Literature. Dissertation Ser.: No. 49). 254p. reprint ed. pap. 72.40 (*0-7837-5443-4*, 2045208) Bks Demand.

***Spirit in Motion...Breath-Stretch: Activating Your Vital Energy Force.** Wendy Gross. 100p. 1996. pap. 19.95 (*0-9655755-0-0*) W Gross.

***Spirit in Paradise: History of the Assemblies of God of Fiji, & Its Ministries to Other Countries of the South Pacific.** Lawrence R. Larson. LC 96-95442. (Illus.). 512p. 1996. 32.95 (*0-9656302-0-X*) L R Larson.

Spirit in Politics. Bob Myers. 208p. 1996. pap. 9.95 (*1-881571-09-2*) Letters Etcetera.

Spirit in the Church. Karl Rahner. 3.95 (*0-8164-2189-7*) Crossroad NY.

Spirit in the Dark: The Spiritual Autobiography of SDiane A. Bogus. SDiane A. Bogus. pap. 25.00 (*0-934172-25-0*) WIM Pubns.

Spirit in the Gospels & Acts: Divine Purity & Power. Craig S. Keener. LC 97-6228. 356p. 1997. 24.95 (*1-56563-169-2*) Hendrickson MA.

Spirit in the Landscape. Bart Testa. (Art Gallery of Ontario Film Bks.). (Illus.). 72p. (C). 1989. pap. 10.00 (*0-919777-73-2*) Wilfrid Laurier.

***Spirit in the Stone: A Handbook of Southwestern Indian Animal Carvings & Beliefs.** Mark Bahti. (Illus.). 224p. (Orig.). 1997. pap. write for info. (*1-887896-09-0*) Treas Chest Bks.

Spirit in the World. Donald L. Gelpi. (Zacchaeus Studies). 127p. 1988. pap. 8.95 (*0-8146-5684-6*) Liturgical Pr.

Spirit in the World. Karl Rahner. 448p. 1994. pap. text ed. 24.95 (*0-8264-0647-5*) Continuum.

Spirit Journey: A Walk Through Matthew. Will Keim. 160p. (Orig.). 1995. pap. 9.99 (*0-8272-3436-8*) Chalice Pr.

Spirit Keepers of the North: Eskimos of Western Alaska. Susan A. Kaplan. (Illus.). 35p. reprint ed. pap. 25.00 (*0-685-24019-3*, 2031612) Bks Demand.

Spirit Lamp: An Aesthetic, Literary & Critical Magazine, Vols. 1-4, No. 2. LC 79-8081. reprint ed. write for info. (*0-404-18390-5*) AMS Pr.

Spirit Led Family. Grace Robley & Rob Robley. 160p. 1974. mass mkt. 4.99 (*0-88368-033-5*) Whitaker Hse.

Spirit-Led Helping. William E. Consiglio. Ed. by Alan Keith-Lucas. (Practice Monograph Ser.: No. 3). 52p. 1987. 6.00 (*0-685-35658-2*) N American Assn.

Spirit Level. David Barber. LC 95-31659. 76p. 1995. pap. 12.95 (*0-8101-5024-7*); text ed. 29.95 (*0-8101-5023-9*) Northwestern U Pr.

Spirit Level. Seamus Heaney. LC 95-42585. 82p. 1995. 18.00 (*0-374-26779-0*) FS&G.

Spirit Level. Seamus Heaney. 1996. 30.00 incl. audio (*0-374-97525-6*) FS&G.

***Spirit Level.** Seamus Heaney. 1997. pap. 11.00 (*0-374-52511-0*, Noonday) FS&G.

***Spirit Level.** Seamus Heaney. 1997. pap. 12.95 (*0-14-086695-7*) Viking Penguin.

Spirit Like a Storm: The Story of Mary Shelley. Calvin C. Miller. (World Writers Ser.). (Illus.). 124p. (YA). (gr. 6 up). 1996. lib. bdg. 18.95 (*1-883846-13-7*) M Reynolds.

Spirit Loose in the World: The Extraordinary Journey of a Beloved Benedictine Abbot in Search of Man's Place in the World & His Relationship with His Creator. Benedict Reid. LC 93-61087. 320p. (Orig.). 1993. pap. 17.95 (*1-879560-20-8*) Harbor Hse West.

Spirit Lost. Nancy Thayer. 192p. 1989. pap. 3.95 (*0-380-70833-7*) Avon.

Spirit Manifestations & the Gift of Tongues. Robert Anderson. LC 86-21495. 32p. 1935. pap. 2.99 (*0-87213-015-0*) Loizeaux.

Spirit Manifestations & the Gift of Tongues, 5 vols., Set. Robert Anderson. LC 86-21495. 1935. Pkg. of 5. pap. 14.95 (*0-87213-560-8*) Loizeaux.

***Spirit Masks & the Art of Shapeshifting.** Ted Andrews. Ed. by Margaret K. Andrews & Pagan Alexander-Harding. (Illus.). 250p. (Orig.). 1997. pap. 14.95 (*1-888767-32-4*) Life Magic.

Spirit Master. John Shea. (Basics of Christian Thought Ser.). 1987. pap. 12.95 (*0-88347-206-6*); pap. 12.95 (*0-88347-264-3*, 7264) Res Christian Liv.

Spirit Meadow. Lauran Paine. 192p. 1987. 15.95 (*0-8027-0970-2*) Walker & Co.

Spirit Medicine: Native American Teachings to Awaken the Spirit. Wolf Moondance. LC 95-20796. (Illus.). 160p. 1995. pap. 12.95 (*0-8069-1368-1*) Sterling.

***Spirit Memories.** (Illus.). 48p. 1997. lib. bdg. 19.95 (*0-9658321-0-4*, Spirit Mems) Memories.

***Spirit Memories.** (Illus.). 48p. 1997. ring bd. 24.95 (*0-9658321-1-2*, Spirit Mems) Memories.

Spirit, Mind & Body. Mary Brook & Ray Brook. 1981. pap. 75.00 (*0-9513312-0-5*, Pub. by R Brooks Pubns UK) St Mut.

Spirit Mound Township in 1984: Campaign Effects in a Rural Electorate. Alan L. Clem. 1985. pap. 1.00 (*1-55614-122-X*) U of SD Gov Res Bur.

Spirit Mound Township Revisited: A Rural View of the 1972 Campaign. Alan L. Clem. 1973. 1.00 (*1-55614-005-3*) U of SD Gov Res Bur.

Spirit Mountain: An Anthology of Yuman Story & Song. Ed. by Leanne Hinton & Lucille Watahomigie. LC 84-112. (Sun Tracks Ser.: No. 10). 344p. 1984. 49.95 (*0-8165-0843-7*); pap. 24.95 (*0-8165-0817-8*) U of Ariz Pr.

Spirit Moves: A Handbook of Dance & Prayer. Carla De Sola. LC 77-89743. (Illus.). 1977. pap. 9.95 (*0-918208-04-1*) Liturgical Conf.

Spirit Moves: A Handbook of Dance & Prayer. Carla De Sola. Ed. & Intro. by Doug Adams. LC 77-89743. (Illus.). 152p. 1986. reprint ed. pap. 9.95 (*0-941500-38-1*) Sharing Co.

Spirit Moves: The Story of Six Generations of Native Women. Loree Boyd. (Illus.). 448p. (Orig.). 1995. pap. 16.95 (*1-880032-59-7*) New Wrld Lib.

Spirit, Nature, & Community: Issues in the Thought of Simone Weil. Diogenes Allen & Eric O. Springsted. LC 93-36973. (SUNY Series, Simone Weil Studies). 241p. (C). 1994. pap. text ed. 19.95 (*0-7914-2018-3*) State U NY Pr.

Spirit, Nature, & Community: Issues in the Thought of Simone Weil. Diogenes Allen & Eric O. Springsted. LC 93-36973. (SUNY Series, Simone Weil Studies). 241p. (C). 1994. text ed. 59.50 (*0-7914-2017-5*) State U NY Pr.

Spirit of a Bear. Susan Harmon. 155p. 1994. 19.95 (*0-8027-4140-1*) Walker & Co.

Spirit of a Bear. large type ed. Susan Harmon. LC 94-33626. 233p. 1995. lib. bdg. 20.95 (*0-7838-1155-1*, GK Hall) Thorndike Pr.

Spirit of a Dog & Other Animal Tales. Edward L. Johnson & Rebecca J. Johnson. LC 92-91105. (Illus.). 188p. (Orig.). 1994. pap. text ed. 9.00 (*1-56002-276-0*, Univ Edtns) Aegina Pr.

Spirit of a Man: A Vision of Transformation for Black Men & the Women Who Love Them. Iyanla Vanzant. LC 96-12258. 240p. 1996. 20.00 (*0-06-251236-6*); pap. write for info. (*0-06-251239-0*) Harper SF.

Spirit of Africa: The Healing Ministry of Archbishop Milingo of Zambia. Gerrie Ter Haar. LC 91-72491. 326p. 1992. 45.00 (*0-86543-268-6*); pap. 12.95 (*0-86543-269-4*) Africa World.

Spirit of African Design. Sharne Algotsson & Denys Davis. LC 95-12992. 176p. 1996. 35.00 (*0-517-59916-3*, Clarkson Potter) Crown Bks Yng Read.

Spirit of Africville. Ed. & Selected by Africville Genealogical Society Staff. (Illus.). 128p. 1995. pap. 19.95 (*0-88780-084-X*) Formac Dist Ltd.

Spirit of Africville. Ed. & Selected by Africville Genealogical Society Staff. (Illus.). 128p. 1995. 34.95 (*0-88780-085-8*) Formac Dist Ltd.

Spirit of Aikido. Kisshomaru Ueshiba. Tr. by Taitetsu Unno from JPN. (Illus.). 126p. (C). 1984. 16.00 (*0-87011-600-2*) Kodansha.

Spirit of Aikido. Kisshomaru Ueshiba. Tr. by Taitetsu Unno from JPN. LC 83-48881. (Illus.). 126p. 1988. pap. 8.00 (*0-87011-850-1*) Kodansha.

Spirit of Akikido. Kisshomaru Uyeshiba. 6.95 (*0-685-05339-3*) Wehman.

Spirit of America: The Biographies of Forty Living Congressional Medal of Honor Recipients. Hugh F. Kayser. LC 81-12533. 1982. 19.95 (*0-88280-087-6*) ETC Pubns.

Spirit of American Government. James A: Smith. Ed. by Seward C. Strout. LC 65-13854. (John Harvard Library). 485p. 1965. 39.95 (*0-674-83220-5*) HUP.

Spirit of American Literature. Darshan S. Maini. viii, 222p. 1988. text ed. 27.50 (*0-938719-27-0*, Envoy Pr) Apt Bks.

Spirit of American Literature. John A. Macy. (BCL1-PS American Literature Ser.). 347p. 1992. reprint ed. lib. bdg. 89.00 (*0-7812-6604-1*) Rprt Serv.

Spirit of American Philosophy. John Smith. LC 82-5612. (SUNY Series in Philosophy). 253p. 1983. reprint ed. pap. text ed. 19.95 (*0-87395-651-6*) State U NY Pr.

***Spirit of Amy.** William A. Clark. Ed. by J. Richards. LC 96-86366. 233p. (Orig.). (J). (gr. 5-10). 1996. pap. 9.98 (*1-887303-23-5*) Blu Lantern Pub.

***Spirit of Ancient Africa.** Virginia L. Starks. (Illus.). 40p. (J). (gr. 1-5). 1997. 16.95 (*0-9656859-1-8*) Blck Pyramid.

***Spirit of Ancient Peru: Treasures from the Musco Arqueologico Rafael Larco Herrera.** Ed. by Kathleen Berrin. LC 97-60322. (Illus.). 216p. 1997. 45.00 (*0-500-01802-2*) Thames Hudson.

Spirit of Anglicanism: Hooker - Maurice - Temple. Ed. by William J. Wolf et al. (Anglican Studies Ser.). 212p. 1979. pap. 9.95 (*0-8192-1263-6*) Morehouse Pub.

Spirit of Atlantis Version 2.1: The Treasure Adventure. rev. ed. Duane K. McCullough. LC 88-92585. 30p. (C). 1994. reprint ed. pap. 20.00 (*0-9621605-3-9*) D K McCullough.

Spirit of Australia: The Crime Fiction of Arthur W. Upfield. Ray B. Browne. LC 87-71998. (Illus.). 292p. (C). 1988. 31.95 (*0-87972-402-1*); pap. 16.95 (*0-87972-403-X*) Bowling Green Univ Popular Press.

Spirit of Beauty...He Holds the Reins. Augustella Clay. 40p. 1995. pap. text ed. 6.00 (*0-8059-3730-7*) Dorrance.

Spirit of Biblical Law. Calum M. Carmichael. LC 96-21568. (Spirit of the Laws Ser.). 1996. 35.00 (*0-8203-1845-0*) U of Ga Pr.

Spirit of Biography. Jeffrey Meyers. Ed. by A. Walton Litz. LC 89-33823. (Studies in Modern Literature: No. 102). 315p. reprint ed. 89.80 (*0-8357-2001-2*, 2070745) Bks Demand.

Spirit of Black Hawk: A Mystery of Africans & Indians. Jason Berry. (Illus.). 128p. 1995. 20.00 (*0-87805-806-0*) U Pr of Miss.

***Spirit of Britain: An Illustrated Guide to Literary Britain.** Ed. & Intro. by Susan Hill. (Illus.). 224p. 1997. pap. 24.95 (*0-7472-7812-1*, Pub. by Headline UK) Trafalgar.

Spirit of Britain's First. Graham Warner. (Illus.). 192p. 1996. 39.95 (*1-85260-533-2*, Pub. by J H Haynes & Co UK) Motorbooks Intl.

Spirit of Buddhism. Hari S. Gour. LC 78-72432. reprint ed. 57.50 (*0-404-17299-7*) AMS Pr.

Spirit of Budo: Old Traditions for Present-Day Life. Trevor P. Leggett. LC 96-14956. 128p. 1996. 29.00 (*0-7103-0562-1*, Pub. by Kegan Paul Intl UK) Col U Pr.

Spirit of Burgundy. Ralph Gibson. (Illus.). 120p. 1994. 50.00 (*0-89381-576-4*) Aperture.

Spirit of "C" An Introduction to Modern Programming. Henry Mullish & Herbert Cooper. 527p. (C). 1987. pap. text ed. 54.25 (*0-314-28500-8*); teacher ed., pap. text ed. write for info. (*0-314-35228-7*) West Pub.

Spirit of Canoe Camping. Harry Drabik. (Illus.). 126p. 1981. pap. 5.95 (*0-931714-11-7*) Nodin Pr.

Spirit of Capitalism & the Protestant Ethic: An Enquiry into the Weber Thesis. Michael H. Lessnoff. 160p. 1994. 65.00 (*1-85278-875-5*) E Elgar.

***Spirit of Cardinal Bernardin.** A. E. Wall. 1996. pap. 8.95 (*0-88347-379-8*) Res Christian Liv.

Spirit of Carnival: Magical Realism & the Grotesque. David K. Danow. 192p. 1995. text ed. 25.95 (*0-8131-1905-7*) U Pr of Ky.

Spirit of Catalonia. J. Trueta. 1976. lib. bdg. 34.95 (*0-8490-2659-8*) Gordon Pr.

***Spirit of Catholicism.** Karl Adam. 1997. pap. text ed. 19.95 (*0-8245-1718-0*) Crossroad NY.

***Spirit of Catholicism.** 2nd ed. Karl Adam. 252p. 1996. reprint ed. pap. 12.95 (*0-940535-85-8*, UP185) Franciscan U Pr.

Spirit of Champions. Del Hessel. 56p. (Orig.). 1982. reprint ed. pap. 8.95 (*0-89279-066-0*) Championship Bks & Vid Prodns.

Spirit of Champions: Great Athletes Reveal How They Integrate Mind, Body & Spirit for Personal Excellence. Lyle Nelson & Thorn Bacon. LC 96-83865. 240p. (Orig.). 1997. pap. 14.95 (*1-885221-32-0*) BookPartners.

Spirit of Change: Voices of Hope for a Better World. Christopher Titmuss. 256p. 1993. lib. bdg. 29.00 (*0-8095-6346-0*) Borgo Pr.

Spirit of Change: Voices of Hope for a Better World. Christopher Titmuss. LC 92-2853. 256p. 1993. reprint ed. pap. 9.95 (*0-89793-094-0*) Hunter Hse.

Spirit of Charles Lindbergh: Another Dimension. T. Willard Hunter. LC 92-42418. 200p. 1993. 19.95 (*1-56833-016-2*) Madison Bks UPA.

Spirit of Chinese Capitalism. S. Gordon Redding. (Studies in Organization: No. 22). xiv, 267p. (C). 1993. pap. text ed. 24.95 (*3-11-013794-1*) De Gruyter.

An Asterisk (*) at the beginning of an entry indicates that the title is appearing in BIP for the first time.

Spirit of Chinese Foreign Policy: A Psychocultural View. Chih-Yu Shih. 210p. 1990. text ed. 49.95 (*0-312-03677-9*) St Martin.

Spirit of Chinese Philosophy. Feng Yu-Lan. Tr. by Ernest R. Hughes. LC 71-98757. 224p. 1970. text ed. 35.00 (*0-8371-2816-1*, FECP, Greenwood Pr) Greenwood.

Spirit of Chinese Politics. 2nd ed. Lucian W. Pye. 264p. (C). 1992. pap. text ed. 17.50 (*0-674-83240-X*) HUP.

***Spirit of Chirstmas Past: Evocative Memories of Years Gone By.** Linda Clements. 1996. 15.98 (*0-7651-9945-9*) Smithmark.

Spirit of Christ. rev. ed. Andrew Murray. LC 79-51335. 288p. 1983. pap. 9.99 (*0-87123-589-7*) Bethany Hse.

Spirit of Christ see Power for Your Life

Spirit of Christmas. Compiled by Evelyn L. Beilenson. (Keepsakes with CDs Ser.). 1995. 11.99 incl. audio compact disk (*0-88088-944-6*) Peter Pauper.

Spirit of Christmas. Henry Van Dyke. 1996. 7.99 (*0-517-14897-8*) Random Hse Value.

***Spirit of Christmas, 11.** Leisure Arts Staff. 1997. 24.95 (*1-57486-064-X*) Oxmoor Hse.

Spirit of Christmas, Bk. 1. 1987. 24.95 (*0-942237-00-5*) Leisure AR.

Spirit of Christmas, Bk. 2. 1988. 24.95 (*0-942237-01-3*) Leisure AR.

Spirit of Christmas, Bk. 3. 1989. 24.95 (*0-942237-04-8*) Leisure AR.

Spirit of Christmas, Bk. 4. 1990. 24.95 (*0-942237-07-2*) Leisure AR.

Spirit of Christmas, Bk. 5. 1991. 24.95 (*0-942237-11-0*) Leisure AR.

Spirit of Christmas, Bk. 6. 1992. 24.95 (*0-942237-17-X*) Leisure AR.

Spirit of Christmas, Bk. 7. Oxmoor House Staff. LC 93-78118. 1993. 24.95 (*0-942237-22-6*) Leisure AR.

Spirit of Christmas, Bk. 8. Leisure Arts Staff. LC 93-80809. 1994. 24.95 (*0-942237-36-6*) Leisure AR.

Spirit of Christmas, Bk. 9. Leisure Arts Staff. 1995. 24.95 (*0-942237-65-X*) Leisure AR.

Spirit of Christmas, Vol. 10. (Illus.). 160p. 1996. 24.95 (*1-57486-009-7*) Leisure AR.

Spirit of Christmas Cookbook. (Illus.). 176p. 1996. 24.95 (*0-942237-79-X*) Oxmoor Hse.

Spirit of Christmas or The Story of Ernestina Scrooge (Playscript) Tom Fuller. 1981. pap. 3.45 (*0-87129-349-8*, S62) Dramatic Pub.

Spirit of Classical Canon Law. R. H. Helmholz. LC 95-46621. (Spirit of the Law Ser.). 1996. 60.00 (*0-8203-1821-3*) U of Ga Pr.

Spirit of Clay. Robert Piepenburg. LC 94-66588. (Illus.). 448p. (Orig.). 1996. pap. text ed. 39.95 (*0-9628481-2-3*) Pebble Pr.

Spirit of Cleveland: Visual Arts Recipients of the Cleveland Arts Prize, 1961-1995. 48p. 1995. 14.95 (*0-9611104-2-2*) Cleveland Institute of Art.

Spirit of Community: Rights, Responsibilities, & the Communitarian Agenda. Amitai Etzioni. LC 92-31527. 1993. 22.00 (*0-517-59277-0*, Crown) Crown Pub Group.

Spirit of Community: Rights, Responsibilities, & the Communitarian Agenda. Amitai Etzioni. (Illus.). 336p. 1994. pap. 12.00 (*0-671-88524-3*, Touchstone Bks) S&S Trade.

Spirit of Counsel. Swainson. 158p. 1977. 8.95 (*0-85435-103-5*, Pub. by C W Daniel UK) Natl Bk Netwk.

Spirit of Counsel. Mary Swainson. 256p. 13.95 (*0-8464-4293-0*) Beekman Pubs.

Spirit of Counsel: Spiritual Perspectives in the Counseling Process. Martin Israel. LC 88-9047. 192p. (Orig.). 1988. pap. 11.95 (*0-8192-1431-0*) Morehouse Pub.

Spirit of D. H. Lawrence: Centenary Studies. Ed. by Gamini Salgado & G. K. Das. LC 86-17385. 272p. 1986. 58.50 (*0-389-20665-2*, N8223) B&N Imports.

Spirit of Delight. George M. Harper. LC 78-76902. (Essay Index Reprint Ser.). 1977. 20.95 (*0-8369-0016-2*) Ayer.

***Spirit of Democracy in America.** John D. Paris. 102p. (J). (gr. 5-8). 1997. pap. 14.95 (*0-9654973-1-3*) Sterling Pr WA.

Spirit of Democratic Capitalism. Michael Novak. LC 90-48169. 449p. 1991. 27.95 (*0-8191-7822-5*); pap. 16.95 (*0-8191-7823-3*) Madison Bks UPA.

Spirit of Denali. Ed. by Edward Bovy. (Mini-Bks.). 24p. (Orig.). 1994. pap. text ed. 4.95 (*0-936425-22-9*) Greatland Graphics.

***Spirit of Dissension: Economics, Politics, & the Revolution in Maryland.** Ronald Hoffman. LC 73-8127. (Maryland Bicentennial Studies). 304p. 1973. reprint ed. pap. 86.70 (*0-608-03733-8*, 2064558) Bks Demand.

Spirit of Dorsai. Gordon R. Dickson. 256p. 1993. mass mkt. 4.99 (*0-8125-0403-8*) Tor Bks.

Spirit of Enquiry: Caleb Hillier Parry MD, FRS. Sholem Glaser. (Illus.). 192p. 1996. pap. 26.95 (*0-7509-0998-6*, Pub. by Sutton Pubng UK) Bks Intl VA.

Spirit of Faith. Billy J. Daugherty. 32p. (Orig.). 1993. pap. 0.50 (*1-56267-087-5*) Victory Ctr OK.

Spirit of False Judgment. Kathie Walters. 80p. 1995. pap. text ed. 5.99 (*0-9629559-5-7*) Good News Min.

***Spirit of Findhorn.** rev. ed. Eileen Caddy. 144p. 1994. pap. 10.95 (*0-905249-97-6*, Pub. by Findhorn Pr UK) Words Distrib.

Spirit of Fire: The Life & Vision of Teilhard de Chardin. Ursula King. LC 96-5978. 250p. 1996. 25.00 (*1-57075-065-3*) Orbis Bks.

Spirit of Flame. Lesia Ukrainka. 320p. 1950. 10.00 (*0-317-36113-9*) UNWLA.

Spirit of Flame. Lesia Ukrainka. Tr. by Percival Cundy from SLA. LC 76-147225. (Illus.). 320p. 1971. reprint ed. text ed. 59.75 (*0-8371-5990-3*, UKSF, Greenwood Pr) Greenwood.

Spirit of Folk Art: The Girard Collection at the Museum of International Folk Art. Henry Glassie. (Illus.). 276p. 1995. pap. 29.95 (*0-8109-2438-2*) Abrams.

Spirit of Freedom: Essays in American History. Ed. by Burton W. Folsom, Jr. 212p. (Orig.). 1994. pap. 14.95 (*0-910614-94-6*) Foun Econ Ed.

Spirit of Freedom: South African Leaders on Religion & Politics. Charles Villa-Vicencio. LC 95-20361. (Perspectives on Southern Africa Ser.: Vol. 52). (Illus.). 325p. 1996. 40.00 (*0-520-20044-6*); pap. 14.95 (*0-520-20045-4*) U CA Pr.

Spirit of French Canada: A Study of the Literature. Ian F. Fraser. LC 70-168135. reprint ed. 20.00 (*0-404-02548-X*) AMS Pr.

Spirit of God: The Exegesis of 1 & 2 Corinthians in the Pneumatomachian Controversy of the Fourth Century. M. A. Haykin. LC 94-26024. (Supplements to Vigiliae Christianae Ser.: 272). 1994. 109.50 (*90-04-09947-6*) E J Brill.

Spirit of God, Spirit of Christ: Ecumenical Reflections on the Filioque Controversy. Ed. by Lukas Vischer. LC 81-157125. (Faith & Order Paper Ser.: No. 103). 192p. 1981. reprint ed. pap. 54.80 (*0-7837-6004-3*, 2045814) Bks Demand.

Spirit of Golf. Ray Ellis & Ben Wright. LC 92-71792. (Illus.). 144p. 1992. 65.00 (*1-56352-041-9*) Longstreet Pr Inc.

Spirit of Golf. Illus. by Ray Ellis. 1996. pap. 24.95 (*1-56352-275-6*) Longstreet Pr Inc.

Spirit of H. H. Richardson on the Midland Prairies. Paul C. Larson et al. (Illus.). 176p. 1988. pap. 24.95 (*0-938713-02-7*) Univ MN Art Mus.

***Spirit of Haida Gwaii: Bill Reid's Masterpiece.** Ulli Steltzer. LC 96-51836. (Illus.). 64p. 1997. pap. 12.95 (*0-295-97624-1*) U of Wash Pr.

Spirit of Han. Southeast Asian Ceramic Society Staff. (Illus.). 190p. 1991. 55.00 (*981-00-2961-6*, Pub. by Sun Tree Pub SI) Art Media Resources.

Spirit of Happiness: Expressions of Emotions. Andrew Shannon. (Illus.). 39p. (Orig.). 1992. pap. 5.95 (*1-56411-035-4*) Untd Bros & Sis.

Spirit of Hebrew Poetry, 2 vols in one. Johann G. Herder. Tr. by James Marsh. LC 70-131583. (Sources in the History of Interpretation Ser.: No. 1). 1971. 35.00 (*0-8401-1065-0*) A R Allenson.

Spirit of Hebrew Poetry. Isaac Taylor. LC 74-30247. (Studies in Poetry: No. 38). 1974. lib. bdg. 56.95 (*0-8383-1988-2*) M S G Haskell Hse.

Spirit of Himalaya: The Story of a Truth Seeker. 2nd rev. ed. Swami Amar Jyoti. LC 85-50206. (Illus.). 128p. 1985. reprint ed. pap. 5.95 (*0-933572-06-9*) Truth Consciousness.

Spirit of Himalaya: The Story of a Truth Seeker. 3rd ed. Swami A. Jyoti. LC 88-50470. (Illus.). 125p. 1988. pap. 7.95 (*0-933572-11-5*) Truth Consciousness.

Spirit of Hope. Bob Graham. (J). 1996. pap. write for info. (*1-57255-201-8*) Kluwer Law Tax Pubs.

Spirit of Hope. Bob Graham. 32p. (J). (gr. 2-6). 1996. 14.95 (*1-57255-202-6*) Kluwer Law Tax Pubs.

Spirit of Hungary: A Panorama of Hungarian History & Culture. 3rd exp. rev. ed. Stephen Sisa. (Illus.). 374p. 1995. 40.00 (*0-9628422-2-2*) Vista Ct Bks.

Spirit of Indian Culture: Saints of India. Vivek Bhattacharya. 622p. 1980. 32.95 (*0-940500-40-X*) Asia Bk Corp.

***Spirit of Intimacy: Ancient Teachings in the Ways of Relationships.** Sobonfu E. Some. 144p. (Orig.). 1997. pap. 12.95 (*0-9653774-2-3*) Berkeley Hills.

Spirit of Iron. Janice J. Shefelman. Ed. by Edwin M. Eakin. (Mina Jordan Ser.: No. 3). 136p. (J). (gr. 4-7). 1987. 12.95 (*0-89015-636-0*); pap. 5.95 (*0-89015-624-7*) Sunbelt Media.

Spirit of Islam. S. Ali. 512p. 1987. 300.00 (*1-85077-179-0*, Pub. by Darf Pubs Ltd UK) St Mut.

Spirit of Islam. S. A. Ali. 19.95 (*0-933511-62-0*) Kazi Pubns.

Spirit of Islam. Afif A. Tabbarah. 479p. 1988. pap. 12.95 (*0-86685-029-5*, LDL0295, Pub. by Librairie du Liban FR); pap. 9.95 (*0-86685-664-1*) Intl Bk Ctr.

Spirit of Islam. Ameer Ali. 1990. reprint ed. 18.50 (*81-85395-91-8*, Pub. by Low Price II) S Asia.

Spirit of Japanese Capitalism. Yamamoto Shichihei. 1991. pap. 24.95 (*0-8191-8294-X*) U Pr of Amer.

Spirit of Japanese Classical Martial Arts: Historical & Philosophical Perspectives. Hiroyuki T. Hamada. 176p. (C). 1990. per., pap. text ed. 27.56 (*0-8403-6039-8*) Kendall-Hunt.

Spirit of Jerusalem. John Pearson. 1995. 10.95 (*0-533-11483-7*) Vantage.

Spirit of Jesus. Vincent M. Walsh. 1984. pap. 5.00 (*0-943374-10-3*) Key of David.

Spirit of Jewish Law: A Brief Account of Biblical & Rabbinical Jurisprudence with a Special Note on Jewish Law & the State of Israel. George Horowitz & David De Sola Pool. LC 93-25578. (Illus.). 1979. reprint ed. pap. 24.95 (*0-8197-0600-0*); reprint ed. lib. bdg. 45.00 (*0-8197-0625-6*) Bloch.

Spirit of Judaism. Josephine Lazarus. LC 77-38031. (Essay Index Reprint Ser.). 1977. reprint ed. 18.95 (*0-8369-2602-1*) Ayer.

Spirit of Judgment. Watchman Nee. Ed. by Herbert L. Fader et al. Tr. by Stephen Kaung from CHI. 158p. (Orig.). 1984. pap. 4.50 (*0-935008-63-2*) Christian Fellow Pubs.

Spirit of Kappa Alpha. Robert S. Tarleton. 384p. 1993. text ed. 60.00 (*0-9636010-0-8*) J H H Educ Fnd.

Spirit of Language in Civilization. Karl Vossler. Tr. by Oscar Oeser. LC 75-41285. reprint ed. 22.50 (*0-404-14625-2*) AMS Pr.

Spirit of Law Librarianship: A Reader. Ed. by Richard A. Leiter. LC 91-19305. ix, 264p. 1991. 37.50 (*0-8377-0865-6*) Rothman.

Spirit of Laws, 2 vols., Set. rev. ed. Charles L. De Secondat Montesquieu. Tr. by Thomas Nugent from FRE. 1991. reprint ed. lib. bdg. 75.00 (*0-8377-0864-8*) Rothman.

Spirit of Laws: Civic Federalism & the Unfinished Project of Republican Modernity. Andrew W. Fraser. 512p. 1990. 75.00 (*0-8020-5836-1*) U of Toronto Pr.

Spirit of Leadership: Inspiring Quotations for Leaders. Compiled by F. C. Harrison. 1989. 17.95 (*0-943703-02-6*) Leader Educ Dev.

Spirit of Liberalism. Harvey C. Mansfield. LC 78-7809. 144p. reprint ed. pap. 41.10 (*0-7837-5936-3*, 2045735) Bks Demand.

***Spirit of Liberation, Vol. 1.** 2nd ed. E. Bernard Jordan. Ed. by Deborah Jones. (Illus.). (Orig.). 1995. reprint ed. pap. 10.00 (*0-939241-09-9*) Faith Print.

Spirit of Life: A Universal Affirmation. Jurgen Moltmann. Tr. by Margaret Kohl. LC 92-18513. (Works of Jurgen Moltmann). 382p. 1992. 27.00 (*0-8006-2737-7*, 1-2737, Fortress Pr) Augsburg Fortress.

Spirit of Life: The Holy Spirit in the Life of the Christian. Luis M. Bermejo. 388p. 1988. 3.00 (*0-8294-0603-4*) Loyola Pr.

Spirit of Light or Darkness? A Casebook for Studying Discernment of Spirits. Jules J. Toner. LC 95-77483. (Original Studies Composed in English: Series III, Vol. 11). (Illus.). iv, 93p. (Orig.). 1995. pap. 14.95 (*1-880810-12-3*) Inst Jesuit.

Spirit of London's River. L. M. Bates. 200p. 1984. 50.00 (*0-905418-43-3*, Pub. by Gresham Bks UK) St Mut.

Spirit of Love. Emma Goldrick. (Presents Ser.). 1993. pap. 2.89 (*0-373-11545-8*, 1-11545-0) Harlequin Bks.

Spirit of Love. large type ed. Emma Goldrick. 1992. lib. bdg. 18.95 (*0-263-13122-X*) Thorndike Pr.

***Spirit of Love: 11 Spiritual Lessons for Creating the Love You Want.** Deepak Chopra. 1997. 16.95 (*0-614-20427-5*, Dutton) NAL-Dutton.

Spirit of Love No. 134. Barbara Cartland. (Camfield Ser.: No. 134). 176p. (Orig.). 1994. mass mkt. 3.99 (*0-515-11479-0*) Jove Pubns.

Spirit of Loveliness. Emilie Barnes. 1992. 14.99 (*0-89081-982-3*) Harvest Hse.

Spirit of Loving. Ed. by Emily H. Sell. LC 94-22605. 160p. (Orig.). 1995. pap. 10.00 (*1-57062-076-8*) Shambhala Pubns.

Spirit of Man. Ed. by Whit Burnett. LC 68-58775. (Essay Index Reprint Ser.). 1977. 24.95 (*0-8369-0036-7*) Ayer.

Spirit of Man & More Barnes' People: Seven Monologues. Peter Barnes. (Methuen Modern Plays Ser.). 104p. (Orig.). (C). 1990. pap. 9.95 (*0-413-63130-3*, A0466, Pub. by Methuen UK) Heinemann.

Spirit of Manufacturing Excellence: An Executive's Guide to the New Mind Set. Ernest C. Huge & Alan D. Anderson. (APICS Ser.). 132p. 1987. text ed. 47.50 (*0-87094-989-6*) Irwin Prof Pubng.

Spirit of Manufacturing Excellence, Market Driven Management, Total Quality, Self-Directed Work Teams, & Competing in World Class Manufacturing Package. Ernst & Young Staff et al. 1991. 165.00 (*1-55623-646-8*) Irwin Prof Pubng.

Spirit of Masonry. 2nd ed. Foster Bailey. 1972. pap. 10.00 (*0-85330-135-2*) Lucis.

Spirit of Medieval Philosophy. Etienne Gilson. LC 90-50958. (C). 1991. reprint ed. pap. text ed. 16.50 (*0-268-01740-9*) U of Notre Dame Pr.

Spirit of Mediterranean Places. Michel Butor. Tr. by Lydia Davis from FRE. LC 85-63763. 160p. 1987. pap. 10.95 (*0-910395-17-9*) Marlboro Pr.

Spirit of Millenium. Winifred Gallagher. Date not set. write for info. (*0-679-44794-6*) Random.

Spirit of Mishnaic Law, Vols. I & II. Reuven Grodner. 560p. (ENG & HEB.). 1992. 25.95 (*965-229-045-9*, Pub. by Gefen Pub Hse IS) Gefen Bks.

Spirit of Modern Philosophy. Josiah Royce. 519p. 1983. reprint ed. pap. 10.95 (*0-486-24432-6*) Dover.

Spirit of Modern Republicanism: The Moral Vision of the American Founders & the Philosophy of Locke. Thomas L. Pangle. LC 87-30885. (Exxon Lectures). x, 344p. 1990. pap. 15.95 (*0-226-64547-9*) U Ch Pr.

Spirit of Montmartre: Cabarets, Humor, & the Avant-Garde, 1875-1905. Phillip D. Cate. Ed. by Mary Shaw. (Illus.). 240p. (C). 1996. pap. 29.95 (*0-8135-2324-9*) Rutgers U Pr.

Spirit of Music. Edward Dickinson. 1973. 59.95 (*0-8490-1111-6*) Gordon Pr.

Spirit of Music. G. P. Green. 128p. 1991. reprint ed. 69.00 (*0-7812-9355-3*) Rprt Serv.

Spirit of Music: How to Find It & How to Share It. Edward Dickinson. (Select Bibliographies Reprint Ser.). 1977. reprint ed. 20.95 (*0-8369-6683-X*) Ayer.

Spirit of Native America: Beauty & Mysticism in American Indian Art. Anna L. Walters. (Illus.). 120p. (C). 1989. 30.00 (*0-87701-651-8*); pap. 18.95 (*0-87701-515-5*) Chronicle Bks.

***Spirit of Naval Aviation: The National Museum of Naval Aviation.** M. Hill Goodspeed. Ed. by E. Earle Rogers & Nancy S. Schwartz. (Illus.). 148p. 1997. 45.00 (*0-9654229-0-9*) Naval Aviation Mus.

***Spirit of Naval Aviation: The Naval Aviation Museum Collection.** Walter M. Schirra. (Illus.). 148p. 1997. 45.00 (*1-55750-836-4*) Naval Inst Pr.

Spirit of Numerology. Joice Ashly. Ed. by Martha Mclellan. (Illus.). 308p. (Orig.). 1996. pap. text ed. 17.90 (*0-9649077-2-0*) J A Winn.

Spirit of Open Adoption. James L. Gritter. LC 97-10333. 1997. 18.95 (*0-87868-637-1*) Child Welfare.

Spirit of Party: Hamilton & Jefferson at Odds. Margaret C. Christman. LC 92-19240. (Illus.). 64p. (C). 1992. pap. 12.95 (*0-8139-1423-X*) U Pr of Va.

***Spirit of Piedmont: The History of Piedmont Airlines.** (Illus.). Date not set. 34.95 (*0-89587-200-5*) Blair.

***Spirit of Place.** Lawrence Durrell. 1997. pap. text ed. 12.95 (*1-56924-722-6*) Marlowe & Co.

Spirit of Place: A Workbook for Sacred Alignment. Loren Cruden. 232p. 1995. pap. 16.95 (*0-89281-511-6*, Destiny Bks) Inner Tradit.

Spirit of Place: Japanese Paintings of the Sixteenth through Nineteenth Centuries. Louisa Cunningham. Ed. by Peter Neill. (Illus.). 80p. (Orig.). 1984. pap. 7.00 (*0-89467-030-1*) Yale Art Gallery.

Spirit of Place: Letters & Essays on Travel. Lawrence Durrell. Ed. by Alan G. Thomas. 432p. 1984. pap. 8.95 (*0-918172-17-9*) Leetes Isl.

Spirit of Place: Nine Neo-Romantic Artists & Their Times. Malcolm Yorke. LC 89-34490. 368p. 1989. text ed. 39.95 (*0-312-03522-5*) St Martin.

Spirit of Place: The Making of an American Literary Landscape. Frederick Turner. LC 92-14384. (Illus.). 370p. 1992. reprint ed. pap. 17.00 (*1-55963-180-5*) Island Pr.

Spirit of Prague & Other Essays. Ivan Klima. Tr. by Paul Wilson. 188p. 1995. pap. 10.95 (*0-9645611-2-3*) Granta USA.

Spirit of Private Government. Grant McConnell. (Reprint Series in Social Sciences). (C). 1993. reprint ed. pap. text ed. 1.00 (*0-8290-2738-6*, PS-196) Irvington.

***Spirit of Progress: Art Deco Architecture in Australia.** Patrick Van Daele & Roy Lumby. (Illus.). 228p. 1997. 75.00 (*90-5703-671-1*, Pub. by Craftsman Hse VB) IPG Chicago.

Spirit of Promise. D. Macleod. 1995. 6.99 (*0-906731-48-8*, Pub. by Christian Focus UK) Spring Arbor Dist.

Spirit of Protestantism. Robert M. Brown. 284p. (YA). (gr. 9 up). 1965. pap. 12.95 (*0-19-500724-7*) OUP.

Spirit of Public Administration. H. George Frederickson. LC 96-1955. (Public Administration Ser.). 1996. write for info. (*0-7879-0295-0*) Jossey-Bass.

Spirit of Quest. D. M. Dooling. (Illus.). 96p. 1994. 12.00 (*0-930407-30-X*) Parabola Bks.

Spirit of Reform: British Literature & Politics, 1832-1867. Patrick Brantlinger. LC 76-30537. (Illus.). 302p. 1977. reprint ed. pap. 86.40 (*0-7837-4450-1*, 2057980) Bks Demand.

Spirit of Renewal: Finding Faith after the Holocaust. Edward Feld. LC 94-30252. 208p. 1995. pap. 16.95 (*1-879045-40-0*) Jewish Lights.

Spirit of Revolt: Anarchism & the Cult of Authority. Richard K. Fenn. LC 86-15430. 192p. 1986. 53.00 (*0-8476-7522-X*) Rowman.

Spirit of Roman Law. Alan Watson. LC 94-5969. (Spirit of the Laws Ser.). 272p. 1995. 45.00 (*0-8203-1669-5*) U of Ga Pr.

Spirit of Romance. Ezra Pound. LC 53-5860. 1968. reprint ed. pap. 12.95 (*0-8112-0163-5*, NDP266) New Directions.

Spirit of Sail. John Dyson. 1990. 17.98 (*0-88365-766-X*) Galahad Bks.

Spirit of Scott. Judi Sturge. 1977. 12.95 (*0-686-10956-2*) J Sturge.

Spirit of Service: How to Reinvent a Customer Focused Service Culture. Thomas D. Hinton. 256p. 1993. per., pap. text ed. 21.95 (*0-8403-9124-2*) Kendall-Hunt.

Spirit of Service: Recollections of a Pioneer. Angus A. Macdonald. Ed. by Eleanor J. Macdonald. (Illus.). 131p. (Orig.). 1988. 20.00 (*0-9637172-0-0*) E J Macdonald.

Spirit of 'Seventy-Six: The Story of the American Revolution As Told by Participants. Ed. by Henry S. Commager & Richard B. Morris. (Illus.). 1436p. 1995. reprint ed. pap. 27.95 (*0-306-80620-7*) Da Capo.

Spirit of Seventy-Six & Other Essays. Carl Becker et al. (Brookings Institution Reprint Ser.). reprint ed. lib. bdg. 27.00 (*0-697-00150-4*) Irvington.

Spirit of Seventy-Six & Other Essays. Carl L. Becker et al. (BCL1 - U. S. History Ser.). 135p. 1991. reprint ed. lib. bdg. 69.00 (*0-7812-6102-3*) Rprt Serv.

Spirit of Sex. Willie C. Hooks. 80p. (Orig.). 1991. pap. 5.95 (*0-9623440-5-2*) JTE Assocs.

Spirit of Shady Side: Peninsula Life 1664-1984. Virginia W. Fitz. LC 84-52251. (Illus.). 122p. 1984. pap. 9.50 (*0-9614295-0-X*) Shady Side Pen.

Spirit of Shaolin. David Carradine. LC 91-65714. (Illus.). 208p. 1991. 19.95 (*0-8048-1751-0*) C E Tuttle.

Spirit of Shaolin: A Kung Fu Philosophy. David Carradine. (Illus.). 192p. 1993. pap. 12.95 (*0-8048-1828-2*) C E Tuttle.

Spirit of Social Work. Edward T. Devine. LC 75-17216. (Social Problems & Social Policy Ser.). 1976. reprint ed. 21.95 (*0-405-07487-5*) Ayer.

***Spirit of Solesmes: Prosper Gueranger, Cecile Bruyere, Paul Delatte.** Mary D. Totah et al. LC 96-50990. (Illus.). (Orig.). Date not set. pap. write for info. (*1-879007-22-3*) St Bedes Pubns.

Spirit of Solitude: Conventions & Continuities in Late Romance. Jay Macpherson. LC 81-11462. (Illus.). 364p. 1982. 47.50 (*0-300-02632-3*) Yale U Pr.

Spirit of Southeast Alaska Vol. 1. Ed. by Edward Bovy. (Mini-Bks.). (Illus.). 24p. (Orig.). 1994. pap. text ed. 5.95 (*0-936425-23-7*) Greatland Graphics.

Spirit of Sport: Essays about Sport & Values. Ed. by John W. Molloy, Jr. & Richard C. Adams. LC 87-50692. 150p. (C). 1987. text ed. 27.95 (*0-317-67979-1*); pap. text ed. 16.95 (*1-55605-012-7*) Wyndham Hall.

Spirit of St. Andrews. Alister Mackenzie. (Illus.). 288p. 1995. 24.95 (*1-886947-00-7*) Sleepng Bear.

Spirit of St. Louis. Charles A. Lindberg. (Illus.). 562p. 1975. 60.00 (*0-684-14421-2*) S&S Trade.

Spirit of St. Louis. R. Conrad Stein. LC 94-9491. (Cornerstones of Freedom Ser.). (Illus.). 32p. (J). 1994. lib. bdg. 18.00 (*0-516-06682-X*) Childrens.

Spirit of St. Louis. Paula Younkin. LC 93-3292. (Those Daring Machines Ser.). (Illus.). 48p. (J). (gr. 5-6). 1994. lib. bdg. 13.95 (*0-89686-832-X*, Crstwood Hse) Silver Burdett Pr.

Spirit of St. Louis. Charles A. Lindbergh. LC 93-4148. xviii, 562p. 1993. reprint ed. pap. 14.95 (*0-87351-288-X*, Borealis Book) Minn Hist.

Spirit of St. Louis. Charles A. Lindbergh. 512p. 1991. reprint ed. lib. bdg. 33.95 (*0-89966-793-7*) Buccaneer Bks.

Spirit of Steam: A Photographic Record of the Golden Age of American Steam. William L. Withuhn. 1995. 15.98 (*0-8317-5511-3*) Smithmark.

Spirit of Student Council. Earl Reum. Ed. by C. Bruce. (J). (gr. 7-9). 1981. pap. 7.00 (*0-88210-117-X*) Natl Assn Principals.

Spirit of Summit County, Colorado: A Photographic Celebration. Christine S. Beck. LC 95-71871. (Illus.). 128p. 1996. 25.95 (*0-9649005-0-5*) PrismLght Pr.

Spirit of Surrealism. Edward B. Henning. LC 79-63387. (Illus.). 196p. reprint ed. pap. 55.90 (*0-317-10524-8*, 2022658) Bks Demand.

Spirit of Sweetwater. Hamlin Garland. (Collected Works of Hamlin Garland). 1988. reprint ed. lib. bdg. 59.00 (*0-7812-1226-X*) Rprt Serv.

Spirit of Sweetwater see Collected Works of Hamlin Garland

Spirit of System: Lamarck & Evolutionary Biology. Richard W. Burkhardt, Jr. 288p. 1990. text ed. 29.00 (*0-674-83317-1*) HUP.

Spirit of System: Lamarck & Evolutionary Biology. Richard W. Burkhardt, Jr. (Illus.). 320p. (C). 1995. pap. text ed. 17.95 (*0-674-83318-X*) HUP.

Spirit of Tao. Tr. by Thomas Cleary from CHI. LC 92-50445. (Pocket Classics Ser.). 228p. (Orig.). 1993. pap. 6.00 (*0-87773-877-7*) Shambhala Pubns.

Spirit of Teaching Excellence. Ed. by David C. Jones. 220p. (Orig.). 1995. pap. text ed. 17.95 (*1-55059-120-7*, Pub. by Detselig CN) Temeron Bks.

Spirit of the Age. Ed. by Caroline Sullivan. 1996. 69.95 (*1-57553-061-9*) Watermrk Pr.

Spirit of the Age. William C. Hazlitt. LC 90-118829. 438p. 1989. reprint ed. 52.00 (*1-85477-021-7*, Pub. by Woodstock Bks UK) Cassell.

Spirit of the Age: The Story of "Old Bushmills" Alf McCreary. 232p. 1983. 25.00 (*0-8159-6837-X*) Devin.

Spirit of the American Revolution. unabridged ed. David Barton. 23p. (Orig.). 1994. pap. 3.95 (*0-925279-43-9*) Wallbuilders.

Spirit of the Andes. Jose S. Chocano. Tr. by Edna W. Underwood. 1977. lib. bdg. 59.95 (*0-8490-2660-1*) Gordon Pr.

Spirit of the Border. Zane Grey. 288p. 1991. mass mkt. 3.99 (*0-06-100293-3*, Harp PBks) HarpC.

Spirit of the Border. Zane Grey. 256p. (Orig.). 1994. mass mkt., pap. text ed. 3.99 (*0-8439-3658-4*) Dorchester Pub Co.

Spirit of the Border. Zane Grey. (Orig.). 1993. mass mkt. 4.99 (*0-8125-3466-2*) Tor Bks.

Spirit of the Border. Zane Grey. 1976. reprint ed. lib. bdg. 24.95 (*0-89190-755-6*, Rivercity Pr) Amereon Ltd.

Spirit of the Border: The Authorized Edition. Zane Grey. LC 95-47620. (Illus.). vi, 274p. (Orig.). 1996. pap. 12.00 (*0-8032-7061-5*, Bison Books) U of Nebr Pr.

Spirit of the Chinese Character: Gifts from the Heart. Barbara Aria & Russell E. Gon. 96p. 1992. 14.95 (*0-8118-0142-X*) Chronicle Bks.

Spirit of the City of San Francisco. (Local History Studies: Vol. 32). 1985. pap. 2.50 (*0-935089-10-1*) CA History Ctr.

Spirit of the Common Law. Roscoe Pound. LC 95-76118. xiv, 224p. 1995. reprint ed. 45.00 (*0-89941-932-1*, 308700) W S Hein.

Spirit of the Constitution: Five Conversations. Robert A. Goldwin & Robert A. Licht. LC 89-18585. (Decade of Study of the Constitution Ser.). 200p. 1990. pap. 9.95 (*0-8447-3720-8*, AEI Pr) Am Enterprise.

Spirit of the Counter-Reformation. H. Outram Evennett. LC 68-11282. 1970. pap. 9.50 (*0-268-00425-0*) U of Notre Dame Pr.

Spirit of the Court: Selected Proceedings of the Fourth Congress of the International Courtly Literature Society, Toronto 1983. Ed. by Glynn S. Burgess et al. 416p. 1985. 90.00 (*0-85991-176-4*) Boydell & Brewer.

Spirit of the Courts. Thomas W. Shelton. xxxvii, 264p. 1995. lib. bdg. 37.50 (*0-8377-2657-3*) Rothman.

Spirit of the Disciplines: Understanding How God Changes Lives. Dallas Willard. LC 86-45033. 288p. 1991. reprint ed. pap. 13.00 (*0-06-069442-4*) Harper SF.

Spirit of the Eagle. Vella Munn. 352p. 1996. 23.95 (*0-312-86096-X*) Forge NYC.

Spirit of the East. Sirdar Ikbal Ali Shah. 277p. 1973. pap. 10.00 (*0-900860-16-2*, Pub. by Octagon Pr UK) ISHK.

Spirit of the Empty Hand. Stan Schmidt. Ed. by Randall G. Hassell & Dale F. Poertner. 192p. (Orig.). 1984. pap. 15.95 (*0-911921-02-8*) Focus Pubns MO.

***Spirit of the Environment: Religion, Value & Environmental Concern.** David E. Cooper & Joy Palmer. LC 97-22308. 1998. write for info. (*0-415-14201-6*); pap. write for info. (*0-415-14202-4*) Routledge.

Spirit of the Father & of the Son. Francois X. Durrwell. 64p. (C). 1990. 39.00 (*0-85439-321-8*, Pub. by St Paul Pubns UK) St Mut.

Spirit of the Game: Exceptional Photographs from the Hockey Hall of Fame. Ed. by Dan Diamond. (Illus.). 240p. 1996. 35.00 (*1-57243-096-6*) Triumph Bks.

***Spirit of the Garden.** Photos by John Hedgecoe. (Illus.). 176p. 1997. 40.00 (*1-85585-292-6*) Coll & Brown.

Spirit of the Ghetto. Hutchins Hapgood. Ed. by Moses Rischin. (Illus.). 355p. 1983. pap. 15.50 (*0-674-83266-3*) Belknap Pr.

Spirit of the Gospel. Watchman Nee. Ed. by Herbert L. Fader. 100p. (Orig.). 1986. pap. 4.50 (*0-935008-67-5*) Christian Fellow Pubs.

Spirit of the Guard. Richard E. Bauer. 122p. 1981. pap. 7.95 (*0-89279-071-7*) R E Bauer.

Spirit of the Harvest: North American Indian Cooking. Beverly Cox. LC 91-12119. (Illus.). 256p. 1991. 35.00 (*1-55670-186-1*) Stewart Tabori & Chang.

***Spirit of the Horse.** Carole Devereux. 242p. 1998. pap. 25.00 (*1-884422-24-1*) Centaur Pubns.

Spirit of the Laws. Charles De Montesquieu. (Library of Classics: No. 9). 768p. 1970. pap. 16.95 (*0-02-849270-6*) Hafner.

Spirit of the Laws. Charles De Montesquieu. Ed. by Anne M. Cohler et al. (Cambridge Texts in the History of Political Thought Ser.). 400p. (C). 1989. text ed. 59.95 (*0-521-36183-4*); pap. text ed. 19.95 (*0-521-36974-6*) Cambridge U Pr.

Spirit of the Laws: A Compendium of the First English Editon with an English Translation of "An Essay on Causes Affecting Mind & Characters", 1737-1743. Charles-Louis De Montesquieu. Ed. by David W. Carrithers. 1978. pap. 16.95 (*0-520-03455-4*) U CA Pr.

Spirit of the Legal Profession. Robert N. Wilkin. viii, 178p. 1981. reprint ed. lib. bdg. 18.50 (*0-8377-1308-0*) Rothman.

Spirit of the Letter: Essays in European Literature. Renato Poggioli. LC 65-22064. 384p. 1965. reprint ed. pap. 109.80 (*0-7837-4179-0*, 2059028) Bks Demand.

Spirit of the Maya: A Boy Explores His People's Mysterious Past. Guy Garcia. LC 94-44813. (Illus.). 48p. (J). (gr. 3-7). 1995. lib. bdg. 17.85 (*0-8027-8380-5*) Walker & Co.

Spirit of the Maya: A Boy Explores His People's Mysterious Past. Guy Garcia. LC 94-44813. (Illus.). 48p. (J). (gr. 3-7). 1995. 16.95 (*0-8027-8379-1*) Walker & Co.

Spirit of the Moon. Earl P. Murray. LC 96-18117. 304p. 1996. 23.95 (*0-312-86189-3*) St Martin.

Spirit of the Mountain. Fela D. Scott. 400p. (Orig.). 1995. mass mkt., pap. text ed. 4.99 (*0-8439-3817-X*) Dorchester Pub Co.

Spirit of the Mountain Man. William W. Johnstone. 256p. 1995. mass mkt. 4.99 (*0-8217-5191-3*, Zebra Kensgtn) Kensgtn Pub Corp.

Spirit of the Mountains. Emma B. Miles. LC 75-19222. (Tennesseana Editions Ser.). (Illus.). 250p. 1975. reprint ed. 26.00 (*0-87049-181-4*); reprint ed. pap. 15.00 (*0-87049-465-1*) U of Tenn Pr.

Spirit of the Nation: Ballads & Songs with Ancient & Original Music. LC 81-81466. 1981. 40.00 (*0-89453-260-X*) Scholarly Res Inc.

***Spirit of the Nation 1845.** Ed. by Charles G. Duffy et al. 368p. 1998. 105.00 (*1-85477-223-6*, Pub. by Woodstock Bks UK) Cassell.

Spirit of the New England Tribes: Indian History & Folklore, 1620-1984. William S. Simmons. LC 85-40936. 343p. 1986. pap. 18.95 (*0-87451-372-3*) U Pr of New Eng.

***Spirit of the Ninja.** Toni Siegel. 1996. pap. text ed. 7.95 (*0-9627746-0-X*) Light Tech Comns Servs.

Spirit of the North. Tom Klein. 1991. 39.95 (*1-55971-085-3*) NorthWord.

Spirit of the Oxford Movement. Christopher H. Dawson. LC 75-30020. reprint ed. 34.50 (*0-404-14025-4*) AMS Pr.

Spirit of the Oxford Movement: Tractarian Essays. Owen Chadwick. 330p. (C). 1992. pap. text ed. 22.95 (*0-521-42440-2*) Cambridge U Pr.

Spirit of the Place: Indiana Hill Country. James A. Thom. LC 95-16713. (Illus.). 144p. 1995. pap. 39.95 (*0-253-32987-6*) Ind U Pr.

Spirit of the Place Vol. 1: The Emerald-Coast Celebrates Its Finest Restaurants, Chefs, & Cuisine. Kurt R. Niland & Scott Armstrong. (Illus.). 154p. 1995. pap. 18.95 (*0-9645334-0-5*) Oracle Pub.

Spirit of the Psalms. Noel Quesson. 1990. pap. 14.95 (*0-8091-3199-4*) Paulist Pr.

Spirit of the Public Journals or, Beauties of the American Newspapers. Ed. by George Bourne. LC 74-125679. (American Journalists Ser.). 1977. reprint ed. 20.95 (*0-405-01654-9*) Ayer.

Spirit of the Rainforest: A Yanomamo Shaman's Story. Mark A. Ritchie. (Illus.). 288p. (Orig.). 1996. pap. 14.95 (*0-9646952-1-9*) Island Lake.

Spirit of the Revolution of 1789: And Other Writings on the Revolutionary Epoch. Pierre L. Roederer. Ed. by Murray Forsyth. 152p. 1989. text ed. 47.95 (*0-85967-813-X*, Pub. by Scolar Pr UK) Ashgate Pub Co.

Spirit of the Scorpion: Conquering the Power of Insurrection. John L. Mastrogiovanni. 78p. (Orig.). 1995. pap. write for info. (*1-885591-53-5*) Morris Pubng.

Spirit of the Season. large type ed. Heather X. Graham. LC 93-31462. 1993. lib. bdg. 19.95 (*0-7862-0050-2*) Thorndike Pr.

Spirit of the Sikhs, 3 vols., Pt. 1. Puran Singh. 1984. reprint ed. Pt.1. 7.50 (*0-8364-1115-3*, Pub. by Punjabi U II) S Asia.

Spirit of the Sikhs, 3 vols., Pt. 2, Vol. 1. Puran Singh. 1984. reprint ed. Pt.2, v.1. 7.50 (*0-8364-1116-1*) S Asia.

Spirit of the Sikhs, 3 vols., Pt. 2, Vol. 2. Puran Singh. 1984. reprint ed. Pt.2, Vol.2. 7.50 (*0-8364-1117-X*) S Asia.

***Spirit of the Sixties: Making of Postwar Radicalism.** James J. Farrell. 256p. (C). 1997. pap. 18.95 (*0-415-91386-1*, Routledge NY) Routledge.

***Spirit of the Sixties: Making of Postwar Radicalism.** James J. Farrell. 256p. (C). 1997. text ed. 69.95 (*0-415-91385-3*, Routledge NY) Routledge.

Spirit of the Sixties see Singing Soldiers: A History of the Civil War in Song

Spirit of the Soil: Agriculture & Environmental Ethics. Paul B. Thompson. LC 94-7196. (Environmental Philosophies Ser.). 144p. (C). 1994. pap. 14.95 (*0-415-08623-X*, B4129) Routledge.

Spirit of the Soil: Agriculture & Environmental Ethics. Paul B. Thompson. LC 94-7196. (Environmental Philosophies Ser.). 144p. (C). (gr. 13). 1994. text ed. 49.95 (*0-415-08622-1*, B4125) Routledge.

Spirit of the Times: Amusements in Nineteenth Century Baltimore, Norfolk, & Richmond. Patricia C. Click. LC 89-5303. (Illus.). 153p. 1989. text ed. 35.00 (*0-8139-1220-2*) U Pr of Va.

Spirit of the Upanishads. Yogi Ramacharaka. 10.00 (*0-911662-11-1*) Yoga.

Spirit of the Waldorf School. Rudolf Steiner. Tr. by Robert F. Lathe & Nancy K. Whittaker. LC 94-45434. 192p. 1995. pap. 14.95 (*0-88010-394-9*) Anthroposophic.

Spirit of the West: Cooking from Ranch House & Range. Beverly Cox. LC 96-21063. (Illus.). 224p. 1996. 35.00 (*1-885183-21-6*) Artisan.

***Spirit of the West - Open Heart Symphony.** Ed. by Michael Lefferts. 68p. (Orig.). (C). 1996. pap. text ed. 18.95 (*0-7692-0473-2*, CCC129) Warner Brothers.

***Spirit of the West Songbook.** Ed. by Michael Lefferts. 80p. (Orig.). (C). 1997. pap. text ed. 19.95 (*0-7692-0494-5*, CCC127) Warner Brothers.

Spirit of the White Bison. Beatrice Culleton. LC 89-32047. (Illus.). 64p. (J). (gr. 5 up). 1989. reprint ed. pap. 5.95 (*0-913990-64-7*) Book Pub Co.

Spirit of the White Bison. Beatrice Culleton. (Illus.). 64p. (J). (gr. 5-9). 1993. reprint ed. pap. 8.00 (*1-895411-43-2*) Peguis Pubs Ltd.

Spirit of the Wind: The Horse in Saudi Arabia. Keith Collie. 112p. (C). 1995. 90.00 (*0-907151-01-9*, Pub. by IMMEL Pubng UK) St Mut.

Spirit of Tio Fernando: A Day of the Dead Story. Janice Levy. Tr. by Teresa Mlawer. LC 95-1318. (Illus.). 32p. (ENG & SPA.). (J). (gr. k-3). 1995. 14.95 (*0-8075-7585-2*) A Whitman.

Spirit of Tio Fernando: A Day of the Dead Story. Janice Levy. Tr. by Morella Fuenmayor. (Illus.). 32p. (J). (gr. k-3). 1995. pap. 6.95 (*0-8075-7586-0*) A Whitman.

Spirit of Tocayo. Steven Gottry & Richard Jacobsen. 1995. 16.95 (*1-886158-01-0*) Macalester.

Spirit of Traditional Chinese Law. Geoffrey MacCormack. LC 94-39610. (Spirit of the Laws Ser.). 1995. 45.00 (*0-8203-1722-5*) U of Ga Pr.

Spirit of Truth. John Breck. LC 90-23505. (Origins of Johannine Pneumatology: Vol. 1). 244p. (Orig.). 1990. pap. 10.95 (*0-88141-081-0*) St Vladimirs.

Spirit of Truth: Ecumenical Perspectives on the Holy Spirit. Theodore G. Stylianopoulos. 197p. 1986. pap. 10.95 (*0-917651-39-1*) Holy Cross Orthodox.

***Spirit of Umunna & the Development of Small Christian Communities in Igboland.** Peter Osuchukwu. LC 95-39195. (European University Studies, Series 23: Vol. 544). 289p. 1996. pap. 54.95 (*0-8204-2933-3*, 68721) P Lang Pubng.

***Spirit of Union: Destiny.** Gordon Ryan. LC 96-27285. 1996. write for info. (*1-57345-215-7*) Deseret Bk.

Spirit of Uppsala. Ed. by Atle Grahl-Madsen & Jiri Toman. xviii, 601p. 1984. 176.95 (*3-11-008822-3*) De Gruyter.

Spirit of Vengeance: Nativism & Louisiana Justice, 1921-1924. John V. Baiamonte, Jr. LC 85-19143. (Illus.). 257p. 1986. text ed. 31.50 (*0-8071-1279-8*) La State U Pr.

Spirit of Wild Places: Ansel Adams & the National Parks. Nash. 1995. 15.98 (*0-8317-8099-1*) Smithmark.

Spirit of Winter Camping. Harry Drabik. (Illus.). 104p. (Orig.). 1985. pap. 5.95 (*0-931714-24-9*) Nodin Pr.

Spirit of Wisdom & Revelation. Watchman Nee. Tr. by Stephen Kaung. 160p. 1980. pap. 4.50 (*0-935008-48-9*) Christian Fellow Pubs.

Spirit of Wit: Reconsiderations of Rochester. Ed. by Jeremy Treglown. 199p. (C). 1982. 33.50 (*0-208-02012-8*, Archon Bks) Shoe String.

Spirit of Yellowstone: The Cultural Evolution of a National Park. Judith L. Meyer. LC 96-15567. 184p. 1996. lib. bdg. 26.95 (*0-8476-8248-X*) Rowman.

***Spirit of Youth & the City Streets.** Lane Addams. LC 78-143047. Date not set. 18.95 (*0-8434-0447-7*, Pub. by McGrath NH) Ayer.

Spirit of Youth & the City Streets. Jane Addams. LC 72-76862. 192p. 1989. reprint ed. pap. text ed. 10.95 (*0-252-00275-X*) U of Ill Pr.

Spirit of Zen: A Way of Life, Work, & Art in the Far East. rev. ed. Alan W. Watts. LC 60-7347. (Illus.). 144p. 1988. pap. 8.95 (*0-8021-3056-9*, Grove) Grove-Atltic.

Spirit of 1848: German Immigrants, Labor Conflict, & the Coming of the Civil War. Bruce S. Levine. (Working Class in American History Ser.). 400p. 1992. text ed. 34.95 (*0-252-01873-7*) U of Ill Pr.

***Spirit of 212: James Hearst Pressly, D. D. 1866-1955.** large type ed. Buford L. Hamilton, Jr. LC 96-95057. (Illus.). 424p. 1997. 50.00 (*0-9654993-0-8*) Belmont Commun.

Spirit of '36: Early History of Virginia Beach Libraries. Ed. by Calvert W. Tazewell. LC 90-61287. (Illus.). 106p. (Orig.). 1991. pap. 11.00 (*1-878515-47-0*) W S Dawson.

Spirit of '69: A Skinhead Bible. George Marshall. (Illus.). 168p. (Orig.). 1991. pap. 19.95 (*0-9518497-0-0*, Pub. by S T Pubng UK) AK Pr Dist.

Spirit of '76 in Rhode Island. Benjamin Cowell. 560p. 1996. reprint ed. lib. bdg. 55.00 (*0-8328-5115-9*) Higginson Bk Co.

Spirit Path. Madeline Baker. (Orig.). 1996. mass mkt. 5.99 (*0-8439-4037-9*) Dorchester Pub Co.

Spirit Path. Judd Cole. (Cheyenne Ser.: No. 11). 176p. (Orig.). 1994. mass mkt., pap. text ed. 3.99 (*0-8439-3656-8*) Dorchester Pub Co.

Spirit Poles & Flying Pigs: Public Art & Cultural Democracy in American Communities. Erika Doss. (Illus.). 288p. 1995. pap. 17.95 (*1-56098-534-8*) Smithsonian.

Spirit Poles & Flying Pigs: Public Art & Cultural Democracy in American Communities. Erika Doss. LC 94-26010. (Illus.). 288p. 1995. text ed. 45.00 (*1-56098-464-3*) Smithsonian.

Spirit Possession & Personhood among the Kel Ewey Tuareg. Susan J. Rasmussen. (Cambridge Studies in Social & Cultural Anthropology: No. 94). 192p. (C). 1995. text ed. 49.95 (*0-521-47007-2*) Cambridge U Pr.

Spirit Possession & Popular Religion: From the Camisards to the Shakers. Clarke Garrett. LC 86-46284. 288p. 1987. text ed. 48.50 (*0-8018-3486-4*) Johns Hopkins.

Spirit Possession in the Nepal Himalayas. Ed. by John T. Hitchcock & Rex L. Jones. (C). 1994. text ed. 34.00 (*0-7069-7867-6*, Pub. by Vikas II) S Asia.

Spirit Possession in the Nepal Himalayas. John T. Hitchcock & Rex L. Jones. 1994. pap. 90.00 (*0-7855-0480-X*, Pub. by Ratna Pustak Bhandar) St Mut.

Spirit Posssesion: The Counterfeit with Many Faces. Theodore E. Wade. Ed. by Theodore Wade, Jr. LC 90-81513. 95p. (Orig.). 1990. pap. 6.95 (*0-930192-24-9*) Gazelle Pubns.

Spirit Prays in Us. Antonio Gentili. Tr. by Joan Fiore. (Orig.). 1994. pap. 5.95 (*0-8198-6956-2*) Pauline Bks.

Spirit Quest. Susan Sharpe. 128p. (J). (gr. 3-7). 1993. pap. 4.99 (*0-14-036282-7*) Puffin Bks.

Spirit Quest. Susan Sharpe. LC 91-4417. (Illus.). 128p. (J). (gr. 4-6). 1991. lib. bdg. 13.95 (*0-02-782355-5*, Bradbury S&S) S&S Childrens.

Spirit Quest: The Initiation of an Indian Boy. Carol Batdorf. (Illus.). 160p. (Orig.). 1997. reprint ed. pap. 9.95 (*0-88839-210-9*) Hancock House.

Spirit-Rapper: An Autobiography. Orestes A. Brownson. (Works of Orestes Augustus Brownson). 1989. reprint ed. lib. bdg. 79.00 (*0-7812-2109-9*) Rprt Serv.

Spirit Releasement Therapy: A Technical Manual. William J. Baldwin. (Illus.). 480p. 1993. pap. 39.95 (*1-882658-00-0*) Human Potent Fnd.

Spirit Releasement Therapy: A Technique Manual. 2nd ed. William J. Baldwin. (Illus.). 480p. 1995. pap. 39.95 (*0-929915-16-X*) Headline Bks.

Spirit Ring. Lois M. Bujold. 384p. 1992. 17.00 (*0-671-72142-9*) Baen Bks.

Spirit Ring. Lois M. Bujold. 384p. 1993. mass mkt. 5.99 (*0-671-72188-7*) Baen Bks.

***Spirit Rock.** Mary Hopkin & Three-D Authors. LC 96-90180. (Illus.). 60p. (Orig.). (J). (gr. 3-9). 1997. pap. 8.95 (*0-533-11941-3*) Vantage.

Spirit Run. Houston A. Baker. LC 81-82664. 38p. (YA). (gr. 9-12). 1982. pap. 3.00 (*0-916418-38-3*) Lotus.

Spirit Said Grow: The Incredible Pentecostal-Charismatic Factor in the Global Expansion of Christianity. Vinson Synan. (Innovations in Mission Ser.). 62p. (Orig.). (C). 1992. pap. 3.95 (*0-912552-73-5*) MARC.

Spirit Seeker. Joan L. Nixon. LC 95-7090. 208p. (YA). (gr. 7 up). 1995. 15.95 (*0-385-32062-0*, Delacorte Pr Bks) BDD Bks Young Read.

***Spirit Seeker.** Joan L. Nixon. 208p. (YA). 1997. mass mkt. 3.99 (*0-440-22685-6*, LLL BDD) BDD Bks Young Read.

Spirit-Seekers: New Religious Movements in Southern Ghana. Robert W. Wyllie. LC 79-20486. (American Academy of Religion. Studies in Religion: No. 21). 147p. reprint ed. pap. 41.90 (*0-7837-5475-2*, 2045240) Bks Demand.

Spirit Seizures. Melissa Pritchard. LC 87-5932. (Flannery O'Connor Award for Short Fiction Ser.). 186p. 1987. 19.95 (*0-8203-0959-1*) U of Ga Pr.

Spirit Song: The Introduction of No-Eyes. Mary S. Rain. LC 85-15894. 160p. (Orig.). 1993. pap. 10.95 (*1-878901-61-3*) Hampton Roads Pub Co.

Spirit, Soul & Body. Lester Sumrall. 176p. 1995. mass mkt. 4.99 (*0-88368-331-8*) Whitaker Hse.

Spirit, Soul, Body: Understanding the Way God Made Us. Jeffrey B. Krall. 40p. (Orig.). 1996. pap. 3.50 (*1-57688-001-X*, 001-X) Branch & Vine.

Spirit, Space & Survival: African American Women in (White) Academe. Ed. by Joy James & Ruth Farmer. 288p. (C). 1993. pap. 17.95 (*0-415-90637-7*, A7457, Routledge NY) Routledge.

Spirit Speaks: The World's Most Insightful Quotes on Religion & Spirituality. Compiled by Claudia Setzer. 248p. 1994. pap. text ed. 14.95 (*0-471-30829-3*) Wiley.

***Spirit Speaks Vol. 1: Daily Spiritual Motivation for Successful African Americans.** Jim Holley. 400p. (Orig.). 1997. pap. 12.00 (*0-913543-51-9*) African Am Imag.

Spirit Speaks in Us. John Sheets. 210p. 1986. pap. 8.95 (*0-87193-250-4*) Dimension Bks.

***Spirit Speaks to Sister: Inspiration & Empowerment for Black Women.** June J. Gatlin. 1997. pap. text ed. 10.95 (*1-879360-51-9*) Noble Pr.

Spirit Speaks to Sisters: Inspiration & Empowerment for Black Women. June Gatlin. 1995. 17.95 (*1-879360-39-X*) Noble Pr.

Spirit Spirit: Shaman Songs. Tr. by David Cloutier. LC 89-7373. (Illus.). 100p. (C). 1980. reprint ed. pap. 8.95 (*0-914278-30-4*) Copper Beech.

Spirit, Spirits & Spirituality. A. E. Knoch. 157p. 1977. pap. text ed. 4.50 (*0-910424-69-1*) Concordant.

Spirit Stones, Vol. I: Cornerstones. Douglas Brodoff. 35p. (Orig.). 1988. pap. 4.25 (*0-317-91169-4*) Spirit Stone Bks.

An Asterisk (*) at the beginning of an entry indicates that the title is appearing in BIP for the first time.

S

Spiritual Aerobics: Spiritual Fitness Through the Disciplined Life. Linda Schott. 1987. pap. 6.99 (*0-89225-298-7*) Gospel Advocate.

Spiritual Aids for Those in Renew: Ponderings, Poems & Promises. Robert F. Morneau. LC 84-12299. 111p. (Orig.). 1984. pap. 4.50 (*0-8189-0473-9*) Alba.

Spiritual Alchemists: Rosicrucians, the Brotherhood of Light. C. E. Lindgren. 70p. (Orig.). 1997. pap. 5.95 (*1-885591-18-7*, PO1351) Morris Pubng.

Spiritual Alchemy. rev. ed. Omraam M. Aivanhov. (Complete Works: Vol. 2). (Illus.). 234p. 1989. pap. 13.95 (*2-85566-371-7*, Pub. by Prosveta FR) Prosveta USA.

Spiritual Alchemy: The Hermetic Art of Spiritual Transformation. C. C. Zain. (Brotherhood of Light Home Study Ser.: Course 3). (Illus.). 144p. 1995. pap. 14.95 (*0-87887-373-2*) Church of Light.

Spiritual America. Richard Prince. (Illus.). 128p. (Orig.). 1989. pap. 24.95 (*0-89381-395-8*) Aperture.

Spiritual & Anabaptist Writers. Ed. by George H. Williams & Angel M. Mergal. LC 57-5003. (Library of Christian Classics). 418p. 1977. pap. 25.00 (*0-664-24150-6*, Westminster) Westminster John Knox.

Spiritual & Intellectual Elements in the Formation of Sisters: Selections from Addresses & Communications on Discussion Topics from the Six Regional Meetings of the Sister Formation Conference, 1955-1956. Sister Ritamary. LC 57-9099. 287p. reprint ed. pap. 81.80 (*0-7837-5580-5*, 2045368) Bks Demand.

Spiritual Applications Of The Tabernacle. Witness Lee. 98p. per. 3.75 (*0-87083-376-6*, 14007001) Living Stream Ministry.

Spiritual Approach to Astrology: A Complete Textbook of Astrology. Myrna Lofthus. LC 78-62936. (Illus.). 444p. 1983. 15.95 (*0-916360-10-5*) CRCS Pubns CA.

Spiritual Aritmetic. Reginald Naish. Ed. by Lynn G. Colson. 125p. 1994. pap. write for info. (*0-318-72815-X*) Peace Pub Co.

Spiritual Art of Creative Silence: Lessons in Christian Meditation. Jeanie Miley. 192p. 1996. pap. 9.99 (*0-87788-140-5*) Shaw Pubs.

Spiritual Art Therapy: An Alternate Path. Ellen G. Horovitz-Darby. LC 94-26380. (Illus.). 186p. (C). 1994. 41.95 (*0-398-05927-6*); pap. 29.95 (*0-398-06513-6*) C C Thomas.

Spiritual Aspects of Indian Music. Simon R. Leopold. 1985. 22.50 (*0-8364-1258-3*, Pub. by Sundeep II) S Asia.

Spiritual Aspects of Psychiatric Practice. Paul R. Fleischman. LC 93-91043. (Illus.). 128p. (Orig.). 1993. pap. 10.95 (*0-9638398-2-9*) Bonne Chance.

Spiritual Aspects of the New Poetry. Amos N. Wilder. LC 68-16988. (Essay Index Reprint Ser.). 1977. 18.95 (*0-8369-0995-X*) Ayer.

Spiritual Assessment in Pastoral Care: A Guide to Selected Resources. George Fitchett. (JPCP Monograph). 38p. (Orig.). 1993. pap. 10.00 (*0-929670-07-8*) JPCP.

Spiritual Astrology: Origins of Astro Mythology & Stellar Religion. C. C. Zain. LC 96-12680. (Brotherhood of Light Home Study Ser.: Course 7). (Illus.). 344p. 1996. pap. 14.95 (*0-87887-377-5*) Church of Light.

Spiritual Astrology: Your Personal Path to Self-Fulfillment. Jan Spiller & Karen McCoy. 452p. 1988. pap. 12.00 (*0-671-66041-1*, Fireside) S&S Trade.

Spiritual Athlete: A Primer for the Inner Life. Ray Berry. (Talking Books Ser.). (Illus.). 109p. 1993. pap. 14.95 (*0-9630839-0-2*) Joshua Pr.

Spiritual Authority. Watchman Nee. Tr. by Stephen Kaung. 191p. 1972. pap. 5.00 (*0-935008-35-7*) Christian Fellow Pubs.

Spiritual Authority: God's Way of Growing Leaders. Stephen B. Bond. LC 94-44045. 1995. 9.99 (*0-89900-727-9*) College Pr Pub.

Spiritual Authority & Temporal Power in the Indian Theory of Government. Amanda K. Comaraswamy. Ed. by Rama P. Comaraswamy & Keshavram N. Iengar. 140p. 1994. 24.00 (*0-19-563253-2*) OUP.

Spiritual Autobiography in Early America. Daniel B. Shea, Jr. LC 87-40375. (Studies in American Autobiography). 304p. (C). 1988. reprint ed. pap. text ed. 12.95 (*0-299-11654-9*) U of Wis Pr.

Spiritual Awakening. Darshan Singh. LC 81-50726. (Illus.). 338p. (Orig.). 1982. pap. 10.00 (*0-918224-11-X*) S K Pubns.

Spiritual Awakening: A Guide to Spiritual Life in Congregations. John Ackerman. 13.95 (*1-56699-135-8*, AL156) Alban Inst.

***Spiritual Awakening - Spiritual Healing: Sunsets...** Beverly J. Hudson. 20p. (Orig.). 1996. pap. 7.50 (*0-9658040-0-3*) Talents From God.

Spiritual Awakenings: Insights of the Near-Death Experience & Other Doorways to the Soul. Barbara H. Whitfield. 205p. (Orig.). 1995. pap. 8.95 (*1-55874-338-3*, 3383) Health Comm.

Spiritual Basis of Steiner Education: The Waldorf School Approach. Roy Wilkinson. 144p. (Orig.). 1996. pap. 16.95 (*1-85584-065-0*, Pub. by Temple Ldge Pub UK) Anthroposophic.

Spiritual Battle for Cuba. Tom White. LC 89-12607. 4.00 (*0-88264-300-2*) Living Sacrifice Bks.

Spiritual Beauty. Constantine Cavarnos. LC 96-75550. (Illus.). 62p. 1996. pap. 5.95 (*1-884729-13-4*) Inst Byzantine.

***Spiritual Being: A User's Guide.** Happy Dobbs. (Illus.). 200p. (Orig.). 1997. pap. 20.00 (*0-85398-415-8*) G Ronald Pub.

Spiritual Beings in the Heavenly Bodies & in the Kingdoms of Nature: A Cycle of 10 Lectures, Helsinki, April 3-14, 1912: with Four Additional Lectures, Two Public Lectures & Two Private Lectures Given to Russian Members. Rudolf Steiner. LC 92-26629. 1992. pap. 16.95 (*0-88010-367-1*) Anthroposophic.

Spiritual Beings in the Heavenly Bodies & in the Realms of Nautre, No. 1: Helsingfors, 1912. Rudolf Steiner. 33p. 1973. reprint ed. spiral bd. 5.50 (*0-7873-0818-8*) Hlth Research.

Spiritual Beings Like You - Like Me. Fredrick A. Johnson. LC 96-68047. (Illus.). 176p. (Orig.). 1996. pap. 11.95 (*0-89716-623-X*) P B Pubng.

***Spiritual Breakthrough: Handbook fo God-Consciousness.** John Van Auken. 170p. 1996. reprint ed. pap. 12.95 (*0-87604-367-8*, 484) ARE Pr.

Spiritual Breakthrough to the Next Millennium. Max Kappeler. LC 85-82058. 84p. 1986. pap. 9.00 (*0-942958-12-8*) Kappeler Inst Pub.

Spiritual Cannibalism. Swami Rudrananda. 182p. (Orig.). 1987. pap. 14.95 (*0-915801-07-8*) Rudra Pr.

Spiritual Canticle. St. John of the Cross. 1990. pap. 12.95 (*0-85574-124-4*, Pub. by E J Dwyer AT) Morehouse Pub.

Spiritual Canticle & Poems. St. John of the Cross. 480p. 1994. pap. 26.00 (*0-86012-061-9*, Pub. by Srch Pr UK) St Mut.

Spiritual Canticle of St. John of the Cross. Tr. by Pascal Pierini. (Illus.). 1991. pap. 25.00 (*0-941179-32-X*) Latitudes Pr.

Spiritual Canticle of St. John of the Cross. 12p. 1990. reprint ed. 90.00 (*0-935072-18-7*) W T Taylor.

Spiritual Canticle of the Soul & the Bridegroom Christ. St. John of the Cross. Tr. by David Lewis. 341p. 1996. pap. 24.95 (*1-56459-550-1*) Kessinger Pub.

Spiritual Care. Dietrich Bonhoeffer. Tr. by Jay C. Rochelle. LC 85-47711. 128p. 1985. pap. 11.00 (*0-8006-1874-2*, 1-1874, Fortress Pr) Augsburg Fortress.

Spiritual Care: The Nurse's Role. 3rd ed. Judith A. Shelly & Sharon Fish. LC 88-871. (Spiritual Perspectives in Nursing Ser.). (Illus.). 251p. 1988. student ed., pap. 12.99 (*0-8308-1254-7*, 1254) InterVarsity.

Spiritual Care of Puerto Rican Migrants. Ed. by Ivan Illich et al. LC 79-6206. (Hispanics in the United States Ser.). 1981. reprint ed. lib. bdg. 25.95 (*0-405-13156-9*) Ayer.

***Spiritual Care of the Dying & Bereaved.** Penelope Wilcock. LC 97-21289. 112p. (Orig.). 1997. pap. 9.95 (*0-8192-1712-3*) Morehouse Pub.

Spiritual Centers in Man. Manly P. Hall. Orig. Title: Operative Occultism. pap. 4.95 (*0-89314-383-9*) Philos Res.

Spiritual Churches of New Orleans: Origins, Beliefs, & Rituals of an African-American Religion. Claude F. Jacobs & Andrew J. Kaslow. LC 90-25402. (Illus.). 272p. (C). 1991. text ed. 26.00 (*0-87049-702-2*) U of Tenn Pr.

Spiritual Cleansing. Draja Mickaharic. 1987. pap. 5.95 (*0-942272-09-9*) Original Pubns.

Spiritual Cleansing. Draja Mickaharic. LC 81-70348. 177p. 1982. pap. 6.95 (*0-87728-531-4*) Weiser.

Spiritual Collection. 9.95 (*0-7935-4649-4*, 50482415) H Leonard.

Spiritual Combat & a Treatise on Peace of Soul. Dom L. Scupoli. Tr. by William Lester & Robert Mohan from ITA. LC 90-70929. 240p. 1993. reprint ed. pap. 9.00 (*0-89555-405-4*) TAN Bks Pubs.

Spiritual Concept: The Real Nature of Things. Roslyn LoPinto. 86p. (Orig.). 1988. pap. 6.95 (*0-9619018-1-0*) Artistech.

Spiritual Conferences. Frederick W. Faber. LC 78-66304. 1988. reprint ed. pap. 15.00 (*0-89555-079-2*) TAN Bks Pubs.

Spiritual Conferences. John Tauler. Tr. by Eric Colledge & M. Jane. LC 78-74568. 1979. reprint ed. pap. 13.00 (*0-89555-082-2*) TAN Bks Pubs.

Spiritual Conflict. Arthur F. Glasser. Ed. by Stephen Hayner & Gordon Aeschliman. (Global Issues Bible Study Ser.). 48p. (Orig.). 1990. wbk. ed., pap. 4.99 (*0-8308-4901-7*, 4901) InterVarsity.

Spiritual Connections: The Journey of Discipleship & Christian Values. Brian P. Hall. (Illus.). 170p. (Orig.). 1992. pap. 9.95 (*0-9630202-1-8*) Values Tech.

Spiritual Conquest: Accomplished by the Religious of the Society of Jesus in the Provinces of Paraguay, Parana & Tape. Antonio R. De Montoya. Tr. by C. J. McNaspy et al. from SPA. LC 92-75537. (Jesuit Primary Sources in English Translation Series I: No. 11). 223p. 1993. 24.95 (*1-880810-02-6*); pap. 17.95 (*1-880810-03-4*) Inst Jesuit.

Spiritual Conquest of Mexico: An Essay on the Apostolate & the Evangelizing Methods of the Mendicant Orders in New Spain, 1523-1572. Robert Ricard. Tr. by Lesley B. Simpson from SPA. (Illus.). 435p. 1974. pap. 14.00 (*0-520-04784-2*) U CA Pr.

Spiritual Counsels of Father John of Kronstadt. W. Jardine Grisbrooke. 230p. (Orig.). 1982. reprint ed. pap. 10.95 (*0-913836-92-3*) St Vladimirs.

Spiritual Counsels of Starets Parfeny. Starets Paefeny. 1991. pap. 1.00 (*0-89981-135-3*) Eastern Orthodox.

Spiritual Crisis: What Really Is Behind Loss, Disease, & Life's Major Hurts. Meredith L. Young-Sowers. 288p. 1993. pap. 13.95 (*0-913299-89-8*) Stillpoint.

Spiritual Crisis of the Gilded Age. Paul A. Carter. LC 72-156938. (Illus.). 295p. 1971. 28.00 (*0-87580-026-2*) N Ill U Pr.

Spiritual Dance & Walk: An Introduction to the Dances of Universal Peace & Walking Meditations of Samuel L. Lewis. rev. ed. Samuel L. Lewis & Neil Douglas-Klotz. Ed. by Marie Demcho-Wagor. (Illus.). 144p. 1990. pap. 9.95 (*0-915424-13-4*) PeaceWks Intl Ntwrk.

Spiritual Dance of Life: Where Two Worlds Meet. M. Teri Daunter. (Illus.). 220p. 1995. 20.00 (*0-9643646-8-9*); pap. 16.00 (*0-9643646-9-7*) Mobius Pubng.

Spiritual Depression: Its Causes & Cure. D. Martyn Lloyd-Jones. 300p. 1965. pap. 15.00 (*0-8028-1387-9*) Eerdmans.

Spiritual Depths. Martha I. Brown. 104p. 1986. pap. 5.00 (*0-9618538-0-8*) Martha I Brown.

Spiritual Development: An Interdisciplinary Study. Daniel A. Helminiak. 256p. 1987. 4.00 (*0-8294-0530-5*) Loyola Pr.

Spiritual Development Guide: An In-Depth Guided Study for Your Spiritual Growth. Keith W. Drury. (Illus.). 24p. (Orig.). 1991. reprint ed. wbk. ed., pap. 3.95 (*0-89827-068-5*, BKE61) Wesleyan Pub Hse.

Spiritual Devotion: Intimacy with God. Nathan H. Nelson. 112p. 1996. pap. 4.95 (*0-88243-107-2*) Gospel Pub.

Spiritual Devotion: Intimacy with God. Nathan H. Nelson. (Spiritual Discovery Ser.). 126p. 1996. teacher ed., pap. 9.95 (*0-88243-207-9*) Gospel Pub.

Spiritual Diary. 380p. 1982. pap. 4.50 (*0-87612-021-4*) Self Realization.

Spiritual Diary. Douglas M. Baker. 1976. pap. 22.00 (*0-906006-88-0*, Pub. by Baker Pubns UK) New Leaf Dist.

Spiritual Diary. Christopher Hills. 370p. 1984. pap. 9.95 (*0-916438-50-3*) Dr Hills Technol.

Spiritual Diary of Emanuel Swedenborg, 6 vols, Set. Emanuel Swedenborg. 1972. lib. bdg. 1,800.00 (*0-87968-560-3*) Krishna Pr.

Spiritual Dilemma of the Jewish People. Arthur W. Kac. 160p. 1984. 5.99 (*0-8010-5456-7*) Baker Bks.

Spiritual Dimensions of Healing: From Native Shamanism to Contemporary Health Care. Stanley Krippner & Patrick Welch. LC 92-159. (Frontiers of Consciousness Ser.). (Illus.). 302p. 1992. 19.95 (*0-8290-2462-X*); text ed. 39.95 incl. audio (*0-8290-3162-6*) Irvington.

Spiritual Dimensions of Healing Addictions. Donna Cunningham & Andrew Ramer. 172p. 1988. 9.95 (*0-9615875-5-5*) Cassandra Pr.

Spiritual Dimensions of Mental Health. Judith A. Shelley & Sandra D. John. LC 83-12769. 179p. (Orig.). (C). 1983. pap. 11.99 (*0-87784-876-9*, 876) InterVarsity.

Spiritual Dimensions of Music: Altering Consciousness for Inner Development. R. J. Stewart. 1990. pap. 12.95 (*0-89281-312-1*) Inner Tradit.

Spiritual Dimensions of Nursing Practice. Carson. 400p. 1989. pap. text ed. 37.50 (*0-7216-2249-6*) Saunders.

Spiritual Dimensions of Psychology. Inayat Khan. 254p. 1988. pap. 15.00 (*0-930872-36-3*) Omega Pubns NY.

Spiritual Dimensions of the Martial Arts. Michael Maliszewski. (Illus.). 224p. 1996. pap. 16.95 (*0-8048-2048-1*) C E Tuttle.

Spiritual Direction: Letters of Starets Macarius of Optina Monastery. pap. 2.95 (*0-89981-097-7*) Eastern Orthodox.

Spiritual Direction: Principles & Practices. Robert F. Morneau. 144p. (Orig.). 1992. pap. 11.95 (*0-8245-1202-2*) Crossroad NY.

Spiritual Direction According to St. Paul of the Cross. Bennet Kelley. LC 93-23863. 172p. (Orig.). 1993. pap. 7.95 (*0-8189-0653-7*) Alba.

Spiritual Direction & Meditation. Thomas Merton. 108p. 1960. pap. 4.95 (*0-8146-0412-9*) Liturgical Pr.

***Spiritual Direction & Spiritual Director.** Joseph Kozlowski. (Orig.). Date not set. pap. write for info. (*1-882972-85-6*) Queenship Pub.

Spiritual Direction & the Encounter with God: A Theological Inquiry. William A. Barry. LC 91-43159. 132p. 1992. pap. 7.95 (*0-8091-3305-9*) Paulist Pr.

***Spiritual Direction for Today's Catholic.** rev. ed. Frederick Schroeder & Craig Meyers. 84p. (Orig.). 1996. pap. 6.95 (*0-89942-139-3*, 140/04) Catholic Bk Pub.

Spiritual Direction in the Dominican Tradition. Benedict M. Ashley. LC 94-46496. (Integration Bks.). 176p. (Orig.). 1995. pap. 12.95 (*0-8091-3567-1*) Paulist Pr.

Spiritual Direction in the Early Eastern Church. Irenee Hausherr. Tr. by Anthony P. Gythiel from FRE. (Cistercian Studies: No. 116). 436p. 49.95 (*0-87907-416-7*) Cistercian Pubns.

Spiritual Discernment: Discernment Begins in the Garden. Jeffrey B. Krall. 40p. (Orig.). 1996. pap. 3.50 (*1-57688-002-8*, 002-8) Branch & Vine.

Spiritual Discernment & Politics: Guidelines for Religious Communities. J. B. Libanio. Tr. by Theodore Morrow from POR. LC 82-2257. Orig. Title: Discernment E politica. 143p. (Orig.). reprint ed. pap. 40.80 (*0-8357-7034-6*, 2033540) Bks Demand.

Spiritual Discernment & the Use of Clearness Committees among Friends. Patricia Loring. LC 92-62676. 32p. (Orig.). 1992. pap. 3.00 (*0-87574-305-6*) Pendle Hill.

Spiritual Discipleship. J. Oswald Sanders. (Commitment to Spiritual Growth Ser.). 1994. pap. 11.99 (*0-8024-6798-9*) Moody.

Spiritual Disciplines. 1984. pap. 8.95 (*0-687-61380-9*) Abingdon.

Spiritual Disciplines. Stephen Eyre. (Discipleship Ser.). 48p. 1992. pap. 4.99 (*0-310-54751-2*) Zondervan.

***Spiritual Disciplines.** Karla Kincannon. (Lifesearch Ser.). 64p. 1996. pap. 4.95 (*0-687-01501-4*) Abingdon.

Spiritual Disciplines for Everyday Living. Ronald V. Wells. LC 87-90606. (Illus.). 260p. 1994. reprint ed. pap. 15.00 (*0-9618701-0-9*) RDC Bks.

Spiritual Disciplines for Ordinary People--Leader's Guide. Keith Drury. (Illus.). 180p. 1990. spiral bd. 14.95 (*0-89827-074-X*, BKM94) Wesleyan Pub Hse.

Spiritual Disciplines for the Christian Life. Donald S. Whitney. LC 91-67293. 240p. 1991. 18.00 (*0-89109-658-2*) NavPress.

Spiritual Disciplines for the Christian Life: A Study Guide Based on the Book. Donald S. Whitney. 96p. (Orig.). 1991. pap. 6.00 (*0-89109-759-7*) NavPress.

Spiritual Disciplines Within the Church: Participating Fully in the Body of Christ. Donald S. Whitney. 1996. pap. 11.99 (*0-8024-7746-1*) Moody.

Spiritual Discourse: Learning with an Islamic Master. Frances Trix. LC 92-32060. (Conduct & Communication Ser.). 208p. (Orig.). (C). 1993. pap. text ed. 15.95 (*0-8122-1439-0*) U of Pa Pr.

Spiritual Discourse & the Meaning of Persons. Patrick Grant. LC 93-39268. 1994. text ed. 55.00 (*0-312-12077-X*) St Martin.

Spiritual Diseases. Craig Tappe. 1993. pap. 5.25 (*0-89137-829-4*) Quality Pubns.

Spiritual Distinction: Perspectives on Havdalah & Melaveh Malkah. Tr. & Compiled by Moshe M. Greebel. LC 93-15795. write for info. (*1-880582-11-2*) Judaica Pr.

Spiritual Doctrine of Blessed Elizabeth of the Trinity: Apostolic Contemplative. Luigi Borriello. Tr. by Jordan Aumann from SPA. LC 86-3446. 154p. (Orig.). 1986. pap. 7.95 (*0-8189-0500-X*) Alba.

Spiritual Doctrine of St. Catherine of Genoa. Don C. Marabotto & St. Catherine of Genoa. LC 88-50267. 328p. 1989. reprint ed. pap. 10.00 (*0-89555-335-X*) TAN Bks Pubs.

Spiritual Drama in the Life of Thackeray. M. Stephenson. 1972. 59.95 (*0-8490-1112-4*) Gordon Pr.

Spiritual Dreaming: A Cross-Cultural & Historical Journey. Kelly Bulkeley. LC 95-22278. 288p. (Orig.). 1995. pap. 16.95 (*0-8091-3592-2*) Paulist Pr.

***Spiritual Dreams: True Stories of Remarkable Encounters with God.** Ann Spangler. LC 96-40873. (Illus.). 176p. 1997. 13.99 (*0-310-20827-0*) Zondervan.

Spiritual Dynamics. G. Raymond Carlson. LC 76-5633. (Radiant Life Ser.). 1976. teacher ed., pap. 5.50 (*0-88243-168-4*, 32-0168) Gospel Pub.

Spiritual Dynamics. G. Raymond Carlson. LC 76-5633. (Radiant Life Ser.). 125p. 1976. pap. 3.95 (*0-88243-894-8*, 02-0894) Gospel Pub.

***Spiritual Economics: Reshaping Your Attitudes about Money, Spirituality, & Personal Property.** abr. ed. Eric Butterworth. 275p. 1998. write for info. (*0-87159-211-8*) Unity Bks.

Spiritual Economics: The Prosperity Process. rev. ed. Eric Butterworth. LC 82-50870. 230p. 1993. pap. 9.95 (*0-87159-196-0*) Unity Bks.

Spiritual Elixir: Timeless Excerpts from Correspondence. 2nd ed. Kirpal Singh. (Illus.). 383p. (C). 1989. reprint ed. pap. 11.00 (*0-942735-02-1*) Ruhani Satsang.

Spiritual Emergency. Ed. by Stanislav Grof & Christina Grof. (New Consciousness Reader Ser.). 272p. (Orig.). 1989. pap. 14.95 (*0-87477-538-8*, Tarcher Putnam) Putnam Pub Group.

Spiritual Empowerment in Afro-American Literature: Frederick Douglass, Rebecca Jackson, Booker T. Washington, Richard Wright, Toni Morrison. James H. Evans, Jr. LC 87-14196. (Studies in Art & Religious Interpretation). 192p. 1987. lib. bdg. 79.95 (*0-88946-560-6*) E Mellen.

Spiritual Empowerment in Pedagogy. Ed. by Regina Foehr & Susan Schiller. LC 96-41585. 1997. pap. text ed. write for info. (*0-86709-413-3*, 0413) Boynton Cook Pubs.

Spiritual Encounter Guides, 8 vols., Set. Stephen D. Eyre & Jacalyn Eyre. (Orig.). 1992. wbk. ed., pap. 39.92 (*0-8308-1175-3*, 1175) InterVarsity.

Spiritual Encounter with the Holy One. Jean Koberlein. LC 84-8938. (Mellen Lives Ser.: Vol. 2). 200p. 1984. pap. 79.95 (*0-88946-012-4*) E Mellen.

Spiritual Enlightener. Dorothy Jones. LC 92-63254. 69p. 1993. 6.95 (*1-55523-587-5*) Winston-Derek.

***Spiritual Entrepreneurs: 6 Principles for Risking Renewal.** Michael Slaughter. (Leadership Insight Ser.). 1996. pap. 13.95 (*0-687-00799-2*) Abingdon.

Spiritual Entrepreneurs: 6 Principles for Risking Renewal. rev. ed. Michael Slaughter. LC 95-230664. (Innovators in Ministry). 176p. (Orig.). 1995. text ed. 16.95 (*0-687-00561-2*) Abingdon.

Spiritual Espousals. Jan Van Ruusbroec. Tr. by H. Rolfson from DUT. LC 94-49569. 128p. 1995. pap. 9.95 (*0-8146-5056-2*, M Glazier) Liturgical Pr.

Spiritual, Ethical & Pastoral Aspects of Death & Bereavement. Ed. by Gerry R. Cox & Ronald J. Fundis. (Death, Value & Meaning Ser.). 289p. 1992. text ed. 36.95 (*0-89503-100-0*); pap. text ed. 27.71 (*0-89503-101-9*) Baywood Pub.

***Spiritual Event of the Twentieth Century: An Imagination: The Occult Significance of the 12 Years 1933-45 in the Light of Spiritual Science.** 2nd rev. ed. Jesaiah Ben-Aharon. 80p. 1996. pap. write for info. (*0-904693-77-5*, Pub. by Temple Ldge Pub UK) Anthroposophic.

Spiritual Exercises. Gertrude the Great of Helfta. Ed. by Gertrud J. Lewis & Jack Lewis. Tr. by Jack Lewis from LAT. (Cistercian Fathers Ser.: No. 49). 192p. 1989. 34.95 (*0-87907-049-8*); pap. 16.95 (*0-87907-449-3*) Cistercian Pubns.

Spiritual Exercises. Robert Kelly. LC 81-10038. 164p. (Orig.). (C). 1981. pap. 10.00 (*0-87685-507-9*) Black Sparrow.

Spiritual Exercises Based on Paul's Epistle to the Romans. Joseph A. Fitzmyer. LC 95-8650. 256p. (Orig.). 1995. pap. 14.95 (*0-8091-3580-9*) Paulist Pr.

***Spiritual Exercises For Couch Potatoes.** Kathy Callahan-Howell. 250p. 1997. pap. text ed. 9.99 (*0-89367-209-2*) Light & Life Comm.

Spiritual Exercises for Today: A Contemporary Presentation of the Classic Exercises of Ignatius Loyola. Tad Dunne. LC 90-55343. 160p. (Orig.). 1991. pap. 9.95 (*0-06-062108-7*) Harper SF.

Spiritual Exercises Made in Everyday Life: A Method & a Biblical Interpretation. Mary A. Roduit. LC 88-83844. (Modern Scholarly Studies about the Jesuits, in English Translations Series II: No. 8). xii, 161p. 1989. 15.95 (*0-912422-90-4*) Inst Jesuit.

Spiritual Exercises of ECK: Your Doorway to Wisdom, Freedom, & Love. Harold Klemp. LC 93-31410. 306p. 1997. pap. 11.00 (*1-57043-001-2*) ECKANKAR.

An Asterisk (*) at the beginning of an entry indicates that the title is appearing in BIP for the first time.

*Spiritual Exercises of Saint Ignatius: A New Translation from the Authorized Latin Text. Tr. & Comment by Pierre Wolff. LC 96-54825. 256p. (Orig.). 1997. 24.00 (0-7648-0028-0, Triumph Books) Liguori Pubns.

*Spiritual Exercises of Saint Ignatius: A New Translation from the Authorized Latin Text. Tr. & Comment by Pierre Wolff. LC 96-54825. 256p. (Orig.). 1997. pap. 15.00 (0-7648-0142-2, Triumph Books) Liguori Pubns.

Spiritual Exercises of Saint Ignatius: A Translation & Commentary. George E. Ganss. LC 91-77119. 232p. (Orig.). 1992. pap. 11.95 (0-8294-0728-6) Loyola Pr.

Spiritual Exercises of St. Ignatius. St. Ignatius Of Loyola. 208p. 1964. pap. 8.95 (0-385-02436-3, D170, Image Bks) Doubleday.

Spiritual Exercises of St. Ignatius. St. Ignatius Of Loyola. 128p. 1991. reprint ed. 12.95 (0-940147-13-0) Source Bks CA.

Spiritual Exercises of St. Ignatius: A Translation & Commentary. George E. Ganss. LC 91-77119. (Jesuit Primary Sources in English Translation Series I: No. 9). xii, 232p. (C). 1992. 22.95 (0-912422-84-X); pap. 11.95 (0-912422-86-6) Inst Jesuit.

Spiritual Exercises of St. Ignatius: Based on Studies in the Language of the Autograph. Louis J. Puhl. (Request Reprint Ser.). 216p. (SPA.). 1968. per., pap. 5.95 (0-8294-0065-6, PUHL) Loyola Pr.

Spiritual Family. John-Roger. 1976. pap. 5.00 (0-914829-21-1, 978-5) Mandeville LA.

Spiritual Feasts. G. D. Watson. 1991. reprint ed. pap. 4.99 (0-88019-278-X) Schmul Pub Co.

Spiritual Fitness. Donnelly. LC 92-53923. 208p. 1993. pap. 14.00 (0-06-061899-X) Harper SF.

Spiritual Fitness. Tom Owen-Towle. LC 89-63710. 394p. (Orig.). 1989. pap. 12.00 (0-931104-27-0) Sunflower Ink.

*Spiritual Fly Fisher. B. Anthony Varga. LC 96-78915. (Illus.). 56p. (Orig.). 1997. pap. 13.50 (0-913559-33-4) Birch Brook Pr.

Spiritual Folk-Songs of Early America. Ed. by George P. Jackson. 1990. 14.50 (0-8446-2297-4) Peter Smith.

Spiritual Food. Wong Ming-Dao. 1983. pap. 8.99 (0-907821-01-4) Revival Lit.

Spiritual Food Gleanings. Ed. by James C. Yu. Tr. by Ming-Tao Wang from ENG. 128p. (Orig.). (CHI.). 1987. pap. text ed. 2.50 (0-940043-28-9) Evangel Lit.

*Spiritual Formation in Seminaries & Instruction on Liturgical Formation in Seminaries. Congregation for Catholic Education Staff. 85p. pap. 2.75 (0-8198-6927-9) Pauline Bks.

Spiritual Formation Journal: A Renovare Resource for Spiritual Formation. Jana Rea. 224p. 1996. pap. 13.00 (0-06-066757-5) Harper SF.

Spiritual Formation Workbook. Renovare. 96p. 1993. pap. 9.00 (0-06-066965-9) Harper SF.

Spiritual Foundation of Morality: Francis of Assisi & the Mission of Love. Rudolf Steiner. 112p. 1995. 10.95 (0-88010-425-2) Anthroposophic.

Spiritual Foundations: Prayer, Meditation & the Devotional Attitude (Extracts from Writings of Baha'u'llah, Abdu'l-Baha & Shoghi Effendi) Universal House of Justice Staff. 20p. 1980. pap. 0.50 (0-87743-140-X) Bahai.

Spiritual Foundations for Social Action. Polly Edgar et al. (Studies in Quakerism: No. 14). 52p. 1987. pap. 4.00 (0-89670-017-8) Progresiv Pub.

Spiritual Foundations of Aikido. William Gleason. (Illus.). 214p. 1995. pap. 19.95 (0-89281-508-6, Destiny Bks) Inner Tradit.

Spiritual Foundations of Society: An Introduction to Social Philosophy. S. L. Frank. Ed. & Tr. by Boris Jakim from RUS. LC 86-12835. 196p. 1986. text ed. 24.95 (0-8214-0848-8) Ohio U Pr.

Spiritual Franciscans. David S. Muzzey. 1972. 59.95 (0-8490-1113-2) Gordon Pr.

Spiritual Freedom: From an Experience of the Ignatian Exercises to the Art of Spiritual Guidance. 2nd ed. John J. English. LC 94-38772. 311p. 1995. pap. 12.95 (0-8294-0823-1) Loyola Pr.

Spiritual Friend: Reclaiming the Gift of Spiritual Direction. Tilden Edwards. LC 79-91408. 272p. 1997. reprint ed. pap. 14.95 (0-8091-2288-X) Paulist Pr.

Spiritual Friendship. Aelred of Rievaulx. (Cistercian Fathers Ser.: No. 5). 144p. 1974. pap. 7.95 (0-87907-705-0) Cistercian Pubns.

Spiritual Friendship: Darkness & Light. Ronda Chervin. LC 92-9890. 96p. (Orig.). 1992. pap. 4.95 (0-8198-6892-2) Pauline Bks.

*Spiritual Genius of Saint Therese of Lisieux. Jean Guitton. LC 97-1640. 128p. 1997. pap. 12.00 (0-7648-0077-9, Triumph Books) Liguori Pubns.

Spiritual Gifts. Neal R. Boese. 1995. pap. 6.95 (0-7880-0615-0, 6150) CSS OH.

Spiritual Gifts. David Hocking. Ed. by M. B. Steele. (Illus.). 160p. (Orig.). 1992. pap. 9.95 (0-939497-28-X) Promise Pub.

Spiritual Gifts. Charles F. Hummel & Anne Hummel. LC 89-15305. (LifeGuide Bible Studies). 64p. (Orig.). 1989. wbk. ed., pap. 4.99 (0-8308-1062-5, 1062) InterVarsity.

Spiritual Gifts. Kent Millard. (Lifesearch Ser.). 64p. (Orig.). 1994. pap. 4.95 (0-687-77866-2) Abingdon.

Spiritual Gifts: A Fresh Look. William W. Menzies. LC 90-23950. 336p. 1991. pap. 8.95 (0-88243-636-8, 02-0636) Gospel Pub.

Spiritual Gifts: A Self Study or Group Study Manual. Bobby Clinton. 219p. 1985. spiral bd. 11.99 (0-88965-071-3) Chr Pubns.

Spiritual Gifts: Ministries & Manifestations. B. E. Underwood. 1984. student ed., pap. 4.95 (0-911866-04-3); teacher ed., pap. 6.95 (0-911866-05-1); pap. text ed. 7.95 (0-911866-03-5) LifeSprings Res.

Spiritual Gifts: Your Job Description from God. Owen C. Weston. 143p. 1996. pap. 9.95 (0-911866-30-2) LifeSprings Res.

Spiritual Gifts: Your Portion of Christ's Bounty, Workbook 1. 4th ed. Robert D. Noble. (Welcome in Ser.). 61p. (Orig.). 1985. pap. 10.00 (0-944687-01-6) Gather Family Inst.

Spiritual Gifts & the Church. D. Bridge. 8.99 (1-85792-141-0, Pub. by Christian Focus UK) Spring Arbor Dist.

Spiritual Gifts & Their Operation. Howard Carter. 96p. 1968. pap. 3.95 (0-88243-593-0, 02-0593) Gospel Pub.

Spiritual Gifts Handbook: A Complete Guide to Discovering & Using Your Spiritual Gift. Bruce W. Black. LC 94-43446. 142p. 1995. pap. 9.99 (0-87213-058-4) Loizeaux.

Spiritual Gifts in the Local Church. David Pytches. LC 87-15128. 288p. (Orig.). 1987. pap. 10.99 (0-87123-984-1) Bethany Hse.

Spiritual Gospel. Jim Lewis. LC 82-51231. 145p. (Orig.). 1982. pap. 8.95 (0-942482-05-0) Unity Church Denver.

Spiritual Greatness: Studies in Exodus. Tom Julien. (Orig.). 1979. pap. 6.99 (0-88469-121-7) BMH Bks.

*Spiritual Growth. Max E. Anders. LC 97-8578. (What You Need to Know Ser.). 1997. pap. write for info. (0-8407-1936-1) Nelson.

Spiritual Growth. Arthur Pink. 200p. (gr. 10). 1996. reprint ed. pap. 10.99 (0-8010-6862-2) Baker Bks.

Spiritual Growth: Being Your Higher Self. Sanaya Roman. Ed. by Elaine Ratner. LC 88-81721. (Earth Life Ser.: Bk. III). 252p. 1989. pap. 12.95 (0-915811-12-X) H J Kramer Inc.

Spiritual Growth: Understanding the Three Levels of Christian Growth. Jeffrey B. Krall. 40p. (Orig.). 1996. pap. 3.50 (1-57688-003-6, 003-6) Branch & Vine.

Spiritual Growth & Development. Robert C. Jiggetts, Jr. 50p. 1993. student ed., wbk. ed. write for info. (0-9632527-3-9) LTUC of Christ.

Spiritual Growth & Maturity. Ed. by R. M. Davis & P. D. Buford. 160p. reprint ed. pap. 5.99 (1-56722-060-6) Word Aflame.

Spiritual Growth in the Congregation. Robert H. Boyte & Kelly Boyte-Peters. 112p. (Orig.). 1988. pap. 7.99 (0-8272-3428-7) Chalice Pr.

Spiritual Growth in Youth Ministry, Bk. 1: Personal Spiritual Growth. J. David Stone. 95p. 1992. pap. text ed. 6.95 (1-882745-03-5) YMTN-Stone.

Spiritual Growth in Youth Ministry, Bk. 2: Spiritual Growth for Youth Groups. J. David Stone. 121p. (Orig.). 1992. pap. text ed. 6.95 (1-882745-04-3) YMTN-Stone.

Spiritual Guidance of the Individual & Humanity: Some Results of Spiritual-Scientific Research into Human History & Development. Rudolf Steiner. Tr. by Samuel Desch from GER. 108p. 1992. pap. 10.95 (0-88010-364-7) Anthroposophic.

Spiritual Guide. Michael Molinos. Ed. by Gene Edwards. 110p. 1982. pap. 8.95 (0-940232-08-1) Seedsowers.

Spiritual Guide for Life. J. Thomas, pseud. 77p. (Orig.). 1993. pap. text ed. 4.95 (0-9637794-1-9) Machia.

*Spiritual Guide Through Pregnancy. Margaret Hammer. 1997. pap. text ed. 10.99 (0-8066-3344-1, Augsburg) Augsburg Fortress.

Spiritual Guides of the Third Century: A Semiotic Study of the Guide-Disciple Relationship in Christianity, Neoplatonism, Hermetism, & Gnosticism. Richard F. Valantasis. LC 91-33295. (Harvard Theological Studies: Vol. 27). 240p. (Orig.). (C). 1990. pap. 17.00 (0-8006-7081-7) TPI PA.

*Spiritual Guides to Holistic Health & Happiness. Robert E. Valett. 1997. per. 12.95 (0-938911-11-2) Indiv Educ Syst.

*Spiritual Healer. Alton E. Joseph. 290p. (Orig.). 1997. mass mkt. 4.99 (1-55197-643-9, Pub. by Comnwlth Pub CN) Partners Pubs Grp.

*Spiritual Healing. John T. Ferrier. 132p. Date not set. pap. text ed. 9.00 (0-900235-66-7) Order Of The Cross.

*Spiritual Healing. Grayson. LC 97-7508. 1997. 23.00 (0-684-82365-9) S&S Trade.

Spiritual Healing. Ed. by Willis H. Kinnear. 110p. (Orig.). 1973. pap. 5.95 (0-911336-50-8) Sci of Mind.

Spiritual Healing. Nelson White & Anne White. LC 85-50745. (Illus.). 65p. (Orig.). 1985. pap. text ed. 18.00 (0-939856-42-5) Tech Group.

Spiritual Healing. 2nd ed. Ed. by Dora Kunz. 320p. 1995. pap. 12.00 (0-8356-0714-3, Quest) Theos Pub Hse.

Spiritual Healing. 4th ed. Swami Paramananda. 1975. pap. 3.95 (0-911564-10-1) Vedanta Ctr.

*Spiritual Healing: A Beginner's Guide. Kristnya Arcarti. (Illus.). 96p. 1997. pap. 11.95 (0-340-67416-4, Pub. by Headway UK) Trafalgar.

*Spiritual Healing: A Patient's Guide. Date not set. pap. write for info. (0-8464-4571-9) Beekman Pubs.

Spiritual Healing: As a Complement to the Art of Medicine. Madeleine Riedel-Michel. 216p. (C). 1988. 35.00 (0-7212-0753-7, Pub. by Regency Press UK) St Mut.

Spiritual Healing: Miracle or Mirage? Alan Young. LC 81-82932. 280p. (Orig.). 1982. pap. 7.95 (0-87516-460-9) DeVorss.

Spiritual Healing: Selections from the Writings of Joel Goldsmith. Joel S. Goldsmith. LC 93-44226. 1994. pap. 12.95 (0-8065-1521-X, Citadel Pr) Carol Pub Group.

Spiritual Healing: Words from Beyond: If Only You Could Hear the Stones & the Eagles. Annette Harris-Rain Bear. Ed. by Nancy Earle. LC 95-76517. 155p. (Orig.). 1996. pap. text ed. 12.95 (1-886836-41-8) Black Diamnd.

Do you feel like your life is stagnant? Are your feelings on a treadmill? Do you wake up every morning & say "Good God, it's morning!?" Then SPIRITUAL HEALING will show you how to learn to wake up & say, "Good morning, God!" & mean it! SPIRITUAL HEALING, WORDS FROM BEYOND offers inspiration, hope, & inner peace. It is a message of love & patience, & of ancient wisdom. The words are simple, the messages are profound. Its short passages cover a variety of themes, all of which help heal the soul through love, closeness to nature, & kindness. The words of the Wise Ones accompany the reader on a journey that binds the past to the future & draws the ages, man, nature, & the earth into a unified whole. This stunning collection of writings on lessons in healing was channeled through Annette Harris-Rain Bear; they are good medicine. Rain Bear - Annette Harris found & developed her spirituality & gift of seeing both past & future through her Native American heritage. She serves as a channel for the spirits of the ancient Native American Wise Ones who impart their message of peace, love, a reverence for nature, & forgiveness. ***Publisher Provided Annotation.***

Spiritual Healing for Today. Raymond C. Barker. LC 88-70091. 136p. (Orig.). 1988. pap. 6.95 (0-87516-607-5) DeVorss.

Spiritual Help Through Simple Prayer Chanting: Aid for the Spirit. Carl M. Schmitthausler. LC 89-84665. (Illus.). 26p. (Orig.). 1989. pap. write for info. (0-9623817-1-3) AOP Lincoln.

Spiritual Heritage of India. Swami Prabhavananda. LC 63-10517. 374p. (C). 1979. reprint ed. pap. 9.95 (0-87481-035-3) Vedanta Pr.

Spiritual Heritage of the Human Race. Suheil Bushrui. 575p. 1997. pap. 14.95 (1-85168-110-8) Onewrld Pubns.

Spiritual Heritage of Tyagaraja. Tyagaraja. Tr. by C. Ramanujachari. Trilingual ed. pap. 12.95 (0-87481-440-5, Pub. by Ramakrishna Math II) Vedanta Pr.

Spiritual Hierarchies & the Physical World: Reality & Illusion. Rudolf Steiner. Tr. by Rene M. Querido & Jan Gates from GER. 256p. (Orig.). (GER.). 1996. pap. 18.95 (0-88010-440-6) Anthroposophic.

Spiritual Hierarchy & the Great White Brotherhood: The Saints Robed in White. Jeremiah. 144p. (Orig.). 1993. pap. 9.95 (0-9639053-0-9) Univ Truth Pr.

Spiritual High Treason. Jimmy Swaggart. 1987. 12.95 (0-935113-07-X) Swaggart Ministries.

Spiritual History: A Reading of William Blake's the Four Zoas. Andrew Lincoln. 344p. 1996. 79.00 (0-19-818314-3) OUP.

Spiritual History of the Dead Sea Sect. David Flusser. 98p. 1989. pap. 12.00 (965-05-0480-X, Pub. by Israel Ministry Def IS) Gefen Bks.

Spiritual Hospitality: A Quaker's Understanding of Outreach. Harvey Gillman. LC 94-65704. 1994. pap. 3.00 (0-87574-314-5) Pendle Hill.

Spiritual Hunger: Filling Your Deepest Longings. Jim Plueddemann & Carol Plueddemann. (Beatitudes Ser.). 48p. 1993. pap. 4.99 (0-310-59633-5) Zondervan.

Spiritual Hunger (John G. Lake Sermons) Gordon Lindsay. 1960. per. 3.95 (0-89985-020-0) Christ for the Nations.

Spiritual Hunger of the Modern Child. J. G. Bennett et al. Ed. by Wendy Addison. LC 87-71204. 220p. 1985. pap. 8.95 (0-934254-06-0) Claymont Comm.

Spiritual Ideal for the Present Age. Swami Vireshwarananda. 167p. 1983. pap. 4.95 (0-87481-578-9, Pub. by Ramakrishna Math II) Vedanta Pr.

Spiritual Image in Modern Art. Compiled by Kathleen J. Regier. LC 87-40127. (Illus.). 215p. (Orig.). (C). 1987. pap. 9.95 (0-8356-0621-X, Quest) Theos Pub Hse.

Spiritual Import of Humanity. John S. Connor. 1990. 13.95 (0-533-08536-5) Vantage.

Spiritual Import of Society. John S. Connor. LC 85-91374. 208p. 1987. 10.95 (0-533-06881-9) Vantage.

Spiritual in Art: Abstract Painting 1890-1985. Maurice Tuchman et al. (Illus.). 436p. 1993. pap. 45.00 (0-7892-0056-2) Abbeville Pr.

Spiritual Initiation see Great Work

Spiritual Insights for Daily Living: A Daybook of Reflections on Ancient Spiritual Truths of Relevance for Our Contemporary Lives. Ed. by Elizabeth W. Fenske. (Illus.). 416p. (Orig.). 1986. pap. 7.50 (0-914071-09-2) Spirit Front Fellow.

Spiritual Instructions of Saint Seraphim of Sarov: A Spirit-Baptizer in the Eastern Christian Church. rev. ed. Donald S. Webley. LC 90-27069. (Basket of Tolerance Ser.). (Illus.). 200p. 1991. pap. 12.95 (0-918801-25-7) Dawn Horse Pr.

*Spiritual Internet: A Guide to the Spiritual & Religious Resources on the Internet. Nickolas Grabovac. (Illus.). 360p. (Orig.). 1998. pap. 14.95 (0-87573-039-6) Jain Pub Co.

Spiritual Interpretation of History. Shailer Mathews. 1977. lib. bdg. 250.00 (0-8490-2661-X) Gordon Pr.

Spiritual Interpretation of Scripture. Joel S. Goldsmith. 235p. 1947. pap. 9.95 (0-87516-310-6) DeVorss.

Spiritual Intimacy: A Study of Counseling in Hasidism. Zalman Schachter-Shalomi. LC 90-43138. 424p. 1991. 35.00 (0-87668-772-9) Aronson.

Spiritual Intimacy: A Study of Counseling in Hasidism. Zalman Schachter-Shalomi. LC 90-43138. 416p. 1996. pap. 30.00 (1-56821-923-7) Aronson.

Spiritual Intimacy for Couples. Charles M. Sell. LC 96-548. 224p. 1996. pap. 10.99 (0-89107-888-6) Crossway Bks.

Spiritual Intimidation. Nelson White & Anne White. LC 84-51476. 65p. (Orig.). (C). 1984. pap. 18.00 (0-939856-39-5) Tech Group.

*Spiritual Intrapreneur: Awakening the Power & Potential Within You. Toni G. Boehm. 112p. 1996. pap. 10.00 (0-8059-3983-0) Dorrance.

Spiritual Journaling: Recording Your Journey Toward God. Richard Peace. (Spiritual Disciplines Ser.). 1996. pap. 7.00 (0-89109-897-6) NavPress.

*Spiritual Journals: Genesee Diary, Gracias!, the Road to Daybreak. Henri J. Nouwen. 288p. 1997. 29.00 (0-8264-1010-3) Continuum.

Spiritual Journey. Anne Bancroft. 160p. 1991. pap. 13.95 (1-85230-239-9) Element MA.

Spiritual Journey. George Carey. LC 93-45516. 148p. (Orig.). 1994. pap. 10.95 (0-8192-1595-3) Morehouse Pub.

Spiritual Journey. Marcel Lefebvre. Tr. by Society of St. Pius X Staff. 73p. (Orig.). 1991. pap. text ed. 7.95 (0-935952-16-0) Angelus Pr.

Spiritual Journey: Augustine's Reflections on the Christian Life. Augustine, Saint et al. LC 96-24008. 1996. pap. 13.95 (0-941491-97-8) Augustinian Pr.

Spiritual Journey: Critical Thresholds & Stages of Adult Spiritual Genesis. Francis K. Nemeck & Marie T. Coombs. LC 85-45664. 230p. (Orig.). 1986. pap. 14.95 (0-8146-5546-7) Liturgical Pr.

Spiritual Journey: Michio Kushi's Guide to Endless Realization & Freedom. Michio Kushi & Edward Esko. (Illus.). 96p. (Orig.). 1994. pap. text ed. 9.95 (1-882984-06-4) One Peaceful World.

Spiritual Journey: The Bar Mitzvah & Bat Mitzvah Handbook. Seymour Rossel. Ed. by William Cutter. (Illus.). 64p. pap. 4.95 (0-87441-551-9) Behrman.

Spiritual Journey No. 15. Esther DeWaal. (Word & Spirit Ser.: No. 15). 108p. 1993. pap. 8.00 (1-879007-02-9) St Bedes Pubns.

Spiritual Journey Life Renewal Devotional: Daily Reflections from the Bible & People of Faith. Ed. by Wightman Weese. LC 93-22492. 404p. 1993. pap. 7.99 (0-8423-5931-1) Tyndale.

Spiritual Journey of a Showbusiness Priest. 2nd ed. Ellwood E. Kieser. LC 95-44285. Orig. Title: Hollywood Priest. 256p. 1996. reprint ed. pap. 14.95 (0-8091-3587-6) Paulist Pr.

*Spiritual Journey of Aikido. Huw Dillon. 1996. pap. 19.95 (1-874250-35-9, Pub. by P H Crompton UK) Talman.

Spiritual Journey of Joel S. Goldsmith. Lorraine Sinkler. reprint ed. pap. 12.95 (0-9629119-2-5) Valor Fndtn.

Spiritual Journey of Newman. Jean Honore. Tr. by Mary C. Ludden. LC 92-26405. 260p. (ENG & FRE.). 1992. pap. 14.95 (0-8189-0654-5) Alba.

*Spiritual Journey to the End of the Rainbow. John Miller. (Illus.). 74p. (Orig.). 1996. pap. 11.95 (0-9656531-0-2) Rainbow Pr ID.

Spiritual Journeys. Ed. by Robert Baram. LC 87-6668. 442p. 1987. pap. 12.95 (0-8198-6876-0) Pauline Bks.

*Spiritual Knowing: Alternative Epistemic Perspective. Tobin Hart et al. (Studies in Social Sciences). 228p. (Orig.). 1997. reprint ed. pap. text ed. write for info. (1-883199-07-7) W GA College.

Spiritual Knowledge. Watchman Nee. Tr. by Stephen Kaung. 124p. 1973. 5.50 (0-935008-36-5); pap. 4.50 (0-935008-37-3) Christian Fellow Pubs.

Spiritual Knowledge see Conhecimento Espiritual

Spiritual Leaders. Paul R. Walker. LC 93-31684. (American Indian Lives Ser.). (Illus.). 160p. (J). (gr. 4-11). 1994. 17.95 (0-8160-2875-3) Facts on File.

Spiritual Leadership: Completely Updated Text with Study Guide. J. Oswald Sanders. (Commitment to Spiritual Growth Ser.). 1994. student ed., pap. 11.99 (0-8024-6799-7) Moody.

Spiritual Leadership & Successful Soulwinning. Ed. by R. M. Davis & P. D. Buford. 160p. reprint ed. pap. 5.99 (1-56722-061-4) Word Aflame.

Spiritual Leadership Begins at Home. Tom Allen. (Contemporary Christian Living Ser.). 19p. (Orig.). 1991. pap. 1.49 (0-87509-463-5) Chr Pubns.

Spiritual Legacies: Holiday Sermons. Isaac Klein. 20.00 (0-87068-276-8) Ktav.

*Spiritual Legacy: Faith for the Next Generation. Winnie Christensen. 1997. pap. text ed. 4.99 (0-87788-612-1) Shaw Pubs.

Spiritual Legacy of American Indian. Joseph E. Brown. 160p. 1984. pap. 12.95 (0-8245-0618-9) Crossroad NY.

Spiritual Legacy of Hans Denck: Interpretation & Translation of Key Texts. Clarence Bauman. LC 90-20241. (Studies in Medieval & Reformation Thought: Vol. 47). ix, 287p. (ENG & GER.). 1990. 100.00 (90-04-09291-9) E J Brill.

*Spiritual Legacy of John Foster Dulles. Henry P. Van Dusen. xxii, 232p. 1972. 18.95 (0-8369-2899-7) Bks for Libraries.

Spiritual Legacy of Sister Mary of the Holy Trinity. Ed. by Silvere Van den Broek. LC 81-82830. 364p. 1988. reprint ed. pap. 10.00 (0-89555-165-9) TAN Bks Pubs.

Spiritual Legacy of the American Indian. Joseph E. Brown. LC 64-17425. (Illus.). (Orig.). 1964. pap. 3.00 (0-87574-135-5) Pendle Hill.

*Spiritual Lemons: Biblical Women, Irreverent Laughter, & Righteous Rage. Lyn Brakeman. LC 96-48354. 128p. (Orig.). 1997. pap. 12.95 (1-880913-22-4) Innisfree Pr.

Spiritual Lessons from an Apple Orchard: A Meditation upon Apple Trees & the Spiritual Life. Fiona MacMath. 48p. 1996. 8.99 (0-7852-7609-2) Nelson.

Spiritual Liberation & Human Freedom in Contemporary Asia. Joseph M. Kitagawa. LC 90-38367. (Rochwell Lectures: Vol. 1). 213p. (C). 1990. text ed. 44.95 (0-8204-1318-6) P Lang Pubng.

Spiritual Liberty. Charles H. Spurgeon. 1978. mass mkt. 0.75 (1-56186-338-6) Pilgrim Pubns.

S

Spiritual Liberty. rev. ed. Inayat Khan. LC 79-67747. (Sufi Message of Hazrat Inayat Khan Ser.: Vol. 5). 256p. 1979. 19.00 (*90-6325-095-9*, Pub. by Sufi Mvemnt NE) Omega Pubns NY.

Spiritual Life. Annie Besant. 243p. 1991. pap. 8.95 (*0-8356-0666-X*, Quest) Theos Pub Hse.

***Spiritual Life.** Andrew Murray. 255p. (Orig.). 1996. mass mkt. 4.99 (*0-88368-304-0*) Whitaker Hse.

Spiritual Life. Edgar S. Brightman. LC 75-3086. (Philosophy in America Ser.). reprint ed. 37.50 (*0-404-59085-3*) AMS Pr.

Spiritual Life. Evelyn Underhill. LC 84-60646. 128p. 1984. reprint ed. pap. 6.95 (*0-8192-1350-0*) Morehouse Pub.

Spiritual Life: A Book of Reflections. Ariel Books Staff. (Illus.). 368p. 1995. pap. 4.95 (*0-8362-0724-6*) Andrews & McMeel.

Spiritual Life: And How to Be Attuned to It. Of Poltava Theophan. 102p. 1996. pap. text ed. 12.95 (*0-938635-36-0*) St Herman Pr.

Spiritual Life: Great Spiritual Truths for Everyday Life. Evelyn Underhill. (Mystical Classics of the World Ser.). 96p. 1994. reprint ed. pap. 6.95 (*1-85168-056-X*) Onewrld Pubns.

Spiritual Life: It's Not What You Think! Douglas Stewart. 120p. (Orig.). 1996. pap. 8.00 (*0-9650904-0-X*) Selah Pubns.

Spiritual Life: Selected Writings of Albert Schweitzer. Albert Schweitzer. Ed. by Charles R. Joy. (Companions Ser.). 256p. 1996. reprint ed. pap. 14.00 (*0-88001-466-0*) Ecco Pr.

Spiritual Life: The Foundation for Preaching & Teaching. John H. Westerhoff. LC 94-10408. 96p. (Orig.). 1994. pap. 10.00 (*0-664-25500-0*) Westminster John Knox.

Spiritual Life - Word of God. Emanuel Swedenborg. 1983. pap. 4.95 (*0-87785-083-6*) Swedenborg.

Spiritual Life, a Guide for Those Seeking Perfection. Joannes Cassianus. 1977. pap. 5.95 (*0-89981-098-5*) Eastern Orthodox.

Spiritual Life Disciplines: A Four Week Study to Help Teenagers Understand & Develop Spiritual Disciplines. Sam Crabtree. Ed. by Gary Swyers et al. (Bible Basics Ser.). (Illus.). 32p. (Orig.). (YA). (gr. 6-12). 1992. wbk. ed., pap. 9.95 (*0-89827-093-6*, BKW13) Wesleyan Pub Hse.

Spiritual Life in Anabaptism. Cornelius J. Dyck. LC 95-31471. 312p. (Orig.). 1996. pap. 16.99 (*0-8361-9024-6*) Herald Pr.

***Spiritual Life in the Congregation: A Guide for Retreats.** Rueben P. Job. LC 97-11425. 128p. (Orig.). 1997. pap. 9.95 (*0-8358-0818-1*, UR 818) Upper Room Bks.

Spiritual Life in the Early Church: The Witness of Acts & Ephesians. Bonnie Thurston. LC 93-11516. 1993. pap. 13.00 (*0-8006-2616-8*, 1-2616) Augsburg Fortress.

Spiritual Life in the Good Ol' U. S. A. Story-Essays on Popular Culture & Christianity. Melvin Hasman. LC 93-34388. (Illus.). 234p. 1994. 23.95 (*0-9638240-8-2*); pap. 15.95 (*0-9638240-9-0*) Potters Bks.

Spiritual Life of Catholics: The Ninth Proceedings of the Fellowship of Catholic Scholars. Ed. by Paul L. Williams. 132p. (Orig.). 1987. pap. 6.95 (*0-317-57615-1*) NE Bks.

Spiritual Life of Children. (Illus.). 384p. 1991. pap. 12.00 (*0-395-59923-7*) HM.

Spiritual Life Songs. 1941. 4.50 (*0-687-39228-4*) Abingdon.

Spiritual Light: New Scripture by Many Authors & Translations from Ancient Manuscripts, Previously Unpublished. John M. Pryse. 193p. 1994. pap. 17.95 (*1-56459-440-8*) Kessinger Pub.

Spiritual Light Journey. Richard Gordon. (Orig.). 1994. audio 10.00 (*0-931892-82-1*) B Dolphin Pub.

Spiritual Lightening. M. Catherine Thomas. 1996. 12.95 (*0-88494-982-6*) Bookcraft Inc.

Spiritual Linkage with Russians. Anthony Manousos. LC 91-68220. 32p. (Orig.). 1992. pap. 3.00 (*0-87574-301-3*, PHP 301) Pendle Hill.

Spiritual Literacy: Reading the Sacred in Everyday Life. Frederic Brussat & Mary A. Brussat. 640p. 1996. 27.50 (*0-684-81533-8*) S&S Trade.

Spiritual Lives of Great Composers. Patrick Kavanaugh. Ed. by Beth Spring. (Illus.). 144p. 1992. 12.95 (*0-917143-08-6*) Sparrow TN.

Spiritual Lives of the Great Composers. Patrick Kavanaugh. 192p. 1996. pap. 10.99 (*0-310-20806-8*) Zondervan.

Spiritual Living for a Skeptical Age: A Psychological Approach to Meditative Practice. J. C. Smith. (Illus.). 265p. 1992. 25.95 (*0-306-44123-3*, Plenum Insight) Plenum.

Spiritual Living in a Secular World: Applying the Book of Daniel Today. 2nd abr. ed. Ajith Fernando. 192p. 1993. pap. 10.99 (*0-310-59501-0*) Zondervan.

***Spiritual Living in Secular Society: The Teachings of Archbishop William D. Borders.** William D. Borders. 160p. 1996. 24.00 (*1-885938-04-7*); pap. 16.00 (*1-885938-06-3*) Cathdrl Fndtn Pr.

Spiritual Magic: Yi King Numerology. Arden C. Rizer, Jr. 180p. (Orig.). 1987. pap. 18.00 (*0-939795-29-9*) Amer Spirit.

Spiritual Man. Watchman Nee. Tr. by Stephen Kaung. 694p. 1968. pap. 10.00 (*0-935008-39-X*) Christian Fellow Pubs.

Spiritual Marriage: Sexual Abstinence in Medieval Wedlock. Dyan Elliott. LC 92-35220. 328p. 1993. text ed. 49.50 (*0-691-08649-4*) Princeton U Pr.

Spiritual Marriage: Sexual Abstinence in Medieval Welock. Dyan Elliott. 390p. (C). 1993. pap. text ed. 16.95 (*0-691-01088-9*) Princeton U Pr.

Spiritual Maturity. J. Oswald Sanders. Tr. by Samuel Chao & Lorna Y. Chao from ENG. (CHI.). 1983. pap. write for info. (*0-941598-08-X*) Living Spring Pubns.

Spiritual Maturity. J. Oswald Sanders. (Commitment to Spiritual Growth Ser.). 1994. pap. 11.99 (*0-8024-6797-0*) Moody.

Spiritual Maturity in the Later Years. Ed. by James J. Seeber. (Journal of Religious Gerontology). 187p. 1990. text ed. 29.95 (*1-56024-050-4*) Haworth Pr.

Spiritual Maturity in the Later Years. Ed. by James J. Seeber. (Journal of Religious Gerontology). 187p. 1990. pap. text ed. 14.95 (*1-56024-051-2*) Haworth Pr.

Spiritual Meadow: The Pratum Spirituale. John Moschus. pap. 1.25 (*0-89981-100-0*) Eastern Orthodox.

Spiritual Meadow (Pratum Spirituale) John Moschos. Tr. & Intro. by John Wortley. (Cistercian Studies). 261p. 1992. pap. 17.95 (*0-87907-539-2*) Cistercian Pubns.

Spiritual Megatrends. Earl Paulk. 293p. 1988. 8.95 (*0-917595-16-5*) Kingdom Pubs.

Spiritual Message of Dante. William B. Carpenter. 1977. 21.95 (*0-8369-7103-5*, 7937) Ayer.

Spiritual Message of Modern English Poetry. Arthur S. Hoyt. LC 67-28753. (Essay Index Reprint Ser.). 1977. 20.95 (*0-8369-0549-0*) Ayer.

Spiritual Messages of a Buffalo Rider, a Man of Tao. rev. ed. Hua-Ching Ni. LC 90-60963. 240p. 1990. pap. 12.95 (*0-937064-34-3*) SevenStar Comm.

Spiritual, Metaphysical & New Trends in Modern Astrology. 2nd ed. Ed. by Joan McEvers. LC 88-6760. (New World Astrology Ser.). 264p. 1988. pap. 9.95 (*0-87542-380-9*) Llewellyn Pubns.

Spiritual Midwifery. 3rd ed. Ina M. Gaskin. LC 89-31060. (Illus.). 480p. 1990. pap. 16.95 (*0-913990-63-9*) Book Pub Co.

Spiritual Moments with the Great Composers: Daily Inspiration from the Lives of Favorite Composers. Patrick Kavanaugh. 176p. 1995. 14.99 (*0-310-20042-3*) Zondervan.

***Spiritual Moments with the Great Hymns: Devotional Readings That Strengthen the Heart.** Evelyn Bence. LC 96-39869. 224p. 1997. 12.99 (*0-310-20840-8*) Zondervan.

Spiritual Mothering: The Titus Two Model for Women Mentoring Women. Susan Hunt. 192p. 1993. reprint ed. pap. 10.99 (*0-89107-719-7*) Crossway Bks.

Spiritual Mothering: The Titus 2 Model for Women Mentoring Women. Susan Hunt. LC 92-18859. 1992. write for info. (*1-880692-01-5*) Legacy Comms.

Spiritual Narratives. Maria W. Stewart et al. (Schomburg Library of Nineteenth-Century Black Women Writers). 495p. 1991. reprint ed. pap. 13.95 (*0-19-506786-X*) OUP.

Spiritual Narratives: Jarena Lee; Zilipha Elaw; Virginia Broughton; Sara Mix; Julia Foote; Maria Stewart; & Rebecca Stewart. Ed. by Sue Houchins. (Schomburg Library of Nineteenth-Century Black Women Writers). 496p. 1988. 29.95 (*0-19-505266-8*) OUP.

Spiritual Needs of Children. Judith A. Shelly. LC 82-7223. 148p. (Orig.). 1982. pap. 10.99 (*0-87784-381-3*, 381) InterVarsity.

***Spiritual Nightlights: Meditations for the Middle of the Night.** Linda DeVries. 120p. 1997. pap. 15.99 (*0-87788-743-8*) Shaw Pubs.

Spiritual Notebook. Paul Twitchell. 245p. 1992. pap. 11.00 (*1-57043-037-3*) ECKANKAR.

Spiritual Notes. pap. 2.95 (*0-89981-101-9*) Eastern Orthodox.

Spiritual Nourishment. Joy A. Clarke. (Illus.). 84p. (Orig.). 1990. pap. 9.95 (*0-9626984-0-7*) Clarke Enterprise.

Spiritual Nurture & Congregational Development. Ed. by Perry D. Lefevre & W. Widick Schroeder. (Studies in Ministry & Parish Life). 186p. 1984. text ed. 21.95 (*0-913552-20-8*) Exploration Pr.

Spiritual Nutrition & the Rainbow Diet. Gabriel Cousens. 239p. 1986. 11.95 (*0-9615875-2-0*) Cassandra Pr.

Spiritual Odyssey: The Unfoldment of a Soul. Lorraine Sinkler. 400p. 1991. pap. 16.95 (*0-9629119-0-9*) Valor Fndtn.

Spiritual Odyssey of Nikos Kazantzakis. Kimon Friar. (Modern Greek History & Culture Ser.). 1979. 10.00 (*0-935476-00-8*) Nostos Bks.

Spiritual or Human Value? An Evaluation-Systematical Reconstruction & Analysis of the Preaching of Jesus in the Synoptical Gospels. Jan Lofberg. (Studia Philosophiae Religionis: No. 10). (Orig.). 1982. pap. 37.50 (*0-317-65795-X*) Coronet Bks.

***Spiritual Origins of Eastern Europe & the Future Mysteries of the Holy Grail.** Sergei O. Prokofieff. Tr. by Simon B. De Lange. (Illus.). 560p. 1993. write for info. (*0-904693-55-4*, Pub. by Temple Ldge Pub UK) Anthroposophic.

Spiritual Parenting. David Carroll. 1994. pap. 12.95 (*1-56924-959-8*) Marlowe & Co.

***Spiritual Parenting.** Hugh Prather & Gayle Prather. 1997. pap. 13.00 (*0-517-88831-9*) Crown Pub Group.

Spiritual Parenting. Charles H. Spurgeon. 170p. 1995. mass mkt. 4.99 (*0-88368-265-6*) Whitaker Hse.

Spiritual Parenting: A Guide to Understanding & Nurturing the Heart of Your Child. Hugh Prather & Gayle Prather. 288p. 1996. 23.00 (*0-517-70385-8*) Random.

Spiritual Parenting: A Sourcebook for Parents & Teachers. Steven M. Rosman. (Illus.). 180p. (Orig.). 1994. pap. 12.00 (*0-8356-0703-8*, Quest) Theos Pub Hse.

Spiritual Passages. Benedict J. Groeschel. LC 82-17139. 210p. 1983. pap. 15.95 (*0-8245-0628-6*) Crossroad NY.

***Spiritual Passages.** Drew Leder. LC 96-6500. 304p. 1997. pap. 15.95 (*0-87477-873-5*, Tarcher Putnam) Putnam Pub Group.

Spiritual Pastels. Julie Du St. Espirit. (Illus.). 10.00 (*0-8159-6821-3*) Devin.

Spiritual Path: Anthology of the Writings of Kirpal Singh. Kirpal Singh. (Illus.). 423p. 1994. 20.00 (*0-685-75214-3*) S K Pubns.

Spiritual Path Guidebook. Dick Sutphen. 128p. (Orig.). 1992. pap. text ed. 5.95 (*0-87554-523-8*, B930) Valley Sun.

Spiritual Path, Sacred Place: Myth, Ritual, & Meaning in Architecture. Thomas Barrie. (Illus.). 240p. (Orig.). 1996. pap. 30.00 (*1-57062-005-9*) Shambhala Pubns.

Spiritual Path to Complete Fulfillment. Philip Harris. (Illus.). 279p. (Orig.). 1994. pap. 18.95 (*0-85572-228-2*, Pub. by Hill Content Pubng AT) Seven Hills Bk.

Spiritual People, Radical Lives: Spirituality & Justice in Four Twentieth Century American Lives. Gary Commins. LC 93-47063. 1996. 69.95 (*1-883255-43-0*); pap. 49.95 (*1-883255-42-2*) Intl Scholars.

Spiritual Perspectives: Essays in Mysticism & Metaphysics. Ed. by T. M. Mahadevan. 303p. 1975. lib. bdg. 12.00 (*0-89253-021-9*) Ind-US Inc.

Spiritual Perspectives & Human Facts. 2nd ed. Frithjof Schuon. Tr. by P. N. Townsend from FRE. 223p. 1987. pap. 21.95 (*0-900588-27-6*) S Perennis.

***Spiritual Philosophy for the New World: The 60-Day Non-Human Program to Rise above the Ego.** 2nd rev. ed. John R. Price. LC 96-53038. 160p. 1997. pap. 10.95 (*1-56170-360-5*, 842) Hay House.

Spiritual Pilgrimage: On Jews & Judaism, 1979-1995. Pope John Paul, II. Ed. & Comment by Eugene J. Fisher. 300p. 1995. pap. 19.95 (*0-8245-1544-7*) Crossroad NY.

Spiritual Pilgrims. fac. ed. Ian Parrott. LC 72-466773. (Illus.). 228p. 1969. pap. 65.00 (*0-7837-7302-1*, AU00451) Bks Demand.

Spiritual Pilgrims: Carl Jung & Teresa of Avila. John W. Welch. LC 82-80164. 208p. 1982. pap. 14.95 (*0-8091-2454-8*) Paulist Pr.

Spiritual Politics: Changing the World from the Inside Out. Corinne McLaughlin & Gordon Davidson. 464p. (Orig.). 1994. pap. 12.95 (*0-345-36983-1*) Ballantine.

Spiritual Portrait of St. John of Kronstadt. Archimandrite Constantine. (Illus.). 94p. (Orig.). 1982. pap. 6.00 (*0-912927-02-X*, X002) St John Kronstadt.

Spiritual Poverty: The Pathway to Riches. Jack Kuhatschek. (Beatitudes Ser.). 48p. 1993. pap. 4.99 (*0-310-59603-3*) Zondervan.

Spiritual Poverty in Sufism. Javad Nurbakhsh. Tr. by Leonard Lewishon. 15p. 1984. pap. 0.95 (*0-933546-11-4*) KNP.

***Spiritual Poverty in Sufism.** Javad Nurbakhsh. 150p. 1996. pap. 8.95 (*0-614-21348-7*, 1161) Kazi Pubns.

***Spiritual Power.** Dwight L. Moody. (Classics Ser.). 128p. (Orig.). 1997. mass mkt. 4.99 (*0-8024-5448-8*) Moody.

Spiritual Power. rev. ed. Don Basham. 92p. 1976. mass mkt. 3.99 (*0-88368-075-0*) Whitaker Hse.

Spiritual Power & Missions: The Related Issues. Ed. by Edward Rommen. (World Evangelical Fellowship Ser.: Vol. 3). 176p. (Orig.). 1995. pap. text ed. 7.95 (*0-87808-377-4*, WCL377-4) William Carey Lib.

***Spiritual Power Points: A Guide to Hidden Oases along the Spiritual Path.** Robert Krajenke. LC 97-1685. 263p. (Orig.). 1997. pap. 14.95 (*0-87604-376-7*, 466) ARE Pr.

Spiritual Practice. Swami Ashokananda. 1972. pap. 4.50 (*0-87481-155-4*, Pub. by Advaita Ashrama II) Vedanta Pr.

Spiritual Precautions. Clay Sterrett. 126p. 1992. pap. 5.00 (*0-9621713-2-8*) CFC Literature.

Spiritual Presence in Psychotherapy: A Guide for Caregivers. David A. Steere. LC 96-87061. 336p. 1997. 39.95 (*0-87630-823-X*) Brunner-Mazel.

Spiritual Primer on Abortion: A Simple Handbook for the Spiritual Truth about Abortion. Michael Luopa. 32p. 1994. pap. 4.95 (*0-9640549-0-6*) Ruby Ray Pubng.

Spiritual Principle of Prayer. Max Kappeler. 28p. 1969. pap. 4.50 (*0-85241-077-8*) Kappeler Inst Pub.

Spiritual Productivity. Jonas Clark. (Illus.). pap. 8.00 (*1-886885-05-2*) Spirit Life.

Spiritual Progression in the Last Days. Blaine M. Yorgason. LC 94-26155. xii, 282p. 1994. 14.95 (*0-87579-913-2*) Deseret Bk.

Spiritual Promise. rev. ed. John Roger. 60p. 1989. lib. bdg. 7.00 (*0-914829-22-X*) Mandeville LA.

Spiritual Properties of Herbs. Gurudas. (Illus.). 288p. (Orig.). 1988. pap. 13.95 (*0-9615875-7-1*) Cassandra Pr.

Spiritual Protection & Healing. William L. Rand. 1995. pap. 16.95 incl. audio (*1-886785-00-7*) Vision Pub.

Spiritual Protection for Your Children: Helping Your Children & Family Find Their Identity, Freedom & Security in Christ. Neil T. Anderson et al. LC 96-30482. 360p. 1996. 18.99 (*0-8307-1868-0*, 5112885); pap. 11.99 (*0-8307-1886-9*, 5112885) Regal.

Spiritual Psalter of St. Ephraim the Syrian. Ed. by Theophan of Poltava. Tr. by Antonina Janda from RUS. 1997. 25.00 (*0-912927-40-2*, X040) St John Kronstadt.

***Spiritual Psychology: A Course for Body, Mind & Spirit.** rev. ed. Jim Morningstar. (Illus.). 119p. Date not set. pap. 10.00 (*0-9604856-3-5*) Transform Inc.

Spiritual Psychology: A New Age Course for Body, Mind & Spirit. 2nd ed. Jim Morningstar. (Illus.). 119p. (C). 1981. pap. 10.00 (*0-9604856-0-0*) Transform Inc.

Spiritual Psychology: A Primer. Meredith J. Sprunger. LC 92-73655. 114p. 1992. 16.00 (*0-9634327-0-2*) Jemenon.

Spiritual Psychology for the Aquarian Age. Arthur C. Lytle. LC 91-68304. 256p. (Orig.). 1992. pap. 12.95 (*1-56184-052-1*) New Falcon Pubns.

Spiritual Quest. Nancy D. Potts. Ed. by Shirlene Bridgewater. 65p. (Orig.). 1995. pap. text ed. 7.00 (*0-9640010-3-9*) Peace Pubng.

Spiritual Quest: Questions & Answers. Tapasyananda. 284p. (Orig.). 1992. pap. 5.95 (*81-7120-456-2*, Pub. by Ramakrishna Math II) Vedanta Pr.

Spiritual Quest: Transcendence in Myth, Religion, & Science. Robert M. Torrance. LC 93-37644. (C). 1994. 35.00 (*0-520-08132-3*) U CA Pr.

***Spiritual Quest: Transcendence in Myth, Religion & Science.** Robert M. Torrance. 1997. pap. text ed. 16.95 (*0-520-21159-6*) U CA Pr.

Spiritual Quest: Variations on a Theme. Donald Pelton. (Illus.). (Orig.). 1986. pap. 8.95 (*0-933169-02-7*) Heldon Pr.

***Spiritual Quest of Francis Wagstaffe.** Tony Foreward. Date not set. pap. 12.95 (*0-85244-298-X*, Pub. by Gracewing UK) Morehouse Pub.

Spiritual Quixote: A Comic Romance, 2 vols. Richard Graves. (BCL1-PR English Literature Ser.). 1992. reprint ed. lib. bdg. 99.00 (*0-7812-7360-9*) Rprt Serv.

Spiritual Re-Awakening of the Great Smoky Mountains. Page Bryant. (Illus.). 264p. (Orig.). 1994. pap. 16.00 (*0-9641390-0-6*) P Bryant.

Spiritual Reality or Obsession. Watchman Nee. Tr. by Stephen Kaung. 64p. 1970. pap. 3.50 (*0-935008-41-1*) Christian Fellow Pubs.

Spiritual Reconstruction. Mary B. Wallace. 168p. 1968. reprint ed. spiral bd. 7.00 (*0-7873-0928-1*) Hlth Research.

Spiritual Reconstruction (1924) Mary B. Wallace. 168p. 1996. pap. 17.95 (*1-56459-970-1*) Kessinger Pub.

***Spiritual Refining: The Anatomy of True & False Conversion.** Anthony Burgess. 288p. 1996. 26.95 (*0-9641803-5-9*) Internat Outreach.

Spiritual Reflections for the Recovering Alcoholic. S. Jack. LC 84-18590. (Illus.). 98p. 1985. pap. 5.95 (*0-8189-0477-1*) Alba.

Spiritual Reflections of a Pro-Life Pilgrim. Michael T. Mannion. LC 86-63590. (Illus.). 60p. (Orig.). 1987. pap. 3.50 (*1-55612-060-5*) Sheed & Ward MO.

Spiritual Reformers of the Sixteenth & Seventeenth Centuries. Rufus M. Jones. 1959. 14.50 (*0-8446-0161-6*) Peter Smith.

Spiritual Regeneration. Torkom Saraydarian. 250p. (Orig.). 1990. pap. write for info. (*0-9624439-1-3*) White Mntn Educ Assn.

Spiritual Relationships: Relationships of Christians, Preachers, Elders, & Teachers. David Roper & Norman R. Martin. 50p. (Orig.). (C). 1995. pap. 6.95 (*0-9646489-1-1*) Martain Pub.

Spiritual Research: Methods & Results. rev. ed. Rudolf Steiner. Tr. by Michael Tapp from GER. 288p. 1982. pap. 12.50 (*0-89345-211-4*, Steinerbks) Garber Comm.

Spiritual Research: Methods & Results, Vol. 18. rev. ed. Rudolf Steiner. Tr. by Michael Tapp from GER. LC 81-51763. 288p. 1982. lib. bdg. 20.00 (*0-89345-010-3*, Spir Sci Lib) Garber Comm.

Spiritual Revelations of the Bible. Brown Landone. 259p. (Orig.). 1972. reprint ed. spiral bd. 14.00 (*0-7873-1097-2*) Hlth Research.

Spiritual Revival. Glenn L. Pace. LC 93-9902. viii, 198p. 1993. 12.95 (*0-87579-733-4*) Deseret Bk.

***Spiritual Revolution: a Seeker's Guide: 52 Powerful Principles for Your Mind & Soul.** Michael Goddart. LC 97-65860. 152p. (Orig.). 1997. pap. 11.95 (*0-87516-706-3*) DeVorss.

Spiritual Rodeo. James Magorian. LC 80-18372. 17p. (Orig.). 1980. pap. 3.00 (*0-915124-37-8*, Toothpaste) Coffee Hse.

Spiritual Roots of Barley. Mary R. Swope. 128p. 1988. pap. 5.00 (*0-936369-24-8*) Son-Rise Pubns.

Spiritual Roots of Human Relations. 2nd ed. Stephen R. Covey. LC 93-2875. 326p. 1993. pap. 11.95 (*0-87579-705-9*) Deseret Bk.

Spiritual Sayings of Kahlil Gibran. Kahlil Gibran. Tr. by Anthony R. Ferris. 1965. pap. 6.95 (*0-8065-0041-7*, 197, Citadel Pr) Carol Pub Group.

Spiritual Science & the Art of Healing: Rudolf Steiner's Anthroposophical Medicine. Victor Bott. (Illus.). 208p. (Orig.). 1996. reprint ed. pap. 12.95 (*0-89281-636-8*, Heal Arts VT) Inner Tradit.

Spiritual Science As a Foundation for Social Forms. Rudolf Steiner. Ed. by Alan Howard. Tr. by Maria St. Goar from GER. 300p. 1986. 30.00 (*0-88010-153-9*); pap. 18.95 (*0-88010-152-0*) Anthroposophic.

Spiritual Science of Kriya Yoga. 2nd ed. Goswami Kriyananda. (Illus.). 393p. reprint ed. pap. text ed. 16.95 (*0-9613099-1-1*) Temple Kriya Yoga.

Spiritual-Scientific Basis of Goethe's Work. Rudolf Steiner. 1982. pap. 2.95 (*0-916786-66-8*, Saint George Pubns) R Steiner Col Pubns.

Spiritual Season: Reflections on Christmas. Ariel Staff. (Illus.). 32p. 1995. 4.95 (*0-8362-3134-1*) Andrews & McMeel.

Spiritual Secret of Hudson Taylor. Howard Taylor & Geraldine Taylor. 396p. (Orig.). 1996. mass mkt. 5.99 (*0-88368-387-3*) Whitaker Hse.

***Spiritual Secrets of Faithful Fathers.** Ken Canfield. 56p. (Orig.). 1997. pap. 2.49 (*0-8341-1663-4*) Beacon Hill.

Spiritual Secrets of George Muller. Selected by Roger Steer. LC 86-28029. 126p. (Orig.). 1987. reprint ed. pap. 7.99 (*0-87788-782-9*) Shaw Pubs.

Spiritual Seeker's Guide: The Complete Source for Religions & Spiritual Groups of the World. Steven Sadleir. LC 91-77865. (Illus.). 343p. (Orig.). 1992. pap. 12.95 (*1-880741-28-8*) Dickens Pr.

Spiritual Self in Everyday Life: The Transformation of Personal Religious Experience in Nineteenth-Century New England. Richard Rabinowitz. (New England Studies). 315p. 1989. text ed. 47.50 (*1-55553-022-2*) NE U Pr.

***Spiritual Serendipity: Cultivating & Celebrating the Art of the Unexpected.** Richard Eyre. LC 96-40114. 1997. 20.00 (*0-684-80786-6*) S&S Trade.

***Spiritual Sex.** Douglas. 1997. pap. 20.00 (*0-671-53739-3*) PB.

Spiritual Sex Manual. Christ Foundation. LC 82-72079. (Illus.). 176p. 1982. pap. 12.95 (*0-910315-01-9*) Pts of Light Distributing.

An Asterisk (*) at the beginning of an entry indicates that the title is appearing in BIP for the first time.

Spiritual Significance of the Body. Ida Mingle. 355p. 1993. reprint ed. spiral bd. 21.00 (0-7873-0619-3) Hlth Research.

Spiritual Significance of the Body (1936) Ida Mingle. 355p. 1996. pap. 24.95 (1-56459-796-2) Kessinger Pub.

***Spiritual Simplicity: Simplify Your Life & Enrich Your Soul.** David Yount. LC 97-4172. 1997. 22.00 (0-684-83813-3) S&S Trade.

Spiritual Situation in Our Technical Society. Paul Tillich. Ed. by J. Mark Thomas. LC 87-34984. (C). 1988. pap. 20.00 (0-86554-293-7, MUP/P064) Mercer Univ Pr.

Spiritual Solution to America's Problems. Bruce Lavan. 150p. 1997. pap. text ed. 10.95 (1-57532-090-8) Press-Tige Pub.

Spiritual Songs. Ed. by Alvin Jennings. 40p. 1980. pap. 0.95 (1-56794-007-2, C1388) Star Bible.

Spiritual Sonnets: Sonetos Espirituales. Juan R. Jimenez. Tr. by Carl W. Cobb from SPA. LC 95-9147. (Hispanic Literature Ser.: Vol. 27). 136p. 1996. 69.95 (0-7734-8889-8) E Mellen.

Spiritual Space: The Religious Architecture of Pietro Belluschi. Meredith L. Clausen. LC 92-14621. (Illus.). 208p. (C). 1992. 50.00 (0-295-97213-0) U of Wash Pr.

Spiritual Spectacles: Vision & Image in Mid-Nineteenth-Century Shakerism. Sally M. Promey. LC 92-19337. (Religion in North America Ser.). 320p. (C). 1993. 37.50 (0-253-34614-2) Ind U Pr.

Spiritual Steps: Affirmations for Self-Discovery. Barton Jay. (Illus.). 96p. 1990. pap. 6.95 (0-9626070-0-2) B Jay Prodns.

Spiritual Storytelling: Discovering & Sharing Your Spiritual Autobiography. Richard Peace. (Spiritual Disciplines Ser.). 1996. pap. 7.00 (0-89109-898-4) NavPress.

***Spiritual Strategy for Counseling & Psychotherapy.** P. Scott Richards & Allen E. Bergin. LC 97-8297. 352p. 1997. text ed. 39.95 (1-55798-434-4) Am Psychol.

Spiritual Struggles of the Early Ascetics. Palladius. 1991. pap. 2.95 (0-89981-115-9) Eastern Orthodox.

***Spiritual Style of Management: Who Is Running This Show Anyway?** James F. McMichael. 202p. (Orig.). 1997. pap. 12.00 (0-9656668-0-8) SFP.

Spiritual Success - Or Something More? Current Issues within Christianity. M. Basilea Schlink. Tr. by Evangelical Sisters of Mary Staff from GER. Orig. Title: Geistlicher Erfolg? - Ein Wort Ze Neuen Stromungen in der Christenheit. 31p. (Orig.). 1989. pap. 0.50 (3-87209-632-X) Evang Sisterhood Mary.

***Spiritual Surrender: Yielding Yourself to a Loving God.** Jim Krishner. LC 96-61816. 96p. (Orig.). 1997. pap. 9.95 (0-89622-721-9) Twenty-Third.

Spiritual Survival in the Last Days. Blaine M. Yorgason & Brenton Yorgason. LC 90-44379. 281p. 1990. 11.95 (0-87579-409-2) Deseret Bk.

Spiritual Symbols for the Astrology of the Soul. Frank Jakubowsky. 57p. (Orig.). 1990. pap. 5.00 (0-932588-14-X) Jesus Bks.

Spiritual Talks. Ramakrishna's Disciples Staff. 1936. pap. 3.95 (0-87481-103-1, Pub. by Advaita Ashrama II) Vedanta Pr.

Spiritual Tarot: 78 Paths to Personal Development. Signe E. Echols et al. LC 95-50112. 304p. 1996. pap. 12.00 (0-380-78206-5) Avon.

***Spiritual Tasks of the Homemaker.** Manfred Schmidt-Brabant. 1997. pap. 9.95 (0-904693-84-8) Anthroposophic.

Spiritual Teaching of Ramana Maharshi. Ramana Maharshi. (Dragon Editions Ser.). 133p. (Orig.). 1989. pap. 12.00 (0-87773-024-5) Shambhala Pubns.

Spiritual Teaching of St. Bernard of Clairvaux. John R. Sommerfeldt. (Cistercian Studies: No. 125). 352p. 1991. 32.95 (0-87907-325-X); pap. 15.95 (0-87907-425-6) Cistercian Pubns.

Spiritual Teachings of Teresa of Avila & Adrian Van Kaam: Formative Spirituality. James Whalen. LC 83-3628. 334p. (Orig.). 1984. pap. text ed. 28.00 (0-8191-3865-7) U Pr of Amer.

Spiritual Theology. Jordan Aumann. 441p. (C). 1980. reprint ed. pap. text ed. 29.95 (0-87061-143-7) Chr Classics.

***Spiritual Theology: The Theology of Yesterday for Spiritual Help Today.** Diogenes Allen. LC 97-623. 172p. 1997. pap. 11.95 (1-56101-130-4) Cowley Pubns.

***Spiritual Thoughts.** Wes Fessler. Ed. by Stephenie Glissmeyer. 133p. (Orig.). 1997. pap. 12.99 (0-9655856-0-3) Better Half.

Spiritual Thoughts & Prayers. Thomas W. Wersell. LC 74-76920. 80p. (Orig.). reprint ed. pap. 25.00 (0-685-16020-3, 2026829) Bks Demand.

Spiritual Thoughts of Jacob Boehme. Jacob Boehme. Ed. by J. D. Holmes. Tr. by Charlotte A. Rainy. 1994. pap. 7.95 (1-55818-301-9, Sure Fire) Holmes Pub.

Spiritual Timing. rev. ed. Roberts Liardon. 64p. (Orig.). 1990. pap. 4.00 (1-879993-07-4) Embassy Pub.

***Spiritual Timing: Discerning Seasons of Change in the Realm of the Spirit.** Roberts Liardon. 1996. pap. 4.99 (1-880089-71-8) Albury Pub.

Spiritual Torrents. rev. ed. Jeanne Guyon. 140p. 1989. reprint ed. pap. 8.95 (0-940232-18-9) Seedsowers.

Spiritual Traditions for the Contemporary Church. Gabriel O'Donnell & Robin Maas. 464p. (Orig.). pap. 24.95 (0-687-39233-0) Abingdon.

Spiritual Traditions of Sex. Richard Craze. 64p. 1996. 12.00 (0-517-70566-4, Harmony) Crown Pub Group.

***Spiritual Training of Your Child.** John MacArthur. 1997. 19.99 (0-8499-1082-X) Word Pub.

Spiritual Traits: A Four Week Study to Help Teenagers Explore God-given Traits. Janet Coates. Ed. by Gary Swyers et al. (Bible Basics Ser.). (Illus.). 32p. (Orig.). (YA). (gr. 6-12). 1992. wbk. ed., pap. 8.95 (0-89827-094-4, BKW14) Wesleyan Pub Hse.

Spiritual Treasures: Letters of Swami Turiyananda. Ed. & Tr. by Swami Chetanananda. LC 92-15574. (Illus.). 288p. 1992. 11.50 (0-916356-77-9) Vedanta Soc St Louis.

Spiritual Truth Using the Enneagram. Alan Fensin. (Illus.). 200p. 1995. per. 11.95 (0-9622183-3-2) Way Enterprises.

Spiritual Truths for Overcoming Adversity. Greg Hinnant. LC 95-78188. 217p. (Orig.). 1996. pap. 7.95 (0-88270-690-X) Bridge-Logos.

Spiritual Unfoldment: A Guide to Liberating Your Soul. Richard Barrett. (Illus.). 160p. (Orig.). 1995. 24.95 (0-9643226-0-9) Fulfilling Bks.

Spiritual Unfoldment 1. White Eagle Staff. 144p. 1942. 11.95 (0-85487-012-1, Pub. by White Eagle UK) DeVorss.

Spiritual Unfoldment 2. White Eagle Staff. 112p. 1969. 11.95 (0-85487-001-6, Pub. by White Eagle UK) DeVorss.

Spiritual Universe: How Quantum Physics Proves the Existence of the Soul. Fred A. Wolf. 400p. 1996. 24.00 (0-684-81200-2) S&S Trade.

Spiritual Value of Gem Stones. Wally G. Richardson & Lenora Huett. LC 79-54728. 176p. 1980. pap. 8.95 (0-87516-383-1) DeVorss.

Spiritual Vampires: The Use & Misuse of Spiritual Power. Marty Raphael. LC 95-75339. 272p. (Orig.). 1996. pap. 14.95 (1-57282-006-3) Message NM.

Spiritual Vandalism: Sins Against the Holy Spirit. Maralene Wesner & Miles Wesner. LC 88-51803. 73p. (Orig.). 1988. pap. 4.95 (0-936715-19-7) Diversity Okla.

Spiritual View of Life. Jakob Lorber. 364p. 1981. pap. 15.00 (0-934616-15-9) Valkyrie Pub Hse.

Spiritual Warfare. (Cross Training Ser.: Vol. 3). 64p. (YA). (gr. 10-12). 1995. pap. 29.95 (1-57405-025-7) CharismaLife Pub.

Spiritual Warfare. Max E. Anders. LC 96-12964. (We Believe! Ser.). 192p. 1996. pap. 8.99 (0-7852-1149-7) Nelson.

Spiritual Warfare. Brian Brodersen. Ed. by Chuck Smith. (Calvary Basics Ser.). 76p. 1995. pap. 3.50 (0-936728-54-X) Word for Today.

***Spiritual Warfare.** J. Gordon Henry. (Illus.). 128p. (Orig.). 1996. pap. 5.00 (0-9656424-0-2) J G H Minist.

Spiritual Warfare. Richard Ing. 304p. 1996. mass mkt. 5.99 (0-88368-385-7) Whitaker Hse.

Spiritual Warfare. A. Scott Moreau. (Fisherman Bible Studyguide Ser.). 96p. 1995. pap. text ed. 4.99 (0-87788-777-2) Shaw Pubs.

Spiritual Warfare. Jessie Penn-Lewis. 1991. pap. 4.95 (0-87508-962-3) Chr Lit.

Spiritual Warfare. Derek Prince. 137p. 1992. mass mkt. 4.99 (0-88368-256-7) Whitaker Hse.

Spiritual Warfare. James Reapsome & Martha Reapsome. (Discipleship Ser.). 48p. 1992. pap. 4.99 (0-310-54771-7) Zondervan.

***Spiritual Warfare, No. 1.** 144p. (J). 1997. write for info. (0-7814-0297-2, Chariot Bks) Chariot Victor.

***Spiritual Warfare, No. 2.** 144p. (J). 1997. write for info. (0-7814-0298-0, Chariot Bks) Chariot Victor.

***Spiritual Warfare, No. 3.** 144p. (J). 1997. write for info. (0-7814-0299-9, Chariot Bks) Chariot Victor.

Spiritual Warfare, No. 12. Charles Stanley. (Guided Growth Ser.). 24p. 1996. pap. 2.50 (1-56476-558-X, 6-3558, Victor Bks) Chariot Victor.

Spiritual Warfare: A Study Guide. Dean Sherman. (Illus.). 80p. 1985. student ed. 6.95 (0-935779-03-5); audio 24.95 (0-935779-04-3); vhs 150.00 (0-935779-05-1) Crown Min.

Spiritual Warfare: Attack Against the Woman. George W. Kosicki. LC 90-85415. 160p. (Orig.). 1990. pap. 5.00 (0-9625975-4-6) Faith Pub OH.

Spiritual Warfare: Fighting to Win. John MacArthur. 75p. 1989. pap. 3.95 (0-318-42572-6) Word Grace.

Spiritual Warfare: The Fight. John White. (Christian Basics Bible Studies). 64p. (Orig.). 1996. wbk. ed., pap. 4.99 (0-8308-2009-4, 2009) InterVarsity.

Spiritual Warfare: The Occult Has Demonic Influence. Donald W. Montrose. 1991. 0.50 (1-56036-014-3, 36492) AMI Pr.

***Spiritual Warfare: The Politics of the Christian Right.** Sara Diamond. 304p. 48.99 (0-921689-65-9, Pub. by Black Rose Bks CN); pap. 19.99 (0-921689-64-0, Pub. by Black Rose Bks CN) Consort Bk Sales.

Spiritual Warfare: The Politics of the Christian Right. Sara Diamond. LC 89-6121. 275p. 1989. 30.00 (0-89608-362-4); pap. 18.00 (0-89608-361-6) South End Pr.

Spiritual Warfare: Understanding the War. Jeffrey B. Krall. 40p. (Orig.). 1996. pap. 3.50 (1-57688-004-4, 004-4) Branch & Vine.

Spiritual Warfare: Victory over the Powers of This Dark World. Timothy M. Warner. 160p. (Orig.). 1991. pap. 8.99 (0-89107-607-7) Crossway Bks.

Spiritual Warfare: You Can Win. Keith Hershey. (Christian Life Ser.). 28p. (Orig.). 1992. pap. 1.95 (0-940487-07-1) Jubilee CA.

Spiritual Warfare - Dynaword Bible Study. Phil Gehlhar. (Illus.). 96p. (Orig.). 1995. pap. 10.00 (1-883893-17-8) WinePress Pub.

Spiritual Warfare & Your Children. Ray Beeson & Kathi Mills. LC 93-8939. 1993. pap. 9.99 (0-8407-3490-5) Nelson.

Spiritual Warfare for Every Christian: How to Live in Victory & Retake the Land. Dean Sherman. 211p. 1990. pap. 9.99 (0-927545-05-5) YWAM Pub.

Spiritual Warfare for the Wounded. Mark Johnson. 212p. (Orig.). 1992. pap. 10.99 (0-89283-753-5, Vine Bks) Servant.

Spiritual Warfare in a Believer's Life. Charles H. Spurgeon. (Believer's Life Ser.). 180p. (Orig.). 1993. pap. 9.99 (1-883002-02-8) Emerald WA.

Spiritual Warfare in the Marriage. Harvey Hester, Jr. Ed. by Tanya C. Stokes. 98p. 1991. pap. 6.00 (0-9627849-0-7) Temperance Pub Hse.

Spiritual Warfare Manual. Barbara J. Beeler. (Illus.). 38p. 1994. student ed. 10.00 (0-9643586-1-1) REED IT.

***Spiritual Warfare Manual.** Mickey Bonner. 1983. pap. 6.95 (1-878578-02-2) M Bonner Evan Assn.

Spiritual Warfare Manual, 3 pts., Set. 259p. 1989. pap. text ed. 21.25 (0-939399-14-8) Bks of Truth.

***Spiritual Warfare Prayer Study Guide.** Mickey Bonner. 1987. pap. 11.95 (1-878578-13-8) M Bonner Evan Assn.

***Spiritual Warfare Prayers: And Pray in the Spirit on All Occasions with All Kinds of Prayers & Requests, Eph. 6:18, 10 bks.** Mark I. Bubeck. 18p. 1997. 12.50 (0-8024-7132-3) Moody.

***Spiritual Warrior.** John-Roger. 1997. 20.00 (0-914829-36-X) Mandeville LA.

***Spiritual Warrior.** Shakura Rei. Ed. by Rodney Charles. LC 97-65709. 250p. (Orig.). 1997. pap. 17.95 (1-887472-28-2) Sunstar Pubng.

Spiritual Warrior: Uncovering Spiritual Truths in Psychic Phenomena. Swami Krishnapada. 200p. (Orig.). 1996. pap. 12.95 (1-885414-01-3) Hari-Nama Pr.

***Spiritual Warrior Vol. II: Transforming Lust into Love.** Swami Krishnapada. 200p. (Orig.). 1998. pap. 12.95 (1-885414-03-X) Hari-Nama Pr.

Spiritual Warrior's Prayer Guide. Quin Sherrer & Ruthanne Garlock. 200p. (Orig.). 1992. pap. 10.99 (0-89283-809-4, Vine Bks) Servant.

Spiritual Weapons to Defeat the Enemy. Rick Renner. 1995. pap. text ed. 4.99 (1-880089-11-4) Albury Pub.

Spiritual Well-Being of Workers: Exploring the Influences of Spirituality in Everyday Work Activities. David C. Trott. (Illus.). 200p. 1996. pap. text ed. write for info. (0-9653106-0-4) D C Trott.

Spiritual Wholeness for Clergy: A New Psychology of Intimacy with God, Self, & Others. Donald R. Hands & Wayne L. Fehr. LC 92-75726. 100p. 1993. pap. 12.95 (1-56699-107-2, AL139) Alban Inst.

Spiritual Wisdom & Practices of Early Christianity. Alphonse Goettmann. Tr. by Theodore J. Nottingham. 135p. 1994. pap. 10.95 (0-9638181-1-2) Inner Life.

Spiritual Wisdom of the Early Christians. large type ed. 1994. pap. 5.00 (0-89981-303-8) Eastern Orthodox.

Spiritual Wisdom of the Native Americans. John Heinerman. (Illus.). 174p. (Orig.). 1989. pap. 9.95 (0-945946-05-8) Cassandra Pr.

Spiritual Witness: Classic Christian Writings of the 20th Century. Ed. by Sherwood E. Wirt. LC 91-12434. (Christian Heritage Classics Ser.). 288p. 1991. pap. 11.99 (0-89107-629-8) Crossway Bks.

Spiritual Work: Consciously Unfolding Spirituality in the Daily Life. Luis F. Zapata & Christopher J. Hibbard. 200p. (Orig.). 1992. pap. 12.00 (0-9623614-6-1) Disciples Pr.

Spiritual Worker's Handbook. Tarostar. (Illus.). 80p. (Orig.). 1985. pap. 3.95 (0-943832-12-8) Intl Imports.

Spiritual Works, 4 vols. Oliver Lodge. 1972. 400.00 (0-8490-1114-0) Gordon Pr.

Spiritual World Laid Open. Emanuel Swedenborg. 1972. lib. bdg. 250.00 (0-87968-561-1) Krishna Pr.

Spiritual Writings of Amir 'Abd al-Kader. Michel Chodkiewicz. Tr. by James Chrestensen & Tom Manning. LC 94-28385. (SUNY Series in Western Esoteric Traditions). 233p. (C). 1995. text ed. 49.50 (0-7914-2445-6); pap. text ed. 16.95 (0-7914-2446-4) State U NY Pr.

***Spiritual Writings of Amir Abd Al-Kader.** Tr. by Michel Chodkiewicz. 233p. 1996. pap. 16.95 (0-614-21349-5, 1485) Kazi Pubns.

***Spiritual Writings of Pierre Favre: The Memoraiale & Selected Letters & Instructions.** Tr. by Edmond C. Murphy & Martin E. Palmer from LAT. (Jesuit Primary Sources in English Translation Ser.: No. 16). xvi, 437p. 1997. 57.95 (1-880810-25-5) Inst Jesuit.

***Spiritual Writings of Pierre Favre: The Memoraiale & Selected Letters & Instructions.** Tr. by Edmond C. Murphy & Martin E. Palmer from LAT. (Jesuit Primary Sources in English Translation Ser.: No. 16). xvi, 437p. 1997. pap. 39.95 (1-880810-26-3) Inst Jesuit.

Spiritual Zest: Finding It & Keeping It. Ed. by Stephen Miller. (Dialog Ser.). 104p. 1992. student ed., pap. 5.95 (0-8341-1448-8); teacher ed., pap. 4.95 (0-8341-1447-X) Beacon Hill.

Spiritualia. Ed. by John W. O'Malley. (Collected Works of Erasmus: No. 66). 406p. 1988. 80.00 (0-8020-2656-7) U of Toronto Pr.

Spiritualism, Vol. 3 of 4. Gordon Lindsay. (Sorcery in America Ser.: Vol. 3). 1969. 2.95 (0-89985-093-6) Christ for the Nations.

Spiritualism among Civilised & Savage Races: A Study in Anthropology. Edward Lawrence. 1977. 19.95 (0-8369-5848-9, 6912) Ayer.

Spiritualism among Civilized & Savage Races. E. Lawrence. 1972. lib. bdg. 250.00 (0-87968-536-0) Krishna Pr.

Spiritualism & Nineteenth-Century Letters. Russell M. Goldfarb & Clare R. Goldfarb. LC 76-19841. 492p. 1978. 29.50 (0-8386-2025-6) Fairleigh Dickinson.

Spiritualism & the Foundations of C. G. Jung's Psychology. F. X. Charet. LC 91-23521. 329p. (C). 1993. pap. text ed. 21.95 (0-7914-1094-3) State U NY Pr.

Spiritualism & the Foundations of C. G. Jung's Psychology. F. X. Charet. LC 91-23521. 329p. (C). 1993. text ed. 64.50 (0-7914-1093-5) State U NY Pr.

Spiritualism I: Spiritualist Thought. Gary L. Ward & J. Gordon Melton. (Cults & New Religions Ser.: Vol. 1). 488p. 1990. reprint ed. text ed. 30.00 (0-8240-4362-6) Garland.

Spiritualism II: The Movement. Gary L. Ward. (Cults & New Religions Ser.: Vol. 2). 456p. 1990. reprint ed. text ed. 35.00 (0-8240-4363-4) Garland.

***Spiritualism in Antebellum America.** Bret E. Carroll. LC 97-7354. (Religion in North America Ser.). 1997. write for info. (0-253-33315-6) Ind U Pr.

Spiritualism in the Bible. E. W. Wallis. 1972. 250.00 (0-8490-1116-7) Gordon Pr.

Spiritualism in the Old Testament. Maurice Elliott. 1972. 59.95 (0-8490-1117-5) Gordon Pr.

Spiritualist Healers in Mexico: Successes & Failures of Alternative Therapeutics. Kaja Finkler. LC 84-14656. (Illus.). 256p. 1984. pap. text ed. 16.95 (0-89789-092-2, Bergin & Garvey) Greenwood.

Spiritualist Healers in Mexico: Successes & Failures of Alternative Therapeutics. Kaja Finkler. 256p. (C). 1994. pap. text ed. 10.95 (1-879215-24-1) Sheffield WI.

Spiritualist Philosophy: The Spirit's Book. Allan Kardec, pseud. LC 75-36918. (Occult Ser.). 1976. reprint ed. 31.95 (0-405-07973-7) Ayer.

Spiritualite de l'Heresie: Le Catharisme. Rene Nelli. LC 78-63189. (Heresies of the Early Christian & Medieval Era Ser.: Second Ser.). reprint ed. 39.50 (0-404-16226-6) AMS Pr.

Spiritualities of the Heart. Ed. by Annice Callahan. 256p. 1990. pap. 10.95 (0-8091-3101-3) Paulist Pr.

Spirituality. Victoria Sherrow. LC 94-5529. (Native American Culture Ser.). 1994. write for info. (0-86625-539-7) Rourke Corp.

Spirituality. Victoria Sherrow. LC 95-8490. (Native Latin American Cultures Ser.). (J). (gr. 2-6). 1995. write for info. (0-86625-557-5) Rourke Pubns.

Spirituality: An Approach Through Descriptive Psychology. Mary M. Shideler. 213p. (Orig.). 1992. pap. 19.95 (0-9625661-2-8) Descriptive Psych Pr.

Spirituality: Christian Life in the World Today. Eugene A. Walsh. (Illus.). 96p. (Orig.). 1993. pap. 4.95 (0-915531-17-8) OR Catholic.

Spirituality: God's RX for Stress. Neil B. Wiseman. 252p. 1992. pap. 11.99 (0-8341-1429-1) Beacon Hill.

Spirituality: God's Spirit Moved. Roger R. Hagwood. 70p. (Orig.). 1995. pap. write for info. (1-57502-018-1) Morris Pub.

Spirituality: Loved by God. Ed. by Gary Wilde. 64p. 1996. pap. 3.99 (1-56476-499-0, 6-3499, Victor Bks) Chariot Victor.

Spirituality: Rooted in Liturgy. Shawn Madigan. 1989. pap. 15.95 (0-912405-56-2) Pastoral Pr.

Spirituality: What It Is. 3rd ed. Kirpal Singh. LC 81-52000. (Illus.). 112p. 1982. reprint ed. pap. 8.00 (0-918224-16-0) S K Pubns.

Spirituality: What It Is Kirpal Singh Explores the Science of Spirituality. 122p. pap. 4.50 (0-942735-78-1) Ruhani Satsang.

***Spirituality: Where Body & Soul Encounter the Sacred.** Carl McColman. 256p. (Orig.). 1997. pap. 14.95 (1-880823-16-0) N Star Pubns.

Spirituality & Addiction: A Bibliography. Steven L. Berg. xiii, 82p. (Orig.). (C). 1993. pap. 12.00 (1-877686-06-9) Bishop Bks.

Spirituality & Administration: The Role of the Bishop in Twelfth-Century Auxerre. Constance B. Bouchard. LC 78-55889. 1979. 20.00 (0-910956-79-0, SAM5); pap. 12.00 (0-910956-67-7) Medieval Acad.

Spirituality & Chemical Dependency. Ed. by Robert J. Kus. 1995. pap. 17.95 (1-56023-069-X) Harrington Pk.

Spirituality & Chemical Dependency. Ed. by Robert J. Kus. 236p. 1995. 39.95 (1-56024-745-2) Haworth Pr.

Spirituality & Chemical Dependency: Guidelines for Treatment. Kitty Joachim. Ed. by Virginia Biegun. 29p. (Orig.). 1988. pap. text ed. 4.00 (0-944335-00-4) Oxford Inst.

Spirituality & Community: An Autobiographical Memoir. Donald Calhoun. (Illus.). 200p. (Orig.). (C). 1995. pap. 14.95 (0-87047-101-5) Schenkman Bks Inc.

Spirituality & Community: Diversity in Lesbian & Gay Experience. Roger J. Corless et al. Ed. by J. Michael Clark & Michael L. Stemmeler. LC 94-4137. (Gay Men's Issues in Religious Studies: Vol. 5). xii, 222p. 1994. pap. 25.00 (0-930383-43-5) Monument Pr.

Spirituality & Couples Therapy: Heart & Soul in the Therapy Process. Pref. by Barbara J. Brothers. LC 93-4262. (Journal of Couples Therapy: Vol. 3, No.1). (Illus.). 158p. 1993. lib. bdg. 29.95 (1-56024-312-0) Haworth Pr.

Spirituality & Emptiness: The Dynamics of Spiritual Life in Buddhism & Christianity. Donald W. Mitchell. 240p. 1991. pap. 12.95 (0-8091-3266-4) Paulist Pr.

***Spirituality & Health, Health & Spirituality: A New Journey of Spirit, Mind, & Body.** Bruce Epperly. LC 97-60029. 136p. (Orig.). 1997. pap. 9.95 (0-89622-723-5) Twenty-Third.

Spirituality & Human Nature. Donald Evans. LC 91-44693. (SUNY Series in Religious Studies). 314p. (C). 1992. pap. 21.95 (0-7914-1280-6) State U NY Pr.

Spirituality & Human Nature. Donald Evans. LC 91-44693. (SUNY Series in Religious Studies). 314p. (C). 1992. text ed. 64.50 (0-7914-1279-2) State U NY Pr.

Spirituality & Justice. Donal Dorr. 264p. (Orig.). 1985. pap. 17.50 (0-88344-449-6) Orbis Bks.

Spirituality & Justice. Tutu. LC 90-55806. 13.95 (0-06-068633-2, HarpT) HarpC.

Spirituality & Liberation: Overcoming the Great Fallacy. Robert M. Brown. LC 87-29425. (Illus.). 160p. (Orig.). 1988. pap. 13.00 (0-664-25002-5, Westminster) Westminster John Knox.

Spirituality & Maturity. Joann W. Conn. 176p. 1994. reprint ed. pap. text ed. 21.00 (0-8191-9569-3) U Pr of Amer.

S

Spirituality & Morality: Integrating Prayer & Action. Ed. by Dennis J. Billy & Donna L. Orsuto. LC 95-37835. 192p. (Orig.). 1996. pap. 14.95 (*0-8091-3611-2*) Paulist Pr.

Spirituality & Pastoral Care. Kenneth Leech. LC 89-22141. 149p. 1989. pap. 10.95 (*0-936384-84-0*) Cowley Pubns.

Spirituality & Prayer: Jewish & Christian Understandings. Ed. by Leon Klenicki & Gabe Huck. LC 82-62966. (Studies in Judaism & Christianity). 160p. reprint ed. pap. 45.60 (*0-7837-1784-9*, 2041983) Bks Demand.

***Spirituality & Recovery: A Guide to Positive Living.** Leo Booth. Orig. Title: Walking on Water. (Illus.). 135p. 1997. pap. 10.00 (*0-9623282-4-3*) SCP Ltd.

Spirituality & Religion in Counseling and Psychotherapy. Eugene W. Kelly, Jr. 325p. 1995. pap. text ed. 34.95 (*1-55620-148-6*, 72572) Am Coun Assn.

Spirituality & Self-Empowerment: How to Open up Your Magical, Mystical Mind Power. Gloria Chadwick. LC 95-32765. 224p. 1995. pap. 12.95 (*0-8092-3441-6*) Contemp Bks.

Spirituality & Self-Esteem. Richard L. Bednar & Scott R. Peterson. LC 90-40728. ix, 157p. 1994. pap. 7.95 (*0-87579-840-3*) Deseret Bk.

Spirituality & Social Liberation: The Message of the Blumhardts & the Light of Wuerttemberg Pietism. Frank D. Macchia. LC 93-27785. (Pietist & Wesleyan Studies: No. 4). 1994. 30.00 (*0-8108-2639-9*) Scarecrow.

Spirituality & Social Responsibility. Intro. by Rosemary S. Keller. LC 92-42140. (Orig.). 1993. pap. 18.95 (*0-687-39236-5*) Abingdon.

Spirituality & Society: Postmodern Visions. Ed. by David R. Griffin. LC 88-1152. (SUNY Series in Constructive Postmodern Thought). 162p. 1988. pap. text ed. 19.95 (*0-88706-854-5*) State U NY Pr.

Spirituality & Society: Postmodern Visions. Ed. by David R. Griffin. LC 88-1152. (SUNY Series in Constructive Postmodern Thought). 162p. 1988. text ed. 59.50 (*0-88706-853-7*) State U NY Pr.

***Spirituality & Stewardship.** Eleanor Snyder & Ken Hawkley. (Living the Vision Ser.: Vol. 1). 60p. 1997. pap. 5.95 (*0-87303-312-4*) Faith & Life.

Spirituality & the Secular Quest. Peter Van Ness. (World Spirituality Ser.: Vol. 22). 536p. (Orig.). 1996. 49.50 (*0-8245-0770-3*) Crossroad NY.

Spirituality & the Secular Quest. Peter Van Ness. (Orig.). 1996. pap. text ed. 29.95 (*0-8245-0774-6*) Crossroad NY.

Spirituality & Total Health. Ishwar C. Puri. Ed. by Edward D. Scott. 29p. (Orig.). 1986. pap. 2.00 (*0-937067-08-3*) Insti Study Aware.

Spirituality, Diversion, & Decadence: The Contemporary Predicament. Peter H. Van Ness. LC 91-38672. (SUNY Series in Religious Studies). 350p. 1992. pap. text ed. 19.95 (*0-7914-1206-7*) State U NY Pr.

Spirituality, Diversion, & Decadence: The Contemporary Predicament. Peter H. Van Ness. LC 91-38672. (SUNY Series in Religious Studies). 350p. 1992. text ed. 59.50 (*0-7914-1205-9*) State U NY Pr.

Spirituality for Active Ministry. Corita Clarke. LC 90-61955. 88p. (Orig.). (C). 1991. pap. 6.95 (*1-55612-361-2*) Sheed & Ward MO.

Spirituality for Contemporary Life: The Jesuit Heritage Today. Ed. by David L. Fleming. xii, 98p. (Orig.). (C). 1991. pap. text ed. 5.95 (*0-924768-02-9*) Review Relig.

Spirituality for Everyday Living: An Adaptation of the Rule of St. Benedict. Brian Taylor. 88p. 1989. pap. 5.95 (*0-8146-1757-3*) Liturgical Pr.

Spirituality for Humanists: Six Capacities of Our Human Spirits. 2nd large type rev. ed. James Park. Orig. Title: Capacities of the Human Spirit: Spirituality for Humanists. 1995. pap. 3.00 (*0-89231-022-7*) Existential Bks.

Spirituality for the Millennium. Sean P. Kealy. 128p. (Orig.). 1995. pap. 9.95 (*0-8146-2369-7*) Liturgical Pr.

Spirituality for the Vulnerable. Charles Davis. LC 89-61233. 120p. 1990. reprint ed. pap. 8.95 (*1-55612-273-X*) Sheed & Ward MO.

***Spirituality in a Mixed Up Age.** H. Mark Abbott. 300p. (Orig.). 1997. pap. 10.99 (*0-89367-208-4*) Light & Life Comm.

***Spirituality in Action.** James Bacik. 1997. pap. text ed. 15.95 (*1-55612-958-0*) Sheed & Ward MO.

Spirituality in an Age of Change: Rediscovering the Spirit of the Reformers. Alister E. McGrath. 240p. 1994. pap. 16.99 (*0-310-42921-8*) Zondervan.

Spirituality in Conflict: Saint Francis & Giotto's Bardi Chapel. Rona Goffen. LC 87-29233. (Illus.). 220p. 1988. lib. bdg. 45.00 (*0-271-00621-8*) Pa St U Pr.

Spirituality in Ecumenical Perspective. Ed. by E. Glenn Hinson. 160p. (Orig.). 1993. pap. 15.00 (*0-664-25385-7*) Westminster John Knox.

Spirituality in Interfaith Dialogue. Ed. by Tosh Arai & Wesley Ariarajah. 120p. 1989. reprint ed. pap. 34.20 (*0-7837-9830-X*, 2060559) Bks Demand.

Spirituality in Nursing: From Traditional to New Age. Barbara S. Barnum. LC 95-25630. 176p. 1996. 29.95 (*0-8261-9180-0*) Springer Pub.

Spirituality in Social Work Practice. Ronald K. Bullis. 200p. 1996. 59.95 (*1-56032-407-4*); pap. 24.95 (*1-56032-406-6*) Hemisp Pub.

Spirituality in Social Work Practice. Ronald K. Bullis. LC 96-7063. 1996. pap. write for info. (*1-56303-240-6*) Taylor & Francis.

***Spirituality in the Lives of Lesbian, Gay & Bisexual People: Spirituality in the Lives of Lesbian, Gay, & Bisexual People.** Peter Sweasey. LC 97-609. (Lesbian & Gay Studies). 288p. 1997. 80.00 (*0-304-33551-7*) Cassell.

***Spirituality in the Lives of Lesbian, Gay & Bisexual People: Spirituality in the Lives of Lesbian, Gay & Bisexual People.** Peter Sweasey. LC 97-609. (Lesbian & Gay Studies). 288p. 1997. pap. 29.95 (*0-304-33552-5*) Cassell.

Spirituality in Transition. James J. Bacik. 226p. (Orig.). 1996. pap. 15.95 (*1-55612-857-6*, LL1857) Sheed & Ward MO.

Spirituality Named Compassion. Matthew Fox. LC 89-45993. 1990. pap. 16.00 (*0-06-254871-9*) Harper SF.

Spirituality of African Peoples: The Search for a Common Moral Discourse. Peter J. Paris. LC 94-32866. 176p. 1995. pap. 15.00 (*0-8006-2854-3*, Fortress Pr) Augsburg Fortress.

Spirituality of Comedy: Comic Heroism in a Tragic World. Conrad Hyers. LC 95-499. 256p. 1995. 34.95 (*1-56000-218-2*) Transaction Pubs.

Spirituality of Compassion. Harriet Finney & Suzanne Martin. LC 96-84192. (Covenant Bible Studies). 88p. (Orig.). 1996. pap. 5.95 (*0-87178-044-5*, 8046) Brethren.

Spirituality of Compassion. Joan Puls. LC 87-51633. 144p. 1988. pap. 7.95 (*0-89622-352-3*) Twenty-Third.

Spirituality of Connelly. Caritas McCarthy. LC 86-21718. (Studies in Women & Religion: Vol. 19). 280p. 1986. lib. bdg. 89.93 (*0-88946-530-4*) E Mellen.

Spirituality of Erasmus of Rotterdam. Richard L. DeMolen. (Bibliotheca Humanistica & Reformatorica Ser.: No. 40). 242p. 1987. lib. bdg. 72.50 (*90-6004-392-8*, Pub. by B De Graaf NE) Coronet Bks.

Spirituality of Fatima & Medjugorje. Edward Carter. LC 94-70239. 144p. (Orig.). 1994. pap. 6.00 (*1-880033-12-7*) Faith Pub OH.

Spirituality of Hope. Segundo Galilea. Tr. by Terrence Cambias from SPA. LC 89-32887. 128p. 1988. reprint ed. pap. 36.50 (*0-7837-9839-3*, 2060568) Bks Demand.

Spirituality of Imperfection: Storytelling & the Journey to Wholeness. Ernest Kurtz & Katherine Ketchum. 304p. 1994. pap. 13.95 (*0-553-37132-0*) Bantam.

Spirituality of Isaac Thomas Hecker: Reconciling the American Character & the Catholic Faith. Martin J. Kirk. (Heritage of American Catholicism Ser.). 408p. 1988. 15.00 (*0-8240-4092-9*) Garland.

Spirituality of Liberation. Pedro Casaldaliga & Jose Maria Vigil. 272p. 1994. pap. 40.00 (*0-86012-215-8*, Pub. by Srch Pr UK) St Mut.

Spirituality of Liberation: Toward Political Holiness. Jon Sobrino. Tr. by Robert R. Barr from SPA. LC 87-34578. 224p. 1988. 40.00 (*0-88344-617-0*); pap. 17.00 (*0-88344-616-2*) Orbis Bks.

Spirituality of Mark: Responding to God. Mitzi Minor. 152p. (Orig.). 1996. pap. 15.00 (*0-664-25679-1*) Westminster John Knox.

Spirituality of Parenting. Maureen Gallagher. (Illus.). 32p. 1985. pap. text ed. 2.95 (*0-934134-18-9*) Sheed & Ward MO.

Spirituality of St. Ignatius Loyola: An Account of Its Historical Development. Hugo Rahner. Tr. by Francis J. Smith. LC 53-5586. 1968. reprint ed. 4.95 (*0-8294-0066-4*) Loyola Pr.

***Spirituality of St. Patrick.** Lesley Whiteside. LC 97-21291. (Illus.). 78p. (Orig.). 1997. pap. 7.95 (*0-8192-1693-3*) Morehouse Pub.

Spirituality of the American Transcendentalists: Selected Writings of Ralph Waldo Emerson, Amos Bronson Alcott, Theodore Parker, & Henry David Thoreau. Ed. by Catherine L Albanese. LC 87-34730. 480p. 1988. pap. 34.95 (*0-86554-323-2*, MUP/P062) Mercer Univ Pr.

Spirituality of the Beatitudes: Matthew's Challenge for First World Christians. Michael H. Crosby. LC 80-24755. 254p. (Orig.). 1981. pap. 13.50 (*0-88344-465-8*) Orbis Bks.

Spirituality of the Body. Alexander Lowen. 224p. 1990. 18.95 (*0-02-575871-3*) Macmillan.

Spirituality of the Catholic Church. William A. Kaschmitter. 980p. 1982. 20.00 (*0-912414-33-2*) Lumen Christi.

Spirituality of the Diocesan Priest. Donald B. Cozzens. LC 96-51709. 200p. (Orig.). 1997. pap. text ed. 14.95 (*0-8146-2421-9*, Liturg Pr Bks) Liturgical Pr.

Spirituality of the Future: A Search Apropos of R. C. Zaehner's Study in Sri-Aurobindo & Teilhard de Chardin. K. D. Sethna. LC 76-14764. 320p. 1981. 40.00 (*0-8386-2028-0*) Fairleigh Dickinson.

Spirituality of the Gospels. Stephen C. Barton. 176p. 1994. pap. 9.95 (*1-56563-147-1*) Hendrickson MA.

Spirituality of the Later English Puritans: An Anthology. Ed. by Dewey D. Wallace, Jr. LC 87-24692. 320p. (C). 1988. 39.95 (*0-86554-275-9*, MUP-H238) Mercer Univ Pr.

Spirituality of the Religious Educator. Ed. by James M. Lee. LC 85-2250. 209p. (Orig.). 1985. pap. 14.95 (*0-89135-045-4*) Religious Educ.

Spirituality of the Road. David J. Bosch. LC 79-10856. (Missionary Studies: No. 6). 96p. reprint ed. pap. 27.40 (*0-7837-5121-4*, 2044820) Bks Demand.

Spirituality of the Third World: A Cry for Life. Ed. by K. C. Abraham & Bernadette Mbuy-Beya. LC 94-23357. 212p. (Orig.). 1994. pap. 19.95 (*0-88344-977-3*) Orbis Bks.

Spirituality of Western Christendom. Ed. by E. Rozanne Elder. LC 76-22615. (Cistercian Studies: No. 30). (Illus.). 1976. pap. 10.95 (*0-87907-987-8*) Cistercian Pubns.

Spirituality of Western Christendom II: The Roots of Modern Christian Spirituality. Ed. by Rozanne E. Elder. Nbr. 55. pap. write for info. (*0-318-56580-3*) Cistercian Pubns.

Spirituality of Work: Business People. William Droel. (Spirituality of Work Ser.). 64p. (Orig.). 1991. pap. 2.95 (*0-914070-75-4*, 134) ACTA Pubns.

Spirituality of Work: Homemakers. William Droel. 64p. (Orig.). 1991. pap. 2.95 (*0-914070-74-6*, 133) ACTA Pubns.

Spirituality of Work: Lawyers. William Droel. 64p. (Orig.). 1991. pap. 2.95 (*0-914070-73-8*, 132) ACTA Pubns.

Spirituality of Work: Nurses. William Droel. (Spirituality of Work Ser.). 48p. (Orig.). 1991. pap. 2.95 (*0-914070-71-1*, 130) ACTA Pubns.

Spirituality of Work: Teachers. William Droel. 64p. (Orig.). 1991. pap. 2.95 (*0-914070-72-X*, 131) ACTA Pubns.

Spirituality of Work: Unemployed Workers. Joseph Gosse. (Spirituality of Work Ser.). 64p. (Orig.). 1993. pap. 2.95 (*0-87946-088-1*, 135) ACTA Pubns.

Spirituality of Work: Visual Artists. John Dylong. 48p. 1995. pap. 2.95 (*0-87946-128-6*) ACTA Pubns.

***Spirituality of Work Vol. 8: Military Personnel.** Ginny Cunningham. 64p. (Orig.). 1996. pap. 2.95 (*0-87946-149-7*, 138) ACTA Pubns.

Spirituality Recharted. Hubert Van Zeller. LC 85-8252. 157p. 1985. pap. 4.95 (*0-932506-39-9*) St Bedes Pubns.

***Spirituality, Sex & Silliness.** Chandler H. Everett. Ed. by Tomi Keitlen. 128p. (Orig.). 1997. pap. 7.00 (*1-886966-08-7*) In Print.

Spirituality, Stress & You. Thomas E. Rodgerson. LC 94-31705. (Illumination Bks.). 80p. 1994. pap. 3.95 (*0-8091-3514-0*) Paulist Pr.

Spiritualizing Everyday Life & Worship of the Spirit by the Spirit. 2nd ed. Swami Ashokananda. 70p. 1987. pap. 3.95 (*0-9612388-0-1*) Vedanta Soc N Cal.

Spiritually Aware Pastoral Care: An Introduction & Training Program. Earle Williams & Elspeth Williams. 1991. pap. 14.95 (*0-8091-3167-6*) Paulist Pr.

Spiritually Beneficial Tales of Paul of Monembasia & of Other Authors. Tr. & Comment by John Wortley. LC 96-7857. (Cistercian Studies: No. 159). 1996. 45.00 (*0-87907-559-7*) Cistercian Pubns.

Spiritually Beneficial Tales of Paul of Monembasia & of Other Authors. Tr. & Comment by John Wortley. LC 96-7857. (Cistercian Studies: No. 159). 1996. 18.95 (*0-87907-659-3*) Cistercian Pubns.

Spiritually Centered Motherhood. Sherrie Johnson. 1995. pap. 5.95 (*0-88494-992-3*) Bookcraft Inc.

Spiritually Correct Bedtime Stories: Parables of Faith for the Modern Reader. Chris Fabry. LC 95-19131. 96p. 1995. 10.99 (*0-8308-1955-X*, 1955) InterVarsity.

Spiritually Yours: Applying Gospel Principles for Personal Progression. S. Brent Farley. LC 81-82054. 160p. 1982. 11.98 (*0-88290-192-3*, 1068) Horizon Utah.

Spirituals. Chelsea House Publishers Staff. (YA). 1995. pap. 16.95 (*0-7910-1854-7*) Chelsea Hse.

Spirituals. Compiled by Jerry Silverman. (Traditional Black Music Ser.). (Illus.). 80p. (YA). (gr. 5 up). 1995. lib. bdg. 18.95 (*0-7910-1838-5*) Chelsea Hse.

Spirituals & Gospels. (Illus.). 64p. 1975. pap. 9.95 (*0-8256-9332-2*, AM15058) Music Sales.

Spirituals & the Blues. 2nd ed. James H. Cone. LC 91-19267. 152p. 1992. reprint ed. pap. 12.50 (*0-88344-843-2*) Orbis Bks.

Spirituals We Play & Sing, Bk. 1. 1993. 7.99 (*0-685-74850-2*, MB-648) Lillenas.

Spirituals We Play & Sing, Bk. 2. 1992. 7.99 (*0-685-74846-4*, MB-649) Lillenas.

Spirituelle: Poems & Prayers of a Woman's Awakening. Christine Tarantino. LC 96-90175. 56p. (Orig.). 1996. pap. 9.95 (*1-887480-02-1*) Wrds Lght Intl.

Spiritus Mundi: Essays on Literature, Myth, & Society. Northrop Frye. LC 76-12364. 314p. reprint ed. pap. 89.50 (*0-7837-3704-1*, 2057882) Bks Demand.

Spiritwalk. Charles DeLint. 416p. 1993. mass mkt. 4.99 (*0-8125-1620-6*) Tor Bks.

Spiritwalk. Smithmark Staff. pap. 3.98 (*0-8317-4173-2*) Smithmark.

Spiritwalker: Messages from the Future. Hank Wesselman. (Illus.). 400p. 1996. pap. 13.95 (*0-553-37837-6*) Bantam.

Spiro Agnew: Controversial Vice-President of the Nixon Administration. Gerald Kurland. Ed. by D. Steve Rahmas. LC 72-190234. (Outstanding Personalities Ser.: No. 16). 32p. (Orig.). (J). (gr. 7-12). 1972. lib. bdg. 7.25 (*0-87157-516-7*) SamHar Pr.

Spiro Ceremonial Center: The Archaeology of Arkansas Valley Caddoan Culture in Eastern Oklahoma. James A. Brown. LC 95-36153. (Memoirs of the Museum of Anthropology, University of Michigan Ser.: No. 29). 1996. pap. 65.00 (*0-915703-39-4*) U Mich Mus Anthro.

***Spiroid Gears.** F. Bohle & O. Saari. (Technical Papers). 1955. pap. text ed. 30.00 (*1-55589-398-8*) AGMA.

Spirometry Quality: The Essentials. Robert Brown & Susan Blonshine. (Illus.). 180p. 1996. spiral bd. 29.95 (*0-932887-11-2*) Health Ed Pubns.

Spirtual Disciplines see Papers from Eranos Yearbooks

Spirulina. Jack J. Challem. (Good Health Guide Ser.). 1982. pap. 3.50 (*0-87983-262-2*) Keats.

Spirulina: Food for a Hungry World; A Pioneer's Story in Aquaculture. Hiroshi Nakamura. Ed. by Christopher Hills. Tr. by Robert Wargo from JPN. LC 82-4816. (Illus.). 224p. (Orig.). 1982. pap. 15.95 (*0-916438-47-3*) Dr Hills Technol.

Spirulina - Nature's Superfood. Helen C. Morgan & Kelly J. Moorhead. 43p. 1993. pap. 2.95 (*0-9637511-3-1*) Nutrex.

Spirulina Cookbook: Recipes for Rejuvenating the Body. Sonia Beasley. LC 81-40027. (Illus.). 184p. (Orig.). 1981. pap. 12.95 (*0-916438-39-2*) Dr Hills Technol.

***Spisok Dvorianam Tsarstva Polskago.** xvii, 326p. (POL & RUS.). 1991. reprint ed. 30.00 (*0-614-25051-X*) Szwede Slavic.

***Spit Delaney's Island.** Jack Hodgins. 1996. pap. text ed. 6.95 (*0-7710-9870-7*) McCland & Stewart.

Spit Nolan. Bill Naughton. (Illustrated Short Stories Ser.). 1987. lib. bdg. 13.95 (*0-88682-122-3*) Creative Ed.

Spit-Shine Syndrome: Organizational Irrationality in the American Field Army. Christopher Bassford. LC 87-37551. (Contributions in Military Studies: No. 76). 192p. 1988. text ed. 49.95 (*0-313-26215-2*, BFP/, Greenwood Pr) Greenwood.

Spitalfields Acts, 1818-28. LC 72-2544. (British Labour Struggles Before 1850 Ser.). 1974. 26.95 (*0-405-04436-4*) Ayer.

Spitalfields & Mile End New Town: The Parishes of Christ Church & All Saints & the Liberties of Norton Folgate & the Old Artillery Ground. P. A. Bezodis. LC 74-6547. (London County Council. Survey of London Ser.: No. 27). 1957. reprint ed. 84.50 (*0-685-00410-4*) AMS Pr.

Spitball Class. Candice F. Ransom. Ed. by Patricia MacDonald. 160p. (Orig.). 1994. pap. 2.99 (*0-671-72910-1*, Minstrel Bks) PB.

Spite Fences. Trudy B. Krisher. 288p. (YA). (gr. 7 up). 1996. mass mkt. 3.99 (*0-440-22016-5*, LLL BDD) BDD Bks Young Read.

Spite Fences. Trudy B. Krisher. LC 94-8665. 288p. (J). (gr. 6 up). 1994. 15.95 (*0-385-32088-4*) Delacorte.

Spite for Spite: El Desden Con el Desden. Augustin Moreto. Tr. by Dakin Matthews. (Great Translations for Actors Ser.). 112p. 1995. pap. 11.95 (*1-57525-002-0*) Smith & Kraus.

Spite House: The Last Secret of the War in Vietnam. Monika Jensen-Stevenson. LC 96-24688. 356p. 1997. 25.00 (*0-393-04041-0*) Norton.

Spite, Malice & Revenge: The Complete Guide to Getting Even. M. Nelson Chunder. 1988. 9.99 (*0-517-67604-4*) Random Hse Value.

Spitfire. Sonya Birmingham. 368p. (Orig.). 1991. pap. 3.95 (*0-380-76294-3*) Avon.

***Spitfire.** Jeffrey L. Ethell. (Illus.). 128p. 1997. pap. 19.95 (*0-7603-0300-2*) Motorbooks Intl.

Spitfire. Deloras Scott. (Historical Ser.). 1994. mass mkt. 3.99 (*0-373-28804-2*, 1-28804-2) Harlequin Bks.

Spitfire. Bertrice Small. 1992. mass mkt. 5.99 (*0-345-37565-3*) Ballantine.

Spitfire: The Combat History. Robert Jackson. (Illus.). 192p. 1995. 34.95 (*0-7603-0193-X*) Motorbooks Intl.

Spitfire: The Fighter Legend. John Dibbs & Tony Holmes. (Illus.). 192p. 1996. 34.95 (*1-85532-594-2*, Pub. by Osprey Pubng Ltd UK) Motorbooks Intl.

Spitfire Diary. rev. ed. E. A. Smith. (Illus.). 238p. 1996. reprint ed. 16.95 (*1-57168-046-2*, Eakin Pr) Sunbelt Media.

Spitfire in Action. Jerry Scutts. (Aircraft in Action Ser.). (Illus.). 1984. pap. 7.95 (*0-89747-092-3*, 1039) Squad Sig Pubns.

Spitfire in Blue. Hugh Smallwood. (Illus.). 168p. 1996. 29.95 (*1-85532-615-9*, Pub. by Osprey Pubng Ltd UK) Motorbooks Intl.

***Spitfire Leader: The Flying Career of Wing Cdr. Evan "Rosie" Mackie, DSO, DFC & BAR, DFC (U. S.), New Zealand Ace.** Max Avery & Christopher Shores. 240p. 1997. 29.95 (*1-898697-58-2*, Pub. by Grub St Pubns UK) Seven Hills Bk.

***Spitfire Log: Sixtieth Anniversary Tribute.** Ed. by Peter Haining. (Illus.). 144p. (Orig.). 1997. pap. 16.95 (*0-285-63363-5*, Pub. by Souvenir UK) IPG Chicago.

Spitfire Mark I/II Aces 1938-41. Alfred Price. (Aircraft of the Aces Ser.: No. 12). (Illus.). 96p. 1996. pap. 15.95 (*1-85532-627-2*, Pub. by Osprey Pubng Ltd UK) Motorbooks Intl.

***Spitfire Mark V Aces 1941-45 - Aircraft of the Aces, No. 16.** Alfred Price. (Aircraft of the Aces Ser.: No. 16). (Illus.). 96p. 1997. pap. 15.95 (*1-85532-635-3*, Pub. by Osprey Pubng Ltd UK) Motorbooks Intl.

Spitfire MK IV Worksh. 71-73. Robert Bentley. 1994. 45.00 (*0-8376-0593-8*) Bentley.

Spitfire Offensive. R. W. Sampson & Norman Franks. (Illus.). 208p. 1994. 29.95 (*1-898697-02-7*, Pub. by Grub St Pubns UK) Seven Hills Bk.

Spitfire-Tug of War. Lori Copeland. 368p. 1995. mass mkt., pap. text ed. 4.99 (*0-505-52022-2*) Dorchester Pub Co.

Spitfires over Israel: The First Authoritative Account of Air Conflict During the Israeli War of Independence, 1948-49. Brian Cull et al. (Illus.). 400p. 1994. 39.95 (*0-948817-74-7*, Pub. by Grub St Pubns UK) Seven Hills Bk.

Spitfires, Thunderbolts & Warm Beer: An American Fighter Pilot Over Europe. Philip D. Caine. (World War II Commemorative Ser.). (Illus.). 192p. 1995. 24.95 (*0-02-881115-1*) Brasseys Inc.

***Spitfires, Thunderbolts, & Warm Beer: An American Fighter Pilot over Europe.** Philip D. Caine. (Illus.). 264p. 1997. reprint ed. pap. 18.95 (*1-57488-116-7*) Brasseys Inc.

***Spitting at Dragons: Towards a Feminist Theology of Sainthood.** Elizabeth Stuart. 144p. (Orig.). 1997. pap. 17.95 (*0-264-67344-1*) Morehouse Pub.

Spitting Cobras of Africa. James Martin. (Animals & the Environment Ser.). 48p. (J). (gr. 3-4). 1994. lib. bdg. 17.80 (*1-56065-239-X*) Capstone Pr.

Spitting Cobras of Africa. James Martin. (Illus.). 48p. (J). (gr. 3-7). 1995. 13.35 (*0-516-35239-3*) Childrens.

Spitting Images. Sean Kelly. (Spitting Image Productions Ser.). (Illus.). 1987. 14.95 (*0-15-184768-1*, Harvest Bks) HarBrace.

Spitting in the Wind. Earl Anthony. LC 89-24310. 208p. 1990. pap. 18.95 (*0-915677-45-8*) Roundtable Pub.

Spitwad Sutras: Classroom Teaching As Sublime Vocation. Robert Inchausti. LC 93-25017. 200p. 1993. text ed. 49.95 (*0-89789-365-4*, H365, Bergin & Garvey) Greenwood.

Spitwad Sutras: Classroom Teaching as Sublime Vocation. Robert Inchausti. LC 93-25017. 1993. pap. text ed. 15.95 (*0-89789-379-4*, Bergin & Garvey) Greenwood.

An Asterisk (*) at the beginning of an entry indicates that the title is appearing in BIP for the first time.

Spitz & Fisher's Medicolegal Investigation of Death: Guidelines for the Application of Pathology to Crime Investigation. 3rd ed. Werner U. Spitz. (Illus.). 856p. (C). 1993. text ed. 86.95 (*0-398-05818-0*) C C Thomas.

Spitzalod. IGOOS Staff. Ed. by Thorguard Templar. 243p. (Orig.). 1993. 25.00 (*1-883147-95-6*) Intern Guild ASRS.

Spitzalod Magic Quest Course. IGOOS Staff. (Illus.). 125p. (Orig.). 1994. 25.00 (*1-883147-88-3*) Intern Guild ASRS.

Spitze. Isobel Drummond. 1989. pap. text ed. 15.28 (*0-582-33206-0*, 72075); audio 22.61 (*0-582-33207-9*, 72076) Longman.

Spivak Reader. Gayatri C. Spivak. Ed. by Donna Landry & Gerald Maclean. LC 95-22222. 320p. (gr. 13). 1995. pap. 17.95 (*0-415-91001-3*, B3879, Routledge NY) Routledge.

Spivak Reader. Gayatri C. Spivak. Ed. by Donna Landry & Gerald Maclean. LC 95-22222. 320p. (C). (gr. 13). 1995. text ed. 62.95 (*0-415-91000-5*, B3875, Routledge NY) Routledge.

***Spizarnia Kosciol - The Parish Pantry Vol. 1: Keepsake Edition.** Judy H. Seikel. 416p. 1996. spiral bd. 16.95 (*0-9619314-1-8*) CDACCK.

Splanchnic Circulation: No Longer a Silent Partner. Ed. by M. R. Pinsky et al. LC 95-37674. (Update in Intensive Care & Emergency Medicine Ser.: Vol. 23). 192p. 1995. 123.00 (*3-540-59198-2*) Spr-Verlag.

Splash! Ann Jonas. LC 94-4110. (Illus.). 24p. (J). (ps up). 1995. 15.00 (*0-688-11051-7*); lib. bdg. 14.93 (*0-688-11052-5*) Greenwillow.

***Splash!** Ann Jonas. 1997. pap. 4.95 (*0-688-15284-8*, Mulberry) Morrow.

Splash. Levinson. 1996. bds. write for info. (*0-15-201254-0*) HarBrace.

Splash. Teddy Teller. 1983. pap. 1.75 (*0-912963-00-X*) Eldridge Pub.

***Splash!** Laura E. Williams. (Let's Have a Party Ser.: No. 2). (J). (gr. 1-4). 1997. pap. 3.99 (*0-380-78922-1*, Camelot) Avon.

Splash! A Little Otter in Big Trouble. Jacqueline Hanks. (Illus.). 24p. (J). (gr. k-3). 1992. pap. 1.99 (*0-87406-600-X*) Willowisp Pr.

***Splash! A Penguin Counting Book.** Kirsty Melville. LC 97-8047. (Illus.). 24p. (J). (ps up). 1997. 12.95 (*1-883672-56-2*) Tricycle Pr.

Splash! Activity Book. 16p. (J). (gr. k-4). 1990. pap. write for info. (*0-89867-517-0*, 70054) Am Water Wks Assn.

Splash! Great Writing about Swimming. Ed. by Laurel Blossom. LC 95-46562. (Companion's Ser.). 272p. 1996. 26.00 (*0-88001-449-0*) Ecco Pr.

Splash-a-Roo & Snowflakes. Michelle Poploff. LC 95-21362. (Illus.). (J). 1996. pap. 3.99 (*0-440-41119-X*, Picture Yearling) BDD Bks Young Read.

Splash-a-Roo & Snowflakes. Michelle Poploff. LC 95-21362. (Yearling First Choice Chapter Book Ser.). (Illus.). 48p. (J). (gr. k-3). 1996. 13.95 (*0-385-32176-7*, YB BDD) BDD Bks Young Read.

Splash & Trickle. Ivah Green. LC 68-56818. (Illus.). 32p. (J). (gr. 2-3). 1968. lib. bdg. 9.95 (*0-87783-037-1*) Oddo.

Splash & Trickle. Ivah Green. (Illus.). (J). (gr. 2-3). 1978. pap. 1.25 (*0-89508-062-1*) Rainbow Bks.

Splash & Trickle. deluxe ed. Ivah Green. LC 68-56818. (Illus.). 32p. (J). (gr. 2-3). 1968. pap. 3.94 (*0-87783-109-2*) Oddo.

***Splash Crash!** Tony Abbott. (Time Surfers Ser.: No. 5). 96p. (J). 1997. mass mkt. 3.50 (*0-553-48462-1*, Skylark BDD) BDD Bks Young Read.

Splash of Fall. Susanne Glover & Georgeann Grewe. (Illus.). 128p. (J). (gr. 2-5). 1987. pap. 12.99 (*0-86653-410-5*, GA1024) Good Apple.

Splash of Fall, Winter & Spring, 3 bks., Set. Susanne Glover & Georgeann Grewe. teacher ed. 37.99 (*1-56417-132-9*, GA1111) Good Apple.

***Splash of Red.** rev. ed. Antonia Fraser. Date not set. pap. 10.00 (*0-393-31687-4*) Norton.

Splash of Spring. Susanne Glover & Georgeann Grewe. (Illus.). 128p. (J). (gr. 2-5). 1987. pap. 12.99 (*0-86653-412-1*, GA1026) Good Apple.

Splash of Winter, Set. Susanne Glover & Georgeann Grewe. (Illus.). 128p. (J). (gr. 2-5). 1987. pap. 12.99 (*0-86653-411-3*, GA1025) Good Apple.

Splash One: Air War Victory over Hanoi. Walter Kross. LC 90-48327. 300p. 1991. 18.95 (*0-685-48178-6*) Macmillan.

***Splash 1: America's Best Watercolors.** Greg Albert. (Illus.). 1997. pap. text ed. 22.99 (*0-89134-849-2*, North Lght Bks) F & W Pubns Inc.

Splash Party. Sharon D. Wyeth. (American Gold Swimmers Ser.: No. 3). 144p. (J). (gr. 4-7). 1996. mass mkt. 3.50 (*0-553-48396-X*, Skylark BDD) BDD Bks Young Read.

Splash, Splash. Jeff Sheppard. LC 92-26163. (Illus.). 40p. (J). (ps-k). 1994. lib. bdg. 15.00 (*0-02-782455-1*, Mac Bks Young Read) S&S Childrens.

Splash 2: FPGAs in a Custom Computing Machine. Ducan A. Buell et al. LC 95-47397. 224p. 1996. 40.00 (*0-8186-7413-X*, BPO7413) IEEE Comp Soc.

Splash 3: Ideas & Inspirations. Ed. by Rachel R. Wolf. (Illus.). 144p. 1994. 29.99 (*0-89134-561-2*, North Lght Bks) F & W Pubns Inc.

Splash 4: The Splendor of Light. Ed. by Rachel R. Wolf. (Illus.). 144p. 1996. 29.99 (*0-89134-677-5*, North Lght Bks) F & W Pubns Inc.

Splashes of Joy: In the Cesspool of Life. B. Johnson. 1994. 4.99 (*0-8499-5070-8*) Word Pub.

Splashes of Joy: In the Cesspools of Life. large type ed. Barbara Johnson. 320p. pap. 14.99 (*0-8499-3941-0*, 2435) Word Dist.

Splashes of Joy in the Cesspools of Life. Barbara Johnson. 192p. 1992. pap. 10.99 (*0-8499-3313-7*) Word Pub.

Splat! Jane O'Connor. LC 93-34127. (All Aboard Reading Ser.). (Illus.). 32p. (J). (ps-1). 1994. pap. 3.95 (*0-448-40219-X*, G&D) Putnam Pub Group.

***Splat in the Hat.** Pat Pollari. (Barf-O-Rama Ser.: No. 11). 128p. (J). 1997. mass mkt. 3.50 (*0-553-48467-2*, Skylark BDD) BDD Bks Young Read.

Splatter Movies: Breaking the Last Taboo of the Screen. John McCarty. LC 83-19134. (Illus.). 192p. 1984. pap. 13.95 (*0-312-75257-1*) St Martin.

Splatterpunks: The Definitive Anthology. Ed. by Paul Sammon. 384p. (Orig.). 1990. pap. 14.95 (*0-312-04581-6*) St Martin.

Splatterpunks II. Ed. by Paul Sammon. 416p. 1995. pap. 14.95 (*0-312-85786-1*) Tor Bks.

Splawn: Genealogy of the Splawn & Collins Family, 1600-1960. Jennie L. Splawn. (Illus.). 86p. 1995. reprint ed. pap. 17.00 (*0-8328-4844-1*); reprint ed. lib. bdg. 27.00 (*0-8328-4843-3*) Higginson Bk Co.

***Spleen.** Ed. by Bowdler. 536p. (C). (gr. 13 up). Date not set. text ed. write for info. (*0-412-29120-7*) Chapman & Hall.

Spleen. Ed. by A. J. Bowdler. (Illus.). 536p. 1990. 159.95 (*0-442-31209-1*) Chapman & Hall.

Spleen. 2nd rev. ed. Olive Moore. LC 96-16131. 136p. 1996. pap. 10.95 (*1-56478-148-8*) Dalkey Arch.

***Spleen & Nostalgia: A Life & Work in Psychoanalysis.** John E. Gedo. LC 97-9834. 1997. text ed. 40.00 (*0-7657-0082-4*) Aronson.

Spleen de Paris. Charles Baudelaire. (FRE.). 1973. pap. 10.95 (*0-8288-9061-7*, F57314) Fr & Eur.

Spleen de Paris - Les Paradis Artificiels. unabridged ed. Charles P. Baudelaire. (FRE.). pap. 7.95 (*2-87714-226-4*, Pub. by Bookking Intl FR) Distribks Inc.

Splendeurs et Miseres des Courtisanes. Honore De Balzac. (Coll. GF). pap. 9.95 (*0-685-34094-5*) Fr & Eur.

Splendeurs et Miseres des Courtisanes. Honore De Balzac. 704p. (FRE.). 1973. pap. 16.95 (*0-7859-1724-1*, 2070364054) Fr & Eur.

Splendeurs et Miseres des Courtisanes. Honore De Balzac. (Folio Ser.: No. 405). 698p. (FRE.). 1973. pap. 12.95 (*2-07-036405-4*) Schoenhof.

Splendeurs et Miseres des Courtisanes. unabridged ed. Honore De Balzac. (FRE.). pap. 7.95 (*2-87714-149-7*, Pub. by Bookking Intl FR) Distribks Inc.

Splendid. Julia Quinn. 400p. (Orig.). 1995. mass mkt. 4.99 (*0-380-78074-7*) Avon.

Splendid Art of Decorating Eggs. Rosemary Disney. 192p. 1986. reprint ed. pap. 6.95 (*0-486-25030-X*) Dover.

Splendid Blond Beast: Money, Law & Genocide in the Twentieth Century. Christopher Simpson. 416p. (C). 1995. reprint ed. pap. 19.95 (*1-56751-062-0*) Common Courage.

***Splendid Century: Life in the France of Louis XIV.** W. H. Lewis. (Illus.). 306p. (C). 1997. reprint ed. pap. text ed. 12.95 (*0-88133-921-0*) Waveland Pr.

Splendid Ceremonies: State Entries & Royal Funerals in the Low Countries, 1515-1791--A Bibliography. John Landwehr. (Illus.). 350p. 1971. text ed. 87.50 (*90-6004-287-5*, Pub. by B De Graaf NE) Coronet Bks.

***Splendid China: Shenzhen Miniature Scenic Spot.** Shen Ping & Cheung Y. Sim. (Illus.). 120p. 1994. pap. 16.95 (*0-8351-2535-1*) China Bks.

Splendid Failure: Hart Crane & the Making of The Bridge. Edward J. Brunner. LC 84-2690. 296p. 1985. text ed. 29.95 (*0-252-01094-9*) U of Ill Pr.

Splendid Family. Margaret Pedler. 14.95 (*0-8488-1444-4*) Amereon Ltd.

Splendid Folly. Margaret Pedler. 1976. lib. bdg. 13.75 (*0-89968-218-9*, Lghtyr Pr) Buccaneer Bks.

Splendid Grain. Rebecca Wood. LC 96-1564. 1997. 30.00 (*0-688-09766-9*) Morrow.

Splendid Hotels of Europe: Photographic Portrait. Photos by Nicholas D'Archimbaud. (Illus.). 1994. 39.95 (*1-57036-111-8*) Turner Pub GA.

Splendid Idle Forties. Gertrude F. Atherton. LC 68-20004. (Americans in Fiction Ser.). (Illus.). reprint ed. pap. text ed. 7.95 (*0-89197-947-6*); reprint ed. lib. bdg. 19.50 (*0-8398-0069-X*) Irvington.

Splendid Innovations: The World of French Design 1650-1785. Henry Joyce. 48p. 1986. pap. text ed. 5.00 (*0-9606718-3-8*) Hyde Collect.

Splendid Isolation: The Curious History of South American Mammals. George G. Simpson. LC 79-17630. (Illus.). 275p. reprint ed. pap. 78.40 (*0-7837-3311-9*, 2057713) Bks Demand.

Splendid Legacy: The Havemeyer Collection. Alice C. Frelinghuysen et al. (Illus.). 432p. 1993. 85.00 (*0-8109-6426-0*) Abrams.

Splendid Legacy: The Havemeyer Collection. Alice C. Frelinghuysen et al. LC 92-45902. 1993. 45.00 (*0-87099-664-9*, 0-8109-6426-0) Metro Mus Art.

Splendid Monarchy: Power & Pageantry in Modern Japan. T. Fujitani. LC 95-38543. (Twentieth-Century Japan Ser.: Vol. 6). (Illus.). 314p. 1996. 40.00 (*0-520-20237-6*) U CA Pr.

***Splendid Needlepoint: 40 Beautiful & Distinctive Designs.** Catherine Reurs. Ed. by Deborah Morgenthal. (Illus.). 128p. 1997. 27.95 (*1-887374-22-1*) Lark Books.

Splendid Samplers to Cross-Stitch: 35 Original Projects. Chris Rankin. LC 95-11548. (Illus.). 144p. (Orig.). 1995. 27.95 (*0-8069-3164-7*) Lark Books.

Splendid Samplers to Cross-Stitch: 35 Original Projects. Chris Rankin. (Illus.). 144p. (Orig.). 1996. pap. 14.95 (*0-8069-3165-5*) Lark Books.

Splendid Scheme. Elizabeth Brodnax. 208p. 1994. reprint ed. mass mkt. 3.99 (*0-515-11406-5*) Jove Pubns.

Splendid Silk Ribbon Embroidery: Embellishing Clothing, Linens & Accessories. Chris Rankin. LC 96-1186. (Illus.). 128p. 1996. 27.95 (*0-8069-4880-9*) Lark Books.

***Splendid Silk Ribbon Embroidery: Embellishing Clothing, Linens & Accessories.** Chris Rankin. 1997. pap. text ed. 14.95 (*0-8069-4881-7*) Sterling.

***Splendid Slippers.** Beverley Jackson. LC 97-22585. 1997. pap. 19.95 (*0-89815-957-1*) Ten Speed Pr.

Splendid Soups. LC 93-11612. (Anne Willan's Look & Cook Ser.). 1994. 16.95 (*1-56458-507-7*) DK Pub Inc.

Splendid Soups. James Peterson. 544p. 1993. 34.95 (*0-553-07505-5*) Bantam.

***Splendid Stutz: The Cars, Companies, People, & Races.** Raymond A. Katzell et al. (Illus.). 392p. 1996. 69.95 (*0-9654709-0-3*) Stutz Club.

Splendid Swedish Recipes. Kerstin O. Van Guilder. 160p. 1988. spiral bd. 5.95 (*0-941016-52-8*) Penfield.

Splendid Symbols: Textiles & Traditions in Indonesia. 2nd rev. ed. Mattiebelle Gittinger. 243p. 1990. reprint ed. pap. 45.00 (*0-19-588956-8*) Textile Mus.

Splendid Table: Five Hundred Years of Eating in Northern Italy. Lynne R. Kasper. (Illus.). 500p. 1992. 35.00 (*0-688-08963-1*) Morrow.

Splendid Torch. Ralph B. Rogers. LC 93-39006. (Illus.). 1993. 25.00 (*0-914659-66-9*) Phoenix Pub.

Splendid Vista. Esther L. Vogt. 1994. reprint ed. pap. 8.99 (*0-88965-105-1*, Pub. by Horizon Books CN) Chr Pubns.

Splendid Was the Trail. rev. ed. Kenneth D. Swan. LC 93-21346. (Sweetgrass Bks.). (Illus.). 144p. 1993. reprint ed. pap. 5.95 (*1-56037-035-1*) Am Wrld Geog.

Splendid Wayfaring: Jedediah Smith & the Ashley-Henry Men, 1822-1831. John G. Neihardt. LC 71-116054. (Illus.). xii, 290p. 1970. reprint ed. pap. 9.95 (*0-8032-5723-6*, Bison Books) U of Nebr Pr.

Splendid Work: The Origins & Development of Williams Baptist College. Kenneth M. Startup. LC 90-83685. (Illus.). (Orig.). 1991. pap. 10.00 (*0-9627911-0-5*) W Baptist Coll.

Splendide-Hotel. deluxe limited ed. Gilbert Sorrentino. LC 73-78786. 64p. 1973. 25.00 (*0-8112-0514-2*) New Directions.

Splendide-Hotel. Gilbert Sorrentino. LC 84-3228. 64p. 1984. reprint ed. 12.00 (*0-916583-00-7*); reprint ed. pap. 5.95 (*0-916583-01-5*) Dalkey Arch.

Splendor. Charlene Cross. Ed. by Carolyn Tolley. 320p. (Orig.). 1995. mass mkt. 5.99 (*0-671-79432-9*) PB.

Splendor. Catherine Hart. 400p. (Orig.). 1993. mass mkt. 4.99 (*0-380-76878-X*) Avon.

Splendor & Wonder: Jesuit Character, Georgetown Spirit, & Liberal Education. Ed. by William J. O'Brien. LC 88-24652. 120p. (Orig.). reprint ed. pap. 34.20 (*0-7837-6703-X*, 2046335) Bks Demand.

Splendor in the Grass. adapted ed. William Inge. 1967. pap. 5.25 (*0-8222-1066-5*) Dramatists Play.

Splendor of American Ceramic Art, 1882-1952. Donald Karshan. (Illus.). 104p. 1991. lib. bdg. 40.00 (*0-685-48758-X*, 91-61272) Museum Art Sciences.

Splendor of Ethnic Jewelry: From the Colette & Jean-Pierre Ghysels Collection. Tr. by I. Mark Paris. LC 94-8417. 1994. 75.00 (*0-8109-4453-7*) Abrams.

Splendor of France. Universe Staff. 1995. pap. 40.00 (*0-7893-0012-5*) Universe.

Splendor of France: Chateaux, Mansions & Country Houses. Roberto Schezen & Laure Murat. LC 91-52882. 420p. 1991. 125.00 (*0-8478-1337-1*) Rizzoli Intl.

Splendor of His Majesty: Award Winning Poems Honoring God. Ed. by Jackson Wilcox. (Illus.). 28p. (Orig.). 1996. pap. 3.50 (*0-944231-20-9*) Slvr Wings CA.

Splendor of His Way. Stephen Kaung. Tr. by Lily Hsu from ENG. (CHI.). 1984. pap. write for info. (*0-941598-14-4*) Living Spring Pubns.

Splendor of His Ways. Stephen Kaung. Ed. by Herbert L. Fader. 171p. 1974. pap. 4.50 (*0-935008-43-8*) Christian Fellow Pubs.

Splendor of Islamic Calligraphy. expanded rev. ed. Abdelkebir Khatibi & Mohammed Sijelmassi. LC 95-78912. (Illus.). 240p. 1996. 65.00 (*0-500-01675-5*) Thames Hudson.

Splendor of Longing in the Tale of Genji. Norma Field. 304p. 1987. pap. text ed. 19.95 (*0-691-01436-1*) Princeton U Pr.

Splendor of Longing in the Tale of Genji. Norma Field. LC 86-21224. 393p. reprint ed. pap. 112.10 (*0-8357-3309-2*, 2039532) Bks Demand.

Splendor of Spain: A Serious Scientific Study of Grammar. Zelda Brooks & Santos J. Garcia. 1994. pap. text ed. write for info. (*0-07-008112-3*) McGraw.

Splendor of the Church. Henri De Lubac. LC 86-82080. 382p. 1986. pap. 16.95 (*0-89870-120-1*) Ignatius Pr.

Splendor of the Light. Reza Saberi. LC 90-70322. 264p. 1990. pap. 8.95 (*1-55523-341-4*) Winston-Derek.

Splendor of the Popes: Treasures from the Sistine Chapel & the Vatican Museums & Library. Robert P. Bergman & Eric M. Zafran. (Illus.). 50p. (Orig.). 1989. pap. text ed. 12.00 (*0-911886-37-0*) Walters Art.

Splendor of Truth: (Latin Title: Veritatis Splendor) Pope John Paul, II. 154p. (Orig.). 1993. pap. 3.95 (*0-8198-6964-3*) Pauline Bks.

Splendor of Truth & Health Care: Proceedings of the Fourteenth Workshop for Bishops, Dallas, Texas. Ed. by Russell E. Smith. LC 95-39696. 250p. 1995. pap. 19.95 (*0-935372-39-3*) Pope John Ctr.

Splendor of Turkish Weaving: An Exhibition of Silks & Carpets of the 13th-18th Centuries. Louise W. Mackie. (Illus.). 86p. 1973. 8.00 (*0-87405-002-2*) Textile Mus.

Splendor of Worship: Women's Fasts, Rituals, Stories & Art. Laxmi Tewari. LC 88-63584. (Illus.). 150p. (C). 29.00 (*0-913215-40-6*) Riverdale Co.

Splendor Sailed the Sound. George H. Foster & Peter C. Weiglin. (Illus.). 384p. 1989. 55.00 (*0-685-29059-X*); boxed 125.00 (*0-685-44856-8*) Potentials Group.

Splendor Solis. Salomin Trisimosin. Tr. by Joscelyn Godwin from GER. LC 90-47417. (Magnum Opus Hermetic Sourceworks Ser.: No. 8). (Illus.). 126p. (Orig.). 1991. 32.00 (*0-933999-91-7*); pap. 18.00 (*0-933999-92-5*) Phanes Pr.

Splendor Solis: A.D. 1582. Solomon Trismosin. (Illus.). 104p. 1976. 16.50 (*0-911662-57-X*) Yoga.

Splendora. Peter Webb et al. 1997. pap. 6.00 (*0-8222-1557-8*) Dramatists Play.

Splendora. Edward Swift. 264p. 1988. reprint ed. pap. 6.95 (*0-8216-2001-0*) Carol Pub Group.

***Splendors of Ancient Egypt.** William H. Peck. LC 97-19806. 1997. pap. write for info. (*0-89558-148-5*) Det Inst Arts.

Splendors of Imperial China: Treasures from the National Palace Museum, Taipei. Maxwell K. Hearn. LC 95-46590. (Illus.). 144p. 1996. 35.00 (*0-8478-1959-0*) Metro Mus Art.

Splendors of Imperial China: Treasures from the National Palace Museum, Taipei. Maxwell K. Hearn. LC 95-46590. 1996. pap. 29.95 (*0-87099-766-1*) Metro Mus Art.

Splendors of Istanbul: Houses & Palaces along the Bosporus. Chris Hellier. (Illus.). 228p. 1993. 75.00 (*1-55859-600-3*) Abbeville Pr.

Splendors of the American West: Thomas Moran's Art of the Grand Canyon & Yellowstone. Anne R. Morand et al. LC 90-1049. (Illus.). 96p. (Orig.). 1991. pap. 19.95 (*0-295-97085-5*) U of Wash Pr.

Splendors of the Past: Lost Cities of the Ancient World. LC 80-7827. (Illus.). 296p. 1981. 19.95 (*0-87044-358-5*) Natl Geog.

Splendors of the Seas: The Photographs of Norbert Wu. Norbert Wu. (Illus.). 256p. 1994. 60.00 (*0-88363-594-1*) H L Levin.

***Splendors of the Universe: A Guide to Photographing the Night Sky.** Terrence Dickinson & Jack Newton. (Illus.). 144p. 1997. 40.00 (*1-55209-141-4*) Firefly Bks Ltd.

Splendour Falla. Susanna Kearsley. 380p. 1996. mass mkt. 7.99 (*0-7704-2718-9*) Bantam.

Splendour Falls. Ed. by Erin E. Kelly. 1995. 5.99 (*1-56504-863-6*, 11400) White Wolf.

Splendour in the Sun. Angela Martell. (Rainbow Romances Ser.). 160p. 1993. 14.95 (*0-7090-4895-5*, Hale-Parkwest) Parkwest Pubns.

Splendour in the Sun. large type ed. Angela Martell. (Linford Romance Ser.). 272p. 1995. pap. 15.99 (*0-7089-7663-8*, Linford) Ulverscroft.

Splendour of Buddhism. A. C. Banerjee. (C). 1991. text ed. 12.75 (*0-685-50091-8*, Pub. by Munshiram Manoharial II) S Asia.

Splendour of Mathura Art & Museum. R. C. Sharma. (Perspectives in Indian Art & Archaeology Ser.: No. 1). (C). 1994. text ed. 50.00 (*81-246-0015-5*, Pub. by DK Pubs Dist II) S Asia.

Splendour of South India. S. Muthiah. (C). 1992. 20.00 (*81-85273-56-1*, Pub. by UBS Pubs Dist II) S Asia.

Splendour of Tipharet. 3rd rev. ed. Omraam M. Aivanhov. (Complete Works: Vol. 10). (Illus.). 319p. (Orig.). 1994. pap. 14.95 (*1-895978-05-X*, Pub. by Prosveta FR) Prosveta USA.

Splendours & Miseries: A Life of Sir Sacheverell Sitwell. Sarah H. Bradford. 1993. 35.00 (*0-374-26789-8*) FS&G.

***Splendours of an Islamic World.** Stierlin. Date not set. write for info. (*1-86064-219-5*) St Martin.

Splendours of Indian Dance. Mohan Kkokar. 102p. (C). 1988. 495.00 (*81-7002-002-6*, Pub. by Himalayan Bks II) St Mut.

Splices for Image Film - Dimensions & Operational Constraints: ANSI-AIIMI MS18-1992. Association for Information & Image Management Staff. 1992. pap. 33.00 (*0-89258-248-0*, MS18) Assn Inform & Image Mgmt.

Splicing Handbook. Barbara Merry. (Illus.). 112p. 1988. pap. text ed. 10.95 (*0-87742-952-9*) Intl Marine.

Splicing Handbook: Techniques for Modern & Traditional Ropes. Barbara Merry & John Darwin. 1988. pap. text ed. 10.95 (*0-07-156371-7*) McGraw.

Splicing of Optical Fibers. rev. ed. IGIC, Inc. Staff. (Fiber Optics Reprint Ser.: Vol. 17). (Illus.). 156p. 1994. pap. 75.00 (*1-56851-066-7*) Info Gatekeepers.

Splicing of Precast Prestressed Concrete Piles: Pt. 1-Review & Performance of Splices, Pt. 2-Tests & Analysis of Cement-Dowel Splice. (PCI Journal Reprints Ser.). 56p. 1974. pap. 18.00 (*0-686-40067-4*, JR149) P-PCI.

Splicing Wire & Fiber Rope. Raoul Graumont & John Hensel. LC 45-3379. (Illus.). 129p. 1945. pap. 7.95 (*0-87033-118-3*) Cornell Maritime.

Spline Functions & Multivariate Interpolations. B. D. Bojanov. (Mathematics & Its Applications Ser.). 292p. (C). 1993. lib. bdg. 155.50 (*0-7923-2229-0*) Kluwer Ac.

Spline Functions Basic Theory. rev. ed. Larry L. Schumaker. LC 92-19422. 570p. (C). 1993. reprint ed. lib. bdg. 86.50 (*0-89464-771-7*) Krieger.

Spline Models for Observational Data. Grace Wahba. LC 89-28687. (CBMS-NSF Regional Conference Ser.: No. 59). xii, 169p. 1990. pap. 29.00 (*0-89871-244-0*) Soc Indus-Appl Math.

Spline Smoothing & Nonparametric Regression. Eubank. (Statistics: Textbooks & Monographs: Vol. 90). 462p. 1987. 150.00 (*0-8247-7869-3*) Dekker.

Splines & Variational Methods. P. M. Prenter. 323p. 1989. pap. text ed. 57.95 (*0-471-50402-5*) Wiley.

Splint Woven Basketry. Robin T. Daugherty. LC 86-80913. (Illus.). 168p. 1986. pap. 17.95 (*0-934026-22-X*) Interweave.

***Splinter of the Mind's Eye.** Dark Horse Comics Staff. (Star Wars Ser.). (Illus.). 1997. pap. text ed. 14.95 (*1-56971-223-9*) Dark Horse Comics.

Splinter of the Mind's Eye. Alan Dean Foster. 1986. mass mkt. 5.99 (*0-345-32023-9*, Del Rey) Ballantine.

S

An Asterisk (*) at the beginning of an entry indicates that the title is appearing in BIP for the first time.

Splintered Classes: Politics & the Lower Middle Classes in Interwar Europe. Ed. by Rudy Koshar. LC 90-4867. 250p. (C). 1990. 39.95 (0-8419-1124-X); pap. 19.95 (0-8419-1243-2) Holmes & Meier.

Splintered Eye. Beth S. Patric. LC 87-12192. 1987. 15.95 (0-88282-031-1) New Horizon NJ.

Splintered Light: Logos & Language in Tolkien's World. Verlyn Flieger. LC 83-14204. 189p. reprint ed. 53.90 (0-685-15872-1, 2027542) Bks Demand.

Splintered Mirror: Chinese Poetry from the Democracy Movement. Tr. by Donald Finkel from CHI. 128p. 1991. 25.00 (0-86547-448-6, North Pt Pr); pap. 10.95 (0-86547-449-4, North Pt Pr) FS&G.

Splintered Party: National Liberalism in Hessen & the Reich, 1867-1918. Dan S. White. LC 75-23213. 332p. 1976. 34.50 (0-674-83320-1) HUP.

***Splintered Sisterhood: Gender & Class in the Campaign Against Woman Suffrage.** Susan E. Marshall. LC 96-43666. (Illus.). 320p. 1997. pap. 21.95 (0-299-15464-5) U of Wis Pr.

***Splintered Sisterhood: Gender & Class in the Campaign Against Woman Suffrage.** Susan E. Marshall. LC 96-43666. (Illus.). 320p. 1997. 55.00 (0-299-15460-2) U of Wis Pr.

***Splintered Soul: Shamanic Journeys to Heal the Inner Darkness.** Mary A. Clare. 272p. (Orig.). 1997. pap. 12.95 (1-57174-070-8) Hampton Roads Pub Co.

***Splintered Vision: An Investigation of U.S. Science & Mathematics Education.** Ed. by William H. Schmidt et al. 1997. pap. text ed. 49.00 (0-7923-4441-3); lib. bdg. 87.00 (0-7923-4440-5) Kluwer Ac.

Splintered Worlds: Fragmentation & the Ideal of Diversity in the Work of Emerson, Melville, Whitman, & Dickinson. Robert M. Greenberg. LC 93-7480. (C). 1993. text ed. 42.50 (1-55553-167-9) NE U Pr.

Splinters & Other Shortness Bids. Max Hardy. 94p. 1987. reprint ed. pap. 9.95 (0-89412-260-6, B-4) Aegean Park Pr.

Splinters from the Past: Discovering History in Old Houses. Alex D. Fowler. Ed. by Lucy Meyer & Anne Adams. (Illus.). 208p. 1984. 15.00 (0-910301-08-5) M C H S.

Splinters of a Nation: German Prisoners of War in Utah. Allan K. Powell. LC 89-4787. (Utah Centennial Ser.). (Illus.). 350p. (C). 1990. text ed. 25.00 (0-87480-330-6) U of Utah Pr.

Splinters of Bone. Tr. by B. M. Bennani. LC 74-25797. Orig. Title: Darweesh. 1974. 2.95 (0-912678-17-8, Greenfld Rev Pr) Greenfld Rev Lit.

Splinters on the Wind. Rodney E. Reinhart. (Illus.). 1985. 3.00 (0-931081-01-7) Operation DOME.

***Splish! Splash!** Joanne Barkan. (J). 1998. write for info. (0-679-89022-X) Random Bks Yng Read.

Splish Splash. Lizi Boyd. (J). 1995. 5.95 (0-8118-0346-5) Chronicle Bks.

Splish Splash. Bobby Darin & Jean Murray. (Sing-a-Song Storybooks Ser.). (Illus.). 24p. (J). 1993. 9.95 (0-7935-1841-5, 00183010) H Leonard.

Splish Splash. Joan B. Graham. LC 94-1237. (Illus.). 32p. (J). (ps-2). 1994. 13.95 (0-395-70128-7) Ticknor & Fields.

Splish, Splash! Yvonne Hooker. (Poke & Look Learning Ser.). (Illus.). (J). (ps-1). 1983. 6.95 (0-448-01454-8, G&D) Putnam Pub Group.

***Splish-Splash: Very First Picture Book.** (Illus.). 20p. (J). (ps). 1997. 3.95 (1-85967-505-0, Lorenz Bks) Anness Pub.

Splish, Splash: Water Fun for Kids. Penny Warner. LC 95-40973. (Illus.). 172p. (Orig.). (J). (ps-7). 1996. pap. 12.95 (1-55652-262-2) Chicago Review.

Splish Splash, Bang Crash! Karen Gundersheimer. LC 94-26354. (My First Busy Preschool Bks.). (Illus.). 24p. (J). (ps). 1995. 5.95 (0-590-48060-X, Cartwheel) Scholastic Inc.

***Splish, Splash, Splosh! A Book about Water.** Mick Manning & Brita G. Om. LC 97-16325. (Wonderwise). (J). 1997. write for info. (0-531-14488-7); pap. write for info. (0-531-15326-6) Watts.

Splish Splashy Day. Liza Alexander. (Golden Super Shape Bks.). (Illus.). 24p. (J). 1989. pap. 1.95 (0-307-10064-2, Golden Pr) Western Pub.

Split. Jim Gove & Edward Mycue. (Took Modern Poetry in English Ser.: No. 40). (Illus.). 28p. (Orig.). 1993. pap. 4.00 (1-879457-35-0) Norton Coker Pr.

Split & the Structure: Twenty-Eight Essays. Rudolf Arnheim. 197p. 1996. 40.00 (0-520-20477-8); pap. 14.95 (0-520-20478-6) U CA Pr.

Split at the Seams? Community, Continuity & Change after the 1984 Coal Dispute. David Waddington et al. 192p. 1990. 90.00 (0-335-09414-7, Open Univ Pr); pap. 32.00 (0-335-09413-9, Open Univ Pr) Taylor & Francis.

Split Britches: Lesbian Practice - Feminist Performance. Ed. by Case. LC 95-47164. 232p. (C). 1996. text ed. 59.95 (0-415-12765-3) Routledge.

Split Britches: Lesbian Practice - Feminist Performance. Ed. by Sue-Ellen Case. LC 95-47164. 232p. 1996. pap. 16.95 (0-415-12766-1) Routledge.

Split Cherry Tree. rev. ed. Jesse H. Stuart. LC 90-62198. (Jesse Stuart Foundation Monograph Ser.). 56p. (YA). (gr. 7 up). 1990. pap. 6.00 (0-945084-20-X) J Stuart Found.

Split Corporatism in Israel. Lev L. Grinberg. LC 90-45047. (SUNY Series in Israeli Studies). 202p. (C). 1991. text ed. 69.50 (0-7914-0705-5); pap. text ed. 24.95 (0-7914-0706-3) State U NY Pr.

***Split Decision.** 187p. (Orig.). 1997. pap. 11.95 (0-614-29849-0) Sterling Hse.

Split Decision. Gabrielle Charbonnet. (American Gold Gymnasts Ser.: No. 3). 144p. (J). (gr. 4-7). 1996. mass mkt. 3.50 (0-553-48298-X, Skylark BDD) BDD Bks Young Read.

Split Decision. John S. Meade. 90p. 1990. 10.95 (0-533-08644-2) Vantage.

***Split Decision.** Leonard Sharkey. 1997. pap. 11.95 (1-56315-047-6) Sterling Hse.

***Split down the Sides: On the Subject of Laughter.** R. D. Glasgow. 264p. 1996. 57.50 (0-7618-0550-8); pap. 32.50 (0-7618-0551-6) U Pr of Amer.

Split Ends. Jill E. Stevens. LC 81-65120. (Illus.). 1982. 9.50 (0-9605818-1-2); pap. 5.95 (0-9605818-0-4) John Alden Bks.

***Split Genes.** Chambon. Date not set. 1.20 (0-7167-9275-3) W H Freeman.

Split Heirs. Lawrence Watt-Evans & Esther Friesner. 320p. 1994. mass mkt. 4.99 (0-8125-2029-7) Tor Bks.

Split Horizon. Thomas Lux. LC 93-46333. 1995. pap. 9.95 (0-395-70097-3) HM.

Split Image. Ron Faust. LC 96-54156. 224p. 1997. 20.95 (0-312-86011-0) St Martin.

Split Image. Charles Winecoff. Date not set. pap. 6.99 (0-451-18641-9) NAL-Dutton.

***Split Image.** Charles Winecoff. 1997. pap. 14.95 (0-452-27839-2, Plume) NAL-Dutton.

Split Image: African Americans in the Mass Media. 2nd ed. Ed. by Jannette L. Dates & William Barlow. LC 92-47367. (C). 1993. 17.95 (0-88258-179-1) Howard U Pr.

Split Image: The Life of Anthony Perkins. Charles Winecoff. 496p. 1996. pap. 24.95 (0-525-94064-2, Dutton) NAL-Dutton.

Split Images. Elmore Leonard. 288p. 1983. mass mkt. 6.50 (0-380-63107-5) Avon.

Split in Two. Michael Daniels. 8.00 (0-89253-680-2) Ind-US Inc.

Split Infinity. Piers Anthony. 368p. 1987. mass mkt. 5.95 (0-345-35491-5, Del Rey) Ballantine.

***Split Just Right.** LC 96-45403. 1997. 14.89 (0-7868-2288-0) Hyprn Child.

***Split Just Right.** Adele Griffin. LC 96-45403. (J). 1997. 14.95 (0-7868-0347-9) Hyprn Child.

Split Level Christians. Vergie McIntyre. Ed. by M. L. Jones. LC 93-87007. 305p. (Orig.). 1994. pap. 9.95 (1-882270-16-9) Old Rugged Cross.

Split-Level Mind. June Shipley. Ed. by Carol Spelius. 88p. (Orig.). 1989. pap. 7.95 (0-941363-05-8) Lake Shore Pub.

Split Minds - Split Brains. Ed. by Jacques M. Quen. LC 86-12532. 224p. (C). 1986. text ed. 32.00 (0-8147-6951-9) NYU Pr.

Split-New Secondary French, Level 1. Bragger. (Miscellaneous/Catalogs Ser.). 1998. lab manual ed., wbk. ed., pap. 7.95 (0-8384-7393-8) Heinle & Heinle.

Split-New Secondary French Text B, Level 1. Bragger. (Miscellaneous/Catalogs Ser.). 1998. text ed. 34.95 (0-8384-7384-9) Heinle & Heinle.

Split Personality. rev. ed. Rusty T. Gooden, Jr. (Illus.). 100p. (C). write for info. (0-9624203-2-8) R Gooden.

Split Personality: After the Fact(s) Rusty T. Gooden, Jr. (Illus.). 250p. write for info. (0-9624203-1-X) R Gooden.

Split-Ply Twining. Virginia I. Harvey. LC 75-4651. (Threads in Action Monographs: No. 1). (Illus.). 44p. (YA). (gr. 7 up). 1976. pap. 7.95 (0-916658-32-5) Shuttle Craft.

***Split Rails.** Carl B. Holmberg. LC 96-53103. 68p. 1997. pap. 12.95 (0-7734-2711-2, Mellen Poetry Pr) E Mellen.

Split Rock see Split Rock Lighthouse

***Split Rock Influence.** Jeanne S. Richardson. LC 96-92827. (Illus.). 140p. (Orig.). 1996. pap. 12.95 (0-9632542-2-7) J S Richardson.

Split Rock Lighthouse. rev. ed. MHS Staff. LC 92-8341. (Minnesota Historic Sites Pamphlet Ser.: No. 15). Orig. Title: Split Rock. (Illus.). 32p. 1993. pap. 7.50 (0-87351-275-8) Minn Hist.

***Split Scene of Reading: Nietzsche/Derrida/Kafka/Bachmann.** Sabine I. Golz. LC 97-1333. (Philosophy & Literary Theory Ser.). 320p. (C). 1997. 60.00 (0-391-04038-3) Humanities.

Split Second. M. R. Meek. 1989. mass mkt. 3.50 (0-373-26035-0) Harlequin Bks.

***Split Second Choice: The Power of Attitude.** James L. Winner & George P. Thompson. LC 96-90824. (Illus.). xvi, 183p. (Orig.). (J). 1996. pap. 17.95 (0-9655042-0-4) Winners LA.

Split Second Decision Making: Winning Strategies for Business Managers. rev. ed. Burdette Hansen. Ed. by Dahk Knox & Josette Rice. (Illus.). 90p. (Orig.). 1992. pap. text ed. 9.95 (1-881116-13-1) Black Forest Pr.

Split Second Selling. Ed. by Joan Kennedy & Ralph Daddio. (Illus.). 145p. (Orig.). 1985. pap. 5.95 (0-9601920-2-6) Younique Pr.

Split Second Society. Thomas B. Cross. (Illus.). 200p. 1991. pap. 24.95 (0-685-34872-5) Smith Micro.

Split Seconds. Kevin Robinson. 208p. 1991. 18.95 (0-8027-5785-5) Walker & Co.

Split Self from Goethe to Broch. Peter B. Waldeck. LC 77-92576. 190p. 1979. 29.50 (0-8387-2214-8) Bucknell U Pr.

Split Self-Split Object: Understanding & Treating Borderline, Narcissistic, & Schizoid Disorders. Philip Manfield. LC 91-44052. 384p. 1992. 47.50 (0-87668-460-6) Aronson.

Split Ticket. H. L. Richardson. 256p. 1996. pap. 12.99 (0-8499-3933-X) Word Pub.

Splits. Jerome McDonough. (Illus.). 17p. (Orig.). 1996. pap. 3.25 (0-88680-422-1) I E Clark.

***Splitter.** George Liebermann. LC 97-65489. 150p. (Orig.). 1997. pap. 7.50 (0-9656987-0-X) Point Conception.

Splitting. Fay Weldon. 256p. 1997. pap. 12.00 (0-87113-636-8, Atlntc Mnthly) Grove-Atltic.

***Splitting: A Case of Female Masculinity.** Robert S. Stoller. 416p. 1997. 35.00 (0-300-07167-1); pap. 18.00 (0-300-06572-8) Yale U Pr.

***Splitting: Reading Group Guide.** Fay Weldon. 1997. pap. 12.00 (0-8021-3470-X) Grove-Atltic.

Splitting & Binding. Pattiann Rogers. LC 88-28065. (Wesleyan Poetry Ser.). 61p. 1989. pap. 11.95 (0-8195-1173-0, Wesleyan Univ Pr) U Pr of New Eng.

Splitting & Projective Identification. James Grotstein. LC 84-45724. 254p. 1993. pap. 30.00 (1-56821-090-6) Aronson.

Splitting Extrapolation Method. Lu Tao et al. LC 95-18449. (Series on Applied Mathematics: Vol. 7). 300p. 1995. text ed. 67.00 (981-02-2217-3) World Scientific Pub.

Splitting Firewood. David Tresemer. (Illus.). 160p. (Orig.). 1981. pap. 6.95 (0-938670-01-8) By Hand & Foot.

***Splitting Heirs.** Rick Hanson. 240p. 1997. 21.95 (1-57566-194-2, Knsington) Kensgtn Pub Corp.

***Splitting Image.** Marty Engle & Johnny R. Barnes, Jr. (Strange Matter Ser.: No. 25). 144p. (Orig.). (J). (gr. 4 up). 1997. pap. 3.99 (1-56714-081-5) Montage Bks.

Splitting in Topological Groups. Karl H. Hofmann & Paul S. Mostert. LC 52-42839. (Memoirs Ser.: No. 1/43). 82p. 1992. reprint ed. pap. 19.00 (0-8218-1243-2, MEMO/1/43) Am Math.

Splitting of Terms in Crystals. Hans A. Bethe. LC 58-2296. (Translated from Annals of Physics Ser.: Vol. 3). (Illus.). 73p. reprint ed. pap. 25.00 (0-317-09920-5, 2003370) Bks Demand.

Splitting the Difference: Compromise & Integrity in Ethics & Politics. Martin Benjamin. LC 89-39224. x, 198p. 1990. 22.50 (0-7006-0414-6); pap. 12.95 (0-7006-0455-3) U Pr of KS.

Splitting the Licks. Janet Davis. 1993. 9.95 (0-87166-913-7, 93998); audio 19.95 (1-56222-615-0, 93998C) Mel Bay.

***Splitting the Licks.** Janet Davis. 1993. 28.95 incl. audio (0-7866-0958-3, 93998P) Mel Bay.

Splitting the Middle: Political Alienation, Acquiescence, & Activism among America's Middle Lawyers. Cedric Herring. LC 89-16080. 159p. 1989. text ed. 45.00 (0-275-93321-0, C3321, Praeger Pubs) Greenwood.

Splitting the Mind: An Experimental Study of Normal Men see Influence of Intuition in the Acquisition of Skill

***Splitting Up.** 3rd ed. David Green. (Personal Finance Ser.). 1995. pap. 15.95 (0-7494-1517-7) Kogan Page Ltd.

Splosh. Levinson. 1996. bds. write for info. (0-15-201253-2) HarBrace.

SPM Hose Ancillary Equipment Guide. OCIMF Staff. (C). 1987. 100.00 (0-948691-54-9, Pub. by Witherby & Co UK) St Mut.

SPM Hose System Design Commentary. OCIMF Staff. 1993. 70.00 (1-85609-027-2, Pub. by Witherby & Co UK) St Mut.

Spock in a Salad Bowl. Jack Merwin. (Firelight Ser.). 64p. (Orig.). 1996. pap. 5.49 (1-885962-70-3) Lincoln Lrning.

Spock's World. Diane Duane. 1989. mass mkt. 5.99 (0-671-66773-4) PB.

Spohady Memoirs. Petro Grigorenko. Ed. by Michael Smyk. Tr. by Dmytro Kyslycia from RUS. LC 84-51852. Orig. Title: Ukranian. 751p. 1984. 30.00 (0-912601-01-9) Ukrainian News.

Spoil of Office. Hamlin Garland. 1988. reprint ed. lib. bdg. 75.00 (0-7812-1219-7) Rprt Serv.

Spoil of Office see Collected Works of Hamlin Garland

***Spoiled: The Dangerous Truth about a Foodchain Gone Haywire.** Nicols Fox. 1997. 24.00 (0-614-28008-7) Basic.

***Spoiled: What Is Happening to Our Food Supply & Why We Are Increasingly at Risk.** Nicols Fox. LC 97-1239. 256p. 1997. 23.00 (0-465-01980-3) Basic.

Spoiled Princess. Piet Wijn & Thom Roep. Tr. by Dwight R. Decker from DUT. (Danny Doodle Ser.). (Illus.). 48p. (Orig.). (J). (gr. 3-7). 1996. pap. 8.95 (1-887911-55-3) Fantsy Flight.

***Spoiled Rich Kids.** Jill R. Klevin. (J). Date not set. write for info. (0-399-21136-5) Putnam Pub Group.

***Spoiled Rotten.** (Barf-o-Rama Ser.). (J). 1997. write for info. (0-614-29174-7) BDD Bks Young Read.

***Spoiled Rotten.** Declement. (J). 1997. 13.89 (0-7868-2317-8) Hyprn Child.

Spoiled Rotten. Barthe DeClements. (Illus.). (J). (gr. 1-3). 1996. pap. 3.95 (0-7868-1145-5) Hyprn Child.

Spoiled Rotten. Fred G. Gosman. 224p. 1993. pap. 12.99 (0-446-39509-9) Warner Bks.

Spoiled Rotten: American Children & How to Change Them. Fred G. Gosman. 196p. 1990. 17.95 (0-9627419-0-6) Bashford & ONeill.

Spoiled System: A Call For Civil Service Reform. Robert G. Vaughn & Ralph Nader. 360p. 1975. 12.95 (0-686-36544-5) Ctr Responsive Law.

Spoilers. Rex E. Beach. LC 71-96874. (Illus.). 324p. reprint ed. lib. bdg. 9.25 (0-8398-0157-2) Irvington.

Spoilers of the Sea. John P. Cranwell. LC 78-93331. (Essay Index Reprint Ser.). 1977. 30.95 (0-8369-1563-1) Ayer.

***Spoiling Childhood: How Well Meaning Parents Are Giving Children Too Much - But Not What They Need.** Ed. by Diane Ehrensaft. 1997. lib. bdg. 18.95 (1-57230-211-9) Guilford Pubns.

Spoiling for a Fight: John S. Roberts & Early Nacogdoches (Texas) Joe E. Ericson & Carolyn R. Ericson. LC 86-82813. (Illus.). 250p. (YA). 1989. lib. bdg. 17.95 (0-911317-41-4) Ericson Bks.

Spoiling Python's Schemes. Bobbie J. Merck. 217p. (Orig.). (C). 1991. pap. text ed. 8.95 (0-929263-02-2) Great Love Church Intl.

Spoils of Famine: Ethiopian Famine Policy & Peasant Agriculture. Jason W. Clay et al. (Cultural Survival Reports: No. 25). 303p. 1988. 29.95 (0-939521-35-0); pap. 15.00 (0-939521-30-X) Cultural Survival.

Spoils of Freedom: Psychoanalysis, Feminism & Idealogy after the Fall of Socialism. Renata Salecl. LC 93-33919. (Opening Out: Feminism for Today Ser.). 192p. (C). (gr. 13). 1994. pap. 16.95 (0-415-07358-8, B2267); text ed. 59.95 (0-415-07357-X, A6558) Routledge.

Spoils of Poynton. Henry James. 1976. 20.95 (0-8488-0543-7) Amereon Ltd.

Spoils of Poynton. Henry James. Ed. by Bernard Richards. (World's Classics Ser.). 224p. (C). 1983. pap. 6.95 (0-19-281605-5) OUP.

Spoils of Poynton. Henry James. Ed. & Intro. by David Lodge. 256p. 1988. pap. 9.95 (0-14-043288-4, Penguin Classics) Viking Penguin.

Spoils of Poynton; A London Life; The Chaperon. Henry James. LC 78-158789. (Novels & Tales of Henry James Ser.: Vol. 10). xxi, 499p. 1976. reprint ed. 45.00 (0-678-02810-9) Kelley.

Spoils of War. Thomas Fleming. 640p. 1986. mass mkt. 4.50 (0-380-70065-4) Avon.

Spoils of War. Alan Dean Foster. (Military Science Fiction Promotion Ser.: Bk. 3). 304p. 1994. mass mkt. 5.99 (0-345-37576-9, Del Rey) Ballantine.

***Spoils of War: The Bright & Bitter Fruits of Human Conflict.** Ed. by Jurgen Kleist & Bruce Butterfield. (Plattsburgh Studies in the Humanities: No. 5). 240p. (C). 1997. text ed. 46.95 (0-8204-3387-X) P Lang Pubng.

***Spoils of War: The Loss, Reappearance & Recovery of Cultural Property.** Ed. by Elizabeth Simpson. LC 96-33258. (Illus.). 328p. 1997. 49.50 (0-8109-4469-3, Abradale Pr) Abrams.

***Spoils of War: Women of Color, Cultures, & Revolutions.** Ed. by T. Denean Sharpley-Whiting & Renee T. White. 208p. 1997. 57.50 (0-8476-8604-3) Rowman.

***Spoils of War: Women of Color, Cultures, & Revolutions.** Ed. by T. Denean Sharpley-Whiting & Renee T. White. 208p. 1997. pap. 22.95 (0-8476-8605-1) Rowman.

Spoils of World War II: The American Military's Role in Stealing Europe's Treasures. Kenneth D. Alford. LC 94-12608. 1994. 19.95 (1-55972-237-1, Birch Ln Pr) Carol Pub Group.

Spoils System in New York. LC 73-19191. (Politics & People Ser.). 187p. 1974. reprint ed. 19.95 (0-405-05900-0) Ayer.

Spoilt Children of Empire: Westerners in Shanghai & the Chinese Revolution of the 1920s. Nicholas R. Clifford. LC 90-50904. (Illus.). 384p. 1991. pap. 21.00 (0-87451-595-5) U Pr of New Eng.

Spoilt Kill. Mary Kelly. 240p. 1993. 18.50 (0-7451-8622-X, Black Dagger) Chivers N Amer.

Spoilt Kill. large type ed. Mary Kelly. 1990. 25.99 (0-7089-2223-6) Ulverscroft.

Spokane: A City for Living. Michael Schmeltzer. LC 96-31221. (Illus.). 104p. 1996. pap. 17.95 (1-56037-105-6) Am Wrld Geog.

Spokane: The Complete Guide to the Hub of the Inland Northwest. M. E. Buckham. LC 95-10103. (Illus.). 256p. (Orig.). 1995. pap. 14.95 (1-881409-13-9) Jhnstn Assocs.

Spokane & the Inland Empire: An Interior Pacific Northwest Anthology. Ed. by David H. Stratton. LC 90-22922. (Illus.). 194p. 1991. 25.00 (0-87422-072-6); pap. 17.95 (0-87422-079-3) Wash St U Pr.

Spokane Centennial Cookbook. Daniel J. Petek. (Illus.). 144p. (Orig.). 1988. pap. 6.95 (0-9615201-5-9) BCG Ltd.

Spokane Child Care Directory. Ed. by Linda Carlson & Donna Lee. 120p. (Orig.). 1988. pap. 5.95 (0-317-93133-4) Parents Info Network.

Spokane Falls Illustrated. Harry H. Hook & Francis J. Maguire. (Illus.). 62p. 1984. 5.95 (0-87770-305-1) Ye Galleon.

Spokane Indians: Children of the Sun. Robert H. Ruby & John A. Brown. LC 79-108797. (Civilization of the American Indian Ser.: Vol. 104). (Illus.). 346p. 1982. pap. 17.95 (0-8061-1757-5) U of Okla Pr.

Spokane Light Cookbook. Daniel J. Petek. (Illus.). 144p. (Orig.). 1987. pap. 5.95 (0-9615201-4-0) BCG Ltd.

Spokane Portland & Seattle. John R. Signor. LC 95-72014. (Illus.). 376p. 1997. 74.50 (0-915713-30-6) Pac Fast Mail.

Spokane Style Cookbook. Daniel J. Petek. (Illus.). 72p. (Orig.). 1985. pap. 4.95 (0-9615201-0-8) BCG Ltd.

Spokane Too! Cookbook. Daniel J. Petek. (Illus.). 120p. (Orig.). 1986. pap. 4.95 (0-9615201-3-2) BCG Ltd.

Spokane Valley Vol. I: A History of the Early Years. Compiled by Florence Boutwell. LC 95-79244. (Illus.). 194p. 1994. 27.50 (0-87062-234-X); pap. 17.50 (0-87062-235-8) A H Clark.

Spokane Valley Vol. II: A History of the Growing Years, 1921-1945. Florence Boutwell. LC 95-79244. (Illus.). 240p. 1995. 27.50 (0-87062-245-5) A H Clark.

Spokane Valley Vol. II: A History of the Growing Years, 1921-1945, Vol. II. Florence Boutwell. LC 95-79244. (Illus.). 240p. 1995. pap. 17.50 (0-87062-246-3) A H Clark.

***Spokane Valley Vol. III: Out in the Gravel - a Supplement.** Florence Boutwell. (Illus.). 112p. 1996. 25.00 (0-87062-269-2); pap. 15.00 (0-87062-268-4) A H Clark.

Spokane's Celebrity Chefs: The MS Cookbook. Patricia Dahmen-Ray et al. (Illus.). 118p. (Orig.). 1990. pap. 15.95 (0-9615201-7-5) BCG Ltd.

Spokane's Street Railways: An Illustrated History. Charles V. Mutschler & Wilmer H. Siegert. 208p. (Orig.). 1987. 30.00 (0-943181-01-1) IERHS.

Spoke. Hannah Weiner. LC 83-40580. 120p. (Orig.). 1984. pap. 6.95 (0-940650-26-6) Sun & Moon CA.

Spoken Albanian. Leonard D. Newmark et al. LC 79-56549. 348p. 1980. pap. 15.00 (0-87950-005-0); audio 75.00 (0-87950-007-7, AFAL10) Spoken Lang Serv.

Spoken Albanian. Leonard D. Newmark et al. LC 79-56549. 348p. 1980. pap. 90.00 (*0-87950-008-5*) Spoken Lang Serv.

Spoken Amharic, Bk. 1. Debebow Zelelie et al. 500p. (AMH.). 1980. pap. 190.00 incl. audio (*0-87950-654-7*) Spoken Lang Serv.

Spoken Amharic, Bk. 1, Units 1-50. Debebow Zelelie et al. 500p. (AMH.). 1980. pap. text ed. 45.00 (*0-87950-650-4*); audio 145.00 (*0-87950-652-0*) Spoken Lang Serv.

Spoken Amharic, Book 2, Units Fifty-One to Sixty. Debebow Zelelie et al. (Spoken Language Ser.). 500p. (AMH.). 1980. pap. text ed. 45.00 (*0-87950-651-2*); audio 65.00 (*0-87950-653-9*) Spoken Lang Serv.

Spoken Amharic, Book 2, Units Fifty-One to Sixty, Bk. 2. Debebow Zelelie et al. (Spoken Language Ser.). 500p. (AMH.). 1980. pap. 110.00 incl. digital audio (*0-87950-655-5*) Spoken Lang Serv.

Spoken Amharic, Book 2, Units Fifty-One to Sixty, Bks. 1 & 2. Debebow Zelelie et al. (Spoken Language Ser.). 500p. (AMH.). 1980. audio 300.00 (*0-87950-656-3*) Spoken Lang Serv.

Spoken Amoy Hokkien: Vocabulary Units 1-30. Nicholas C. Bodman. (Spoken Language Ser.). 630p. 1987. pap. text ed. 45.00 (*0-87950-450-1*); pap. text ed. 170.00 incl. audio (*0-87950-452-8*); audio 125.00 (*0-87950-451-X*) Spoken Lang Serv.

Spoken & Unspoken Thanks: Some Comparative Soundings. Ed. by John B. Carman. LC 88-71649. (Center for the Study of World Religions Ser.: No. 5). 170p. (Orig.). (C). 1989. 29.95 (*0-945454-00-7*, 03 00 05); pap. 19.95 (*0-945454-01-5*) Harvard U Wrld Relig.

***Spoken & Unspoken Thanks: Some Comparative Soundings.** John B. Carman & Frederick Streng. 170p. 1989. pap. 20.95 (*1-55540-282-8*) Scholars Pr GA.

Spoken & Written Hindi. fac. ed. Gordon H. Fairbanks & Bal G. Misra. LC 66-13345. 504p. 1966. reprint ed. pap. 143.70 (*0-608-01014-6*, 2061872) Bks Demand.

Spoken & Written Language. M. A. Halliday. (Language Education Ser.). 128p. 1989. pap. 14.95 (*0-19-437153-0*) OUP.

Spoken & Written Language. M. A. Halliday. 109p. (C). 1995. pap. 34.00 (*0-7300-0309-4*, ECS805, Pub. by Deakin Univ AT) St Mut.

Spoken & Written Language. Deborah Tannen. Ed. by Roy O. Freedle. LC 81-12865. (Advances in Discourse Processes Ser.: Vol. 9). 288p. (Orig.). (C). 1982. pap. 42.50 (*0-89391-099-6*) Ablex Pub.

Spoken & Written Language. Ed. by Deborah Tannen & Roy O. Freedle. LC 81-12865. (Advances in Discourse Processes Ser.: Vol. 9). 288p. (Orig.). (C). 1982. text ed. 78.50 (*0-89391-094-5*) Ablex Pub.

Spoken Arabic. rev. ed. Said Salah. 364p. 1991. pap. 14.95 incl. audio (*1-887584-04-8*) Intl Prom Art.

Spoken Arabic (Iraqi) Merrill Y. Van Wagoner. LC 75-11338. (Spoken Language Ser.). 294p. 1975. pap. 15.00 (*0-87950-010-7*); student ed., pap. 90.00 incl. audio (*0-87950-017-4*); audio 75.00 (*0-87950-016-6*) Spoken Lang Serv.

Spoken Arabic of Cairo. Maurice Salib. 1985. pap. 25.00 (*977-424-054-5*, Pub. by Am Univ Cairo Pr UA) Col U Pr.

Spoken Arabic of the Arabian Gulf. Librarie Du Liban. 1976. pap. 4.50 (*0-86685-042-2*) Intl Bk Ctr.

Spoken Arabic (Saudi) Merrill Y. Van Wagoner et al. LC 76-17389. (Spoken Language Ser.). 160p. 1979. pap. 15.00 (*0-87950-410-2*); student ed., pap. 90.00 incl. audio (*0-87950-412-9*); audio 75.00 (*0-87950-411-0*) Spoken Lang Serv.

Spoken Arabic-Self Taught. A. M. Ashiurakis. 118p. 1985. pap. 55.00 (*1-85077-090-5*, Pub. by Darf Pubs Ltd UK) St Mut.

Spoken Brockhaus, Germany Dictionary: Der Sprach Brockhaus: Deutsches Bildwoerterbuch von A-Z. 9th ed. Brockhaus. 972p. (GER.). 1984. 85.00 (*0-8288-1970-X*, M15507) Fr & Eur.

Spoken Bulgarian. Carleton T. Hodge. 493p. 1980. pap. text ed. 45.00 (*0-87950-658-X*); pap. text ed. 170.00 incl. audio (*0-87950-662-8*); audio 125.00 (*0-87950-660-1*) Spoken Lang Serv.

Spoken Burmese. William S. Cornyn. (Spoken Language Ser.). 165p. 1979. audio 75.00 (*0-87950-025-5*) Spoken Lang Serv.

Spoken Burmese, Bk. 1. William S. Cornyn. (Spoken Language Ser.). 165p. 1979. pap. 90.00 incl. audio (*0-87950-026-3*) Spoken Lang Serv.

Spoken Burmese, Bk. 1, Units 1-12. William S. Cornyn. (Spoken Language Ser.). 165p. 1979. pap. 15.00 (*0-87950-020-4*) Spoken Lang Serv.

Spoken Cambodian. F. E. Huffman. (Spoken Language Ser.). 464p. 1985. pap. 25.00 (*0-87950-471-4*); pap. 130.00 incl. audio (*0-87950-473-0*); audio 105.00 (*0-87950-472-2*) Spoken Lang Serv.

Spoken Cantonese, Bk I. Elisabeth L. Boyle & Pauline N. Delbridge. 410p. 1980. pap. 25.00 (*0-87950-675-X*); audio 105.00 (*0-87950-677-6*) Spoken Lang Serv.

Spoken Cantonese, Bk. I. Elisabeth L. Boyle & Pauline N. Delbridge. 410p. 1980. pap. 130.00 incl. audio (*0-87950-679-2*) Spoken Lang Serv.

Spoken Cantonese, Bk. 2. Elisabeth L. Boyle & Pauline N. Delbridge. 410p. 1980. pap. 140.00 incl. audio (*0-87950-680-6*) Spoken Lang Serv.

Spoken Cantonese, Bk. II. Elisabeth L. Boyle & Pauline N. Delbridge. 410p. 1980. pap. 35.00 (*0-87950-676-8*); audio 105.00 (*0-87950-678-4*) Spoken Lang Serv.

Spoken Cantonese, Bks. I & II. Elisabeth L. Boyle & Pauline N. Delbridge. 410p. 1980. pap. 270.00 incl. audio (*0-87950-681-4*) Spoken Lang Serv.

Spoken Cantonese: Context & Performance, Vol. 1. Xiaobin Jian. (Kaleidoscope Ser.). 1995. 175.00 incl. audio, vhs (*0-87415-265-8*, 113B) OSU Foreign Lang.

Spoken Cantonese: Performance & Acquisition. Matthew B. Christensen & Xiaobin Jian. (Kaleidoscope Ser.). (Illus.). (Orig.). 1995. 135.00 incl. audio, vhs (*0-87415-268-2*, 114B) OSU Foreign Lang.

Spoken Cantonese: Performance & Acquisition, Vol. 2. Matthew B. Christensen & Xiaobin Jian. (Kaleidoscope Ser.). (Illus.). 315p. (Orig.). 1995. pap. 35.00 (*0-87415-267-4*, 114E) OSU Foreign Lang.

Spoken Cantonese Vol. I: Context & Performance: Kaleidoscope. Xiaobin Jian. Ed. by Galal Walker. (Kaleidoscope Ser.). (Illus.). 320p. (Orig.). (C). 1994. student ed., pap. text ed. 35.00 (*0-87415-264-X*, 113E) OSU Foreign Lang.

Spoken Chamorro. 2nd ed. Donald M. Topping. LC 80-14596. (PALI Language Texts, Micronesia Ser.). 376p. (Orig.). 1980. pap. text ed. 16.00 (*0-8248-0417-1*) UH Pr.

Spoken Chinese. Charles F. Hockett. LC 76-767. (Spoken Language Ser.). 1976. audio 75.00 (*0-87950-036-0*) Spoken Lang Serv.

Spoken Chinese, Bk. 1. Charles F. Hockett. LC 76-767. (Spoken Language Ser.). 1976. pap. 90.00 incl. audio (*0-87950-037-9*) Spoken Lang Serv.

Spoken Chinese, Bk. 1, Units 1-12. Charles F. Hockett. LC 76-767. (Spoken Language Ser.). 268p. 1976. pap. 15.00 (*0-87950-031-X*) Spoken Lang Serv.

Spoken Chinese, Bk. 2, Units 13-30. Charles F. Hockett. LC 76-767. (Spoken Language Ser.). 393p. 1976. pap. 20.00 (*0-87950-032-8*) Spoken Lang Serv.

***Spoken Czech: Czech Fast Course.** Radovan Pletka. (Spoken Language Ser.). 250p. (Orig.). 1995. pap. text ed. 30.00 (*0-87950-630-X*) Spoken Lang Serv.

***Spoken Czech: Czech Fast Course.** Radovan Pletka. 1995. pap. 135.00 incl. audio (*0-87950-632-6*) Spoken Lang Serv.

Spoken Danish. Jeannette Dearden & Karin Stig-Nielsen. audio 75.00 (*0-87950-050-6*) Spoken Lang Serv.

Spoken Danish, Bk. I. Jeannette Dearden & Karin Stig-Nielsen. pap. 90.00 (*0-87950-051-4*) Spoken Lang Serv.

Spoken Danish, Bk. I, Units 1-12. Jeannette Dearden & Karin Stig-Nielsen. 341p. pap. 15.00 (*0-87950-044-1*) Spoken Lang Serv.

Spoken Danish, Bk. II, Units 13-30. Jeannette Dearden & Karin Stig-Nielsen. 567p. pap. 20.00 (*0-87950-045-X*) Spoken Lang Serv.

***Spoken Discourse: A Model for Analysis.** Willis Edmondson. LC 80-41190. (Longman Linguistics Library: Vol. 27). 227p. 1981. reprint ed. pap. 64.70 (*0-608-03583-1*, 2064406) Bks Demand.

Spoken Dutch. Leonard Bloomfield. LC 75-15107. (Spoken Language Ser.). 266p. 1975. pap. 15.00 (*0-87950-054-9*); student ed., pap. 90.00 incl. audio (*0-87950-061-1*); audio 75.00 (*0-87950-060-3*) Spoken Lang Serv.

Spoken East Armenian. Gordon H. Fairbanks & Earl W. Stevick. LC 75-15932. (Spoken Language Ser.). 428p. (C). 1975. reprint ed. pap. 20.00 (*0-87950-420-X*); reprint ed. audio 75.00 (*0-87950-421-8*) Spoken Lang Serv.

Spoken East Armenian. Gordon H. Fairbanks & Earl W. Stevick. LC 75-15932. (Spoken Language Ser.). 428p. (C). 1975. reprint ed. student ed., pap. 95.00 incl. audio (*0-87950-422-6*) Spoken Lang Serv.

Spoken English: A Practical Guide. Christine Cheepen & James Monaghan. 240p. 1990. text ed. 49.00 (*0-685-61124-8*) St Martin.

Spoken English: A Practical Guide. Christine Cheepen & James Monaghan. 224p. 1992. pap. text ed. 14.95 (*0-86187-754-3*) St Martin.

Spoken English As a Foreign Language. William E. Welmers. 31p. 1979. reprint ed. pap. 2.50 (*0-87950-289-4*) Spoken Lang Serv.

Spoken English Illuminated. Wilkinson et al. 1990. 27.00 (*0-335-09349-3*, Open Univ Pr) Taylor & Francis.

Spoken Fijian: An Intensive Course in Bauan Fijian, with Grammatical Notes & Glossary. Albert J. Schutz & Rusiate T. Komaitai. LC 76-157881. (PALI Language Texts: Melanesia Ser.). 304p. reprint ed. pap. 86.70 (*0-317-58205-4*, 2029724) Bks Demand.

Spoken Finnish. Thomas A. Sebeok. LC 74-164345. (Spoken Language Ser.). 502p. 1977. pap. 70.00 incl. audio (*0-87950-076-X*); audio 55.00 (*0-87950-075-1*) Spoken Lang Serv.

Spoken Finnish, Units 1-30. Thomas A. Sebeok. LC 74-164345. (Spoken Language Ser.). 502p. 1977. pap. 15.00 (*0-87950-070-0*) Spoken Lang Serv.

Spoken French. Francois Denoeu & R. A. Hall, Jr. LC 74-152740. (Spoken Language Ser.). 230p. 1973. pap. 90.00 incl. audio (*0-87950-086-7*); audio 75.00 (*0-87950-085-9*) Spoken Lang Serv.

Spoken French, Units 1-12. Francois Denoeu & R. A. Hall, Jr. LC 74-152740. (Spoken Language Ser.). 230p. 1973. pap. 15.00 (*0-87950-080-8*) Spoken Lang Serv.

Spoken French for Students & Travelers. 2nd ed. Bernard F. Uzan et al. 277p. (FRE.). (C). 1978. pap. text ed. 26.36 (*0-669-00878-8*) HM College Div.

Spoken German. William G. Moulton & Jenni K. Moulton. LC 76-416. (Spoken Language Ser.). 290p. 1971. pap. 90.00 incl. audio (*0-87950-097-2*); audio 75.00 (*0-87950-096-4*) Spoken Lang Serv.

Spoken German, Units 1-12. William G. Moulton & Jenni K. Moulton. LC 76-416. (Spoken Language Ser.). 290p. 1971. pap. 15.00 (*0-87950-091-3*) Spoken Lang Serv.

Spoken German for Students & Travelers. Renate Hiller. 274p. (ENG & GER.). (C). 1980. pap. text ed. 27.56 (*0-669-03022-8*) HM College Div.

Spoken Greek. Henry Kahane et al. LC 74-150404. (Spoken Language Ser.). 1976. audio 75.00 (*0-87950-105-7*) Spoken Lang Serv.

Spoken Greek. Henry Kahanes et al. LC 74-150404. (Spoken Language Ser.). 1976. pap. 90.00 incl. audio (*0-87950-106-5*) Spoken Lang Serv.

Spoken Greek. rev. ed. Evris Tsakirides. (Illus.). 200p. (C). 1992. text ed. 37.50 (*0-472-09488-2*); pap. text ed. 21.95 (*0-472-06488-6*) U of Mich Pr.

Spoken Greek, Units 1-12. Henry Kahane et al. LC 74-150404. (Spoken Language Ser.). 305p. 1976. pap. 15.00 (*0-87950-100-6*) Spoken Lang Serv.

Spoken Hausa. J. Ronayne Cowan & Russell G. Schuh. LC 75-15184. (Spoken Language Ser.). 350p. 1976. pap. text ed. 15.00 (*0-87950-401-3*); pap. text ed. 90.00 incl. audio (*0-87950-403-X*); audio 75.00 (*0-87950-402-1*); audio 105.00 (*0-87950-404-8*) Spoken Lang Serv.

Spoken Hawaiian. Samuel H. Elbert. LC 77-98134. (Illus.). 266p. (Orig.). 1970. pap. text ed. 15.00 (*0-87022-216-3*) UH Pr.

Spoken Heart: Poetry & Prose by Nathan Vern Herman. Nathan V. Herman. 70p. (Orig.). 1995. pap. write for info. (*1-57502-015-7*) Morris Pub.

Spoken Hindustani. Henry Hoenigswald. LC 74-175966. (Spoken Language Ser.). 270p. (gr. 9-12). 1976. audio 75.00 (*0-87950-115-4*) Spoken Lang Serv.

Spoken Hindustani. Henry Hoenigswald. LC 74-175966. (Spoken Language Ser.). 270p. (YA). (gr. 9-12). 1976. pap. 90.00 incl. audio (*0-87950-116-2*) Spoken Lang Serv.

Spoken Hindustani, Bk. 1, Units 1-12. Henry Hoenigswald. LC 74-175966. (Spoken Language Ser.). 270p. (gr. 9 up). 1971. pap. 15.00 (*0-87950-110-3*) Spoken Lang Serv.

Spoken Hungarian. Thomas A. Sebeok. LC 74-176085. (Spoken Language Ser.). 230p. (gr. 9-12). 1983. reprint ed. audio 75.00 (*0-87950-126-X*) Spoken Lang Serv.

Spoken Hungarian. Thomas A. Sebeok. LC 74-176085. (Spoken Language Ser.). 230p. (YA). (gr. 9-12). 1983. reprint ed. pap. 90.00 incl. audio (*0-87950-127-8*) Spoken Lang Serv.

Spoken Hungarian, Units 1-12. Thomas A. Sebeok. LC 74-176085. (Spoken Language Ser.). 230p. (gr. 9-12). 1983. reprint ed. pap. 15.00 (*0-87950-120-0*) Spoken Lang Serv.

***Spoken in Darkness.** Ann Imbrie. 262p. 3.98 (*0-8317-6933-5*) Smithmark.

Spoken in Darkness: A Friendship Remembered, a Life Reclaimed, & the Anatomy of a Small-Town Murder. Ann E. Imbrie. LC 93-47325. 272p. 1994. pap. 10.95 (*0-452-27217-3*, Plume) NAL-Dutton.

Spoken in Jest. Ed. by Gillian Bennett. 305p. 1991. 42.50 (*1-85075-257-5*, Pub. by Sheffield Acad UK) CUP Services.

Spoken Korean. Fred Lukoff. LC 73-17223. (Spoken Language Ser.). 370p. (gr. 9-12). 1975. audio 75.00 (*0-87950-155-3*) Spoken Lang Serv.

Spoken Korean, Bk. 1. Fred Lukoff. LC 73-17223. (Spoken Language Ser.). 370p. (gr. 9-12). 1975. pap. 90.00 incl. audio (*0-87950-156-1*) Spoken Lang Serv.

Spoken Korean, Bk, 1, Units 1-12. Fred Lukoff. LC 73-17223. (Spoken Language Ser.). 370p. (gr. 9-12). 1975. pap. 15.00 (*0-87950-150-2*) Spoken Lang Serv.

Spoken Korean, Bk. 2, Units 13-30. Fred Lukoff. LC 73-17223. (Spoken Language Ser.). 305p. (gr. 9-12). 1975. pap. 20.00 (*0-87950-151-0*) Spoken Lang Serv.

Spoken Language Comprehension: An Experimental Approach to Disordered & Normal Processing. Lorraine K. Tyler. (Bradford Bks.). (Illus.). 288p. 1992. 44.00 (*0-262-20088-0*) MIT Pr.

Spoken Language Systems Technology (SL'96) Ed. by ARPA Staff. 300p. (Orig.). 1996. pap. 50.00 (*1-55860-422-7*) Morgan Kaufmann.

Spoken-Language Technology: Proceedings of the 1994 Conference. ARPA Staff. 153p. 1995. pap. 40.00 (*1-55860-358-1*) Morgan Kaufmann.

Spoken-Language Technology: Proceedings of the 1995 Conference. ARPA Staff. 305p. 1995. pap. 50.00 (*1-55860-374-3*) Morgan Kaufmann.

Spoken Language Tests see Language Classroom

Spoken Malay. Isidore Dyen. Incl. Units 1-12: . LC 74-176207. v, 192p. 1974. pap. 15.00 (*0-87950-160-X*); Cassettes, Six Dual Track. LC 74-176207. 1974. 75.00 (*0-87950-165-0*); Cassette Course - Bk. 1 & Cassettes. LC 74-176207. 1974. pap. 90.00 (*0-87950-166-9*); LC 74-176207. (Spoken Language Ser.). (C). 1974. Set pap. (*0-685-04718-0*) Spoken Lang Serv.

Spoken Marshallese: An Intensive Language Course with Grammatical Notes & Glossary. Byron W. Bender. (PALI Language Texts, Micronesia Ser.). 464p. (Orig.). 1978. pap. text ed. 17.00 (*0-87022-070-5*) UH Pr.

Spoken Ministry among Friends: Three Centuries of Progress & Development. Seth B. Hinshaw. (Illus.). 160p. (Orig.). 1987. pap. 7.50 (*0-942585-14-3*) NC Frnds Hist Soc.

Spoken Modern Hebrew. Joseph A. Reif & Hanna Levinson. (Spoken Language Ser.). 590p. 1980. pap. 30.00 (*0-87950-683-0*); pap. 220.00 incl. audio (*0-87950-685-7*); audio 190.00 (*0-87950-684-9*) Spoken Lang Serv.

Spoken Modern Italian. Robert A. Hall, Jr. LC 75-312677. (Spoken Language Ser.). xiv, 428p. 1974. reprint ed. pap. 20.00 (*0-87950-320-3*); reprint ed. student ed., pap. 100.00 incl. audio (*0-87950-322-X*); reprint ed. audio 80.00 (*0-87950-321-1*) Spoken Lang Serv.

Spoken Natural Language Dialog Systems: A Practical Approach. Ronnie Smith & Richard Hipp. (Illus.). 304p. 1995. text ed. 60.00 (*0-19-509187-6*) OUP.

Spoken Norwegian. Einar Haugen. LC 75-15152. (Spoken Language Ser.). 312p. (gr. 9-12). 1976. audio 75.00 (*0-87950-175-8*) Spoken Lang Serv.

Spoken Norwegian. 3rd ed. Einar Haugen & Kenneth Chapman. 450p. (C). 1982. text ed. 45.25 (*0-03-060013-8*) HB Coll Pubs.

Spoken Norwegian, Bk. 1. Einar Haugen. LC 75-15152. (Spoken Language Ser.). 312p. (gr. 9-12). 1976. pap. 90.00 incl. audio (*0-87950-176-6*) Spoken Lang Serv.

Spoken Norwegian, Bk. 1, Units 1-12. Einar Haugen. LC 75-15152. (Spoken Language Ser.). 312p. (gr. 9-12). 1976. pap. 15.00 (*0-87950-170-7*) Spoken Lang Serv.

Spoken Norwegian, Bk. 2, Units 13-30. Einar Haugen. LC 75-15152. (Spoken Language Ser.). 312p. (gr. 9-12). 1978. pap. 20.00 (*0-87950-171-5*) Spoken Lang Serv.

Spoken Pangasinan. Richard A. Benton. LC 79-152457. (University of Hawaii, Honolulu. Pacific & Asian Linguistics Institute Ser.). 729p. reprint ed. pap. 180.00 (*0-317-10118-8*, 2017214) Bks Demand.

Spoken Persian. Serge Obolinsky. Ed. by Kambiz Y. Panah & Fereidoun K. Nouri. Incl. Book, Units 1-12. LC 73-15155. 401p. 1973. pap. 20.00 (*0-87950-295-9*); Cassettes, Five Dual Track. LC 73-15155. 1973. audio 100.00 (*0-87950-297-5*); Cassette Course, Bk. & Cassettes. LC 73-15155. 1973. pap. 120.00 incl. audio (*0-87950-299-1*); LC 73-15155. (Spoken Language Ser.). (C). 1973. (*0-318-55757-6*) Spoken Lang Serv.

Spoken Polish. Alexander M. Schenker. (Spoken Language Ser.). 487p. 1981. pap. 35.00 (*0-87950-040-9*); pap. 165.00 incl. audio (*0-87950-042-5*); audio 130.00 (*0-87950-041-7*) Spoken Lang Serv.

Spoken Portuguese, Bk. I. Margarida F. Reno et al. (ENG & POR.). 1978. pap. 90.00 incl. audio (*0-87950-186-3*); audio 75.00 (*0-87950-185-5*) Spoken Lang Serv.

Spoken Portuguese, Bk. I, Units 1-12. Margarida F. Reno et al. 218p. (ENG & POR.). 1978. Bk. I, units 1-12, 218 p. 15.00 (*0-87950-180-4*) Spoken Lang Serv.

Spoken Portuguese, Bk. II, Units 13-30. Margarida F. Reno et al. 307p. (ENG & POR.). 1978. Bk. II, units 13-30, 307 p. 15.00 (*0-87950-181-2*) Spoken Lang Serv.

Spoken Romanian. F. B Agard. LC 74-1000. (Spoken Language Ser.). 342p. (gr. 9-12). 1976. audio 75.00 (*0-87950-317-3*) Spoken Lang Serv.

Spoken Romanian. F. B Agard. LC 74-1000. (Spoken Language Ser.). 342p. (YA). (gr. 9-12). 1976. pap. 95.00 incl. audio (*0-87950-314-9*) Spoken Lang Serv.

Spoken Romanian, Units 1-30. F. B Agard. LC 74-1000. (Spoken Language Ser.). 342p. (gr. 9-12). 1976. pap. 20.00 (*0-87950-315-7*) Spoken Lang Serv.

Spoken Russian. Leonard Bloomfield et al. audio 75.00 (*0-87950-196-0*); audio 115.00 (*0-87950-200-2*); audio 110.00 (*0-87950-201-0*) Spoken Lang Serv.

Spoken Russian, Bk. I. Leonard Bloomfield et al. pap. 95.00 incl. audio (*0-87950-197-9*) Spoken Lang Serv.

Spoken Russian, Bk. I, Units 1-12. Leonard Bloomfield et al. 481p. 20.00 (*0-87950-190-1*) Spoken Lang Serv.

Spoken Russian, Bk. II, Units 13-30. Leonard Bloomfield et al. 398p. 20.00 (*0-87950-191-X*) Spoken Lang Serv.

Spoken Russian, Bk. IE. Leonard Bloomfield et al. pap. 135.00 incl. audio (*0-87950-202-9*) Spoken Lang Serv.

Spoken Russian, Bk. IIE. Leonard Bloomfield et al. pap. 130.00 incl. audio (*0-87950-203-7*) Spoken Lang Serv.

Spoken Russian, Bks. I & II. Leonard Bloomfield et al. pap. 265.00 incl. audio (*0-87950-204-5*) Spoken Lang Serv.

Spoken Seen: Film & the Romantic Imagination. Frank D. McConnell. LC 75-11342. 214p. reprint ed. pap. 61.00 (*0-317-42067-4*, 2025886) Bks Demand.

Spoken Serbo-Croatian. Carleton T. Hodge. LC 74-150403. (Spoken Language Ser.). 276p. (gr. 9 up). 1973. audio 75.00 (*0-87950-215-0*) Spoken Lang Serv.

Spoken Serbo-Croatian, Bk. 1. Carleton T. Hodge. LC 74-150403. (Spoken Language Ser.). 276p. (gr. 9 up). 1973. pap. 90.00 incl. audio (*0-87950-216-9*) Spoken Lang Serv.

Spoken Serbo-Croatian, Bk. 1, Units 1-12. Carleton T. Hodge. LC 74-150403. (Spoken Language Ser.). 276p. (gr. 9-12). 1973. pap. 15.00 (*0-87950-210-X*) Spoken Lang Serv.

Spoken Serbo-Croatian, Bk. 2, Units 13-30. Carleton T. Hodge. LC 74-150403. (Spoken Language Ser.). 432p. (gr. 9-12). 1973. pap. 15.00 (*0-87950-211-8*) Spoken Lang Serv.

Spoken Sinhalese. G. H. Fairbanks et al. (Spoken Language Ser.). 1979. audio 135.00 (*0-87950-441-2*); audio 115.00 (*0-87950-443-9*) Spoken Lang Serv.

Spoken Sinhalese, Bk. I, Lessons 1-24. G. H. Fairbanks et al. (Spoken Language Ser.). 415p. 1979. pap. 25.00 (*0-87950-440-4*) Spoken Lang Serv.

Spoken Sinhalese, Bk. II, Lessons 25-36. G. H. Fairbanks et al. (Spoken Language Ser.). 260p. 1979. Bk. II Lessons 25-36, 260 p. pap. 25.00 (*0-87950-442-0*) Spoken Lang Serv.

Spoken Sinhalese, Bks. I, II & Cassettes I, II. G. H. Fairbanks et al. (Spoken Language Ser.). 1980. pap. 300.00 incl. audio (*0-87950-446-3*) Spoken Lang Serv.

Spoken Sinhalese, Set. G. H. Fairbanks et al. (Spoken Language Ser.). 1980. pap. 160.00 incl. audio (*0-87950-444-7*); pap. 140.00 incl. audio (*0-87950-445-5*) Spoken Lang Serv.

Spoken Spanish. S. N. Trevino. LC 75-15933. (Spoken Language Ser.). 1975. student ed., pap. 90.00 incl. audio (*0-87950-226-6*); audio 75.00 (*0-87950-225-8*) Spoken Lang Serv.

Spoken Spanish, Units 1-12. S. N. Trevino. LC 75-15933. (Spoken Language Ser.). 276p. 1975. pap. 15.00 (*0-87950-220-7*) Spoken Lang Serv.

Spoken Standard Chinese, Vol. 1. Hugh M. Stimson & Huang P. Po-Fei. 1976. 17.95 (*0-88710-107-0*); audio 81.95 (*0-88710-108-9*) Yale Far Eastern Pubns.

Spoken Standard Chinese, Vol. 2. Hugh M. Stimson & Huang P. Po-Fei. 1976. 17.95 (*0-88710-110-0*); audio 89.95 (*0-88710-111-9*) Yale Far Eastern Pubns.

Spoken Standard Chinese Workbook, Vol. I. Lu V. Wong-Quincey & Hugh M. Stimson. (Standard Chinese Ser.). 136p. (CHI.). 1982. 14.95 (*0-88710-109-7*) Yale Far Eastern Pubns.

S

S

Spoken Standard Chinese Workbook, Vol. II. Lu V. Wong-Quincey & Hugh M. Stimson. (Standard Chinese Ser.). 114p. 1982. 14.95 (*0-88710-112-7*) Yale Far Eastern Pubns.

Spoken Swahili. Anthony J. Vitale. LC 79-92846. 310p. 1979. Bk. & Cassettes. pap. 90.00 incl. audio (*0-87950-365-3*); pap. 15.00 (*0-87950-363-7*); audio 75.00 (*0-87950-364-5*) Spoken Lang Serv.

Spoken Swedish. Fritz Frauchiger & William R. Van Buskirk. 261p. 1980. pap. text ed. 15.00 (*0-87950-704-7*); pap. text ed. 160.00 incl. audio (*0-87950-706-3*); audio 145.00 (*0-87950-705-5*) Spoken Lang Serv.

Spoken Tagalog. J. Donald Bowen. LC 65-25321. (Spoken Language Ser.). 551p. (Orig.). (C). 1982. pap. 135.00 incl. audio (*0-87950-407-2*); pap. text ed. 40.00 (*0-87950-465-X*) Spoken Lang Serv.

Spoken Tagalog, Bks. I & II. J. Donald Bowen. LC 65-25321. (Spoken Language Ser.). 551p. (Orig.). (C). 1982. Book & Cassette I & II. pap. 245.00 incl. audio (*0-87950-469-2*) Spoken Lang Serv.

Spoken Tagalog, No. I, Units 1-12. J. Donald Bowen. LC 65-25321. (Spoken Language Ser.). 551p. (Orig.). (C). 1982. Cassettes I, Units 1-12. audio 95.00 (*0-87950-466-8*) Spoken Lang Serv.

Spoken Tagalog, No. II, Exercise Tests. J. Donald Bowen. LC 65-25321. (Spoken Language Ser.). 551p. (Orig.). (C). 1982. Cassettes II, Exercise Tests. audio 110.00 (*0-87950-468-4*) Spoken Lang Serv.

Spoken Taiwanese. Nicholas C. Bodman & Wu Su-Chu. (Spoken Language Ser.). 208p. (CHI.). 1980. pap. 15.00 (*0-87950-460-9*); pap. 120.00 incl. audio (*0-87950-462-5*); audio 105.00 (*0-87950-461-7*) Spoken Lang Serv.

***Spoken Tear: The Story of Ivan.** Muntaha A. Hannawa. LC 96-70674. 136p. 1997. 16.95 (*1-882792-35-1*) Proctor Pubns.

Spoken Telugu. Leigh Lisker. LC 63-12992. (Spoken Language Ser.). xxvii, 345p. (gr. 9-12). 1976. audio 100.00 (*0-87950-377-7*) Spoken Lang Serv.

Spoken Telugu. Leigh Lisker. LC 63-12992. (Spoken Language Ser.). xxvii, 345p. (YA). (gr. 9-12). 1976. pap. 120.00 incl. audio (*0-87950-378-5*) Spoken Lang Serv.

Spoken Telugu. Leigh Lisker. LC 63-12992. (Spoken Language Ser.). xxvii, 345p. (YA). (gr. 9-12). 1976. audio 55.00 (*0-87950-379-3*) Spoken Lang Serv.

Spoken Telugu, Bk. 1, Units 1-30. Leigh Lisker. LC 63-12992. (Spoken Language Ser.). xxvii, 345p. (gr. 9-12). 1976. pap. 20.00 (*0-87950-376-9*) Spoken Lang Serv.

Spoken Text. Alison Knowles. 152p. 1993. 40.00 (*1-880516-11-X*); pap. 18.00 (*1-880516-09-8*) Left Hand Bks.

Spoken Thai. Mary R. Haas & Heng R. Subhanka. LC 74-166349. (Spoken Language Ser.). 307p. (gr. 9-12). 1978. pap. 15.00 (*0-87950-229-0*); audio 75.00 (*0-87950-235-5*) Spoken Lang Serv.

Spoken Thai. Mary R. Haas & Heng R. Subhanka. LC 74-166349. (Spoken Language Ser.). 307p. (YA). (gr. 9-12). 1978. pap. 90.00 incl. audio (*0-87950-236-3*) Spoken Lang Serv.

Spoken Thai, Bk. 2. Mary R. Haas & Heng R. Subhanka. LC 74-166349. (Spoken Language Ser.). 410p. (gr. 9-12). 1978. pap. 20.00 (*0-87950-230-4*) Spoken Lang Serv.

Spoken Turkish. Norman A. McQuown. LC 74-152747. (Spoken Language Ser.). 378p. (gr. 9-12). 1971. audio 75.00 (*0-87950-245-2*) Spoken Lang Serv.

Spoken Turkish, Bk. 1. Norman A. McQuown. LC 74-152747. (Spoken Language Ser.). 378p. (gr. 9-12). 1971. pap. 95.00 incl. audio (*0-87950-246-0*) Spoken Lang Serv.

Spoken Turkish, Bk. 1, Units 1-12. Norman A. McQuown. LC 74-152747. (Spoken Language Ser.). 378p. (gr. 9-12). 1971. pap. 20.00 (*0-87950-240-1*) Spoken Lang Serv.

Spoken Turkish, Bk. 2, Units 13-30. Norman A. McQuown. LC 74-152747. (Spoken Language Ser.). 378p. (gr. 9-12). 1971. pap. 20.00 (*0-87950-241-X*) Spoken Lang Serv.

Spoken Urdu. Muhammad A. Barker. LC 75-15183. (Spoken Language Ser.). 530p. (YA). (gr. 9-12). 1975. audio 100.00 (*0-87950-344-0*); audio 85.00 (*0-87950-345-9*) Spoken Lang Serv.

Spoken Urdu, Bk. 1. Muhammad A. Barker. LC 75-15183. (Spoken Language Ser.). 530p. (YA). (gr. 9-12). 1975. pap. 20.00 (*0-87950-340-8*); pap. 120.00 incl. audio (*0-87950-347-5*) Spoken Lang Serv.

Spoken Urdu, Bk. 2. Muhammad A. Barker. LC 75-15183. (Spoken Language Ser.). 576p. (YA). (gr. 9-12). 1975. pap. 20.00 (*0-87950-341-6*); pap. 105.00 incl. audio (*0-87950-348-3*) Spoken Lang Serv.

Spoken Urdu, Bk. 3. Muhammad A. Barker. LC 75-15183. (Spoken Language Ser.). 230p. (YA). (gr. 9-12). 1975. pap. 10.00 (*0-87950-342-4*) Spoken Lang Serv.

Spoken Urdu, Bks. 1 & 2. Muhammad A. Barker. LC 75-15183. (Spoken Language Ser.). 530p. (YA). (gr. 9-12). 1975. pap. 225.00 incl. audio (*0-87950-349-1*) Spoken Lang Serv.

***Spoken Urdu, Nos. 1, 2 & 3.** Muhammad A. Barker. 1000p. 1996. pap. 59.95 (*0-614-21655-9*, 1162) Kazi Pubns.

Spoken Urdu, 3 bks., Set. Muhammad A. Barker. LC 75-15183. (Spoken Language Ser.). 530p. (YA). (gr. 9-12). 1975. 50.00 (*0-87950-343-2*) Spoken Lang Serv.

Spoken Uyghur. Reinhard F. Hahn. LC 90-35851. 656p. (C). 1991. text ed. 35.00 (*0-295-97015-4*) U of Wash Pr.

Spoken Vietnamese. Robert B. Jones & Huynh S. Thong. LC 79-3165. (Spoken Language Ser.). xiii, 295p. (gr. 9-12). 1976. pap. 15.00 (*0-87950-371-8*); audio 75.00 (*0-87950-372-6*) Spoken Lang Serv.

Spoken Vietnamese. Robert B. Jones & Huynh S. Thong. LC 79-3165. (Spoken Language Ser.). xiii, 295p. (YA). (gr. 9-12). 1976. pap. 90.00 incl. audio (*0-87950-373-4*) Spoken Lang Serv.

***Spoken Vietnamese for Beginners: Instructors Manual for Activities.** LePham Thuy-Kim. 59p. 1996. teacher ed., lib. bdg. 15.00 (*1-877979-32-5*) SE Asia.

Spoken Vietnamese for Beginners, with 3 Audio Tapes. Nguyen Long et al. (Southeast Asian Language Text Ser.). (Illus.). 401p. (Orig.). (C). 1994. pap. text ed. 31.00 incl. audio (*1-877979-45-7*) SE Asia.

Spoken Word. Harry H. Schanker. Ed. by John A. Rothermich. LC 80-24143. (Illus.). 384p. 1982. text ed. 23.20 (*0-07-055135-9*) McGraw.

Spoken Word & the Work of Interpretation. Dennis Tedlock. LC 82-40489. (Conduct & Communication Ser.). (Illus.). 400p. 1983. pap. 22.00 (*0-8122-1143-X*) U of Pa Pr.

Spoken Words: Effects of Situation & Social Group on Oral Word Usage & Frequency. William S. Hall et al. (Psychology of Reading & Reading Instruction Ser.). 504p. 1984. pap. 59.95 (*0-89859-387-5*) L Erlbaum Assocs.

Spokesman for the Minority: A Bibliography of Sidney Lanier, William Vaughn Moody, Henry Timrod, Frederick Goddard Tuckerman, & Jones Very, with Selective Annotations. Jeanetta Boswell. LC 86-24828. x, 296p. 1987. 32.50 (*0-8108-1944-9*) Scarecrow.

Spokesmen. Thomas K. Whipple. LC 70-142711. (Essay Index Reprint Ser.). 1977. 21.95 (*0-8369-2179-8*) Ayer.

Spokesmen for the Despised: Fundamentalist Leaders of the Middle East. Ed. by R. Scott Appleby. LC 96-20600. 424p. 1996. pap. 19.95 (*0-226-02125-4*) U Ch Pr.

Spokesmen for the Despised: Fundamentalist Leaders of the Middle East. Ed. by R. Scott Appleby. LC 96-20600. 424p. 1996. lib. bdg. 55.00 (*0-226-02124-6*) U Ch Pr.

***Spokesongs: Bicycle Adventures on Three Continents.** Willie Weir. LC 97-65213. (Illus.). 144p. (Orig.). 1997. pap. 11.95 (*0-9656792-6-8*) Pineleaf Prodns.

Spokesperson: A Public Appearance Primer. 2nd ed. Ken W. Huskey. (Illus.). 150p. 1986. pap. 10.00 (*0-9604840-1-9*) K W Huskey.

Spokesperson Milton: Voices in Contemporary Criticism. Ed. by Charles W. Durham & Kristin P. McColgan. LC 93-47329. 1995. 42.50 (*0-945636-65-2*) Susquehanna U Pr.

Spomenica Palih Srba Vazduhoplovaca. Milos Acin-Kosta. 300p. (SER.). 1975. pap. 10.00 (*0-931931-10-X*) Ravnogorski.

Spondyloarthropathies. Ed. by Morris Ziff & Stanley B. Cohen. LC 84-42721. (Advances in Inflammation Research Ser.: Vol. 9). 288p. 1985. reprint ed. pap. 82.10 (*0-608-00435-9*, 2061150) Bks Demand.

Spondylotherapy Simplified. Alva E. Gregory. 84p. 1979. reprint ed. spiral bd. 14.50 (*0-7873-0357-7*) Hlth Research.

Sponemann Site, No. 11-Ms-517: The Formative Emergent Mississippian Sponemann Phase Occupations. Andrew C. Fortier et al. (American Bottom Archaeology Ser.: Selected FAI-270 Site Reports: Vol. 23). (Illus.). 584p. 1992. pap. text ed. 39.95 (*0-252-01113-9*) U of Ill Pr.

***Sponges: Filters of the Sea.** Andreu Llamas. LC 97-8485. (Secrets of the Animal World Ser.). (Illus.). (J). 1997. lib. bdg. write for info. (*0-8368-1645-5*) Gareth Stevens Inc.

Sponges & Spongiomorphs: Notes for a Short Course Organized by J. K. Rigby & C. W. Stearn. Ed. by T. W. Broadhead. (Studies in Geology). (Illus.). 220p. (C). 1983. pap. 12.00 (*0-910249-06-7*) U of Tenn Geo.

Sponges Are Skeletons. Barbara J. Esbensen. LC 92-9740. (Let's-Read-&-Find-Out Science Bk.: Stage 2). (Illus.). 32p. (J). (gr. k-4). 1993. 15.00 (*0-06-021034-6*); lib. bdg. 14.89 (*0-06-021037-0*) HarpC Child Bks.

Sponges in Time & Space: Proceedings of the 4th International Porifera Congress, Amsterdam, Netherlands, April 1993. Ed. by R. W. Van Soest et al. (Illus.). 544p. (C). 1994. text ed. 95.00 (*90-5410-097-4*, Pub. by A A Balkema NE) Ashgate Pub Co.

Spongeware & Spatterware. Kevin McConnell. LC 90-60599. (Illus.). 128p. 1990. pap. 14.95 (*0-88740-253-4*) Schiffer.

Sponging: A Guide to Living off Those You Love. Anthony E. Marsh. 112p. 1996. mass mkt. 6.99 (*0-06-101054-5*, Harp PBks) HarpC.

SPONGING: A Guide to Living Off Those You Love. Robert Moritz et al. (Illus.). 112p. 1995. pap. 9.95 (*1-886186-00-6*) Dune Rd Bks.

Sponging Etc. Cy DeCosse Incorporated Staff. LC 96-15848. (Creative Touches Ser.). (Illus.). 64p. 1996. pap. 9.95 (*0-86573-996-X*) Cowles Creative.

Spon's Architects' & Builders Book, 1995. 120th ed. 1994. 112.00 (*0-419-19350-2*, E & FN Spon) Routledge Chapman & Hall.

Spon's Architects' & Builders' Price Book 1992. 117th ed. Ed. by Davis Langdon & Everest Staff. 1050p. 1991. write for info. (*0-419-17360-9*, E & FN Spon) Routledge Chapman & Hall.

***Spon's Architects' & Builders' Price Book 1997.** Davis Langdon & Everest Staff. Date not set. write for info. (*0-419-22190-5*, E & FN Spon) Routledge Chapman & Hall.

Spon's Budget Estimating Handbook. Spain. 1990. text ed. 58.95 (*0-442-31176-1*) Van Nos Reinhold.

Spon's Budget Estimating Handbook. 2nd ed. Tweed. 1994. 69.00 (*0-419-19250-6*, E & FN Spon); 69.00 (*0-419-19380-4*, E & FN Spon) Routledge Chapman & Hall.

***Spon's Building Costs Guide for Educational Premises.** Ed. by Tweeds, Chartered Quantity Surveyors Staff. 256p. 1995. text ed. 60.50 (*0-419-18860-6*, E & FN Spon) Routledge Chapman & Hall.

Spon's Civil Engineering & Highway Works Price Book 1992. 6th ed. Ed. by Davis Langdon & Everest Staff. 850p. 1991. write for info. (*0-419-17380-3*, E & FN Spon) Routledge Chapman & Hall.

***Spon's Civil Engineering & Highway Works Price Book 1997.** Davis Langdon & Everest Staff. Date not set. write for info. (*0-419-22200-6*, E & FN Spon) Routledge Chapman & Hall.

***Spon's Construction Cost & Price Indices Handbook.** Fleming & B. A. Tysoe. 370p. text ed. 63.00 (*0-419-15330-6*, E & FN Spon) Routledge Chapman & Hall.

Spon's Construction Output Manual. T. Johnson. 200p. 1991. write for info. (*0-419-16850-8*, E & FN Spon) Routledge Chapman & Hall.

***Spon's European Construction Costs Handbook.** 2nd ed. Ed. by Davis Langdon & Everest Staff. (Illus.). 608p. 1995. text ed. 129.50 (*0-419-19650-1*, E & FN Spon) Routledge Chapman & Hall.

***Spon's Fabrication Norms for Offshore Structures: A Handbook for the Oil Gas & Petrochemical Industries.** Franklin. (Illus.). 304p. 1993. text ed. 225.95 (*0-419-14160-X*, E & FN Spon) Routledge Chapman & Hall.

Spon's Grounds Maintenance Contract Handbook. R. M. Chadwick. 190p. 1990. 44.95 (*0-442-31235-0*) Chapman & Hall.

Spon's International Construction Costs Handbook. Everest Staff. Ed. by Davis & Belfield. 300p. 1988. lib. bdg. 89.50 (*0-419-14210-X*, E & FN Spon) Routledge Chapman & Hall.

***Spon's Landscape & External Works Price Book 1997.** Derek Lovejoy Partnership Staff & Davis Langdon & Everest Staff. Date not set. write for info. (*0-419-22220-0*, E & FN Spon) Routledge Chapman & Hall.

Spon's Landscape & External Works Price Book 1992. 11th ed. Ed. by Lovejoy Derek & Patrners Staff & Davis Langdon & Everest Staff. 240p. 1991. write for info. (*0-419-17390-0*, E & FN Spon) Routledge Chapman & Hall.

Spon's Landscape & External Works Price Book, 1995. 14th ed. 1994. 91.00 (*0-419-19370-7*, E & FN Spon) Routledge Chapman & Hall.

***Spon's Mechanical & Electrical Services Price Book.** Davis Langdon & Everest Staff. Date not set. write for info. (*0-419-22210-3*, E & FN Spon) Routledge Chapman & Hall.

Spon's Mechanical & Electrical Services Price Book 1992. 23th ed. Ed. by Davis Langdon & Everest Staff. 700p. 1991. write for info. (*0-419-17370-6*, E & FN Spon) Routledge Chapman & Hall.

Spon's Mechanical & Electrical Services Price Book, 1995. 26th ed. 1994. 117.00 (*0-419-19360-X*, E & FN Spon) Routledge Chapman & Hall.

Sponsor: Notes on a Modern Potentate. Erik Barnouw. (Illus.). 220p. 1979. pap. 10.95 (*0-19-502614-4*) OUP.

Sponsor Couple Program for Chirstian Marriage Preparation - Manual. Robert Ruhnke. 32p. 1981. pap. 4.95 (*0-89243-143-1*) Liguori Pubns.

Sponsor Couple Program for Christian Marriage Preparation - Dialogue Packet. Robert Ruhnke. 96p. 1981. pap. 4.95 (*0-89243-144-X*) Liguori Pubns.

***Sponsored Identities: Culture, Politics in Puerto Rico.** Arlene M. Davila. LC 97-1942. (Puerto Rican Studies). 1997. write for info. (*1-56639-548-8*); pap. write for info. (*1-56639-549-6*) Temple U Pr.

Sponsored Life: Ads, TV, & American Culture. Leslie Savan. (Culture & the Moving Image Ser.). (Illus.). 272p. (C). 1994. pap. 16.95 (*1-56639-245-4*) Temple U Pr.

Sponsoring Someone with HIV Infection see Mart Series

Sponsors' Handbook: Junior Historian & Walter Prescott Webb Historical Society. rev. ed. David C. De Boe. iv, 86p. (J). pap. text ed. 5.00 (*0-87611-120-7*) Tex St Hist Assn.

Sponsors Report Almanac 1992 Edition: Exposure Analysis, Trends & Projections. Ed. by Robert J. Cotman et al. LC 91-1164. 175p. 1992. pap. 87.50 (*0-9630140-0-5*) J Julius Assocs.

Sponsorship. Richard Bagehot. (Waterlow Practitioner's Library). 192p. 1990. pap. 50.00 (*0-08-040116-3*, Waterlow) Macmillan.

Sponsorship: Its Role & Effects. Global Media Commission Staff. 1988. 40.00 (*0-317-02011-0*) Intl Advertising Assn.

***Sponsorship, Colleagueship & Service: A Conversation about the Future of Religious Communities & American Catholic High Schools.** Ed. by Dale McDonald. 59p. (Orig.). 1996. pap. 10.00 (*1-55833-179-4*) Natl Cath Educ.

***Sponsorship Guide for Twelve Step.** Mira T. Date not set. pap. write for info. (*0-312-18182-5*) St Martin.

Sponsorship Strategy: Evidentiary Tactics for Winning Jury Trials. Robert H. Klonoff & Paul L. Colby. 350p. 1990. 55.00 (*0-87473-577-7*) MICHIE.

Spontaneity in Prophetic Realms: Spontaneous Combustion. Marilyn J. Wright. (Illus.). 55p. (C). 1994. pap. 5.00 (*0-9632748-3-X*) Majesty Pubns.

Spontaneous Abortion: Diagnosis & Treatment. Isabel Stabile. (Illus.). xiv, 231p. 1992. 174.00 (*0-387-19712-5*) Spr-Verlag.

Spontaneous Activity in Education. Maria Montessori. (Basic Montessori Library). (Illus.). 384p. 1984. pap. 12.95 (*0-916011-02-X*) Ed Sys Pub.

Spontaneous Alternation Behavior. Ed. by W. N. Dember. (Illus.). 175p. 1989. 70.95 (*0-387-96963-2*) Spr-Verlag.

Spontaneous & Induced Abortion: Proceedings of the WHO Scientific Group, Geneva, 1970. WHO Staff. (Technical Report Ser.: No. 461). 51p. 1970. pap. text ed. 5.00 (*92-4-120461-3*, 1100461) World Health.

Spontaneous & Induced Intima Formation in Blood Vessels. Mark M. Kockx. (Medical Intelligence Unit Ser.). 107p. 1995. 59.00 (*1-57059-220-9*) R G Landes.

Spontaneous Animal Models of Human Disease, Vol. 2. Ed. by Edwin J. Andrews et al. LC 78-20039. (American College of Laboratory Animal Medicine Ser.). 1980. text ed. 99.00 (*0-12-058502-2*) Acad Pr.

Spontaneous Cognitive Processes in Handicapped Children. M. Cherkes-Julkowski & N. Gertner. (Disorders of Human Learning, Behavior, & Communication Ser.). (Illus.). 175p. 1988. 80.95 (*0-387-96801-6*) Spr-Verlag.

Spontaneous Combustion. David B. Feinberg. (Contemporary American Fiction Ser.). 240p. 1992. reprint ed. pap. 10.95 (*0-14-014862-0*, Penguin Bks) Viking Penguin.

***Spontaneous Combustion, Vol. 844.** Janis R. Hudson. (Loveswept Ser.). 1997. mass mkt. 3.50 (*0-553-44543-X*) Bantam.

***Spontaneous Combustion: Amazing True Stories of Mysterious Fires.** Damon Wilson. (Strange but True Ser.). 1997. pap. text ed. 5.95 (*0-8069-0587-5*) Sterling.

Spontaneous Combustion: Grass Roots Christianity, Latin American Style. Clayton L. Berg, Jr. & Paul E. Pretiz. LC 95-49639. 1996. pap. 9.95 (*0-87808-265-4*) William Carey Lib.

Spontaneous Combustion of Coal & Mine Fires. Ed. by Sudhish C. Banerjee. 180p. (C). 1985. text ed. 105.00 (*90-6191-574-0*, Pub. by A A Balkema NE) Ashgate Pub Co.

Spontaneous Creative Imagery: Problem-Solving & Life-Enhancing Skills. Aina O. Nucho. LC 95-20397. (Illus.). 174p. 1995. pap. 25.95 (*0-398-06550-0*); text ed. 41.95 (*0-398-06549-7*) C C Thomas.

Spontaneous Current Sheets in Magnetic Fields: With Applications to Stellar X-Rays. Eugene N. Parker. (International Series in Astronomy & Astrophysics). (Illus.). 400p. 1994. 75.00 (*0-19-507371-1*) OUP.

Spontaneous Descriptions, Bk. 1. Harris Winitz & Douglas Moore. (Illus.). 125p. (Orig.). (C). 1985. pap. text ed. 32.50 incl. audio (*0-939990-39-3*) Intl Linguistics.

Spontaneous Descriptions, Bk. 2. Harris Winitz & Douglas Moore. 125p. (Orig.). 1985. pap. text ed. 32.50 incl. audio (*0-939990-42-3*) Intl Linguistics.

Spontaneous Emission & Laser Oscillation in Microcavities. Ed. by Hiroyuki Yokoyama & Kikuo Ujihara. LC 95-4016. (Laser Science & Technology Ser.). 384p. 1995. 200.00 (*0-8493-3786-0*, 3786) CRC Pr.

Spontaneous Formation of Space-Time Structures & Criticality. Ed. by Tormod Riste & D. Sherrington. 464p. (C). 1991. lib. bdg. 182.00 (*0-7923-1452-2*) Kluwer Ac.

Spontaneous Generation Controversy from Descartes to Oparin. John Farley. LC 76-47379. 240p. reprint ed. pap. 68.40 (*0-8357-6911-9*, 2037969) Bks Demand.

Spontaneous Gesture: Selected Letters of D. W. Winnicott. Ed. by F. Robert Rodman. LC 86-18483. (Illus.). 256p. 1987. pap. 32.00 (*0-674-83336-8*) HUP.

Spontaneous Healing: How to Discover & Enchance Your Body's Natural Ability to Maintain & Heal Itself. Andrew Weil. 320p. 1996. pap. 12.95 (*0-449-91064-4*) Fawcett.

Spontaneous Healing: How to Discover & Enhance Your Body's Natural Ability to Maintain & Heal Itself. large type ed. Andrew Weil. LC 95-47853. (Large Print Ser.). 400p. 1995. lib. bdg. 25.95 (*1-57490-034-X*, Beeler LP Bks) T T Beeler.

Spontaneous Healing: How to Enlist & Enhance the Body's Own Gifts for Maintaining & Healing Itself. Andrew Weil. 1995. 23.00 (*0-679-43607-3*) Knopf.

Spontaneous Intracerebral Haematomas: Advances in Diagnosis & Therapy. Ed. by H. W. Pia et al. (Illus.). 500p. 1981. 158.00 (*0-387-10146-2*) Spr-Verlag.

Spontaneous Joy. D. G. Blore. (Orig.). 1996. pap. write for info. (*1-57553-203-4*) Watermrk Pr.

Spontaneous Melodramas: Twenty-Four Fun, No-Prep, Melodramas Your Kids Will Love to Perform. Doug Fields et al. LC 95-48256. 104p. 1996. pap. 12.99 (*0-310-20775-4*) Zondervan.

Spontaneous Play in Early Childhood. M. C. Pugmire-Stoy. 128p. 1992. pap. text ed. 24.95 (*0-8273-3660-8*) Delmar.

Spontaneous Play in Early Childhood. M. C. Pugmire-Stoy. 128p. 1992. teacher ed. 10.50 (*0-8273-3661-6*) Delmar.

Spontaneous Poetics of Jack Kerouac. Regina Weinreich. 1994. pap. 9.95 (*1-56924-971-7*) Marlowe & Co.

Spontaneous PSI, Depth Psychology & Parapsychology: Proceedings of an International Conference Held in Berkeley, California, October 31-November 1, 1987. Ed. by Betty Shapin & Lisette Coly. LC 92-82653. 287p. 1992. 20.00 (*0-912328-42-8*) Parapsych Foun.

Spontaneous Recovery: Unexpected Health after Chronic or Incurable Illness. Claire Warga. 1994. write for info. (*0-201-62209-2*) Addison-Wesley.

Spontaneous Self: Viable Alternatives to Free Will. Paul Breer. LC 89-84648. 300p. (Orig.). (C). 1989. pap. 20.00 (*0-9623589-0-8*) Inst Naturalistic Philos.

Spontaneous Shelter: International Perspectives & Prospects. Ed. by Carl V. Patton. LC 87-10002. (Illus.). 256p. (C). 1987. 39.95 (*0-87722-507-9*) Temple U Pr.

Spontaneous Symmetry Breakdown & Related Subjects: XXI Karpacz Winter School on Theoretical Physics, Poland, 1985. Ed. by L. Michel et al. 504p. 1985. 78.00 (*9971-978-54-7*) World Scientific Pub.

Spook. (J). Date not set. pap. 3.95 (*0-590-20752-0*) Scholastic Inc.

Spook. Steve Vance. LC 90-40469. 234p. 1990. 18.95 (*0-939149-38-9*) Soho Press.

Spook: Tales of a Bird Dog. David Henderson. LC 95-10778. (Illus.). 136p. 1995. 22.95 (*1-55821-402-X*) Lyons & Burford.

An Asterisk (*) at the beginning of an entry indicates that the title is appearing in BIP for the first time.

Spook Book: A Strange & Dangerous Look at Forbidden Technology. Mick Tyner. (Illus.). 258p. 1989. pap. 29.95 (0-940401-72-X) Trentland Pr.
Spook House. Don Whittington. (Orig.). (J). 1995. pap. 3.50 (0-380-77937-4, Camelot) Avon.
Spook House. M. C. Helldorfer. Ed. by Patricia MacDonald. 160p. 1992. reprint ed. pap. 2.99 (0-671-72326-X, Minstrel Bks) PB.
Spook Matinee: And Other Scary Poems for Kids. George Ulrich. 32p. (J). 1994. pap. 3.50 (0-440-40956-X) Dell.
Spook Stories. Douglas A. Menville. LC 75-46252. (Supernatural & Occult Fiction Ser.). 1976. reprint ed. lib. bdg. 23.95 (0-405-08112-X) Ayer.
Spook Who Sat by the Door. Sam Greenlee. LC 89-40227. (African American Life Ser.). 182p. (C). 1989. reprint ed. pap. 15.95 (0-8143-2246-8) Wayne St U Pr.
Spooker. Dean Ing. 320p. 1995. 23.95 (0-312-85740-3) Forge NYC.
***Spooker.** Dean Ing. 1997. mass mkt. 6.99 (0-8125-4842-6) Tor Bks.
Spookiest Day. David Gantz. (Illus.). 32p. (Orig.). (J). (gr. k-3). 1986. pap. 2.50 (0-590-40325-7) Scholastic Inc.
Spooks. David Thomson. LC 97-5066. 1997. 25.00 (0-679-45115-3) Knopf.
***Spooks.** David Thomson. 1998. pap. write for info. (0-679-77291-X, Vin) Random.
Spooks of the Valley: Ghost Stories for Boys & Girls. Louis C. Jones. (Illus.). 111p. (YA). reprint ed. pap. 11.95 (0-910746-10-9, SOT01) Hope Farm.
Spooks, Spies, & Private Eyes: Black Mystery, Crime, & Suspense Fiction of the 20th Century. Paula L. Woods. 368p. 1995. 22.95 (0-385-48082-2) Doubleday.
Spooks, Spies, & Private Eyes: Black Mystery, Crime, & Suspense Fiction of the 20th Century. Paula L. Woods. 368p. 1996. pap. 12.95 (0-385-47955-7) Doubleday.
Spook's Surprise. Karen Dolby. (Young Puzzle Adventures Ser.). (Illus.). 32p. (J). (ps-1). 1996. pap. 4.95 (0-7460-2296-4, Usborne); lib. bdg. 12.95 (0-88110-837-5, Usborne) EDC.
Spooksville, No. 16. Christopher Pike. (J). 1997. mass mkt. 3.99 (0-671-00264-3) PB.
Spooky Eerie Night Noise. Mona R. Reeves. LC 89-447. (Illus.). 32p. (J). (ps-2). 1989. lib. bdg. 13.95 (0-02-775732-3, Bradbury S&S) S&S Childrens.
Spooky Halloween Party. Annabelle Prager. LC 81-1945. (I Am Reading Bks.). (Illus.). 48p. (J). (gr. 1-4). 1981. lib. bdg. 7.99 (0-394-94370-8) Pantheon.
Spooky Halloween Party: A Step 2 Book. Annabelle Prager. LC 88-37571. (Step into Reading Bks.). (Illus.). 48p. (J). (gr. 1-3). 1989. lib. bdg. 7.99 (0-394-94961-7) Random Bks Yng Read.
Spooky Halloween Party: A Step 2 Book. Annabelle Prager. LC 88-37571. (Step into Reading Bks.). (Illus.). 48p. (J). (gr. 1-3). 1989. pap. 3.99 (0-394-84961-2) Random Bks Yng Read.
Spooky Halloween Sticker Fun. (Sticker Bks.). 16p. (J). 1995. pap. 3.95 (0-7894-0323-4, 5-70673) DK Pub Inc.
Spooky Haunted House Puzzles. Elvira Gamiello. (Illus.). 64p. (Orig.). (J). (gr. 4-6). 1987. pap. 1.95 (0-942025-06-7) Kidsbks.
Spooky House: Glow in the Dark. Joanne Barkan. (Illus.). 24p. (J). (ps-3). 1990. 6.50 (0-307-06252-X, Golden Pr) Western Pub.
Spooky Jokes & Riddles. Jeffrey S. Nelson. LC 89-123851. (J). 1988. pap. 1.95 (0-02-689070-4, Mac Bks Young Read) S&S Childrens.
Spooky Jokes & Riddles Books. Jeffrey S. Nelson. (Illus.). 24p. (J). (gr. 3 up). 1988. pap. 1.95 (1-56288-344-5) Checkerboard.
Spooky Kids: Strange but True Tales. Bruce Nash & Allan Zullo. LC 93-44029. (Illus.). 128p. (J). (gr. 1-6). 1996. pap. 2.95 (0-8167-3447-X) Troll Communs.
Spooky Magic. Date not set. pap. 1.75 (0-590-08099-7) Scholastic Inc.
Spooky Magic Tricks. David Knoles. (Illus.). 128p. (J). 1994. pap. 4.95 (0-8069-0419-4) Sterling.
Spooky Ohio: Thirteen Traditional Tales. Chris Woodyard. (Illus.). 96p. (Orig.). (J). (gr. 4-7). 1995. pap. 8.95 (0-9628472-3-2); lib. bdg. 12.95 (0-9628472-4-0) Kestrel Pubns.
Spooky Poems. Ed. by Jill Bennett. (Illus.). 32p. 1990. 14.95 (0-7737-2350-1) Genl Dist Srvs.
Spooky Riddles. Marc T. Brown. LC 83-6051. (Illus.). 48p. (J). (gr. k-3). 1983. 7.99 (0-394-86093-4) Beginner.
Spooky Riddles. Katy Hall & Lisa Eisenberg. LC 94-37524. (J). 1998. lib. bdg. write for info. (0-8037-1685-0); trans. write for info. (0-8037-1684-2) Dial Bks Young.
Spooky Riddles & Jokes. Joseph Rosenbloom. LC 87-17972. (Illus.). 128p. (J). (gr. 4 up). 1988. pap. 4.95 (0-8069-6736-6) Sterling.
Spooky Sea Stories. Ed. by Charles G. Waugh & Frank D. McSherry, Jr. 192p. 1991. pap. 11.95 (0-89909-337-X, 80-450-8) Yankee Bks.
Spooky Sleepover. Susan Pearson. (Eagle-Eye Ernie Mysteries Ser.). (Illus.). 64p. (J). (gr. 1-3). 1991. pap. 12.00 (0-671-74070-9, S&S Bks Young Read) S&S Childrens.
Spooky Stories & Other Scary Stuff. Mary Packard. (Illus.). 32p. (Orig.). (J). (gr. k-3). 1996. pap. 6.95 (0-8167-3833-5) Troll Communs.
Spooky Stories for a Dark & Stormy Night. Ed. by Alice Low. LC 93-33638. (Illus.). 128p. (J). (gr. 3 up). 1994. 19.95 (0-7868-0012-7) Hyprn Child.
Spooky Stories for a Dark & Stormy Night. Ed. by Alice Low. 128p. (J). (gr. 3 up). 1996. pap. 7.95 (0-7868-1114-5) Hyprn Child.
Spooky Tail of Prewitt Peacock. Bill Peet. LC 72-7930. (Illus.). 32p. (J). (gr. k-3). 1973. 14.95 (0-395-15494-4) HM.
Spooky Tail of Prewitt Peacock. Bill Peet. (Illus.). (J). (gr. k-3). 1979. pap. 5.95 (0-395-28159-8) HM.
Spooky Tales from Gullah Gullah Island: A Glow-in-the-Dark Book. Hettie Jones. (J). 1996. pap. 11.95 (0-689-80829-1) S&S Childrens.
***Spooky Things.** Penny King & Clare Roundhill. (Making Pictures Ser.). (J). 1997. write for info. (1-57572-195-3) Rigby Educ.
***Spooky Towers.** (Activity Fun Packs Ser.). (Illus.). (YA). (gr. 6 up). 1996. pap. 6.95 (0-7894-1162-8) DK Pub Inc.
***Spooky Tree.** Arthur Ruolo. (Story Shapes Ser.). (Illus.). 24p. (Orig.). (J). (gr. k up). 1997. pap. 2.25 (1-56293-944-0) McClanahan Bk.
Spooky Tricks. Rose Wyler & Gerald Ames. LC 92-47501. (I Can Read Bk.). (Illus.). 64p. (J). (gr. k-3). 1994. 14.00 (0-06-023025-8); lib. bdg. 14.89 (0-06-023026-6) HarpC Child Bks.
Spooky Tricks. Rose Wyler & Gerald Ames. LC 92-47501. (Trophy I Can Read Bk.). (Illus.). 64p. (J). (ps-3). 1994. pap. 3.75 (0-06-444172-5, Trophy) HarpC Child Bks.
Spool of Blue: New & Selected Poems. Carolyn Stoloff. LC 82-6006. (Poets Now Ser.: No. 5). 194p. 1983. 13.50 (0-8108-1563-X) Scarecrow.
Spool of Thread. Rogene L. Jados. LC 85-51407. 64p. 1986. 6.95 (0-938232-91-6, Baker & Taylor) Winston-Derek.
Spools & Tools Wallhanging. Wendy Gilbert. (Illus.). 20p. 1991. 5.95 (0-922705-27-5) Quilt Day.
Spoon. Mark Dunster. 20p. (Orig.). 1994. pap. 5.00 (0-89642-234-8) Linden Pubs.
Spoon Fed Christian. Melvin E. McQueen. 144p. 1993. 14.95 (0-926099-01-9) Netcom.
Spoon Fishing for Steelhead. William T. Herzog. (Illus.). 64p. 1993. pap. 16.95 (1-878175-30-0) F Amato Pubns.
Spoon for Every Bite. Joe Hayes. LC 95-22019. (Illus.). 32p. (J). (ps-2). 1996. 15.95 (0-531-09499-5); lib. bdg. 16.99 (0-531-08799-9) Orchard Bks Watts.
Spoon River Anthology. Edgar L. Masters. 1976. 20.95 (0-8488-1430-4) Amereon Ltd.
Spoon River Anthology. Edgar L. Masters. 320p. 1962. pap. 7.00 (0-02-070010-5) Macmillan.
Spoon River Anthology. Edgar L. Masters. 320p. 1992. pap. 4.95 (0-451-52530-2, Sig Classics) NAL-Dutton.
Spoon River Anthology. Edgar L. Masters. 328p. 1987. 35.00 (0-02-581780-9) S&S Trade.
***Spoon River Anthology.** Edgar L. Masters. 22.95 (1-56723-075-X) Yestermorrow.
Spoon River Anthology. unabridged ed. Edgar L. Masters. 144p. 1992. reprint ed. pap. text ed. 1.00 (0-486-27275-3) Dover.
Spoon River Anthology. Edgar L. Masters. 345p. 1983. reprint ed. lib. bdg. 21.95 (0-89966-456-3) Buccaneer Bks.
Spoon River Anthology: An Annotated Edition. Edgar L. Masters. Ed. by John E. Hallwas. (Prairie State Bks.). (Illus.). 464p. 1992. 29.95 (0-252-01561-4); pap. text ed. 14.95 (0-252-06363-5) U of Ill Pr.
Spoon with Every Course: In Search of the Legendary Food of France. Mirabel Osler. (Illus.). 224p. 1996. 29.95 (1-85793-766-X, Pub. by Pavilion UK) Trafalgar.
Spoonbill Swamp. Brenda Z. Guiberson. LC 91-8555. (J). (ps-3). 1994. pap. 4.95 (0-8050-3385-8) H Holt & Co.
Spoonbread & Strawberry Wine: Recipes & Reminiscences of a Family. Norma Jean & Carole Darden. LC 93-34264. (Illus.). 352p. 1994. pap. 17.95 (0-385-47270-6) Doubleday.
Spooner's Moving Animals: The Zoo of Tranquility. Paul Spooner. (Illus.). 64p. 1986. pap. 16.95 (0-8109-2331-9) Abrams.
Spoonful of Luger. large type ed. Roger Ormerod. (Linford Mystery Library). 288p. 1994. pap. 15.99 (0-7089-7476-7, Linford) Ulverscroft.
Spoonhandle. Ruth Moore. 1986. pap. 10.95 (0-942396-49-9) Blackberry ME.
Spoonproof Jello & Other Poems. James Magorian. LC 90-81004. (Illus.). 16p. (J). (gr. 2-5). 1990. pap. 3.00 (0-930674-34-0) Black Oak.
Spoons from Around the World. Dorothy T. Rainwater & Donna H. Felger. LC 92-60628. (Illus.). 288p. 1992. text ed. 59.95 (0-88740-425-1) Schiffer.
Spoons 1650-1930. Simon Moore. 1989. pap. 25.00 (0-85263-910-4, Pub. by Shire UK) St Mut.
Sporadic Groups. Michael Aschbacher. (Cambridge Tracts in Mathematics Ser.: No. 104). (Illus.). 328p. (C). 1994. text ed. 54.95 (0-521-42049-0) Cambridge U Pr.
***Spore Morphology of Chinese Pteridophytes.** Zhang Yu-Long. (ENG & LAT.). 1990. 188.00 (0-7855-0529-6, Pub. by Wanhai Books CH) St Mut.
Spores of Indian Ferns. Santha Devi. (Illus.). 129p. 1973. 15.00 (0-88065-190-3, Messers Today & Tomorrow) Scholarly Pubns.
Spores of the Pteridophyta: Surface, Wall Structure & Diversity Based on Electron Microscope Studies. Alice F. Tryon & B. Lugardon. (Illus.). 672p. 1990. 172.95 (0-387-97218-8) Spr-Verlag.
Spork of the Ayor. Perry A. Chapdelaine, Sr. 208p. 1978. 7.50 (0-7091-6528-5) AC Projects.
Sporopollenin Dinoflagellate Cysts: Their Morphology & Interpretation. William R. Evitt. LC 84-72457. (Illus.). 349p. (C). 1985. 30.00 (0-931871-00-X) Am Assn Strat.
Sport: A Cultural History. Richard D. Mandell. LC 83-20017. (Illus.). 384p. 1984. text ed. 52.50 (0-231-05470-X) Col U Pr.
Sport: A Cultural History. Richard D. Mandell. LC 83-20017. (Illus.). 384p. 1986. pap. text ed. 18.50 (0-231-05471-8) Col U Pr.
Sport: A Philosophic Inquiry. Paul Weiss. LC 69-15326. 286p. 1969. 29.95 (0-8093-0358-2) S Ill U Pr.
Sport: A Philosophic Inquiry. Paul Weiss. LC 69-15326. (Arcturus Books Paperbacks). 286p. 1971. pap. 19.95 (0-8093-0501-1) S Ill U Pr.
Sport: Creative Image Bank. 96p. 1991. pap. 19.95 (88-7070-154-9) Belvedere USA.
***Sport: Eine Kulturgeschichte Im Spiegel der Kunst.** Peter Kuhnst. 1996. text ed. 120.00 (90-5705-001-3) Gordon & Breach.
Sport A. S. I. S. T. A Student Athlete's Guide to Collegiate Athletics. rev. ed. James P. Britt et al. LC 96-92001. 140p. 1996. pap. 19.95 (1-881013-11-1) Sports Sci.
Sport & a Pastime. James Salter. 196p. 1995. 12.50 (0-679-60156-2) Random.
Sport & a Pastime. James Salter. LC 85-60855. 192p. 1985. reprint ed. pap. 10.95 (0-86547-210-6, North Pt Pr) FS&G.
Sport & American Mentality, 1880-1910. Donald J. Mrozek. LC 83-3667. (Illus.). 304p. (C). 1983. text ed. 36.00 (0-87049-394-9); pap. text ed. 18.00 (0-87049-395-7) U of Tenn Pr.
Sport & British Politics since 1960. John F. Coghlan. 240p. 1990. 80.00 (1-85000-809-4, Falmer Pr); pap. 38.00 (1-85000-810-8, Falmer Pr) Taylor & Francis.
Sport & Canadian Diplomacy. Donald Macintosh & Michael Hawes. 248p. 1994. 34.95 (0-7735-1161-X, Pub. by McGill CN) U of Toronto Pr.
Sport & Exercise Science: Essays in the History of Sports Medicine. Ed. by Jack W. Berryman & Roberta J. Park. 392p. (C). 1992. text ed. 44.95 (0-252-01896-6); pap. text ed. 18.95 (0-252-06242-6) U of Ill Pr.
Sport & Fitness Management: Career Strategies & Professional Skills. Ed. by Janet B. Parks & Beverly R. Zanger. LC 89-71722. (Illus.). 288p. (C). 1990. text ed. 40.00 (0-87322-269-5, BPAR0269) Human Kinetics.
Sport & Higher Education. Ed. by Donald Chu et al. LC 85-143. 440p. 1985. text ed. 39.00 (0-87322-000-5, BCHU0000) Human Kinetics.
Sport & International Politics. Barrie Houlihan. 256p. 1994. pap. text ed. 50.00 (0-13-302589-6) P-H.
***Sport & International Politics.** Riordan. (Illus.). 224p. 1996. text ed. write for info. (0-419-21160-8, E & FN Spon) Routledge Chapman & Hall.
Sport & Leisure. Central Office of Info. (Aspects of Britain Ser.). (Illus.). 115p. 1997. pap. 9.95 (0-11-701740-X, HM1740X, Pub. by Statnry Ofc UK) Seven Hills Bk.
Sport & Leisure in Social Thought. Grant Jarvie & Joseph A. Maguire. LC 94-7261. 304p. (C). 1994. pap. 19.95 (0-415-07704-4, B4397) Routledge.
Sport & Leisure in the Civilizing Process: Critique & Counter-Critique. Ed. by Eric Dunning & Chris Rojek. 320p. (Orig.). 1992. 50.00 (0-8020-2804-7); pap. 19.95 (0-8020-7679-3) U of Toronto Pr.
Sport & Medicine. 2nd ed. Peter N. Sperryn. Date not set. write for info. (0-7506-1260-6) Buttrwrth-Heinemann.
Sport & Medicine. 2nd ed. Peter N. Sperryn. Date not set. pap. write for info. (0-7506-1258-4) Buttrwrth-Heinemann.
Sport & Physical Education: Past, Present & Future. Earle F. Zeigler. 350p. 1991. pap. text ed. 18.80 (0-87563-367-6) Stipes.
Sport & Play in American Life: A Textbook in the Sociology of Sport. 2nd ed. Stephen K. Figler & Gail Whitaker. 368p. (C). 1990. per. write for info. (0-697-10690-X) Brown & Benchmark.
Sport & Play in American Life: A Textbook in the Sociology of Sport. 3rd ed. Stephen K. Figler & Gail Whitaker. 384p. (C). 1994. per. write for info. (0-697-15242-1) Brown & Benchmark.
Sport & Political Ideology. John M. Hoberman. 327p. (C). 1984. pap. 12.95 (0-292-77588-1) U of Tex Pr.
Sport & Politics: The Olympics & the Los Angeles Games. Bill Shaikin. LC 87-17660. 125p. 1988. text ed. 42.95 (0-275-92786-5, C2786, Praeger Pubs) Greenwood.
Sport & Politics in Canada: Federal Government Involvement since 1961. Donald Macintosh et al. 210p. (C). 1988. pap. text ed. 22.95 (0-7735-0665-9, Pub. by McGill CN) U of Toronto Pr.
Sport & Religion. Ed. by Shirl J. Hoffman. LC 91-685. (Illus.). 304p. (Orig.). 1992. text ed. 32.00 (0-87322-341-1, BHOF0341) Human Kinetics.
***Sport & Remedial Massage Therapy.** Mel Cash. (Illus.). 288p. 1997. pap. 24.95 (0-09-180956-8, Pub. by Ebury Pr UK) Trafalgar.
Sport & Social Organization. Howard L. Nixon, III. LC 75-31742. (Studies in Sociology). 64p. 1976. pap. text ed. write for info. (0-672-61337-9) Macmillan.
***Sport & Society: A Contemporary History.** Martin Polley. LC 97-24974. 1998. write for info. (0-415-14216-4); pap. write for info. (0-415-14217-2) Routledge.
Sport & Society in Latin America: Diffusion, Dependency, & the Rise of Mass Culture. Ed. by Joseph L. Arbena. LC 87-32271. (Contributions to the Study of Popular Culture Ser.: No. 20). 171p. 1988. text ed. 45.00 (0-313-24774-9, ARS/) Greenwood.
Sport & the Artist: Ball Games, Vol. 1. Mary A. Wingfield. (Illus.). 360p. 1988. 59.50 (1-85149-071-X) Antique Collect.
Sport & the Artist: Horse Racing, Vol. 2. Mary A. Wingfield. (Horse Racing Ser.). (Illus.). 250p. 1997. 59.50 (1-85149-094-9) Antique Collect.
Sport & the British: A Modern History. Richard Holt. (Oxford Studies in Social History). (Illus.). 424p. 1990. reprint ed. pap. 26.00 (0-19-285229-9) OUP.
Sport & the English Middle Classes, 1870-1914. John Lowerson. (International Studies in the History of Sport). (Illus.). 304p. (C). 1993. text ed. 69.95 (0-7190-3777-8, Pub. by Manchester Univ Pr UK) St Martin.
Sport & the English Middle Classes, 1870-1914. John Lowerson. (International Studies in the History of Sport). 320p. 1996. text ed. 24.95 (0-7190-4651-3, Pub. by Manchester Univ Pr UK) St Martin.
Sport & the Law. Edward Grayson. 1988. U.K. pap. 48.00 (0-406-25300-5, U.K.) MICHIE.
***Sport & the Law.** 2nd ed. Deborah Healy. 200p. 1996. pap. 29.95 (0-86840-199-4, Pub. by New South Wales Univ Pr AT) Intl Spec Bk.
Sport & the Law: A Guide for Everyone Involved in Sport. Deborah Healey. (Illus.). 144p. 1989. pap. 19.95 (0-86840-291-5, Pub. by New South Wales Univ Pr AT) Intl Spec Bk.
Sport & the Law: An Australian Perspective. G. M. Kelly. xlviii, 472p. 1987. pap. 79.50 (0-455-20712-7, Pub. by Law Bk Co AT) Gaunt.
Sport & the Making of Britain. Derek Birley. LC 93-81. (International Studies in the History of Sport). 1993. text ed. 75.00 (0-7190-3758-1, Pub. by Manchester Univ Pr UK) St Martin.
Sport & the Making of Britain. Derek Birley. LC 93-81. (International Studies in the History of Sport). 1993. text ed. 27.95 (0-7190-3759-X, Pub. by Manchester Univ Pr UK) St Martin.
Sport & the Mass Media: National & European Identities. Neil Blain et al. (Sport, Politics & Culture Ser.). 256p. 1993. pap. text ed. 29.00 (0-7185-1451-3) St Martin.
Sport & the Spirit of Play in Contemporary American Fiction. Christian K. Messenger. 456p. 1990. text ed. 39.50 (0-231-07094-2) Col U Pr.
Sport & Travel. Frederick C. Selous. 1988. 29.00 (0-935632-71-9) Wolfe Pub Co.
Sport & Work. Bero Rigauer. Ed. by Allen Guttmann. LC 81-793. 110p. (ENG.). 1981. text ed. 32.50 (0-231-05200-6) Col U Pr.
Sport Brockhaus. 576p. (GER.). 85.00 (3-7653-0021-7, M7626) Fr & Eur.
Sport-Brockhaus. 4th ed. Brockhaus. 576p. (GER.). 1984. 110.00 (0-8288-2346-4, M7626) Fr & Eur.
Sport Business: Operational & Theoretical Aspects. Peter J. Graham. 304p. (C). 1993. per. write for info. (0-697-16648-1) Brown & Benchmark.
***Sport Business Management.** Lori K. Miller. LC 97-7553. 1997. write for info. (0-8342-0942-X) Aspen Pub.
Sport Climber's Guide to Skyline Boulevard: Featuring Castle Rock State Park, Sanborn Skyline County Park & Mid-Peninsula Regional Open Space District Preserves. expanded ed. Bruce Morris. (Illus.). 123p. 1995. 17.50 (0-9650234-1-9) MorComm Pr.
Sport Climber's Guide to the Castle Rock Area: Featuring Stevens Canyon Boulder, Summit & Indian Rocks, the Western Addition, & Castle Rock Falls. Bruce Morris. (Illus.). 64p. (Orig.). 1992. pap. 10.95 (0-9650234-0-0) MorComm Pr.
***Sport Climbing.** John Long & Gia P. Franklin. (How to Rock Climb Ser.). (Illus.). (Orig.). 1997. pap. 12.95 (1-57540-078-2) Chockstone Pr.
***Sport Climbing Competition Handbook.** rev. ed. Peter Darmi. (Illus.). 64p. 1992. pap. write for info. (0-614-30359-1) Chockstone Pr.
Sport Climbing with Robyn Erbesfield. Robyn Erbesfield & Steven Boga. (Illus.). 112p. 1997. pap. 14.95 (0-8117-2930-3) Stackpole.
Sport Coach Manual for Competitive Cycling. USAC (Niederpruem) Staff. 252p. 1996. pap. text ed. 23.99 (0-7872-2114-7) Kendall-Hunt.
Sport Competition Structures. Charles F. Cicciarella. 72p. 1992. pap. 15.00 (0-926152-72-6) Persimmon Soft.
Sport, Culture & Society: A Reader on the Sociology of Sport. 2nd rev. ed. John W. Loy et al. LC 81-3692. (Illus.). 385p. reprint ed. pap. 109.80 (0-8357-7649-2, 2056975) Bks Demand.
Sport, Culture, & the Modern State. Ed. by Hart Cantelon & Richard Gruneau. LC 83-143220. 332p. reprint ed. pap. 94.70 (0-8357-6376-5, 2035730) Bks Demand.
Sport, Culture, & the Modern State: Papers Presented at a Conference Held at Queen's University, Kingston, Ont., Oct. 1979. Ed. by Hart Cantelon & Richard Gruneau. 315p. 1982. pap. 15.95 (0-8020-6493-0) U of Toronto Pr.
***Sport, Cultures, & Identities in South Africa.** John Nauright. LC 97-20139. (Sport & Nation Ser.). 1997. write for info. (0-7185-0049-0, Pub. by Leicester Univ Pr); pap. write for info. (0-7185-0072-5, Pub. by Leicester Univ Pr) Bks Intl VA.
Sport Diver's Guide to Sunken Treasure. unabridged ed. David Finnern. LC 96-67625. (Illus.). 151p. (Orig.). 1996. pap. 12.95 (0-9651204-0-6) Pearl Pub CA.
Sport Diving Catalog. Compiled by Herb Taylor. (Illus.). 320p. 1982. pap. 14.95 (0-312-75323-3) St Martin.
Sport Education: Quality PE Through Positive Sport Experiences. Ed. by Daryl Siedentop. LC 93-42450. 152p. 1994. pap. text ed. 16.00 (0-87322-435-3, BSIE0435) Human Kinetics.
Sport Ethics: Applications for Fair Play. Sharon K. Stoll & Jennifer M. Beller. Ed. by Angela Lumpkin et al. 1994. write for info. (0-318-72915-6) Mosby Yr Bk.
***Sport Facility Planning & Management.** Peter J. Farmer et al. LC 96-84609. 345p. (C). 1996. text ed. 41.00 (1-885693-05-2) Fit Info Tech.
Sport First Aid Updated Edition. rev. ed. Melinda J. Flegel. LC 96-22584. 1996. pap. 18.95 (0-88011-556-4, PFLE0556) Human Kinetics.
***Sport Fishing & Aquatic Resources Handbook: AL Version.** F. F. Hayden. 112p. 1996. per., pap. text ed. 0.20 (0-7872-2989-X) Kendall-Hunt.
Sport Fishing & Aquatic Resources Handbook: Student Manual, AK Version. American Fishing & Tackle Manufacturer's Association Staff. 112p. 1991. per., pap. text ed. 3.50 (0-8403-6930-1) Kendall-Hunt.
Sport Fishing & Aquatic Resources Handbook: Student Manual, CT Version. American Fishing & Tackle Manufacturer's Association Staff. 112p. 1991. per., pap. text ed. 3.50 (0-8403-6932-8) Kendall-Hunt.

Sport Fishing & Aquatic Resources Handbook: Student Manual, NM Version. American Fishing & Tackle Manufacturer's Association Staff. 112p. 1991. per., pap. text ed. 3.50 (*0-8403-6935-2*) Kendall-Hunt.

Sport Fishing & Aquatic Resources Handbook: Student Manual, WA Version. American Fishing & Tackle Manufacturer's Association Staff. 120p. 1991. per., pap. text ed. 3.50 (*0-8403-6929-8*) Kendall-Hunt.

Sport Fishing for Yellowfin Tuna. Dave Preble. Ed. by Bob Rhodes. (Fisherman Library). (Illus.). 136p. (Orig.). 1988. pap. text ed. 9.95 (*0-923155-07-4*) Fisherman Lib.

Sport Fishing in the Virgin Islands: Everything You Need to Know. Carol Bareuther. (Illus.). 113p. (Orig.). 1992. pap. 10.00 (*0-9631060-3-1*) Am Paradise.

Sport Governance in the Global Community. James E. Thoma & Laurence Chalip. 242p. (C). 1996. text ed. 36.00 (*1-885693-03-6*) Fit Info Tech.

Sport, Identity & Ethnicity. Ed. by Jeremy MacClancy et al. (Ethnic Identity Ser.). 256p. 1996. 45.95 (*1-85973-140-6*); pap. 19.95 (*1-85973-145-7*) Berg Pubs.

Sport in Africa: Essays in Social History. Ed. by William J. Baker & James A. Mangan. LC 87-1804. 320p. 1987. 49.50 (*0-8419-0906-7*) Holmes & Meier.

Sport in America: From Wicked Amusement to National Obsession. Ed. by David K. Wiggins. LC 94-16363. 360p. 1994. pap. text ed. 25.00 (*0-87322-520-1*, BWIG0520) Human Kinetics.

Sport in America: New Historical Perspectives. Ed. by Donald Spivey. LC 84-25265. (Contributions to the Study of Popular Culture Ser.: No. 12). (Illus.). x, 282p. 1985. text ed. 42.95 (*0-313-24705-6*, SSI/, Greenwood Pr) Greenwood.

Sport in Art. William A. Baillie-Grohman. LC 69-18532. (Illus.). 445p. 1978. 49.95 (*0-405-08228-2*, Pub. by Blom Pubns UK) Ayer.

Sport in Asia & Africa: A Comparative Handbook. Ed. by Eric A. Wagner. LC 89-7490. 312p. 1989. text ed. 69.50 (*0-313-25767-1*, WNS, Quorum Bks) Greenwood.

Sport in Australia: A Social History. Ed. by Wray Vamplew & Brian Stoddart. (Illus.). 280p. (C). 1995. text ed. 59.95 (*0-521-43513-7*) Cambridge U Pr.

Sport in Australian Drama. Richard Fotheringham. (Illus.). 272p. (C). 1992. text ed. 69.95 (*0-521-40156-9*) Cambridge U Pr.

***Sport in Australian History.** Daryl Adair & Wray Vamplew. (Australian Retrospectives). 176p. (Orig.). 1997. pap. 39.95 (*0-19-553590-1*) OUP.

Sport in China. Ed. by Howard G. Knuttgen et al. LC 89-49271. (Illus.). 240p. 1990. text ed. 29.00 (*0-87322-193-1*, BKNU0193) Human Kinetics.

Sport in Cuba: The Diamond in the Rough. Paula J. Pettavino & Geralyn Pye. LC 93-24372. (Latin American Ser.). 320p. (C). 1994. 49.95 (*0-8229-3764-6*); pap. 19.95 (*0-8229-5512-1*) U of Pittsburgh Pr.

Sport in Greece & Rome. H. A. Harris. Ed. by Howard H. Scullard. LC 77-39824. (Aspects of Greek & Roman Life Ser.). (Illus.). 288p. 1972. 35.00 (*0-8014-0718-4*) Cornell U Pr.

Sport in Schools. John Evans. 148p. (C). 1990. pap. 66.00 (*0-7300-0729-4*, ECT458, Pub. by Deakin Univ AT) St Mut.

Sport in Social Development: Traditions, Transitions, & Transformations. Ed. by Alan G. Ingham & John W. Loy. LC 92-38866. 296p. 1993. text ed. 45.00 (*0-87322-467-1*, BING0467) Human Kinetics.

Sport in Society: Equal Opportunity or Business As Usual? Ed. by Richard E. Lapchick & Jeffrey R. Benedict. LC 95-35477. 332p. 1995. 49.95 (*0-8039-7280-6*); pap. 23.95 (*0-8039-7281-4*) Sage.

Sport in Soviet Society. James Riordan. LC 76-9729. (Cambridge Russian, Soviet & Post-Soviet Studies: No. 22). (Illus.). 448p. 1980. pap. text ed. 24.95 (*0-521-28023-0*) Cambridge U Pr.

Sport in the Classroom: Teaching Sport-Related Courses in the Humanities. Ed. by David L. Vanderwerken. LC 88-46148. 328p. 1990. 45.00 (*0-8386-3354-4*) Fairleigh Dickinson.

Sport in the Global Village. Ed. by Ralph C. Wilcox. LC 94-70170. 556p. (C). 1994. text ed. 46.00 (*0-9627926-4-0*) Fit Info Tech.

Sport in the Industrial Age, 1850-1920. Steven A. Riess. Ed. by John H. Franklin & A. S. Eisenstadt. (American History Ser.). 150p. (C). 1995. pap. text ed. write for info. (*0-88295-916-6*) Harlan Davidson.

Sport in the West. Ed. by Donald J. Mrozek. (Illus.). 71p. (Orig.). 1983. pap. 15.00 (*0-89745-041-8*) Sunflower U Pr.

Sport Inside Out: Readings in Literature & Philosophy. Ed. by David L. Vanderwerken & Spencer K. Wertz. LC 84-23951. 782p. (C). 1985. pap. text ed. 14.95 (*0-87565-006-6*) Tex Christian.

Sport Instruction for Individuals with Disabilities: The Best of Practical Pointers. Ed. by Sue Grosse. (Illus.). 314p. (Orig.). (C). 1991. pap. 21.00 (*0-88314-507-3*) AAHPERD.

Sport Karate. Charles. pap. 12.95 (*0-901764-63-9*, 93224, Pub. by P H Crompton UK) Talman.

Sport Kite Magic! Vol. 1: Advanced Flying Techniques for More Kiting Fun! David Gomberg. (Illus.). (Orig.). (YA). 1996. pap. 14.00 (*1-884496-03-2*) Gomberg Kite.

Sport Law. Linda A. Sharp. 1990. 15.50 (*1-56534-025-6*) Ed Law Assn.

***Sport Law for Sports Managers.** T. Jesse Wilde & Doyice Cotten. 576p. (C). 1996. per., pap. text ed. 56.95 (*0-7872-3228-9*) Kendall-Hunt.

Sport Law Study Guide. Stephen C. Jefferies. 1985. ring bd. 26.00 (*0-931250-95-1*, ACEP0200) Human Kinetics.

Sport Lawyer's Guide to Legal Periodicals. Glenn M. Wong & Jesse T. Wilde. LC 93-8942. xx, 678p. 1994. lib. bdg. 85.00 (*0-89941-850-3*, 306400) W S Hein.

Sport Lawyer's Guide to Legal Periodicals 1995 Supplement. Glenn M. Wong & Jesse T. Wilde. 189p. 1995. 20.00 (*0-89941-989-5*) W S Hein.

Sport Machines. Norman Barrett. LC 93-33236. (Visual Guides Ser.). (Illus.). 48p. (J). (gr. 5-7). 1994. lib. bdg. 22.00 (*0-531-14299-X*) Watts.

***Sport Management.** 2nd ed. Davis. 1990. pap. text ed. 28.00 (*0-697-29508-7*) McGraw.

Sport Management: Successful Private Sector Business Strategies. Kathleen A. Davis. 320p. (C). 1994. text ed. write for info. (*0-697-13995-6*) Brown & Benchmark.

Sport Management Field Experiences. Jacquelyn Cuneen & M. Joy Sidwell. LC 94-72328. 142p. (Orig.). (C). 1994. pap. text ed. 26.00 (*1-885693-01-X*) Fit Info Tech.

Sport Marketing. Bernard J. Mullin et al. LC 92-36331. (Illus.). 312p. 1993. text ed. 42.00 (*0-87322-449-3*, BMUL0449) Human Kinetics.

***Sport Marketing: The Money Side of Sports.** Kermit Pemberton. Ed. by Kevin Myfois & DeAnn Steele. 344p. Date not set. pap. 29.95 incl. vhs (*0-9656421-8-6*) Sports Servs.

Sport Medicine: Incidence & Treatment of Athletic Injuries. E. C. Percy et al. LC 73-10382. (Sport Medicine Ser.: Vol. 1). 1973. 29.00 (*0-8422-7142-2*) Irvington.

Sport Medicine: Pathology. Olof Ringertz et al. LC 73-10369. (Sport Medicine Ser.: Vol. 3). 1973. 29.00 (*0-8422-7141-4*) Irvington.

Sport Medicine: Physiology. Kenneth D. Rose et al. LC 73-11032. (Sport Medicine Ser.: Vol. 4). 202p. 1974. text ed. 29.00 (*0-8422-7139-2*) Irvington.

Sport Medicine: Protection, Treatment & Nutrition. Russel M. Lane et al. LC 73-10420. (Sport Medicine Ser.: Vol. 2). 1974. 29.00 (*0-8422-7140-6*) Irvington.

Sport, Men, & the Gender Order: Critical Feminist Perspectives. Ed. by Michael A. Messner & Donald F. Sabo. LC 90-31880. (Illus.). 296p. 1990. pap. text ed. 22.00 (*0-87322-421-3*, BMES0421) Human Kinetics.

Sport of Bicycling - Helmet Laws, Head, & Body Injuries & Accident Prevention: Index & Reference Book of New Information. Ross R. Cabutan. 150p. 1996. 47.50 (*0-7883-0902-1*); pap. 44.50 (*0-7883-0903-X*) ABBE Pubs Assn.

Sport of Hope. Robert Selby. 134p. 1993. 14.95 (*0-9637626-0-5*) Support Our Srs.

Sport of Judo. K. Kobayashi. 9.95 (*0-685-38453-5*) Wehman.

Sport of Judo: As Practiced in Japan. Kiyoshi Kobayashi & Harold E. Sharp. LC 57-75. (Illus.). 104p. (J). (gr. 9 up). 1957. pap. 11.95 (*0-8048-0542-3*) C E Tuttle.

Sport of Kings & Other Stories. Tom Griffith. 60p. (C). 1990. 35.00 (*1-875238-00-X*, Pub. by Pascoe Pub AT) St Mut.

***Sport of Learning.** Fudzie. Date not set. 24.95 (*1-56743-069-4*); pap. 17.95 (*1-56743-070-8*) St Martin.

Sport of Learning: The First Comprehensive Guide for African-American Student-Athletes. Vince Fudzie & Andre Hayes. (Illus.). 224p. (Orig.). (YA). (gr. 9-12). 1996. pap. 12.95 (*0-9652824-0-6*) African Amer.

Sport of Nature. Nadine Gordimer. 352p. 1988. pap. 11.95 (*0-14-008470-3*, Penguin Bks) Viking Penguin.

Sport of Racing Pigeons: Everything One Needs to Know When Organizing, Participating in, Or Breeding & Grading Racing Pigeons for Entering Them in a Futurity Race. 2nd rev. ed. Herman Simpson. (Illus.). 296p. 1995. 75.00 (*0-9635180-0-3*) BayouView Pr.

Sport of Skin Diving. Charles F. Cicciarella. (Illus.). 68p. (Orig.). (C). 1982. pap. text ed. 8.95 (*0-89641-100-1*) American Pr.

Sport of the Gods. Paul Dunbar. (Masterworks of Literature Ser.). 1995. pap. 13.95 (*0-614-05585-7*) NCUP.

Sport of the Gods. Paul L. Dunbar. 15.00 (*1-56675-008-3*); pap. 12.00 (*1-56675-009-1*) Mnemosyne.

Sport of the Gods. Paul L. Dunbar. LC 69-18588. (American Negro: His History & Literature. Series 2). 262p. (C). 1978. reprint ed. 38.95 (*0-405-01859-2*) Ayer.

Sport of the Gods. Paul L. Dunbar. LC 69-18588. (American Negro: His History & Literature. Series 2). 262p. (C). 1991. reprint ed. pap. 27.95 (*0-88143-136-2*) Ayer.

Sport of the Gods. Paul L. Dunbar. (Notable American Authors Ser.). 1992. reprint ed. lib. bdg. 75.00 (*0-7812-2714-3*) Rprt Serv.

Sport on Film & Video: The North American Society for Sport History Guide. Ed. by Daryl Alder. LC 93-27967. 204p. 1993. pap. 32.50 (*0-8108-2739-5*) Scarecrow.

Sport, Physical Activity, & the Law. Neil J. Dougherty et al. LC 93-21763. (Illus.). 316p. 1993. text ed. 38.00 (*0-87322-512-0*, BDOU0512) Human Kinetics.

Sport Physiology Study Guide: A Manual to Accompany the Coaches Guide to Sport Physiology. Stephen C. Jefferies. 1986. pap. text ed. 32.00 (*0-87322-061-7*, ACEP0202) Human Kinetics.

***Sport, Policy & Politics: A Comparative Analysis.** Barrie Houlihan. LC 97-3355. 1997. write for info. (*0-415-12918-4*); pap. write for info. (*0-415-12919-2*) Routledge.

Sport, Power & Culture: A Social & Historical Analysis of Popular Sports in Britain. John Hargreaves. LC 86-15503. 288p. 1986. text ed. 39.95 (*0-312-75324-1*) St Martin.

Sport Preparticipation Fitness Examination. W. Ben Kibler. LC 90-33236. (Illus.). 120p. 1990. spiral bd. 25.00 (*0-87322-297-0*, BKIB0297) Human Kinetics.

Sport Psychology. Arnold LeUnes & Jack R. Nation. 477p. 1996. write for info. (*0-8304-1445-2*) Nelson-Hall.

Sport Psychology. Robert A. Mechikoff. 1996. text ed. write for info. (*0-205-16265-7*) Allyn.

***Sport Psychology.** Daniel L. Wann. LC 96-38684. (Illus.). 464p. (C). 1996. text ed. 46.33 (*0-02-424512-7*) Macmillan.

***Sport Psychology.** 4th ed. Cox. 1997. pap. text ed. 26.00 (*0-697-29507-9*) McGraw.

***Sport Psychology: An Analysis of Athlete Behavior.** 3rd ed. Ed. by Keith P. Henschen & William F. Straub. 1996. pap. 34.95 (*0-614-24659-8*) Mouvement Pubns.

Sport Psychology: An Introduction. 2nd ed. Arnold LeUnes & Jack R. Nation. LC 95-41298. (Nelson-Hall Series in Psychology). 592p. 1996. text ed. 45.95 (*0-8304-1306-5*) Nelson-Hall.

Sport Psychology: Concepts & Applications. 2nd ed. Steven M. Cox. 496p. (C). 1989. per. write for info. (*0-697-01340-5*) Brown & Benchmark.

Sport Psychology: Concepts & Applications. 3rd ed. Richard H. Cox. 464p. (C). 1993. per. write for info. (*0-697-12621-8*) Brown & Benchmark.

Sport Psychology: From Theory to Practice. 2nd ed. Mark H. Anshel. LC 93-32165. 1993. pap. text ed. 37.95 (*0-89787-626-1*) Gorsuch Scarisbrick.

Sport Psychology: From Theory to Practice. 3rd ed. Mark H. Anshel. LC 96-29200. 480p. (C). 1997. pap. text ed. write for info. (*0-89787-634-2*) Gorsuch Scarisbrick.

Sport Psychology: Psychological Consideration in Maximizing Sport Psychology. Ed. by L. K. Bunker & R. J. Rotella. 1985. 34.95 (*0-932392-20-2*) Mouvement Pubns.

Sport Psychology: The Psychological Health of the Athlete. Ed. by Jerry R. May & Michael J. Asken. LC 87-787361. 315p. 1987. 35.00 (*0-89335-304-3*) PMA Pub Corp.

Sport Psychology Interventions. Ed. by Shane M. Murphy. LC 94-10390. (Illus.). 392p. 1995. text ed. 42.00 (*0-87322-659-3*, BMUR0659) Human Kinetics.

Sport Psychology Study Guide. Linda A. Bump. (Illus.). 1989. pap. text ed. 32.00 (*0-87322-023-4*, ACEP0204) Human Kinetics.

Sport Psychs: Yes, I Can! Beasey S. Hendrix, III. 208p. 1996. pap. 16.95 (*1-888397-10-1*) High Prfmnce Athltcs.

Sport, Racism & Ethnicity. Ed. by Grant Jarvie. 224p. 1991. 65.00 (*1-85000-916-3*, Falmer Pr); pap. 27.00 (*1-85000-917-1*, Falmer Pr) Taylor & Francis.

Sport Record. Ed. by Richard Wyszynski. 120p. 1974. 75.00 (*0-318-13787-9*) Consol Athletic Comm.

Sport Rehabilitation Study Guide. Steven R. Tippett. (Illus.). 168p. 1991. spiral bd. 32.00 (*0-88011-447-9*, ACEP0208) Human Kinetics.

***Sport Safety Training.** American Red Cross Staff. (Illus.). 192p. (C). (gr. 13). 1997. spiral bd. 12.50 (*0-8151-0983-0*, 29435) Mosby Yr Bk.

***Sport Safety Training Course Text Package.** American Red Cross Staff. (C). (gr. 13). 1997. pap. text ed. 15.75 (*0-8151-0998-9*, 29483) Mosby Yr Bk.

Sport Safety Training "Trade" Handbook. American Red Cross Staff. (C). (gr. 13). 1996. 99.95 (*0-8151-2022-2*) Mosby Yr Bk.

Sport Scuba Diving in Depth. 2nd ed. Tom Griffiths. LC 90-53350. (Illus.). 256p. 1990. pap. 15.95 (*0-916622-85-1*) Princeton Bk Co.

Sport Sculpture of R. Tait McKenzie. 2nd ed. Andrew J. Kozar. LC 91-33632. (Illus.). 160p. 1992. text ed. 19.95 (*0-87322-336-5*, BKOZ0336) Human Kinetics.

Sport, Sectarianism, & Society in Ireland. John Sugden & Alan Bairner. LC 92-42149. (Sport, Politics & Culture Ser.). 240p. (C). 1993. 69.00 (*0-7185-1457-2*, Pub. by Leicester Univ Pr) St Martin.

Sport Signs. Incl. Signs & Printed Words, General Vocabulary. Harley Hamilton & Nancy K. Jones. 64p. 1985. pap. 6.00 (*0-317-42767-9*); Football. 48p. pap. 5.00 (*0-317-42768-7*); Basketball. Harley Hamilton & Nancy K. Jones. 48p. 1985. pap. 5.00 (*0-317-42769-5*); Baseball-Softball. Harley Hamilton & Nancy K. Jones. 48p. 1985. pap. 5.00 (*0-317-42770-9*); Track & Field. Harley Hamilton & Nancy K. Jones. 40p. 1985. pap. 4.00 (*0-317-42771-7*); Set. Volley Ball. Harley Hamilton & Nancy K. Jones. 28p. 1985. pap. 3.00 (*0-317-42772-5*); (Six Book Series in Sign Language). (J). 1985. Set pap. 20.00 (*0-317-42766-0*) Modern Signs.

Sport Sociology: Contemporary Themes. 4th ed. Andrew Yiannakis. 640p. (C). 1995. per., pap. text ed. 47.19 (*0-8403-9612-0*) Kendall-Hunt.

***Sport Source Official Athletic College Guide: Soccer 1997 Edition.** Ed. by Charlie Kadupski. (YA). (gr. 8-12). pap. 22.45 (*0-614-20345-7*) Spt Source TX.

Sport Specific Aerobic Routines. Leon Greene. 151p. 1989. pap. 18.95 (*0-912855-91-6*) E Bowers Pub.

Sport Summit Sports Business Directory. 2nd rev. ed. 906p. 1996. write for info. (*0-9644259-1-2*) E J Krause.

Sport Under Communism: A Comparative Study. Ed. by James Riordan. 1978. 24.95 (*0-7735-0505-9*, Pub. by McGill CN) U of Toronto Pr.

Sport under Communism: A Comparative Study. Ed. by James Riordan. 1982. pap. 24.95 (*0-7735-0533-4*, Pub. by McGill CN) U of Toronto Pr.

Sport Vehicle Blue Book, 1996. Intertec Publishing Staff. Date not set. 34.95 (*0-87288-597-6*, SMG961) Intertec Pub.

***Sportbike Performance Handbook.** Kevin Cameron. (Cyclepro Ser.). (Illus.). 160p. 1997. pap. 19.95 (*0-7603-0229-4*) Motorbooks Intl.

***Sportfish, Cruisers, Yachts: Owner's Manual.** TAL Marketing Services Staff. (Illus.). 104p. (Orig.). 1996. pap. 6.95 (*1-887960-01-5*, 596-207G) TotalConcepts.

Sportfishing Boats 28'-82' 1975-Current, 1996 Edition: A McKnew & Parker Buyer's Guide, 1996 Edition. M. Parker & Ed McKnew. 1996. pap. text ed. 17.95 (*0-07-045496-5*) Intl Marine.

Sportfishing Log. Weems & Plath Staff. (Illus.). 98p. (Orig.). 1991. pap. 15.95 (*1-878797-09-3*) C Plath North Amer.

Sportflier's Guide to RC Soaring. Jeff Troy. 1991. pap. 12.95 (*0-07-065288-0*) McGraw.

Sportflier's Guide to RC Soaring. Jeff Troy. (Doug Pratt's Modeling Guides Ser.). (Illus.). 160p. 1991. pap. 12.95 (*0-8306-3519-X*, 3519) McGraw-Hill Prof.

***Sportin' a 'Tude.** Patsy Clairmont. 1996. audio 22.99 (*1-56179-491-0*) Focus Family.

Sportin' a 'Tude: What Your Attitude Says When You're Not Looking. Patsy Clairmont. LC 96-15378. 1996. pap. 15.99 (*1-56179-470-8*) Focus Family.

Sporting Alien: English Sport's Lost Camelot. Mihir Bose. (Illus.). 224p. 1996. 29.95 (*1-85158-745-4*, Pub. by Mnstream UK) Trafalgar.

Sporting & Athletic Equipment Market. 370p. 1990. 995.00 (*0-318-00538-7*) Busn Trend.

Sporting Art & English Society. Stephen Deuchar. LC 88-165. (C). 1988. text ed. 50.00 (*0-300-04116-0*) Yale U Pr.

Sporting Art of Cecil Aldin. Roy Heron. (Illus.). 192p. 1990. 45.00 (*0-948253-50-9*, Pub. by Sportmans Pr UK) Trafalgar.

Sporting Ballistics Book. Charles W. Matthews. (Illus.). 184p. (Orig.). 1991. pap. 19.95 (*0-9613734-2-3*) B Matthews Inc.

Sporting Body. Mervyn Cross et al. (Illus.). 200p. 1991. pap. text ed. 29.00 (*0-07-452830-0*) McGraw-Hill HPD.

Sporting Body, Sporting Mind: An Athlete's Guide to Mental Training. John Syer & Christopher Connolly. (Illus.). 160p. 1988. 15.50 (*0-13-835539-8*) P-H.

Sporting Chance. Elizabeth Moon. 416p. (Orig.). 1994. mass mkt. 5.99 (*0-671-87619-8*) Baen Bks.

Sporting Chance: Sports & Gender. Andy Steiner. LC 94-47584. (Sports Issues Ser.). (Illus.). 96p. (J). (gr. 4-8). 1995. lib. bdg. 16.13 (*0-8225-3300-6*) Lerner Group.

Sporting Chef's Favorite Wild Game Recipes. Scott Leysath. Ed. by Donald A. Gazzaniga. (Illus.). 112p. (C). Date not set. text ed. 14.95 (*1-886571-02-3*) Arrowhead Classics.

Sporting Clays. A. J. Smith & Philip Upton. (Illus.). 156p. 1989. 19.50 (*0-932558-48-8*) Willow Creek Pr.

Sporting Clays: Expert Techniques for Every Kind of Clays Course. Michael Pearce. LC 91-8655. (Illus.). 160p. 1991. 16.95 (*0-8117-1914-6*) Stackpole.

Sporting Clays Handbook. Jerry Meyer. (Illus.). 144p. 1990. pap. 15.95 (*1-55821-066-0*) Lyons & Burford.

Sporting Club. Thomas McGuane. 1994. lib. bdg. 24.95 (*1-56849-401-7*) Buccaneer Bks.

Sporting Club. Thomas McGuane. 224p. 1996. pap. 11.00 (*0-679-75290-0*) Random.

***Sporting Collectibles.** Stephen Irwin. (Illus.). 288p. 1997. pap. 19.95 (*0-88317-200-3*) Stoeger Pub Co.

Sporting Collectibles. Vivien Karsnitz & James Karsnitz. LC 91-67009. (Illus.). 160p. 1992. pap. 29.95 (*0-88740-385-9*) Schiffer.

Sporting Craftsmen: A Complete Guide to Contemporary Makers of Custom- Built Sporting Equipment. Art Carter. (Illus.). 256p. 1994. 49.00 (*0-924357-46-0*, 61100-A) Countrysport Pr.

Sporting Craftsmen: A Complete Guide to Contemporary Makers of Custom- Built Sporting Equipment. deluxe limited ed. Art Carter. (Illus.). 256p. 1994. lthr. 95.00 (*0-924357-47-9*, 61100-B) Countrysport Pr.

Sporting Days. John T. Foote. LC 72-121544. (Short Story Index Reprint Ser.). (Illus.). 1977. 18.95 (*0-8369-3500-4*) Ayer.

Sporting Dogs. Barbara J. Patten. LC 96-23078. (Read All about Dogs Ser.). 1996. write for info. (*0-86593-460-6*) Rourke Corp.

Sporting Epicure: The Tradition of Great Game Cookery. Ronald Eden. (Illus.). 208p. 1992. 29.95 (*1-85626-015-1*) Trafalgar.

Sporting Females: Critical Issues in the History & Sociology of Women's Sports. Jennifer Hargreaves. 352p. (C). 1994. pap. 25.00 (*0-415-07028-7*) Routledge.

Sporting Fords Vol. 1: Cortinas. 2nd ed. Graham Robson. (Collector's Guide Ser.). (Illus.). 136p. 1990. 27.95 (*0-947981-39-X*, Pub. by Motor Racing UK) Motorbooks Intl.

Sporting Fords Vol. 4: Sierras. Graham Robson. (Illus.). 128p. 1991. 27.95 (*0-947981-55-1*, Pub. by Motor Racing UK) Motorbooks Intl.

Sporting Gentlemen: Men's Tennis from the Age of Honor to the Cult of the Superstar. E. Digby Baltzell. (Illus.). 420p. 1995. 30.00 (*0-02-901315-1*, Free Press) Free Pr.

Sporting Goods Agent: A Vital Link. Elmer A. Blasco. LC 91-157234. (Illus.). 168p. (Orig.). 1991. pap. 25.00 (*0-9630922-0-0*) Spt Gds Agents.

Sporting Goods Buyers 1996. Ed. by Edgar Adcock et al. 880p. 1995. pap. 185.00 (*0-87228-083-7*) Salesmans.

Sporting Goods Buyers 1997. Ed. by Elizabeth Onaran et al. 1996. pap. 195.00 (*0-87228-096-9*) Salesmans.

***Sporting Goods Buyers 1998.** Salesman's Guide Staff. 1997. 199.95 (*0-87228-108-6*) Salesmans.

Sporting Image: A Pictorial History of Queensland at Play. Maxwell L. Howell et al. 1989. pap. 34.95 (*0-7022-2206-2*, Pub. by Univ Queensland Pr AT) Intl Spec Bk.

Sporting Injuries. 2nd ed. Peter Dornan & Richard Dunn. (Illus.). 256p. 1988. pap. text ed. 19.95 (*0-7022-2064-7*, Pub. by Univ Queensland Pr AT) Intl Spec Bk.

Sporting Life: A Passion for Hunting & Fishing. Larry Sheehan et al. (Illus.). 1992. 40.00 (*0-517-58166-3*, C P Pubs) Crown Pub Group.

Sporting Life at Birch Brook Press Series. (Illus.). 1997. write for info. (*0-913559-16-4*) Birch Brook Pr.

Sporting Life Gourmet. Kathleen Krenzel & Robyn Heckendorf. (Illus.). 74p. (Orig.). 1980. 9.95 (*0-9605410-0-4*) R Louis Pub.

Sporting Lives. Michael Parkinson. 160p. 1996. pap. 15.95 (*1-85793-089-4*, Pub. by Pavilion UK) Trafalgar.

An Asterisk (*) at the beginning of an entry indicates that the title is appearing in BIP for the first time.

Sporting Minis: Mini Cooper, Mini Coopers 1275GT. John Brigden. (Illus.). 128p. 1990. 27.95 (*0-947981-40-3*, Pub. by Motor Racing UK) Motorbooks Intl.

Sporting News' This Day in Sports: A Day-by-Day Record of America's Sporting Year. Ron Smith. LC 94-20098. 1994. 75.00 (*0-02-897264-3*) Macmillan.

Sporting Profiles. Michael Parkinson. 160p. 1996. 35.00 (*1-85793-404-0*, Pub. by Pavilion UK) Trafalgar.

***Sporting Profiles.** Michael Parkinson. (Illus.). 240p. 1997. pap. 16.95 (*1-85793-878-X*, Pub. by Pavilion UK) Trafalgar.

***Sporting Rifle Takedown & Reassembly Guide.** J. B. Wood. (Illus.). 480p. (Orig.). 1997. pap. 19.95 (*0-87349-201-3*, SRAT) Krause Pubns.

Sporting Rileys: The Forgotten Champions. David G. Styles. 288p. 1988. 64.95 (*0-901564-70-2*) Auto Quarterly.

Sporting Scotland. John Burnett. (Illus.). 88p. 1995. pap. 6.95 (*0-948636-66-1*, 36661, Pub. by Natl Mus Scotland UK) A Schwartz & Co.

Sporting Scots of Nineteenth-Century Canada. Gerald Redmond. LC 80-67124. (Illus.). 352p. 1982. 40.00 (*0-8386-3069-3*) Fairleigh Dickinson.

Sporting Set: An Original Anthology. Ed. by Leon Stein. LC 75-1877. (Leisure Class in America Ser.). (Illus.). 1975. 23.95 (*0-405-06941-3*) Ayer.

Sporting Spite: Rebels & Rebellion in World Sport. Evening Standard Sports Writers Staff. (Illus.). 144p. pap. 14.95 (*0-7063-7078-3*, Pub. by Ward Lock UK) Sterling.

Sporting Success in Ancient Greece & Rome. Audrey Briers. 48p. (Orig.). 1995. pap. 8.95 (*1-85444-055-1*, 0551, Pub. by Natl Mus Scotland UK) A Schwartz & Co.

Sporting the Right Right: Surviving Family Violence. Walter H. Jackson. 102p. 1992. pap. 9.95 (*0-9634086-0-7*) Self Expansion.

Sporting Time: New York City & the Rise of Modern Athletics, 1820-1870. Melvin L. Adelman. LC 85-13967. (Sport & Society Ser.). (Illus.). 408p. 1986. pap. text ed. 14.95 (*0-252-06121-7*) U of Ill Pr.

Sporting Way to Reading Comprehension. Katherine Oana. Ed. by William H. Cooper. LC 84-51195. (Illus.). 68p. (Orig.). (J). (gr. 3-8). 1984. 3.95 (*0-914127-17-9*) Univ Class.

Sporting with Amaryllis. Paul West. LC 96-22766. 144p. 1996. 19.95 (*0-87951-666-6*) Overlook Pr.

Sporting with the Gods: The Rhetoric of Play & Game in American Literature. Michael Oriard. (Cambridge Studies in Latin American LIterature & Culture: No. 45). (Illus.). 500p. (C). 1991. text ed. 69.95 (*0-521-39113-X*) Cambridge U Pr.

Sportive Rhythmic Gymnastics. Maureen Vyse & Meryl Papas. 226p. (C). 1990. pap. 90.00 (*0-86439-137-4*, Pub. by Boolarong Pubns AT) St Mut.

Sportmanship. John S. Bowman. (Values Library). (Illus.). 64p. (YA). (gr. 7-12). 1990. lib. bdg. 15.95 (*0-8239-1110-1*) Rosen Group.

Sportometrics. Ed. by Brian L. Goff & Robert D. Tollison. LC 89-49065. (Economics Ser.: No. 11). (Illus.). 336p. 1990. 49.95 (*0-89096-425-4*) Tex A&M Univ Pr.

***Sportoons.** Larry Lambert & Dave Carpenter. Ed. by Stan Silliman. (Illus.). 88p. (Orig.). 1997. pap. text ed. 6.50 (*1-886682-03-8*) Comedy Emp Pr.

Sportparent. American Sport Education Program Staff. LC 94-3914. 96p. 1994. pap. 8.95 (*0-87322-696-8*, ACEP0452) Human Kinetics.

SportParent Course Package. American Sport Education Program Staff. (Illus.). 1994. pap. text ed. 95.00 incl. vhs (*0-87322-799-9*, ACEP0457) Human Kinetics.

SportParent Survival Guide: The Thinking Parent's Guide to Not Just Surviving Youth Sport-but Thriving in It! American Sport Education Program Staff. (Illus.). 16p. 1994. pap. text ed. 10.00 (*0-87322-697-6*, ACEP0453) Human Kinetics.

Sportplane Builder. rev. ed. Tony Bingelis. Ed. by David A. Rivers. (Illus.). 320p. 1992. pap. 19.95 (*0-940000-30-X*) EAA Aviation.

Sportplane Builder: Aircraft Construction Methods. Tony Bingelis. Ed. by David A. Rivers. (Tony Bingelis Ser.). (Illus.). 319p. 1992. reprint ed. pap. 17.95 (*0-940000-57-1*) EAA Aviation.

Sportplane Construction: A Builder's Handbook. Tony Bingelis. Ed. by Teresa Hawkins. (Illus.). 366p. 1986. reprint ed. pap. 20.95 (*0-940000-92-X*, 21-01395) EAA Aviation.

Sportplane Construction Techniques: A Builder's Handbook. Tony Bingelis. Ed. by Tressa Hawkins. (Tony Bingelis Ser.). (Illus.). 368p. 1992. reprint ed. pap. 20.95 (*0-940000-31-8*) EAA Aviation.

Sports. (Encyclopaedia Britannica Fascinating Facts Ser.). (Illus.). 32p. (J). 1993. 8.98 (*1-56173-323-7*) Pubns Intl Ltd.

***Sports.** (Illus.). 80p. (YA). (gr. 6-12). 1996. pap. 2.40 (*0-8395-5007-3*, 35007) BSA.

***Sports.** Ed. by Eleanor C. Goldstein. (Social Issues Resources Ser.: Vol. 5). 1996. 19.00 (*0-89777-201-6*) Sirs Inc.

Sports. Ian Graham. LC 94-34206. (Science Spotlight Ser.). (J). 1995. lib. bdg. 22.83 (*0-8114-3842-2*) Raintree Steck-V.

Sports. Tim Hammond. LC 88-1573. (Eyewitness Bks.). (Illus.). 64p. (J). (gr. 5 up). 1988. 19.00 (*0-394-89616-5*) Knopf Bks Yng Read.

Sports. Tim Hammond. LC 88-1573. (Eyewitness Bks.). (Illus.). 64p. (J). (gr. 5 up). 1988. lib. bdg. 20.99 (*0-394-99616-X*) Knopf Bks Yng Read.

Sports. Neil M. Jameson. LC 95-53698. (Discoveries Ser.). (Illus.). 64p. (J). (gr. 4-7). 1997. write for info. (*0-7835-4800-1*) Time-Life.

Sports. Jeffry Jensen. LC 95-2029. (Growing up Latino Ser.). (J). (gr. 2-6). 1995. write for info. (*0-86625-544-3*) Rourke Pubns.

Sports. Julie Rigby. LC 94-15315. 96p. (J). 1994. 13.95 (*0-8442-4361-2*, VGM Career Bks) NTC Pub Grp.

***Sports.** Julian Rowe. LC 96-33351. (Science Encounters Ser.). (J). 1997. write for info. (*1-57572-089-2*) Rigby Interact Libr.

Sports. Nigel Smith. LC 96-21834. (Then & Now Ser.). (Illus.). 32p. (J). (gr. 4 up). 1996. lib. bdg. 16.40 (*0-7613-0492-4*, Copper Beech Bks) Millbrook Pr.

Sports, Incl. 1986-1990 Supplements. Ed. by Eleanor C. Goldstein. LC Vol. 3. (Social Issues Resources Ser.). 1991. 95.00 (*0-89777-087-0*) Sirs Inc.

Sports: A Multimedia Guide for Children & Young Adults. Calvin Blickle & Frances Corcoran. LC 80-13519. (Selection Guide Ser.: No. 6). 245p. 1980. 27.95 (*0-87436-283-0*) Neal-Schuman.

Sports: A Pictorial Archive of Contemporary Illustrations. Typony Inc. 1989. pap. 7.95 (*0-486-26010-0*) Dover.

Sports: A Reference Guide. Robert J. Higgs. LC 81-20320. (American Popular Culture Ser.). xi, 317p. 1982. text ed. 49.95 (*0-313-21361-5*, HSR/, Greenwood Pr) Greenwood.

Sports: An Integrated Unit. Kathy Rogers. (Primary Thematic Units Ser.). (Illus.). 96p. (Orig.). 1993. pap. 12. 95 (*0-944459-84-6*) ECS Lrn Systs.

Sports: As Reported by the New York Times. Ed. by Gene Brown & Arleen Keylin. LC 76-2450. (Illus.). 1976. 16. 95 (*0-405-06689-9*) Ayer.

***Sports: Bobsledding & the Luge.** Childrens Press Staff. (New True Books Ser.). 1997. pap. 6.95 (*0-516-26203-3*) Childrens.

Sports: Careers in Sports. Staci Bonner. LC 93-9887. (Now Hiring Ser.). (Illus.). 48p. (J). (gr. 5-6). 1994. lib. bdg. 14.95 (*0-89686-789-7*, Crstwood Hse) Silver Burdett Pr.

***Sports: Figure Skating.** Childrens Press Staff. (New True Books). 1997. pap. 6.95 (*0-516-26204-1*) Childrens.

Sports: Guidebook for Reference & Research. Hugo H. Bronsen. LC 88-47627. 150p. 1988. 44.50 (*0-88164-652-0*); pap. 39.50 (*0-88164-653-9*) ABBE Pubs Assn.

Sports: Index of Modern Developments for Prompt Applications. Benard F. Parr. LC 90-56308. 160p. 1991. 44.50 (*1-55914-390-8*); pap. 39.50 (*1-55914-391-6*) ABBE Pubs Assn.

Sports: My Life's Track Record. Mae Mary. 1995. pap. 9.95 (*1-887679-52-9*) Foxglove Found.

Sports: Research & Medical Guidebook with Bibliography. Riley N. Wiseman. LC 87-47660. 150p. 1987. 44.50 (*0-88164-678-4*); pap. 39.50 (*0-88164-679-2*) ABBE Pubs Assn.

***Sports: Skiing.** Childrens Press Staff. (New True Books Ser.). 1997. pap. 6.95 (*0-516-26205-X*) Childrens.

***Sports: Speed Skating.** Childrens Books Staff. (New True Books Ser.). 1997. pap. 6.95 (*0-516-26206-8*) Childrens.

Sports: Superdoodles. LC 92-74098. (J). (gr. 1-6). 1993. pap. 4.95 (*0-88160-221-3*, LW305) Learning Wks.

***Sports: The Winter Olympics.** Childrens Press Staff. (New True Books Ser.). 1997. pap. 6.95 (*0-516-26207-6*) Childrens.

Sports Vol. 4: (Incl. 1991-94 Supplements) Ed. by Eleanor C. Goldstein. (Social Issues Resources Ser.). 1995. 95.00 (*0-89777-169-9*) Sirs Inc.

***Sports - Mental Health, Psychic Stress & Emotional Reactions: Index of New Information with Authors, Subjects, Research Categories & References.** rev. ed. Hugo H. Bronsen. 147p. 1997. 49.50 (*0-7883-1560-9*); pap. 39.50 (*0-7883-1561-7*) ABBE Pubs Assn.

Sports - Mental Health, Psychic Stress & Emotional Reactions: Index of New Information with References. Hugo H. Bronsen. 150p. 1996. 47.50 (*0-7883-0818-1*); pap. 44.50 (*0-7883-0819-X*) ABBE Pubs Assn.

Sports - Performance & Circadian Rhythms: Index of Modern Authors & Subjects with Guide for Rapid Research. Riley N. Wiseman. 200p. 1991. 44.50 (*1-55914-278-2*); pap. 39.50 (*1-55914-279-0*) ABBE Pubs Assn.

***Sports - the Importance of Oxygen & Anaerobic Thresholds in Training, Performance & Competition: Index of New Information with Authors, Subjects, Research Categories & References.** Max L. Mikker. 166p. 1997. 47.50 (*0-7883-1518-8*); pap. 44.50 (*0-7883-1519-6*) ABBE Pubs Assn.

Sports-a-Thon. Kathryn Lay. 18p. (J). (ps-2). 1993. 10.95 (*1-879680-17-3*) About You.

Sports Address Bible: The Comprehensive Directory of Sports Addresses. 8th ed. Ed Kobak, Jr. 348p. 1996. pap. text ed. 21.95 (*0-9619181-6-0*) Global Sports Prodns.

Sports, Adventure, & God's Power. 19p. (J). 1996. pap. 5.95 (*0-87510-309-X*) Christian Sci.

Sports Afield Fishing Almanac. Ed. by Frank Golad. (Illus.). 160p. (Orig.). 1989. pap. 17.95 (*1-55821-020-2*) Lyons & Burford.

Sports Afield Freshwater Fishing: A Comprehensive Guide for Beginners & Experts. Ed. by Frank S. Golad. (Illus.). 192p. 1992. pap. 15.00 (*0-688-11538-1*) Hearst Bks.

Sports Afield's Deer Hunter's Almanac: A Complete Guide to Finding, Taking, & Preparing America's Favorite Game Animals. Sid Evans. 288p. 1996. pap. text ed. 15. 00 (*0-87113-643-0*, Atlntc Mnthly) Grove-Atltic.

***Sports Afield's Eat Like a Wild Man: The Ultimate Game & Fish Cookbook.** Rebecca Gray. 1997. 25.00 (*0-614-27967-4*) Willow Crk Pr.

***Sports Afield's Eat Like a Wildman: 110 Years of Great Game & Fish Recipes.** Rebecca Gray. 1997. 25.00 (*1-57223-088-6*) Idyll Arbor.

***Sports Afield's Guide to North America's Greatest Fishing Lodges.** John E. Ross. LC 97-16540. 1997. pap. text ed. 18.95 (*1-57223-105-X*) Idyll Arbor.

Sports after Fifty: Fit Yourself into Fun Sports. Ted Overton. LC 88-70544. (Illus.). 224p. 1988. 17.95 (*0-913179-20-5*) Azimuth Pr.

Sports & Adventure Photography. Sean Hargrave. LC 95-12914. (Point & Shoot Ser.). (Illus.). 96p. 1995. pap. 11. 95 (*0-8174-5489-6*, Amphoto) Watsn-Guptill.

Sports & Anabolic Steroids: Index of Modern Information. Hugo H. Bronsen. LC 88-47866. 150p. 1988. 37.50 (*0-88164-924-4*); pap. 34.50 (*0-88164-925-2*) ABBE Pubs Assn.

Sports & Blood Pressure: Medical Subject Index with Bibliography. Jerry B. Holtz. LC 88-47625. 150p. 1988. 44.50 (*0-88164-664-4*); pap. 39.50 (*0-88164-665-2*) ABBE Pubs Assn.

Sports & Competitive Behavior: Index of Modern Information. Vicky W. Holibrook. LC 90-31768. 141p. 1990. 44.50 (*1-55914-226-X*); pap. 39.50 (*1-55914-227-8*) ABBE Pubs Assn.

Sports & Exercise for Children with Chronic Health Conditions. Ed. by Barry Goldberg. LC 95-30663. (Illus.). 381p. 1995. text ed. 49.00 (*0-87322-873-1*, BGOL0873) Human Kinetics.

Sports & Exercise in Midlife. Ed. by Stephan L. Gordon et al. 570p. 1994. pap. 65.00 (*0-89203-078-X*) Amer Acad Ortho Surg.

Sports & Exercise Injuries: Conventional, Homeopathic & Alternative Treatments. Steven I. Subotnick. LC 91-20892. 393p. 1991. pap. 18.95 (*1-55643-114-7*) North Atlantic.

Sports & Exercise Medicine. Ed. by Wood & Roach. (Lung Biology in Health & Disease Ser.: Vol. 76). 314p. 1994. 125.00 (*0-8247-9190-8*) Dekker.

Sports & Fitness: An Information Guide. Raymond J. Prytherch. 200p. 1988. text ed. 21.95 (*0-566-03569-3*, Pub. by Gower UK) Ashgate Pub Co.

Sports & Fitness Equipment Design. Ed. by Ellen F. Kreighbaum & Mark A. Smith. LC 95-33993. (Illus.). 232p. 1995. text ed. 45.00 (*0-87322-695-X*, BKRE0695) Human Kinetics.

Sports & Fitness Success from 6 to 16: A Guide for Parents & Educators. Michael Yessis. LC 96-51754. 256p. (Orig.). 1997. pap. 19.95 (*1-57028-108-4*) Masters Pr IN.

Sports & Freedom: The Rise of Big-Time College Athletics. Ronald A. Smith. (Sports History & Society Ser.). (Illus.). 320p. 1990. reprint ed. pap. 18.95 (*0-19-506582-4*) OUP.

***Sports & Games.** Neil Jamison. (Nature Company Discoveries Library). (J). (gr. 4-7). 1997. 16.00 (*0-614-29120-8*) Time-Life.

***Sports & Games.** Penny King. LC 97-24692. (Artists' Workshop Ser.). 1997. 19.96 (*0-86505-854-7*); pap. text ed. 8.95 (*0-86505-864-4*) Crabtree Pub Co.

Sports & Games in the Middle Ages: An Annotated Bibliography. John M. Carter. (Medieval Bibliographies Ser.: Vol. 12). 175p. 22.00 (*0-8240-7184-0*, H1369) Garland.

Sports & Heart Rate: Medical Subject Index with Bibliography. Alfred H. Irving. LC 88-47626. 150p. 1988. 44.50 (*0-88164-666-0*); pap. 39.50 (*0-88164-667-9*) ABBE Pubs Assn.

Sports & Law: Contemporary Issues. Ed. by Herb Appenzeller. 295p. 1985. 32.00 (*0-87215-929-9*) MICHIE.

Sports & Money: It's a Sellout! Karen Judson. LC 95-12174. (Issues in Focus Ser.). (Illus.). 112p. (YA). (gr. 6 up). 1995. lib. bdg. 18.95 (*0-89490-622-4*) Enslow Pubs.

Sports & New Exercise Research: Index of Current Information. Lindy H. Price. 150p. 1994. 44.50 (*0-7883-0068-7*); pap. 39.50 (*0-7883-0069-5*) ABBE Pubs Assn.

***Sports & New Exercise Research: Index of Current Information.** Lindy H. Price. 171p. 1997. 44.50 (*0-7883-1608-7*) ABBE Pubs Assn.

***Sports & New Exercise Research: Index of Current Information.** Lindy H. Price. 171p. 1997. pap. 39.50 (*0-7883-1609-5*) ABBE Pubs Assn.

Sports & Physical Education: A Guide to the Reference Resources. Compiled by Bonnie Gratch et al. LC 82-24159. xxi, 198p. 1983. text ed. 47.95 (*0-313-23433-7*, GED/, Greenwood Pr) Greenwood.

Sports & Play. 2nd rev. ed. Donna Martin. (Love 'n Hug Notes Ser.). (Illus.). 10p. (J). 1993. write for info. (*1-879127-44-X*) Lighten Up Enter.

Sports & Politics. Andrew Langley. (World Issues Ser.). (Illus.). 48p. (J). (gr. 5 up). 1990. lib. bdg. 18.60 (*0-86592-117-2*); lib. bdg. 13.95 (*0-685-46458-X*) Rourke Corp.

Sports & Psycho-Physiology: Index of Modern Information with Guide for Rapid Research. Hugo H. Bronsen. LC 92-26129. 1992. 49.50 (*1-55914-754-7*); pap. 39.50 (*1-55914-755-5*) ABBE Pubs Assn.

Sports & Psychological Influences: Index of Modern Authors & Subjects with Guide for Rapid Research. rev. ed. Hugo H. Bronsen. LC 94-34382. 145p. 1994. 44. 50 (*0-7883-0250-7*); pap. 39.50 (*0-7883-0251-5*) ABBE Pubs Assn.

Sports & Recreation. (Life in America 100 Years Ago Ser.). (Illus.). 104p. (YA). (gr. 5 up). 1995. lib. bdg. 19.95 (*0-7910-2848-8*) Chelsea Hse.

Sports & Recreation Fads. Frank W. Hoffman & William G. Bailey. (Fads Ser.). (Illus.). 397p. 1991. pap. 14.95 (*0-918393-92-2*); text ed. 49.95 (*1-56024-056-3*) Haworth Pr.

Sports & Recreation for the Disabled. 2nd ed. Jeffery Jones. (Illus.). 550p. (C). 1994. pap. 20.00 (*1-884125-04-2*) Cooper Pubng.

Sports & Recreation for the Disabled. Michael J. Paciorek & Jeffery A. Jones. (Illus.). 468p. 1994. reprint ed. pap. 19.95 (*1-57028-012-6*) Masters Pr IN.

Sports & Recreational Prov for Disabled People. Thompson. 1984. pap. 64.95 (*0-85139-620-8*) Buttrwrth-Heinemann.

Sports & Society. Ed. by Dwight W. Hoover & John T. Koumoulides. (Conspectus of History Ser.). (Orig.). 1983. pap. 5.95 (*0-937994-03-0*) Ball State Univ.

Sports & Society. Robert Lipsyte & Gene Brown. (Great Contemporary Issues Ser.). 35.00 (*0-405-13143-7*) Ayer.

Sports & Sporting Goods. Euromonitor Staff. 124p. 1987. 705.00 (*0-86338-202-9*, Pub. by Euromonitor Pubns UK) Gale.

Sports & Stress Therapy: Athletic Rehabilitation on Massage, Stretching & Strengthening. Eskay Shazryl & Jarrod Hanks. Ed. by Judy LeBlanc & Dave Henley. LC 93-74515. (Illus.). 144p. 1994. 19.95 (*0-9639757-8-1*) Eskay.

***Sports & the American Jew.** Steven A. Riess. LC 97-20930. (Sports & Entertainment Ser.). 1997. write for info. (*0-8156-2754-8*); pap. write for info. (*0-8156-2761-0*) Syracuse U Pr.

Sports & the Courts. Herb Appenzeller & H. Thomas Appenzeller. 423p. 1980. 19.50 (*0-87215-243-X*) MICHIE.

Sports & the Humanities: A Symposium. Ed. by William J. Baker & James A. Rog. LC 83-50027. 126p. (Orig.). (C). 1983. pap. 10.95 (*0-89101-055-6*) U Maine Pr.

Sports & the Law. Herb Appenzeller et al. (Illus.). 200p. (J). 1984. pap. text ed. 26.75 (*0-314-79386-0*) West Pub.

Sports & the Law: Major Legal Cases. Ed. by Charles E. Quirk. LC 94-35594. (American Law & Society Ser.: Vol. 04). 336p. 1996. text ed. 55.00 (*0-8153-0220-7*, SS765) Garland.

Sports & the Law in Canada. 2nd ed. Barnes. 368p. 1988. 75.00 (*0-409-81181-5*) MICHIE.

Sports & the Macho Male. 2nd ed. John Mitzel. 1976. pap. 2.50 (*0-915480-06-9*) Fag Rag.

Sports & the Spirit of Play in American Fiction: Hawthorne to Faulkner. Christian K. Messenger. LC 81-4843. 352p. 1981. text ed. 49.50 (*0-231-05168-9*) Col U Pr.

Sports & the Spirit of Play in American Fiction: Hawthorne to Faulkner. Christian K. Messenger. LC 81-4843. 352p. 1983. pap. text ed. 19.50 (*0-231-05169-7*) Col U Pr.

***Sports Architecture.** Sheard. (Illus.). 208p. 1997. text ed. write for info. (*0-419-21220-5*, E & FN Spon) Routledge Chapman & Hall.

***Sports Biomechanics.** Bartlett. (Illus.). 304p. (Orig.). 1997. pap. text ed. write for info. (*0-419-18440-6*, E & FN Spon) Routledge Chapman & Hall.

Sports Book. Joseph DiPalma. (Illus.). 52p. (YA). 1995. 11. 95 (*0-936459-30-1*) Stained Glass.

Sports Book: Everything You Need to Be a Fan in Philadelphia. Stan Hochman. 116p. (Orig.). 1995. pap. 6.95 (*0-9647806-0-7*) PB Pubns.

Sports Books for Children: An Annotated Bibliography. Barbara K. Harrah. LC 78-18510. 540p. 1978. 37.50 (*0-8108-1154-5*) Scarecrow.

Sports Broadcasting. John R. Catsis. LC 95-1215. 1995. pap. text ed. 27.95 (*0-8304-1379-0*) Nelson-Hall.

***Sports Buildings.** Allan Konya. LC 86-233552. (Briefing & Design Guide Ser.: No. 2). (Illus.). 182p. 1986. reprint ed. pap. 51.90 (*0-608-04412-1*, 2065193) Bks Demand.

Sports Car: Its Design & Performance. 4th ed. Colin Campbell. LC 77-94089. (Illus.). 306p. 1979. 24.95 (*0-8376-0158-4*) Bentley.

Sports Car & Competition Driving. Paul Frere. LC 92-54694. (Illus.). 156p. 1992. 17.95 (*0-8376-0202-5*) Bentley.

Sports Cards. Robert S. Young. LC 92-33761. (Collectibles Ser.). (Illus.). 72p. (YA). (gr. 5 up). 1993. lib. bdg. 13.95 (*0-87518-519-3*, Dillon Silver Burdett) Silver Burdett Pr.

Sports Cars. Consumer Guide Editors. 1990. 9.99 (*0-517-02734-8*) Random Hse Value.

Sports Cars. Ian Dussek. 1989. pap. 25.00 (*0-85263-850-7*, Pub. by Shire UK) St Mut.

Sports Cars. Sallie Stephenson. (Cruisin' Ser.). 48p. (J). (gr. 3-4). 1991. lib. bdg. 17.80 (*1-56065-078-8*) Capstone Pr.

***Sports Cars.** Sallie Stephenson. (Cruisin' Ser.). (Illus.). 48p. (J). (gr. 3-6). 1991. 18.40 (*0-516-35078-1*) Childrens.

Sports Cars. rev. ed. Jackson Jay. (Rollin' Ser.). 48p. (J). (gr. 3-9). 1996. lib. bdg. 17.80 (*1-56065-367-1*) Capstone Pr.

Sports Champs in Action. (J). pap. 1.95 (*0-590-31340-1*) Scholastic Inc.

Sports Coaching & Teaching. Gummerson. pap. 23.95 (*0-7136-3575-4*, 92774, Pub. by A&C Black UK) Talman.

Sports Collector's Bible. 4th rev. ed. Bert R. Sugar. LC 82-45889. 578p. 1983. pap. write for info. (*0-672-52741-3*) Macmillan.

Sports Collectors Digest: Baseball Card Pocket Guide, 1993. Sports Collectors Digest Editors. 576p. (Orig.). 1993. mass mkt. 5.99 (*0-446-36406-1*) Warner Bks.

Sports Collectors Digest Baseball Card Pocket Price Guide, 1992. Sports Collectors Digest Editors. 576p. (Orig.). 1992. mass mkt. 5.99 (*0-446-36283-2*) Warner Bks.

***Sports, Convention, & Entertainment Facilities.** David C. Petersen. LC 95-62037. 331p. 1996. pap. text ed. 59.95 (*0-87420-781-9*, S04) Urban Land.

Sports Curmudgeon. George Sullivan & Barbara Lagowski. 192p. (Orig.). 1993. mass mkt. 7.99 (*0-446-39399-1*) Warner Bks.

Sports Curriculum, Vols. I-VII. rev. ed. (Illus.). 645p. (YA). (gr. 7-12). 1994. pap. text ed. write for info. (*1-884480-50-0*) Spts Curriculum.

S

Sports Curriculum, Vol. 1: Footmatics, with an Academic Emphasis upon Football. rev. ed. Laurence A. Frame. (Illus.). 84p. 1993. teacher ed. 2.00 (*1-884480-62-4*); student ed. 12.50 (*1-884480-63-2*); pap. text ed. 14.50 (*1-884480-55-1*, A902896) Spts Curriculum.

Sports Curriculum, Vol. 2: Basematics with an Academic Emphasis upon Baseball. rev. ed. Laurence A. Frame. (Illus.). 66p. 1993. teacher ed. 2.00 (*1-884480-64-0*); student ed. 10.75 (*1-884480-65-9*) Spts Curriculum.

Sports Curriculum, Vol. 2: Basematics with an Academic Emphasis upon Baseball. rev. ed. Laurence A. Frame. (Illus.). 66p. (J). (gr. 5-9). 1993. pap. text ed. 12.75 (*1-884480-56-X*, TX36-187) Spts Curriculum.

Sports Curriculum, Vol. 3: Socmaticas, with an Academic Emphasis upon Soccer, Spanish-English, a Maintenance Bilingual Program. rev. ed. Laurence A. Frame. (Illus.). 132p. (ENG & SPA.). 1992. teacher ed. 14.00 (*1-884480-66-7*); student ed. 14.00 (*1-884480-67-5*) Spts Curriculum.

Sports Curriculum, Vol. 3: Socmaticas, with an Academic Emphasis upon Soccer, Spanish-English, a Maintenance Bilingual Program. rev. ed. Laurence A. Frame. (Illus.). 132p. (ENG & SPA.). (YA). (gr. 7-12). 1992. pap. text ed. 19.00 (*1-884480-57-8*, TX612-875) Spts Curriculum.

Sports Curriculum, Vol. 4: Sock, With an Academic Emphasis upon Soccer, ESL, a Transitional Bilingual Program. rev. ed. Laurence A. Frame. (Illus.). 101p. (YA). (gr. 7-12). 1993. pap. text ed. 14.00 (*1-884480-58-6*, TX1-245-033) Spts Curriculum.

Sports Curriculum, Vol. 5: Basketmatics with an Academic Emphasis upon Basketball. rev. ed. Laurence A. Frame. (Illus.). 100p. (J). (gr. 4-8). 1993. teacher ed. 2.00 (*1-884480-68-3*); student ed. 22.00 (*1-884480-69-1*); pap. text ed. 24.00 (*1-884480-59-4*, TX-2-400-454) Spts Curriculum.

Sports Curriculum, Vol. 6: With an Emphasis upon Computers, Phase II. Laurence A. Frame. (Illus.). 32p. (J). (gr. 3-12). 1993. pap. text ed. 9.25 (*1-884480-60-8*) Spts Curriculum.

Sports Curriculum, Vol. 7: With an Emphasis upon Computers, Phase I. Laurence A. Frame. (Illus.). 100p. (ENG & SPA.). (J). (gr. 3-12). 1995. pap. text ed. 15.00 (*1-884480-61-6*) Spts Curriculum.

Sports Day. (Tales from Fern Hollow Ser.). (Illus.). 22p. (J). (ps-1). 1985. 1.98 (*0-517-42789-3*) Random Hse Value.

Sports Day. (Read with Me Key Words to Reading Ser.: No. 9010-9). (Illus.). (J). (ps-2). 1990. 3.50 (*0-7214-1322-6*, Ladybrd); teacher ed. 3.95 (*0-317-04760-4*, Ladybrd) Penguin.

Sports Doctor, Vol. 1. abr. ed. Charles Ngwu. Ed. by Mrchido Nwangwu. (Illus.). 80p. 1997. pap. 5.95 (*0-9656754-0-8*) Concept Cascade. Charles Ngwu belongs to the new breed of writers who combine provocative inquiry & unvarnished commentary on the social interactions including the varied indiscretions of today's youth through fiction. He approaches romance, sex, crime & behind the scene pressures that sports figures & medical professionals face in a plot that involves a compelling cast of characters. Charles will, surely, provoke thousands of nurses with his portrayal of their romantic escapades with doctors in & out of their clinics. This is largely the story of the sexual escapades & the struggle by one gifted athlete & medical doctor who gets caught in the crossfire of his own perennial flirtation & infidelity. The lessons are very lucid.** ***Publisher Provided Annotation.

Sports, Drugs & Doping: Index of Modern Information. Hugo H. Bronsen. LC 89-77608. 175p. 1990. 44.50 (*1-55914-126-3*); pap. 39.50 (*1-55914-127-1*) ABBE Pubs Assn.

Sports Encyclopedia: Baseball. 8th ed. David S. Neft & Richard M. Cohen. LC 85-1833. 610p. 1988. 29.95 (*0-685-20014-0*) St Martin.

Sports Encyclopedia: Baseball, 1994. David S. Neft & Richard M. Cohen. (Illus.). 688p. (Orig.). 1994. pap. 19.99 (*0-312-10551-7*) St Martin.

Sports Encyclopedia: Baseball 1995. David S. Neft. 1995. pap. 19.99 (*0-312-11897-X*) St Martin.

***Sports Encyclopedia: Baseball 1997.** David S. Neft. 1997. pap. 19.99 (*0-312-15213-2*) St Martin.

***Sports Encyclopedia: Pro Football.** David S. Neft. 1997. pap. 19.99 (*0-312-15662-6*, Griffin) St Martin.

Sports Encyclopedia: Pro Football. 13th ed. David S. Neft. 1995. pap. 21.99 (*0-312-13186-0*) St Martin.

Sports Encyclopedia: Pro Football. 14th ed. David S. Neft. 784p. 1996. pap. 21.99 (*0-312-14424-5*) St Martin.

Sports Encyclopedia Vol. 1-10: Index & Reference Book of New Information, Set. Ed. by John C. Barton. 1500p. (YA). 1996. 335.00 (*0-7883-1075-5*); pap. 275.00 (*0-7883-1076-3*) ABBE Pubs Assn.

Sports Encyclopedia Baseball. David S. Neft. 720p. 1996. pap. 19.99 (*0-312-14135-1*) St Martin.

***Sports Encyclopedia: Index & Reference Books of New Information Vol. 1: Anaerobic Thresholds.** Max L. Mikker. Ed. by John C. Bartone. 150p. 1996. 44.50 (*0-7883-1077-1*); pap. 39.50 (*0-7883-1078-X*) ABBE Pubs Assn.

***Sports Encyclopedia: Index & Reference Books of New Information Vol. 2: Male & Female Athletes.** Allen Z. Buckner. Ed. by John C. Bartone. 150p. 1996. 44.50 (*0-7883-1080-1*); pap. 39.50 (*0-7883-1081-X*) ABBE Pubs Assn.

***Sports Encyclopedia: Index & Reference Books of New Information Vol. 3: Sports, Drugs & Doping.** Hugo H. Bronsen. Ed. by John C. Bartone. 150p. 1996. 44.50 (*0-7883-1082-8*); pap. 39.50 (*0-7883-1083-6*) ABBE Pubs Assn.

***Sports Encyclopedia: Index & Reference Books of New Information Vol. 4: Sports & Psychological Influences.** Hugo H. Bronsen. Ed. by John C. Bartone. 150p. 1996. 44.50 (*0-7883-1084-4*); pap. 39.50 (*0-7883-1085-2*) ABBE Pubs Assn.

***Sports Encyclopedia: Index & Reference Books of New Information Vol. 5: Sports Performance.** Jerry B. Holtz. Ed. by John C. Bartone. 150p. 1996. 44.50 (*0-7883-1086-0*); pap. 39.50 (*0-7883-1087-9*) ABBE Pubs Assn.

***Sports Encyclopedia: Index & Reference Books of New Information Vol. 6: Sports & Psycho-Physiology.** Hugo H. Bronsen. Ed. by John C. Bartone. 150p. 1996. 44.50 (*0-7883-1088-7*); pap. 39.50 (*0-7883-1089-5*) ABBE Pubs Assn.

***Sports Encyclopedia: Index & Reference Books of New Information Vol. 7: Sports & Competitive Behavior.** Vicky W. Holibrook. Ed. by John C. Bartone. 150p. 1996. 44.50 (*0-7883-1090-9*); pap. 39.50 (*0-7883-1091-7*) ABBE Pubs Assn.

***Sports Encyclopedia: Index & Reference Books of New Information Vol. 8: Sports, Exercise & Energy Metabolism in Men & Women.** Estee V. Valpone. Ed. by John C. Bartone. 150p. 1996. 44.50 (*0-7883-1092-5*); pap. 39.50 (*0-7883-1093-3*) ABBE Pubs Assn.

***Sports Encyclopedia: Index & Reference Books of New Information Vol. 9: Sports, Prevention & Control of Athletic Injuries.** Hugo H. Bronsen. Ed. by John C. Bartone. 150p. 1996. 44.50 (*0-7883-1094-1*); pap. 39.50 (*0-7883-1095-X*) ABBE Pubs Assn.

***Sports Encyclopedia: Index & Reference Books of New Information Vol. 10: Sports & Heart Rate.** Alfred H. Irving. Ed. by John C. Bartone. 150p. 1996. 44.50 (*0-7883-1096-8*); pap. 39.50 (*0-7883-1097-6*) ABBE Pubs Assn.

Sports Encyclopedia North America, Vols. 1-5. Ed. by John D. Windhausen. 1987. 36.00 (*0-87569-094-7*) Academic Intl.

Sports Encyclopedia of Baseball. David S. Neft. 1989. 29.95 (*0-312-02033-3*) St Martin.

Sports Encyclopedia of Pro Football. David S. Neft et al. (Illus.). 768p. (Orig.). 1994. pap. 19.99 (*0-312-11073-1*) St Martin.

Sports Encyclopedia, Pro Football. David S. Neft & Richard M. Cohen. 1989. pap. 18.95 (*0-318-42737-0*) St Martin.

Sports Equipment. 1990. 210.00 (*0-686-71957-3*, Pub. by Euromonitor Pubns UK) St Mut.

Sports Equipment Management. Walker. (Fitness & Health Ser.). 232p. (C). 1992. pap. text ed. 28.75 (*0-86720-281-5*) Jones & Bartlett.

Sports Equipment Price Guide. David Bushing. LC 95-79728. (Illus.). 336p. 1995. pap. text ed. 16.95 (*0-87341-349-0*, SEP01) Krause Pubns.

Sports Ethics. Gough. (C). 1996. pap. text ed. write for info. (*0-15-503528-2*) HB Coll Pubs.

Sports Ethics: A Reference Handbook. Lawrence H. Berlow. (Contemporary World Issues Ser.). 204p. (YA). (gr. 7 up). 1994. lib. bdg. 39.50 (*0-87436-769-7*) ABC-CLIO.

Sports Ethics in America: A Bibliography, 1970-1990. Donald G. Jones. LC 91-47538. (Bibliographies & Indexes in American History Ser.: No. 21). 320p. 1992. text ed. 55.00 (*0-313-27767-2*, JSE, Greenwood Pr) Greenwood.

Sports, Everyone! Recreation & Sports for the Physically Challenged of All Ages. Conway Greene Publishing Co. Editorial Staff et al. (Illus.). 272p. (Orig.). 1995. pap. 16.95 (*1-884669-10-7*) Conway Greene.

Sports, Exercise & Energy Metabolism in Men & Women: Index of New Information with Authors & Subjects. rev. ed. Estee V. Valpone. LC 94-34385. 167p. 1994. 47.50 (*0-7883-0378-3*); pap. 44.50 (*0-7883-0379-1*) ABBE Pubs Assn.

***Sports Facility Management.** Walker & Stotlar. LC 96-39659. 1997. write for info. (*0-7637-0283-8*) Jones & Bartlett.

Sports Facts. (Pocket Guides Ser.: No. 24). (Illus.). 128p. (J). 1996. pap. 6.95 (*0-7894-1021-4*) DK Pub Inc.

Sports Fan's Connection. 2nd ed. Morgan. Date not set. 62.00 (*0-8103-8512-0*) Gale.

Sports Fan's Connection: 1991. 91th ed. Morgan. 1991. 62.00 (*0-8103-7954-6*) Gale.

***Sports Fans Who Made Headlines.** Rick Wolf & Dale Ratermann. LC 97-16786. (Illus.). 128p. (Orig.). 1997. pap. text ed. 12.95 (*1-57028-117-3*) Masters Pr IN.

Sports Figures. Patrick Spielman & Brian Dahlen. LC 93-48073. (Woodworker's Pattern Library). (Illus.). 155p. 1994. pap. 10.95 (*0-8069-0485-2*) Sterling.

Sports Films: A Complete Reference. Ed. by Lawrence J. Babich. LC 85-43601. (Illus.). 622p. 1987. lib. bdg. 62.50 (*0-89950-227-X*) McFarland & Co.

Sports for Children: A Guide for Adults. James H. Humphrey. LC 93-28285. (Illus.). 218p. (C). 1994. pap. 29.95 (*0-398-06168-8*); text ed. 41.95 (*0-398-05890-3*) C C Thomas.

***Sports for Fun & Profit: Baseball, Basketball, Football, Softball, Tennis, Volleyball, Soccer & Bowling.** (Illus.). 350p. (Orig.). 1998. pap. 24.95 (*1-56559-918-7*) HGI Mrktng.

Sports for the Athletically Impaired. Tom Raabe. LC 92-54764. (Illus.). 256p. (Orig.). 1993. pap. 4.99 (*1-55591-133-1*) Fulcrum Pub.

Sports Franchise Game: Cities in Pursuit of Sports Franchises, Events, Stadiums, & Arenas. Kenneth L. Shropshire. LC 94-46405. 102p. 1995. text ed. 24.95 (*0-8122-3121-X*) U of Pa Pr.

***Sports Games & Pastimes.** (Information Guide Ser.). 1979. 62.00 (*0-8103-4393-2*, 00009582, Gale Res Intl) Gale.

Sports, Games, & Play: Social & Psychological Viewpoints. 2nd ed. Jeffrey H. Goldstein. 392p. 1988. text ed. 79.95 (*0-89859-875-3*) L Erlbaum Assocs.

Sports Games Play Book. Bradygames Staff. 1996. 9.99 (*1-56686-537-9*) Brady Pub.

Sports Geography. John Bale. 262p. 1989. pap. 24.95 (*0-419-14390-4*, E & FN Spon) Routledge Chapman & Hall.

Sport's Golden Age, a Closeup of the Fabulous Twenties. Ed. by Allison Danzig & Peter Brandwein. LC 68-58784. (Essay Index Reprint Ser.). 1977. 24.95 (*0-8369-0013-8*) Ayer.

Sports Graphics. (Illus.). 224p. 1994. 69.95 (*4-938586-53-3*, Pub. by PIE Bks JA) Bks Nippan.

***Sports Great: Brett Favre.** Jeff Savage. LC 97-22843. (Sports Great Books Ser.). 1998. write for info. (*0-7660-1000-7*) Enslow Pubs.

Sports Great Alonzo Mourning. Frank Fortunato. LC 95-49719. (Sports Great Bks.). (Illus.). 64p. (J). (gr. 4-10). 1997. lib. bdg. 15.95 (*0-89490-875-8*) Enslow Pubs.

Sports Great Anfernee Hardaway. George R. Rekela. LC 95-20298. (Sports Great Bks.). 64p. (J). (gr. 4-10). 1996. lib. bdg. 15.95 (*0-89490-758-1*) Enslow Pubs.

Sports Great Barry Bonds. Michael J. Sullivan. LC 94-37930. (Sports Great Bks.). (Illus.). 64p. (J). (gr. 4-10). 1995. lib. bdg. 15.95 (*0-89490-595-3*) Enslow Pubs.

Sports Great Barry Sanders. Ron Knapp. LC 92-38432. (Sports Great Bks.). (Illus.). 64p. (J). (gr. 4-10). 1993. lib. bdg. 15.95 (*0-89490-418-3*) Enslow Pubs.

Sports Great Bo Jackson. Ron Knapp. LC 89-29059. (Sports Great Bks.). (Illus.). 64p. (J). (gr. 4-10). 1990. lib. bdg. 15.95 (*0-89490-281-4*) Enslow Pubs.

Sports Great Bobby Bonilla. Ron Knapp. LC 92-38431. (Sports Great Bks.). (Illus.). 64p. (J). (gr. 4-10). 1993. lib. bdg. 15.95 (*0-89490-417-5*) Enslow Pubs.

Sports Great Books Series, 41 bks., Set. (Illus.). (J). (gr. 4-10). 1990. lib. bdg. 653.95 (*0-89490-342-X*) Enslow Pubs.

Sports Great Cal Ripken, Jr. Glen Macnow. LC 92-24158. (Sports Great Bks.). (Illus.). 64p. (J). (gr. 4-10). 1993. lib. bdg. 15.95 (*0-89490-387-X*) Enslow Pubs.

Sports Great Charles Barkley. Glen Macnow. LC 91-45827. (Sports Great Bks.). (Illus.). 64p. (J). (gr. 4-10). 1992. lib. bdg. 15.95 (*0-89490-386-1*) Enslow Pubs.

Sports Great Darryl Strawberry. John A. Torres & Michael J. Sullivan. LC 89-28918. (Sports Great Bks.). (Illus.). 64p. (J). (gr. 4-10). 1990. lib. bdg. 15.95 (*0-89490-291-1*) Enslow Pubs.

Sports Great David Robinson. Nathan Aaseng. LC 91-41532. (Sports Great Bks.). (Illus.). 64p. (J). (gr. 4-10). 1992. lib. bdg. 15.95 (*0-89490-373-X*) Enslow Pubs.

***Sports Great, David Robinson.** Nathan Aaseng. LC 97-14982. (Sports Great Books Ser.). (J). 1998. write for info. (*0-7660-1077-5*) Enslow Pubs.

Sports Great Dennis Rodman. Stew Thornley. LC 95-9229. (Sports Great Bks.). (Illus.). 64p. (J). (gr. 4-10). 1996. lib. bdg. 15.95 (*0-89490-759-X*) Enslow Pubs.

Sports Great Dominique Wilkins. Peter C. Bjarkman. (Sports Great Bks.). (Illus.). 64p. (J). (gr. 4-10). 1996. lib. bdg. 15.95 (*0-89490-754-9*) Enslow Pubs.

***Sports Great Eric Lindros.** Ken Rappoport. LC 96-52884. (Sports Great Bks.). (Illus.). 64p. (J). (gr. 4-10). 1997. lib. bdg. 15.95 (*0-89490-871-5*) Enslow Pubs.

Sports Great Greg Maddox. Stew Thornley. LC 95-49720. (Sports Great Bks.). (Illus.). 64p. (J). (gr. 4-10). 1997. lib. bdg. 15.95 (*0-89490-873-1*) Enslow Pubs.

Sports Great Hakeem Olajuwon. Ron Knapp. LC 91-41526. (Sports Great Bks.). (Illus.). 64p. (J). (gr. 4-10). 1992. lib. bdg. 15.95 (*0-89490-372-1*) Enslow Pubs.

Sports Great Herschel Walker. Jim Benagh. LC 89-28385. (Sports Great Bks.). (Illus.). 64p. (J). (gr. 4-10). 1990. lib. bdg. 15.95 (*0-89490-207-5*) Enslow Pubs.

Sports Great Isiah Thomas. Ron Knapp. LC 91-41528. (Sports Great Bks.). (Illus.). 64p. (J). (gr. 4-10). 1992. lib. bdg. 15.95 (*0-89490-374-8*) Enslow Pubs.

Sports Great Jerome Bettis. Stephen Majewski. LC 96-25400. (Sports Great Bks.). 64p. (J). (gr. 4-10). 1997. lib. bdg. 15.95 (*0-89490-872-3*) Enslow Pubs.

Sports Great Jerry Rice. Glenn Dickey. LC 93-19997. (Sports Great Bks.). (Illus.). 64p. (J). (gr. 4-10). 1993. lib. bdg. 15.95 (*0-89490-419-1*) Enslow Pubs.

Sports Great Jim Abbott. Jeff Savage. LC 92-522. (Sports Great Bks.). (Illus.). 64p. (J). (gr. 4-10). 1993. lib. bdg. 15.95 (*0-89490-395-0*) Enslow Pubs.

Sports Great Jim Kelly. Denis J. Harrington. LC 95-14144. (Illus.). 64p. (J). (gr. 4-10). 1996. lib. bdg. 15.95 (*0-89490-670-4*) Enslow Pubs.

Sports Great Joe Montana. Jack Kavanagh. LC 91-41527. (Sports Great Bks.). (Illus.). 64p. (J). (gr. 4-10). 1992. lib. bdg. 15.95 (*0-89490-371-3*) Enslow Pubs.

Sports Great John Elway. Larry Fox. LC 89-28465. (Sports Great Bks.). (Illus.). 64p. (J). (gr. 4-10). 1990. lib. bdg. 15.95 (*0-89490-282-2*) Enslow Pubs.

Sports Great John Stockton. Nathan Aaseng. LC 94-34940. (Sports Great Bks.). (Illus.). 64p. (J). (gr. 4-10). 1995. lib. bdg. 15.95 (*0-89490-598-8*) Enslow Pubs.

Sports Great Karl Malone. Jeff Savage. LC 94-3709. (Sports Great Bks.). (Illus.). 64p. (J). (gr. 4-10). 1995. lib. bdg. 15.95 (*0-89490-599-6*) Enslow Pubs.

Sports Great Kirby Puckett. Nathan Aaseng. LC 92-38433. (Sports Great Bks.). (Illus.). 64p. (J). (gr. 4-10). 1993. lib. bdg. 15.95 (*0-89490-392-6*) Enslow Pubs.

Sports Great Larry Bird. Jack Kavanagh. LC 91-41525. (Sports Great Bks.). (Illus.). 64p. (J). (gr. 4-10). 1992. lib. bdg. 15.95 (*0-89490-368-3*) Enslow Pubs.

Sports Great Magic Johnson. expanded rev. ed. James Haskins. LC 92-9188. (Sports Great Bks.). (Illus.). 80p. (J). (gr. 4-10). 1992. lib. bdg. 15.95 (*0-89490-348-9*) Enslow Pubs.

Sports Great Mario Lemieux. Ron Knapp. LC 94-21990. (Sports Great Bks.). (Illus.). 64p. (J). (gr. 4-10). 1995. lib. bdg. 15.95 (*0-89490-596-1*) Enslow Pubs.

Sports Great Michael Jordan. Nathan Aaseng. LC 92-11607. (Sports Great Bks.). (Illus.). 64p. (J). (gr. 4-10). 1992. lib. bdg. 15.95 (*0-89490-370-5*) Enslow Pubs.

***Sports Great Michael Jordan.** rev. ed. Nathan Aaseng. LC 97-5539. (Sports Great Books Ser.). (Illus.). (J). (gr. 4-10). 1997. lib. bdg. 15.95 (*0-89490-978-9*) Enslow Pubs.

Sports Great Muggsy Bogues. George R. Rekela. LC 96-14170. (Sports Great Bks.). (Illus.). 64p. (J). (gr. 4-10). 1997. lib. bdg. 15.95 (*0-89490-876-6*) Enslow Pubs.

Sports Great Nolan Ryan. William W. Lace. LC 92-41693. (Sports Great Bks.). (Illus.). 64p. (J). (gr. 4-10). 1993. lib. bdg. 15.95 (*0-89490-394-2*) Enslow Pubs.

Sports Great Orel Hershiser. Ron Knapp. LC 92-11329. (Sports Great Bks.). (Illus.). 64p. (J). (gr. 4-10). 1993. lib. bdg. 15.95 (*0-89490-389-6*) Enslow Pubs.

Sports Great Patrick Ewing. Jack Kavanagh. LC 91-41531. (Sports Great Bks.). (Illus.). 64p. (J). (gr. 4-10). 1992. lib. bdg. 15.95 (*0-89490-369-1*) Enslow Pubs.

Sports Great Pete Sampras. Victoria Sherrow. LC 95-19101. (Sports Great Bks.). (Illus.). 64p. (J). (gr. 4-10). 1996. lib. bdg. 15.95 (*0-89490-756-5*) Enslow Pubs.

Sports Great Reggie Miller. Stew Thornley. LC 95-51447. (Sports Great Bks.). (Illus.). 64p. (J). (gr. 4-10). 1996. lib. bdg. 15.95 (*0-89490-874-X*) Enslow Pubs.

Sports Great Scottie Pippen. Peter C. Bjarkman. LC 95-51440. (Sports Great Bks.). (Illus.). 64p. (J). (gr. 4-10). 1996. lib. bdg. 15.95 (*0-89490-755-7*) Enslow Pubs.

Sports Great Shaquille O'Neal. Michael J. Sullivan. LC 94-30536. (Sports Great Bks.). (Illus.). 64p. (J). (gr. 4-10). 1995. lib. bdg. 15.95 (*0-89490-594-5*) Enslow Pubs.

Sports Great Steffi Graf. Ron Knapp. LC 94-30538. (Sports Great Bks.). (Illus.). 64p. (J). (gr. 4-10). 1995. lib. bdg. 15.95 (*0-89490-597-X*) Enslow Pubs.

Sports Great Troy Aikman. Glen Macnow. LC 94-30537. (Sports Great Bks.). (Illus.). 64p. (J). (gr. 4-10). 1995. lib. bdg. 15.95 (*0-89490-593-7*) Enslow Pubs.

Sports Great Wayne Gretzky. Ken Rappoport. LC 95-18840. (Sports Great Bks.). (Illus.). 64p. (J). (gr. 4-10). 1996. lib. bdg. 15.95 (*0-89490-757-3*) Enslow Pubs.

Sports Guide: A Planning Guide for Cardiovascular Risk Reduction Projects at Sporting Events. (Illus.). 64p. (Orig.). 1996. pap. text ed. 25.00 (*0-7881-2823-X*) DIANE Pub.

Sports Gynecology: Problems & Care of the Athletic Female. Mona M. Shangold. LC 96-48787. (Illus.). 265p. (Orig.). 1996. pap. text ed. 34.95 (*0-86542-463-2*) Blackwell Sci.

Sports Hall of Fame. Bruce Nash & Allan Zullo. 1987. write for info. (*0-318-62709-4*) PB.

Sports Hall of Oblivion. Chuck Hershberger. LC 86-159616. 111p. (Orig.). 1985. pap. 3.95 (*0-938455-00-1*) Sports Hall Oblivion.

Sports Hall of Shame: Young Fans Edition. Bruce Nash & Allan Zullo. Ed. by Patricia MacDonald. 176p. (J). (gr. 5 up). reprint ed. pap. 2.95 (*0-671-69355-7*, Archway) PB.

Sports Hall of Shame's Funtastic Trivia & Sticker Book. Bruce Nash & Allan Zullo. (Illus.). 24p. (J). (gr. 1 up). 1992. pap. 3.95 (*0-671-74438-0*, Litl Simon S&S) S&S Childrens.

***Sports Heroes.** Jean Lacouture. (Illus.). 200p. 1997. pap. 12.95 (*2-85025-569-6*) Dist Art Pubs.

Sports Heroes, Feats & Facts. 1994. write for info. (*1-886614-00-8*) Intl Masters Pub.

Sports Hidden Pictures. Ed. by Jody Taylor. LC 92-76173. (Illus.). 32p. (Orig.). (J). (ps-5). 1993. pap. 3.95 (*1-56397-255-7*) Boyds Mills Pr.

Sports Illusion, Sports Reality: A Reporter's View of Sports, Journalism, & Society. Leonard Koppett. LC 94-12175. 312p. 1994. reprint ed. 13.95 (*0-252-06415-1*) U of Ill Pr.

Sports Illustrated: Great Moments in Pro Football. Bill Gutman. Ed. by Lisa Clancy. 128p. (J). (gr. 5 up). pap. 2.99 (*0-671-70969-0*, Archway) PB.

Sports Illustrated: The World Series. Ron Fimrite. 1996. 24.99 (*0-517-18303-X*) Random Hse Value.

Sports Illustrated Backpacking. Jack McDowell. 1989. pap. 9.95 (*1-56800-064-2*, Sports Illus Bks) Natl Bk Netwk.

Sports Illustrated Baseball: Play the Winning Way. rev. ed. Jerry Kindall. LC 87-32394. (Winner's Circle Ser.). (Illus.). 256p. 1993. pap. 11.95 (*1-56800-000-6*, Sports Illus Bks) Natl Bk Netwk.

Sports Illustrated Baseball Records Breakers. Bill Gutman. Ed. by Lisa Clancy. 144p. (gr. 5 up). pap. 2.99 (*0-671-70217-3*, Archway) PB.

Sports Illustrated Basketball. Neil D. Isaacs. 1988. pap. 9.95 (*1-56800-065-0*, Sports Illus Bks) Natl Bk Netwk.

Sports Illustrated Bowling. Herm Weiskopf. 1987. pap. 9.95 (*1-56800-066-9*, Sports Illus Bks) Natl Bk Netwk.

Sports Illustrated Competitive Swimming. Mark Schubert. 1990. pap. 10.95 (*1-56800-068-5*, Sports Illus Bks) Natl Bk Netwk.

Sports Illustrated Cross Country Skiing. Casey Sheahan. 1989. pap. 9.95 (*1-56800-069-3*, Sports Illus Bks) Natl Bk Netwk.

Sports Illustrated Figure Skating. John M. Petkevich. 1989. pap. 10.95 (*1-56800-070-7*, Sports Illus Bks) Natl Bk Netwk.

Sports Illustrated Fly Fishing: Learn from a Master. Bill Mason. (Orig.). 1994. pap. 11.95 (*1-56800-033-2*, Sports Illus Bks) Natl Bk Netwk.

Sports Illustrated Golf. Mark Mulvoy. 1988. pap. 9.95 (*1-56800-036-7*, Sports Illus Bks) Natl Bk Netwk.

An Asterisk (*) at the beginning of an entry indicates that the title is appearing in BIP for the first time.

Sports Illustrated Golf: Play Like a Pro. Mark Mulvoy. 1993. pap. 12.95 (*1-56800-007-3*, Sports Illus Bks) Natl Bk Netwk.

Sports Illustrated Hockey. Jack Falla. 1987. pap. 9.95 (*1-56800-037-5*, Sports Illus Bks) Natl Bk Netwk.

Sports Illustrated Lacrosse. Sports Illustrated Staff. (Illus.). 1991. pap. 10.95 (*1-56800-071-5*, Sports Illus Bks) Natl Bk Netwk.

Sports Illustrated Mountain Biking. Bob Woodward. 1991. pap. 10.95 (*1-56800-072-3*, Sports Illus Bks) Natl Bk Netwk.

Sports Illustrated 100 Years of Hoops. Alexander Wolff. (Illus.). 208p. 1995. 19.99 (*0-517-14690-8*) Random Hse Value.

Sports Illustrated Pitching. Pat Jordan. 1988. pap. 9.95 (*1-56800-073-1*, Sports Illus Bks) Natl Bk Netwk.

Sports Illustrated Pitching: The Keys to Excellence. rev. ed. Pat Jordan. LC 87-35639. (Winner's Circle Ser.). (Illus.). 140p. 1993. pap. 10.95 (*1-56800-001-4*, Sports Illus Bks) Natl Bk Netwk.

Sports Illustrated Putting. John Garrity. 1992. pap. 9.95 (*1-56800-074-X*, Sports Illus Bks) Natl Bk Netwk.

Sports Illustrated Racquetball. Victor I. Spear. 1988. pap. 9.95 (*1-56800-025-1*, Sports Illus Bks) Natl Bk Netwk.

Sports Illustrated Sailing. David Dellenbaugh. 1990. pap. 10.95 (*1-56800-029-4*, Sports Illus Bks) Natl Bk Netwk.

Sports Illustrated Scuba Diving. Hank Ketels. 1988. pap. 9.95 (*1-56800-027-8*, Sports Illus Bks) Natl Bk Netwk.

Sports Illustrated Skiing. Tim Petrick. (Illus.). 1989. pap. 9.95 (*1-56800-028-6*, Sports Illus Bks) Natl Bk Netwk.

Sports Illustrated Soccer. Dan Herbst. 1988. pap. 9.95 (*1-56800-038-3*, Sports Illus Bks) Natl Bk Netwk.

***Sports Illustrated Sports Almanac.** Sports Illustrated Staff. 1998. pap. text ed. 13.95 (*0-316-80008-2*) Little.

Sports Illustrated Sports Almanac, 1994. Ed. by Sports Illustrated Editors. 1993. pap. 10.95 (*0-316-80838-5*) Little.

Sports Illustrated Sports Almanac 1995. Sports Illustrated Editors. (Illus.). 1994. pap. 11.95 (*0-316-80860-1*) Little.

Sports Illustrated Strange & Amazing Baseball Stories. Bill Gutman. 128p. (J). (gr. 5 up). 1990. pap. 2.99 (*0-671-70120-7*, Archway) PB.

Sports Illustrated Strange & Amazing Football Stories. Bill Gutman. Ed. by Lisa Clancy. 128p. (J). (gr. 5 up). 1989. pap. 2.99 (*0-671-70716-7*, Archway) PB.

Sports Illustrated Strength Training. John Garhammer. (Orig.). 1987. pap. 11.95 (*1-56800-030-8*, Sports Illus Bks) Natl Bk Netwk.

Sports Illustrated Tennis: Strokes for Success. Doug MacCurdy & Shawn Tully. LC 93-28170. (Illus.). 1993. pap. 12.95 (*1-56800-006-5*, Sports Illus Bks) Natl Bk Netwk.

Sports Illustrated Track: Championship Running. Mel Rosen & Karen Rosen. LC 93-28169. (Illus.). 1993. pap. 12.95 (*1-56800-008-1*, Sports Illus Bks) Natl Bk Netwk.

Sports Illustrated Track & Field. Jim Santos. 1991. pap. 10.95 (*1-56800-031-6*, Sports Illus Bks) Natl Bk Netwk.

Sports Illustrated Tracking - Running. Mel Rosen. 1988. pap. 9.95 (*1-56800-040-5*, Sports Illus Bks) Natl Bk Netwk.

Sports Illustrated Training with Weights. Robert B. Parker. (Orig.). 1990. pap. 8.95 (*1-56800-032-4*, Sports Illus Bks) Natl Bk Netwk.

Sports Illustrated Volleyball: The Keys to Excellence. Doug Beal. (Orig.). 1993. pap. 12.95 (*1-56800-009-X*, Sports Illus Bks) Natl Bk Netwk.

Sports Illustrated 1996 Sports Almanac, Vol. 1. Sports Illustrated Staff. 1995. pap. text ed. 11.95 (*0-316-80883-0*) Little.

Sports Illustrated, 1997 Sports Almanac. Sports Illustrated Editors. 1996. pap. text ed. 12.95 (*0-316-80882-2*) Little.

Sports Imitated: The Swimsuit Issue Parody. Steve Lavapies. 80p. (Orig.). 1996. pap. 10.00 (*1-57297-071-5*) Blvd Books.

Sports Immortals: Defying the American Athlete. Peter Williams. (Sports & Culture Ser.). 161p. (C). 1994. 35.95 (*0-87972-669-5*); pap. text ed. 17.95 (*0-87972-670-9*) Bowling Green Univ Popular Press.

Sports in America. Sarah Flowers. LC 96-3430. (Lucent Overview Ser.). 80p. (J). 1996. lib. bdg. 17.96 (*1-56006-178-2*) Lucent Bks.

Sports in America. James A. Michener. 1987. mass mkt. 6.99 (*0-449-21450-8*, Crest) Fawcett.

Sports in America. James A. Michener. LC 75-40549. 1976. 15.95 (*0-394-40646-X*) Random.

Sports in America. Ed. by Peter Stine. LC 95-11556. 200p. (Orig.). 1995. pap. text ed. 14.95 (*0-8143-2557-2*) Wayne St U Pr.

Sports in America: Opposing Viewpoints. William Dudley. LC 93-30961. (Opposing Viewpoints Ser.). (Illus.). 264p. (YA). (gr. 10 up). 1994. pap. text ed. 12.96 (*1-56510-104-9*); lib. bdg. 20.96 (*1-56510-105-7*) Greenhaven.

Sports in America: Paradise Lost? Ed. by Oliver C. Trager. (Editorials on File Bk.). 224p. (YA). 1990. 29.95 (*0-8160-2412-X*) Facts on File.

Sports in American Life. Frederick W. Cozens & Florence S. Stumpf. LC 75-22810. (America in Two Centuries Ser.). 1976. reprint ed. 31.95 (*0-405-07681-9*) Ayer.

Sports in Cleveland: An Illustrated History. Text by John J. Grabowski. LC 92-7904. (Encyclopedia of Cleveland History Ser.). (Illus.). 168p. 1992. 29.95 (*0-253-32620-6*); pap. 9.95 (*0-253-20747-9*) Ind U Pr.

Sports in Contemporary Society. 5th ed. Eitzen. 1995. pap. text ed. 24.00 (*0-312-11985-2*) St Martin.

Sports in Dayton: A Bicentennial Celebration of the Dayton Area. Ritter Collett. LC 96-75102. (Bicentennial Bookshelf Ser.: Vol. 3). (Illus.). 376p. 1996. 34.95 (*0-913428-78-7*) Landfall Pr.

Sports in 5-D Stereograms. Ed. by Stephen Schutz & Susan P. Schutz. 1995. 12.95 (*0-88396-413-9*) Blue Mtn Pr CO.

Sports in Literature: Experiencing Literature Through Poems, Stories & Non-Fiction. Bruce Emra. 384p. 1994. pap. 20.95 (*0-8442-5498-3*, Natl Textbk) NTC Pub Grp.

Sports in North America Vol. 2: A Documentary History. Ed. by Larry Menna. 1995. 95.00 (*0-87569-136-6*) Academic Intl.

Sports in North America Vol. 4: A Documentary History. Ed. by George B. Kirsch. 1995. 95.00 (*0-87569-135-8*) Academic Intl.

Sports in North America, Vol. 3: A Documentary History. Ed. by George B. Kirsh. 1992. 72.00 (*0-87569-156-0*) Academic Intl.

Sports in the Twentieth Century. Tom Raabe. Ed. by Bob Baron. LC 95-8767. (Millennium 2000 Ser.). 144p. 1995. 12.95 (*1-55591-276-1*) Fulcrum Pub.

Sports in the Western World. rev. ed. William J. Baker. (Sport & Society Ser.). (Illus.). 368p. 1988. pap. text ed. 14.95 (*0-252-06042-3*) U of Ill Pr.

Sports-Induced Inflammation: Clinical & Basic Science Concepts. Ed. by Wayne B. Leadbetter et al. LC 90-1055. 799p. 1990. 95.00 (*0-89203-037-2*) Amer Acad Ortho Surg.

Sports Industry & Collective Bargaining. 2nd ed. Paul D. Staudohar. LC 89-1831. 224p. 1989. pap. 12.95 (*0-87546-151-4*, ILR Press) Cornell U Pr.

***Sports Injuries.** Fuller & Oakes. Date not set. pap. text ed. write for info. (*0-85896-143-1*) Addison-Wesley.

Sports Injuries. Ed. by Vivian Grisogono. (Illus.). 264p. 1989. pap. text ed. 29.00 (*0-443-03175-4*) Churchill.

Sports Injuries. Leslie J. Speight. 197p. 1989. pap. 5.95 (*0-85207-213-9*, Pub. by C W Daniel UK) Natl Bk Netwk.

Sports Injuries: A Self-Help Guide. Vivian Grisogono. LC 94-19341. 1994. pap. 16.95 (*0-89594-716-1*) Crossing Pr.

Sports Injuries: A Self-Help Guide. Vivian Grisogono. (Illus.). 294p. 1989. pap. 29.95 (*0-7195-4111-5*, Pub. by John Murray UK) Trafalgar.

Sports Injuries: Basic Principles of Prevention & Care. 2nd ed. Ed. by P. A. Renstrom. (Encyclopaedia of Sports Medicine Ser.: Vol. 4). (Illus.). 165p. 1993. text ed. 59.95 (*0-632-03331-2*, BREN3331, Pub. by Blackwell UK) Human Kinetics.

Sports Injuries: Causes, Diagnosis, Treatment & Prevention. S. Bird et al. (Illus.). 220p. (Orig.). 1997. pap. 47.75 (*1-56593-196-3*, 0511) Singular Publishing.

Sports Injuries: Diagnosis & Management for Physiotherapists. Christopher M. Norris. LC 92-22841. (Illus.). 327p. 1993. pap. 55.00 (*0-7506-0156-6*) Buttrwrth-Heinemann.

Sports Injuries: Diagnosis & Mgmt. Garrick & Webb. 368p. 1990. text ed. 65.00 (*0-7216-2127-9*) Saunders.

Sports Injuries: Diagnosis & Treatment. 2nd ed. Garrick. 1998. text ed. write for info. (*0-7216-4434-1*) HarBrace.

Sports Injuries: Mechanisms, Prevention, & Treatment. Ed. by Freddie H. Fu & David A. Stone. LC 93-31440. (Illus.). 1040p. 1994. 149.00 (*0-683-03388-3*) Williams & Wilkins.

Sports Injuries: Recognition & Management. 2nd ed. Ed. by Michael A. Hutson. (Illus.). 252p. 1996. 98.00 (*0-19-262676-0*); pap. 45.00 (*0-19-262675-2*) OUP.

Sports Injuries: The Unthwarted Epidemic. Ed. by Paul F. Vinger & Earl F. Hoerner. LC 79-22195. 429p. reprint ed. pap. 122.30 (*0-8357-7867-3*, 2036284) Bks Demand.

Sports Injuries: Their Treatment by Homeopathy & Acupressure. Leslie J. Speight. 76p. (Orig.). 1991. pap. 11.95 (*0-8464-1535-6*) Beekman Pubs.

***Sports Injuries & Their Treatment.** Ed. by Helal et al. (Illus.). 520p. (C). (gr. 13 up). 1987. text ed. 158.95 (*0-412-23950-7*) Chapman & Hall.

Sports Injuries of the Ankle & Foot. George J. Lian & Richard A. Marder. LC 96-7605. (Illus.). 224p. 1996. 135.00 (*0-387-94687-X*) Spr-Verlag.

Sports Injuries of the Lower Extremity. McNerney. 1996. text ed. write for info. (*0-7216-3746-9*) Saunders.

Sports Injuries of the Shoulder: Conservative Management. Ed. by Thomas Souza. (Illus.). 640p. 1993. text ed. 129. 95 (*0-443-08844-6*) Churchill.

Sports Injuries Sourcebook. Ed. by Heather Aldred. (Health Reference Ser.). 1996. lib. bdg. 75.00 (*0-7808-0218-7*) Omnigraphics Inc.

Sports Injury Assessment & Rehabilitation. David C. Reid. (Illus.). 1269p. 1992. text ed. 134.00 (*0-443-08662-1*) Churchill.

Sports Injury Care. Thomas E. Abdenour. (Fitness & Health Ser.). 256p. 1993. spiral bd. 17.50 (*0-86720-282-3*) Jones & Bartlett.

Sports Injury Handbook: Professional Advice for Amateur Athletes. Allan M. Levy & Mark L. Fuerst. LC 92-29435. 304p. 1993. pap. text ed. 18.95 (*0-471-54737-9*) Wiley.

Sports Injury Management. Marcia K. Anderson & Susan J. Hall. LC 94-12487. 1995. 45.95 (*0-683-01752-7*); 45. 95 (*0-683-00175-2*) Williams & Wilkins.

Sports Injury Management. Maria K. Anderson & Susan J. Hall. 1994. 43.95 (*0-8121-1754-9*) Williams & Wilkins.

Sports Jingo. Gary Grimm & Phoebe Wear. 32p. (J). (gr. k-6). 1995. 12.00 (*1-56490-012-6*) G Grimm Assocs.

***Sports, Jobs & Taxes: The Economic Impact of Sports Teams & Facilities.** Ed. by Roger G. Noll & Andrew Zimbalist. 420p. 1997. 49.95 (*0-8157-6110-4*); pap. 22.95 (*0-8157-6111-2*) Brookings.

Sports Jokes. Gary Chmielewski. (Smile-a-While Ser.). (Illus.). (J). (gr. 2-3). 1986. 13.27 (*0-86592-683-2*); lib. bdg. 9.95 (*0-685-58364-3*) Rourke Corp.

Sports Jokes. Bill Stott. Ed. by Helen Exley & Samantha Armstrong. (Joke Bks.). (Illus.). 60p. 1993. 6.99 (*1-85015-403-1*) Exley Giftbooks.

Sports Jokes. Viki Woodworth. (Funny Side up Ser.). (Illus.). 32p. (J). (gr. 1-4). 1991. lib. bdg. 19.93 (*0-89565-727-9*) Childs World.

Sports Journalism at Its Best: Pulitzer Prize-Winning Articles, Cartoons & Photographs. Heinz-Dietrich Fischer. LC 94-27374. (Illus.). 1995. pap. text ed. 19.95 (*0-8304-1365-0*) Nelson-Hall.

Sports Jumbles: Word Power Workouts. (Jumble Ser.). (Illus.). 192p. (Orig.). 1996. pap. 9.95 (*1-57243-113-X*) Triumph Bks.

Sports Junkies Rejoice! The Birth of ESPN. Bill Rasmussen. 256p. 1983. 14.95 (*0-318-00106-3*) QV Pub.

Sports Lab. Robert Sheely. LC 93-41621. (Science Lab Ser.). 64p. (J). (gr. 4-6). 1994. lib. bdg. 13.95 (*1-881889-49-1*) Silver Moon.

Sports Lab see Police Lab; Sports Lab; Entertainment Lab

Sports Law. Robert McCormick et al. 588p. (C). 1996. ring bd. 49.50 (*1-879581-26-4*) Lupus Pubns.

Sports Law. George W. Schubert et al. 395p. 1986. text ed. 29.00 (*0-314-99967-1*) West Pub.

Sports Law: A Practical Guide. Ed. by Mark Fewell. 1995. pap. 75.00 (*0-455-21366-6*) Gaunt.

***Sports Law: Cases & Materials.** Michael J. Cozzillio & Mark S. Levinstein. 900p. (C). 1997. text ed. 75.00 (*0-89089-835-9*) Carolina Acad Pr.

Sports Law: Cases & Materials. Raymond L. Yasser et al. 498p. 1990. 49.00 (*0-87084-789-9*) Anderson Pub Co.

Sports Law: Cases & Materials. 2nd ed. James R. McCurdy et al. LC 93-40229. 1993. 56.00 (*0-87084-799-6*) Anderson Pub Co.

***Sports Law: Cases & Materials.** 3rd ed. Ray L. Yasser et al. 876p. (C). 1997. text ed. 57.95 (*0-87084-798-8*) Anderson Pub Co.

Sports Law & Legislation: An Annotated Bibliography. Compiled by John Hladczuk et al. LC 91-30204. (Bibliographies & Indexes in Law & Political Science Ser.: No. 15). 344p. 1991. text ed. 59.95 (*0-313-26499-6*, HIZ/, Greenwood Pr) Greenwood.

Sports Law for Educational Institutions. Steven C. Wade & Robert D. Hay. LC 87-37573. 216p. 1988. text ed. 55.00 (*0-89930-335-8*, HSL/, Quorum Bks) Greenwood.

Sports Law in a Nutshell. Walter T. Champion. (Nutshell Ser.). 325p. 1993. pap. 16.50 (*0-314-01642-2*) West Pub.

Sports Law Practice, 2 vols., Set. Martin J. Greenberg. 1992. 180.00 (*0-87473-961-6*) MICHIE.

Sports Leagues & Teams: An Encyclopedia, 1871-1996. Mark Pollack. LC 96-50084. 664p. 1996. lib. bdg. 65.00 (*0-7864-0252-0*) McFarland & Co.

***Sports, Leisure & Ergonomics.** Ed. by Atkinson & T. Reilly. (Illus.). 336p. 1995. text ed. 89.95 (*0-419-20600-0*, E & FN Spon) Routledge Chapman & Hall.

***Sports Life.** J. Ennis Kirkland. (Illus.). 104p. (Orig.). 1986. pap. 7.50 (*0-9657093-0-2*) Copperline Pub.

Sports Lighting. rev. ed. IES Committee on Sports & Recreational Areas Lighting Staff. (Recommended Practices Ser.). (Illus.). 107p. 1989. pap. 40.00 (*0-87995-028-5*, RP-6-88) Illum Eng.

Sports Logo Guide: Premiere Edition. John M. Fulgaro. LC 94-92185. (Illus.). 290p. (Orig.). 1994. pap. 16.95 (*1-885497-00-8*) Sports Fanatic.

***Sports Logos.** Carter. Date not set. 35.00 (*0-688-15349-6*) Morrow.

***Sports Management & Administration.** Watt. (Illus.). 256p. 1996. text ed. 77.50 (*0-419-19640-4*, E & FN Spon) Routledge Chapman & Hall.

Sports Market Place. 16th ed. Richard A. Lipsey. 1350p. 1996. pap. 199.00 (*0-935644-02-4*) Sportsguide.

Sports Market Place Register 1995. Richard A. Lipsey. 600p. 1996. pap. 59.00 (*0-935644-03-2*) Sportsguide.

Sports Marketing. Howard Schlossberg. 200p. 1996. pap. 22.95 (*1-55786-590-6*) Blackwell Pubs.

Sports Marketing: Competitive Business Strategies for Sport. Christine Brooks. 333p. 1994. text ed. 56.00 (*0-13-835893-1*) P-H.

Sports Marketing: It's Not Just a Game Anymore. Phil Schaaf. (Illus.). 355p. 1995. 25.95 (*1-57392-019-3*) Prometheus Bks.

***Sports Marketing: The Money Side of Sports. Kermit Pemberton. 330p. (Orig.). 1997. pap. 22. 95 (*0-9656421-9-4*) Sports Servs.**
Finally there is a book that provides an easy-to-understand, step-by-step explanation of the multibillion dollar business of sports! Over $26 billion is spent on health & fitness-themed events. Six of the top-rated television programs in history have been sporting events. Estimates suggest that the sports market totals $174 billion annually; $40 million is spent per year for Michael Jordan to endorse products & up to $500,000 has been paid for a single baseball. Introduction; Chapter 1 - Sports Marketing, Chapter 2 - Marketing Products Through Sports, Chapter 3 - Sponsorship, Chapter 4 - Promotion, Chapter 5 - Endorsements; Chapter 6 - Athlete Marketing, Chapter 7 - Broadcasting & Media, Chapter 8 - The Development of a Special Event, Chapter 9 - The Women's Sport Market, Chapter 10 - Marketing Sports Event Tickets, Chapter 11 - Operation Costs & Ownership, Chapter 12 - An Inside Look at Bijian & Michael Jordan, Chapter 13 - Operating a Sports Marketing Firm. "This is a must read book for any student, instructor, or any person looking to expand knowledge in sports marketing. Step-by-step outlines & real-life examples of sports promotions are the key to learning how to tie in professional sports with products & services." ***Publisher Provided Annotation.***

***Sports Marketing: The Money Side of Sports (Educational Program; includes video "Famous People Sell Famous Products" & tapes "Media Attention with Sports Celebrity" & "Increase Profits, Motivate Customers, Employees & Distributors through Sports")** Kermit Pemberton. 330p. 1997. pap. 177.50 incl. audio, vhs (*0-9656421-6-X*) Sports Servs.

Sports Marketing Europe: The Legal & Tax Aspects. Ed. by Ian S. Blackshaw & Gillian Hogg. LC 93-5893. 1993. write for info. (*90-6544-678-8*) Kluwer Law Tax Pubs.

Sports Marketing Guide. Terence R. Wascovich. LC 93-85421. (Illus.). 318p. (Orig.). (C). 1995. pap. text ed. 39. 00 (*0-9638238-0-9*) Pts Ahead.

***Sports Massage.** Hungerford. 1997. pap. text ed. 34.95 (*0-8385-8653-8*) P-H.

Sports Massage. Jari Ylinen & Mel Cash. (Illus.). 192p. 1989. pap. 24.95 (*0-09-173746-X*, Pub. by S Paul UK) Trafalgar.

Sports Math. Frank Schaffer Publications, Inc. Staff. (Middle School Bks.). (Illus.). 1996. wbk. ed. 12.95 (*0-7647-0024-3*, FS-10201) Schaffer Pubns.

Sports Math Mania! Lorrainne J. Hipping & Christopher Egan. Ed. by Jill Safro. (Illus.). 64p. (Orig.). pap. write for info. (*1-886749-18-3*, Spts Illus Kids) Little.

Sports Medicine. William R. Heitzmann. (Opportunities in.. .Ser.). (Illus.). 160p. 1988. 13.95 (*0-8442-6240-4*, VGM Career Bks) NTC Pub Grp.

Sports Medicine. William R. Heitzmann. (Opportunities in.. .Ser.). (Illus.). 160p. 1993. pap. 10.95 (*0-8442-6241-2*, VGM Career Bks) NTC Pub Grp.

Sports Medicine. Nathan J. Smith. (Blue Bk.). (Illus.). 238p. 1987. pap. text ed. 35.00 (*0-7216-1167-2*) Saunders.

Sports Medicine. 2nd ed. Richard H. Strauss. (Illus.). 656p. 1991. text ed. 80.00 (*0-7216-3734-5*) Saunders.

Sports Medicine: A Practical Guide for Youth Sports Coaches & Parents. Jerald D. Hawkins. 105p. 1992. pap. text ed. 10.95 (*0-944183-09-3*) Prof Reports Corp.

***Sports Medicine: Common Problems & Practical Management.** Ed. by Eugene Sherry & Des J. Bokor. (Greenwich Medical Media Ser.). (Illus.). 480p. 1997. pap. 85.00 (*1-900151-55-3*) OUP.

Sports Medicine: Curriculum Guide for Family Practice Residencies. STFM Task Force on Sports Medicine Staff. 41p. (Orig.). 1990. pap. 10.00 (*0-942295-21-8*, 85) Soc Tchrs Fam Med.

Sports Medicine: Ethics & the Law. Edward Grayson & Catherine Bond. 288p. 1996. pap. write for info. (*0-7506-1576-1*) Buttrwrth-Heinemann.

Sports Medicine: Health Care for Young Athletes. 2nd ed. American Academy of Pediatrics Staff. 328p. 1991. pap. 42.95 (*0-910761-28-0*) Am Acad Pediat.

Sports Medicine: Primary Care & Rehabilitation. Scuderi & McCann. 800p. (C). (gr. 13). 1996. text ed. 89.95 (*0-8151-7771-2*) Mosby Yr Bk.

Sports Medicine: The School Age Athlete. 2nd ed. Bruce Reuder. Ed. by Richard Lampert. LC 95-36916. (Saunders Text & Review Ser.). (Illus.). 704p. 1996. text ed. 142.50 (*0-7216-5673-0*) Saunders.

Sports Medicine & Athletic Injuries. Alfred F. Morris. 396p. (C). 1984. pap. write for info. (*0-697-00087-7*) Brown & Benchmark.

Sports, Medicine & Health. G. P. Hermans & W. L. Mostrerd. (International Congress Ser.: Vol. 921). 1991. 289.50 (*0-444-81168-0*, ICS 921) Elsevier.

Sports Medicine & Rehabilitation: A Sport-Specific Approach. Ed. by Ralph Buschbacker & Randall L. Braddom. 400p. 1994. 50.00 (*1-56053-133-9*) Hanley & Belfus.

Sports Medicine Bible: Prevent, Detect, & Treat Your Sports Injuries Through the Latest Medical Techniques. Lyle J. Micheli & Mark Jenkins. LC 95-2316. (Illus.). 352p. 1995. pap. 20.00 (*0-06-273143-2*, Harper Ref) HarpC.

Sports Medicine for Coaches & Athletes - Soccer. Adil E. Shamoo. 120p. 1995. text ed. 24.95 (*3-7186-0600-3*, Harwood Acad Pubs); pap. text ed. 12.95 (*3-7186-0601-1*, Harwood Acad Pubs) Gordon & Breach.

Sports Medicine for Coaches & Trainers. 2nd ed. Edward J. Shahady & Michael J. Petrizzi. LC 91-2604. (Illus.). xvi, 192p. 1991. pap. 19.95 (*0-8078-4331-8*) U of NC Pr.

Sports Medicine for Primary Care. John C. Richmond et al. LC 95-32073. 608p. 1995. 79.95 (*0-86542-348-2*) Blackwell Sci.

Sports Medicine for the Primary Care Physician. 2nd ed. Ed. by Richard B. Birrer. LC 93-45708. 656p. 1994. 65. 00 (*0-8493-2741-5*) CRC Pr.

Sports Medicine in General Practice. Randell K. Wexler. (Illus.). 130p. (Orig.). 1995. pap. text ed. 22.95 (*0-9646891-1-1*) Anadem Pubng.

Sports Medicine of the Lower Extremity. Ed. by Steven I. Subotnick. LC 88-25550. (Illus.). 699p. reprint ed. pap. 180.00 (*0-7837-6231-3*, 2045945) Bks Demand.

Sports Medicine Prevention Evaluation Management & Rehabilitation. Steven P. Roy & Richard F. Irvin. (Illus.). 560p. 1983. text ed. 72.00 (*0-13-837807-X*) P-H.

***Sports Medicine Roles & Responsibilities for High School Team Physicians & Athletic Trainers.** Joint Advisory Committee on Sports Medicine of Ohio State Medical Association, Ohio Athletic Association & Ohio High School Athletic Association. LC 96-70418. 90p. (Orig.). 1997. pap. 12.95 (*0-944183-20-4*) PRC Pubng.

Sports Medicine Secrets: Questions You Will Be Asked on Rounds, in the Clinic, & on Oral Exams. Ed. by Morris B. Mellion. (Secrets Ser.). (Illus.). 450p. (Orig.). 1993. pap. text ed. 35.95 (*1-56053-074-X*) Hanley & Belfus.

S

Sports Medicine Standards Book. David L. Herbert. LC 91-68119. 50p. 1993. pap. 29.95 (*0-944183-10-7*) Prof Reports Corp.

Sports Minded. 366p. (Orig.). 1988. spiral bd. 7.00 (*1-882835-03-4*) STA-Kris.

Sports Mix. (World Textile Collection Ser.: No. 5). (Illus.). 84p. 1993. pap. 39.95 (*4-7636-8101-X*, Pub. by Kyoto Shoin JA) Bks Nippan.

Sports Movie Posters. Bruce Hershenson. (Illustrated History of Movies Through Posters Ser.: Vol. 4). (Illus.). 84p. 1996. pap. 20.00 (*1-887893-15-6*) B Hershenson.

Sports Movie Posters. Bruce Hershenson. (Illustrated History of Movies Through Posters Ser.: Vol.4). (Illus.). 84p. 1996. 50.00 (*1-887893-16-4*) B Hershenson.

Sports Movies. CineBooks Staff. LC 89-60763. (CineBooks Home Library Ser.: No. 5). 256p. (Orig.). 1997. pap. 9.95 (*0-933997-24-8*) CineBks.

Sports Neurology. Ed. by Barry D. Jordan et al. 327p. 1989. text ed. 86.50 (*0-8342-0055-4*) Lppncott-Raven.

***Sports Neurology.** 2nd ed. Ed. by Barry D. Jordan et al. (Illus.). 450p. 1997. text ed. 89.00 (*0-397-51629-0*) Lppncott-Raven.

Sports Nutrition. Walt C. Evans. (Sports & Fitness Library). (Illus.). 40p. (Orig.). 1989. pap. 2.95 (*0-87983-493-5*) Keats.

Sports Nutrition. Joyce Sorenson & Nancy Murray. (Menus for Better Health Ser.). 36p. (Orig.). 1982. pap. 1.95 (*0-911638-13-X*) Witkower.

***Sports Nutrition.** 2nd ed. Berning & Steen. 1997. 52.00 (*0-8342-0882-2*) Aspen Pub.

Sports Nutrition: A Guide for Professionals Working with Active People. 2nd ed. Dan Benardot. LC 92-49945. 1992. pap. 35.00 (*0-88091-110-7*) Am Dietetic Assn.

Sports Nutrition: Minerals & Electrolytes. Ed. by Constance V. Kies & Judy A. Driskell. LC 94-18438. 352p. 1995. 83.95 (*0-8493-7916-4*) CRC Pr.

***Sports Nutrition: Vitamins & Trace Minerals.** Ira Wolinsky & Judy A Driskell. LC 96-27158. (Nutrition in Exercise & Sport Ser.). 256p. 1996. 79.95 (*0-8493-8192-4*) CRC Pr.

***Sports Nutrition for the Child Athlete.** Debbie S. Jennings & Suzanne N. Steen. LC 93-23145. 79p. 1993. reprint ed. pap. 25.00 (*0-608-03032-5*, 2063483) Bks Demand.

Sports Nutrition for the Nineties: The Health Professional's Handbook. rev. ed. Jacqueline Berning & Suzanne N. Steen. 300p. 1991. 45.00 (*0-8342-0216-6*) Aspen Pub.

Sports Nutrition for Women. Anita Bean & Wellington. pap. 22.95 (*0-7136-4066-9*, 93384, Pub. by A&C Black UK) Talman.

Sports Nutrition Self Study Course. King Helm. 60p. 1994. 72.00 (*0-8342-0561-0*, 20561) Aspen Pub.

Sports of the Times: Great Moments in Sports History. Gene Brown. Ed. by Arleen Keylin & Daniel Lundy. 1982. 18.95 (*0-405-14225-0*, 19816) Ayer.

Sports on Television: A New Ball Game for Broadcasters. Mark C. Wyche et al. 99p. (Orig.). 1990. pap. 80.00 (*0-89324-089-3*) Natl Assn Broadcasters.

***Sports 100: A Ranking of the Greatest Athletes of All Time.** Bert R. Sugar. LC 97-2184. 464p. 1997. pap. 19.95 (*0-8065-1872-3*, Citadel Pr) Carol Pub Group.

Sports Ophthalmology. Bruce M. Zagelbaum. LC 95-42108. (Illus.). 256p. 1996. 85.00 (*0-86542-365-2*) Blackwell Sci.

Sports Page. Ed. by Peter Beilenson. LC 89-60649. (Illus.). 64p. 1989. 7.99 (*0-88088-256-5*) Peter Pauper.

Sports Page. Dale Tobias. 168p. (Orig.). 1993. pap. 5.95 (*1-56245-039-5*) Great Quotations.

Sports Page. Stanley Woodward. LC 68-55638. (Illus.). 229p. 1970. reprint ed. text ed. 55.00 (*0-8371-0762-8*, WOSP, Greenwood Pr) Greenwood.

Sports Pages. Arnold Adoff. LC 85-45169. (Illus.). 80p. (J). (gr. 3-7). 1986. lib. bdg. 14.89 (*0-397-32103-1*, Lipp Jr Bks) HarpC Child Bks.

Sports Pages. Arnold Adoff. LC 85-45169. (Trophy Nonfiction Bk.). (Illus.). 80p. (J). (gr. 3 up). 1990. pap. 5.95 (*0-06-446098-3*, Trophy) HarpC Child Bks.

Sports Pages: A Critical Bibliography of Twentieth-Century American Novels & Stories Featuring Baseball, Basketball, Football & Other Pursuits. Grant Burns. LC 86-31388. 284p. 1987. 27.50 (*0-8108-1966-X*) Scarecrow.

Sports Patterns for Cake Decorating. Roland A. Winbeckler. (Illus.). 24p. (Orig.). 1985. pap. 4.95 (*0-930113-03-9*) Winbeckler.

Sports People in the News, 1996. David Brownstone & Irene Franck. 253p. 1996. 85.00 (*0-02-864525-1*, Hall Reference) Macmillan.

***Sports People in the News 1997.** Brownstone & Franck. 1997. 85.00 (*0-02-864778-5*) S&S Trade.

Sports Performance - Analysis, Skills, Conditions, Training, & Human Factors: Index to New Information with Authors & Subjects. rev. ed. Jerry B. Holtz. LC 94-34141. 155p. 1994. 49.50 (*0-7883-0497-6*); pap. 39.50 (*0-7883-0498-4*) ABBE Pubs Assn.

Sports Photography, No. I: Wills Book of Excellence. Ashok Kamath. (Illus.). 204p. 1990. text ed. 40.00 (*0-685-34691-9*, Pub. by Orient Longman Ltd II) Apt Bks.

Sports Photography of Robert Riger. Robert Riger. (Illus.). 176p. 1995. 45.00 (*0-679-44513-7*) Random.

Sports Physical Therapy. Ed. by Donna B. Bernhardt. (Clinics in Physical Therapy Ser.: Vol. 10). (Illus.). 223p. (C). 1986. text ed. 39.95 (*0-443-08444-0*) Churchill.

Sports Physical Therapy. Barbara Sanders. (Illus.). 535p. (C). 1990. text ed. 65.00 (*0-8385-8652-X*, A8652-8) Appleton & Lange.

Sports Physiology. 3rd ed. Richard Bowers & Edward L. Fox. 464p. (C). 1992. text ed. write for info. (*0-697-13008-8*) Brown & Benchmark.

***Sports Physiology.** 3rd ed. Richard Bowers & Edward L. Fox. 464p. (C). 1992. pap. text ed. write for info. (*0-697-20864-8*) Brown & Benchmark.

***Sports Physiology.** 5th ed. Bowers & Fox. 1992. pap. text ed. 33.00 (*0-697-29501-X*) McGraw.

Sports Physiotherapy: Applied Science & Practice. Joan McMeeken et al. 1994. write for info. (*0-443-04804-5*) Churchill.

***Sports Pocket Power Guide.** Ed. by Judie Svabik. 96p. 1997. per. 7.99 (*0-7615-1119-9*) Prima Pub.

Sports Poop: The All Time Greatest Sports Quotes. Great Quotations Staff. 78p. (Orig.). 1991. pap. 7.95 (*1-56245-021-2*) Great Quotations.

Sports, Prevention & Control of Athletic Injuries: Index of New Information with Authors & Subjects. rev. ed. Hugo H. Bronsen. LC 94-24773. 157p. 1994. 47.50 (*0-7883-0264-7*); pap. 44.50 (*0-7883-0265-5*) ABBE Pubs Assn.

Sports Process: A Comparative & Developmental Approach. Ed. by Eric G. Dunning et al. LC 92-29998. (Illus.). 334p. (Orig.). 1996. reprint ed. pap. text ed. 24.00 (*0-88011-624-2*, BDUN0624) Human Kinetics.

Sports Psyching: Playing Your Best Game All of the Time. Thomas A. Tutko & Umberto Tosi. LC 75-27975. 240p. 1980. pap. 10.95 (*0-87477-136-6*, Tarcher Putnam) Putnam Pub Group.

Sports Psychology: A Self Help Guide. Stephen J. Bull. (Illus.). 1992. 29.95 (*1-85223-568-3*, Pub. by Crowood Pr UK) Trafalgar.

Sports Psychology in Action. Richard J. Butler. (Illus.). 160p. 1996. pap. 30.00 (*0-7506-2436-1*) Buttrwrth-Heinemann.

Sports Quotes. Joe Klein. (Illus.). 192p. (Orig.). 1995. pap. 14.95 (*1-57028-035-5*, Spalding Sports) Masters Pr IN.

***Sports Quotes & Anecdotes.** Robert Harrison. (Illus.). 144p. 1997. pap. 16.00 (*0-8059-4110-X*) Dorrance.

Sports Radio. (Stereo Boom Box Ser.: Vol. 2). 160p. (J). (gr. 1-6). 1994. ring bd. 149.95 (*1-57405-049-4*) CharismaLife Pub.

***Sports Report - Baseball: Index of New Information with Authors, Subjects & References.** rev. ed. Hugo H. Bronsen. 171p. 1997. 47.50 (*0-7883-1460-2*); pap. 44.50 (*0-7883-1461-0*) ABBE Pubs Assn.

Sports Report - Football: Index of New Information with Authors, Subjects & References. Hugo H. Bronsen. 1994. 47.50 (*1-55914-730-X*); pap. 44.50 (*1-55914-731-8*) ABBE Pubs Assn.

Sports Report - Soccer: Index of New Information with Authors, Subjects & References. Hugo H. Bronsen. 1994. 47.50 (*1-55914-732-6*); pap. 44.50 (*1-55914-733-4*) ABBE Pubs Assn.

Sports Report - Swimming: Index of New Information with Authors, Subjects & References. Hugo H. Bronsen. 1994. 47.50 (*1-55914-734-2*); pap. 44.50 (*1-55914-735-0*) ABBE Pubs Assn.

Sports Report - Tennis: Index of New Information with Authors, Subjects & References. Hugo H. Bronsen. 1994. 47.50 (*1-55914-736-9*); pap. 44.50 (*1-55914-737-7*) ABBE Pubs Assn.

Sports Report - Tennis Elbow: Index of New Information with Authors, Subjects & References. Hugo H. Bronsen. 1994. 47.50 (*1-55914-738-5*); pap. 44.50 (*1-55914-739-3*) ABBE Pubs Assn.

Sports Report - Track & Field: Index of New Information with Authors, Subjects, & References. Hugo H. Bronsen. 160p. 1995. 47.50 (*0-7883-0456-9*); pap. 44.50 (*0-7883-0457-7*) ABBE Pubs Assn.

Sports Reporting. 2nd ed. Bruce Garrison & Mark J. Sabljak. LC 92-40403. (Illus.). 368p. (C). 1993. text ed. 32.95 (*0-8138-1692-0*) Iowa St U Pr.

Sports Reports Series, 20 bks., Set. (Illus.). (J). (gr. 4-10). 1994. lib. bdg. 379.00 (*0-89490-568-6*) Enslow Pubs.

***Sports Rules Book.** Thomas Hanlon. 1997. pap. 19.95 (*0-88011-807-5*) Human Kinetics.

***Sports Rules Book.** Tom Hanlon. (Illus.). 400p. (Orig.). 1997. pap. 19.95 (*0-614-30999-9*) Human Kinetics.

***Sports Scan: The Baseball Fan's Superhighway Survival Guide.** Mel West & Glen Greene. 228p. (Orig.). 1997. pap. 8.95 (*0-9657971-3-9*) Emerald Cty Pubns.

Sports Scandals. Hank Nuwer. LC 93-26317. (Social Issues Ser.). (Illus.). 144p. (YA). (gr. 9-12). 1994. lib. bdg. 22.70 (*0-531-11183-0*) Watts.

***Sports Science.** Snape & Rowlands. (Science at Work Ser.). 1992. pap. text ed. write for info. (*0-582-07826-1*, Pub. by Longman UK) Longman.

***Sports Science: Molding Superstar Athletes.** Elaine Pascoe. LC 96-50962. (New Explorers Ser.). (Illus.). 48p. 1997. lib. bdg. 16.95 (*1-56711-227-7*) Blackbirch.

Sports Science for Young People. George Barr. (YA). 1990. pap. 3.95 (*0-486-26527-7*) Dover.

Sports, Sex, Drugs...& Other American Pastimes. Judd Biasiotto. (Illus.). 175p. (Orig.). 1988. pap. 10.00 (*0-933079-09-5*) World Class Enterprises.

Sports Shorts: Two Thousand of Sports' Funniest One-Liners. Glenn Liebman. LC 93-2776. 432p. 1993. 14.95 (*0-8092-3768-7*) Contemp Bks.

Sports Shots: Deion Sanders. Jimmy Preller. (J). 1995. 1.49 (*0-590-62328-1*) Scholastic Inc.

Sports Shots: Michael Jordan. James Preller. (J). 1995. 1.49 (*0-590-62327-3*) Scholastic Inc.

Sports Shots: Steve Young. Jimmy Preller. (J). 1995. 1.49 (*0-590-62326-5*) Scholastic Inc.

Sports Shots Box, 6 bks., Set. (J). 1991. pap. 7.50 (*0-590-63964-1*) Scholastic Inc.

***Sports Slump Busting: 10 Steps to Mental Toughness & Peak Performance.** Alan S. Goldberg. LC 97-22402. 1997. pap. 16.95 (*0-88011-653-6*, PGOL0653) Human Kinetics.

Sports Spectators. Allen Guttmann. LC 86-8268. 224p. 1988. pap. text ed. 16.00 (*0-231-06401-2*) Col U Pr.

Sports Spectrum, A Flow of Work Simplified Equations. 2nd ed. Warren. (KM - Office Procedures Ser.). 1986. wbk. ed., pap. 11.95 (*0-538-25711-3*) S-W Pub.

Sports Spectrum, a Flow of Work Simulation. 2nd ed. Warren. (KM - Office Procedures Ser.). 1986. wbk. ed., pap. 40.95 (*0-538-25712-1*) S-W Pub.

***Sports Speed.** 2nd rev. ed. George B. Dintiman et al. LC 96-47831. (Illus.). 224p. 1997. pap. 16.95 (*0-88011-607-2*, PDIN0607) Human Kinetics.

Sports Spots, No. 1458. (Illus.). 48p. 5.95 (*1-878259-13-X*) Neibauer Pr.

Sports Stadium As a Municipal Investment. Dean V. Baim. LC 93-21501. (Contributions in Economics & Economic History Ser.). 264p. 1994. text ed. 55.00 (*0-313-27816-4*, Greenwood Pr) Greenwood.

Sports Stars, 2 vols. Michael A. Pare. LC 94-21835. (J). 1994. 49.95 (*0-8103-9859-1*, UXL) Gale.

***Sports Stars.** 3rd ed. Michael A. Pare. LC 97-622. (J). 1997. 49.95 (*0-7876-1749-0*, UXL) Gale.

Sports Stars, Vol. 1. Michael A. Pare. LC 94-21835. 1994. write for info. (*0-8103-9860-5*, UXL) Gale.

Sports Stars, Vol. 2. Michael A. Pare. LC 94-21835. 1994. write for info. (*0-8103-9861-3*, UXL) Gale.

Sports Stars Cookbook. Harvey Shapiro. (Illus.). 1976. spiral bd. 5.95 (*0-915088-11-8*) C Hungness.

Sports Stars II, 2 vols., Set. 2nd ed. Michael A. Pare. LC 96-10646. (J). 1996. 49.95 (*0-7876-0867-X*, UXL) Gale.

Sports Stars II, Vol. 1, A-K. Michael A. Pare. LC 96-10646. (J). 1996. write for info. (*0-7876-0868-8*, UXL) Gale.

Sports Stars II, Vol. 2, L-Z. Michael A. Pare. LC 96-10646. (J). 1996. write for info. (*0-7876-0869-6*, UXL) Gale.

Sports Strength: Strength Training Routines to Improve Power, Speed, & Flexibility for Virtually Every Sport. Ken Sprague. LC 92-21472. (Illus.). 224p. (Orig.). 1993. pap. 16.95 (*0-399-51802-9*, Perigee Bks) Berkley Pub.

Sports Stretch. Michael J. Alter. LC 89-27880. (Illus.). 168p. 1990. pap. 15.95 (*0-88011-381-2*, PALT0381) Human Kinetics.

***Sports Stretch.** 2nd ed. Michael J. Alter. LC 97-14591. (Illus.). 200p. 1997. pap. 15.95 (*0-88011-823-7*) Human Kinetics.

Sports Style Guide & Reference Manual: The Complete Reference for Sports Editors, Writers, & Broadcasters. Jennifer Swan. 375p. (Orig.). 1996. pap. 18.95 (*1-57243-101-6*) Triumph Bks.

Sports Style Guide & Reference Manual: The Complete Reference for Sports Editors, Writers, & Broadcasters. Jennifer Swan. 400p. 1996. lib. bdg. 24.95 (*1-57243-117-2*) Triumph Bks.

Sports Talk: A Dictionary of Sports Metaphors. Robert A. Palmatier & Harold L. Ray. LC 88-24646. 245p. 1989. text ed. 45.00 (*0-313-26426-0*, PSK, Greenwood Pr) Greenwood.

Sports Teacher's Resource Guide. Irene Welch. Ed. by Liz Parker. (Take Ten Bks.). 35p. (Orig.). 1993. pap. text ed. 16.95 (*1-56254-077-7*) Saddleback Pubns.

***Sports Technology.** T. Reilly. 1995. pap. text ed. write for info. (*0-419-12130-7*, E & FN Spon) Routledge Chapman & Hall.

Sports Top Ten Series, 17 bks., Set. (Illus.). (J). (gr. 4-10). 1994. lib. bdg. 305.15 (*0-89490-582-1*) Enslow Pubs.

Sports Touch: The Athletic Ritual. Kate Montgomery. Ed. by Beverly Trainer. (Illus.). 162p. (Orig.). 1990. Wkbk. student ed. 24.95 (*1-878069-00-4*) Sports Touch.

Sports Tough Guys. (J). pap. 1.95 (*0-590-31893-4*) Scholastic Inc.

Sports-Training, Endurance, Discipline & Psycho-Stress: Index of New Information & Bibliography. Harold H. Zenker. 150p. 1997. 47.50 (*0-7883-1006-2*); pap. 44.50 (*0-7883-1007-0*) ABBE Pubs Assn.

Sports Trip. Lee Mountain. (Attention Span Stories Ser). (Illus.). 48p. (Orig.). 1978. pap. text ed. 8.65 (*0-89061-147-5*, 583) Jamestown Pubs.

Sports Varieties - Studies of Exercise Using Human Saliva As a Diagnostic Instrument: Index of New Information & Bibliography. Boris A. Mormons. 150p. 1997. 39.50 (*0-7883-0988-9*); pap. 34.50 (*0-7883-0989-7*) ABBE Pubs Assn.

Sports Violence: The Interaction Between Private Lawmaking & the Criminal Law. Richard B. Horrow. LC 80-65053. 266p. 1980. text ed. 45.00 (*0-313-27069-4*, U7069, Greenwood Pr) Greenwood.

Sports Vision. D. F. Loran & C. J. MacEwen. (Illus.). 240p. 1995. 75.00 (*0-7506-1578-8*) Buttrwrth-Heinemann.

Sports Vision. Michael W. Stoner & Alan W. Reichow. Ed. by Timothy G. Ramage. (Introduction to Behavioral Optometry Ser.). (Illus.). 80p. (Orig.). lib. bdg. 18.00 (*0-943599-64-4*) OEPF.

***Sports Widow.** Sherri Weaver. Ed. by Patrick Caton. LC 96-78974. 168p. 1997. pap. 5.95 (*1-56245-282-7*) Great Quotations.

Sports with Racquets (Badminton, Lacross, Racquetball & Squash) Index of New Data & Information. Hugo H. Bronsen. (Illus.). 160p. 1995. 47.50 (*0-7883-0644-8*); pap. 44.50 (*0-7883-0645-6*) ABBE Pubs Assn.

Sports Without Pressure: A Guide for Parents & Coaches of Young Athletes. Eric Margenau. LC 89-16998. 156p. 1992. pap. 12.95 (*0-89876-165-4*) Brunner-Mazel.

Sports Women. Ed. by M. J. Adrian. (Medicine & Sport Science Ser.: Vol. 24). (Illus.). viii, 160p. 1987. 118.50 (*3-8055-4501-0*) S Karger.

Sports World. write for info. (*1-879104-00-8*) Overly Pub.

Sports World...in a Nutshell. Leo Ewing. (Nutshell Ser.). 60p. 1994. pap. 5.49 (*1-885962-59-2*) Lincoln Lrning.

Sports Writing Handbook. Thomas Fensch. (Communications Textbook Ser.). 272p. (C). 1988. 49.95 (*0-8058-0263-0*); pap. 29.95 (*0-8058-0396-3*) L Erlbaum Assocs.

Sports Writing Handbook. 2nd ed. Thomas Fensch. (LEA's Communication Ser.). 272p. 1995. pap. 19.95 (*0-8058-1529-5*); text ed. 49.95 (*0-8058-1528-7*) L Erlbaum Assocs.

Sports 100: The 100 Most Important People in American Sports History. Brad Herzog. LC 95-40968. 1996. 14.95 (*0-02-860427-X*) Macmillan.

Sports 100: The 100 Most Important People in Sports History. Brad Herzog. 320p. 1996. 16.95 (*0-02-860402-4*) Macmillan.

Sportsayings. James Charlton. 1999. pap. 4.95 (*0-14-006936-4*, Viking) Viking Penguin.

Sportscape. John R. Gleeson, III. LC 84-52105. (Illus.). 176p. (Orig.). 1984. pap. 12.95 (*0-912661-04-6*) Woodsong Graph.

Sportscard Counterfeit Detector. Bob Lemke. LC 91-77563. (Illus.). 272p. 1994. pap. text ed. 17.95 (*0-87341-284-2*, BD03) Krause Pubns.

Sportscasting. John R. Hitchcock. (Electronic Media Management Ser.). 116p. 1991. pap. 19.95 (*0-240-80062-1*, Focal) Buttrwrth-Heinemann.

Sportsdykes: Stories from on & off the Field. Ed. by Susan F. Rogers. LC 95-5497. 1995. pap. 8.95 (*0-312-13187-9*) St Martin.

Sportshots. Wally Neibart & Mickey Charles. (Illus.). 120p. 1982. pap. 4.95 (*0-943588-00-6*) Baron-Scott Enterp.

***Sportslang.** Bill Coppell. (Illus.). 100p. 1997. pap. write for info. (*1-86452-001-9*) D W Thorpe.

Sportsmanlike Driving. rev. ed. American Automobile Association Staff. Ed. by Carolyn E. Cranford. (Illus.). (gr. 10-12). 1980. text ed. 22.56 (*0-07-001330-6*); pap. text ed. 14.80 (*0-07-001331-4*) McGraw.

Sportsmanlike Driving. 7th ed. American Automobile Association Staff. (J). 1975. text ed. 25.24 (*0-07-001292-X*) McGraw.

Sportsmanlike Driving. 9th ed. American Automobile Association Staff. 352p. (J). (gr. 9-12). 1987. text ed. 22.16 (*0-07-001338-1*); pap. text ed. 14.48 (*0-07-001339-X*) McGraw.

***Sportsmans Cook Book: With Some Old Country Favorites.** (Illus.). 86p. 1992. pap. 15.00 (*0-9657836-0-X*, 2844A) C Sherman.

***Sportsman's Guide to Recipes.** Frank Davern. Ed. by Stephanie Wirkkala. (Illus.). 104p. 1996. pap. 9.95 (*1-889694-00-2*) Wolf Pr.

Sportsman's Legacy. William G. Tapply. 144p. 1993. 17.95 (*1-55821-244-2*) Lyons & Burford.

***Sportsman's Lodge in Poudre Canyon: A Colorado Resort "A Home Away from Home"** F. Bernedene Toms. (Illus.). 120p. (Orig.). 1996. pap. 16.95 (*0-9615226-9-0*) Giddings Studio Pub.

Sportsman's Notebook. Ivan S. Turgenev. Tr. by Charles Hepburn & Natasha Hepburn from RUS. 398p. 1986. reprint ed. pap. 10.50 (*0-88001-119-X*) Ecco Pr.

Sportsman's Quotes of Wisdom. Cotton Cordell. 61p. (Orig.). 1994. pap. text ed. 4.95 (*0-914917-11-0*) Folk-Life.

Sportsmassage: A Complete Program for Increasing Performance in Fifteen Popular Exercises. Jack Meagher. 1990. pap. 14.95 (*0-685-34812-1*) Station Hill Pr.

Sportsmassage: A Complete Program for Increasing Performance in Fifteen Popular Exercises. rev. ed. Jack Meagher & Pat Boughton. (Illus.). 224p. 1990. pap. 16.95 (*0-88268-096-X*) Station Hill Pr.

Sportsmedicine Book. Gabe Mirkin & Marshall Hoffman. LC 78-14908. 1978. 24.95 (*0-316-57434-1*) Little.

SportsMedicine for the Combat Arts. Joseph J. Estwanik. LC 96-83747. (Illus.). 288p. (Orig.). 1996. pap. 24.95 (*1-888926-00-7*) Boxergenics.

Sportsmen. Ed. by Christopher Morgan. (Orig.). 1996. mass mkt. 5.95 (*1-56333-385-6*, Badboy) Masquerade.

Sportsmen in a Landscape. Aubrey Noakes. LC 72-134122. (Essay Index Reprint Ser.). 1977. 26.95 (*0-8369-2005-8*) Ayer.

***Sportsmen United: The Story of the Tennessee Conservation League.** Marge Davis. LC 96-79647. (Illus.). xvi, 354p. (Orig.). 1997. pap. 12.95 (*0-9654561-8-8*) Bench Top Bks.

Sportspeak: An Encyclopedia of Sport. Ed. by Thorpe, D. W., Staff. (Illus.). 600p. 1996. pap. 25.00 (*1-875589-73-2*) D W Thorpe.

Sportswomen Towards Two Thousand: A Celebration. Ed. by Ken Dyer. 286p. (C). 1989. pap. 115.00 (*0-909120-93-5*, Pub. by U of Adelaide AT) St Mut.

Sportsworks: More Than Fifty Fun Games & Activities That Explore the Science of Sports. Ontario Science Centre Staff. 1989. pap. 9.95 (*0-201-15296-7*) Addison-Wesley.

Sportswriter. Richard Ford. LC 85-40537. (Vintage Contemporaries Ser.). 432p. 1986. pap. 12.00 (*0-394-74325-3*, Vin) Random.

Sportswriter. Richard Ford. 1995. pap. 12.00 (*0-679-76210-8*) Random.

Sportswriter. Richard Ford. 1996. 25.00 (*0-679-45451-9*) Knopf.

Sportswriter: The Life & Times of Grantland Rice. Charles Fountain. LC 92-46146. 352p. (C). 1993. 27.50 (*0-19-506176-4*) OUP.

***Sportswriter Signed Edition.** Richard Ford. 1996. 25.00 (*0-676-51863-X*) Knopf.

Sportswriter Joe. Joe E. Palmer. 280p. (Orig.). (C). Date not set. pap. 11.00 (*0-9622549-3-2*) Remlap Pub.

Sporty Course. Jack Swayze. (Illus.). 180p. 1993. pap. 16.95 (*0-89745-163-5*) Sunflower U Pr.

Sporty Game. John Newhouse. LC 81-48123. 1982. 22.95 (*0-394-51447-5*) Knopf.

Sporty Riddles. Joanne E. Bernstein & Paul Cohen. Ed. by Judith Mathews. LC 89-5294. (Illus.). 32p. (J). (gr. 1-5). 1989. lib. bdg. 8.95 (*0-8075-7590-9*) A Whitman.

S

An Asterisk (*) at the beginning of an entry indicates that the title is appearing in BIP for the first time.

Spot. Russell Collins. 160p. 1996. pap. 12.95 (*0-684-83421-9*) S&S Trade.
Spot: The Rise of Political Advertising on Television. 3rd ed. Edwin Diamond & Stephen Bates. (Illus.). 432p. 1992. 32.50 (*0-262-04130-8*); pap. 17.50 (*0-262-54065-7*) MIT Pr.
Spot a Cat. Lucy Micklethwait. LC 94-44797. (Illus.). 32p. (J). (ps-7). 1995. 9.95 (*0-7894-0144-4*, 5-70595) DK Pub Inc.
Spot a Dog. Lucy Micklethwait. LC 94-48608. (Illus.). 32p. (J). (ps-7). 1995. 9.95 (*0-7894-0145-2*, 5-70596) DK Pub Inc.
Spot & Friends Dress Up. Eric Hill. LC 95-43725. (J). 1996. bds. 7.95 (*0-399-23031-9*, Putnam) Putnam Pub Group.
Spot & Friends Play. Eric Hill. LC 95-43718. (J). 1996. bds. 7.95 (*0-399-23032-7*, Putnam) Putnam Pub Group.
Spot at Home. Eric Hill. (Board Bk.). (Illus.). 14p. (J). (ps). 1991. bds. 3.95 (*0-399-21774-6*, Putnam) Putnam Pub Group.
Spot Bakes a Cake. Eric Hill. (Lift-the-Flap Bks.). (Illus.). 22p. (J). (ps-1). 1994. 12.95 (*0-399-22701-6*, Putnam) Putnam Pub Group.
***Spot Bakes a Cake.** Eric Hill. 1997. pap. 5.99 (*0-14-055529-3*) Viking Penguin.
Spot Counts from One to Ten. Eric Hill. (Little Spot Board Bks.). (Illus.). 14p. (J). (ps). 1989. bds. 3.95 (*0-399-21672-3*, Putnam) Putnam Pub Group.
Spot Drills, Bk. 1. Rayner W. Markley. (Illus.). 142p. 1983. pap. text ed. 8.95 (*0-19-434125-9*) OUP.
Spot Drills, Bk. 2. Rayner W. Markley. (Illus.). 142p. 1987. pap. text ed. 8.95 (*0-19-434126-7*) OUP.
Spot Drills, Bk. 3. Rayner W. Markley. (Illus.). 142p. 1987. pap. text ed. 8.95 (*0-19-434127-5*) OUP.
Spot Goes Splash! Eric Hill. (Soft Spots Ser.). (Illus.). 8p. (J). (gr. k-1). 1984. 4.95 (*0-399-21068-7*, Putnam) Putnam Pub Group.
Spot Goes to a Party. Eric Hill. (Illus.). 22p. (J). (ps). 1992. 12.95 (*0-399-22409-2*, Putnam) Putnam Pub Group.
***Spot Goes to a Party.** Eric Hill. (J). Date not set. pap. 5.99 (*0-14-055521-8*) Viking Penguin.
Spot Goes to a Party. Eric Hill. 1997. pap. 5.99 (*0-14-055321-5*) NAL-Dutton.
Spot Goes to School. Eric Hill. (Lift-the-Flap Ser.). (Illus.). 24p. (ARA & ENG.). (J). (ps-2). 1988. 11.95 (*0-940793-06-7*, Crocodile Bks) Interlink Pub.
Spot Goes to School. Eric Hill. (Lift-the-Flap Bks.). 22p. (J). (ps). 1994. pap. 5.99 (*0-14-055282-0*) Puffin Bks.
Spot Goes to School. Eric Hill. LC 84-42695. (Soft Spots Ser.). (Illus.). 22p. (J). (ps-2). 1984. 12.95 (*0-399-21073-3*, Putnam) Putnam Pub Group.
Spot Goes to the Beach. Eric Hill. LC 84-18291. (Illus.). 22p. (J). (gr. k). 1985. 12.95 (*0-399-21247-7*, Putnam) Putnam Pub Group.
Spot Goes to the Beach. Eric Hill. (Spot Ser.). (Illus.). 20p. (J). (ps-1). 1995. pap. 5.99 (*0-14-055281-2*) Puffin Bks.
Spot Goes to the Circus. Eric Hill. (Lift-the-Flap Bks.). 22p. (J). (ps). 1994. pap. 5.99 (*0-14-055297-9*) Puffin Bks.
Spot Goes to the Circus. Eric Hill. LC 85-24471. (Spot Lift-the-Flap Bks.). (Illus.). 22p. (J). (ps). 1986. 12.95 (*0-399-21317-1*, Putnam) Putnam Pub Group.
Spot Goes to the Farm. Eric Hill. (Lift-the-Flap Bks.). (Illus.). 22p. (J). (ps-1). 1987. 12.95 (*0-399-21434-8*, Putnam) Putnam Pub Group.
Spot Goes to the Park. Eric Hill. (Illus.). 22p. (J). 1991. 12.95 (*0-399-21833-5*, Putnam) Putnam Pub Group.
Spot Goes to the Park. Eric Hill. (Illus.). 20p. (J). (ps-1). 1996. pap. 5.99 (*0-14-055320-7*, Puffin) Puffin Bks.
Spot Hace un Pastel. Eric Hill. (Illus.). (SPA.). (J). 1995. 12.95 (*0-399-22806-3*, Putnam) Putnam Pub Group.
Spot Illustrations from Women's Magazines of the Teens & Twenties. Ed. by Judy M. Johnson. 64p. 1989. pap. 5.95 (*0-486-26116-6*) Dover.
"Spot-It" Guide to Nature. Rosy Border. (FunFax Ser.). (Illus.). 48p. (J). (gr. 3-6). 1992. pap. 2.95 (*1-56680-012-9*) Mad Hatter Pub.
Spot Looks at Colors. Eric Hill. (Little Spot Board Bks.). (Illus.). 14p. (J). (ps). 1986. 3.95 (*0-399-21349-X*, Putnam) Putnam Pub Group.
Spot of Tea: The California Guide to Afternoon Tea. Linda Wexler. LC 95-83100. (Spot of Tea Ser.). (Illus.). 300p. (Orig.). 1995. pap. 19.95 (*1-888230-00-2*) Chelsea St Prods.
***Spot of Tea: The West Coast Guide to Afternoon Teas.** 2nd rev. ed. Linda R. Wexler. Ed. by Howard B. Raff. (Illus.). 400p. 1997. per. 22.95 (*1-888230-02-9*) Chelsea St Prods.
***Spot of Tea & Teatime Recipes.** Linda R. Wexler. Ed. by Howard B. Raff. (Illus.). 64p. (Orig.). 1997. per. 5.95 (*1-888230-07-X*) Chelsea St Prods.
***Spot of Tea at Home: How to Host a Tea Party with Style.** Linda R. Wexler. Ed. by Howard B. Raff. (Illus.). 72p. (Orig.). 1997. per. 5.95 (*1-888230-09-6*) Chelsea St Prods.
***Spot of Tea/Tea Shirt Gift Combination.** Linda R. Wexler. (Illus.). 400p. 1997. per. 38.95 (*1-888230-10-X*) Chelsea St Prods.
***Spot On! Correspondence & Report Writing with Guidelines on Plain English.** unabridged ed. George Stern. LC 95-13922. 40p. (Orig.). 1996. pap. 11.95 (*0-644-46277-9*, Pub. by AGPS Pr AT) Intl Spec Bk.
***Spot on Skits: 12 Short Plays on Life Issues.** Tony Llewellyn & Allison Llewellyn. 48p. (Orig.). 1997. pap. 15.95 (*1-86407-134-6*, Pub. by JBCE AT) Morehouse Pub.
Spot on the Ground. Ralph F. Parkison. Ed. by Marion O. Withrow. (Illus.). 83p. (Orig.). (J). (gr. 2-8). 1988. pap. write for info. (*0-318-63997-1*) Little Wood Bks.
***Spot Puppy Love Mini.** Eric Hill. (J). Date not set. pap. 6.95 (*0-399-21825-4*) Putnam Pub Group.
Spot Sleeps Over. Eric Hill. (Illus.). 20p. (J). 1996. pap. 5.99 (*0-14-055301-0*) Puffin Bks.
Spot Sleeps Over. Eric Hill. (Lift-the-Flap Bks.). (Illus.). 22p. (J). (ps). 1990. 11.95 (*0-399-21815-7*, Putnam) Putnam Pub Group.
Spot Test Analysis: Clinical, Environmental, Forensic, & Geochemical Applications. 2nd ed. Ervin Jungreis. LC 96-2780. (Chemical Analysis Ser.). 1996. text ed. 69.95 (*0-471-12412-5*) Wiley.
Spot Test Analysis: Clinical,Environmental, Forensic & Geochemical Applications. Ervin Jungreis. LC 84-15176. (Chemical Analysis: A Series of Monographs on Analytical Chemistry & Its Applications: No. 1-075). 315p. 1985. text ed. 132.00 (*0-471-86524-9*) Wiley.
Spot Tests in Inorganic Analysis. 6th ed. F. Feigl & Y. Anger. 670p. 1982. 281.00 (*0-444-40929-7*) Elsevier.
***Spot Tests in Organic Analysis.** F. Feigl & V. Anger. 772p. 1966. 290.25 (*0-444-40209-8*) Elsevier.
Spot the Warships. 3rd ed. James Goss. 56p. 1987. 55.00 (*0-85937-294-4*, Pub. by K Mason Pubns Ltd UK) St Mut.
Spot Va a la Escuela (Spot Goes to School) Eric Hill. (Illus.). 22p. (SPA.). (J). (gr. 3-7). 1985. 12.95 (*0-399-21223-X*, Putnam) Putnam Pub Group.
Spot Va a la Granja. Eric Hill. (Spot Goes to the Farm Ser.). (Illus.). 22p. (SPA.). (J). (ps-1). 1987. 12.95 (*0-399-21463-1*, Putnam) Putnam Pub Group.
Spot Va a una Fiesta. Eric Hill. (Illus.). (SPA.). (J). 1995. 12.95 (*0-399-22438-6*, Putnam) Putnam Pub Group.
Spot Va Al Parque. Eric Hill. (Illus.). 22p. (SPA.). (J). (ps). 1993. 12.95 (*0-399-22345-2*, Putnam) Putnam Pub Group.
Spot Visits His Grandparents. Eric Hill. LC 96-5222. (Illus.). 22p. (J). (ps-1). 1996. 12.95 (*0-399-23033-5*, Putnam) Putnam Pub Group.
Spotlight. pap. 0.67 (*0-590-08726-6*) Scholastic Inc.
Spotlight. Peter Chilver. 207p. (C). 8700. pap. 15.95 (*0-85950-567-7*) Dufour.
Spotlight. Stewart M. Venit. Date not set. teacher ed., pap. text ed. write for info. (*0-314-08398-7*); teacher ed., pap. text ed. write for info. (*0-314-08399-5*) West Pub.
Spotlight. Patricia Wentworth. 22.95 (*0-88411-722-7*) Amereon Ltd.
Spotlight: English & Communication for the Certificate. Peter Chilver. 208p. (C). 1987. 60.00 (*0-685-33829-0*, Pub. by S Thornes Pubs UK) St Mut.
Spotlight: Solo Scenes for Student Actors. Stephanie Fairbanks. Ed. by Theodore O. Zapel. 144p. (Orig.). 1996. pap. text ed. 12.95 (*1-56608-020-7*, B176) Meriwether Pub.
Spotlight: Teacher's Book. Stanley Thornes. (C). 1987. 65.00 (*0-85950-568-5*, Pub. by S Thornes Pubs UK) St Mut.
Spotlight-Mode Synthetic Aperture Radar: A Signal Processing Approach. Charles V. Jakowatz et al. LC 95-47486. 448p. (C). 1996. lib. bdg. 125.00 (*0-7923-9677-4*) Kluwer Ac.
Spotlight on Computer Literacy. Ellen Richman. (J). (gr. 6-8). 1984. pap. 14.00 (*0-07-480653-X*) McGraw.
Spotlight on Construction Productivity. Louis E. Alfeld. 98.00 (*0-317-59584-9*) Constr Ind Pr.
Spotlight on Effective Communication. 20p. (Orig.). 1993. pap. 2.00 (*1-884048-07-2*) Natl Assn Parliamentarians.
Spotlight on Films. S. Larsen. 1976. lib. bdg. 69.95 (*0-8490-2662-8*) Gordon Pr.
***Spotlight on Los Angeles.** Crabtree Publishing Co. Staff. (Cities of North America Ser.). 1997. 19.96 (*0-86505-927-6*); pap. text ed. 7.95 (*0-86505-941-1*) Crabtree Pub Co.
Spotlight on Love. Julie Cahn. (Dream Your Own Romance Ser.: No. 3). (J). (gr. 2-7). 1984. pap. 2.95 (*0-671-52625-1*) S&S Trade.
Spotlight on Male Female Relations. Mba Mbulu & Bomani Sekou. 29p. 1993. pap. 4.00 (*1-883885-00-0*) ASET Pubns.
Spotlight on Meeting Management. 20p. (Orig.). 1993. pap. 2.00 (*1-884048-08-0*) Natl Assn Parliamentarians.
***Spotlight on Mexico City.** Crabtree Publishing Co. Staff. (Cities of North America Ser.). 1997. 19.96 (*0-86505-929-2*); pap. text ed. 7.95 (*0-86505-943-8*) Crabtree Pub Co.
Spotlight on New Jersey Government. 6th ed. Ed. by Barbara W. Prabhu. LC 91-45493. 400p. (C). 1992. text ed. 42.00 (*0-8135-1843-1*); pap. text ed. 16.95 (*0-8135-1844-X*) Rutgers U Pr.
***Spotlight on New Orleans.** Crabtree Publishing Co. Staff. (Cities of North America Ser.). 1997. 19.96 (*0-86505-930-6*) Crabtree Pub Co.
***Spotlight on New Orleans.** Crabtree Publishing. Co. Staff. (Cities of North America Ser.). 1997. pap. text ed. 7.95 (*0-86505-944-6*) Crabtree Pub Co.
***Spotlight on New York.** Crabtree Publishing Co. Staff. (Cities of North America Ser.). 1997. 19.96 (*0-86505-926-8*); pap. text ed. 7.95 (*0-86505-940-3*) Crabtree Pub Co.
***Spotlight on Ottawa.** Crabtree Publishing Co. Staff. (Cities of North America Ser.). 1997. 19.96 (*0-86505-932-2*); pap. text ed. 7.95 (*0-86505-946-2*) Crabtree Pub Co.
***Spotlight on Parliamentary Terminology.** 16p. (Orig.). 1997. pap. 2.00 (*1-884048-18-8*) Natl Assn Parliamentarians.
Spotlight on Program Planning. 20p. (Orig.). 1993. pap. 2.00 (*1-884048-09-9*) Natl Assn Parliamentarians.
Spotlight on Public Relations. 17p. (Orig.). 1993. pap. 2.00 (*1-884048-04-8*) Natl Assn Parliamentarians.
***Spotlight on Security for Real Estate Managers.** Lawrence J. Fennelly & John H. Lombardi. LC 96-38549. (Illus.). 238p. 1997. 62.95 (*1-57203-052-6*, 723) Inst Real Estate.
Spotlight on Speech - Language Services. Janet M. Shaw. (Illus.). 96p. 1990. pap. text ed. 25.00 (*0-937857-15-7*, 1578) Speech Bin.
Spotlight on Spiders. Densey Clyne. (Illus.). 32p. (Orig.). (J). (gr. 2-6). 1996. pap. 6.95 (*1-86373-862-2*, Pub. by Allen & Unwin Aust Pty AT) IPG Chicago.
***Spotlight on Strings Bk. 1: Cello.** Doris Gazda & Albert Stoutamire. (Illus.). 32p. (J). 1996. pap. 4.95 (*0-8497-3343-X*, 92CO) Kjos.
***Spotlight on Strings Bk. 1: Full Conductor Score.** Doris Gazda & Albert Stoutamire. (Illus.). 104p. (J). 1996. pap. 9.95 (*0-8497-3340-5*, 92F) Kjos.
***Spotlight on Strings Bk. 1: String Bass.** Doris Gazda & Albert Stoutamire. (Illus.). 32p. (J). 1996. pap. 4.95 (*0-8497-3344-8*, 92SB) Kjos.
***Spotlight on Strings Bk. 1: Viola.** Doris Gazda & Albert Soutamire. (Illus.). 32p. (J). 1996. pap. 4.95 (*0-8497-3342-1*, 92VA) Kjos.
***Spotlight on Strings Bk. 1: Violin.** Doris Gazda & Albert Stoutamire. (Illus.). 32p. (J). 1996. pap. 4.95 (*0-8497-3341-3*, 92VN) Kjos.
Spotlight on Structured Programming with Turbo Pascal. Stewart M. Venit & P. K. Subramanian. Ed. by Mixter. 689p. (C). 1992. pap. text ed. 47.25 (*0-314-91104-9*) West Pub.
Spotlight on the Child: Studies in the History of American Children's Theatre. Ed. by Roger L. Bedard & C. John Tolch. LC 88-21336. (Contributions in Drama & Theatre Studies: No. 28). 207p. 1989. text ed. 49.95 (*0-313-25793-0*, BDT/, Greenwood Pr) Greenwood.
Spotlight on the Cities: Improving Urban Health in Developing Countries. I. Tabibzadeh et al. iv, 174p. (ENG, FRE & SPA.). 1989. pap. text ed. 27.00 (*92-4-156131-9*, 1150329) World Health.
Spotlight on the Family: Public Policy & Private Responsibility. Steven Bayme & David Biale. LC 88-70021. 60p. (Orig.). 1988. pap. 7.00 (*0-87495-098-8*) Am Jewish Comm.
Spotlight on the Transfer Function: A National Study of State Policies & Practices. Louis W. Bender. 1990. 18.50 (*0-87117-213-5*, 1132) Am Assn Comm Coll.
Spotlight on the U. S. A. Randee Falk. LC 92-32456. 1994. 12.95 (*0-19-434235-2*) OUP.
***Spotlight on Toronto.** Crabtree Publishing Co. Staff. (Cities of North America Ser.). 1997. 19.96 (*0-86505-928-4*); pap. text ed. 7.95 (*0-86505-942-X*) Crabtree Pub Co.
Spotlight on Turkey: Continuity & Change. Ed. by Linda Arkin. 200p. (C). 1992. ring bd. 30.00 (*0-944675-49-2*) Amer Forum.
***Spotlight on Voting.** 16p. (Orig.). 1997. pap. 2.00 (*1-884048-17-X*) Natl Assn Parliamentarians.
***Spotlight on Washington.** Crabtree Publishing Co. Staff. (Cities of North America Ser.). 1997. 19.96 (*0-86505-931-4*); pap. text ed. 7.95 (*0-86505-945-4*) Crabtree Pub Co.
Spotlight on Workshops That Work. 20p. (Orig.). 1993. pap. 2.00 (*1-884048-10-2*) Natl Assn Parliamentarians.
Spotlight on You the Board of Directors. 20p. (Orig.). 1993. pap. 2.00 (*1-884048-05-6*) Natl Assn Parliamentarians.
Spotlight on You the Delegate. 20p. (Orig.). 1993. pap. 2.00 (*1-884048-06-4*) Natl Assn Parliamentarians.
***Spotlight on You the President.** 16p. (Orig.). 1997. pap. 2.00 (*1-884048-15-3*) Natl Assn Parliamentarians.
Spotlight Synthetic Aperture Radar: Signal Processing Algorithms. Walter C. Carrara et al. LC 95-19078. 554p. 1995. 89.00 (*0-89006-728-7*) Artech Hse.
Spotlights: level 3. Ndir. 1985. teacher ed., pap. write for info. (*0-395-34134-5*) HM.
***Spots.** Patricia T. Cousin et al. (Visions: African-American Experiences: No. 40). (Illus.). 8p. (Orig.). (J). (gr. k-1). 1995. pap. text ed. 3.00 (*1-57518-039-1*) Arborlake.
***Spots.** Lesser. Date not set. write for info. (*0-15-200666-4*) HarBrace.
Spot's Baby Sister. Eric Hill. (Lift-the-Flaps Ser.). (Illus.). 20p. (J). (ps). 1995. pap. 5.99 (*0-14-055298-7*) Puffin Bks.
Spot's Baby Sister: A Lift-the-Flap Book. Eric Hill. (Illus.). 22p. (J). (ps). 1989. 12.95 (*0-399-21640-5*, Putnam) Putnam Pub Group.
***Spot's Big Book of Colors.** Eric Hill. (J). 1997. pap. 5.99 (*0-14-055531-5*) Viking Penguin.
Spot's Big Book of Colors, Shapes, & Numbers. Eric Hill. (Illus.). 22p. (J). (ps-1). 1994. 10.95 (*0-399-22679-6*, Putnam) Putnam Pub Group.
Spot's Big Book of Colors, Shapes & Numbers-El Libro Grande De Spot: Colores, Formas y Numeros. Eric Hill. (Illus.). 28p. (ENG & SPA.). (J). (ps-2). 1994. 11.95 (*0-399-22782-2*, Putnam) Putnam Pub Group.
Spot's Big Book of Words. Eric Hill. 32p. (J). (gr. 2 up). 1988. 10.95 (*0-399-21563-8*, Putnam) Putnam Pub Group.
Spot's Big Book of Words. Eric Hill. (Spot Ser.). (Illus.). 24p. (J). (ps-1). 1995. pap. 5.99 (*0-14-055532-3*) Puffin Bks.
Spot's Big Book of Words - El Libro Grande de las Palabras de Spot. Eric Hill. (Illus.). 32p. (ENG & SPA.). (J). (ps-1). 1989. 12.95 (*0-399-21689-8*, Putnam) Putnam Pub Group.
Spot's Birthday Party. Eric Hill. (Illus.). 22p. (J). (ps up). 1982. 12.95 (*0-399-20903-4*, Putnam) Putnam Pub Group.
Spot's Birthday Party: Mini Book. Eric Hill. (Illus.). 48p. (J). 1991. 5.95 (*0-399-21770-3*, Putnam) Putnam Pub Group.
Spot's Busy Year. Eric Hill. (Spot's Color-a-Story Bks.). (Illus.). 14p. (J). (ps-2). 1983. pap. 1.95 (*0-399-20987-5*, Putnam) Putnam Pub Group.
Spot's Christmas Activity Book. Eric Hill. (Illus.). 24p. (J). (ps-k). 1995. pap. 4.99 (*0-14-055757-1*) Puffin Bks.
***Spot's Favorite Baby Animals.** Eric Hill. LC 96-43547. (Illus.). 10p. (J). (ps). 1997. 4.95 (*0-399-23157-9*, Putnam) Putnam Pub Group.
***Spot's Favorite Colors.** Eric Hill. LC 96-43553. (Illus.). 10p. (J). (ps). 1997. 4.95 (*0-399-23177-3*, Putnam) Putnam Pub Group.
***Spot's Favorite Numbers.** Eric Hill. LC 96-43548. (Illus.). 10p. (J). (ps). 1997. 4.95 (*0-399-23155-2*, Putnam) Putnam Pub Group.
***Spot's Favorite Words.** Eric Hill. (Illus.). 10p. (J). (ps). 1997. 4.95 (*0-399-23156-0*, Putnam) Putnam Pub Group.
Spots, Feathers, & Curly Tails. Nancy Tafuri. LC 87-15638. (Illus.). 32p. (J). (ps-1). 1988. 16.00 (*0-688-07536-3*); lib. bdg. 15.93 (*0-688-07537-1*) Greenwillow.
Spot's First Easter. Eric Hill. 20p. (J). 1995. pap. 5.99 (*0-14-055299-5*) Puffin Bks.
Spot's First Easter. Eric Hill. (Lift-the-Flap Bks.). (Illus.). 22p. (J). (ps-1). 1988. 12.95 (*0-399-21435-6*, Putnam) Putnam Pub Group.
Spot's First Easter: A Lift-the-Flap Book. Eric Hill. (Illus.). 22p. (J). (ps-k). 1993. 5.95 (*0-399-22424-6*, Putnam) Putnam Pub Group.
Spot's First Walk. Eric Hill. (Lift-the-Flap Ser.). (Illus.). 24p. (ARA & ENG.). (J). (ps-2). 1988. 11.95 (*0-940793-05-9*, Crocodile Bks) Interlink Pub.
Spot's First Walk. Eric Hill. (Illus.). 16p. (J). (ps-1). 1994. pap. 5.99 (*0-14-050725-6*) Puffin Bks.
Spot's First Walk. Eric Hill. (Lift-the-Flap Bks.). (Illus.). 22p. (J). (ps). 1981. 12.95 (*0-399-20838-0*, Putnam) Putnam Pub Group.
Spot's First Walk see Primer Paseo de Spot
Spot's First 1-2-3 Frieze. Eric Hill. (Illus.). 22p. (J). (ps-1). 1994. pap. 5.95 (*0-399-22773-3*, Putnam) Putnam Pub Group.
Spot's Friends. Eric Hill. (Soft Spots Ser.). (Illus.). 8p. (J). (gr. k-1). 1984. 4.95 (*0-399-21066-0*, Putnam) Putnam Pub Group.
Spot's Magical Christmas. Eric Hill. LC 95-8259. (Illus.). 32p. (J). (ps-1). 1995. 11.95 (*0-399-22912-4*, Putnam) Putnam Pub Group.
***Spot's Magical Christmas Big Coloring Book.** Eric Hill. 1997. pap. 2.99 (*0-14-056321-0*) Viking Penguin.
Spots on My Shoes. John Clementson. LC 95-80316. (Illus.). 10p. (J). (ps). 1995. pap. 4.00 (*0-15-200313-4*, Red Wagon Bks) HarBrace.
Spot's Sticker Story Book. Eric Hill. (Illus.). 22p. (J). (ps-1). 1996. pap. 5.99 (*0-14-055680-X*, Puffin) Puffin Bks.
***Spot's Touch & Feel Day.** Eric Hill. (Illus.). 10p. (J). (ps). 1997. 11.95 (*0-399-23209-5*) Putnam Pub Group.
Spot's Toys. Eric Hill. (Soft Spots Ser.). (Illus.). 8p. (J). (gr. k-1). 1984. 4.95 (*0-399-21067-9*, Putnam) Putnam Pub Group.
Spot's Walk in the Woods. Hill Eric. 1997. pap. 6.99 (*0-14-055530-7*) NAL-Dutton.
Spot's Walk in the Woods. Eric Hill. (Lift-the-Flap Rebus Book Ser.). (Illus.). 22p. (J). (ps-2). 1993. 12.95 (*0-399-22528-5*, Putnam) Putnam Pub Group.
Spotswood. Max Dann & Andrew Knight. 82p. 1992. pap. 17.95 (*0-86819-315-1*) Aubrey Bks.
***Spotsylvania Campaign: May 7-19, 1864.** John Cannan. (Great Campaigns Ser.). (Illus.). 256p. 1997. 24.95 (*0-938289-47-0*, Combined Bks) Combined Pub.
Spotsylvania County: Virginia Publick Claims. Janice L. Abercrombie & Richard Slatten. (Virginia Publick Claims Ser.). ix, 52p. 1991. pap. 8.00 (*0-8095-8694-0*) Borgo Pr.
Spotsylvania County: Virginia Publick Claims. Janice L. Abercrombie & Richard Slatten. (Virginia Publick Claims Ser.). ix, 52p. (C). 1991. reprint ed. lib. bdg. 25.00 (*0-8095-8362-3*) Borgo Pr.
Spotsylvania County Records. W. A. Crozier. (Virginia County Records Ser.: Vol. I). (Illus.). 576p. 1996. reprint ed. lib. bdg. 49.00 (*0-8328-5134-5*) Higginson Bk Co.
Spotsylvania County Records. William A. Crozier. (Virginia County Records Ser.: Vol. I). 576p. 1990. reprint ed. 35.00 (*0-614-10539-0*, 1235) Genealog Pub.
Spotted Bear. Hanneke Ippisch. (J). Date not set. 17.00 (*0-689-80557-8*) S&S Childrens.
Spotted Cow. Schomer Lichtner. LC 81-81117. (Illus.). 48p. (Orig.). 1969. pap. 4.50 (*0-941074-01-3*) Lichtner.
Spotted Dick, S'il Vous Plait: An English Restaurant in France. Tom Higgins. 256p. 1996. pap. 10.00 (*0-449-91047-4*) Fawcett.
Spotted Dick, S'il Vous Plait: An English Restaurant in France. Tom Higgins. LC 94-43484. 256p. 1995. 22.00 (*1-56947-032-4*) Soho Press.
Spotted Dolphins. John F. Prevost. LC 95-12365. (Dolphins Ser.). (J). 1995. lib. bdg. 13.98 (*1-56239-495-9*) Abdo & Dghtrs.
Spotted Dragon Visits Romp-er-Roo Land. Tedi T. Wixom. (Illus.). 20p. (Orig.). (J). (ps-8). 1995. lib. bdg. 14.95 (*1-885227-28-0*) TNT Bks.
Spotted Dragon Visits Romp-er-Roo Land. Tedi T. Wixom. (Illus.). 20p. (Orig.). (J). (ps-8). 1995. pap. 4.95 (*1-885227-29-9*) TNT Bks.
Spotted Horse. Henry Tall Bull & Tom Weist. (Indian Culture Ser.). (J). (gr. 2-10). 1970. pap. 4.95 (*0-89992-002-0*) Coun India Ed.
Spotted Horses. limited ed. Boyd Saunders. 100p. 1989. 150.00 (*0-87249-522-1*) U of SC Pr.
Spotted Horses see Three Famous Short Novels
Spotted Owl. Brenda Z. Guiberson. (J). 1994. 14.95 (*0-8050-3171-5*) H Holt & Co.
Spotted Owl. Virginia B. Silverstein et al. LC 93-42624. (Endangered in America Ser.). (Illus.). 64p. (J). (gr. 4-6). 1994. lib. bdg. 16.90 (*1-56294-415-0*) Millbrook Pr.
Spotted Owl. Virginia B. Silverstein et al. (Endangered in America Ser.). (Illus.). 64p. (J). (gr. 4-6). 1996. pap. 6.95 (*0-7613-0164-X*) Millbrook Pr.
Spotted Owlets. Victoria Miles. (Illus.). 24p. (Orig.). (J). (gr. 1-4). 1995. pap. 5.95 (*1-55143-004-5*) Orca Bk Pubs.

S

An Asterisk (*) at the beginning of an entry indicates that the title is appearing in BIP for the first time.

Spotted Owls. James E. Gerholdt. LC 95-48187. (J). 1997. lib. bdg. 13.98 (*1-56239-589-0*) Abdo & Dghtrs.

Spotted Plume. large type ed. Yvonne Whittal. (Linford Romance Library). 296p. 1984. pap. 15.99 (*0-7089-6023-5*) Ulverscroft.

Spotted Pony: A Collection of Hanukkah Stories. Illus. by Leonard E. Fisher. LC 91-24214. 72p. (J). (gr. 2-6). 1992. 15.95 (*0-8234-0936-8*) Holiday.

Spotting the Leopard. Anna Myers. LC 96-13697. 1996. 15.95 (*0-8027-8459-3*) Walker & Co.

***Spotting the Leopard.** Anna Myers. LC 97-15202. (J). 1997. pap. 3.99 (*0-14-038728-5*, Puffin) Puffin Bks.

***Spotty.** Margaret Rey. 1997. pap. 5.95 (*0-395-83732-4*) HM.

Spotty. Margaret Rey. LC 96-26818. 1997. 14.95 (*0-395-83736-7*) HM.

***Spotty Can't Sleep!** Sarah Albee. (Fisher-Price Playbooks). (Illus.). 12p. (J). (ps up). 1997. bds. 6.99 (*1-57584-179-7*) Rdrs Dgst Yng Fam.

***Spotty Pig.** Dick King-Smith. (Illus.). 32p. (J). (ps-1). 1997. 15.00 (*0-374-37154-7*) FS&G.

Spotty Spotty Jones. Bill Gillespie. (Illus.). 22p. (Orig.). (J). 1986. pap. 3.50 (*0-940859-03-3*) Snd Dollar Pub.

Spotty's Adventures. Decatur Celebration Writers. (Wee Write Bks.: No. 26). (Illus.). 43p. (J). (ps-3). 1995. pap. 8.95 (*1-884987-88-5*) WeWrite.

Spotz v. GCM, Inc. 3rd ed. James H. Seckinger. 198p. 1992. pap. 18.95 (*1-55681-334-1*) Natl Inst Trial Ad.

Spotz v. GCM, Inc. Teaching Notes. 3rd ed. Joseph J. Kalo & James H. Seckinger. 104p. 1992. pap. 8.95 (*1-55681-350-3*) Natl Inst Trial Ad.

Spousage of a Virgin to Christ. John Alcock. LC 74-80158. (English Experience Ser.: No. 638). (Illus.). 19p. 1974. reprint ed. 15.00 (*90-221-0638-1*) Walter J Johnson.

Spousal Property Rights under the Ontario Family Law Act. Payne. 280p. 1987. 72.00 (*0-409-80936-5*) MICHIE.

Spouse Abuse: A Treatment Program for Couples. Peter H. Neidig & Dale H. Friedman. LC 84-61187. 256p. (Orig.). 1984. pap. text ed. 17.95 (*0-87822-234-0*, 2340) Res Press.

Spouse Abuse: An Annotated Bibliography of Violence Between Mates. Eugene A. Engeldinger. LC 85-14546. 331p. 1986. 35.00 (*0-8108-1838-8*) Scarecrow.

Spouse Abuse: Assessing & Treating Battered Women, Batterers, & Their Children. Michele Harway & Marsali Hansen. LC 94-29476. 114p. (Orig.). 1994. pap. 19.70 (*1-56887-005-1*, SABP, Prof Resc Pr) Pro Resource.

***Spouse & Child Support in New York.** Jeffrey H. Gallet & Maureen M. Finn. Ed. by Mary E. West & Eliot J. Katz. LC 95-82082. 650p. 1996. text ed. write for info. (*0-7620-0032-5*) Lawyers Cooperative.

Spouse for a Mouse see Magic Badgerkettle & A Spouse for A Mouse

***Spouse for Hire.** 1999. pap. 5.99 (*0-373-20155-9*, 1-20155-7) Harlequin Bks.

Spouse, Parent, Worker: On Gender & Multiple Roles. Faye J. Crosby. 216p. (C). 1990. reprint ed. pap. 14.00 (*0-300-04744-4*) Yale U Pr.

Spouse-Partner Abuse: A Categorized Bibliography & Reference List. R. Geffner et al. 371p. 1990. 40.00 (*1-882948-02-5*) Family Violence.

Spouse-Partner Physical/Psychological Maltreatment: A Categorized Bibliography & Reference List, Update 1996. R. Geffner & C. Lloyd. 1997. 16.95 (*0-614-04196-1*) Family Violence.

Spouse Survival: Personal & Financial Organization. Ray H. Weinrub. 1994. pap. 8.95 (*0-9615390-8-9*) Aspen West Pub.

Spouse Survival Handbook. (Illus.). 104p. (Orig.). 1990. pap. 8.95 (*0-9626726-0-2*) R H Weinrub.

Spoyle of Antwerpe Faithfully Reported by a True Englishman. George Gascoigne. LC 74-25952. (English Experience Ser.: No. 180). 52p. 1969. reprint ed. 15.00 (*90-221-0180-0*) Walter J Johnson.

SPQR. John M. Roberts. 224p. 1990. mass mkt. 3.99 (*0-380-75993-4*) Avon.

***SPQR: The Official Strategy Guide.** John Waters. 240p. 1996. per. 19.99 (*0-7615-1034-6*) Prima Pub.

SPQR Two: The Catiline Conspiracy. John M. Roberts. 224p. 1991. pap. 3.50 (*0-380-75995-0*) Avon.

Sprach-Vebung, Rosen-Mand, Helikonische Hechell, Sendeschreiben a Den Kreutztragenden see Saemtliche Werke: Ausgaben Deutscher Literatur des 15 bis 18 Jahrhunderts

Sprachbruecke Level 1: Cassette zu den Eisprchigen Arbeitsheften. (GER.). (C). 1989. audio 33.50 (*3-12-557151-0*, Pub. by Klett Edition GW) Intl Bk Import.

Sprachbruecke Level 1: Cassetten zum Lehrbuch, 2 cass. (GER.). (C). 1988. audio 47.00 (*3-12-557170-7*, Pub. by Klett Edition GW) Intl Bk Import.

Sprachbruecke Level 1: Einspr. Arbeitsheft 1 (Lektionen 1-7) Abel et al. 129p. (GER.). (C). 1988. pap. text ed. 14.50 (*3-12-557150-2*, Pub. by Klett Edition GW) Intl Bk Import.

Sprachbruecke Level 1: Einspr. Arbeitsheft 2 (Lektionen 8-15) Abel et al. 144p. (GER.). (C). 1989. pap. text ed. 14.50 (*3-12-557160-X*, Pub. by Klett Edition GW) Intl Bk Import.

Sprachbruecke Level 1: Glossar Englisch. Jenkins. 145p. (ENG & GER.). (C). 1989. pap. text ed. 11.75 (*3-12-557510-9*, Pub. by Klett Edition GW) Intl Bk Import.

Sprachbruecke Level 1: Handbuch fuer den Unterricht. Marlene Rall. 296p. (GER.). (C). 1990. pap. text ed. 23.50 (*3-12-557130-8*, Pub. by Klett Edition GW) Intl Bk Import.

Sprachbruecke Level 1: Lehrbuch. Dietmar Roesler et al. 251p. (GER.). (C). 1987. pap. text ed. 23.50 (*3-12-557100-6*, Pub. by Klett Edition GW) Intl Bk Import.

Sprachbruecke Level 2: Einspr. Arbeitsheft 1 (Lektionen 1-5) Jenkins et al. 118p. (GER.). (C). 1992. pap. text ed. 14.50 (*3-12-557250-9*, Pub. by Klett Edition GW) Intl Bk Import.

Sprachbruecke Level 2: Einspr. Arbeitsheft 2 (Lektionen 6-10) Jenkins et al. 118p. (GER.). (C). 1992. pap. text ed. 14.50 (*3-12-557255-X*, Pub. by Klett Edition GW) Intl Bk Import.

Sprachbruecke Level 2: Handbuch fuer den Unterricht. Dietmar Roesler. 119p. (GER.). (C). 1994. pap. text ed. 20.25 (*3-12-557230-4*, Pub. by Klett Edition GW) Intl Bk Import.

Sprachbruecke Level 2: Lehrbuch. D. Roesler et al. 175p. (GER.). (C). 1989. pap. text ed. 22.50 (*3-12-557200-2*, Pub. by Klett Edition GW) Intl Bk Import.

Sprachbruecke Level 2: Lehrbuch, 2 cass. D. Roesler et al. (GER.). (C). 1990. audio 45.00 (*3-12-557215-0*, Pub. by Klett Edition GW) Intl Bk Import.

Sprachdenken im Ubersetzen. Franz Rosenzweig & Rafael Rosenzweig. 286p. 1984. lib. bdg. 143.50 (*90-247-2695-6*, Pub. by M Nijhoff NE) Kluwer Ac.

Sprachdenken im Ubersetzen: Band-Arbeitspapiere zur Verdeutschung der Schrift, Vol. 4. F. Rosenzweig. 396p. 1984. lib. bdg. 186.00 (*90-247-2854-1*) Kluwer Ac.

***Sprache - System und Funktion: Festschrift fur Gunter Weise.** Rudolf Beier. Ed. by Gerhard Augst. (Theorie und Vermittlung der Sprache Ser.: Bd. 25). (Illus.). x, 262p. (GER.). 1996. 51.95 (*3-631-49815-2*) P Lang Pubng.

Sprache der Ahiqarspruche. Ingo Kottsieper. (Beiheft zur Zeitschrift fuer die Alttestamentliche Wissenschaft Ser.: Vol. 194). xii, 302p. (C). 1990. lib. bdg. 95.40 (*3-11-012331-2*) De Gruyter.

Sprache der DDR im Spiegel Ihrer Literatur: Studien zum DDR-Typischen Wortschatz. Sabina Schroeter. (Sprache, Politik, Oeffentlichkeit Ser.: Band 2). x, 241p. (GER.). (C). 1994. lib. bdg. 100.00 (*3-11-013808-5*) De Gruyter.

Sprache der Guang in Togo und auf der Goldkuste und Funf Andere Togosprachen. Diedrich Westermann. (GER.). 1922. 25.00 (*0-8115-3093-0*) Periodicals Srv.

Sprache der Massenmedien: Eine Einfuhrung. 2nd rev. ed. Harald Burger. (Sammlung Goschen Ser.: No. 2225). 388p. (C). 1990. pap. 22.95 (*3-11-012306-1*) De Gruyter.

Sprache des Parlaments und Semiotik der Demokratie: Studien zur Politischen Kommunikation in der Moderne. Ed. by Andreas Doerner & Ludgera Vogt. (Sprache, Politik, Oeffentlichkeit Ser.: Bd. 6). iv, 400p. (GER.). (C). 1995. lib. bdg. 144.60 (*3-11-014496-4*) De Gruyter.

Sprache Huldrych Zwinglis im Kontrast zur Sprache Luthers. Walter Schenker. (Studia Linguistica Germanica: Vol. 14). (Illus.). (C). 1977. 169.25 (*3-11-006605-X*) De Gruyter.

Sprache Im Konflikt: Zur Rolle der Sprache in Sozialen, Politischen und Militaerischen Auseinandersetzung. Ed. by Ruth Reiher. (Sprache, Politik, Oeffentlichkeit Ser.: No. 5). 480p. (GER.). (C). 1994. lib. bdg. 204.65 (*3-11-013958-8*) De Gruyter.

Sprache Im Umbruch: Politischer Sprachwandel Im Zeichen Von "Wende" und "Vereinigung" Ed. by Armin Burkhardt & K. Peter Fritzsche. (Sprache, Politik, Oeffentlichkeit Ser.: Bd. 1). xxi, 314p. (GER.). (C). 1992. lib. bdg. 113.85 (*3-11-013613-9*) De Gruyter.

Sprache Ohne Worte: Idee Einer Allgemeinen Wissenschaft der Sprache. Rudolph Kleinpaul. (Approaches to Semiotics Ser.: No. 19). 456p. 1972. reprint ed. text ed. 90.80 (*90-279-2047-8*) Mouton.

Sprache und Evolution: Grundlagen der Evolution und Ansatze einer Evolutionstheoretischen Sprachwissenschaft. Horst M. Muller. (Grundlagen der Kommunikation & Kognition (Foundations of Communication & Cognition) Ser.). (Illus.). x, 137p. (C). 1990. lib. bdg. 98.50 (*3-11-011041-5*) De Gruyter.

***Sprache und Kommunikation Im Kulturkontext: Beitrage Zum Ehrenkolloquium asu Anlab des 60. Geburtstages von Gotthard Lerchner.** Volker Hertel et al. (Leipziger Arbetien zur Sprach- und Kommunikationsgeschichte Ser.: Bd. 4). ix, 428p. (GER.). 1996. 63.95 (*3-631-50050-5*) P Lang Pubng.

Sprache und Literatur bis zum Ende des see Aufstieg und Niedergang der romischen Welt: Section 1, von den Anfangen Roms bis zum Ausgang der Republik

Sprache und Literatur (Literatur der Augusteischen Zeit: Allgemeines, Einzelne Autoren), Vol. 30, Pt. I see Aufstieg und Niedergang der Roemischen Welt: Selection 2, Principat

Sprache und Literatur (Literatur der Augusteischen Zeit: Allgemeines, Einzelne Autoren, Fortsetzung), Vol. 30, Pt. II see Aufstieg und Niedergang der Roemischen Welt: Selection 2, Principat

Sprache und Literatur (Literatur der Augusteischen Zeit: Allgemeines, Einzule Autoren Fortsetzung), Vol. 30, Pt. III see Aufstieg und Niedergang der Roemischen Welt: Selection 2, Principat

Sprache und Literatur (Literatur der augusteischen Zeit: Einzelne Autoren, Fortsetzung Vergil, Horaz, Ovid), Vol. 31, Pt. IV see Aufstieg und Niedergang der Roemischen Welt: Selection 2, Principat

Sprache und Literatur (Literatur der Ausgusteischen Zeit: Einzelne Autoren- Vergil, Horaz, Ovid), Vol. 31, Pt. I see Aufstieg und Niedergang der Roemischen Welt: Selection 2, Principat

Sprache und Literatur (Literatur der Julisch-Claudischen und der Flavischen Zeit), Vol. 32, Pt. I see Aufstieg und Niedergang der Roemischen Welt: Selection 2, Principat

Sprache und Literatur (Literatur der Julisch-Claudischen und der Flavischen Zeit- Fortsetzung), Vol. 32, Pt. II see Aufstieg und Niedergang der Roemischen Welt: Selection 2, Principat

Sprache und Literatur (Literatur der Julsich-Claudischen und der Flavischen Zeit- Fortsetzung), Vol. 32, Pt. III see Aufstieg und Niedergang der Roemischen Welt: Selection 2, Principat

Sprache und Literatur (Sprachen und Schriften Fortsetzung), Vol. 29, Pt. II see Aufstieg und Niedergang der Roemischen Welt: Selection 2, Principat

Sprache und Literatur (Sprachen und Schriften), Vol. 29, Pt. I see Aufstieg und Niedergang der Roemischen Welt: Selection 2, Principat

Sprache und Literatur 1 see Aufstieg und Niedergang der romischen Welt: Section 1, von den Anfangen Roms bis zum Ausgang der Republik

Sprache und Litertur (Literatur der Augsteischen Zeit: Einzelne Autoren- Fortsetzung, Vergil, Horaz, Ovid), Vol. 31, Pt. III see Aufstieg und Niedergang der Roemischen Welt: Selection 2, Principat

Sprache und Litertur(Literatur ser Augusteischen Zeit: Einzelne Autoren, Fortstzung Vergil, Horaz, Ovid), Vol. 31, Pt. II see Aufstieg und Niedergang der Roemischen Welt: Selection 2, Principat

Sprache und Politik: Untersuchungen zum Sprachgebrauch der "Paulskirche" Horst Gruenert. LC 74-80634. (Studia Linguistica Germanica: Vol. 10). 1974. 89.25 (*3-11-003609-6*) De Gruyter.

***Sprache: Verstehen und Verstandlichkeit: KongreBbeitrage Zur 25. Jahrestagung der Gesellschaft Fur Angewandte Linguistik GAL e. V.** Bernd Spillner. (Forum Angewandte Linguistik Ser.: Bd. 28). 353p. (GER.). 1995. 61.95 (*3-631-49109-3*) P Lang Pubng.

Sprachen der Logik und die Logik der Sprache. M. J. Cresswell. (Grundlagen der Kommunikation De Gruyter Studienbuch Ser.). (C). 1979. 33.85 (*3-11-004923-6*) De Gruyter.

Sprachen Europas in Systematischer Uebersicht (Bonn, 1850) Linguistische Untersuchungen. August Schleicher. (Amsterdam Classics in Linguistics Ser.: 4). viii, 270p. 1983. 78.00 (*90-272-0875-1*) Benjamins North Am.

Sprachforschung der Aufklaerung Im Spiegel der Grossen Franzoesischen Enzyklopaedie. Irene Monreal-Wickert. 210p. (GER.). 1977. 59.95 (*0-8288-5518-8*, M7054) Fr & Eur.

Sprachfuehrer fuer die Krankenpflege. Deutsche Schwestergemeinschaft Staff. 253p. 1968. pap. 19.95 (*0-8288-6662-7*, M-7627, Pub. by Wissenschaftliche Buchgesellschaft) Fr & Eur.

***Sprachgebrauch - Sprachvariation - Sprachwissen: Eine Familienfallstudie.** Evelyn Ziegler. (Variolingua, Nonstandard - Standard - Substandard Ser.: Bd. 2). (Illus.). 292p. (GER.). 1996. 54.95 (*3-631-49750-4*) P Lang Pubng.

Sprachgebrauch Des Cornelius Nepos. Bernhard Lupus. vii, 224p. 1972. reprint ed. write for info. (*3-487-04508-7*) G Olms Pubs.

Sprachgeschichte: Ein Handbuch zur Geschichte der Deutschen Sprache und Ihrer Erforschung, 2 pts., Pt. 1. Ed. by Stefan Sonderegger et al. (Handbooks of Linguistics & Communication Science). (Illus.). xxxiiii, 948p. (GER.). 1984. 488.50 (*3-11-007396-X*) De Gruyter.

Sprachgeschichte und Sprachkritik: Festschrift Fuer Peter von Polenz Zum 65. Geburtstag. Ed. by Hans Juergen & Georg Stoezel. viii, 378p. (GER.). 1993. lib. bdg. 150.80 (*3-11-013583-3*) De Gruyter.

Sprachgitter/Die Niemandsrose: Gedichte. Paul Celan. 158p. (GER.). 1986. 18.00 (*3-10-010504-4*, Pub. by S Fischer GW) Intl Bk Import.

Sprachhelden Und Sprachverderber: Dokumente Zur Erforschung Des Fremdwortpurismus Im Deutschen (1478-1750) Ed. by William J. Jones. (Studia Linguistica Germanica: Bd. 38). x, 687p. (GER.). (C). 1995. lib. bdg. 229.25 (*3-11-014480-8*) De Gruyter.

Sprachherkunftsforschung, Vol. I: Einleitung & Phonogenese. Gyula Decsy. (Bibliotheca Nostratica Ser.: Vol 2). 87p. 1977. 22.00 (*3-447-01861-5*) Eurolingua.

Sprachherkunftsforschung, Vol. II: Semogenese-Palaosemiotik. Gyula Decsy. (Bibliotheca Nostratica Ser.: Vol. 2). 78p. 1981. 22.00 (*0-931922-06-2*) Eurolingua.

Sprachkurs Deutsch 1. Ulrich Haussermann et al. 21p. (GER.). 1993. trans. 162.00 (*3-425-08324-4*, Pub. by Verlag Moritz Diesterweg GW) Intl Bk Import.

Sprachkurs Deutsch 1. Ulrich Haussermann et al. 69p. (C). 1994. teacher ed. 9.00 (*3-425-05951-3*, Pub. by Verlag Moritz Diesterweg GW) Intl Bk Import.

Sprachkurs Deutsch 1. Ulrich Haussermann et al. 1995. audio 88.25 (*3-425-05941-6*, Pub. by Verlag Moritz Diesterweg GW) Intl Bk Import.

Sprachkurs Deutsch 1. 4th ed. Ulrich Haussermann et al. viii, 296p. (GER.). 1995. pap. text ed. 27.00 (*3-425-05901-7*, Pub. by Verlag Moritz Diesterweg GW) Intl Bk Import.

Sprachkurs Deutsch 1: German-English Glossary. Frances Zwicky-Schon & Gerhard Koller. 99p. (ENG & GER.). 1995. pap. text ed. 14.00 (*3-425-05911-4*, Pub. by Verlag Moritz Diesterweg GW) Intl Bk Import.

Sprachkurs Deutsch 2. Ulrich Haussermann & Georg Dietrich. (Illus.). (GER.). (C). audio 72.00 (*3-425-05942-4*, Pub. by Verlag Moritz Diesterweg GW) Intl Bk Import.

Sprachkurs Deutsch 2. Ulrich Haussermann & Georg Dietrich. (Illus.). 20p. (GER.). (C). 1993. trans. 162.00 (*3-425-08325-2*, Pub. by Verlag Moritz Diesterweg GW) Intl Bk Import.

Sprachkurs Deutsch 2. 2nd ed. Ulrich Haussermann & Georg Dietrich. (Illus.). 71p. (GER.). (C). 1993. teacher ed. 9.00 (*3-425-05952-1*, Pub. by Verlag Moritz Diesterweg GW) Intl Bk Import.

Sprachkurs Deutsch 2. 3rd ed. Ulrich Haussermann & Georg Dietrich. (Illus.). 216p. (GER.). (C). 1995. pap. text ed. 27.00 (*3-425-05902-5*, Pub. by Verlag Moritz Diesterweg GW) Intl Bk Import.

Sprachkurs Deutsch 2: German-English Glossary. 2nd ed. Frances Zwicky-Schon & Gerhard Koller. 114p. (ENG & GER.). (C). 1993. pap. text ed. 14.50 (*3-425-05921-1*, Pub. by Verlag Moritz Diesterweg GW) Intl Bk Import.

Sprachkurs Deutsch 3. Ulrich Haussermann & Georg Dietrich. (GER.). (C). 1991. audio 72.00 (*3-425-05943-2*, Pub. by Verlag Moritz Diesterweg GW) Intl Bk Import.

Sprachkurs Deutsch 3. Ulrich Haussermann & Georg Dietrich. 21p. (GER.). (C). 1993. trans. 162.00 (*3-425-08326-0*, Pub. by Verlag Moritz Diesterweg GW) Intl Bk Import.

Sprachkurs Deutsch 3. 2nd ed. Ulrich Haussermann & Georg Dietrich. 96p. (GER.). (C). 1993. teacher ed. 11.75 (*3-425-05953-X*, Pub. by Verlag Moritz Diesterweg GW) Intl Bk Import.

Sprachkurs Deutsch 3. 3rd ed. Ulrich Haussermann & Georg Dietrich. 324p. (GER.). (C). 1995. pap. text ed. 27.00 (*3-425-05903-3*, Pub. by Verlag Moritz Diesterweg GW) Intl Bk Import.

Sprachkurs Deutsch 3: German-English Glossary. Frances Zwicky-Schon & Gerhard Koller. 195p. (ENG & GER.). (C). 1992. pap. text ed. 17.00 (*3-425-05931-9*, Pub. by Verlag Moritz Diesterweg GW) Intl Bk Import.

Sprachkurs Deutsch 4. Ulrich Haussermann & Georg Koller. (Illus.). 103p. (GER.). (C). 1992. teacher ed. 13.50 (*3-425-05954-8*, Pub. by Verlag Moritz Diesterweg GW); pap. text ed. 27.00 (*3-425-05904-1*, Pub. by Verlag Moritz Diesterweg GW); audio 72.00 (*3-425-05944-0*, Pub. by Verlag Moritz Diesterweg GW) Intl Bk Import.

Sprachkurs Deutsch 5. Ulrich Haussermann & Georg Koller. (Illus.). 288p. (GER.). (C). 1993. teacher ed., pap. text ed. 10.75 (*3-425-05955-6*, Pub. by Verlag Moritz Diesterweg GW); audio 72.00 (*3-425-05945-9*, Pub. by Verlag Moritz Diesterweg GW) Intl Bk Import.

Sprachkurs Deutsch 5. Ulrich Haussermann & Georg Koller. (Illus.). 288p. (GER.). (C). 1994. pap. text ed. 27.00 (*3-425-05905-X*, Pub. by Verlag Moritz Diesterweg GW) Intl Bk Import.

Sprachkurs Deutsch 6. Ulrich Haussermann & Georg Koller. (Illus.). (GER.). (C). 1994. teacher ed. 13.50 (*3-425-05956-4*, Pub. by Verlag Moritz Diesterweg GW); pap. text ed. 27.00 (*3-425-05906-8*, Pub. by Verlag Moritz Diesterweg GW); audio 72.00 (*3-425-05946-7*, Pub. by Verlag Moritz Diesterweg GW) Intl Bk Import.

Sprachlicher und Historischer Kommenter zu Amianus Marcellinus XIV. P. De Jonge. 148p. (GER.). 1972. 38.00 (*0-318-41850-9*, Pub. by Egbert Forsten NE) Benjamins North Am.

Sprachliches Handbuch Zur Biblischen Vulgata. Franz Kaulen. xvi, 332p. 1973. reprint ed. write for info. (*3-487-05012-9*) G Olms Pubs.

Sprachphilosophie - Philosophy of Language - La Philosophie Du Langage: An International Handbook of Contemporary Research. Ed. by Marcelo Dascal et al. (Handbooks of Linguistics & Communication Science: No. 7.1). xxxvi, 872p. (ENG, FRE & GER.). (C). 1992. lib. bdg. 523.10 (*3-11-009583-1*) De Gruyter.

Sprachphilosophie des Hl, Thomas Von Aquin. F. Manthey. (Philosophy Reprints Ser.). (GER.). reprint ed. lib. bdg. 45.00 (*0-697-00042-7*) Irvington.

***Sprachphilosophie Hilary Putnams.** Rainer Noske. (Europaische Hochschulschriften Ser.: Reihe 20, Bd. 524). 90p. (GER.). 1997. 29.95 (*3-631-31036-6*) P Lang Pubng.

Sprachphilosophie in Antike und Mittelalter: Bochumer Kolloquim, 2-4, June 1982. Burkhard Mojsisch. (Bochum Studies in Philosophy: No. 3). 448p. (GER.). 1986. 58.00 (*90-6032-233-9*, Pub. by B R Gruener NE) Benjamins North Am.

Sprachpilosophie/Philosophy of Language/la Philosophie du Langage Vol. 2: Ein Internationales Handbuch Zeitgenoessischer Forschung, an International Handbook of Contemporary Research Manuel International des Recherches Contemporaines. Ed. by Marcelo Dascal et al. (Handbooks of Linguistics & Communication Science: Bd. 7.2). xii, 1216p. (ENG, FRE & GER.). (C). 1995. lib. bdg. 676.95 (*3-11-013991-X*) De Gruyter.

Sprachpolitik In der Romania: Zur Geschichte Sprachpolitischen Denkens und Handelns Von der Franzoesischen Revolution Bis Zur Gegenwart. Ed. by Klaus Bochmann. xvi, 528p. (GER.). 1993. lib. bdg. 206.15 (*3-11-013614-7*) De Gruyter.

Sprachreflexion in Barock und Fruehaufklaerung: Entwuerfe von Boehme bis Leibniz. Andreas Gardt. (Quellen und Forschungen zur Sprach und Kulturgeschichte der Germanischen Voelker, NF 108 (232)). 530p. (GER.). (C). 1994. lib. bdg. 184.65 (*3-11-014282-1*, 182-94) De Gruyter.

Sprachschatze der Angelsachsischen Dichter. Christian W. Grein. 1973. 100.00 (*0-8490-1118-3*) Gordon Pr.

***Sprachspiele und Sprachkomik Jeux de Mots & Comique Verbal.** Michael Herrmann & Karl Holz. (FRE.). 1996. 51.95 (*3-631-49162-X*) P Lang Pubng.

Sprachspielereien Fur Deutschlernende. Rainer Bohn & Ina Schreiter. 168p. 1993. 15.95 (*3-324-00483-7*) Langenscheidt.

An Asterisk (*) at the beginning of an entry indicates that the title is appearing in BIP for the first time.

Sprachstrategien und Dialogblockaden: Linguistische und Politikwissenschaftliche Studien zur Politischen Kommunikation. Ed. by Josef Klein & Hajo Diekmannshenke. (Sprache, Politik, Oeffentlichkeit Ser.: Vol. 7). (Illus.). x, 214p. (C). 1996. lib. bdg. 100.75 (*3-11-015077-8*) De Gruyter.

***Sprachtherapie Bei Laryngektomie Entwicklung und Uberprufung Prognostisch Relevanter Kriterien Fur die Stimmliche Rehabilitation Kehlkopfektomierter Patienten: Ein Betrag Zur Therapieforschung.** Axel Kurvers. (Europaische Hochschulschriften Ser.: Reihe 11, Bd. 705). (Illus.). ix, 370p. (GER.). 1997. 63.95 (*3-631-31128-1*) P Lang Pubng.

Sprachtraumata in den Texten Wolfgang Hilbigs. Gabriele Eckart. LC 94-26825. (DDR Studien - East German Studies: Vol. 10). 216p. (GER.). (C). 1996. text ed. 52.95 (*0-8204-2645-8*) P Lang Pubng.

***Sprachvarianten und Ihr Status in Den Sprachsystemen.** Leopold Auburger. (Philosophische Texte und Studien: Vol. 36). iv, 382p. (GER.). 1993. write for info. (*3-487-09768-0*) G Olms Pubs.

Sprachvergleichung und Urgeschichte. Otto Schrader. xii, 795p. 1980. reprint ed. write for info. (*3-487-07000-6*) G Olms Pubs.

***Sprachwahlverhalten Bei Deutschfranzosischer Mehrsprachigkeit.** Thomas Biegel. (Studien zur Allgemeinen und Romanischen Sprachwissenschaft Ser.: Bd. 4). (Illus.). xii, 252p. (GER.). 1996. 51.95 (*3-631-31074-9*) P Lang Pubng.

Sprachwandel: Reader Zur diachronischen Sprachwissenschaft. Ed. by Dieter Cherubim. (Grundlagen der Kommunikation Ser.). x, 362p. (C). 1975. pap. 27.70 (*3-11-004330-0*) De Gruyter.

Sprachwandel im Dialekt von Krefeld. Helga Bister-Broosen. (Berkeley Insights in Linguistics & Semiotics Ser.: Vol. 3). 200p. (GER.). (C). 1989. text ed. 31.95 (*0-8204-1006-3*) P Lang Pubng.

***Sprachwissenschaft: Ein Reader.** Ed. by Ludger Hoffmann. xii, 778p. (GER.). (C). 1996. text ed. 83.00 (*3-11-015529-X*); pap. text ed. 50.40 (*3-11-014701-7*) De Gruyter.

Sprague: Genealogy, in Part, of the Sprague Families in America, as Descended from Edward Sprague of England, from 1614, with the Descendant of Edward Sprague & That of His Son William Who Settled in Hingham MA in 1636. A. B. Sprague. 49p. 1994. reprint ed. pap. 10.00 (*0-8328-4095-5*) Higginson Bk Co.

Sprague: Part of the 1940-1 Supplement to "Sprague Families in America", Francus Sprague of Duxbury, Massachusetts, 1913. W. V. Sprague. 35p. 1994. reprint ed. pap. 7.00 (*0-8328-4181-1*) Higginson Bk Co.

Sprague Family in America. (Illus.). 578p. 1989. reprint ed. pap. 87.00 (*0-8328-1105-X*); reprint ed. lib. bdg. 95.00 (*0-8328-1104-1*) Higginson Bk Co.

Sprained Ankle! Pam Jarnell. (HRL Big Bks.). (Illus.). 8p. (Orig.). (J). (ps). 1995. pap. 10.95 (*1-57332-062-5*) HighReach Lrning.

Sprang: Language & Techniques. 2nd ed. Jules Kliot. 16p. 1974. pap. 7.00 (*0-916896-03-X*) Lacis Pubns.

***Sprat Morrison.** D'Costa. Date not set. pap. text ed. write for info. (*0-582-05207-6*, Pub. by Longman UK) Longman.

Spratling Silver. Sandraline Cederwall & Hal Riney. (Illus.). 128p. 1991. 32.50 (*0-87701-845-6*) Chronicle Bks.

***Spratlys: The Dispute in the South China Sea.** Bob Catley & Makmur Keliat. 232p. (C). 1997. text ed. 63.95 (*1-85521-995-6*, Pub. by Dartmth Pub UK) Ashgate Pub Co.

Sprawlgangs & Megacorps. Terry K. Amthor & Kevin Barrett. (Cyberspace Ser.). (Illus.). 56p. (C). 1990. pap. 12.00 (*1-55806-086-3*, 5101) Iron Crown Ent Inc.

Spray. Robert J. Blake. LC 94-32514. 32p. (J). (ps-3). 1996. 15.95 (*0-399-22770-9*, Philomel Bks) Putnam Pub Group.

Spray: The Ultimate Cruising Boat. R. Bruce Roberts-Goodson. (Illus.). 224p. 1995. 29.95 (*0-924486-87-2*) Sheridan.

***Spray: The Work of Howard Arkley.** Ashley Crawford & Ray Edgar. (Illus.). 156p. 1997. 72.00 (*976-641-028-3*, Pub. by Craftsman Hse VB) IPG Chicago.

***Spray & Stitch: Over 30 Projects Combining Cross Stitch with Easy Spray Paint Techniques.** Sally Harman. 1997. 24.95 (*0-7153-0460-7*) Sterling.

Spray Application Using Flammable & Combustible Materials. National Fire Protection Association Staff. 27p. 1989. 20.25 (*0-317-63067-9*, 33-89) Natl Fire Prot.

Spray Dryers. Ed. by AIChE's Equipment Testing Procedure Committee Staff. 24p. 1988. pap. 60.00 (*0-8169-0462-6*, E 26) Am Inst Chem Eng.

Spray Finishing. Andy Charron. LC 96-33748. (Illus.). 176p. 1996. pap. 19.95 (*1-56158-114-3*) Taunton.

Spray Forming: Science, Technology & Applications: Preprint of a Seminar Held at the 1992 Powder Metallurgy World Congress, San Francisco, California, June 23-24, 1992. Powder Metallurgy World Congress Staff. (Illus.). 178p. reprint ed. pap. 50.80 (*0-7837-6978-4*, 2046789) Bks Demand.

Spray Forming 2: Proceedings of the Second International Conference on Spray Forming (ICSF 2) Ed. by J. V. Wood. 446p. 1994. pap. 255.00 (*1-85573-146-0*, Pub. by Woodhead Pubng UK) Am Educ Systs.

Spray Nozzles. 12p. 1993. 16.75 (*0-685-64955-5*, 1964-93) Natl Fire Prot.

Spray-Paint Mystery. Angela S. Medearis. (J). (gr. 2-5). 1996. pap. 2.99 (*0-590-48474-5*) Scholastic Inc.

Spray Painting License. (Career Examination Ser.: C-3766). pap. 23.95 (*0-8373-3766-6*) Nat Learn.

Spraycan Art. Henry Chalfant & James Prigoff. LC 87-50389. (Illus.). 96p. (Orig.). 1987. pap. 15.95 (*0-500-27469-X*) Thames Hudson.

Sprayed Concrete: Properties, Design, & Applications. Simon A. Austin. LC 94-24425. 1995. text ed. 60.00 (*0-07-057148-1*) McGraw.

Sprayed Zinc Galvanic Anodes for Concrete Marine Bridge Substructures. Alberto A. Sagues & Rodney G. Powers. (SHRP Ser.: S-405). (Illus.). 85p. (Orig.). (C). 1994. pap. text ed. 10.00 (*0-309-05819-8*) Natl Res Coun.

Spraying under the Bed for Wolves. Anne George. (Illus.). 40p. (Orig.). 1985. pap. 5.00 (*0-945301-02-2*) Druid Pr.

SprayPaint Conference Proceedings, 1993. Products Finishing Staff. 316p. (C). 1993. pap. text ed. 45.00 (*1-56990-079-5*) Hanser-Gardner.

***Sprays of Salt: Reminiscences of a Native Shoaler.** John W. Downs. (Illus.). 192p. 1997. reprint ed. 24.00 (*0-914339-59-1*) P E Randall Pub.

Spread a Little Christmas Cheer. Berta Poorman & Sonja Poorman. 1982. pap. 4.95 (*0-686-38388-5*) Eldridge Pub.

Spread Mooring Systems. (Rotary Drilling Ser.: Unit V, Lesson 2). (Illus.). 47p. (Orig.). 1976. pap. text ed. 14.00 (*0-88698-070-4*, 2.50210) PETEX.

Spread Mooring Systems. Ed. by Celina Henderson. Tr. by Marcela Rossman. (Rotary Drilling Ser.: Unit V, Lesson 2). (Illus.). 53p. (Orig.). (SPA.). 1982. pap. text ed. 14.00 (*0-88698-045-3*, 2.50212) PETEX.

Spread My Wings. Eugenia Collier. 1992. pap. 8.00 (*0-88378-090-9*) Third World.

***Spread My Wings: A Message in the Music.** Leotha A. Stanley. (Illus.). 52p. (Orig.). (J). (gr. k-8). 1996. pap. 14.99 (*0-9654945-0-0*) Musical-Lee Yours Inc.

Spread of AIDS. Ed. by Daniel Leone. LC 96-42912. (At Issue Ser.). 96p. (J). (gr. 5-12). 1997. pap. 8.96 (*1-56510-537-0*) Greenhaven.

Spread of AIDS. Ed. by Daniel Leone. LC 96-42912. (At Issue Ser.). (J). (gr. 5-12). 1997. lib. bdg. 14.96 (*1-56510-538-9*) Greenhaven.

Spread of British Printing - 1557 to 1695. Sessions, William Ltd., Staff. 204p. (C). 1988. 146.00 (*1-85072-036-3*, Pub. by W Sessions UK) St Mut.

Spread of Deserts. Ewan McLeish. LC 90-10018. (Conserving Our World Ser.). (Illus.). 48p. (J). (gr. 4-9). 1990. pap. 5.95 (*0-8114-3456-7*); lib. bdg. 24.26 (*0-8114-2390-5*) Raintree Steck-V.

Spread of Economic Ideas. Ed. by David Colander & A. W. Coats. (Illus.). 288p. (C). 1989. text ed. 54.95 (*0-521-36233-4*) Cambridge U Pr.

Spread of Economic Ideas. Ed. by David Colander & A. W. Coats. (Illus.). 288p. (C). 1993. pap. text ed. 18.95 (*0-521-44650-3*) Cambridge U Pr.

Spread of English: The Sociology of English As an Additional Language. Ed. by Joshua A. Fishman et al. LC 77-11068. 350p. 1977. reprint ed. pap. 99.80 (*0-608-00001-9*, AU00467) Bks Demand.

Spread of Islam. John Dunn. LC 95-51795. (World History Ser.). 112p. (YA). (gr. 9 up). 1996. lib. bdg. 17.96 (*1-56006-285-1*) Lucent Bks.

Spread of Islam to India + Teacher's Guide. pap. text ed. 4.95 (*1-878099-15-9*) Vidya Bks.

Spread of Machinery, 1793-1806. LC 72-2545. (British Labour Struggles Before 1850 Ser.). 1974. 25.95 (*0-405-04437-2*) Ayer.

Spread of Nuclear Weapons. Leonard Beaton & John Maddox. LC 76-16061. (Studies in International Security: No. 5). 216p. 1976. reprint ed. text ed. 35.00 (*0-8371-8949-7*, BENW, Greenwood Pr) Greenwood.

Spread of Nuclear Weapons: A Debate. Scott D. Sagan & Kenneth N. Waltz. LC 94-24470. 120p. (C). 1995. pap. text ed. 8.95 (*0-393-96716-6*) Norton.

***Spread of Religion, Bk. 4.** Paul Russell. Date not set. write for info. (*0-688-13908-6*) Morrow.

***Spread of Sponsorship in the Arts & Sport: Education, the Health Service & Broadcasting.** Roy Shaw. 125p. 1993. pap. 16.95 (*1-85224-190-X*, Pub. by Bloodaxe Bks UK) Dufour.

Spread of Terror: Plus Lots of Cartoons We Could Have Put on the Cover but Didn't. P. S. Mueller. 137p. 1986. pap. 5.95 (*0-933893-15-9*) Bonus Books.

Spread of Tumors in the Human Body. 3rd ed. Rupert A. Willis. LC 75-312789. (Illus.). 429p. reprint ed. pap. 122.30 (*0-317-41709-6*, 2025722) Bks Demand.

Spread of Vaisnavism in Gujarat up to 1600 AD: A Study with Special Reference to the Iconic Forms of Visnu. Haripriya Rangarajan. (C). 1991. 72.00 (*81-7039-192-X*, Pub. by Somaiya II) S Asia.

Spread Sheet Application for Health Care & Business Professionals: A Self Aided Instruction. Edward Khiwa-Kiwuwa. 75p. 1994. student ed., text ed. 30.95 (*0-9643899-1-6*) E K Kiwuwa.

***Spread Spectrum CDMA Systems for Wireless Communications.** Savo Glisic & Branka Vucetic. LC 97-860. (Wireless Communications Ser.). 442p. 1997. 89.00 (*0-89006-858-5*) Artech Hse.

Spread Spectrum Communications Handbook. rev. ed. Marvin K. Simon. 1994. text ed. 99.50 (*0-07-057629-7*) McGraw.

Spread Spectrum Signal Design: LPE & AJ Systems. David L. Nicholson. Ed. by Sandy Kahl. LC 87-38218. (Electrical Engineering, Telecommunications, & Signal Processing Ser.). 291p. (C). 1995. text ed. write for info. (*0-7167-8150-6*) W H Freeman.

Spread Spectrum Sourcebook. 1991. pap. 20.00 (*0-87259-317-7*) Am Radio.

Spread Spectrum Systems: With Commercial Applications. 3rd ed. Robert C. Dixon. LC 93-8378. 573p. 1994. text ed. 85.95 (*0-471-59342-7*) Wiley.

Spread Spectrum Techniques: Overview Summary. Dave Adamy. (Overview Summaries Ser.). 32p. 1994. pap. 8.00 (*1-885897-06-5*) Lynx Pubng.

Spread the Flame: Missions Education in the Local Church. David A. Womack. LC 92-75953. 128p. (Orig.). 1993. pap. text ed. 2.95 (*0-88243-687-2*, 02-0687) Gospel Pub.

Spread the Word: How to Promote Nonprofits with a Network of Speakers. Terri Horvath. (Orig.). 1995. pap. text ed. 14.95 (*0-9644364-0-X*) Publishing Res.

***Spread Trading: Low Risk Strategies for Profiting from Market Relationships.** Howard Abell. LC 97-8296. 1997. 40.00 (*0-7931-2425-5*) Dearborn Trade.

Spreading Depression. Ed. by R. J. Do Carmo. (Experimental Brain Research Ser.: Vol. 23). (Illus.). 125p. 1992. 82.95 (*0-387-55532-3*) Spr-Verlag.

***Spreading Depression: A Retinal Model.** V. M. Fernandes De Lima et al. LC 96-47969. (Biological Techniques Ser.). (Illus.). 300p. 1997. text ed. 84.95 (*0-12-209035-7*) Acad Pr.

Spreading Flame: The Rise & Progress of Christianity from Its Beginnings to the Conversion of the English. F. F. Bruce. 432p. 1985. reprint ed. pap. 15.00 (*0-8028-1805-6*) Eerdmans.

Spreading Flame: The Stories of the Churches of Troy Annual Conference. Charles D. Schwartz & Ouida D. Schwartz. LC 85-70363. (Illus.). 360p. 1986. text ed. 25.00 (*0-914960-57-1*); pap. text ed. 18.00 (*0-914960-61-X*) Academy Bks.

Spreading My Wings: Wartime ATA Flying Adventures by One of Britain's Top Women Pilots. Diana B. Walker. (Illus.). 224p. 1994. 36.95 (*1-85260-473-5*, Pub. by J H Haynes & Co UK) Motorbooks Intl.

Spreading Resistance Symposium: Proceedings of a Symposium Held At the National Bureau of Standards, Gaithersburg, Md., June 13-14, 1974. Spreading Resistance Symposium Staff. Ed. by James R. Ehrstein. LC 75-600857. (Semiconductor Measurement Technology Ser., Special Technical Paper: No. 572). 293p. reprint ed. pap. 83.60 (*0-317-29813-5*, 2016595) Bks Demand.

Spreading Rhythm Round: African American Pop Music. David A. Jasen. Date not set. 35.00 (*0-02-864742-4*) Mac Lib Ref.

Spreading the American Dream: American Economic & Cultural Expansion 1890-1945. Emily Rosenberg. (American Century Ser.). 264p. 1982. pap. 11.00 (*0-8090-0146-2*) Hill & Wang.

***Spreading the Fire.** Wagner. 16.30 (*0-8307-1711-0*) Regal.

Spreading the Gospel. Bernard R. Youngman. (Background to the Bible Ser.). 102p. (J). (gr. 8-12). 7900. pap. 9.95 (*0-7175-0420-4*) Dufour.

***Spreading the Gospel of the Modern Dance: Newspaper Dance Criticism in the United States, 1850-1934.** Lynne Conner. LC 96-45868. 180p. 1997. 35.00 (*0-8229-3963-0*); pap. 17.95 (*0-8229-5617-9*) U of Pittsburgh Pr.

***Spreading the News.** unabridged ed. Lady A. Gregory. Ed. by William-Alan Landes. LC 97-17287. 55p. 1997. pap. 6.00 (*0-88734-399-6*) Players Pr.

Spreading the News: A Guide to Media Reform. Frank Allaun. 112p. 1988. 42.50 (*0-85124-488-2*, Pub. by Spokesman Bks UK); pap. 21.50 (*0-85124-498-X*, Pub. by Spokesman Bks UK) Coronet Bks.

Spreading the News: Sharing the Stories of Early Childhood Education. Margie Carter & Deb Curtis. LC 96-6995. 64p. 1996. pap. 13.95 (*1-884834-14-0*, 1327) Redleaf Pr.

Spreading the News: The American Postal System from Franklin to Morse. Richard R. John. LC 95-20067. (Illus.). 384p. (C). 1996. 49.95 (*0-674-83338-4*) HUP.

Spreading the Word. Ed. by Suzanne Lummis. 1993. 7.00 (*0-9622847-7-7*) Red Wind Bks.

Spreading the Word: Distribution Networks of Print 1550-1850. Ed. by Robin Myers & Michael Harris. 241p. 1990. lib. bdg. 28.00 (*0-906795-87-7*) Oak Knoll.

Spreading the Word: Editors on Poetry. Warren Slesinger. 112p. 1990. 24.95 (*0-930769-19-8*); pap. 14.95 (*0-930769-10-4*) Bench Pr SC.

Spreading the Word: Editors on Poetry. Ed. by Warren Slesinger. 1990. 24.95 (*0-930769-09-0*) Bench Pr SC.

Spreading the Word: Groundings in the Philosophy of Language. Simon Blackburn. (Illus.). 378p. (C). 1984. pap. 24.00 (*0-19-824651-X*) OUP.

Spreading the Word: Poetry & the Survival of Community in America. Ross Talarico. LC 94-36497. 168p. 1995. text ed. 29.95 (*0-8223-1562-9*); pap. text ed. 13.95 (*0-8223-1589-0*) Duke.

Spreading the Word: The Bible Business in Nineteenth-Century America. Peter J. Wosh. (Illus.). 288p. 1994. 35.00 (*0-8014-2928-5*) Cornell U Pr.

Spreading Your Wings: A Young Woman's Introduction to Life. Linda Bairstow. LC 87-92072. 1988. 8.95 (*0-87212-210-7*) Libra.

Spreads & Toppers. Diane Rozas. LC 96-39679. 1997. 16.00 (*0-02-861003-2*) Macmillan.

Spreads Set & Card Titles. Iain McLaren-Owens. LC 94-96298. (Astro-Cards System Ser.). 138p. 1994. pap. text ed. 15.00 (*1-885500-01-7*, AC2) Astro-Cards.

Spreadsheet Accounting for the Microcomputer. Dale H. Klooster. (BA - Accounting - First Year Ser.). 1990. pap. 17.95 (*0-538-02771-1*) S-W Pub.

Spreadsheet Accounting for the Microcomputer. Dale H. Klooster. (BA - Accounting - First Year Ser.). 1990. pap. 17.95 (*0-538-02782-7*) S-W Pub.

Spreadsheet Accounting for the Microcomputer. Dale H. Klooster. (BA - Accounting - First Year Ser.). 1992. pap. 22.95 (*0-538-61361-0*) S-W Pub.

Spreadsheet Activities in Middle School Mathematics. John C. Russell. LC 92-9414. (Illus.). 42p. (Orig.). 1992. pap. 22.50 (*0-87353-343-7*) NCTM.

Spreadsheet Activities to Reinforce Math Skills. Steffe. (DF - Computer Applications Ser.). 1997. pap. 11.95 (*0-538-71465-4*) S-W Pub.

Spreadsheet Analysis for Engineers & Scientists. Sylvan C. Bloch. LC 95-10234. 320p. 1995. text ed. 39.95 (*0-471-12683-7*, Wiley-Interscience) Wiley.

Spreadsheet Analysis with Visi-Calc & Flash-Calc. Lewis M. Elia & Comley. 1987. teacher ed. 34.95 (*0-87350-284-1*) Milady Pub.

Spreadsheet & Database Cases for Information Systems. Raymond W. Knab. LC 92-9907. (C). 1992. 21.50 (*0-201-58177-9*) Addison-Wesley.

Spreadsheet Applications: Job-Based Tasks. Joseph C. Otto. 160p. (C). 1993. pap. text ed. 13.95 (*1-56118-447-0*); pap. text ed. 13.95 (*1-56118-448-9*) Paradigm MN.

Spreadsheet Applications for Accounting. Gregory E. Anders. 1994. pap. 27.00 (*0-02-800729-8*) Glencoe.

Spreadsheet Applications in Chemistry Using Microsoft Excel. Dermot Diamond & Venita C. Hanratty. LC 96-26223. 1997. pap. text ed. 29.50 (*0-471-14087-2*, Wiley-Interscience) Wiley.

Spreadsheet Applications in Intermediate Accounting, Vol. 1. Angelo E. DiAntonio. (Illus.). 256p. (C). 1986. pap. text ed. write for info. (*0-8359-6948-7*, Reston) P-H.

Spreadsheet Applications in Practice. 2nd ed. Kenneth S. Close. LC 92-46647. 1994. pap. 27.95 (*0-538-61550-8*) S-W Pub.

Spreadsheet Applied Engineer Econ. Kahl. (West - Engineering Ser.). 1992. text ed. 35.95 (*0-534-93825-6*) PWS Pubs.

Spreadsheet Geomechanics: An Introduction. Burt Look. (Illus.). 256p. (C). 1994. pap. text ed. 28.50 (*90-5410-152-0*, Pub. by A A Balkema NE) Ashgate Pub Co.

Spreadsheet Investigations. 4th ed. Raymond A. Serway. (C). 1995. pap. text ed. 19.50 incl. disk (*0-03-018129-1*) HB Coll Pubs.

Spreadsheet Mod - Principles of Physics. Raymond A. Serway. (C). 1994. pap. text ed. 22.50 (*0-03-008444-X*) HB Coll Pubs.

Spreadsheet Modeling & Decision Analysis. 2nd ed. Ragsdale. (Miscellaneous/Catalogs Ser.). 1998. pap. 65.95 (*0-538-86756-6*) S-W Pub.

Spreadsheet Modeling for Engineers & Scientists Using 1-2-3. David Cress & James A. Murtha. 200p. text ed. write for info. (*0-13-838020-1*) P-H.

Spreadsheet Models for Investments. Richard A. Followill. LC 92-75219. 405p. (C). pap. text ed. 29.95 (*1-878975-20-X*) Blackwell Pubs.

Spreadsheet Models for Urban & Regional Analysis. Ed. by Richard E. Klosterman et al. LC 92-18834. 487p. (C). 1993. text ed. 39.95 incl. disk (*0-88285-142-X*) Ctr Urban Pol Res.

***Spreadsheet Physics.** Charles Misner. (C). 1998. pap. text ed. write for info. (*0-201-83437-5*) Addison-Wesley.

Spreadsheet Physics. Charles W. Misner. (C). 1991. pap. text ed. 24.50 (*0-201-16410-8*) Addison-Wesley.

Spreadsheet Skills. Roger Carter & Jill Gray. (Made Simple Ser.). 200p. 1993. pap. write for info. incl. disk (*0-7506-1567-2*) Buttrwrth-Heinemann.

Spreadsheet Software for Farm Business Management. Dick Landis & Edward Schmisseur. 1985. pap. text ed. 22.00 (*0-8359-6955-X*, Reston) P-H.

Spreadsheet Style Manual. David Harrison & John W. Yu. 200p. 1990. pap. 30.00 (*1-55623-267-5*) Irwin Prof Pubng.

Spreadsheet Tools for Engineers: Excel 5.0 Version. Byron S. Gottfried. (Illus.). 341p. 1996. text ed. 19.75 (*0-07-024018-3*) McGraw.

Spreadsheet Usage for Geotechnical Engineering. Wolff. (General Engineering Ser.). 1995. pap. 36.95 (*0-534-93441-2*) PWS Pubs.

Spreadsheet/Database Activities to Build Science Skills. Steffe. (DF - Computer Applications Ser.). 1997. pap. 11.95 (*0-538-66572-6*) S-W Pub.

Spreadsheeting on the TRS-80 Color Computer. Harry Anbarlian. (Personal Computing Ser.). 320p. 1983. write for info. (*0-07-001595-3*, BYTE Bks) McGraw.

Spreadsheeting on the TRS-80 Color Computer. Harry Anbarlian. (Personal Computing Ser.). 320p. 1983. text ed. write for info. (*0-07-079110-4*, BYTE Bks) McGraw.

Spreadsheets for Agriculture. David Noble & Charles Course. 259p. (Orig.). 1993. pap. text ed. 54.95 (*0-470-22067-8*) Halsted Pr.

Spreadsheets for Agriculture. Ed. by David Noble & Charles Course. LC 92-41099. (Orig.). 1993. pap. text ed. write for info. (*0-582-05389-7*) Longman.

Spreadsheets for Architects: Swiss Army Knife Software. Leonard R. Bachman & David J. Thaddeus. LC 94-23795. 1995. pap. 52.95 (*0-442-01950-5*) Van Nos Reinhold.

Spreadsheets for Business: Concepts, Examples, Applications & Cases. Norman E. Sondak. 528p. 1990. Incl. text & software (avail. on 5.25" & 3.5"). write for info. incl. disk (*0-318-67293-6*) Holden-Day.

Spreadsheets for Chemists. Gordon Filby. LC 94-30442. 1994. 60.00 (*3-527-28570-9*, VCH) Wiley.

Spreadsheets for Small Business 2-3. Conaster. 1991. pap. 24.95 (*0-13-785874-4*) P-H.

Spreadsheets Go to School: Applications for Administrators. Edward Caffarella. 1985. pap. text ed. 30.00 (*0-8359-7060-4*, Reston) P-H.

Spreadsheets in Mathematics & Science Teaching. John C. Whitmer. (Classroom Activities Ser.). (Illus.). (Orig.). (C). 1992. pap. text ed. 15.00 (*0-912047-09-7*) Sch Sci Math.

Spreadsheets in Structural Design. S. R. Davies. (C). 1992. text ed. 94.95 (*0-582-22698-8*) Longman.

Spreadsheets Skill Building Exercises & Applications. Iris Blanc & Cathy Vento. 124p. 1986. 20.00 (*0-936862-22-X*, 369); teacher ed. 10.00 (*0-936862-45-9*, SAE/TM); student ed. 20.00 incl. disk (*1-56243-056-4*, 10-TESP); trans. 250.00 (*0-936862-19-X*, 1359); trans. 250.00 (*1-56243-055-6*, S-124); disk 65.00 (*0-936862-43-2*, T-L34/LW4/EX40); disk 65.00 (*0-936862-48-3*, SS10SL) DDC Pub.

Spreadsheets Skill Building Exercises & Applications, Solutions Booklet. Cathy Vento & Iris Blanc. 80p. 1986. pap. text ed. 1.00 (*1-56243-005-X*, 369-SOL) DDC Pub.

Spreadsheets with Lotus One-Two-Three. Bruce J. McLaren. (C). 1991. text ed. 18.00 (*0-06-500530-9*) Addson-Wesley Educ.

Spreadsheets with Lotus 1-2-3: Productivity Software Guide Module. 4th ed. Charles S. Parker. 96p. (C). 1993. pap. text ed. 9.75 (*0-03-097122-5*) Dryden Pr.

Spreadsheets with Lotus 1-2-3 & Joe Spreadsheet. Charles S. Parker. 80p. (C). 1991. pap. text ed. 9.50 (*0-03-072287-X*) Dryden Pr.

Spreadsheets with Lotus 1-2-3 Release 4.0-5 Windows Productivity Software Guide. 95th ed. Edward G. Martin & Charles Kee. 128p. (C). 1995. pap. text ed. 9.75 (*0-03-010813-6*) Dryden Pr.

Spreadsheets with Quattro Pro 6.0 for Windows Productivity Software Guide. 95th ed. Edward G. Martin & Marilyn Meyer. 112p. (C). 1995. pap. text ed. 9.75 (*0-03-010814-4*) Dryden Pr.

Spreadshet WorkBook for Quantitative Chemical Analysis. Robert De Levie. 1992. pap. text ed. write for info. (*0-07-016274-3*) McGraw.

***Sprech- und Gespraechsstile.** Barbara Sandig. Ed. by Margret Selting. 480p. (GER.). (C). 1997. lib. bdg. 178.00 (*3-11-014604-5*) De Gruyter.

***Sprechakte und Sprechaktanalyse im Alten Testament: Untersuchungen im Biblischen Hebraeisch an der Nahtstelle Zwischen Handlungsebene und Grammatik.** Andreas Wagner. (Beihefte zur Zeitschrift fuer die Alttestamentliche Wissenschaft Ser.: Vol. 253). 336p. (GER.). (C). 1997. lib. bdg. 125.00 (*3-11-015549-4*) De Gruyter.

Sprechen. Vasiliauska. (College German Ser.). 1994. pap. 87.95 (*0-8384-3595-5*); wbk. ed., pap. 25.95 (*0-8384-3596-3*) Heinle & Heinle.

Sprechen Wir Daruber: German Conversation - A Functional Approach. Werner Haas & Heimy F. Taylor. LC 83-19793. 181p. 1984. Net. pap. text ed. 23.50 (*0-471-87125-7*) Wiley.

Sprechen wir Deutsch! 2nd ed. Kathryn A. Corl et al. LC 88-19105. (Illus.). 528p. (GER.). (C). 1989. teacher ed. write for info. (*0-03-014102-8*); text ed. 44.75 (*0-03-014099-4*); 23.50 (*0-03-014103-6*); audio write for info. (*0-318-64064-3*) HB Coll Pubs.

Sprechen Wir Deutsch! 3rd ed. Barbara S. Jurasek et al. 496p. (GER.). (C). 1992. teacher ed. write for info. (*0-03-076629-X*); text ed. 45.25 (*0-03-055974-X*); write for info. (*0-318-69160-4*); IBM. disk 17.50 (*0-03-055954-5*); Mac. disk 17.50 (*0-03-055958-8*) HB Coll Pubs.

Sprechen Wir Deutsch! 3rd ed. Barbara S. Jurasek et al. 496p. (GER.). (C). 1992. pap. text ed. 27.75 (*0-03-055963-4*); 6.00 (*0-03-055953-7*) HB Coll Pubs.

***Sprecherausschusse fur Leitende Angestellte im Rahmen der Unternehmungsverfassung: Ergebnisse einer Empirischen Untersuchung aus Organisatorischer Sicht.** Stefan Luczak. (Europaische Hochschulschriften: Reihe 5: Bd. 2008). (Illus.). 261p. (GER.). 1996. pap. 51.95 (*3-631-30669-5*) P Lang Pubng.

Spree Killers. Art Crockett. 1991. mass mkt. 4.95 (*1-55817-461-3*, Pinncle Kensgtn) Kensgtn Pub Corp.

Sprich Deutsch! 3rd ed. Philip Grundlehner & Steven De Hart. LC 88-19102. (Illus.). 208p. (GER.). (C). 1989. pap. text ed. 24.00 (*0-03-008039-8*) HB Coll Pubs.

Sprichwoerter und Zitate. Franz Eppert. 80p. (GER.). (C). 1990. pap. text ed. 15.25 (*3-12-675338-8*, Pub. by Klett Edition GW) Intl Bk Import.

Sprichwoertersammlungen, 2 vols. Johannes Agricola. Ed. by Sander L. Gilman. (Ausgaben Deutscher Literatur des XV bis XVIII Jahrhunderts Ser.). 989p. (C). 1971. 707.70 (*3-11-003710-6*) De Gruyter.

Sprichwoertlich. Hans Hunfeld. 160p. (GER.). (C). 1989. pap. text ed. 19.00 (*3-12-675339-6*, Pub. by Klett Edition GW) Intl Bk Import.

Sprichwort und Sprache: Am Beispiel des Sprichworts im Schweizerdeutschen. Hans Ruef. (Studia Linguistica Germanica: No. 36). x, 303p. (GER.). (C). 1995. lib. bdg. 124.60 (*3-11-014494-8*) De Gruyter.

Sprichworter der Germanischen und Romanischen Sprachen, 2 vo.s., Set. Ida Von Duringsfeld & Otto Von Reinsberg-Duringsfeld. (Volkskundliche Quellen Ser.: Vol. VII). xxii, 1160p. 1973. reprint ed. write for info. (*3-487-04764-0*) G Olms Pubs.

***Sprichworter und Handeln: Eine Psychologische Untersuchung.** Frank Detje. (GER.). 1996. 40.95 (*3-906756-35-1*) P Lang Pubng.

Sprichworter und Sprichwortlichen Redensarten der Romer. August Otto. xlv, 436p. 1988. reprint ed. write for info. (*3-487-00240-X*) G Olms Pubs.

Sprig Muslin. Georgette Heyer. 1976. 23.95 (*0-8488-0815-0*) Amereon Ltd.

Sprig Muslin. Georgette Heyer. 340p. 1983. reprint ed. lib. bdg. 16.95 (*0-89966-128-9*) Buccaneer Bks.

Sprig of Sea Lavender. large type ed. J. R. Anderson. 324p. 1979. 25.99 (*0-7089-0364-9*) Ulverscroft.

***Sprigs of Lilacs.** 1997. write for info. (*0-614-30150-5*) Wind-Blown.

***Sprigs of Lilacs.** Muriel Kaltman. Incl. Constant Interest. 50p. 1997. pap. Not sold separately (*0-9657573-1-5*); Scenes in Memory. 50p. Date not set. pap. Not sold separately (*0-9657573-2-3*); In Reflection. 50p. Date not set. pap. Not sold separately (*0-9657573-3-1*); And the Stone Was Turned. Date not set. pap. Not sold separately (*0-9657573-4-X*); write for info. (*0-9657573-0-7*) Wind-Blown.

Spring. 1995. 3.98 (*0-7858-0297-5*) Bk Sales Inc.

Spring. Richard L. Allington & Kathleen Krull. LC 80-25093. (Beginning to Learn about Ser.). (Illus.). 32p. (J). (gr. k-3). 1985. pap. 3.95 (*0-8114-8244-8*) Raintree Steck-V.

Spring. Nicola Baxter. LC 95-50046. (Toppers Ser.). 24p. (J). 1996. lib. bdg. 15.00 (*0-516-09274-X*) Childrens.

***Spring.** Nicola Baxter. (Toppers Ser.). 24p. (J). 1997. pap. 4.95 (*0-516-26086-3*) Childrens.

***Spring.** Karen Bryant-Mole. (Picture This! Ser.). (J). 1997. lib. bdg. write for info. (*1-57572-055-8*) Rigby Interact Libr.

***Spring.** Gillian Chapman. LC 97-17159. (Seasonal Crafts Ser.). (J). 1998. write for info. (*0-8172-4872-2*) Raintree Steck-V.

Spring. Chris L. Demarest. 1997. pap. 4.95 (*0-15-201390-3*) HarBrace.

Spring. Mark Dunster. 10p. (Orig.). 1993. pap. 4.00 (*0-89642-225-9*) Linden Pubs.

Spring. Ron Hirschi. LC 89-49039. (Illus.). (J). (ps-3). 1990. pap. 14.99 (*0-525-65037-7*, Cobblehill Bks) Dutton Child Bks.

Spring. Ron Hirschi. (Illus.). 32p. (J). (ps-3). 1996. pap. 4.99 (*0-14-055786-5*) Puffin Bks.

Spring. Clifford Irving. 288p. 1996. 23.00 (*0-684-81076-X*, S&S) S&S Trade.

***Spring.** Judy Nayer. Ed. by Jennifer Mooney. (Newbridge Links Ser.). 8p. (J). (gr. k up). 1997. pap. 2.75 (*1-56784-909-1*) Newbridge Comms.

Spring. Louis Santrey. LC 82-19381. (Discovering the Seasons Ser.). (Illus.). 32p. (J). (gr. 4-7). 1983. lib. bdg. 11.50 (*0-89375-909-0*) Troll Communs.

Spring. Lynne M. Stone. LC 93-41104. (As the World Turns Ser.). (J). 1994. write for info. (*1-55916-018-7*) Rourke Bk Co.

Spring. Ruth Thomson. LC 94-16916. (Get Set...Go! Ser.). (Illus.). 24p. (J). (ps-3). 1994. pap. 4.95 (*0-516-47994-6*); lib. bdg. 15.40 (*0-516-07994-8*) Childrens.

Spring. David Webster. (Exploring Nature Around the Year Ser.). (Illus.). 48p. (J). (gr. 2-4). 1990. pap. 4.95 (*0-671-65983-9*, Julian Messner) Silver Burdett Pr.

***Spring.** Joanne Weir. (Williams-Sonoma Celebration Ser.). 1997. 21.95 (*0-614-27961-5*) Time-Life.

Spring. Alana Willoughby. Ed. by Alton Jordan. (I Can Eat an Elephant Ser.). (Illus.). (J). (gr. k-3). 1984. 7.95 (*0-89868-019-0*, Read Res); pap. 3.95 (*0-89868-052-2*, Read Res) ARO Pub.

Spring. rev. ed. Marlene J. McCracken & Robert A. McCracken. (Themes Ser.). (Illus.). 92p. (J). (gr. k-4). 1987. pap. 12.00 (*0-920541-14-3*) Peguis Pubs Ltd.

Spring. Don Coyhis. LC 95-79096. (Meditations with Native American Elders Ser.). 112p. 1995. reprint ed. pap. 9.95 (*1-887874-00-3*) Moh-He-Con-Nuck.

Spring: A Haiku Story. George Shannon. LC 95-2265. (Illus.). 32p. (J). Date not set. lib. bdg. 15.93 (*0-688-13889-6*) Greenwillow.

Spring: A Haiku Story. George Shannon. LC 95-2265. (Illus.). 32p. (J). (gr. k up). 1996. 16.00 (*0-688-13888-8*) Greenwillow.

Spring: New Life Everywhere. Janet McDonnell. LC 93-10309. (Four Seasons Ser.). (Illus.). 32p. (J). (ps-2). 1993. lib. bdg. 17.40 (*0-516-00677-0*) Childrens.

***Spring: Recipes Inspired by Nature's Bounty.** Joanne Weir. LC 96-33476. (Williams-Sonoma Seasonal Celebration Ser.). (Illus.). 1997. write for info. (*0-7835-4606-8*) Time-Life.

Spring see Growing Strong in the Seasons of Life: A Season of Reverance

***Spring a Buzz'n.** Peggy Laurie. (Illus.). 52p. 1997. pap. text ed. write for info. (*1-57377-010-8*) Easl Pubns.

Spring Across America. Seymour Simon. LC 95-8184. (Illus.). 32p. (J). (gr. k-5). 1996. lib. bdg. 15.89 (*0-7868-2056-X*) Hyprn Child.

Spring Across America. Seymour Simon. LC 95-8184. (Illus.). 32p. (J). (gr. k-5). 1996. 15.95 (*0-7868-0069-0*) Hyprn Child.

Spring & May. Nancy M. Davis et al. (Davis Teaching Units Ser.: Vol. 1, No. 9). (Illus.). 46p. (Orig.). (J). (ps-4). 1986. pap. 5.95 (*0-937103-11-X*) DaNa Pubns.

Spring & Summer in N.C. Forests. Rosa K. Mullet. 238p. 1982. pap. 6.45 (*0-686-35755-8*) Rod & Staff.

***Spring & Summer Sonatas.** Ramon Del Valle-Inclan. Tr. by Margaret J. Costa from SPA. (Empire of the Senses Ser.). 176p. (Orig.). 1997. pap. 11.99 (*1-873982-03-8*, Pub. by Dedalus UK) Subterranean Co.

Spring & the Spectacle. Margaret Chatterjee. 4.80 (*0-89253-555-5*); text ed. 4.00 (*0-89253-556-3*) Ind-US Inc.

Spring at the Villa. large type ed. Rosalind Brett. 1991. 25.99 (*0-7089-2404-2*) Ulverscroft.

Spring Awakening. Ted Hughes & Frank Wedekind. 96p. 1996. pap. text ed. 10.95 (*0-571-17791-3*) Faber & Faber.

Spring Awakening. Frank Wedekind. Tr. & Adapted by Edward Bond. 1979. 5.95 (*0-87129-425-7*, S61) Dramatic Pub.

Spring Awakening. Frank Wedekind. Tr. by Edward Bond. 96p. (C). 1988. pap. 8.95 (*0-413-47620-0*, A0270, Pub. by Methuen UK) Heinemann.

Spring Awakening. Frank Wedekind. Tr. by Tom Osborn from GER. 1979. pap. 10.95 (*0-7145-0634-6*) Riverrun NY.

Spring Awakening: An Account of the 1990 Revolution in Nepal. Kceper Willia & Martin Hoftun. (C). 1990. 47.00 (*0-7855-0213-0*, Pub. by Ratna Pustak Bhandar) St Mut.

Spring Bamboo. Ed. by Jeanne Tai. 1989. write for info. (*0-318-64949-7*) Random.

Spring Blossom. Jill Metcalf. (Homespun Ser.). 336p. (Orig.). 1992. mass mkt. 4.99 (*1-55773-751-7*) Diamond.

Spring Bouquet. Janet Dailey et al. 1996. pap. text ed. 6.99 (*0-8217-5309-6*, Zebra Kensgtn) Kensgtn Pub Corp.

Spring Bouquet. large type ed. Janet Dailey. LC 96-24246. 1996. 25.95 (*0-7862-0799-X*, Thorndike Lrg Prnt) Thorndike Pr.

Spring Break. Johanna Hurwitz. LC 96-20032. (J). 1997. 15.00 (*0-688-14937-5*, Morrow Junior) Morrow.

***Spring Break.** Peter Lerangis. (J). 1997. mass mkt. 3.99 (*0-590-69771-4*) Scholastic Inc.

Spring Break. Melissa Lowell. (Silver Blades Ser.: No. 9). 144p. (J). (gr. 4-7). 1995. pap. 3.50 (*0-553-48309-9*) Bantam.

Spring Break. Bernie Sheahan. LC 96-43528. (Palisades University Ser.: No. 3). 208p. (YA). (gr. 7-11). 1996. pap. 5.99 (*0-88070-950-2*, Palisades OR) Multnomah Pubs.

Spring Break. Barbara Steiner. (J). 1996. mass mkt. 3.99 (*0-590-54419-5*) Scholastic Inc.

Spring Break at Pokeweed Public School. John Bianchi. (Illus.). 24p. (J). (gr. 1-4). 1994. pap. 4.95 (*0-921285-32-9*, Pub. by Bungalo Bks CN); lib. bdg. 14.95 (*0-921285-33-7*, Pub. by Bungalo Bks CN) Firefly Bks Ltd.

Spring Break Missionaries: Growing up in Christian America, 1976-1983. Dwayne Walker. 160p. 1994. pap. text ed. 15.00 (*0-9641893-0-5*) Corinthian Prods.

Spring Break Nineteen Eighty-Six. Starlog Editors. 1986. pap. 3.95 (*0-317-40172-6*, Sig) NAL-Dutton.

Spring Bride. Sandra Marton. (Harlequin Presents Ser.: No. 1825). 1996. mass mkt. 3.50 (*0-373-11825-2*, 1-11825-6) Harlequin Bks.

Spring Bride. large type ed. Sandra Marton. (Harlequin Romance Ser.). 1996. 19.95 (*0-263-14668-5*) Thorndike Pr.

Spring Bulletin Boards. Imogene Forte. (Easy-To-Make-&-Use Ser.). 64p. (J). (gr. k-6). 1987. pap. text ed. 7.95 (*0-86530-169-7*, IP-113-0) Incentive Pubns.

Spring Came on Forever. large type ed. Bess S. Aldrich. LC 92-41150. 418p. 1993. reprint ed. lib. bdg. 20.95 (*1-56054-503-8*) Thorndike Pr.

Spring Came on Forever. Bess S. Aldrich. LC 84-19671. vii, 333p. 1985. reprint ed. pap. 13.95 (*0-8032-5907-7*, Bison Books) U of Nebr Pr.

Spring Canyon. 2nd ed. Jennie Tennant. Ed. by Roberta Debono. 252p. (Orig.). 1991. pap. 9.95 (*0-9613901-2-3*) Ankh Pr CA.

Spring Cleaning. Clean Team Staff & Jeff Campbell. 200p. (Orig.). (YA). (gr. 7 up). 1997. pap. 7.99 (*0-440-50162-8*, Dell Trade Pbks) Dell.

Spring Cleaning: Household Poisons. Jacquie Milligan. (Child Safety Ser.). (Illus.). 48p. 1986. 4.95 (*0-513-01829-8*) Denison.

***Spring Cleaning for Your Soul: Stories That Polish the Spirit.** 125p. (Orig.). 1997. pap. 10.95 (*0-9657864-4-7*) Abbodanza.

Spring Clip Art a la Carte. Compiled & Concept by Imogene Forte. (Illus.). 80p. (Orig.). 1990. pap. text ed. 8.95 (*0-86530-202-2*, IP 191-5) Incentive Pubns.

***Spring Collection.** Judith Krantz. 416p. 1997. mass mkt. 7.50 (*0-553-56136-7*) Bantam.

Spring Collection. Judith Krantz. 352p. 1996. 24.00 (*0-517-59334-3*, Crown) Crown Pub Group.

Spring Collection. large type ed. Judith Krantz. LC 95-50063. 1996. pap. 24.00 (*0-679-75880-1*) Random.

Spring Collection: A Novel. large type ed. Judith Krantz. 768p. 1996. pap. 24.00 (*0-7838-1680-4*, GK Hall) Thorndike Pr.

Spring Comes Again to Arnet. Patrick W. Gray. Ed. by John M. Gogol & Robert A. Davies. (Poetry Chapbook Ser.). (Illus.). 38p. (Orig.). 1987. pap. 10.00 (*0-932191-08-8*) Mr Cogito Pr.

Spring Comes to Chicago: Poems. Campbell McGrath. 96p. (Orig.). 1996. pap. 12.95 (*0-88001-484-9*) Ecco Pr.

Spring Conference Paper Summaries Book, 1993. (Illus.). 156p. 1992. pap. 31.00 (*0-931403-13-8*, 1337) Am Soc Nondestructive.

Spring Creek. Nick Lyons. LC 92-13026. (Illus.). 176p. 1995. pap. 11.00 (*0-87113-612-0*, Atlntc Mnthly) Grove-Atltic.

Spring Design Manual. 2nd ed. 421p. 1995. 95.00 (*1-56091-680-X*, AE-21) Soc Auto Engineers.

Spring Designer's Handbook. Carlson. (Mechanical Engineering Ser.: Vol. 1). 368p. 1978. 145.00 (*0-8247-6623-7*) Dekker.

***Spring Dreams.** Lydia Browne. (Homespun Ser.). 320p. 1997. mass mkt. 5.99 (*0-515-12068-5*) Jove Pubns.

Spring Enchantment. Christina Cordaire. 1996. mass mkt. 5.99 (*0-515-11876-1*) Jove Pubns.

Spring Evenings, Summer Afternoons: A Little Collection of Warm-Weather Recipes. Barbara Scott-Goodman & Mary Goodbody. LC 93-8850. (Illus.). 72p. 1994. 9.95 (*0-8118-0487-9*) Chronicle Bks.

Spring Fancy. LaVryle Spencer. 1995. pap. 17.95 (*0-7871-0553-8*, Dove Bks) Dove Audio.

Spring Fancy. LaVyrle Spencer. 256p. (Orig.). 1989. pap. text ed. 6.99 (*0-515-10122-2*) Jove Pubns.

Spring Fancy '94. Dixie Browning. 1994. mass mkt. 4.99 (*0-373-48266-3*, 5-48266-6) Silhouette.

Spring Fever. Peter Lerangis. (J). 1996. pap. text ed. 2.99 (*0-590-25471-5*) Scholastic Inc.

***Spring Fever.** Mary Mackie. 192p. 1996. 22.00 (*0-7278-5156-X*) Severn Hse.

Spring Fever. Tom Smario. 64p. (Orig.). 1985. pap. 6.00 (*0-940584-09-3*) Gull Bks.

Spring Fever. P. G. Wodehouse. 18.95 (*0-8488-0681-6*) Amereon Ltd.

***Spring Fever.** large type ed. Mary Mackie. (Ulverscroft Large Print Ser.). 288p. 1997. 27.50 (*0-7089-3778-0*) Ulverscroft.

Spring Fever: Spring Super Edition, No. 2. Francine Pascal. (Sweet Valley High Ser.). 240p. (Orig.). (YA). (gr. 7-12). 1987. 4.50 (*0-553-26420-6*) Bantam.

Spring Fevers. Martin Pyx. 1992. mass mkt. 5.95 (*1-56201-027-1*, 124) Blue Moon Bks.

Spring Fifty-Three - Pagans, Christians, Jews: A Journal of Archetype & Culture. Ed. by James Hillman & Charles Boer. 176p. 1992. pap. 17.50 (*1-882670-00-0*) Spring Jrnl.

Spring Fires Love. Cynthia C. Richardson. 1980. pap. 1.50 (*0-373-58055-X*) Harlequin Bks.

Spring Flora of Wisconsin. 4th ed. Norman C. Fassett. LC 74-27307. (Illus.). 430p. 1976. 18.50 (*0-299-06750-5*); pap. 9.95 (*0-299-06754-8*) U of Wis Pr.

Spring Flowers. 2nd ed. Mabel J. Cuthbert & Susan Verhoek. (Pictured Key Nature Ser.). 256p. (C). 1982. spiral bd. write for info. (*0-697-04782-2*) Wm C Brown Pubs.

Spring Flowers Own & The Manifestations of the Voyage. Etel Adnan. (Illus.). 101p. (Orig.). 1990. pap. 12.00 (*0-942996-14-3*) Post Apollo Pr.

Spring Forest. Geoffrey Lehmann. 192p. (Orig.). 1994. pap. 10.95 (*0-571-17246-6*) Faber & Faber.

Spring Garden: New & Selected Poems. Fred Chappell. LC 95-22425. (C). 1995. pap. 14.95 (*0-8071-1949-0*); text ed. 24.95 (*0-8071-1948-2*) La State U Pr.

Spring Geese & Other Poems. Denise Low. Ed. by Joseph T. Collins. (Illus.). 84p. 1984. pap. 4.00 (*0-89338-024-5*) U KS Nat Hist Mus.

Spring Gobbler Fever: Your Complete Guide to Spring Turkey Hunting. Michael Hanback. LC 95-82122. (Illus.). 256p. 1996. pap. 15.95 (*0-87341-423-3*, SGF) Krause Pubns.

Spring Has Returned & I Am Renewed. Gabrielle David. (Illus.). 48p. 1996. pap. 12.95 (*1-889033-01-4*, 01-951996) Chimeara Communs.

Spring Hat. Gill. (J). 1998. pap. 4.95 (*0-671-88245-7*, Atheneum Bks Young) S&S Childrens.

Spring Hat. Madelaine Gill. LC 91-30556. (Illus.). 40p. (J). (ps-1). 1993. pap. 13.00 (*0-671-75666-4*, S&S Bks Young Read) S&S Childrens.

Spring Hill Plantation. Jane Gandy. 60p. pap. 5.00 (*1-878096-09-5*) Best E TX Pubs.

Spring Hill Resprung. Boolarong Publications Staff. 64p. (C). 1990. 44.00 (*0-908175-13-2*, Pub. by Boolarong Pubns AT) St Mut.

***Spring I Would Like to Save.** Mongbie Ngo. 120p. Date not set. pap. text ed. 8.00 (*1-888065-13-3*) New Wrld Poetry.

Spring Idea Book: A Creative Idea Book for the Elementary Teacher, Ps-6. Karen Sevaly & Margaret Bolz. (Illus.). 112p. (Orig.). 1990. pap. text ed. 9.95 (*0-943263-16-6*, TF-1603) Teachers Friend Pubns.

***Spring in Henry Street.** Eva Bourke. 1996. 18.95 (*1-873790-91-0*) Dufour.

***Spring in Henry Street.** Eva Bourke. 88p. 9700. pap. 11.95 (*1-873790-90-2*) Dufour.

Spring in the Enchanted Forest. (Enchanted Forest Ser.). (Illus.). (J). (ps-1). 1985. 2.98 (*0-517-46980-4*) Random Hse Value.

Spring in the Wood. Janet Fitzgerald. (Science Through the Seasons Ser.). (Illus.). 32p. (J). (gr. 1-3). 1991. 15.95 (*0-237-60218-0*, Pub. by Evans Bros Ltd UK) Trafalgar.

Spring in Washington. Louis J. Halle. LC 87-46315. (Illus.). 248p. 1988. reprint ed. 18.95 (*0-8018-3688-3*) Johns Hopkins.

Spring in Winter: The Nineteen Eighty-Nine Revolutions. Ed. by Gwyn Prins. 160p. 1991. 29.95 (*0-685-38699-6*, Pub. by Manchester Univ Pr UK); text ed. 19.95 (*0-7190-3445-0*, Pub. by Manchester Univ Pr UK) St Martin.

Spring into Love. large type ed. Margaret A. Carr. (Linford Romance Library). 1991. pap. 15.99 (*0-7089-7054-0*) Ulverscroft.

Spring into Math & Science. (J). (gr. k-1). 1987. 16.95 (*1-881431-16-9*, 1103) AIMS Educ Fnd.

Spring into Winter. Margot G. Massey. (Orig.). 1994. pap. 12.95 (*0-925917-01-X*) Wyman Hse Pubns.

Spring Is a New Beginning. Joan W. Anglund. LC 63-7892. (Illus.). 32p. (J). (ps up). 1963. 8.95 (*0-15-278161-7*, HB Juv Bks) HarBrace.

Spring Is Here. Taro Gomi. 40p. (J). (ps-3). 1995. pap. 4.95 (*0-8118-1022-4*) Chronicle Bks.

Spring Jaunts: Some Walks, Excursions, & Personal Explorations of City, Country, & Seashore. Anthony Bailey. LC 86-80347. 256p. 1986. 16.95 (*0-374-26799-5*) FS&G.

***Spring Lake, NJ.** P. Colrick. (Images of America Ser.). 1997. pap. 16.99 (*0-7524-0583-7*, Arcdia) Chalford.

Spring Like Any Other: A Novel. Takashi Tsujii. Tr. by Beth Cary from JPN. 272p. 1992. 19.95 (*4-7700-1550-X*) Kodansha.

Spring Manufacturing Handbook. Harold Carlson. LC 82-12750. (Mechanical Engineering Ser.: No. 15). (Illus.). 384p. reprint ed. pap. 109.50 (*0-7837-0939-0*, 2041244) Bks Demand.

Spring Meeting, Boston, 1987: Proceedings. Industrial Relations Research Association. 1987. 5.00 (*0-913447-35-8*) Indus Relations Res.

Spring Meeting, 1982, Milwaukee: Proceedings. 1982. 5.00 (*0-913447-20-X*) Indus Relations Res.

Spring Meeting, 1983, Honolulu: Proceedings. 1983. 5.00 (*0-913447-23-4*) Indus Relations Res.

Spring Meeting, 1984, Cleveland: Proceedings. 1984. 5.00 (*0-913447-27-7*) Indus Relations Res.

Spring Meeting, 1985, Detroit: Proceedings. Industrial Relations Research Association Staff. 1985. 5.00 (*0-913447-29-3*) Indus Relations Res.

Spring Meeting, 1986,. Atlanta, GA: Proceedings. 1986. 5.00 (*0-913447-32-3*) Indus Relations Res.

Spring Meeting, 1988, Cincinnati: Proceedings. 1988. 5.00 (*0-913447-40-4*) Indus Relations Res.

Spring Meeting, 1989, Anaheim, CA: Proceedings. 1989. 5.00 (*0-913447-43-9*) Indus Relations Res.

Spring Meeting, 1990, Buffalo, NY: Proceedings. 1990. 5.00 (*0-913447-46-3*) Indus Relations Res.
Spring Meeting, 1991, Chicago, IL: Proceedings. 1991. 5.00 (*0-913447-50-1*) Indus Relations Res.
Spring Meeting, 1992, Denver CO: Proceedings. 1992. 5.00 (*0-913447-52-8*) Indus Relations Res.
Spring Meeting, 1994, Philadelphia: Proceedings. 1994. 5.00 (*0-913447-58-7*) Indus Relations Res.
Spring Meeting, 1995, Washington D.C. Proceedings. 1995. 5.00 (*0-614-06238-1*) Indus Relations Res.
Spring Moon. Bette Bao Lord. 1982. mass mkt. 4.95 (*0-380-59923-6*) Avon.
Spring Moon. Bette Bao Lord. 592p. 1990. mass mkt. 5.99 (*0-06-100105-8*, Harp PBks) HarpC.
Spring of Chinese North American Literature: Collected Writings of Sui Sin Far. Sui Sin Far. Ed. by Amy Ling & Annette White-Parks. LC 94-14202. (Asian American Experience Ser.). 296p. 1995. 15.95 (*0-252-06419-4*) U of Ill Pr.
Spring of Chinese North American Literature: Collected Writings of Sui Sin Far. Sui Sin Far. Ed. by Amy Ling & Annette White-Parks. LC 94-14202. (Asian American Experience Ser.). 312p. 1995. text ed. 39.95 (*0-252-02133-9*) U of Ill Pr.
Spring of Contemplation: A Retreat at the Abbey of Gethsemani. Thomas Merton. 1992. 22.00 (*0-374-12893-6*) FS&G.
Spring of Criticism. Cecil Cragg. (C). 1989. 60.00 (*0-86303-481-0*, Pub. by Merlin Bks UK) St Mut.
***Spring of My Life.** Sam Hamill. LC 97-7530. 1997. pap. 14.00 (*1-57062-144-6*) Shambhala Pubns.
Spring of Nations: Churches in the Rebirth of Central & Eastern Europe. J. Martin Bailey. (Orig.). 1991. pap. 10.95 (*0-377-00224-0*) Friendship Pr.
Spring of Prosperity. 2nd rev. ed. Torkom Saraydarian. LC 80-67685. 1995. pap. 8.95 (*0-911794-12-3*) Aqua Educ.
Spring of Second Comings. James I. McGovern. LC 92-91048. 152p. (Orig.). 1994. pap. 9.00 (*1-56002-226-4*, Univ Edtns) Aegina Pr.
Spring of Springs. Michael J. Rosen & Thomas Wharton. LC 96-23865. 1999. write for info. (*0-15-201532-9*) HarBrace.
Spring of the Ram. Dorothy Dunnett. 1992. reprint ed. lib. bdg. 33.95 (*0-89966-964-6*) Buccaneer Bks.
Spring of the Tiger. Victoria Holt. 384p. 1985. mass mkt. 5.99 (*0-449-20845-1*, Crest) Fawcett.
***Spring of '68.** Chris Cawood. Ed. by Gaynell Seale. 240p. (Orig.). 1998. pap. 9.95 (*0-9642231-7-1*) Magnolia Hill.
***Spring Offensive 1918.** Gerald Gliddon. (VCs of the First World War Ser.). (Illus.). 224p. 1997. 31.95 (*0-7509-1107-7*, Pub. by Sutton Pubng UK) Bks Intl VA.
Spring on the Farm. Julie Fitzgerald. (Science Through the Seasons Ser.). (Illus.). 32p. (J). (gr. 1-3). 1991. 15.95 (*0-237-60220-2*, Pub. by Evans Bros Ltd UK) Trafalgar.
Spring Pick-a-Project. Linda Milliken. (Illus.). 52p. 1989. student ed., pap. 5.95 (*1-56472-038-1*) Edupress.
Spring Planting. Rita Kohn. LC 94-38377. (Woodland Adventures Ser.). (Illus.). 32p. (J). (ps-2). 1995. lib. bdg. 19.30 (*0-516-05203-9*) Childrens.
Spring Planting. Rita Kohn. (Woodland Adventures Ser.). (Illus.). 32p. (J). (ps-2). 1995. pap. 4.95 (*0-516-45203-7*) Childrens.
Spring Pools. Robert Frost. (Illus.). 64p. 1983. boxed 295.00 (*0-317-31386-X*) Lime Rock Pr.
Spring Prairie. E. Robert Bayley, Jr. LC 90-55259. 214p. (Orig.). 1991. pap. 8.00 (*1-56002-068-7*) Aegina Pr.
Spring Programming: An Introduction to Distributed Objects. Tony Hillman. (C). 1996. pap. text ed. 28.50 (*0-13-461930-7*) P-H.
Spring Rabbit. Joyce Dunbar. (Illus.). (J). (ps-3). 1994. 13.00 (*0-688-13191-3*) Lothrop.
Spring Rain. Susan Weldon. 352p. (Orig.). 1996. mass mkt. 5.50 (*0-380-78068-2*) Avon.
Spring Rainbow. large type ed. Leila Mackinlay. 384p. 1987. 25.99 (*0-7089-1702-X*) Ulverscroft.
Spring Science Projects. John Williams. LC 96-17530. (Seasonal Science Projects Ser.). (J). 1996. pap. 5.95 (*0-382-39708-8*, Julian Messner); lib. bdg. 11.95 (*0-382-39707-X*, Julian Messner) Silver Burdett Pr.
Spring Shade: Poems 1931-1970. Robert Fitzgerald. LC 74-145931. 1971. 6.50 (*0-8112-0280-1*); pap. 2.75 (*0-8112-0052-3*, NDP311) New Directions.
Spring Silkworms & Other Stories. 2nd ed. Mao Dun. 1980. 9.95 (*0-8351-0615-2*) China Bks.
Spring Silkworms & Other Stories. 2nd ed. Dun Mao Tun. Tr. by Sidney Shapiro from CHI. 240p. (C). 1979. 9.95 (*0-917056-90-6*, Pub. by Foreign Lang Pr CH) Cheng & Tsui.
Spring Silkworms & Other Stories. Yen-Ping Shen, pseud. Tr. by Sidney Shapiro. LC 75-36238. reprint ed. 39.50 (*0-404-14486-1*) AMS Pr.
Spring Sketches. Harriet L. Smith et al. (Humor Ser.). (Illus.). 50p. (Orig.). 1973. pap. 5.00 (*0-913626-01-5*) S S S Pub Co.
Spring Snow. Yukio Mishima. LC 89-40565. (Vintage International Ser.). 400p. 1990. pap. 13.00 (*0-679-72241-6*, Vin) Random.
Spring Snow: The Seasons of New England from The Old Farmer's Alamanac. Castle Freeman, Jr. LC 95-17170. (Illus.). 167p. 1995. 21.95 (*0-395-73098-8*) HM.
Spring Snowman. Jill Barnes & Fusako Ishinabe. Ed. by Caroline Rubin. Tr. by Japan Foreign Rights Centre Staff from JPN. LC 90-37748. (Dragonfly Tales Ser.). (Illus.). 32p. (J). (gr. k-3). 1990. lib. bdg. 14.60 (*0-944483-83-6*) Garrett Ed Corp.
***Spring Song & Other Stories.** Joyce Cary. 285p. 1970. 19.95 (*0-8369-3448-2*) Ayer.
Spring Sowing. Liam O'Flaherty. LC 72-10748. (Short Story Index Reprint Ser.). 1977. reprint ed. 21.95 (*0-8369-4221-3*) Ayer.
Spring Sparkers: To Perk up Primary Programs. Imogene Forte. Ed. by Jan Keeling. (Illus.). 80p. (Orig.). 1993. teacher ed. 8.95 (*0-86530-246-4*) Incentive Pubns.
Spring Sprouts. Judy Delton. (Pee Wee Scouts Ser.: No. 9). 80p. (Orig.). (J). (gr. k-6). 1989. mass mkt. 3.99 (*0-440-40160-7*, YB BDD) BDD Bks Young Read.
Spring Story. David Updike. (Illus.). 40p. (J). (gr. 2 up). 1989. lib. bdg. 15.95 (*0-945912-06-4*) Pippin Pr.
Spring Surprise. Kenneth E. Sibley. (Illus.). 19p. (Orig.). (YA). (gr. 7 up). 1989. pap. 6.95 (*0-9619934-1-3*) K E Sibley.
Spring Surprises, Set. Toni Bauman & June Zinkgraf. 240p. (J). (gr. k-6). 1979. 13.99 (*0-916456-54-4*, GA109) Good Apple.
***Spring Tender.** Catherine M. Feldman. 660p. (Orig.). 1998. mass mkt. 10.99 (*1-889501-19-0*, SV 501-19-0, Appaloosa) Sovereign.
Spring Thaw. S. L. Stebel. 252p. 1989. 17.95 (*0-8027-1068-9*) Walker & Co.
Spring Thing: The 52nd Street Project Plays. Ed. by Willie Reale. 1995. spiral bd. 15.00 (*0-8222-1445-8*) Dramatists Play.
Spring Thunder: Awaken the Hibernating Power of Your Life. Hua-Ching Ni. LC 95-49229. 176p. (Orig.). 1996. pap. 14.95 (*0-937064-77-7*) SevenStar Comm.
Spring Tide. Pia Tafdrup. Tr. by Anne Born from DAN. LC 89-82068. 96p. 9000. pap. 16.95 (*0-948259-55-8*, Pub. by Forest Bks UK) Dufour.
Spring Tides. Jacques Poulin. Tr. by Sheila Fischman from FRE. 166p. (Orig.). 1986. reprint ed. pap. 9.95 (*0-88784-149-X*, Pub. by Hse of Anansi Pr CN) Genl Dist Srvs.
***Spring Tides: Memories of Alaskan Towboats.** Edward C. Larson. LC 96-94798. (Illus.). 130p. (Orig.). 1996. pap. 13.95 (*0-9654376-0-4*) E Larson.
***Spring to Stardom, Vol. 5.** Linda J. Singleton. (Cheer Squad Ser.). 1997. pap. 3.99 (*0-380-78509-9*) Avon.
Spring Torrents. Ivan S. Turgenev. (Classics Ser.). 240p. 1980. pap. 9.95 (*0-14-044369-X*, Penguin Classics) Viking Penguin.
Spring Training. Mark Freeman. (Rookies Ser.: No. 3). 144p. (J). (gr. 4 up). 1989. mass mkt. 4.99 (*0-345-35904-6*) Ballantine.
Spring Training. William K. Zinsser. (Spectator Ser.). 1990. pap. 9.95 (*0-685-46180-7*) P-H.
Spring Turkey Hunting: The Serious Hunter's Guide. John M. McDaniel. LC 85-27723. (Illus.). 224p. 1986. 21.95 (*0-8117-1688-0*) Stackpole.
Spring Wild Flowers of West Virginia. Earl L. Core. LC 81-50933. 104p. 1981. 7.50 (*0-937058-02-5*) West Va U Pr.
Spring Wildflowers. Randy Olson. (Field Guide Ser.). (Illus.). 156p. 1993. pap. 9.95 (*1-55109-050-3*, Pub. by Nimbus Publishing Ltd CN) Chelsea Green Pub.
Spring Wildflowers of the San Francisco Bay Region. Helen K. Sharsmith. (California Natural History Guides Ser.: No. 11). (Illus.). 1965. pap. 10.95 (*0-520-01168-6*) U CA Pr.
Spring Will Come. Sherry Deborde. 384p. 1987. mass mkt. 3.95 (*0-373-97046-3*) Harlequin Bks.
***Spring Will Follow.** large type ed. Dee Wyatt. (Linford Romance Large Print Ser.). 224p. 1997. pap. 16.99 (*0-7089-5087-6*, Linford) Ulverscroft.
Spring Wind of the Silent Administrator. Myrna L Etheridge. 80p. (Orig.). 1987. pap. 4.00 (*0-937417-02-5*) Etheridge Minist.
Spring Winds of Beijing. Gail Copeland. LC 92-73014. (Illus.). 330p. 1993. 21.95 (*0-944435-20-3*) Glenbridge Pub.
Spring Within. Robert F. Mainone. (Haiku Series: Vol. 10). (Illus.). 52p. 1989. pap. 10.00 (*1-888693-10-X*) Wnderlnd MI.
Spring 1995 Seasonal. (J). 1995. pap. write for info. (*0-590-47944-X*) Scholastic Inc.
Spring 54 - Reality: A Journal of Archetype & Culture. 176p. (Orig.). 1993. pap. 17.50 (*1-882670-01-9*) Spring Jrnl.
Springboard for College Writers. Maggy Smith & Douglas Meyers. LC 94-29864. (Illus.). 560p. (C). 1996. text ed. 25.50 (*0-06-501158-9*) Addson-Wesley Educ.
Springboard to French: Introduction to the French Language. rev. ed. American Cultural Exchange, Language School Staff & Ulrike Criminale. (Springboard Ser.). (Illus.). 32p. (J). (gr. k-4). 1991. 21.95 incl. audio (*1-880770-00-8*) Brdgstn Multimed Grp.
Springboard to German: Introduction to the German Language. American Cultural Exchange, Language School Staff & Ulrike Criminale. (Springboard Ser.). (Illus.). 32p. (J). (gr. k-4). 1991. 21.95 incl. audio (*1-880770-01-6*) Brdgstn Multimed Grp.
Springboard to Love. large type ed. Grace Lang. (Linford Romance Library). 1991. pap. 15.99 (*0-7089-7062-1*) Ulverscroft.
Springboard to Spanish: Introduction to the Spanish Language. American Cultural Exchange, Language School Staff & Ulrike Criminale. (Springboard Ser.). (Illus.). (J). (gr. k-4). 1991. 21.95 incl. audio (*1-880770-02-4*) Brdgstn Multimed Grp.
Springboard to the Future-Yearbook Compendium. 140p. 1987. pap. 4.95 (*0-86544-041-7*) Salv Army Suppl South.
Springboard Women's Development Workbook. 2nd ed. L. Willis & J. Daisley. (Biography & Self-Development). (Illus.). 277p. 1990. pap. 34.95 (*1-869890-19-1*) Anthroposophic.
Springboards: Interacting in English. Richard Yorkey. 1984. text ed. 11.78 (*0-201-09910-1*) Addison-Wesley.
Springboards see Ideas for Spelling
Springboards for English: Thirty-Three Creative & Cooperative Lessons for Grades 6-12. Marion Horton. 96p. 1992. pap. text ed. 11.95 (*0-944459-49-8*) ECS Lrn Systs.
Springboards for Reading, Grades 3-6: 48 Strategic Reading Lessons. Lori Mammen. (ECS Activity Book for Language Arts Ser.). 96p. 1993. pap. text ed. 11.95 (*0-944459-69-2*) ECS Lrn Systs.
Springboards for Reading, Grades 7-12: 38 Strategic Reading Lessons. Lori Mammen. (ECS Activity Book for Language Arts Ser.). 80p. 1993. pap. text ed. 10.95 (*0-944459-70-6*) ECS Lrn Systs.
Springboards for Today's Children. E. Rosalie Cempura. LC 92-74214. 222p. (Orig.). 1993. pap. 14.95 (*0-9633919-9-2*) Hells Canyon.
Springboards for Writing. Brenda McNeal. (gr. 8-12). 1979. pap. text ed. 15.00 (*0-87879-222-8*) Acad Therapy.
Springboards of Superstition. Joseph Lantiere. (Illus.). 58p. (Orig.). 1990. pap. 7.00 (*0-9627695-0-9*) J Lantiere Bks.
Springboards to Creative Thinking. Patricia T. Muncy. LC 85-11389. 237p. 1985. pap. 27.95 (*0-87628-775-5*) Ctr Appl Res.
Springer Texts in Mechanical Engineering. Ed. by Frederick F. Ling. 1991. text ed. write for info. (*0-318-68929-4*) Spr-Verlag.
Springer Tracts in Modern Physics. Ed. by G. Hohler et al. 220p. 1994. 75.95 (*0-387-57946-X*) Spr-Verlag.
Springer Tracts in Modern Physics, Vol. 37. Ed. by G. Hoehler. (Illus.). iv, 180p. (ENG & GER.). 1965. 39.00 (*0-387-03404-8*) Spr-Verlag.
Springer Tracts in Modern Physics, Vol. 119: Chemical Lasers. V. A. Shcheglov et al. (Illus.). 392p. 1990. 127.95 (*0-387-16185-6*) Spr-Verlag.
Springer Tracts in Modern Physics, Vol. 119: Rigorous Methods in Particle Physics. Ed. by G. Hohler et al. (Illus.). 232p. 1991. 99.95 (*0-387-52902-0*) Spr-Verlag.
Springer Tracts in Modern Physics, Vol. 121: Current-Induced Nonequilibrium Phenomena in Quasi-One-Dimensional Superconductors. Ed. by G. Hohler et al. (Illus.). 368p. 1990. 96.00 (*0-387-53127-0*) Spr-Verlag.
Springer Tracts in Modern Physics, Vol. 123: Particle Induced Electron Emission II. P. S. Varga & Joachim Treusch. (Illus.). 212p. 1992. 104.95 (*0-387-54147-0*) Spr-Verlag.
Springer Tracts in Modern Physics, Vol. 125: Inelastic Scattering of X-Rays with Very High Resolution. E. Burkel. Ed. by G. Hohler & E. A. Niekisch. (Illus.). 130p. 1991. 97.95 (*0-387-54418-6*) Spr-Verlag.
***Springer-Verlag: History of a Scientific Publishing House, 2 pts.** Heinz Sarkowski. Tr. by G. R. Graham. Incl. Pt. I. 1842-1945. Foundation - Maturation - Adversity. LC 96-30570. (Illus.). xviii, 449p. 1996. 59.50 (*3-540-61560-1*); 99.50 (*3-540-61744-2*) Spr-Verlag.
Springer's Progress. David Markson. LC 90-2731. 240p. 1990. reprint ed. pap. 9.95 (*0-916583-57-0*) Dalkey Arch.
Springerville. Brian Young. 36p. (Orig.). 1994. pap. write for info. (*0-930502-10-8*) Pine Pr.
Springfellow's Parade see Bunny's Nutshell Library
Springfield: Prairies of Promise. Edward J. Russo. 1983. 19.95 (*0-89781-084-8*) Am Historical Pr.
Springfield & Clark County: An Illustrated History. William A. Kinnison. 152p. 1985. 22.95 (*0-89781-146-1*) Am Historical Pr.
Springfield & Clark County: An Illustrated History. William A. Kinnison. 152p. 1988. pap. 14.95 (*0-89781-312-X*) Am Historical Pr.
***Springfield Armory Shoulder Weapons, 1795-1968.** Robert W. Ball. (Illus.). 240p. (Orig.). 1997. pap. 34.95 (*0-930625-74-9*, Antque Trdr Bks) Antique Trader Bks.
***Springfield Entertainment: A Pictorial History.** Melinda Garvert et al. (Illinois Pictorial History Ser.). (Illus.). 1996. write for info. (*0-943963-56-7*) G Bradley.
Springfield, MA. Historical Briefs, Inc. Staff. Ed. by Thomas Antonucci & Michael Antonucci. 176p. 1993. pap. 11.95 (*0-89677-018-4*) Hist Briefs.
Springfield Model 1903 Service Rifle: Production & Alteration 1905-1910. C. S. Ferris & John Beard. LC 95-90656. (Illus.). 72p. (Orig.). 1995. pap. 12.50 (*0-9634123-1-0*) C S Ferris.
Springfield Reader. David Cavitch. 1997. pap. text ed. 12.50 (*0-312-15040-7*); pap. text ed. 5.00 (*0-312-15041-5*) St Martin.
***Springfield Reader.** David Cavitch. 1997. pap. text ed. 12.50 (*0-312-14912-3*) St Martin.
Springfield Saga: The Thompsons of Fort Thompson on New River Pulaski County, Virginia. Patricia G. Johnson. (Illus.). 74p. (Orig.). 1985. pap. 15.00 (*0-9614765-0-8*) Walpa Pub.
Springfield Sharpshooters. Jon Sharpe. (Trailsman Ser.: No. 149). 176p. (Orig.). 1994. pap. 3.50 (*0-451-17885-8*, Sig) NAL-Dutton.
Springfield, 1636-1886, History of Town & City, Including an Account of the Quarter-Millenial Celebration. Mason A. Green. (Illus.). 645p. 1995. reprint ed. lib. bdg. 67.00 (*0-8328-4698-8*) Higginson Bk Co.
Springfield 1903 Rifles. William S. Brophy. LC 84-16154. (Illus.). 624p. 1985. 75.00 (*0-8117-0872-1*) Stackpole.
Springhouse: Poems. Norman Dubie. 1986. pap. 6.95 (*0-393-30323-3*) Norton.
Springhouse Certification Review: Critical Care Nursing. Springhouse Publishing Co. Editors. LC 95-35911. 400p. 1995. 24.95 (*0-87434-782-3*) Springhouse Pub.
Springhouse Certification Review: Emergency Nursing. Ed. by Springhouse Publishing Company Staff & June Norris. (Illus.). 416p. (Orig.). 1996. 27.95 (*0-87434-846-3*) Springhouse Pub.
***Springhouse Notes: Anatomy & Physiology.** Cecelia G. Grindel & Leonard V. Crowley. 296p. 1997. 22.95 incl. cd-rom (*0-87434-901-X*) Springhouse Pub.
Springhouse Nurse's Drug Guide 97. Springhouse Publishing Company Staff. Ed. by June Norris. (Illus.). 1440p. (Orig.). 1996. pap. 27.95 incl. disk (*0-87434-837-4*) Springhouse Pub.
***Springhouse Nurse's Drug Guide 98.** SPC Staff. (Illus.). 1536p. 1997. 28.95 incl. disk (*0-87434-892-7*) Springhouse Pub.
Springing up Puppies. 5p. 1995. pap. 6.98 (*1-57082-121-6*) Mouse Works.
SpringPoem No. 3,719,242. Bob Grumman. 18p. (Orig.). 1990. pap. 1.00 (*0-926935-39-9*) Runaway Spoon.
Springs. David Glover. LC 96-15799. (Simple Machines Ser.). (J). 1997. lib. bdg. write for info. (*1-57572-082-5*) Rigby Interact Libr.
Springs: Troubleshooting & Failure Analysis. Carlson. (Engineering Troubleshooting Ser.: Vol. 1). 192p. 1980. 110.00 (*0-8247-1003-7*) Dekker.
Spring's Awakening: English Version with an Introduction by Eric Bentley. Frank Wedekind. Tr. by Eric Bentley. 160p. 1996. pap. 9.95 (*1-55783-245-5*) Applause Theatre Bk Pubs.
Spring's Fury. Denise Domning. 384p. (Orig.). 1995. mass mkt., pap. 4.99 (*0-451-40521-8*, Topaz) NAL-Dutton.
Spring's Game. Warner Tchan. 100p. 1996. pap. text ed. 5.00 (*0-614-13435-8*) New Wrld Poetry.
Spring's Gentle Promise. Janette Oke. LC 89-22. (Seasons of the Heart Ser.). 224p. (Orig.). (YA). (gr. 10 up). 1989. pap. 8.99 (*1-55661-059-9*) Bethany Hse.
Spring's Gentle Promise. large type ed. Janette Oke. LC 89-22. (Seasons of the Heart Ser.: Vol. 4). 224p. (Orig.). (YA). (gr. 10 up). 1989. pap. 10.99 (*1-55661-074-2*) Bethany Hse.
Springs-In the Old Days: A History of Long Island Village. Ferris Talmage. (Illus.). 48p. 1983. write for info. (*0-910425-05-1*) Starchand Pr.
Springs in the Valley. Cowman. 384p. 1988. 12.99 (*0-310-35380-7*, 6814) Zondervan.
Springs of Action: Understanding Intentional Behavior. Alfred R. Mele. 288p. 1992. 49.95 (*0-19-507114-X*) OUP.
***Springs of Affection.** Brennan. 1997. 24.00 (*0-395-87046-1*) HM.
Springs of Carmel: An Introduction to Carmelite Spirituality. Peter O. Slattery. LC 91-17926. 152p. (Orig.). 1991. pap. 7.95 (*0-8189-0604-9*) Alba.
Springs of Colorado. Richard M. Pearl. (Illus.). 36p. 1994. reprint ed. pap. 2.95 (*0-9624008-7-4*) Pulpit Rock.
***Springs of Contemplation: A Retreat at the Abbey of Gethsemani.** Thomas Merton. Ed. by Jane M. Richardson. LC 96-47761. 208p. 1997. reprint ed. pap. 9.95 (*0-87793-598-X*) Ave Maria.
Springs of Florida. Doug Stamm. LC 93-33773. (Illus.). 112p. 1994. 29.95 (*1-56164-054-9*); pap. 19.95 (*1-56164-048-4*) Pineapple Pr.
***Springs of Joy.** Tudor. (J): 1998. pap. 18.00 (*0-689-81882-3*) S&S Childrens.
Springs of Joy: A Biblical Treasury. Ed. by Lyn Scaramanga. 160p. 1995. 24.95 (*0-8245-1502-1*) Crossroad NY.
Springs of Scientific Creativity: Essays on Founders of Modern Science. Ed. by Rutherford Aris et al. LC 82-23715. 353p. 1983. reprint ed. pap. 100.70 (*0-608-00784-6*, 2059333) Bks Demand.
Springs of Sinhala Civilization: An Illustrated Survey of Ancient Irrigation System of Sri Lanka. Anuradha Seneviratna. (C). 1989. 77.50 (*0-685-37823-3*, Pub. by Navrang) S Asia.
Springs of Spirituality: Essentials of Catholic Tradition & Practice. Mary A. Huddleston. LC 94-38530. 224p. 1995. pap. 12.95 (*0-89243-781-2*, Triumph Books) Liguori Pubns.
Springs of Stillness & Solitude. 22p. 1986. 4.95 (*3-85788-326-X*) Natl Bk Netwk.
Springs of Texas, Vol. 1. Gunnar Brune. LC 80-71016. (Illus.). 584p. 1981. 35.00 (*0-9604766-0-1*); (*0-318-52335-3*) G Brune.
Springs of Water in a Dry Land: Spiritual Survival for Catholic Women Today. Mary J. Weaver. 176p. 1994. pap. 14.00 (*0-8070-1219-X*) Beacon Pr.
Spring's Return. Carolyn T. Feagans. LC 94-90083. 440p. 1994. pap. 7.95 (*0-9634627-2-5*) C T Feagans.
***Springside Seasons: The Way We Cook Today.** Springside School Community Members. (Illus.). 224p. 1996. spiral bd. 16.95 (*0-9653152-0-7*) Sprngside Schl.
Springsigns. Gerald Cox. (Illus.). 80p. pap. 5.95 (*0-935576-20-7*) Kesend Pub Ltd.
Springsteen: Blinded by the Light. Patrick Humphries & Hunt. 176p. 1994. per. 14.95 (*0-85965-086-3*, Pub. by Plexus UK) Publishers Group.
Springtime. Judy Beach & Kathleen Spencer. (Teachers' Holiday Helpers Ser.). (J). (gr. 1-3). 1987. pap. 6.99 (*0-8224-6775-5*) Fearon Teach Aids.
Springtime. Ann Schweninger. (Illus.). 32p. (J). 1995. pap. 4.99 (*0-14-054054-7*) Puffin Bks.
Springtime & Harvest. Upton Sinclair. 1992. reprint ed. lib. bdg. 18.95 (*0-89966-955-7*) Buccaneer Bks.
Springtime, & Other Essays. Francis Darwin. LC 67-23201. (Essay Index Reprint Ser.). 1977. 19.95 (*0-8369-0364-1*) Ayer.
***Springtime Friends: Big Fat Coloring Book.** (Illus.). 352p. (Orig.). (J). (gr. k-5). 1997. pap. write for info. (*1-889372-21-8*) Sweetwtr Pr AL.
***Springtime Fun: Big Fat Coloring Book.** (Illus.). 352p. (Orig.). (J). (gr. k-5). 1997. pap. write for info. (*1-889372-22-6*) Sweetwtr Pr AL.
Springtime Ghost. Brown. (Kate & Tracy Ser.). (J). (gr. 4-8). 1989. pap. 1.95 (*0-87386-063-2*); lib. bdg. 8.49 (*0-87386-059-4*) Jan Prods.
Springtime in My Very Own Dollhouse. Playskool Staff. 1996. pap. 4.99 (*0-525-45544-2*) NAL-Dutton.
Springtime Jingo. Gary Grimm & Phoebe Wear. 32p. (J). (gr. k-6). 1993. 12.00 (*1-56490-008-8*) G Grimm Assocs.
Springtime of Faith. Jeanette Lockerbie. 150p. (Orig.). 1990. pap. 4.99 (*0-8024-7696-1*) Moody.

S

An Asterisk (*) at the beginning of an entry indicates that the title is appearing in BIP for the first time.

Springtime of Love & Marriage: Guidance for the Early Years of Marriage. James R. Hine. LC 85-14664. (Judson Family Life Ser.). 159p. 1985. reprint ed. pap. 45.40 (*0-608-00220-8*, 2061015) Bks Demand.

Springtime of the Liturgy. rev. ed. Lucien Deiss. Tr. by Matthew J. O'Connell from FRE. LC 79-15603. 307p. (C). 1979. pap. 14.95 (*0-8146-1023-4*) Liturgical Pr.

Springtime on the Via Condotti. Gustav Ernst. Tr. by Todd C. Hanlin. LC 96-9579. (Studies in Austrian Literature, Culture, & Thought). 1997. pap. 13.95 (*1-57241-034-5*) Ariadne CA.

Springtime Romance. Donna S. Lee. 1996. 7.95 (*0-533-09574-3*) Vantage.

Springtime Special: The Good News Kids Learn about Patience. Dorothy K. Mock. LC 92-27010. (Good News Kids Ser.). (Illus.). 32p. (Orig.). (J). (ps-2). 1993. pap. 4.99 (*0-570-04736-6*, 56-1693) Concordia.

Springtime Surprises: Things to Make & Do. Judith Conaway. LC 85-16497. (Illus.). 48p. (J). (gr. 1-5). 1986. lib. bdg. 12.50 (*0-8167-0670-0*) Troll Communs.

Springville Summers. Joseph A. Schufle. (Illus.). 131p. 1989. 29.95 (*0-945407-02-5*) Meadow Pr NM.

Springwood. Larry Parr. 170p. 1981. 11.95 (*0-940812-00-2*) Plantagenet Hse.

***Sprinkle & Trickle Irrigation.** Keller & Bliesner. (Illus.). 584p. (C). (gr. 13 up). 1990. text ed. 112.95 (*0-412-07591-1*) Chapman & Hall.

***Sprinkle of Fairy Dust.** Maggie B. Shayne. 1996. mass mkt. 5.99 (*0-312-96035-2*) St Martin.

Sprinkle of Nutmeg: Letters to Christopher Fry, 1943-45. Phyl Fry. (Illus.). 64p. 9300. pap. 19.95 (*1-870612-58-2*, Pub. by Enitha Pr UK) Dufour.

Sprinkler Experience in High-Rise Buildings. W. Robert Powers. 1979. 3.25 (*0-686-26148-8*, TR 79-1) Society Fire Protect.

Sprinkler Fitter, Level 1. National Center for Construction Education & Research Staff. (Wheels of Learning Ser.). 1996. teacher ed., ring bd. 50.00 (*0-13-265638-8*) P-H.

***Sprinkler Fitter, Level 2.** 1996. student ed., ring bd. 80.00 (*0-13-266008-3*, Prentice Hall) P-H.

Sprinkler Fitter, Level 2. National Center for Construction Education & Research Staff. (Wheels of Learning Ser.). 1996. teacher ed., ring bd. 80.00 (*0-13-265646-9*) P-H.

Sprinkler Fitter: Level 1. Ed. by National Center for Construction Staff. 1996. pap. text ed. 50.00 (*0-13-462821-7*) P-H.

Sprinkler Fitter: Level 1. Ed. by National Center for Construction Staff. 1996. teacher ed., pap. text ed. 50.00 (*0-13-462839-X*) P-H.

***Sprinkler Fitter Level 2 Trainee Guide.** 1996. pap. 80.00 (*0-13-490020-0*) P-H.

***Sprinkler Fitter Level 3 Trainee Guide.** 1996. pap. 80.00 (*0-13-490038-3*) P-H.

***Sprinkler Fitterder, Level 3.** 1996. student ed., ring bd. 80.00 (*0-13-266016-4*, Prentice Hall) P-H.

***Sprinkler Fitters Guide, Level 3.** 1996. ring bd. 80.00 (*0-13-265653-1*, Prentice Hall) P-H.

Sprinkler Fittter: Trainee, Level 1. National Center for Construction Education & Research Staff. (Wheels of Learning Ser.). 1996. student ed., pap. text ed. 50.00 (*0-13-266487-9*) P-H.

Sprinkler Irrigation. R. K. Sivannappan. (C). 1987. 12.50 (*81-204-0232-4*, Pub. by Oxford IBH II) S Asia.

Sprinkler Irrigation see Irrigation

Sprinkler Irrigation System. 3rd rev. ed. Virgil E. Young. (Illus.). 200p. (Orig.). (C). 1976. reprint ed. pap. text ed. 4.98 (*0-916970-01-9*) Mist'er Rain.

Sprinkler Systems Design: Past, Present & Future. C. F. Averill. 1979. 2.50 (*0-685-04683-4*, TR 79-3) Society Fire Protect.

Sprinkler Systems License. (Career Examination Ser.: C-3767). pap. 23.95 (*0-8373-3767-4*) Nat Learn.

Sprint Car Chassis Set-Up. Steve Smith. (Illus.). 104p. (Orig.). 1990. pap. text ed. 15.95 (*0-936834-74-9*) S S Autosports.

Sprint Handicapping Explained. Jim Adams. 208p. 1990. 46.00 (*0-85131-407-4*, Pub. by J A Allen & Co UK) St Mut.

SPRINT Simplified. Douglas J. Wolf. (Illus.). 220p. 1988. pap. 19.95 (*0-8306-3113-5*, 3113) McGraw-Hill Prof.

Sprinting & Hurdling. Peter Warden. (Skills of the Game Ser.). (Illus.). 109p. 1990. pap. 19.95 (*1-85223-299-4*, Pub. by Crowood Pr UK) Trafalgar.

***Sprinting from the Graveyard.** Goran Simic. Tr. by David Harsent. 64p. 1997. pap. 11.95 (*0-19-288023-3*) OUP.

Sprinting into Sun. Jim Dewitt. (Illus.). 64p. (Orig.). 1979. pap. 3.95 (*0-915199-98-X*) Pen-Dec.

Sprints & Hurdles see Modern Drills for Track & Field

***Sprints & Relays.** 4th ed. Ed. by Jess Jarver. (Contemporary Theory, Technique & Training Ser.). (Illus.). 160p. 1995. pap. 16.00 (*0-911521-29-1*) Tafnews.

Sprite Graphics: For the Commodore C-64 & C-128, Vol. II. James L. Farvour. (Commodore Information Ser.). (Illus.). 112p. 1985. pap. 9.95 (*0-932679-03-X*) Blue Cat.

Sprite Midget Twelve Seventy-Five CC, 1967-1974, the Complete Official: Comprising the Official Driver's Handbook, Workshop Manual, Emission Control Supplement. British Leyland Motors Staff. LC 75-37232. (Illus.). 400p. (Orig.). 1975. pap. 45.00 (*0-8376-0127-4*) Bentley.

Sprite-Midget 948cc & 1098cc, 1961-1966, the Complete Official: Comprising the Official Driver's Handbook, Workshop Manual, Special Tuning Manual. British Leyland Motors Staff. LC 67-28432. (Illus.). 256p. (Orig.). 1968. pap. 40.00 (*0-8376-0023-5*) Bentley.

Sprites & Midgets: Collector's Guide. Eric Dymock. (Collector's Guide Ser.). (Illus.). 112p. 1982. 27.95 (*0-900549-53-X*, Pub. by Motor Racing UK) Motorbooks Intl.

Sprituality & Nursing Practice. Judy Harrison & Philip Burnard. 218p. 1993. 58.95 (*1-85628-509-X*, Pub. by Avebury Pub UK) Ashgate Pub Co.

Sproget see Language: An Introduction

Sprouse's Income Tax Handbook, 1986. Mary L. Sprouse. (Handbook Ser.). 592p. 1985. pap. 7.95 (*0-685-43121-5*, Penguin Bks) Viking Penguin.

Sprouse's Two-Earner Money Book. Mary L. Sprouse. Date not set. pap. 10.00 (*0-14-012887-5*, Viking) Viking Penguin.

Sprout. Richard Gleason. LC 86-51074. (Illus.). 84p. (J). (gr. 3-8). 1987. 7.95 (*1-55523-052-0*) Winston-Derek.

Sprout for the Love of Everybody: Nutritional Evaluation of Sprouts & Grasses. Viktoras Kulvinskas. 1978. pap. 8.95 (*0-933278-03-9*) Twen Fir Cent.

Sprout Garden. Mark M. Braunstein. LC 93-1155. (Illus.). 128p. 1993. pap. 8.95 (*0-913990-96-5*) Book Pub Co.

Sprouting Book: How to Grow & Use Sprouts to Maximize Your Health & Vitality. Ann Wigmore. LC 86-10713. (Illus.). 128p. pap. 7.95 (*0-89529-246-7*) Avery Pub.

Sprouting for All Seasons: How & What to Sprout, Including Delicious Easy-to-Prepare Recipes. Bertha B. Larimore. LC 75-23564. (Illus.). 140p. (Orig.). 1993. reprint ed. pap. 11.98 (*0-88290-055-2*) Horizon Utah.

Sproutman's Kitchen Garden Cookbook: Sprout Breads, Cookies, Salads, Soups & 250 Other Low Fat, Dairy-Free, Vegetarian Recipes. 4th ed. Steve Meyerowitz. (Illus.). 336p. 1994. pap. 14.95 (*1-878736-84-1*) Sprout Hse.

Sprouts: A Diary for the Foster Child. Beverly Amstutz. (Illus.). 38p. (Orig.). (J). (gr. k-7). 1982. pap. 2.50 (*0-937836-07-9*) Precious Res.

Sprouts: Nurturing Children through Covenant Discipleship. Edie G. Harris & Shirley L. Ramsey. LC 95-69440. 72p. 1996. pap. 9.95 (*0-88177-143-0*, DR143) Discipleship Res.

***Sprouts - The Miracle Food: A Complete Guide to Sprouting.** Steve Meyerowitz. 224p. 1997. pap. 12.95 (*1-878736-03-5*) Sprout Hse.

Sprouts & Saplings: Gardening with a Difference. Monica M. Brandies. LC 86-14341. (Illus.). 208p. (Orig.). 1986. pap. 9.95 (*0-89407-066-5*) Strawberry Hill.

Spruce Root Basketry of the Alaska Tlingit. Frances Paul. 80p. 1991. pap. text ed. 5.95 (*1-880475-02-2*) Friends of SJM.

***Sprucey, the Blue Christmas Tree.** Donna Abear. (Illus.). 36p. (J). (gr. k-8). 1997. pap. 3.50 (*0-88680-439-6*) I E Clark.

Sprung from Some Common Source: Investigations into the Prehistory of Languages. Ed. by Sydney M. Lamb & E. Douglas Mitchell. LC 90-46495. (Illus.). 432p. 1991. 52.50 (*0-8047-1897-0*) Stanford U Pr.

Sprungbrett. D. Bonnyman & K. Oberheid. (C). 1990. 60.00 (*0-7487-0489-2*, Pub. by Stanley Thornes UK); teacher ed. 40.00 (*0-7487-0490-6*, Pub. by Stanley Thornes UK); audio 125.00 (*0-7487-0491-4*, Pub. by Stanley Thornes UK) Trans-Atl Phila.

SPSE Handbook of Photographic Science & Engineering. Ed. by Woodlief Thomas. LC 72-10168. (Wiley Series on Photographic Science & Technology & the Graphic Arts). 1428p. reprint ed. pap. 180.00 (*0-685-20939-3*, 2056550) Bks Demand.

SPSF Merger. Joseph W. Shine. 128p. (Orig.). 1986. 25.95 (*0-9616874-0-1*) Four Ways.

SPSS - PC: Graphics from Tri Metrix. 2nd ed. SPSS Inc. Staff. pap. text ed. 6.00 (*0-13-108879-3*) P-H.

SPSS - PC Plus Advanced Statistics, Version 5.0. Marija J. Norusis. LC 92-85165. 592p. 1992. pap. 21.95 (*0-923967-68-0*) SPSS Inc.

SPSS - PC Plus Base System User's Guide, Version 5.0. Marija J. Norusis. LC 92-85164. 800p. 1992. pap. 29.95 (*0-923967-66-4*) SPSS Inc.

SPSS - PC Plus Graphics from TriMetrix. LC 92-63023. 600p. (Orig.). 1992. pap. 21.95 (*0-923967-79-6*) SPSS Inc.

SPSS - PC Plus Professional Statistics, Version 5.0. Marija J. Norusis. LC 92-85163. 272p. (Orig.). 1992. pap. 21.95 (*0-923967-67-2*) SPSS Inc.

SPSS - PC Plus Studentware for Business. Marija J. Norusis. Ed. by SPSS Inc. Staff. LC 91-62550. 604p. (Orig.). 1991. pap. text ed. 44.95 incl. disk (*0-923967-30-3*); pap. text ed. 44.95 incl. disk (*0-923967-31-1*) SPSS Inc.

SPSS - PC Plus Studentware Plus. rev. ed. Marija J. Norusis. LC 91-62551. 483p. 1991. pap. text ed. 39.95 incl. disk (*0-923967-28-1*); pap. text ed. 39.95 incl. disk (*0-923967-29-X*) SPSS Inc.

SPSS - PCplus Advanced Statistics 4.0. SPSS Inc. Staff & Marija J. Norusis. LC 90-70750. 400p. 1990. pap. text ed. 19.95 (*0-923967-13-3*) SPSS Inc.

SPSS - PCplus Graphics 4.0 Featuring Harvard Graphics. SPSS Inc. Staff. LC 90-70753. 72p. (Orig.). 1990. pap. text ed. 5.95 (*0-923967-25-7*) SPSS Inc.

SPSS - PCplus Statistics 4.0 for the IBM PC - XT & PS - 2. rev. ed. SPSS Inc. Staff & Marija J. Norusis. LC 90-70749. 400p. 1990. pap. text ed. 19.95 (*0-923967-12-5*) SPSS Inc.

SPSS - PCplus Tables 4.0 for the IBM - PC - XT & PS - 2. SPSS Inc. Staff. LC 90-70752. 240p. 1990. pap. text ed. 19.95 (*0-923967-20-6*) SPSS Inc.

SPSS - PCplus Trends 4.0. rev. ed. SPSS Inc. Staff. LC 90-70751. 352p. 1990. pap. text ed. 19.95 (*0-923967-14-1*) SPSS Inc.

SPSS - PCplus 4.0 Base Manual for the IBM PC - XT & PS - 2. rev. ed. SPSS Inc. Staff & Marija J. Norusis. LC 90-70748. 640p. 1990. pap. text ed. 19.95 (*0-923967-11-7*) SPSS Inc.

SPSS Advanced Statistics Student Guide. LC 90-60790. 480p. (C). 1990. pap. 21.95 (*0-923967-03-6*) SPSS Inc.

SPSS Advanced Statistics User's Guide. SPSS, Inc. Staff. LC 89-62959. 304p. (Orig.). 1990. pap. 19.95 (*0-918469-90-2*) SPSS Inc.

***SPSS Advanced Statistics 7.5.** SPSS Inc., Staff. (C). 1996. pap. text ed. 41.00 (*0-13-656927-7*) P-H.

SPSS Base System Syntax Reference Guide, Release 5.0. SPSS Inc. Staff. LC 92-60766. 768p. 1992. pap. 32.95 (*0-923967-53-2*) SPSS Inc.

SPSS Base System User's Guide. SPSS Inc. Staff & Marija J. Norusis. LC 89-62958. 528p. 1990. pap. 24.95 (*0-918469-63-5*) SPSS Inc.

SPSS Base System User's Guide for SPSS 4.0. SPSS, Inc. Staff. 1993. pap. text ed. 42.00 (*0-13-177866-8*) P-H.

SPSS Base Sys7.0: Application Guide. 1996. pap. text ed. 21.00 (*0-13-476318-1*) P-H.

SPSS Base 7.0 Syntax Reference Guide. Prentice Hall Editorial Staff. 1996. pap. text ed. 42.00 (*0-13-476326-2*) P-H.

***SPSS Base 7.5: Applications Guide.** SPSS Inc., Staff. (C). 1996. pap. text ed. 25.20 (*0-13-656992-7*) P-H.

***SPSS Base 7.5: Syntax Reference Guide.** SPSS Inc., Staff. 1996. pap. text ed. 41.00 (*0-13-656943-9*) P-H.

***SPSS Base 7.5 for Windows: User's Guide.** SPSS Inc., Staff. (C). 1996. pap. text ed. 41.00 (*0-13-657214-6*) P-H.

SPSS Categories. SPSS, Inc. Staff. LC 89-62961. 320p. (Orig.). 1990. pap. 24.95 (*0-918469-93-7*) SPSS Inc.

SPSS Data Entry Two. rev. ed. SPSS Inc. Staff. LC 90-70756. 192p. 1990. pap. text ed. 19.95 (*0-923967-19-2*) SPSS Inc.

SPSS for IBM - MVS: Operations Guide. SPSS Inc. Staff. LC 90-62544. 140p. (Orig.). 1990. pap. text ed. 10.95 (*0-923967-09-5*) SPSS Inc.

SPSS for IBM-CMS: Operations Guide. SPSS, Inc. Staff. LC 89-62963. 128p. (Orig.). 1990. pap. text ed. 10.95 (*0-918469-96-1*) SPSS Inc.

SPSS for OS-2, Operations Guide Release 4.1. rev. ed. SPSS Inc. Staff. LC 90-64048. 235p. 1991. pap. text ed. 8.95 (*0-923967-27-3*) SPSS Inc.

SPSS for the Macintosh: Operations Guide. SPSS Inc. Staff. LC 89-62964. 160p. (Orig.). 1990. pap. 10.95 (*0-918469-98-8*) SPSS Inc.

SPSS for Unix: Operations Guide. SPSS, Inc. Staff. LC 89-62962. 176p. (Orig.). 1990. pap. 10.95 (*0-918469-97-X*) SPSS Inc.

SPSS for VAX - VMS: Operations Guide. SPSS Inc. Staff. LC 90-62543. 258p. (Orig.). 1990. pap. text ed. 10.95 (*0-923967-07-9*) SPSS Inc.

SPSS for Windows: Advanced Statistics Release 5. Marija J. Norusis. LC 92-85019. 400p. (Orig.). pap. 24.95 (*0-923967-56-7*) SPSS Inc.

SPSS for Windows: Base System User's Guide, Release 5.0. Marija J. Norusis. Ed. by SPSS Inc. Staff. LC 91-68310. 768p. 1992. pap. 32.95 (*0-923967-49-4*) SPSS Inc.

SPSS for Windows: Help for SPSS - PC Plus Users. SPSS Inc. Staff. 16p. 1992. pap. 2.95 (*0-923967-55-9*) SPSS Inc.

SPSS for Windows: Professional Statistics User's Guide, Release 5.0. Marija J. Norusis & SPSS Inc. Staff. LC 91-68311. 400p. pap. 24.95 (*0-923967-50-8*) SPSS Inc.

SPSS for Windows Base System User's Guide 6.0. SPSS Inc. Staff. 1993. pap. text ed. 42.00 (*0-13-178856-6*) P-H.

SPSS for Windows Base System Users Guide 6.0 Bundle. SPPSS Inc. Staff. 1995. pap. text ed. 46.00 (*0-13-185208-6*) P-H.

SPSS for Windows Tables, Release 5. LC 93-83235. 276p. 1993. pap. text ed. 24.95 (*0-923967-85-0*) SPSS Inc.

SPSS Graphics. SPSS Inc. Staff. LC 84-42995. (Illus.). 343p. 1991. pap. 32.95 (*0-923967-35-4*) SPSS Inc.

SPSS Guide. Kilman Shin. 288p. (C). 1994. 19.75 (*0-256-15925-4*) Irwin.

SPSS Guide. 2nd ed. Kilman Shin. (Irwin Statistical Software Ser.). 400p. (C). 1995. 20.54 (*0-256-20652-X*) Irwin.

SPSS Guide to Data Analysis for Release 4. Marija J. Norusis. Ed. by SPSS Inc. Staff. LC 90-63465. (Illus.). 470p. 1991. pap. text ed. 16.95 (*0-923967-08-7*) SPSS Inc.

SPSS Guide to Data Analysis for SPSS-PC Plus. 2nd rev. ed. SPSS Inc. Staff & Marija J. Norusis. LC 91-66147. 499p. 1991. pap. text ed. 16.95 (*0-923967-34-6*) SPSS Inc.

SPSS Guide to Data Analysis for SPSS-X. rev. ed. Marija J. Norusis. Ed. by SPSS Inc. Staff. LC 87-60776. (Illus.). 448p. (C). 1988. pap. text ed. 16.95 (*0-918469-42-2*) SPSS Inc.

SPSS Guide to Data Analysis for SPSS 4.0. SPSS, Inc. Staff. 1993. pap. text ed. 42.00 (*0-13-178096-4*) P-H.

***SPSS Guide to the New Statistical Analysis of Data by T. W. Anderson & Jeremy D. Finn.** Susan B. Gerber et al. LC 96-47394. 216p. 1997. text ed. 29.95 (*0-387-94821-X*) Spr-Verlag.

SPSS Introductory Statistics Student Guide. SPSS Inc. Staff & Marija J. Norusis. LC 90-60795. 444p. (Orig.). (C). 1990. pap. 16.95 (*0-923967-02-8*) SPSS Inc.

Spss Lisrel 7 & Prelis. SPSS Inc. Staff. 1993. pap. text ed. 27.00 (*0-13-112384-X*) P-H.

SPSS Made Simple. 2nd ed. John Hedderson & Melinda Fisher. 283p. (C). 1993. pap. 26.95 (*0-534-19992-5*) Wadsworth Pub.

SPSS PC: Students 3.5 & SPSS Guide to Data 4.0 Package. SPSS Inc. Staff. 1993. pap. text ed. 92.80 (*0-13-125931-8*) P-H.

SPSS PC Plus Base System User's Guide 5.0. SPSS, Inc. Staff. 1992. pap. text ed. 42.00 (*0-13-177692-4*) P-H.

SPSS-PC Plus Codebook. SPSS Inc. Staff. LC 91-66146. 144p. (Orig.). 1991. pap. text ed. 24.95 (*0-923967-38-9*) SPSS Inc.

SPSS PC Plus Guide to Data Analysis. 2nd ed. SPSS, Inc. Staff. 1991. pap. text ed. 42.00 (*0-13-178443-9*) P-H.

SPSS-PC Plus Made Simple. John Hedderson. 271p. (C). 1991. pap. 26.95 (*0-534-14376-8*) Wadsworth Pub.

SPSS-PC Plus Map 4.0 from MapInfo. SPSS Inc. Staff. LC 90-70754. 201p. (Orig.). 1990. pap. text ed. 24.95 (*0-923967-15-X*) SPSS Inc.

SPSS-PC Plus Step by Step: A Simple Guide & Reference. Darren George & Paul Mallery. 320p. 1995. pap. 26.95 incl. 3.5 hd (*0-534-22068-1*) Wadsworth Pub.

SPSS-PC Plus Studentware. Marija J. Norusis. Ed. by SPSS Inc. Staff. LC 88-80965. 416p. (Orig.). (C). 1988. pap. text ed. 34.95 (*0-918469-73-2*) SPSS Inc.

SPSS Prelis & LISREL 7: User's Guide & Reference. SPSS Inc. Staff. LC 89-69859. 300p. (Orig.). 1990. pap. 24.95 (*0-918469-70-8*) SPSS Inc.

***SPSS Professional Statistics 7.5.** SPSS Inc., Staff. (C). 1997. pap. text ed. 41.00 (*0-13-656935-8*) P-H.

SPSS Reference Guide. SPSS, Inc. Staff. LC 89-43279. 944p. (Orig.). 1990. pap. text ed. 36.95 (*0-918469-62-7*) SPSS Inc.

SPSS Statistical Algorithms. 2nd rev. ed. SPSS Inc. Staff. LC 89-69858. 290p. (Orig.). 1991. pap. text ed. 24.95 (*0-918469-89-9*) SPSS Inc.

SPSS Trends II. SPSS Inc. Staff. LC 88-80964. 512p. (Orig.). 1988. pap. text ed. 29.95 (*0-918469-72-4*) SPSS Inc.

SPSS-X Advanced Statistics Guide. 2nd ed. Marija J. Norusis. Ed. by SPSS Inc. Staff. LC 88-61671. 544p. 1988. pap. text ed. 19.95 (*0-918469-81-3*) SPSS Inc.

SPSS-X Data Entry for VAX-VMS. SPSS Inc. Staff. LC 88-63757. 160p. (Orig.). 1988. pap. text ed. 17.95 (*0-918469-84-8*) SPSS Inc.

SPSS-X Introductory Statistics Guide for SPSS-X Release 3. rev. ed. Marija J. Norusis. LC 87-62352. 384p. (C). 1988. pap. text ed. 16.95 (*0-918469-54-6*) SPSS Inc.

SPSS-X Tables. 2nd ed. SPSS Inc. Staff. LC 87-62351. 240p. (C). 1988. pap. 19.95 (*0-918469-53-8*) SPSS Inc.

SPSS-X Trends. SPSS Inc. Staff. LC 87-62350. 352p. (Orig.). (C). 1987. pap. text ed. 19.95 (*0-918469-52-X*) SPSS Inc.

SPSS-X User's Guide. 3rd ed. SPSS Inc. Staff. LC 87-62349. 1088p. (C). 1987. pap. text ed. 34.95 (*0-918469-51-1*) SPSS Inc.

***SPSS 6.1 Base System User's Guide, Pts. 1 & 2.** SPSS Inc. Staff. (C). 1996. pap. 42.00 (*0-13-628066-8*) P-H.

***SPSS 7.5 for Windows: Brief Guide.** SPSS Inc., Staff. (C). 1997. pap. text ed. 21.33 (*0-13-656885-8*) P-H.

***SPSS 7.5 Guide to Data Analysis.** Marija J. Norusis. (C). 1997. pap. text ed. 31.50 (*0-13-656877-7*) P-H.

***Spud in Winter.** Brian Doyle. (J). (gr. 4-6). 1996. pap. 5.95 (*0-88899-250-5*, Pub. by Groundwood-Douglas & McIntyre CN) Firefly Bks Ltd.

Spud Johnson & "Laughing Horse" Sharyn R. Udall. LC 93-42070. (Illus.). 430p. (C). 1994. 16.95 (*0-8263-1469-4*) U of NM Pr.

***Spud Sweetgrass.** Brian Doyle. (J). (gr. 4-6). 1996. pap. 5.95 (*0-88899-251-3*, Pub. by Groundwood-Douglas & McIntyre CN) Firefly Bks Ltd.

Spuds, Buds, & Tots: Chronicle of the Lowly Potato That Nurtured the Poor, the Solider & the Mighty. Ruth M. Snyder. (Illus.). 88p. (Orig.). 1995. pap. write for info. (*1-57502-074-2*) Morris Pubng.

Spumco Comic Book. John Kricfalusi. 1995. pap. 24.95 (*0-7851-0088-1*) Marvel Entmnt.

Spun by the Moon. large type ed. Leslie Lance. 336p. 1988. 25.99 (*0-7089-1900-6*) Ulverscroft.

Spun-Yarn. Morgan Robertson. LC 76-98592. (Short Story Index Reprint Ser.). 1977. 19.95 (*0-8369-3166-1*) Ayer.

***Spunk.** Romy Rosen. (Orig.). 1997. mass mkt. 6.95 (*1-56333-492-5*, Rhinoceros) Masquerade.

Spunk: The Selected Stories of Zora Neale Hurston. Zora Neale Hurston. 106p. (Orig.). 1985. pap. 9.95 (*0-913666-79-3*) Turtle Isl Foun.

Spunk: Three Tales by Zora Neale Hurston. George C. Wolfe. LC 90-29040. 1991. 17.95 (*1-55936-023-2*); pap. 8.95 (*1-55936-024-0*) Theatre Comm.

Spunk: Three Tales by Zora Neale Hurston. adapted ed. Zora Neale Hurston. 1992. spiral bd. 9.95 (*0-8222-1067-3*) Dramatists Play.

Spunky Spot: A Tale of One Smart Fish. Suzanne Tate. LC 88-63784. (Suzanne Tate's Nature Ser.: No. 4). (Illus.). 28p. (Orig.). (J). (gr. k-4). 1989. pap. 3.95 (*0-9616344-6-4*) Nags Head Art.

Spunky Spot: Un Cuento De Un Pez Inteligente. Suzanne Tate. LC 90-61966. (Suzanne Tate de la Natural Serie: Numero 4). (Illus.). 28p. (Orig.). (J). (gr. k-4). 1990. pap. 3.95 (*1-878405-02-0*) Nags Head Art.

Spunky the Monkey. Tom LaFleur & Gale Brennan. (Illus.). 16p. (Orig.). (J). (gr. k-6). 1981. pap. 1.25 (*0-685-02457-1*) Brennan Bks.

Spunky's Diary. Janette Oke. (Illus.). 100p. (J). (gr. 3 up). pap. 4.99 (*0-934998-11-6*) Bethel Pub.

Spur. Jerry Evans. LC 94-77005. 135p. (Orig.). (YA). (gr. 11 up). 1995. pap. 7.95 (*0-9623698-2-9*) Magnum Pr.

***Spur & Helical Gear Geometry Factors.** AGMA Technical Committee & J. H. Hitchcock. (Technical Papers: Vol. 229.07). 87p. 1963. pap. text ed. 30.00 (*1-55589-143-8*) AGMA.

***Spur Gear Bending Strength Geometry Factors.** E. R. Teraa. (1993 Fall Technical Meeting Ser.: Vol. 1). 1993. pap. text ed. 30.00 (*1-55589-626-X*) AGMA.

***Spur Gear Durability Based on Critical Stress in Region of Single Tooth Contact.** AGMA Technical Committee. (Technical Papers: Vol. 102B). 1941. pap. text ed. 30.00 (*1-55589-133-0*) AGMA.

***Spur Gears - A New Approach to Tooth Design.** B. Srinivasulu. (1992 Fall Technical Meeting Ser.). 1992. pap. text ed. 30.00 (*1-55589-593-X*) AGMA.

An Asterisk (*) at the beginning of an entry indicates that the title is appearing in BIP for the first time.

Spur of Fame: Dialogues of John Adams & Benjamin Rush, 1805-1813. John Adams & Benjamin Rush. Ed. by John A. Schutz & Douglass Adair. LC 66-15694. (Huntington Library Publications). (Illus.). 321p. reprint ed. pap. 91.50 (0-7837-6684-X, 2046300) Bks Demand.

Spur-Of-The-Cock. Ed. by J. Frank Dobie. LC 34-1434. (Texas Folklore Society Publications: No. 11). 112p. 1965. reprint ed. 11.95 (0-87074-043-1) UNTX Pr.

***Spur-of-the-Moment Crafts.** Mary Davis. (Illus.). 96p. 1996. 9.95 (0-89636-327-9) Accent CO.

***Spur-of-the-Moment Games & Learning Activities.** Mary Davis. 80p. 1996. 9.95 (0-89636-328-7) Accent CO.

***Spur-of-the-Moment Marriage.** Cathy G. Thacker. 1997. mass mkt. 3.75 (0-373-16697-4, 1-16697-4) Harlequin Bks.

Spur Tracks & Buffalo Chips. Bob Schild. (Illus.). 96p. (Orig.). 1985. pap. 9.95 (0-9616569-0-5) B-B Leather.

***Spuren in die Zukunft: Zukunftsorientierte Problemlosungen auf dem Prufstand, Beitrage zum 60, Geburtstag von Carl Bohret.** Michael Hofmann et al. (Beitrage zur Politikwissenschaft Ser.: Bd. 65). 321p. (GER.). 1996. pap. 51.95 (3-631-30032-8) P Lang Pubng.

***Spurensicherung: Eine Revision.** Gunter Metken. (GER.). 1996. text ed. 18.00 (90-5705-019-6) Gordon & Breach.

Spurgeon: A New Biography. Arnold A. Dallimore. 272p. (C). 1985. reprint ed. pap. 14.99 (0-85151-451-0) Banner of Truth.

Spurgeon: The Prince of Preachers. Lewis A. Drummond. LC 92-15242. (Illus.). 950p. 1992. pap. 26.99 (0-8254-2473-9) Kregel.

Spurgeon: The Prince of Preachers. Lewis A. Drummond. LC 92-15242. (Illus.). 950p. 1992. 32.99 (0-8254-2472-0) Kregel.

Spurgeon Family. Eric W. Hayden. 1993. pap. 4.00 (1-56186-206-1) Pilgrim Pubns.

Spurgeon, Glorious Spurgeon. James A. Stewart. pap. 1.49 (1-56632-072-0) Revival Lit.

Spurgeon un Principe Olvidado. 2nd ed. Iain H. Murray. 156p. (SPA.). 1984. reprint ed. pap. 5.50 (0-85151-439-1) Banner of Truth.

Spurgeon vs. Hyper-Calvinism: The Battle for Gospel Preaching. Iain H. Murray. 164p. 1995. pap. 5.99 (0-85151-692-0) Banner of Truth.

***Spurgeon's Daily Treasures in the Psalms.** Roger Campbell. 1997. 14.99 (0-7852-7536-3) Nelson.

Spurgeon's Expository Encyclopedia: Sermons by Charles H. Spurgeon, Classified & Arranged for Ready Reference, 8 vols. Charles H. Spurgeon. (Sermon Ser.). 8p. (YA). (gr. 10). 1996. reprint ed. 300.00 (0-8010-1114-0) Baker Bks.

Spurgeon's Gold. 2nd ed. Ed. by Edmond H. Swem. 200p. 1996. reprint ed. 20.95 (1-57358-039-2) Soli Deo Gloria.

Spurgeon's Prayers. (Spurgeon Collection). 1995. 6.99 (1-85792-041-4, Pub. by Christian Focus UK) Spring Arbor Dist.

Spurgeon's Proverbs & Sayings. Charles H. Spurgeon. 720p. (YA). (gr. 10). 1996. reprint ed. 32.99 (0-8010-1107-8) Baker Bks.

Spurgeon's Sermon Illustrations. Charles H. Spurgeon. LC 90-36549. 144p. 1990. reprint ed. pap. 7.99 (0-8254-3767-9) Kregel.

***Spurgeon's Sermon Notes.** Charles H. Spurgeon. 800p. 1997. 24.95 (1-56563-304-0) Hendrickson MA.

Spurgeon's Sermon Notes. Charles H. Spurgeon. LC 90-36550. 336p. 1990. reprint ed. pap. 10.99 (0-8254-3768-7) Kregel.

Spurgeon's Sermons, 5 vols. Charles H. Spurgeon. (Illus.). 5p. (YA). (gr. 10). 1996. reprint ed. 150.00 (0-8010-1113-2) Baker Bks.

Spurgeon's Sermons on Angels. Charles H. Spurgeon. LC 95-24909. (C. H. Spurgeon Sermon Ser.). 160p. 1996. pap. 8.99 (0-8254-3690-7) Kregel.

Spurgeon's Sermons on Christmas & Easter. Charles H. Spurgeon. 160p. 1995. pap. 8.99 (0-8254-3689-3) Kregel.

Spurgeon's Sermons on Family & Home. Charles H. Spurgeon. (Spurgeon's Sermons Ser.). 160p. 1995. pap. 8.99 (0-8254-3688-5, 95-029) Kregel.

Spurgeon's Sermons on Great Prayers of the Bible. Charles H. Spurgeon. LC 95-24910. (C. H. Spurgeon Sermon Ser.). 160p. 1996. pap. 8.99 (0-8254-3691-5) Kregel.

Spurgeon's Sermons on New Testament Men, Bk. 1. Charles H. Spurgeon. 160p. 1994. pap. 8.99 (0-8254-3783-0) Kregel.

Spurgeon's Sermons on New Testament Men, Bk. 2. Charles H. Spurgeon. 160p. 1996. pap. 8.99 (0-8254-3791-1) Kregel.

Spurgeon's Sermons on New Testament Miracles. Charles H. Spurgeon et al. (Spurgeon's Sermons Ser.). 160p. 1995. pap. 8.99 (0-8254-3784-9) Kregel.

Spurgeon's Sermons on New Testament Women, Bk. 1. Charles H. Spurgeon. 160p. 1994. pap. 8.99 (0-8254-3782-2) Kregel.

Spurgeon's Sermons on New Testament Women, Bk. 2. Charles H. Spurgeon. 160p. 1996. pap. 8.99 (0-8254-3792-X) Kregel.

Spurgeon's Sermons on Old Testament Men, No. 2. Charles H. Spurgeon. 160p. 1995. pap. 8.99 (0-8254-3789-X) Kregel.

Spurgeon's Sermons on Old Testament Men Bk. 1, Bk. 1. Charles H. Spurgeon. 160p. 1993. pap. 8.99 (0-8254-3772-5) Kregel.

Spurgeon's Sermons on Old Testament Women, Bk. 1. Charles H. Spurgeon. 160p. 1993. pap. 8.99 (0-8254-3781-4) Kregel.

Spurgeon's Sermons on Old Testament Women, No. 2. Charles H. Spurgeon. (Spurgeon's Sermons Ser.: Bk. 2). 160p. 1995. pap. 8.99 (0-8254-3790-3) Kregel.

***Spurgeon's Sermons on Proverbs.** Charles H. Spurgeon. LC 96-53065. 1997. pap. 8.99 (0-8254-3794-6) Kregel.

Spurgeon's Sermons on Soul-Winning. Charles H. Spurgeon. 160p. 1995. pap. 8.99 (0-8254-3787-3) Kregel.

Spurgeon's Sermons on Special Days & Occasions. Charles H. Spurgeon. 160p. 1995. pap. 8.99 (0-8254-3786-5) Kregel.

Spurgeon's Sermons on the Cross of Christ. Charles H. Spurgeon. LC 93-13811. 160p. 1993. pap. 8.99 (0-8254-3687-7) Kregel.

Spurgeon's Sermons on the Parables of Christ. Charles H. Spurgeon. 160p. 1995. pap. 8.99 (0-8254-3785-7, 95-020) Kregel.

***Spurgeon's Sermons on the Prayers of Christ.** Charles H. Spurgeon. 1997. pap. 8.99 (0-8254-3793-8) Kregel.

Spurgeon's Sermons on the Resurrection. Charles H. Spurgeon. LC 93-13812. 160p. 1993. pap. 8.99 (0-8254-3686-9) Kregel.

Spurious & Doubtful Works. William Shakespeare. (BCL1-PR English Literature Ser.). 455p. 1992. reprint ed. lib. bdg. 99.00 (0-7812-7276-9) Rprt Serv.

Spurious Books of the Bible. Gar Baybrook. 224p. 1994. per. 9.95 (0-945383-61-4) Teach Servs.

Spurious Texts of Philo of Alexandria: A Study of Textual Transmission & Corruption with Indexes to the Major Collections of Greek Fragments. James R. Royse. (Arbeiten zur Literatur und Geschichte des Hellenistischen Judentums Ser.: No. 22). xiii, 252p. 1991. 93.00 (90-04-09511-X) E J Brill.

***SPURPLOT: Mixer Spurious-Response Analysis with Tunable Filtering - Software & User's Manual.** Robert Kyle. (Microwave Engineering Ser.). 125p. 1997. 125.00 incl. disk (0-89006-956-5) Artech Hse.

Spurr's Boatbook: Upgrading the Cruising Sailboat. 2nd ed. Daniel Spurr. (Illus.). 1993. pap. 24.95 (0-87742-411-X) Intl Marine.

Spurr's Boatbook: Upgrading the Cruising Sailboat. 2nd ed. Daniel Spurr. 1993. pap. text ed. 24.95 (0-07-060554-8) McGraw.

Spurs: Nietzsche's Styles. Jacques Derrida. Tr. by Barbara Harlow from FRE. LC 79-31. vi, 172p. (C). 1981. reprint ed. pap. text ed. 8.95 (0-226-14333-3) U Ch Pr.

Spurs West. Western Writers of America Staff. LC 70-113692. (Short Story Index Reprint Ser.). 1977. 24.95 (0-8369-3421-0) Ayer.

Sputnik & Other Poems. Ulick O'Connor. (Orig.). pap. 4.95 (0-8159-6822-1) Devin.

Sputnik Rock & Roll: Cincinnati Rockabilly & Country Performers of the 1950s. Gene Johnston. (Labels of History Ser.). (Illus.). 54p. 1995. spiral bd. 14.95 (0-940152-06-1, HHP Bks) Hamilton Hobby.

Sputniks Crisis & Early United States Space Policy: A Critique of the Historiography of Space. Rip Bulkeley. LC 90-46786. 304p. 1991. 12.95 (0-253-31281-7) Ind U Pr.

Sputtering by Particle Bombardment III: Characteristics of Sputtered Particles, Technical Applications. Ed. by K. Wittmaack et al. (Illus.). xv, 410p. 1991. 107.95 (0-387-53428-8) Spr-Verlag.

Spy. James Fenimore Cooper. 1976. lib. bdg. 28.95 (0-89968-161-1, Lghtyr Pr) Buccaneer Bks.

Spy. James Fenimore Cooper. Ed. by James H. Pickering. (Masterworks of Literature Ser.). 1971. pap. 17.95 (0-8084-0027-4) NCUP.

***Spy.** James Fenimore Cooper. LC 97-12074. 1997. pap. 12.95 (0-14-043628-6) Viking Penguin.

Spy. Richard Platt. LC 96-11003. (Eyewitness Bks.). (J). 1996. 19.00 (0-679-88122-0) Knopf.

Spy. Richard Platt. LC 96-11003. (Eyewitness Bks.). (J). 1996. lib. bdg. 20.99 (0-679-98122-5) Knopf.

***Spy.** unabridged ed. James Fenimore Cooper. 250p. 1997. reprint ed. pap. 14.95 (1-57002-045-0) Univ Publng Hse.

Spy. James Fenimore Cooper. (Works of James Fenimore Cooper Ser.). 1990. reprint ed. lib. bdg. 79.00 (0-7812-2370-9) Rprt Serv.

Spy & Thriller Guide. Stone. LC 96-40454. 1997. 45.00 (0-8161-1800-0, Hall Library) G K Hall.

Spy at Ticonderoga. 2nd rev. ed. Clavin Fisher. LC 96-68290. (Illus.). 144p. (J). (gr. 3-6). 1996. pap. 6.95 (0-9651667-0-8) Simsbry Hist.

Spy at Twilight. Bryan Forbes. 448p. 1991. reprint ed. pap. 5.99 (0-451-40263-4, Onyx) NAL-Dutton.

Spy Book. Norman Polmar & Thomas B. Allen. 1996. 30.00 (0-614-96930-1, Random Ref) Random.

Spy Book: The Encyclopedia of Espionage. Norman Polmer & Thomas B. Allen. 608p. 1996. 30.00 (0-679-42514-4) Random.

Spy Catchers of the U. S. Army: The Story of the Counter Intelligence Corps in the War with Japan. Duval A. Edwards. LC 93-87777. 250p. 1994. 17.00 (1-880222-14-0) Red Apple Pub.

Spy Code Caper. Susan Pearson. (Eagle-Eye Ernie Mysteries Ser.). (Illus.). 64p. (J). (gr. 1-3). 1991. pap. 12.00 (0-671-74071-7, S&S Bks Young Read) S&S Childrens.

Spy Craft: The Great Game Guide. James Adams. (Illus.). 300p. (Orig.). 1996. pap. 19.99 (1-56686-425-9) Brady Pub.

Spy Development, 1985. Ed. & Tr. by Robert C. Sandness. (Orig.). 1997. pap. 8.50 (0-9614076-0-3) Sandness.

Spy Development, 1985. limited ed. Ed. & Tr. by Robert C. Sandness. (Orig.). 1997. write for info. (0-9614076-2-X) Sandness.

Spy Fiction, Spy Films & Real Intelligence. Ed. by Wesley K. Wark. 225p. 1991. text ed. 27.50 (0-7146-3411-5, Pub. by F Cass Pubs UK) Intl Spec Bk.

***Spy File Organizer.** (FunFax Spy Ser.). (Illus.). 80p. (J). (gr. 3-9). 1996. pap. 8.95 (0-7894-0740-X) DK Pub Inc.

***Spy Flights of the Cold War.** Paul Lashmar. (Illus.). 256p. 1997. 29.95 (1-55750-837-2) Naval Inst Pr.

Spy for a Spy: A Mystery Jigsaw Puzzle. Karen L. Richardson. (BePuzzled Ser.). (C). 1989. 20.00 (0-922242-44-5) Bepuzzled.

Spy for All Seasons. Duane R. Clarridge. 1997. 27.50 (0-684-80068-3) S&S Trade.

Spy for Hannibal: A Novel of Carthage. Elisabeth R. Craft. LC 95-13835. 290p. 1996. 21.95 (0-910155-33-X) Bartleby Pr.

Spy for the Night Riders. Dave Jackson & Neta Jackson. (Trailblazer Bks.: Vol. 3). 128p. (J). (gr. 3-8). 1992. pap. 5.99 (1-55661-237-0) Bethany Hse.

***Spy from Israel.** Dan. Date not set. pap. 12.50 (0-85303-015-4, Pub. by Vallentine Mitchell UK) Intl Spec Bk.

Spy Game. John McNeil. 1982. mass mkt. 2.95 (0-686-97470-0, Zebra Kensgtn) Kensgtn Pub Corp.

***Spy Game: Espionage for Fun & Profit.** Victor Ostrovsky. 250p. 1997. 24.95 (0-89526-424-2, Gateway Editions) Regnery Pub.

***Spy Girl.** Created by Francine Pascal. (Sweet Valley University Ser.: No. 34). 240p. (Orig.). (YA). (gr. 9 up). 1997. mass mkt. 3.99 (0-553-57058-7) BDD Bks Young Read.

Spy Hook. Len Deighton. 352p. 1990. mass mkt. 5.99 (0-345-36520-8) Ballantine.

***Spy Hook.** Len Deighton. 1997. pap. 12.00 (0-345-42016-0) Ballantine.

Spy Hook. large type ed. Len Deighton. LC 89-4673. 454p. 1990. pap. 14.95 (0-89621-943-7) Thorndike Pr.

Spy in a Catcher's Mask. Kurt Willinger. LC 95-1867. 282p. 1995. 19.95 (1-879094-45-2, Sabre Pr); pap. 12.95 (1-879094-44-4, Sabre Pr) Momentum Bks.

***Spy in Camera.** large type ed. Richard Grayson. (Linford Mystery Large Print Ser.). 400p. 1997. pap. 16.99 (0-7089-5096-5, Linford) Ulverscroft.

Spy in Canaan: My Life As a Jewish American Businessman Who Spied for Israel in Arab Lands. Howard H. Schack & H. Paul Jeffers. LC 92-21113. 1993. 19.95 (1-55972-178-2, Birch Ln Pr) Carol Pub Group.

Spy in Canaan: My Secret Life As a Jewish-American Businessman Spying for Israel in Arab Lands. large type ed. Howard H. Schack & Paul H. Jeffers. LC 93-39260. 1994. lib. bdg. 18.95 (0-7862-0119-3) Thorndike Pr.

Spy in My Mouth. (J). Date not set. pap. 2.50 (0-590-40444-X) Scholastic Inc.

Spy in Petticoats. large type ed. Katrina Wright. (Linford Romance Library). 208p. 1993. pap. 15.99 (0-7089-7328-0, Linford) Ulverscroft.

Spy in Question. Amanda K. Williams. (Madison McGuire Novel Ser.). 234p. 1993. pap. 9.95 (1-56280-037-X) Naiad Pr.

Spy in Question. large type ed. Tim Sebastian. 1989. 25.99 (0-7089-2095-0) Ulverscroft.

***Spy in the Attic.** Ursel Scheffler. LC 96-44510. (Illus.). 64p. (J). (gr. 2-4). 1997. 13.95 (1-55858-727-6); lib. bdg. 13.88 (1-55858-728-4) North-South Bks NYC.

Spy in the Enemy's Country: The Emergence of Modern Black Literature. Donald A. Petesch. LC 88-37391. 299p. 1989. reprint ed. pap. 12.95 (0-87745-322-5) U of Iowa Pr.

Spy in the House of Love. Anais Nin. LC 66-6833. 140p. 1959. pap. 8.95 (0-8040-0280-0) Swallow.

Spy in the House of Love. Anais Nin. Ed. by Julie Rubenstein. 176p. 1994. reprint ed. mass mkt. 5.50 (0-671-87139-0) PB.

Spy in the King's Colony. Lisa Banim. (Mysteries in Time Ser.). (Illus.). 80p. (J). (gr. 4-6). 1994. lib. bdg. 13.95 (1-881889-54-8) Silver Moon.

Spy in the King's Colony see Spy in the King's Colony; A Thief on Morgan's Plantation; An Art Bandit on Sugar Hill; A Conspiracy in Washington

Spy in the King's Colony; A Thief on Morgan's Plantation; An Art Bandit on Sugar Hill; A Conspiracy in Washington. Bd. with Spy in the King's Colony. (J). (gr. 4-6).; Thief on Morgan's Plantation. (Illus.). (J). (gr. 4-6).; Art Bandit on Sugar Hill. (Illus.). (J). (gr. 4-6).; Conspiracy in Wilmington. (Illus.). (J). (gr. 4-6). (Mysteries in Time Ser.). 51.80 (1-881889-78-5) Silver Moon.

Spy in the Russian Club. Ronald Kessler. Ed. by Paul McCarthy. 272p. 1992. reprint ed. mass mkt. 5.99 (0-671-73890-9) PB.

Spy in the Sky. Kathleen Karr. LC 96-45073. 64p. (J). (gr. 3). 1997. pap. 3.95 (0-7868-1165-X); lib. bdg. 13.89 (0-7868-2239-2) Hyprn Child.

Spy in the Vatican. Branko Bokun. 224p. (Orig.). 1988. pap. 9.95 (0-9510525-2-7) Riverrun NY.

Spy in Their Midst: The World War II Struggle of a Japanese-American Hero. Wayne S. Kiyosaki. LC 94-46954. 1995. 22.95 (1-56833-044-8) Rowman.

Spy is Dead. large type ed. Terrence Kelly. (Adventure Suspense Ser.). 464p. 1992. 25.99 (0-7089-2772-6) Ulverscroft.

Spy Line. Len Deighton. 1989. 18.95 (0-394-55179-6) Knopf.

***Spy Line.** Len Deighton. 1997. pap. 12.00 (0-345-42017-9) Ballantine.

Spy Line. large type ed. Len Deighton. 1990. reprint ed. pap. 15.95 (0-89621-983-6) Thorndike Pr.

Spy Line. Len Deighton. 336p. 1991. reprint ed. mass mkt. 5.99 (0-345-37006-6) Ballantine.

Spy Machine. Esther A. Peterson. LC 94-72207. 64p. (J). (gr. 4-7). 1994. pap. 3.99 (0-8066-2719-0, Augsburg) Augsburg Fortress.

***Spy of the Rebellion: Being a True History of the Spy System of the United States Army During the Late Rebellion, Revealing Many Secrets of the War Hitherto Not Made Public.** Allan Pinkerton. LC 89-33081. 680p. 1989. reprint ed. pap. 180.00 (0-608-02670-0, 2063323) Bks Demand.

***Spy on the Roof of the World.** Sydney Wignall. LC 96-47350. (Illus.). 288p. 1997. reprint ed. 25.00 (1-55821-558-1) Lyons & Burford.

Spy on Third Base. Matt Christopher. LC 88-8914. (Springboard Bks.). (Illus.). (J). (gr. 2-4). 1988. 12.95 (0-316-13996-3) Little.

Spy on Third Base, Vol. 1. Matt Christopher. (J). (ps-3). 1990. mass mkt. 3.95 (0-316-14008-2) Little.

Spy Overhead: The Story of Industrial Espionage. Clinch Calkins. LC 70-156408. (American Labor Ser., No. 2). 1975. reprint ed. 35.95 (0-405-02917-9) Ayer.

Spy Paramount. E. Phillips Oppenheim. reprint ed. lib. bdg. 23.95 (0-89190-414-X, Rivercity Pr) Amereon Ltd.

Spy Planes. David Baker. (Military Aircraft Library). (Illus.). 48p. (J). (gr. 3-8). 1987. lib. bdg. 18.60 (0-86592-353-1); lib. bdg. 13.95 (0-685-67592-0) Rourke Corp.

Spy Planes. Jay Schleifer. (Wings Ser.). (Illus.). 48p. (J). (gr. 3-9). 1996. 17.80 (1-56065-302-7) Capstone Pr.

Spy Planes. Jay Schleifer. (Illus.). 48p. (J). (gr. 3-7). 1995. 13.35 (0-516-35302-0) Childrens.

Spy Science: 40 Secret-Sleuthing, Code-Cracking, Spy-Catching Activities for Kids. Jim Wiese. LC 96-7019. (Illus.). 128p. (J). (gr. 3-7). 1996. pap. text ed. 12.95 (0-471-14620-X) Wiley.

Spy Shadow. large type ed. Tim Sebastian. 1991. 25.99 (0-7089-2414-X) Ulverscroft.

Spy Sinker. Len Deighton. 448p. 1991. mass mkt. 5.99 (0-06-109928-7, Harp PBks) HarpC.

Spy Sinker. large type ed. Len Deighton. LC 90-29907. 556p. 1991. reprint ed. lib. bdg. 22.95 (1-56054-121-0) Thorndike Pr.

Spy Sinker. large type ed. Len Deighton. LC 90-29907. 556p. 1991. pap. 16.95 (1-56054-992-0) Thorndike Pr.

Spy Story. John G. Cawelti & Bruce A. Rosenberg. LC 86-30716. x, 272p. 1987. 27.00 (0-226-09868-0) U Ch Pr.

Spy Story. Len Deighton. 272p. 1985. mass mkt. 4.95 (0-345-31569-3) Ballantine.

Spy Story. Len Deighton. 304p. 1991. mass mkt. 5.50 (0-06-100265-8, Harp PBks) HarpC.

***Spy Sub.** Roger Dunham. 1997. mass mkt. 5.99 (0-451-40797-0, Onyx) NAL-Dutton.

Spy Sub: A Top Secret Mission to the Bottom of the Pacific. Roger C. Dunham. (Illus.). 256p. 1996. 27.95 (1-55750-178-5) Naval Inst Pr.

Spy System of Soviet Russia: From Their Very Beginning to the Present Day. Joseph D. Lowe. LC 90-91681. (Illus.). xxvi, 560p. 1994. text ed. 90.00 (0-930325-16-8) Lowe Pub.

Spy-Tech. Graham Yost. LC 84-13769. (Illus.). 302p. reprint ed. pap. 86.10 (0-7837-1566-8, 2041858) Bks Demand.

Spy Thrillers: From Buchan to le Carre. Ed. by Clive Bloom. LC 89-49608. 200p. 1991. text ed. 39.95 (0-312-04245-0) St Martin.

Spy vs. Spy. Ronald Kessler. 384p. 1989. mass mkt. 5.99 (0-671-67967-8) PB.

Spy Wars. Tom Bower. Date not set. pap. write for info. (0-670-84886-7) Viking Penguin.

Spy Wednesday's Kind. Francis Sullivan. LC 79-65678. 108p. (Orig.). 1979. pap. 6.00 (0-912292-60-1) Smith.

Spy Went Dancing. Aline Countess of Romanones. 1991. mass mkt. 5.95 (0-515-10507-4) Jove Pubns.

Spy Who Came In From the Cold. John Le Carre. 1992. mass mkt. 6.99 (0-345-37737-0) Ballantine.

***Spy Who Came in from the Cold.** John Le Carre. 1997. pap. 12.00 (0-345-41833-6) Ballantine.

Spy Who Came in from the Cold, 2 cassettes, Set. (Read-Along Ser.). (YA). 1985. student ed., pap. 34.95 incl. audio (0-88432-970-4, S23911) Audio-Forum.

Spy Who Came in from the Cold, 2 vols., Set. large type ed. John Le Carre. (YA). (gr. 10-12). reprint ed. 10.00 (0-89064-058-0) NAVH.

Spy Who Came in from the Cold Notes. Franz G. Blaha. (Cliffs Notes Ser.). 59p. (Orig.). 1993. pap. 4.25 (0-8220-1221-9) Cliffs.

Spy Who Came in with the Gold. Henry A. Zeiger. 19.95 (0-8488-0355-8) Amereon Ltd.

Spy Who Came North from the Pole. Mary E. Monsell. Ed. by Alexandria Childs. (Mr. Rogers' First Experience Bks.: Vol. III). 64p. 1995. pap. 3.50 (0-671-88399-2, Minstrel Bks) PB.

Spy Who Came North from the Pole: Mr. Pin, Vol. 3. Mary E. Monsell. LC 92-24646. (Mr. Pin Ser.: Vol. 3). (Illus.). 64p. (J). (gr. 1-4). 1993. lib. bdg. 12.95 (0-689-31754-9, Atheneum Bks Young) S&S Childrens.

Spy Who Drank Blood. Gordon Linzner. LC 84-14127. 144p. (Orig.). 1984. pap. 5.95 (0-917053-01-X) Space And.

Spy Who Got Away. David Wise. 320p. 1989. mass mkt. 4.95 (0-380-70772-1) Avon.

Spy Who Knew Too Much: The Government Plot to Silence Jonathan Pollard. Elliot Goldenberg. 1993. pap. 5.50 (1-56171-230-2, S P I Bks) Sure Seller.

***Spy Who Loved Children: The Enigma of Herbert Dyce Murphy.** Moira Watson. (Illus.). 184p. 1997. pap. 17.95 (0-522-84767-6, Pub. by Melbourne Univ Pr AT) Paul & Co Pubs.

Spy Who Loved Her. Sheryl Danson. (Temptation Ser.). 1994. mass mkt. 2.99 (0-373-25579-9, 1-25579-3) Harlequin Bks.

Spy Who Loved Me. Ian Fleming. (FRE.). pap. 9.95 (0-685-11575-5) Fr & Eur.

Spy Who Loved Me. Ian Fleming. (James Bond Ser.). 1995. 6.98 (1-56731-052-4, MJF Bks) Fine Comms.

Spy Who Saved the World: How a Soviet Colonel Changed the Course of the Cold War. Jerrold L. Schecter & Peter S. Deriabin. (Intelligence & National Security Library). (Illus.). 506p. 1996. reprint ed. pap. 21.95 (1-57488-046-2) Brasseys Inc.

S

An Asterisk (*) at the beginning of an entry indicates that the title is appearing in BIP for the first time.

Spy Wore Red. Aline Countess of Romanones. 1990. mass mkt. 5.99 (*0-515-10653-4*) Jove Pubns.
Spy Wore Red: My Adventures As an Undercover Agent in World War II. Aline - Countess of Romanones. LC 86-29644. 288p. 1987. 18.95 (*0-394-55665-8*) Random.
Spy Wore Silk. Aline Countess of Romanones. 1992. mass mkt. 5.99 (*0-515-10876-6*) Jove Pubns.
Spycomm: Covert Communication Techniques of the Underground. Lawrence W. Myers. (Illus.). 256p. 1991. pap. 19.95 (*0-87364-643-6*) Paladin Pr.

***Spyder Web. Tom Grace. LC 96-93029. 305p. 1997. 24.95 (*0-9656040-0-4*) Seanachaoi Pr.**
For Western intelligence agencies, industrial espionage has grown into the single largest threat to a nation's economic security - eclipsing both military & political espionage. Adding to the difficulty in dealing with this dangerous trend, the Chinese takeover of Hong Kong has created an intelligence blind spot for the West at a time when the PRC is emerging as a dominant player on the world stage. The CIAs response to the loss of agents in China is an ambitious project, code-named SPYDER. Nolan Kilkenny knew nothing of these secret worlds when he returned home, to Ann Arbor, to pursue a doctorate. Nor did he suspect that his new job, tending the computers at the Michigan Applied Research Consortium, would place him in the center of a world wide web of intrigue. For the decorated former SEAL, an apparently harmless technical problem rapidly unravels into lethal situation. Kilkenny's efforts to isolate an unusual signal, buried deep within MARCs network put him on the trail & in the sites of a ruthless trio of information age pirates. Blending an intimate knowledge of high-tech research with powerful characters & riveting suspense, SPYDER WEB grips the reader from its opening sentence to its explosive climax. ISBN 0- 9656040-0-4. ***Publisher Provided Annotation.***

Spyglass: An Autobiography. Helene Deschamps-Adams. LC 94-39233. (YA). (gr. 7 up). 1995. 16.95 (*0-8050-3536-2*) H Holt & Co.
Spyglass Tree. Albert Murray. LC 92-50077. 1992. pap. 12.00 (*0-679-73085-0*, Vin) Random.
Spying Electronically: A Manual. 1991. lib. bdg. 79.95 (*0-8490-4767-6*) Gordon Pr.
***Spying for America: The Hidden History of U. S. Intelligence.** 2nd ed. Nathan Miller. 1997. pap. text ed. 14.95 (*1-56924-721-8*) Marlowe & Co.
Spying in Guru Land: Inside Britain's Cults. William Shaw. 224p. 1995. 34.95 (*1-85702-152-5*, Pub. by Fourth Estate UK) Trafalgar.
***Spying in Guru Land: Inside Britain's Cults.** William Shaw. 215p. 1996. reprint ed. pap. 14.95 (*1-85702-329-3*) Trafalgar.
Spying on America: The FBI's Domestic Counterintelligence Program. James K. Davis. LC 91-23131. 208p. 1992. text ed. 35.00 (*0-275-93407-1*, C3407, Praeger Pubs) Greenwood.
Spying on Miss Muller. Eve Bunting. LC 94-15003. (J). 1995. 14.95 (*0-395-69172-9*, Clarion Bks) HM.
Spying on Miss Muller. Eve Bunting. 1996. mass mkt. 4.50 (*0-449-70455-6*) Fawcett.
***Spying on Your Spouse: Guide for Anyone Who Suspects a Partner Is Cheating.** Kelly Squires. 1996. pap. text ed. 9.95 (*0-8065-1810-3*, Citadel Pr) Carol Pub Group.
Spying Without Spies: Origins of America's Secret Nuclear Surveillance System. Charles A. Ziegler & David Jacobson. LC 94-33263. 256p. 1995. text ed. 49.95 (*0-275-95049-2*, Praeger Pubs) Greenwood.
Spymaster: The Real-Life Karla, His Moles & the East German Secret Police. Leslie R. Colitt. LC 95-25065. 304p. 1995. 23.00 (*0-201-40738-8*) Addison-Wesley.
Spy's London: A Walk Book of One Hundred Thirty-Six Sites in Central London Relating to Spies, Spycatchers, & Subversives from More Than a Century of London's Secret History. Roy Berkeley. (Illus.). 192p. 1994. pap. 29.50 (*0-85052-113-0*, Pub. by L Cooper Bks UK) Trans-Atl Phila.
Spy's Workshop: America's Clandestine Weapons. Don McLean. (Illus.). 288p. 1989. pap. 30.00 (*0-87364-512-X*) Paladin Pr.
SQC-SPC Manufacturing Experiences. Ed. by T. Drozda. LC 89-61109. 275p. 1989. 44.00 (*0-87263-362-4*) SME.
SQL: DS Performance. Dov Gilor. 325p. 1991. text ed. 49.95 (*0-471-52624-X*) Wiley.
SQL: Self Teaching Guide. Peter Stephenson. LC 92-7098. 240p. 1992. pap. text ed. 24.95 (*0-471-54544-9*) Wiley.
SQL: The Standard Handbook. Stephen J. Cannan & Gerard A. Otten. LC 92-28176. 1992. 29.95 (*0-07-707664-8*) McGraw.
SQL & Relational Databases. Soren Vang. Ed. by Lance A. Leventhal. LC 90-53257. (Lance A. Leventhal Microtrend Ser.). 350p. (Orig.). 1990. pap. 24.95 (*0-915391-42-2*, Microtrend) Slawson Comm.
SQL Applications Programming. Nicolas Nierenberg. (Illus.). 304p. (Orig.). 1989. pap. 21.95 (*0-8306-3214-X*, Windcrest) TAB Bks.
SQL-Based Fourth Generation Languages. George Feuerlicht. 1991. text ed. 54.80 (*0-13-840067-9*) P-H.
***SQL Developer's Guide.** Hans Ladanyi. 1997. 59.99 (*0-672-31133-X*) Macmillan.
SQL for DB2 & SQL-DS Application Developers. Jonathan S. Sayles. 473p. 1993. pap. text ed. 39.95 (*0-471-58813-X*) Wiley.
SQL for Dummies. Allen G. Taylor. 400p. 1995. pap. 19.99 (*1-56884-336-4*) IDG Bks.
***SQL for Dummies.** 2nd ed. Allen G. Taylor. 400p. 1997. pap. 24.99 (*0-7645-0105-4*) IDG Bks.
SQL Guide for dBase IV. Van. (C). 1991. text ed. 32.95 (*0-201-54410-5*) Addison-Wesley.
SQL Guide for Oracle. Rick Van Der Lans. (C). 1992. pap. text ed. 36.75 (*0-201-56545-5*) Addison-Wesley.
SQL-I Training Manual. Revelation Technologies Staff. 90p. 1990. 50.00 (*0-923387-39-0*) Rev Tech Inc.
SQL Instant Reference. Martin Gruber. LC 93-84817. 350p. 1993. 14.95 (*0-7821-1148-3*) Sybex.
SQL Programming. Steven Feuerstein. Ed. by Deborah Russell. (Illus.). (Orig.). 1995. pap. 44.95 (*1-56592-142-9*) OReilly & Assocs.
SQL Server Handbook: A Guide to Microsoft Database Computing. Ken England & Nigel Stanley. LC 95-71210. 480p. 1996. pap. 36.95 (*1-55558-152-8*, QA76.73, Digital DEC) Buttrwrth-Heinemann.
***SQL Server 6.5 Performance Optimization & Tuning Handbook.** Ken England. LC 97-10627. 1997. pap. write for info. (*1-55558-180-3*, Digital DEC) Buttrwrth-Heinemann.
SQL Server 6.5 Secrets. David K. Rensin. 1996. pap. 44.99 (*1-56884-698-3*) IDG Bks.
***SQL Server 7.0 Bible.** Arthur Knowles. 1998. pap. 49.99 (*0-7645-3161-1*) IDG Bks.
SQL Solutions for IBM DBMSS. Bruce L. Larson. 1991. text ed. 49.95 (*0-442-00119-3*) Van Nos Reinhold.
SQL 400: A Professional Programmer's Guide. Tim Martyn et al. 1995. text ed. 45.00 (*0-07-040799-1*) McGraw.
Squad: The U.S. Government's Secret Alliance with Organized Crime. Michael Milan. (Illus.). 1989. 19.95 (*0-933503-36-9*) Sure Seller.
Squad Leader. Bobby Owens. LC 93-93623. 147p. 1993. pap. text ed. 25.00 (*1-884308-05-8*); pap. text ed. 14.95 (*1-884308-06-6*) Enlisted Ldrship.
Squaddies. Robert V. Hockey. 192p. 1986. pap. text ed. 25.00 (*0-85989-248-4*) Northwestern U Pr.
***Squadron.** Spencer Dunmore. 1996. mass mkt. 6.99 (*0-7710-2919-5*) McCland & Stewart.
Squadron Alert. Roland J. Green. (Starcruiser Shenandoah Ser.: No. 1). 320p. 1989. pap. 4.99 (*0-451-16156-4*, Sig) NAL-Dutton.
Squadron Ninety-Five. Harold Buckley. LC 78-169409. (Literature & History of Aviation Ser.). 1972. reprint ed. 25.95 (*0-405-03754-6*) Ayer.
Squadron Supreme: Death - Universe. Ryan et al. 80p. 1989. 9.95 (*0-87135-598-1*) Marvel Entmnt.
Squall Across the Atlantic: American Civil War Prize Cases & Diplomacy. Stuart L. Bernath. LC 76-79042. 239p. reprint ed. pap. 68.20 (*0-318-34910-8*, 2031425) Bks Demand.
Squall Line. Judy Collins. 44p. (Orig.). 1995. pap. write for info. (*0-936563-17-6*) Signpost.
Squall Line. James Magorian. LC 85-73614. 52p. 1986. pap. 3.00 (*0-930674-19-7*) Black Oak.
***Squamish/Skaha.** Laird Davis. (Classic Rock Climbs Ser.). (Illus.). (Orig.). 1997. pap. 10.95 (*1-57540-049-9*) Chockstone Pr.
***Squandered Computer.** unabridged ed. Ed. by Paul A. Strassmann. (Business Alignment of Information Technologies Ser.). (Illus.). 460p. 1997. 49.00 (*0-9620413-1-9*) Info Econ Pr.
Squandered Fortune. Lisa R. Gubernick. 328p. 1992. mass mkt. 5.50 (*0-380-71724-7*) Avon.
Squandered Victory: The American First Army at St. Mihiel. James H. Hallas. LC 94-21060. 320p. 1995. text ed. 55.00 (*0-275-95022-0*, Praeger Pubs) Greenwood.
Squanicook Eclogues. Melissa Green. 1988. pap. 7.95 (*0-393-30495-7*) Norton.
Squanto. rev. ed. James R. Rothaus. (We the People Ser.). (J). (gr. 2-4). 1987. lib. bdg. 14.95 (*0-88682-161-4*) Creative Ed.
Squanto. Feenie Ziner. LC 88-13982. ix, 158p. (YA). (gr. 7 up). 1988. reprint ed. pap. 15.00 (*0-208-02274-0*, Linnet Bks) Shoe String.
Squanto: A Warrior's Tale. Ron Fontes & Justine Korman. LC 93-48122. (Illus.). 32p. (J). (gr. k-3). 1994. pap. 3.50 (*0-8167-2502-0*) Troll Communs.
***Squanto: First Friend to the Pilgrims.** Cathy E. Dubowski. LC 96-30712. (Famous Lives Ser.). (Illus.). 100p. (J). (gr. 3 up). 1997. lib. bdg. 19.93 (*0-8368-1474-6*) Gareth Stevens Inc.
Squanto, a Warrior's Tale Picture Book. Ron Fontes. (Illus.). (J). (ps-3). 1996. pap. 2.95 (*0-8167-3535-2*) Troll Communs.
Squanto & the First Thanksgiving. Teresa N. Celsi. (Real Readers Ser.: Level Red). (Illus.). 32p. (J). (gr. 1-4). 1989. lib. bdg. 21.40 (*0-8172-3511-6*) Raintree Steck-V.
Squanto & the First Thanksgiving. Teresa N. Celsi. (Real Readers Ser.: Level Red). (Illus.). 32p. (J). (gr. 1-4). 1989. pap. 4.95 (*0-8114-6710-4*) Raintree Steck-V.
Squanto & the First Thanksgiving. Joyce K. Kessel. LC 82-10313. (Carolrhoda On My Own Bks.). (Illus.). 48p. (J). (gr. k-3). 1983. pap. 5.95 (*0-87614-452-0*, Carolrhoda); lib. bdg. 13.13 (*0-87614-199-8*, Carolrhoda) Lerner Group.
Squanto & the First Thanksgiving. Rabbit. 1996. pap. 19.95 (*0-689-80234-X*) Macmillan.
Squanto, Friend of the Pilgrims. Clyde R. Bulla. 112p. (J). 1990. pap. 3.50 (*0-590-44055-1*) Scholastic Inc.
Squanto, the Pilgrim Adventure. Kate Jassem. LC 78-18042. (Illus.). 48p. (J). (gr. 4-6). 1979. lib. bdg. 11.89 (*0-89375-161-8*) Troll Communs.
Squanto, the Pilgrim Adventure. Kate Jassem. LC 78-18042. (Illus.). 48p. (J). (gr. 4-6). 1997. pap. 3.50 (*0-89375-151-0*) Troll Communs.
Squantum, in the State of Massachusetts. Ed. by H. Hobart Holly. (Illus.). 72p. 1992. 20.00 (*0-88492-051-8*) W S Sullwold.
Square. Marguerite Duras. (FRE.). 1990. pap. 10.95 (*0-8288-3642-6*, F42630) Fr & Eur.
Square. Marguerite Duras. Ed. by Claude M. Begue. 1965. pap. text ed. write for info. (*0-685-16005-X*) Macmillan.
Square. Marguerite Duras. (Folio Ser.: No. 2158). (FRE.). 1990. pap. 6.95 (*2-07-038224-9*) Schoenhof.
***Square & Slant Fatigue Crack Growth in Al 2024.** Jan Zuidema. (Illus.). ix, 177p. (Orig.). 1995. pap. 59.50 (*90-407-1191-7*, Pub. by Delft U Pr NE) Coronet Bks.
Square Beak. Chyng F. Sun. LC 92-19093. (Illus.). 40p. (J). (gr. k-3). 1993. 13.95 (*0-395-64567-0*) HM.
Square Ben Drew see Circle Sarah Drew
Square Dance: Fancy Quilts from Plain Squares. Martha Thompson. LC 95-38723. 1995. pap. 16.95 (*1-56477-121-0*, B238) That Patchwork.
Square Dance & Contra Dance Handbook: Calls, Dance Movements, Music, Glossary, Bibliography, Discography, & Directories. Margot Gunzenhauser. LC 92-56646. (Illus.). 320p. 1996. pap. 30.00 (*0-89950-855-3*) McFarland & Co.
Square Dance Saturday Night: Music & Figures for Traditional Square Dances. 1991. lib. bdg. 79.95 (*0-8490-5187-8*) Gordon Pr.
Square Dances of Today, & How to Teach & Call Them. Richard G. Kraus. LC 50-10717. 134p. reprint ed. pap. 38.20 (*0-317-28453-3*, 2055152) Bks Demand.
Square Dancing in the Ice Age. Abbie Hoffman. LC 81-19174. 250p. 1982. reprint ed. pap. 8.00 (*0-89608-194-X*) South End Pr.
Square Deal. David Drake. 224p. (Orig.). 1992. pap. 8.99 (*0-8125-1989-2*) Tor Bks.
Square Deal. David Drake. 224p. (Orig.). 1993. mass mkt. 4.99 (*0-8125-3030-6*) Tor Bks.
Square Feet: The Autobiography of Jack Rose. Jack Rose & M. Phil. 160p. 1993. pap. 59.00 (*0-85406-565-2*, Pub. by R-I-C-S Bks UK) St Mut.
Square Foot Estimating. 2nd ed. Bill J. Cox & F. William Horsley. 1996. boxed 67.95 (*0-87629-418-2*, 67145A) ACMDG Co.
Square Halo & Other Mysteries in Art: Images & the Stories That Inspired Them. Sally Fisher. LC 94-48284. 1995. write for info. (*0-8109-2621-0*) Abrams.
Square Halo & Other Mysteries of Western Art: Images & the Stories That Inspired Them. Sally Fisher. LC 94-48284. (Illus.). 176p. 1995. 29.95 (*0-8109-4463-4*) Abrams.
Square John: The Story of Ex-Con Tony McGilvary & the HELP Program. Marlene Webber & Tony McGilvary. 1988. 14.95 (*0-8020-6687-9*) U of Toronto Pr.
Square Meals: Taste Thrills of Only Yesterday-From Mom's Best Pot Roast & Tuna Noodle Casserole to the Perfect Tea Time Chocolate Bread. Jane Stern & Michael Stern. LC 84-47527. (Illus.). 1984. 17.95 (*0-394-53112-4*) Knopf.
Square Meets Circle: A Love Story. Shelley. (Illus.). 1992. 5.95 (*965-229-072-6*, Pub. by Gefen Pub Hse IS) Gefen Bks.
Square Meter Construction Costs: For Mexico & South America/Bilingual. 10th ed. Leopoldo Varela. Orig. Title: Costos Por Metro Cuadrado De Construccion. (Illus.). 207p. (Orig.). (ENG & SPA.). 1996. pap. 145.00 (*968-7585-00-5*, Pub. by Bimsa Southam MX) ACMDG Co.
***Square of Sevens.** 3rd ed. Robert Antrobus. Ed. by E. Irenaeus Stevenson. (Astro-Cards Reprints Ser.). 97p. 1996. reprint ed. pap. text ed. 13.00 (*1-885500-07-6*, AR5) Astro-Cards.
Square One. C. G. Donahue. 1995. 8.95 (*0-533-11130-7*) Vantage.
Square One. Steve Tesich. Ed. by Glenn Young. 160p. 1990. pap. 7.95 (*1-55783-076-2*) Applause Theatre Bk Pubs.
Square One: A Chess Drill Book for Beginners. Bruce Pandolfini. LC 94-17956. 1994. pap. 12.00 (*0-671-88424-7*, Fireside) S&S Trade.
Square Peg: A Tight Fit in a Tin Can. Jesse E. Pond, Jr. Ed. by Lilja B. Powell. LC 92-85443. 208p. (Orig.). 1992. pap. 19.95 (*0-9634347-0-5*) Pearl Harbor Hist.
Square Peg for a Round Hole. J. W. Hughes. 444p. 1993. text ed. 30.00 (*0-9639503-0-4*) J W Hughes.
Square Peg in a Round Hole: Coping with Learning Differences at Home, in School & at Work. Jimmie Shreve. 450p. (Orig.). 1993. pap. 35.00 (*0-9639421-0-7*) Sq Peg Enter.
Square Pegs, Round Holes: The Learning-Disabled Child in the Classroom & at Home. Harold B. Levy. LC 73-3422. (Illus.). 288p. 1974. 8.95 (*0-316-52232-5*) Little.
Square Persimmon & Other Stories. Takashi Atoda. Tr. by Millicent Horton. LC 89-51723. 180p. (Orig.). 1991. 12.95 (*0-8048-1678-6*) C E Tuttle.
Square Riggers in the United States & Canada: A Current Directory of Sailing Ships. Dana T. Parker. Ed. by Marion Harris. LC 94-4536. (Illus.). 72p. 1994. pap. 9.50 (*0-933449-19-4*) Transport Trails.
Square Root of Wonderful. Carson McCullers. LC 90-47728. 169p. 1990. reprint ed. 29.95 (*0-87797-188-9*) Cherokee.
Square Rounds. Tony Harrison. 96p. (Orig.). 1993. pap. 8.95 (*0-571-16868-X*) Faber & Faber.
Square Trap. Irving Shulman. Ed. by Carlos E. Cortes. LC 76-1585. (Chicano Heritage Ser.). 1977. reprint ed. 25.95 (*0-405-09525-2*) Ayer.
Square, Triangle, Round, Skinny: Four Books in a Box. Eugenia Radunsky. (J). (ps). 1992. 19.95 (*0-8050-2205-8*, Bks Young Read) H Holt & Co.
Square Wheels: How Russian Democracy Got Derailed. Boris Kagarlitsky. Tr. by Leslia A. Auerbach from RUS. 224p. 1994. 30.00 (*0-85345-891-X*); pap. 18.00 (*0-85345-892-8*) Monthly Rev.
Squared Circle. James W. Bennett. LC 94-42283. 288p. (YA). (gr. 7 up). 1995. 14.95 (*0-590-48671-3*, Scholastic Hardcover) Scholastic Inc.
Squared Squares Who's Who What's What. Jasper D. Skinner, II. (Illus.). (C). 1993. text ed. 75.00 (*0-9636569-0-2*) J D Skinner.
Squarerigging. Frank Brookesmith. (Illus.). 270p. 1981. 12.95 (*0-89182-038-8*); pap. 7.95 (*0-89182-039-6*) Charles River Bks.
Squares. Mary C. Penders. LC 91-34659. (Quilts from Simple Shapes Ser.). (Illus.). 32p. 1992. pap. 9.95 (*0-8442-2633-5*) Quilt Digest Pr.
Squares. A. R. Rajwade. (London Mathematical Society Lecture Note Ser.: No. 171). 300p. (C). 1993. pap. text ed. 44.95 (*0-521-42668-5*) Cambridge U Pr.
***Squares.** unabridged ed. Catherine S. Ross. (Shapes in Math, Science & Nature Ser.). (Illus.). 64p. (J). (gr. 4-9). 1996. pap. 9.95 (*1-55074-273-6*, Pub. by Kids Can Pr CN) Genl Dist Srvs.
Squares: Active Graphic Design. 80p. 1991. pap. 18.95 (*88-7070-163-8*) Belvedere USA.
Squares & Rectangles see Key to Geometry Series
***Squares Everywhere.** Brenda Parkes. Ed. by Susan Evento. (Newbridge Links Ser.). 8p. (J). (gr. k up). 1997. pap. 2.75 (*1-56784-903-2*) Newbridge Comms.
Squares of the City. John Brunner. 320p. 1992. reprint ed. pap. 5.95 (*0-02-017511-6*) Macmillan.
Squares of the Natural Numbers in Radiation Protection. Herbert M. Parker. LC 77-81781. (Taylor Lectures: No. 1). 1977. pap. 20.00 (*0-913392-39-1*) NCRP Pubns.
Squaring Accounts. Patricia Rosemoor. (Intrigue Ser.: No. 163). 1991. pap. 2.75 (*0-373-22163-0*) Harlequin Bks.
Squaring Off. Leonard Todd. Date not set. pap. 4.95 (*0-14-034458-6*, Viking) Viking Penguin.
Squaring the Circle. Tom Stoppard. LC 84-28732. 179p. 1985. pap. 8.95 (*0-571-12538-7*) Faber & Faber.
Squaring the Waves. Geoffrey F. Dutton. 60p. 8600. pap. 11.95 (*1-85224-007-5*, Pub. by Bloodaxe Bks UK) Dufour.
***Squash.** LC 97-13667. (Know the Sport Ser.). (Illus.). 48p. 1997. pap. 5.95 (*0-8117-2839-0*) Stackpole.
***Squash: A Country Garden Cookbook.** Regina Schrambling. 1995. 7.53 (*0-00-225140-X*) HarperColl Wrld.
***Squash: Steps to Success.** Philip Yarrow. LC 97-10150. (Steps to Success Ser.). (Illus.). 160p. (Orig.). 1997. pap. 16.95 (*0-88011-541-6*, PYAR0541) Human Kinetics.
Squash: Technique, Tactics, & Training. Eric Sommers. (Crowood Sports Guides Ser.). (Illus.). 128p. 1992. pap. 22.95 (*1-85223-543-8*, Pub. by Crowood Pr UK) Trafalgar.
Squash Family Cookbook. Marjorie B. Zucker. (Illus.). 1977. pap. 5.50 (*0-686-23105-8*) M B Zucker.
***Squash It!** Eric A. Kimmel. LC 96-48128. (Illus.). 32p. (J). 1997. lib. bdg. 15.95 (*0-8234-1299-7*) Holiday.
Squash Rackets. Tony Swift. (EP Sports Ser.). (Illus.). 1974. 6.95 (*0-7158-0584-3*) Charles River Bks.
Squash Racquets. Margaret V. Bloss & Norman B. Bramall. (Physical Education Activities Ser.). 80p. (C). 1967. per. write for info. (*0-697-07027-1*) Brown & Benchmark.
Squash Racquets: The Khan Game. Hashim Khan & Richard E. Randall. LC 68-12250. (Illus.). 170p. 1972. reprint ed. pap. 15.95 (*0-8143-1469-4*) Wayne St U Pr.
Squash Workshop: A Complete Game Guide. Ian McKenzie. (Illus.). 272p. 1993. 39.95 (*1-85223-115-7*, Pub. by Crowood Pr UK) Trafalgar.
Squash Workshop: A Complete Game Guide. Ian McKenzie. (Illus.). 272p. 1993. pap. 29.95 (*1-85223-728-7*, Pub. by Crowood Pr UK) Trafalgar.
Squashed. Joan Bauer. LC 91-44905. 208p. (J). (gr. 7 up). 1992. 15.95 (*0-385-30793-4*) Delacorte.
Squashed. Joan Bauer. 208p. (J). 1994. mass mkt. 3.99 (*0-440-21912-4*) Dell.
Squashed. large type ed. Joan Bauer. LC 93-6722. 243p. 1993. Alk. paper. pap. 15.95 (*1-56054-685-9*) Thorndike Pr.
Squashed in the Middle. Elizabeth Winthrop. LC 93-46834. (Illus.). (J). 1994. 13.95 (*0-06-024489-5*); lib. bdg. 13.89 (*0-06-024490-9*) HarpC.
Squatter & the Don. Amparo Ruiz de Burton. Ed. by Rosaura Sanchez & Beatriz Pita. LC 92-33829. 386p. 1993. pap. 14.00 (*1-55885-055-4*) Arte Publico.
Squatters & Oligarchs: Authoritarian Rule & Policy Change in Peru. David Collier. LC 75-34112. 200p. reprint ed. pap. 57.00 (*0-7837-1617-6*, 2041910) Bks Demand.
Squatters & the Roots of Mau-Mau 1905-1963. Tabitha Kanogo. LC 87-11201. 206p. 1987. pap. text ed. 14.95 (*0-8214-0874-7*) Ohio U Pr.
Squatter's Rights. large type ed. Frank C. Robertson. (Linford Western Library). 352p. 1985. pap. 15.99 (*0-7089-6184-3*) Ulverscroft.
Squatters' Rites. Tim Bascom. 98p. (Orig.). (C). 1991. pap. 10.00 (*971-10-0414-3*, Pub. by New Day Pub PH) Cellar.
Squattin' Pigeon. Eugene Smith. LC 95-78805. 296p. 1995. pap. 12.95 (*1-885487-04-5*) Brownell & Carroll.
Squaw Dance. Lee McAllister. Ed. by John Seginski. 245p. 1991. write for info. (*1-879586-00-2*) TJE NV.
Squaw Man. Edwin M. Doyle & Julie O. Faversham. LC 77-104559. 294p. (C). 1988. reprint ed. pap. text ed. 7.95 (*0-8290-2142-6*); reprint ed. lib. bdg. 28.00 (*0-8398-1769-X*) Irvington.
Squaw Man: A Comedy Drama in Four Acts. Edwin M. Royle. (BCL1-PS American Literature Ser.). 90p. 1992. reprint ed. lib. bdg. 59.00 (*0-7812-6847-8*) Rprt Serv.
Squaw Men. Lauran Paine. 192p. 1992. 19.95 (*0-8027-4126-6*) Walker & Co.
***Squaw Peak - A Hikers Guide.** Jack San Felice. (Illus.). (Orig.). 1997. pap. write for info. (*1-890216-05-4*) Millsite Canyon.

An Asterisk (*) at the beginning of an entry indicates that the title is appearing in BIP for the first time.

Squaw Peak Parkway Archaeology. LC 93-144219. 31p. 1993. pap. 2.00 (1-882572-00-9) Pueblo Grande Mus.

***Squaw Winter.** Wilford W. Berard. 230p. (Orig.). 1997. mass mkt. 4.99 (1-55237-093-3, Pub. by Comnwlth Pub CN) Partners Pubs Grp.

Squeak Abu! (Squeeze Me Ser.). (J). 1998. 6.98 (1-57082-391-X) Mouse Works.

Squeak Abu: Aladdin. Disney Studios Staff. (Illus.). (J). (ps). 1994. 6.98 (0-453-03243-5) NAL-Dutton.

Squeak & Roar. Sally Hewitt. LC 94-12309. (Get Set...Go! Ser.). (Illus.). 24p. (J). (ps-3). 1994. pap. 4.95 (0-516-47995-4); lib. bdg. 15.40 (0-516-07995-6) Childrens.

Squeak Carnwath: Lists, Observations & Counting. Squeak Carnwath. LC 95-23315. 108p. 1996. 29.95 (0-8118-1220-0); pap. 18.95 (0-8118-1171-9) Chronicle Bks.

Squeak the Dinosaur. Marcus Donnely. (Illus.). 32p. (J). (ps-2). 1987. 9.00 (0-938715-02-X) Toy Works Pr.

Squeak the Mouse. Massimo Mattioli. (Illus.). (Orig.). 1989. pap. 10.95 (0-87416-070-7) Catalan Communs.

Squeakeasy. Dan Garrett. (Illus.). 64p. (Orig.). 1992. pap. 8.00 (0-941599-22-1) Piccadilly Bks.

Squeaker the Dog. Wendy Kanno. (Funny Farm Ser.). (Illus.). (J). (gr. k-3). 1994. pap. 3.50 (0-89868-215-0, Read Res); lib. bdg. 9.95 (0-89868-214-2, Read Res) ARO Pub.

Squeakers. Stephen Cosgrove. (Serendipity Ser.). (Illus.). 32p. (Orig.). (J). (ps-4). 1996. pap. 3.95 (0-8431-3925-0) Price Stern Sloan.

***Squeaky: The Life & Times of Lynette Alice Fromme - Runaway.** Jess Bravin. LC 96-54514. 1997. 25.95 (0-312-15663-4) St Martin.

Squeaky Blue & the Cat. Betsy Brown. 16p. (J). (gr. 1-3). 1995. write for info. (1-888479-01-9) Tarpley Pubng.

***Squeaky Clean.** large type ed. James A. Pattinson. (Large Print Ser.). 336p. 1997. 27.50 (0-7089-3689-X) Ulverscroft.

***Squeaky Clean Jokes for Kids.** Bob Phillips & Steve Russo. 176p. (J). (gr. 3-7). 1997. mass mkt. 3.99 (1-56507-719-9) Harvest Hse.

Squeaky Shoes. Morgan Matthews. LC 85-14014. (Illus.). 48p. (Orig.). (J). (gr. 1-3). 1997. pap. 3.50 (0-8167-0643-3) Troll Communs.

Squeaky Wheel. Robert K. Smith. 192p. (J). (gr. 3-7). 1992. 3.99 (0-440-40631-5, YB BDD) BDD Bks Young Read.

Squeeze. Ellen Steiber. (X-Files Ser.: No. 4). 128p. (YA). (gr. 5 up). 1996. pap. 3.95 (0-06-440621-0, Trophy) HarpC Child Bks.

Squeeze & Squeak Gentle Donkey. Illus. by Bori Weissman. (Squeeze & Squeak Ser.). 9p. (J). (ps up). 1996. bds. 7.99 (1-57584-051-0, Little Lambs) Rdrs Dgst Yng Fam.

Squeeze & Squeak Gentle Lion. Illus. by Bori Weissman. (Squeeze & Squeak Ser.). 9p. 1996. bds. 7.99 (1-57584-050-2, Little Lambs) Rdrs Dgst Yng Fam.

Squeeze at Bridge. Chien-Hwa Wang. 204p. 1993. pap. 12.95 (1-85744-507-4, Pub. by Cadogan Books UK) Macmillan.

Squeeze Me. Random House Staff. (J). 1996. write for info. (0-679-87196-9) Random Bks Yng Read.

Squeeze Play. Mark Freeman. (Rookies Ser.). 144p. (J). (gr. 7-9). 1989. mass mkt. 4.50 (0-345-35903-8) Ballantine.

Squeeze Play. Carolyn Keene. Ed. by Ruth Ashby. (Nancy Drew Files Series, Passport to Romance Trilogy: No. 97). 160p. (Orig.). (YA). (gr. 6 up). 1994. mass mkt. 3.99 (0-671-79489-2, Archway) PB.

***Squeeze Play: The United States, Cuba, & the Helms Burton Act.** Patrick Kiger. 96p. 1997. pap. write for info. (1-882583-08-6) Ctr Public Integrity.

Squeeze Your Home for Cash. Ruth Rejnis. 224p. 1994. pap. 14.95 (0-7931-0991-4, 191325-01, Real Estate Ed) Dearborn Finan.

Squeezed & Correlated States of Quantum Systems. Ed. by M. A. Markov. (Proceedings of the Lebedev Physics Institute Ser.: Vol. 205). 242p. (C). 1993. lib. bdg. 125.00 (1-57072-117-3) Nova Sci Pubs.

Squeezed & Correlated States of Quantum Systems. Ed. by M. A. Markov. Tr. by V. V. Dodonov et al. LC 93-20853. (Proceedings of the Lebedev Physics Institute Ser.: Vol. 205). 242p. 1993. 125.00 (1-56072-117-0) Nova Sci Pubs.

Squeezed & Nonclassical Light. Ed. by P. Tombesi & E. R. Pike. 332p. 1988. 95.00 (0-306-43084-3, Plenum Pr) Plenum.

Squeezed Light. Ed. by Osamu Hirota. LC 92-36404. 268p. 1992. 185.25 (0-444-89453-5) Elsevier.

Squeezed Light: Special Issue of Journal of Modern Optics, Vol 34: 6/7. Ed. by Rodney Loudon & P. L. Knight. 310p. 1987. 51.00 (0-85066-922-7) Taylor & Francis.

Squeezing a Dry Sponge: Water Planning in Texas. Susan G. Hadden & William P. Hobby. (Policy Research Project Report: No. 111). 180p. 1994. pap. 12.50 (0-89940-719-6) LBJ Sch Pub Aff.

Squeezing a New Service into a Crowded Market. Dennis J. Cahill. LC 94-45865. 175p. 1995. lib. bdg. 29.95 (1-56024-939-0) Haworth Pr.

Squibbles & Quotes. Susie S. Piper. (Orig.). 1983. pap. write for info. (0-9618280-0-5) S S Piper.

Squibob: An Early California Humorist. Ed. by Richard D. Reynolds. LC 89-61831. (Illus.). 256p. 1989. 15.95 (0-9618577-5-7); pap. 10.95 (0-9618577-6-5) Squibob Pr.

SQUID: Superconducting Quantum Interference Devices & Their Applications. Ed. by Hans-Dieter Hahlbohm & Heinz Lubbig. 724p. 1980. 176.95 (3-11-008063-X) De Gruyter.

SQUID Applications to Geophysics. Ed. by Harold Weinstock & William C. Overton, Jr. LC 81-51399. (Illus.). 208p. 1981. 12.00 (0-931830-18-4, 523) Soc Expl Geophys.

Squid As Experimental Animals. Ed. by D. L. Gilbert et al. LC 90-6849. (Illus.). 548p. 1990. 115.00 (0-306-43513-6, Plenum Pr) Plenum.

SQUID Sensors. Richard K. Miller & Terri C. Walker. LC 88-81653. (Survey on Technology & Markets Ser.: No. 62). 50p. 1989. pap. text ed. 200.00 (1-55865-061-X) Future Tech Surveys.

***SQUID Sensors: Fundamentals, Fabrication & Applications.** Harold Weinstock. LC 96-49522. 1996. lib. bdg. 349.00 (0-7923-4350-6) Kluwer Ac.

SQUID '85: Superconducting Quantum Interference Devices & Their Applications: Proceedings of the Third International Conference on Superconducting Quantum Interference Devices, Berlin (West), June 25-28, 1985. Ed. by H. D. Hahlbohm & H. Luebbig. xxxi, 1236p. 1986. 338.50 (3-11-010330-3) De Gruyter.

SQUIDS, the Josephson Effects & Superconducting Electronics. J. C. Gallop. (Measurement Science & Technology Ser.). (Illus.). 240p. 1991. 112.00 (0-7503-0051-5) IOP Pub.

Squiggle. Carole L. Schaefer. LC 95-2299. (Illus.). 1996. 17.00 (0-517-70047-6, Crown) Crown Pub Group.

Squiggle. Carole L. Schaefer. LC 95-2299. (Illus.). (J). 1996. lib. bdg. 18.99 (0-517-70048-4, Crown) Crown Pub Group.

Squiggley Line & Other Oddities: Investigations into the Corners of the World. Frank J. Lombardo. (Illus.). 130p. (Orig.). 1988. pap. 6.95 (0-945702-00-0) Vertizon Bks.

Squiggly Wiggly Head Family. Dwight A. Osborne. (Illus.). 16p. (J). 1992. pap. 5.95 (0-9632817-0-4) Osborne Bks.

Squim: The Untold Story. Michael Yaeger & Brian Dunn. (Illus.). 64p. (Orig.). 1986. pap. 5.95 (0-931693-03-9, 04299) Studio Solstone.

Squire. Enid Bagnold. 1988. 23.95 (0-8488-0421-X) Amereon Ltd.

Squire: The Legendary Golfing Life of Gene Sarazen. John M. Olman. LC 87-5714. (Illus.). 176p. 1987. 29.95 (0-942117-00-X) Market St Pr.

Squire: The Legendary Golfing Life of Gene Sarazen. deluxe limited ed. John M. Olman. LC 87-5714. (Illus.). 176p. 1987. lthr. 140.00 (0-942117-01-8) Market St Pr.

Squire Gullible & the Dragon. rev. ed. Camilla H. Wolak. LC 89-43530. (J). (gr. 3-12). 1985. pap. 6.00 (0-88734-508-5) Players Pr.

Squire of East Hampton: The Life of Evan M. Frankel. Allen Appel. LC 89-80476. (Illus.). 280p. 1989. write for info. (0-9622459-0-9) Jewish Ctr Hamptons.

Squire Simmons Family, Seventeen Forty-Six to Nineteen Eighty-Six. Dorothy G. Skelton. LC 85-63456. (Illus.). 985p. 1986. 68.00 (0-9616290-0-2); ring bd. write for info. (0-318-60852-9) D G S Skelton.

Squire Takes a Wife. Eve Feldman. (Ready-Set-Read Ser.). (Illus.). 24p. (J). (ps-2). 1990. lib. bdg. 21.40 (0-8172-3580-9) Raintree Steck-V.

Squire Takes a Wife. Eve Feldman. 1995. pap. text ed. 4.95 (0-8114-6747-3) Raintree Steck-V.

Squire's Blood. Peter Telep. 464p. 1995. mass mkt. 4.99 (0-06-105478-X, HarperPrism) HarpC.

Squire's Daughter. Deborah Simmons. (Historical Ser.). 1994. mass mkt. 3.99 (0-373-28808-5, 1028808-3) Harlequin Bks.

***Squire's Fundamentals of Radiology.** 5th ed. Robert A. Novelline & Lucy F. Squire. LC 96-36574. 1997. write for info. (0-674-83339-2) HUP.

Squire's Tale. Geoffrey Chaucer. Ed. by Donald C. Baker. LC 89-24928. (Variorum Edition of the Works of Geoffrey Chaucer, The Canterbury Tales Ser.: Vol. II, Pt. 12). (Illus.). 304p. 1990. 49.95 (0-8061-2154-8) U of Okla Pr.

***Squire's Tale.** Gerald Morris. LC 97-12447. (J). 1998. write for info. (0-395-86959-5) HM.

Squirmasters! David Jacobs. (Bug Files Ser.: No. 1). 1996. mass mkt. 4.50 (0-425-15320-7) Berkley Pub.

Squirmy Wormy Composters. Bobbie Kalman & Janine Schaub. (Primary Ecology Ser.). (Illus.). 32p. (J). (gr. k-8). 1992. pap. 7.95 (0-86505-581-5); lib. bdg. 19.16 (0-86505-555-6) Crabtree Pub Co.

Squirmy's Big Secret. Robert Kraus & Bonnie Brook. (Miss Gator's Schoolhouse Ser.). (Illus.). 48p. (J). (ps-3). 1990. pap. 2.95 (0-671-70852-X, Silver Pr NJ) Silver Burdett Pr.

Squirrel. Margaret Lane. LC 81-1229. (Illus.). 32p. (J). (gr. k-4). 1981. pap. 13.99 (0-8037-8230-6) Dial Bks Young.

Squirrel. Margaret Lane. (Illus.). 32p. (J). (gr. k-4). 1993. pap. 4.99 (0-14-054926-9, Puff Pied Piper) Puffin Bks.

Squirrel. Western Promotional Books Staff. (Nature Shape Bks.). (Illus.). 12p. (J). (ps). 1993. bds. 2.49 (0-307-13252-8, Golden Books) Western Pub.

Squirrel, Reading Level 3-4. Dalmais. (World Animal Library). (Illus.). 28p. (J). (gr. 2-5). 1983. 12.50 (0-685-58826-2); lib. bdg. 16.67 (0-86592-857-6) Rourke Corp.

Squirrel & the Frog. Mildred McDowell. LC 76-133256. (Story & Its Verse Ser.). (Illus.). 44p. (J). (gr. 1-2). 1971. 2.50 (0-87884-007-9) Unicorn Ent.

Squirrel & the Moon. Eleonore Schmid. Tr. by Rosemary Lanning. LC 95-43716. (Illus.). 32p. (J). (gr. k-3). Date not set. 15.95 (1-55858-530-3) North-South Bks NYC.

Squirrel & the Moon. Eleonore Schmid. Tr. by Rosemary Lanning. 32p. (J). (ps-3). 1996. lib. bdg. 15.88 (1-55858-531-1) North-South Bks NYC.

Squirrel & the Nut. James Swartzentruber. (God Is Good Ser.). 1989. 2.50 (0-318-41784-7) Rod & Staff.

***Squirrel Family Who Lived with Us.** Mary C. Farran. (Illus.). 64p. (Orig.). (J). (ps-5). 1996. pap. 8.00 (1-56002-623-5, Univ Edtns) Aegina Pr.

***Squirrel from the Moon - & Other Stories...Wild but True.** Penny Porter. (Illus.). 140p. 1997. pap. 10.95 (0-9656923-0-2) Singing Valley.

Squirrel Is Hungry. Satoshi Kitamura. 14p. (J). 1996. 4.95 (0-374-37171-7) FS&G.

Squirrel Jumped Out of the Tree. Johnette Downing. (Illus.). (J). (ps). 1990. pap. 2.50 (0-938991-57-4) Colonial Pr AL.

Squirrel Nutkin. (Beatrix Potter Coloring Bks.: No. S884-2). (Illus.). (J). (ps-2). 1989. 1.95 (0-7214-5139-X, Ladybrd) Penguin.

Squirrel Nutkin. (Classic Tales Ser.). (Illus.). 24p. (J). 1993. 4.98 (1-56173-476-4) Pubns Intl Ltd.

Squirrel Nutkin. Illus. by Pat Schoonover & Anita Nelson. (Classic Tales Ser.). 24p. (J). (gr. 2-4). 1992. lib. bdg. 10.95 (1-56674-009-6, HTS Bks) Forest Hse.

Squirrel Nutkin. deluxe ed. (Beatrix Potter Collector Ser.). 224p. Date not set. text ed. 5.95 (1-56987-341-0) Landoll.

Squirrel Wars: Adventures in Bird Feeding. Ary Renaud. 100p. 1996. pap. 14.95 (0-9645708-7-4) Sea of Fanta Pubns.

Squirrels. Jessica Holm. (Illus.). 128p. text ed. 19.95 (1-873580-17-7, Pub. by Whittet Bks UK) Diamond Farm Bk.

Squirrels. Emilie U. Lepthien. LC 92-9207. (New True Bks.). (Illus.). 48p. (J). (gr. k-4). 1992. lib. bdg. 19.00 (0-516-01947-3) Childrens.

Squirrels. Emilie U. Lepthien. LC 92-9207. (New True Bks.). (Illus.). 48p. (J). (gr. k-4). 1993. pap. 5.50 (0-516-41947-1) Childrens.

Squirrels. Kim Long. LC 95-43163. (Nature Ser.). (Illus.). 192p. (Orig.). 1995. pap. 15.95 (1-55566-152-1) Johnson Bks.

Squirrels. Brian Wildsmith. (Illus.). 32p. (J). 1987. pap. 11.95 (0-19-272105-4) OUP.

Squirrel's Adventure in Alphabet Town. Laura Alden. LC 92-1314. (Read Around Alphabet Town Ser.). (Illus.). 32p. (J). (ps-2). 1992. lib. bdg. 17.50 (0-516-05419-8) Childrens.

Squirrels All Year Long. Melvin Berger. (Early Science Big Bks.). (Illus.). 16p. (J). (ps-2). 1992. pap. 14.95 (1-56784-003-5) Newbridge Comms.

Squirrels All Year Long: Mini Books. Melvin Berger. Ed. by Natalie Lunis. (Early Science Big Bks.). (Illus.). 16p. (J). (ps-2). 1993. pap. 2.95 (1-56784-028-0) Newbridge Comms.

Squirrels All Year Round Theme Pack. Melvin Berger. Ed. by Susan Evento. (Macmillan Early Science Big Bks.). (Illus.). (J). (ps-2). 1995. pap. write for info. (1-56784-135-X) Newbridge Comms.

***Squirrels & Chipmunks.** Allan Fowler. LC 96-28769. (Rookie Read-About Science Ser.). (J). 1997. lib. bdg. 17.50 (0-516-20323-1) Childrens.

***Squirrels & Chipmunks.** Allan Fowler. (Rookie Read-About Science Ser.). 1997. pap. 4.95 (0-516-26158-4) Childrens.

Squirrels & Other Fur Bearers. John Burroughs. (Works of John Burroughs). 1989. reprint ed. lib. bdg. 79.00 (0-7812-2188-9) Rprt Serv.

***Squirrel's Friends.** Gaby Goldsack. (Little Spring Window Bks.). 1998. 3.99 (1-57584-070-7) Rdrs Dgst Yng Fam.

Squirrels on the Move (EV) Independent Reader 5-Pack, Unit 8. (Networks Ser.). (J). (gr. 2). 1991. 15.00 (0-88106-765-2) Charlesbridge Pub.

Squirrel's Party. Stewart Cowley. LC 93-77348. (Magic Window Bks.). (Illus.). 22p. (J). (ps-3). 1993. 6.99 (0-89577-514-X, Random) RD Assn.

Squirrel's Tale. Richard Fowler. (Slot Bks.). 24p. (J). (ps-3). 1984. 10.95 (0-88110-157-5) EDC.

Squirrels' Thanksgiving. Steven Kroll. LC 89-77513. (Illus.). 32p. (J). (ps-3). 1991. lib. bdg. 15.95 (0-8234-0823-X) Holiday.

***Squirrel's Thanksgiving.** Steven Kroll. (J). 1997. pap. text ed. 4.99 (0-590-10837-9) Scholastic Inc.

Squirt & the Super Soldier. Bruce Porter. (Illus.). 40p. (Orig.). (J). (gr. 3 up). 1987. pap. 3.95 (0-939925-16-8) R C Law & Co.

Squirt Book: The Manual of Squirt Kayaking Technique. James E. Snyder. LC 87-22120. (Illus.). 176p. 1987. pap. 9.95 (0-89732-075-1) Menasha Ridge.

Squirts & Snails & Skinny Green Tails: Seashore Nature Activities for Kids. Diane Swanson. (J). (gr. 2 up). 1994. pap. 5.95 (1-55850-389-7) Adams Media.

SQUISH! A Wetland Walk. Nancy Luenn. LC 93-22628. (Illus.). 32p. (J). 1994. text ed. 15.00 (0-689-31842-1, Atheneum Bks Young) S&S Childrens.

Squish, Sort, Paint & Build: Over 200 Easy Learning Center Activities. Sharon MacDonald. LC 96-9099. (Illus.). 254p. (Orig.). 1996. pap. 19.95 (0-87659-180-2) Gryphon Hse.

Squishy, Misty, Damp, & Muddy: The in-between World of Wetlands. Molly Cone. (Illus.). 32p. (J). (gr. 1-4). 1996. 15.95 (0-87156-480-7) Sierra Club Childrens.

Squitter-Wits & Muse-Haters: Sidney, Spenser, Milton & Renaissance Antipoetic Sentiment. Peter C. Herman. (Illus.). 284p. (Orig.). 1996. pap. 28.95 (0-8143-2571-8) Wayne St U Pr.

Squyr of Lowe Degre: A Middle English Metrical Romance Edited in All Extant Forms, with Introduction, Notes & Glossary. Ed. by William E. Mead. LC 76-178506. reprint ed. 27.50 (0-404-56676-6) AMS Pr.

SR French: Parlons Francais, Bk. 1. Incl. Text 1. 1984. pap. 17.25 (0-8325-9662-0); Text 2. 1984. pap. 17.25 (0-8325-9665-5); Tape 3. 1994. pap. 17.25 (0-8325-9669-8); 1995. Tapebook 1. 10.00Set incl. audio (0-8442-9663-5, Natl Textbk) NTC Pub Grp.

SR French: Parlons Francais, Bk. 2. Incl. Text 1. 1984. pap. 17.25 (0-8325-9662-0); Text 2. 1984. pap. 17.25 (0-8325-9665-5); Tape 3. 1994. pap. 17.25 (0-8325-9669-8); 1994. Tapebook 2. Set pap. 10.60 (0-8325-9666-3, Natl Textbk) NTC Pub Grp.

SR French: Parlons Francais, Level 1. Incl. Text 1. 1984. pap. 17.25 (0-8325-9662-0); Text 2. 1984. pap. 17.25 (0-8325-9665-5); Tape 3. 1994. pap. 17.25 (0-8325-9669-8); 1991. Set audio 20.00 (0-8442-9662-7, Natl Textbk) NTC Pub Grp.

SR French: Parlons Francais, Level 2. Incl. Text 1. 1984. pap. 17.25 (0-8325-9662-0); Text 2. 1984. pap. 17.25 (0-8325-9665-5); Tape 3. 1994. pap. 17.25 (0-8325-9669-8); 1995. Set audio 233.35 (0-8325-9668-X, Natl Textbk) NTC Pub Grp.

SR French: Parlons Francais, Reader 1. Incl. Text 1. 1984. pap. 17.25 (0-8325-9662-0); Text 2. 1984. pap. 17.25 (0-8325-9665-5); Tape 3. 1994. pap. 17.25 (0-8325-9669-8); 1984. Set pap. 10.60 (0-8325-9664-7, Natl Textbk) NTC Pub Grp.

SR French: Parlons Francais, Reader 2. Incl. Text 1. 1984. pap. 17.25 (0-8325-9662-0); Text 2. 1984. pap. 17.25 (0-8325-9665-5); Tape 3. 1994. pap. 17.25 (0-8325-9669-8); 1985. Set pap. 10.60 (0-8325-9667-1, Natl Textbk) NTC Pub Grp.

SR Italian: Lo Dica in Italiano. Incl. Text 1. 1985. text ed. 17.25 (0-8325-9674-4); Tapebook 1. 1988. pap. 10.60 (0-8325-9675-2); Reader 1. 1991. audio 20.00 (0-8442-9676-7); Set text ed. write for info. (0-318-53535-1, Natl Textbk) NTC Pub Grp.

SR Japanese. Nubuo Akiyama. (SR Japanese Ser.). 1990. pap. 6.60 (0-8325-9649-3, Natl Textbk); pap. text ed. 7.95 (0-8325-9648-5, Natl Textbk) NTC Pub Grp.

SR Russian. 1990. pap. 6.60 (0-8325-9645-0, Natl Textbk) NTC Pub Grp.

SR Russian. 1994. pap. 7.95 (0-8325-9643-4, Natl Textbk) NTC Pub Grp.

SR Russian. 69th ed. 1990. student ed. 6.60 (0-8325-9644-2, Natl Textbk) NTC Pub Grp.

Sr. Texas Deals: A Shopper's Bonanza for the 50 & Better Generation. Ed. by Frank Kelly. (Illus.). (Orig.). 1989. pap. text ed. 3.95 (0-685-29097-2) Liberty M Inc.

Sr. Texas Deals, Vol. 1: A Shopper's Bonanza for the 50 - & - Better Generation. Ed. by Frank Kelly & Sue Goldstein. LC 89-92261. 150p. (Orig.). 1990. pap. text ed. 3.95 (0-9624211-0-3) Liberty M Inc.

***Sr. Thea: Songs of My People.** 96p. 7.95 (0-8198-6888-4) Pauline Bks.

SR-71 Blackbird. Jim Goodall. (Aircraft Specials Ser.). (Illus.). 80p. 1995. pap. 12.95 (0-89747-338-8) Squad Sig Pubns.

SR-71 Blackbird in Action. Lou Drendel. (Illus.). 50p. 1982. 7.95 (0-89747-136-9, 1055) Squad Sig Pubns.

SR-71 Revealed: The Untold Story. Rich Graham. (Illus.). 224p. 1996. pap. 16.95 (0-7603-0122-0) Motorbooks Intl.

Sraddha-Sagara of Kullukabhatta: With a Critical Exposition & Introduction. S. G. Moghe. 1994. 29.00 (81-246-0016-3, Pub. by DK Pubs Dist II) S Asia.

Sraffa & the Theory of Prices. Alessandro Roncaglia. Tr. by J. A. Kregel from ITA. LC 77-7241. 196p. reprint ed. pap. 55.90 (0-685-23761-3, 2032835) Bks Demand.

Sraffian Economics, 2 vols., Set, Vols. I & II. Ed. by Ian Steedman. (Schools of Thought in Economics Ser.: Vol. 4). 848p. 1989. Set. text ed. 285.00 (1-85278-118-1) E Elgar.

Srbija Gori! Milos Acin-Kosta. 220p. (Orig.). (SER.). 1960. pap. 3.00 (0-317-61882-2) Ravnogorski.

Src Family of Tyrosine Kinases in Leukocytes. Tomas Mustelin. (Molecular Biology Intelligence Unit Ser.). 118p. 1994. 89.95 (1-57059-113-X, LN9113) R G Landes.

Srdce a Korene Duse. 2nd ed. Vladimir Uhri. 46p. (Orig.). (SLO.). 1995. pap. 2.75 (1-56983-034-7) New Creat WI.

***Srebrenica: Record of a War Crime.** Norbert Both & Jan W. Honig. 1997. pap. 11.95 (0-14-026632-1) Viking Penguin.

Sredi Veshchei i Golosov. Grigorii Mark. LC 95-2466. 128p. (Orig.). (RUS.). 1995. pap. 9.00 (1-55779-075-2) Hermitage.

Sredni Vashtar & Other Stories. unabridged ed. Saki, pseud. (Thrift Editions Ser.). 96p. (Orig.). 1995. pap. text ed. 1.00 (0-486-28521-9) Dover.

Sri Arrobindo Ghose. Ed. by Verinder Grover. (Political Thinkers of Modern India Ser.: No. 1). (C). 1993. 52.00 (81-7100-422-9, Pub. by Deep II) S Asia.

Sri Aurobindo. G. H. Langley. 1972. 59.95 (0-8490-1119-1) Gordon Pr.

Sri Aurobindo. 3rd ed. Manoj Das. 1982. reprint ed. pap. 4.00 (0-8364-1585-X, Pub. by National Sahitya Akademi II) S Asia.

Sri Aurobindo: A Critical Introduction. Prema Nandakumar. 128p. 1989. text ed. 18.95 (81-207-0765-6, Pub. by Sterling Pubs II) Apt Bks.

Sri Aurobindo: His Life Unique. Rishabchand. (Illus.). 427p. 1981. 18.75 (0-89071-326-X, Pub. by SAA II); pap. 15.00 (0-89071-325-1, Pub. by SAA II) Aurobindo Assn.

Sri Aurobindo: His Life Unique. Rishabhchand. 427p. (Orig.). 1982. pap. 14.95 (0-89744-147-8) Auromere.

Sri Aurobindo & His Yoga. M. P. Pandit. LC 87-80572. 196p. (Orig.). 1987. pap. 6.95 (0-941524-25-6) Lotus Light.

Sri Aurobindo & Karl Marx: Integral Sociology & Dialectical Sociology. 2nd ed. Debiprasad Chattopadhyaya. (C). 1988. 38.50 (81-208-0388-4, Pub. by Motilal Banarsidass II) S Asia.

Sri Aurobindo & the Mother on Collective Yoga. Ed. by Eric Hughes. 75p. 1974. pap. 1.00 (0-89071-000-7) Aurobindo Assn.

Sri Aurobindo & the Mother on Education. Sri Aurobindo & Mother. 168p. 1986. pap. 5.95 (81-7058-028-5) Aurobindo Assn.

Sri Aurobindo & the Mother on Education. 6th ed. Sri Aurobindo. 1978. 3.95 (0-89744-955-X) Auromere.

S

Sri Aurobindo & the Mother on Love. Sri Aurobindo & Mother. 49p. 1988. pap. 1.95 (81-7058-104-4) Aurobindo Assn.

Sri Aurobindo & Vedanta Philosophy. Sheojee Pandey. (C). 1987. 21.00 (81-7100-028-2, Pub. by Deep II) S Asia.

Sri Aurobindo As a Political Thinker: An Interdisciplinary Study. Som P. Ranchan & K. D. Gupta. 113p. 1989. text ed. 15.95 (81-220-0111-4, Pub. by Konark Pubs Pvt Ltd II) Advent Bks Div.

Sri Aurobindo on Himself. Sri Aurobindo. 512p. 1985. 15.95 (0-89071-317-0, Pub. by SAA II); pap. 12.00 (0-89071-316-2, Pub. by SAA II) Aurobindo Assn.

Sri Aurobindo on Himself. Sri Aurobindo. 1979. 11.50 (0-89744-917-7) Auromere.

Sri Aurobindo on Shakespeare. 2nd ed. K. D. Sethna. 134p. 1991. 4.75 (81-7058-236-9) Aurobindo Assn.

Sri Aurobindo's Ideal of Human Life. M. Rafique. 127p. (C). 1987. 17.50 (81-7024-074-3, Pub. by Ashish II) S Asia.

Sri Aurobindo's Plays: A Thematic Study. S. S. Jaiswal. (C). 1993. text ed. 27.00 (81-7054-170-0, Pub. by Classical Pub II) S Asia.

Sri Aurobindo's Prose Style. Goutam Ghosal. 254p. 1991. 7.00 (81-900160-0-8) Aurobindo Assn.

Sri Aurobindo's Vision of the Supermind: Its Indian & Non-Indian Interpreters. Anil K. Sarkar. (C). 1989. 16.00 (81-7003-100-1, Pub. by S Asia Pubs II) S Asia.

Sri Bala-Krsna-Sahasra-Nama: A Thousand Names of Child Krsna Taken by Srila Bhaktivinoda Thakura from Sri Narada-Pancaratra. Nardamuni & Bhaktivinodathakura. Tr. by Kusakrathadasa from SAN. (Krsna Library: Vol. 97). 64p. (Orig.). 1990. pap. text ed. 8.00 (1-56130-004-7) Krsna Inst.

Sri Brahma-samhita, Chapter Five with the Commentary of Srila Jiva Gosvami. Brahmadeva. Tr. by Kusakrathadasa from SAN. (Krsna Library: Vol. 180). 144p. (C). 1992. pap. text ed. 10.00 (1-56130-093-4) Krsna Inst.

Sri Brahma-Sanihita. Bhaktisiddhanta S. Thakura. 157p. 1990. pap. 6.95 (0-89213-145-4) Bhaktivedanta.

Sri Brahma-Vaivarta Purana Canto Four Sri Krsna-Janma-Khanda: The Birth of Lord Krsna, Vol. 2. Tr. by Kusakrathadasa from SAN. (Krsna Library: Vol. 136). 177p. (C). 1991. pap. text ed. 10.00 (1-56130-048-9) Krsna Inst.

Sri Brahma-Vaivarta Purana Canto Four Sri Krsna-Janma-Khanda: The Birth of Lord Krsna, Vol. 3. Tr. by Kusakrathadasa from SAN. (Krsna Library: Vol. 137). 168p. (C). 1991. pap. text ed. 10.00 (1-56130-049-7) Krsna Inst.

Sri Brahma-Vaivarta Purana Canto Four Sri Krsna-Janma-Khanda: The Birth of Lord Krsna, Vol. 4. Tr. by Kusakrathadasa from SAN. (Krsna Library: Vol. 138). 152p. (C). 1991. pap. text ed. 10.00 (1-56130-050-0) Krsna Inst.

Sri Brahma-Vaivarta Purana Canto Four Sri Krsna-Janma-Khanda: The Birth of Lord Krsna, Vol. 5. Tr. by Kusakrathadasa from SAN. (Krsna Library: Vol. 139). 156p. (C). 1991. pap. text ed. 10.00 (1-56130-051-9) Krsna Inst.

Sri Brahma-Vaivarta Purana Canto Four Sri Krsna-Janma-Khanda: The Birth of Lord Krsna, Vol. 6. Tr. by Kusakrathadasa from SAN. (Krsna Library: Vol. 141). 176p. (C). 1991. pap. text ed. 10.00 (1-56130-052-7) Krsna Inst.

Sri Brahma-Vaivarta Purana Canto Four Sri Krsna-Janma-Khanda: The Birth of Lord Krsna, Vol. 7. Tr. by Kusakrathadasa from SAN. (Krsna Library: Vol. 142). 212p. (C). 1991. pap. text ed. 10.00 (1-56130-053-5) Krsna Inst.

Sri Brahma-Vaivarta Purana Canto Four Sri Krsna-Janma-Khanda: The Birth of Lord Krsna, Vol. 8. Tr. by Kusakrathadasa from SAN. (Krsna Library: Vol. 143). 109p. 1991. pap. text ed. 10.00 (1-56130-054-3) Krsna Inst.

Sri Brahma-Vaivarta Purana Canto Four Sri Krsna-Janma-Khanda: The Birth of Lord Krsna, Vol. 9. Tr. by Kusakrathadasa from SAN. (Krsna Library: Vol. 144). 112p. 1991. pap. text ed. write for info. (1-56130-055-1) Krsna Inst.

Sri Brahma-Vaivarta Purana Canto Four Sri Krsna-Janma-Khanda: The Birth of Lord Krsna, Vol. 10. Vyasadeva. Tr. by Kusakrathadasa from SAN. (Krsna Library: Vol. 145). 148p. (C). 1991. pap. text ed. 10.00 (1-56130-057-8) Krsna Inst.

Sri Brahma-Vaivarta Purana Canto Four Sri Krsna-Janma-Khanda: The Birth of Lord Krsna, Vol. 18. Vyasadeva. Tr. by Kusakrathadasa from SAN. (Krsna Library: Vol. 146). 158p. (C). 1991. pap. text ed. 10.00 (1-56130-058-6) Krsna Inst.

Sri Brahma-Vaivarta Purana Canto Four Sri Krsna-Janma-Khanda: The Birth of Lord Krsna, Vol. 22. Vyasadeva. Tr. by Kusakrathadasa from SAN. (Krsna Library: Vol. 148). 132p. (C). 1991. pap. text ed. 10.00 (1-56130-060-8) Krsna Inst.

Sri Brahma-Vaivarta Purana Canto Four, Sri Krsna-Janma-Khanda, the Birth of Lord Krsna, Vol. 1. Vyasadeva. Tr. by Kusakratha Dasa from SAN. (Krsna Library: Vol. 115). 190p. (Orig.). 1990. pap. text ed. 12.00 (1-56130-024-1) Krsna Inst.

Sri Caitanya-Candrodaya Complete in Ten Volumes, 10 vols. Kavi Karnapura. Tr. by Kusakrathadasa from SAN. (Krsna Library: Vol. 69-78). (Orig.). 1989. pap. text ed. 80.00 (0-944833-79-9) Krsna Inst.

Sri Caitanya-Caritamrta: Madhya-Lila, 9 vols. Swami A. C. Bhaktivedanta. (Illus.). 7300p. 1975. Vol. 5. 450.00 (0-912776-67-6) Bhaktivedanta.

Sri Caitanya Mahaprabhu's Incarnation Predicted in Scripture. Tr. by Kusakrathadasa from SAN. (Krsna Library). 87p. (C). 1992. pap. text ed. 8.00 (1-56130-073-X) Krsna Inst.

Sri Ganesh Puja (Worship of God of Obstacles) Panduranga R. Malyala. (Illus.). 56p. 1982. 5.00 (0-938924-03-6) Sri Shirdi Sai.

Sri Garga-Samhita, Canto 2, Vol. 1. Gargamuni. Tr. by Kusakrathadasa from SAN. (Krsna Library: Vol. 116). 187p. (Orig.). 1991. pap. text ed. 10.00 (1-56130-026-8) Krsna Inst.

Sri Garga-Samhita, Canto 2, Vol. 2. Gargamuni. Tr. by Kusakrathadasa from SAN. (Krsna Library: Vol. 117). 153p. (Orig.). 1991. pap. text ed. 10.00 (1-56130-027-6) Krsna Inst.

Sri Garga-Samhita, Canto 2, Vol. 3. Gargamuni. Tr. by Kusakrathadasa from SAN. (Krsna Library: Vol. 118). 155p. (Orig.). 1991. pap. text ed. 10.00 (1-56130-028-4) Krsna Inst.

Sri Garga-Samhita, Canto 3. Gargamuni. Tr. by Kusakrathadasa from SAN. (Krsna Library: Vol. 121). 172p. (Orig.). 1991. pap. text ed. 10.00 (1-56130-033-0) Krsna Inst.

Sri Garga-Samhita, Canto 4, Vol. 1. Gargamuni. Tr. by Kusakrathadasa from SAN. (Krsna Library: Vol. 122). 148p. (Orig.). 1991. pap. text ed. 10.00 (1-56130-034-9) Krsna Inst.

Sri Garga-Samhita, Canto 4, Vol. 2. Gargamuni. Tr. by Kusakrathadasa from SAN. (Krsna Library: Vol. 123). 180p. (Orig.). 1991. pap. text ed. 10.00 (1-56130-035-7) Krsna Inst.

Sri Garga-Samhita, Canto 5, Vol. 1. Gargamuni. Tr. by Kusakrathadasa from SAN. (Krsna Library: Vol. 125). 156p. (Orig.). 1991. pap. text ed. 10.00 (1-56130-036-5) Krsna Inst.

Sri Garga-Samhita, Canto 5, Vol. 2. Gargamuni. Tr. by Kusakrathadasa from SAN. (Krsna Library: Vol. 126). 165p. (Orig.). 1991. pap. text ed. 10.00 (1-56130-037-3) Krsna Inst.

Sri Garga-Samhita, Canto 5, Vol. 3. Gargamuni. Tr. by Kusakrathadasa from SAN. (Krsna Library: Vol. 127). 184p. (Orig.). 1991. pap. text ed. 10.00 (1-56130-038-1) Krsna Inst.

Sri Garga-samhita Canto Eight, Vol. 2: Sri Balarama. Gargamuni. Tr. by Kusakrathadasa from SAN. (Krsna Library: Vol. 151). 108p. (C). 1991. pap. text ed. 10.00 (1-56130-065-9) Krsna Inst.

Sri Garga-Samhita Canto One, Sri Goloka, Vol. 1. Gargamuni. Tr. by Kusakrathadasa from SAN. (Krsna Library: Vol. 106). 166p. (Orig.). 1990. pap. text ed. 10.00 (1-56130-015-2) Krsna Inst.

Sri Garga-Samhita Canto One, Sri Goloka, Vol. 2. Gargamuni. Tr. by Kusakrathadasa from SAN. (Krsna Library: Vol. 107). 157p. (Orig.). 1990. pap. text ed. 10.00 (1-56130-016-0) Krsna Inst.

Sri Garga-Samhita Canto One, Sri Goloka, Vol. 3. Gargamuni. Tr. by Kusakrathadasa from SAN. (Krsna Library: Vol. 108). 131p. (Orig.). 1990. pap. text ed. 10.00 (1-56130-017-9) Krsna Inst.

Sri Garga-Samhita, Canto Six, Vol. 1: Sri Dvaraka. Gargamuni. Tr. by Kusakrathadasa from SAN. (Krsna Library: Vol. 130). 136p. (Orig.). 1991. pap. text ed. 10.00 (1-56130-041-1) Krsna Inst.

Sri Garga-Samhita, Canto Six, Vol. 2: Sri Dvaraka. Gargamuni. Tr. by Kusakrathadasa from SAN. (Krsna Library: Vol. 131). 136p. (Orig.). 1991. pap. text ed. 10.00 (1-56130-042-X) Krsna Inst.

Sri Garga-Samhita, Canto Six, Vol. 3: Sri Dvaraka. Gargamuni. Tr. by Kusakrathadasa from SAN. (Krsna Library: Vol. 132). 144p. (Orig.). 1991. pap. text ed. 10.00 (1-56130-043-8) Krsna Inst.

***Sri Gaura-Govindarcana - Smarana-Paddhati.** Sripada D. Goswami & Haridhama Dasa. 123p. 1993. pap. 12.00 (1-889756-26-1) Sanskrit Relgns Inst.

Sri Gaura-Kirtana: The Glories of Lord Gaura. Kusakrathadasa. (Krsna Library: No. 2, Vol. 4). 56p. (C). 1993. pap. text ed. 4.00 (1-56130-104-3) Krsna Inst.

Sri Gaura Lila, Vol. I: Nimai of Nadia. rev. ed. Varsana Swami. (Illus.). 190p. 1992. pap. text ed. 15.00 (0-9628590-2-8) Gaura Lila Bks.

Sri Gopala-sahasra-nama: A Thousand Names of Lord Gopala. Vyasadeva. Tr. by Kusakrathadasa from SAN. (Krsna Library: Vol. 167). 83p. (C). 1992. pap. text ed. 6.00 (1-56130-092-6) Krsna Inst.

Sri Govinda-Vrndavana. Sadasiva. Tr. by Kusakrathadasa from SAN. (Krsna Library: Vol. 163). 124p. (C). 1992. pap. text ed. 10.00 (1-56130-080-2) Krsna Inst.

Sri Guru Granth Sahib, 2. Ed. by Talib. (C). 1989. 24.00 (0-8364-2548-0, Pub. by Punjabi U II) S Asia.

Sri Guru Granth Sahib, 3. Ed. by Talib. (C). 1989. 24.00 (0-8364-2549-9, Pub. by Punjabi U II) S Asia.

Sri Guru Granth Sahib, 4. Ed. by Talib. (C). 1989. 26.00 (0-8364-2550-2, Pub. by Punjabi U II) S Asia.

Sri Guru Granth Sahib in English Translation, Vol. 1. Tr. by Gurbachan S. Talib. 1985. 30.00 (0-8364-1507-8, Pub. by Punjabi U II) S Asia.

Sri Guru Granth Sahib with Complete Index, 2 vols., Set. Winand M. Callewaert. (C). 1996. 200.00 (81-208-1379-0, Pub. by Motilal Banarsidass II) S Asia.

Sri Hanumaan Chaaleesa. 2.00 (0-938924-22-2) Sri Shirdi Sai.

Sri Hari-Bhakti-Kalpa-Latika: The Flowering Vine of Devotion to Lord Hari. Tr. by Kusaratha Dasa from SAN. (Krsna Library: Vol. 14). 275p. (Orig.). (C). 1988. pap. text ed. 12.00 (0-944833-13-6) Krsna Inst.

Sri Hayagriva Upanisad: And Other Vaisnava Upanisads. Vedavyasa. Tr. by Kusakrathadasa from SAN. (Krsna Library: Vol. 187). 106p. (C). 1993. pap. text ed. 10.00 (1-56130-107-8) Krsna Inst.

Sri Isopanisad: Discovering the Original Person. Bhaktivedanta Swami. 182p. 1985. pap. 2.95 (0-89213-138-1) Bhaktivedanta.

Sri Krsna Caitanya: A Historical Study of Gaudiya Vaisnavism. A. N. Chatterjee. 1985. 22.00 (0-8364-1321-0, Pub. by Assoc Bks IA) S Asia.

Sri Krsna-Kathamrta-Vyakarana: An Introduction to Sanskrit, Vol. 1. Kusakrathadasa. (Krsna Library: Vol. 114). 124p. (Orig.). 1990. pap. text ed. 10.00 (1-56130-023-3) Krsna Inst.

Sri Krsna-Kathamrta-Vyakarana: An Introduction to Sanskrit, Vol. 2. Kusakrathadasa. (Krsna Library: Vol. 119). 125p. (Orig.). 1991. pap. text ed. 10.00 (1-56130-029-2) Krsna Inst.

Sri Krsna-Kathamrta-Vyakarana: An Introduction to Sanskrit, Vol. 3. Kusakrathadasa. (Krsna Library: Vol. 120). 140p. (Orig.). 1991. pap. text ed. 10.00 (1-56130-030-6) Krsna Inst.

Sri Krsna-Kirtana: The Glories of Lord Krsna. Kusakrathadasa. (Krsna Library: No. 2, Vol. 5). 60p. (C). 1993. pap. text ed. 4.00 (1-56130-105-1) Krsna Inst.

Sri Krsna-Sahasra-Nama: A Thousand Names of Lord Krsna from the Visnu-Dharma Purana. Vedavyasa. Tr. by Kusakratha Dasa from SAN. (Krsna Library). 81p. (Orig.). 1995. pap. text ed. 6.00 (1-56130-162-0) Krsna Inst.

Sri Krsna-Stavastakavali: Prayers Glorifying Lord Krsna. Kusakrathadasa. (Krsna Library: No. 2, Vol. 6). 98p. (C). 1993. pap. text ed. 10.00 (1-56130-115-9) Krsna Inst.

Sri Krsna Upanisad & Other Vaisnava Upanisads. Vyasadeva & Baladevavidyabhusana. Tr. by Kusakrathadasa from SAN. (Krsna Library: Vol. 165). 44p. (C). 1992. pap. text ed. 4.00 (1-56130-078-0) Krsna Inst.

Sri Krsnakrstih: Attraction to Krsna. Kusakrathadasa. Tr. by Kusakratha Dasa from SAN. (Krsna Library: No. 2, Vol. 1). 56p. (Orig.). 1991. pap. text ed. 6.00 (1-56130-046-2) Krsna Inst.

Sri Lalita Sahasranam. 5.95 (81-7120-104-0) Vedanta Pr.

Sri Lanka. (Insight Guides Ser.). 1993. pap. 22.95 (0-395-66310-5) HM.

Sri Lanka. P. C. Chaudhury. (Lands & Peoples of the World Ser.). 150p. 1985. text ed. 12.95 (0-86590-732-3, Pub. by Sterling Pubs II) Apt Bks.

Sri Lanka. Vijaya Samaraweera. (World Bibliographical Ser.: No. 20). 194p. 1987. lib. bdg. 40.50 (0-903450-33-X) ABC-CLIO.

Sri Lanka. Robert Zimmermann. LC 91-35252. (Enchantment of the World Ser.). 128p. (J). (gr. 5-9). 1992. lib. bdg. 30.00 (0-516-02606-2) Childrens.

Sri Lanka. 6th ed. Christine Niven. (Illus.). 282p. 1996. pap. 14.95 (0-86442-476-0) Lonely Planet.

Sri Lanka: A Country Study. 2nd ed. Ed. by Russell R. Ross & Andrea M. Savada. LC 89-600470. (Illus.). 360p. 1990. 22.00 (0-16-024055-7, 008-020-01216-5) USGPO.

Sri Lanka: A History. Chandra R. De Silva. Ed. by B. N. Pandley & David Taylor. 325p. 1987. text ed. 35.00 (0-7069-3294-3) Advent Bks Div.

Sri Lanka: A Survey. K. M. De Silva. LC 77-73917. 516p. 1977. reprint ed. pap. 147.10 (0-608-00535-5, 2061414) Bks Demand.

Sri Lanka: Ethnic Fratricide & the Dismantling of Democracy. Stanley J. Tambiah. (Illus.). xii, 210p. 1991. pap. text ed. 12.95 (0-226-78952-7) U Ch Pr.

Sri Lanka: Its Company Law Stock Exchange Company Secretarian Practice. H. M. Fernando. xxvii, 353p. Date not set. pap. 40.00 (955-95760-0-3) Gaunt.

Sri Lanka: The Conflict Within. Somasundaram Vanniasingham. (C). 1988. 34.00 (0-317-93136-9, Pub. by Lancer II) S Asia.

Sri Lanka: The Ethnic Conflict: Myths, Realities & Perspectives. Rational Development Committee Staff. 1985. 35.00 (0-8364-1292-3, Pub. by Navrang) S Asia.

Sri Lanka: The Invention of Enmity. David Little. LC 94-1061. 1994. pap. text ed. 14.95 (1-878379-15-1) US Inst Peace.

Sri Lanka: War-Torn Island. Lawrence J. Zweir. LC 96-24898. (World in Conflict Ser.). (J). 1997. lib. bdg. write for info. (0-8225-3550-5) Lerner Group.

***Sri Lanka: What Went Wrong.** V. P. Vittachi. (C). 1995. 20.00 (81-7013-146-4, Pub. by Navrang) S Asia.

Sri Lanka see Cultures of the World - Group 3

Sri Lanka by Rail. Royston Ellis. (Bradt Rail Guides Ser.). (Illus.). 240p. 1994. pap. 15.95 (1-56440-536-2, Pub. by Bradt Pubns UK) Globe Pequot.

Sri Lanka, Extrajudicial Executions, "Disappearances" & Torture, 1987 to 1990. 71p. 1990. 6.00 (0-939994-57-7) Amnesty Intl USA.

Sri Lanka Handbook with the Maldives. Robert Bradnock. (Handbooks of the World Ser.). 1996. 19.95 (0-8442-4902-5, Passport Bks) NTC Pub Grp.

Sri Lanka in Pictures. Ed. by Lerner Publications, Department of Geography Staff. (Visual Geography Ser.). (Illus.). 64p. (YA). (gr. 5 up). 1988. lib. bdg. 19.95 (0-8225-1853-8, Lerner Publctns) Lerner Group.

Sri Lanka Journal of International Law, 1989-1994, 2 bks., Set, Vols. 1-6. 1996. Set. 325.00 (0-685-69183-7) Gaunt.

Sri Lanka Phrasebook. Margit Meinhold. 80p. (Orig.). 1987. pap. 2.95 (0-908086-94-6) Lonely Planet.

Sri Lanka with the Maldives. (Handbooks of the World Ser.). 1996. 19.95 (0-614-97029-6) NTC Pub Grp.

Sri Lankan Crisis & India's Response. Ed. by V. Suryanarayan. (C). 1991. 10.00 (81-7050-141-5, Pub. by Patriot II) S Asia.

Sri Lankan Fisherman: Rural Capitalism & Peasant Society. Paul Alexander. (C). 1995. 36.00 (0-614-06779-0, Pub. by Sterling Plns Pvt II) S Asia.

Sri Mad Devi Bhagavatam. Vijnanananda. LC 73-3819. (Sacred Books of the Hindus: No. 26, Bks. 1-12). reprint ed. 87.50 (0-404-57826-8) AMS Pr.

Sri Nandanandanabhinandana: Welcoming Lord Krsna with Prayers. Kusakrathadasa. (Krsna Library: No. 2, Vol. 3). 52p. (C). 1991. pap. text ed. 4.00 (1-56130-064-0) Krsna Inst.

Sri Narada Pancharatnam, the Jnanamrita Sara Samhita. Narada-Pancaratra Pancaratra. Tr. by Swami Vijnanananda. LC 73-3816. (Sacred Books of the Hindus: No. 23). reprint ed. 32.50 (0-404-57823-3) AMS Pr.

Sri Neelakanta's Prasna Tantra: Horary Astrology. Bangalore V. Raman. Ed. by Astrological Magazine Staff. (Orig.). (C). 1993. pap. text ed. 6.50 (81-85674-66-3, Pub. by UBS Pubs Dist II) S Asia.

Sri Nityanandabhinandana: Welcoming Lord Nityananda with Prayers. Kusakrathadasa. (Krsna Library: Series 2, Vol. 15). 56p. (Orig.). 1994. pap. text ed. 4.00 (1-56130-151-5) Krsna Inst.

Sri Nrsimha-palana-prarthana: Prayers to Lord Nrsimha for Protection. Kusakrathadasa. (Krsna Library: No. 2, Vol. 2). 52p. (C). 1991. pap. text ed. 4.00 (1-56130-063-2) Krsna Inst.

Sri Nrsimha-Sahasra-Nama: A Thousand Names of Lord Nrsimha, Taken from the Nrsimha Purana. Vedavyasa. Tr. by Kusakrathadasa from SAN. (Krsna Library: Vol. 181). 72p. (C). 1993. pap. text ed. 6.00 (1-56130-103-5) Krsna Inst.

Sri Nrsimha-stava: Prayers to Lord Nrsimha. Vyasadeva et al. Tr. by Kusakrathadasa from SAN. (Krsna Library: Vol. 179). 67p. (C). 1992. pap. text ed. 4.00 (1-56130-094-2) Krsna Inst.

Sri Radha-kirti: The Glories of Sri Radha. Kusakrathadasa. (Krsna Library: No. 2, Vol. 9). 53p. (C). 1993. pap. text ed. 4.00 (1-56130-118-3) Krsna Inst.

Sri Radha-Krsna-Sahasra-Nama: A Thousand Names of Sri Radha-Krsna from Sri Narada Purana. Naradamuni. Tr. by Kusakrathadasa from SAN. (Krsna Library: Vol. 140). 78p. (C). 1991. pap. text ed. 6.00 (1-56130-047-0) Krsna Inst.

Sri Radha-Sahasra-Nama-Stotra: A Thousand Names of Sri Radha. Naradamuni. Tr. by Kusakrathadasa from SAN. (Krsna Library: Vol. 105). 84p. (Orig.). 1990. pap. text ed. 6.00 (1-56130-014-4) Krsna Inst.

Sri Ramacharitamansa: Holy Lake of Rama (Epic on Indian Ramayana) Tulsidasa. Ed. & Tr. by R. C. Prasad. (C). 1989. 48.50 (81-208-0443-0, Pub. by Motilal Banarsidass II) S Asia.

Sri Ramakrishna in the Eyes of Brahma & Christian Admirers. Ed. by Nanda Mookerjee. LC 76-904430. 1976. 6.50 (0-88386-791-5) S Asia.

Sri Ramakrishna's Life & Message in the Present Age: With the Author's Reminiscences of Holy Mother & Some Direct Disciples. Swami Satprakashananda. LC 75-46386. 208p. 1976. 7.95 (0-916356-54-X) Vedanta Soc St Louis.

Sri Sanatkumara-Samhita. Sanatkumara. Tr. by Kusakrathadasa from SAN. (Krsna Library: Vol. 164). 148p. (C). 1992. pap. text ed. 10.00 (1-56130-079-9) Krsna Inst.

Sri Sankara Vijayam. Ramachandran. 1977. pap. 1.50 (0-89744-123-0) Auromere.

Sri Sarada Devi: Consort of Sri Ramakrishna. Ed. by Nanda Mookerjee. 1978. 6.00 (0-8364-0173-5) S Asia.

Sri Sarada Devi: The Great Wonder. 526p. 13.50 (81-7120-486-4) Vedanta Pr.

Sri Sarasvati Puja: Goddess of Knowledge & Education. Panduranga R. Malyala. (Illus.). 28p. 1982. 2.00 (0-938924-10-9) Sri Shirdi Sai.

***Sri Sarbarthachintamani, 3 pts.** B. Suryanarain Rao. 1996. 36.00 (81-208-1351-0, Pub. by Motilal Banarsidass II) S Asia.

Sri Satvata Tantra: The Devotees of the Lord, 2 vols., Set. Naradamuni & Sivadeva. Tr. by Kusakrathadasa from SAN. (Krsna Library: Vols. 109-110). 330p. (Orig.). 1990. pap. text ed. 20.00 (1-56130-025-X) Krsna Inst.

Sri Satvata Tantra: The Devotees of the Lord, Vol. 1. Naradamuni & Sivadeva. Tr. by Kusakrathadasa from SAN. (Krsna Library: Vol. 109). 170p. (Orig.). 1990. pap. text ed. 10.00 (1-56130-018-7) Krsna Inst.

Sri Satvata Tantra: The Devotees of the Lord, Vol. 2. Naradamuni & Sivadeva. Tr. by Kusakrathadasa from SAN. (Krsna Library: Vol. 110). 160p. (Orig.). 1990. pap. text ed. 10.00 (1-56130-019-5) Krsna Inst.

Sri Satyanarayana Katha see Model Building of Solar Systems

Sri Satyanarayana Puja. Satguru S. Keshavadas. (Illus.). 172p. (Orig.). 1984. pap. 12.00 (0-942508-17-3) Vishwa.

Sri Shirdi Sai Baba. 1989. 5.00 (0-938924-34-6) Sri Shirdi Sai.

Sri Shirdi Sai Baba: Universal Master. S. P. Ruhela. (C). 1994. pap. 8.00 (81-207-1624-8, Pub. by Sterling Plns Pvt II) S Asia.

Sri Skanda Purana's, Sri Vasudeva-Mahatmya's & Sri Narada's Visit to Goloka Vrndavana. Vyasadeva. Tr. by Kusakrathadasa from SAN. (Krsna Library: Vol. 177). 87p. (C). 1992. pap. text ed. 8.00 (1-56130-091-8) Krsna Inst.

Sri Sri Radha-Giridhari-Gitavatamsa: A Garland of Songs Glorifying Sri Sri Radha-Giridhari. Kusakrathadasa. (Krsna Library: No. 2, Vol. 10). 98p. (C). 1993. pap. text ed. 10.00 (1-56130-130-2) Krsna Inst.

Sri Sri Radha-Govinda-lilaravindatavi-manda-vayv-avali Vol. 1: Breezes Carrying the Fragrance of the Lotus Forest of Sri Sri Radha-Krsna's Pastimes. Kusakrathadasa. (Krsna Library: Series 2, Vol. 14). 120p. (Orig.). 1994. pap. text ed. 8.00 (1-56130-150-7) Krsna Inst.

Sri Sri Radha-Madhava-Keli-Cintamani-Victira-Citravali: Colorful Pictures of Sr. Sri Radha-Krsna's Cintamani Jewel Pastimes. Kusakrathadasa. (Krsna Library). 93p. (Orig.). 1995. pap. text ed. 6.00 (1-56130-164-7) Krsna Inst.

Sri Sukhmani Sahib: A Part of Sikh Scriptures. Ujagar S. Bawa. LC 89-51589. (Books on Sikhism Ser.). 304p. (J). 1997. reprint ed. pap. 15.00 (0-942245-05-9) Wash Sikh Ctr.

An Asterisk (*) at the beginning of an entry indicates that the title is appearing in BIP for the first time.

Sri Surabhi-Pankajangi-Stava: Prayers Glorifying Lord Krsna, Whose Limbs Are Like Lotus Petals. Kusakrathadasa. (Krsna Library). 50p. (Orig.). 1995. pap. text ed. 4.00 (*1-56130-163-9*) Krsna Inst.

Sri Svetasvatara Upanisad. Svetasvataramuni & Vedavyasa. Tr. by Kusakrathadasa from SAN. (Krsna Library: Vol. 79). 65p. (Orig.). 1989. pap. text ed. 6.00 (*0-944833-45-4*) Krsna Inst.

Sri Swami Satchidananda: Apostle of Peace. Sita Bordow et al. LC 86-10533. (Illus.). 454p. (Orig.). 1986. pap. 14.95 (*0-932040-31-4*) Integral Yoga Pubns.

Sri Vedanta-Rahasya: The Secrets of Vedanta. Kusakrathadasa. (Krsna Library: No. 2, Vol. 11). 57p. (C). 1994. pap. text ed. 4.00 (*1-56130-127-2*) Krsna Inst.

Sri Vedanta-sutra: With the Sri Govinda-bhasya Commentary of Srila Baladeva Vidyabhusana, 6 vols., Set. Vyasadeva & Baladevavidyabhusana. Tr. by Kusakrathadasa from SAN. (Krsna Library). (C). 1992. pap. text ed. 62.00 (*1-56130-100-0*) Krsna Inst.

Sri Visnu-Sahasra-Nama-Stotra: A Thousand Names of Lord Visnu with the Commentary of Srila Baladeva Vidyabhusana. Vyasadeva & Baladeva Vidyabhusana. Tr. by Kusakrathadasa from SAN. (Krsna Library: Vol. 15). 178p. (Orig.). (C). 1988. pap. text ed. 10.00 (*0-944833-25-X*) Krsna Inst.

Sri Vraja-Mandala-Kavita: The Poetry of Vraja-mandala. Kusakrathadasa. (Krsna Library). 116p. (C). 1994. pap. text ed. 8.00 (*1-56130-141-8*) Krsna Inst.

Sri Vrajavira-virudavali: Calling Out to Lord Krsna. Kusakrathadasa. (Krsna Library: No. 2, Vol. 7). 40p. (C). 1993. pap. text ed. write for info. (*1-56130-116-7*) Krsna Inst.

Sri Vrndavana-Kirtana: The Glories of Sri Vrndavana. Kusakrathadasa. (Krsna Library: No. 2, Vol. 8). 55p. (C). 1993. pap. text ed. 4.00 (*1-56130-117-5*) Krsna Inst.

Srihastamuktavali: A Text of Ancient Indian Aescetics. Maheswar Neog. (C). 1991. 30.00 (*81-208-0829-0*, Pub. by Motilal Banarsidass II) S Asia.

Srikanthacarita: A Mahakavya of Mankhaka. Bankim C. Mandal. (C). 1992. 24.00 (*0-8364-2798-X*, Pub. by Sanskrit Pustake) S Asia.

Srila Baladeva Vidyabhusana's Sri Aisvarya-kadambini: The Monsoon of Lord Krsna's Opulence. Baladeva Vidyabhusana. Tr. by Kusakratha Dasa from SAN. (Krsna Library: Vol. 5). 110p. (Orig.). (C). 1987. pap. text ed. 8.00 (*0-944833-04-7*) Krsna Inst.

Srila Baladeva Vidyabhusana's Sri Prameya-Ratnavali: The Jewel Necklace of Truths. Kusakratha Dasa. Tr. by Baladeva Vidyabhusana from SAN. (Krsna Library: Vol. 21). 107p. (Orig.). (C). 1988. pap. text ed. 8.00 (*0-944833-14-4*) Krsna Inst.

Srila Baladeva Vidyabhusana's Sri Vedanta-Syamantaka: The Syamantaka Jewel of Vedanta. Baladevavidyabhusana. Tr. by Kusakratha Dasa from SAN. (Krsna Library). 85p. (Orig.). 1995. pap. text ed. 8.00 (*1-56130-160-4*) Krsna Inst.

Srila Bhaktivinoda Thakura's Gita-Mala: A Garland of Songs. Bhaktivinodathakura. Tr. by Kusakrathadasa from BEN. (Krsna Library: Vol. 216). 248p. (Orig.). 1994. pap. text ed. 15.00 (*1-56130-142-6*) Krsna Inst.

Srila Bhaktivinoda Thakura's Gitavali: Songs. Bhaktivinodathakura. Tr. by Kusakrathadasa from SAN. (Krsna Library). 211p. (C). 1994. pap. text ed. 12.00 (*1-56130-138-8*) Krsna Inst.

Srila Bhaktivinoda Thakura's Kalyana-Kalpataru: The Desire-Tree of Auspiciousness. Bhaktivinodathakura. Tr. by Kusakrathadasa from BEN. (Krsna Library). 250p. (C). 1994. pap. text ed. 15.00 (*1-56130-139-6*) Krsna Inst.

Srila Bhaktivinoda Thakura's Prema-Pradipa: The Lamp of Love. Bhaktivinodathakura. Tr. by Kusakrathadasa from BEN. (Krsna Library: Vol. 218). 112p. (Orig.). 1994. pap. text ed. 8.00 (*1-56130-152-3*) Krsna Inst.

Srila Bhaktivinoda Thakura's Saranagati: Surrender. Bhaktivinoda Thakura. Tr. by Kusakratha Dasa from BEN. (Krsna Library). 159p. (C). 1994. pap. text ed. 10.00 (*1-56130-137-X*) Krsna Inst.

Srila Bhaktivinoda Thakura's Sri Amnaya-sutra: The Teachings of the Scriptures. Bhaktivinodathakura. Tr. by Kusakrathadasa from SAN. (Krsna Library: Vol. 166). 238p. (C). 1992. pap. text ed. 12.00 (*1-56130-090-X*) Krsna Inst.

Srila Bhaktivinoda Thakura's Sri Datta-kaustubha: The Gift of a Kaustubha Jewel. Bhaktivinodathakura. Tr. by Kusakrathadasa from SAN. (Krsna Library: Vol. 178). 101p. (C). 1992. pap. text ed. 10.00 (*1-56130-089-6*) Krsna Inst.

Srila Bhaktivinoda Thakura's Sri Hari-Nama-Cintamani: The Cintamani Jewel of Lord Krsna's Holy Name. Bhaktivinodathakura. Tr. by Kusakrathadasa from BEN. (Krsna Library: Vol. 217). 192p. (Orig.). 1994. pap. text ed. 10.00 (*1-56130-145-0*) Krsna Inst.

Srila Bhaktivinoda Thakura's Sri Jaiva-dharma: The Universal Religion. Bhaktivinodathakura. Tr. by Kusakrathadasa from BEN. (Krsna Library: Vol. 196). 115p. (C). 1993. pap. text ed. 10.00 (*1-56130-119-1*) Krsna Inst.

Srila Bhaktivinoda Thakura's Sri Jaiva-dharma, Vol. 2: The Universal Religion. Bhaktivinodathakura. Tr. by Kusakrathadasa from BEN. (Krsna Library: Vol. 197). 111p. (C). 1993. pap. text ed. 10.00 (*1-56130-120-5*) Krsna Inst.

Srila Bhaktivinoda Thakura's Sri Jaiva-dharma, Vol. 3: The Universal Religion. Bhaktivinodathakura. Tr. by Kusakrathadasa from BEN. (Krsna Library: Vol. 198). 124p. (C). 1993. pap. text ed. 10.00 (*1-56130-121-3*) Krsna Inst.

Srila Bhaktivinoda Thakura's Sri Jaiva-dharma, Vol. 4: The Universal Religion. Bhaktivinodathakura. Tr. by Kusakrathadasa from BEN. (Krsna Library: Vol. 199). 124p. (C). 1993. pap. text ed. 10.00 (*1-56130-122-1*) Krsna Inst.

Srila Bhaktivinoda Thakura's Sri Jaiva-dharma, Vol. 5: The Universal Religion. Bhaktivinodathakura. Tr. by Kusakrathadasa from BEN. (Krsna Library: 200). 119p. (C). 1993. pap. text ed. 10.00 (*1-56130-123-X*) Krsna Inst.

Srila Bhaktivinoda Thakura's Sri Jaiva-dharma, Vol. 6: The Universal Religion. Bhaktivinodathakura. Tr. by Kusakrathadasa from BEN. (Krsna Library: Vol. 201). 132p. (C). 1993. pap. text ed. 10.00 (*1-56130-124-8*) Krsna Inst.

Srila Bhaktivinoda Thakura's Sri Jaiva-dharma, Vols. 1-6: The Universal Religion, 6 vols., Set. Bhaktivinodathakura. Tr. by Kusakrathadasa from BEN. (Krsna Library: Vols. 196-201). (C). 1993. pap. text ed. 10.00 (*1-56130-125-6*) Krsna Inst.

Srila Bhaktivinoda Thakura's Sri Navadvipa-dhama-mahatmya Pramana-khanda: The Glories of Sri Navadvipa: Evidence from Scripture. Bhaktivinoda Thakura. Tr. by Kusakratha dasa. (Krsna Library: Vol. 61). 203p. (Orig.). 1989. pap. text ed. 12.00 (*0-944833-61-6*) Krsna Inst.

Srila Bhaktivinoda Thakura's Sri Tattva-Sutra: The Truth. Bhaktivinodathakura. Tr. by Kusakrathadasa from SAN. (Krsna Library: Vol. 182). 184p. (C). 1993. pap. text ed. 12.00 (*1-56130-102-7*) Krsna Inst.

Srila Bhaktivinoda Thakura's Srila Gauranga-Smarana-Mangala-Stotra. Bhaktivinoda Thakura. Tr. by Kusakratha Dasa from SAN. (Krsna Library: Vol. 16). 64p. (Orig.). (C). 1988. pap. text ed. 8.00 (*0-944833-26-8*) Krsna Inst.

Srila Bhaktivinoda Thakura's Tattva-viveka - Discerning the Truth. Bhaktivinoda Thakura. Tr. by Kusakratha dasa from SAN. (Krsna Library). 90p. (Orig.). 1995. pap. text ed. 10.00 (*1-56130-165-5*) Krsna Inst.

Srila Gopala-tapani Upanisad. Vyasadeva. Tr. by Kusakratha dasa from SAN. (Krsna Library: Vol. 24). 94p. (Orig.). 1989. pap. text ed. 8.00 (*0-944833-29-2*) Krsna Inst.

Srila Jiva Gosvami's Songs from Sri Gopala-campu. Jiva Gosvami. Tr. by Kusakratha dasa from SAN. (Krsna Library: Vol. 23). 89p. (Orig.). 1989. pap. text ed. 8.00 (*0-944833-28-4*) Krsna Inst.

Srila Jiva Gosvami's Songs from Sri Gopala-campu, Vol. 2. Tr. by Kusakrathadasa from SAN. (Krsna Library: Vol. 152). 91p. (C). 1992. pap. text ed. 8.00 (*1-56130-069-1*) Krsna Inst.

Srila Jiva Gosvami's Sri Bhagavat-Sandarbha: An Essay on Bhagavan, Vol. 1. Jivagosvami. Tr. by Kusakrathadasa from SAN. (Krsna Library: Vol. 64). (Orig.). (C). 1990. pap. text ed. 12.00 (*0-944833-81-0*) Krsna Inst.

Srila Jiva Gosvami's Sri Bhagavat-Sandarbha: An Essay on Bhagavan, Vol. 2. Jivagosvami. Tr. by Kusakrathadasa from SAN. (Krsna Library: Vol. 65). (Orig.). (C). 1990. pap. text ed. 12.00 (*0-944833-82-9*) Krsna Inst.

Srila Jiva Gosvami's Sri Bhagavat-Sandarbha: An Essay on Bhagavan, Vol. 3. Jivagosvami. Tr. by Kusakrathadasa from SAN. (Krsna Library: Vol. 66). (Orig.). (C). 1990. pap. text ed. 12.00 (*0-944833-83-7*) Krsna Inst.

Srila Jiva Gosvami's Sri Bhagavat-Sandarbha: An Essay on Bhagavan, Vol. 4. Jivagosvami. Tr. by Kusakrathadasa from SAN. (Krsna Library: Vol. 67). (Orig.). (C). 1990. pap. text ed. 12.00 (*0-944833-84-5*) Krsna Inst.

Srila Jiva Gosvami's Sri Bhagavat-Sandarbha: An Essay on Bhagavan, Vol. 5. Jivagosvami. Tr. by Kusakrathadasa from SAN. (Krsna Library: Vol. 68). (Orig.). (C). 1990. pap. text ed. 12.00 (*0-944833-85-3*) Krsna Inst.

Srila Jiva Gosvami's Sri Bhagavat-Sandarbha, Complete in Six Volumes: An Essay on Bhagavan, Vols. 1-6. Jivagosvami. Tr. by Kusakrathadasa from SAN. (Krsna Library: Vol. 64). (Orig.). (C). 1990. pap. text ed. 60.00 (*0-944833-86-1*) Krsna Inst.

Srila Jiva Gosvami's Sri Bhakti-sandarbha: An Essay on Devotional Service, 12 vols., Set. Jivagosvami. Tr. by Kusakrathadasa from SAN. (Krsna Library). (C). 1992. pap. text ed. 128.00 (*1-56130-101-9*) Krsna Inst.

Srila Jiva Gosvami's Sri Bhakti-Sandarbha: An Essay on Devotional Service, Vol. 1. Jivagosvami. Tr. by Kusakrathadasa from SAN. (Krsna Library: Vol. 112). 200p. (Orig.). 1990. pap. text ed. 12.00 (*1-56130-021-7*) Krsna Inst.

Srila Jiva Gosvami's Sri Bhakti-Sandarbha: An Essay on Devotional Service, Vol. 2. Jivagosvami. Tr. by Kusakrathadasa from SAN. (Krsna Library: Vol. 113). 202p. (Orig.). 1990. pap. text ed. 12.00 (*1-56130-022-5*) Krsna Inst.

Srila Jiva Gosvami's Sri Bhakti-sandarbha, Vol. 10: An Essay on Devotional Service. Jivagosvami. Tr. by Kusakrathadasa from SAN. (Krsna Library: Vol. 174). 128p. (C). 1992. pap. text ed. 10.00 (*1-56130-086-1*) Krsna Inst.

Srila Jiva Gosvami's Sri Bhakti-sandarbha, Vol. 11: An Essay on Devotional Service. Jivagosvami. Tr. by Kusakrathadasa from SAN. (Krsna Library: Vol. 175). 132p. (C). 1992. pap. text ed. 10.00 (*1-56130-087-X*) Krsna Inst.

Srila Jiva Gosvami's Sri Bhakti-sandarbha, Vol. 12: An Essay on Devotional Service. Jivagosvami. Tr. by Kusakrathadasa from SAN. (Krsna Library: Vol. 176). 128p. (C). 1992. pap. text ed. 10.00 (*1-56130-088-8*) Krsna Inst.

Srila Jiva Gosvami's Sri Bhakti-Sandarbha, Vol. 3: An Essay on Devotional Service. Jivagosvami. Tr. by Kusakrathadasa from SAN. (Krsna Library: Vol. 124). 202p. (Orig.). 1991. pap. text ed. 12.00 (*1-56130-032-2*) Krsna Inst.

Srila Jiva Gosvami's Sri Bhakti-Sandarbha, Vol. 4: An Essay on Devotional Service. Jivagosvami. Tr. by Kusakrathadasa from SAN. (Krsna Library: Vol. 133). 202p. (Orig.). 1991. pap. text ed. 12.00 (*1-56130-044-6*) Krsna Inst.

Srila Jiva Gosvami's Sri Bhakti-sandarbha, Vol. 5: An Essay on Devotional Service. Jivagosvami. Tr. by Kusakrathadasa from SAN. (Krsna Library: Vol. 169). 141p. (C). 1992. pap. text ed. 10.00 (*1-56130-081-0*) Krsna Inst.

Srila Jiva Gosvami's Sri Bhakti-sandarbha, Vol. 6: An Essay on Devotional Service. Jivagosvami. Tr. by Kusakrathadasa from SAN. (Krsna Library: Vol. 170). 111p. (C). 1992. pap. text ed. 10.00 (*1-56130-082-9*) Krsna Inst.

Srila Jiva Gosvami's Sri Bhakti-sandarbha, Vol. 7: An Essay on Devotional Service. Jivagosvami. Tr. by Kusakrathadasa from SAN. (Krsna Library: Vol. 171). 109p. (C). 1992. pap. text ed. 10.00 (*1-56130-083-7*) Krsna Inst.

Srila Jiva Gosvami's Sri Bhakti-sandarbha, Vol. 8: An Essay on Devotional Service. Jivagosvami. Tr. by Kusakrathadasa from SAN. (Krsna Library: Vol. 172). 132p. (C). 1992. pap. text ed. 10.00 (*1-56130-084-5*) Krsna Inst.

Srila Jiva Gosvami's Sri Bhakti-sandarbha, Vol. 9: An Essay on Devotional Service. Jivagosvami. Tr. by Kusakrathadasa from SAN. (Krsna Library: Vol. 173). 140p. (C). 1992. pap. text ed. 10.00 (*1-56130-085-3*) Krsna Inst.

Srila Jiva Gosvami's Sri Gopala-Campu, Vol. 1. Jivagosvami. Tr. by Kusakrathadasa from SAN. (Krsna Library). 130p. (Orig.). 1993. pap. text ed. 8.00 (*1-56130-161-2*) Krsna Inst.

Srila Jiva Gosvami's Sri Krsna-Sandarbha: An Essay on Sri Krsna, Set. Jivagosvami. Tr. by Kusakrathadasa from SAN. (Krsna Library: Vols. 43-48). 1254p. (Orig.). (C). 1989. pap. text ed. 72.00 (*0-944833-68-3*) Krsna Inst.

Srila Jiva Gosvami's Sri Krsna-Sandarbha: An Essay on Sri Krsna, Vol. 1. Jivagosvami. Tr. by Kusakrathadasa from SAN. (Krsna Library: Vol. 43). 211p. (Orig.). (C). 1989. pap. text ed. 12.00 (*0-944833-62-4*) Krsna Inst.

Srila Jiva Gosvami's Sri Krsna-Sandarbha: An Essay on Sri Krsna, Vol. 2. Jivagosvami. Tr. by Kusakrathadasa from SAN. (Krsna Library: Vol. 44). 217p. (Orig.). (C). 1989. pap. text ed. 12.00 (*0-944833-63-2*) Krsna Inst.

Srila Jiva Gosvami's Sri Krsna-Sandarbha: An Essay on Sri Krsna, Vol. 3. Jivagosvami. Tr. by Kusakrathadasa from SAN. (Krsna Library: Vol. 45). 228p. (Orig.). (C). 1989. pap. text ed. 12.00 (*0-944833-64-0*) Krsna Inst.

Srila Jiva Gosvami's Sri Krsna-Sandarbha: An Essay on Sri Krsna, Vol. 4. Jivagosvami. Tr. by Kusakrathadasa from SAN. (Krsna Library: Vol. 46). 216p. (Orig.). (C). 1989. pap. text ed. 12.00 (*0-944833-65-9*) Krsna Inst.

Srila Jiva Gosvami's Sri Krsna-Sandarbha: An Essay on Sri Krsna, Vol. 5. Jivagosvami. Tr. by Kusakrathadasa from SAN. (Krsna Library: Vol. 47). 201p. (Orig.). (C). 1989. pap. text ed. 12.00 (*0-944833-66-7*) Krsna Inst.

Srila Jiva Gosvami's Sri Krsna-Sandarbha: An Essay on Sri Krsna, Vol. 6. Jivagosvami. Tr. by Kusakrathadasa from SAN. (Krsna Library: Vol. 48). 181p. (Orig.). (C). 1989. pap. text ed. 12.00 (*0-944833-67-5*) Krsna Inst.

Srila Jiva Gosvami's Sri Paramatma - Sandarbha, Vol. 1: An Essay on the Supersoul. Jivagosvami. Tr. by Kusakrathadasa from SAN. (Krsna Library: Vol. 188). 110p. (C). 1993. pap. text ed. 10.00 (*1-56130-109-4*) Krsna Inst.

Srila Jiva Gosvami's Sri Paramatma - Sandarbha, Vol. 2: An Essay on the Supersoul. Jivagosvami. Tr. by Kusakrathadasa from SAN. (Krsna Library: Vol. 191). 132p. (C). 1993. pap. text ed. 10.00 (*1-56130-110-8*) Krsna Inst.

Srila Jiva Gosvami's Sri Paramatma - Sandarbha, Vol. 3: An Essay on the Supersoul. Jivagosvami. Tr. by Kusakrathadasa from SAN. (Krsna Library: Vol. 192). 120p. (C). 1993. pap. text ed. 10.00 (*1-56130-111-6*) Krsna Inst.

Srila Jiva Gosvami's Sri Paramatma - Sandarbha, Vol. 4: An Essay on the Supersoul. Jivagosvami. Tr. by Kusakrathadasa from SAN. (Krsna Library: Vol. 193). 116p. (C). 1993. pap. text ed. 10.00 (*1-56130-112-4*) Krsna Inst.

Srila Jiva Gosvami's Sri Paramatma - Sandarbha, Vol. 5: An Essay on the Supersoul. Jivagosvami. Tr. by Kusakrathadasa from SAN. (Krsna Library: Vol. 194). 121p. (C). 1993. pap. text ed. 10.00 (*1-56130-113-2*) Krsna Inst.

Srila Jiva Gosvami's Sri Paramatma - Sandarbha, Vol. 6: An Essay on the Supersoul. Jivagosvami. Tr. by Kusakrathadasa from SAN. (Krsna Library: Vol. 195). 158p. (C). 1993. pap. text ed. 10.00 (*1-56130-114-0*) Krsna Inst.

Srila Jiva Gosvami's Sri Priti-sandarbha: An Essay on Love of Lord Krishna. Jivagosvami. Tr. by Kusakrathadasa from SAN. (Krsna Library: Vol. 225). 500p. (Orig.). 1995. pap. text ed. 50.00 (*1-56130-172-8*) Krsna Inst.

Srila Jiva Gosvami's Sri Sankalpa-Kalpadruma, Vol. 1: The Kalpadruma Tree That Fulfills All Desires. Jivagosvami. Tr. by Kusakrathadasa from SAN. (Krsna Library: Vol. 134). 128p. (Orig.). 1991. pap. text ed. 10.00 (*1-56130-045-4*) Krsna Inst.

Srila Jiva Gosvami's Sri Sankalpa-kalpadruma, Vol. 2: The Tree That Fulfills All Desires. Jivagosvami. Tr. by Kusakrathadasa from SAN. (Krsna Library: Vol. 149). 97p. (C). 1991. pap. text ed. 10.00 (*1-56130-061-6*) Krsna Inst.

Srila Jiva Gosvamis Sri Tattva-Sandarbha: An Essay on Truth. Jivagosvami. Tr. by Kusakrathadasa from SAN. (Krsna Library: Vol. 6). 257p. (C). 1987. pap. text ed. 12.00 (*0-944833-06-3*) Krsna Inst.

Srila Kavi-Karnapura's: Sri Gaura-ganoddesa-dipika. Kavikarnapura. Tr. by Kusakrathadasa from SAN. (Krsna Library: Vol. 11). 126p. (Orig.). (C). 1987. pap. 8.00 (*0-944833-10-1*) Krsna Inst.

Srila Kavi Karnapura's Sri Caitanya-Candrodaya: The Rising of the Moon of Sri Caitanya - Act Eight Prataparudrahugrahah, Mercy to King Prataparudra. Kavikarnapura. Tr. by Kusakrathadasa from SAN. (Krsna Library: Vol. 76). 110p. (Orig.). 1989. pap. text ed. 8.00 (*0-944833-76-4*) Krsna Inst.

Srila Kavi Karnapura's Sri Caitanya-Candrodaya: The Rising of the Moon of Sri Caitanya - Act Four Sannyasa-parigrahah, Acceptance of Sannyasa. Kavikarnapura. Tr. by Kusakrathadasa from SAN. (Krsna Library: Vol. 72). 74p. (Orig.). 1989. pap. text ed. 8.00 (*0-944833-72-1*) Krsna Inst.

Srila Kavi Karnapura's Sri Caitanya-Candrodaya: The Rising of the Moon of Sri Caitanya - Act Four Sannyasa-parigrahah, Acceptance of Sannyasa. Kavikarnapura. Tr. by Kusakrathadasa from SAN. (Krsna Library: Vol. 73). 54p. (Orig.). 1989. pap. text ed. 8.00 (*0-944833-73-X*) Krsna Inst.

Srila Kavi Karnapura's Sri Caitanya-Candrodaya: The Rising of the Moon of Sri Caitanya - Act Nine Mathuragamanam, Journey to Mathura. Kavikarnapura. Tr. by Kusakrathadasa from SAN. (Krsna Library: Vol. 77). 83p. (Orig.). 1989. pap. text ed. 8.00 (*0-944833-77-2*) Krsna Inst.

Srila Kavi Karnapura's Sri Caitanya-Candrodaya: The Rising of the Moon of Sri Caitanya - Act One Svanandavesah, The Entrance of His Bliss. Kavikarnapura. Tr. by Kusakrathadasa from SAN. (Krsna Library: Vol. 69). 110p. (Orig.). 1989. pap. text ed. 8.00 (*0-944833-69-1*) Krsna Inst.

Srila Kavi Karnapura's Sri Caitanya-Candrodaya: The Rising of the Moon of Sri Caitanya - Act Six Sarvabhaumanugrahah, Mercy to Sarvabhauma. Kavikarnapura. Tr. by Kusakrathadasa from SAN. (Krsna Library: Vol. 74). 116p. (Orig.). 1989. pap. text ed. 8.00 (*0-944833-74-8*) Krsna Inst.

Srila Kavi Karnapura's Sri Caitanya-Candrodaya: The Rising of the Moon of Sri Caitanya - Act Six Sarvabhaumanugrahah, Mercy to Sarvabhauma. Kavikarnapura. Tr. by Kusakrathadasa from SAN. (Krsna Library: Vol. 75). 62p. (Orig.). 1989. pap. text ed. 8.00 (*0-944833-75-6*) Krsna Inst.

Srila Kavi Karnapura's Sri Caitanya-Candrodaya: The Rising of the Moon of Sri Caitanya - Act Two Sarvavatara-darsanah, The Revelation of All Incarnations. Kavikarnapura. Tr. by Kusakrathadasa from SAN. (Krsna Library: Vol. 70). 78p. (Orig.). 1989. pap. text ed. 6.00 (*0-944833-70-5*) Krsna Inst.

Srila Kavi Karnapura's Sri Caitanya-Candrodaya: The Rising of the Moon of Sri Caitanya - Act Two Sarvavatara-darsanah, The Revelation of All Incarnations. Kavikarnapura. Tr. by Kusakrathadasa from SAN. (Krsna Library: Vol. 71). 107p. (Orig.). 1989. pap. text ed. 8.00 (*0-944833-71-3*) Krsna Inst.

Srila Kavi Karnapura's Sri Caitanya-Candrodaya: The Rising of the Moon of Sri Caitanya - Act Two Sarvavatara-darsanah, The Revelation of All Incarnations. Kavikarnapura. Tr. by Kusakrathadasa from SAN. (Krsna Library: Vol. 78). 134p. (Orig.). 1989. pap. text ed. 8.00 (*0-944833-78-0*) Krsna Inst.

Srila Kavi-Karnapura's Sri Caitanya-Sahasra-Nama-Stotra: A Thousand Names of Lord Caitanya. Kavikarnapura. Tr. by Kusakrathadasa from SAN. (Krsna Library: Vol. 12). 65p. (Orig.). (C). 1988. pap. 6.00 (*0-944833-11-X*) Krsna Inst.

Srila Kavikarnapura's Sri Caitanya-Carita, Vol. 1: The Pastimes of Lord Caitanya. Kavikarnapura. Tr. by Kusakrathadasa from SAN. (Krsna Library: Vol. 162). 156p. (C). 1992. pap. text ed. 10.00 (*1-56130-077-2*) Krsna Inst.

Srila Locana Dasa Thakura's Sri Caitanya-Mangala. Locanadasathakura. Tr. by Kusakrathadasa from BEN. (Krsna Library: Vol. 224). 270p. 1995. pap. text ed. 28.00 (*1-56130-171-X*) Krsna Inst.

Srila Madhvacarya's Sri Tattva-Muktavali or Mayavada-Sata-Dusani: The Pearl Necklace of Truths, or 100 Refutations of the Mayavada Fallacy. Madhvacarya. Tr. by Kusakrathadasa from SAN. (Krsna Library: Vol. 13). 110p. (Orig.). (C). 1988. pap. 8.00 (*0-944833-12-8*) Krsna Inst.

Srila Narottama Dasa Thakura's Sri Prarthana: Prayers. Narottamadasa. Tr. by Kusakrathadasa from BEN. (Krsna Library: Vol. 128). 152p. (Orig.). 1991. pap. text ed. 10.00 (*1-56130-039-X*) Krsna Inst.

Srila Narottama Dasa Thakura's Sri Prema-Bhakti-Candrika: The Moonlight of Loving Devotion. Narottamadasa. Tr. by Kusakrathadasa from BEN. (Krsna Library: Vol. 129). 76p. (Orig.). 1991. pap. text ed. 8.00 (*1-56130-040-3*) Krsna Inst.

Srila Prabodhananda Sarasvatis: Sri Vrndavana Mahimamrta Sataka Seventeen. Prabodhanandasarasvati. Tr. by Kusakrathadasa from SAN. (Krsna Library: Vol. 186). 78p. (C). 1993. pap. text ed. 6.00 (*1-56130-106-X*) Krsna Inst.

Srila Prabodhananda Sarasvati's Sri Caitanya-candramrta: The Nectar Moon of Sri Caitanya. Prabodhanandasarasvati. Tr. by Kusakrathadasa from SAN. (Krsna Library: Vol. 2). 156p. (C). 1987. pap. text ed. 10.00 (*0-944833-07-1*) Krsna Inst.

Srila Prabodhananda Sarasvati's Sri Navadvipa-sataka: A Hundred Verses Glorifying Sri Navadvipa. Bhaktivinoda Thakura. Tr. by Kusakrathadasa from SAN. (Krsna Library: Vol. 43). 61p. (Orig.). 1989. pap. text ed. 6.00 (*0-944833-39-X*) Krsna Inst.

Srila Prabodhananda Sarasvati's Sri Radha-Rasa-Sudha-Nidhi: The Nectar Moon of Sri Radha's Sweetness. Prabodhanandasarasvati. Tr. by Kusakrathadasa from SAN. (Krsna Library: Vol. 204). 180p. (C). 1993. pap. text ed. 10.00 (*1-56130-129-9*) Krsna Inst.

Srila Prabodhananda Sarasvati's Sri Vrndavana-Mahimamrta: The Nectar Glory of Sri Vrndavana, Vol. 1. Prabodhanandasarasvati. Tr. by Kusakrathadasa from SAN. (Krsna Library: Vol. 17). 166p. (Orig.). (C). 1988. pap. text ed. 6.00 (*0-944833-16-0*) Krsna Inst.

Srila Prabodhananda Sarasvati's Sri Vrndavana-Mahimamrta: The Nectar Glory of Sri Vrndavana, Vol. 2. Prabodhanandasarasvati. Tr. by Kusakrathadasa from SAN. (Krsna Library: Vol. 18). 166p. (Orig.). (C). 1988. pap. text ed. 6.00 (*0-944833-17-9*) Krsna Inst.

Srila Prabodhananda Sarasvati's Sri Vrndavana-Mahimamrta: The Nectar of Glory Sri Vrndavana, Vol. 3. Prabodhanandasarasvati. Tr. by Kusakrathadasa from SAN. (Krsna Library: Vol. 19). 150p. (Orig.). (C). 1988. pap. text ed. 6.00 (*0-944833-18-7*) Krsna Inst.

Srila Prabodhananda Sarasvati's Sri Vrndavana-Mahimamrta, Vol. 10: The Nectar Glory of Sri Vrndavana. Prabodhanandasarasvati. Tr. by Kusakrathadasa from SAN. (Krsna Library: Vol. 31). 80p. (Orig.). (C). 1988. pap. text ed. 6.00 (*0-944833-40-3*) Krsna Inst.

Srila Prabodhananda Sarasvati's Sri Vrndavana-Mahimamrta, Vol. 11: The Nectar Glory of Sri Vrndavana. Prabodhanandasarasvati. Tr. by Kusakrathadasa from SAN. (Krsna Library: Vol. 32). 72p. (Orig.). (C). 1988. pap. text ed. 6.00 (*0-944833-41-1*) Krsna Inst.

Srila Prabodhananda Sarasvati's Sri Vrndavana-Mahimamrta, Vol. 12: The Nectar Glory of Sri Vrndavana. Prabodhanandasarasvati. Tr. by Kusakrathadasa from SAN. (Krsna Library: Vol. 36). (Orig.). (C). 1988. pap. text ed. 6.00 (*0-944833-42-X*) Krsna Inst.

Srila Prabodhananda Sarasvati's Sri Vrndavana-Mahimamrta, Vol. 13: The Nectar Glory of Sri Vrndavana. Prabodhanandasarasvati. Tr. by Kusakrathadasa from SAN. (Krsna Library: Vol. 37). (Orig.). (C). 1988. pap. text ed. 6.00 (*0-944833-43-8*) Krsna Inst.

Srila Prabodhananda Sarasvati's Sri Vrndavana-Mahimamrta, Vol. 14: The Nectar Glory of Sri Vrndavana. Prabodhanandasarasvati. Tr. by Kusakrathadasa from SAN. (Krsna Library: Vol. 38). (Orig.). (C). 1988. pap. text ed. 6.00 (*0-944833-44-6*) Krsna Inst.

Srila Prabodhananda Sarasvati's Sri Vrndavana-Mahimamrta, Vol. 4: The Nectar Glory of Sri Vrndavana. Prabodhanandasarasvati. Tr. by Kusakrathadasa from SAN. (Krsna Library: Vol. 25). 80p. (Orig.). (C). 1988. pap. text ed. 6.00 (*0-944833-19-5*) Krsna Inst.

Srila Prabodhananda Sarasvati's Sri Vrndavana-Mahimamrta, Vol. 5: The Nectar Glory of Sri Vrndavana. Prabodhanandasarasvati. Tr. by Kusakrathadasa from SAN. (Krsna Library: Vol. 26). 72p. (Orig.). (C). 1988. pap. text ed. 6.00 (*0-944833-20-9*) Krsna Inst.

Srila Prabodhananda Sarasvati's Sri Vrndavana-Mahimamrta, Vol. 6: The Nectar Glory of Sri Vrndavana. Prabodhanandasarasvati. Tr. by Kusakrathadasa from SAN. (Krsna Library: Vol. 27). 72p. (Orig.). (C). 1988. pap. text ed. 6.00 (*0-944833-21-7*) Krsna Inst.

Srila Prabodhananda Sarasvati's Sri Vrndavana-Mahimamrta, Vol. 7: The Nectar Glory of Sri Vrndavana. Prabodhanandasarasvati. Tr. by Kusakrathadasa from SAN. (Krsna Library: Vol. 28). 64p. (Orig.). (C). 1988. pap. text ed. 6.00 (*0-944833-22-5*) Krsna Inst.

Srila Prabodhananda Sarasvati's Sri Vrndavana-Mahimamrta, Vol. 8: The Nectar Glory of Sri Vrndavana. Prabodhanandasarasvati. Tr. by Kusakrathadasa from SAN. (Krsna Library: Vol. 29). 72p. (Orig.). (C). 1988. pap. text ed. 6.00 (*0-944833-23-3*) Krsna Inst.

Srila Prabodhananda Sarasvati's Sri Vrndavana-Mahimamrta, Vol. 9: The Nectar Glory of Sri Vrndavana. Prabodhanandasarasvati. Tr. by Kusakrathadasa from SAN. (Krsna Library: Vol. 30). 80p. (Orig.). (C). 1988. pap. text ed. 6.00 (*0-944833-24-1*) Krsna Inst.

Srila Raghava Gosvami's Sri Krsna-Bhakti-Ratna-Prakasa: The Jewel of Krsna-Bhakti, 2 vols. Raghavagosvami. Tr. by Kusakrathadasa from SAN. (Krsna Library: Vols. 34-35). 432p. (Orig.). (C). 1988. pap. text ed. 24.00 (*0-944833-33-0*) Krsna Inst.

Srila Raghava Gosvami's Sri Krsna-Bhakti-Ratna-Prakasa, Vol. 1: The Jewel of Krsna-Bhakti. Raghavagosvami. Tr. by Kusakrathadasa from SAN. (Krsna Library: Vol. 34). 184p. (Orig.). (C). 1988. pap. text ed. 12.00 (*0-944833-31-4*) Krsna Inst.

Srila Raghava Gosvami's Sri Krsna-Bhakti-Ratna-Prakasa, Vol. 2: The Jewel of Krsna-Bhakti. Raghavagosvami. Tr. by Kusakrathadasa from SAN. (Krsna Library: Vol. 35). 248p. (Orig.). (C). 1988. pap. text ed. 12.00 (*0-944833-32-2*) Krsna Inst.

Srila Raghunatha dasa Gosvami's Sri Stavavali, Collected Prayers, 4 Vols. Raghunathadasagosvami. Tr. by Kuskrathadasa from SAN. (Krsna Library: Vols. 93, 4, 94, 95). (Orig.). 1990. pap. text ed. 32.00 (*1-56130-002-0*) Krsna Inst.

Srila Raghunatha dasa Gosvami's Sri Stavavali, Vol. 4: Collected Praayers. Raghunathadasagosvami. Tr. by Kusakrathadasa from SAN. (Krsna Library: Vol. 95). 136p. (Orig.). 1990. pap. text ed. 8.00 (*0-944833-98-5*) Krsna Inst.

Srila Raghunatha dasa Gosvami's Sri Stavavali, VOl. 1: Collected Prayers. Raghunathadasagosvami. Tr. by Kusakrathadasa from SAN. (Krsna Library: Vol. 93). 112p. (Orig.). 1990. pap. text ed. 8.00 (*0-944833-96-9*) Krsna Inst.

Srila Raghunatha dasa Gosvami's Sri Stavavali, Vol. 3: Collected Prayers. Raghunathadasagosvami. Tr. by Kusakrathadasa from SAN. (Krsna Library: Vol. 94). 128p. (Orig.). 1990. pap. text ed. 8.00 (*0-944833-97-7*) Krsna Inst.

Srila Raghunatha dasa Gosvami's Sri Vraja-vilasa-stava: Prayers Glorifying the Lord's Pastimes in Vraja. Raghunathadasagosvami. Tr. by Kusakrathadasa from SAN. (Krsna Library: Vol. 4). 97p. (Orig.). (C). 1987. pap. text ed. 8.00 (*0-944833-03-9*) Krsna Inst.

Srila Ragunatha dasa Gosvami's Sri Dana-Keli-Cintamani: The Cintamani Jewel of the Toll Pastime. Raghunathadasagosvami. Tr. by Kusakrathadasa from SAN. (Krsna Library: Vol. 111). 103p. (Orig.). 1990. pap. text ed. 8.00 (*1-56130-020-9*) Krsna Inst.

Srila Rasikananda's Sri Syamananda-Sataka: A Hundred Verses Glorifying Sri Syamahanda. Rasikananda. Tr. by Kusakrathadasa from SAN. (Krsna Library). 77p. (Orig.). 1995. pap. text ed. 6.00 (*1-56130-159-0*) Krsna Inst.

Srila Rupa Gosvami's Sri Astadasa-cchandah-stava: Eighteen Chandah Prayers. Rupagosvami. Tr. by Kusakrathadasa from SAN. (Krsna Library: Vol. 9). 121p. (Orig.). (C). 1987. pap. text ed. 8.00 (*0-944833-00-4*) Krsna Inst.

Srila Rupa Gosvami's Sri Dana-Keli-Kaumudi: The Moonlight of the Dana-Keli Pastime. Rupagosvami. Tr. by Kusakrathadasa from SAN. (Krsna Library: Vol. 215). 64p. (Orig.). 1994. pap. text ed. 6.00 (*1-56130-144-2*) Krsna Inst.

Srila Rupa Gosvami's Sri Govinda-virudavali: Calling Out to Lord Krsna. Rupagosvami. Tr. by Kusakrathadasa from SAN. (Krsna Library: Vol. 8). 123p. (C). 1987. pap. text ed. 6.00 (*0-944833-08-X*) Krsna Inst.

Srila Rupa Gosvami's Sri Hamsaduta: The Swan Messenger. Rupagosvami. Tr. by Kusakrathadasa from SAN. (Krsna Library: Vol. 98). 96p. (Orig.). 1990. pap. text ed. 8.00 (*1-56130-005-5*) Krsna Inst.

Srila Rupa Gosvami's Sri Laghu-Bhagavatamrta: A Little Nectar of the Supreme Personality of Godhead & His Devotees, Vols. 99-101. Rupagosvami. Tr. by Kusakrathadasa from SAN. (Orig.). 1990. pap. text ed. 30.00 (*1-56130-009-8*) Krsna Inst.

Srila Rupa Gosvami's Sri Laghu-Bhagavatamrta, Vol. 1: A Little Nectar of the Supreme Personality of Godhead & His Devotees, Vol. 99. Rupagosvami. Tr. by Kusakrathadasa from SAN. 176p. (Orig.). 1990. pap. text ed. 10.00 (*1-56130-006-3*) Krsna Inst.

Srila Rupa Gosvami's Sri Laghu-Bhagavatamrta, Vol. 2: A Little Nectar of the Supreme Personality of Godhead & His Devotees, Vol. 100. Rupagosvamai. Tr. by Kusakrathadasa from SAN. 152p. (Orig.). 1990. pap. text ed. 10.00 (*1-56130-007-1*) Krsna Inst.

Srila Rupa Gosvami's Sri Laghu-Bhagavatamrta, Vol. 3: A Little Nectar of the Supreme Personality of Godhead & His Devotees, Vol. 101. Rupagosvami. Tr. by Kusakrathadasa from SAN. 159p. (Orig.). 1990. pap. text ed. 10.00 (*1-56130-008-X*) Krsna Inst.

Srila Rupa Gosvami's Sri Lalita-Madhava: Playful Krsna. Rupagosvami. Tr. by Kusakrathadasa from SAN. (Krsna Library: Vol. 209). 182p. (C). 1994. pap. text ed. 10.00 (*1-56130-135-3*) Krsna Inst.

Srila Rupa Gosvami's Sri Lalita-Madhava (Playful Krsna) Act Eight; Nava-vrndavana-vihara (Pastimes in New Vrndavana) Rupagosvami. Tr. by Kusakrathadasa from SAN. (Krsna Library: Vol. 58). 66p. (Orig.). 1989. pap. text ed. 8.00 (*0-944833-58-6*) Krsna Inst.

Srila Rupa Gosvami's Sri Lalita-Madhava (Playful Krsna) Act Five; Candravali-labha (the Attainment of Candravali) Rupagosvami. Tr. by Kusakrathadasa from SAN. (Krsna Library: Vol. 55). 72p. (Orig.). 1989. pap. text ed. 8.00 (*0-944833-55-1*) Krsna Inst.

Srila Rupa Gosvami's Sri Lalita-Madhava (Playful Krsna) Act Four; Radhabhisaranka-garbhanka-garbha (the Play "Meeting Radha") Rupagosvami. Tr. by Kusakrathadasa from SAN. (Krsna Library: Vol. 54). 77p. (Orig.). 1989. pap. text ed. 8.00 (*0-944833-54-3*) Krsna Inst.

Srila Rupa Gosvami's Sri Lalita-Madhava (Playful Krsna) Act Nine; Citra-darsana (Looking at Pictures) Rupagosvami. Tr. by Kusakrathadasa from SAN. (Krsna Library: Vol. 59). 98p. (Orig.). 1989. pap. text ed. 8.00 (*0-944833-59-4*) Krsna Inst.

Srila Rupa Gosvami's Sri Lalita-Madhava (Playful Krsna) Act Seven; Nava-vrndavana-sangama (Meeting in New Vrndavana) Rupagosvami. Tr. by Kusakrathadasa from SAN. (Krsna Library: Vol. 57). 74p. (Orig.). 1989. pap. text ed. 8.00 (*0-944833-57-8*) Krsna Inst.

Srila Rupa Gosvami's Sri Lalita-Madhava (Playful Krsna) Act Six; Lalitopalabdhi (the Attainment of Lalita) Rupagosvami. Tr. by Kusakrathadasa from SAN. (Krsna Library: Vol. 56). 66p. (Orig.). 1989. pap. text ed. 8.00 (*0-944833-56-X*) Krsna Inst.

Srila Rupa Gosvami's Sri Lalita-Madhava (Playful Krsna) Act Ten; Purna-manoratha (All Desires Are Fulfilled) Rupagosvami. Tr. by Kusakrathadasa from SAN. (Krsna Library: Vol. 60). 106p. (Orig.). 1989. pap. text ed. 8.00 (*0-944833-60-8*) Krsna Inst.

Srila Rupa Gosvami's Sri Lalita-Madhava (Playful Krsna) Act Three; Unmatta-Radhika (Maddened Radhika) Rupagosvami. Tr. by Kusakrathadasa from SAN. (Krsna Library: Vol. 53). 71p. (Orig.). 1989. pap. text ed. 8.00 (*0-944833-53-5*) Krsna Inst.

Srila Rupa Gosvami's Sri Lalita-Madhava (Playful Krsna) Act Two; Sankhacuda-vadha (The Killing of Sankhacuda) Rupagosvami. Tr. by Kusakrathadasa from SAN. (Krsna Library: Vol. 52). 71p. (Orig.). 1989. pap. text ed. 8.00 (*0-944833-52-7*) Krsna Inst.

Srila Rupa Gosvami's Sri Lalita-Madhava (Playful Krsna), Act One: Sayam Utsava (An Evening Festival) Rupagosvami. Tr. by Kusakrathadasa from SAN. (Krsna Library: Vol. 51). 86p. (Orig.). 1989. pap. text ed. 8.00 (*0-944833-51-9*) Krsna Inst.

Srila Rupa Gosvami's Sri Mathura-Mahatmya: The Glories of Mathura. Rupagosvami. Tr. by Kusakrathadasa from SAN. (Krsna Library). 226p. (Orig.). (C). 1989. pap. text ed. 12.00 (*0-944833-35-7*) Krsna Inst.

Srila Rupa Gosvami's Sri Nikunja-Rahasya-Stava & Srila Visvanatha Cakravartis Sri Gitavali & Other Poems. Rupagosvami & Visvanathacakravarti. Tr. by Kusakrathadasa from SAN. (Krsna Library: Vol. 208). 64p. (C). 1994. pap. text ed. 4.00 (*1-56130-134-5*) Krsna Inst.

Srila Rupa Gosvami's Sri Padyavali: A Verse Anthology. Rupagosvami. Tr. by Kusakrathadasa from SAN. (Krsna Library: Vol. 63). (Orig.). (C). 1990. pap. text ed. 15.00 (*0-944833-80-2*) Krsna Inst.

Srila Rupa Gosvami's Sri Radha-Krsna-gaoddesa-dipka: A Lamp to See the Associates of Sri Sri Radha Krsna. Rupagosvami. Tr. by Kusakrathadasa. (Krsna Library: Vol. 7). 304p. 1987. pap. text ed. 12.00 (*0-944833-05-5*) Krsna Inst.

Srila Rupa Gosvami's Sri Stava-mala, Vol. 1: A Garland of Prayers. Rupagosvami. Tr. by Kusakrathadasa from SAN. (Krsna Library: Vol. 88). 116p. (Orig.). 1990. pap. text ed. 8.00 (*0-944833-49-7*) Krsna Inst.

Srila Rupa Gosvami's Sri Stava-mala, Vol. 2: A Garland of Prayers. Rupagosvami. Tr. by Kusakrathadasa from SAN. (Krsna Library: Vol. 89). 119p. (Orig.). 1990. pap. text ed. 8.00 (*0-944833-47-0*) Krsna Inst.

Srila Rupa Gosvami's Sri Stava-mala, Vol. 5: A Garland of Prayers. Rupagosvami. Tr. by Kusakrathadasa from SAN. (Krsna Library: Vol. 90). 78p. (Orig.). 1990. pap. text ed. 8.00 (*0-944833-87-X*) Krsna Inst.

Srila Rupa Gosvami's Sri Stava-mala, Vol. 6: A Garland of Prayers. Rupagosvami. Tr. by Kusakrathadasa from SAN. (Krsna Library: Vol. 91). 127p. (Orig.). 1990. pap. text ed. 8.00 (*0-944833-88-8*) Krsna Inst.

Srila Rupa Gosvami's Sri Uddhava-Sandesa: A Message for Uddhava. Rupagosvami. Tr. by Kusakrathadasa from SAN. (Krsna Library: Vol. 207). 85p. (C). 1994. pap. text ed. 6.00 (*1-56130-133-7*) Krsna Inst.

Srila Sanatana Gosvami's Sri Brhad-Bhagavatamrta: The Nectar of the Supreme Personality of Godhead, Vols. 81-87 & 102-104. Santanagosvami. Tr. by Kusakrathadasa from SAN. (Orig.). 1990. pap. text ed. 100.00 (*1-56130-013-6*) Krsna Inst.

Srila Sanatana Gosvami's Sri Brhad-Bhagavatamrta, Pt. 1, Chapters 1-3: The Nectar of the Supreme Personality of Godhead, Vol. 102. Santanagosvami. Tr. by Kusakrathadasa from SAN. 122p. (Orig.). 1990. pap. text ed. 10.00 (*1-56130-010-1*) Krsna Inst.

Srila Sanatana Gosvami's Sri Brhad-Bhagavatamrta, Pt. 1, Chapters 4 & 5: The Nectar of the Supreme Personality of Godhead, Vol. 103. Santanagosvami. Tr. by Kusakrathadasa from SAN. 119p. (Orig.). 1990. pap. text ed. 10.00 (*1-56130-011-X*) Krsna Inst.

Srila Sanatana Gosvami's Sri Brhad-Bhagavatamrta, Pt. 1, Chapters 6 & 7: The Nectar of the Supreme Personality of Godhead, Vol. 104. Santanagosvami. Tr. by Kusakrathadasa from SAN. (Orig.). 1990. pap. text ed. 10.00 (*1-56130-012-8*) Krsna Inst.

Srila Sanatana Gosvami's Sri Brhad-Bhagavatamrta, Part 2, Chapter 1: The Great Nectar of the Supreme Personality of Godhead. Santanagosvami & Kusakrathadasa. (Krsna Library: Vol. 81). 109p. (Orig.). 1990. pap. text ed. 10.00 (*0-944833-89-6*) Krsna Inst.

Srila Sanatana Gosvami's Sri Brhad-Bhagavatamrta, Part 2, Chapter 3: The Great Nectar of the Supreme Personality of Godhead. Santanagosvami. Tr. by Kusakrathadasa from SAN. (Krsna Library: Vol. 83). 94p. (Orig.). 1990. pap. text ed. 10.00 (*0-944833-91-8*) Krsna Inst.

Srila Sanatana Gosvami's Sri Brhad-Bhagavatamrta, Part 2, Chapter 4: The Great Nectar of the Supreme Personality of Godhead. Santanagosvami. Tr. by Kusakrathadasa from SAN. (Krsna Library: Vol. 84). (Orig.). 1990. pap. text ed. 10.00 (*0-944833-92-6*) Krsna Inst.

Srila Sanatana Gosvami's Sri Brhad-Bhagavatamrta, Part 2, Chapter 5: The Great Nectar of the Supreme Personality of Godhead. Santanagosvami. Tr. by Kusakrathadasa from SAN. (Krsna Library: Vol. 85). (Orig.). 1990. pap. text ed. 10.00 (*0-944833-93-4*) Krsna Inst.

Srila Sanatana Gosvami's Sri Brhad-Bhagavatamrta, Part 2, Chapter 6: The Great Nectar of the Supreme Personality of Godhead. Santanagosvami. Tr. by Kusakrathadasa from SAN. (Krsna Library: Vol. 86). (Orig.). 1990. pap. text ed. 10.00 (*0-944833-94-2*) Krsna Inst.

Srila Sanatana Gosvami's Sri Brhad-Bhagavatamrta, Part 2, Chapter 7: The Great Nectar of the Supreme Personality of Godhead. Santanagosvami. Tr. by Kusakrathadasa from SAN. (Krsna Library: Vol. 87). (Orig.). 1990. pap. text ed. 10.00 (*0-944833-95-0*) Krsna Inst.

Srila Sanatana Gosvami's Sri Hari-Bhakti-Vilasa: The Pastimes of Devotion to Lord Hari Fifteenth Vilasa-Divyavirbhava-Transcendental Appearance Days, Vol. 2. Sanatanagosvami. Tr. by Kusakrathadasa from SAN. (Krsna Library: Vol. 183). 113p. (C). 1993. pap. text ed. 10.00 (*1-56130-097-7*) Krsna Inst.

Srila Sanatana Gosvami's Sri Hari-Bhakti-Vilasa: The Pastimes of Devotion to Lord Hari Fifteenth Vilasa-Divyavirbhava-Transcendental Appearance Days, Vol. 3. Sanatanagosvami. Tr. by Kusakrathadasa from SAN. (Krsna Library: Vol. 184). 107p. (C). 1993. pap. text ed. 10.00 (*1-56130-098-5*) Krsna Inst.

Srila Sanatana Gosvami's Sri Hari-Bhakti-Vilasa: The Pastimes of Devotion to Lord Hari Fourteenth Vilasa, San-Masika, Holy Days of Six Months, Vol. 1. Sanatanagosvami. Tr. by Kusakrathadasa from SAN. (Krsna Library: Vol. 189). 119p. (C). 1993. pap. text ed. 10.00 (*1-56130-096-9*) Krsna Inst.

Srila Sanatana Gosvami's Sri Hari-bhakti-vilasa, the Pastimes of Devotion to Lord Hari, Eighth Vilasa, Pratar-arca-samapana, Worship in the Early Morning, Vol. 1. Santanagosvami. Tr. by Kusakrathadasa from SAN. (Krsna Library: Vol. 154). 128p. (C). 1992. pap. text ed. 10.00 (*1-56130-070-5*) Krsna Inst.

Srila Sanatana Gosvami's Sri Hari-bhakti-vilasa, the Pastimes of Devotion to Lord Hari, Eighth Vilasa, Pratar-arca-samapana, Worship in the Early Morning, Vol. 2. Tr. by Kusakrathadasa from SAN. (Krsna Library: Vol. 156). 146p. (C). 1992. pap. text ed. 10.00 (*1-56130-072-1*) Krsna Inst.

Srila Sanatana Gosvami's Sri Hari-bhakti-vilasa, the Pastimes of Devotion to Lord Hari, Ninth Vilasa, Maha-prasada, the Great Mercy of the Lord, Vol. 1. Sanatanagosvami. Tr. by Kusakrathadasa from SAN. (Krsna Library: Vol. 147). 117p. (C). 1992. pap. text ed. 10.00 (*1-56130-071-3*) Krsna Inst.

Srila Sanatana Gosvami's Sri Hari-bhakti-vilasa, the Pastimes of Devotion to Lord Hari, Sixteenth Vilasa, Sri Damodara-priya-Duties That Please Lord Damodara, Vol. 1. Sanatanagosvami. Tr. by Kusakrathadasa from SAN. (Krsna Library: Vol. 158). 121p. (C). 1992. pap. text ed. 10.00 (*1-56130-068-3*) Krsna Inst.

Srila Sanatana Gosvami's Sri Hari-bhakti-vilasa the Pastimes of Devotional Service: First Vilasa, Sri Gaurava, the Spiritual Master. Sanatanagosvami. Tr. by Kusakrathadasa from SAN. (Krsna Library: Vol. 152). 144p. (C). 1991. pap. text ed. 10.00 (*1-56130-066-7*) Krsna Inst.

Srila Sanatana Gosvami's Sri Hari-bhakti-vilasa the Pastimes of Devotional Service, Vol. 2: Eleventh Vilasa, Nitya-krtya-samapana Regular Duties. Sanatanagosvami. Tr. by Kusakrathadasa from SAN. (Krsna Library: Vol. 153). 221p. (C). 1991. pap. text ed. 12.00 (*1-56130-067-5*) Krsna Inst.

Srila Sanatana Gosvami's Sri Krsna-Lila-Stava: Prayers Glorifying Sri Krsna. Sanatanagosvami. Tr. by Kusakrathadasa from SAN. (Krsna Library). 217p. (Orig.). (C). 1989. pap. text ed. 12.00 (*0-944833-34-9*) Krsna Inst.

Srila Santana Gosvami's Sri Brhad-Bhagavatamrta, Part 2, Chapter 2: The Great Nectar of the Supreme Personality of Godhead. Santanagosvami. Tr. by Kusakrathadasa from SAN. (Krsna Library: Vol. 82). 124p. (Orig.). 1990. pap. text ed. 10.00 (*0-944833-90-X*) Krsna Inst.

Srila Visvanatha Cakravarti's Sri Ksanada-Gita-Cintamani (Selections) Tr. by Kusakrathadasa from BEN. (Krsna Library). 49p. (Orig.). 1996. pap. text ed. 4.00 (*1-56130-181-7*) Krsna Inst.

Srila Visvanatha Cakravarti's Sri Rupa-cintamani (the Cintamani Jewel of Beauty) & Sri Radhika-dhyanamrta (the Nectar of Meditation on Sri Radhika) Visvanathacakravarti. Tr. by Kusakrathadasa from SAN. (Krsna Library: Vol. 62). 31p. (Orig.). 1989. pap. text ed. 4.00 (*0-944833-50-0*) Krsna Inst.

Srila Visvanatha Cakravarti's Sri Sankalpa-Kalpadruma: The Tree That Fulfills All Desires. Visvanathacakravarti. Tr. by Kusakrathadasa from SAN. (Krsna Library: Vol. 135). 60p. (C). 1991. pap. text ed. 8.00 (*1-56130-056-X*) Krsna Inst.

Srila Visvanatha Cakravarti's Sri Vraja-Riti-Cintamani: The Cintamani Jewel of Vraja. Visvanathacakravarti. Tr. by Kusakrathadasa from SAN. (Krsna Library: Vol. 33). 136p. (Orig.). (C). 1988. pap. text ed. 8.00 (*0-944833-30-6*) Krsna Inst.

Srila Vrndavana Dasa Thakura's Sri Caitanya- Bhagavata, Antya-Khanda. Vrndavanadasathakura. Tr. by Kusakrathadasa from BEN. (Krsna Library: Vol. 210). 249p. (C). 1994. pap. text ed. 12.00 (*1-56130-136-1*) Krsna Inst.

Srila Vrndavana Dasa Thakura's Sri Caitanya-Bhagavata: Madhya-Khanda, Vol. 2. Vrndavanadasathakura. Tr. by Kusakrathadasa from BEN. (Krsna Library: Vol. 206). 226p. (C). 1994. pap. text ed. 12.00 (*1-56130-132-9*) Krsna Inst.

Srila Vrndavana Dasa Thakura's Sri Cartanya-Bhagavata: Madhya-Khanda, Vol. 1. Vrndavanadasathakura. Tr. by Kusakrathadasa from BEN. (Krsna Library: Vol. 205). 188p. (C). 1994. pap. text ed. 12.00 (*1-56130-131-0*) Krsna Inst.

Srila Vrndavanadasa Thakura's Sri Caitanya-Bhagavata: Adi-Khanda. Vrndavanadasathakura. Tr. by Kusakrathadasa from BEN. (Krsna Library: Vol. 203). 244p. (C). 1993. pap. text ed. 15.00 (*1-56130-128-0*) Krsna Inst.

Srila Vyasadeva's Sri Vedanta-Sutra: With the Govinda-Bhasya Commentary of Srila Baladeva Vidyabhusana, Vol. 4, Chap. 3, Padas 1 & 2. Vyasadeva & Baladevavidyabhusana. Tr. by Kusakrathadasa from SAN. (Krsna Library: Vol. 160). 124p. (C). 1992. pap. text ed. 10.00 (*1-56130-075-6*) Krsna Inst.

An Asterisk (*) at the beginning of an entry indicates that the title is appearing in BIP for the first time.

Srila Vyasadeva's Sri Vedanta-Sutra: With the Govinda-Bhasya Commentary of Srila Baladeva Vidyabhusana, Vol. 5, Chap. 3, Pada 3. Vyasadeva & Baladevavidyabhusana. Tr. by Kusakrathadasa from SAN. (Krsna Library: Vol. 161). 154p. (C). 1992. pap. text ed. 10.00 (*1-56130-076-4*) Krsna Inst.

Srila Vyasadeva's Sri Vedanta-Sutra: With the Sri Govinda-Bhasya Commentary of Srila Baladeva Vidyabhusana. Vyasadeva & Baladevavidyabhusana. Tr. by Kusakrathadasa from SAN. (Krsna Library). 220p. (Orig.). (C). 1989. pap. text ed. 12.00 (*0-944833-36-5*) Krsna Inst.

Srila Vyasadeva's Sri Vedanta-sutra, Vol. 2: Chapter Two, Padas One & Two with the Sri Govinda-bhasya Commentary of Srila Baladeva Vidyabhusana. Vyasadeva & Baladevavidyabhusana. Tr. by Kusakrathadasa from SAN. (Krsna Library: Vol. 150). 132p. (C). 1991. pap. text ed. 10.00 (*1-56130-062-4*) Krsna Inst.

Srila Vyasadeva's Sri Vedanta-sutra, Vol. 6: Chapter Three, Pada Four, & Chapter Four, Padas One, Two, Three, & Four with the Sri Govinda-bhasya Commentary of Srila Baladeva Vidyabhusana. Vyasadeva & Baladevavidyabhusana. Tr. by Kusakrathadasa from SAN. (Krsna Library: Vol. 168). 218p. (C). 1992. pap. text ed. 10.00 (*1-56130-095-0*) Krsna Inst.

Srimad Bhagavad Gita. 161p. 1994. pap. 12.00 (*0-923569-10-3*, D-06) Maharishi U Mgmt Pr.

Srimad-Bhagavad-Gita. 7th ed. Swami Paramananda. Orig. Title: Bhagavad-Gita, Srimad. 1981. 5.95 (*0-911564-03-9*); 3.95 (*0-685-05240-0*) Vedanta Ctr.

Srimad Bhagavad Gita: Pocket Book Edition. Swami Jyotir Maya Nanda. (Illus.). 384p. 1986. pap. 4.00 (*0-934664-44-7*) Yoga Res Foun.

Srimad Bhagavad Gita - The Song Celestial: An English Rendering of Original Sanskrit Verses. H. K. Kewalramani. 160p. (Orig.). 1994. pap. 8.95 (*1-881338-11-8*) Nataraj Bks.

Srimad Bhagavata, 4 vols., Set. Tapasyananda. (ENG & SAN.). 84.00 (*0-87481-550-9*) Vedanta Pr.

***Srimad-Bhagavatam: Bhagavata Purana, 18 vols.** 595.00 (*0-89213-264-7*) Bhaktivedanta.

Srimad Bhagavatam: The Beautiful Narrations of the Supreme Lord. Krsna B. Swami. (Ganto Ten Ser.). 450p. 1994. write for info. (*0-9631403-0-2*) H H K B S.

Srimad Bhagavatam: The Beautiful Narrations of the Supreme Lord, Vol. 2. Mahant Krsna Balaram Swami. 350p. 1995. write for info. (*0-9631403-1-0*) H H K B S.

Srimad Bhagavatam: The Beautiful Narrations of the Supreme Lord, Vol. 3. Mahant Krsna Balaram Swami. 350p. 1995. write for info. (*0-9631403-2-9*) H H K B S.

Srimad Bhagavatam: The Wisdom of God. Bhagavatam. Tr. by Swami Prabhavananda from SAN. 329p. 1979. pap. 5.95 (*0-87481-490-1*, Pub. by Ramakrishna Math II) Vedanta Pr.

Srimad-Bhagavatam, Canto Ten, Chapter Fourteen with the Commentaries of Srila Sridhara Svami, Srila Sanatana Gosvami, & Srila Visvanatha Cakravarti. Vedavyasa et al. Tr. by Kusakrathadasa from SAN. (Krsna Library: Vol. 185). 204p. (C). 1993. pap. text ed. 12.00 (*1-56130-099-3*) Krsna Inst.

Srimad Ramayana. D. S. Sarma. 385p. pap. 5.95 (*81-7120-222-5*) Vedanta Ctr.

Srimadbhagavatam: A Concise Narrative. Gunada C. Sen. 1987. 26.00 (*81-215-0036-2*, Pub. by Munshiram Manoharial II) S Asia.

Srivaisnava Theological Dispute - Manavalamamuni & Bedanta Desika. Patricia Y. Mumme. (C). 1988. 25.00 (*0-8364-2453-0*, Pub. by New Era Pubns) S Asia.

Sriyukteswar: A Biography. 2nd ed. Swami S. Giri. LC 94-68385. (Illus.). 168p. (Orig.). 1994. pap. text ed. 15.00 (*1-877854-28-X*) Sanskrit Classics.

Srngara-Prakasa of Bhoja, 2 vols., Set. Bhoja. Ed. by V. Raghavan. LC 87-33908. (Oriental Ser.). 1888p. (SAN.). 1988. 90.00 (*0-674-83340-6*) HUP.

SRS-A & Leukotrienes: Proceedings of the Annual Symposium of the Institute of Basic Medical Sciences, Royal College of Surgeons of England, 24th September 1980. Priscilla J. Piper. LC 80-41758. (Prostaglandins Research Studies Ser.: No. 1). (Illus.). 296p. reprint ed. pap. 84.40 (*0-8357-3549-4*, 2034232) Bks Demand.

SRT Diver. (Illus.). 360p. 1989. 20.00 (*0-939235-02-1*) Spec Trning Unit.

Sruti Gita: The Song of the Srutis. Tr. by Gambhirananda from SAN. 99p. (C). 1982. pap. 4.50 (*0-87481-510-X*, Pub. by Advaita Ashrama II) Vedanta Pr.

***Srzednicki Lesniewski's System.** 1997. lib. bdg. write for info. (*0-7923-4504-5*) Kluwer Ac.

***SS: Roll of Infamy.** A. D. Gooch. (Illus.). 1997. 24.95 (*0-7603-0409-2*) Motorbooks Intl.

SS: The SS Blood-Soaked Soil. Gordon Williamson. (Illus.). 192p. 1995. 24.95 (*0-7603-0185-9*, Zenith Aviation) Motorbooks Intl.

SS - Hitler's Instrument of Terror: The Full Story from Street Fighters to the Waffen-SS. Gordon Williamson. (Illus.). 256p. 1994. 24.95 (*0-87938-905-2*) Motorbooks Intl.

SS Cygni Light Curves, 1985-1990. Janet A. Mattei et al. (AAVSO Monograph: No. 1, Supplement 1). (Illus.). 36p. 1991. pap. text ed. 7.50 (*1-878174-05-3*) Am Assn Var Star.

SS Cygni Light Curves 1991-1995: AAVSO Monography 1, Supplement 2. Janet A. Mattei et al. (Illus.). 21p. 1996. pap. text ed. 10.00 (*1-878174-14-2*) Am Assn Var Star.

SS Headgear: A Collector's Guide. Kit Wilson. Ed. by J. Rex Reddick. (Illus.). 72p. (Orig.). 1989. pap. 16.50 (*0-9624883-0-5*) Reddick Enterp.

SS Helmets: A Collector's Guide. Kelly Hicks. Ed. by J. Rex Reddick & Ed Wells. (Illus.). 96p. 1993. pap. 17.50 (*0-9624883-5-6*) Reddick Enterp.

SS Regalia. Schrick. 1995. 17.98 (*0-7858-0228-2*) Bk Sales Inc.

SS-Sturmbannfuhrer Ernst August Krag: Trager des Ritterkreuzes Mit Eichenlaub Kommandeur SS-Sturmgeschutzabteilung 2/SS-Panzer-Aufklarungsabteilung 2 "Das Reich" Mark C. Yerger. (Illus.). 64p. 1996. 19.95 (*0-7643-0049-0*) Schiffer.

SS Totenkopf H. Himmler Honor Ring 1933-1945. Don Boyle. (Illus.). 73p. 1995. 44.50 (*0-685-72342-9*) Johnson Ref Bks.

***SS Uniforms, Insignia & Accoutrements: A Study in Photographs.** Compiled by A. Hayes. (Illus.). 248p. 69.95 (*0-7643-0046-6*) Schiffer.

***SSA Disability: Program Redesign Necessary to Encourage Return to Work.** (Illus.). 84p. (Orig.). (C). 1996. pap. 25.00 (*0-7881-3608-9*) DIANE Pub.

***SSA Disability: Return-to-Work Strategies from Other Systems May Improve Federal Programs.** (Illus.). 88p. (Orig.). (C). 1996. pap. 25.00 (*0-7881-3491-4*) DIANE Pub.

SSADM: A Practical Handbook. Colin Bentley. (Illus.). 300p. 1995. pap. 47.95 (*0-7506-1811-6*) Buttrwrth-Heinemann.

SSADM & Application Packages. HMSO Staff. 74p. 1994. pap. 60.00 (*0-11-330626-1*, HM06261, Pub. by Stationery Ofc UK) Bernan Associates.

SSADM & Client/Server Applications. 130p. 1995. pap. 85.00 (*0-11-330624-5*, HM06245, Pub. by Stationery Ofc UK) Bernan Associates.

SSADM & GRAPES: A Comparison of Two Major European Methodologies for Information Systems Engineering. A. Aue et al. Ed. by R. Duschl & N. C. Hopkins. LC 92-11653. 324p. 1992. 82.95 (*0-387-55380-0*) Spr-Verlag.

SSADM & GUI Design: A Project Manager's Guide. 118p. 1994. pap. 35.00 (*0-11-330650-4*, HM06504, Pub. by Stationery Ofc UK) Bernan Associates.

SSADM for Handling Geographic Information Systems. HMSO Staff. 90p. 1994. pap. 60.00 (*0-11-330613-X*, HM0613X, Pub. by Stationery Ofc UK) Bernan Associates.

SSADM for the Advanced Practitioner. John Hares. LC 90-12494. 298p. 1990. text ed. 60.00 (*0-471-92739-2*) Wiley.

SSADM 4+ for Rapid Systems Development. David Hargrave. LC 95-37896. 1995. pap. write for info. (*0-07-709082-9*) McGraw.

SSADM Version 4: A User's Guide. Malcom Eva. LC 93-46575. (McGraw-Hill International Series in Software Engineering). 1994. write for info. (*0-07-707959-0*) McGraw.

***SSADM Version 4: The Advanced Practitioner's Guide.** John S. Hares. LC 93-10575. (Wiley Series in Software Engineering Practice). (Illus.). 405p. reprint ed. pap. 115.50 (*0-608-05279-5*, 2065817) Bks Demand.

SSADM Version 4 Project: Manager's Handbook. Martin H. Hammer. LC 92-24292. (McGraw-Hill International Series in Software Engineering). 1992. write for info. (*0-07-707659-1*) McGraw.

SSAT, 1998. Princeton Review Publishing Staff. Date not set. pap. write for info. (*0-679-76938-2*, Random Ref) Random.

SSC Low Energy Booster: Design & Component Prototypes for the First Injector Synchrotron. Hans-Ulrich Wienands. LC 95-50603. 1996. 149.95 (*0-7803-1164-7*) Inst Electrical.

SSC 200 Soil Science Lab Manual. H. Joseph Kleiss. (Illus.). 246p. (C). Date not set. lab manual ed., pap. text ed. 12.40 (*1-886855-15-3*) Tavenner Pub.

SSC 200 Soil Science Lecture Notes. H. Joseph Kleiss. 192p. (C). 1995. pap. text ed. 10.65 (*1-886855-16-1*) Tavenner Pub.

Ssh, Don't Wake the Baby! Yvonne Winer. LC 92-34160. (Voyages Ser.). (Illus.). (J). 1993. 3.75 (*0-383-03655-0*) SRA McGraw.

Sshaboom! Brian Mangas. LC 91-24764. (Illus.). 40p. (J). (ps-1). 1993. pap. 14.00 (*0-671-75538-2*, S&S Bks Young Read) S&S Childrens.

SSI Instructor Manual. 6th ed. 1990. pap. text ed. 110.00 (*0-943717-82-5*) Concept Sys.

SSI Student Study Guide for Open Water Certification. rev. ed. 24p. 1988. reprint ed. pap. text ed. 3.95 (*0-943717-58-2*) Concept Sys.

***SSN.** Tom Clancy. 1996. pap. text ed. 15.00 (*0-425-15911-6*) Berkley Pub.

SSN-21 Sea Wolf Official Strategy Guide. Ed Dille. 1994. pap. 19.95 (*1-55958-527-7*) Prima Pub.

***S+SpatialStats: User's Manual for Windows & UNIX.** S. P. Kaluzny & Silvia C. Vega. LC 97-10093. 1997. pap. write for info. (*0-387-98226-4*) Spr-Verlag.

SSRC Fiftieth Anniversary Conference Proceedings, 1994: SSRC - Link Between Research & Practice. Ed. by James M. Ricles. 407p. 1994. text ed. 50.00 (*1-879749-56-4*) Structural Stability.

SSS Newsletter, 11 vols. Ed. by Rado L. Lencek et al. 238p. 1978. write for info. (*0-318-60013-7*) Soc Slovene Studies.

SS7 Basics. Toni Beninger. (Illus.). 80p. (Orig.). 1991. pap. 29.95 (*0-917845-16-1*) Intertec IL.

***St. Agnes, Virgin & Martyr.** 1997. pap. 2.50 (*0-89981-168-X*) Eastern Orthodox.

St. Anthony of Padua: Friend of All the World. Sheilah W. Ling. 158p. 1994. pap. 15.95 (*0-85439-503-2*, Pub. by St Paul Pubns UK) St Mut.

St. Anthony, the Wonder-Worker of Padua. 2nd ed. Charles W. Stoddard. 1992. reprint ed. pap. 5.00 (*0-89555-039-3*) TAN Bks Pubs.

***St. Anthony 1996 HCPCS: Level II Codes.** spiral bd. 39.95 (*0-614-19640-X*, OP057196WE) AMA.

***St. Anthony/BISI Disease Management Directory.** Ed. by Susan Namovicz-Peat. 250p. (C). 1996. 299.00 (*1-56329-335-8*) St Anthony Pub.

***St. Anthony's Ambulatory Surgery Editor: A Guide for Benchmarking Coding Compliance & Financial Performance.** St. Anthony Publishing Staff. Ed. & Intro. by Lolita Jones. 500p. (C). 1998. 299.00 (*1-56329-436-2*) St Anthony Pub.

***St. Anthony's APG Implementation Guide: A Task Force Action Plan.** Lolita M. Jones. Ed. by Kathy Brouch & Carol Endehe. (Illus.). 375p. Date not set. 349.00 (*1-56329-402-8*) St Anthony Pub.

***St. Anthony's APG Sourcebook.** Lolita Jones & Karen Farrow. Date not set. ring bd. 269.00 (*1-56329-418-4*) St Anthony Pub.

***St. Anthony's Clinical Coder.** Karen M. Schmidt. 210p. (C). 1996. write for info. (*1-56329-347-1*) St Anthony Pub.

St. Anthony's Coding Assistant for GI Endoscopic Procedures: An Illustrated Guide to Coding & Billing. Deborah C. Hall & Connie Johnson. Ed. by Paul Hickey & Pete Kelly. (Illus.). 350p. 1996. 149.00 (*1-56329-329-3*) St Anthony Pub.

***St. Anthony's Color-Coded Compact ICD-9-CM Code Book for Physician Payment.** Ed. by Laurie Castillo & Catherine Hopkins. 1418p. 1996. 49.95 (*1-56329-356-0*) St Anthony Pub.

***St. Anthony's Color-Coded Compact ICD-9-CM Codebook for Physician Payment.** Ed. by Laurie Castillo & Catherine Hopkins. 1418p. 1997. 49.95 (*1-56329-425-7*) St Anthony Pub.

***St. Anthony's Color-Coded ICD-9-CM Code Book 1996, Vols. 1 & 2.** pap. 59.95 (*0-614-19630-2*, OP565696WE) AMA.

***St. Anthony's Color-Coded Illustrated 1996 ICD-9-CM, Vols. 1 & 2.** (Illus.). pap. 79.95 (*0-614-19631-0*, OP054096WE) AMA.

***St. Anthony's Compact ICD-9-CM Code Book for Physician Payment.** Ed. by Laurie Castillo & Catherine Hopkins. 1418p. 1996. 39.95 (*1-56329-355-2*) St Anthony Pub.

***St. Anthony's CPT Coding Companion for Ophthalmology (ATEY) A Guide to Understanding Selected Procedure Codes.** Ed. by Karen Kachur. (Illus.). 650p. (C). 159.00 (*1-56329-338-2*) St Anthony Pub.

***St. Anthony's CPT-4 Clinic: Emergency Room Coding for Hospital Reimbursement.** Lolita M. Jones. Ed. by Andrea Clark. (Illus.). 300p. (C). write for info. (*1-56329-343-9*) St Anthony Pub.

St. Anthony's CPT-4 Hospital Clinic: Basic Procedural Coding for Hospitals. Karen Kachner. (Illus.). 220p. (C). 149.00 (*1-56329-324-2*) St Anthony Pub.

***St. Anthony's Data Quality for Coding.** Lolita M. Jones & Kathy L. Broach. 128p. (C). Date not set. write for info. (*1-56329-346-3*) St Anthony Pub.

***St. Anthony's DRG Guidebook.** Connie Johnson & Charlotte Bowers. Ed. by Regina M. Kukucka & Keith Swann. 515p. (C). 69.00 (*1-56329-365-X*) St Anthony Pub.

***St. Anthony's DRG Optimizer.** Cay Moriarity & Julia Palmer. Ed. by Regina M. Kukucka & Keith Swann. 363p. (C). 129.00 (*1-56329-366-8*) St Anthony Pub.

***St. Anthony's Forms That Work.** St. Anthony Publishing Staff. Ed. by Cathy Hopkins. (C). Date not set. 199.00 (*1-56329-414-1*) St Anthony Pub.

***St. Anthony's Guide to Ambulatory Surger Center Payment Groups: A Clinical Coding & Reimbursement Reference for Hospitals & ASCs.** Marleeta K. Jones & Julia R. Palmer. Ed. by Lolita M. Jones. (ASC Ser.). (Illus.). 650p. Date not set. 169.00 (*1-56329-401-X*) St Anthony Pub.

St. Anthony's Guide to Chiropractic Managed Care. Ed. by Jay Leditman. 150p. (C). Date not set. 149.00 (*1-56329-326-9*) St Anthony Pub.

***St. Anthony's Guide to Code Linkage.** Ed. by Cathy Hopkins & Laurie Castillo. Date not set. 199.00 (*1-56329-435-4*) St Anthony Pub.

***St. Anthony's HCPCS Level II Code Book.** Marleeta Jones. Ed. by Laurie Castillo & Carol Endahl. 500p. (C). Date not set. 75.00 (*1-56329-376-5*) St Anthony Pub.

***St. Anthony's HCPCS Level III Code Book.** Marleeta Jones. Ed. by Laurie Castillo & Carol Endahl. 450p. (C). Date not set. 39.95 (*1-56329-377-3*) St Anthony Pub.

St. Anthony's HCPCS Reference Manual for Outpatient Services. E. Lorenz. 350p. (C). 1992. ring bd. 329.00 (*1-56329-133-9*) St Anthony Pub.

***St. Anthony's Home Health Agency Policy & Procedure Manual (HHPP)** Marilyn Seiler. 300p. (C). 1996. 349.00 (*1-56329-336-6*) St Anthony Pub.

St. Anthony's ICD-9-CM Annotated Code Book for Physicians, 2 vols. E. Lorenz. (Illus.). 285p. (C). 1992. ring bd. 180.00 (*1-56329-100-2*, PAB) St Anthony Pub.

St. Anthony's ICD-9-CM Basic Diagnostic Coding Seminar Manual. Ed. by Gay M. Boughton-Barnes. 200p. 1992. 149.00 (*1-56329-047-2*, 19CM) St Anthony Pub.

***St. Anthony's ICD-9-CM Code Book.** Ed. by Karen Schmidt et al. 1300p. 1997. pap. 69.95 (*1-56329-432-X*) St Anthony Pub.

St. Anthony's ICD-9-CM Code Book, Vols. I, II, & III. Ed. by Charlotte Bowers. 1985. 139.00 (*1-56329-000-6*) St Anthony Pub.

St. Anthony's ICD-9-CM Code Book for AMA, '94, 2 vols. E. Lorenz. 300p. (Orig.). 1993. pap. 20.00 (*1-56329-167-3*) St Anthony Pub.

***St. Anthony's ICD-9-CM Code Book for Home Health Services, Nursing Homes & Hospices.** Ed. by Karen Schmidt & Anita Hart. 1250p. 1997. 125.00 (*1-56329-427-3*) St Anthony Pub.

St. Anthony's ICD-9-CM Code Book for Home Health Services, Nursing Homes & Hospices: 1992 Edition. Ed. by Marleeta K. Jones. 1000p. 1991. 107.00 (*1-56329-052-9*) St Anthony Pub.

St. Anthony's ICD-9-CM Code Book for Outpatient Services, 3 vols. E. Lorenz. 278p. (C). 1993. ring bd. 139.00 (*1-56329-136-3*) St Anthony Pub.

St. Anthony's ICD-9-CM Code Book for Outpatient Services, Vols. I, II, & III. Ed. by Charlottte Bowers. 1989. 139.00 (*1-56329-013-8*) St Anthony Pub.

St. Anthony's ICD-9-CM Code Book for Physician Payment, Vols. I & II. Ed. by Deborah Hall. 1989. 129.00 (*1-56329-023-5*) St Anthony Pub.

St. Anthony's ICD-9-CM Code Book for Physician Payment, Vols. I & II: 1992 Edition, 2 vols., Set. Ed. by Deborah Hall. 800p. 1991. pap. 89.00 (*1-56329-053-7*) St Anthony Pub.

St. Anthony's ICD-9-CM Code Book for Physicians. E. Lorenz. 250p. (C). 1994. ring bd. 129.00 (*1-56329-131-2*) St Anthony Pub.

St. Anthony's ICD-9-CM Code Book for Physicians - B-W. E. Lorenz. 185p. (Orig.). (C). 1993. pap. 39.95 (*1-56329-168-1*) St Anthony Pub.

St. Anthony's ICD-9-CM Code Book, Vols. I-III: 1992 Edition, 3 vols., Set. Ed. by Charlotte Bowers. 1000p. 1991. pap. 97.00 (*1-56329-063-4*) St Anthony Pub.

St. Anthony's ICD-9-CM Code Book, '94, 3 vols. E. Lorenz. 300p. (Orig.). (C). 1993. pap. 49.95 (*1-56329-166-5*); pap. 59.95 (*1-56329-163-0*) St Anthony Pub.

St. Anthony's ICD-9-CM Questions & Answers: 1992 Edition. Ed. by Charlotte Bowers. 200p. 1992. 137.00 (*1-56329-067-7*) St Anthony Pub.

***St. Anthony's Illustrated ICD-9-CM Code Book.** Ed. by Laurie Castillo & Catherine Hopkins. (Illus.). 1110p. 1996. write for info. (*1-56329-350-1*) St Anthony Pub.

***St. Anthony's Illustrated ICD-9-CM Code Book.** Ed. by Karen Schmidt & Anita Hart. (Illus.). 1630p. 1997. pap. 89.95 (*1-56329-429-X*) St Anthony Pub.

***St. Anthony's Illustrated ICD-9-CM Code Book.** Ed. by Karen Schmidt & Anita Hart. (Illus.). 1630p. 1997. 195.00 (*1-56329-430-3*) St Anthony Pub.

***St. Anthony's Illustrated ICD-9-CM Code Book.** Ed. by Karen Schmidt & Anita Hart. (Illus.). 1630p. 1997. spiral bd. 195.00 (*1-56329-431-1*) St Anthony Pub.

***St. Anthony's Illustrated ICD-9-CM Code Book for Physician Payment.** Ed. by Laurie Castillo & Catherine Hopkins. (Illus.). 1110p. 1996. 79.95 (*1-56329-351-X*) St Anthony Pub.

***St. Anthony's Illustrated ICD-9-CM Codebook.** Ed. by Laurie Castillo & Catherine Hopkins. (Illus.). 1110p. 1997. write for info. (*1-56329-423-0*) St Anthony Pub.

***St. Anthony's Illustrated ICD-9-CM Codebook for Physician Payment.** Ed. by Laurie Castillo & Catherine Hopkins. (Illus.). 1110p. 1997. pap. 79.95 (*1-56329-424-9*) St Anthony Pub.

St. Anthony's Integrated Health Care Directory. Ed. by Susan Namovicz-Peat & Mary Darby. 600p. (C). Date not set. 595.00 (*1-56329-319-6*) St Anthony Pub.

St. Anthony's Management for Profitable Outcomes: Concurrent Review of the '90's Seminar Manual. Ed. by Gay M. Boughton-Barnes. 200p. 1992. write for info. (*1-56329-084-7*, CCRC) St Anthony Pub.

***St. Anthony's Medical Managed Care & Capitation Manual.** Ed. by Mike Grambo. Date not set. ring bd. 597.00 (*1-56329-434-6*) St Anthony Pub.

St. Anthony's Medicare Billing Compliance Guide. Carol F. Endahl. Ed. by Karen M. Schmidt & Paul H. Hubbard. 200p. Date not set. 259.00 (*1-56329-323-4*) St Anthony Pub.

***St. Anthony's Medicare Billing Compliance Guide.** Carol F. Endahl. 350p. Date not set. 259.00 (*1-56329-406-0*) St Anthony Pub.

***St. Anthony's Medicare Billing Compliance Source Book: The Official Reference for Inpatient & Outpatient Coding, Documentation & Billing.** St. Anthony Publishing Staff. Ed. by Carol Endahl & Miriam Weiss. 500p. (C). 1997. 399.00 (*1-56329-438-9*) St Anthony Pub.

St. Anthony's Medicare Coverage Manual. Ed. by Mike Grambo et al. 1990. 129.00 (*1-56329-009-X*) St Anthony Pub.

St. Anthony's Medicare Coverage Manual. E. Lorenz. 147p. 1993. ring bd. 129.00 (*1-56329-135-5*) St Anthony Pub.

St. Anthony's Medicare Payment Guide for Orthopaedics. E. Lorenz. 187p. (C). 1993. ring bd. 138.00 (*1-56329-157-6*) St Anthony Pub.

St. Anthony's Medicare Payment Guide to Cardiology. E. Lorenz. 188p. (C). 1993. ring bd. 197.00 (*1-56329-156-8*) St Anthony Pub.

St. Anthony's Medicare Secondary Payer - Billing & Reimbursement Guide. E. Lorenz. 200p. (C). 1994. ring bd. 149.00 (*1-56329-181-9*) St Anthony Pub.

***St. Anthony's Medicare Unbundling Guide for Anesthesiology.** Ed. by Sheila R. Parvis. 300p. (C). write for info. (*1-56329-339-0*) St Anthony Pub.

***St. Anthony's OASIS Implementation Package: Integrating OASIS into Home Health Assessments.** Marilyn Seiler. 90p. (C). Date not set. 149.00 (*1-56329-349-8*) St Anthony Pub.

St. Anthony's Orthopaedic Training Guide-Seminar Manual. Ed. by Gay M. Boughton-Barnes. 200p. 1992. 149.00 (*1-56329-099-5*, ORTC) St Anthony Pub.

St. Anthony's Outpatient PPS Seminar Manual. Ed. by Gay M. Boughton-Barnes. 200p. 1992. 149.00 (*1-56329-079-0*, APCM) St Anthony Pub.

***St. Anthony's Physician Capitation & Managed Care Reference Manual.** Ed. by Mike Grambo & Jay Lechtman. 400p. (C). Date not set. 349.00 (*1-56329-344-7*) St Anthony Pub.

S

St. Anthony's Physician Medicaid Service Utilization Data Library. Michael Grambo. 150p. Date not set. 5.95 (*1-56329-327-7*) St Anthony Pub.

St. Anthony's Physician Questions & Answers. Ed. by Debbie Hall. 150p. 1992. 117.00 (*1-56329-069-3*) St Anthony Pub.

St. Anthony's Physician Reimbursement Seminar Manual. Ed. by Gay M. Boughton-Barnes. 200p. 1992. 149.00 (*1-56329-043-X*, PHCM) St Anthony Pub.

***St. Anthony's Prosthetic Billing Guide for Freestanding Ambulatory Surgery Centers.** 20p. (C). Date not set. write for info. (*1-56329-437-0*) St Anthony Pub.

***St. Anthony's Provider Stop Loss Solutions: The Guide to Understanding Provider Stop Loss Arrangements.** St. Anthony Publishing Staff. Ed. by Mike Grambo. 500p. Date not set. 299.00 (*1-56329-416-8*) St Anthony Pub.

St. Anthony's RBRVS Step-by-Step, Pts. 1-2. Ed. by Ryan Teel. 200p. 1991. 200.00 (*1-56329-062-6*) St Anthony Pub.

St. Anthony's Reengineering the Medical Practice: Profit Through Efficiency in a Medical Office Environment. rev. ed. Jon Hultman. (Illus.). 206p. 1996. 199.00 (*1-56329-308-0*) St Anthony Pub.

***St. Anthony's Reimbursement Guide for Radiology Services: The Coding, Billing & Coverage Reference.** Kathy L. Brouch. Ed. by Sheila R. Parvis et al. 624p. Date not set. 189.00 (*1-56329-378-1*) St Anthony Pub.

St. Anthony's Reimbursement Guide to Radiology Services, 1992. E. Lorenz. 340p. (C). 1992. ring bd. 177.00 (*1-56329-093-6*, SRA) St Anthony Pub.

***St. Anthony's Roadmap for Medicaid Managed Care: A Clinical & Financial Tour of Unmanaged, Managed & Highly Managed Markets.** Sean Hopkins. Ed. by Michael Grambo. 300p. (C). 1996. 345.00 (*1-56329-373-0*) St Anthony Pub.

***St. Anthony's Softbound ICD-9-CM Code Book for Physician Payment.** Ed. by Laurie Castillo & Catherine Hopkins. 982p. 1996. 59.95 (*1-56329-353-6*) St Anthony Pub.

St. Anthony's Specialty Coding Seminar Manual: Cardiovascular. Ed. by Gay M. Boughton-Barnes. 200p. 1992. 149.00 (*1-56329-072-3*, CARM) St Anthony Pub.

St. Anthony's Specialty Coding Seminar Manual-Opthamology. Ed. by Gay M. Boughton-Barnes. 200p. 1992. 149.00 (*1-56329-078-2*, EYSM) St Anthony Pub.

***St. Anthony's Spiral ICD-9-CM Code Book for Physician Payment.** Ed. by Laurie Castillo & Catherine Hopkins. 982p. 1996. 59.95 (*1-56329-354-4*) St Anthony Pub.

***St. Anthony's Standard ICD-9-CM Code Book.** Ed. by Karen Schmidt & Anita Hart. 1250p. 1997. 49.95 (*1-56329-426-5*) St Anthony Pub.

St. Anthony's Three-in-One Code Book: Dermatology 1993 Edition. Ed. by Kathy Brouch. 1992. 159.00 (*1-56329-111-8*, SDM) St Anthony Pub.

St. Anthony's Three-in-One Code Book: Ear, Nose, Throat 1993 Edition. Ed. by Kathy Brouch. 1992. 167.00 (*1-56329-110-X*, SEN) St Anthony Pub.

St. Anthony's Three-in-One Code Book: Neurology 1993 Edition. Ed. by Kathy Brouch. 1992. 135.00 (*1-56329-107-X*) St Anthony Pub.

St. Anthony's Three-in-One Code Book: OB - GYN 1993 Edition. Ed. by Kathy Brouch. 1992. 139.00 (*1-56329-104-5*, SBG) St Anthony Pub.

St. Anthony's Three-in-One Code Book: Oncology - Hematology 1993 Edition. Ed. by Kathy Brouch. 1992. 169.00 (*1-56329-113-4*, SOH) St Anthony Pub.

St. Anthony's Three-in-One Code Book: Ophthalmology 1993 Edition. Ed. by Kathy Brouch. 1992. 115.00 (*1-56329-112-6*, SPH) St Anthony Pub.

St. Anthony's Three-in-One Code Book: Orthopaedics 1993 Edition. Ed. by Kathy Brouch. 1992. 149.00 (*1-56329-108-8*) St Anthony Pub.

St. Anthony's Three-in-One Code Book: Urology 1993 Edition. Ed. by Kathy Brouch. 1992. 115.00 (*1-56329-109-6*, SUR) St Anthony Pub.

St. Anthony's Three-in-One Code Book for Cardiology. E. Lorenz. 1993. ring bd. 125.00 (*1-56329-106-1*, SCR) St Anthony Pub.

St. Anthony's Three-in-One Code Book for Cardiology - CPT, HCPCS Level II & ICD-9-CM: 1992 Edition. Ed. by Kathy Brouch. 300p. 1992. 125.00 (*1-56329-055-3*) St Anthony Pub.

St. Anthony's Three-in-One Code Book for Dermatology & Plastic Reconstructive Surgery - CPT, HCPCS Level II, ICD-9-CM: 1992 Edition. Ed. by Kathy Brouch. 300p. 1992. 159.00 (*1-56329-056-1*) St Anthony Pub.

St. Anthony's Three-in-One Code Book for ENT - CPT, HCPCS Level II, ICD-9-CM: 1992 Edition. Ed. by Kathy Brouch. 300p. 1992. 167.00 (*1-56329-066-9*) St Anthony Pub.

St. Anthony's Three-in-One Code Book for General Surgery: 1993 Edition. Ed. by Kathy Brouch. 1992. 119.00 (*1-56329-105-3*, SGS) St Anthony Pub.

St. Anthony's Three-in-One Code Book for General Surgery - CPT, HCPCS Level II, ICD-9-CM: 1992 Edition. Ed. by Kathy Brouch. 300p. 1992. 119.00 (*1-56329-057-X*) St Anthony Pub.

St. Anthony's Three-in-One Code Book for Neurology - CPT, HCPCS Level II, ICD-9-CM: 1992 Edition. Ed. by Kathy Brouch. 300p. 1992. 135.00 (*1-56329-064-2*) St Anthony Pub.

St. Anthony's Three-in-One Code Book for OB-GYN. E. Lorenz. 147p. (C). 1993. 139.00 (*1-56329-119-3*) St Anthony Pub.

St. Anthony's Three-in-One Code Book for OB-GYN - CPT, HCPCS Level II, ICD-9-CM: 1992 Edition. Ed. by Kathy Brouch. 300p. 1992. 139.00 (*1-56329-054-5*) St Anthony Pub.

St. Anthony's Three-in-One Code Book for Oncology & Hematology - CPT, HCPCS Level II, ICD-9-CM: 1992 Edition. Ed. by Kathy Brouch. 300p. 1992. 169.00 (*1-56329-058-8*) St Anthony Pub.

St. Anthony's Three-in-One Code Book for Ophthalmology - CPT, HCPCS Level II, ICD-9-CM: 1992 Edition. Ed. by Kathy Brouch. 300p. 1992. 115.00 (*1-56329-059-6*) St Anthony Pub.

St. Anthony's Three-in-One Code Book for Orthopaedics. E. Lorenz. 140p. (C). 1993. ring bd. 149.00 (*1-56329-120-7*) St Anthony Pub.

St. Anthony's Three-in-One Code Book for Orthopaedics - CPT, HCPCS Level II, ICD-9-CM: 1992 Edition. Ed. by Kathy Brouch. 300p. 1992. 149.00 (*1-56329-060-X*) St Anthony Pub.

St. Anthony's Three-in-One Code Book for Physical. E. Lorenz. 250p. 1993. ring bd. 175.00 (*1-56329-144-4*) St Anthony Pub.

St. Anthony's Three-in-One Code Book for Urology - CPT, HCPCS Level II, ICD-9-CM: 1992 Edition. Ed. by Kathy Brouch. 300p. 1992. 115.00 (*1-56329-065-0*) St Anthony Pub.

St. Anthony's Three-in-One Coding Seminar Manual. Kim R. Stafford. 200p. 1992. 180.00 (*1-56329-073-1*, TREM) St Anthony Pub.

St. Anthony's Training Manual for Physician Coding. Ed. by Marleeta K. Jones & Gay Boughton-Barnes. 150p. 1990. 75.00 (*1-56329-001-4*) St Anthony Pub.

St. Anthony's Training Resource for OB-GYN Coding. Ed. by Marleeta K. Jones et al. 150p. 1990. 75.00 (*1-56329-021-9*) St Anthony Pub.

St. Anthony's Training Resource for Orthopaedic Coding. Ed. by Marleeta K. Jones & Gay Boughton-Barnes. 150p. 1990. 75.00 (*1-56329-017-0*) St Anthony Pub.

St. Anthony's UB-82 Editor. Ed. by Lotita Dickerson et al. 400p. 1991. 195.00 (*1-56329-048-0*) St Anthony Pub.

***St. Anthony's UB-92 Editor.** Ed. by Carol Endahl & Karen Schmidt. Date not set. ring bd. 249.00 (*1-56329-417-6*) St Anthony Pub.

***St. Anthony's UB-92 Editor.** Carol F. Endahl. Ed. by Greg Britt & Julia Palmer. 600p. (C). 1996. 199.00 (*1-56329-348-X*) St Anthony Pub.

St. Anthony's UB-92 Editor, '93. E. Lorenz. 200p. (C). 1992. ring bd. 195.00 (*1-56329-114-2*) St Anthony Pub.

***St. Anthony's Updatable ICD-9-CM Code Book.** Ed. by Karen Schmidt et al. 1300p. 1997. 139.00 (*1-56329-433-8*) St Anthony Pub.

***St. Anthony's Updatable ICD-9-CM Code Book for Outpatient Services.** Ed. by Karen Schmidt & Lolita Jones. 1282p. 1997. 139.00 (*1-56329-428-1*) St Anthony Pub.

***St. Anthony's Updatable ICD-9-CM Code Book for Physician Payment.** Ed. by Laurie Castillo & Catherine Hopkins. 982p. 1996. 129.00 (*1-56329-352-8*) St Anthony Pub.

***St. Anthony's Updatable ICD-9-CM Codebook for Physician Payment.** Ed. by Laurie Castillo & Catherine Hopkins. 982p. Date not set. 129.00 (*1-56329-420-6*) St Anthony Pub.

***St. Anthony's Updatable ICD-9-CM Codebook for Physician Payment.** Ed. by Laurie Castillo & Catherine Hopkins. 982p. 1997. pap. 59.95 (*1-56329-421-4*) St Anthony Pub.

***St. Anthony's Updatable ICD-9-CM Codebook for Physician Payment.** Ed. by Laurie Castillo & Catherine Hopkins. 982p. 1997. spiral bd. 59.95 (*1-56329-422-2*) St Anthony Pub.

***St. Anthony's 1996 ICD-9-CM, Vols. 1 & 2.** (Illus.). pap. 39.95 (*0-614-19629-9*, OP051996WE) AMA.

***St. Anthony's 1997-1998 Health Insurance Directory.** Ed. by Susan Peat. 400p. (C). 1996. 129.00 (*1-56329-372-2*) St Anthony Pub.

***St. Anthony's 1997-98 Health Insurance Directory (NAIC)** Ed. by Susan Namovicz-Peat. 300p. (C). 129.00 (*1-56329-341-2*) St Anthony Pub.

St. Antony of the Desert. Athanasius The Great. 106p. 1995. pap. 5.00 (*0-89555-525-5*) TAN Bks Pubs.

St. Athanasius: Defender of the Faith. Michael Davies. 1995. pap. 4.25 (*0-935952-12-8*) Angelus Pr.

St. Athanasius: The Life of St. Antony. Ed. by W. J. Burghardt et al. LC 78-62454. (Ancient Christian Writers Ser.: No. 10). 155p. 1950. 14.95 (*0-8091-0250-1*) Paulist Pr.

St. Athanasius on the Incarnation. St. Anthanasius. 120p. 1977. pap. 7.95 (*0-913836-40-0*) St Vladimirs.

St. Augustine. Adolphe Hatzfeld. LC 71-168252. 155p. 1975. reprint ed. 34.50 (*0-404-03155-2*) AMS Pr.

St. Augustine: America's Oldest City. Linda R. Wade. (Doors to America's Past Ser.). (J). 1991. 11.95 (*0-86592-468-6*) Rourke Enter.

St. Augustine: Aspects of His Life & Thought. W. Montgomery. 1977. lib. bdg. 34.95 (*0-8490-2556-7*) Gordon Pr.

St. Augustine: Man, Pastor, Mystic. Augustine Trape. (Orig.). 1985. reprint ed. pap. 7.95 (*0-89942-172-5*, 172/04) Catholic Bk Pub.

St. Augustine: On Faith & Works. Gregory J. Lombardo. (Ancient Christian Writers Ser.: No. 48). 128p. 1988. 14.95 (*0-8091-0406-7*) Paulist Pr.

St. Augustine: The Literal Meaning of Genesis, Vol. 1. Tr. & Anno. by John H. Taylor. (Ancient Christian Writers Ser.: No. 41). 292p. 1983. 19.95 (*0-8091-0326-5*) Paulist Pr.

St. Augustine: The Literal Meaning of Genesis, Vol. 2. Tr. & Anno. by John H. Taylor. (Ancient Christian Writers Ser.: No. 42). 358p. 1983. 22.95 (*0-8091-0327-3*) Paulist Pr.

St. Augustine, Against the Academics. Ed. by W. J. Burghardt et al. LC 78-62461. (Ancient Christian Writers Ser.: No. 12). 220p. 1950. 16.95 (*0-8091-0252-8*) Paulist Pr.

St. Augustine & the Donatist Controversy. Geoffrey G. Willis. LC 82-45826. (Orthodoxies & Heresies in the Early Church Ser.). reprint ed. 39.50 (*0-404-62397-2*) AMS Pr.

***St. Augustine Coloring Book & Historical Text.** rev. ed. Patricia A. Dolan. (Illus.). 34p. 1991. pap. text ed. 2.75 (*0-9657376-0-8*) Creat By PAD.

St. Augustine, Faith, Hope & Charity. Ed. by J. Kuasten & J. Plumpe. Tr. by Louis A. Arand. LC 78-62450. (Ancient Christian Writers Ser.: No. 3). 165p. 1947. 15.95 (*0-8091-0045-2*) Paulist Pr.

St. Augustine Grass & Home-Made Mayonnaise. Allene Goldman. 104p. (Orig.). 1993. pap. 12.00 (*0-9623167-2-5*) Odenwald Pr.

***St. Augustine in 90 Minutes.** LC 96-40321. (Philosophers in 90 Minutes Ser.). 1997. text ed. 12.95 (*1-56663-149-1*) I R Dee.

***St. Augustine in 90 Minutes.** LC 96-40321. (Philosophers in 90 Minutes Ser.). 1997. pap. 5.95 (*1-56663-150-5*) I R Dee.

***St. Augustine of Canterbury.** Michael A. Green. 42p. 1997. pap. 9.95 (*1-85756-366-2*, Pub. by Janus Pubng UK) Paul & Co Pubs.

St. Augustine of Hippo: Life & Controversies. Gerald I. Bonner. 1995. pap. 19.95 (*0-907547-52-4*, Pub. by Canterbury Press Norwich UK) Morehouse Pub.

St. Augustine of Hippo: Life & Controversies. Gerald I. Bonner. LC 82-45807. (Orthodoxies & Heresies in the Early Church Ser.). 1985. reprint ed. 42.50 (*0-404-62376-X*) AMS Pr.

St. Augustine on Marriage & Sexuality. Ed. by Elizabeth Clark. LC 96-8089. (Fathers of the Church Ser.: Vol. 1). 112p. 1996. text ed. 29.95 (*0-8132-0866-1*); pap. text ed. 13.95 (*0-8132-0867-X*) Cath U Pr.

St. Augustine on the End of the World. Ed. by George N. Thompson. 55p. (Orig.). reprint ed. pap. text ed. 5.95 (*0-940564-15-7*) Mayflower Pilgrim.

St. Augustine, the Lord's Sermon on the Mount. Ed. by W. J. Burghardt et al. LC 78-62451. (Ancient Christian Writers Ser.: No. 5). 227p. 1948. 16.95 (*0-8091-0246-3*) Paulist Pr.

St. Augustine, the Problem of Free Choice. Ed. by W. J. Burghardt et al. LC 78-62469. (Ancient Christian Writers Ser.: No. 22). 298p. 1955. 19.95 (*0-8091-0259-5*) Paulist Pr.

St. Augustine's Abbey: Report on Excavations, 1960-78. D. Sherlock & H. Woods. (Illus.). 400p. 1993. text ed. 66.00 (*0-907746-11-X*, Pub. by Sutton Pubng UK) Bks Intl VA.

St. Augustine's Confessions. Date not set. pap. text ed. 8.50 (*0-674-78515-0*) HUP.

***St. Augustine's Dilemma: Grace & Eternal Law in the Major Works of Augustine of Hippo.** Dennis R. Creswell. (Studies in Church History: Vol. 5). 176p. (C). 1997. 39.95 (*0-8204-2843-4*) P Lang Pubng.

St. Augustine's Early Theory of Man, A. D. 386-391. Robert J. O'Connell. LC 68-21981. 323p. 1969. reprint ed. pap. 92.10 (*0-7837-4173-1*, 2059022) Bks Demand.

St. Augustine's Theory of Knowledge: A Contemporary Analysis. Bruce Bubacz. LC 81-18754. (Texts & Studies in Religion: Vol. 11). 234p. (C). 1981. lib. bdg. 89.95 (*0-88946-959-8*) E Mellen.

***St. B. Life at St. Barnabas Hospital School of Medicine.** Elizabeth Crawford. Ed. by Dan Benedict. (Illus.). 80p. (Orig.). 1997. per. 20.00 (*0-89716-756-2*) P B Pubng.

***St. Barth: French West Indies.** Charles Didcott. LC 97-13684. (Illus.). 144p. (ENG & FRE.). 1997. 35.00 (*0-393-04612-5*) Concepts Pub.

St. Bartholomew's Church in the City of New York. Christine Smith. (Illus.). 232p. 1988. 45.00 (*0-19-505406-7*) OUP.

St. Basil & Monasticism. M. Gertrude Murphy. LC 70-144661. reprint ed. 29.50 (*0-404-04543-X*) AMS Pr.

St. Basil on the Value of Greek Literature. Ed. by N. Wilson. 1986. pap. 13.95 (*0-7156-0924-6*, Pub. by Duckworth UK) Focus Pub-R Pullins.

St. Basil the Great & Apollinaris of Laodicea. George L. Prestige. LC 82-45832. (Orhtodoxies & Heresies in the Early Church Ser.). reprint ed. 32.50 (*0-404-62399-9*) AMS Pr.

St. Basil the Great on The Forty Martyrs of Sebaste, Paradise, & the Catholic Faith. Basil. 1979. pap. 3.95 (*0-89981-083-7*) Eastern Orthodox.

***St. Benedict - A Rule for Beginners: Excerpts from the Life & Rule.** 3rd ed. Ed. by Julian Stead. 160p. 1993. pap. 8.95 (*1-56548-098-8*) New City.

St. Benedict & Christianity in England. Patrick Barry. 40p. (Orig.). 1996. pap. 4.95 (*0-85244-338-2*, Pub. by Gracewing UK) Morehouse Pub.

St. Benedict & the Sixth Century. John Chapman. LC 79-109719. 239p. 1971. reprint ed. text ed. 55.00 (*0-8371-4209-1*, CHSB, Greenwood Pr) Greenwood.

St. Benedict for the Laity. Eric Dean. 88p. 1989. pap. 5.95 (*0-8146-1595-3*) Liturgical Pr.

St. Benedict of Nursia: Life from the Menology of St. Dimitri of Rostov, Orthodox Liturgical Service, Akathist Hymn, Rule for Monasteries. Tr. by Isaac E. Lambertsen from LAT. (Illus.). 80p. (Orig.). 1989. reprint ed. pap. 5.00 (*0-912927-38-0*, X038) St John Kronstadt.

St. Benedict's Rule for Monasteries. Tr. by Leonard J. Doyle. 106p. (Orig.). 1950. pap. 2.95 (*0-8146-0644-X*) Liturgical Pr.

St. Bernadette, Vol. 7. Rene Berthier & Marie Sigault. Tr. by Marianne L. Trouve' from FRE. (Saints Ser.). (Illus.). 32p. (J). (gr. 3-8). 1995. pap. 1.95 (*0-8198-6977-5*) Pauline Bks.

St. Bernadette Soubirous. Francois Trochu. LC 84-51819. 432p. 1985. reprint ed. pap. 18.50 (*0-89555-253-1*) TAN Bks Pubs.

St. Bernard of Clairvaux. Leon Cristiani. LC 77-4942. 1977. 4.50 (*0-8198-0463-0*); pap. 3.50 (*0-8198-0464-9*) Pauline Bks.

St. Bernard of Clairvaux: Essays Commemorating the Eighth Centenary of His Canonization. Ed. by M. Basil Pennington. LC 77-4487. (Cistercian Studies: No. 28). 1977. 14.95 (*0-87907-828-6*) Cistercian Pubns.

St. Bernard of Clairvaux: Oracle of the 12th Century (1091-1153) Abbot, Confessor & Doctor of the Church. Theodore Ratisbonne. LC 91-67795. Orig. Title: The Life & Times of St. Bernard. 437p. 1991. reprint ed. pap. 18.50 (*0-89555-453-4*) TAN Bks Pubs.

St. Bernard of Clairvaux (1090-1153) Michael Casey et al. (Word & Spirit Ser.: No. 12). 192p. (Orig.). 1990. pap. 8.00 (*0-932506-84-4*) St Bedes Pubns.

St. Bernard of Claivaux, Vol. 9. Monk of Citeaux Staff. Tr. by Marianne L. Trouve' from FRE. (Saints Ser.). (Illus.). 32p. (J). (gr. 3-8). 1995. pap. 1.95 (*0-8198-6979-1*) Pauline Bks.

St. Bernard on Women. Jean Leclercq. 1989. 34.95 (*0-318-41660-3*); pap. 16.95 (*0-318-41661-1*) Cistercian Pubns.

St. Bonaventure. Efrem Bettoni. Tr. by Scuola, Editrice, Brescia, Italy La from ITA. LC 81-13371. (Notre Dame Pocket Library). 127p. 1981. reprint ed. text ed. 49.75 (*0-313-23271-7*, BESB, Greenwood Pr) Greenwood.

St. Bonaventure's Writings Concerning the Franciscan Order, Vol. V. Bonaventure Staff. (Works of Saint Bonaventure). 281p. 1994. pap. 15.00 (*1-57659-047-X*) Franciscan Inst.

***St. Brieuc City Plan.** (Grafocarte Maps Ser.). 1995. 8.95 (*2-7416-0069-4*, 80069) Michelin.

***St. Brieuc/St. Malo/Rennes Map.** 1996. 6.95 (*2-06-700059-4*, 59) Michelin.

St. Brigid: The Girl Who Loved to Give. Patricia Egan. (Illus.). 24p. (Orig.). (J). (gr. 4-7). 1994. pap. 4.50 (*1-85390-222-5*, Pub. by Veritas Pubns IE) Irish Bks Media.

St. Camber, Vol. 2. Katherine Kurtz. (Legends of Camber of Culdi Ser.). 464p. 1987. mass mkt. 5.99 (*0-345-34768-4*, Del Rey) Ballantine.

St. Catharines: Garden on the Canal. Robert Shipley. (Illus.). 176p. 1987. 28.95 (*0-89781-219-0*) Am Historical Pr.

St. Catherine de'Ricci: Selected Letters. Catherine De'Ricci. Ed. by Simon Tugwell. Tr. by Jennifer Petrie. (Dominican Sources: New Editions in English Ser.). 71p. 1985. pap. 4.00 (*0-9511202-2-0*, Pub. by Dominican Sources UK) Parable.

St. Catherine Laboure of the Miraculous Medal. Joseph I. Dirvin. LC 84-50466. 245p. 1984. reprint ed. pap. 13.50 (*0-89555-242-6*) TAN Bks Pubs.

St. Catherine of Siena. Alice Curtayne. LC 80-53745. 1980. reprint ed. pap. 13.50 (*0-89555-162-4*) TAN Bks Pubs.

St. Catherine of Siena: A Study in the Religion, Literature & History of the Fourteenth Century in Italy. E. Gardner. 1976. lib. bdg. 59.95 (*0-8490-2557-5*) Gordon Pr.

St. Catherines: An Island in Time. David H. Thomas. (Georgia Humanities Council Publications). (Illus.). 94p. 1991. pap. 9.95 (*0-8203-1316-5*) U of Ga Pr.

St. Catherine's House. (C). 1987. 35.00 (*0-317-89822-1*, Pub. by Birmingham Midland Soc UK) St Mut.

St. Catherine's Parish, Dublin, 1840-1900: A Portrait of a Church of Ireland Community. John Crawford. 64p. 1996. pap. 9.95 (*0-7165-2593-3*, Pub. by Irish Acad Pr IE) Intl Spec Bk.

St. Cecilia's Hall in the Niddry Wynd. David F. Harris. LC 81-12628. (Music Reprint Ser.). (Illus.). 303p. 1983. reprint ed. lib. bdg. 35.00 (*0-306-76142-4*) Da Capo.

St. Christopher. Mary F. Windeatt. (Catholic Story Coloring Bks.). (Illus.). 32p. (J). (gr. 1-5). 1992. reprint ed. student ed. 3.00 (*0-89555-376-7*) TAN Bks Pubs.

***St. Ciaran, Patron of Ossory, a Memoir of His Life & Times.** John Hogan. 1997. reprint ed. pap. 10.00 (*0-89979-093-3*) British Am Bks.

St. Clair: A Nineteenth-Century Coal Town's Experience with a Disaster-Prone Industry. Anthony F. Wallace. LC 88-47772. 544p. 1988. reprint ed. pap. 16.95 (*0-8014-9900-3*) Cornell U Pr.

St. Clair County, Alabama Genealogical Notes, Vol. 1. Mildred S. Wright. LC 74-82803. (Illus.). 1984. pap. 12.50 (*0-917016-01-7*) M S Wright.

St. Clair County, Alabama Genealogical Notes, Vol. 2. Mildred S. Wright. LC 74-82803. (Illus.). viii, 67p. 1982. pap. 15.00 (*0-917016-25-4*) M S Wright.

St. Clair Papers: The Life & Public Services of Arthur St. Clair, 2 Vols, Set. William H. Smith. LC 77-117894. (Select Bibliographies Reprint Ser.). 1977. 68.95 (*0-8369-5347-9*) Ayer.

St. Clair Tunnel: Rails Beneath the River. Clare Gilbert. (Illus.). 96p. (Orig.). pap. 14.95 (*1-55046-045-5*, Pub. by Boston Mills Pr CN) Genl Dist Srvs.

St. Clare Catholic Church Records, Colesburg, Kentucky, 1813-1899. Dolores Y. Kennedy. 143p. 1987. pap. 17.00 (*1-889221-17-1*) Ancestral Trails.

St. Clare of Assisi. Nesta DeRobeck. 242p. (Orig.). 1980. reprint ed. pap. 7.95 (*0-8199-0808-8*, Frncscn Herld) Franciscan Pr.

St. Clare of Assisi, Vol. 5. Pierre Dhombre. Tr. by Marianne L. Trove' from FRE. (Saints Ser.). (Illus.). 32p. (J). (gr. 3-8). 1995. pap. 1.95 (*0-8198-6976-7*) Pauline Bks.

St. Clements: The Chronicle of a Connecticut River Castle. Prudence T. Palmer & T. J. Palmer. (Illus.). 208p. (Orig.). 1992. pap. 25.00 (*0-9634150-0-X*) Paper Rock Pub.

St. Cloud: The Triplet City. John J. Doninik. 1983. 22.95 (*0-89781-091-0*, 5072) Am Historical Pr.

St. Collectibles V3 R-Z. Chris Gentry. 1993. pap. 29.95 (*0-08-978217-8*, Pergamon Pr) Elsevier.

St. Croix: Midwest Border River. James T. Dunn. LC 79-52970. (Illus.). xv, 310p. 1979. reprint ed. pap. 9.95 (*0-87351-141-7*) Minn Hist.

St. Croix Avenue. Lauri Lemberg. Tr. by Miriam Eldridge. 424p. 1992. pap. 14.95 (*0-9633780-0-7*) Tyomies Soc.

St. Croix in Another Time: Rapping with George Alexander Cornelius - Count Your Blessings: The Night Hurricane Hugo Lashed St. Croix. Richard A. Schrader, Sr. LC 89-92742. (Illus.). 95p. (Orig.). 1990. pap. text ed. 12.95 (*0-9622987-1-9*) R A Schrader.

St. Croix under French Dominion: 1650-1733. Aimery P. Caron & Arnold R. Highfield. (Illus.). 200p. (Orig.). 1984. pap. text ed. 10.00 (*0-916611-00-0*) Antilles Pr.

St. Croix Valley. Debra M. Chial. (Illus.). 48p. (Orig.). 1993. pap. 3.95 (*0-89658-183-7*) Voyageur Pr.

St. Croix 1493: An Encounter of Two Worlds. Arnold R. Highfield. (Illus.). 173p. (Orig.). (C). 1995. pap. write for info. (*1-886007-01-2*) VI Human Coun.

St. Cyprian, the Lapsed, the Unity of the Catholic Church. Ed. by W. J. Burghardt et al. LC 57-7364. (Ancient Christian Writers Ser.: No. 25). 132p. 1957. 12.95 (*0-8091-0260-9*) Paulist Pr.

St. Cyril of Jerusalem on the Christian Sacraments. Cyril of Jerusalem. 83p. 1977. pap. 7.95 (*0-913836-39-7*) St Vladimirs.

St. David of Dewisland. Nona Rees. (Illus.). (C). 1993. pap. 21.00 (*0-86383-856-1*, Pub. by Gomer Pr UK) St Mut.

St. David's Parish, (Cheraw) South Carolina: Minutes of the Vestry, 1768-1832, & Parish Register, 1819-1924. Brent H. Holcomb. 165p. 1991. reprint ed. 25.00 (*0-89308-144-2*, SC 9) Southern Hist Pr.

St. Dominic. Mary J. Dorcy. LC 82-50978. 173p. 1993. reprint ed. pap. 10.00 (*0-89555-195-0*) TAN Bks Pubs.

St. Dominic & the Rosary. Catherine Beebe. LC 95-79886. 216p. (J). (gr. 4-8). 1996. reprint ed. pap. 9.95 (*0-89870-518-5*) Ignatius Pr.

St. Dominic Savio. Mary F. Windeatt. (Catholic Story Coloring Bks.). (Illus.). 32p. (J). (gr. 1-5). 1992. reprint ed. student ed. 3.00 (*0-89555-370-8*) TAN Bks Pubs.

St. Dominic's Family. Mary J. Dorcy. LC 83-70219. 631p. 1983. reprint ed. pap. 24.00 (*0-89555-208-6*) TAN Bks Pubs.

St. Dunstan: His Life, Times & Cult. Ed. by Nigel Ramsay et al. (Illus.). 360p. (C). 1992. 130.00 (*0-85115-301-1*) Boydell & Brewer.

St. Edmund, King & Martyr. Brian Houghton. (C). 1988. 22.00 (*0-900963-18-2*, Pub. by T Dalton UK) St Mut.

St. Edward's University: A Centennial History. William Dunn. LC 80-53738. (Illus.). 444p. 1986. 34.95 (*0-938472-01-1*) St Edwards Univ.

St. Elizabeth, Vol. 3. Justin Lang & Juliette Wehrung. Tr. by Marianne L. Trouve' from FRE. (Saints Ser.). (Illus.). 32p. (J). (gr. 3-8). 1995. pap. 1.95 (*0-8198-6981-3*) Pauline Bks.

St. Elizabeth Hospital: Looking Back, Looking Forward. Margaret Finnerty. Ed. by Rodney Nelson & Amy Phillips. 110p. (C). 1993. 25.00 (*0-929690-18-4*) Herit Pubs AZ.

***St. Elizabeth's Three Crowns.** Blanche J. Thompson. 165p. 1996. pap. text ed. 9.95 (*0-89870-596-7*) Ignatius Pr.

St. Elias. Jacques Ferron. Tr. by Pierre Cloutier. LC 75-322403. (French Writers of Canada Ser.). 145p. reprint ed. pap. 41.40 (*0-685-23645-5*, 2026117) Bks Demand.

St. Elmo. Augusta J. Evans. 1976. 29.95 (*0-8488-1307-3*) Amereon Ltd.

***St. Elmo.** Augusta J. Evans. Date not set. lib. bdg. 30.95 (*0-8488-1973-X*) Amereon Ltd.

St. Elmo. Augusta J. Evans. 440p. 1980. reprint ed. lib. bdg. 32.95 (*0-89968-210-3*, Lghtyr Pr) Buccaneer Bks.

St. Elmo. Augusta J. Evans. 415p. 1984. reprint ed. lib. bdg. 32.95 (*0-89966-487-3*) Buccaneer Bks.

St. Elmo. Augusta J. Evans. LC 91-41589. (Library of Alabama Classics). 392p. (C). 1992. reprint ed. pap. 19.95 (*0-8173-0577-7*) U of Ala Pr.

St. Elmo: A Novel. Augusta J. Evans. LC 74-15736. (Popular Culture in America Ser.). 576p. 1975. reprint ed. 41.95 (*0-405-06371-7*) Ayer.

St. EOM in the Land of Pasaquan: The Life & Times & Art of Eddie Owens Martin. Photos by Jonathan Williams et al. (Illus.). 260p. 1987. 30.00 (*0-912330-60-0*) Jargon Soc.

***St. Etienne City Plan.** (Grafocarte Maps Ser.). 1993. 8.95 (*2-7416-0036-8*, 80036) Michelin.

St. Eustatius: The Treasure Island of the Caribbean. Eric O. Ayisi. LC 92-14520. (Illus.). 250p. 1992. 45.00 (*0-86543-347-X*); pap. 12.95 (*0-86543-348-8*) Africa World.

St. Eustatius, St. Christopher (St. Kitts) & Nevis. Wilson Ltd. Staff & Imray L. Norie. (C). 1986. 53.00 (*0-685-40401-3*, Pub. by Imray Laurie Norie & Wilson UK) St Mut.

St. Frances Cabrini. Mary F. Windeatt. (Catholic Story Coloring Bks.). (Illus.). 32p. (J). (gr. 1-5). 1991. reprint ed. student ed. 3.00 (*0-89555-375-9*) TAN Bks Pubs.

St. Francis: Poet of Creation. Susan Saint Sing. 110p. 1985. pap. 2.95 (*0-8199-0877-0*, Frncscn Herld) Franciscan Pr.

St. Francis & His Four Ladies. Joan M. Erikson. LC 71-127178. (Illus.). 1970. 6.95 (*0-393-05427-6*) Norton.

St. Francis & the Christmas Miracle. Chester Wrzaszczak. LC 86-62619. 96p. 1986. pap. 7.95 (*0-89390-091-5*) Resource Pubns.

St. Francis & the Foolishness of God. Maire Dennis et al. LC 93-28727. 175p. (Orig.). 1993. pap. 13.50 (*0-88344-899-8*) Orbis Bks.

St. Francis & the Third Order. Raffaele Pazzelli. 235p. 1989. pap. 14.95 (*0-8199-0953-X*, Frncscn Herld) Franciscan Pr.

St. Francis de Sales: Don Bosco's Patron. Arnold Pedrini. Ed. by Francis J. Klauder. Tr. by Wallace L. Cornell. 149p. 1988. 13.95 (*0-89944-096-7*); pap. 8.95 (*0-89944-092-4*) Salesiana Pubs.

St. Francis Hotel Cookbook. Victor Hirtzler. 460p. 1988. 25.00 (*0-915269-06-6*) Windgate Pr.

St. Francis Murals of Santa Fe. Carl Sheppard. Ed. by James C. Smith, Jr. LC 89-39446. (Illus.). 96p. (Orig.). 1990. pap. 9.95 (*0-86534-137-0*) Sunstone Pr.

St. Francis, Nature Mystic: The Derivation & Significance of the Nature Stories in the Franciscan Legend. Edward A. Armstrong. LC 74-149949. (Hermeneutics, Studies in the History of Religions: No. 2). (Illus.). 296p. reprint ed. pap. 84.40 (*0-685-23646-3*, 2029036) Bks Demand.

***St. Francis of Assisi.** Margaret Bunson & Matthew Bunson. (Saints You Should Know Ser.). 56p. 1996. pap. 5.95 (*0-87973-557-0*) Our Sunday Visitor.

St. Francis of Assisi. Thomas Celano. 405p. 1963. pap. 15.00 (*0-8199-0554-2*, Frncscn Herld) Franciscan Pr.

St. Francis of Assisi. Gilbert K. Chesterton. LC 57-1230. 160p. 1987. pap. 9.95 (*0-385-02900-4*, Image Bks) Doubleday.

St. Francis of Assisi. Leon Christiani. LC 74-79802. 1975. pap. 4.95 (*0-8198-2623-5*) Pauline Bks.

St. Francis of Assisi. Raoul Manselli. Tr. by Paul Duggan. 363p. 1988. 24.95 (*0-8199-0880-0*, Frncscn Herld) Franciscan Pr.

St. Francis of Assisi. John R. Moorman. 118p. 1986. pap. 4.95 (*0-8199-0904-1*, Frncscn Herld) Franciscan Pr.

St. Francis of Assisi. Mary F. Windeatt. (Catholic Story Coloring Bks.). (Illus.). 32p. (J). (gr. 1-5). 1991. reprint ed. student ed. 3.00 (*0-89555-368-6*) TAN Bks Pubs.

St. Francis of Assisi, Vol 2. Justin Lang & Juliette Wehrung. Tr. by Marianne L. Trouve' from FRE. (Saints Ser.). (Illus.). 32p. (J). (gr. 3-8). 1995. pap. 1.95 (*0-8198-6983-X*) Pauline Bks.

St. Francis of Assisi, Vol. 9. Monks of New Skete Staff. (Liturgical Music Ser.: No. I). 40p. 1996. pap. 20.00 (*0-935129-34-0*) Monks of New Skete.

St. Francis of Assisi: A Biography. abr. ed. Omer Englebert. 256p. 1979. pap. 7.99 (*0-89283-071-9*) Servant.

St. Francis of Assisi: Essays in Commemoration, 1982. Ed. by Maurice W. Sheehan. (Franciscan Pathways Ser.). xiii, 194p. 1982. pap. 10.00 (*1-57659-063-1*) Franciscan Inst.

St. Francis of Assisi: Omnibus of Sources of the Life of St. Francis. Ed. by Marion A. Habig. Tr. by Leo Sherley-Price et al. (Illus.). 1665p. 1991. 64.95 (*0-8199-0862-2*, Frncscn Herld) Franciscan Pr.

St. Francis of Assisi: Writings for a Gospel Life. Regis J. Armstrong. (Spiritual Legacy Ser.). 240p. 1993. pap. 12.95 (*0-8245-2501-9*) Crossroad NY.

St. Francis of Assisi: Writings for a Gospel Life. Regis J. Armstrong. 240p. 1994. pap. 40.00 (*0-85439-484-2*, Pub. by St Paul Pubns UK) St Mut.

St. Francis of Paola: God's Miracle Worker Supreme. Gino J. Simi & Mario M. Segreti. LC 77-78097. 1993. pap. 8.00 (*0-89555-065-2*) TAN Bks Pubs.

St. Genevieve Watching over Paris. Leonard Gontarek. Ed. by Maureen Owen. 1984. pap. 4.00 (*0-916382-32-X*) Telephone Bks.

St. George. E. O. Gordon. (Illus.). 160p. 1989. reprint ed. pap. 7.00 (*0-934666-32-6*) Artisan Sales.

St. George & St. Michael. George MacDonald. (George MacDonald Original Works: Series VIII). 432p. 1997. 18.00 (*1-881084-49-3*) Johannesen.

St. George & the Dandelion: Forty Years of Practice As a Jungian Analyst. Joseph B. Wheelwright & Audrey H. Blodgett. 109p. 1982. 15.00 (*0-932630-04-9*) C G Jung Frisco.

St. George & the Dragon. Margaret Hodges. (J). (ps-4). 1990. mass mkt. 6.95 (*0-316-36795-8*) Little.

St. George & the Dragon. Illus. by Trina S. Hyman. LC 83-19980. (J). (gr. 6-8). 1984. 16.95 (*0-316-36789-3*) Little.

St. George & the Dragon. Esther Porter-Lane. (Orig.). (J). (gr. 4 up). 1985. pap. 5.00 (*0-87602-249-2*) Anchorage.

St. George & the Dragon. Calvin Tomkins. 1996. 19.50 (*0-8050-0824-1*) H Holt & Co.

St. George & the Dragon & the Quest for the Holy Grail. Edward Hays. LC 85-82568. (Illus.). 184p. 1986. pap. 10.95 (*0-939516-07-1*) Forest Peace.

***St. George's Cathedral: Two Hundred Years of Tradition.** Ed. by Donald Swainson. 272p. 1991. pap. 39.95 (*1-55082-030-3*, Pub. by Quarry Pr CN) LPC InBook.

***St. George's Cathedral: Two Hundred Years of Tradition.** Ed. by Donald Swainson. 272p. 1991. pap. 26.95 (*1-55082-031-1*, Pub. by Quarry Pr CN) LPC InBook.

St. George's Channel: Wales to the East Coast of Ireland. Wilson Ltd. Staff & Imray L. Norie. (C). 1990. 60.00 (*0-685-40430-7*, Pub. by Imray Laurie Norie & Wilson UK) St Mut.

St. George's Episcopal Church, Germantown, Tennessee: The First Twenty Years. Leonard V. Hughes, Jr. Ed. by James D. Russell. LC 83-50804. (Illus.). 224p. 1984. 6.00 (*0-9613533-0-9*) St Georges Episcopal.

St. Gertrude the Great: Herald of Divine Love. Benedictine Sisters of Clyde, Missouri Staff. 1994. pap. 1.50 (*0-89555-026-1*) TAN Bks Pubs.

St. Gorbachev & Other Neo-Missionary Position. John Hatch. LC 90-60732. (Illus.). 54p. 1990. pap. 6.95 (*0-932693-03-2*) Jukebox Press.

St. Gregoire de Nazianze. Alphonse Benoit. vi, 788p. 1973. reprint ed. 200.00 (*3-487-04695-4*) G Olms Pubs.

St. Gregory of Nyssa on the Origin & Destiny of the Soul. John P. Cavarnos. 12p. 1996. pap. 1.75 (*0-914744-01-1*) Inst Byzantine.

St. Gregory of Nyssa, the Lord's Prayer, the Beatitudes. Ed. by W. J. Burghardt & T. C. Lawler. LC 78-62466. (Ancient Christian Writers Ser.: No. 18). 216p. 1954. 16.95 (*0-8091-0255-2*) Paulist Pr.

St. Gregory Palamas & Orthodox Spirituality. John Meyendorff. LC 96-23233. (Illus.). 184p. 1996. pap. 11.95 (*0-913836-11-7*) St Vladimirs.

St. Gregory the Great: Pastoral Care. Ed. by W. J. Burghardt et al. (Ancient Christian Writers Ser.: No. 11). 282p. 1950. 19.95 (*0-8091-0251-X*) Paulist Pr.

St. Helens: The Changing Mountain. Larry D. Ikenberry. (Illus.). 34p. 1980. pap. 3.95 (*0-935818-03-0*) Cascade Photo.

St. Herman, Ascetic & Enlightner of Alaska. Frank A. Golder. 1992. pap. 0.75 (*0-89981-141-8*) Eastern Orthodox.

St. Herman of Alaska. Vladimir S. Borichevsky. (Illus.). 80p. (Orig.). 1970. pap. 4.50 (*1-878997-06-8*) St Tikhons Pr.

St. Hugh of Lincoln. David H. Farmer. (Cistercian Studies: No. 87). xi, 114p. 1986. pap. 7.95 (*0-87907-887-1*) Cistercian Pubns.

St. Hugh of Lincoln. Ed. by Henry Mayr-Harting. (Illus.). 144p. 1987. 45.00 (*0-19-820120-6*) OUP.

St. Ignatius & the Ratio Studiorum. Ed. by Edward A. Fitzpatrick. Tr. by Mary H. Mayer & A. R. Ball. LC 83-45593. reprint ed. 31.50 (*0-404-19886-4*) AMS Pr.

St. Ignatius' Idea of a Jesuit University. 2nd ed. George E. Ganss. LC 56-13077. (Illus.). 1956. pap. 20.00 (*0-87462-437-1*) Marquette.

St. Ignatius of Loyola. Paul Dudon. Tr. by William J. Young. LC 83-45591. reprint ed. 49.50 (*0-404-19884-8*) AMS Pr.

St. Ignatius of Loyola. Henri Joly. LC 70-170821. reprint ed. 42.50 (*0-404-03597-3*) AMS Pr.

St. Ignatius's Own Story. Tr. by William Young. 138p. 1980. reprint ed. per., pap. 5.95 (*0-8294-0359-0*, SIOS, Jesuit Way) Loyola Pr.

St. Irenaeus: Proof of the Apostolic Preaching. Ed. by W. J. Burghardt & T. C. Lawler. LC 78-62503. (Ancient Christian Writers Ser.: No. 16). 242p. 1952. 16.95 (*0-8091-0254-4*) Paulist Pr.

St. Irenaeus of Lyons, Bk. 1: Against the Heresies, Bk. 1. Tr. & Anno. by Dominic J. Unger. LC 91-40838. (Ancient Christian Writers Ser.: No. 55). 288p. 1992. pap. 24.95 (*0-8091-0454-7*) Paulist Pr.

St. Ives Mining District, Vol. 1. Cyril Noall. (C). 1989. 50.00 (*0-907566-33-2*, Pub. by Dyllansow Truran UK) St Mut.

St. Ives Mining District, Vol. 11. Cyril Noall. Ed. by Philip Payton. (C). 1993. 39.00 (*1-85022-067-0*, Pub. by Dyllansow Truran UK) St Mut.

St. Ives, 1890-1990: History of an Art Colony. Marion Whybrow. (Illus.). 200p. 1994. pap. 39.50 (*1-85149-170-8*) Antique Collect.

St. Ives 1939-64: Twenty-Five Years of Painting, Sculpture, & Pottery. Ed. by David Brown. (Illus.). 248p. 1996. 75.00 (*1-85437-190-8*, Pub. by Tate Gallery UK) U of Wash Pr.

St. James: Critical & Exegetical Commentary. James H. Ropes. LC 16-6543. (International Critical Commentary Ser.). 336p. 1916. 39.95 (*0-567-05035-1*, Pub. by T & T Clark UK) Bks Intl VA.

St. James Encyclopedia of Banking & Finance. Ed. by Charles J. Woelfel. 1300p. 1991. 115.00 (*1-55862-141-5*) St James Pr.

St. James Encyclopedia of Mortgage & Real Estate Finance. Ed. by James Newell. 400p. 1991. 55.00 (*1-55862-154-7*) St James Pr.

St. James Fashion Encyclopedia: A Survey of Style from 1945 to the Present. Martin. LC 96-22878. (Illus.). 450p. 1996. 29.95 (*0-7876-1036-4*) Visible Ink Pr.

St. James Guide to Biography. Ed. by Paul Schellinger. LC 90-63663. 870p. 1991. 140.00 (*1-55862-146-6*, 200103) St James Pr.

***St. James Guide to Black Artists.** 750p. 1997. 155.00 (*1-55862-220-9*, 00155964) St James Pr.

St. James Guide to Science Fiction Writers. 3rd ed. Ed. by Jay P. Pederson. (St. James Guide Ser.). 1300p. (C). 1991. 135.00 (*1-55862-111-3*, 200195) St James Pr.

St. James in the Streets: The Religious Processions of Loiza, Puerto Rico. Edward C. Zaragoza. LC 95-35832. (Drew Studies in Liturgy: No. 2). 198p. 1995. 32.50 (*0-8108-3070-1*) Scarecrow.

St. James Mutual Fund Directory. Ed. by Investment Company Institute Staff. 540p. 1991. 50.00 (*1-55862-148-2*) St James Pr.

St. James Northam Parish Vestry Book, 1744-1850. William L. Hopkins. 129p. 1987. pap. 17.00 (*0-8095-8695-9*); lib. bdg. 43.00 (*0-8095-8286-4*) Borgo Pr.

St. James Opera Encyclopedia: A Guide to People & Works. Larue. LC 96-22877. (Illus.). 600p. 1996. 29.95 (*0-7876-1035-6*) Visible Ink Pr.

St. James Reference Guide to American Literature. 2nd ed. Ed. by Daniel L. Kirkpatrick. 1987. 130.00 (*0-912289-61-9*) St James Pr.

St. James United Church of Christ Church Register, Reformed Church: Loudoun County, Virginia, Sept. 17, 1789-August 23, 1823. Jerry Mower & Tedi J. Mower. 53p. 1993. pap. 7.00 (*1-55856-130-7*) Closson Pr.

St. James World Directory of Futures & Options. 91th ed. Ed. by Nick Battley. 700p. 1991. 95.00 (*1-55862-143-1*) St James Pr.

St. James's Park Encyclopedia. Paul Harrison. (Illus.). 208p. 1996. pap. 17.95 (*1-85158-750-0*, Pub. by Mnstream UK) Trafalgar.

St. Jean De Crevecoeur. Julia P. Mitchell. LC 71-181959. reprint ed. 37.50 (*0-404-04347-X*) AMS Pr.

St. Jean de Crevecoeur. Julia P. Mitchell. (BCL1-PS American Literature Ser.). 362p. 1992. reprint ed. lib. bdg. 89.00 (*0-7812-6660-2*) Rprt Serv.

St. Jeanne de Chantal: Noble Lady, Holy Woman. Andre Ravier. LC 89-84205. (Illus.). 231p. (Orig.). 1989. pap. text ed. 12.95 (*0-89870-267-4*) Ignatius Pr.

St. Joan: Playing with Fire. Arnold Silver. (Masterwork Studies). 160p. 1993. 23.95 (*0-8057-9436-0*, Twayne); pap. 13.95 (*0-8057-8578-7*, Twayne) Scribnrs Ref.

St. Joan, Major Barbara, Androcles. George Bernard Shaw. Bd. with Major Barbara. LC 56-5413.; Androcles & the Lion. LC 56-5413. LC 56-5413. 1979. 16.50 (*0-394-60480-6*, Modern Lib) Random.

***St. Joan of Arc.** Margaret Bunson & Matthew Bunson. (Saints You Should Know Ser.). 56p. 1996. pap. 5.95 (*0-87973-558-9*) Our Sunday Visitor.

***St. Joan of Arc.** Margaret Bunson & Matthew Bunson. (Saints You Should Know Ser.). 56p. 1996. 7.95 (*0-87973-784-0*) Our Sunday Visitor.

St. Joan of Arc. Vita Sackville-West. 400p. 1991. pap. 13.95 (*0-385-42109-5*) Doubleday.

St. Joan of Arc. John Beevers. 1995. reprint ed. pap. 9.00 (*0-89555-043-1*) TAN Bks Pubs.

St. Joan of Arc. Mary F. Windeatt. (Catholic Story Coloring Bks.). (Illus.). 32p. (J). (gr. 1-5). 1989. reprint ed. student ed. 3.00 (*0-89555-367-8*) TAN Bks Pubs.

St. Joan of Arc, Vol. 4. Rene Berthier & Marie Segault. Tr. by Marianne L. Trouve' from FRE. (Saints Ser.). (Illus.). 32p. (J). (gr. 3-8). 1995. pap. 1.95 (*0-8198-6975-9*) Pauline Bks.

St. Joan of Arc, Virgin-Soldier. Leon Cristiani. 1995. pap. 4.95 (*0-8198-0466-5*) Pauline Bks.

St. Joan of the Stockyards. Bertolt Brecht. Tr. by Frank Jones. LC 69-16006. 128p. 1970. pap. 8.95 (*0-253-20127-6*, MB 127) Ind U Pr.

***St. Job of Pochaev: Life, Service & Akathist Hymn.** Tr. by Isaac Lambertsen from RUS. 96p. 1997. pap. 5.00 (*0-912927-79-8*, X050) St John Kronstadt.

St. Joe Road. Willard Gellis. 12p. 1989. pap. 4.00 (*0-917455-11-8*) Big Foot NY.

St. Joe Road: Emigration Mid Eighteen Hundreds. Jacqueline A. Lewin & Marilyn S. Taylor. 64p. 1992. pap. 12.00 (*1-884483-00-3*) St Joseph Mus.

St. John. Members of the Faculty of Theology of the University of Navarre. (Navarre Bible Ser.). pap. 14.95 (*1-85182-094-9*, Pub. by Four Cts Pr IE) Intl Spec Bk.

St. John: Feet, Fins, & Four-Wheel Drive. Pam Gaffin. 140p. 1994. pap. 10.50 (*0-9631060-7-4*) Am Paradise.

St. John: The Making of a Colonial Urban Community. T. W. Acheson. 310p. 1985. 35.00 (*0-8020-2586-2*) U of Toronto Pr.

St. John: Two Hundred Years Proud. George W. Schuyler. (Illus.). 208p. 1984. 27.95 (*0-89781-108-9*) Am Historical Pr.

St. John see Expository Thoughts on the Gospels

St. John & the Seven Veils. William Babula. 1991. 15.95 (*1-55972-071-9*, Birch Ln Pr) Carol Pub Group.

St. John Backtime. Ed. by Ruth H. Low & Lito Valls. LC 80-68089. (Illus.). 96p. (Orig.). 1985. pap. 14.95 (*0-9614355-0-X*) Eden Hill Pr.

St. John Chrysostom, Baptismal Instructions. Ed. by W. J. Burghardt et al. LC 62-21489. (Ancient Christian Writers Ser.: No. 31). 381p. 1963. 22.95 (*0-8091-0262-5*) Paulist Pr.

St. John Chrysostom on the Priesthood. John Chrysostom. 160p. 1977. pap. 7.95 (*0-913836-38-9*) St Vladimirs.

St. John Fisher. E. E. Reynolds. 328p. 1993. reprint ed. pap. 11.95 (*0-940147-21-1*) Source Bks CA.

St. John Genealogy: Descendants of Matthias of Dorchester, Massachusetts, 1634, of Windsor, Connecticut, 1640 (& Wethersfield & Norwalk) O. Alexander. (Illus.). 639p. 1989. reprint ed. pap. 96.00 (*0-8328-1107-6*); reprint ed. lib. bdg. 104.00 (*0-8328-1106-8*) Higginson Bk Co.

St. John Hankin: Edwardian Mephistopheles. William H. Phillips. LC 77-89783. 150p. 1979. 24.50 (*0-8386-2155-4*) Fairleigh Dickinson.

St. John of Kronstadt: Life, Service, & Akathist Hymn. Tr. by Isaac E. Lambertsen from RUS. 64p. (Orig.). 1996. pap. 3.50 (*0-912927-03-8*, X003) St John Kronstadt.

St. John of Patmos & the Seven Churches of the Apocalypse. Otto F. Meinardus. LC 78-51245. (In the Footsteps of the Saints Ser.). (Illus.). 160p. 1979. 17.50 (*0-89241-070-1*); pap. 6.95 (*0-89241-043-4*) Caratzas.

St. John of the Cross. Steven K. Payne. 264p. (C). 1990. lib. bdg. 129.00 (*0-7923-0707-0*, Pub. by Klwr Acad Pubs NE) Kluwer Ac.

St. John of the Cross: Alchemist of the Soul. Antonio T. De Nicolas. 288p. (Orig.). 1996. pap. 18.00 (*0-87728-859-3*) Weiser.

St. John of the Cross: An Appreciation. Daniel A. Dombrowski. LC 90-28577. (SUNY Series in Latin American & Iberian Thought & Culture). 223p. (C). 1992. pap. 24.95 (*0-7914-0888-4*); text ed. 67.50 (*0-7914-0887-6*) State U NY Pr.

St. John of the Cross: Doctor of Divine Love, an Introduction to His Philosophy, Theology & Spirituality. Bede Frost. 1977. lib. bdg. 250.00 (*0-8490-2559-1*) Gordon Pr.

St. John of the Cross: His Life & Poetry. Gerald Brenan. LC 72-83577. 245p. reprint ed. pap. 69.90 (*0-317-26068-5*, 2024428) Bks Demand.

St. John of the Cross: Selected Poems. Tr. by Mary Rae from SPA. LC 90-19808. 94p. (C). 1991. text ed. 14.95 (*0-89341-644-4*, Longwood Academic) Hollowbrook.

St. John of the Cross & Dr. C. G. Jung: Christian Mysticism in the Light of Jungian Psychology. James Arraj. LC 86-11315. 200p. (Orig.). 1986. pap. 12.00 (*0-914073-02-8*) Inner Growth Bks.

St. John of the Cross & Other Lectures & Addresses. E. Allison Peers. 1977. lib. bdg. 250.00 (*0-8490-2558-3*) Gordon Pr.

St. John of the Cross, & Other Lectures & Addresses, 1920-1945. Edgar A. Peers. LC 70-136650. (Biography Index Reprint Ser.). 1977. 18.95 (*0-8369-8045-X*) Ayer.

St. John People: A Dozen St. John Writers Profile 22 St. John Residents. Ed. by Gary M. Goodlander. (Illus.). 233p. (Orig.). 1993. pap. 20.00 (*0-9631060-5-8*) Am Paradise.

S

St. John Perse: Letters. John Perse. Ed. by Arthur J. Knodel. LC 79-9080. (Bollingen Ser.: LXXXVII: 2). (Illus.). 712p. 1979. reprint ed. pap. text ed. 25.00 (*0-691-01836-7*) Princeton U Pr.

St. John the Evangelist Church, Indianapolis, Indiana: A Photographic Essay of the Oldest Catholic Church in Indianapolis & Marion County. William F. Stineman & Jack W. Porter. LC 85-63564. (Illus.). 80p. 1986. 19.95 (*0-9616134-0-8*) St John Evang.

St. John, Vols. 1 & 2: Critical & Exegetical Commentary. J. H. Bernard. Ed. by Samuel R. Driver et al. write for info. (*0-318-50940-7*, Pub. by T & T Clark UK) Bks Intl VA.

St. John, Vols. 1 & 2: Critical & Exegetical Commentary, Vol. I. J. H. Bernard. Ed. by Samuel R. Driver et al. (International Critical Commentary Ser.). 480p. 39.95 (*0-567-05024-6*, Pub. by T & T Clark UK) Bks Intl VA.

St. John, Vols. 1 & 2: Critical & Exegetical Commentary, Vol. II. J. H. Bernard. Ed. by Samuel R. Driver et al. (International Critical Commentary Ser.). 456p. 39.95 (*0-567-05025-4*, Pub. by T & T Clark UK) Bks Intl VA.

St. John West, Canada. D. Goss. 1995. pap. 16.99 (*0-7524-0230-7*, Arcdia) Chalford.

St. John's Baptism. William Babula. 256p. 1988. 14.95 (*0-8184-0461-2*) Carol Pub Group.

St. John's Eve & Other Stories. Nikolai V. Gogol. Tr. by Isabel F. Hapgood from RUS. LC 70-152941. (Short Story Index Reprint Ser.). 1977. reprint ed. 19.95 (*0-8369-3800-3*) Ayer.

St. John's Home: From Brooklyn to Rockaway Park. Joe Cunningham. 128p. 1993. pap. write for info. (*0-9636989-0-7*) SJH Pr.

***St. John's Lutheran Church Near Berrysburg, Mifflin Twp., Dauphin County, Pennsylvania.** Tr. by Phillip A. Rice from GER. LC 96-85598. 139p. (Orig.). 1996. pap. 15.00 (*1-55856-239-7*) Closson Pr.

St. John's Tower & Health Care Facility: An Architectural Evaluation. William F. Gartz et al. Ed. by Gary T. Moore. (Publications in Architecture & Urban Planning: No. R81-7). (Illus.). iv, 135p. 1987. reprint ed. 9.50 (*0-938744-20-8*) U of Wis Ctr Arch-Urban.

St. John's Wood. large type ed. Nancy Fitzgerald. 1989. 25.99 (*0-7089-2054-3*) Ulverscroft.

St. Joseph: Shadow of the Father. Andrew Doze. Tr. by Florentine Audett. LC 92-15022. 196p. (Orig.). 1992. pap. 9.95 (*0-8189-0644-8*) Alba.

St. Joseph - St. Mauritus Cemetery at Ashland, Schuylkill County, Pa. Compiled by Schuylkill Roots Staff. 65p. 1989. pap. text ed. 8.50 (*1-55856-018-1*) Closson Pr.

St. Joseph Altar Traditions of South Louisiana. Ethelyn G. Orso. LC 90-82375. (Louisiana Life Ser.: No. 4). 57p. 1990. pap. 5.00 (*0-940984-59-8*) U of SW LA Ctr LA Studies.

***St. Joseph Beginner Book of Saints.** Lawrence G. Lovasik. (J). 1996. 5.50 (*0-89942-152-0*) Catholic Bk Pub.

***St. Joseph Beginner's Book of Prayers.** Lawrence G. Lovasik. (Pocket-Size Ser.). (Illus.). 64p. (J). (gr. k-2). 1997. pap. 5.75 (*0-89942-148-2*, 148/22) Catholic Bk Pub.

St. Joseph Cafasso: Priest of the Gallows. Saint John Bosco. LC 82-50979. Orig. Title: A Saint Speaks for Another Saint. 80p. 1993. reprint ed. pap. 4.50 (*0-89555-194-2*) TAN Bks Pubs.

St. Joseph Children's Missal Boxed Gift Set. Catholic Book Staff. pap. text ed. 17.25 (*0-89942-744-8*, B806/82W); pap. text ed. 17.25 (*0-89942-745-6*, B806/82B) Catholic Bk Pub.

St. Joseph Children's Missal Boxed Gift Set. Catholic Book Staff. 1996. pap. text ed. 10.50 (*0-89942-743-X*, B806/42B) Catholic Bk Pub.

St. Joseph Concise Bible History. 1976. pap. 2.95 (*0-89942-770-7*, 770/04) Catholic Bk Pub.

***St. Joseph County Cemetery Inscriptions Vol. 4: Union, Center, Madison Townships.** 325p. 1997. pap. 35.00 (*1-888005-06-8*) S Bend Area Geneol Soc.

St. Joseph County Indiana Cemetery Inscriptions Vol. 1: Greene, Liberty, & Lincoln Townships. South Bend Area Genealogical Society Staff. 369p. 1992. pap. 33.00 (*1-888005-03-3*) S Bend Area Geneol Soc.

St. Joseph County Indiana Cemetery Inscriptions Vol. 2: Penn Township, Pt. 1. South Bend Area Genealogical Society Staff. 312p. 1995. pap. 38.00 (*1-888005-04-1*) S Bend Area Geneol Soc.

St. Joseph County, Indiana Cemetery Inscriptions Vol. 3: Penn Township, Pt. 2. South Bend Area Genealogical Society Staff. 353p. 1995. pap. text ed. 38.00 (*1-888005-05-X*) S Bend Area Geneol Soc.

***St. Joseph Daily Prayer Book.** Ed. by John Murray. (Illus.). 256p. 1997. pap. 4.95 (*0-89942-142-3*) Catholic Bk Pub.

St. Joseph, Fatima & Fatherhood: Reflections on the Miracle of the Sun. Joseph A. Cirrincione & Thomas A. Nelson. LC 89-50766. 62p. (Orig.). 1989. pap. 1.50 (*0-89555-384-8*) TAN Bks Pubs.

St. Joseph of Copertino. Angelo Pastrovicchi. LC 79-91298. 135p. 1994. reprint ed. pap. 6.00 (*0-89555-135-7*) TAN Bks Pubs.

***St. Joseph Pocket Prayer Book.** (Orig.). 1997. pap. 0.75 (*0-89942-030-3*, 30/04) Catholic Bk Pub.

***St. Joseph Sunday Missal & Hymnal 1998.** (Orig.). 1997. pap. write for info. (*0-89942-898-3*, 898/04) Catholic Bk Pub.

***St. Joseph Sunday Missal & Hymnal 1998.** (Orig.). 1997. pap. write for info. (*0-89942-998-X*, 998/04) Catholic Bk Pub.

St. Josephs-Blatt: 1896-1919. Steven W. Harmon. (American University Studies: History: Ser. IX, Vol. 78). 200p. (C). 1989. text ed. 37.95 (*0-8204-1100-0*) P Lang Pubng.

St. Joseph's Children: A True Story of Terror & Justice. Terry Ganey. Ed. by Hillel Black. (Illus.). 256p. 1989. 17.95 (*0-8184-0509-0*) Carol Pub Group.

St. Joseph's First One Hundred Years. Trudy T. Rice. 104p. 1991. write for info. (*0-929690-12-5*) Herit Pubs AZ.

St. Joseph's Mass Book. Stephanie Clifford. 32p. pap. 1.95 (*0-8146-1556-2*) Liturgical Pr.

St. Juliana of Nicomedia. Tr. by Charles W. Kennedy. 1992. pap. 1.95 (*0-89981-130-2*) Eastern Orthodox.

St. Justin Martyr: The First & Second Apologies. Leslie W. Barnard. LC 96-3012. (Ancient Christian Writers Ser.: No. 56). 192p. 1996. 29.95 (*0-8091-0472-5*) Paulist Pr.

St. Katherine of Alexandria: The Late Middle English Prose Legend in Southwell Minster MS 7. Ed. by Saara Nevanlinna & Irma Taavitsainen. LC 93-36296. (Illus.). 174p. (C). 1994. 53.00 (*0-85991-391-0*, DS Brewer) Boydell & Brewer.

St. Kilda. David Quine. (Colin Baxter Island Guides Ser.). (Illus.). 160p. 1995. 19.95 (*0-948661-58-5*, Pub. by Colin Baxter Ltd UK) Voyageur Pr.

St. Kilda. George Seton. 384p. (C). 1986. 65.00 (*0-901824-60-7*, Pub. by Mercat Pr Bks UK) St Mut.

St. Kitts-Nevis. Verna P. Moll. (World Bibliographical Ser.: Vol. 174). 185p. 1995. 62.00 (*1-85109-222-6*) ABC-CLIO.

St. Kitts Vervet. Ed. by M. T. McGuire. (Contributions to Primatology Ser.: Vol. 1). 202p. 1974. 45.00 (*3-8055-1692-4*) S Karger.

St Law Lesson Plans. Arbetman. Date not set. write for info. (*0-314-04649-6*) West Pub.

St. Lawrence Seaway. Ann Armbruster. LC 96-2086. (True Bk.). 48p. (J). 1996. lib. bdg. 19.00 (*0-516-20016-X*) Childrens.

St. Lawrence Seaway. Gennifer Sussman. LC 78-71332. (Canadian-U. S. Prospect Ser.). 90p. 1978. 5.00 (*0-88806-041-6*) Natl Planning.

St. Lawrence University. Photos by John DeVisser. (Illus.). 112p. 1991. 39.00 (*0-916509-72-9*) Harmony Hse Pub.

St. Leon. William Godwin. LC 93-29771. (World's Classics Ser.). 512p. (C). 1994. 12.95 (*0-19-282833-9*) OUP.

St. Leon: A Tale of the Sixteenth Century. William Godwin. LC 74-162884. (Illus.). reprint ed. 45.00 (*0-404-54405-3*) AMS Pr.

St. Leon: A Tale of the Sixteenth Century. William Godwin. LC 70-131318. (Gothic Novels Ser.). 1976. reprint ed. 51.95 (*0-405-00802-3*) Ayer.

St. Lo. Ed. by Historical Section European Theater of Operations Staff. (Combat Arms Ser.: No. 10). (Illus.). 128p. 1984. reprint ed. 29.95 (*0-89839-080-X*) Battery Pr.

St. Louis. Barbara Ford. LC 88-35912. (Downtown America Bks.). (Illus.). 60p. (J). (gr. 3 up). 1989. lib. bdg. 13.95 (*0-87518-402-2*, Dillon Silver Burdett) Silver Burdett Pr.

St. Louis. Stephan A. Thernstrom. LC 77-5907. (Documentary History of American Cities Ser.). 220p. (C). 1977. reprint ed. pap. text ed. 6.95 (*0-531-05603-1*) Wiener Pubs Inc.

St. Louis: And the Court Style in Gothic Architecture. Robert Branner. Ed. by John Harris & Alastair Laing. (Studies in Architecture: No. VII). (Illus.). 158p. 1986. pap. 39.95 (*0-302-02753-X*, Pub. by Zwemmer Bks UK) Sothebys Pubns.

St. Louis: Louis IX of France, the Most Christian King. Frederick Perry. LC 73-14462. reprint ed. 49.50 (*0-404-58280-X*) AMS Pr.

St. Louis: 1870 Census Index. Ed. by Bradley W. Steuart. 1181p. 1989. lib. bdg. 175.00 (*1-877677-04-3*) Precision Indexing.

St. Louis & Its Streetcars: The Way It Was. Andrew D. Young. 52p. 1996. pap. 21.95 (*0-9647279-1-9*) Archway Pub.

St. Louis & the Mighty Mississippi in the Steamboat Age: The Collected Writings of Ruth Ferris. Ruth Ferris. (Illus.). 140p. (Orig.). 1993. pap. 20.00 (*0-9639804-0-8*) St Louis Mercantile.

St. Louis at War. Betty Burnett. LC 87-15591. (Illus.). 175p. 1987. 14.95 (*0-935284-52-4*) Patrice Pr.

St. Louis Attractions. Victor R. Oddo, Jr. 108p. (Orig.). 1994. pap. 9.95 (*1-883562-01-5*) Natl Pub MO.

St. Louis Blues & Other Song Hits of 1914. Sandy Marrone. 1990. pap. 7.95 (*0-486-26383-5*) Dover.

St. Louis Cardinals. Michael E. Goodman. (Baseball: The Great American Game Ser.). 48p. (J). (gr. 4-10). 1992. lib. bdg. 14.95 (*0-88682-461-3*) Creative Ed.

St. Louis Cardinals. Chris W. Sehnert. LC 96-5576. (America's Game Ser.). (J). 1997. lib. bdg. 15.98 (*1-56239-662-5*) Abdo & Dghtrs.

***St. Louis Cardinals.** rev. ed. Michael E. Goodman. LC 97-1870. (Baseball Ser.). (Illus.). 32p. (YA). (gr. 4 up). 1998. lib. bdg. 15.95 (*0-88682-922-4*) Creative Ed.

St. Louis Cardinals: Great Baseball Club. Lieb. 1976. 24.95 (*0-8488-1579-3*) Amereon Ltd.

St. Louis Cardinals Baseball Trivia "for the Greatest Fans" Morris Jenkins. 108p. (Orig.). 1990. pap. 6.95 (*0-9629623-0-9*) Cook Dist.

St. Louis Church Survey: A Religious Investigation with a Social Background. Harlan P. Douglass. LC 77-112540. (Rise of Urban America Ser.). (Illus.). 1978. reprint ed. 23.95 (*0-405-02449-5*) Ayer.

St. Louis Clock Company 1904. 1983. pap. 7.95 (*0-915706-08-3*) Am Reprints.

St. Louis Gardeners' Directory Vol. 1. Gary Abbott & Gail Abbott. (Illus.). 1994. 2.25 (*0-9643007-0-2*) Flora Fauna MO.

St. Louis Germans, 1850-1920: The Nature of an Immigrant Community & Its Relation to the Assimilation Process. Audrey L. Olson. Ed. by Francesco Cordasco. LC 80-886. (American Ethnic Groups Ser.). 1981. lib. bdg. 42.95 (*0-405-13447-9*) Ayer.

St. Louis Illustrated: Nineteenth-Century Engravings & Lithographs of a Mississippi River Metropolis. John W. Reps. LC 88-20914. (Illus.). 208p. (C). 1989. 44.95 (*0-8262-0698-0*) U of Mo Pr.

St. Louis in the Gilded Age. Katharine T. Corbett & Howard S. Miller. LC 93-79982. (Illus.). 102p. 1993. pap. 12.95 (*1-883982-01-4*) MO Hist Soc.

St. Louis in Your Pocket: The Definitive Guide to the Gateway City. Saunders. 1992. pap. 8.95 (*0-935031-58-8*) Terrell Missouri.

St. Louis in 1884. William H. Bishop. Ed. by William R. Jones. (Illus.). 24p. 1977. reprint ed. pap. 2.95 (*0-89646-024-X*) Vistabooks.

St. Louis Interior Design Resources. Suzanne Ponder. (Design Registry Ser.: Vol. 2). (Illus.). 200p. 1990. 17.95 (*0-9622567-6-5*); pap. 8.95 (*0-9622567-7-3*) Design Registry.

St. Louis Mary Grignion deMontfort & the Marion Consecration. J. Patrick Gaffney. 1991. 2.00 (*0-911988-90-4*, 48697) AMI Pr.

St. Louis Movement in Philosophy: Some Source Material. Ed. by Charles M. Perry. LC 31-8773. (Illus.). 150p. reprint ed. pap. 42.80 (*0-317-09234-0*, 2016248) Bks Demand.

St. Louis Rams. Bob Italia. LC 95-43595. (Inside the NFL Ser.). (J). 1996. lib. bdg. 15.98 (*1-56239-541-6*) Abdo & Dghtrs.

St. Louis Rams. 2nd rev. ed. Chip Lovitt. (NFL Today Ser.). (Illus.). 32p. (J). (gr. 4-8). 1996. lib. bdg. 14.95 (*0-88682-790-6*) Creative Ed.

St. Louis Rams Facts & Trivia. Linda Everson. (Illus.). 96p. (Orig.). 1995. pap. 6.99 (*0-938313-13-4*) E B Houchin.

St. Louis Street Atlas. Gousha. 1992. 6.95 (*0-671-84997-2*) S&S Trade.

St. Louis Street Atlas. Gousha. 1992. 6.95 (*0-671-84998-0*) S&S Trade.

St. Louis Union Station & Its Railroads. rev. ed. Norbury L. Wayman. LC 86-217654. (Illus.). 176p. 1988. pap. 12.95 (*0-9616356-1-4*) E E Newman.

St. Louis Woman. Helen Traubel & Richard G. Hubler. Ed. by Andrew Farkas. LC 76-29974. (Opera Biographies Ser.). (Illus.). 1977. reprint ed. lib. bdg. 28.95 (*0-405-09712-3*) Ayer.

St. Louise de Marillac: Servant of the Poor. Sr. Vincent Regnault. LC 83-50058. 136p. 1984. pap. 6.00 (*0-89555-215-9*) TAN Bks Pubs.

***St. Lucia, Vol. 185.** Janet H. Momsen. (World Bibliographical Ser.). 214p. 1996. 62.00 (*1-85109-136-X*) ABC-CLIO.

St. Lucia: Caribbean Sunseekers. Don Philpott. (Caribbean Sunseekers Ser.). (Illus.). 160p. (Orig.). 1996. pap. 10.95 (*0-8442-4927-0*, Passport Bks) NTC Pub Grp.

St. Lucia see Statements of the Laws of the OAS Member States in Matters Affecting Business

St. Lucia Diary. Hazel Eggleston. 1977. pap. 10.00 (*0-8159-6839-6*) Devin.

***St. Lucie County's Performanced Based Diploma Program Case Study Report.** Ivan Charner. (Cross Case Report & Case Studies). 50p. 1995. teacher ed., text ed. 20.00 (*0-614-24536-2*); teacher ed., pap. text ed. 10.00 (*0-614-24537-0*) Natl Inst Work.

St. Luke: Critical & Exegetical Commentary. Alfred Plummer. Ed. by Samuel R. Driver & Charles A. Briggs. (International Critical Commentary Ser.). 688p. 1901. 39.95 (*0-567-05023-8*, Pub. by T & T Clark UK) Bks Intl VA.

St. Luke see Expository Thoughts on the Gospels

St. Luke's Missiology: A Cross-Cultural Challenge. Harold E. Dollar. LC 96-8292. 208p. (Orig.). 1996. pap. text ed. 9.95 (*0-87808-267-0*, WCL267-0) William Carey Lib.

St. Lydwine of Schiedam. J. K. Huysmans. Tr. by Agnes Hastings from FRE. LC 79-87551. 1979. reprint ed. pap. 9.00 (*0-89555-087-3*) TAN Bks Pubs.

St. Magnus. Robert of Orkney. Ed. by Iain MacDonald. (Celtic Studies Ser.). 62p. 1994. pap. 4.95 (*0-86315-164-7*) Dufour.

St. Magnus Cathedral: Orkney's Twelfth-Century Renaissance. B. E. Crawford. (Illus.). 400p. 1989. text ed. 25.00 (*0-08-036580-9*, Pergamon Pr) Elsevier.

***St. Malo - Dinard City Plan.** (Grafocarte Maps Ser.). 1995. 8.95 (*2-7416-0077-5*, 80077) Michelin.

St. Margaret. Turgot. Ed. by Iain MacDonald. (Celtic Studies Ser.). 62p. 1994. pap. 4.95 (*0-86315-165-5*) Dufour.

St. Margaret of Antioch. 1993. pap. 1.25 (*0-89981-138-8*) Eastern Orthodox.

St. Margaret's Cave: or The Nun's Story, 4 Vols., Set. Elizabeth Helme. Ed. by Devendra P. Varma. LC 77-2040. (Gothic Novels III Ser.). 1977. lib. bdg. 101.95 (*0-405-10139-2*) Ayer.

St. Maria Goretti. Mary F. Windeatt. (Catholic Story Coloring Bks.). (Illus.). 32p. (J). (gr. 1-5). 1993. reprint ed. student ed. 3.00 (*0-89555-374-0*) TAN Bks Pubs.

St. Mark. Members of the Faculty of Theology of the University of Navarre. (Navarre Bible Ser.). pap. 14.95 (*1-85182-092-2*, Pub. by Four Cts Pr IE) Intl Spec Bk.

St. Mark: Critical & Exegetical Commentary. Ezra P. Gould. Ed. by Samuel R. Driver et al. (International Critical Commentary Ser.). 376p. 1896. 39.95 (*0-567-05022-X*, Pub. by T & T Clark UK) Bks Intl VA.

St. Mark's Rest, the History of Venice. John Ruskin. (BCL1-PR English Literature Ser.). 236p. 1992. reprint ed. lib. bdg. 79.00 (*0-7812-7635-7*) Rprt Serv.

St. Martial Mehrstimmigkeitl - Polyphony. Bryan Gillingham. (Wissenschaftliche Abhandlungen-Musicological Studies: Vol. 44). 240p. (ENG & GER.). 1983. lib. bdg. 54.00 (*0-931902-38-X*) Inst Mediaeval Mus.

St. Martin, Vol. 6. Tr. by Marianne L. Trouve' & Raymond Maric from FRE. (Saints Ser.). (Illus.). 32p. (J). (gr. 3-8). 1995. pap. 1.95 (*0-8198-6980-5*) Pauline Bks.

St. Martin de Porres - Apostle of Charity. Giuliana Cavallini. Tr. by Caroline Holland from ITA. LC 79-65530. (Cross & Crown Series of Spirituality). 1979. reprint ed. pap. 12.50 (*0-89555-092-X*) TAN Bks Pubs.

St. Martin's Anthologies of English Literature, 5 vols., Set. Ed. by Michael Alexander et al. 2985p. 1991. text ed. 85.00 (*0-312-04474-7*) St Martin.

St Martin's Guide to Contemporary British History. Cook. 1994. text ed. 75.00 (*0-312-12076-1*) St Martin.

St. Martin's Guide to Sources in Contemporary British History, Vol. 1. Ed. by David Waller. LC 93-11678. 1993. text ed. 75.00 (*0-312-10303-4*) St Martin.

St Martin's Guide to Writing. 4th ed. Axelrod. 1994. teacher ed., pap. text ed. 2.44 (*0-312-11164-9*) St Martin.

St. Martin's Guide to Writing. 4th ed. Rise B. Axelrod & Charles R. Cooper. 788p. 1994. pap. text ed. 27.50 (*0-312-07541-3*) St Martin.

St. Martin's Guide to Writing: Shorter Version. 3rd ed. Rise B. Axelrod & Charles R. Cooper. 611p. (C). 1991. teacher ed. write for info. (*0-318-68120-X*) St Martin.

St. Martin's Guide to Writing Short. 4th ed. Rise B. Axelrod & Charles R. Cooper. 704p. 1994. pap. text ed. 25.50 (*0-312-10372-7*) St Martin.

St. Martin's Handbook. 2nd annot. ed. Andrea A. Lunsford & Robert J. Connors. 848p. (C). 1992. teacher ed. write for info. (*0-318-68814-X*) St Martin.

St. Martin's Workbook. 3rd ed. Runciman. 1995. teacher ed., pap. text ed. 5.00 (*0-312-10245-3*) St Martin.

St. Mary at Hill Church: The Medieval Records of a London City Church A.D. 1420-1559, Set, Pts. 1 & 2. Ed. by Henry Littlehales. (EETS, OS Ser.: Nos. 125, 128). 1974. reprint ed. Set. 80.00 (*0-527-00121-X*) Periodicals Srv.

St. Mary Magdalene in Medieval Literature. Helen M. Garth. LC 78-64210. (Johns Hopkins University. Studies in the Social Sciences. Thirtieth Ser. 1912: 3). reprint ed. 37.50 (*0-404-61315-2*) AMS Pr.

St. Mary Mazzarello. Domenica Agasso. 180p. (Orig.). 1996. pap. 9.95 (*0-8198-6989-9*) Pauline Bks.

St. Mary's & Royal Oak Cemeteries, Oakland County, Michigan. Intro. by Joan Pate. 136p. (Orig.). 1990. pap. 11.00 (*1-879766-16-7*) OCG Society.

St. Mary's Bay, 1818-1829: Catalog of Families. Ed. by Leonard H. Smith, Jr. pap. 16.00 (*0-932022-07-3*, 1482) Picton Pr.

St. Mary's Church, Deerhurst, Gloucestershire: Fieldwork, Excavations & Structural Analysis, 1971-1984. Ed. by Philip Rahtz et al. LC 96-19670. (Report Research Committee Ser.: Vol. 55). (Illus.). 224p. 1997. 135.00 (*0-85115-687-8*) Boydell & Brewer.

St Mary's County, Maryland, Administrative Accounts, 1674-1720. T.L.C. Genealogy Staff. 224p. (Orig.). 1994. spiral bd., pap. 20.00 (*1-886633-25-8*) TLC Genealogy.

St. Mary's County, Maryland, Rent Rolls, 1639-1771. T. L.C. Genealogy Staff. 145p. (Orig.). 1993. spiral bd., pap. 14.00 (*1-886633-26-6*) TLC Genealogy.

***St. Mary's, Hamilton: A Social History 1846-1996.** T. M. Devine. 208p. 1996. pap. 30.00 (*0-85976-429-X*, Pub. by J Donald UK) St Mut.

St. Mary's in ths Mountains. Virgil A. Bucchianeri. (Illus.). 52p. 1984. pap. 5.95 (*0-940936-01-1*) Gold Hill.

St. Mary's Law Journal: 1969-1995/96, 27 vols., Set. Bound set. 1,232.50 (*0-8377-9140-5*) Rothman.

St. Matthew: St. Matthew. Members of the Faculty of Theology of the University of Navarre. (Navarre Bible Ser.). 236p. pap. 14.95 (*1-85182-058-2*, Pub. by Four Cts Pr IE) Intl Spec Bk.

St. Matthew & St. Mark. 2nd ed. Farrer. 238p. 1966. 69.50 (*0-614-00157-9*) Elliots Bks.

St. Matthew & St. Mark see Expository Thoughts on the Gospels

St. Mawr. David H. Lawrence. Bd. with Man Who Died. 1959. Set pap. 8.00 (*0-394-70071-6*, Vin) Random.

St. Mawr & the Man Who Died. D. H. Lawrence. 1976. 21.95 (*0-8488-0560-7*) Amereon Ltd.

St. Maximilian Kolbe. Antonio Ricciardi. Tr. by Daughters of St. Paul from ITA. LC 82-18316. (Illus.). 314p. 1982. pap. 7.95 (*0-8198-6837-X*) Pauline Bks.

St. Maximilian Kolbe, Vol. 1. Jean-Marie Laferte & Brigitte Jeanson. Tr. by Marianne L. Trouve' from FRE. (Saints Ser.). (Illus.). 32p. (J). (gr. 3-8). 1995. pap. 1.95 (*0-8198-6978-3*) Pauline Bks.

St. Maximus the Confessor: The Ascetic Life, the Four Centuries on Charity. Ed. by W. J. Burghardt et al. LC 55-8642. (Ancient Christian Writers Ser.: No. 21). 293p. 1955. 19.95 (*0-8091-0258-7*) Paulist Pr.

St. Meinrad. Mary F. Windeatt. (Catholic Story Coloring Bks.). (Illus.). 32p. (J). (gr. 1-5). 1992. reprint ed. student ed. 3.00 (*0-89555-377-5*) TAN Bks Pubs.

St. Methodius, the Symposium: A Treatise on Chastity. Ed. by W. J. Burghardt et al. (Ancient Christian Writers Ser.: No. 27). 256p. 1958. 16.95 (*0-8091-0143-2*) Paulist Pr.

St. Michael & the Angels. LC 82-62040. Orig. Title: The Precious Blood & the Angels. 133p. 1995. reprint ed. pap. 7.00 (*0-89555-196-9*) TAN Bks Pubs.

***St. Michael the Archangel: Celestial Friends vs. Demonic Enemies.** 2nd ed. Sonja B. Blankenship. (Illus.). 1997. pap. 11.00 (*1-888516-03-8*) Apostlte Our Lady.

***St. Michael's Fall.** Raymond Luczak. 86p. 1995. pap. 12.95 (*0-9634016-8-8*, Deaf Life Pr) MSM Prods.

***St. Molaissi of Devenish Island, County Fermanagh, Ireland.** John Hanlon. 1997. pap. 3.95 (*0-89979-096-8*) British Am Bks.

St. Mungo. Jocelinus of Furness. Ed. by Iain MacDonald. (Celtic Studies Ser.). 62p. 1994. pap. 4.95 (*0-86315-166-3*) Dufour.

***St. Murphy's Commandments.** Ron Birk. (Illus.). 104p. (Orig.). 1998. pap. 10.00 (*1-880292-57-2*) LangMarc.

An Asterisk (*) at the beginning of an entry indicates that the title is appearing in BIP for the first time.

***St. Nazaire City Plan.** (Grafocarte Maps Ser.). 1996. 8.95 (*2-7416-0078-3*, 80078) Michelin.

St. Nectarios Orthodox Conference 1980. Ed. by Neketas S. Palassis. LC 80-53258. 176p. (Orig.). 1981. pap. 15.00 (*0-913026-14-X*) St Nectarios.

***St. Nerses Shnorhali: General Epistle.** Arakel Aljalian. (Illus.). (Orig.). 1997. pap. text ed. 15.00 (*1-885011-02-4*) St Nersess.

***St. Nersess Theological Review.** 115p. 1996. pap. 8.00 (*0-614-30090-8*) St Nersess.

***St. Nicholas Anthology.** Henry S. Commager. Date not set. lib. bdg. 31.95 (*0-8488-1896-2*) Amereon Ltd.

St. Ninian. Aelred of Rievaulx. Ed. by Iain MacDonald. (Celtic Studies Ser.). 62p. 1994. pap. 4.95 (*0-86315-167-1*) Dufour.

St. Olaf College - Then & Now. Photos by Mitch Kezar. (Illus.). 112p. 1991. 39.00 (*0-916509-74-5*) Harmony Hse Pub.

St. Panteleimon. Sebastian Dabovich. pap. 0.25 (*0-89981-086-1*) Eastern Orthodox.

St. Patrick. Margaret Bunson & Matthew Bunson. LC 92-61547. (Saints You Should Know Ser.). (Illus.). 56p. (Orig.). (J). 1993. 7.95 (*0-87973-785-9*, 785); pap. 5.95 (*0-87973-559-7*, 559) Our Sunday Visitor.

St. Patrick & the Daughters of Loegaire. pap. 1.50 (*0-89981-087-X*) Eastern Orthodox.

***St. Patrick, the Green Revolution, & the Hydrogen Conversion Project: Featuring the International Alliance for Sustainable Agriculture Purple Database.** Patrick A. O'Dougherty. (Illus.). 116p. 1996. lib. bdg. 19.99 (*0-9626665-7-2*) Hellenist Amer Co.

St. Patrick's: The First One Hundred Years. William J. Hoover. Ed. by Malinda R. Crumley & Kay Fialho. (Illus.). 112p. (C). 1988. 20.00 (*0-9621410-0-3*) St Patrick Cathedral.

St. Patrick's Day. Dorothy R. Freeman. LC 91-43098. (Best Holiday Bks.). (Illus.). 48p. (J). (gr. 1-4). 1992. lib. bdg. 17.95 (*0-89490-383-7*) Enslow Pubs.

St. Patrick's Day. Gail Gibbons. LC 93-29570. (Illus.). 32p. (J). (ps-3). 1994. lib. bdg. 15.95 (*0-8234-1119-2*) Holiday.

St. Patrick's Day. Bob Reese. Ed. by Alton Jordan. (Holiday Set). (Illus.). (J). (gr. k-3). 1984. 7.95 (*0-89868-030-1*, Read Res); pap. 3.95 (*0-89868-063-8*, Read Res) ARO Pub.

St. Patrick's Day in the Morning. Eve Bunting. LC 79-15934. (Illus.). 32p. (J). (ps-3). 1980. 15.00 (*0-395-29098-8*, Clarion Bks) HM.

St. Patrick's Day in the Morning. Eve Bunting. LC 79-15934. (Illus.). 32p. (J). (ps-3). 1983. pap. 5.95 (*0-89919-162-2*, Clarion Bks) HM.

St. Patrick's Day Murder. Lee Harris. (Orig.). 1994. mass mkt. 5.50 (*0-449-14872-6*, GM) Fawcett.

St. Patrick's Purgatory: Two Versions of Owayne Miles & the Vision of William Stranton. Ed. by Robert Easting. (Early English Text Society Original Ser.: No. 298). (Illus.). 500p. 1992. 70.00 (*0-19-722300-1*) OUP.

St. Patrick's World: The Christian Culture of Ireland's Apostolic Age. Tr. & Comment by Liam De Paor. LC 93-21717. (C). 1993. text ed. 42.50 (*0-268-01749-2*) U of Notre Dame Pr.

St. Paul. Mireille Brisebois. (C). 1988. 45.00 (*0-85439-243-2*, Pub. by St Paul Pubns UK) St Mut.

St. Paul: He Created Christianity from Jesus' Religion. George Drew. 60p. (Orig.). 1984. pap. 7.95 (*0-940754-22-3*) Ed Ministries.

St. Paul & Epicurus. Norman W. De Witt. LC 54-12314. 211p. reprint ed. pap. 60.20 (*0-8357-7035-4*, 2033217) Bks Demand.

St. Paul & His Gospel. G. P. Tasker. 87p. 1982. reprint ed. pap. 1.00 (*0-686-36256-X*) Faith Pub Hse.

St. Paul & Paganism. Thomas Wilson. 1977. lib. bdg. 250.00 (*0-8490-2560-5*) Gordon Pr.

St. Paul & the Mystery Religions. H. A. Kennedy. 1977. lib. bdg. 59.95 (*0-8490-2561-3*) Gordon Pr.

St. Paul in Britain. R. W. Morgan. LC 83-73168. 128p. 1984. reprint ed. pap. 4.50 (*0-934666-12-1*) Artisan Sales.

St. Paul in Ephesus & the Cities of Galatia & Cyprus. Otto F. Meinardus. LC 78-51246. (In the Footsteps of the Saints Ser.). (Illus.). 160p. 1979. 17.50 (*0-89241-071-X*); pap. 6.95 (*0-89241-044-2*) Caratzas.

St. Paul in Greece. Otto F. Meinardus. LC 78-51244. (In the Footsteps of the Saints Ser.). 160p. 1979. 17.50 (*0-89241-072-8*); pap. 6.95 (*0-89241-045-0*) Caratzas.

St. Paul Metro Business Directory 1996-97. rev. ed. American Sales Leads Staff. 1392p. 1996. boxed 215.00 (*1-56105-897-1*) Am Busn Direct.

St. Paul or "White" Church at Ringtown, Union Township. Compiled by Schuylkill Roots Staff. 135p. 1990. pap. text ed. 15.00 (*1-55856-056-4*) Closson Pr.

St. Paul, Oregon, Eighteen Thirty to Eighteen Ninety. Harvey J. McKay. LC 80-69228. (Illus.). 340p. 1980. 15.00 (*0-8323-0384-4*) Binford Mort.

St. Paul Prayer Book. St. Paul Publications Staff. 209p. (C). 1990. text ed. 39.00 (*0-85439-420-6*, Pub. by St Paul Pubns UK) St Mut.

St. Paul Pumping Station. (PCI Journal Reprints Ser.). 16p. 1981. pap. 10.00 (*0-686-40156-5*, JR254) P-PCI.

St. Paul Sunday Missal, 1993. St. Paul Publications Staff. 447p. (C). 1990. text ed. 39.00 (*0-85439-419-2*, Pub. by St Paul Pubns UK) St Mut.

St. Paul, the Three Missing Years. Leo M. Brown. LC 92-80783. 491p. 1993. pap. 12.95 (*1-55523-528-X*) Winston-Derek.

St. Paul's Corinth: Texts & Archaeology. Jerome Murphy-O'Connor. LC 83-80110. (Good News Studies: Vol. 6). 192p. 1983. pap. 14.95 (*0-8146-5303-0*) Liturgical Pr.

St. Paul's Epistle to the Ephesians. (Theosis Group Studies). 74p. (Orig.). 1986. student ed., pap. 4.50 (*1-56125-007-4*) Educ Services.

St. Paul's Epistle to the Ephesians. (Theosis Group Studies). 25p. (Orig.). 1986. teacher ed. 2.50 (*1-56125-008-2*) Educ Services.

St. Paul's Last Journey. Otto F. Meinardus. LC 78-51247. (In the Footsteps of the Saints Ser.). (Illus.). 160p. 1979. 17.50 (*0-89241-073-6*); pap. 6.95 (*0-89241-046-9*) Caratzas.

St. Paul's Schubert Club: A Century of Music 1882-1982. James T. Dunn. 103p. 1983. 5.00 (*0-912373-02-4*) Schubert.

St. Paul's Theology of Proclamation: 1 Corinthians 1-4 & Greco-Roman Rhetoric. Duane Litfin. (Society for New Testament Studies Monographs: No. 79). 310p. (C). 1994. text ed. 65.00 (*0-521-45178-7*) Cambridge U Pr.

St. Paul's (White Church) Cemetery & Reformed Congregation Records (1874-1913) with Collected Cemeteries of Union Township & North Union Township, Schuylkill County, PA. Phillip A. Rice & Jean A. Dellock. 260p. 1994. pap. text ed. 24.95 (*1-55856-161-7*) Closson Pr.

St. Pauls Within-the-Walls: Rome, a History. Judith Millon. LC 81-8055. 1982. 9.95 (*0-87233-058-3*) Bauhan.

St. Peter Icon of Dumbarton Oaks. Kurt Weitzmann. (Byzantine Collection Publications: No. 6). (Illus.). 48p. 1983. pap. 6.00 (*0-88402-133-5*) Dumbarton Oaks.

St. Peter Relates an Incident: Selected Poems. James Weldon Johnson. LC 73-18558. reprint ed. 27.50 (*0-404-11371-0*) AMS Pr.

St. Peter's Episcopal Church, Delaware, Ohio - The First 100 Years, 1817-1918: A Collection of Documents & Genealogical Data. Ed. by MaryAnne D. Cummins. 389p. (Orig.). 1994. pap. text ed. 28.50 (*1-55613-926-8*) Heritage Bk.

St. Peter's Fair. Ellis Peters. 224p. 1992. mass mkt. 5.99 (*0-446-40301-6*, Mysterious Paperbk) Warner Bks.

***St. Peter's Fair: The Cadfael Chronicles IV.** large type ed. Ellis Peters. LC 97-1202. 1998. pap. write for info. (*0-7862-1074-5*) Thorndike Pr.

St. Peter's (Fetterhoff's) Evangelical Lutheran & German Reformed (Now United Church of Christ) Church Record. Compiled by Schuylkill Roots Staff. 112p. 1990. pap. text ed. 12.75 (*1-55856-049-1*) Closson Pr.

St. Peter's Just for Fun Bridge: In Five Easy Lessons. Robert C. Jacobson. (Illus.). 72p. 1995. pap. 8.00 (*0-8059-3615-7*) Dorrance.

St. Petersburg. (New Essential Guides Ser.). 1996. pap. 7.95 (*0-614-97913-7*) NTC Pub Grp.

St. Petersburg. Andrei Biely. Tr. by John Cournos from RUS. LC 59-5417. 342p. (Orig.). 1989. pap. 12.95 (*0-8021-3158-1*, Grove) Grove-Atltic.

***St. Petersburg.** Deborah Kent. LC 97-6161. (Cities of the World Ser.). (J). 1997. write for info. (*0-516-20467-X*) Childrens.

St. Petersburg: Architecture of the Tsars. Dmitri Shvidkovsky. LC 96-17849. (Illus.). 360p. 1996. 95.00 (*0-7892-0217-4*) Abbeville Pr.

***St. Petersburg: Economy, Industry, Government, Business.** 2nd rev. ed. Russian Information & Business Center, Inc. Staff. (Russian Regional Business Directories Ser.). (Illus.). 200p. 1997. pap. 99.00 (*1-57751-372-X*) Russ Info & Busn Ctr.

St. Petersburg & Moscow: A Visit to the Court of the Czar. Richard S. Bourke. LC 70-115508. (Russia Observed, Series I). 1970. reprint ed. 31.95 (*0-405-03005-3*) Ayer.

St. Petersburg & the Florida Dream, 1888-1950. Raymond Arsenault. LC 96-3863. (Illus.). 1996. reprint ed. pap. write for info. (*0-8130-1446-8*) U Press Fla.

St. Petersburg & the Florida Dream, 1888-1950. Raymond Arsenault. (Illus.). 360p. (C). 1996. reprint ed. 34.95 (*0-8130-1442-5*) U Press Fla.

St. Petersburg Between the Revolutions: Workers & Revolutionaries, June 1907-February 1917. Robert B. McKean. 600p. (C). 1990. text ed. 52.50 (*0-300-04791-6*) Yale U Pr.

St. Petersburg Dialogues: Or Conversations on the Temporal Government of Providence. Joseph De Maistre. Ed. by Richard A. Lebrun. 448p. 1993. 55.00 (*0-7735-0982-8*, Pub. by McGill CN) U of Toronto Pr.

St. Petersburg Fragments. Steve Scott. LC 93-11125. 25p. 1993. pap. 4.00 (*0-940895-11-0*) Cornerstone IL.

St. Petersburg International Chess Tournament, 1914. S. Tarrasch. Tr. by Robert Maxham from GER. (World's Greatest Chess Tournaments Ser.). (Illus.). 267p. 32.00 (*0-939433-17-6*) Caissa Edit.

St. Philip Neri. V. J. Matthews. LC 84-50406. 120p. 1984. reprint ed. pap. 5.50 (*0-89555-237-X*) TAN Bks Pubs.

St. Philip's. Miriam C. Harris. LC 70-164399. (American Fiction Reprint Ser.). 1977. reprint ed. 28.95 (*0-8369-7042-X*) Ayer.

St. Philomena. Mary F. Windeatt. (Catholic Story Coloring Bks.). (Illus.). 32p. (J). (gr. 1-5). 1993. reprint ed. student ed. 3.00 (*0-89555-373-2*) TAN Bks Pubs.

St. Philomena: Powerful with God. Marie H. Mohr. LC 88-50160. 136p. 1993. reprint ed. pap. 8.00 (*0-89555-332-5*) TAN Bks Pubs.

St. Philomena, the Wonder-Worker. Paul O'Sullivan. LC 93-61563. 155p. 1927. text ed. 7.00 (*0-89555-501-8*) TAN Bks Pubs.

St. Photios: The Mystagogy of the Holy Spirit. Joseph P. Farrell. 116p. (C). 1987. pap. 5.00 (*0-917651-09-X*) Holy Cross Orthodox.

St. Photios the Great. Asterios Gerostergios. LC 80-82285. (Illus.). 125p. 1988. pap. 6.95 (*0-914744-51-8*) Inst Byzantine.

St. Pitirim of Tambov. 1989. pap. 1.00 (*0-89981-209-0*) Eastern Orthodox.

St. Pius V - A Brief Account of His Life, Times, Virtues & Miracles. Robin Anderson. LC 78-55637. 1992. reprint ed. pap. 5.00 (*0-89555-068-7*) TAN Bks Pubs.

St. Pius X. Mary F. Windeatt. (Catholic Story Coloring Bks.). (Illus.). 32p. (J). (gr. 1-5). 1993. reprint ed. student ed. 3.00 (*0-89555-371-6*) TAN Bks Pubs.

St. Prosper of Aquitaine, Defense of St. Augustine. Ed. by W. J. Burghardt et al. LC 78-62463. (Ancient Christian Writers Ser.: No. 32). 235p. 1963. 16.95 (*0-8091-0263-3*) Paulist Pr.

St. Prosper of Aquitaine, the Call of All Nations. Ed. by W. J. Burghardt et al. (Ancient Christian Writers Ser.: No. 14). 250p. 1952. 16.95 (*0-8091-0253-6*) Paulist Pr.

***St. Raphael City Plan.** (Grafocarte Maps Ser.). 1995. 8.95 (*2-7416-0037-6*, 80037) Michelin.

St. Rita of Cascia: Saint of the Impossible & Model of Maidens, Wives, Mothers, Widows, & Nuns. rev. ed. Joseph A. Sicardo. Tr. by Dan J. Murphy from SPA. LC 90-71100. Orig. Title: Life of Sister St. Rita of Cascia. 182p. 1994. reprint ed. pap. 7.00 (*0-89555-407-0*) TAN Bks Pubs.

St. Rose of Lima. Mary Alphonsus. LC 81-86444. 304p. 1993. reprint ed. pap. 15.00 (*0-89555-172-1*) TAN Bks Pubs.

St. Seraphim of Sarov. Valentine Zander. LC 75-24136. Orig. Title: Seraphim of Sarov. 150p. 1975. pap. 10.95 (*0-913836-28-1*) St Vladimirs.

St. Seraphim of Sarov: A Spiritual Biography. Archimandrite L. Moore. 504p. 1994. pap. write for info. (*1-880364-13-1*) New Sarov.

St. Sergius & Russian Spirituality. Pierre Kovalevsky. LC 76-13018. (Illus.). 190p. 1976. pap. 10.95 (*0-913836-24-9*) St Vladimirs.

St. Sharbel, Mystic of the East. Clare M. Benedict. 1990. reprint ed. 11.95 (*0-911218-11-4*); reprint ed. pap. 5.95 (*0-911218-12-2*) Ravengate Pr.

St. Simeon's Shrine in Zadar, Croatia. Ivo Petricioli. 108p. 1983. 30.00 (*0-918660-93-9*) Ragusan Pr.

St. Stanislaus Parish, Meriden, Connecticut: A Century of Connecticut Polonia. Stanislaus A. Blejwas. 215p. 1991. 20.00 (*0-910179-01-8*) CCSU Polish.

***St. Stephen Rural Cemetery - St. Stephen N. B. Tombstone Inscriptions of Charlotte County, N. B. Canada.** Ed. by Charlotte Branch. LC 96-69777. 368p. 1996. 39.50 (*0-89725-273-X*, 1754) Picton Pr.

St. Stephen's Green: Generous Lovers. William Philips. 112p. 8000. 22.00 (*0-85105-367-X*, Pub. by Colin Smythe Ltd UK) Dufour.

St. Stephen's Handbook for Altar Servers. Edward Mattlews. 1994. pap. 4.95 (*0-85244-277-7*, Pub. by Gracewing UK) Morehouse Pub.

St. Susanna. J. A. Fastre. pap. 1.95 (*0-89981-088-8*) Eastern Orthodox.

St. Symeon: The New Theologian & Spiritual Fatherhood. H. J. Turner. LC 90-39223. (Byzantina Neerlandica Ser.: No. 11). xvi, 257p. 1990. 89.00 (*90-04-09166-1*) E J Brill.

St. Symeon, the New Theologian: Theological & Practical Discourses & Three Theological Discourses. St. Symeon The New Theologian. (Cistercian Studies: No. 41). 1982. write for info. (*0-87907-841-3*); pap. 8.00 (*0-87907-941-X*) Cistercian Pubns.

St. Tammany Parish: L'Autre Cote du Lac. Frederick S. Ellis. LC 80-63. (Illus.). 304p. 1982. 27.95 (*0-88289-252-5*) Pelican.

St. Teresa of Avila. rev. ed. Giorgio Papasogil. Tr. by Gloria I. Anzilotti from ITA. LC 58-12223. 1988. reprint ed. pap. 9.95 (*0-8198-6880-9*) Pauline Bks.

St. Teresa of Avila. Marcelle Auclair. Tr. by Kathleen Pond from FRE. LC 53-6126. (Illus.). 454p. 1988. reprint ed. pap. 12.95 (*0-932506-67-4*) St Bedes Pubns.

St. Teresa of Avila. Mary F. Windeatt. (Catholic Story Coloring Bks.). (Illus.). 32p. (J). (gr. 1-5). 1992. reprint ed. student ed. 3.00 (*0-89555-372-4*) TAN Bks Pubs.

St. Teresa of Avila: A Biography. William T. Walsh. LC 87-50928. 592p. 1994. reprint ed. pap. 21.50 (*0-89555-325-2*) TAN Bks Pubs.

St. Theodore the Studite on the Holy Icons. Tr. by Catharine P. Roth. LC 81-18319. 115p. (Orig.). 1981. pap. 7.95 (*0-913836-76-1*) St Vladimirs.

St. Theresa, the Little Flower. Gesualda Of The Holy Spirit. 1986. 7.95 (*0-8198-6817-5*) Pauline Bks.

St. Therese of Lisieux: By Those Who Knew Her. Ed. & Tr. by Christopher O'Mahony from FRE. 287p. (Orig.). 1975. pap. 14.95 (*0-901810-84-3*, Pub. by Veritas Publns IE) Ignatius Pr.

St. Therese of Lisieux: Her Last Conversations. Intro. by John Clarke. LC 76-27207. (Illus.). 352p. 1977. pap. 11.95 (*0-9600876-3-X*) ICS Pubns.

***St. Therese of Lisieux: Her Life, Times & Teaching, Centenary Edition.** Ed. by Conrad De Meester. LC 96-52134. Orig. Title: My Vocation Is Love. (Illus.). 300p. 1997. 44.95 (*0-935216-61-8*) ICS Pubns.

St. Therese, the Little Flower: The Making of a Saint. John Beevers. LC 73-80147. (Orig.). 1994. pap. 6.00 (*0-89555-035-0*) TAN Bks Pubs.

St. Thomas & Analogy. Gerald B. Phelan. (Aquinas Lectures). 1941. 15.00 (*0-87462-105-4*) Marquette.

St. Thomas & Epistemology. Louis-Marie Regis. (Aquinas Lectures). 1946. 15.00 (*0-87462-110-0*) Marquette.

St. Thomas & Historicity. Armand A. Maurer. LC 79-84278. (Aquinas Lectures). 1979. 15.00 (*0-87462-144-5*) Marquette.

St. Thomas & Philosophy. Anton C. Pegis. LC 64-17418. (Aquinas Lectures). 1964. 15.00 (*0-87462-129-1*) Marquette.

St. Thomas & the Future of Metaphysics. Joseph C. Owens. LC 57-7374. (Aquinas Lectures). 1957. 15.00 (*0-87462-122-4*) Marquette.

St. Thomas & the Gentiles. Mortimer J. Adler. (Aquinas Lectures). 1938. 15.00 (*0-87462-102-X*) Marquette.

St. Thomas & the Greek Moralists. Vernon J. Bourke. (Aquinas Lectures). 1947. 15.00 (*0-87462-111-9*) Marquette.

St. Thomas & the Greeks. Anton C. Pegis. (Aquinas Lectures). 1939. 15.00 (*0-87462-103-8*) Marquette.

St. Thomas & the Life of Learning. John F. McCormick. (Aquinas Lectures). 1937. 15.00 (*0-87462-101-1*) Marquette.

St. Thomas & the Object of Geometry. Tr. by Vincent E. Smith. (Aquinas Lectures). 1953. 15.00 (*0-87462-118-6*) Marquette.

St. Thomas & the Problem of Evil. Jacques Maritain. (Aquinas Lectures). 1942. 15.00 (*0-87462-106-2*) Marquette.

St. Thomas & the World State. Robert M. Hutchins. (Aquinas Lectures). 1949. 15.00 (*0-87462-114-3*) Marquette.

St. Thomas Aquinas. 37p. 1995. pap. 1.25 (*0-89555-513-1*) TAN Bks Pubs.

St. Thomas Aquinas. Gilbert K. Chesterton. 200p. 1974. pap. 10.00 (*0-385-09002-1*, Image Bks) Doubleday.

St. Thomas Aquinas: On Charity. St. Thomas Aquinas. Tr. by Lottie H. Kendzierski. (Medieval Philosophical Texts in Translation Ser.: No. 10). 1960. pap. 15.00 (*0-87462-210-7*) Marquette.

St. Thomas Aquinas: On Spiritual Creatures. St. Thomas Aquinas. Tr. by Mary C. Fitzpatrick. (Medieval Philosophical Texts in Translation Ser.: No. 5). 1949. pap. 15.00 (*0-87462-205-0*) Marquette.

St. Thomas Aquinas: On the Unity of the Intellect Against the Averroists. Ed. by Beatrice H. Zedler. LC 68-28029. (Medieval Philosophical Texts in Translation Ser.: No. 19). 1968. pap. 10.00 (*0-87462-219-0*) Marquette.

St. Thomas Aquinas: Questions on the Soul. James H. Robb. LC 84-61636. (Medieval Philosophical Texts in Translation Ser.). 1984. 25.00 (*0-87462-226-3*) Marquette.

St. Thomas Aquinas: Teacher of Truth. Francis Selman. 116p. 1994. pap. text ed. 17.95 (*0-567-29245-2*, Pub. by T & T Clark UK) Bks Intl VA.

St. Thomas Aquinas on Analogy: A Textual Analysis & Systematic Synthesis. George P. Klubertanz. LC 60-9602. (Jesuit Studies). 327p. reprint ed. pap. 93.20 (*0-317-09004-6*, 2000813) Bks Demand.

St. Thomas Aquinas on Politics & Ethics. St. Thomas Aquinas. Ed. by Paul E. Sigmund. (Critical Editions Ser.). (C). 1987. pap. text ed. 9.95 (*0-393-95243-6*) Norton.

St. Thomas Aquinas, the Angel of the Schools: A Book for Children & the Child-Like. Raissa Maritain. (Illus.). 127p. (Orig.). (J). (gr. 3-7). 1993. pap. 5.50 (*0-935952-95-0*) Angelus Pr.

St. Thomas Aquinas (1225-1274) Ed. by Mark Blaug. (Pioneers in Economics Ser.: Vol. 3). 320p. 1991. text ed. 120.00 (*1-85278-465-2*) E Elgar.

St. Thomas et le Pseudo-Denis. J. Durantel. (Medieval Studies Ser.). (FRE.). reprint ed. lib. bdg. 45.00 (*0-697-00036-2*) Irvington.

St. Thomas in Early Danish Times. Johan L. Carstens. Ed. & Tr. by Arnold R. Highfield. (Orig.). 1997. pap. write for info. (*1-886007-04-7*) VI Human Coun.

St. Thomas More: Action & Contemplation: Proceedings of the Symposium Held at St. John's University, October 9-10, 1970. St. Thomas More Symposium Staff. LC 77-179478. 194p. reprint ed. pap. 55.30 (*0-8357-8332-4*, 2033834) Bks Demand.

St. Thomas More: Selected Letters. Thomas More. Ed. by Elizabeth F. Rogers. LC 61-14944. (Yale Edition of the Works of St. Thomas More: Modernized Ser.). 297p. reprint ed. pap. 84.70 (*0-8357-8331-6*, 2033876) Bks Demand.

St. Thomas More: Vol. 3, Pt. 2 - Latin Poems. Thomas More. Ed. by Clarence H. Miller et al. LC 63-7949. (Yale Edition of the Complete Works of St. Thomas More Ser.). 800p. 1984. text ed. 90.00 (*0-300-02591-2*) Yale U Pr.

St. Thomas of Canterbury. W. H. Hutton. 1973. 59.95 (*0-8490-0983-9*) Gordon Pr.

St. Thomas of Canterbury: His Death & Miracles, 2 vols. in 1. Edwin A. Abbott. LC 80-18216. (Crusades & Military Orders Ser.: Second Series). reprint ed. 74.50 (*0-404-16366-1*) AMS Pr.

St. Thomas, Siger de Brabant, St. Bonaventure: On the Eternity of the World. Tr. by Cyril Vollert et al. (Medieval Philosophical Texts in Translation Ser.). 1965. pap. 15.00 (*0-87462-216-6*) Marquette.

St. Thomas's Eve. Jean Plaidy. 22.95 (*0-8488-0610-7*) Amereon Ltd.

St. Tiggywinkles Wildcare Handbook: First Aid & Care for Wildlife. Les Stocker. (Illus.). 224p. 1993. 22.95 (*0-7011-3775-4*, Pub. by Chatto & Windus UK) Trafalgar.

St. Tikhon of Zadonsk: Inspirer of Dostoevsky. Nadejda Gorodetzky. LC 76-49919. 320p. 1977. pap. 10.95 (*0-913836-32-X*) St Vladimirs.

St. Tos 78 Rings of Tautee. Dean W. Smith. 1996. mass mkt. 5.99 (*0-671-00171-X*, PB Trade Paper) PB.

St. Valentine's Night. large type ed. Andrew M. Greeley. 756p. 1990. reprint ed. lib. bdg. 15.95 (*0-89621-980-1*) Thorndike Pr.

St. Veronica Gig Stories. Jack Pulaski. LC 86-50657. 178p. (Orig.). 1986. 15.95 (*0-939010-10-0*); pap. 8.95 (*0-939010-09-7*) Zephyr Pr.

St. Veronica Gig Stories. deluxe ed. Jack Pulaski. LC 86-50657. 178p. (Orig.). 1986. 25.00 (*0-685-13535-7*) Zephyr Pr.

St. Vincent & Grenadines: Caribbean Sunseekers. Don Philpott. (Caribbean Sunseekers Ser.). (Illus.). 160p. (Orig.). 1996. pap. 10.95 (*0-8442-4928-9*, Passport Bks) NTC Pub Grp.

St. Vincent & the Grenadines. Robert B. Potter. (World Bibliographical Ser.). 1992. lib. bdg. 79.00 (*1-85109-183-1*) ABC-CLIO.

St. Vincent & the Grenadines: A Plural Country. 4th ed. Jill R. Bobrow. (Illus.). 130p. 1993. reprint ed. 35.00 (*0-393-03309-0*) Concepts Pub.

St. Vincent De Paul, Vol. 8. Roland Garel. Tr. by Marianne L. Trouve' from FRE. (Saints Ser.). (Illus.). 32p. (J). (gr. 3-8). 1995. pap. 1.95 (*0-8198-6982-1*) Pauline Bks.

St. Vincent De Paul & the Fruits of His Life. Jedediah V. Huntington. (Notable American Authors Ser.). 1992. reprint ed. lib. bdg. 75.00 (*0-7812-3291-0*) Rprt Serv.

St. Vith: Lion in the Way: The 106th Infantry Division in World War II. R. Ernest Dupuy. (Divisional Ser.: 30th). (Illus.). 284p. 1986. reprint ed. 34.95 (*0-89839-092-3*) Battery Pr.

Sta Oni Nazivaju Demokratijom? Milos Acin-Kosta. 210p. (Orig.). (SER.). 1953. pap. 1.00 (*0-317-61884-9*) Ravnogorski.

Staat Im Wachstum Versucheiner Finanzwirthschaftlichen Analyse der Preussischen Haushaltsrechungen, 1871-1913, 2 Vols. Peter-Michael Prochnow. Ed. by Stuart Bruchey. LC 80-2825. (Dissertations in European Economic History Ser.). (Illus.). 1981. lib. bdg. 35.95 (*0-405-14009-6*) Ayer.

Staat und Gesellschaft der Griechen und Romer. Von Ulrich & B. Niese Wiliamovitz-Moellendorff. Ed. by J. P. Mayer. LC 78-67398. (European Political Thought Ser.). (GER.). 1980. reprint ed. lib. bdg. 21.95 (*0-405-11750-7*) Ayer.

Staat und Handel Im Alten Griechenland. Johannes Hasebroek. x, 200p. 1966. reprint ed. write for info. (*0-318-70931-7*) G Olms Pubs.

Staat und Manufaktur im Romischen Reiche. Axel W. Persson. Ed. by Moses Finley. LC 79-4998. (Ancient Economic History Ser.). (GER.). 1979. reprint ed. lib. bdg. 17.95 (*0-405-12387-6*) Ayer.

***Staatliche Viehhaltung im Altbablonischen Lande Larsa.** F. R. Kraus. 67p. pap. 18.75 (*0-7204-8430-8*) Elsevier.

***Staatsdiskurs und Selbstbewusstein: Sprachlich-Rhetorische Formen Ihrer Institutionalisierung.** Alexander Thumfart. (GER.). 1996. text ed. 57.00 (*90-5708-015-X*); pap. text ed. 25.00 (*90-5708-016-8*) Gordon & Breach.

Staatsgalerie Stuttgart. (Illus.). 360p. (GER.). 1991. 80.00 (*3-7757-0333-0*, Pub. by Gerd Hatje GW) Dist Art Pubs.

Staatslehre des Franz Suarez, S. J. Heinrich A. Rommen. Ed. by J. P. Mayer. LC 78-67381. (European Political Thought Ser.). (GER.). 1980. reprint ed. lib. bdg. 30.95 (*0-405-11731-0*) Ayer.

***Staatsordnung und Kommunalverfassung: Die Formierung Moderner Gemeindekonzeptionen in Wurttemberg Zwischen Ancien Regime und Fruhkonstitutionalismus.** Ulrich Speck. (Europaische Hochschulschriften: Reihe 3: Bd. 723). 263p. (GER.). 1997. pap. 51.95 (*3-631-30549-4*) P Lang Pubng.

Staatsverwaltung der Beserzten Gebiete, Erster Band, Belgien. Ludwig Von Kohler. (Wirtschafts-Und Sozialgeschichte des Weltkrieges (Osterreichische Und Ungarische Serie)). (GER.). 1927. 100.00 (*0-317-27587-9*) Elliots Bks.

***Stab in the Bach.** Roy Gilligan. LC 96-85135. (Pat Riordan Mysteries Ser.: Vol. 8). 200p. 1996. write for info. (*0-9626136-6-5*) Brendan Bks.

Stab in the Back. large type ed. Malcolm Gray. (Linford Mystery Library). 337p. 1989. pap. 15.99 (*0-7089-6638-1*, Linford) Ulverscroft.

Stab in the Dark. Lawrence Block. (Matthew Scudder Novel Ser.). 192p. 1992. reprint ed. mass mkt. 5.99 (*0-380-71574-0*) Avon.

***Stab Your Way to the Top.** Martin Wakeman. 1997. pap. text ed. 9.95 (*0-7494-1718-8*, Kogan Pg Educ) Stylus Pub VA.

Stabat Mater: Noble Icon of the Outcast & the Poor. Peter Daino. LC 87-30633. 80p. 1988. pap. 4.95 (*0-8189-0526-3*) Alba.

Stabbing of George Harry Storrs. Jonathan Goodman. LC 83-8267. (Illus.). 254p. 1983. 35.00 (*0-8142-0349-3*) Ohio St U Pr.

Stabbing the Water. Marshall Draper. 1994. 17.95 (*0-533-10977-9*) Vantage.

***Stabilitatseinbuben Durch die Europaische Wahrungsunion: Theoretische und Empirische Untersuchungen.** Christoph Knoppik. (Europaische Hochschulschriften: Reihe 5: Bd. 2011). (Illus.). 245p. (GER.). 1997. pap. 44.95 (*3-631-50058-0*) P Lang Pubng.

Stability Analysis: Nonlinear Mechanical Equations. A. A. Martynyuk. (Stability & Control: Theory, Methods Ser.). 336p. 1995. text ed. 120.00 (*2-88449-023-X*) Gordon & Breach.

Stability Analysis for Linear Repetitive Processes. E. T. Rogers & D. H. Owens. (Lecture Notes in Control & Information Sciences Ser.: Vol. 175). (Illus.). 201p. 1992. 63.95 (*0-387-55264-2*) Spr-Verlag.

Stability Analysis in Terms of Two Measures. V. Lakshmikantham & Xinzhi Liu. LC 93-14063. 250p. 1993. text ed. 61.00 (*981-02-1389-1*) World Scientific Pub.

Stability Analysis of Earth Slopes. Yang Huang. 316p. (gr. 13). 1983. text ed. 60.95 (*0-442-23689-1*) Chapman & Hall.

Stability Analysis of Nonlinear Systems. Lakshmikantham et al. (Pure & Applied Mathematics Ser.: Vol. 125). 336p. 1988. 160.00 (*0-8247-8067-1*) Dekker.

Stability & Ballast Control, Vol. 7. Michael Hancox. (Oilfield Seamanship Ser.). (Illus.). 350p. 1995. pap. 125.00 (*1-870945-76-X*, Pub. by Oilfld Pubns Ltd UK) Am Educ Systs.

Stability & Change: Innovation In an Educational Context. S. Rosenblum & K. S. Louis. LC 80-28291. (Environment, Development, & Public Policy & Social Services Ser.). 370p. 1981. 55.00 (*0-306-40665-9*, Plenum Pr) Plenum.

Stability & Change in American Politics: The Coming of Age of the Generation of the 1960's. Michael X. Delli Carpini. 304p. (C). 1986. text ed. 44.00 (*0-8147-1780-2*) NYU Pr.

Stability & Change in American Politics: The Coming of Age of the Generation of the 1960's. Michael X. Delli Carpini. 304p. (C). 1987. pap. text ed. 14.00 (*0-8147-1784-5*) NYU Pr.

Stability & Change in Australian Politics. Aitkin. (Australian National University Press Ser.). 1982. pap. text ed. 37.00 (*0-08-032822-9*, Pergamon Pr) Elsevier.

Stability & Change in Highland Chiapas, Mexico. Henning Siverts. (Bergen Studies in Social Anthropology: No. 4). 152p. (Orig.). 1985. pap. text ed. 11.95 (*0-936508-51-5*, Pub. by Bergen Univ Dept Social Anthro NO) Barber Pr.

Stability & Change in Literacy Learning. Don Holdaway. LC 83-22636. 67p. (C). 1984. pap. text ed. 13.50 (*0-435-08209-4*, 08209) Heinemann.

Stability & Change in Revolutionary Pennsylvania: Banking, Politics, & Social Structure. George D. Rappaport. 288p. 1996. 37.50 (*0-271-01531-4*) Pa St U Pr.

Stability & Characterization of Protein & Peptide Drugs: Case Histories. Ed. by Y. J. Wang & Rodney Pearlman. (Pharmaceutical Biotechnology Ser.: Vol. 5). (Illus.). 351p. (C). 1993. 75.00 (*0-306-44365-1*, Plenum Pr) Plenum.

Stability & Complexity in Model Ecosystems. Robert M. May. (Population Biology Monographs: No. 6). 150p. 1961. pap. text ed. 24.95 (*0-691-08130-1*) Princeton U Pr.

Stability & Constancy in Visual Perception: Mechanisms & Processes. Ed. by William Epstein. LC 76-28769. (Wiley Series in Behavior). 477p. reprint ed. pap. 136.00 (*0-317-55551-0*, 2056335) Bks Demand.

Stability & Continuity in Mental Development: Behavioral & Biological Perspectives. Norman A. Krasnegor. 352p. (C). 1989. text ed. 69.95 (*0-8058-0203-7*) L Erlbaum Assocs.

Stability & Control of Discrete Processes. J. P. Lasalle. (Applied Mathematical Sciences Ser.: Vol. 62). (Illus.). 610p. 1986. 52.95 (*0-387-96411-8*) Spr-Verlag.

Stability & Ductility of Steel Structures under Cyclic Loading. Fukumato. 384p. 1991. 110.00 (*0-8493-0144-0*, TA) CRC Pr.

Stability & Dynamic Systems. M. I. Al'muhamedov et al. (Translations Ser.: Series 1, Vol. 5). 510p. 1962. pap. 38.00 (*0-8218-1605-5*, TRANS1/5) Am Math.

Stability & Flexibility: An Analysis of Natural Systems. N. D. Cook. (Systems Science & World Order Library). (Illus.). 246p. 1982. 32.00 (*0-317-66881-1*, Pub. by Pergamon Repr UK) Franklin.

Stability & Inflation: A Volume of Essays to Honour the Memory of A. W. H. Phillips. Ed. by Abram R. Bergstrom et al. LC 77-4420. (Illus.). 341p. reprint ed. pap. 97.20 (*0-8357-4318-7*, 2037117) Bks Demand.

Stability & Operations of Jackups: Design Guides for Offshore Structures. CLAROM Staff. Ed. by C. Perol & Pierre Le Tirant. (Design Guides for Offshore Structures Ser.: Vol. 4). (Illus.). 350p. (C). 1993. 540.00 (*2-7108-0636-3*, Pub. by Edits Technip FR) St Mut.

Stability & Optimization of Flexible Space Structures. S. J. Britvec. LC 93-16441. (Illus.). 312p. 1995. 134.00 (*0-8176-2864-9*) Birkhauser.

Stability & Oscillations in Delay Differential Equations of Population Dynamics. K. Gopalsamy. (Mathematics & Its Applications Ser.). (C). 1992. lib. bdg. 231.50 (*0-7923-1594-4*) Kluwer Ac.

Stability & Perfection of Nash Equilibria. E. Van Damme. (Illus.). 370p. 1987. 99.00 (*0-387-17101-0*) Spr-Verlag.

Stability & Perfection of Nash Equilibria. 2nd enl. rev. ed. E. Van Damme. (Illus.). 368p. 1996. pap. 69.95 (*0-387-53800-3*) Spr-Verlag.

Stability & Performance of Slopes & Embankments, No. Two: Proceedings of a Specialty Conference. Ed. by Raymond B. Seed & Ross W. Boulanger. LC 92-14707. (Geotechnical Special Publications: No. 31). 1560p. 1992. pap. text ed. 96.00 (*0-87262-872-8*) Am Soc Civil Eng.

Stability & Protein Pharmaceuticals Pt. A: Chemical & Physical Pathways of Protein Degradation. Ed. by T. J. Ahern & M. C. Manning. (Pharmaceutical Biotechnology Ser.: Vol. 2). (Illus.). 400p. 1992. 89.50 (*0-306-44152-7*, Plenum Pr) Plenum.

Stability & Robustness of Multivariable Feedback Systems. Michael G. Safonov. (Signal Processing, Optimization, & Control Ser.). 171p. (C). 1980. 42.00 (*0-262-19180-6*) MIT Pr.

Stability & Seismic Resistance of Buttress Dams. N. S. Motsonelidze. Tr. by V. S. Kothekar from RUS. 293p. (C). 1987. text ed. 90.00 (*90-6191-490-6*, Pub. by A A Balkema NE) Ashgate Pub Co.

Stability & Seismic Resistance of Buttress Dams. N. S. Motsonelidze. 278p. (C). 1987. 30.00 (*81-204-0207-3*, Pub. by Oxford IBH II) S Asia.

Stability & Stabilization of Enzymes: Proceedings of an International Symposium Held in Maastrich, The Netherlands, 22-25 November, 1992. Ed. by W. J. Van Den Tweel et al. (Studies in Organic Chemistry: Vol. 47). 534p. 1993. 295.25 (*0-444-89372-5*) Elsevier.

Stability & Strategic Defenses. Ed. by Jack N. Barkenbus & Alvin M. Weinberg. LC 88-39748. (Illus.). 305p. 1989. pap. 13.95 (*0-88702-050-X*); text ed. 22.95 (*0-88702-046-1*) Washington Inst Pr.

Stability & Strife: England 1714-1760. W. A. Speck. (New History of England Ser.). 224p. (C). 1979. reprint ed. pap. 14.50 (*0-674-83350-3*) HUP.

Stability & the Industrial Elite in China & the Soviet Union. Constance S. Meaney. LC 87-83158. (China Research Monographs: No. 34). 160p. (Orig.). 1988. pap. 15.00 (*0-912966-98-X*) IEAS.

Stability & Trim for the Ship's Officer. 3rd rev. ed. Ed. by William E. George. LC 82-74137. (Illus.). 359p. 1983. text ed. 25.00 (*0-87033-297-X*) Cornell Maritime.

Stability & Variation in Hopi Song. George List. LC 92-73156. (Memoirs Ser.: Vol. 204). 205p. 1993. 28.00 (*0-87169-204-X*, M204-LIG) Am Philos.

Stability & Wave Propagation in Fluids & Solids. Ed. by Giovanni P. Galdi. (CISM International Centre for Mechanical Sciences Ser.: No. 344). (Illus.). 154p. 1995. pap. 53.95 (*3-211-82687-4*) Spr-Verlag.

Stability, Bifurcation & Postcritical Behaviour of Structures. M. Pignataro et al. (Developments in Civil Engineering Ser.: Vol. 39). 358p. 1991. 153.75 (*0-444-88140-9*) Elsevier.

Stability Concept of Evolutionary Game Theory: A Dynamic Approach. R. Cressman. Ed. by S. A. Levin. (Lecture Notes in Biomathematics Ser.: Vol. 94). viii, 128p. 1992. 39.95 (*0-387-55419-X*) Spr-Verlag.

Stability Constants Metal Ion Complexes, Pt. A: Inorganic Ligands. E. Hogfeldt. (IUPAC Chemical Data Ser.: Vol. 21, Pt. A). 1982. 147.00 (*0-08-020959-9*, Pub. by Pergamon Repr UK) Franklin.

Stability Constants of Metal-Ion Complexes, Pt. B: Organic Ligands. Ed. by D. D. Perrin. (Chemical Data Ser.: No. 22). 1280p. 1979. 552.00 (*0-08-020958-0*, Pub. by Pergamon Repr UK) Franklin.

Stability, Democracy, & Peace Through Cooperation: The New NATO. Ed. by George A. Joulwan et al. (Workshops on Political-Military Decision Making Ser.). 128p. (Orig.). (C). 1995. pap. 25.00 (*0-9631515-7-6*) Strat Dec Pr.

Stability Design of Semi-Rigid Frames. Wai-Fah Chen et al. LC 95-10783. 496p. 1995. text ed. 79.95 (*0-471-07670-8*) Wiley.

***Stability Design of Semi-Rigid Frames.** Wai-Fah Chen et al. 1995. pap. text ed. 0.01 (*0-471-15214-5*) Wiley.

Stability Design of Steel Frames. Chen & Lui. 400p. 1991. 89.00 (*0-8493-8606-3*, TA) CRC Pr.

Stability for Fishermen: A Self-Study Course for the Commercial Fishing Industry of the United States. Intro. by William E. George. (Illus.). 231p. (C). 1990. pap. text ed. 150.00 (*0-9627009-0-8*) Natl Cargo Bureau.

***Stability in Central Europe: Weakening & Strengthening Factors.** Ed. by Bengt-Goran Bergstrand & Ingmar Oldberg. (Illus.). 157p. (C). 1996. reprint ed. pap. 35.00 (*0-7881-3052-8*) DIANE Pub.

Stability in Modules for Classical Lie Algebras - A Constructive Approach. G. Benkart et al. LC 90-31825. (Memoirs Ser.: No. 85/430). 165p. 1990. pap. text ed. 22.00 (*0-8218-2492-9*, MEMO/85/430) Am Math.

Stability in Nonlinear Control Systems. A. M. Letov. 336p. 1961. text ed. 65.00 (*0-691-08040-2*) Princeton U Pr.

***Stability in Nonlinear Control Systems.** Aleksandr M. Letov. Tr. by J. George Adashko. LC 59-5599. 332p. 1961. reprint ed. pap. 94.70 (*0-608-02933-5*, 2063999) Bks Demand.

Stability in the Dynamics of Metal Cutting. S. T. Chiriacescu. (Studies in Applied Mechanics: No. 22). 200p. 1990. 141.25 (*0-444-98868-8*) Elsevier.

Stability in the Financial System. Ed. by Dimitri B. Papadimitriou. (Jerome Levy Economics Institute Ser.). 448p. 1996. text ed. 79.95 (*0-312-15935-8*) St Martin.

Stability in Underground Mining, First International Conference, August 16-18, 1982, Vancouver, British Columbia, Canada. International Conference on Stability in Open Pit Mining Staff. Ed. by C. O. Brawner. LC 82-73915. 1083p. reprint ed. pap. 180.00 (*0-8357-3417-X*, 2039674) Bks Demand.

Stability in Viscoelasticity. Aleskey D. Drozdov & Vladimir B. Kolmanovskii. LC 94-39063. (Applied Mathematics & Mechanics Ser.: Vol. 38). 622p. 1994. 191.50 (*0-444-81951-7*, North Holland) Elsevier.

Stability, Instability & Chaos. Paul Glendinning. (Texts in Applied Mathematics Ser.: No. 11). (Illus.). 350p. (C). 1994. text ed. 80.00 (*0-521-41553-5*); pap. text ed. 32.95 (*0-521-42566-2*) Cambridge U Pr.

***Stability, Instability & Direct Integrals.** Bruno Scarpellini. LC 96-31184. (Pitman Research Notes in Mathematics Ser.). 1998. write for info. (*0-582-30271-4*) Longman.

Stability of a Macroeconomic System with Quantity Constraints. P. Van den Heuvel. (Lecture Notes in Economics & Mathematical Systems Ser.: Vol. 211). 169p. 1983. 31.00 (*0-387-11992-2*) Spr-Verlag.

Stability of Amorphous Silicon Alloy Materials & Devices. Ed. by B. L. Stafford & E. Sabisky. LC 87-70990. (Conference Proceeding Ser.: No. 157). 408p. 1987. 65.00 (*0-88318-357-9*) Am Inst Physics.

Stability of Collisionless Stellar Systems: Mechanisms for the Dynamical Structure of Galaxies. P. L. Palmer. LC 94-32551. (Astrophysics & Space Science Library: Vol. 185). 360p. (C). 1994. lib. bdg. 151.50 (*0-7923-2455-2*) Kluwer Ac.

Stability of Constants: Second Supplement. International Union of Pure & Applied Chemistry Staff. 1976. write for info. (*0-318-55230-2*, Pergamon Pr) Elsevier.

Stability of Convective Flows. Ed. by P. G. Simpkins & A. Liakopoulos. (HTD Ser.: Vol. 219). 72p. 1992. 27.50 (*0-7918-1061-5*, G00705) ASME.

Stability of Critical Equilibrium States. L. G. Khazin & E. E. Schnol. Ed. by Arun V. Holden. Tr. by Catherine Waterhouse. (Nonlinear Science: Theory & Applications Ser.). 220p. 1992. text ed. 309.00 (*0-471-93523-9*) Wiley.

Stability of Dynamical Systems. J. P. LaSalle. (CBMS-NSF Regional Conference Ser.: No. 25). v, 76p. (Orig.). 1976. pap. text ed. 20.50 (*0-89871-022-7*) Soc Indus-Appl Math.

Stability of Dynamical Systems: Theory & Applications. John R. Graef. (Lecture Notes in Pure & Applied Mathematics Ser.: Vol. 28). 232p. 1977. 130.00 (*0-8247-6410-2*) Dekker.

Stability of Elastic Systems. Horst Leipholz. (Mechanics of Elastic Stability Ser.: No. 7). 492p. 1980. lib. bdg. 200.00 (*90-286-0050-7*) Kluwer Ac.

Stability of Functional Differential Equations. V. R. Nosov & Vladimir B. Kolmanovski. 1986. text ed. 142.00 (*0-12-417940-1*); pap. text ed. 69.00 (*0-12-417941-X*) Acad Pr.

Stability of Heavy Minerals. E. Nickel et al. Ed. by H. Fuechtbauer. (Contributions to Sedimentology Monograph: No. 1). (Illus.). 125p. 1973. pap. text ed. 34.00 (*3-510-57001-4*) Lubrecht & Cramer.

Stability of Insulin. Jens Brange. 128p. (C). 1995. lib. bdg. 45.50 (*0-7923-8874-7*) Kluwer Ac.

Stability of Linear Systems: Some Aspects of Kinematic Similarity. C. J. Harris & J. F. Miles. (Mathematics in Science & Engineering Ser.). 1980. text ed. 103.00 (*0-12-328250-0*) Acad Pr.

Stability of Mappings of Hyers-Ulam Type. Ed. by Themistocles M. Rassias & Jozef Tabor. 160p. 1994. text ed. 90.00 (*0-911767-82-7*); pap. text ed. 60.00 (*0-911767-64-9*) Hadronic Pr Inc.

Stability of Materials: Proceedings of a NATO ASI Held in Corfu, Greece, June 25-July 7, 1994, Vol. 355. Ed. by A. Gonis et al. LC 96-18486. (NATO ASI Series B: Vol. 355). (Illus.). 750p. (C). 1996. 159.50 (*0-306-45311-8*, Plenum Pr) Plenum.

Stability of Matter: From Atoms to Stars: Selecta of Elliott H. Lieb. Elliott H. Lieb. Ed. by W. Thirring. viii, 565p. 1991. 89.00 (*0-387-53039-8*) Spr-Verlag.

***Stability of Matter: From Atoms to Stars: Selecta of Elliott H. Lieb.** 2nd ed. Elliott H. Lieb & Walter E. Thirring. LC 96-35788. 653p. 1997. 74.95 (*3-540-61565-2*) Spr-Verlag.

Stability of Metal Structures: A World View. 2nd ed. Lynn S. Beedle. 940p. 1991. 85.00 (*1-879749-50-5*) Structural Stability.

Stability of Microstructure in Metallic Systems. 2nd ed. J. W. Martin et al. (Solid State Science Ser.). (Illus.). 368p. 1997. text ed. 110.00 (*0-521-41160-2*); pap. text ed. 44.95 (*0-521-42316-3*) Cambridge U Pr.

Stability of Minerals. Ed. by G. Price & N. Ross. (Mineralogical Society Ser.: No. 3). (Illus.). 352p. (gr. 13). 1992. text ed. 182.95 (*0-412-44150-0*, A9494) Chapman & Hall.

Stability of Motion. W. Hahn. Tr. by A. P. Baartz. (Grundlehren der Mathematischen Wissenschaften Ser.: Vol. 138). (Illus.). 1968. 147.95 (*0-387-03829-9*) Spr-Verlag.

Stability of Motion: Applications of Lyapunov's Second Method to Differential Systems & Equations with Delay. Nikolai N. Krasovskii. Tr. by J. L. Brenner. vi, 188p. 1963. 29.50 (*0-8047-0098-2*) Stanford U Pr.

Stability of Motion of Nonautonomous Systems (Methods of Limiting Equations) J. Kato & A. A. Martynyuk. (Stability & Control: Theory, Methods Ser). 304p. 1996. text ed. 120.00 (*2-88449-035-3*) Gordon & Breach.

Stability of Multi-Dimensional Shock Fronts. Andrew Majda. LC 82-20636. (Memoirs Ser.: No. 41/275). 95p. 1982. pap. 16.00 (*0-8218-2275-6*, MEMO/41/275) Am Math.

Stability of Nonlinear Systems. Derek P. Atherton. LC 80-40947. (Control Theory & Applications Studies: No. 1). (Illus.). 243p. reprint ed. pap. 69.30 (*0-8357-4552-X*, 2037451) Bks Demand.

Stability of Particle Motion in Storage Rings. Ed. by Alessandro G. Ruggiero. (AIP Conference Proceedings Ser.: Vol. 292, No. 54). 516p. 1993. text ed. 502.00 (*1-56396-225-X*) Am Inst Physics.

Stability of Planetary Systems: Reprinted from Celestial Mechanics, Vol. 34, Nos. 1-4. Raynor L. Duncombe et al. 1985. lib. bdg. 243.00 (*90-277-1961-6*) Kluwer Ac.

Stability of Protein Pharmaceuticals Pt. B: In Vivio Pathways of Degradation & Strategies for Protein Stability. Ed. by T. J. Ahern & M. C. Manning. (Pharmaceutical Biotechnology Ser.: Vol. 3). (Illus.). 300p. 1992. 75.00 (*0-306-44153-5*, Plenum Pr) Plenum.

Stability of Rock Slopes: Proceedings of the Symposium on Rock Mechanics, 13th, University of Illinois, Urbana, August 30-September 1, 1971. Rock Mechanics Symposium Staff. Ed. by Edward J. Cording. LC 76-380975. (Illus.). 922p. reprint ed. pap. 180.00 (*0-317-08305-8*, 2019553) Bks Demand.

Stability of Runge-Kutta Methods for Stiff Nonlinear Differential Equations. K. Dekker & J. G. Verwer. (CWI Monographs: No. 2). 308p. 1984. 88.25 (*0-444-87634-0*, North Holland) Elsevier.

Stability of Slopes. E. N. Bromhead. (Illus.). 450p. 1992. 125.00 (*0-216-93175-4*, A9753, Pub. by Blackie Acad & Prof UK) Routledge Chapman & Hall.

Stability of Solutions of Differential Equations in Banach Space. Ju. L. Daleckii & M. G. Krein. LC 74-8403. (Translations of Mathematical Monographs: Vol. 43). 386p. 1974. 97.00 (*0-8218-1593-8*, MMONO/43) Am Math.

Stability of Solutions to Convex Problems of Optimization. K. Malanowski. (Lecture Notes in Control & Information Sciences Ser.: Vol. 93). ix, 137p. 1987. 31.95 (*0-387-17589-X*) Spr-Verlag.

Stability of Steel Structures. M. Klos Ivanyi. 1106p. (C). 1988. 570.00 (*0-569-09166-7*, Pub. by Collets) St Mut.

Stability of Steel Structures, Set, Vols. 1 & 2. M. Klos Ivanyi. (Illus.). 1698p. (C). 1988. 300.00 (*963-05-5222-1*, Pub. by Akad Kiado HU) St Mut.

Stability of Steel Structures: Proceedings & Final Report of the International Conference on Stability of Steel Structures Held in Budapest, Hungary, April 25-27, 1990, 2 vols., Set. Miklos Ivanyi. 1865p. (C). 1991. 414.00 (*963-05-6073-9*, Pub. by Akad Kiado HU) St Mut.

***Stability of Steel Structures 1995, Budapest Vol. 1-2: Further Direction in Stability Research & Design, 2 vols.** M. Ivansfkfkf. 1144p. 1996. 180.00 (*963-05-6966-3*, Pub. by A K HU) Intl Spec Bk.

Stability of Structures. Mehdi Farshad. LC 93-47575. 438p. 1994. 194.50 (*0-444-81698-4*) Elsevier.

Stability of Structures: Elastic, Inelastic & Damage Theories. Zdenek P. Bazant & Luigi Cedolin. (Oxford Engineering Science Ser.: No. 26). (Illus.). 1014p. (C). 1991. text ed. 85.00 (*0-19-505529-2*) OUP.

Stability of Structures by Finite Element Methods. Zenon Waszczyszyn et al. (Studies in Applied Mechanics: 40). 482p. 1994. 223.50 (*0-444-82123-6*) Elsevier.

***Stability of Structures in Two Dimensions: Straight Bars, Frames, Curved Bars, & Arches.** John V. Huddleston. LC 96-35383. (Illus.). 140p. (Orig.). (C). 1997. pap. text ed. 24.00 (*0-945261-08-X*) Exchange Pub Div.

Stability of Structures under Static & Dynamic Loads. Compiled by American Society of Civil Engineers Staff. 820p. 1977. pap. 33.00 (*0-87262-095-6*) Am Soc Civil Eng.

Stability of Superconductors. Lawrence Dresner. LC 95-17274. (Selected Topics in Superconductivity Ser.). 225p. 1995. 49.50 (*0-306-45030-5*, Plenum Pr) Plenum.

Stability of the International Monetary System. W. M. Scammell. 176p. 1987. pap. 22.00 (*0-8476-7541-6*) Rowman.

Stability of the Solar System & Its Minor Natural & Artificial Bodies. Ed. by Victor G. Szebehely. (NATO Advanced Study Institutes Series C, Mathematical & Physical Sciences). 1985. lib. bdg. 162.50 (*90-277-2046-0*) Kluwer Ac.

Stability of the Solar System & Small Stellar Systems: Proceedings of the I.A.U. Symposium, No. 62, Warsaw, Poland, Sept. 5-8, 1973. Yoshihide Kozai. LC 74-76475. (Symposia of the International Astronomical Union Ser.: No. 62). 1974. lib. bdg. 129.50 (*90-277-0458-9*) Kluwer Ac.

Stability of Thermodynamic Systems, Barcelona, Spain, 1981: Proceedings. Ed. by J. C. Vazquez & G. Lebon. (Lecture Notes in Physics Ser.: Vol. 164). 321p. 1982. 36.95 (*0-387-11581-1*) Spr-Verlag.

Stability of Unfoldings. G. Wasserman. (Lecture Notes in Mathematics Ser.: Vol. 393). xxix, 164p. 1986. 30.95 (*0-387-06794-9*) Spr-Verlag.

Stability Problems for Stochastic Models. Ed. by Vladimir V. Kalashnikov & V. M. Zolotarev. (Lecture Notes in Mathematics Ser.: Vol. 1412). x, 380p. 1989. 46.00 (*0-387-51948-3*) Spr-Verlag.

Stability Problems for Stochastic Models. Ed. by V. M. Zolotarev et al. (Frontiers in Pure & Applied Probability Ser.: No. 3). 322p. 1994. 197.50 (*90-6764-159-6*, Pub. by VSP NE) Coronet Bks.

Stability Problems for Stochastic Models. Ed. by V. M. Zolotarev & Vladimir V. Kalashnikov. (Lecture Notes in Mathematics Ser.: Vol. 1155). 447p. 1985. 59.95 (*0-387-15985-1*) Spr-Verlag.

Stability Problems for Stochastic Models: Proceedings, Moscow 1982. Ed. by Vladimir V. Kalashnikov & V. M. Zolotarev. (Lecture Notes in Mathematics Ser.: Vol. 982). 295p. 1983. 42.95 (*0-387-12278-8*) Spr-Verlag.

Stability Problems for Stochastic Models: Proceedings of the International Seminar, Held in Suzdal, Russia, Jan. 27-Feb. 2, 1991. Ed. by Vladimir V. Kalashnikov & V. M. Zolotarev. LC 93-15959. (Lecture Notes in Mathematics Ser.: Vol. 1546). 1993. 45.95 (*0-387-56744-5*) Spr-Verlag.

Stability Problems for Stochastic Models: Proceedings of the Ninth International Seminar held in Varna, Bulgaria, May 13-19, 1985. Ed. by V. V. Kalshnikov et al. (Lecture Notes in Mathematics Ser.: Vol. 1233). vi, 223p. 1987. 33.50 (*0-387-17204-1*) Spr-Verlag.

Stability Problems in Fracture Mechanics. Vladimir V. Bolotin. LC 95-17501. (Nonlinear Science Ser.). (Illus.). 192p. 1996. text ed. 64.95 (*0-471-12546-6*, Wiley-Interscience) Wiley.

Stability Problems of Steel Structures. Ed. by M. Klos Ivanyi & M. Skaloud. (CISM International Centre for Mechanical Sciences Ser.: Vol. 323). (Illus.). v, 415p. 1992. 110.95 (*0-387-82398-0*) Spr-Verlag.

Stability, Security & Continuity: Mr. Justice Burton & Decision-Making in the Supreme Court, 1945-1958. Mary F. Berry. LC 77-84772. (Contributions in Legal Studies: No. 1). (Illus.). viii, 296p. 1978. text ed. 59.95 (*0-8371-9798-8*, BSS/) Greenwood.

Stability, Stabilization & Control of Delay Large Scale Systems. Liu Yongging & Feng Zhaoshu. Ed. by Ronald V. Book & Du Dingzhu. (Applied Discrete Mathematics & Theoretical Computer Science Ser.). (Illus.). 196p. 1996. text ed. 38.95 (*1-880132-20-6*) Sci Pr NY.

Stability, Structures & Chaos in Nonlinear Synchronization Networks. V. D. Shalfeev et al. (Series on Nonlinear Science: Vol. 6). 260p. 1995. text ed. 59.00 (*981-02-1822-2*) World Scientific Pub.

Stability Techniques for Continuous Linear Systems. Allan M. Krall. x, 150p. 1967. text ed. 156.00 (*0-677-01420-1*) Gordon & Breach.

Stability Testing in the E. C., Japan & the U. S. A. Grimm & Krummen. 1993. 73.00 (*3-8047-1215-0*) CRC Pr.

Stability Theorems in Geometry and Analysis, 304. Iurii G. Reshetniak. LC 94-33303. (Mathematics & Its Applications Ser.). (ENG.). 1994. lib. bdg. 208.00 (*0-7923-3118-4*) Kluwer Ac.

Stability Theory: An Introduction to the Stability of Dynamic Systems & Rigid Bodies. 2nd ed. Horst Leipholz. 359p. 1987. text ed. 119.95 (*0-471-91181-X*) Wiley.

***Stability Theory: Hurwitz Centenary Conference, Centro Stefano Franscini, Ascona, 1995.** Rolf Jeltsch & M. Mansour. LC 96-35956. 1996. 122.95 (*0-8176-5474-7*) Birkhauser.

***Stability Theory: Hurwitz Centenary Conference, Centro Stefano Franscini, Ascona, 1995, Vol. 121.** Ed. by Rolf Jeltsch & M. Mansour. LC 96-35956. (International Series of Numerical Mathematics). 264p. 1996. 122.95 (*3-7643-5474-7*) Birkhauser.

Stability Theory & Existence of Periodic Solutions & Almost Periodic Solutions. T. Yoshizawa. LC 74-28140. (Applied Mathematical Sciences Ser.: Vol. 14). vii, 233p. 1975. 31.95 (*0-387-90112-4*) Spr-Verlag.

Stability Theory & Related Topics in Dynamical Systems. Ed. by K. Shiraiwa & G. Ikegami. (Advanced Series in Dynamical Systems: Vol. 6). 192p. (C). 1989. text ed. 81.00 (*9971-5-0904-0*) World Scientific Pub.

***Stability Theory of Elastic Rods.** T. M. Atanackovic. (Series on Stability Vibration & Control of Systems). 400p. 1997. 68.00 (*981-02-3054-0*) World Scientific Pub.

Stability Theory of Stream Ciphers. C. S. Ding et al. Ed. by G. Goos & J. Hartmanis. (Lecture Notes in Computer Science Ser.: Vol. 561). ix, 187p. 1991. 31.00 (*0-387-54973-0*) Spr-Verlag.

Stability under Seismic Loading. Ed. by Franklin Y. Cheng. (Sessions Proceedings Ser.). 80p. 1986. 13.00 (*0-87262-556-7*) Am Soc Civil Eng.

Stability, Vibration, & Control of Structures, Vol. I. A. Guran & Daniel J. Inman. 324p. 1995. text ed. 81.00 (*981-02-2981-X*) World Scientific Pub.

Stability, Vibration, & Control of Structures, Vol. II. A. Guran & Daniel J. Inman. 300p. 1997. text ed. 147.00 (*981-02-2982-8*) World Scientific Pub.

***Stabilization - Solidification.** Paul Kalb et al. Ed. by William C. Anderson. (Innovative Site Remediation Technology Ser.: Vol. 4). (Illus.). 200p. 1997. 70.00 (*1-883767-20-2*) Am Acad Environ.

Stabilization & Adjustment. 164p. 1991. 19.50 (*92-1-126021-3*, 91.III.B.3) UN.

***Stabilization & Degradation of Polymers.** Ed. by David L. Allara & Walter L. Hawkins. LC 78-10600. (Advances in Chemistry Ser.: Vol. 169). 455p. 1978. reprint ed. pap. 129.70 (*0-608-03866-0*, 2064313) Bks Demand.

Stabilization & Growth in Developing Countries: A Structuralist Approach, Vol. 29. L. Taylor. 98, viiip. 1989. pap. text ed. 43.00 (*3-7186-4871-7*) Gordon & Breach.

Stabilization & Growth in the EC Periphery. John Bradley et al. (Study of the Irish Economy Ser.). 210p. 1993. 59. 95 (*1-85628-539-1*, Pub. by Avebury Pub UK) Ashgate Pub Co.

Stabilization & Privatization in Poland: An Economic Evaluation of the Shock Therapy Program. Kazimierz A. Poznanski. LC 93-885. 1993. lib. bdg. 114.50 (*0-7923-9341-4*) Kluwer Ac.

Stabilization & Solidification of Hazardous, Radioactive, & Mixed Wastes: 2nd Volume. Ed. by T. Michael Gilliam & W. C. Wiles. (Special Technical Publication Ser.: No. 1123). (Illus.). 520p. 1992. text ed. 69.00 (*0-8031-1443-5*, 04-011230-16) ASTM.

Stabilization & Structural Adjustment: Macroeconomic Frameworks for Analysing the Crisis in Sub-Saharan Africa. Finn Tarp. 256p. (C). (gr. 13). 1992. text ed. 110.00 (*0-415-08179-3*, B0146) Routledge.

Stabilization & Structural Adjustment: Macroeconomic Frameworks for Analyzing the Crisis in Sub-Saharan Africa. Finn Tarp. 232p. (C). 1994. pap. 18.95 (*0-415-08180-7*, B4694) Routledge.

Stabilization & Structural Adjustment in Poland. Ed. by Henryk Kierzkowski et al. LC 93-16560. 288p. (C). (gr. 13). 1993. text ed. 74.95 (*0-415-10024-0*) Routledge.

Stabilization & Structural Reform in the Czech & Slovak Federal Republic: First Stage. Bijan B. Aghevli et al. LC 92-7788. (Occasional Paper Ser.: No. 92). vi, 46p. 1992. pap. 15.00 (*1-55775-226-5*) Intl Monetary.

Stabilization, Debt & Reform: Policy Analysis for Developing Countries. Rudiger Fornbusch. 407p. (C). 1993. text ed. 63.00 (*0-13-097395-5*) P-H.

Stabilization of Arsenic Wastes. Max Taylor & Robert Fuessle. (Illus.). 120p. (Orig.). (C). 1995. pap. text ed. 35.00 (*0-7881-1947-8*) DIANE Pub.

Stabilization of Business. Ed. by Lionel D. Edie. LC 73-2503. (Big Business; Economic Power in a Free Society Ser.). 1973. reprint ed. 29.95 (*0-405-05085-2*) Ayer.

Stabilization of Colloidal Dispersions by Polymer Adsorption. Tatsuo Sato & Richard Ruch. LC 80-15650. (Surfactant Science Ser.: No. 9). 171p. reprint ed. pap. 48.80 (*0-7837-5177-X*, 2044907) Bks Demand.

Stabilization of Control Systems, Vol. 20. O. Hijab. (Applications of Mathematics Ser.). (Illus.). 160p. 1986. 71.95 (*0-387-96384-7*) Spr-Verlag.

Stabilization of Flexible Structures: Proceedings of the Comcon Workshop, Montpellier, France, December 1987. Ed. by A. V. Balakrishnan & J. P. Zolesio. LC 88-34517. (Comcon Conferences Proceedings Ser.). 320p. (Orig.). 1988. pap. text ed. 90.00 (*0-911575-37-5*) Optimization Soft.

Stabilization of Flexible Structures: Third Working Conference Montpellier, France, January 1989. Ed. by J. P. Zolesio et al. (Lecture Notes in Control & Information Sciences Ser.: Vol. 147). (Illus.). 367p. 1991. 72.95 (*0-387-53161-0*) Spr-Verlag.

Stabilization of International Commodity Markets. Paul Hallwood. Ed. by Edward I. Altman & Ingo Walter. LC 77-7793. (Contemporary Studies in Economic & Financial Analysis: Vol. 18). 230p. 1979. 73.25 (*0-89232-086-9*) Jai Pr.

***Stabilization of Linear Systems.** V. Dragan & A. Halanay. (Systems & Control Ser.). 250p. 1997. 64.50 (*0-8176-3970-5*) Birkhauser.

Stabilization of Pavement Subgrades & Base Courses with Lime. NLA (Potter) Staff. 256p. 1995. 39.95 (*0-8403-9632-5*) Kendall-Hunt.

Stabilization of the Mark. Hjalmar H. Schacht. Ed. by Mira Wilkins. LC 78-3946. (International Finance Ser.). 1979. reprint ed. lib. bdg. 24.95 (*0-405-11246-7*) Ayer.

Stabilization Policy in an Exchange Rate Union: Transmission, Coordination & Influence on the Union Cohesion. V. De Bonis. 172p. 1994. 61.95 (*3-7908-0789-3*) Spr-Verlag.

Stabilization/Solidification. W. C. Anderson. (Innovative Site Remediation Technology Ser.: Vol. 4). 146p. 1995. 75.95 (*3-540-59064-1*) Spr-Verlag.

Stabilization Solidification of Hazardous, No. 1240. Ed. by T. Michael Gilliam & Carlton C. Wiles. (Special Technical Publication Ser.). (Illus.). 730p. 1996. text ed. 89.00 (*0-8031-2020-6*) ASTM.

***Stabilization/Solidification: Design & Application.** Paul Kalb et al. (Innovative Site Remediation Technology: Vol. 4). (Illus.). 180p. 1997. write for info. (*0-614-30717-1*) Am Acad Environ.

Stabilized Accounting. Henry W. Sweeney. Ed. by Richard P. Brief. LC 77-87288. (Development of Contemporary Accounting Thought Ser.). 1978. reprint ed. lib. bdg. 37. 95 (*0-405-10916-4*) Ayer.

Stabilizing Cardiocervical Operations, Calcium Antagonists in SAH: Current Legal Issues. Ed. by K. A. Bushe et al. (Advances in Neurosurgery Ser.: Vol. 18). (Illus.). 384p. 1990. pap. 86.00 (*0-387-51967-X*) Spr-Verlag.

Stabilizing Dynamics: Constructing Economic Knowledge. E. Roy Weintraub. (Historical Perspectives on Modern Economics Ser.). 176p. (C). 1991. text ed. 20.95 (*0-521-39346-9*) Cambridge U Pr.

Stabilizing Effects of Government Employment. Walter Ebanks. (Explorations in Economic Research Three Ser.: No. 4). 20p. 1976. reprint ed. 35.00 (*0-685-61406-9*) Natl Bur Econ Res.

Stabilizing Fragile Democractics: New Party Systems in Southern & Eastern Europe. Geoffrey Pridham & Paul Lewis. LC 95-25092. 272p. 1995. text ed. 62.95 (*0-415-11802-6*) Routledge.

Stabilizing Fragile Democractics: New Party Systems in Southern & Eastern Europe. Geoffrey Pridham & Paul Lewis. LC 95-25092. 272p. (C). 1995. pap. 22.95 (*0-415-11803-4*) Routledge.

Stabilizing Speculative Commodity Markets. Shyamal K. Ghosh et al. (Illus.). 452p. 1987. 98.00 (*0-19-828472-1*) OUP.

Stabilizing the Workforce: A Complete Guide to Controlling Turnover. James E. Gardner. LC 86-9394. 200p. 1986. text ed. 55.00 (*0-89930-167-3*, GSZ/, Quorum Bks) Greenwood.

Stable & Barn Fixtures. Ed. by J. W. Fiske Iron Works, NYC Staff. 182p. 1987. reprint ed. 50.00 (*0-938290-07-X*) Apollo.

Stable Carbocation Chemistry. Ed. by Paul V. Schleyer & G. K. Praskash. LC 95-33695. 420p. 1996. text ed. 79.95 (*0-471-59462-8*, Wiley-Interscience) Wiley.

Stable Cat. Garrison Allen. 304p. 1996. 18.95 (*1-57566-042-3*) Kensgtn Pub Corp.

***Stable Cat.** Garrison Allen. 304p. 1997. mass mkt. 5.50 (*1-57566-188-8*, Knsington) Kensgtn Pub Corp.

Stable Colloidal Dispersions of Copper. Clarkson College of Technology Staff. 73p. 1972. 10.95 (*0-317-34547-8*, 174) Intl Copper.

Stable External Currency for Europe. Jacques Riboud. Tr. by Stephen Harrison. 190p. 1991. text ed. 69.95 (*0-312-05363-0*) St Martin.

Stable Farewell. Bonnie Bryant. (The Saddle Club Ser.: Vol. 49). 144p. (J). (gr. 3-7). 1995. pap. 3.50 (*0-553-48267-X*, Skylark BDD) BDD Bks Young Read.

Stable Fixation of the Hand & Wrist. A. E. Freeland et al. (Illus.). 295p. 1986. 155.00 (*0-387-96300-6*) Spr-Verlag.

Stable for Nightmares or Weird Tales: Anthology. Joseph S. Le Fanu. LC 75-46286. (Supernatural & Occult Fiction Ser.). (Illus.). 1976. reprint ed. lib. bdg. 23.95 (*0-405-08147-2*) Ayer.

Stable Groom. Bonnie Bryant. (Saddle Club Ser.: No. 45). 144p. (J). (gr. 4-7). 1995. pap. 3.99 (*0-553-48263-7*) Bantam.

***Stable Groups.** F. Wagner. (London Mathematical Society Lecture Note Ser.: Vol. 240). 300p. (C). 1997. pap. text ed. 39.95 (*0-521-59839-7*) Cambridge U Pr.

***Stable Hearts.** Bonnie Bryant. (The Saddle Club Ser.: No. 63). 144p. (J). 1997. pap. 3.99 (*0-553-48418-4*, Skylark BDD) BDD Bks Young Read.

Stable Homotopy & Generalised Homology. J. Frank Adams. (Chicago Lectures in Mathematics). 384p. 1974. pap. text ed. 30.00 (*0-226-00524-0*) U Ch Pr.

Stable Homotopy Groups of Spheres: A Computer-Assisted Approach. S. D. Kochman. Ed. by A. Dold et al. (Lecture Notes in Mathematics Ser.: Vol. 1423). viii, 330p. 1990. 48.95 (*0-387-52468-1*) Spr-Verlag.

Stable in Bethlehem: A Christmas Counting Story. (First Little Golden Bks.). (Illus.). 24p. (J). 1995. bds. 1.09 (*0-307-80125-X*, Golden Pr) Western Pub.

Stable Internal Fixation in Maxillofacial Bone Surgery. R. R. Schmoker. (Illus.). 105p. 1986. 65.00 (*0-387-13593-6*) Spr-Verlag.

Stable Isotope Geochemistry. 3rd enl. rev. ed. Jochen Hoefs. (Minerals & Rocks Ser.: Vol. 9). (Illus.). 240p. 1995. 70.00 (*0-387-17341-2*) Spr-Verlag.

***Stable Isotope Geochemistry.** 4th enl. rev. ed. Jochen Hoefs. LC 96-31362. (Illus.). 232p. 1996. 59.95 (*3-540-61126-6*) Spr-Verlag.

Stable Isotope Geochemistry: A Tribute to Samuel Epstein. H. P. Taylor, Jr. et al. LC 91-76040. (Special Publication: No. 3). 550p. 1991. 65.00 (*0-941809-02-1*) Geochemical Soc.

Stable Isotope Pharmaceuticals for Clinical Research & Diagnosis, Vol. 18: Drug Development & Evaluation. Peter Krumbiegel. (Illus.). 210p. (Orig.). 1992. pap. 62. 00 (*1-56081-327-X*) G F Verlag.

Stable Isotopes: Natural & Anthropogenic Sulphur in the Environment. Ed. by H. R. Krouse & V. A. Grinenko. (Scientific Committee on Problems of the Environment Ser.: No. 43). 440p. 1991. text ed. 285.00 (*0-471-92646-9*) Wiley.

***Stable Isotopes: The Integration of Biological, Ecological & Geological Processes.** Ed. by H. Griffiths et al. (Environmental Planning Ser.). (Illus.). 448p. 1997. 120. 00 (*1-85996-135-5*, Pub. by Bios Scientific UK) Bks Intl VA.

S

Stable Isotopes & Plant Carbon - Water Relations. Ed. by James R. Ehleringer et al. LC 93-1090. (Physiological Ecology Ser.). (Illus.). 555p. 1993. text ed. 99.00 (*0-12-233380-2*) Acad Pr.

Stable Isotopes in Ecological Research. Ed. by P. W. Rundekl et al. (Ecological Studies: Vol. 68). (Illus.). 545p. 1988. 108.00 (*0-387-96712-5*) Spr-Verlag.

Stable Isotopes in Ecology and Environmental Science. K. Lajtha & R. Michener. (Illus.). 250p. 1994. 39.95 (*0-632-03154-9*) Blackwell Sci.

Stable Isotopes in High Temperature Geological Processes. Ed. by H. P. Taylor, Jr. et al. (Reviews in Mineralogy Ser.: Vol. 16). 570p. 1986. per. 24.00 (*0-939950-20-0*) Mineralogical Soc.

Stable Isotopes in Human Nutrition Studies. Ed. by Fred Mellon & Brittmarie Sanstrom. (Food Science & Technology International Ser.). (Illus.). 172p. 1996. text ed. 56.00 (*0-12-490540-4*) Acad Pr.

Stable Isotopes in Nutrition. Judith R. Turnlund & Phyllis E. Johnson. LC 84-12430. (Symposium Ser.: No. 258). 240p. 1984. 43.95 (*0-8412-0855-7*) Am Chemical.

***Stable Isotopes in Nutrition.** Ed. by Judith R. Turnlund & Phyllis E. Johnson. LC 84-12430. (ACS Symposium Ser.: No. 258). (Illus.). 239p. 1984. reprint ed. pap. 68.20 (*0-608-03139-9*, 2063592) Bks Demand.

Stable Isotopes in Plant Nutrition, Soil Fertility & Environmental Studies. IAEA Staff. 670p. 1991. pap. 200.00 (*92-0-010391-X*, STI/PUB/845, Pub. by IAEA AU) Bernan Associates.

Stable Isotopes in Sedimentary Geology. Michael A. Arthur. (Society of Economic Paleontologists & Mineralogists, Special Publication Ser.: No. 10). (Illus.). 458p. reprint ed. pap. 130.60 (*0-317-58124-4*, 2029676) Bks Demand.

Stable Isotopes in the Life Sciences. (Panel Proceedings Ser.). 456p. 1977. pap. 105.00 (*92-0-011077-0*, ISP442, Pub. by IAEA AU) Bernan Associates.

Stable Management for the Owner-Groom. George Wheatly. 1977. pap. 7.00 (*0-87980-258-8*) Wilshire.

Stable Manners. Bonnie Bryant. (Saddle Club Ser.: No. 28). 144p. (J). (gr. 4-6). 1993. pap. 3.50 (*0-553-48075-8*) Bantam.

Stable Mappings & Their Singularities: Second Corrected Printing. Martin Golubitsky & V. W. Guillemin. (Graduate Texts in Mathematics Ser.: Vol. 14). (Illus.). 209p. (C). 1986. 59.95 (*0-387-90072-1*) Spr-Verlag.

***Stable Marriage & Its Relation to Other Combinatorial Problems: An Introduction to the Mathematical Analysis of Algorithms.** Donald E. Knuth. LC 96-27510. (CRM Proceedings & Lecture Notes Ser.: Vol. 10). 1996. 19.00 (*0-8218-0603-3*, CRMP/10) Am Math.

Stable Marriage Problem: Structure & Algorithms. Dan Gusfield & Robert W. Irving. (Foundations of Computing Ser.). 150p. 1989. 34.00 (*0-262-07118-5*) MIT Pr.

Stable Module Theory. M. Auslander & M. Bridger. LC 52-42839. (Memoirs Ser.: No. 1/94). 146p. 1969. pap. 17. 00 (*0-8218-1294-7*, MEMO/1/94) Am Math.

Stable Money. W. E. Turner. 1979. lib. bdg. 59.95 (*0-8490-3008-0*) Gordon Pr.

Stable Networks & Product Graphs. Tomas Feder. LC 95-15926. (Memoirs Ser.: No. 555). 223p. 1995. pap. 45.00 (*0-8218-0347-6*, MEMO/116/555) Am Math.

Stable Non-Gaussian Random Processes: Stochastic Models With Infinite Variance. Gennady Samorodnitsky & Murad S. Taqqu. LC 94-13685. (Stochastic Modeling Ser.). 632p. (gr. 13). 1994. text ed. 66.95 (*0-412-05171-0*) Chapman & Hall.

Stable Processes & Related Topics: A Selection of Papers from the Mathematical Sciences Institute Workshop, January 9-13, 1990. Ed. by Stamatis Cambanis et al. (Progress in Probability Ser.: Vol. 25). 330p. 1991. 86.50 (*0-8176-3485-1*) Spr-Verlag.

Stable Radicals. Anatolii L. Buchachenko. Tr. by C. Nigel Turton & Tatiana I. Turton from RUS. LC 65-900. (Illus.). 188p. reprint ed. pap. 53.60 (*0-317-09364-9*, 2020670) Bks Demand.

Stable Relationship. Sandi Haddad. 192p. 1994. 17.95 (*0-8034-9053-4*) Bouregy.

Stable Where Jesus Was Born. Greene. 1998. 17.00 (*0-689-81258-2*) S&S Childrens.

Stable Witch. Bonnie Bryant. (Saddle Club Ser.: No. 41). 144p. (J). (gr. 4-7). 1995. mass mkt. 3.99 (*0-553-48259-9*) Bantam.

Stable Yard. British Horse Society Staff. (British Horse Society Manual of Stable Management Ser.: Bk. 6). (Illus.). 128p. 1989. pap. 15.95 (*1-872082-28-9*) Half Halt Pr.

***StableMotion: A Progressive Home Exercise Program.** Beth J. Dana. LC 96-90970. (Illus.). iv, 75p. 1996. spiral bd. 18.95 (*0-9655783-0-5*) TheraTool.

Stables & Shelters Sheds & Shelters. Toni Webber. (Threshold Picture Guides Ser.). (Illus.). 24p. (Orig.). 1989. pap. 12.00 (*1-872082-68-8*, Pub. by Kenilworth Pr UK) Half Halt Pr.

Stables & Stable Blocks. Christopher Powell. 1989. pap. 25.00 (*0-7478-0105-3*, Pub. by Shire UK) St Mut.

Stably Stratified Flows: Flows & Dispersion over Topography. Ed. by I. P. Castro & N. J. Rockliffe. 372p. 1994. 95.00 (*0-19-853698-4*) OUP.

***Stacey & Cheerleaders.** Ann M. Martin. (Baby-Sitters Club Ser.). (J). 1997. pap. text ed. 3.99 (*0-590-92601-2*) Scholastic Inc.

Stacey & Mystery, Vol. 1. Martin. 1994. 7.98 (*1-57042-143-9*) Warner Bks.

Stacey & the Bad Girls. Ann M. Martin. (Baby-Sitters Club Ser.: No. 87). 192p. (J). (gr. 4-6). 1995. pap. 3.50 (*0-590-48237-8*) Scholastic Inc.

Stacey & the Cheerleaders. Ann M. Martin. (Baby-Sitters Club Ser.: No. 70). 192p. (J). (gr. 4-6). 1993. pap. 3.50 (*0-590-47008-6*) Scholastic Inc.

***Stacey & the Fashion Victim.** Ann M. Martin. (Baby-Sitters Club Mystery Ser.: No. 29). (J). (gr. 4-7). 1997. pap. 3.99 (*0-590-69177-5*, 691540) Scholastic Inc.

Stacey & the Haunted Masquerade. Ann M. Martin. (Baby-Sitters Club Mystery Ser.: No. 22). 176p. (gr. 4-6). 1995. pap. text ed. 3.50 (*0-590-22866-8*) Scholastic Inc.

Stacey & the Missing Ring. Ann M. Martin. (Baby-Sitters Club Mystery Ser.: No. 1). 176p. (J). (gr. 4-6). 1991. pap. 3.99 (*0-590-44084-5*) Scholastic Inc.

Stacey & the Mystery at the Empty House. Ann M. Martin. (Baby-Sitters Club Mystery Ser.: No. 18). 176p. (J). (gr. 4-6). 1994. pap. 3.50 (*0-590-48233-5*) Scholastic Inc.

Stacey & the Mystery at the Mall. Ann M. Martin. (Baby-Sitters Club Mystery Ser.: No. 14). 176p. (J). (gr. 4-6). 1994. pap. 3.99 (*0-590-47052-3*) Scholastic Inc.

Stacey & the Mystery Money. Ann M. Martin. (Baby-Sitters Club Ser.: No. 10). 176p. (J). (gr. 4-6). 1993. pap. 3.50 (*0-590-45696-2*) Scholastic Inc.

Stacey & the Mystery of Stoneybrook. Ann M. Martin. (Baby-Sitters Club Ser.: No. 35). 192p. (J). (gr. 4-6). 1990. pap. 3.50 (*0-590-42508-0*) Scholastic Inc.

Stacey & the Mystery of Stoneybrook, Vol. 35. large type ed. Ann M. Martin. LC 95-21213. (Baby-Sitters Club Ser.: Vol. 35). 144p. (J). (gr. 4 up). 1995. lib. bdg. 15.93 (*0-8368-1415-0*) Gareth Stevens Inc.

Stacey McGill, Super Sitter. Ann M. Martin. (Baby-Sitters Club Mystery Ser.: Vol. 94). (J). 1996. pap. text ed. 3.99 (*0-590-22878-1*) Scholastic Inc.

Stacey vs. the BSC. Ann M. Martin. (Baby-Sitters Club Ser.: No. 83). 192p. (J). (gr. 4-6). 1995. pap. 3.99 (*0-590-48235-1*) Scholastic Inc.

Stacey's Big Crush. Ann M. Martin. (Baby-Sitters Club Ser.: No. 65). 192p. (J). (gr. 4-6). 1993. pap. 3.50 (*0-590-45667-9*) Scholastic Inc.

Stacey's Book. Ann M. Martin. (Baby-Sitters Club Portrait Collection). 160p. (J). (gr. 4-6). 1994. pap. 3.50 (*0-590-48399-4*) Scholastic Inc.

Stacey's Choice. Ann M. Martin. (Baby-Sitters Club Ser.: No. 58). 192p. (J). (gr. 4-6). 1992. 3.50 (*0-590-45659-8*) Scholastic Inc.

***Stacey's Choice, Vol. 58.** Ann M. Martin. (Baby Sitter's Club Ser.). 1997. pap. text ed. 3.50 (*0-590-92584-9*) Scholastic Inc.

Stacey's Emergency. Ann M. Martin. LC 96-17010. (Baby-Sitters Club Ser.: Vol. 43). (J). 1996. lib. bdg. 15.93 (*0-8368-1567-X*) Gareth Stevens Inc.

Stacey's Emergency. Ann M. Martin. (Baby-Sitters Club Ser.: No. 43). 192p. (J). (gr. 4-6). 1991. pap. 3.50 (*0-590-43572-8*) Scholastic Inc.

***Stacey's Emergency, Vol. 43.** Ann M. Martin. (Baby-Sitters Club Mystery Ser.). 1991. pap. 3.99 (*0-590-74243-4*) Scholastic Inc.

Stacey's Ex-Best Friend. Ann M. Martin. (Baby-Sitters Club Ser.: No. 51). 192p. (J). (gr. 4-6). 1992. pap. 3.50 (*0-590-44968-0*) Scholastic Inc.

Stacey's Lie. Ann M. Martin. (Baby-Sitters Club Ser.: No. 76). 192p. (J). (gr. 4-6). 1994. pap. 3.50 (*0-590-47014-0*) Scholastic Inc.

Stacey's Mistake. Ann M. Martin. 192p. (J). (gr. 4-6). 1988. pap. 3.99 (*0-590-43718-6*) Scholastic Inc.

Stacey's Mistake. Ann M. Martin. (Baby-Sitters Club Ser.: No. 18). (J). (gr. 4-7). 1996. pap. text ed. 3.99 (*0-590-60534-8*) Scholastic Inc.

Stacey's Mistake. large type ed. Ann M. Martin. LC 93-8086. (Baby-Sitters Club Ser.: Vol. 18). 176p. (J). (gr. 4 up). 1993. lib. bdg. 15.93 (*0-8368-1022-8*) Gareth Stevens Inc.

***Stacey's Secret Friend, Vol. 111.** Ann M. Martin. (Baby-Sitters Club Ser.). (J). 1997. pap. text ed. 3.99 (*0-590-05989-0*) Scholastic Inc.

Stacey's Story. Robert L. Perea. 70p. (Orig.). 1995. pap. 8.95 (*0-931122-80-5*) West End.

Stacions of Rome. F. J. Furnivall. (EETS, OS Ser.: No. 25). 1974. reprint ed. 30.00 (*0-527-00025-6*) Periodicals Srv.

Stack A. Dollar. Denver Warbash. 224p. (Orig.). 1985. mass mkt. 2.50 (*0-87067-264-9*) Holloway.

***Stack the Deck.** Robert B. Cahill & Herbert J. Hrebic. (Writing Program Ser.). (YA). (gr. 9-12). 1973. pap. 14.95 (*0-933282-26-5*) Stack the Deck.

Stack the Deck. Robert B. Cahill & Herbert J. Hrebic. (Writing Program Ser.). (YA). (gr. 9-12). 1973. text ed. 9.00 (*0-933282-11-7*); pap. text ed. 10.95 (*0-933282-25-7*) Stack the Deck.

Stack the Deck. rev. ed. Robert B. Cahill & Herbert J. Hrebic. (Illus.). 1980. reprint ed. pap. 6.00 (*0-933282-00-1*) Stack the Deck.

Stackelberg Differential Games in Economic Models. Amiya K. Bagchi. (Lecture Notes in Control & Information Sciences Ser.: Vol. 64). viii, 203p. 1984. pap. 27.00 (*0-387-13587-1*) Spr-Verlag.

Stacker: An Illustrated Tutorial. 2nd ed. Dan Gookin. LC 92-44682. 1993. pap. 19.95 (*0-8306-4487-3*, Windcrest) TAB Bks.

Stacker Multimedia. Stuart J. Stuple. 1995. pap. text ed. 19.95 (*0-7615-0093-6*) Prima Pub.

Stacker(TM) An Illustrated Tutorial. Dan Gookin. LC 92-10428. 176p. 1992. pap. 19.95 (*0-8306-4213-7*, 4268, Windcrest) TAB Bks.

Stacking the Deck: A Social Skills Game for Adults with Developmental Disabilities. Richard M. Foxx & Martin J. McMorrow. (Orig.). (C). 1983. pap. text ed. 19.95 (*0-87822-231-6*, 2316) Res Press.

Stacking Wood. Photos by Mimi Lipton & Thorsten Dueser. LC 92-62137. (Illus.). 124p. 1993. pap. 19.95 (*0-500-97407-1*) Thames Hudson.

Stackpole's History of Winthrop, Maine, with Genealogical Notes. David C. Young & Elizabeth K. Young. (Illus.). 993p. (Orig.). 1994. pap. text ed. 57.00 (*1-55613-991-8*) Heritage Bk.

Stacs 86. Ed. by B. Monien & G. Vidal-Naquet. (Lecture Notes in Computer Science Ser.: Vol. 210). ix, 368p. 1986. pap. 42.00 (*0-387-16078-7*) Spr-Verlag.

STACS 88. Ed. by R. Cori & M. Wirsing. (Lecture Notes in Computer Science Ser.: Vol. 294). ix, 404p. 1988. 46.00 (*0-387-18834-7*) Spr-Verlag.

STACS, 89. Ed. by B. Monien & R. Cori. (Lecture Notes in Computer Science Ser.: Vol. 349). 544p. 1989. 54.00 (*0-387-50840-6*) Spr-Verlag.

STACS, '91: Proceedings of the 8th Annual Symposium on Theoretical Aspects of Computer Science Hamburg, Germany, February 14-16, 1991, Vol. 480. Ed. by C. Choffrut & M. Jantzen. (Lecture Notes in Computer Science Ser.). x, 549p. 1991. 64.00 (*0-387-53709-0*) Spr-Verlag.

STACS 92: Ninth Annual Symposium on Theoretical Aspects of Computer Science Cachan, France, February 13-15, 1992 Proceedings. Ed. by A. Finkel et al. (Lecture Notes in Computer Science Ser.: Vol. 577). xiv, 621p. 1992. 90.95 (*0-387-55210-3*) Spr-Verlag.

STACS '93: Tenth Annual Symposium on Theoretical Aspects of Computer Science, Wurzburg, Germany, February 25-27, 1993 Proceedings, Vol. 665. Ed. by P. Enjalbert et al. (Lecture Notes in Computer Science Ser.). xiv, 274p. 1993. 102.95 (*0-387-56503-5*) Spr-Verlag.

STACS 94: Eleventh Annual Symposium on Theoretical Aspects of Computer Science, Caen, France, February 24-26, 1994 Proceedings. Ed. by Ernst W. Mayr et al. LC 94-2919. (Lecture Notes in Computer Science Ser.: Vol. 775). xiv, 782p. 1994. 108.95 (*0-387-57785-8*) Spr-Verlag.

STACS 95: Proceedings of the Twelfth Annual Symposium on Theoretical Aspects of Computer Science, Held in Munich, Germany, March 2-4, 1995. Symposium on Theoretical Aspects of Computer Science Staff et al. LC 95-2779. (Lecture Notes in Computer Science Ser.: Vol. 900). 1995. 100.00 (*0-387-59042-0*) Spr-Verlag.

STACS 95: Proceedings of the Twelfth Annual Symposium on Theoretical Aspects of Computer Science, Held in Munich, Germany, March 2-4, 1995. Symposium on Theoretical Aspects of Computer Science Staff et al. LC 95-2779. (Lecture Notes in Computer Science Ser.: Vol. 900). 1995. 100.00 (*3-540-59042-0*) Spr-Verlag.

STACS 96: 13th Annual Symposium on Theoretical Aspects of Computer Science, Grenoble, France, February 22-24, 1996: Proceedings. Ed. by Claude Puech & Rudiger Reischuk. LC 96-6926. (Lecture Notes in Computer Science Ser.: Vol. 1046). xii, 690p. 1996. pap. 106.00 (*3-540-60922-9*) Spr-Verlag.

***STACS 97 Vol. 120: 14th Annual Symposium on Theoretical Aspects of Computer Science, Lubeck, Germany, February-March 1997: Proceedings.** R. Udiger Reischuk & Michel Morvan. LC 97-7674. (Lecture Notes in Computer Science Ser.). 1997. 91.00 (*3-540-62616-6*) Spr-Verlag.

STACS, '99, Vol. 415. Ed. by C. Choffrut & Thomas Lengauer. (Lecture Notes in Computer Science Ser.). vi, 312p. 1990. 38.00 (*0-387-52282-4*) Spr-Verlag.

Stacy Had a Little Sister: A Concept Book. Wendie Old. Ed. by Christy Grant. (Illus.). 32p. (J). (ps-3). 1994. lib. bdg. 14.95 (*0-8075-7598-4*) A Whitman.

Stacy Says Good-Bye. Patricia R. Giff. (New Kids at the Polk Street School Ser.). (Illus.). 80p. (J). (gr. k-3). 1989. mass mkt. 3.99 (*0-440-40135-6*, YB BDD) BDD Bks Young Read.

Stadelhofen Train Station, Zurich. Santiago Calatrava. (Opus Ser.). (Illus.). 72p. 1993. 45.00 (*3-8030-2710-1*, Pub. by Ernst Wasmuth GW) Dist Art Pubs.

Stadia: A Design & Development Guide. Geraint John & Rod Sheard. LC 94-3608. (Illus.). 128p. 1995. 69.95 (*0-7506-1854-X*, Butterwrth Archit) Buttrwrth-Heinemann.

***Stadia: A Design & Development Guide.** 2nd ed. Geraint John & Rod Sheard. LC 96-52384. 260p. 1997. pap. 39.95 (*0-7506-3217-8*) Buttrwrth-Heinemann.

Stadium: Microcomputer Word Processing Program. D. Gioffre. 272p. 1987. pap. text ed. 9.32 (*0-07-023328-4*) McGraw.

Stadt. Meyers K. Kinderbibliothek. 24p. (GER.). (J). 1994. 13.25 (*3-411-08691-2*) Langenscheidt.

Stadt des Glaubens. Franz D. Lucas & Margret Heitmann. (Wissenschaftliche Abhandlungen des Salomon Ludwig Steinheim-Instituts fur Deutsch-Judische Geschichte Ser.: Bd. 3). viii, 583p. (GER.). 1992. write for info. (*3-487-09495-9*) G Olms Pubs.

Stadt Des Schwarz: Eighteen Photographs of Berlin. limited ed. Photos by John Gossage. (Illus.). 24p. 1987. 130.00 (*0-614-06482-1*) RAM Publications.

Stadt Im Spiegel der Descriptiones und Laudes Urbium in der Antiken und Mittelalterlichen Literatur. Carl J. Classen. (Beitrage Zur Altertumswissenschaft Ser.: Band 2). 131p. (GER.). 1986. 20.00 (*3-487-07060-X*) G Olms Pubs.

Stadt und Eidgenossenschaft im Alten Testament: Eine Auseinandersetzung mit Max Webers Studie "Das Antike Judentum" Christa Schaefer-Lichtenberger. 485p. (GER.). 1983. 97.70 (*3-11-008591-7*) De Gruyter.

Stadte Kleinasiens im 7. und 8. Jahrlundert. Wolfram Brandes. 244p. 1989. pap. 64.00 (*90-5063-012-X*, Pub. by Gieben NE) Benjamins North Am.

Stadte-Villes-Towns see Glossarium Artis, a Specialized & Systematic Dictionary

Stadtlexikon Dresden von A-Z. Folke Stimmer & Rainer Tittmann. 640p. 1994. text ed. 74.00 (*3-364-00304-1*) Gordon & Breach.

Stadtmauer von Resafa in Syrien. Walter Karnapp. (Denkmaeler Antiker Architektur Ser.: Vol. 11). (Illus.). (C). 1976. 150.00 (*3-11-006535-5*) De Gruyter.

Stadtrechtsbuch von Sillein: Einleitung Edition und Glossar. Ilpo T. Piirainen. (Quellen und Forschungen zur Sprach und Kulturgeschichte der Germanischen Voelker Ser.: No. 46). (C). 1972. 109.25 (*3-11-003543-X*) De Gruyter.

Staedt Suedamerikas, Pt. 2: Die Urbanen Zentren und Ihre Regionen. H. Wilhelmy & A. Borsdorf. (Urbanisierung der Erde Ser.: Vol. 3-2). (Illus.). 486p. (GER.). 1985. lib. bdg. 131.00 (*3-443-37004-7*) Lubrecht & Cramer.

Staedte des Suedlichen Afrika. K. G. Scheider. (Urbanisierung der Erde Ser.: Vol. 2). (Illus.). 175p. (GER.). 1983. lib. bdg. 68.60 (*3-443-37001-2*) Lubrecht & Cramer.

Staedte des Tropischen Afrika. W. Manshard. (Urbanisierung der Erde Ser.: Vol. 1). (Illus.). 258p. (GER.). 1977. lib. bdg. 68.60 (*3-443-39070-6*) Lubrecht & Cramer.

Staedte Indonesiens: Staedte und Andere Nich-Landwirtschaftliche Siedlungen, Ihre Entwicklung und Gegenwaertige Stellung in Verwaltung und Wirtschaft. Werner Rutz. (Urbanisierung der Erde Ser.: Vol. 4). (Illus.). 286p. (GER.). 1985. lib. bdg. 72.80 (*3-443-37005-5*) Lubrecht & Cramer.

Staedte Suedamerikas, Teil 1: Wesen und Wandel. H. Wilhelmy & A. Borsdorf. Vol. 3-1. (Illus.). 233p. (GER.). 1984. write for info. (*0-318-70297-5*) Lubrecht & Cramer.

Staefcraeft: Studies in Germanic Linguistics. Selected Papers from the First & Second Symposium on Germanic Linguistics. Ed. by Elmer H. Antonsen & Hans H. Hock. LC 91-24743. (Current Issues in Linguistic Theory Ser.: Vol. 79). viii, 217p. 1991. 56.00 (*1-55619-134-0*) Benjamins North Am.

Staehling Family Tree, 1598-1939. W. E. Staehling. 37p. 1994. reprint ed. pap. 7.00 (*0-8328-4149-8*) Higginson Bk Co.

Staerke see Rohstoffe des Pflanzenreichs

Staerke (Starch) 5th ed. E. Samec & M. Bling. Ed. by C. Von Regel. (Rohstoffe des Pflanzenreichs Ser.: Pt. 6). 192p. (GER.). 1966. pap. text ed. 48.00 (*3-7682-0428-6*, Pub. by Cramer GW) Lubrecht & Cramer.

Staff Analyst. Jack Rudman. (Career Examination Ser.: C-1551). 1994. pap. 34.95 (*0-8373-1551-4*) Nat Learn.

Staff & Student Supervision: A Task-Centered Approach. Dorothy E. Pettes. 1979. 35.00 (*0-317-05776-6*, Pub. by Natl Inst Soc Work) St Mut.

***Staff & the Serpent: Pertinent & Impertinent Observations on the World of Medicine.** Allen B. Weisse. LC 97-5480. 1997. write for info. (*0-8093-2149-1*) S Ill U Pr.

Staff Appraisal: A First Step to Effective Leadership. rev. ed. Gerry Randell et al. 128p. (C). 1984. 48.00 (*0-85292-333-3*, Pub. by IPM Hse UK) St Mut.

Staff Appraisal in Schools & Colleges. Brian Fidler. Ed. by Robert Cooper. 204p. (Orig.). (C). 1987. pap. text ed. write for info. (*0-582-02070-0*) Longman.

Staff Burnout: Job Stress in the Human Services. Cary Cherniss. LC 80-19408. (Sage Studies in Community Mental Health: No. 2). 199p. reprint ed. pap. 56.80 (*0-8357-8486-X*, 2034754) Bks Demand.

Staff Cars. David Fletcher. 1989. pap. 25.00 (*0-7478-0058-8*, Pub. by Shire UK) St Mut.

Staff Development. Howard Bradley. (School Development & the Management of Change Ser.). 224p. 1991. 65.00 (*1-85000-827-2*, Falmer Pr); pap. 27.00 (*1-85000-828-0*, Falmer Pr) Taylor & Francis.

Staff Development: A Humanistic Approach. Russell Dobson et al. LC 80-67254. 175p. 1980. pap. text ed. 19.00 (*0-8191-1131-7*) U Pr of Amer.

Staff Development: A Practical Guide. 2nd ed. LAMA Development Committee Staff. Ed. by Anne G. Lipow & Deborah A. Carver. LC 91-18962. 104p. (C). 1991. pap. text ed. 25.00 (*0-8389-3402-1*) ALA.

Staff Development: How to Assess Staff Needs, Choose Training Models & Plan Development Cycles. Cook Communications Ministries International Staff. (Interlit Imprint Ser.: Vol. 16). (Illus.). 40p. (Orig.). 1996. pap. 5.95 (*1-884752-25-X*, 44313) Cook Min Intl.

Staff Development: The Director of Staff Development in Long Term Care, a 24 Hour Course. Jimmie R. Rankin & Marifi Aquino. (Illus.). 150p. (Orig.). 1995. ring bd. 49.95 (*1-883938-19-8*) Dry Bones Pr.

Staff Development: The Key to School Renewal. Michele A. Woods-Houston et al. 56p. 1990. pap. 16.95 (*1-56602-034-4*) Research Better.

Staff Development & Clinical Intervention in Brain Injury Rehabilitation. Nancy D. Schmidt & Jeanne Fryer. Ed. by Charles J. Durgin et al. 410p. 1993. 74.00 (*0-8342-0359-6*, 20359) Aspen Pub.

Staff Development & Educational Change. Ed. by W. Robert Houston & Roger Panbratz. LC 80-68586. 1980. pap. 6.25 (*0-686-38077-0*) Assn Tchr Ed.

Staff Development Coordinator. Jack Rudman. (Career Examination Ser.: C-2171). 1994. reprint ed. pap. 34.95 (*0-8373-2171-9*) Nat Learn.

Staff Development for Education in the 90s: New Demands, New Realities, New Perspectives. 2nd ed. Ed. by Ann Lieberman & Lynne Miller. (Series on School Reform). 288p. (C). 1991. text ed. 46.00 (*0-8077-3100-5*); pap. text ed. 20.95 (*0-8077-3099-8*) Tchrs Coll.

Staff Development for School Improvement: A Focus on the Teacher. Ed. by Marvin F. Wideen & Ian Andrews. 250p. 1987. 60.00 (*1-85000-171-5*, Falmer Pr); pap. 32.50 (*1-85000-172-3*, Falmer Pr) Taylor & Francis.

Staff Development for the Practitioner: Planning - Procedures - Practices - Assessment. Margaret E. Fitch & O. W. Kopp. (Illus.). 134p. 1990. pap. 23.95 (*0-398-06122-X*) C C Thomas.

Staff Development for the Practitioner: Planning - Procedures - Practices - Assessment. Margaret E. Fitch & O. W. Kopp. (Illus.). 134p. (C). 1990. text ed. 32.95 (*0-398-05661-7*) C C Thomas.

Staff Development for the Psychiatric Nurse. 2nd ed. Anita W. Finkelman. 222p. 1992. ring bd. 59.95 (*0-944132-78-2*) Skidmore Roth Pub.

Staff Development Handbook for Long-Term Care Facilities. 2nd ed. Charlotte Eliopoulos. 109p. 1997. 39.95 (*1-882515-03-X*) Hlth Educ Netwk.

Staff Development HB: An Action Guide for Managers & Supervisors. Peter R. Sheal. 234p. (C). 1993. pap. text ed. 33.95 (*0-89397-380-7*) Nichols Pub.

***Staff Development in Academic Libraries: Present Practice & Future Challenges.** Margaret Oldroyd. 192p. 1996. 60.00 (*1-85604-174-3*, LAP1743, Pub. by Library Association UK) Bernan Associates.

Staff Development in the Secondary School: Management Perspectives. Chris Day & Roger Morre. 320p. 1987. 49.95 (*0-7099-0895-4*, Pub. by Croom Helm UK); pap. 17.00 (*0-7099-4539-6*, Pub. by Croom Helm UK) Routledge Chapman & Hall.

Staff Development in Tomorrow's Finance Industry, 1989. M. Morison et al. 146p. (C). 1990. pap. 125.00 (*0-85297-262-8*, Pub. by Inst Bankers UK) St Mut.

Staff Development Manager: A Guide to Professional Growth. Marjorie K. Bradley et al. 244p. 1990. text ed. 39.95 (*0-205-12795-9*, H27956) Allyn.

Staff Development, Organization Development. fac. ed. Ed. by Betty Dillon-Peterson. LC 80-70653. 157p. 1981. reprint ed. pap. 44.80 (*0-608-01025-1*, 2082501) Bks Demand.

Staff Development Programs: A Guide to Evaluation. Terry W. Mullins. LC 94-21623. (Program Evaluation Guides for Schools Ser.). 112p. 1994. pap. 19.95 (*0-8039-6045-X*) Corwin Pr.

Staff Development Specialist. Jack Rudman. (Career Examination Ser.: C-2489). 1994. pap. 34.95 (*0-8373-2489-0*) Nat Learn.

Staff Development Training Program for Nursing Homes & ACLF's. Alan Meyers. 150p. 1995. wbk. ed. 89.95 (*0-937119-03-2*) Meyers Pub.

Staff Esteem Builders: The Administrator's Bible for Enhancing Self-Esteem. Michele Borba. 336p. 1993. pap. 44.95 (*1-880396-04-1*, JP 9604-1) Jalmar Pr.

Staff Evaluation Phrases: Examples of Commendations & Constructive Suggestions for Thorough Evaluation. Donald R. Wilson. 41p. 1992. lib. bdg. 12.95 (*0-939136-11-2*) School Admin.

Staff for the President: The Executive Office, 1921-1952. Alfred D. Sander. LC 88-21339. (Contributions in Political Science Ser.: No. 229). 404p. 1989. text ed. 65.00 (*0-313-26526-7*, SRJ/, Greenwood Pr) Greenwood.

***Staff Growth Program for Child Care Centers.** Polly Greenberg & Bea Epstein. LC 87-1021. 1987. pap. 35.00 (*0-87491-829-4*) Acrpls Bks CO.

Staff Making & Pivoting. Eugene E. Hall. (Illus.). 48p. 1993. pap. 5.95 (*0-930163-73-7*) Arlington Bk.

Staff Management: Material for Management Training in Agricultural Cooperatives (MATCOM, Vienna) 133p. 1991. 31.50 (*92-2-102939-5*) Intl Labour Office.

Staff Management in Human Services: Behavioral Research & Application. Dennis H. Reid et al. (Illus.). 248p. 1989. pap. 39.95 (*0-398-06343-5*) C C Thomas.

Staff Management in Human Services: Behavioral Research & Application. Dennis H. Reid et al. (Illus.). 248p. (C). 1989. text ed. 59.95 (*0-398-05547-5*) C C Thomas.

Staff Nurse. Jack Rudman. (Career Examination Ser.: C-756). 1994. pap. 23.95 (*0-8373-0756-2*) Nat Learn.

Staff Officers of the Confederate States Army. John M. Carroll. Date not set. pap. 19.95 (*0-8488-0045-1*, J M C & Co); lib. bdg. 29.95 (*0-8488-0008-7*, J M C & Co) Amereon Ltd.

Staff Physician. Jack Rudman. (Career Examination Ser.: C-1493). 1994. pap. 44.95 (*0-8373-1493-3*) Nat Learn.

Staff Reaction to Building Energy Management Systems. J. G. Levermore. 1989. 80.00 (*0-86022-233-0*, Pub. by Build Servs Info Assn UK) St Mut.

Staff Relations in the Civil Service: The Canadian Experience. Saul J. Frankel. LC 63-4271. 344p. reprint ed. pap. 98.10 (*0-317-20715-6*, 2023829) Bks Demand.

Staff Report Readings for Credit Executives. 153p. 1982. 40.00 (*0-939050-35-8*) Credit Res NYS.

***Staff Services Analyst.** Jack Rudman. (Career Examination Ser.: Vol. C-3810). 1997. pap. 34.95 (*0-8373-3810-7*) Nat Learn.

Staff Studies for the World Economic Outlook. International Monetary Fund Staff. (World Economic & Financial Surveys Ser.). xi, 195p. 1986. pap. 15.00 (*0-939934-73-6*) Intl Monetary.

S

An Asterisk (*) at the beginning of an entry indicates that the title is appearing in BIP for the first time.

Staff Studies for the World Economic Outlook. International Monetary Fund Staff. (World Economic & Financial Surveys Ser.). 195p. 1987. pap. 15.00 (0-939934-86-8) Intl Monetary.

Staff Studies for the World Economic Outlook. International Monetary Fund Staff. (World Economic & Financial Surveys Ser.). 104p. 1988. pap. 15.00 (1-55775-023-8) Intl Monetary.

Staff Studies for the World Economic Outlook. International Monetary Fund Staff. (World Economic & Financial Surveys Ser.). ix, 125p. 1989. pap. 15.00 (1-55775-120-X) Intl Monetary.

Staff Studies for the World Economic Outlook. International Monetary Fund Staff. (World Economic & Financial Surveys Ser.). 63p. 1990. pap. 20.00 (1-55775-168-4) Intl Monetary.

Staff Studies for the World Economic Outlook. International Monetary Fund Staff. (World Economic & Financial Surveys July 1986 Ser.). 207p. reprint ed. pap. 59.00 (0-685-44442-2, 2029092) Bks Demand.

***Staff Supervision in a Turbulent Environment: Managing Process & Task in Front-Line Services.** Ed. by Lynette Hughes & Paul Pengelly. 172p. 1996. pap. 26.95 (1-85302-327-2, Pub. by J Kingsley Pubs UK) Taylor & Francis.

Staff Supervision in Child Protection Work. Margaret Richards et al. (C). 1990. 95.00 (0-7855-0072-3, Pub. by Natl Inst Soc Work); pap. 38.00 (0-902789-70-8, Pub. by Natl Inst Soc Work) St Mut.

Staff Supervision in Services for Sensory Impaired Children & Adults: A European Perspective. Geoff Aplin & Chris Payne. 1994. pap. 58.00 (0-902789-92-9, Pub. by Natl Inst Soc Work) St Mut.

***Staff Support in Health Care.** David J. Stoter. LC 97-10863. 224p. (Orig.). 1997. pap. text ed. 24.95 (0-632-04098-X) Blackwell Sci.

Staff Training: An Annotated Review of the Literature, 1980-1988. William Crimando & T. F. Riggar. LC 90-3254. (Research & Information Guides in Business, Industry & Economic Institutions Ser.: Vol. 3). 358p. 1990. text ed. 52.00 (0-8240-7385-1, SS662) Garland.

Staff Training & Assessment. David Osborne. LC 95-31896. 1996. 70.00 (0-304-33119-8); pap. 24.95 (0-304-33124-4) Cassell.

Staff Training & Special Education Needs. Ed. by Graham Upton. 192p. 1991. 69.00 (1-85346-172-5, Pub. by D Fulton UK) Taylor & Francis.

Staff Training & User Awareness in Preservation Management. W. Boomgaarden. 89p. pap. 15.00 (0-918006-64-3) ARL.

Staff Training in Mental Handicap. Ed. by James Hogg & Peter Mittler. 459p. 1987. text ed. 15.00 (0-914797-35-2) Brookline Bks.

Staff Training Manual. Lynn E. Robbins. 324p. 1995. lib. bdg. 80.00 (1-888143-12-6) Robbins Mgmt.

***Staffing: Survey Results.** Urban Libs. Council Staff. (Frequent Fast Facts Ser.). 1993. pap. 45.00 (0-614-29738-9) Urban Libraries.

Staffing & Management for Social, Economic, & Environmental Impact Assessments. (National Cooperative Highway Research Program Report Ser.: No. 40). 43p. 1977. 4.00 (0-309-02541-9) Transport Res Bd.

Staffing Commercial Credit Functions: A Survey. Roger K. Nordgren. Ed. by Daphne Smith & Shelley Geehr. (Illus.). 64p. (Orig.). 1994. pap. text ed. 58.00 (1-57070-008-7, 32191) Robt Morris Assocs.

Staffing for Success: A Guide for Health & Human Service Professionals. M. J. Schmidt et al. (Illus.). 160p. (C). 1992. text ed. 39.95 (0-8039-4500-0); pap. text ed. 17.50 (0-8039-4501-9) Sage.

Staffing in Residential Care Homes. Wagner Development Group Staff. (C). 1990. 85.00 (0-7855-0084-7, Pub. by Natl Inst Soc Work) St Mut.

Staffing in Residential Care Homes: A Handbook of Guidance on the Calculation of Staffing Establishments & the Deployment of Staff for Managers, Proprietors, Employers & Trade Union Officers. Wagner Development Group Staff. (C). 1990. pap. 35.00 (0-902789-69-4, Pub. by Natl Inst Soc Work) St Mut.

Staffing Industry Resource Guide, 1994. Staffing Industry Analysts, Inc. Staff. 248p. (Orig.). 1994. pap. 35.00 (1-883814-02-2) Staff Ind Analysts.

Staffing of Nuclear Power Plants & Recruitment, Training, & Authorization of Operation Personnel. IAEA Staff. (Safety Ser.: No. 50-SG-01, Rev. 1). 60p. 1991. pap. 30.00 (92-0-123391-4, STI/PUB/874, Pub. by IAEA AU) Bernan Associates.

Staffing Organizations. Herbert G. Heneman & Rob Heneman. 500p. (C). 1993. text ed. 71.75 (0-256-14142-8) Irwin.

***Staffing Organizations.** 2nd ed. Herbert G. Heneman & Robert Heneman. 752p. (C). 1996. text ed. 71.75 (0-256-20806-9) Irwin.

Staffing Organizations. 2nd ed. Benjamin Schneider & Neal Schmitt. (Illus.). 478p. (C). 1992. reprint ed. text ed. 38.95 (0-88133-672-6) Waveland Pr.

Staffing Policies & Procedures. Beverly Kilmer. (Cosmetology Ser.). (Illus.). 176p. 1996. text ed. 19.95 (1-56253-314-2) Milady Pub.

Staffing Problem Solver for Human Resource Professionals & Managers. Marc Dorio. 288p. 1994. text ed. 75.00 (0-471-00630-0) Wiley.

Staffing, Scheduling, & Workforce Planning: A Help Desk Institute White Paper. Steven J. Murtagh. Ed. by Patrick Bultema et al. (Illus.). (Orig.). (C). pap. write for info. (1-57125-002-6) Help Desk Inst.

Staffing Standards for Art Libraries & Visual Resources Collections. ARLIS-NA Staffing Standards Task Force. (Occasional Papers: No. 11). 16p. (Orig.). 1995. pap. 7.50 (0-942740-16-5) Art Libs Soc.

Staffing the Child Welfare Agency: Recruitment & Retention. Child Welfare League of America Staff. 1991. pap. 8.95 (0-87868-475-1) Child Welfare.

Staffing the Contemporary Organization: A Guide to Planning, Recruiting, & Selecting for Human Resource Professionals. Donald L. Caruth et al. LC 87-13092. 323p. 1988. text ed. 59.95 (0-89930-236-X, CFG/, Quorum Bks) Greenwood.

Staffing the Contemporary Organization: A Guide to Planning, Recruiting, & Selecting for Human Resource Professionals. Donald L. Caruth et al. LC 90-7760. 328p. 1990. pap. text ed. 22.95 (0-275-93804-2, B3804, Praeger Pubs) Greenwood.

***Staffing the Contemporary Organization: A Guide to Planning, Recruiting & Selecting for Human Resource Professionals.** Donald L. Caruth & Gail D. Handlogten. LC 97-8858. 1997. text ed. write for info. (1-56720-056-7, Quorum Bks) Greenwood.

***Staffing the Contemporary Organization: A Guide to Planning, Recruiting & Selecting for Human Resource Professionals.** 2nd ed. Donald L. Caruth & Gail D. Handlogten. LC 97-8858. 1997. pap. text ed. write for info. (0-275-95523-0, Praeger Pubs) Greenwood.

***Staffing the New Workplace.** 562p. 1996. 48.00 (0-614-26844-3, 06896BLS01) Commerce.

Staffing the New Workplace: Selecting & Promoting for Quality Improvement. Ronald B. Morgan & Jack E. Smith. (Illus.). 577p. 1996. 40.00 (0-87389-361-1, H0865) ASQC Qual Pr.

Staffing Tomorrow's Parishes: Experiences & Issues in Evolving Forms of Pastoral Leadership. Ed. by Institute for Pastoral Life Staff & Maurice L. Monette. 84p. (Orig.). (C). 1990. pap. 5.95 (1-55612-366-3) Sheed & Ward MO.

Stafford County: Virginia Publick Claims. Janice L. Abercrombie & Richard Slatten. (Virginia Publick Claims Ser.). ix, 45p. 1991. pap. 7.00 (0-8095-8696-7) Borgo Pr.

Stafford County: Virginia Publick Claims. Janice L. Abercrombie & Richard Slatten. (Virginia Publick Claims Ser.). ix, 45p. (C). 1991. reprint ed. lib. bdg. 25.00 (0-8095-8363-1) Borgo Pr.

Stafford County Virginia Tithables: Quit Rents, Personal Property Taxes & Related Lists & Petitions, 1723-1790, 2 vols. John Vogt & T. William Kethley. xviii, 612p. (C). 1990. reprint ed. Set. lib. bdg. 60.00 (0-8095-8175-2) Borgo Pr.

Stafford County Virginia Tithables: Quit Rents, Personal Property Taxes & Related Lists & Petitions, 1723-1790, 2 vols., Set. John Vogt & T. William Kethley. 1990. pap. 30.00 (0-935931-50-3) Borgo Pr.

Stafford Cripps' Mission to Moscow, 1940-42. Gabriel Gorodetsky. (Illus.). 377p. 1985. text ed. 59.95 (0-521-23866-8) Cambridge U Pr.

Stafford's Road: An Anthology of Poems for William Stafford. Ed. by Thomas L. Ferte. (Illus.). 70p. (Orig.). 1991. pap. 15.00 (0-9629194-1-1) Adrienne Lee.

Staffordshire. Ed. by M. W. Greenslade. (Victoria History of the Counties of England Ser.: Vol. VI). (Illus.). 314p. 1979. 135.00 (0-19-722733-3) OUP.

Staffordshire Bull Terrier Champions, 1975-1986. Camino E. E. & Bk. Co. Staff. (Illus.). 128p. 1988. pap. 36.95 (0-940808-72-2) Camino E E & Bk.

Staffordshire Bull Terrier Champions, 1988-1993. Camino E. E. & Bk. Co. Staff. (Illus.). 85p. 1996. pap. 32.95 (1-55893-038-8) Camino E E & Bk.

Staffordshire Bull Terriers. Anna K. Nicholas. 1996. 9.95 (0-7938-1191-0, KW-157) TFH Pubns.

Staffordshire Bull Terriers: An Owner's Companion. V. H. Pounds & Lilian V. Rant. (Illus.). 240p. 1995. 39.95 (1-85223-365-6, Pub. by Crowood Pr UK) Trafalgar.

Staffordshire Christmas. Compiled by Robin Pearson. LC 93-33710. 1993. 15.00 (0-7509-0312-0, Pub. by Sutton Pubng UK) Bks Intl VA.

Staffordshire Figures. Amoret Scott & Christopher Scott. 1989. pap. 25.00 (0-85263-793-4, Pub. by Shire UK) St Mut.

Staffordshire of One Hundred Years Ago. David Buxton. (One Hundred Years Ago Ser.). (Illus.). 1994. 38.00 (0-7509-0419-4, Pub. by Sutton Pubng UK) Bks Intl VA.

Staffordshire Portrait Figures of the Victorian Era. P. D. Pugh. (Illus.). 1987. 99.50 (1-85149-010-8) Antique Collect.

Staffordshire Romantic Transfer Patterns: Cup Plates & Early Victorian China. Petra Williams. LC 78-55047. (Illus.). 763p. 1978. 35.00 (0-914736-05-1) Fountain Hse East.

Staffordshire Romantic Transfer Patterns Vol. III: Cup, Plates, 2nd Early Victorian China L'Envoie. Petra Williams & Marguerite R. Weber. (Illus.). 250p. 1997. write for info. (0-914736-10-8) Fountain Hse East.

Staffordshire Romantic Transfer Patterns II: Cup Plates, & Early Victorian China. Marguerite R. Weber. LC 78-55047. (Illus.). 700p. 1986. 35.00 (0-914736-09-4) Fountain Hse East.

***Staffordshire Spaniels.** Adele Kenny. LC 96-70727. (Illus.). 144p. 1997. 39.95 (0-7643-0216-7) Schiffer.

Staffordshire Terriers: American Staffordshire Terrier & Staffordshire Bull Terrier. Anna K. Nicholas. (TS Ser.). (Illus.). 256p. 1991. text ed. 47.95 (0-86622-637-0, TS-143) TFH Pubns.

Staffroom: Observing the Professional Culture of Teachers. Anat Kainan. LC 94-22345. 190p. 1994. 51.95 (1-85628-974-5, Pub. by Avebury Pub UK) Ashgate Pub Co.

Stage Am I? Raping Lucrece in Early Modern England. Mercedes M. Camino. LC 96-140957. 228p. 1996. 89.95 (0-7734-4220-0) E Mellen.

Stage & School. 6th ed. Harry H. Schanker. 1989. 43.25 (0-07-055145-6) McGraw.

Stage & Screen. Ian Graham. LC 94-36560. (Science Spotlight Ser.). (J). 1995. lib. bdg. 24.26 (0-8114-3845-7) Raintree Steck-V.

Stage & Screen Science Anytime Guide. HB Staff. 1995. pap. 8.00 (0-15-306068-9) HB Schl Dept.

Stage & Set Design. Rodolfo Di Giammarco. (Illus.). 24p. 5.00 (0-930209-04-4) Otis Gallery.

Stage & Social Struggle in Early Modern England. Jean E. Howard. LC 93-8068. 224p. (C). 1993. pap. 16.95 (0-415-09553-0) Routledge.

Stage & Social Struggle in Early Modern England. Jean E. Howard. LC 93-8068. 224p. (C). (gr. 13). 1993. text ed. 62.95 (0-415-04258-5) Routledge.

Stage & Structure: Reopening the Debate. Ed. by Iris Levin & Sidney Strauss. LC 85-15624. (Human Development Ser.: Vol. 1). 336p. 1986. text ed. 73.25 (0-89391-224-7) Ablex Pub.

Stage & the School. 5th ed. K. A. Ommanney & Harry H. Schanker. 1982. text ed. 29.76 (0-07-047671-3) McGraw.

Stage Attacked. Northbrooke & Gosson: A Treatise Against Dicing, Dancing, Plays & Interludes. Bd. with School of Abuse: A Pleasant Invective Against Poets, Pipers, Players, Jesters, Etc. (Shakespeare Society of London Publications: Vol. 15). 1974. reprint ed. Set pap. (0-8115-0177-9) Periodicals Srv.

Stage Blood: Vampires of the Nineteenth-Century Stage. Roxana Stuart. LC 94-72404. (Illus.). 381p. (C). 1995. 49.95 (0-87972-659-8); pap. 25.95 (0-87972-660-1) Bowling Green Univ Popular Press.

Stage Clown in Shakespeare's Theater. Bente A. Videbaek. LC 95-20556. (Contributions in Drama & Theatre Studies: No. 69). 224p. 1996. text ed. 55.00 (0-313-29872-6, Greenwood Pr) Greenwood.

Stage Coach. Bonnie Bryant. (Saddle Club Ser.: No. 37). 144p. (J). (gr. 4-7). 1994. pap. 3.99 (0-553-48153-3) Bantam.

Stage Coach. Maurice De Bevere & Rene De Goscinny. (Lucky Luke Ser.: No. 1). (Illus.). 48p. (J). (gr. 2-7). 1996. reprint ed. pap. 8.95 (1-887911-52-9) Fantsy Flight.

Stage-Coach & Tavern Days. A. M. Earle. LC 68-26351. (American History & Americana Ser.: No. 47). (Illus.). 1969. reprint ed. lib. bdg. 75.00 (0-8383-0280-7) M S G Haskell Hse.

Stage-Coach & Tavern Days. Alice Earle. (BCL1 - U. S. History Ser.). 449p. 1991. reprint ed. lib. bdg. 99.00 (0-7812-6007-8) Rprt Serv.

Stage Coach & Tavern Days. Alice M. Earle. LC 70-81558. (Illus.). 499p. 1972. reprint ed. 27.95 (0-405-08476-5, Pub. by Blom Pubns UK) Ayer.

Stage-Coach Days in the Bluegrass. J. Winston Coleman, Jr. LC 95-21201. (Illus.). 304p. 1995. 24.95 (0-8131-1914-6) U Pr of Ky.

Stage-Coach Days in the Bluegrass. J. Winston Coleman, Jr. (Illus.). 226p. 1989. reprint ed. 12.50 (0-935680-25-X) Kentucke Imprints.

Stage Controversy in France from Corneille to Rousseau. Moses Barras. LC 78-159116. 365p. 1973. reprint ed. text ed. 75.00 (0-87753-051-3) Phaeton.

Stage Costume Handbook. Berneice Prisk. LC 78-27695. 198p. 1979. reprint ed. text ed. 62.50 (0-313-20912-X, PRSC, Greenwood Pr) Greenwood.

Stage Costume Step-by-Step. Mary T. Kidd. (Illus.). 144p. 1996. 21.99 (1-55870-406-X, Betrwy Bks) F & W Pubns Inc.

Stage Deaths: A Biographical Guide to International Theatrical Obituaries, 1850 to 1990. Compiled by George B. Bryan. LC 91-10304. (Bibliographies & Indexes in the Performing Arts Ser.: No. 9). 1376p. 1991. text ed. 195.00 (0-313-27593-9, BDH/, Greenwood Pr) Greenwood.

Stage Deaths: A Biographical Guide to International Theatrical Obituaries, 1850-1990, Vol. 1, A-J. George B. Bryan. LC 91-10304. (Bibliographies & Indexes in the Performing Arts Ser.: Vol. 9). 704p. 1991. text ed. 195.00 (0-313-28037-1, Greenwood Pr) Greenwood.

Stage Deaths: A Biographical Guide to International Theatrical Obituaries, 1850-1990, Vol. 2. George B. Bryan. LC 91-10304. (Bibliographies & Indexes in the Performing Arts Ser.: Vol. 9). 688p. 1991. text ed. 195.00 (0-313-28038-X, Greenwood Pr) Greenwood.

Stage Decoration. Sheldon W. Cheney. LC 66-29421. (Illus.). 1972. reprint ed. 23.95 (0-405-08357-2, Pub. by Blom Pubns UK) Ayer.

Stage Design & Properties. rev. ed. Michael Holt. (Theater Manuals Ser.). (Illus.). 128p. 1995. reprint ed. pap. 14.95 (0-7148-2515-8, Pub. by Phaidon Press UK) Chronicle Bks.

Stage Design, Photography & Film see Encyclopedie Des Arts Decoratifs et Industriels Modernes

Stage Designs of Inigo Jones: The European Context. John Peacock. (Illus.). 400p. (C). 1995. text ed. 145.00 (0-521-41812-7) Cambridge U Pr.

Stage Designs of Leslie Hurry. Raymond Ingram. (Theatre in Focus Ser.). 1990. pap. 105.00 incl. sl. (0-85964-223-2) Chadwyck-Healey.

Stage Dialects. Jerry Blunt. 1994. pap. 18.95 (0-87129-331-5, SA5) Dramatic Pub.

Stage Directions. John Gielgud. 1979. pap. 12.95 (0-87830-568-8, Thtre Arts Bks) Routledge.

Stage Directions. John Gielgud. LC 78-23580. 1979. reprint ed. text ed. 65.00 (0-313-21035-7, GISD, Greenwood Pr) Greenwood.

Stage Directions & Spared: The Quannapowit Quartet, Parts Three & Four. Israel Horovitz. 1977. pap. 5.25 (0-8222-1068-1) Dramatists Play.

Stage Directors in Modern France. David Whitton. 1988. text ed. 79.95 (0-7190-2467-6, Pub. by Manchester Univ Pr UK) St Martin.

Stage Door. Charles B. Davis. LC 74-122693. (Short Story Index Reprint Ser.). 1977. 20.95 (0-8369-3526-8) Ayer.

Stage Door. Edna Ferber & George S. Kaufman. 1943. pap. 5.25 (0-8222-1069-X) Dramatists Play.

Stage Favorites of the Eighteenth Century. Lewis S. Benjamin. LC 68-57303. (Essay Index Reprint Ser.). 1977. 20.95 (0-8369-0060-X) Ayer.

Stage Fights: A Simple Handbook of Techniques. Gilbert E. Gordon. LC 73-75918. (Illus.). 1974. 9.95 (0-87830-580-7, Thtre Arts Bks) Routledge.

Stage Flying: 431 B. C. to Modern Times. John A. McKinven. LC 95-5936. 1995. 35.00 (0-916638-81-2) Meyerbooks.

Stage for a Nation: The Story of the National Theatre. Douglas B. Lee et al. LC 85-22761. (Illus.). 152p. (C). 1986. 30.75 (0-8191-5021-5, National Theatre) U Pr of Amer.

Stage for Poets: Studies in the Theatre of Hugo & Musset. Charles Affron. LC 75-153847. (Princeton Essays in European & Comparative Literature Ser.). 274p. reprint ed. pap. 78.10 (0-8357-7036-2, 2033407) Bks Demand.

***Stage Fright.** C. Archer & Catherine Marshall. LC 96-45388. (Christy Fiction Ser.: Vol. 10). (Illus.). (J). 1997. 4.99 (0-8499-3961-5) Tommy Nelson.

Stage Fright. Erica Field. (J). 1995. pap. 2.95 (0-8167-3517-4) Troll Communs.

Stage Fright. Ellen Hart. LC 92-14966. 261p. 1992. 9.95 (1-878067-21-4) Seal Pr WA.

Stage Fright. Ellen Hart. (Midwest Mysteries Ser.). 1994. mass mkt. 5.99 (0-345-38142-4) Ballantine.

Stage Fright. James Howe. (YA). 1987. pap. 2.95 (0-380-70173-1, Flare) Avon.

Stage Fright. James Howe. 144p. (J). 1991. pap. 3.99 (0-380-71331-4, Camelot) Avon.

Stage Fright. James Howe. (J). 1995. pap. 3.95 (0-689-80338-9, Aladdin Paperbacks) S&S Childrens.

Stage Fright. Carolyn Keene. Ed. by Anne Greenberg. (Nancy Drew Files Ser.: No. 90). 160p. (Orig.). (YA). (gr. 6 up). 1993. mass mkt. 3.99 (0-671-79482-5, Archway) PB.

Stage Fright. Clare McNally. 256p. (Orig.). 1995. 5.99 (0-8125-4839-6) Tor Bks.

Stage Fright. Paul Stewart. (Spinechillers Ser.). (Illus.). 48p. (J). (gr. 3 up). 1996. pap. 4.95 (0-7460-2087-2, Usborne) EDC.

Stage Fright. Paul Stewart. (Spinechillers Ser.). (J). (gr. 4-7). 1996. lib. bdg. 13.95 (0-88110-797-2) EDC.

Stage Fright: A Sebastian Barth Mystery. 2nd ed. James Howe. LC 85-20025. 160p. (J). (gr. 3-7). 1990. lib. bdg. 15.00 (0-689-31701-8, Atheneum Bks Young) S&S Childrens.

Stage Fright: Health & Safety in the Theater. Monona Rossol. LC 85-28080. (Illus.). 128p. 1986. pap. text ed. 12.95 (0-918875-02-1) Ctr Occupational Hazards.

Stage Fright: Health Hazards in Theater. Monona Rossol. LC 90-85553. (Illus.). 144p. (Orig.). 1991. pap. 16.95 (0-9607118-3-X) Allworth Pr.

Stage Fright: Its Role in Acting. Stephen Aaron. LC 85-24649. 176p. 1986. 13.95 (0-226-00018-4) U Ch Pr.

Stage Fright: Its Role in Acting. Ann M. Martin. (J). 1986. pap. text ed. 2.50 (0-590-33758-0) Scholastic Inc.

***Stage Frightened.** Judy Delton. (Pee Wee Scouts Ser.: No. 32). (J). 1997. mass mkt. 3.99 (0-440-41327-3) BDD Bks Young Read.

Stage from Deadwood. Ray Toepfer. (Novel of the West Ser.). 192p. 1993. 18.95 (0-87131-743-5) M Evans.

Stage History of Shakespeare's "King Richard the Third" Alice I. Wood. LC 09-25746. reprint ed. 27.50 (0-404-07024-8) AMS Pr.

Stage II Relationships. Earnie Larsen. LC 86-45815. 1987. pap. 12.00 (0-06-254808-5, PL-4199) Harper SF.

Stage Images & Traditions: Shakespeare to Ford. Marion Lomax. LC 86-31062. (Illus.). 220p. 1987. text ed. 54.95 (0-521-32659-1) Cambridge U Pr.

Stage in Action. Helen Manfull. 672p. 1996. per. 34.59 (0-8403-7624-3) Kendall-Hunt.

Stage in the Twentieth Century. Robert Grau. LC 68-54536. (Illus.). 1972. 30.95 (0-405-08572-9, Pub. by Blom Pubns UK) Ayer.

Stage Irishman. George C. Duggan. LC 70-91899. (Illus.). 1972. 23.95 (0-405-08468-4, Pub. by Blom Pubns UK) Ayer.

Stage Is All the World: The Theatrical Designs of Tanya Moiseiwitsch. Robertson Davies et al. LC 93-85974. (Illus.). 134p. 1994. pap. 29.95 (0-935573-14-3) D & A Smart Museum.

Stage Is Set. Lee Simonson. LC 62-12338. (Illus.). 1963. pap. 12.95 (0-87830-508-4, Thtre Arts Bks) Routledge.

Stage Is Set. Lee Simonson. (New Reprints in Essay & General Literature Index Ser.). 1977. reprint ed. 38.95 (0-518-10206-8, 10206) Ayer.

Stage It with Music: An Encyclopedic Guide to the American Musical Theatre. Thomas S. Hischak. LC 92-35321. 328p. 1993. text ed. 49.95 (0-313-28708-2, GR8708) Greenwood.

Stage Left: The Development of the American Social Drama in the Thirties. Richard C. Reynolds. LC 85-52030. 175p. 1986. 22.50 (0-87875-311-7) Whitston Pub.

Stage Lighting. Theodore Fuchs. 1972. 27.95 (0-405-07249-X, 1721) Ayer.

Stage Lighting: Practice & Design. W. Oren Parker. 256p. (C). 1987. text ed. 37.25 (0-03-011912-X) HB Coll Pubs.

Stage Lighting Design: The Art - the Process - the Life. Richard Pilbrow. LC 97-26071. (Illus.). 488p. 1997. text ed. write for info. (0-89676-139-8, By Design Pr) QSMG Ltd.

Stage Lighting for Theatre Designers. Nigel Morgan. (Orig.). 1995. pap. 21.95 (0-435-08685-5, 08685) Heinemann.

S

Stage Lighting Handbook. Francis Reid. LC 76-8319. (Illus.). 1976. pap. 13.95 (*0-87830-988-8*, Thtre Arts Bks) Routledge.

Stage Lighting Handbook. Francis Reid. 1987. pap. 10.45 (*0-87830-156-9*) Routledge Chapman & Hall.

***Stage Lighting Handbook.** 5th ed. Francis Reid. (Theatre Studies). 208p. 1996. pap. 22.95 (*0-87830-064-3*) Routledge.

Stage Lighting in the Boondocks. 4th rev. ed. James H. Miller. Ed. by Arthur L. Zapel. LC 95-22366. (Illus.). 144p. (Orig.). 1995. pap. 10.95 (*1-56608-017-7*, B141) Meriwether Pub.

Stage Lighting Revealed: A Design & Execution Handbook. Glen Cunningham. (Illus.). 176p. (Orig.). 1993. pap. 18.99 (*1-55870-290-3*, Betrwy Bks) F & W Pubns Inc.

Stage Lights. Katerina Evanova. 160p. 1995. lib. bdg. 39.00 (*0-8095-4844-5*) Borgo Pr.

Stage Lights. Katerina Evanova. 160p. 14.95 (*0-88962-567-0*) Mosaic.

Stage Lights. Katerina Evanova. 203p. 1994. pap. text ed. 15.00 (*0-88962-572-7*) Mosaic.

Stage Lives: A Bibliography & an Index to Theatrical Biographies in English. George B. Bryan. LC 84-19833. (Bibliographies & Indexes in the Performing Arts Ser.: No. 2). xvi, 368p. 1985. text ed. 75.00 (*0-313-24577-0*, BSV/, Greenwood Pr) Greenwood.

Stage Make-up Techniques: A Players Press Guide. Martin Jans & William-Alan Landes. LC 92-56429. (Illus.). 112p. (Orig.). 1993. pap. 24.00 (*0-88734-621-9*) Players Pr.

Stage Makeup. 8th ed. Richard Corson. 400p. 1990. text ed. 78.00 (*0-13-840539-5*) P-H.

Stage Makeup Step-by-Step. Rosemarie Swinfield. (Illus.). 128p. 1995. 21.99 (*1-55870-390-X*, Betrwy Bks) F & W Pubns Inc.

Stage Management. Peter Bax. 1977. 24.95 (*0-405-09118-4*, 1700) Ayer.

Stage Management. 5th ed. Lawrence Stern. 1995. pap. text ed. 42.95 (*0-205-17084-6*, H70840) Allyn.

***Stage Management.** 6th ed. Stern. LC 97-17047. 1997. pap. text ed. 42.95 (*0-205-27303-3*) P-H.

Stage Management: A General Art. Daniel Bond. 160p. (gr. 13). 1991. pap. 15.95 (*0-87830-010-4*, Thtre Arts Bks) Routledge.

Stage Management: A Guide Book of Practical Techniques. 3rd ed. Nancy B. Stern. 264p. 1986. pap. text ed. 35.95 (*0-205-10287-5*, H02876) Allyn.

Stage Management & Theater Administration. rev. ed. Pauline Menear & Terry Hawkins. (Theater Manuals Ser.). (Illus.). 128p. 1995. reprint ed. pap. 14.95 (*0-7148-2516-6*, Pub. by Phaidon Press UK) Chronicle Bks.

Stage Management & Theatrecraft: A Stage Manager's Handbook. 4th ed. Hendrik Baker. LC 68-16449. (Illus.). 392p. 1988. pap. 20.00 (*0-85343-556-1*) Players Pr.

Stage Management Forms & Formats. Barbara Dilker. LC 79-16689. 200p. 1991. reprint ed. pap. 19.95 (*0-910482-85-3*, Drama Pubs) QSMG Ltd.

Stage Management Handbook. Daniel A. Ionazzi. (Illus.). 192p. (Orig.). 1992. pap. 17.99 (*1-55870-235-0*, Betrwy Bks) F & W Pubns Inc.

Stage Manager's Handbook. rev. ed. Bert Gruver. LC 72-190641. (Illus.). 240p. 1972. pap. 12.95 (*0-89676-007-3*, Drama Pubs) QSMG Ltd.

Stage of Dreams: The Dramatic Art of Alfred de Musset (1828-1834) Gochberg. (Hist. des Idees et Crit. Litt. Ser.). 27.50 (*0-685-34954-3*, F69260) Fr & Eur.

Stage of Their Own: Feminist Playwrights of the Suffrage Era. Sheila Stowell. 176p. 1994. pap. text ed. 14.95 (*0-472-08273-6*) U of Mich Pr.

Stage One: Minirus. ACTR Staff. 256p. 1996. per., pap. 29.95 (*0-7872-1692-5*) Kendall-Hunt.

Stage One Validation of the Relationship Between Asphalt Properties & Asphalt-Aggregate Mixes. Compiled by SHRP Staff. (SHRP Ser.: No. A-398). 253p. (Orig.). (C). 1994. pap. text ed. 15.00 (*0-309-05814-7*) SHRP.

Stage: or Recollections of Actors & Acting. James E. Murdoch. LC 79-81213. 1972. 24.95 (*0-405-08810-8*) Ayer.

Stage Plays from the Classics. Joellen Bland. LC 87-14669. (Orig.). (YA). (gr. 7-12). 1987. pap. 15.95 (*0-8238-0281-7*) Plays.

Stage Production Handbook: Job Responsibilities for All Technical Backstage Crews. Kathryn M. Busti. (Illus.). 178p. 1994. 40.00 (*0-9642913-0-4*) Theatre Things.

Stage-Quarrel Between Ben Jonson & the So-Called Poetasters. Roscoe A. Small. LC 02-25126. reprint ed. 36.50 (*0-404-06099-4*) AMS Pr.

Stage Rigging Handbook. Jay O. Glerum. LC 86-13834. (Illus.). 128p. (Orig.). (C). 1987. pap. 19.95 (*0-8093-1318-9*) S Ill U Pr.

Stage Rigging Handbook. 2nd rev. ed. Jay O. Glerum. LC 96-7589. (Illus.). 224p. (Orig.). (C). 1997. pap. 24.95 (*0-8093-1744-3*) S Ill U Pr.

Stage Right: Crisis & Recovery in British Contemporary Mainstream Theatre. John Bull. LC 93-36479. 1994. text ed. 45.00 (*0-312-12026-5*); text ed. 18.95 (*0-312-12029-X*) St Martin.

Stage Scenery, Machinery & Lighting: A Guide to Information Sources. Ed. by Richard Stoddard. LC 76-13574. (Performing Arts Information Guide Ser.: Vol. 2). 288p. 1977. 68.00 (*0-8103-1374-X*) Gale.

Stage Specs: A Guide to Legit Theatres. Ed. by Robert B. Gould. LC 90-60537. 625p. (Orig.). 1990. pap. 65.00 (*0-9625844-0-1*) Lea Amer Theatre.

Stage-Struck in Coaltown. Jack E. Smith. (Orig.). 1996. pap. 10.00 (*1-888836-03-2*) Shenango River.

***Stage-Struck Yankee.** Oliver E. Durivage. Ed. & Intro. by Walter J. Meserve. (On Stage, America! Ser.). 17p. 1996. spiral bd. 2.95 (*0-937657-25-5*) Feedbk Theabks & Prospero.

Stage-Structured Populations: Sampling, Analysis & Simulation. Bryan F. Manly. (Population & Community Biology Ser.). (Illus.). 160p. 1990. 49.95 (*0-412-35060-2*, A4128) Chapman & Hall.

Stage System for Talented & Gifted Education. Roberta Edwards et al. (Illus.). 62p. (Orig.). (C). 1984. pap. 3.50 (*0-9613243-0-9*) Trinity County.

Stage Theories of Cognitive & Moral Development: Criticisms & Application. Intro. by Deanna Kuhn. LC 77-91693. (HER Reprint Ser.: No. 13). 204p. 1978. pap. 6.95 (*0-916690-16-4*) Harvard Educ Rev.

Stage to Screen: Theatrical Method from Garrick to Griffith. A. Nicholas Vardac. LC 68-20251. (Illus.). 1972. reprint ed. 20.95 (*0-405-09039-0*) Ayer.

Stage to Studio: Musicians & the Sound Revolution, 1890-1950. James P. Kraft. LC 95-43923. (Studies in Industry & Society: No. 9). (Illus.). 248p. (C). 1996. text ed. 35.00 (*0-8018-5089-4*) Johns Hopkins.

Stage to Yosemite: Recollections of Wawona's Albert Gordon. Annie Reynolds & Albert Gordon. Ed. by Mary Vocelka & Jane Bentle. (Illus.). 180p. (Orig.). 1994. pap. 19.95 (*0-9639148-0-4*) A L Reynolds.

***Stage 2.** Betty Berzon. Date not set. pap. write for info. (*0-525-93991-1*) NAL-Dutton.

Stage Two: Poetic Lives. Stage Two Poets. Ed. by E. D. Klein. (Anthology Ser.). (Illus.). 97p. 1993. pap. 8.95 (*0-9639612-0-9*) Journey Edit.

Stage Two Recovery: Life Beyond Addiction. Earnie Larsen. LC 85-51017. 96p. 1984. pap. 12.00 (*0-86683-460-5*) Harper SF.

Stage Whispers. Elise Title. (Intrigue Ser.: No. 180). 1992. pap. 2.79 (*0-373-22180-0*, 1-22180-3) Harlequin Bks.

***Stage-Wrights: Shakespeare, Jonson, Middleton, & the Making of Theatrical Value.** Paul E. Yachnin. LC 96-54900. (New Cultural Studies). 216p. 1997. text ed. 36.50 (*0-8122-3395-6*) U of Pa Pr.

Stage Write: Playwriting Curriculum for Kids & Teachers. Norman Delue & Thomas B. Hayward. 64p. teacher ed. 8.99 (*1-56417-870-6*, GA1563) Good Apple.

Stage Writers Handbook: A Complete Business Guide for Playwrights, Composers, Lyricists, & Librettists. Dana Singer. LC 96-7093. 1996. pap. text ed. 15.95 (*1-55936-116-6*) Theatre Comm.

Stagecoach: BFI Film Classics. Edward Buscombe. (Illus.). 96p. 1992. pap. 9.95 (*0-85170-299-6*, Pub. by British Film Inst UK) Ind U Pr.

***Stagecoach & Tavern Tales of the Old Northwest.** Harry E. Cole. Ed. by Louise P. Kellogg. LC 96-51161. (Shawnee Classics Ser.). (Illus.). 382p. 1997. pap. 12.95 (*0-8093-2125-4*) S Ill U Pr.

Stagecoach Days in Santa Barbara County. Walker A. Tompkins. (Illus.). 136p. pap. 7.50 (*0-87461-048-6*) McNally & Loftin.

Stagecoach Heyday. W. Harland Boyd. (Illus.). 1983. 12.00 (*0-943500-10-9*) Kern Historical.

Stagecoach Inns of Texas. Kathryn Carter. 280p. 22.95 (*0-89015-914-9*) Sunbelt Media.

Stagecoach Pioneers of the Southwest. Robert N. Mullin. (Southwestern Studies: No. 71). 64p. 1983. pap. 5.00 (*0-87404-131-7*) Tex Western.

Stagecoach Santa. Randall A. Reinstedt. Ed. by John Bergez. LC 86-81735. (History & Happenings of California Ser.). (Illus.). 46p. (J). (gr. 3-6). 1986. pap. 8.95 (*0-933818-75-0*); boxed 12.95 (*0-933818-20-3*) Ghost Town.

Stagecoach to Birdsville. Helen Ferber. (Illus.). 112p. (Orig.). 1995. pap. 16.95 (*0-86417-694-5*, Pub. by Kangaroo Pr AT) Seven Hills Bk.

Stagecoach Towns. Arch Merrill. (Arch Merrill's New York Ser.: Vol. 6). 208p. 1991. reprint ed. pap. 12.95 (*1-55787-002-0*, 76040, Empire State Bks) Hrt of the Lakes.

Stagecoach 22-San Antonio-El Paso Line. Rudolph Mellard. (Illus.). 1977. 15.00 (*0-685-87381-1*) A Jones.

Stagecraft. Roy A. Beck. 93p. 1994. pap. 10.95 (*0-8442-5134-8*, Natl Textbk) NTC Pub Grp.

Stagecraft: A Handbook for Organization Construction & Management. 2nd ed. David Welker. 1986. text ed. 47.95 (*0-205-10286-7*, H02868) Allyn.

Stagecraft for Christmas & Easter Plays: A Method of Simplified Staging for the Church. James H. Miller. Ed. by Arthur L. Zapel & Theodore O. Zapel. LC 89-49383. (Illus.). 96p. (Orig.). 1989. pap. 9.95 (*0-916260-64-X*, B170) Meriwether Pub.

Stagecraft for Nonprofessionals. rev. ed. F. A. Buerki. LC 83-1244. 192p. 1983. reprint ed. pap. 54.80 (*0-608-01923-2*, 2062578) Bks Demand.

Stagecraft Handbook. Daniel A. Ionazzi. LC 96-22964. (Illus.). 208p. 1996. pap. 21.99 (*1-55870-404-3*, Betrwy Bks) F & W Pubns Inc.

Stagecraft I: A Teacher's Guide. 2nd ed. William H. Lord. Ed. by Arthur L. Zapel. (Illus.). 160p. 1991. reprint ed. teacher ed., pap. 14.95 (*1-56608-018-5*, B116) Meriwether Pub.

Stagecraft in Euripides. Michael R. Halleran. LC 84-12314. 138p. 1984. 48.50 (*0-389-20513-3*, BNB 08069) B&N Imports.

Stagecraft One: A Complete Guide to Backstage Work. 2nd ed. William H. Lord. Ed. by Arthur L. Zapel. LC 90-26462. (Illus.). 160p. (C). 1991. reprint ed. pap. text ed. 14.95 (*0-916260-76-3*, B116) Meriwether Pub.

Stagecraft 1: A Complete Guide to Backstage Work. 2nd ed. William H. Lord. (Illus.). 67p. (C). 1991. student ed., pap. 5.00 (*0-9606320-4-2*); teacher ed., ring bd. 20.00 (*0-9606320-5-0*); per. 14.95 (*0-9606320-3-4*) W H Lord.

Stagecrafters' Handbook. 2nd ed. I. E. Clark. (Illus.). 56p. 1977. pap. 5.00 (*0-88680-182-6*) I E Clark.

Stagecrafters' Handbook: A Guide for Theatre Technicians. 3rd ed. I. E. Clark. LC 94-39528. (Illus.). 96p. (Orig.). 1995. pap. 10.00 (*0-88734-649-9*) Players Pr.

***Staged Art.** Maurizio F. Dell'Arco et al. (Illus.). 256p. 1997. pap. 55.00 (*88-8158-112-4*) Dist Art Pubs.

Staged Diabetes Management: DecisionPaths. Roger Mazze et al. 1995. ring bd. write for info. (*1-885115-03-2*) IDC Pub.

Stagefright: Letting It Work for You. Robert Triplett. LC 82-14205. (Illus.). 208p. 1983. 29.95 (*0-88229-720-1*); pap. text ed. 19.95 (*0-8304-1202-6*) Nelson-Hall.

Stager, Freundschaft: Facts, Incidents & Tradition Relating to the Stager-Rudy Families & Lineage, from 1717. Ed. by H. J. Stager. 144p. 1992. reprint ed. pap. 23.00 (*0-8328-2737-1*); reprint ed. lib. bdg. 33.00 (*0-8328-2736-3*) Higginson Bk Co.

Stages. Gillian Hall. 416p. 1987. mass mkt. 3.95 (*0-373-97036-6*) Harlequin Bks.

Stages. Jerome McDonough. (Illus.). 52p. 1979. pap. 3.25 (*0-88680-183-4*) I E Clark.

Stages: Director's Script. Jerome McDonough. (Illus.). 52p. 1979. pap. 10.00 (*0-88680-184-2*) I E Clark.

Stages: Norman Lloyd. Norman Lloyd. LC 89-77810. (Directors Guild of American Oral History Ser.: No. 9). (Illus.). 296p. 1990. 34.50 (*0-8108-2290-3*) Scarecrow.

Stages: Of Life in Theatre, Film & Television. Norman Lloyd. LC 92-30285. (Illus.). 278p. 1993. reprint ed. pap. 14.95 (*0-87910-166-0*) Limelight Edns.

Stages & Views. Penny Harter. Ed. by Thomas Fitzsimmons. LC 93-38840. (Reflections Ser.: No. 5). (Illus.). 128p. 1994. pap. text ed. 15.00 (*0-942668-42-1*) Katydid Bks.

Stages in the Revolution: Political Theatre in Britain since 1968. Catherine Itzin. 399p. (C). 1989. pap. 14.95 (*0-413-61505-7*, A0384, Pub. by Methuen UK) Heinemann.

Stages of Acting. Mack Owen. 194p. 1994. pap. text ed. 32.50 (*0-8230-4952-3*, Back Stage Bks) Watsn-Guptill.

Stages of Acting: A Practical Approach for Beginning Actors. Mack Owen. LC 92-20698. (C). 1993. text ed. 42.50 (*0-06-500632-1*) Addson-Wesley Educ.

Stages of Annihilation: Theatrical Representations of the Holocaust. Edward R. Isser. LC 96-20310. 208p. 1997. 33.50 (*0-8386-3674-8*) Fairleigh Dickinson.

Stages of Consciousness: Meditations on the Boundaries of the Soul. Georg Kuhlewind. Tr. by Maria St. Goar from GER. 160p. (Orig.). 1985. pap. 8.95 (*0-940262-08-8*) Lindisfarne Bks.

Stages of Desire: Male & Female Homosexuality in British & American Theatre. Carl Miller. Date not set. pap. 17.95 (*0-304-32817-0*, Pub. by Cassell Pubng UK) LPC InBook.

Stages of Desire: Male & Female Homosexuality in British & American Theatre. Carl Miller. (Lesbian & Gay Studies). 256p. 1995. 60.00 (*0-304-32815-4*, Pub. by Cassell Pubng UK) LPC InBook.

Stages of Drama: Classical to Contemporary Theater. Carl H. Klaus et al. 1349p. 1994. pap. text ed. 31.00 (*0-312-10135-X*) St Martin.

Stages of Economic Growth: A Non-Communist Manifesto. 3rd ed. Walt W. Rostow. 320p. 1991. pap. text ed. 21.95 (*0-521-40928-4*) Cambridge U Pr.

Stages of Economic Growth: A Non-Communist Manifesto. 3rd ed. Walt W. Rostow. 320p. 1991. text ed. 69.95 (*0-521-40070-8*) Cambridge U Pr.

Stages of Faith: The Psychology of Human Development. James W. Fowler. LC 80-7757. 352p. 1995. pap. 15.00 (*0-06-062866-9*) Harper SF.

Stages of Higher Knowledge. Rudolf Steiner. 64p. 1990. reprint ed. pap. 6.95 (*0-910142-37-8*) Anthroposophic.

Stages of History: Shakespeare's English Chronicles. Phyllis Rackin. LC 90-55196. 264p. 1990. 37.50 (*0-8014-2430-5*); pap. 14.95 (*0-8014-9698-5*) Cornell U Pr.

Stages of Human Evolution. 5th ed. C. Loring Brace. LC 94-35681. 371p. 1994. pap. text ed. 35.40 (*0-13-125485-5*) P-H.

Stages of Human Life: A Biography of Entire Man. James K. Feibleman. 270p. 1975. pap. text ed. 82.50 (*90-247-1692-6*, Pub. by M Nijhoff NE) Kluwer Ac.

Stages of Life: A Groundbreaking Look at How We Mature. Clifford Anderson. LC 94-43724. 240p. 1995. 23.00 (*0-87113-481-0*, Atlntc Mnthly) Grove-Atltic.

Stages of Management. August W. Smith. (Systems Inquiry Ser.). 164p. 1987. pap. text ed. 10.95 (*0-914105-37-X*) Intersystems Pubns.

***Stages of Play: Shakespeare's Theatrical Energies in Elizabethan Performance.** Michael W. Shurgot. LC 97-12163. 1997. write for info. (*0-87413-614-8*) U Delaware Pr.

Stages of Reading Development. 2nd ed. Chall. (C). 1995. pap. text ed. 30.00 (*0-15-503081-7*) HB Coll Pubs.

Stages of Religious Faith in the Classical Reformation Tradition: The Covenant Approach to the Ordo Salutis. David N. Poole. LC 95-7267. (Illus.). 336p. 1995. text ed. 99.95 (*0-7734-8890-1*) E Mellen.

Stages of Self: The Dramatic Monologues of Laforgue, Valery & Mallarme. Elisabeth A. Howe. LC 90-30675. 220p. (C). 1990. text ed. 24.95 (*0-8214-0953-0*) Ohio U Pr.

***Stages of Stress Leading to Disease: Predict It, Prevent It, What to Do.** Eileen B. Curns & Gladys T. McGarey. (Illus.). 32p. (Orig.). 1997. pap. 10.00 (*0-942968-04-2*) ACCORD IL.

Stages of Terror: Terrorism, Ideology, & Coercion As Theatre History. Anthony Kubiak. LC 90-25521. 228p. 1991. 39.95 (*0-253-33146-3*); pap. 13.95 (*0-253-20663-4*, MB-663) Ind U Pr.

Stages of the Development of a Feminist Consciousness in Perez Galdos (1843-1920) A Biographical Sketch. Lisa P. Conde. LC 90-35014. (Hispanic Literature Ser.: Vol. 7). 392p. 1990. lib. bdg. 99.95 (*0-88946-375-1*) E Mellen.

Stages of Translation: Translators on Translating for the Stage. Ed. by David Johnston. 224p. 1996. pap. 24.95 (*0-948230-75-4*, Pub. by N Hern Bks UK) Theatre Comm.

Stages of Twilight. Alice Derry. LC 86-17554. 74p. 1987. 14.95 (*0-932576-38-9*); pap. 7.95 (*0-932576-39-7*) Breitenbush Bks.

Stages on Life's Way. Soren Kierkegaard. Ed. by Howard V. Hong & Edna H. Hong. Tr. by Edna H. Hong. 866p. 1989. text ed. 95.00 (*0-691-07323-6*); pap. text ed. 24.95 (*0-691-02049-3*) Princeton U Pr.

Stages on the Road. Sigrid Undset. Tr. by A. G. Chater. LC 70-80404. (Essay Index Reprint Ser.). 1977. 18.95 (*0-8369-1068-0*) Ayer.

Stagflation: An International Problem. Ed. by Randall W. Hinshaw. LC 77-21824. (Business Economics & Finance Ser.: No. 10). 160p. reprint ed. pap. 45.60 (*0-7837-0631-6*, 2040975) Bks Demand.

Stagflation in the U. S. S. R. Isaak Adirim. Ed. by Maureen Young. (Illus.). 122p. (Orig.). 1983. pap. text ed. 75.00 (*1-55831-003-7*) Delphic Associates.

Staggered Lights. Dennis Nurkse. 1990. pap. 9.00 (*0-937669-42-3*) Owl Creek Pr.

Staggerford. Jon Hassler. 304p. 1986. mass mkt. 6.99 (*0-345-33375-6*) Ballantine.

***Staggerford.** Jon Hassler. 1997. pap. 12.00 (*0-345-41824-7*) Ballantine.

Stagg's University: The Rise, Decline & Fall of Big-Time Football at The University of Chicago. Robin Lester. LC 94-34018. (Sport & Society Ser.). (Illus.). 344p. 1995. 32.95 (*0-252-02128-2*) U of Ill Pr.

Staging a Children's Musical. 1987. pap. text ed. 24.95 (*0-7935-2887-9*) H Leonard.

Staging a Pantomime. Gill Davies. (Illus.). 128p. 1996. pap. 20.95 (*0-7136-4120-7*, Pub. by A&C Black UK) Talman.

Staging a Sanskrit Drama: Bhasa's Vision of Vasavadatta. John D. Mitchell & Mrinalini Sarabhai. LC 92-70319. (Illus.). 240p. (Orig.). (ENG & SAN.). (C). 1992. pap. 19.95 (*1-882763-02-5*) IASTA.

Staging a Snazzy Senior Showcase. Bob Dryden. Ed. by Mary Trone. LC 89-92203. (Illus.). 168p. (Orig.). 1989. pap. 9.95 (*0-9624834-0-0*) Cent Lakas Coll.

Staging a Spanish Classic: The House of Fools. Hugh A. Hareter. 1995. pap. text ed. 15.95 (*0-87359-053-8*) Northwood Univ.

Staging & Treatment of Gastric Cancer. C. Cordiano & D. De Manzoni. 330p. 1991. text ed. 60.00 (*1-57235-016-4*) Piccin NY.

Staging Areas for Persons with Mobility Limitations. (Illus.). 178p. (Orig.). (C). 1993. pap. text ed. 35.00 (*1-56806-777-1*) DIANE Pub.

Staging Chekhov: Cherry Orchard. John D. Mitchell. LC 91-73015. (Illus.). 416p. (Orig.). (ENG & RUS.). (C). 1991. pap. 19.95 (*1-882763-00-9*) IASTA.

Staging Den & Pack Ceremonies. 152p. 1986. 7.50 (*0-8395-3212-1*, 33212) BSA.

Staging Depth: The Politics of Psychological Discourse in the Drama of O'Neill. Joel Pfister. LC 94-26336. (Cultural Studies of the United States). (Illus.). 350p. 1995. pap. text ed. 17.95 (*0-8078-4496-9*); lib. bdg. 45.00 (*0-8078-2186-1*) U of NC Pr.

Staging Difference: Cultural Pluralism in American Theatre & Drama. Ed. by Marc Maufort. (American University Studies: Ser. XXVI, Vol. 25). 408p. (C). 1995. text ed. 60.95 (*0-8204-2732-2*) P Lang Pubng.

Staging Diversity: Plays & Practice in American Theater. Wolcott & Quinn. 464p. (C). 1992. pap. text ed. 44.04 (*0-8403-8050-X*) Kendall-Hunt.

Staging Fascism: 18 BL & the Theater for Masses. Jeffrey T. Schnapp. LC 95-12797. 384p. 1996. pap. 16.95 (*0-8047-2608-6*) Stanford U Pr.

Staging Fascism: 18 BL & the Theater for Masses. Jeffrey T. Schnapp. LC 95-12797. (Illus.). 384p. 1996. 49.50 (*0-8047-2607-8*) Stanford U Pr.

Staging Gay Lives: An Anthology of Contemporary Gay Theater. Ed. by John M. Clum. (Illus.). 496p. (C). 1996. pap. text ed. 30.00 (*0-8133-2505-6*) Westview.

Staging Handbook. Francis Reid. (Illus.). 1978. 14.95 (*0-87830-160-7*, Thtre Arts Bks) Routledge.

Staging Handbook. Francis Reid. 1996. pap. 16.95 (*0-435-08682-0*, 08682) Heinemann.

Staging Japanese Theatre: Noh & Kabuki. John D. Mitchell et al. (Illus.). 245p. (Orig.). (C). pap. text ed. 24.95 (*1-882763-06-8*) IASTA.

Staging Masculinity: Male Identity in Contemporary Drama. Carla J. McDonough. LC 96-44555. 192p. 1996. lib. bdg. 29.50 (*0-7864-0268-7*) McFarland & Co.

Staging Musical Theatre: A Complete Guide for Directors, Choreographers & Producers. Elaine A. Novak & Deborah Novak. LC 96-18158. (Illus.). 192p. 1996. pap. 19.99 (*1-55870-407-8*, Betrwy Bks) F & W Pubns Inc.

Staging of Language & Languages of the Stage: Mallarme's Poeme Critique & Artaud's Poetry-Minus-Text, Vol. 15. Dominique D. Fisher. LC 93-11439. (Reading Plus Ser.: Vol. 15). 151p. (C). 1994. text ed. 41.95 (*0-8204-2298-3*) P Lang Pubng.

Staging of Religious Drama in Europe in the Middle Ages: Texts & Documents in English Translation. 2nd ed. Ed. by Peter Meredith & John Tailby. (Early Drama, Art & Music Ser.: No. 4). 1989. reprint ed. boxed 24.95 (*0-918720-23-0*) Medieval Inst.

Staging of Shakespeare's 'Romeo & Juliet' As a Ballet. Camille C. Howard. LC 92-4981. 156p. 1992. 69.95 (*0-7734-9856-7*) E Mellen.

An Asterisk (*) at the beginning of an entry indicates that the title is appearing in BIP for the first time.

Staging O'Neill: The Experimental Years, 1920-1934. Ronald H. Wainscott. LC 87-34056. (C). 1988. text ed. 47.00 (0-300-04152-7) Yale U Pr.

Staging Place: The Geography of Modern Drama. Una Chaudhuri. LC 95-13373. (Theater: Theory - Text - Performance Ser.). 1995. text ed. 34.50 (0-472-09589-7) U of Mich Pr.

*Staging Place: The Geography of Modern Drama. Una Chaudhuri. (C). 1997. pap. 16.95 (0-472-06589-0) U of Mich Pr.

Staging Politics: The Lasting Impact of Shakespeare's Historical Plays. Wolfgang Iser. Tr. by David Henry Wilson. LC 93-19730. (ENG & GER.). 1994. 39.50 (0-231-07588-X) Col U Pr.

Staging Premodern Drama: A Guide to Production Problems. Lee Mitchell. LC 83-5624. xiv, 239p. 1984. text ed. 52.95 (0-313-23685-2, MSD/, Greenwood Pr) Greenwood.

Staging Real Things: The Performance of Ordinary Events. Geoff Pywell. LC 93-44701. 1994. 32.50 (0-8387-5274-8) Bucknell U Pr.

*Staging Reform, Reforming the Stage: Protestantism & Popular Theater in Early Modern England. Huston Diehl. LC 96-41169. (Illus.). 256p. 1996. 39.95 (0-8014-3303-7) Cornell U Pr.

Staging Strikes: Workers' Theatre & the American Labor Movement. LC 96-24739. (Critical Perspectives on the Past Ser.). 1997. 39.95 (1-56639-504-6) Temple U Pr.

Staging the Gaze: Postmodernism, Psychoanalysis & Shakespearean Comedy. Barbara Freedman. LC 90-55117. (Illus.). 264p. 1991. 42.50 (0-8014-2279-5); pap. 16.95 (0-8014-9737-X) Cornell U Pr.

Staging the Impossible: The Fantastic Mode in Modern Drama. Ed. by Patrick D. Murphy. LC 92-10678. (Contributions to the Study of Science Fiction & Fantasy Ser.: No. 54). 256p. 1992. text ed. 55.00 (0-313-27270-0, MIJ/, Greenwood Pr) Greenwood.

*Staging the Jew: The Performance of an American Ethnicity, 1860-1920. Harley Erdman. LC 97-6968. (Illus.). 224p. (C). 1997. text ed. 50.00 (0-8135-2413-X); pap. text ed. 19.95 (0-8135-2414-8) Rutgers U Pr.

Staging the Musical: Planning, Rehearsing, & Marketing the Amateur Production. David Grote. 1986. 10.95 (0-13-840182-9) S&S Trade.

*Staging the Nation. Wilmeth. Date not set. pap. text ed. write for info. (0-312-17091-2) St Martin.

Staging the Renaissance: Reinterpretations of Elizabethan & Jacobean Drama. Ed. by David S. Kastan & Peter Stallybrass. 256p. (C). (gr. 13). 1991. pap. 16.95 (0-415-90166-9, A3571, Routledge NY) Routledge.

Staging Women: The Lysistrata, Women at the Thesmophoria, & Assemblywomen of Aristophanes. Jeffrey Henderson. LC 96-1810. 300p. 1996. pap. 16.95 (0-415-90744-6) Routledge.

Staging Women: The Lysistrata, Women at the Thesmophoria, & Assemblywomen of Aristophanes. Jeffrey Henderson. LC 96-1810. 300p. (C). 1996. text ed. 59.95 (0-415-90743-8) Routledge.

Stagings: Short Scripts for Middle & High School Students. Joan Garner. xiii, 233p. 1995. pap. text ed. 27.00 (1-56308-343-4) Teacher Ideas Pr.

Stagnant Thoughts. Sajan Gunesekere. (Orig.). 1996. pap. write for info. (1-57553-272-7) Watermrk Pr.

Stagnating Metropolis: The Economy & Demography of Stockholm, 1750-1850. Johan Soderberg et al. (Studies in Population, Economy & Society in Past Time: No. 13). 248p. (C). 1991. text ed. 64.95 (0-521-39046-X) Cambridge U Pr.

Stagnation & Renewal in Social Policy. Martin Rein et al. LC 86-20380. (Comparative Public Policy Analysis Ser.). 244p. (C). (gr. 13). 1987. text ed. 66.95 (0-87332-390-4) M E Sharpe.

Stagnation & the Financial Explosion. Harry Magdoff & Paul M. Sweezy. 224p. 1987. 24.00 (0-85345-716-6); pap. 10.00 (0-85345-715-8) Monthly Rev.

Stagnation Oder Ruckschritt? Autopsie Zweier Padagogischer Idole. Harald Hirschfeld et al. 439p. 1987. 60.80 (3-8204-9445-6) P Lang Pubng.

Stagnation or Healthy Growth? The Economic Challenge to the United States in the Nineties. James J. O'Leary. 162p. (C). 1992. lib. bdg. 42.50 (0-8191-8839-5) U Pr of Amer.

Stahleisen-Woerterbuch. 4th ed. Eisenbuettenleut Verein Deutsch. 411p. (ENG & GER.). 1987. 75.00 (0-8288-0634-9, M15533) Fr & Eur.

Stahleisen-Woerterbuch: German-French, French-German. 3rd ed. Centre de Recherches Metallurgiques Staff. 555p. (FRE & GER.). 1991. 75.00 (0-7859-7101-7) Fr & Eur.

Stahleisen Woerterbuch German-Spanish, Spanish-German. 3rd ed. Centre de Recherches Metallurgiques Staff. 569p. (GER & SPA.). 1991. 75.00 (0-7859-6945-4) Fr & Eur.

Stahl's Wild Edibles. rev. ed. Mary Lou Stahl. (Illus.). 46p. 1990. reprint ed. pap. 5.00 (1-886075-06-9) Grass Rt Ent.

Stahmer Family: The Stahmer Family from Hasenburen & Bremerhaven, Germany & the U.S.A. Meg Thompson. (Illus.). 200p. (Orig.). 1992. pap. 25.00 (0-685-51144-8) Pac Family Hist Pub.

*Stain. Harry L. Kraus, Jr. LC 97-16775. 424p. (Orig.). 1997. pap. 12.99 (0-89107-972-6) Crossway Bks.

Stain. rev. ed. Fred Viebahn. Tr. by Karin Isbell from GER. 284p. 18.00 (0-934257-17-5); pap. 8.00 (0-934257-18-3) Story Line.

Stain. Rikki Ducornet. LC 95-16365. 230p. 1995. reprint ed. pap. 11.95 (1-56478-085-6) Dalkey Arch.

Stain & Spot Remover Handbook. Jean Cooper. LC 95-12056. 160p. 1995. pap. 12.95 (0-88266-811-0, Garden Way Pub) Storey Comm Inc.

Stain Buster's Bible: The Complete Guide to Spot Removal. Don A. Aslett. 192p. 1990. pap. 11.95 (0-452-26385-9, Plume) NAL-Dutton.

Stain Removal Guide for Stone. Frederick M. Hueston. LC 94-23814. 1995. 29.95 (1-885863-04-7) Busn News.

Staindrop Quaker Meeting House. J. C. Mann. (C). 1988. 25.00 (1-85072-118-1, Pub. by W Sessions UK) St Mut.

Stained Cross. Don Abernathy. Ed. by Melanie Pompey. 250p. (Orig.). 1996. pap. 9.95 (1-878567-08-X, P40) D A Pub.

Stained Glass. William F. Buckley, Jr. 352p. 1981. pap. 3.95 (0-380-54791-0) Avon.

*Stained Glass. Concetta Principe. 96p. 1997. pap. text ed. 12.00 (1-55071-062-1) Guernica Editions.

Stained Glass. Rosanna Warren. LC 92-37194. 80p. 1993. 17.95 (0-393-03486-0) Norton.

*Stained Glass. William F. Buckley, Jr. LC 97-14254. 320p. 1997. reprint ed. pap. 10.95 (1-888952-29-6) Cumberland Hse.

Stained Glass: A Guide to Information Sources. Ed. by Darlene Brady & William Serban. LC 79-23712. (Art & Architecture Information Guide Ser.: Vol. 10). 586p. 1980. 68.00 (0-8103-1445-2) Gale.

Stained Glass: An Illustrated History. Sarah Browne. (Illus.). 1992. 19.99 (0-517-06967-9) Random Hse Value.

Stained Glass: How to Make Stunning Stained Glass Items Using Modern Materials... Marc Gerstein. 1995. pap. 16.95 (0-8050-4266-0) H Holt & Co.

Stained Glass: Poems. Rosanna Warren. 1994. pap. 8.95 (0-393-31174-0) Norton.

Stained Glass: Poems. fac. ed. William Mills. LC 78-11893. 69p. 1979. reprint ed. pap. 25.00 (0-7837-7808-2, 2047564) Bks Demand.

Stained Glass: Projects & Patterns. George Shannon & Pat Torlen. LC 95-34184. (Illus.). 128p. 1995. pap. 24.95 (1-895569-40-0, Pub. by Tamos Bks CN) Sterling.

*Stained Glass: Projects & Patterns. George Shannon. 1997. pap. 14.95 (1-895569-13-3) Sterling.

Stained Glass: Worldviews & Social Science. Ed. by Paul A. Marshall et al. 188p. (Orig.). (C). 1989. pap. text ed. 19.50 (0-8191-7254-5, Inst Christ Stud) U Pr of Amer.

Stained Glass Art of William Jay Bolton. Willene B. Clark. LC 91-18456. (Illus.). 308p. 1992. 49.95 (0-8156-2553-7) Syracuse U Pr.

Stained Glass Basics: Techniques - Tools - Projects. Chris Rich et al. (Illus.). 128p. 1996. 24.95 (0-8069-4876-0) Lark Books.

*Stained Glass Basics: Techniques, Tools, Projects. Chris Rich. 1997. pap. text ed. 14.95 (0-8069-4877-9) Sterling.

Stained Glass Before 1700 in American Collections: Silver-Stained Roundels & Unipartite Panels. Timothy B. Husband. (Monograph Series I: Vol. 39). (Illus.). 277p. 1991. pap. 30.00 (0-89468-175-3) Natl Gallery Art.

Stained Glass Bouquet. Terra Parma. Ed. by Stained Glass Images Inc. Staff. (Illus.). 64p. 1989. text ed. 11.95 (0-936459-12-3) Stained Glass.

Stained-Glass Ceiling: Churches & Their Women Pastors. Sally B. Purvis. 112p. (Orig.). 1995. pap. 12.00 (0-664-25608-2) Westminster John Knox.

Stained Glass Coloring Book. William H. Mackintosh & Ruth M. Goliwas. (Illus.). 48p. (J). (ps-2). 1990. pap. 2.95 (0-671-69477-4, Litl Simon S&S) S&S Childrens.

Stained Glass Craft. Nancy E. Krulik. (J). 1996. pap. 9.95 (0-590-20251-0) Scholastic Inc.

Stained Glass Craft. J. A. Divine & G. Blachford. 115p. 1972. reprint ed. pap. 3.50 (0-486-22812-6) Dover.

Stained Glass Craft Made Simple: Step-by-Step Instructions Using the Modern Copper-Foil Method. James McDonell. 32p. 1985. pap. 3.95 (0-486-24963-8) Dover.

Stained Glass Delightful Designs. Randy DeMello. (Illus.). 56p. 1986. pap. 8.95 (0-935133-06-2) CKE Pubns.

Stained Glass Elegies. Shusaku Endo. 166p. 8400. 30.00 (0-7206-0629-2, Pub. by P Owen Ltd UK) Dufour.

Stained Glass Elegies. Shusaku Endo. Tr. by Van C. Gessel from JPN. LC 90-6026. (New Directions Classics Ser.). 176p. 1990. pap. 10.95 (0-8112-1142-8, NDP699) New Directions.

Stained Glass Gift Shoppe. Terra Parma. Ed. by Stained Glass Images Inc. Staff. (Illus.). 1988. 11.95 (0-936459-08-5) Stained Glass.

Stained Glass Guide. Kay B. Weiner. (Illus.). 144p. 1994. 24.95 (0-8230-4913-2, Watsn-Guptill) Watsn-Guptill.

*Stained Glass in England. June Osborne. (History Handbooks Ser.). (Illus.). 288p. (Orig.). 1997. pap. 26.95 (0-7509-1613-3, Pub. by Sutton Pubng UK) Bks Intl VA.

Stained Glass in England. 2nd rev. ed. June Osbourne. LC 92-43356. (Illus.). 288p. 1993. 38.00 (0-7509-0234-5, Pub. by Sutton Pubng UK) Bks Intl VA.

Stained Glass in England During the Middle Ages. Richard Marks. (Illus.). 376p. 1993. 85.00 (0-8020-0592-6) U of Toronto Pr.

*Stained Glass of the Church of St. Mary, Fairford, Glos. Hilary Wayment. (Illus.). 189p. 1985. pap. 15.98 (0-85431-240-4, Pub. by Soc Antiquaries UK) David Brown.

Stained Glass of William Morris & His Circle: A Catalogue, Vol. 2. A. Charles Sewter. LC 72-91307. (Studies in British Art). 730p. 1975. 195.00 (0-300-01836-3) Yale U Pr.

Stained Glass Pattern Book: Eighty-Eight Designs for Workable Projects. Ed Sibbett, Jr. LC 76-15447. (Pictorial Archive Ser.). (Illus.). (Orig.). 1976. pap. 4.95 (0-486-23360-X) Dover.

*Stained Glass Patterns: Patterns for All Uses. Patricia L. MacKenzie. (Illus.). 95p. (Orig.). 1997. pap. 10.95 (0-9657552-8-2) P L Mackenzie.

Stained Glass Photo Frames. Alex Spatz. (Illus.). 48p. (Orig.). 1994. pap. 4.19 (0-9641597-1-6) Cliffside Studio.

Stained Glass Primer, Vol 1. Peter Mollica. 1971. pap. 6.95 (0-9601306-1-6) Mollica Stained Glass.

Stained Glass Projects for the Home. Nikolaus Koppel. (Illus.). 80p. 1991. pap. 14.95 (0-7137-2230-4, Pub. by Blandford Pr UK) Sterling.

Stained Glass Rain: A Novel of the Sixties. Bruce Boston. 464p. 1994. lib. bdg. 39.00 (0-8095-6014-3) Borgo Pr.

Stained Glass Rain: A Novel of the Sixties. Bruce Boston. LC 93-5326. 460p. 1993. pap. 14.95 (0-938075-30-6) Ocean View Bks.

Stained Glass Rain: A Novel of the Sixties. deluxe limited ed. Bruce Boston. LC 93-5326. 460p. 1993. Signed ltd. ed. 50.00 (0-938075-29-2) Ocean View Bks.

Stained Glass Shades for Small Lamps: With Full-Size Templates. Ed Sibbett, Jr. (Illus.). 64p. (Orig.). 1988. pap. 6.95 (0-486-25628-6) Dover.

Stained Glass to Go. Daniel Donovan. (Illus.). 20p. 1989. pap. 7.95 (0-935133-32-1) CKE Pubns.

Stained Glass Treasures. Donna Schulze. (Illus.). 48p. (Orig.). 1985. pap. 6.50 (0-940353-00-8, VA 192-640) Papillon Texas.

Stained Glass Village. Vicki F. Morrison. (Illus.). 52p. 1993. 11.95 (0-936459-21-2) Stained Glass.

Stained Glass Village, Bk. 2. Vicki Ford-Morrison. (Illus.). 52p. 1994. 11.95 (0-936459-23-9) Stained Glass.

Stained Glass Window. Charlotte M. Stein. Ed. by Jennifer Sakurai. LC 88-70883. (Illus.). 150p. (Orig.). (YA). 1996. student ed., pap. 11.95 (0-916634-12-4) Double M Pr.

*Stained Glass Window: With Imagery Workbook. Charlotte M. Stein. Ed. by Jennifer Sakurai. LC 88-70883. (Illus.). 150p. (Orig.). (YA). (gr. 7-12). 1997. student ed., pap. 11.95 (0-916634-15-9) Double M Pr.

*Stained Glass Window: With Imagery Workbook. Charlotte M. Stein. Ed. by Jennifer Sakurai. (Illus.). 200p. (YA). (gr. 7-12). 1997. write for info. (0-916634-16-7) Double M Pr.

Stained Radiance. J. Leslie Mitchell. 240p. (Orig.). 1993. pap. 16.00 (0-7486-6141-7, Pub. by Polygon UK) Subterranean Co.

Stained White Radiance. James Lee Burke. 336p. 1993. reprint ed. mass mkt. 6.99 (0-380-72047-7) Avon.

Staining Technique in Botany. B. K. Prasad. 107p. 1986. 45.00 (81-7089-081-0, Pub. by Intl Bk Distr II) St Mut.

Stainless. Todd Grimson. LC 95-32702. 265p. 1996. pap. 12.00 (0-06-105321-X, HarpT) HarpC.

*Stainless. Todd Grimson. 1997. mass mkt. 5.99 (0-06-105775-4, Harp PBks) HarpC.

Stainless & Heat Resisting Steels. LC 90-71018. 267p. 1990. 45.00 (0-932897-56-8) Iron & Steel.

Stainless Steel Angle from Japan: An International Trade Investigation. (Illus.). 80p. (Orig.). (C). 1995. pap. text ed. 30.00 (0-7881-1911-7) DIANE Pub.

Stainless Steel Bar from Brazil, India, Japan, & Spain: An International Trade Investigation. Jim McClure. (Illus.). 229p. (Orig.). (C). 1995. pap. text ed. 50.00 (0-7881-2368-8) DIANE Pub.

Stainless Steel Castings - STP 756. Albert S. Melilli. 454p. 1982. 45.00 (0-8031-0740-4, 04-756000-01) ASTM.

Stainless Steel Hearts. Harry L. Kraus, Jr. LC 94-8019. 416p. (Orig.). 1994. pap. 12.99 (0-89107-810-X) Crossway Bks.

*Stainless Steel in Concrete: State of the Art Report. Ed. by Ulf Nurnberger. (European Federation of Corrosion Publications: No. 18). 48p. 1996. pap. 20.00 (1-86125-008-8, Pub. by Inst Materials UK) Ashgate Pub Co.

Stainless Steel Rat for President. Harry Harrison. 192p. 1988. mass mkt. 4.99 (0-553-27612-3, Spectra) Bantam.

Stainless Steel Rat Gets Drafted. Harry Harrison. 288p. 1988. mass mkt. 4.99 (0-553-27307-8, Spectra) Bantam.

Stainless Steel Rat Goes to Hell, Vol. 1. Harry Harrison. 1996. 21.95 (0-312-86063-3) Tor Bks.

Stainless Steel Rat Is Born. Harry Harrison. 224p. (Orig.). 1985. mass mkt. 4.99 (0-553-27942-4, Spectra) Bantam.

Stainless Steel Rat Sings the Blues. Harry Harrison. 256p. 1995. mass mkt. 5.50 (0-553-56939-2) Bantam.

Stainless Steel Rule. Jean Ferris. LC 85-45731. 192p. (J). (gr. 7 up). 1986. 13.95 (0-374-37212-8) FS&G.

Stainless Steel Soprano. Kathryn B. Gurkin. 69p. (Orig.). 1990. pap. 9.95 (0-932662-92-7) St Andrews NC.

Stainless Steel Visions. Harry Harrison. 256p. 1994. mass mkt. 4.99 (0-8125-3529-4) Tor Bks.

Stainless Steels. Ed. by Joseph R. Davis. LC 94-23392. (ASM Specialty Handbook Ser.). (Illus.). 576p. 1994. 173.00 (0-87170-503-6, 6398) ASM.

Stainless Steels. Ed. by P. Lacombe et al. 978p. 1993. 156.00 (2-86883-189-3, 6547) ASM.

Stainless Steels '84. 587p. 1985. pap. text ed. 50.00 (0-904357-68-6, Pub. by Inst Materials UK) Ashgate Pub Co.

Stainless Steels '87: Proceedings of Conference, University of York, 14-16 September '87. 392p. 1988. text ed. 94.50 (0-901462-42-X, Pub. by Inst Materials UK) Ashgate Pub Co.

Stains Cytochemical Methods. M. A. Hayat. (Illus.). 430p. (C). 1993. 95.00 (0-306-44294-9, Plenum Pr) Plenum.

Stains on a White Collar. Peter Grabosky & Adam Sutton. 308p. 1989. pap. 29.00 (1-86287-009-8, Pub. by Federation Pr AU) Gaunt.

Stains on My Name, War in My Veins: Guyana & the Politics of Cultural Struggle. Brackette F. Williams. LC 90-47529. 343p. 1991. text ed. 39.95 (0-8223-1114-3); pap. text ed. 19.95 (0-8223-1119-4) Duke.

Stair Builders Handbook. T. W. Love. LC 74-4298. (Illus.). 1974. pap. 15.50 (0-910460-07-8) Craftsman.

Stair-Building Made Easy. Fred T. Hodgson. 1994. reprint ed. lib. bdg. 18.95 (1-56849-525-0) Buccaneer Bks.

*Stair Layout. Stanley Badzinski, Jr. (Illus.). 172p. 1996. pap. 16.96 (0-8269-0701-6) Am Technical.

Stair-Step Wit. Agnes McGaha. Ed. by Michael McGaha. (Took Modern Poetry in English Ser.: No. 15). (Illus.). 28p. (Orig.). 1991. pap. 5.00 (1-879457-18-0) Norton Coker Pr.

Staircase, Set. John Templer. (Illus.). 195p. 1992. 65.00 (0-262-20090-2) MIT Pr.

Staircase: History & Theories. John Templer. 1992. 32.00 (0-262-20082-1) MIT Pr.

Staircase: History & Theories. John Templer. (Illus.). 200p. 1995. pap. 14.95 (0-262-70055-7) MIT Pr.

Staircase: Studies of Hazards, Falls & Safer Design. John Templer. (Illus.). 210p. 1992. 37.50 (0-262-20083-X) MIT Pr.

Staircase: Studies of Hazards, Falls, & Safer Design, 2 vols., Set. John Templer. (Illus.). 1995. 29.95 (0-262-70057-3) MIT Pr.

Staircase: Studies of Hazards, Falls, & Safer Design, Vol. 2. John Templer. (Illus.). 216p. 1995. 16.95 (0-262-70056-5) MIT Pr.

Staircase Seventeen. Gauri Pant. (Writers Workshop Redbird Ser.). 1975. 8.00 (0-88253-644-3); pap. text ed. 4.00 (0-88253-643-5) Ind-US Inc.

Staircases. Maritz Vandenburg. 1996. pap. 25.00 (1-85490-416-7) Academy Ed UK.

StairMaster Fitness Handbook: A User's Guide to Exercise Testing & Prescription. Ed. by James A. Peterson & Cedric X. Bryant. LC 95-70429. (Health, Fitness, & Wellness Ser.). (Illus.). 340p. (Orig.). 1995. pap. 19.95 (1-57167-050-5) Sagamore Pub.

StairMaster Weekly Planner & Training Diary. Cedric X. Bryant & James A. Peterson. (Health, Fitness, & Wellness Ser.). 140p. (Orig.). 1995. spiral bd., pap. 9.95 (1-57167-024-6) Sagamore Pub.

*Stairs. FHB Editors. LC 96-37612. (Builder's Library). (Illus.). 128p. 1997. 24.95 (1-56158-207-7, 070335) Taunton.

Stairs: The Best of Fine Homebuilding. Taunton Press Staff. LC 95-47080. (Best of Fine Homebuilding Ser.). (Illus.). 128p. (Orig.). 1996. pap. 14.95 (1-56158-131-3, 070263) Taunton.

Stairs & Railings. Jeff Beneke. Ed. by Rich Ziegner. LC 96-84681. (Quick Guide Ser.). (Illus.). 80p. (Orig.). 1996. pap. 7.95 (1-880029-88-X) Creative Homeowner.

Stairs-Geneva-the Location. Peter Greenaway. 228p. 1995. pap. 35.00 (1-85894-010-9) Dist Art Pubs.

Stairs of Sand. Zane Grey. 304p. 1992. mass mkt. 3.99 (0-06-100468-5, Harp PBks) HarpC.

Stairs, Steps & Ramps. Alan Blanc. (Illus.). 192p. 1996. pap. 89.95 (0-7506-1526-5) Buttrwrth-Heinemann.

Stairway. rev. ed. Alice A. Chown. (Illus.). 351p. 1988. 30.00 (0-8020-5769-1); pap. 14.95 (0-8020-6683-6) U of Toronto Pr.

Stairway from Here to There. Betty K. Schultz. LC 94-68949. (Illus.). 78p. (J). (gr. 5-6). 1995. per., pap. 8.95 (0-929568-03-6) Raspberry IL.

Stairway over the Brandywine: A Love Story. Ed Okonowicz. 24p. (Orig.). pap. 5.00 (0-9643244-2-3) Myst & Lace.

Stairway to Destiny. large type ed. Miriam Macgregor. 303p. 1994. 25.99 (0-7505-0661-X) Ulverscroft.

Stairway to Doom. Robert Quackenbush. LC 82-21484. (Miss Mallard Mystery Ser.). (Illus.). 48p. (J). (gr. 2-6). 1998. pap. 5.95 (0-671-67053-0, S&S Bks Young Read) S&S Childrens.

Stairway to Doom: A Miss Mallard Mystery. Robert Quackenbush. LC 82-21484. (Illus.). 48p. (J). (ps-5). 1983. lib. bdg. 9.95 (0-13-804595-X) P-H.

Stairway to Heaven. Zecharia Sitchin. 336p. 1983. mass mkt. 6.99 (0-380-63339-6) Avon.

Stairway to Heaven: Led Zeppelin Uncensored. Richard Cole. 464p. 1993. mass mkt. 6.99 (0-06-109021-2, Harp PBks) HarpC.

Stairway to Heaven: The Second Book of The Earth Chronicles. Zecharia Sitchin. (Earth Chronicles Ser.). (Illus.). 336p. 1993. reprint ed. 21.95 (0-939680-89-0) Bear & Co.

Stairway to Hell: The Well-Planned Destruction of Teens. Rick Jones. LC 88-72362. (Illus.). 206p. (Orig.). (YA). (gr. 7-12). 1988. pap. 8.50 (0-937958-30-1) Chick Pubns.

*Stairway to Success: The Complete Blueprint for Personal & Professional Achievement. Nido R. Qubein. LC 97-7567. 256p. 1997. pap. text ed. 16.95 (0-471-15494-6) Wiley.

Stairway to the Mind: The Controversial New Science of Consciousness. Alwyn C. Scott. (Illus.). 248p. 1995. 25.00 (0-387-94381-1) Spr-Verlag.

*Stairway to the Stars: Skywatching in Three Great Ancient Cultures. Anthony F. Aveni. LC 96-36517. 1997. text ed. 24.95 (0-471-15942-5) Wiley.

Stairway to the Stars: The Story of the World's Largest Observatory. B. Parker. (Illus.). 360p. 1994. 27.95 (0-306-44763-0, Plenum Pr) Plenum.

Stairway Walks in Los Angeles. Adah Bakalinsky & Larry Gordon. LC 90-41027. (Illus.). 128p. (Orig.). 1990. pap. 9.95 (0-89997-112-1) Wilderness Pr.

Stairway Walks in San Francisco. 3rd rev. ed. Adah Bakalinsky. (Illus.). 148p. (Orig.). 1995. pap. 9.95 (0-89997-184-9) Wilderness Pr.

Stairways Level 7: HBJ Reading 1987. Early. (J). 1987. student ed., pap. 30.00 (0-15-330507-X) HB Schl Dept.

Stake. J. F. Freedman. Date not set. 16.95 (0-453-00958-1, NAL Bks) NAL-Dutton.

*Stake in the Future: Redefining the Canadian Mineral Industry. Mary L. McAllister & Cynthia J. Alexander. 248p. 1997. 75.00 (0-7748-0603-6, Pub. by U BC Pr) U of Wash Pr.

*Stake in the Future: The Stakeholder Solution. John Plender. LC 97-6369. (Illus.). 288p. 1997. 25.00 (1-85788-175-3) Nicholas Brealey.

Stake in the Kingdom. Nigel Tranter. 384p. 1996. pap. 10.95 (0-340-63765-X, Pub. by H & S UK) Trafalgar.

Stake in the Land see Americanization Studies: The Acculturation of Immigrant Groups into American Society

Stake Your Claim: Exploring the Gold Mine Within. Emmet Fox. LC 52-11683. 112p. 1992. reprint ed. pap. 10.00 (*0-06-250537-8*) Harper SF.

***Stake Your Claim! How to Find Gold & Stake a Mining Claim.** 2nd rev. ed. Mark Silva. (Illus.). 124p. 1997. pap. 17.95 (*0-9627347-3-X*) M Silva.

Stake Your Claim! The Tale of America's Enduring Mining Laws. Charles W. Miller, Jr. (Illus.). 1991. 34.95 (*0-87026-080-4*) Westernlore.

Staked Goat. Jeremiah Healy. 320p. 1991. mass mkt. 5.99 (*0-671-74284-1*) PB.

Staked Plain. Frank X. Tolbert. LC 87-9754. (Southwest Life & Letters Ser.). 292p. 1987. reprint ed. 22.50 (*0-87074-252-3*); reprint ed. pap. 10.95 (*0-87074-253-1*) SMU Press.

Stakeholder Approach to Corporate Governance Managing in a Dynamic Environment. Abbass F. Alkhafaji. LC 88-32489. 302p. 1989. text ed. 69.50 (*0-89930-447-8*, ACA, Quorum Bks) Greenwood.

***Stakeholder Capitalism.** Kelly. LC 96-29602. 1997. text ed. 69.95 (*0-312-17346-6*) St Martin.

***Stakeholder Corporation: A Blueprint for Maximizing Stakeholder Value.** David Wheeler & Maria Sillanpaa. 320p. 1997. 25.00 (*0-273-62661-2*) Pitman Pubing.

Stakeholder Negotiations: Exercise in Sustainable Development. Matthew Arnold. 184p. (C). 1995. 16.25 (*0-256-18806-8*) Irwin.

Stakeholders of the Organizational Mind: Toward a New View of Organizational Policy Making. Ian J. Mitroff. LC 83-48161. (Management Ser.). 203p. text ed. 32.95 (*0-87589-580-8*) Jossey-Bass.

Stakeholders/Allies/Adversaries: Module 9, Module 9. Ancona et al. (GI - Organizational Behavior Ser.). (Illus.). 1996. text ed. 7.95 (*0-538-85889-3*) S-W Pub.

Stakes Annual for 1993. Ed. by Raymond S. Paulick. (Illus.). 480p. (Orig.). 1994. pap. 24.95 (*0-939049-57-0*) Blood-Horse.

Stakes Annual for 1994: Annual Supplement to the Blood-Horse. Ed. by Raymond S. Paulick & Dan Mearns. (Blood-Horse Supplement Ser.). (Illus.). 475p. (Orig.). 1995. pap. 35.00 (*0-939049-65-1*) Blood-Horse.

Stakes Annual for 1995. Ed. by Raymond S. Paulick & Dan Mearns. (Illus.). 500p. (Orig.). 1996. pap. 35.00 (*0-939049-71-6*) Blood-Horse.

Stakes Winners 1991. (Annual Supplement Ser.). 900p. (Orig.). 1992. pap. 42.00 (*0-939049-45-7*) Blood-Horse.

Stakhanovism & the Politics of Productivity in the U. S. S. R., 1935-1941. Lewis H. Siegelbaum. (Cambridge Russian, Soviet & Post-Soviet Studies: No. 59). (Illus.). 288p. (C). 1990. pap. text ed. 20.95 (*0-521-39556-9*) Cambridge U Pr.

Stakhanovism & the Politics of Productivity in the USSR, 1935-1941. Lewis H. Siegelbaum. (Cambridge Russian, Soviet & Post-Soviet Studies: No. 59). 275p. 1988. text ed. 59.95 (*0-521-34548-0*) Cambridge U Pr.

Staking a Claim: Feminism, Bureacracy & the State. Suzanne Franzway et al. 240p. 1989. pap. text ed. 19.95 (*0-04-352239-4*, Pub. by Allen Unwin AT) Paul & Co Pubs.

Staking Claims. Page Edwards, Jr. LC 79-66572. 160p. 1980. 11.95 (*0-7145-2689-4*); pap. 7.95 (*0-7145-2774-2*) M Boyars Pubs.

Staking Out the Terrain: Power & Performance among Natural Resource Agencies. 2nd ed. Jeanne N. Clarke & Daniel C. McCool. LC 85-12663. 279p. (C). 1996. text ed. 59.50 (*0-7914-2945-8*); pap. text ed. 19.95 (*0-7914-2946-6*) State U NY Pr.

Staking Tools & How to Use Them. K & D Manufacturing Corp. Staff. (Illus.). 108p. 1988. pap. 11.95 (*0-930163-16-8*) Arlington Bk.

Staking Your Claim on Healing. C. C. Cribb. LC 79-83919. (If God Has It I Want It! Ser.). 1979. pap. 2.95 (*0-932046-14-2*) Manhattan Ltd NC.

Stalag Luft III. Spellmount Ltd. Publishers Staff. (C). 1986. 129.00 (*0-685-60237-0*, Pub. by Spellmount UK) St Mut.

Stalag Luft III: The Full Story. Charles Rollings. 1000p. (C). 1992. 125.00 (*0-946771-58-8*, Pub. by Spellmount UK) St Mut.

Stalag Seventeen. Donald Bevan. 1952. pap. 5.25 (*0-8222-1070-3*) Dramatists Play.

Stale Food vs. Fresh Food: Cause & Cure of Choked Arteries. 6th ed. Robert S. Ford. 48p. 1977. student ed., ring bd. 7.00 (*0-686-09051-9*) Magnolia Lab.

***Stalemate.** John Philpin. 1997. mass mkt. 6.50 (*0-553-56999-6*) Bantam.

Stalemate: Political Economic Origins of Supply-Side Policy. Howard A. Winant. LC 87-15157. 224p. 1988. text ed. 55.00 (*0-275-92806-3*, C2806, Praeger Pubs) Greenwood.

***Stalemate! The Great Trench Warfare Battles, 1915-1917.** J. H. Johnson. 1997. pap. text ed. 16.95 (*1-85409-412-2*, Pub. by Arms & Armour UK) Sterling.

Stalemate at Panmunjon. Wilbert L. Walker. LC 79-90648. 158p. 1980. 9.00 (*0-935428-00-3*) Heritage Pr.

Stalemate in Korea: And How We Coped. Colin H. Brown. (Illus.). 160p. 1997. 35.00 (*0-646-22368-2*) Letter of Marque.

Stalemates: The Truth about Extramarital Affairs. Marcella B. Weiner & Bernard D. Starr. LC 89-43163. 237p. 1989. 19.95 (*0-88282-036-2*) New Horizon NJ.

Stalemates: The Truth about Extramarital Affairs. Marcella B. Weiner & Bernard D. Starr. Ed. by Joan S. Dunphy. 237p. 1991. pap. 12.95 (*0-88282-071-0*) New Horizon NJ.

***Staley McBrayer & the Offset Newspaper Revolution.** Otha C. Spencer. (Illus.). 200p. 1997. 24.50 (*0-9637092-1-6*) E TX Mayo Pr.

***Stalin.** Edward Radzinsky. 1997. pap. 15.95 (*0-385-47954-9*, Anchor NY) Doubleday.

Stalin, 2 Vol. Set. Leon Trotsky. 626p. (RUS.). 1985. pap. 60.00 (*0-87348-799-0*) Pathfinder NY.

Stalin: A Critical Survey of Bolshevism. Boris Souvarine. LC 72-4300. (World Affairs Ser.: National & International Viewpoints). 704p. 1972. reprint ed. 44.95 (*0-405-04591-3*) Ayer.

Stalin: A Time for Judgement. Jonathan Lewis. 1990. 22.45 (*0-394-58058-3*) Pantheon.

Stalin: An Annotated Guide to Books in English. Marty Bloomberg & Buckley B. Barrett. Ed. by Michael Burgess & Paul D. Seldis. LC 92-43368. (Borgo Reference Guides Ser.: No. 1). 128p. 1993. pap. 17.00 (*0-8095-1701-9*); lib. bdg. 27.00 (*0-8095-0701-3*) Borgo Pr.

Stalin: Breaker of Nations. Robert Conquest. 368p. 1992. reprint ed. pap. 13.95 (*0-14-016953-9*, Penguin Bks) Viking Penguin.

Stalin: Man & Ruler. Robert H. McNeal. LC 88-15525. (Illus.). 400p. (C). 1988. text ed. 36.00 (*0-8147-5443-0*) NYU Pr.

Stalin: Man & Ruler. Robert H. McNeal. LC 88-15525. (Illus.). 400p. (C). 1990. pap. 18.50 (*0-8147-5455-4*) NYU Pr.

Stalin: Man of Contradiction. Kenneth N. Cameron. 200p. 1990. text ed. 21.95 (*0-920053-97-1*, Pub. by NC Press CN) U of Toronto Pr.

Stalin: Man of Steel. Derek Chapman. 1988. pap. text ed. 11.64 (*0-582-85749-X*, 75156) Longman.

Stalin: Russia's Man of Steel. Albert Marrin. LC 93-3798. 256p. (J). (gr. 7 up). 1993. pap. 5.99 (*0-14-032605-7*, Puffin) Puffin Bks.

Stalin: The First In-Depth Biography Based on Explosive New Documents from Russia's Secret Archives. Edvard Radzinsky. (Illus.). 608p. 1996. 30.00 (*0-385-47397-4*) Doubleday.

Stalin: The History of a Dictator. H. Montgomery Hyde. (Quality Paperbacks Ser.). (Illus.). 679p. (C). 1982. reprint ed. pap. 18.95 (*0-306-80167-1*) Da Capo.

Stalin: The Iron Fisted Dictator of Russia. Alan L. Paley. Ed. by D. Steve Rahmas. LC 76-185663. (Outstanding Personalities Ser.: No. 7). 32p. 1972. lib. bdg. 7.25 (*0-87157-507-8*) SamHar Pr.

Stalin: Triumph & Tragedy. Dmitri Volkogonov. Tr. by Harry Shukman. (Illus.). 672p. 1992. pap. 19.00 (*1-55958-216-2*) Prima Pub.

Stalin: Triumph & Tragedy. Dmitri Volkogonov. 672p. 1996. per., pap. 22.00 (*0-7615-0718-3*) Prima Pub.

Stalin Account. large type ed. Kenneth Royce. 576p. 1986. 27.99 (*0-7089-8328-6*, Charnwood) Ulverscroft.

Stalin & German Communism: A Study in the Orgins of the State Party. Ruth Fischer. LC 81-3418. (Social Science Classics Ser.). 700p. (C). 1982. reprint ed. pap. 29.95 (*0-87855-822-5*) Transaction Pubs.

Stalin & His Times. Arthur E. Adams. (Illus.). 243p. (C). 1986. reprint ed. pap. text ed. 12.50 (*0-88133-250-X*) Waveland Pr.

Stalin & Stalinism. Ed. by Alexander Dallin & Bertrand M. Patenaude. LC 91-44952. (Articles on Russian & Soviet History, 1500-1991 Ser.: Vol. 7). 408p. 1992. text ed. 25.00 (*0-8153-0564-8*) Garland.

Stalin & Stalinism. Alan Wood. 64p. (C). 1990. pap. text ed. 10.95 (*0-415-03721-2*, A4337) Routledge.

Stalin & Stalinism. 2nd ed. Martin McCauley. LC 95-10104. (Seminar Studies in History). 128p. (C). 1996. pap. text ed. 13.50 (*0-582-27658-6*) Longman.

Stalin & the Bomb. David Holloway. 1996. pap. 18.00 (*0-614-97877-7*) Yale U Pr.

Stalin & the Bomb: The Soviet Union & Atomic Energy, 1939-1956. David Holloway. (Illus.). 1996. pap. 18.00 (*0-300-06664-3*) Yale U Pr.

Stalin & the Bomb: The Soviet Union & Atomic Energy, 1939-56. David Holloway. LC 94-8216. (Illus.). 464p. 1994. 35.00 (*0-300-06056-4*) Yale U Pr.

Stalin & the European Communists. Paulo Spriano. Tr. by Jon Rothschild from ITA. 315p. 1985. text ed. 29.95 (*0-86091-103-9*, Pub. by Verso UK) Routledge Chapman & Hall.

Stalin & the Kirov Murder. Robert Conquest. 192p. 1990. reprint ed. pap. 7.95 (*0-19-506337-6*) OUP.

Stalin As Revolutionary, 1879-1929: A Study in History & Personality. Robert C. Tucker. (Illus.). 1992. pap. 12.95 (*0-393-00738-3*) Norton.

Stalin, Churchill, & Roosevelt Divide Europe, Vol. 3. Remi Nadeau. LC 90-7413. 272p. 1990. text ed. 59.95 (*0-275-93450-0*, C3450, Praeger Pubs) Greenwood.

Stalin Embattled, Nineteen Forty-Three to Nineteen Forty-Eight. William O. McCagg. LC 77-28286. 424p. reprint ed. pap. 120.90 (*0-685-20906-7*, 2032034) Bks Demand.

Stalin Era. Stuart A. Kallen. Ed. by Rosemary Wallner. LC 92-13474. (Rise & Fall of the Soviet Union Ser.). (J). 1992. lib. bdg. 14.98 (*1-56239-102-X*) Abdo & Dghtrs.

Stalin in October: The Man Who Missed the Revolution. Robert M. Slusser. LC 87-3666. 304p. 1987. text ed. 45.00 (*0-8018-3457-0*) Johns Hopkins.

Stalin in October: The Man Who Missed the Revolution. Robert M. Slusser. LC 87-3666. 296p. 1990. reprint ed. pap. text ed. 16.95 (*0-8018-4112-7*) Johns Hopkins.

Stalin in Power: The Revolution from above, 1928-1941. Robert C. Tucker. (Illus.). 752p. 1992. pap. 17.95 (*0-393-30869-3*) Norton.

Stalin Letters to Molotov. Stalin. (RUS.). 1995. 30.00 (*0-300-06385-7*) Yale U Pr.

Stalin over Wisconsin: The Making & Unmaking of Militant Unionism, 1900-1950. Stephen Meyer. LC 91-32610. 275p. (C). 1992. text ed. 45.00 (*0-8135-1798-2*) Rutgers U Pr.

Stalin Phenomenon. Giuseppe Boffa. LC 91-813. (Williams College Center for the Humanities & Social Sciences Ser.). 224p. 1992. 37.50 (*0-8014-2576-X*); pap. 14.95 (*0-8014-9799-X*) Cornell U Pr.

Stalin Phenomenon. Ed. by Alexander Proskurin. 1990. text ed. 22.50 (*81-207-1141-6*, Pub. by Sterling Pubs II) Apt Bks.

Stalin (R) The Man & His Era. Adam B. Ulam. 1989. pap. 21.00 (*0-8070-7005-X*) Beacon Pr.

Stalin Revolution: Foundations of the Totalitarian Era. 3rd ed. Ed. by Robert V. Daniels. LC 89-84257. (Problems in European Civilization Ser.). 269p. (C). 1990. pap. text ed. 18.36 (*0-669-21165-6*) HM College Div.

***Stalin Revolution: Foundations of the Totalitarian Era.** 4th ed. Robert V. Daniels. 288p. (C). 1996. pap. text ed. 18.36 (*0-669-41693-2*) HM College Div.

Stalin School of Falsification. Leon Trotsky. Tr. by John G. Wright. LC 74-156381. (Illus.). 338p. 1972. reprint ed. pap. 25.95 (*0-87348-216-6*); reprint ed. lib. bdg. 65.00 (*0-87348-215-8*) Pathfinder NY.

Stalin, Siberia & the Crisis of the New Economic Policy. James J. Hughes. (Cambridge Russian, Soviet & Post-Soviet Studies: No. 81). (Illus.). 288p. (C). 1991. text ed. 69.95 (*0-521-38039-1*) Cambridge U Pr.

Stalin und der Aufstieg Hitlers: Die Deutschlandpolitik der Kommunistischen Internationale, 1929-1934. Thomas Weingartner. (Beitraege zur Auswaertigen und Internationalen Politik Ser.: No. 4). (C). 1970. 50.80 (*3-11-002702-X*) De Gruyter.

Stalin Years, 1929-1953: PB see Resolutions & Decisions of the Communist Party of the Soviet Union

***Stalingrad.** Antony Beevor. 1998. pap. 27.95 (*0-670-87095-1*) Viking Penguin.

Stalingrad. Theodore Plievier. Tr. by Richard Winston & Clara Winston. 460p. 1984. pap. 8.95 (*0-88184-108-0*) Carroll & Graf.

Stalingrad: Memories & Reassessments. Joachim Wieder & Henrich G. Von Einsiedel. 384p. 1996. 27.95 (*1-85409-303-7*, Pub. by Arms & Armour UK) Sterling.

Stalingrad: Mythos und Wirklichkeit Einer Schlacht. Ed. by Gerd R. Ueberschaer & Wolfram Wette. 320p. (GER.). 1992. pap. 17.25 (*3-596-11097-1*, Pub. by Fischer Taschbch Verlag GW) Intl Bk Import.

Stalingrad: The Defeat of the German 6th Army. Paul Carell. LC 92-62188. (Illus.). 352p. 1992. 29.95 (*0-88740-469-3*) Schiffer.

Stalingrad to Berlin: The German Defeat in the East, 2 vols., Set. 1994. lib. bdg. 626.95 (*0-8490-6445-7*) Gordon Pr.

***Stalinism.** Gill. Date not set. text ed. 10.95 (*0-312-17764-X*) St Martin.

Stalinism. Gill. 1996. text ed. 10.95 (*0-333-46473-7*) St Martin.

Stalinism: Essays in Historical Interpretation. Ed. by Richard C. Tucker. 1978. pap. 12.95 (*0-393-00892-4*) Norton.

Stalinism: Its Impact on Russia & the World. George R. Urban. 464p. 1986. pap. text ed. 13.50 (*0-674-83366-X*) HUP.

Stalinism - Its Nature & Aftermath: Essays in Honor of Moshe Lewin. Ed. by Nick Lampert & Gabor T. Rittersporn. LC 91-15051. 200p. (gr. 13). 1991. text ed. 72.95 (*0-87332-876-0*) M E Sharpe.

Stalinism & After: The Road to Gorbachev. 3rd ed. Alec Nove. LC 92-36715. 1992. 19.95 (*0-415-09445-3*) Routledge.

Stalinism & After: The Road to Gorbachev. 3rd ed. Alec Nove. LC 92-36715. 224p. (C). 1988. pap. 24.95 (*0-04-445112-1*) Routledge Chapman & Hall.

***Stalinism & Nazism: Dictatorships in Comparison.** Ed. by Ian Kershaw & Moshe Lewin. 296p. (C). 1997. text ed. 59.95 (*0-521-56345-3*); pap. text ed. 22.95 (*0-521-56521-9*) Cambridge U Pr.

Stalinism & Seeds Soviet: The Debates of the 1960's. Moshe Lewin. (C). pap. 22.00 (*0-7453-0427-3*, Pub. by Pluto Pr UK) LPC InBook.

Stalinism & Soviet Cinema. Ed. by Richard Taylor & Derek Spring. LC 92-32301. (Soviet Cinema Ser.). (Illus.). 304p. (C). (gr. 13). 1993. text ed. 62.95 (*0-415-07285-9*, A7925) Routledge.

Stalinism & Soviet Rail Transport, 1928-41. E. A. Rees. LC 94-30652. (Studies in Soviet History & Society Ser.). 307p. 1994. text ed. 69.95 (*0-312-12381-7*) St Martin.

Stalinism & the Seeds of Soviet Reform: The Debates of the 1960s. Moshe Lewin. LC 91-8701. 414p. (C). (gr. 13). 1991. pap. text ed. 31.95 (*0-87332-858-2*) M E Sharpe.

Stalinism in a Russian Province: A Study in Collectivization & Dekulakization in Siberia. James Hughes. (Studies in Russian & East European History & Society). 288p. 1997. text ed. 65.00 (*0-312-15948-X*) St Martin.

Stalinism in Crisis. Rob Knight. 209p. (C). 66.50 (*0-7453-0464-8*, Pub. by Pluto Pr UK); pap. 22.00 (*0-7453-0465-6*, Pub. by Pluto Pr UK) LPC InBook.

Stalinism in Ukraine in the 1940s. David R. Marples. LC 92-2295. 1992. text ed. 65.00 (*0-312-08401-3*) St Martin.

Stalinist Command Economy. Timothy Dunmore. LC 79-26712. 224p. 1980. text ed. 29.95 (*0-312-75516-3*) St Martin.

Stalinist Legacy: Its Impact on Twentieth-Century World Politics. Ed. by Tariq Ali. LC 85-14300. 551p. 1985. reprint ed. lib. bdg. 49.95 (*0-931477-56-5*) Lynne Rienner.

***Stalinist Penal System: A History of Soviet Repression & Terror, 1930-1953.** J. Otto Pohl. LC 97-26939. 184p. 1997. lib. bdg. 35.00 (*0-7864-0336-5*) McFarland & Co.

Stalinist Planning for Economic Growth, 1933-1952. Eugene Zaleski. Ed. by Marie-Christine MacAndrew & John H. Moore. LC 78-31453. xxxiv, 788p. 1980. text ed. 70.00 (*0-8078-1370-2*) U of NC Pr.

Stalinist Science. N. L. Krementosov. LC 96-14404. 368p. 1997. text ed. 45.00 (*0-691-02877-X*) Princeton U Pr.

Stalinist Simplications & Soviet Complications: Social Tensions & Political Conflicts in the U. S. S. R. 1933-1953, Vol. Gabor T. Rittersporn. (Social Orders Ser.). xii, 334p. 1991. text ed. 65.00 (*3-7186-5107-6*, Harwood Acad Pubs) Gordon & Breach.

Stalinist Terror: New Perspectives. Ed. by J. Arch Getty & Roberta T. Manning. LC 92-2472. (Illus.). 352p. (C). 1993. text ed. 69.95 (*0-521-44125-0*); pap. text ed. 19.95 (*0-521-44670-8*) Cambridge U Pr.

Stalin's American Policy. William S. Taubman. 304p. 1983. pap. 11.95 (*0-393-30130-3*) Norton.

Stalin's Apologist: Walter Duranty, the New York Time's Man in Moscow. S. J. Taylor. (Illus.). 404p. 1990. 30.00 (*0-19-505700-7*) OUP.

Stalin's Aviation Gulag: A Memoir of Andrei Tupolev & the Purge Era. L. L. Kerber et al. Ed. by Von Hardesty. Tr. by Paul Mitchell. LC 96-17488. (Smithsonian History of Aviation Ser.). (Illus.). 464p. 1996. text ed. 45.00 (*1-56098-640-9*) Smithsonian.

Stalin's Captive: Nikolaus Riehl & the Soviet Race for the Bomb. Nikolaus Riehl. Ed. by Frederick Seitz. (History of Modern Chemical Sciences Ser.). (Illus.). 242p. 1995. 34.95 (*0-8412-3310-1*) Am Chemical.

***Stalin's Carnival.** Steven Heighton. 96p. 1989. pap. 12.95 (*0-919627-21-8*, Pub. by Quarry Pr CN) LPC InBook.

Stalin's Cold War: Soviet Strategies in Europe, 1943 to 1956. Caroline Kennedy-Pipe. LC 94-36785. 1995. text ed. 24.95 (*0-7190-4202-X*, Pub. by Manchester Univ Pr UK) St Martin.

Stalin's Doctor, Stalin's Nurse: A Personal Memoir. N. Petrova. 107p. 1984. 9.50 (*0-940670-22-4*) Kingston Pr.

Stalin's Drive to the West, 1938-1945: The Origins of the Cold War. Richard C. Raack. LC 95-4990. xii, 265p. 1995. 45.00 (*0-8047-2415-6*) Stanford U Pr.

Stalin's Famine & Roosevelt's Recognition of Russia. M. Wayne Morris. LC 93-45822. 234p. (C). 1994. lib. bdg. 39.50 (*0-8191-9379-8*) U Pr of Amer.

***Stalin's Forgotten Zion: Birobidzhan & the Making of a Soviet Jewish Homeland: An Illustrated History, 1928-1996.** Robert Weinberg. LC 97-5052. 1998. write for info. (*0-520-20989-3*); pap. write for info. (*0-520-20990-7*) U CA Pr.

***Stalin's Ghosts.** King. LC 97-20832. 1997. 40.00 (*0-8050-5294-1*); pap. 16.95 (*0-8050-5295-X*) H Holt & Co.

Stalin's Giants - The KV-I & KV-II. Horst Scheibert. Tr. by Edward Force from GER. (Illus.). 48p. 1992. pap. 8.95 (*0-88740-404-9*) Schiffer.

Stalin's Industrial Revolution: Politics & Workers, 1928-1932. Hiroaki Kuromiya. (Soviet & East European Studies: No. 60). (Illus.). 364p. (C). 1990. pap. text ed. 19.95 (*0-521-38741-8*) Cambridge U Pr.

Stalin's Letters to Molotov, 1925-1936. Lars T. Lih. 1996. pap. 16.00 (*0-300-06861-1*) Yale U Pr.

Stalin's Letters to Molotov, 1925-1936. Ed. by Oleg V. Naumov & Lars T. Lih. Tr. by Catherine A. Fitzpatrick from RUS. LC 94-44050. (Annals of Communism Ser.). 1995. 30.00 (*0-300-06211-7*) Yale U Pr.

***Stalin's Lieutenants.** William J. Spahr. LC 97-12329. 1997. 24.95 (*0-89141-564-5*) Presidio Pr.

Stalin's Nose. large type ed. Roy MacLean. 1993. 39.95 (*0-7066-1002-4*, Pub. by Remploy Pr CN) St Mut.

Stalin's Peasants: Resistance & Survival in the Russian Village After Collectivization. Shelia Fitzpatrick. (Illus.). 416p. (C). 1996. pap. 18.95 (*0-19-510459-5*) OUP.

Stalin's Reluctant Soldiers: A Social History of the Red Army, 1925-1941. Roger R. Reese. LC 96-4252. (Modern War Studies). (Illus.). 288p. 1996. 35.00 (*0-7006-0772-2*) U Pr of KS.

Stalin's Revolution from Abov: An Interpretive History. Robert C. Tucker. (Illus.). 1990. 29.95 (*0-393-02881-X*) Norton.

Stalin's Russia. Chris Ward. LC 93-3565. (Reading History Ser.). 224p. 1995. text ed. 16.95 (*0-340-54464-3*, A9526, Pub. by E Arnld UK) St Martin.

Stalin's Slave Camps. Charles A. Orr. LC 74-22754. (Labor Movement in Fiction & Non-Fiction Ser.). reprint ed. 27.50 (*0-404-58507-8*) AMS Pr.

Stalin's Successors: Leadership, Stability & Change in the Soviet Union. Seweryn Bialer. LC 80-12037. 416p. 1982. pap. text ed. 21.95 (*0-521-28906-8*) Cambridge U Pr.

***Stalins Unwanted Child.** Loth. Date not set. text ed. 65.00 (*0-312-21028-0*) St Martin.

Stalin's War: A Radical New Theory of the Origins of the Second World War. Ernst Topitsch. LC 87-16332. 160p. 1987. text ed. 24.95 (*0-312-00989-5*) St Martin.

Stalin's War Against the Jews: The Doctor's Plot & the Soviet Solution. Louis Rapoport. (Illus.). 1990. text ed. 27.95 (*0-02-925821-9*, Free Press) Free Pr.

***Stalin's War Through the Eyes of His Commanders.** Albert Axell. 1997. 27.95 (*1-85409-402-5*, Pub. by Arms & Armour UK) Sterling.

Stalk. Janet Morris & Chris Morris. 256p. 1994. 4.99 (*0-451-45307-7*, ROC) NAL-Dutton.

***Stalk & Kill.** Gilbert. LC 97-23220. 1997. 24.95 (*0-312-17030-0*) St Martin.

***Stalk & Kill: The Sniper Experience.** Adrian Gilbert. (Illus.). 300p. 1997. 42.50 (*0-283-06284-3*, Pub. by Sidgwick & Jackson UK) Trans-Atl Phila.

Stalk Line. 1995. mass mkt. 4.99 (*0-373-61442-X*, 1-61442-9) Harlequin Bks.

Stalked, Vol. 1. La Vonne Skalias. 1995. mass mkt. 5.50 (*0-312-95631-2*) St Martin.

Stalked: A True Story. LaVonne Skaliasi & Barbara Davis. Ed. by Mike Towle & June Ford. LC 94-26270. (Illus.). 1994. 19.95 (*1-56530-146-3*) Summit TX.

S

An Asterisk (*) at the beginning of an entry indicates that the title is appearing in BIP for the first time.

Stalked! Breaking the Silence on the Crime Epidemic of the Nineties. Melita C. Schaum. 256p. (Orig.). 1995. mass mkt. 5.99 (*0-671-88710-6*) PB.

Stalked in the Catacombs. Peter R. Doyle. (Daring Adventure Ser.: Vol. 3). 1993. pap. 5.99 (*1-56179-144-X*) Focus Family.

Stalker. Chester Ballard. Date not set. pap. 6.99 (*0-9646070-0-X*) Seacab.

Stalker. Nicole Davidson. 176p. (Orig.). 1992. pap. 3.50 (*0-380-76645-0*, Flare) Avon.

Stalker. Carol Ellis. (J). 1996. mass mkt. 3.99 (*0-590-25520-7*) Scholastic Inc.

***Stalker.** Tom Nelson. 185p. (Orig.). 1997. mass mkt. 4.99 (*1-55197-996-9*, Pub. by Comnwlth Pub CN) Partners Pubs Grp.

Stalker. Joan L. Nixon. 192p. (YA). (gr. 7 up). 1987. mass mkt. 3.99 (*0-440-97753-3*, LLL BDD) BDD Bks Young Read.

Stalker Affair & the Press. David Murphy. 276p. (C). 1990. pap. text ed. 18.95 (*0-04-445412-0*) Routledge Chapman & Hall.

Stalker Affair & the Press. David Murphy. 276p. (C). (gr. 13). 1990. text ed. 52.95 (*0-04-445411-2*) Routledge Chapman & Hall.

Stalker Analog. Mel Odom. 352p. (Orig.). 1993. pap. 5.50 (*0-451-45257-7*, ROC) NAL-Dutton.

Stalkers. Ed. by Ed Gorman & Martin Greenberg. 1991. 20.00 (*0-7278-4275-7*) Severn Hse.

Stalkers. Dean R. Koontz et al. Ed. by Edward Gorman & Martin Greenberg. 352p. 1992. mass mkt. 5.99 (*0-451-45148-1*, ROC) NAL-Dutton.

Stalker's Life of Christ see Bible Reference Library: Value Pack

Stalker's Life of Paul see Bible Reference Library: Value Pack

Stalker's Moon. Bruce Jones. 240p. (Orig.). 1993. mass mkt. 4.99 (*0-380-76243-9*) Avon.

Stalkers of Pestilence: The Story of Man's Ideas of Infection. Wade W. Oliver. LC 77-119210. 1930. 21.95 (*0-8434-0092-7*, Pub. by McGrath NH) Ayer.

Stalking. Elaine Landau. LC 96-5088. (Individual Titles Ser.). 120p. (J). (gr. 2-7). 1996. lib. bdg. 22.70 (*0-531-11295-0*) Watts.

Stalking Big Game. Walter Prothero. LC 92-754. (Illus.). 224p. 1992. 19.95 (*0-8117-0282-0*) Stackpole.

Stalking Big Ideas in the Advertising Jungle. Don Mix. LC 85-81845. (Illus.). 144p. (Orig.). 1986. 16.50 (*0-937884-11-1*, Bennington Bks) Hystry Mystry.

***Stalking Darkness.** Lynn Flewelling. 572p. 1997. mass mkt. 5.99 (*0-553-57543-0*, Spectra) Bantam.

Stalking Horse. 1993. pap. 16.95 (*0-7871-0025-0*, Dove Bks) Dove Audio.

***Stalking Horse.** Miriam G. Monfredo. LC 97-21547. 352p. 1997. 21.95 (*0-425-15783-0*, Prime Crime) Berkley Pub.

Stalking Horse. Bill Shoemaker. (Los Angeles Mysteries Ser.). 1995. mass mkt. 5.99 (*0-449-14936-6*, GM) Fawcett.

Stalking-Horse. large type ed. Michael Delahaye. 496p. 1988. 25.99 (*0-7089-1896-4*) Ulverscroft.

Stalking-Horse. large type ed. James Pattinson. LC 94-12704. 272p. 1994. lib. bdg. 16.95 (*0-8161-7420-2*, GK Hall) Thorndike Pr.

Stalking Horse. large type ed. Willie Shoemaker. LC 95-7483. 481p. 1995. pap. 19.95 (*0-7838-1296-5*, GK Hall) Thorndike Pr.

Stalking Horse. large type ed. Terence Strong. (Magna Large Print Ser.). 1994. 25.99 (*0-7505-0721-7*) Ulverscroft.

***Stalking Joy.** Margaret Benbow. LC 96-47109. (Walt McDonald First-Book Poetry Ser.). 94p. 1997. 17.95 (*0-89672-375-5*) Tex Tech Univ Pr.

Stalking Justice. Paul Mones. 1996. mass mkt. 6.99 (*0-671-00201-5*) PB.

Stalking Justice: The Dramatic True Story of the Detective Who First Used DNA Testing to Catch a Serial Killer. Paul Mones. Ed. by Claire Zion. 320p. 1995. 23.00 (*0-671-70348-X*) PB.

Stalking Laws. Donna Hunzeker. (State Legislative Reports: Vol. 17, No. 19). 6p. 1992. 5.00 (*1-55516-291-6*, 7302-1719) Natl Conf State Legis.

Stalking Louis Curtiss. Wilda Sandy & Larry K. Hancks. 115p. 1991. 39.95 (*0-9629847-0-1*) Ward Pkwy Pr.

***Stalking Moon.** Theodore V. Olsen. 256p. 1997. reprint ed. mass mkt. 4.50 (*0-8439-4180-4*) Dorchester Pub Co.

***Stalking of Kristin.** George Lardner. 1997. pap. 5.99 (*0-451-40731-8*, Onyx) NAL-Dutton.

Stalking the Academic Communist: Intellectual Freedom & the Firing of Alex Novikoff. David R. Holmes. LC 88-40129. (Illus.). 302p. 1988. pap. 19.95 (*0-87451-469-X*) U Pr of New Eng.

Stalking the Angel. Robert Crais. 272p. 1992. mass mkt. 5.99 (*0-553-28644-7*) Bantam.

Stalking the Blue-Eyed Scallop. Euell Gibbons. (Illus.). 1987. pap. 3.95 (*0-679-50236-X*) McKay.

Stalking the Florida Panther. 2nd ed. Enid Shomer. LC 87-50707. 125p. 1990. pap. 10.00 (*0-915380-21-8*) Word Works.

Stalking the Healthful Herbs. Euell Gibbons. (Illus.). 303p. 1989. reprint ed. pap. 17.50 (*0-911469-06-0*) A C Hood.

Stalking the Ice Dragon: An Alaskan Journey. Susan Zwinger. LC 91-11627. (Illus.). 219p. 1991. 16.95 (*0-8165-1202-7*) U of Ariz Pr.

Stalking the Motorsports Sponsor. Pat Bentley. (Illus.). 49p. (Orig.). 1984. pap. text ed. 9.95 (*0-936834-19-6*) S S Autosports.

Stalking the Nightmare. Harlan Ellison. 300p. 1982. 16.00 (*0-932096-16-6*) Phantasia Pr.

Stalking the Past: Prehistory at Petrified Forest. Anne T. Jones. (Illus.). 48p. (Orig.). (C). 1993. pap. 8.95 (*0-945695-04-7*) Petrified Forest Mus Assn.

***Stalking the Shark: Pressure & Passion on the Pro Golf Tour.** Carl A. Vigeland. LC 96-52869. 1997. pap. 14.95 (*0-8092-3032-1*) Contemp Bks.

Stalking the Shark: Pressure & Passion on the Pro Golf Tour. Carl A. Vigeland. (Illus.). 256p. 1996. 25.00 (*0-393-03795-9*) Norton.

Stalking the Side Hill Salmon. Heather Marks. LC 96-75494. (Illus.). 143p. (Orig.). 1996. pap. 12.95 (*0-614-14404-3*) Great Wave AK.

Stalking the U-boat: USAAF Offensive Antisubmarine Operations in World War II. Max Schoenfeld. LC 93-41041. (History of Aviation Ser.). (Illus.). 272p. 1994. text ed. 37.50 (*1-56098-403-1*) Smithsonian.

Stalking the Unicorn. Mike Resnick. 320p. (Orig.). 1990. mass mkt. 3.95 (*0-8125-0985-4*) Tor Bks.

***Stalking the Vietcong: Inside Operation Phoenix, a Personal Account.** Stuart A. Herrington. LC 81-17901. Orig. Title: Silence Was a Weapon. (Illus.). 240p. 1997. reprint ed. pap. 14.95 (*0-89141-641-2*) Presidio Pr.

Stalking the Wild Asparagus. Euell Gibbons. LC 87-16933. (Illus.). 303p. 1988. reprint ed. 19.95 (*0-911469-04-4*); reprint ed. pap. 17.50 (*0-911469-03-6*) A C Hood.

Stalking the Wild Asparagus. Euell Gibbons. 1978. reprint ed. teacher ed., pap. 6.95 (*0-679-50223-8*) McKay.

Stalking the Wild Golf Ball: A Guide to Finding, & Not Losing, Golf Balls. Thomas A. Lee. 128p. 1994. pap. 16.95 (*0-9638807-4-8*) Fairway Pubng.

Stalking the Wild Pendulum: On the Mechanics of Consciousness. Itzhak Bentov. 208p. 1988. pap. 12.95 (*0-89281-202-8*, Destiny Bks) Inner Tradit.

Stalking the Wild Resnick. limited ed. Mike Resnick. (Boskone Bks.). (Illus.). viii, 216p. 1991. 15.00 (*0-915368-45-5*); boxed 30.00 (*0-915368-96-X*) New Eng SF Assoc.

Stalking the Wild Solution: A Problem Finding Approach to Creative Problem Solving. Arthur B. VanGundy. 194p. (Orig.). 1987. pap. 14.95 (*0-943456-19-3*) Bearly Ltd.

Stalking the Wild Verb Phrase: A Self-Paced Self-Correcting Adventure into the Grammar of English for English-Speaking Learners of Other Languages. Robert Fradkin. LC 90-22539. 395p. (Orig.). (C). 1991. pap. text ed. 24.50 (*0-8191-8103-X*); lib. bdg. 53.50 (*0-8191-8102-1*) U Pr of Amer.

Stalking Trophy Mule Deer. Walter Prothero. 240p. 1993. 18.98 (*0-88290-476-0*, 1240) Horizon Utah.

Stalky & Co. Rudyard Kipling. (World's Classics Ser.). 384p. 1987. pap. 5.95 (*0-19-281660-8*) OUP.

Stalky & Co. Rudyard Kipling. 1976. 26.95 (*0-8488-0174-1*) Amereon Ltd.

Stalky & Company. Rudyard Kipling. (J). (gr. 5 up). 1988. pap. 2.25 (*0-317-69643-2*, Puffin) Puffin Bks.

Stalky & Company. Rudyard Kipling. Date not set. pap. write for info. (*0-14-043300-7*) Viking Penguin.

Stallard's Eye Surgery. 7th ed. Michael J. Roper-Hall. 457p. 1989. 225.00 (*0-7236-0714-1*) Buttrwrth-Heinemann.

Stallcup's Electrical Calculations Simplified. James G. Stallcup. LC 96-76764. (Illus.). 478p. 1996. wbk. ed. 38.95 (*1-885341-13-X*) Grayboy Pubng.

***Stallcup's Electrical Design Book.** James G. Stallcup. Ed. by James W. Stallcup. LC 96-94456. (Illus.). 648p. (Orig.). (C). 1996. wbk. ed. 44.95 (*1-885341-14-8*); teacher ed. 10.95 (*1-885341-15-6*) Grayboy Pubng.

***Stallcup's Generator, Transformer & Motor Book.** James G. Stallcup. Ed. by James W. Stallcup. LC 96-94803. (Illus.). 352p. (Orig.). (C). 1996. wbk. ed., pap. text ed. 34.95 (*1-885341-19-9*) Grayboy Pubng.

***Stallcup's Generator, Transformer & Motor Book.** James G. Stallcup. Ed. by James W. Stallcup. (Illus.). 35p. (C). 1996. teacher ed., pap. 9.95 (*1-885341-20-2*) Grayboy Pubng.

***Stallcup's One & Two Family Dwelling.** James G. Stallcup & James W. Stallcup. LC 96-77830. (Illus.). 456p. (Orig.). (C). 1996. wbk. ed., pap. 38.95 (*1-885341-16-4*); teacher ed., pap. 10.95 (*1-885341-21-0*) Grayboy Pubng.

Stalled Ox & Other Stories. 1995. 5.25 (*0-19-585383-0*) OUP.

Stalling's Island Mound, Columbia County, Georgia. W. H. Claflin. (HU PMP Ser.). 1931. 25.00 (*0-527-01232-7*) Periodicals Srv.

Stallion. Georgina Brown. (Black Lace Ser.). 1995. mass mkt. 5.95 (*0-352-33005-8*, Pub. by Virgin Pub UK) London Brdge.

Stallion. Gordon Mcgill. 1991. pap. 3.95 (*1-55773-449-6*) MICHIE.

Stallion. Harold Robbins. 1997. mass mkt. 6.99 (*0-671-87294-X*) PB.

Stallion: A Breeding Guide for Owners & Handlers. James P. McCall. (Illus.). 1994. pap. 29.95 (*0-87605-987-6*) Howell Bk.

Stallion: A Novel. Harold Robbins. 368p. 1996. 23.00 (*0-684-81067-0*) S&S Trade.

Stallion Finder 1995: Premier Publishing Equine. Ed. by Andrea L. Mattson. 328p. 1995. pap. 34.95 (*1-879984-50-4*) Premier KS.

Stallion Finder 1996: Premier Publishing Equine. Ed. by Andrea L. Mattson. 328p. 1995. pap. 34.95 (*1-879984-51-2*) Premier KS.

Stallion Gate. Martin C. Smith. 384p. 1987. mass mkt. 6.99 (*0-345-31079-9*) Ballantine.

Stallion Gate. Martin Cruz Smith. LC 85-24444. 336p. 1986. 17.95 (*0-394-53006-3*) Random.

Stallion Man. large type ed. Judith Glover. 528p. 1985. 27.99 (*0-7089-8235-2*) Ulverscroft.

Stallion Management. A. C. Leighton-Hardman. 1975. pap. 5.00 (*0-87980-297-9*) Wilshire.

Stallion on a Frozen Lake: Love Poems of the Sixth Dalai Lama. Dalai Lama. Tr. & Intro. by Coleman Barks. 95p. (C). 1993. pap. 8.00 (*0-9618916-5-3*) Maypop.

Stallion Register for 1994. (Illus.). 1500p. 1993. pap. 29.95 (*0-939049-55-4*) Blood-Horse.

Stallion Register for 1995. Ed. by Raymond S. Paulick & Dan Mearns. (Illus.). 1500p. (Orig.). 1994. pap. 29.95 (*0-939049-60-0*) Blood-Horse.

Stallion Register for 1996: Annual Supplement to the Blood Horse. Ed. by Raymond S. Paulick & Dan Mearns. (Blood Horse Supplement Ser.). (Illus.). 1500p. (Orig.). 1995. pap. 29.95 (*0-939049-68-6*) Blood-Horse.

Stallion Register for 1997. Ed. by Raymond S. Paulick & Dan Mearns. (Illus.). 1500p. (Orig.). 1996. pap. 29.95 (*0-939049-74-0*) Blood-Horse.

***Stallion Register for 1998.** Ed. by Raymond S. Paulick & Dan Mearns. (Illus.). 1600p. (Orig.). 1997. pap. 39.95 (*0-939049-88-0*) Blood-Horse.

Stallion Road: A Screenplay by William Faulkner. William Faulkner. Ed. by Louis D. Brodsky & Robert W. Hamblin. LC 89-16668. 176p. 1990. 21.95 (*0-87805-371-9*) U Pr of Miss.

Stallions: Their Management & Handling. Neil Dougall. 102p. 1990. pap. 30.00 (*0-85131-256-X*, Pub. by J A Allen & Co UK) St Mut.

***Stallion's Call.** Lynn Salem & Josie Stewart. (Illus.). 8p. (Orig.). (J). (gr. k-1). 1997. pap. 3.50 (*1-80661-257-7*) Seedling Pubns.

Stallions of Love. Kimberly Wittman. 200p. (Orig.). (YA). 1994. pap. 9.95 (*1-885351-88-7*) Cheval Intl.

Stalls & Spins. Paul Craig. 1992. text ed. 26.95 (*0-07-013421-9*) McGraw.

Stalls & Spins. Paul A. Craig. (Illus.). 304p. 1993. 24.95 (*0-8306-4019-3*, 4174); pap. 16.95 (*0-8306-4020-7*, 4174) McGraw-Hill Prof.

Stalls, Spins & Safety. Sammy Mason. (Illus.). 25.95 (*0-614-13214-2*, 31-13160) EAA Aviation.

Stalsby-Wilson's Petrochemicals: Spring & Fall. 1997. pap. text ed. 95.00 (*0-911299-89-0*) Oil Price Info Serv.

***Stamberg Aferiat Architecture.** Intro. by Paul Goldberger. LC 96-47014. (Illus.). 160p. 1997. pap. 35.00 (*0-8478-2011-4*) Rizzoli Intl.

***Stamboul Intrigue.** large type ed. Robert Charles. (Linford Mystery Library). 400p. 1997. pap. 16.99 (*0-7089-5059-0*, Linford) Ulverscroft.

Stamboul Train. Graham Greene. 224p. 1983. mass mkt. 4.95 (*0-14-001898-0*, Penguin Bks) Viking Penguin.

Stamboul Train. Graham Greene. 224p. 1992. pap. 11.95 (*0-14-018532-1*, Penguin Classics) Viking Penguin.

Stamford Bridge Encyclopedia. Paul Harrison. (Illus.). 208p. 1996. pap. 17.95 (*1-85158-749-7*, Pub. by Mnstream UK) Trafalgar.

Stamford, Connecticut - a Bibliography: An Annotated, Indexed Compiliation of Books - Pamphlets - Special Editions of Newspapers - Atlas - Articles in Periodicals - Motion Picture Film - Containing Information Relating to the History of Stamford, CT. Ronald Marcus. xxii, 284p. (Orig.). 1995. pap. 49.95 (*1-886054-13-4*) Stamford Hist Soc.

Stamford, CT. Historical Briefs, Inc. Staff. Ed. by Thomas Antonucci & Michael Antonucci. 176p. 1992. pap. 14.95 (*0-89677-016-8*) Hist Briefs.

Stamford Street Railroad Co. Ed Martin. (Transportation Bulletin Ser.: No. 83). (Illus.). 1978. 9.00 (*0-910506-19-1*) De Vito.

Stamm 'Abad in Alten Testament. Ingrid Riesener. (Beiheft zur Zeitschrift fuer die Alttestamentliche Wissenschaft Ser.: Vol. 149). (C). 1979. 165.40 (*3-11-007260-2*) De Gruyter.

Stamme der Insel Hainan,, 2 vols. Hans Stubel. (Asian Folklore & Social Life Monographs: Nos. 83 & 84). (GER & JPN.). 1935. 35.00 (*0-89986-293-4*) Oriental Bk Store.

Stamme der Insel Hainan, 2 vols. Hans Stubel & Shimizu Mitsuo. (Asian Folklore & Social Life Monographs: Nos. 85 & 86). (GER & JPN.). 1935. 35.00 (*0-89986-294-2*) Oriental Bk Store.

Stammering Century. Gilbert Seldes. 414p. 1993. reprint ed. lib. bdg. 99.00 (*0-7812-5315-2*) Rprt Serv.

Stammeslehren der Dschagga, 3 vols., 2. Bruno Gutmann. (B. E. Ser.: No. 123). (GER.). 1938. write for info. (*0-8115-3051-5*) Periodicals Srv.

Stammeslehren der Dschagga, 3 vols., 3. Bruno Gutmann. (B. E. Ser.: No. 123). (GER.). 1938. write for info. (*0-8115-3052-3*) Periodicals Srv.

Stammverbesserung Biotechnologisch Relevanter Hyphenpilze durch Gentechnik: Integrative Transformation von Aspergillus Niger. Georg Mohr. (Dissertationes Botanicae Ser.: Vol. 131). (Illus.). 116p. (GER.). 1989. spiral bd. 40.00 (*3-443-64043-5*, Pub. by Cramer GW) Lubrecht & Cramer.

Stamp: A Tool for Dialect Adaptation. David J. Weber et al. Ed. by Gary F. Simons. (Occasional Publications in Academic Computing: No. 15). 235p. 1990. pap. 20.00 (*0-88312-638-9*) Summer Instit Ling.

Stamp-A-Christmas Book & Kit. Judy Ritchie. 1995. 25.00 (*0-88363-319-1*) H L Levin.

Stamp-a-Christmas TM Book & Kit. Judy Ritchie. (Illus.). 96p. 1995. pap. 25.00 (*0-88363-895-9*, Scrbnr) Scribnrs Ref.

Stamp Act Congress: With an Exact Copy of the Complete Journal. C. A. Weslager. LC 75-21514. (Illus.). 279p. 38.50 (*0-87413-111-1*) U Delaware Pr.

Stamp Act Crisis: Prologue to Revolution. Edmund S. Morgan & Helen M. Morgan. LC 94-31357. (Institute of Early American History & Culture Ser.). 350p. 1995. pap. text ed. 14.95 (*0-8078-4513-2*) U of NC Pr.

***Stamp Collecting.** Boy Scouts of America Staff. (Illus.). 40p. (YA). (gr. 6-12). 1993. pap. 2.40 (*0-8395-3296-2*, 33296) BSA.

Stamp Collecting. Neill Granger. LC 94-6390. (First Guide Ser.). (Illus.). 96p. (J). (gr. 3-6). 1994. pap. 9.95 (*1-56294-734-6*); lib. bdg. 17.90 (*1-56294-399-5*) Millbrook Pr.

Stamp Collecting for Beginners. Burton H. Hobson. 1979. pap. 7.00 (*0-87980-148-4*) Wilshire.

Stamp Decorating. Stewart Walton. 160p. 1996. 27.50 (*1-85967-306-6*, Lorenz Bks) Anness Pub.

Stamp Decorating Kit. Stewart Walton & Sally Walton. (Illus.). 160p. 1996. 32.50 (*1-85967-200-0*, Lorenz Bks) Anness Pub.

Stamp Duties, Aspects of Trusts, Settlements & Gifts in Australia. E. W. Wallace & F. P. Zipfinger. 1983. Australia. 74.00 (*0-409-49421-6*, A.T.) MICHIE.

Stamp Magic: Inspired Effects with the Easiest New Decorating Technique. Stewart Walton & Sally Walton. (Illus.). 160p. 1995. 27.50 (*1-85967-140-3*, Lorenz Bks) Anness Pub.

Stamp of the School: Reminiscences of the Thacher School, 1949-1992. John S. Huyler. LC 94-34951. 1994. 30.00 (*0-87562-111-2*) Spec Child.

Stamp Your Greeting. Judy Ritchie. 104p. 1996. pap. 25.00 (*0-88363-896-7*) H L Levin.

***Stamp 5.0: Structural Time Series Analyser, Modeller & Predictor-Tutorial Guide.** Harvey. 112p. 1995. text ed. 18.50 (*0-412-73410-9*, Chap & Hall NY) Chapman & Hall.

***Stamp 5.0: Structured Time Series Analyser & Modeller & Predictor.** Koopman et al. 408p. (Orig.). 1995. pap. text ed. 899.00 incl. disk (*0-412-72220-8*, Chap & Hall NY) Chapman & Hall.

***Stamp 5.0: Structured Time Series Analyser, Modeller & Predictor.** Koopman et al. 408p. 1995. pap. text ed. 46.00 (*0-412-72230-5*, Chap & Hall NY) Chapman & Hall.

Stampability: Hearts. Stewart Walton & Sally Walton. (Illus.). 32p. (Orig.). 1996. pap. 14.95 (*1-85967-173-X*, Lorenz Bks) Anness Pub.

Stampability: Roses. Stewart Walton & Sally Walton. (Illus.). 32p. (Orig.). 1996. pap. 14.95 (*1-85967-178-0*, Lorenz Bks) Anness Pub.

Stampability: Seashore. Stewart Walton & Sally Walton. (Illus.). 32p. (Orig.). 1996. pap. 14.95 (*1-85967-168-3*, Lorenz Bks) Anness Pub.

Stampability: Stars. Stewart Walton & Sally Walton. (Illus.). 32p. (Orig.). 1996. pap. 14.95 (*1-85967-163-2*, Lorenz Bks) Anness Pub.

Stampability Kits: Cherubs: Interior Decorating Effects with Stamps. Stewart Walton. 1996. pap. text ed. 14.95 (*1-85967-302-3*, Lorenz Bks) Anness Pub.

Stampability Kits: Folk Art: Interior Decorating Effects with Stamps. Stewart Walton. 1996. pap. text ed. 14.95 (*1-85967-301-5*, Lorenz Bks) Anness Pub.

Stampability Kits: Heraldic: Interior Decorating Effects with Stamps. Stewart Walton. 1996. pap. text ed. 14.95 (*1-85967-300-7*, Lorenz Bks) Anness Pub.

Stampability Kits: Vineyard: Interior Decorating Effects with Stamps. Stewart Walton. 1996. pap. text ed. 14.95 (*1-85967-303-1*, Lorenz Bks) Anness Pub.

Stampcraft: Dozens of Creative Ideas for Stamping on Cards, Clothing, Furniture & More. Carl Haysom. 1996. pap. text ed. 19.95 (*0-8019-8850-0*) Chilton.

***Stampede!** Laban C. Hill. (Choose Your Own Adventure Ser.: No. 180). (Illus.). 112p. (J). (gr. 3-7). 1997. pap. 3.50 (*0-553-56756-X*) BDD Bks Young Read.

Stampede. Robert Sabbag. 1985. 16.45 (*0-671-42196-4*) S&S Trade.

Stampede Kid. Norman A. Fox. 176p. 1989. reprint ed. pap. 2.75 (*0-380-70645-8*) Avon.

Stampede, the First Really Big Book. Jerry Palen. (Illus.). 54p. (Orig.). 1986. pap. 6.95 (*0-941803-00-7*) Stampede Cartoons.

Stampede to Timberline: The Ghost Towns & Mining Camps of Colorado. 2nd rev. ed. Muriel S. Wolle. LC 74-6940. (Illus.). 583p. 1974. pap. 34.95 (*0-8040-0946-5*) Swallow.

Stampede to Timberline: The Ghost Towns & Mining Camps of Colorado. 2nd rev. ed. Muriel S. Wolle. LC 74-6940. 583p. 1974. pap. 34.95 (*0-8040-0672-5*) Swallow.

Stamper Footprints: Eleven Generations. Betty S. Latham. (Illus.). 154p. (Orig.). 1995. pap. 24.00 (*0-7884-0320-6*) Heritage Bk.

Stamping, Design Through Maintenance. Ed. by Karl A. Keyes. LC 82-61302. 268p. reprint ed. pap. 76.40 (*0-317-30172-1*, 2025354) Bks Demand.

Stamping Fun. Lorenz Books Staff. 64p. (J). 1996. 7.95 (*1-85967-225-6*, Lorenz Bks) Anness Pub.

***Stamping Ground.** Loren D. Estleman. 1997. mass mkt. 5.99 (*0-8125-3569-3*) Tor Bks.

Stamping Made Easy. Nancy Ward. LC 93-46572. (Craft Kaleidoscope Ser.). 128p. 1994. pap. 16.95 (*0-8019-8506-4*) Chilton.

Stamping Our History: The Story of the United States Portrayed on Its Postage Stamps. Charles Davidson & Lincoln Diamant. 1990. 49.95 (*0-8184-0532-5*) Carol Pub Group.

Stamping Our History: The Story of the United States Portrayed on Its Postage Stamps. 2nd ed. Charles S. Davidson & Lincoln Diamant. (Illus.). 272p. 1995. pap. 24.95 (*0-8065-1691-7*, Citadel Pr) Carol Pub Group.

***Stamps.** LC 96-39410. (Cool Collections Ser.). (J). 1997. write for info. (*1-57572-113-9*) Rigby Interact Libr.

Stamps. Eric Arnold. LC 94-12739. (J). (gr. 4 up). 14.95 (*0-689-31911-8*, Atheneum S&S) S&S Trade.

Stamps & Philately Honors in Science & Medicine: Index of Modern Authors & Subjects with Guide for Rapid Research. Pauline N. Operkola. LC 90-56321. 170p. 1991. 44.50 (*1-55914-436-X*); pap. 39.50 (*1-55914-437-8*) ABBE Pubs Assn.

Stamps, Coins, Postcards & Related Materials: A Directory of Periodicals. Ed. by Doris Robinson. 150p. (Orig.). 1991. pap. text ed. 29.00 (*0-9617844-7-4*) Peri Press.

Stamps of Alderney. Picton Publishing (Chippenham) Ltd. Staff. (C). 1987. 50.00 (*0-948251-33-6*, Pub. by Picton UK) St Mut.

Stamps of British North America. Fred Jarrett. LC 74-82308. (Illus.). 624p. 1975. reprint ed. 40.00 (*0-88000-052-X*) Quarterman.

Stamps of Jammu & Kashmir. Fritz Staal. (Illus.). 360p. 1984. 125.00 (*0-912574-37-2*) Collectors.

Stamps on Stamps. Bunny Kaplan. (Illus.). 176p. 1992. pap. text ed. 17.00 (*0-935991-17-4*) Am Topical Assn.

Stan: The Life of Stan Laurel. Fred L. Guiles. LC 80-5806. 272p. 1991. pap. 12.95 (*0-8128-8528-7*, Scrbrough Hse) Madison Bks UPA.

Stan & Jan Barenstain. Julie Berg. LC 93-12959. (Young at Heart Ser.). (J). 1993. lib. bdg. 14.98 (*1-56239-224-7*) Abdo & Dghtrs.

***Stan Getz.** Donald L. Maggin. 1997. pap. write for info. (*0-688-15555-3*, Quill) Morrow.

Stan Getz: A Life in Jazz. Donald L. Maggin. 1996. 25.00 (*0-614-95806-7*) Morrow.

Stan Getz B Flat Tenor Saxophone Artist Transcriptions. 88p. 1993. otabind 14.95 (*0-7935-1947-0*, 00699375) H Leonard.

Stan Kenton: The Early Years. Edward F. Gabel. 120p. 1993. pap. 17.95 (*0-936653-51-5*, Balboa Books) Tiare Pubns.

Stan Kenton: The Man & His Music. Lillian Arganian. (Illus.). 220p. (Orig.). 1989. pap. 22.50 (*0-9621116-0-0*) Artistry Pr.

Stan Lee's Riftworld: Crossover. Bill McCay. 256p. 1993. pap. 4.50 (*0-451-45274-7*, ROC) NAL-Dutton.

Stan Lee's Riftworld, Odyssey. Stan Lee & Bill McCay. 432p. 1996. mass mkt. 5.99 (*1-57297-069-3*) Blvd Books.

Stan Mack's Out-Takes. Stanley Mack. LC 84-42756. (Illus.). 128p. 1985. pap. 7.95 (*0-87951-997-5*) Overlook Pr.

Stan Mack's Real Life American Revolution. Stanley Mack. LC 94-17808. (Illus.). 144p. (Orig.). 1994. pap. 10.00 (*0-380-77223-X*) Avon.

Stan Musial. John F. Grabowski. (Baseball Legends Ser.). (Illus.). (J). 1994. lib. bdg. 15.95 (*0-7910-1184-4*) Chelsea Hse.

Stan Musial Story. Gene Schoor. 20.95 (*0-8488-1585-8*) Amereon Ltd.

Stan Shaw, Master Cutler: The Story of a Sheffield Craftsman. Geoffrey Tweedale. 96p. 1993. pap. 39.00 (*1-874718-20-2*, Pub. by Hallamshire Pr UK) St Mut.

Stan the Hot Dog Man. Ethel Kessler & Leonard Kessler. LC 89-34474. (I Can Read Bk.). (Illus.). 64p. (J). (gr. k-3). 1990. lib. bdg. 14.89 (*0-06-023280-3*) HarpC Child Bks.

Stan the Hot Dog Man. Ethel Kessler. LC 89-34474. (I Can Read Bk.). (Illus.). 64p. (J). (ps-3). 1995. pap. 3.75 (*0-06-444192-X*, Trophy) HarpC Child Bks.

Stan "The Man" Musial: Born to Be a Ball Player. Jerry Lansche. LC 93-45459. 240p. 1994. 19.95 (*0-87833-846-2*) Taylor Pub.

Stan Veit's History of the Personal Computer. Stan Veit. LC 93-60161. (Illus.). 306p. (Orig.). 1993. 27.95 (*1-56664-030-X*); pap. 19.95 (*1-56664-023-7*) WorldComm.

Stan Weinstein's Secrets for Profiting in Bull & Bear Markets. Stan Weinstein. 220p. 1988. text ed. 30.00 (*1-55623-079-6*) Irwin Prof Pubng.

Stan Weinstein's Secrets for Profiting in Bull & Bear Markets. Stan Weinstein. 320p. 1992. per. 19.00 (*1-55623-683-2*) Irwin Prof Pubng.

Stance & Motion: Facts & Concepts. Ed. by V. S. Gurfinkel et al. (Illus.). 270p. 1989. 69.50 (*0-306-43108-4*, Plenum Pr) Plenum.

Stance of Plato. Albert Cook. 266p. 1996. 62.50 (*0-8226-3048-6*); pap. 24.95 (*0-8226-3049-4*) Littlefield.

Stances a Sophie. Christiane Rochefort. 250p. (FRE.). 1978. 11.95 (*0-686-55231-8*, 2246005892); pap. 24.95 (*0-7859-1452-8*) Fr & Eur.

Stand. Stephen King. LC 77-16928. 1994. pap. 6.99 (*0-451-17928-5*) NAL-Dutton.

Stand. Stephen King. LC 77-16928. 1994. reprint ed. lib. bdg. 45.95 (*1-56849-571-4*) NAL-Dutton.

Stand: The Complete & Uncut Edition. Stephen King. 1200p. 1990. 34.95 (*0-385-19957-0*) Doubleday.

Stand: The Complete & Uncut Edition. Stephen King. 1168p. 1991. reprint ed. pap. 7.99 (*0-451-16953-0*, Sig) NAL-Dutton.

***Stand! Victory in Praise Music & Arts Seminar Mass Choir.** Ed. by Jeannette DeLisa. 52p. (Orig.). (YA). 1996. pap. text ed. 16.95 (*1-57623-537-8*, PF9625) Warner Brothers.

Stand Against Tyranny: Norway's Physicians & the Nazis. Maynard M. Cohen. LC 96-14957. (Illus.). 380p. 1996. 39.95 (*0-8143-2603-X*) Wayne St U Pr.

Stand Alone Blues. Robert Brown. (Stand Alone Ser.). 32p. (YA). 1992. reprint ed. pap. 9.95 (*0-88284-543-8*, 4428) Alfred Pub.

Stand Alone Fusion. Mark Dziuba. (Stand Alone Ser.). 32p. 1992. reprint ed. pap. 9.95 (*0-88284-542-X*, 4429) Alfred Pub.

Stand Alone, Inventor! And Make Money with Your New Product Ideas! Robert G. Merrick. (Illus.). 310p. (Orig.). 1997. pap. 19.95 (*0-9643832-0-9*) Lee Pubng.

Stand Alone Rock. Chris Amelar. (Stand Alone Ser.). 32p. (YA). 1992. reprint ed. pap. 9.95 (*0-88284-544-6*, 4430) Alfred Pub.

***Stand & Be Counted.** David Crosby. 1997. 50.00 (*0-00-225214-7*); pap. 25.00 (*0-00-649149-9*) HarperColl Wrld.

Stand & Be Counted. rev. ed. Robert Dugan. 280p. 1995. pap. 9.99 (*0-88070-783-6*, Multnomah Bks) Multnomah Pubs.

***Stand & Deliver.** Andrew Clark. 256p. 1997. 29.95 (*0-385-25602-7*) Doubleday.

***Stand & Deliver.** Neil Heyen. (Longman American Business English Skills Ser.). 1994. pap. text ed. 12.60 (*0-582-08420-2*, Pub. by Longman UK) Longman.

***Stand & Deliver.** Ramon Menendez & Tom Musca. 112p. 1997. pap. 5.25 (*0-87129-740-X*, SB3) Dramatic Pub.

Stand & Deliver: The Fine Art of Presentation. Ralph L. Kliem & Irwin S. Ludin. LC 95-1064. 286p. 1995. 37.95 (*0-566-07574-1*, Pub. by Gower UK) Ashgate Pub Co.

Stand & Deliver That Speech: Guide to Effective Public Speaking. Larry Gruman. (Illus.). (C). 1992. pap. text ed. 9.95 (*0-9632594-0-7*) Lowell Pr OR.

***Stand at the Cross & Be Changed.** E. Lonnie Melashenko & John McLarty. LC 96-48568. 1997. write for info. (*0-8163-1384-9*) Pacific Pr Pub Assn.

Stand B-y-y-y to Start Engines - Now, Hear This! 5th ed. Daniel V. Gallery. (Illus.). 218p. 1996. reprint ed. 21.95 (*0-930926-21-8*) Calif Fin Pubns.

Stand Back, I Think I'm Gonna Laugh: Cartoons by Rina Piccolo. Rina Piccolo. (Illus.). 96p. (Orig.). 1994. pap. 7.95 (*0-9632526-3-1*) Laugh Lines.

Stand Back, Said the Elephant, I'm Going to Sneeze! Patricia Thomas. LC 89-43215. (Illus.). 32p. (J). (ps-2). 1990. 16.00 (*0-688-09338-8*); lib. bdg. 15.93 (*0-688-09339-6*) Lothrop.

Stand Before Your God. Paul Watkins. LC 92-44885. 1994. 22.00 (*0-679-42056-8*) Random.

Stand Before Your God. Paul Watkins. LC 92-44885. 1995. pap. 11.00 (*0-679-75941-7*, Vin) Random.

***Stand by Faith or Not at All.** Orville Anvik. 368p. (Orig.). 1996. pap. 12.99 (*1-883893-65-8*) WinePress Pub.

***Stand by Me.** 1998. pap. 5.99 (*0-373-20151-6*, 1-20151-6) Harlequin Bks.

Stand-By Nurse. large type ed. Peggy O'Moore. (Linford Romance Library). 1995. pap. 15.99 (*0-7089-7682-4*, Linford) Ulverscroft.

Stand by Your Man. Kathy Clark. (Crystal Creek Ser.). 1993. mass mkt. 3.99 (*0-373-82522-6*, 1-82522-3) Harlequin Bks.

Stand by Your Man. B. J. Daniels. (Intrigue Ser.). 1995. pap. 3.50 (*0-373-22312-9*, 1-22312-2) Harlequin Bks.

Stand by Your Man: And Other One-Handed, Two-Fisted Stories. Jack Fritscher. 160p. (Orig.). 1987. pap. 10.00 (*0-943595-02-9*) Leyland Pubns.

Stand by Your Pan: Country Music Cookbook. Diane Pfeifer. (Illus.). 160p. 1994. pap. 9.95 (*0-9618306-3-8*) Strawberry GA.

Stand Density & Stem Taper in Pinus Patula: Schiede & Deppe. P. G. Adlard & K. F. Richardson. 1978. 30.00 (*0-85074-047-9*) St Mut.

Stand Facing the Stove: The Story of the Woman Who Gave America the Joy of Cooking. Anne Mendelson. (Illus.). 474p. 1996. 29.95 (*0-8050-2904-4*) H Holt & Co.

Stand Fast in Liberty. James E. Bristol. LC 61-18784. (C). 1961. pap. 3.00 (*0-87574-119-3*) Pendle Hill.

Stand Fast in Liberty: An Expression of Freedom Through Music. Jerilynn Carter. 24p. 1996. pap. text ed. 8.95 (*1-57636-011-3*) SunRise Pbl.

Stand Fast in the Truth. 2nd rev. ed. Abp. Averky of Syracuse. Ed. by Demetrios Serfes. Tr. by Seraphim Johnson. (Illus.). 24p. 1995. pap. 4.00 (*0-912927-63-1*, D030) St John Kronstadt.

Stand Firm: A Survival Guide for the New Jewish Believer. rev. ed. Eliezer Maass. Ed. by Fran Anderson. 202p. 1995. reprint ed. pap. 8.00 (*1-878678-02-7*) A M F Intl.

Stand Firm Ye Boys from Maine: The 20th Maine & the Gettysburg Campaign. Thomas A. Desjardin. (Illus.). 256p. (C). 1995. text ed. 28.00 (*0-939631-89-X*) Thomas Publications.

***Stand for Children: A Parent's Guide to Child Advocacy.** 36p. 1996. pap. 4.95 (*1-881985-05-9*) Childrens Defense.

Stand Hunting for Whitetails. Richard P. Smith. LC 95-82427. (Illus.). 250p. 1996. pap. 14.95 (*0-87341-439-X*, GSH) Krause Pubns.

***Stand-In.** Deborah Moggach. 390p. 4.98 (*0-8317-7126-7*) Smithmark.

Stand-In. large type ed. Vanessa Graham. LC 94-20477. (Nightingale Ser.). 1995. pap. 16.95 (*0-8161-7451-2*, GK Hall) Thorndike Pr.

Stand-In Bride. Barbara Boswell. (Fortune's Children Ser.). 1996. mass mkt. 4.50 (*0-373-50180-3*, 1-50180-8) Harlequin Bks.

Stand-In for Love. large type ed. Irene Ord. (Linford Romance Library). 1989. pap. 15.99 (*0-7089-6787-6*) Ulverscroft.

Stand-in for Murder. Lynn Bradley. (WWL Mystery Ser.). 1996. mass mkt. 4.99 (*0-373-26199-3*, 1-26199-9, Wrldwide Lib) Harlequin Bks.

Stand-in for Murder: A Cole January Mystery. Lynn Bradley. 214p. 1994. 19.95 (*0-8027-3189-9*) Walker & Co.

***Stand-In Groom.** Suzann Brockmann. (Loveswept Ser.: No. 840). 1997. mass mkt. 3.50 (*0-553-44598-7*, Loveswept) Bantam.

Stand-in Husband. Anne Peters. 1995. mass mkt. 2.99 (*0-373-19110-3*, 1-19110-5) Silhouette.

Stand-In Mom. Susan Meier. (Romance Ser.). 1994. pap. 2.75 (*0-373-19022-0*, 1-19022-2) Harlequin Bks.

***Stand in the Gap.** Bill McCartney. 64p. 1997. pap. 2.99 (*0-8499-4047-8*) Word Pub.

Stand in the Gap for Your Children. rev. ed. Norvel Hayes. 64p. (Orig.). 1991. pap. 4.99 (*0-89274-886-9*, HH886) Harrison Hse.

Stand in the Mountains. Peter Taylor. LC 85-70509. 113p. 1985. 45.00 (*0-913720-60-7*) Beil.

Stand into Danger. large type ed. Alexander Kent. 1982. 15.95 (*0-7089-0753-9*) Ulverscroft.

Stand into Danger. Alexander Kent. 1992. reprint ed. lib. bdg. 25.95 (*0-89966-972-7*) Buccaneer Bks.

***Stand Like Mountain, Flow Like Water: Reflections on Stress & Human Spirituality.** Brian L. Seaward. LC 96-6525. 1997. pap. 10.95 (*1-55874-462-2*) Health Comm.

Stand on It: A Novel by Stroker Ace. William Neely. LC 73-10414. 294p. 1990. reprint ed. pap. 12.95 (*0-89404-081-2*) Aztex.

Stand on the Crooked & Cut Straight. Elisha A. Colgram. 1994. 16.95 (*0-533-10763-2*) Vantage.

Stand on Zanzibar. John Brunner. 672p. 1987. reprint ed. mass mkt. 5.99 (*0-345-34787-0*, Del Rey) Ballantine.

Stand on Zanzibar. John Brunner. LC 79-19062. 1979. reprint ed. lib. bdg. 30.00 (*0-8376-0438-9*) Bentley.

Stand Out: How You Can Become a Strong Leader. Bill Sanders. LC 94-28907. (Illus.). 224p. (Orig.). (YA). (gr. 9-12). 1994. pap. 7.99 (*0-8007-5533-2*) Revell.

Stand Out Service! Talk Straight, Think Positive & Smile! Dartnell Corp. Staff. (Customer Service Rep's Survival Guide Ser.). 227p. 1995. pap. 13.95 (*0-85013-204-5*) Dartnell Corp.

Stand Proud. Elmer Kelton. LC 89-20386. (Texas Tradition Ser.: No. 13). 286p. 1990. reprint ed. pap. 10.95 (*0-87565-044-9*) Tex Christian.

Stand Still Like the Hummingbird. Henry Miller. LC 62-10408. 1967. reprint ed. pap. 9.95 (*0-8112-0322-0*, NDP236) New Directions.

Stand Still Summer. Betty K. Thomae. LC 85-71083. 1987. 8.95 (*0-8158-0431-8*) Chris Mass.

Stand Tall. P. C. Erickson. (Illus.). (Orig.). (J). (gr. 4-8). 1978. pap. 2.95 (*0-89036-111-8*) Hawkes Pub Inc.

Stand Tall! The Informed Woman's Guide to Preventing Osteoporosis. 2nd rev. ed. Morris Notelovitz et al. (Illus.). 224p. 1998. write for info. (*0-937404-38-1*) Triad Pub FL.

***Stand the Storm: A History of the Atlantic Slave Trade.** Edward Reynolds. 1989. pap. 6.95 (*0-85031-586-7*, Pub. by A & B UK) London Brdge.

Stand the Storm: A History of the Atlantic Slave Trade. Edward Reynolds. 192p. 1993. reprint ed. pap. text ed. 8.95 (*1-56663-020-7*) I R Dee.

Stand to a Diary of the Trenches 1915-18. F. C. Hitchcock. 358p. 1988. 79.00 (*0-947893-05-9*, Pub. by Gliddon Bks UK) St Mut.

Stand und Aufgaben der Deutschen Dialektlexikographie Vol. II: Brueder-Grimm-Symposium Zur Historischen Wortforschung. Ed. by Ernst Bremer & Reiner Hildebrandt. (Historische Wortforschung Ser.). (Illus.). viii, 293p. (GER.). (C). 1996. lib. bdg. 133.35 (*3-11-014464-6*) De Gruyter.

***Stand Up.** Edelman. LC 97-10831. (J). 1998. 14.95 (*0-7868-0365-7*); lib. bdg. 14.89 (*0-7868-2310-0*) Hyprn Child.

Stand Up. Kahaner. Date not set. pap. 3.50 (*0-679-85427-4*) Random.

Stand-Up: A Miles Jacoby Mystery. Robert J. Randisi. LC 94-18377. 1994. 20.95 (*0-8027-3196-1*) Walker & Co.

Stand Up! On Being a Comedian. Double. 1995. pap. 25.95 (*0-413-70310-X*, Pub. by Methuen UK) Heinemann.

Stand Up & Be a Voice: Eight Poetic Voice Plays. Pepper Worthington. (Illus.). 373p. 1991. pap. 14.95 (*0-9627087-2-0*) Mt Olive Coll Pr.

Stand Up & Be Counted: Math Jokes for Those Who Count. Renee Ewing. 104p. (Orig.). (J). (gr. k-12). 1994. pap. 10.95 (*1-884340-00-8*) MathAmer Math.

Stand Up & Die: A Captain Heimrich Mystery. large type ed. Richard Lockridge & Frances Lockridge. LC 94-19359. 296p. 1994. lib. bdg. 17.95 (*1-56054-305-1*) Thorndike Pr.

Stand up & Fight Back: A Young Persons Guide to Spiritual Warfare. Ken Abraham. 180p. (Orig.). 1993. pap. 10.99 (*0-89283-812-4*, Vine Bks) Servant.

Stand Up & Hook Up. Buck Dawson. 185p. 1990. 21.95 (*1-880236-01-X*) Hoffman FL.

***Stand up & Hook Up: WW II Novel.** Buck Dawson. 186p. 1997. pap. 16.95 (*1-57168-155-8*, Eakin Pr) Sunbelt Media.

***Stand up & Talk to 1000 People (& Enjoy It!)** Marion Witz. 176p. 1997. pap. 12.95 (*0-919292-02-X*, Pub. by McLeod Pub CN) Genl Dist Srvs.

Stand-up Comedians on Television. Pref. by Larry Gelbart. LC 95-37222. (Illus.). 175p. 1996. 39.95 (*0-8109-4467-7*) Abrams.

Stand-up Comedy: The Book. Judy Carter. 208p. 1989. pap. 13.95 (*0-440-50243-8*, Dell Trade Pbks) Dell.

Stand-up Flip over Cookbooks: Morocco. 1994. write for info. (*1-870049-87-X*) Oliver Bks.

Stand-Up Flip-Over Cookbooks: Northern Italy. 1994. Wire-o bdg. spiral bd. write for info. (*1-870049-85-3*) Oliver Bks.

Stand-up Flip over Cookbooks: Southwest France. 1994. write for info. (*1-870049-86-1*) Oliver Bks.

Stand Up Math: 180 Challenging Problems for Kids, Budding Genius Level, Ages 8-10. James Riley et al. (Illus.). 184p. (Orig.). 1994. spiral bd. 9.95 (*0-673-36144-6*, GoodYrBooks) Addson-Wesley Educ.

Stand Up Math: 180 Challenging Problems for Kids, Genius Level, Ages 9-11. James Riley et al. (Illus.). 184p. (Orig.). 1994. spiral bd. 9.95 (*0-673-36145-4*, GoodYrBooks) Addson-Wesley Educ.

Stand Up Math: 180 Challenging Problems for Kids, Super Genius Level, Ages 10 Up. James Riley et al. (Illus.). 184p. (Orig.). 1994. spiral bd. 9.95 (*0-673-36146-2*, GoodYrBooks) Addson-Wesley Educ.

Stand up, Mr. Dickens: A Dickens Anthology. Edward Blishen. LC 95-18237. (Illus.). 96p. (YA). (gr. 5 up). 1995. 16.95 (*0-395-75656-1*) HM.

Stand up Poetry: The Poetry of Los Angeles & Beyond. Ed. & Intro. by Charles H. Webb. 84p. 1990. pap. 7.95 (*0-9622847-2-6*) Red Wind Bks.

Stand Up, Shake Hands, Say "How Do You Do" What Boys Need to Know about Today's Manners News. rev. ed. Marjabelle Y. Stewart & Ann Buchwald. LC 77-8159. (YA). (gr. 7 up). 1988. 14.95 (*0-88331-100-3*) Luce.

Stand up, Speak out, Talk Back. Robert E. Alberti. 1990. mass mkt. 5.50 (*0-671-73588-8*) PB.

Stand up to the IRS: How to Handle Audits, Tax Bills & Tax Court. 3rd ed. Frederick W. Daily. Ed. by Robin Leonard. LC 96-16422. 368p. 1996. 24.95 (*0-87337-337-5*) Nolo Pr.

***Stand Your Ground.** unabridged ed. Eric Walters. 160p. (YA). (gr. 7 up). 1994. mass mkt. 4.95 (*0-7736-7421-7*, Pub. by Stoddart Kids CN) Genl Dist Srvs.

Standalone Facsimile Equipment Market (U. S.) Market Intelligence Staff. 200p. 1992. 2,900.00 (*1-56753-827-4*, A2515) Frost & Sullivan.

Standard. Carman Walker & Walter Walker. 1994. 14.95 (*0-917143-33-7*) Sparrow TN.

Standard, 20 vols., Vols. 15-35. Ed. by Frank S. Murray. Incl. Vol. 15. Standard 1963. LC 49-3353. 1963. 3.00 (*0-910840-63-6*); Vol. 16. Standard 1964. 1964. 3.00 (*0-910840-64-4*); Vol. 17. Standard 1965. 1965. 3.00 (*0-910840-65-2*); Vol. 18. Standard 1966. 1966. 3.00 (*0-910840-66-0*); Vol. 19. Standard 1967. 1967. 3.00 (*0-910840-67-9*); Vol. 20. Standard 1968. 1968. 3.00 (*0-910840-68-7*); Vol. 21. Standard 1969. 1969. 3.00 (*0-910840-69-5*); Vol. 22. Standard 1970. 1970. 3.00 (*0-910840-70-9*); Vol. 23. Standard 1971. 1971. 3.00 (*0-910840-71-7*); Vol. 24. Standard 1972. 4p. 1995. pap. 3.00 (*0-910840-72-5*); Vol. 25. Standard 1973. 4p. 1995. pap. 3.00 (*0-910840-73-3*); Vol. 26. Standard 1974. 4p. 1995. pap. 3.00 (*0-910840-74-1*); Vol. 27. Standard 1975. 4p. 1995. pap. 3.00 (*0-910840-75-X*); Vol. 28. Standard 1976. 4p. 1995. pap. 3.00 (*0-910840-76-8*); Vol. 29. Standard 1977. 4p. 1995. pap. 3.00 (*0-910840-77-6*); Vol. 30. Standard 1978. 4p. 1995. pap. 3.00 (*0-910840-78-4*); Vol. 31. Standard 1979. 4p. 1995. pap. 3.00 (*0-910840-79-2*); Vol. 32. Standard 1980. 4p. 1995. pap. 3.00 (*0-910840-80-6*); Vol. 33. Standard 1981. 4p. 1995. pap. 3.00 (*0-910840-81-4*); Vol. 34. Standard 1982. 4p. 1995. pap. 3.00 (*0-910840-82-2*); Vol. 35. Standard 1983. 1995. pap. 3.00 (*0-910840-83-0*); Vol. 26. Standard 1974. 4p. 1995. pap. 3.00 (*0-910840-74-1*); Vol. 24. Standard 1972. 4p. 1995. pap. 3.00 (*0-910840-72-5*); write for info. (*0-318-53986-1*) Kingdom.

Standard Abbreviations for Image Descriptions for Use in Fine Arts Visual Resources Collections. Nancy S. Schuller. 1987. 10.00 (*0-685-54076-6*) Visual Resources Assn.

Standard Accounting System for Lutheran Congregations. Neal D. Meitler & Linda M. La Porte. 1981. 7.50 (*0-8100-0129-2*, 21N2001) Northwest Pub.

Standard Achievement Tests. Raji M. Rammuny. 118p. 1994. pap. text ed. 11.00 (*1-57074-141-7*) Greyden Pr.

Standard Acupuncture Nomenclature. 2nd ed. iii, 266p. 1993. pap. text ed. 16.00 (*92-9061-105-7*, 1512001) World Health.

Standard Address Number (SAN) for the Publishing Industry, Z39.43-1993. rev. ed. National Information Standards Organization Staff. LC 95-39985. (National Information Standards Ser.). 19p. 1995. reprint ed. 30.00 (*1-880124-14-9*, 1041-5653) NISO.

Standard Aircraft Handbook. (Illus.). 232p. 11.95 (*0-614-13173-1*, 21-37077) EAA Aviation.

Standard Aircraft Handbook. 4th ed. Ed. by Larry W. Reithmaier. (Illus.). 240p. 1987. 11.95 (*0-8306-8812-9*, 28512V, TAB-Aero) TAB Bks.

Standard Aircraft Handbook. 5th ed. Larry W. Reithmaier. (Illus.). 232p. 1991. pap. text ed. 12.95 (*0-07-157642-8*) McGraw.

Standard Aircraft Handbook. 5th ed. Larry W. Reithmaier. (Illus.). 256p. 1991. vinyl bd. 11.95 (*0-8306-8634-7*, 3634, TAB-Aero) TAB Bks.

Standard Aircraft Workers' Manual. 15th ed. Fletcher Aircraft Company Staff. 190p. 1989. spiral bd. 9.95 (*0-911721-29-0*) Aviation.

Standard Albanian: A Reference Grammar for Students. Leonard D. Newmark et al. LC 81-52125. 368p. 1982. 55.00 (*0-8047-1129-1*) Stanford U Pr.

Standard Alphabet for Reducing Unwritten Languages & Foreign Graphic Systems to a Uniform Orthography in European Letters. 2nd ed. Richard Lepsius. Ed. by J. Alan Kemp. (Amsterdam Classics in Linguistics Ser.: Vol. 5). xvii, 336p. 1981. 87.00 (*90-272-0876-X*) Benjamins North Am.

***Standard (American) Bridge Flipper.** Ron Klinger. 1997. pap. 3.95 (*0-575-05121-3*, Pub. by V Gollancz UK) Trafalgar.

Standard American Bridge Updated. Norma Sands. pap. 6.95 (*0-9605648-0-2*) Rocky Mtn Bks.

Standard American Foxtrot. (Ballroom Dance Ser.). 1985. lib. bdg. 72.00 (*0-87700-740-3*) Revisionist Pr.

Standard American Waltz. (Ballroom Dance Ser.). 1986. lib. bdg. 79.95 (*0-8490-3414-0*) Gordon Pr.

Standard American Waltz. (Ballroom Dance Ser.). 1985. lib. bdg. 64.50 (*0-87700-813-2*) Revisionist Pr.

Standard & Mental Handicap. Thompson. 1992. text ed. 38.00 (*0-7020-1566-0*) HarBrace.

Standard & Policies Manual. rev. ed. (C). 1996. reprint ed. ring bd. 49.95 (*1-57743-003-4*, 12902) NAUI.

Standard & Poor's How to Invest: A Guide for Buying Stocks, Bonds & Mutual Funds. D. Rachman. 1992. pap. text ed. write for info. (*0-07-051337-6*) McGraw.

Standard & Poor's Midcap 400 Guide, 1997 Edition. Standar & Poors Staff. 1996. pap. text ed. 24.95 (*0-07-052501-3*) McGraw.

***Standard & Poor's Midcap 400 Guide, 1998.** Standard & Poor's Staff. 1997. pap. text ed. 24.95 (*0-07-052620-6*) McGraw.

Standard & Poor's Nineteen Ninety-Five Insurance Company Ratings Guide. Standard & Poors Staff. 384p. 1995. pap. text ed. 19.95 (*0-07-052101-8*) McGraw.

Standard & Poor's Smallcap 600 Guide, 1995. 1995. pap. text ed. 27.95 (*0-07-052098-4*) McGraw.

An Asterisk (*) at the beginning of an entry indicates that the title is appearing in BIP for the first time.

Standard & Poor's Smallcap 600 Guide, 1997 Edition. Standard & Poors Staff. 1996. pap. text ed. 24.95 (*0-07-052503-X*) McGraw.

***Standard & Poor's Stock & Bond Guide, 1997.** Standard & Poors Staff. 1997. pap. text ed. 22.95 (*0-07-052553-6*) McGraw.

***Standard & Poor's 100 Top Dividend-Paying Stocks.** (Illus.). 224p. 1997. pap. text ed. 19.95 (*0-07-052556-0*) McGraw.

***Standard & Poor's 100 Top Growth Stocks.** (Illus.). 224p. 1997. pap. text ed. 19.95 (*0-07-052555-2*) McGraw.

Standard & Poor's 1995 Guide to Sector Investing. Standard & Poors Staff. 288p. 1996. pap. text ed. 24.95 (*0-07-061717-1*) McGraw.

Standard & Poor's 401K Planning Guide: Every Employee's Guide to Making 401K Decisions. Alan J. Miller. LC 94-40808. 1995. pap. text ed. 12.95 (*0-07-042197-8*) McGraw.

Standard & Poor's 500. Carol Mull. LC 83-72385. 100p. 1984. 31.00 (*0-86690-261-9*, M2400-014) Am Fed Astrologers.

Standard & Poor's 500 Guide, 1997 Edition. Standard & Poors Staff. 1996. pap. text ed. 24.95 (*0-07-052502-1*) McGraw.

Standard Arabic for Beginners. Wafaa' M. Salman. 49p. 1994. student ed., pap. text ed. 50.00 incl. audio (*0-9641767-0-X*) Cambrdge Inst Tech.

Standard Aviation Maintenance Handbook. (Illus.). 7.00 (*0-614-13166-9*, 21-37713) EAA Aviation.

Standard Aviation Maintenance Handbook. 3rd ed. LC 88-142641. (Illus.). 235p. 1985. pap. text ed. 10.95 (*0-89100-282-0*, EA-282-0) IAP.

Standard BASIC Dictionary for Programming. John P. Steiner. LC 84-11436. 256p. 1986. 24.95 (*0-13-841560-9*, Busn); pap. 19.95 (*0-13-841552-8*, Busn) P-H.

Standard BASIC Programming with True BASIC. Avery Catlin. (Illus.). 400p. (C). 1987. pap. text ed. 34.00 (*0-13-841578-1*) P-H.

Standard Bearer: A Story of Army Life in the Time of Caesar. Albert C. Whitehead. (Illus.). (J). (gr. 7-11). 1943. 21.00 (*0-8196-0116-0*) Biblo.

***Standard Bible Atlas.** 2nd ed. (Illus.). 32p. 1997. reprint ed. pap. 7.99 (*0-7847-0596-8*, 03166) Standard Pub.

Standard Bid Evaluation Form: Procurement of Goods or Works. 48p. 1996. pap. 7.95 (*0-8213-3588-X*) World Bank.

Standard Biphasic-Contrast Examination of the Stomach & Duodenum: Method Results & Radiological Atlas. J. Odo Op den Orth. 182p. 1979. lib. bdg. 146.00 (*90-247-2159-8*) Kluwer Ac.

Standard Bodhran. 120.00 (*0-685-75037-X*, 95193IWW) Mel Bay.

Standard Book of British & American Verse: Preface by Christopher Morley. Ed. by Nella Braddy. LC 72-38594. (Granger Index Reprint Ser.). 1977. reprint ed. 37.95 (*0-8369-6326-1*) Ayer.

Standard Book of Dog Breeding: A New Look. rev. ed. Alvin Grossman. Ed. by Luana Luther. LC 91-70232. (Illus.). 300p. 1992. 26.50 (*0-944875-18-1*) Doral Pub.

Standard Book of Dog Grooming. Diane Fenger & Arlene F. Steinle. LC 95-26629. (Illus.). 224p. 1996. reprint ed. spiral bd. 29.95 (*0-931866-84-7*) Alpine Pubns.

Standard Book of Quilt-Making & Collecting. Marguerite Ickis. (Illus.). 1990. 20.00 (*0-8446-0720-7*) Peter Smith.

Standard Book of Quiltmaking & Collecting. Marguerite Ickis. (Illus.). 1949. pap. 6.95 (*0-486-20582-7*) Dover.

Standard Bridge Flipper. Ron Klinger. 1991. pap. 9.95 (*0-685-40072-7*) HM.

Standard C. P. L. Plauger & Jim Brodie. LC 95-15055. 256p. 1995. pap. 29.95 (*0-13-436411-2*) P-H.

Standard C Library. P. J. Plauger. 1991. text ed. 62.00 (*0-13-838012-0*); pap. text ed. 49.00 (*0-13-131509-9*) P-H.

Standard California Codes (Penal) annuals 1961. Annual. write for info. (*0-8205-1698-8*) Bender.

Standard California Codes (5-in-1) write for info. (*0-8205-1700-3*) Bender.

***Standard Candles: The Best Short Fiction of Jack McDevitt.** Jack McDevitt. 250p. 1996. 25.00 (*0-9648320-4-6*) Tachyon Pubns.

Standard Catalog of American Cars, 1805-1942. Beverly R. Kimes. LC 85-50390. (Illus.). 1598p. 1996. pap. 55.00 (*0-87341-428-4*, AB03) Krause Pubns.

Standard Catalog of American Cars, 1946-1975. 3rd ed. Ed. by John Gunnell. LC 82-84065. (Standard Catalog of American Cars Ser.). (Illus.). 864p. 1992. pap. 27.95 (*0-87341-204-4*, AC03) Krause Pubns.

***Standard Catalog of American Cars, 1946-75.** 4th ed. Ed. by Ron Kowalke. (Illus.). 928p. 1997. pap. 34.95 (*0-87341-521-3*, AC04) Krause Pubns.

Standard Catalog of American Cars, 1976-1986. 2nd ed. James M. Flammang. LC 88-81627. (Illus.). 468p. 1990. pap. 19.95 (*0-87341-133-1*, AD02) Krause Pubns.

Standard Catalog of American Light Duty Trucks. 2nd ed. John Gunnell. LC 86-83144. (Standard Catalog of American Cars Ser.). (Illus.). 800p. 1993. pap. 29.95 (*0-87341-238-9*, PT02) Krause Pubns.

Standard Catalog of American Motors 1902-1987. Ed. by John Gunnell. LC 92-74794. (Standard Catalog of American Cars Ser.). (Illus.). 320p. (Orig.). 1993. pap. 19.95 (*0-87341-232-X*, AS01) Krause Pubns.

Standard Catalog of Baseball Cards. 6th ed. Sports Collectors Digest Staff. 1552p. 1997. pap. text ed. 37.95 (*0-87341-467-5*) Krause Pubns.

***Standard Catalog of Basketball Cards.** Sports Collectors Digest Staff. (Illus.). 288p. (Orig.). 1997. pap. 19.95 (*0-87341-551-5*, SCBC01) Krause Pubns.

Standard Catalog of Buick 1903-1990. Ed. by Mary Sieber & Ken Buttolph. LC 91-61302. (Standard Catalog of American Cars Ser.). (Illus.). 304p. (Orig.). 1991. pap. 18.95 (*0-87341-173-0*, AK01) Krause Pubns.

Standard Catalog of Cadillac 1903-1990. Ed. by Mary Sieber & Ken Buttolph. LC 91-61301. (Standard Catalog of American Cars Ser.). (Illus.). 272p. 1991. pap. 18.95 (*0-87341-174-9*, AL01) Krause Pubns.

Standard Catalog of Cessna Single Engine Aircraft. 2nd rev. ed. Jim Cavangh. LC 95-77239. (Illus.). 840p. 1959. pap. text ed. 49.95 (*1-879825-18-X*) Jones Publish.

Standard Catalog of Chevrolet Light-Duty Trucks, 1918-1995. John Gunnell. LC 95-60365. (Illus.). 288p. 1995. pap. text ed. 24.95 (*0-87341-364-4*, ACT01) Krause Pubns.

Standard Catalog of Chevrolet, 1912-1990. Pat Chappell. LC 90-60576. (Illus.). 480p. 1990. pap. 19.95 (*0-87341-141-2*, AV01) Krause Pubns.

Standard Catalog of Chrysler 1924-1990. John Lee. LC 90-60577. (Illus.). 480p. (Orig.). 1990. pap. 19.95 (*0-87341-142-0*, AY01) Krause Pubns.

Standard Catalog of Depression Scrip of U. S. Ralph Mitchell & Neil Shafer. LC 85-52834. (Illus.). 320p. 1985. pap. 27.50 (*0-87341-047-5*, DS01) Krause Pubns.

***Standard Catalog of Firearms.** 7th ed. Ed. by Ned Schwing. (Illus.). 1116p. 1997. pap. 29.95 (*0-87341-480-2*, GG07) Krause Pubns.

Standard Catalog of Football, Basketball & Hockey Cards. Sports Collectors Digest Editors. LC 95-76859. (Illus.). 640p. 1995. pap. text ed. 19.95 (*0-87341-356-3*, SFH01) Krause Pubns.

Standard Catalog of Football, Basketball & Hockey Cards. Sports Collectors Digest Staff. 1996. pap. text ed. 21.95 (*0-87341-431-4*) Krause Pubns.

***Standard Catalog of Football Cards.** Sports Collectors Digest Staff. (Illus.). 400p. (Orig.). 1997. pap. 24.95 (*0-87341-550-7*, SCFC01) Krause Pubns.

Standard Catalog of Ford 1903-1990. Bob Lichty. LC 90-60574. (Standard Catalog of American Cars Ser.). (Illus.). 480p. (Orig.). 1990. pap. 19.95 (*0-87341-140-4*, AF01) Krause Pubns.

Standard Catalog of German Coins, 1601 - Present. Douglas Nicol. LC 93-77549. (Illus.). 952p. 1995. pap. text ed. 59.00 (*0-87341-272-9*, GE01) Krause Pubns.

Standard Catalog of Imported Cars: 1946-1990. James M. Flammang. LC 90-63914. (Standard Catalog of American Cars Ser.). (Illus.). 512p. 1992. pap. 24.95 (*0-87341-158-7*, AI01) Krause Pubns.

Standard Catalog of Military Vehicles, 1940-1965. Thomas Berndt. LC 92-72123. (Illus.). 400p. 1993. pap. 29.95 (*0-87341-223-0*, MV01) Krause Pubns.

***Standard Catalog of Oldsmobile: 1897-1997.** John Chevedden & Ron Kowalke. (Illus.). 304p. (Orig.). 1997. pap. 21.95 (*0-87341-484-5*, OLDS) Krause Pubns.

Standard Catalog of Piper Single Engine Aircraft. Jim Cavanagh. Ed. by David C. Sakrison. (Illus.). 528p. (Orig.). 1993. pap. 49.95 (*1-879825-08-2*) Jones Publish.

Standard Catalog of Piper Twin Engine Aircraft. Jim Cavanagh. Ed. by David C. Sakrison. (Illus.). 248p. (Orig.). 1994. pap. 29.95 (*1-879825-10-4*) Jones Publish.

Standard Catalog of Pontiac, 1926-1995. John Gunnell. LC 95-79461. (Illus.). 304p. 1995. pap. 19.95 (*0-87341-369-5*, APO01) Krause Pubns.

Standard Catalog of Provincial Banks & Banknotes. G. L. Grant. 1978. 30.00 (*0-686-52192-7*) S J Durst.

Standard Catalog of Smith & Wesson. Jim Supica. LC 96-75277. (Illus.). 256p. 1996. pap. 29.95 (*0-87341-404-7*, FSW01) Krause Pubns.

***Standard Catalog of U. S. Paper Money.** 16th ed. Ed. by Chet Krause et al. (Illus.). 248p. 1997. 24.95 (*0-87341-536-1*, SP16) Krause Pubns.

Standard Catalog of U. S. Tokens 1700-1900. Russell Rulau. LC 93-80096. (Illus.). 284p. 1994. pap. text ed. 45.00 (*0-87341-246-X*, ST01) Krause Pubns.

***Standard Catalog of U. S. Tokens 1700-1900.** 2nd ed. Russell Rulau. (Illus.). 304p. 1997. pap. 47.95 (*0-87341-479-9*, ST02) Krause Pubns.

Standard Catalog of United States Altered & Counterfeit Coins. Virgil Hancock & Larry Spanbauer. (Illus.). 1979. lib. bdg. 30.00 (*0-915262-26-6*) S J Durst.

Standard Catalog of United States Paper Money. 14th ed. Robert E. Wilhite. LC 81-81876. (Illus.). 216p. 1995. 24.95 (*0-87341-376-8*, SP14) Krause Pubns.

Standard Catalog of World Coins, 2 vols., Set. 19th ed. Chester Krause & Clifford Mishler. Ed. by Colin R. Bruce, II. LC 79-640940. (Illus.). 3016p. 1991. 145.00 (*0-87341-151-X*, SC19) Krause Pubns.

Standard Catalog of World Coins: Eighteenth Century 1701-1800. Ed. by Colin R. Bruce, III. LC 79-640940. (Illus.). 1000p. 1993. pap. 45.00 (*0-87341-260-5*, SE01) Krause Pubns.

Standard Catalog of World Coins, 17th Century 1601-1700. Chester L. Krause. LC 79-640940. (Illus.). 800p. 1995. pap. text ed. 65.00 (*0-87341-271-0*, C401) Krause Pubns.

***Standard Catalog of World Coins, 18th Century.** 2nd ed. Chester L. Krause et al. (Illus.). 1248p. 1997. pap. 65.00 (*0-87341-526-4*, SE02) Krause Pubns.

Standard Catalog of World Coins 1801-Present. 23th ed. LC 79-640940. (Illus.). 1995. pap. text ed. 49.95 (*0-87341-357-1*, SC23) Krause Pubns.

Standard Catalog of World Coins, 19th Century. Chester L. Krause. Ed. by Colin R. Bruce, II. LC 79-640940. (Illus.). 1152p. 1996. pap. 45.00 (*0-87341-427-6*, SCN01) Krause Pubns.

Standard Catalog of World Coins 1901-Present. 24th ed. Chester L. Krause. Ed. by Colin R. Bruce, II. LC 79-640940. (Illus.). 1344p. 1996. pap. 45.00 (*0-87341-426-8*, SC24) Krause Pubns.

Standard Catalog of World Crowns & Talers, 1601-Date. Ed. by Colin R. Bruce, II. LC 92-71448. (Illus.). 1360p. 1993. pap. 75.00 (*0-87341-211-7*, CW01) Krause Pubns.

Standard Catalog of World Gold Coins. 3rd ed. Chester L. Krause & Clifford Mishler. Ed. by Colin R. Bruce, II. LC 85-61548. (Illus.). 848p. 1992. pap. 60.00 (*0-87341-213-3*, GC03) Krause Pubns.

Standard Catalog of World Paper Money Vol. 2: General Issues. Albert Pick. 1996. 55.00 (*0-87341-469-1*) Krause Pubns.

Standard Catalog of World Paper Money Vol. I: Specialized Issues. 7th ed. Colin R. Bruce. LC 83-83100. (Illus.). 1096p. 1995. 60.00 (*0-87341-208-7*, PS07) Krause Pubns.

Standard Catalog of World Paper Money Vol. III: Modern Issues. 2nd ed. Colin R. Bruce. Ed. by George Cuhaj. LC 95-76858. (Illus.). 800p. 1996. pap. 32.95 (*0-87341-425-X*, WP02) Krause Pubns.

Standard Catalog of 4 x 4's. Robert C. Ackerson. LC 92-71443. (Illus.). 528p. 1993. pap. 24.95 (*0-87341-203-6*, FX01) Krause Pubns.

Standard Cataloging for School & Public Libraries. 2nd ed. Sheila S. Intner & Jean Weihs. LC 95-53186. 360p. 1996. lib. bdg. 32.50 (*1-56308-349-3*) Libs Unl.

***Standard Catalogue of British Coinage 1997.** 32th ed. Ed. by Stephen Mitchell & Brian Reeds. (Illus.). 290p. 1996. 24.95 (*0-7134-8052-1*, Pub. by Batsford UK) Trafalgar.

Standard Catalogue of British Orders, Decorations & Medals. E. C. Joslin. 1984. 30.00 (*0-685-51506-0*) S J Durst.

Standard Catalogue of Encased Postage Stamps. Michael J. Hodder & Q. David Bowers. (Illus.). 192p. 1989. 27.95 (*0-943161-24-X*); pap. 19.95 (*0-943161-20-7*) Bowers & Merena.

***Standard Chess Openings: The Complete & Definitive Chess Player's Guide.** Eric Schiller. LC 96-71754. (Illus.). 816p. 1997. pap. 24.95 (*0-940685-72-8*) Cardoza Pub.

Standard Christmas Program Book: Includes Material for Thanksgiving. Ed. by Pat Fittro. 48p. (Orig.). 1996. pap. 3.99 (*0-7847-0494-5*, 08657) Standard Pub.

***Standard Christmas Program Book: Includes Thanksgiving Material.** Ed. & Compiled by Patt Fittro. 48p. (Orig.). 1997. pap. 3.99 (*0-7847-0700-6*, 21-08658) Standard Pub.

Standard Citation Forms for Published Bibliographies & Catalogs Used in Rare Book Cataloging. 2nd ed. Compiled by Peter M. Van Wingen & Belinda D. Urquiza. LC 94-45780. 1995. write for info. (*0-8444-0872-7*) Lib Congress.

Standard Clauses in a Licensing Agreement. 47p. (Orig.). 1981. pap. text ed. 12.50 (*0-911378-36-7*) Sheridan.

Standard Code of Parliamentary Procedure. 3rd rev. ed. Alice F. Sturgis. 275p. 1993. pap. text ed. 12.95 (*0-07-062522-0*) McGraw.

Standard Common & Scientific Names. Collins. 1990. pap. write for info. (*0-916984-21-4*) SSAR.

***Standard Conditions of Sale.** 5th ed. Frances Silverman. 280p. 1996. pap. 175.00 (*1-86012-162-4*, Pub. by Tolley Pubng UK) St Mut.

Standard Conditions of Sale: A Conveyancer's Guide. 4th ed. Frances Silverman. 280p. 1992. 100.00 (*1-85190-184-1*, Pub. by Tolley Pubng UK) St Mut.

Standard Contract for Sale of Land in N. S. W. P. J. Butt. lxxxiv, 948p. 1985. suppl. ed. 168.50 (*0-455-20697-X*, Pub. by Law Bk Co AT); suppl. ed., pap. 55.00 (*0-685-50927-3*, Pub. by Law Bk Co AT) Gaunt.

Standard Contracts for Building. Dennis F. Turner. LC 83-11670. (Godwin Study Guides Ser.). 244p. reprint ed. pap. 69.60 (*0-8357-2981-8*, 2039243) Bks Demand.

Standard Costing. B. Batty. 1990. pap. 26.00 (*0-7463-0483-8*, Pub. by Northcote UK) St Mut.

Standard Costing. Colin Drury. (Advanced Management Accounting & Finance Ser.). (Illus.). 198p. 1992. pap. text ed. 17.00 (*0-12-222355-1*) Acad Pr.

Standard Costs & Variance Analysis - a Summary. Thomas F. George. Ed. by Mary E. George. (Illus.). 34p. (Orig.). (C). 1987. pap. text ed. 9.98 (*0-317-91276-3*) Servs by George.

Standard Costs & Variance Analysis - a Summary: Using Appleworks Or IBM Spreadsheets. Thomas F. George. Ed. by Mary E. George. (Illus.). 40p. (Orig.). (C). 1989. pap. text ed. 12.95 (*0-929683-11-0*) Servs by George.

Standard Curves & Surfaces: A Mathematica Notebook. 8p. 1992. 56.95 (*0-8493-0761-9*) CRC Pr.

Standard Data Encryption Algorithm. Harry Katzan, Jr. LC 77-13582. (Illus.). 1977. text ed. 14.00 (*0-89433-016-0*) Petrocelli.

Standard Deviations: Change & the Modern British Novel. Leland Monk. LC 92-38358. 216p. (C). 1993. 35.00 (*0-8047-2174-2*) Stanford U Pr.

Standard Dialogues. Ed. by Alexander Clark. LC 77-109137. (Granger Index Reprint Ser.). 1977. 18.95 (*0-8369-6121-8*) Ayer.

Standard Dictionary of Advertising, Mass Media & Marketing. Wolfgang J. Koschnick. (ENG & GER.). 1987. 275.00 (*0-8288-0096-0*, M4446) Fr & Eur.

***Standard Dictionary of Electrical & Electronics Terms, 100-1992.** 95.00 (*1-55937-240-0*, SH15594) IEEE Standards.

Standard Dictionary of the Social Sciences, Vol. 2. Wolfgang J. Koschnick. 664p. (ENG & GER.). 1984. 150.00 (*0-8288-2360-X*, M 5000) Fr & Eur.

Standard Dictionary of the Social Sciences, English - German, Vol. 1. Wolfgang J. Koschnick. 664p. (ENG & GER.). 1984. 225.00 (*0-7859-4785-X*) Fr & Eur.

Standard Dictionary of the Social Sciences English-German, Vol. 1. Wolfgang J. Koschnick. 674p. 1983. lib. bdg. 92.50 (*3-598-10526-6*) K G Saur.

Standard Dictionary of the Social Sciences German-English, Vol. 2. Wolfgang J. Koschnick. 2291p. 1993. lib. bdg. 190.00 (*3-598-10527-4*) K G Saur.

Standard Dictionary of the Social Sciences, German-English, Vol. 2. Wolfgang J. Koschnick. 785p. 1992. 150.00 (*0-7859-3721-8*, F90030) Fr & Eur.

Standard Directory of Advertisers: Business Classifications Edition. Ed. by National Register Publishing Editorial Staff. 1960p. 1996. 499.95 (*0-87217-244-9*) Natl Register.

***Standard Directory of Advertisers: Business Classifications Edition.** Ed. by National Register Publishing Editorial Staff. 1930p. 1997. 499.95 (*0-87217-276-7*) Natl Register.

Standard Directory of Advertisers: Geographic Edition. National Register Publishing Editorial Staff. 1860p. 1996. 499.95 (*0-87217-245-7*) Natl Register.

***Standard Directory of Advertisers: Geographic Edition.** Ed. by National Register Publishing Editorial Staff. 1830p. 1997. 499.95 (*0-87217-277-5*) Natl Register.

Standard Directory of Advertisers: Indexes. National Register Publishing Editorial Staff. 1066p. 1996. write for info. (*0-87217-246-5*) Natl Register.

***Standard Directory of Advertisers: Indexes.** Ed. by National Register Publishing Editorial Staff. 1056p. 1997. write for info. (*0-87217-278-3*) Natl Register.

Standard Directory of Advertisers 1995: Business Classifications Edition with Supplements. 3030p. 1995. 579.00 (*0-87217-242-2*) K G Saur.

Standard Directory of Advertisers 1995: Geographic Edition with Supplements. 2992p. 1995. 579.00 (*0-87217-243-0*) K G Saur.

Standard Directory of Advertisers 1996: Business Classifications Edition with Supplements. Ed. by National Register Publishing Co. Staff. 1996. 599.00 (*0-87217-249-X*) Natl Register.

Standard Directory of Advertisers 1996: Geographic Edition with Supplements. Ed. by National Register Publishing Co. Staff. 1996. 599.00 (*0-87217-275-9*) Natl Register.

Standard Directory of Advertisers 1996: January & July with Supplements. Ed. by National Register Publishing Co. Staff. 1996. 599.00 (*0-87217-036-5*) Natl Register.

Standard Directory of Advertising Agencies, January 1996: The Agency Red Book. Ed. by National Register Publishing Editorial Staff. 1563p. 1996. pap. 499.95 (*0-87217-034-9*) Natl Register.

***Standard Directory of Advertising Agencies, January 1997: The Agency Red Book.** Ed. by National Register Publishing Editorial Staff. 1660p. 1997. pap. 499.95 (*0-87217-350-X*) Natl Register.

***Standard Directory of Advertising Agencies, July 1996: The Agency Red Book.** Ed. by National Register Publishing Editorial Staff. LC 66-6149. 1647p. 1996. pap. 499.95 (*0-87217-035-7*) Natl Register.

Standard Directory of International Advertisers & Agencies: The International Red Book. Ed. by National Register Publishing Editorial Staff. 1310p. 1996. pap. 399.95 (*0-87217-147-7*) Natl Register.

***Standard Directory of International Advertisers & Agencies: The International Red Book.** Ed. by National Register Publishing Editorial Staff. 1300p. 1997. pap. 399.95 (*0-87217-148-5*) Natl Register.

Standard Distribution in Texture Analysis: Maps for the Case of Cubic - Orthorhombic Symmetry, Vol. 2. S. Matthies et al. 256p. 1988. lib. bdg. 70.00 (*3-05-500248-2*, Pub. by Akademie Verlag GW) Wiley.

Standard Distribution in Texture Analysis: Maps for the Case of Cubic - Orthorhombic Symmetry, Vol. 3. S. Matthies et al. 480p. 1990. lib. bdg. 103.00 (*3-05-500249-0*, Pub. by Akademie Verlag GW) Wiley.

Standard Documentary Credit Forms. rev. ed. Ed. by Charles Del Busto. 88p. 1994. pap. 29.95 (*92-842-1160-3*, 516) ICC Pub.

Standard Doyle Company: Christopher Morley on Sherlock Holmes. Ed. by Steven Rothman. LC 90-82073. (Illus.). 429p. 1990. reprint ed. 19.95 (*0-8232-1292-0*) Fordham.

Standard Easter Program Book: Includes Material for Mother's Day & Father's Day. Compiled by Pat Fittro. 48p. (Orig.). 1996. pap. 3.99 (*0-7847-0422-8*, 08716) Standard Pub.

Standard Emergency Medicine. Wigder. 1994. 125.00 (*0-316-93925-0*) Little.

Standard Emergency Procedures for the Small Animal Veterinarian. Signe J. Plunkett. LC 92-39992. 1993. pap. text ed. 31.00 (*0-7216-6781-3*) Saunders.

Standard EMT Record & Log. Joseph Trudo. 74p. (Orig.). (C). 1993. student ed. 39.95 (*0-9635599-2-3*) Talley Pr.

Standard Encyclopedia of Carnival Glass. 5th ed. Bill Edwards. 352p. 1996. 24.95 (*0-89145-689-9*, 4634) Collector Bks.

Standard Encyclopedia of Carnival Glass. 10th ed. Bill Edwards. 64p. 1996. pap. 9.95 (*0-89145-690-2*, 4635) Collector Bks.

Standard Encyclopedia of Opalescent Glass. Bill Edwards. 160p. 1995. 19.95 (*0-89145-645-7*) Collector Bks.

***Standard Encyclopedia of Opalescent Glass: Identification & Values.** 2nd ed. Bill Edwards. (Illus.). 224p. 1997. 19.95 (*0-89145-787-9*, 4875) Collector Bks.

Standard English - Macedonian, Macedonian - English Dictionary. Crvenkovski et al. 1000p. (ENG & MAC.). 1990. 95.00 (*0-8288-8225-8*, F131370) Fr & Eur.

Standard English & the Politics of Language. Tony Crowley. LC 88-27887. 312p. 1989. pap. 15.95 (*0-252-06082-2*); text ed. 34.95 (*0-252-01639-4*) U of Ill Pr.

Standard English Grammar & Composition. Abdullah H. Ghandhistani. LC 89-92075. (Illus.). 341p. (Orig.). (C). 1991. pap. text ed. 20.00 (*0-9623534-0-X*) Private Tutor.

Standard English in the United States & England. Aleksandr D. Svejcer. (Janua Linguarum: Ser. Minor: No. 159). 1978. pap. 48.50 (*90-279-7566-3*) Mouton.

Standard English-Korean & Korean-English Dictionary for Foreigners: Romanized. B. J. Jones & Gene S. Rhie. LC 90-86084. 780p. (Orig.). (ENG & KOR.). (C). 1992. 23.95 (0-930878-06-X) Hollym Intl.

Standard English-Korean Dictionary for Foreigners. Gene S. Rhie & B. J. Jones. LC 81-84204. (Illus.). 386p. (ENG & KOR.). 1982. 14.95 (0-930878-21-3) Hollym Intl.

Standard English-Korean Dictionary for Foreigners. 6th ed. B. J. Jones. 386p. (ENG & KOR.). 1986. 14.95 (0-8288-1613-1, M5850) Fr & Eur.

Standard English Poems. Ed. by Henry S. Pancoast. LC 72-149107. (Granger Index Reprint Ser.). 1977. 42.95 (0-8369-6232-X) Ayer.

Standard English-Urdu, Urdu-English Dictionary, 2 vols. Abdul Haq. 1467p. (ENG & URD.). 1993. reprint ed. 95.00 (0-8288-1110-5, M 14107) Fr & Eur.

Standard Fabrication Practices for Cane Sugar Mills. E. Delden. (Sugar Ser.: Vol. 1). 254p. 1981. 165.00 (0-444-41958-6) Elsevier.

***Standard Facility Report.** 2nd ed. AAM Registrars Committee. 50p. 1996. pap. text ed. 15.00 (0-614-19239-0) Am Assn Mus.

Standard Factory-Built Chimneys for Residential Type & Building Heating Appliances UL 103. 9th ed. (C). 1995. pap. text ed. 135.00 (1-55989-946-8) Underwrtrs Labs.

Standard File Format for Electronic Transfer of Data. (Lighting Measurements Ser.). (Illus.). 8p. 1991. pap. 18.00 (0-87995-085-4, LM-63-91) Illum Eng.

Standard First Aid. 2nd ed. American Red Cross Staff. (gr. 13). 1997. write for info. (0-8151-1001-4) Mosby Yr Bk.

Standard Flourescence Spectra. J. N. Miller. 600p. 1995. text ed. 138.95 (0-13-841636-2) P-H.

Standard for Air Leakage Tests of Door Assemblies UL 1784. 2nd ed. (C). 1995. pap. text ed. 95.00 (1-55989-907-7) Underwrtrs Labs.

Standard for Alarm Accessories for Automatic Water-Supply Control Valves for Fire Protection Service, UL 753. 6th ed. (C). 1995. pap. text ed. 95.00 (1-55989-819-4) Underwrtrs Labs.

Standard for Attachment Plugs & Receptacles: UL 498. 13th ed. (C). 1996. pap. text ed. 330.00 (0-7629-0028-8) Underwrtrs Labs.

Standard for Audio-Video Products & Accessories: UL 1492. 2nd ed. (C). 1996. pap. text ed. 175.00 (1-55989-990-5) Underwrtrs Labs.

Standard for Automated Teller Systems U. L. 291. 2nd ed. (C). 1995. pap. text ed. 175.00 (1-55989-866-6) Underwrtrs Labs.

***Standard for Automatic Sprinklers for Fire-Protection Service: UL 199.** 10th ed. 1997. pap. text ed. 264.00 (0-7629-0167-5) Underwrtrs Labs.

Standard for Automatic Sprinklers for Fire-Protection Service UL 199. 9th ed. (C). 1995. pap. text ed. 330.00 (1-55989-937-9) Underwrtrs Labs.

Standard for Brazing Procedures & Performance Qualification (B2.2-91) (Illus.). 59p. 1991. pap. 27.00 (0-87171-356-X) Am Welding.

Standard for Burglary-Resistant Safes UL 687. 12th ed. (C). 1995. pap. text ed. 330.00 (1-55989-804-6) Underwrtrs Labs.

Standard for Cables for Power-Limited Fire-Alarm Circuits: UL 1424. 2nd ed. (C). 1996. pap. text ed. 95.00 (0-7629-0031-8) Underwrtrs Labs.

Standard for Capacitors. 5th ed. (C). 1995. pap. text ed. 95.00 (1-55989-833-X) Underwrtrs Labs.

Standard for Cellular Metal Floor Raceways & Fittings UL 209. 7th ed. (C). 1995. pap. text ed. 135.00 (1-55989-902-6) Underwrtrs Labs.

***Standard for Central-Station Alarm Services: UL827.** 6th ed. (C). 1996. pap. text ed. 95.00 (0-7629-0067-9) Underwrtrs Labs.

Standard for Chimney Liners: UL 1777. 3rd ed. (C). 1996. pap. text ed. 290.00 (1-55989-981-6) Underwrtrs Labs.

Standard for Christmas-Tree & Decorative-Lighting Outfits. 17th ed. (C). 1996. pap. text ed. 175.00 (1-55989-985-9, UL 588) Underwrtrs Labs.

Standard for Closure Systems for Use with Flexible Air Ducts & Air Connectors UL 181B. 1995. pap. 95.00 (1-55989-926-3) Underwrtrs Labs.

Standard for Coated Electrical Sleeving, No. UL1441. 3rd ed. (C). 1995. pap. text ed. 95.00 (1-55989-897-6) Underwrtrs Labs.

***Standard for Commercial Audio Equipment: UL 813.** 7th ed. (C). 1996. pap. text ed. 330.00 (0-7629-0072-5) Underwrtrs Labs.

Standard for Commercial Closed Circuit Television Equipment, UL 2044. (C). 1993. pap. text ed. 135.00 (1-55989-347-8) Underwrtrs Labs.

***Standard for Commercial Filters for Cooking Oil: UL 1889.** (C). 1996. pap. text ed. 135.00 (0-7629-0034-2, UL 1889) Underwrtrs Labs.

Standard for Communications Circuit Accessories UL 1863. 2nd ed. (C). 1995. pap. text ed. 330.00 (1-55989-090-8) Underwrtrs Labs.

Standard for Component Connectors for Use in Data, Signal Control & Power Applications UL 1977. (C). 1995. pap. text ed. 95.00 (1-55989-948-4) Underwrtrs Labs.

***Standard for Components for Personal Flotation Devices UL 1191.** 3rd ed. (C). 1997. pap. text ed. 264.00 (0-7629-0195-0) Underwrtrs Labs.

Standard for Components of Robotic & Automatic Welding Installations (D16.2-94) (Illus.). 10p. 1994. pap. 27.00 (0-87171-446-9) Am Welding.

Standard for Compressed Gas Regulator Accessories: UL 252A. 2nd ed. (C). 1996. pap. text ed. 330.00 (0-7629-0020-2) Underwrtrs Labs.

Standard for Compressed Gas Regulators: UL 252. 7th ed. (C). 1996. pap. text ed. 95.00 (1-55989-903-4) Underwrtrs Labs.

Standard for Connectors & Switches for Use with Burglar-Alarm Systems UL 634. 7th ed. (C). 1995. pap. text ed. 135.00 (1-55989-752-X) Underwrtrs Labs.

***Standard for Constant-Level Oil Valves: UL 352.** 7th ed. (C). 1997. pap. text ed. 264.00 (0-7629-0151-9) Underwrtrs Labs.

***Standard for Control Cables.** 41.00 (0-614-18708-7, S-73-532) Insulated Cable.

***Standard for Control Centers for Changing Message Type Electric Signs UL 1433.** 3rd ed. (C). 1996. 330.00 (0-7629-0058-X) Underwrtrs Labs.

Standard for Control Equipment for Use with Flammable Liquid Dispensing Devices: UL 1238. 2nd ed. (C). 1996. pap. text ed. 95.00 (1-55989-977-8) Underwrtrs Labs.

***Standard for Control Units for Fire-Protective Signaling Systems UL 864.** 8th ed. (C). 1996. pap. text ed. 135.00 (0-7629-0060-1) Underwrtrs Labs.

Standard for Cylinder Valves: UL 1769. 2nd ed. (C). 1996. pap. text ed. 330.00 (0-7629-0002-4) Underwrtrs Labs.

Standard for Diesel Engines for Driving Centrifugal Fire Pumps UL 1247. 3rd ed. (C). 1995. pap. text ed. 95.00 (1-55989-715-5) Underwrtrs Labs.

Standard for Digital Alarm Communicator System Units UL 1635. 3rd ed. (C). 1996. pap. text ed. 135.00 (1-55989-121-1) Underwrtrs Labs.

Standard for Direct Acting Pressure Reducing & Pressure Restricting Values UL 1468. 3rd ed. (C). 1995. pap. text ed. 95.00 (1-55989-847-X) Underwrtrs Labs.

***Standard for Door Closer-Holders, with or Without Integral Smoke Detectors UL 228.** 9th ed. (C). 1997. pap. text ed. 76.00 (0-7629-0147-0) Underwrtrs Labs.

Standard for Dry Chemical Fire Extinguishers UL 299. 9th ed. (C). 1995. pap. text ed. 95.00 (1-55989-839-9) Underwrtrs Labs.

Standard for Ducted Heat Recovery Ventilators UL 1812. 2nd ed. (C). 1995. pap. text ed. 330.00 (1-55989-836-4) Underwrtrs Labs.

***Standard for Edison-Base Lampholders: UL 496.** 11th ed. Underwriters Laboratories Staff. (C). 1996. pap. text ed. 95.00 (0-7629-0083-0) Underwrtrs Labs.

Standard for Electric Aquarium Equipment: UL 1018. 4th ed. (C). 1995. pap. text ed. 230.00 (1-55989-877-1) Underwrtrs Labs.

Standard for Electric Booster & Commercial Storage Tank Water Heaters UL 1453. 4th ed. (C). 1995. pap. text ed. 175.00 (1-55989-883-6) Underwrtrs Labs.

***Standard for Electric Heating Appliances UL 499.** 12th ed. (C). 1997. pap. text ed. 76.00 (0-7629-0161-6) Underwrtrs Labs.

Standard for Electric Heating Pads: UL 130. 11th ed. (C). 1996. pap. text ed. 330.00 (0-7629-0014-8) Underwrtrs Labs.

Standard for Electric Hobby & Sports Equipment UL 961. 3rd ed. (C). 1995. pap. text ed. 215.00 (1-55989-805-4) Underwrtrs Labs.

Standard for Electric Household Cooking & Food Appliances UL 1026. 4th ed. (C). 1995. pap. text ed. 95.00 (1-55989-889-5) Underwrtrs Labs.

Standard for Electric Lighting Fixtures for Use in Hazardous (Classified) Locations UL 844. 11th ed. 1995. pap. 195.00 (1-55989-911-5) Underwrtrs Labs.

***Standard for Electric Oil Heaters UL 574.** 7th ed. (C). 1996. pap. text ed. 95.00 (0-7629-0022-9) Underwrtrs Labs.

Standard for Electric Signs: UL 48. 14th ed. (C). 1996. pap. text ed. 95.00 (1-55989-974-3) Underwrtrs Labs.

Standard for Electric Space Heating Cables: UL 1673. 2nd ed. (C). 1996. pap. text ed. 330.00 (0-7629-0041-5) Underwrtrs Labs.

***Standard for Electric Spas, Equipment Assemblies, & Associated Equipment UL 1563.** 4th ed. (C). 1996. pap. text ed. 330.00 (0-7629-0026-1) Underwrtrs Labs.

***Standard for Electric Toys UL 696.** 9th ed. (C). 1996. pap. text ed. 330.00 (1-55989-976-X) Underwrtrs Labs.

***Standard for Electric Water Bed Heaters UL 1445.** 5th ed. (C). 1996. pap. text ed. 230.00 (0-7629-0057-1) Underwrtrs Labs.

Standard for Electric Water Heaters for Pools & Tubs UL 1261. 4th ed. (C). 1996. pap. text ed. 135.00 (1-55989-919-0) Underwrtrs Labs.

Standard for Electrical Power & Control Tray Cables with Optional Optical-Fiber Members: UL 1277. 3rd ed. (C). 1996. pap. text ed. 95.00 (0-7629-0015-6) Underwrtrs Labs.

***Standard for Electrically Isolated Semiconductor Devices: UL 1557.** 3rd ed. (C). 1997. pap. text ed. 76.00 (0-7629-0180-2) Underwrtrs Labs.

***Standard for Electrode Receptacles for Gas-Tube Signs UL 879.** 7th ed. (C). 1997. pap. text ed. 76.00 (0-7629-0076-8) Underwrtrs Labs.

Standard for Electronic Manuscript Preparation & Markup: Version 2.0. 1988. 100.00 (0-318-35246-X) AAP.

Standard for Electrostatic Air Cleaners UL 867. 3rd ed. (C). 1995. pap. text ed. 95.00 (1-55989-722-8) Underwrtrs Labs.

Standard for Emergency Vault Ventilators & Vault-Ventilating Ports UL 680. 7th ed. (C). 1996. pap. text ed. 330.00 (1-55989-995-6) Underwrtrs Labs.

Standard for Enclosures for Electrical Equipment UL 50. 11th ed. (C). 1995. pap. text ed. 330.00 (1-55989-909-3) Underwrtrs Labs.

Standard for Exhaust Hoods for Commercial Cooking Equipment UL 710. 5th ed. (C). 1995. pap. text ed. 135.00 (1-55989-855-0) Underwrtrs Labs.

Standard for Factory-Built Fireplaces: UL 127. 7th ed. (C). 1996. pap. text ed. 135.00 (1-55989-980-8) Underwrtrs Labs.

Standard for Factory-Made Air Ducts & Air Connectors: UL 181. 9th ed. (C). 1996. pap. text ed. 330.00 (1-55989-979-4) Underwrtrs Labs.

Standard for Fire Dampers UL 555. 5th ed. (C). 1995. pap. text ed. 330.00 (1-55989-828-3) Underwrtrs Labs.

Standard for Fire Extinguishers, Rating & Fire Testing of UL 711. 5th ed. (C). 1995. pap. text ed. 95.00 (1-55989-838-0) Underwrtrs Labs.

Standard for Fire Extinguishing Systems for Protection of Restaurant Cooking Areas, Fire Testing of UL 300. 2nd ed. (C). 1996. pap. text ed. 95.00 (1-55989-940-9) Underwrtrs Labs.

Standard for Fire Protection for Nuclear Power Plants: 1988. 1993. 20.25 (0-317-07395-8, NFPA 803) Natl Fire Prot.

Standard for Fire Protection of Vessels During Construction, Repair & Lay-up: 1990. 16.75 (0-317-07390-7, 312-90) Natl Fire Prot.

Standard for Fire Pump Controllers UL 218. (C). 1996. pap. text ed. 95.00 (1-55989-945-X) Underwrtrs Labs.

Standard for Fire Pump Relief Valves, UL 1478. 3rd ed. (C). 1995. pap. text ed. 330.00 (1-55989-810-0) Underwrtrs Labs.

***Standard for Fire Test of Plastic Sprinkler Pipe for Visible Flame & Smoke Characteristics UL 1887.** 2nd ed. (C). 1996. pap. text ed. 330.00 (0-7629-0025-3) Underwrtrs Labs.

***Standard for Fire Tests for Foamed Plastics Used for Decorative Purposes: UL 1975.** 2nd ed. Underwriters Laboratories Editors. (C). 1996. pap. text ed. 330.00 (0-7629-0056-3) Underwrtrs Labs.

***Standard for Fire Tests of Door Assemblies UL 10B.** 9th ed. (C). 1997. pap. text ed. 76.00 (0-7629-0170-5) Underwrtrs Labs.

Standard for Fire Tests of Surgical Fabrics: UL 2154. (C). 1996. pap. text ed. 175.00 (1-55989-998-0) Underwrtrs Labs.

Standard for Fireplace Stoves: UL 737. 8th ed. (C). 1996. pap. text ed. 290.00 (1-55989-978-6) Underwrtrs Labs.

***Standard for Fixed & Location-Dedicated Electric Room Heaters UL 2021.** 2nd ed. (C). 1997. pap. text ed. 264.00 (0-7629-0171-3) Underwrtrs Labs.

Standard for Fluorescent Lighting Fixtures, UL 1570. 4th ed. (C). 1995. pap. text ed. 250.00 (1-55989-871-2) Underwrtrs Labs.

Standard for Fully Inflatable Recreational Personal Flotation Devices UL 1180. (C). 1995. pap. text ed. 95.00 (1-55989-754-6) Underwrtrs Labs.

Standard for Gas-Tube-Sign & Ignition Cable U. L. 814. 10th ed. (C). 1995. pap. text ed. 135.00 (1-55989-931-X) Underwrtrs Labs.

Standard for Gearmotors Using Spur, Helical, Herringbone, Straight Bevel or Spiral Bevel Gears. 7th ed. (ANSI - AGMA Ser.: No. 6019-E89). (Illus.). 103p. 1989. pap. text ed. 90.00 (1-55589-526-3) AGMA.

Standard for General-Use Snap Switches UL 20. 11th ed. (C). 1995. pap. text ed. 215.00 (1-55989-821-6) Underwrtrs Labs.

Standard for Hair Clipping & Shaving Appliances: UL 1028. 4th ed. (C). 1995. pap. text ed. 95.00 (1-55989-894-1) Underwrtrs Labs.

Standard for Halogenated Agent Extinguishing Systems Units UL 1058. 3rd ed. (C). 1995. pap. text ed. 135.00 (1-55989-820-8) Underwrtrs Labs.

Standard for Halogenated Agent Fire Extinguishers UL 1093. 5th ed. (C). 1995. pap. text ed. 95.00 (1-55989-840-2) Underwrtrs Labs.

Standard for Halon 1211 Recovery-Recharge Equipment UL 2006. 2nd ed. (C). 1995. pap. text ed. 330.00 (1-55989-835-6) Underwrtrs Labs.

***Standard for Hand-Held Torches for Fuel Gases.** 5th ed. (C). 1996. pap. text ed. 330.00 (0-7629-0043-1, UL 147) Underwrtrs Labs.

Standard for High Intensity Discharge Lighting Fixtures, UL 1572. 4th ed. (C). 1995. pap. text ed. 95.00 (1-55989-873-9) Underwrtrs Labs.

***Standard for Holdup Alarm Units & Systems: UL 636.** 10th ed. (C). 1996. pap. text ed. 95.00 (0-7629-0061-X) Underwrtrs Labs.

Standard for Hose Valves for Fire-Protection Service UL 668. 9th ed. (C). 1995. pap. text ed. 95.00 (1-55989-857-7) Underwrtrs Labs.

***Standard for Hospital Signaling & Nurse Call Equipment: UL1069.** 5th ed. (C). 1996. pap. text ed. 135.00 (0-7629-0046-6) Underwrtrs Labs.

***Standard for Household & Commercial Furnishings UL 962.** (C). 1996. pap. text ed. 135.00 (0-7629-0053-9) Underwrtrs Labs.

***Standard for Household, Commercial, & Professional-Use Carts & Stands UL 1678.** 2nd ed. (C). 1996. pap. text ed. 264.00 (0-7629-0137-3) Underwrtrs Labs.

***Standard for Household Electric Coffee Makers & Brewing-Type Appliances UL 1082.** 5th ed. (C). 1996. pap. text ed. 230.00 (0-7629-0126-8) Underwrtrs Labs.

Standard for Household Electric Skillets & Frying-Type Appliances UL 1083. 4th ed. (C). 1995. pap. text ed. 95.00 (1-55989-890-9) Underwrtrs Labs.

Standard for Household Electric Storage Tank Water Heaters UL 174. 10th ed. (C). 1996. pap. text ed. 330.00 (1-55989-850-X) Underwrtrs Labs.

Standard for Ice Makers UL 563. 7th ed. (C). 1995. pap. text ed. 175.00 (1-55989-882-8) Underwrtrs Labs.

Standard for Immersion-Detection Circuit-Interrupters, No. UL1664. 2nd ed. (C). 1995. pap. text ed. 330.00 (1-55989-930-1) Underwrtrs Labs.

***Standard for Immersion Suits.** 2nd ed. (C). 1996. pap. text ed. 250.00 (1-55989-989-1, UL 1197) Underwrtrs Labs.

Standard for Incandescent Lighting Fixtures, UL 1571. 4th ed. (C). 1995. pap. text ed. 95.00 (1-55989-872-0) Underwrtrs Labs.

Standard for Indicating Pressure Gauges for Fire-Protection Service: UL 393. 7th ed. (C). 1996. pap. text ed. 330.00 (1-55989-994-8) Underwrtrs Labs.

Standard for Industrial Control Equipment for Use in Hazardous (Classified) Locations UL 698. 12th ed. (C). 1995. pap. text ed. 195.00 (1-55989-876-3) Underwrtrs Labs.

Standard for Insect-Control Equipment-Electrocution Type, UL 1559. 3rd ed. (C). 1995. pap. text ed. 175.00 (1-55989-891-7) Underwrtrs Labs.

***Standard for Instrumentation Tay Cable UL 2250.** (C). 1996. pap. text ed. 108.00 (0-7629-0138-1) Underwrtrs Labs.

***Standard for Insulating Bushings: UL 635.** (C). 1996. pap. text ed. 135.00 (0-7629-0030-X) Underwrtrs Labs.

***Standard for Intermediate Metal Conduit UL 1242.** 2nd ed. (C). 1996. pap. text ed. 135.00 (0-7629-0037-7) Underwrtrs Labs.

***Standard for Intrusion-Detection Units: UL 639.** 7th ed. (C). 1997. pap. text ed. 76.00 (0-7629-0088-1) Underwrtrs Labs.

Standard for Isolating Signal & Feedback Transformers for Use in Electronic Equipment UL 1876. 2nd ed. (C). 1995. pap. text ed. 175.00 (1-55989-853-4) Underwrtrs Labs.

Standard for Light Water Reactor Coolant Pressure Boundary Leak Detection: ANSI-ISA Standard S67.03. 27p. 1982. pap. text ed. 30.00 (0-87664-734-4, 1734-4) ISA.

Standard for Liquid-Level Indicating Gauges for Oil Burner Fuels: UL 180. 6th ed. (C). 1996. pap. text ed. 135.00 (0-7629-0001-6) Underwrtrs Labs.

Standard for Lithium Batteries UL 1642. 3rd ed. (C). 1995. pap. text ed. 330.00 (1-55989-829-1) Underwrtrs Labs.

Standard for Load Resistance Factor Design (LRFD) for Engineered Wood Construction: ASCE-16-95. American Society of Civil Engineers Staff. 1996. 36.00 (0-7844-0041-5) Am Soc Civil Eng.

***Standard for Local Burglar Alarm Units & Systems, UL609.** 11th ed. (C). 1996. pap. text ed. 95.00 (0-7629-0039-3) Underwrtrs Labs.

***Standard for Low Level Marking & Lighting System UL 1994.** 2nd ed. (C). 1997. pap. text ed. 264.00 (0-7629-0145-4) Underwrtrs Labs.

***Standard for Low-Voltage AC & DC Power Circuit Breakers Used in Enclosures UL 1066.** 3rd ed. (C). 1997. pap. text ed. 76.00 (0-7629-0179-9) Underwrtrs Labs.

Standard for Marine Buoyant Devices: UL 1123. 6th ed. (C). 1996. pap. text ed. 330.00 (0-7629-0029-6) Underwrtrs Labs.

***Standard for Marine Gear Units: Rating.** AGMA Technical Committee Staff. (ANSI/AGMA Standard Ser.). 1994. pap. text ed. 95.00 (1-55589-633-2) AGMA.

***Standard for Marine Propulsion Gear Units.** AGMA Technical Committee Staff. (ANSI/AGMA Standard Ser.). 1988. pap. text ed. 65.00 (1-55589-500-X) AGMA.

Standard for Marine Shipboard Cable, UL 1309. (C). 1995. pap. text ed. 95.00 (1-55989-874-7) Underwrtrs Labs.

Standard for Medium Heat Appliances Factory-Built Chimneys UL 959. 7th ed. (C). 1995. pap. text ed. 250.00 (1-55989-941-7) Underwrtrs Labs.

Standard for Medium-Voltage Power Cables UL 1072. 2nd ed. (C). 1995. pap. text ed. 135.00 (1-55989-869-0) Underwrtrs Labs.

Standard for Metal-Clad Cables UL 1569. 2nd ed. (C). 1995. pap. text ed. 135.00 (1-55989-870-4) Underwrtrs Labs.

Standard for Metal Waste Paper Containers. (C). 1995. pap. text ed. 95.00 (1-55989-912-3, UL 1315) Underwrtrs Labs.

Standard for Meters for Flammable & Combustible Liquids & LP-Gas: UL 25. 7th ed. (C). 1996. pap. text ed. 230.00 (0-7629-0000-8) Underwrtrs Labs.

***Standard for Molded-Case Circuit Breakers, Molded-Case Switches, & Circuit-Breaker Enclosures: UL 489.** 9th ed. Underwriters Laboratories Staff. (C). 1996. pap. text ed. 330.00 (0-7629-0091-1) Underwrtrs Labs.

Standard for Motor-Operated Water Pumps: UL 778. 3rd ed. (C). 1996. pap. text ed. 135.00 (1-55989-992-1) Underwrtrs Labs.

***Standard for Neon Transformers & Power Supplies: UL2161.** (C). 1996. pap. text ed. 135.00 (1-55989-908-5, UL 2161) Underwrtrs Labs.

Standard for Nightlights, UL 1786. 2nd ed. (C). 1995. pap. text ed. 330.00 (1-55989-856-9) Underwrtrs Labs.

Standard for Nonducted Heat Recovery Ventilators Ul 1815. 2nd ed. (C). 1995. pap. text ed. 175.00 (1-55989-837-2) Underwrtrs Labs.

***Standard for Nonmetallic-Sheathed Cables UL 719.** 10th ed. (C). 1996. pap. text ed. 95.00 (0-7629-0063-6) Underwrtrs Labs.

***Standard for Nonrefillable (Disposable) Type Fuel Gas Cylinder Assemblies.** (C). 1996. pap. text ed. 175.00 (0-7629-0044-X, UL 147A) Underwrtrs Labs.

***Standard for Nonrefillable (Disposable) Type Metal Container Assemblies for Butane.** 2nd ed. (C). 1996. pap. text ed. 175.00 (0-7629-0045-8, UL 147B) Underwrtrs Labs.

Standard for Oil-Fired Boiler Assemblies UL 726. 7th ed. (C). 1995. pap. text ed. 95.00 (1-55989-858-5) Underwrtrs Labs.

Standard for Oil-Fired Storage Tank Water Heaters UL 732. 5th ed. (C). 1995. pap. text ed. 95.00 (1-55989-818-6) Underwrtrs Labs.

Standard for Oil-Fired Unit Heaters UL 731. 5th ed. (C). 1995. pap. 135.00 (1-55989-817-8) Underwrtrs Labs.

Standard for Optical Fiber Cable Raceway UL 2024. (C). 1995. pap. text ed. 95.00 (1-55989-951-4) Underwrtrs Labs.

An Asterisk (*) at the beginning of an entry indicates that the title is appearing in BIP for the first time.

***Standard for Overheating Protection for Motors UL2111.** (C). 1997. pap. text ed. 156.00 (*0-7629-0166-7*) Underwriters Labs Canada.
Standard for Oxy-Fuel Gas Torches UL 123. 9th ed. (C). 1995. pap. text ed. 95.00 (*1-55989-916-6*) Underwrtrs Labs.
***Standard for Panic Hardware UL 305.** 5th ed. (C). 1997. pap. text ed. 76.00 (*0-7629-0074-1*) Underwrtrs Labs.
***Standard for Personal Hygiene & Health Care Appliances UL 1431.** 2nd ed. (C). 1996. pap. text ed. 135.00 (*0-7629-0127-6*) Underwrtrs Labs.
Standard for Pipe Connectors for Petroleum Products & LP-Gas: UL 567. 8th ed. (C). 1996. pap. text ed. 330.00 (*0-7629-0021-0*) Underwrtrs Labs.
***Standard for Pipe Hangere Equipment for Fire Protection Service, UL203.** 8th ed. (C). 1996. pap. text ed. 175.00 (*0-7629-8040-0*) Underwrtrs Labs.
***Standard for Polymeric Materials - Long Term Property Evaluations UL 746B.** 3rd ed. (C). 1996. pap. text ed. 95.00 (*0-7629-0065-2*) Underwrtrs Labs.
Standard for Polymeric Materials-Electrical Equipment Evaluations UL 746C. 4th ed. (C). 1995. pap. text ed. 95.00 (*1-55989-949-2*) Underwrtrs Labs.
Standard for Polymeric Materials-Short Term Property Evaluations UL 746A. 4th ed. (C). 1995. pap. text ed. 95.00 (*1-55989-936-0*) Underwrtrs Labs.
***Standard for Portable Electric Hand Lamps UL 298.** 4th ed. (C). 1996. pap. text ed. 95.00 (*0-7629-0124-1*) Underwrtrs Labs.
Standard for Portable Electric Lamps UL153. 11th ed. (C). 1995. pap. text ed. 95.00 (*1-55989-842-9*) Underwrtrs Labs.
***Standard for Portable Marine Fuel Tanks UL 1185.** 4th ed. (C). 1996. pap. text ed. 330.00 (*1-55989-988-3*) Underwrtrs Labs.
***Standard for Power Conversion Equipment, UL 508C.** 2nd ed. (C). 1996. pap. text ed. 95.00 (*0-7629-0093-8*) Underwrtrs Labs.
Standard for Power-Limited Circuit Cables UL 13. 2nd ed. (C). 1996. pap. text ed. 215.00 (*1-55989-997-2*) Underwrtrs Labs.
Standard for Power-Operated Dispensing Devices for Petroleum Products UL 87. 10th ed. (C). 1995. per. 95.00 (*1-55989-884-4*) Underwrtrs Labs.
Standard for Power-Operated Pumps for Ammonia & LP-Gas UL 51. 8th ed. (C). 1995. pap. text ed. 230.00 (*1-55989-915-8*) Underwrtrs Labs.
Standard for Pre-Engineered Dry Chemical Extinguishing System Units UL 1254. 2nd ed. (C). 1996. pap. text ed. 330.00 (*1-55989-066-5*) Underwrtrs Labs.
Standard for Pressure Cookers: UL 136. 6th ed. (C). 1995. pap. text ed. 175.00 (*1-55989-901-8*) Underwrtrs Labs.
***Standard for Professional Video & Audio Equipment UL 1419.** 2nd ed. (C). 1997. pap. text ed. 108.00 (*0-7629-0162-4*) Underwrtrs Labs.
Standard for Proprietary Burglar Alarm Units & Systems UL 1076. 5th ed. (C). 1995. pap. text ed. 95.00 (*1-55989-878-X*) Underwrtrs Labs.
Standard for Protection of Electrical Overstress - Electrostatic Discharge Susceptible Items-Surface Resistance Measurement of Dissipative Planar Materials: EOS - ESD S11.11-1993. (Illus.). 1993. pap. text ed. 37.50 (*1-878303-40-6*, ESDS11-11) EOS ESD.
Standard for Protection of Electrostatic Discharge Susceptible Items: Personnel Grounding Wrist-Straps: EOS-ESD Standard No. 1. (Illus.). 13p. (Orig.). 1987. pap. text ed. 10.00 (*1-878303-01-5*, ESD S1.0-1987) EOS ESD.
Standard for Protectors for Paired Conductor Communications Circuits, UL 497. 6th ed. (C). 1995. pap. text ed. 95.00 (*1-55989-825-9*) Underwrtrs Labs.
Standard for Radiant Heating Panels & Heating Panel Sets UL 1693. (C). 1995. pap. text ed. 95.00 (*1-55989-861-5*) Underwrtrs Labs.
Standard for Receptacle-Plug Combinations for Use in Hazardous (Classified) Locations, UL1010. 6th ed. 1995. pap. text ed. 290.00 (*1-55989-879-8*) Underwrtrs Labs.
***Standard for Relocatable Power Taps: UL 1363.** 2nd ed. (C). 1996. pap. text ed. 330.00 (*0-7629-0073-3*) Underwrtrs Labs.
Standard for Repair: The Establishment Clause, Equality, & Natural Rights. T. Jeremy Gunn. LC 92-15941. (Distinguished Studies in American Legal & Constitutional History). 240p. 1992. text ed. 43.00 (*0-8153-0893-0*) Garland.
Standard for Safety for Access Control System Units, UL 294. 4th ed. (C). 1994. pap. text ed. 95.00 (*1-55989-604-3*) Underwrtrs Labs.
Standard for Safety for Acetylene Generators, Portable, Medium-Pressure, UL 297. 6th ed. (C). 1994. pap. text ed. 95.00 (*1-55989-697-3*) Underwrtrs Labs.
Standard for Safety for Acetylene Generators, Stationary, Low-Pressure, UL 409. 5th ed. (C). 1993. pap. text ed. 95.00 (*1-55989-427-X*) Underwrtrs Labs.
Standard for Safety for Acetylene Generators, Stationary, Medium-Pressure, UL 408. 5th ed. (C). 1993. pap. text ed. 95.00 (*1-55989-424-5*) Underwrtrs Labs.
Standard for Safety for Across-the-Line, Antenna-Coupling & Line-by-Pass Capacitors for Radio- & Television-Type Appliances, UL 1414. 5th ed. (C). 1994. pap. text ed. 95.00 (*1-55989-570-5*) Underwrtrs Labs.
Standard for Safety for Adjustable Drop Nipples for Sprinkler Systems. 4th ed. (C). 1996. pap. text ed. 330.00 (*1-55989-938-7*, UL 1474) Underwrtrs Labs.
Standard for Safety for Adjustable Drop Nipples for Sprinkler Systems, UL 1474. 4th ed. (C). 1996. pap. text ed. 330.00 (*1-55989-104-1*) Underwrtrs Labs.
Standard for Safety for Air Filter Units, UL 900. 6th ed. (C). 1994. pap. text ed. 95.00 (*1-55989-692-2*) Underwrtrs Labs.
Standard for Safety for Air Leakage Tests of Door Assemblies, UL 1784. 2nd ed. (C). 1995. pap. text ed. 95.00 (*1-55989-115-7*) Underwrtrs Labs.
Standard for Safety for Alarm Accessories for Automatic Water-Supply Control Valves for Fire Protection Service, UL 753. 6th ed. (C). 1995. pap. text ed. 95.00 (*1-55989-029-0*) Underwrtrs Labs.
Standard for Safety for Alarm Valves for Fire-Protection Service, UL 193. 9th ed. 1993. pap. 215.00 (*1-55989-320-6*) Underwrtrs Labs.
Standard for Safety for Alcohol & Kerosene Cooking Appliances for Marine Use, UL 1100. (C). 1989. pap. text ed. 135.00 (*1-55989-040-1*) Underwrtrs Labs.
Standard for Safety for Amateur Movie Lights, UL 1230. 4th ed. (C). 1994. pap. text ed. 95.00 (*1-55989-719-8*) Underwrtrs Labs.
Standard for Safety for Amplifiers for Fire Protective Signaling Systems, UL 1711. 2nd ed. (C). 1994. pap. text ed. 135.00 (*1-55989-645-0*) Underwrtrs Labs.
Standard for Safety for Amusement & Gaming Machines, UL 22. 4th ed. (C). 1994. pap. text ed. 175.00 (*1-55989-572-1*) Underwrtrs Labs.
Standard for Safety for Antenna-Discharge Units, UL 452. 6th ed. (C). 1993. pap. text ed. 95.00 (*1-55989-421-0*) Underwrtrs Labs.
Standard for Safety for Antenna Rotators, UL 150. 3rd ed. 330p. (C). 1994. pap. text ed. 330.00 (*1-55989-633-7*) Underwrtrs Labs.
Standard for Safety for Antitheft Alarms & Devices, UL 1037. 4th ed. (C). 1994. pap. text ed. 230.00 (*1-55989-618-3*) Underwrtrs Labs.
Standard for Safety for Armored Cable. 14th ed. (C). 1996. pap. text ed. 330.00 (*1-55989-986-7*, UL 4) Underwrtrs Labs.
Standard for Safety for Asbestos-Cement Pipe & Couplings, UL 107. 4th ed. 1993. pap. 95.00 (*1-55989-318-4*) Underwrtrs Labs.
Standard for Safety for Attachment Plug Blades for Use in Cord Sets & Power-Supply Cords, UL 1659. (C). 1993. pap. text ed. 95.00 (*1-55989-464-4*) Underwrtrs Labs.
Standard for Safety for Attachment Plugs & Receptacles, UL 498. 13th ed. (C). 1996. pap. text ed. 330.00 (*1-55989-159-9*) Underwrtrs Labs.
Standard for Safety for Audible Signal Appliances, UL 464. 7th ed. (C). 1996. pap. text ed. 95.00 (*1-55989-056-8*) Underwrtrs Labs.
Standard for Safety for Audio-Video Products & Accessories, UL 1492. (C). 1992. pap. text ed. 250.00 (*1-55989-266-8*) Underwrtrs Labs.
Standard for Safety for Automatic Drain Valves for Standpipe Systems, UL 1726. 2nd ed. (C). 1993. pap. text ed. 95.00 (*1-55989-481-4*) Underwrtrs Labs.
Standard for Safety for Automatic Electrical Controls for Household & Similar Use: Particular Requirements for Timers & Time Switches, UL 8730-2-7. (C). 1995. pap. text ed. 35.00 (*1-55989-746-5*) Underwrtrs Labs.
Standard for Safety for Automatic Sprinklers for Fire-Protection Service, UL 199. 9th ed. (C). 1995. pap. text ed. 330.00 (*1-55989-069-X*) Underwrtrs Labs.
Standard for Safety for Automatic Transfer Switches, UL 1008. 4th ed. (C). 1989. pap. text ed. 330.00 (*1-55989-000-2*) Underwrtrs Labs.
Standard for Safety for Automotive Fuel Tanks, UL 395. 5th ed. 1993. pap. 95.00 (*1-55989-301-X*) Underwrtrs Labs.
Standard for Safety for Automotive Glass-Tube Fuses, UL 275. 9th ed. (C). 1993. pap. text ed. 95.00 (*1-55989-495-4*) Underwrtrs Labs.
Standard for Safety for Battery Chargers for Charging Engine-Starter Batteries, UL 1236. 5th ed. (C). 1994. pap. text ed. 250.00 (*1-55989-588-8*) Underwrtrs Labs.
Standard for Safety for Battery Contactors for Use in Diesel Engines Driving Centrifugal Fire Pumps, UL 218A. 2nd ed. (C). 1994. pap. text ed. 330.00 (*1-55989-433-4*) Underwrtrs Labs.
Standard for Safety for Bullet-Resisting Equipment, UL 752. 8th ed. (C). 1991. pap. text ed. 135.00 (*1-55989-139-4*) Underwrtrs Labs.
Standard for Safety for Bullet-Resisting Equipment, UL 752. 9th ed. (C). 1995. pap. text ed. 135.00 (*1-55989-714-7*) Underwrtrs Labs.
Standard for Safety for Burglary-Resistant Electric Locking Mechanisms, UL 1034. 4th ed. (C). 1994. pap. text ed. 95.00 (*1-55989-619-1*) Underwrtrs Labs.
Standard for Safety for Burglary Resistant Safes, UL 687. 12th ed. (C). 1995. pap. text ed. 330.00 (*1-55989-234-X*) Underwrtrs Labs.
Standard for Safety for Burglary Resistant Vault Doors & Modular Panels, UL 608. 5th ed. (C). 1994. pap. text ed. 95.00 (*1-55989-651-5*) Underwrtrs Labs.
Standard for Safety for Burglary Resisting Glazing Material, UL 972. 4th ed. (C). 1995. pap. text ed. 95.00 (*1-55989-721-X*) Underwrtrs Labs.
Standard for Safety for Busways & Associated Fittings, UL 857. 11th ed. (C). 1996. pap. text ed. 290.00 (*1-55989-047-9*) Underwrtrs Labs.
Standard for Safety for Busways & Associated Fittings, UL 857. 11th ed. (C). 1994. pap. text ed. 290.00 (*1-55989-671-X*) Underwrtrs Labs.
Standard for Safety for Butterfly Valves for Fire-Protection Service, UL 1091. 5th ed. (C). 1994. pap. text ed. 95.00 (*1-55989-626-4*) Underwrtrs Labs.
Standard for Safety for Cables for Power-Limited Fire-Alarm Circuits, UL 1424. 2nd ed. (C). 1996. pap. text ed. 95.00 (*1-55989-137-8*) Underwrtrs Labs.
Standard for Safety for Carbon-Dioxide Fire Extinguishers, UL 154. 8th ed. (C). 1995. pap. text ed. 95.00 (*1-55989-106-8*) Underwrtrs Labs.
Standard for Safety for Carbon-Dioxide Fire Extinguishers, UL 154. 8th ed. (C). 1995. pap. text ed. 95.00 (*1-55989-845-3*) Underwrtrs Labs.
Standard for Safety for Carbon Monoxide Gas Detectors for Marine Use, UL 1524. (C). 1989. pap. text ed. 330.00 (*1-55989-048-7*) Underwrtrs Labs.
Standard for Safety for Ceiling Dampers, UL 555C. (C). 1992. pap. text ed. 135.00 (*1-55989-348-6*) Underwrtrs Labs.
Standard for Safety for Central-Station Alarm Services UL 827. 6th ed. (C). 1996. pap. text ed. 95.00 (*1-55989-449-0*) Underwrtrs Labs.
Standard for Safety for Central Station Automation Systems, UL 1981. (C). 1994. pap. text ed. 95.00 (*1-55989-677-9*) Underwrtrs Labs.
Standard for Safety for Central-Station Burglar-Alarm Systems, UL 611. 13th ed. (C). 1994. pap. text ed. 95.00 (*1-55989-607-8*) Underwrtrs Labs.
Standard for Safety for Central-Station Burglar-Alarm Units, UL 1610. 2nd ed. (C). 1994. pap. text ed. 95.00 (*1-55989-594-2*) Underwrtrs Labs.
Standard for Safety for Check Valves for Fire Protection Service, UL 312. 8th ed. (C). 1993. pap. text ed. 175.00 (*1-55989-335-4*) Underwrtrs Labs.
Standard for Safety for Chimney Liners, UL 1777. 3rd ed. (C). 1996. pap. text ed. 290.00 (*1-55989-760-0*) Underwrtrs Labs.
Standard for Safety for Chimneys, Factory-Built, Residential Type & Building Heating Appliance, UL 103. 9th ed. (C). 1995. pap. text ed. 135.00 (*1-55989-567-5*) Underwrtrs Labs.
Standard for Safety for Christmas-Tree & Decorative-Lighting Outfits, UL 588. 17th ed. (C). 1996. pap. text ed. 175.00 (*1-55989-122-X*) Underwrtrs Labs.
Standard for Safety for Circuit Breakers & Circuit-Breaker Enclosures for Use in Hazardous (Classified) Locations, UL 877. 4th ed. 1993. pap. 95.00 (*1-55989-305-2*) Underwrtrs Labs.
Standard for Safety for Class 2 & Class 3 Transformers UL 1585. 3rd ed. (C). 1993. pap. text ed. 95.00 (*1-55989-388-5*) Underwrtrs Labs.
Standard for Safety for Class 2 Power Units, UL 1310. 4th ed. (C). 1994. pap. text ed. 135.00 (*1-55989-589-6*) Underwrtrs Labs.
Standard for Safety for Clock-Operated Switches, UL 917. 4th ed. (C). 1994. pap. text ed. 95.00 (*1-55989-639-6*) Underwrtrs Labs.
Standard for Safety for Closure Systems for Use with Rigid Air Ducts & Air Connectors, UL 181A. (C). 1991. pap. text ed. 330.00 (*1-55989-118-1*) Underwrtrs Labs.
Standard for Safety for Closure Systems for Use with Rigid Air Ducts & Air Connectors, UL 181A. 2nd ed. (C). 1994. pap. text ed. 330.00 (*1-55989-702-3*) Underwrtrs Labs.
Standard for Safety for Coated Electrical Sleeving UL 1441. 3rd ed. (C). 1995. pap. text ed. 95.00 (*1-55989-157-2*) Underwrtrs Labs.
Standard for Safety for Coin & Currency Changers & Actuators, UL 756. 4th ed. (C). 1993. pap. text ed. 330.00 (*1-55989-370-2*) Underwrtrs Labs.
Standard for Safety for Combination Locks, UL 768. 6th ed. (C). 1994. pap. text ed. 175.00 (*1-55989-553-5*) Underwrtrs Labs.
Standard for Safety for Commercial Audio Equipment, UL 813. 6th ed. (C). 1992. pap. text ed. 330.00 (*1-55989-270-6*) Underwrtrs Labs.
Standard for Safety for Commercial Dry-Cleaning Machines (Type IV), UL 664. 4th ed. (C). 1993. pap. text ed. 175.00 (*1-55989-422-9*) Underwrtrs Labs.
Standard for Safety for Commercial Electric Dishwashers, No. UL 921. 4th ed. (C). 1992. pap. text ed. 330.00 (*1-55989-261-7*) Underwrtrs Labs.
Standard for Safety for Commercial Electric Personal Grooming Appliances, UL 1727. 3rd ed. (C). 1994. pap. text ed. 330.00 (*1-55989-564-0*) Underwrtrs Labs.
Standard for Safety for Commercial-Industrial Gas & or Oil-Burning Assemblies with Emission Reduction Equipment, UL 2096. (C). 1993. pap. text ed. 135.00 (*1-55989-498-9*) Underwrtrs Labs.
Standard for Safety for Commercial-Industrial Gas Heating Equipment, UL 795. 4th ed. (C). 1994. pap. text ed. 215.00 (*1-55989-568-3*) Underwrtrs Labs.
Standard for Safety for Commercial Refrigerators & Freezers, UL 471. 8th ed. (C). 1995. pap. text ed. 135.00 (*1-55989-275-7*) Underwrtrs Labs.
Standard for Safety for Communications Cables, UL 444. (C). 1990. pap. text ed. 195.00 (*1-55989-098-3*) Underwrtrs Labs.
Standard for Safety for Communications Cables, UL 444. 2nd ed. (C). 1994. pap. text ed. 195.00 (*1-55989-622-1*) Underwrtrs Labs.
Standard for Safety for Components for Personal Flotation Devices, UL 1191. 2nd ed. (C). 1993. pap. text ed. 330.00 (*1-55989-396-6*) Underwrtrs Labs.
Standard for Safety for Compressed Gas Regulator Accessories, UL 252A. 2nd ed. 1996. pap. 330.00 (*1-55989-197-1*) Underwrtrs Labs.
Standard for Safety for Concrete Masonry Units, UL 618. 9th ed. (C). 1995. pap. text ed. 95.00 (*1-55989-757-0*) Underwrtrs Labs.
Standard for Safety for Connectors & Switches for Use with Burglar-Alarm Systems, UL 634. 7th ed. (C). 1995. pap. text ed. 135.00 (*1-55989-116-5*) Underwrtrs Labs.
Standard for Safety for Constant-Level Oil Valves, UL 352. 6th ed. (C). 1993. pap. text ed. 330.00 (*1-55989-293-5*) Underwrtrs Labs.
Standard for Safety for Container Assemblies for LP-Gas, UL 644. 7th ed. (C). 1994. pap. text ed. 330.00 (*1-55989-710-4*) Underwrtrs Labs.
Standard for Safety for Control Centers for Changing Message Type Electric Signs, UL 1433. 3rd ed. (C). 1996. pap. text ed. 330.00 (*1-55989-230-7*) Underwrtrs Labs.
Standard for Safety for Control Units for Fire-Protective Signaling Systems, UL 864. 7th ed. (C). 1991. pap. text ed. 135.00 (*1-55989-182-3*) Underwrtrs Labs.
Standard for Safety for Cord Reels, UL 355. 9th ed. (C). 1996. pap. text ed. 95.00 (*1-55989-272-2*) Underwrtrs Labs.
Standard for Safety for Cord Sets & Power-Supply Cords, UL817. 10th ed. (C). 1994. pap. text ed. 290.00 (*1-55989-548-9*) Underwrtrs Labs.
Standard for Safety for Couplings for Fire Hose, UL 236. 7th ed. 1992. pap. 95.00 (*1-55989-310-9*) Underwrtrs Labs.
Standard for Safety for Cylinder Valves, UL 1769. 2nd ed. (C). 1996. pap. text ed. 330.00 (*1-55989-008-8*) Underwrtrs Labs.
Standard for Safety for Data-Processing Cable, UL 1690. (C). 1993. pap. text ed. 135.00 (*1-55989-510-1*) Underwrtrs Labs.
Standard for Safety for Dead-Front Switchboards, UL 891. 9th ed. (C). 1994. pap. text ed. 250.00 (*1-55989-450-4*) Underwrtrs Labs.
Standard for Safety for Dehumidifiers, UL 474. 7th ed. 1993. pap. 95.00 (*1-55989-415-6*) Underwrtrs Labs.
Standard for Safety for Delayed-Action Timelocks, UL 887. 7th ed. (C). 1994. pap. text ed. 250.00 (*1-55989-593-4*) Underwrtrs Labs.
Standard for Safety for Diesel Engines for Driving Centrifugal Fire Pumps, UL 1247. 3rd ed. (C). 1995. pap. text ed. 95.00 (*1-55989-021-5*) Underwrtrs Labs.
Standard for Safety for Direct-Acting Pressure-Reducing & Pressure-Control Valves, UL 1468. 3rd ed. (C). 1995. pap. text ed. 95.00 (*1-55989-189-0*) Underwrtrs Labs.
Standard for Safety for Discharge Path Resistors, UL 1676. 2nd ed. (C). 1995. pap. text ed. 95.00 (*1-55989-119-X*) Underwrtrs Labs.
Standard for Safety for Door Closers-Holders, with or Without Integral Smoke Detectors, UL 228. 3rd ed. (C). 1993. pap. text ed. 95.00 (*1-55989-313-3*) Underwrtrs Labs.
Standard for Safety for Double Insulation Systems for Use in Electrical Equipment, UL 1097. 3rd ed. (C). 1993. pap. text ed. 195.00 (*1-55989-414-8*) Underwrtrs Labs.
Standard for Safety for Draft Equipment, UL 378. 3rd ed. (C). 1993. pap. text ed. 95.00 (*1-55989-416-4*) Underwrtrs Labs.
Standard for Safety for Drinking-Water Coolers, UL 399. 6th ed. (C). 1993. pap. text ed. 330.00 (*1-55989-432-6*) Underwrtrs Labs.
Standard for Safety for Dry Chemical Fire Extinguishers UL 299, UL 299. 9th ed. (C). 1995. pap. text ed. 95.00 (*1-55989-107-6*) Underwrtrs Labs.
Standard for Safety for Dry Pipe & Deluge Valves for Fire-Protection Service, UL 260. 6th ed. (C). 1994. pap. text ed. 95.00 (*1-55989-584-5*) Underwrtrs Labs.
Standard for Safety for Dry-Type General Purpose & Power Transformers, UL 1561. 2nd ed. (C). 1994. pap. text ed. 330.00 (*1-55989-514-4*) Underwrtrs Labs.
Standard for Safety for Duct Heaters, UL 1996. (C). 1992. pap. text ed. 135.00 (*1-55989-299-4*) Underwrtrs Labs.
Standard for Safety for Ducted Heat Recovery Ventilators, UL 1812. 2nd ed. (C). 1995. pap. text ed. 330.00 (*1-55989-093-2*) Underwrtrs Labs.
Standard for Safety for Early-Suppression Fast-Response Sprinklers, UL 1767. 2nd ed. (C). 1995. pap. text ed. 330.00 (*1-55989-705-8*) Underwrtrs Labs.
Standard for Safety for Electric Aquarium Equipment, UL 1018. 4th ed. 1995. pap. text ed. 230.00 (*1-55989-143-2*) Underwrtrs Labs.
Standard for Safety for Electric Baseboard Heating Equipment, UL 1042. 4th ed. (C). 1994. pap. text ed. 95.00 (*1-55989-549-7*) Underwrtrs Labs.
Standard for Safety for Electric-Battery-Powered Industrial Trucks, UL 583. 9th ed. (C). 1996. pap. text ed. 95.00 (*1-55989-207-2*) Underwrtrs Labs.
Standard for Safety for Electric Chain Saws, UL 1662. 2nd ed. (C). 1994. pap. text ed. 175.00 (*1-55989-676-0*) Underwrtrs Labs.
Standard for Safety for Electric Clothes Dryers, UL 2158. (C). 1994. pap. text ed. 95.00 (*1-55989-506-3*) Underwrtrs Labs.
Standard for Safety for Electric Clothes Washing Machines & Extractors, UL 2157. (C). 1994. pap. text ed. 95.00 (*1-55989-505-5*) Underwrtrs Labs.
Standard for Safety for Electric Coin-Operated Clothes-Drying Equipment, UL 1556. 3rd ed. (C). 1990. pap. text ed. 95.00 (*1-55989-064-9*) Underwrtrs Labs.
Standard for Safety for Electric Coin-Operated Clothes-Washing Equipment, UL 1555. 3rd ed. (C). 1990. pap. text ed. 95.00 (*1-55989-063-0*) Underwrtrs Labs.
Standard for Safety for Electric Commercial Clothes-Drying Equipment, UL 1240. 3rd ed. (C). 1994. pap. text ed. 95.00 (*1-55989-571-3*) Underwrtrs Labs.
Standard for Safety for Electric Commercial Clothes-Washing Equipment, UL 1206. 3rd ed. (C). 1994. pap. text ed. 95.00 (*1-55989-520-9*) Underwrtrs Labs.
Standard for Safety for Electric Dry Bath Heaters, UL 875. 6th ed. (C). 1994. pap. text ed. 330.00 (*1-55989-027-4*) Underwrtrs Labs.
Standard for Safety for Electric Dry Bath Heaters, UL 875. 6th ed. (C). 1994. pap. text ed. 330.00 (*1-55989-646-9*) Underwrtrs Labs.
Standard for Safety for Electric Fans, UL 507. 8th ed. (C). 1994. pap. text ed. 230.00 (*1-55989-439-3*) Underwrtrs Labs.
Standard for Safety for Electric-Fence Controllers, UL 69. 8th ed. (C). 1993. pap. 330.00 (*1-55989-368-0*) Underwrtrs Labs.
Standard for Safety for Electric Flashlights & Lanterns for Use in Hazardous (Classified) Locations, UL 783. 5th ed. (C). 1993. pap. text ed. 330.00 (*1-55989-296-X*) Underwrtrs Labs.

S

Standard for Safety for Electric Flatirons, UL 1005. 3rd ed. (C). 1993. pap. text ed. 135.00 (*1-55989-369-9*) Underwrtrs Labs.

Standard for Safety for Electric Gardening Appliances, UL 82. 6th ed. (C). 1994. pap. text ed. 330.00 (*1-55989-573-X*) Underwrtrs Labs.

Standard for Safety for Electric Heaters for Use in Hazardous (Classified) Locations, UL 823. 8th ed. (C). 1995. pap. text ed. 175.00 (*1-55989-141-6*) Underwrtrs Labs.

Standard for Safety for Electric Heating Pads, UL 130. 11th ed. (C). 1996. pap. text ed. 330.00 (*1-55989-103-3*) Underwrtrs Labs.

Standard for Safety for Electric Hedge Trimmers, UL 1448. 4th ed. (C). 1994. pap. text ed. 175.00 (*1-55989-583-7*) Underwrtrs Labs.

Standard for Safety for Electric Home-Laundry Equipment, UL 560. 7th ed. (C). 1993. pap. text ed. 330.00 (*1-55989-460-1*) Underwrtrs Labs.

Standard for Safety for Electric Household Clocks UL 826. 9th ed. (C). 1995. pap. text ed. 250.00 (*1-55989-822-4*) Underwrtrs Labs.

Standard for Safety for Electric Lawn Mowers, UL 1447. 3rd ed. (C). 1994. pap. text ed. 175.00 (*1-55989-582-9*) Underwrtrs Labs.

Standard for Safety for Electric Lighting Fixtures for Use in Hazardous (Classified) Locations, UL 844. 11th ed. (C). 1995. pap. text ed. 195.00 (*1-55989-120-3*) Underwrtrs Labs.

Standard for Safety for Electric Motors & Generators for Use in Division 1 Hazardous (Classified) Locations, UL 674. 3rd ed. (C). 1994. pap. text ed. 95.00 (*1-55989-609-4*) Underwrtrs Labs.

Standard for Safety for Electric Motors & Generators for Use in Hazardous (Classified) Locations, UL 674. 2nd ed. (C). 1989. pap. text ed. 95.00 (*1-55989-019-3*) Underwrtrs Labs.

Standard for Safety for Electric Motors, UL 1004. 4th ed. (C). 1989. pap. text ed. 95.00 (*1-55989-017-7*) Underwrtrs Labs.

Standard for Safety for Electric Motors, UL 1004. 5th ed. (C). 1994. pap. text ed. 95.00 (*1-55989-608-6*) Underwrtrs Labs.

Standard for Safety for Electric Oil Heaters, UL 574. 7th ed. (C). 1996. pap. text ed. 95.00 (*1-55989-184-X*) Underwrtrs Labs.

Standard for Safety for Electric Plumbing Accessories, UL 1951. (C). 1994. pap. text ed. 95.00 (*1-55989-566-7*) Underwrtrs Labs.

Standard for Safety for Electric Scales, UL 466. 7th ed. (C). 1994. pap. text ed. 95.00 (*1-55989-516-0*) Underwrtrs Labs.

Standard for Safety for Electric Snow Movers, UL 1090. 4th ed. (C). 1994. pap. text ed. 175.00 (*1-55989-621-3*) Underwrtrs Labs.

Standard for Safety for Electric Space Heating Cables, UL 1673. 2nd ed. 1996. pap. text ed. 330.00 (*1-55989-138-6*) Underwrtrs Labs.

Standard for Safety for Electric Spas, Equipment Assemblies, & Associated Equipment, UL 1563. 4th ed. (C). 1996. pap. text ed. 330.00 (*1-55989-326-5*) Underwrtrs Labs.

Standard for Safety for Electric Toys, UL 696. 9th ed. (C). 1996. pap. text ed. 330.00 (*1-55989-238-2*) Underwrtrs Labs.

Standard for Safety for Electric Water Bed Heaters, UL 1445. 4th ed. (C). 1991. pap. text ed. 230.00 (*1-55989-181-5*) Underwrtrs Labs.

Standard for Safety for Electric Water Heaters for Pools & Tubs, UL 1261. 4th ed. (C). 1996. pap. text ed. 135.00 (*1-55989-269-2*) Underwrtrs Labs.

Standard for Safety for Electrical Analog Instruments - Panel Board Types, UL 1437. 2nd ed. (C). 1993. pap. text ed. 95.00 (*1-55989-392-3*) Underwrtrs Labs.

Standard for Safety for Electrical & Electronic Measuring & Testing Equipment, UL 1244. 3rd ed. (C). 1993. pap. text ed. 290.00 (*1-55989-508-X*) Underwrtrs Labs.

Standard for Safety for Electrical Cables for Boats, UL 1426. 2nd ed. (C). 1994. pap. text ed. 95.00 (*1-55989-600-0*) Underwrtrs Labs.

Standard for Safety for Electrical Controls for Household & Similar Use, Pt. 1: General Requirements, UL 8730-1. (C). 1993. pap. text ed. 195.00 (*1-55989-437-7*) Underwrtrs Labs.

Standard for Safety for Electrical Equipment for Laboratory Use, Pt. 1: General Requirements, UL 3101-1. (C). 1993. pap. text ed. 135.00 (*1-55989-475-X*) Underwrtrs Labs.

Standard for Safety for Electrical Equipment for Use in Class I & II, Division 2, & Class III Hazardous (Classified) Locations, UL 1604. 3rd ed. (C). 1994. pap. text ed. 95.00 (*1-55989-610-8*) Underwrtrs Labs.

Standard for Safety for Electrical Measuring & Test Equipment, Pt. 1: General Requirements, UL 3111-1. (C). 1994. pap. text ed. 95.00 (*1-55989-634-5*) Underwrtrs Labs.

Standard for Safety for Electrical Metallic Tubing, UL 797. 6th ed. (C). 1993. pap. text ed. 95.00 (*1-55989-420-2*) Underwrtrs Labs.

Standard for Safety for Electrical Quick-Connect Terminals, UL 310. 6th ed. (C). 1995. pap. text ed. 95.00 (*1-55989-200-5*) Underwrtrs Labs.

Standard for Safety for Electrical Wires, Cables & Flexible Cords, UL 1581. 2nd ed. (C). 1991. pap. text ed. 95.00 (*1-55989-222-6*) Underwrtrs Labs.

Standard for Safety for Electrically-Actuated Transmitters, UL 632. 5th ed. (C). 1991. pap. text ed. 175.00 (*1-55989-142-4*) Underwrtrs Labs.

Standard for Safety for Electrically-Actuated Transmitters, UL 632. 6th ed. (C). 1994. pap. text ed. 175.00 (*1-55989-652-3*) Underwrtrs Labs.

Standard for Safety for Electrically Conductive Floorings, UL 779. 6th ed. (C). 1990. pap. text ed. 175.00 (*1-55989-071-1*) Underwrtrs Labs.

Standard for Safety for Electrically Conductive Floorings, UL 779. 7th ed. (C). 1995. pap. text ed. 95.00 (*1-55989-816-X*) Underwrtrs Labs.

Standard for Safety for Electrically Heated Bedding, UL 964. 10th ed. (C). 1994. pap. text ed. 330.00 (*1-55989-708-2*) Underwrtrs Labs.

Standard for Safety for Electrically Isolated Semiconductor Devices, UL 1557. 2nd ed. 1993. pap. 95.00 (*1-55989-418-0*) Underwrtrs Labs.

Standard for Safety for Electrically Operated Valves for Use in Hazardous (Classified) Locations, UL 1002. 6th ed. (C). 1994. pap. text ed. 95.00 (*1-55989-559-4*) Underwrtrs Labs.

Standard for Safety for Electrically Operated Valves, UL 429. 4th ed. (C). 1994. pap. text ed. 135.00 (*1-55989-644-2*) Underwrtrs Labs.

Standard for Safety for Electrode Receptacles for Gas - Tube Signs, UL 879. 6th ed. (C). 1993. pap. text ed. 95.00 (*1-55989-375-3*) Underwrtrs Labs.

Standard for Safety for Electromagnetic Interference Filters, UL 1283. 3rd ed. (C). 1993. pap. text ed. 95.00 (*1-55989-436-9*) Underwrtrs Labs.

Standard for Safety for Electrostatic Air Cleaners, UL 867. 3rd ed. (C). 1995. pap. text ed. 135.00 (*1-55989-049-5*) Underwrtrs Labs.

Standard for Safety for Elevator Door Locking Devices & Contacts, UL 104. 9th ed. (C). 1994. pap. text ed. 95.00 (*1-55989-696-5*) Underwrtrs Labs.

Standard for Safety for Emergency Lighting & Power Equipment, UL 924. 8th ed. 1995. pap. text ed. 290.00 (*1-55989-140-8*) Underwrtrs Labs.

Standard for Safety for Emergency Lighting & Power Equipment, UL 924. 8th ed. (C). 1995. pap. text ed. 290.00 (*1-55989-830-5*) Underwrtrs Labs.

Standard for Safety for Emergency Vault Ventilators & Vault-Ventilating Ports, UL 680. 7th ed. (C). 1996. pap. text ed. 330.00 (*1-55989-208-0*) Underwrtrs Labs.

Standard for Safety for Enclosed & Dead-Front Switches, UL 98. 12th ed. (C). 1994. pap. text ed. 95.00 (*1-55989-612-4*) Underwrtrs Labs.

Standard for Safety for Enclosures for Electrical Equipment, UL 50. 11th ed. (C). 1995. pap. text ed. 330.00 (*1-55989-282-X*) Underwrtrs Labs.

Standard for Safety for Energy Management Equipment, UL 916. 2nd ed. (C). 1994. pap. text ed. 135.00 (*1-55989-576-4*) Underwrtrs Labs.

Standard for Safety for Engine-Generator Assemblies for Use in Recreational Vehicles, UL 1248. 2nd ed. (C). 1993. pap. 95.00 (*1-55989-430-X*) Underwrtrs Labs.

Standard for Safety for Equipment Wiring Terminals for Use with Aluminum & - or Copper Conductors, UL 486E. 3rd ed. (C). 1994. pap. text ed. 95.00 (*1-55989-690-6*) Underwrtrs Labs.

Standard for Safety for Exhaust Hoods for Commercial Cooking Equipment, UL 710. 5th ed. (C). 1995. pap. text ed. 135.00 (*1-55989-123-8*) Underwrtrs Labs.

Standard for Safety for Explosion-Proof & Dust-Ignition-Proof Electrical Equipment for Use in Hazardous (Classified) Locations, UL 1203. 2nd ed. (C). 1994. pap. text ed. 95.00 (*1-55989-641-8*) Underwrtrs Labs.

Standard for Safety for External Corrosion Protection Systems for Steel Underground Storage Tanks, UL 1746. 2nd ed. 1993. pap. 330.00 (*1-55989-328-1*) Underwrtrs Labs.

Standard for Safety for Extruded Insulating Tubing, UL 224. 4th ed. (C). 1992. pap. text ed. 215.00 (*1-55989-263-3*) Underwrtrs Labs.

Standard for Safety for Fabricated Scaffold Planks & Stages, UL 1322. 4th ed. (C). 1993. pap. text ed. 250.00 (*1-55989-376-1*) Underwrtrs Labs.

Standard for Safety for Factory Follow-Up on Third Party Certified Portable Fire Extinguishers, UL 1803. 2nd ed. (C). 1994. pap. text ed. 95.00 (*1-55989-717-1*) Underwrtrs Labs.

Standard for Safety for Factory-Made Air Ducts & Air Connectors, UL 181. 8th ed. (C). 1994. pap. text ed. 330.00 (*1-55989-701-5*) Underwrtrs Labs.

Standard for Safety for Factory-Made Air Ducts & Air Connectors, UL 181. 9th ed. (C). 1996. pap. text ed. 330.00 (*1-55989-100-9*) Underwrtrs Labs.

Standard for Safety for Field Conversion-Retrofit of Products to Change to an Alternative Refrigerant - Construction & Operation, UL 2170. (C). 1993. pap. text ed. 95.00 (*1-55989-478-4*) Underwrtrs Labs.

Standard for Safety for Field Conversion-Retrofit of Products to Change to an Alternative Refrigerant - Insulating Material & Refrigerant Compatibility, UL 2171. (C). 1993. pap. text ed. 95.00 (*1-55989-479-2*) Underwrtrs Labs.

Standard for Safety for Field Conversion-Retrofit of Products to Change to an Alternative Refrigerant - Procedures & Methods, UL 2172. (C). 1993. pap. text ed. 95.00 (*1-55989-480-6*) Underwrtrs Labs.

Standard for Safety for Field Erected Boiler Assemblies, UL 2106. (C). 1994. pap. text ed. 95.00 (*1-55989-688-4*) Underwrtrs Labs.

Standard for Safety for Fire Dampers, UL 555. 5th ed. (C). 1995. pap. text ed. 330.00 (*1-55989-088-6*) Underwrtrs Labs.

Standard for Safety for Fire Department Connections, UL 405. 3rd ed. (C). 1993. pap. text ed. 95.00 (*1-55989-345-1*) Underwrtrs Labs.

Standard for Safety for Fire Extinguisher & Booster Hose, UL 92. 10th ed. (C). 1993. pap. text ed. 175.00 (*1-55989-349-4*) Underwrtrs Labs.

Standard for Safety for Fire Extinguishers, Rating & Fire Testing of, UL 711. 5th ed. (C). 1995. pap. text ed. 95.00 (*1-55989-096-7*) Underwrtrs Labs.

Standard for Safety for Fire Extinguishing Systems for Protection of Restaurant Cooking Areas, Fire Testing of, UL 300. 2nd ed. (C). 1996. pap. text ed. 95.00 (*1-55989-265-X*) Underwrtrs Labs.

Standard for Safety for Fire Test of Interior Finish Material, UL 1715. 2nd ed. (C). 1994. pap. text ed. 230.00 (*1-55989-556-X*) Underwrtrs Labs.

Standard for Safety for Fire Test of Mattresses, UL 1895. (C). 1991. pap. text ed. 330.00 (*1-55989-156-4*) Underwrtrs Labs.

Standard for Safety for Fire Test of Mattresses, UL 1895. 2nd ed. (C). 1995. pap. text ed. 330.00 (*1-55989-747-3*) Underwrtrs Labs.

Standard for Safety for Fire Test of Mattresses with Bedclothes Using a Furniture Calorimeter, UL 2060. (C). 1994. pap. text ed. 95.00 (*1-55989-614-0*) Underwrtrs Labs.

Standard for Safety for Fire Test of Pneumatic Tubing for Flame & Smoke Characteristics, UL 1820. 2nd ed. (C). 1994. pap. text ed. 330.00 (*1-55989-629-9*) Underwrtrs Labs.

Standard for Safety for Fire Test of Roof Deck Constructions, UL 1256. 2nd ed. (C). 1993. pap. text ed. 95.00 (*1-55989-434-2*) Underwrtrs Labs.

Standard for Safety for Fire Tests for Foamed Plastics Used for Decorative Purposes, UL 1975. 2nd ed. (C). 1996. pap. text ed. 330.00 (*1-55989-130-0*) Underwrtrs Labs.

Standard for Safety for Fire Tests of Building Construction & Materials, UL 263. 11th ed. (C). 1992. pap. text ed. 95.00 (*1-55989-267-6*) Underwrtrs Labs.

Standard for Safety for Fire Tests of Door Assemblies, UL 10B. 8th ed. (C). 1993. pap. text ed. 95.00 (*1-55989-446-6*) Underwrtrs Labs.

Standard for Safety for Fire Tests of Through-Penetration Firestops, UL 1479. 2nd ed. (C). 1994. pap. text ed. 330.00 (*1-55989-624-8*) Underwrtrs Labs.

Standard for Safety for Fire Tests of Window Assemblies, UL 9. 6th ed. (C). 1994. pap. text ed. 95.00 (*1-55989-669-8*) Underwrtrs Labs.

Standard for Safety for Fireplace Accessories, UL 907. 2nd ed. (C). 1994. pap. text ed. 330.00 (*1-55989-647-7*) Underwrtrs Labs.

Standard for Safety for Fireplace Stoves, UL 737. 8th ed. (C). 1996. pap. text ed. 290.00 (*1-55989-755-4*) Underwrtrs Labs.

Standard for Safety for Fixed & Location-Dedicated Electric Room Heaters, UL 2021. (C). 1992. pap. text ed. 330.00 (*1-55989-229-3*) Underwrtrs Labs.

Standard for Safety for Flame Arresters, UL 525. 6th ed. (C). 1994. pap. text ed. 330.00 (*1-55989-712-0*) Underwrtrs Labs.

Standard for Safety for Flammable Liquid Storage Cabinets, UL 1275. 2nd ed. (C). 1994. pap. text ed. 135.00 (*1-55989-596-9*) Underwrtrs Labs.

Standard for Safety for Flat-Plate Photovoltaic Modules & Panels, UL 1703. 2nd ed. (C). 1993. pap. text ed. 330.00 (*1-55989-390-7*) Underwrtrs Labs.

Standard for Safety for Flexible Cord & Fixture Wire, UL 62. 15th ed. (C). 1991. pap. text ed. 95.00 (*1-55989-231-5*) Underwrtrs Labs.

Standard for Safety for Flexible Metal Conduit, UL 1. 9th ed. (C). 1993. pap. text ed. 95.00 (*1-55989-453-9*) Underwrtrs Labs.

Standard for Safety for Flexible Metallic Hose, UL 536. 8th ed. (C). 1993. pap. text ed. 95.00 (*1-55989-496-2*) Underwrtrs Labs.

Standard for Safety for Flexible Nonmetallic Tubing for Electric Wiring, UL 3. 9th ed. (C). 1994. pap. text ed. 95.00 (*1-55989-707-4*) Underwrtrs Labs.

Standard for Safety for Floor-Finishing Mcachines, UL 561. 4th ed. 1993. pap. 330.00 (*1-55989-403-2*) Underwrtrs Labs.

Standard for Safety for Fluorescent-Lamp Ballasts, UL 935. 9th ed. (C). 1995. pap. text ed. 230.00 (*1-55989-809-7*) Underwrtrs Labs.

Standard for Safety for Foam Equipment & Liquid Concentrates, UL 162, UL162. 7th ed. (C). 1994. pap. text ed. 330.00 (*1-55989-561-6*) Underwrtrs Labs.

Standard for Safety for Foam Fire Extinguishers, UL 8. 4th ed. (C). 1990. pap. text ed. 330.00 (*1-55989-105-X*) Underwrtrs Labs.

Standard for Safety for Foam Fire Extinguishers, UL 8. 5th ed. (C). 1995. pap. text ed. 330.00 (*1-55989-756-2*) Underwrtrs Labs.

Standard for Safety for Fused Power-Circuit Devices, UL 977. 4th ed. (C). 1994. pap. text ed. 215.00 (*1-55989-709-0*) Underwrtrs Labs.

Standard for Safety for Fuseholders, UL 512. 10th ed. (C). 1993. pap. text ed. 95.00 (*1-55989-379-6*) Underwrtrs Labs.

Standard for Safety for Fusing Resistors & Temperature-Limited Resistors for Radio- & Television-Type Appliances, UL 1412. 4th ed. (C). 1994. pap. text ed. 175.00 (*1-55989-640-X*) Underwrtrs Labs.

Standard for Safety for Garage Equipment, UL 201. (C). 1994. pap. text ed. 135.00 (*1-55989-687-6*) Underwrtrs Labs.

Standard for Safety for Garment Finishing Appliances, UL 141. 7th ed. (C). 1996. pap. text ed. 135.00 (*1-55989-223-4*) Underwrtrs Labs.

Standard for Safety for Gas-Burning Heating Appliances for Manufactured Homes & Recreational Vehicles, UL 307B. 4th ed. (C). 1995. pap. text ed. 230.00 (*1-55989-716-3*) Underwrtrs Labs.

Standard for Safety for Gas Burning Heating Appliances for Mobile Homes & Recreational Vehicles, UL 307B. 4th ed. 1995. pap. 230.00 (*1-55989-319-2*) Underwrtrs Labs.

Standard for Safety for Gas-Fired Cooking Appliances for Recreational Vehicles, UL 1075. 2nd ed. (C). 1993. pap. 175.00 (*1-55989-405-9*) Underwrtrs Labs.

Standard for Safety for Gas Vents, UL 441. 7th ed. (C). 1991. pap. text ed. 330.00 (*1-55989-213-7*) Underwrtrs Labs.

Standard for Safety for Gas Vents, UL 441. 8th ed. (C). 1996. pap. text ed. 330.00 (*1-55989-637-X*) Underwrtrs Labs.

Standard for Safety for Gas Vents UL 441. 9th ed. (C). 1996. pap. text ed. 330.00 (*1-55989-947-6*) Underwrtrs Labs.

Standard for Safety for Gasketed Joints for Ductile-Iron Pipe & Fittings for Fire Protection Service, UL 194. 5th ed. (C). 1996. pap. text ed. 95.00 (*1-55989-002-9*) Underwrtrs Labs.

Standard for Safety for Gaskets & Seals, UL 157. 2nd ed. (C). 1996. pap. text ed. 135.00 (*1-55989-180-7*) Underwrtrs Labs.

Standard for Safety for Gasoline Hose, UL 330. 6th ed. (C). 1993. pap. text ed. 215.00 (*1-55989-332-X*) Underwrtrs Labs.

Standard for Safety for Gate Valves for Fire-Protection Service, UL 262. 7th ed. (C). 1994. pap. text ed. 230.00 (*1-55989-585-3*) Underwrtrs Labs.

Standard for Safety for Gauges, Indicating Pressure, for Compressed Gas Service, UL 404. 5th ed. (C). 1993. pap. text ed. 95.00 (*1-55989-342-7*) Underwrtrs Labs.

Standard for Safety for Glass-Fiber-Reinforced Plastic Underground Storage Tanks for Petroleum Products, UL 1316. 2nd ed. (C). 1994. pap. text ed. 95.00 (*1-55989-462-8*) Underwrtrs Labs.

Standard for Safety for Graphic Arts Equipment UL 775. 2nd ed. (C). 1994. pap. text ed. 95.00 (*1-55989-563-2*) Underwrtrs Labs.

Standard for Safety for Grease Ducts, UL 1978. (C). 1995. pap. text ed. 95.00 (*1-55989-762-7*) Underwrtrs Labs.

Standard for Safety for Ground-Fault Circuit-Interrupters, UL 943. 3rd ed. (C). 1993. pap. text ed. 330.00 (*1-55989-465-2*) Underwrtrs Labs.

Standard for Safety for Ground-Fault Sensing & Relaying Equipment, UL 1053. 5th ed. (C). 1994. pap. text ed. 95.00 (*1-55989-649-3*) Underwrtrs Labs.

Standard for Safety for Grounding & Bonding Equipment, UL 467. 7th ed. (C). 1993. pap. text ed. 95.00 (*1-55989-491-1*) Underwrtrs Labs.

Standard for Safety for Hair Clipping & Shaving Appliances, UL 1028. 4th ed. (C). 1995. pap. text ed. 95.00 (*1-55989-112-2*) Underwrtrs Labs.

Standard for Safety for Halogenated Agent Extinguishing System Units, UL 1058. 3rd ed. (C). 1995. pap. text ed. 135.00 (*1-55989-024-X*) Underwrtrs Labs.

Standard for Safety for Halogenated Agent Fire Extinguishers UL 1093. 5th ed. (C). 1995. pap. text ed. 95.00 (*1-55989-109-2*) Underwrtrs Labs.

Standard for Safety for Halon 1211 Recovery-Recharge Equipment, UL 2006. 2nd ed. (C). 1995. pap. text ed. 330.00 (*1-55989-178-5*) Underwrtrs Labs.

Standard for Safety for Halon 1301 Recovery - Recycling Equipment UL 2083. 2nd ed. (C). 1996. pap. text ed. 135.00 (*1-55989-459-8*) Underwrtrs Labs.

Standard for Safety for Hand-Held Torches for Fuel Gases, UL 147. 5th ed. (C). 1996. pap. text ed. 330.00 (*1-55989-279-X*) Underwrtrs Labs.

Standard for Safety for Heat Detectors for Fire Protective Signaling Systems, UL 521. 6th ed. (C). 1993. pap. text ed. 95.00 (*1-55989-513-6*) Underwrtrs Labs.

Standard for Safety for Heat Reclaimers for Gas-, Oil-, or Solid Fuel-Fired Appliances, UL 462. 2nd ed. (C). 1993. pap. text ed. 175.00 (*1-55989-470-9*) Underwrtrs Labs.

Standard for Safety for Heat Responsive Links for Fire-Protection Service, UL 33. 6th ed. (C). 1993. pap. text ed. 95.00 (*1-55989-443-1*) Underwrtrs Labs.

Standard for Safety for Heating & Cooling Equipment, UL 1995. 2nd ed. (C). 1995. pap. text ed. 330.00 (*1-55989-152-1*) Underwrtrs Labs.

Standard for Safety for Heating, Water Supply, & Power Boilers - Electric, UL 834. 3rd ed. (C). 1991. pap. text ed. 95.00 (*1-55989-227-7*) Underwrtrs Labs.

Standard for Safety for Heating, Water Supply, & Power Boilers-Electric, UL 834. 4th ed. (C). 1995. pap. text ed. 95.00 (*1-55989-631-0*) Underwrtrs Labs.

Standard for Safety for Hermetic Refrigerant Motor-Compressors, UL 984. 7th ed. (C). 1996. pap. text ed. 290.00 (*1-55989-070-3*) Underwrtrs Labs.

Standard for Safety for High-Efficiency, Particulate, Air Filter Units, UL 586. 7th ed. (C). 1990. pap. text ed. 175.00 (*1-55989-129-7*) Underwrtrs Labs.

Standard for Safety for High-Intensity-Discharge Lamp Ballasts, UL 1029. 5th ed. (C). 1994. pap. text ed. 95.00 (*1-55989-578-0*) Underwrtrs Labs.

Standard for Safety for High Intensity Discharge Lighting Fixtures, UL 1572. 4th ed. (C). 1995. pap. text ed. 95.00 (*1-55989-236-6*) Underwrtrs Labs.

Standard for Safety for High-Pressure Cleaning Machines, UL 1776. 2nd ed. (C). 1995. pap. text ed. 175.00 (*1-55989-264-1*) Underwrtrs Labs.

Standard for Safety for High-Voltage Components for Television-Type Appliances, UL 1413. 5th ed. (C). 1994. pap. text ed. 95.00 (*1-55989-694-9*) Underwrtrs Labs.

Standard for Safety for High Voltage Industrial Control Equipment, UL 347. 4th ed. (C). 1993. pap. text ed. 215.00 (*1-55989-468-7*) Underwrtrs Labs.

Standard for Safety for Highway Emergency Signals, UL 912. 5th ed. 1993. pap. 95.00 (*1-55989-317-6*) Underwrtrs Labs.

Standard for Safety for Hobby & Sports Equipment, UL 961. 3rd ed. (C). 1995. pap. text ed. 215.00 (*1-55989-053-3*) Underwrtrs Labs.

Standard for Safety for Home Health Care Signaling Equipment, UL1637. 2nd ed. (C). 1993. pap. text ed. 330.00 (*1-55989-451-2*) Underwrtrs Labs.

An Asterisk (*) at the beginning of an entry indicates that the title is appearing in BIP for the first time.

Standard for Safety for Hose Valves for Fire-Protection Service, UL 668. 9th ed. (C). 1995. pap. text ed. 95.00 (*1-55989-022-3*) Underwrtrs Labs.

Standard for Safety for Hospital Signaling & Nurse Call Equipment, UL 1069. 5th ed. (C). 1996. pap. text ed. 135.00 (*1-55989-012-6*) Underwrtrs Labs.

Standard for Safety for Household Burglar-Alarm System Units, UL 1023. 5th ed. (C). 1991. pap. text ed. 250.00 (*1-55989-204-8*) Underwrtrs Labs.

Standard for Safety for Household, Commercial, & Professional-Use Carts & Stands, UL 1678. 1991. pap. text ed. 330.00 (*1-55989-144-0*) Underwrtrs Labs.

Standard for Safety for Household Diswashers, UL 749. 6th ed. (C). 1995. pap. text ed. 95.00 (*1-55989-518-7*) Underwrtrs Labs.

Standard for Safety for Household Electric Clocks, UL 826. 9th ed. (C). 1995. pap. text ed. 250.00 (*1-55989-114-9*) Underwrtrs Labs.

Standard for Safety for Household Electric Coffee Makers & Brewing-Type Appliances, UL 1082. 4th ed. (C). 1991. pap. text ed. 230.00 (*1-55989-206-4*) Underwrtrs Labs.

Standard for Safety for Household Electric Personal Grooming Appliances, UL 859. 9th ed. (C). 1995. pap. text ed. 330.00 (*1-55989-149-1*) Underwrtrs Labs.

Standard for Safety for Household Electric Ranges, UL 858. 14th ed. (C). 1993. pap. text ed. 330.00 (*1-55989-452-0*) Underwrtrs Labs.

Standard for Safety for Household Electric Storage Tank Water Heaters, UL 174. 10th ed. (C). 1996. pap. text ed. 330.00 (*1-55989-052-5*) Underwrtrs Labs.

Standard for Safety for Household Fire Warning System Units, UL 985. 4th ed. (C). 1994. pap. text ed. 95.00 (*1-55989-615-9*) Underwrtrs Labs.

Standard for Safety for Household Refrigerators & Freezers, UL 250. 10th ed. (C). 1993. pap. text ed. 95.00 (*1-55989-461-X*) Underwrtrs Labs.

Standard for Safety for Household Trash Compactors, UL 1086. 4th ed. (C). 1996. pap. text ed. 135.00 (*1-55989-210-2*) Underwrtrs Labs.

Standard for Safety for Hydrants for Fire-Protection Service, UL 246. 7th ed. 1993. pap. 95.00 (*1-55989-308-7*) Underwrtrs Labs.

Standard for Safety for Hydromassage Bathtubs, UL 1795. 2nd ed. (C). 1993. pap. text ed. 330.00 (*1-55989-489-X*) Underwrtrs Labs.

Standard for Safety for Ice Cream Makers, UL 621. 5th ed. (C). 1993. pap. text ed. 330.00 (*1-55989-393-1*) Underwrtrs Labs.

Standard for Safety for Ice Makers, UL 563. 7th ed. (C). 1995. pap. text ed. 175.00 (*1-55989-241-2*) Underwrtrs Labs.

Standard for Safety for Immersion-Detection Circuit-Interrupters, UL 1664. 2nd ed. (C). 1995. pap. text ed. 330.00 (*1-55989-091-6*) Underwrtrs Labs.

Standard for Safety for Impedance-Protected Motors, UL 519. 2nd ed. (C). 1994. pap. text ed. 230.00 (*1-55989-581-0*) Underwrtrs Labs.

Standard for Safety for Incandescent Lighting Fixtures, UL 1571. 4th ed. (C). 1995. pap. text ed. 95.00 (*1-55989-235-8*) Underwrtrs Labs.

Standard for Safety for Indicating Pressure Gauges for Fire Protection Service, UL 393. 7th ed. (C). 1996. pap. text ed. 330.00 (*1-55989-146-7*) Underwrtrs Labs.

Standard for Safety for Indicator Posts for Fire-Protection Service, UL 789. 9th ed. 1993. pap. 215.00 (*1-55989-303-6*) Underwrtrs Labs.

Standard for Safety for Industrial Battery Chargers, UL 1564. 2nd ed. (C). 1993. pap. text ed. 135.00 (*1-55989-504-7*) Underwrtrs Labs.

Standard for Safety for Industrial Control Equipment for Use in Hazardous (Classified) Locations, UL 698. 12th ed. (C). 1995. pap. text ed. 195.00 (*1-55989-192-0*) Underwrtrs Labs.

Standard for Safety for Industrial Control Equipment, UL 508. 16th ed. (C). 1993. pap. text ed. 330.00 (*1-55989-037-1*) Underwrtrs Labs.

Standard for Safety for Industrial Trucks, Internal Combustion Engine-Powered, UL 558. 9th ed. 1996. pap. 175.00 (*1-55989-196-3*) Underwrtrs Labs.

Standard for Safety for Information Technology Equipment, Including Electrical Business Equipment, UL 1950. 3rd ed. 1995. pap. 195.00 (*1-55989-383-4*) Underwrtrs Labs.

Standard for Safety for Installation & Classification of Burglar & Holdup Alarm Systems, UL 681. 12th ed. (C). 1994. pap. text ed. 95.00 (*1-55989-630-2*) Underwrtrs Labs.

Standard for Safety for Installation & Classification of Residential Burglar Alarm Systems, UL 1641. 3rd ed. (C). 1994. pap. text ed. 95.00 (*1-55989-653-1*) Underwrtrs Labs.

Standard for Safety for Installation Requirements for Lightning Protection Systems, UL 96A. 10th ed. (C). 1993. pap. text ed. 35.00 (*1-55989-429-6*) Underwrtrs Labs.

Standard for Safety for Insulated Aboveground Tanks for Flammable & Combustible Liquids, UL 2085. (C). 1994. pap. text ed. 95.00 (*1-55989-711-2*) Underwrtrs Labs.

Standard for Safety for Insulated Wire Connectors for Use with Underground Conductors, UL 486D. 3rd ed. 1993. pap. 95.00 (*1-55989-408-3*) Underwrtrs Labs.

Standard for Safety for Insulation Coordination Including Clearances & Creepage Distances for Electrical Equipment, UL 840. 2nd ed. (C). 1993. pap. text ed. 95.00 (*1-55989-391-5*) Underwrtrs Labs.

Standard for Safety for Intrusion-Detection Units, UL 639. 6th ed. (C). 1993. pap. text ed. 95.00 (*1-55989-431-8*) Underwrtrs Labs.

Standard for Safety for Isolated Power Systems Equipment, UL 1047. 3rd ed. (C). 1995. pap. text ed. 175.00 (*1-55989-761-9*) Underwrtrs Labs.

Standard for Safety for Isolating Signal & Feedback Transformers for Use in Electronic Equipment, UL 1876. 2nd ed. (C). 1995. pap. text ed. 175.00 (*1-55989-043-6*) Underwrtrs Labs.

Standard for Safety for Junction Boxes for Swimming Pool Lighting Fixtures, UL 1241. 5th ed. (C). 1994. pap. text ed. 330.00 (*1-55989-020-7*) Underwrtrs Labs.

Standard for Safety for Key-Locked Safes (Class KL), UL 786. 5th ed. (C). 1994. pap. text ed. 95.00 (*1-55989-698-1*) Underwrtrs Labs.

Standard for Safety for Key Locks, UL 437. 6th ed. (C). 1994. pap. text ed. 95.00 (*1-55989-678-7*) Underwrtrs Labs.

Standard for Safety for Knife Switches, UL 363. 9th ed. (C). 1994. pap. text ed. 95.00 (*1-55989-718-X*) Underwrtrs Labs.

Standard for Safety for Laboratory Equipment, UL 1262. 3rd ed. (C). 1990. pap. text ed. 95.00 (*1-55989-126-2*) Underwrtrs Labs.

Standard for Safety for Lampholders, Starters, & Starter Holders for Fluorescent Lamps, UL 542. 7th ed. (C). 1994. pap. text ed. 95.00 (*1-55989-683-3*) Underwrtrs Labs.

Standard for Safety for Leakage Current Protection Devices, UL 943A. (C). 1993. pap. text ed. 135.00 (*1-55989-521-7*) Underwrtrs Labs.

Standard for Safety for Leakage Rated Dampers for Use in Smoke Control Systems, UL 555S. 3rd ed. (C). 1996. pap. text ed. 95.00 (*1-55989-483-0*) Underwrtrs Labs.

Standard for Safety for Lightning Protection Components, UL 96. 4th ed. (C). 1994. pap. text ed. 35.00 (*1-55989-602-7*) Underwrtrs Labs.

Standard for Safety for Limit Controls, UL 353. 5th ed. (C). 1994. pap. text ed. 95.00 (*1-55989-655-8*) Underwrtrs Labs.

Standard for Safety for Line Isolation Monitors, UL 1022. 3rd ed. (C). 1994. pap. text ed. 135.00 (*1-55989-558-6*) Underwrtrs Labs.

Standard for Safety for Lined Fire Hose for Interior Standpipes, UL 219. 2nd ed. (C). 1993. pap. text ed. 95.00 (*1-55989-399-0*) Underwrtrs Labs.

Standard for Safety for Linings & Screens for Use with Burglar-Alarm Systems, UL 606. 3rd ed. (C). 1994. pap. text ed. 95.00 (*1-55989-670-1*) Underwrtrs Labs.

Standard for Safety for Liquid Fuel-Burning Heating Appliances for Manufactured Homes & Recreational Vehicles, UL 307A. 7th ed. (C). 1995. pap. text ed. 330.00 (*1-55989-704-X*) Underwrtrs Labs.

Standard for Safety for Liquid-Level Gauges & Indicators for Anhydrous Ammonia & LP-Gas, UL 565. 4th ed. (C). 1993. pap. text ed. 95.00 (*1-55989-497-0*) Underwrtrs Labs.

Standard for Safety for Liquid-Level Indicating Gauges & Tank-Filling Signals for Petroleum Products, UL 180. 6th ed. (C). 1996. pap. text ed. 135.00 (*1-55989-202-1*) Underwrtrs Labs.

Standard for Safety for Liquid-Tight Flexible Nonmetallic Conduit, UL 1660. 2nd ed. (C). 1994. pap. text ed. 330.00 (*1-55989-720-1*) Underwrtrs Labs.

Standard for Safety for Lithium Batteries, UL 1642. 3rd ed. (C). 1995. pap. text ed. 330.00 (*1-55989-276-5*) Underwrtrs Labs.

Standard for Safety for Local Burglar Alarm Units & Systems, UL 609. 11th ed. (C). 1996. pap. text ed. 95.00 (*1-55989-111-4*) Underwrtrs Labs.

Standard for Safety for Low Level Path Marking & Lighting Systems, UL 1994. (C). 1991. pap. text ed. 330.00 (*1-55989-201-3*) Underwrtrs Labs.

Standard for Safety for Low-Temperature Venting Systems, Type L, UL 641. 7th ed. (C). 1995. pap. text ed. 135.00 (*1-55989-565-9*) Underwrtrs Labs.

Standard for Safety for Low-Voltage AC & DC Power Circuit Breakers Used in Enclosures, UL 1066. 2nd ed. (C). 1993. pap. text ed. 95.00 (*1-55989-373-7*) Underwrtrs Labs.

Standard for Safety for Low-Voltage Fuses Pt. 1: General Requirements, UL 248-1. (C). 1994. pap. text ed. 95.00 (*1-55989-662-0*) Underwrtrs Labs.

Standard for Safety for Low-Voltage Fuses Pt. 4: Class CC Fuses, UL 248-4. (C). 1994. pap. text ed. 95.00 (*1-55989-663-9*) Underwrtrs Labs.

Standard for Safety for Low-Voltage Fuses Pt. 8: Class J Fuses, UL248-8. (C). 1994. pap. text ed. 95.00 (*1-55989-664-7*) Underwrtrs Labs.

Standard for Safety for Low-Voltage Fuses Pt. 10: Class L Fuses, UL 248-10. (C). 1994. pap. text ed. 95.00 (*1-55989-665-5*) Underwrtrs Labs.

Standard for Safety for Low-Voltage Fuses Pt. 12: Class R Fuses, UL 248-12. (C). 1994. pap. text ed. 95.00 (*1-55989-666-3*) Underwrtrs Labs.

Standard for Safety for Low-Voltage Fuses Pt. 14: Supplemental Fuses, UL 248-14. (C). 1994. pap. text ed. 95.00 (*1-55989-667-1*) Underwrtrs Labs.

Standard for Safety for Low-Voltage Fuses Pt. 15: Class T Fuses, UL 248-15. (C). 1994. pap. text ed. 95.00 (*1-55989-668-X*) Underwrtrs Labs.

Standard for Safety for Low Voltage Landscape Lighting Systems, UL 1838. 2nd ed. (C). 1996. pap. text ed. 95.00 (*1-55989-575-6*) Underwrtrs Labs.

Standard for Safety for Low Voltage Lighting Fixtures for Use in Recreational Vehicles, UL 234. 4th ed. (C). 1994. pap. text ed. 95.00 (*1-55989-519-5*) Underwrtrs Labs.

Standard for Safety for Low Voltage Marine Lighting Fixtures, UL 1149. (C). 1994. pap. text ed. 95.00 (*1-55989-611-6*) Underwrtrs Labs.

Standard for Safety for LP-Gas Hose, UL 21. 9th ed. (C). 1995. pap. text ed. 230.00 (*1-55989-233-1*) Underwrtrs Labs.

Standard for Safety for Machine-Tool Wires & Cables, UL 1063. 5th ed. (C). 1993. pap. text ed. 95.00 (*1-55989-484-9*) Underwrtrs Labs.

Standard for Safety for Manifolds for Compressed Gases, UL 407. 5th ed. (C). 1993. pap. text ed. 95.00 (*1-55989-423-7*) Underwrtrs Labs.

Standard for Safety for Manually Actuated Signaling Boxes for Use with Fire-Protective Signaling Systems, UL 38. 6th ed. (C). 1994. pap. text ed. 95.00 (*1-55989-515-2*) Underwrtrs Labs.

Standard for Safety for Manufactured Wiring Systems, UL 183. 2nd ed. (C). 1993. pap. text ed. 95.00 (*1-55989-448-2*) Underwrtrs Labs.

Standard for Safety for Marking & Labeling Systems, UL 969. 4th ed. (C). 1995. pap. text ed. 95.00 (*1-55989-339-7*) Underwrtrs Labs.

Standard for Safety for Materials for Built-up Roof Coverings, UL 55A. 12th ed. (C). 1993. pap. text ed. 95.00 (*1-55989-447-4*) Underwrtrs Labs.

Standard for Safety for Mechanically & Electrically Operated Fuel Pumps for Marine Use, UL 1130. (C). 1990. pap. text ed. 95.00 (*1-55989-131-9*) Underwrtrs Labs.

Standard for Safety for Medical & Dental Equipment, UL 544. 3rd ed. (C). 1993. pap. text ed. 215.00 (*1-55989-469-5*) Underwrtrs Labs.

Standard for Safety for Medical Electrical Equipment Pt. 1: General Requirements for Safety, UL 2601-1. (C). 1994. pap. text ed. 175.00 (*1-55989-660-4*) Underwrtrs Labs.

Standard for Safety for Medium Heat Appliance Factory-Built Chimneys, UL 959. 7th ed. (C). 1995. pap. text ed. 250.00 (*1-55989-673-6*) Underwrtrs Labs.

Standard for Safety for Metal-Enclosed Low-Voltage Power Circuit Breaker Switchgear, UL 1558. 3rd ed. (C). 1993. pap. text ed. 95.00 (*1-55989-493-8*) Underwrtrs Labs.

Standard for Safety for Metal Safety Cans, UL 30. 9th ed. (C). 1995. pap. text ed. 330.00 (*1-55989-187-4*) Underwrtrs Labs.

Standard for Safety for Metal Waste Cans, UL 32. 5th ed. (C). 1994. pap. text ed. 175.00 (*1-55989-628-0*) Underwrtrs Labs.

Standard for Safety for Metallic Outlet Boxes, UL 514A. 8th ed. (C). 1991. pap. text ed. 330.00 (*1-55989-220-X*) Underwrtrs Labs.

Standard for Safety for Meter Sockets, UL 414. 6th ed. (C). 1994. pap. text ed. 330.00 (*1-55989-592-6*) Underwrtrs Labs.

Standard for Safety for Meters for Flammable & Combustible Liquid & LP-Gas, UL 25. 7th ed. (C). 1996. pap. text ed. 230.00 (*1-55989-132-7*) Underwrtrs Labs.

Standard for Safety for Microwave Cooking Appliances, UL 923. 4th ed. (C). 1995. pap. text ed. 175.00 (*1-55989-099-1*) Underwrtrs Labs.

Standard for Safety for Mine-Duty Fuses, UL 198M. 3rd ed. (C). 1995. pap. text ed. 95.00 (*1-55989-661-2*) Underwrtrs Labs.

Standard for Safety for Molded-Case Circuit-Breakers, Molded-Case Switches & Circuit Breaker Enclosures, UL 489. 9th ed. (C). 1996. pap. text ed. 330.00 (*1-55989-151-3*) Underwrtrs Labs.

Standard for Safety for Molded-Case Switches, UL 1087. 2nd ed. (C). 1993. pap. text ed. 290.00 (*1-55989-494-6*) Underwrtrs Labs.

Standard for Safety for Motor Control Centers, UL 845. 4th ed. (C). 1995. pap. text ed. 215.00 (*1-55989-713-9*) Underwrtrs Labs.

Standard for Safety for Motor-Operated Air Compressors, Vacuum Pumps, & Painting Equipment, UL 1450. 2nd ed. (C). 1993. pap. text ed. 230.00 (*1-55989-371-0*) Underwrtrs Labs.

Standard for Safety for Motor-Operated Appliances, UL 73. 8th ed. (C). 1993. pap. text ed. 95.00 (*1-55989-273-0*) Underwrtrs Labs.

Standard for Safety for Motor-Operated Commercial Food Preparing Machines, UL 763. 2nd ed. (C). 1993. pap. text ed. 95.00 (*1-55989-490-3*) Underwrtrs Labs.

Standard for Safety for Motor-Operated Household Food Preparing Machines, UL 982. 4th ed. (C). 1995. pap. text ed. 95.00 (*1-55989-799-6*) Underwrtrs Labs.

Standard for Safety for Motor-Operated Massage & Exercise Machines, UL 1647. 2nd ed. (C). 1991. pap. text ed. 215.00 (*1-55989-188-2*) Underwrtrs Labs.

Standard for Safety for Motor-Operated Water Pumps, UL 778. 3rd ed. (C). 1996. pap. text ed. 135.00 (*1-55989-226-9*) Underwrtrs Labs.

Standard for Safety for Movable & Wall- or Ceiling-Hung Electric Room Heaters, UL 1278. 2nd ed. (C). 1994. pap. text ed. 290.00 (*1-55989-684-1*) Underwrtrs Labs.

Standard for Safety for Musical Instruments & Accessories, UL 469. 2nd ed. (C). 1993. pap. text ed. 195.00 (*1-55989-386-9*) Underwrtrs Labs.

Standard for Safety for Night Depositories, UL 771. 7th ed. (C). 1994. pap. text ed. 95.00 (*1-55989-605-1*) Underwrtrs Labs.

Standard for Safety for Nonducted Heat Recovery Ventilators UL 1815. 2nd ed. (C). 1995. pap. text ed. 175.00 (*1-55989-095-9*) Underwrtrs Labs.

Standard for Safety for Nonintegral Marine Fuel Tanks, UL 1102. 4th ed. (C). 1996. pap. text ed. 230.00 (*1-55989-242-0*) Underwrtrs Labs.

Standard for Safety for Nonmetallic Containers for Waste Paper, UL 242. 3rd ed. 1993. pap. 250.00 (*1-55989-321-4*) Underwrtrs Labs.

Standard for Safety for Nonmetallic Safety Cans for Petroleum Products UL 1313. 2nd ed. (C). 1993. pap. text ed. 290.00 (*1-55989-455-5*) Underwrtrs Labs.

Standard for Safety for Nonmetallic Surface Raceways & Fittings, UL 5A. (C). 1994. pap. text ed. 95.00 (*1-55989-598-5*) Underwrtrs Labs.

Standard for Safety for Nonrefillable (Disposable) Type Fuel Gas Cylinder Assemblies, UL 147A. 2nd ed. (C). 1996. pap. text ed. 135.00 (*1-55989-280-3*) Underwrtrs Labs.

Standard for Safety for Nonrefillable (Disposable) Type Metal Container Assemblies for Butane, UL 147B. 2nd ed. (C). 1996. pap. text ed. 135.00 (*1-55989-281-1*) Underwrtrs Labs.

Standard for Safety for Nonreusable Plastic Containers for Flammable & Combustible Liquids UL 1853. 2nd ed. (C). 1995. pap. text ed. 175.00 (*1-55989-177-7*) Underwrtrs Labs.

Standard for Safety for Office Furnishings, UL 1286. 3rd ed. (C). 1993. pap. text ed. 330.00 (*1-55989-271-4*) Underwrtrs Labs.

Standard for Safety for Oil Burners, UL 296. 9th ed. (C). 1994. pap. text ed. 195.00 (*1-55989-627-2*) Underwrtrs Labs.

Standard for Safety for Oil-Burning Stoves, UL 896. 5th ed. (C). 1993. pap. text ed. 330.00 (*1-55989-438-5*) Underwrtrs Labs.

Standard for Safety for Oil-Fired Air Heaters & Direct-Fired Heaters, UL 733. 4th ed. (C). 1993. pap. text ed. 95.00 (*1-55989-457-1*) Underwrtrs Labs.

Standard for Safety for Oil-Fired Boiler Assemblies, UL 726. 7th ed. (C). 1995. pap. text ed. 95.00 (*1-55989-124-6*) Underwrtrs Labs.

Standard for Safety for Oil-Fired Central Furnaces, UL 727. 8th ed. (C). 1994. pap. text ed. 195.00 (*1-55989-577-2*) Underwrtrs Labs.

Standard for Safety for Oil-Fired Floor Furnaces, UL 729. 5th ed. (C). 1994. pap. text ed. 330.00 (*1-55989-706-6*) Underwrtrs Labs.

Standard for Safety for Oil-Fired Wall Furnaces, UL 730. 4th ed. (C). 1994. pap. text ed. 330.00 (*1-55989-569-1*) Underwrtrs Labs.

Standard for Safety for Optical Fiber Cable, UL 1651. (C). 1993. pap. text ed. 95.00 (*1-55989-472-5*) Underwrtrs Labs.

Standard for Safety for Optical Isolators, UL 1577. 3rd ed. (C). 1995. pap. text ed. 95.00 (*1-55989-832-1*) Underwrtrs Labs.

Standard for Safety for Organic Coatings for Steel Enclosures for Outdoor Use Electrical Equipment, UL 1332. 3rd ed. (C). 1995. pap. text ed. 95.00 (*1-55989-753-8*) Underwrtrs Labs.

Standard for Safety for Outlet Boxes & Fittings for Use in Hazardous (Classified) Locations, UL 886. 10th ed. (C). 1994. pap. text ed. 135.00 (*1-55989-522-5*) Underwrtrs Labs.

Standard for Safety for Outlet Circuit Testers & Similar Indicating Devices, UL 1436. 3rd ed. (C). 1993. pap. text ed. 215.00 (*1-55989-381-8*) Underwrtrs Labs.

Standard for Safety for Overcurrent & Overtemperature Protectors for Radio- & Television-Type Appliances, UL 1416. 5th ed. (C). 1994. pap. text ed. 95.00 (*1-55989-685-X*) Underwrtrs Labs.

Standard for Safety for Oxy-Fuel Gas Torches, UL 123. 9th ed. (C). 1995. pap. text ed. 95.00 (*1-55989-337-0*) Underwrtrs Labs.

Standard for Safety for Panelboards, UL 67. 11th ed. (C). 1993. pap. text ed. 290.00 (*1-55989-579-9*) Underwrtrs Labs.

Standard for Safety for Panic Hardware, UL 305. 4th ed. (C). 1993. pap. text ed. 95.00 (*1-55989-487-3*) Underwrtrs Labs.

Standard for Safety for Photographic Equipment, UL 122. 3rd ed. (C). 1993. pap. text ed. 95.00 (*1-55989-435-0*) Underwrtrs Labs.

Standard for Safety for Pigtails & Flexible Hose Connectors for LP-Gas, UL 569. 7th ed. (C). 1995. pap. text ed. 135.00 (*1-55989-827-5*) Underwrtrs Labs.

Standard for Safety for Pilot-Operated Pressure-Control Valves for Fire-Protection Service, UL 1739. 3rd ed. (C). 1994. pap. text ed. 330.00 (*1-55989-643-4*) Underwrtrs Labs.

Standard for Safety for Pin & Sleeve Configurations, UL 1686, UL1686. (C). 1993. pap. text ed. 135.00 (*1-55989-547-0*) Underwrtrs Labs.

Standard for Safety for Pipe & Couplings, Polyvinyl Chloride (PVC), for Underground Fire Service, UL 1285. 3rd ed. (C). 1995. pap. text ed. 175.00 (*1-55989-807-0*) Underwrtrs Labs.

Standard for Safety for Pipe Connectors for Flammable & Combustible Liquids & LP-Gas, UL 567. 8th ed. (C). 1996. pap. text ed. 330.00 (*1-55989-004-5*) Underwrtrs Labs.

Standard for Safety for Pipe Hanger Equipment for Fire Protection Service, UL 203. 8th ed. (C). 1996. pap. text ed. 175.00 (*1-55989-044-4*) Underwrtrs Labs.

Standard for Safety for Pipe Unions for Flammable & Combustible Fluids & Fire-Protection Service, UL 860. 6th ed. (C). 1993. pap. text ed. 95.00 (*1-55989-341-9*) Underwrtrs Labs.

Standard for Safety for Play Pipes for Water Supply Testing in Fire Protection Service, UL 385. 9th ed. (C). 1994. pap. text ed. 135.00 (*1-55989-700-7*) Underwrtrs Labs.

Standard for Safety for Plug-in, Locking Type Photocontrols for Use with Area Lighting, UL 773. 4th ed. (C). 1995. pap. text ed. 95.00 (*1-55989-748-1*) Underwrtrs Labs.

S

S

Standard for Safety for Plugs, Receptacles, & Cable Connectors, of the Pin & Sleeve Type, UL 1682. (C). 1993. pap. text ed. 135.00 (*1-55989-546-2*) Underwrtrs Labs.

Standard for Safety for Police Station Connected Burglar Alarm Units & Systems, UL 365. 3rd ed. (C). 1993. pap. text ed. 95.00 (*1-55989-409-1*) Underwrtrs Labs.

Standard for Safety for Polymeric Materials - Fabricated Parts, UL 746D. 5th ed. 1993. pap. 95.00 (*1-55989-417-2*) Underwrtrs Labs.

Standard for Safety for Polymeric Materials - Industrial Laminaets, Filament Wound Tubing, Vulcanized Fibre, & Materials Used in Printed Wiring Boards, UL 746E. 2nd ed. (C). 1994. pap. text ed. 95.00 (*1-55989-500-4*) Underwrtrs Labs.

Standard for Safety for Polymeric Materials - Short Term Property Evaluations, UL 746A. 4th ed. (C). 1995. pap. text ed. 95.00 (*1-55989-113-0*) Underwrtrs Labs.

Standard for Safety for Polymeric Materials--Use in Electrical Equipment Evaluations, UL 746C. 4th ed. (C). 1995. pap. text ed. 95.00 (*1-55989-018-5*) Underwrtrs Labs.

Standard for Safety for Polymeric Materials-Coil Forms, UL 1692. (C). 1994. pap. text ed. 95.00 (*1-55989-599-3*) Underwrtrs Labs.

Standard for Safety for Polyvinyl Chloride, Polyethelene, & Rubber Insulating Tape, UL 510. 7th ed. (C). 1994. pap. text ed. 95.00 (*1-55989-623-X*) Underwrtrs Labs.

Standard for Safety for Porcelain Cleats, Knobs, & Tubes, UL 511. 6th ed. (C). 1994. pap. text ed. 95.00 (*1-55989-745-7*) Underwrtrs Labs.

Standard for Safety for Portable Electric Hand Lamps, UL 298. 3rd ed. (C). 1991. pap. text ed. 95.00 (*1-55989-232-3*) Underwrtrs Labs.

Standard for Safety for Portable Electric Lamps, UL 153. 11th ed. (C). 1995. pap. text ed. 95.00 (*1-55989-562-4*) Underwrtrs Labs.

Standard for Safety for Portable Electric Lighting Units for Use in Hazardous (Classified) Locations, UL 781. 6th ed. (C). 1993. pap. text ed. 215.00 (*1-55989-297-8*) Underwrtrs Labs.

Standard for Safety for Portable Electric Tools, UL 45. 7th ed. (C). 1991. pap. text ed. 330.00 (*1-55989-185-8*) Underwrtrs Labs.

Standard for Safety for Portable Metal Ladders, UL 184. 5th ed. 1993. pap. 95.00 (*1-55989-316-8*) Underwrtrs Labs.

Standard for Safety for Portable Spray Hose Nozzles for Fire-Protection Service, UL 401. 3rd ed. (C). 1993. pap. text ed. 290.00 (*1-55989-428-8*) Underwrtrs Labs.

Standard for Safety for Portable Sun-Heat Lamps, UL 482. 7th ed. (C). 1994. pap. text ed. 95.00 (*1-55989-616-7*) Underwrtrs Labs.

Standard for Safety for Portable Wood Ladders, UL 112. 7th ed. 1993. pap. 135.00 (*1-55989-312-5*) Underwrtrs Labs.

Standard for Safety for Power Conversion Equipment, UL 508C. (C). 1993. pap. text ed. 95.00 (*1-55989-517-9*) Underwrtrs Labs.

Standard for Safety for Power Converters/Inverters & Power Converter/Inverter Systems for Land Vehicles & Marine Crafts. 4th ed. (C). 1993. pap. text ed. 330.00 (*1-55989-212-9*) Underwrtrs Labs.

Standard for Safety for Power-Limited Circuit Cables, UL 13. 2nd ed. (C). 1996. pap. text ed. 215.00 (*1-55989-134-3*) Underwrtrs Labs.

Standard for Safety for Power-Operated Dispensing Devices for LP-Gas, UL 495. 2nd ed. (C). 1994. pap. text ed. 230.00 (*1-55989-679-5*) Underwrtrs Labs.

Standard for Safety for Power-Operated Dispensing Devices for Petroleum Products, UL 87. 10th ed. (C). 1995. pap. text ed. 95.00 (*1-55989-128-9*) Underwrtrs Labs.

Standard for Safety for Power-Operated Pumps for Petroleum Dispensing Products, UL 79. 7th ed. (C). 1992. pap. text ed. 135.00 (*1-55989-290-0*) Underwrtrs Labs.

Standard for Safety for Power-Operated Pumps for Anhydrous Ammonia & LP-Gas, UL 51. 8th ed. (C). 1995. pap. text ed. 230.00 (*1-55989-287-0*) Underwrtrs Labs.

Standard for Safety for Power Outlets, UL 231. 7th ed. (C). 1994. pap. text ed. 290.00 (*1-55989-591-8*) Underwrtrs Labs.

Standard for Safety for Power Supplies for Fire Protective Signaling Systems, UL 1481. 3rd ed. (C). 1994. pap. text ed. 95.00 (*1-55989-554-3*) Underwrtrs Labs.

Standard for Safety for Power Supplies for Use with Burglar-Alarm Systems, UL 603. 3rd ed. (C). 1993. pap. text ed. 290.00 (*1-55989-377-X*) Underwrtrs Labs.

Standard for Safety for Power Units Other Than Class 2, UL 1012. 6th ed. (C). 1994. pap. text ed. 175.00 (*1-55989-587-X*) Underwrtrs Labs.

Standard for Safety for Power Ventilators, UL 705. 5th ed. (C). 1994. pap. text ed. 175.00 (*1-55989-574-8*) Underwrtrs Labs.

Standard for Safety for Pressure Cookers, UL 136. 6th ed. (C). 1995. pap. text ed. 175.00 (*1-55989-136-X*) Underwrtrs Labs.

Standard for Safety for Pressure Pipe & Couplings, Glass Fiber-Reinforced, for Underground Fire Service, UL 1713. 2nd ed. (C). 1995. pap. text ed. 95.00 (*1-55989-802-X*) Underwrtrs Labs.

Standard for Safety for Pressure Regulating Valves for LP-Gas, UL 144. 6th ed. (C). 1994. pap. text ed. 135.00 (*1-55989-597-7*) Underwrtrs Labs.

Standard for Safety for Primary Safety Controls, UL 372. 5th ed. (C). 1994. pap. text ed. 330.00 (*1-55989-524-1*) Underwrtrs Labs.

Standard for Safety for Printed-Wiring Boards, UL 796. 7th ed. (C). 1993. pap. text ed. 95.00 (*1-55989-440-7*) Underwrtrs Labs.

Standard for Safety for Professional Video & Audio Equipment, UL 1419. (C). 1992. pap. text ed. 135.00 (*1-55989-262-5*) Underwrtrs Labs.

Standard for Safety for Protectors for Data Communication & Fire Alarm Circuits, UL497B. 2nd ed. (C). 1993. pap. text ed. 95.00 (*1-55989-512-8*) Underwrtrs Labs.

Standard for Safety for Protectors for Paired Conductor Communication Circuits, UL 497. 6th ed. (C). 1995. pap. text ed. 95.00 (*1-55989-158-0*) Underwrtrs Labs.

Standard for Safety for Pullout Switches, UL 1429. 3rd ed. (C). 1994. pap. text ed. 135.00 (*1-55989-695-7*) Underwrtrs Labs.

Standard for Safety for Pumps for Fire-Protection Service, UL 448. 8th ed. (C). 1994. pap. text ed. 135.00 (*1-55989-636-1*) Underwrtrs Labs.

Standard for Safety for Pumps for Oil-Burning Appliances, UL 343. 7th ed. 1993. pap. 195.00 (*1-55989-300-1*) Underwrtrs Labs.

Standard for Safety for Quick Opening Devices for Dry Pipe Valves for Fire Protection Service, UL 1486. 2nd ed. (C). 1993. pap. text ed. 135.00 (*1-55989-442-3*) Underwrtrs Labs.

Standard for Safety for Rapid Rise Fire Tests of Protection Materials for Structural Steel, UL 1709. 2nd ed. (C). 1994. pap. text ed. 330.00 (*1-55989-557-8*) Underwrtrs Labs.

Standard for Safety for Receptacle-Plug Combinations for Use in Hazardous (Classified) Locations, UL 1010. 6th ed. (C). 1995. pap. text ed. 290.00 (*1-55989-179-3*) Underwrtrs Labs.

Standard for Safety for Receptacles & Switches Intended for Use with Aluminum Wire, UL 1567. 2nd ed. (C). 1993. pap. text ed. 95.00 (*1-55989-454-7*) Underwrtrs Labs.

Standard for Safety for Reference Standard for Double Insulation Systems for Use in Electronic Equipment, UL 2097. 2nd ed. (C). 1994. pap. text ed. 135.00 (*1-55989-590-X*) Underwrtrs Labs.

Standard for Safety for Refrigerant-Containing Components & Accessories, Nonelectrical, UL 207. 6th ed. (C). 1993. pap. text ed. 95.00 (*1-55989-346-X*) Underwrtrs Labs.

Standard for Safety for Refrigerant Recovery-Recycling Equipment, UL 1963. 2nd ed. (C). 1995. pap. text ed. 330.00 (*1-55989-054-1*) Underwrtrs Labs.

Standard for Safety for Refrigerated Medical Equipment, UL 416. 4th ed. (C). 1993. pap. text ed. 175.00 (*1-55989-466-0*) Underwrtrs Labs.

Standard for Safety for Refrigerating Units, UL 427. 2nd ed. (C). 1989. pap. text ed. 95.00 (*1-55989-055-X*) Underwrtrs Labs.

Standard for Safety for Refrigerating Units, UL 427. 3rd ed. (C). 1994. pap. text ed. 95.00 (*1-55989-691-4*) Underwrtrs Labs.

Standard for Safety for Refrigeration Unit Coolers, UL 412. 3rd ed. (C). 1993. pap. text ed. 135.00 (*1-55989-482-2*) Underwrtrs Labs.

Standard for Safety for Reinforced Thermosetting Resin Conduit, UL 1684. (C). 1993. pap. text ed. 135.00 (*1-55989-471-7*) Underwrtrs Labs.

Standard for Safety for Relocking Devices for Safes & Vaults, UL 140. 9th ed. 1993. pap. 95.00 (*1-55989-311-7*) Underwrtrs Labs.

Standard for Safety for Repackaged Products, UL 1442. (C). 1994. pap. text ed. 95.00 (*1-55989-601-9*) Underwrtrs Labs.

Standard for Safety for Residential Gas Detectors, UL 1484. 3rd ed. (C). 1994. pap. text ed. 330.00 (*1-55989-680-9*) Underwrtrs Labs.

Standard for Safety for Residential Incinerators, UL 791. 4th ed. (C). 1993. pap. text ed. 95.00 (*1-55989-419-9*) Underwrtrs Labs.

Standard for Safety for Residential Sprinklers for Fire-Protection Service, UL 1626. 2nd ed. (C). 1994. pap. text ed. 330.00 (*1-55989-648-5*) Underwrtrs Labs.

Standard for Safety for Rigid Metal Conduit, UL 6. 10th ed. (C). 1993. pap. text ed. 330.00 (*1-55989-394-X*) Underwrtrs Labs.

Standard for Safety for Roof Jacks for Manufactured Homes & Recreational Vehicles, UL 311. 8th ed. (C). 1994. pap. text ed. 290.00 (*1-55989-551-9*) Underwrtrs Labs.

Standard for Safety for Roof Trusses for Manufactured Homes, UL 1298. 4th ed. (C). 1995. pap. text ed. 95.00 (*1-55989-811-9*) Underwrtrs Labs.

Standard for Safety for Room Air Conditioners, UL 484. 7th ed. 1993. pap. 135.00 (*1-55989-302-8*) Underwrtrs Labs.

Standard for Safety for Room Air Conditioners UL 484. 7th ed. (C). 1993. pap. text ed. 95.00 (*1-55989-975-1*) Underwrtrs Labs.

Standard for Safety for Room Heaters, Solid-Fuel Type, UL 1482. 5th ed. (C). 1996. pap. text ed. 175.00 (*1-55989-681-7*) Underwrtrs Labs.

Standard for Safety for Rosettes, UL 351. 7th ed. (C). 1995. pap. text ed. 330.00 (*1-55989-797-X*) Underwrtrs Labs.

Standard for Safety for Rubber Gasketed Fittings for Fire Protection Service, UL 213. 2nd ed. (C). 1993. pap. text ed. 290.00 (*1-55989-329-X*) Underwrtrs Labs.

Standard for Safety for Rubber-Insulated Wires & Cables, UL 44. 13th ed. (C). 1991. pap. text ed. 95.00 (*1-55989-214-5*) Underwrtrs Labs.

Standard for Safety for Safety-Related Software, UL 1998. (C). 1994. pap. text ed. 95.00 (*1-55989-550-0*) Underwrtrs Labs.

Standard for Safety for Safety-Related Solid-State Controls for Household Electric Ranges, UL 858A. 2nd ed. (C). 1995. pap. text ed. 330.00 (*1-55989-658-2*) Underwrtrs Labs.

Standard for Safety for Safety Relief Valves for Anhydrous Ammonia & LP-Gas, UL 132. 5th ed. 1993. pap. 95.00 (*1-55989-309-5*) Underwrtrs Labs.

Standard for Safety for Scaffold Hoists, UL 1323. 2nd ed. (C). 1995. pap. text ed. 330.00 (*1-55989-456-3*) Underwrtrs Labs.

Standard for Safety for Schedule 40 & 80 Rigid PVC Conduit, UL 651. 6th ed. (C). 1995. pap. text ed. 95.00 (*1-55989-015-0*) Underwrtrs Labs.

Standard for Safety for Self-Ballasted Lamps & Lamp Adapters, UL 1993. (C). 1993. pap. text ed. 135.00 (*1-55989-486-5*) Underwrtrs Labs.

Standard for Safety for Semiautomatic Fire Hose Storage Devices, UL 47. 5th ed. (C). 1993. pap. text ed. 330.00 (*1-55989-441-5*) Underwrtrs Labs.

Standard for Safety for Septic Tanks, Bituminous Coated Metal, UL 70. 6th ed. (C). 1993. pap. text ed. 95.00 (*1-55989-340-0*) Underwrtrs Labs.

Standard for Safety for Service-Entrance Cables, UL 854. 8th ed. (C). 1996. pap. text ed. 95.00 (*1-55989-190-4*) Underwrtrs Labs.

Standard for Safety for Service Equipment, UL 869A. 2nd ed. (C). 1993. pap. text ed. 95.00 (*1-55989-412-1*) Underwrtrs Labs.

Standard for Safety for Sewage Pumps for Use in Hazardous (Classified) Locations, UL 1207. 2nd ed. (C). 1994. pap. text ed. 95.00 (*1-55989-642-6*) Underwrtrs Labs.

Standard for Safety for Sewing & Cutting Machines, UL 1594. 2nd ed. (C). 1995. pap. text ed. 330.00 (*1-55989-749-X*) Underwrtrs Labs.

Standard for Safety for Shear Resistance Tests for Ceiling Boards for Manufactured Homes, UL 1296. 5th ed. (C). 1996. pap. text ed. 95.00 (*1-55989-286-2*) Underwrtrs Labs.

Standard for Safety for Sheathed Heating Elements, UL 1030. 6th ed. (C). 1994. pap. text ed. 95.00 (*1-55989-686-8*) Underwrtrs Labs.

Standard for Safety for Signaling Devices for the Hearing Impaired, UL 1971. 2nd ed. (C). 1995. pap. text ed. 135.00 (*1-55989-268-4*) Underwrtrs Labs.

Standard for Safety for Single & Multiple Station Smoke Detectors, UL 217. 4th ed. 1993. pap. 135.00 (*1-55989-402-4*) Underwrtrs Labs.

Standard for Safety for Sliding Hardware for Standard, Horizontally Mounted Tin-Clad Fire Doors, UL 14B. 7th ed. (C). 1993. pap. text ed. 95.00 (*1-55989-502-0*) Underwrtrs Labs.

Standard for Safety for Slip Resistance of Floor Surface Materials, UL 410. 2nd ed. (C). 1996. pap. text ed. 135.00 (*1-55989-277-3*) Underwrtrs Labs.

Standard for Safety for Smoke Detector Monitors & Accessories for Individual Living Units of Multifamily Residences & Hotel-Motel Rooms, UL 1730. 2nd ed. (C). 1994. pap. text ed. 290.00 (*1-55989-654-X*) Underwrtrs Labs.

Standard for Safety for Smoke Detectors for Duct Application, UL 268A. 2nd ed. (C). 1993. pap. text ed. 175.00 (*1-55989-378-8*) Underwrtrs Labs.

Standard for Safety for Smoke Detectors for Fire Protective Signaling Systems, UL 268. 3rd ed. (C). 1989. pap. text ed. 95.00 (*1-55989-010-X*) Underwrtrs Labs.

Standard for Safety for Solid-Fuel & Combination-Fuel Central & Supplementary Furnaces, UL 391. 3rd ed. (C). 1995. pap. text ed. 135.00 (*1-55989-801-1*) Underwrtrs Labs.

Standard for Safety for Solid-State Controls for Appliances, UL 244A. 2nd ed. (C). 1994. pap. text ed. 95.00 (*1-55989-444-X*) Underwrtrs Labs.

Standard for Safety for Solid-State Fan Speed Controls, UL 1917. 2nd ed. (C). 1994. pap. text ed. 175.00 (*1-55989-511-X*) Underwrtrs Labs.

Standard for Safety for Solidified Fuel Cooking Appliances for Marine Use, UL 1101. (C). 1989. pap. text ed. 135.00 (*1-55989-041-X*) Underwrtrs Labs.

Standard for Safety for Speakers for Fire Protective Signaling Systems, UL 1480. 3rd ed. (C). 1994. pap. text ed. 95.00 (*1-55989-488-1*) Underwrtrs Labs.

Standard for Safety for Special Fuses for Radio- & Television-Type Appliances, UL 1417. 5th ed. (C). 1994. pap. text ed. 95.00 (*1-55989-659-0*) Underwrtrs Labs.

Standard for Safety for Special-Purpose Containers, UL 1314. 3rd ed. (C). 1995. pap. text ed. 230.00 (*1-55989-006-1*) Underwrtrs Labs.

Standard for Safety for Special-Use Switches, UL 1054. 5th ed. (C). 1995. pap. text ed. 95.00 (*1-55989-153-X*) Underwrtrs Labs.

Standard for Safety for Specialty Transformers, UL 506. 11th ed. (C). 1994. pap. text ed. 95.00 (*1-55989-617-5*) Underwrtrs Labs.

Standard for Safety for Splicing Wire Connectors, UL 486C. 2nd ed. (C). 1991. pap. text ed. 95.00 (*1-55989-216-1*) Underwrtrs Labs.

Standard for Safety for Stage & Studio Lighting Units, UL 1573. 3rd ed. (C). 1996. pap. text ed. 95.00 (*1-55989-555-1*) Underwrtrs Labs.

Standard for Safety for Standby Batteries, UL 1989. (C). 1992. pap. text ed. 135.00 (*1-55989-288-9*) Underwrtrs Labs.

Standard for Safety for Stationary & Fixed Electric Tools, UL 987. 6th ed. (C). 1994. pap. text ed. 330.00 (*1-55989-635-3*) Underwrtrs Labs.

Standard for Safety for Steel Aboveground Tanks for Flammable & Combustible Liquids, UL 142. 7th ed. (C). 1993. pap. text ed. 195.00 (*1-55989-385-0*) Underwrtrs Labs.

Standard for Safety for Steel Auxiliary Tanks for Oil-Burner Fuel, UL 443. 5th ed. (C). 1995. pap. text ed. 330.00 (*1-55989-094-0*) Underwrtrs Labs.

Standard for Safety for Strainers for Flammable Fluids & Anhydrous Ammonia, UL 331. 6th ed. (C). 1993. pap. text ed. 95.00 (*1-55989-221-8*) Underwrtrs Labs.

Standard for Safety for Strength of Body & Hydraulic Pressure Loss Testing of Backflow Special Check Valves, UL 1469. (C). 1995. pap. text ed. 95.00 (*1-55989-846-1*) Underwrtrs Labs.

Standard for Safety for Supplementary Protectors for Use in Electrical Equipment, UL 1077. 4th ed. (C). 1994. pap. text ed. 95.00 (*1-55989-613-2*) Underwrtrs Labs.

Standard for Safety for Surveillance Camera Units UL 983. 5th ed. (C). 1993. pap. text ed. 95.00 (*1-55989-413-X*) Underwrtrs Labs.

Standard for Safety for Surveillance Closed Circuit Television Equipment, UL 3044. (C). 1994. pap. text ed. 135.00 (*1-55989-699-X*) Underwrtrs Labs.

Standard for Safety for Swimming Pool Pumps, Filters, & Chlorinators, UL 1081. 4th ed. (C). 1993. pap. text ed. 330.00 (*1-55989-477-6*) Underwrtrs Labs.

Standard for Safety for Swinging Hardware for Standard Tin-Clad Fire Doors Mounted Singly & in Pairs, UL 14C. 6th ed. (C). 1993. pap. text ed. 95.00 (*1-55989-509-8*) Underwrtrs Labs.

Standard for Safety for Switches for Use in Hazardous (Classified) Locations, UL 894. 7th ed. (C). 1993. pap. text ed. 135.00 (*1-55989-285-4*) Underwrtrs Labs.

Standard for Safety for Systems of Insulating Materials-General, UL 1446. 4th ed. (C). 1994. pap. text ed. 95.00 (*1-55989-703-1*) Underwrtrs Labs.

Standard for Safety for Tall Institutional Carts for Use with Audio-, Video-, & Television-Type Equipment, UL 1667. 3rd ed. (C). 1996. pap. text ed. 95.00 (*1-55989-038-X*) Underwrtrs Labs.

Standard for Safety for Temperature-Indicating & -Regulating Equipment, UL 873. 11th ed. (C). 1994. pap. text ed. 330.00 (*1-55989-682-5*) Underwrtrs Labs.

Standard for Safety for Temporary Lighting Strings, UL 1088. 4th ed. (C). 1995. pap. text ed. 95.00 (*1-55989-831-3*) Underwrtrs Labs.

Standard for Safety for Temporary Power Taps, UL 1363. (C). 1991. pap. text ed. 330.00 (*1-55989-194-7*) Underwrtrs Labs.

Standard for Safety for Terminal Blocks, UL 1059. 3rd ed. (C). 1993. pap. text ed. 175.00 (*1-55989-372-9*) Underwrtrs Labs.

Standard for Safety for Termination Boxes, UL 1773. 2nd ed. (C). 1993. pap. text ed. 230.00 (*1-55989-406-7*) Underwrtrs Labs.

Standard for Safety for Test for Flame-Propagation & Smoke-Density Values for Electrical & Optical-Fiber Cables Used in Spaces Transporting Environmental Air, UL 910. 4th ed. (C). 1995. pap. text ed. 95.00 (*1-55989-798-8*) Underwrtrs Labs.

Standard for Safety for Test for Flame Propagation Height of Electrical & Optical-Fiber Cables Installed Vertically in Shafts, UL 1666. 2nd ed. (C). 1991. pap. text ed. 95.00 (*1-55989-147-5*) Underwrtrs Labs.

Standard for Safety for Test for Sharpness of Edges on Equipment, UL 1439. 3rd ed. (C). 1993. pap. text ed. 95.00 (*1-55989-374-5*) Underwrtrs Labs.

Standard for Safety for Test for Surface Burning Characteristics of Building Materials, UL 723. 8th ed. (C). 1996. pap. text ed. 95.00 (*1-55989-333-8*) Underwrtrs Labs.

Standard for Safety for Tests for Comparative Flammability of Liquids, UL 340. 3rd ed. (C). 1993. pap. text ed. 95.00 (*1-55989-338-9*) Underwrtrs Labs.

Standard for Safety for Tests for Fire Resistance of Building Joint Systems, UL 2079. (C). 1994. pap. text ed. 135.00 (*1-55989-689-2*) Underwrtrs Labs.

Standard for Safety for Tests for Fire Resistance of Record Protection Equipment, UL 72. 14th ed. (C). 1995. pap. text ed. 95.00 (*1-55989-154-8*) Underwrtrs Labs.

Standard for Safety for Tests for Fire Resistance of Vault & File Room Doors, UL 155. 7th ed. (C). 1995. pap. text ed. 95.00 (*1-55989-068-1*) Underwrtrs Labs.

Standard for Safety for Tests for Flame-Propagation of Fabrics & Films, UL 214. 5th ed. (C). 1993. pap. text ed. 95.00 (*1-55989-330-3*) Underwrtrs Labs.

Standard for Safety for Tests for Flammability of Plastic Materials for Parts in Devices & Appliances, UL 94. 5th ed. (C). 1996. pap. text ed. 95.00 (*1-55989-150-5*) Underwrtrs Labs.

Standard for Safety for Tests for Uplift Resistance of Roof Assemblies, UL 580. 4th ed. (C). 1994. pap. text ed. 95.00 (*1-55989-620-5*) Underwrtrs Labs.

Standard for Safety for Thermal Cutoffs in Electrical Appliances & Components, UL 1020. 5th ed. (C). 1994. pap. text ed. 95.00 (*1-55989-638-8*) Underwrtrs Labs.

Standard for Safety for Thermal Protectors for Motors, UL 547. 7th ed. (C). 1991. pap. text ed. 175.00 (*1-55989-237-4*) Underwrtrs Labs.

Standard for Safety for Thermoplastic-Insulated Wires & Cables, UL 83. 11th ed. (C). 1996. pap. text ed. 135.00 (*1-55989-217-X*) Underwrtrs Labs.

Standard for Safety for Thermoplastic Sprinkler Pipe & Fittings for Fire Protection Service, UL 1821. (C). 1994. pap. text ed. 95.00 (*1-55989-693-0*) Underwrtrs Labs.

Standard for Safety for Time-Indicating & -Recording Appliances, UL 863. 6th ed. (C). 1993. pap. text ed. 135.00 (*1-55989-387-7*) Underwrtrs Labs.

Standard for Safety for Tin-Clad Fire Doors, UL 10A. 19th ed. 1993. pap. 290.00 (*1-55989-306-0*) Underwrtrs Labs.

An Asterisk (*) at the beginning of an entry indicates that the title is appearing in BIP for the first time.

Standard for Safety for Toy Transformers, UL 697. 4th ed. (C). 1993. pap. 95.00 (*1-55989-410-5*) Underwrtrs Labs.

Standard for Safety for Transformer-Type Arc-Welding Machines, UL 551. 7th ed. (C). 1994. pap. text ed. 135.00 (*1-55989-503-9*) Underwrtrs Labs.

Standard for Safety for Transformers & Motor Transformers for Use in Audio-, Radio, & Television-Types Appliances, UL 1411. 4th ed. 1993. pap. 95.00 (*1-55989-382-6*) Underwrtrs Labs.

Standard for Safety for Transformers, Distribution, Dry-Type - over 600 Volts, UL 1562. 2nd ed. (C). 1994. pap. text ed. 330.00 (*1-55989-552-7*) Underwrtrs Labs.

Standard for Safety for Tube Fittings for Flammable & Combustible Fluids, Refrigeration Service, & Marine Use, UL 109. 5th ed. 1993. pap. 95.00 (*1-55989-307-9*) Underwrtrs Labs.

Standard for Safety for Two & One-Half Gallon Stored-Pressure Water-Type Fire Extinguishers, UL 626. 7th ed. (C). 1995. pap. text ed. 95.00 (*1-55989-108-4*) Underwrtrs Labs.

Standard for Safety for Type EB & A Rigid PVC Conduit & HDPE Conduit, UL 651A. 3rd ed. (C). 1995. pap. text ed. 95.00 (*1-55989-016-9*) Underwrtrs Labs.

Standard for Safety for Underfloor Raceways & Fittings, UL 884. 9th ed. (C). 1994. pap. text ed. 95.00 (*1-55989-632-9*) Underwrtrs Labs.

Standard for Safety for Underwater Lighting Fixtures, UL 676. 6th ed. (C). 1993. pap. text ed. 135.00 (*1-55989-476-8*) Underwrtrs Labs.

Standard for Safety for Uninterruptible Power Supply Equipment, UL 1778. 2nd ed. (C). 1994. pap. text ed. 330.00 (*1-55989-674-4*) Underwrtrs Labs.

Standard for Safety for Unit Substations, UL 1062. 2nd ed. 1993. pap. 330.00 (*1-55989-404-0*) Underwrtrs Labs.

Standard for Safety for Unvented Kerosene-Fired Room Heaters & Portable Heaters, UL 647. 2nd ed. 1993. pap. 330.00 (*1-55989-395-8*) Underwrtrs Labs.

Standard for Safety for Uplift Tests for Roof Covering Systems, UL 1897. 3rd ed. (C). 1995. pap. text ed. 135.00 (*1-55989-397-4*) Underwrtrs Labs.

Standard for Safety for Vacuum Cleaners, Blower Cleaners, & Household Floor Finishing Machines, UL 1017. 5th ed. (C). 1996. pap. text ed. 135.00 (*1-55989-191-2*) Underwrtrs Labs.

Standard for Safety for Valves for Anhydrous Ammonia & LP-Gas (Other Than Safety Relief), UL 125. 5th ed. (C). 1993. pap. text ed. 95.00 (*1-55989-389-3*) Underwrtrs Labs.

Standard for Safety for Valves for Flammable Fluids, UL 842. 7th ed. (C). 1993. pap. text ed. 95.00 (*1-55989-294-3*) Underwrtrs Labs.

Standard for Safety for Vehicle Battery Adapters, UL 2089. (C). 1994. pap. text ed. 95.00 (*1-55989-595-0*) Underwrtrs Labs.

Standard for Safety for Vending Machines, UL 751. 6th ed. (C). 1995. pap. text ed. 95.00 (*1-55989-060-6*) Underwrtrs Labs.

Standard for Safety for Vent or Chimney Connector Dampers for Oil-Fired Appliances, UL 17. 3rd ed. (C). 1994. pap. text ed. 95.00 (*1-55989-586-1*) Underwrtrs Labs.

Standard for Safety for Venting Systems for Gas-Burning Appliances, Categories II, III, & IV, UL 1738. 2nd ed. (C). 1993. pap. text ed. 95.00 (*1-55989-499-7*) Underwrtrs Labs.

Standard for Safety for Vertical-Tray Fire-Propagation & Smoke-Release Test for Electrical & Optical-Fiber Cables, UL 1685. (C). 1992. pap. text ed. 330.00 (*1-55989-215-3*) Underwrtrs Labs.

Standard for Safety for Visual Signaling Appliances, UL 1638. 3rd ed. (C). 1995. pap. text ed. 95.00 (*1-55989-117-3*) Underwrtrs Labs.

Standard for Safety for Waste Disposers, UL 430. 5th ed. (C). 1994. pap. text ed. 330.00 (*1-55989-657-4*) Underwrtrs Labs.

Standard for Safety for Waste-Oil Burning Air-Heating Appliances, UL 296A. 2nd ed. (C). 1995. pap. text ed. 330.00 (*1-55989-133-5*) Underwrtrs Labs.

Standard for Safety for Waterflow Indicators for Fire Protective Signaling Systems, UL 346. 4th ed. (C). 1994. pap. text ed. 95.00 (*1-55989-560-8*) Underwrtrs Labs.

Standard for Safety for Wind Resistance of Prepared Roof Covering Materials, UL 997. 5th ed. 1995. pap. 135.00 (*1-55989-304-4*) Underwrtrs Labs.

Standard for Safety for Wire Connectors & Soldering Lugs for Use with Copper Conductors, UL 486A. 8th ed. 1991. pap. 135.00 (*1-55989-195-5*) Underwrtrs Labs.

Standard for Safety for Wire Connectors for Use with Aluminum Conductors, UL 486B. 3rd ed. (C). 1991. pap. text ed. 95.00 (*1-55989-209-9*) Underwrtrs Labs.

Standard for Safety for Wire Positioning Devices, UL 1565. 2nd ed. (C). 1994. pap. text ed. 95.00 (*1-55989-675-2*) Underwrtrs Labs.

Standard for Safety for Wired Cabinets, UL 65. 5th ed. (C). 1993. pap. text ed. 95.00 (*1-55989-384-2*) Underwrtrs Labs.

Standard for Safety for Wireways, Auxiliary Gutters, & Associated Fittings, UL 870. 7th ed. (C). 1995. pap. text ed. 95.00 (*1-55989-145-9*) Underwrtrs Labs.

Standard for Safety for Wiring Device Configurations, UL 1681. 2nd ed. (C). 1996. pap. text ed. 175.00 (*1-55989-186-6*) Underwrtrs Labs.

Standard for Safety for X-Ray Equipment, UL 187. 6th ed. (C). 1993. pap. text ed. 215.00 (*1-55989-401-6*) Underwrtrs Labs.

Standard for Safety of Information Technology Equipment, Including Electrical Business Equipment: UL 1950. 3rd ed. (C). 1995. pap. text ed. 195.00 (*1-55989-881-X*) Underwrtrs Labs.

Standard for Scaffold Hoists, UL 1323. 2nd ed. (C). 1995. pap. text ed. 330.00 (*1-55989-826-7*) Underwrtrs Labs.

Standard for Secondary Protectors for Communications Circuits. 2nd ed. (C). 1996. pap. text ed. 95.00 (*1-55989-067-3*, UL 497A) Underwrtrs Labs.

*__Standard for Service-Entrance Cables UL 854.__ 9th ed. (C). 1996. pap. text ed. 95.00 (*0-7629-0040-7*) Underwrtrs Labs.

Standard for Shaft Mounted & Screw Conveyor Drives Using Spur, Helical & Herringbone Gears. 5th ed. (ANSI - AGMA Ser.: No. 6021-E89). (Illus.). 93p. 1989. pap. text ed. 90.00 (*1-55589-531-X*) AGMA.

Standard for Signaling Devices for the Hearing Impaired, No. UL1971. 2nd ed. (C). 1995. pap. text ed. 135.00 (*1-55989-852-6*) Underwrtrs Labs.

*__Standard for Single & Multiple Station Carbon Monoxide Detectors: UL 2034.__ 2nd ed. (C). 1996. pap. text ed. 330.00 (*0-614-24603-2*) Underwrtrs Labs.

Standard for Single & Multiple Station Heat Detectors UL 539. 4th ed. (C). 1995. pap. text ed. 195.00 (*1-55989-824-0*) Underwrtrs Labs.

*__Standard for Single & Multiple Station Smoke Alarms.__ 5th ed. (C). 1997. pap. text ed. 108.00 (*0-7629-0062-8*, UL 217) Underwrtrs Labs.

Standard for Solid-Fuel Type Room Heaters. 5th ed. (C). 1996. pap. text ed. 175.00 (*1-55989-984-0*, UL 1482) Underwrtrs Labs.

Standard for Spur, Helical, Herringbone, & Bevel Enclosed Drives. 5th ed. (Illus.). 107p. 1988. pap. text ed. 110.00 (*1-55589-523-9*, 6010E88) AGMA.

*__Standard for Stage & Studio Lighting Units, UL1573.__ (C). 1996. pap. text ed. 95.00 (*0-7629-0077-6*) Underwrtrs Labs.

Standard for Steel Auxiliary Tanks for Oil-Burner Fuel UL 443. 5th ed. (C). 1995. pap. text ed. 330.00 (*1-55989-913-1*) Underwrtrs Labs.

*__Standard for Steel Tanks for Oil-Burner Fuel UL 80.__ 10th ed. (C). 1996. pap. text ed. 135.00 (*0-7629-0123-3*) Underwrtrs Labs.

*__Standard for Surface Metal Raceways & Fittings: UL 5.__ 12th ed. Underwriters Laboratories Editors. (C). 1996. pap. text ed. 230.00 (*1-55989-917-4*) Underwrtrs Labs.

Standard for Surface Metal Raceways & Fittings UL 5. 12th ed. (C). 1996. pap. text ed. 230.00 (*1-55989-843-7*) Underwrtrs Labs.

*__Standard for Swimming Pool Pumps, Filters, & Chlorinators: UL 1081.__ 5th ed. (C). 1997. pap. text ed. 264.00 (*0-7629-0140-3*) Underwrtrs Labs.

*__Standard for Systems of Insulating Materials - General UL 1446.__ 5th ed. (C). 1997. pap. text ed. 76.00 (*0-7629-0169-1*) Underwrtrs Labs.

*__Standard for Test for Flame Propagation Height of Electrical & Optical-Fiber Cables Installed Vertically in Shafts UL 1666.__ 3rd ed. (C). 1997. pap. text ed. 76.00 (*0-7629-0157-8*) Underwriters Labs Canada.

*__Standard for Test for Flammability of Plastic Materials for Parts in Devices & Appliances: UL 94.__ 5th ed. Underwriters Laboratories Editors. (C). 1996. pap. text ed. 95.00 (*0-7629-0082-2*) Underwrtrs Labs.

Standard for Tests for Fire Resistance of Record Protection Equipment U. L. 72. 14th ed. (C). 1995. pap. text ed. 95.00 (*1-55989-900-X*) Underwrtrs Labs.

Standard for Tests for Flammability of Small Polymeric Component Materials UL 1694. (C). 1995. pap. text ed. 95.00 (*1-55989-862-3*) Underwrtrs Labs.

Standard for the Exchange of Digital Information on CD-ROM. Ed. by Marcia Siedschlag. 105p. (Orig.). (YA). (gr. 12 up). 1994. pap. text ed. 35.00 (*0-7881-0785-2*) DIANE Pub.

Standard for the Installation of Centrifugal Fire Pumps. 61p. 22.25 (*0-686-68287-4*, 20-90) Natl Fire Prot.

Standard for the Manufacture of Aluminum or Magnesium Powder. (Sixty Ser.). 1993. pap. 16.75 (*0-685-58073-3*, 651-87) Natl Fire Prot.

Standard for the Structural Design of Composite Slabs. American Society of Civil Engineers Staff. LC 94-3855. (ASCE Standard Ser.). 1994. 44.00 (*0-87262-954-6*) Am Soc Civil Eng.

*__Standard for Thermoplastic-Insulated Wires & Cables: UL83.__ 11th ed. (C). 1996. pap. text ed. 135.00 (*0-7629-0081-4*) Underwrtrs Labs.

*__Standard for Thermoset-Insulated Wire & Cables: UL 44.__ 14th ed. (C). 1997. pap. text ed. 76.00 (*0-7629-0144-6*) Underwrtrs Labs.

Standard for Track Lighting Systems UL 1574. 2nd ed. (C). 1995. pap. text ed. 330.00 (*1-55989-864-X*) Underwrtrs Labs.

*__Standard for Transfer Switch Equipment UL 1008.__ 5th ed. (C). 1996. pap. text ed. 264.00 (*0-7629-0125-X*) Underwrtrs Labs.

*__Standard for Transient Voltage Surge Suppressors, UL 1449.__ (C). 1985. pap. text ed. 175.00 (*0-7629-0064-4*) Underwrtrs Labs.

*__Standard for Tube Fittings for Flammable & Combustible Fluids, Refrigeration Service, & Marine Use UL 109.__ 6th ed. (C). 1997. pap. text ed. 76.00 (*0-7629-0159-4*) Underwrtrs Labs.

Standard for Type E. B. & A. Rigid P. V. C. Conduit & H. D. P. E. Conduit U. L. 651A. 3rd ed. (C). 1995. pap. text ed. 95.00 (*1-55989-868-2*) Underwrtrs Labs.

Standard for Type L Low-Temperature Venting Systems. 7th ed. (C). 1995. pap. text ed. 95.00 (*1-55989-935-2*) Underwrtrs Labs.

*__Standard for Unit Substations UL 1062.__ 3rd ed. (C). 1997. pap. text ed. 264.00 (*0-7629-0089-X*) Underwrtrs Labs.

Standard for Uplift Tests for Roof Covering Systems UL 1897. 3rd ed. (C). 1995. pap. text ed. 135.00 (*1-55989-750-3*) Underwrtrs Labs.

*__Standard for Valves for Anhydrous Ammonia & LP-Gas (Other Than Safety Relief)__ 6th ed. (C). 1997. pap. text ed. 76.00 (*0-7629-0087-3*, UL 125) Underwrtrs Labs.

*__Standard for Valves for Flammable Fluids UL 842.__ 8th ed. (C). 1997. pap. text ed. 76.00 (*0-7629-0148-9*) Underwrtrs Labs.

*__Standard for Vertical-Tray Fire-Propagation & Smoke-Release Test for Electrical & Optical-Fiber Cables UL 1685.__ 2nd ed. (C). 1997. pap. text ed. 264.00 (*0-7629-0156-X*) Underwriters Labs Canada.

Standard for Visual Signaling Appliances - Private Mode Emergency & General Utility Signaling UL 1638. 3rd ed. (C). 1995. pap. text ed. 95.00 (*1-55989-806-2*) Underwrtrs Labs.

Standard for Waste Oil-Burning Air-Heating Appliances UL 296A. 2nd ed. (C). 1995. pap. text ed. 330.00 (*1-55989-859-3*) Underwrtrs Labs.

Standard for Welding Procedure & Performance Qualification (B2.1-84) (Illus.). 132p. 1984. pap. 66.00 (*0-87171-235-0*) Am Welding.

Standard for Wind Resistance of Prepared Roof Covering Materials UL 997. 5th ed. (C). 1995. pap. text ed. 135.00 (*1-55989-844-5*) Underwrtrs Labs.

*__Standard for Wire Positioning Devices UL 1565.__ 3rd ed. (C). 1997. pap. text ed. 76.00 (*0-7629-0181-0*) Underwrtrs Labs.

*__Standard for Wired Cabinets: UL65.__ 6th ed. (C). 1997. pap. text ed. 76.00 (*0-7629-0117-9*) Underwrtrs Labs.

Standard for Wiring Device Configurations: UL 1681. 2nd ed. (C). 1996. pap. text ed. 175.00 (*0-7629-0032-6*) Underwrtrs Labs.

Standard for 2 1-2-Gallon Stored-Pressure Water-Type Fire Extinguishers UL 626. 7th ed. (C). 1995. pap. text ed. 95.00 (*1-55989-841-0*) Underwrtrs Labs.

Standard Form of Contract: Consultants' Services: Complex Time-Based Assignments. 62p. 1995. 7.95 (*0-8213-3403-4*, 13403) World Bank.

Standard Form of Contract: Consultants' Services: Lump Sum Renumeration. 30p. 1995. 6.95 (*0-8213-3404-2*, 13404) World Bank.

Standard Format Test Bank for Mathematics Today Level 1. Abbott. 1987. suppl. ed., teacher ed., pap. 14.50 (*0-15-350121-9*) HB Schl Dept.

Standard Format Test Bank for Mathematics Today Level 2. Abbott. 1987. suppl. ed., teacher ed., pap. 14.50 (*0-15-350122-7*) HB Schl Dept.

Standard Format Test Bank for Mathematics Today Level 3. Abbott. 1987. suppl. ed., teacher ed., pap. 11.50 (*0-15-350123-5*) HB Schl Dept.

Standard Format Test Bank for Mathematics Today Level 4. Abbott. 1987. suppl. ed., teacher ed., pap. 11.50 (*0-15-350124-3*) HB Schl Dept.

Standard Format Test Bank for Mathematics Today Level 5. Abbott. 1987. suppl. ed., teacher ed., pap. 12.00 (*0-15-350125-1*) HB Schl Dept.

Standard Format Test Bank for Mathematics Today Level 6. Abbott. 1987. suppl. ed., teacher ed., pap. 12.00 (*0-15-350126-X*) HB Schl Dept.

Standard Format Test Bank for Mathematics Today Level 7. Abbott. 1987. suppl. ed., teacher ed., pap. 12.75 (*0-15-350127-8*) HB Schl Dept.

Standard Format Test Bank for Mathematics Today Level 8. Abbott. 1987. suppl. ed., teacher ed., pap. 12.75 (*0-15-350128-6*) HB Schl Dept.

Standard Freemasonry. (Illus.). pap. 13.00 (*0-685-19501-5*) Powner.

Standard Freemasonry. J. Blanchard. 15.95 (*0-685-22116-4*) Wehman.

Standard French Dictionary. 16.95 (*0-395-53770-3*); pap. 9.95 (*0-395-53771-1*) HM.

Standard German-Serbocroatian, Serbocroatian-German Dictionary: Standardni Recnik Nemacko-Srpskohrvatski-Nemacki. 838p. (GER & SER.). 1983. 19.95 (*0-8288-1048-6*, M14516) Fr & Eur.

Standard Glossary of Terms Relating to Chimneys, Vents, & Heat-Producing Appliances. National Fire Protection Association Staff. 1992. 16.75 (*0-317-63300-7*, 97-92) Natl Fire Prot.

Standard Guide for Describing Arc Welds in Computerized Material Property & Nondestructive Examination Databases (A9.1-92) 9p. 1992. pap. 24.00 (*0-87171-397-7*) Am Welding.

Standard Guide for Recording Arc Weld Material Property & Nondestructive Examination Data in Computerized Databases (A9.2-92) 9p. 1992. pap. 24.00 (*0-87171-398-5*) Am Welding.

Standard Guide to American Muscle Cars, 1949-1995. 2nd ed. Ron Kowalke. LC 92-74075. (Illus.). 300p. 1996. pap. 21.95 (*0-87341-429-2*, AM02) Krause Pubns.

Standard Guide to Automotive Restoration. Matt Joseph. LC 91-77562. (Illus.). 384p. 1992. pap. 24.95 (*0-87341-188-9*, AJ01) Krause Pubns.

Standard Guide to Cars & Prices 1996. James T. Lenzke & Ken Buttolph. LC 89-80091. (Illus.). 656p. 1995. pap. text ed. 15.95 (*0-87341-378-4*, CG08) Krause Pubns.

Standard Guide to Razors. Roy Ritchie. 1995. pap. 9.95 (*0-89145-658-9*) Collector Bks.

*__Standard Guide to Small Size U. S. Paper Money.__ Dean Oakes. 1997. pap. text ed. 24.95 (*0-87341-494-2*, HP04) Krause Pubns.

Standard Guide to the Jewish & Civil Calendars: A Parallel Jewish & Civil Calender from 1899-2050. Ed. by Frederick Reiss. 160p. 1986. pap. text ed. 14.95 (*0-87441-428-8*) Behrman.

Standard Guide to Workers Compensation. Ed. by Standard Publishing Corporation Staff. 160p. 1994. pap. 57.50 (*0-923240-09-8*) Stndrd Publishing.

*__Standard Guidelines for Air Supported Structures.__ American Society of Civil Engineers Staff. LC 97-13560. 1997. write for info. (*0-7844-0116-0*) Am Soc Civil Eng.

*__Standard Guidelines for In-Process Oxygen Transfer Testing.__ American Society of Civil Engineers Staff. LC 97-8344. 1997. write for info. (*0-7844-0114-4*) Am Soc Civil Eng.

*__Standard Guidelines for the Design & Installation of Pile Foundations.__ LC 96-30072. 1997. write for info. (*0-7844-0219-1*) Am Soc Civil Eng.

*__Standard Guidelines for the Structural Applications of Steel Cables for Buildings.__ LC 97-16275. 1997. write for info. (*0-7844-0245-0*) Am Soc Civil Eng.

Standard Guitar Method, Bk. 1. D. Bennett. (Easy Play Ser.). 48p. 1986. pap. 4.95 (*0-7935-2551-9*, 50393970) H Leonard.

Standard Guitar Method, Bk. 2. D. Bennett. (Easy Play Ser.). 48p. 1986. pap. 4.95 (*0-7935-2583-7*, 50393980) H Leonard.

Standard Guitar Method, Bk. 3. D. Bennett. (Easy Play Ser.). 48p. 1986. pap. 4.95 (*0-7935-5521-3*, 50393990) H Leonard.

Standard Guitar Method, Bk. 4. D. Bennett. (Easy Play Ser.). 48p. 1986. pap. 5.95 (*0-7935-5534-5*, 50394000) H Leonard.

Standard Guitar Method, Bk. 7. D. Bennett. (Easy Play Ser.). 40p. 1986. pap. 5.95 (*0-7935-5563-9*, 50394030) H Leonard.

Standard Guitar Method: Beacon, Bk. 5. D. Bennett. (Easy Play Ser.). 40p. 1986. pap. 5.95 (*0-7935-5549-3*, 50394010) H Leonard.

Standard Guitar Method: Beacon, Bk. 6. D. Bennett. (Easy Play Ser.). 40p. 1986. pap. 5.95 (*0-7935-5553-1*, 50394020) H Leonard.

Standard Guitar Theory Workbook Puzzles Exercises Theory. D. Bennett. (Easy Play Ser.). 32p. 1986. pap. 3.50 (*0-7935-5528-0*, 50394060) H Leonard.

Standard Haematology Practice 2. 2nd ed. J. K. Wood. (Illus.). 304p. 1994. 99.95 (*0-632-03739-3*, Pub. by Blckwell Sci Pubns UK) Blackwell Sci.

Standard Hair Coloring Workbook. (Illus.). 16p. 1991. teacher ed. write for info. (*1-56253-010-0*); pap. 16.95 (*1-56253-009-7*) Milady Pub.

Standard Haircutting Manual. Pylant. (Cosmetology Ser.). 1997. student ed. 17.95 (*1-56253-335-5*) Milady Pub.

Standard Handbook - Solid & Hazardous Waste Facility Assessment. Martin N. Sara. 976p. 1993. 89.95 (*0-87371-318-4*, L318) Lewis Pubs.

Standard Handbook for Civil Engineers. 4th ed. Ed. by Frederick S. Merritt et al. LC 95-11425. 1600p. 1995. text ed. 120.00 (*0-07-041597-8*) McGraw.

Standard Handbook for Electrical Engineers. 13th ed. Donald G. Fink. 2304p. 1993. text ed. 125.00 (*0-07-020984-7*) McGraw.

Standard Handbook of Consulting Engineering Practice. 2nd ed. Tyler G. Hicks & Jerome F. Mueller. (Illus.). 640p. 1996. text ed. 74.95 (*0-07-028782-1*) McGraw.

Standard Handbook of Engineering Calculations. 3rd ed. T. G. Hicks. 1500p. 1994. text ed. 110.00 (*0-07-028812-7*) McGraw.

Standard Handbook of Environmental Engineering. R. A. Corbitt. 1990. text ed. 110.00 (*0-07-013158-9*) McGraw.

Standard Handbook of Fastening & Joining. 3rd ed. Ed. by Robert O. Parmley. LC 96-27689. (Illus.). 992p. 1996. text ed. 99.95 (*0-07-048589-5*) McGraw.

Standard Handbook of Hazardous Waste Treatment & Disposal. Harry M. Freeman. 1136p. 1989. text ed. 115.00 (*0-07-022042-5*) McGraw.

*__Standard Handbook of Hazardous Waste Treatment & Disposal.__ 2nd expanded rev. ed. Ed. by Harry M. Freeman. LC 97-17300. (Illus.). 1300p. 1997. text ed. 125.00 (*0-07-022044-1*) McGraw.

Standard Handbook of Heavy Construction. 3rd ed. Ed. by James J. O'Brien et al. LC 95-45878. 1996. text ed. 115.00 (*0-07-047971-2*) McGraw.

Standard Handbook of Machine Design. 2nd ed. Joseph E. Shigley & Charles R. Mishchke. 1700p. 1996. text ed. 125.00 (*0-07-056958-4*) McGraw.

Standard Handbook of Petroleum & Natural Gas Engineering, Vol. 1. 6th ed. Ed. by William C. Lyons. LC 96-13965. 1440p. 1996. 275.00 (*0-88415-642-7*, 5642) Gulf Pub.

Standard Handbook of Petroleum & Natural Gas Engineering, Vol. 2. 6th ed. Ed. by W. Lyons. 1088p. 1996. 220.00 (*0-88415-643-5*, 5643) Gulf Pub.

Standard Handbook of Plant Engineering. 2nd ed. Robert C. Rosaler. 1994. text ed. 104.50 (*0-07-052164-6*) McGraw.

Standard Handbook of Powerplant Engineering. 2nd ed. Thomas C. Elliott. LC 97-26055. 1997. text ed. 115.00 (*0-07-019435-1*) McGraw.

Standard Handbook of Structural Details for Building Contruction. 2nd ed. Morton Newman. 1993. text ed. 99.95 (*0-07-046352-2*) McGraw.

Standard Hematology Practice 1. Ed. by B. E. Roberts. 272p. 1991. 115.00 (*0-632-02623-5*) Blackwell Sci.

Standard Highway Signs. (Illus.). 376p. (Orig.). (YA). (gr. 12 up). 1994. pap. text ed. 75.00 (*0-7881-0851-4*) DIANE Pub.

Standard History of Adams & Wells County, Indiana, 2 vols. in 1. Ed. by John W. Tyndall & O. E. Lesh. (Illus.). 985p. 1992. reprint ed. lib. bdg. 98.50 (*0-8328-2568-9*) Higginson Bk Co.

*__Standard History of Allen County: Authentic Narrative of the Past, with Particular Attention to the Modern Era, 2 vols.__ Ed. by William Rusler. (Illus.). 1997. reprint ed. lib. bdg. 100.00 (*0-8328-6290-8*) Higginson Bk Co.

Standard History of Champaign County: An Authentic Narrative of the Past, with Particular Attention to the Modern Era...with Family Lineage & Memoirs, 2 vols., Set. Ed. by J. R. Stewart. (Illus.). 1072p. 1995. reprint ed. lib. bdg. 109.00 (*0-8328-4681-3*) Higginson Bk Co.

S

***Standard History of Fulton County: Authentic Narrative of the Past, with an Extended Survey of Modern Developments in the Progress of Town & County. With Modern Every-Name Index Compiled by the Fulton County Chapter, Ohio Genealogical Society, 2 vols.** Ed. by Reighard, Frank H., & Assistants Staff. (Illus.). 1205p. 1997. reprint ed. lib. bdg. 121.00 (*0-8328-6317-3*) Higginson Bk Co.

Standard History of Lorain County, Ohio, 2 vols., Set. George F. Wright. (Illus.). 1062p. 1994. reprint ed. lib. bdg. 105.00 (*0-8328-3973-6*) Higginson Bk Co.

Standard History of Music. J. F. Cooke. 1972. 59.95 (*0-8490-1120-5*) Gordon Pr.

***Standard History of Springfield & Clark County: Authentic Narrative of the Past, with Particular Attention to the Modern Era in the Commercial, Industrial, Educational, Civic & Social Development.** Ed. by Benjamin F. Prince. (Illus.). 999p. 1997. reprint ed. lib. bdg. 106.00 (*0-8328-6363-7*) Higginson Bk Co.

***Standard History of Stark County: Authentic Narrative of the Past, with Particular Attention to the Modern Era; Chronicle of the People, with Family Lineag & Memoirs, 3 vols.** Ed. by John H. Lehman. (Illus.). 1114p. 1997. reprint ed. lib. bdg. 123.00 (*0-8328-6364-5*) Higginson Bk Co.

S

Standard History of the Medical Profession of Philadelphia. 2nd enl. ed. Burton A. Konkle. LC 75-17803. reprint ed. 115.00 (*0-404-13201-4*) AMS Pr.

Standard Hits, Vol. 194. 148p. 1984. per. 15.95 (*0-7935-0727-8*, 00101941) H Leonard.

Standard in Practice: Grades 3-5. Martha Sierra-Perry. LC 95-49756. (Illus.). 97p. (Orig.). 1996. teacher ed., pap. 15.95 (*0-8141-4693-7*) NCTE.

Standard in South African English & Its Social History. L. W. Lanham & C. A. MacDonald. (Varieties of English Around the World General Ser.: Vol. G1). 96p. (Orig.). 1979. pap. 33.00 (*3-87276-210-9*) Benjamins North Am.

Standard Industrial Classification Manual. 1991. lib. bdg. 499.95 (*0-8490-5061-8*) Gordon Pr.

Standard Industrial Classification Manual. Executive Office of the President, Office of Management & Budget Staff. 705p. 1992. pap. 24.95 (*1-56370-064-6*, SICS) JIST Works.

Standard Industrial Classification Manual, 1987. 2nd ed. 1987. 29.00 (*0-16-004329-8*, S/N 041-001-00314-2) USGPO.

Standard Industrial Classification of Economic Activities, 1992. HMSO Staff. 246p. 1992. pap. 40.00 (*0-11-620550-4*, HM05504, Pub. by Stationery Ofc UK) Bernan Associates.

Standard Information Technology - Test Methods for Measuring Conformance to Directory Services C Language Interfaces - Binding for Application Program Interface (API) Institute of Electrical & Electronics Engineers, Inc. 68p. (Orig.). 1994. pap. text ed. 43.00 (*1-55937-316-4*, SH16261) IEEE Standards.

Standard Interchange Language (SIL) Data Dictionary. 1996. 30.00 (*0-614-15376-X*) Uniform Code.

Standard Interchange Language (SIL) General Overview. 1995. write for info. (*0-614-15375-1*) Uniform Code.

Standard Interchange Language (SIL) Manuals, 3 vols., Set. 75.00 (*0-614-15377-8*) Uniform Code.

Standard Interchange Language (SIL) Manuals, 4 vols., Set. 100.00 (*0-614-15378-6*) Uniform Code.

Standard International Trade Classification. 3rd rev. ed. (Statistical Papers, Series M: No. 34). 12.50 (*92-1-161265-9*, E.86.XVII.12) UN.

Standard Journal - Blue. (Masquerade Ser.). 128p. 1995. 6.95 (*0-8069-3950-8*) Sterling.

Standard Journal - Green. (Masquerade Ser.). 128p. 1995. 6.95 (*0-8069-3953-2*) Sterling.

Standard Journal - Pink. (Masquerade Ser.). 128p. 1995. 6.95 (*0-8069-3951-6*) Sterling.

Standard Journal - Yellow. (Masquerade Ser.). 128p. 1995. 6.95 (*0-8069-3952-4*) Sterling.

Standard Jury Instructions in Misdemeanor Cases with Grand Jury Handbook & Instructions. Florida Bar Staff. LC 81-67759. 84p. 1991. pap. 15.00 (*0-910373-42-6*, 266) FL Bar Legal Ed.

Standard Knife Collectors Guide. 3rd rev. ed. Roy Ritchie & Ron Stewart. (Illus.). 688p. 1996. pap. 12.95 (*0-89145-737-2*, 4730) Collector Bks.

Standard Korean-English Dictionary for Foreigners. B. J. Jones. 394p. (ENG & KOR.). 1986. 14.95 (*0-8288-1614-X*, M14671) Fr & Eur.

Standard Korean-English Dictionary for Foreigners: Romanized. Gene S. Rhie & B. J. Jones. LC 85-80494. 394p. 1986. 14.95 (*0-930878-49-3*) Hollym Intl.

Standard Land Contract in Queensland. 3rd ed. W. D. Duncan & H. A. Weld. c, 370p. 1990. pap. 65.00 (*0-455-20952-9*, Pub. by Law Bk Co AT) Gaunt.

Standard Languages: Spoken & Written. Ed. by W. Haas. 200p. (C). 1982. text ed. 48.50 (*0-389-20291-6*, 07121) B&N Imports.

Standard Legal Forms & Agreements for Canadian Business. Ed. by Steve Sanderson. (Legal Ser.). 160p. (Orig.). 1989. Canadian Edition. pap. 14.95 (*0-88908-865-9*) Self-Counsel Pr.

Standard Legal Forms & Agreements for Small Business: Do It Yourself - Save Time & Money. Steve Sanderson. (National Legal Ser.). (Illus.). 208p. (Orig.). 1990. pap. 14.95 (*0-88908-925-6*) Self-Counsel Pr.

***Standard Lesson Commentary 1997-98.** Ed. by D. Redford. 456p. (Orig.). 1997. text ed. 16.99 (*0-614-26979-2*, 11-01998) Standard Pub.

***Standard Lesson Commentary 1997-98.** Ed. by D. Redford. 456p. (Orig.). 1997. pap. text ed. 12.99 (*0-7847-0618-2*, 11-74028) Standard Pub.

Standard Lesson Plans for Private, Commercial & Flight Instructor: Airplane Single Engine Land. Martin Selph & Jim Easton. 320p. write for info. (*0-9641922-0-9*) Johannsen Grp.

Standard Letters in Architectural Practice. 2nd ed. David Chappell. 320p. 1994. 59.95 (*0-632-03451-3*, Pub. by Blckwell Sci Pubns UK) Blackwell Sci.

Standard Lexikon fur Marketing, 2. 1996. 425.00 (*3-598-11185-1*) K G Saur.

Standard-Lexikon fur Marketing: Marktkommunication, Markt-und Mediforschung. Wolfgang J. Koschnick. vi, 940p. 1987. lib. bdg. 85.00 (*3-598-10583-5*) K G Saur.

Standard Lexikon fur Markt-und Konsumforschung, 2. Wolfgang J. Koschnick. 1052p. 1995. 300.00 (*3-598-11247-5*) K G Saur.

Standard-Lexikon fur Mediaplanung und Mediaforschung, 2 vols. Wolfgang J. Koschnick. 1000p. 1995. lib. bdg. 90.00 (*3-598-11170-3*) K G Saur.

Standard Life of a Temporary Pantyhose Salesman. Aldo Busi. 448p. 1990. pap. 9.95 (*0-571-14162-5*) Faber & Faber.

Standard Macrobiotic Diet: A Guide to Balanced Eating with Endless Variety & Satisfaction. 2nd rev. ed. Michio Kushi. Ed. by Alex Jack. (Illus.). 64p. (Orig.). 1996. pap. 6.95 (*1-882984-21-8*) One Peaceful World.

Standard Manicure Techniques. Lisa Hansen. (Orig.). student ed. write for info. (*0-940039-01-X*); pap. text ed. write for info. (*0-940039-00-1*) Ttl Concepts Ltd.

Standard Manual & Constitution & By-Laws of the United Holy Church of America, Inc. rev. ed. Ed. by Thomas E. Talley et al. LC 88-6867. 221p. 1988. pap. 9.95 (*0-9616056-6-9*) Mid Atl Reg Pr.

Standard Manual of Quality Auditing. Gregory Hutchins. LC 92-22636. 1992. 89.95 (*0-13-554627-3*) P-H Gen Ref & Trav.

Standard Marine Navigational Vocabulary. IMO Staff. (C). 1985. English ed. 90.00 (*0-7855-0029-4*, IMO 985E, Pub. by Intl Maritime Org UK); French ed. 90.00 (*0-318-69907-9*, IMO 986F, Pub. by Intl Maritime Org UK); Spanish ed. 90.00 (*0-685-74534-1*, IMO 988S, Pub. by Intl Maritime Org UK) St Mut.

***Standard Marketing Procedures for Dentists.** Gordon Burgett. (Illus.). 224p. (Orig.). 1997. pap. 129.00 (*0-910167-36-2*, Dental Commun) Comm Unltd CA.

Standard Masonic Monitor. George E. Simons. 248p. 1996. reprint ed. pap. 9.50 (*0-88053-010-3*, M-033) Macoy Pub.

***Standard Math Live!** Ed. by Daniel Zwillinger. 1996. 99.95 incl. cd-rom (*0-8493-9701-4*) CRC Pr.

Standard Mathamatical Tables. 28th ed. Beyer. 1986. pap. 34.95 (*0-8493-0625-6*, CRC Reprint) Franklin.

Standard Mathematical Tables. 28th ed. 680p. 1987. 44.00 (*0-8493-0628-0*, QA) CRC Pr.

Standard Mathematical Tables & Formulae. 29th ed. William H. Beyer. 725p. 1991. 39.95 (*0-8493-0629-9*, QA) CRC Pr.

Standard Mathematical Tables & Formulae. 30th rev. ed. Ed. by Daniel Zwillinger. 832p. 1995. 39.95 (*0-8493-2479-3*, 2479) CRC Pr.

Standard Method for Evaluating the Strength of Brazed Joints in Shear (C3.2-82) (Illus.). 7p. 1982. pap. 27.00 (*0-87171-221-0*) Am Welding.

Standard Method of Detailing Structural Concrete. Ed. by Institution of Structural Engineers Staff & Concrete Society Staff. 138p. 1989. pap. 84.00 (*0-685-32921-6*, S033, Pub. by Inst Civil Eng UK) Am Soc Civil Eng.

Standard Method of Specifying for Minor Works. 3rd ed. L. Gardiner. (Illus.). 260p. 1991. 59.95 (*0-419-15520-1*, E & FN Spon) Routledge Chapman & Hall.

Standard Method of Test for Critical Radiant Flux of Floor Covering Systems Using a Radiant Heat Energy Source. National Fire Protection Association Staff. 1990. 16.75 (*0-317-63364-3*, 253-90) Natl Fire Prot.

Standard Method of Test for Determining Resistance of Mock-Up Upholstered Furniture Material Assemblies to Ignition by Smoldering Cigarettes. National Fire Protection Association Staff. 99p. 1994. 16.75 (*0-317-63383-X*, 261-89) Natl Fire Prot.

Standard Method of Test for Fire & Smoke Characteristics of Wires & Cables. National Fire Protection Association Staff. 1994. 16.75 (*0-685-18990-2*, 262-90) Natl Fire Prot.

***Standard Methods for Analysis & Testing of Petroleum & Related Products - 1997, 2 vols., Vol. 2.** Institute of Petroleum Staff. text ed. 450.00 (*0-471-97094-8*) Wiley.

Standard Methods for Analysis & Testing of Petroleum & Related Products, 1991, 2 vols, Vols. 1 & 2. Institute of Petroleum Staff. (Institute of Petroleum Standards for Petroleum & Its Products Ser.). 1160p. 1991. text ed. 750.00 (*0-471-92949-2*) Wiley.

Standard Methods for Analysis Testing of Petroleum & Related Products 1994: Methods IP 1 to 402, 2 vols. Institute of Petroleum Staff. (Institute of Petroleum Standards for Petroleum & Its Products Ser.: Vols. 1 & 2). 13606p. 1994. text ed. 400.00 (*0-471-94343-6*) Wiley.

Standard Methods for Determination of the Diffusable Hydrogen Content of Martensitic, Bainitic, & Ferritic Steel Weld Metal Produced by Arc Welding (A4.3-93) 17p. 1993. pap. 27.00 (*0-87171-401-9*) Am Welding.

Standard Methods for Mechanical Testing of Welds (B4.0-92) (Illus.). 61p. 1992. 39.00 (*0-87171-393-4*) Am Welding.

Standard Methods for the Examination of Dairy Products. 16th ed. Ed. by Gary H. Richardson. 450p. 1992. 55.00 (*0-87553-208-X*); pap. 45.00 (*0-87553-210-1*) Am Pub Health.

Standard Methods for the Examination of Water & Wastewater. 17th ed. 1644p. 1989. 120.00 (*0-685-50829-3*, 10047) Am Pub Health.

Standard Methods for the Examination of Water & Wastewater. 18th ed. Ed. by Arnold E. Greenberg et al. (Illus.). 1100p. 1992. 160.00 (*0-87553-207-1*) Am Pub Health.

Standard Methods for the Examination of Water & Wastewater. 19th ed. Ed. by Arnold E. Greenberg. (Illus.). 1100p. 1995. 180.00 (*0-87553-223-3*) Am Pub Health.
The best compilation of water & wastewater analysis methods available anywhere! This reorganized reference source is written for many scientific fields, including chemistry, engineering, biology, health, the environment & geo-sciences. More than 340 methods are presented, each with step-by-step procedures for precise analysis of water & wastewater chemical constituents, sanitary quality, & physical & biological characteristics. Twenty-three new methods have been added & 26 methods have been revised to reflect the very latest technical advances. You'll find a revised method for turbidity, new information on UV-absorbing organic constituents cited in the Information Collection Rule (ICR), new procedures for laboratory occupational health & safety, & much more. Incorporates the methods published in the 18th Edition Supplement. CONTENTS INCLUDE : Physical Examination, Determination of Metals & Other Inorganic Nonmetallic Constituents, Determination of Organic Constituents, Examination of Water & Wastewater Radioactivity, Toxicity Test Methods for Aquatic Organisms, Microbiological Examination of Water, Biological Examination of Water. $180.00 Nonmembers, $140.00 APHA, AWWA & WEF members. ***Publisher Provided Annotation.***

Standard Methods of Chemical Analysis, 5 vols., Set. Ed. by N. Howell Furman. LC 74-23465. 6202p. 1975. 598.00 (*0-88275-940-X*) Krieger.

Standard Methods of Chemical Analysis: Instrumental Methods, Vol. IIIA. 6th ed. Ed. by Frank J. Welcher. LC 74-23465. 996p. 1975. reprint ed. 108.00 (*0-88275-342-8*) Krieger.

Standard Methods of Chemical Analysis: The Elements, Vol. 1. 6th ed. Ed. by N. Howell Furman. LC 74-23465. 1426p. 1975. reprint ed. 148.00 (*0-88275-254-5*) Krieger.

Standard Methods of Chemical Analysis: Vol. IIA Industrial & Natural Products & Noninstrumental Methods. 6th ed. Ed. by Frank J. Welcher. LC 74-23465. 1372p. 1975. reprint ed. 148.00 (*0-88275-340-1*) Krieger.

Standard Methods of Chemical Analysis: Vol. IIIB, Instrumental Methods. 6th ed. Ed. by Frank J. Welcher. LC 74-23465. 1060p. 1975. reprint ed. 115.00 (*0-88275-253-7*) Krieger.

Standard Methods of Chemical Analysis Vol. 2B: Industrial & Natural Products & Noninstru. 6th ed. Ed. by Frank J. Welcher. LC 74-23465. 1348p. 1975. reprint ed. 148.00 (*0-88275-333-9*) Krieger.

Standard Methods of Fire Tests for Flame-Resistant Textiles & Films. National Fire Protection Association Staff. 1989. 15.50 (*0-317-63499-2*, 701-89) Natl Fire Prot.

Standard Methods of Fire Tests of Building Construction & Materials. (Two Hundred Ser.). 1990. pap. 20.25 (*0-685-58174-8*, 251-90) Natl Fire Prot.

Standard Methods of Fire Tests of Door Assemblies. National Fire Protection Association Staff. 1990. 16.75 (*0-317-63362-7*, 252-90) Natl Fire Prot.

Standard Methods of Hydraulic Design for Power Boilers. Ed. by V. A. Lokshin et al. Tr. by Henri A. Bronstein from RUS. 345p. 1988. 264.00 (*0-89116-359-X*) Hemisp Pub.

Standard Methods of Tests & Classification System for Cigarette Ignition Resistance of Components of Upholstered Furniture. National Fire Protection Association Staff. 1994. 16.75 (*0-317-63378-3*, 260-89) Natl Fire Prot.

Standard Model & Beyond. Ed. by M. Zralek & R. Manka. 182p. (C). 1992. text ed. 125.00 (*1-56072-027-1*) Nova Sci Pubs.

Standard Model & Beyond: First International Triangle Workshop. Ed. by D. Ebert et al. 324p. (C). 1991. text ed. 89.00 (*981-02-0594-5*) World Scientific Pub.

Standard Model & Beyond: Ninth Symposium on Theoretical Physics. Ed. by J. E. Kim. 480p. (C). 1991. text ed. 118.00 (*981-02-0610-0*) World Scientific Pub.

Standard Model & Beyond: The Fifth Lake Louise Winter Inst. of Frontiers in Physics. Ed. by A. Astbury et al. 428p. (C). 1990. text ed. 118.00 (*981-02-0318-7*) World Scientific Pub.

Standard Model & Just Beyond. F. L. Navarria & P. G. Pelfer. 520p. 1993. text ed. 121.00 (*981-02-1319-0*) World Scientific Pub.

Standard Model at the Energy of Present. Ed. by F. Csikor & G. Pocsik. 165p. 1992. 115.00 (*1-56072-021-2*) Nova Sci Pubs.

Standard Model Designs for Rural Water Supply. (Illus.). 235p. 1986. pap. text ed. 60.00 (*92-890-1030-4*, 1340031) World Health.

Standard Model, Hadron Phenomenology & Weak Decays on the Lattice: Dir in HEP, Vol. 8. G. Martinelli. 350p. 1997. pap. 61.00 (*981-02-0468-X*); text ed. 130.00 (*981-02-0467-1*) World Scientific Pub.

Standard Model Higgs Boson: Selections & Comments. Ed. by M. B. Einhorn. (Current Physics Sources & Comments Ser.: Vol. 8). 380p. 1991. 127.50 (*0-444-88807-1*, North Holland); pap. 65.75 (*0-444-88808-X*, North Holland) Elsevier.

Standard Monitor. George E. Simons. pap. 8.00 (*0-685-19502-3*) Powner.

Standard Mortgage Clause: Protecting All Parties. LC 87-71808. 200p. 1987. pap. 29.95 (*0-89707-319-3*, 519-0069-01) Amer Bar Assn.

Standard MUMPS Pocket Guide. Ed. by Thomas Salander. 1990. pap. 4.00 (*0-918118-38-7*) M Technol.

Standard Object-Oriented COBOL. Ned Chapin. LC 96-28543. 352p. 1996. pap. text ed. 34.95 (*0-471-12974-7*) Wiley.

Standard Occupational Classification Manual. 1991. lib. bdg. 499.95 (*0-8490-5062-6*) Gordon Pr.

Standard of Care: California Edition. James B. McKenney. Ed. by Paul Chaffee et al. (Illus.). 165p. 1994. per. 19.50 (*1-885104-00-6*) Prof Pubng.

Standard of Care: The Law of American Bioethics. George J. Annas. 304p. 1993. 28.95 (*0-19-507247-2*) OUP.

***Standard of Care: The Law of American Bioethics.** George J. Annas. 304p. 1997. reprint ed. pap. 22.95 (*0-19-512006-X*) OUP.

Standard of Excellence: Full Score, Bk. 1. Bruce Pearson. 1994. audio 8.95 (*0-614-03107-9*); audio compact disk 12.95 (*0-614-03108-7*, W22CD1) Kjos.

Standard of Excellence: Full Score, Bk. 1. Bruce Pearson. 660p. 1995. 49.95 (*0-8497-5948-X*, W21F) Kjos.

Standard of Excellence: Full Score, Bk. 2. Bruce Pearson. 1994. audio 8.95 (*0-614-03111-7*); audio compact disk 12.95 (*0-318-72755-2*, W22CD2) Kjos.

Standard of Excellence: Full Score, Bk. 2. Bruce Pearson. 640p. 1995. 49.95 (*0-8497-5950-1*, W22F) Kjos.

Standard of Excellence: Full Score, Bk. 2: Theory & History Workbook. Bruce Pearson. 640p. 1995. 5.95 (*0-8497-0516-9*, L22) Kjos.

Standard of Excellence, Bk. 1: Theory & History Workbook. Chuck Elledge et al. 32p. 1993. 5.95 (*0-8497-0515-0*, L21) Kjos.

Standard of Living. Mildred B. Young. (C). 1941. pap. 3.00 (*0-87574-012-X*) Pendle Hill.

Standard of Living Among Workingmen's Families in New York City. Robert C. Chapin. LC 72-137159. (Poverty U. S. A. Historical Record Ser.). 1971. reprint ed. 35.95 (*0-405-03097-5*) Ayer.

Standard of Living in Japan. Kokichi Morimoto. LC 78-63963. (Johns Hopkins University. Studies in the Social Sciences. Thirtieth Ser. 1912: No. 2). reprint ed. 32.50 (*0-404-61210-5*) AMS Pr.

Standard of Perfection. 206p. 10.00 (*0-318-32888-7*) Am Rabbit Breeders.

Standard of the West: The Justin Story. Irvin Farman. LC 96-14897. (Texas Biography Ser.). 260p. 1996. 26.95 (*0-87565-167-4*) Tex Christian.

Standard Oil: The First 125 Years. Scott Benjamin & Wayne Henderson. (Illus.). 128p. 1996. pap. 19.95 (*0-7603-0086-0*) Motorbooks Intl.

Standard Oil Company (Indiana) Oil Pioneer of the Middle West. Paul H. Giddens. LC 75-41757. (Companies & Men: Business Enterprises in America Ser.). (Illus.). 1976. reprint ed. 70.95 (*0-405-08073-5*) Ayer.

Standard Old Bottle Price Guide. Carlo Sellari & Dot Sellari. (Illus.). 256p. 1989. pap. 14.95 (*0-89145-383-0*) Collector Bks.

Standard on Assessment Appeal. 1981. 8.00 (*0-88329-108-8*) IAAO.

Standard on Cadastral Maps & Parcel Identifiers. 1988. 8.00 (*0-88329-101-0*) IAAO.

Standard on Certification of Assessing Officers & Valuation Personnel. 3p. 1979. pap. 8.00 (*0-88329-105-3*) IAAO.

Standard on Contracting for Assessment Services. 9p. 1986. pap. 8.00 (*0-88329-060-X*) IAAO.

Standard on Education & Training for Assessing Agencies. 1996. 8.00 (*0-88329-069-3*) IAAO.

Standard on Facilities, Computers, Equipment, & Supplies. 1989. 8.00 (*0-88329-068-5*) IAAO.

Standard on Live Fire Training Evolutions in Structures. National Fire Protection Association Staff. 1992. 16.75 (*0-317-63545-X*, 1403-92) Natl Fire Prot.

Standard on Mass Appraisal of Real Property. 1984. 8.00 (*0-88329-131-2*) IAAO.

Standard on Property Use Codes. 3p. 1980. pap. 8.00 (*0-88329-106-1*) IAAO.

Standard on Public Relations. 9p. 1988. pap. 8.00 (*0-88329-102-9*) IAAO.

Standard on Ratio Studies. 1990. 8.00 (*0-88329-070-7*) IAAO.

Standard on the Application of the Three Approaches to Value in Mass Appraisal. rev. ed. 23p. 1985. pap. 8.00 (*0-88329-149-5*) IAAO.

Standard on Urban Land Valuation. 5p. 1987. pap. 8.00 (*0-88329-063-4*) IAAO.

Standard on Valuation of Personal Property. 9p. 1996. pap. 8.00 (*0-88329-139-8*) IAAO.

Standard Operas: Their Plots, Their Music, Their Composers, a Handbook. George P. Upton. 1980. lib. bdg. 72.95 (*0-8490-3173-7*) Gordon Pr.

Standard Operating Procedures. 3rd ed. Kenneth C. Gass. (Illus.). 37p. (C). 1992. lib. bdg. 42.00 (*0-9634906-0-5*); spiral bd. 28.00 (*0-9634906-1-3*) Special Qual.

Standard Operating Procedures, Aircraft Rescue & Fire Fighting. (Four Hundred Ser.). 110p. 1991. pap. 26.50 (*0-685-44137-7*, 402M-91) Natl Fire Prot.

Standard Operating Procedures for Dentists. Marsha Freeman. 384p. (Orig.). 1995. pap. 169.00 incl. disk (*0-910167-33-8*, Dental Commun) Comm Unltd CA.

***Standard Operating Procedures for Investigators.** Paul Meng et al. pap. text ed. write for info. (*0-471-96936-2*) Wiley.

An Asterisk (*) at the beginning of an entry indicates that the title is appearing in BIP for the first time.

Standard Operating Procedures for Pediatric Dentists. Marsha Freeman. 256p. 1995. pap. 129.00 incl. disk (*0-910167-28-1*, Dental Commun) Comm Unltd CA.

Standard Operating Procedures for Pediatric Dentists. 2nd rev. ed. Marsha Freeman. (Illus.). 304p. 1996. pap. write for info. incl. disk (*0-910167-34-6*, Dental Commun) Comm Unltd CA.

Standard Operating Procedures for Primary Care Physicians. Robyn Freeman & Leila Chambers. (Illus.). 384p. (Orig.). 1997. pap. 169.00 incl. disk (*0-910167-35-4*) Comm Unltd CA.

Standard Operating Safety Guides. U. S. Environmental Protection Agency, Office of Wetlands, Oceans, & Watersheds Staff. 184p. (Orig.). 1994. pap. text ed. 79.00 (*0-86587-374-7*) Gov Insts.

Standard Operations Manual for Mounting District-Wide Invention Convention. Melvin L. Fuller & Maggie Weisberg. (Illus.). 80p. 1989. pap. 50.00 (*0-685-25990-0*) M&M Assocs.

Standard or Head-Dress? Zelia Nuttall. (HU PMP Ser.). 1888. 25.00 (*0-527-01183-5*) Periodicals Srv.

Standard Orthopaedic Operations. 4th ed. John C. Adams & Clifford A. Stossel. (Illus.). 485p. 1992. text ed. 145.00 (*0-443-04351-5*) Churchill.

Standard Pascal User Reference Manual. Doug Cooper. 1983. pap. 15.95 (*0-393-30121-4*) Norton.

Standard Pennsylvania Practice, 35 vols. 2nd ed. LC 80-84968. 1991. Suppl. 1991. suppl. ed. 3,990.00 (*0-318-57161-7*) Lawyers Cooperative.

Standard Periodical Directory. 15th ed. 1992. 445.00 (*0-8103-9957-1*) Oxbridge Comm.

Standard Periodical Directory. 16th ed. 1993. write for info. (*0-8103-9657-2*, 070219) Gale.

Standard Periodical Directory. 16th ed. 1993. 584.50 (*0-917460-44-8*) Oxbridge Comm.

Standard Periodical Directory. 19th ed. 1995. 645.00 (*0-917460-63-4*) Gale.

Standard Periodical Directory 1991. 14th ed. Ed. by Matthew Manning. 1782p. 1991. 425.00 (*0-917460-30-8*, 070217-M99348) Gale.

*__Standard Periodical Directory 1997.__ 20th ed. 2000p. 1996. 695.00 incl. cd-rom (*0-917460-76-6*) Oxbridge Comm.

Standard Perm Waving Manual. Milady Publishing Company Staff. (Cosmetology Ser.). 1997. pap. text ed. 18.95 (*1-56253-365-7*) Milady Pub.

Standard Personal Directory DOS. 8th ed. 1995. 795.00 (*0-917460-57-X*) Gale.

Standard Personal Directory DOS. 19th ed. 1996. 695.00 (*0-917460-64-2*) Gale.

Standard Personal Directory Windows. 18th ed. 1995. 795.00 (*0-917460-58-8*) Gale.

Standard Pesticide: User Guide. 4th ed. Bert L. Bohmont. 560p. (C). 1996. text ed. 82.00 (*0-13-442443-3*) P-H.

Standard Phonographic Dictionary. Andrew J. Graham. 1991. reprint ed. lib. bdg. 119.00 (*0-7812-9363-4*) Rprt Serv.

Standard Pilot Log Black. ASA Staff. (Logbook Ser.). 68p. 1990. 6.95 (*1-56027-052-7*, ASA-SP-30) Av Suppl & Acad.

Standard Pilot Log Blue. ASA Staff. (Logbook Ser.). (Illus.). 110p. 1985. 10.95 (*1-56027-054-3*, ASA-SP-57) Av Suppl & Acad.

Standard Pilot Log Red. ASA Staff. (Logbook Ser.). (Illus.). 206p. 1985. 9.95 (*1-56027-053-5*, ASA-SP-40) Av Suppl & Acad.

Standard Plans for Public Construction, 1997: Metric Edition. BNI Building News Staff. 375p. 1996. pap. text ed. 59.95 (*1-55701-149-4*) BNI Pubns.

Standard Potentials in Aqueous Solution. Allen J. Bard et al. (Monographs in Electroanalytical Chemistry & Electrochemistry: Vol. 6). 848p. (C). 1985. 49.75 (*0-8247-7291-1*) Dekker.

Standard Practical Workbook: 91 Edition. 2nd ed. Milady Publishing Company Staff. (Standard Texts of Cosmetology Ser.). 1991. pap. 20.25 (*1-56253-007-0*) Delmar.

Standard Practice for Design & Construction of Concrete Silos & Stacking Tubs for Storing Granular Materials & Commentary. 22p. 1991. 44.25 (*0-685-62961-9*, 313/313R-91BOW6) ACI.

Standard Practice for Direct Design of Precast Concrete Pipe Using Standards Installation. American Society of Civil Engineers Staff. LC 94-3852. (ASCE Standard Ser.). 1994. 32.00 (*0-87262-995-3*) Am Soc Civil Eng.

Standard Practice for Shotcrete Vol. 11: Technical Engineering & Design Guides As Adapted from the U. S. Army Corps of Engineers. American Society of Civil Engineers Staff. LC 95-11427. (Technical Engineering & Design Guides As Adapted from the U. S. Army Corps of Engineers Ser.: No. 11). 72p. 1995. pap. 24.00 (*0-7844-0068-7*) Am Soc Civil Eng.

Standard Practice for the Design & Construction of Reinforced Concrete Chimneys & Commentary. 30p. 1995. 31.75 (*0-614-11130-7*, 307-95/307R-95) ACI.

Standard Practice for Use of the International System of Units (SI) (The Modernized Metric System) American Society for Testing & Materials Staff. (ASTM Ser.: E 380-91a). 37p. reprint ed. pap. 25.00 (*0-7837-4703-9*, 2044850) Bks Demand.

Standard Pressure-Volume-Temperature Data for Polymers. Paul Zoller & David Walsh. LC 95-60846. 420p. 1995. 249.95 (*1-56676-328-2*) Technomic.

Standard Prestressed Box Beams for Highway Bridge Spans to 103 Ft. see Standards for Selected Prestressed Units

Standard Prestressed Concrete Beams for Highway Bridge Spans 30 to 140 Ft. see Standards for Selected Prestressed Units

Standard Prestressed Concrete Piles, Square, Octagonal & Cylinder see Standards for Selected Prestressed Units

Standard Prestressed Concrete Slabs for Highway Bridge Spans to 55 Ft. see Standards for Selected Prestressed Units

Standard Probability & Statistics Tables & Formulae. Beyer. 520p. 1990. 41.95 (*0-8493-0680-9*, QA276) CRC Pr.

*__Standard Procedure in Determining the Size & Horsepower Capacities of Gears of Different Materials.__ G. E. Katzenmeyer. (Technical Papers). 1936. pap. text ed. 30.00 (*1-55589-241-8*) AGMA.

Standard Procedures for Calibrating Magnetic Instruments to Measure the Delta Ferrite Content of Austenitic & Duplex Austenitic Ferritic Stainless Steel Weld Metal (A4.2-91) 18p. 1991. 21.00 (*0-87171-361-6*) Am Welding.

*__Standard Program Book for Easter: Includes Materials for Mother's Day & Father's Day.__ Compiled by Pat Fittro. 48p. 1996. pap. 3.99 (*0-7847-0467-8*) Standard Pub.

Standard Propeller Logbook. ASA Staff. (Logbook Ser.). (Illus.). 20p. 1988. pap. 4.95 (*1-56027-202-3*, ASA-SP-L) Av Suppl & Acad.

Standard Ptolemaic Silver. Edward T. Newell. LC 80-70056. (Illus.). 1981. reprint ed. pap. 6.00 (*0-915262-49-5*); reprint ed. suppl. ed. (*0-318-55575-1*) S J Durst.

Standard Radio Communications Manual: With Instrumentation & Testing Techniques. R. Harold Kinley. 432p. 1988. 16.95 (*0-13-842386-5*) P-H.

Standard Rate in American Trade Unions. David A. McCabe. LC 70-156435. (American Labor Ser., No. 2). 1971. reprint ed. 19.95 (*0-405-02932-2*) Ayer.

Standard Reference Tables for Metric Conversion of Transportation Tariffs. rev. ed. ANMC Tariff Task Group Staff. 90p. 1982. 19.00 (*0-686-47622-0*) Am Natl.

Standard Relational & Network Database Languages. E. J. Yannakoudakis & C. P. Cheng. (Illus.). ix, 148p. 1989. 59.00 (*0-387-19537-8*) Spr-Verlag.

Standard Research Test Method for Determining Smoke Generation of Solid Materials. National Fire Protection Association Staff. 20p. 1989. 18.75 (*0-317-63373-2*, 258-89) Natl Fire Prot.

*__Standard Schnauzer: AKC Rank #100.__ Barbara Dille. (Rare Breed Ser.). (Illus.). 96p. 1997. 19.95 (*0-7938-0756-5*, RX-106) TFH Pubns.

Standard Securities Calculation Methods: Fixed Income Securities Formulas for Analytic Measures, Vol. 2. Jan Mayle. 1994. write for info. (*0-318-72505-3*) Securities Industry.

Standard Selections. Ed. by Robert I. Fulton et al. LC 79-152150. (Granger Index Reprint Ser.). 1977. reprint ed. 26.95 (*0-8369-6253-2*) Ayer.

Standard Setting & Financing in Postsecondary Education: Eight Recommendations for Change in Federal & State Policies. James R. Mingle & Arthur M. Hauptman. 1994. 15.00 (*1-881543-04-8*) SHEEO.

Standard Setting As Educational Reform. Gary Sykes & Peter Plastrik. 1993. 15.00 (*0-89333-108-2*) AACTE.

Standard Setting for Complex Performance Tasks: A Special Issue of "Applied Measurement in Education", Vol. 8, No. 1, 1995. Ed. by James C. Impara & Barbara S. Plake. 112p. 1995. pap. 20.00 (*0-8058-9954-5*) L Erlbaum Assocs.

Standard Speaker: Containing Exercises in Prose & Poetry. Epes Sargent. LC 75-37020. (Granger Index Reprint Ser.). 1977. reprint ed. 27.95 (*0-8369-6319-9*) Ayer.

Standard Specification for Latex-Modified Concrete (LCM) Overlays. 6p. 1993. 6.50 (*0-614-11136-6*, 548.4R-93. BOW6) ACI.

Standard Specification for Plain Concrete Parking Lots. 7p. 1994. pap. 9.50 (*0-614-02501-X*, 330.1-94BOW6) ACI.

Standard Specification for the Construction of Drilled Piers. 11p. 1994. 14.75 (*0-614-02502-8*, 336.1-94BOW6) ACI.

Standard Specifications for BEMS, 2 pts., Pt. 1. 1990. 90.00 (*0-86022-259-4*, Pub. by Build Servs Info Assn UK) St Mut.

Standard Specifications for BEMS, 2 pts., Pt. 2. 1990. 90.00 (*0-86022-260-8*, Pub. by Build Servs Info Assn UK) St Mut.

*__Standard Specifications for Construction & Maintenance of Trails.__ 1997. lib. bdg. 251.99 (*0-8490-8130-0*) Gordon Pr.

Standard Specifications for Construction of Roads & Bridges on Federal Highway Projects, 2 vols. 1995. lib. bdg. 599.99 (*0-8490-6512-7*) Gordon Pr.

*__Standard Specifications for Construction of Roads & Bridges on Federal Highway Projects, 2 vols.__ 1997. lib. bdg. 600.75 (*0-8490-6119-9*) Gordon Pr.

Standard Specifications for Highway Bridges. 15th rev. ed. AASHTO Staff. (Bridges & Structures Ser.). (Illus.). 752p. 1992. 62.25 (*1-56051-014-5*, HB-15) AASHTO.

Standard Specifications for Movable Highway Bridges. 1987. pap. 16.00 (*0-686-27096-7*, MHB-5) AASHTO.

Standard Specifications for Public Works Construction: 1997 Metric Edition. BNI Building News Staff. 730p. 1996. 49.95 (*1-55701-148-6*) BNI Pubns.

Standard Specifications for Structural Supports for Highway Signs, Luminaires & Traffic Signals. 1994. pap. 20.00 (*1-56051-065-X*, LTS-3) AASHTO.

Standard Steel Pocketbook. 36p. 1996. 12.00 (*1-886362-09-2*) Iron & Steel.

Standard Swahili-English Dictionary. Ed. by Frederick Johnson. 558p. (ENG & SWA.). 1955. 59.00 (*0-19-864403-5*) OUP.

Standard Symbols for Welding Brazing & Nondestructive Examination (A2.4-94) (Illus.). 101p. 1993. pap. 72.00 (*0-87171-370-5*) Am Welding.

*__Standard Technical Report Number Format & Creation: An American National Standard.__ National Information Standards Organization Staff & American National Standards Institute Staff. (National Information Standards Ser.). 1997. write for info. (*1-880124-30-0*) NISO.

Standard Technical Report Number (STRN) Format & Creation, Z39.23-1990. rev. ed. National Information Standards Organization Staff. LC 95-39984. (National Information Standards Ser.). 18p. 1995. reprint ed. 30.00 (*1-880124-13-0*, 1041-5653) NISO.

Standard Template Library: A Definitive Approach to C++ Programming Using STL. P. J. Plauger & Stepanov. 1996. pap. text ed. 38.00 (*0-13-437633-1*) P-H.

Standard Terms for Handwriting Analysts: English Terms, Document Examiners' Terms, Health Terms, International Terms. (Illus.). 106p. (C). 1991. pap. 15.95 (*1-877772-04-6*) AHAF.

Standard Terms of Energy Economy: Ruttley. World Energy Conference Staff. 1978. 126.00 (*0-08-022445-8*, Pub. by Pergamon Repr UK) Franklin.

Standard Test Bank. Milady Publishing Company Staff. (Standard Texts of Cosmetology Ser.). 1993. 49.95 (*1-56253-202-2*) Van Nos Reinhold.

Standard Test Method for Comparative Performance of Flammable Gas Detectors Against Poisoning. EEMUA Staff. 1988. 125.00 (*0-85931-059-0*, Pub. by EEMUA UK) St Mut.

Standard Test Method for Comparative Performance of Flammable Gas Detectors Against Poisoning. EEMUA Staff. 1988. 90.00 (*0-685-22642-5*, Pub. by EEMUA UK) St Mut.

Standard Test Method for Measuring the Smoke Generated by Solid Materials. 1989. pap. 18.75 (*0-685-58190-X*, 258-89) Natl Fire Prot.

Standard Test Method for Potential Heat of Building Materials. National Fire Protection Association Staff. 1993. 16.75 (*0-317-63377-5*, 259-93) Natl Fire Prot.

Standard Test Methods for Metal Powders & Metallurgy Products, 1996. MPIF Standards Committee Staff. (Illus.). 1996. student ed. 35.00 (*1-878954-55-5*) Metal Powder.

Standard Tests for Fire Resistance of Vault & File Room Doors, UL 155. 7th ed. (C). 1995. pap. text ed. 95.00 (*1-55989-803-8*) Underwrtrs Labs.

*__Standard Text of Electricity Transparency Masters.__ Herman. 128p. 1996. text ed. 12.95 (*0-8273-8375-4*) Delmar.

Standard Text of Professional Estheticians. Gerson. (Skin Ser.). 1986. text ed. 35.95 (*0-87350-366-X*) Milady Pub.

Standard Textbook for Professional Barber-Styling: Lesson Plans. rev. ed. Milady Publishing Company Staff. 184p. 1993. 49.95 (*1-56253-163-8*) Milady Pub.

Standard Textbook for Professional Barber-Styling: State Exam Review. 2nd rev. ed. Milady Publishing Company Staff. 152p. 1993. pap. text ed. 13.50 (*1-56253-144-1*) Milady Pub.

Standard Textbook of Cosmetology. rev. ed. Constance V. Kibbe. (Illus.). 547p. 1985. text ed. 34.50 (*0-87350-363-5*) Milady Pub.

Standard Textbook of Cosmetology. 9th deluxe ed. Milady Publishing Company Staff. (Standard Texts of Cosmetology Ser.). 1992. text ed. 41.95 (*1-56253-173-5*) Milady Pub.

Standard Textbook of Professional Barber Styling. Milady Editors. 1983. text ed. 34.50 (*0-87350-501-8*) Milady Pub.

Standard Theatre of Victorian England. Allan S. Jackson. LC 89-46134. (Illus.). 360p. 1993. 55.00 (*0-8386-3392-7*) Fairleigh Dickinson.

Standard Trade Index of Japan, 1988-89. 32th ed. 1445p. 1988. 227.00 (*0-8002-4204-1*) Taylor & Francis.

Standard Trade Index of Japan 1995-96. 39th ed. 1400p. 1995. 275.00 (*0-8002-4331-5*) Intl Pubns Serv.

Standard Trust Income Tax Guide 1992-93. Price Waterhouse Staff. 230p. 1993. pap. 28.00 (*0-409-07654-6*, SA) MICHIE.

Standard Turns: Cross Turns, Spot Turns, Pivots, Twinkles. (Ballroom Dance Ser.). 1986. lib. bdg. 79.95 (*0-8490-3401-9*) Gordon Pr.

Standard Types of Building Construction. National Fire Protection Association Staff. 1992. 16.75 (*0-317-07387-7*, 220-92) Natl Fire Prot.

Standard Urdu-English Dictionary. Abdul Haq. 696p. (ENG & URD.). 95.00 (*0-7859-9263-4*) Fr & Eur.

Standard-Vacuum Oil Company & United States East Asian Policy, 1933-1941. Irvine H. Anderson. LC 74-25611. 273p. reprint ed. pap. 77.90 (*0-685-23408-8*, 2032632) Bks Demand.

Standard Vocal Repertoire, Bk. 2: For High Voice. Ed. by Richard D. Row. (Illus.). 80p. 1963. pap. 10.50 (*0-8258-0253-9*, RB-71) Fischer Inc NY.

Standard Welding Procedure Specification for Gas Metal Arc Welding of Austenitic Stainless Steel, (M-8 or P-8), 10 Through 18 Gauge, in the As-Welded Condition, with or Without Backing (B2.1.005-90) 6p. 1990. 39.00 (*0-87171-334-9*) Am Welding.

Standard Welding Procedure Specification for Gas Metal Arc Welding of Carbon Steel, (M-1, Group 1), 10 Through 18 Gauge, in the As-Welded Condition, with or Without Backing (B2.1.004-90) 6p. 1990. 39.00 (*0-87171-333-0*) Am Welding.

Standard Welding Procedure Specification for Gas Metal Arc Welding of Carbon Steel to Austenitic Stainless Steel, (M-I to M-8 or P.8), 10 Through 18 Gauge, in the As-Welded Condition, with or Without Backing (B2.1.006-90) 6p. 1990. 39.00 (*0-87171-335-7*) Am Welding.

Standard Welding Procedure Specification for Gas Metal Arc Welding of Galvanized Steel, 10 Through 18 Gauge, in the As-Welded Condition, with or Without Backing (B2.1.003-90) 6p. 1990. 39.00 (*0-87171-332-2*) Am Welding.

Standard Welding Procedure Specification for Gas Tungsten Arc Welding of Aluminum, (M-22 or P-22), 10 Through 18 Gauge, in the As-Welded Condition, with or Without Backing (B2.1.015-91) 6p. 1991. 39.00 (*0-87171-369-1*) Am Welding.

Standard Welding Procedure Specification for Gas Tungsten Arc Welding of Austenitic Stainless Steel, (M.8 - P-8), 10 Through 18 Gauge, in the As-Welded Condition, with or Without Backing (B2.1.009-90) 6p. 1990. 39.00 (*0-87171-338-1*) Am Welding.

Standard Welding Procedure Specification for Gas Tungsten Arc Welding of Carbon Steel, (M-I, Group 1), 10 Through 18 Gauge, in the As-Welded Condition, with or Without Backing (B2.1.008-90) 6p. 1990. 39.00 (*0-87171-337-3*) Am Welding.

Standard Welding Procedure Specification for Gas Tungsten Arc Welding of Carbon Steel, (M-1 - P-1, Group 1 or 2), 3-16 Through 7-8 Inch, in the As-Welded Condition, with or Without Backing (B2.1.002-90) 6p. 1990. 39.00 (*0-87171-340-3*) Am Welding.

S

Standard Welding Procedure Specification for Gas Tungsten Arc Welding of Carbon Steel to Austenitic Stainless Steel, (M-1 to M-8 or P-8), 10 Through 18 Gauge, in the As-Welded Condition, with or Without Backing (B2.1.010-90) 6p. 1990. 39.00 (*0-87171-339-X*) Am Welding.

Standard Welding Procedure Specification for Gas Tungsten Arc Welding of Galvanized Steel, 10 Through 18 Gauge, in the As-Welded Condition, with or Without Backing (B2.1.007-90) 6p. 1990. 39.00 (*0-87171-336-5*) Am Welding.

Standard Welding Procedure Specification for Shielded Metal Arc Welding of Austenitic Stainless Steel, (M-8 or P-8), 10 Through 18 Gauge, in the As-Welded Condition, with or Without Backing (B2.1.013-91) 6p. 1991. 39.00 (*0-87171-367-5*) Am Welding.

Standard Welding Procedure Specification for Shielded Metal Arc Welding of Carbon Steel, (M-1 - P-1, Group 1 or 2), 3-16 Through 3-4 Inch, in the As-Welded Condition, with Backing (B2.1.001-90) 4p. 1990. 39.00 (*0-87171-318-7*) Am Welding.

Standard Welding Procedure Specification for Shielded Metal Arc Welding of Carbon Steel to Austenitic Stainless Steel, (M-1 to M-8 or P-8), 10 Through 18 Gauge, in the As-Welded Condition, with or Without Backing (B2.1.014-91) 6p. 1991. 39.00 (*0-87171-368-3*) Am Welding.

Standard Welding Procedure Specification for Shielded Metal Arc Welding of Galvanized Steel, 10 Through 18 Gauge, in the As-Welded Condition, with or Without Backing (B2.1.011-91) 6p. 1991. 39.00 (*0-87171-365-9*) Am Welding.

Standard Welding Procedure Specification for Shielded Metal, (M-1, Group 10), 10 Through 18 Gauge, in the As-Welded Condition, with or Without Backing (B2.1.012-91) 6p. 1991. 39.00 (*0-87171-366-7*) Am Welding.

Standard Welding Terms & Definitions (A3.0-94) (Illus.). 109p. 1994. 66.00 (*0-87171-455-8*) Am Welding.

Standard Wine Cookbook. Anne Director. (Culinary Arts Ser.). (Illus.). 192p. 1979. reprint ed. pap. 9.95 (*0-89496-013-X*) Ross Bks.

Standard Woerterbuch fuer Werbung, Massenmedien und Marketing. Deutsch-English-Standard Dictionary of Advertising, Mass Media & Marketing. German-English. Wolfgang J. Koschnick. Orig. Title: Standardwoerterbuch fuer Werbung, Massenmedien und Marketing, Deutsch-English. x, 592p. (GER.). 1987. lib. bdg. 113.85 (*3-11-008985-8*) De Gruyter.

Standard Work on Cutting: Ladies Tailor Made Garments - 1908. S. S. Gorden. Ed. by Jules Kliot & Kaethe Kliot. (Illus.). 240p. (C). 1993. reprint ed. pap. 22.00 (*0-916896-45-5*) Lacis Pubns.

Standard Work on Cutting (Men's Garments), 1886. Intro. by Jules Kliot & Kaethe Kliot. 128p. (C). 1990. reprint ed. pap. 12.00 (*0-916896-33-1*) Lacis Pubns.

Standard Worterbuch fur die Sozialwissenschaften, Vol. 2, Pt. 1. Wolfgang J. Koschnick. 1506p. (ENG & GER.). 1993. 150.00 (*0-7859-3722-6*, F90030) Fr & Eur.

Standard Worterbuch fur die Sozialwissenschaften, Vol. 2, Pt. 2. 17th ed. 1638p. (FRE.). 1993. 160.00 (*0-7859-4849-X*) Fr & Eur.

*__Standard 14.5 Inch Spur Gear Teeth.__ AGMA Technical Committee. (Technical Papers: Vol. P90B). 1930. pap. text ed. 30.00 (*1-55589-127-6*) AGMA.

Standard 1963 see Standard

Standard 1964 see Standard

Standard 1965 see Standard

Standard 1966 see Standard

Standard 1967 see Standard

Standard 1968 see Standard

Standard 1969 see Standard

Standard 1970 see Standard

Standard 1971 see Standard

Standard 1972. (FAO Rice Report). 39p. 1973. pap. 5.75 (*0-685-12490-8*, F165); pap. 110.00 (*92-0-010272-7*, ISP310) Bernan Associates.

Standard 1972. (United Nations Statistical Yearbook). 35.00 (*0-685-13073-8*, E.73.XVII.1); Supplement. suppl. ed., pap. 17.00 (*0-685-43497-4*, E.74.XVII.2); pap. 30.00 (*0-685-12871-7*, E.75.XIV.1) UN.

Standard 1972. (Yearbook of Labor Statistics). 1972. 21.00 (*0-685-12995-0*, ILO42) UN.

Standard 1972, No. 2. (Evaluation of Some Pesticide Residues in Food 1971). 1973. pap. 25.00 (*92-4-166502-5*) World Health.

Standard 1972, No. 205. (Official Records of the World Health Organization; Work of WHO). 1973. pap. 6.00 (*92-4-160205-8*) World Health.

Standard 1972, 3 Vols., Set. (Yearbook of National Accounts Statistics). 2139p. 1979. pap. 50.00 (*0-685-12748-6*, UN74/17/3) UN.

Standard 1972, Vol. 2. (Ethnies). 1972. pap. 23.50 (*90-279-7156-0*) Mouton.

Standard 1972 see Ethnies: Proceedings

Standard 1972 see Official Records of the World Health Organization; Work of WHO: Reports

Standard 1972 see Evaluation of Some Pesticide Residues in Food 1971: Monographs

Standard 1972 see Standard

Standard 1974. (Bulletin of Statistics on World Trade in Engineering Products). pap. 17.00 (*0-686-93347-8*, E.76. 11.E.7); pap. 7.00 (*0-685-12627-7*, E.75.XI.5); pap. 5.00 (*0-685-12648-X*, EFR.75.II.E.15); pap. 36.00 (*0-685-13077-0*, E.75.XVII.1) UN.

Standard 1974. 34th ed. (Yearbook of Labor Statistics). 34.50 (*92-2-001216-2*, ILO45) Bernan Associates.

Standard 1974. 34th ed. (Yearbook of Labor Statistics). pap. 28.75 (*92-2-001217-0*, ILO44) Fr & Eur.

Standard 1974, No. 4. (Evaluation of Some Pesticide Residues in Food 1971). 1975. pap. 48.00 (*92-4-166504-1*) World Health.

Standard 1974, No. 221. (Official Records of the World Health Organization; Work of WHO). 1975. pap. 7.20 (*92-4-160221-X*) World Health.

Standard 1974, 2 Pts., Pt. 1: Mid-Term Review. (World Economic Survey). pap. 11.00 (*0-686-93634-5*, UN75/2C1) UN.

Standard 1974, 2 Pts., Pt. 2: Current Economic Developments. (World Economic Survey). pap. 9.50 (*0-686-99154-0*, UN75/2C3) UN.

Standard 1974, 3 Vols., Set. (Yearbook of National Accounts Statistics). pap. 70.00 (*0-685-12750-8*, UN75/17/5) UN.

Standard 1974 see Official Records of the World Health Organization; Work of WHO: Reports

Standard 1974 see Evaluation of Some Pesticide Residues in Food 1971: Monographs

Standard 1974 see Standard

Standard 1975 see Standard

Standard 1976 see Standard

Standard 1977 see Standard

Standard 1978 see Standard

Standard 1979 see Standard

Standard 1980 see Standard

Standard 1981 see Standard

Standard 1982 see Standard

Standard 1983 see Standard

Standard 90.1 Users Manual. 1992. 73.00 (*0-910110-92-1*) Am Heat Ref & Air Eng.

*__Standardbred Horse.__ Charlotte Wilcox. LC 96-46930. (Learning about Horses Ser.). (J). 1997. write for info. (*1-56065-467-8*) Capstone Pr.

*__Standardbred Horse.__ Charlotte Wilcox. (Learning about Horses Ser.). (Illus.). (J). 1997. 18.40 (*0-516-20520-X*) Childrens.

Standardfornlierungen Fur Deutsche Vertragstexte: Mit Ubersetzungen in Englischer, Franzososcher und Spanischer Sprache. (Terminological Series Issued by the Foreign Office of the Federal Republic of Germany: Vol. 4). viii, 430p. (GER.). (C). 1992. pap. text ed. 60.00 (*3-11-012824-1*) De Gruyter.

Standardisation of Manifolds for Refrigerated Liquefied Gas Carriers (LNG) OCIMF Staff. (C). 1979. 55.00 (*0-685-26148-4*, Pub. by Witherby & Co UK) St Mut.

Standardization: A New Discipline. Lal C. Verman. LC 72-8370. (Illus.). 481p. reprint ed. pap. 137.10 (*0-317-10688-0*, 2015419) Bks Demand.

Standardization: Mathematical Methods in Assortment Determination. C. Bongers. 265p. 1980. lib. bdg. 70.50 (*0-89838-029-4*) Kluwer Ac.

Standardization & Control of Biologicals Produced by Recombinant DNA Technology. Ed. by F. T. Perkins & W. Hennessen. (Developments in Biological Standardization Ser.: Vol. 59). (Illus.). viii, 216p. 1985. pap. 56.00 (*3-8055-4027-2*) S Karger.

*__Standardization & Design Optimization of Flexible Piping Elements.__ Anatolii P. Gusenkov et al. LC 96-34051. 1996. write for info. (*1-56700-069-X*) Begell Hse.

Standardization & Orthography in the Balochi Language. Carina Jahani. (Studia Iranica Upsaliensia: No. 1). 268p. (Orig.). 1989. pap. 53.00 (*91-554-2487-2*) Coronet Bks.

Standardization in Blood Fractionation Including Coagulation Factors: Joint IABS-CSL Symposium, Melbourne, May 1986. Ed. by P. Schiff & W. Hennessen. (Developments in Biological Standardization Ser.: Vol. 67). (Illus.). viii, 388p. 1987. pap. 160.00 (*3-8055-4607-6*) S Karger.

Standardization of Albumin, Plasa Substitutes & Plasmapheresis. Ed. by W. Hennessen. (Developments in Biological Standardization Ser.: Vol. 48). (Illus.). viii, 326p. 1981. pap. 60.00 (*3-8055-2496-X*) S Karger.

Standardization of Cell Substrates for the Production of Virus Vaccines: Proceedings of the Joint WHO-IABS, Geneva, 1976. Joint WHC-IABS Staff. Ed. by International Association of Biological Standardization Staff & R. H. Regamey. (Developments in Biological Standardization Ser.: Vol. 37). (Illus.). 1977. 35.25 (*3-8055-2784-5*) S Karger.

Standardization of Epidemiological Studies of Host Susceptibility. Ed. by Janice Dorman. LC 94-48569. (NATO ASI Ser.: Series A, Life Sciences: Vol. 270). 290p. 1995. 89.50 (*0-306-44892-0*, Plenum Pr) Plenum.

Standardization of Fretting Fatigue Test Methods & Equipment. Ed. by M. Helmi Attia & R. B. Waterhouse. LC 92-17237. (Special Technical Publication Ser.: No. 1159). (Illus.). 275p. 1992. text ed. 82.00 (*0-8031-1448-6*, 04-011590-30) ASTM.

Standardization of Liberian Ethnic Nomenclature. Svend E. Holsoe. (Liberian Research Working Papers: No. 6). 1979. 7.00 (*0-317-00235-X*) Arden Assocs.

Standardization of Nomenclature: International Journal of the Sociology of Language, No. 23. Ed. by J. C. Sager. 1980. pap. text ed. 60.00 (*90-279-3028-7*) Mouton.

Standardization of Radiation Dosimetry in the Soviet Union, France, the United Kingdom, the Federal Republic of Germany & Czechoslavakia. (Illus.). 101p. (Orig.). 1973. pap. 17.00 (*92-0-117073-4*, ISTR4, Pub. by IAEA AU) Bernan Associates.

Standardization of Radioactive Waste Categories. (Technical Reports: No. 101). (Illus.). (Orig.). 1970. pap. 15.00 (*92-0-125070-3*, IDC101, Pub. by IAEA AU) Bernan Associates.

*__Standardization of Sodium & Potassium Ion-Selective Electrode Systems to the Flame Photometric Reference Method: Approved Standard (1995)__ Contrib. by Gary A. Graham & Paul D'Orazio. 1995. 75.00 (*1-56238-264-0*, C29-A) Natl Comm Clin Lab Stds.

Standardization of Technical Terminology: Principles & Practices - STP 806. Ed. by C. G. Interrante & F. J. Heymann. LC 82-73769. 146p. 1983. text ed. 24.00 (*0-8031-0247-X*, 04-806000-42) ASTM.

Standardization of Technical Terminology, Vol. 2: Principles & Practices STP 991. Richard A. Strehlow. (Special Technical Publication (STP) Ser.). (Illus.). 136p. 1988. text ed. 30.00 (*0-8031-1183-5*, 04-991000-42) ASTM.

Standardization of Tests for Defective Children see On the Function of the Cerebrum

Standardization of the Immunopharmacology of Natural & Synthetic Immunomodulators. Ed. by F. Brown & J. P. Revillard. (Developments in Biological Standardization Ser.: Vol. 77). (Illus.). x, 254p. 1992. pap. 182.75 (*3-8055-5619-5*) S Karger.

Standardized Facilitation Forms (FAL Forms) International Maritime Organization Staff. 1991. text ed. 70.00 (*0-89771-887-9*, Pub. by Intl Maritime Org UK) St Mut.

Standardized Nursing Care Plans for Emergency Departments. Bourg et al. 400p. (C). (gr. 13). 1986. spiral bd. 31.95 (*0-8016-1257-8*) Mosby Yr Bk.

Standardized Protocol for the Evaluation of GAC. (Illus.). 176p. 1992. pap. 58.00 (*0-89867-626-6*, 90615) Am Water Wks Assn.

Standardized Reasoning Tests in Arithmetic & How to Utilize Them. 2nd enl. rev. ed. Cliff W. Stone. LC 70-177817. (Columbia University. Teachers College. Contributions to Education Ser.: No. 83). reprint ed. 37.50 (*0-404-55083-5*) AMS Pr.

*__Standardized RFPs: Effective Tools for Selecting Cash Management Banks.__ Bank Administration Institute Staff. LC 96-84784. 149p. (Orig.). 1996. pap. 100.00 (*0-614-30099-1*) Treasry Mgmt.

Standardized Survey Interviewing: Minimizing Interviewer-Related Error. Floyd J. Fowler, Jr. & Thomas W. Mangione. (Applied Social Research Methods Ser.: Vol. 18). (Illus.). 160p. (C). 1989. text ed. 39.95 (*0-8039-3092-5*); pap. text ed. 17.95 (*0-8039-3093-3*) Sage.

Standardized System for Evaluating Waste Disposal Sites. Harry LeGrand. 42p. 1983. 15.00 (*1-56034-043-6*, T005) Natl Grnd Water.

Standardized Tests. 1981. pap. 2.95 (*0-590-49062-1*, Scholastic Hardcover) Scholastic Inc.

Standardized Tests: A Practical Handbook. LC 91-65016. 1991. pap. text ed. 28.50 (*0-317-05384-1*) EDITS Pubs.

Standardized Tests: A Practical Handbook. Robert H. Bavernfeind et al. LC 91-65016. x, 150p. (C). 1991. pap. text ed. 28.50 (*0-9632550-0-2*) DMore Pubs.

Standardizing a Hydrochloric Acid Solution. Norman E. Griswold. (Modular Laboratory Program in Chemistry Ser.). 8p. (C). 1988. pap. text ed. 1.35 (*0-87540-349-2*, ANAL 349-2) Chem Educ Res.

Standardizing a Sodium Hydroxide Solution. Norman E. Griswold. Ed. by H. Anthony Neidig. (Modular Laboratory Program in Chemistry Ser.). 8p. (C). 1988. pap. text ed. 1.35 (*0-87540-350-6*, ANAL 350-6) Chem Educ Res.

Standardizing a Sodium Hydroxide Solution with a Standard Solution of Hydrochloric Acid. Andrew W. Zanella. Ed. by H. Anthony Neidig. (Modular Laboratory Program in Chemistry Ser.). 12p. (C). 1993. pap. text ed. 1.35 (*0-87540-426-X*, ANAL 426-X) Chem Educ Res.

Standardizing a Sodium Hydroxide Solution with Oxalic Acid. Norman E. Griswold. Ed. by H. Anthony Neidig. (Modular Laboratory Program in Chemistry Ser.). 12p. (C). 1993. pap. text ed. 1.35 (*0-87540-424-3*, ANAL 424-3) Chem Educ Res.

Standardizing a Sodium Hydroxide Solution & Using It To Analyze Vinegar. Marcia L. Gillette. (Modular Laboratory Program in Chemistry Ser.). 12p. (C). 1995. pap. text ed. 1.35 (*0-87540-466-9*, ANAL 466-9) Chem Educ Res.

Standardizing & Harmonizing Terminology: Theory & Practice, STP 1223. Ed. by Sue E. Wright & Richard A. Strehlow. LC 94-27794. (STP Ser.: No. 1223). (Illus.). 257p. 1995. 85.00 (*0-8031-1984-4*, 04-012230-42) ASTM.

Standardizing Behavioral Measurements Across Cultures, Nations & Time. Richard H. Pfau. (TWEC World Education Monographs). 31p. 1984. 3.50 (*0-685-09458-8*) I N Thut World Educ Ctr.

Standardizing English: Essays in the History of Language Change. Ed. by Joseph B. Trahern, Jr. LC 88-26029. (Tennessee Studies in Literature: Vol. 31). 208p. 1989. text ed. 26.00 (*0-87049-600-X*) U of Tenn Pr.

Standardizing Methods of Assessing Causality of Adverse Drug Reactions. Ed. by J. Venulet et al. 1982. text ed. 89.00 (*0-12-717350-1*) Acad Pr.

Standardizing Terminology for Better Communication: Practice, Applied Theory, & Results. Ed. by Richard A. Strehlow & Ellen Wright. LC 92-41098. (Special Technical Publication Ser.: No. STP 1166). (Illus.). 395p. 1993. text ed. 77.00 (*0-8031-1493-1*, 04-011660-42) ASTM.

Standardizing Written English: Diffusion in the Case of Scotland, 1520-1659. Amy J. Devitt. (Illus.). 136p. (C). 1989. text ed. 49.95 (*0-521-36446-9*) Cambridge U Pr.

Standards. William C. Brownell. (BCL1-PS American Literature Ser.). 151p. 1992. reprint ed. lib. bdg. 69.00 (*0-7812-6680-7*) Rprt Serv.

Standards, Vol. 2. (Ultimate Ser.). 256p. 1983. pap. 17.95 (*0-7935-1186-0*, 00361422) H Leonard.

*__Standards: European Telecommunications Standards & Liberalisation Guides.__ 595.00 (*0-614-18411-8*) Info Gatekeepers.

Standards: One Hundred All-Time Favorites, Vol. 1. (Ultimate Ser.). 256p. 1983. pap. 17.95 (*0-88188-161-9*, 00361421) H Leonard.

Standards: One Hundred All-Time Favorites, Vol. 3. (Ultimate Ser.). 256p. 1983. pap. 17.95 (*0-88188-606-8*, 00361423) H Leonard.

Standards: The Rough Road to the Common Byte. Martin C. Libicki. (Illus.). 46p. (Orig.). 1994. pap. text ed. write for info. (*1-879716-15-1*, P-94-6) Ctr Info Policy.

Standards Activities of Organizations in the U. S. Ed. by Robert B. Toth. 729p. (Orig.). (C). 1994. pap. text ed. 75.00 (*0-7881-0679-1*) DIANE Pub.

Standards & APEC: An Action Agenda. John S. Wilson. LC 95-24851. (Policy Analyses in International Economics Ser.: Vol. 42). (Illus.). 176p. (Orig.). 1995. pap. 12.95 (*0-88132-223-7*) Inst Intl Eco.

Standards & Certification in Europe. Brian Rothery. 216p. 1996. 69.95 (*0-566-07644-6*, Pub. by Gower UK) Ashgate Pub Co.

Standards & Common Interfaces for Video Information Systems: Proceedings of a Conference Held 25-26 October 1995, Philadelphia, Pennsylvania. Ed. by K. R. Rao. (Critical Reviews of Optical Science & Technology Ser.: Vol. CR60). 1995. pap. 66.00 (*0-8194-1983-4*) SPIE.

Standards & Criteria in Higher Education: Proceedings of Annual Conference Held December 1986. G. C. Moodie. 170p. 1986. pap. 45.00 (*1-85059-015-X*) Taylor & Francis.

Standards & Ethics for Counselling in Action. Tim Bond. (Counselling in Action Ser.: Vol. 17). (Illus.). 160p. (C). 1993. text ed. 49.95 (*0-8039-8645-9*); pap. text ed. 21.50 (*0-8039-8646-7*) Sage.

Standards & Ethics in Clinical Psychology. Richard E. Jenson. 374p. (Orig.). (C). 1992. lib. bdg. 64.00 (*0-8191-8523-X*) U Pr of Amer.

Standards & Guidance for Disclosure. Ed. by Deborah E. Kelly & Samuel B. Jones. viii, 30p. (Orig.). 1996. pap. 10.00 (*0-9652339-0-1*) Nat Invest Relat.

Standards & Guidelines for Adult Day Care. 2nd ed. National Institute on Adult Daycare, a Constituent Unit of the National Council on the Aging, Inc. Staff. LC 90-13518. 224p. 1990. pap. text ed. 25.00 (*0-910883-54-8*, 2042) Natl Coun Aging.

Standards & Guidelines for Adult Day Care: A Self-Assessment Workbook. 54p. 1990. pap. text ed., spiral bd. 12.50 (*0-910883-55-6*, 2043) Natl Coun Aging.

Standards & Guidelines of Service for the Library of Congress Network of Libraries for the Blind & Physically Handicapped, 1995. ASCLA Staff. 48p. 1995. 12.00 (*0-8389-7797-9*) ASCLA.

Standards & Illustrated Guidelines for Rehabilitating Historic Buildings. rev. ed. (Illus.). 175p. (C). 1994. pap. text ed. 30.00 (*0-7881-0481-0*) DIANE Pub.

Standards & IS Strategy. HMSO Staff. 64p. 1994. pap. 70.00 (*0-11-330653-9*, HM06539, Pub. by Stationery Ofc UK) Bernan Associates.

*__Standards & Liberalisation: European Telecommunications Standards & Liberalisation Guides.__ 795.00 (*0-614-18415-0*) Info Gatekeepers.

Standards & Practice of Homecare Therapeutics. 2nd ed. Michael M. Rothkopf. LC 96-20733. 441p. 1996. pap. 49.00 (*0-683-07375-3*) Williams & Wilkins.

Standards & Practices Guidebook: An Operating Manual for Land Trusts. LC 93-12360. 500p. (Orig.). 1993. pap. 69.00 (*0-943915-09-0*) Land Trust DC.

Standards & Review Manual for Certification in Knowledge Engineering: Handbook of Theory & Practice. Milton White & Joe Goldsmith. 600p. (C). 1990. pap. 50.00 (*0-938801-04-X*) Systemsware.

*__Standards & Scope of Advanced Rehabilitation Nursing Practice.__ Association of Rehabilitation Nurses Staff. 25p. (Orig.). (C). 1996. pap. text ed. 7.00 (*1-884278-06-X*) Rehab Nursing.

Standards & Specifications Information Sources. Ed. by Erasmus J. Struglia. LC 65-24659. (Management Information Guide Ser.: No. 6). 190p. 1973. 68.00 (*0-8103-0806-1*) Gale.

Standards & Standardization: Basic Principles & Applications. Sullivan. 112p. 1983. 55.00 (*0-8247-1919-0*) Dekker.

*__Standards & Standards Lists: European Telecommunications Standards & Liberalisation Guides.__ 695.00 (*0-614-18414-2*) Info Gatekeepers.

*__Standards & Variation in Urban Speech: Some Examples from Lowland Scots.__ Ronald K. Macaulay. LC 97-23074. (Varieties of English Around the World Ser.: No. 20). 1997. lib. bdg. write for info. (*1-55619-717-9*) Benjamins North Am.

*__Standards-Based Education.__ Tucker & Codding. 1998. 25.00 (*0-7879-3894-7*) Jossey-Bass.

Standards-Based Procurement. Kevin M. Lewis. 31p. (Orig.). 1993. pap. 10.00 (*0-936593-19-9*) UniForum.

Standards Compliance Analyst. Jack Rudman. (Career Examination Ser.: C-3109). 1994. pap. 27.95 (*0-8373-3109-9*) Nat Learn.

Standards, Conformity Assessment, & Trade: Into the 21st Century. National Research Council Staff. 238p. (Orig.). (C). 1995. pap. text ed. 37.95 (*0-309-05236-X*) Natl Acad Pr.

Standards for Adult Community Residential Services,3rd Edition. 3rd ed. American Correctional Association Staff & Commission on Accreditation for Corrections Staff. 133p. 1995. pap. 30.00 (*0-569-91011-0*) Am Correctional.

Standards for Adult Correctional Boot Camp Programs. American Correctional Association Staff & Commission on Accreditation for Corrections Staff. 155p. 1995. pap. 30.00 (*1-56991-019-7*) Am Correctional.

Standards for Adult Correctional Institutions. 3rd ed. American Correctional Association. 199p. (Orig.). 1990. pap. 43.00 (*0-929310-26-8*, 303R) Am Correctional.

Standards for Adult Local Detention Facilities. 3rd ed. 156p. 1991. pap. 35.00 (*0-929310-47-0*, 316) Am Correctional.

Standards for Adult Parole Authorities. 2nd ed. American Correctional Association Staff & Commission on Accreditation for Corrections Staff. 53p. 1981. pap. 12.00 (*0-942974-28-X*, 301) Am Correctional.

Standards for Adult Probation & Parole Field Services. 2nd ed. 65p. 1981. pap. 12.00 (*0-942974-29-8*, 304) Am Correctional.

Standards for Agency Management & Service Delivery. Council on Accreditation of Services for Families & Children Staff. LC 91-77979. 232p. 1991. per. 50.00 (*1-880853-00-0*); disk 60.00 (*0-685-59102-6*) Coun Accred Srvs Fam & Child.

Standards for Animal-Assisted Activities & Animal-Assisted Therapy. Delta Society Staff. (Illus.). 1995. pap. text ed. 10.00 (*0-9627802-5-1*) Delta Soc.

Standards for Archival Description: A Handbook. 320p. 1994. pap. 25.00 (*0-931828-96-1*) Soc Am Archivists.

Standards for Art Libraries & Fine Arts Slide Collections. Ed. by William C. Bunce. (Occasional Papers: No. 2). 48p. (Orig.). 1983. pap. 10.00 (*0-942740-01-7*) Art Libs Soc.

Standards for Art Teacher Preparation. Ed. by Foster L. Wygant. 24p. 1980. pap. 2.50 (*0-937652-28-8*) Natl Art Ed.

Standards for Auditing Computer Applications. 2nd ed. William E. Perry. 1990. Supplemented semi-annually. suppl. ed., ring bd. 182.00 (*0-87769-288-2*) Warren Gorham & Lamont.

Standards for Auditing Computer Applications, No. 1. 2nd ed. William E. Perry. 1991. Supplement, 1991-1. suppl. ed. 49.00 (*0-685-45022-8*) Warren Gorham & Lamont.

Standards for Auditing Computer Applications, No. 2. 2nd ed. William E. Perry. 1991. Supplement, 1991-2. suppl. ed. 54.00 (*0-685-45023-6*) Warren Gorham & Lamont.

Standards for Blood Banks & Transfusion Services. 17th rev. ed. Ed. by Harvey G. Klein. 86p. (Orig.). 1996. pap. text ed. 40.00 (*1-56395-061-8*, PC97-ST9617) Am Assn Blood.

Standards for Church & Synagogue Libraries. LC 77-6634. (Guide Ser.: No. 6). 20p. 1993. pap. 7.00 (*0-614-03056-0*) CSLA.

Standards for Church & Synagogue Libraries: Guidelines for Measuring Effectiveness & Progress. rev. ed. Church & Synagogue Library Association Staff. (Guide Ser.: No. 6). 24p. 1993. reprint ed. pap. 7.00 (*0-915324-36-9*) CSLA.

Standards for Conference & Retreat Centers: An Accreditation Program of the American Camping Association. LC 93-27409. 102p. 1993. pap. 19.95 (*0-87603-134-3*) Am Camping.

Standards for Cooperative Multitype Library Organizations. Association of Specialized & Cooperative Library Agencies, Headquaters Staff. 1990. 10.00 (*0-8389-7399-X*) ASCLA.

Standards for Correctional Industries. American Correctional Association Staff & Commission on Accreditation for Corrections Staff. 26p. 1981. 14.00 (*0-942974-39-5*, 306) Am Correctional.

Standards for Correctional Training Academies. American Correctional Association Staff. 136p. (Orig.). 1993. pap. text ed. 28.00 (*0-929310-94-2*, 324) Am Correctional.

Standards for Data Collection from Human Skeletal Remains: Proceedings of a Seminar at the Field Museum of Natural History. Jonathan Haas. Ed. by Jane E. Buikstra et al. LC 94-36389. (Arkansas Archeological Survey Research Ser.). (Illus.). 272p. 1994. pap. 25.00 (*1-56349-075-7*, RS44) AR Archaeol.

Standards for Day & Resident Camps: An Accreditation Program of the American Camping Association. 234p. 1993. pap. 19.95 (*0-87603-123-8*) Am Camping.

Standards for Educational & Psychological Testing. American Educational Research Association & American Psychological Association Staff. LC 85-71493. 98p. (Orig.). 1985. pap. 23.95 (*0-912704-95-0*) Am Psychol.

An Asterisk (*) at the beginning of an entry indicates that the title is appearing in BIP for the first time.

Standards for Educational & Psychological Tests Prepared by a Joint Committee of the American Psychological Association, American Educational Research Association & National Council on Measurement in Education. American Psychological Association Staff. LC 74-75734. 78p. reprint ed. pap. 25.00 (*0-7837-0495-X*, 2040819) Bks Demand.

Standards for Electronic Imaging Systems: Critical Reviews. Ed. by M. E. Courtot & M. Nier. 1991. pap. 20.00 (*0-8194-0567-1*, VOL. CR37) SPIE.

Standards for Electronic Imaging Technologies, Devices, & Systems: Proceedings of a Conference Held 1-2 February 1996, San Jose, California. Ed. by M. C. Nier. LC 95-49185. (Critical Reviews of Optical Science & Technology Ser.: Vol. CR61). 1996. pap. 70.00 (*0-8194-2016-6*) SPIE.

Standards for Electronic Monitoring Programs. American Correctional Association Staff & Commission on Accreditation for Corrections Staff. 159p. 1995. 30.00 (*1-56991-022-7*, 291) Am Correctional.

Standards for Emergency Nursing Practice. 2nd ed. National Emergency Nurses' Association Staff. 101p. (C). (gr. 13). 1993. pap. text ed. 21.00 (*0-8016-8094-8*) Mosby Yr Bk.

Standards for Employee Assistance Programs. ALMACA Staff. pap. 20.00 (*0-318-22967-6*) EAPA.

Standards for Epoxies Used in Microelectronics. NASA Staff & MSFC Staff. 115p. 1990. reprint ed. pap. 58.00 (*0-938648-17-9*) T-C Pr CA.

Standards for Equipment Employed in the Mooring & Ships at Single Point Moorings. OCIMF Staff. 1978. 36.00 (*0-317-61485-1*, Pub. by Witherby & Co UK) St Mut.

Standards for Establishing an Effective Contingency Planning & Disaster Recovery Function. Contingency Planning & Recovery Institute Staff. Ed. by Javier F. Kuong. (Illus.). 100p. 1990. student ed., ring bd. 179.00 (*0-685-34662-5*) Management Advisory Pubns.

Standards for Evaluations of Educational Programs, Projects & Materials. Joint Committee on Standards for Educational Programs Staff. LC 80-12192. 224p. 1980. text ed. 15.00 (*0-07-032725-4*) McGraw.

Standards for Excellence in Business Education. 124p. 1985. write for info. (*0-933964-28-5*) Natl Busn Ed Assoc.

Standards for Fats & Oils. 2nd ed. Harry W. Lawson. 1992. text ed. write for info. (*0-442-01053-2*) Chapman & Hall.

Standards for Fire Tests of Window Assemblies. (Two Hundred Ser.). 1990. pap. 16.75 (*0-685-58055-5*, 257-90) Natl Fire Prot.

Standards for Health Services in Correctional Institutions. 2nd ed. American Public Health Association, Jails & Prisons Task Force Staff. Ed. by Nancy N. Dubler. LC 86-14078. 160p. 1986. 15.00 (*0-87553-143-1*) Am Pub Health.

Standards for Health Services in Jails, 1992. 208p. 1992. pap. 25.00 (*0-929561-02-3*) NCCHC.

Standards for Health Services in Juvenile Detention & Confinement Facilities, 1992. 136p. 25.00 (*0-929561-01-5*) NCCHC.

Standards for Health Services in Prisons, 1992. 206p. 1992. pap. 25.00 (*0-929561-03-1*) NCCHC.

***Standards for Hematopoietic Progenitor Cells.** Ed. by Jay E. Menitove. 36p. 1996. pap. text ed. 30.00 (*1-56395-071-5*, PC97-935720) Am Assn Blood.

Standards for Hospital Libraries. Compiled by Hospital Library Standards & Practices Committee. 1984. 12.00 (*0-912176-17-2*) Med Lib Assn.

Standards for Imposing Lawyer Sanctions. ABA, Center for Professional Responsibility Staff. 63p. 1991. pap. 12. 95 (*0-318-36471-9*, 561-0104) Amer Bar Assn.

Standards for Juvenile Community Residential Facilities. 3rd ed. American Correctional Association & Commission on Accreditation for Corrections Staff. 112p. 1993. pap. 28.00 (*1-56991-004-9*, 338) Am Correctional.

Standards for Juvenile Correctional Boot Camp Programs. American Correctional Association Staff & Commission on Accreditation for Corrections Staff. 155p. 1995. 28. 00 (*1-56991-018-9*, 293) Am Correctional.

Standards for Juvenile Day Treatment Programs. American Correctional Association & Commission on Accreditation for Corrections Staff. 240p. (Orig.). 1993. pap. 28.00 (*0-929310-99-3*, 336) Am Correctional.

Standards for Juvenile Detention Facilities. 3rd ed. American Correctional Association Staff & Commission on Accreditation for Corrections Staff. 147p. 1991. pap. 28.00 (*0-929310-52-7*, 334) Am Correctional.

Standards for Juvenile Probation & Aftercare Services. 2nd ed. 69p. 1983. pap. 16.00 (*0-942974-45-X*, 333) Am Correctional.

Standards for Juvenile Training Schools. 3rd ed. American Correctional Association Staff & Commission on Accreditation for Corrections Staff. 160p. 1991. pap. 28. 00 (*0-929310-44-6*, 307) Am Correctional.

Standards for Libraries at Institutions for the Mentally Retarded. Standards for Libraries at Institutions for the Mentally Retarded Subcommittee. 32p. 1981. 5.00 (*0-8389-6460-5*) ASCLA.

Standards for Library Services in Health Care Institutions. Association of Hospital & Institution Libraries, Hospital Library Standards Committee. LC 74-124576. 31p. reprint ed. pap. 25.00 (*0-317-27838-X*, 2024220) Bks Demand.

Standards for Measuring Shoreline Changes. Ed. by William F. Tanner. 87p. 1978. pap. 5.00 (*0-686-36732-4*) FSU Geology.

Standards for Monitoring & Evaluation of the Providers of Civil Legal Services to the Poor. 113p. 1992. 10.00 (*0-685-29728-4*, 419-0009-01) Amer Bar Assn.

Standards for Nursing Professional Development: Continuing Education & Staff Development. American Nurses Association Staff. 20p. 1994. pap. 10.95 (*0-614-02737-3*, COE-17) Am Nurses Pub.

Standards for Oil Tanker Manifolds & Associated Equipment. OCIMF Staff. (C). 1981. 95.00 (*0-900886-64-1*, Pub. by Witherby & Co UK) St Mut.

***Standards for Online Communication.** Joann T. Hackos & Dawn M. Steven. LC 96-39029. 1997. pap. text ed. 44. 95 incl. cd-rom (*0-471-15695-7*) Wiley.

Standards for Parentage Testing Laboratories. 2nd rev. ed. Ed. by AABB Parentage Testing Committee. 24p. 1994. pap. text ed. 20.00 (*1-56395-037-5*) Am Assn Blood.

Standards for Preservation & Rehabilitation, No. 1258. Ed. by Stephen J. Kelley. LC 95-50874. (Special Technical Publication Ser.: Vol. 1258). (Illus.). 450p. 1996. text ed. 119.00 (*0-8031-2006-0*, Q4-012580-10) ASTM.

Standards for Publicity Programs in State Supported Colleges & Universities Derived from the Institutions Responsibility for Reporting to Its Constituents. Melvin W. Hyde. LC 73-176893. (Columbia University. Teachers College. Contributions to Education Ser.: No. 506). reprint ed. 37.50 (*0-404-55506-3*) AMS Pr.

Standards for Reading Professionals. 52p. 1992. pap. 7.95 (*0-87207-749-7*) Intl Reading.

Standards for Selected Prestressed Units, 5 units, Set. Incl. Standard Prestressed Concrete Beams for Highway Bridge Spans 30 to 140 Ft. 7p. 1985. (*0-318-60679-8*, STD 101-68); Standard Prestressed Box Beams for Highway Bridge Spans to 103 Ft. 7p. 1985. (*0-318-60680-1*, STD-107-59); Standard Prestressed Concrete Slabs for Highway Bridge Spans to 55 Ft. 7p. 1985. (*0-318-60681-X*, STD-108-59); Standard Prestressed Concrete Piles, Square, Octagonal & Cylinder. 7p. 1985. (*0-318-60682-8*, STD-112-81); Prestressed Concrete Channel Slabs for Short Span Bridges. 7p. 1985. (*0-318-60683-6*, STD-114-62); 1985. 20.00 (*0-318-19729-4*, STD-1) P-PCI.

Standards for Small Jail Facilities. American Correctional Association & Commission on Accreditation for Corrections Staff. 89p. (Orig.). 1989. pap. 23.00 (*0-929310-04-7*, 382) Am Correctional.

Standards for Small Juvenile Detention Facilities. American Correctional Association Staff & Commission on Accreditation for Corrections Staff. 131p. 1991. 28. 00 (*0-929310-60-8*, 320) Am Correctional.

Standards for Specialized Courts Dealing with Children. United States Children's Bureau Staff. LC 78-10186. (Children's Bureau Publication: 546). vi, 99p. 1978. reprint ed. lib. bdg. 22.50 (*0-313-20678-3*, CBSS, Greenwood Pr) Greenwood.

Standards for Suicide Prevention & Crisis Centers. Jerome A. Motto et al. LC 73-17029. 114p. 1974. 32.95 (*0-87705-105-4*) Human Sci Pr.

Standards for Teachers. Linda Darby-Hammond. 1994. 12. 00 (*0-89333-126-0*) AACTE.

Standards for the Accreditation of Home Care. 109p. 1988. pap. 30.00 (*0-86688-147-6*) Joint Comm Hlthcare.

Standards for the Administration of Correctional Agencies. 2nd ed. American Correctional Association & Commission on Accreditation for Corrections Staff. 172p. 1993. pap. text ed. 28.00 (*0-929310-79-9*, 335) Am Correctional.

Standards for the Assessment of Reading & Writing. International Reading Association Staff & National Council of Teachers of English Staff. 44p. 1994. pap. 8.95 (*0-87207-674-1*) Intl Reading.

Standards for the English Language Arts. LC 96-3238. (Illus.). 131p. (Orig.). (J). (gr. k-12). 1996. pap. 18.00 (*0-8141-4676-7*) NCTE.

Standards for the Practice of Therapeutic Recreation & Self Assessment Guide. American Training Association Staff. 32p. (Orig.). 1993. pap. text ed. 18.75 (*1-889435-02-3*) Am Therapeutic.

***Standards for the Professional Practice of Internal Auditing.** Institute of Internal Auditors Staff. Ed. by Lee A. Campbell. 109p. 1995. pap. 15.00 (*0-89413-367-5*, A319) Inst Inter Aud.

***Standards for Thermal Comfort: Indoor Air Temperature Standards for the 21st Century.** Humphreys et al. (Illus.). 264p. 1995. text ed. 77.50 (*0-419-20420-2*, E & FN Spon) Routledge Chapman & Hall.

Standards for Traffic Justice. 12p. 1975. pap. write for info. (*0-318-59433-1*, 523-0011) Amer Bar Assn.

Standards for Vocational Automotive Service Instruction. 118p. 1979. write for info. (*0-943350-07-7*) Motor Veh Man.

Standards for Vocational Truck-Tractor-Trailer Service Instruction. 84p. 1982. write for info. (*0-943350-06-9*) Motor Veh Man.

Standards in Electronics. Ray L. Tricker. (Illus.). 208p. 1996. 56.95 (*0-7506-2531-7*) Buttrwrth-Heinemann.

Standards in Information Technology & Industrial Control: Contributions from IFIP Working Group 5.4 1988. Ed. by N. E. Malagardis & T. J. Williams. 294p. 1988. 109. 50 (*0-444-70403-5*, North Holland) Elsevier.

Standards in Laboratory Animal Management, 2 vols. UFAW Staff. (C). 1983. 75.00 (*0-900767-36-7*) St Mut.

Standards in Pediatric Orthopedics: Tables, Charts, & Graphs Illustrating Growth. Robert N. Hensinger. (Illus.). 416p. 1986. text ed. 89.00 (*0-88167-183-5*) Lppncott-Raven.

Standards in Practice: Grades K-2. Linda K. Crafton. LC 95-26593. (Illus.). 121p. (Orig.). 1996. teacher ed., pap. 15.95 (*0-8141-4691-0*) NCTE.

Standards in Practice: Grades 6-8. Jeffrey D. Wilhelm. LC 95-49758. (Illus.). 120p. (Orig.). 1996. teacher ed., pap. 15.95 (*0-8141-4694-5*) NCTE.

Standards in Practice: Grades 9-12. Peter Smagorinsky. LC 95-49757. (Illus.). 135p. (Orig.). 1996. teacher ed., pap. 15.95 (*0-8141-4695-3*) NCTE.

Standards, Innovations & Competitiveness: The Politics & Economics of Standards in Natural & Technical Environments. Ed. by Richard Hawkins et al. (Illus.). 288p. 1995. 80.00 (*1-85898-037-2*) E Elgar.

Standards, Interpretations & Audit Criteria for Performance of Occupational Health Programs. Occupational Safety & Health Administration Staff. 218p. 1976. 50.00 (*0-932627-15-3*) Am Indus Hygiene.

Standards Library for Measurement & Control: Guidelines for Quality, Safety, & Productivity, 5 vols., Set. 12th ed. 2900p. 1995. pap. 550.00 (*1-55617-527-2*) ISA.

***Standards Lists: European Telecommunications Standards & Liberalisation Guides.** 295.00 (*0-614-18412-6*) Info Gatekeepers.

Standards Management: A Handbook for Profits. Illus. by Jim Garber. 512p. (Orig.). 1990. pap. 99.00 (*1-878129-00-7*) ANSI.

Standards of a Hospice Program of Care. National Hospice Organization Staff. 40p. 1993. ring bd. 31.50 (*0-931207-20-7*) Natl Hospice.

Standards of Bibliographical Description. Curt F. Buhler. LC 73-1431. 120p. 1973. reprint ed. text ed. 49.75 (*0-8371-6796-5*, BUBD, Greenwood Pr) Greenwood.

Standards of Care for the Health Care Professional. Meridith B. Cox. (Legal Aspects of Medical & Health Records Ser.). (Illus.). xiii, 130p. (C). 1984. pap. 40.00 (*0-912665-05-X*) Cox Pubns.

Standards of Care for the Health Care Professional. 2nd ed. Meredith B. Cox. (Illus.). xiii, 130p. 1997. spiral bd. 65.00 (*0-912665-53-X*) Cox Pubns.

Standards of Care in Anaesthesia. Thomas H. Taylor & David R. Goldhill. 192p. 1992. pap. 75.00 (*0-7506-0063-2*) Buttrwrth-Heinemann.

Standards of Care in Emergency Medicine. Herbert Wigder & Mark S. Grotefeld. 1989. write for info. (*0-318-63273-X*) Little.

Standards of Child Welfare: A Report of the Children's Bureau Conferences, May & June, 1919. Ed. by William L. Chenery & Ella A. Merrit. LC 74-1672. (Children & Youth Ser.: Vol. 6). 464p. 1974. reprint ed. 36.95 (*0-405-05952-3*) Ayer.

Standards of Emergency Nursing Practice. 109p. 17.95 (*0-318-17557-6*) Emerg Nurses IL.

Standards of Emergency Nursing Practice. 3rd ed. Emergency Nurses Association Staff. LC 94-9563. 109p. 1994. 17.95 (*0-8151-3048-1*) Emerg Nurses IL.

Standards of Ethical Conduct for Employees of the Executive Branch. 80p. (Orig.). (C). 1994. pap. text ed. 30.00 (*0-7881-0302-4*) DIANE Pub.

Standards of Flight Nursing Practice. 2nd ed. National Flight Nurses Association Staff. 128p. (C). (gr. 13). 1994. 52.95 (*0-8151-6294-4*) Mosby Yr Bk.

Standards of Human Occlusal Development. Moyers et al. (Craniofacial Growth Ser.: Vol. 5). (Illus.). 371p. 1976. 65.00 (*0-929921-03-8*) UM CHGD.

Standards of Living in the Later Middle Ages. Christopher Dyer. (Cambridge Medieval Textbooks Ser.). (Illus.). 288p. (C). 1989. text ed. 59.95 (*0-521-25127-3*); pap. text ed. 19.95 (*0-521-27215-7*) Cambridge U Pr.

Standards of Nursing Care: A Model for Clinical Practice. Wesorick. (Illus.). 400p. 1989. text ed. 41.50 (*0-397-54640-8*) Lppncott-Raven.

Standards of Oncology Nursing Practice. Mary H. Brown et al. LC 86-11102. 622p. 1989. pap. text ed. 39.95 (*0-8273-4212-8*) Delmar.

Standards of Professional Appraisal Practice & Ethics. Henry S. Harrison. (Illus.). (Orig.). 1996. pap. text ed. 34.95 (*0-927054-13-2*) H Sq Co.

Standards of Professional Conduct for Lawyers & Judges. Norman Redlich. (C). 1984. pap. 16.00 (*0-316-73658-9*) Little.

Standards of Public Morality. Arthur T. Hadley. LC 73-2509. (Big Business; Economic Power in a Free Society Ser.). 1973. reprint ed. 16.95 (*0-405-05090-9*) Ayer.

Standards of Reasonableness in Local Freight Discriminations. John M. Clark. LC 68-56651. (Columbia University. Studies in the Social Sciences: No. 97). reprint ed. 32.50 (*0-404-51097-3*) AMS Pr.

Standards of Success. Teresina R. Havens. (C). 1948. pap. 3.00 (*0-87574-043-X*) Pendle Hill.

Standards of Tax Practice: Professional Responsibility & Ethics. 2nd ed. Wolfman et al. 400p. 1992. pap. 49.50 (*0-685-67032-5*, 4805) Commerce.

Standards of the Expansion Joint Manufacturers Association. 5th ed. Expansion Joint Manufacturers Association Staff. 180p. 1993. vinyl bd. 200.00 (*0-318-16766-2*) Tubular Exch.

Standards of the Tubular Exchange Manufacturers Association. 6th ed. 242p. 1988. 200.00 (*0-318-16767-0*) Tubular Exch.

Standards of the 50's. 1990. pap. 5.95 (*0-7935-0149-0*, 00001248) H Leonard.

Standards Organizer. 353p. 1993. pap. 49.95 (*0-87603-124-6*) Am Camping.

Standards Policy for Information Infrastructure. Ed. by Brian Kahin & Janet Abbate. LC 95-8809. (Publication of the Information Infrastructure Project). 1995. 60.00 (*0-262-11206-X*); pap. 35.00 (*0-262-61117-1*) MIT Pr.

Standards, Principles & Techniques in Quantity. 4th ed. Lendal H. Kotschevar. (Hospitality, Travel & Tourism Ser.). 1989. teacher ed. 22.95 (*0-442-31911-8*) Van Nos Reinhold.

***Standards Q&A.** Music Educators National Conference Staff. 4p. (Orig.). (C). 1994. pap. write for info. (*1-56545-074-4*, 4016) Music Ed Natl.

***Standards, Recommended Practices, & Guidelines.** 313p. (Orig.). 1997. pap. text ed. 48.75 (*0-939583-97-6*) Assn Oper Rm Nurses.

***Standards, Regulations & Federal Programs for Noise Control: NOISE-CON 75.** Ed. by William W. Lang. (Noise-Con Ser.). ix, 458p. Date not set. pap. 30.00 (*0-614-25016-1*) Noise Control.

Standards Relating to Court Delay Reduction. National Conference of State Trial Judges Judical Benchbook Committee. LC 85-62250. 22p. 1985. pap. write for info. (*0-89707-181-6*, 484-0002-01) Amer Bar Assn.

***Standards, Standards List, & Liberalisation: European Telecommunications Standards & Liberalisation Guides, 3 vols., Set.** 995.00 (*0-614-18416-9*) Info Gatekeepers.

Standards, Strategy, & Policy: A Casebook. Peter Grindley. (Illus.). 266p. 1995. 59.00 (*0-19-828807-7*) OUP.

***Standards Supplement, 1996.** rev. ed. American Correctional Association Staff. 225p. 1996. pap. 35.00 (*1-56991-043-X*) Am Correctional.

Standardwoerterbuch fuer Werbung, Massenmedien und Marketing, Deutsch-English see Standard Woerterbuch fuer Werbung, Massenmedien und Marketing. Deutsch-English-Standard Dictionary of Advertising, Mass Media & Marketing. German-English

Standasrd for Telephone Equipment. 3rd ed. (C). 1995. pap. text ed. 330.00 (*1-55989-892-5*, UL 1459) Underwrtrs Labs.

***Standby & Commercial Letters of Credit.** 2nd ed. Brooke Wunnicke. (Business Practice Library). 1996. text ed. 135.00 (*0-471-12800-7*) Wiley.

Standby Arnold. Chesty Arnold. 104p. 1992. pap. 5.00 (*0-9634288-0-2*) R M C Arnold.

Standby Arnold. rev. ed. Chesty Arnold. (Illus.). 116p. 1994. pap. 9.95 (*0-9634288-1-0*) R M C Arnold.

Standby Letters of Credit. Brooke Wunnicke & Diane B. Wunnicke. 480p. 1989. text ed. 125.00 (*0-471-62289-3*) Wiley.

***Standby Letters of Credit: 1996 Cumulative Supplement.** Brooke Wunnicke & Diane B. Wunnicke. LC 89-14798. 264p. 1995. pap. 63.00 (*0-471-14486-X*, LA15) Wiley.

Standby Power Systems. Richard K. Miller & Marcia E. Rupnow. LC 90-83920. (Survey on Technology & Markets Ser.: No. 115). 50p. 1991. pap. text ed. 200.00 (*1-55865-138-1*) Future Tech Surveys.

Standby Vessels of the World. Oilfield Publications Limited Staff. (Vessels of the World Ser.). (Illus.). 300p. (C). 1992. pap. 195.00 (*1-870945-24-7*, Pub. by Oilfld Pubns Ltd UK) Am Educ Systs.

Standen: West Sussex. Oliver Garnett. (Illus.). 64p. 1993. pap. 10.95 (*0-7078-0165-6*, Pub. by Natl Trust UK) Trafalgar.

Standin' Tall Cleanliness. Janeen Brady. (Illus.). 22p. (Orig.). (J). (ps-6). 1984. student ed., pap. text ed. 1.50 (*0-944803-54-7*); pap. text ed. 9.95 incl. audio (*0-944803-55-5*) Brite Music.

Standin' Tall Courage. Janeen Brady. (Illus.). 22p. (Orig.). (J). (ps-6). 1982. student ed., pap. text ed. 1.50 (*0-944803-43-1*); pap. text ed. 9.95 incl. audio (*0-944803-45-8*) Brite Music.

Standin' Tall Dependability. Janeen Brady & Diane Woolley. (Illus.). 22p. (Orig.). (J). (ps-6). 1984. student ed., pap. text ed. 1.50 (*0-944803-59-8*); pap. text ed. 9.95 incl. audio (*0-944803-60-1*) Brite Music.

Standin' Tall Forgiveness. Janeen Brady. (Illus.). 22p. (Orig.). (J). (ps-6). 1981. student ed., pap. text ed. 1.50 (*0-944803-39-3*); pap. text ed. 9.95 incl. audio (*0-944803-40-7*) Brite Music.

Standin' Tall Gratitude. Janeen Brady & Diane Woolley. (Illus.). 22p. (Orig.). (J). (ps-6). 1982. student ed., pap. text ed. 1.50 (*0-944803-48-2*); pap. text ed. 9.95 incl. audio (*0-944803-49-0*) Brite Music.

Standin' Tall Happiness. Janeen Brady & Diane Woolley. (Illus.). 22p. (Orig.). (J). (ps-6). 1982. student ed., pap. text ed. 1.50 (*0-944803-46-6*); pap. text ed. 9.95 incl. audio (*0-944803-47-4*) Brite Music.

Standin' Tall Honesty. Janeen Brady. (Illus.). 22p. (Orig.). (J). (ps-6). 1981. student ed., pap. text ed. 1.50 (*0-944803-37-7*); pap. text ed. 9.95 incl. audio (*0-944803-38-5*) Brite Music.

Standin' Tall Love. Janeen Brady & Diane Woolley. (Illus.). 22p. (Orig.). (J). (ps-6). 1982. student ed., pap. text ed. 1.50 (*0-944803-50-4*); pap. text ed. 9.95 incl. audio (*0-944803-51-2*) Brite Music.

Standin' Tall Obedience. Janeen Brady. (Illus.). 22p. (Orig.). (J). (ps-6). 1981. student ed., pap. text ed. 1.50 (*0-944803-35-0*); pap. text ed. 9.95 incl. audio (*0-944803-36-9*) Brite Music.

Standin' Tall Self-Esteem. Janeen Brady & Diane Woolley. (Illus.). 22p. (Orig.). (J). (ps-6). 1984. student ed., pap. text ed. 1.50 (*0-944803-56-3*); pap. text ed. 9.95 incl. audio (*0-944803-57-1*) Brite Music.

Standin' Tall Service. Janeen Brady & Diane Woolley. (Illus.). 22p. (Orig.). (J). (ps-6). 1984. student ed., pap. text ed. 1.50 (*0-944803-52-0*); pap. text ed. 9.95 incl. audio (*0-944803-53-9*) Brite Music.

Standin' Tall Songbook, Vol. 1. Janeen Brady. 52p. (J). (ps-6). 1987. pap. text ed. 7.95 (*0-944803-62-8*) Brite Music.

Standin' Tall Songbook, Vol. 2. Janeen Brady. 71p. (J). (ps-6). 1988. pap. text ed. 7.95 (*0-944803-63-6*) Brite Music.

Standin' Tall Songbook, Vol. 3. Janeen Brady. 72p. (J). (ps-6). 1989. pap. text ed. 7.95 (*0-944803-64-4*) Brite Music.

Standin' Tall Work. Janeen Brady. (Illus.). 22p. (Orig.). (J). (ps-6). 1981. student ed., pap. text ed. 1.50 (*0-944803-41-5*); pap. text ed. 9.95 incl. audio (*0-944803-42-3*) Brite Music.

Standing Accused: The Organization & Practices of Criminal Defence Lawyers in Britain. Michael McConville et al. (Oxford Monographs on Criminal Law & Justice). 328p. 1994. 59.00 (*0-19-825868-2*) OUP.

S

S

***Standing Advisory Commission on Human Rights - Annual Report for 1995-96.** HMSO Staff. 368p. 1996. pap. 45.00 (*0-10-276096-9*, HM60969, Pub. by Stationery Ofc UK) Bernan Associates.

Standing Again at Sinai: Judaism from a Feminist Perspective. Judith Plaskow. LC 89-45559. 272p. 1991. reprint ed. pap. 16.00 (*0-06-066684-6*) Harper SF.

Standing Against the Whirlwind: Evangelical Episcopalians in Nineteenth-Century America. Diana H. Butler. LC 93-34323. (Religion in America Ser.). 320p. (C). 1995. 45.00 (*0-19-508542-6*) OUP.

Standing & Understanding: A Re-Appraisal of the Christian Faith. Stanley B. Frost. LC 68-59095. 187p. reprint ed. pap. 53.30 (*0-317-26033-2*, 2023834) Bks Demand.

Standing & Walking with Functional Electrical Stimulation (FES) for People with Paralysis. Carole Kantor. 5p. 1992. pap. text ed. 5.00 (*1-888470-02-X*) FES Info Ctr.

Standing at Armageddon: The United States, 1877-1919. Nell I. Painter. LC 86-33111. 1989. pap. 15.95 (*0-393-30588-0*) Norton.

Standing at the Crossroads: Southern Life in the Twentieth Century. Pete Daniel. LC 96-34839. 259p. 1996. reprint ed. pap. text ed. 14.95 (*0-8018-5495-4*) Johns Hopkins.

Standing Bear & the Ponca Chiefs. Thomas H. Tibbles. Ed. & Intro. by Kay Graber. LC 94-42222. Orig. Title: The Ponca Chief. xiv, 143p. 1995. pap. 7.95 (*0-8032-9426-3*, Bison Books) U of Nebr Pr.

Standing Before God: Studies on Prayer in Scripture & in Essays in Honor of John M. Oesterreicher. Asher Finkel & Lawrence Frizzell. 1981. 49.50 (*0-87068-708-5*) Ktav.

Standing Before the Shouting Mob: Lenoir Chambers & Virginia's Massive Resistance to Public-School Integration. Lenoir Chambers & Alexander S. Leidholdt. LC 96-19043. 29.95 (*0-8173-0858-X*) U of Ala Pr.

Standing Beside You: A Book for Bereaved Parents. Linda K. Maurer. LC 97-93340. 88p. (Orig.). 1996. pap. 9.95 (*0-9636977-1-4*) L K Maurer.

Standing by & Making Do: Women of Wartime Los Alamos. Ed. by Jane S. Wilson & Charlotte Serber. LC 88-26761. (Illus.). 130p. (Orig.). 1988. pap. 8.95 (*0-941232-08-5*) Los Alamos Hist Soc.

Standing Commissions of the Supreme Soviet: Effective Co-optation. Robert W. Siegler. LC 81-19925. 304p. 1982. text ed. 55.00 (*0-275-90902-6*, C0902, Praeger Pubs) Greenwood.

Standing Committee on Federal Judiciary: What It Is & How It Works. 5th ed. 13p. 1991. pap. write for info. (*0-89707-621-4*, 373-0001) Amer Bar Assn.

Standing Day by Day. Marilyn Phillipps. 1994. write for info. (*1-884794-13-0*) Eden Pubng.

***Standing Fast: Battles of a Champion.** Michelle Akers & Tim Nash. (Orig.). 1997. pap. 12.95 (*1-887791-04-3*) JTC Sports.

Standing Fast: Ministry in an Unfriendly World. Ed. by Ed Dobson et al. (Pressure Points Ser.). 168p. 1994. 15.99 (*0-88070-646-5*, Multnomah Bks) Multnomah Pubs.

Standing Fast: The Autobiography of Roy Wilkins. Roy Wilkins & Tom Mathews. (Illus.). 384p. 1994. reprint ed. pap. 14.95 (*0-306-80566-9*) Da Capo.

***Standing Female Nude.** Carol A. Duffy. 62p. 1993. pap. 14.95 (*0-85646-150-4*, Pub. by Anvil Press UK) Dufour.

Standing Firm: Reclaiming Christian Faith in Times of Controversy. Parker T. Williamson. 221p. (Orig.). 1996. pap. 12.00 (*0-9652602-0-8*) PLC Publns.

Standing Firm in Jesus: A Daily Guide for Spiritual Warfare. 2nd ed. abr. ed. Sarah Hornsby. (Illus.). 368p. (gr. 10). 1994. spiral bd. 9.99 (*0-8007-9217-3*) Chosen Bks.

Standing Firm in These Last Days: First & Second Thessalonians. Kay Arthur & Bob Vereen. (International Inductive Study Ser.). 120p. 1996. pap. 4.99 (*1-56507-387-8*) Harvest Hse.

Standing Firmly upon God's Word. Gene Steiner. 1994. pap. 5.95 (*1-886045-13-5*) Covenant Marriages.

Standing for God, the Story of Elijah. Roger Ellsworth. 138p. 1994. pap. 7.99 (*0-85151-665-3*) Banner of Truth.

Standing Guard: Protecting Foreign Capital in the 19th & 20th Centuries. Charles Lipson. LC 83-24260. (Studies in International Political Economy: Vol. 11). 330p. 1985. pap. 16.00 (*0-520-05327-3*) U CA Pr.

Standing in Heat: The Myth of the Corporate Slut. Jessica Flemming & Bill Tyson. LC 93-85262. (Illus.). 160p. (Orig.). 1993. pap. 12.95 (*1-883445-04-3*) Plain Brown.

Standing in Line. Jerry D. Miley. 20p. (Orig.). 1990. pap. 3.00 (*0-916397-08-4*) Manic D Pr.

Standing in Love: A Guide to Repairing Broken Marriages. Bob Christensen & Lynne Christensen. (Illus.). 73p. (Orig.). 1990. pap. 5.95 (*1-886045-01-1*) Covenant Marriages.

Standing in the Doorway of Life. Tyrone Parnell. 80p. 1995. pap. 12.00 (*0-9645299-0-4*) Inspired Images.

Standing in the Gap. Don Gilmore. 104p. (Orig.). 1991. mass mkt. 4.95 (*0-87508-178-9*, 178) Chr Lit.

Standing in the Gap. Essex Hemphill. Date not set. pap. 19.95 (*0-525-93816-8*) NAL-Dutton.

Standing in the Gap. Marilyn Hickey. 37p. (Orig.). pap. 1.00 (*1-56441-167-2*) M Hickey Min.

Standing in the Light: A Lakota Way of Seeing. Richmond. 1994. 30.00 (*0-939185-00-8*) General Communications Inc.

Standing in the Light: A Lakota Way of Seeing. Severt Young Bear & R. D. Theisz. LC 93-50834. (American Indian Lives Ser.). (Illus.). xxxii, 210p. (C). 1994. pap. 12.00 (*0-8032-9912-5*, Bison Books) U of Nebr Pr.

Standing in the Light: A Lakota Way of Seeing. Severt Young Bear & R. D. Theisz. LC 93-50834. (American Indian Lives Ser.). (Illus.). xxxii, 210p. 1994. text ed. 35.00 (*0-8032-4911-X*) U of Nebr Pr.

Standing in the Shadows of Motown: The Life & Music of Legendary Bassist James Jamerson. Dr. Licks. 208p. 1989. pap. 32.95 incl. audio compact disk (*0-88188-882-6*, 00698960) H Leonard.

Standing in the Tempest: Painters of the Hungarian Avante-Garde, 1908-1930. Ed. by Steven A. Mansbach. (Illus.). 240p. 1991. 47.50 (*0-262-13274-5*) MIT Pr.

Standing in Your Own Way: Tales on the Nature of Ego. Anthony Damiani. 270p. 1992. pap. 15.95 (*0-943914-60-4*) Larson Pubns.

Standing Invitation: To Gracious Southern Living. Dawson United Methodist Women's Staff. Ed. by Lynette Cowart & Mary Tuck. (Illus.). 400p. 1990. 16.95 (*0-9627311-0-2*) Dawson United Methodist.

***Standing Liberty Quarters.** 3rd rev. ed. J. H. Cline. (Illus.). 192p. Date not set. 34.95 (*1-880731-55-X*); pap. 24.95 (*1-880731-54-1*) DLRC Pr.

Standing of Psychoanalysis. Brian A. Farrell. (Oxford Paperbacks University Ser.). 240p. 1982. pap. 10.95 (*0-19-289120-0*) OUP.

Standing on High Places: The Story of Hannah Hurnard & Hinds' Feet on High Places. Isabel Anders. LC 94-18881. 128p. 1994. pap. 8.99 (*0-8423-5933-8*) Tyndale.

Standing on My Knees. John Olive. 1983. pap. 5.25 (*0-8222-1071-1*) Dramatists Play.

Standing on One Foot. large type ed. Ed. & Intro. by Kenneth Jernigan. (Kernel Bk.: No. 6). (Illus.). 84p. (Orig.). 1994. pap. 3.00 (*0-9624122-8-7*) Natl Fed Blind.

***Standing on the Promises.** 1995. pap. 1.20 (*0-8341-9383-3*) Lillenas.

Standing on the Promises, or Sitting on the Premises. James W. Moore. LC 95-8274. 144p. (Orig.). 1995. pap. 10.00 (*0-687-00807-7*) Dimen for Liv.

Standing on the Rock: Biblical Authority in a Secular Age. rev. ed. James M. Boice. LC 93-36780. 200p. (C). 1994. pap. 9.99 (*0-8010-1076-4*) Baker Bks.

Standing on the Shoulders of Geniuses: They Will Rob & Cheat You, & Kill You. Ricardo A. Scott. (Ras Cardo Speaks Ser.). (Illus.). 75p. (Orig.). Date not set. pap. write for info. (*1-883427-71-1*) Crnerstone GA.

Standing on the Shoulders of Giants: A Longer View of Newton & Halley. Ed. by Norman J. Thrower. LC 90-10715. 408p. 1990. 48.00 (*0-520-06589-1*) U CA Pr.

Standing Orders of House of Lords Relating to Public Business 1994. 62p. 1995. pap. 20.00 (*0-10-401595-0*, HM15950, Pub. by Stationery Ofc UK) Bernan Associates.

Standing Outside on the Inside: Black Adolescents & the Construction of Academic Identity. Olga M. Welch & Carolyn R. Hodges. LC 96-21039. (SUNY Series, the Social Context of Education). 144p. (C). 1997. text ed. 44.50 (*0-7914-3341-2*); pap. text ed. 14.95 (*0-7914-3342-0*) State U NY Pr.

Standing Outside the Fire & Other Hot Country Singles. Ed. by Carol Cuellar. 44p. (Orig.). (YA). 1994. pap. text ed. 7.95 (*0-89898-886-1*, F3421SMX) Warner Brothers.

Standing Ovation: Appreciating the Success You Are! Peter D. Burns. 256p. (Orig.). 1995. pap. 12.95 (*0-9646035-0-0*) Paradigm WI.

Standing Ovations. Tri-City Symphony Orchestra Board Editors. (Illus.). 308p. reprint ed. spiral bd. 9.50 (*0-317-00009-8*) Bawden Bros.

Standing Ovations...Devi Dja: Woman of Java. Leona M. Merrin. Ed. by Mary Baum. (Illus.). 417p. (Orig.). 1990. pap. 8.95 (*0-9624120-0-7*) Lee & Lee Pub.

Standing Room Only. Beth Cruise. (Saved by the Bell Ser.: No. 24). (J). 1996. pap. text ed. 3.50 (*0-689-80625-6*, Aladdin Paperbacks) S&S Childrens.

***Standing Room Only.** Philip De Courcey. Ed. by Tomm Knutson. 200p. 1997. pap. 10.99 (*1-889893-12-9*) Emerald House Group Inc.

Standing Room Only? Edward A. Ross. Ed. by Gerald Grob. LC 76-46101. (Anti-Movements in America Ser.). 1977. reprint ed. lib. bdg. 31.95 (*0-405-09972-X*) Ayer.

Standing Room Only: Strategies for Marketing the Performing Arts. Philip Kotler & Joanne Scheff. LC 96-10225. 576p. 1996. 60.00 (*0-87584-737-4*) Harvard Busn.

***Standing Room Only: Strategies for Marketing the Performing Arts.** Philip Kotler & Joanne Scheff. 1996. text ed. 45.00 (*0-07-103849-3*) McGraw.

Standing Room Only: The World's Exploding Population. Karl Sax. LC 83-1757. Orig. Title: The Challenge of Overpopulation, 1955 edition. xviii, 206p. (C). 1983. reprint ed. text ed. 35.00 (*0-313-23968-1*, SAST, Greenwood Pr) Greenwood.

Standing Room. Stories. Hollis S. Summers. LC 84-10004. 104p. 1984. pap. 9.95 (*0-8071-1200-3*) La State U Pr.

***Standing Soldiers, Kneeling Slaves: Race, War, & Monument in Nineteenth-Century America.** Kirk Savage. LC 97-9731. 1997. write for info. (*0-691-01616-X*) Princeton U Pr.

Standing Still & Walking in New York. Frank O'Hara. Ed. by Donald Allen. LC 74-75455. 192p. 1975. reprint ed. pap. 6.95 (*0-912516-12-7*) Grey Fox.

Standing Still While Traffic Moved about Me. Robert Hutchinson. LC 79-165697. 1971. 20.00 (*0-87130-028-1*); pap. 12.50 (*0-87130-029-X*) Eakins.

Standing Stones & Other Monuments of Early Ireland. Kenneth McNally. (Illus.). 128p. 1991. reprint ed. pap. 14.95 (*0-86281-201-1*, Pub. by Appletree Pr IE) Irish Bks Media.

***Standing Stones of Europe: A Guide to the Great Megalithic Monuments.** Jean Bradbery & Alastair Service. (Illus.). 288p. 1997. pap. 15.95 (*0-297-83545-9*, Pub. by Orion Bks UK) Trafalgar.

Standing Strong: Notes from Joseph's Journal. Sandy Larsen. (Bible Discovery Guide Ser.). (Illus.). 32p. (Orig.). 1986. student ed., pap. text ed. 1.50 (*0-87788-784-5*); teacher ed., pap. text ed. 3.50 (*0-87788-785-3*) Shaw Pubs.

Standing Tall: How a Man Can Protect His Family. Steve Farrar. 224p. 1994. 17.99 (*0-88070-618-X*, Multnomah Bks) Multnomah Pubs.

Standing Tall: The Shawn Bradley Story. Shawn Bradley & Brenton Yorgason. 1993. 11.95 (*0-88494-912-5*) Bookcraft Inc.

Standing Tall: The Stories of Ten Hispanic Americans. Argentina Palacios. 192p. (J). (gr. 4-6). 1994. pap. 3.50 (*0-590-47140-6*) Scholastic Inc.

***Standing Tall: Unusually Tall People.** Elaine Landau. LC 96-41681. (First Bk.). (J). 1997. lib. bdg. 21.00 (*0-531-20257-7*) Watts.

Standing the Gaff: The Life & Hard Times of a Minor League Umpire. Harry S. Johnson. Ed. by Larry R. Gerlach. LC 93-30952. (Illus.). xlvi, 148p. 1994. reprint ed. pap. 6.95 (*0-8032-7579-X*, Bison Books) U of Nebr Pr.

Standing Timber, Pt. 1. U. S. Dept. of Commerce & Labor-Bureau of Corporations. LC 72-2873. (Lumber Industry). 1972. reprint ed. text ed. write for info. (*0-318-50840-0*) Ayer.

Standing Timber see Lumber Industry

Standing to Change - Changing to Stand. Danny A. Dixon. 122p. (Orig.). 1993. pap. 5.95 (*1-56794-034-X*, C2293) Star Bible.

Standing Together. Howard Hendricks. 1995. 17.99 (*1-885305-31-1*) Multnomah Pubs.

***Standing Together When Life's Falling Apart.** abr. ed. Dennis Rainey & Barbara Rainey. Ed. by Julie Denker. 20p. (Orig.). (C). 1994. 1.95 (*1-57229-000-5*) FamilyLife.

Standing up, Standing Together: The Emergence of the National Association of Evangelicals. Arthur H. Matthews. (Illus.). xiv, 187p. (Orig.). 1992. pap. 8.95 (*1-880844-00-1*) Nat Assn Evan.

Standing upon the Mouth of a Volcano: New South Georgia. Ed. by Mills Lane. (A Documentary History Ser.). 245p. 1993. 35.00 (*0-88322-018-0*) Beehive GA.

Standing Wave. John Taggart. (Lost Roads Ser.: No. 38). 88p. (Orig.). 1993. pap. 10.95 (*0-918786-43-6*) Lost Roads.

***Standing Without Apology: The History of Bob Jones University.** Daniel Turner. Ed. by Steve Skaggs. LC 96-52624. 1997. pap. 19.95 (*0-89084-930-7*, 102673) Bob Jones Univ Pr.

Standing Witnesses. Thorbjorn Campbell. (Illus.). 200p. (C). 1993. text ed. 35.00 (*0-85976-381-1*, Pub. by J Donald UK) St Mut.

Standing Witnesses. Thorbjorn Campbell. (C). 1995. pap. 39.95 (*0-85411-061-5*, Pub. by Saltire Soc) St Mut.

Standing Your Ground: Principles to Help You Stand in Your Marriage Covenant. Linda Harrower. (Illus.). 22p. 1994. pap. 2.00 (*1-886045-05-4*) Covenant Marriages.

Standing Your Ground: Territorial Disputes & International Conflict. Paul K. Huth. LC 95-48856. (C). 1995. 47.50 (*0-472-10689-9*) U of Mich Pr.

Standish: The Families of Standish of Standish, Lancashire, England; & Standish of Dusbury, Arley, Ormskirk, Gathurst, Croston, Park Brook & Wantage; Prescott of Standish & Prescott of Driby. Frederick L. Weis. 77p. 1994. reprint ed. pap. 15.00 (*0-8328-4240-0*); reprint ed. lib. bdg. 25.00 (*0-8328-4239-7*) Higginson Bk Co.

Standish Chronicles. Robert Singleton. 154p. (Orig.). 1993. pap. 6.95 (*1-56043-107-5*) Destiny Image.

Standish of Standish. Jane G. Austin. (Works of Jane (Goodin) Austin). 1989. reprint ed. lib. bdg. 79.00 (*0-7812-1831-4*) Rprt Serv.

Standish O'Grady. Phillip L. Marcus. LC 74-124647. (Irish Writers Ser.). 92p. 1975. 8.50 (*0-8387-7751-1*); pap. 1.95 (*0-8387-7660-4*) Bucknell U Pr.

Standoff. Chuck Hogan. 368p. 1996. mass mkt. 6.50 (*0-553-57446-9*) Bantam.

Standoff. Lee Magner. (Intimate Moments Ser.). 1993. mass mkt. 3.50 (*0-373-07507-3*, 5-07507-2) Silhouette.

Standoff. large type ed. Chuck Hogan. LC 95-17111. 1995. 25.95 (*1-56895-231-7*) Wheeler Pub.

Standoff at Sunrise Creek. Stephen A. Bly. LC 92-33517. (Stuart Brannon Western Ser.). 192p. 1993. pap. 7.99 (*0-89107-695-6*) Crossway Bks.

Standoff at Sunrise Creek. large type ed. Stephen A. Bly. LC 95-3703. 270p. 1995. 20.95 (*0-7838-1275-2*, GK Hall) Thorndike Pr.

Standoff at the Border: A Failure of Microdiplomacy. Thomas J. Price. (Southwestern Studies: No. 87). (Orig.). 1989. pap. 10.00 (*0-87404-173-2*) Tex Western.

Standortkatalog der Sammlung Welding. Armin Hetzer. Ed. by Staats- & Universitatsbibliothek Bremen Staff. xi, 214p. (GER.). 1990. lib. bdg. 100.00 (*3-598-10931-8*) K G Saur.

Standpipe & Hose Systems. National Fire Protection Association Staff. 1993. 20.25 (*0-317-63051-2*, 14-93) Natl Fire Prot.

Standpipe Systems License. (Career Examination Ser.: C-3768). pap. 23.95 (*0-8373-3768-2*) Nat Learn.

***Standridge: Caddoan Settlement in a Mountain Environment.** Ann M. Early et al. (Illus.). 195p. 1988. pap. 10.00 (*1-56349-056-0*, RS29) AR Archaeol.

Stands A Calder Man. Janet Dailey. Incl. This Calder Range. (*0-318-57963-4*); This Caldor Sky. (*0-318-57964-2*); Calder Born, Calder Bred. (*0-318-57965-0*); boxed 15.80 (*0-671-90082-X*) PB.

Stands a Calder Man. Janet Dailey. 1983. mass mkt. 6.99 (*0-671-87516-7*) PB.

Standup Shakespeare. Ray Leslee & Kenneth Welsh. 1997. pap. 6.00 (*0-8222-1526-8*) Dramatists Play.

***Stanford: Home of Champions.** Gary Migdol. 1997. 39.95 (*1-57167-116-1*) Sagamore Pub.

Stanford Album: A Photographic History, 1885-1945. Margo Davis & Roxanne Nilan. (Illus.). 320p. 1989. 24.95 (*0-8047-1639-0*) Stanford U Pr.

Stanford Bank Game, Version 10. George G. Parker & Terrence Beals. 124p. (C). 1988. Teaching notes. teacher ed. write for info. (*0-89426-130-4*) Course Tech.

Stanford Bank Game: Version 11. George G. Parker & Terry Beals. LC 94-43533. 1996. pap. 26.50 (*0-87709-876-X*) Course Tech.

Stanford Bank Game Version 11 International Manual. Parker. (GC - Principles of Management Ser.). 1996. pap. 36.95 (*0-87709-877-8*) S-W Pub.

Stanford Bank Game Version 11 International Manual: International Commercial Manual. Parker. (GC - Principles of Management Ser.). 1995. pap. 26.50 (*0-7895-0095-7*) Course Tech.

Stanford Bank Game 11: Commercial Manual. Parker. (Principles of Management Ser.). 1995. pap. 26.50 (*0-7895-0094-9*) Course Tech.

Stanford Binet. 4th ed. John R. Whitworth & Dorothy L. Sutton. 240p. 1989. pap. 38.00 (*0-87879-637-1*) Acad Therapy.

Stanford-Binet Intelligence Scale. Lewis M. Terman & M. A. Merrill. 1973. 189.00 (*0-395-15925-3*); student ed. 20.88 incl. lp (*0-395-09542-5*); student ed. 21.93 (*0-395-15936-9*) HM.

Stanford Companion to Victorian Fiction. John Sutherland. LC 88-61462. 695p. (C). 1989. 79.50 (*0-8047-1528-9*); pap. 22.50 (*0-8047-1842-3*) Stanford U Pr.

Stanford Environmental Law Journal, Vol. 12. Linda A. Malone et al. 220p. (C). 1993. pap. 15.00 (*0-942007-36-0*) Stanford Enviro.

Stanford Environmental Law Journal, Vol. 13. Intro. by Johanna Wald. 260p. (Orig.). (C). 1994. pap. 15.00 (*0-942007-32-8*) Stanford Enviro.

Stanford Environmental Law Journal, Vol. 14, Issue 2. Intro. by Raymond Austin. 250p. (Orig.). pap. text ed. 15.00 (*0-942007-40-9*) Stanford Enviro.

Stanford Environmental Law Journal, Vol. 14, No. 1. Intro. by Luke W. Cole. 211p. (Orig.). 1995. pap. text ed. 15.00 (*0-942007-39-5*) Stanford Enviro.

Stanford Environmental Law Journal, 1990, Vol. 9. Dunne et al. 197p. (Orig.). 1990. pap. 15.00 (*0-942007-34-4*) Stanford Enviro.

Stanford Environmental Law Journal, 1991, Vol. 10. Ed. by Judith G. Tracy. 240p. (Orig.). 1991. pap. 15.00 (*0-685-53633-5*) Stanford Enviro.

Stanford Environmental Law Journal, 1992, Vol. 11. Ed. by Tracey George. 1992. pap. 15.00 (*0-685-53634-3*) Stanford Enviro.

Stanford Graphbase: A Platform for Combinatorial Computing. Donald E. Knuth. (Illus.). 608p. (C). 1994. text ed. 45.25 (*0-201-54275-7*) Addison-Wesley.

***Stanford Handbook: Stories, Stats & Stuff about Cardinal Football.** Dave Kellogg. (Illus.). 160p. (Orig.). 1996. pap. 9.95 (*1-880652-86-2*) Wichita Eagle.

Stanford House Staff Auxiliary Guidebook to the Bay Area: A Guide for Finding Your Way Around the Bay from Napa to Monterey. Sheila K. Robinson. LC 93-86355. (Illus.). 170p. (Orig.). 1994. pap. 9.95 (*0-9637673-3-X*) Napa Sonoma.

Stanford Intramural Law Review, 1 Vol. 1948. ring bd. 37.50 (*0-8377-9218-5*) Rothman.

Stanford Journal of International Law: 1966-1996, 32 vols., Set. Bound set. 1,092.50 (*0-8377-9151-0*) Rothman.

Stanford Law Review: 1948-1995/96, 48 vols., Set. Bound set. 2,630.00 (*0-8377-9152-9*) Rothman.

Stanford Legal Essays. Ed. by John H. Merryman. LC 75-182. 480p. 1975. 57.50 (*0-8047-0884-3*) Stanford U Pr.

Stanford Life Plan for a Healthy Heart: The 25 Gram Plan plus Over 200 Low-Fat Recipes from the World-Renowned Stanford University Medical Center. John S. Schroeder et al. LC 95-17132. 608p. 1996. 29.95 (*0-8118-1045-3*) Chronicle Bks.

Stanford Manual of Cardiopulmonary Transplantation. Ed. by Julian A. Smith et al. (Illus.). 320p. 1996. 65.00 (*0-87993-637-1*) Futura Pub.

Stanford Mathematics Problem Book: With Hints & Solutions. George Polya et al. LC 73-86270. 72p. reprint ed. pap. 25.00 (*0-317-09309-6*, 2019663) Bks Demand.

Stanford Museum Centennial Handbook: One Hundred Works of Art. Carol M. Osborne et al. LC 90-72067. (Illus.). 128p. (Orig.). (C). 1991. 20.00 (*0-937031-07-0*); pap. 10.00 (*0-937031-00-3*) Stanford Art.

Stanford Skull, a Probable Early Man from Santa Clara County, California. fac. ed. R. F. Heizer & T. D. McCown. (Reports of the University of California Archaeological Survey: No. 6). 20p. (Orig.). 1950. reprint ed. pap. 2.15 (*1-55567-332-5*) Coyote Press.

Stanford Slavic Studies, Vol. 1. Ed. by Lazar Fleishman et al. 385p. (ENG & RUS.). 1987. pap. text ed. 30.00 (*0-926953-00-1*) Berkeley Slavic.

Stanford Stories: Tales of a Young University. Charles K. Field & William H. Irwin. LC 71-121541. (Short Story Index Reprint Ser.). 1977. 23.95 (*0-8369-3497-0*) Ayer.

Stanford Studies in Language & Literature 1941: Fiftieth Anniversary of the Founding of Stanford University. Stanford University, School of Letters Staff. Ed. by Hardin Craig. LC 67-30232. (Essay Index Reprint Ser.). 1977. 30.95 (*0-8369-0901-1*) Ayer.

Stanford Two-Mile Accelerator. Ed. by Richard B. Neal. LC 68-24364. (Illus.). 1183p. reprint ed. pap. 180.00 (*0-8357-3820-5*, 2057030) Bks Demand.

Stanford University: The First Twenty-Five Years. Orrin L. Elliott. Ed. by Walter P. Metzger. LC 76-55191. (Academic Profession Ser.). (Illus.). 1977. reprint ed. lib. bdg. 54.95 (*0-405-10013-2*) Ayer.

***Stanford University Healthy Heart Cookbook & Life Plan: Over 200 Delicious Low-Fat Recipes.** Helen C. Page. 1997. pap. 17.95 (*0-8118-1750-4*) Chronicle Bks.

Stanford University Medical Center Auxiliary Cookbook. SUMC Auxiliary Staff. Ed. by Molly Huckins. 268p. (Orig.). 1988. pap. 14.50 (*0-9621781-0-1*) SUMC Aux.

Stanford University Museum of Art: The Drawing Collection. Lorenz Eitner et al. (Illus.). 420p. 1993. 60.00 (*0-295-97294-7*) U of Wash Pr.

Stanford University Museum of Art, the Drawing Collection. Carol M. Osborne et al. LC 92-44797. (Illus.). 1993. 60.00 (*0-937031-02-X*); pap. 40.00 (*0-937031-01-1*) Stanford Art.

Stanford University, Nineteen Sixteen to Forty-One. John P. Mitchell. LC 58-59714. 120p. reprint ed. pap. 30.00 (*0-317-30440-2*, 2024927) Bks Demand.

Stanford White. Charles C. Baldwin. LC 78-150512. (Architecture & Decorative Art Ser.: Vol. 39). 1971. reprint ed. pap. 6.95 (*0-306-80031-4*); reprint ed. lib. bdg. 49.50 (*0-306-70138-3*) Da Capo.

***Stanford White: Letters to His Family.** Stanford White. Ed. by Claire N. White. LC 96-37364. (Illus.). 192p. 1997. 29.95 (*0-8478-2022-X*) Rizzoli Intl.

Stanforth Secrets. Jo Beverley. 256p. 1991. mass mkt. 3.99 (*0-380-71438-8*) Avon.

Stanforth Secrets. large type ed. Jo Beverley. LC 90-10728. 386p. 1990. lib. bdg. 18.95 (*0-89621-971-2*) Thorndike Pr.

Stangl & Pennsbury Birds. Mike Schneider. LC 94-65630. (Illus.). 144p. (Orig.). 1994. pap. 19.95 (*0-88740-612-2*) Schiffer.

Stangl Pottery. Harvey Duke. LC 92-50192. (Illus.). 160p. 1992. pap. 19.95 (*0-87069-674-2*) Chilton.

Stanhope. Elms College Staff. (Nursing Texts Ser.). (C). (gr. 13). 1996. 69.45 (*0-8151-4494-6*) Mosby Yr Bk.

Stanislaski Sisters: Taming Natasha, Falling for Rachel. Nora Roberts. 1997. mass mkt. 5.99 (*0-373-20134-6*, 1-20134-2) Harlequin Bks.

Stanislaus: With Feet in the World. Barbaralie Stiefermann. LC 89-85494. (Illus.). 320p. (Orig.). 1990. pap. 9.00 (*0-9625781-0-X*) Schl Sisters St Francis.

Stanislaus County: An Illustrated History. Kathleen M. Gooch. (Illus.). 176p. (YA). (gr. 7 up). 1988. 27.95 (*0-89781-245-X*) Am Historical Pr.

Stanislaus Indian Wars. Thorne B. Gray. 302p. 1993. 29.95 (*0-930349-02-4*); pap. 19.95 (*0-930349-01-6*) McHenry Mus Soc.

Stanislaus River: From Camp Nine to Parrots Ferry. Keith Robinson & Fred Lehman. (Whitewater Ser.). (Illus.). 1982. pap. 3.95 (*0-941838-01-3*) Lore Unlim.

Stanislaus, the Struggle for a River. Tim Palmer. LC 81-43692. (Illus.). 311p. reprint ed. pap. 88.70 (*0-7837-4696-2*, 2044443) Bks Demand.

Stanislav Libensky & Jaroslava Brychtova: A 40 Year Collaboration in Glass. Thomas Buechner et al. (Illus.). 224p. 1995. 99.95 (*3-7913-1252-9*, Pub. by Prestel GW) te Neues.

Stanislav Libensky & Jaroslava Brychtova: Paintings, Drawings & Sculpture. Kate Elliott. 32p. 1995. 20.00 (*0-9647982-0-4*) Elliott Brown Gall.

Stanislavski: A Biography. Jean Benedetti. (Illus.). 320p. 1988. 29.95 (*0-87830-984-5*, Thtre Arts Bks) Routledge.

Stanislavski: An Introduction. Jean Benedetti. 79p. 1987. pap. 7.95 (*0-87830-578-5*, Thtre Arts Bks) Routledge.

Stanislavski in Rehearsal: The Final Years. V. O. Toporkov. Tr. by Christine Edwards. 224p. (C). 1987. text ed. 18.95 (*0-87830-162-3*, Thtre Arts Bks) Routledge.

Stanislavski on Opera. Constantin Stanislavski & P. I. Rumyantsev. Tr. by Elizabeth R. Hapgood. LC 72-87119. (Illus.). 374p. 1987. pap. 14.95 (*0-87830-552-1*, Thtre Arts Bks) Routledge.

Stanislavski System: The Professional Training of an Actor. 2nd rev. ed. Sonia Moore. 144p. 1984. pap. 11.95 (*0-14-046660-6*, Penguin Bks) Viking Penguin.

Stanislavski's Encounter with Shakespeare: The Evolution of a Method. Joyce V. Morgan. LC 83-17979. (Theater & Dramatic Studies: No. 14). (Illus.). 186p. reprint ed. pap. 53.10 (*0-8357-1485-3*, 2070485) Bks Demand.

Stanislavskis Legacy. Stanislavskis. 1985. pap. 4.95 (*0-87830-504-1*) Routledge Chapman & Hall.

Stanislavski's Legacy. rev. ed. Constantin Stanislavski. Tr. by Elizabeth R. Hapgood. LC 68-16450. 209p. (Orig.). 1987. pap. 9.95 (*0-87830-127-5*, Thtre Arts Bks) Routledge.

Stanislavsky: A Life. David Magarshack. 432p. 1986. pap. 13.95 (*0-571-13791-1*) Faber & Faber.

Stanislavsky Directs. Nikolai Gorchakov. Tr. by Marina Goldina. LC 85-18214. 416p. (C). 1985. reprint ed. pap. 17.95 (*0-87910-051-6*) Limelight Edns.

Stanislavsky Directs. Nikolai M. Gorchakov. Tr. by Miriam Goldina. LC 73-15243. 402p. 1974. reprint ed. text ed. 45.00 (*0-8371-7164-4*, GOSD, Greenwood Pr) Greenwood.

Stanislavsky, Konstantin: Selected Works. Compiled by Oksana Korneva. 310p. 1984. 45.00 (*0-317-42834-9*) St Mut.

Stanislavsky on the Art of the Stage. 2nd ed. Konstantin Stanislavsky. 320p. 1988. pap. 11.95 (*0-571-08172-X*) Faber & Faber.

Stanislavsky Revealed: The Actor's Guide to Spontaneity on Stage. Sonia Moore. (Acting Ser.). 256p. 1991. pap. 10.95 (*1-55783-103-3*) Applause Theatre Bk Pubs.

Stanislavsky Technique: Russia: A Workbook for Actors. Mel Gordon. 264p. 1988. pap. 12.95 (*0-936839-08-2*) Applause Theatre Bk Pubs.

Stanislaw Lem. J. Madison Davis. LC 87-17646. (Starmont Reader's Guide Ser.: No. 32). x, 116p. 1990. pap. 17.00 (*1-55742-026-2*) Borgo Pr.

Stanislaw Lem. J. Madison Davis. LC 87-17646. (Starmont Reader's Guide Ser.: No. 32). x, 116p. 1990. lib. bdg. 27.00 (*1-55742-027-0*) Borgo Pr.

Stankevich & His Moscow Circle, 1830-1840. Edward J. Brown. 149p. 1966. 25.00 (*0-8047-0295-0*) Stanford U Pr.

Stanley. (J). Date not set. pap. 1.50 (*0-590-38027-3*) Scholastic Inc.

Stanley. Pam Gems. 96p. (Orig.). 1996. pap. 14.95 (*1-85459-254-8*, Pub. by N Hern Bks UK) Theatre Comm.

Stanley. Syd Hoff. LC 91-12266. (Trophy I Can Read Bk.). (Illus.). 64p. (J). (gr. k-3). 1992. pap. 3.75 (*0-06-444010-9*, Trophy); lib. bdg. 12.89 (*0-06-022536-X*) HarpC Child Bks.

Stanley: Behind Barbed Wire. Jean Gittins. 176p. (C). 1982. pap. text ed. 27.00 (*962-209-061-3*, Pub. by Hong Kong U Pr HK) St Mut.

Stanley & Kilcullen's Federal Income Tax Law. Stephan R. Leimberg. 1994. pap. text ed. 95.00 (*0-7913-1988-1*) Warren Gorham & Lamont.

Stanley & Kilcullen's Federal Income Tax Law (SK) Stephan R. Leimberg et al. LC 84-50708. 1991. pap. 95.00 (*0-7913-0971-1*, SK) Warren Gorham & Lamont.

Stanley & Livingstone: Expeditions Through Africa. Clint Twist. LC 94-21642. (Beyond the Horizons Ser.). (J). (gr. 1-8). 1995. lib. bdg. 24.26 (*0-8114-3976-3*) Raintree Steck-V.

Stanley & Rhoda. Rosemary Wells. LC 78-51874. (Pied Piper Bks.). (Illus.). 40p. (J). (ps-2). 1981. pap. 4.95 (*0-8037-7995-X*, 0383-120) Dial Bks Young.

Stanley & Rhoda. Rosemary Wells. (J). 1993. pap. 5.99 (*0-14-054707-X*, Puff Pied Piper) Puffin Bks.

Stanley & the Magic Lamp. Jeff Brown. LC 95-23158. (Trophy Chapter Bk.). (Illus.). 96p. (J). (gr. 1-5). 1996. pap. 3.95 (*0-06-442028-0*, Trophy) HarpC Child Bks.

***Stanley Bleifeld.** Stanley Bleifeld et al. LC 96-3191. 1996. write for info. (*1-56833-083-9*) Madison Bks UPA.

Stanley Book of Woodworking Tools, Techniques & Projects. Mark Finney. (Illus.). 160p. (Orig.). 1995. pap. 19.95 (*1-55870-379-9*, Betrwy Bks) F & W Pubns Inc.

Stanley Boxer: Forty Years of Drawing. Stanley Boxer. (Illus.). (Orig.). 1991. write for info. (*0-925941-03-4*) Dorsky Gallery.

Stanley Burnshaw Reader. Stanley Burnshaw. LC 89-48330. 328p. 1990. pap. 20.00 (*0-8203-1196-0*) U of Ga Pr.

Stanley Catalog Collection. Emil S. Pollak. (Illus.). 400p. 1989. 29.50 (*0-9618088-4-5*) Astragal Pr.

***Stanley Catalog Collection.** Illus. by Emil S. Pollak. 400p. 1989. reprint ed. pap. 22.50 (*1-879335-74-3*) Astragal Pr.

Stanley Cavell: Philosophy's Recounting of the Ordinary. Stephen Mulhall. 376p. 1994. 65.00 (*0-19-824074-0*) OUP.

Stanley Cavell & Literary Skepticism. Michael Fischer. LC 88-30312. 180p. 1989. pap. text ed. 13.95 (*0-226-25141-1*); lib. bdg. 33.00 (*0-226-25140-3*) U Ch Pr.

Stanley Clarke Collection. 19.95 (*0-7935-4443-2*, 00672307) H Leonard.

Stanley Cobb: A Builder of the Modern Neurosciences. Benjamin V. White. (Illus.). 445p. 1984. 29.50 (*0-318-04637-7*) F A Countway.

Stanley Combination Plane. rev. ed. Kenneth D. Roberts. (Illus.). 80p. 1989. pap. 8.50 (*0-9618088-3-7*) Astragal Pr.

Stanley Complete Step-by-Step Book of Home Repair & Improvement. James A. Hufnagel. Ed. by William L. Broecker. LC 93-16746. (Illus.). 480p. 1993. 25.00 (*0-671-74442-9*) S&S Trade.

Stanley Cup. Jonathan Bliss. LC 93-50579. (J). 1994. write for info. (*1-55916-012-8*) Rourke Bk Co.

Stanley Cup. William McGuire. (Great Moments in Sports Ser.). 32p. (J). (gr. 4). 1990. lib. bdg. 14.95 (*0-88682-316-1*) Creative Ed.

Stanley Cup: Old Time Hockey Trivia. Don Weekes. (Illus.). 144p. 1996. pap. 9.95 (*1-55054-509-4*, Pub. by Greystone Bks) Sterling.

***Stanley Cup: One Hundred Years of Hockey at Its Best.** Darcy Jenish. 1996. pap. text ed. 16.99 (*0-7710-4407-0*) McCland & Stewart.

Stanley Cup Fever: One Hundred Years of Hockey Greatness. Brian McFarlane. 271p. 1992. pap. 15.95 (*0-7737-5554-3*) Genl Dist Srvs.

Stanley Donen. John A. Casper. LC 83-2913. (Filmmakers Ser.: No. 5). 300p. 1983. 25.00 (*0-8108-1615-6*) Scarecrow.

Stanley Elkin to Patricia Highsmith see Library of Literary Criticism

***Stanley Elkin/Alasdair Gray.** (Review of Contemporary Fiction Ser.: Vol. 15, No. 2). 1995. pap. 8.00 (*1-56478-128-3*) Dalkey Arch.

Stanley Family of America as Descended from John, Timothy & Thomas Stanley of Hartford, Connecticut, 1636. I. P. Warren. (Illus.). 352p. 1989. reprint ed. pap. 52.50 (*0-8328-1109-2*); reprint ed. lib. bdg. 60.50 (*0-8328-1108-4*) Higginson Bk Co.

Stanley K. Hornbeck & the Open Door Policy 1919-1937. Shizhang Hu. LC 94-29834. (Contributions to the Study of World History Ser.). 280p. 1995. text ed. 62.95 (*0-313-29394-5*, Greenwood Pr) Greenwood.

Stanley Kramer Film Maker. 2nd ed. Donald Spoto. LC 90-3190. (Illus.). 367p. 1990. reprint ed. pap. 14.95 (*0-573-60609-9*) S French Trade.

***Stanley Kubrick: A Biography.** John Baxter. (Illus.). 384p. 1997. pap. 13.95 (*0-7867-0485-3*) Carroll & Graf.

Stanley Kubrick: A Biography. Vincent LoBrutto. LC 96-35737. (Illus.). 480p. 1996. pap. 29.95 (*1-55611-492-3*) D I Fine.

Stanley Kubrick: A Narrative & Stylistic Analysis. Mario Falsetto. LC 93-49620. (Contributions to the Study of Popular Culture Ser.). 232p. 1994. text ed. 59.95 (*0-313-29246-9*, Greenwood Pr); pap. text ed. 17.95 (*0-275-95082-4*, Praeger Pubs) Greenwood.

Stanley Kubrick & the Art of Adaptation: Three Novels, Three Films. Greg Jenkins. (Illus.). 216p. 1996. lib. bdg. 35.00 (*0-7864-0281-4*) McFarland & Co.

Stanley Kunitz: An Introduction to the Poetry. Gregory Orr. LC 84-23213. (Columbia Introductions to Twentieth Century American Poetry Ser.). 296p. 1985. text ed. 37.50 (*0-231-05234-0*) Col U Pr.

Stanley M. Isaacs, the Conscience of New York. Terry J. Ruderman. 1981. 38.95 (*0-405-14105-X*) Ayer.

Stanley Marcus: A Life with Books. David Farmer. LC 95-7570. (Illus.). 150p. 1995. pap. 17.95 (*0-87565-147-X*) Tex Christian.

Stanley Marcus Collection of Christmas Books. Illus. by David Price. (Orig.). 1968. pap. 10.00 (*0-87959-029-7*) U of Tex H Ransom Ctr.

Stanley Morison. Nicolas J. Barker. LC 76-189157. (Illus.). 566p. 1972. 45.00 (*0-674-83425-9*) HUP.

Stanley Morison. Beatrice Warde. 1967. 2.00 (*0-910330-15-8*) Grant Dahlstrom.

Stanley Morison & D. B. Updike: Selected Correspondence. Ed. by David J. McKitterick. LC 79-87761. (Illus.). 1979. 25.00 (*0-89679-001-0*) Moretus Pr.

Stanley Roseman & the Dance: Drawings from the Paris Opera. Stanley Roseman. (Illus.). 256p. 1996. 75.00 (*0-9652950-0-1*) R Davis NY.

Stanley Saitowitz. Ed. by Michael Bell. (Architecture at Rice Ser.: Vol. 33). (Illus.). 136p. 1996. 27.95 (*1-885232-03-9*) Princeton Arch.

Stanley Saitowitz. Stanley Saitowitz. LC 94-18117. (Architecture at Rice University Ser.: Vol. 33). 1994. write for info. (*1-885232-00-4*) Rice U Sch Archit.

Stanley Saitowitz: A House in the Transvaal. George Wagner. (Illus.). 88p. 1996. pap. 24.95 (*1-56898-034-5*) Princeton Arch.

Stanley Spencer. Duncan Robinson. (Illus.). 128p. (C). 1993. reprint ed. pap. 24.95 (*0-7148-2810-6*, Pub. by Phaidon Press UK) Chronicle Bks.

***Stanley Spencer: A Biography.** Kenneth Pople. (Illus.). 576p. 1997. pap. 24.00 (*0-00-255664-2*) HarperColl Wrld.

***Stanley Spencer: A Complete Catalogue of the Paintings.** Keith Bell. (Illus.). 545p. 1992. 195.00 (*0-7148-2735-5*, Pub. by Phaidon Press UK) Chronicle Bks.

***Stanley Spencer: English Visions.** Fiona MacCarthy. 1997. 45.00 (*0-300-07337-2*) Yale U Pr.

Stanley the Sleuth Uncovers the Story of Casimir Pulaski. Rochelle A. Carman. LC 94-93853. (Illus.). 40p. (J). (gr. k-4). 1995. 14.95 (*1-886325-18-9*) DanNiall Pubng.

Stanley, the Talking Parrot. Ronald W. Robinson. LC 89-60801. (Illus.). 22p. (Orig.). (J). (gr. 3-4). 1989. Incl. cassette & filmstrip pkg. 12.95 incl. audio, flmstrp (*0-9622692-2-0*); Incl. cassette pkg. 8.95 incl. audio (*0-9622692-1-2*); pap. 4.95 (*0-9622692-0-4*) R W Robinson.

***Stanley Truman - Fifty Years of Photography: Images from 1936-1986.** Marvin A. Schenck. (Illus.). 20p. (Orig.). 1996. pap. 8.95 (*1-886091-13-7*) Hearst Art Gal.

Stanley's Story or Through the Wilds of Africa. D. M. Kelsey. 1988. 37.00 (*0-935632-74-3*) Wolfe Pub Co.

Stanleyville: An African Urban Community under Belgian Administration. Valdo Pons. LC 70-396468. 383p. reprint ed. pap. 109.20 (*0-8357-3222-3*, 2057116) Bks Demand.

Stannic Oxide Gas Sensor: Principles & Applications. Kousuke Ihokura. LC 93-35554. 208p. 1994. 59.95 (*0-8493-2604-4*) CRC Pr.

Stanstead, Forest & Clearings: History of Stanstead Co., Province of Quebec, with Sketches of More Than 500 Families. B. F. Hubbard. Ed. by John Lawrence. (Illus.). 367p. 1995. reprint ed. lib. bdg. 42.50 (*0-8328-4612-0*) Higginson Bk Co.

Stansted: Norman Foster & the Architecture of Flight. Ken Powell. (Illus.). 112p. 1992. 29.95 (*1-872180-99-X*, Pub. by Fourth Estate UK) Trafalgar.

Stanton: The Life & Times of Lincoln's Secretary of War. Benjamin P. Thomas & Harold M. Hyman. LC 80-18970. (Illus.). xvii, 642p. 1980. reprint ed. text ed. 89.50 (*0-313-22581-8*, THSL, Greenwood Pr) Greenwood.

Stanton White. Asa Z. Hall. LC 72-39086. (Black Heritage Library Collection). 1977. reprint ed. 22.95 (*0-8369-9024-2*) Ayer.

Stanvac in Indonesia. National Planning Association Staff. Ed. by Stuart Bruchey & Eleanor Bruchey. LC 76-5022. (American Business Abroad Ser.). (Illus.). 1976. reprint ed. 19.95 (*0-405-09289-X*) Ayer.

Stanwyck. Axel Madsen. 496p. 1995. mass mkt. 6.99 (*0-06-109067-0*) HarpC.

Stanyan Street & Other Sorrows. Rod McKuen. 1994. lib. bdg. 25.95 (*1-56849-474-2*) Buccaneer Bks.

Stanzaic Morte: A Verse Translation of "Le Morte Arthur" Sharon Kahn. LC 86-9175. 144p. (Orig.). (C). 1986. pap. text ed. 16.00 (*0-8191-5427-X*) U Pr of Amer.

Stanzas: The Word & the Phantasm in Western Culture. Giorgio Agamben. Tr. by Ronald L. Martinez from FRE. (Theory & History of Literature Ser.: Vol. 89). 224p. (C). 1992. text ed. 39.95 (*0-8166-2037-7*); pap. text ed. 16.95 (*0-8166-2038-5*) U of Minn Pr.

Stanzas for an Evening Out: Poems 1968-1977. Curtis Favile. 1977. 7.50 (*0-685-04175-1*); 4.00 (*0-685-04176-X*) L Pubns.

Stanzas in Meditation. Gertrude Stein. (Sun & Moon Classics Ser.: No. 44). 232p. (Orig.). 1994. pap. 11.95 (*1-55713-169-4*) Sun & Moon CA.

Stanzas in Meditation & Other Poems, (Nineteen Twenty-Nine to Nineteen Thirty-Three), Vol. Six Of Unpublished Works Of Gertrude Stein In. Gertrude Stein. LC 70-103666. (Select Bibliographies Reprint Ser.). 1980. 30.95 (*0-8369-5166-2*) Ayer.

Stanzas of Dzyan: Notes for Study on Cosmogenesis & Anthropogenesis. Elsie Benjamin. (Study Ser.: No. 5). 45p. 1981. pap. 6.00 (*0-913004-40-5*) Point Loma Pub.

Stanzas on Vibration: The SpandaKarika with Four Commentaries. Tr. by Mark S. Dyczkowski. LC 91-36928. (SUNY Series in the Shaiva Traditions of Kashmir). 427p. 1992. text ed. 24.50 (*0-7914-1261-X*) State U NY Pr.

Stanze of Angelo Poliziano. Tr. by David Quint from ITA. LC 92-35532. 128p. (C). 1993. reprint ed. pap. 14.95 (*0-271-00937-3*) Pa St U Pr.

Stanzi: A Magic Christmas Story. John L. Oberleitner. Tr. by Teresa McMahon-Ehalt. 33p. (J). 1995. 16.95 (*1-884889-11-5*) Suarez.

Staphlocci & Staphylococcal Infections: Proceedings of the International Symposium, Stockholm, June 29-July 3, 1992. Ed. by Roland Mollry & Jan-Ingmar Flock. (Zentralblatt fur Bakteriologie Supplement Ser.: No. 26). (Illus.). xxiv, 571p. 1994. 160.00 (*3-437-11541-3*, Pub. by G Fischer Verlag GW) Lubrecht & Cramer.

Staphylococcal Disease in the Soviet Union - Epidemiology & Response to a National Epidemic. Daivd Shrayer. Ed. by Michael Oxman. (Illus.). 144p. (Orig.). 1989. pap. 75.00 (*1-55831-113-0*) Delphic Associates.

Staphylococci. Ed. by Janusz Jeljaszewicz. (Zentralblatt fur Bakteriologie Supplements Ser.: Vol. 14). (Illus.). 706p. 1985. lib. bdg. 195.00 (*0-89574-216-0*, Pub. by G Fischer Verlag GW) Lubrecht & Cramer.

Staphylococci: Proceedings of the Sixth International Symposium on Staphylocci & Staphylococcal Infections, Warsaw, Sept. 4-8, 1989. Ed. by Janusz Jeliaszewicz & Pawel Ciborowski. (Zentralblatt fur Bakteriologie Supplements Ser.: Vol. 21). 450p. 1991. text ed. 225.00 (*1-56081-304-0*, Pub. by G Fischer Verlag GW) Lubrecht & Cramer.

Staphylococci & Staphylococcal Infections, 1. Charles S. Easmon & Chris A. Easman. 1984. text ed. 149.00 (*0-12-228101-2*) Acad Pr.

***Staphylococci in Human Disease.** Kent B. Crossley & Gordon Archer. LC 96-49803. 1996. write for info. (*0-443-07644-8*) Churchill.

Staple Food Economies of Western Tropical Africa. Bruce F. Johnston. xi, 305p. 1958. 45.00 (*0-8047-0537-2*) Stanford U Pr.

***Staple Foods.** Ed. by Harlan Walker. (Proceedings of the Oxford Symposium on Food Ser.). (Illus.). 248p. (Orig.). 1990. pap. 35.00 (*0-907325-44-0*, Pub. by Prospect UK) Food Words.

Staple of News. Ben Jonson. Ed. by A. N. Parr. (Revels Plays Ser.). 256p. 1990. text ed. 17.95 (*0-7190-1631-2*, Pub. by Manchester Univ Pr UK) St Martin.

Staple of News. Ben Jonson. Ed. by Devra R. Kifer. LC 74-76133. (Regents Renaissance Drama Ser.). 197p. 1975. reprint ed. pap. 56.20 (*0-608-02045-1*, 2062698) Bks Demand.

Staple State: Canadian Industrial Resources in Cold War. Melissa Clark-Jones. 38.50 (*0-8020-5700-4*); pap. 19.95 (*0-8020-6626-7*) U of Toronto Pr.

Stapled Duplexing Job Analysis. Juneann Kasper. Ed. by Thomas A. Minnella. (Copier Productivity Ser.). 71p. (Orig.). 1994. pap. 95.00 (*0-9629936-1-1*) Minnella Ent.

Staples - CIG Making Money on Wall Street. 1994. 16.95 (*1-56761-643-7*, Alpha Ref) Macmillan Gen Ref.

Staples - CIG to Buying Selling a Home. 1994. 16.95 (*1-56761-642-9*, Alpha Ref) Macmillan Gen Ref.

Staples - Elements of Grammar PPR. 1986. 7.00 (*0-02-860546-2*) Macmillan.

Staples - OMR Lotus 1-2-3. 1993. 6.99 (*1-56761-633-X*, Alpha Ref) Macmillan Gen Ref.

Staples - OMR WordPerfect 6.0. 1993. 6.99 (*1-56761-628-3*, Alpha Ref) Macmillan Gen Ref.

Staples - Oops! PC Problem Solver. 1992. 16.95 (*0-7897-0332-7*) Que.

Staples - Organize Yourself PPR. 1986. 8.95 (*0-02-860543-8*) Macmillan.

Staples - Using Microsoft Office. 1994. student ed. 29.99 (*0-7897-0309-2*) Que.

Staples - Using the Internet. William Eager. 1994. 19.99 (*0-7897-0712-8*) Que.

Staples - Using Your PC. 1994. 19.99 (*0-7897-0316-5*) Que.

Staples for Success. Ed. by Thomas G. Stemberg. 160p. 1996. 22.95 (*1-888232-24-2*) Knowldge Exchange.

Staples, Markets, & Cultural Change: Selected Essays. Harold A. Innis. Ed. by Daniel Drache. (Innis Centenary Ser.). 552p. 1995. 55.00 (*0-7735-1299-3*, Pub. by McGill CN); pap. 24.95 (*0-7735-1302-7*, Pub. by McGill CN) U of Toronto Pr.

Stapling in Gastrointestinal Surgery. Boulds. Date not set. write for info. (*0-7506-1394-7*) Buttrwrth-Heinemann.

Star. Mark Dunster. 11p. (Orig.). 1991. pap. 4.00 (*0-89642-202-X*) Linden Pubs.

Star. Peter Mills. (Window Bks.). (Illus.). 16p. (J). 1995. pap. text ed. 1.99 (*0-88070-789-5*, Gold & Honey) Multnomah Pubs.

Star. Danielle Steel. 456p. 1989. 19.95 (*0-440-50072-9*) Delacorte.

Star. Jane Walker. (Little Christmas Window Book Ser.). (Illus.). 14p. (J). (gr. k-3). 1996. bds. 3.99 (*1-57584-045-6*) Rdrs Dgst Yng Fam.

Star. deluxe limited ed. Danielle Steel. 1989. 100.00 (*0-440-50172-5*) Delacorte.

Star. large type ed. Danielle Steel. 1993. 21.95 (*0-385-50170-6*, Delacorte LT) BDD LT Grp.

Star. large type ed. Danielle Steel. LC 93-9259. (General Ser.). 1993. pap. 20.95 (*0-8161-5769-3*, GK Hall) Thorndike Pr.

Star. Danielle Steel. 480p. 1990. reprint ed. mass mkt. 6.50 (*0-440-20557-3*, Dell Trade Pbks) Dell.

Star: And Other Korean Short Stories. Tr. by Agnita Tennant from KOR. LC 95-43446. 160p. 1996. 29.00 (*0-7103-0533-8*, Pub. by Kegan Paul Intl UK) Col U Pr.

Star Almanac for Land Surveyors, No. 1995. 80p. 1994. pap. 11.95 (*0-11-886501-3*, HM65013, Pub. by Stationery Ofc UK) Bernan Associates.

S

Star & the Garter. Aleister Crowley. 1973. lib. bdg. 250.00 (*0-87968-175-6*) Krishna Pr.

Star & the Lily: Native American Story Pak. Retold by K. Hollenbeck. (Graphic Learning Literature Program Series: Folk Tales). (Illus.). (ENG & SPA.). 1992. 43.00 (*0-87746-269-0*) Graphic Learning.

Star & the Scared Little Creature, Bk. 2. Sharon L. Karim. (Unicorn Ser.: Bk. 2). (Illus.). 32p. (J). (ps-3). 1995. 12.95 (*1-883703-01-8*) Big Heart Pub.

Star & the Sword. Pamela Melnikoff. LC 94-5813. (Illus.). 140p. (J). (gr. 3 up). 1994. 8.95 (*0-8276-0528-5*) JPS Phila.

Star & the Wreath. Bobby Owens. 227p. (Orig.). 1993. 33.95 (*1-884308-00-7*) Enlisted Ldrship.

Star Ascendant. Louise Cooper. 352p. 1995. 23.95 (*0-312-85871-X*) Tor Bks.

***Star Ascendant, Vol. 1.** Louise Cooper. 1996. mass mkt. 5.99 (*0-8125-5175-3*) Tor Bks.

***Star Babies.** Mary S. Rain. (Illus.). (J). (gr. k-6). 1997. bds. 12.95 (*1-57174-069-4*) Hampton Roads Pub Co.

Star Bear. Rhyk Gilbar. LC 95-92813. (Illus.). 32p. (J). 1997. pap. 6.95 (*1-888588-08-X*, Star Bear); lib. bdg. 14.95 (*1-888588-07-1*, Star Bear) Positive Press.

Star Beast. Robert A. Heinlein. 256p. 1987. mass mkt. 5.99 (*0-345-35059-6*, Del Rey) Ballantine.

Star Beast. Robert A. Heinlein. 1984. 15.00 (*0-684-15329-7*) S&S Trade.

Star-Bones Weep the Blood of Angels. Sue Storm. 60p. 1995. pap. text ed. 5.00 (*1-886988-01-3*) Jasmine Sail.

Star Book for Ministers. rev. ed. Edward T. Hiscox. 1967. 11.00 (*0-8170-0167-0*) Judson.

Star-Borne: A Remembrance for the Awakened Ones. Solara. (Illus.). 346p. (Orig.). 1989. pap. 14.95 (*1-878246-00-3*) Star-Borne.

Star Boy. Paul Goble. LC 91-8694. (Illus.). 32p. (J). (gr. k-3). 1991. reprint ed. pap. 5.99 (*0-689-71499-8*, Aladdin Paperbacks) S&S Childrens.

***Star Bright!** Greeley. LC 97-13846. 1997. 13.95 (*0-312-86387-X*) St Martin.

Star-Bright Lie. Coleman Dowell. LC 92-30873. (Illus.). 192p. 1993. 19.95 (*1-56478-022-8*) Dalkey Arch.

***Star Brothers.** Mary Wells-Noyes. 1996. 19.95 (*1-887361-02-2*) Wolf Wise Pub.

Star by Star. 2nd ed. Naomi L. Madgett. LC 77-143900. 61p. (YA). (gr. 7-12). 1970. reprint ed. per. 5.00 (*0-916418-00-6*) Lotus.

Star Cafe. Mary Caponegro. 192p. 1991. pap. 8.95 (*0-393-30791-3*) Norton.

Star Caster: Cast the Stars & Read Your Future. 2nd ed. Jannine Palmer. 72p. 1993. pap. text ed. 30.00 (*0-9636085-0-9*) Jasmine Prods.

Star Catalogues: A Centennial Tribute to A. N. Vyssotsky. Ed. by A. G. Davis Philip & A. R. Upgren. 100p. 1989. 20.00 (*0-933485-10-7*) L Davis Pr.

Star-Chamber Cases, Shewing What Causes Properly Belong to the Cognizance of That Court. Richard Crompton. LC 74-28842. (English Experience Ser.: No. 723). 1975. reprint ed. 20.00 (*90-221-0723-X*) Walter J Johnson.

Star Chart. Colorprint Staff. 1988. pap. 4.95 (*0-8416-9574-1*, 695741) Am Map.

Star Children. Clara Asscher-Pinkhof. Tr. by Terese Edelstein & Inez Smidt from DUT. LC 86-24543. Orig. Title: Sterrekinderen. (Illus.). 268p. 1987. reprint ed. 29.95 (*0-8143-1846-0*) Wayne St U Pr.

Star Children: The True Story of Alien Offspring among Us. Jenny Randles. LC 95-30212. 224p. 1995. pap. 10.95 (*0-8069-3856-0*) Sterling.

Star Clusters: Proceedings of the International Astronomical Union, 85th Symposium, Victoria, B.C., Canada, Aug. 27-30, 1979. Astronomical Union Symposium Staff. Ed. by James E. Hesser. (International Astronomical Union Symposia Ser.: No. 85). 540p. 1980. lib. bdg. 158.50 (*90-277-1087-2*) Kluwer Ac.

Star Connection. Philip S. Berg. 256p. (ITA.). 1994. pap. write for info. (*0-924457-65-1*) Res Ctr Kabbalah.

Star Connection. rev. ed. Philip S. Berg. 224p. 1992. write for info. (*0-318-70374-2*); write for info. (*0-318-70375-0*); write for info. (*0-318-70376-9*); write for info. (*0-318-70377-7*); write for info. (*0-318-70378-5*); write for info. (*0-318-70379-3*); pap. 14.95 (*0-924457-11-2*) Res Ctr Kabbalah.

Star Control: Interbellum: A Novel. W. T. Quick. 1996. mass mkt. 5.99 (*0-7615-0196-7*) Prima Pub.

Star Control 3: The Official Strategy Guide. Daniel Greenberg. 1996. pap. 19.99 (*0-7615-0156-8*) Prima Pub.

Star Country. Jill Robinson. 352p. 1996. 23.00 (*0-449-90861-5*) Fawcett.

***Star Country.** Jill Robinson. 1997. mass mkt. 6.50 (*0-8041-1551-6*) Ivy Books.

***Star Creek Papers.** Horace M. Bond & Julia W. Bond. Ed. by Adam Fairclough. LC 96-48851. 1997. 19.95 (*0-8203-1904-X*) U of Ga Pr.

***Star Crock: Reality: the Final Frontier.** David J. Richardson. 260p. 1997. pap. 12.95 (*1-889120-05-7*) StarsEnd Creations.

Star-Crossed. Saranne Dawson. 448p. (Orig.). 1994. mass mkt., pap. text ed. 4.99 (*0-505-51982-8*, Love Spell) Dorchester Pub Co.

Star-Crossed. Jillian Grey. 448p. 1994. mass mkt. 4.50 (*0-8217-4558-1*, Zebra Kensgtn) Kensgtn Pub Corp.

Star-Crossed Lovers. Joann Ross. (Temptation Ser.). 1993. mass mkt. 2.99 (*0-373-25532-2*, 1-25532-2) Harlequin Bks.

Star Crossed Renaissance. Allen. 35.00 (*0-7146-1029-1*, Pub. by F Cass Pubs UK) Intl Spec Bk.

Star Crown Empire & the Sea of Lotas. Mike Cremer et al. Ed. by John D. Ruemmler. (Shadow World Ser.). (Illus.). 64p. (Orig.). (C). 1989. pap. 12.00 (*1-55806-074-X*) Iron Crown Ent Inc.

Star Crusader: A Novel. Bruce Balfour. 1995. mass mkt. 5.99 (*0-7615-0067-7*) Prima Pub.

Star Crusader: The Official Strategy Guide. Ed Dille. 1995. pap. 19.95 (*1-55958-778-4*) Prima Pub.

Star Cycles: The Life & Death of Stars. Isaac Asimov. LC 95-7892. (Isaac Asimov's Library of the Universe). (J). (gr. 3 up). 1995. lib. bdg. 18.60 (*0-8368-1227-1*) Gareth Stevens Inc.

***Star Dancers.** Spider Robinson & Jeanne Robinson. 416p. 1997. mass mkt. 5.99 (*0-671-87802-6*) Baen Bks.

Star Diaries. Stanislaw Lem. Tr. by Michael Kandel. LC 83-26385. (Illus.). 286p. 1985. pap. 8.95 (*0-15-684905-4*, Harvest Bks) HarBrace.

***Star Drive Campaign Setting.** TSR Inc. Staff. 1997. 30.00 (*0-7869-0738-X*) TSR Inc.

Star Dwarves Travesty see Star Dwarves Trilogy

***Star Dwarves Trilogy.** 2nd rev. ed. David J. Richardson. LC 96-72269. Orig. Title: The Star Dwarves Travesty. 256p. 1996. pap. 12.95 (*1-889120-06-5*) StarsEnd Creations.

Star Fall to the Raw Law of Worship & Other Select Poems. Robert Guinther. LC 87-91025. 46p. (Orig.). (C). 1989. pap. 3.00 (*0-9619248-0-2*) R Guinther.

Star Fiction. Erik Belgum. 1996. write for info. (*1-886214-01-8*) Detour Pr.

Star Fighter Battle Books. (Star Wars Supplements Ser.). 444p. 25.00 (*0-87431-092-X*, 40011) West End Games.

Star Film Ranch Presents Texas' First Picture Show. Frank Thompson. 272p. 1995. pap. 12.95 (*1-55622-481-8*, Rep of TX Pr) Wordware Pub.

Star Finder: Guide to the Northern Sky. Larry Deckman. 1995. pap. 11.99 (*0-945200-02-1*) Star Finders.

Star Fisher. Laurence Yep. 160p. (J). (gr. 5 up). 1992. pap. 3.99 (*0-14-036003-4*, Puffin) Puffin Bks.

Star Fisher. Laurence Yep. LC 90-23785. 150p. (J). (gr. 3 up). 1991. 16.00 (*0-688-09365-5*, Morrow Junior) Morrow.

Star Fleet Academy Entrance Exam: Tantalizing Trivia from Classic Star Trek Voyager. Bill Adler, Jr. & Peggy Robin. 224p. 1995. pap. 9.95 (*0-8065-1695-X*, Citadel Pr) Carol Pub Group.

Star Fleet Technical Manual. Franz Joseph. 194p. (Orig.). 1986. pap. 14.00 (*0-345-34074-4*, Ballantine Trade) Ballantine.

Star Flight. Phyllis A. Whitney. 1993. 20.00 (*0-517-59499-4*, Crown) Crown Pub Group.

Star Flight. Phyllis A. Whitney. 1994. mass mkt. 5.99 (*0-449-22258-6*, Expression) Fawcett.

Star Food. Carole A. Travis. Ed. by Peggy Brooks & Barbara Woods. (Illus.). 336p. (Orig.). 1981. boxed 10.95 (*0-9606622-0-0*) Teton Pub Hse.

Star for a Day. Effin Older. (Silver Blades Figure Eight Ser.: No. 2). 80p. (J). 1996. pap. 3.50 (*0-553-48492-3*) Bantam.

Star for a Day see Heinemann Guided Readers

Star for All Seasons Table Runner & Placemats, Quilt in a Day. Wendy Gilbert. (Illus.). 24p. 1992. 6.95 (*0-922705-37-2*) Quilt Day.

Star for Buster. Gordon Greene. LC 93-93950. (Illus.). 112p. 1994. pap. 8.00 (*1-56002-354-6*, Univ Edtns) Aegina Pr.

Star for Christmas. Barbra Askinosie. (Illus.). 26p. (J). (ps-1). 1988. pap. 2.95 (*0-671-66870-6*, Litl Simon S&S) S&S Childrens.

Star Formation. Mary Barsony. (C). 1997. write for info. (*0-201-57696-1*) Addison-Wesley.

Star Formation. Mary Barsony. (C). 1997. pap. write for info. (*0-201-57697-X*) Addison-Wesley.

Star Formation. Ed. by T. De Jong & Andre Maeder. (Symposia of the International Astronomical Union Ser.: No. 75). 1977. pap. text ed. 67.00 (*90-277-0797-9*); lib. bdg. 104.50 (*90-277-0796-0*) Kluwer Ac.

Star Formation, Galaxies & the Interstellar Medium. Guillermo Tenorio-Tagle. (Illus.). 410p. (C). 1993. 64.95 (*0-521-44412-8*) Cambridge U Pr.

Star Formation in Stellar Systems: Third Canary Islands Winter School of Astrophysics. Guillermo Tenorio-Tagle. (Illus.). 593p. (C). 1993. 74.95 (*0-521-44230-3*) Cambridge U Pr.

***Star Formation, Near & Far: Seventh Astrophysics Conference.** Ed. by Stephen S. Holt & Lee G. Mundy. (AIP Conference Proceedings Ser.: No. 393). (Illus.). 672p. 1997. text ed. 155.00 (*1-56396-678-6*, AIP) Am Inst Physics.

Star Forming Regions. Ed. by Manuel Peimbert & Jun Jugaku. 1986. pap. text ed. 110.00 (*90-277-2389-3*); lib. bdg. 259.00 (*90-277-2388-5*) Kluwer Ac.

***Star Fox 64: Unauthorized Game Secrets.** Prima Publishing Staff. 96p. 1997. per. 12.99 (*0-7615-1093-1*) Prima Pub.

***Star Fox 64 Survival Guide.** J. Douglas Arnold. 176p. 1997. pap. 12.95 (*1-884364-41-1*) Sandwich Islands.

Star Frontiers Mod, No. 1. M. Acres & Tom Moldvay. 1982. 5.50 (*0-394-52593-0*) Random.

Star Frontiers Reference Scroll. Tom Moldvay. 1983. 5.50 (*0-394-53156-6*) Random.

Star Gates. Corinne Heline. (Illus.). 204p. 1986. reprint ed. pap. text ed. 10.95 (*0-933963-09-2*) New Age Bible.

Star Gazer. Jeanne McCafferty. 208p. 1994. 19.95 (*0-312-11074-X*) St Martin.

Star Gazer. Jeanne McCafferty. (Worldwide Library Mystery). 1996. mass mkt. 4.99 (*0-373-26211-6*, 1-26211-2, Wrldwide Lib) Harlequin Bks.

***Star Gazer.** large type ed. Jeanne McCafferty. (Large Print Ser.). 416p. 1996. 25.99 (*0-7089-3591-5*) Ulverscroft.

Star Gazer's Guide. rev. ed. Greg Walz-Chojnacki et al. (Library of the Universe). (Illus.). (J). (gr. 3 up). 1995. lib. bdg. 18.60 (*0-8368-1197-6*) Gareth Stevens Inc.

Star-Gazing: Hollywood Cinema & Female Spectatorship. Jackie Stacey. LC 93-10970. 296p. (C). (gr. 13). 1994. pap. 16.95 (*0-415-09179-9*); text ed. 62.95 (*0-415-09178-0*) Routledge.

Star Gazing for Cats: Jill Davies Wood Engravings. Jill Davies. 1995. 9.95 (*1-885061-11-0*) Adventure Pubns.

Star-Gazy Pie: Two Plays. James Stock. 192p. (Orig.). 1996. pap. 18.95 (*1-85459-293-9*, Pub. by N Hern Bks UK) Theatre Comm.

***Star General: The Official Strategy Guide.** Michael Knight. 240p. 1996. pap. 16.99 (*0-7615-0966-6*) Prima Pub.

Star Ghost. Bard Strickland. Ed. by Lisa Clancy. (Star Trek: Deep Space Nine Ser.: No. 1). (Illus.). 128p. (Orig.). (J). (gr. 3-6). mass mkt. 3.99 (*0-671-87999-5*, Minstrel Bks) PB.

Star Gone Nova. W. Edward Smalls, Jr. (Illus.). 155p. (Orig.). 1994. pap. 8.95 (*1-56411-077-X*) Untd Bros & Sis.

***Star Group.** Pike. (YA). 1997. mass mkt. 3.99 (*0-671-55057-8*, Archway) PB.

***Star Group.** Christopher Pike. 1997. 14.00 (*0-671-55058-6*, Archway) PB.

Star Guide: A Unique System for Identifying the Brightest Stars in the Night Sky. Steven L. Beyer. LC 85-13039. (Illus.). 404p. 1986. pap. 12.95 (*0-316-09268-1*) Little.

Star Guide: Learn How to Read the Night Sky Star by Star. Robin Kerrod. LC 93-4818. (Illus.). 160p. 1993. 27.50 (*0-671-87467-5*) P-H Gen Ref & Trav.

Star Guide 1997-1998: Where to Contact over 3200 Movie Stars, TV Stars, Rock Stars, Sports Stars, & Other Famous Celebrities. rev. ed. Axiom Information Resources Staff. Ed. by Terry Robinson. 208p. 1997. pap. 12.95 (*0-943213-22-3*) Axiom Info Res.

***Star Guide 1998-1999.** Air Staff. 1998. pap. text ed. 12.95 (*0-943213-28-2*) Axiom Info Res.

Star Guitars: Guitars & Players That Have Helped Shape Modern Music. Neville Marten. (Illus.). 106p. (Orig.). (YA). (gr. 9-12). 1994. pap. 24.95 (*0-931759-83-8*, HL00000168) Centerstream Pub.

Star Hatchling. Margaret Bechard. (Illus.). 160p. (J). (gr. 3-7). 1995. pap. 13.99 (*0-670-86149-9*) Viking Child Bks.

***Star Hatchling.** Margaret Bechard. (J). 1997. pap. 3.99 (*0-14-037581-3*) Viking Penguin.

Star Healing: Your Sun Sign, Your Health & Your Success. David Lawson & Jennifer Griffiths. 352p. 1995. pap. 11.95 (*0-340-60646-0*, Pub. by Hodder & Stoughton Ltd UK) Trafalgar.

Star-Hopping: Your Visa to Viewing the Universe. Robert Garfinkle. (Illus.). 352p. (C). 1994. text ed. 25.95 (*0-521-41590-X*) Cambridge U Pr.

***Star-Hopping: Your Visa to Viewing the Universe.** Robert Garfinkle. (Illus.). 352p. 1997. pap. text ed. 16.95 (*0-521-59889-3*) Cambridge U Pr.

Star-Hopping for Backyard Astronomers. Alan M. MacRobert. LC 93-25106. (Illus.). 160p. 1993. 21.95 (*0-933346-68-9*) Sky Pub.

Star Horse. Margaret Greaves. (J). (ps-3). 1995. pap. text ed. 5.95 (*0-8120-9270-8*) Barron.

Star in My Heart: Experiencing Sophia, Inner Wisdom. Joyce Rupp. LC 90-41108. (Illus.). 96p. (Orig.). 1990. pap. 11.95 (*0-931055-75-X*) Innisfree Pr.

Star in the Breaking, Vol. 2. Bill Myers & Ken Johnson. (McGee & Me! Ser.: Vol. 2). (J). 1989. pap. 5.99 (*0-8423-4168-4*) Tyndale.

Star in the Saddle. Ann Sheldon. (Linda Craig Adventures Ser.: No. 8). (Orig.). (J). (gr. 3-6). 1989. pap. 2.75 (*0-318-41208-X*, Minstrel Bks) PB.

Star in the Shed Window: Collected Poems. James Hayford. LC 89-9279. 304p. 1989. 24.95 (*0-933050-66-6*) New Eng Pr VT.

Star in the West: A Critical Essay upon the Works of Aleister Crowley. J. F. Fuller. 327p. 1969. reprint ed. spiral bd. 12.00 (*0-7873-0338-0*) Hlth Research.

Star in the West: A Humble Attempt to Discover the Long Lost Ten Tribes of Israel. Elias Boudinot. LC 79-121499. (Select Bibliographies Reprint Ser.). 1977. 19.95 (*0-8369-5457-2*) Ayer.

Star in the West: A Study of Aleister Crowley. J. F. Fuller. 1992. lib. bdg. 250.00 (*0-8490-9904-8*) Gordon Pr.

Star in the Window: Reminiscences of the Years 1941-1945 & the Personal Impact of World War II. Arizona's Senior Adults Staff. Ed. by Nadine L. Smith et al. LC 95-25960. (Illus.). 154p. (Orig.). 1995. pap. write for info. (*0-9617772-5-7*) Scottsdale Cmnty Coll.

Star Is Born. Dale Bringman. (Orig.). 1987. pap. 4.25 (*0-89536-881-1*, 7867) CSS OH.

***Star Is Born, 25 booklets.** Jill Briscoe & Stuart Briscoe. (Baker Interactive Books for Lively Education). (Illus.). (J). 1996. pap. text ed. 49.75 (*0-8010-8198-X*) Baker Bks.

Star Is Born: The Story of the Making of the 1954 Movie & Its 1983 Restoration. Ronald Haver. LC 88-45214. (Illus.). 320p. 1988. 24.95 (*0-394-53714-9*) Knopf.

Star Is Born: Vocal Selections. (Illus.). 024p. 1983. pap. 7.95 (*0-88188-542-8*, 00384828) H Leonard.

***Star Is Born: Vocal Selections.** Ed. by Carol Cuellar. 36p. (Orig.). (C). 1995. pap. text ed. 9.95 (*0-7692-0853-3*, SF0064) Warner Brothers.

Star-Junior First Aid. rev. ed. Sheila Greeley. LC 89-51922. (Illus.). 50p. (Orig.). 1989. per. 8.95 (*0-936029-19-6*) Western Bk Journ.

Star Lake Archaeological Project: Anthropology of a Headwaters Area of Chaco Wash, New Mexico. Ed. by Walter K. Wait & Ben A. Nelson. LC 81-13596. (Publications in Archaeology). (Illus.). 480p. (C). 1983. 24.95 (*0-8093-0949-1*) S Ill U Pr.

Star Ledger. Lynda Hull. LC 90-49398. (Edwin Ford Piper Poetry Award Cowinner Ser.). 107p. (Orig.). 1991. pap. 10.95 (*0-87745-319-5*) U of Iowa Pr.

Star Light, Star Bright. Karen Davis. LC 92-17120. (J). (ps-2). 1993. 15.00 (*0-671-79455-8*, Green Tiger S&S) S&S Childrens.

Star Light, Star Bright. Angela E. Hunt. LC 92-18796. (Cassie Perkins Ser.: Vol. 7). (YA). 1993. pap. 4.99 (*0-8423-1117-3*) Tyndale.

Star Light, Star Bright. Marian Wells. LC 86-6102. (Starlight Trilogy Ser.: Vol. 2). 256p. (Orig.). 1986. pap. 8.99 (*0-87123-883-7*) Bethany Hse.

Star Light, Star Bright. large type ed. Stanley Ellin. (Keating's Choice Ser.). 257p. 1992. 21.95 (*1-85089-529-5*, Pub. by ISIS UK) Transaction Pubs.

Star Light, Star Bright: Whole Language Activities Through Nursery Rhymes. Beth R. Neiderman. 1992. pap. 18.95 (*0-201-81537-0*) Addison-Wesley.

Star Lit Kitchens. Contrib. by Dotti Turkot. (Illus.). 96p. (Orig.). 1996. pap. 12.95 (*0-9651564-0-0*) D Turkot.

Star, Little Star. Lonnie George. (Poke & Look Bks.). (Illus.). 16p. (J). (ps). 1992. bds., spiral bd. 9.95 (*0-448-40487-7*, G&D) Putnam Pub Group.

Star Log Cabin Quilt. Eleanor Burns. (Illus.). 92p. 1995. per. 14.95 (*0-922705-86-0*) Quilt Day.

Star Lord. Donald G. Phillips. (Battletech Ser.: No. 23). 288p. 1996. mass mkt., pap. 5.50 (*0-451-45386-7*, ROC) NAL-Dutton.

***Star Lore Handbook: An Essential Guide to the Night Sky.** Geoffrey Cornelius. LC 96-28301. 1997. pap. 14.95 (*0-8118-1604-4*) Chronicle Bks.

Star Lore of All Ages. William T. Olcott. 452p. 1985. reprint ed. spiral bd. 38.00 (*0-7873-1096-4*) Hlth Research.

Star Lore of All Ages: A Collection of Myths, Legends, & Facts Concerning the Constellations of the Northern Hemisphere (1911) William T. Olcott. 475p. 1996. pap. 29.95 (*1-56459-770-9*) Kessinger Pub.

Star Magic. Suzanne Weyn. LC 90-11151. (Sitting Pretty Ser.). 128p. (J). (gr. 4-8). 1997. pap. 2.95 (*0-8167-2014-2*) Troll Communs.

Star Maiden: An Ojibway Tale. Barbara J. Esbensen. (J). (ps-3). 1988. 15.95 (*0-316-24951-3*) Little.

Star Maiden: An Ojibway Tale. Barbara J. Esbensen. (Illus.). (J). (ps-3). 1991. mass mkt. 5.95 (*0-316-24955-6*) Little.

***Star-Man: And Other Tales.** Basil H. Johnston et al. (Illus.). 64p. 1996. 19.95 (*0-88854-419-7*, Pub. by Royal Ont Mus CN) U of Toronto Pr.

Star-Mapped. Geraldine C. Little. 72p. 1989. 6.00 (*0-943710-02-2*) Silver App Pr.

Star Maps for Beginners: Fiftieth Anniversary Edition. 50th anniversary ed. I. M. Levitt & Roy K. Marshall. (Illus.). 64p. 1992. pap. 10.00 (*0-671-79187-7*, Fireside) S&S Trade.

***Star Mates for Aquarius.** Celeste Longacre. Ed. by Lesle Lewis. (Illus.). 44p. (Orig.). 1996. pap. 6.95 (*0-930043-11-1*) Sweet Fern.

Star Mates for Aries. Celeste Longacre. Ed. by Lesle Lewis. (Illus.). (Orig.). 1994. pap. 6.95 (*0-930043-01-4*) Sweet Fern.

Star Mates for Cancer. Celeste Longacre. Ed. by Lesle Lewis. (Illus.). (Orig.). 1994. pap. 6.95 (*0-930043-04-9*) Sweet Fern.

Star Mates for Capricorn. Celeste Longacre. Ed. by Lesle Lewis. (Illus.). (Orig.). 1995. pap. 6.95 (*0-930043-10-3*) Sweet Fern.

Star Mates for Gemini. Celeste Longacre. Ed. by Lesle Lewis. (Illus.). (Orig.). 1994. pap. 6.95 (*0-930043-03-0*) Sweet Fern.

Star Mates for Leo. Celeste Longacre. Ed. by Lesle Lewis. (Illus.). (Orig.). 1994. pap. 6.95 (*0-930043-05-7*) Sweet Fern.

Star Mates for Libra. Celeste Longacre. Ed. by Lesle Lewis. (Illus.). (Orig.). 1994. pap. 6.95 (*0-930043-07-3*) Sweet Fern.

***Star Mates for Pisces.** Celeste Longacre. Ed. by Lesle Lewis. (Illus.). 44p. 1996. pap. 6.95 (*0-930043-12-X*) Sweet Fern.

Star Mates for Sagittarius. Celeste Longacre. Ed. by Lesle Lewis. (Illus.). (Orig.). 1995. pap. 6.95 (*0-930043-09-X*) Sweet Fern.

Star Mates for Scorpio. Celeste Longacre. Ed. by Lesle Lewis. (Illus.). (Orig.). 1994. pap. 6.95 (*0-930043-08-1*) Sweet Fern.

Star Mates for Taurus. Celeste Longacre. Ed. by Lesle Lewis. (Illus.). (Orig.). 1994. pap. 6.95 (*0-930043-02-2*) Sweet Fern.

Star Mates for Virgo. Celeste Longacre. Ed. by Lesle Lewis. (Illus.). (Orig.). 1994. pap. 6.95 (*0-930043-06-5*) Sweet Fern.

***Star Medicine: Native American Path to Emotional Healing.** Wolf Moondance. LC 97-1003. (Illus.). 160p. 1997. pap. 12.95 (*0-8069-9547-5*) Sterling.

Star Menu: A Professional Menu & System Management Program for the IBM PC-XT-AT-PS2. rev. ed. Charles F. Severance. (Illus.). 80p. (C). 1990. 79.95 incl. disk (*0-9626641-0-3*) AstroSoft Data.

Star Mother's Youngest Child. Louise Moeri. (Illus.). 48p. (J). (ps-2). 1975. 14.95 (*0-395-21406-8*, Sandpiper) HM.

Star Mother's Youngest Child. Louise Moeri. (Illus.). 48p. (J). (ps-2). 1980. pap. 5.95 (*0-395-29929-2*, Sandpiper) HM.

Star Myths: Show-Business Biographies on Film. Robert M. Miller. LC 83-14292. 416p. 1983. 32.50 (*0-8108-1643-1*) Scarecrow.

***Star Myths of the Greeks & Romans: A Sourcebook.** Theony Condos. 1997. pap. 18.95 (*1-890482-93-5*) Phanes Pr.

Star Names: Their Lore & Meaning. Richard H. Allen. 1990. 22.50 (*0-8446-1527-7*) Peter Smith.

Star Names: Their Lore & Meaning. rev. ed. Richard H. Allen. 563p. 1963. pap. 8.95 (*0-486-21079-0*) Dover.

S

An Asterisk (*) at the beginning of an entry indicates that the title is appearing in BIP for the first time.

Star of Argence. large type ed. Margaret Astridge. (Linford Romance Library). 288p. 1993. pap. 15.99 (*0-7089-7461-9*, Trailtree Bookshop) Ulverscroft.

Star of Bethlehem. Elisabeth D. Gauerke. 1989. 11.00 (*0-86690-336-4*, G2808-014) Am Fed Astrologers.

Star of Bethlehem. Laura Nownes. LC 90-41883. (Classic Quilt Ser.). (Illus.). 20p. (Orig.). 1990. pap. text ed. 6.95 (*0-8442-2613-0*) Quilt Digest Pr.

Star of Bethlehem. 2nd ed. Frank E. Stranges. 21p. (Orig.). 1994. pap. text ed. 4.95 (*0-933470-06-1*) Intl Evang.

Star of Bethlehem: The Birth of Jesus. abr. ed. Joe Loesch. Ed. by Cheryl J. Hutchinson. (Parable Ser.: Vol. 4). (Illus.). 52p. (Orig.). (J). (gr. 1-5). 1996. pap. 16.95 incl. audio compact disk (*1-887729-13-5*) Toy Box Prods.

Star of Bethlehem: The Birth of Jesus. unabridged ed. Joe Loesch. Ed. by Cheryl J. Hutchinson. (Parable Ser.: Vol. 4). (Illus.). 52p. (Orig.). (J). (gr. 1-5). 1996. pap. 14.95 incl. audio (*1-887729-12-7*) Toy Box Prods.

Star of Danger. Marion Zimmer Bradley. 224p. 1994. mass mkt. 4.99 (*0-88677-607-4*) DAW Bks.

Star of Danger. Marion Zimmer Bradley. 192p. 1993. lib. bdg. 20.00 (*0-7278-4513-6*) Severn Hse.

Star of Destiny: The Private Life of Sam & Margaret Houston. Madge T. Roberts. LC 92-31587. 432p. 1993. 29.50 (*0-929398-51-3*) UNTX Pr.

Star of Fear, Star of Hope. Jo Hoestlandt. Tr. by Mark Polizzotti from FRE. LC 94-32378. (Illus.). 32p. (J). (gr. 2-5). 1995. 15.95 (*0-8027-8373-2*) Walker & Co.

Star of Fear, Star of Hope. Jo Hoostlandt. Tr. by Mark Polizzotti from FRE. LC 94-32378. (Illus.). 32p. (J). (gr. 2-5). 1995. lib. bdg. 16.85 (*0-8027-8374-0*) Walker & Co.

Star of Fortune. large type ed. Juliet Gray. 1990. 25.99 (*0-7089-2210-4*) Ulverscroft.

Star of Free Will. Maria L. Spaziani. Tr. by Carol Lettieri & Irene Marchegiani from ITA. (Essential Poets Ser.: No. 63). 136p. 1995. 15.00 (*1-55071-002-8*) Guernica Editions.

Star of Gettysburg. Joseph Altsheler. 1990. reprint ed. lib. bdg. 22.95 (*0-89968-469-6*) Buccaneer Bks.

Star of Gypsie. 1999. pap. 3.95 (*0-445-73864-2*) Warner Bks.

Star of Honor. Ron Moyne. LC 89-273. 1990. 21.95 (*0-87949-302-X*) Ashley Bks.

Star of Jacob: Insights into the Birth of Jesus of Nazareth. Wayne D. Leeper. 164p. 1988. pap. 8.99 (*0-89225-345-2*) Gospel Advocate.

Star of Light. Patricia M. St. John. (Patricia St. John Bks.). (J). (gr. 5-8). 1953. mass mkt. 5.99 (*0-8024-0004-3*) Moody.

Star of Oudh. large type ed. Alex Stuart. 496p. 1985. 25.99 (*0-7089-1344-X*) Ulverscroft.

Star of Peace. large type ed. Jan De Hartog. 560p. 1986. 27.99 (*0-7089-8314-6*, Charnwood) Ulverscroft.

Star of Redemption. Franz Rosenzweig. Tr. by William W. Hallo from GER. LC 84-40833. 464p. (C). 1985. reprint ed. pap. text ed. 19.50 (*0-268-01718-2*) U of Notre Dame Pr.

Star of Return: Judaism after the Holocaust. Dow Marmur. LC 90-19911. (Contributions to the Study of Religion Ser.: No. 29). 176p. 1991. text ed. 49.95 (*0-313-27604-8*, MRJ/, Greenwood Pr) Greenwood.

***Star of Shadowbrook.** Joanna Campbell. 192p. mass mkt. 3.99 (*0-06-106483-1*, Harp PBks) HarpC.

Star of Shadowbrook Farm. Joanna Campbell. 192p. (YA). 1992. mass mkt. 3.50 (*0-06-106783-0*, Harp PBks) HarpC.

Star of Song: The Life of Christina Nilsson. Guy Charnace. LC 80-2264. 1981. reprint ed. 27.50 (*0-404-18817-6*) AMS Pr.

Star of Sutherland. Gene Breaznell. 192p. 1990. 18.95 (*0-8027-5754-5*) Walker & Co.

Star of Texas Cookbook. Junior League of Houston, Inc., Staff. LC 82-45328. 384p. 1983. reprint ed. 19.95 (*0-9632421-1-3*) Jr Leag Houston.

***Star of the Circus.** Mary B. Sampson & Michael R. Sampson. LC 96-28806. (Illus.). (J). 1997. 14.95 (*0-8050-4284-9*) H Holt & Co.

Star of the Guardians, Vol. 2: King's Test. Margaret Weis. 448p. 1991. mass mkt. 6.50 (*0-553-28907-1*, Spectra) Bantam.

Star of the Parade. Francine Pascal. (Sweet Valley Kids Ser.: No. 54). 80p. (J). (ps-3). 1994. pap. 3.50 (*0-553-48111-8*) Bantam.

Star of the Show. Lael J. Littke. LC 93-27258. (Bee There Ser.). 162p. (Orig.). (J). (gr. 5-9). 1993. pap. 4.95 (*0-87579-785-7*) Deseret Bk.

Star of Wonder. Daniel M. Epstein. LC 86-16301. 144p. 1986. 19.95 (*0-87951-257-1*) Overlook Pr.

Star of Wonder. Daniel M. Epstein. 124p. 1991. reprint ed. pap. 13.95 (*0-87951-435-3*) Overlook Pr.

Star of 2000: Our Journey Toward Hope. Jay Gary. LC 97-21828. 176p. 1994. pap. 10.95 (*0-9641388-0-8*) Bimillennial.

Star on His Shoulder. Fanny K. DeVine. 88p. 1962. 12.50 (*1-886796-00-9*) DEramo Pub.

Star on Many a Battlefield: Brevet Brigadier General Joseph Karge in the Civil War. Francis C. Kajencki. LC 77-89781. 1980. 38.50 (*0-8386-2149-X*) Fairleigh Dickinson.

Star on the Door. Maggie Teyte. Ed. by Andrew Farkas. LC 76-29971. (Opera Biographies Ser.). (Illus.). 1977. reprint ed. lib. bdg. 19.95 (*0-405-09710-7*) Ayer.

***Star on the Pole.** R. W. Thompson. (Illus.). 16p. (J). (ps-3). 1996. 8.95 (*0-9636442-3-8*) N Pole Chron.

Star over Bethlehem & Other Stories. Agatha Christie. 1991. pap. 6.95 (*0-425-13229-3*, Berkley Trade) Berkley Pub.

Star Papers: Experience of Art & Nature. Henry W. Beecher. (Works of Henry Ward Beecher). vi, 359p. reprint ed. lib. bdg. 49.00 (*0-932051-01-4*) Rprt Serv.

Star Papers: Or, Experiences of Art & Nature. Henry W. Beecher. LC 75-39679. (Essay Index Reprint Ser.). 1977. reprint ed. 26.95 (*0-8369-2745-1*) Ayer.

Star Particle Theory: An Introductory Survey. James S. Hughes, Jr. (Illus.). 16p. 1974. 15.00 (*0-915386-00-3*) Arctinurus Co.

S.T.A.R. Patrol. Sheila Greeley. 90p. (Orig.). (J). (ps-6). 1997. pap. text ed. 19.95 (*0-9622812-1-2*) FAFCTPC.

Star Poems & Other Poems. Clifford Davidson. LC 76-27932. (Illus.). 1976. pap. 5.00 (*0-87423-021-7*) Westburg.

Star Point Series & Ceremonies. enl. rev. ed. Ottillies S. Brunke. 96p. 1994. pap. 6.50 (*0-88053-362-5*, S-307) Macoy Pub.

***Star Power for Preschoolers: Learning Life Skills Through Physical Play.** Andrew Oser. (Illus.). 1997. pap. write for info. (*1-884834-35-3*, 3048) Redleaf Pr.

Star Prey. Ehren M. Ehly. 1992. mass mkt. 4.50 (*0-8217-3751-1*, Zebra Kensgtn) Kensgtn Pub Corp.

Star Quality. (Girl Talk Ser.). (YA). 1991. write for info. (*0-307-22017-6*, Golden Pr) Western Pub.

***Star Quality.** Janet Quin-Harkin. 1997. mass mkt. 3.99 (*0-671-00285-6*, Minstrel Bks) PB.

Star Quality: A Seven-Point Program to Turn Your Inner Strength into Your Outer Power. Christen Brown. 384p. 1996. 22.00 (*0-345-38886-0*) Ballantine.

Star Quest. Ed. by Paul M. Miller. 1989. 5.99 (*0-685-68459-8*, MC-71); audio 10.99 (*0-685-68460-1*, TA-9118C) Lillenas.

Star Quest for Quilters. Betty Boyink. 80p. (Orig.). 1986. pap. 13.50 (*0-9612608-7-4*) B Boyink.

Star Quilt. Roberta H. Whiteman. LC 83-80591. (Illus.). 96p. (Orig.). 1984. pap. 6.95 (*0-930100-17-4*) Holy Cow.

Star Quilt Designs. Doreen L. Saunders. (Illus.). 48p. (Orig.). pap. 3.95 (*0-486-26912-4*) Dover.

Star Quilts. Mary E. Johnson. LC 96-22658. (Illus.). 192p. 1996. pap. 24.95 (*0-8442-2604-1*) Quilt Digest Pr.

Star Rangers Strategies & Secrets. Dan Irish. (Illus.). 242p. (Orig.). 1996. pap. text ed. 19.99 incl. cd-rom (*0-7821-1870-4*, Strategies & Secrets) Sybex.

Star Requiem No. 1: Mother of Storms. Adrian Cole. 384p. (Orig.). 1992. mass mkt. 4.99 (*0-380-76767-8*, AvoNova) Avon.

Star Requiem No. 2: Thief of Dreams. Adrian Cole. 384p. (Orig.). 1993. mass mkt. 4.99 (*0-380-76768-6*, AvoNova) Avon.

Star Requiem No. 3: Warlord of Heaven. Adrian Cole. 368p. (Orig.). 1993. mass mkt. 4.99 (*0-380-76769-4*, AvoNova) Avon.

Star Requiem No. 4: Labyrinth of Worlds. Adrian Cole. 352p. (Orig.). 1993. mass mkt. 4.99 (*0-380-76770-8*, AvoNova) Avon.

Star Rhythms. 2nd ed. Ed. by William Lonsdale. (Io Ser.: No. 27). (Illus.). 180p. 1982. pap. 8.95 (*0-938190-00-8*) North Atlantic.

Star Rider. Bonnie Bryant. (Saddle Club Ser.: No. 19). 144p. (J). (gr. 4-7). 1991. pap. 3.99 (*0-553-15938-0*) Bantam.

Star Riders. Josephin Pullein-Thompson. 127p. (C). 1990. pap. 21.00 (*0-85131-519-4*, Pub. by J A Allen & Co UK) St Mut.

Star Rigger's Way. Jeffrey A. Carver. 1994. pap. 4.99 (*0-8125-3444-1*) Tor Bks.

Star Rookie. Krista Bell. (Illus.). 64p. (J). (gr. 3-5). 1996. pap. 4.95 (*1-86373-857-6*, Pub. by Allen & Unwin Aust Pty AT) IPG Chicago.

Star Rover. Jack London. 348p. 1983. pap. 8.95 (*0-911842-31-4*, B914) Valley Sun.

Star Rover. Jack London. 1976. 23.95 (*0-8488-1082-1*) Amereon Ltd.

Star Rover. Jack London. 320p. (C). reprint ed. pap. 12.95 (*0-904526-10-0*, Pub. by Pluto Pr UK) LPC InBook.

Star Sapphire. Rebecca Danton. 1980. pap. 1.75 (*0-449-50058-6*, Coventry) Fawcett.

***Star Science Program.** unabridged ed. Clifford Russell. (Illus.). (C). 1997. teacher ed., ring bd. 48.00 (*0-9657270-1-7*) Germane Pubs.

Star Scorers of AVAA. Dennis DeNure. (Illus.). 125p. 1984. 19.95 (*0-915659-01-8*) Video Athlete.

Star Scroll. Melanie Rawn. (Dragon Prince Ser.: Bk. 2). 592p. 1989. reprint ed. mass mkt. 6.99 (*0-88677-349-0*) DAW Bks.

Star Search. Judy McGorray. 25p. 1993. pap. text ed. write for info. (*1-888200-04-9*) JayMac Commun.

Star Seed. Mary A. Fontenot. LC 86-12171. (Illus.). 32p. (J). (gr. k-4). 1986. reprint ed. 7.95 (*0-88289-628-8*) Pelican.

Star Sets: Vintage & Custom Drum Kits of the Great Drummers. Jon Cohan. (Illus.). 160128p. (Orig.). 1995. pap. 22.95 (*0-7935-3489-5*, HL00330113) H Leonard.

Star Shall Fall: India 1857. P. J. Taylor. (C). 1993. pap. text ed. 10.00 (*81-7223-066-4*, Pub. by Indus Pub II) S Asia.

Star Shapes. Peter Malone. LC 95-38256. (Illus.). (J). 1997. 14.95 (*0-8118-0726-6*) Chronicle Bks.

***Star Shines for Me: How to Maximize Any Child's Education.** James P. Thompson. LC 96-90696. 276p. (Orig.). 1997. pap. text ed. 29.95 incl. audio (*1-889869-00-7*) T C & A Pub.

Star Shone. Christopher Stasheff. (Saga Ser.: Bk. 2). 1997. mass mkt. 5.99 (*0-345-39244-2*) Ballantine.

Star Shots. (J). 1992. boxed, pap. 7.50 (*0-590-66216-3*) Scholastic Inc.

Star Signs. Kristyna Arcarti. (For Beginners Ser.). (Illus.). 103p. 1995. pap. 11.95 (*0-340-59553-1*, Pub. by Headway UK) Trafalgar.

Star Signs the Secret Codes of the Universe: A Practical Guide for the New Age. Linda Goodman. 1988. pap. write for info. (*0-318-63948-3*) St Martin.

Star Slammers. Walter Simonson. (Illus.). 64p. 1983. pap. 5.95 (*0-939766-21-3*) Marvel Entmnt.

Star Soldier. Steve Tymon. LC 84-52308. (Illus.). 128p. (Orig.). 1985. 7.95 (*0-931683-03-3*); pap. 3.95 (*0-931683-01-7*) Sci Fict & Fant Prodns.

Star Songs: A Book of Inspired Astrology. Velma Swann. LC 87-80999. (Illus.). 64p. (Orig.). 1987. pap. 5.50 (*0-9615149-8-1*) Fenton Valley Pr.

Star-Spangled Banana: And Other Revolutionary Riddles. Ed. by Richard E. Baker & Tomie De Paola. (Illus.). 62p. (J). (gr. 2 up). 1978. 3.95 (*0-13-842971-5*, S&S) S&S Trade.

Star-Spangled Banner. Stuart A. Kallen. LC 94-12222. (Famous Illustrated Speeches Ser.). (J). 1994. lib. bdg. 15.98 (*1-56239-317-0*) Abdo & Dghtrs.

Star-Spangled Banner. Deborah Kent. LC 95-836. (Cornerstones of Freedom Ser.). (Illus.). 32p. (J). (gr. 3-6). 1995. lib. bdg. 18.00 (*0-516-06630-7*) Childrens.

Star-Spangled Banner. Peter Spier. (Illus.). 56p. (J). (ps-3). 1992. pap. 7.99 (*0-440-40697-8*, YB BDD) BDD Bks Young Read.

Star Spangled Banner. Deborah Kent. (Cornerstones of Freedom Ser.). (Illus.). 32p. (J). (gr. 3-6). 1996. reprint ed. pap. 4.95 (*0-516-46630-5*) Childrens.

Star-Spangled Banner. Oscar G. Sonneck. LC 68-16245. (Music Reprint Ser.). (Illus.). 1969. reprint ed. lib. bdg. 29.50 (*0-306-71108-7*) Da Capo.

Star-Spangled Banner: Our Nation & Its Flag. Margaret Sedeen. LC 93-15173. (Illus.). 232p. 1993. 37.50 (*0-87044-944-3*); 52.50 (*0-87044-945-1*) Natl Geog.

Star-Spangled Banner: Words & Music Issued Between 1814-1864. Joseph Muller. LC 79-169653. (Music Ser.). (Illus.). 1973. reprint ed. lib. bdg. 35.00 (*0-306-70263-0*) Da Capo.

Star Spangled Beer: A Guide to America's New Microbreweries & Brewpubs. Jack Erickson. (Illus.). 156p. (Orig.). 1987. pap. 13.95 (*0-941397-00-9*) Redbrick Pr.

Star-Spangled Bride. Iris Johansen. (Loveswept Ser.: No. 622). 1993. pap. 3.50 (*0-553-44184-1*, Loveswept) Bantam.

Star Spangled Contract. Jim Garrison. 384p. 1992. mass mkt. 4.99 (*0-446-36355-3*) Warner Bks.

Star-Spangled Girl. Neil Simon. 1968. pap. 5.25 (*0-8222-1073-8*) Dramatists Play.

Star Spangled Heresy: Americanism. Solange Hertz. 187p. 1992. pap. 12.50 (*1-883511-01-1*) Veritas Pr CA.

Star-Spangled Mirror: America's Image of Itself & the World. Richard J. Kerry. 176p. (C). 1990. lib. bdg. 39.00 (*0-8476-7649-8*) Rowman.

Star-Spangled Murder. Valerie Wolzien. 1993. mass mkt. 4.50 (*0-449-14834-3*, GM) Fawcett.

***Star-Spangled Quote Book.** Bob Phillips. 336p. (Orig.). 1997. pap. 9.99 (*1-56507-725-3*) Harvest Hse.

Star Spangled Salute. Aurand Harris. (J). (gr. 1-12). 1974. 5.00 (*0-87602-205-0*) Anchorage.

Star Spangled Sampler Quilts: The Art of the States. Quilter's Newsletter Magazine Editors & Bonnie Leman. (Illus.). 64p. (Orig.). 1993. pap. 16.95 (*0-943721-12-1*) Leman Pubns.

Star-Spangled Science: Inside the Policies & Politics of Science in Washington. Stanley D. Schneider. LC 92-30195. 1992. 19.95 (*0-87949-369-0*) Ashley Bks.

Star-Spangled Screen: The American World War II Film. Bernard F. Dick. LC 85-9205. 304p. 1985. 32.00 (*0-8131-1531-0*) U Pr of Ky.

Star-Spangled Screen: The American World War II Film. Bernard F. Dick. (Illus.). 304p. 1996. pap. 15.95 (*0-8131-0885-3*) U Pr of Ky.

Star-Spangled Specter: The Adventures of George Washington in the Twentieth Century. Donald A. Weatherby. 160p. (Orig.). 1995. pap. 9.95 (*1-56474-127-3*) Fithian Pr.

Star-Spangled Summer. Ilene Cooper. (Holiday Five, Ser.: 4). (Illus.). 128p. (J). (gr. 5-8). 1996. pap. 14.99 (*0-670-85655-X*) Viking Child Bks.

***Star Spangled Summer.** Ilene Cooper. Date not set. pap. 3.99 (*0-14-037086-2*) Penguin.

***Star Spangled Summertime.** Becky Daniel. (Illus.). 192p. (Orig.). 1996. pap. text ed. 12.95 (*1-56490-027-4*) G Grimm Assocs.

Star Sparks in the Sky. Lenore Warren. 44p. (Orig.). 1991. pap. 3.50 (*0-9644346-0-1*) KR Syst.

Star Spells. Sarah Holcombe. 224p. (Orig.). 1996. mass mkt. 5.50 (*0-380-77995-1*, Cosmopolitan) Avon.

Star-Spider Speaks: The Teachings of the Native American Tarot. Magda W. Gonzalez & J. A. Gonzalez. LC 89-50587. (Illus.). 224p. 1990. pap. 9.95 (*0-88079-369-4*) US Games Syst.

Star Stalkers. George Mair. 352p. 1995. pap. 4.99 (*0-7860-0138-0*, Pinncle Kensgtn); pap. 4.99 (*0-7860-0162-3*) Kensgtn Pub Corp.

Star Stone Bk. 1: The Shaman. Christopher Stasheff. 1996. mass mkt. 5.99 (*0-345-39247-7*, Del Rey) Ballantine.

Star Strike: Vessel Compendium, No. 1. Tony Van Liew. Ed. by Kevin Barrett & Terry K. Amthor. (Space Master Ser.). (Illus.). 64p. (Orig.). (C). 1989. pap. 12.00 (*1-55806-057-X*, 9011) Iron Crown Ent Inc.

Star Strike: Vessel Compendium, No. 2. Tony Van Liew. Ed. by Kevin Barrett. (Space Master Ser.). (Illus.). 64p. (Orig.). (C). 1989. pap. 12.00 (*1-55806-059-6*, 9012) Iron Crown Ent Inc.

Star Strike: Vessel Compendium, No. 3. Tony Van Liew. Ed. by Kevin Barrett. (Space Master Ser.). (Illus.). 64p. (Orig.). (C). 1989. pap. 12.00 (*1-55806-037-5*, 9013) Iron Crown Ent Inc.

Star Struck. Meg F. Schneider. (You Choose the Romance Ser.: Bk. 2). 128p. (YA). 1994. write for info. (*0-307-22601-8*, Whitman) Western Pub.

Star Style: Hollywood Legends As Fashion Icons. Patty Fox. LC 95-32222. (Illus.). 128p. 1995. 23.95 (*1-883318-03-3*) Angel City Pr.

Star Tales: North American Indian Stories about the Stars. Gretchen W. Mayo. 96p. (J). (gr. 5 up). 1987. 12.95 (*0-8027-6672-2*); lib. bdg. 13.85 (*0-8027-6673-0*) Walker & Co.

Star Teachers of Children in Poverty. Martin Haberman. (Illus.). 128p. (Orig.). 1995. pap. 15.00 (*0-912099-08-9*) Kappa Delta Pi.

Star Testing Astronomical Telescopes: A Practical Guide to Optical Evaluation & Adjustment. Richard H. Suiter. LC 94-30450. (ENG.). 1994. 24.95 (*0-943396-44-1*) Willmann-Bell.

Star Texts: Image & Performance in Film & Television. Ed. by Jeremy G. Butler. LC 90-23964. (Contemporary Film & Television Ser.). 384p. 1991. 39.95 (*0-8143-2311-1*); pap. 21.95 (*0-8143-2312-X*) Wayne St U Pr.

Star that Astonished the World. Ernest L. Martin. (Illus.). 220p. (Orig.). (YA). (gr. 10). 1991. pap. 14.95 (*0-945657-88-9*) Acad Scriptural Knowledge.

***Star That Astonished the World: "Star of Bethlehem"** 2nd rev. ed. (Illus.). 280p. 1996. pap. 14.95 (*0-945657-87-0*) Acad Scriptural Knowledge.

Star Thistle Control with Grasses. Craig C. Dremann. 4p. (Orig.). (C). 1993. pap. 3.00 (*0-933421-49-4*) Redwood Seed.

Star Thrower. Loren Eiseley. LC 79-10406. 319p. 1979. pap. 10.00 (*0-15-684909-7*, Harvest Bks) HarBrace.

Star to Steer By. Gladys Taber. 20.95 (*0-8488-1197-6*) Amereon Ltd.

Star to Steer Her By: A Self-Teaching Guide to Offshore Navigation. Edward J. Bergin. LC 83-71313. 216p. 1983. pap. 18.50 (*0-87033-309-7*) Cornell Maritime.

Star Track. David A. Wilson. (Illus.). 152p. (Orig.). 1994. pap. 12.00 (*0-934852-38-3*) Lorien Hse.

Star Track Reading & Spelling: A Training Manual for Low Flyers. Cosette Beadle & Joan Hampshire. 250p. 1997. pap. 95.00 (*1-56593-606-X*, 1258) Singular Publishing.

Star Tracks: Principles for Success in the Music & Entertainment Business. Larry E. Wacholtz. Ed. by Kathy Hartlove & April Higuera. (Illus.). xv, 304p. 1996. pap. 21.95 (*0-9652341-0-X*) Thumbs Up.

***Star Trak.** Anton Corbijn. 144p. 1996. 55.00 (*3-88814-857-X*) Stewart Tabori & Chang.

Star Treatment. Dick Stelzer. LC 77-76868. 1977. 7.95 (*0-672-52290-X*, Bobbs) Macmillan.

***Star Tree.** Gisela Colle & Rosemary Lanning. LC 97-7542. (Illus.). (J). 1997. write for info. (*1-55858-741-1*); lib. bdg. write for info. (*1-55858-742-X*) North-South Bks NYC.

Star Trek. 1990. mass mkt. 5.99 (*0-671-72300-6*) PB.

Star Trek, 4 vols. 1991. pap. 18.00 (*0-671-96368-6*) S&S Trade.

Star Trek, 4 vols., Set. 1990. Boxed set. boxed 18.00 (*0-671-96369-4*) PB.

Star Trek: An Annotated Guide to Resources on the Development, the Phenomenon, the People, the Television Series, the Films, the Novels & the Recordings. Susan R. Gibberman. LC 91-52502. 445p. 1991. lib. bdg. 43.50 (*0-89950-547-3*) McFarland & Co.

***Star Trek: Chronology.** Michael Okuda & Denise Okuda. 1996. pap. 25.00 (*0-614-20458-5*) PB.

Star Trek: Crew Member's Exploration Pack. Sarah Hewetson. (J). 1996. 19.95 (*0-689-80906-9*, S&S Bks Young Read) S&S Childrens.

Star Trek: Death's Angel. Kathleen Sky. 224p. 1995. mass mkt. 4.99 (*0-553-24983-5*, Spectra) Bantam.

Star Trek: Debt of Honor. Chris Claremont. Ed. by Bob Greenberger. (Illus.). 96p. 1992. pap. 14.95 (*1-56389-031-3*) DC Comics.

***Star Trek: Deep Space Nine Legends of the Ferengi.** Ira S. Behr. (U Ser.). 1997. pap. 12.00 (*0-671-00728-9*) PB.

Star Trek: Deep Space Nine: The Ferengi Rules of Acquisition. Quark. Ed. by Kevin Ryan. 96p. 1995. pap. 6.00 (*0-671-52936-6*) PB.

Star Trek: Devil World. Gordon Eklund. 160p. 1995. mass mkt. 4.99 (*0-553-24677-1*, Spectra) Bantam.

***Star Trek: First Contact: Movie Tie-In.** John Vornholt. 1996. pap. 3.99 (*0-614-19124-6*, Minstrel Bks) PB.

***Star Trek: Logs Five & Six.** Alan Dean Foster. 1996. pap. 11.00 (*0-345-40941-8*, Del Rey) Ballantine.

***Star Trek: Logs Nine & Ten.** Alan Dean Foster. 1996. pap. 11.00 (*0-345-40943-4*, Del Rey) Ballantine.

***Star Trek: Logs One & Two.** Alan Dean Foster. 1996. pap. 11.00 (*0-345-40939-6*, Del Rey) Ballantine.

***Star Trek: Logs Seven & Eight.** Alan Dean Foster. 1996. pap. 11.00 (*0-345-40942-6*, Del Rey) Ballantine.

***Star Trek: Logs Three & Four.** Alan Dean Foster. 1996. pap. 11.00 (*0-345-40940-X*, Del Rey) Ballantine.

Star Trek: Revisitations. Howard Weinstein. Ed. by Bob Kahan. (Illus.). 176p. 1995. pap. 19.95 (*1-56389-223-5*) DC Comics.

Star Trek: Tests of Courage. R. Whigham. (Illus.). 160p. 1994. pap. 17.95 (*1-56389-151-4*) DC Comics.

Star Trek: The Ashes of Eden. William Shatner. Ed. by M. Clark. (Illus.). 96p. 1995. pap. 14.95 (*1-56389-235-9*) DC Comics.

Star Trek: The Ashes of Eden. William Shatner. Ed. by Kevin Ryan. 384p. 1995. 23.00 (*0-671-52035-0*) PB.

Star Trek: The Ashes of Eden. William Shatner. 1996. mass mkt., pap. 5.99 (*0-671-52036-9*) PB.

Star Trek: The First Twenty-Five Years. Gene Roddenberry & Susan Sackett. 256p. 1991. 45.00 (*0-671-73233-1*) PB.

Star Trek: The Klingon Way: A Warrior's Guide. Marc Okrand. 192p. 1996. pap. 12.00 (*0-671-53755-5*, PB Trade Paper) PB.

Star Trek: The Last Conversation. Yvonne Fern. 256p. 1996. pap. 14.00 (*0-671-52299-X*) PB.

S

Star Trek: The Making of Deep Space Nine. Judith Reeves-Stevens & Garfield Reeves-Stevens. Ed. by Kevin Ryan. (Orig.). 1994. pap. 16.00 (*0-671-87430-6*) PB.

Star Trek: The Mirror Universe Saga. Mike W. Barr. Ed. by Bob Greenberger. (Illus.). 192p. 1991. pap. 19.95 (*0-930289-96-X*) DC Comics.

Star Trek: The New Voyages. Culbreath & Marsh. 256p. 1996. mass mkt. 4.99 (*0-553-24636-4*, Spectra) Bantam.

Star Trek: The Next Generation. Michael J. Friedman. 1996. 23.00 (*0-614-96946-8*, PB Hardcover) PB.

Star Trek: The Next Generation-Beginnings. Mike Carlin. Ed. by Bob Kahan. (Illus.). 160p. 1995. pap. 19.95 (*1-56389-200-6*) DC Comics.

Star Trek: The Next Generation Companion. Larry Nemecek. 1995. pap. 18.00 (*0-671-88340-2*) PB.

Star Trek: The Next Generation: Kahless. Michael J. Friedman. 1996. 23.00 (*0-614-96776-7*, PB Hardcover) PB.

Star Trek: The Next Generation: Technical Manual. Rick Sternbach & Michael Okuda. 1991. pap. 16.00 (*0-671-70427-3*) PB.

***Star Trek: The Next Generation 45 Intellivore.** Diane Duane. 1997. mass mkt. 5.99 (*0-671-56832-9*) PB.

Star Trek: The Return. William Shatner. 1996. 22.00 (*0-614-96775-9*, PB Hardcover); 23.00 (*0-614-96945-X*, PB Hardcover) PB.

Star Trek: The Return. William Shatner et al. (Star Trek Ser.). 288p. 1996. 22.00 (*0-671-52610-3*, Star Trek) PB.

***Star Trek: The Return.** William Shatner. 1997. mass mkt. 5.99 (*0-671-52609-X*) PB.

***Star Trek: The Return.** large type ed. William Shatner. LC 96-32272. (Large Print Bks.). 1996. 23.95 (*1-56895-359-3*, Compass) Wheeler Pub.

***Star Trek: Voyager: The Official Strategy Guide.** Rick Barba. 240p. 1998. per., pap. 19.99 (*0-7615-0945-3*) Prima Pub.

***Star Trek: Vulcan's Forge.** Josepha Sherman & Susan Schwartz. 1997. 23.00 (*0-671-00926-5*) PB.

Star Trek: Where No One Has Gone Before. J. M. Dillard. 192p. 1996. pap. 25.00 (*0-671-00206-6*, Pocket Books) PB.

Star Trek: Who Killed Captain Kirk? Peter David. Ed. by Bob Kahan. 176p. 1993. pap. 16.95 (*1-56389-096-8*) DC Comics.

Star Trek No. 37: The Next Generation: The Last Stand. Brad Ferguson. 1995. mass mkt. 5.99 (*0-671-50105-4*) PB.

***Star Trek & History: Race-Ing Toward a White Future.** Daniel Bernardi. LC 97-17665. 1998. pap. write for info. (*0-8135-2466-0*) Rutgers U Pr.

***Star Trek & History: Race-Ing Toward a White Future.** Daniel Bernardi. LC 97-17665. 1998. write for info. (*0-8135-2465-2*) Rutgers U Pr.

Star Trek Atari. 1988. 39.95 (*0-13-842857-3*) P-H.

Star Trek Chronology. Michael Okuda. (Star Trek Ser.). 1996. pap. 25.00 (*0-671-53610-9*, Star Trek) PB.

Star Trek Chronology: The History of the Future. Michael Okuda & Denise Okuda. Ed. by Dave Stern. (Orig.). 1993. pap. 14.00 (*0-671-79611-9*) PB.

Star Trek Classic Episodes, No. 1. James Blish. 656p. 1991. mass mkt. 5.99 (*0-553-29138-6*, Spectra) Bantam.

Star Trek Classic Episodes, No. 3. James Blish. 608p. 1991. mass mkt. 5.99 (*0-553-29140-8*, Spectra) Bantam.

Star Trek Compendium. rev. ed. Allan Asherman. Ed. by Kevin Ryan. 192p. 1993. pap. 14.00 (*0-671-79612-7*) PB.

Star Trek Concordance: The A-to-Z Guide to the Classic Original Television Series & Films. Rev. by Bjo Trimble. (Illus.). 288p. 1995. pap. 19.95 (*0-8065-1610-0*, Citadel Pr) Carol Pub Group.

***Star Trek Cookbook.** 1996. pap. 12.00 (*0-614-19378-8*) PB.

***Star Trek Cookbook: Recipes from the 23rd Century & Beyond.** Theresa Robberson. 1997. 16.95 (*1-55972-439-0*, Birch Ln Pr); pap. text ed. 12.00 (*0-8065-1904-5*, Citadel Pr) Carol Pub Group.

Star Trek Creator: The Authorized Biography of Gene Roddenberry. David Alexander. 672p. 1995. pap. 6.99 (*0-451-45440-5*, ROC) NAL-Dutton.

Star Trek Deep Space Nine: Dimensional Poster & Booklet. Smith. (J). 1995. pap. 19.95 (*0-689-80413-X*, Litl Simon S&S) S&S Childrens.

Star Trek Deep Space Nine: The Way of the Warrior. Diane Carey. 1995. mass mkt. 5.99 (*0-671-56813-2*) PB.

Star Trek Deep Space 9: Warped. K. W. Jeter. Ed. by Kevin Ryan. 352p. 1995. 22.00 (*0-671-87252-4*) PB.

Star Trek Deep Space 9 No. 11: Devil in the Sky. Greg Cox. (Illus.). (J). 1995. mass mkt. 5.50 (*0-671-88114-0*) PB.

***Star Trek Encyclopedia.** Okuda. 1997. 50.00 (*0-671-53607-9*, PB Hardcover) PB.

Star Trek Encyclopedia. Ed. by Michael Okuda. (Illus.). 1994. 30.00 (*0-671-88684-3*) PB.

Star Trek Fans & Costume Art. Heather R. Joseph-Witham. (Folk Art & Artists Ser.). (Illus.). 72p. 1996. 32.50 (*0-87805-919-9*); pap. 16.95 (*0-87805-920-2*) U Pr of Miss.

Star Trek Federation Passport: A Mini Travel Guide & Star Trek Passport. J. M. Dillard. 1996. pap. 6.00 (*0-671-00317-8*) PB.

***Star Trek Federation Travel Guide.** Michael J. Friedman. 64p. 1997. pap. 6.00 (*0-671-00978-8*) PB.

Star Trek First Contact. 1987. 39.95 (*0-13-842907-3*) P-H.

***Star Trek First Contact: A Novel by J. M. Dillard Based on the Film Star Trek Generations II.** Contrib. by Rick Berman et al. (Illus.). 256p. 1996. 27.00 (*0-614-19273-0*) PB.

Star Trek Generations. J. M. Dillard. 1994. pap. 17.00 (*0-671-51996-4*) PB.

Star Trek Generations. John Vornholt. (YA). (gr. 3-6). 1994. mass mkt. 3.99 (*0-671-51901-8*, Minstrel Bks) PB.

Star Trek Generations: Star Trek: The Next Generations. J. M. Dillard. 1995. mass mkt. 5.99 (*0-671-53753-9*) PB.

***Star Trek Generations II.** J. M. Dillard. 1996. 20.00 (*0-614-20656-1*, PB Hardcover) PB.

***Star Trek Generations II.** John Vornholt. (J). (gr. 3-7). Date not set. pap. 3.99 (*0-614-19320-6*) PB.

Star Trek Generations Official Guide. Bradygames Staff. 216p. 1997. 19.99 (*1-56686-589-1*) Brady Pub.

Star Trek II: The Wrath of Khan. Vonda N. McIntyre. 1991. mass mkt. 5.50 (*0-671-74149-7*) PB.

Star Trek II Gift Set, 3 vols., Set. William Rotsler. (J). boxed 9.50 (*0-317-12429-3*) S&S Trade.

Star Trek III: The Search for Spock. Vonda N. McIntyre. (Star Trek Ser.: No. 17). 1990. mass mkt. 5.50 (*0-671-73133-5*) PB.

Star Trek Interview Book. Allan Asherman. 1988. pap. 13.00 (*0-671-61794-X*) PB.

Star Trek Kobayshi Com64. 1986. 29.95 (*0-13-842642-2*) P-H.

Star Trek Log Eight. Alan Dean Foster. 1976. lib. bdg. 22.95 (*0-88411-088-5*) Amereon Ltd.

Star Trek Log Five. Alan Dean Foster. 1975. reprint ed. lib. bdg. 22.95 (*0-88411-085-0*) Amereon Ltd.

Star Trek Log Four. Alan Dean Foster. 1975. reprint ed. lib. bdg. 22.95 (*0-88411-084-2*) Amereon Ltd.

Star Trek Log Nine. Alan Dean Foster. 195p. reprint ed. lib. bdg. 21.95 (*0-88411-089-3*) Amereon Ltd.

Star Trek Log One. Alan Dean Foster. 1975. reprint ed. lib. bdg. 22.95 (*0-88411-081-8*) Amereon Ltd.

Star Trek Log Seven. Alan Dean Foster. 1976. lib. bdg. 22.95 (*0-88411-087-7*) Amereon Ltd.

Star Trek Log Six. Alan Dean Foster. 1976. reprint ed. lib. bdg. 22.95 (*0-88411-086-9*) Amereon Ltd.

Star Trek Log Ten. Alan Dean Foster. 215p. reprint ed. lib. bdg. 22.95 (*0-88411-090-7*) Amereon Ltd.

Star Trek Log Three. Alan Dean Foster. 224p. 1985. mass mkt. 4.99 (*0-345-33318-7*, Del Rey) Ballantine.

Star Trek Log Three. Alan Dean Foster. 1975. reprint ed. lib. bdg. 22.95 (*0-88411-083-4*) Amereon Ltd.

Star Trek Log Two. Alan Dean Foster. 1975. reprint ed. lib. bdg. 19.95 (*0-88411-082-6*) Amereon Ltd.

Star Trek Logs Four, Five, & Six. Alan Dean Foster. 1993. mass mkt. 5.99 (*0-345-38522-5*, Del Rey) Ballantine.

Star Trek Logs One, Two & Three. Alan Dean Foster. 1993. mass mkt. 4.99 (*0-345-38247-1*, Del Rey) Ballantine.

Star Trek Logs Seven, Eight, & Nine. Alan Dean Foster. 1993. mass mkt. 5.99 (*0-345-38561-6*, Del Rey) Ballantine.

Star Trek Memories. William Shatner. 432p. 1994. mass mkt. 6.99 (*0-06-109235-5*) HarpC.

Star Trek Movie Magazine Presents: Star Trek 30th Anniversary Crosswords. annuals (YA). 1996. pap. text ed. 6.99 (*0-934551-07-3*) Starlog Pr.

Star Trek Movie Memories. William Shatner. 464p. 1995. mass mkt. 6.99 (*0-06-109329-7*, HarperPrism) HarpC.

Star Trek Movie Story Book. (J). (gr. k-3). 1996. 9.99 (*0-689-80899-2*, S&S Bks Young Read) S&S Childrens.

Star Trek Movie Tie-in #1. (J). 1996. 3.25 (*0-689-80897-6*) S&S Trade.

Star Trek Movie Tie-in #2. LC 96-41588. (J). (ps-2). 1996. pap. 3.25 (*0-689-80898-4*) S&S Trade.

Star Trek Next Generation Card Game Bundle. Bradygames Staff. 1996. pap. text ed. 16.99 (*1-56686-516-6*) Brady Pub.

Star Trek Next Generation Unification. Jeri Taylor. 1991. mass mkt. 5.50 (*0-671-77056-X*) PB.

Star Trek, No. 3: Klingon Gambit. Robert E. Vardeman. 1990. pap. 4.50 (*0-671-70767-1*) S&S Trade.

Star Trek, No. 42: Memory Prime. Garfield Reeves-Stevens & Judith Reeves-Stevens. 1991. mass mkt. 5.50 (*0-671-74359-7*) PB.

***Star Trek, Phase II.** Judith Reeves-Stevens. (Lost Ser.). 1997. pap. 128.00 (*0-671-84007-X*) PB.

Star Trek Phase II: The Lost Series. Judith Reeves-Stevens & Garfield Reeves-Stevens. (Illus.). 288p. 1997. pap. 16.00 (*0-671-56839-6*) S&S Trade.

***Star Trek Reader's Reference.** Alva Underwood. 294p. (Orig.). 1997. mass mkt. 4.99 (*1-55237-098-4*, Pub. by Comnwlth Pub CN) Partners Pubs Grp.

***Star Trek Sketchbook.** Herbert F. Solow & Yvonne F. Fern. 256p. 1997. pap. 20.00 (*0-671-00219-8*) PB.

Star Trek-the Motion Picture. Gene Roddenberry. 1980. 9.95 (*0-686-60888-7*) S&S Trade.

Star Trek the Next Generation Giant Novel No. 2: Vendetta. Peter David. 1991. mass mkt. 5.99 (*0-671-74145-4*) PB.

Star Trek the Next Generation U. S. S. Enterprise NCC-1701-D Blueprints. Rick Sternbach. 16p. 1996. pap. 24.00 (*0-671-50093-7*) PB.

Star Trek V: Final Frontier. J. M. Dillard. 1989. mass mkt. 4.50 (*0-671-68008-0*) PB.

Star Trek VI: The Undiscovered Country. J. M. Dillard. Ed. by Dave Stern. (Orig.). 1992. mass mkt. 5.50 (*0-671-75883-7*) PB.

Star Trek Voyager Flashback. Diane Carey. (Star Trek: Voyager Ser.). 1996. mass mkt. 5.99 (*0-671-00383-6*, Star Trek) PB.

Star Trek with Latin. Rudolph Masciantonio. 39p. (Orig.). 1991. spiral bd. 3.55 (*0-939507-27-7*, B 311) Amer Classical.

Star Trek 1. James Blish. 18.95 (*0-8488-0431-7*) Amereon Ltd.

Star Trek #2. 1989. pap. 15.80 (*0-671-92163-0*) PB.

Star Trek 2. James Blish. 18.95 (*0-8488-0738-3*) Amereon Ltd.

Star Trek 3. James Blish. 18.95 (*0-8488-0739-1*) Amereon Ltd.

Star Trek 4. James Blish. 18.95 (*0-8488-0740-5*) Amereon Ltd.

Star Trek 5. James Blish. 18.95 (*0-8488-0741-3*) Amereon Ltd.

***Star Tribune Basketball Souvenir Book.** (Illus.). 96p. 1997. pap. 12.95 (*0-9647179-4-8*) Star MN.

Star Trip. Lee Mountain. (Attention Span Stories Ser). (Illus.). 48p. (Orig.). 1978. pap. text ed. 8.65 (*0-89061-149-1*, 585) Jamestown Pubs.

Star Twenty One: Strategic Technologies for the Army of the Twenty-First Century Technology Forecast Assessment, 2 vols., Set. 1994. lib. bdg. 625.95 (*0-8490-5802-3*) Gordon Pr.

***Star Viking: Planetfal.** Date not set. 30.00 (*1-55878-111-0*) Game Designers.

Star Vision. Samanthe Parker. (Illus.). 64p. (Orig.). 1992. pap. 4.95 (*0-910241-00-7*) ShaunTar Ent.

Star Voyager Academy. William R. Forstchen. 288p. (Orig.). 1994. mass mkt. 5.99 (*0-671-87608-2*) Baen Bks.

Star Walk. Ed. by Seymour Simon. LC 94-16643. (Illus.). 32p. (J). (gr. k up). 1995. 15.00 (*0-688-11887-9*, Morrow Junior) Morrow.

Star Ware: The Amateur Astronomer's Ultimate Guide to Choosing & Buying Telescopes & Accessories. Philip S. Harrington. 373p. 1994. pap. text ed. 24.95 (*0-471-57671-9*) Wiley.

Star Ware: The Amateur Astronomer's Ultimate Guide to Choosing, Buying & Using Telescopes & Accessories. Philip S. Harrington. 373p. 1994. text ed. 47.95 (*0-471-10593-7*) Wiley.

Star Warrior: The Story of SwiftDeer. Bill Wahlburg. LC 93-3038. (Illus.). 196p. (Orig.). 1993. pap. 12.95 (*1-879181-07-X*) Bear & Co.

***Star Wars.** (J). 1997. pap. 2.99 (*0-307-10577-6*, Golden Books) Western Pub.

***Star Wars.** Walt Disney. (J). 1997. 8.98 (*1-57082-567-X*) Mouse Works.

Star Wars. Phil Dusenberry. 1998. pap. 24.95 (*0-670-86309-2*) Viking Penguin.

***Star Wars.** Bruce Jones. 1997. pap. 9.95 (*1-56971-213-1*) Dark Horse Comics.

***Star Wars.** expanded ed. 30.00 (*0-87431-268-X*, 40120) West End Games.

***Star Wars: A New Hope.** Adapted by Michael Teitelbaum. (New Look-Look Books & Tattoos). (Illus.). (J). (ps-3). 1997. pap. 3.99 (*0-614-28799-5*, Golden Books) Western Pub.

Star Wars: A New Hope. John Whitman. LC 96-52906. (Little Chronicles Ser.). (Illus.). 432p. 1997. 9.95 (*0-8118-1480-7*) Chronicle Bks.

Star Wars: Battle of the Bounty Hunters. unabridged ed. Illus. by Christopher Moeller. 12p. (J). (gr. 2 up). 1996. 17.95 (*1-56971-129-1*) Dark Horse Comics.

Star Wars: Before the Storm. Michael P. Kube-McDowell. (The Black Fleet Crisis Ser.: Vol. 1). 1996. audio 16.99 (*0-553-47422-7*) Bantam.

Star Wars: Before the Storm: Book 1 of the Black Fleet Crisis. Michael P. Kube-McDowell. 1996. pap. 5.99 (*0-614-98033-X*) Bantam.

***Star Wars: Coloring Book.** (J). 1997. pap. 2.29 (*0-307-05653-8*, Golden Books) Western Pub.

***Star Wars: Dark Empire.** Tom Veitch. 1997. pap. 16.95 (*1-56511-201-6*) D I Fine.

***Star Wars: Dark Force.** Bill Dietz. 1997. pap. 16.95 (*1-56511-202-4*) D I Fine.

***Star Wars: Dark Lords.** Kevin J. Anderson. 1997. pap. 16.95 (*1-56511-199-0*) D I Fine.

Star Wars: Darksaber. Kevin J. Anderson. 1995. 22.95 (*0-614-15489-8*) Bantam.

Star Wars: From Concept to Screen to Collectible. Stephen J. Sansweet. Ed. by Nion McEvoy. (Illus.). 132p. 1992. 29.95 (*0-8118-0101-2*); pap. 19.95 (*0-8118-0096-2*) Chronicle Bks.

Star Wars: From the Adventures of Luke Skywalker. George Lucas. LC 77-88169. 224p. 1986. mass mkt. 5.99 (*0-345-34146-5*, Del Rey) Ballantine.

Star Wars: Heir to the Empire. Timothy Zahn. (Illus.). 160p. (Orig.). 1996. pap. 17.95 (*1-56971-202-6*) Dark Horse Comics.

Star Wars: Jedi Academy Trilogy, 3 vols. in 1. Kevin J. Anderson. 720p. 1994. 14.98 (*1-56865-120-1*, GuildAmerica) Dblday Direct.

***Star Wars: Pilots & Spacecraft.** Margaret Snyder. (Glow-in-the-Dark Bks.). (J). (gr. 3-6). 1997. pap. 3.99 (*0-614-28802-9*, Golden Books) Western Pub.

***Star Wars: Planet of Twilight.** Hambly. 1997. 16.99 (*0-553-47196-1*) Bantam.

***Star Wars: Planet of Twilight.** Barbara Hambly. 1997. 22.95 (*0-614-27885-6*) Bantam.

***Star Wars: Return of the Jedi.** James Kahn. 1997. mass mkt. 5.99 (*0-345-91184-9*, Del Rey) Ballantine.

***Star Wars: Return of the Jedi.** Justine Korman. (New Look-Look Books & Tattoos). (Illus.). (J). (ps-3). 1997. pap. 3.99 (*0-614-28800-2*, Golden Books) Western Pub.

***Star Wars: Return of the Jedi.** George Lucas. 1997. mass mkt. 3.99 (*0-345-41356-3*, Del Rey) Ballantine.

***Star Wars: Return of the Jedi.** John Whitman. 1997. 9.95 (*0-8118-1494-7*) Chronicle Bks.

Star Wars: Shadows of the Empire. Steve Perry. 1996. 22.95 (*0-614-96771-6*) Bantam.

Star Wars: Shadows of the Empire. Steve Perry. 1996. 22.95 (*0-614-96941-7*) Bantam.

***Star Wars: Shadows of the Empire.** Steve Perry. 1997. mass mkt. 5.99 (*0-614-27717-5*) Bantam.

Star Wars: Shield of Lies. Michael P. Kube-McDowell. (Black Fleet Crisis Ser.: Bk. 2). 352p. 1996. mass mkt. 5.99 (*0-553-57277-6*) Bantam.

Star Wars: Showdown at Centerpoint. Roger M. Allen. (Orig.). 1995. mass mkt. 5.99 (*0-614-15538-X*) Bantam.

Star Wars: Tales From Jabba's Palace. Ed. by Kevin J. Anderson. (Star Wars Anthologies Ser.). 384p. (YA). 1996. mass mkt. 5.99 (*0-553-56815-9*, Spectra) Bantam.

***Star Wars: Tales of the Jedi.** Tom Veitch. 1997. pap. 16.95 (*1-56511-198-2*) D I Fine.

Star Wars: Tales of the Jedi. 2nd ed. Tom Veitch. (Illus.). 136p. 1994. pap. 14.95 (*1-56971-060-0*) Dark Horse Comics.

Star Wars: Tales of the Jedi: Dark Cords of the Sith. unabridged ed. Tom Veitch & Kevin J. Anderson. (Illus.). 160p. (Orig.). (YA). (gr. 7 up). 1996. pap. 17.95 (*1-56971-095-3*) Dark Horse Comics.

Star Wars: Tales of the Jedi: Dark Lords of the Sith. Kevin Anderson. (Illus.). 160p. (Orig.). 1996. pap. 17.95 (*1-56971-173-9*) Dark Horse Comics.

***Star Wars: The Art of Dave Dorman.** Ed. by Stephen D. Smith & Lurene Haines. (Illus.). 128p. (Orig.). 1996. 75.00 (*1-887569-38-3*); pap. 24.95 (*1-887569-37-5*) FPG.

Star Wars: The Art of Ralph Mcquarrie. Ralph Mcquarrie. 1996. 18.95 (*0-8118-1320-7*) Chronicle Bks.

Star Wars: The Crystal Star. Vonda N. McIntyre. (Star Wars Ser.). 368p. (YA). 1995. reprint ed. mass mkt., pap. 5.99 (*0-553-57174-5*) Bantam.

***Star Wars: The Death Star.** John Whitman. (Illus.). 1997. 15.95 (*0-614-28839-8*) Little.

Star Wars: The Economic Fallout. Rosy Nimroody. 350p. 1988. 19.95 (*0-614-16165-7*) CEP.

***Star Wars: The Empire Strikes Back.** Donald F. Glut. 1997. pap. 5.99 (*0-345-91183-0*, Del Rey) Ballantine.

***Star Wars: The Empire Strikes Back.** John Whitman. LC 96-52904. 1997. 9.95 (*0-8118-1482-3*) Chronicle Bks.

Star Wars: The Essential Guide to Vehicles & Vessels. Bill Smith. (Illus.). 225p. (J). 1996. pap. 18.00 (*0-345-39299-X*) Ballantine.

***Star Wars: The Magic of Myth.** Mary S. Henderson. LC 97-13039. 1997. write for info. (*0-553-10206-0*); pap. write for info. (*0-553-37810-4*) Broadway BDD.

Star Wars: The Mos Eisley Cantina Pop-Up Book. Kevin J. Anderson. (J). 1995. 19.95 (*0-316-53511-7*) Little.

Star Wars: The National Public Radio Dramatization. Brian Daley. (Illus.). 304p. (Orig.). 1994. pap. 11.00 (*0-345-39109-8*, Del Rey) Ballantine.

***Star Wars: The New Rebellion.** Kristine K. Rusch. 1996. 22.95 (*0-614-20653-7*) Bantam.

***Star Wars: The Paradise Snare.** A. C. Crispin. (Orig.). 1997. mass mkt. 5.99 (*0-614-27719-1*) Bantam.

Star Wars: The Roleplaying Game. 144p. 20.00 (*0-87431-065-2*, 40001) West End Games.

Star Wars: The Strategic Defense Initiative Debates in Congress. Larry Pressler. LC 86-809. 193p. 1986. text ed. 55.00 (*0-275-92052-6*, C2052, Praeger Pubs) Greenwood.

Star Wars: The Truce at Bakura. Kathleen M. Tyers. (Star Wars Ser.). 352p. (YA). 1994. mass mkt. 5.99 (*0-553-56872-8*) Bantam.

Star Wars: The Young Jedi Knights: The Lost Ones. Kevin J. Anderson & Rebecca Moesta. (Star Wars Ser.). 240p. (Orig.). 1995. mass mkt. 4.99 (*1-57297-052-9*) Blvd Books.

***Star Wars: Tyrant's Test.** Michael P. Kube-McDowell. (The Black Fleet Crisis Ser.: Bk. 3). 1997. mass mkt. 5.99 (*0-614-20501-8*) Bantam.

Star Wars: Vintage Toys: Postcard Book. Chronicle Books Staff. (Star Wars Ser.). 1995. pap. 12.95 (*0-8118-1153-0*) Chronicle Bks.

Star Wars Bk. 1: Dark Empire. 2nd ed. Tom Veitch. (Illus.). 184p. (J). 1995. pap. 17.95 (*1-56971-073-2*) Dark Horse Comics.

Star Wars Bk. 1: Droids. Dan Thorsland & Ryder Windham. (Illus.). 200p. (J). (gr. 4 up). 1995. pap. 17.95 (*1-56971-064-3*) Dark Horse Comics.

Star Wars Bk. 2: Dark Empire II. Tom Veitch. (Illus.). 168p. (J). 1995. pap. 17.95 (*1-56971-119-4*) Dark Horse Comics.

Star Wars No. 3: Young Jedi Knights: Heir of the Force. Kevin J. Anderson & Rebecca Moesta. 240p. (Orig.). (YA). 1995. mass mkt. 4.99 (*1-57297-000-6*) Blvd Books.

Star Wars No. 4: Young Jedi Knights: Light Saber. Kevin J. Anderson & Rebecca Moesta. 240p. (Orig.). (J). 1996. mass mkt. 5.99 (*1-57297-091-X*) Blvd Books.

***Star Wars - The Adventure Continues.** (J). 1997. boxed, pap. 11.97 (*0-553-62866-6*) BDD Bks Young Read.

Star Wars: A Defense Insider's Case Against the Strategic Defense Initiative: A Defense Expert's Case Against the Strategic Defense Initiative. Robert Bowman. 192p. 1986. reprint ed. pap. 7.95 (*0-87477-377-6*, Tarcher Putnam) Putnam Pub Group.

Star Wars Adventure. George Lucas. 1994. 8.98 (*1-57042-153-6*) Warner Bks.

***Star Wars Adventure Journal, Vol. 1, No. 4.** 12.00 (*0-87431-403-8*, 41004) West End Games.

***Star Wars Adventure Journal, Vol. 1, No. 5.** 12.00 (*0-87431-404-6*, 41005) West End Games.

***Star Wars Adventure Journal, Vol. 1, No. 6.** 12.00 (*0-87431-405-4*, 41006) West End Games.

***Star Wars Adventure Journal, Vol. 1, No. 7.** 12.00 (*0-87431-406-2*, 41007) West End Games.

***Star Wars Adventure Journal, Vol. 1, No. 8.** 12.00 (*0-87431-407-0*, 41008) West End Games.

***Star Wars Adventure Journal, Vol. 1, No. 9.** 12.00 (*0-87431-408-9*, 41009) West End Games.

***Star Wars Adventure Journal, Vol. 1, No. 10.** 12.00 (*0-87431-409-7*, 41010) West End Games.

***Star Wars Adventure Journal, Vol. 1, No. 11.** 12.00 (*0-87431-410-0*, 41011) West End Games.

***Star Wars Adventure Journal, Vol. 1, No. 12.** 12.00 (*0-87431-411-9*, 41012) West End Games.

***Star Wars Adventure Journal, Vol. 1, No. 13.** 1997. 12.00 (*0-87431-412-7*, 41013) West End Games.

Star Wars & European Defence: European Perceptions & Assessments. Ed. by Hans G. Brauch. LC 85-19593. 280p. 1987. text ed. 49.95 (*0-312-30786-1*) St Martin.

An Asterisk (*) at the beginning of an entry indicates that the title is appearing in BIP for the first time.

***Star Wars & 20 Great Movie Hits.** Ed. by Sy Feldman. 96p. (Orig.). (YA). 1997. pap. text ed. 12.95 (*0-7692-0030-3*) Warner Brothers.

***Star Wars Annotated Scripts.** Laurent Bouzereau. 1997. pap. text ed. 12.95 (*0-345-40981-7*, Del Rey) Ballantine.

Star Wars Chronicles. deluxe limited ed. Deborah Fine & Aeon Incorporated Staff. LC 96-51019. (Illus.). 320p. 1997. 150.00 (*0-8118-1498-X*) Chronicle Bks.

Star Wars Controversy: An International Security Reader. Ed. by Steven E. Miller et al. LC 86-4280. (Illus.). 350p. reprint ed. pap. 99.80 (*0-8357-4201-6*, 2036980) Bks Demand.

Star Wars Customizable Card Game Players Guide. Bradygames Staff. 1995. 14.99 (*1-56686-500-X*) Brady Pub.

***Star Wars, Dark Forces: Soldier for the Empire.** William C. Dietz. (Illus.). 128p. 1997. 23.95 (*0-399-14198-7*) Blvd Books.

***Star Wars Diplomatic Corps Entrance Exam.** Kristine Rusch. 1997. pap. 12.00 (*0-345-41412-8*, Del Rey) Ballantine.

***Star Wars Diplomatic Corps Entrance Exam.** Kristine K. Rusch. 1997. pap. 12.00 (*0-614-27311-0*, Del Rey) Ballantine.

***Star Wars: Empire Strikes Back: From the Adventures of Luke Skywalker.** George Lucas. 1997. mass mkt. 3.99 (*0-614-27736-1*, Del Rey) Ballantine.

Star Wars Encyclopedia. LC 97-15066. (Illus.). 1997. write for info. (*0-345-40227-8*) Ballantine.

Star Wars Encyclopedia. (Illus.). Date not set. pap. write for info. (*0-345-40228-6*) Ballantine.

Star Wars Junior Jedi Knights No. 2: Lyric's World. Nancy A. Richardson. 128p. (Orig.). (J). 1996. mass mkt. 4.50 (*1-57297-068-5*) Blvd Books.

Star Wars Miniatures Battles. 128p. 1991. 18.00 (*0-87431-144-6*, 40044) West End Games.

***Star Wars Movie Story.** 1997. mass mkt. 5.99 (*0-590-06654-4*) Scholastic Inc.

Star Wars Now! 1988. 9.25 (*0-914119-20-6*) Tesla Bk Co.

***Star Wars: Return of the Jedi: From the Adventures of Luke Skywalker.** George Lucas. 1997. mass mkt. 3.99 (*0-614-27737-X*, Del Rey) Ballantine.

Star Wars Rules Companion. 80p. 15.00 (*0-87431-147-0*, 40043) West End Games.

Star Wars Sourcebook. 144p. 20.00 (*0-87431-066-0*, 40002) West End Games.

***Star Wars Sourebook.** (Star Wars Ser.). 22.00 (*0-87431-211-6*, 40093) West End Games.

Star Wars Technical Journal. Shane Johnson. (Illus.). 144p. 1995. 35.00 (*0-345-40182-4*, Del Rey) Ballantine.

Star Wars Treasury. (J). Date not set. pap. 4.95 (*0-590-39635-8*) Scholastic Inc.

Star Wars Trilogy, 3 vols. 480p. 1987. pap. 10.00 (*0-345-34806-0*, Del Rey) Ballantine.

***Star Wars Trilogy.** George Lucas et al. 1997. mass mkt. 6.99 (*0-345-91126-1*) Ballantine.

***Star Wars Trilogy: Alto Sax.** Ed. by Tony Esposito. 20p. (Orig.). (YA). 1997. pap. text ed. 10.95 (*0-7692-0010-9*) Warner Brothers.

***Star Wars Trilogy: Clarinet.** Ed. by Tony Esposito. 20p. (Orig.). (YA). 1997. pap. text ed. 10.95 (*0-7692-0009-5*) Warner Brothers.

***Star Wars Trilogy: Flute.** Ed. by Tony Esposito. 20p. (Orig.). (YA). 1997. pap. text ed. 10.95 (*0-7692-0008-7*) Warner Brothers.

Star Wars Trilogy: Stars Wars; The Empire Strikes Back; Return of the Jedi, 3 vols. in 1. George Lucas et al. 1993. mass mkt. 5.99 (*0-345-38438-5*, Del Rey) Ballantine.

***Star Wars Trilogy: Tenor Sax.** Ed. by Tony Esposito. 20p. (Orig.). (YA). 1997. pap. text ed. 10.95 (*0-7692-0011-7*) Warner Brothers.

***Star Wars Trilogy: Trombone.** Ed. by Tony Esposito. 20p. (Orig.). (YA). 1997. pap. text ed. 10.95 (*0-7692-0013-3*) Warner Brothers.

***Star Wars Trilogy: Trumpet.** Ed. by Tony Esposito. 20p. (Orig.). (YA). 1997. pap. text ed. 10.95 (*0-7692-0012-5*) Warner Brothers.

***Star Wars Trilogy: Violin.** Ed. by Tony Esposito. (Orig.). (YA). 1997. pap. text ed. 10.95 (*0-7692-0063-X*) Warner Brothers.

Star Western. Ed. by Jon Tuska. LC 95-14139. 1995. 12.99 (*0-517-14688-6*, Pub. by Gramercy) Random Hse Value.

***Star Wisdom.** Gene Andrade. Ed. by Eileen Maceri. (Illus.). 153p. (Orig.). 1997. pap. 15.00 (*1-885757-10-7*) Pleiades Proj.

***Star Witness.** J. F. Freedman. 1997. 23.95 (*0-614-27941-0*) NAL-Dutton.

***Star Witness.** Lia Matera. LC 97-1196. 1997. 22.00 (*0-684-83469-3*) S&S Trade.

Star Woman: We Are Made From Stars & to the Stars We Must Return. Lynn V. Andrews. 256p. 1987. pap. 12.99 (*0-446-38566-2*) Warner Bks.

Star Wormwood. Curtis Bok. LC 84-45877. (Capital Punishment Ser.). 1983. reprint ed. 30.00 (*0-404-62402-2*, 8675) AMS Pr.

Star Wreck: The Generation Gap. Leah Rewolinski. 1990. pap. 3.50 (*0-312-92359-7*) St Martin.

Star Wreck Four: Live Long & Profit. Leah Rewolinski. 1993. mass mkt. 4.50 (*0-312-92985-4*) St Martin.

Star Wreck II: The Attack of the Jargonites. Leah Rewolinski. 1992. mass mkt. 3.99 (*0-312-92737-1*) St Martin.

Star Wreck the Generation Gap. Leah Rewolinski. 1992. mass mkt. 3.99 (*0-312-92802-5*) St Martin.

Star Wreck Three: Time Warped. Leah Rewolinski. 1992. mass mkt. 3.99 (*0-312-92891-2*) St Martin.

Star Wreck V: The Undiscovered Nursing Home. Leah Rewolinski. 1993. mass mkt. 3.99 (*0-312-95122-1*) St Martin.

Star 21: Strategic Technologies for the Army in the Twenty-First Century. National Research Council Staff. 334p. 1992. text ed. 34.95 (*0-309-04629-7*) Natl Acad Pr.

Star 21, Strategic Technologies for the Army of the 21st Century: Technology Forecast Assessments. (Illus.). 697p. (Orig.). (C). 1994. text ed. 95.00 (*0-7881-1194-9*) DIANE Pub.

Starbase Earth: Guide to Science Anytime 1995. annuals 95th ed. 1995. pap. text ed. 9.00 (*0-15-306065-4*) HarBrace.

Starbird: Genealogy of the Starbird - Starbard Family. A. A. Starbird. 179p. 1992. reprint ed. pap. 27.00 (*0-8328-2290-6*); reprint ed. lib. bdg. 37.00 (*0-8328-2289-2*) Higginson Bk Co.

Starbook Music Hall of Fame, 1985. 1985. pap. 4.95 (*0-317-01181-2*, Sig) NAL-Dutton.

Starborn. John Nelson. (Mystical Tale Ser.). 136p. 1993. pap. 8.95 (*1-878901-59-1*) Hampton Roads Pub Co.

Starborn. Brad Steiger & Sherry H. Steiger. 1992. mass mkt. 4.99 (*0-425-13308-7*) Berkley Pub.

Starborne. Robert Silverberg. LC 95-44862. 304p. 1996. 22.95 (*0-553-10264-8*, Spectra) Bantam.

***Starborne.** Robert Silverberg. 1997. mass mkt. 6.50 (*0-553-57334-9*, Spectra) Bantam.

Starbound. (Voyage Through the Universe Ser.). (Illus.). 144p. 1991. 19.93 (*0-8094-6941-3*); lib. bdg. 25.93 (*0-8094-6942-1*) Time-Life.

Starbridge. A. C. Crispin. 1989. mass mkt. 4.99 (*0-441-78329-5*) Ace Bks.

Starbridge, No. 3: Shadow World. A. C. Crispin. 1991. mass mkt. 4.99 (*0-441-78332-5*) Ace Bks.

Starbridge, No. 4: Serpent's Gift. A. C. Crispin & Deborah A. Marshall. 1992. mass mkt. 4.50 (*0-441-78331-7*) Ace Bks.

Starbright: Meditations for Children. Maureen Garth. LC 90-56458. 96p. (Orig.). (J). 1991. pap. 11.00 (*0-06-250398-7*) Harper SF.

StarBrothers. Mary W. Noyes. Date not set. write for info. (*0-614-17662-X*) Southern Pubs Grp.

Starbuck. Wilma Fletcher. 108p. 1982. 12.00 (*0-87770-271-3*) Ye Galleon.

Starbuck Essays of Henry Stommel. Henry M. Stommel. Ed. by Vicky Cullen. 96p. (Orig.). 1992. pap. 15.00 (*1-880224-06-2*) Woods Hole Ocean.

Starbuck's Brand. large type ed. Theodore V. Olsen. LC 92-19929. (Nightingale Ser.). 311p. 1992. pap. 14.95 (*0-8161-5594-1*, GK Hall) Thorndike Pr.

***Starbuck's Brand.** T. V. Olsen. 192p. 1997. reprint ed. mass mkt. 4.99 (*0-8439-4326-2*, Leisure Bks) Dorchester Pub Co.

***Starburst.** Charles J. Palmer & Jacqueline Palmer. (Journal of the International Society of Authors & Artists Ser.: Vol. 4, No. 3). (Illus.). 60p. 1996. pap. 7.00 (*1-881808-30-0*) Creat Arts & Sci.

Starburst. Frederik Pohl. 1986. mass mkt. 5.99 (*0-345-33928-2*, Del Rey) Ballantine.

***Starburst Vol. V, No. 1: Journal of the International Society of Authors & Artists.** Jacqueline Palmer. (Illus.). 60p. (Orig.). 1997. pap. 7.00 (*1-881808-32-7*) Creat Arts & Sci.

Starburst, A Conversation on Man & Nature. Kenneth M. Sayre. LC 76-30423. 120p. reprint ed. pap. 34.20 (*0-317-08185-3*, 2015540) Bks Demand.

Starburst Mosaic. Camille Remme. (Illus.). (Orig.). pap. 14.95 (*0-929950-12-7*) ME Pubns.

Starcarbon: A Meditation on Love. Ellen Gilchrist. 1995. pap. 11.95 (*0-316-31462-5*) Little.

Starch: Chemistry & Technology. 2nd ed. Roy L. Whistler et al. LC 82-25311. 1984. text ed. 169.00 (*0-12-746270-8*) Acad Pr.

Starch: Properties & Potential. Ed. by T. Galliard. (Critical Reports on Applied Chemistry). 151p. 1987. text ed. 159.95 (*0-471-91326-X*) Wiley.

Starch & Starch Products in Paper Coating. Ed. by R. L. Kearney & H. W. Maurer. 246p. 1990. reprint ed. pap. 96.00 (*0-89852-050-9*, 0102B050) TAPPI.

Starch & Starch Products in Paper Coating. Ed. by Robert L. Kearney & Hans W. Maurer. LC 90-32718. reprint ed. pap. 66.30 (*0-8357-4303-9*, 2037100) Bks Demand.

Starch Hydrolysis Products: Worldwide Technology, Production & Application. Ed. by Fred W. Schenck & Ronald E. Habeda. (Illus.). 650p. 1991. 165.00 (*1-56081-055-6*, VCH) Wiley.

Starch Manufacturing & Handling. 1989. pap. 20.25 (*0-685-58081-4*, 61A-89) Natl Fire Prot.

Starchild Trilogy. Frederik Pohl & Jack Williamson. 448p. 1986. reprint ed. mass mkt. 4.99 (*0-671-65558-2*) Baen Bks.

***Starck.** O. Boissiere. 1994. pap. 24.99 (*3-8228-9752-3*) Taschen Amer.

Starclimber: The Literary Adventures & Autobiography of Raymond Z. Gallun. Raymond Z. Gallun & Jeffrey M. Elliot. LC 89-82175. (Borgo Bioviews Ser.: No. 1). 168p. 1991. pap. 21.00 (*0-89370-448-2*); lib. bdg. 31.00 (*0-89370-348-6*) Borgo Pr.

***StarCraft: The Official Strategy Guide.** Bart Farkas. 240p. 1997. per., pap. 19.99 (*0-7615-0496-6*) Prima Pub.

Starcrossed. Ben Bova. 224p. 1988. pap. 2.95 (*0-8125-3231-7*) Tor Bks.

Starcrossed. Susan Krinard. 432p. 1995. mass mkt. 5.99 (*0-553-56917-1*, Fanfare) Bantam.

***Stardancer.** Jean Cummings. 299p. (Orig.). 1997. mass mkt. 4.99 (*1-55197-936-5*, Pub. by Comnwlth Pub CN) Partners Pubs Grp.

Stardark Songs. Nancy Springer. LC 91-75680. (Illus.). 96p. 1993. 20.00 (*0-932445-58-6*); pap. 7.95 (*0-932445-49-7*) Ganley Pub.

Stardark Songs. deluxe limited ed. Nancy Springer. LC 91-75680. (Illus.). 96p. 1993. boxed 35.00 (*0-932445-50-0*) Ganley Pub.

Stardom: Industry of Desire. Ed. by Christine Gledhill. 272p. (C). (gr. 13). 1991. pap. 17.95 (*0-415-05218-1*, A5098); text ed. 85.00 (*0-415-05217-3*, A5094) Routledge.

Stardream Chronicles, No. 1. large type ed. Astara. 96p. (J). (ps-12). 1996. pap. 11.95 (*1-885226-46-2*) StarLineage.

***Stardream Chronicles, Vol. 2.** Astara L. Leopold. 128p. (Orig.). (J). (gr. 1-8). 1997. pap. 12.95 (*1-885226-45-4*) StarLineage.

Stardrift & Other Fantastic Flotsam. Emil Petaja. 6.50 (*0-686-00172-9*) Fantasy Pub Co.

Stardust. Alane Ferguson. LC 92-33011. 160p. (J). (gr. 3-7). 1993. lib. bdg. 14.00 (*0-02-734527-0*, Bradbury S&S) S&S Childrens.

Stardust. Alane Ferguson. 128p. (J). 1995. pap. 3.99 (*0-380-72321-2*, Camelot) Avon.

Stardust. Walter Kerr. 1946. 5.00 (*0-87129-441-9*, S50) Dramatic Pub.

***Stardust.** Shari MacDonald. 286p. 1997. pap. 8.99 (*1-57673-109-X*, Palisades OR) Multnomah Pubs.

Stardust. Robert B. Parker. 1991. mass mkt. 6.99 (*0-425-12723-0*) Berkley Pub.

Stardust. large type ed. Robert B. Parker. LC 90-11276. 306p. 1991. lib. bdg. 13.95 (*1-56054-996-3*) Thorndike Pr.

Stardust: I Climbed a Rainbow Once. Christopher Lane. (Illus.). 1993. 4.50 (*0-8378-5304-4*) Gibson.

Stardust: I Saw an Angel Yesterday. Christopher Lane. (Illus.). 1993. 4.50 (*0-8378-5305-2*) Gibson.

Stardust & Whirlwinds. Pamela Litton. (Historical Ser.: No. 69). 1991. mass mkt. 3.95 (*0-373-28669-4*) Harlequin Bks.

Stardust Book, Tooth Fairy. George Kelly. (Illus.). 24p. 1994. 4.50 (*0-8378-6987-0*) Gibson.

Stardust Bound. Karen Cadora. LC 94-29814. 152p. (Orig.). 1994. pap. 8.95 (*1-56341-052-4*); lib. bdg. 18.95 (*1-56341-053-2*) Firebrand Bks.

Stardust Dreams. Marilyn Campbell. 384p. (Orig.). 1993. pap. 4.99 (*0-451-40413-0*, Topaz) NAL-Dutton.

Stardust of Yesterday. Lynn Kurland. 368p. (Orig.). 1996. mass mkt. 5.99 (*0-515-11839-7*) Jove Pubns.

Stardust Otel. Paul B. Janeczko. LC 92-44514. (Illus.). 64p. (YA). (gr. 7 up). 1993. 15.95 (*0-531-05498-5*) Orchard Bks Watts.

***Stardust Quilt.** Kaye Wood. (Illus.). 16p. (Orig.). 1996. pap. 8.00 (*0-944588-31-X*) K Wood.

Stardust Road. Hoagy Carmichael. (American Autobiography Ser.). 156p. 1995. reprint ed. lib. bdg. 69.00 (*0-7812-8474-0*) Rprt Serv.

Stardust Road: Music Book Index. Hoagy Carmichael. 1993. reprint ed. lib. bdg. 69.00 (*0-7812-9575-0*) Rprt Serv.

Stardust to Planets: A Geological Tour of the Solar System. Harry Y. McSween, Jr. 256p. 1993. 22.95 (*0-312-09394-2*) St Martin.

Stardust to Planets: A Geological Tour of the Universe. Harry Y. McSween. LC 95-17153. 1995. pap. 14.95 (*0-312-13188-7*, Griffin) St Martin.

Stardust to Twilight: A Collection of Poems. Jude B. Paat. (Illus.). 75p. (Orig.). 1992. pap. 7.50 (*971-10-0495-X*, Pub. by New Day Pub PH) Cellar.

Stare Decisis. Gale Nelson. (Burning Deck Poetry Ser.). 144p. (Orig.). 1991. pap. 9.00 (*0-930901-72-X*) Burning Deck.

Stare Decisis. limited ed. Gale Nelson. (Burning Deck Poetry Ser.). 144p. (Orig.). 1991. Signed. pap. 15.00 (*0-930901-73-8*) Burning Deck.

Stare Decisis. William O. Douglas. (Reprint Series in Social Sciences). (C). 1993. reprint ed. pap. text ed. 1.00 (*0-8290-2818-8*, PS-66) Irvington.

Stare Indecisis: The Alteration of Precedent on the Supreme Court, 1946-1992. Saul Brenner & Harold J. Spaeth. 163p. (C). 1995. text ed. 54.95 (*0-521-45188-4*) Cambridge U Pr.

Stare on the Donkey's Face. John Wheatcroft. LC 89-42841. 120p. 1990. 16.95 (*0-8453-4823-X*, Cornwall Bks) Assoc Univ Prs.

***Starfall.** (Star Wars Adventures Ser.). 10.00 (*0-87431-105-5*, 40016) West End Games.

Starfall. John Cunningham. 352p. 1993. mass mkt. 4.99 (*0-8125-1361-4*) Tor Bks.

Starfall. Brad Strickland. (Starfleet Academy Ser.: No. 8). (J). (gr. 3-6). 1995. mass mkt. 3.99 (*0-671-51010-X*) PB.

Starfarer's Dozen: Stories of Things to Come. Ed. by Michael Stearns. LC 95-8455. (Illus.). 224p. (YA). (gr. 5 up). 1995. 17.00 (*0-15-299871-3*, J Yolen Bks) HarBrace.

Starfinder Book. David Burch. (Illus.). 86p. 1990. pap. 12.95 (*0-939837-08-0*) Paradise Cay Pubns.

Starfire. Barbara Bretton. (Mira Bks.). 1996. mass mkt. 5.50 (*0-614-08420-2*, 1-66066-1, Mira Bks) Harlequin Bks.

Starfire. Phoebe Conn. 448p. 1994. mass mkt. 5.99 (*0-7860-0033-3*, Pinncle Kensgtn) Kensgtn Pub Corp.

Starfire. Jayne Ann Krentz. 1996. mass mkt. 5.50 (*1-55166-066-0*, Mira Bks) Harlequin Bks.

***Starfire.** Julian J. Savarin. 1997. mass mkt. write for info. (*0-06-101060-X*, Harp PBks) HarpC.

***Starfire.** Sybil Von Cannon. 312p. 1997. pap. 17.00 (*0-8059-4219-X*) Dorrance.

Starfire Accounting. Gersich. Date not set. teacher ed., pap. text ed. write for info. (*0-314-09662-0*) West Pub.

Starfish. Edith T. Hurd. LC 62-7742. (Let's-Read-&-Find-Out Science Bk.). (Illus.). 40p. (J). (gr. k-2). 1962. lib. bdg. 13.89 (*0-690-77069-3*, Crowell Jr Bks) HarpC Child Bks.

Starfish. Rebecca Stefoff. LC 96-2080. (Living Things Ser.). (Illus.). 32p. (J). (gr. 1 up). 1996. lib. bdg. 14.95 (*0-7614-0117-2*, Benchmark NY) Marshall Cavendish.

Starfish Floats & Motorboats: A Child's Primer for Beginning Swimming. Irene M. Kolbisen. Ed. by John Reiter. (I Can Swim Ser.: Vol. 2). (Illus.). 20p. (J). (ps). 1990. 12.95 (*1-877863-01-7*); pap. 8.95 (*0-685-26750-4*) I Think I Can.

Starfish, Jellyfish, & the Order of Life: Issues in Nineteenth-Century Science. Mary P. Winsor. LC 74-29739. (Yale Studies in the History of Science & Medicine: No. 10). (Illus.). 238p. reprint ed. pap. 67.90 (*0-8357-8333-2*, 2033924) Bks Demand.

Starfish, Seashells, & Crabs. George S. Fichter. (Junior Guides Ser.). (Illus.). 36p. (J). (gr. k-3). 1993. 5.50 (*0-307-11430-9*, 11430, Golden Pr) Western Pub.

Starfish, Seashells, & Crabs. Georges S. Fichter. 1993. 14.60 (*0-307-61430-1*) Western Pub.

***Starfish Summer.** Ona Gritz-Gilbert. (Illus.). 96p. (J). (gr. 2-5). 13.95 (*0-06-027193-0*); lib. bdg. 13.89 (*0-06-027194-9*) HarpC Child Bks.

Starfishes of the Atlantic: An Illustrated Key. A. M. Clark & M. E. Downey. (Identification Guides Ser.). (Illus.). 576p. (gr. 13). 1992. text ed. 295.95 (*0-412-43280-3*, A6312) Chapman & Hall.

StarFixer: The Ultimate WordStar Enhancement. Stephen Manes & Paul Somerson. (Business Productivity Library). 1994. pap. 29.95 incl. disk (*0-553-34462-5*) Bantam.

***Starfleet Academy.** Carey. (Star Trek Ser.). 1997. mass mkt. 5.99 (*0-671-01550-8*, Star Trek) PB.

Starfleet Academy, No. 2: Worf's Mission. Peter David. (Star Trek: The Next Generation Ser.). 128p. (Orig.). (J). (gr. 3-8). pap. 3.99 (*0-671-87085-8*, Minstrel Bks) PB.

Starfleet Academy Student Handbook. 2nd rev. ed. W. Paul Hollingsworth. (Starfleet Guides Ser.: No. I). (Illus.). 128p. (Orig.). 1996. pap. 16.95 (*1-886810-02-8*) Parsec Publ.

Starfleet Marine Corps Manual: Peacekeeping Operations in the 24th Century. W. Paul Hollingsworth & Ronald U. Murray. (Illus.). 256p. (Orig.). Date not set. pap. 17.95 (*1-886810-04-4*) Parsec Publ.

Starfleet Operations Manual: An Operational Guide to the 24th Century. W. Paul Hollingsworth. (Illus.). 300p. (Orig.). Date not set. pap. 19.95 (*1-886810-03-6*) Parsec Publ.

Starfleet Personnel Manual. W. Paul Hollingsworth. (Illus.). 256p. (Orig.). Date not set. pap. 17.95 (*1-886810-05-2*) Parsec Publ.

Starflight Handbook: A Pioneer's Guide to Interstellar Travel. Eugene F. Mallove & Gregory L. Matloff. LC 88-31933. (Wiley Science Editions Ser.). 274p. 1989. text ed. 29.95 (*0-471-61912-4*) Wiley.

***Starfox 64 Totally Unauthorized Guide.** Brady Games Staff. 1997. 11.99 (*1-56686-718-5*) Brady Pub.

Stargate. Dean Devlin. 128p. (J). (gr. 4-7). 1994. pap. 3.99 (*0-14-037540-6*) Puffin Bks.

Stargate. Dean Devlin. 1994. pap. 4.99 (*0-451-18410-6*, Sig) NAL-Dutton.

Stargate: Rebellion. Bill McCay. 272p. 1995. pap. 4.99 (*0-451-45502-9*, ROC) NAL-Dutton.

***Stargate: Retaliation.** Bill McCay. 1996. mass mkt. 5.99 (*0-614-20519-0*, ROC) NAL-Dutton.

Stargate of the Heart. Patricia D. Cota-Robles. 263p. 1989. pap. 14.00 (*0-9615287-4-5*) New Age Study Human.

Stargate to Past Lives: Healing Through Past Life Regression. 2nd ed. John H. Goode. Ed. by Mae R. Ludlam. (Wholistic Approach to Perfect Health Ser.). (Illus.). 209p. 1992. 22.00 (*0-9629362-2-7*); pap. 12.95 (*0-9629362-1-9*) Goode Insights.

Stargate 2. Bill McCay. 1996. pap. 5.99 (*0-451-45516-9*) NAL-Dutton.

***Stargate 3: Retribution.** Bill McCay. 1997. mass mkt. 5.99 (*0-451-45556-8*, ROC) NAL-Dutton.

***Stargazer.** Miguel O. Conner. (Orig.). 1997. pap. write for info. (*0-614-19754-6*, Aspect) Warner Bks.

Stargazer. Gerald Hausman. LC 88-81626. (Stargazer Trilogy Ser.: Bk. 1). 219p. (Orig.). 1989. pap. 9.95 (*0-914955-03-9*) Lotus Light.

***Stargazer.** Robin Kerrod. LC 97-16213. (Fact Packs Ser.). (J). 1997. pap. text ed. 14.95 (*0-7641-7044-9*) Barron.

***Stargazer, Vol. 1.** Baker. 1997. mass mkt. write for info. (*0-312-96316-5*) St Martin.

Stargazer: The Life, World & Films of Andy Warhol. 3rd ed. Stephen Koch. (Illus.). 192p. 1990. pap. 14.95 (*0-7145-2920-6*) M Boyars Pubs.

Stargazers. Ed. by S. Dunlop & M. Gerbaldi. (Illus.). xvii, 232p. 1989. 42.95 (*0-387-50230-0*) Spr-Verlag.

Stargazers. Gail Gibbons. LC 92-52713. (Illus.). 32p. (J). (ps-3). 1992. lib. bdg. 15.95 (*0-8234-0983-X*) Holiday.

Stargazers: An Historical Drama in Two Acts. Joseph G. Cowley. 100p. (Orig.). 1996. pap. 11.95 (*1-57502-259-1*, P0941) Morris Pubng.

***Stargazer's Diary: An Intimate Journal of the Cruising Lifestyle from California to Florida.** (Illus.). 250p. 1997. mass mkt. 16.95 (*0-9658551-0-4*) Spellbinders Pub.

Stargazer's Guide to the Galaxy. Querida L. Pearce. 1991. mass mkt. 4.99 (*0-8125-9423-1*) Tor Bks.

***Stargazers Touchstone.** George E. Soroka. 1997. 25.00 (*1-889122-23-8*) Ariel Starr.

***Stargazers Tribebook.** Elizabeth Ditchburn & Mark Cenczyk. (Werewolf). (Illus.). (Orig.). 1997. pap. write for info. (*1-56504-332-4*, 3061) White Wolf.

StarGazing. John R. Smith & Linda Abbott. (Illus.). 52p. (YA). 1995. 11.95 (*0-936459-29-8*) Stained Glass.

Stargone John. Ellen K. McKenzie. LC 90-34119. (Illus.). 80p. (J). (gr. 2-4). 1990. 13.95 (*0-8050-1451-9*, Redfeather BYR) H Holt & Co.

Stargone John. Ellen K. McKenzie. LC 90-34119. (Illus.). 64p. (J). (gr. 2-4). 1992. pap. 4.95 (*0-8050-2069-1*, Redfeather BYR) H Holt & Co.

Staring at the Sun. Julian Barnes. LC 93-15509. 1993. pap. 11.00 (0-679-74820-2, Vin) Random.

Staring at Variations: The Concept of 'Self' in Breyten Breytenbach's Mouroir. Hans-Georg Colz. LC 95-40803. (Aachen British & American Studies: Vol. 5). 103p. 1995. 29.95 (0-8204-2910-4) P Lang Pubng.

Staring at Variations: The Concept of 'Self' in Breyten Breytenbach's Mouroir, Mirrornotes of a Novel. Hans-Georg Golz. LC 95-40803. (Aachen British & American Studies: Vol. 5). 1995. write for info. (3-631-49192-1) P Lang Pubng.

***Staring Back.** Kenny Fries. 1999. pap. 23.95 (0-525-94187-8) Viking Penguin.

***Staring Back: An Anthology of Writers with Disabilities.** Ed. by Kenny Fries. LC 97-15209. 1997. pap. 15.95 (0-452-27913-5, Plume) NAL-Dutton.

***Staring into Chaos: Explorations in the Decline of Western Culture.** B. G. Brander. 1997. write for info. (0-9653208-5-5) Spence Pub.

Staring Match. Jerry McNeely. 1957. pap. 3.25 (0-8222-1072-X) Dramatists Play.

Stark: For Those Who Dream He Dares the Impossible. Paul Stamas. LC 93-84785. (Illus.). 352p. (Orig.). 1996. pap. 12.95 (0-9636325-0-7) P&K Stark Prods.

Stark Decency: German Prisoners of War in a New England Village. Allen V. Koop. LC 88-5550. (Illus.). 150p. 1988. pap. 13.95 (0-87451-468-1) U Pr of New Eng.

Stark Drama. Michael V. McGee. (Illus.). 20p. (Orig.). 1992. pap. 3.25 (0-88680-375-6) I E Clark.

Stark Impressions: Graphic Production in Germany, 1918-1933. Reinhold Heller. (Illus.). 300p. (Orig.). (C). 1994. pap. 35.00 (0-941680-12-6) M&L Block.

Stark Munro Letters. Arthur Conan Doyle. LC 79-8259. (Illus.). reprint ed. 44.50 (0-404-61840-5) AMS Pr.

Stark Naked. Ric Masten. LC 80-51980. 1980. pap. 6.00 (0-931104-40-8) Sunflower Ink.

Stark Naked on a Cold Irish Morning. Gabriele Glang. LC 90-53236. (Illus.). (Orig.). 1990. pap. 9.95 (0-930526-13-9) SCOP Pubns.

***Stark Raving Elvis.** William M. Henderson. 272p. 1997. mass mkt. 6.99 (0-425-15935-3) Berkley Pub.

Stark Reality: Health Care. Roest & Folk. 150-200p. 1996. 139.00 (0-8342-0802-4) Aspen Pub.

Stark Truth. Peter Freeborn. 1990. mass mkt. 4.95 (0-380-71162-1) Avon.

Stark White Paper. Colleen M. Gilmore. 32p. 1994. pap. 4.95 (0-9643922-0-8) W G Writing.

Starken Verben Im Sprachgebrauch: Syntax-Valenz-Kollokationen. H. Griesbach & G. Uhlig. 448p. (GER.). 1996. 36.95 (3-324-00604-X) Langenscheidt.

Starke's International Law. 11th ed. Ivan Shearer. 560p. 1994. pap. 52.00 (0-406-01623-2, U.K.) MICHIE.

***Starkey Sacrifice: The Allied Bombing of le Portel, 1943.** Michael Cumming. (Illus.). 192p. 1996. 33.95 (0-7509-1253-7, Pub. by Sutton Pubng UK) Bks Intl VA.

StarKist Sensational Tuna. (Favorite All Time Recipes Ser.). (Illus.). 96p. 1993. spiral bd. 3.50 (1-56173-387-3, 2009000) Pubns Intl Ltd.

Stark's Justice. James Reasoner. 1994. mass mkt. 3.99 (0-671-87140-4) PB.

Stark's Justice: A Judge Earl Stark Western. large type ed. James Reasoner. LC 94-35471. 1994. 21.95 (1-56895-153-1) Wheeler Pub.

Starkweather: A Story of Mass Murder on the Great Plains. Jeff O'Donnell & Kevin Oliver. (Illus.). 208p. (Orig.). 1993. pap. 10.00 (0-934904-31-6) J & L Lee.

Starless Night. R. A. Salvatore. 336p. 1994. pap. 5.99 (1-56076-880-0) TSR Inc.

Starlet: Biographies, Filmographies, TV Credits & Photos of 54 Famous & Not So Famous Leading Ladies of the Sixties. Kim R. Holston. LC 87-43209. (Illus.). 320p. 1988. lib. bdg. 45.00 (0-89950-307-1) McFarland & Co.

Starlight. Patrick N. Hayden. LC 96-8454. 320p. 1996. 24.95 (0-312-86214-8); pap. 13.95 (0-312-86215-6) St Martin.

Starlight. Debbie Macomber. 1995. pap. 4.99 (1-55166-021-0, Mira Bks) Harlequin Bks.

Starlight: Beholding the Christmas Miracle All Year Long. John Shea. 192p. 1993. reprint ed. pap. 10.95 (0-8245-1272-3) Crossroad NY.

Starlight: Seven Address Given for Love of the Star. C. W. Leadbeater. 104p. 1985. reprint ed. spiral bd. 9.00 (0-7873-1245-2) Hlth Research.

Starlight: Seven Addresses Given for Love of the Star. C. W. Leadbeater. 104p. 1992. pap. 9.95 (1-56459-244-8) Kessinger Pub.

Starlight: The Great Short Fiction of Alfred Bester. Alfred Bester. 1993. reprint ed. lib. bdg. 18.95 (1-56849-249-9) Buccaneer Bks.

Starlight & Candles: The Joys of the Sabbath. Marion M. Markham. (Illus.). 46p. (J). (ps up). 1995. 15.00 (0-689-80274-9) S&S Childrens.

Starlight & Splendor. Janelle Taylor. 512p. 1994. mass mkt. 5.99 (0-7860-0042-2, Pinncle Kensgtn) Kensgtn Pub Corp.

***Starlight & Time: Solving the Puzzle of Distant Starlight in a Young Universe.** D. Russell Humphreys. 133p. 1996. pap. 6.95 (0-89051-202-7, STATIM) Master Bks.

***Starlight Barking.** Smith. LC 97-16438. (J). 1997. pap. 8.95 (0-312-15664-2) St Martin.

Starlight Bride. Paul O. Lewis. (Illus.). 40p. (J). (ps-6). 1988. 14.95 (0-941831-33-7); pap. 9.95 (0-941831-25-6) Beyond Words Pub.

Starlight Child. Nancy Cane. 400p. (Orig.). 1995. mass mkt., pap. text ed. 4.99 (0-505-52019-2) Dorchester Pub Co.

Starlight Christmas. Bonnie Bryant. (Saddle Club Ser.: No. 13). 144p. (J). (gr. 4-7). 1990. mass mkt. 3.99 (0-553-15832-5) Bantam.

Starlight Crystal. Christopher Pike. (YA). (gr. 9 up). 1996. 14.00 (0-671-55029-2, Archway) PB.

Starlight Crystal. Christopher Pike. (YA). (gr. 9 up). 1996. pap. 3.99 (0-671-55028-4, Archway) PB.

Starlight Elixers & Cosmic Vibrational Healing. Michael Smulkis & Fred Rubenfeld. 352p. (Orig.). pap. 31.95 (0-8464-4294-9) Beekman Pubs.

Starlight Elixirs & Cosmic Vibrational Healing. Michael Smulkis & Fred Rubenfeld. 17p. 1992. pap. 21.00 (0-85207-258-9, Pub. by C W Daniel UK) Natl Bk Netwk.

***Starlight Escape.** Adapted by Brian Brown & Andrew Melrose. (Storykeepers Juvenile Ser.: Bk. 6). (Illus.). 64p. (J). (gr. 2-5). 1997. mass mkt. 3.99 (0-310-20337-6) Zondervan.

***Starlight Escape.** Adapted by Brian Brown & Andrew Melrose. (Storykeepers Easy Reader Ser.: Bk. 6). (J). (ps-3). 1997. mass mkt. 3.99 (0-310-20339-2) Zondervan.

Starlight Express: Vocal Selections. (Illus.). 88p. 1987. pap. 12.95 (0-88188-578-9, HL 00361185) H Leonard.

Starlight Passage. Anita Bunkley. 1997. pap. 5.99 (0-451-19037-8, Sig) NAL-Dutton.

***Starlight Passage.** Anita R. Bunkley. Date not set. pap. 5.99 (0-451-18482-3, Sig) NAL-Dutton.

Starlight Passage. Anita R. Bunkley. LC 95-47908. 352p. 1996. pap. 23.95 (0-525-94009-X, Dutton) NAL-Dutton.

***Starlight Passage.** large type ed. Anita R. Bunkley. LC 96-43569. (Romance Ser.). 650p. 1996. lib. bdg. 24.95 (0-7862-0922-4) Thorndike Pr.

Starlight Poets One. Ed. by Ira Rosenstein. 32p. (Orig.). 1990. pap. 4.00 (0-9605438-4-8) Starlight Pr.

Starlight Poets Two: Sonnets. Ed. by Ira Rosenstein. 40p. (Orig.). 1992. pap. 5.00 (0-9605438-5-6) Starlight Pr.

Starlight Ranch & Other Stories of Army Life on the Frontier. Charles King. LC 73-94737. (Short Story Index Reprint Ser.). 1977. 19.95 (0-8369-3117-3) Ayer.

Starlight Through the Shadows. large type ed. F. Ridley Havergal. Date not set. 5.99 (1-871676-56-8, Pub. by Christian Focus UK) Spring Arbor Dist.

Starlights. Ruth Dyer. LC 89-51255. 50p. (J). (gr. k-3). 1992. pap. 5.95 (1-55523-258-2) Winston-Derek.

Starliner. David Drake. 288p. (Orig.). 1992. mass mkt. 5.99 (0-671-72121-6) Baen Bks.

Starling: Genealogy & Family Memorial (of Starling, Sullivant & Related Families. Joseph Sullivant. 375p. 1993. reprint ed. pap. 58.50 (0-8328-3411-4); reprint ed. lib. bdg. 68.50 (0-8328-3410-6) Higginson Bk Co.

Starling's Law of the Heart Revisited. Ed. by H. E. Ter Keurs & M. I. Noble. (Developments in Cardiovascular Medicine Ser.). 168p. (C). 1988. lib. bdg. 133.00 (0-89838-382-X) Kluwer Ac.

Starlink: The Book of Knowledge of Anton--Communique from the Pleiades. Joy Whitney. (Anton Materials Ser.: Vol. I). 166p. (Orig.). 1989. pap. 12.95 (0-317-93870-3) Starset Pub.

Starlist Two Thousand: A Quick Reference Star Catalog for Astronomers. Richard Dibon-Smith. LC 92-2907. 416p. 1992. pap. text ed. 29.95 (0-471-55895-8) Wiley.

***Starlit Garden.** large type ed. Patricia Hemstock. (Linford Romance Library). 256p. 1997. pap. 16.99 (0-7089-5036-1) Ulverscroft.

Starlit Somersault Downhill. Nancy Willard. (J). (ps-3). 1993. 15.95 (0-316-94113-1) Little.

Starlit Somersault Downhill. Nancy Willard. (Illus.). 32p. (J). (gr. 1-5). 1996. pap. text ed. 6.95 (0-316-94129-8) Little.

Starlit Tomorrow. Lynda Trent. (Superromance Ser.). 1993. mass mkt. 3.50 (0-373-70569-7, 1-70569-8) Harlequin Bks.

***Starlite Drive-In: A Novel.** Marjorie Reynolds. 224p. 1997. 23.00 (0-688-15389-5) Morrow.

***Starlog: Star Trek's Greatest Guest Stars.** David Mcdonnell. 256p. 1997. mass mkt. 5.50 (0-06-105662-6, HarperPrism) HarpC.

Starlog Movie Magazine Presents: Star Trek 30th Anniversary. annuals (YA). 1996. pap. text ed. 12.99 (0-934551-08-1) Starlog Pr.

Starlog Movie Magazine Presents: The Island of Dr. Moreau. annuals (YA). 1996. pap. text ed. 5.99 (0-934551-06-5) Starlog Pr.

Starlog Movie Series Presents: Species, No. 3. 1995. pap. 4.99 (0-934551-00-6) Starlog Pr.

Starlog Presents: Action Heroes. 1995. pap. 4.99 (0-934551-02-2) Starlog Pr.

Starlog Presents: Beatles Forever. 1995. pap. text ed. 4.99 (0-934551-03-0) Starlog Pr.

Starlog Presents: Skateboarding. (YA). 1996. pap. text ed. write for info. (0-934551-11-1) Starlog Pr.

***Starlog Presents: Spawn.** (Illus.). 1997. pap. 5.99 (0-934551-21-9) Starlog Pr.

***Starlog Presents - A Salute to Batman & Other Heroes.** (YA). 1997. pap. 4.99 (0-934551-17-0) Starlog Pr.

***Starlog Presents Hanson & Today's Top Teens.** (Illus.). 72p. (YA). 1997. pap. 3.99 (0-934551-25-1) Starlog Pr.

***Starlog Presents Legendary Heroes.** (Illus.). (YA). 1997. pap. 5.99 (0-934551-24-3) Starlog Pr.

Starlord: The Conquest of Earth. Stuart D. Waymire. (Illus.). 1989. 19.95 (0-929256-17-4) Thundblt Pr NV.

Starluck. Donald Wismer. LC 81-43375. 186p. (YA). 1982. 20.00 (0-89366-255-0) Ultramarine Pub.

***Starmaker Design Concepts.** Kaye Wood. 16p. (Orig.). 1996. pap. 4.95 (0-614-30957-3) K Wood.

Starmakers Ablaze: Log Cabin Diamonds, Vol. 2. Kaye Wood. (Illus.). 87p. (Orig.). 1987. pap. 19.95 (0-944588-00-X, STR2) K Wood.

Starmakers Ablaze I: Log Cabin Triangles. Kaye Wood. (Illus.). (Orig.). 1988. reprint ed. pap. 19.95 (0-944588-01-8) K Wood.

Starmaking: Realism, Anti-Realism, & Irrealism. Ed. by Peter J. McCormick. LC 95-48929. (Representation & Mind Ser.). (Illus.). 208p. (C). 1996. 30.00 (0-262-13320-2, Bradford Bks) MIT Pr.

Starman: Night & Day. James Robinson. (Illus.). 240p. 1997. pap. text ed. 14.95 (1-56389-270-7) DC Comics.

Starman: Sins of the Father. James Robinson. Ed. by Bob Kahan. (Illus.). 160p. 1995. pap. 12.95 (1-56389-248-0) DC Comics.

Starman Jones. Robert A. Heinlein. Ed. by Judy-Lynn Del Rey. 252p. 1985. mass mkt. 5.99 (0-345-32811-6, Del Rey) Ballantine.

Starman Jones. Robert A. Heinlein. 1994. reprint ed. lib. bdg. 29.95 (1-56849-289-8) Buccaneer Bks.

Starmind. Spider Robinson & Jeanne Robinson. LC 94-33374. 304p. (Orig.). 1995. pap. 21.95 (0-441-00209-9) Ace Bks.

Starmind. Spider Robinson & Jeanne Robinson. (Orig.). 1996. mass mkt. 5.99 (0-441-00305-2) Ace Bks.

***Starovery - Old Believers: Studies on Old Ritualism in Eastern Christianity.** Ed. by Juha Pentikainen. 192p. 1997. 70.00 (1-874312-34-6, Pub. by Drake Intl Serv UK) Intl Spec Bk.

Starpacker. large type ed. David Whitehead. (Linford Western Library). 272p. 1992. pap. 15.99 (0-7089-7184-9, Traittree Bookshop) Ulverscroft.

Starpilot's Grave. Debra Doyle & James D. MacDonald. (MageWorlds Ser.: No. 2). 448p. (Orig.). 1993. mass mkt. 4.50 (0-8125-1705-9) Tor Bks.

***Starplex.** Robert J. Sawyer. 304p. 1996. mass mkt. 5.99 (0-441-00372-9) Ace Bks.

Starquake. deluxe ed. Robert L. Forward. 340p. 1985. 25.00 (0-938075-64-0) Ocean View Bks.

Starr: Early Starrs in Kent & New England. H. S. Ballou. (Illus.). 140p. 1992. reprint ed. pap. 23.00 (0-8328-2739-8); reprint ed. lib. bdg. 33.00 (0-8328-2738-X) Higginson Bk Co.

Starr Tracks: Belle & Pearl Starr. Phillip W. Steele. LC 88-30309. (Illus.). 112p. (Orig.). 1989. pap. 7.95 (0-88289-723-3) Pelican.

Starr Zoo. 1993. pap. 5.25 (0-19-422706-5) OUP.

Starring Betty Boop. Rick Hackney. LC 83-72944. (Illus.). 1984. 3.95 (0-915696-85-1) Determined Prods.

Starring Demi Moore As Hester Prynne: Hollywood's All-Time Worst Casting Bounders. Damien Bona. LC 95-48047. (Illus.). 192p. 1996. pap. 12.95 (0-8065-1802-2, Citadel Pr) Carol Pub Group.

Starring Dorothy Kane. Judith Caseley. LC 90-24172. (J). (gr. 1 up). 1992. 13.00 (0-688-10182-8) Greenwillow.

Starring Dorothy Kane. Judith Caseley. LC 93-6992. (Illus.). 160p. (J). (gr. 3 up). 1994. pap. 4.95 (0-688-12548-4) Morrow.

Starring First Grade: Welcome to First Grade! Miriam Cohen. (Illus.). 32p. (J). (gr. k-3). 1996. pap. 4.99 (0-440-41154-8, Picture Yearling) BDD Bks Young Read.

Starring First Grade: Welcome to First Grade! Miriam Cohen. LC 84-5929. (Illus.). 32p. (J). (gr. k-3). 1985. lib. bdg. 16.93 (0-688-04030-6) Greenwillow.

Starring Fred & Ursulina. Suzy-Jane Tanner. (Illus.). 32p. (J). (ps-1). 1994. 17.95 (0-09-176436-X, Pub. by Hutchinson UK) Trafalgar.

Starring Jessica. Francine Pascal. (Sweet Valley High Ser.: No. 71). 160p. (YA). (gr. 9-12). 1991. pap. 3.25 (0-553-28796-6) Bantam.

Starring John Wayne As Genghis Khan: Hollywood's All-Time Worst Casting Blunders. Damien Bona. LC 95-48048. (Illus.). 192p. 1996. pap. 12.95 (0-8065-1797-2, Citadel Pr) Carol Pub Group.

Starring Mirette & Bellini. Emily A. McCully. (J). 1997. 15.95 (0-399-22636-2, Putnam) Putnam Pub Group.

Starring Miss Seeton. Hamilton Crane. 256p. (Orig.). 1994. pap. 4.99 (0-425-14044-X) Berkley Pub.

***Starring Quincy Rumpel.** 2nd ed. Betty Waterton. (Quincy Rumpel Ser.). (J). (gr. 2-5). 1996. pap. 5.95 (0-88899-196-7, Pub. by Groundwood-Douglas & McIntyre CN) Firefly Bks Ltd.

***Starring Rosie.** Patricia R. Giff. (Illus.). (J). 1997. pap. 13.99 (0-670-86967-8) Viking Penguin.

Starring Sally J. Freedman As Herself. Judy Blume. 240p. (J). (gr. 4 up). 1986. pap. 4.50 (0-440-48253-4, LLL BDD) BDD Bks Young Read.

Starring Sally J. Freedman As Herself. Judy Blume. LC 76-57805. 296p. (J). (gr. 4-7). 1982. lib. bdg. 17.00 (0-02-711070-2, Bradbury S&S) S&S Childrens.

Starring Sally J. Freedman As Herself see Judy Blume Collection

Starring the Baby-Sitters Club. Ann M. Martin. (Baby-Sitters Club Super Special Ser.: No. 9). 256p. (J). (gr. 4-6). 1992. pap. 3.95 (0-590-45661-X) Scholastic Inc.

Starr's Guide to the John Muir Trail & the High Sierra Region. 12th rev. ed. Walter A. Starr, Jr. Ed. by Douglas Robinson. LC 67-25840. (Totebook Ser.). (Illus.). 224p. 1982. pap. 14.00 (0-87156-172-7) Sierra.

Starr's Showdown. large type ed. G. Clifton Wisler. (Linford Western Library). (Orig.). 1991. pap. 15.99 (0-7089-7096-6) Ulverscroft.

Starry Messenger: Galileo Galilei. Illus. & Created by Peter Sis. LC 95-44986. 40p. (J). (gr. 1 up). 1996. 16.00 (0-374-37191-1) FS&G.

Starry Night. Marjorie Agosin. Tr. by Mary G. Berg. 112p. (Orig.). 1996. pap. 12.00 (1-877727-66-0) White Pine.

Starry Night. Robin J. Gunn. LC 93-15030. (Christy Miller Ser.: Vol. 8). (YA). 1993. pap. 5.99 (1-56179-163-6) Focus Family.

Starry Night: A Speculative Alternate Cosmology. Gavin Immermann. LC 93-74669. (Illus.). 48p. (Orig.). 1993. pap. 5.95 (0-9637108-1-8) Demiurge Edits.

Starry Place Between the Antlers: Why I Live in South Carolina. James Dickey. 1981. 5.00 (0-89723-030-2) Bruccoli.

Starry Place Between the Antlers: Why I Live in South Carolina. deluxe limited ed. James Dickey. 1981. 30.00 (0-89723-031-0) Bruccoli.

Starry Rift. James Tiptree, Jr. 256p. 1994. pap. 12.95 (0-312-89021-4) Orb NYC.

Starry Sky. Patrick Moore. (Illus.). 96p. (J). (gr. k-3). 1995. 9.95 (1-56294-181-X, Copper Beech Bks) Millbrook Pr.

Starry Sky. Rose Wyler. Ed. by Jane Steltenpohl. (Outdoor Science Ser.). (Illus.). 32p. (J). (gr. k-2). 1989. pap. 4.95 (0-671-66349-6, Julian Messner) Silver Burdett Pr.

Starry Sky to Starry Sky: Poems by Mary Jane White with Translations from Marina Tsvetaeva. Mary J. White. LC 87-80785. 96p. (Orig.). 1988. 15.00 (0-930100-26-3); pap. 7.95 (0-930100-25-5) Holy Cow.

Starry Wisdom: A Tribute to H. P. Lovecraft. William S. Burroughs et al. Ed. by D. M. Mitchell. (Illus.). 192p. (Orig.). 1996. pap. 15.95 (1-871592-32-1) Creation Bks.

Stars. Ed. by Applewood Books Staff. (Wonderlings Ser.). (Illus.). 32p. (J). (ps up). 1996. pap. 1.50 (1-55709-379-2) Applewood.

Stars! Daphne Davis. 1985. 14.98 (0-517-47980-X) Random Hse Value.

Stars. Robin Dexter. LC 95-4869. (First Start Science Ser.). (Illus.). 32p. (J). (gr. k-3). 1995. lib. bdg. 9.79 (0-8167-3858-0) Troll Communs.

Stars. Robin Dexter. (First Start Science Ser.). (Illus.). 32p. (J). (gr. k-3). 1996. pap. 2.95 (0-8167-3859-9) Troll Communs.

Stars. Jennifer Dussling. (All Aboard Reading Ser.: Level 1). (Illus.). 32p. (J). (ps-1). 1996. pap. 3.95 (0-448-41148-2, G&D) Putnam Pub Group.

Stars. Jennifer Dussling. (All Aboard Reading Ser.). (Illus.). 32p. (J). (ps-1). 1996. lib. bdg. 13.99 (0-448-41149-0, G&D) Putnam Pub Group.

Stars. Richard Dyer. (Illus.). 204p. 1982. pap. 12.95 (0-85170-085-3, Pub. by British Film Inst UK) Ind U Pr.

Stars. Robert Estalella. (Window on the Universe Ser.). (Illus.). 32p. (J). (gr. 4-8). 1993. 12.95 (0-8120-6371-6); pap. 6.95 (0-8120-1738-2) Barron.

Stars. Michael George. (Images Ser.). (J). 1992. lib. bdg. 16.95 (0-88682-400-1) Creative Ed.

Stars. Kathryn Harvey. 592p. 1993. mass mkt. 5.99 (0-380-71504-X) Avon.

Stars. James Kaler. (Scientific American Library). 1995. text ed. write for info. (0-7167-5033-3) W H Freeman.

Stars. Andres L. Ruiz. (Sequences of Earth & Space Ser.). (Illus.). 32p. (J). 1996. 12.95 (0-8069-9337-5) Sterling.

Stars. Evry L. Schatzman & Francoise Praderie. Tr. by A. R. King. LC 92-38500. (Astronomy & Astrophysics Library). 1993. 98.00 (0-387-54196-9) Spr-Verlag.

Stars. Seymour Simon. LC 85-32012. (Illus.). 32p. (J). (ps-3). 1986. 17.00 (0-688-05855-8); lib. bdg. 16.93 (0-688-05856-6) Morrow.

Stars. Seymour Simon. LC 85-32012. (Illus.). 32p. (J). (ps-3). 1989. pap. 5.95 (0-688-09237-3) Morrow.

***Stars.** Paul P. Sipiera. LC 96-36150. (True Bk.). (J). 1997. lib. bdg. 19.00 (0-516-20341-X) Childrens.

Stars. Lynda Sorensen. LC 93-10475. (Solar System Ser.). (J). 1993. write for info. (0-86593-276-X) Rourke Corp.

***Stars.** Stewart Walton & Sally Walton. (Stampability Bks.). (Illus.). 32p. 1997. pap. 6.95 (1-85967-230-2, Lorenz Bks) Anness Pub.

Stars. Roy Wandelmaier. LC 84-8642. (Now I Know Ser.). (Illus.). 32p. (J). (gr. k-2). 1994. pap. 3.50 (0-8167-0442-2) Troll Communs.

Stars. rev. ed. (Voyage Through the Universe Ser.). 144p. 1992. write for info. (0-8094-9075-7); lib. bdg. write for info. (0-8094-9076-5) Time-Life.

Stars. rev. ed. Herbert S. Zim & Robert H. Baker. (Golden Guide Ser.). (Illus.). 160p. (YA). (gr. 6 up). 1985. pap. 5.50 (0-307-24493-8, Golden Pr) Western Pub.

Stars. 2nd ed. Joachim Ekrutt. (Mini Fact Finders Ser.). 80p. (Orig.). 1996. pap. 5.95 (0-8120-9642-8) Barron.

Stars: A New Way to See Them. H. A. Rey. (J). (gr. 4 up). 1976. pap. 11.95 (0-395-24830-2) HM.

Stars: A New Way to See Them. 3rd ed. H. A. Rey. (Illus.). (J). (gr. 8 up). 1973. 25.00 (0-395-08121-1) HM.

Stars: How & Where They Influence. L. Edward Johndro. 120p. 1991. pap. 15.00 (0-89540-187-8, SB-187, Sun Bks) Sun Pub.

Stars: Lights in the Night Sky. Jeanne Bendick. (Early Bird Astronomy Ser.). (Illus.). 32p. (J). (gr. k-2). 1991. lib. bdg. 14.90 (1-878841-00-9) Millbrook Pr.

Stars: Lights in the Night Sky. Jeanne Bendick. (Early Bird Astronomy Ser.). (Illus.). 32p. (J). (gr. k-2). 1996. lib. bdg. 4.95 (1-878841-48-3) Millbrook Pr.

Stars: Poems. C. G. Hanzlicek. LC 77-270. (Breakthrough Bks.). 80p. 1977. text ed. 18.95 (0-8262-0226-8) U of Mo Pr.

Stars: The Art of Making Stellar Gifts & Radiant Crafts. Katy Brown. LC 93-23144. (Illus.). 128p. 1994. 23.00 (0-671-88436-0) S&S Trade.

Stars: Their Structure & Evolution. Roger J. Tayler. 220p. 1970. pap. 18.00 (0-85109-110-5) Taylor & Francis.

Stars: Their Structure & Evolution. 2nd ed. Roger J. Taylor. (Illus.). 240p. (C). 1994. text ed. 59.95 (0-521-46063-8); pap. text ed. 25.95 (0-521-45885-4) Cambridge U Pr.

Stars: Their Structure & Evolution. Roger J. Tayler & A. S. Everest. (Wykeham Science Ser.: No. 10). 220p. (C). 1970. reprint ed. 18.00 (0-8448-1112-2, Crane Russak) Taylor & Francis.

Stars: Whimsy, Wisdom, & Light from the Other Side of the Day. Norm Kohn. LC 92-25247. (Illus.). 1992. 14.00 (1-56145-064-2) Peachtree Pubs.

Stars: 20 Practical Inspirations. Joanne Rippin. 1996. 12.95 (1-85967-277-9, Lorenz Bks) Anness Pub.

***Stars Across America.** Eleanor Burns. Ed. by Loretta Smith. (Quilt Block Party Ser.: No. 7). (Illus.). 120p. (Orig.). 1996. 24.95 (0-922705-89-5) Quilt Day.

An Asterisk (*) at the beginning of an entry indicates that the title is appearing in BIP for the first time.

Stars & Atoms: From the Big Bang to the Solar System. Stuart Clark. LC 94-30783. (New Encyclopedia of Science Ser.). (Illus.). 160p. 1995. text ed. 39.95 (0-19-521087-5) OUP.

Stars & Bars: A Tribute to the American Fighter Ace 1920-1973. Frank Olynyk. (Illus.). 698p. 1995. 69.95 (1-898697-17-5, Pub. by Grub St Pubns UK) Seven Hills Bk.

Stars & Clusters. Cecilia H. Gaposchkin. LC 79-4472. (Harvard Books on Astronomy). (Illus.). 272p. reprint ed. pap. 77.60 (0-7837-3847-1, 2043669) Bks Demand.

Stars & Featured Players of Paramount of 1930-1931. Ed. by R. Gordon. 1976. lib. bdg. 80.00 (0-8490-2663-6) Gordon Pr.

Stars & Films of 1937 & 1938, 2 vols. Ed. by Stephen Watts. 1976. lib. bdg. 200.00 (0-8490-2664-4) Gordon Pr.

Stars & Flowers: Three-Sided Patchwork. Sara A. Nephew. LC 88-72380. (Illus.). 56p. (Orig.). 1989. pap. 12.95 (0-9621172-0-X) Clearview Triangle.

Stars & Galaxies: Astronomy's Guide to Exploring the Cosmos. Astronomy Magazine Staff. Ed. by David Eicher. (Illus.). 192p. (Orig.). 1992. per. 29.95 (0-913135-05-4, 18536) Kalmbach.

Stars & Galaxies (SAR) Citizens of the Universe. Donald E. Osterbrock. LC 89-48325. (Readings from Scientific American Ser.). (Illus.). 184p. (C). 1995. text ed. write for info. (0-7167-2069-8) W H Freeman.

Stars & Planets. (Secrets of Science Ser.). (Illus.). 32p. (J). (gr. 3-8). 1991. lib. bdg. 10.95 (1-85435-272-5) Marshall Cavendish.

Stars & Planets. (Discover Ser.). (Illus.). 48p. (J). 1993. 9.98 (1-56173-105-6) Pubns Intl Ltd.

***Stars & Planets.** 1997. write for info. (0-8069-9906-3) Sterling.

Stars & Planets. Joachim Ekrutt. (Illus.). 160p. 1992. pap. 12.95 (0-8120-4776-1) Barron.

Stars & Planets. David Lambert. LC 93-28282. (New View Ser.). (Illus.). (J). 1994. lib. bdg. 21.40 (0-8114-9246-X) Raintree Steck-V.

Stars & Planets. David Lambert. (New View Ser.). (J). 1995. pap. text ed. 6.95 (0-8114-6449-0) Raintree Steck-V.

Stars & Planets. David Levy. LC 95-32799. (Discoveries Ser.). 64p. (J). (gr. 3 up). 1996. 15.00 (0-8094-9246-6) Time-Life.

Stars & Planets. Maynard. (Young Scientist Ser.). (Illus.). 32p. (J). (gr. 4-8). 1976. lib. bdg. 14.95 (0-88110-313-6) EDC.

Stars & Planets. Christopher Maynard. (Young Scientist Ser.). (Illus.). 32p. (J). (gr. 4-8). 1976. pap. 6.95 (0-86020-094-9) EDC.

Stars & Planets. James Muirden. LC 93-20104. (Visual Factfinders Ser.). (Illus.). 96p. (J). (gr. 5 up). 1993. pap. 10.95 (1-85697-851-6, Kingfisher LKC) LKC.

Stars & Planets. James Muirden. (Visual Factfinders Ser.). (Illus.). 96p. (J). 1993. lib. bdg. 16.90 (1-85697-693-9, Kingfisher LKC) LKC.

Stars & Planets. Mary Packard. (J). (ps-3). 1995. pap. 6.95 (0-8167-3563-8) Troll Communs.

Stars & Planets. Ian Ridpath. 384p. 1994. pap. 16.00 (0-00-219979-3, Pub. by HarpC UK) HarpC.

Stars & Planets: An Integrated Unit. Kathy Rogers. (Primary Thematic Units Ser.). (Illus.). 96p. (Orig.). 1993. pap. 12.95 (0-944459-85-4) ECS Lrn Systs.

Stars & Planets: The Sierra Club Guide to Sky Watching & Direction Finding. William S. Kals. LC 90-33711. 1990. pap. 15.00 (0-87156-671-0) Sierra.

***Star's & Planets Atlas.** rev. ed. Ian Ridpath. LC 97-15966. (Atlas Ser.). (Illus.). 80p. (J). 1997. 18.95 (0-8160-3716-7) Facts on File.

***Stars & Relativity.** unabridged ed. Ya B. Zel'Dovich. (Illus.). 540p. 1997. reprint ed. pap. text ed. 13.95 (0-486-69424-0) Dover.

Stars & Star Handlers. Whitney Stine. LC 84-60759. (Illus.). 426p. (C). 1985. 17.95 (0-915677-08-3) Roundtable Pub.

Stars & Star Systems. Ed. by Bengt E. Westerlund. (Astrophysics & Space Science Library: No. 75). 1979. lib. bdg. 88.00 (90-277-0983-1) Kluwer Ac.

Stars & Stepping Stones. Marsha R. McCloskey. (Orig.). 1993. pap. 6.95 (0-486-27416-0) Dover.

Stars & Strife: Inside the Dallas Cowboys' Reemergence As America's Team. Mike Fisher. Ed. by Mike Towle. (Illus.). 332p. 1993. 21.95 (1-56530-064-5) Summit TX.

Stars & Strikes: Unionization of Hollywood. Murray Ross. LC 41-24783. reprint ed. 20.00 (0-404-05408-0) AMS Pr.

Stars & Stripes. Leonard E. Fisher. LC 93-20176. (Illus.). (J). (ps-3). 1993. lib. bdg. 15.95 (0-8234-1053-6) Holiday.

Stars & Stripes: Doughboy Journalism in World War I. Alfred E. Cornebise. LC 83-12863. (Contributions in Military History Ser.: No. 37). (Illus.). xiii, 221p. 1984. text ed. 55.00 (0-313-24230-5, COS/, Greenwood Pr) Greenwood.

***Stars & Stripes: Stories about the U.S.A., Yesterday & Today.** Pamela McPartland-Fairman. 1997. pap. text ed. write for info. (0-07-045993-2) McGraw.

Stars & Stripes: The Early Years. Ken Zumwalt. (Illus.). 288p. 1989. 16.95 (0-89015-658-1) Sunbelt Media.

Stars & Stripes: The Official Newspaper of the A. E. F., Vol. 19. U. S. Army A. E. F., 1917-1920 Staff. 1971. reprint ed. 220.95 (0-405-00290-4, 19521) Ayer.

Stars & Stripes & Soldiers. Richard Roseblum. 32p. (J). (ps-3). 1993. pap. 3.95 (0-590-45222-3) Scholastic Inc.

Stars & Stripes Forever. John W. Adams. (Illus.). 60p. 1994. 9.98 (0-8317-6658-1) Smithmark.

Stars & Stripes Forever. Elliot H. Paul. LC 74-22802. reprint ed. 32.50 (0-404-58459-4) AMS Pr.

Stars & Swastikas: The Boy Who Wore Two Uniforms. Walter K. Schroder. LC 92-5564. (Illus.). xiv, 202p. (C). 1992. lib. bdg. 28.00 (0-208-02322-4, Archon Bks) Shoe String.

Stars & the Chakras. Joan Hodgson. (Illus.). 176p. 1990. 14.50 (0-85487-082-2, Pub. by White Eagle UK) DeVorss.

Stars & the Land. Grace B. Freeman. 16p. (Orig.). 1983. pap. 4.95 (0-9607730-7-X) Johns Pr.

Stars & the Mind: A Study of the Impact of Astronomical Development on Human Thought. M. Davidson. 1972. 59.95 (0-8490-1121-3) Gordon Pr.

Stars & Their Spectra: An Introduction to the Spectral Sequence. James B. Kaler. (Illus.). 300p. (C). 1989. text ed. 42.95 (0-521-30494-6) Cambridge U Pr.

***Stars & Their Spectra: An Introduction to the Spectral Sequence.** James B. Kaler. (Illus.). 320p. 1997. pap. text ed. 24.95 (0-521-58570-8) Cambridge U Pr.

Stars Appear. Richard D. MacCann. LC 91-42748. (American Movies: The First Thirty Years Ser.: No. 3). (Illus.). 339p. 1992. 42.50 (0-8108-2527-9); pap. 22.50 (0-8108-2528-7) Scarecrow.

Stars Are Also Fire. Poul Anderson. 544p. 1995. 5.99 (0-8125-3022-5) Tor Bks.

***Stars Are Birds: And Other Writings.** MariJo Moore. LC 96-92712. (Illus.). 32p. (Orig.). (J). (gr. 1-12). 1996. pap. 8.95 (0-9654921-1-7) Renegade Planets.

Stars Are for Eagles: The Original Adventure. Sydney G. DeFraites, III. (Stareagle Adventures Ser.: No. 1). 320p. (Orig.). 1992. pap. 5.95 (0-9640160-0-1) JK Books.

Stars Are My Children. large type ed. Phyllis Hastings. 1974. 25.99 (0-85456-268-0) Ulverscroft.

Stars Are Waiting. Murray. 1997. 14.95 (0-689-80543-8) S&S Childrens.

Stars as Laboratories for Fundamental Physics: The Astrophysics of Neutrinos, Axions, & Other Weakly Interacting Particles. Georg G. Raffelt. LC 95-39684. (Theoretical Astrophysics Ser.). 1996. pap. text ed. 42.00 (0-226-70272-3); lib. bdg. 77.00 (0-226-70271-5) U Ch Pr.

Stars at Noon. Denis Johnson. LC 86-45274. 192p. 1986. 15.95 (0-394-53840-4) Knopf.

Stars at Noon. Jacqueline Cochran & Floyd Odlum. Ed. by James B. Gilbert. LC 79-7241. (Flight: Its First Seventy-Five Years Ser.). (Illus.). 1980. reprint ed. lib. bdg. 32.95 (0-405-12156-3) Ayer.

***Stars at War.** Michael Munn. (Illus.). 294p. 1996. 28.95 (0-86051-954-6, Pub. by BBC UK) Parkwest Pubns.

Stars Burn On. large type ed. Denise A. Robertson. (Magna General Fiction Ser.). 575p. 1992. 25.99 (0-7505-0300-9) Ulverscroft.

***Stars by Kruger.** Illus. by Sebastian Kruger. Date not set. 34.95 (1-883398-27-4) Morpheus Intl.

Stars, Clusters, & Galaxies. John R. Gustafson. LC 92-11228. (Young Stargazer's Guide to the Galaxy Ser.). (J). (gr. 3-7). 1993. pap. 6.95 (0-671-72537-8, Julian Messner); lib. bdg. 12.98 (0-671-72536-X, Julian Messner) Silver Burdett Pr.

Stars Come down to Earth & Other Essays on the Irrational in Culture. Theodor Adorno. Ed. by Stephen Crook. LC 94-12151. 240p. (C). (gr. 13). 1994. text ed. 49.95 (0-415-10567-6, B4753) Routledge.

Stars Come down to Earth & Other Essays on the Irrational in Culture. Theodor W. Adorno. Ed. by Stephen Crook. LC 94-12151. 240p. (gr. 13). 1994. pap. 17.95 (0-415-10568-4, B4757) Routledge.

Stars' Desserts. Emily Luchetti. LC 90-56386. (Illus.). 288p. 1991. 35.00 (0-06-016688-6, HarpT) HarpC.

Stars Desserts. Emily Luchetti. LC 90-56386. (Illus.). 272p. 1993. reprint ed. pap. 22.50 (0-06-092218-4, PL) HarpC.

Stars Dispose No. 1: De Medici Fantasy Book. Michaela Roessner. LC 96-42995. (De Medici Fantasy Bks.: No. 1). 1997. 23.95 (0-312-85754-3) Tor Bks.

Stars Fell on Alabama. Carl Carmer. LC 85-8107. (Library of Alabama Classics). 320p. (Orig.). 1985. reprint ed. pap. 19.95 (0-8173-0235-2) U of Ala Pr.

Stars for a Light. Lynn Morris & Gilbert Morris. 320p. 1994. pap. 9.99 (1-55661-422-5) Bethany Hse.

Stars for Lincoln, Doctors & Dogs. J. Benbow Bullock. LC 80-66936. (Illus.). 100p. (Orig.). 1981. pap. 4.95 (0-937024-00-7) Gourmet Guides.

***Stars for the Toff.** large type ed. John Creasey. LC 96-43101. (Nightingale Ser.). 1997. pap. 18.95 (0-7838-1990-0) G K Hall.

Stars, Galaxies, Cosmos. William R. Corliss. LC 87-60007. (Catalog of Astronomical Anomalies Ser.). (Illus.). 246p. 1987. 17.95 (0-915554-21-6) Sourcebook.

Stars Galore & Even More: Speed-Cut Designs Using Hexagons & Octagons. Donna Paster. LC 95-7314. (Contemporary Quilting Ser.). 192p. 1995. pap. 22.95 (0-8019-8615-X) Chilton.

***Stars in Blue: Movie Actors in America's Sea Services.** James E. Wise, Jr. & Anne C. Rehill. (Illus.). 352p. 1997. 32.95 (1-55750-937-9) Naval Inst Pr.

Stars in De Elements: A Study of Negro Folk Music. Willis L. James. 1995. pap. text ed. 19.95 (0-8223-6432-8) Duke.

***Stars in Heaven & Stars on Earth.** Myungkark Park. 1995. pap. write for info. (1-877974-26-9) Prompter Pubns.

Stars in My Eyes. Edward Field. LC 77-95137. (Illus.). 91p. 1978. pap. 7.95 (0-8180-1537-3) Sheep Meadow.

Stars in the Dark: Coal Mines of Southwestern Oregon. Dow Bechham. (Illus.). 226p. (C). 1995. pap. text ed. 15.95 (0-930998-06-5) Arago Bks.

***Stars in the Firmament: Tangier Characters 1660-1960.** David S. Woolman. LC 96-10624. 203p. 1997. 20.00 (1-57889-068-3); pap. 14.00 (1-57889-067-5) Passeggiata.

***Stars in the Galley: Star of India Auxiliary Cookbook.** Star of India Auxiliary Staff. (Illus.). 194p. (Orig.). 1996. pap. 10.00 (0-944580-09-2) Maritime Mus Assn.

Stars in the Morning Sky: New Soviet Plays. Intro. by Michael Glenny. 329p. 1989. pap. 18.95 (1-85459-020-0, Pub. by N Hern Bks UK) Theatre Comm.

Stars in the Night. Don Summers. 1971. pap. 1.95 (0-915374-33-1, 33-1) Rapids Christian.

Stars in the Sky. Allan Fowler. LC 95-39677. (Rookie Read-about Science Ser.). (Illus.). 32p. (J). (ps-2). 1996. lib. bdg. 17.30 (0-516-06055-4) Childrens.

Stars in the Sky. Allan Fowler. (Rookie Read-About Science Ser.). (J). 1996. pap. 3.95 (0-516-20220-0) Childrens.

Stars in Their Courses. Harry Brown. 1995. reprint ed. lib. bdg. 24.95 (1-56849-664-8) Buccaneer Bks.

Stars in Their Courses, Vol. 8. Gilbert Morris. LC 95-35086. (Appomattox Saga Ser.). 350p. 1995. pap. 10.99 (0-8423-1674-4) Tyndale.

Stars in Their Courses: The Gettysburg Campaign. Shelby Foote. 252p. 1994. 14.50 (0-679-60112-0) Random.

Stars in Their Courses Audio. Shelby Foote. 1994. Three Cassettes. 25.00 (0-679-43466-6, Modern Lib) Random.

Stars in Your Bones. Bozarth et al. LC 90-35127. 112p. 1990. pap. 19.95 (0-87839-057-X) North Star.

Stars in Your Eyes: A Guide to the Northern Skies. Upper Willamette Valley Project Office Staff. (Illus.). 23p. 1985. reprint ed. pap. 1.50 (0-16-001802-1, S/N 008-022-00155-7) USGPO.

Stars in Your Family: How Astrology Affects Relationships Between Parents & Children. Sylvia Friedman. LC 95-14485. 400p. (Orig.). 1995. pap. 14.95 (1-56170-139-4, 121) Hay House.

Stars, Minds & Fate: Essays on Ancient & Medieval Cosmology. J. D. North. 460p. 1989. text ed. 60.00 (0-907628-94-X) Hambledon Press.

Stars, Moon & Clouds: Glow in the Dark. Eugene B. Coco. (Illus.). 24p. (J). (ps-3). 1990. 6.50 (0-307-06253-8, Golden Pr) Western Pub.

Stars My Destination. Alfred Bester. 1996. pap. 11.00 (0-679-76780-0) Random.

Stars My Destination. Alfred Bester & Howard Chaykin. 192p. 1992. 21.95 (0-87135-881-6) Marvel Entmnt.

Stars My Destination. Alfred Bester. 1993. reprint ed. lib. bdg. 25.95 (0-89968-328-2, Lghtyr Pr) Buccaneer Bks.

Stars, Nebulae & the Interstellar Medium: Observational Physics & Astrophysics. C. R. Kitchin. (Illus.). 376p. 1987. 149.00 (0-85274-580-X); pap. 47.00 (0-85274-581-8) IOP Pub.

Stars Notes. Valerie Coursen. (Notes Ser.). 1996. pap. text ed. 3.95 (1-56138-758-4) Running Pr.

Stars of Country Music. 14.98 (0-7853-0872-5) Pubns Intl Ltd.

Stars of Country Music. Ed. by Bill C. Malone & Judith McCulloh. (Quality Paperbacks Ser.). (Illus.). 476p. 1991. reprint ed. pap. 14.95 (0-306-80444-1) Da Capo.

Stars of Country Music: Uncle Dave Macon to Johnny Rodriguez. Ed. by Bill C. Malone & Judith McCulloh. LC 75-15848. (Music in American Life Ser.). 488p. 1975. 29.95 (0-252-00527-9) U of Ill Pr.

Stars of David: Jewish Science Fiction. Joe Sampliner et al. Ed. by D. J. Kessler. 416p. (Orig.). 1996. pap. 18.00 (0-9650294-0-9) DLZ Media.

Stars of Destiny: The Ancient Science of Astrology & How to Make Use of it Today. Katherine T. Craig. 312p. 1981. pap. 27.00 (0-89540-115-0, SB-115) Sun Pub.

***Stars of Hollywood Remembered: Career Biographies of 81 Actors & Actresses of the Golden Era, 1920s-1950s.** J. G. Ellrod. LC 97-9338. 232p. 1997. pap. 38.50 (0-7864-0294-6) McFarland & Co.

Stars of Jade. Julius D. Staal. LC 84-50263. (Chinese Astronomy Ser.). (Illus.). 225p. (Orig.). (C). 1984. pap. text ed. 24.95 (0-914653-00-8) Writ Pr.

***Stars of Magic Cookbook.** Harry Monti & Trudy Monti. (Illus.). 256p. Date not set. pap. 24.95 (0-9649321-6-4) Tiger Press.

Stars of Obron: Chambo Returns. Alta M. Rymer. (Tales of Planet Artembo Ser.: Bk. 3). (Illus.). 56p. (Orig.). (J). (gr. 5-7). pap. text ed. 20.00 (0-9600792-3-8) Rymer Bks.

Stars of Promise. 1990. 4.95 (0-86508-056-9) BCM Pubn.

Stars of Stand-up Comedia Encyclopedia: A Biographical Encyclopedia. Ronald L. Smith. LC 84-48408. (Library of Humanities Reference Bks.). 227p. 1986. text ed. 15.00 (0-8240-8803-4) Garland.

Stars of the American Ballet Theatre in Performance Photographs. Fred Fehl. 144p. 1984. pap. 10.95 (0-486-24755-4) Dover.

Stars of the American Musical Theater in Historic Photographs: 361 Portraits from the 1860s to 1950. Stanley Appelbaum & James Camner. (Illus.). 176p. 1981. pap. 11.95 (0-486-24209-9) Dover.

Stars of the Ballet. Ellen Jacob. (Learn-by-Coloring Ser.). (Illus.). 48p. (J). (ps-7). 1991. pap. 4.95 (0-937180-06-8) Variety Arts.

Stars of the Ballet & Dance in Performance Photographs. Fred Fehl. (Illus.). 144p. (Orig.). (gr. 6 up). 1983. pap. 10.95 (0-486-24492-X) Dover.

Stars of the Broadway Stage, 1940-1970. Fred Fehl. (Illus.). 144p. (Orig.). pap. 9.95 (0-486-24398-2) Dover.

Stars of the Curfew. Ben Okri. 1990. pap. 11.95 (0-14-011745-8, Viking) Viking Penguin.

Stars of the First Magnitude. 1983. pap. 7.99 (0-88019-147-3) Schmul Pub Co.

Stars of the First People. Docas S. Miller. LC 97-20052. (Orig.). 1997. pap. 20.00 (0-87108-858-4) Pruett.

Stars of the Major Leagues. Dave Klein. LC 73-18739. (Illus.). 160p. (YA). (gr. 7-12). 1974. lib. bdg. 3.69 (0-394-92762-1) Random Bks Yng Read.

Stars of the Nineteen Fifties Baseball Cards. Carol B. Grafton. 1985. pap. 3.95 (0-486-24848-8) Dover.

Stars of the Opera: The Great Opera Singers. Enrico Stinchelli. 1994. 39.95 (88-7301-007-5, Pub. by Gremese Intl IT) Natl Bk Netwk.

Stars of the Opera, 1950-1985, in Photographs. Ed. by James Camner. 128p. 1986. pap. 10.95 (0-486-25240-X) Dover.

Stars of the Screen 1931. Cedric O. Bermingham. 1976. lib. bdg. 75.00 (0-8490-3065-X) Gordon Pr.

Stars of the Silents. Edward Wagenknecht. LC 87-4508. (Filmmakers Ser.: No. 19). (Illus.). 180p. 1987. 22.50 (0-8108-1992-9) Scarecrow.

Stars of the South. Julian Green. Tr. by Robin Buss from FRE. 656p. 1996. 29.95 (0-7145-2985-0) M Boyars Pubs.

Stars of the Twilight. Mada Scott. LC 84-51156. 161p. 1984. pap. 4.95 (0-931117-00-3) Univ Pub.

Stars of the 80's. Julie A. Waterman. 7p. (Orig.). 1982. The Stars of the Eighties. pap. 1.25 (0-943334-07-1) Carmonelle Pubns.

***Stars over England.** Mark Penfield. 1996. spiral bd. 10.95 (0-86690-453-0, P3589-014) Am Fed Astrologers.

Stars over Hawaii. Edwin H. Bryan, Jr. (Illus.). 1977. reprint ed. pap. 6.95 (0-912180-30-7) Petroglyph.

***Stars Over Texas.** Virginia G. Messer. LC 96-33289. (Illus.). 1996. write for info. (1-57168-072-1, Eakin Pr) Sunbelt Media.

Stars over Texas. rev. ed. Carolyn Adams. (Illus.). 128p. (J). (gr. 1-6). 1983. 9.95 (0-89015-411-2) Sunbelt Media.

Stars Principal. J. D. McClatchy. 80p. 1986. pap. 9.95 (0-02-070030-X) Macmillan.

***Stars Register of Yachts, Clubs & Flags.** Sarah Marsh & Atle Moe. (Illus.). 1000p. 1997. 89.50 (0-9651781-1-0) Stars Reg Yachts.

Stars Register of Yachts 1996. Ed. by Atle Moe & Kristina Thyrre. (Illus.). 1000p. 1996. 100.00 (0-5651781-0-2) Stars Reg Yachts.

***Stars Screaming.** John Kaye. LC 97-9368. 304p. 1997. 25.00 (0-87113-691-0, Atlntc Mnthly) Grove-Atltic.

Stars Shine Down. Sidney Sheldon. (Sheldon Continuity Ser.). 320p. 1992. 12.95 (1-56865-026-4, GuildAmerica) Dblday Direct.

Stars Shine Down. Sidney Sheldon. 416p. 1993. mass mkt. 6.99 (0-446-36476-2) Warner Bks.

Stars Shine Down. Sidney Sheldon. LC 92-25280. 1992. 23.00 (0-688-08490-7) Morrow.

Stars Shine Down. Sidney Sheldon. 1994. pap. 16.95 (1-55800-492-0, Dove Bks) Dove Audio.

Stars Smile at You: Star Sign Astrology for a Child & a Lay Person. Milo Kovar. (Illus.). 55p. (Orig.). 1996. mass mkt. write for info. (0-941208-17-6) Milo Kovar.

Stars Speak: Astronomy in the Bible. Stewart Custer. (Illus.). 203p. (Orig.). 1977. pap. 9.95 (0-89084-059-8, 001255) Bob Jones Univ Pr.

***Stars, Stars, Stars: Off the Screen.** Photos by Edward Quinn. (Illus.). 336p. 1996. 75.00 (3-931141-28-4, 620041, Pub. by Scalo Pubs) Dist Art Pubs.

Stars, States & Historic Dates: Activities, Research & Readings in American History. Hilda K. Weisburg & Ruth Toor. 1987. 17.50 (0-931315-03-4) Lib Learn Res.

Stars, Stripes, & Italian Tricolor: The U. S. & Italy (1946-1989) Leo J. Wollemborg. LC 89-16217. 336p. 1990. text ed. 59.95 (0-275-93141-2, C3141, Praeger Pubs) Greenwood.

Stars, Stripes & Statutes: A Compendium of State Flag & Related Laws. Ed. by Patricia Artimovich et al. 68p. (Orig.). 1992. pap. 4.95 (0-934021-25-2) Natl Flag Foun.

STARS Telecommunications Regions Development Study. 95p. (Orig.). (C). 1993. pap. text ed. 25.00 (1-56806-771-2) DIANE Pub.

***Stars, the Earth, the River: Short Stories by Le Minh Khue.** Le Minh Khue. Ed. by Wayne Karlin. Tr. by Bac Hoai Tran & Dana Sachs from VIE. LC 96-45139. 256p. (Orig.). 1997. pap. 12.95 (1-880684-47-0) Curbstone.

Stars, the Snow, the Fire. John Haines. LC 88-37719. (Memoir Ser.). 200p. 1989. 17.95 (1-55597-117-2) Graywolf.

***Stars Through the Mist.** Betty Neels. 1997. mass mkt. 3.99 (0-373-83336-9) Harlequin Bks.

Stars to Steer By: A Galaxy of Poetry. deluxe limited ed. Mary C. Snotherly. Ed. by MaryBelle Campbell. (Persephone Press Poetry Ser.: No. 1). (Illus.). 24p. (Orig.). 1989. pap. 8.00 (0-9624737-5-8) S P-Persephone Pr.

Stars' Trip to Earth. (Kids Are Authors Picture Book Ser.). (Illus.). 24p. (J). (gr. k-3). 1993. 5.99 (0-87406-650-6) Willowisp Pr.

Stars Upstream: Life Along an Ozark River. Leonard Hall. LC 59-5772. (Illus.). 272p. 1983. reprint ed. pap. 16.95 (0-8262-0074-5) U of Mo Pr.

***Stars We Know: Crow Indian Astronomy & Lifeways.** Timothy P. McCleary. (Illus.). 127p. (Orig.). (C). 1996. pap. text ed. 9.95 (0-88133-924-5) Waveland Pr.

Stars Which See, Stars Which Do Not See. 2nd ed. Marvin Bell. (Classic Contemporaries Ser.). 56p. 1992. reprint ed. pap. 12.95 (0-88748-138-8) Carnegie-Mellon.

Stars, Wings, & Fun Things: Three Hundred Sixty-Five Activities for Children. Marilyn Neil. (Illus.). 68p. (Orig.). (J). (gr. k-3). 1991. pap. text ed. 8.95 (0-945301-05-7) Druid Pr.

Stars Without Garters! The Memoirs of Two Gay GI's in WWII. C. Tyler Carpenter & Edward H. Yentts. (Illus.). 160p. 1996. 20.00 (1-886360-03-0) Alamo Sq Pr.

Stars Without Garters: The Memoirs of Two Gay GI's in WWII. C. Tyler Carpenter & Edward H. Yeatts. LC 96-13649. 1996. pap. write for info. (1-886360-04-9) Alamo Sq Pr.

Starsailing: Solar Sails & Interstellar Space Travel. Louis Friedman. LC 87-14229. (Illus.). 146p. 1988. pap. text ed. 9.95 (0-471-62593-0) Wiley.

Starseed. Spider Robinson & Jeanne Robinson. 256p. 1992. mass mkt. 4.99 (0-441-78360-0) Ace Bks.

S

Starseed: An Introduction (for children) to the World. Michael Bridge. (Illus.). 32p. (J). 1992. 22.95 (*0-944963-34-X*); pap. 16.95 (*0-685-60191-9*); lib. bdg. 20.95 (*0-944963-15-3*) Glastonbury Pr.

Starseed Transmissions. Ken Carey. LC 90-56461. 112p. 1991. reprint ed. pap. 11.00 (*0-06-250189-5*) Harper SF.

Starshield Bk. 1: Sentinels. Margaret Weis & Tracy Hickman. LC 96-27414. 544p. 1996. 24.00 (*0-345-39760-6*, Del Rey) Ballantine.

Starshine! Ellen Schwartz. 160p. (Orig.). (YA). (gr. 4-8). 1987. pap. 5.95 (*0-919591-24-8*, Pub. by Polestar Bk Pubs CN) Orca Bk Pubs.

Starshine: Motivation & Courage Comes from Within. Kaye M. Jeters. 52p. (J). (gr. 4-6). 1995. pap. 12.99 (*1-886663-02-5*) Chatman Pub.

***Starshine & Sunglow.** Betty Levin. (J). Date not set. lib. bdg. write for info. (*0-688-12807-6*) Greenwillow.

Starshine & Sunglow. Betty Levin. LC 93-26672. (J). (gr. 4-7). 1994. 14.00 (*0-688-22806-2*) Greenwillow.

Starshine & Sunglow. Betty Levin. LC 93-26672. (Illus.). 96p. (J). (gr. 4-7). 1994. 14.00 (*0-688-12806-8*) Greenwillow.

Starshine at Camp Crescent Moon. Ellen Schwartz. 160p. (Orig.). (YA). (gr. 4-8). 1994. pap. 5.95 (*0-919591-02-7*, Pub. by Polestar Bk Pubs CN) Orca Bk Pubs.

Starship & the Canoe. Kenneth Brower. LC 82-48519. 256p. 1983. pap. 12.00 (*0-06-091030-5*, CN 1030, PL) HarpC.

Starship Trap. Mel Gilden. (Star Trek Ser.: No. 64). (Orig.). 1993. mass mkt. 5.50 (*0-671-97754-7*) PB.

Starship Trap. Mel Gilden. Ed. by Dave Stern. (Star Trek Ser.: No. 64). 256p. (Orig.). 1993. mass mkt. 5.50 (*0-671-79324-1*) PB.

Starship Troopers. Robert A. Heinlein. 272p. 1997. mass mkt. 5.99 (*0-441-78358-9*) Ace Bks.

Starship Troopers. Robert A. Heinlein. 1976. 24.95 (*0-8488-1045-7*) Amereon Ltd.

Starship Troopers. Robert A. Heinlein. 1994. reprint ed. lib. bdg. 27.95 (*1-56849-287-1*) Buccaneer Bks.

Starsource: Uncommon Ground Rules for Enlightenment. David J. Hainge. LC 96-1077. Orig. Title: Ground Rules. (Illus.). 80p. (Orig.). 1997. spiral bd., pap. 24.00 (*0-934172-44-7*) WIM Pubns.

Starspawn of Volturnus. Mark Acres. 1983. 5.50 (*0-394-53068-3*) Random.

***Starstone.** Donna M. Robb. LC 95-91015. 184p. (Orig.). 1996. pap. 8.00 (*1-56002-646-4*, Univ Edtns) Aegina Pr.

Starstrike. W. Michael Gear. 1990. mass mkt. 6.99 (*0-88677-427-6*) DAW Bks.

Starstruck. Richie T. Cusick. (YA). (gr. 7 up). 1996. mass mkt. 3.99 (*0-671-55104-3*) PB.

Starstruck. E. Lee et al. 85p. (Orig.). 1985. pap. 11.95 (*0-88145-023-5*) Broadway Play.

Starstruck. Elain Lee & Michael W. Kaluta. 80p. (Orig.). 1984. 6.95 (*0-87135-001-7*) Marvel Entmnt.

Starstruck. Anne McAllister. (Men Made in America Ser.). 1994. pap. 3.99 (*0-373-45199-7*, 1-45199-6) Harlequin Bks.

Starstruck: Celebrity Performers & the American Public. Jib Fowles. LC 91-23702. (Illus.). 300p. 1992. 29.95 (*1-56098-123-7*) Smithsonian.

Starstruck: Images from Hollywood's Golden Age. Anne Timpano. 33p. 1992. pap. write for info. (*1-882650-01-8*) Colmbs Mus GA.

***Starstruck: The Expanding Universe.** Elaine Lee & Michael W. Kaluta. (Illus.). 256p. 1996. pap. 16.95 (*1-56924-795-1*) Marlowe & Co.

***Starstruck: The Expanding Universe, Vol. 1.** 2nd ed. Elaine Lee. 1996. 22.95 (*1-56924-769-2*) Marlowe & Co.

***Starstruck Vol. 1: The Expanding Universe.** limited ed. Elaine Lee & Michael W. Kaluta. (Illus.). 1997. 50.00 (*1-56924-794-3*) Marlowe & Co.

Start a Business Without Borrowing. D. Kelly Irvin. LC 94-62185. 276p. (Orig.). 1995. 26.95 (*1-885373-05-8*) Emerald Ink.

Start a Business Without Borrowing. D. Kelly Irvine. LC 94-62185. (Illus.). 275p. (Orig.). 1995. pap. 14.95 (*1-885373-06-6*) Emerald Ink.

Start a Craft: Basket Making. Polly Pollock. 1994. 7.98 (*0-7858-0060-3*) Bk Sales Inc.

Start a Craft: Christmas Craft. Alison Jenkins. 1995. 7.98 (*0-7858-0481-1*) Bk Sales Inc.

Start a Craft: Decoupage. Lesley Player. 1996. 8.98 (*0-7858-0572-9*) Bk Sales Inc.

***Start a Craft: Greeting Cards.** S. McSwiney. 1996. 8.98 (*0-7858-0611-3*) Bk Sales Inc.

Start a Craft: Magic Tricks. Peter Eldin. 1996. 14.95 (*0-7858-0570-2*) Bk Sales Inc.

Start a Craft: Stained Glass. Lynette Wrigley. 1994. 7.98 (*0-7858-0056-5*) Bk Sales Inc.

***Start a Craft: Toleware.** A. Witchell. 1996. 8.98 (*0-7858-0610-5*) Bk Sales Inc.

***Start a Craft: Wood Carving.** P. Berry. 1996. 8.98 (*0-7858-0612-1*) Bk Sales Inc.

Start a Garden. Redefinition, Inc. Staff. LC 93-2179. (Do It! Ser.). 112p. 1994. ring bd. 9.95 (*0-8118-0561-1*) Chronicle Bks.

***Start a Health Service Business on Your PC & Make a Bundle.** 2nd ed. Rick Benzel. LC 96-29742. (Illus.). 256p. 1997. pap. text ed. 34.95 incl. cd-rom (*0-07-913139-5*) McGraw.

Start a Successful Business. Rosemary Phipps. 1996. pap. 9.95 (*0-563-36962-0*, BBC-Parkwest) Parkwest Pubns.

Start All over - an American's Experience: People, Places, & Lessons Learned. Peter Viemeister. (Illus.). 462p. 1995. lib. bdg. 32.00 (*1-883912-01-6*) Hamiltons.

Start & Run a Money-Making Bar. 2nd ed. Bruce Fier. 1993. pap. text ed. 16.95 (*0-07-020796-8*) McGraw.

Start & Run a Money-Making Bar. 2nd ed. Bruce Fier. 1993. pap. 15.95 (*0-8306-4246-3*) McGraw-Hill Prof.

Start & Run a Profitable Bed & Breakfast: Your Step-by-Step Business Plan. Monica Taylor & Richard Taylor. (Business Ser.). 216p. (Orig.). 1992. pap. 14.95 (*0-88908-989-2*) Self-Counsel Pr.

Start & Run a Profitable Catering Business: From Thyme to Timing: Your Step-by-Step Business Plan. George Erdosh. (Business Ser.). 184p. 1994. pap. 14.95 (*0-88908-772-5*) Self-Counsel Pr.

***Start & Run a Profitable Coffee Bar.** Tom Matzen & Marybeth Harrison. 208p. 1997. pap. 14.95 (*1-55180-098-5*) Self-Counsel Pr.

Start & Run a Profitable Consulting Business: A Step-by-Step Business Plan. 4th ed. Douglas Gray. (Business Ser.). 184p. 1995. pap. 14.95 (*1-55180-106-X*) Self-Counsel Pr.

***Start & Run a Profitable Craft Business.** 6th ed. William G. Hynes. 1996. pap. 14.95 (*1-55180-071-3*) Self-Counsel Pr.

***Start & Run a Profitable Desktop Publishing Business.** Barbara A. Fanson. 160p. (Orig.). 1997. pap. 14.95 (*1-55180-134-5*) Self-Counsel Pr.

Start & Run a Profitable Freelance Writing Business: Your Step-by-Step Business Plan. Christine Adamec. (Business Ser.). 112p. (Orig.). 1994. pap. 14.95 (*0-88908-523-4*) Self-Counsel Pr.

Start & Run a Profitable Gift Basket Business: Your Step-by-Step Business Plan. Mardi Foster-Walker. (Business Ser.). 144p. (Orig.). 1995. pap. 14.95 (*0-88908-846-2*) Self-Counsel Pr.

***Start & Run a Profitable Home-Based Business: Your Step-by-Step, First-Year Guide.** Edna Sheedy. (Orig.). Date not set. pap. 29.95 incl. audio (*1-55180-005-5*) Self-Counsel Pr.

Start & Run a Profitable Home-Based Business: Your Step-by-Step, First-Year Guide. 2nd ed. Edna Sheedy. (Business Ser.). 152p. (Orig.). 1994. pap. 12.95 (*0-88908-522-6*) Self-Counsel Pr.

Start & Run a Profitable Home Cleaning Business: Your Step-by-Step Business Plan. Susan Bewsey. (Business Ser.). 128p. (Orig.). 1995. pap. 12.95 (*1-55180-006-3*) Self-Counsel Pr.

Start & Run a Profitable Home Daycare: Your Step-by-Step Business Plan. Catherine Pruissen. (Business Ser.). 216p. 1993. pap. 14.95 (*0-88908-294-4*) Self-Counsel Pr.

Start & Run a Profitable Mail-Order Business: Getting Started for under $500: Your Step-by-Step Business Plan. Robert W. Bly. 160p. (Orig.). 1996. pap. 14.95 (*1-55180-065-9*) Self-Counsel Pr.

Start & Run a Profitable Office Service Business from Your Home: Secretarial Support, Word Processing, Desktop Publishing; Your Step-by-Step Business Plan. Louise Hagan. (Business Ser.). 112p. (Orig.). 1995. pap. 12.95 (*1-55180-028-4*) Self-Counsel Pr.

Start & Run a Profitable Restaurant: A Step by Step Business Plan. 3rd ed. Michael M. Coltman. 152p. 1993. pap. 12.95 (*0-88908-787-3*) Self-Counsel Pr.

***Start & Run a Profitable Retail Business.** 3rd ed. Michael M. Coltman. 1993. pap. text ed. 14.95 (*0-88908-767-9*) Self-Counsel Pr.

Start & Run a Profitable Retail Business: A Step-by-Step Business Plan. 4th ed. Jim Dion & Ted Topping. (Business Ser.). 184p. 1997. pap. 14.95 (*1-55180-100-0*, 9520) Self-Counsel Pr.

***Start & Run a Profitable Secondhand Bookstore.** Richard Cropp et al. (Start & Run Ser.). 200p. (Orig.). 1997. pap. 15.95 (*1-55180-136-1*) Self-Counsel Pr.

Start & Run a Profitable Student-Run Business: Your Step-by-Step Plan for Turning Bright Ideas into Big Bucks. David Schincariol. (Business Ser.). 144p. (Orig.). 1995. pap. 12.95 (*1-55180-026-8*) Self-Counsel Pr.

Start & Run a Profitable Tour Guiding Business: Part-Time, Full-Time, at Home, or Abroad: Your Step-by-Step Business Plan. Barbara Braidwood et al. 160p. (Orig.). 1996. pap. 14.95 (*1-55180-057-8*) Self-Counsel Pr.

Start & Run Your Own Profitable Service Business. Irving Burstiner. LC 92-31197. 1993. pap. text ed. 19.95 (*0-13-842733-X*) P-H.

START & the Future of Deterrence. Michael J. Mazarr. LC 90-8881. 208p. 1991. text ed. 65.00 (*0-312-05330-4*) St Martin.

***Start at Square One: Starting & Managing the Planned Gift Program.** Lynda S. Moerschbaecher. 200p. 1997. 40.00 (*1-56625-089-7*) Bonus Books.

Start at the Top. Burton D. Morgan. (Illus.). 131p. (C). 1982. 14.95 (*0-9609310-0-7*) Summit Pub OH.

***Start Collecting: Coins.** Margo Russell. (Illus.). 112p. 1996. 12.95 (*1-56138-762-2*) Running Pr.

***Start Collecting: Stamps.** Samuel Grossman. (Illus.). 121p. 1996. 12.95 (*1-56138-761-4*) Running Pr.

***Start Cooking: The Guide for the Newly Be-Kitchened.** John Morearty. LC 96-72122. (Illus.). 1997. spiral bd. 8.95 (*1-56875-190-7*, 190-7) R & E Pubs.

Start Early for an Early Start: You & the Young Child. Ed. by Ferne Johnson. LC 76-44237. 191p. reprint ed. pap. 54.50 (*0-317-26575-X*, 2023956) Bks Demand.

Start Expenses. Javaras. 1995. 125.00 (*0-316-46099-0*) Little.

Start Exploring Architecture: A Fact-Filled Coloring Book. Peter Dobrin. (Start Exploring Ser.). (Illus.). 128p. (Orig.). (J). (gr. 3 up). 1993. pap. 8.95 (*1-56138-237-X*) Running Pr.

***Start Exploring Ballet: A Fact Filled Coloring Book.** Trudy Garfunkel. (Illus.). (J). 1996. pap. 8.95 (*1-56138-749-5*) Running Pr.

Start Exploring Bulfinch's Mythology: Classic Tales of Heroes, Gods, & Magic. Retold by Steven Zorn. (Start Exploring Ser.). (Illus.). 128p. (Orig.). (J). (gr. 2 up). 1989. pap. 8.95 (*0-89471-710-3*) Running Pr.

Start Exploring Folktales of Native Americans: A Story-Filled Coloring Book. David Borgenicht. (Start Exploring Ser.). (Illus.). 128p. (Orig.). (J). (gr. 3 up). 1993. pap. 8.95 (*1-56138-303-1*) Running Pr.

Start Exploring Forests: A Fact-Filled Coloring Book. Elizabeth Dudley. (Start Exploring Ser.). (Illus.). (Orig.). (J). 1989. pap. 8.95 (*0-89471-782-0*) Running Pr.

Start Exploring Natural Wonders: A Fact-Filled Coloring Book. Elizabeth C. Dudley. (Illus.). 128p. (J). 1996. pap. 8.95 (*1-56138-695-2*) Running Pr.

Start Exploring Oceans: A Fact-Filled Coloring Book. Diane M. Tyler & James C. Tyler. (Start Exploring Ser.). (Illus.). 128p. (Orig.). (J). (gr. 3 up). 1990. pap. 8.95 (*0-89471-759-6*) Running Pr.

***Start Exploring the Civil War.** Blake A. Magner. (Start Exploring Ser.). (Illus.). 128p. (J). (gr. 3-6). 1997. 8.95 (*0-7624-0163-X*) Running Pr.

Start Fencing. A. T. Simmonds & E. D. Morton. (Illus.). 96p. 1990. 19.95 (*0-948253-40-1*, Pub. by Sportmans Pr UK) Trafalgar.

***Start Here.** (Whizz Bang Bumper Bk.). (J). Date not set. pap. text ed. write for info. (*0-582-19331-1*, Pub. by Longman UK) Longman.

***Start Karate!** J. Allen Queen. LC 96-50442. (Illus.). 128p. (J). 1997. pap. 5.95 (*0-8069-9306-5*) Sterling.

***Start Keyboarding & Information Processing.** Reilly. 1995. pap. text ed. write for info. (*0-582-80693-3*, Pub. by Longman UK) Longman.

Start Mushrooming. Stan Tekiela. 1993. 11.95 (*1-885061-03-X*) Adventure Pubns.

Start Mushrooming. Stan Tekiela. 1993. pap. 7.95 (*0-934860-96-3*) Adventure Pubns.

Start Now in Pastel. Tom Robb. (Start Now Ser.). (Illus.). 96p. 1996. 14.95 (*1-85410-241-9*, Pub. by Aurum Pr UK) London Brdge.

Start Now in Watercolour. Tom Robb. (Illus.). 96p. 1995. 14.95 (*1-85410-206-0*, Pub. by Piatkus Bks UK) London Brdge.

Start Now to Draw. Tom Robb. 96p. 1995. 14.95 (*1-85410-323-7*, Pub. by Piatkus Bks UK) London Brdge.

Start of a Glacial. Ed. by George J. Kukla & Ellen Went. LC 92-26367. (NATO ASI Series I: Global Environmental Change: Vol. 3). 368p. 1992. 272.95 (*0-387-54585-9*) Spr-Verlag.

Start of Something Big: Your Ultimate Guide to Writing a Dynamic Business Plan. K. L. Johnson. 308p. 1996. 22.95 (*1-884933-00-9*); lib. bdg. 23.95 (*1-884933-01-7*) Noted Concepts.

Start of the End of It All. Carol Emschwiller. LC 90-49563. 216p. 1991. pap. 10.95 (*1-56279-002-1*) Mercury Hse Inc.

Start Over. Bill Berkson. (Desert Island Chapbook Ser.). 32p. 1983. pap. 3.50 (*0-939180-24-3*) Tombouctou.

Start Over Every Morning. Harvey Jackins. 1989. 16.00 (*0-913937-36-3*); pap. 13.00 (*0-913937-35-5*) Rational Isl.

Start Playing Chess. Rosalyn B. Katz. LC 96-24656. (Illus.). 96p. 1996. pap. 7.95 (*0-8069-9349-9*) Sterling.

Start Playing Keyboard: Collection One. Peter Lavender. (Illus.). 48p. 1988. pap. 7.95 (*0-7119-1623-3*, AM72216) Music Sales.

Start Playing Keyboard: Omnibus Edition, 2 bks. in 1. Peter Lavender. (Illus.). 96p. 1987. pap. 12.95 (*0-8256-1187-3*, AM67588) Music Sales.

***Start Quilting with Alex Anderson: Six Projects for First-Time Quilters.** Alex Anderson. Ed. by Elizabeth Aneloski & Diana Roberts. (Illus.). 40p. (Orig.). 1997. pap. 12.95 (*1-57120-029-0*, 10154) C & T Pub.

Start Reading: A Basic Reader in English. Franklin I. Bacheller. 192p. (C). 1990. pap. text ed. 15.45 (*0-13-753724-7*) P-H.

Start Reading Music. Amy Appleby. (Illus.). 64p. 1992. pap. 4.95 (*0-8256-1246-2*, AM80219) Music Sales.

Start Reading Series: Instructor's Manual. E. Reid et al. 36p. 1986. teacher ed. 12.95 (*1-56422-030-3*) Start Reading.

Start Reading with Ann: Short "A" Sound. P. Newbold et al. (Start Reading Ser.: No. A1). 8p. (J). (ps-3). 1986. pap. text ed. 2.99 (*1-56422-000-1*) Start Reading.

Start Reading with Get Set: Short "e" Sound. E. Reid et al. (Start Reading Ser.: No. A5). 8p. (J). (ps-3). 1986. pap. text ed. 2.99 (*1-56422-004-4*) Start Reading.

Start Reading with Red Plane: Long "a" Sound. E. Reid et al. (Start Reading Ser.: No. B1). 8p. (J). (ps-3). 1986. pap. text ed. 2.99 (*1-56422-005-2*) Start Reading.

Start Reading with the Blue Boat: Long "o" Sound. E. Reid et al. (Start Reading Ser.: No. B2). 8p. (J). (ps-3). 1986. pap. text ed. 2.99 (*1-56422-006-0*) Start Reading.

Start Reading with the Brown Mule: Long "u" Sound. E. Reid et al. (Start Reading Ser.: No. B5). 8p. (J). (ps-3). 1986. pap. text ed. 2.99 (*1-56422-009-5*) Start Reading.

Start Reading with the Chimp: Ch Sound. E. Reid et al. (Start Reading Ser.: No. C3). 8p. (J). (ps-3). 1986. pap. text ed. 2.99 (*1-56422-012-5*) Start Reading.

Start Reading with the Green Jeep: Long "e" Sound. E. Reid et al. (Start Reading Ser.: No. B3). 8p. (J). (ps-3). 1986. pap. text ed. 2.99 (*1-56422-007-9*) Start Reading.

Start Reading with the Queen: Qu Sound. E. Reid et al. (Start Reading Ser.: No. C4). 8p. (J). (ps-3). 1986. pap. text ed. 2.99 (*1-56422-013-3*) Start Reading.

Start Reading with the Shark: Sh Sound. E. Reid et al. (Start Reading Ser.: No. C2). 8p. 1986. pap. text ed. 2.99 (*1-56422-011-7*) Start Reading.

Start Reading with the Thing: Th Sound. E. Reid et al. (Start Reading Ser.: No. C5). 8p. (J). (ps-3). 1986. pap. text ed. 2.99 (*1-56422-010-9*) Start Reading.

Start Reading with the Whale: Wh Sound. E. Reid et al. (Start Reading Ser.: No. C1). 8p. (J). (ps-3). 1986. pap. text ed. 2.99 (*1-56422-014-1*) Start Reading.

Start Reading with the White Bike: Long "i" Sound. E. Reid et al. (Start Reading Ser.: No. B4). 8p. (J). (ps-3). 1986. pap. text ed. 2.99 (*1-56422-008-7*) Start Reading.

Start Reading with Tip: Short "i" Sound. E. Reid et al. (Start Reading Ser.: No. A2). 8p. (J). (ps-3). 1986. pap. text ed. 2.99 (*1-56422-001-X*) Start Reading.

Start Reading with Top Dog: Short "o" Sound. E. Reid et al. (Start Reading Ser.: No. A3). 8p. (J). (ps-3). 1986. pap. text ed. 2.99 (*1-56422-002-8*) Start Reading.

Start Reading with up & Up: Short "u" Sound. E. Reid et al. (Start Reading Ser.: No. A4). 8p. (J). (ps-3). 1986. pap. text ed. 2.99 (*1-56422-003-6*) Start Reading.

Start Right: A Positive Approach to Literacy. Karen Brinkman & Joanie Walker. 176p. (C). 1991. pap. text ed. 12.00 (*0-13-068271-3*, 640302) P-H.

***Start, Run & Grow a Successful Small Business.** CCH Editorial Staff. Ed. by Susan Jacksack. (CCH Business Owner's Toolkit Ser.). 720p. (Orig.). 1997. pap. 39.95 (*0-8080-0176-0*) Commerce.

Start, Run & Profit from Your Own Home-Based Business. Gregory F. Kishel & Patricia G. Kishel. 194p. 1991. text ed. 34.95 (*0-471-52588-X*); pap. text ed. 19.95 (*0-471-52587-1*) Wiley.

***Start Sailing Right!** 2nd rev. ed. Derrick Fries. Ed. & Illus. by Mark Smith. 128p. 1997. pap. text ed. 14.95 (*1-882502-48-5*) US Sail Assn.

Start Sculpting. John Plowman. 1995. 17.98 (*0-7858-0354-8*) Bk Sales Inc.

Start Smart: Answers to Questions Asked by First Year College Students. Melinda Dalgran. 94p. (YA). (gr. 11-12). 1994. pap. text ed. 12.95 (*0-07-015190-3*) McGraw.

Start Smart: The Young Adult's Guide to Independent Living. Lavern R. Weathers. Ed. by Patty Davis. (Illus.). 70p. (Orig.). (YA). (gr. 9-12). 1994. pap. 8.95 (*0-9638608-0-1*) Strt Smart.

Start Smart: Your Home-Based Business. Bernadette Tiernan. 304p. 1996. 16.95 (*0-02-860330-3*, 96-21526) Macmillan.

***Start Supervising.** 3rd ed. Howard F. Shout. LC 84-12105. (Illus.). 155p. 1984. reprint ed. pap. 44.20 (*0-608-04276-5*, 2065028) Bks Demand.

Start the Conversation: The Book about Death You Were Hoping to Find. Ganga Stone. (Illus.). 208p. 1996. 22.95 (*0-446-51959-6*) Warner Bks.

Start the Conversation: The Book about Death You Were Hoping to Find. Kay Willis & Maryann B. Brinley. 240p. 1997. 12.99 (*0-446-67280-7*) Warner Bks.

Start the Fire. Lee Roberson. 385p. 1986. pap. 7.95 (*0-931117-04-6*) Univ Pub.

Start Them Thinking: A Handbook of Classroom Strategies for the Early Years. Robin Fogarty & Kay Opeka. (Illus.). 176p. (Orig.). 1988. pap. text ed. 23.95 (*0-932935-52-4*) IRI-SkyLght.

Start Thinking Export! Jack S. Wolf & Jean B. Romeo. 92p. (Orig.). (C). 1993. pap. text ed. 30.00 (*0-7881-0002-5*) DIANE Pub.

Start-to-Finish Cabinetmaking. Peter Jones. 1986. 18.50 (*0-8359-7062-0*, Reston) P-H.

Start-to-Finish Fund Raising. William Cumerford. 340p. 1993. 50.00 (*0-944496-33-4*) Precept Pr.

Start to Navigate. Conrad Dixon. (Illus.). 120p. 1977. 11.95 (*0-8464-1139-3*) Beekman Pubs.

Start to Navigate. 2nd ed. Conrad Dixon. (Illus.). 128p. 1983. pap. 11.95 (*0-229-11706-6*, Pub. by Adlard Coles UK) Sheridan.

Start to Plant: Container Gardens. Graham Pavey. 1996. 7.98 (*0-7858-0368-8*) Bk Sales Inc.

Start to Plant: Flower Gardens. Graham Pavey. 1996. 7.98 (*0-7858-0366-1*) Bk Sales Inc.

Start to Plant: Herb Garden. Graham Pavey. 1996. 7.98 (*0-7858-0458-7*) Bk Sales Inc.

Start to Plant: Rock & Alping Gardens. Graham Pavey. 1996. 7.98 (*0-7858-0369-6*) Bk Sales Inc.

Start to Ride. Holger Heck. 154p. (C). 1990. 60.00 (*0-85131-536-4*, Pub. by J A Allen & Co UK) St Mut.

***Start Typing.** K. Reilly. 1983. pap. text ed. write for info. (*0-85896-014-1*) Addison-Wesley.

***Start Typing & Word Processing.** Reilly. Date not set. pap. text ed. write for info. (*0-7299-0098-3*) Addison-Wesley.

Start Up. 4th ed. William J. Stolze. 288p. (Orig.). 1996. pap. 16.99 (*1-56414-252-3*) Career Pr Inc.

Start-up! A Guide to Getting off on the Right Foot. Donald F. Barkman. (Illus.). 74p. (Orig.). 1991. pap. 13.95 (*1-883655-00-5*) Busn Ctr.

***Start Up! Preparing to Lead Your Small Group.** (YouthSearch: Small-Group Resources Ser.). 64p. 1995. pap. 4.95 (*0-687-00836-0*) Abingdon.

***Start-Up! The Entrepreneur's Guide to the Art of New Business Finance & Planning.** T. Jefferson Straub. (Orig.). 1996. pap. 34.95 (*0-9651660-0-7*) Profit Mgnt.

Start up - Survival & Success of Your Small Business, 2 vols. Max Fallek. (Illus.). 793p. 1993. ring bd. 99.95 (*0-939069-49-0*) Amer Inst Small Bus.

Start-up & Shutdown Procedures: Subcritical Units. Center for Occupational Research & Development Staff. (EUTEC Power Plant Operator Curriculum Ser.). (Illus.). 32p. (C). 1985. pap. text ed. write for info. (*1-55502-253-7*) CORD Commns.

Start-up & Shutdown Procedures: Supercritical Units. Center for Occupational Research & Development Staff. (EUTEC Power Plant Operator Curriculum Ser.). (Illus.). 28p. (C). 1985. pap. text ed. write for info. (*1-55502-254-5*) CORD Commns.

Start-up Business Plan. William M. Luther. 240p. 1991. pap. 15.95 (*0-13-842543-4*, Lasser) Macmillan Gen Ref.

Start-up Companies: Planning, Financing, & Operating the Successful Business, 2 vols., Set. Ed. by Richard D. Harroch. 1500p. 1985. ring bd. 140.00 (*0-318-20273-5*, 00592) NY Law Pub.

An Asterisk (*) at the beginning of an entry indicates that the title is appearing in BIP for the first time.

Start-Up Entrepreneur: How You Can Succeed at Building Your Own Company or Enterprise Starting from Scratch. James R. Cook. 1997. pap. 13.95 (*0-452-27800-7*, Plume) NAL-Dutton.

Start-up Entrepreneur: How You Can Succeed in Building Your Own Company into a Major Enterprise Starting from Scratch. James R. Cook. LC 86-45650. 320p. 1987. reprint ed. pap. 13.50 (*0-06-097070-7*, PL 7070, PL) HarpC.

***Start up Financing: Hundreds of Ways to Get the Cash You Need to Start or Expand Your Business.** William J. Stolze. LC 97-17795. 288p. 1997. pap. 16.99 (*1-56414-271-X*) Career Pr Inc.

Start up Guide. David H. Bangs. 1995. pap. text ed. 34.95 incl. cd-rom (*0-7931-1664-3*, 1800-1001) Dearborn Trade.

Start up Guide: A One-Year Plan for Entrepreneurs. 2nd ed. David H. Bangs, Jr. 160p. 1994. pap. 19.95 (*0-936894-57-1*) Upstart Pub.

Start up Marketing: An Entrepreneur's Guide to Launching, Advertising, Marketing &... Philip R. Nulman. 288p. (Orig.). 1996. pap. 16.99 (*1-56414-256-6*) Career Pr Inc.

Start Where You Are: A Guide to Compassionate Living. Pema Chodron. LC 93-39135. 1994. pap. 12.00 (*0-87773-880-7*) Shambhala Pubns.

Start Where You Are: Matching Your Strategy to Your Marketplace. William B. Rouse. LC 95-47030. (Business & Management Ser.). 222p. 1996. 28.95 (*0-7879-0247-0*) Jossey-Bass.

Start Windsurfing Right. United States Yacht Racing Union Staff. 160p. (gr. 13). 1991. pap. text ed. 21.00 (*0-8016-9054-4*) Mosby Yr Bk.

Start with a Hull: Fitting Out a GRP Hull from Start to Finish. Loris Goring. (Illus.). 224p. 1992. pap. 30.00 (*0-7136-3563-0*) Sheridan.

Start with a Scan. Janet Ashford & John Odam. (Illus.). 144p. (C). 1996. pap. text ed. 34.95 (*0-201-88456-9*) Peachpit Pr.

Start with a Story: Literature & Learning in Your Classroom. Linda Wason-Ellam. LC 91-11268. 158p. 1991. pap. text ed. 17.50 (*0-435-08591-3*, 08591) Heinemann.

Start with Listening. Pat Dunkel & Christine Gorder. 256p. 1987. pap. 19.95 (*0-8384-2820-7*, Newbury); pap. 7.95 (*0-8384-2821-5*, Newbury) Heinle & Heinle.

Start with Rhymes, Nos. 7-12: Little Miss Muffett; Baa Baa Black Sheep; 1, 2 Buckle My Shoe; Rain; In a Dark Dark Wood & Round the Moon, 6 bks., Set. Ed. by Aidan Warlow. (Illus.). 48p. (Orig.). (J). (gr. k-1). 1988. pap. text ed. 29.60 (*1-55624-518-1*) Wright Group.

***Start with Soil.** Gershumy. Date not set. pap. 13.95 (*0-87596-697-7*) St Martin.

Start with Song! Two Hundred Ready-to-Use Interdisciplinary Activities for Young Learners. Audrey J. Adair-Hauser. LC 92-13259. (Illus.). 1992. write for info. (*0-13-832734-3*, Parker Publishing Co) P-H.

Start with Squares: Speedy Square Piecing for Scrap Quilts. Martha Thompson. Ed. by Janet White. LC 96-17670. (Illus.). 65p. (Orig.). 1996. pap. 12.95 (*1-56477-122-9*, B239) That Patchwork.

***Start with the Soil: The Organic Gardner's Guide to Improving the Soil for Higher Yields, More Beautiful Flowers & a Healthy, Easy-Care Garden.** Grace Gershuny. 1997. pap. 14.95 (*0-87596-960-7*) Rodale Pr Inc.

Start with the Sun: Studies in the Whitman Tradition. James E. Miller et al. LC 60-5493. (Bison Book Ser.: No. 165). 269p. reprint ed. pap. 76.70 (*0-7837-7047-2*, 2046858) Bks Demand.

Start Worrying: Details to Follow. Albert Vorspan. LC 91-22708. 1991. pap. 7.95 (*0-8074-0462-4*, 160002) UAHC.

Start Your Business: A Beginner's Guide. 2nd ed. (Illus.). 265p. ring bd. 24.95 incl. disk (*1-55571-332-7*) Oasis Pr OR.

Start Your Business: A Beginner's Guide. 2nd ed. PSI Research Staff. Ed. by Vickie Reierson. (Successful Business Library). (Illus.). 224p. 1995. pap. 9.95 (*1-55571-363-7*) Oasis Pr OR.

***Start Your New Business Now!** Arlene Appelbaum. 164p. 1997. per., pap. 48.00 (*1-885750-04-8*, SB97) Visions Communs.

Start Your Own At-Home Childcare Business. 2nd expanded rev. ed. Patricia C. Gallagher. 160p. (Orig.). (C). 1994. reprint ed. pap. 19.95 (*0-943135-08-7*) Young Sparrow Pr.

***Start Your Own Band: Everything You Need to Know to Take Your Band to the Top.** Marty Jourard. LC 96-53285. (Jet Lambert's Gumption Guides Ser.). (Illus.). 240p. 1997. pap. 9.95 (*0-7868-8216-6*) Hyperion.

Start Your Own Business: After Fifty - or Sixty - or Seventy! Lauraine Snelling. (Mature Reader Ser.). 228p. 1990. pap. 8.95 (*1-55867-007-6*) Bristol Pub Ent CA.

Start Your Own Business for One Thousand Dollars or Less. Will Davis. 280p. 1994. pap. 17.95 (*0-936894-70-9*, 610063-01, Upstart) Dearborn Finan.

Start Your Own Catering Business. LC 95-33367. (Start Your Own Ser.). 256p. 1995. pap. 12.95 (*0-89384-285-0*) P-H.

***Start Your Own Catering Business.** Prentice Hall Editorial Staff. (Start Your Own Ser.). 1996. pap. text ed. 12.95 (*0-13-603309-1*) P-H.

Start Your Own Childcare Business. LC 95-33974. (Start Your Own Ser.). 256p. 1995. pap. 12.95 (*0-89384-287-7*) P-H.

***Start Your Own Childcare Business.** Prentice Hall Editorial Staff. (Start Your Own Ser.). 1995. pap. text ed. 12.95 (*0-13-603325-3*) P-H.

***Start Your Own Coffee & Tea Store.** Prentice Hall Editorial Staff. (Start Your Own Ser.). 1996. pap. text ed. 12.95 (*0-13-603275-3*) P-H.

Start Your Own Computer Repair Business. Linda Rohrbough. 1995. pap. text ed., pap. 32.95 incl. disk (*0-07-911901-8*) McGraw.

Start Your Own Construction & Land Development Business. Adam Starchild. LC 83-2366. 232p. 1983. lib. bdg. 39.95 (*0-8304-1013-9*) Nelson-Hall.

Start Your Own Construction & Land Development Business. Adam Starchild. LC 83-2366. 222p. reprint ed. pap. 63.30 (*0-8357-3613-X*, AU00398) Bks Demand.

***Start Your Own Desktop Publishing Business.** Prentice Hall Editorial Staff. (Start Your Own Ser.). 1994. pap. text ed. 12.95 (*0-13-603283-4*) P-H.

Start Your Own Gift Basket Business. 181p. (Orig.). 1993. pap. 14.95 (*1-57327-002-4*, M Pr CA) Busn Concepts.

***Start Your Own Gift Basket Business.** Prentice Hall Editorial Staff. (Start Your Own Ser.). 1994. pap. text ed. 12.95 (*0-13-603291-5*) P-H.

***Start Your Own Import-Export Business.** Prentice Hall Editorial Staff. (Start Your Own Ser.). 1994. pap. text ed. 12.95 (*0-13-603028-9*) P-H.

Start Your Own Information Broker Service. LC 95-24326. (Start Your Own Ser.). 235p. 1995. pap. 12.95 (*0-89384-286-9*) P-H.

***Start Your Own Information Broker Service.** Prentice Hall Editorial Staff. (Start Your Own Ser.). 1996. pap. text ed. 12.95 (*0-13-603317-2*) P-H.

Start Your Own Interior Design Business & Keep It Growing! Your Guide to Business Success. Linda M. Ramsay. Ed. by Faren Bachelis. LC 93-93833. 384p. (Orig.). (C). 1994. pap. text ed. 39.99 (*0-9629918-0-5*, Baker & Taylor) Touch Design.

Start Your Own Latchkey Program. Ed. by Miriam Charnow. (Illus.). 32p. 1989. 4.00 (*0-910883-48-3*, 2037) Natl Coun Aging.

Start Your Own Lemonade Stand. Steven Caney. LC 89-40724. (Steven Caney's Kids' America Kits Ser.). (Illus.). 64p. (Orig.). (J). (gr. 2-6). 1991. pap. 12.95 (*0-89480-398-0*, 1398) Workman Pub.

***Start Your Own Mail Order Business.** Prentice Hall Editorial Staff. (Start Your Own Ser.). 1996. pap. text ed. 12.95 (*0-13-603051-3*) P-H.

***Start Your Own Money-Making Computer Business.** Prentice Hall Editorial Staff. (Start Your Own Ser.). 1994. pap. text ed. 12.95 (*0-13-603226-5*) P-H.

Start Your Own Newsletter from Scratch. Jim Terhune. (Illus.). 68p. 1996. pap. 9.95 (*0-614-16626-8*, 9565) Clearfield Co.

Start Your Own Newsletter Publishing Business. LC 95-4757. (Start Your Own Ser.). 264p. 1995. pap. 12.95 (*0-89384-284-2*) P-H.

***Start Your Own Newsletter Publishing Business.** Prentice Hall Editorial Staff. (Start Your Own Ser.). 1995. pap. text ed. 12.95 (*0-13-603333-4*) P-H.

***Start Your Own 101 Extra Income Ideas.** Prentice Hall Editorial Staff. (Start Your Own Ser.). 1994. pap. text ed. 12.95 (*0-13-603267-2*) P-H.

Start Your Own Private School-Legally!, 2 vols., Set Incl. Alternate Education. Dorie Erickson. LC 80-51385. (Illus.). 65p. (Orig.). (J). (gr. k-12). 1980. Set incls. Alternate Education, K-12. pap. 11.95 (*0-937242-00-4*) Scandia Pubs.

***Start Your Own Resume Writing Service.** Prentice Hall Editorial Staff. (Start Your Own Ser.). 1994. pap. text ed. 12.95 (*0-13-603234-6*) P-H.

***Start Your Own Secretarial Service Business.** Prentice Hall Editorial Staff. (Start Your Own Ser.). 1994. pap. text ed. 12.95 (*0-13-603242-7*) P-H.

Start Your Own Software Company: A Step-by-Step Guide to Setting up a Computer Software Business. David J. Cracas. LC 95-61394. 280p. (Orig.). Date not set. pap. 24.95 (*0-9640945-8-4*) Pierpoint-Martin.

***Start Your Own Temporary Help Agency.** Prentice Hall Editorial Staff. (Start Your Own Ser.). 1994. pap. text ed. 12.95 (*0-13-603259-1*) P-H.

***Start Your Own Zine: Everything You Need to Know to Put It in Print.** Veronika Kalmar. (Jet Lambert's Gumption Guides Ser.). (Illus.). 160p. 1997. pap. 9.95 (*0-7868-8217-4*) Hyperion.

Start Your Trip with a Full Tank: An Other Spiritual Jump Starts. Ron Hutchcraft. LC 95-37014. (Illus.). 256p. (YA). (gr. 10). 1996. pap. 13.99 (*0-8010-5298-X*) Baker Bks.

Starter Garden: The Guide for the Horticulturally Hapless. Cheryl Merser. (Illus.). 256p. (Orig.). 1994. pap. 14.00 (*0-06-096933-4*, PL) HarpC.

Starter Homes. 1994. pap. 8.95 (*1-881955-14-1*) Home Planners.

Starter Kit for the AS/400: Thirty-Three Fundamental Concepts. 2nd ed. Wayne Madden. 429p. 1994. pap. 89.00 (*1-882419-09-X*) Duke Commns Intl.

***Starter Library, 350 titles in 14 vols., Set.** 1993. spiral bd. 366.50 (*0-87063-484-4*, SL93) Vocational Biographies.

***Starter Library, 350 titles in 14 vols., Set.** 1993. 366.50 (*0-87063-485-2*, SL93) Vocational Biographies.

***Starter Library, 350 titles in 14 vols., Set.** 1994. spiral bd. 366.50 (*0-87063-601-4*, SL94) Vocational Biographies.

***Starter Library, 350 titles in 14 vols., Set.** 1994. 366.50 (*0-87063-602-2*, SL94) Vocational Biographies.

Starter One Hundred One, Bk. 8. Ruth A. O'Keefe. Ed. by AEVAC, Inc. Staff. (Structured Beginning Reading Program Ser.). 96p. student ed. 3.50 (*0-913356-14-X*) AEVAC.

Starter Tennis. rev. ed. 1985. 5.00 (*0-938822-67-5*) USTA.

***Starter Trainer's Package.** Pfeiffer & Company Staff. (Enneagram Personality Portraits Ser.). 1997. 29.95 (*0-7879-0891-6*, Pfffr & Co) Jossey-Bass.

Starters, Etc. LC 96-18131. (Meals for Life Ser.). (Illus.). 1996. spiral bd. 14.95 (*0-86573-994-3*) Cowles Creative.

Startide Rising. David Brin. (Uplift Trilogy Ser.). 352p. 1984. mass mkt. 6.50 (*0-553-27418-X*, Bantam Classics) Bantam.

Startime Theatre - Five Three Act Plays. 35.00 (*0-930061-61-6*) Interspace Bks.

Starting a Business in New York State. 4th ed. David Coleman. LC 92-74156. (For the Proprietor Ser.). 110p. 1995. pap. 20.00 (*0-930726-12-X*) Concept Pub.

Starting a Business in Oregon: The Required Steps to Open a Business in Oregon. Mary A. Turner. 65p. (Orig.). 1994. pap. 19.95 (*0-9638951-6-8*) Adella Pr.

Starting a Business in Pittsburgh. Neil F. Fogarty. (Orig.). 1988. pap. 7.95 (*0-929260-01-5*) Cricklewood Pr.

Starting a Business Made Simple. Rosie Milligan. 66p. 1991. pap. text ed. 20.00 (*1-881524-02-7*) Prof Busn Cnslt.

Starting a Business on a Budget. William C. Talman. v, 102p. (Orig.). 1996. pap. 19.95 (*0-9651848-0-3*) Lakemoor.

Starting a Business to Sell Your Artwork. Business of Your Own Staff. 240p. 1988. 59.95 (*0-943267-11-0*) Busn Your Own.

Starting a Business to Sell Your Craft Items. Business of Your Own Staff. 230p. 1988. 59.95 (*0-943267-08-0*) Busn Your Own.

Starting a Career. Peter Carpenter & John Western. (C). 1990. 75.00 (*0-86431-052-8*, Pub. by Aust Council Educ Res AT) St Mut.

Starting a Child Care Business, a Rewarding Career: A Home Study Course. Wendy Pfeffer. (Home Study Ser.). 1989. 33.00 (*0-939926-45-8*); audio (*0-939926-44-X*) Fruition Pubns.

Starting a Chiropractic Practice: A Comprehensive Guide to Clinic Management. rev. ed. Gayle A. Jensen & Rudolf P. Vrugtman. LC 90-63189. (Illus.). 213p. (C). 1990. pap. text ed. 29.95 (*0-945213-02-6*) Rudi Pub.

Starting a Clothing Boutique. Business of Your Own Staff. 230p. 1988. 59.95 (*0-943267-07-2*) Busn Your Own.

Starting a Day Care Center. Business of Your Own Staff. 240p. 1988. 59.95 (*0-943267-06-4*) Busn Your Own.

Starting a Design Firm. Frank A. Stasiowski & Julia Willard. 35p. 1994. text ed. 59.95 (*0-471-58576-9*) Wiley.

Starting a Driver-Owned & Operated Vanpool. (Energy Conservation Ser.). 1990. lib. bdg. 79.95 (*0-87700-902-3*) Revisionist Pr.

Starting a Flower Shop. Business of Your Own Staff. 240p. 1988. 59.95 (*0-943267-05-6*) Busn Your Own.

Starting a Franchise. Business of Your Own Staff. 240p. 1988. 59.95 (*0-943267-09-9*) Busn Your Own.

Starting a Gift Shop. Business of Your Own Staff. 240p. 1988. 59.95 (*0-943267-01-3*) Busn Your Own.

Starting a High-Income Consultancy. James Essinger. 192p. (Orig.). 1994. pap. 42.50 (*0-273-60506-2*, Pub. by Pitman Pub Ltd UK) Trans-Atl Phila.

Starting a High Tech Company. Michael L. Baird. LC 95-16795. (IEEE Engineers Guide to Business Ser.: vol. 7). 1995. 19.95 (*0-7803-2293-2*, EG107) Inst Electrical.

Starting a Home Based Business. Business of Your Own Staff. 240p. 1988. 59.95 (*0-943267-03-X*) Busn Your Own.

Starting a Home Based Business (Full or Part-Time) A Learning Annex Book. Irene Korn & Bill Zanker. 1993. pap. 8.95 (*0-8065-1472-8*, Citadel Pr) Carol Pub Group.

Starting a Home Sewing - Craft School. Allan Smith. 50p. (Orig.). 1994. pap. 7.00 (*0-931113-47-4*) Success Publ.

Starting a Human Resources Function: The Basics. Joseph P. Bacarro, Sr. (Illus.). 1996. pap. 30.00 (*0-939900-69-6*) Soc Human Resc Mgmt.

Starting a Job. Richard H. Turner. (Follet Success Skills Ser.). 64p. 1988. pap. text ed. 5.00 (*0-8428-2273-9*) Cambridge Bk.

Starting a Land Trust: A Guide to Forming a Land Conservation Organization. Land Trust Alliance Staff. 200p. (Orig.). 1990. pap. 16.00 (*0-943915-06-6*) Land Trust DC.

Starting a Limited Liability Company. Martin M. Shenkman et al. LC 95-26492. 256p. 1996. pap. text ed. 19.95 (*0-471-13365-5*) Wiley.

Starting a Limited Liability Company. Martin M. Shenkman et al. LC 95-26492. 256p. 1996. text ed. 55.00 (*0-471-13357-4*) Wiley.

Starting a Mail Order Business. Business of Your Own Staff. 240p. 1988. 59.95 (*0-943267-10-2*) Busn Your Own.

Starting a Marine Aquarium. Craig Barker. 1972. 8.95 (*0-87666-751-5*, PS-305) TFH Pubns.

***Starting a Medical Practice: The Physician's Handbook for Successful Start-Up.** American Medical Association Staff. (Practice Success Ser.). pap. 44.95 (*0-614-19649-3*, OP315296WE) AMA.

Starting a Mini-Business: A Guidebook for Seniors. rev. ed. Nancy Olsen. LC 88-81194. (Illus.). 144p. 1988. pap. 8.95 (*0-933271-02-6*) Fair Oaks CA.

***Starting a Nursery.** H. Jameson. 160p. 1997. 39.95 (*1-56593-783-X*, 1528) Singular Publishing.

***Starting a Nursery or Herb Farm.** John Mason. (Illus.). 180p. 1998. pap. 10.95 (*0-86417-843-3*, Pub. by Kangaroo Pr AT) Seven Hills Bk.

Starting a Pet Sitting Business. William S. Foster. 1990. pap. 12.95 (*0-88839-241-9*) Hancock House.

Starting a Private Practice see Becoming an Entrepreneur in Your Own Setting

Starting a Public Relations Firm. Ed. by Ruth Q. Smith. 240p. 1988. 59.95 (*0-943267-04-8*) Busn Your Own.

Starting a Secretarial Service. Business of Your Own Staff. Ed. by Emily Miller. 230p. 1988. 59.95 (*0-943267-12-9*) Busn Your Own.

Starting a Seeker-Sensitive Service. Ed Dobson. 160p. 1993. pap. 12.99 (*0-310-38481-8*) Zondervan.

Starting a Single Adult Ministry: Includes Ideas for the Small Church. Sue Nilson & Andy Morgan. 18.99 (*0-7814-5061-6*, 87866) Cook.

Starting a Small Business Handbook: How to Start & Operate Your Own Small Business. 2nd rev. ed. Andrew J. Lynn. (Illus.). 190p. (Orig.). 1992. pap. 24.95 (*1-877983-05-5*) Data-Lynn Bk.

Starting a Small Business in Connecticut. 2nd ed. CAAS Inc. Staff. Ed. by John Purtill, Jr. (Illus.). 264p. 1994. pap. text ed. 24.95 (*0-9639309-0-7*) Commun Account.

Starting a Small Business of Your Own-with "No" Money. David F. Cox. LC 89-82744. 83p. (Orig.). 1990. pap. 8.95 (*0-9616213-1-1*) Empire Pub.

Starting a Small Food-Processing Enterprise. Peter Fellows et al. 128p. (Orig.). 1996. pap. 15.50 (*1-85339-323-1*, Pub. by Intermed Tech UK) Women Ink.

Starting a Small Restaurant: A Guide to Excellence in the Purveying of Public Victuals. rev. ed. Daniel Miller. LC 83-6188. 224p. (Orig.). 1983. pap. 12.95 (*0-916782-37-9*) Harvard Common Pr.

Starting a Successful Business on the West Coast. 4th ed. Douglas L. Clark. (Business Ser.). 216p. 1994. pap. 14.95 (*0-88908-940-X*) Self-Counsel Pr.

Starting a Swan Dive. Patricia C. Miller. LC 93-18474. 64p. (Orig.). 1993. pap. 9.00 (*0-933532-91-1*) BkMk.

Starting a Technology Business. John C. Allen. 192p. 1992. 98.00 (*0-273-03671-8*, Pub. by Pitman Pubng UK) St Mut.

Starting Again: Early Rehabilitation after Traumatic Brain Injury or Other Severe Brain Lesion. Patricia M. Davies. LC 94-9131. 1994. 42.00 (*0-387-55934-5*) Spr-Verlag.

Starting America: The Story of Independence Hall. rev. ed. Edward M. Riley. (Illus.). 64p. (YA). 1990. reprint ed. pap. text ed. 4.95 (*0-939631-23-7*) Thomas Publications.

Starting an Agricultural Marketing Cooperative. 56p. (Orig.). 1994. pap. 10.00 (*1-885641-07-9*) U CA Ctr Cooperatives.

Starting an Antique Shop. Business of Your Own Staff. 240p. 1988. 59.95 (*0-943267-02-1*) Busn Your Own.

Starting an Archives. Elizabeth Yakel. LC 94-14408. 1994. 25.00 (*0-8108-2864-2*) Scarecrow.

Starting an Indexing Business. American Society of Indexers Staff. LC 93-40013. 1994. 30.00 (*0-936547-20-0*) Am Soc Index.

Starting an Indexing Business. 2nd ed. LC 95-21593. 106p. 1995. pap. text ed. 30.00 (*0-936547-31-6*) Am Soc Index.

Starting an Unemployment Benefits Clinic: A How to Guide. 15.00 (*0-685-14949-8*) Natl Lawyers Guild.

Starting & Building Your Catal. Herman R. Holtz. 288p. 1990. text ed. 27.95 (*0-471-50816-0*) Wiley.

Starting & Building Your Own Accounting Business. 2nd ed. Jack Fox. (Ronald National Association of Accounting Ser.). 416p. 1991. text ed. 69.00 (*0-471-52643-6*) Wiley.

Starting & Building Your Own Accounting Business. 2nd ed. Jack Fox. LC 90-37154. 416p. 1996. pap. text ed. 24.95 (*0-471-15380-X*) Wiley.

Starting (& Ending) a Small Group. Dan Williams. (LifeGuide Bible Studies). 61p. (Orig.). 1996. wbk. ed., pap. 4.99 (*0-8308-1075-7*, 1075) InterVarsity.

***Starting & Growing a Personal Training Business.** (Illus.). (Orig.). 1996. pap. write for info. (*0-9618161-7-1*) Am Coun Exer.

Starting & Managing a Business from Your Home. 1991. lib. bdg. 69.95 (*0-8490-4224-0*) Gordon Pr.

Starting & Managing a Business from Your Home. 1990. lib. bdg. 75.00 (*0-87700-905-8*) Revisionist Pr.

Starting & Managing a Business from Your Home. 1995. lib. bdg. 255.95 (*0-8490-6777-4*) Gordon Pr.

Starting & Managing a Business from Your Home. Lynne Waymon. 52p. (Orig.). (C). 1993. pap. text ed. 25.00 (*1-56806-368-7*) DIANE Pub.

Starting & Managing a Small Business. Frans Bekker & Gavin Staude. 553p. (C). 1994. reprint ed. pap. text ed. 41.50 (*0-7021-2128-2*, Pub. by Juta & Co SA) Intl Spec Bk.

Starting & Managing a Small Business of Your Own. 1984. lib. bdg. 79.95 (*0-87700-528-1*) Revisionist Pr.

***Starting & Managing Fee-Based Information Services in Academic Libraries.** Suzanne M. Ward. LC 97-4997. (Foundations in Library & Information Science Ser.). 1997. write for info. (*0-7623-0225-9*) Jai Pr.

Starting & Managing the Small Business. Arthur H. Kuriloff & John M. Hemphill, Jr. (Illus.). 608p. 1983. text ed. write for info. (*0-07-035662-9*) McGraw.

Starting & Managing the Small Business. 3rd ed. Arthur H. Kuriloff. 1992. text ed. write for info. (*0-07-035825-7*) McGraw.

***Starting & Managing Your Business.** Daniel E. Harn. 175p. Date not set. ring bd. write for info. (*0-9653749-0-4*) Harn Cnslting.

Starting & Managing Your Own Business: A Freelancing Guide for Paralegals. Dorothy Secol. (Paralegal Law Library). 280p. 1994. text ed. 60.00 (*0-471-04302-8*) Wiley.

***Starting & Managing Your Own Business: A Freelancing Guide for Paralegals - 1997 Cumulative Supplement.** Dorothy Secol. 1996. pap. text ed. 27.00 (*0-471-17498-X*) Wiley.

Starting & Operating a Business, 11 vols., Set. Michael D. Jenkins. Ed. by Vickie Reierson & Rosanno Alejandro. (Illus.). 1994. ring bd. 295.00 (*1-55571-182-0*) Oasis Pr OR.

Starting & Operating a Business after You Retire: What You Need to Know to Succeed. Bess R. May. LC 93-23063. (Illus.). 256p. pap. 12.95 (*0-89529-567-9*) Avery Pub.

S

S

Starting & Operating a Business in Alabama. 3rd ed. Ernst & Young Staff & Michael D. Jenkins. Ed. by Vickie Reierson & Rosanno Alejandro. (Successful Business Library). 310p. 1994. pap. 27.95 (*1-55571-201-0*); ring bd. 29.95 (*1-55571-200-2*) Oasis Pr OR.

Starting & Operating a Business in Alaska. 2nd ed. Michael D. Jenkins & PSI Research Staff. (Successful Business Library). 296p. (Orig.). 1994. pap. 27.95 (*1-55571-203-7*); ring bd. 29.95 (*1-55571-202-9*) Oasis Pr OR.

Starting & Operating a Business in Arizona. 3rd ed. Michael D. Jenkins & Ernst & Young Staff. Ed. by Vickie Reierson et al. (Successful Business Library). 310p. 1995. pap. 24.95 (*1-55571-205-3*) Oasis Pr OR.

Starting & Operating a Business in Arizona. 3rd ed. Michael D. Jenkins & Ernst & Young Staff. Ed. by Vickie Reierson et al. (Successful Business Library). 310p. 1995. ring bd. 29.95 (*1-55571-204-5*) Oasis Pr OR.

Starting & Operating a Business in Arkansas. 3rd ed. Michael D. Jenkins. (Successfull Business Library). 300p. 1994. pap. 27.95 (*1-55571-207-X*); ring bd. 29.95 (*1-55571-206-1*) Oasis Pr OR.

Starting & Operating a Business in California. 9th ed. Michael D. Jenkins. 346p. 1995. pap. 27.95 (*1-55571-372-6*) Oasis Pr OR.

Starting & Operating a Business in California. 9th ed. Michael D. Jenkins & Ernst & Young Staff. Ed. by Vickie Reierson et al. (Successful Business Library). 346p. 1995. ring bd. 29.95 (*1-55571-208-8*) Oasis Pr OR.

Starting & Operating a Business in Colorado. 4th ed. Michael D. Jenkins et al. Ed. by Vickie Reierson & Rosanno Alejandro. (Successful Business Library). 306p. 1994. pap. 27.95 (*1-55571-211-8*); ring bd. 29.95 (*1-55571-210-X*) Oasis Pr OR.

Starting & Operating a Business in Connecticut. 3rd ed. Michael D. Jenkins & Ernst & Young Staff. Ed. by Vickie Reierson et al. (Successful Business Library). 304p. 1995. pap. 27.95 (*1-55571-213-4*); ring bd. 29.95 (*1-55571-212-6*) Oasis Pr OR.

Starting & Operating a Business in Delaware. 3rd ed. Michael D. Jenkins & PSI Research Staff. (Successful Business Library). 312p. 1994. pap. 27.95 (*1-55571-215-0*); ring bd. 29.95 (*1-55571-214-2*) Oasis Pr OR.

Starting & Operating a Business in District of Columbia. 2nd ed. Michael D. Jenkins & Steven M. Ferguson. (Successful Business Library). 320p. 1994. pap. 27.95 (*1-55571-217-7*); ring bd. 29.95 (*1-55571-216-9*) Oasis Pr OR.

Starting & Operating a Business in Florida. 5th ed. Michael D. Jenkins & Jonathan H. Warner. Ed. by Vickie Reierson & Rosanno Alejandro. (Successful Business Library). 276p. 1994. pap. 27.95 (*1-55571-219-3*); ring bd. 29.95 (*1-55571-218-5*) Oasis Pr OR.

Starting & Operating a Business in Georgia. 4th ed. Michael D. Jenkins et al. Ed. by Vickie Reierson et al. (Successful Business Library). 314p. 1995. pap. 27.95 (*1-55571-221-5*); ring bd. 29.95 (*1-55571-220-7*) Oasis Pr OR.

Starting & Operating a Business in Hawaii. 3rd ed. Michael D. Jenkins. Ed. by Vickie Reierson & Rosanno Alejandro. (Successful Business Library). 312p. 1994. pap. 27.95 (*1-55571-223-1*); ring bd. 29.95 (*1-55571-222-3*) Oasis Pr OR.

Starting & Operating a Business in Idaho. 2nd ed. Michael D. Jenkins & PSI Research Staff. Ed. by Vickie Reierson et al. (Successful Business Library). 300p. 1995. pap. 27.95 (*1-55571-225-8*); ring bd. 29.95 (*1-55571-224-X*) Oasis Pr OR.

Starting & Operating a Business in Illinois. 3rd ed. Ernst & Young Staff & Michael D. Jenkins. LC 80-83053. (Successful Business Library). 310p. 1994. pap. 27.95 (*1-55571-098-0*); ring bd. 29.95 (*1-55571-044-1*) Oasis Pr OR.

Starting & Operating a Business in Indiana. Michael D. Jenkins. (Successful Business Library). 310p. 1994. ring bd. 29.95 (*1-55571-228-2*) Oasis Pr OR.

Starting & Operating a Business in Indiana. 4th ed. Michael D. Jenkins. (Successful Business Library). 310p. 1994. pap. 27.95 (*1-55571-229-0*) Oasis Pr OR.

Starting & Operating a Business in Iowa. 3rd ed. Michael D. Jenkins. (Successful Business Library). 310p. 1994. pap. 27.95 (*1-55571-231-2*); ring bd. 29.95 (*1-55571-230-4*) Oasis Pr OR.

Starting & Operating a Business in Kansas. 4th ed. Michael D. Jenkins & Ernst & Young Staff. Ed. by Vickie Reierson et al. (Successful Business Library). 308p. 1995. ring bd. 29.95 (*1-55571-232-0*) Oasis Pr OR.

Starting & Operating a Business in Kansas. 4th ed. Michael D. Jenkins & Ernst & Young Staff. Ed. by Vickie Reierson et al. (Successful Business Library). 308p. 1995. pap. 27.95 (*1-55571-233-9*) Oasis Pr OR.

Starting & Operating a Business in Kentucky. 3rd ed. Michael D. Jenkins & Ernst & Young Staff. Ed. by Vickie Reierson et al. (Successful Business Library). 306p. 1995. pap. 27.95 (*1-55571-235-5*); ring bd. 29.95 (*1-55571-234-7*) Oasis Pr OR.

Starting & Operating a Business in Louisiana. 3rd ed. Ernst & Young Staff & Michael D. Jenkins. Ed. by Vickie Reierson & Rosanno Alejandro. (Successful Business Library). 304p. 1994. pap. 27.95 (*1-55571-237-1*); ring bd. 29.95 (*1-55571-236-3*) Oasis Pr OR.

Starting & Operating a Business in Maine. 3rd ed. Michael D. Jenkins & PSI Research Staff. Ed. by Vickie Reierson et al. (Successful Business Library). 294p. 1995. pap. 27.95 (*1-55571-239-8*); ring bd. 29.95 (*1-55571-238-X*) Oasis Pr OR.

Starting & Operating a Business in Maryland. 3rd ed. Michael D. Jenkins & Ernst & Young Staff. Ed. by Vickie Reierson et al. (Successful Business Library). 326p. 1995. pap. 27.95 (*1-55571-241-X*); ring bd. 29.95 (*1-55571-240-1*) Oasis Pr OR.

Starting & Operating a Business in Massachusetts. 4th ed. Ernst & Young Staff & Michael D. Jenkins. Ed. by Vickie Reierson & Rosanno Alejandro. (Successful Business Library). 306p. 1994. pap. 27.95 (*1-55571-243-6*); ring bd. 29.95 (*1-55571-242-8*) Oasis Pr OR.

Starting & Operating a Business in Michigan. 3rd ed. Ernst & Young Staff & Michael D. Jenkins. Ed. by Vickie Reierson & Rosanno Alejandro. (Successful Business Library). 314p. 1994. pap. 27.95 (*1-55571-245-2*); ring bd. 29.95 (*1-55571-244-4*) Oasis Pr OR.

Starting & Operating a Business in Minnesota. 4th ed. Michael D. Jenkins et al. (Successful Business Library). 334p. 1994. pap. 27.95 (*1-55571-247-9*); ring bd. 29.95 (*1-55571-246-0*) Oasis Pr OR.

Starting & Operating a Business in Mississippi. 3rd ed. Michael D. Jenkins & PSI Research Staff. Ed. by Vickie Reierson et al. (Successful Business Library). 304p. 1995. pap. 27.95 (*1-55571-249-5*); ring bd. 29.95 (*1-55571-248-7*) Oasis Pr OR.

Starting & Operating a Business in Missouri. 3rd ed. Michael D. Jenkins & Rodney Hipp. Ed. by Vickie Reierson et al. (Successful Business Library). 310p. 1995. pap. 27.95 (*1-55571-251-7*); ring bd. 29.95 (*1-55571-250-9*) Oasis Pr OR.

Starting & Operating a Business in Montana. 2nd ed. Michael D. Jenkins & PSI Research Staff. (Successful Business Library). 288p. 1994. pap. 27.95 (*1-55571-253-3*); ring bd. 29.95 (*1-55571-252-5*) Oasis Pr OR.

Starting & Operating a Business in Nebraska. 3rd ed. Michael D. Jenkins & Franklin S. Forbes. (Successful Business Library). 322p. 1994. pap. 27.95 (*1-55571-255-X*); ring bd. 29.95 (*1-55571-254-1*) Oasis Pr OR.

Starting & Operating a Business in Nevada. 2nd ed. Ernst & Young Staff & Michael D. Jenkins. LC 80-83053. (Successful Business Library). 302p. 1994. pap. 27.95 (*1-55571-143-X*); ring bd. 29.95 (*0-916378-81-0*) Oasis Pr OR.

Starting & Operating a Business in New Hampshire. 3rd ed. Michael D. Jenkins & Ernst & Young Staff. Ed. by Vickie Reierson et al. (Successful Business Library). 306p. 1995. pap. 27.95 (*1-55571-259-2*); ring bd. 29.95 (*1-55571-258-4*) Oasis Pr OR.

Starting & Operating a Business in New Jersey. 5th ed. Michael D. Jenkins & Ernst & Young Staff. Ed. by Vickie Reierson et al. (Successful Business Library). 314p. 1995. pap. 27.95 (*1-55571-261-4*); ring bd. 29.95 (*1-55571-260-6*) Oasis Pr OR.

Starting & Operating a Business in New Mexico. 3rd ed. Michael D. Jenkins. Ed. by Vickie Reierson & Rosanno Alejandro. (Successful Business Library). 312p. 1994. pap. 27.95 (*1-55571-263-0*); ring bd. 29.95 (*1-55571-262-2*) Oasis Pr OR.

Starting & Operating a Business in New York. 4th ed. Michael D. Jenkins et al. (Successful Business Library). 346p. 1994. pap. 27.95 (*1-55571-265-7*); ring bd. 29.95 (*1-55571-264-9*) Oasis Pr OR.

Starting & Operating a Business in North Carolina. 3rd ed. Michael D. Jenkins et al. (Successful Business Library). 302p. 1994. pap. 27.95 (*1-55571-267-3*); ring bd. 29.95 (*1-55571-266-5*) Oasis Pr OR.

Starting & Operating a Business in North Dakota. 2nd ed. Michael D. Jenkins & PSI Research Staff. Ed. by Vickie Reierson et al. (Successful Business Library). 298p. 1995. pap. 27.95 (*1-55571-269-X*) Oasis Pr OR.

Starting & Operating a Business in North Dakota. 3rd ed. Michael D. Jenkins & PSI Research Staff. Ed. by Vickie Reierson et al. (Successful Business Library). 298p. 1995. ring bd. 29.95 (*1-55571-268-1*) Oasis Pr OR.

Starting & Operating a Business in Ohio. 4th ed. Ernst & Young Staff & Michael D. Jenkins. Ed. by Vickie Reierson & Rosanno Alejandro. (Successful Business Library). 314p. 1994. pap. 27.95 (*1-55571-271-1*); ring bd. 29.95 (*1-55571-270-3*) Oasis Pr OR.

Starting & Operating a Business in Oklahoma. 4th ed. Michael D. Jenkins et al. (Successful Business Library). 286p. 1994. pap. 27.95 (*1-55571-273-8*); ring bd. 29.95 (*1-55571-272-X*) Oasis Pr OR.

Starting & Operating a Business in Oregon. 3rd ed. Michael D. Jenkins & Carl R. Sniffen. Ed. by Vickie Reierson & Rosanno Alejandro. (Successful Business Library). 312p. 1994. pap. 27.95 (*1-55571-275-4*); ring bd. 29.95 (*1-55571-274-6*) Oasis Pr OR.

Starting & Operating a Business in Pennsylvania. Michael D. Jenkins et al. (Successful Business Library). 310p. 1994. ring bd. 29.95 (*1-55571-276-2*) Oasis Pr OR.

Starting & Operating a Business in Pennsylvania. 4th ed. Michael D. Jenkins et al. (Successful Business Library). 310p. 1994. pap. 27.95 (*1-55571-277-0*) Oasis Pr OR.

Starting & Operating a Business in Rhode Island. 3rd ed. Michael D. Jenkins et al. (Successful Business Library). 310p. 1994. pap. 27.95 (*1-55571-279-7*) Oasis Pr OR.

Starting & Operating a Business in Rhode Island. 3rd ed. Michael D. Jenkins et al. LC 80-83053. (Successful Business Library). 310p. 1994. ring bd. 29.95 (*1-55571-278-9*) Oasis Pr OR.

Starting & Operating a Business in South Carolina. 3rd ed. Ernst & Young Staff & Michael D. Jenkins. LC 80-83053. (Successful Business Library). 294p. 1995. pap. 27.95 (*1-55571-146-4*); ring bd. 29.95 (*0-916378-55-1*) Oasis Pr OR.

Starting & Operating a Business in South Dakota. 2nd ed. Michael D. Jenkins & PSI Research Staff. Ed. by Vickie Reierson et al. (Successful Business Library). 302p. 1995. pap. 27.95 (*1-55571-283-5*); ring bd. 29.95 (*1-55571-282-7*) Oasis Pr OR.

Starting & Operating a Business in Tennessee. 3rd ed. Ernst & Young Staff & Michael D. Jenkins. Ed. by Vickie Reierson & Rosanno Alejandro. (Successful Business Library). 310p. 1994. pap. 27.95 (*1-55571-285-1*); ring bd. 29.95 (*1-55571-284-3*) Oasis Pr OR.

Starting & Operating a Business in Texas. 4th ed. Michael D. Jenkins & Donald L. Sexton. LC 80-83053. (Successful Business Library). 314p. 1994. pap. 27.95 (*1-55571-115-4*); ring bd. 29.95 (*0-916378-24-1*) Oasis Pr OR.

Starting & Operating a Business in Utah. 3rd ed. Ernst & Young Staff & Michael D. Jenkins. Ed. by Vickie Reierson & Rosanno Alejandro. (Successful Business Library). 304p. 1994. pap. 27.95 (*1-55571-289-4*); ring bd. 29.95 (*1-55571-288-6*) Oasis Pr OR.

Starting & Operating a Business in Vermont. 2nd ed. Ernst & Young Staff & Michael D. Jenkins. LC 80-83053. (Successful Business Library). 294p. 1994. pap. 27.95 (*1-55571-082-4*); ring bd. 29.95 (*1-55571-034-4*) Oasis Pr OR.

Starting & Operating a Business in Virginia. 2nd ed. Ernst & Young Staff & Michael D. Jenkins. LC 80-83053. (Successful Business Library). 324p. 1994. pap. 27.95 (*1-55571-148-0*); ring bd. 29.95 (*0-916378-21-7*) Oasis Pr OR.

Starting & Operating a Business in Washington. 5th ed. Michael D. Jenkins & Ernst & Young Staff. Ed. by Vickie Reierson et al. (Successful Business Library). 308p. 1995. pap. 27.95 (*1-55571-295-9*); ring bd. 29.95 (*1-55571-294-0*) Oasis Pr OR.

Starting & Operating a Business in West Virginia. 2nd ed. Michael D. Jenkins & Steven Ferguson. LC 80-83053. (Successful Business Library). 316p. 1994. pap. 27.95 (*1-55571-083-2*); ring bd. 29.95 (*0-916378-72-1*) Oasis Pr OR.

Starting & Operating a Business in Wisconsin. 3rd ed. Ernst & Young Staff & Michael D. Jenkins. Ed. by Vickie Reierson & Rosanno Alejandro. (Successful Business Library). 304p. 1994. pap. 27.95 (*1-55571-299-1*); ring bd. 29.95 (*1-55571-298-3*) Oasis Pr OR.

Starting & Operating a Business in Wyoming. 3rd ed. Michael D. Jenkins & PSI Research Staff. Ed. by Vickie Reierson et al. (Successful Business Library). 298p. 1995. pap. 27.95 (*1-55571-301-7*); ring bd. 29.95 (*1-55571-300-9*) Oasis Pr OR.

Starting & Operating a Child Care Center. Jean Billman. 272p. (C). 1992. spiral bd. write for info. (*0-697-14550-6*) Brown & Benchmark.

Starting & Operating A Child Care Center: A Guide. Lillie M. Robinson. 1994. 29.95 (*0-9637908-6-2*) Readers Press.

Starting & Operating a Clipping Service. rev. ed. Demaris C. Smith. LC 80-10477. 62p. 1987. pap. 3.95 (*0-87576-133-X*) Pilot Bks.

Starting & Operating a Landscape Maintenance Business. Laurence W. Price. (Illus.). 133p. (Orig.). (C). 1989. pap. text ed. 8.95 (*0-9611966-1-0*) Botany Bks.

Starting & Operating a Playgroup for Profit. Susan Chidakel. LC 75-44029. 47p. 1985. pap. 3.95 (*0-87576-055-4*) Pilot Bks.

Starting & Operating a Vintage Clothing Shop. Rose F. Whitis. LC 83-8170. 46p. 1983. pap. 3.50 (*0-87576-104-6*) Pilot Bks.

Starting & Operating a Word Processing Service. Jean W. Murray. LC 83-2229. 32p. 1983. pap. 3.50 (*0-87576-102-X*) Pilot Bks.

Starting & Operating an Employee Leasing Firm. T. Joe Willey. 1989. write for info. (*0-944308-04-X*) Aegis Consulting.

Starting & Running a Money-Making Bar. Bruce Fier. 230p. 1988. 15.95 (*0-318-33266-3*, 119) Am Bartenders.

Starting & Running a Money-Making Bar. Bruce Fier. (Illus.). 240p. 1986. pap. 14.95 (*0-8306-2661-1*, 2661P) McGraw-Hill Prof.

Starting & Running a Nonprofit Organization. Joan M. Hummel. LC 80-15210. 160p. 1980. pap. 14.95 (*0-8166-0989-6*) U of Minn Pr.

Starting & Running a Nonprofit Organization. 2nd rev. ed. Joan M. Hummel. LC 95-53699. 168p. (C). 1996. pap. 14.95 (*0-8166-2777-0*) U of Minn Pr.

Starting & Running a Profitable Investment Club: The Official Guide from the National Association of Investment Clubs. Thomas E. O'Hara & Kenneth S. Janke. 256p. 1996. 23.00 (*0-8129-2686-2*, Times Business) Random.

Starting & Running a Successful Newsletter or Magazine. Cheryl Woodard. LC 96-50915. 320p. 1996. pap. text ed. 24.95 (*0-87337-357-X*) Nolo Pr.

***Starting & Running Your Own Horse Business.** Mary A. McDonald. LC 96-49470. 160p. (Orig.). 1997. pap. 19.95 (*0-88266-960-5*) Storey Comm Inc.

Starting & Sustaining Genetic Support Groups. Joan O. Weiss & Jayne S. Mackta. 152p. (C). 1996. text ed. 40.00 (*0-8018-5023-1*); pap. text ed. 18.95 (*0-8018-5264-1*) Johns Hopkins.

Starting Ballet. H. Edom. (First Skills Ser.). (Illus.). 32p. (J). (gr. k-3). 1993. pap. 4.95 (*0-7460-0982-8*); lib. bdg. 12.95 (*0-88110-634-8*) EDC.

Starting Blocks: Running the Race A-G Style. Terry Raburn. LC 88-80813. (Radiant Life Ser.). (Orig.). (YA). (gr. 7 up). 1988. teacher ed., pap. 5.50 (*0-88243-200-1*, 32-0200) Gospel Pub.

Starting Blocks: Running the Race A-G Style. Terry Raburn. LC 88-80813. (Radiant Life Ser.). 128p. (Orig.). (YA). (gr. 7 up). 1988. pap. 3.95 (*0-88243-860-3*, 02-0860) Gospel Pub.

Starting Bluegrass Banjo from Scratch. Wayne Erbsen. 80p. (Orig.). 1978. pap. 7.95 (*0-8258-0001-3*, PCB 104) Fischer Inc NY.

Starting Business English. Christine Johnson & Jack Lonergan. 1994. pap. 72.50 incl. audio (*962-209-368-X*, Pub. by Hong Kong Univ Pr HK) Coronet Bks.

Starting Business Studies. F. Frain. 1990. pap. 24.00 (*0-7463-0302-5*, Pub. by Northcote UK) St Mut.

Starting Chess. Harriet Castor. (First Skills Ser.). (Illus.). 32p. (J). (ps-2). 1995. pap. 4.95 (*0-7460-1386-8*, Usborne) EDC.

Starting Chess. Harriet Castor. (First Skills Ser.). (Illus.). 32p. (J). (ps-2). 1995. lib. bdg. 12.95 (*0-88110-768-9*, Usborne) EDC.

Starting College. Robert V. Iosue. (Illus.). 126p. 1992. pap. 9.00 (*0-940844-72-9*) Wellspring.

Starting College on the Right Foot. Melanie M. Lemaster. 96p. (C). 1992. per. 12.54 (*0-8403-7903-X*) Kendall-Hunt.

Starting Colts. Mike Kevil. Ed. by Pat Close. (Illus.). 168p. (Orig.). 1990. pap. 12.95 (*0-911647-21-X*) Western Horseman.

Starting Commerce. T. A. Shafto. (Illus.). 192p. (C). 1981. 45.00 (*0-7175-0797-1*, Pub. by S Thornes Pubs UK) St Mut.

Starting Cooking. Gill Harvey. (First Skills Ser.). (Illus.). (J). (gr. k-2). 1996. pap. 4.95 (*0-7460-1991-2*, Usborne) EDC.

Starting Cooking. Gill Harvey. (First Skills Ser.). (J). (ps-3). 1996. lib. bdg. 12.95 (*0-88110-793-X*) EDC.

***Starting Design & Communication.** Light. Date not set. pap. text ed. write for info. (*0-582-00429-2*, Pub. by Longman UK) Longman.

***Starting Drawing.** Anna Claybourne. (First Skills Ser.). (Illus.). 32p. (J). (gr. k-2). 1997. pap. 4.95 (*0-7460-2377-4*, Usborne); lib. bdg. 12.95 (*0-88110-891-X*, Usborne) EDC.

Starting Early with Study Skills: A Week by Week Guide for Elementary Students. Judith L. Irvin & Elaine O. Rose. LC 94-346. 1994. pap. text ed. 35.95 (*0-205-13943-4*, Longwood Div) Allyn.

Starting Economics. F. Davies. 144p. (C). 1979. 45.00 (*0-7175-0542-1*, Pub. by S Thornes Pubs UK) St Mut.

***Starting Economics.** Stanlake. Date not set. pap. text ed. write for info. (*0-582-02189-8*, Pub. by Longman UK) Longman.

***Starting Electronic Keyboard Bk. 1.** Longman Publishing Staff. Date not set. pap. text ed. write for info. (*0-582-03795-6*, Pub. by Longman UK) Longman.

***Starting Electronic Keyboard Bk. 2.** Longman Publishing Staff. Date not set. pap. text ed. write for info. (*0-582-03796-4*, Pub. by Longman UK) Longman.

Starting Electronics: All You Need To Get a Grounding in Practical Electronics. Keith Brindley. (Maplin Ser.). 240p. 1994. pap. 21.95 (*0-7506-2053-6*) Buttrwrth-Heinemann.

Starting English for Business. D. Adamson. 208p. 1991. pap. text ed. 17.95 (*0-13-842519-1*) P-H.

Starting English with a Smile. Barbara Zaffran & David Krulik. (English with a Smile Ser.: Bk. 1). 144p. 1995. pap. 10.60 (*0-8442-0575-3*, Natl Textbk) NTC Pub Grp.

Starting English with a Smile. Barbara Zaffran & David Krulik. (English with a Smile Ser.: Bk. 1). 144p. 1995. audio 20.00 (*0-8442-0586-9*, Natl Textbk) NTC Pub Grp.

Starting English with a Smile. 2nd ed. Barbara Zaffran & David Krulik. (English with a Smile Ser.: Bk. 1). 176p. 1994. teacher ed. 9.25 (*0-8442-0589-3*, Natl Textbk) NTC Pub Grp.

Starting from Ellis Island. Frank Higgins. LC 79-7740. 1979. pap. 3.25 (*0-933532-01-6*) BkMk.

***Starting from Here: Dakota Poetry, Pottery, & Caring.** Jerome W. Freeman. Ed. by Mary W. Freeman & Ronald L. Robinson. LC 96-61600. (Illus.). 108p. (Orig.). 1996. pap. 12.95 (*0-944287-16-6*) Ex Machina.

Starting from Paumanok: Five Long Island Poets. David B. Axelrod et al. 118p. 1971. 20.00 (*0-685-25233-7*); pap. 10.00 (*0-685-25234-5*) Writers Ink Pr.

Starting from Pyron. Jane G. Rushing. (Illus.). xi, 153p. (C). 1992. 25.00 (*0-89672-283-X*) Tex Tech Univ Pr.

Starting from San Francisco. enl. rev. ed. Lawrence Ferlinghetti. LC 67-23492. (C). 1967. pap. 6.95 (*0-8112-0046-9*, NDP220) New Directions.

Starting from Scratch. Colin Morris. 96p. (Orig.). (C). 1991. pap. 9.95 (*0-7162-0473-8*, Epworth Pr) TPI PA.

Starting from Scratch: A Different Kind of Writers' Manual. Rita Mae Brown. 272p. 1989. pap. 11.95 (*0-553-34630-X*) Bantam.

Starting from Scratch: A for Better or for Worse Collection. Lynn Johnston. (Illus.). 128p. 1995. pap. 8.95 (*0-8362-0424-7*) Andrews & McMeel.

Starting from Scratch: How to Begin Your Own R. E. Program. Ann Fields et al. Ed. by Mary J. Curry. (Illus.). 64p. (Orig.). 1994. 15.00 (*1-55896-125-9*) Unitarian Univ.

Starting from Scratch: One Classroom Builds an Authentic Curriculum. LC 96-4126. 205p. 1996. pap. text ed., pap. 22.00 (*0-435-07205-6*) Heinemann.

***Starting from the Child? Teaching & Learning from 4 to 8.** Julie Fisher. 160p. 1996. 59.00 (*0-335-19557-1*, Open Univ Pr); pap. 18.95 (*0-335-19556-3*, Open Univ Pr) Taylor & Francis.

An Asterisk (*) at the beginning of an entry indicates that the title is appearing in BIP for the first time.

Starting From Zero. Barbara Crooker. 28p. 1987. pap. 3.50 (*0-9613465-8-2*) Great Elm.

***Starting Gardening.** Sue Johnson & Cheryl Evans. (First Skills Ser.). (Illus.). 32p. (J). (gr. k-2). 1997. pap. 4.95 (*0-7460-2383-9*, Usborne); lib. bdg. 12.95 (*0-88110-892-8*, Usborne) EDC.

Starting Home: The Story of Horace Pippin, Painter. Mary E. Lyons. LC 92-26990. (African-American Artists & Artisans Ser.). (Illus.). 48p. (J). (gr. 3-6). 1993. lib. bdg. 15.95 (*0-684-19534-8*, C Scribner Sons Young) S&S Childrens.

Starting in Heating & Air Conditioning Service. L. E. LaRocque. Ed. by Joanna Turpin. LC 92-11928. (Illus.). 180p. (C). 1992. 24.95 (*0-912524-63-4*) Busn News.

Starting in Medical Pracrtice. Morton Walker & John P. Trowbridge. 192p. (Orig.). 1987. pap. 33.95 (*0-87489-473-5*) Med Econ.

***Starting in Taekwondo: Training for Competition & Self-Defense.** Joe Fox & Art Michaels. LC 96-35886. 1997. 16.95 (*0-8069-6104-X*) Sterling.

Starting in Video: The Costs & Resources Needed, Including a Directory of Christian Video Producers. Kenneth E. Acton. (C). 1989. 29.00 (*0-9510086-4-1*, Pub. by Jay Bks UK) St Mut.

***Starting Lettering.** Fiona M. Watt. (First Skills Ser.). (Illus.). 32p. (J). (gr. k-2). 1997. pap. 4.95 (*0-7460-2379-0*, Usborne); lib. bdg. 12.95 (*0-88110-893-6*, Usborne) EDC.

Starting, Lighting, Ignition & Generating Systems. 10th ed. 1987. 8.00 (*0-685-12354-5*) IBMA Pubns.

Starting Line. Community of Jesus, Inc. Staff. (Illus.). 118p. 1989. student ed. 19.95 (*0-685-29183-9*) Community Jesus.

Starting Lines. David Blot. (College ESL Ser.). 1995. suppl. ed., pap. 6.95 (*0-8384-5259-0*) Heinle & Heinle.

Starting Lines: A Beginning Writing Text. David Blot & David Davidson. LC 94-39153. 144p. 1995. pap. 21.95 (*0-8384-5258-2*) Heinle & Heinle.

Starting Management Science. D. R. Snaddon. (Illus.). 130p. (C). 1991. pap. text ed. 25.15 (*0-7021-2636-5*, Pub. by Juta & Co SA) Intl Spec Bk.

Starting, Managing, & Promoting the Small Library. Robert Berk. LC 89-10704. 160p. (gr. 13). 1990. text ed. 59.95 (*0-87332-576-1*) M E Sharpe.

***Starting Millionaire Success Kit.** 9th ed. Tyler G. Hicks. 361p. 1998. pap. 99.50 (*1-56150-245-6*) Intl Wealth.

Starting Millionaire Success Kit, 12 bks., Set. 8th ed. Tyler G. Hicks. 361p. 1996. pap. 99.50 (*1-56150-195-6*) Intl Wealth.

Starting Needlecraft. H. Castor. (First Skills Ser.). (Illus.). 32p. (J). (ps-2). 1994. pap. 4.95 (*0-7460-1664-6*, Usborne); lib. bdg. 12.96 (*0-88110-706-9*, Usborne) EDC.

Starting Needlepoint Lace: A Course for Beginners. Valerie Grimwood. (Illus.). 1996. pap. 24.95 (*0-7134-5807-0*, Pub. by Batsford UK) Trafalgar.

Starting off Right: A Resource Guide for Employee Orientation. Ora Spaid. 144p. 1991. ring bd. 39.95 (*0-87425-156-7*) HRD Press.

***Starting Off Right in Law School.** Carolyn Nygren. LC 97-12484. 128p. (C). 1997. pap. 12.50 (*0-89089-877-4*) Carolina Acad Pr.

Starting on a Shoestring: Building a Business Without a Bankroll. 3rd ed. Arnold S. Goldstein. LC 95-11207. 320p. 1995. text ed. 29.95 (*0-471-13413-9*); pap. text ed. 16.95 (*0-471-13415-5*) Wiley.

Starting on the Harpsichord: A First Book for the Beginner. Jean Nandi & Leonie Jenkins. LC 88-92718. (Illus.). 212p. (Orig.). (C). 1989. pap. 22.95 (*0-9622023-0-4*) Bon Gout Pub.

Starting Out: Class & Community in the Lives of Working-Class Youth. Victoria A. Steinitz & Ellen R. Solomon. LC 86-5808. 296p. 1986. 34.95 (*0-87722-430-7*) Temple U Pr.

Starting Out: Class & Community in the Lives of Working-Class Youth. Victoria A. Steinitz & Ellen R. Solomon. LC 86-5808. 296p. 1989. pap. 18.95 (*0-87722-620-2*) Temple U Pr.

Starting Out: Step-by-Step Guide for Teens Succeeding in the '90s. Terilyn A. Davenport. LC 93-87661. 320p. (Orig.). (YA). (gr. 11 up). 1994. 29.95 (*1-884573-09-6*); pap. 19.95 (*1-884573-10-X*) S-By-S Pubns.

Starting Out: The Complete Home Buyer's Guide. Dian Hymer. (Illus.). 250p. 1997. pap. 17.95 (*0-8118-1272-3*) Chronicle Bks.

Starting Out Vol. 1: Visions & Nightmares, Ends & Beginnings. rev. ed. Mary M. Shideler. LC 95-92737. (Visions & Nightmares, Ends & Beginnings Ser.: Vol. 1). 352p. 1996. 22.95 (*0-9649509-6-0*); pap. 14.95 (*0-9649509-4-4*) Scribendi Pr.

Starting Out in Futures Trading. 5th ed. Mark J. Powers. 1993. per. 24.95 (*1-55738-506-8*) Irwin Prof Pubng.

***Starting Out in the Evening.** Brian Morton. LC 97-10797. 1998. 25.00 (*0-517-70862-0*) Crown Pub Group.

Starting out in the Thirties. Alfred Kazin. LC 88-31709. 176p. 1989. pap. 10.95 (*0-8014-9562-8*) Cornell U Pr.

***Starting Out Right: Development Assets for Children.** Jolene L. Roehlkepartain et al. (Orig.). 1996. pap. 14.95 (*1-57482-364-7*) Search Inst.

Starting Out Right: Guidelines for Organizing a New Retail Cooperative. Jesse Singerman. 1986. pap. 5.75 (*0-9608298-0-6*) NCBA.

Starting Out Right: How to Turn Your Preorder into a Retail Food Comparative. Jesse Singerman. 79p. 1982. 5.00 (*0-318-17052-3*) NASCO.

Starting Out, Starting Over: Finding the Work That's Waiting for You. Linda Peterson. LC 95-4177. 208p. (Orig.). 1995. pap. 14.95 (*0-89106-073-1*, 7230) Davies-Black.

Starting Out Suburban: A Frosh Year Survival Guide. Linda P. Puner. LC 96-67384. 240p. (Orig.). (YA). 1996. pap. 16.95 (*0-9651403-0-X*) New Forge.

Starting Over. Nicole Grey. (Girl Friends Ser.: No. 7). 224p. 1994. mass mkt. 3.50 (*0-8217-4451-8*, Zebra Kensgtn) Kensgtn Pub Corp.

Starting Over. Jacqueline Lapidus. (Illus.). 1990. pap. 3.50 (*0-918314-03-8*) Out & Out.

Starting Over. Ellen S. Stern. (Clear & Simple Ser.). 384p. (Orig.). 1995. pap. 8.95 (*0-440-50595-X*, Dell Trade Pbks) Dell.

Starting Over. Joyce J. Tyra. LC 92-10901. 96p. (Orig.). 1992. pap. 6.99 (*0-8361-3587-3*) Herald Pr.

Starting Over: Feminism & the Politics of Cultural Critique. Judith Newton. LC 94-10225. (Critical Perspectives on Women & Gender Ser.). 1994. text ed. 42.50 (*0-472-09482-3*); pap. text ed. 15.95 (*0-472-06482-7*) U of Mich Pr.

Starting Over: How to Change Careers or Start Your Own Business. Stephen M. Pollan & Mark Levine. 256p. (Orig.). 1997. pap. 10.99 (*0-446-67166-5*) Warner Bks.

Starting Over: Learning to Cook with Natural Foods. Delia Quigley & Polly Pitchford. LC 87-33007. (Illus.). 144p. (Orig.). 1988. pap. 10.95 (*0-913990-55-8*) Book Pub Co.

Starting Over: The Task of the Protagonist in the Contemporary Bildungsroman. Ed. by Susan Gohlman. LC 90-34445. (Studies in Comparative Literature). 272p. 1990. reprint ed. 20.00 (*0-8240-0004-8*) Garland.

Starting Over: You in the New Workplace. rev. ed. Jo Danna. LC 90-6119. (Illus.). 272p. (Orig.). 1990. pap. 12.95 (*0-9610036-3-4*) Palomino Pr.

Starting over Again. Joanne Wallace. 226p. 1991. pap. text ed. 10.95 (*0-8407-3048-9*) J Wallace Sem.

Starting over but Not from Scratch: Spiritual & Mental Health Between Jobs. Richard Kew. LC 93-33343. 144p. (Orig.). 1994. pap. 2.69 (*0-687-27702-7*) Abingdon.

Starting over in Eastern Europe: Entrepreneurship & Economic Renewal. Simon Johnson. 1995. 27.95 (*0-87584-569-X*) Harvard Busn.

Starting over in Eastern Europe: Entrepreneurship & Economic Renewal. Simon Johnson & Gary W. Loveman. 1995. text ed. 27.95 (*0-07-103618-0*) McGraw.

Starting over Single: Life & Hope after the Death of a Marriage. Mervin E. Thompson. LC 85-3638. 160p. 1985. 4.95 (*0-933173-00-8*) Chging Church Forum.

Starting Painting. Susan Mayes. (First Skills Ser.). (Illus.). 32p. (J). (gr. k-2). 1996. pap. 4.95 (*0-7460-2375-8*, Usborne); lib. bdg. 12.95 (*0-88110-847-2*, Usborne) EDC.

Starting Photography. 2nd ed. Michael J. Langford. (Illus.). 160p. (YA). (gr. 7 up). 1993. pap. 19.95 (*0-240-51348-7*, Focal) Buttrwrth-Heinemann.

***Starting Point: Science, Vol. 4.** Kate Needham. 1996. 12.95 (*0-7460-1307-8*) EDC.

Starting Point Science, Vol. 2. Susan Mayes et al. (J). (gr. 4-7). 1992. 12.95 (*0-7460-0655-1*, Usborne) EDC.

Starting Point Science, Vol. 3. Sue Meredith. (Illus.). 96p. (J). (gr. 2-7). 1992. 12.95 (*0-7460-0970-4*, Usborne) EDC.

Starting Point Science IV. (Illus.). 96p. (J). (gr. 1 up). 1994. pap. 12.95 (*0-7460-1306-X*, Usborne) EDC.

Starting Point 1996: The AVA Guide to 1,100 Plus Trails in America. 232p. 1995. pap. 5.00 (*0-9644794-1-9*) Am Volkssport Assoc.

***Starting Point 1997: The AVA Guide to 1,100 + Trails in America.** 232p. 1997. pap. 10.95 (*0-9644794-2-7*) Am Volkssport Assoc.

***Starting Points.** Arnold & Scott. Date not set. pap. text ed. write for info. (*0-582-55483-7*, Pub. by Longman UK) Longman.

Starting Points: For Implementing Visual Mathematics. Linda C. Foreman. 86p. 1995. teacher ed., spiral bd. 10.00 (*1-886131-28-7*, SP95) Math Lrning.

Starting Points: How to Set up & Run a Writing Workshop. Dan Rothermel. LC 96-20406. 1996. pap. write for info. (*1-56090-109-8*) Natl Middle Schl.

Starting Points: Meeting the Needs of Our Youngest Children. Carnegie Task Force Staff. LC 94-8825. 1994. write for info. (*1-885039-00-X*) Carnegie Corp.

Starting-Points in Social Science. A. G. Keller. LC 76-136073. 183p. 1971. reprint ed. text ed. 49.75 (*0-8371-5223-2*, KESP, Greenwood Pr) Greenwood.

Starting Research: A New Guide to Researching & Writing Up. Roy Preece. 264p. 1994. 48.00 (*1-85567-090-9*, Pub. by Pntr Pubs UK); pap. text ed. 16.00 (*1-85567-091-7*, Pub. by Pntr Pubs UK) Bks Intl VA.

Starting Riding. H. Edom. (First Skills Ser.). (Illus.). 32p. (J). (gr. k-3). 1992. pap. 4.95 (*0-7460-0980-1*); lib. bdg. 12.95 (*0-88110-022-6*) EDC.

Starting Right: A Basic Guide to Museum Planning. Gerald George & Cindy Sherrell-Leo. LC 95-43382. (American Association for State & Local History Book Ser.). (Illus.). 160p. 1986. pap. 19.95 (*0-7619-9148-4*) AltaMira Pr.

Starting Right: How America Neglects Its Youngest Children & What We Can Do about It. Sheila B. Kamerman & Alfred J. Kahn. 192p. 1995. text ed. 25.00 (*0-19-509675-4*) OUP.

Starting Right in Your New Business. 2nd ed. Robert Clements & Wilfred F. Tetreault. LC 81-512. 1981. pap. 17.95 (*0-201-07795-7*) Addison-Wesley.

Starting Right in Your New Business. 2nd ed. Wilfred F. Tetreault & Robert W. Clements. LC 80-66118. (Illus.). 198p. 1979. pap. 14.00 (*0-937152-01-3*) Am Busn Consult.

Starting Right with Rabbits. Mervin F. Roberts. (Illus.). 128p. 1983. 11.95 (*0-87666-814-7*, PS-796) TFH Pubns.

Starting Salaries of Chemists & Chemical Engineers, 1989. 105p. 1989. pap. 24.95 (*0-8412-1732-7*) Am Chemical.

Starting School. (Talkabouts Ser.: No. 735-9). (Illus.). (J). (ps). 3.50 (*0-7214-1086-3*, Ladybrd) Penguin.

Starting School. Janet Ahlberg. (J). 1990. pap. 4.99 (*0-14-050843-0*, Puffin) Puffin Bks.

***Starting School.** Johanna Hurwitz. (Illus.). (J). Date not set. write for info. (*0-688-15685-1*, Morrow Junior) Morrow.

Starting School: From Separation to Independence - a Guide for Early Childhood Teachers. Nancy Balaban. (Early Childhood Education Ser.). 160p. (C). 1985. pap. text ed. 15.95 (*0-8077-2793-8*) Tchrs Coll.

***Starting School: The Vital Years.** Henry Pluckrose. 121p. (Orig.). 1993. pap. 29.50 (*0-7501-0673-5*, Pub. by Stanley Thornes UK) Trans-Atl Phila.

***Starting School: Three Programs to Help Young Students Develop a Positive Attitude Toward School.** Laura Weitzman et al. LC 95-81945. (Illus.). 48p. (J). (gr. k-1). 1996. 14.95 (*1-57543-000-2*) Mar Co Prods.

Starting School at 4: A Joint Endeavor. Marion Dowling. 192p. 1995. pap. 19.95 (*1-85396-270-8*, Pub. by Paul Chapman UK) Taylor & Francis.

***Starting School with an Enemy.** Elise Carbone. (J). 1998. write for info. (*0-679-88639-7*); pap. write for info. (*0-679-88640-0*) Knopf Bks Yng Read.

***Starting School with an Enemy.** Elise Carbone. 1998. lib. bdg. write for info. (*0-679-98639-1*) Random Bks Yng Read.

Starting Seeds Indoors. Reilly. 1989. pap. 2.95 (*0-88266-519-7*) Storey Comm Inc.

Starting Shoestring Businesses: Steady Profits on a Full-Time Or Part-Time Basis. 1992. lib. bdg. 88.00 (*0-8490-5517-2*) Gordon Pr.

Starting Small - Thinking Big: Practical Strategies for School Success. Chris Alexiou. 200p. 1995. pap. 12.95 (*0-88962-579-4*) Mosaic.

***Starting Small Groups: Building Communities That Matter.** Jeffrey Arnold. 1997. pap. text ed. 13.95 (*0-687-01856-0*) Abingdon.

Starting Small Groups & Keeping Them Going. (Small Group Ser.). 144p. 1995. pap. text ed. 17.80 (*0-8066-0125-6*, 15-160) Augsburg Fortress.

Starting Small, Investing Smart: What to Do with Five Dollars to Five Thousand. 2nd ed. Donald R. Nichols. 156p. 1990. per. 17.00 (*1-55623-381-7*) Irwin Prof Pubng.

Starting Small, Investing Smart: What to Do with Five to Five Thousand Dollars. 2nd rev. ed. Donald R. Nichols. 200p. 1987. text ed. 26.00 (*1-55623-041-9*) Irwin Prof Pubng.

Starting Small, Thinking Big: Practical Strategies for School Success. Chris Alexiou. 200p. 1995. lib. bdg. 35.00 (*0-8095-4857-7*) Borgo Pr.

Starting Soccer. Edward F. Dolan, Jr. 1978. pap. 5.00 (*0-87980-352-5*) Wilshire.

Starting Soccer. H. Edom et al. (First Skills Ser.). (Illus.). 32p. (J). (gr. k-3). 1994. pap. 4.95 (*0-7460-1384-1*, Usborne); lib. bdg. 12.95 (*0-88110-671-2*, Usborne) EDC.

Starting Sociology. 4th ed. James L. Spates. 528p. (C). 1990. pap. text ed. 37.50 (*0-06-044078-3*) Addson-Wesley Educ.

Starting Something. Carol Montgomery. LC 91-73630. 90p. (Orig.). 1992. pap. 6.95 (*1-879603-01-2*) Los Hombres.

Starting SPSS - PC Plus & SPSS for Windows: A Beginner's Guide to Data Analysis. 2nd ed. Jeremy Foster. 292p. (Orig.). 1993. pap. 42.50 (*1-85058-509-1*, Pub. by Sigma Press UK) Coronet Bks.

Starting Statistics. E. L. Hanson & G. A. Brown. (Illus.). 96p. (C). 1983. 45.00 (*0-7175-0176-0*, Pub. by S Thornes Pubs UK) St Mut.

Starting System Explained. George Chrestionson. LC 80-730402. (Orig.). 1979. student ed. 6.00 (*0-8064-0135-4*, 435); audio, vhs 219.00 (*0-8064-0136-2*) Bergwall.

Starting the Colt. Mary Twelveponies. (Illus.). 128p. 1992. pap. 11.95 (*0-395-63127-0*) HM.

Starting the Western Horse. LC 96-33104. 1997. 22.95 (*0-87605-926-4*) Howell Bk.

Starting Time: A True Account of the Origins of Creation, Sex, Death, & Golf. Gray Kochhar-Lindgren. (Illus.). 132p. (Orig.). 1995. pap. 12.00 (*1-883991-11-0*) Whte Cloud Pr.

Starting to Add. J. Tyler & K. Bryant-Mole. (First Learning Ser.). (Illus.). 24p. (J). (ps up). 1989. pap. 3.95 (*0-7460-0455-9*, Usborne) EDC.

Starting to Collect Silver. John Luddington. (Illus.). 1984. 49.50 (*0-907462-48-0*) Antique Collect.

Starting to Count. J. Tyler & G. Round. (First Learning Ser.). (Illus.). 24p. (J). (ps up). 1987. pap. 3.95 (*0-7460-0216-5*) EDC.

Starting to Draw. Wendon Blake. (Artist's Painting Library). (Illus.). 80p. 1981. pap. 9.95 (*0-8230-4916-7*, Watsn-Guptill) Watsn-Guptill.

Starting to Drive. Sallie Walrond. (Threshold Picture Guides Ser.). 24p. 1994. pap. 12.00 (*1-872082-47-5*, Pub. by Kenilworth Pr UK) Half Halt Pr.

Starting to Manage: The Essential Skills. Gerard Blair. (IEEE Engineers Guide to Business Ser.: Vol. 8). 1995. pap. 19.95 (*0-7803-2295-9*, EG108) Inst Electrical.

Starting to Measure. J. Tyler & G. Round. (First Learning Ser.). (Illus.). 24p. (J). (ps up). 1991. pap. 3.95 (*0-7460-0624-1*, Usborne) EDC.

Starting to Plan for Lifetime Financial Independence. Elmo A. Peterle. 1993. pap. 17.95 (*1-882180-10-0*) Griffin CA.

Starting to Play Guitar. 1994. pap. 17.95 incl. audio (*0-89724-223-8*, XW1703) Astor Bks.

Starting to Subtract. J. Tyler & K. Bryant-Mole. (First Learning Ser.). (Illus.). 24p. (J). (ps up). 1989. pap. 3.95 (*0-7460-0456-7*, Usborne) EDC.

Starting to Teach in the Secondary School: A Companion for the Newly Qualified Teacher. Susan Anne Capel et al. LC 96-21557. 320p. (C). 1997. pap. text ed. write for info. (*0-415-13278-9*) Routledge.

Starting Today... Steps to Success for Beginning Bilingual Educators. Frank Gonzales. 130p. (Orig.). 1994. pap. text ed. 25.00 (*1-878550-51-9*) Inter Dev Res Assn.

Starting Up. Rita Abrams. 1990. bds. 9.95 (*0-938971-46-8*) JTG Nashville.

Starting Up. Gary Jones. 208p. (Orig.). 1991. pap. 36.00 (*0-273-03514-2*, Pub. by Pitman Pubng UK) St Mut.

Starting Up. 3rd ed. Gary Jones. (Pitman Small Business Bookshelf Ser.). 256p. (Orig.). 1995. 33.50 (*0-273-61701-X*, Pub. by Pitman Pub Ltd UK) Trans-Atl Phila.

***Starting Up: An Interactive Adventure That Challenges Your Entrepreneurial Skills.** David E. Rye & Craig R. Hickman. LC 97-19720. 1997. write for info. (*0-13-312240-9*) P-H.

Starting Up: How to Begin Your Professional Business. Marvin Banasky. (Illus.). 72p. (Orig.). (C). student ed., pap. text ed. 15.00 (*1-880932-04-0*) Lovergy Prods.

Starting-Up Without Big Bucks: Creating a New Business with Small Capital. Lawrence Schulz. (Illus.). 102p. (Orig.). 1996. pap. 11.99 (*0-614-13693-8*) CA Entrprnr Pub.

Starting up Your Own Small Business: Expert Advice from the Small Business Administration. G. Howard Poteet. 264p. 1990. pap. 19.95 (*0-8306-3548-3*, 3548) McGraw-Hill Prof.

***Starting with AutoCAD LT.** write for info. (*0-340-62543-0*, Pub. by E Arnold UK) Routledge Chapman & Hall.

Starting with Books: An Activities Approach to Children's Literature. Emilie P. Sullivan. (Illus.). 159p. 1990. pap. text ed. 19.50 (*0-87287-792-2*) Teacher Ideas Pr.

***Starting with Budgerigars.** Kurt Kolar. (Starting with Pets Ser.). 1997. pap. text ed. 6.95 (*0-7137-2683-0*, Pub. by Blandford Pr UK) Sterling.

***Starting with Cats.** Birgit Gollman. (Starting with Pets Ser.). 1997. pap. text ed. 6.95 (*0-7137-2682-2*, Pub. by Blandford Pr UK) Sterling.

Starting with Christ. David Larsen & Sandy Larsen. (Teamwork Discipleship Guides Ser.). 96p. (Orig.). 1993. wbk. ed., pap. 4.99 (*0-8308-1126-5*, 1126) InterVarsity.

Starting with COMAL. Ingvar Gratte. 224p. 1985. 25.95 (*0-13-843003-9*) P-H.

Starting with Coquille. Geranna Fleming. Ed. by Vi Gale. LC 77-95426. (First Bk.). (Illus.). 1978. pap. 5.00 (*0-915986-08-6*) Prescott St Pr.

Starting with Coquille. limited ed. Geranna Fleming. Ed. by Vi Gale. LC 77-95426. (First Bk.). (Illus.). 1978. 20.00 (*0-915986-07-8*) Prescott St Pr.

Starting with Foucault: An Introduction to Genealogy. C. G. Prado. 160p. 1995. text ed. 49.00 (*0-8133-1790-8*) Westview.

Starting with Foucault: An Introduction to Genealogy. C. G. Prado. 160p. (C). 1995. pap. text ed. 17.95 (*0-8133-1791-6*) Westview.

***Starting with Hamsters.** George Gassner. (Starting with Pets Ser.). 1997. pap. text ed. 6.95 (*0-7137-2680-6*, Pub. by Blandford Pr UK) Sterling.

***Starting with "I" Personal Essays by Teenagers.** Youth Communication Staff. Ed. by Andrea Estepa & Philip Kay. LC 96-48606. 240p. (Orig.). (YA). (gr. 7 up). 1997. pap. 13.95 (*0-89255-228-X*) Persea Bks.

***Starting with Space: The Earth.** Cynthia P. Nicolson & Bill Slavin. (Illus.). (FRE.). (J). pap. 8.99 (*0-590-16009-5*) Scholastic Inc.

***Starting with Space: The Moon.** Paulette Bourgeois & Bill Slavin. (Illus.). (FRE.). (J). pap. 8.99 (*0-590-16020-6*) Scholastic Inc.

***Starting with Space: The Sun.** Paulette Bourgeois & Bill Slavin. (Illus.). (FRE.). (J). pap. 8.99 (*0-590-16019-2*) Scholastic Inc.

Starting with the New Testament, Vol. 2. Stephen Travis. 64p. 1996. pap. 5.95 (*0-687-06696-4*) Abingdon.

Starting with the Old Testament, Vol. 1. Stephen Travis. 64p. 1996. 5.95 (*0-687-06684-0*) Abingdon.

Starting with the Unit Circle: Background to Higher Analysis. L. K. Hua. (Illus.). 192p. 1981. 107.95 (*0-387-90589-8*) Spr-Verlag.

Starting Work in Sales. Sheila McCallum & Anne Strong. 128p. (C). 1987. 80.00 (*0-946139-27-X*, Pub. by Elm Pubns UK) St Mut.

Starting Yoga: A Step-by-Step Program for Health & Wellbeing. Doriel Hall. (Illus.). 128p. 1996. pap. 14.95 (*0-7063-7457-6*, Pub. by Ward Lock UK) Sterling.

Starting Young: School-Based Health Centers at the Elementary Level. National Health & Education Consortium Staff. 50p. 1995. 10.00 (*0-937846-42-2*) Inst Educ Lead.

Starting Your Business: Decide if Proprietorship, Partnership, or Corporation. 2nd rev. ed. Holmes F. Crouch. Ed. by Irma J. Crouch. LC 95-80857. (Series 200 Tax Guides: Vol. 203). (Illus.). 224p. 1996. pap. 18.95 (*0-944817-27-0*, T/G 203) Allyear Tax.

Starting Your Business, Vol. 1: Planning & Organization. Frank L. Bouquet. 125p. 1992. 35.00 (*1-56216-008-7*); pap. 25.00 (*1-56216-064-8*) Systems Co.

Starting Your Business, Vol. 2: Operating Techniques & Pitfalls Procedures. Frank L. Bouquet. (Illus.). 125p. (C). 1992. 35.00 (*1-56216-052-4*); pap. 25.00 (*1-56216-065-6*) Systems Co.

Starting Your Child on the Computer: A Guidebook for Parents & Teachers. Peter Silton. (Illus.). 150p. (Orig.). 1994. pap. 14.95 (*1-882758-01-3*) N P Finan Systs.

Starting Your Home Based Business. Linda Pinson. 1995. pap. text ed. 34.95 incl. cd-rom (*0-7931-1693-7*, 1800-2801) Dearborn Trade.

S

S

Starting Your New Business: A Guide for Entrepreneurs. rev. ed. Charles L. Martin. Ed. by Michael G. Crisp. LC 91-77079. (Fifty-Minute Ser.). (Illus.). 103p. 1992. pap. 10.95 (*1-56052-144-9*) Crisp Pubns.

Starting Your New Job. Los Angeles Unified School District Staff. (Project Get That Job Ser.). (Illus.). 48p. (Orig.). (YA). (gr. 7-12). 1990. student ed. 4.95 (*1-56119-096-9*); teacher ed. 1.95 (*1-56119-097-7*) Educ Pr MD.

Starting Your New Job, Set. Los Angeles Unified School District Staff. (Project Get That Job Ser.). (Illus.). 48p. (Orig.). (YA). (gr. 7-12). 1990. student ed., teacher ed. 44.95 (*1-56119-098-5*) Educ Pr MD.

Starting Your Own Big Business with Venture Capital. William A. Gilmartin. LC 95-61389. (Illus.). 128p. (Orig.). 1995. pap. 24.95 (*0-936029-39-0*) Western Bk Journ.

Starting Your Own Business. Granary Pr Ltd Staff. 30p. (C). 1986. 75.00 (*0-86236-030-7*, Pub. by Granary UK) St Mut.

Starting Your Own Business. LMP, Inc. Staff & Love. 140p. 1996. per., pap. text ed. 29.95 (*0-7872-1873-1*) Kendall-Hunt.

***Starting Your Own Business.** James J. Pearce. (Orig.). 1996. pap. 15.95 (*0-9640133-6-3*) Rhapsody.

Starting Your Own Business: An Easy-To-Follow Guide for the New Entrepreneur. Joan Sotkin. (Orig.). 1993. pap. 11.95 (*1-881002-84-5*) Build Your Busn.

Starting Your Own Business: No Money Down. M. John Storey. 266p. 1988. pap. text ed. 19.95 (*0-471-63839-0*) Wiley.

Starting Your Own Garment Graphics Business. Robert T. Jordan. 74p. 1995. pap. 19.95 (*0-944094-12-0*) ST Pubns.

Starting Your Own Law Firm: Costs, Space Alternatives, Client Development, & Income Techniques. (Commercial Law & Practice Course Handbook Ser.: Vol. 642). 186p. 1992. 70.00 (*0-685-65487-7*, A4-4401) PLI.

Starting Your Own Marketing Business. 2nd ed. Vivian K. Ely & Michael Barnes. Ed. by Eugene L. Dorr. (Occupational Manuals & Projects in Marketing Ser.). (Illus.). (J). (gr. 11-12). 1978. text ed. 12.28 (*0-07-019307-X*) McGraw.

Starting Your Own Mediation Practice: A Workbook. Sarah C. Grebe et al. 1985. 29.95 (*0-9617319-0-7*) CasaMar Ent.

Starting Your Own Mediation Practice: A Workbook. rev. ed. Martin Kranitz et al. (C). 1992. write for info. (*0-9617319-1-5*) CasaMar Ent.

Starting Your Own Patient Advisory Council. Francine Early & Milton H. Seifert, Jr. 39p. (Orig.). 1981. pap. text ed. 9.00 (*0-9617590-0-3*) MD Pub.

Starting Your Own Software Company. Mirbach. 1991. pap. 49.95 (*0-13-845504-X*) P-H.

Starting Your Own Successful Indian Business. Steve Robinson & Stephen Hogan. 160p. 1991. pap. 45.00 (*0-945253-08-7*) Thornsbury Bailey Brown.

Starting Your Personal Fitness Program. Ann Ward & James M. Rippe. LC 65-10408. (Illus.). 32p. 1988. pap. text ed. 1.20 (*0-397-50875-1*, Lippnctt) Lppncott-Raven.

Starting Your Tropical Aquarium. Herbert R. Axelrod. (Illus.). 288p. 1986. 11.95 (*0-86622-697-4*, PS-840) TFH Pubns.

Startling Jungle: Colour & Scent in the Romantic Garden. Stephen Lacey. LC 88-46166. (Illus.). 253p. 1989. reprint ed. 19.95 (*0-87923-712-0*) Godine.

Startling New Facts about Osteoporosis: Why Calcium Alone Does Not Prevent Bone Disease. rev. ed. Betty Kamen. (Illus.). 42p. 1989. pap. 2.95 (*0-944501-02-8*) Nutrition Encounter.

Startup: A Silicon Valley Adventure. Jerry Kaplan. LC 94-45110. (Illus.). 322p. 1995. 22.95 (*0-395-71133-9*) HM.

Startup: A Silicon Valley Adventure. Jerry Kaplan. 352p. 1996. pap. 12.95 (*0-14-025731-4*) Viking Penguin.

Startup: An Entrepreneur's Guide to Launching & Managing a New Venture. LC 88-92349. 200p. (C). 1989. pap. 19.95 (*0-9621634-1-4*); text ed. 24.95 (*0-9621634-0-6*) Rock Beach Pr.

Starvation Camp. Bill Pronzini. LC 93-8123. (Mystery Scene Bks.). 192p. 1994. pap. 21.00 (*0-913960-25-X*); lib. bdg. 31.00 (*0-913960-24-1*) Borgo Pr.

Starvation Heights: The True Story of an American Doctor & the Murder of a British Heiress. Gregg Olsen. 440p. (Orig.). 1997. mass mkt. 6.50 (*0-446-60341-4*) Warner Bks.

Starvation in Bacteria. Ed. by Staffan Kjelleberg. LC 93-21918. 1993. 75.00 (*0-306-44430-5*, Plenum Pr) Plenum.

Starved Rock Murders. Steve Stout. (Illus.). 210p. 1982. pap. 6.95 (*0-9609296-0-6*) Utica Hse.

Starved Rock Stories: Selected Histories of North Central Illinois. Steve Stout. (Illus.). 240p. (Orig.). 1996. pap. 19.99 (*0-9609296-1-4*) Utica Hse.

Starving Artists' Cookbook. Betty Guernsey & Richard Dorian. LC 93-93611. (Illus.). 144p. (Orig.). 1993. pap. 14.95 (*0-9691172-1-3*) Marincourt Pr.

Starving Artists' Cookbook: Food, Sex, Art. Paul Lamarre & Melissa Wolf. (Illus.). 162p. (Orig.). (C). 1991. pap. 60.00 (*0-9619021-1-6*, TXU 290827) Eidia Bks.

Starving for Attention: A Young Woman's Struggle with & Triumph over Anorexia Nervosa. 2nd rev. ed. Cherry B. O'Neill. Ed. by Nathan Unseth. 240p. 1992. pap. 12.95 (*0-89638-274-5*) Hazelden.

Starving in the Silences: An Exploration of Anorexia Nervosa. Matra Robertson. LC 92-16188. 125p. (C). 1992. pap. 15.00 (*0-8147-7435-0*); text ed. 28.00 (*0-8147-7434-2*) NYU Pr.

Starving People: Life & Death in West Clare, 1845-1851. Ignatius Murphy. 112p. 1996. pap. 13.50 (*0-7165-2582-8*, Pub. by Irish Acad Pr IE) Intl Spec Bk.

***Starving People: Life & Death in West Clare, 1845-1851.** Ignatius Murphy. (Illus.). 112p. 1996. pap. 11.95 (*0-7165-2587-9*, Pub. by Irish Acad Pr IE) Intl Spec Bk.

Starving Poets' Cookbook. Ed. by Ron Offen. LC 94-90594. 68p. 1994. per., pap. 10.00 (*0-9643296-0-3*) Free Lunch.

Starving Students' Cookbook. Dede Napoli & Bill Reynolds. 144p. 1984. mass mkt. 6.95 (*0-446-38145-4*) Warner Bks.

Starving Students' Cookbook. rev. ed. Dede Hall. (Illus.). 192p. (Orig.). 1994. pap. 9.99 (*0-446-39530-7*) Warner Bks.

Starving to Death in a Sea of Objects: The Anorexia Nervosa Syndrome. John A. Sours. LC 80-68043. 464p. 1992. pap. 30.00 (*0-87668-435-5*) Aronson.

***Starwalking: Shamanic Practices for Traveling into the Night Sky.** Page Bryant. LC 97-13044. (Illus.). 408p. (Orig.). 1997. pap. 18.95 (*1-879181-36-3*) Bear & Co.

Starwalking with Sarah: And Other Essays. Steve Pollick. (Illus.). 144p. (Orig.). 1994. pap. 7.95 (*0-9614554-1-1*) Toledo Blade.

Starwatch. David Baker. (Today's World in Space Bks.: Set 11). (Illus.). 48p. (J). (gr. 3-8). 1989. lib. bdg. 18.60 (*0-86592-400-7*); lib. bdg. 13.95 (*0-685-58637-5*) Rourke Corp.

Starweb - Heroic Fantasy Set. Rick Loomis. 1988. 5.00 (*0-940244-79-9*) Flying Buffalo.

Starweb Rulebook. Rich Loomis. 1988. 2.00 (*0-940244-76-4*) Flying Buffalo.

Starwick Episodes. Thomas Wolfe. Ed. by Richard S. Kennedy. LC 94-10619. (Southern Literary Studies). (Illus.). xi, 128p. 1994. pap. 11.95 (*0-8071-1975-X*); text ed. 25.00 (*0-8071-1929-6*) La State U Pr.

Starwolves: Battle of the Ring. Thorarinn Gunnarsson. 240p. (Orig.). 1989. mass mkt. 4.50 (*0-445-20908-9*) Warner Bks.

Staryi Parizh, Monmartr. 2nd ed. Andrei Sedykh, pseud. LC 85-60443. (Illus.). 365p. (RUS.). 1985. reprint ed. pap. 16.00 (*0-89830-096-7*) Russica Pubs.

Stasi: The East German Intelligence & Security Service, 1917-89. David Childs & Richard Popplewell. LC 96-35553. 253p. (C). 1996. 45.00 (*0-8147-1551-6*) NYU Pr.

Stasi Slut. (Orig.). 1992. mass mkt. 4.95 (*1-56333-050-4*) Masquerade.

Stasimon. Walther Kranz. vi, 325p. 1988. write for info. (*3-615-00035-8*) G Olms Pubs.

Stat! Medical Office Emergency Manual. Jeryll A. Tuttle-Yoder & Susan A. Fraser-Nobbe. LC 95-14211. 304p. 1996. text ed. 24.95 (*0-8273-6489-X*) Delmar.

STAT: The Laboratory's Role. Kathleen Sazama & Mary G. Haugh. LC 86-17353. 89p. 1986. pap. text ed. 28.00 (*0-89189-210-9*) Am Soc Clinical.

Stat, Dynam & Kinetic Theory. Hecht. (C). 1995. text ed. write for info. (*0-7167-2058-2*) W H Freeman.

STAT Facts: The Clinical Pocket Reference for Nurses. Ed. by Brenda W. Holloway et al. LC 95-10795. (Illus.). 508p. (C). 1995. pap. text ed. 19.95 (*0-8036-0023-2*) Davis Co.

STAT for Women in the Health Professions: Special Techniques in Assertiveness Training. 4th rev. ed. Melodie Chenevert. LC 93-26505. Orig. Title: STAT Special Techniques in Assertiveness Training for Women in the Health Professions. 192p. (C). (gr. 13). 1993. pap. text ed. 19.95 (*0-8016-7233-3*) Mosby Yr Bk.

Stat Jordan: The Complete Statistical Career of Michael Jordan & Other Basketball Facts. J. James Patrick. 1995. pap. 7.95 (*0-533-11322-9*) Vantage.

STAT! Medical Office Emergency Manual. Jeryll A. Tuttle-Yoder. (Medical Assisting Ser.). 1996. teacher ed. 14.95 (*0-8273-7090-3*) Delmar.

Stat-Power: Statistical Design Analysis System. James L. Bavry. 1991. ring bd. 30.00 (*0-89498-031-9*) Sci Ware.

STAT Special Techniques in Assertiveness Training for Women in the Health Professions see STAT for Women in the Health Professions: Special Techniques in Assertiveness Training

Stat Star Workbook. (C). 24.95 (*0-9627565-0-4*) Academy SW.

Stat Star Workbook & Laboratory Manual. 2nd ed. (C). 19.95 (*0-9627565-1-2*) Academy SW.

Stat 101: Software for Statistics Instruction. Minitab Inc. Staff. 200p. (C). 1993. pap. text ed. write for info. incl. disk (*0-201-59087-5*); pap. text ed. write for info. incl. disk (*0-201-59088-3*) Addison-Wesley.

Stata Graphics Editor Reference Manual. (Illus.). 79p. (Orig.). 1989. pap. 25.00 (*1-881228-04-5*) Stata Corp.

***Stata Reference Manual Vol. I A-F: Release 5.0.** (Illus.). 465p. 1996. pap. text ed. write for info. (*1-881228-27-4*) Stata Corp.

***Stata Reference Manual Vol. II G-O: Release 5.0.** (Illus.). 661p. 1996. pap. text ed. write for info. (*1-881228-28-2*) Stata Corp.

***Stata Reference Manual Vol. III P-Z: Release 5.0.** (Illus.). 691p. 1996. pap. text ed. write for info. (*1-881228-29-0*) Stata Corp.

Stata Reference Manual: Release 4.0, 3 vols. Incl. Vol. I. . 458p. (Orig.). 1995. pap. text ed. 25.00 (*1-881228-15-0*); Vol. II. . 604p. 1995. pap. text ed. 25.00 (*1-881228-16-9*); Vol. III. . 578p. (Orig.). 1995. pap. text ed. 25.00 (*1-881228-17-7*); 1995. 75.00 (*1-881228-14-2*) Stata Corp.

Stata Technical Bulletin Reprints, Vol. I. (Illus.). 228p. (Orig.). 1992. pap. 25.00 (*1-881228-05-3*) Stata Corp.

Stata Technical Bulletin Reprints, Vol. 2. (Illus.). 271p. (Orig.). 1993. pap. text ed. 25.00 (*1-881228-07-X*) Stata Corp.

Stata Technical Bulletin Reprints, Vol. III. (Illus.). 269p. (Orig.). 1994. reprint ed. pap. text ed. 25.00 (*1-881228-12-6*) Stata Corp.

Stata Technical Bulletin Reprints, Vol. 4. (Illus.). 269p. (Orig.). 1995. pap. text ed. write for info. (*1-881228-19-3*) Stata Corp.

***Stata Technical Bulletin Reprints, Vol. 5.** (Illus.). 238p. 1996. pap. text ed. write for info. (*1-881228-21-5*) Stata Corp.

***Stata Technical Bulletin Reprints, Vol. 6.** (Illus.). 1997. pap. text ed. write for info. (*1-881228-30-4*) Stata Corp.

***Stata User's Guide.** (Illus.). 385p. 1996. pap. text ed. write for info. (*1-881228-25-8*) Stata Corp.

StataQuest. J. Theodore Anagnoson & Richard E. DeLeon. 253p. 1994. pap. 17.95 (*0-534-23676-6*); pap. 18.75 incl. 3.5 hd (*0-534-23677-4*); pap. 26.95 incl. 5.25 hd (*0-534-23678-2*); pap. 25.95 incl. disk (*0-534-23679-0*) Wadsworth Pub.

StataQuest 4. J. Theodore Anagnoson & Richard E. DeLeon. (Statistics Software Ser.). (C). 1997. pap. text ed. 26.95 (*0-534-52137-1*) Wadsworth Pub.

StataQuest 4. 2nd ed. J. Theodore Anagnoson & Richard E. DeLeon. (C). 1996. pap. text ed. 26.95 incl. 3.5 hd (*0-534-26545-6*); pap. text ed. 27.95 incl. disk (*0-534-26546-4*) Wadsworth Pub.

StataQuest 4. 2nd ed. J. Theodore Anagnoson & Richard E. DeLeon. (C). 1997. pap. text ed., pap. 27.95 incl. mac hd (*0-534-26544-8*) Wadsworth Pub.

StataQuest 4 Text Companion. J. Theodore Anagnoson & Richard E. DeLeon. (Statistics Software Ser.). (C). 1997. pap. text ed. 11.95 (*0-534-52138-X*) Wadsworth Pub.

Stataquest 4 Text Companion Dos Version. 2nd ed. J. Theodore Anagnoson. (Statistics Software Ser.). 1996. pap. 11.95 (*0-534-26548-0*) Wadsworth Pub.

Stataquest 4 Text Companion Mac Version. 2nd ed. J. Theodore Anagnoson. (Statistics Software Ser.). 1997. pap. 11.95 (*0-534-26549-9*) Wadsworth Pub.

StatChoice: The Statistical Consulting Program. Lee Baer & David K. Ahern. 50p. 1988. student ed., ring bd. 189.00 incl. disk (*0-88416-590-6*, Yr Bk Med Pubs); student ed., ring bd. 189.00 incl. disk (*0-88416-589-2*, Yr Bk Med Pubs) Mosby Yr Bk.

StatConcepts: Visual Tour of Statistical Ideas. H. Joseph Newton & Jane Harvill. (Statistics Software Ser.). (C). 1997. pap. 29.95 (*0-534-26552-9*) Wadsworth Pub.

***State.** John Hall & John Ikenberry. Ed. by Frank Parkin. (Concepts in the Social Sciences Ser.). 136p. 1989. pap. 9.99 (*0-335-15574-X*, Open Univ Pr) Taylor & Francis.

State. Franz Oppenheimer. Tr. by John Gitterman from GER. 122p. 1975. pap. 12.95 (*0-919618-59-6*, Pub. by Black Rose Bks CN) Consort Bk Sales.

State. Franz Oppenheimer. 1984. lib. bdg. 250.00 (*0-87700-647-4*) Revisionist Pr.

***State.** Franz Oppenheimer. Tr. by John Gitterman from GER. 148p. 1997. reprint ed. 22.95 (*0-930073-22-3*) Fox & Wilkes.

***State.** Franz Oppenheimer. Tr. by John Gitterman from GER. 148p. 1997. reprint ed. pap. 12.95 (*0-930073-23-1*) Fox & Wilkes.

State, 3 vols., Set. John Hall. (Critical Concepts Ser.). 1772p. (C). (gr. 13). 1993. text ed. 465.00 (*0-415-08683-3*, B3792) Routledge.

State: Concepts in Social Thought. John A. Hall & G. John Ikenberry. 107p. (Orig.). 1989. pap. text ed. 13.95 (*0-8166-1796-1*) U of Minn Pr.

State: Its Historic Role. rev. ed. Peter Kropotkin. Tr. by Vernon Richards from FRE. 60p. (C). 1987. pap. 3.00 (*0-900384-33-6*) Left Bank.

State: Its History & Development Viewed Sociologically. Franz Oppenheimer. Tr. by John M. Gitterman. LC 73-172224. (Right Wing Individualist Tradition in America Ser.). 1978. reprint ed. 25.95 (*0-405-00433-8*) Ayer.

State: Its Nature, Development & Prospects. Gianfranco Poggi. LC 90-70700. 222p. 1991. 35.00 (*0-8047-1849-0*); pap. 11.95 (*0-8047-1877-6*) Stanford U Pr.

State Accounts Auditor/Examiner of Municipal Affairs. Jack Rudman. (Career Examination Ser.: C-2367). 1994. pap. 39.95 (*0-8373-2367-3*) Natl Learn.

State Accounts of the County Lieutenants During the War of the Revolution, 1777-1789, Vol. 1, Pt. A. Ed. by William H. Egle. 387p. (Orig.). 1995. reprint ed. pap. text ed. 26.00 (*0-7884-0157-2*) Heritage Bk.

State Actions to Restructure Schools: The First Steps. Jane L. David & Michael Cohen. 51p. (Orig.). 1990. pap. text ed. 7.50 (*1-55877-101-8*) Natl Governor.

State-Administered Locally-Shared Taxes. Ruth G. Hutchinson. LC 68-58593. (Columbia University. Studies in the Social Sciences: No. 355). reprint ed. 20.00 (*0-404-51355-7*) AMS Pr.

State Administration in South Carolina. James K. Coleman. LC 70-76647. (Columbia University. Studies in the Social Sciences: No. 406). reprint ed. 29.50 (*0-404-51406-5*) AMS Pr.

State Administrative Law. L. Harold Levinson. write for info. (*0-318-59313-0*) Little.

State Administrative Officials Classified by Function 1991-92. Council of State Governments Staff. 300p. 1992. pap. 30.00 (*0-87292-962-0*, D-003-91) Coun State Govts.

State Administrative Officials Classified by Function, 1993-94. 336p. 1993. pap. 30.00 (*0-87292-979-5*, D-024-92) Coun State Govts.

State Administrative Rule Making. Arthur E. Bonfield. 704p. 1986. Lawyer's bk. 145.00 (*0-316-10122-2*) Little.

State Administrative Rule Making of Books & Supplies, Set. Arthur E. Bonfield. 1988. 145.00 (*0-316-10124-9*) Little.

State Against Democracy: In Search of Humane Governance. Rajni Kothari. 322p. 1989. 28.50 (*0-945257-16-3*) Apex Pr.

State Against Democracy in Search of Humane Governance. Rajni Kothari. (C). 1988. 41.00 (*81-202-0193-0*, Pub. by Ajanta II) S Asia.

State Against Development: The Experience of Post-1965 Zaire. Mondonga M. Mokoli. LC 91-47973. (Contributions in Afro-American & African Studies: No. 150). 168p. 1992. text ed. 47.95 (*0-313-28213-7*, MKD, Greenwood Pr) Greenwood.

State Against Society: Political Crises & Their Aftermath in East Central Europe. Grzegorz Ekiert. 448p. 1996. text ed. 59.50 (*0-691-01114-1*); pap. text ed. 19.95 (*0-691-01113-3*) Princeton U Pr.

***State Against the State: The Theory & Practice of the Coup d'Etat.** Eric Carlton. LC 96-43351. 256p. 1997. text ed. 68.95 (*1-85928-231-8*, Pub. by Ashgate UK) Ashgate Pub Co.

State Aid & the Division of Schooling in Australia. Dean Ashenden. 129p. (C). 1989. 65.00 (*0-7300-0672-7*, Pub. by Deakin Univ AT) St Mut.

State Aid for Educational Projects in the Public Schools. Lester N. Neulen. LC 73-177117. (Columbia University. Teachers College. Contributions to Education Ser.: No. 308). reprint ed. 37.50 (*0-404-55308-7*) AMS Pr.

State Aid to Local Governments in the 1980s. Steven D. Gold & Brenda M. Erickson. (Legislative Finance Papers: No. 63). 1988. pap. text ed. 10.00 (*1-55516-063-8*, 5101-63) Natl Conf State Legis.

State Aid to Railways in Missouri. John W. Million. Ed. by Stuart Bruchey. LC 80-1331. (Railroads Ser.). (Illus.). 1981. reprint ed. lib. bdg. 27.95 (*0-405-13805-9*) Ayer.

State Aide to Higher Education. Herbert B. Adams. (Principle Works of Herbert Baxter Adams). 1989. reprint ed. lib. bdg. 79.00 (*0-7812-1480-7*) Rprt Serv.

State Aids & Public Enterprises. Daniel Alexander et al. 300p. 1994. pap. text ed. 193.00 (*0-406-00638-5*, UK) MICHIE.

***State & Administration in Japan & Germany: A Comparative Perspective on Continuity & Change.** Ed. by Michio Muramatsu & Frieder Naschold. LC 96-30384. (Studies in Organization: Vol. 75). xiv, 349p. (C). 1996. text ed. 78.95 (*3-11-014462-X*) De Gruyter.

State & Agrarian Change in Zimbabwe's Communal Areas. Michael Drinkwater. LC 90-8934. 330p. 1991. text ed. 69.95 (*0-312-05350-9*) St Martin.

State & American Foreign Economic Policy. Ed. by G. John Ikenberry et al. LC 88-47736. (Cornell Studies in Political Economy). 256p. 1988. 39.95 (*0-8014-2229-9*); pap. 14.95 (*0-8014-9524-5*) Cornell U Pr.

State & Business in India: A Historical Perspective. Dwijendra Tripathi. (C). 1987. 26.00 (*81-85054-26-6*, Pub. by Manohar II) S Asia.

State & Business in Modern Turkey: A Comparative Study. Ayse Bugra. LC 93-18517. (SUNY Series in Social & Economic History of the Middle East). 328p. 1994. text ed. 64.50 (*0-7914-1787-5*); pap. text ed. 21.95 (*0-7914-1788-3*) State U NY Pr.

State & Capital: A Marxist Debate. Ed. by John Holloway & Sol Picciotto. LC 78-65361. 226p. 1979. text ed. 18.95 (*0-292-77551-2*) U of Tex Pr.

State & Capital Accumulation in Latin America: Brazil, Chile, Mexico. Ed. by Christian Anglade & Carlos Fortin. LC 84-12015. (Latin American Ser.). (Illus.). 272p. 1985. 49.95 (*0-8229-1144-2*) U of Pittsburgh Pr.

State & Capital Accumulation in Latin America, Vol. 2: Argentina, Bolivia, Colombia, Ecuador, Peru, Uruguay, Venezuela. Ed. by Christian Anglade & Carlos Fortin. LC 84-12015. (Latin American Ser.). 304p. 1990. 49.95 (*0-8229-1158-2*) U of Pittsburgh Pr.

State & Capital in Chile. Eduardo Silva. 272p. (C). 1996. text ed. 59.00 (*0-8133-2751-2*) Westview.

State & Capitalism in Israel. Amir Ben-Porat. LC 92-42670. (Contributions in Economics & Economic History Ser.: No. 147). 224p. 1993. text ed. 59.95 (*0-313-28149-1*, BEZ, Greenwood Pr) Greenwood.

State & Capitalist Development in Africa: Declining Political Economies. Julius E. Nyang Oro. LC 88-34030. 189p. 1989. text ed. 49.95 (*0-275-93120-X*, C3120, Praeger Pubs) Greenwood.

State & Church in Early Russia, from the Tenth to the Thirteenth Centuries. Yaroslav N. Shchapov. Tr. by Vic Shneyerson from RUS. LC 93-1941. 248p. (C). 1993. lib. bdg. 50.00 (*0-89241-499-5*) Caratzas.

State & City Guide Books, 61 vols., Set. Federal Writers' Project Staff. (American Guidebook Ser.). reprint ed. lib. bdg. 5,201.00 (*0-403-02249-5*) Somerset Pub.

State & Civil Authority in Pakistan: Politics of Authority, Ideology, & Ethnicity. Iftikhar H. Malik. LC 96-27847. (St. Antony's Ser.). 1997. text ed. 65.00 (*0-312-16421-1*) St Martin.

State & Civil Society: Explorations in Political Theory. Neera Chandhoke. 1995. 26.00 (*0-8039-9246-7*) Sage.

State & Class in Africa. Ed. by Nelson Kasfir. 132p. 1984. 45.00 (*0-7146-3239-2*, BHA-03239, Pub. by F Cass Pubs UK) Intl Spec Bk.

State & Class in Turkey: A Study in Capitalist Development. Caglar Keyder. 252p. 1987. text ed. 39.95 (*0-86091-165-9*, Pub. by Verso UK) Routledge Chapman & Hall.

State & Class in Turkey: A Study in Capitalist Development. Caglar Keyder. 252p. (C). 1987. pap. text ed. 20.00 (*0-86091-877-7*, Pub. by Vrso UK) Norton.

State & Community During the Aftermath of Mexico City's 1984 Gas Explosion. Kirsten Johnson. (Special Publications Ser.: No. 13). 48p. 1985. 4.00 (*0-614-01775-0*) Natural Hazards.

State & Conflict in the Middle East: Emergence of the Post-Colonial State. Gabriel Ben-Dor. LC 82-24616. 288p. 1983. text ed. 34.95 (*0-275-90946-8*, C0946, Praeger Pubs) Greenwood.

State & Cosmos in the Art of Tenochtitlan. Richard F. Townsend. LC 79-63726. (Studies in Pre-Columbian Art & Archaeology: No. 20). (Illus.). 78p. 1992. reprint ed. pap. 12.00 (*0-88402-083-5*, TOSCP) Dumbarton Oaks.

An Asterisk (*) at the beginning of an entry indicates that the title is appearing in BIP for the first time.

State & Countryside: Development Policy & Agrarian Politics in Latin America. Merilee S. Grindle. LC 85-8081. (Studies in Development). 272p. 1986. text ed. 42.50 (*0-8018-3278-0*); pap. text ed. 15.95 (*0-8018-2935-6*) Johns Hopkins.

State & County Detailed Population Estimates, 1991: Pennsylvania. Pennsylvania State Data Center Staff. 100p. 1993. pap. 25.00 (*0-939667-21-5*) Penn State Data Ctr.

State & Cultural Transformation. 1991. write for info. (*0-318-68405-5*, 91.III.A.5) UN.

State & Democracy: Revitalizing America's Government. Jeff Faux et al. (Alternative Policies for America Ser.). 256p. 1988. text ed. 49.95 (*0-415-90045-X*, Routledge NY); pap. text ed. 17.95 (*0-415-90076-X*, Routledge NY) Routledge.

State & Development in Ethiopia. Girma Kebbede. LC 91-18846. 184p. (C). 1992. text ed. 45.00 (*0-391-03731-5*) Humanities.

***State & Development in the Third World.** Ed. by Atul Kohli. LC 86-5045. (World Politics Reader Ser.). 297p. 1986. reprint ed. pap. 84.70 (*0-608-02939-4*, 2064005) Bks Demand.

State & Diplomacy in Early Modern Japan: Asia in the Development of the Tokugawa Bakufu. 2nd ed. Ronald P. Toby. LC 91-65279. (Illus.). 341p. 1992. 47.50 (*0-8047-1951-9*); pap. 15.95 (*0-8047-1952-7*) Stanford U Pr.

State & Diplomatic Immunity. 3rd rev. ed. Charles Lewis. 224p. 1990. 120.00 (*1-85044-254-1*) LLP.

State & Discrimination: The Other Side of the Cold War. Lynn Turgeon. LC 89-6437. (Illus.). 168p. (C). (gr. 13). 1989. text ed. 53.95 (*0-87332-532-X*) M E Sharpe.

State & Domestic Agricultural Markets in Nicaragua: From Interventionism to Neo-Liberalism. Max Spoor. LC 94-47458. 298p. 1995. text ed. 65.00 (*0-312-12610-7*) St Martin.

State & Economic Development: Lessons from the Far East. Ed. by Robert Fitzgerald. LC 94-44155. (Studies in Far Eastern Business). (Illus.). 152p. 1995. 35.00 (*0-7146-4638-5*, Pub. by F Cass Pubs UK); pap. 19.50 (*0-7146-4159-6*, Pub. by F Cass Pubs UK) Intl Spec Bk.

State & Economic Enterprise in Japan. Ed. by William W. Lockwood. LC 65-15386. (Studies in the Modernization of Japan). 763p. reprint ed. pap. 180.00 (*0-8357-9514-4*, 2015225) Bks Demand.

State & Economic Knowledge: The American & British Experiences. Barry E. Supple. (Woodrow Wilson Center Ser.). 500p. (C). 1990. text ed. 74.95 (*0-521-39424-4*) Cambridge U Pr.

State & Economic Transformation: The Taiwan Case. Chien-Kuo Pang. LC 91-41620. (Developing Economies of the Third World Ser.). 336p. 1992. text ed. 50.00 (*0-8153-0635-0*) Garland.

State & Economics in the Middle East. Alfred Bonne. LC 72-11325. (Illus.). 452p. 1973. reprint ed. text ed. 79.50 (*0-8371-6661-6*, BOSE, Greenwood Pr) Greenwood.

State & Economy in New Zealand. Ed. by Brian Roper & Chris Rudd. (Oxford Readings in New Zealand Politics Ser.: No. 2). (Illus.). 292p. 1993. pap. 45.00 (*0-19-558273-X*) OUP.

State & Educational Change: Essays in the History of Education & Pedagogy. Simon. (C). 1995. pap. 29.95 (*0-85315-806-1*, Pub. by Lawrence & Wishart UK) NYU Pr.

State & Educational Policy. Roger Dale. 176p. 1989. 90.00 (*0-335-09553-4*, Open Univ Pr); pap. 32.00 (*0-335-09552-6*, Open Univ Pr) Taylor & Francis.

State & Enterprise: Canadian Manufacturing & the Federal Government, 1917-1931. Tom Traves. (State & Economic Life Ser.). 1979. pap. 11.95 (*0-8020-6353-5*) U of Toronto Pr.

***State & Ethnic Politics in South East Asia.** David Brown. 376p. (C). 1997. pap. 19.95 (*0-415-12792-0*) Routledge.

State & Family in Singapore: Restructuring an Industrial Society. Janet W. Salaff. LC 87-47962. (Anthropology of Contemporary Issues Ser.). (Illus.). 320p. 1988. 45.00 (*0-8014-2140-3*) Cornell U Pr.

State & Fate of Publishing: A "Flair" Symposium. Ed. by Dave Oliphant. (Illus.). 1995. pap. 15.00 (*0-87959-134-X*) U of Tex H Ransom Ctr.

State & Federal Administrative Law: Cases & Materials. Arthur E. Bonfield & Michael R. Asimow. (American Casebook Ser.). 826p. 1989. reprint ed. text ed. 44.00 (*0-314-50388-9*) West Pub.

State & Federal Administrative Law: 1993 Supplement. Arthur E. Bonfield & Michael R. Asimow. (American Casebook Ser.). 185p. 1993. pap. text ed. 12.00 (*0-314-02697-5*) West Pub.

State & Federal Corrupt-Practices Legislation. Earl R. Sikes. reprint ed. 42.50 (*0-404-06004-8*) AMS Pr.

State & Federal EEO Compliance Encyclopedia, 3 vols., Set. Ed. by Lynn Atkinson. 1989. ring bd. 200.00 (*0-685-53350-6*, P998) Busn Legal Reports.

State & Federal Environmental Criminal Enforcement Statutes, 2 vols. 434p. 1991. 50.00 (*0-317-05912-2*) Natl Attys General.

State & Federal Environmental Criminal Enforcement Statutes. 2 vols. 434p. 1991. 100.00 (*0-317-05911-4*, PB13) Natl Attys General.

State & Federal Exploratory Wells & Core Holes Drilled off the West Coast of Continental U. S. A. Prior to 1974. 1975. 35.00 (*0-686-28277-9*) Munger Oil.

State & Federal Government in Switzerland. John M. Vincent. LC 78-64253. (Johns Hopkins University. Studies in the Social Sciences. Thirtieth Ser. 1912: 9). reprint ed. 42.50 (*0-404-61357-8*) AMS Pr.

State & Federal OSHA: What You Need to Know. 24p. 1994. pap. 7.50 (*0-88711-212-9*) Am Trucking Assns.

State & Federal Prisons: Factors That Affect Construction & Operations Costs. (Illus.). 40p. (Orig.). (C). 1993. pap. text ed. 20.00 (*1-56806-897-2*) DIANE Pub.

State & Federal Regulation of National Advertising. J. Howard Beales & Timothy J. Muris. LC 92-38187. (Studies in Regulation & Federalism). 150p. (Orig.). 1993. pap. 9.75 (*0-8447-3824-7*, AEI Pr) Am Enterprise.

***State & Federal Regulation of Private Schools.** Keene. 1997. 125.00 (*0-8342-0948-9*) Aspen Pub.

State & Future Directions of Acute Myocardial Infarction. A. Raineri et al. 484p. 1988. text ed. 287.00 (*3-7186-4808-3*) Gordon & Breach.

State & Government Employee Unions in France. Frederic Meyers. LC 73-634398. (Comparative Studies in Public Employment Labor Relations Ser.). 1971. 10.00 (*0-87736-007-3*); pap. 5.00 (*0-87736-008-1*) U of Mich Inst Labor.

State & Government in Medieval Islam: An Introduction to the Study of Islamic Political Theory; the Jurists. Ann K. Lambton. (London Oriental Ser.: No. 36). 382p. 1981. 65.00 (*0-19-713600-1*) OUP.

State & Government in the Federal Republic of Germany: The Executive at Work. N. Johnson. (Governments of Western Europe Ser.). 240p. 1983. text ed. 131.00 (*0-08-030188-6*, CRC Reprint) Franklin.

State & Higher Education. Brian Salter & Ted Tapper. LC 93-32137. (Woburn Education Ser.). 242p. (C). 1994. 40.00 (*0-7130-0190-9*, Pub. by Woburn Pr UK) Intl Spec Bk.

State & Higher Education. Brian Salter & Ted Tapper. LC 93-32137. (Woburn Education Ser.). (C). 1994. pap. 20.00 (*0-7130-4021-1*, Pub. by Woburn Pr UK) Intl Spec Bk.

State & Higher Education. Herbert B. Adams. (Principle Works of Herbert Baxter Adams). 1989. reprint ed. lib. bdg. 79.00 (*0-7812-1474-2*) Rprt Serv.

State & Ideology in the Middle East & Pakistan. Ed. by Fred Halliday & Hamza Alavi. 320p. (C). 1988. 27.00 (*0-85345-734-4*); pap. 16.00 (*0-85345-735-2*) Monthly Rev.

State & Industry in South Korea: The Limits of the Authoritarian State. Jong-Chen Rhee. LC 93-43156. 224p. (C). (gr. 13). 1994. text ed. 85.00 (*0-415-11102-1*, B4408, Routledge NY) Routledge.

State & Instability in the South. Ed. by Caroline Thomas & Paikiasothy Saravanamuttu. LC 88-28312. 208p. 1989. text ed. 45.00 (*0-312-02447-9*) St Martin.

State & Intellectual in Imperial Japan: The Public Man in Crisis. Andrew E. Barshay. 335p. 1991. pap. 16.00 (*0-520-07393-2*) U CA Pr.

State & International Aviation in India: Performance & Policy on the Eve of Aviation Globalization. Baldev R. Nayar. (C). 1994. 34.00 (*81-7304-093-1*, Pub. by Manohar II) S Asia.

State & Its Critics, 2 vols., Set. Ed. by Andrew Levine. (Schools of Thought in Politics Ser.: Vol. 3). 832p. 1992. text ed. 250.00 (*1-85278-413-X*) E Elgar.

State & Its Enemies in Papua New Guinea: Fighting Lucifer. Alexander Wanek. (SIAS Monographs: No. 64). (Illus.). 352p. (C). 1996. pap. text ed. 45.00 (*0-7007-0304-7*, Pub. by Curzon Press UK) UH Pr.

State & Its Servants: Administration in Ottoman & Modern Egypt. Ed. by Nelly Hanna. 160p. 1996. 35.00 (*977-424-364-1*, Pub. by Am Univ Cairo Pr UA) Col U Pr.

State & Justice: An Essay in Political Theory. Milton Fisk. 408p. (C). 1989. text ed. 80.00 (*0-521-37473-1*) Cambridge U Pr.

State & Justice: An Essay in Political Theory. Milton Fisk. 408p. (C). 1989. pap. text ed. 32.95 (*0-521-38966-6*) Cambridge U Pr.

State & Labor in Modern America. Melvyn Dubofsky. LC 93-21404. xx, 322p. 1994. 37.50 (*0-8078-2125-X*); pap. 16.95 (*0-8078-4436-5*) U of NC Pr.

State & Labor in Modern Japan. Sheldon Garon. LC 86-30890. 326p. 1987. 50.00 (*0-520-05983-2*); pap. 16.95 (*0-520-06838-6*) U CA Pr.

State & Labor Market. Ed. by S. Rosenberg. LC 89-33437. (Studies & Work & Industry). (Illus.). 276p. 1989. 42.50 (*0-306-43170-X*, Plenum Pr) Plenum.

State & Law in Eastern Asia. Ed. by Leslie Palmier. LC 96-21350. 166p. 1996. text ed. 62.95 (*1-85521-781-3*, Pub. by Dartmth Pub UK) Ashgate Pub Co.

State & Law in the Development Process: Problem Solving & Institutional Change. Ann Seidman. 1995. text ed. 22.95 (*0-333-60148-3*, Pub. by Macm UK) St Martin.

State & Local Administration of School Transportation. Roe L. Johns. LC 76-176911. (Columbia University. Teachers College. Contributions to Education Ser.: No. 330). reprint ed. 37.50 (*0-404-55330-3*) AMS Pr.

State & Local Experience with Drug Paraphernalia Laws. Kerry M. Healey. 139p. (Orig.). (C). 1993. pap. text ed. 35.00 (*0-7881-0012-2*) DIANE Pub.

State & Local Finance. Oliver S. Oldman. Date not set. text ed. 22.00 (*0-88277-396-8*) West Pub.

State & Local Finance. Ed. by William E. Mitchell & Ingo Walter. LC 77-110554. 380p. reprint ed. pap. 108.30 (*0-317-09323-1*, 2012396) Bks Demand.

State & Local Finance: The Pressures of the 1980s: Proceedings of a Symposium Sponsored by the Committee on Taxation, Resources & Economic Development (TRED) at the Lincoln Institute of Land Policy, Cambridge MA, 1980. Ed. by George F. Break. LC 83-47757. (Publications of the Committee on Taxation, Resources & Economic Development: Vol. 12). 255p. 1983. reprint ed. pap. 72.70 (*0-608-01984-4*, 2062639) Bks Demand.

State & Local Government, 3 Vols. Bowman. (C). 1995. suppl. ed., teacher ed., pap. 11.96 (*0-395-73042-2*) HM.

State & Local Government, 3 Vols. Bowman. (C). 1995. text ed. 52.76 (*0-395-73041-4*) HM.

State & Local Government: Politics & Public Policies. 2nd ed. David C. Saffell. (Political Science Ser.). 384p. 1981. pap. text ed. write for info. (*0-201-06568-1*) Addison-Wesley.

State & Local Government: Politics & Public Policies. 5th ed. David C. Saffell. LC 92-23653. 1992. pap. text ed. write for info. (*0-07-054477-8*) McGraw.

***State & Local Government: Politics & Public Policies.** 6th ed. David C. Saffell & Harry Basehart. LC 97-18734. 1997. write for info. (*0-07-057192-9*) McGraw.

State & Local Government Administration. Jack Rabin & Don Dodd. (Public Administration & Public Policy Ser.: Vol. 28). 464p. 1985. 59.75 (*0-8247-7355-1*) Dekker.

State & Local Government & Politics: A Simulation. 3rd ed. Morris J. Levitt. 136p. 1993. spiral bd. 20.94 (*0-8403-8741-5*) Kendall-Hunt.

State & Local Government & Politics: Essential Readings. Ed. by Harry A. Bailey, Jr. & Jay M. Shafritz. LC 92-61960. 350p. (C). 1993. pap. text ed. 30.00 (*0-87581-372-0*) Peacock Pubs.

State & Local Government & Public-Private Partnerships: A Policy Issues Handbook. William G. Colman. LC 88-24627. (Illus.). 451p. 1989. text ed. 99.50 (*0-313-26206-3*, CLL, Greenwood Pr) Greenwood.

State & Local Government Civil Rights Liability, 2 vols. Ivan E. Bodensteiner & Rosalie B. Levinson. 1992. 185.00 (*0-318-36193-0*) Clark Boardman Callaghan.

State & Local Government Debt Financing, 3 vols., Set. Ed. by M. David Gelfand. LC 85-25550. 1992. 350.00 (*0-685-43446-X*) Clark Boardman Callaghan.

State & Local Government Environmental Liability. Joel A. Mintz. (Liability Prevention Ser.). 1994. write for info. (*0-615-00167-X*) Clark Boardman Callaghan.

State & Local Government Finance: A Selectively Annotated Bibliography, No. 783. Ed. by James J. Brown. 1975. 5.50 (*0-686-20351-8*, Sage Prdcls Pr) Sage.

State & Local Government Finance & Financial Management: A Compendium of Current Research. Municipal Finance Officers Association, Government Finance Research Center Staff. LC 78-70328. 690p. 1978. 18.00 (*0-686-84363-0*) Municipal.

State & Local Government Finance for the 1990's: A Case Study of Arizona. Ed. by Therese J. McGuire & Dana W. Naimark. 500p. (C). 1991. pap. text ed. write for info. (*1-879286-01-7*) AZ Bd Regents.

State & Local Government Fiscal Almanac 1982-MFOA Membership Directory. Municipal Finance Officers Association Staff. 400p. 1982. pap. 50.00 (*0-686-84339-8*) Municipal.

State & Local Government in a Changing Society. 2nd ed. Richard D. Bingham & David M. Hedge. 1991. text ed. write for info. (*0-07-005303-0*) McGraw.

State & Local Government in a Federal System. 3rd ed. Daniel R. Mandelker & Dawn Clark Netsch. (Contemporary Legal Education Ser.). 828p. 1990. 40.00 (*0-87473-584-X*) MICHIE.

State & Local Government in a Federal System. 3rd ed. Daniel R. Mandelker & Dawn Clark Netsch. (Contemporary Legal Education Ser.). 828p. 1992. Supplement 1992. suppl. ed. 6.00 (*0-685-57756-2*) MICHIE.

State & Local Government in America. 5th ed. Daniel R. Grant & Lloyd Omdahl. 576p. (C). 1987. text ed. write for info. (*0-697-06802-1*) Brown & Benchmark.

State & Local Government in America. 6th ed. Daniel R. Grant & Lloyd Omdahl. 480p. (C). 1992. student ed. write for info. (*0-697-13981-6*) Brown & Benchmark.

State & Local Government in America. 6th ed. Daniel R. Grant & Lloyd Omdahl. 480p. (C). 1992. text ed. write for info. (*0-697-11116-4*) Brown & Benchmark.

State & Local Government Political Dictionary. Jeffrey M. Elliot & Sheikh R. Ali. LC 87-18722. (Clio Dictionaries in Political Science Ser.: No. 12). 325p. 1987. lib. bdg. 49.00 (*0-87436-417-5*) ABC-CLIO.

State & Local Government Political Dictionary. Jeffrey M. Elliot & Sheikh R. Ali. LC 95-11397. (Reference Guides Ser.: No. 7). x, 325p. 1995. pap. 31.00 (*0-8095-1703-5*); lib. bdg. 41.00 (*0-8095-0703-X*) Borgo Pr.

State & Local Government Procurement: Developments in Legislation & Litigation. Louis F. DelDuca et al. LC 87-108173. 67p. 1986. pap. 8.95 (*0-89707-253-7*, 533-0025) Amer Bar Assn.

State & Local Government Purchasing. Council of State Governments Staff. LC 83-621513. (Publication Ser.: No. C3). 295p. (Orig.). reprint ed. pap. 84.10 (*0-7837-2661-9*, 2043023) Bks Demand.

State & Local Government Relations in North Carolina: Their Evolution & Current Status. 2nd ed. Ed. by Charles D. Liner. 251p. (C). 1995. pap. text ed. 30.00 (*1-56011-244-1*) Institute Government.

State & Local Government Responsibilities to Provide Medical Care for Indigents. Michael Dowell. (Illus.). 384p. (Orig.). 1985. pap. 25.00 (*0-941077-02-0*, 40,275) NCLS Inc.

State & Local Highway Finance: Where Does the Money Come from & Why Isn't There Enough? Ronald K. Snell. Ed. by Karen Hansen. (Legislative Finance Papers: No. 78). (Illus.). 24p. 1991. pap. text ed. 15.00 (*1-55516-078-6*, 5101-78) Natl Conf State Legis.

State & Local Industrial Policy Question. Ed. by Harvey A. Goldstein. LC 86-72373. (Illus.). 195p. (Orig.). (C). 1987. pap. 33.95 (*0-918286-46-8*) Planners Pr.

State & Local Influence over Offshore Oil Decisions. Marc J. Hershman et al. (Washington State & Offshore Oil & Gas Ser.). (Illus.). 297p. (Orig.). 1988. pap. 10.00 (*0-934539-06-5*, WSG88-4) Wash Sea Grant.

State & Local Issues in Transportation of Hazardous Waste Materials: Toward a National Strategy. Ed. by Mark D. Abkowitz & Kostas D. Zografos. LC 91-18477. 297p. 1991. pap. text ed. 33.00 (*0-87262-796-9*) Am Soc Civil Eng.

State & Local Law Enforcement Training Catalog. 55p. (Orig.). (C). 1993. pap. text ed. 20.00 (*1-56806-834-4*) DIANE Pub.

***State & Local Levels: FY 1993.** Arturo Perez. (Legislative Finance Papers). 12p. 1996. 30.00 (*1-55516-522-2*, 5101-0105) Natl Conf State Legis.

State & Local Money Laundering Prosecution: A Profile. 80p. 1993. 15.00 (*0-317-05916-5*, PB18) Natl Attys General.

State & Local Politics. Charles R. Adrian & Michael R. Fine. (Political Science Ser.). 420p. (Orig.). (C). 1991. text ed. 35.95 (*0-8304-1285-9*) Nelson-Hall.

State & Local Politics. Steven A. Peterson & Thomas H. Rasmussen. 352p. 1993. pap. text ed. 12.95 (*0-07-049671-4*) McGraw.

***State & Local Politics.** Schultze. (Miscellaneous/Catalogs Ser.). (C). 1988. pap. 33.00 (*0-314-28601-2*) West Pub.

State & Local Politics. Straayer. 1994. teacher ed., pap. text ed. 5.00 (*0-312-11142-8*) St Martin.

State & Local Politics. John A. Straayer et al. 512p. 1994. pap. text ed. 29.00 (*0-312-09104-4*) St Martin.

***State & Local Politics.** 2nd ed. Cole. Date not set. pap. text ed. write for info. (*0-312-17084-X*) St Martin.

State & Local Politics. 2nd ed. Straayer. Date not set. pap. text ed. write for info. (*0-312-14989-1*) St Martin.

***State & Local Politics.** 2nd ed. Straayer. Date not set. pap. text ed. write for info. (*0-312-15361-9*) St Martin.

State & Local Politics. 6th ed. David R. Berman. 432p. (C). 1990. pap. write for info. (*0-697-11130-X*) Brown & Benchmark.

State & Local Politics. 7th ed. David R. Berman. 464p. (C). 1993. per. write for info. (*0-697-12696-X*) Brown & Benchmark.

State & Local Politics. 8th ed. David R. Berman. LC 96-19264. 464p. (C). 1996. pap. text ed. 32.00 (*1-56324-767-4*) M E Sharpe.

State & Local Politics: Government by the People. 8th ed. James M. Burns et al. LC 95-23798. 1995. pap. text ed. 35.20 (*0-13-455866-9*) P-H.

State & Local Politics: The Great Entanglement. 5th ed. Robert S. Lorch. LC 94-17182. 448p. 1994. text ed. 62.00 (*0-13-109117-4*) P-H.

State & Local Politics: The Individual & the Governments. 2nd ed. W. B. Stouffer et al. (C). 1995. teacher ed. write for info. (*0-673-97072-8*) Addson-Wesley Educ.

State & Local Politics: The Individual & the Governments. 2nd ed. W. B. Stouffer et al. LC 95-31706. 576p. (C). 1996. text ed. 41.50 (*0-673-99661-1*) Addson-Wesley Educ.

State & Local Politics & Policy: Change & Reform. Michael J. Ross. (Illus.). 352p. (C). 1987. pap. text ed. write for info. (*0-13-843384-4*) P-H.

State & Local Politics in the New Nation. Intro. by Peter S. Onuf. LC 91-15466. (New American Nation, 1775-1820 Ser.: Vol. 10). 600p. 1991. text ed. 45.00 (*0-8153-0445-5*) Garland.

State & Local Public Finance: Institutions, Theory, Policy. 2nd ed. Ronald C. Fisher. LC 95-23204. 704p. (C). 1995. text ed. 69.75 (*0-256-16062-7*) Irwin Prof Pubng.

State & Local Public Finances. 2nd ed. Ronald Fisher. 538p. (C). 1993. per. 35.25 (*0-256-16079-1*) Irwin.

State & Local Response to Money Laundering Program Manual. 235p. 1993. 30.00 (*0-317-05780-4*, PB17) Natl Attys General.

State & Local Statistics Sources. 2nd ed. Sarojini Balachandran. 1993. 145.00 (*0-8103-5468-3*) Gale.

State & Local Statistics Sources, 1989-1990: A Subject Guide to Data on Industrial, Business, Social, Educational, Financial, & Other Topics Presented on the State, City & Local Levels. 800p. 1990. 135.00 (*0-8103-2798-8*) Gale.

State & Local Tax Levels: Fiscal Year 1991. Scott R. Mackey. (Legislative Finance Papers: No. 80). 24p. 1992. pap. text ed. 25.00 (*1-55516-080-8*, 5101-80) Natl Conf State Legis.

State & Local Tax Performance Nineteen Seventy-Eight. rev. ed. Kenneth E. Quindry & Niles Schoening. 1980. pap. 3.00 (*0-686-29037-2*) S Regional Ed.

State & Local Tax Policies: A Comparative Handbook. Ronald J. Hy & William L. Waugh. LC 94-30931. 320p. 1995. text ed. 85.00 (*0-313-28529-2*, Greenwood Pr) Greenwood.

State & Local Tax Policy & the Telecommunications Industry. Karl E. Case. LC 92-43833. 1992. 13.95 (*0-934842-13-2*) CSPA.

State & Local Tax Revolt: New Directions for the 80's. Dean Tipps & Lee Webb. 380p. 1980. 29.95 (*0-89788-010-2*) Transaction Pubs.

State & Local Tax Service. Prentice Hall Editorial Staff. write for info. (*0-318-62096-0*) P-H.

***State & Local Taxation.** rev. ed. Oliver S. Oldman & Richard D. Pomp. 881p. (Orig.). 1995. pap. text ed. 51.50 (*0-9653722-0-0*) R D Pomp.

***State & Local Taxation: Cases & Materials.** 6th ed. Jerome R. Hellerstein & Walter Hellerstein. LC 97-25340. (American Casebook Ser.). 1997. write for info. (*0-314-21126-8*) West Pub.

State & Local Taxation & Finance in a Nutshell. M. David Gelfand. LC 85-20283. (Nutshell Ser.). 309p. 1986. pap. 15.50 (*0-314-95571-2*) West Pub.

State & Local Taxation of Natural Resources in the Federal System: Legal, Economic & Political Perspectives. LC 85-52446. 420p. 1986. 79.00 (*0-89707-216-2*, 547-0088-01) Amer Bar Assn.

State & Local Taxes. ring bd. write for info. (*0-318-57356-3*) P-H.

State & Locality: A Comparative Perspective on State Restructuring. C. G. Pickvance & Edmond Preteceille. 224p. 1991. text ed. 39.00 (*0-86187-983-X*) St Martin.

S

State & Market: Aspects of Modern European Development. Ed. by John Sheldrake & Paul D. Webb. 192p. 1993. 59.95 (*1-85521-318-4*, Pub. by Dartmth Pub UK) Ashgate Pub Co.

State & Market in Development: Synergy or Rivalry? Ed. by Louis Putterman & Dietrich Rueschemeyer. LC 92-17038. (Emerging Global Issues Ser.). 277p. 1992. lib. bdg. 45.00 (*1-55587-311-1*) Lynne Rienner.

***State & Metropolitan Area Data Book, 2 vols., Set.** 1996. lib. bdg. 645.95 (*0-8490-6380-9*) Gordon Pr.

State & Movement of Water in Living Organisms. Society for Experimental Biology (Great Britain). LC 65-27550. (Symposia of the Society for Experimental Biology Ser.: No. 19). 448p. reprint ed. pap. 127.70 (*0-685-15299-5*, 2014957) Bks Demand.

State & Nation Building. Rajni Kothari. 336p. 1976. 16.95 (*0-318-37219-3*) Asia Bk Corp.

***State & Nation Building in East Central Europe.** Ed. by John S. Micgiel. xxii, 369p. (Orig.). (C). 1996. pap. 19.95 (*0-9654520-0-X*) Col U Inst E Cntrl Eur.

State & Nation in Multi-Ethnic Societies: The Breakup of Multinational States. Keith Armes et al. 1992. 39.95 (*0-685-61137-X*, Pub. by Manchester Univ Pr UK) St Martin.

***State & Nobility in Early Modern Germany: The Knightly Feud in Franconia, 1440-1567.** Hillay Zmora. (Studies in Early Modern History). 400p. (C). 1997. text ed. 69.95 (*0-521-56179-5*) Cambridge U Pr.

State & Opposition in Military Brazil. Maria H. Alves. (Latin American Monographs: No. 63). 368p. 1988. reprint ed. pap. 12.95 (*0-292-77617-9*) U of Tex Pr.

***State & Organized Labour in Botswana, 1966-1990: "Liberal Democracy" in Emergent Capitalism.** Monageng Mogalakwe. (Making of Modern Africa Ser.). (Illus.). 180p. 1997. text ed. 59.95 (*1-85972-344-6*, Pub. by Ashgate UK) Ashgate Pub Co.

State & Peasant in Contemporary China: The Political Economy of Village Government. Jean C. Oi. 1989. 45.00 (*0-520-06105-5*) U CA Pr.

State & Peasant in Contemporary China: The Political Economy of Village Government. Jean C. Oi. (Illus.). 308p. 1991. reprint ed. pap. 15.00 (*0-520-07637-0*) U CA Pr.

State & Peasant in the Ottoman Empire: Agrarian Power Relations & Regional Economic Development in Ottoman Anatolia during the Sixteenth Century. Huri Islamoglu-Inan. LC 94-2819. (Ottoman Empire & Its Heritage Ser.: Vol. 1). 1994. 89.50 (*90-04-10028-8*) E J Brill.

State & Policy Outcomes in the Latin American Vortex: Politics in Latin America. Lawrence S. Graham. LC 89-29653. 224p. 1990. text ed. 49.95 (*0-275-93494-2*, C3494, Greenwood Pr) Greenwood.

State & Political Mobilization: A Radical Critique of Political Sociology. Peter Burnham et al. 256p. Date not set. 62.00 (*1-85567-228-6*, Pub. by Pntr Pubs UK); pap. 21.95 (*1-85567-229-4*, Pub. by Pntr Pubs UK) Bks Intl VA.

***State & Politics in India.** Ed. by Partha Chatterjee. (Oxford in India Readings Ser.). (Illus.). 544p. 1997. 42.00 (*0-19-563950-2*) OUP.

State & Politics in the U. S. S. R. David Lane. 418p. (C). 1985. text ed. 40.00 (*0-8147-5013-3*); pap. text ed. 20.00 (*0-8147-5014-1*) NYU Pr.

State & Private Education: An Evaluation of the Assisted Places Scheme. Tony Edwards et al. 220p. 1989. 75.00 (*1-85000-567-2*, Falmer Pr); pap. 35.00 (*1-85000-568-0*, Falmer Pr) Taylor & Francis.

State & Province Vital Records Guide. Michael Burgess et al. LC 87-6312. (Borgo Reference Guides Ser.: No. 5). 96p. 1993. pap. 15.00 (*0-89370-915-8*); lib. bdg. 25.00 (*0-89370-815-1*) Borgo Pr.

***State & Provincial Society in the Early Modern Ottoman Empire: Mosul, 1540-1834.** Dina R. Khoury. (Studies in Islamic Civilization). 328p. (C). 1997. text ed. 59.95 (*0-521-59060-4*) Cambridge U Pr.

State & Public Bureaucracies: A Comparative Perspective. Ed. by Metin Heper. LC 87-15059. (Contributions in Political Science Ser.: No. 193). 232p. 1987. text ed. 55.00 (*0-313-25438-9*, HSK/, Greenwood Pr) Greenwood.

State & Public Welfare in Nineteenth-Century America: Five Investigations, 1833-1877. Gerald N. Grob. LC 75-17244. (Social Problems & Social Policy Ser.). (Illus.). 1976. 51.95 (*0-405-07515-4*) Ayer.

***State & Regional Associations of the U. S., 1997.** 9th ed. Ed. by John J. Russell et al. 1997. pap. 65.00 (*1-880873-23-0*) Columbia Bks.

State & Regional Initiatives for Managing Development: Policy Issues & Practical Concerns. Ed. by Douglas R. Porter. LC 92-606688. 259p. 1992. pap. text ed. 45.95 (*0-87420-727-4*, S28) Urban Land.

State & Regional Patterns in American Manufacturing, 1860-1900. Albert W. Niemi, Jr. LC 73-13289. (Contributions in Economics & Economic History Ser.: No. 10). 209p. 1974. text ed. 69.50 (*0-8371-7148-2*, NAM, Greenwood Pr) Greenwood.

State & Repressive Culture: A Case Study of Gujarat. A. R. Desai & Wilfred D'Costa. (C). 1994. text ed. 18.00 (*81-7154-702-8*, Pub. by Popular Prakashan II) S Asia.

State & Reservation: New Perspectives on Federal Indian Policy. Ed. by George P. Castile & Robert L. Bee. LC 92-8229. 259p. (Orig.). (C). 1992. 42.00 (*0-8165-1319-8*); pap. text ed. 21.50 (*0-8165-1325-2*) U of Ariz Pr.

State & Resistance in South Africa, 1939-1965. Yvonne Muthien. (Making of Modern Africa Ser.). 233p. 1994. 68.95 (*1-85628-501-4*, Pub. by Avebury Pub UK) Ashgate Pub Co.

State & Revolution. Vladimir I. Lenin. 1965. pap. 3.95 (*0-8351-0372-2*) China Bks.

State & Revolution. Vladimir I. Lenin. 103p. (C). 1932. pap. text ed. 2.75 (*0-7178-0196-9*) Intl Pubs Co.

State & Revolution. Robert W. Service. 192p. 1993. pap. 11.95 (*0-14-018435-X*, Penguin Classics) Viking Penguin.

State & Revolution: Marxist Teachings about the Theory of the State & the Tasks of the Proletariat in the Revolution. Vladimir I. Lenin. LC 78-2228. 104p. 1978. reprint ed. text ed. 35.00 (*0-313-20351-2*, LESTR, Greenwood Pr) Greenwood.

State & Revolution in East Africa. John S. Saul. LC 79-11458. 454p. 1979. 26.00 (*0-85345-487-6*); pap. 12.00 (*0-85345-508-2*) Monthly Rev.

State & Revolution in Finland. Risto Alapuro. 320p. (C). 1988. 45.00 (*0-520-05813-5*) U CA Pr.

State & Rural Class Formation in Ghana: A Comparative Analysis. Piet Konigs. (Monographs from the African Studies Centre, Leiden). 420p. 1987. lib. bdg. 75.00 (*0-7103-0117-0*) Routledge Chapman & Hall.

***State & Rural Society in Medieval Islam: Sultans, Muqta's & Fallahun.** Tsugitaka Sato. LC 96-45396. (Islamic History & Civilization, Studies & Texts Ser.: Vol. 17). (Illus.). 300p. 1997. text ed. 94.00 (*90-04-10649-9*, NLG145) E J Brill.

State & Rural Transformation in Northern Somalia, 1884-1986. Abdi I. Samatar. LC 88-40443. (Illus.). 224p. (Orig.). (C). 1989. text ed. 24.95 (*0-299-11990-4*); pap. text ed. 11.95 (*0-299-11994-7*) U of Wis Pr.

State & Salvation: The Jehovah's Witnesses & Their Fight for Civil Rights. William Kaplan. 352p. 1989. 35.00 (*0-8020-5842-6*) U of Toronto Pr.

State & Scholars in T'ang China. D. L. McMullen. (Cambridge Studies in Chinese History, Literature & Institutions). 448p. 1988. 75.00 (*0-521-32991-4*) Cambridge U Pr.

State & Social Investigation in Britain & the United States. Ed. by Michael J. Lacey & Mary O. Furner. (Woodrow Wilson Center Ser.). 500p. (C). 1993. text ed. 59.95 (*0-521-41638-8*) Cambridge U Pr.

State & Social Power in Global Environmental Politics. Ed. by Ronnie D. Lipschutz & Ken Conca. LC 93-15878. (New Directions in World Politics Ser.). 363p. 1993. 49.50 (*0-231-08106-5*); pap. 18.50 (*0-231-08107-3*) Col U Pr.

State & Social Transformation in Tunisia & Libya, 1830-1980. Lisa Anderson. LC 85-43266. (Near East Studies). (Illus.). 320p. 1987. pap. text ed. 19.95 (*0-691-00819-1*) Princeton U Pr.

***State & Social Welfare.** Wilson. 1992. pap. text ed. write for info. (*0-582-08513-6*, Pub. by Longman UK) Longman.

State & Society. Richard Taylor. LC 91-61777. 1992. 17.95 (*0-8158-0473-3*) Chris Mass.

State & Society: British Political & Social History, 1870-1992. Martin Pugh. 384p. 1995. text ed. 74.95 (*0-340-50711-X*, B2315, Pub. by E Arnld UK); text ed. 19.95 (*0-340-50710-1*, B2319, Pub. by E Arnld UK) St Martin.

State & Society: Emergence & Developement of Social Hierarchy & Political Centralization. B. Bender. Ed. by J. Gledhill et al. (One World Archaeology Ser.). 272p. (C). 1995. pap. 25.00 (*0-415-12255-4*, Routledge NY) Routledge.

State & Society: Peru in Comparative Perspective. Alfred C. Stepan. LC 77-85567. 368p. reprint ed. pap. 104.90 (*0-7837-1419-X*, 2041774) Bks Demand.

State & Society in Africa: Perspectives on Continuity & Change. Ed. by Feraidoon Shams. LC 95-12677. 168p. (Orig.). (C). 1995. 49.00 (*0-8191-9977-X*); pap. 28.50 (*0-8191-9978-8*) U Pr of Amer.

State & Society in China: Japanese Perspectives on Ming-Qing Social & Economic Theory. Linda Grove & Christian Daniels. 507p. 1984. 77.50 (*0-86008-356-X*, Pub. by U of Tokyo JA) Col U Pr.

State & Society in China's Political Economy: The Cultural Dynamics of Socialist Reform. Chih-yu Shih. LC 94-23749. 207p. 1995. lib. bdg. 45.00 (*1-55587-580-7*) Lynne Rienner.

State & Society in Contemporary China. Ed. by David Mozingo & Victor G. Nee. LC 82-46010. 269p. 1983. pap. 17.95 (*0-8014-9253-X*) Cornell U Pr.

State & Society in Contemporary Korea. Ed. by Hagen Koo. 272p. 1993. 37.50 (*0-8014-2867-X*); pap. 14.95 (*0-8014-8106-6*) Cornell U Pr.

State & Society in Dar Fur. R. S. O'Fahey. LC 80-13372. 1980. text ed. 35.00 (*0-312-75606-2*) St Martin.

***State & Society in Early Medieval China.** Ed. by Albert Dien. 420p. 1990. write for info. (*962-209-244-6*, Pub. by Hong Kong Univ Pr HK) Coronet Bks.

State & Society in Early Medieval China. Ed. by Albert E. Dien. LC 89-60727. 272p. 1991. 47.50 (*0-8047-1745-1*) Stanford U Pr.

State & Society in Early Modern Austria. Ed. by Charles W. Ingrao. LC 93-33879. 360p. 1994. 35.00 (*1-55753-047-5*) Purdue U Pr.

State & Society in Eighteenth-Century China: The Ch'ing Empire in Its Glory. Albert Feuerwerker. (Michigan Monographs in Chinese Studies: No. 27). 1976. pap. text ed. 15.00 (*0-89264-027-8*) Ctr Chinese Studies.

State & Society in Europe. Percy Allum. (Illus.). 619p. (C). 1995. text ed. 66.95 (*0-7456-0409-9*); pap. text ed. 27.95 (*0-7456-0410-2*) Blackwell Pubs.

State & Society in Fatimid Egypt. Yaacov Lev. LC 90-24522. (AHC Ser.: No. 1). xi, 217p. 1991. 77.00 (*90-04-09344-3*) E J Brill.

State & Society in France, 1661-1789. Tim J. Le Goff. 288p. 1993. pap. 18.95 (*0-7131-6527-8*, A9527, Pub. by E Arnold UK) Routledge Chapman & Hall.

State & Society in Francophone Africa since Independence. Ed. by Anthony H. Kirk-Greene & Daniel Bach. LC 94-33765. 1995. text ed. 69.95 (*0-312-12112-1*) St Martin.

State & Society in India: Studies in Nation Building. T. K. Oommen. 210p. (C). 1990. text ed. 26.00 (*0-8039-9656-X*) Sage.

State & Society in International Relations. Ed. by Michael A. Banks & Martin Shaw. LC 91-21399. 256p. 1991. text ed. 49.95 (*0-312-06762-3*) St Martin.

State & Society in Medieval Europe: Gwynedd & Languedoc under Outside Rule. James B. Given. Ed. by David Laitin. LC 90-31274. (Wilder House Series in Politics, History, & Culture). (Illus.). 312p. 1990. pap. 18.95 (*0-8014-9774-4*) Cornell U Pr.

State & Society in Mid-Nineteenth-Century Egypt. Ehud R. Toledano. (Cambridge Middle East Library: No. 22). (Illus.). 328p. (C). 1990. text ed. 69.95 (*0-521-37194-5*) Cambridge U Pr.

State & Society in Post War. Bernard Eccleston. 270p. 1990. pap. 27.95 (*0-7456-0166-9*) Blackwell Pubs.

State & Society in Pre-Colonial Asante. T. C. McCaskie. (African Studies: No. 79). (Illus.). 512p. (C). 1995. text ed. 74.95 (*0-521-41009-6*) Cambridge U Pr.

State & Society in Seventeenth-Century France. Ed. & Tr. by Raymond F. Kierstead from FRE. Tr. by Marilyn J. Kierstead from FRE. LC 74-32202. (Modern Scholarship on European History Ser.). 284p. (Orig.). (C). 1975. pap. text ed. 8.95 (*0-531-05573-6*) Wiener Pubs Inc.

State & Society in Syria & Lebanon, 1919-1991. Ed. by Youssef M. Choueiri. LC 93-7555. 208p. 1994. text ed. 49.95 (*0-312-09586-4*) St Martin.

State & Society in the Dominican Republic. Emelio Betances. (C). 1995. pap. text ed. 18.95 (*0-8133-8682-9*) Westview.

State & Society in the Taiwan Miracle. Thomas B. Gold. LC 85-2350. (Taiwan in the Modern World Ser.). 176p. (gr. 13). 1986. pap. text ed. 23.95 (*0-87332-399-8*, East Gate Bk) M E Sharpe.

***State & Society in Transition: The Politics of Institutional Reform in the Eastern Townships, 1838-1852.** J. I. Little. (Studies on the History of Quebec/Etudes d'Histoire du Quebec). (Illus.). 344p. 1997. 55.00 (*0-7735-1544-5*, Pub. by McGill CN) U of Toronto Pr.

***State & Society in Transition: The Politics of Institutional Reform in the Eastern Townships, 1838-1852.** J. I. Little. (Studies on the History of Quebec/Etudes d'Histoire du Quebec). (Illus.). 344p. 1997. pap. 24.95 (*0-7735-1545-3*, Pub. by McGill CN) U of Toronto Pr.

***State & Society in Twentieth-Century America.** Robert Harrison. LC 97-14180. 1997. write for info. (*0-582-27000-6*); pap. write for info. (*0-582-26772-2*) Longman.

State & Statecraft in Old Java No. 43: A Study of the Later Mataram Period, 16th to 19th Century. 2nd rev. ed. Soemarsaid Moertono. 181p. 1981. pap. 9.00 (*0-87763-017-8*) Cornell Mod Indo.

State & Statistics in France, Seventeen Eighty-Nine to Eighteen Fifteen. Jean-Claude Perrot & Stuart J. Woolf. (Social Orders Ser.: Vol. 2). 206p. 1984. text ed. 92.00 (*3-7186-0201-6*) Gordon & Breach.

State & Status: The Rise of State & Aristocratic Power in Western Europe. Samuel Clark. 520p. 1996. pap. 29.95 (*0-7083-1299-3*, Pub. by Univ Wales Pr UK) Paul & Co Pubs.

State & Status: The Rise of the State & Aristocratic Power in Western Europe. Samuel Clark. 502p. 1995. pap. 24.95 (*0-7735-1249-7*, Pub. by McGill CN) U of Toronto Pr.

***State & Status: The Rise of the State & Aristocratic Power in Western Europe.** Samuel Clark. 1995. 55.00 (*0-7735-1226-8*, Pub. by McGill CN) U of Toronto Pr.

State & the Academic Library. Ed. by Vicki L. Gregory. LC 93-13013. (Contributions in Librarianship & Information Science Ser.: No. 76). 208p. 1993. text ed. 59.95 (*0-313-28108-4*, GVA/, Greenwood Pr) Greenwood.

State & the Church in a Free Society. Albert V. Murray. LC 77-27134. (Hibbert Lectures: 1957). reprint ed. 37.50 (*0-404-60433-1*) AMS Pr.

State & the City. Ted R. Gurr & Desmond S. King. LC 87-5015. (Illus.). 251p. (C). 1987. pap. text ed. 18.00 (*0-226-31091-4*); lib. bdg. 42.00 (*0-226-31090-6*) U Ch Pr.

State & the Economic Process. Ed. by C. W. Naastepad & Servaas Storm. LC 95-42421. (Belgian-Dutch Post-Keynesian Association for Post-Keynesian Economics Ser.). (Illus.). 288p. 1996. 80.00 (*1-85898-168-9*) E Elgar.

State & the Economy under Capitalism, Vol. 31. Adam Przeworski. (Fundamentals of Pure & Applied Economics Ser.). 126, viiip. 1990. pap. text ed. 47.00 (*3-7186-5006-1*, Harwood Acad Pubs) Gordon & Breach.

State & the Family: A Comparative Analysis of Family Policies in Industrialized Countries. Anne H. Gauthier. 248p. 1996. 65.00 (*0-19-828804-2*) OUP.

State & the Market. Ed. by Clive Dewey. LC 85-62582. 353p. (C). 1987. 34.00 (*0-913215-09-0*) Riverdale Co.

State & the Market Economy: Industrial Patriotism & Economic Intervention in France. Jack Hayward. 256p. (C). 1986. text ed. 30.00 (*0-8147-3435-9*) NYU Pr.

State & the Market Economy: Industrial Patriotism & Economic Intervention in France. Jack Hayward. 256p. (C). 1991. pap. text ed. 13.20 (*0-8147-3476-6*) NYU Pr.

State & the Mass Media in Japan, 1918-1945. Gregory J. Kasza. (C). 1988. pap. 14.00 (*0-520-08273-7*) U CA Pr.

State & the Nation. Edward Jenks. LC 73-14159. (Perspectives in Social Inquiry Ser.). 324p. 1974. reprint ed. 20.95 (*0-405-05505-6*) Ayer.

State & the Non-Public School, 1825-1925. Lloyd P. Jorgenson. LC 86-30776. (Illus.). 248p. 1987. text ed. 34.95 (*0-8262-0633-6*) U of Mo Pr.

State & the Poor: Public Policy & Political Development in India & the United States. John Echeverri-Gent. LC 92-28991. 1993. 45.00 (*0-520-08082-3*) U CA Pr.

State & the Poor in the Nineteen Eighties. Ed. by Manuel Carballo & Mary J. Bane. 352p. (C). 1984. text ed. 49.95 (*0-86569-064-2*, T064, Auburn Hse) Greenwood.

State & the Rule of Law. Blandine Kriegel. Tr. by Marc A. LePain & Jeffrey C. Cohen. LC 95-17976. (New French Thought Ser.). 176p. (ENG & FRE.). 1995. text ed. 19.95 (*0-691-03291-2*) Princeton U Pr.

State & the School: An International Perspective. Ed. by John D. Turner. LC 95-23595. 208p. 1995. 78.95 (*0-7507-0477-2*, Falmer Pr); pap. 26.95 (*0-7507-0478-0*, Falmer Pr) Taylor & Francis.

State & the Spatial Management of Industrial Change. Ed. by D. C. Rich & Godfrey J. Linge. 256p. (C). (gr. 13). 1990. text ed. 62.95 (*0-415-03851-0*, A5125) Routledge.

State & the Unions: Labor Relations, Law, & the Organized Labor Movement in America, 1880-1960. Christopher L. Tomlins. LC 85-414. 1985. pap. 19.95 (*0-521-31452-6*) Cambridge U Pr.

State & the Visual Arts. Nicholas M. Pearson. 128p. 1982. pap. 32.00 (*0-335-10109-7*, Open Univ Pr) Taylor & Francis.

State & Transnational Corporations: A Network Approach to Industrial Policy in India. Hans Jansson et al. LC 95-5519. (New Horizons in International Business Ser.). 264p. 1995. 80.00 (*1-85898-255-3*) E Elgar.

***State & Tribe in Nineteenth-Century Afghanistan: The Reign of Amir Dost Muhammad Khan 1826-1863.** Christine Noelle. 380p. 1997. 75.00 (*0-7007-0629-1*, Pub. by Curzon Pr UK) Paul & Co Pubs.

State & Village Society. Shakeeb A. Khan. (C). 1989. 26.00 (*81-85054-81-9*, Pub. by Manohar II) S Asia.

State & Welfare, U. S. A. - U. S. S. R. Contemporary Policy & Practice. Ed. by Gail W. Lapidus & Guy E. Swanson. LC 88-15444. (Research Ser.: No. 71). (Illus.). xxii, 467p. 1988. pap. text ed. 22.50 (*0-87725-171-1*) U of Cal IAS.

State & Women in the Economy: Lessons from Sex Discrimination in the Republic of Ireland. Jean L. Pyle. LC 89-26160. (Series on Women & Work). 202p. 1990. pap. text ed. 21.95 (*0-7914-0380-7*) State U NY Pr.

State & Women in the Economy: Lessons from Sex Discrimination in the Republic of Ireland. Jean L. Pyle. LC 89-26160. (SUNY Series on Women & Work). 202p. 1990. text ed. 64.50 (*0-7914-0379-3*) State U NY Pr.

State & Working Women: A Comparative Study of Britain & Sweden. Mary Ruggie. LC 84-42563. 376p. 1984. reprint ed. pap. 107.20 (*0-7837-9283-2*, 2060022) Bks Demand.

State Antitrust Law. William J. Haynes, Jr. (Corporate Practice Ser.: No. 52). 1988. 92.00 (*1-55871-006-X*) BNA Books.

State Antitrust Law. William T. Lifland. 350p. 1984. ring bd. 95.00 (*0-318-12030-5*, 00583) NY Law Pub.

State Antitrust Laws. William J. Haynes, Jr. 436p. 1988. text ed. 92.00 (*0-87179-585-X*, 0585) BNA Books.

State Antitrust Laws. William J. Haynes. LC 88-24275. 437p. 1989. reprint ed. pap. 124.60 (*0-608-02230-6*, 2061479) Bks Demand.

State-Approved Schools of Nursing - RN (Annual) 128p. 1992. 23.95 (*0-88737-555-3*) Natl League Nurse.

State-Approved Schools of Nursing LPN-LVN: Annual. 96p. 1992. 23.95 (*0-88737-556-1*) Natl League Nurse.

State, Army & Society in Byzantium: Approaches to Military, Social & Administrative History, 6th-12th Centuries. John Haldon. (Collected Studies: Vol. CS504). 336p. 1995. 87.50 (*0-86078-497-5*, Pub. by Variorum UK) Ashgate Pub Co.

State Art Museum of the Moldavian SSR. E. V. Barashkov. (Illus.). 1982. 175.00 (*0-317-57447-7*) St Mut.

State As Charade: V. P. Singh, Chandra Shekhar & the Rest. Arun Shourie. (C). 1991. 22.00 (*0-8364-2756-4*, Pub. by Manohar II) S Asia.

State As Defendant: Governmental Accountability & the Redress of Individual Grievances. Leon Hurwitz. LC 80-657. (Contributions in Political Science Ser.: No. 51). (Illus.). xv, 211p. 1981. text ed. 55.00 (*0-313-21257-0*, HSD/, Greenwood Pr) Greenwood.

State As Employer: Labour Law in the Public Services. Sandra Fredman & Gillian S. Morris. Ed. by Bob Hepple & Paul O'Higgins. (Studies in Labour & Social Law). 542p. 1989. text ed. 55.00 (*0-7201-1978-2*, Mansell Pub) Cassell.

State As Parent. Ed. by J. Hudson & Burt Galaway. (C). 1989. lib. bdg. 220.50 (*0-7923-0492-6*) Kluwer Ac.

State As Terrorist: The Dynamics of Governmental Violence & Repression. Ed. by Michael Stohl & George A. Lopez. LC 83-5631. (Contributions to the Study of Political Science Ser.: No. 103). (Illus.). 256p. 1984. text ed. 55.00 (*0-313-23726-3*, STH) Greenwood.

State Asbestos Programs Related to the Asbestos Hazard Emergency Response Act: A Survey Update of State Laws & Regulations. Ed. by Doug Farquhar. 358p. 1992. pap. text ed. 125.00 (*1-55516-494-3*, 4636) Natl Conf State Legis.

State Atlas of Political & Cultural Diversity. William Lilley, 3rd & William M. Diefenderfer, 3rd. 298p. 1996. 210.00 (*1-56802-177-1*) Congr Quarterly.

State Attorneys General: Powers & Responsibilities. 445p. 1990. 72.00 (*0-317-05904-1*) Natl Attys General.

State Attorneys General Guide to Environmental Law. 174p. 1990. 25.00 (*0-317-05907-6*, PB09) Natl Attys General.

State Attorneys General Guide to the Clean Air Act Amendments of 1990. 181p. 1992. 25.00 (*0-317-05910-6*, PB12) Natl Attys General.

An Asterisk (*) at the beginning of an entry indicates that the title is appearing in BIP for the first time.

State Attorneys General, Powers & Responsibilities. Ed. by Lynne M. Ross. LC 89-71288. 471p. 1990. reprint ed. pap. 134.30 (0-608-00707-2, 2061480) Bks Demand.

State Autonomy or Class Dominance? Case Studies on Policy Making in America. G. William Domhoff. 312p. 1996. pap. text ed. 24.95 (0-202-30512-0); lib. bdg. 49.95 (0-202-30511-2) Aldine de Gruyter.

State Average Auto Insurance Expenditure & Premiums. 20p. (C). 1993. pap. 25.00 (0-89382-223-X) Nat Assn Insurance.

State Average Auto Insurance Expenditures & Premiums. annuals 35p. (C). 1995. pap. 25.00 (0-89382-319-8) Nat Assn Insurance.

***State Average Expenditures & Premiums for Personal Automobile Insurance in 1995.** 7th rev. ed. Ed. by Steve Lamberty. 32p. (C). 1997. pap. 35.00 (0-89382-447-X, AUS-PB) Nat Assn Insurance.

State Bait. Debby Head & Libby Pollett. (Curiosity Bait Ser.). 72p. 1994. teacher ed., pap. 9.95 (1-885775-06-7) BBY Pubns.

State Banking in the United States. George E. Barnett. 1972. 59.95 (0-8490-1122-1) Gordon Pr.

State Banking in the United States Since the Passage of the National Bank Act. George E. Barnett. LC 78-63887. (Johns Hopkins University. Studies in the Social Sciences. Thirtieth Ser. 1912: Nos. 2-3). reprint ed. 39.50 (0-404-61141-9) AMS Pr.

State Banks & the Economic Development of the West, 1830-1844. Carter H. Golembe. LC 77-14780. (Dissertations in American Economic History Ser.). 1978. 47.95 (0-405-11035-9) Ayer.

State Banks & Trust Companies: Since the Passage of the National Bank Act. George E. Barnett. LC 68-30516. (Reprints of Economic Classics Ser.). 366p. 1969. reprint ed. 45.00 (0-678-00503-6) Kelley.

State Birds: An Educational Coloring Book. Spizzirri Publishing Co. Staff. Ed. by Linda Spizzirri. (Illus.). 32p. (J). (gr. 1-8). 1983. pap. 1.99 (0-86545-050-1) Spizzirri.

State Birds: Including the Commonwealth of Puerto Rico. Elaine Landau. LC 92-8949. (State Symbols Ser.). (Illus.). 64p. (J). 1992. lib. bdg. 22.10 (0-531-20058-2) Watts.

State Birds & Flowers Coloring Book. Annika Bernhard. (Illus.). (J). (gr. k-3). 1990. pap. 2.95 (0-486-26456-4) Dover.

***State Birds in Stained Glass.** Carolyn Kyle. (Illus.). 60p. 1997. pap. 16.95 (0-935133-61-5, 20133615) CKE Pubns.

State Board Exam Review for Skin Care Specialist. 1980. pap. 12.95 (0-87350-094-6) Milady Pub.

State Board Review Questions: The Professional Cosmetologist. 3rd ed. John W. Dalton. 361p. (C). 1991. reprint ed. pap. text ed. 13.00 (0-314-77882-9) West Pub.

State Boundary Changes in India: Constitutional Provisions & Consequenses. Suman Sharma. (C). 1995. 31.00 (81-7100-706-6, Pub. by Deep II) S Asia.

State Bridge - Burns, CO. rev. ed. Ed. by Trails Illustrated Staff. 1994. 8.99 (0-925873-41-1) Trails Illustrated.

State Budget Actions in 1989. Martha A. Fabricius et al. (Legislative Finance Papers: No. 69). 101p. 1989. pap. text ed. 35.00 (1-55516-069-7, 5101-69) Natl Conf State Legis.

State Budget Actions, 1994. Corina L. Eckl. (Legislative Finance Papers: No. YY). 40p. 1994. 35.00 (1-55516-000-X, 5101-95) Natl Conf State Legis.

State Budget Actions 1995. Ronald K. Snell. 48p. Date not set. 35.00 (1-55516-035-2, 5101-00YY) Natl Conf State Legis.

State Budget & Tax Actions 1990. (Legislative Finance Papers: No. 74). 97p. 1990. 35.00 (1-55516-074-3, 5101-74) Natl Conf State Legis.

State Budget & Tax Actions, 1991. Corina L. Eckl et al. (Legislative Finance Papers: No. 79). 110p. 1991. pap. text ed. 35.00 (1-55516-079-4, 5101-79) Natl Conf State Legis.

State Budget Control of State Institutions of Higher Education. Oscar W. Irvin. LC 78-176897. (Columbia University. Teachers College. Contributions to Education Ser.: No. 271). reprint ed. 37.50 (0-404-55271-4) AMS Pr.

State Budget Update: April 1992. NCSL Fiscal Staff. (State Legislative Reports: Vol. 17, No. 7). 13p. 1992. pap. text ed. 5.00 (1-55516-279-7, 7302-1707) Natl Conf State Legis.

State Budget Update: March 1994. Arturo Perez. (Legislative Finance Papers: No. 93). 18p. 1994. 15.00 (1-55516-007-7, 5101-93) Natl Conf State Legis.

State Budgeting in Florida: A Handbook for Budget Analysts. Ed. by Thomas C. Foss & Thomas D. Sutberry. 272p. 1984. 25.00 (0-932143-00-8) FL Ctr Public.

State Budgeting in South Dakota. Loren M. Carlson. 1967. 1.00 (1-55614-006-1) U of SD Gov Res Bur.

State Building & Democracy in Southern Africa: Botswana, Zimbabwe, & South Africa. Pierre Du Toit. LC 95-22653. 1995. 37.50 (1-878379-50-X); pap. text ed. 19.95 (1-878379-46-1) US Inst Peace.

State-Building in Medieval France: Studies in Early Angevin History. Bernard S. Bachrach. LC 94-42647. (Collected Studies Ser.: No. CS486). 336p. 1995. 89.95 (0-86078-468-1, Pub. by Variorum UK) Ashgate Pub Co.

State, Bureaucracy, & Revolution in Modern Iran: Agrarian Reforms & Regime Politics. Ali Farazmand. LC 88-29268. 303p. 1989. text ed. 55.00 (0-275-92855-1, C2855, Praeger Pubs) Greenwood.

State, Bureaucracy, & the Cuban Schools: Power & Participation. Sheryl Lutjens. LC 96-8395. (Latin American Perspectives Ser.: No. 17). 239p. (C). 1996. text ed. 62.50 (0-8133-8241-6) Westview.

State by State. Davis. 1994. 59.00 (1-56706-014-5) Aspen Pub.

State by State Analysis of EPA's Acute Hazardous Events Data Base. Deborah Sheiman & Ken Silver. 1986. 3.00 (0-318-23633-8) NRDC Newsletter.

***State-by-State Biotechnology Directory.** 4th ed. Inst. for Biotechnology Info. Staff. 206p. 1996. pap. text ed. 149.00 (1-886041-10-5) Inst Biotech Info.

State-by-State Biotechnology Directory: Centers, Companies & Contacts. 2nd ed. Biotechnology Information Division of North Carolina Biotechnology Service Staff. 189p. 1991. 79.00 (1-55871-228-3, RDSB) BNA Books.

***State-by-State, City-by-City Web Directory.** Bryan Hiquet. 1996. pap. text ed. 29.99 incl. cd-rom (1-56276-464-0, Ziff-Davis Pr) Que.

State by State Compendium of Energy Efficiency Programs Using Oil Overcharge Funds. 650p. 1991. 500.00 (0-317-04971-2) Consumer Energy Coun.

State by State Guide to Budget Motels, 1995: Your National Guide to the Best Low-Cost Lodgings. Loris G. Bree. 336p. 1995. pap. 11.95 (0-943400-79-1) Marlor Pr.

State-by-State Guide to Children's & Young Adult Authors & Illustrators. David V. Loertscher & Lance Castle. 344p. 1991. ring bd. 37.50 (0-931510-33-3); disk 23.00 (0-931510-37-6); Apple II 22.00 (0-931510-35-X); mac hd 22.50 (0-931510-36-8) Hi Willow.

State by State Guide to Human Resources Law. Ronald M. Green et al. Ed. by Laura B. Kaiser. 600p. 1991. pap. text ed. 125.00 (1-878375-67-9) Panel Pubs.

State by State Guide to Human Resources Law. Ronald M. Green et al. 579p. 1991. reprint ed. pap. text ed. 136.00 (1-878375-10-5) Panel Pubs.

***State by State, Guide to Human Resources Law, 1997 Edition.** Ronald M. Green et al. 904p. pap. write for info. (1-56706-406-X, S91) Panel Pubs.

***State-By-State Laws & Regulations on Workers' Compensation Managed Care: 1997 Edition.** 3rd ed. Jane Anderson. Ed. by Ashli Towler. 150p. 1996. pap. 79.00 (1-56925-059-6, SBS3) Capitol Publns.

***State by State with the State: An Uninformed, Poorly Researched Guide to United States.** LC 96-46335. (Illus.). 288p. 1997. 10.95 (0-7868-8213-1) Hyperion.

State Capacity to Use UI Wage Records: The Vocational Education Experience. Lorraine Amico. Ed. by Karen Glass. 71p. (Orig.). 1993. pap. text ed. 15.00 (1-55877-205-7) Natl Governor.

State Capital & Private Enterprise: The Case of the UK National Enterprise Board. Daniel C. Kramer. 320p. 1989. lib. bdg. 57.50 (0-415-00915-4) Routledge.

State Capitalism: Public Enterprise in Canada. Jeanne K. Laux & Maureen A. Molot. LC 86-47600. (Cornell Studies in Political Economy). (Illus.). 272p. (C). 1988. pap. 16.95 (0-8014-9469-9) Cornell U Pr.

State, Capitalism, & Democracy in Latin America. Atilio A. Boron. 220p. 1995. lib. bdg. 49.95 (1-55587-508-4) Lynne Rienner.

State Capitalism & Marx's Humanism, or Philosophy & Revolution: China, Russia, U. S. A. Raya Dunayevskaya. 62p. (Orig.). 1967. pap. 0.50 (0-914441-10-8) News & Letters.

State Capitalism & Working-Class Radicalism in the French Aircraft Industry. Herrick Chapman. LC 90-10790. (Illus.). 480p. 1990. 55.00 (0-520-05953-0); pap. 17.95 (0-520-07125-5) U CA Pr.

State Capitalism & World Revolution. Intro. by Paul Buhle. (Revolutionary Classics Ser.). 160p. 1985. pap. 12.00 (0-88286-079-8) C H Kerr.

State Capitals Quilt Blocks: Fifty Patchwork Patterns from "Hearth & Home Magazine" 1912-1916. Ed. by Barbara Bannister & Edna P. Ford. (Orig.). 1977. pap. 3.95 (0-486-23557-2) Dover.

State Case Names Citators. Shepard's Citation, Inc. Staff. 1992. write for info. (0-318-64274-3) Shepards.

State Censorship & the Academic Process in South Africa. Christopher Merrett. (Occasional Papers: No. 192). 1991. pap. 5.00 (0-685-56565-3) U of Ill Grad Sch.

State Census of North Carolina, 1784-1787. 2nd ed. Alvaretta K. Register. LC 73-3664. 233p. 1993. reprint ed. 20.00 (0-8063-0556-8) Genealog Pub.

State Census Records. Ann S. Lainhart. 116p. 1992. 17.95 (0-8063-1362-5, 3275) Genealog Pub.

State Centennial History of Ohio, Covering the Periods of Indian, French & British Dominion, the Territory Northwest, & the Hundred Years of Statehood. Rowland H. Rerick. 425p. 1995. reprint ed. lib. bdg. 45.00 (0-8328-4616-3) Higginson Bk Co.

State Champions: The Story of the Buhl Bulldogs' Rise to Glory in 1941 & 1942. George R. Rekela. (Orig.). 1991. pap. 5.95 (0-9619505-0-1) Milkees Pr.

State, Class, & Bureaucracy: Canadian Unemployment Insurance & Public Policy. Leslie A. Pal. 365p. 1988. 49.95 (0-7735-0623-3, Pub. by McGill CN) U of Toronto Pr.

State, Class, & Ethnicity in Nicaragua: Capitalist Modernization & Revolutionary Change on the Atlantic Coast. Carlos M. Vilas. LC 89-3604. 223p. 1989. lib. bdg. 40.00 (1-55587-163-1) Lynne Rienner.

State, Class & the Nationalization of the Mexican Banks. Russell N. White. (International Political Economy Ser.). 285p. 1991. 52.00 (0-8448-1698-1, Crane Russak) Taylor & Francis.

State, Class, & the Recession. Ed. by Paul Boreham et al. LC 83-2915. 335p. 1983. text ed. 39.95 (0-312-75609-7) St Martin.

State, Class & Underdevelopment in Nigeria & Early Meiji Japan. Sakah S. Mahmud. 176p. 1996. text ed. 59.95 (0-312-15932-3) St Martin.

State, Class Formation, & Development in Bangladesh. S. M. Alam. 262p. Date not set. lib. bdg. 48.00 (0-7618-0079-4) U Pr of Amer.

State Codes on Domestic Violence: Analysis, Commentary & Recommendations. Barbara J. Hart. 81p. (Orig.). (C). 1994. pap. text ed. 20.00 (0-7881-0886-7) DIANE Pub.

State Coinage of Connecticut. Henry C. Miller. (Illus.). 1981. reprint ed. lib. bdg. 30.00 (0-915262-64-9) S J Durst.

State College, PA. Historical Briefs, Inc. Staff. Ed. by Thomas Antonucci & Michael Antonucci. 176p. 1992. pap. 14.95 (0-89677-043-5) Hist Briefs.

State College, Pennsylvania: A Photographic Celebration. Ed. by Maryann Curione & Lurene Frantz. (Illus.). 124p. 1995. 34.95 (0-9647274-1-2); pap. 24.95 (0-9647274-6-3) State Col Cent.

***State, Community, & Local Development in Nigeria.** Paul Francis et al. (World Bank Technical Papers: No. 336). 72p. 1996. 7.95 (0-8213-3733-5, 13733) World Bank.

***State Compacts for Community Service.** 67p. 1993. pap. 7.50 (0-614-30596-9) Ed Comm States.

State Compensation for Criminal Injuries. David Miers. 319p. 1997. pap. 54.00 (1-85431-505-6, Pub. by Blackstone Pr UK) Gaunt.

State Competitive Research Grant Programs. John Forrer. Ed. by Mark Miller. 80p. (Orig.). 1989. pap. text ed. 10.00 (1-55877-047-X) Natl Governor.

State Computer Law: Commentary, Cases, & Statutes. Virginia V. Shue & James V. Vergari. LC 92-20419. (IP Ser.). 1992. 140.00 (0-87632-902-4) Clark Boardman Callaghan.

State, Conceptual Chaos, & the Future of International Relations Theory. Yale H. Ferguson & Richard W. Mansbach. LC 88-29387. (GSIS Monograph in World Affairs). 127p. 1989. lib. bdg. 20.00 (1-55587-144-5) Lynne Rienner.

State Concerns in the Future Development of Vocational Education. Anne Lindeman. 22p. 1984. 3.00 (0-318-22201-9, OC98) Ctr Educ Trng Employ.

State Constitutional Amendment & Interpretation in the American System. Lawrence Schlam. LC 93-42753. 250p. 1997. 69.95 (1-880921-73-1); pap. 49.95 (1-880921-72-3) Austin & Winfield.

State Constitutional & Statutory Restrictions upon the Structural, Functional, & Personnel Powers of Local Government. United States Advisory Commission on Intergovernmental Relations. LC 78-13964. 1979. reprint ed. text ed. 39.75 (0-313-20674-0, ACSC, Greenwood Pr) Greenwood.

State Constitutional Criminal Law. Barry Latzer. LC 94-69102. 1995. ring bd. 135.00 (0-614-07299-9) Clark Boardman Callaghan.

State Constitutional Criminal Procedure. Neil McCabe & Catherine Burnett. LC 94-78748. 630p. 1994. pap. 60.00 (0-916081-34-6) J Marshall Pub Co.

State Constitutional Law in a Nutshell. Thomas C. Marks, Jr. & John F. Cooper. (Nutshell Ser.). 329p. 1988. pap. text ed. 18.50 (0-314-41748-6) West Pub.

State Constitutional Limitations on Solutions of Metropolitan Area Problems. John M. Winters. (Michigan Legal Publications). ix, 169p. 1986. reprint ed. lib. bdg. 37.50 (0-89941-493-1, 304200) W S Hein.

State Constitutionalism in Maryland. Michael C. Tolley. LC 92-18777. (Distinguished Studies in American Legal & Constitutional History). 196p. 1992. text ed. 38.00 (0-8153-0892-2) Garland.

State Constitutions & Criminal Justice, No. 65. Barry Latzer. LC 91-3249. (Contributions in Legal Studies). 232p. 1991. text ed. 59.95 (0-313-26112-1, LLF, Greenwood Pr) Greenwood.

State Constitutions in a Federal System. Ed. by John Kincaid. (Annals Ser.: Vol. 496). 1988. 26.00 (0-8039-3010-0); pap. 17.00 (0-8039-3011-9) Sage.

State Control in Soviet Russia: The Rise & Fall of the Workers' & Peasants' Inspectorate, 1920-1934. E. A. Rees. LC 87-4777. 320p. 1987. text ed. 45.00 (0-312-00767-1) St Martin.

State Control of Textbooks with Special Reference to Florida. Clyde J. Tidwell. LC 77-177710. (Columbia University. Teachers College. Contributions to Education Ser.: No. 299). reprint ed. 37.50 (0-404-55299-4) AMS Pr.

***State Corporatism & Proto-Industry: The Wuttemberg Black Forest, 1580-1797.** Sheilagh C. Ogilvie. (Cambridge Studies in Population, Economy & Society in Past Time: No. 33). 500p. (C). 1997. text ed. 80.00 (0-521-37209-7) Cambridge U Pr.

State, Corporatist Politics & Educational Policy Making in Mexico. Daniel A. Morales-Gomez & Carlos A. Torres. LC 89-29986. 224p. 1990. text ed. 49.95 (0-275-93484-5, C3484, Praeger Pubs) Greenwood.

***State Court Caseload Statistics, 1995: Supplement to Examining the Work of State Courts, 1995.** Court Statistics Project Staff. (Illus.). 252p. 1996. pap. 12.00 (0-89656-173-9, R-192) Natl Ctr St Courts.

State Court Organization (1993) David B. Rottman et al. (Illus.). 399p. (Orig.). (C). 1995. pap. text ed. 45.00 (0-7881-2267-3) DIANE Pub.

***State Court Sentencing of Convicted Felons (1992)** Patrick A. Langan & Robyn L. Cohen. (Illus.). 64p. (Orig.). (C). 1996. pap. 20.00 (0-7881-3138-9) DIANE Pub.

State Credentialing of the Health Occupations & Professions. Council of State Governments Staff. (Publication Ser.: No. C40). 244p. reprint ed. pap. 69.60 (0-7837-2656-2, 2043014) Bks Demand.

State Crime, the Media, & the Invasion of Panama. Christina J. Johns & P. Ward Johnson. LC 93-19092. (Criminology & Crime Control Policy Ser.). 168p. 1993. text ed. 57.95 (0-275-94314-3, C4314, Praeger Pubs) Greenwood.

State Currency System: How to Free Ourselves from International Finance. 1991. lib. bdg. 75.00 (0-8490-4469-3) Gordon Pr.

State Curriculum Frameworks in Mathematics & Science: How Are They Changing Across the States? Rolf Blank & Ellen M. Perryman. 132p. 1995. pap. 15.00 (1-884037-11-9) Coun Chief St Schl Offs.

State Cutback Management: Prospects for Fiscal Year 1991 & Fiscal Year 1992. (State Legislative Reports: Vol. 16, No. 3). 14p. 1991. 5.00 (1-55516-302-5, 7302-1603) Natl Conf State Legis.

State D Coaching Course: Workbook. Karl R. Nystrom. (Illus.). 50p. (Orig.). (C). 1989. pap. 3.50 (1-879397-03-X) Kanvi.

State D Soccer Coaching Course: Instructor's Manual. Karl R. Nystrom. 51p. (Orig.). (C). 1989. pap. 3.50 (1-879397-02-1) Kanvi.

State Debate. Ed. by Simon Clarke. LC 90-25328. 280p. 1991. text ed. 49.95 (0-312-06073-4) St Martin.

State Deficit Management Strategies: LFP, No. 60. Corina L. Eckl. 1987. pap. 10.00 (1-55516-060-3, 5101-60) Natl Conf State Legis.

State, Democracy, & the Military: Turkey in the 1980s. Ed. by Metin Heper & Ahmet Evin. 265p. (C). 1988. lib. bdg. 95.75 (3-11-011344-9) De Gruyter.

***State Department: Actions Needed to Improve Embassy Management.** (Illus.). 32p. (Orig.). 1996. pap. 20.00 (0-7881-3264-4) DIANE Pub.

***State Department: Options for Addressing Possible Budget Reductions.** (Illus.). 108p. (Orig.). (C). 1996. pap. 30.00 (0-7881-3667-4) DIANE Pub.

State Department: Survey of Administrative Issues Affecting Embassies. (Illus.). 70p. (Orig.). (C). 1994. pap. text ed. 20.00 (0-7881-0589-2) DIANE Pub.

***State Department Novel.** Allen Drury. Date not set. write for info. (0-688-12742-8) Morrow.

State Department Policy Planning Staff Papers, 3 vols., Set. George F. Kennan. Ed. by Anna K. Nelson. LC 83-14212. 880p. 1983. lib. bdg. 75.00 (0-8240-5500-4) Garland.

***State, Development Planning & Liberalisation in India.** Terence J. Byres. (Shool of Oriental & African Studies). 448p. 1997. 35.00 (0-19-563973-1) OUP.

State Directory, Three Times Yearly. (Government Directories Ser.). 1997. pap. 210.00 (0-8103-7478-1) Carroll Pub.

State Divided: Opposition in Pennsylvania to the American Revolution. Anne M. Ousterhout. LC 86-29573. (Contributions in American History Ser.: No. 123). 358p. 1987. text ed. 59.95 (0-313-25728-0, OUS/, Greenwood Pr) Greenwood.

State Document Checklists: A Historical Bibliography. Susan L. Dow. LC 90-33881. 224p. 1990. lib. bdg. 40.00 (0-89941-739-6, 306370) W S Hein.

***State DOT Market for AIEIP & Environmental Consulting Firms.** write for info. (1-885002-30-0) Zweig White.

State Drug Resources National Directory (1992) 130p. (Orig.). (C). 1993. pap. text ed. 30.00 (0-7881-0164-1) DIANE Pub.

State Drug Resources National Directory (1994) 142p. (Orig.). (C). 1995. pap. text ed. 35.00 (0-7881-0223-0) DIANE Pub.

State Early Retirement Programs in Fiscal Years 1992 & 1993. Ronald K. Snell. (State Legislative Reports: Vol. 18, No. 5). 6p. 1993. 5.00 (1-55516-225-8, 7302-1805) Natl Conf State Legis.

***State Economic Agencies.** Date not set. text ed. write for info. (0-582-90253-3, Pub. by Longman UK) Longman.

State Economic Development: Wisconsin's Planning Methods & Potentials. Richard B. Andrews. LC 68-9014. (Land Economics Monographs: No. 2). 116p. reprint ed. pap. 33.10 (0-8357-6796-5, 2035476) Bks Demand.

State Economic Development Case Studies: Recent Changes. 121p. 1991. 13.00 (0-317-05055-9) Natl Coun Econ Dev.

State, Economic Transformation, & Political Change in the Philippines, 1946-1972. Amando Doronila. (Illus.). 224p. 1992. 39.95 (0-19-588577-5) OUP.

State, Economy & Public Policy in Australia. Ed. by Stephen Bell & Brian W. Head. 288p. 1994. pap. 38.00 (0-19-553401-8) OUP.

State, Economy & Society. Rene B. Bertramsen et al. 272p. (C). 1990. pap. text ed. 22.95 (0-04-445431-7) Routledge Chapman & Hall.

State, Economy, & Society. Rene B. Bertramsen et al. 272p. (C). 1990. text ed. 55.00 (0-04-445433-3) Routledge Chapman & Hall.

State, Economy & Society in Western Europe, 1815-1975: A Data Handbook, 2 vols. Peter Flora. Incl. Vol. 1. Growth of Mass Democracies & Welfare States. 1983. 65.00 (0-912289-00-7); Vol. 2. Growth of Industrial Societies & Capitalist Economies. 1986. 5.00 (0-685-73560-5); write for info. (0-685-06729-7) St James Pr.

State, Economy & Society in Western Europe, 1815-1975: A Data Handbook, 2 vols. Peter Flora. Incl. Vol. 1. Growth of Mass Democracies & Welfare States. 1983. 65.00 (0-912289-00-7); Vol. 2. Growth of Industrial Societies & Capitalist Economies. 1986. 5.00 (0-685-73560-5); 1987. 65.00 (0-912289-06-6) St James Pr.

State, Education, & Social Class in Mexico, 1880-1928. Mary K. Vaughan. LC 81-18733. (Origins of Modern Mexico Ser.). 316p. 1982. 29.00 (0-87580-079-3) N Ill U Pr.

State Education Documents: A State-by-State Directory for Their Acquisition & Use. EBSS Education-Related Government Publications Subcommittee Staff. 54p. 1989. pap. 21.95 (0-8389-7327-2) Assn Coll & Res Libs.

S

***State Education Governance Structures.** 123p. 1993. pap. 12.50 (*0-614-30591-8*, EG-93-1) Ed Comm States.

State Education in Canada: Public Policy & Public Philosophy. Ronald A. Manzer. 367p. 1994. 50.00 (*0-8020-0604-3*); pap. 19.95 (*0-8020-7209-7*) U of Toronto Pr.

State Elections in India Vol. 1, Pt. 1: Data Handbook on Vidhan Sabha Elections, 1952-85, The North: Haryana, Himachal Pradesh, Jammu & Kashmir, Punjab, Rajasthan, & Delhi. V. B. Singh & Shankar Bose. LC 87-905480. 500p. reprint ed. pap. 142.50 (*0-8357-4856-1*, 2037788) Bks Demand.

State Elections in India, Vol. 4: The North: Data Handbook on Vidhan Sabha Elections, 1952-1985. V. B. Singh & Shankar Bose. (Elections in India Ser.). 728p. (C). 1988. text ed. 75.00 (*0-8039-9549-0*) Sage.

State Elections in India, Vol. 5: The South: Data Handbook on Vidhan Sabhan Sabha Elections, 1952-1985. V. B. Singh & Shankar Bose. (Elections in India Ser.). 750p. (C). 1988. text ed. 75.00 (*0-8039-9558-X*) Sage.

State Elective Officials & the Legislatures, 1989-90. 160p. 1989. 30.00 (*0-87292-085-2*) Coun State Govts.

State Elective Officials & the Legislatures 1991-92. Council of State Governments Staff. 176p. 1991. pap. 30.00 (*0-87292-960-4*, D-001-91) Coun State Govts.

State Elective Officials & the Legislatures, 1993-94. 176p. 1993. pap. 35.00 (*0-87292-977-9*, D-022-92) Coun State Govts.

S

State Elective Officials, 1995. Council of State Government Staff. 1995. 59.50 (*0-87292-998-1*) Coun State Govts.

State Employment Policy in Hard Times. Ed. by Michael Barker & Robert N. Wise. LC 83-5674. (Duke Press Policy Studies). xxix, 252p. 1983. text ed. 46.95 (*0-8223-0538-0*) Duke.

State Energy Data Report, 2 vols., Set. 1995. lib. bdg. 599.99 (*0-8490-6503-8*) Gordon Pr.

State Energy Data Report: Consumption Estimates, 1960-1988. 1992. lib. bdg. 88.95 (*0-8490-5534-2*) Gordon Pr.

State Energy Data Report, 1992-Consumption Estimates. (Illus.). 532p. (Orig.). (C). 1994. pap. text ed. 75.00 (*0-7881-1078-0*) DIANE Pub.

***State Energy Data Report 1993: Consumption Estimates.** (Illus.). 518p. (Orig.). (C). 1997. pap. text ed. 60.00 (*0-7881-3898-7*) DIANE Pub.

State Enterprises in Developing Countries: The Indian Experience. R. C. Dutt. 1990. 33.00 (*81-7017-272-1*, Pub. by Abhinav II) S Asia.

***State Entrepreneur.** Stuyck. 1993. pap. text ed. 61.00 (*90-6544-773-3*) Kluwer Ac.

State Environmental Law. Daniel P. Selmi & Kenneth A. Manaster. LC 89-37142. (Environmental Law Ser.). 1989. ring bd. 145.00 (*0-87632-692-0*) Clark Boardman Callaghan.

State Estimation for Dynamic Systems: Methods of Ellipsoids. Felix L. Chernusko. 320p. 1993. 160.00 (*0-8493-4458-1*) CRC Pr.

State Exam Review for Cosmetology. Milady Publishing Company Staff. 126p. 1995. pap. 13.50 (*1-56253-237-5*) Milady Pub.

State Exam Review for Nail Technology. Milady Publishing Company Staff. 63p. 1993. pap. 13.50 (*1-56253-170-0*) Milady Pub.

State Exam Review for the Theory & Practice of Therapeutic Massage. 2nd ed. Ed. by Barbara Jewett. 94p. 1994. pap. 13.50 (*1-56253-223-5*) Milady Pub.

State Export Programs: A Resource Guide. 179p. 1987. 60.00 (*0-87179-932-4*) BNA Plus.

State Fact Finder 1996: Rankings Across America. Hal Hovey. 454p. 1996. 76.95 (*1-56802-216-6*) Congr Quarterly.

State Failure: The Impotence of Politics in Industrial Society. Martin Janicke. Tr. by Alan Braley from GER. 200p. 1990. lib. bdg. 32.50 (*0-271-00714-1*) Pa St U Pr.

State Fair. Phil Stong. LC 96-60644. (Bur Oak Bk.). 280p. 1996. pap. 12.95 (*0-87745-569-4*) U of Iowa Pr.

State Fair: Vocal Selections. (Illus.). 048p. 1981. pap. 8.95 (*0-88188-116-3*, 00312403) H Leonard.

State Fair Blue Ribbon Cookbook. Opal M. Hayes. LC 76-7358. (Illus.). 1976. 12.95 (*0-88280-046-9*) ETC Pubns.

State, Federal, & C. I. T. E. S. Regulations for Herpetologists. Norman Frank & Erica Ramus. 64p. 1994. pap. 4.50 (*0-9641032-1-4*) Reptile & Amphibian.

State-Federal Collaboration on Rural Development. Thomas Unruh & Jay Kayne. Ed. by Karen Glass. 66p. (Orig.). 1992. pap. text ed. 15.00 (*1-55877-200-6*) Natl Governor.

State Fiscal Agenda for the 1990s. 180p. 1990. 35.00 (*1-55516-547-8*, 5317) Natl Conf State Legis.

State Fiscal Conditions. Steven D. Gold. (Legislative Finance Papers: No. 55). 32p. 1987. pap. 6.25 (*1-55516-055-7*, 5101-55) Natl Conf State Legis.

State Fiscal Outlook: Nineteen Ninety & the Coming Decade. Ronald K. Snell. (State Legislative Reports: Vol. 15, No. 5). 10p. 1990. pap. text ed. 5.00 (*1-55516-261-4*, 7302-1505) Natl Conf State Legis.

State Fiscal Outlook for 1991. (Legislative Finance Papers: No. 76). 30p. 1991. 25.00 (*1-55516-076-X*, 5101-76) Natl Conf State Legis.

State Fiscal Outlook for 1992. Fiscal Affairs Department Staff. (State Legislative Reports: Vol. 17, No. 1). 19p. 1992. pap. text ed. 5.00 (*1-55516-309-2*, 7302-1701) Natl Conf State Legis.

State Fiscal Outlook for 1993. Arturo Perez. (Legislative Finance Papers: No. 84). 28p. 1993. pap. text ed. 25.00 (*1-55516-082-4*, 5101-84) Natl Conf State Legis.

State Fiscal Outlook for 1995. Arturo Perez & Ronald K. Snell. (Legislative Finance Papers: No. 97). 21p. 1994. 25.00 (*1-55516-006-9*, 5101-90) Natl Conf State Legis.

State Flags. Janet A. Bloss. 80p. (J). (gr. 5-8). 1994. pap. 2.50 (*0-87406-183-0*) Willowisp Pr.

State Flags: Including the Commonwealth of Puerto Rico. Sue R. Brandt. LC 92-8948. (Our State Symbols Ser.). (YA). 1992. lib. bdg. 22.10 (*0-531-20001-9*) Watts.

State Flowers. Anne O. Dowden. LC 78-41927. (Illus.). 96p. (J). (gr. 5 up). 1978. lib. bdg. 14.89 (*0-690-03884-4*, Crowell Jr Bks) HarpC Child Bks.

State Flowers: An Educational Coloring Book. Spizzirri Publishing Co. Staff. (Illus.). 32p. (J). (gr. 1-8). 1989. pap. 1.99 (*0-86545-142-7*) Spizzirri.

State Flowers: Including the Commonwealth of Puerto Rico. Elaine Landau. LC 92-8950. (Our State Symbols Ser.). 64p. (YA). 1992. lib. bdg. 22.10 (*0-531-20059-0*) Watts.

***State Flowers in Stained Glass.** Carolyn Kyle. (Illus.). 60p. 1997. pap. 16.95 (*0-935133-62-3*, 20133623) CKE Pubns.

State Formation among Tribals: A Quest for Santal Identity. A. B. Chaudhuri. (C). 1993. 20.00 (*81-212-0422-4*, Pub. by Gian Publng Hse II) S Asia.

State Formation & Political Legitimacy. Ed. by Myron J. Aronoff et al. (Political Anthropology Ser.: Vol. 6). 340p. 1987. 39.95 (*0-88738-161-8*) Transaction Pubs.

State Formation in Central America: The Struggle for Autonomy, Development, & Democracy. Howard H. Lentner. LC 93-12603. (Contributions in Latin American Studies: No. 2). 264p. 1993. text ed. 59.95 (*0-313-28921-2*, GM8921) Greenwood.

State Formation in Eastern Africa. Ed. by Ahmed I. Salim. LC 84-15103. 260p. 1986. text ed. 35.00 (*0-312-75614-3*) St Martin.

State Formation, Nation-Building, & Mass Politics in Europe. Stein Rokkan. Ed. by Stein Kuhnle et al. LC 96-24645. (Comparative European Politics Ser.). (Illus.). 360p. 1997. 59.00 (*0-19-828032-7*) OUP.

State Games. Larry R. Leichter. LC 89-62823. 1990. 20.00 (*0-87212-232-8*); pap. 15.00 (*0-87212-247-6*) Libra.

State Geographic Information Activities Compendium. Warnecke et al. 1992. 79.00 (*0-87292-098-4*, C-002-91) Coun State Govts.

State Government: CQ's Guide to Current Issues & Activities 1994-1995. Ed. by Thad L. Beyle. LC 85-9657. 250p. 1994. pap. 22.95 (*0-87187-802-X*) Congr Quarterly.

State Government: CQ's Guide to Current Issues & Activities 1995-96. Ed. by Thad L. Beyle. LC 85-9657. 253p. 1995. pap. 22.95 (*0-87187-824-0*) Congr Quarterly.

State Government & Economic Development. Gerald D. Nash. Ed. by Stuart Bruchey. LC 78-56676. (Management of Public Lands in the U. S. Ser.). 1979. reprint ed. lib. bdg. 31.95 (*0-405-11346-3*) Ayer.

State Government & Economic Performance. Paul Brace. LC 92-24177. 192p. 1993. text ed. 35.00 (*0-8018-4494-0*) Johns Hopkins.

State Government & Economic Performance. Paul Brace. 176p. 1994. reprint ed. pap. text ed. 14.95 (*0-8018-4971-3*) Johns Hopkins.

State Government Associations: A Reconnaissance. National League of Cities Staff et al. LC 86-146573. (National League of Cities State-Local Backgrounder Ser.). (Illus.). 1986. write for info. (*0-933729-07-3*) Natl League Cities.

State Government Export Promotion: An Exporter's Guide. Alan R. Posner. LC 84-1999. x, 192p. 1984. text ed. 49.95 (*0-89930-042-1*, PGE/, Quorum Bks) Greenwood.

State Government Finances. 1994. lib. bdg. 250.00 (*0-8490-8434-2*) Gordon Pr.

State Government Finances (1992) (Illus.). 82p. (Orig.). (C). 1994. pap. text ed. 25.00 (*0-7881-0466-7*) DIANE Pub.

State Government in Georgia. Lawrence R. Hepburn. LC 86-29433. 1991. text ed. 12.25 (*0-89854-151-4*) U of GA Inst Govt.

State Government in Iowa. 5th ed. Brian Carter. Ed. by Institute of Public Affairs Staff. (Illus.). (YA). (gr. 10). 1990. pap. text ed. 7.00 (*0-317-02886-3*) U Iowa IPA.

State Government Policy. Dennis Judd et al. (Orig.). 1981. pap. 15.00 (*0-918592-49-6*) Pol Studies.

State Government Research Directory. Kay Gill & Susan E. Tufts. 349p. 1986. 175.00 (*0-8103-1591-2*) Gale.

State Government 1996-1997: CQ's Guide to Current Issues & Activities. Thad L. Beyle. LC 85-9657. 260p. 1996. pap. 22.95 (*0-87187-891-7*) Congr Quarterly.

State Governments. Barbara S. Feinberg. LC 92-27368. (First Bks.). 64p. (J). 1993. lib. bdg. 21.00 (*0-531-20154-6*) Watts.

State Governments Turn to New Taxes. Stephen Moore. 1990. pap. 5.00 (*0-943802-85-7*, BG106) Natl Ctr Pol.

State Groundwater Protection Legislation: A Proposed Comprehensive Policy Framework. 28p. 1990. 10.00 (*1-55516-458-7*, 4327) Natl Conf State Legis.

State Groundwater Regulation: Guide to Laws, Standards & Risk Assessment. Sally Benjamin & David Belluck. LC 94-2393. 650p. 1994. 105.00 (*0-87179-795-X*, 0795) BNA Books.

State Guide to Cleanup & Compliance Issues at Federal Facilities. Christine O'Donnell & Paul Thompson. Ed. by Gerry Feinstein & Mark Miller. 195p. (Orig.). 1991. pap. text ed. 15.00 (*1-55877-095-X*) Natl Governor.

State Guide to the Uniform Hazardous Waste Manifest. Ed. by Karen Glass. 106p. (Orig.). 1991. pap. text ed. 15.00 (*1-55877-127-1*) Natl Governor.

State Hazardous Waste Regulation, 1991-1992, 2 vols. Mitchell L. Lathrop. 1992. suppl. ed., ring bd. 62.00 (*0-685-74334-9*); ring bd. 160.00 (*0-88063-361-1*) MICHIE.

State Health Care Plans. 1994. lib. bdg. 250.95 (*0-8490-5697-7*) Gordon Pr.

State Health Care Reform Under the Clinton Administration. John C. Goodman & Gerald L. Musgrave. 1992. pap. 10.00 (*0-943802-76-8*, 173) Natl Ctr Pol.

State Hermitage: Proceedings, Vol. 22. Collet's Holdings, Ltd. Staff. 1982. 42.00 (*0-317-57355-1*) St Mut.

State Higher Education Appropriations, 1991-92. State Higher Education Executive Officers Staff. 1993. 6.00 (*1-881543-00-5*) SHEEO.

State Higher Education Appropriations 1992-93. 1993. 6.00 (*1-881543-01-3*) SHEEO.

State Higher Education Appropriations 1994-95. 1995. 9.00 (*1-881543-06-4*) SHEEO.

State Higher Education Appropriations 1995-96. Edward R. Hines & Gwen Pruyne. 1996. 9.00 (*1-881543-08-0*) SHEEO.

***State Higher Education Appropriations, 1996-97.** SHEEO Staff. 1997. 16.00 (*1-881543-09-9*) SHEEO.

***State History Chronicles Notebook.** Gladys Whitted. 75p. (J). (gr. 1-8). 1996. ring bd. 14.95 (*0-913717-61-4*, 2308) Hewitt Res Fnd.

State Holding Companies & Public Enterprise in Transition. Anjali Kumar. 1993. text ed. 75.00 (*0-312-10172-4*) St Martin.

State Hospitals in the Depression. National Committee for Mental Health. Ed. by Gerald N. Grob. LC 78-22579. (Historical Issues in Mental Health Ser.). 1980. reprint ed. lib. bdg. 17.95 (*0-405-11931-3*) Ayer.

State Houses of Rhode Island. Patrick T. Conley et al. (Illus.). 79p. (Orig.). 1988. pap. 9.95 (*0-932840-04-3*) RI Hist Soc.

State, Identity, & the National Question in China & Japan. Germaine A. Hoston. LC 93-50669. 640p. 1994. text ed. 85.00 (*0-691-07873-4*); pap. text ed. 24.95 (*0-691-02334-4*) Princeton U Pr.

***State Immunity: Some Recent Developments.** 224p. 1993. text ed. 59.95 (*0-521-46319-X*) Cambridge U Pr.

State Immunity: Some Recent Developments. Chrisoph Schreuer. 224p. (C). 1988. 110.00 (*0-949009-14-8*, Pub. by Grotius Pubns UK) St Mut.

***State Immunity & the Violation of Human Rights.** J. Urgen Brohmer. LC 96-47876. (International Studies in Human Rights). 1997. write for info. (*90-411-0322-8*) Kluwer Law Tax Pubs.

State in Action: Public Policy & Politics. Ed. by James Simmie & Roger King. 224p. 1992. text ed. 45.00 (*0-86187-748-9*); pap. text ed. 17.50 (*0-86187-749-7*) St Martin.

State in Africa: The Politics of the Belly. Jean-Francois Bayart. Tr. by Chris Harrison et al. LC 92-28666. 400p. (C). 1994. text ed. 69.95 (*0-582-06422-8*, 79465); pap. text ed. 40.95 (*0-582-06421-X*, 79464) Longman.

State in Capitalist Europe: A Casebook. Ed. by Stephen Bornstein et al. (Casebook Series on European Politics & Society: No. 3). 1987. pap. text ed. 24.95 (*0-04-350059-5*) Routledge Chapman & Hall.

State in Catholic Thought: A Treatise in Political Philosophy. Heinrich A. Rommen. LC 74-91770. 747p. 1970. reprint ed. text ed. 38.50 (*0-8371-2437-9*, ROCT, Greenwood Pr) Greenwood.

State in Constitutional & International Law. Robert T. Crane. LC 78-63921. (Johns Hopkins University. Studies in the Social Sciences. Thirtieth Ser. 1912: 6-7). reprint ed. 37.50 (*0-404-61172-9*) AMS Pr.

State in Contemporary Society: An Introduction. John Schwarzmantel. 1995. pap. text ed. 34.95 (*0-13-320730-7*) P-H.

State in Early Modern France. James B. Collins. (New Approaches to European History Ser.: Vol. 5). (Illus.). 296p. (C). 1995. text ed. 49.95 (*0-521-38284-X*); pap. text ed. 15.95 (*0-521-38724-8*) Cambridge U Pr.

State in India 1000-1700. Ed. by Hermann Kulke. (Oxford in India Readings Ser.: Themes in Indian History). 450p. 1995. 29.95 (*0-19-563127-7*) OUP.

***State in India 1000-1700.** Ed. by Hermann Kulke. (Oxford in India Readings). 380p. 1997. reprint ed. pap. 11.95 (*0-19-564267-8*) OUP.

State in Indian Tradition. Hartmut Scharfe. LC 89-25233. (Handbuch der Orientalistik. Zweite Abteilung Ser.). ix, 265p. 1990. pap. 92.00 (*90-04-09060-6*) E J Brill.

State in Modern Society: New Directions in Political Sociology. Roger King. LC 86-23320. 296p. (C). 1987. pap. text ed. 14.95 (*0-934540-60-8*) Chatham Hse Pubs.

State in Question: Transformations of the Australian State. Ed. by Paul James. 272p. 1996. pap. 24.95 (*1-86373-673-5*, Pub. by Allen Unwin AT) Paul & Co Pubs.

State in Relation to Labour. 4th ed. William S. Jevons. LC 67-16344. (Reprints of Economic Classics Ser.). xviii, 174p. 1968. reprint ed. 35.00 (*0-678-00434-X*) Kelley.

State in Socialist Society. Ed. by Neil Harding. LC 83-15339. 316p. 1984. text ed. 64.50 (*0-87395-838-1*); pap. text ed. 21.95 (*0-87395-839-X*) State U NY Pr.

State in the American Political Economy: Public Policy & the Evolution of State-Economy Relations. Marc A. Eisner. LC 94-16789. 416p. 1994. text ed. 58.00 (*0-13-294810-9*) P-H.

State in the Making: Myth, History, & Social Transformation in Pre-Colonial Ufipa. Roy G. Willis. LC 80-8155. (American Systems of Thought Ser.). 347p. reprint ed. pap. 99.80 (*0-685-23903-9*, 2056725) Bks Demand.

State in Theory & Practice. Harold J. Laski. 336p. 1967. 49.50 (*0-614-01806-4*) Elliots Bks.

State in Transition: Reimagining Political Space. Ed. by Joseph A. Camilleri et al. LC 94-38877. (Critical Perspectives on World Politics Ser.). 250p. 1995. lib. bdg. 49.95 (*1-55587-538-6*) Lynne Rienner.

State in Western Europe: Retreat or Redefinition? Ed. by Wolfgang C. Muller & Vincent Wright. LC 94-22208. 199p. 1994. 35.00 (*0-7146-4594-X*, Pub. by F Cass Pubs UK) Intl Spec Bk.

State Income Differentials, 1919-1954. Frank A. Hanna. LC 76-39841. 1977. reprint ed. text ed. 69.50 (*0-8371-9352-4*, HASD, Greenwood Pr) Greenwood.

State Income Tax Checkoff Programs: 1986 Update. (Legislative Finance Papers: No. 57). 1987. 6.25 (*1-55516-057-3*, 5101-57) Natl Conf State Legis.

State Income Taxation. Clara Penniman. LC 79-20081. 1980. 47.50 (*0-8018-2290-4*) Johns Hopkins.

State Income Taxes. ring bd. write for info. (*0-318-57359-8*) P-H.

State Indicators of Science & Mathematics Education 1995. Rolf Blank & Dorreen Gruebel. 130p. 1995. pap. 18.00 (*1-884037-13-5*) Coun Chief St Schl Offs.

State Individual Income Taxes. Emanuel O. Melichar. LC 94-76234. xxii, 424p. 1994. reprint ed. 52.00 (*0-89941-885-6*, 308490) W S Hein.

***State Information Book 1987-1988.** 1987. 75.00 (*0-8103-7796-9*, 00010269, Gale Res Intl) Gale.

State Initiatives on Industry-Based Skill Standards & Credentials. Evelyn Ganzglass & Martin Simon. Ed. by Karen Glass. 88p. (Orig.). 1993. pap. text ed. 15.00 (*1-55877-215-4*) Natl Governor.

State Initiatives to Establish Basic Health Insurance Plans. Matthew D. Pierce. (Working Paper Ser.: No. 61). 23p. 1992. pap. 5.50 (*0-89940-543-6*) LBJ Sch Pub Aff.

State Initiatives to Improve Rural Health Care. Amanda H. McCloskey & John Luehrs. Ed. by Karen Glass. 129p. (Orig.). 1990. pap. text ed. 15.00 (*1-55877-081-X*) Natl Governor.

State Input-Output Models for Transportation Impact Analysis. Benjamin H. Stevens et al. (Discussion Paper Ser.: No. 128). 21p. (Orig.). 1981. pap. 10.00 (*1-55869-005-0*) Regional Sci Res Inst.

State Insurance Department Resources Report. rev. ed. Ed. by Steve Lamberty. 74p. (C). 1995. pap. 35.00 (*0-89382-376-7*, STA-BB94) Nat Assn Insurance.

State Insurance Guarantee Funds. Roger A. Kessinger. 160p. (Orig.). 1991. pap. 24.95 (*1-56459-025-9*) Kessinger Pub.

State Insurance Regulation. Kathleen H. Ettlinger et al. LC 95-77157. (Illus.). 281p. (C). 1995. pap. text ed. 26.00 (*0-89462-088-6*, IR201) IIA.

State Interest in Cable Communications. Thomas A. Muth. Ed. by Christopher H. Sterling. LC 78-21728. (Dissertations in Broadcasting Ser.). 1980. lib. bdg. 30.95 (*0-405-11767-1*) Ayer.

State Intervention in British Industry, 1964-68. Frank Broadway. LC 79-115974. 191p. 1975. 25.00 (*0-8386-7690-1*) Fairleigh Dickinson.

State Intervention in Great Britain. Samuel J. Hurwitz. LC 70-76655. (Columbia University. Studies in the Social Sciences: No. 546). reprint ed. 20.00 (*0-404-51546-0*) AMS Pr.

State Intervention in Industry: A Worker's Inquiry. 2nd ed. Ed. by Spokesman, Bertrand Russell House Staff. (Illus.). 215p. 1982. pap. 28.50 (*0-85124-363-0*, Pub. by Spokesman Bks UK) Coronet Bks.

State Intervention in Medical Care: Consequences for Britain, France, Sweden, & the United States, 1890-1970. J. Rogers Hollingsworth et al. LC 89-25155. (Illus.). 320p. 1990. pap. 17.95 (*0-8014-9615-2*) Cornell U Pr.

State Investment Companies in Western Europe: Picking Winners or Backing Losers? Ed. by Brian Hindley. LC 83-13968. 293p. 1984. text ed. 39.95 (*0-312-75611-9*) St Martin.

State Is Your Enemy: Selections from the Anarchist Journal Freedom 1965-1986. Ed. by Freedom Press Staff. (Centenary Ser.: Vol. 6). 270p. (Orig.). 1991. pap. 10.00 (*0-900384-57-3*) Left Bank.

State Issues, 1992: A Survey of Priority Issues for State Legislatures. 116p. 1992. pap. text ed. 35.00 (*1-55516-987-2*, 9354) Natl Conf State Legis.

State Job Opportunities for Anthropologists. Compiled by D. B. Givens. 1986. 3.00 (*0-317-66270-8*) Am Anthro Assn.

State Justice Sourcebook of Statistics & Research. (Illus.). 250p. (Orig.). (C). 1993. pap. text ed. 45.00 (*1-56806-716-X*) DIANE Pub.

State, Labor, Capital: Democratizing Class Relations in the Southern Cone. Paul G. Buchanan. (Latin American Ser.). 328p. (C). 1996. 49.95 (*0-8229-3910-X*) U of Pittsburgh Pr.

State Land-Use Planning & Regulation: Florida, the Model Code, & Beyond. Thomas G. Pelham. LC 79-2390. 224p. reprint ed. pap. 63.90 (*0-7837-5773-5*, 2045438) Bks Demand.

State, Landlords & Peasants: Rajasthan in the 19th Century. Dilbagh Singh. 1990. 22.00 (*0-945921-14-4*, Pub. by S Asia Pubs II) S Asia.

State, Law, & Development: Problem Solving & Institutional Change in the Third World. Ann Seidman & Robert B. Seidman. LC 94-1156. (International Political Economy Ser.). 1994. text ed. 49.95 (*0-312-12171-7*) St Martin.

State, Law & Religion: Pagan Rome. Alan Watson. LC 91-14391. 192p. 1992. 30.00 (*0-8203-1387-4*) U of Ga Pr.

***State Law Challenges to School Discipline: An Outline of Claims & Case Summaries - Updated Edition.** 3rd ed. Robert Pressman. 116p. 1995. 20.00 (*0-912585-15-3*) Ctr Law & Ed.

State Laws see Securities Regulation Series

State Laws & Ordinances on Firearms. 60p. (Orig.). (C). 1993. pap. text ed. 25.00 (*1-56806-844-1*) DIANE Pub.

An Asterisk (*) at the beginning of an entry indicates that the title is appearing in BIP for the first time.

State Laws & Regulations on Truck Size & Weight. (National Cooperative Highway Research Program Report Ser.: No. 198). 117p. 1979. 7.20 (*0-309-02900-7*) Transport Res Bd.

State Lead Poisoning Prevention Directory 1992. Ed. by Doug Farquhar. 92p. 1992. pap. text ed. 12.00 (*1-55516-492-7*, 4631) Natl Conf State Legis.

State Leadership in Education: On Being a Chief State School Officer. Jerome T. Murphy. 144p. 1980. 12.00 (*0-318-03017-9*); pap. 7.00 (*0-318-03018-7*) Inst Educ Lead.

State Leadership in Improving Instruction: A Study of the Leadership Service Function of State Education Departments, with Special Reference to Louisiana, Tennessee & Virginia. William M. Alexander. LC 71-176508. (Columbia University. Teachers College. Contributions to Education Ser.: No. 820). reprint ed. 37.50 (*0-404-55820-8*) AMS Pr.

State Legislation & Programs in the Southeast: Child Abuse. 2nd ed. Clara L. Johnson. 162p. 1978. 5.00 (*0-318-16357-8*, B16) Regional Inst Social Welfare.

State Legislation Relating to Native Americans, 1991. James B. Reed. (State Legislative Reports: Vol. 16, No. 9). 19p. 1991. pap. text ed. 5.00 (*1-55516-308-4*, 7302-1609) Natl Conf State Legis.

State Legislative Committees: A Study in Procedure. Clinton I. Winslow. LC 74-2797. 158p. 1974. reprint ed. text ed. 49.75 (*0-8371-7435-X*, WISL, Greenwood Pr) Greenwood.

State Legislative Compilations: Selected Summaries of Real Estate Finance Law. LC 83-126340. 1994. 345.00 (*0-945359-62-4*) Mortgage Bankers.

State Legislative Elections: Voting Patterns & Demographics. Michael Barone et al. 400p. 1996. 125.00 (*1-56802-200-X*) Congr Quarterly.

State Legislative Leaders - 95. 1995. 59.50 (*0-87292-995-7*) Coun State Govts.

State Legislative Leaders, 1996. Council of State Government Staff. 1996. pap. text ed. 59.50 (*0-87292-905-1*) Coun State Govts.

State Legislative Leadership, Committees & Staff, 1989-90. 279p. 1989. 30.00 (*0-87292-087-9*) Coun State Govts.

State Legislative Leadership, Committees, & Staff 1991-92. Council of State Governments Staff. 290p. 1991. pap. 30.00 (*0-87292-961-2*, D-002-91) Coun State Govts.

State Legislative Leadership, Committees & Staff, 1993-94. 288p. 1993. pap. 30.00 (*0-87292-978-7*, D-023-92) Coun State Govts.

State Legislative Perceptions of Vocational Education. Ronald H. Field. 16p. 1984. 2.75 (*0-318-22202-7*, OC102) Ctr Educ Trng Employ.

State Legislative Potential: Challenge to American Federalism. Terry L. Sanford. 1974. 1.00 (*1-55614-007-X*) U of SD Gov Res Bur.

State Legislative Response to Crimes Against the Elderly. 25p. 1990. 10.00 (*1-55516-976-7*, 9333) Natl Conf State Legis.

***State Legislative Sourcebook (1997 Edition) A Resource Guide to Legislative Information in the Fifty States.** annuals 12th ed. Ed. by Lynn Hellebust. 496p. 1997. pap. 155.00 (*1-879929-20-1*) Govt Res Serv.

State Legislative Staff Directory 1993: Key Policy & Fiscal Contacts. Ed. by Jennifer Weberg. 167p. 1992. pap. text ed. 35.00 (*1-55516-988-0*); pap. text ed. 35.00 (*1-55516-991-0*, 9352) Natl Conf State Legis.

State Legislative Staff Directory, 1994. Denise Griffin & Valerie Jackson. 200p. 1994. 35.00 (*1-55516-994-5*, 9356) Natl Conf State Legis.

State Legislative Summary of Child & Maternal Health Legislation: 1992. Melissa K. Hough et al. 75p. 1993. pap. text ed. 15.00 (*1-55516-699-7*, 6644) Natl Conf State Legis.

***State Legislative Summary of Maternal & Child Health Legislation: 1993.** 1994. 15.00 (*1-55516-657-1*) Natl Conf State Legis.

State Legislative Summary, 1989: Children, Youth, & Family Issues. CYF Program Staff. 171p. 1990. pap. 15.00 (*1-55516-628-8*, 6116) Natl Conf State Legis.

State Legislative Summary, 1991: Children, Youth, & Family Issues. 125p. 1991. pap. text ed. 15.00 (*1-55516-644-X*, 6127) Natl Conf State Legis.

State Legislative Summary, 1993: Children, Youth, & Family Issues. NCSL Children, Youth & Families Program Staff. 192p. 1993. pap. text ed. 20.00 (*1-55516-647-4*, 6130) Natl Conf State Legis.

State Legislators' Occupations, 1994: A Survey. NCSL Legislative Management Staff. 35p. 1994. 20.00 (*1-55516-746-2*, 7138) Natl Conf State Legis.

State Legislature in India: (Bihar) Dayadhar Jha. 1977. 12.50 (*0-88386-969-1*) S Asia.

State Legislature Summary 1986: Children & Youth Issues. Children & Youth Program Staff. Ed. by Susan D. Robison. 138p. (Orig.). 1986. pap. 15.00 (*1-55516-619-9*) US HHS.

State Legislature Use of Information Technology: Proceedings of the U. S. Library of Congress, Science Policy Research Division, 9th Congress, 1st Session, 1977. U. S. Library of Congress, Science Policy Research Division Staff et al. LC 78-18915. (House Document Ser.: No. 271). 304p. 1978. reprint ed. text ed. 59.75 (*0-313-20519-1*, CHSL) Greenwood.

State-Level Data Book on Health Care Access & Financing. Pamela J. Loprest & Michael Gates. LC 93-14692. (Illus.). 190p. (Orig.). (C). 1993. pap. text ed. 35.00 (*0-87766-597-4*) Urban Inst.

State-Level Databook on Health Care Access & Financing. 2nd ed. Colin Winterbottom et al. 262p. (C). 1995. pap. text ed. 42.50 (*0-87766-633-4*) Urban Inst.

State Level Disclosure Guidelines see Securities Regulation Series

***State-Level K-12 Education Reform Activities.** 60p. 1994. pap. 8.00 (*0-614-30576-4*, SI-94-2) Ed Comm States.

State Liability for Outer Space Activities in Accordance with the 1972 Convention on International Liability for Damage Caused by Space Objects. Bruce A. Hurwitz. (Utrecht Studies in Air & Space Law). 264p. (C). 1992. lib. bdg. 119.00 (*0-7923-1463-8*) Kluwer Ac.

State Library Agencies: A Survey Project Report, 1991. 10th ed. Ed. by Amy L. Kellerstrass. 38p. 1991. 32.50 (*0-8389-7663-8*) ASCLA.

State Library Policy: Its Legislative & Environmental Contexts. Douglass St. Angelo et al. LC 71-171256. 128p. reprint ed. pap. 36.50 (*0-317-26369-2*, 2024221) Bks Demand.

State Library Services & Issues: Facing Future Challenges. Ed. by Charles R. McClure. LC 85-2287. 320p. 1986. text ed. 73.25 (*0-89391-317-0*) Ablex Pub.

State Licensure Reference Guide. 304p. (Orig.). 1995. pap. 21.00 (*0-614-10392-4*, A-7) Am Phys Therapy Assn.

State Limited Partnership Laws: Practice Guides, Statutes, Annotations & Official Forms. Michael A. Bamberger & Joseph J. Basile. LC 86-30532. write for info. (*0-15-004391-0*) P-H.

State Lines. Illus. by Rolf Laub. LC 93-3512. (Wardlaw Bk.). 240p. (C). 1993. 29.50 (*0-89096-557-9*); pap. 14.95 (*0-89096-562-5*) Tex A&M Univ Pr.

State-Local Fiscal Indicators. Steven D. Gold & Judy A. Zelio. 103p. (Orig.). 1990. pap. 25.00 (*1-55516-546-X*, 5316) Natl Conf State Legis.

State-Local Relations: A Partnership Approach. 2nd ed. Joseph F. Zimmerman. LC 95-2209. 272p. 1995. text ed. 65.00 (*0-275-95069-7*, Praeger Pubs); pap. text ed. 18.95 (*0-275-95235-5*, Praeger Pubs) Greenwood.

State-Local Tax Levels: Fiscal Year 1992. Scott R. Mackey. (Legislative Finance Papers: No. 92). 7p. 1994. 10.00 (*1-55516-552-4*, 5105-92) Natl Conf State Legis.

State Lotteries & Legalized Gambling: Painless Revenue or Painful Mirage. Richard McGowan. LC 94-15884. 192p. 1994. text ed. 55.00 (*0-89930-859-7*, Quorum Bks) Greenwood.

State Magazine Index 1966-1986. Ed. by Robert S. Bridgers et al. 300p. 1989. 59.50 (*0-916107-75-2*) Broadfoot.

***State Manufacturing Enterprise in a Mixed Economy: The Turkish Case.** Bertil Walstedt. LC 78-21398. 380p. 1980. reprint ed. pap. 108.30 (*0-608-03663-3*, 2064489) Bks Demand.

State Maps on File, 7 vols., Set. (Illus.). 1200p. 1989. ring bd. 425.00 (*0-8160-0116-2*) Facts on File.

State Maps on File: Mid-Atlantic. (Illus.). 142p. 1985. ring bd. 85.00 (*0-8160-0118-9*) Facts on File.

State Maps on File: Midwest. (Illus.). 182p. 1985. ring bd. 85.00 (*0-8160-0120-0*) Facts on File.

State Maps on File: Mountain & Prairie. (Illus.). 180p. 1985. ring bd. 85.00 (*0-8160-0121-9*) Facts on File.

State Maps on File: New England. (Illus.). 146p. 1985. ring bd. 85.00 (*0-8160-0117-0*) Facts on File.

State Maps on File: Southeast. (Illus.). 242p. 1985. ring bd. 85.00 (*0-8160-0119-7*) Facts on File.

State Maps on File: Southwest. (Illus.). 160p. 1985. ring bd. 85.00 (*0-8160-0122-7*) Facts on File.

State Maps on File: West. (Illus.). 160p. 1985. ring bd. 85.00 (*0-8160-0123-5*) Facts on File.

***State, Market & Organizational Form.** Ayse Bugra & Behlul Usdiken. LC 97-20076. (De Gruyter Studies in Organization). 1997. write for info. (*3-11-015468-4*) De Gruyter.

State, Market & Social Regulation: New Perspectives on Italy. Ed. by Peter Lange & Marino Regini. (Illus.). 320p. (C). 1989. text ed. 59.95 (*0-521-35453-6*) Cambridge U Pr.

State, Markets & Development: Beyond the Neoclassical Dichotomy. Ed. by Amitava K. Dutt et al. 240p. 1994. 80.00 (*1-85278-929-8*) E Elgar.

***State Medical Licensure Guidelines, 1997: Information Manual for MD & DO Physicians in the United States of America.** rev. ed. 150p. 1997. reprint ed. pap. 89.00 (*1-887617-53-1*) St Bart Pr Ltd.

State Mental Hospitals: Problems & Potentials. Ed. by John Talbott. LC 79-21928. 219p. 1980. 35.95 (*0-87705-394-4*) Human Sci Pr.

State Mental Hospitals & the Elderly: A Task Force Report of the American Psychatric Association. Task Force on Geriatric Psychiatry in the Public Health Sector. LC 93-6585. 110p. 1993. 21.50 (*0-89042-242-7*, 2242) Am Psychiatric.

State Mental Patient & Urban Life: Moving in & Out of the Institution. Dan A. Lewis & Arthur J. Lurigio. 146p. 1994. pap. 24.95 (*0-398-06238-2*) C C Thomas.

State Mental Patient & Urban Life: Moving in & Out of the Institution. Dan A. Lewis & Arthur J. Lurigio. 146p. (C). 1994. text ed. 37.95 (*0-398-05901-2*) C C Thomas.

State Methadone Treatment Guidelines: A Treatment Improvement Protocol. (Illus.). 393p. (Orig.). (C). 1994. pap. text ed. 50.00 (*0-7881-1166-3*) DIANE Pub.

State Mineral Enterprises: An Investigation into Their Impact on International Mineral Markets. Marian Radetzki. LC 85-2346. 150p. 1985. pap. text ed. 15.00 (*0-915707-16-0*) Resources Future.

State Mineral Summaries. 1994. lib. bdg. 256.75 (*0-8490-5790-6*) Gordon Pr.

State Minimum Teacher's Salary Schedule: A Part of Florida's State Minimum Educational Program. Paul R. Spencer. LC 77-177753. (Columbia University. Teachers College. Contributions to Education Ser.: No. 519). reprint ed. 37.50 (*0-404-55519-5*) AMS Pr.

State Municipal League Directory. 225p. 1985. 25.00 (*0-317-35181-8*, 2003) Natl League Cities.

State Murder Exposed: The Truth about the Killing of Joy Gardner. (Illus.). 150p. (Orig.). 1996. pap. 14.95 (*1-873045-12-3*, Pub. by IWB UK) Labor Pubns Inc.

State Museum of Ukrainian Folk Decorative Art. (ENG & RUS.). 1983. 231.00 (*0-317-57451-5*) St Mut.

State Names, Flags, Seals, Songs, Birds, Flowers, & Other Symbols: A Study Based on Historical Documents. George E. Shankle. 1971. reprint ed. 79.00 (*0-403-00784-4*) Scholarly.

State Names, Seals, Flags, & Symbols: A Historical Guide. expanded rev. ed. Benjamin F. Shearer & Barbara S. Shearer. LC 93-49552. 440p. 1994. text ed. 49.95 (*0-313-28862-3*, Greenwood Pr) Greenwood.

State, Nation, Ethnicity & the Rise of Separatist Movements in Contemporary South Asia. Ishtiaq Ahmed. LC 95-36993. 288p. 1996. 90.00 (*0-86187-747-0*, Pub. by Pntr Pubs UK) Bks Intl VA.

***State Nobility: 'Grandes Ecoles' & Esprit de Corps.** Pierre Bourdieu. 1996. 55.00 (*0-8047-1778-8*) Stanford U Pr.

State Nursing Boards for Practical Nurse (SNB-PN) Jack Rudman. (Admission Test Ser.: ATS-46). 1994. pap. 29.95 (*0-8373-5046-8*) Nat Learn.

State Nursing Boards for Registered Nurse (SNB-RN) Jack Rudman. (Admission Test Ser.: ATS-45). 1994. pap. 29.95 (*0-8373-5045-X*) Nat Learn.

***State Nursing Licensure Guidelines, 1997: Information Manual for Nurses in the United States of America.** Jason F. Janoulis & Brenda H. Janoulis. 224p. 1997. pap. 89.00 (*1-887617-54-X*) St Bart Pr Ltd.

State of Academic Science: Background Papers, Vol. 2. Bruce L. Smith & Joseph J. Karlesky. LC 77-72979. 1977. pap. 21.95 (*0-915390-13-2*, Pub. by Change Mag) Transaction Pubs.

State of Academic Science: The Role of the Universities in the Nation's R & D Effort, Vol. 1. Bruce L. Smith & Joseph J. Karlesky. LC 77-72979. (Orig.). 1977. pap. 21.95 (*0-915390-09-4*, Pub. by Change Mag) Transaction Pubs.

State of Afro-American History: Past, Present & Future. Ed. by Darlene C. Hine. LC 85-24138. xi, 301p. 1986. pap. text ed. 16.95 (*0-8071-1581-9*) La State U Pr.

***State of Alternative Fuel Technologies, 1997.** 1997. 93.00 (*0-7680-0002-5*) Soc Auto Engineers.

State of American Education. Ed. & Pref. by Robert E. Long. LC 84-22110. (Reference Shelf Ser.: Vol. 56, No. 5). 231p. 1984. pap. 15.00 (*0-8242-0699-1*) Wilson.

State of Americans. Urie Bronfenbrenner et al. (Illus.). 192p. 1996. 22.00 (*0-684-82336-5*) Free Pr.

State of America's Children Yearbook 1995. Children's Defense Fund Staff. 144p. 1995. pap. 14.95 (*1-881985-10-5*) Childrens Defense.

State of America's Children Yearbook 1996. Children's Defense Fund Staff. 110p. (Orig.). 1996. pap. 14.95 (*1-881985-11-3*) Childrens Defense.

***State of America's Children Yearbook 1997.** 1997. write for info. (*1-881985-13-X*) Childrens Defense.

State of Asia. Lawrence K. Rosinger et al. LC 76-134131. (Essay Index Reprint Ser.). 1977. 30.95 (*0-8369-2069-4*) Ayer.

State of Asian America: Activism & Resistance in the 1990s. Ed. by Karin Aguilar-San Juan. (Race & Resistance Ser.). (Illus.). 460p. (Orig.). 1993. 40.00 (*0-89608-477-9*) South End Pr.

State of Asian America: Activism & Resistance in the 1990s. Ed. by Karin Aguilar-San Juan. (Race & Resistance Ser.). (Illus.). 460p. (Orig.). 1993. pap. 16.00 (*0-89608-476-0*) South End Pr.

State of Asian America: Reframing the Immigration Debate. Ed. by Bill O. Hing & Ronald Lee. 322p. (C). 1996. text ed. write for info. (*0-934052-26-3*) UCLA Asian Am Studies Ctr.

State of Bihar: An Economic History Without Footnotes. Arvind Das. 116p. 1993. pap. text ed. 20.00 (*90-5383-135-5*, Pub. by VU Univ Pr NE) Paul & Co Pubs.

State of Black America: 1989, Vol. 13. Ed. by Janet Dewart. 257p. 1989. pap. 24.00 (*0-914758-10-1*) Transaction Pubs.

State of Black America 1980, Vol. 4. Ed. by James D. Williams. 287p. 1980. pap. 24.95 (*0-87855-891-8*) Transaction Pubs.

State of Black America 1981, Vol. 5. Ed. by James D. Williams. 340p. 1981. pap. 24.95 (*0-87855-892-6*) Transaction Pubs.

State of Black America, 1982, Vol. 6. Ed. by James D. Williams. 324p. 1982. pap. 24.95 (*0-87855-890-X*) Transaction Pubs.

State of Black America, 1983, Vol. 7. Ed. by James D. Williams. LC 77-647469. (Illus.). 325p. 1983. pap. 24.95 (*0-87855-937-X*) Transaction Pubs.

State of Black America, 1986. Ed. by Janet Dewart. 235p. 1986. pap. text ed. 24.00 (*0-914759-37-X*) Transaction Pubs.

State of Black America, 1987, Vol. 11. Ed. by Janet Dewart. 261p. 1988. pap. 24.00 (*0-914758-07-1*) Transaction Pubs.

State of Black America, 1988, Vol. 12. Ed. by Janet Dewart. 239p. 1988. pap. 24.00 (*0-914758-08-X*) Transaction Pubs.

State of Black America, 1989, Vol. 10. Ed. by Janet Dewart. 325p. 1986. pap. 18.00 (*0-685-35028-2*) Natl Urban Leag DC.

State of Black America, 1990. Ed. by Janet Dewart. 332p. 1990. pap. 24.00 (*0-914758-11-X*) Transaction Pubs.

State of Black Cleveland, 1989. Ed. by Willa M. Hemmons & Margaret Thoren. 180p. (Orig.). (C). 1989. pap. 19.00 (*0-9622700-8-3*); pap. text ed. 19.00 (*0-9622700-9-1*) Urban Lea Greater Cleve.

State of Black Cleveland, 1990. Ed. by Margaret L. Thoren. (Illus.). 100p. (Orig.). 1990. pap. 19.00 (*0-9622700-1-6*) Urban Lea Greater Cleve.

State of California Commission on Judicial Performance: 1993 Annual Report. (Illus.). 61p. (Orig.). (C). 1994. pap. text ed. 25.00 (*0-7881-0873-5*) DIANE Pub.

State of Canada's Forests (1994) A Balancing Act. (Illus.). 112p. (Orig.). (C). 1995. pap. text ed. 30.00 (*0-7881-1837-4*) DIANE Pub.

***State of Canada's Forests 1995-1996: Sustaining Forests at Home & Abroad.** (Illus.). 112p. (Orig.). 1996. pap. text ed. 35.00 (*0-7881-3626-7*) DIANE Pub.

State of Change. Christopher Bulis. (Dr. Who Missing Adventures Ser.). (Illus.). 1995. mass mkt. 5.95 (*0-426-20431-X*, Pub. by Virgin Pub UK) London Brdge.

***State of Child Health in the Eastern Mediterranean Region.** (EMRO Technical Publications: Vol. 13). 213p. 1995. pap. 20.00 (*92-9021-187-3*, 1450009) World Health.

State of Church Giving Through 1991. John L. Ronsvalle. 88p. 1993. pap. 12.00 (*0-9639962-2-3*) Empty Tomb.

State of Church Giving Through 1992. John L. Ronsvalle. 74p. 1994. pap. 13.00 (*0-9639962-3-1*) Empty Tomb.

State of Church Giving Through 1993. John L. Ronsvalle. (State of Church Giving Ser.). 124p. (Orig.). 1995. pap. 14.00 (*0-9639962-4-X*) Empty Tomb.

***State of Church Giving Through 1994.** John L. Ronsvalle & Sylvia Ronsvalle. (State of Church Giving Ser.). 90p. (Orig.). 1996. pap. 14.00 (*0-9639962-5-8*) Empty Tomb.

State of Colorado Archaeology. Ed. by Philip Duke & Gary Matlock. (Memoir Ser.: No. 5). 1992. pap. text ed. 12.95 (*1-888400-02-1*) Colo Archaeol.

***State of Corrections: Proceedings - ACA Annual Conferences, 1995.** 290p. 1996. pap. 25.00 (*1-56991-039-1*) Am Correctional.

State of Corrections: Proceedings of the American Correctional Association, 1994. 280p. 1995. 25.00 (*1-56991-023-5*) Am Correctional.

***State of Cybernation: Cultural, Political & Economic Implications of the Internet.** Neil Barratt. (Business & Management Ser.). 1996. 19.95 (*0-7494-2053-7*) Kogan Page Ltd.

State of Deference: Ragusa - Dubrovnik in the Medieval Centuries. Susan M. Stuard. LC 92-12164. (Middle Ages Ser.). (Illus.). 288p. (C). 1992. 33.50 (*0-8122-3178-3*) U of Pa Pr.

State of Denmark. Derek Raymond. (Mask Noir Ser.). 272p. (Orig.). 1995. pap. 12.99 (*1-85242-315-3*) Serpents Tail.

State of Deseret. Dale L. Morgan. LC 87-21632. 215p. reprint ed. pap. 61.30 (*0-7837-7063-4*, 2046875) Bks Demand.

State of Disorder. Tirso de Molina. Ed. by Round. write for info. (*0-85668-503-8*, Pub. by Aris & Phillips UK); pap. write for info. (*0-85668-504-6*, Pub. by Aris & Phillips UK) David Brown.

State of Distance & Flexible Learning Today: ILI Special Report. Lieve Van den Brande. 263p. 1993. text ed. 195.00 (*0-471-93015-6*) Wiley.

State of Earth Science from Space: Past Progress, Future Prospects. Ed. by Ghassem Asrar & David Dokken. (Illus.). 170p. 1995. 75.00 (*1-56396-492-9*) Am Inst Physics.

State of Economic Science: Views of Six Nobel Laureates. Ed. by Werner Sichel. LC 89-27443. 115p. 1989. text ed. 20.00 (*0-88099-084-8*); pap. text ed. 10.00 (*0-88099-083-X*) W E Upjohn.

State of Education in Canada. Thomas T. Schweitzer. 142p. 1996. pap. 15.95 (*0-88645-159-0*, Pub. by Inst Res Pub CN) Ashgate Pub Co.

***State of Emergency.** Steve Pieczenik. LC 97-24400. 288p. 1997. 23.95 (*0-399-14323-8*) Putnam Pub Group.

State of Emergency. Floyd Salas. LC 95-45264. 394p. 1996. 22.95 (*1-55885-093-7*); pap. 11.95 (*1-55885-155-0*) Arte Publico.

State of Emergency: Nyasaland 1959. Colin Baker. 208p. 1997. text ed. 59.50 (*1-86064-068-0*, Pub. by I B Tauris UK) St Martin.

***State of European Cinema: A New Dose of Reality.** Angus Finney. (Cassell Film Studies). (Illus.). 224p. 1997. 75.00 (*0-304-33300-X*); pap. 21.95 (*0-304-33302-6*) Cassell.

State of Extremes: Guide to the Wild Weather of South Dakota. Jay Trobec. (Illus.). 200p. 1995. pap. 14.95 (*0-9648410-5-3*) Wheres ware.

State of Families Four: Family, Employment & Reconstruction - Policy Based on What Works. Lynn A. Curtis. LC 87-24374. 158p. 1995. pap. 16.95 (*0-87304-270-0*) Families Intl.

State of Families, One: 1984-85. Family Service America Staff. LC 84-18792. (Illus.). 88p. reprint ed. pap. 25.10 (*0-7837-1631-1*, 2041924) Bks Demand.

State of Families Three: Losing Direction: Families, Human Resource Development, & Economic Performance. Ray Marshall. LC 87-24374. 160p. 1991. pap. 15.00 (*0-87304-249-2*) Families Intl.

State of Families Two: Work & Family. R. Morton Darrow. LC 87-24374. 96p. (Orig.). 1987. pap. 10.00 (*0-87304-226-3*) Families Intl.

***State of Food & Agriculture 1990.** (Agriculture Ser.: No. 23). 223p. 1991. 50.00 (*92-5-102989-X*, F989X, Pub. by FAO IT) Bernan Associates.

State of Food & Agriculture, 1992. FAO Staff. 280p. 1993. pap. 50.00 (*92-5-103226-2*, F32262, Pub. by FAO IT) Bernan Associates.

***State of Food & Agriculture 1993.** (Agriculture Ser.: No. 26). 328p. 1993. 50.00 (*92-5-103360-9*, F33609, Pub. by FAO IT) Bernan Associates.

***State of Food & Agriculture 1995 - Agricultural Trade: Entering a New Era?** 280p. 1995. pap. 55.00 (*92-5-103700-0*, F37000, Pub. by FAO IT) Bernan Associates.

S

An Asterisk (*) at the beginning of an entry indicates that the title is appearing in BIP for the first time.

State of Germany: The National Idea in the Making, Unmaking & Remaking of a Modern Nation State. Ed. by John Brevilly. 243p. (C). 1992. pap. text ed. 22.75 (*0-685-72534-0*, 79344) Longman.

State of Germany: The National Idea in the Making, Unmaking & the Remaking of a National State. John Breuilly. (C). 1992. pap. text ed. 27.50 (*0-582-07865-2*) Addison-Wesley.

State of Grace. Joy Williams. 1990. pap. 12.00 (*0-679-72619-5*, Vin) Random.

State of Graduate Education. Ed. by Bruce L. Smith. LC 85-72214. (Dialogues on Public Policy Ser.). 193p. 1985. pap. 11.95 (*0-8157-7995-X*) Brookings.

State of Granite: What Makes New Hampshire Work? unabridged ed. Jack Falvey. 223p. (Orig.). 1995. pap. 16. 95 (*0-9650616-0-4*) Intermark.

***State of Hawai'i Coloring Book.** Illus. by Wren. 32p. (Orig.). (J). (gr. k-8). 1997. pap. 4.95 (*1-57306-058-5*) Bess Pr.

State of Health Atlas. Judith MacKay et al. LC 92-27298. 128p. 1993. pap. 16.00 (*0-671-79375-6*, Touchstone Bks) S&S Trade.

State of Health Care in America (1995) (Illus.). 66p. (Orig.). (C). 1995. pap. text ed. 20.00 (*0-7881-2451-X*) DIANE Pub.

***State of Health Care in America (1996)** (Illus.). 66p. (Orig.). 1996. pap. text ed. 25.00 (*0-7881-3709-3*) DIANE Pub.

***State of Health in America.** Michael Scigliano. (Illus.). 160p. 1997. pap. write for info. (*0-9656924-1-8*) Uptime Sprts Nutrit.

State of High Energy Physics, No. 134. Ed. by Melvin Month et al. LC 85-73170. 382p. 1985. lib. bdg. 46.00 (*0-88318-333-1*) Am Inst Physics.

State of Humanity. Julian L. Simon. LC 94-31956. 694p. 1996. pap. 26.95 (*1-55786-585-X*) Blackwell Pubs.

State of Illinois Application & Statewide Strategy to Control Drug & Violent Crime. (Illus.). 125p. (Orig.). (C). 1993. pap. text ed. 35.00 (*1-56806-911-1*) DIANE Pub.

State of Independence. Caryl Phillips. 158p. 1986. 13.95 (*0-374-26976-9*) FS&G.

State of Independence. Caryl Phillips. LC 94-31112. 1995. pap. 10.00 (*0-679-75930-1*, Vin) Random.

State of Interpretation of Keynes. Ed. by John B. Davis. LC 94-34751. (Recent Economic Thought Ser.). 272p. (C). 1994. lib. bdg. 93.00 (*0-7923-9508-5*) Kluwer Ac.

State of Intrigue: The Epic of Bamana Segu According to Tayiru Banbera. Ed. by David C. Conrad. Tr. by Soumaila Diakite. (Fontes Historiae Africanae, Series Varia: Vol. VI). (Illus.). 372p. 1990. pap. 85.00 (*0-19-726088-8*) OUP.

***State of Israel, Diaspora, & Jewish Continuity: Essays on the Ever-Dying People.** Simon Rawidowicz. Ed. by Benjamin C. Ravid. (Tauber Institute for the Study of European Jewry Ser.: Vol. 26). 256p. 1997. pap. 22.00 (*0-87451-846-6*) U Pr of New Eng.

State of Israel in Jewish Public Thought: The Quest for Collective Identity. Yosef Gorny. LC 93-27378. (C). 1994. 40.00 (*0-8147-3055-8*) NYU Pr.

State of Israel, the Land of Israel: The Statist & Ethnonational Dimensions of Foreign Policy. Shmuel Sandler. LC 92-37518. (Contributions in Political Science Ser.: No. 321). 320p. 1993. text ed. 57.95 (*0-313-28822-4*, GM8822) Greenwood.

State of Jefferson & Other Yarns. Thomas K. Worcester. (Illus.). 80p. (Orig.). 1982. pap. 7.95 (*0-911518-65-7*) Touchstone Oregon.

State of Jewish Studies. Ed. by Shaye J. Cohen & Edward L. Greenstein. LC 89-39860. 280p. (C). 1990. pap. text ed. 19.95 (*0-8143-2195-X*) Wayne St U Pr.

State of Jewish Studies. Ed. by Shaye J. Cohen & Edward L. Greenstein. LC 89-39860. 280p. (C). 1990. text ed. 39.95 (*0-8143-2194-1*) Wayne St U Pr.

State of Literacy in San Antonio in the 1990's. Maria R. Montecel et al. (Illus.). 24p. (Orig.). 1994. pap. text ed. 10.00 (*1-878550-50-0*) Inter Dev Res Assn.

State of Martial Rule: The Origins of Pakistan's Political Economy of Defence. Ayesha Jalal. (Cambridge South Asian Studies: No. 46). (Illus.). 350p. (C). 1990. text ed. 65.00 (*0-521-37348-4*) Cambridge U Pr.

State of Mathematics Achievement: NAEP's 1990 Assessment of the Nation & the Trial Assessment of the States (Complete Report) Ina V. Mullis et al. (Illus.). 532p. (Orig.). (C). 1993. pap. text ed. 75.00 (*0-7881-0107-2*) DIANE Pub.

State of Mathematics Achievement: NAEP's 1990 Assessment of the Nation & the Trial Assessment of the States (Executive Summary) Ina V. Mullis et al. (Illus.). 51p. (Orig.). (C). 1993. pap. text ed. 25.00 (*0-7881-0106-4*) DIANE Pub.

State of Matter: A Volume Dedicated to E. H. Lieb. M. Aizenman & H. Araki. (Advanced Series in Mathematical Physics). 500p. 1994. text ed. 109.00 (*981-02-1669-6*) World Scientific Pub.

State of Matter: A Volume Dedicated to E. H. Lieb. Ed. by M. Aizenman & H. Araki. (Advanced Series in Mathematical Physics: Vol. 20). 500p. 1994. pap. 109.00 (*981-02-1721-8*) World Scientific Pub.

***State of Mind.** John Katzenbach. LC 97-1415. 1997. 24.00 (*0-345-38631-0*, Ballantine Epiphany) Ballantine.

State of Mind. Martha Ronk. (New American Poetry Ser.: No. 21). 120p. (Orig.). 1996. pap. 10.95 (*1-55713-236-4*) Sun & Moon CA.

State of Mind. Ed. by Robert N. Linscott. LC 72-8483. (Essay Index Reprint Ser.). 1977. reprint ed. 28.95 (*0-8369-7321-6*) Ayer.

State of Minority Languages: International Perspectives on Survival & Decline. Ed. by W. Fase et al. (European Studies on Multilingualism: Vol. 5). vi, 318p. 1995. pap. 48.00 (*90-265-1414-X*) Swets.

State of Monetary Economics. Universities-National Bureau Staff. (Conference Ser.: No. 16). 159p. 1965. reprint ed. 41.40 (*0-87014-307-7*) Natl Bur Econ Res.

State of Monetary Economics: Proceedings. Conference of the Universities. LC 75-19702. (National Bureau of Economic Research Ser.). (Illus.). 1975. reprint ed. 19.95 (*0-405-07582-0*) Ayer.

State of Native America: Genocide, Colonization, & Resistance. Ed. by M. Annette Jaimes. (Race & Resistance Ser.). 480p. (Orig.). 1992. 40.00 (*0-89608-425-6*); pap. 18.00 (*0-89608-424-8*) South End Pr.

State of Nature: Ecology, Community & American Social Thought, 1900-1950. Gregg Mitman. (Science & Its Conceptual Foundations Ser.). (Illus.). 304p. (C). 1992. pap. text ed. 26.50 (*0-226-53237-2*) U Ch Pr.

State of Nature: Ecology, Community & American Social Thought, 1900-1950. Gregg Mitman. (Science & Its Conceptual Foundations Ser.). (Illus.). 304p. (C). 1992. lib. bdg. 67.00 (*0-226-53236-4*) U Ch Pr.

***State of New Jersey: Final Report of the Gettysburg Battlefield Monument Commission.** Ed. by David G. Martin. (Illus.). 165p. 1997. reprint ed. 20.00 (*0-944413-41-2*, 209) Longstreet Hse.

State of New York City's Municipal Hospital System, Fiscal Year 1995: Report of the City Hospital Visiting Committee. United Hospital Fund, City Hospital Visiting Committee Staff. 56p. 1995. pap. 10.00 (*1-881277-26-7*) United Hosp Fund.

***State of New York City's Municipal Hospital System, Fiscal Year 1996: Report of the City Hospital Visiting Committee.** United Hospital Fund, City Hospital Visiting Committee Staff. 48p. 1996. pap. 10.00 (*1-881277-30-5*) United Hosp Fund.

***State of N.J. Index of Wills, Inventories, Etc., in the Office of the Secretary of State Prior to 1901, 3 vols., Set.** Compiled by Office of the Secretary of State Staff. 1452p. 1996. reprint ed. lib. bdg. 156.00 (*0-8328-5213-9*) Higginson Bk Co.

State of North Carolina vs Christian Liberty. Kent Kelly. 112p. (Orig.). 1978. pap. 2.95 (*0-9604138-3-9*) Calvary Pr.

State of Ohio vs. Isaac Milton Smith, Murder. Ottie W. Reno. LC 90-55329. (Illus.). 376p. 1991. 24.95 (*0-8453-4832-9*, Cornwall Bks) Assoc Univ Prs.

State of Our Prisons. Roy King & Kathleen McDermott. (Clarendon Studies in Criminology). 300p. 1996. text ed. 69.00 (*0-19-825449-0*) OUP.

State of Particle Accelerators & High Energy Physics (Fermilab Summer School, 1981) Ed. by Melvin Month et al. LC 82-73861. (AIP Conference Proceedings Ser.: No. 92). 337p. 1982. lib. bdg. 33.75 (*0-88318-191-6*) Am Inst Physics.

State of Peace: The Women Speak. Ed. by Elaine Starkman et al. 88p. 1987. pap. 8.00 (*0-940584-12-3*) Gull Bks.

State of Philosophy: An Invitation to a Reading in Three Parts of Stanley Cavell's "The Claim of Reason" Richard Fleming. LC 92-54948. (C). 1993. 33.50 (*0-8387-5253-5*) Bucknell U Pr.

State of Play Eight: INDECS. 304p. 1995. 24.95 (*1-86373-879-7*) Paul & Co Pubs.

State of Police Education: Policy Direction for the 21st Century. David Carter et al. LC 89-60695. 172p. (Orig.). (C). 1988. pap. text ed. 16.50 (*1-878734-00-8*) Police Exec Res.

State of Prisons & of Child-Saving Institutions in the Civilized World. Enoch C. Wines. LC 68-55784. (Criminology, Law Enforcement, & Social Problems Ser.: No. 24). 1968. reprint ed. 30.00 (*0-87585-024-3*) Patterson Smith.

State of Prisons in England & Wales. 4th ed. John Howard. 1973. reprint ed. write for info. (*0-318-62184-3*) Patterson Smith.

State of Prisons in England & Wales see Prisons & Lazarettos

State of Public Bureaucracy. Ed. by Larry B. Hill. LC 91-39830. (Bureaucracies, Public Administration & Public Policy Ser.). 248p. (C). (gr. 13). 1992. text ed. 59.95 (*1-56324-007-6*); pap. text ed. 24.95 (*1-56324-008-4*) M E Sharpe.

State of Public Management. Ed. by Donald F. Kettl & H. Brinton Milward. LC 95-50984. 336p. 1996. pap. text ed. 16.95 (*0-8018-5276-5*) Johns Hopkins.

State of Public Management. Ed. by Donald F. Kettl & H. Brinton Milward. LC 95-50984. 336p. (C). 1996. text ed. 45.00 (*0-8018-5275-7*) Johns Hopkins.

State of Quality in Logistics: Findings from the Cleveland Consulting Associates' Survey of Logistics Professionals. (Illus.). 34p. (Orig.). (C). 1993. pap. text ed. 25.00 (*1-56806-380-6*) DIANE Pub.

State of Rebellion: Reconstruction in South Carolina, 1865-1877. Richard Zuczek. LC 95-50219. (Illus.). 260p. 1996. text ed. 29.95 (*1-57003-105-3*) U of SC Pr.

State of Robeson County, North Carolina. Robert C. Lawrence. 279p. 1994. reprint ed. lib. bdg. 32.50 (*0-8328-4154-4*) Higginson Bk Co.

State of Science & Research: Some New Indicators. Ed. by Nestor E. Terleckyj. (Illus.). 200p. 1977. 22.00 (*0-89158-124-3*) Natl Planning.

State of Sequoyah: An Impressionistic Look at Eastern Oklahoma. Jerald C. Walker. LC 85-11362. (Illus.). 116p. 1985. 25.00 (*0-913504-95-5*) Lowell Pr.

***State of Siege.** Eric Ambler. 3.95 (*0-7867-0717-8*) Carroll & Graf.

State of Siege. Eric Ambler. 160p. 1991. pap. 3.95 (*0-88184-717-8*) Carroll & Graf.

State of Siege. Janet Frame. LC 66-20188. 1981. pap. 10.95 (*0-8076-0986-2*) Braziller.

State of Siege: Ukraine's National Predicament. Yuriy Badzyo. Ed. by Roman Senkus. LC 81-67209. (Illus.). 130p. (Orig.). 1981. 9.95 (*0-86725-001-1*); pap. 3.75 (*0-86725-000-3*) ERUHG.

State of Siege see Caligula & Three Other Plays

***State of Small Business, 2 vols.** 1997. lib. bdg. 600.95 (*0-8490-6234-9*) Gordon Pr.

State of Social Psychology: Issues, Themes, & Controversies. Mark R. Leary. 152p. (C). 1989. text ed. 36.00 (*0-8039-3621-4*); pap. text ed. 16.95 (*0-8039-3622-2*) Sage.

State of Sociology: Problems & Prospects. Ed. by James F. Short. LC 81-8576. 303p. reprint ed. pap. 86.40 (*0-8357-4854-5*, 2037786) Bks Demand.

State of State: An Inquiry Concerning the Role of Invisible Hands in Political & Civil Society. Nils Karlson. (Skrifter Stat for Uppsala Ser.: No. 117). 234p. (Orig.). 1993. pap. 43.00 (*91-554-3104-6*, Pub. by Uppsala Universitet SW) Coronet Bks.

State of Strategy. Harvard Business Review Staff. (Strategy in Action Ser.). 151p. 1991. pap. 19.95 (*0-87584-271-2*) Harvard Busn.

State of Strategy. Harvard Business School Press Staff. 1991. pap. text ed. 19.95 (*0-07-103331-9*) McGraw.

***State of Terror.** Annamarie Oliverio. LC 97-17274. (SUNY Series in Deviance & Social Control). 192p. (C). 1998. text ed. 59.50 (*0-7914-3707-8*); pap. text ed. 19.95 (*0-7914-3708-6*) State U NY Pr.

***State of the Apostate.** James D. Spinnati. 96p. (Orig.). 1995. pap. 5.95 (*1-56794-086-2*, C-2383) Star Bible.

State of the Art. Iain M. Banks. 1989. 16.00 (*0-929480-06-6*) Mark Ziesing.

State of the Art. limited ed. Iain M. Banks. 1989. 40.00 (*0-929480-07-4*) Mark Ziesing.

State of the Art: Irrigation Drainage & Flood Control, No. 1. 676p. 1978. 27.00 (*0-318-16938-X*) US Comm Irrigation.

State of the Art: Irrigation Drainage & Flood Control, No. 2. 264p. 1981. 27.00 (*81-85068-02-X*) US Comm Irrigation.

State of the Art: Irrigation Drainage & Flood Control, No. 3. 1984. 25.00 (*81-85068-08-9*) US Comm Irrigation.

State of the Art: Issues in Contemporary Mass Communication. David Shimkin et al. LC 91-61131. 512p. (Orig.). (C). 1992. pap. text ed. 27.25 (*0-312-05543-9*) St Martin.

State of the Art: Small Scale (to 50 kw) Gas Producer Engine Systems. A. Kaupp & J. R. Goss. (Illus.). 278p. (Orig.). 1983. 40.00 (*0-942914-03-1*); pap. 20.00 (*0-942914-02-3*) Tipi Wkshp Bks.

***State of the Art: Transforming Ideas for Teaching & Learning Mathematics.** 1997. lib. bdg. 250.95 (*0-8490-8110-6*) Gordon Pr.

State of the Art: Wisconsin Painting & Drawing. (Illus.). 20p. 1982. pap. 5.00 (*0-932718-11-6*) Kohler Arts.

State-of-the-Art Computer Applications in Concrete Technology. Ed. by Fernando E. Fagundo. LC 88-83275. (American Concrete Institute Publication Ser.: No. SP-111). 123p. 1988. reprint ed. pap. 35.10 (*0-608-01423-0*, 2062186) Bks Demand.

State of the Art in Community-Based Education in the American Community College. Kenneth B. McGuire. Ed. by Ervin L. Harlacher. LC 88-151056. 83p. reprint ed. pap. 25.00 (*0-7837-2482-9*, 2042638) Bks Demand.

State-of-the-Art in Computer Animation. Ed. by N. Magnenat-Thalmann & Daniel Thalmann. (Illus.). viii, 227p. 1989. 109.00 (*0-387-70046-3*) Spr-Verlag.

State-of-the-Art in Computer Graphics: Aspects of Visualization. Ed. by David F. Rogers & Rae A. Earnshaw. LC 93-33016. 1993. 199.95 (*0-387-94164-9*) Spr-Verlag.

State of the Art in Computer Graphics: Visualization & Modeling. Ed. by D. F. Rogers & P. A. Earnshaw. (Illus.). 368p. 1991. 118.95 (*0-387-97560-8*) Spr-Verlag.

State of the Art in Digital Mammographic Image Analysis. K. W. Bowyer & S. Astley. (Series in Machine Perception & Artificial Intelligence: Vol. 9). 308p. 1994. text ed. 109.00 (*981-02-1509-6*) World Scientific Pub.

State of the Art in Family Therapy Research: Controversies & Recommendations. Ed. by Lyman C. Wynne. (Orig.). 1987. text ed. 30.00 (*0-9615519-2-5*) Family Process.

State of the Art in Family Therapy Research: Controversies & Recommendations. Intro. by Lyman C. Wynne. LC 87-951. 312p. (Orig.). 1988. pap. 18.00 (*0-9615519-3-3*) Family Process.

State of the Art in Global Optimization: Computational Methods & Applications. Ed. by Christodoulos A. Floudas & Panos M. Pardalos. LC 95-43930. (Nonconvex Optimization & Its Applications Ser.: No. 7). 1996. lib. bdg. 299.00 (*0-7923-3838-3*) Kluwer Ac.

***State of the Art in Numerical Analysis.** Ed. by I. S. Duff & G. A. Watson. (The Institute of Mathematics & Its Applications Conference Ser.: No. 63). (Illus.). 1997. 185.00 (*0-19-850014-9*) OUP.

State of the Art in Quantitative Coronary Arteriography. Ed. by Johan H. Reiber & Patrick W. Serruys. (Developments in Cardiovascular Medicine Ser.). 1986. lib. bdg. 208.50 (*0-89838-804-X*) Kluwer Ac.

***State of the Art in Small Business & Entrepreneurship: GREPME - Research Group in the Economy & Management of Small & Medium Sized Enterprises.** Pierre-Andre Julien. 492p. 1997. text ed. 59.95 (*1-85972-409-4*, Pub. by Ashgate UK) Ashgate Pub Co.

State of the Art in Wind Engineering: Davenport Sixtieth Birthday Anniversary Volume. International Association Wind Engineering Staff. 1994. write for info. (*81-224-0718-8*, Pub. by Wiley Estrn II) Franklin.

State of the Art Marketing Research. A. B. Blankinship. 608p. 1994. 44.95 (*0-8442-3457-5*, NTC Busn Bks) NTC Pub Grp.

State of the Art of Computer Aided Environmental Design. Kaiman Lee. LC 76-358975. (Illus.). 309p. 1975. 50.00 (*0-915250-14-4*) Environ Design.

State of the Art of Energy Efficiency: Future Directions. Ed. by Edward Vine & Drury Crawley. 287p. (C). 1991. pap. 29.00 (*0-918249-11-2*) Am Coun Energy.

***State of the Art of Entrepreneurship.** Donald L. Sexton & Raymond W. Smilor. LC 96-43653. 1996. write for info. (*1-57410-064-5*) Upstart Pub.

State of the Art of Entrepreneurship. Donald L. Sexton & John D. Kasarda. 512p. 1992. text ed. 73.95 (*0-534-92868-4*) S-W Pub.

State of the Art of Precast Prestressed Concrete Tank Construction. 50p. 1983. 22.00 (*0-318-17393-X*, JR283) P-PCI.

***State-of-the-Art of Spliced Girder Bridges.** 134p. 1994. pap. text ed. 30.00 (*0-614-25741-7*, SG-92) P-PCI.

State of the Art of Surgery, Nineteen Seventy-Nine to Nineteen Eighty. Ed. by M. Allgower & F. Arder. 116p. 1980. 18.95 (*0-387-10136-5*) Spr-Verlag.

State of the Art of the IUD: Liber Amicorum Professor Thiery. Ed. by H. Van Der Pas. 240p. 1990. lib. bdg. 120.50 (*0-7923-8922-0*) Kluwer Ac.

State-of-the-Art Portfolio Selection: Using Knowledge-Based Systems to Enhance Investment Portfolios. Robert R. Trippi & Jae K. Lee. 350p. 1992. text ed. 60. 00 (*1-55738-295-6*) Irwin Prof Pubng.

State-of-the-Art Program on Compound Semiconductors XXI. P. Van Daele, pseud. et al. 312p. 1995. pap. 40.00 (*1-56677-093-9*, PV 94-34) Electrochem Soc.

***State-of-the-Art Program on Compound Semiconductors XXIV.** Ed. by F. Ren et al. (Illus.). 278p. 1996. 53.00 (*1-56677-152-8*, PV96-2) Electrochem Soc.

***State-of-the-Art Program on Compound Semiconductors XXVI.** Ed. by D. N. Buckley et al. (Illus.). 332p. 1997. 55.00 (*1-56677-128-5*, PV97-1) Electrochem Soc.

***State-of-the-Art Program on Compound Semiconductors XXVII.** Ed. by S. N. Chu et al. Date not set. 66.00 (*1-56677-149-8*, PV97-21) Electrochem Soc.

State of the Art Regarding the Problem of Residual Stresses in Welds of LMFBR. V. De Angelis & C. Sampietri. 467p. 1995. 70.00 (*92-826-8906-9*, CR-NA-15895-ENC, Pub. by Commiss Europ Commun BE) Bernan Associates.

State-of-the-Art Report on Air-Supported Structures. American Society of Civil Engineers Staff. LC 79-125997. (Illus.). 103p. reprint ed. pap. 29.40 (*0-317-10911-1*, 2019556) Bks Demand.

State-of-the-Art Report on Composite or Mixed Steel Concrete Construction for Buildings. H. S. Iyengar. 160p. pap. 45.60 (*0-317-42235-9*, 2026069) Bks Demand.

State-of-the-Art Report on High Strength Concrete. 55p. 1992. 57.75 (*0-685-62960-0*, 363R-92BOW6) ACI.

State-of-the-Art Report on Polymer Modified Concrete. 37p. 1995. reprint ed. 48.75 (*0-614-11135-8*) ACI.

State-of-the-Art Report on Prestressed Concrete Ties for North American Railroads. (PCI Journal Reprints Ser.). 16p. 1985. pap. 14.00 (*0-318-19778-2*, JR213) P-PCI.

State-of-the-Art Report on Roller-Compacted Concrete Pavements. 32p. 1995. pap. 36.75 (*0-614-11132-3*, 325. 10R-95.BOW6) ACI.

State of the Art Report on Seismic Resistance of Prestressed & Precast Concrete Structures. (PCI Journal Reprints Ser.). 52p. 1978. pap. 16.00 (*0-685-06908-7*, JR194) P-PCI.

State of the Art Selling. Barry Farber. 240p. (Orig.). 1994. pap. 16.95 (*1-56414-131-4*) Career Pr Inc.

State of the Art Symposium: Bioinorganic Chemistry. Journal of Chemical Education Staff. (Journal of Chemical Education Ser.: No. 62). (Illus.). 86p. 1985. reprint ed. pap. 25.00 (*0-7837-9768-0*, 2060496) Bks Demand.

State of the Art Symposium: Polymer Chemistry, Atlanta, 1981. State of the Art Chemical Educators III, Polymer Chemistry Symposium Staff. 120p. reprint ed. pap. 34.20 (*0-317-26617-9*, 2025425) Bks Demand.

State of the Art TESOL Essays: Celebrating 25 Years of the Discipline. Ed. by Sandra Silberstein. 414p. 1993. pap. 29.95 (*0-939791-48-X*) Tchrs Eng Spkrs.

State of the Arts: From Bezalel to Mapplethorpe. Gene E. Veith, Jr. LC 90-25447. (Turning Point Christian Worldview Ser.). (Illus.). 256p. (Orig.). 1991. pap. 12.99 (*0-89107-608-5*) Crossway Bks.

State of the Baltic. G. Kullenberg. (Marine Pollution Bulletin Ser.: Vol. 12, No. 6). 48p. 1981. pap. 6.00 (*0-08-026283-X*, Pergamon Pr) Elsevier.

State of the Black Economy. Lloyd Hogan. LC 80-53746. 128p. (Orig.). 1980. pap. 21.95 (*0-87855-816-0*) Transaction Pubs.

State of the Blindness System Today: 1987-1990 Helen Keller Seminar. 48p. 1992. pap. 19.00 (*0-89128-239-4*); audio 19.00 (*0-89128-250-5*) Am Foun Blind.

State of the Blindness System Today: 1987-1990 Helen Keller Seminar. braille ed. 48p. 1992. 19.00 (*0-89128-251-3*) Am Foun Blind.

State of the Child: A Profile of Pennsylvania's Children (A 1993 Factbook) Frederick K. Richmond & Martha W. Steketee. (Illus.). 192p. (Orig.). 1993. pap. 20.00 (*0-9637063-0-6*) PA Ptnership.

State of the Child in Pennsylvania: A 1995 Kidscount Fact Book. Frederick K. Richmond & Martha W. Steketee. 260p. 1995. pap. 29.00 (*0-9645008-1-7*) PA Ptnership.

State of the Child in Pennsylvania: A 1996 Program & Economic Guide to Child Well-Being in Pennsylvania Counties. 2nd ed. Martha W. Steketee & Frederick K. Richmond. 268p. 1996. pap. 29.00 (*0-9645008-2-5*) PA Ptnership.

An Asterisk (*) at the beginning of an entry indicates that the title is appearing in BIP for the first time.

***State of the Child in Pennsylvania: A 1997 Guide to Child Well-Being in Pennsylvania Counties.** 3rd ed. Martha C. Bergsten & Martha W. Steketee. (Fact Book Ser.). 256p. 1997. pap. 29.00 (*0-9645008-3-3*) PA Ptnership.

State of the Church. Andrew Murray. (Orig.). 1989. reprint ed. pap. 4.95 (*0-87508-407-9*) Chr Lit.

***State of the Cybernation: The Future of the Internet.** Neil Barrett. 1997. 19.95 (*0-7494-2054-5*, Pub. by Kogan Page UK) Nichols Pub.

State of the Discipline, 1970's-1980's: A Special Issue of the ADE Bulletin. fac. ed. J. Paul Hunter et al. LC 80-116944. (ADE Bulletin Ser.: No. 62). 114p. 1979. reprint ed. pap. 32.50 (*0-7837-8031-1*, 2047787) Bks Demand.

***State of the Earth: Contemporary Geographic Perspectives.** Akin L. Mabogunje. LC 96-36188. (Contemporary Social Sciences Ser.). 1997. write for info. (*0-631-20243-9*); pap. 29.95 (*0-631-20244-7*) Blackwell Pubs.

State of the Economy, 1991. Mark Boleat. (C). 1991. text ed. 65.00 (*0-255-36243-9*, Pub. by Inst Economic Affairs UK) St Mut.

State of the Economy, 1992. Giles Keating. 160p. (C). 1992. text ed. 59.95 (*0-255-36304-4*, Pub. by Inst Economic Affairs UK) St Mut.

State of the Environment. 297p. 1991. 38.00 (*92-64-13442-5*) OECD.

State of the Environment. Essam El-Hinnawi & Manzur H. Hashmi. (Illus.). 182p. 1987. 105.00 (*0-408-02183-7*) Buttrwrth-Heinemann.

***State of the Environment Reporting: Source Book of Methods & Approaches.** Paul C. Rump. 135p. pap. 20.00 (*92-807-1583-6*) UN.

State of the European Community, Vol. 2: The Maastricht Debates & Beyond. Ed. by Alan W. Cafruny & Glenda G. Rosenthal. LC 93-7665. (European Community Studies Association). 438p. 1993. lib. bdg. 49.95 (*1-55587-359-6*) Lynne Rienner.

State of the European Union Vol. 3: Building a European Polity? Ed. by Carolyn Rhodes & Sonia Mazey. LC 95-9034. 520p. 1995. 49.95 (*1-55587-605-6*) Lynne Rienner.

***State of the European Union Vol. 4: Deepening & Widening.** Ed. by Pierre-Henri Laurent & Marc Maresceau. (European Community Studies Association). 410p. 1997. 55.00 (*1-55587-720-6*) Lynne Rienner.

State of the Expedition from Canada, As Laid Before the House of Commons. John Burgoyne. LC 70-77104. (Eyewitness Accounts of the American Revolution Ser., No. 1). 1969. reprint ed. 23.95 (*0-405-01146-6*) Ayer.

State of the Fantastic: Studies in the Theory & Practice of Fantastic Literature & Film: Selected Essays from the Eleventh International Conference on the Fantastic in the Arts, 1990. Ed. by Nicholas Ruddick. LC 91-46867. (Contributions to the Study of Science Fiction & Fantasy Ser.: No. 50). 232p. 1992. text ed. 55.00 (*0-313-27853-9*, RSF, Greenwood Pr) Greenwood.

State of the Government: A View Toward the Nineties. Conservation Foundation Staff. LC 87-15193. (Illus.). 664p. reprint ed. pap. 180.00 (*0-8357-2931-1*, 2039170) Bks Demand.

***State of the History of Economics: Proceedings of the History of Economics Society.** James P. Henderson & History of Economics Society Staff. LC 97-4159. 272p. (C). 1997. text ed. write for info. (*0-415-13354-8*) Routledge.

State of the Laboratory: Lawrence Livermore National Laboratory. Ed. by William A. Bookless. (Illus.). 106p. (Orig.). (C). 1995. pap. text ed. 30.00 (*0-7881-2614-8*) DIANE Pub.

State of the Language, 1990 Edition. Ed. by Christopher Ricks & Leonard Michaels. 600p. 1989. 40.00 (*0-520-05906-9*) U CA Pr.

State of the Marine Environment. GESAMP Staff. (Illus.). 128p. 1991. pap. 39.95 (*0-632-03198-0*) Blackwell Sci.

State of the Masses. Richard F. Hamilton & James D. Wright. LC 85-20127. (Social Institutions & Social Change Ser.). (Illus.). 482p. (Orig.). 1986. pap. text ed. 31.95 (*0-202-30325-X*); lib. bdg. 58.95 (*0-202-30324-1*) Aldine de Gruyter.

State of the Nation. John R. Dos Passos. LC 73-718. (Illus.). 333p. 1973. reprint ed. text ed. 38.50 (*0-8371-6782-5*, DOSN, Greenwood Pr) Greenwood.

State of the Nation: A Conference of the Committee for the Free World. Ed. by Steven C. Munson. LC 84-23444. 126p. (Orig.). 1985. pap. text ed. 11.50 (*0-8191-4391-X*); lib. bdg. 27.00 (*0-8191-4390-1*) U Pr of Amer.

State of the Nation: Government & the Quest for a Better Society, 1960-1995. Derek Bok. LC 96-22881. 480p. 1996. 35.00 (*0-674-29210-3*) HUP.

***State of the Nation: Thailand.** Suchit Bunbongkarn. (Illus.). 118p. (Orig.). (C). 1997. pap. 35.00 (*0-7881-3708-5*) DIANE Pub.

State of the Nation & the Agenda for Higher Education. Howard R. Bowen. LC 81-20746. (Jossey-Bass Series in Higher Education). 232p. reprint ed. pap. 66.20 (*0-8357-4860-X*, 2037792) Bks Demand.

***State of the Net.** Peter Clemente. 1997. pap. text ed. 24.95 (*0-07-011979-1*) McGraw.

State of the Northwest, No. 1. John C. Ryan & Northwest Environment Watch Staff. LC 94-61323. (New Reports: No. 1). 80p. (Orig.). 1995. pap. 9.95 (*1-886093-00-8*) NW Environ Watch.

State of the Novel: Dying Art or New Science. Walker Percy. (Illus.). 20p. 1988. 50.00 (*0-917905-05-9*); 125.00 (*0-317-66751-3*) Faust Pub Co.

State of the Park 1995. John F. Sheehan. (State of the Park Ser.: No. 8). (Illus.). 16p. 1995. pap. write for info. (*0-614-14001-3*) Adirondack Council.

State of the Park 1996, No. 9. John F. Sheehan. (Illus.). 16p. 1996. pap. 1.09 (*0-614-14003-X*) Adirondack Council.

State of the Parties: The Changing Role of Contemporary American Parties. 2nd ed. Daniel M. Shea & John C. Green. 296p. 1996. 62.50 (*0-8476-8265-X*); pap. 22.95 (*0-8476-8266-8*) Rowman.

State of the Parties: The Changing Role of Contemporary American Party Organizations. Ed. by Daniel M. Shea & John C. Green. 288p. 1994. pap. text ed. 22.95 (*0-8476-7980-2*); lib. bdg. 62.50 (*0-8476-7979-9*) Rowman.

State of the Peoples: A Global Human Rights Report on Societies in Danger. Cultural Survival Staff. LC 93-24013. (Illus.). 256p. 1993. pap. 18.00 (*0-8070-0221-6*) Beacon Pr.

State of the Poor. Frederick M. Eden. Ed. by A. G. Rogers. LC 68-56502. 432p. 1972. reprint ed. 26.95 (*0-405-08485-4*, Pub. by Blom Pubns UK) Ayer.

***State of the Poor: 1797 Edition, 3 vols., Set.** Frederic M. Eden. 2028p. 1996. reprint ed. write for info. (*1-85506-262-3*) Bks Intl VA.

State of the Prisons - Two Hundred Years On. Ed. by Richard Whitfield. 208p. (C). (gr. 13). 1991. text ed. 49.95 (*0-415-05187-8*, A5258) Routledge.

State of the Rio Grande-Rio Bravo: A Study of Water Resource Issues Along the Texas-Mexico Border. David J. Eaton & John M. Andersen. LC 87-10748. (PROFMEX Ser.). 331p. 1986. 38.50 (*0-8165-0990-5*) U of Ariz Pr.

State of the Scene: Science Education in the Nation. 1994. lib. bdg. 250.75 (*0-8490-5786-8*) Gordon Pr.

State of the Scene: Science Education in the Nation. 1995. lib. bdg. 251.95 (*0-8490-6843-6*) Gordon Pr.

State of the Society Address: Selected Writings, Musings & Poetry of a Curmudgeon (Including Armenia & Kuwait) Gerald E. Ottenbreit, Jr. 113p. 1992. pap. 12.00 (*0-9634509-0-5*) Bookshelf Pubs.

State of the South. George B. Autry et al. LC 96-94245. (Illus.). xiv, 80p. (Orig.). 1996. pap. 20.00 (*0-9651907-0-6*) MDC.

State of the States. 3rd ed. Carl E. Van Horn. LC 96-12559. 234p. 1996. pap. 24.95 (*1-56802-158-5*) Congr Quarterly.

State of the States: Current Conditions, Future Directions. rev. ed. Council of State Governments Staff. Ed. by Frank Hersman. 1986. pap. 22.50 (*0-87292-064-X*, C-33) Coun State Govts.

State of the States' Children. Lynne Fender & David Shaw. 60p. (Orig.). 1990. pap. text ed. 15.00 (*1-55877-119-0*) Natl Governor.

State of the States' Environmental Planning. Heidi Snow. Ed. by Mary Houghton & Gerry Feinstein. 90p. (Orig.). 1991. pap. text ed. 15.00 (*1-55877-097-6*) Natl Governor.

State of the U. S. A. Atlas. Doug Henwood. 1994. 30.00 (*0-671-79696-8*); pap. 17.00 (*0-671-79695-X*) S&S Trade.

State of the Union. Light. 1997. pap. text ed. 33.00 (*0-312-08969-4*) St Martin.

State of the Union. Howard Lindsey & Russel Crouse. 1947. pap. 5.25 (*0-8222-1074-6*) Dramatists Play.

***State of the Union: A Novel.** David Callahan. LC 96-47114. 1997. 23.95 (*0-316-12490-7*) Little.

State of the Union: A Report on President Clinton's First Four Years in Office. Thomas Blood. (Illus.). 160p. 1996. pap. 14.95 (*1-57544-008-3*) Genl Pub Grp.

State of the Union: Essays in Social Criticism. Albert J. Nock. LC 90-22412. 342p. (Orig.). 1991. pap. 7.50 (*0-86597-093-9*); text ed. 18.00 (*0-86597-092-0*) Liberty Fund.

State of the Union Vol. 1: America in the 1990s: Economic Trends. Ed. by Reynolds Farley. LC 94-40284. (1990 Census Research Ser.: Vol. 1). (Illus.). 375p. 1995. 39.95 (*0-87154-240-4*) Russell Sage.

State of the Union Vol. 2: America in the 1990s: Social Trends. Ed. by Reynolds Farley. LC 94-40284. (1990 Census Research Ser.: Vol. 2). (Illus.). 377p. 1995. 39.95 (*0-87154-241-2*) Russell Sage.

State of the Union see Best American Plays: Third Series, 1945-51

State of the Union of Europe: Report of the CADMOS Group to the European People. Ed. by Denis De Rougemont. 1979. pap. 56.00 (*0-08-024476-9*, Pub. by Pergamon Repr UK) Franklin.

State of the Unions. 1991. 20.00 (*0-913447-49-8*) Indus Relations Res.

State of the Unions. George G. Higgins. (Benjamin Aaron Annual Lecture Ser.). 19p. 1993. reprint ed. 7.00 (*0-89215-176-5*) U Cal LA Indus Rel.

State of the Unions. Barrie Sherman. LC 86-13329. 189p. reprint ed. pap. 53.90 (*0-7837-5207-5*, 2044935) Bks Demand.

State of the United Nations: Decline or Regeneration in the Next 50 Years: 29th U. N. of the Next Decade Conference 1994. 40p. (Orig.). 1995. pap. text ed. 20.00 (*0-7881-2622-9*) DIANE Pub.

State of the United Nations: 1992. Craig N. Murphy et al. (Reports & Papers). 92p. (C). 1992. pap. text ed. 10.00 (*1-880660-04-0*) Acad Coun UN Syst.

State of the United Nations, 1993: North-South Perspectives. Gerald Dirks et al. (Reports & Papers). 110p. (C). 1993. pap. 10.00 (*1-880660-07-5*) Acad Coun UN Syst.

***State of the World.** Mikhail S. Gorbachev. write for info. (*0-06-251339-7*); write for info. (*0-06-251340-0*) HarpC.

State of the World Atlas: A Unique Visual Survey of Global Political, Economic & Social Trends. 5th ed. Michael Kidron & Ronald Segal. (Illus.). 160p. 1995. pap. 29.95 (*0-670-86545-1*, Viking) Viking Penguin.

State of the World Atlas: A Unique Visual Survey of Global Political, Economic, & Social Trends. 5th ed. Michael Kidron & Ronald Segal. 160p. 1995. pap. 16.95 (*0-14-025204-5*, Penguin Bks) Viking Penguin.

State of the World Environment, 1989. 43p. 1991. 15.00 (*92-807-1218-7*, 89.III.D.1) UN.

State of the World Environment 1990: Children & the Environment. 74p. 1990. 15.00 (*92-806-0034-6*, 90.XX.USA.2) UN.

State of The World, 1984. Lester R. Brown et al. LC 83-25123. (Worldwatch Book Series). 1984. 10.95 (*0-393-01835-0*) Worldwatch Inst.

State of the World, 1991. 253p. 1991. 10.95 (*1-86373-018-4*) Worldwatch Inst.

State of the World, 1994: A Worldwatch Institute Report on Progress Toward a Sustainable Society. Lester R. Brown et al. 256p. 1993. 19.95 (*0-393-03439-9*) Norton.

State of the World, 1995. Lester Brown. 288p. 1995. 23.00 (*0-393-03717-7*) Norton.

State of the World 1996. Worldwatch Staff. 1996. pap. text ed. 30.50 (*5-556-65603-7*) Norton.

State of the World 1996: A Worldwatch Institute Report on Progress Toward a Sustainable Society. Lester R. Brown et al. (Illus.). 288p. 1996. pap. write for info. (*1-85383-327-4*, Pub. by Erthscan Pubns UK) Island Pr.

State of the World 1996: A Worldwatch Institute Report on Progress Toward a Sustainable Society. Lester R. Brown et al. (Illus.). 288p. 1996. 23.00 (*0-393-03851-3*); pap. 11.95 (*0-393-31339-5*, Norton Paperbks) Norton.

State of the World 1997: A Worldwatch Institute Report on Progress Toward a Sustainable Society. Lester Brown. 288p. 1997. 25.00 (*0-393-04008-9*) Norton.

State of the World 1997: A Worldwatch Institute Report on Progress Toward a Sustainable Society. Lester Brown. 288p. 1997. pap. 13.95 (*0-393-31569-X*) Norton.

***State of the World 1998.** Lester Brown. Date not set. 25.00 (*0-393-04565-X*); pap. 13.95 (*0-393-31727-7*) Norton.

State of the World's Children 1996. Ed. by Carol Bellamy. (Illus.). 96p. (C). 1996. pap. 10.95 (*0-19-262747-3*) OUP.

***State of the World's Children 1997.** Ed. by Carol Bellamy. (Illus.). 108p. 1997. pap. 12.95 (*0-19-262871-2*) OUP.

State of the World's Mountains: A Global Report. Peter B. Stone. (Illus.). 384p. (C). 1992. pap. 25.00 (*1-85649-116-1*, Pub. by Zed Bks Ltd UK); text ed. 60.00 (*1-85649-115-3*, Pub. by Zed Bks Ltd UK) Humanities.

State of the World's Refugees: The Search for Solutions. United Nations High Commissioner for Refugees Staff. (Illus.). 264p. 1995. pap. 16.95 (*0-19-828043-2*) OUP.

State of the World's Refugees 1995: The Search for Solutions. United Nations High Commissioner for Refugees Staff. (Illus.). 224p. 1995. 49.95 (*0-19-828044-0*) OUP.

***State of the World's Refugees, 1997.** (Illus.). 224p. 1998. pap. 18.95 (*0-19-829309-7*) OUP.

***State of the World's Refugees, 1997.** (Illus.). 224p. 1998. 60.00 (*0-19-829310-0*) OUP.

State of Theory: Essays on Literary Theory & Literary Criticism. Ed. by Richard Bradford. LC 93-14827. 208p. (C). 1993. pap. text ed. 17.95 (*0-415-07324-3*, B0379) Routledge.

State of Theory: Essays on Literary Theory & Literary Criticism. Ed. by Richard Bradford. LC 93-14827. 208p. (C). (gr. 13). 1993. text ed. 69.95 (*0-415-07323-5*, B0375) Routledge.

State of Trade in the Northern Colonies Considered. Otis Little. LC 79-141124. (Research Library of Colonial Americana). 1972. reprint ed. 20.95 (*0-405-03336-2*) Ayer.

State of Transboundary Air Pollution, No. 5. 104p. 1989. 25.00 (*92-1-116460-5*, 89-II.E.25) UN.

State of Transboundary Air Pollution: 1989 Update. 1989. 25.00 (*92-1-116489-3*, 90.II.E.33) UN.

***State of Violent Crime in America: First Report of the Council on Crime in America.** (Illus.). 58p. (Orig.). 1996. pap. 25.00 (*0-7881-3655-0*) DIANE Pub.

State of War: Michigan in World War II. Alan Clive. LC 79-10213. (Illus.). 1979. text ed. 32.50 (*0-472-10001-7*) U of Mich Pr.

***State of War & Peace Atlas.** Dan Smith. 1997. pap. 16.95 (*0-14-051373-6*); pap. 29.95 (*0-670-10007-2*) Viking Penguin.

State of Water in the Cell. Ed. by L. Edelmann. (Illus.). vi, 114p. 1988. pap. text ed. 19.00 (*0-931288-40-1*) Scanning Microscopy.

State of Welfare. Gilbert Y. Steiner. LC 70-150952. 346p. 1971. pap. 11.95 (*0-8157-8121-0*) Brookings.

State of Welfare: The Welfare State in Britain since 1974. Ed. by John Hills. (Illus.). 412p. 1992. pap. 35.00 (*0-19-828763-1*) OUP.

State of Western European Studies: Implications for Collection Development. Ed. by Anthony M. Angiletta et al. LC 84-12803. (Collection Management: Vol. 6, No. 1-2). 273p. 1984. text ed. 49.95 (*0-86656-354-7*) Haworth Pr.

State of Workers' Compensation. Brenda Trolin. 91p. 1994. pap. text ed. 35.00 (*1-55516-335-1*, 3302) Natl Conf State Legis.

State of Working America. Lawrence R. Mishel & Jacqueline Simon. LC 88-82263. 53p. 1988. 12.00 (*0-944826-04-0*) Economic Policy Inst.

State of Working America, 1992-1993. Lawrence R. Mishel & Jared Bernstein. LC 91-641696. (Economic Policy Institute Ser.). 520p. (gr. 13). 1993. text ed. 65.95 (*1-56324-211-7*); pap. text ed. 25.95 (*1-56324-212-5*) M E Sharpe.

State of Working America 1994-95. Lawrence R. Mishel & Jared Bernstein. (Economic Policy Institute Ser.). (Illus.). 410p. (C). (gr. 13). 1994. 65.95 (*1-56324-532-9*); pap. 25.95 (*1-56324-533-7*) M E Sharpe.

***State of Working America, 1996-97.** Lawrence R. Mishel et al. (Economic Policy Institute Ser.). 464p. (C). (gr. 13). 1996. pap. 24.95 (*0-7656-0024-2*) M E Sharpe.

***State of Working America, 1996-97: 1996-97.** Lawrence R. Mishel et al. (Economic Policy Institute Ser.). 464p. (C). (gr. 13). 1996. 62.95 (*0-7656-0023-4*) M E Sharpe.

***State of World Fisheries & Aquaculture 1996.** FAO Staff. 1997. pap. 20.00 (*92-5-103941-0*, F39410, Pub. by FAO IT) Bernan Associates.

State of World Population. 66p. 1994. pap. 9.95 (*0-89714-195-4*, E.94.XIII.9) UN.

State of World Rural Poverty. (Illus.). 450p. (C). 1993. 75.00 (*0-8147-3753-6*); pap. 25.00 (*0-8147-3754-4*) NYU Pr.

State Offshore: Petroleum, Politics, & State Intervention on the British & Norwegian Continental Shelves. Brent F. Nelsen. LC 90-21037. 272p. 1991. text ed. 59.95 (*0-275-93835-2*, C3835, Praeger Pubs) Greenwood.

State, Oil, & Agriculture in Nigeria. Ed. by Michael Watts. LC 87-2941. (Research Ser.: No. 66). (Illus.). xiv, 328p. (C). 1987. pap. text ed. 16.95 (*0-87725-166-5*) U of Cal IAS.

State or the Market: Politics & Welfare in Contemporary Britain. Ed. by Martin Loney et al. 288p. (C). 1987. text ed. 35.00 (*0-8039-8104-X*); pap. text ed. 16.50 (*0-8039-8105-8*) Sage.

State Outlines & Political Divisions. (Regional Map Packages Ser.). (Illus.). 1989. Incl. 102 maps. ring bd. 50.00 (*0-8160-1341-1*) Facts on File.

***State Oversight of Integrated Health Systems.** Intro. by Carmen H. Buell. 258p. (Orig.). 1997. pap. write for info. (*1-887748-11-3*) Milbank Memorial.

State-Owned Enterprise in the Western Economies. Ed. by Raymond Vernon & Yair Aharoni. 1981. text ed. 35.00 (*0-312-75623-2*) St Martin.

***State-Owned Enterprise Reform in Vietnam: Lessons from Asia.** Ed. by Ng Chee Yuen et al. (Illus.). 182p. (Orig.). (C). 1997. pap. 50.00 (*0-7881-3707-7*) DIANE Pub.

State-Owned Enterprises in Africa. Barbara Grosh & Rwekaza Mukandala. LC 93-8957. 259p. 1994. lib. bdg. 50.00 (*1-55587-453-3*) Lynne Rienner.

State-Owned Enterprises in High Technology Industries: Studies in India & Brazil. Ravi Ramaurti. LC 85-30751. 319p. 1987. text ed. 65.00 (*0-275-92156-5*, C2156, Praeger Pubs) Greenwood.

State Owned Multinationals. Jean-Pierre Anastassopoulos et al. LC 87-2033. (IRM Series in Multinationals). 200p. 1987. text ed. 100.00 (*0-471-91502-5*) Wiley.

State Papers & Speeches on the Tariff. Compiled by Frank W. Taussig. LC 68-18604. (Reprints of Economic Classics Ser.). vii, 385p. 1972. reprint ed. 49.50 (*0-678-00555-9*) Kelley.

State Papers on Nullification. LC 69-16649. (American Constitutional & Legal History Ser). 1970. reprint ed. lib. bdg. 42.50 (*0-306-71126-5*) Da Capo.

State Papers Relating to the Defeat of the Spanish Armada Anno, 1588. Ed. by J. K. Laughton. 418p. 1987. text ed. 93.95 (*0-566-05540-6*, Pub. by Scolar Pr UK) Ashgate Pub Co.

State Park System in Illinois. John E. Trotter. LC 62-6256. (University of Chicago, Department of Geography, Research Paper Ser.: No. 74). (Illus.). 166p. reprint ed. pap. 47.40 (*0-8357-3716-0*, 2036438) Bks Demand.

State Parks of North Carolina. Walter C. Biggs, Jr. & James F. Parnell. LC 89-6976. (Illus.). 339p. (Orig.). 1989. pap. 14.95 (*0-89587-071-1*) Blair.

State Parks of the Northeast: America's Colonial Frontier: A Guide to Camping, Fishing, Hiking, & Sightseeing. Vici DeHaan. LC 94-43534. (Illus.). 320p. (Orig.). 1995. pap. 16.95 (*1-55566-143-2*) Johnson Bks.

State Parks of the South. Blair Howard. (Illus.). 256p. (Orig.). 1995. pap. 13.95 (*1-55650-655-4*) Hunter NJ.

State Parks of the South: America's Historic Paradise: A Guide to Camping, Fishing, Hiking, & Sightseeing. Vici DeHaan. LC 96-1303. (Illus.). 480p. (Orig.). 1996. pap. 16.95 (*1-55566-167-X*) Johnson Bks.

State Parks of Utah: A Guide & History. John V. Young. LC 89-31524. (Illus.). 256p. 1989. pap. 14.95 (*0-87480-315-2*) U of Utah Pr.

***State Parks on the Great Lakes.** Dean Miller. 370p. 1997. pap. 15.95 (*1-881139-17-4*) Glovebox Guidebks.

State Parties & National Politics: North Carolina, 1815-1861. Thomas E. Jeffrey. LC 88-25998. (Illus.). 424p. 1989. 50.00 (*0-8203-1090-5*) U of Ga Pr.

State, Party, & Policy: Industry & Agriculture in America's New Deal. Kenneth Finegold & Theda Skocpol. LC 95-5709. 356p. 1995. 54.00 (*0-299-14760-6*); pap. 19.95 (*0-299-14764-9*) U of Wis Pr.

State Party Profiles: A 50-State Guide to Development, Organization, & Resources. Ed. by Andrew M. Appleton & Daniel S. Ward. LC 96-25500. 375p. 1996. 80.00 (*1-56802-150-X*) Congr Quarterly.

State Patronage in a Rural County. Frank J. Sorauf. (Reprint Series in Social Sciences). (C). 1993. reprint ed. pap. text ed. 1.00 (*0-8290-2758-0*, PS-271) Irvington.

State Per-Capita Income Change Since 1950: Sharecropping's Collapse & Other Causes of Convergence. Leonard F. Wheat & William H. Crown. LC 95-7437. (Contributions in Economics & Economic History Ser.: No. 167). 248p. 1995. text ed. 59.95 (*0-313-29694-4*, Greenwood Pr) Greenwood.

State Personal Income, 1929-1987: Estimates, Sources, & Methods. 1992. lib. bdg. 99.95 (*0-8490-5535-0*) Gordon Pr.

State Personal Income, 1929-1993, 2 vols., Set. 1996. lib. bdg. 613.95 (*0-8490-5992-5*) Gordon Pr.

State Personnel Office: Roles & Functions. Council of State Governments Staff. Ed. by Linda Carroll. 39p. (Orig.). 1987. pap. 20.00 (*0-87292-072-0*, C-74) Coun State Govts.

An Asterisk (*) at the beginning of an entry indicates that the title is appearing in BIP for the first time.

State Petroleum Enterprises in Developing Countries. United Nations Centre for Natural Resources, Energy & Transport Staff. LC 79-20681. (Policy Studies). 185p. 1980. 74.00 (*0-08-025126-9*, Pergamon Pr) Elsevier.

***State Police & State Highway Patrol Badge Guide.** 4th rev. ed. (Illus.). 140p. 1997. pap. 25.00 (*0-9653262-0-9*) W Mauldin Prods.

State Police Exam California. LC 96-11258. (Law Enforcement Library). 192p. 1996. pap. 35.00 (*1-57685-005-6*) LrningExprss.

State Police Exam Massachusetts. Ed. by Jim Gish. LC 97-22840. (Law Enforcement Library). 256p. (Orig.). (C). 1997. pap. 30.00 (*1-57685-058-7*) LrningExprss.

State Police Exam Texas. LC 96-11291. (Law Enforcement Library). 192p. 1996. pap. 35.00 (*1-57685-006-4*) LrningExprss.

State Police in the United States: A Socio-Historical Analysis. H. Kenneth Bechtel. LC 94-30929. (Contributions in Criminology & Penology Ser.: Vol. 47). 192p. 1995. text ed. 55.00 (*0-313-26380-9*, Greenwood Pr) Greenwood.

State Police New Jersey. LC 96-4718. (Law Enforcement Library). 192p. 1996. pap. 30.00 (*1-57685-022-6*) LrningExprss.

State Police New York. LC 96-4720. (Law Enforcement Library). 192p. 1996. pap. 30.00 (*1-57685-004-8*) LrningExprss.

State Police, Organization & Administration. Bruce Smith. LC 69-14946. (Criminology, Law Enforcement, & Social Problems Ser.: No. 64). 1969. reprint ed. 24.00 (*0-87585-064-2*) Patterson Smith.

State Policewoman. Jack Rudman. (Career Examination Ser.: C-1692). 1994. pap. 23.95 (*0-8373-1692-8*) Nat Learn.

State Policies & Techno-Industrial Innovation. Ed. by Ulrich Hilpert. LC 90-8779. 384p. (C). 1991. text ed. 79.95 (*0-415-04268-2*, A5217) Routledge.

***State Policies for School Restructuring.** Theodor Rebarber. 20p. 1992. pap. 10.00 (*1-55516-324-6*, 3114) Natl Conf State Legis.

State Policies, State Penetration & Ecology: Comparative Analysis of Uneven Development & Underdevelopment in Mexico's Micro Agrarian Regions. Manuel L. Carlos. (Research Reports: No. 19). 39p. (Orig.). (C). 1981. pap. 5.00 (*0-935391-18-5*, RR-19) UCSD Ctr US-Mex.

State Policies to Improve the Teacher Workforce: Shaping the Profession That Shapes America's Future. Recruiting New Teachers, Inc. Staff. (Illus.). 48p. 1993. 6.95 (*1-884139-00-0*) Recruit New Tchrs.

***State Policy & Economic Development in Oklahoma: A Report to Oklahoma 2000, Inc., 1996.** unabridged ed. Kent W. Olson et al. (Illus.). 69p. (Orig.). 1996. mass mkt. write for info. (*1-890100-01-3*) OK Two-Thousand.

State Policy Choices: The Wisconsin Experience. Ed. by Sheldon Danziger & John F. Witte. LC 88-40232. (La Follette Public Policy Ser.). 312p. 1988. reprint ed. pap. 89.00 (*0-608-01967-4*, 2062622) Bks Demand.

State Policy Formation & the Origin of the Poll Tax. Allan McConnell. 256p. 1995. text ed. 59.95 (*1-85521-488-1*, Pub. by Dartmth Pub UK) Ashgate Pub Co.

State Policy Formation in Illinois Higher Education. Franklin G. Matsler & Edward R. Hines. (Orig.). (C). 1987. pap. text ed. 7.50 (*0-944498-00-0*) ISU Ctr High Educ.

State Policy Making for the Public Schools. Roald F. Campbell & Tim L. Mazzoni, Jr. LC 75-31311. 476p. 1976. 37.30 (*0-8211-0224-9*) McCutchan.

State Policy Problems. Ed. by Fred Meyer & Ralph Baker. 250p. 1993. text ed. 31.95 (*0-8304-1337-5*) Nelson-Hall.

State Policy Problems. Ed. by Fred Meyer & Ralph Baker. 1992. pap. 15.00 (*0-944285-28-7*) Pol Studies.

State, Political Processes & Identity: Reflections on Modern India. Ed. by S. N. Zoya Hasan & Rasheeduddin Khan. 320p. (C). 1989. text ed. 27.50 (*0-8039-9577-6*) Sage.

State Politics. David C. Saffell. LC 83-2590. (Illus.). 352p. (C). 1983. write for info. (*0-201-06444-8*) Addison-Wesley.

State, Politics, & Health: Essays for Rudolf Klein. Ed. by Patricia Day et al. LC 95-36573. 1995. 52.95 (*1-55786-868-9*) Blackwell Pubs.

State Politics in Islam. Mumtaz Ahmad. 160p. (Orig.). 1986. pap. 8.00 (*0-89259-058-0*) Am Trust Pubns.

State Politics in Zimbabwe. Jeffrey Herbst. 1990. 47.50 (*0-520-06818-1*) U CA Pr.

State Politics of Judicial & Congressional Reform: Legitimizing Criminal Justice Policies. Thomas C. Dalton. LC 84-29763. (Contributions in Political Science Ser.: No. 135). (Illus.). xxi, 320p. 1985. text ed. 59.95 (*0-313-24549-5*, DSP/) Greenwood.

State Population Estimates by Age & Sex: 1980-1992. (Illus.). 120p. (Orig.). (C). 1994. pap. text ed. 40.00 (*0-7881-0464-0*) DIANE Pub.

State Postsecondary Education Structures Handbook. 174p. 1991. 23.90 (*0-318-22549-2*, PS-91-1) Ed Comm States.

State Power & Black Politics in South Africa, 1912-51. Paul B. Rich. LC 95-14921. 1996. text ed. 59.95 (*0-312-12756-1*) St Martin.

State Power & Culture in Thailand. Ed. by E. Paul Durrenberger. LC 95-61260. (Southeast Asia Studies Monographs: Vol. 44). 216p. 1996. pap. 20.00 (*0-614-14928-2*); lib. bdg. 32.00 (*0-938692-59-3*) Yale U SE Asia.

State, Power & Democracy: Contentious Concepts in Practical Political Theory. John Hoffman. LC 87-35304. 256p. 1988. text ed. 55.00 (*0-312-01950-5*) St Martin.

State, Power & Politics in the Making of the Modern Middle East. Roger Owen. LC 91-41501. (Illus.). 288p. (C). 1992. pap. 18.95 (*0-415-07591-2*, A7080) Routledge.

State, Power & Politics in the Making of the Modern Middle East. Roger Owen. LC 91-41501. (Illus.). 288p. (C). (gr. 13). 1992. text ed. 69.95 (*0-415-07590-4*, A7076) Routledge.

State Power & Social Forces: Domination & Transformation in the Third World. Ed. by Joel S. Migdal et al. LC 93-48757. (Studies in Comparative Politics). 320p. (C). 1994. text ed. 59.95 (*0-521-46166-9*); pap. text ed. 20.95 (*0-521-46734-9*) Cambridge U Pr.

State Printing Activities. 1992. pap. 29.95 (*0-87292-973-6*, C-043-92) Coun State Govts.

State, Private Enterprise, & Economic Change in Egypt, 1918-1952. Robert L. Tignor. LC 83-43097. (Princeton Studies on the New East). 334p. 1984. reprint ed. pap. 95.20 (*0-7837-9461-4*, 2060203) Bks Demand.

State, Private Life & Political Change. Ed. by Lynn Jamieson & Helen Corr. 320p. 1990. text ed. 49.95 (*0-312-03676-0*) St Martin.

State Procurement Practices. 78p. 1993. 20.00 (*0-317-05616-6*) NARUC.

State Professional Standards-Practices Commissions or Boards: A Policy Analysis Paper. 1989. 12.00 (*0-89333-058-2*) AACTE.

State Programs to Assist Distressed Local Governments. Scott R. Mackey. (Legislative Finance Papers: No. 86). 37p. 1993. 15.00 (*1-55516-083-2*, 5101-86) Natl Conf State Legis.

State Progress in Health Care Reform, 1992: Strategic Investments: Tough Choices for America's Future. Timothy Curley et al. Ed. by Karen Glass. 70p. (Orig.). 1993. pap. text ed. 15.00 (*1-55877-202-2*) Natl Governor.

State Property Tax Relief Programs for Homeowners & Renters. Scott R. Mackey. (Legislative Finance Papers: No. 81). 21p. 1992. pap. text ed. 15.00 (*1-55516-081-6*, 5101-81) Natl Conf State Legis.

State Public Welfare Legislation. Robert C. Lowe. LC 75-165602. (Research Monographs: Vol. 20). 1971. reprint ed. lib. bdg. 49.50 (*0-306-70352-1*) Da Capo.

State Publications & Depository Libraries: A Reference Handbook. Margaret T. Lane. LC 80-24688. (Illus.). 560p. 1981. text ed. 105.00 (*0-313-22118-9*, LSP/, Greenwood Pr) Greenwood.

State Punishment: Political Principles & Community Values. Nicola Lacey. (International Library of Philosophy). 256p. 1988. text ed. 49.95 (*0-415-00171-4*) Routledge.

State Punishment: Political Principles & Community Values. Nicola Lacey. LC 94-17878. (International Library of Philosophy Ser.). 256p. (C). 1994. pap. 17.95 (*0-415-10938-8*, B4695) Routledge.

State Railroad Control with a History of Its Development in Iowa. Frank H. Dixon. Ed. by Stuart Bruchey. LC 80-1303. (Railroads Ser.). 1981. reprint ed. lib. bdg. 24.95 (*0-405-13772-9*) Ayer.

State Rankings 1995. Ed. by Kathleen O. Morgan et al. 612p. 1995. pap. 43.95 (*1-56692-303-4*) Morgan Quitno Corp.

State Rankings 1995. Ed. by Kathleen O. Morgan et al. 612p. 1995. 67.95 (*1-56692-304-2*) Morgan Quitno Corp.

State Rankings 1996. Ed. by Kathleen O. Morgan et al. 608p. 1996. 49.95 (*1-56692-310-7*) Morgan Quitno Corp.

***State Rankings 1997.** Ed. by Kathleen O. Morgan & Scott E. Morgan. 608p. 1997. 49.95 (*1-56692-316-6*) Morgan Quitno Corp.

State Rating Law Survey - 1996. annuals 118p. 1996. lib. bdg. 95.00 (*0-614-13251-7*) Am Ins NY.

State Recordkeeping Requirements. BNA PLUS Staff. 1993. 95.00 (*1-55871-295-X*) BNA Plus.

State Records of North Carolina, Vol. 11: 1776 & Supplement - 1730-1776. Ed. by Walter Clark. (Colonial & State Records of North Carolina Ser.). 850p. 1994. reprint ed. 50.00 (*1-56837-211-6*) Broadfoot.

State Records of North Carolina, Vol. 12: 1777-1778. Ed. by Walter Clark. (Colonial & State Records of North Carolina Ser.). 886p. 1994. reprint ed. 50.00 (*1-56837-212-4*) Broadfoot.

State Records of North Carolina, Vol. 13: 1778-1779. Ed. by Walter Clark. (Colonial & State Records of North Carolina Ser.). 1000p. 1994. reprint ed. 50.00 (*1-56837-213-2*) Broadfoot.

State Records of North Carolina, Vol. 14: 1779-1780. Ed. by Walter Clark. (Colonial & State Records of North Carolina Ser.). 876p. 1994. reprint ed. 50.00 (*1-56837-214-0*) Broadfoot.

State Records of North Carolina, Vol. 15: 1780-1781. Ed. by Walter Clark. (Colonial & State Records of North Carolina Ser.). 789p. 1994. reprint ed. 50.00 (*1-56837-215-9*) Broadfoot.

State Records of North Carolina, Vol. 16: 1782-1783. Ed. by Walter Clark. (Colonial & State Records of North Carolina Ser.). 1204p. 1994. reprint ed. 50.00 (*1-56837-216-7*) Broadfoot.

State Records of North Carolina, Vol. 17: 1781-1785. Ed. by Walter Clark. (Colonial & State Records of North Carolina Ser.). 1061p. 1994. reprint ed. 50.00 (*1-56837-217-5*) Broadfoot.

State Records of North Carolina, Vol. 18: 1786 & Supplement, 1779. Ed. by Walter Clark. (Colonial & State Records of North Carolina Ser.). 825p. 1994. reprint ed. 50.00 (*1-56837-218-3*) Broadfoot.

State Records of North Carolina, Vol. 19: 1782-1784 & Supplement, 1771-1782. Ed. by Walter Clark. (Colonial & State Records of North Carolina Ser.). 1001p. 1994. reprint ed. 50.00 (*1-56837-219-1*) Broadfoot.

State Records of North Carolina, Vol. 20: 1785-1788. Ed. by Walter Clark. (Colonial & State Records of North Carolina Ser.). 793p. 1994. reprint ed. 50.00 (*1-56837-220-5*) Broadfoot.

State Records of North Carolina, Vol. 21: 1788-1790. Ed. by Walter Clark. (Colonial & State Records of North Carolina Ser.). 1083p. 1994. reprint ed. 50.00 (*1-56837-221-3*) Broadfoot.

State Records of North Carolina, Vol. 22: Miscellaneous. Ed. by Walter Clark. (Colonial & State Records of North Carolina Ser.). 1049p. 1994. reprint ed. 50.00 (*1-56837-222-1*) Broadfoot.

State Records of North Carolina, Vol. 23: Laws 1715-1776. Ed. by Walter Clark. (Colonial & State Records of North Carolina Ser.). 1000p. 1994. reprint ed. 50.00 (*1-56837-223-X*) Broadfoot.

State Records of North Carolina, Vol. 24: Laws 1777-1788. Ed. by Walter Clark. (Colonial & State Records of North Carolina Ser.). 994p. 1994. reprint ed. 50.00 (*1-56837-224-8*) Broadfoot.

State Records of North Carolina, Vol. 25: Laws 1789-1790 & Supplement Omitted Laws 1669-1783, with Index to Vols. 23-25. Ed. by Walter Clark. (Colonial & State Records of North Carolina Ser.). 741p. 1994. reprint ed. 50.00 (*1-56837-250-7*) Broadfoot.

State Records of North Carolina, Vol. 26: Census 1790, Names of Heads of Families. Ed. by Walter Clark. (Colonial & State Records of North Carolina Ser.). 1313p. 1994. reprint ed. 50.00 (*1-56837-251-5*) Broadfoot.

State Records of North Carolina, 1777-1790, 16 Vols, Set. North Carolina General Assembly Staff. Ed. by Walter Clark. LC 72-1798. reprint ed. 2,880.00 (*0-404-07470-7*) AMS Pr.

***State Reference Guide to Work-Family Program for State Employees.** Michele Lord & Margaret King. 126p. 1991. pap. 27.00 (*0-614-22667-8*, W91-02) Families & Work.

***State Reference Publications (1996-1997) A Bibliographic Guide to State Blue Books, Legislative Manuals, & Other General Reference Sources.** rev. ed. Ed. by Lynn Hellebust. 230p. 1996. spiral bd. 67.50 (*1-879929-19-8*) Govt Res Serv.

State Regulation: Housing Prices. James C. Nicholas. 140p. 1982. pap. text ed. 12.95 (*0-88285-075-X*) Transaction Pubs.

State Regulation of Railroads in the South. Maxwell Ferguson. LC 75-76711. (Columbia University. Studies in the Social Sciences: No. 162). reprint ed. 29.50 (*0-404-51162-7*) AMS Pr.

State Regulation of the Health Occupations & Professions, 1985-86: Final Report, March 10, 1987. Council of State Governments Staff. (Publication Ser.: No. C76). 249p. reprint ed. pap. 71.00 (*0-7837-2654-6*, 2043009) Bks Demand.

State, Religion, & Ethnic Politics: Afghanistan, Iran, & Pakistan. Ed. by Ali Banuazizi & Myron Weiner. LC 86-6048. (Contemporary Issues in the Middle East Ser.). 464p. 1988. reprint ed. pap. text ed. 16.95 (*0-8156-2448-4*) Syracuse U Pr.

State Reporters. write for info. (*0-318-57504-3*) West Pub.

State Resistance & Change in South Africa. Ed. by Phillip Frankel et al. 256p. 1988. lib. bdg. 45.00 (*0-7099-4900-6*, Pub. by Croom Helm UK) Routledge Chapman & Hall.

State Resources & Services Related to Alcohol & Drug Problems for Fiscal Year 1993: An Analysis of State Alcohol & Drug Abuse Profile Data. John S. Gustafson et al. 395p. (Orig.). 1996. pap. text ed. 45.00 (*0-7881-2799-3*) DIANE Pub.

State Responsibility & the Direct Broadcast Satellite. Marika N. Taishoff. 220p. 1992. 45.00 (*0-86187-700-4*) St Martin.

State Responsibility & the Marine Environment: The Rules of Decision. Brian D. Smith. (Oxford Monographs in International Law). (Illus.). 304p. 1988. 75.00 (*0-19-825581-0*) OUP.

State Responsibility for the Support of Education in Georgia. Gordon G. Singleton. LC 73-177779. (Columbia University. Teachers College. Contributions to Education Ser.: No. 181). reprint ed. 37.50 (*0-404-55181-5*) AMS Pr.

State Responsiveness & State Activism. Jerald Hage et al. 256p. 1989. text ed. 55.00 (*0-04-445043-5*) Routledge Chapman & Hall.

State Retirement Guides Series. Thomas Myers, Jr. et al. Ed. by William L. Bowman & David A. Wilson. (Orig.). 1995. pap. 39.90 (*1-886429-02-2*) Retirement Info.

State, Revolution & Superpowers in Afghanistan. Hafizullah Emadi. LC 89-22853. 173p. 1990. text ed. 45.00 (*0-275-93460-8*, C3460, Greenwood Pr) Greenwood.

State Rights in the Confederacy. Frank L. Owsley. 1990. 14.50 (*0-8446-1337-1*) Peter Smith.

State Road Use Taxes: A Guide to Fuel Uses & Weight-Distance Taxes. 236p. 1996. pap. text ed. 24.00 (*0-88711-325-7*) Am Trucking Assns.

State Role in Public Transportation. (Transportation Research Circular Ser.: No. 343). 84p. 1988. 7.00 (*0-685-38587-6*) Transport Res Bd.

State Roots of National Politics: Congress & the Tax Agenda, 1978-1986. Michael B. Berkman. LC 93-16227. (Policy & Institutional Studies). 216p. (C). 1993. text ed. 49.95 (*0-8229-3761-1*); pap. text ed. 15.95 (*0-8229-5508-3*) U of Pittsburgh Pr.

State Rural Transportation Programs in an Era of Contraction. Thomas G. Johnson. (New Alliances for Rural America Ser.). (Orig.). 1988. pap. text ed. 6.00 (*1-55877-032-1*) Natl Governor.

***State Sacrifices & Music in Ming China: Orthodoxy, Creativity, & Expressiveness.** Joseph S. Lam. (SUNY Series in Chinese Studies). (Illus.). 256p. (C). 1998. text ed. 74.50 (*0-7914-3705-1*) State U NY Pr.

***State Sacrifices & Music in Ming China: Orthodoxy, Creativity, & Expressiveness.** Joseph S. Lam. (SUNY Series in Chinese Studies). (Illus.). 256p. (C). 1998. pap. text ed. 24.95 (*0-7914-3706-X*) State U NY Pr.

***State Sales Handbook.** unabridged ed. Woody Tutcove & Gloria Leacox. 300p. (Orig.). 1996. pap. 295.00 (*1-890299-01-4*) Gov Technology.

State Sanitation: A Review of the Work of the Massachusetts State Board of Health, 2 Vols. George C. Whipple. Ed. by Barbara G. Rosenkrantz. LC 76-40652. (Public Health in America Ser.). (Illus.). 1977. reprint ed. lib. bdg. 69.95 (*0-405-09835-9*) Ayer.

State Scholarship Students at Hunter College of the City of New York. A. Bildersee. LC 77-176563. (Columbia University. Teachers College. Contributions to Education Ser.: No. 540). reprint ed. 37.50 (*0-404-55540-3*) AMS Pr.

State School Finance Litigation: A Summary & Analysis. Terry N. Whitney & Faith E. Crampton. 8p. 1995. 5.00 (*1-55516-395-5*, 7302-2009) Natl Conf State Legis.

State School Reports. Frank L. Shaw. LC 72-177792. (Columbia University. Teachers College. Contributions to Education Ser.: No. 242). reprint ed. 37.50 (*0-404-55242-0*) AMS Pr.

State Science & Technology Policies: An Assessment. Jurgen Schmandt & Robert Wilson. (Working Paper Ser.: No. 40). 40p. 1987. pap. 5.00 (*0-89940-521-5*) LBJ Sch Pub Aff.

State Secrets. Linda L. Miller. 1995. pap. 4.99 (*1-55166-014-8*, Mira Bks) Harlequin Bks.

State Secrets. Linda L. Miller. 1994. mass mkt. 4.50 (*0-373-48307-4*, 5-48307-8) Silhouette.

State Secrets: A French President's Experiences with Power & Private Life. Valery G. D'Estang. 320p. 1998. 25.00 (*0-394-57624-1*) Random.

State Security & the League of Nations. Bruce S. Williams. LC 75-177845. reprint ed. 47.50 (*0-404-06959-2*) AMS Pr.

State Security in South Africa: Civil-Military Relations under P W Botha. James M. Roherty. LC 91-14446. 240p. (gr. 13). 1992. text ed. 62.95 (*0-87332-877-9*) M E Sharpe.

State Security, Privacy & Information. John D. Baxter. LC 90-42654. 240p. 1990. text ed. 49.95 (*0-312-05375-4*) St Martin.

State-Selected & State-to-State Ion-Molecule Reaction Dynamics: Experiment, Vol. 82. Ed. by Cheuk-Yiu Ng & Michael Baer. (Advances in Chemical Physics Ser.: Vol. 82, Pt. 1). 704p. 1992. text ed. 209.00 (*0-471-53258-4*) Wiley.

State-Selected & State-to-State Ion-Molecule Reaction Dynamics: Theoretical Aspects, Vol. 82. Ed. by Michael Baer & Cheuk-Yiu Ng. (Advances in Chemical Physics Ser.: Vol. 82, Pt. 2). 576p. 1992. text ed. 195.00 (*0-471-53263-0*) Wiley.

State Shrinking: A Comparative Inquiry into Privatization. Frwd. by William P. Glade. LC 86-10631. (Special Publications). x, 326p. 1987. pap. 14.95 (*0-86728-016-6*) U TX Inst Lat Am Stud.

State Smart! Over 130 Ready-to-Use Puzzle Activities Based on the Geography & History of the 50 United States. John H. Thompson. LC 95-6468. 292p. 1995. spiral bd. 27.95 (*0-87628-881-6*) Ctr Appl Res.

State, SMSA, ADI, City, County Data & Indices see **Nineteen Eighty U. S. Census Population & Housing Characteristics**

State, Social Policy & Social Change in Germany, 1880-1994. rev. ed. Ed. by W. R. Lee & Eve Rosenhaft. 320p. 1997. 39.95 (*1-85973-197-X*) Berg Pubs.

State Socialism & Anarchism & Other Essays: Including the Attitude of Anarchism Toward Industrial Combinations & Why I Am an Anarchist. Benjamin R. Tucker. LC 72-77201. (Libertarian Broadsides Ser.: No. 4). 40p. 1985. pap. 2.15 (*0-87926-015-7*) R Myles.

***State, Society & Big Business in South Korea.** Yeon-Ho Lee. (Routledge Studies in the Growth Economies of Asia Ser.). 224p. (C). 1997. text ed. write for info. (*0-415-14583-X*) Routledge.

State, Society, & Corporate Power. 2nd rev. ed. Ed. by Marc R. Tool & Warren J. Samuels. 608p. 1989. pap. 24.95 (*0-88738-759-4*) Transaction Pubs.

***State, Society & Democratic Change in Pakistan.** Ed. by Rasul B. Rais. 309p. 1997. 29.95 (*0-19-577759-X*) OUP.

***State, Society, & Human Rights in South Asia.** Stig T. Madsen. (C). 1996. 38.00 (*81-7304-138-5*, Pub. by Manohar II) S Asia.

State, Society, & Law in Islam: Ottoman Law in Comparative Perspective. Haim Gerber. LC 93-8076. 233p. 1994. text ed. 64.50 (*0-7914-1877-4*); pap. text ed. 21.95 (*0-7914-1878-2*) State U NY Pr.

State, Society & Liberty: Studies in Political Theory & Constitutional Law. Ernst-Wolfgang Bockenforde. Tr. by J. A. Underwood from GER. LC 90-37046. (State, Law & Society Ser.). 266p. 1991. 19.95 (*0-85496-595-5*) Berg Pubs.

State, Society, & Limited Nuclear War. Eric Mlyn. LC 94-10966. (SUNY Series in the Making of Foreign Policy). 241p. (C). 1995. text ed. 59.50 (*0-7914-2347-6*); pap. text ed. 19.95 (*0-7914-2348-4*) State U NY Pr.

State, Society & Market: A Guide to Competing Theories of Development. John Martinussen. LC 96-24005. 400p. 1997. 65.00 (*1-85649-441-1*, Pub. by Zed Bks Ltd UK); pap. 25.00 (*1-85649-442-X*, Pub. by Zed Bks Ltd UK) Humanities.

***State, Society & Mobilization in Europe During the First World War.** Ed. by John Horne. (Studies in the Social & Cultural History of Modern Warfare: No. 3). 296p. (C). 1997. text ed. 59.95 (*0-521-56112-4*) Cambridge U Pr.

State, Society, & Popular Leaders in Mid-Republican Rome, 241-167 B.C. Rachel F. Vishnia. LC 95-39442. 280p. (C). 1996. text ed. 65.00 (*0-415-10512-9*) Routledge.

State, Society, & Privitization in Turkey, 1979-1990. Sallama Shaker. 112p. 1995. pap. text ed. 13.00 (*0-943875-75-7*) Johns Hopkins.

State, Society, & the Elementary School in Imperial Germany. Marjorie Lamberti. 302p. 1989. 55.00 (*0-19-505611-6*) OUP.

State-Society Relations in Yugoslavia: 1945-1992. Ed. by Jill A. Irvine et al. LC 95-12886. 275p. 1997. text ed. 55.00 (*0-312-12690-5*) St Martin.

State-Society Struggle: Zaire in Comparative Perspective. Thomas M. Callaghy. LC 84-5865. 515p. 1984. pap. text ed. 27.50 (*0-231-05721-0*) Col U Pr.

***State-Society Synergy: Government & Social Capital in Development.** Peter B. Evans. LC 97-1327. (Research Ser.). 1997. pap. write for info. (*0-87725-194-0*) U of Cal IAS.

***State Sovereigns & Society.** Carlton. Date not set. text ed. 55.00 (*0-312-21045-0*) St Martin.

***State Sovereignty: Change & Persistence in International Relations.** Schail H. Hashmi. LC 96-50181. 1997. write for info. (*0-271-01696-5*); pap. write for info. (*0-271-01697-3*) Pa St U Pr.

State Sovereignty As Social Construct. Ed. by Thomas J. Biersteker & Cynthia Weber. (Studies in International Relations: No. 46). 320p. (C). 1996. text ed. 59.95 (*0-521-56252-X*); pap. text ed. 19.95 (*0-521-56599-5*) Cambridge U Pr.

State Space & Input-Output Linear Systems. D. F. Delchamps. (Illus.). 425p. 1987. 72.00 (*0-387-96659-5*) Spr-Verlag.

State-Space Methods for Contro System. F. Csaki. 650p. (C). 1976. 120.00 (*963-05-0862-1*, Pub. by Akad Kiado HU) St Mut.

State Space Modeling of Time Series. Masahiko Aoki. (Illus.). 330p. 1986. 69.00 (*0-387-17256-4*) Spr-Verlag.

State Space Modeling of Time Series. Masahiko Aoki. (Universitext Ser.). (Illus.). xi, 314p. 1987. pap. 25.00 (*0-387-17257-2*) Spr-Verlag.

State Space Modeling of Time Series. enl. rev. ed. Masahiko Aoki. (Illus.). xviii, 323p. 1990. pap. 32.00 (*0-387-52870-9*) Spr-Verlag.

State Space Modeling of Time Series. 2nd enl. rev. ed. Masahiko Aoki. (Illus.). xviii, 323p. 1990. 79.95 (*0-387-52869-5*) Spr-Verlag.

State-Space Models of Lumped & Distributed Systems. V. Kecman. (Lecture Notes in Control & Information Sciences Ser.: Vol. 112). (Illus.). ix, 280p. 1988. 59.95 (*0-387-50082-0*) Spr-Verlag.

State Space Theory of Systems. 2nd enl. rev. ed. A. V. Balakrishnan. LC 88-25591. (Series in Communication & Control Systems). 224p. 1988. text ed. 65.00 (*0-911575-54-5*) Optimization Soft.

***State Staff Directory, 1997 Spring(Subscription Only)** annuals Ed. by P. Wayne Walker. (YA). (gr. 7 up). 1997. pap. 175.00 (*0-87289-126-7*) C Q Staff.

State Standards & Local Planning Regulation for Farmland Preservation in Oregon. Robert E. Coughlin. Ed. by Benjamin H. Stevens. (Discussion Paper Ser.: No. 124). 67p. (Orig.). 1981. pap. 10.00 (*1-55869-001-8*) Regional Sci Res Inst.

State Sticker Book. Justine Korman. 64p. (J). (gr. 1-5). 1995. pap. 6.95 (*1-56293-814-2*) McClanahan Bk.

State Strategic Planning under the Drug Formula Grant Program: An Evaluation. Terence Dunworth & Aaron J. Saiger. 137p. (Orig.). (YA). (gr. 12 up). 1994. pap. text ed. 30.00 (*0-7881-0781-X*) DIANE Pub.

State Strategies in the Global Political Economy. Ronan Palan & Jason Abbott. 256p. 1996. 90.00 (*1-85567-342-8*, Pub. by Pntr Pubs UK) Bks Intl VA.

***State Strategies to Manage Budget Shortfalls.** Fiscal Affairs Department Staff. 55p. 1996. 35.00 (*1-55516-557-5*, 5333) Natl Conf State Legis.

State Succession Relating to Unequal Treaties. Lung-Fong Chen. LC 74-9820. xiii, 324p. (C). 1974. lib. bdg. 37.50 (*0-208-01433-0*, Archon Bks) Shoe String.

State Supervision & Regulation of Budgetary Procedure in Public School Systems: An Evaluation of State Provisions for Budget-Making in Local School Systems. R. G. Campbell. LC 73-176625. (Columbia University. Teachers College. Contributions to Education Ser.: No. 637). reprint ed. 37.50 (*0-404-55637-X*) AMS Pr.

State Supervision of Local Finance: Proceedings of a Conference, December 4, 5, 6, 1941. Municipal Finance Officers Association Staff & United States, Bureau of the Census Staff. 127p. write for info. (*0-318-59326-2*) Municipal.

State Supreme Courts: Policymakers in the Federal System. Ed. by Mary P. Cornelia & G. Alan Tarr. LC 81-13431. (Contributions in Legal Studies: No. 24). (Illus.). xxvii, 221p. 1982. text ed. 59.95 (*0-313-22942-2*, PSC/, Greenwood Pr) Greenwood.

State Supreme Courts in Nation & State. G. Alan Tarr & Mary C. Porter. LC 87-2303. 288p. (C). 1988. 42.50 (*0-300-03912-3*) Yale U Pr.

State Supreme Courts in State & Nation. G. Alan Tarr et al. 295p. (C). 1990. reprint ed. pap. 17.00 (*0-300-04590-5*) Yale U Pr.

State Takeover Statutes & Poison Pills. Robert H. Winter et al. 85.00 (*0-318-36197-3*) P-H.

State Tax Actions, 1994. Scott R. Mackey. (Legislative Finance Papers: No. ZZ). 56p. 1994. 35.00 (*1-55516-001-8*, 5101-94) Natl Conf State Legis.

State Tax Actions 1995. Scott R. Mackey. 55p. Date not set. 35.00 (*1-55516-014-X*, 5101-00ZZ) Natl Conf State Legis.

***State Tax Actions 1996.** Scott R. Mackey. 56p. 1996. 35.00 (*1-55516-555-9*, 5101-0102) Natl Conf State Legis.

***State Tax & Expenditure Limits.** Mandy Rafool. (Legislative Finance Papers). 30p. 1996. pap. 20.00 (*1-55516-558-3*, 5104-0104) Natl Conf State Legis.

State Tax Consequences of IRA Distributions for Nonresidents. Anthony P. Curatola. 41p. (Orig.). 1990. pap. 20.00 (*0-89154-399-6*) Intl Found Employ.

State Tax Expenditure Review Mechanisms. (Legislative Finance Papers: No. 47). 30p. 1985. 6.25 (*1-55516-047-6*, 5101-47) Natl Conf State Legis.

State Tax Handbook: As of October, 1992. 336p. 1992. pap. 24.50 (*0-685-67079-1*, 4714) Commerce.

***State Tax Handbook, 1997.** 386p. 1997. pap. 32.00 (*0-614-26834-6*, 12396BLS05) Commerce.

State Tax Policy: Evaluating the Issues. Andrew Reschovsky et al. (Illus.). 300p. 1983. pap. 15.00 (*0-943142-04-0*) St Local Inter.

State Tax Policy & Senior Citizens. 2nd ed. Scott R. Mackey & Karen Carter. 78p. 1994. 25.00 (*1-55516-523-0*, 5323) Natl Conf State Legis.

State Tax Policy & the Development of Small & New Business. Roger Vaughan. LC 83-179310. 144p. 1983. pap. 10.00 (*0-914193-01-5*) Coalition NE Govn.

State Tax Relief for the Poor. 2nd ed. Steven D. Gold & David S. Liebschutz. LC 96-1621. 1996. write for info. (*0-914341-44-8*) Nelson Rockefeller Inst Govt.

State Tax Study Commissions: An Overview of Four Approaches. (Legislative Finance Papers: No. 48). 68p. 1985. 6.25 (*1-55516-048-4*, 5101-48) Natl Conf State Legis.

State Tax Treatment of LLCs. Francis X. Mellon. 52p. (Orig.). Date not set. pap. text ed. 25.95 (*0-7811-0113-1*) Res Inst Am.

State Taxation, Vols. I & II. rev. ed. Jerome R. Hellerstein & Walter Hellerstein. 1993. ring bd. 275.00 (*0-685-69558-1*, ST2) Warren Gorham & Lamont.

State Taxation: Corporate Income & Franchise Taxes, 2 vols., 2. Jerome R. Hellerstein. 800p. 1983. 155.00 (*0-685-53913-X*) Warren Gorham & Lamont.

State Taxation: Corporate Income & Franchise Taxes, 2 vols., Set. Jerome R. Hellerstein. 800p. 1983. 265.00 (*0-685-53914-8*) Warren Gorham & Lamont.

State Taxation: Corporate Income & Franchise Taxes, 2 vols., Vol. 1. Jerome R. Hellerstein. 800p. 1983. 155.00 (*0-88262-748-1*, ST) Warren Gorham & Lamont.

State Taxation Manual. annuals 1996. ring bd. write for info. (*0-614-13254-1*) Am Ins NY.

State Taxation of Business: Issues & Policy Options. Ed. by Thomas F. Pogue. LC 92-15767. 360p. 1992. text ed. 59.95 (*0-275-94125-6*, C4125, Praeger Pubs) Greenwood.

State Taxation of Geothermal Resources Compared with State Taxation of Other Energy Minerals. Sharon C. Wagner. (Special Reports: No. 4). (Illus.). 86p. (Orig.). 1979. pap. 4.00 (*0-934412-04-9*) Geothermal.

State Taxation of Interstate Commerce. Paul J. Hartman. LC 53-11622. xi, 323p. 1953. lib. bdg. 38.50 (*0-89941-358-7*, 500390) W S Hein.

State Taxation of Public Pensions: The Impact of Davis vs. Michigan. Corina Eckl et al. (Legislative Finance Papers: No. 70). (Illus.). 30p. 1989. pap. text ed. 10.00 (*1-55516-070-0*, 5101-70) Natl Conf State Legis.

State Taxation Policy & Economic Growth. Ed. by Michael Barker. LC 83-1551. (Duke Press Policy Studies). xix, 284p. 1983. text ed. 46.95 (*0-8223-0535-6*) Duke.

State, Technology & Industrialization in Africa. Jeffrey James. LC 94-31256. 1995. text ed. 75.00 (*0-312-12491-0*) St Martin.

State Technology Programs: A Preliminary Analysis of Lessons Learned. David Osborne. 75p. 1989. 12.00 (*0-934892-50-4*) CSPA.

State, the Investor, & the Railroad: The Boston & Albany, 1825-1867. Stephen Salsbury. LC 67-20881. (Publication of the Center for the Study of the History of Liberty in America, Harvard University Ser.). (Illus.). 424p. reprint ed. pap. 120.90 (*0-7837-4188-X*, 2059038) Bks Demand.

State the State: More Than 2,500 Questions & Answers from Alabama to Wyoming. Gilbert W. Davies. LC 94-75126. 118p. (Orig.). (C). 1994. pap. 7.95 (*0-9634413-4-5*) HiSt Ink Bks.

State Theory: Putting the Capitalist State in Its Place. Bob Jessop. 380p. 1991. 45.00 (*0-271-00735-4*); pap. 17.95 (*0-271-00745-1*) Pa St U Pr.

State Theory & State History. Ed. by Rolf Torstendahl. (Swedish Collegium for Advanced Study in the Social Sciences Ser.). (Illus.). 256p. (C). 1992. text ed. 65.00 (*0-8039-8780-3*) Sage.

State Theory of Money. Georg F. Knapp. Tr. by H. M. Lucas & James Bonar. LC 75-140544. xviii, 306p. 1973. reprint ed. lib. bdg. 39.50 (*0-678-00831-0*) Kelley.

State Theory, State Autonomy & the Pre-Modern State. John Haldon. 240p. (C). (gr. 13). 1993. text ed. 60.00 (*0-86091-496-8*, B2503, Pub. by Vrso UK) Norton.

State Theory, State Autonomy & the Pre-Modern State. John Haldon. 240p. (C). 1994. pap. text ed. 19.00 (*0-86091-661-8*, B2507, Pub. by Vrso UK) Norton.

State-to-State Chemistry. Ed. by Philip R. Brooks & Edward F. Hayes. LC 77-14164. (ACS Symposium Ser.: No. 56). 1977. 35.95 (*0-8412-0386-5*) Am Chemical.

***State-to-State Chemistry.** Ed. by Philip R. Brooks & Edward F. Hayes. LC 77-14164. (ACS Symposium Ser.: Vol. 56). 271p. 1977. reprint ed. pap. 77.30 (*0-608-03939-X*, 2064386) Bks Demand.

State, Trade Unions, & Self-Management: Issues of Competence & Control. Ed. by Paul Blyton et al. (Studies in Organization: No. 16). x, 362p. (C). 1989. 74.95 (*0-89925-475-6*) De Gruyter.

State, Trade Unions, & Self-Management: Issues of Competence & Control. Ed. by Gyorgy Szell et al. (Studies in Organization: No. 16). x, 362p. (C). 1989. lib. bdg. 82.95 (*3-11-011667-7*) De Gruyter.

State Trademark & Unfair Competition Law. United States Trademark Association Staff. LC 87-17637. 1996. ring bd. 145.00 (*0-87632-556-8*, T7) Intl Trademark.

State Trading in International Markets: Theory & Practice of Industrialized & Developing Countries. M. M. Kostecki. 1982. text ed. 39.95 (*0-312-75693-3*) St Martin.

State Training Resource Directory, 1989. 1989. 95.00 (*0-685-38252-4*, C-147) Coun State Govts.

State Transportation Finance Within the Context of Energy Constraints. (National Cooperative Highway Research Program Report Ser.: No. 231). 86p. 1981. 7.60 (*0-309-03156-7*) Transport Res Bd.

State Trees: Including the Commonwealth of Puerto Rico. Sue R. Brandt. LC 92-8946. (Our State Symbols Ser.). 64p. (YA). 1992. lib. bdg. 22.10 (*0-531-20000-0*) Watts.

State Tretyakov Gallery. E. N. Atsarkina & V. M. Volodarskii. (Illus.). 720p. (RUS.). 1984. 63.00 (*0-317-57452-3*) St Mut.

State Tribal Legislation: 1992 & 1993 Legislations. Judy A. Zelio et al. 26p. 1994. 10.00 (*1-55516-926-0*, 9364) Natl Conf State Legis.

State Trooper. Jack Rudman. (Career Examination Ser.: C-757). 1994. pap. 23.95 (*0-8373-0757-0*) Nat Learn.

State Trooper. 11th ed. Hy Hammer. 1995. 14.95 (*0-02-860021-5*) Macmillan.

State Trooper. 11th ed. Edward Scheinkman. 1995. pap. 13.00 (*0-671-89915-5*) PB.

***State Trooper: Highway Patrol Officer - State Traffic Officer.** 12th ed. Hy Hammer & Edward Scheinkman. 240p. 1997. pap. 13.95 (*0-02-861523-9*, Arco) Macmillan Gen Ref.

State Troops & Volunteers: A Photographic Record of North Carolina's Civil War Soldiers. Greg Mast. (Illus.). 381p. 1995. reprint ed. 50.00 (*0-86526-264-0*) NC Archives.

State Trust Lands: History, Management, & Sustainable Use. Jon A. Souder & Sally K. Fairfax. LC 95-31165. (Development of Western Resources Ser.). (Illus.). 360p. (C). 1996. 40.00 (*0-7006-0731-5*) U Pr of KS.

State Under Seige. Philip Mauceri. LC 96-20662. (C). 1996. text ed. 52.00 (*0-8133-2753-9*) Westview.

State Under Siege: The Establishment of Northern Ireland, 1920-1925. Bryan A. Follis. 232p. 1995. text ed. 55.00 (*0-19-820305-5*) OUP.

State under Stress: Can the Hollow State Be Good Government? Christopher D. Foster & F. J. Plowden. LC 96-21865. (Public Policy & Management Ser.). 256p. 1996. 89.00 (*0-335-19714-0*, Open Univ Pr); pap. 28.95 (*0-335-19713-2*, Open Univ Pr) Taylor & Francis.

State under Timur. Syed Jamaluddin. (C). 1995. text ed. 27.00 (*81-241-0258-9*, Pub. by Har-Anand Pubns II) S Asia.

State Universities & Democracy. Allan Nevins. LC 77-9308. 171p. 1977. reprint ed. text ed. 38.50 (*0-8371-9705-8*, NESU, Greenwood Pr) Greenwood.

State University Program Aide. Jack Rudman. (Career Examination Ser.: C-3541). 1994. pap. 27.95 (*0-8373-3541-8*) Nat Learn.

State University Surveys the Humanities. University of North Carolina, Division of the Humanities Staff. Ed. by Loren C. MacKinney. LC 72-3386. (Essay Index Reprint Ser.). 1977. reprint ed. 21.95 (*0-8369-2916-0*) Ayer.

State v. Burns. 5th rev. ed. Anthony J. Bocchino & Donald H. Beskind. 140p. 1992. pap. 18.95 (*1-55681-297-3*) Natl Inst Trial Ad.

State v. Burns Teaching Notes. 5th rev. ed. Anthony J. Bocchino & Donald H. Beskind. 54p. 1992. teacher ed., pap. 8.95 (*1-55681-437-2*) Natl Inst Trial Ad.

State v. Cramden. Joseph E. Taylor & Michael S. Sands. 81p. 1995. pap. 18.95 (*1-55681-464-X*) Natl Inst Trial Ad.

State v. Diamond. 4th rev. ed. James H. Seckinger. 116p. 1992. pap. 18.95 (*1-55681-315-5*) Natl Inst Trial Ad.

State v. Lawrence. William Burnham & James H. Seckinger. 28p. 1992. pap. 18.95 (*1-55681-339-2*) Natl Inst Trial Ad.

State v. O'Neill. 5th rev. ed. James H. Seckinger. 142p. 1992. pap. 18.95 (*1-55681-305-8*) Natl Inst Trial Ad.

State v. O'Neill Teaching Notes. 5th rev. ed. James H. Seckinger. 30p. 1992. teacher ed., pap. 8.95 (*1-55681-435-6*) Natl Inst Trial Ad.

State v. Stone. 4th rev. ed. James H. Seckinger. 160p. 1992. pap. 18.95 (*1-55681-311-2*) Natl Inst Trial Ad.

State v. Stone Teaching Notes. 4th rev. ed. James H. Seckinger. 30p. pap. 8.95 (*1-55681-440-2*) Natl Inst Trial Ad.

State v. Wyatt. David S. Rudolf & Thomas K. Maher. 100p. 1995. pap. 18.95 (*1-55681-476-3*) Natl Inst Trial Ad.

State Variable Methods in Automatic Control. Katsuhisa Furuta & Akira Sano. LC 87-35481. 212p. 1988. text ed. 98.00 (*0-471-91877-6*) Wiley.

State Verdict Survey. 1996. 29.50 (*0-685-14933-1*) Jury Verdict.

State, Village, & Ritual in Bali: An Historical Perspective. Henk S. Nordholt. (Comparative Asian Studies: No. 6). 58p. (Orig.). 1992. pap. text ed. 14.50 (*90-5383-023-5*, Pub. by VU Univ Pr NE) Paul & Co Pubs.

State, Violence & Development: The Political Economy of War in Mozambique, 1975-1992. Mark Chingono. (Making of Modern Africa Ser.). 303p. 1996. 68.95 (*1-85972-077-3*, Pub. by Avebury Pub UK) Ashgate Pub Co.

State Violence & Ethnicity. Ed. by Pierre L. Van den Berghe. (Illus.). 228p. (C). 1990. text ed. 29.95 (*0-87081-217-3*) Univ Pr Colo.

State vs. Diamond Teaching Notes. 4th rev. ed. James H. Seckinger. 42p. teacher ed., pap. 8.95 (*1-55681-444-5*) Natl Inst Trial Ad.

State vs. Elinor Norton. Mary R. Rinehart. 288p. 1988. mass mkt. 3.50 (*0-8217-2412-6*, Zebra Kensgtn) Kensgtn Pub Corp.

State vs. Elinor Norton. Mary R. Rinehart. 21.95 (*0-8488-0618-2*) Amereon Ltd.

State vs. Justice. Gallatin Warfield. 384p. 1993. mass mkt. 5.99 (*0-446-36477-0*) Warner Bks.

State Wage Assignment & Garnishment Handbook, 1994 Edition. Ed. by Robert S. Teachout. 400p. 1994. text ed. 55.00 (*0-87179-826-3*) BNA Books.

State, War, & the State of War. Kalevi J. Holsti. LC 96-3881. (Studies in International Relations: No. 51). 270p. (C). 1996. text ed. 59.95 (*0-521-57113-8*) Cambridge U Pr.

State, War, & the State of War. Kalevi J. Holsti. LC 96-3881. (Cambridge Studies in International Relations: No. 51). 270p. (C). 1996. pap. 18.95 (*0-521-57790-X*) Cambridge U Pr.

State Water Policies: A Study of Six States. Jurgen Schmandt et al. LC 88-15257. 205p. 1988. text ed. 55.00 (*0-275-93132-3*, C3132, Praeger Pubs) Greenwood.

State Weights & Measures Laboratories: State Standards Program Description & Directory. 1994. lib. bdg. 250.00 (*0-8490-8560-8*) Gordon Pr.

State Weights & Measures Laboratories: State Standards Program Description & Directory. 1995. lib. bdg. 250.75 (*0-8490-6696-4*) Gordon Pr.

State Weights & Measures Laboratories: State Standards Program Description & Directory. 115p. (Orig.). (C). 1994. pap. text ed. 30.00 (*0-7881-1125-6*) DIANE Pub.

State Welfare-to-Work Programs: Four Case Studies. Jose R. Figueroa et al. 75p. (Orig.). 1990. pap. text ed. 15.00 (*1-55877-107-7*) Natl Governor.

State Welfare Waiver Evaluations: Will They Increase Our Understanding of the Impact of Welfare Reform on Children? Ann Collins & J. Lawrence Aber. 37p. 1996. pap. 10.00 (*0-926582-16-X*) NCCP.

State We're In: Why Britain Is in Crisis & How to Overcome It. Will Hutton. 352p. 1996. 35.00 (*0-224-03688-2*) Trafalgar.

State Wildlife Laws Handbook: Center for Wildlife Law at the Institute of Public Law, University of New Mexico, Albuquerque, New Mexico. Ruth Musgrave & Mary A. Stein. LC 93-23418. 840p. 1993. text ed. 94.00 (*0-86587-357-7*) Gov Insts.

State Within a State: Industrial Relations in Israel, 1965-1987. Ran Chermesh. LC 92-9264. (Contributions in Labor Studies: No. 43). 320p. 1993. text ed. 55.00 (*0-313-28547-0*, CWT, Greenwood Pr) Greenwood.

State Within the State: The KGB & Its Hold on Russia--Past, Present & Future. Yevgenia Albats. 1994. 25.00 (*0-374-18104-7*) FS&G.

Statecraft. William Sanderson. 1972. 59.95 (*0-8490-1123-X*) Gordon Pr.

Statecraft & Agriculture in Mexico, 1980-1982: Domestic & Foreign Policy Considerations in the Making of Mexican Agricultural Policy. John J. Bailey & John E. Link. (Research Reports: No. 23). 40p. (Orig.). (C). 1981. pap. 5.00 (*0-935391-22-3*, RR-23) UCSD Ctr US-Mex.

Statecraft & Political Economy on the Taiwan Frontier, 1600-1800. John R. Shepherd. LC 91-46158. (Illus.). 624p. (C). 1993. 67.50 (*0-8047-2066-5*) Stanford U Pr.

Statecraft & Power: Essays in Honor of Harold W. Rood. Ed. by Christopher C. Harman & David Tucker. LC 93-35904. 296p. (Orig.). (C). 1994. pap. 26.00 (*0-8191-8718-6*); lib. bdg. 57.50 (*0-8191-8717-8*) U Pr of Amer.

Statecraft in the Middle East: Historical Memory & Popular Culture. Ed. by Eric Davis & Nicolas Gavrielides. 304p. 1991. pap. text ed. 22.95 (*0-8130-1058-6*); lib. bdg. 49.95 (*0-8130-1046-2*) U Press Fla.

Stategem & Other Stories. Aleister Crowley. 1993. reprint ed. lib. bdg. 18.95 (*0-89968-422-X*, Lghtyr Pr) Buccaneer Bks.

Stategic Change. Colin Carnall. (Management Reader Ser.). 280p. 1996. pap. 37.95 (*0-7506-1932-5*) Buttrwrth-Heinemann.

Statehood. Marilyn Brown. 304p. (Orig.). 1995. pap. 9.95 (*1-56236-308-5*) Aspen Bks.

Statehood & Union: A History of the Northwest Ordinance. Peter S. Onuf. LC 86-43046. (Midwestern History & Culture Ser.). (Illus.). 224p. 1987. 31.50 (*0-253-35482-X*) Ind U Pr.

Statehood & Union: A History of the Northwest Ordinance. Peter S. Onuf. LC 86-43046. (Midwestern History & Culture Ser.). 224p. 1992. reprint ed. pap. 5.95 (*0-253-20758-4*, MB-758) Ind U Pr.

Statehouse Democracy: Public Opinion & the American States. Robert S. Erikson et al. LC 93-7076. (Illus.). 256p. (C). 1994. text ed. 69.95 (*0-521-41349-4*); pap. text ed. 19.95 (*0-521-42405-4*) Cambridge U Pr.

Stateless in Gaza. Paul Cossali & Clive Robson. (Illus.). 172p. (C). 1986. pap. 9.95 (*0-86232-509-9*, Pub. by Zed Bks Ltd UK); text ed. 29.95 (*0-86232-508-0*, Pub. by Zed Bks Ltd UK) Humanities.

Stateless Market: European Dilemma of Integration & Civilization. Paul Kapteyn. (European Public Policy Ser.). 224p. (C). 1995. text ed. 69.95 (*0-415-12232-5*, Routledge NY) Routledge.

Stateless Market: European Dilemma Of Integration & Civilization. Paul Kapteyn. (European Public Policy Ser.). 194p. (C). 1995. pap. 18.95 (*0-415-12233-3*) Routledge Chapman & Hall.

***Stately President Liners Pt. 1: American Passenger Liners of the Interwar Years: The "SOL's"** Mark H. Goldberg. (American Merchant Marine History Ser.: Vol. 5). (Illus.). 550p. (Orig.). 1996. pap. 24.95 (*1-879180-11-1*) AMM Mus Found.

Stately Science Pauses Not... (Mary Baker Eddy) Max Kappeler. 54p. 1992. reprint ed. pap. 6.00 (*0-942958-15-2*) Kappeler Inst Pub.

Stately Secrets: Behind-the-Scene Stories from the Stately Homes of Britain. Richard Earl of Bradford. 211p. 1995. 23.95 (*0-86051-917-1*, Robson-Parkwest) Parkwest Pubns.

***Stately Secrets: Behind-the-Scenes Stories from the Stately Homes of Britain.** 1997. pap. text ed. 11.95 (*1-86105-035-6*) Parkwest Pubns.

Statemaking & Social Movements: Essays in History & Theory. Ed. by Charles C. Bright & Susan F. Harding. LC 84-7430. 404p. 1984. text ed. 39.50 (*0-472-10050-5*) U of Mich Pr.

Statement. Brian Moore. LC 95-43885. 250p. 1996. pap. 22.95 (*0-525-94128-2*, Dutton) NAL-Dutton.

***Statement.** Brian Moore. 1997. pap. 11.95 (*0-452-27632-2*, Plume) NAL-Dutton.

***Statement.** Brian Moore. 1997. pap. 11.95 (*0-614-27293-9*, Plume) NAL-Dutton.

Statement & Referent: An Inquiry into the Foundations of Our Conceptual Order: Statements Are Products of Assertion. D. S. Shwayder. LC 92-16652. (Synthese Library: Vol. 224). 480p. (C). 1992. lib. bdg. 177.00 (*0-7923-1803-X*, Pub. by Klwr Acad Pubs NE) Kluwer Ac.

Statement by the Krishnamurti Foundation of America about the Radha Sloss Book "Lives in the Shadow" with J. Krishnamurti. Krishnamurti Foundation of America Staff. 16p. 1995. spiral bd. write for info. (*1-888004-07-X*) Krishnamurti.

Statement of Accounting Principles. Thomas H. Sanders et al. 138p. 1938. 12.00 (*0-86539-009-6*) Am Accounting.

Statement of Basic Accounting Theory. Basic Accounting Theory Committee. 100p. 1966. 12.00 (*0-86539-008-8*) Am Accounting.

Statement of Basic Auditing Concepts, Vol. 6. Basic Auditing Concepts Committee. (Studies in Accounting Research). 58p. 1973. 12.00 (*0-86539-018-5*) Am Accounting.

***Statement of Federal Financial Accounting Programs, 6 vols.** 1997. lib. bdg. 1,995.95 (*0-8490-7679-X*) Gordon Pr.

Statement of Financial Accounting Standards No. 5: Impact on Corporate Risk & Insurance Management. Robert C. Goshay. LC 78-65314. (Financial Accounting Standards Board Research Report Ser.). (Illus.). 68p. (Orig.). 1978. pap. 2.50 (*0-910065-05-5*) Finan Acct Found.

Statement of Some New Principles on the Subject of Political Economy: Exposing the Fallacies of the System of Free Trade. John Rae. LC 65-10366. (Reprints of Economic Classics Ser.). xvi, 414p. 1964. 49.50 (*0-678-00065-4*) Kelley.

Statement of the Laws of Argentina in Matters Affecting Business. Carlos Alurralde. 1976. lib. bdg. 134.95 (*0-8490-2666-0*) Gordon Pr.

Statement of the Laws of Honduras in Matters Affecting Business. 4th ed. OAS, General Secretariat for Legal Affairs. 292p. (C). 1981. pap. text ed. 10.00 (*0-8270-1421-X*) OAS.

Statement on Accounting Theory & Theory Acceptance. Concepts & Standards for External Financial Reports Committee. 61p. 1977. 12.00 (*0-86539-010-X*) Am Accounting.

Statement on Competencies in Languages Other Than English Expected of Entering Freshmen, Phase I: French, German, Spanish. California Department of Education Staff. 74p. 1986. pap. 5.50 (*0-8011-0807-1*) Calif Education.

Statement on Competencies in Mathematics Expected of Entering Freshmen. California Department of Education Staff. 64p. 1989. pap. 5.50 (*0-8011-0836-5*) Calif Education.

Statement on Psychiatric-Mental Health Clinical Nursing Practice & Standards of Psychiatric-Mental Health Clinical Nursing Practice. American Nurses Association Staff. 47p. (C). 1994. text ed. 13.95 (*1-55810-098-9*, PMH-12) Am Nurses Pub.

Statement on Race: An Annotated Elaboration & Exposition of the Four Statements on Race Issued by the United Nations Educational, Scientific & Cultural Organization. 3rd ed. Ashley Montagu. LC 80-27835. xii, 278p. 1981. reprint ed. text ed. 55.00 (*0-313-22739-X*, MOSR) Greenwood.

Statement on School-Based Clinics. National Conference of Catholic Bishops. (Orig.). 1987. pap. 0.95 (*1-55586-196-2*) US Catholic.

Statement on the Scope & Standards of Otorhinolaryngology Nursing Practice. American Nurses Association Staff & Society of Otorhinolaryngology Staff. 20p. 1994. pap. 11.50 (*0-614-02739-X*, NP-95) Am Nurses Pub.

Statement on the Scope & Standards of Respiratory Nursing Practice. American Nurses Association Staff & Respiratory Nursing Society Staff. 20p. 1994. pap. 11.50 (*0-614-02738-1*, NP-96) Am Nurses Pub.

Statement on the Scope & Standards on Oncology Nursing Practice. American Nurses Association Staff & Oncology Nursing Society Staff. LC 96-2450. 50p. (Orig.). 1996. pap. 13.95 (*1-55810-121-7*, MS-23) Am Nurses Pub.

Statements, 3 plays. Athol Fugard et al. 124p. 1986. pap. 8.95 (*0-930452-61-5*) Theatre Comm.

Statements in Stone: Monuments & Society in Neolithic Europe. Mark Patton. LC 92-30505. (Illus.). 272p. (C). (gr. 13). 1993. text ed. 69.95 (*0-415-06729-4*, B0308) Routledge.

Statements of Fact in Traditional Chinese Medicine. Bob Flaws. 120p. (Orig.). 1994. pap. 12.95 (*0-936185-52-X*) Blue Poppy Pr.

Statements of Financial Accounting Concepts. Financial Accounting Standards Board Staff. 1996. pap. text ed. write for info. (*0-471-16023-7*) Wiley.

Statements of Financial Accounting Concepts 1-6 see Accounting Standards: Original Pronouncements, July 1973-June 1986

Statements of the Laws of the OAS Member States in Matters Affecting Business. Incl. Brazil. 308p. (*0-8270-5470-X*); Colombia. 303p. (*0-8270-5480-7*); Dominica. (*0-318-54743-0*); Grenada. (*0-318-54744-9*); St. Lucia. 1980. (*0-318-54745-7*); Suriname. 1980. (*0-318-54746-5*); Argentina. 317p. 1975. 10.00 (*0-8270-5635-4*); Bolivia. 366p. 1974. 10.00 (*0-8270-5465-3*); Chile. 350p. 1977. 10.00 (*0-8270-5560-9*); Costa Rica. 332p. 1978. 10.00 (*0-8270-5590-0*); Dominican Republic. 300p. 1964. 10.00 (*0-8270-5490-4*); Ecuador. 296p. 1975. 10.00 (*0-8270-5495-5*); Salvador. 230p. 1979. 10.00 (*0-8270-5500-5*); Guatemala. 367p. 1975. 10.00 (*0-8270-5505-6*); Haiti. 116p. 1974. 10.00 (*0-8270-5510-2*); Honduras. 275p. 1965. 10.00 (*0-8270-5515-3*); No. 1. Honduras. 54p. 1979. suppl. ed. 2.00 (*0-8270-5651-6*); Mexico. 300p. 1970. 10.00 (*0-8270-5520-X*); Nicaragua. 325p. 1978. 10.00 (*0-8270-5570-6*); Panama. 306p. 1974. 10.00 (*0-8270-5530-7*); Paraguay. 300p. 1973. 10.00 (*0-8270-5595-1*); No. 1. Paraguay. 42p. 1979. suppl. ed. 2.00 (*0-8270-5650-8*); Peru. 290p. 1973. 10.00 (*0-8270-5640-0*); Uruguay. 275p. 1971. 10.00 (*0-8270-5630-3*); Venezuela. 350p. 1977. 10.00 (*0-8270-5555-2*); write for info. (*0-318-54747-3*) OAS.

Statements on Management Accounting, No. 4K. National Association of Accountants Staff. 36p. 1990. pap. 9.95 (*0-13-844465-X*) P-H.

Statements on Writing: A Compilation of Baha'i Scriptures & Other Sources. Duane L. Herrmann. 53p. 1993. pap. 4.00 (*1-879448-07-6*) Buffalo Pr KS.

Statements Two. Ed. by Jonathan Baumbach & Peter Spielberg. LC 76-56053. 1977. 10.95 (*0-914590-36-7*); pap. 6.95 (*0-914590-37-5*) Fiction Coll.

Staten Island Ferry. Theodore Scull. 1982. pap. 9.95 (*0-915276-37-2*) Quadrant Pr.

Staten Island Ferry International Poetry Festival. Ed. by Stanley H. Barkan. 48p. 1989. pap. 5.00 (*0-89304-068-1*) Cross-Cultrl NY.

Staten Island, Fifteen Twenty-Four to Eighteen Ninety-Eight. Henry G. Steinmeyer. (Illus.). 1987. reprint ed. 17.50 (*0-686-20334-8*) Staten Island.

Staten Island Patroons. Theodora Dubois & Dorothy V. Smith. (Illus.). 1961. pap. 1.50 (*0-686-23393-X*) Staten Island.

Staten Island Wills & Letters of Administration, Richmond County, New York, 1670-1800. Charlotte M. Hix. vi, 269p. (Orig.). 1993. pap. 22.00 (*1-55613-811-3*) Heritage Bk.

States. (Regional Map Packages Ser.). (Illus.). 1989. Incl. 50 maps. ring bd. 50.00 (*0-8160-1342-X*) Facts on File.

***States.** LC 97-2071. (Discovering Geography Ser.). (Illus.). 32p. (YA). (gr. 3 up). 1997. lib. bdg. 14.95 (*0-7614-0541-0*, Benchmark NY) Marshall Cavendish.

States Against Markets. Ed. by Boyer. 464p. (C). 1996. pap. 24.95 (*0-415-13726-8*); text ed. 79.95 (*0-415-13725-X*) Routledge.

States & Anti-Nuclear Movements. Ed. by Helena Flam. (Environment, Politics, & Society Ser.). 450p. 1994. text ed. 85.00 (*0-7486-0396-4*, Pub. by Edinburgh U Pr UK) Col U Pr.

States & Capitals. Kim M. Thompson & Karen M. Hilderbrand. (Rhythm, Rhyme & Read Ser.). (Illus.). 24p. (J). (gr. 3-6). 1993. student ed. 9.98 incl. audio (*1-882331-24-9*, TWIN 406) Twin Sisters.

States & Capitals: Individual Sets. Marion W. Stuart. text ed. write for info. (*0-943343-05-4*) Lrn Wrap-Ups.

States & Capitals Curriculum Activities. Harold Silvani. (Illus.). 74p. 1994. pap. text ed. 12.95 (*1-878669-59-1*) Crea Tea Assocs.

States & Capitals Rap. Brad Caudle & Richard Caudle. (Rock 'N Learn Ser.). (Illus.). 24p. (J). (gr. 4-12). 1993. pap. 9.95 incl. audio (*1-878489-15-1*, RL915) Rock n Learn.

States & Collective Action: The European Experience. Pierre Birnbaum. (Illus.). 228p. 1988. text ed. 54.95 (*0-521-32548-X*) Cambridge U Pr.

States & Companies: Political Risks in the International Oil Industry. Howard L. Lax. LC 88-15227. (Illus.). 209p. 1988. text ed. 55.00 (*0-275-93074-2*, C3074, Praeger Pubs) Greenwood.

States & Development in the Pacific Rim. Ed. by Richard P. Appelbaum & Jeffrey Henderson. (Illus.). 320p. (C). 1992. 48.00 (*0-8039-4034-3*); pap. 22.50 (*0-8039-4035-1*) Sage.

States & Economic Development: A Comparative Historical Analysis. Linda Weiss. 1995. pap. text ed. 24.95 (*0-7456-1457-4*) Blackwell Pubs.

States & Firms: Multinational Enterprises in Institutional Competition. Razeen Sally. LC 95-6974. 264p. (C). (gr. 13). 1995. text ed. 79.95 (*0-415-10379-7*) Routledge.

States & Higher Education: A Proud Past & a Vital Future: A Commentary of the Carnegie Foundation for the Advancement of Teaching Staff. Carnegie Foundation for the Advancement of Teaching Staff. LC 76-11958. (Carnegie Council Ser.). 112p. reprint ed. pap. 32.00 (*0-317-26531-8*, 2023982) Bks Demand.

States & Manufactured Housing. Thomas E. Nutt-Powell et al. (Illus.). 231p. 1980. pap. 10.00 (*0-943142-02-4*) St Local Inter.

States & Markets. Guoli Liu. (C). 1994. text ed. 59.50 (*0-8133-8799-X*) Westview.

States & Markets. 2nd ed. Susan Strange. LC 94-7274. 1994. 60.00 (*1-85567-244-8*) St Martin.

States & Markets: An Introduction to International Political Economy. 2nd ed. Susan Strange. 272p. 1994. pap. text ed. 19.00 (*1-85567-236-7*, Pub. by Pntr Pubs UK) Bks Intl VA.

States & Private Higher Education: Problems & Policies in a New Era. Carnegie Council on Policy Studies in Higher Education. LC 77-90808. (Carnegie Council Ser.). reprint ed. pap. 55.50 (*0-317-26050-2*) Bks Demand.

States & Provinces in the International Economy. Ed. by Douglas M. Brown & Earl H. Fry. LC 92-44595. 248p. (C). 1993. pap. 24.95 (*0-87772-335-4*) UCB IGS.

States & Regions. Harcourt Brace Staff. (J). (gr. 4). 1985. 74.50 (*0-15-373211-3*) HB Schl Dept.

States & Regions: Grade 4. Harcourt Brace Staff. 1985. 38.75 (*0-15-373204-0*) HB Schl Dept.

States & Regions: Landmark Edition. 88th ed. Stephanie Hirsh. 1988. text ed. 42.00 (*0-15-372904-X*) HarBrace.

States & Regions: Social Studies 1995. Harcourt Brace Staff. 1985. wbk. ed., pap. 10.25 (*0-15-373236-9*) HB Schl Dept.

States & Regions: Tests - Social Studies 1985. Harcourt Brace Staff. 1985. pap. 6.00 (*0-15-373244-X*) HB Schl Dept.

States & Small Business: A Directory of Programs & Activities. 1993. lib. bdg. 269.95 (*0-8490-9013-X*) Gordon Pr.

States & Small Business: A Directory of Programs & Activities, 2 vols., Set. 1995. lib. bdg. 600.95 (*0-8490-6774-X*) Gordon Pr.

States & Social Evolution: Coffee & the Rise of National Governments in Central America. Robert G. Williams. LC 93-44709. (Illus.). 350p. 1994. pap. text ed. 15.95 (*0-8078-4463-2*); lib. bdg. 45.00 (*0-8078-2154-3*) U of NC Pr.

States & Social Revolutions. Theda Skocpol. LC 78-14314. 448p. 1979. pap. text ed. 21.95 (*0-521-29499-1*) Cambridge U Pr.

States & Societies. Ed. by David Held et al. 640p. (C). 1983. text ed. 44.00 (*0-8147-3421-9*); pap. text ed. 16.00 (*0-8147-3422-7*) NYU Pr.

States & the Economy: Policymaking & Decentralization. Robert H. Wilson. LC 92-33329. 304p. 1993. text ed. 65.00 (*0-275-94506-5*, C4506, Praeger Pubs) Greenwood.

States & the Indian Gaming Regulating Act. Judy A. Zelio. (State Legislative Reports: Vol. 17, No. 16). 17p. 1992. pap. text ed. 5.00 (*1-55516-288-6*, 7302-1716) Natl Conf State Legis.

States & the Interstates. AASHTO Staff. (Reference Books & Proceedings). (Illus.). 236p. (Orig.). (C). 1991. pap. text ed. 48.00 (*1-56051-011-0*, TSI) AASHTO.

States & the Metropolis. Patricia S. Florestano & Vincent L. Marando. (Public Administration & Public Policy Ser.: Vol. 9). 176p. 1981. 85.00 (*0-8247-1287-0*) Dekker.

States & the Reemergence of Global Finance: From Bretton Woods to the 1990s. Eric Helleiner. 264p. 1994. 37.50 (*0-8014-2859-9*) Cornell U Pr.

States & the Reemergence of Global Finance: From Bretton Woods to the 1990s. Eric Helleiner. 256p. 1996. pap. 15.95 (*0-8014-8333-6*) Cornell U Pr.

States & the Violent Crime Control & Law Enforcement Act of 1994. Jon Felde et al. (State-Federal Issue Brief Ser.: Vol. 7, No. 1). 43p. 1995. pap. 6.50 (*1-55516-900-7*, 8500-0701) Natl Conf State Legis.

States & Tribes: Building New Traditions. James B. Reed & Judy A. Zelio. 99p. 1996. 25.00 (*1-55516-929-5*, 9354) Natl Conf State Legis.

States & Urban-Based Revolutions: Iran & Nicaragua. Farideh Farhi. 160p. 1990. text ed. 29.95 (*0-252-01710-2*) U of Ill Pr.

States As Water Quality Financiers: Legislative Options for the 1990s. 40p. 1991. 10.00 (*1-55516-457-9*, 4330) Natl Conf State Legis.

***States, Citizens, & Questions of Significance: Tenth Round Table on Law & Semiotics.** Ed. by John Brigham & Roberta Kevelson. (Semiotics & the Human Sciences Ser.: Vol. 11). 272p. (C). 1997. text ed. 48.95 (*0-8204-3020-X*) P Lang Pubng.

***States Coloring Book.** (Illus.). (J). Date not set. pap. 5.95 (*0-910119-45-7*) SOCO Pubns.

States Dyckman: American Loyalist. James T. Flexner. LC 92-8063. (Illus.). 238p. 1992. reprint ed. pap. 19.95 (*0-8232-1369-2*) Fordham.

States, Effects & Operations. K. Kraus. Ed. by A. Boehm et al. (Lecture Notes in Physics Ser.: Vol. 190). 151p. 1983. 18.00 (*0-387-12732-1*) Spr-Verlag.

States, Firms, & Raw Materials: The World Economy & Ecology of Aluminum. Ed. by Bradford L. Barham et al. LC 94-14005. 1995. 50.00 (*0-299-14110-1*); pap. 22.50 (*0-299-14114-4*) U of Wis Pr.

States in a Changing World: A Contemporary Analysis. Alan James. Ed. by Robert H. Jackson. (Illus.). 396p. (C). 1993. 65.00 (*0-19-827394-0*, 8955); pap. 26.00 (*0-19-827923-X*) OUP.

States in Profile: The State Policy Reference Book, 1991. State Policy Research, Inc. Staff et al. 300p. 1991. pap. text ed. 79.00 (*1-880077-00-0*) U S Data Demand.

States in West German Federalism. Roger H. Wells. 1961. 19.95 (*0-8084-0282-X*); pap. 14.95 (*0-8084-0283-8*) NCUP.

States, Labor Markets & the Future of Old Age Policy. Ed. by John Myles & Jill Quadagno. 340p. 1991. 59.95 (*0-87722-790-X*) Temple U Pr.

States' Laws on Race & Color. Davison M Douglas & Pauli Murray. LC 96-9128. (Studies in the Legal History of the South). 1997. 65.00 (*0-8203-1883-3*) U of Ga Pr.

States Manual of Spinal, Pelvic & Extravertebral Technics. 2nd ed. C. R. Kirk et al. (Illus.). 245p. (C). 1986. text ed. 35.00 (*0-9615849-0-4*) Natl Coll Chiro.

States, Nations & Nationalism: From the Middle Ages to the Present. Hagan Schulze. Tr. by W. E. Yuill from GER. LC 95-36139. (Making of Europe Ser.). 352p. (C). 1996. 29.95 (*0-631-19633-1*) Blackwell Pubs.

States, Nations, Sovereignty: Sri Lanka, India, & the Tamil Eelam Movement. Sumantra Bose. LC 93-49452. 1994. 33.50 (*0-8039-9170-3*) Sage.

States of Arabia. Z. H. Kour. (Afro-Asian Nations: History & Culture Ser.). 1991. text ed. 35.00 (*0-7069-5554-4*, Pub. by Vikas II) S Asia.

States of Awareness: An Annotated Bibliography. Compiled by John J. Miletich. LC 88-24733. (Bibliographies & Indexes in Psychology Ser.). 320p. 1988. text ed. 55.00 (*0-313-26194-6*, MSR, Greenwood Pr) Greenwood.

States of Belonging: German-American Intellectuals & the First World War. Phyllis Keller. LC 78-27544. 324p. reprint ed. pap. 92.40 (*0-7837-4159-6*, 2059007) Bks Demand.

States of Brain & Mind. Allan J. Hobson. (Readings from the Encyclopedia of Neuroscience Ser.). 144p. 1988. 38.00 (*0-8176-3409-6*) Birkhauser.

States of Central America: Honduras, San Salvador, Nicaragua, Costa Rica, & Guatemala. Ephraim G. Squier. 1977. lib. bdg. 95.00 (*0-8490-2667-9*) Gordon Pr.

States of Consciousness. American Psychological Association Staff et al. (Human Behavior Curriculum Project Ser.). 55p. 1981. teacher ed. 9.95 (*0-8077-2616-8*); pap. text ed. 3.95 (*0-8077-2615-X*) Tchrs Coll.

States of Consciousness. Ed. by Raghavan N. Iyer. 115p. (Orig.). 1983. pap. 8.75 (*0-88695-017-1*) Concord Grove.

States of Desire: Travels in Gay America. Edmund White. 360p. 1983. pap. 8.95 (*0-525-48223-7*, 0869-260, Obelisk) NAL-Dutton.

States of Disarray: The Social Effects of Globalization. United Nations Research Institute for Social Development (UNRISD) Staff. (Illus.). 172p. 1995. pap. 22.00 (*1-85383-318-5*, Pub. by Erthscan Pubns UK) Island Pr.

***States of Eastern Europe.** Francis W. Carter & David Turnock. LC 97-26185. 1997. spiral bd. write for info. (*1-85521-512-8*) Ashgate Pub Co.

States of Estrangement: The Novels of D. H. Lawrence, 1912-1917. Wayne D. Templeton. LC 88-50652. 316p. 1989. 38.50 (*0-87875-362-1*) Whitston Pub.

States of Exile. Young-Mason. 1995. 37.95 (*0-88737-626-6*) Natl League Nurse.

States of Fantasy. Jacqueline Rose. (Clarendon Lectures in English Literature). 200p. (C). 1996. 35.00 (*0-19-818280-5*, Clarendon Pr) OUP.

***States of Grace: Senegalese in Italy & the New European Immigration.** Donald M. Carter. LC 97-25951. 1997. write for info. (*0-8166-2542-5*); pap. write for info. (*0-8166-2543-3*) U of Minn Pr.

States of Grace: Spiritual Grounding in the Postmodern Age. Charlene Spretnak. LC 90-55076. 352p. 1993. reprint ed. pap. 12.00 (*0-06-250697-8*) Harper SF.

States of Injury: Power & Freedom in Late Modernity. Wendy Brown. LC 94-24068. 219p. 1995. text ed. 45.00 (*0-691-02990-3*); pap. text ed. 13.95 (*0-691-02989-X*) Princeton U Pr.

States of Injustice: A Guide to Human Rights & Civil Liberties in the European Union. Michael Spencer. 1995. pap. 19.95 (*0-7453-0980-1*, Pub. by Pluto Pr UK) LPC InBook.

States of Injustice: A Guide to Human Rights & Civil Liberties in the European Union. Michael Spencer. (C). 1995. 65.00 (*0-7453-0979-8*, Pub. by Pluto Pr UK) LPC InBook.

States of Matter. David L. Goodstein. 512p. 1985. reprint ed. pap. 10.95 (*0-486-64927-X*) Dover.

States of Mind: A Personal Journey through the Mid-Atlantic. Jonathan Yardley. LC 92-246900. 1993. 23.00 (*0-394-58911-4*, Villard Bks) Random.

***States of Mind: American & Post-Soviet Perspectives on Contemporary Issues in Psychology.** Ed. by Diane F. Halpern & Alexander E. Voiskounsky. LC 96-28089. (Illus.). 432p. 1997. 55.00 (*0-19-510350-5*); pap. 29.95 (*0-19-510351-3*) OUP.

States of Mind: Configurational Analysis of Individual Psychology. 2nd ed. Mardi J. Horowitz. LC 87-2571. (Critical Issues in Psychiatry Ser.). 292p. 1987. 59.50 (*0-306-42449-5*, Plenum Pr) Plenum.

States of Mind: Dialogues with Contemporary Thinkers. Richard Kearney. 336p. (C). 1995. 55.00 (*0-8147-4672-1*); pap. 18.95 (*0-8147-4673-X*) NYU Pr.

States of Mind Analysis of C. Mardi J. Horowitz. 1979. pap. 35.00 (*0-306-40088-X*) Da Capo.

States of Perfect Freedom: Autobiography & American Political Thought. Philip Abbott. LC 86-16248. 226p. 1987. 30.00 (*0-87023-542-7*) U of Mass Pr.

States of Rage: Emotional Eruption, Violence, & Social Change. Ed. by Renee R. Curry & Terry L. Allison. (Illus.). 233p. (C). 1996. 55.00 (*0-8147-1525-7*); pap. 18.95 (*0-8147-1530-3*) NYU Pr.

States of Shock. Sam Shepard. 1992. pap. 5.25 (*0-8222-1075-4*) Dramatists Play.

An Asterisk (*) at the beginning of an entry indicates that the title is appearing in BIP for the first time.

States of Shock, Far North, Silent Tongue. Sam Shepard. 1990. 22.50 (*0-8446-6752-8*) Peter Smith.

States of Shock, Far North, Silent Tongue. Sam Shepard. LC 92-50639. 1993. pap. 12.00 (*0-679-74218-2*, Vin) Random.

States of Siege: U. S. Prison Riots, 1971-1986. Bert Useem & Peter Kimball. (Illus.). 288p. 1991. reprint ed. pap. 16. 95 (*0-19-507271-5*) OUP.

***States of Sympathy: Democracy & Feeling in the Early American Novel.** Elizabeth Barnes. LC 96-53284. 1997. write for info. (*0-231-10878-8*); pap. write for info. (*0-231-10879-6*) Col U Pr.

States of "Theory" History, Art, & Critical Discourse. Intro. by David Carroll. (Irvine Studies in the Humanities). 320p. 1989. text ed. 39.50 (*0-231-07086-1*) Col U Pr.

States of "Theory" History, Art & Critical Discourse. David Carroll. x, 316p. 1994. pap. 16.95 (*0-8047-2254-4*) Stanford U Pr.

States of Unconsciousness in Three Tales by C. F. Meyer. Dennis McCort. LC 87-47786. 136p. 1988. 28.50 (*0-8387-5130-X*) Bucknell U Pr.

States of Wonder: Puzzles for Learning State Facts. Jeanne Cheyney & Arnold B. Cheyney. (Illus.). 128p. (Orig.). (J). (gr. 4-6). 1991. pap. 9.95 (*0-673-46352-4*, GoodYrBooks) Addson-Wesley Educ.

States or Markets? Neo-Liberalism & the Development Policy Debate. Ed. by Christopher Colclough & James Manor. (IDS Development Studies Ser.). (Illus.). 376p. (C). 1993. reprint ed. pap. 21.00 (*0-19-828811-5*, 5133) OUP.

States-Plus-Nations: A New Approach to Ethnic Conflicts, the Decline of Sovereignty, & the Dilemmas of Collective Security. Gidon Gottlieb. 148p. 1993. pap. 14.95 (*0-87609-156-7*) Coun Foreign.

States, Regulation & the Medical Profession. Michael Moran & Bruce Wood. LC 92-23833. 1993. 90.00 (*0-335-15749-1*, Open Univ Pr); pap. 32.50 (*0-335-15748-3*, Open Univ Pr) Taylor & Francis.

States' Rights & Vested Interests. Robert J. Harris. (Reprint Series in Social Sciences). (C). 1993. reprint ed. pap. text ed. 1.00 (*0-8290-3311-4*, PS-122) Irvington.

States Rights Gist: A South Carolina General of the Civil War. Walter B. Cisco. LC 91-30467. (First Edition Library). (Illus.). 208p. (C). 1991. 27.95 (*0-942597-28-1*) White Mane Pub.

States Rights Gist: A South Carolina General of the Civil War. deluxe ed. Walter B. Cisco. LC 91-30467. (First Edition Library). (Illus.). 208p. (C). 1991. 39.95 (*0-942597-29-X*) White Mane Pub.

***State's Role in Effective Technology Transfer.** (Hazardous, Nuclear & Solid Waste Environmental Management Ser.: No. 2). 1996. pap. 10.00 (*1-55516-512-5*, 4659) Natl Conf State Legis.

State's Role in Incubator Planning & Operation. 42p. 1989. 20.00 (*0-317-05043-5*) Natl Coun Econ Dev.

States, Special Knowledge, & the Origins of Modern Social Policies. Ed. by Dietrich Rueschemeyer & Theda Skocpol. LC 95-17924. 328p. 1996. text ed. 55.00 (*0-691-03444-3*); pap. text ed. 18.95 (*0-691-00112-X*) Princeton U Pr.

State's Supervision of Its Elementary Schools. Murphy P. Rogers. LC 73-177204. (Columbia University. Teachers College. Contributions to Education Ser.: No. 679). reprint ed. 37.50 (*0-404-55679-5*) AMS Pr.

States System of Europe, 1640-1990: Peacemaking & the Conditions of International Stability. Andreas Osiander. 360p. 1994. 75.00 (*0-19-827887-X*) OUP.

States Versus Markets: History, Geography, & the Development of the International Political Economy. Herman M. Schwartz. 368p. 1994. pap. text ed. 20.00 (*0-312-06594-9*) St Martin.

States vs. Markets. Herman M. Schwartz. 336p. 1994. text ed. 39.95 (*0-312-10271-2*) St Martin.

***States vs. Markets in the World-System.** Ed. by Peter Evans et al. LC 85-11716. (Political Economy of the World-System Annuals Ser.: Vol. 8). 295p. 1985. reprint ed. pap. 84.10 (*0-608-02793-6*, 2063860) Bks Demand.

States, Waves & Photons: A Modern Introduction to Light. Joseph W. Simmons & Mark J. Guttmann. LC 73-102998. (Addison-Wesley Series in Physics). 291p. reprint ed. pap. 83.00 (*0-317-08759-2*, 2051972) Bks Demand.

***States Yearbook 97-98.** 134th ed. Hunter. Date not set. text ed. 110.00 (*0-312-17437-3*) St Martin.

Stateside. James A. Kleman & MaryLouise Kleman. (J). (gr. 4 up). 1982. 14.00 (*0-938464-06-X*) JML Enter MD.

Stateside Aim Manual. Mark Schaufler. 32p. 1994. 2.00 (*1-886904-17-0*) MST Minist.

Statesman. Piers Anthony. (Bio of a Space Tyrant Ser.: No. 5). 320p. 1986. mass mkt. 4.99 (*0-380-89835-7*) Avon.

Statesman. Plato. Ed. by Martin Ostwald. Tr. by B. J. Skemp. LC 57-14633. 1957. pap. 3.95 (*0-672-60230-X*, LLA57, Bobbs) Macmillan.

Statesman. Plato. Ed. by Julia Annas & Robin Waterfield. (Cambridge Texts in the History of Political Thought Ser.). 128p. (C). 1995. text ed. 44.95 (*0-521-44262-1*); pap. text ed. 14.95 (*0-521-44778-X*) Cambridge U Pr.

Statesman. Plato. Tr. by J. B. Skemp. LC 92-26568. 136p. (C). 1992. reprint ed. 29.95 (*0-87220-139-2*); reprint ed. pap. 7.95 (*0-87220-138-4*) Hackett Pub.

Statesman: By Sir Henry Taylor. rev. ed. Henry Taylor. LC 92-12718. 208p. 1992. text ed. 55.00 (*0-275-94285-6*, C4285, Praeger Pubs); pap. text ed. 17. 95 (*0-275-94403-4*, B4403, Praeger Pubs) Greenwood.

Statesman & Builder of the New Bulgaria. Todor Zhivkov. 1982. text ed. 20.00 (*0-08-028205-9*, Pergamon Pr) Elsevier.

Statesman & Philebus, Vol. VIII. Plato. Ed. by E. H. Warmington. Bd. with Ion. (Loeb Classical Library: No. 164). (ENG & GRE.). 15.50 (*0-674-99182-6*) HUP.

Statesman & Pragmatic Humanist - In Honor of Takeo Fukuda on the Occasion of His 90th Birthday. Ed. by Hans D'Orville. 175p. (C). 1995. 15.00 (*1-885060-02-5*) H dOrville.

Statesman As Historians: The White House & the Kremlin. Michael Fry. 1991. text ed. 45.00 (*0-86187-129-4*) St Martin.

Statesman of Harper's Ferry. Charles E. Ranson. LC 95-68286. 180p. 1995. 14.95 (*0-9636320-3-5*) Nuggets Wisdom.

Statesman, Patriot & General in Ancient China. Ch'Ien Ssu-Ma. Tr. by D. Bodde. (American Oriental Ser.: No. 17). 1940. pap. 25.00 (*0-527-02691-3*) Periodicals Srv.

Statesman's Year-Book. 129th rev. ed. Ed. by Brian Hunter. 1730p. 1992. text ed. 79.95 (*0-312-07975-3*) St Martin.

Statesman's Year-Book: Historical Companion. Ed. by John Paxton. 350p. 1988. text ed. 45.00 (*0-312-00047-2*) St Martin.

Statesman's Year-Book: 1983-1984. 120th ed. Ed. by John Paxton. 1749p. 1983. 37.50 (*0-317-03872-9*) St Martin.

Statesman's Year-Book World Gazetteer. 4th ed. Ed. by John Paxton. LC 85-26263. 680p. 1991. 49.95 (*0-312-05597-8*) St Martin.

Statesman's Year-Book 1987-88. 124th ed. Ed. by John Paxton. LC 04-3776. 1691p. 1987. 55.00 (*0-312-00235-1*) St Martin.

Statesman's Year-Book, 1988-89. 125th ed. Ed. by John Paxton. LC 04-3376. 1700p. 1988. 59.95 (*0-312-02094-5*) St Martin.

Statesman's Year-Book, 1991-92. 128th rev. ed. Ed. by Brian Hunter. 1724p. 1991. text ed. 75.00 (*0-312-06497-7*) St Martin.

Statesman's Year-Book 1994-95. 131th ed. Ed. by Brian Hunter. 1704p. 1994. 89.95 (*0-312-12194-6*) St Martin.

Statesman's Year-Book, 1995-1996. 132th ed. Brian Hunter. 1704p. 1995. text ed. 95.00 (*0-312-12749-9*) St Martin.

Statesman's Yearbook, 1989-90. 126th rev. ed. Ed. by John Paxton. LC 04-3776. 1700p. 1989. 65.00 (*0-312-03235-8*) St Martin.

Statesman's Yearbook, 1993-94. 130th ed. Ed. by Brian Hunter. 1730p. 1993. text ed. 85.00 (*0-312-09701-8*) St Martin.

Statesman's Yearbook 1996-1997. 133th ed. Ed. by Brian Hunter. 1800p. 1996. text ed. 100.00 (*0-312-16123-9*) St Martin.

Statesmanship: Essays in Honor of Sir Winston S. Churchill. Ed. by Harry V. Jaffa. LC 80-68075. 296p. 1981. lib. bdg. 29.75 (*0-89089-165-6*) Carolina Acad Pr.

Statesmanship: Six Modern Illustrations of a Modified Ancient Ideal. Wendell J. Coats, Jr. LC 95-14824. 152p. 1996. 29.50 (*0-945636-84-9*) Susquehanna U Pr.

Statesmanship of Jesus. W. Pascoe Goard. LC 89-83501. 160p. 1989. reprint ed. pap. 6.00 (*0-934666-35-0*) Artisan Sales.

Statesmen & Gentlemen: The Elite of Fu-Chou Chang-Hsi in Northern & Southern Sung. Robert Hymes. (Cambridge Studies in Chinese History, Literature & Institutions). (Illus.). 320p. 1987. 69.95 (*0-521-30631-0*) Cambridge U Pr.

Statesmen of the Old South. William E. Dodd. 1994. pap. 22.00 (*0-8196-1897-7*) Biblo.

Statesmen of the War in Retrospect, 1918-1928. William Martin. LC 75-105029. (Essay Index Reprint Ser.). 1977. 23.95 (*0-8369-1675-1*) Ayer.

Statesmen Who Changed the World: A Bio-Bibliographical Dictionary of Diplomacy. Ed. by Frank W. Thackeray & John E. Findling. LC 92-14616. 696p. 1993. text ed. 89.50 (*0-313-27380-4*, FST, Greenwood Pr) Greenwood.

***Statesmen Who Were Never President.** Ed. by Kenneth W. Thompson. LC 96-41082. (Miller Center Series on Statesmen Defeated for President: Vol. II). 162p. 1996. pap. text ed. 20.50 (*0-7618-0533-8*); lib. bdg. 49.50 (*0-7618-0532-X*) U Pr of Amer.

Stateswoman to the World: A Story about Eleanor Roosevelt. Maryann N. Weidt. LC 90-23216. (Creative Minds Ser.). (Illus.). 64p. (J). (gr. 3-6). 1991. lib. bdg. 14.21 (*0-87614-663-9*, Carolrhoda) Lerner Group.

Stateswoman to the World: A Story about Eleanor Roosevelt. Maryann N. Weidt. (J). (gr. 3-6). 1992. pap. 2.98 (*0-87614-562-4*, Carolrhoda) Lerner Group.

Stateville: The Penitentiary in Mass Society-Studies in Crime & Justice. James B. Jacobs. LC 76-22957. 310p. 1978. pap. text ed. 12.95 (*0-226-38977-4*, P788) U Ch Pr.

Statewide Computing Systems: Coordinating Academic Computer Planning. Ed. by Charles J. Mosmann. LC 74-24337. (Books in Library & Information Science: Vol. 10). 215p. reprint ed. pap. 61.30 (*0-685-16299-0*, 2027119) Bks Demand.

Statewide Coordination & Governance of Post Secondary Education: Quality, Costs & Accountability: Major Issues of the '80s. Spring Hill Center Staff. Ed. by Martha Levin & John Ziegenhagen. LC 78-65390. 1978. pap. text ed. 4.50 (*0-932676-05-7*) Spring Hill.

***Statewide Geographic Information Systems Implementation Plan: Building Texas GIS Infrastructure.** (Illus.). 160p. 1996. pap. 35.00 (*0-7881-3085-4*) DIANE Pub.

Statewide Strategy for Drug & Violent Crime Control in Texas. (Illus.). 111p. (Orig.). (C). 1993. pap. text ed. 35. 00 (*1-56806-500-0*) DIANE Pub.

Statewide Systemic Change to Improve Math, Science, & Technology Education. 16p. 1991. 4.00 (*0-317-05350-7*) NASBE.

Statewide Transportation Planning. (National Cooperative Highway Research Program Report Ser.: No. 95). 54p. 1982. 7.20 (*0-309-03456-6*) Transport Res Bd.

Statewide Wetlands Strategies: A Guide to Protecting & Managing the Resource. World Wildlife Fund Staff. LC 92-3563. 268p. 1992. 60.00 (*1-55963-205-4*); pap. 40.00 (*1-55963-206-2*) Island Pr.

Statgraphics Plus Guide. Kilman Shin. 440p. (C). 1995. text ed. 20.54 (*0-256-20648-1*) Irwin.

Stat'i o Pushkine. Mikhail O. Gershenzon. 122p. (RUS.). 1983. reprint ed. pap. 7.00 (*0-933884-37-0*) Berkeley Slavic.

Stati Uniti d'America et l'Emigrazione Italiana: The United States & Italian Immigration. Luigi Villari. LC 74-17959. (Italian American Experience Ser.). (Illus.). 326p. 1975. reprint ed. 23.95 (*0-405-06428-4*) Ayer.

Static Analysis: Proceedings of the First International Static Analysis Symposium, SAS '94, Namur, Belgium, September 28-30, 1994. Ed. by B. Le Charlier. (Lecture Notes in Computer Science Ser.: Vol. 864). xii, 465p. 1994. 65.95 (*3-540-58485-4*) Spr-Verlag.

Static Analysis: Second International Symposium, SAS '95, Glasgow, U. K. September 1995. Ed. by Alan Mycroft. LC 95-38035. (Lecture Notes in Computer Science Ser.: No. 983). 423p. 1995. 68.00 (*3-540-60360-3*) Spr-Verlag.

***Static Analysis: Third International Symposium, SAS '96, Aachen, Germany, September 24-26, 1996 - Proceedings, Vol. 114.** Radhia Cousot & David A. Schmidt. LC 96-35936. (Lecture Notes in Computer Science Ser.). 1996. 62.00 (*3-540-61739-6*) Spr-Verlag.

Static Analysis: Third International Workshop, WSA '93, Padova, Italy, September 1993: Proceedings. Patrick Cousot et al. LC 93-23377. (Lecture Notes in Computer Science Ser.: Vol. 724). 1993. 44.95 (*0-387-57264-3*) Spr-Verlag.

Static Analysis of Operating & Disconnected Risers with or Without Articulations. J. E. Kokarakis & M. M. Bernitsas. (University of Michigan, Dept. of Naval Architecture & Marine Engineering, Report Ser.: No. 286). 119p. reprint ed. pap. 34.00 (*0-317-27123-7*, 2024685) Bks Demand.

Static & Applied Strength Mathematics. Raymond F. Neathery. 1987. text ed. 69.80 (*0-13-844606-7*) P-H.

Static & Dynamic Analysis of Plates & Shells. H. K. Huang. (Illus.). 176p. 1989. 241.95 (*0-387-19538-6*) Spr-Verlag.

Static & Dynamic Analysis of Structures: With Emphasis on Mechanics & Computer Matrix Methods. James F. Doyle. (C). 1991. pap. text ed. 69.00 (*0-7923-1208-2*); lib. bdg. 157.50 (*0-7923-1124-8*) Kluwer Ac.

***Static & Dynamic Aspects of General Disequilibrium Theory.** Jean-Jacques Herings. (Theory & Decision Library: Series C). 520p. (C). 1996. lib. bdg. 159.95 (*0-614-22048-3*) Kluwer Ac.

Static & Dynamic Behavior of Kurobe Dam: Record of Measurements & Observations on a High Arch Dam. Ed. by Shunzo Okamoto et al. LC 88-206004. 437p. 1988. reprint ed. pap. 124.60 (*0-608-01259-9*, 2061947) Bks Demand.

Static & Dynamic Considerations in Rock Engineering: Proceedings of the ISRM International Symposium, Swaziland, 10-12 September 1990. Ed. by Richard Brummer. (Illus.). 410p. (C). 1990. text ed. 125.00 (*90-6191-153-2*, Pub. by A A Balkema NE) Ashgate Pub Co.

Static & Dynamic Electricity. 3rd ed. William B. Smythe. (Summa Bks.). (Illus.). 623p. 1989. pap. 53.95 (*0-89116-917-2*) Hemisp Pub.

Static & Dynamic Fracture Mechanics. Ed. by C. A. Brebbia et al. LC 93-72573. (Computational Engineering Ser.). 365p. 1994. 117.00 (*1-56252-175-6*) Computational Mech MA.

Static & Dynamic Properties of Gravelly Soils: Proceedings of Sessions Sponsored by the Soil Properties Committee of the Geotechnical Engineering Division of the American Society of Civil Engineers in Conjunction with the ASCE Convention, San Diego, California, October 23-27, 1995. Ed. by Mark D. Evans & Richard J. Fragaszy. LC 95-41130. (Geotechnical Special Publications: No. 56). 168p. 1995. 23.00 (*0-7844-0130-6*) Am Soc Civil Eng.

Static & Dynamic Properties of the Polymeric Solid State. R. W. Richards & Richard A. Pethrick. 1982. lib. bdg. 152.00 (*90-277-1481-9*) Kluwer Ac.

Static & Rotating Electromagnetic Devices. Engelmann. (Electrical Engineering & Electronics Ser.: Vol. 14). 544p. 1982. 175.00 (*0-8247-1697-3*) Dekker.

Static Demand Theory. Donald W. Katzner. LC 74-96742. x, 242p. 1970. 24.95 (*0-02-362070-6*, Macmillan Coll) P-H.

Static Electrical Equipment Testing. 1987. 75.00 (*0-85083-068-0*) St Mut.

Static Electrical Equipment Winding & Building One, 2 vols., Set. 1987. 75.00 (*0-685-05786-0*) St Mut.

Static Electricity. 1996. lib. bdg. 250.95 (*0-8490-8314-1*) Gordon Pr.

Static Electricity. National Fire Protection Association Staff. 30p. 1993. 20.25 (*0-317-63227-2*, 77-88) Natl Fire Prot.

Static Electricity in Building, LB 9-87. BSRIA Staff. (C). 1987. 80.00 (*0-86022-184-9*, Pub. by Build Servs Info Assn UK) St Mut.

Static Encephalopathies of Infancy & Childhood. Geoffrey Miller & Jeanette C. Ramer. 384p. 1992. text ed. 121.00 (*0-88167-872-4*) Lppncott-Raven.

Static Microeconomic Model of Pure Competition. C. Klein. (Lecture Notes in Economics & Mathematical Systems Ser.: Vol. 306). 139p. 1988. 28.40 (*0-387-19358-8*) Spr-Verlag.

Static SIMS Handbook of Polymer Analysis. J. G. Newman et al. LC 90-62564. (Illus.). 200p. (Orig.). 1991. write for info. (*0-9627026-0-9*); pap. write for info. (*0-9627026-1-7*) Perkin-Elmer.

Static Strength of Uniplanar & Multiplanar T- & X-Joints. G. J. Van Der Vegte. 392p. 1995. pap. 82.50 (*90-407-1081-3*, Pub. by Delft U Pr NE) Coronet Bks.

Statical & Geomechanical Models. E. Fumagalli. (Illus.). xv, 182p. 1973. 75.95 (*0-387-81096-X*) Spr-Verlag.

Statically Indeterminant Structures. Wadi S. Rumman. LC 90-22897. 504p. 1991. text ed. 99.95 (*0-471-09345-9*) Wiley.

Statically Indeterminate Structures: Their Analysis & Design. Paul Andersen. LC 52-11520. (Illus.). 326p. reprint ed. pap. 93.00 (*0-317-10804-2*, 2012568) Bks Demand.

Statics. Anthony Bedford & Wallace L. Fowler. (Illus.). 576p. (C). 1995. text ed. 64.50 (*0-201-58193-0*) Addison-Wesley.

***Statics.** Mcgill. (Illus.). 600p. 1997. text ed. write for info. (*0-412-73190-8*, Chap & Hall NY) Chapman & Hall.

Statics. 2nd ed. Ginsberg. (General Engineering Ser.). 1995. text ed. 35.95 (*0-534-94604-6*) PWS Pubs.

Statics. 2nd ed. Ginsberg. Date not set. pap. text ed. 34.25 (*0-314-04765-4*) West Pub.

Statics. 2nd ed. James L. Meriam. LC 71-136719. (Illus.). 394p. reprint ed. pap. 112.30 (*0-317-08359-7*, 2019288) Bks Demand.

Statics: Windows Version. A. Marc Bedford. (C). 1995. pap. text ed. write for info. (*0-201-84558-X*) Addison-Wesley.

Statics see Engineering Mechanics

Statics & Dynamics. Anthony Bedford et al. (Illus.). 1152p. (C). 1995. text ed. 79.75 (*0-201-18197-5*) Addison-Wesley.

***Statics & Dynamics.** Downie Plum. LC 97-19518. (C). 1997. pap. text ed. 39.95 (*0-582-21060-7*, Pub. by Longman UK) Longman.

Statics & Dynamics of Alloy Phase Transformations. P. E. Turchi. (NATO ASI Ser.: Series B, Physics: Vol. 319). (Illus.). 724p. 1994. 149.50 (*0-306-44626-X*, Plenum Pr) Plenum.

Statics & Dynamics of Nonlinear Systems. Ed. by G. Benedek et al. (Solid-State Sciences Ser.: Vol. 47). (Illus.). 311p. 1983. 75.95 (*0-387-12841-7*) Spr-Verlag.

Statics & Kinematics of Granular Materials. R. M. Nedderman. (Illus.). 424p. (C). 1992. text ed. 110.00 (*0-521-40435-5*) Cambridge U Pr.

Statics & Kinematics with Applications to Robotics. Joseph Duffy. (Illus.). 224p. (C). 1996. text ed. 49.95 (*0-521-48213-5*) Cambridge U Pr.

Statics & Mechanics of Materials. Beer & Johnson. 1992. pap. text ed. write for info. (*0-07-004597-6*) McGraw.

Statics & Mechanics of Materials. Russell C. Hibbeler. LC 92-28506. (Illus.). 832p. (C). 1995. text ed. 91.00 (*0-02-354091-5*, Macmillan Coll) P-H.

Statics & Mechanics of Materials: An Integrated Approach. William F. Riley et al. LC 95-4072. 768p. 1996. text ed. 48.00 (*0-471-01334-X*) Wiley.

Statics & Mechanics of Materials: Including 400 Solved Problems. William A. Nash. 1992. pap. text ed. 13.95 (*0-07-045896-0*) McGraw.

Statics & Strength of Materials. Irving J. Levinson. (C). 1970. text ed. 93.00 (*0-13-844506-0*) P-H.

Statics & Strength of Materials. 2nd ed. Fa-Hwa Cheng. 1995. 50.06 (*0-02-803067-2*) Glencoe.

Statics & Strength of Materials. 2nd ed. Fa-Hwa Cheng. 1995. write for info. (*0-02-803068-0*) Glencoe.

Statics & Strength of Materials. 2nd ed. Harold W. Morrow. 640p. 1992. text ed. 92.00 (*0-13-845835-9*) P-H.

Statics & Strength of Materials. 3rd ed. Milton G. Bassin et al. (Illus.). 1979. text ed. 41.50 (*0-07-004030-3*) McGraw.

***Statics & Strength of Materials.** 3rd ed. H. W. Morrow. LC 97-11183. 1997. 64.00 (*0-13-453201-5*) P-H.

Statics & Strength of Materials. 4th ed. Milton G. Bassin. 496p. 1988. text ed. 41.50 (*0-07-004023-0*) McGraw.

Statics & Strength of Materials: A Parallel Approach. Lawrence Wolf. 512p. (C). 1990. text ed. 61.51 (*0-675-20622-7*, Merrill Coll) P-H.

Statics & Strength of Structures. Mario G. Salvadori. LC 70-138821. (C). 1971. 50.00 (*0-685-03908-0*) P-H.

Statics & Strengths Materials. Towers. (Mechanical Technology Ser.). Date not set. text ed. 59.95 (*0-8273-7191-8*) Delmar.

Statics & Strengths of Materials. George Kraut. (C). 1984. teacher ed. write for info. (*0-8359-7113-9*, Reston) P-H.

Statics & Strengths of Materials. 4th ed. Alfred E. Jensen & Harry H. Chenoweth. LC 82-12642. (C). 1983. text ed. 43.95 (*0-07-032494-8*) McGraw.

Statics Engineering Mechanics: SI Version. A. Marc Bedford. LC 97-18607. (C). 1996. pap. text ed. write for info. (*0-201-40340-4*) Addison-Wesley.

Statics Exam File. Ed. by Charles E. Smith. LC 84-21141. (Exam File Ser.). 346p. (Orig.). (C). 1985. pap. 16.50 (*0-910554-47-1*) Engineering.

Statics for Architects & Architectural Engineers. David A. Fanella & Robert W. Gerstner. LC 92-26644. 1993. text ed. 56.95 (*0-442-01297-7*) Van Nos Reinhold.

Statics for Engineers. Bichara B. Muvdi et al. LC 96-13159. (Illus.). 936p. 1997. 84.95 incl. disk (*0-387-94779-5*) Spr-Verlag.

Statics, Formfinding & Dynamics of Air-Supported Membrane Structures. Vladimir Firt. 1983. lib. bdg. 222.50 (*90-247-2672-7*) Kluwer Ac.

***Statics of Deformable Solids.** Bisplinghoff et al. pap. 10.95 (*0-486-66360-4*) Dover.

Statics of Suspension Cable Roofs. Jaroslav Kadlcak. (Illus.). 295p. (C). 1995. 140.00 (*90-5410-618-2*, Pub. by A A Balkema NE) Ashgate Pub Co.

Statics Problems Solved in BASIC. 1988. 39.50 (*0-685-24858-5*, 84-0-B); disk 24.00 (*0-685-24859-3*, 84-0-ID) Kern Intl.

S

An Asterisk (*) at the beginning of an entry indicates that the title is appearing in BIP for the first time.

Statics, Strengths & Structures for Architects. 3rd ed. B. S. Benjamin. (Illus.). 332p. (C). 1992. text ed. 50.00 (*0-942387-07-4*) AB Lit Hse.

Statics, Structure & Stress: A Teaching Text for Problem-Solving in Theory of Structures & Strength of Materials. W. Fisher Cassie. LC 74-158981. (Longman Text Ser.). 565p. reprint ed. pap. 161.10 (*0-317-09285-5*, 2016309) Bks Demand.

Stating Objectives for Classroom Instruction see How to Write Instructional Objectives

Stating the Gospel: Formulations & Declarations of Faith from the Heritage of the United Reformed Church. Ed. by David M. Thompson. 256p. 1990. 43.95 (*0-567-09508-8*, Pub. by T & T Clark UK) Bks Intl VA.

***Stating the Gospel: Formulations & Declarations of Faith from the Heritage of the United Reformed Church.** Ed. by David M. Thompson. 272p. 1997. pap. 25.95 (*0-567-08563-5*, Pub. by T & T Clark UK) Bks Intl VA.

Station Agent. (Career Examination Ser.: Vol. C-3807). 1997. pap. 23.95 (*0-8373-3807-7*) Nat Learn.

Station Balneaire. Christian Giudicelli. 214p. (FRE.). 1988. pap. 10.95 (*0-7859-2555-4*, 2070379418) Fr & Eur.

Station Champbaudet. Eugene Labiche. 9.95 (*0-686-54251-7*); pap. 4.95 (*0-686-54252-5*) Fr & Eur.

Station Commissioning see Modern Power Station Practice

Station Hospital Saigon: A Navy Nurse in Vietnam, 1963-1964. Bobbi Hovis. LC 91-45414. (Illus.). 224p. 1992. 26.95 (*1-55750-376-1*) Naval Inst Pr.

Station Installation & Maintenance. rev. ed. Frank E. Lee. LC 73-85629. (ABC of the Telephone Ser.: Vol. 2). (Illus.). 104p. (C). 1986. pap. text ed. 16.95 (*1-56016-001-2*) ABC TeleTraining.

Station Island. Seamus Heaney. LC 84-21067. 123p. 1985. 20.00 (*0-374-26978-5*) FS&G.

Station Island. Seamus Heaney. 124p. 1986. pap. 12.00 (*0-374-51935-8*) FS&G.

Station J: An American Play. Richard France. LC 82-14936. 170p. (Orig.). 1983. pap. 9.95 (*0-8290-0538-2*) Irvington.

Station KBOE. 3rd ed. O. Church. 240p. 1984. text ed. 7.56 (*0-07-010837-4*) McGraw.

Station Master on the Underground Railroad: The Life & Letters of Thomas Garrett. James McGowan. LC 77-84816. (Illus.). 181p. 1977. 7.95 (*0-916178-00-5*) Whimsie Pr.

Station Now Standing. Bill Pertwee. (Illus.). 128p. 1992. 34.95 (*0-340-54685-9*, Pub. by H & S UK) Trafalgar.

Station Operation & Maintenance see Modern Power Station Practice

Station Planning & Design see Modern Power Station Practice

Station Protectors. James H. Miller. (ABC Pocket Guide for the Field Ser.). 44p. (Orig.). (C). 1983. pap. 6.95 (*1-56016-026-8*) ABC TeleTraining.

Station Rage. Diane Carey. (Star Trek: Deep Space Nine Ser.: No. 13). 1995. mass mkt. 5.99 (*0-671-88561-8*) PB.

Station Supervisor. Jack Rudman. (Career Examination Ser.: C-2105). 1994. reprint ed. pap. 23.95 (*0-8373-2105-0*) Nat Learn.

***Station to Station.** Steven Parissien. (Illus.). 240p. 1997. 59.95 (*0-7148-3467-X*, Pub. by Phaidon Press UK) Chronicle Bks.

Station to Station. Susan R. Simms. (Travel Traxx Ser.). 10p. (J). (ps-2). 1994. write for info. (*1-883366-54-2*) YES Ent.

Station Wagon in Spain. Frances P. Keyes. 256p. 1977. mass mkt. 1.50 (*0-449-23193-3*, Crest) Fawcett.

Station West. large type ed. Luke Short. (Nightingale Ser.). 309p. (Orig.). 1992. pap. 14.95 (*0-8161-5406-6*, GK Hall) Thorndike Pr.

Station-Work Uniforms for Fire Fighters. National Fire Protection Association Staff. 1990. 16.75 (*0-317-63572-7*, 1975-90) Natl Fire Prot.

***Stationary Battery: 1993 Edition.** 97.00 (*1-55937-363-6*, SH16725) IEEE Standards.

Stationary Bicycles. Michael T. Cannell & Judith Zimmer. Ed. by Susan Wallach. LC 84-40600. (AT Home Gym Ser.). 64p. 1985. pap. 2.95 (*0-394-72973-0*, Villard Bks) Random.

Stationary Combustion Engines & Gas Turbines. National Fire Protection Association Staff. 1994. 16.75 (*0-317-63071-7*, 37-90) Natl Fire Prot.

Stationary Engineer. Jack Rudman. (Career Examination Ser.: C-758). 1994. pap. 27.95 (*0-8373-0758-9*) Nat Learn.

Stationary Engineer (Electric) Jack Rudman. (Career Examination Ser.: C-759). 1994. pap. 27.95 (*0-8373-0759-7*) Nat Learn.

Stationary Engineer 1. Jack Rudman. (Career Examination Ser.: C-1903). 1994. pap. 27.95 (*0-8373-1903-X*) Nat Learn.

Stationary Engineer 2. Jack Rudman. (Career Examination Ser.: C-1904). 1994. pap. 29.95 (*0-8373-1904-8*) Nat Learn.

Stationary Engineering. Theodore B. Sauselien. LC 89-22383. 1990. 17.95 (*0-912524-53-7*) Busn News.

***Stationary Engineering.** 2nd ed. F. M. Steingress & H. J. Frost. (Illus.). 586p. 1996. 59.96 (*0-8269-4445-0*) Am Technical.

Stationary Engineering Handbook. Kenneth L. Petrocelly. LC 88-45795. 300p. 1989. text ed. 67.00 (*0-88173-078-5*) Fairmont Pr.

Stationary Engineers, Testbook. California Department of Education Staff. (Apprenticeship Instructional Materials Ser.). 174p. 1972. pap. 3.75 (*0-8011-0643-5*) Calif Education.

Stationary Engineers, Workbook. California Department of Education Staff. (Apprenticeship Instructional Materials Ser.). (Illus.). 380p. 1972. pap. 5.25 (*0-8011-0642-7*) Calif Education.

Stationary Fireman. Jack Rudman. (Career Examination Ser.: C-760). 1994. pap. 27.95 (*0-8373-0760-0*) Nat Learn.

Stationary Gas Turbine Alternative Fuels - STP 809. Ed. by J. S. Clark & S. M. De Corso. LC 82-73767. 360p. 1983. 43.00 (*0-8031-0258-5*, 04-809000-13) ASTM.

Stationary Marked Point Processes: An Intuitive Approach. Karl Sigman. LC 94-22450. 200p. (gr. 13). 1994. text ed. 47.95 (*0-412-98431-8*) Chapman & Hall.

Stationary Marked Point Processes: An Intuitive Approach. Karl Sigman. 1994. 44.95 (*0-412-05651-8*) Chapman & Hall.

Stationary Motions & Stability of Flexible Satellites. LC 96-18902. (Advanced Series in Mathematical Science & Engineering). 1996. write for info. (*1-885978-06-5*) Wrld Fed Pubs.

Stationary Motions & Stability of Flexible Satellites, Vol. 4. M. K. Nabiulin. LC 95-32737. (Advanced Series in Mathematical Science & Engineering). 1995. write for info. (*1-885978-03-0*) Wrld Fed Pubs.

Stationary Phases in Gas Chromatography. H. Rotzsche. (Journal of Chromatography Library: Vol. 48). 410p. 1991. 250.75 (*0-444-98733-9*) Elsevier.

Stationary Random Processes Associated with Point Processses. T. Rolski. (Lecture Notes in Statistics Ser.: Vol. 5). 152p. 1981. 45.95 (*0-387-90575-8*) Spr-Verlag.

Stationary Semiconductor Device Equations. P. A. Markovich. (Computational Microelectronics Ser.). (Illus.). 210p. 1986. 87.95 (*0-387-81892-8*) Spr-Verlag.

Stationary Sequences & Random Fields. Murray Rosenblatt. 288p. 1985. 52.00 (*0-8176-3264-6*) Birkhauser.

Stationary Steam Engines. Geoffrey Hayes. (Album Ser.). (Illus.). 32p. 1979. pap. text ed. 5.25 (*0-85263-652-0*, Pub. by Shire Pubns UK) Lubrecht & Cramer.

Stationary Stochastic Models. Andreas Brandt et al. LC 89-22544. 344p. 1990. text ed. 199.00 (*0-471-92132-7*) Wiley.

Stationary Stochastic Processes. Takeyuki Hida. LC 79-105271. (Mathematical Notes Ser.). 173p. reprint ed. pap. 49.40 (*0-8357-7037-0*, 2033373) Bks Demand.

Stationary Subdivision. A. Cavaretta et al. LC 91-22743. (Memoirs Ser.). 186p. 1991. pap. 25.00 (*0-8218-2507-0*, MEMO/93/453) Am Math.

Stationers' Company: A History, 1403-1959. Cyprian Blagden. LC 76-48000. 320p. 1960. 39.50 (*0-8047-0935-1*) Stanford U Pr.

Stationers' Company Archive: An Account of the Records 1554-1984. Ed. by Robin Myers & Michael Harris. 376p. 1990. lib. bdg. 60.00 (*0-906795-71-0*) Oak Knoll.

Stationing & Stability of Semi-Submersibles. Ed. by Society for Underwater Technology Staff. (C). 1986. lib. bdg. 152.00 (*0-86010-831-7*, Pub. by Graham & Trotman UK) Kluwer Ac.

***StationMasters: Pocket Guide to Metrorail Station Neighborhoods.** 4th rev. ed. Larry A. Bowring. LC 96-86611. (Illus.). 84p. 1997. pap. 4.95 (*0-9618322-3-1*) Bowring Cartograph.

***Stations.** (St. Joseph's Coloring Bks.). (Illus.). 32p. (Orig.). (J). (ps-3). 1990. pap. 0.99 (*0-89942-689-1*, 689/00) Catholic Bk Pub.

***Stations.** Keith Bosley. 112p. 1979. pap. 14.95 (*0-85646-055-9*, Pub. by Anvil Press UK) Dufour.

Stations. Jerome McDonough. (Illus.). 32p. (Orig.). 1988. pap. 3.25 (*0-88680-291-1*) I E Clark.

Stations. Jay Meek. 80p. 1989. pap. 11.95 (*0-88748-081-0*) Carnegie-Mellon.

Stations: An Imagined Journey. Michael Flanagan. LC 94-7596. 1994. 21.00 (*0-679-43547-6*) Pantheon.

Stations: Paintings & Poems of Spiritual Journey. 1995. per. 12.00 (*0-943594-12-X*) Cardinal Pr.

Stations in a Dream. Michael S. Weaver. 68p. (Orig.). pap. 9.95 (*0-614-05295-5*) Dolphin-Moon.

Stations in Life: The Andomus Material Three. Andomus & Powell. Ed. by Krueger. 224p. (Orig.). 1992. pap. 12.95 (*0-9625738-2-5*) Gala Pub.

Stations of the Air. John Ciardi. LC 92-8657. 64p. 1993. 10.50 (*0-933532-86-5*) BkMk.

***Stations of the Cross.** Lawrence G. Lovasik. (Saint Joseph Picture Bks.). (Illus.). 1978. pap. 1.25 (*0-89942-299-3*, 299-00) Catholic Bk Pub.

Stations of the Cross. John R. Reed. (Illus.). 32p. (Orig.). 1992. pap. text ed. 5.00 (*1-56439-012-8*) Ridgeway.

Stations of the Cross: A Latin American Pilgrimage. Dorothee Soelle. Tr. by Joyce L. Irwin. LC 92-34220. 160p. 1993. pap. 13.00 (*0-8006-2688-5*, Fortress Pr) Augsburg Fortress.

Stations of the Cross: Arranged for Readers Theatre. Anne Bedessem & Peter B. McIver. (Orig.). 1994. pap. text ed. 5.95 (*1-56929-023-7*) Pastoral Pr.

Stations of the Cross, an AIDS Poem. Robert T. Webb. (Amelia Chapbooks Ser.). 16p. (Orig.). 1994. pap. 5.00 (*0-936545-20-8*) Amelia.

Stations of the Cross for Children. Rita Coleman. 24p. (Orig.). 1992. pap. 1.95 (*0-8146-2062-0*) Liturgical Pr.

Stations of the Cross for Teenagers. Gwen Costello. (Illus.). 32p. (YA). 1988. pap. 1.95 (*0-89622-386-8*) Twenty-Third.

Stations of the Cross with Pope John Paul II. Joseph M. Champlin. (Illus.). 40p. (Orig.). 1994. pap. 2.95 (*0-89243-679-4*) Liguori Pubns.

Stations of the Divided Subject: Contestation & Ideological Legitimation in German Bourgeois Literature, 1770-1914. Richard T. Gray. LC 94-33723. xviii, 390p. 1995. 55.00 (*0-8047-2402-4*) Stanford U Pr.

Stations of the Lost: The Treatment of Skid Row Alcoholics. Jacqueline P. Wiseman. LC 79-13632. 368p. 1979. reprint ed. pap. text ed. 16.95 (*0-226-90307-9*, P853) U Ch Pr.

Stations of the Resurrection. Ronald C. Gibbins. (C). 1988. 39.00 (*0-85439-268-8*, Pub. by St Paul Pubns UK) St Mut.

Stations of the Spirit. Victor Carpenter. LC 89-52162. 148p. (Orig.). 1990. pap. 10.00 (*0-931104-28-9*) Sunflower Ink.

Stations of the Sun: A History of the Ritual Year in Britain. Ronald Hutton. (Illus.). 560p. 1996. 35.00 (*0-19-820570-8*) OUP.

***Stations of the Sun: A History of the Ritual Year in Britain.** Ronald Hutton. LC 97-22955. (Illus.). 560p. 1997. reprint ed. pap. 18.95 (*0-19-288045-4*) OUP.

Stations of the Tide. Michael Swanwick. 1992. mass mkt. 4.50 (*0-380-71524-4*, AvoNova) Avon.

***Stations of the Tide.** Michael Swanwick. 1997. pap. text ed. 13.00 (*0-380-73045-6*) Avon.

Stations of Wisdom. rev. ed. Frithjof Schuon. LC 94-34053. (Library of Traditional Wisdom). 110p. (Orig.). 1995. pap. 12.00 (*0-941532-18-6*) Wrld Wisdom Bks.

Statira by Pietro Ottoboni & Alessandro Scarlatti: The Textual Sources, with a Documentary Postscript. William Holmes. LC 82-12357. (Monographs in Musicology: No. 2). 120p. 1983. lib. bdg. 32.00 (*0-918728-18-5*) Pendragon NY.

Statis Analysis: Proceedings of the First International Symposium, SAS '94, Namur, Belgium, September 28-30, 1994. SAS Staff. Ed. by Baudouin Le Charlier. LC 94-35446. (Lecture Notes in Computer Science Ser.: Vol. 864). 1994. 62.00 (*0-387-58485-4*) Spr-Verlag.

***Statische Preisentscheidungen im Rahmen Eines Wettbewerbsorientierten Krankenhausfinanzierungssystems: Eine Untersuchung vor dem Hintergrund des Gesundheitsstrukturgesetzes 1993 & der Bundespflegesatzverordnung 1995.** Christian J. Glasmacher. (Illus.). xxv, 294p. (GER.). 1996. 57.95 (*3-631-30683-0*) P Lang Pubng.

Statisical Record of Older Americans. Ed. by Arsen Darnay. 1993. 99.00 (*0-8013-9198-9*) Gale.

Statism & Anarchy. Mikhail Bakunin. Ed. by J. Frank Harrison. 1974. lib. bdg. 250.00 (*0-87700-219-3*) Revisionist Pr.

Statism & Anarchy. Marshall S. Shatz. (Cambridge Texts in the History of Political Thought Ser.). 288p. (C). 1990. text ed. 59.95 (*0-521-36182-6*); pap. text ed. 19.95 (*0-521-36973-8*) Cambridge U Pr.

***Statisphere: Web Traffic Analyzer.** 135p. Date not set. 399.00 incl. disk (*1-56592-233-6*) OReilly & Assocs.

Statist & Statistician. Ed. by Victor L. Hilts & I. Bernard Cohen. LC 80-2091. (Development of Science Ser.). (Illus.). 1981. lib. bdg. 60.95 (*0-405-13856-3*) Ayer.

Statistic Report on Profits, Sales, Production & Marketing Trends for the Men's & Boys' Tailored Clothing Industry. Robert A. Kaplan. 17p. 1989. 25.00 (*0-685-45066-X*) Clothing Mfrs.

***Statistica: Benutzerhandbuch.** (Illus.). 700p. (ENG & GER.). 1996. pap. text ed. 25.00 (*1-884233-38-4*) StatSoft.

***Statistica: Guide de l'Utilisateur.** 525p. (C). 1997. pap. text ed. 70.00 (*1-884233-40-6*) StatSoft.

***Statistica: Quick Reference.** 240p. 1997. pap. text ed. 25.00 (*1-884233-39-2*) StatSoft.

STATISTICA - QC for Windows: Industrial Statistics Modules. 600p. (C). 1995. pap. write for info. (*1-884233-16-3*) StatSoft.

STATISTICA for DOS: Addendum. 44p. (C). 1992. pap. write for info. (*1-884233-27-9*) StatSoft.

STATISTICA for DOS: Quick Start. 40p. (C). 1991. pap. write for info. (*1-884233-23-6*) StatSoft.

STATISTICA for DOS, Vol. III: Graphics. 346p. (C). 1991. pap. write for info. (*1-884233-25-2*) StatSoft.

STATISTICA for DOS, Vols. I & II: Basic & Advanced Statistics. 968p. (C). 1991. pap. write for info. (*1-884233-24-4*) StatSoft.

STATISTICA for the Macintosh: Quick Reference. 18p. (C). 1994. pap. write for info. (*1-884233-22-8*) StatSoft.

STATISTICA for the Macintosh: Time Series & Forecasting Module. 100p. (C). 1994. pap. write for info. (*1-884233-21-X*) StatSoft.

STATISTICA for the Macintosh, Vol. I: Statistics & Graphics. 518p. (C). 1993. pap. write for info. (*1-884233-17-1*) StatSoft.

STATISTICA for the Macintosh, Vol. II: Advanced Statistics. 309p. (C). 1993. pap. write for info. (*1-884233-18-X*) StatSoft.

Statistica for Windows Vol. V: Languages: Basic & SCL. (Illus.). 496p. (C). 1995. pap. text ed. 30.00 (*1-884233-37-6*) StatSoft.

STATISTICA for Windows, Vol. III: Advanced Statistics. 600p. (C). 1995. pap. write for info. (*1-884233-13-9*) StatSoft.

STATISTICA for Windows, Vols. I & II: Statistics & Graphics. 1000p. (C). 1995. pap. write for info. (*1-884233-12-0*) StatSoft.

Statistica (Release 5) Quick Reference. (Illus.). 196p. (C). 1995. pap. text ed. 30.00 (*1-884233-30-9*) StatSoft.

Statistical Abstract of Latin America, Vol. 22. Ed. by James W. Wilkie & Stephen Haber. LC 56-63569. 1983. 75.00 (*0-87903-241-3*) UCLA Lat Am Ctr.

Statistical Abstract of Latin America, Vol. 23. Ed. by James W. Wilkie & Adam Perkal. LC 56-63569. 1984. 100.00 (*0-87903-244-8*) UCLA Lat Am Ctr.

Statistical Abstract of Latin America, Vol. 24. Ed. by James W. Wilkie & Adam Perkal. LC 56-63569. 700p. 1986. 100.00 (*0-87903-245-6*) UCLA Lat Am Ctr.

Statistical Abstract of Latin America, Vol. 29, Pts. 1 & 2. Ed. by James W. Wilkie & Carlos A. Contreras. LC 56-63569. 1992. 225.00 (*0-87903-253-7*) UCLA Lat Am Ctr.

Statistical Abstract of Latin America, Vol. 30, Pt. 1. Christof A. Weber. LC 56-63569. 1993. 125.00 (*0-87903-255-3*) UCLA Lat Am Ctr.

Statistical Abstract of Latin America, Vol. 31, Pts. 1-2. Ed. by James W. Wilkie et al. LC 56-63569. 1995. 275.00 (*0-87903-258-8*) UCLA Lat Am Ctr.

***Statistical Abstract of Latin America, Vol. 32.** Ed. by James W. Wilkie et al. 1139p. 1997. 295.00 (*0-87903-259-6*) UCLA Lat Am Ctr.

Statistical Abstract of Latin America, 1981, Vol. 21. Ed. by James W. Wilkie. LC 56-63569. 1981. 50.00 (*0-87903-239-1*) UCLA Lat Am Ctr.

Statistical Abstract of Latin America, 1991, Vol. 28. Ed. by James W. Wilkie et al. 1260p. 1991. 175.00 (*0-87903-252-9*) UCLA Lat Am Ctr.

***Statistical Abstract of the ESCWA Region, 1984-1993.** Economic & Social Commission for Western Asia Staff. LC 95-571. 456p. 1996. pap. 49.00 (*92-1-128153-9*, 68722) UN.

Statistical Abstract of the United States. United States Department of Commerce, Bureau of the Census Staff. 1045p. 1995. lib. bdg. 42.00 (*0-89059-050-8*) Bernan Pr.

***Statistical Abstract of the United States: The National Data Book: 1996.** annuals 116th ed. U. S. Dept. of Commerce, Economics & Statistics Administration, Bureau of the Census Staff. (Illus.). 1044p. 1996. 35.00 (*0-934213-49-6*, PB96-965301); pap. 30.00 (*0-934213-50-X*, PB96-965801) Natl Tech Info.

Statistical Abstract of the United States-Mexico Borderlands. Peter L. Reich. (Statistical Abstract of Latin America Supplement Ser.: Vol. 9). 204p. 1984. 45.00 (*0-87903-243-X*) UCLA Lat Am Ctr.

Statistical Abstract of the United States, 1992. 112th ed. Ed. by U. S. Bureau of the Census Staff. (Illus.). 979p. 1992. 19.95 (*1-878753-08-8*) Hoovers TX.

***Statistical Abstract of the United States, 1992: The National Data Book.** 112th ed. Commerce Dept., Census Bureau, Economics & Statistics Administration Staff. (Illus.). 1992. per., pap. 38.00 (*0-16-038080-4*, 003-024-08159-8) USGPO.

Statistical Abstract of the United States, 1993. 113th ed. Ed. by U. S. Bureau of the Census Staff. (Illus.). 1009p. 1993. 19.95 (*1-878753-31-2*) Hoovers TX.

Statistical Abstract of the United States, 1993: The National Data Book. Intro. by U. S. Department of Commerce, Bureau of the Census Staff. (Illus.). 1000p. 1993. lib. bdg. 38.00 (*0-89059-020-6*) Bernan Pr.

Statistical Abstract of the United States, 1994. 114th ed. Commerce Dept., Economics & Statistics Administration Staff. (Illus.). 1035p. 1994. boxed 49.00 (*0-16-045173-6*, 003-024-08757-0) USGPO.

Statistical Abstract of the United States, 1994. 114th ed. Commerce Dept., Economics & Statistics Administration Staff. (Illus.). 1035p. 1994. per., pap. 42.00 (*0-16-045174-4*, 003-024-08756-1) USGPO.

Statistical Abstract of the United States, 1994. 114th ed. Ed. by U. S. Bureau of the Census Staff. 1000p. 1994. lib. bdg. 24.95 (*1-878753-67-3*) Hoovers TX.

Statistical Abstract of the United States 1994: The National Data Book. enl. ed. Ed. by U. S. Department of Commerce Staff & Bureau Of the Census Staff. (Illus.). 1000p. 1994. lib. bdg. 38.00 (*0-89059-029-X*) Bernan Pr.

***Statistical Abstract of the United States 1995.** (Illus.). 1046p. 1995. pap. text ed. 45.00 (*1-57979-205-7*) BPI Info Servs.

Statistical Abstract of the United States 1995. 115th ed. 1040p. 1995. lib. bdg. 24.95 (*1-878753-92-4*) Hoovers TX.

Statistical Abstract of the United States, 1995: The National Data Book. U. S. Bureau of Census Staff. 1045p. 1995. lib. bdg. 28.00 (*0-89059-055-9*) Bernan Pr.

Statistical Abstract of the United States, 1995: The National Data Book. U. S. Bureau of Census Staff. 1045p. 1995. lib. bdg. 32.00 (*0-89059-056-7*) Bernan Pr.

Statistical Abstract of the United States, 1995: The National Data Book. U. S. Department of Commerce Staff et al. (Orig.). 1995. pap. 28.00 (*0-934213-47-X*, PB95-965800); text ed. 30.75 (*0-934213-46-1*, PB95-965300) Natl Tech Info.

***Statistical Abstract of the United States, 1995: The National Data Book.** 115th ed. Commerce Dept., Economics & Statistics Administration Staff. (Illus.). 1059p. 1995. 54.00 (*0-16-048288-7*, 003-024-08788-0) USGPO.

***Statistical Abstract of the United States, 1995: The National Data Book.** 115th ed. Commerce Dept., Economics & Statistics Administration Staff. (Illus.). 1059p. 1995. per., pap. 48.00 (*0-16-048289-5*, 003-024-08787-1) USGPO.

***Statistical Abstract of the United States 1996.** 116th ed. 1040p. 1996. 27.95 (*1-57311-015-9*) Hoovers TX.

***Statistical Abstract of the United States, 1996: The National Data Book.** 116th ed. Commerce Dept., Economics & Statistics Administration Staff. 1036p. 1996. per., pap. 40.00 (*0-614-24572-9*, 003-024-08809-6) USGPO.

***Statistical Abstract of the United States, 1996: The National Data Book.** 116th ed. Commerce Dept., Economics & Statistics Administration Staff. (Illus.). 1036p. 1996. per. 47.00 (*0-16-048837-0*, 003-024-08810-0) USGPO.

***Statistical Abstract of the United States 1997.** 1022p. 1997. lib. bdg. 29.95 (*1-57311-036-1*) Hoovers TX.

***Statistical Abstract of the United States, 1997: The National Data Book.** Bernan Press Staff. 1996. 42.00 (*0-89059-068-0*) Bernan Pr.

***Statistical Abstract of the World.** 3rd ed. 1997. 60.00 (*0-8103-6434-4*, 00001939, Gale Res Intl) Gale.

***Statistical Abstract of the World.** 4th ed. 1998. 60.00 (*0-7876-0081-4*, 00108714, Gale Res Intl) Gale.

Statistical Abstract of the World 1. Ed. by Arsen J. Darnay. 950p. 1994. 60.00 (*0-8103-9199-6*) Gale.

An Asterisk (*) at the beginning of an entry indicates that the title is appearing in BIP for the first time.

***Statistical Abstract of U. S. '92.** U. S. Census Bureau Staff. 1992. 34.00 (*0-87511-979-4*, UST90H) Claitors.
***Statistical Abstract of U. S. '92.** U. S. Census Bureau Staff. 1992. pap. 29.00 (*0-87511-980-8*, UST90P) Claitors.
***Statistical Abstract of U. S. '93.** U. S. Census Bureau Staff. 1993. 38.00 (*0-614-30838-0*) Claitors.
***Statistical Abstract of U. S. '93.** U. S. Census Bureau Staff. 1993. pap. 32.00 (*0-614-30839-9*) Claitors.
***Statistical Abstract of U. S. '94.** U. S. Census Bureau Staff. 1994. pap. 32.00 (*0-614-30840-2*) Claitors.
***Statistical Abstract of U. S. '94.** U. S. Census Bureau Staff. 1994. 40.00 (*0-614-30841-0*) Claitors.
***Statistical Abstract of U. S. '95.** U. S. Census Bureau Staff. 1995. pap. 37.00 (*0-87511-735-X*, UST95P) Claitors.
***Statistical Abstract of U. S. '95.** U. S. Census Bureau Staff. 1995. 42.00 (*0-87511-748-1*, UST95H) Claitors.
***Statistical Abstract of U. S. '96.** U. S. Census Bureau Staff. 1996. 47.00 (*0-614-30817-8*, UST96H) Claitors.
***Statistical Abstract of U. S. '96.** U. S. Census Bureau Staff. 1996. pap. 40.00 (*0-614-30818-6*, UST96P) Claitors.
Statistical Abstract of Utah: 1990. 11th ed. University of Utah Bureau of Economic & Business Research Staff. (Illus.). (Orig.). 1990. pap. 40.00 (*0-942486-07-2*) Univ Utah.
Statistical Abstract of Utah - 1987. 10th ed. Ed. by University of Utah, Bureau of Economic & Business Research Staff. 1987. pap. 40.00 (*0-942486-05-6*) Univ Utah.
Statistical Abstract of Utah, 1993. University of Utah, Bureau of Economic & Business Research Staff. (Illus.). 500p. 1993. pap. 40.00 (*0-942486-08-0*) Univ Utah.
***Statistical Abstract of Utah 1996: Centennial Edition.** 13th ed. Bureau of Econ & Bus Research Staff. Ed. by Diane S. Gillam. 518p. (Orig.). (C). 1996. pap. 40.00 (*0-942486-11-0*) Univ Utah.
***Statistical Abstracts of the U. S., 1996: The National Data Book.** (Illus.). 1015p. 1997. 70.00 (*0-7881-3843-X*) DIANE Pub.
***Statistical Abstracts of the U. S., 1996: The National Data Book.** (Illus.). 1015p. (Orig.). 1997. pap. 60.00 (*0-7881-3844-8*) DIANE Pub.
Statistical Abstracts of the World 2. 2nd ed. Darnay. 1996. 60.00 (*0-8103-6433-6*) Gale.
Statistical Account of the City of New Haven. Timothy Dwight. (Connecticut Academy of Arts & Sciences Ser., Trans.: Vol. 1, No. 1). 1811. pap. 300.00 (*0-685-22873-8*) Elliots Bks.
Statistical Account of the Parish of St. Just-In-Penwith. Buller. (C). 1989. 80.00 (*0-907566-61-8*, Pub. by Dyllansow Truran UK) St Mut.
Statistical Adjustment of Data. William E. Deming. 261p. 1984. reprint ed. pap. 9.95 (*0-486-64685-8*) Dover.
***Statistical Agencies: Adherence to Guidelines & Coordination of Budgets.** Ed. by James M. McDermott et al. (Illus.). 56p. 1997. reprint ed. pap. text ed. 30.00 (*0-7881-4107-4*) DIANE Pub.
***Statistical Agencies: Statutory Requirements Affecting Government Policies & Programs.** (Illus.). 40p. (Orig.). (C). 1996. pap. 25.00 (*0-7881-3472-8*) DIANE Pub.
Statistical Agencies of the Federal Government: A Report to the Commission on Organization of the Executive Branch of the Government. Frederick C. Mills & Clarence D. Long. (General Ser.: No. 50). 215p. 1949. reprint ed. 60.40 (*0-87014-049-3*); reprint ed. mic. film 30.20 (*0-685-61276-7*) Natl Bur Econ Res.
Statistical Analysis: A Computer Oriented Approach. 2nd ed. Abdelmonem A. Afifi & Stanley P. Azen. 1979. text ed. 108.00 (*0-12-044460-7*) Acad Pr.
Statistical Analysis: An Interdisciplinary Introduction to Univariate & Multivariate Methods. Sam K. Kachigan. LC 85-61811. (Illus.). 589p. (C). 1986. text ed. 49.95 (*0-942154-99-1*) Radius Pr.
Statistical Analysis: For Business & Economics. 3rd ed. Harnet. 1985. 59.25 (*0-201-10683-3*) Addison-Wesley.
Statistical Analysis & Control of Dynamic Systems. H. Akaike & T. Nakagawa. (C). 1989. lib. bdg. 167.50 (*90-277-2786-4*) Kluwer Ac.
Statistical Analysis & Mathematical Modelling of AIDS. J. C. Jager & E. J. Ruitenberg. (Illus.). 192p. 1988. 56.50 (*0-19-261745-1*) OUP.
Statistical Analysis for Business & Economics. Y. L. Chou. 856p. 1989. 48.00 (*0-444-01301-6*) P-H.
Statistical Analysis for Decision-Makers in Healthcare: Understanding & Evaluating Critical Information in a Competitive Market. Jeffrey C. Bauer. 225p. (C). 1995. text ed. 55.00 (*1-55738-633-1*) Irwin Prof Pubng.
Statistical Analysis for Decision Making. Jeffrey E. Jarrett & Arthur Kraft. 736p. 1989. teacher ed. write for info. (*0-318-63857-6*, H18088) P-H.
Statistical Analysis for Decision Making. 5th ed. Morris Hamburg. 900p. (C). 1990. text ed. 57.75 (*0-15-583459-2*) Dryden Pr.
Statistical Analysis for Decision Making. 6th ed. Morris Hamburg & Peg Young. LC 93-71261. 812p. (C). 1993. text ed. 57.75 (*0-03-096914-X*) Dryden Pr.
Statistical Analysis for Decision Making. 6th ed. Morris Hamburg & Peg Young. 812p. (C). 1994. text ed. 75.95 (*0-534-51037-X*) Wadsworth Pub.
Statistical Analysis for Education & Psychology Researchers. Ian Peers. LC 96-12659. 224p. 1996. 69.95 (*0-7507-0505-1*, Falmer Pr); pap. 25.95 (*0-7507-0506-X*, Falmer Pr) Taylor & Francis.
Statistical Analysis for Engineers & Scientists: A Computer-Based Approach, IBM Version. J. Wesley Barnes. 1994. text ed. write for info. (*0-07-839608-5*) McGraw.
Statistical Analysis for Engineers & Scientists: A Computer-Based Approach, Macintosh Version. J. Wesley Barnes. 1994. text ed. write for info. (*0-07-839605-0*) McGraw.
Statistical Analysis for Geographers. Daniel A. Griffith et al. 496p. 1990. text ed. 77.00 (*0-13-844184-7*) P-H.
Statistical Analysis for Public Administration. Lawrence L. Giventer. LC 95-2886. 527p. (C). 1995. pap. text ed. 38.25 (*0-534-15222-8*) HarBrace.
Statistical Analysis for Public & Non-Profit Managers. Leanna Stiefel. LC 89-16131. 226p. 1990. text ed. 59.95 (*0-275-93301-6*, C3301, Praeger Pubs) Greenwood.
Statistical Analysis in Art Conservation Research. Terry J. Reedy & Chandra L. Reedy. LC 88-2994. (Research in Conservation Ser.). 108p. 1988. pap. 20.00 (*0-89236-097-6*, Getty Conservation Inst) J P Getty Trust.
Statistical Analysis in Chemistry & the Chemical Industry. Carl A. Bennett et al. LC 54-11428. (Wiley Publications in Statistics). 724p. reprint ed. pap. 180.00 (*0-317-09349-5*, 2055153) Bks Demand.
Statistical Analysis in Psychology & Education. 6th ed. George A. Ferguson. (Illus.). 576p. 1989. text ed. write for info. (*0-07-020485-3*) McGraw.
Statistical Analysis in Water Resources Engineering. Mamdouth Shahin et al. (Applied Hydrology Monographs: Vol. I). (Illus.). 280p. (C). 1993. text ed. 60.00 (*90-5410-162-8*, Pub. by A A Balkema NE); pap. text ed. 35.00 (*90-5410-163-6*, Pub. by A A Balkema NE) Ashgate Pub Co.
Statistical Analysis of Behavioural Data: An Approach Based on Time-Structured Models. Patsy Haccou & Evert Meelis. (Illus.). 416p. 1994. reprint ed. pap. 45.00 (*0-19-854850-8*) OUP.
Statistical Analysis of Categorical Data. E. B. Andersen. (Illus.). ix, 523p. 1990. pap. 104.70 (*0-387-52139-9*) Spr-Verlag.
Statistical Analysis of Categorical Data. 2nd ed. Erling B. Andersen. LC 94-3807. 1994. 125.00 (*0-387-57696-7*) Spr-Verlag.
Statistical Analysis of Categorical Data. 2nd enl. rev. ed. E. B. Andersen. (Illus.). xi, 532p. 1991. 108.00 (*0-387-54463-1*) Spr-Verlag.
Statistical Analysis of Circular Data. N. I. Fisher. (Illus.). 384p. (C). 1993. text ed. 74.95 (*0-521-35018-2*) Cambridge U Pr.
Statistical Analysis of Circular Data. N. I. Fisher. (Illus.). 295p. 1996. pap. text ed. 30.95 (*0-521-56890-0*) Cambridge U Pr.
Statistical Analysis of Compositional Data. J. Aitchison. (Monographs on Statistics & Applied Probability). 400p. 1986. text ed. 49.95 (*0-412-28060-4*, 9864) Chapman & Hall.
Statistical Analysis of Data-Set Quality. V. V. Shvyrkov. LC 85-20211. (Illus.). 190p. (Orig.). 1985. pap. text ed. 33.10 (*0-942004-13-2*) Throwkoff Pr.
Statistical Analysis of Discrete Data. D. E. Duffy & Thomas J. Santner. (Texts in Statistics Ser.). (Illus.). 305p. 1989. 61.95 (*0-387-97018-5*) Spr-Verlag.
Statistical Analysis of DNA Sequence Data. Ed. by Bruce S. Weir. LC 83-5137. (Statistics, Textbooks & Monographs: No. 47). 271p. reprint ed. pap. 77.30 (*0-7837-3420-4*, 2052466) Bks Demand.
Statistical Analysis of Epidemiological Data. 2nd ed. Steve Selvin. (Monographs in Epidemiology & Biostatistics: No. 25). (Illus.). 488p. 1996. text ed. 45.00 (*0-19-509760-2*) OUP.
Statistical Analysis of Experimental Data. John Mandel. LC 83-20599. (Mathematics Ser.). 448p. 1984. reprint ed. pap. 9.95 (*0-486-64666-1*) Dover.
Statistical Analysis of Experimental Density Data. Clyde R. Metz. Ed. by H. Anthony Neidig. (Modular Laboratory Program in Chemistry Ser.). 11p. (C). 1988. pap. text ed. 1.35 (*0-87540-353-0*, PROP 353-0) Chem Educ Res.
***Statistical Analysis of Extreme Values.** R. D. Reiss & M. Thomas. LC 97-23442. 1997. write for info. (*0-8176-5768-1*) Birkhauser.
Statistical Analysis of Failure Time Data. J. D. Kalbfleisch & R. L. Prentice. LC 79-21889. (Probability & Mathematical Statistics: Applied Probability & Statistics Section Ser.). 321p. 1980. text ed. 99.95 (*0-471-05519-0*, Wiley-Interscience) Wiley.
Statistical Analysis of Fatigue Data - STP 744. Ed. by R. E. Little & J. C. Ekvall. 151p. 1981. 16.50 (*0-8031-0716-1*, 04-744000-30) ASTM.
Statistical Analysis of Finite Mixture Distributions. D. M. Titterington et al. LC 85-6434. (Probability & Mathematical Statistics Ser.). 243p. 1986. text ed. 255.00 (*0-471-90763-4*) Wiley.
Statistical Analysis of Geological Data. George S. Koch, Jr. & Richard F. Link. 850p. 1981. reprint ed. pap. 15.95 (*0-486-64040-X*) Dover.
Statistical Analysis of Measurement Error Models & Applications. Brown & Fuller. LC 90-44278. (Contemporary Mathematics Ser.: Vol. 112). 248p. 1990. pap. text ed. 55.00 (*0-8218-5117-9*, CONM/112) Am Math.
Statistical Analysis of Nonnormal Data. J. V. Deshpande et al. 370p. 1995. text ed. 40.95 (*0-470-22057-0*) Halsted Pr.
Statistical Analysis of Observations of Increasing Dimension. Vyacheslav L. Girko. LC 95-5546. (Theory & Decision Library B: Vol. 28). 308p. (C). 1995. lib. bdg. 120.00 (*0-7923-2886-8*) Kluwer Ac.
Statistical Analysis of Rainfall & Runoff. Ed. by Vijay P. Singh. LC 81-71289. 1982. 42.00 (*0-918334-44-6*) WRP.
Statistical Analysis of Random Fields. Alexander V. Ivanov & N. N. Leonenko. (C). 1989. lib. bdg. 151.00 (*90-277-2800-3*) Kluwer Ac.
Statistical Analysis of Regional Yield Trials: AMMI Analysis of Factorial Designs. Ed. by Hugh G. Gauch, Jr. LC 92-32306. 278p. 1992. 200.00 (*0-444-89240-0*) Elsevier.
Statistical Analysis of Reliability & Life-Testing Models: Theory & Methods. 2nd expanded rev. ed. Lee J. Bain. (Statistics: Textbooks & Monographs: Vol. 115). 520p. 1991. 160.00 (*0-8247-8506-1*) Dekker.
Statistical Analysis of Reliability Data. M. J. Crowder et al. 256p. 1991. 49.95 (*0-412-30560-7*, A6119) Chapman & Hall.
Statistical Analysis of Reliability Data. M. J. Crowder. 1994. pap. 43.00 (*0-412-59480-3*) Chapman & Hall.
Statistical Analysis of Sand Gain Size in San Salvador, Bahamas. Robert B. Gardner. 11p. (Orig.). (C). 1993. pap. text ed. 4.00 (*0-935909-45-1*) Bahamian.
Statistical Analysis of Spherical Data. N. I. Fisher et al. (Illus.). 300p. 1987. text ed. 80.00 (*0-521-24273-8*) Cambridge U Pr.
Statistical Analysis of Spherical Data. N. I. Fisher et al. (Illus.). 352p. (C). 1993. pap. text ed. 36.95 (*0-521-45699-1*) Cambridge U Pr.
Statistical Analysis of Stationary Time Series. 2nd ed. Ulf Grenander & Murray Rosenblatt. LC 83-62687. 308p. 1984. text ed. 19.95 (*0-8284-0320-1*) Chelsea Pub.
Statistical Analysis of the Functional & Spatial Structure of the London Region. Allen J. Scott. (Discussion Paper Ser.: No. 21). 1968. pap. 10.00 (*1-55869-121-9*) Regional Sci Res Inst.
Statistical Analysis of Time Series. T. W. Anderson. 720p. 1994. pap. text ed. 46.95 (*0-471-04745-7*) Wiley.
Statistical Analysis of Weather Modification Experiments. Wegman & DePriest. (Lecture Notes in Statistics Ser.: Vol. 3). 160p. 1980. 89.75 (*0-8247-1177-7*) Dekker.
Statistical Analysis Software System. Mel Tainiter. 250p. 1985. 295.00 incl. disk (*0-934577-09-9*) Softext Pub.
Statistical Analysis with Missing Data. Roderick Little. LC 86-19075. 304p. 1987. text ed. 79.95 (*0-471-80254-9*) Wiley.
Statistical & Chronological History of the United States Navy, 1775-1907, 2 vols., Set. Robert W. Neeser. (BCL1 - U. S. History Ser.). 1991. reprint ed. lib. bdg. 150.00 (*0-7812-6044-2*) Rprt Serv.
Statistical & Commercial History of the Kingdom of Guatemala. Domingo Juarros. LC 76-128432. reprint ed. 72.50 (*0-404-03622-8*) AMS Pr.
Statistical & Comparative Studies of the Australian Aboriginal Dentition. Ed. by Kazuro Hanihara. 57p. 1976. 24.50 (*0-86008-171-0*, Pub. by U of Tokyo JA) Col U Pr.
Statistical & Computational Methods in Data Analysis. rev. ed. S. Brandt. 416p. 1983. pap. 80.00 (*0-444-86615-9*, North Holland) Elsevier.
Statistical & Mathematical Aspects of Pollution Problems: Papers. Satellite Symposium on Statistical Aspects of Pollution Problems (1971: Harvard Business School) Staff. Ed. by John W. Pratt. LC 73-90771. (Statistics, Textbooks & Monographs: No. 6). 424p. reprint ed. pap. 120.90 (*0-318-35012-2*, 2030872) Bks Demand.
Statistical & Mathematical Methods in Population Dynamics & Pest Control: Proceedings of a Meeting of the EC Experts Group, Parma, 26-28th October 1983. Ed. by R. Cavalloro. 256p. (C). 1984. text ed. 85.00 (*90-6191-548-1*, Pub. by A A Balkema NE) Ashgate Pub Co.
Statistical & Methodological Advances in Psychiatric Research. Ed. by Robert D. Gibbons & Dysken. 184p. 1983. 29.95 (*0-88331-203-4*) Luce.
Statistical & Scientific Database Management. Ed. by Zbigniew Michalewicz. (Lecture Notes in Computer Science Ser.: Vol. 420). v, 256p. 1990. 35.00 (*0-387-52342-1*) Spr-Verlag.
Statistical & Scientific Database Management. Ed. by M. Rafanelli et al. (Lecture Notes in Computer Science Ser.: Vol. 339). ix, 454p. 1989. 55.00 (*0-387-50575-X*) Spr-Verlag.
Statistical & Thermal Physics, Pt. 1. Shugeji Fujita. LC 83-22250. 540p. 1986. pap. 42.50 (*0-89874-689-2*) Krieger.
Statistical & Thermal Physics, Pt. 2. Shugeji Fujita. LC 83-22250. 550p. 1986. pap. 42.50 (*0-89874-866-6*) Krieger.
Statistical Annals. Adam Seybert. LC 68-18229. (Library of Early American Business & Industry: No. 26). xxvii, 803p. 1970. reprint ed. 87.50 (*0-678-00553-2*) Kelley.
Statistical Antenna Theory. A. S. Shifrin. Tr. by Petr Beckmann from RUS. LC 73-158655. (Electromagnetics Ser.: Vol. 7). (Illus.). 1971. 25.00 (*0-911762-11-6*) Golem.
Statistical Applications. 75p. 1972. 10.00 (*0-318-12575-7*, 031) Am Feed Industry.
Statistical Applications for the Behavioral Sciences. L. G. Grimm et al. 1128p. 1993. student ed. 56.00 (*0-471-31047-6*) Wiley.
Statistical Applications for the Behavioral Sciences. L. G. Grimm et al. 540p. 1992. wbk. ed., pap. 17.00 (*0-471-55046-9*) Wiley.
Statistical Applications for the Behavioral Sciences. Lawrence G. Grimm. LC 00-29. 588p. 1993. Net. text ed. 44.50 (*0-471-50982-5*) Wiley.
Statistical Applications in Criminal Justice. Gennaro F. Vito & Edward J. Latessa. (Law & Criminal Justice Ser.: Vol. 10). 160p. 1989. text ed. 39.95 (*0-8039-2982-X*); pap. text ed. 17.95 (*0-8039-2983-8*) Sage.
Statistical Applications in Process Control. Ed. by J. Bert Keats & Douglas C. Montgomery. LC 96-958. (Quality & Reliability Ser.: Vol. 47). 528p. 1996. 150.00 (*0-8247-9711-6*) Dekker.
Statistical Applications of Jordan Algebras. James D. Malley. LC 94-28225. (Lecture Notes in Statistics Ser.: Vol. 91). 1994. 35.95 (*0-387-94341-2*) Spr-Verlag.
Statistical Applications Using Fuzzy Sets. Kenneth G. Manton et al. (Probability & Mathematical Statistics Ser.). 312p. 1994. text ed. 69.95 (*0-471-54561-9*) Wiley.
Statistical Approach to Social Measurement. David J. Bartholmew. (Illus.). 239p. 1996. boxed 54.95 (*0-12-079860-3*) Acad Pr.
Statistical Approach to VLSI. Ed. by S. W. Director & W. Maly. LC 93-46624. (Advances in CAD for VLSI Ser.: Vol. 8). 402p. 1994. 191.50 (*0-444-88371-1*, North Holland) Elsevier.
Statistical Aspects of Quality Control. Cyrus Derman & Sheldon M. Ross. LC 96-25651. (Statistical Modeling & Decision Science Ser.). (Illus.). 200p. 1996. boxed 59.95 (*0-12-210010-7*) Acad Pr.
Statistical Aspects of the Microbiological Analysis of Foods. B. Jarvis. (Progress in Industrial Microbiology Ser.: No. 21). 180p. 1989. 108.25 (*0-444-42570-5*) Elsevier.
Statistical Assessment of National Significant Industrial User Noncompliance for Pre-Treatment of Wastewater Discharges. 110p. (Orig.). (C). 1993. pap. text ed. 35.00 (*1-56806-599-X*) DIANE Pub.
Statistical Auditing: Review, Concepts & Problems. Andrew D. Bailey, Jr. 308p. (C). 1981. 2.20 (*0-15-583759-1*) HB Coll Pubs.
Statistical Bases of Reference Values in Laboratory Medicine. Eugene K. Harris & James C. Boyd. LC 95-9589. (Statistics: Textbooks & Monographs: Vol. 146). 384p. 1995. 165.00 (*0-8247-9339-0*) Dekker.
Statistical Business Economics 5. Anderson. Date not set. student ed., pap. text ed. write for info. (*0-314-01708-9*) West Pub.
Statistical Business Economics 5. Anderson. Date not set. wbk. ed., pap. text ed. 21.00 (*0-314-01711-9*) West Pub.
***Statistical Case Studies for Industrial Process Improvement.** Ed. by A. Veronica Czitrom & Patrick Spagon. LC 97-12582. (ASA-SIAM Series on Statistics & Applied Probability: Vol. 1). (Illus.). 500p. (Orig.). 1997. pap. text ed. write for info. (*0-89871-394-3*) Soc Indus-Appl Math.
Statistical Challenges in Modern Astronomy. Eric D. Feigelson & Gutti J. Babu. LC 92-27811. (Illus.). 520p. 1995. 69.95 (*0-387-97911-5*) Spr-Verlag.
***Statistical Challenges in Modern Astronomy II.** Gutti J. Babu & Eric D. Feigelson. LC 97-5785. 1997. write for info. (*0-387-98203-5*) Spr-Verlag.
Statistical Chart on Children: Early Child Development & Learning Achievement 1990. 1990. 5.95 (*0-685-39209-0*, 90.XVII.14) UN.
Statistical Charts & Indicators on the Situation of Youth. (Illus.). 50p. 1990. pap. 10.95 (*92-1-161343-4*, E.92. XVII.4) UN.
Statistical Clerk. Jack Rudman. (Career Examination Ser.: C-762). 1994. pap. 23.95 (*0-8373-0762-7*) Nat Learn.
Statistical Compendium for Series. (Virginia's Local Economies Ser.). 1990. 15.68 (*0-685-61068-3*) U VA Ctr Pub Serv.
Statistical Compendium on the Ukrainians in Canada, 1891-1976. Ed. by William Darcovich & Paul Yuzyk. LC 82-176005. 869p. 1980. reprint ed. pap. 180.00 (*0-608-01995-X*, 2062651) Bks Demand.
Statistical Compilation & Market Share Reports: For Accident & Health Insurance Companies in 1994. 92p. (C). 1995. per. 50.00 (*0-89382-358-9*) Nat Assn Insurance.
***Statistical Compilation & Market Share Reports: For Accident & Health Insurance Companies in 1995.** 2nd rev. ed. 92p. (C). 1996. pap. 75.00 (*0-89382-432-1*, STA-HB) Nat Assn Insurance.
Statistical Compilation & Market Share Reports for Accident & Health Insurance Companies in 1993. (Annual Ser.). 93p. (C). 1995. per. 50.00 (*0-89382-347-3*, STA-HB93) Nat Assn Insurance.
***Statistical Compilation of Annual Statement Information: For Life Insurance Companies in 1995.** 3rd rev. ed. 286p. (C). 1996. pap. 175.00 (*0-89382-420-8*, STA-LS) Nat Assn Insurance.
***Statistical Compilation of Annual Statement Information: For Property/Casualty Insurance Companies in 1995.** 3rd rev. ed. 441p. (C). 1996. pap. 175.00 (*0-89382-419-4*, STA-PS) Nat Assn Insurance.
Statistical Compilation of Annual Statement Information for Life - Health Insurance Companies. 178p. 1994. per. 150.00 (*0-89382-251-5*) Nat Assn Insurance.
Statistical Compilation of Annual Statement Information for Life - Health Insurance Companies. annuals 224p. (C). 1995. per. 150.00 (*0-89382-301-5*) Nat Assn Insurance.
Statistical Compilation of Annual Statement Information for Life/Health Insurance Companies in 1994. annuals 290p. (Orig.). (C). 1995. 150.00 (*0-89382-366-X*) Nat Assn Insurance.
Statistical Compilation of Annual Statement Information for Property - Casualty Insurance Companies. 1994. per. 150.00 (*0-89382-250-7*) Nat Assn Insurance.
Statistical Compilation of Annual Statement Information for Property - Casualty Insurance Companies. annuals 325p. (C). 1994. per. 150.00 (*0-89382-300-7*) Nat Assn Insurance.
Statistical Compilation of Annual Statement Information for Property/Casualty Insurance Companies in 1994. annuals 432p. (Orig.). (C). 1995. 150.00 (*0-89382-367-8*) Nat Assn Insurance.
Statistical Computerized Electrocardiogram Norm for Males & Females 26 Yrs. Old to 65 Yrs. Old. Ralph H. Kapilian. 79p. (Orig.). 1984. spiral bd. 29.95 (*0-916311-00-7*) R H Kapilian.
Statistical Computing Environments for Social Research. Robert Stine & John Fox. LC 96-9978. 224p. 1996. 49.95 (*0-7619-0269-4*); pap. 24.95 (*0-7619-0270-8*) Sage.

S

Statistical Concepts. 3rd ed. Foster Brown et al. LC 94-35670. (C). 1995. text ed. 23.95 (*0-673-99440-6*) Addson-Wesley Educ.

Statistical Concepts: A Basic Foundation for Social Science Research. Laura Poole. (Illus.). pap. 10.00 (*0-533-11433-0*) Vantage.

Statistical Concepts & Applications in Medicine. J. Aitchison & I. J. Lauder. (Monographs on Statistics & Applied Probability). (Illus.). 400p. 1993. text ed. 60.00 (*0-412-30430-9*) Chapman & Hall.

Statistical Concepts & Methods. Gouri K. Bhattacharyya & Richard A. Johnson. (Probability & Mathematical Statistics Ser.). 656p. 1977. text ed. 56.00 (*0-471-07204-4*) Wiley.

Statistical Concepts for Attorneys: A Reference Guide. Wayne C. Curtis. LC 82-24068. xviii, 230p. 1983. text ed. 49.95 (*0-89930-033-2*, CSA/, Quorum Bks) Greenwood.

Statistical Concepts for the Behavioral Sciences. 2nd ed. Harold O. Kiess. LC 95-12845. 1995. text ed. 69.00 (*0-205-16648-2*) Allyn.

Statistical Concepts in Geography. John Silk. (Illus.). 1979. pap. text ed. 16.95 (*0-04-910066-1*) Routledge Chapman & Hall.

Statistical Concepts with Applications to Business & Economics. 2nd ed. Richard W. Madsen & Melvin L. Moeschberger. (Illus.). 672p. (C). 1986. text ed. 33.95 (*0-317-38353-1*) P-H.

Statistical Consultant in Action. Ed. by D. J. Hand & B. S. Everitt. (Illus.). 200p. 1987. text ed. 59.95 (*0-521-30717-1*) Cambridge U Pr.

***Statistical Control by Monitoring & Feedback Adjustment.** George E. Box & Alberto Luceno. LC 97-459. (Series in Probability & Statistics). 1997. 69.95 (*0-471-19046-2*) Wiley.

Statistical Data Analysis: Proceedings of Symposia in Applied Mathematics, Vol. 28. Ed. by Ram Gnanadesikan. LC 82-24308. (Proceedings of Symposia in Applied Mathematics Ser.: Vol. 28). 141p. 1983. pap. 25.00 (*0-8218-0040-X*, PSAPM/28) Am Math.

Statistical Data Analysis & Inference. Ed. by Yadolah Dodge. 618p. 1989. 190.75 (*0-444-88029-1*, North Holland) Elsevier.

Statistical Data Analysis for Ocean & Atmospheric Sciences. Ed. by H. Jean Thiebaux. (Illus.). 247p. 1994. boxed 74.95 (*0-12-686925-1*) Acad Pr.

Statistical Data Bank Systems: Socio-Economic Database & Model Building in Japan. Ed. by K. Uno & S. Shishido. 364p. 1988. 153.25 (*0-444-70397-7*, North Holland) Elsevier.

Statistical Data Editing Vol. 1: Methods & Techniques. (Statistical Standards & Studies: No. 44). 219p. 1994. 20.00 (*92-1-116614-4*) UN.

Statistical Deception at Work. John B. Mauro. (Communication Textbook Ser.). 128p. (C). 1992. pap. 17.50 (*0-8058-1232-6*) L Erlbaum Assocs.

Statistical Decision: Models for Management. John E. Hanke et al. (C). 1983. teacher ed. 7.00 (*0-685-07779-9*, H80864) P-H.

Statistical Decision Rules & Optimal Inference. N. N. Cencov. LC 81-15039. (Translations of Mathematical Monographs: Vol. 53). 499p. 1982. 119.00 (*0-8218-4502-0*, MMONO/53) Am Math.

Statistical Decision Theory & Bayesian Analysis. 2nd ed. J. O. Berger. (Series in Statistics). (Illus.). xvi, 617p. 1997. 64.95 (*0-387-96098-8*) Spr-Verlag.

Statistical Decision Theory & Bayesian Analysis. 3rd ed. J. O. Berger. (Series in Statistics). (Illus.). xvi, 617p. 1993. write for info. (*3-540-96098-8*) Spr-Verlag.

Statistical Decision Theory & Related Topics IV. Ed. by S. S. Gupta & J. O. Berger. (Illus.). xii, 418p. 1987. 91.95 (*0-387-96661-7*) Spr-Verlag.

Statistical Decision Theory & Related Topics IV, Vol. 2. Ed. by S. S. Gupta & J. O. Berger. (Illus.). xvi, 399p. 1987. 71.95 (*0-387-96662-5*) Spr-Verlag.

Statistical Decision Theory & Related Topics V. S. S. Gupta & J. O. Berger. 552p. 1993. 79.95 (*0-387-94143-6*) Spr-Verlag.

Statistical Decomposition of Industrial Fire Loss. David Shpilberg. LC 80-52616. (S. S. Huebner Foundation Monographs: No. 11). 102p. (Orig.). 1982. pap. 17.95 (*0-918930-11-1*) Huebner Foun Insur.

Statistical Description of Transport in Plasma, Astro & Nuclear Physics. Ed. by J. Misguich et al. (Houches Ser.). (Illus.). 437p. (C). 1993. lib. bdg. 145.00 (*1-56072-152-9*) Nova Sci Pubs.

Statistical Design - Analysis of Experiments: An App. Approach. Leonard Onyiah. 1995. write for info. (*0-8493-8632-2*) CRC Pr.

Statistical Design Analysis of Experiments with Applications to Engineering & Science. Robert L. Mason et al. LC 88-20893. (Probability & Mathematical Statistics Ser.). 692p. 1989. text ed. 94.95 (*0-471-85364-X*) Wiley.

Statistical Design & Analysis for Intercropping Experiments. Walter T. Federer. LC 92-29586. (Series in Statistics). 1993. 79.95 (*0-387-97923-9*) Spr-Verlag.

Statistical Design & Analysis of Engineering Experiments. Charles Lipson & N. J. Sheth. (Illus.). 544p. (C). 1973. text ed. write for info. (*0-07-037991-2*) McGraw.

Statistical Design & Analysis of Industrial Experiments. Ed. by Ghosh. (Statistics: Textbooks & Monographs: Vol. 109). 440p. 1990. 65.00 (*0-8247-8251-8*) Dekker.

Statistical Design & Analysis of Pharmaceutical Sciences: Validation, Process Controls, & Stability. Ed. by Chow & Liu. (Statistics: Textbooks & Monographs: Vol. 143). 580p. 1995. 150.00 (*0-8247-9336-6*) Dekker.

Statistical Design for Research. J. Leslie Kish. LC 86-28084. (Probability & Mathematical Statistics Ser.). 296p. 1987. text ed. 94.95 (*0-471-08359-3*) Wiley.

Statistical Design of Integrated Circuits. Ed. by Andrzej J. Strojwas. 160p. 1987. pap. 39.95 (*0-87942-226-2*, PP02220) Inst Electrical.

Statistical Determination of Affiliation in the Landmark Manuscripts of the 'Canterbury Tales' Charles W. Moorman. LC 93-413. 224p. 1993. text ed. 89.95 (*0-7734-9276-3*) E Mellen.

Statistical Digital Signal Processing & Modeling. Mason H. Hayes. LC 96-10241. 608p. 1996. text ed. 86.95 (*0-471-59431-8*) Wiley.

Statistical Disclosure Control in Practice. L. Willenborg & T. De Waal. (Lecture Notes in Statistics Ser.: Vol. 111). 176p. 1996. pap. 34.95 (*0-387-94722-1*) Spr-Verlag.

Statistical Distributions. 2nd ed. Merran Evans et al. LC 92-40419. 192p. 1993. pap. text ed. 36.95 (*0-471-55951-2*) Wiley.

Statistical Distributions for Flood Frequency Analysis. World Meteorological Organization Staff. (WMO, No. 718 & Operational Hydrology Reports: No. 33). 1989. pap. 22.00 (*92-63-10718-1*, Pub. by Wrld Meteorological SZ) Am Meteorological.

Statistical Distributions in Ecological Work. Ed. by G. P. Patil et al. (Statistical Ecology Ser.: Vol. 4). 1979. 45.00 (*0-89974-001-4*) Intl Co-Op.

Statistical Distributions in Scientific Work, 3 vols., Vol. 1. 1975. lib. bdg. 141.50 (*90-277-0606-9*) Kluwer Ac.

Statistical Distributions in Scientific Work, 3 vols., Vol. 2. 1975. lib. bdg. 141.50 (*90-277-0607-7*) Kluwer Ac.

Statistical Distributions in Scientific Work, 3 vols., Vol. 3. 1975. lib. bdg. 141.50 (*90-277-0608-5*) Kluwer Ac.

Statistical Distributions in Scientific Work, Vol. 4, Models, Structures & Characterizations. xxii, 456p. 1981. lib. bdg. 158.50 (*90-277-1332-4*) Kluwer Ac.

Statistical Distributions in Scientific Work, Vol. 6. xxii, 439p. 1981. lib. bdg. 158.50 (*90-277-1333-2*); lib. bdg. 158.50 (*90-277-1334-0*) Kluwer Ac.

Statistical Distributions Software Sourcebook. R. Christensen. (Entropy Minimax Sourcebook Ser.: Vol. 9). 1985. lib. bdg. 149.00 (*0-938876-20-1*) Entropy Ltd.

***Statistical Dynamics.** 350p. 1997. 33.00 (*1-86094-045-5*); pap. text ed. 16.00 (*1-86094-046-3*) World Scientific Pub.

Statistical Dynamics - A Stochastic Approach to Nonequilibrium Thermodynamics. Raymond F. Streater. 250p. 1995. text ed. 44.00 (*1-86094-002-1*); pap. text ed. 29.00 (*1-86094-004-8*) World Scientific Pub.

Statistical Dynamics of Nonlinear & Time Varying Systems. M. F. Dimentberg. LC 88-16936. 609p. 1988. text ed. 385.00 (*0-471-92056-8*) Wiley.

Statistical Ecology: A Primer on Methods & Computing. John A. Ludwig & James F. Reynolds. LC 87-26348. 337p. 1988. text ed. 69.95 (*0-471-83235-9*) Wiley.

Statistical Energy Analysis: An Overview, with Applications in Structural Dynamics. Ed. by W. G. Price & A. J. Keane. LC 95-49979. (Illus.). 150p. (C). 1997. text ed. 47.95 (*0-521-55175-7*) Cambridge U Pr.

Statistical Engineering & Science. 4th ed. Boudreau & Mendenhall. 1995. student ed., pap. text ed. 24.00 (*0-02-312718-X*, Macmillan Coll) P-H.

Statistical Epidemiology in Veterinary Science. F. B. Leech & K. C. Sellers. 1979. 30.00 (*0-85264-211-3*) Lubrecht & Cramer.

Statistical Estimation: Asymtotic Theory. I. A. Ibragimov & R. Z. Has'Minskii. (Applications of Mathematics Ser.: Vol. 16). 420p. 1981. 98.00 (*0-387-90523-5*) Spr-Verlag.

Statistical Evaluation of Mutagenicity Test Data. Ed. by David J. Kirkland. (Illus.). 320p. (C). 1990. text ed. 69.95 (*0-521-36605-4*) Cambridge U Pr.

***Statistical Evaluations in Exploration for Mineral Deposits.** Friederich-Welmer Wellmer. LC 96-3338. 1996. write for info. (*3-540-61242-4*) Spr-Verlag.

Statistical Evidence. David W. Barnes. 1986. 125.00 (*0-316-08148-5*) Little.

***Statistical Evidence: A Likelihood Paradigm.** R. Royall. 192p. 1997. 54.95 (*0-412-04411-0*) Chapman & Hall.

Statistical Evidence in Litigation: Methodology, Procedure, & Practice. David W. Barnes & John M. Conley. 1986. 85.00 (*0-316-08145-0*) Little.

Statistical Exercises. Porter. Date not set. pap. text ed. 21.50 (*0-314-04748-4*) West Pub.

Statistical Exorcist: Dispelling Statistics Anxiety. Hollander & Proschan. (Popular Statistics Ser.: Vol. 3). 264p. 1984. 49.75 (*0-8247-7225-3*) Dekker.

Statistical Explanation & Statistical Relevance. Wesley C. Salmon. LC 77-158191. (Pitt Paperback Ser.: Vol. 69). 127p. 1971. reprint ed. pap. 36.20 (*0-608-02054-0*, 2062707) Bks Demand.

Statistical Factor Analysis & Related Methods: Theory & Applications. Alexander Basilevsky. (Probability & Mathematical Statistics Ser.). 737p. 1994. text ed. 99.95 (*0-471-57082-6*) Wiley.

Statistical Field Theory. Giorgio Parisi. (C). 1988. text ed. 48.50 (*0-317-69757-9*) Addison-Wesley.

Statistical Field Theory, Vol. 1: From Brownian Motion to Renormalization & Lattice Gauge Theory. Jean-Michel Drouffe & Claude Itzykson. (Cambridge Monographs on Mathematical Physics). 400p. (C). 1989. 64.95 (*0-521-34058-6*) Cambridge U Pr.

Statistical Field Theory, Vol. 1: From Brownian Motion to Renormalization & Lattice Gauge Theory. Claude Itzykson & Jean-Michel Drouffe. (Monographs on Mathematical Physics). 432p. (C). 1991. pap. text ed. 37.95 (*0-521-40805-9*) Cambridge U Pr.

Statistical Field Theory, Vol. 2: Strong Coupling, Monte Carlo Methods, Conformal Field Theory, & Random Systems. Jean-Michel Drouffe & Claude Itzykson. (Cambridge Monographs on Mathematical Physics). 400p. (C). 1989. text ed. 105.00 (*0-521-37012-4*) Cambridge U Pr.

Statistical Field Theory, Vol. 2: Strong Coupling, Monte Carlo Methods, Conformal Field Theory, & Random Systems. Claude Itzykson & Jean-Michel Drouffe. (Monographs on Mathematical Physics). 432p. (C). 1991. pap. text ed. 38.95 (*0-521-40806-7*) Cambridge U Pr.

Statistical First Aid: Instructor's Guide. R. P. Hirsch & Richard K. Riegelman. (Illus.). 80p. 1992. teacher ed. write for info. (*0-86542-192-7*) Blackwell Sci.

Statistical First Aid: Interpretation of Medical Research Data. R. P. Hirsch & Richard K. Riegelman. (Illus.). 80p. 1992. pap. 36.95 (*0-86542-138-2*) Blackwell Sci.

Statistical Forecast for the United States. 2nd ed. Ed. by Sean Pollack. 850p. 1995. 95.00 (*0-8103-8935-5*, 101635) Gale.

***Statistical Forecast United States.** 3rd ed. 1997. 95.00 (*0-8103-9983-0*, 00007743, Gale Res Intl) Gale.

Statistical Forecasts of the United States. Ed. by James E. Person, Jr. & Sean R. Pollock. LC 93-7565. 1993. Acid-free paper. 95.00 (*0-8103-8922-3*) Gale.

Statistical Foundation of Inference in Medicine: Rationale - Technique - Strategy. rev. ed. Raymond Jonnard. Ed. by Karel B. Absolon. (Illus.). 518p. (C). 1994. pap. 39.50 (*0-685-71254-0*) Kabel Pubs.

Statistical Foundation of Inference in Medicine: Rationale - Technique - Strategy, 3 vols., Set. 2nd rev. ed. Raymond Jonnard. Ed. by Karel B. Absolon. (Illus.). 737p. (C). 1993. pap. text ed. 59.50 (*0-930329-61-9*) Kabel Pubs.

Statistical Foundations for Econometric Techniques. Asad Zaman. (Illus.). 355p. 1996. pap. 44.95 (*0-12-775415-6*) Acad Pr.

***Statistical Foundations for Econometrics.** Ed. by Omar F. Hamouda & J. C. Rowley. (Foundations of Probability, Econometrics & Economic Games Ser.: Vol. 5). 512p. 1997. 150.00 (*1-85898-437-8*) E Elgar.

Statistical Foundations of Econometric Modelling. Aris Spanos. (Illus.). 718p. (C). 1989. pap. text ed. 34.95 (*0-521-26912-1*) Cambridge U Pr.

Statistical Games & Human Affairs: The View from Within. R. J. Bowden. (Illus.). 336p. 1989. text ed. 64.95 (*0-521-36178-8*) Cambridge U Pr.

***Statistical Genomics: Linkage, Mapping, & QTL Analysis.** Ben-Hui Liu. LC 97-1863. 1997. write for info. (*0-8493-3166-8*) CRC Pr.

Statistical Geography: Problems in Analyzing Areal Data. Otis D. Duncan et al. LC 77-7890. (Illus.). 190p. 1977. reprint ed. text ed. 35.00 (*0-8371-9676-0*, DUSG, Greenwood Pr) Greenwood.

Statistical Graphics: Design Principles & Practices. Calvin F. Schmid. LC 91-45331. 224p. (C). 1992. reprint ed. pap. 44.50 (*0-89464-709-1*) Krieger.

***Statistical Graphics for Univariate & Bivariate Data.** William G. Jacoby. LC 96-45892. (Quantitative Applicatons in the Social Sciences Ser.: Vol. 117). 96p. (C). 1997. pap. 10.95 (*0-7619-0083-7*, 00837) Sage.

Statistical Handbook. annuals 135p. (C). 1994. ring bd. 100.00 (*0-89382-308-2*) Nat Assn Insurance.

***Statistical Handbook for the Graphic Arts Industry 1996.** 700p. 1996. 167.00 (*0-614-25550-3*, 00BT54021) Print Indus Am.

Statistical Handbook of Data Available to Insurance Regulators. 156p. (C). 1992. ring bd. 100.00 (*0-89382-213-2*) Nat Assn Insurance.

Statistical Handbook of Japan. 1991. lib. bdg. 79.95 (*0-8490-5116-9*) Gordon Pr.

Statistical Handbook of Social & Economic Indicators for the Former Soviet Union. Compiled by Center for Human Values, CIS Committee for Statistics Staff. LC 94-33435. 1996. lib. bdg. 75.00 (*0-88354-378-8*) N Ross.

***Statistical Handbook of Working America.** 2nd ed. 1997. 99.00 (*0-7876-0849-1*, 00155708, Gale Res Intl) Gale.

Statistical Handbook of Working America 1. Charity Dorjan. 1300p. 1995. 99.00 (*0-7876-0087-3*, 108804) Gale.

Statistical Handbook on Adolescents in America. Bruce A. Chadwick & Tim B. Heaton. LC 96-10514. (Illus.). 344p. 1996. boxed 54.50 (*0-89774-922-7*) Oryx Pr.

Statistical Handbook on Aging Americans. 2nd ed. Renee Schnick. LC 93-36711. (Illus.). 360p. 1994. 54.50 (*0-89774-721-6*) Oryx Pr.

Statistical Handbook on the American Family. Bruce A. Chadwick & Tim B. Heaton. LC 91-44175. (Illus.). 312p. 1992. 59.50 (*0-89774-687-2*) Oryx Pr.

Statistical Handbook on U. S. Hispanics. Ed. by Frank L. Schick & Renee Schick. LC 90-48167. (Illus.). 272p. 1991. 49.50 (*0-89774-554-X*) Oryx Pr.

Statistical Handbook on Violence in America. Adam Dobrin et al. LC 95-42437. (Illus.). 424p. 1995. boxed 54.50 (*0-89774-945-6*) Oryx Pr.

Statistical Handbook on Women in America. 2nd ed. Ed. by Cynthia M. Taeuber. LC 96-1521. (Illus.). 384p. (C). 1996. boxed 54.50 (*1-57356-005-7*) Oryx Pr.

***Statistical Handbook 1995: States of the Former U. S. S. R.** (Studies of Economics in Transformation: No. 19). 656p. 1996. 25.95 (*0-8213-3508-1*, 13508) World Bank.

***Statistical Handbook 1996: States of the Former U. S. S. R.** (Studies of Economies in Transformation: No. 21). 584p. 1996. 50.00 (*0-8213-3845-5*, 13845) World Bank.

Statistical History of the American Presidential Elections: With Supplementary Tables Covering 1968 to 1980. Svend Petersen & Louis Filler. LC 81-6348. xxiii, 275p. 1981. reprint ed. text ed. 41.50 (*0-313-22952-X*, PESH, Greenwood Pr) Greenwood.

Statistical Ideas for Managers. Hildebrand. (Business Statistics Ser.). 1996. student ed., pap. 17.95 (*0-534-25526-4*) Wadsworth Pub.

Statistical Image Processing & Graphics. Wegman & DePriest. (Statistics: Textbooks & Monographs: Vol. 72). 368p. 1986. 125.00 (*0-8247-7600-3*) Dekker.

Statistical Imperative-Practical Quantitative Tools for Healthcare Managers. 2nd ed. Eric Joseph. Ed. by Ellen Crowhurst. 124p. 1994. pap. text ed. 50.00 (*0-916499-66-9*) Care Educ Grp.

Statistical Independence in Probability Analysis & Number Theory. Mark Kac. (Carus Mathematical Monograph: No. 12). 112p. 1969. pap. 14.00 (*0-88385-025-7*, CAM-12) Math Assn.

Statistical Indicators for Asia & Pacific Vol. XXIII, No. 1: March 1993. 77p. 1993. 12.00 (*92-1-119615-9*) UN.

Statistical Indicators for Asia & Pacific Vol. XXIII, No. 2: June 1993. 96p. 1993. 15.00 (*92-1-119622-1*) UN.

Statistical Indicators for Asia & Pacific Vol. XXIII, No. 3: September 1993. 96p. 1993. 15.00 (*92-1-119625-6*) UN.

Statistical Indicators for Asia & Pacific Vol. XXIII, No. 4: December 1993. 98p. 1994. 15.00 (*92-1-119631-0*) UN.

Statistical Indicators for Asia & Pacific Vol. XXIV, No. 1: March 1994. 98p. 1994. 15.00 (*92-1-119643-4*) UN.

Statistical Indicators for Asia & the Pacific, Vol. 18, No. 1. 80p. 1988. 10.00 (*92-1-119462-8*, 88.II.F.6) UN.

Statistical Indicators for Asia & the Pacific, Vol. 18, No. 2. 80p. 1988. 10.00 (*92-1-119464-4*, 88.II.F.8) UN.

Statistical Indicators for Asia & the Pacific, Vol. 18, No. 3. 80p. 1988. 10.00 (*0-685-54406-0*) UN.

Statistical Indicators for Asia & the Pacific, Vol. XIX, No. 1. 80p. 1989. No. 1, 03/1989, 80p. 10.00 (*92-1-119544-6*, E.89.II.F.6) UN.

Statistical Indicators for Asia & the Pacific, Vol. XIX, No. 3. 95p. No. 3, 95p. 10.00 (*92-1-119547-0*, E.89.II.F.13) UN.

Statistical Indicators for Asia & the Pacific, Vol. XIX, No.2. 90p. 1989. No. 2, 06/1989, 90p. 10.00 (*92-1-119546-2*, E.89.II.F.10) UN.

Statistical Indicators for Asia & the Pacific, Vol. XX, No. 2. 88p. 1990. 10.00 (*92-1-119569-1*) UN.

Statistical Indicators for Asia & the Pacific, Vol. XX, No. 3. 88p. 1990. 10.00 (*92-1-119571-3*) UN.

Statistical Indicators for Asia & the Pacific, Vol. XX, No. 4. 79p. 1990. 10.00 (*92-1-119578-0*) UN.

Statistical Indicators for Asia & the Pacific, Vol. XXI, No. 1. 88p. 1991. 15.00 (*92-1-119584-5*, 91.II.F.13) UN.

Statistical Indicators for Asia & the Pacific Vol. 24: Number 4 December 1994. 79p. 1995. pap. 17.50 (*92-1-119692-2*, UN95 2F 28) UN Inst Train & Res.

***Statistical Indicators for Asia & the Pacific Vol. 25, No. 1: 1995.** Economic & Social Commission for Asia & the Pacific. 107p. Date not set. pap. 17.50 (*92-1-119694-9*, HC412) UN.

Statistical Indicators for Asia & the Pacific, 1989, Vol. XIX, No. 4. 80p. 1989. 10.00 (*92-1-119554-3*, 89.II.F. 19) UN.

Statistical Indicators for Asia & the Pacific, 1990, Vol. XX, No. 1. 88p. 1990. 10.00 (*92-1-119566-7*, 90.II.F.6) UN.

***Statistical Indicators for Asia & the Pacific, 1996, Vol. 26, No. 3.** Economic & Social Commission for Asia & the Pacific. 81p. 1996. pap. 17.50 (*92-1-119728-7*, HC412) UN.

Statistical Indicators for the Economic & Social Sciences. Robert V. Horn. LC 92-23005. (Illus.). 256p. (C). 1993. text ed. 59.95 (*0-521-41333-8*); pap. text ed. 18.95 (*0-521-42399-6*) Cambridge U Pr.

Statistical Indicators for the Planning & Evaluation of Public Health Programmes: Proceedings of the WHO Expert Committee on Health Statistics, 14th, Geneva, 1970. WHO Staff. 1971. pap. text ed. 5.00 (*92-4-120472-9*, 1100472) World Health.

Statistical Indicators of Cyclical Revivals. Wesley C. Mitchell & Arthur F. Burns. (NBER Bulletin Ser.: No. 69). 1938. reprint ed. 20.00 (*0-685-61191-4*) Natl Bur Econ Res.

Statistical Indicators of Cyclical Revivals & Recessions. Geoffrey H. Moore. (Occasional Papers: No. 31). 104p. 1950. reprint ed. 27.10 (*0-87014-346-8*) Natl Bur Econ Res.

Statistical Indicators of Short-Term Economic Changes in ECE Countries - Supplement: Sources & Definitions. 415p. 1990. 65.00 (*92-1-116466-4*, 90.II.E.2) UN.

Statistical Indicators of Short-Term Economic Changes in ECE Countries, 1990, Vol. XXXII, No. 8. 1990. 6.00 (*0-685-74316-0*) UN.

Statistical Indicators on Youth. 202p. 1986. 15.50 (*92-1-061099-7*, E.85.XVII.12) UN.

Statistical Indices of Family Health: Report. WHO Staff. (Technical Report Ser.: No. 587). 1976. pap. text ed. 8.00 (*92-4-120587-3*, 1100587) World Health.

Statistical Inference. Paul H. Garthwaite et al. LC 95-7038. 336p. 1995. pap. text ed. 65.00 (*0-13-847260-2*) P-H.

***Statistical Inference.** Kay. (Illus.). 320p. (Orig.). 1997. pap. text ed. 37.00 (*0-412-57610-4*, Chap & Hall NY) Chapman & Hall.

Statistical Inference. Michael Oakes. LC 90-2834. 185p. (Orig.). (C). 1990. pap. text ed. 24.00 (*0-917227-04-2*) Epidemiology.

Statistical Inference. S. D. Silvey. (Monographs on Statistics & Applied Probability). 192p. (gr. 13). 1975. pap. text ed. 34.95 (*0-412-13820-4*, 6248) Chapman & Hall.

Statistical Inference. 2nd ed. Casella. (Statistics - Ser.). Date not set. text ed. 69.95 (*0-534-24312-6*) Wadsworth Pub.

Statistical Inference: Theory & Practice. Ed. by Tadeusz Bromek & Elzbieta Pleszczynska. (C). 1991. lib. bdg. 230.50 (*0-7923-0718-6*) Kluwer Ac.

Statistical Inference for Spatial Processes. Brian D. Ripley. 154p. 1991. pap. text ed. 24.95 (*0-521-42420-8*) Cambridge U Pr.

Statistical Inference for Stochastic Processes. Ed. by Ishwar V. Basawa & Prakasa Rao. LC 79-50533. (Probability & Mathematical Statistics Ser.). 1980. text ed. 95.00 (*0-12-080250-3*) Acad Pr.

An Asterisk (*) at the beginning of an entry indicates that the title is appearing in BIP for the first time.

Statistical Inference from Stochastic Processes. Ed. by N. Prabhu. LC 88-31369. (Contemporary Mathematics Ser.: No. 80). 386p. 1988. pap. 44.00 (*0-8218-5087-3*, CONM/80) Am Math.

Statistical Inference in Elliptically Contoured & Related Distributions. Ed. by Kai-Tai Fang & T. W. Anderson. (Illus.). xiii, 498p. 1990. 95.00 (*0-89864-048-2*) Allerton Pr.

Statistical Inference in Linear Models, Vol. 1: Statistical Methods of Model Building. Ed. by Helga Bunke & Olaf Bunke. Tr. by John Bibby & Michal Basch. LC 83-21675. (Wiley Series in Probability & Mathematical Statistics). 614p. reprint ed. pap. 175.00 (*0-8357-3395-5*, 2039652) Bks Demand.

Statistical Inference in Stochastic Processes. Ed. by N. U. Prabhu & I. V. Basawa. (Probability Ser.: Vol. 6). 288p. 1990. 135.00 (*0-8247-8417-0*) Dekker.

Statistical Inference under Order Restrictions: The Theory & Application of Isotonic Regression. Richard E. Barlow et al. LC 74-39231. (Wiley Series in Probability & Mathematical Statistics: No. 8). 400p. reprint ed. pap. 114.00 (*0-685-15432-7*, 2026680) Bks Demand.

Statistical Information. Ghosh. 1988. 65.95 (*0-387-96751-6*) Spr-Verlag.

Statistical Intervals: A Guide for Practitioners. Gerald J. Hahn & William Q. Meeker. LC 91-8728. (Probability & Mathematical Statistics: Applied Probability & Statistics Section Ser.). 416p. 1991. text ed. 82.95 (*0-471-88769-2*) Wiley.

Statistical Issues in Analyzing the NHANES I Epidemiologic Followup Study. LC 93-46586. (Vital & Health Statistics Ser. 2: Data Evaluation & Methods Research: No. 121). 1994. write for info. (*0-8406-0487-4*) Natl Ctr Health Stats.

Statistical Issues in Analyzing the NHANES I Epidemiologic Followup Study. National Center for Health Statistics Staff. LC 94-1395. (Series Reports: Series 2, No. 121). 30p. 2.75 (*0-614-02904-X*, 017-022-01258-8) Natl Ctr Health Stats.

Statistical Issues in Drug Research & Development. Peace. (Statistics: Textbooks & Monographs: Vol. 106). 416p. 1989. 155.00 (*0-8247-8290-9*) Dekker.

Statistical Language Learning. Eugene Charniak. LC 93-28080. (Language, Speech, & Communication Program Ser.). 208p. 1994. 28.00 (*0-262-03216-3*, Bradford Bks) MIT Pr.

Statistical Language Learning. Eugene Charniak. (Language, Speech, Computation & Communication Program Ser.). (Illus.). 192p. 1996. pap. 14.00 (*0-262-53141-0*, Bradford Bks) MIT Pr.

Statistical Law Set. Phillip I. Blumberg. 1991. 155.00 (*0-316-10074-9*) Little.

Statistical Linguistic Analysis of American English. A. Hood Roberts. (Janua Linguarum, Series Practica: No. 8). 1965. text ed. 89.25 (*90-279-0627-0*) Mouton.

Statistical Literacy for Business & Economics Casebook. Roger C. Pfaffenberger. 1996. pap. text ed. write for info. (*0-201-42177-1*) Addison-Wesley.

Statistical Management. Hoffman. Date not set. teacher ed., pap. text ed. write for info. (*0-314-01738-0*) West Pub.

Statistical Manual of the AOAC. W. J. Youden et al. (Illus.). 96p. 1987. 34.00 (*0-935584-15-3*) AOAC Intl.

Statistical Mechanic & Thermodynamics with Software for Macintosh. Claude Garrod. (Illus.). 720p. (C). 1995. text ed. 53.50 incl. disk (*0-19-509775-0*) OUP.

Statistical Mechanics, 2 pts. Ed. by Bruce J. Berne. Incl. Equilibrium Techniques. LC 76-46977. 242p. 1977. (*0-306-33505-0*); Time-Dependent Processes. LC 76-46977. 362p. 1977. 89.50 (*0-306-33506-9*); LC 76-46977. (Modern Theoretical Chemistry Ser.: Vols. 5 & 6). (Illus.). 1977. write for info. (*0-318-55337-6*, Plenum Pr) Plenum.

Statistical Mechanics. R. Kubo. Ed. by H. Ichimura et al. 426p. 1990. pap. 61.75 (*0-444-87103-9*, North Holland) Elsevier.

Statistical Mechanics. Shang-Keng Ma. 576p. 1985. text ed. 38.00 (*9971-966-06-9*); pap. text ed. 53.00 (*9971-966-07-7*) World Scientific Pub.

Statistical Mechanics. Donald A. McQuarrie. (Chemistry Ser.). 640p. (C). 1975. text ed. 101.95 (*0-06-044366-9*) Addison-Wesley Educ.

***Statistical Mechanics.** Pathria. 1972. 57.95 (*0-7506-2811-1*) Buttrwrth-Heinemann.

***Statistical Mechanics.** Siddhartha Sen. 1996. pap. text ed. 45.00 (*0-13-126152-5*) P-H.

Statistical Mechanics. 2nd ed. Kerson Huang. LC 86-32466. 493p. 1987. Net. text ed. 51.00 (*0-471-81518-7*, Wiley-Interscience) Wiley.

Statistical Mechanics. 2nd ed. R. K. Pathria. LC 96-1679. (Illus.). 529p. 1996. pap. text ed. 66.95 (*0-7506-2469-8*, Q175, Prgamon Press) Buttrwrth-Heinemann.

Statistical Mechanics. Ryuzo Abe. Tr. by Yasushi Takahashi. LC 74-84826. 188p. 1975. reprint ed. pap. 53.60 (*0-608-01193-2*, 2061882) Bks Demand.

Statistical Mechanics: A Set of Lectures. Richard P. Feynman. (Frontiers in Physics Ser.). 354p. (C). 1972. pap. 45.95 (*0-8053-2509-3*, Adv Bk Prog) Addison-Wesley.

Statistical Mechanics: An Intermediate Course. Giuseppe Morandi. LC 95-24957. 650p. 1995. text ed. 78.00 (*981-02-2299-8*) World Scientific Pub.

Statistical Mechanics: Foundations, Problems, Perspectives. Angelo Baracca et al. 700p. 1998. text ed. 78.00 (*981-02-1693-9*) World Scientific Pub.

***Statistical Mechanics: Fundamentals & Modern Applications.** Richard E. Wilde & Sujit Singh. LC 97-3287. 544p. 1997. 64.95 (*0-471-16165-9*) Wiley.

Statistical Mechanics: New Concepts, New Problems, New Applications. Ed. by Stuart A. Rice & Karl F. Freed. LC 72-85434. 434p. reprint ed. pap. 123.70 (*0-317-08081-4*, 2019965) Bks Demand.

Statistical Mechanics: Principles & Selected Applications. Terrell L. Hill. 448p. 1987. reprint ed. pap. text ed. 9.95 (*0-486-65390-0*) Dover.

Statistical Mechanics: Proceedings of the 10th Annual Open University Conference on Statistical Mechanics. Ed. by Allan I. Solomon. 170p. (C). 1988. text ed. 51.00 (*9971-5-0554-1*) World Scientific Pub.

Statistical Mechanics & Field Theory: Mathematical Aspects. Ed. by T. C. Dorlas et al. (Lecture Notes in Physics Ser.: Vol. 257). vii, 328p. 1986. 48.95 (*0-387-16777-3*) Spr-Verlag.

Statistical Mechanics & Field Theory: Proceedings of the 7th Physics Summer School. V. V. Bazhanov & C. J. Burden. 450p. 1995. text ed. 86.00 (*981-02-2397-8*) World Scientific Pub.

Statistical Mechanics & Fractals. R. L. Dobrushin & S. Kusukoa. LC 93-44952. 1994. 27.95 (*0-387-57516-2*) Spr-Verlag.

Statistical Mechanics & Manybody Problems. rev. ed. K. M. Khanna. (Illus.). 450p. 1986. 45.00 (*1-55528-067-6*, Pub. by Today & Tomorrows P & P II) Scholarly Pubns.

Statistical Mechanics & Stability of Macromolecules: Application to Bond Disruption, Base Pair Separation, Melting, & Drug Dissociation of the DNA Double Helix. Earl Prohofsky. (Illus.). 275p. (C). 1995. text ed. 52.95 (*0-521-45184-1*) Cambridge U Pr.

Statistical Mechanics & the Theory of Dynamical Systems: Collection of Papers. Ed. by N. N. Bogolyubov, Jr. LC 92-16440. (Proceedings of the Steklov Institute of Mathematics Ser.: Vol. 191). 243p. 1992. pap. 160.00 (*0-8218-3144-5*, STEKLO/191) Am Math.

Statistical Mechanics & Thermodynamics. Claude Garrod. (Illus.). 720p. (C). 1995. text ed. 53.50 (*0-19-508523-X*) OUP.

Statistical Mechanics at the Turn of the Decade. Ed. by E. G. Cohen. LC 70-134789. (Illus.). 245p. reprint ed. pap. 69.90 (*0-7837-0762-2*, 2041076) Bks Demand.

Statistical Mechanics, Deformation, Ultrasonic & Spectroscopy. Contrib. by C. F. Curtis et al. (Advances in Polymer Science Ser.: Vol. 125). (Illus.). viii, 206p. 1996. 133.00 (*3-540-60483-9*) Spr-Verlag.

***Statistical Mechanics for Chemists.** Jerry Goodisman. LC 96-44749. text ed. 69.95 (*0-471-16812-2*) Wiley.

Statistical Mechanics for Thermophysical Property Calculations. Richard L. Rowley. LC 93-45530. 512p. 1994. text ed. 90.00 incl. disk (*0-13-030818-8*) P-H.

***Statistical Mechanics in Physics & Biology.** Ed. by D. Wirtz et al. LC 97-20743. (Materials Research Society Symposium Proceedings Ser.: No. 463). 1997. text ed. 75.00 (*1-55899-367-3*) Materials Res.

Statistical Mechanics of Chain Molecules. Paul J. Flory. 432p. (C). 1989. text ed. 52.50 (*1-56990-019-1*) Hanser-Gardner.

Statistical Mechanics of Elasticity. Jerome H. Weiner. LC 82-20056. 454p. 1986. reprint ed. 59.95 (*0-471-09773-X*) Krieger.

Statistical Mechanics of Irreversible Change: Proceedings of the IUPAP Conference on Statistical Mechanics, 6th, 1971. IUPAP Conference Staff. LC 55-8426. 140p. reprint ed. pap. 39.90 (*0-317-08501-8*, 2010184) Bks Demand.

Statistical Mechanics of Lattice Gases, Vol. 1. Barry Simon. LC 92-36714. (Illus.). 456p. (C). 1993. text ed. 79.50 (*0-691-08779-2*) Princeton U Pr.

Statistical Mechanics of Magnetically Ordered Systems. Y. A. Izyumov & Yu. N. Skryabin. Tr. by Roger Cooke from RUS. LC 88-23770. (Illus.). 308p. 1988. 95.00 (*0-306-11015-6*, Consultants) Plenum.

Statistical Mechanics of Membranes & Surfaces: 5th Jerusalem Winter School for Theoretical Physics. Ed. by David Nelson et al. 272p. (C). 1989. text ed. 53.00 (*9971-5-0722-6*); pap. text ed. 36.00 (*9971-5-0734-X*) World Scientific Pub.

Statistical Mechanics of Neural Networks: Proceedings of the XIth Sitges Conference Sitges, Barcelona, Spain, 3-7 June 1990. Ed. by Luis Garrido. (Lecture Notes in Physics Ser.: Vol. 368). vi, 477p. 1990. 70.95 (*0-387-53267-6*) Spr-Verlag.

Statistical Mechanics of Nonequilibrium Liquids. Ed. by D. J. Evans. (Theoretical Chemistry Ser.). 302p. 1990. text ed. 98.00 (*0-12-244090-0*) Acad Pr.

Statistical Mechanics of Nonequilibrium Processes, Vol. 2. D. Zubarev et al. 300p. 1996. write for info. (*3-05-501709-9*, VCH) Wiley.

***Statistical Mechanics of Nonequilibrium Processes Vol. 1: Basic Concepts, Kinetic Theory.** D. Zubarev et al. 270p. 1996. 70.00 (*3-05-501708-0*, Pub. by Akademie Verlag GW) Wiley.

Statistical Mechanics of Periodic Frustrated Ising Systems. R. Liebmann. (Lecture Notes in Physics Ser.: Vol. 251). vii, 142p. 1986. 29.95 (*0-387-16473-1*) Spr-Verlag.

Statistical Mechanics of Phase Transitions. J. M. Yeomans. (Illus.). 160p. 1992. pap. 26.00 (*0-19-851730-0*) OUP.

***Statistical Mechanics of Phases, Interfaces & Thin Films.** H. T. Davis. 1995. text ed. 95.00 (*0-471-18562-0*) Wiley.

Statistical Mechanics of Phases, Interfaces, & Thin Films. H. Ted Davis. Ed. by D. F. Evans. LC 95-14941. (Advances in Interfacial Engineering Ser.). (Illus.). 750p. 1995. 95.00 (*1-56081-513-2*, VCH) Wiley.

Statistical Mechanics of the Liquid Surface. Clive A. Croxton. LC 79-40819. (Illus.). 367p. reprint ed. pap. 104.60 (*0-685-20738-2*, 2030376) Bks Demand.

Statistical Mechanics, Protein Structure & Protein Substrate Interactions. Ed. by S. Doniach. (NATO ASI, Series B, Physics: Vol. 325). (Illus.). 408p. (C). 1994. text ed. 115.00 (*0-306-44728-2*, Plenum Pr) Plenum.

Statistical Method for Large Scale Stochastic Linear Programming. Julia L. Higle & Suvrajeet Sen. LC 95-46322. (Nonconvex Optimization & Its Applications Ser.: Vol. 8). 248p. (C). 1996. lib. bdg. 112.00 (*0-7923-3840-5*) Kluwer Ac.

Statistical Method from the Viewpoint of Quality Control. Walter A. Shewhart. 192p. 1986. reprint ed. pap. text ed. 7.95 (*0-486-65232-7*) Dover.

Statistical Methodology in the Pharmaceutical Sciences. Berry. (Statistics: Textbooks & Monographs: Vol. 104). 560p. 1989. 180.00 (*0-8247-8117-1*) Dekker.

Statistical Methods. John D. Williams. LC 95-44362. 384p. (Orig.). (C). 1995. pap. text ed. 37.50 (*0-7618-0173-1*) U Pr of Amer.

Statistical Methods. 2nd rev. ed. Rudolph J. Freund & William J. Wilson. (Illus.). 684p. 1996. boxed 52.50 (*0-12-267472-3*) Acad Pr.

Statistical Methods. 8th rev. ed. George W. Snedecor & William G. Cochran. LC 89-15405. 524p. 1989. text ed. 54.95 (*0-8138-1561-4*) Iowa St U Pr.

Statistical Methods: A Geometric Primer. David J. Saville & Graham R. Wood. LC 96-10598. (Illus.). 280p. 1996. pap. 39.95 (*0-387-94705-1*) Spr-Verlag.

Statistical Methods: Concepts, Application & Computation. Y. P. Agarwal. (C). 1986. text ed. 37.50 (*81-207-0157-7*, Pub. by Sterling Pubs II) Apt Bks.

Statistical Methods: For Business & Economics. 3rd ed. Roger C. Pfaffenberger & James H. Patterson. (C). 1987. text ed. 60.95 (*0-256-03664-0*) Irwin.

Statistical Methods: Games & Songs. George E. Gardenier. Ed. by T. K. Gardenier. (Gardenier Math-Stat Ser.). 99p. 1989. 89.00 (*0-685-29043-3*) Teka Trends.

Statistical Methods: Quantity & Quality. rev. ed. LC 91-75167. 230p. 1994. student ed. 28.95 (*0-942004-60-4*) Throwkoff Pr.

Statistical Methods: The Geometric Approach. D. J. Saville & G. R. Wood. (Texts in Statistics Ser.). (Illus.). 576p. 1997. 64.95 (*0-387-97517-9*) Spr-Verlag.

Statistical Methods & Financial Calculations. 2nd rev. ed. Isabel Willemse. (Illus.). 328p. (C). 1994. pap. text ed. 37.00 (*0-7021-3128-8*, Pub. by Juta & Co SA) Intl Spec Bk.

Statistical Methods by Marascuilo & Serlin. Serlin. (C). 1995. pap. write for info. (*0-7167-1969-X*) W H Freeman.

Statistical Methods, Experimental Design, & Scientific Inference. R. A. Fisher. Ed. by J. H. Bennett. (Illus.). 872p. 1990. pap. 65.00 (*0-19-852229-0*) OUP.

Statistical Methods for Business & Economics. 4th ed. Donald Harnett. (C). 1991. student ed., pap. text ed. 18.95 (*0-201-55830-0*) Addison-Wesley.

Statistical Methods, for Business & Economics. 4th ed. Donald L. Harnett. 1991. 62.50 (*0-201-51395-1*) Addison-Wesley.

Statistical Methods for Cancer Studies. Cornell. (Statistics: Textbooks & Monographs: Vol. 51). 496p. 1984. 150.00 (*0-8247-7169-9*) Dekker.

Statistical Methods for Comparative Studies: Techniques for Bias Reduction. Sharon Anderson et al. LC 79-27220. (Probability & Mathematical Statistics: Applied Probability & Statistics Section Ser.). 289p. 1980. text ed. 118.00 (*0-471-04838-0*) Wiley.

Statistical Methods for Criminology & Criminal Justice. Ronet Bachman & Raymond Pasternoster. 1996. text ed. write for info. (*0-07-003000-6*) McGraw.

***Statistical Methods for Engineers.** Vining. 1998. student ed., pap. 15.95 (*0-534-35362-2*) Brooks-Cole.

Statistical Methods for Engineers. Geoffrey Vining. LC 97-10101. (Statistics). (Illus.). 200p. 1998. text ed. 63.95 (*0-534-23706-1*) Wadsworth Pub.

Statistical Methods for Engineers & Scientists. 3rd ed. Bethea. (Statistics - Textbooks & Monographs: Vol. 144). 680p. 1995. 69.75 (*0-8247-9335-8*) Dekker.

***Statistical Methods for Environmental & Agricultural Sciences.** 2nd ed. Reza A. Hoshmand. LC 97-80. 1997. write for info. (*0-8493-3152-8*) CRC Pr.

Statistical Methods for Environmental Pollution Monitoring. Richard Gilbert. (Professional Bks.). (Illus.). 384p. (C). 1987. text ed. 72.95 (*0-442-23050-8*) Van Nos Reinhold.

Statistical Methods for Food & Agriculture. Ed. by Larry W. Douglass & Amihud Kramer. (Illus.). 345p. 1989. reprint ed. pap. text ed. 39.95 (*1-56022-000-7*) Haworth Jrnl Co-Edits.

Statistical Methods for Forecasting. Bovas Abraham & Johannes Ledolter. LC 83-7006. (Probability & Mathematics Statistics Ser.). 464p. 1983. text ed. 84.95 (*0-471-86764-0*, 1-346) Wiley.

Statistical Methods for Geographers. W. A. Clark & P. L. Hosking. LC 85-20309. 528p. 1986. Net. text ed. 46.00 (*0-471-81807-0*) Wiley.

Statistical Methods for Ground-Water Monitoring. Robert D. Gibbons. 286p. 1994. text ed. 79.95 (*0-471-58707-9*) Wiley.

Statistical Methods for Health Care Research. 3rd ed. Barbara Munro. LC 96-46123. 464p. 1997. pap. text ed. 37.95 (*0-397-55365-X*) Lppncott-Raven.

Statistical Methods for Health Sciences. M. M. Shoukri & V. L. Edge. 320p. 1995. 59.95 (*0-8493-7644-0*) CRC Pr.

Statistical Methods for Long-Memory Processes. Jan Beran. LC 94-14144. 1994. write for info. (*0-412-98681-7*) Chapman & Hall.

Statistical Methods for Long Memory Processes. Jan Beran. 326p. (gr. 13). 1994. text ed. 57.95 (*0-412-04901-5*) Chapman & Hall.

***Statistical Methods for Materials Testing & Evaluation: Practical Statistics.** (C). 1998. write for info. (*0-614-26940-7*) ASM.

***Statistical Methods for Materials Testing & Evaluation Vol. 1: Practical Statistics.** (C). 1997. write for info. (*0-614-19997-2*) ASM.

Statistical Methods for Medical Investigations. 2nd ed. Brian S. Everitt. 241p. 1994. pap. text ed. 39.95 (*0-470-23383-4*) Halsted Pr.

Statistical Methods for Medical Investigations. 2nd ed. Brian S. Everitt. LC 94-8091. 1994. write for info. (*0-340-61431-5*) Routledge Chapman & Hall.

Statistical Methods for Meta-Analysis. Larry V. Hedges & Ingram Olkin. 1985. text ed. 63.00 (*0-12-336380-2*) Acad Pr.

Statistical Methods for Motor Efficiency Data. 1978p. 2.00 (*0-318-17070-1*) Natl Elec Mfrs.

Statistical Methods for Non-Precise Data. Reinhard Viertl. LC 95-38137. 208p. 1995. 49.95 (*0-8493-8242-4*) CRC Pr.

Statistical Methods for Pharmaceutical Research Planning. Bergman & Gittins. (Statistics: Textbooks & Monographs: Vol. 67). 272p. 1985. 125.00 (*0-8247-7146-X*) Dekker.

Statistical Methods for Planners. Thomas R. Willemain. (Illus.). 352p. 1980. 29.95 (*0-262-23101-8*) MIT Pr.

***Statistical Methods for Plant Variety Evaluation.** Ed. by Kempton et al. (Plant Breeding Ser.). 180p. 1997. text ed. 99.00 (*0-412-54750-3*, Chap & Hall NY) Chapman & Hall.

Statistical Methods for Psychology. 3rd ed. David C. Howell. 693p. 1992. text ed. 50.50 (*0-534-92955-9*) Wadsworth Pub.

Statistical Methods for Psychology. 4th ed. David C. Howell. (Business Statistics Ser.). (C). 1997. text ed. 69.95 (*0-534-51993-8*) Wadsworth Pub.

Statistical Methods for Psychology: Solutions Manual. 3rd ed. David C. Howell. Date not set. teacher ed. write for info. (*0-534-92956-7*) Brooks-Cole.

Statistical Methods for Quality: With Applications to Engineering & Management. Irwin Miller & Marylees Miller. LC 94-4684. 416p. 1994. text ed. 79.00 (*0-13-013749-9*) P-H.

Statistical Methods for Quality Design & Control: Contemporary Concepts & Methods. R. E. Devor et al. (Illus.). 832p. (C). 1992. text ed. 89.33 (*0-02-329180-X*, Macmillan Coll) P-H.

Statistical Methods for Quality Improvement. Alan Ryan. LC 88-14230. 446p. 1989. text ed. 79.95 (*0-471-84337-7*) Wiley.

Statistical Methods for Quality Improvement. Ed. by Hitoshi Kume. 231p. 1987. reprint ed. pap. 29.50 (*4-906224-34-2*, Pub. by Three A JA) Qual Resc.

Statistical Methods for Rates & Proportions. 2nd ed. Joseph L. Fleiss. LC 80-26382. (Probability & Mathematical Statistics Ser.). 352p. 1981. text ed. 84.95 (*0-471-06428-9*) Wiley.

Statistical Methods for Social Scientists. Eric Hanushek & John Jackson. (Quantitative Studies in Social Relations). 374p. 1977. text ed. 58.00 (*0-12-324350-5*) Acad Pr.

Statistical Methods for Software Quality. A. Burr & M. Owen. (Illus.). 224p. 1996. pap. 37.95 (*1-85032-171-X*) ITCP.

Statistical Methods for SPC & TQM. Derek Bissell. LC 93-74454. (Texts in Statistical Science Ser.). 373p. (C). (gr. 13). 1994. text ed. 63.95 (*0-412-39440-5*) Chapman & Hall.

Statistical Methods for Survival Data Analysis. 2nd ed. Elisa T. Lee. LC 91-27926. (Probability & Mathematical Statistics: Applied Probability & Statistics Section Ser.). 496p. 1992. text ed. 76.95 (*0-471-61592-7*) Wiley.

Statistical Methods for Testing, Development & Manufacturing. Forrest W. Breyfogle. LC 91-14539. 544p. 1992. text ed. 89.95 (*0-471-54035-8*) Wiley.

Statistical Methods for Textile Technologists. T. Murphy et al. 107p. 1979. 40.00 (*0-686-63797-6*) St Mut.

Statistical Methods for the Analysis of Biomedical Data. Robert F. Woolson. LC 87-6069. (Probability & Mathematical Statistics Ser.). 513p. 1987. text ed. 125.00 (*0-471-80615-3*) Wiley.

Statistical Methods for the Assessment of Point Source Pollution: Proceedings of a Workshop on Statistical Methods for the Assessment of Point Source Polution, Held in Burlington, Ontario, Canada, September 12-14, 1988. Ed. by D. T. Chapman & A. H. El-Sharrawi. (C). 1990. lib. bdg. 171.50 (*0-7923-0619-8*) Kluwer Ac.

Statistical Methods for the Process Industries. William McNeese & R. A. Klein. (Quality & Reliability Ser.: Vol. 28). 528p. 1991. 65.00 (*0-8247-8524-X*) Dekker.

Statistical Methods for the Social & Behavioral Sciences. Ronald C. Serlin & Leonard A. Marascuilo. LC 87-398. (Psychology Ser.). (Illus.). 885p. (C). 1995. text ed. write for info. (*0-7167-1824-3*) W H Freeman.

Statistical Methods for the Social Sciences. Alan Agresti & Barbara F. Agresti. (Illus.). 554p. (C). 1979. text ed. write for info. (*0-02-301100-9*, Macmillan Coll) P-H.

***Statistical Methods for the Social Sciences.** 3rd ed. Alan Agresti & Barbara Finlay. LC 96-38408. 1997. 68.67 (*0-13-526526-6*) P-H.

***Statistical Methods for the Textile Industry.** M. Bona. 1993. pap. 81.00 (*1-870812-57-3*, Pub. by Textile Inst UK) St Mut.

Statistical Methods in Agriculture & Experimental Biology. 2nd ed. R. Mead et al. (Statistical Textbooks Ser.). 352p. 1993. 99.95 (*0-412-35470-5*, A9669) Chapman & Hall.

Statistical Methods in Agriculture & Experimental Biology. 2nd ed. R. Mead et al. (Statistical Textbooks Ser.). 352p. (gr. 13). 1993. pap. text ed. 49.95 (*0-412-35480-2*, A9673) Chapman & Hall.

Statistical Methods in Analytical Chemistry. Peter C. Meier & Richard E. Zund. LC 92-27288. (Chemical Analysis Ser.: Vol. 123). 352p. 1993. text ed. 69.95 (*0-471-58454-1*) Wiley.

Statistical Methods in Biology. 3rd ed. Norman T. Bailey. (Illus.). 216p. (C). 1995. pap. text ed. 16.95 (*0-521-46983-X*) Cambridge U Pr.

S

Statistical Methods in Biology. 3rd ed. Norman T. Bailey. (Illus.). 216p. (C). 1995. text ed. 49.95 (*0-521-47032-3*) Cambridge U Pr.

Statistical Methods in Cancer Research Vol. 1: The Analysis of Case-Control Studies. N. E. Breslow & N. E. Day. (IARC Scientific Publications: No. 32). (Illus.). 360p. (C). 1993. reprint ed. pap. 32.50 (*92-832-0132-9*, 11877) OUP.

Statistical Methods in Cancer Research Vol. 2: The Design & Analysis of Cohort Studies. N. E. Breslow & N. E. Day. (IARC Scientific Publications: No. 82). (Illus.). 452p. 1994. reprint ed. pap. 47.00 (*92-832-0182-5*) OUP.

***Statistical Methods in Cancer Research Vol. 3: The Design & Analysis of Long-Term Animal Experiments.** J. J. Gart et al. (IARC Scientific Publications: No. 79). 240p. 1987. text ed. 45.00 (*92-832-1179-0*) OUP.

Statistical Methods in Cancer Research Vol. 4: Descriptive Epidemiology. Ed. by Jacques Esteve et al. (IARC Scientific Publications: No. 128). (Illus.). 300p. 1995. pap. text ed. 52.00 (*92-832-2128-1*) OUP.

S

***Statistical Methods in Clinical Trials.** (Texts in Statistical Science Ser.). (C). (gr. 13 up). 1997. text ed. 54.95 (*0-412-06361-1*) Chapman & Hall.

***Statistical Methods in Control & Signal Processing, Vol. 103.** Ed. by Katayama & Sugimoto. LC 97-22476. (Electrical Engineering & Electronics Ser.: Vol. 103). 576p. 1997. 175.00 (*0-8247-9948-8*) Dekker.

Statistical Methods in Cryptanalysis. Solomon Kullback. 206p. 1977. pap. 25.80 (*0-89412-006-9*) Aegean Park Pr.

Statistical Methods in Discrimination Litigation. D. H. Kaye & Mikel Aicken. (Statistics: Textbooks & Monographs: Vol. 69). 232p. 1986. 115.00 (*0-8247-7514-7*) Dekker.

Statistical Methods in Econometrics. Ramu Ramanathan. (Illus.). 405p. 1993. text ed. 58.00 (*0-12-576830-3*) Acad Pr.

Statistical Methods in Econometrics. 3rd rev. ed. A. Malinvaud. (Studies in Mathematical & Managerial Economics: Vol. 6). 770p. 1980. 132.25 (*0-444-85473-8*, North Holland) Elsevier.

Statistical Methods in Education & Psychology. A. K. Kurtz & S. T. Mayo. 1979. 54.95 (*0-387-90265-1*) Spr-Verlag.

Statistical Methods in Education & Psychology. 3rd ed. Gene V. Glass & Kenneth D. Hopkins. LC 95-13309. 1995. text ed. 66.00 (*0-205-14212-5*) Allyn.

Statistical Methods in Engineering & Quality Assurance. Peter John. LC 90-33718. (Probability & Mathematical Statistics Ser.). 373p. 1990. text ed. 97.95 (*0-471-82986-2*) Wiley.

Statistical Methods in Environmental Health. Anthony Turton & James C. Pearson. LC 93-17174. 184p. (gr. 13). 1993. pap. text ed. 39.95 (*0-412-48450-1*) Chapman & Hall.

Statistical Methods in Epidemiology. Harold A. Kahn & Christopher T. Sempos. (Monographs in Epidemiology & Biostatistics: No. 12). (Illus.). 320p. 1989. pap. 29.95 (*0-19-505049-5*) OUP.

Statistical Methods in Food & Consumer Research. Maximo C. Gacula, Jr. & Jagbir Singh. (Food Science & Technology Ser.). 1984. text ed. 174.00 (*0-12-272050-4*) Acad Pr.

Statistical Methods in Geology: For Field & Lab Decisions. R. F. Cheeney. (Illus.). 192p. 1983. pap. text ed. 24.95 (*0-04-550030-4*) Routledge Chapman & Hall.

Statistical Methods in Hydrology. C. T. Haan. (Illus.). 378p. 1977. reprint ed. pap. text ed. 29.95 (*0-8138-1510-X*) Iowa St U Pr.

Statistical Methods in Laboratory Medicine. 2nd ed. P. W. Strike. (Monographs in Medical Laboratory Science). (Illus.). 541p. 1991. 175.00 (*0-7506-1345-9*) Buttrwrth-Heinemann.

Statistical Methods in Longitudinal Research, Vol. 1: Principles & Structuring Change. Ed. by Alexander Von Eye. 256p. 1990. pap. text ed. 45.00 (*0-12-724962-1*) Acad Pr.

Statistical Methods in Medical Research. 3rd ed. P. Armitage & G. Berry. LC 93-22118. (Illus.). 640p. 1994. 69.95 (*0-632-03695-8*, Pub. by Blckwell Sci Pubns UK) Blackwell Sci.

Statistical Methods in Nuclear Material Control. AEC Technical Information Center Staff & John L. Jaech. LC 73-600241. 409p. 1973. 18.25 (*0-87079-343-8*, TID-26298); fiche 9.00 (*0-87079-344-6*, TID-26298) DOE.

Statistical Methods in Psychology. Arthur Aron & Elaine N. Aron. LC 92-45260. 612p. (C). 1993. text ed. 66.00 (*0-13-845637-2*) P-H.

Statistical Methods in Reliability Theory & Practice. Brian Bunday. (Mathematics & Its Applications Ser.). 1991. pap. 66.00 (*0-13-853797-6*, 540502) P-H.

Statistical Methods in the Atmospheric Sciences: An Introduction. Daniel S. Wilks. (International Geophysics Ser.: Vol. 59). (Illus.). 467p. 1995. boxed 75.00 (*0-12-751965-3*) Acad Pr.

Statistical Methods in the Biological & Health Sciences. 2nd ed. J. Susan Milton. 1992. text ed. write for info. (*0-07-042506-X*) McGraw.

Statistical Methods in the Social Sciences. 2nd ed. Agresti. 1986. text ed. 79.00 (*0-02-301120-3*, Macmillan Coll) P-H.

***Statistical Methods in Water Resources.** D. R. Helsel & R. M. Hirsch. (Studies in Environmental Science: Vol. 49). 522p. 1992. 232.25 (*0-444-88528-5*) Elsevier.

Statistical Methods in Water Resources. D. R. Helsel & R. M. Hirsch. (Studies in Environmental Science: Vol. 49). 522p. 1993. Incl. disk. pap. 92.00 (*0-444-81463-9*) Elsevier.

Statistical Methods of Discrimination & Classification: Advances in Theory & Applications. Ed. by S. C. Choi. (International Series in Modern Applied Mathematics & Computer Science). 135p. 1986. 39.00 (*0-08-034000-8*, A110,C110,D110,D130,H100, Pergamon Pr) Elsevier.

Statistical Methods of Management. Roger Johnson. (C). 1993. student ed. 10.00 (*1-881592-22-7*) Hayden-McNeil.

***Statistical Methods of Quality Assurance.** Mittag & Rinne. (Illus.). 680p. 1993. text ed. 60.95 (*0-412-55980-3*, Chap & Hall NY) Chapman & Hall.

Statistical Model: Frederick Mosteller's Contributions to Statistics, Science, & Public Policy. Ed. by Stephen E. Fienberg et al. (Illus.). xviii, 283p. 1990. 52.95 (*0-387-97223-4*) Spr-Verlag.

Statistical Modeling: Applications in Contemporary Issues. William S. Mallios. LC 89-31303. (Illus.). 248p. (C). 1989. text ed. 44.95 (*0-8138-0307-1*) Iowa St U Pr.

Statistical Modeling for Computer-Aided Design of MOS VLSI Circuits. Christopher Michael & Mohammed I. Ismail. LC 92-35702. (Kluwer International Series in Engineering & Computer Science). 208p. (C). 1993. lib. bdg. 86.50 (*0-7923-9299-X*) Kluwer Ac.

Statistical Modeling in Hydrology. Robin T. Clarke. 412p. 1994. text ed. 95.00 (*0-471-95016-5*) Wiley.

Statistical Modeling Techniques. Shapiro & Gross. (Statistics: Textbooks & Monographs: Vol. 38). 384p. 1981. 99.75 (*0-8247-1387-7*) Dekker.

Statistical Modelling. Ed. by A. Decarli et al. (Lecture Notes in Statistics Ser.: Vol. 57). ix, 343p. 1989. 63.95 (*0-387-97097-5*) Spr-Verlag.

Statistical Modelling. Warren Gilchrist. LC 83-21584. (Illus.). 355p. reprint ed. pap. 101.20 (*0-8357-6432-X*, 2035803) Bks Demand.

Statistical Modelling: A Selection of Papers from the Sixth International Workshop on Statistical Modelling, Utrecht, The Netherlands, 15-19 July 1991. Ed. by P. G. Van Der Heijden et al. LC 92-25107. 344p. 1992. 165.00 (*0-444-89399-7*, North Holland) Elsevier.

Statistical Modelling: Proceedings of the 10th International Workshop on Statistical Modelling, Innsbruck, Austria, July 10-14, 1995. N. Wermuth et al. (Lecture Notes in Statistics Ser.: Vol. 104). (Illus.). 327p. 1995. 54.95 (*0-387-94565-2*) Spr-Verlag.

Statistical Modelling & Latent Variables. Ed. by Klaus Haagen et al. LC 93-13660. 366p. 1993. 197.75 (*0-444-89832-8*, North Holland) Elsevier.

Statistical Modelling in GLIM. Murray Aitken et al. (Oxford Statistical Science Ser.). (Illus.). 392p. 1989. 90.00 (*0-19-852204-5*); pap. 45.00 (*0-19-852203-7*) OUP.

***Statistical Models: Yang-Baxter EQ & Related Topics - Symmetry, Statistical Mechanical Models, & Applications.** 450p. 1996. lib. bdg. 60.00 (*981-02-2756-6*) World Scientific Pub.

Statistical Models & Methods for Lifetime Data. J. F. Lawless. LC 81-11446. (Probability & Mathematical Statistics Ser.). 580p. 1982. text ed. 110.00 (*0-471-08544-8*) Wiley.

Statistical Models & Their Experimental Applications. P. Ottestad. (Griffin's Statistical Monographs: No. 25). 88p. 1970. pap. text ed. 25.00 (*0-85264-166-4*) Lubrecht & Cramer.

Statistical Models Based on Counting Processes. Per K. Andersen et al. Ed. by J. O. Berger et al. LC 92-11354. (Series in Statistics). (Illus.). 832p. 1993. 69.00 (*0-387-97872-0*) Spr-Verlag.

Statistical Models Based on Counting Processes. P. K. Anderson et al. (Statistics Ser.). 767p. 1995. 39.95 (*3-540-94519-9*) Spr-Verlag.

Statistical Models for Causal Analysis. Robert D. Retherford & Minja K. Choe. 258p. 1993. text ed. 54.95 (*0-471-55802-8*) Wiley.

Statistical Models for Longitudinal Studies of Health. James H. Dwyer et al. (Monographs in Epidemiology & Biostatistics: No. 16). (Illus.). 400p. 1992. 59.50 (*0-19-505473-3*, 7312) OUP.

Statistical Models for Optimizing Mineral Exploration. T. K. Wignall & J. G. De Geoffroy. 446p. 1987. 120.00 (*0-306-42542-4*, Plenum Pr) Plenum.

Statistical Models for Ordinal Variables. Clifford C. Clogg & Edward S. Shihadeh. (Advanced Quantitative Techniques in the Social Sciences Ser.: Vol. 4). (C). 1994. text ed. 38.95 (*0-8039-3676-1*) Sage.

***Statistical Models for Strategic Management.** Michel Ghertman et al. LC 97-25698. 1997. write for info. (*0-7923-9970-6*) Kluwer Ac.

Statistical Models for the Fracture of Disordered Media. Ed. by H. J. Hermann & S. Roux. (Random Materials & Processes Ser.: Vol. 1). 354p. 1990. 141.50 (*0-444-88551-X*, RAP 2, North Holland); pap. 65.00 (*0-444-88550-1*, RAP 1, North Holland) Elsevier.

***Statistical Models for the Social & Behavioral Sciences: Multiple Regression & Limited-Dependent Variable Models.** William H. Crown. LC 97-5583. 1997. text ed. write for info. (*0-275-95316-5*, Praeger Pubs) Greenwood.

Statistical Models in Behavioral Research. W. K. Estes. 168p. 1991. pap. 19.95 (*0-8058-0688-1*) L Erlbaum Assocs.

Statistical Models in Engineering. Gerald J. Hahn & Samuel S. Shapiro. 355p. 1994. pap. text ed. 39.95 (*0-471-04065-7*) Wiley.

Statistical Models in Epidemiology. David Clayton & Michael Hills. (Illus.). 376p. (C). 1993. 54.95 (*0-19-852221-5*, 7713) OUP.

Statistical Models in Psychological & Educational Testing. D. N. De Gruijter & Leo J. Van der Kamp. x, 294p. 1984. pap. 59.00 (*90-265-0517-5*) Swets.

***Statistical Models in S.** Chambers & Hastie. (C). (gr. 13 up). 1991. text ed. 60.95 (*0-412-05291-1*); pap. text ed. 43.00 (*0-412-05301-2*) Chapman & Hall.

Statistical Models in S. John M. Chambers & Trevor J. Hastie. LC 91-17646. 600p. (C). 1992. text ed. 52.50 (*0-534-16764-0*) Chapman & Hall.

Statistical Models of the Temperature & Gaseous Components of the Atmosphere. Vladimir E. Zuev. (C). 1987. lib. bdg. 167.00 (*90-277-2466-0*) Kluwer Ac.

Statistical Multiple Integration. N. Flournoy & R. Tsutakawa. LC 90-27134. (Contemporary Mathematics Ser.: Vol. 115). 276p. 1991. pap. 74.00 (*0-8218-5122-5*, CONM/115) Am Math.

Statistical Operations: Analysis of Health Research Data. R. Hirsch & Richard K. Riegelman. LC 94-33711. (Illus.). 500p. 1995. pap. 49.95 incl. disk (*0-86542-258-3*) Blackwell Sci.

Statistical Optics. Joseph W. Goodman. LC 84-13160. (Pure & Applied Optics Ser.). 550p. 1985. text ed. 89.95 (*0-471-01502-4*, Wiley-Interscience) Wiley.

Statistical Optimization for Geometric Computation: Theory & Practice. Kenichi Kanatani. LC 96-207. 524p. 1996. 200.75 (*0-444-82427-8*) Elsevier.

Statistical Pattern Classification Using Contextual Information. King Fu & T. S. Yu. LC 80-40949. (Electronic & Electrical Engineering Research Ser.: Vol. 1). 201p. reprint ed. pap. 57.30 (*0-317-26335-8*, 2025199) Bks Demand.

Statistical Pattern of Instalment Debt. Ralph A. Young & Blanche Bernstein. (NBER Bulletin Ser.: No. 76/77). 1939. reprint ed. 20.00 (*0-685-61201-5*) Natl Bur Econ Res.

Statistical Physics. Tony Guenault. (Student Physics Ser.). 256p. 1988. pap. text ed. 17.95 (*0-415-00259-1*) Routledge.

Statistical Physics. Yu. L. Klimontovich. Tr. by G. Pontercorvo from RUS. xxvi, 734p. 1986. text ed. 484.00 (*3-7186-0323-3*) Gordon & Breach.

Statistical Physics. Ed. by R. Peralta & C. Varea. 248p. (C). 1988. text ed. 66.00 (*9971-5-0776-5*) World Scientific Pub.

Statistical Physics. Ed. by F. Ramos-Gomez. 160p. (C). 1991. text ed. 59.00 (*981-02-0584-8*) World Scientific Pub.

***Statistical Physics.** 2nd ed. Guenault. (Physics & Its Applications Ser.). (Illus.). 240p. (Orig.). 1995. pap. text ed. 22.00 (*0-412-57920-0*, Chap & Hall NY) Chapman & Hall.

Statistical Physics. 2nd ed. Franz Mandl. LC 87-8283. (Manchester Physics Ser.). (Illus.). 406p. reprint ed. pap. 115.80 (*0-8357-3091-3*, 2039348) Bks Demand.

Statistical Physics. 2nd ed. Franz Mandl. LC 87-8283. (Manchester Physics Ser.). 386p. 1988. pap. text ed. 49.95 (*0-471-91533-5*) Wiley.

Statistical Physics. Gregory H. Wannier. xii, 532p. 1987. reprint ed. pap. text ed. 12.95 (*0-486-65401-X*) Dover.

Statistical Physics: A Probabilistic Approach. Beranrd H. Lavenda. LC 91-15687. 384p. 1991. text ed. 115.00 (*0-471-54607-0*) Wiley.

Statistical Physics see Berkeley Physics Course

Statistical Physics & Chaos in Fusion Plasmas. Ed. by C. W. Horton, Jr. & L. E. Reichl. 378p. 1984. 105.00 (*0-471-88310-7*) Krieger.

Statistical Physics & Condensed Matter Theory: Proceedings of the Sino-Japan Bilateral Workshop on Statistical Physics & Condensed Matter Theory, Shanghai, China, April 8-12, 1986. Ed. by Xide D. Xie. 396p. 1986. text ed. 100.00 (*9971-5-0148-1*) World Scientific Pub.

Statistical Physics & the Atomic Theory of Matter: From Boyle & Newton to Landau & Onsager. Stephen G. Brush. LC 82-61357. (Princeton Series in Physics). 367p. reprint ed. pap. 104.60 (*0-7837-0247-7*, 2040556) Bks Demand.

Statistical Physics & Thermodynamics of Nonlinear Equilibrium Systems. W. Muschik & W. Ebeling. 268p. 1993. text ed. 95.00 (*981-02-1134-1*) World Scientific Pub.

Statistical Physics, Automata Networks & Dynamical Systems. Ed. by Eric Goles. (Mathematics & Its Applications, West Ser.). 220p. (C). 1992. lib. bdg. 126.00 (*0-7923-1595-2*) Kluwer Ac.

Statistical Physics for Students of Science & Engineering. Robert D. Reed & R. R. Roy. (Illus.). xi, 320p. 1995. pap. text ed. 10.95 (*0-486-68568-3*) Dover.

Statistical Physics I: Equilibrium Statistical Mechanics. 2nd rev. ed. Morikazu Toda et al. Ed. by M. Cardona et al. (Series in Solid-State Sciences: Vol. 30). 252p. 1995. 49.95 (*0-387-53662-0*) Spr-Verlag.

Statistical Physics II: Nonequilibrium Statistical Mechanics, Vol. XVI. 2nd rev. ed. R. Kubo et al. Ed. by M. Cardona et al. Tr. by N. Saito et al. from JPN. (Series in Solid-State Sciences: Vol. 31). (Illus.). 279p. 1995. 49.95 (*0-387-53833-X*) Spr-Verlag.

***Statistical Physics of Crystal Growth.** Yukio Saito. LC 96-27446. 1996. write for info. (*981-02-2834-1*) World Scientific Pub.

***Statistical Physics of Fracture & Breakdown in Disordered Systems.** Bikas K. Chakrabarti & L. Gilles Benuigui. (Monographs on the Physics & Chemistry of Materials: No. 55). (Illus.). 176p. 1997. 85.00 (*0-19-852056-5*) OUP.

Statistical Physics of Macromolecules. A. R. Khoklov & A. Grosberg. (Polymers & Complex Materials Ser.). (Illus.). 400p. 1994. text ed. 80.00 (*1-56396-071-0*, AIP) Am Inst Physics.

Statistical Physics 2. R. Kubo et al. (Solid-State Sciences Ser.: Vol. 31). (Illus.). 295p. 1985. 59.00 (*0-387-11461-0*) Spr-Verlag.

Statistical Pioneers. James W. Tankard, Jr. 168p. 1984. 19.95 (*0-87073-408-3*); pap. 13.95 (*0-87073-409-1*) Schenkman Bks Inc.

Statistical Plasma Physics, Vol. 2: Condensed Particles. Setsuo Ichimaru. (C). 1994. 55.95 (*0-201-55491-7*) Addison-Wesley.

Statistical Plasma Physics 1: Basic Principles: Frontiers in Physics, Vol. 87. Setsuo Ichimaru. (C). 1992. 50.95 (*0-201-55490-9*) Addison-Wesley.

Statistical Pocket Book Nepal 1994. 1994. pap. 25.00 (*0-7855-0484-2*, Pub. by Ratna Pustak Bhandar) St Mut.

Statistical Pocket Book of Nepal 1992. Ed. by Ratna P. Bhandar. (C). 1992. 30.00 (*0-7855-0214-9*, Pub. by Ratna Pustak Bhandar) St Mut.

Statistical Pocket Book 1994. 1994. pap. 25.00 (*0-7855-0482-6*, Pub. by Ratna Pustak Bhandar) St Mut.

Statistical Power Analysis: A Computer Program. 2nd ed. Michael Borenstein & Jacob Cohen. 1989. disk 10.00 (*1-56321-006-1*); disk 125.00 (*1-56321-008-8*); disk 10.00 (*1-56321-010-X*) L Erlbaum Assocs.

Statistical Power Analysis: A Computer Program. 2nd ed. Michael Borenstein & Jacob Cohen. 567p. 1989. Incl. 3 1/2" disk. student ed. 140.00 incl. disk (*1-56321-009-6*) L Erlbaum Assocs.

Statistical Power Analysis for the Behavioral Sciences. Jacob Cohen. 567p. (C). 1988. 89.95 (*0-8058-0283-5*) L Erlbaum Assocs.

Statistical Prediction by Discriminant Analysis. Robert G. Miller. (Meteorological Monograph: Vol. 4. No. 25). (Illus.). 54p. (Orig.). 1962. pap. 17.00 (*0-933876-13-0*) Am Meteorological.

Statistical Primer for Real Estate Problem Solving. 88p. 1989. 12.50 (*0-685-45283-2*) Couns Real Estate.

Statistical Principles in Experimental Design, Third Edition. 3rd ed. Benjamin J. Winer et al. (Psychology Ser.). 1991. text ed. write for info. (*0-07-070982-3*) McGraw.

Statistical Principles of Research Design & Analysis. Robert O. Kuehl. 686p. 1994. text ed. 75.95 (*0-534-18804-4*) Wadsworth Pub.

Statistical Problem Solving in Quality Engineering. T. J. Kazmierski. LC 95-12017. 1995. 59.00 (*0-07-034048-X*) McGraw.

Statistical Problem Solving (SPS) A Team Process for Identifying & Resolving Problems. Hans J. Bajaria & Richard P. Copp. (Illus.). 300p. 1991. 44.95 (*0-9629223-0-7*) Multiface Pub.

***Statistical Problems in Modern Life.** 5th ed. Newmark. (C). 1992. suppl. ed., pap. write for info. (*0-03-076299-5*) HB Coll Pubs.

Statistical Problems with Nuisance Parameters. Jurii V. Linnik. Tr. by S. Technica. LC 67-30101. (Translations of Mathematical Monographs: Vol. 20). 258p. 1968. 44.00 (*0-8218-1570-9*, MMONO/20) Am Math.

***Statistical Procedures Analysis.** McBean & Rovers. 1997. text ed. 70.00 (*0-13-675018-4*) P-H.

Statistical Procedures for Agricultural Research. 2nd ed. Kwanchai A. Gomez & Arturo A. Gomez. LC 83-14556. 680p. 1984. text ed. 99.95 (*0-471-87092-7*) Wiley.

Statistical Procedures for Engineering, Management & Science. Leland T. Blank. (Industrial Engineering & Management Science Ser.). (Illus.). 1980. text ed. write for info. (*0-07-005851-2*) McGraw.

***Statistical Process Control.** Alwan. 1998. text ed. 54.80 (*0-256-11939-2*) McGraw.

Statistical Process Control. Ed. by Charles L. Mamzic. LC 94-9020. (Practical Guides for Measurement & Control Ser.). 325p. 1994. 145.00 (*1-55617-511-6*) ISA.

Statistical Process Control. Multimedia Development Services Staff. (Plant Fundamentals Ser.: Vol. X, Module II). (Illus.). 1995. teacher ed. 65.00 (*1-57431-072-0*); student ed. 30.00 (*1-57431-032-1*) Tech Trng Systs.

Statistical Process Control. 2nd ed. Leonard A. Doty. LC 95-44408. 1996. 38.95 (*0-8311-3069-5*) Indus Pr.

Statistical Process Control. 2nd ed. John S. Oakland & Roy F. Followell. (Illus.). 431p. 1990. 74.95 (*0-434-91484-3*) Buttrwrth-Heinemann.

Statistical Process Control. 3rd ed. John S. Oakland. (Illus.). 352p. 1996. 74.95 (*0-7506-2464-7*) Buttrwrth-Heinemann.

Statistical Process Control: How to Implement in a Corrugated Box Plant Seminar, Chicago, IL, October 29-30, 1987. Technical Association of the Pulp & Paper Industry Staff. (TAPPI Notes Ser.). (Illus.). 331p. reprint ed. pap. 94.40 (*0-685-23334-0*, 2032260) Bks Demand.

Statistical Process Control: Theory & Practice. 3rd ed. G. Barrie Wetherill & Don W. Brown. 320p. (gr. 13). 1991. text ed. 78.95 (*0-412-35700-3*, A5026) Chapman & Hall.

Statistical Process Control & Beyond. Richard R. Clements. LC 87-4086. 314p. 1988. lib. bdg. 31.50 (*0-89874-992-1*) Krieger.

Statistical Process Control & Quality Improvement. 2nd ed. Gerald Smith. LC 94-11705. 573p. (C). 1994. text ed. 77.00 (*0-02-412552-0*, Macmillan Coll) P-H.

***Statistical Process Control & Quality Improvement.** 3rd ed. Smith. LC 97-13326. (C). 1997. text ed. 65.00 (*0-13-617846-4*) P-H.

***Statistical Process Control Explained: The Easy-To-Understand Guide to SPC.** H. James Harrington. (Illus.). 300p. 1997. pap. text ed., pap. 29.95 incl. cd-rom (*0-07-856636-3*) McGraw.

Statistical Process Control for Quality Improvement. James R. Thompson & Jacek Koronacki. LC 92-21144. 391p. (gr. 13). 1992. pap. text ed. 36.95 (*0-412-03431-X*) Chapman & Hall.

Statistical Process Control for Quality Improvement. James R. Thompson & Jacek Koronacki. LC 92-21144. 391p. (gr. 13). 1993. text ed. 84.95 (*0-412-03421-2*) Chapman & Hall.

Statistical Process Control for Quality Improvement: A Training Guide to Learning SPC. James R. Evans. 224p. 1991. text ed. 65.00 (*0-13-558990-8*, 140301) P-H.

An Asterisk (*) at the beginning of an entry indicates that the title is appearing in BIP for the first time.

Statistical Process Control in Automated Manufacturing. Keats & Hubele. (Quality & Reliability Ser.: Vol. 15). 312p. 1988. 125.00 (*0-8247-7889-8*) Dekker.

Statistical Process Control in Manufacturing. Keats & Montgomery. (Quality & Reliability Ser.: Vol. 23). 392p. 1991. 99.75 (*0-8247-8467-7*) Dekker.

Statistical Process Control in the Steel Industry: International Symposium, August 18-21, 1985, Vancouver, BC, Canada. International Symposium on Statistical Process Control in the Steel Industry (1985: Vancouver, BC) Staff. LC 85-196851. (Illus.). 219p. reprint ed. pap. 62.50 (*0-8357-3713-6*, 2036435) Bks Demand.

Statistical Process Control Methods for Long & Short Runs. 2nd ed. Gary K. Griffith. 250p. 1995. pap. 37.00 (*0-87389-345-X*, H0900) ASQC Qual Pr.

Statistical Process Control Technologies: State of the Art for the Forest Products Industry. 101p. 1995. 45.00 (*0-935018-73-5*, 7307) Forest Prod.

Statistical Process Control, 1990: An Introduction for Box Makers Seminar. Technical Association of the Pulp & Paper Industry Staff. (TAPPI Notes Ser.). (Illus.). 383p. reprint ed. pap. 109.20 (*0-8357-4083-8*, 2036773) Bks Demand.

Statistical Profile of the Chinese in the United States. Betty L. Sung. Ed. by Roger Daniels. LC 78-54832. (Asian Experience in North America Ser.). 1979. reprint ed. lib. bdg. 15.95 (*0-405-11289-0*) Ayer.

Statistical Profile on Nepalese Women: An Update in the Policy Context. Madhu R. Acharya. 1994. pap. 30.00 (*0-7855-0486-9*, Pub. by Ratna Pustak Bhandar) St Mut.

Statistical Proof of Discrimination. David C. Baldus & James L. Cole. 386p. 1980. text ed. 95.00 (*0-07-003470-2*) Shepards.

Statistical Properties of the Generalized Inverse Gaussian Distribution. B. Jorgensen. (Lecture Notes in Statistics Ser.: Vol. 9). (Illus.). 188p. 1981. 47.95 (*0-387-90665-7*) Spr-Verlag.

Statistical Quality Assurance. Francis J. Guldner. LC 86-6387. 298p. (C). 1987. teacher ed. 16.00 (*0-8273-2666-1*); text ed. 49.50 (*0-8273-2665-3*) Delmar.

Statistical Quality Control. Miles O. Weaver. (C). pap. 25.00 (*0-923231-27-7*) Mohican Pub.

Statistical Quality Control. 7th ed. Eugene L. Grant & Richard S. Leavenworth. (Series in Industrial Engineering & Management Science). 720p. 1995. 56.00 (*0-07-024162-7*) McGraw.

Statistical Quality Control. 7th ed. Eugene L. Grant & Richard S. Leavenworth. 1996. text ed. write for info. (*0-07-844354-7*) McGraw.

Statistical Quality Control. Ed. by Warren H. Klippel. LC 84-50170. (Illus.). 277p. reprint ed. pap. 79.00 (*0-7837-6272-0*, 2045987) Bks Demand.

***Statistical Quality Control: A Loss Minimization Approach.** (Applied Mathematics Ser.). 400p. 1998. 46.00 (*981-02-3031-1*) World Scientific Pub.

Statistical Quality Control for Manufacturing Managers. William S. Messina. LC 86-34022. (Engineering Management Ser.). 331p. 1987. text ed. 89.95 (*0-471-85774-2*) Wiley.

Statistical Quality Control for the Food Industry. 2nd ed. Merton R. Hubbard. LC 95-44229. 344p. (gr. 13). 1996. text ed. 64.95 (*0-412-07661-6*) Chapman & Hall.

Statistical Quality Control Handbook. Ed. by Bonnie B. Small. (Illus.). 328p. (C). 1956. text ed. 29.95 (*0-932764-12-6*, 700-444) AT&T Customer Info.

Statistical Quality Control in High Reliability Systems. Lance A. Matheson. LC 93-34976. (Studies on Industrial Productivity). 120p. 1993. text ed. 44.00 (*0-8153-1628-3*) Garland.

Statistical Quality Control Methods. Irving Burr. (Statistics: Textbooks & Monographs: Vol. 16). 536p. 1976. 69.75 (*0-8247-6344-0*) Dekker.

Statistical Quality Control Using the SAS System. Dennis W. King. 383p. (C). 1996. pap. 38.95 (*1-55544-280-3*, BR55232) SAS Inst.

Statistical Quality Control with Microcomputer Applications. Larry E. Shirland. (Series in Production-Operations Management). 416p. 1993. pap. text ed. 29.50 (*0-471-61984-1*); pap. text ed. 29.50 (*0-471-58246-8*) Wiley.

Statistical Reasoning. 3rd ed. Smith. 1994. pap. text ed. write for info. (*0-07-059227-6*) McGraw.

Statistical Reasoning: Lab Manual with Excel 5. Lehmann. (Statistics Ser.). 1998. lab manual ed., pap. 20.95 incl. disk (*0-534-51611-4*) Wadsworth Pub.

Statistical Reasoning for the Behavioral Sciences. 3rd ed. Richard J. Shavelson. 1996. text ed. 69.00 (*0-205-18460-X*) Allyn.

Statistical Reasoning in Law & Public Policy, Vol. 1: Statistical Concepts & Issues of Fairness. Joseph L. Gastwirth. (Statistical Modeling & Decision Science Ser.). 465p. 1988. text ed. 83.00 (*0-12-277160-5*) Acad Pr.

Statistical Reasoning in Law & Public Policy, Vol. 2: Tort Law, Evidence & Health. Joseph L. Gastwirth. (Statistical Modeling & Decision Science Ser.). 450p. 1988. text ed. 83.00 (*0-12-277161-3*) Acad Pr.

Statistical Reasoning in Psychology & Education. 3rd ed. E. W. Minium et al. 280p. 1993. student ed., wbk. ed., pap. 17.00 (*0-471-82473-9*) Wiley.

Statistical Reasoning in Psychology & Education. 3rd ed. Edward W. Minium. LC 92-33570. 608p. (C). 1993. text ed. 44.50 (*0-471-82188-8*) Wiley.

Statistical Reasoning with Imprecise Probabilities. P. Walley. (Monographs on Statistics & Applied Probability: No. 42). 600p. (gr. 13). 1991. text ed. 166.95 (*0-412-28660-2*, A5015) Chapman & Hall.

Statistical Record: Of the Armies of the United States. fac. ed. Frederick Phisterer. Ed. & Intro. by John D. Kallmann. 343p. 1996. 29.95 (*0-9650926-1-5*, L-1002) J Kallmann.

Statistical Record of Asian-Americans: Comprehensive Coverage of Americans & Canadians of Asian-Pacific Islander Descent. Ed. by Susan B. Gall & Timothy L. Gall. 750p. 1993. 105.00 (*0-8103-8918-5*, 101609) Gale.

Statistical Record of Black America. 4th ed. Horton. 1996. 109.00 (*0-8103-9252-6*) Gale.

Statistical Record of Black America, 1990. Ed. by Carrell Horton & Jessie C. Smith. (Illus.). 1000p. 1990. 89.50 (*0-8103-7724-1*) Gale.

Statistical Record of Black Americans, 1993, Vol. 1. 2nd ed. Horton. 1992. 95.00 (*0-8103-8351-9*) Gale.

Statistical Record of Black Americans 1995. 3rd ed. Horton. 1994. 99.00 (*0-8103-8419-1*) Gale.

Statistical Record of Children. Ed. by Linda Schmittroth. 900p. 1994. 109.00 (*0-8103-9196-1*) Gale.

Statistical Record of Children. 2nd ed. Linda Schmittroth. 1998. 109.00 (*0-8103-6430-1*) Gale.

***Statistical Record of Health & Medicine.** 2nd ed. Ed. by Charity A. Dorgan. 1200p. 1997. 115.00 (*0-614-27180-0*) Gale.

Statistical Record of Health & Medicine. 94th ed. Ed. by Charity Anne Dorgan. (Illus.). 1218p. 1994. 109.00 (*0-8103-9745-5*) Gale.

Statistical Record of Hispanic Americans. Ed. by Peggy Bessette. 1224p. 1993. 99.00 (*0-8103-8962-2*, 101756) Gale.

Statistical Record of Hispanic Americans. 2nd ed. Ed. by Marlita A. Reddy. 1100p. 1995. 109.00 (*0-8103-6422-0*, 102121) Gale.

***Statistical Record of Hispanic Americans.** 3rd ed. 1998. 109.00 (*0-7876-0072-5*, 00108723, Gale Res Intl) Gale.

Statistical Record of Native North Americans. 2nd ed. Ed. by Marlita A. Reddy. 1400p. 1995. 109.00 (*0-8103-6421-2*, 102120) Gale.

***Statistical Record of Native North Americans.** 3rd ed. 1998. 109.00 (*0-7876-0618-9*, 00153072, Gale Res Intl) Gale.

Statistical Record of Native North Americans: Current & Historical Data. Ed. by Marlita A. Reddy. 750p. 1993. 99.00 (*0-8103-8963-0*, 101755) Gale.

Statistical Record of Older Americans. Ed. by Arsen J. Darnay. 800p. 1993. 109.00 (*0-8103-9198-8*, M89334-101911) Gale.

Statistical Record of Older Americans. 2nd ed. Darnay. 1996. 109.00 (*0-8103-6431-X*) Gale.

Statistical Record of Religions in America, 1. J. Gordon Melton. 1996. 105.00 (*0-8103-9197-X*) Gale.

***Statistical Record of the Environment.** 4th ed. 1997. 109.00 (*0-7876-0071-7*, 00108722, Gale Res Intl) Gale.

Statistical Record of the Environment Worldwide. 1991. 89.50 (*0-8103-8374-8*) Gale.

Statistical Record of the Environment Worldwide 2. 2nd ed. Ed. by Arsen J. Darnay. 850p. 1993. 105.00 (*0-8103-8863-4*, 101555) Gale.

Statistical Record of the Environment 3. 3rd ed. Ed. by Charity Anne Dorgan. 1118p. 1995. 109.00 (*0-8103-6432-8*) Gale.

Statistical Record of Women Worldwide. 2nd ed. Ed. & Compiled by Linda Schmittroth. LC 95-37853. 1047p. 1995. 99.00 (*0-8103-8872-3*) Gale.

Statistical Record of Women Worldwide 1. John Schmittroth, Jr. 1991. 99.00 (*0-8103-8349-7*) Gale.

Statistical Reference Index Annual, 1994, 2 vols. Ed. by Congressional Information Service, Inc., Staff. 1912p. 1995. write for info. (*0-88692-321-2*) Cong Info.

Statistical Reference Index Annual, 1994 Abstracts Volume. Ed. by Congressional Information Service, Inc., Staff. 1995. write for info. (*0-88692-323-9*) Cong Info.

Statistical Reference Index Annual, 1994 Index Volume. Ed. by Congressional Information Service, Inc., Staff. 1995. write for info. (*0-88692-322-0*) Cong Info.

Statistical Reference Index 1980, 2 vols. Ed. by Congressional Information Service, Inc., Staff. 1981. write for info. (*0-912380-86-1*) Cong Info.

Statistical Reference Index 1980, Abstracts Volume. Ed. by Congressional Information Service, Inc., Staff. 1981. write for info. (*0-912380-88-8*) Cong Info.

Statistical Reference Index 1980, Index Volume. Ed. by Congressional Information Service, Inc., Staff. 1981. write for info. (*0-912380-87-X*) Cong Info.

Statistical Reference Index 1980-1985 Cumulative Index, 4 vols. Ed. by Congressional Information Service, Inc., Staff. 1986. write for info. (*0-88692-101-5*) Cong Info.

Statistical Reference Index 1980-1985 Cumulative Index (A-E) Ed. by Congressional Information Service, Inc., Staff. 1986. write for info. (*0-88692-102-3*) Cong Info.

Statistical Reference Index 1980-1985 Cumulative Index (F-N) Ed. by Congressional Information Service, Inc., Staff. 1986. write for info. (*0-88692-103-1*) Cong Info.

Statistical Reference Index 1980-1985 Cumulative Index (O-Z) Ed. by Congressional Information Service, Inc., Staff. 1986. write for info. (*0-88692-104-X*) Cong Info.

Statistical Reference Index 1980-1985 Cumulative Index (Supp.) Ed. by Congressional Information Service, Inc., Staff. 1986. write for info. (*0-88692-105-8*) Cong Info.

Statistical Reference Index 1981, 2 vols. Ed. by Congressional Information Service, Inc., Staff. 1982. write for info. (*0-912380-89-6*) Cong Info.

Statistical Reference Index 1981, Abstracts Volume. Ed. by Congressional Information Service, Inc., Staff. 1982. write for info. (*0-912380-91-8*) Cong Info.

Statistical Reference Index 1981, Index Volume. Ed. by Congressional Information Service, Inc., Staff. 1982. write for info. (*0-912380-90-X*) Cong Info.

Statistical Reference Index 1982, 2 vols. Ed. by Congressional Information Service, Inc., Staff. 1983. write for info. (*0-912380-06-3*) Cong Info.

Statistical Reference Index 1982, Abstracts Volume. Ed. by Congressional Information Service, Inc., Staff. 1983. write for info. (*0-912380-08-X*) Cong Info.

Statistical Reference Index 1982, Index Volume. Ed. by Congressional Information Service, Inc., Staff. 1983. write for info. (*0-912380-07-1*) Cong Info.

Statistical Reference Index 1983, 2 vols. Ed. by Congressional Information Service, Inc., Staff. 1984. write for info. (*0-88692-014-0*) Cong Info.

Statistical Reference Index 1983, Abstracts Volume. Ed. by Congressional Information Service, Inc., Staff. 1984. write for info. (*0-88692-015-9*) Cong Info.

Statistical Reference Index 1983, Index Volume. Ed. by Congressional Information Service, Inc., Staff. 1984. write for info. (*0-88692-016-7*) Cong Info.

Statistical Reference Index 1984, 2 vols. Ed. by Congressional Information Service, Inc., Staff. 1985. write for info. (*0-88692-040-X*) Cong Info.

Statistical Reference Index 1984, Abstracts Volume. Ed. by Congressional Information Service, Inc., Staff. 1985. write for info. (*0-88692-041-8*) Cong Info.

Statistical Reference Index 1984, Index Volume. Ed. by Congressional Information Service, Inc., Staff. 1985. write for info. (*0-88692-042-6*) Cong Info.

Statistical Reference Index 1985, 2 vols. Ed. by Congressional Information Service, Inc., Staff. 1986. write for info. (*0-88692-082-5*) Cong Info.

Statistical Reference Index 1985, Abstracts Volume. Ed. by Congressional Information Service, Inc., Staff. 1986. write for info. (*0-88692-083-3*) Cong Info.

Statistical Reference Index 1985, Index Volume. Ed. by Congressional Information Service, Inc., Staff. 1986. write for info. (*0-88692-084-1*) Cong Info.

Statistical Reference Index 1986, 2 vols. Ed. by Congressional Information Service, Inc., Staff. 1987. write for info. (*0-88692-111-2*) Cong Info.

Statistical Reference Index 1986, Abstracts Volume. Ed. by Congressional Information Service, Inc., Staff. 1987. write for info. (*0-88692-112-0*) Cong Info.

Statistical Reference Index 1986, Index Volume. Ed. by Congressional Information Service, Inc., Staff. 1987. write for info. (*0-88692-113-9*) Cong Info.

Statistical Reference Index 1986-1989 Cumulative Index, 4 vols. Ed. by Congressional Information Service, Inc., Staff. 1990. write for info. (*0-88692-201-1*) Cong Info.

Statistical Reference Index 1987, 2 vols. Ed. by Congressional Information Service, Inc., Staff. 1988. write for info. (*0-88692-135-X*) Cong Info.

Statistical Reference Index 1987, Abstracts Volume. Ed. by Congressional Information Service, Inc., Staff. 1988. write for info. (*0-88692-136-8*) Cong Info.

Statistical Reference Index 1987, Index Volume. Ed. by Congressional Information Service, Inc., Staff. 1988. write for info. (*0-88692-137-6*) Cong Info.

Statistical Reference Index 1988, 2 vols. Ed. by Congressional Information Service, Inc., Staff. 1989. write for info. (*0-88692-160-0*) Cong Info.

Statistical Reference Index 1988, Abstracts Volume. Ed. by Congressional Information Service, Inc., Staff. 1989. write for info. (*0-88692-162-7*) Cong Info.

Statistical Reference Index 1988, Index Volume. Ed. by Congressional Information Service, Inc., Staff. 1989. write for info. (*0-88692-161-9*) Cong Info.

Statistical Reference Index 1989, 2 vols. Ed. by Congressional Information Service, Inc., Staff. 1990. write for info. (*0-88692-182-1*) Cong Info.

Statistical Reference Index 1989, Abstracts Volume. Ed. by Congressional Information Service, Inc., Staff. 1990. write for info. (*0-88692-184-8*) Cong Info.

Statistical Reference Index 1989, Index Volume. Ed. by Congressional Information Service, Inc., Staff. 1990. write for info. (*0-88692-183-X*) Cong Info.

Statistical Reference Index 1990, 2 vols. Ed. by Congressional Information Service, Inc., Staff. 1991. write for info. (*0-88692-208-9*) Cong Info.

Statistical Reference Index 1990, Abstracts Volume. Ed. by Congressional Information Service, Inc., Staff. 1991. write for info. (*0-88692-210-0*) Cong Info.

Statistical Reference Index 1990, Index Volume. Ed. by Congressional Information Service, Inc., Staff. 1991. write for info. (*0-88692-209-7*) Cong Info.

Statistical Reference Index 1990-1993 Cumulative Index, 4 vols. Ed. by Congressional Information Service, Inc., Staff. 1994. write for info. (*0-88692-305-0*) Cong Info.

Statistical Reference Index 1991, 2 vols. Ed. by Congressional Information Service, Inc., Staff. 1992. write for info. (*0-88692-233-X*) Cong Info.

Statistical Reference Index 1991, Abstracts Volume. Ed. by Congressional Information Service, Inc., Staff. 1992. write for info. (*0-88692-235-6*) Cong Info.

Statistical Reference Index 1991, Index Volume. Ed. by Congressional Information Service, Inc., Staff. 1992. write for info. (*0-88692-234-8*) Cong Info.

Statistical Reference Index 1992, 2 vols. Ed. by Congressional Information Service, Inc., Staff. 1993. write for info. (*0-88692-259-3*) Cong Info.

Statistical Reference Index 1992, Abstracts Volume. Ed. by Congressional Information Service, Inc., Staff. 1993. write for info. (*0-88692-261-5*) Cong Info.

Statistical Reference Index 1992, Index Volume. Ed. by Congressional Information Service, Inc., Staff. 1993. write for info. (*0-88692-260-7*) Cong Info.

Statistical Reference Index 1993, 2 vols. Ed. by Congressional Information Service, Inc., Staff. 1994. write for info. (*0-88692-290-9*) Cong Info.

Statistical Reference Index 1993, Abstracts Volume. Ed. by Congressional Information Service, Inc., Staff. 1994. write for info. (*0-88692-292-5*) Cong Info.

Statistical Reference Index 1993, Index Volume. Ed. by Congressional Information Service, Inc., Staff. 1994. write for info. (*0-88692-291-7*) Cong Info.

Statistical Reliability Theory. I. B. Gertsbakh. (Probability Ser.: Vol. 4). 352p. 1988. 140.00 (*0-8247-8019-1*) Dekker.

Statistical Report on Profit, Sales, Production & Marketing Trends for the Men's & Boys' Tailored Clothing Industry - November, 1985. 21p. 1985. 20.00 (*0-318-19704-9*) Clothing Mfrs.

Statistical Report on Profit, Sales, Production & Marketing Trends for the Men's & Boys' Tailored Clothing Industry - October, 1984. 21p. 1984. 20.00 (*0-318-19700-6*) Clothing Mfrs.

Statistical Report on Profits, Sales, Production & Marketing Trends for the Men's & Boy's Tailored Clothing Industry. 21p. 1986. 20.00 (*0-318-41804-5*) Clothing Mfrs.

Statistical Report on Profits, Sales, Production & Marketing Trends for the Men's & Boy's Tailored Clothing Industry. 20p. 1988. 20.00 (*0-318-41807-X*) Clothing Mfrs.

Statistical Report on Profits, Sales, Production & Marketing Trends for the Men's & Boy's Tailored Clothing Industry. 1994. 25.00 (*0-685-72039-X*) Clothing Mfrs.

Statistical Report on Profits, Sales, Production & Marketing Trends for the Men's & Boy's Tailored Clothing Industry. 1995. 25.00 (*0-614-05675-6*) Clothing Mfrs.

***Statistical Report on Profits, Sales, Production & Marketing Trends for the Men's & Boy's Tailored Clothing Industry.** 1998. pap. 25.00 (*0-614-30634-5*) Clothing Mfrs.

Statistical Report on Profits, Sales, Production & Marketing Trends for the Men's & Boy's Tailored Clothing Industry. 21p. 1987. 20.00 (*0-318-41805-3*) Clothing Mfrs.

Statistical Report on Profits, Sales, Production & Marketing Trends for the Men's & Boys' Tailored Clothing Industry. 1993. 25.00 (*0-685-69524-7*) Clothing Mfrs.

Statistical Report on Profits, Sales, Production & Marketing Trends for the Men's & Boy's Tailored Clothing Industry, 1989. 1989. 25.00 (*0-685-64979-2*) Clothing Mfrs.

Statistical Report on Profits, Sales, Production & Marketing Trends for the Men's & Boy's Tailored Clothing Industry, 1990. 1990. 25.00 (*0-685-64980-6*) Clothing Mfrs.

Statistical Report on Profits, Sales, Production & Marketing Trends for the Men's & Boy's Tailored Clothing Industry, 1991. 1991. 25.00 (*0-685-64981-4*) Clothing Mfrs.

Statistical Report on Profits, Sales, Production & Marketing Trends for the Men's & Boy's Tailored Clothing Industry, 1992. 1992. 25.00 (*0-685-64982-2*) Clothing Mfrs.

Statistical Report on Road Accidents in 1990. OECD Staff. 80p. (Orig.). 1992. pap. 27.00 (*92-821-0174-6*) OECD.

Statistical Report on Road Accidents in 1991. OECD Staff. 81p. (Orig.). (ENG & FRE.). 1993. pap. 23.00 (*92-821-0176-2*) OECD.

Statistical Report on the Languages of the World as of 1985, Part III: Languages of the World Arranged According to Continents & Countries. (Bibliotheca Nostratica Ser.: Vol. 6: 3). 224p. 1988. pap. 26.00 (*0-931922-31-3*) Eurolingua.

Statistical Report on the Languages of the World As of 1985, Pt. I. 2nd ed. Ed. by Gyula Decsy. (Bibliotheca Nostratica Ser.: Vol. 6: 1). 98p. 1990. 26.00 (*0-931922-41-0*) Eurolingua.

Statistical Report on the Languages of the World As of 1985, Pt. II. (Bibliotheca Nostratica Ser.: Vol. 6: 2). 112p. 1987. 26.00 (*0-8315-2227-5*) Eurolingua.

Statistical Reports on Road Accidents in 1992. OECD Staff. 68p. (Orig.). 1994. pap. 25.00 (*92-64-04267-9*) OECD.

Statistical Risk Model for Forecasting Nuclear Proliferation. Stephen M. Meyer. (CISA Working Papers: No. 41). 29p. (Orig.). 1983. pap. 15.00 (*0-86682-053-1*) Ctr Intl Relations.

Statistical Sampling: Past, Present & Future Theoretical & Practical. Milton J. Kowalewski & John B. Tye. LC 90-45081. (Special Technical Publication Ser.: No. 1097). (Illus.). 96p. 1990. text ed. 19.00 (*0-8031-1400-1*, 04-010970-34) ASTM.

Statistical Sampling for Audit & Control. Thomas W. McRae. LC 73-19329. (Wiley-Interscience Publications). 299p. reprint ed. pap. 85.30 (*0-7837-4518-4*, 2044297) Bks Demand.

Statistical Science in Economics, Vol. I. 4th ed. V. V. Shvyrkov. LC 83-50656. (Illus.). 187p. (C). 1983. student ed. 19.20 (*0-942004-08-6*) Throwkoff Pr.

Statistical Science in Economics, Vol. II. V. V. Shvyrkov. LC 84-90294. (Illus.). 188p. (C). 1984. student ed. 19.99 (*0-942004-11-6*) Throwkoff Pr.

Statistical Sciences & Data Analysis: Proceedings of the Third Pacific Area Statistica Conference. Ed. by K. Matusita et al. x, 570p. 1993. 295.00 (*90-6764-150-2*) Coronet Bks.

Statistical Sequential Analysis. A. N. Sirjaev. Tr. by L. Rosenblatt & J. Rosenblatt. LC 73-445. (Translations of Mathematical Monographs: Vol. 38). 174p. 1973. 58.00 (*0-8218-1588-1*, MMONO/38) Am Math.

Statistical Services Directory. 2nd ed. 464p. 1984. 200.00 (*0-8103-0668-9*) Gale.

Statistical Signal Characterization. Herbert L. Hirsch. (Radar Library). 296p. 1991. text ed. 59.00 (*0-89006-515-2*) Artech Hse.

Statistical Signal Characterization Algorithms & Analysis Programs. Herbert L. Hirsch. 1992. 70.00 (*0-89006-631-0*) Artech Hse.

S

Statistical Signal Processing: Detection, Estimation, & Time Series Analysis. Louis L. Scharf. (A-E Series in Electrical Engineering, Digital Signal Processing). (Illus.). (C). 1991. text ed. 76.50 (*0-201-19038-9*) Addison-Wesley.

Statistical Significance: Rationale, Validity & Unity. Siu L. Chow. 208p. 1996. 69.95 (*0-7619-5204-7*) Sage.

***Statistical Significance: Rationale, Validity, & Utility.** Siu L. Chow. 208p. 1996. pap. 26.95 (*0-7619-5205-5*) Sage.

***Statistical Sleuth: A Course in Methods of Data Analysis.** Fred L. Ramsey & Daniel W. Schafer. LC 96-35423. (C). 1997. text ed. 74.95 (*0-534-25380-6*) Wadsworth Pub.

Statistical Software: A Comparative Review. Ivor Francis. LC 81-12568. 560p. reprint ed. pap. 159.60 (*0-685-20507-X*, 2029965) Bks Demand.

Statistical Software Engineering. National Research Council, Panel on Statistical Methods in Software Engineering. 84p. (Orig.). 1996. pap. text ed. 29.00 (*0-309-05344-7*) Natl Acad Pr.

Statistical Sources & Methods, Vol. 4: Employment, Unemployment, Wages & Hours of Work (Administrative Records & Related Sources) xi, 180p. (Orig.). 1989. pap. 29.25 (*92-2-106406-9*) Intl Labour Office.

Statistical Sources & Methods, Vol. 6: Household Income & Expenditure Surveys. ix, 305p. (Orig.). 1992. pap. 31.50 (*92-2-107752-7*) Intl Labour Office.

Statistical Sources on the California Hispanic Population. Ed. by Roberta Medford. 210p. 1990. 14.95 (*0-685-47549-2*) Floricanto Pr.

Statistical Sources on the California Hispanic Population: Update. Compiled by Eudora Loh & Roberta Medford. pap. 25.00 (*0-915745-06-2*) Floricanto Pr.

Statistical Study of Certain Aspects of the Time Factor in Intelligence. Frederick C. Walters. LC 77-177666. (Columbia University. Teachers College. Contributions to Education Ser.). reprint ed. 37.50 (*0-404-55248-X*) AMS Pr.

Statistical Study of Literary Vocabulary. G. Udny Yule. LC 68-8027. viii, 306p. (C). 1968. reprint ed. lib. bdg. 39.50 (*0-208-00689-3*, Archon Bks) Shoe String.

Statistical Study of the Middle East: Demographics & Population. 1991. lib. bdg. 248.95 (*0-8490-5094-4*) Gordon Pr.

Statistical Survey of Museums in the United States & Canada. American Association of Museums Staff. LC 75-21957. (America in Two Centuries Ser.). 1976. reprint ed. 16.95 (*0-405-07735-1*) Ayer.

Statistical Survey on Insurance & Reinsurance Operations in Developing Countries 1983-1990. 468p. 1994. 50.00 (*92-1-112368-2*) UN.

Statistical Tables. 2nd ed. F. James Rohlf & Robert R. Sokal. LC 81-2576. (Illus.). 219p. (C). 1995. pap. text ed. write for info. (*0-7167-1258-X*) W H Freeman.

Statistical Tables. 3rd ed. F. James Rolf & Robert R. Sokal. LC 94-11121. (C). 1995. pap. text ed. write for info. (*0-7167-2412-X*) W H Freeman.

***Statistical Tables for Economic, Business & Social Studies.** 2nd ed. Z. W. Kmietowicz. 1988. pap. 7.95 (*0-582-44070-X*, Pub. by Longman UK) Longman.

Statistical Tables for the Social, Biological & Physical Sciences. F. C. Powell. LC 80-42241. (Illus.). 96p. 1982. pap. 7.95 (*0-521-28473-2*) Cambridge U Pr.

Statistical Techniques & Applications for Engineers. Ranesh Sircar. (C). 1989. 40.00 (*0-89771-385-0*, Pub. by Current Dist II) St Mut.

Statistical Techniques for Analytical Review. 2nd rev. ed. Trevor R. Stewart & Kenneth W. Stringer. LC 95-37321. 350p. 1996. text ed. 95.00 (*0-471-11816-8*) Wiley.

Statistical Techniques for Data Analysis. John K. Taylor. (Illus.). 216p. 1990. 87.00 (*0-87371-250-1*, L250) Lewis Pubs.

Statistical Techniques for Manpower Planning. 2nd ed. David J. Bartholomew et al. LC 90-28589. (Probability & Mathematical Statistics: Applied Probability & Statistics Section Ser.). 350p. 1991. text ed. 155.00 (*0-471-92879-8*) Wiley.

Statistical Techniques for Social Research. Anthony A. Hickey. 362p. 1986. text ed. write for info. (*0-07-554340-0*) McGraw.

Statistical Techniques for the Study of Language & Language Behaviour. A. C. Rietveld & R. Van Hout. LC 92-35677. 1993. 44.65 (*3-11-013663-5*) Mouton.

Statistical Techniques in Bioassay. Z. Govindarajulu. (Illus.). xiv, 166p. 1988. 55.25 (*3-8055-4630-0*) S Karger.

Statistical Techniques in Business & Economics. Douglas A. Lind & Robert D. Mason. LC 95-16497. 1995. teacher ed. write for info. (*0-256-18904-8*) Irwin Prof Pubng.

Statistical Techniques in Business & Economics. 7th ed. Robert D. Mason & Douglas A. Lind. 1024p. (C). 1989. text ed. 66.95 (*0-256-07696-0*) Irwin.

Statistical Techniques in Business & Economics. 7th ed. Robert D. Mason & Douglas A. Lind. (C). 1989. student ed. 18.95 (*0-256-08054-2*) Irwin.

Statistical Techniques in Business & Economics. 8th ed. Douglas A. Lind & Robert D. Mason. 360p. (C). 1992. per. 22.75 (*0-256-12680-1*) Irwin.

Statistical Techniques in Business & Economics. 8th ed. Robert D. Mason & Douglas A. Lind. LC 92-9933. 896p. (C). 1992. text ed. 71.25 (*0-256-10338-0*) Irwin.

Statistical Techniques in Business & Economics. 9th ed. Robert D. Mason & Douglas A. Lind. LC 95-16497. 912p. (C). 1995. text ed. 71.25 (*0-256-13901-6*) Irwin Prof Pubng.

Statistical Techniques in Business & Economics. 9th ed. Robert D. Mason & Douglas A. Lind. 352p. (C). 1995. student ed., pap. text ed. 22.75 (*0-256-17371-0*) Irwin.

Statistical Techniques in Business & Economics. 91th ed. Robert D. Mason & Douglas A. Lind. (C). 1995. per. 36.00 (*0-256-21877-3*) Irwin.

***Statistical Techniques in Business & Economics: Business Statistics Software.** 9th ed. Robert D. Mason et al. (C). 1996. pap. 77.50 incl. disk (*0-256-21184-1*) Irwin.

Statistical Techniques in Geographical Analysis. 2nd ed. Gareth Shaw & Dennis Wheeler. 359p. 1994. pap. 29.95 (*0-470-23402-4*) Halsted Pr.

Statistical Techniques in Geographical Analysis. 2nd ed. Gareth Shaw & Dennis Wheeler. 288p. 1994. pap. 36.00 (*1-85346-229-2*, Pub. by D Fulton UK) Taylor & Francis.

Statistical Techniques in Simulation, Pt. 2. Jack P. Kleijnen. LC 74-79920. (Statistics, Textbooks & Monographs: No. 9). 509p. reprint ed. pap. 145.10 (*0-318-35006-8*, 2030866) Bks Demand.

Statistical Techniques for Studying Genotype-Environment Interactions. V. T. Prabhakaran. (C). 1994. 24.00 (*81-7003-168-0*, Pub. by S Asia Pubs II) S Asia.

Statistical Tests: An Introduction with Minitab Commentary. A. P. Beaumont & J. D. Knowles. LC 95-30474. 200p. (C). 1995. pap. text ed. 38.00 (*0-13-842576-0*) P-H.

Statistical Tests & Experimental Design: A Guidebook. David Sheskin. 325p. 1984. text ed. 30.00 (*0-89876-094-1*) Gardner Pr.

***Statistical Tests in Mixed Linear Models.** Andre I. Khuri et al. (Series in Probability & Statistics). 352p. 1998. 69.95 (*0-471-15653-1*, Wiley-Interscience) Wiley.

Statistical Theories of Turbulence. Chia-Ch'iao Lin. (Princeton Aeronautical Paperbacks Ser: No. 10). 67p. reprint ed. pap. 25.00 (*0-317-09284-7*, 2001133) Bks Demand.

Statistical Theory. 4th ed. Bernard W. Lindgren. LC 93-1042. 633p. (gr. 13). 1993. text ed. 63.95 (*0-412-04181-2*) Chapman & Hall.

Statistical Theory: An Introduction. Delmar Crabill. 296p. (Orig.). (C). 1984. pap. text ed. 24.00 (*0-8191-3796-0*) U Pr of Amer.

Statistical Theory & Applications: Papers in Honor of Herbert A. David, Vol. XVII. Pranab K. Sen. (Illus.). 334p. 1995. 65.95 (*0-387-94591-1*) Spr-Verlag.

Statistical Theory & Methodology: In Science & Engineering. 2nd ed. K. A. Brownlee. LC 84-3941. 608p. (C). 1984. reprint ed. lib. bdg. 66.50 (*0-89874-748-1*) Krieger.

Statistical Theory & Modelling: In Honour of Sir David Cox FRS. E. Joyce Snell. 300p. (gr. 13). 1990. text ed. 54.95 (*0-412-30590-9*, A5021) Chapman & Hall.

Statistical Theory & Random Matrices. Carmeli. (Pure & Applied Mathematics Ser.: Vol. 74). 224p. 1983. 125.00 (*0-8247-1779-1*) Dekker.

Statistical Theory of Heat. W. Brenig. (Illus.). xii, 296p. 1990. 49.95 (*0-387-51036-2*) Spr-Verlag.

Statistical Theory of Linear Systems. E. J. Hannan & M. Deistler. LC 87-19863. (Probability & Mathematical Statistics Ser.). 380p. 1988. text ed. 127.00 (*0-471-80777-X*) Wiley.

Statistical Theory of Liquids. Iosif Z. Fisher. Tr. by Theodore M. Switz. LC 64-22249. 347p. reprint ed. suppl. ed., pap. 98.90 (*0-317-08823-8*, 2020284) Bks Demand.

Statistical Theory of Reliability. Ed. by Marvin Zelen. LC 63-9061. (U. S. Army. Mathematical Research Center. Madison, Wis. Ser.: No. 9). 184p. reprint ed. pap. 52.50 (*0-317-09139-5*, 2015375) Bks Demand.

Statistical Theory of Shape. Christopher G. Small. LC 96-13587. (Statistics Ser.). 240p. 1996. 52.95 (*0-387-94729-9*) Spr-Verlag.

Statistical Theory of Signal Detection. 2nd ed. C. W. Helmstrom. 1968. 222.00 (*0-08-013265-0*, Pub. by Pergamon Repr UK) Franklin.

Statistical Theory of the Analysis of Experimental Designs. Junjiro Ogawa. LC 73-90769. (Statistics, Textbooks & Monographs: Vol. 8). 475p. reprint ed. pap. 135.40 (*0-685-15685-0*, 2027339) Bks Demand.

Statistical Thermodynamics. M. C. Gupta. LC 88-14810. 404p. 1991. text ed. 62.95 (*0-470-21151-2*) Halsted Pr.

Statistical Thermodynamics. Donald A. McQuarrie. 343p. (C). 1985. pap. text ed. 44.00 (*0-935702-18-0*) Univ Sci Bks.

Statistical Thermodynamics. Erwin Schrodinger. 1989. pap. 4.95 (*0-486-66101-6*) Dover.

Statistical Thermodynamics. rev. ed. Chang L. Tien & John H. Lienhard. 397p. 1979. pap. 76.95 (*0-89116-828-1*) Hemisp Pub.

Statistical Thermodynamics: A Version of Statistical Mechanics for Students of Physics & Chemistry. Ralph H. Fowler & E. A. Guggenheim. 711p. reprint ed. pap. 180.00 (*0-317-08661-8*, 2051495) Bks Demand.

Statistical Thermodynamics & Differential Geometry of Microstructured Materials. Ed. by H. T. Davis & J. C. Nitsche. LC 93-12274. (IMA Volumes in Mathematics & Its Applications Ser.: Vol. 51). 1993. 52.95 (*0-387-94027-8*) Spr-Verlag.

Statistical Thermodynamics & Stochastic Theory. W. Ebeling & L. Schimansky-Geier. (Advances in Statistical Mechanics Ser.: Vol. 8). 200p. 1998. text ed. 48.00 (*981-02-1382-4*) World Scientific Pub.

Statistical Thermodynamics for Chemists & Biochemists. Arieh Ben-Naim. (Illus.). 590p. 1991. 95.00 (*0-306-43848-8*, Plenum Pr) Plenum.

Statistical Thermodynamics of Alloys. N. A. Gokcen. 320p. 1986. 85.00 (*0-306-42177-1*, Plenum Pr) Plenum.

Statistical Thermodynamics of Nonequilibrium Processes. J. Keizer. (Illus.). 520p. (C). 1987. 118.95 (*0-387-96501-7*) Spr-Verlag.

Statistical Thermodynamics of Surfaces, Interfaces, & Membranes. Samuel A. Safran. LC 93-40842. (Frontiers in Physics Ser.: Vol. 90). (C). 1994. 55.95 (*0-201-62633-0*) Addison-Wesley.

Statistical Thermophysics. Harry S. Robertson. LC 92-17052. 592p. 1992. text ed. 94.00 (*0-13-845603-8*) P-H.

Statistical Thinking & Data Analysis Methods for Managers. Wynn A. Abranovic. (C). 1997. text ed. 67.95 (*0-673-99296-9*) Addson-Wesley Educ.

Statistical Thinking for Managers. 3rd ed. Hildebrand. (Business Statistics Ser.). 1991. student ed., pap. 22.95 (*0-534-92594-4*) Wadsworth Pub.

Statistical Thinking for Managers. 3rd ed. David K. Hildebrand & R. Lyman Ott. 950p. (C). 1991. text ed. 71.95 (*0-534-92561-8*) Wadsworth Pub.

***Statistical Thinking for Managers.** 4th ed. Hildebrand. 1998. pap. 14.95 (*0-534-35372-X*) Brooks-Cole.

Statistical Thinking for Managers. 4th ed. Hildebrand. (Business Statistics Ser.). 1998. text ed. 68.95 (*0-534-20406-6*) Wadsworth Pub.

Statistical Tools for Nonlinear Regression: A Practical Guide with S-PLUS Examples. S. Huet et al. LC 96-13753. (Springer Series in Statistics). (Illus.). 168p. 1996. 44.95 (*0-387-94727-2*) Spr-Verlag.

Statistical Tools for Simulation Practitioners. Jack P. Kleijnen. (Statistics: Textbooks & Monographs: Vol. 76). 448p. 1986. 125.00 (*0-8247-7333-0*) Dekker.

Statistical Tools for Total Quality Management: Using Lotus 1-2-3, Version D-1.0. Gordon H. Otto & James G. Soules. LC 94-60523. (Illus.). 140p. (Orig.). 1994. pap. 29.00 (*0-9639553-2-2*) Verenikia Pr.

Statistical Tools in Human Biology: Proceedings of the 17th Course of the Internatioanl School of Mathematics. M. Di Bacco et al. (Science & Culture Series, Mathematics). 350p. 1994. text ed. 99.00 (*981-02-1782-X*) World Scientific Pub.

Statistical Tools of Safety Management. Walters. (Industrial Health & Safety Ser.). 1995. text ed. 51.95 (*0-442-02125-9*) Van Nos Reinhold.

Statistical Treatment of Data on Environmental Isotopes in Precipitation. IAEA Staff. (Technical Reports: No. 331). 597p. 1992. pap. 220.00 (*92-0-100892-9*, STI/DOC/331, Pub. by IAEA AU) Bernan Associates.

Statistical Treatment of Experimental Data. rev. ed. J. R. Green & D. Margerison. (Physical Sciences Data Ser.: Vol. 2). 382p. 1983. 236.00 (*0-444-41725-7*) Elsevier.

***Statistical Treatment of Experimental Data: An Introduction to Statistical Methods.** Hugh D. Young. (Illus.). 186p. (C). 1996. reprint ed. pap. text ed. 9.95 (*0-88133-913-X*) Waveland Pr.

Statistical Trends in Transport 1965-1990. OECD ECMT Staff. 148p. (Orig.). 1995. pap. 42.00 (*92-821-0204-1*, Pub. by Org for Econ FR) OECD.

***Statistical Trends in Transport 1965-1992.** ECMT Staff. 260p. (Orig.). 1997. pap. 45.00 (*92-821-0219-X*, 75-96-08-3, Pub. by Org for Econ FR) OECD.

Statistical Tutor Data Analysis for Social Scientists. Lawrence C. Hamilton. (Business Statistics Ser.). 1996. pap. 17.95 (*0-534-24723-7*) Wadsworth Pub.

Statistical Typing. 4th ed. Wanous. (TA - Typing/Keyboarding Ser.). 1991. text ed. 15.95 (*0-538-60346-1*) S-W Pub.

Statistical View of the Commerce of the United States of America. Timothy Pitkin. LC 65-26374. (Library of Early American Business & Industry: No. 13). xii, 407p. 1967. reprint ed. 57.50 (*0-678-00219-3*) Kelley.

Statistical View of the Trusts: A Manual of Large American Industrial & Mining Corporations Active Around 1900. David Bunting. LC 72-9824. (Contributions in Economics & Economic History Ser.: No. 9). 311p. 1974. text ed. 69.50 (*0-8371-6624-1*, BOM/) Greenwood.

***Statistical Visions in Time: A History of Time Series Analysis, 1662-1938.** Judy L. Klein. (Illus.). 328p. (C). 1997. text ed. 59.95 (*0-521-42046-6*) Cambridge U Pr.

Statistical Work of the National Government. Laurence F. Schmeckebier. (Brookings Institution Reprint Ser.). reprint ed. lib. bdg. 39.00 (*0-697-00167-9*) Irvington.

Statistical Yearbook. (ENG & FRE.). 1986. pap. 75.00 (*92-1-061106-3*) UN.

***Statistical Yearbook.** 40th ed. 1996. 120.00 (*92-1-061163-2*) UN.

Statistical Yearbook, No. 38. 1130p. 1991. 100.00 (*92-1-061141-1*, 91.XVII.1) UN.

Statistical Yearbook No. 39: 1992. 1055p. 1994. 110.00 (*92-1-061159-4*) UN.

Statistical Yearbook No. 39: 1992. 1055p. 1995. 249.00 incl. cd-rom (*92-1-161377-9*) UN.

Statistical Yearbook for Asia & the Pacific: 1993. 502p. 1994. 70.00 (*92-1-119636-1*) UN.

Statistical Yearbook for Asia & the Pacific, 1988. 1990. 49.00 (*92-1-119469-5*) UN.

Statistical Yearbook for Asia & the Pacific, 1989. 483p. 1990. 49.00 (*92-1-119553-5*, 90.II.F.1) UN.

Statistical Yearbook for Asia & the Pacific, 1990. 465p. 1991. 60.00 (*92-1-119577-2*, E/F.91.II.F.1) UN.

Statistical Yearbook for Asia & the Pacific, 1994. 470p. 1995. pap. 70.00 (*92-1-119674-4*, UN95 2F 1) UN.

Statistical Yearbook for Latin America & the Caribbean. 790p. 1995. 70.00 (*92-1-021034-4*) UN.

Statistical Yearbook for Latin America & the Caribbean: 1991. 774p. 1992. 65.00 (*92-1-021030-1*) UN.

Statistical Yearbook for Latin America & the Caribbean: 1993. 774p. 1994. 65.00 (*92-1-021033-6*) UN.

***Statistical Yearbook for Latin America & the Caribbean: 1995 Edition.** 775p. 1996. pap. 75.00 (*92-1-021035-2*, JX1977) UN.

Statistical Yearbook for Latin America & the Caribbean, 1987. 716p. (ENG & SPA.). 1988. 65.00 (*92-1-021025-5*, ES.88.II.G.1) UN.

Statistical Yearbook for Latin America & the Caribbean, 1988. United Nations Staff. 786p. 1989. pap. 65.00 (*92-1-021026-3*) UN.

Statistical Yearbook for Latin America & the Caribbean, 1990. 782p. 1991. 65.00 (*92-1-021029-8*, 91.II.G.1) UN.

***Statistical Yearbook of China 1981.** 1983. 60.00 (*0-8103-1592-0*, 00001698, Gale Res Intl) Gale.

***Statistical Yearbook of China 1996.** 900p. (CHI.). 1996. 255.00 (*7-5037-2141-3*, C1266, Pub. by HUWEI Cnslts CH) Am Overseas Bk Co.

Statistical Yearbook 1983-1984: ST-ESA-STAT-SER.S-10. 1137p. 70.00 (*92-1-061103-9*, E/F.85.XVII.1); pap. 60.00 (*92-1-061104-7*) UN.

Statistical Yearbook 1987. 36th ed. United Nations Staff. 1100p. 1991. 100.00 (*92-1-061131-4*) UN.

statistical Yearbook, 1990-91. 1109p. 1993. 110.00 (*92-1-061152-7*) UN.

Statistical Yearbooks: An Annotated Bibliography of the General Statistical Yearbooks of Major Political Subdivisions of the World. United States Library of Congress Staff. LC 78-10213. 123p. 1979. reprint ed. text ed. 45.00 (*0-313-20676-7*, CAST) Greenwood.

Statistically-Based Natural Language Programming Techniques: Papers from the 1992 AAAI Workshop. Ed. by Carl Weir. (Technical Reports). (Illus.). 114p. (Orig.). 1993. spiral bd. 25.00 (*0-929280-33-4*) AAAI Pr.

***Statistically Speaking: A Collection of Quotes, Quips from the Improbable to the Infinite.** Carl C. Gaither & Alma E. Cavazos-Gaither. 416p. 1996. pap. text ed. 39.00 (*0-7503-0401-4*) IOP Pub.

Statistician. Jack Rudman. (Career Examination Ser.: C-761). 1994. pap. 29.95 (*0-8373-0761-9*) Nat Learn.

Statistics. 1979. teacher ed. 20.95 (*0-387-90377-1*) Spr-Verlag.

***Statistics.** 1996. 16.50 (*0-340-63194-5*, Pub. by E Arnold UK) Routledge Chapman & Hall.

Statistics. Victoria L. Armstrong. LC 94-18819. 576p. 1994. text ed. 62.00 (*0-13-101320-3*) P-H.

Statistics. Joseph Balkin. (Illus.). 152p. (Orig.). (C). 1988. pap. text ed. 20.00 (*0-940524-04-X*) G Handwerk.

***Statistics.** Ed. by Boot. (C). Date not set. text ed. write for info. (*0-321-01613-0*) Addson-Wesley Educ.

***Statistics.** David E. Brigham. (Illus.). 68p. (Orig.). (YA). 1996. student ed., pap. text ed. 12.95 (*1-889403-01-6*) Regnts College.

Statistics. Norman H. Crowhurst. 110p. (Orig.). 1981. pap. text ed. 11.95 (*0-89420-111-5*, 413040); audio 103.95 (*0-89420-202-2*, 413000) Natl Book.

Statistics. Devore. Date not set. teacher ed., pap. text ed. write for info. (*0-314-97130-0*); teacher ed., pap. text ed. 19.50 (*0-314-97131-9*) West Pub.

Statistics. Andrew Edmondson. 380p. (C). 1991. pap. 60.00 (*1-85352-930-3*, Pub. by HLT Pubns UK) St Mut.

Statistics. Fox et al. (C). 1992. student ed. 18.00 (*0-06-500617-8*) Addson-Wesley Educ.

***Statistics.** Ed. by Gleason. (C). Date not set. text ed. write for info. (*0-321-01614-9*) Addson-Wesley Educ.

Statistics. Alan Graham. 256p. 1995. pap. 9.95 (*0-8442-3684-5*, Teach Yourslf) NTC Pub Grp.

Statistics. William Harkness. 296p. (C). 1994. pap. text ed., spiral bd. 27.24 (*0-8403-9250-8*) Kendall-Hunt.

Statistics. W. M. Harper. 387p. (Orig.). (C). 1988. 110.00 (*0-685-39818-8*, Pub. by Inst Pur & Supply UK) St Mut.

Statistics. Keller. (Statistics Ser.). 1994. lab manual ed., pap. 22.95 (*0-534-21864-4*) Wadsworth Pub.

Statistics. Alan H. Kvanli. Date not set. student ed., pap. text ed. write for info. (*0-314-65687-1*); student ed., pap. text ed. 21.75 (*0-314-65692-8*) West Pub.

Statistics. Richard J. Larsen & Morris L. Marx. 800p. (C). 1990. text ed. 87.00 (*0-13-844085-9*) P-H.

Statistics. M. Martin & F. Firth. (Core Business Studies). 1990. 35.00 (*0-7463-0048-4*, Pub. by Northcote UK) St Mut.

Statistics. Moore & McCabe. (C). 1995. text ed. write for info. (*0-7167-2450-2*) W H Freeman.

***Statistics.** Research & Education Association Staff. 1997. pap. text ed. 19.95 (*0-87891-082-4*) Res & Educ.

Statistics. Jack Rudman. (ACT Proficiency Examination Program Ser.: PEP-57). 1994. pap. 23.95 (*0-8373-5907-4*) Nat Learn.

Statistics. Jack Rudman. (College Level Examination (CLEP) Ser.: Vol. CLEP-26). 1994. pap. 23.95 (*0-8373-5326-2*) Nat Learn.

Statistics. Jack Rudman. (Regents College Proficiency Examination Ser.: Vol. CPEP-15). 1994. pap. 23.95 (*0-8373-5415-3*) Nat Learn.

***Statistics.** Jack Rudman. (Advanced Placement Test (AP) Ser.: Vol. AP-21). 1997. pap. 23.95 (*0-8373-6221-0*) Nat Learn.

Statistics. Anthony A. Salvia. (C). 1994. text ed. write for info. (*0-03-033704-6*) HB Coll Pubs.

***Statistics.** School Mathematics Project Staff. (School Mathematics Project 16-19). 512p. (C). 1997. pap. 29.95 (*0-521-56616-9*) Cambridge U Pr.

Statistics. Marion Smoothey. LC 92-35574. (Let's Investigate Ser.). (Illus.). 64p. (J). (gr. 4-8). 1993. text ed. 17.95 (*1-85435-468-X*) Marshall Cavendish.

Statistics. Martin Sternstein. LC 94-4069. (EZ-101 Study Keys Ser.). 200p. (Orig.). 1994. student ed., pap. 6.95 (*0-8120-1869-9*) Barron.

Statistics. Martin Sternstein. LC 95-40545. (College Review Ser.). 1996. pap. 13.95 (*0-8120-9311-9*) Barron.

Statistics. Summers. (C). Date not set. text ed. write for info. (*0-15-505200-4*) HarBrace.

Statistics. Summers. (C). 1998. teacher ed., pap. text ed. 21.00 (*0-15-505208-X*) HarBrace.

***Statistics.** rev. ed. Walter Antoniotti. (Quick Notes Learning System Ser.). (Illus.). 265p. (C). 1995. pap. text ed. write for info. (*0-9632772-5-1*) Twen Frst Cent Lrn.

An Asterisk (*) at the beginning of an entry indicates that the title is appearing in BIP for the first time.

Statistics. 2nd ed. David Freedman et al. 550p. (C). 1991. text ed. 52.95 (*0-393-96043-9*) Norton.

Statistics. 2nd ed. David Freeman. Date not set. teacher ed., pap. text ed. write for info. (*0-393-96045-5*) Norton.

Statistics. 2nd ed. Richard C. Weimer. 800p. (C). 1992. student ed., per. write for info. (*0-697-12356-1*); student ed., spiral bd. write for info. (*0-697-16344-X*) Wm C Brown Pubs.

Statistics. 2nd ed. Richard C. Weimer. 800p. (C). 1992. student ed., per. write for info. (*0-697-15397-5*) Wm C Brown Pubs.

Statistics. 2nd ed. Richard C. Weimer. 800p. (C). 1992. text ed. write for info. (*0-697-12146-1*) Wm C Brown Pubs.

***Statistics.** 3rd ed. David Freedman et al. LC 97-21345. 1997. write for info. (*0-393-97083-3*) Norton.

Statistics. 3rd ed. Donald J. Koosis. LC 85-6292. 282p. 1985. pap. text ed. 17.95 (*0-471-82720-7*) Wiley.

Statistics. 3rd ed. Robert S. Witte. (Illus.). 500p. (C). 1989. text ed. 46.75 (*0-03-014128-1*) HB Coll Pubs.

Statistics. 4th ed. William L. Hays. 750p. (C). 1988. text ed. 50.75 (*0-03-002464-1*) HB Coll Pubs.

Statistics. 4th ed. Ron Jones & Frank F. Owen. 512p. (Orig.). 1994. pap. 47.50 (*0-273-60320-5*, Pub. by Pitman Pub Ltd UK) Trans-Atl Phila.

***Statistics.** 4th ed. Kirk. (C). 1998. student ed., pap. text ed. 21.00 (*0-03-019328-1*) HB Coll Pubs.

Statistics. 4th ed. Witte. (C). 1993. student ed., wbk. ed., pap. text ed. 24.00 (*0-03-072387-6*) HB Coll Pubs.

Statistics. 4th ed. Robert S. Witte. LC 91-54563. 1992. 46.75 (*0-03-072243-8*) HB Coll Pubs.

Statistics. 5th ed. James T. McClave, II. 1991. write for info. (*0-02-379185-3*, Macmillan Coll) P-H.

Statistics. 5th ed. Statsoft. Date not set. write for info. (*0-314-09773-2*) West Pub.

Statistics. 5th ed. Witte. (C). 1996. text ed. write for info. (*0-03-017888-6*) HB Coll Pubs.

Statistics. 5th ed. Witte. (C). 1996. suppl. ed., teacher ed., text ed. 42.00 (*0-03-017889-4*) HB Coll Pubs.

Statistics. 5th ed. Witte. (C). 1996. wbk. ed., text ed. 20.00 (*0-03-017899-1*) HB Coll Pubs.

Statistics. 6th ed. Freund. 1995. student ed., pap. text ed. 25.00 (*0-13-149980-7*) P-H.

***Statistics.** 7th ed. McClave. 1996. student ed., pap. text ed. 25.00 (*0-13-471666-3*) P-H.

Statistics. 7th ed. James T. McClave et al. 1996. write for info. (*0-13-471657-4*) P-H.

Statistics. 7th ed. James T. McClave & Dietrich. 1000p. (C). 1996. text ed. 73.00 (*0-13-471542-X*) P-H.

Statistics: A Bayesian Perspective. Donald A. Berry. (Statistics Ser.). 1996. student ed., pap. 17.95 (*0-534-23476-3*) Wadsworth Pub.

Statistics: A Bayesian Perspective. Donald A. Berry. (C). 1996. text ed. 60.95 (*0-534-23472-0*) Wadsworth Pub.

Statistics: A Biomedical Introduction. Byron W. Brown, Jr. & Myles Hollander. (Probability & Mathematical Statistics Ser.). 456p. 1977. text ed. 125.00 (*0-471-11240-2*) Wiley.

Statistics: A Component of the Research Process. Peter Hernon. Ed. by Charles R. McClure. LC 90-25781. (Information Management, Policies & Services Ser.: Vol. 22). 264p. (C). 1991. pap. 39.50 (*0-89391-759-1*) Ablex Pub.

Statistics: A Component of the Research Process. rev. ed. Peter Hernon. (Information Management, Policies & Services Ser.). 264p. 1994. pap. 39.50 (*1-56750-093-5*) Ablex Pub.

Statistics: A Component of the Research Process. 2nd rev. ed. Peter Hernon. (Information Management, Policies & Services Ser.). 264p. 1994. text ed. 73.25 (*1-56750-092-7*) Ablex Pub.

Statistics: A Computer Integrated Approach. Alan H. Kvanli. 935p. (C). 1988. text ed. 60.25 (*0-314-60541-X*) West Pub.

Statistics: A Conceptual Approach. K. Laurence Weldon. (Illus.). 528p. (C). 1986. text ed. write for info. (*0-13-845819-7*) P-H.

Statistics: A First Course. 5th ed. John A. Banks. 1995. student ed., pap. text ed. write for info. (*0-07-054942-7*) McGraw.

Statistics: A First Course. 5th ed. John E. Freund & Gary A. Simon. 592p. (C). 1991. text ed. 73.00 (*0-13-844523-0*) P-H.

Statistics: A First Course. 5th ed. Donald H. Sanders. LC 94-32146. 1995. text ed. write for info. (*0-07-054900-1*) McGraw.

Statistics: A First Course. 5th ed. Robert K. Smidt. 1994. student ed., pap. text ed. write for info. (*0-07-054943-5*) McGraw.

Statistics: A First Course. 6th ed. John E. Freund & Gary A. Simon. LC 94-27691. 573p. 1994. text ed. 68.00 (*0-13-083024-0*) P-H.

Statistics: A Fresh Approach. 4th rev. ed. Donald H. Sanders. 736p. 1990. text ed. write for info. (*0-07-054881-1*) McGraw.

Statistics: A Guide & Reference to the Use of Statistical Methods in the Physical Sciences. Roger Barlow. LC 88-33908. (Manchester Physics Ser.). 204p. 1989. text ed. 69.95 (*0-471-92294-3*) Wiley.

Statistics: A Guide for Therapists. John McCall. (Skills for Practice Ser.). 268p. 1996. pap. 35.00 (*0-7506-2104-4*) Buttrwrth-Heinemann.

Statistics: A Guide to Biological & Health Sciences. Richard S. Pieters & Gerald R. Rising. LC 76-50856. 1977. reprint ed. pap. text ed. 8.95 (*0-8162-8564-0*) Holden-Day.

Statistics: A Guide to Political & Social Issues. Richard S. Pieters & Gerald F. Rising. LC 76-50852. 1977. reprint ed. pap. text ed. 8.95 (*0-8162-8574-8*) Holden-Day.

Statistics: A Guide to the Unknown. 3rd ed. Judith M. Tanur et al. LC 88-25889. 284p. (C). 1989. pap. 27.95 (*0-534-09492-9*) Wadsworth Pub.

Statistics: A Guide to the Use of Statistical Methods in the Physical Sciences. Roger Barlow. LC 88-33908. (Manchester Physics Ser.). 204p. 1993. pap. text ed. 42.95 (*0-471-92295-1*) Wiley.

Statistics: A Health Sciences Introduction Minitab. Biles. 160p. 1993. pap. 16.95 (*0-8016-6534-5*) Mosby Yr Bk.

Statistics: A Health Sciences Orientation. Charles M. Biles. 544p. (C). 1994. text ed. write for info. (*0-697-21608-X*) Wm C Brown Pubs.

Statistics: A Model for Uncertainty. Soler. 306p. (C). 1996. text ed. 49.29 (*0-7872-2522-3*) Kendall-Hunt.

Statistics: A Second Course in Statistics. 2nd ed. Robert Loveday. LC 74-96095. (Illus.). 1970. pap. 14.95 (*0-521-07234-4*) Cambridge U Pr.

***Statistics: A Self-Teaching Guide.** 4th ed. Donald J. Koosis. LC 96-50887. 1997. pap. text ed. 17.95 (*0-471-14688-9*) Wiley.

Statistics: A Spectator Sport. 2nd ed. Richard M. Jaeger. (Illus.). 404p. (C). 1990. text ed. 52.00 (*0-8039-3420-3*); pap. text ed. 25.00 (*0-8039-3421-1*) Sage.

Statistics: A Tool for Social Research. 3rd ed. Joseph F. Healey. 555p. (C). 1993. text ed. 40.50 (*0-534-17742-5*) Wadsworth Pub.

Statistics: A Tool for Social Research. 4th ed. Joseph F. Healey. 551p. 1996. pap. 58.95 (*0-534-25152-8*) Wadsworth Pub.

Statistics: A Tool for the Social Sciences. 5th ed. R. Lyman Ott et al. 634p. (C). 1992. text ed. 64.95 (*0-534-92931-1*) Wadsworth Pub.

Statistics: A Tool for Understanding Society. Ivy Lee & Minako Maykovich. LC 94-4804. 1994. text ed. 69.00 (*0-205-13961-2*) Allyn.

Statistics: An Applied Approach. Neil R. Ullman. LC 77-171918. 624p. (C). reprint ed. 177.90 (*0-8357-9982-4*, 2055154) Bks Demand.

Statistics: An Introduction. Robert D. Mason et al. 700p. (C). 1990. text ed. 52.00 (*0-15-583536-X*) SCP.

Statistics: An Introduction. A. D. Rickmers & H. N. Todd. 1967. text ed. write for info. (*0-07-052616-8*) McGraw.

Statistics: An Introduction. 3rd ed. Roger E. Kirk. 480p. (C). 1990. text ed. 46.75 (*0-03-020424-0*) HB Coll Pubs.

***Statistics: An Introduction.** 4th ed. Kirk. (C). 1998. pap. text ed. 49.00 (*0-03-019337-0*) HB Coll Pubs.

Statistics: An Introduction. 4th ed. Robert D. Mason et al. 660p. (C). 1994. text ed. 71.95 (*0-534-51070-1*) Wadsworth Pub.

***Statistics: An Introduction.** 5th ed. Mason & Lind. 1998. student ed., pap. 14.95 (*0-534-35383-5*); text ed. 55.95 (*0-534-35379-7*) Brooks-Cole.

Statistics: An Introduction for Non-Statisticians. Contrib. by S. C. Pearce & P. M. North. 200p. 1993. 49.00 (*1-85070-420-1*) Prthnon Pub.

Statistics: An Introduction to Numerical Reasoning. Ray A. Waller. LC 78-60357. 1979. Pilot ed. pap. 19.95 (*0-8162-9314-7*) Holden-Day.

Statistics: An Introduction to Quantitative Economic Research. rev. ed. Daniel B. Suits. LC 63-8246. (Illus.). xix, 288p. (C). 1985. reprint ed. pap. text ed. 15.00 (*0-916717-01-1*) Halyburton.

Statistics: An Intuitive Approach. 4th ed. George H. Weinberg et al. LC 80-18474. 470p. (C). 1981. text ed. 46.95 (*0-8185-0426-9*) Brooks-Cole.

Statistics: Art or Science? V. V. Shvyrkov. LC 82-61951. (Illus.). 105p. (Orig.). (C). 1982. text ed. 13.40 (*0-942004-05-1*) Throwkoff Pr.

Statistics: Basic Principles & Applications. William J. Adams. 808p. (C). 1994. boxed, pap. text ed. 63.99 (*0-8403-8964-7*) Kendall-Hunt.

Statistics: Concepts & Applications. Amir D. Aczel. LC 94-41399. 533p. (C). 1995. text ed. 65.85 (*0-256-11935-X*) Irwin.

Statistics: Concepts & Applications. Harry Frank & Steven C. Althoen. LC 92-275020. (Illus.). 1064p. (C). 1994. text ed. 54.95 (*0-521-44554-X*); pap. text ed. 0.01 (*0-521-46599-0*) Cambridge U Pr.

Statistics: Concepts & Applications. William C. Schefler. 520p. (C). 1988. teacher ed. 10.95 (*0-8053-8781-1*); text ed. 54.95 (*0-8053-8780-3*) Addison-Wesley.

Statistics: Concepts & Controversies. 3rd ed. David S. Moore. (C). 1995. pap. text ed. 17.95 (*0-7167-2199-6*) W H Freeman.

Statistics: Descriptive Statistics & Probability, Vol. I. Elliot A. Tanis. (College Outline Ser.). 257p. (C). 1987. pap. text ed. 11.25 (*0-15-601616-8*) HB Coll Pubs.

Statistics: Difficult Concepts Understandable Explanations. Mattson. LC 80-24947. 1984. 24.00 (*0-86516-056-2*) Bolchazy-Carducci.

Statistics: Elementary Study Units. James J. O'Donnell. 292p. (C). 1995. spiral bd. 28.29 (*0-8403-9231-1*) Kendall-Hunt.

Statistics: Elementary Units. 2nd ed. James O'Donnell. 272p. (C). 1995. pap. text ed., ring bd. 29.34 (*0-7872-0982-1*) Kendall-Hunt.

Statistics: Essentials of Research. 3rd ed. Ed. by Henry E. Klugh. 456p. 1986. text ed. 45.00 (*0-89859-627-0*) L Erlbaum Assocs.

Statistics: Estimation & Tests of Hypothesis, Vol. II. Elliot A. Tanis. (College Outline Ser.). 388p. (C). 1987. pap. text ed. 13.25 (*0-15-601617-6*) HB Coll Pubs.

Statistics: Exploration & Analysis. 2nd ed. Devore & Peck. (Statistics Ser.). 1993. student ed., pap. 16.50 (*0-534-19616-0*) Wadsworth Pub.

Statistics: Exploration/Analysis. 3rd ed. Devore. (Statistics Ser.). 1997. student ed., pap. 19.95 (*0-534-22899-2*) Wadsworth Pub.

Statistics: Learning in the Presence of Variation. Robert L. Wardrop. 736p. 42.95 (*0-8016-7505-7*) Mosby Yr Bk.

Statistics: Learning in the Presence of Variation. Robert L. Wardrop. 1993. 75.00 (*0-8016-5684-2*); 250.00 (*0-8016-5682-6*); 250.00 (*0-8016-5690-7*); pap. 16.95 (*0-8016-7506-5*) Mosby Yr Bk.

Statistics: Learning in the Presence of Variation. Robert L. Wardrop. 224p. (C). 1994. teacher ed., per. write for info. (*0-697-22421-X*) Wm C Brown Pubs.

Statistics: Learning in the Presence of Variation. Robert L. Wardrop. 1993. 100.00 (*0-8016-5681-8*) Mosby Yr Bk.

***Statistics: Learning in the Presence of Variation, Student Study Guide.** unabridged ed. Robert L. Wardrop. 116p. (Orig.). (C). 1996. pap. text ed. 20.00 (*0-9654104-0-4*) R Wardrop.

Statistics: Principles & Methods. 2nd ed. R. A. Johnson et al. 312p. 1992. student ed., pap. 17.00 (*0-471-55549-5*) Wiley.

Statistics: Principles & Methods. 3rd ed. Richard A. Johnson & Gouri K. Bhattacharyya. LC 95-39204. 720p. 1996. text ed. 40.00 (*0-471-04194-7*) Wiley.

Statistics: The Conceptual Approach. Gudmund Iversen & Mary Gergen. LC 96-23148. (Textbooks in Mathematical Sciences Ser.). (Illus.). 752p. 1997. 54.95 (*0-387-94610-1*) Spr-Verlag.

Statistics: The Exploration & Analysis of Data. 2nd ed. Jay Devore & Roxy L. Peck. LC 92-18203. 881p. 1993. text ed. 50.75 (*0-534-19614-4*) Wadsworth Pub.

Statistics: Theory & Methods. Jyoti P. Medhi. 438p. 1993. text ed. 84.95 (*0-470-22085-6*) Halsted Pr.

Statistics: Theory & Practice in the Social Sciences. Ed. by Norman Schofield et al. LC 85-28173. (Praeger Studies in Ethnographic Perspectives on American Education). (Illus.). 304p. 1986. text ed. 65.00 (*0-275-92076-3*, C2076, Praeger Pubs) Greenwood.

Statistics: Tool of the Behavioral Sciences. Margaret H. Johnson & Robert M. Liebert. 1977. text ed. write for info. (*0-13-844704-7*) P-H.

Statistics: Tools for Social Research. 4th ed. Healey. (Sociology Ser.). 1996. student ed., pap. 17.95 (*0-534-25156-0*) Wadsworth Pub.

Statistics--Asia & Australasia: Sources for Market Research. 2nd ed. Ed. by Joan M. Harvey. 240p. 1984. 145.00 (*0-900246-41-3*, 070096) Gale.

Statistics, Africa: Sources for Social, Economic, & Market Research. 2nd ed. Ed. by Joan M. Harvey. 1978. 80.00 (*0-900246-26-X*, Pub. by CBD Res Ltd UK) Gale.

Statistics America: Sources for Social, Economic, & Marketing Research. 2nd ed. Joan M. Harvey. 300p. 1979. 72.00 (*0-900246-16-2*) Gale.

Statistics, an Appraisal: Proceedings of a Conference Marking the 50th Anniversary of the Statistical Laboratory, Iowa State University, Ames, IA, June 13-15, 1983. Ed. by H. A. David & H. T. David. LC 84-4669. (Illus.). 674p. 1984. reprint ed. pap. 180.00 (*0-608-00010-8*, 2060776) Bks Demand.

Statistics & Control of Stochastic Processes: Steklov Seminar 1984. Ed. by N. V. Krylov et al. LC 85-8851. (Translations Series in Mathematics & Engineering). 575p. 1985. text ed. 70.00 (*0-911575-18-9*) Optimization Soft.

Statistics & Control of Stochastic Processes, Steklov Seminar, 1985-1986. Ed. by A. N. Shiryaev et al. LC 88-8851. (Translations Series in Mathematics & Engineering). 256p. 1989. text ed. 84.00 (*0-911575-51-0*) Optimization Soft.

Statistics & Data Analysis. Vell & M. Moore. (C). 1995. text ed. write for info. (*0-7167-2249-6*) W H Freeman.

Statistics & Data Analysis: An Introduction. 2nd ed. Andrew F. Siegel & Charles J. Morgan. LC 95-12110. 635p. 1995. text ed. 67.95 (*0-471-57424-4*) Wiley.

Statistics & Data Analysis for Social Workers. 2nd ed. John L. Craft. LC 89-63450. 194p. (Orig.). (C). 1990. pap. text ed. 25.00 (*0-87581-343-7*) Peacock Pubs.

Statistics & Data Analysis in Geochemical Prospecting. Ed. by R. J. Howarth. (Handbook of Exploration Geochemistry Ser.: Vol. 2). 438p. 1983. 224.75 (*0-444-42038-X*) Elsevier.

Statistics & Data Analysis in Geology. 2nd ed. John C. Davis. LC 85-12331. 656p. 1986. text ed. 55.50 (*0-471-08079-9*) Wiley.

Statistics & Decisions: An Introduction to Foundations. Steven H. Kim. 352p. (gr. 13). 1992. text ed. 60.95 (*0-442-01006-0*) Chapman & Hall.

Statistics & Econometric Models, 2 vols., Set. Christian Gourieroux & Alain Monfort. (Themes in Modern Econometrics Ser.). (Illus.). 1062p. (C). 1996. pap. 44.95 (*0-521-47837-5*) Cambridge U Pr.

Statistics & Econometric Models, Vol. 1. Christian Gourieroux & Alain Monfort. (Themes in Modern Econometrics Ser.). (Illus.). 475p. (C). 1995. text ed. 69.95 (*0-521-40551-3*); pap. text ed. 25.95 (*0-521-47744-1*) Cambridge U Pr.

Statistics & Econometric Models, Vol. 2. Christian Gourieroux & Alain Monfort. (Themes in Modern Econometrics Ser.). (Illus.). 542p. (C). 1996. text ed. 69.95 (*0-521-47162-1*); pap. text ed. 25.95 (*0-521-47745-X*) Cambridge U Pr.

Statistics & Econometrics: A Guide to Information Sources. Ed. by Joseph Zaremba. (Economics Information Guide Ser.: Vol. 15). 720p. 1980. 68.00 (*0-8103-1466-5*) Gale.

***Statistics & Experimental Design.** 3rd ed. write for info. (*0-340-59324-5*, Pub. by E Arnold UK) Routledge Chapman & Hall.

Statistics & Experimental Design: An Introduction for Biologists & Biochemists. 3rd ed. Geoffrey M. Clarke. 208p. 1994. pap. text ed. 28.95 (*0-470-23409-1*) Wiley.

Statistics & Experimental Design for Toxicologists. 2nd ed. Shayne C. Gad & Carrol S. Weil. 380p. 1989. 83.00 (*0-936923-17-2*, RA1199); 53.00 (*0-936923-18-0*) CRC Pr.

Statistics & Indicators on Women in Africa, 1986. 225p. 1989. 23.50 (*92-1-061133-0*, E/F 89.XV11.11) UN.

Statistics & Measurement: An Introduction for MBTI Users. 2nd ed. Ray M. Zeisset. 62p. 1996. pap. 8.00 (*0-935652-27-2*) Ctr Applications Psych.

Statistics & Optimization: The Interface. Ed. by Bruce L. Golden et al. LC 84-72719. (American Sciences Press Series in Mathematical & Management Sciences: Vol. 11). 1984. 125.00 (*0-935950-08-7*) Am Sciences Pr.

Statistics & Probabilities. 5th ed. Joseph Newmark. (C). 1992. student ed., pap. text ed. 22.50 (*0-03-076298-7*) HB Coll Pubs.

Statistics & Probability. J. H. Durran. LC 70-96086. (School Mathematics Project Handbooks). 1984. 27.95 (*0-521-06933-5*) Cambridge U Pr.

Statistics & Probability. Dennis C. Gilliland. student ed. 10.00 (*1-881592-42-1*) Hayden-McNeil.

Statistics & Probability. Ed. by J. Mogyorodi. 1984. lib. bdg. 192.00 (*90-277-1675-7*) Kluwer Ac.

Statistics & Probability & Their Applications. Patrick Brockett & Arnold Levine. 624p. (C). 1985. text ed. 52.00 (*0-03-053406-2*) SCP.

Statistics & Probability in Civil Engineering: Proceedings. International Conference on Applications of Statistics & Probabilities to Soil & Structural Engineering Staff. Ed. by Peter Lamb. LC 78-322289. (Illus.). 685p. reprint ed. pap. 180.00 (*0-8357-6664-0*, 2035332) Bks Demand.

Statistics & Probability in Modern Life. 5th ed. Joseph Newmark. 736p. (C). 1992. text ed. 56.00 (*0-03-072867-3*) SCP.

Statistics & Probability, Management/Monitoring/Policy/Law, Statistics: Environmental Statistics. Ed. by G. P. Patil & C. R. Rao. LC 93-33430. (Handbook of Statistics Ser.: No. 12). 948p. 1994. 190.00 (*0-444-89803-4*, North Holland) Elsevier.

S

***Statistics & Problems in Modern Life.** 6th ed. Newmark. (C). 1997. student ed. write for info. (*0-03-019487-3*) HB Coll Pubs.

***Statistics & Problems in Modern Life.** 6th ed. Newmark. (C). 1997. lab manual ed. write for info. (*0-03-019489-X*) HB Coll Pubs.

***Statistics & Problems in Modern Life.** 6th ed. Newmark. (C). 1997. pap. write for info. (*0-03-020338-4*) HB Coll Pubs.

***Statistics & Problems in Modern Life.** 6th ed. Newmark. (C). 1997. write for info. (*0-03-006393-0*) HB Coll Pubs.

***Statistics & Public Policy.** B. D. Spencer. 320p. 1997. 36.95 (*0-19-852341-6*) OUP.

Statistics & Quality Control for the Workplace. Frank C. Kaminsky et al. LC 93-12053. 116p. 1993. 10.98 (*0-87389-205-4*, H0752) ASQC Qual Pr.

Statistics & Research Design in the Behavioral Sciences. Richard S. Lehman. 550p. (C). 1991. text ed. 59.95 (*0-534-13878-0*) Brooks-Cole.

Statistics & Research Design in the Behavioral Sciences: Answer Book. Richard S. Lehman. Date not set. write for info. (*0-534-13879-9*) Brooks-Cole.

Statistics & Society: Data Collection & Interpretation. 2nd ed. Walter T. Federer. (Statistics: Textbooks & Monographs: Vol. 117). 600p. 1991. 45.00 (*0-8247-8249-6*) Dekker.

Statistics & Society: Data Collection & Interpretation. Walter T. Federer. LC 73-79457. (Statistics, Textbooks & Monographs: No. 3). (Illus.). 413p. reprint ed. pap. 117.80 (*0-8357-3550-8*, 2034530) Bks Demand.

Statistics & Sociology. Gudmund R. Iverson. LC 72-86045. (Studies in Sociology). 46p. (C). 1972. pap. text ed. write for info. (*0-672-61218-6*, Bobbs) Macmillan.

Statistics & Strength of Materials. Dr. Harris. 1987. text ed. 94.00 (*0-13-844754-3*) P-H.

Statistics & the Evaluation of Evidence for Forensic Scientists. C. G. Aitken. (Statistics in Practice Ser.). 290p. 1995. text ed. 62.95 (*0-471-95532-9*) Wiley.

Statistics & the Law. Ed. by Morris H. Degroot et al. (Probability & Mathematical Statistics Ser.). 484p. 1986. text ed. 121.00 (*0-471-09435-8*) Wiley.

Statistics & the Law. Ed. by Morris H. DeGroot et al. (Classics Library). 484p. 1994. pap. text ed. 45.95 (*0-471-05538-7*) Wiley.

***Statistics & Truth, Putting Chance to Work.** LC 97-10349. 240p. 1997. text ed. 25.00 (*981-02-3111-3*) World Scientific Pub.

Statistics Applied to Canadian Issues. Clarence Bayne et al. 1991. 22.50 (*0-536-58107-X*) Ginn Pr.

Statistics As Principled Argument. Robert P. Abelson. 232p. 1995. 49.95 (*0-8058-0527-3*) L Erlbaum Assocs.

Statistics As Principled Argument. Robert P. Abelson. 232p. 1995. pap. 24.95 (*0-8058-0528-1*) L Erlbaum Assocs.

***Statistics at Square One.** 9th rev. ed. Ed. by T. D. Swinscow. 152p. 1996. pap. text ed. 22.00 (*0-7279-0916-9*, Pub. by BMJ Pubng Grp UK) Amer Coll Phys.

Statistics Business Economics. 6th ed. Anderson. Date not set. wbk. ed., pap. text ed. 22.25 (*0-314-08459-2*); student ed., pap. text ed. write for info. (*0-314-08588-2*) West Pub.

Statistics by Example. 5th ed. Boudreau. 1993. student ed., pap. text ed. 25.00 (*0-02-312716-3*, Macmillan Coll) P-H.

Statistics by Example. 5th ed. Terry Sincich. LC 92-42330. 960p. (C). 1993. text ed. 78.00 (*0-02-410981-9*, Macmillan Coll) P-H.

***Statistics, Concepts & Controversies.** 4th ed. David S. Moore. 1997. pap. text ed. 32.95 (*0-7167-2863-X*) W H Freeman.

Statistics Easystat Manual: An Introduction. 4th ed. Mason. (Statistics Ser.). 1994. pap. 23.95 (*0-534-51072-8*) Wadsworth Pub.

Statistics Economized: Basic Statistics for Economics & Business. Walter D. Fisher. LC 81-40114. (Illus.). 282p. (Orig.). (C). 1981. pap. text ed. 24.00 (*0-8191-1745-5*) U Pr of Amer.

An Asterisk (*) at the beginning of an entry indicates that the title is appearing in BIP for the first time.

***Statistics Emerging Lab Market.** Chernyshev. LC 97-13477. 1997. text ed. 69.95 (*0-312-17620-1*) St Martin.

Statistics Europe. 6th ed. 1995. write for info. (*0-8103-9951-2*, 070093) Gale.

***Statistics Explained.** J. P. Lewis. (C). 1998. pap. text ed. write for info. (*0-201-17802-8*) Addison-Wesley.

Statistics Explained: An Easy Guide for Students. Perry R. Hinton. LC 94-41830. 344p. (C). 1995. pap. 17.95 (*0-415-10286-3*) Routledge.

Statistics Explained: An Easy Guide for Students. Perry R. Hinton. LC 94-41830. 344p. (C). (gr. 13). 1995. text ed. 59.95 (*0-415-10285-5*) Routledge.

Statistics for Analytical Chemistry. 3rd ed. Jane C. Miller & James N. Miller. LC 93-4521. 256p. 1993. pap. text ed. 74.00 (*0-13-030990-7*) P-H.

Statistics for Analytical Chemists. R. Caulcutt & R. Boddy. 264p. (gr. 13). 1983. text ed. 100.95 (*0-412-23730-X*, NO. 6806) Chapman & Hall.

Statistics for Applied Problem Solving & Decision Making. Richard Larsen et al. LC 96-35368. (Business Statistics Ser.). (C). 1997. text ed. 62.95 (*0-534-93084-0*) Wadsworth Pub.

Statistics for Archaeologists: A Commonsense Approach. R. D. Drennan. (Interdisciplinary Contributions to Archaeology Ser.). (Illus.). 273p. (C). 1996. 42.50 (*0-306-45327-4*, Plenum Pr) Plenum.

Statistics for Archaeologists: A Commonsense Approach. R. D. Drennan. (Interdisciplinary Contributions to Archaeology Ser.). (Illus.). 273p. (C). 1996. 24.50 (*0-306-45326-6*, Plenum Pr) Plenum.

***Statistics for Bahaverial & Social Sciences: Custom Edition.** Ed. by Kenny. (C). 1994. text ed. 51.95 (*0-673-52430-2*) Addison-Wesley.

Statistics for Behavioral & Social Sciences. Aron. LC 96-41285. 1996. pap. text ed. 51.00 (*0-13-458902-5*) P-H.

Statistics for Biologists. 3rd ed. R. Campbell. 400p. (C). 1989. 69.95 (*0-521-36095-1*) Cambridge U Pr.

Statistics for Biologists. 3rd ed. R. Campbell. 400p. (C). 1989. pap. text ed. 27.95 (*0-521-36932-0*) Cambridge U Pr.

Statistics for Biologists: A Study Guide. N. R. Webb. 106p. 1985. pap. 11.95 (*0-521-31712-6*) Cambridge U Pr.

Statistics for Business. 2nd ed. Cryer. (Business Statistics Ser.). 1994. student ed., pap. 19.95 (*0-534-20391-4*) Wadsworth Pub.

Statistics for Business. 2nd ed. Cryer & Lovelace. (Business Statistics Ser.). 1994. suppl. ed., pap. 18.95 (*0-534-20393-0*) Wadsworth Pub.

Statistics for Business. 2nd ed. Geoffrey Whitehead. 256p. (Orig.). 1992. pap. 42.50 (*0-273-03810-9*, Pub. by Pitman Pub Ltd UK) Trans-Atl Phila.

Statistics for Business. 4th ed. Derek Gregory et al. LC 92-43484. 336p. (Orig.). 1993. pap. 46.50 (*0-07-707610-9*, Pub. by Stanley Thornes UK) Trans-Atl Phila.

Statistics for Business: Data Analysis & Modeling. 2nd ed. Jonathan D. Cryer & Robert B. Miller. 883p. 1994. text ed. 75.95 (*0-534-20388-4*) Wadsworth Pub.

Statistics for Business: Data Analysis & Modelling. Jonathan D. Cryer & Robert B. Miller. 848p. (C). 1991. text ed. 54.95 (*0-534-92239-2*) Wadsworth Pub.

***Statistics for Business & Economics.** Anderson & Sweeney. (ME - Statistics Ser.). Date not set. student ed., pap. 18.95 (*0-538-87594-1*) S-W Pub.

Statistics for Business & Economics. Becker. (HB - Economics Ser.). 1995. student ed., pap. 22.95 (*0-538-84100-1*) S-W Pub.

Statistics for Business & Economics. William E. Becker. LC 94-18153. 900p. 1995. text ed. 68.95 (*0-538-84033-1*) S-W Pub.

Statistics for Business & Economics. John A. Ingram & Joseph G. Monks. 1049p. (C). 1989. teacher ed. 5.00 (*0-15-583546-7*); disk write for info. (*0-318-64933-0*) HB Coll Pubs.

Statistics for Business & Economics. P. S. Mann. 1995. student ed., pap. write for info. (*0-471-11617-3*) Wiley.

Statistics for Business & Economics. Prem S. Mann. 976p. 1994. text ed. 46.00 (*0-471-58969-1*) Wiley.

***Statistics for Business & Economics.** Prem S. Mann. 1995. pap. text ed. 25.00 (*0-471-11745-5*) Wiley.

Statistics for Business & Economics. Lawrence B. Morse. (C). 1993. 76.95 (*0-06-044617-X*) Addison-Wesley Educ.

Statistics for Business & Economics. Paul Newbold. (Illus.). 864p. (C). 1984. text ed. write for info. (*0-13-845140-0*) P-H.

Statistics for Business & Economics. Deborah O. Oltman. (Business Statistics Ser.). 1991. student ed., pap. 26.95 (*0-534-14433-0*) Wadsworth Pub.

Statistics for Business & Economics. Debra O. Oltman & James R. Lackritz. LC 90-2148. 984p. (C). 1991. text ed. 80.95 (*0-534-14430-6*) Wadsworth Pub.

Statistics for Business & Economics. Paulson. (QM - Quantitative Methods Ser.). Date not set. text ed. 51.00 (*0-87709-368-7*) Course Tech.

Statistics for Business & Economics. Paulson. (QM - Quantitative Methods Ser.). Date not set. student ed., pap. 16.00 (*0-87709-369-5*) Course Tech.

Statistics for Business & Economics. 2nd ed. John A. Ingram & Joseph G. Monks. 925p. (C). 1992. text ed. 52.25 (*0-15-583549-1*) Dryden Pr.

Statistics for Business & Economics. 2nd ed. John A. Ingram & Joseph G. Monks. 907p. (C). 1992. text ed. 68.95 (*0-534-51047-7*) Wadsworth Pub.

Statistics for Business & Economics. 3rd ed. Heinz Kohler. LC 93-12512. (Illus.). (C). 1994. text ed. 76.95 (*0-673-46325-7*); Study guide. student ed., pap. text ed. 21.95 (*0-673-46326-5*) Addison-Wesley Educ.

Statistics for Business & Economics. 4th ed. Paul Newbold. LC 94-33610. 1994. text ed. 91.00 (*0-13-181595-4*) P-H.

Statistics for Business & Economics. 5th ed. David R. Anderson et al. Ed. by Schiller. LC 92-18129. 950p. (C). 1993. text ed. 65.25 (*0-314-01244-3*) West Pub.

Statistics for Business & Economics. 5th ed. James T. McClave, II et al. (Illus.). 1248p. (C). 1991. text ed. write for info. (*0-02-379182-9*, Macmillan Coll) P-H.

Statistics for Business & Economics. 6th ed. David R. Anderson et al. LC 95-41209. 950p. (C). 1996. text ed. write for info. (*0-314-06378-1*) West Atlantic.

Statistics for Business & Economics. 6th ed. James T. McClave & George Benson. LC 93-33416. (Illus.). 935p. (C). 1994. text ed. 77.00 (*0-02-379201-9*, Macmillan Coll) P-H.

Statistics for Business & Economics. 6th ed. Susan L. Reiland. 352p. (C). 1994. pap. text ed. 25.00 (*0-02-399207-7*, Macmillan Coll) P-H.

***Statistics for Business & Economics.** 7th ed. Anderson & Sweeney. (ME - Statistics Ser.). Date not set. student ed., pap. 18.95 (*0-538-87597-6*); text ed. 62.95 (*0-538-87593-3*) S-W Pub.

Statistics for Business & Economics: Back to Basics, 3.5 IBM. Lawrence B. Morse. (C). 1993. pap. text ed. 7.50 (*0-06-501661-0*) Addison-Wesley Educ.

Statistics for Business & Economics: International Edition. John A. Ingram & Joseph G. Monks. 1049p. (C). 1989. write for info. (*0-318-64934-9*) HB Coll Pubs.

Statistics for Business & Economics: Methods & Applications. 5th ed. Edwin Mansfield. LC 93-7702. (C). 1994. text ed. 62.95 (*0-393-96460-4*) Norton.

Statistics for Business & Economics: Problems. 5th ed. Edwin Mansfield. (C). Date not set. pap. text ed. 71.90 (*0-393-96655-0*) Norton.

Statistics for Business & Economics: Problems, Exercises, & Case Studies. 5th ed. Edwin Mansfield. LC 93-22745. (C). 1994. pap. text ed. 18.95 (*0-393-96488-4*) Norton.

Statistics for Business & Economics: Stat Workbook. Lawrence B. Morse. (C). 1994. pap. text ed. 21.95 (*0-06-501762-5*) Addison-Wesley Educ.

Statistics for Business & Economics, Minitab Computer Supplement. 6th ed. Ruth K. Meyer & David D. Krueger. 416p. (C). 1994. pap. text ed. 24.00 (*0-02-380840-3*, Macmillan Coll) P-H.

Statistics for Business & Economics, Student's Solutions Manual. 6th ed. N. Shafer-Boudreau. 1994. pap. text ed. 25.00 (*0-02-312721-X*, Macmillan Coll) P-H.

Statistics for Business & Economy. Becker. (HB - Economics Ser.). 1995. pap. 22.95 (*0-538-84398-5*) S-W Pub.

Statistics for Business & Financial Economics. C. F. Lee. 864p. (C). 1993. text ed. 73.16 (*0-669-24598-4*); Instr.'s manual & test bank. teacher ed. 2.66 (*0-669-24600-X*); Study guide. student ed. 23.56 (*0-669-24599-2*); Minitab manual. student ed. 15.16 (*0-669-32684-4*) HM College Div.

Statistics for Business Problem Solving. Harvey J. Brightman & Howard Schneider. 700p. (C). 1991. text ed. write for info. (*0-538-80286-3*, ME60AA) S-W Pub.

Statistics for Business with Minitab: Text & Cases. P. C. Bell & E. F. Newson. 374p. (Orig.). (C). 1987. teacher ed. (*0-89426-095-2*) Course Tech.

Statistics for Business with Spreadsheets. 2nd ed. Peter C. Bell & E. F. Newson. (Illus.). 410p. (C). 1992. Instr. manual. teacher ed. write for info. (*0-89426-208-4*) Course Tech.

Statistics for Clinicians. Puri. 1996. pap. text ed. 27.00 (*0-7020-1876-7*) Saunders.

Statistics for Decision Making. Larsen & Marx. (Business Statistics Ser.). 1997. pap. 17.95 (*0-534-51730-7*) Wadsworth Pub.

Statistics for Economics. Caniglia. (C). 1992. text ed. 72.95 (*0-06-041168-6*) Addison-Wesley Educ.

Statistics for Economics, Accountancy & Business Studies. Michael Barrow. 1996. pap. text ed. write for info. (*0-582-23953-2*, Pub. by Longman UK) Longman.

Statistics for Economics & Business. David Bowers. 448p. (C). 1991. text ed. 44.00 (*0-8147-1158-8*) NYU Pr.

Statistics for Economics, Business Administration & the Social Sciences. E. B. Andersen et al. (Illus.). 455p. 1987. 50.95 (*0-387-17720-5*) Spr-Verlag.

***Statistics for Education & Psychology.** (C). 1990. pap. write for info. (*0-15-601691-5*) HB Coll Pubs.

Statistics for Educators & Social Scientists with Computer Applications. Archie W. Earl, Sr. (Probability & Statistics Ser.). 580p. (C). 1994. lib. bdg. 62.95 (*1-884169-08-2*) Intl Educ Improve.

Statistics for Educators & Social Scientists with Computer Applications. Archie W. Earl, Sr. (Probability & Statistics Ser.). 580p. (C). 1994. pap. text ed. 47.95 (*1-884169-09-0*) Intl Educ Improve.

Statistics for Engineering & the Sciences. 3rd ed. William Mendenhall. 963p. (C). 1991. text ed. 70.00 (*0-02-380552-8*, Macmillan Coll) P-H.

Statistics for Engineering & the Sciences. 4th ed. William Mendenhall & Terry Sincich. LC 94-41303. 1008p. 1995. text ed. 86.00 (*0-02-380581-1*, Macmillan Coll) P-H.

Statistics for Engineering & the Sciences, Student's Solutions Manual. 3rd ed. N. Shafer-Boudreau. 400p. (C). 1991. pap. text ed. 23.40 (*0-02-379243-4*, Macmillan Coll) P-H.

Statistics for Engineering Problem Solving. Stephen B. Vardeman. 832p. 1994. text ed. 81.95 (*0-534-92871-4*) PWS Pubs.

Statistics for Engineers. A. Greer. 144p. (C). 1988. pap. 52.00 (*0-85950-495-6*, Pub. by S Thornes Pubs UK) St Mut.

Statistics for Engineers. A. Greer. (C). 1990. text ed. 50.00 (*0-85950-574-X*, Pub. by Stanley Thornes UK) Trans-Atl Phila.

***Statistics for Environmental Biology & Toxicology.** John Bailer & W. Piegorsch. (Interdisciplinary Statistics Ser.). 352p. (C). (gr. 13 up). 1997. 59.95 (*0-412-04731-4*) Chapman & Hall.

Statistics for Environmental Engineers. P. Mac Berthouex & Linfield C. Brown. 352p. 1994. 69.95 (*1-56670-031-0*, L1031) Lewis Pubs.

Statistics for Experimenters: An Introduction to Design, Data Analysis & Model Building. George E. Box et al. (Probability & Mathematical Statistics Ser.). 653p. 1978. text ed. 69.95 (*0-471-09315-7*) Wiley.

Statistics for Geoscientists. D. Marsal. (Illus.). 186p. 1987. 74.95 (*0-08-026268-6*, Prgamon Press) Buttrwrth-Heinemann.

Statistics for Health & the Life Sciences. Goteti B. Krishnamurty et al. (Life Science Ser.). 500p. (C). 1994. pap. text ed. 48.75 (*0-86720-868-6*) Jones & Bartlett.

Statistics for Health Professionals. Shott. (Illus.). 432p. 1990. text ed. 41.00 (*0-7216-8254-5*) Saunders.

***Statistics for Health Professionals.** Susan Shott. (Illus.). 1990. teacher ed., pap. write for info. (*0-7216-3472-9*) Saunders.

Statistics for Lawyers. Michael O. Finkelstein & B. Levin. Ed. by Stephen E. Fienberg & Ingram Olkin. (Texts in Statistics Ser.). (Illus.). xxii, 608p. 1990. 76.95 (*0-387-97136-X*); 42.95 (*0-387-97140-8*) Spr-Verlag.

Statistics for Library Decision Making: A Handbook. Peter Hernon et al. Ed. by Charles R. McClure. LC 89-6744. (Information Management, Policies & Services Ser.: Vol. 15). 216p. (C). 1989. pap. 39.50 (*0-89391-605-6*); text ed. 73.25 (*0-89391-586-6*) Ablex Pub.

Statistics for Life Sciences. Samuels. 1988. text ed. 79.00 (*0-02-405501-8*, Macmillan Coll) P-H.

Statistics for Management. John Ashford. 464p. (C). 1980. 78.00 (*0-85292-271-X*) St Mut.

Statistics for Management. 6th ed. Stinson. 1994. pap. text ed. 26.40 (*0-13-847815-5*) P-H.

Statistics for Management. 7th ed. Richard I. Levin & David S. Rubin. LC 96-17344. 1024p. 1997. 73.33 (*0-13-476292-4*) P-H.

Statistics for Management: A Practical Introduction to Statistics. 6th rev. ed. B. J. Mandel & Robert E. Laessig. LC 95-83928. 538p. 1996. text ed. 49.50 (*0-910484-00-7*) Dangary Pub.

***Statistics for Management: One Color.** 6th ed. Levin & David S. Rubin. (C). 1997. pap. text ed. 60.00 (*0-13-633349-4*) P-H.

Statistics for Management & Economics. abr. ed. Gerald Keller et al. 849p. (C). 1994. pap. 53.95 (*0-534-17775-1*) Wadsworth Pub.

Statistics for Management & Economics. 2nd ed. (Business Statistics Ser.). 1992. student ed., pap. 19.95 (*0-534-51048-5*) Wadsworth Pub.

Statistics for Management & Economics. 3rd ed. Keller. (Business Statistics Ser.). 1994. student ed., pap. 18.75 (*0-534-17776-X*) Wadsworth Pub.

Statistics for Management & Economics. 3rd ed. Keller. (Business Statistics Ser.). 1994. student ed., pap. 14.00 (*0-534-17777-8*) Wadsworth Pub.

Statistics for Management & Economics. 3rd ed. Gerald Keller et al. 1016p. (C). 1994. text ed. 55.00 (*0-534-17772-7*) Wadsworth Pub.

Statistics for Management & Economics. 4th ed. Gerald Keller. (Business Statistics Ser.). 1997. pap. 18.95 (*0-534-51586-X*) Wadsworth Pub.

Statistics for Management & Economics. 4th ed. Gerald Keller. (Business Statistics Ser.). 1997. student ed., pap. 25.95 (*0-534-51587-8*) Wadsworth Pub.

Statistics for Management & Economics. 4th ed. Collin J. Watson et al. 950p. 1990. teacher ed. write for info. (*0-318-66348-1*, H21868); teacher ed. write for info. incl. trans. (*0-318-66349-X*, H21850); student ed. 19.00 (*0-685-29829-9*, H22742); write for info. (*0-318-66350-3*, H22221); trans. write for info. (*0-318-66351-1*, H21892) P-H.

Statistics for Management & Economics. 5th ed. Collin J. Watson et al. LC 92-37332. 1000p. (C). 1993. text ed. 61.60 (*0-205-14094-7*) Allyn.

Statistics for Management & Economics. 7th ed. Mendenhall. (Business Statistics Ser.). 1993. student ed., pap. 18.95 (*0-534-93301-7*) Wadsworth Pub.

Statistics for Management & Economics. 7th ed. Mendenhall & Beaver. (Business Statistics Ser.). 1993. student ed., pap. 26.95 (*0-534-93304-1*) Wadsworth Pub.

Statistics for Management & Economics. 7th ed. William Mendenhall et al. LC 92-30933. 1062p. 1993. text ed. 73.95 (*0-534-93299-1*) Wadsworth Pub.

Statistics for Management & Economics: A Systematic Approach. 2nd ed. Gerald Keller et al. 1050p. (C). 1990. text ed. 58.95 (*0-534-12678-2*) Wadsworth Pub.

Statistics for Managers. Ulrich Menzefricke. 682p. 1995. text ed. 71.95 incl. 3.5 hd (*0-534-23538-7*) Wadsworth Pub.

***Statistics for Managers Using Microsoft Excel.** David M. Levine et al. LC 96-34706. 1997. 76.00 (*0-13-462912-4*) P-H.

Statistics for Managing Libarary Acquisitions. Eileen D. Hardy. (Acquisitions Guidelines Ser.: No. 6). 14p. 1989. pap. text ed. 10.00 (*0-8389-3374-2*) ALA.

Statistics for Marketing & Business. R. L. Galloway. (C). 1989. 130.00 (*0-09-172958-0*, Pub. by S Thornes Pubs UK) St Mut.

Statistics for Mathematicians: An Introduction. D. J. Finney. 1968. 15.00 (*0-934454-74-4*) Lubrecht & Cramer.

Statistics for Modern Business: A First Course. Lawrence L. Lapin. 678p. (C). 1995. pap. 48.95 (*0-534-51117-1*) Wadsworth Pub.

Statistics for Modern Business Decisions. 5th ed. Lawrence L. Lapin. 1021p. (C). 1990. text ed. 56.00 (*0-15-583705-2*); disk write for info. (*0-318-67019-4*) Dryden Pr.

Statistics for Modern Business Decisions. 6th ed. Lawrence L. Lapin. LC 92-70669. 1263p. (C). 1993. text ed. 58.75 (*0-15-500004-7*) Dryden Pr.

Statistics for Modern Business Decisions. 6th ed. Lawrence L. Lapin. 1265p. (C). 1993. text ed. 76.95 (*0-534-51062-0*) Wadsworth Pub.

Statistics for Modern Business Decisions. 6th ed. Lapino. (Business Statistics Ser.). 1993. student ed., pap. 23.95 (*0-534-51063-9*) Wadsworth Pub.

Statistics for Modern Business Decisions. 6th ed. Lapino. (Business Statistics Ser.). 1993. suppl. ed., pap. 23.95 (*0-534-51064-7*) Wadsworth Pub.

Statistics for Modern Business Decisions: International Edition. 5th ed. Lawrence L. Lapin. 1021p. (C). 1990. write for info. (*0-318-67020-8*) Dryden Pr.

Statistics for Non-Statisticians: A Primer for Professionals. 2nd ed. Farrell E. Bloch. (Illus.). 188p. 1993. pap. 30.00 (*0-916559-45-9*) EPF.

Statistics for Petroleum Engineers & Geoscientists. Jerry Jensen & Patrick Corbett. 1996. 70.00 (*0-13-131855-1*) P-H.

***Statistics for Pharmacists.** Alain W. Li. LC 97-20887. 1997. pap. write for info. (*0-632-04881-6*) Blackwell Sci.

Statistics for Public Managers. William F. Matlack. LC 91-68073. 536p. (Orig.). (C). 1993. boxed 50.00 (*0-87581-365-8*) Peacock Pubs.

Statistics for Real Estate Professionals. Rebecca F. Guy & Louis G. Pol. LC 88-23660. 211p. 1989. text ed. 59.95 (*0-89930-324-2*, GYS/, Quorum Bks) Greenwood.

Statistics for Research. 2nd ed. Shirley Dowdy & Stanley Wearden. LC 90-42104. (Series in Probability & Mathematics). 629p. 1991. text ed. 72.95 (*0-471-85703-3*) Wiley.

Statistics for Research & Development. 2nd ed. R. Caulcutt. (Illus.). 416p. (gr. 13). 1991. text ed. 72.95 (*0-412-35890-5*, A5899) Chapman & Hall.

***Statistics for Social Change.** Lucy Horwitz & Lou Ferlerger. 341p. 47.99 (*0-920057-12-8*, Pub. by Black Rose Bks CN); pap. 18.99 (*0-920057-11-X*, Pub. by Black Rose Bks CN) Consort Bk Sales.

Statistics for Social Data Analysis. 3rd ed. George W. Bohrnstedt & David Knoke. LC 93-86174. 574p. (C). 1994. teacher ed., boxed 52.00 (*0-87581-381-X*) Peacock Pubs.

***Statistics for Social Research.** George Argyrous. 336p. 1997. 79.95 (*0-7329-3936-4*, Pub. by Macmill Educ AT); pap. 39.95 (*0-7329-3939-9*, Pub. by Macmill Educ AT) Paul & Co Pubs.

Statistics for Social Scientists. Frank J. Kohout. LC 84-5643. 464p. (C). 1984. reprint ed. lib. bdg. 47.50 (*0-89874-759-7*) Krieger.

Statistics for Social Workers. 3rd ed. Robert W. Weinbach. LC 94-6160. 272p. (C). 1995. pap. text ed. 31.50 (*0-8013-1388-0*, 76372) Longman.

***Statistics for Social Workers.** 4th ed. Robert W. Weinbach. (C). 1998. pap. text ed. write for info. (*0-8013-1826-2*) Addison-Wesley.

Statistics for Spatial Data. rev. ed. Noel A. Cassie. 928p. 1993. text ed. 105.00 (*0-471-00255-0*) Wiley.

Statistics for Technicians. J. O. Bird & A. J. May. LC 79-41681. (Longman Technician Series, Mathematics & Sciences). 133p. reprint ed. pap. 38.00 (*0-8357-3551-6*, 2034469) Bks Demand.

Statistics for Technology: A Course in Applied Statistics. 3rd ed. Christopher Chatfield. 384p. (gr. 13). 1983. pap. text ed. 24.95 (*0-412-25340-2*, NO. 6845) Chapman & Hall.

Statistics for the Behavioral & Social Sciences. Sharon L. Weinberg & Kenneth P. Goldberg. (Illus.). 453p. (C). 1990. 74.95 (*0-521-37089-2*) Cambridge U Pr.

Statistics for the Behavioral Sciences. 34.95 (*0-521-40873-3*) Cambridge U Pr.

Statistics for the Behavioral Sciences. Kenneth M. Rosenberg. 496p. (C). 1990. boxed write for info. (*0-697-09740-4*); write for info. (*0-318-66913-7*) Brown & Benchmark.

Statistics for the Behavioral Sciences. Kenneth M. Rosenberg. 496p. (C). 1990. student ed., per. write for info. (*0-697-11257-8*) Brown & Benchmark.

***Statistics for the Behavioral Sciences.** Steve Slane & B. Michael Thorne. 324p. (Orig.). 1997. pap. text ed. 17.95 (*1-55934-639-6*, 1639) Mayfield Pub.

Statistics for the Behavioral Sciences. B. Michael Thorne. LC 88-13349. 363p. (C). 1989. text ed. 51.95 (*0-87484-813-X*, 813) Mayfield Pub.

Statistics for the Behavioral Sciences. 2nd ed. James Jaccard & Michael A. Becker. 520p. (C). 1990. text ed. 47.50 (*0-534-10326-X*) Brooks-Cole.

***Statistics for the Behavioral Sciences.** 2nd ed. B. Michael Thorne & Steve Slane. LC 96-32313. 1997. text ed. 59.95 incl. disk (*1-55934-805-4*) Mayfield Pub.

Statistics for the Behavioral Sciences. 3rd ed. Frederick J. Gravetter & Larry B. Wallnau. Ed. by Baxter. 632p. (C). 1992. text ed. 63.00 (*0-314-90876-5*) West Pub.

Statistics for the Behavioral Sciences. 3rd ed. James Jaccard & Michael A. Becker. (C). 1997. teacher ed., text ed. write for info. (*0-534-17408-6*) Brooks-Cole.

Statistics for the Behavioral Sciences. 3rd ed. James Jaccard & Michael A. Becker. (Psychology Ser.). 646p. (C). 1997. text ed. 64.95 (*0-534-17406-X*) Brooks-Cole.

Statistics for the Behavioral Sciences. 3rd ed. James Jaccard & Michael A. Becker. (Psychology Ser.). (C). 1997. student ed., text ed. 21.95 (*0-534-17407-8*) Brooks-Cole.

Statistics for the Behavioral Sciences. 4th ed. Frederick J. Gravetter & Larry B. Wallnau. LC 95-44462. 650p. (C). 1996. text ed. 63.00 (*0-314-06806-6*) West Pub.

Statistics for the Behavioral Sciences: Instructor's Manual. 2nd ed. James Jaccard & Michael A. Becker. Date not set. teacher ed. write for info. (*0-534-10328-6*) Brooks-Cole.

S

Statistics for the Behavioral Sciences: Study Guide. 2nd ed. Jaccard. (Psychology Ser.). 1990. student ed., pap. 22.95 (*0-534-10327-8*) Brooks-Cole.

Statistics for the Behavioral Sciences, Instructor's Manual. B. Michael Thorne. (C). 1989. teacher ed., pap. text ed. write for info. (*0-87484-932-2*, 932) Mayfield Pub.

***Statistics for the Behavioral Sciences Instructor's Manual.** 2nd rev. ed. Steve Slane & B. Michael Thorne. 71p. 1997. pap. text ed. write for info. (*1-55934-638-8*, 1638) Mayfield Pub.

Statistics for the Behavioral Sciences Workbook. B. Michael Thorne. (C). 1989. student ed., pap. text ed. 16.95 (*0-87484-816-4*, 816) Mayfield Pub.

***Statistics for the Behavioral Sciences, 1989: Including Labstat Pkg.** B. Michael Thorne. 384p. 56.95 (*1-55934-766-X*) Mayfield Pub.

***Statistics for the Behavioral Sciences, 1989: Including Workbook.** B. Michael Thorne. 384p. 56.95 (*1-55934-408-3*) Mayfield Pub.

Statistics for the Biological Sciences. 2nd ed. William C. Schefler. LC 78-55830. (Illus.). 1979. text ed. write for info. (*0-201-07500-8*) Addison-Wesley.

***Statistics for the Biosciences 3: Data Analysis Using Minitab Software.** LC 96-48475. 1997. 55.00 (*0-13-447582-8*) P-H.

Statistics for the Environment. Ed. by Vic Barnett & K. Feridun Turkman. LC 92-21239. 427p. 1993. text ed. 115.00 (*0-471-93467-4*) Wiley.

Statistics for the Environment: Water Related Issues. Ed. by Vic Barnett & K. Feridun Turkman. 391p. 1995. text ed. 57.95 (*0-471-95048-3*) Wiley.

Statistics for the Health Professional. 2nd ed. Shott. Date not set. pap. text ed. write for info. (*0-7216-5979-9*) HarBrace.

Statistics for the Health Sciences. Richard J. Larsen. (Illus.). (C). 1986. reprint ed. pap. text ed. 14.95 (*0-935005-04-8*); reprint ed. lib. bdg. 21.95 (*0-935005-10-2*) Lincoln-Rembrandt.

Statistics for the Helping Professions. Frank P. Besag & Peter L. Besag. LC 84-13399. 375p. 1985. reprint ed. pap. 106.90 (*0-608-01482-6*, 2059526) Bks Demand.

Statistics for the Real World. Heiner Thiessen. LC 96-21458. 200p. 1996. pap. text ed. 35.00 incl. disk (*0-471-94988-4*) Wiley.

Statistics for the Social & Behavioral Science: Univariate, Bivariate, & Multivariate. George M. Diekhoff. 448p. (C). 1992. boxed write for info. (*0-697-12116-X*) Brown & Benchmark.

Statistics for the Social & Behavioral Sciences. George M. Diekhoff. 448p. (C). 1994. per. write for info. (*0-697-28514-6*) Brown & Benchmark.

Statistics for the Social Sciences. Leroy C. Gould. Ed. by Marshall. 450p. (C). text ed. write for info. (*0-314-02839-0*) West Pub.

Statistics for the Social Sciences. R. Mark Sirkin. LC 94-18897. 1994. 69.95 (*0-8039-5144-2*); pap. 36.50 (*0-8039-5145-0*) Sage.

Statistics for the Social Sciences. Ed. by Rand R. Wilcox. (Illus.). 430p. 1995. 59.95 incl. disk (*0-12-751540-2*) Acad Pr.

***Statistics for the Social Sciences Workbook.** Walsh. (C). 1991. text ed. 16.95 (*0-06-046903-X*) Addison-Wesley.

Statistics for the Terrified. Gerald D. Kranzler & Janet P. Moursund. LC 94-34406. 176p. 1994. pap. text ed. 23.00 (*0-13-183831-8*) P-H.

Statistics for the Twenty-First Century. Ed. by Florence Gordon & Sheldon Gordon. LC 91-60194. (MAA Notes Ser.: Vol. 26). 318p. 1992. pap. 29.95 (*0-88385-078-8*, NTE-26) Math Assn.

Statistics for the 21st Century: Proposals for Improving Statistics for Better Decision Making. Joseph W. Duncan & Andrew C. Gross. 230p. (Orig.). 1993. pap. 14.95 (*1-56203-310-7*) Irwin Prof Pubng.

Statistics for the 21st Century: Proposals for Improving Statistics for Better Decision Making. Joseph W. Duncan & Andrew Grass. 336p. (Orig.). 1995. text ed. 45.00 (*0-7863-0328-X*) Irwin Prof Pubng.

Statistics for Toxicologists. Salsburg. (Drug & Chemical Toxicology Ser.: Vol. 4). 216p. 1986. 110.00 (*0-8247-7590-2*) Dekker.

Statistics from Scratch: An Introduction for Health Care Professionals. David Bowers. LC 95-49518. 1996. pap. text ed. 19.95 (*0-471-96325-9*) Wiley.

***Statistics Further from Scratch.** LC 96-47783. 1997. pap. write for info. (*0-471-97136-7*) Wiley.

Statistics in a World of Applications. 4th ed. Ramakant Khazanie. LC 95-23434. 768p. (C). 1996. text ed. 63.95 (*0-673-46768-6*) Addson-Wesley Educ.

Statistics in a World of Applications. 4th ed. Khoury. (C). 1995. teacher ed. write for info. (*0-673-55118-0*) Addson-Wesley Educ.

Statistics in a World of Applications. 4th ed. Khoury. LC 95-23434. (C). 1996. student ed., pap. text ed. 22.50 (*0-673-46770-8*) Addson-Wesley Educ.

Statistics in Britain, Eighteen Sixty-Five to Nineteen Thirty: The Social Construction of Scientific Knowledge. Donald Mackenzie. 306p. 1981. 26.50 (*0-85224-369-3*, Pub. by Edinburgh U Pr UK) Col U Pr.

***Statistics in Clinical Practice.** Ed. by David Coggan. 120p. (Orig.). 1995. pap. text ed. 26.00 (*0-7279-0907-X*, Pub. by BMJ Pubng Grp UK) Amer Coll Phys.

***Statistics in Criminal Justice.** David Weisburd. (Criminal Justice Ser.). (C). 1998. student ed., pap. 15.95 (*0-534-51842-7*) Wadsworth Pub.

***Statistics in Criminal Justice: Macintosh Version.** David Weisburd. (Criminal Justice Ser.). (C). 1997. text ed. 60.95 (*0-534-51841-9*) Wadsworth Pub.

Statistics in Criminal Justice: Windows Version. David Weisburd. (Criminal Justice Ser.). (C). 1997. text ed. 60.95 (*0-534-51840-0*) Wadsworth Pub.

Statistics in Dialectology. Lawrence M. Davis. LC 90-35856. 104p. 1990. pap. text ed. 14.95 (*0-8173-0510-6*) U of Ala Pr.

Statistics in Engineering: A Practical Approach. A. V. Metcalfe. 1994. pap. 26.95 (*0-412-49220-2*, Blackie & Son-Chapman NY) Routledge Chapman & Hall.

Statistics in Epidemiology: Methods, Techniques, & Applications. Hardeo Sahai & Anwer Khurshid. 352p. 1995. 59.95 (*0-8493-9444-9*, 9444) CRC Pr.

Statistics in Geography: A Practical Approach. 2nd ed. David Ebdon. 240p. 1993. pap. text ed. 25.95 (*0-631-13688-6*) Blackwell Pubs.

***Statistics in Human Genetics.** write for info. (*0-340-66241-7*, Pub. by E Arnold UK) Routledge Chapman & Hall.

***Statistics in Industry Case Studies of Semiconductor Process-Equipment Characterization.** Ed. by A. Veronica Czitrom & Spagon. (Interdisciplinary Statistics Ser.). 330p. text ed. 59.95 (*0-412-99701-0*, Chap & Hall NY) Chapman & Hall.

Statistics in Kinesiology. William J. Vincent. LC 94-1643. 272p. 1994. pap. text ed. 24.00 (*0-87322-699-2*, BVIN0699) Human Kinetics.

Statistics in Language Studies. Anthony Woods et al. (Cambridge Textbooks in Linguistics Ser.). (Illus.). 350p. 1986. text ed. 89.95 (*0-521-25326-8*); pap. text ed. 31.95 (*0-521-27312-9*) Cambridge U Pr.

Statistics in Litigation. Richard A. Wehmhoefer. 506p. 1985. text ed. 95.00 (*0-07-017857-7*) Shepards.

Statistics in Medical Research: Developments in Clinical Trials. E. A. Gehan & N. A. Lemak. (Illus.). 224p. (C). 1995. 39.50 (*0-306-44863-7*, Plenum Pr) Plenum.

Statistics in Medicine. Theodore Colton. LC 73-1413. 400p. 1975. pap. text ed. 43.95 (*0-316-15250-1*) Lppncott-Raven.

Statistics in Medicine. Ed. by F. Dunstan & J. Pickles. (Institute of Mathematics & Its Applications Conference Series, New Ser.: New Series 29). (Illus.). 288p. 1991. 79.00 (*0-19-853662-3*) OUP.

Statistics in Ornithology. Ed. by B. J. Morgan & P. M. North. LC 85-10052. (Lecture Notes in Statistics Ser.: Vol. 29). xxv, 418p. 1997. pap. 59.00 (*0-387-96189-5*) Spr-Verlag.

Statistics in Plain English. Harvey J. Brightman. (C). 1986. pap. 23.95 (*0-538-13210-8*, M21) S-W Pub.

Statistics in Political & Behavioral Science. 2nd ed. Dennis J. Palumbo. LC 76-15572. 469p. 1977. text ed. 57.50 (*0-231-04010-5*) Col U Pr.

***Statistics in Practice.** Blaisde. (C). 1993. student ed. write for info. (*0-03-032227-8*) HB Coll Pubs.

***Statistics in Practice.** Blaisde. (C). 1993. write for info. (*0-03-032229-4*) HB Coll Pubs.

Statistics in Practice. 2nd ed. Blaisdell. (C). 1997. text ed. write for info. (*0-03-019374-5*) HarBrace.

***Statistics in Practice.** 2nd ed. Blaisdell. (C). 1996. teacher ed., pap. text ed. 28.00 (*0-03-019849-6*) HB Coll Pubs.

***Statistics in Practice.** 2nd ed. Blaisdell. (C). 1998. pap. text ed. 21.00 (*0-03-019843-7*); student ed., pap. text ed. 17.00 (*0-03-019844-5*) HB Coll Pubs.

***Statistics in Practice: An Illustrated Guide to SPSS.** Basant K. Puri. (Illus.). 144p. 1996. text ed. 24.95 (*0-340-66209-3*, Pub. by Ed Arnold UK) OUP.

Statistics in Psychology: An Historical Perspective. Michael Cowles. 224p. (C). 1989. text ed. 49.95 (*0-8058-0031-X*) L Erlbaum Assocs.

Statistics in Psychology & Education. Henry E. Garrett. LC 82-15599. xii, 491p. (C). 1982. reprint ed. text ed. 99.75 (*0-313-23653-4*, GAST, Greenwood Pr) Greenwood.

Statistics in Research: Basic Concepts & Techniques for Research Workers. 4th ed. Bernard Ostle & Linda C. Malone. (Illus.). 682p. 1987. text ed. 56.95 (*0-8138-1569-X*) Iowa St U Pr.

Statistics in Science: A Students' & Teachers' Manual for Science, Math & Computer Science, Projects & Experiments. Judy Beauford. LC 91-66670. 135p. 1992. pap. text ed. 14.95 (*0-88247-905-9*, 905) R & E Pubs.

Statistics in Science: The Foundations of Statistical Methods in Biology, Physics & Economics. Ed. by Roger Cooke & Domenico Costantini. 200p. (C). 1990. lib. bdg. 115.50 (*0-7923-0797-6*, Pub. by Klwr Acad Pubs NE) Kluwer Ac.

Statistics in Small Doses. 2nd rev. ed. Winifred M. Castle. LC 76-8430. (Illus.). 226p. (C). 1977. pap. text ed. 23.00 (*0-443-01491-4*) Churchill.

Statistics in Small Doses. 3rd ed. Win M. Castle & Philip M. North. LC 95-9992. 1995. write for info. (*0-443-04542-9*) Churchill.

Statistics in Spectroscopy. Howard Mark & Jerry Workman. (Illus.). 313p. 1991. text ed. 73.00 (*0-12-472530-9*) Acad Pr.

Statistics in the Behavioral Sciences: A Conceptual Introduction. Richard S. Lehman. LC 94-22175. 538p. 1995. text ed. 67.95 (*0-534-25320-2*) Brooks-Cole.

Statistics in the Behavioral Sciences: A Conceptual Introduction. Richard S. Lehman. Date not set. teacher ed. write for info. (*0-534-25321-0*) Brooks-Cole.

***Statistics in the Environmental & Earth Sciences.** write for info. (*0-340-54530-5*, Pub. by E Arnold UK) Routledge Chapman & Hall.

Statistics in the Environmental & Earth Sciences: New Developments. Andrew Walden & Peter Guttorp. 306p. 1992. text ed. 195.00 (*0-470-21946-7*) Halsted Pr.

Statistics in the Environmental Sciences - STP 845. ASTM Committee D-19 on Water. Ed. by Steven M. Gertz & M. D. London. LC 83-73430. 115p. 1984. pap. 24.00 (*0-8031-0206-2*, 04-845000-16) ASTM.

Statistics in the Labor Market: The Role in Planning & Policy Formulation. Trewin. (Lecture Notes in Statistics Ser.: Vol. 5). 176p. 1983. 75.00 (*0-8247-1912-3*) Dekker.

Statistics in the Pharmaceutical Industry. 2nd ed. Ed. by C. Ralph Buncher & Jia-Yeong Tsay. LC 93-6362. (Statistics: Textbooks & Monographs: Vol. 140). 592p. 1993. 165.00 (*0-8247-9073-1*) Dekker.

Statistics in Theory & Practice. Robert Lupton. LC 92-36396. (Illus.). 128p. (C). 1993. text ed. 29.95 (*0-691-07429-1*) Princeton U Pr.

Statistics in Toxicology. Ed. by D. Krewski & C. Franklin. 677p. 1991. text ed. 337.00 (*2-88124-340-1*) Gordon & Breach.

Statistics in Toxicology: A Volume in Memory of David A. Williams. Ed. by Byron J. Morgan. (Royal Statistical Society Lecture Notes Ser.: No. 3). (Illus.). 248p. 1996. 65.00 (*0-19-852329-7*) OUP.

Statistics Inference for Branching Processes. Peter Guttorp. LC 90-22224. (Series in Probability & Mathematical Statistics). 211p. 1991. text ed. 93.95 (*0-471-82291-4*) Wiley.

Statistics Lab, No. 123: Using Electronic Spreadsheet. Tower Chen. 60p. (C). 1993. student ed. write for info. (*0-9630276-5-4*) Jern Charng.

***Statistics Lecture Notes.** 2nd ed. Alex Waigandt. 152p. (C). 1997. per. 22.95 (*0-7872-3670-5*) Kendall-Hunt.

Statistics Made Simple. H. T. Hayslett, Jr. LC 67-10414. (Made Simple Ser.). 192p. 1968. pap. 12.00 (*0-385-02355-3*) Doubleday.

Statistics Management. 5th ed. Watson & Billingsley. 1993. wbk. ed., pap. text ed. 22.20 (*0-205-14864-6*) Allyn.

Statistics Manual. Edwin L. Crow et al. (Illus.). (C). 1955. pap. 6.95 (*0-486-60599-X*) Dover.

Statistics, Minitab Computer Supplement. 6th ed. Ruth K. Meyer & David D. Krueger. 352p. (C). 1994. pap. text ed. 25.00 (*0-02-380833-0*, Macmillan Coll) P-H.

Statistics Minitab Manual. Amir D. Aczel & Michael Doviak. 120p. (C). 1995. 10.50 (*0-256-20064-5*) Irwin.

Statistics of Bivariate Extreme Values. H. Xin. (Tinbergen Institute Research Ser.). 94p. 1992. pap. 25.00 (*90-5170-127-6*, Pub. by Thesis Pubs NE) IBD Ltd.

Statistics of Deadly Quarrels. Lewis F. Richardson. Ed. by Quincy Wright & C. C. Lienau. (Illus.). 1960. 45.00 (*0-910286-10-8*) Boxwood.

***Statistics of Education: Schools in England 1996.** Stationery Office. 240p. 1997. pap. 45.00 (*0-11-271004-2*, HM10042, Pub. by Stationery Ofc UK) Bernan Associates.

Statistics of Extremes. Emil J. Gumbel. LC 57-10160. 397p. reprint ed. pap. 113.20 (*0-8357-7038-9*, 2033593) Bks Demand.

Statistics of Health Services & of Their Activities: Proceedings of the WHO Expert Committee on Health Statistics, 13th, Geneva, 1968. WHO Staff. (Technical Report Ser.: No. 429). 1969. pap. text ed. 5.00 (*92-4-120429-X*, 1100429) World Health.

Statistics of Insanity see On the Different Forms of Insanity in Relation to Jurisprudence

***Statistics of Knots & Entangled Random Walks.** 200p. 1996. text ed. 20.00 (*981-02-2519-9*) World Scientific Pub.

Statistics of Natural Selection. Bryan F. Manly. 500p. 1987. pap. text ed. 37.50 (*0-412-30700-6*) Chapman & Hall.

Statistics of Quality, Vol. 153. Ed. by Ghosh et al. LC 96-31579. (Statistics: Textbooks & Monographs: Vol. 153). 456p. 1996. 69.75 (*0-8247-9763-9*) Dekker.

Statistics of Road Traffic Accidents in Europe, Vol. 34. (Transport Ser.). 83p. 1987. 22.00 (*92-1-016219-6*, EFR. 88.II.E.13) UN.

Statistics of Road Traffic Accidents in Europe, Vol. XXXV. 80p. 1988. 25.00 (*92-1-016226-9*, 89.II.E.3) UN.

Statistics of Road Traffic Accidents in Europe, Vol. XXXVI. 1991. 25.00 (*92-1-016261-7*, 91.II.E.16) UN.

Statistics of Road Traffic Accidents in Europe Vol. XLI: 1996. 113p. 1995. 25.00 (*92-1-016305-2*) UN.

Statistics of Road Traffic Accidents in Europe Vol. XXXIX: 1994. 113p. 1993. 25.00 (*92-1-016278-1*) UN.

Statistics of Road Traffic Accidents in Europe & North America. 121p. 1994. 25.00 (*92-1-016295-1*) UN.

Statistics of Road Traffic Accidents in Europe, 1989, Vol. XXXVI. 86p. 1991. 25.00 (*92-1-016247-1*, 90.II.E.22) UN.

Statistics of School Library Media Centers, 1985. David V. Loertscher. 1990. 30.00 (*0-931510-31-7*) Hi Willow.

***Statistics of the Boolean Model for Practitioners & Mathematicians.** Ilya Molchanov. (Series in Probability & Statistics). 160p. 1997. 49.95 (*0-471-97102-2*, PR10) Wiley.

Statistics of the United States, 1860. U. S. Census Office Staff. LC 75-22852. (America in Two Centuries Ser.). 1976. reprint ed. 53.95 (*0-405-07719-X*) Ayer.

Statistics of World Trade in Steel. 93p. 1988. 25.00 (*92-1-016231-5*, 89.II.E.8) UN.

Statistics of World Trade in Steel. 1990. 25.00 (*92-1-016257-9*, 91.II.E.12) UN.

Statistics of World Trade in Steel: 1993. 155p. 1994. 28.00 (*92-1-016302-8*, T.94.II.E.37) UN.

Statistics of World Trade in Steel, 1987. 63p. (ENG, FRE & RUS.). 1988. pap. 17.00 (*92-1-016215-3*, 88.II.E.10) UN.

Statistics of World Trade in Steel, 1989. 1990. 25.00 (*92-1-016242-0*, TR90.II.E.17) UN.

Statistics on Alcohol, Drug, & Tobacco Use: A Selection of Statistical Charts, Graphs & Tables about Alcohol, Drug & Tobacco Use from a Variety of Published Sources with Explanatory Comments. Ed. by Timothy L. Gall & Daniel M. Lucas. LC 95-32413. (Statistics for Students Ser.). 254p. 1995. 55.00 (*0-7876-0526-3*, 109567) Gale.

Statistics on American Business Abroad, 1950-1975: An Original Anthology. U. S. Department of Commerce Staff. Ed. by Stuart Bruchey & Eleanor Bruchey. LC 76-5035. (American Business Abroad Ser.). (Illus.). 1976. 30.95 (*0-405-09301-2*) Ayer.

Statistics on Children in UNICEF Assisted Countries. rev. ed. (Illus.). 285p. 1992. 45.00 (*92-806-1084-8*, E.92.XX. USA.2) UN.

Statistics on Crime & Punishment. Gall. 1996. 55.00 (*0-7876-0528-X*) Gale.

Statistics on Military Expenditure in Developing Countries: Concepts, Methodological Problems, & Sources. OECD Staff. 76p. (Orig.). 1994. pap. 12.00 (*92-64-14230-4*) OECD.

Statistics on Outdoor Recreation, Pts. 1 & 2. Ed. by Marion Clawson & Carlton S. Van Doren. 368p. 1984. 16.50 (*0-318-37304-1*) Resources Future.

Statistics on Outdoor Recreation Pt. 1: The Record Through 1956, Pt. 1. Ed. by Marion Clawson & Carlton S. Van Doren. 368p. 1984. pap. write for info. (*0-318-63350-7*) Resources Future.

Statistics on Outdoor Recreation Pt. 2: The Record since 1956, Pt. 2. Ed. by Marion Clawson & Carlton S. Van Doren. 368p. 1984. pap. write for info. (*0-318-63351-5*) Resources Future.

***Statistics on Poverty & Income Distribution: An ILO Compendium of Data.** Hamid Tabatabai. 150p. 1996. pap. 24.75 (*92-2-109505-3*) Intl Labour Office.

Statistics on Psychotropic Substances. 196p. (Orig.). 1989. 22.00 (*92-1-048048-1*) UN.

Statistics on Psychotropic Substances for 1988. 116p. 19.00 (*92-1-048046-5*, EFS.89.XI.4) UN.

Statistics on Psychotropic Substances, 1990. 196p. 1991. 38.00 (*92-1-048051-1*, 91.XI.3) UN.

Statistics on Social Work Education in the U. S. 1994. Todd M. Lennon. 131p. (Orig.). (C). 1994. pap. text ed. 13.00 (*0-87293-047-5*) Coun Soc Wk Ed.

Statistics on the IBM: Introduction, Practial Applications, Ready to Run Programs. Sam D. Roberts. (Illus.). 200p. 1985. pap. 12.95 (*3-88963-047-2*) Elcomp.

Statistics on U. S. Immigration: An Assessment of Data Needs for Future Research. National Research Council Staff. Ed. by Barry Edmonston. 100p. (Orig.). 1996. pap. text ed. 24.00 (*0-309-05275-0*) Natl Acad Pr.

Statistics on Weapons & Violence: A Selection of Statistical Charts, Graphs & Tables about Weapons & Violence from a Variety of Published Sources with Explanatory Comments. Ed. by Timothy L. Gall et al. LC 95-44897. (Statistics for Students Ser.). (Illus.). 250p. 1995. 55.00 (*0-7876-0527-1*, 109568) Gale.

Statistics Primer for Managers: How to Ask the Right Questions About Forecasting, Control & Investment. John J. Clark & Margaret T. Clark. (Illus.). 272p. write for info. (*0-318-56699-0*) Macmillan.

Statistics, Probability, & Graphing: A "Hands On" Approach to Teaching . . . Andy Heidemann et al. (Illus.). 202p. 1988. teacher ed. 17.95 (*0-927726-00-9*) Hands On CA.

***Statistics, Probability & Reliability for Civil & Environmental Engineers.** Nathabandu T. Kottegoda & Renzo Rosso. LC 96-52333. 1997. write for info. (*0-07-035966-0*) McGraw.

Statistics Problem Solver. rev. ed. Research & Education Association Staff. LC 78-64581. (Illus.). 1056p. 1996. pap. text ed. 23.95 (*0-87891-515-X*) Res & Educ.

Statistics Quick Review. David H. Voelker & Peter Z. Orton. (Cliffs Quick Reviews Ser.). (Illus.). 164p. (Orig.). (C). 1993. pap. text ed. 7.95 (*0-8220-5349-7*) Cliffs.

Statistics "Reading in Statistics" Amir D. Aczel. 128p. (C). 1995. 11.85 (*0-256-18929-3*) Irwin.

Statistics Sources. 11th ed. Ed. by Jacqueline W. O'Brien & Steven R. Wasserman. 1550p. 1987. 280.00 (*0-8103-4398-3*) Gale.

Statistics Sources, 2 vols. 13th ed. Wasserman. 1989. 305.00 (*0-8103-4699-0*) Gale.

Statistics Sources, 2 vols. 15th ed. Wasserman. 1991. 335.00 (*0-8103-7378-5*) Gale.

Statistics Sources, 2 vols. 16th ed. Wasserman. 1992. 345.00 (*0-8103-7665-2*) Gale.

Statistics Sources, 2 Vols. 17th ed. Wasserman. 1993. 375.00 (*0-8103-8162-1*) Gale.

Statistics Sources, 2 vols. 18th ed. Wasserman. 1994. 375.00 (*0-8103-8533-3*) Gale.

***Statistics Sources, 2 vols.** 20th ed. 1996. 400.00 (*0-8103-5782-8*, 00010156, Gale Res Intl) Gale.

***Statistics Sources, 2 vols.** 21th ed. 1997. 415.00 (*0-7876-0162-4*, 00108856, Gale Res Intl) Gale.

Statistics Sources, Vol. 1. 18th ed. Wasserman. 1994. write for info. (*0-8103-8534-1*) Gale.

Statistics Sources, Vol. 2. 18th ed. Wasserman. 1994. write for info. (*0-8103-8535-X*) Gale.

***Statistics Sources, Vol. 2.** 22th ed. 1998. 415.00 (*0-7876-2459-4*, 00158121) Gale.

Statistics Sources: A Subject Guide to Data on Industrial, Business, Social, Educational, Financial, & Other Topics for the United States & Internationally. 14th ed. Ed. by Jacqueline W. O'Brien & Steven R. Wasserman. 3524p. 1990. 320.00 (*0-8103-7375-0*, 009381) Gale.

Statistics Sources: A Subject Guide to Data on Industrial, Business, Social, Educational, Financial & Other Topics for the United States & Internationally, 2 Vols. 19th ed. Ed. by Jacqueline W. O'Brien & Steven R. Wasserman. (Statistics Sources Ser.). 3000p. 1995. 385.00 (*0-8103-9091-4*) Gale.

Statistics Sources, 1989. 12th ed. Ed. by Steven R. Wasserman. 1988. 290.00 (*0-8103-2586-1*) Gale.

Statistics Students Companion. Amir D. Aczel. 136p. (C). 1995. 20.55 (*0-256-18928-5*) Irwin.

Statistics, Student's Solutions Manual. 5th ed. N. Shafer-Boudreau. 1991. pap. write for info. (0-02-379242-6, Macmillan Coll) P-H.

Statistics, Student's Solutions Manual. 6th ed. N. Shafer-Boudreau. 368p. (C). 1994. pap. text ed. 25.00 (0-02-312723-6, Macmillan Coll) P-H.

Statistics, Study Guide. 6th ed. Susan L. Reiland. 240p. (C). 1994. pap. text ed. 25.00 (0-02-399210-7, Macmillan Coll) P-H.

Statistics Subject Indexed from Mathematical Reviews, 1980-84, 1973-79, 1959-72, 1940-58, 2 vols. LC 86-26460. (Probability of Statistics Cumulative Index Ser.: No. 40-84). 508p. 1987. pap. text ed. 82.00 (0-8218-0107-4, STATIN/40/84) Am Math.

Statistics the Easy Way. 2nd ed. Douglas Downing & Jeff Clark. (Easy Way Ser.). 270p. 1989. pap. 12.95 (0-8120-4196-8) Barron.

***Statistics the Easy Way.** 3rd ed. Douglas Downing & Jeff Clark. LC 96-41827. 1997. pap. 11.95 (0-8120-9392-5) Barron.

Statistics Today: A Comprehensive Introduction. D. R. Byrkit. 850p. 1987. teacher ed. 12.95 (0-8053-0743-5) Addison-Wesley.

Statistics Today: A Comprehensive Introduction. D. R. Byrkit. 850p. (C). 1987. text ed. 54.95 (0-8053-0740-0); student ed., pap. text ed. 12.95 (0-8053-0741-9) Addison-Wesley.

Statistics Tutor: Computational Software for the Behavioral Sciences. Joseph D. Allen & David J. Pittenger. 240p. 1991. Net. pap. text ed. 19.50 (0-471-50280-4) Wiley.

Statistics Tutor: Tutorial & Computational Software for the Behavioral Sciences, Student Edition. Joseph D. Allen & David J. Pittenger. 215p. 1991. Net. pap. text ed. 19.50 (0-471-57142-3) Wiley.

Statistics Two Hundred Ninety-One Supplements. A. L. France. 152p. (C). 1984. pap. text ed. 12.95 (0-89917-427-2) Tichenor Pub.

Statistics Unraveled: A Practical Guide to Using Data in Decision Making. Tari Renner. 198p. (Orig.). 1988. pap. text ed. 28.00 (0-87326-934-9) Intl City-Cnty Mgt.

Statistics with a Sense of Humor: A Humorous Workbook & Guide to Study Skills. Fred Pyrczak. Ed. by Linda Sasser & Deborah Finkle. (Illus.). 132p. (C). 1989. student ed., pap. text ed. 18.95 (0-9623744-0-7) Pyrczak Pub.

Statistics with a Sense of Humor: Concise Key & Step-by-Step Key. Fred Pyrczak. Ed. by Robert Morman. 60p. (C). 1989. teacher ed., pap. text ed. 5.50 (0-9623744-1-5) Pyrczak Pub.

Statistics with Minitab. Fassil Nebebe. 1990. 9.25 (0-685-51813-2) Ginn Pr.

Statistics with Stata. Lawrence C. Hamilton. 171p. (C). 1990. pap. text ed. 38.95 incl. 5.25 hd (0-534-12850-5) Wadsworth Pub.

Statistics with Stata 3. 2nd ed. Lawrence C. Hamilton. LC 92-39339. 194p. (C). 1993. text ed. 26.95 (0-534-18918-0); pap. text ed. 46.95 incl. 3.5 hd (0-534-18920-2) Wadsworth Pub.

Statistics with Stata 3. 2nd ed. Lawrence C. Hamilton. LC 92-39339. 194p. (C). 1993. pap. text ed. 46.95 incl. mac hd (0-534-18919-9) Wadsworth Pub.

Statistics with Stata 5. 3rd ed. Lawrence C. Hamilton. (C). 1998. pap. 26.95 (0-534-26559-6) Wadsworth Pub.

***Statistics with the TI-83.** Gloria Barrett. Ed. by Steve Nichols. (Illus.). 202p. (J). (gr. 11 up). 1997. pap. text ed. 25.00 (1-887050-31-0) Meridian Creative.

Statistics Without Tears: A Primer for Non-Mathematicians. Derek Rowntree. 199p. (C). 1981. pap. text ed. 36.00 (0-02-404090-8, Macmillan Coll) P-H.

Statistics Without Tears: A Primer for Non-Mathematicians. Derek Rowntree. LC 82-3157. (Illus.). 200p. 1982. pap. write for info. (0-684-17502-9) S&S Trade.

Statistics 100 Workbook. University of Michigan, Department of Statistics Staff. (C). 1993. student ed. 15.00 (1-881592-39-1) Hayden-McNeil.

Statistics 402 Workbook. University of Michigan, Department of Statistics Staff. (C). 1993. student ed. 15.00 (1-881592-40-5) Hayden-McNeil.

Statistik Analyse System, Vol. 1. F. Faulbaum et al. 268p. (GER.). 1983. pap. text ed. 35.00 (3-437-40124-6) Lubrecht & Cramer.

Statistik-Software Three: Konferenz Ueber die Wissenschaftliche Anwendung von Statistik-Software, 1985. Ed. by W. Lehmacher & A. Hoermann. 393p. (GER.). 1986. pap. 37.70 (3-437-40170-X) Lubrecht & Cramer.

Statistix Users Guide. Marie Coffin & Herman Senter. 54p. (C). 1995. wbk. ed., pap. text ed. 6.00 (1-886855-17-X) Tavenner Pub.

Statius Achilled. Ed. by W. R. Connor & O. A. Dilke. LC 78-67127. (Latin Texts & Commentaries Ser.). (ENG & LAT.). 1979. reprint ed. lib. bdg. 23.95 (0-405-11598-9) Ayer.

Statius Silvae (Selections) Stephen T. Newmyer. (Latin Commentaries Ser.). 117p. (Orig.). (C). 1987. pap. text ed. 7.00 (0-929524-52-7) Bryn Mawr Commentaries.

Statius Theibaid VII: A Commentary. J. J. Smolenaars. LC 94-2817. (Mnemosyne, Bibliotheca Classica Batava Ser.: Vol. 134). 1994. 135.00 (90-04-10029-6) E J Brill.

Statler Brothers Anthology. 1986. 14.95 (0-89524-186-2, 02509951) Cherry Lane.

Statler Brothers Anthology. Ed. by Milton Okun. pap. 14.95 (0-89524-044-0) Cherry Lane.

***Statler Brothers Discography.** Alice Y. Holtin. LC 97-5301. (Discographies Ser.: Vol. 17). 256p. 1997. text ed. 65.00 (0-313-29663-4, Greenwood Pr) Greenwood.

Statler Brothers Songbook. 1991. pap. 7.95 (0-7935-0573-9, 00001561) H Leonard.

Statlib: A Statistical Computing Library. William M. Brelsford & Daniel A. Relles. 448p. (C). 1981. pap. text ed. 48.00 (0-13-846220-8) P-H.

Statokinetic Reflexes in Equilibrium & Movement. Tadashi Fukuda. Tr. by Hitoshi Okhubo & Shinya Ushio. 311p. 1984. 82.50 (0-86008-343-8, Pub. by U of Tokyo JA) Col U Pr.

***Statphys 19: Proceedings of the 19th IUPAP International Conference on Statistical Physics.** 596p. 1996. 51.00 (981-02-2579-2) World Scientific Pub.

Statphys 19: Proceedings of the 19th IUPAP International Conference on Statistical Physics. B. L. Hao. 450p. 1996. text ed. 118.00 (981-02-2314-5) World Scientific Pub.

StatQuest Text Companion: DOS. J. Theodore Anagnoson. (Statistical Software Ser.). 1994. pap. 7.50 incl. 3.5 hd (0-534-23680-4) Wadsworth Pub.

StatQuest Text Companion: With MAC. J. Theodore Anagnoson. (Statistical Software Ser.). 1994. pap. 10.95 incl. mac hd (0-534-23682-0) Wadsworth Pub.

***Stats: The Conceptual Approach.** Iverson & Gergen. 49.00 (0-7637-0249-8) Jones & Bartlett.

Stats Analysis for Publication. Giventer. (C). 1995. pap. text ed. 35.00 (0-534-15223-6) HarBrace.

STATS Baseball Scoreboard, 1991. John Dewan et al. (Illus.). 325p. (Orig.). 1991. pap. 12.95 (0-9625581-2-5) STATS.

STATS Baseball Scoreboard, 1993. John Dewan & Don Zminda. (Illus.). 330p. 1993. 12.95 (0-9625581-8-4) STATS.

Stats Baseball Scoreboard 1995. John Dewan. 1995. pap. 15.00 (1-884064-11-6) STATS.

Stats Basketball Scoreboard 1994-95. 2nd ed. John Dewan. 1994. pap. 15.00 (1-884064-06-X) STATS.

Stats Batter vs. Pitcher Match-Ups! 1994. Bill James. 1994. pap. 6.99 (1-884064-03-5) STATS.

STATS Batter vs. Pitcher Match Ups 1995. Bill James. 1995. pap. text ed. 6.99 (1-884064-10-8) STATS.

Stats Canadian Players Encyclopedia: The Complete Statistical Record of the Canadians Who... Neil Munro. 252p. (Orig.). 1996. pap. 17.95 (1-884064-29-9) STATS.

***Stats Diamond Chronicles, 1997.** Stats Publications Staff. 1997. pap. text ed. 14.95 (1-884064-41-8) STATS.

STATS for Those in the Know! Susie McAuley. LC 88-90536. 76p. (Orig.). 1988. pap. text ed. write for info. (0-9619964-0-4) S McAuley.

***Stats Hockey Handbook 1997-98.** (Orig.). 1997. pap. 19.95 (1-884064-40-X) STATS.

Stats Minor League Handbook, 1994. Bill James. 1993. pap. 17.95 (1-884064-01-9) STATS.

Stats Minor League Scouting Notebook 1995. Eddie Epstein. 1995. pap. 12.95 (1-884064-13-2) STATS.

Stats Nineteen Ninety-One Major League Handbook. Stats Inc., Staff & Bill James. 319p. 1990. pap. 17.95 (0-9625581-1-7) STATS.

Stats. on Psychotrpoic Substances 1987. 1988. 19.00 (92-1-048043-0, TR88.XI.3) UN.

STATS Player Profiles, 1993. STATS, Inc. Staff. Ed. by John Dewan. 375p. 1992. 14.95 (0-9625581-9-2) STATS.

Stats Player Profiles 1995. Tim Kurkjian. 1994. pap. 17.95 (1-884064-09-4) STATS.

Stats Pro Basketball Handbook, 1995-96. 1995. pap. 17.95 (1-884064-16-7) STATS.

***Stats Pro Basketball Handbook 1997-98.** (Orig.). 1997. pap. 19.95 (1-884064-39-6) STATS.

***Stats Pro Football Handbook, 1997.** (Orig.). 1997. pap. 19.95 (1-884064-37-X) STATS.

***Stats Pro Football Revealed: The 100 Yard War.** (Illus.). 18.95p. (Orig.). 1997. pap. 18.95 (1-884064-38-8) STATS.

Stats Pro Football Revealed 1996: The 100-Yard War. 3rd ed. STATS Publishing Staff. (Illus.). 358p. 1996. pap. 18.95 (1-884064-26-4) STATS.

Stats 1992 Baseball Scoreboard. John Dewan & Don Zminda. (Illus.). 330p. (Orig.). (C). 1992. per. 12.95 (0-9625581-4-1) STATS.

Stats 1995 Major League Handbook. Bill James. 1994. pap. 17.95 (1-884064-07-8) STATS.

Stats 1996 Baseball Scoreboard. Stats Publishing Staff. 1996. pap. 16.95 (1-884064-21-3) STATS.

Stats 1996 Batter Versus Pitcher Match-Ups. Stats Publishing Staff. 1996. pap. 12.95 (1-884064-20-5) STATS.

Stats 1996 Major League Handbook. Bill James. 1995. pap. 17.95 (1-884064-17-5) STATS.

Stats 1996 Minor League Handbook. Bill James. 1995. pap. 17.95 (1-884064-18-3) STATS.

Stats 1996 Minor League Scouting Notebook. Stats Publishing Staff. 1996. pap. 16.95 (1-884064-23-X) STATS.

Stats 1996 Player Profiles. Stats Publishing Staff. 1995. pap. 17.95 (1-884064-19-1) STATS.

Stats 1996 Pro Football Handbook. 2nd ed. Stats Publishing Staff. 521p. 1996. pap. 19.95 (1-884064-24-8) STATS.

Stats 1996-97 Hockey Handbook. STATS Publishing Staff. 360p. (Orig.). 1996. pap. 17.95 (1-884064-28-0) STATS.

Stats 1996-97 Pro Basketball Handbook. 2nd ed. 352p. 1996. pap. 19.95 (1-884064-25-6) STATS.

Stats 1997 Baseball Scoreboard. 8th ed. 315p. 1997. pap. 18.95 (1-884064-34-5) STATS.

Stats 1997 Batter vs. Pitcher Match-Ups! 4th ed. 350p. 1997. pap. 14.95 (1-884064-33-7) STATS.

Stats 1997 Major League Handbook. 8th ed. 380p. 1996. pap. 19.95 (1-884064-30-2) STATS.

Stats 1997 Minor League Handbook. 6th ed. 343p. 1996. pap. 19.95 (1-884064-31-0) STATS.

Stats 1997 Minor League Scouting Notebook. 3rd ed. 234p. 1997. pap. 18.95 (1-884064-36-1) STATS.

Stats 1997 Player Profiles. 5th ed. 520p. 1996. pap. 19.95 (1-884064-32-9) STATS.

Statue. Arnold Bennett. LC 74-17141. (Collected Works of Arnold Bennett: Vol. 75). 1977. reprint ed. 22.95 (0-518-19156-7) Ayer.

Statue de Sel. Albert Memmi. (Folio Ser.: No. 206). 377p. (FRE.). 1984. pap. 9.95 (2-07-036206-X) Schoenhof.

Statue Interieure. Francois Jacob. 442p. (FRE.). 1990. pap. 13.95 (0-7859-2662-3, 207038246X) Fr & Eur.

Statue of Glaucus: Rosseau's Modern Quest for Authenticity. Patrizia L. Heckle. LC 91-15829. (American University Studies: Political Science: Ser. X, Vol. 33). 178p. 1992. 35.95 (0-8204-1626-6) P Lang Pubng.

Statue of Liberty. Craig A. Doherty & Katherine M. Doherty. Ed. by Nicole Bowman. LC 95-20921. (Building America Ser.). (Illus.). 48p. (J). (gr. 3-7). 1996. lib. bdg. 15.95 (1-56711-111-4) Blackbirch.

Statue of Liberty. Leonard E. Fisher. LC 85-42878. (Illus.). 64p. (J). (gr. 3-7). 1985. lib. bdg. 15.95 (0-8234-0586-9) Holiday.

Statue of Liberty. Natalie Miller. LC 91-44647. (Cornerstones of Freedom Ser.). (Illus.). 32p. (J). (gr. 3-6). 1992. lib. bdg. 18.00 (0-516-06655-2) Childrens.

Statue of Liberty. Natalie Miller. LC 91-44647. (Cornerstones of Freedom Ser.). (Illus.). 32p. (J). (gr. 3-6). 1993. pap. 4.95 (0-516-46655-0) Childrens.

Statue of Liberty. Lucille R. Penner. LC 95-1854. (Step into Reading: Step 1 Bks.). (Illus.). 32p. (J). (gr. k-4). 1995. pap. 3.99 (0-679-86928-X) Random.

Statue of Liberty. Lucille R. Penner. (Illus.). (J). (gr. k-4). 1995. lib. bdg. 11.99 (0-679-96928-4) Random Bks Yng Read.

***Statue of Liberty.** Patricia R. Quiri. LC 97-12216. (True Book Ser.). (J). 1998. write for info. (0-516-20628-1) Childrens.

Statue of Liberty. Lynda Sorensen. LC 94-7052. (American Symbols Ser.). (J). 1994. write for info. (1-55916-046-2) Rourke Bk Co.

***Statue of Liberty.** Gina Strazzabosco-Hayn. LC 97-14513. (Library of American Landmarks). (J). 1997. write for info. (0-8239-5018-2, PowerKids) Rosen Group.

Statue of Liberty: America's Proud Lady. Jim Haskins. LC 85-18061. (American Landmarks Ser.). (Illus.). 48p. (J). (gr. 4 up). 1986. lib. bdg. 1,595.00 (0-8225-1706-X, Lerner Publctns) Lerner Group.

Statue of Liberty: The New Colossus. Stuart A. Kallen. LC 94-13309. (Famous Illustrated Speeches Ser.). (J). (gr. 3 up). 1994. lib. bdg. 15.98 (1-56239-315-4) Abdo & Dghtrs.

Statue of Liberty: The Story Behind the Scenery. rev. ed. Paul Weinbaum. LC 88-80652. (Illus.). 48p. (Orig.). 1988. pap. 7.95 (0-88714-023-8) KC Pubns.

Statue of Liberty & Ellis Island. Gabriele. (J). 1986. pap. 1.95 (0-911211-79-9) Penny Lane Pubns.

Statue of Liberty Catalogue. 1986. 29.95 (0-317-40603-5); pap. 14.95 (0-317-40604-3) HM.

Statue of Liberty on Stamps. Ed. by Donald Brenke. 32p. 1988. pap. 5.00 (0-935991-04-2) Am Topical Assn.

Statue of Liberty Restoration. Ed. by R. Baboian et al. LC 90-61053. (Illus.). 149p. 1990. 79.00 (1-877914-12-6) NACE Intl.

Statue of Liberty Revisited: Making a Universal Symbol. Ed. by Wilton S. Dillon & Neil G. Kotler. LC 92-37913. (Illus.). 192p. (Orig.). 1993. pap. text ed. 17.95 (1-56098-252-7) Smithsonian.

Statue of Library: Its First Hundred Years. Bernard A. Wiesberger. (Illus.). 192p. 1985. 29.95 (0-685-11137-7) HM.

Statue Walks at Night. Joan L. Nixon. LC 94-71791. (Disney Adventures Casebusters Ser.: No. 1). (Illus.). 96p. (J). (gr. 2-6). 1995. pap. 3.95 (0-7868-4018-8) Disney Pr.

Statue Within: An Autobiography. Francois Jacob. Tr. by Franklin Philip. LC 87-47780. (Sloan Foundation Science Ser.). 336p. 1988. pap. 10.95 (0-685-19488-4) Basic.

Statue Within: An Autobiography. expanded ed. Francois Jacob. Tr. by Franklin Philip from FRE. 326p. (C). 1995. reprint ed. pap. 19.95 (0-87969-476-9) Cold Spring Harbor.

Statues in the Park. Frank J. Valentino. 50p. (Orig.). 1997. pap. text ed. 5.00 (1-880764-03-2) Northwind NJ.

Statues of Paris: Open Air Pantheon. limited ed. June Hargrove. (Illus.). 382p. 1990. 150.00 (0-86565-121-3) Vendome.

Stature, Living Standards & Economic Development: Essays in Anthropometric History. Ed. by John Komlos. LC 94-8700. 264p. 1994. 36.50 (0-226-45092-9) U Ch Pr.

Stature of Dickens: A Centenary Bibliography. Joseph Gold. LC 70-151368. 276p. reprint ed. pap. 78.70 (0-317-27040-0, 2023625) Bks Demand.

Stature of Man. Colin Wilson. LC 68-23338. 171p. 1968. reprint ed. text ed. 59.75 (0-8371-0273-1, WISM, Greenwood Pr) Greenwood.

Stature of Thomas Mann. Ed. by Charles Neider. LC 68-16961. (Essay Index Reprint Ser.). 1977. 29.95 (0-8369-0737-X) Ayer.

***Status.** Bryan Turner. Ed. by Frank Parkin. (Concepts in the Social Sciences Ser.). 112p. (Orig.). 1988. 32.50 (0-335-15370-4, Open Univ Pr); pap. 9.99 (0-335-15369-0, Open Univ Pr) Taylor & Francis.

Status. Bryan Turner. LC 88-27717. (Concepts in Social Thought Ser.). 96p. (Orig.). 1989. pap. text ed. 13.95 (0-8166-1723-6) U of Minn Pr.

Status & Applications of Diamond & Diamond-Like Materials: An Emerging Technology. National Research Council Staff. 114p. 1990. pap. text ed. 15.00 (0-309-04196-1) Natl Acad Pr.

***Status & Appraisal of Classic Texts: An Essay on Political Theory, Its Inheritance, & the History of Ideas.** Conal Condren. LC 83-43065. 318p. 1985. reprint ed. pap. 90.70 (0-608-03314-6, 2064026) Bks Demand.

Status & Control: The Dynamics of Personal & Social Power. Jack Friedland. 340p. 1997. 25.00 (0-9642390-5-1) New Gateway Pr.

Status & Distribution of New Jersey's Birds. Charles F. Leck. LC 83-17655. 210p. 1984. text ed. 30.00 (0-8135-1033-3) Rutgers U Pr.

Status & Function of Languages & Language Varieties. Ed. by Ulrich Ammon. (Foundations of Communication & Cognition Ser.). x, 665p. (C). 1989. lib. bdg. 223.10 (3-11-011299-X) De Gruyter.

Status & Future Developments in the Study of Transport Properties. Ed. by W. A. Wakeham et al. (C). 1992. lib. bdg. 137.50 (0-7923-1612-6) Kluwer Ac.

Status & Health in Prehistory: A Case Study of the Moundville Chiefdom. Mary L. Powell. LC 87-23318. (Series in Archaeological Inquiry). (Illus.). 352p. (C). 1988. text ed. 37.00 (0-87474-756-2) Smithsonian.

Status & Identity in West Africa: Nyamakalaw of Mande. Ed. by David C. Conrad & Barbara E. Frank. LC 94-20215. (African Systems of Thought Ser.). 224p. 1995. 29.95 (0-253-31409-7); pap. 12.95 (0-253-20929-3) Ind U Pr.

Status & Management of Interior Stocks of Cutthroat Trout. Ed. by R. E. Gresswell. LC 88-72021. (AFS Symposium Ser.: No. 4). 140p. 1988. pap. 18.00 (0-913235-56-3); text ed. 25.00 (0-913235-55-5) Am Fisheries Soc.

Status & Ministry of the Laity in the Orthodox Church. John N. Karmiris. Tr. by Evie Zachariades-Holmberg from GRE. 52p. (Orig.). (C). 1994. pap. text ed. 5.95 (0-917651-95-2) Holy Cross Orthodox.

Status & Perspectives of Nuclear Energy: Fission & Fusion, Varenna on Lake Como, Villa Monastero, 10-20 July 1990. Ed. by C. Salvetti et al. LC 92-9918. 1992. 230.00 (0-444-89425-X, North Holland) Elsevier.

Status & Potential of Aquaculture & the Caribbean. Ed. by John A. Hargreaves & Dallas E. Alston. (Advances in World Aquaculture Ser.: Vol. 5). (Illus.). 274p. 1991. text ed. 45.00 (0-9624529-4-7) World Aquaculture.

***Status & Potential of Aquaculture in Small Waterbodies (Ponds & Ditches) in Bangladesh.** M. Ahmed. (ICLARM Technical Reports: No. 37). 36p. 1992. write for info. (971-8709-28-2, Pub. by ICLARM PH) Intl Spec Bk.

Status & Power in Rural Jamaica: A Study of Educational & Political Change. Nancy Foner. LC 72-5943. (Publications of the Center for Education in Africa). 192p. reprint ed. pap. 54.80 (0-685-20392-1, 2030153) Bks Demand.

Status & Power in Verbal Interaction: A Study of Discourse in a Close-Knit Social Network. Julie Diamond. LC 96-4154. (Pragmatics & Beyond Ser.: Vol. 40). viii, 184p. 1996. lib. bdg. 55.00 (1-55619-801-9) Benjamins North Am.

Status & Prospects for Dairying, 1992-1995. Ronald D. Knutson et al. (Illus.). 57p. (Orig.). (C). 1993. pap. text ed. 20.00 (1-56806-454-3) DIANE Pub.

Status & Sacredness: A General Theory of Status Relations & An Analysis of Indian Culture. Murray Milner, Jr. LC 93-20052. 352p. 1994. pap. 26.00 (0-19-508489-6) OUP.

Status & Work of the Training Supervisor. N. L. Garrison. LC 70-176797. (Columbia University. Teachers College. Contributions to Education Ser.: No. 280). reprint ed. 37.50 (0-404-55280-3) AMS Pr.

Status, Authority & Regional Power: Aquitaine & France, 9th-12th Centuries. Jane Martindale. LC 95-30953. (Collected Studies: Vol. CS488). 350p. Date not set. 89.95 (0-86078-480-0, Pub. by Variorum UK) Ashgate Pub Co.

Status Change of Languages. Ed. by Ulrich Ammon & Marlis Hellinger. (Foundations of Communication & Cognition Ser.). (Illus.). ix, 547p. (C). 1991. lib. bdg. 190.80 (3-11-012668-0, 256-91) De Gruyter.

Status Crystallization: A Non-Vertical Dimension of Social Status. Gerhard E. Lenski. (Reprint Series in Social Sciences). (C). 1993. reprint ed. pap. text ed. 1.00 (0-8290-3968-6, S-168) Irvington.

Status, Distribution & Biogeography of the Birds of Paraguay. Floyd E. Hayes. Ed. by Kenneth P. Able. LC 95-75102. (Monographs in Field Ornithology). (Illus.). 232p. (Orig.). 1995. pap. 29.95 (1-878788-30-2, 041) Amer Birding Assn.

Status Epilepticus. DeLorenzo. 1997. write for info. (0-7506-9413-0) Buttrwrth-Heinemann.

Status Epilepticus: Its Clinical Features & Treatment in Children & Adults. Simon D. Shorvon. (Illus.). 250p. (C). 1994. text ed. 90.00 (0-521-42065-2) Cambridge U Pr.

Status Epilepticus, Mechanisms of Brain Damage & Treatment. Ed. by Antonio V. Delgado-Escueta et al. LC 80-6214. (Advances in Neurology Ser.: No. 34). (Illus.). 579p. 1983. reprint ed. pap. 165.10 (0-608-00604-1, 2061191) Bks Demand.

Status for Sale: The Complete Guide to Instant Prestige. Wayne Yeager. LC 92-70454. 128p. 1992. student ed. 4.95 (1-881248-01-1); pap. 8.95 (1-881248-00-3); audio 8.95 (1-881248-02-X) Charter Pubns.

Status Generalization: New Theory & Research. Ed. by Murray Webster, Jr. & Martha Foschi. LC 88-2297. 552p. 1988. 57.50 (0-8047-1421-5) Stanford U Pr.

Status Inequality: The Self in Culture. George A. De Vos. (Cross-Cultural Research & Methodology Ser.: Vol. 15). 312p. (C). 1990. text ed. 48.00 (0-8039-3962-0) Sage.

An Asterisk (*) at the beginning of an entry indicates that the title is appearing in BIP for the first time.

Status Influences in Third World Labor Markets: Caste, Gender & Custom. Ed. by James G. Scoville. (Studies in Organization: No. 32). vii, 329p. (C). 1991. lib. bdg. 72.95 (3-11-012647-8, 170-91) De Gruyter.

Status, Management & Commercialization of the American Black Bear (Ursus Americanus) Catherine McCracken. LC 95-6971. 1995. pap. 16.00 (0-89164-143-2) World Wildlife Fund.

***Status, Network, & Structure: Theory Development in Group Processes.** Jacek Szmatka et al. LC 97-2429. 1997. write for info. (0-8047-2844-5) Stanford U Pr.

Status of Advanced Reactors & Developments in Advanced Reactor Instrumentation & Control. J. M. Yedidia & J. Kunze. LC 93-73004. (NE Ser.: Vol. 12). 92p. 1993. 30.00 (0-7918-0999-4, H00831) ASME.

Status of Aliens in China. Vi K. Koo. LC 68-56665. (Columbia University. Studies in the Social Sciences: No. 126). reprint ed. 35.00 (0-404-51126-0) AMS Pr.

Status of Alternative Methods in Toxicology. Anderson. Date not set. 95.00 (0-85404-404-3) CRC Pr.

Status of Animals in the Christian Religion. C. W. Hume. 1980. 35.00 (0-317-43856-5) St Mut.

Status of Aquaculture in the U. S. Ed. by Peter Allen. 300p. (Orig.). 1981. pap. 795.00 (0-931634-21-0) FIND-SVP.

Status of Arms Regulations & Disarmament Agreements, Vol. I & II. 4th ed. 740p. 1992. 75.00 (92-1-142196-9, E.93.IX.11) UN.

Status of Arts Education in American Public Schools. Charles Leonhard. 1992. 15.00 (0-317-05162-8) U IL Sch Music.

Status of Arts Education in American Public Schools: Summary & Conclusions. Charles Leonhard. 1992. 5.00 (0-317-05163-6) U IL Sch Music.

Status of Blacks in Higher Education. Ed. by Ada M. Elam. LC 88-39410. (Illus.). 120p. (Orig.). (C). 1989. pap. text ed. 15.00 (0-8191-7287-1, NAEOHE) U Pr of Amer.

Status of Cadmium, Lead, Cobalt & Selenium in Soils & Plants of 30 Countries. Mikko Sillanpaa & Hakan Jensson. (Soils Bulletins Ser.: No. 65). 207p. 1993. pap. 25.00 (92-5-103238-6, F32386, Pub. by FAO IT) Bernan Associates.

Status of Civil Science in Eastern Europe. Ed. by Craig Sinclair. (C). 1989. lib. bdg. 171.50 (0-7923-0267-2) Kluwer Ac.

Status of Coal Research: Combustion Chemistry & Soot Formation; Storch Award Symposium on Coal Maceral Characterizations & Separation; SO2 & NOx Removal Techniques; Preprints of Papers Presented at the 207th ACS National Meeting, San Diego, CA, March 13-17, 1994. American Chemical Society, Division of Fuel Chemistry Staff. (Preprints of Papers: Vol. 39, No. 1). 280p. reprint ed. pap. 79.80 (0-7837-6801-X, 2046633) Bks Demand.

Status of Common Sense in Psychology. Ed. by Jurg Siegfried. LC 92-48700. 388p. 1994. text ed. 78.50 (0-89391-873-3) Ablex Pub.

Status of Competition in Intrastate Telecommunication. 203p. 1995. 45.00 (0-317-05197-0) NARUC.

***Status of Conservation Areas in the Brazilian Amazon.** Anthony B. Rylands. LC 92-232849. 156p. pap. 44.50 (0-608-04963-8, 2065542) Bks Demand.

Status of Deer in Kansas. Donald D. Anderson. (Miscellaneous Publications: No. 39). 36p. 1964. pap. 2.00 (0-317-04916-X) U KS Nat Hist Mus.

Status of Education in Nepal, 8 papers. ANEF Staff. 76p. 1982. 14.00 (0-318-17089-2, 71) Am-Nepal Ed.

Status of Everyday Life: A Sociological Excavation of the Prevailing Framework of Perception. Fiona Mackie. (International Library of Sociology). 288p. 1985. 49.95 (0-7102-0154-0, RKP) Routledge.

Status of Fish Stocks & Fisheries of 13 Medium-Sized African Reservoirs. Martin Van der Knaap. (CIFA Technical Paper Ser.: No. 26). 118p. 1995. pap. 15.00 (92-5-103581-4, F35814, Pub. by FAO IT) Bernan Associates.

Status of Forest Remnants in the Cordillera de la Costa & Adjacent Areas of Southwestern Ecuador. Ed. by Theodore A. Parker, 3rd & John L. Carr. LC 92-73741. 172p. 1992. pap. 10.00 (1-881173-04-6) Conser Intl.

***Status of General Practioners in America.** R. Cantafio. 268p. 1996. lib. bdg. 59.00 (1-56072-382-3) Nova Sci Pubs.

Status of Girl Child & Women in India. Niranjan Pant. (Illus.). xxxiii, 175p. 1995. 22.00 (81-7024-708-X, Pub. by Ashish Pub Hse II) Nataraj Bks.

Status of Girls in Development Strategies. Neerakuckrejasohoni. (C). 1994. text ed. 28.00 (81-241-0019-5, Pub. by Har-Anand Pubns II) S Asia.

Status of Harvest Mechanization of Horticultural Crops. 78p. 1984. pap. 15.00 (0-916150-50-X, CO383) Am Soc Ag Eng.

Status of Health in Nepal. A. Ali. (C). 1991. text ed. 60.00 (0-7855-0156-8, Pub. by Ratna Pustak Bhandar) St Mut.

Status of Health of Blacks in the United States of America: A Prescription for Improvement. Valiere Alcena. 256p. 1992. pap. text ed. 30.95 (0-8403-7394-5) Kendall-Hunt.

Status of Illiteracy in San Antonio. Jose A. Cardenas et al. (Illus.). 80p. (Orig.). 1983. pap. text ed. 8.00 (1-878550-08-X) Inter Dev Res Assn.

Status of Indian Women: A Historical Perspective. B. R. Sharan. (C). 1992. 17.50 (81-85565-02-3, Pub. by Uppal Pub Hse II) S Asia.

Status of Inter-American Treaties & Conventions. rev. ed. Ed. by OAS, General Secretariat, Bureau of Legal Affairs Staff. (Treaty Ser.: No. 5). 53p. (C). text ed. 5.00 (0-8270-1147-4) OAS.

Status of Invertebrate Paleontology, 1953, Vol. 112. Ed. by Bernhard Kummel & Stephen J. Gould. LC 79-8351. (History of Paleontology Ser.). (Illus.). 1980. reprint ed. lib. bdg. 21.95 (0-405-12715-4) Ayer.

***Status of ISDN in North America.** 30p. 1993. 95.00 (0-614-18399-5, 126NO2) Info Gatekeepers.

Status of Ketamine in Anesthesiology: Pros & Cons. Ed. by E. F. Domino. LC 89-92147. (Illus.). 583p. 1990. 95.00 (0-916182-07-X) NPP Bks.

Status of Legal Instruments: Supplement 8. 1981. pap. 9.00 (0-685-12799-0, G145, Pub. by Wrld Trade SZ) Bernan Associates.

***Status of Legal Instruments GATT.** 500p. 1997. 190.00 (0-614-27216-5, WTO/648, Pub. by Wrld Trade SZ) Bernan Associates.

Status of Morality. Thomas L. Carson. (Philosophical Studies: No. 31). 216p. 1984. lib. bdg. 97.00 (90-277-1691-9, D Reidel) Kluwer Ac.

Status of Multilateral Arms Regulation & Disarmament Agreements, 1987. 3rd ed. 190p. 1988. 18.00 (92-1-142140-3, E.88.IX.5) UN.

Status of Near Field Modelling. OECD Staff. 360p. (Orig.). (ENG & FRE.). 1993. pap. 59.00 (92-64-03974-0) OECD.

Status of Pattern Analysis: Identification of Problems in the Statistical Analysis of Spatial Arrangement. Michael F. Dacey. (Discussion Paper Ser.: No. 3.). 1963. pap. 10.00 (1-55869-122-7) Regional Sci Res Inst.

Status of Puerto Rico. United States-Puerto Rico Commission on the Status of Puerto Rico. LC 74-14253. (Puerto Rican Experience Ser.). 984p. 1975. reprint ed. 23.95 (0-405-06238-9) Ayer.

Status of Rare Fish: A Literature Review of Freshwater Fish in the U. K. 64p. 1995. pap. 17.00 (0-11-886511-0, HM65110, Pub. by Stationery Ofc UK) Bernan Associates.

Status of Reading Subject in the "Libro de Buen Amor" Marina S. Brownlee. (Studies in the Romance Languages & Literatures: No. 224). 136p. (Orig.). (C). 1985. pap. 19.95 (0-8078-9228-9) U of NC Pr.

Status of Refugees in Asia. Ed. by Vitit Muntarbhorn. 226p. 1992. 55.00 (0-19-825668-X) OUP.

Status of Rural Women in India. Mumtaz A. Khan & Noor Aysha. 1983. 17.50 (0-8364-0978-7, Pub. by Uppal Pub Hse II) S Asia.

Status of Scheduled Castes. S. Selvanathan. (C). 1988. 35.00 (81-7024-229-0, Pub. by Ashish II) S Asia.

Status of School Desegregation: The Next Generation. Gary Orfield & Franklin Monfort. 39p. (Orig.). 1992. pap. 25.00 (0-88364-174-7) Natl Sch Boards.

Status of School Desegregation 1968-1986: Segregation, Integration, & Public Policy: National, State, & Metropolitan Trends in Public Schools. Gary Orfield et al. 31p. (Orig.). 1989. pap. text ed. 10.00 (0-88364-171-2) Natl Sch Boards.

Status of Seabirds in Britain & Ireland. Clare S. Lloyd et al. (Illus.). 384p. 1991. text ed. 37.00 (0-85661-061-5, 784661) Acad Pr.

Status of Small Business in Retail Trade (1948-1958) U. S. House of Representatives Select Committee on Small Business. Ed. by Stuart Bruchey & Vincent P. Carosso. LC 78-18992. (Small Business Enterprise in America Ser.). (Illus.). 1979. reprint ed. lib. bdg. 17.95 (0-405-11505-9) Ayer.

Status of Social Science Research in Borneo. Ed. by George N. Appell & Leigh R. Wright. (Cornell University, Southeast Asia Program, Data Paper Ser.: No. 109). 134p. reprint ed. pap. 38.20 (0-8357-3681-4, 2036405) Bks Demand.

Status of Technology for Volume Reduction & Treatment of Low & Intermediate Level. International Atomic Energy Agency Staff. (Technical Reports: No. 360). 98p. 1994. pap. 40.00 (92-0-100494-X, STI/DOC/360, Pub. by IAEA AU) Bernan Associates.

***Status of the Aegean Sea According to International Law.** Angelos M. Syrigos. (Illus.). 400p. 1997. pap. text ed. 40.00 (0-89241-573-8) Caratzas.

***Status of the Aegean Sea According to International Law.** Angelos M. Syrigos. (Illus.). 400p. 1997. text ed. 70.00 (0-89241-582-7) Caratzas.

Status of the American Public School Teacher, 1990-91. 238p. 1992. pap. 29.95 (0-8106-3258-6) NEA.

Status of the Arab Woman: A Select Bibliography. Samira R. Meghdessian. LC 80-1028. 176p. 1980. text ed. 49.95 (0-313-22548-6, MEA/, Greenwood Pr) Greenwood.

Status of the Beginning Calculus Students in Pre-Calculus College Mathematics: Study Carried Out with Students in Brooklyn College & City College of New York. M. Boeker. LC 76-176690. (Columbia University. Teachers College. Contributions to Education Ser.: No. 922). reprint ed. 37.50 (0-404-55922-0) AMS Pr.

***Status of the Curability of Childhood Cancers: The University of Texas System Cancer Center, M. D. Anderson Hospital & Tumor Institute 24th Annual Clinical Conference on Cancer.** Clinical Conference on Cancer Staff. Ed. by Jan Van Eys & Margaret P. Sullivan. LC 79-5469. 349p. 1980. reprint ed. pap. 99.50 (0-608-03457-6, 2064158) Bks Demand.

Status of the Individual & Contemporary International Law: Promotion, Protection & Restoration of Human Rights at National, Regional & International Levels. (Human Rights Studies: No. 4). 68p. 1991. 30.00 (92-1-154084-4) UN.

Status of the Individual in East & West. East-West Philosophers Conference (4th: 1964, University of Hawaii). Ed. by Charles A. Moore. LC 67-14717. 628p. reprint ed. pap. 179.00 (0-317-55712-2, 2029583) Bks Demand.

Status of the Industry, 1986-87. Smith Bucklin & Association - Statistics Division. 1987. write for info. (0-318-58986-9) AMOA.

Status of the Inter-American Treaties & Conventions. (Treaty Ser.). 52p. 1972. 1.00 (0-8270-0290-4) OAS.

***Status of Tribal Women in Tripura.** Ed. by Malabika Das Gupta. (C). 1993. 14.00 (0-614-18156-9, Pub. by Vikas II) S Asia.

Status of U. S. A. Nuclear Reactor Pressure Vessel Surveillance for Radiation Effects- STP 784. Ed. by L. E. Steele. LC 82-71751. 277p. 1983. text ed. 29.50 (0-8031-0229-1, 04-784000-35) ASTM.

Status of Woman in Islam. Jamal A. Badawi. 28p. (Orig.). 1980. pap. write for info. (1-882837-13-4) W A M Y Intl.

Status of Woman in Islam. Jamal A. Badawi. Ed. by Abdussamad Al-Jarrahi. Tr. by Muhammad Bekkari from ENG. (Illus.). 28p. (Orig.). 1982. pap. 1.50 (0-89259-036-X) Am Trust Pubns.

Status of Women: Household & Non-Household Economic Activity. A. Mitra. 78p. 1979. 6.95 (0-318-37312-2) Asia Bk Corp.

Status of Women: Literacy & Employment. A. Mitra. (Illus.). 74p. 1979. 6.95 (0-318-37313-0) Asia Bk Corp.

***Status of Women & Children in India.** Ed. by Sunit Gupta & Mukta Mittal. (C). 1995. 22.00 (81-7488-128-X, Pub. by Anmol II) S Asia.

Status of Women & Children in Slums: A Study of Hyderabad City. S. Vasudeva Rao. (C). 1992. 15.00 (81-7013-094-8, Pub. by Navarang II) S Asia.

Status of Women & Population Growth in India. K. P. Singh. 165p. 1979. 14.95 (0-318-37074-3) Asia Bk Corp.

Status of Women in Foreign Policy. Nancy E. McGlen & Meredith R. Sarkees. Ed. by Nancy L. Hoepli-Phalon. (Headline Ser.: No. 307). (Illus.). 72p. (Orig.). 1995. pap. 5.95 (0-87124-165-X) Foreign Policy.

Status of Women in Georgia, 1783-1860. Eleanor M. Boatwright. LC 94-16767. (Scholarship in Women's History Ser.: Vol. 2). 1994. 50.00 (0-926019-63-5) Carlson Pub.

Status of Women in India, 2 vols., Set. H. C. Upadhyay. (C). 1991. 72.00 (0-685-53623-8, Pub. by Anmol II) S Asia.

Status of Women in Islam. Ed. by Asghar Ali Engineer. (C). 1987. 17.50 (81-202-0190-6, Pub. by Ajanta II); pap. 11.00 (0-317-89626-1, Pub. by Ajanta II) S Asia.

Status of Women in Islam. Mohammad S. Khan. (C). 1996. 27.00 (0-614-13258-4, Pub. by Ashish II) S Asia.

Status of Women in Islam. Mohammad S. Khan. (C). 1996. 27.00 (81-7024-732-2, Pub. by Ashish II) S Asia.

Status of Women in Islam. M. T. Mesbah et al. vi, 57p. 1990. text ed. 10.95 (0-685-35772-4, Pub. by Radiant Pubs II) S Asia.

Status of Women in Islam. Qamaruddin Khan. 1989. text ed. 10.95 (81-207-1060-6, Pub. by Sterling Pubs II) Apt Bks.

Status of Women in Librarianship: Historical, Sociological, & Economic Issues. Ed. by Kathleen M. Heim. LC 82-7887. 483p. 1983. 42.50 (0-918212-62-6) Neal-Schuman.

Status of Women in Preindustrial Societies. Martin K. Whyte. LC 77-85574. 235p. 1978. reprint ed. 67.00 (0-7837-9483-5, 2060225) Bks Demand.

Status of Women in South Asia. Ed. by Angadipuram Appadorai. LC 75-38654. 1976. reprint ed. 23.95 (0-89201-026-6) Zenger Pub.

Status of Women under Islam. Jamal J. Nasir. (Arab & Islamic Laws Ser.). 1995. lib. bdg. 80.00 (1-85966-084-3) Kluwer Ac.

Status, Power & Conflict in the Kibbutz. Eliezer Ben-Rafael. 200p. 1988. text ed. 63.95 (0-566-05506-6, Pub. by Avebury Pub UK) Ashgate Pub Co.

Status Quo Vadis. Donald Driver. 1973. pap. 5.25 (0-8222-1076-2) Dramatists Play.

Status Report Energy from Biomass: Direct & Reduced Combustion. (GATE Ser.). (Illus.). 73p. 1986. pap. 11.00 (3-528-02027-X, Pub. by Vieweg & Sohn GW) Informatica.

Status Report on Contemporary Criminal Justice Education: A Definition of the Discipline & an Assessment of Its Curricula, Faculty & Program Characteristics. Charles P. Nemeth. LC 88-7998. (Mellen Studies in Education: Vol. 3). 250p. 1989. lib. bdg. 89.95 (0-88946-938-5) E Mellen.

Status Report Solar Energy. (GATE Ser.). (Illus.). 54p. 1986. pap. 9.00 (3-528-02029-6, Pub. by Vieweg & Sohn GW) Informatica.

Status Report Wind Energy. (GATE Ser.). (Illus.). 54p. 1985. pap. 7.00 (3-528-02019-9, Pub. by Vieweg & Sohn GW) Informatica.

Status, Reputation & Image of the Library & Information Profession: Proceedings of the IFLA Pre-Session Seminar, Delhi, 24-28 August 1992. Ed. by Russel Bowden & Donald Wijasuriya. (IFLA Publications: Vol. 68). 228p. 1994. 60.00 (3-598-21795-1) K G Saur.

Status, Resources & Needs of Systematic Collections. 1995. 15.00 (0-942924-18-5) Assn Syst Coll.

Status, Rewards & Influence. Ed. by Joseph Berger & Morris Zelditch, Jr. LC 84-47979. (Jossey-Bass Social & Behavioral Science Ser.). 513p. reprint ed. pap. 146.30 (0-8357-4966-5, 2037899) Bks Demand.

Status Seekers. Ed. by Vance Packard & Daniel Horowitz. 224p. 1995. pap. text ed. 7.50 (0-312-11180-0) St Martin.

Status Seekers Buyers' Guide. Richard M. Greene, Jr. (Illus.). 56p. 1973. pap. 2.95 (0-934487-14-6) R M Greene.

Status System of a Modern Community. William L. Warner & Paul S. Lunt. LC 73-8153. (Illus.). 246p. 1974. reprint ed. text ed. 59.75 (0-8371-6959-3, WASM, Greenwood Pr) Greenwood.

Status Terminology & the Social Structure of North American Indians. Munro S. Edmonson. LC 84-45527. (American Ethnological Society Monographs: No. 30). 1988. reprint ed. 20.00 (0-404-62929-6) AMS Pr.

Status Warriors: War, Violence & Society in Homer & History. Hans Van Wees. (Dutch Monographs on Ancient History & Archaeology: No. 9). 455p. 1992. pap. 87.00 (90-5063-075-8, Pub. by Gieben NE) Benjamins North Am.

Status 1996: A Report on the Integrated Circuit Industry. 396p. 1996. 795.00 (1-877750-47-6) ICE Corp.

***Status 1997: A Report on the Integrated Circuit Industry.** 398p. 1997. 795.00 (1-877750-56-5) ICE Corp.

Statut Personnel et Famille Au Maghreb De 1940 a Nos Jours. M. Borrmans. 107.70 (90-279-7713-5) Mouton.

Statut Personnel et Liens de Famille dans les Droits de l'Antiquite. Joseph Meleze-Modrzejewski. (Collected Studies: Vol. 411). 320p. 1993. 89.95 (0-86078-376-6, Pub. by Variorum UK) Ashgate Pub Co.

Statute Law in New Zealand. J. F. Burrows. 200p. 1992. pap. 99.00 (0-409-78844-9, NZ) MICHIE.

Statute Law Review: 1980-1985, 6 vols., Set. 225.00 (0-8377-9244-4) Rothman.

Statute of Limitations & Adverse Possession: With an Appendix Containing the English Acts of Limitation. Henry F. Buswell. lxvi, 623p. 1991. reprint ed. lib. bdg. 57.50 (0-8377-1951-8) Rothman.

Statute of Limitations in American Conflicts of Law. Alejo De Cervera. LC 65-23494. 189p. (C). 1966. 4.00 (0-8477-3001-8) U of PR Pr.

Statute of the International Law Commission. 12p. 1982. pap. 6.00 (92-1-133250-8, E.82.V.8) UN.

Statute of Virginia for Religious Freedom. Thomas Jefferson. 1979. pap. text ed. 9.95 (0-8139-0878-7) U Pr of Va.

Statute of York & the Interest of the Commons. George L. Haskins. LC 77-4920. 129p. 1977. reprint ed. text ed. 57.50 (0-8371-9610-8, HASY, Greenwood Pr); reprint ed. fiche write for info. (0-8371-9612-4, Greenwood Pr) Greenwood.

Statutere Sakereg. N. J. Olivier et al. 700p. 1988. ring bd. write for info. (0-7021-1994-6, Pub. by Juta SA) Gaunt.

Statutes. 3rd ed. A. I. MacAdam. 360p. 1993. pap. 63.00 (0-409-30504-9, Austral) MICHIE.

Statutes see Pimsleur's Checklists of Basic American Legal Publications

Statutes & Conventions on International Trade. 2nd ed. Indira Carr & Richard Kidner. 554p. 1995. pap. 25.00 (1-85941-280-7, Pub. by Cavendish UK) Gaunt.

Statutes & Conventions on Private International Law. Jason C. Chuah. 327p. 1996. pap. 32.00 (1-85941-034-0, Pub. by Cavendish UK) Gaunt.

Statutes & Their Interpretation in the First Half of the 14th Century. Theodore F. Plucknett. LC 85-81796. (Cambridge Studies in English Legal History). 244p. 1986. reprint ed. 59.00 (0-912004-49-5) Gaunt.

Statutes at Large, Being a Collection of All the Laws of Virginia from the First Session of the Legislature in the Year 1619, 13 Vols, Set. Ed. by William W. Hening. LC 69-18889. (Jamestown Foundation of the Commonwealth of VA Ser.). 1969. text ed. 400.00 (0-8139-0254-1) U Pr of Va.

Statutes at Large of Pennsylvania from 1682-1801, 17 vols., Set. Compiled by James T. Mitchell. LC 74-19615. reprint ed. 875.00 (0-404-12413-5) AMS Pr.

Statutes at Large of the Provisional Government of the Confederate States of America. James Matthews. LC 87-83739. 922p. 1988. reprint ed. lib. bdg. 95.00 (0-89941-629-2, 305500) W S Hein.

Statutes at Large of Virginia from October Session 1792, to December Session 1806, 3 Vols, Set. Ed. by Samuel Shepherd. LC 79-119153. reprint ed. lib. bdg. 145.00 (0-404-06010-2) AMS Pr.

Statutes-at-Large of Virginia 1619 to 1792, 13 vols., Set. Ed. by William W. Hening. reprint ed. 390.00 (0-404-19571-7) AMS Pr.

Statutes Compared: A U. S., Canadian, Multinational Research Guide. rev. ed. Ed. by Jon S. Schultz. 374p. 1991. ring bd. 65.00 (0-89941-760-4, 301380) W S Hein.

Statutes of India: A Manual of Central Acts & Rules. Khetrapal Publications Staff. (C). 1988. 540.00 (0-685-27944-8) St Mut.

Statutes of India: A Manual of Central Acts & Rules: Exhaustive Comm. on All Central Acts with Important Central Rules 1988 Edition, 4 vols. Khetrapal Publications Staff. (C). 1988. 210.00 (0-685-46481-4) St Mut.

Statutes of the Realm, 11 vols., 12 bks., Set. 1993. reprint ed. 2,400.00 (1-57588-365-1, 307950) W S Hein.

Statutes on Employment Law. 5th ed. Richard Kidner. 397p. 1995. pap. 26.00 (1-85431-419-X, Pub. by Blackstone Pr UK) Gaunt.

Statutes on Intellectual Property. A. Christie. (C). 1992. 45.00 (1-85431-186-7, Pub. by Blackstone Pr UK) Gaunt.

Statutes, Regulations & Case Law Protecting Individuals with Disabilities. LC 93-39443. 1994. pap. 91.25 (0-939675-39-0) Data Res MN.

Statutes Requiring the Use of Criminal History Record Information. (Illus.). 71p. (Orig.). (C). 1995. pap. text ed. 25.00 (0-7881-1898-6) DIANE Pub.

Statutory Agricultural Liens: Rapid Finder Charts. Martha L. Noble. 174p. 1993. lib. bdg. 35.00 (1-882461-01-0) Natl Ctr Agricult LR&I.

Statutory Construction in Georgia: The Doctrine of in Pari Materia. R. Perry Sentell, Jr. LC 96-21850. 88p. 1996. pap. 7.95 (0-89854-185-9) U of GA Inst Govt.

***Statutory Instruments Pt. I, Sections 1-4: 1st January - 30th April 1995.** 1453p. 1996. 1,040.00 (0-11-840350-8, HM03508, Pub. by Stationery Ofc UK) Bernan Associates.

***Statutory Instruments Pt. III, Sections 1-4: 1st September - 31st December 1994.** 1453p. 1996. 990.00 (0-11-840349-4, HM03494, Pub. by Stationery Ofc UK) Bernan Associates.

S

Statutory Instruments Pt. 11, Sections 1 & 2: May 1 - August 31, 1992. (Statutory Instruments Ser.). 1453p. 1994. 435.00 (*0-11-840335-4*, HM03354, Pub. by Stationery Ofc UK) Bernan Associates.
Statutory Instruments - Bound Volumes Sections 1-4, 1st September-December 31st 1992, 4 vols., Set. 1453p. 1995. 825.00 (*0-11-840336-2*, HM03362, Pub. by Stationery Ofc UK) Bernan Associates.
Statutory Instruments, Part II Sections 1, 2 & 3. 1453p. 1994. 510.00 (*0-11-840326-5*, HM03265) Her Majesty s Stationery Office.
Statutory Interpretation. D. J. Gifford. xxxi, 210p. 1990. pap. 39.00 (*0-455-20939-1*, Pub. by Law Bk Co AT) Gaunt.
Statutory Interpretation. 2nd ed. F. A. Bennion. 1006p. 1992. U. K. 260.00 (*0-406-00341-6*, U.K.) MICHIE.
Statutory Interpretation: An Introduction for Students. C. R. Botha. 132p. 1991. pap. write for info. (*0-7021-2676-4*, Pub. by Juta SA) Gaunt.
Statutory Interpretation in Australia. 3rd ed. D. C. Pearce. 1988. pap. 55.00 (*0-409-30810-2*) MICHIE.
Statutory Intervention in Agricultural Marketing: A New Zealand Perspective. Dorothy V. Jacobsen et al. (Technical Paper Ser.: No. 283). 84p. 1995. 7.95 (*0-8213-3247-3*, 13247) World Bank.
Statutory Materials on Family Law. Walter J. Wadlington. 1981. 10.95 (*0-88277-485-9*) Foundation Pr.
Statutory Murder. Dicey Thomas. 189p. 1989. 14.95 (*0-936389-14-1*) Tudor Pubs.
Statutory Planning in Victoria. D. Eccles & T. L. Bryant. 200p. 1991. pap. 54.00 (*0-409-30174-4*, Austral) MICHIE.
Statutory Supplement. 2nd ed. Ed. by Teresa Donohue. 240p. 1995. pap. 42.00 (*0-934914-93-1*) NACM.
Statutory Supplement on Commericial Paper. William D. Hawkland. 1967. 8.25 (*0-88277-388-7*) Foundation Pr.
Statutory Supplement to Case & Materials on Labor Law. Leslie. 1992. 17.95 (*0-316-52167-1*) Little.
***Statutory Supplement to Cases & Materials on Labor Law.** 12th ed. Archibald Cox et al. (University Casebook Ser.). 130p. suppl. ed., pap. text ed. write for info. (*1-56662-437-1*) Foundation Pr.
Statutory Supplement to Labor Law: Cases, Materials & Problems. Bernard D. Meltzer & Stanley D. Henderson. LC 84-81751. (C). 1985. pap. 11.95 (*0-316-56648-9*) Little.
Statutory Time Limitations, 1981-1991: Colorado. Butterworths Staff. LC 81-66550. 265p. 1991. ring bd. 50.00 (*0-409-20218-5*) MICHIE.
Statutory Time Limitations, 1981-1991: Colorado. Butterworths Staff. LC 81-66550. 265p. 1992. suppl. ed. 45.00 (*1-56257-806-5*) MICHIE.
***Statutory Valuations.** 3rd ed. Andrew Baum & Gary Sams. 288p. 1996. pap. 25.95 (*0-415-13762-4*) Routledge.
Staubach Corp, Practice Problem 1. James Benjamin & Stanley H. Kratchman. (C). 1989. pap. text ed. 17.50 (*0-256-06909-3*) Irwin.
Staubach Corp, Practice Problem II. 3rd ed. James Benjamin & Stanley H. Kratchman. 72p. (C). 1989. per. 22.95 (*0-256-06911-5*) Irwin.
***Stauffenberg: A Family History, 1905-1944.** 442p. 1997. pap. text ed. 19.95 (*0-521-62988-8*) Cambridge U Pr.
Stauffenberg: A Family History, 1905-1944. Peter Hoffmann. (Illus.). 412p. (C). 1995. text ed. 39.95 (*0-521-45307-0*) Cambridge U Pr.
Staunton Artillery - McClanahan's Battery. Robert J. Driver, Jr. (Virginia Regimental Histories Ser.). (Illus.). 127p. 1988. 19.95 (*0-930919-63-7*) H E Howard.
Stauton - Waynesboro. San Antonio Cartographers Staff. 1996. 2.95 (*0-671-56292-4*) Macmillan.
Stavelot Triptych: Mosan Art & the Legend of the True Cross. William Voelkle. LC 80-8970. (Illus.). 80p. 1980. pap. 12.00 (*0-87598-071-6*) Pierpont Morgan.
Staves Calends Legends. Thomas Meyer. 1979. 20.00 (*0-912330-36-8*, Inland Bk); pap. 12.50 (*0-912330-37-6*, Inland Bk) Jargon Soc.
Staves for Louisville. William Carigan. LC 81-81067. 1981. 10.95 (*0-9605986-0-X*) Juniper Pubs.
***Staving off Rapture.** Ava L. Hayman. 1994. pap. 7.00 (*0-9613984-9-3*) Flume Pr.
Stavrogin's Confession & the Plan of the Life of a Great Sinner. Fyodor Dostoyevsky. LC 72-2556. (Studies in Fiction: No. 34). 1972. reprint ed. lib. bdg. 75.00 (*0-8383-1494-5*) M S G Haskell Hse.
***Stavropol Kray: Economy, Industry, Government, Business.** 2nd rev. ed. Russian Information & Business Center, Inc. Staff. (Russian Regional Business Directories Ser.). (Illus.). 200p. 1997. pap. 99.00 (*1-57751-378-9*) Russ Info & Busn Ctr.
Stax Record Story. Bowman. LC 97-19812. 1997. 25.00 (*0-02-860268-4*) Macmillan.
Stay Alive: How to Street Fight with a Pistol. Wayne R. Lippert. LC 95-90017. (Illus.). 270p. (Orig.). pap. text ed. write for info. (*0-9645362-0-X*) Fair Winds.
Stay Alive All Your Life. Norman Vincent Peale. 1983. mass mkt. 5.99 (*0-449-20480-4*) Fawcett.
***Stay Alive All Your Life.** Norman Vincent Peale. 1996. pap. 10.00 (*0-449-91204-3*) Fawcett.
***Stay-at-Home Mom: For Women at Home & Those Who Want to Be.** expanded rev. ed. Donna Otto. LC 96-45434. 224p. 1997. pap. 8.99 (*1-56507-638-9*) Harvest Hse.
***Stay-at-Home Mom's Guide to Making Money/Busy Women's Guide/Earning.** Liz Folger. LC 97-5569. 304p. 1997. per., pap. 12.00 (*0-7615-0793-0*) Prima Pub.
***Stay-at-Home Mom's Survival Guide.** Anne V. Palumbo. Ed. by Laurie Boucke. LC 97-10761. (Illus.). 230p. (Orig.). 1997. pap. 15.00 (*1-888580-05-4*) White-Boucke.
Stay Away from Simon! Carol Carrick. (Illus.). (J). (gr. 3-6). 1989. pap. 5.95 (*0-89919-849-X*, Clarion Bks) HM.
Stay Away from That City They Call It Cheyenne. Stephen A. Bly. LC 95-26675. 192p. 1996. pap. 8.99 (*0-89107-890-8*) Crossway Bks.
Stay Away from the Junkyard! Tricia Tusa. LC 87-15274. (Illus.). 40p. (J). (gr. k-3). 1988. lib. bdg. 14.95 (*0-02-789541-6*, Mac Bks Young Read) S&S Childrens.
Stay Away from the Junkyard! Tricia Tusa. LC 91-38498. 32p. (J). (gr. k-3). 1992. reprint ed. pap. 4.95 (*0-689-71626-5*, Aladdin Paperbacks) S&S Childrens.
***Stay Away from the Swamp.** Fred E. Katz. (SpineChillers Ser.). (Orig.). (J). 1997. pap. 5.99 (*0-8499-4064-8*) Nelson.
Stay Away from the Treehouse. R. L. Stine. (Ghosts of Fear Street Ser.: No. 5). (J). (gr. 3-6). 1996. pap. 3.99 (*0-671-52945-5*, Minstrel Bks) PB.
Stay Away, Joe. Dan Cushman. LC 52-12887. 1968. 21.95 (*0-911436-01-4*) Stay Away.
Stay Awhile: A New Mexico Sojourn. Toby Smith. LC 91-31144. (Illus.). 160p. 1992. pap. 9.95 (*1-878610-07-4*) Red Crane Bks.
Stay Carl Stay - Best Half Foot Forward - Pillow Talk: Three One-Act Plays. Peter Tolan. 1991. pap. 5.25 (*0-8222-1077-0*) Dramatists Play.
***Stay Close & Do Nothing: A Spiritual & Practical Guide to Caring for the Dying at Home.** Merrill J. Collett. LC 97-13464. (Illus.). 256p. 1997. 22.95 (*0-8362-3583-5*) Andrews & McMeel.
Stay, Fang. Barbara S. Hazen. LC 89-32359. (Illus.). 32p. (J). (gr. k-3). 1990. lib. bdg. 13.95 (*0-689-31599-6*, Atheneum Bks Young) S&S Childrens.
Stay Fit: Build a Strong Body. Catherine Reef. LC 93-19349. (Good Health Guidelines Ser.). (Illus.). 64p. (J). (gr. 4-7). 1993. 15.98 (*0-8050-2441-7*) TFC Bks NY.
Stay Fit & Healthy until You're Dead. Dave Barry. Ed. by Roger B. Yepsen. LC 85-11931. (Illus.). 96p. 1985. pap. 8.95 (*0-87857-570-7*, 10-136-1) Rodale Pr Inc.
***Stay Focused: A Practical Message for Leaders & Laymen.** Randy Borders. 100p. (Orig.). 1997. pap. 9.95 (*1-57502-433-0*, PO1321) Morris Pubng.
***Stay Here with Me.** large type ed. Robert Olmstead. (Niagara Large Print Ser.). 332p. 1997. 29.50 (*0-7089-5872-9*) Ulverscroft.
Stay Here With Me: A Memoir. Robert Olmstead. 207p. 1996. 23.00 (*0-8050-4162-1*) H Holt & Co.
***Stay Here with Me: A Memoir.** Robert Olmstead. 1997. pap. text ed. 12.00 (*0-8050-5358-1*, Owl) H Holt & Co.
Stay Home & Get Rich. Stewart Kime. (Illus.). 176p. (Orig.). 1994. pap. 19.95 (*0-9639124-0-2*) Mtn Pubng.
Stay Home & Make Money. Russ Von Hoelscher. 120p. 1981. pap. write for info. (*0-940398-17-6*) Profit Ideas.
Stay Home & Star: A Step-by-Step Guide to Starting Your Regional Acting Career. Bill Steele. LC 91-14981. 154p. (C). 1992. pap. 13.95 (*0-435-08603-0*, 08603) Heinemann.
Stay in Control: How to Cope & Still Get the Job You Really Want. Carla-Krystin Andrade. 212p. 1994. pap. text ed. 14.95 (*1-880030-27-6*) DBM Pub.
Stay in Line. Teddy Slater. LC 95-13234. (Hello Math Reader Ser.: Level 2). (Illus.). 32-40p. (J). 1996. pap. 3.50 (*0-590-22713-0*, Cartwheel) Scholastic Inc.
***Stay in School, Stay out of Prison.** David S. Schofield. LC 97-11268. (Illus.). 96p. (Orig.). 1997. teacher ed., pap. 15.95 (*0-89390-366-3*) Resource Pubns.
Stay in the Game: It's Too Soon to Quit! Van Crouch. 224p. (Orig.). Date not set. pap. 9.99 (*1-56292-583-0*, HB-583) Honor Bks OK.
Stay Love until Autumn. Ann C. Brown. 245p. 1989. pap. 9.95 (*0-89697-288-7*) Intl Univ Pr.
Stay Me, Oh Comfort Me: Journals & Stories, 1933-1941. M. F. K. Fisher. 1995. pap. 13.00 (*0-679-75825-9*) Pantheon.
Stay of Execution. William P. Wood. LC 93-6815. 1993. write for info. (*0-671-73178-5*) PB.
Stay of Execution. William P. Wood. Ed. by Claire Zion. 416p. 1994. mass mkt. 5.99 (*0-671-73179-3*) PB.
***Stay on a Farm 1997.** Holiday Bureau Staff. 1997. pap. text ed. 12.95 (*0-7117-0871-1*, Pub. by Jarrold Pub UK) Seven Hills Bk.
Stay Out of Court: The Manager's Guide to Preventing Employee Lawsuits. Rita Risser. LC 93-6799. 1993. write for info. (*0-13-845561-9*); pap. write for info. (*0-13-845553-8*) P-H.
***Stay Out of Court & in Business: Every Manager's Guide to Minimizing Legal Troubles.** Stafford et al. (Illus.). 225p. (Orig.). 1997. pap. 19.95 (*1-888925-10-8*) Archipligo Pub.
Stay Out of Court & Stay in Business. Clarance Hogglund et al. (Stay Out of Court Ser.). 156p. 1995. pap. 22.50 (*0-9631290-3-1*) Common Law.
Stay Out of Politics: A Philosopher Views South Africa. Ronald Aronson. LC 89-20291. 178p. 1990. pap. text ed. 18.00 (*0-226-02803-8*); lib. bdg. 38.50 (*0-226-02801-1*) U Ch Pr.
***Stay Out of the Basement.** R. L. Stine. LC 97-13831. (Goosebumps Ser.). (J). 1997. lib. bdg. write for info. (*0-8368-1974-8*) Gareth Stevens Inc.
Stay Out of the Basement. R. L. Stine. (Goosebumps Ser.). 160p. (J). (gr. 4-6). 1992. pap. 3.99 (*0-590-45366-1*, Apple Paperbacks) Scholastic Inc.
Stay out of the Basement see No Bajes Al Sotano - Stay Out of the Basement
Stay Out of the Bathroom. R. U. Slime. (Gooflumps Ser.: No. 2.5). 1995. pap. 3.99 (*0-679-87908-0*, Bullseye Bks) Random Bks Yng Read.
Stay Out of the Wheat Field. James F. Rayle. Ed. by Diana M. Montague. 269p. (Orig.). 1993. pap. 10.95 (*1-883868-00-9*) Am Vision Pub.
Stay Put, Robbie McAmis. Frances G. Tunbo. LC 87-18123. (Chaparral Bks.). (Illus.). 160p. (J). (gr. 4 up). 1988. lib. bdg. 15.95 (*0-87565-025-2*) Tex Christian.
Stay Slim God's Way. Shirley B. Johnson. 120p. (Orig.). 1996. pap. write for info. (*1-57502-219-2*, P6873) Morris Pubng.
***Stay the Course: European Unity & Atlantic Solidarity.** Andrew S. Natsios. LC 96-54065. (Washington Papers: Vol. 171). 210p. 1997. text ed. 49.95 (*0-275-95932-5*, Praeger Pubs); pap. text ed. 14.95 (*0-275-95933-3*, Praeger Pubs) Greenwood.
Stay This Moment: The Photographs of Sam Abell. Sam Abell. LC 90-38328. (Illus.). 172p. 1990. 50.00 (*0-934738-72-6*) Lickle Pubng.
Stay Tooned. Rhonda Dicksion. (Illus.). 144p. 1993. pap. 9.95 (*1-56280-045-0*) Naiad Pr.
***Stay True: Short Stories for Strong Girls.** Marilyn Singer. LC 97-14709. (J). 1998. write for info. (*0-590-36031-0*) Scholastic Inc.
Stay Tuned: A Guide to Communion in the Age of Communication. Leonard A. Sroka. LC 93-30965. 1994. pap. 6.95 (*0-8189-0686-3*) Alba.
***Stay Tuned: My Life & the Business of Running the ABC Television Network.** James E. Duffy. 1996. 24.95 (*0-935016-07-4*, Dunhill Pub Co) Zinn Pub Grp.
Stay Tuned: Raising Media-Savvy Kids in the Age of the Channel-Surfing Couch Potato. Jane Murphy & Karen Tucker. 224p. 1996. 11.95 (*0-385-47690-6*, Main St Bks) Doubleday.
Stay Tuned for Danger. Carolyn Keene. (Nancy Drew Files Ser.: No. 17). 160p. (Orig.). (YA). (gr. 7 up). 1991. pap. 3.50 (*0-671-73667-1*, Archway) PB.
***Stay Tuned for Terror.** Fred E. Katz. LC 97-11090. (Spinechillers Ser.). (J). 1997. write for info. (*0-8499-4053-2*) Word Pub.
***Stay Tuned for Terror.** Fred E. Katz. (SpineChillers Mysteries Ser.: Vol. 10). 144p. (Orig.). (J). (gr. 5-8). 1997. pap. 5.99 (*0-614-30894-1*) Tommy Nelson.
Stay Tuned for the Greatest Spectacle in Racing. Ron Dorson. (Illus.). 260p. 1980. lib. bdg. 9.95 (*0-915088-21-5*) C Hungness.
Stay Up: I Within. Arnold Bathersfield. LC 90-84864. 140p. 1991. 12.50 (*0-9613919-1-X*) Evergreen Prods.
Stay Well: A Nationally Acclaimed Family Doctor Tells You How. Robert T. Johnson. LC 85-60510. 1985. 18. 98 (*0-685-09964-4*, 1236) Horizon Utah.
Stay Well Without Going Broke: Winning the War Over Medical Bills. Pattie Vargas et al. 384p. 1993. 22.95 (*0-914984-52-7*) Starburst.
Stay with Us: Praying as Disciples. John Mullin. (Spirit Life Ser.). 48p. (Orig.). 1995. pap. 3.95 (*1-878718-28-2*) Resurrection.
Stay Young Reduce Your Rate of Aging. John K. Beddow. 101p. (Orig.). 1986. pap. 9.95 (*0-9617531-0-2*) Am Univ Sci & Tech.
Stay Young the Melatonin Way: The Natural Plan for Better Sex, Better Sleep, Better Health & Longer Life. Stephen J. Bock & Michael Boyette. 224p. 1996. pap. 10.95 (*0-452-27525-3*, Plume) NAL-Dutton.
***Stayin' Over Songbook.** Peter Alsop et al. (J). 1994. 11.00 (*1-877942-01-4*) Moose Schl Records.
***Staying Afloat in the Construction Industry: Economic & Political Trends for the 1900's...** Quinn Mills. 1996. pap. text ed. 29.95 (*1-55701-168-0*) BNI Pubns.
***Staying after School: At-Risk Students in a Compensatory Education Program.** Bram A. Hamovitch. LC 96-36368. 144p. 1997. text ed. 55.00 (*0-275-95701-2*, Praeger Pubs) Greenwood.
Staying Ahead. Morris Macarz. LC 95-83304. (Illus.). 448p. 1997. 19.95 (*0-8158-0522-5*) Chris Mass.
***Staying Ahead Activity Book.** Lynda Lawson. 72p. 1997. pap. text ed. 7.95 (*0-521-57817-5*) Cambridge U Pr.
Staying Ahead of CRA: What Financial Institutions Must Know to Win at Community Reinvestment. Jeffrey Marshall. 276p. 1991. text ed. 45.00 (*1-55623-448-1*) Irwin Prof Pubng.
Staying Alive: The Complete Guide to Energy Renewal. Marylil K. Humphreys. LC 89-82616. (Illus.). 184p. (Orig.). 1990. pap. 12.95 (*0-9625645-0-8*) Avocet Pub.
Staying Alive: Women, Ecology & Development. Vandana Shiva. LC 88-29783. 224p. (C). 1989. pap. 19.95 (*0-86232-823-3*, Pub. by Zed Bks Ltd UK) Humanities.
Staying Alive & Other Poems. Jaqueline H. Becker. 56p. 1994. pap. 9.95 (*0-9644685-0-6*) Intrcult Commun.
Staying Alive in Alaska's Wild. Andy Nault. Ed. by Tee Loftin. (Illus.). 224p. (Orig.) (J). 1980. pap. 8.95 (*0-934812-01-2*) Tee Loftin.
Staying at the Top. Evelyn Rothstein et al. Ed. by Joan Ostacher. LC 86-80111. (Illus.). 175p. 1986. 9.95 (*0-913935-42-5*) ERA-CCR.
Staying Clean: Living Without Drugs. 76p. (Orig.). 1989. pap. 8.00 (*0-89486-447-5*, 5150A) Hazelden.
Staying Close. Dennis Rainey. 1992. pap. 12.99 (*0-8499-3343-9*) Word Pub.
Staying Close to the River: Travel, Politics & Letters. Ken Worpole. 192p. (C). 1995. pap. 18.50 (*0-85315-820-7*, Pub. by Lawrence & Wishart UK) NYU Pr.
***Staying Competitive on Federal IT Buys.** Rand L. Allen et al. 1997. ring bd. 156.00 (*1-56726-052-7*) Holbrook & Kellogg.
Staying Dry: A Practical Guide to Bladder Control. Kathryn L. Burgio et al. LC 89-45480. 176p. 1989. pap. 12.95 (*0-8018-3909-2*); text ed. 30.00 (*0-8018-3912-2*) Johns Hopkins.
Staying Employed: The Work Manual for the Eighties...& Beyond. William Homolka. LC 84-60968. 100p. (Orig.). 1984. pap. 9.95 (*0-917601-00-9*) New World NY.
Staying Faithful. Andrea S. Louthan & Howard Louthan. (Christian Character Bible Studies). 64p. (Orig.). 1992. wbk. ed., pap. 4.99 (*0-8308-1146-X*, 1146) InterVarsity.
Staying Fat for Sarah Byrnes. Chris Crutcher. 224p. (YA). 1995. mass mkt. 4.50 (*0-440-21906-X*) Dell.
Staying Fat for Sarah Byrnes. Chris Crutcher. LC 91-40097. (J). (gr. 7 up). 1993. 16.00 (*0-688-11552-7*) Greenwillow.
Staying Fat for Sarah Byrnes. large type ed. Chris Crutcher. (Teen Scene Ser.). (YA). (gr. 9-12). 1993. pap. 15.95 (*0-7862-0062-6*) Thorndike Pr.
Staying Flexible. (Fitness, Health & Nutrition Ser.). (Illus.). 144p. 1987. 17.27 (*0-8094-6167-6*); lib. bdg. 23.27 (*0-8094-6168-4*) Time-Life.
Staying Focused: Practical Advice for Writers. Stephanie Stearns et al. (Illus.). 42p. (Orig.). 1992. pap. 3.75 (*0-929614-04-6*) Dubless Pubns.
Staying for Sarah Byrnes. Chris Crutcher. 224p. (J). 1996. pap. 2.49 (*0-440-22009-2*) Dell.
Staying Found: The Complete Map & Compass Handbook. 2nd ed. June Fleming. LC 94-10541. (Orig.). 1994. pap. 12.95 (*0-89886-397-X*) Mountaineers.
***Staying Friends with Your Kids.** Kathy C. Miller & Darcy Miller. LC 97-2827. 1997. write for info. (*0-87788-800-0*) Shaw Pubs.
Staying Healthy. Ruth C. Rosen. (Life Skills Library). (Illus.). 48p. (YA). (gr. 7-12). 1993. lib. bdg. 14.95 (*0-8239-1471-2*) Rosen Group.
Staying Healthy: A Bibliography of Health Promotion Materials. 1986. lib. bdg. 79.95 (*0-8490-3807-3*) Gordon Pr.
Staying Healthy: A Bibliography of Health Promotion Materials. 1984. lib. bdg. 25.00 (*0-87700-550-8*) Revisionist Pr.
***Staying Healthy: Dental Care.** LC 96-37360. (Library of Healthy Living Ser.). (J). 1997. lib. bdg. 11.95 (*0-8239-5139-1*, PowerKids) Rosen Group.
***Staying Healthy: Eating RIght.** A. B. McGinry. LC 96-44287. (Library of Healthy Living Ser.). (J). 1996. lib. bdg. 11.95 (*0-8239-5136-7*, PowerKids) Rosen Group.
***Staying Healthy: Good Hygiene.** Alice B. McGinty. LC 96-53252. (Library of Healthy Living). (J). 1997. lib. bdg. 11.95 (*0-8239-5141-3*, PowerKids) Rosen Group.
***Staying Healthy: Let's Exercise.** A. B. McGinry. LC 96-47208. (Library of Healthy Living Ser.). (J). 1996. lib. bdg. 11.95 (*0-8239-5137-5*, PowerKids) Rosen Group.
***Staying Healthy: Personal Safety.** LC 96-39985. (Library of Healthy Living). (J). 1997. lib. bdg. 11.95 (*0-8239-5140-5*, PowerKids) Rosen Group.
***Staying Healthy: Sleep & Rest.** LC 96-37359. (Library of Healthy Living Ser.). 1996. lib. bdg. 11.95 (*0-8239-5138-3*, PowerKids) Rosen Group.
Staying Healthy: 10 Easy Steps for Women. Carolle Jean-Murat. (Illus.). 120p. (Orig.). 1994. pap. 14.94 (*0-9627145-7-7*) Waterside Prodns.
Staying Healthy in Asia, Africa, & Latin America. 4th ed. Dirk G. Schroeder. (Moon Travel Handbooks Ser.). (Illus.). 197p. 1995. pap. 11.95 (*1-56691-026-9*) Moon Trvl Hdbks.
Staying Healthy in Asia, Africa & Latin America: Your Complete Health Guide to Traveling & Living in Less-Developed Regions of the World. 4th rev. ed. Dirk G. Schroeder. (Illus.). 208p. 1995. pap. 11.95 (*0-917704-19-3*) Volunteers Asia Pr.
Staying Healthy with Nutrition: The Complete Guide to Diet & Nutritional Medicine. Elson M. Haas. LC 90-38517. 1200p. (Orig.). 1995. pap. 34.95 (*0-89087-481-6*) Celestial Arts.
Staying Healthy with the Seasons. Elson M. Haas. LC 80-69469. (Illus.). 260p. (Orig.). 1995. pap. 12.95 (*0-89087-306-2*) Celestial Arts.
Staying Healthy Without Medicine: A Manual of Home Prevention & Treatment. Daniel P. Marshall et al. LC 83-2297. (Illus.). 312p. 1983. lib. bdg. 40.95 (*0-88229-635-3*) Nelson-Hall.
Staying Home. Elisabeth Nonas. 320p. 1994. pap. 10.95 (*1-56280-076-0*) Naiad Pr.
Staying Home: From Full-Time Professional to Full-Time Parent. Darcie Sanders. 1993. pap. 11.95 (*0-316-77066-3*) Little.
Staying Home Instead: Alternatives to the Two-Paycheck Family. rev. ed. Christine Davidson. LC 92-31463. 225p. 24.95 (*0-02-906945-9*, Free Press) Free Pr.
Staying Human in Seattle & the Puget Sound Area: Sustainable Family Giving When You're Sick of Being Hassled & Too Tired to Save the World. Ed. by Mark Rothman & Patricia Rothman. (Staying Human Ser.). (Orig.). 1994. pap. 16.00 (*1-884749-05-4*) Careful Contrib.
Staying Human in the Organization: Our Biological Heritage & the Workplace. J. Gary Bernhard & Kalman Glantz. LC 92-892. (Human Evolution, Behavior & Intelligence Ser.). 176p. 1992. text ed. 49.95 (*0-275-94295-3*, C4295, Praeger Pubs) Greenwood.
Staying in... John E. Biegert. (Looking up Ser.). 1985. pap. 1.95 (*0-8298-0567-2*) Pilgrim OH.
Staying In. Grey Brown. 24p. 1992. pap. 5.00 (*0-9624274-7-0*) NC Writers Network.
Staying in Love. Norton F. Kristy. 1985. pap. 7.00 (*0-87980-414-9*) Wilshire.
Staying in Love for a Lifetime. Ed Wheat. 544p. 1994. 12. 98 (*0-88486-097-3*) Arrowood Pr.
Staying in School: Partnerships for Educational Change. Ian M. Evans et al. (Children, Youth & Change Ser.). 272p. 1995. pap. 25.00 (*1-55766-173-1*) P H Brookes.
Staying in Shape: An Insider's View of the Great Spas. Carleton Varney. LC 83-3794. (Illus.). 224p. 1983. write for info. (*0-672-52722-7*) Macmillan.
***Staying in Style: Clothing & Adornment.** Sheila Henrikson. (Our Human Family Ser.). (Illus.). 80p. (YA). (gr. 5 up). Date not set. lib. bdg. 21.95 (*1-56711-137-8*) Blackbirch.
Staying in the Loop: International Alliances for Sharing Technology, No. 61. Ashoka Mody. (Discussion Paper Ser.). 22p. 1989. 6.95 (*0-8213-1344-4*, 11344) World Bank.

An Asterisk (*) at the beginning of an entry indicates that the title is appearing in BIP for the first time.

Staying in the Right Lane. (Power Tool Box Ser.: Vol. 4). 116p. (J). (gr. 1-6). 1993. ring bd. 149.95 (*1-57405-046-X*) CharismaLife Pub.

Staying in Touch. J. W. Duggar. 96p. 1990. pap. 4.00 (*0-89114-174-X*) Baptist Pub Hse.

Staying in Touch: A Novel Idea for Sex Education at Home & Family Relations. D. R. Hall. 372p. 1995. pap. 16.00 (*0-8059-3802-8*) Dorrance.

***Staying Intact.** John Palen. 24p. Date not set. pap. 6.00 (*0-932412-11-4*) Mayapple Pr.

Staying Is Nowhere: An Anthology of Kondh & Paraja Poetry. Sitakant Mahapatra & Norman H. Zide. (Saffronbird Ser.). 1976. 6.75 (*0-89253-142-8*); lib. bdg. 12.00 (*0-89253-126-6*) Ind-US Inc.

Staying Jewish & Surviving College: Survival Guide for the Jewish Student at College. Paul A. Silverman. 90p. (Orig.). 1995. pap. write for info. (*1-57502-024-6*) Morris Pub.

***Staying Married.** Anita Diggs & Vera S. Paster. 240p. 1998. 23.00 (*1-57566-248-5*, Knsington) Kensgtn Pub Corp.

Staying Married Is the Best Revenge. Michael Moore. 96p. 1987. 3.95 (*1-55601-006-0*) Great Sky.

***Staying Married...& Loving It! How to Get What You Want from Your Man Without Asking.** Patricia Allen & Sandra Harmon. LC 96-53066. 272p. 1997. 23.00 (*0-688-05291-6*) Morrow.

Staying Nine. Pam Conrad. LC 87-45862. (Illus.). 80p. (J). (gr. 2-5). 1988. 13.95 (*0-06-021319-1*); lib. bdg. 13.89 (*0-06-021320-5*) HarpC Child Bks.

Staying Nine. Pam Conrad. LC 87-45862. (Trophy Bk.). (Illus.). 80p. (J). (gr. 2-5). 1990. pap. 3.95 (*0-06-440377-7*, Trophy) HarpC Child Bks.

***Staying off the Beaten Track in England & Wales 1997.** Elizabeth Gundrey & Walter Gundrey. (Illus.). 432p. 1997. pap. 14.95 (*0-09-936031-4*, Pub. by Arrow Bks UK) Trafalgar.

Staying Off the Beaten Track in Scotland. Elizabeth Gundrey & Nancy Webber. (Illus.). 176p. 1996. pap. 11.95 (*0-09-966931-5*, Pub. by Arrow Bks UK) Trafalgar.

Staying OK. Amy B. Harris & Thomas A. Harris. 272p. 1986. mass mkt. 4.95 (*0-380-70130-8*) Avon.

***Staying On.** Scott. Date not set. pap. text ed. write for info. (*0-582-07718-4*, Pub. by Longman UK) Longman.

Staying On. Paul Scott. 240p. 1979. pap. 3.50 (*0-380-46045-9*) Avon.

Staying on Alone: Letters of Alice B. Toklas. rev. ed. Alice B. Toklas. Ed. by Edward Burns. 1982. reprint ed. pap. 8.95 (*0-87140-131-2*) Liveright.

Staying on Course. H. Paul Bauer. 53p. (Orig.). 1984. pap. 3.50 (*0-8100-0181-0*, 22N0791) Northwest Pub.

Staying on the Line: Blue-Collar Women in Contemporary Japan. Glenda S. Roberts. LC 93-27346. 1994. pap. text ed. 17.00 (*0-8248-1579-3*) UH Pr.

Staying on the Path. Wayne W. Dyer. Ed. by Jill Kramer. LC 94-38239. 208p. (Orig.). 1995. pap. 6.95 (*1-56170-126-2*, 152) Hay House.

Staying on Top: A Survival Handbook for the Ages of Our Lives. Margo Piper. LC 91-17592. 80p. 1991. pap. 9.95 (*0-942963-14-8*) Distinctive Pub.

***Staying on Track: An Educational Leader's Guide to Preventing Derailment & Ensuring Personal & Organizational Success.** Dale L. Brubaker & Larry D. Coble. (Illus.). 152p. 1996. 42.95 (*0-8039-6537-0*); pap. 18.95 (*0-8039-6538-9*) Corwin Pr.

Staying Out of Court: A Self-Assessment Guide for Nurses. 4th ed. Barbara E. Calfee. 90p. 1994. per., pap. text ed., ring bd. 19.95 (*0-9633540-3-5*) ARC Pub.

Staying Out of Hell. James A. Thom. 1985. mass mkt. 5.99 (*0-345-30665-1*) Ballantine.

Staying Poor: Ghana's Political Economy 1950-1990. Rimmer. 256p. 1992. 49.95 (*0-08-041032-4*, Prgamon Press) Buttrwrth-Heinemann.

Staying Poor: How the Job Training Partnership Act Fails Women. Jo Sanders. LC 88-23913. 193p. 1988. pap. 17.50 (*0-8108-2067-6*) Scarecrow.

***Staying Positive in a Negative World: Biblical Alternatives to Attitudes That Steal the Joy of Life.** Roger Campbell. 1997. pap. 7.99 (*0-8254-2346-5*) Kregel.

Staying Power. Van Crouch. 160p. Date not set. pap. 6.99 (*1-56292-228-9*) Honor Bks OK.

Staying Power. Peter Fryer. (C). 77.50 (*0-86104-774-5*, Pub. by Pluto Pr UK) LPC InBook.

Staying Power: How to Get the B. S. Out of College (or the B. A. or the Degree of Your Choice) Thom Murray & Linda Wiley. LC 93-35802. (Practical Guide Ser.: No. 2). 167p. (Orig.). 1994. pap. 18.95 (*0-929398-65-3*) UNTX Pr.

Staying Power: Long Term Lesbian Couples. Susan E. Johnson. 352p. 1990. pap. 14.95 (*0-941483-75-4*) Naiad Pr.

Staying Power: Reflections on Gender, Justice & Compassion. Carter Heyward. LC 94-39963. 188p. (Orig.). 1995. pap. 12.95 (*0-8298-1027-7*) Pilgrim OH.

Staying Power: The History of Black People in Britain. Fryer. 648p. (C). pap. 19.95 (*0-86104-749-4*, Pub. by Pluto Pr UK) LPC InBook.

Staying Put: Adapting the Places Instead of the People. Ed. by Susan Lanspery & Joan Hyde. LC 95-51473. (Society & Aging Ser.). 295p. 1996. 39.95 (*0-89503-133-7*) Baywood Pub.

Staying Put: Making a Home in a Restless World. Scott R. Sanders. LC 92-35629. 224p. 1994. pap. 12.95 (*0-8070-6341-X*) Beacon Pr.

Staying Put! The Art of Anchoring. Brian Fagan. (Illus.). 124p. (Orig.). 1993. pap. 12.95 (*0-9634635-2-7*) Caractacus.

Staying Rational in an Irrational World: Albert Ellis & Rational Emotive Therapy. Michael Bernard. 288p. 1991. pap. 9.95 (*0-8184-0559-7*, L Stuart) Carol Pub Group.

Staying Safe: Preventing Child Abuse. Girl Scouts of the U. S. A. Staff. (Contemporary Issues Ser.). 16p. 1986. pap. 1.50 (*0-88441-461-2*, 26-821) Girl Scouts USA.

Staying Safe at Home. Donna Chaiet. LC 95-8492. (Get Prepared Library of Violence Prevention for Young Women). (Illus.). 64p. (YA). (gr. 7-12). 1995. lib. bdg. 16.95 (*0-8239-1863-7*) Rosen Group.

Staying Safe at School. Donna Chaiet. LC 95-8493. (Get Prepared Library of Violence Prevention for Young Women). (Illus.). 64p. (YA). (gr. 7-12). 1995. lib. bdg. 16.95 (*0-8239-1864-5*) Rosen Group.

Staying Safe at School. Chester L. Quarles. LC 93-6441. (New Survival Skills for Teachers Ser.). 96p. 1993. pap. 11.95 (*0-8039-6086-7*) Corwin Pr.

Staying Safe at Work. Donna Chaiet. LC 95-8481. (Get Prepared Library of Violence Prevention for Young Women). (Illus.). 64p. (YA). (gr. 7-12). 1995. lib. bdg. 16.95 (*0-8239-1867-X*) Rosen Group.

Staying Safe on Dates. Donna Chaiet. LC 95-8475. (Get Prepared Library of Violence Prevention for Young Women). (Illus.). 64p. (YA). (gr. 7-12). 1995. lib. bdg. 16.95 (*0-8239-1862-9*) Rosen Group.

Staying Safe on Public Transportation. Donna Chaiet. LC 95-8476. (Get Prepared Library of Violence Prevention for Young Women). (Illus.). 64p. (YA). (gr. 7-12). 1995. lib. bdg. 16.95 (*0-8239-1866-1*) Rosen Group.

Staying Safe on the Streets. Donna Chaiet. (Get Prepared Library). (Illus.). 64p. (YA). (gr. 7-12). 1995. lib. bdg. 16.95 (*0-8239-1865-3*) Rosen Group.

Staying Safe while Shopping. Donna Chaiet. LC 95-8478. (Get Prepared Library of Violence Prevention for Young Women). (Illus.). 64p. (YA). (gr. 7-12). 1995. lib. bdg. 16.95 (*0-8239-1869-6*) Rosen Group.

Staying Safe while Traveling. Donna Chaiet. LC 95-8477. (Get Prepared Library of Violence Prevention for Young Women). (Illus.). 64p. (YA). (gr. 7-12). 1995. lib. bdg. 16.95 (*0-8239-1868-8*) Rosen Group.

Staying Sane in a Crazy World: A Guide to Rational Living. Sherwin T. Wine. 276p. 1996. 22.00 (*0-9648016-0-4*) Ctr New Thinking.

Staying Small Successfully: A Guide for Architects & Other Design Professionals. Frank A. Stasiowski. LC 90-29887. 297p. 1991. text ed. 59.95 (*0-471-50652-4*) Wiley.

Staying Sober: A Guide for Relapse Prevention. Terence T. Gorski & Merlene Miller. 228p. 1986. pap. 12.00 (*0-8309-0459-X*, 17-0120-7) Herald Hse.

Staying Sober: Recovery & Education Modular Dependencies. Terence T. Gorski & Marlene Miller. 1989. pap. 150.00 (*0-8309-0542-1*, 17-0166-5); student ed., pap. 7.50 (*0-8309-0602-9*, 17-0188-6) Herald Hse.

Staying Sober Workbook. rev. ed. Terence T. Gorski. 293p. (YA). (gr. 7 up). 1992. pap. text ed. 25.00 (*0-8309-0621-5*) Herald Hse.

Staying Straight: A Relapse Prevention Workbook for Young People. Emil Chiauzzi & Steven K. Liljegren. 1991. pap. 11.50 (*1-55691-069-X*, 69x) Learning Pubns.

Staying Straight: Adolescent Recovery. Mary Montagne. 32p. (Orig.). 1987. pap. 3.95 (*0-9613416-6-1*) Comm Intervention.

Staying the Course: Henry M. Jackson & National Security. Ed. by Dorothy Fosdick. LC 87-2015. (Illus.). 206p. 1987. 20.00 (*0-295-96498-7*); pap. 9.95 (*0-295-96501-0*) U of Wash Pr.

Staying the Course: The Emotional & Social Lives of Men Who Do Well at Work. Robert S. Weiss. 314p. 1990. text ed. 24.95 (*0-02-934090-X*, Free Press) Free Pr.

Staying the Distance: A Novel. Franci McMahon. LC 93-49793. 200p. (Orig.). 1994. pap. 9.95 (*1-56341-046-X*); lib. bdg. 20.95 (*1-56341-047-8*) Firebrand Bks.

Staying Together. William Glasser. LC 95-5745. 144p. 1995. 16.00 (*0-06-017247-9*, HarpT) HarpC.

Staying Together: A Control Theory Guide to a Lasting Marriage. William Glasser. 144p. 1996. pap. 10.00 (*0-06-092699-6*) HarpC.

Staying Together: Forty Ways to Make your Marriage Work. Tom Owen-Towle. LC 87-62585. (Illus.). 108p. (Orig.). 1987. pap. 7.95 (*0-931104-21-1*) Sunflower Ink.

Staying Tuned. Daniel Schorr. 1997. write for info. (*0-201-48913-9*) Addison-Wesley.

Staying Tuned: Contemporary Soap Opera Criticism. Ed. by Suzanne Frentz. LC 91-76365. (C). 1992. 26.95 (*0-87972-537-0*) Bowling Green Univ Popular Press.

Staying up for Love. Leslie A. Miller. 68p. (Orig.). (C). 1990. pap. 11.95 (*0-88748-096-9*) Carnegie-Mellon.

Staying Well. American Institute for Preventive Medicine (AIPM) Staff. LC 93-34773. (For Your Information Ser.). 1993. 8.95 (*1-56420-027-2*); audio 16.00 (*1-56420-028-0*) New Readers.

***Staying Well in a Toxic World: Understanding Environmental Illness, Multiple Chemical Sensitivities, Chemical Injuries, & Sick Building Syndrome.** Lynn Lawson. LC 96-94641. 488p. (Orig.). 1996. pap. 15.95 (*0-9653659-0-5*) Lynnwrd Pr.

Staying Well with Guided Imagery. Belleruth Naparstek. 240p. 1994. 19.95 (*0-446-51821-2*) Warner Bks.

Staying Well with Guided Imagery. Belleruth Naparstek. 1995. pap. write for info. (*0-446-67159-2*); pap. 11.99 (*0-446-67134-7*) Warner Bks.

Staying Well with the Gentle Art of Verbal Self-Defense. Suzette H. Elgin. 1995. 7.98 (*1-56731-081-8*, MJF Bks) Fine Comms.

Staying with Grandma Norma. Lynn Salem & Josie Stewart. (Illus.). 16p. (J). (gr. k-1). 1993. pap. 3.50 (*1-880612-08-9*) Seedling Pubns.

Staying with Grandmother. Barbara Baker. LC 93-13749. (Illus.). 48p. (J). (gr. 1-4). 1994. pap. 12.99 (*0-525-44603-6*) Dutton Child Bks.

Staying with Relations. Rose Macaulay. 320p. 1987. pap. 9.50 (*0-88001-148-3*) Ecco Pr.

***Staying Young.** Tom Monte. 1996. pap. 6.99 (*0-425-15483-1*) Berkley Pub.

Staying Young. Liz Renay. 192p. 11.95 (*0-8184-0329-2*) Carol Pub Group.

Staying Young: How to Look Good, Feel Better & Live Longer. Frances S. Goulart. (Illus.). 228p. 1987. 21.95 (*0-13-846213-5*); 9.95 (*0-13-846205-4*) P-H.

Staying Young: How to Prevent, Slow or Reverse More than 60 Signs of Aging. Prevention Magazine Health Book Editors & Tom Monte. LC 93-39905. (Illus.). 352p. 1994. 24.95 (*0-87596-209-2*) Rodale Pr Inc.

Staying Young: How to Prevent, Slow or Reverse More Than 60 Signs of Aging. Tom Monte. Tr. by Christine Grimm. 400p. 1996. reprint ed. mass mkt. 6.99 (*0-425-15251-0*, Berkley Trade) Berkley Pub.

***Staying Young, Looking Great.** Michael Lafavore. 1997. pap. 12.95 (*0-87596-391-9*) Rodale Pr Inc.

Stazwoerterbuch des Buch und Verlagswesens. Ulrich Stiehl. 1000p. (ENG & GER.). 1977. 250.00 (*0-8288-3396-6*, M7619) Fr & Eur.

STCW Amendments 1991. IMO Staff. (C). 1991. English ed. 50.00 (*0-7855-0018-9*, IMO 997E, Pub. by Intl Maritime Org UK); French ed. 50.00 (*0-685-74504-X*, IMO 998F, Pub. by Intl Maritime Org UK); Spanish ed. 50.00 (*0-685-74505-8*, 999S, Pub. by Intl Maritime Org UK) St Mut.

STD: Health Facts. Lucas Stang & Kathleen R. Miner. LC 93-43843. 1996. 12.95 (*1-56071-183-3*, H303) ETR Assocs.

STD: Sexually Transmitted Diseases, Including HIV - AIDS. 3rd rev. ed. John T. Daugirdas. 1992. 14.95 (*0-9629279-1-0*) Medtext.

STD & HIV: A Guide for Today's Young Adults. William L. Yarber. (Illus.). 106p. (Orig.). (YA). 1992. pap. text ed. 9.00 (*0-88314-533-2*) AAHPERD.

STD Blues. rev. ed. Judy Ismach. 1997. pap. 0.50 (*0-89230-185-6*) Do It Now.

STD Counseling & Treatment Guide. Linda Alexander et al. (Illus.). 256p. (Orig.). 1995. pap. write for info. (*1-885833-02-4*) Am Social Health.

Std 959-1987: IEEE Standard Specifications for an I-O Expansion Bus, IEEE SBX Bus. IEEE Computer Society, Technical Committee on Microprocessors. LC 88-83218. (Illus.). (Orig.). 1989. pap. 44.00 (*1-55937-001-7*, SH12187) IEEE Standards.

STDs & HIV: A Guide for Today's Young Adults. William L. Yarber. 103p. (Orig.). 1992. teacher ed., pap. text ed. 17.00 (*0-88314-534-0*) AAHPERD.

Stead. Cid Corman. 1966. pap. 6.00 (*0-685-00990-4*) Elizabeth Pr.

Stead. Lady Light. 208p. 1993. write for info. (*1-56167-116-9*) Am Literary Pr.

Steadfast & Immovable: Striving for Spiritual Maturity. Robert L. Millet. LC 92-18727. 166p. 1992. 11.95 (*0-87579-635-4*) Deseret Bk.

Steadfast Christianity. (Swindoll Bible Study Guide Ser.). 1986. pap. 5.99 (*0-8499-8286-3*) Word Pub.

Steadfast Faith in Times of Turmoil. Michelle Booth. (Tapestry Collection). 108p. (Orig.). 1995. pap. 6.50 (*1-56476-326-9*, 6-3326, Victor Bks) Chariot Victor.

Steadfast Heart. Dorothy Mack. 224p. 1988. pap. 3.99 (*0-451-15601-3*, Sig) NAL-Dutton.

Steadfast Love: The Third Passage of Marriage. Brian Newman et al. LC 92-23733. 1993. 9.99 (*0-8407-4551-6*) Nelson.

Steadfast Stream: An Introduction to Jewish Social Values. Arthur Lelyveld. LC 94-39947. 120p. 1995. pap. 10.95 (*0-8298-1023-4*) Pilgrim OH.

Steadfast Tin Soldier. (Timeless Tales from Hallmark Fairy Tale Classics Ser.). 24p. (J). Date not set. text ed. 4.95 (*1-56987-215-5*) Landoll.

Steadfast Tin Soldier. Hermann Ammann. (Illus.). 29p. (J). (gr. 1 up). 1968. 7.50 (*0-88680-187-7*) I E Clark.

Steadfast Tin Soldier. Hermann Ammann. (Illus.). 29p. (J). (gr. 1 up). 1969. pap. 3.25 (*0-88680-186-9*) I E Clark.

Steadfast Tin Soldier. Hans Christian Andersen. LC 86-2787. (Knopf Book & Cassette Classics Ser.). (Illus.). 48p. 1986. 13.95 incl. audio (*0-394-88299-7*) Knopf.

Steadfast Tin Soldier. Hans Christian Andersen. (Children's Classics Ser.). (Illus.). 32p. (J). 1991. 6.95 (*0-8362-4929-1*) Andrews & McMeel.

Steadfast Tin Soldier. Hans Christian Andersen. (Creative's Collection of Fairy Tales). (Illus.). 32p. (J). 1983. lib. bdg. 13.95 (*0-87191-948-6*) Creative Ed.

Steadfast Tin Soldier. Hans Christian Andersen. LC 91-71342. (From the Disney Archives Ser.). (Illus.). 32p. (J). (gr. 1-4). 1991. 13.95 (*1-56282-016-8*); lib. bdg. 13.89 (*1-56282-073-7*) Disney Pr.

Steadfast Tin Soldier. Hans Christian Andersen. LC 92-52690. (Michael di Capua Bks.). (Illus.). 32p. (J). (ps-3). 1992. 15.00 (*0-06-205000-1*); lib. bdg. 14.89 (*0-06-205001-X*) HarpC Child Bks.

***Steadfast Tin Soldier.** Hans Christian Andersen. LC 92-52690. (Michael di Capua Bks.). (Illus.). 32p. (J). 1997. pap. 5.95 (*0-06-205900-9*, Trophy) HarpC Child Bks.

Steadfast Tin Soldier. Hans Christian Anderson. (Illus.). 32p. (J). 1996. 14.95 (*1-56458-310-4*) DK Pub Inc.

Steadfast Tin Soldier. Illus. & Retold by Rachel Isadora. LC 95-15816. (J). (ps-3). 1996. 15.95 (*0-399-22676-1*, Putnam) Putnam Pub Group.

Steading of Hill Giant. Gary Gygax. 1981. 6.00 (*0-394-52185-4*) Random.

***Steadwell, Stedwell, Studwell: Descendants of Thomas Studwell I, ca. 1620-1669.** Marion J. Stedwell. 306p. (Orig.). 1996. pap. 45.00 (*0-7884-0515-2*, 5711) Heritage Bk.

Steady, Axially Symmetric Flow of a Viscous Fluid in a Deep Rotating Cylinder Heated from Below. G. N. Lance & E. C. Deland. LC 58-9085. (California University Publications in Engineering: Vol. 5, No. 6). 20p. reprint ed. pap. 25.00 (*0-317-10229-X*, 2021188) Bks Demand.

Steady Digression to a Fixed Point. Rose Hobart. LC 94-1535. (Filmmakers Ser.: No. 40). (Illus.). 186p. 1994. 27.50 (*0-8108-2862-6*) Scarecrow.

Steady Flow in Gas Pipelines: Testing-Measurement-Behavior-Computation. A. E. Uhl et al. (Technical Reports: No. 10). vi, 257p. 1965. pap. 5.00 (*0-685-43364-1*) Inst Gas Tech.

Steady Longing for Flight. Joannie Kervran. Ed. by T. Clear et al. 32p. (Orig.). 1995. pap. text ed. 6.00 (*0-9647199-0-8*) Floating Bridge Pr.

Steady Nerves & Stout Hearts: The Enterprise (CVG) Air Group & Pearl Harbor, 7 December, 1941. Robert J. Cressman & J. Michael Cressman. LC 90-60875. (Illus.). 80p. (Orig.). 1990. pap. 9.95 (*0-929521-25-0*) Pictorial Hist.

Steady Revolutions: The Australian Institute of Marine & Power Engineers 1881-1990. Rosemary Broomham. (Illus.). 296p. 41.95 (*0-86840-324-5*, Pub. by New South Wales Univ Pr AT) Intl Spec Bk.

S

Steady State Economics: With New Essays. 2nd ed. Herman Daly. LC 91-6512. 297p. (Orig.). 1991. 34.95 (*1-55963-072-8*); pap. 19.95 (*1-55963-071-X*) Island Pr.

Steady State Flow Computation Manual for Natural Gas Transmission Lines. 94p. 1964. 2.50 (*0-318-12703-2*, L20020) Am Gas Assn.

Steady-State Methods for Simulating Analog & Microwave Circuits. Kenneth S. Kundert et al. (C). 1990. lib. bdg. 97.00 (*0-7923-9069-5*) Kluwer Ac.

Steady Trade: A Boyhood at Sea. Tristan Jones. (Illus.). 280p. 1996. pap. 16.50 (*1-57409-018-6*) Sheridan.

Steadying the Landscape. Jeanne Lohmann. (Illus.). 102p. 1982. pap. 5.95 (*0-9607688-1-5*) J A Lohmann.

Steak Lover's Cookbook. William Rice. LC 96-38749. 304p. 1996. 23.95 (*0-7611-0631-6*, 10631); pap. 13.95 (*0-7611-0080-6*, 10080) Workman Pub.

Steakhouse Cookbook. Joe Foley & Joan Foley. LC 85-27549. 152p. 1986. 17.95 (*0-88191-021-X*) Freundlich.

***Steaklover's Companion: 170 Savory Recipes from America's Greatest Chefs.** Frederick J. Simon et al. LC 96-51609. 1997. write for info. (*0-06-018781-6*) HarpC.

Steal Away. Jennifer Armstrong. LC 91-18504. 224p. (YA). (gr. 6 up). 1992. 15.95 (*0-531-05983-9*) Orchard Bks Watts.

Steal Away. Jennifer Armstrong. 224p. (J). (gr. 3-7). 1993. pap. 3.99 (*0-590-46921-5*, Apple Paperbacks) Scholastic Inc.

Steal Away. Timothy Watts. LC 96-15573. 272p. 1996. 22.00 (*1-56947-067-7*) Soho Press.

Steal Away Home. pap. 1.95 (*0-590-03322-0*) Scholastic Inc.

Steal Away Home. Lois Ruby. LC 93-47300. (J). 1994. text ed. 16.00 (*0-02-777883-5*) Macmillan.

Steal Away Home: Musical. Aurand Harris. (J). (gr. 1-9). 1972. 5.00 (*0-87602-206-9*) Anchorage.

***Steal Me, Sweet Thief.** Carole Howey. 368p. (Orig.). 1997. mass mkt. 5.50 (*0-8439-4251-7*, Leisure Bks) Dorchester Pub Co.

Steal the Bacon. Charles Martin. LC 86-46285. (Johns Hopkins Poetry & Fiction Ser.). 88p. 1987. pap. 7.95 (*0-8018-3494-5*); text ed. 14.95 (*0-8018-3493-7*) Johns Hopkins.

Steal the Dragon. Patricia Briggs. 288p. (Orig.). 1995. mass mkt. 4.99 (*0-441-00273-0*) Ace Bks.

Steal the Stars. Miranda Jarrett. (Historical Ser.: No. 715). 1992. mass mkt. 3.99 (*0-373-28715-1*, 1-28715-0) Harlequin Bks.

Steal These Homes! As Well As Vacation Houses, Retirement & Investment Real Estate & Commercial Property. Laurence Leichman. 1995. pap. 14.95 (*0-9636867-4-7*) Leichman Assocs.

Steal This Book. Abbie Hoffman. 1976. 25.95 (*0-8488-1368-5*) Amereon Ltd.

Steal This Book. Abbie Hoffman. LC 95-4840. (Illus.). 336p. 1995. pap. 9.95 (*1-56858-053-3*) FWEW.

Steal This Book. Abbie Hoffman. (Illus.). 320p. 1991. reprint ed. lib. bdg. 35.95 (*0-89966-777-5*) Buccaneer Bks.

Steal This Code! Create Reusable Components for Windows 95. Al Williams. LC 95-37111. 400p. 1995. pap. 34.95 incl. disk (*0-201-40998-4*) Addison-Wesley.

***Steal This Computer Book: All the Stuff They Never Tell You about the Internet.** Wallace Wang. 1997. pap. text ed. 16.95 (*1-886411-21-2*) No Starch Pr.

Steal This Handbook! A Template for Creating a Museum's Emergency Preparedness Plan. Allyn Lord et al. LC 94-92256. 240p. (Orig.). 1994. pap. 25.00 (*0-9621348-1-3*) SERA LA.

Steal This Plot: A Writer's Guide to Story Structure & Plagiarism. William Noble & June Noble. 224p. 1985. 19.95 (*0-8397-7880-5*) Eriksson.

Steal This Plot: A Writer's Guide to Story Structure & Plagiarism. 2nd ed. William Noble & June Noble. LC 85-6878. 224p. 1991. reprint ed. pap. 12.95 (*0-8397-7881-3*) Eriksson.

Steal This Urine Test. Abbie Hoffman. 1994. reprint ed. lib. bdg. 32.95 (*1-56849-292-8*) Buccaneer Bks.

Steal This Urine Test: Fighting the Drug Hysteria in America. Abbie Hoffman & Jonathan Silvers. 192p. 1987. pap. 11.95 (*0-14-010400-3*, Penguin Bks) Viking Penguin.

Stealing. Bernadine. 1993. pap. text ed. write for info. (*0-07-005154-2*) McGraw.

Stealing a Little Freedom: Advertisements for Slave Runaways in North Carolina, 1791-1840. Ed. by Freddie L. Parker. LC 93-36958. 912p. 1994. text ed. 99.00 (0-8153-1532-5, H1812) Garland.

Stealing Beauty. Susan Minot. LC 96-19178. 224p. (Orig.). 1996. pap. 11.00 (0-8021-3492-0, Grove) Grove-Atltic.

***Stealing Fire.** Claudia Mauro. 54p. (Orig.). 1996. pap. 12.95 (0-9653800-0-9) Whiteaker Pr.

Stealing Fire: The Atomic Bomb as Symbolic Body. Peter C. Reynolds. (Illus.). 304p. 1991. 19.95 (0-9629261-0-8) Iconic Anthro.

Stealing First in a Two-Team Town: The White Sox from Comiskey to Reinsdorf. Richard Lindberg. LC 94-65137. (Illus.). 275p. 1994. 19.95 (0-915611-93-7) Sagamore Pub.

Stealing from America: A History of Corruption from Jamestown to Whitewater. Nathan Miller. 450p. 1995. pap. 13.95 (1-56924-820-6) Marlowe & Co.

Stealing from the Rich: The Home Stake Oil Swindle. David McClintick. LC 77-22103. 336p. 1977. 10.00 (0-87131-240-9) M Evans.

Stealing Heaven. Kimberly Cates. (Illus.). (J). 1995. mass mkt. 5.99 (0-671-89745-4) PB.

Stealing Heaven. Marion Meade. LC 79-1182. (Hera Ser.). 415p. 1994. pap. 15.00 (1-56947-011-1) Soho Press.

Stealing Heaven. Jaclyn Reding. 1996. pap. 5.99 (0-451-40649-4, Onyx) NAL-Dutton.

Stealing Home. Peter Simpson. LC 84-72898. 64p. 1984. pap. 5.25 (0-933532-43-1) BkMk.

Stealing Home. Mary Stolz. LC 92-5226. 160p. (J). (gr. 3-6). 1992. 14.95 (0-06-021154-7); lib. bdg. 14.89 (0-06-021157-1) HarpC Child Bks.

***Stealing Home: An Intimate Family Portrait by the Daughter of Jackie Robinson.** Sharon Robinson. LC 97-5868. 256p. 1997. pap. 13.00 (0-06-092840-9, PL) HarpC.

Stealing Home: An Intimate Family Portrait by the Daughters of Jackie Robinson. Sharon Robinson. (Illus.). 288p. 1996. 24.00 (0-06-017191-X) HarpC.

Stealing Home: How to Leave Your Job & Become a Successful Consultant. Peter C. Brown. LC 93-28941. 1994. pap. 12.00 (0-517-88157-8, Crown) Crown Pub Group.

Stealing Home: Israel Bound & Rebound. Haim Chertok. LC 87-80546. xii, 295p. (C). 1988. 19.95 (0-8232-1188-6) Fordham.

Stealing Home: Israel Bound & Rebound. Haim Chertok. LC 87-80546. xii, 295p. 1991. pap. 12.95 (0-8232-1306-4) Fordham.

Stealing Home: The Story of Jackie Robinson. Barry Denenberg. 128p. (J). (gr. 3-7). 1997. pap. 3.99 (0-590-42560-9) Scholastic Inc.

Stealing into Print: Fraud, Plagiarism, & Misconduct in Scientific Publishing. Marcel C. LaFollette. 1992. 37.50 (0-520-07831-4) U CA Pr.

Stealing into Print: Fraud, Plagiarism, & Misconduct in Scientific Publishing. Marcel C. LaFollette. LC 91-41669. 293p. (C). 1996. pap. 13.95 (0-520-20513-8) U CA Pr.

Stealing Jesus: How Fundamentalism Betrays Christianity. Bruce Bawer. LC 97-20111. 1997. 26.00 (0-517-70682-2) Random Hse Value.

***Stealing Mangoes.** Sydney March. (Premeri Ser.: Vol. 4). (Illus.). 28p. (Orig.). 1997. 5.00 (0-9654421-9-5) Mica Press.

Stealing Midnight. Sonia Simone. 256p. (Orig.). 1996. mass mkt. 4.99 (0-06-108458-1, HarperPrism) HarpC.

Stealing People's Names: History & Politics in a Sepik River Community. Simon J. Harrison. (Cambridge Studies in Social & Cultural Anthropology: No. 71). (Illus.). 264p. (C). 1990. text ed. 74.95 (0-521-38504-0) Cambridge U Pr.

***Stealing Samantha.** Charlotte Maclay. (American Romance Ser.: No. 684). 1997. mass mkt. 3.75 (0-373-16684-2, 1-16684-2) Harlequin Bks.

Stealing Savannah. Donna Carlisle. (Desire Ser.). 1994. mass mkt. 2.99 (0-373-05852-7, 5-05852-4) Silhouette.

Stealing the Borders. Elliot Rais. 1994. pap. 5.50 (1-56171-325-2, S P I Bks) Sure Seller.

Stealing the Children. 4th ed. Carolyne L. Wright. Ed. by Dale K. Boyer. LC 78-60226. (Ahsahta Press Modern & Contemporary Poets of the West Ser.). 64p. 1978. pap. 6.95 (0-916272-09-5) Ahsahta Pr.

Stealing the Dragon's Fire: A Personal Guide & Resource for Dealing with Breast Cancer. Clo Wilson-Hashiguchi. Ed. by Margaret D. Smith et al. LC 93-94147. (Illus.). 334p. (Orig.). 1995. pap. 19.95 (0-9638590-0-5) Wilson Pubng.

Stealing the Fire: The Art & Protest of James Baldwin. Horace A. Porter. LC 88-27806. 240p. 1990. pap. 17.95 (0-8195-6239-4, Wesleyan Univ Pr) U Pr of New Eng.

Stealing the Language: The Emergence of Women's Poetry in America. Alicia S. Ostriker. LC 85-73368. 336p. 1987. pap. 17.00 (0-8070-6303-7, BP 763) Beacon Pr.

Stealing the Mona Lisa. Chris Greenhalgh. 64p. 9500. pap. 14.95 (1-85224-286-8, Pub. by Bloodaxe Bks UK) Dufour.

Stealing the National Parks. Don Hummel. Ed. by Ron Arnold. (Free Enterprise Battle Bks.). 403p. 1987. 19.95 (0-939571-01-3) Free Enter Pr.

Stealing the Show: Seven Women Artists in Canadian Public Art. Gunda Lambton. (Illus.). 240p. 1994. 55.00 (0-7735-1188-1, Pub. by McGill CN); pap. 24.95 (0-7735-1189-X, Pub. by McGill CN) U of Toronto Pr.

Stealing the Show No. 9. B. B. Calhoun. Date not set. 3.99 (0-679-87470-4) Random.

***Stealing the State: Control & Collapse in Soviet Institutions.** Steven L. Solnick. LC 97-13909. (Russian Research Center Studies). 1997. write for info. (0-674-83680-4) HUP.

Stealing Time. Glenna Sloan. (YA). (gr. 7 up). 1997. pap. 6.99 (0-88092-266-4) Royal Fireworks.

Stealth. M. E. Morris. 352p. (Orig.). 1996. mass mkt. 5.99 (0-380-78488-2) Avon.

Stealth at Sea. Hagan. 1997. 25.00 (0-02-913472-2, Free Press) Free Pr.

Stealth at Sea: The History of the Submarine. Dan Van der Vat. (Illus.). 384p. 1995. 30.00 (0-395-65242-1) HM.

Stealth Fighter Pilot. D. M. Giangreco. (Power Ser.). (Illus.). 128p. 1993. pap. 16.95 (0-87938-716-5) Motorbooks Intl.

Stealth Liposomes. Ed. by F. J. Martin & Danilo D. Lasic. LC 94-32683. (Pharmacology & Toxicology Ser.). 320p. 1995. 136.95 (0-8493-8383-8) CRC Pr.

Stealth Management: With Shared Goals They Will Hardly Know You Are Leading Them. Sheldon Miller. LC 92-90895. (Illus.). 300p. 1993. 39.00 (0-9635316-0-3) Stealth Mgmt.

Stealth PACs: How Israel's American Lobby Took Control of U. S. Middle East Policy. Richard H. Curtiss. (Illus.). 170p. (Orig.). (C). 1990. pap. 9.95 (0-937165-03-4) Am Educ Trust.

***Stealth PACs: Lobbying Congress for Control of U. S. Middle East Policy.** 4th ed. Richard H. Curtiss. 1996. pap. 14.95 (0-937165-05-0) Am Educ Trust.

Stealth PACs: Lobbying Congress for Control of U.S. Middle East Policy. 3rd ed. Richard H. Curtiss. 1991. 14.95 (0-937165-04-2) Am Educ Trust.

Stealth Strike. Frank J. O'Brien. 264p. 1990. 16.95 (0-8306-3472-X, 3472, TAB-Aero) TAB Bks.

Stealth Technology. Clifford Williams. (Illus.). 40p. (Orig.). 1997. pap. 24.00 (0-934274-21-5) Consumertronics.

Stealth Technology: The Art of Black Magic. J. Jones. Ed. by Matt Thurber. (Illus.). 160p. (Orig.). 1989. 22.95 (0-8306-8281-3, TAB-Aero); pap. 14.95 (0-8306-8381-X, TAB-Aero) TAB Bks.

Stealworks: The Graphic Details of John Yates. John Yates. (Illus.). 136p. 1994. pap. 11.95 (1-873176-51-1, AK Pr San Fran) AK Pr Dist.

Steam. Jay B. Laws. 398p. (Orig.). 1991. pap. 9.95 (1-55583-184-2) Alyson Pubns.

Steam: Its Generation & Use. 40th ed. S. C. Stultz & J. B. Kitto. LC 92-74123. (Illus.). 1064p. 1992. lib. bdg. 80.00 (0-9634570-0-4) Babcock & Wilcox.

Steam Age. Paul Lidberg et al. (Castle Falkenstein Ser.). (Illus.). 104p. (Orig.). 1995. pap. 14.00 (0-937279-56-0, CF6021) R Talsorian.

Steam Alive: The Story of Bressingham Steam Museum. Ed. by Alan Bloom. 208p. 1990. 60.00 (0-948251-56-5, Pub. by Picton UK) St Mut.

Steam & Air Tables in SI Units. Thomas F. Irvine, Jr. & James P. Hartnett. 1975. 9.50 (0-07-032054-3) McGraw.

Steam & Air Tables, SI Units. Thomas F. Irvine, Jr. & James P. Hartnett. LC 75-34007. (Illus.). 125p. (C). 1976. pap. text ed. 38.95 (0-89116-004-3) Hemisp Pub.

***Steam & Diesel Power Plant Operators Examinations.** 2nd ed. James Russell. LC 82-2198. (Illus.). 106p. 1995. pap. 34.95 (0-916367-05-3, CU47-SD2) J R Pub.

Steam & Gas Turbines for Marine Propulsion. 2nd ed. Maido Saarlas. 241p. 1987. 29.95 (0-87021-690-2) Naval Inst Pr.

Steam & Stirling: Engines You Can Build. Ed. by William C. Fitt. LC 80-50602. (Illus.). 160p. 1980. 24.95 (0-914104-06-3) Wildwood Pubns MI.

Steam & the Sea: A Guide to the Steamship Collections of the Peabody Museum of Salem. Paul F. Johnston. (Illus.). 1983. 25.00 (0-87577-074-6, Peabody Museum); pap. 15.00 (0-87577-073-8, Peabody Museum) Peabody Essex Mus.

Steam at Oakville. Dick George & Allan Paterson. (Illus.). 268p. 35.00 (0-919783-55-4, Pub. by Boston Mills Pr CN) Genl Dist Srvs.

***Steam at Sea: Two Centuries of Steam-Powered Ships.** Denis Griffiths. (Illus.). 256p. 1997. 43.95 (0-85177-666-3, Pub. by Brasseys UK) Brasseys Inc.

Steam Beneath the Red Star. Ron Ziel. 36.95 (0-8488-0929-7) Amereon Ltd.

Steam Blowing. (Fossil Power Plant Startup Training Ser.: Module 6). (Illus.). 88p. 1984. spiral bd. 34.50 (0-87683-363-6) GP Courseware.

Steam Boiler Operation: Principles & Practice. James J. Jackson. (Illus.). 1980. text ed. 39.00 (0-13-846311-5) P-H.

Steam Boiler Operation: Principles & Practice. 2nd ed. James J. Jackson. (Illus.). 256p. 1987. text ed. 47.00 (0-13-846346-8) P-H.

Steam Charts: S1-10. Ed. by J. H. Potter. 128p. 1976. 25.00 (0-317-33617-7, E00090) ASME.

Steam Conquers the Atlantic. David B. Tyler. LC 72-5082. (Technology & Society Ser.). (Illus.). 504p. 1972. reprint ed. 31.95 (0-405-04731-2) Ayer.

Steam Cooking Now! Barbara S. Brauer. LC 80-82174. (Illus.). 1980. pap. 2.95 (0-915942-15-1) SF Design.

Steam Dummy & Fragments from the Fire: Poems. rev. ed. Chris Llewellyn. (Midwest Writers Ser.). (Illus.). 124p. (Orig.). pap. 8.95 (0-933087-29-2) Bottom Dog Pr.

Steam Engine. Beatrice Siegel. LC 86-5616. (Inventions That Changed Our Lives Ser.). (Illus.). 64p. (J). (gr. 5 up). 1986. 10.95 (0-8027-6655-2); lib. bdg. 10.85 (0-8027-6656-0) Walker & Co.

Steam Engine Design. 1983. reprint ed. pap. 9.95 (0-917914-10-4) Lindsay Pubns.

Steam Engine, 1888. D. Lardner. (Illus.). 135p. 1989. pap. 20.00 (0-87556-165-9) Saifer.

Steam Era of Lehigh Valley. Chuck Yungkurth. Ed. by Mike Schafer. (Illus.). 128p. (Orig.). 1991. pap. 29.95 (0-944119-07-7) Andover Junction.

Steam Explosion Techniques: Fundamentals & Industrial Applications. B. Focher. 412p. 1991. text ed. 105.00 (2-88124-457-2) Gordon & Breach.

Steam Fireman. Jack Rudman. (Career Examination Ser.: C-1035). 1994. pap. 27.95 (0-8373-1035-0) Nat Learn.

Steam Fireman - Stationary Fireman. Jack Rudman. (Career Examination Ser.: C-1902). 1994. pap. 29.95 (0-8373-1902-1) Nat Learn.

Steam Fitter. Jack Rudman. (Career Examination Ser.: C-763). 1994. pap. 27.95 (0-8373-0763-5) Nat Learn.

Steam Fitter's Helper. Jack Rudman. (Career Examination Ser.: C-764). 1994. pap. 23.95 (0-8373-0764-3) Nat Learn.

Steam Gauge. Christopher Morgan. (Orig.). 1996. mass mkt. 6.50 (1-56333-473-9, Badboy) Masquerade.

Steam Generator & Auxiliaries. (Principles of Steam Generation Ser.: Module 11). (Illus.). 175p. 1982. spiral bd. 59.50 (0-87683-261-3) GP Courseware.

Steam Generator Thermal Hydraulics. Ed. by Y. A. Hassan & S. M. Cho. (HTD Ser.: Vol. 251). 64p. 1992. 30.00 (0-7918-1164-6, G00808) ASME.

Steam in the Alleghenies: Western Maryland. Krause & Grenard. (Hobby Bks.: No. C37). (Illus.). 1981. reprint ed. pap. 9.95 (0-911868-37-2) Carstens Pubns.

Steam in the Redwoods. Lynwood Carranco & Henry L. Sorensen. LC 87-730. (Illus.). (Orig.). 1988. 27.95 (0-87004-321-8) Caxton.

Steam in Wartime Britain. Kenneth Oldham. LC 92-45036. 1993. 30.00 (0-7509-0325-2, Pub. by Sutton Pubng UK) Bks Intl VA.

Steam Intellect Societies: Essays on Culture, Education & Industry Circa 1820-1914. Ed. by I. Inkster. (C). 1985. 60.00 (1-85041-008-9, Pub. by Univ Nottingham UK) St Mut.

Steam Jet Ejectors for the Process Industries. Robert B. Power. 400p. 1994. text ed. 85.00 (0-07-050618-3) McGraw.

Steam Launch. Richard M. Mitchell. Ed. by Bill Durham. (Classics Ser.). (Illus.). 342p. 1995. 49.95 (0-9641204-0-2) Boat Hse.

Steam Lines. Picton Publishing Staff. 1987. 30.00 (0-317-90393-4, Pub. by Picton UK) St Mut.

Steam Locomotive. Edgar A. Haine. LC 82-46082. (Illus.). 672p. 1990. 60.00 (0-8453-4763-2, Cornwall Bks) Assoc Univ Prs.

Steam Locomotive Directory of North America, 2 vols., Set, Vols. 1&2. J. David Conrad. Set. 47.00 (0-933449-06-2) Transport Trails.

Steam Locomotive Directory of North America, Vol. 1. Ed. by Jackie Plachno. LC 87-30098. (Illus.). 192p. 1988. pap. 25.00 (0-933449-04-6) Transport Trails.

Steam Locomotive Directory of North America, Vol. 2. Ed. by Jackie Plachno. LC 87-30098. (Illus.). 176p. 1988. pap. 25.00 (0-933449-05-4) Transport Trails.

Steam Locomotives of the Baltimore & Ohio: An All-Time Roster. William D. Edson. LC 92-90239. (Illus.). 250p. (Orig.). 1992. pap. 22.00 (0-9632913-0-0) Edson Pubns.

***Steam Locomotives 1955: 40000-59999 - London, the Midlands, North Wales & Western Scotland.** Eric Sawford. (Illus.). 192p. 1997. 35.95 (0-7509-1313-4, Pub. by Sutton Pubng UK) Bks Intl VA.

Steam Locomotives 1955, 1-39999: Southern & Western. Eric H. Sawford. (Illus.). 192p. Date not set. 33.95 (0-7509-1002-X, Pub. by Sutton Pubng UK) Bks Intl VA.

Steam Machine Cuisine. Stephanie Lyness. LC 95-2328. 1996. 19.95 (0-688-13814-4) Hearst Bks.

Steam over Macedonia: Socio-Economic Change & the Railway Factor. Vassilios Gounaris. 372p. 1994. 40.00 (0-88033-277-8, 380) East Eur Monographs.

Steam Packet Ships. rev. ed. F. Henry. (C). 1987. 60.00 (0-85174-511-3, Pub. by Brwn Son Ferg) St Mut.

Steam Packets on the Chesapeake: A History of the Old Bay Line since 1840. Alexander C. Brown. LC 61-12580. (Illus.). 208p. reprint ed. pap. 59.30 (0-7837-6726-9, 2046354) Bks Demand.

Steam Passenger Service Directory. annuals Ed. by Michelle Giroux. 356p. write for info. (0-614-10783-0) Great Eastern.

Steam Passenger Service Directory. Mark Smith. Ed. by Christianson. (Illus.). 1996. per. 14.95 (0-89024-307-7, 01078) Kalmbach.

***Steam Passenger Service Directory (1997) 32nd Annual: A Guide to Tourist Railroads & Railroad Museums.** Ed. by Julie LaFountain. (Railroad Reference Ser.: Vol. 19). (Illus.). 464p. (Orig.). 1997. pap. 14.95 (0-89024-309-3, 01082, Kalmbach Books) Kalmbach.

Steam Picket Boats & Other Small Steam Craft of the Royal Navy. N. B. Stapleton. 120p. (C). 1988. 90.00 (0-900963-63-8, Pub. by T Dalton UK) St Mut.

Steam Plant Calculations Manual. 2nd expanded rev. ed. Ganapathy. (Mechanical Engineering Ser.: Vol.87). 448p. 1993. 75.00 (0-8247-9147-9) Dekker.

Steam Plant Errors. Frank Browning. (Shorey Lost Arts Ser.). 90p. reprint ed. pap. 4.00 (0-8466-6010-5, U10) Shorey.

Steam Power of the New York Central System 1915-1955. Alvin F. Staufer. LC 61-11846. (Illus.). 224p. 1961. 40.00 (0-944513-00-X) Staufer Bks.

Steam, Steel & Shellfire: The Warship, 1840-1905. Ed. by Robert Gardiner & Andrew D. Lambert. (Conway's History of the Ship Ser.). (Illus.). 192p. 1993. 46.95 (1-55750-774-0) Naval Inst Pr.

Steam, Steel & Stars: America's Last Steam Railroad. O. Winston Link. 1994. pap. 19.95 (0-8109-2587-7) Abrams.

Steam Tables: Thermodynamic Properties of Water Including Vapor, Liquid & Solid Phases. Joseph H. Keenan et al. 162p. 1969. text ed. 125.00 (0-471-46501-1) Wiley.

Steam Tables: Thermodynamic Properties of Water Including Vapor, Liquid & Solid Phases. 2nd ed. Joseph H. Keenan et al. LC 91-39064. 182p. (C). 1992. reprint ed. lib. bdg. 64.50 (0-89464-685-0) Krieger.

Steam Tables in SI-Units - Wasserdampftafeln. 3rd enl. ed. Ed. by U. Grigull et al. (Illus.). 140p. 1990. 25.95 (0-387-51888-6) Spr-Verlag.

Steam Tables in SI-Units Wasserdampftafeln: Concise Steam Tables in SI-Units (Student's Tables)-Properties of Ordinary Water Substance up to 1000 degrees & 100 Megapascal. 2nd rev. ed. Ed. by U. Grigull et al. (Illus.). 96p. 1984. pap. 17.00 (0-387-13503-0) Spr-Verlag.

Steam Thrashing in the Cotswolds. Michael Thexton. 116p. 1986. pap. 39.00 (0-7212-0707-3, Pub. by Regency Press UK) St Mut.

Steam Through Five Continents. Keith Strickland. 1996. 19.95 (0-7509-0627-8, Pub. by Sutton Pubng UK) Bks Intl VA.

Steam Towards the Sunset: The Railroads of Lincoln County. Lloyd Palmer. LC 82-84454. (Lincoln County Historical Society Ser.: No. 23). (Illus.). 192p. (Orig.). 1982. pap. 19.95 (0-911443-00-2) Lincoln Coun Hist.

Steam Toys: A Symphony in Motion. Morton Hirschberg. LC 96-18028. (Illus.). 256p. 1996. 69.95 (0-7643-0009-1) Schiffer.

***Steam Tractors.** Patrick Ertel. LC 97-13758. (Illus.). 96p. 1997. pap. 14.95 (0-7603-0097-6) Motorbooks Intl.

Steam Tractors. Hans Halberstadt. (Farm Tractor Color History Ser.). (Illus.). 128p. (YA). 1996. pap. 19.95 (0-7603-0140-9) Motorbooks Intl.

Steam Train Ride. Evelyn C. Mott. (Illus.). 32p. (J). (gr. 4-8). 1991. 13.95 (0-8027-6995-0); lib. bdg. 14.85 (0-8027-6996-9) Walker & Co.

Steam Train Ride. Evelyn C. Mott. LC 90-49223. 32p. (J). (gr. k-4). 1995. pap. 5.95 (0-8027-7452-0) Walker & Co.

***Steam Trains.** Chelsea House Staff. (Concise Collection). 1997. 15.95 (1-85627-743-7) Chelsea Hse.

Steam Trains of the World. Colin Garratt. 1987. 16.98 (0-671-08642-1) S&S Trade.

Steam Trap Handbook. McCauley & Fairmount Press Staff. 1995. text ed. 74.00 (0-13-450990-0) P-H.

Steam Trap Handbook. James F. McCauley. LC 95-13399. 1995. write for info. (0-88173-187-0) Fairmont Pr.

Steam Traps. Richard K. Miller & Marcia E. Rupnow. LC 89-85440. (Survey on Technology & Markets Ser.: No. 132). 50p. 1991. pap. text ed. 200.00 (1-55865-155-1) Future Tech Surveys.

Steam Traps. Multimedia Development Services Staff. (Plant Fundamentals Ser.). (Illus.). 62p. (Orig.). 1995. student ed. 30.00 (1-57431-011-9) Tech Trng Systs.

Steam Traps, Vol. III, Module IV. Multimedia Development Services Staff. (Plant Fundamentals Ser.). (Illus.). (Orig.). 1995. teacher ed. 65.00 (1-57431-051-8) Tech Trng Systs.

Steam Turbine-Generator Today: Materials Flow Path Design Repair & Refurbishment. B. R. King. LC 93-73002. (PWR Ser.: Vol. 21). 236p. 1993. 45.00 (0-7918-0996-X, H00828) ASME.

***Steam Turbine Generators: Process Control & Diagnostics - Modern Instrumentation for the Greatest Economy of Power Plants.** U. Sill & W. Zorner. 1996. text ed. 129.00 (3-89578-040-5) Wiley.

Steam Turbine Theory & Practice: A Text-Book for Engineering Students. 7th ed. William J. Kearton. reprint ed. pap. 160.00 (0-317-10952-9, 20151555) Bks Demand.

Steam Turbines & Their Cycles. J. Kenneth Salisbury. LC 73-89694. 670p. 1974. reprint ed. 74.50 (0-88275-138-7) Krieger.

***Steam Wagons in Colour.** Eric Sawford. (Illus.). 80p. 1997. 31.95 (0-7110-2495-2, Pub. by Ian Allan UK) Motorbooks Intl.

Steam-Water Cycle. Center for Occupational Research & Development Staff. (EUTEC Power Plant Operator Curriculum Ser.). (Illus.). 28p. (C). 1985. pap. text ed. write for info. (1-55502-225-1) CORD Commns.

Steam Yachts & Launches, Their Machinery & Management. C. P. Kuhnhardt. (Illus.). 240p. 1994. reprint ed. lib. bdg. 32.50 (0-8328-3961-2) Higginson Bk Co.

Steamboat: Virginia V. M. S. Kline. (Illus.). 98p. 1994. pap. 14.95 (0-295-96371-9) U of Wash Pr.

Steamboat Adventures, Recipes & Stories of Early-Day Settlers. Kenneth C. Weyand. (Woodsmoke Ser.: Vol. 2). (Illus.). 154p. (Orig.). 1991. pap. 7.95 (1-878496-02-6) Discovery MO.

Steamboat Bill: Cumulative Index to Years 1940 thru 1974. 64p. 1975. pap. 5.50 (0-913423-05-X) Steamship Hist Soc.

Steamboat Bill: Cumulative Index to Years 1975-1989. 56p. (Orig.). 1991. pap. 5.50 (0-913423-09-2) Steamship Hist Soc.

Steamboat Bill: Nineteen Forty-Four to Nineteen Forty-Six, Vol. III. (Illus.). 208p. 1968. reprint ed. pap. 7.00 (0-913423-04-1) Steamship Hist Soc.

Steamboat Bill: Nineteen Forty-Seven - Nineteen Forty-Eight. (Illus.). 200p. 1990. reprint ed. pap. 29.75 (0-913423-08-4) Steamship Hist Soc.

Steamboat Calliopes. Leslie C. Swanson. 1981. pap. 4.00 (0-911466-12-6) Swanson.

***Steamboat Echoes.** Phil Cole. 140p. 1996. pap. write for info. (0-9648916-1-1) Three Star Invstmnts.

Steamboat Entertains: Winning Recipes from Ski Town U. S. A. Steamboat Entertains Staff. 1991. 17.95 (0-9631010-2-1) Steamboat SWSC.

Steamboat Era in the Muskokas, Vol. 1: To the Golden Years. Richard Tatley. (Illus.). 304p. 45.00 (1-919822-50-X, Pub. by Boston Mills Pr CN) Genl Dist Srvs.

Steamboat-Inspection Service: Its History, Activities & Organization. Lloyd M. Short. LC 72-3021. (Brookings Institution. Institute for Government Research. Service Monographs of the U. S. Government: No. 18). reprint ed. 24.50 (0-404-57108-5) AMS Pr.

An Asterisk (*) at the beginning of an entry indicates that the title is appearing in BIP for the first time.

Steamboat Legacy: The Life & Times of a Steamboat Family. Dorothy H. Shrader. 288p. 1993. 27.95 (*0-9638589-0-4*); pap. 12.95 (*0-9638589-1-2*) Wein Pr.

Steamboat, Legendary Bucking Horse: His Life & Times, & the Cowboys Who Tried to Tame Him. Candy V. Moulton & Flossie Moulton. LC 92-8507. 1992. pap. 11. 95 (*0-931271-19-3*) Hi Plains Pr.

Steamboat Single Tracks: The Mountain Biking Guide to Steamboat Springs, Colorado. Tom Barnhart. LC 93-73409. 68p. (Orig.). 1993. pap. 10.95 (*0-9638419-5-5*) Fat Tire Pr.

Steamboat Ski Area Trail Map Jigsaw Puzzle. (Ski Area in a Box Ser.). 1995. write for info. (*1-888270-02-0*) Teewinot Ent.

Steamboat Springs. Tracy Salcedo. (Twelve Short Hikes Ser.). (Illus.). 32p. (Orig.). 1995. pap. 4.95 (*0-934641-85-4*) Chockstone Pr.

Steamboat Springs - Rabbit Ears Pass, CO. rev. ed. Ed. by Trails Illustrated Staff. (Illus.). 1994. Folded topographical map. 8.99 (*0-925873-39-X*) Trails Illustrated.

Steamboat to the Shore: A Pictorial History of the Steamboat Era in Monmouth County New Jersey. George H. Moss, Jr. LC 66-28794. (Illus.). 102p. 1991. reprint ed. 29.95 (*0-912396-02-4*) Ploughshare Pr.

***Steamboat Treasures: The Inadvertent Autobiography of a Steamboatman.** Dorothy H. Shrader. (Illus.). 264p. 1997. 27.95 (*0-9638589-2-0*) Wein Pr.

***Steamboat Treasures: The Inadvertent Autobiography of a Steamboatman.** Dorothy H. Shrader. (Illus.). 264p. 1997. pap. 12.95 (*0-9638589-3-9*) Wein Pr.

Steamboat Virginia. Kline. 1985. pap. 14.95 (*0-935503-00-5*) Document Bk.

Steamboat Visions: A Photographic View of the Yampa Valley. Karen Schulman & Joe Rife. (Illus.). 112p. 1993. 39.95 (*0-9638546-1-5*); pap. 22.50 (*0-9638546-0-7*) Icon Pr CO.

Steamboat Yesterdays on Casco Bay. William Frappier. (Illus.). 196p. 40.00 (*1-55046-086-2*, Pub. by Boston Mills Pr CN) Genl Dist Srvs.

Steamboater's Handbook V: Steamboating. Ed. by Bill W. Mueller. (Illus.). 288p. (Orig.). 1995. pap. 25.00 (*0-933847-12-2*) Wooden Porch Bks.

***Steamboater's Handbook VI: Steamboating.** Ed. by Bill W. Mueller. (Illus.). 304p. 1996. pap. 25.00 (*0-933847-14-9*) Wooden Porch Bks.

Steamboatin' Days. Compiled by Mary Wheeler. LC 70-75718. (Granger Index Reprint Ser.). 1977. 22.95 (*0-8369-6048-3*) Ayer.

Steamboatin' Days: Folksongs of the River Packet Era. Mary Wheeler. LC 45-1486. 131p. reprint ed. pap. 37.40 (*0-317-09639-7*, 2055318) Bks Demand.

Steamboating on the Upper Mississippi. unabridged ed. William J. Petersen. (Illus.). 640p. 1995. reprint ed. pap. 15.95 (*0-486-28844-7*) Dover.

Steamboats & Sailors of the Great Lakes. Mark L. Thompson. LC 91-12663. (Great Lakes Bks.). (Illus.). 232p. 1991. 32.95 (*0-8143-2359-6*, Great Lks Bks) Wayne St U Pr.

Steamboats & the Cotton Economy: River Trade in the Yazoo-Mississippi Delta. Harry P. Owens. LC 90-33067. 250p. 1990. 37.50 (*0-87805-436-7*) U Pr of Miss.

Steamboats Come True: American Inventors in Action. James T. Flexner. LC 92-20062. (Illus.). xxii, 406p. (C). 1992. reprint ed. pap. 20.00 (*0-8232-1376-5*) Fordham.

Steamboats for Rondout: Passenger Service Between New York & Rondout Creek, 1829-1863. Donald C. Ringwald. LC 81-51099. (Illus.). 145p. 1981. 25.00 (*0-913423-00-9*) Steamship Hist Soc.

***Steamboats in Ice.** James Donahue. Date not set. pap. 14. 00 (*0-9626947-3-8*) J L Donahue.

Steamboats on the Chena: The Founding & Development of Fairbanks, Alaska. Basil C. Hedrick & Susan Savage. LC 87-83742. (Orig.). (YA). (gr. 9-12). 1988. pap. 9.95 (*0-945397-00-3*) Epicenter Pr.

Steamboats on the Colorado River, 1852-1916. Richard E. Lingenfelter. LC 78-16241. (Illus.). 211p. reprint ed. pap. 60.20 (*0-7837-1908-6*, 2042112) Bks Demand.

Steamboats on the Fox River: A Pictorial History of Navigation in Northeastern Wisconsin. D. C. Mitchell. (Illus.). 208p. 1986. 29.95 (*0-9640937-1-5*) Steamboat Pr.

Steamboats on the Ganges. Henry T. Bernstein. xvi, 230p. 1988. text ed. 35.00 (*0-86131-756-4*, Pub. by Orient Longman Ltd II) Apt Bks.

Steamboats on the Green. Agnes S. Harralson. LC 81-90284. (Illus.). 343p. 1981. 12.95 (*0-935680-07-1*) Kentucke Imprints.

Steamboats on the St. Croix. Anita A. Buck. LC 90-7915. (Illus.). 170p. 1990. pap. 19.95 (*0-87839-060-X*) North Star.

Steamboats on the Western Rivers: An Economic & Technological History. Louis C. Hunter. LC 93-31494. (Illus.). 684p. 1994. reprint ed. pap. text ed. 14.95 (*0-486-27863-8*) Dover.

Steamer Cookbook. Coleen Simmons & Bob Simmons. 176p. 1993. pap. 8.95 (*1-55867-080-7*, Nitty Gritty Ckbks) Bristol Pub Ent CA.

Steamer William Irvin. Jody Aho. LC 95-78442. 88p. 1995. pap. 9.95 (*0-932212-85-9*) Avery Color.

Steamers of the Clyde: Memories of the Clyde. Hart, Maclagan & Will Publishers Staff. 1992. pap. 60.00 (*0-9516140-1-0*, Pub. by Hart Maclagan & Will UK) St Mut.

Steamflood Reservoir Management: Thermal Enhanced Oil Recovery. K. C. Hong. LC 93-28351. 528p. 1993. 99.95 (*0-87814-405-6*) PennWell Bks.

Steaming. Donald Rawley. LC 93-19965. 1993. pap. 12.50 (*0-941749-30-4*) Black Tie Pr.

Steaming as Before. Richard Bovbjerg. LC 94-18875. 259p. 1996. 59.95 (*1-883255-12-0*); pap. 39.95 (*1-883255-05-8*) Intl Scholars.

Steaming Through Smoke & Fire: True Stories of Shipwreck & Disaster on the Great Lakes. 2nd ed. James L. Donahue. (Illus.). 192p. 1996. reprint ed. pap. 14.95 (*1-882376-30-7*) Thunder Bay Pr.

Steaming Through Smoke & Fire 1871: True Stories of Shipwreck & Disaster on the Great Lakes, Vol. 1. James L. Donahue. LC 90-93084. (Illus.). 192p. (Orig.). 1990. pap. text ed. 12.00 (*0-9626947-0-3*) J L Donahue.

***Steampunk Trilogy.** Paul Di Filippo. 354p. 1997. pap. 13. 95 (*1-56858-102-5*) FWEW.

Steampunk Trilogy. Paul DiFilippo. LC 94-42282. 360p. 1995. 20.00 (*1-56858-028-2*) FWEW.

Steamship Accounting. Philip C. Cheng. LC 70-80637. (Illus.). 192p. 1969. reprint ed. pap. 54.80 (*0-7837-9071-6*, 2049820) Bks Demand.

Steamship Conquest of the World, 1812-1912. Frederick Talbot. 1977. lib. bdg. 59.95 (*0-8490-2668-7*) Gordon Pr.

Steamy December. Ann Charlton. 1995. mass mkt. 3.25 (*0-373-11782-5*, 1-11782-9) Harlequin Bks.

Steamy December. large type ed. Ann Charlton. (Harlequin Romance Ser.). 1996. 19.95 (*0-263-14506-9*) Thorndike Pr.

***Steamy Dreamer: The Saga of Dr. Hartley O. Baker & the Baker Steamer Motor Car.** Barbara P. Baker. 176p. 1996. 29.95 (*1-882418-22-0*) Centenn Pubns.

***Steamy Dreamer: The Saga of Dr. Hartley O. Baker & the Baker Steamer Motor Car.** Barbara P. Baker. 176p. 1996. pap. 22.95 (*1-882418-23-9*) Centenn Pubns.

***Stearman.** Martin W. Bowman. 1997. 39.95 (*0-7603-0479-3*) Motorbooks Intl.

Stearns & Todd Counties Fishing Map Guide. James F. Billig. 1995. spiral bd. 16.95 (*1-885010-10-9*) Sptsmans Connect.

Stearns County, Minnesota, 1896 Plat Book Index. St. Cloud Area Genealogists, Inc. Staff. 110p. 1993. pap. text ed. 16.50 (*0-9637127-0-5*) St Cloud Area.

Stearn's Dictionary of Plant Names for Gardeners. William T. Stearn. (Illus.). 384p. 1996. pap. 17.95 (*0-304-34782-5*, Pub. by Cassell UK) Sterling.

Stearns Wharf: Surviving Change on the California Coast. Otis L. Graham, Jr. et al. (South Coast Historical Ser.). (Illus.). (Orig.). 1994. pap. 8.95 (*1-883535-15-8*) U CA Dept Hist.

Stebbins. J. A. Stebbins. (Illus.). 190p. 1991. reprint ed. pap. 29.00 (*0-8328-2174-8*); reprint ed. lib. bdg. 39.00 (*0-8328-2173-X*) Higginson Bk Co.

Stebbins Genealogy, 2 vols., Set. R. S. Greenlee. (Illus.). 1386p. 1989. reprint ed. pap. 199.00 (*0-8328-1125-4*); reprint ed. lib. bdg. 207.00 (*0-8328-1124-6*) Higginson Bk Co.

Steber, Eleanor: An Autobiography. Eleanor Steber & Marcia Sloat. LC 92-85436. (Illus.). 277p. 1992. 29.95 (*0-9634174-0-1*) Wordswrth.

Stecheson Classified Song Directory: With Supplement Thru 1978. Anne Stecheson & Anthony Stecheson. 1961. 40.00 (*0-910468-08-7*) Criterion Mus.

Stechlin. Theodor Fontane. Tr. & Intro. by William L. Zwiebel. (GERM Ser.). xvii, 340p. (C). 1995. 49.00 (*1-57113-024-1*) Camden Hse.

Stechlin. unabridged ed. Fontane. (World Classic Literature Ser.). (GER.). pap. 7.95 (*3-89507-025-4*, Pub. by Bookking Intl FR) Distribks Inc.

Steck-Vaughn GED: Literature & the Arts. rev. ed. Ed. by Steck-Vaughn Co., Staff. 320p. 1990. pap. 8.95 (*0-8114-4704-9*) Raintree Steck-V.

Steck-Vaughn GED: Mathematics. rev. ed. Ed. by Steck-Vaughn Co., Staff. (Illus.). 400p. 1990. pap. 8.95 (*0-8114-4703-0*) Raintree Steck-V.

Steck-Vaughn GED: Science. rev. ed. Ed. by Steck-Vaughn Co., Staff. (Illus.). 320p. 1990. pap. 8.95 (*0-8114-4701-4*) Raintree Steck-V.

Steck-Vaughn GED: Social Studies. rev. ed. Ed. by Steck-Vaughn Co., Staff. (Illus.). 304p. 1990. pap. 8.95 (*0-8114-4702-2*) Raintree Steck-V.

Steck-Vaughn GED: The Essay. Ed. by Steck-Vaughn Co., Staff. 128p. (Orig.). 1988. pap. 8.95 (*0-8114-4705-7*) Raintree Steck-V.

Steck-Vaughn GED: Writing Skills. rev. ed. Ed. by Steck-Vaughn Co., Staff. 304p. 1990. pap. 8.95 (*0-8114-4700-6*) Raintree Steck-V.

***Steck Vaughn GED Mathematics.** Steck-Vaughn Co., Staff. 1990. pap. text ed. 8.95 (*0-8114-7364-3*) Raintree Steck-V.

***Steck Vaughn GED Writing Skills.** Steck-Vaughn Co., Staff. 1990. pap. text ed. 8.95 (*0-8114-7361-9*) Raintree Steck-V.

Stedman & Joanna: A Love in Bondage - Dedicated Love in the Eighteenth Century. Beryl Gilroy. 1991. 15.95 (*0-533-09498-4*) Vantage.

Stedman Pocket Dictionary. 832p. 1987. pap. text ed. 21. 95 (*0-683-07921-2*) Williams & Wilkins.

***Stedman Portuguese/English-English/Portuguese Medical Dictionary.** 25th ed. 1658p. (ENG & POR.). 295.00 (*0-7859-9348-7*) Fr & Eur.

Stedman's - Bergey Bacteria Word Book. 392p. 1992. pap. 28.00 (*0-683-07945-X*) Williams & Wilkins.

Stedman's Abbreviations, Acronyms, Symbols. 674p. 1991. 24.00 (*0-683-07926-3*) Williams & Wilkins.

Stedman's ASP Parasite Names. John E. Ubelaker. LC 93-18764. 208p. 1993. 28.00 (*0-683-07958-1*) Williams & Wilkins.

Stedman's ATCC Fungus Names. Shung-Chang Jong et al. LC 92-22845. 272p. 1992. pap. 28.00 (*0-683-07957-3*) Williams & Wilkins.

***Stedman's Cardiology & Pulmonary Words.** 2nd ed. Helen E. Littrell & Thomas L. Stedman. LC 96-45978. (Stedman's Word Book Ser.). 1996. write for info. (*0-683-40081-9*) Williams & Wilkins.

Stedman's Cardiology Words. LC 92-21067. 256p. 1992. 28.00 (*0-683-07953-0*) Williams & Wilkins.

***Stedman's Cardiology Words.** (Stedman's Specialty Word Bks.). 16.95 (*0-614-19708-2*, OP993992WE) AMA.

Stedman's Concise Medical Dictionary. Ed. by Stedman Medical Dictionary Staff. LC 93-21060. 1994. 25.00 (*0-671-87473-X*, Webstrs New) Macmillan Gen Ref.

Stedman's Concise Medical Dictionary. 2nd ed. LC 93-41724. (Illus.). 1286p. 1994. pap. 24.95 (*0-683-07917-4*) Williams & Wilkins.

***Stedman's Concise Medical Dictionary.** 2nd ed. (Illus.). 1000p. 1994. 24.95 (*0-614-19690-6*, OP494993WE) AMA.

***Stedman's Concise Medical Dictionary.** 3rd ed. John H. Dirckx & Thomas L. Stedman. LC 96-3192. (Illus.). 1996. write for info. (*0-683-40019-3*) Williams & Wilkins.

Stedman's Dentistry Words. LC 93-15222. (Stedman's Word Bks.). 350p. 1993. 28.00 (*0-683-07964-6*) Williams & Wilkins.

***Stedman's Dentistry Words.** (Stedman's Specialty Word Bks.). 16.95 (*0-614-19703-1*, OP949393WE) AMA.

***Stedman's Dermatology & Immunology Words.** Darla Haberer. LC 96-36759. (Stedman's Word Book Ser.). 1996. write for info. (*0-683-40080-0*) Williams & Wilkins.

Stedman's Diccionario de Ciencas Medicas Illustrado. 25th ed. (Illus.). 1568p. (SPA.). 1993. 59.95 (*0-683-07912-3*) Williams & Wilkins.

Stedman's English-Japanese-English Medical Dictionary. 2nd ed. Medical View Staff. 1973p. 1984. 250.00 (*0-8288-1850-9*) Fr & Eur.

Stedman's English-Portuguese Medical Dictionary, 2 vols. Stedman. (ENG & POR.). 1979. 195.00 (*0-7859-7528-4*, 8522602247) Fr & Eur.

Stedman's ENT Words. LC 93-17042. 350p. 1993. 28.00 (*0-683-07963-8*) Williams & Wilkins.

***Stedman's ENT Words.** (Stedman's Specialty Word Bks.). 16.95 (*0-614-19702-3*, OP949193WE) AMA.

***Stedman's GI & GU Words: Including: Nephrology.** 2nd ed. Ed. by Darla Haberer. 731p. 1996. pap. 34.95 (*0-683-18145-9*) Williams & Wilkins.

Stedman's GI Words. 360p. 1992. 28.00 (*0-683-07943-3*) Williams & Wilkins.

Stedman's ICTV Virus Words. Charles H. Calisher & Claude M. Fauquet. LC 92-12319. 304p. 1992. pap. 28. 00 (*0-683-07956-5*) Williams & Wilkins.

Stedman's Medical & Surgical Equipment Words. 2nd ed. Ed. by Catherine S. Baxter. LC 96-5666. 861p. 1996. 35. 95 (*0-683-18144-0*) Williams & Wilkins.

Stedman's Medical Dictionary. 22th ed. Stedman. 1586p. 1976. reprint ed. 9.95 (*0-683-07919-0*, Williams & Wilkins) Krieger.

***Stedman's Medical Dictionary.** 26th deluxe ed. (Illus.). 2240p. 89.95 (*0-614-19689-2*, OP984794WE) AMA.

Stedman's Medical Dictionary. 26th ed. (Illus.). 1995. 44. 95 (*0-683-07922-0*) Williams & Wilkins.

***Stedman's Medical Dictionary.** 26th ed. (Illus.). 2240p. 44. 95 (*0-614-19688-4*, OP982994WE) AMA.

Stedman's Medical Dictionary: Deluxe Version. 25th ed. (Illus.). 1920p. 1990. 89.95 (*0-683-07925-5*) Williams & Wilkins.

Stedman's Medical Equipment Words. 608p. 1993. 34.00 (*0-683-07954-9*) Williams & Wilkins.

Stedman's Medical Speller. 2nd ed. LC 96-7785. 1013p. 1996. 28.95 (*0-683-40023-1*) Williams & Wilkins.

Stedman's Neurosurgery Words. LC 93-16861. (Stedman's Word Bks.). 350p. 1993. 28.00 (*0-683-07962-X*) Williams & Wilkins.

***Stedman's Neurosurgery Words.** (Stedman's Specialty Word Bks.). 16.95 (*0-614-19701-5*, OP948993WE) AMA.

Stedman's OB-GYN Words. 272p. 1992. pap. 28.00 (*0-683-07942-5*) Williams & Wilkins.

***Stedman's OB-GYN Words.** (Stedman's Specialty Word Bks.). 16.95 (*0-614-19707-4*, OP989692WE) AMA.

Stedman's OB-GYN Words: Including Neonatology, Pediatrics, Genetics. 2nd ed. Ed. by Helen E. Littrell. LC 95-4488. 478p. 1995. pap. 34.95 (*0-683-07967-0*) Williams & Wilkins.

Stedman's Oncology Words. LC 92-49350. 300p. 1992. 28. 00 (*0-683-07951-4*) Williams & Wilkins.

***Stedman's Ophthalmology Words.** (Stedman's Specialty Word Bks.). 16.95 (*0-614-19709-0*, OP994992WE) AMA.

Stedman's Ophthalmology Words. Thomas L. Stedman. LC 92-22886. 300p. 1992. 28.00 (*0-683-07952-2*) Williams & Wilkins.

Stedman's Orthopaedic & Rehab Words. 2nd ed. LC 94-38151. (Stedman's Word Book Ser.). 1994. 34.00 (*0-683-07959-X*) Williams & Wilkins.

Stedman's Pathology & Lab Medicine. 688p. 1992. pap. 28. 00 (*0-683-07939-5*) Williams & Wilkins.

***Stedman's Pathology & Lab Medicine Words.** (Stedman's Specialty Word Bks.). 16.95 (*0-614-19705-8*, OP988092WE) AMA.

***Stedman's Pathology & Lab Medicine Words.** 2nd ed. LC 97-15929. 1997. write for info. (*0-683-40191-2*) Williams & Wilkins.

Stedman's Podiatry Words. 350p. 1995. 28.00 (*0-683-07961-1*) Williams & Wilkins.

Stedman's Psychiatry Words. 272p. 1992. pap. 28.00 (*0-683-07944-1*) Williams & Wilkins.

***Stedman's Psychiatry Words.** (Stedman's Specialty Word Bks.). 16.95 (*0-614-19706-6*, OP989292WE) AMA.

Stedman's Radiology & Oncology Words: Including HIV-AIDS, Hematology. 2nd rev. ed. Ed. by Catherine S. Baxter. LC 95-24138. (Stedman's Word Book Ser.). 620p. 1995. 34.95 (*0-683-07966-2*) Williams & Wilkins.

Stedman's Radiology Words. 308p. 1992. 28.00 (*0-683-07940-9*) Williams & Wilkins.

***Stedman's Surgery Words.** Sandy Kovacs. LC 97-20704. (Stedman's Word Book Ser.). 1997. write for info. (*0-683-40190-4*) Williams & Wilkins.

Stedman's Surinam: Life in an Eighteenth-Century Slave Society. John G. Stedman. Ed. by Richard Price & Sally Price. (Illus.). 512p. 1992. pap. 19.95 (*0-8018-4260-3*); text ed. 60.00 (*0-8018-4259-X*) Johns Hopkins.

Stedman's Urology Words. 350p. 1993. 28.00 (*0-683-07960-3*) Williams & Wilkins.

***Stedman's Urology Words.** (Stedman's Specialty Word Bks.). 16.95 (*0-614-19704-X*, OP949593WE) AMA.

Steel. David Drake & S. M. Stirling. (General Ser.: Bk. IV). 400p. (Orig.). 1993. mass mkt. 5.99 (*0-671-72189-5*) Baen Bks.

***Steel.** Kenneth Johnson. (J). 1997. pap. 3.95 (*0-8167-4339-8*) Troll Communs.

***Steel.** Tor Books Staff. 1997. mass mkt. 6.99 (*0-8125-3931-1*) Tor Bks.

Steel: Diary of a Furnace Worker. Charles R. Walker. Ed. by Leon Stein. LC 77-70544. 1977. reprint ed. lib. bdg. 19.95 (*0-405-10213-5*) Ayer.

Steel - a Handbook for Materials Research & Engineering Vol. 1: Fundamentals. German Iron & Steel Institute Staff. 758p. 1992. 785.00 (*3-514-00377-7*, Pub. by Woodhead Pubng UK) Am Educ Systs.

Steel - a Handbook for Materials Research & Engineering Vol. 2: Applications. German Iron & Steel Institute Staff. (Illus.). 862p. 1993. 785.00 (*3-514-00378-5*, Pub. by Woodhead Pubng UK) Am Educ Systs.

Steel - A Handbook for Materials Research & Engineering, Vol. 1: Fundamentals. Ed. by Verein D. Eisenhuttenleute. (Illus.). 760p. 1992. 510.95 (*0-387-52968-3*) Spr-Verlag.

Steel - A Handbook for Materials Research & Engineering, Vol. 2: Applications. Ed. by Verein D. Eisenhuttenleute. (Illus.). 880p. 1993. 479.95 (*0-387-54075-X*) Spr-Verlag.

Steel - Bars, Forgings, Bearing, Chain, Springs see 1997 Annual Book of ASTM Standards: Iron & Steel Products, Section 1

Steel - City: A Docudrama in Three Acts. E. Favorini & Gillette Elvgren. LC 91-50874. (Illus.). 128p. (C). 1992. 39.95 (*0-8229-3707-7*); pap. 12.95 (*0-8229-5470-2*) U of Pittsburgh Pr.

Steel - Piping, Tubing, Fittings see 1997 Annual Book of ASTM Standards: Iron & Steel Products, Section 1

Steel - Plate, Sheet Strip, Wire - Stainless Steel Bar see 1997 Annual Book of ASTM Standards: Iron & Steel Products, Section 1

Steel - Structural, Reinforcing, Pressure Vessel, Railway see 1997 Annual Book of ASTM Standards: Iron & Steel Products, Section 1

***Steel Across the Plains.** Pierre Berton. (Canada Moves West Ser.). 88p. (J). (gr. 6-9). pap. 4.99 (*0-7710-1441-4*) McCland & Stewart.

***Steel Across the Shield.** Pierre Berton. (Canada Moves West Ser.). 88p. (J). (gr. 6-9). pap. 4.99 (*0-7710-1422-8*) McCland & Stewart.

Steel Albatross. Scott Carpenter. Ed. by Jane Chelius. 384p. 1992. reprint ed. mass mkt. 5.99 (*0-671-67314-9*) PB.

Steel Alloying Handbook: The Definitive Reference Source to the Steel-Alloying Metals. Ed. by Angus MacMillan. (Illus.). 302p. 1994. 635.00 (*1-85573-048-0*, Pub. by Woodhead Pubng UK) Am Educ Systs.

Steel & Bone. Jeff Grubb. 1996. pap. 5.99 (*0-7869-0474-7*) TSR Inc.

Steel & Flame. (Executioner Ser.: No. 159). 1992. mass mkt. 3.50 (*0-373-61159-5*, 1-61159-9) Harlequin Bks.

Steel & Metal Workers-It Takes a Fight to Win! 2nd ed. Gus Hall. (Illus.). 64p. 1972. pap. 0.25 (*0-87898-094-6*) New Outlook.

***Steel Armor & Associated Coverings for Impregnated-Paper-Insulated Cables.** 13.00 (*0-614-18696-X*, S-67-401) Insulated Cable.

***Steel Ashes.** Karen R. Cercone. 272p. 1997. mass mkt. 5.99 (*0-425-15856-X*, Prime Crime) Berkley Pub.

Steel at the Sault: Francis H. Clergue, Sir James Dunn, & the Algoma Steel Corporation, 1901-1956. Duncan McDowall. 352p. 1988. pap. text ed. 18.95 (*0-8020-6736-0*) U of Toronto Pr.

Steel at the Sault: Francis H. Clergue, Sir James Dunn, & the Algoma Steel Corporation, 1901-1956. Duncan McDowall. LC 85-115719. (Illus.). 348p. reprint ed. pap. 99.20 (*0-8357-3768-3*, 2036497) Bks Demand.

Steel Away: A Guidebook to the World of Steel Sailboats. LeCain W. Smith & Sheila Moir. (Illus.). 432p. (Orig.). 1986. pap. 28.00 (*0-9615508-0-5*) Windrose Prods.

Steel Band. John Bartholomew. (Topics in Music Ser.). 48p. 1985. pap. 12.95 (*0-19-321329-X*) OUP.

Steel Beach. John Varley. 576p. 1993. mass mkt. 5.99 (*0-441-78565-4*) Ace Bks.

Steel-Belted Grimm. Mike Peters. 128p. 1988. pap. 6.95 (*0-88687-366-5*, Pharos) Wrld Almnc.

***Steel Boatbuilding: From Plans to Launching.** Thomas E. Colvin. 1996. pap. text ed. 34.95 (*0-07-012121-4*) McGraw.

Steel Bonnets. George M. Fraser. 1994. lib. bdg. 26.95 (*1-56849-425-4*) Buccaneer Bks.

Steel Bonnets: The Story of the Anglo-Scottish Border Reivers. George M. Fraser. 404p. 1993. pap. 15.00 (*0-00-272746-3*, Pub. by HarpC UK) HarpC.

Steel Brother. Gordon R. Dickson. (Orig.). 1991. mass mkt. 3.99 (*0-8125-1547-1*) Tor Bks.

Steel Buildings: Analysis & Design. 4th ed. Stanley W. Crawley & Robert M. Dillon. LC 92-27769. 736p. 1993. text ed. 79.95 (*0-471-84298-2*) Wiley.

S

***Steel Butterflies: Japanese Women & the American Experience.** Nancy B. Diggs. LC 97-11077. 160p. (C). 1998. text ed. 56.50 (*0-7914-3623-3*) State Univ of New York.

***Steel Butterflies: Japanese Women & the American Experience.** Nancy B. Diggs. LC 97-11077. 160p. (C). 1998. pap. 18.95 (*0-7914-3624-1*) State Univ of New York.

Steel Cables: Love Poems from Adam Rib. Brod Bagert. (Illus.). 49p. (Orig.). 1991. pap. 12.95 (*0-9614228-8-2*) Juliahouse Pubs.

Steel Canvas: The Art of American Arms. R. L. Wilson. LC 94-19344. 1995. 65.00 (*0-679-40673-5*) Random.

Steel Casting Handbook Supplements, Set. Incl. Supplement 2. Summery of Standard Specifications for Steel Castings. 15.00 (*0-686-44966-5*); Supplement 3. Tolerances. 10.00 (*0-686-44967-3*); Supplement 4. Drafting Practices for Castings. 10.00 (*0-686-44968-1*); Supplement 5. General Properties of Steel Castings. 10.00 (*0-686-44969-X*); Supplement 6. Repair Welding & Fabrication Welding of Steel Castings. 10.00 (*0-686-44970-3*); Supplement 7. Welding of High Alloy Castings. 10.00 (*0-686-44971-1*); Supplement 8. High Alloy Data Sheets, Corrosion Series. 10.00 (*0-686-44972-X*); Supplement 9. High Alloy Data Sheets, Heat Series. 10.00 (*0-686-44973-8*); Supplement 10. Glossary of Foundry Terms. 10.00 (*0-686-44974-6*); Supplement 11. Hardenability & Heat Treatment. 10.00 (*0-686-44975-4*); 100.00 (*0-685-55664-6*) Steel Founders.

Steel Castings Handbook. 5th ed. 450p. 1980. 20.00 (*0-317-59786-8*, OS8100) Am Foundrymen.

Steel Castings Handbook. 6th ed. Ed. by Malcolm Blair et al. 500p. 1995. 182.00 (*0-87170-556-7*, 6820) ASM.

Steel City: Entrepreneurship, Strategy, & Technology in Sheffield 1743-1993. Geoffrey Tweedale. (Illus.). 350p. 1995. 75.00 (*0-19-828866-2*) OUP.

Steel City: Hamilton & Region. Ed. by M. J. Dear et al. 308p. 1987. 38.50 (*0-8020-2563-3*); pap. 16.95 (*0-8020-6582-1*) U of Toronto Pr.

Steel City: Urban & Ethnic Patterns in Gary, Indiana, 1906-1950. Raymond A. Mohl & Neil Betten. LC 85-963. (Illus.). 227p. 1986. 34.95 (*0-8419-1010-3*); pap. 23.50 (*0-8419-1077-4*) Holmes & Meier.

Steel Claws. Don Pendleton. (Executioner Ser.: No. 211). 1996. mass mkt. 3.75 (*0-373-64211-3*, 1-64211-5, Wrldwide Lib) Harlequin Bks.

Steel Cold Destiny. Kenneth D. Kay. 280p. (Orig.). 1995. pap. 11.95 (*0-9646532-0-6*) PPG.

Steel, Concrete, & Composite Design of Tall Buildings. 2nd ed. Bungale S. Taranath. LC 96-49612. (Illus.). 768p. 1997. text ed. 79.95 (*0-07-062914-5*) McGraw.

Steel Concrete Structures for Multistorey Buildings. J. Kozak. (Developments in Civil Engineering Ser.: Vol. 35). 402p. 1991. 210.00 (*0-444-98820-3*, DCE 35) Elsevier.

Steel Construction Inspector. Jack Rudman. (Career Examination Ser.: C-765). 1994. pap. 29.95 (*0-8373-0765-1*) Nat Learn.

***Steel Corrosion in Concrete: Fundamentals in Civil Engineering Practice.** S. Diamond & N. Berke. 208p. 1997. 92.00 (*0-419-22530-7*, E & FN Spon) Routledge Chapman & Hall.

***Steel Cricket: Versions: 1958-1997.** Stephen Berg. LC 97-4653. 1997. pap. text ed. 16.00 (*1-55659-075-X*) Copper Canyon.

Steel Crisis: The Economics & Politics of a Declining Industry. William E. Scheuerman. LC 85-28100. 235p. 1986. text ed. 49.95 (*0-275-92124-7*, C2124, Praeger Pubs) Greenwood.

Steel Decisions & the National Economy. Henry W. Broude. LC 63-13958. (Yale Studies in Economics: No. 16). 347p. reprint ed. pap. 98.90 (*0-317-29591-8*, 2021983) Bks Demand.

***Steel Deep.** Mayfair Games Staff. 1996. 18.00 (*1-56905-015-5*) Mayfair Games.

Steel Design. rev. ed. William T. Segui. (General Engineering Ser.). 560p. 1996. pap. 85.95 (*0-534-95478-2*) PWS Pubs.

Steel Design: For the P. E. Examination. Frank Talania. (Illus.). 150p. 1995. pap. 22.95 (*0-929176-15-4*) Burdick & Landreth Co.

Steel Design for Engineers & Architects. 2nd ed. David A. Fanella & Rene Amon. (Illus.). 544p. (gr. 13). 1992. text ed. 79.95 (*0-442-00927-5*) Chapman & Hall.

Steel Design Handbook: LRFD Method. Ed. by Akbar R. Tamboli. (Illus.). 600p. 1996. text ed. 89.00 incl. cd-rom (*0-07-061400-8*) McGraw.

Steel Design Review Manual. Frank Talania. (Illus.). 400p. 1995. pap. 37.50 (*0-929176-19-7*) Burdick & Landreth Co.

***Steel Designer's Handbook.** Branko Gorenc et al. 320p. 1995. pap. 39.95 (*0-86840-366-0*, Pub. by New South Wales Univ Pr AT) Intl Spec Bk.

Steel Designer's Handbook. 5th ed. B. Gorenc & R. Tinyou. (Illus.). 336p. 36.95 (*0-86840-248-6*, Pub. by New South Wales Univ Pr AT) Intl Spec Bk.

Steel Designers' Manual. 5th ed. Steel Construction Institute Staff. (Illus.). 1328p. 1992. 150.00 (*0-632-02488-7*) Blackwell Sci.

Steel Detailers' Manual. Alan Hayward & Frank Weare. (Illus.). 216p. 1992. pap. 46.95 (*0-632-03523-4*) Blackwell Sci.

Steel Detailing in CAD Format. Kamal A. Zayat. 270p. 1995. text ed. 79.95 (*0-471-10992-4*) Wiley.

Steel Drug: Cocaine & Crack in Perspective. 2nd ed. Patricia G. Erickson et al. LC 94-20173. 284p. 30.00 (*0-02-909645-6*, Free Press) Free Pr.

Steel Erection Safety. Center for Occupational Research & Development Staff. (Job Safety & Health Instructional Materials Ser.). (Illus.). 44p. (C). 1981. pap. text ed. 3.75 (*1-55502-141-7*) CORD Commns.

Steel Eye. Chet Gottfried. LC 84-5444. 160p. (Orig.). 1984. pap. 5.95 (*0-917053-00-1*) Space And.

Steel Fabrication Safety Manual. 120p. 1981. 16.00 (*1-56424-027-4*, F502) Am Inst Steel Construct.

Steel Fabricator's Handbook. Robert Pardun. (Illus.). 99p. (Orig.). 1991. student ed., spiral bd. 9.50 (*0-9630780-0-3*) Pardun Pub.

Steel Fiber Concrete: U. S.-Sweden Joint Seminar. Ed. by Surendra P. Shah & Ake Skarendahl. (Illus.). 520p. (Orig.). 1985. pap. text ed. 83.50 (*91-970408-4-3*) Coronet Bks.

Steel Fiber Reinforced Concrete. 76p. 1994. pap. 36.25 (*0-614-02509-5*, C27BOW6) ACI.

Steel for the Mind: Samuel Johnson & Critical Discourse. Charles H. Hinnant. LC 93-766. 1994. Alk. paper. 39.50 (*0-87413-492-7*, Assoc Univ Prs) U Delaware Pr.

Steel Forgings: STP 903. Ed. by E. G. Nisbett & Albert S. Melilli. LC 86-14066. (Illus.). 610p. 1986. text ed. 59.00 (*0-8031-0465-0*, 04-903000-02) ASTM.

Steel Foundry Melting Practice. 1973. 30.00 (*0-686-44984-3*) Steel Founders.

Steel Glory: The Life of Shipbuilder Arthur Sewall (1835-1900) Susie Yakowicz. LC 96-90236. (Illus.). x, 80p. (Orig.). 1996. pap. 11.95 (*0-9652546-0-7*) S Yakowicz.

Steel Guitar. Linda Barnes. 272p. 1991. 18.50 (*0-385-30013-1*) Delacorte.

Steel Guitar: A Carlotta Carlyle Mystery. Linda Barnes. 272p. 1993. mass mkt. 5.99 (*0-440-21268-5*) Dell.

Steel Hardening, Tempering, & Forging Made Easy. Joseph V. Woodworth. (Illus.). 288p. 1991. reprint ed. pap. 13.00 (*1-877767-22-0*) Univ Publng Hse.

Steel Hawk & Other Stories. Bhabani Bhattacharya. 143p. 1968. pap. 2.95 (*0-88253-020-8*) Ind-US Inc.

***Steel Heat Treatment Handbook.** George E. Totten & Maurice A. Howes. LC 96-52020. 1997. 195.00 (*0-8247-9750-7*) Dekker.

***Steel Illusions.** R. Z. Crompton. 400p. 1996. pap. text ed. 15.95 (*0-9649438-1-6*) Zoller Pubng.

***Steel in Automotive Applications.** 1997. 49.00 (*1-56091-971-X*) Soc Auto Engineers.

***Steel in His Soul: The Dick Hillis Story.** Jan Winebrenner. 288p. (Orig.). 1996. pap. 8.99 (*1-883893-53-4*) WinePress Pub.

***Steel in the Field: A Farmer's Guide to Weed-Management Tools.** Greg Bowman & Christopher Shirley. LC 97-8406. (Sustainable Agriculture Network Handbook Ser.: Vol. 2). (Illus.). 112p. 1997. pap. write for info. (*1-888626-02-X*) Sustnble Agri.

Steel in the Twenty-First Century: Competition Forges a New World Order. William T. Hogan. LC 94-10301. 1994. 40.00 (*0-02-914795-6*, Free Press) Free Pr.

Steel Industry & the Energy Crisis: Proceedings of the Fourth C. C. Furnas Memorial Conference. Furnas (C C) Memorial Conference Staff. Ed. by Julian Szekely. LC 74-30737. (Illus.). 134p. reprint ed. pap. 38.20 (*0-7837-0720-7*, 2041046) Bks Demand.

Steel Industry & the Environment: Proceedings of the C. C. Furnas Memorial Conference. Furnas (C C) Memorial Conference Staff. Ed. by Julian Szekely. LC 72-86613. (Illus.). 301p. reprint ed. pap. 85.80 (*0-7837-0771-1*, 2041085) Bks Demand.

Steel Industry I: Manufacturing System, Vol. 1. Tadao Kawaguchi & Kenji Sugiyama. Ed. by Toshiaki Ikoma. (Japanese Technology Reviews Ser.: Vol. 6). 130p. 1989. pap. text ed. 113.00 (*2-88124-329-0*) Gordon & Breach.

Steel Industry II: Control System, Vol. 2. Tadao Kawaguchi & Takatsugu Ueyama. Ed. by Toshiaki Ikoma. (Japanese Technology Reviews Ser.: Vol. 7). 130p. 1989. pap. text ed. 129.00 (*2-88124-331-2*) Gordon & Breach.

Steel Industry in Japan: A Comparison with Britain. H. Hasegawa. LC 95-34926. 368p. (C). 1996. text ed. 75.00 (*0-415-10386-X*) Routledge.

Steel Industry of India. William A. Johnson. LC 66-23471. (Rand Corporation Research Studies). 355p. 1966. 34.50 (*0-674-83715-0*) HUP.

Steel Industry Wage Structure: A Study of the Joint Union-Management Job Evaluation Program in the Basic Steel Industry. Jack Steiber. LC 59-12977. (Wertheim Publications in Industrial Relations). (Illus.). 403p. 1959. text ed. 27.50 (*0-674-83760-6*) HUP.

***Steel Inferno: The 1st S. S. Panzer Corps in Normandy.** Michael Reynolds. (Illus.). 320p. 1997. 27.50 (*1-885119-44-5*) Sarpedon.

Steel Lightning Slash & Burn. Kevin Sherrill. 1992. mass mkt. 3.99 (*0-8217-3633-7*, Zebra Kensgtn) Kensgtn Pub Corp.

Steel Magnolias. Robert Harling. 1988. pap. 5.25 (*0-8222-1078-9*) Dramatists Play.

Steel Manual. Ed. by German Iron & Steel Institute Staff. (Illus.). 136p. 1992. pap. 54.95 (*3-514-00455-2*, Pub. by Woodhead Pubng UK) Am Educ Systs.

Steel Market in 1988. 180p. 30.00 (*92-1-116458-3*, E.89.II.E.23) UN.

Steel Market in 1993 & Prospects for 1994: 1993. 155p. 1994. 35.00 (*92-1-116605-5*) UN.

Steel Market in 1994 & the Outlook for 1995 & 1996. OECD Staff. 48p. (Orig.). 1995. pap. 31.00 (*92-64-14531-1*, Pub. by Org for Econ FR) OECD.

***Steel Market in 1995 & Prospects for 1996.** United Nations Economic Commission for Europe. 175p. pap. 52.00 (*92-1-116652-7*) UN.

***Steel Market in 1995 & the Outlook for 1996 & 1997.** OECD Staff. 52p. (Orig.). 1996. pap. 24.00 (*92-64-15306-3*, 58-96-02-1) OECD.

Steel Market, 1987. (Energy, Environment, Metals & Natural Resources Ser.). 198p. 1989. 28.00 (*92-1-116435-4*, E.88.II.E.29) UN.

Steel Market, 1989. 181p. 1990. 30.00 (*92-1-116490-7*, E 90.II.E.34) UN.

Steel Mill Lubrication. 150p. 1984. 25.00 (*0-318-17685-8*, SP-18) Soc Tribologists.

Steel Mill or Treadmill? How to Stop the Big Steel Steal. Communist Party Steel & Metal Workers Commission. 1971. pap. 0.15 (*0-87898-069-5*) New Outlook.

***Steel My Soldier's Heart.** James Gritz. Date not set. write for info. (*0-688-13565-X*) Morrow.

***Steel My Soldiers' Hearts.** James Gritz. 352p. 1997. 21.00 (*0-06-017197-9*) HarpC.

Steel on Immigration Law. 2nd ed. Richard D. Steel. LC 92-18583. (Immigration Ser.). 1992. ring bd. 135.00 (*0-87632-899-0*) Clark Boardman Callaghan.

***Steel Panthers III.** Michael Knight. 1997. pap. 19.99 (*0-7615-1150-4*) Prima Pub.

***Steel Panthers 2: The Official Strategy Guide.** Michael Knight. 128p. 1996. per., pap. 16.99 (*0-7615-0893-7*) Prima Pub.

Steel Penstocks. American Society of Civil Engineers, Task Committee on Marines 2000 Staff. LC 93-13346. (Manual & Report on Engineering Practice Ser.: No. 79). 1993. 49.00 (*0-87262-951-1*) Am Soc Civil Eng.

Steel Phoenix: Fall & Fall the U.S. Steel Industry. Hall. LC 96-46909. 420p. 1997. text ed. 49.95 (*0-312-16198-0*) St Martin.

Steel Pipe, No. M11: A Guide for Design & Installation. 182p. pap. 60.00 (*0-89867-329-1*, 30011) Am Water Wks Assn.

Steel Plated Structures. Ed. by M. Klos Ivanyi & M. Skaloud. (CISM International Centre for Mechanical Sciences Ser.: No. 358). (Illus.). 373p. 1995. pap. 101.95 (*3-211-82742-0*) Spr-Verlag.

Steel Producers. Ed. by ICC Information Group Staff. 1987. 695.00 (*1-85319-045-4*, Pub. by ICC Info Group Ltd UK) St Mut.

Steel Product Quality & Maximum Utilization of Scrap: 1992. (ECE Steel Ser.). 197p. 1992. 55.00 (*92-1-116550-4*) UN.

Steel Production, Processes, Products, & Residuals. Clifford S. Russell & William J. Vaughan. LC 75-36945. 328p. 1976. 26.50 (*0-8018-1824-9*) Resources Future.

Steel Rails to the Sunrise. Ron Ziel. 61.95 (*0-8488-0368-X*) Amereon Ltd.

Steel Rails to Victory. Ron Ziel. Date not set. 14.99 (*0-517-14877-3*) Random Hse Value.

Steel Rain. Nyx Smith. (Shadowrun Ser.: No. 24). Orig. Title: Shadowrun Twenty-Four. 1997. pap. 5.99 (*0-451-45593-2*, ROC) NAL-Dutton.

Steel-Rolling Technology: Theory & Practice. Ginzburg. (Manufacturing Engineering & Materials Processing Ser.: No. 30). 804p. 1989. 225.00 (*0-8247-8124-4*) Dekker.

***Steel Rose.** Kara Dalkey. 1997. mass mkt. 5.99 (*0-451-45639-4*, ROC) NAL-Dutton.

***Steel Shards.** Bidwell Moore. 576p. (Orig.). 1997. mass mkt. 5.99 (*1-55237-010-0*, Pub. by Comnwlth Pub CN) Partners Pubs Grp.

Steel Ship Building. Fred M. Walker. 1989. pap. 25.00 (*0-85263-569-9*, Pub. by Shire UK) St Mut.

Steel Ships, Iron Crosses & Refugees: The Germany Navy in the Baltic, 1939-1945. Charles W. Koburger, Jr. LC 89-3871. 160p. 1989. text ed. 49.95 (*0-275-93260-5*, C3260, Praeger Pubs) Greenwood.

Steel Skeleton, Vol. 2: Plastic Behaviour & Design. John F. Baker et al. LC 54-3769. 447p. reprint ed. pap. 127.40 (*0-317-26067-7*, 2024427) Bks Demand.

Steel, Smoke & Steam: A Guide to America's Most Scenic Railroads. Margery Read. LC 91-77860. (Illus.). 120p. (Orig.). 1992. pap. 12.95 (*0-9630646-3-0*) Country Rds.

Steel Specialty Tubular Products. 118p. 1980. 8.00 (*0-614-05636-5*) Iron & Steel.

Steel Specification for Fixed Offshore Structure. EEMUA Staff. 1987. 125.00 (*0-85931-128-7*, Pub. by EEMUA UK) St Mut.

Steel Spine, Iron Will. Rod Lewin. LC 91-78105. 320p. (Orig.). 1992. pap. 18.95 (*0-9632031-0-X*) Boomerang Bks.

Steel Square. 2nd ed. G. Townsend. (Illus.). 172p. 1947. pap. 9.96 (*0-8269-0685-0*) Am Technical.

Steel, State & Labor: Mobilization & Adjustment in France. Anthony Daley. LC 95-23147. 341p. (Orig.). (C). 1996. pap. 22.95 (*0-8229-5602-0*); text ed. 49.95 (*0-8229-3918-5*) U of Pittsburgh Pr.

Steel Steeds Christie: A Memoir of J. Walter Christie. J. Edward Christie. (Illus.). 86p. 1985. pap. text ed. 16.00 (*0-89745-059-0*) Sunflower U Pr.

Steel String Guitar: Construction & Repair. David R. Young. (Bold Strummer Guitar Ser.). (Illus.). 188p. (Orig.). 1988. 24.95 (*0-933224-11-7*); pap. 15.95 (*0-933224-08-7*) Bold Strummer Ltd.

Steel String Guitar: Its History & Construction. 2nd rev. ed. Donald Brosnac. (Illus.). 112p. (C). 1976. pap. 7.95 (*0-915572-26-5*) Panjandrum.

Steel-String Guitar Construction: Acoustic Six-String, Twelve-String, & Arched-Top Guitars. Irving Sloane. 1990. reprint ed. pap. 21.00 (*0-933224-16-8*) Bold Strummer Ltd.

Steel, Structure, & Architecture: A Survey of the Material & Its Applications. Peter Eggen & Bjorn N. Sandaker. (Illus.). 256p. 1995. 35.00 (*0-8230-5020-3*) Watson-Guptill.

Steel Structures. Ed. by Jerome S. Iffland. LC 89-6775. 792p. 1989. pap. text ed. 65.00 (*0-87262-697-0*, 697) Am Soc Civil Eng.

Steel Structures: Controlling Behavior Through Design. Robert Englekirk. 832p. 1994. text ed. 84.95 (*0-471-58458-4*) Wiley.

Steel Structures: Design & Behavior. 4th ed. Charles G. Salmon & John E. Johnson. LC 95-37679. (Illus.). 1024p. (C). 1996. text ed. 72.95 (*0-673-99786-3*) Addson-Wesley Educ.

Steel Structures: Design & Behavior with LRFD Methods. 3rd ed. Charles G. Salmon & John E. Johnson. 1040p. (C). 1990. text ed. 84.50 (*0-06-045703-1*) Addson-Wesley Educ.

***Steel Structures: Practical Design Studies.** 2nd ed. T. J. Macginley. (Illus.). 352p. (Orig.). 1993. pap. text ed. 45.95 (*0-419-17930-5*, E & FN Spon) Routledge Chapman & Hall.

Steel Structures - Eurosteel '95: Proceedings of the 1st European Conference on Steel Structures, Athens, Greece, 18-20 May 1995. Anthony N. Kounadis. (Illus.). 524p. (C). 1995. text ed. 165.00 (*90-5410-554-2*, Pub. by A A Balkema NE) Ashgate Pub Co.

Steel Structures Painting Manual, 2 vols., Set. 3rd ed. Ed. by John D. Keane et al. (Illus.). 649p. 1993. 175.00 (*0-938477-84-6*) SSPC.

Steel Structures Painting Manual Vol. 1: Good Painting Practice. 3rd ed. Ed. by John D. Keane et al. (Illus.). 649p. 1993. 90.00 (*0-938477-81-1*) SSPC.

Steel Structures Painting Manual Vol. 2: Systems & Specifications. 460p. 1991. 100.00 (*0-938477-60-9*) SSPC.

Steel Structures Painting Manual Vols. 1 & 2, 2 vols., Set. Ed. by John D. Keane. (Illus.). 935p. 1989. 175.00 (*0-614-02632-6*) NACE Intl.

Steel Summers. William F. Keefe. Ed. by Keith Irvine. (Illus.). 119p. (Orig.). 1986. pap. 11.95 (*0-917256-31-X*) Action Res.

Steel Terror: Iron Man Super Thriller. David Seidman. 1996. mass mkt. 4.99 (*0-671-00321-6*) PB.

Steel Tiger. Mark Berent. 1990. pap. 5.99 (*0-515-10467-1*) Jove Pubns.

Steel Tiger. large type ed. Kay Thorpe. 1990. reprint ed. lib. bdg. 18.95 (*0-263-12233-6*, Pub. by Mills & Boon UK) Thorndike Pr.

Steel Titan: The Life of Charles M. Schwab. Robert Hessen. LC 90-33958. 376p. 1990. reprint ed. pap. 19.95 (*0-8229-5906-2*) U of Pittsburgh Pr.

Steel to the South - Fabulous Gunman. Wayne D. Overholser. 416p. 1994. mass mkt., pap. text ed. 4.99 (*0-8439-3700-9*) Dorchester Pub Co.

Steel Toe Boots. David Lawrence. LC 96-8328. 80p. (Orig.). 1996. pap. 9.50 (*1-56474-188-5*) Fithian Pr.

Steel Town Story. Brian Apelt. (Illus.). 160p. (Orig.). 1995. pap. write for info. (*0-614-07231-X*) J Szilagyi.

Steel Traders of the World. 5th ed. Ed. by Richard Serjeantson. 700p. 1990. text ed. 188.40 (*0-947671-37-4*) Metal Bulletin.

Steel Valley: Postcards & Letters. Larry Smith. LC 92-62452. 64p. 1992. pap. 5.95 (*0-917530-32-2*) Pig Iron Pr.

Steel Valley Klan: The Ku Klux Klan in Ohio's Mahoning Valley. William D. Jenkins. LC 90-34701. (Illus.). 236p. 1990. 27.50 (*0-87338-415-6*) Kent St U Pr.

Steel Web. large type ed. Ronald Tierney. LC 92-40636. (General Ser.). 321p. 1993. pap. 17.95 (*0-8161-5458-9*, GK Hall) Thorndike Pr.

Steel Will: The Life of Tad Sendzimir. Vanda Sendzimir. 520p. 1993. 24.95 (*0-7818-0169-9*) Hippocrene Bks.

Steel Wind: Colonel Georg Bruchm Uller & the Birth of Modern Artillery. David T. Zabecki & J. B. A. Bailey. LC 94-7658. (Military Profession Ser.). 224p. 1994. text ed. 65.00 (*0-275-94749-1*, Praeger Pubs) Greenwood.

Steel Wind: Colonel George Bruchmuller & the Birth of Modern Artillery. David T. Zabecki. LC 94-7658. (Military Profession Ser.). 224p. 1994. pap. text ed. 19.95 (*0-275-94750-5*, Praeger Pubs) Greenwood.

Steel Wire & Wire Products Industry: An Analysis of Current Markets & Prospects for Future Growth. 320p. 1995. 1,095.00 (*0-317-55179-5*) Busn Trend.

Steel Wire Handbook, Vol. 1. Ed. by Allan B. Dove. (Illus.). 318p. 1965. 50.00 (*0-685-26423-8*) Wire Assn Intl.

Steel Wire Handbook, Vol. 2. Ed. by Allan B. Dove & Dartrey B. Lewis. (Illus.). 388p. 1969. 50.00 (*0-685-26424-6*) Wire Assn Intl.

Steel Wire Handbook, Vol. 3. Allan B. Dove. (Illus.). 495p. 1972. 50.00 (*0-685-26425-4*) Wire Assn Intl.

Steel Wire Handbook, Vol. 4. Ed. by Allan B. Dove. (Illus.). 202p. 1980. 50.00 (*0-685-26427-0*) Wire Assn Intl.

Steel Wire Handbooks, 4 vols., Set. Ed. by Allan B. Dove. (Illus.). 1965. 170.00 (*0-685-26426-2*) Wire Assn Intl.

Steel Wire in America. 2nd ed. Kenneth B. Lewis. 1989. 30.00 (*0-685-26880-2*) Wire Assn Intl.

Steel Worker. John A. Fitch. LC 70-89757. (American Labor, from Conspiracy to Collective Bargaining Ser., No. 1). 393p. 1972. reprint ed. 23.95 (*0-405-02121-6*) Ayer.

Steel Workers. John A. Fitch. LC 88-19813. (Social & Labor History Ser.). (Illus.). 432p. 1989. reprint ed. pap. 19.95 (*0-8229-6091-5*) U of Pittsburgh Pr.

Steel Workers Rank & File. Philip Nyden. LC 83-22462. 192p. 1984. text ed. 45.00 (*0-275-91236-1*, C1236, Praeger Pubs) Greenwood.

Steelband Movement: The Forging of a National Art in Trinidad & Tobago. Stephen Stuempfle. (Illus.). 312p. 1996. text ed. 38.95 (*0-8122-3329-8*); pap. text ed. 16.95 (*0-8122-1565-6*) U of Pa Pr.

Steele - Carriage by Sea. 2nd ed. A. Sparks. 250p. 1995. 140.00 (*1-85044-834-5*) LLP.

Steele Rudd Selection: The Best Dad & Dave Stories with Other Rudd Classics. Steele Rudd. Ed. by Frank Moorhouse. LC 86-975. (Illus.). 240p. (Orig.). 1987. pap. 15.95 (*0-7022-1978-9*, Pub. by Univ Queensland Pr AT) Intl Spec Bk.

An Asterisk (*) at the beginning of an entry indicates that the title is appearing in BIP for the first time.

Steeleglas, Fifteen Seventy-Five & the Complaynte of Philomene Fifteen Seventy-Six. George Gascoigne. Ed. by EDward Arber. 1983. pap. 12.50 (*0-87556-496-8*) Saifer.

Steele's Answers. Daniel Steele. 1980. 13.99 (*0-88019-302-6*) Schmul Pub Co.

Steelhead. David Campiche. (Illus.). 24p. (Orig.). 1994. pap. 5.95 (*0-9634294-2-6*) C&D Pub OR.

Steelhead. Barry M. Thornton. 1995. pap. 17.95 (*0-88839-370-9*) Hancock House.

Steelhead. limited ed. Barry M. Thornton. 1995. pap. 17.95 (*0-88839-371-7*) Hancock House.

Steelhead & the Floating Line. Bob Arnold. (Illus.). 181p. 1995. pap. 15.95 (*1-57188-040-2*) F Amato Pubns.

Steelhead Country. Steve Raymond. (Illus.). 224p. 1991. 19.95 (*1-55821-126-8*) Lyons & Burford.

Steelhead Country: Angling in Northwest Waters. Steve Raymond. 208p. 1994. reprint ed. pap. 9.95 (*1-57061-014-2*) Sasquatch Bks.

Steelhead Fly Fishing. Trey Combs. (Illus.). 512p. 1991. 45.00 (*1-55821-119-5*) Lyons & Burford.

Steelhead Fly Fishing & Flies. Trey Combs. (Illus.). 118p. (Orig.). 1976. pap. 19.95 (*0-936608-03-X*) F Amato Pubns.

Steelhead Fly Fishing in Low Water. Dick Van DeMark. Ed. & Photos by Daniel B. Homel. (Illus.). 132p. (Orig.). 1996. pap. 16.95 (*1-879522-05-5*) Forrest Pk.

Steelhead Fly Tying Guide. H. Kent Helvie. (Illus.). 80p. 1995. 34.95 (*1-878175-86-6*); pap. 24.95 (*1-878175-85-8*) F Amato Pubns.

***Steelhead Jig Fishing: Techniques & Tackle.** Dave Vedder & Drew Harthorn. 48p. 1996. pap. 8.95 (*1-57188-073-9*) F Amato Pubns.

Steelhead Paradise. John F. Fennelly. (Illus.). 128p. 1989. 21.95 (*0-936608-87-0*) F Amato Pubns.

Steelhead Savvy. Jim Bedford. (Illus.). 88p. 1995. pap. 12.95 (*1-878175-94-7*) F Amato Pubns.

Steelhead Trout. Trey Combs. (Illus.). 187p. 1988. reprint ed. pap. 9.95 (*0-936608-77-3*) F Amato Pubns.

Steelhead Water. Bob Arnold. 300p. 1993. 24.95 (*1-878175-60-2*) F Amato Pubns.

Steelheading for the Simple-Minded. Bob Ellsberg. (Illus.). 96p. (Orig.). 1987. pap. 7.95 (*0-944294-00-6*) Outdoor Enterprises.

Steelheading for the Simple-Minded. 2nd ed. Bob Ellsberg. (Illus.). 96p. (Orig.). 1989. reprint ed. pap. 6.95 (*0-916473-04-X*) Flying Pencil.

Steelheart. 96p. 1991. otabind 19.95 (*0-7935-1016-3*, 00694796) H Leonard.

Steeling the Mind of America. Ed. by Bill Perkins. 300p. (Orig.). 1995. pap. 11.95 (*0-89221-294-2*) New Leaf.

***Steeling the Mind of America, Vol. II.** John Ankerberg et al. Ed. & Compiled by Bill Perkins. LC 96-69689. 224p. 1996. pap. 11.95 (*0-89221-334-5*) New Leaf.

Steelmakers & Knotted String. H. Brearley. 276p. 1995. 40.00 (*0-901716-65-0*, Pub. by Inst Materials UK) Ashgate Pub Co.

Steelmaking Capacity in Non-OECD Countries: Two-Yearly Report 1995 Edition. OECD Staff. 154p. (Orig.). 1995. pap. 32.00 (*92-64-14487-0*, Pub. by Org for Econ FR) OECD.

Steelmaking Conference: Proceedings of the Annual ISS Steelmaking Conferences, Vol. 76. 744p. 1993. 80.00 (*0-932897-86-X*) Iron & Steel.

***Steelmaking Conference: Proceedings of the Annual ISS Steelmaking Conferences, Vol. 79.** LC 83-111773. 787p. 1996. pap. 90.00 (*1-886362-11-4*) Iron & Steel.

Steelmaking Conference: Proceedings of the Annual Steelmaking Conferences, Vol. 77. LC 83-111773. 764p. 1994. 90.00 (*0-932897-93-2*) Iron & Steel.

Steelmaking Conference Proceedings: Detroit Meeting, April 14-17, 1985, Vol. 68-1985. Iron & Steel Society of AIME Staff. LC 83-111773. (Illus.). 510p. reprint ed. pap. 145.40 (*0-685-24020-7*, 2032244) Bks Demand.

Steelmaking Conference Proceedings: Toronto Meeting, April 17-20, 1988. Steelmaking Conference Staff. LC 83-111773. 512p. pap. 146.00 (*0-8357-7874-6*, 2036292) Bks Demand.

Steelmaking Conference Proceedings, Seventy-Second: Chicago Meeting, April 2-5, 1989. Iron & Steel Society of AIME Staff. LC 83-111773. (Illus.). 574p. reprint ed. pap. 163.60 (*0-7837-1663-X*, 2041960) Bks Demand.

Steelmaking Conference Proceedings, 1991: Washington Meeting, April 14-17 - Sponsored by the Steelmaking Division, the Iron & Steel Society. Steelmaking Conference Staff. LC 83-111773. (Illus.). 875p. reprint ed. pap. 180.00 (*0-7837-4781-0*, 2044536) Bks Demand.

Steelmaking Conference Proceedings, 1992: Toronto Meeting, April 5-8, 75th, Sponsored by the Steelmaking Division, the Iron & Steel Society. Steelmaking Conference Staff. LC 83-111773. 993p. reprint ed. pap. 180.00 (*0-7837-5728-X*, 2045388) Bks Demand.

Steelmaking Conference Proceedings, 64th: Toronto, Ontario Meeting, March 29-April 1, 1981. Iron & Steel Society of AIME Staff. LC 83-111773. (Illus.). 321p. reprint ed. pap. 91.50 (*0-7837-6112-0*, 2045647) Bks Demand.

Steelmaking Conference Proceedings, 65th, Pittsburgh Meeting, March 28-31, 1982, Sponsored by the Steelmaking Division, the Iron & Steel Society of Aime. Iron & Steel Society of AIME Staff. 388p. reprint ed. pap. 110.60 (*0-317-26839-2*, 2023494) Bks Demand.

Steelmaking Conference Proceedings, 66th: Atlanta Meeting, April 17-20, 1983. Iron & Steel Society of AIME Staff. LC 83-111773. (Illus.). 417p. reprint ed. pap. 118.90 (*0-7837-6113-9*, 2045648) Bks Demand.

Steelmaking Conference Proceedings, 67th: Chicago Meeting, April 1-4, 1984. Iron & Steel Society of AIME Staff. LC 83-111773. (Illus.). 381p. reprint ed. pap. 108.60 (*0-7837-6114-7*, 2045649) Bks Demand.

Steelmaking Conference Proceedings, 69th: Washington Meeting, April 6-9, 1986. Iron & Steel Society of AIME Staff. LC 83-111773. (Illus.). 1067p. reprint ed. pap. 180.00 (*0-7837-6115-5*, 2045650) Bks Demand.

Steelmaking Conference Proceedings, 70th: Pittsburgh Meeting, March 29-April 1, 1987. Iron & Steel Society of AIME Staff. LC 83-111773. (Illus.). 480p. reprint ed. pap. 136.80 (*0-7837-6116-3*, 2045651) Bks Demand.

Steelmaking Conferences: Proceedings of the Annual ISS Steelmaking Conferences, Vol. 78. LC 83-111773. 776p. 1995. 90.00 (*1-886362-00-9*) Iron & Steel.

Steelmaking Data Sourcebook: The Japan Society for the Promotion of Science, the 19th Committee on Steelmaking. 326p. 1988. text ed. 190.00 (*2-88124-153-0*) Gordon & Breach.

Steelmaking Eighteen Fifty to Nineteen Hundred. K. C. Barraclough. 320p. 1990. text ed. 64.00 (*0-901462-71-3*, Pub. by Inst Materials UK) Ashgate Pub Co.

***Steelman: Jonathan & Hannah Steelman Family.** Sarah R. Lawyer. (Illus.). 106p. 1996. reprint ed. pap. 18.50 (*0-8328-5607-X*); reprint ed. lib. bdg. 28.50 (*0-8328-5606-1*) Higginson Bk Co.

Steelmasters & Labor Reform, 1886-1923. Gerald G. Eggert. LC 81-50636. 232p. 1981. 49.95 (*0-8229-3801-4*) U of Pittsburgh Pr.

***Steels.** 2nd ed. write for info. (*0-340-58946-9*, Pub. by E Arnold UK) Routledge Chapman & Hall.

Steels: Heat Treatment & Processing Principles. 497p. 1990. 128.00 (*0-87170-370-X*, 6936) ASM.

Steels: Microstructure & Properties. 2nd ed. Robert Honeycombe & H. Bhadshia. 324p. 1996. pap. text ed. 44.95 (*0-470-23568-3*) Halsted Pr.

Steels: Microstructure & Properties. Robert W. Honeycombe. LC 81-17681. (Metallurgy & Materials Science Ser.). 256p. reprint ed. pap. 73.00 (*0-685-15619-2*, 2027039) Bks Demand.

Steels Metallurgy & Applications. 2nd ed. D. T. Llewellyn. 320p. 1994. pap. 42.95 (*0-7506-2086-2*) Buttrwrth-Heinemann.

***Steelton: Immigration & Industrialization, 1870-1940.** John E. Bodnar. LC 90-33284. (Pittsburgh Series in Social & Labor History). 237p. pap. 67.60 (*0-608-05087-3*, 2065641) Bks Demand.

Steeltown, U. S. S. R. A Soviet Society in the Gorbachev Era. Stephen Kotkin. 1992. pap. 14.00 (*0-520-07354-1*) U CA Pr.

Steeltown, U. S. S. R. Glasnost, Destalinization & Perestroika in the Provinces. Stephen Kotkin. Ed. by Reginald Zelnik. (Center for Slavic & East European Studies Occasional Papers). 72p. (Orig.). (C). 1989. pap. text ed. 5.00 (*0-9622629-0-0*) UCB CFSEES.

Steeltown, U. S. S. R. Soviet Society in the Gorbachev Era. Stephen Kotkin. LC 90-11310. (Illus.). 269p. 1991. 35.00 (*0-520-07353-3*) U CA Pr.

Steelwork. Gilbert Sorrentino. LC 79-119484. 1970. 30.00 (*0-685-46841-0*) SPD-Small Pr Dist.

Steelwork. Gilbert Sorrentino. LC 92-9095. 179p. 1992. reprint ed. pap. 9.95 (*1-56478-004-X*) Dalkey Arch.

Steelworkers Rank & File: The Political Economy of a Union Reform Movement. Philip Nyden. (Illus.). 176p. 1984. text ed. 34.95 (*0-03-063370-2*, Bergin & Garvey) Greenwood.

Steely Blue. Dennis Smith. 1994. lib. bdg. 25.95 (*1-56849-576-5*) Buccaneer Bks.

Steely Dan: Reelin' in the Years. Brian Sweet. (Illus.). 200p. pap. 17.95 (*0-7119-3551-3*, OP 47400) Omnibus NY.

Steenburgen Diagnostic-Prescriptive Math Program, Levels I & II. Fran S. Gelb. (J). (gr. 1-6). 1978. Level I (gr. 1-3); Level II (gr. 4-6). 18.00 (*0-87879-209-0*) Acad Therapy.

Steenis Flora Males, Vol. 1. 1985. lib. bdg. 391.00 (*90-247-3116-X*, Pub. by M Nijhoff NE) Kluwer Ac.

Steenrod Connections & Connectivity in H Spaces. J. Lin. LC 87-12589. (Memoirs Ser.: No. 68-369). 87p. 1987. pap. text ed. 18.00 (*0-8218-2431-7*, MEMO/68/369) Am Math.

Steen's Mountain in Oregon's High Desert Country. E. R. Jackman & John Scharff. LC 67-24205. (Illus.). 1967. 49.95 (*0-87004-028-6*) Caxton.

Steens Mt. Scrapbook. Janice P. Gutenberg. LC 23-939860. 1982. 24.95 (*0-939860-05-8*) Tremaine Graph & Pub.

Steep Holm Through the Centuries. Stan Randall & Joan Randall. 256p. 1993. pap. 19.99 (*0-7509-0323-6*, Pub. by Sutton Pubng UK) Bks Intl VA.

Steep Trails. John Muir. LC 93-25661. (John Muir Library). 304p. 1994. pap. 10.00 (*0-87156-535-8*) Sierra.

Steep Trails. John Muir. (BCL1 - United States Local History Ser.). 390p. 1991. reprint ed. lib. bdg. 89.00 (*0-7812-6326-3*) Rprt Serv.

Steepe & the Sown see Corridors of Time: New Haven & London, 1927-1956

***Steepland Forests of New Zealand: Their Conservation & Management.** Peter McKelvey. (Illus.). 296p. (Orig.). (C). 1995. pap. 49.50 (*0-908812-38-8*, Pub. by Canterbury Univ NZ) Aubrey Bks.

Steepland Geomorphology. Ed. by Olav Slaymaker. LC 95-5284. (International Association of Geomorphologists Publications: No. 3). 264p. 1995. text ed. 110.00 (*0-471-95752-6*) Wiley.

Steeple Chase. Jeff Hagen. 1996. pap. text ed. 10.95 (*1-57025-130-4*) Pfeifer-Hamilton.

Steeple Chase: Ontario's Historic Churches. James Preyde & Susan Preyde. (Illus.). 72p. 20.00 (*1-55046-030-7*, Pub. by Boston Mills Pr CN) Genl Dist Srvs.

Steeplechasing. John Hislop. 250p. 1990. 60.00 (*0-85131-375-2*, Pub. by J A Allen & Co UK) St Mut.

Steeplejack, 2 vols., Set. James G. Huneker. (BCL1-PS American Literature Ser.). 1992. reprint ed. lib. bdg. 150.00 (*0-7812-6751-X*) Rprt Serv.

Steeplejack, 2 vols., Set. James G. Huneker. 1993. reprint ed. lib. bdg. 150.00 (*0-7812-5471-X*) Rprt Serv.

Steeples & Smokestacks: A Collection of Essays on the Franco-American Experience in New England. Ed. by Claire Quintal. 683p. 1996. pap. 24.95 (*1-880261-03-0*) FI Assump Coll.

Steeples & Stacks: Religion & Steel Crisis in Youngstown, Ohio. Thomas G. Fuechtmann. (Studies in Religion & American Public Life). (Illus.). 300p. (C). 1989. text ed. 69.95 (*0-521-33481-0*) Cambridge U Pr.

Steeples on the Riverbend. Sue Davidson. 352p. 1991. write for info. (*0-942407-16-4*) Father & Son.

***Steer Clear: A Christian Guide to Teen Temptations.** Kathleen Winkler. LC 96-41165. 1997. 6.99 (*0-570-04957-1*) Concordia.

Steer Clear of Haunted Hill. Eric Weiner. (Ghostwriter Ser.). 112p. (J). (gr. 1-3). 1993. pap. 3.50 (*0-553-48087-1*) Bantam.

Steerage & Ten Other Stories. Raymond S. Sayers. LC 82-84530. (Illus.). 224p. (Orig.). 1983. pap. 6.00 (*0-943722-06-3*) Gavea-Brown.

Steered by the Falling Stars: A Father's Journey. Daniel Spurr. 240p. 1992. 19.95 (*0-87742-332-6*, 60324) Intl Marine.

Steering a New Course: Transportation, Energy, & the Environment. Deborah Gordon. LC 91-24401. 245p. (Orig.). 1991. 34.95 (*1-55963-135-X*); pap. 19.95 (*1-55963-134-1*) Island Pr.

Steering & Suspension. 2nd ed. John Remling. (Automotive Ser.). 422p. 1983. pap. text ed. 34.95 (*0-471-87614-3*) P-H.

Steering & Suspension. 2nd ed. John Remling. 1989. pap. text ed. 65.00 (*0-13-859398-1*) P-H.

***Steering & Suspensions Technology.** 1997. 86.00 (*1-56091-935-3*) Soc Auto Engineers.

Steering Clear of Highway Madness: A Driver's Guide to Curbing Stress & Strain. John A. Larson. LC 96-83183. (Illus.). 176p. (Orig.). 1996. pap. 14.95 (*1-885221-38-X*) BookPartners.

Steering Gear: Test Routines & Check List Card. ICS Staff. 1978. 22.00 (*0-317-61493-2*, Pub. by Witherby & Co UK) St Mut.

Steering Gear Systems. (C). 1989. 100.00 (*0-89771-703-1*, Pub. by Lorne & MacLean Marine) St Mut.

Steering Gear Systems. Lorne & MacLean Marine & Offshore Publications Staff. (C). 1987. 75.00 (*0-685-33868-1*, Pub. by Lorne & MacLean Marine) St Mut.

Steering Gear Systems. OCS Marine Staff. (C). 1989. text ed. 150.00 (*0-685-63531-7*) St Mut.

Steering Locks! Top Secret Lethal Defect. Wilson Sherman. LC 94-70054. (Illus.). 80p. (Orig.). 1994. pap. write for info. (*0-9639964-8-7*) ASF Pubns.

Steering the Polity: Communication & Politics in Israel. Itzhak Galnoor. LC 81-21485. (Illus.). 423p. reprint ed. pap. 120.60 (*0-8357-8463-0*, 2034731) Bks Demand.

Steering Them Straight: A Parental Plan for Conquering Today's Temptations. Stephen F. Arterburn & Jim Burns. LC 95-30774. 1995. pap. 10.99 (*1-56179-406-6*) Focus Family.

***Stefan Grossman's Complete Fingerpicking Guitar Exercises & Hot Licks.** Stefan Grossman. 1993. 24.95 incl. audio (*0-7866-1229-0*, 95216P) Mel Bay.

Stefan Heym: Perpetual Dissident. Peter Hutchinson. (Studies in German). 240p. (C). 1992. text ed. 69.95 (*0-521-40438-X*) Cambridge U Pr.

Stefan in Love: A Novel. Joseph Machlis. 240p. 1991. 19.95 (*0-393-03005-9*) Norton.

Stefan Problem. L. I. Rubenstein. Tr. by A. Solomon. LC 75-168253. (Translations of Mathematical Monographs: Vol. 27). 419p. 1971. 77.00 (*0-8218-1577-6*, MMONO/27) Am Math.

Stefan Stambolov & the Emergence of Modern Bulgaria, 1870-1895. Duncan M. Perry. LC 92-34704. (Illus.). 328p. 1993. text ed. 41.95 (*0-8223-1313-8*) Duke.

Stefan Zweig: An International Bibliography. Randolph J. Klawiter. (Studies in Austrian Literature, Culture, & Thought). 934p. 1991. 65.00 (*0-929497-35-X*) Ariadne CA.

Stefan Zweig: Exil und Suche nach dem Weltfrieden. Ed. by Mark H. Gelber & Klaus Zelewitz. (Studies in Austrian Literature, Culture & Thought; Translation Ser.). 348p. (GER.). 1995. 42.00 (*1-57241-011-6*) Ariadne CA.

Stefan Zweig-Heute. Ed. by Mark H. Gelber. (New Yorker Studien zur Neueren Deutschen Literaturgeschichte Ser.: Band 7). 226p. (GER.). 1987. text ed. 45.00 (*0-8204-0378-4*) P Lang Pubng.

Stefanchik Method: Earn Ten Thousand Dollars a Month for the Rest of Your Life, in Your Spare Time. John Stefanchik. LC 93-46111. 1994. 20.00 (*0-688-12741-X*) Morrow.

Stefanie Hero. Mark Medoff. 1994. pap. 5.25 (*0-8222-1370-2*) Dramatists Play.

Stefano Bernardi: Sonatas & Sinfonias from the "Motetti in Cantilena a Quattro Voci, con Alcune Canzoni per Sonare con Ogni Sorte di Strumenti" (Venice, 1613) & the "Concerti Academici con Varia di Sinfonie a Sei Voci...Libro Primo" (Venice, 1615-1616) Ed. by James Ladewig. LC 91-761355. (Italian Instrumental Music of the Sixteenth & Early Seventeenth Centuries Ser.: Vol. 23). 192p. 1992. text ed. 75.00 (*0-8240-4522-X*) Garland.

Stefansson: Ambassador of the North. Donat M. Le Bourdais. LC 63-17243. (Emulation Bks). 206p. reprint ed. pap. 58.80 (*0-317-28425-8*, 2022307) Bks Demand.

Stefansson & the Canadian Arctic. Richard J. Diubaldo. LC 79-304078. 296p. reprint ed. pap. 84.40 (*0-7837-1020-8*, 2041331) Bks Demand.

Stefansson-Anderson Arctic Expedition: Preliminary Ethnological Report. Vilhjalmur Stefansson. LC 74-5880. (Anthropological Papers of the American Museum of Natural History: Vol. 14.). reprint ed. 72.50 (*0-404-11688-4*) AMS Pr.

Steffi. Roberts & Davis. LC 96-17576. 1997. 16.00 (*0-689-81166-7*) S&S Childrens.

Steffi. Roberts & Davis. 1998. 4.50 (*0-689-81167-5*) S&S Childrens.

Steffi: Public Power, Personal Pain. Sue Heady. 228p. 1995. 19.95 (*1-85227-516-2*, Pub. by Virgin Pub UK) London Brdge.

Steffi: Public Power, Private Pain. rev. ed. Sue Heady. (Illus.). 204p. 1996. mass mkt. 5.95 (*0-86369-944-8*, Pub. by Virgin Pub UK) London Brdge.

Steffi Graf. James R. Rothaus. (Sports Superstars Ser.). (Illus.). 32p. (J). (gr. 2-6). 1991. lib. bdg. 21.36 (*0-89565-734-1*) Childs World.

Steffi Graf: Tennis Champ. Philip Brooks. LC 95-40244. (Sports Stars Ser.). (Illus.). 48p. (J). (gr. 2-8). 1996. lib. bdg. 17.50 (*0-516-04397-8*) Childrens.

Stege Mounds at Richmond, California. fac. ed. Llewellyn L. Loud. (University of California Publications in American Archaeology & Ethnology: Vol. 17: 6). 22p. (C). 1924. reprint ed. pap. text ed. 2.50 (*1-55567-231-0*) Coyote Press.

S

Steggall Family in America: John Steggall & Some of His Descendants, with Brief Information on the Families of Baldry & Hasner. Mary A. Thies. (Illus.). 280p. 1993. pap. 39.50 (*0-8328-3581-1*); lib. bdg. 49.50 (*0-8328-3580-3*) Higginson Bk Co.

Steggie Saurus: Kindergartener in Korea. Bonnie J. Dryer. LC 92-60813. 44p. (J). (gr. k-3). 1993. pap. 5.95 (*1-55523-547-6*) Winston-Derek.

Stegner: Conversations on History & Literature. Wallace Stegner & Richard W. Etulain. (Western Literature Ser.). Orig. Title: Conversations with Wallace Stegner on Western History Literatrue. (Illus.). 248p. 1996. reprint ed. pap. 15.95 (*0-87417-274-8*) U of Nev Pr.

Stegosaurus. Stuart A. Kallen. Ed. by Julie Berg. LC 94-4532. (If the Dinosaurs Could Talk Ser.). (J). 1994. 14.98 (*1-56239-285-9*) Abdo & Dghtrs.

Stegosaurus. Janet Riehecky. LC 88-15347. (Dinosaur Bks.). (Illus.). 32p. (J). (gr. k-4). 1988. lib. bdg. 21.36 (*0-89565-385-0*) Childs World.

Stegosaurus. J. F. Rifkin. Date not set. pap. 4.50 (*0-451-45270-4*, Onyx) NAL-Dutton.

Stegosaurus. Sheehan. (Dinosaur Library: Set I). (Illus.). 24p. (J). 1981. lib. bdg. 14.00 (*0-86592-112-1*) Rourke Enter.

Stegosaurus: The Dinosaur with the Smallest Brain. Elizabeth Sandell. Ed. by Marjorie Oelerich & Howard Schroeder. LC 88-995. (Dinosaur Discovery Era Ser.). (Illus.). 32p. (J). (gr. k-5). 1988. pap. 5.95 (*0-944280-08-0*); lib. bdg. 12.95 (*0-944280-02-1*) Bancroft-Sage.

***Stegosaurus: The Plated Dinosaur.** Janet Riehecky. LC 96-49419. (Dinosaur Days Ser.: Group 1). (Illus.). (J). (ps up). 1997. lib. bdg. 14.95 (*0-7614-0604-2*, Benchmark NY) Marshall Cavendish.

Stegosaurus & Other Jurassic Plant-Eaters. Daniel Cohen. (Dinosaurs of North America Ser.). (Illus.). 48p. (J). (gr. 3-9). 1996. 17.80 (*1-56065-287-X*) Capstone Pr.

Stegosaurus & Other Jurassic Plant-Eaters. Daniel Cohen. (Illus.). 48p. (J). (gr. 3-7). 1995. 13.35 (*0-516-35287-3*) Childrens.

Stehekin: A Guide to the Enchanted Valley. 2nd ed. Fred T. Darvill, Jr. (Illus.). 100p. 1996. pap. 9.95 (*0-915740-00-1*) Darvill Outdoor.

***Steichen: A Biography.** Penelope Niven. 1997. 35.00 (*0-517-59373-4*, C P Pubs) Crown Pub Group.

Steidlmayer on Markets: A New Approach to Trading. J. Peter Steidlmayer. LC 88-36683. (Illus.). 184p. 1989. text ed. 55.00 (*0-471-62115-3*) Wiley.

Steiff: Sensational Teddy Bears, Animals & Dolls. Christel Pistorius & Rolf Pistorius. (Illus.). 160p. 1991. 19.95 (*0-87588-356-7*) Hobby Hse.

***Steiff Sortiment: 1947-1995.** Gunther Peiffer. (Illus.). 480p. (GER.). 1996. 90.00 (*0-614-23851-X*, C5234) Hobby Hse.

***Steiff Teddy Bears.** Jurgen Cieslik & Marianne Cieslik. (Illus.). 184p. 1996. 60.00 (*0-614-23852-8*, C4897) Hobby Hse.

Stein & Day Handbook of Magic. Marvin Kaye. LC 83-42966. (Illus.). 310p. (C). 1983. pap. 8.95 (*0-8128-6203-1*, Scrbrough Hse) Madison Bks UPA.

Stein & Day Handbook of Magic. Marvin Kaye. LC 73-817930. 1973. pap. 3.95 (*0-8128-1803-2*, Scrbrough Hse) Madison Bks UPA.

Stein, Bishop, & Rich: Lyrics of Love, War, & Place. Margaret Dickie. LC 96-9615. 272p. (C). 1997. 16.95 (*0-8078-4622-8*) U of NC Pr.

Stein, Bishop, & Rich: Lyrics of Love, War, & Place. Margaret Dickie. LC 96-9615. 272p. (C). (gr. 13). 1997. 45.00 (*0-8078-2308-2*) U of NC Pr.

***Stein on Probate: Administration of Decedents' Estates under the Uniform Code As Enacted in Minnesota, 2 vols.** 3rd ed. Robert A. Stein. 1995. 160.00 (*1-55834-282-6*, 81889-11) MICHIE.

Stein on Probate: Administration of Decedents' Estates under the Uniform Probate Code As Enacted in Minnesota, 1986-1991, 2 vols. 2nd ed. Robert A. Stein. 1300p. 1993. suppl. ed., ring bd. 67.00 (*0-614-02556-7*) MICHIE.

Stein on Probate: Administration of Decedents' Estates under the Uniform Probate Code As Enacted in Minnesota, 1986-1991, 2 vols., Set. 2nd ed. Robert A. Stein. 1300p. 1994. ring bd. 225.00 (*0-86678-540-X*) MICHIE.

Stein on the Problem of Empathy. 1970. pap. text ed. 41.50 (*90-247-0150-3*, Pub. by M Nijhoff NE) Kluwer Ac.

Stein on Writing: A Master Editor of Some of the Most Successful Writers of Our Century Shares His Craft Techniques & Strategies. Sol Stein. LC 95-31793. 320p. 1995. 23.95 (*0-312-13608-0*) St Martin.

Stein Personal Injury Damages Service, 5 vols., Set. Jacob A. Stein. LC 91-78048. 1992. ring bd. 635.00 (*0-685-59916-7*) Clark Boardman Callaghan.

Stein Reader. Gertrude Stein. Ed. & Intro. by Ulla Dydo. (Illus.). 700p. (Orig.). 1993. 64.95 (*0-8101-1058-X*); pap. 24.95 (*0-8101-1083-0*) Northwestern U Pr.

***Steinaker Gap: An Early Fremont Farmstead.** Richard K. Talbot & Lane Richens. (Museum of Peoples & Cultures Occasional Papers: Vol. 2). (Illus.). 239p. Date not set. 20.00 (*0-614-26091-4*) U of Utah Pr.

Steinbeck. F. Watt. (Writers & Critics Ser.). 117p. 1978. 24.50 (*0-912378-06-9*) Chips Bksearch.

Steinbeck: A Life in Letters. John Steinbeck & Elaine A. Steinbeck. Ed. by Robert Wallsten. 928p. 1989. pap. 19.95 (*0-14-004288-1*, Penguin Bks) Viking Penguin.

Steinbeck & Hemingway: Dissertation Abstracts & Research Opportunities. Ed. by Tetsumaro Hayashi. LC 80-15540. 242p. 1980. 20.00 (*0-8108-1321-1*) Scarecrow.

Steinbeck & His Critics: A Record of 25 Years: An Anthology. Ernest W. Tedlock & C. V. Wickev. LC 56-12746. 352p. reprint ed. pap. 100.40 (*0-685-15520-X*, 2026752) Bks Demand.

***Steinbeck & the Environment: Interdisciplinary Approaches.** Ed. by Susan F. Beegel et al. LC 96-36276. 384p. 1997. text ed. 29.95 (*0-8173-0846-6*) U of Ala Pr.

Steinbeck Bibliographies: An Annotated Guide. Robert B. Harmon. LC 86-33830. 145p. 1987. 20.00 (*0-8108-1963-5*) Scarecrow.

Steinbeck Country. Steve Crouch. 192p. 1995. reprint ed. text ed. 35.00 (*0-9645311-0-0*) Pilothse Pub.

Steinbeck Question: New Essays in Criticism. Ed. by Donald R. Noble. LC 91-75026. 278p. 1993. 29.50 (*0-87875-424-5*) Whitston Pub.

Steinbeck's Literary Dimension, Pt. II. Ed. by Tetsumaro Hayashi. LC 72-7457. (Guide to Comparative Studies: No. II). 198p. 1991. 22.50 (*0-8108-2444-2*) Scarecrow.

Steinbeck's The Grapes of Wrath: "Essays in Criticism" Ed. by Hayashi Tetsumaro. (Steinbeck Essay Ser.: No. 3). 77p. 1990. 20.00 (*0-937994-16-2*) Ball State Univ.

Steinbeck's Typewriter: Essays on Creative Dimensions of His Art. Robert DeMott. LC 93-60806. 362p. 1996. 35.00 (*0-87875-446-6*) Whitston Pub.

Steiner: Genealogy of the Steiner Family in Germany & America, Especially the Descendants of Jacob Steiner. L. H. Steiner & B. C. Steiner. 99p. 1994. reprint ed. pap. 19.00 (*0-8328-4383-0*); reprint ed. lib. bdg. 29.00 (*0-8328-4382-2*) Higginson Bk Co.

Steiner: The Lyran Commonwealth. (BattleTech Ser.). (Illus.). 80p. (Orig.). 1987. pap. 15.00 (*1-55560-033-6*, 1621) FASA Corp.

Steiner Brothers. Edward R. Ricciuti. Ed. by Bruce Glassman. (Face to Face Ser.). 25p. (Orig.). (J). (gr. 5 up). 1994. pap. text ed. 6.95 (*1-56711-073-8*, Topdog) Blackbirch.

Steiner Tree Problem. Frank K. Hwang et al. LC 92-25345. (Annals of Discrete Mathematics Ser.: No. 53). 340p. 1992. 158.25 (*0-444-89098-X*, North Holland) Elsevier.

Steiner's How to Talk Mortgage Talk. Clyde Steiner & Shari Steiner. (Illus.). 64p. 1997. pap. 3.95 (*0-614-13914-7*) Computing.

Steingass Learner's Arabic-English Dictionary. F. Steingass. 1243p. (ARA & ENG.). 45.00 (*0-86685-091-0*, LDL0910, Pub. by Librairie du Liban FR) Intl Bk Ctr.

Steingass Learner's English-Arabic Dictionary. F. Steingass. 466p. (ARA & ENG.). 1984. 24.95 (*0-86685-081-3*, LDL0813, Pub. by Librairie du Liban FR) Intl Bk Ctr.

***Steinhardt.** Mike Steinhardt & Ron Insana. 288p. 1997. 29.95 (*0-471-18152-8*, FN20) Wiley.

Steinlen: The Graphic Work. E. De Crauzat. (Illus.). 248p. (FRE.). 1983. reprint ed. 95.00 (*0-915346-71-0*) A Wofsy Fine Arts.

Steinlen Cats. Theophile-Alexandre Steinlen. (Illus.). 48p. 1980. pap. 4.95 (*0-486-23950-0*) Dover.

Steinlen's Lithographs: One Hundred Twenty-One Plates from "Gil Blas Illustre" Theophile-Alexandre Steinlen. (Illus.). 128p. 1980. pap. 8.95 (*0-486-23943-8*) Dover.

Steinlen's Posters. Rejane Bargiel & Christophe Zagrodski. 120p. (FRE.). 1986. 95.00 (*1-55660-110-7*) A Wofsy Fine Arts.

Steinmetz: Engineer & Socialist. Ronald Kline. (Studies in the History of Technology, New Ser.: No. 13). (Illus.). 376p. 1992. text ed. 48.00 (*0-8018-4298-0*) Johns Hopkins.

Steinmetz: The Philosopher. Ed. by P. L. Alger. viii, 188p. 1965. 70.00 (*0-677-65170-8*) Gordon & Breach.

Steinmetz in Schenectady: A Picture Story of Three Memorable Decades. Larry Hart. (Illus.). 331p. (Orig.). 1978. pap. text ed. 10.00 (*0-932035-06-X*) Old Dorp Bks.

***Steins.** Linda Wagner-Martin. Date not set. write for info. (*0-688-09853-3*) Morrow.

Steinway. Ronald Ratcliffe. (Illus.). 196p. 1989. 45.00 (*0-87701-592-9*) Chronicle Bks.

Steinway & Sons. Richard K. Lieberman. LC 95-17330. 1995. 35.00 (*0-300-06364-4*) Yale U Pr.

***Steinway & Sons.** Richard K. Lieberman. 1997. pap. text ed. 18.00 (*0-300-06850-6*) Yale U Pr.

Steinway Saga: The Family That Created the World's Most Famous Piano. D. W. Fostle. LC 94-7842. 1995. 35.00 (*0-684-19318-3*) S&S Trade.

Steklov Seminar, 1984: Statistics & Control of Stochastic Processes. Ed. by N. V. Krylov et al. xiii, 507p. 1985. 107.95 (*0-387-96101-1*) Spr-Verlag.

Stelaluna - Stellaluna. Janell Cannon. 1996. 15.95 (*84-261-2849-1*) Lectorum Pubns.

Steles. Victor Segalen. Ed. by Michael Taylor. LC 87-80272. (Illus.). 144p. 1987. pap. 12.50 (*0-932499-21-X*) Lapis Pr.

Stell & Maran's Head & Neck Surgery. 3rd ed. Arnold G. Maran et al. (Illus.). 336p. 1993. 80.00 (*0-7506-0916-8*) Buttrwrth-Heinemann.

***Stella.** Asher. Date not set. write for info. (*0-15-201613-9*) HarBrace.

Stella. Peter Wyden. 384p. 1993. pap. 12.95 (*0-385-47179-3*, Anchor NY) Doubleday.

Stella: On the Edge of Popularity. Lauren Lee. LC 93-43917. (J). 1994. 10.95 (*1-879965-08-9*) Polychrome Pub.

Stella: One Woman's Victory over Cancer. Stella Andres & Brad Steiger. 160p. 1986. 14.95 (*0-86700-015-5*, Synergy Bks) P Walsh Pr.

Stella & Roy. Ashley Wolff. LC 92-27005. (Illus.). 32p. (J). (ps up). 1993. pap. 12.99 (*0-525-45081-5*) Dutton Child Bks.

Stella & Roy. Ashley Wolff. (Illus.). 32p. (J). (ps-1). 1996. pap. 4.99 (*0-14-055884-5*, Puff Unicorn) Puffin Bks.

Stella Landry. Robin McCorquodale. 320p. 1993. reprint ed. pap. 8.00 (*0-380-71882-0*) Avon.

Stella Manhattan. Silviano Santiago. Tr. by George Yudice. LC 94-9342. 224p. 1994. text ed. 45.95 (*0-8223-1486-X*); pap. text ed. 14.95 (*0-8223-1498-3*) Duke.

***Stella Natura: Gardening with Cosmic Rhythms.** Ed. by Sherry Wildfeuer. (Illus.). 40p. 1996. 10.95 (*0-938250-45-0*) Bio-Dynamic Farm.

Stella-Natura: Kimberton Hills Agricultural Cal. Ed. by Sherry Wildfeuer. (Gardening with Zodiac & Plants Ser.). (Illus.). 40p. 1995. student ed., pap. 10.95 (*0-938250-44-2*) Bio-Dynamic Farm.

Stella Parton's Country Cookin' Stella Parton. (Illus.). 180p. (Orig.). 1995. pap. 7.95 (*1-55850-473-7*) Adams Media.

Stellaluna. Cannon. 1997. pap. 22.00 (*0-15-201540-X*) HarBrace.

Stellaluna. Janell Cannon. LC 92-16439. (Illus.). 48p. (J). (ps-3). 1993. 16.00 (*0-15-280217-7*) HarBrace.

***Stellaluna: A Pop-Up Book & Mobile.** Janell Cannon. LC 96-47338. 1997. write for info. (*0-15-201530-2*) HarBrace.

Stellaluna: Plush Doll. Cannon. 1994. pap. 13.00 (*0-15-200286-3*) HarBrace.

Stellaluna-Book & Finger Puppet. Janell Cannon. (J). 1996. 21.00 (*0-15-201302-4*) HarBrace.

Stellar Almanac: A History & Tour Guide of the Infernal Kingdom of Hades. P. Scott Hollander. LC 73-94036. 1974. 18.95 (*0-87707-137-3*) Infernal Artists.

Stellar & Circumstellar Astrophysics No. 57. Ed. by George Wallerstein & Alberto Noriega-Crespo. 232p. 1994. 28.00 (*0-937707-76-7*) Astron Soc Pacific.

Stellar Astrophysics. Ed. by Roger J. Tayler. (Graduate Series in Astronomy). (Illus.). 368p. 1992. 152.00 (*0-7503-0200-3*) IOP Pub.

Stellar Atmospheres: Beyond Classical Models. Ed. by Lucio Crivellari et al. (C). 1991. lib. bdg. 186.00 (*0-7923-1343-7*) Kluwer Ac.

Stellar Attraction. Eugenia Riley. (Temptation Ser.: No. 391). 1992. mass mkt. 2.99 (*0-373-25491-1*, 1-25491-1) Harlequin Bks.

Stellar Attractions: Replacement Set. 5th ed. Kenton E. Ross. (BA-Accounting-First Year Ser.). 1992. 411.95 (*0-538-60649-5*) S-W Pub.

Stellar Attractions: Simplified Pegboard Payroll. 5th ed. Kenton E. Ross. (BA-Accounting-First Year Ser.). 1992. 26.95 (*0-538-60647-9*) S-W Pub.

Stellar Cable Company -- Computerized Bill. 2nd ed. Taylor. (BB - Record Keeping I Ser.). 1990. pap. 20.95 (*0-538-60088-8*) S-W Pub.

Stellar Complexes, Open Clusters & Associations, Vol. 7. Yu. N. Efremov. (Soviet Scientific Reviews Ser.: Vol. 7, Pt. 2). 82p. 1989. pap. text ed. 75.00 (*3-7186-4926-8*) Gordon & Breach.

Stellar Dynamics. Ivan R. King. 1998. 38.00 (*0-935702-39-3*) Univ Sci Bks.

Stellar Evolution. Amos Harpaz. LC 93-38857. (Illus.). 272p. 1994. text ed. 44.00 (*1-56881-012-1*) AK Peters.

Stellar Evolution. 2nd ed. A. J. Meadows. 1978. text ed. 87.00 (*0-08-021668-4*, Pub. by Pergamon Repr UK) Franklin.

Stellar Healing: Astrological Predisposition, Diagnosis & Treatment of Disease. C. C. Zain. (Brotherhood of Light Home Study Ser.: Course 16). (Illus.). 1976. pap. 15.95 (*0-87887-355-4*) Church of Light.

Stellar Instability & Evolution: Proceedings of the International Astronomical Union Symposium, No. 59, Mount Stromlo, Canberra, Australia, Aug. 16-18, 1973. International Astronomical Union Staff. Ed. by P. Ledoux et al. LC 74-80520. 200p. 1974. pap. text ed. 70.50 (*90-277-0480-5*); lib. bdg. 100.50 (*90-277-0479-1*) Kluwer Ac.

Stellar Interiors: Physical Principles, Structure & Evolution. Carl J. Hansen & Steven D. Kawaler. LC 93-27498. (Astronomy & Astrophysics Library). (Illus.). xiii, 445p. 1995. 49.95 incl. 3.5 hd (*0-387-94138-X*) Spr-Verlag.

Stellar Jets & Bipolar Outflows: Proceedings of the Sixth International Workshop of the Astronomical Observatory of Capodimonte (OAC 6), Held at Capri, Italy, September 18-21, 1991. Ed. by L. Errico. LC 93-33131. (Astrophysics & Space Science Library). 448p. (C). 1993. lib. bdg. 214.50 (*0-7923-2521-4*) Kluwer Ac.

Stellar Magnitude to Zwitter Ion see Encyclopaedic Dictionary of Physics

Stellar Man. John Baines. Ed. by Judith Hipskind. Tr. by Margaret L. Nunez from SPA. LC 84-48085. (Hermetic Philosophy Ser.: Bk. 2). (Illus.). 288p. (Orig.). 1985. pap. 9.95 (*0-87542-026-5*) J Baines Inst.

Stellar Missiles. Repp. 5.00 (*0-686-00483-3*); pap. 2.00 (*0-686-00484-1*) Fantasy Pub Co.

Stellar Nucleosynthesis. Ed. by Cesare Chiosi & Alvio Renzini. 1984. lib. bdg. 153.50 (*90-277-1729-X*) Kluwer Ac.

Stellar Paths: Photographic Astrometry with Long-Focus Instruments. Peter Van de Kamp. xix, 149p. 1981. lib. bdg. 82.50 (*90-277-1256-5*) Kluwer Ac.

Stellar Photometry - Current Techniques & Future Developments. C. J. Butler & I. Elliott. (Illus.). 370p. (C). 1994. text ed. 69.95 (*0-521-41866-6*) Cambridge U Pr.

Stellar Populations. Ed. by C. A. Norman et al. (Space Telescope Science Institute Symposium Ser.: No. 1). 270p. 1987. text ed. 64.95 (*0-521-33380-6*) Cambridge U Pr.

Stellar Populations: Proceedings of the 164th Symposium of the International Astronomical Union, held in The Hague, The Netherlands, August 15-19, 1994. Ed. by P. C. van der Kruit & G. Gilmore. (International Astronomical Union Symposia Ser.). 496p. (C). 1995. lib. bdg. 174.00 (*0-7923-3537-6*) Kluwer Ac.

Stellar Populations of Galaxies: Proceedings of the 149th Symposium of the International Astronomical Union, Held in Angro dos Reis, Brazil, August 5-9, 1991. Ed. by B. Barbuy. (International Astronomical Union Symposia Ser.). 540p. (C). 1992. pap. text ed. 94.00 (*0-7923-1699-1*); lib. bdg. 188.00 (*0-7923-1698-3*) Kluwer Ac.

Stellar Pulsation. Ed. by A. N. Cox et al. (Lecture Notes in Physics Ser.: Vol. 274). xii, 422p. 1987. 59.95 (*0-387-17668-3*) Spr-Verlag.

Stellar Radial Velocities. Ed. by A. G. Davis Philip & D. W. Latham. (IAU Colloquium Ser.: No. 88). 1985. 31.00 (*0-933485-01-8*); pap. 32.00 (*0-933485-00-X*) L Davis Pr.

Stellar Ranger. Steve Perry. 224p. (Orig.). 1994. mass mkt. 4.99 (*0-380-77301-5*, AvoNova) Avon.

***Stellar Remnants, Vol. 199.** Steven D. Kawaler et al. LC 96-45985. (SAAS-Fee Advanced Course 25 Lecture Notes). 1996. 79.00 (*3-540-61520-2*) Spr-Verlag.

Stellar Structure & Evolution. Rudolph Kippenhahn & A. Weigert. (Astronomy & Astrophysics Library). (Illus.). xvi, 468p. 1991. 54.50 (*0-387-50211-4*) Spr-Verlag.

Stellar Structure & Evolution. Rudolph Kippenhahn & A. Weigert. LC 94-19141. (Astronomy & Astrophysics Library). 1996. 49.95 (*0-387-58013-1*) Spr-Verlag.

Stellar Surface Structure: Proceedings of the 176th Symposium of the International Astronomical Union, Held in Vienna, Austria, October 9-13, 1995. Ed. by Klaus G. Strassmeier & Jeffrey L. Linsky. 598p. 1996. lib. bdg. 199.00 (*0-7923-4026-4*) Kluwer Ac.

Stellar Theology & Masonic Astronomy. Robert H. Brown. 120p. 1993. pap. 16.95 (*1-56459-357-6*) Kessinger Pub.

Stellar Theology & Masonic Astronomy. Robert H. Brown. 117p. 1969. reprint ed. spiral bd. 12.00 (*0-7873-1222-3*) Hlth Research.

Stellar Turbulence: Proceedings of Colloquium 51 of the International Astronomical Union, Held at the University of Western Ontario, London, Ontario, Canada, August 27-30, 1979. Ed. by David F. Gray. (Lecture Notes in Physics Ser.: Vol. 114). 308p. 1980. pap. 26.00 (*3-540-09737-6*) Spr-Verlag.

Stellar Twenty-Eight Constellation Game. Comlit Inc. Staff. (C). 1995. pap. text ed. 25.14 (*0-8403-8189-1*) Kendall-Hunt.

Stellarian. Alice Morrey-Bailey. LC 86-81777. 158p. 1986. 10.98 (*0-88290-279-2*) Horizon Utah.

Stellas & Stratocasters. Willie G. Moseley. (Illus.). 292p. 1994. pap. 19.95 (*0-7935-3492-5*, HL00330115) H Leonard.

Stellas & Stratocasters. Willie G. Moseley. 292p. pap. 19.95 (*1-884883-00-1*) Vintage Guitar.

Stella's Bull. Frances Arrington. LC 93-29068. (Illus.). (J). 1994. 14.95 (*0-395-67345-3*) HM.

***Stella's Story: The Last.** Ann Hodgman. mass mkt. 3.50 (*0-06-106370-3*, Harp PBks) HarpC.

Stellen, Legen und Setzen. Sigrid S. Hildebrand & Eckart Hildebrand. Ed. by Josef Rohrer. (Illus.). 80p. (Orig.). (GER.). (YA). (gr. 7 up). 1990. Incls. cass. tape. 22.00 incl. audio (*0-939990-65-2*) Intl Linguistics.

Steller Ranger: Lone Star. Steve Perry. (Steller Ranger Ser.). 224p. (Orig.). 1995. mass mkt. 4.99 (*0-380-77302-3*) Avon.

Stello. Alfred De Vigny. (FRE.). 1984. pap. 11.95 (*0-7859-3050-7*) Fr & Eur.

Stello. Alfred De Vigny. Ed. by Sylvie Germain. Bd. with Consultations du Docteur Noir.; Daphne. (Class. Garnier Ser.). Set pap. 22.95 (*0-685-37142-5*) Fr & Eur.

***Stello.** unabridged ed. Alfred D. Vigny. (FRE.). Date not set. reprint ed. pap. 7.95 (*2-87714-344-9*, Pub. by Bookking Intl FR) Distribks Inc.

Stello: A Session with Doctor Noir. Alfred De Vigny. Tr. by Irving Massey. LC 68-48328. 216p. reprint ed. pap. 61.60 (*0-317-20719-9*, 2023828) Bks Demand.

Stellung des Alexander Von Aphrodisias Zur Aristotelischen Schlublehre. Georges Volait. 99p. 1975. reprint ed. write for info. (*3-487-05635-6*) G Olms Pubs.

***Stellung des Elohisten Zur Kanaanaischen Religion.** 2nd ed. Karl Jaros. (Orbis Biblicus et Orientalis Ser.: Vol. 4). 1982. 58.50 (*3-7278-0276-6*) Eisenbrauns.

Stellwagen Bank: A Guide to the Whales, Sea Birds, & Marine Life of the Stellwagen Bank National Marine Sanctuary. Nathalie Ward. LC 94-31840. (Illus.). 240p. 1995. pap. 17.95 (*0-89272-336-X*) Down East.

Stem Cell Proliferation & Differentiation. C. A. Macken et al. (Lecture Notes in Biomathematics Ser.: Vol. 76). viii, 113p. 1988. 31.95 (*0-387-50183-5*) Spr-Verlag.

Stem Cells. Ed. by C. S. Potten. (Illus.). 496p. 1996. boxed 99.95 (*0-12-563455-2*) Acad Pr.

Stem Cells & Tissue Homeostasis. Ed. by Brian I. Lord et al. LC 77-80844. (Symposium of the British Society for Cell Biology Ser.: No. 2). 376p. reprint ed. pap. 107.20 (*0-685-15671-0*, 2027336) Bks Demand.

Stem Dictionary of the English Language. John Kennedy. 1971. reprint ed. 51.00 (*1-55888-227-8*) Omnigraphics Inc.

Stem Doctor. Anthony D. Chant. (C). 1989. 45.00 (*0-89771-933-6*, Pub. by A Chant UK) St Mut.

Stem of Jesse: Costs of Community at a 1960s Southern School. Will D. Campbell. LC 94-25708. 1994. 25.00 (*0-86554-449-2*, MUP/H356) Mercer Univ Pr.

Stem Vocabulary of the Navaho Language, 2 vols., Set. Berard Haile. LC 73-15403. (NAV.). reprint ed. 105.00 (*0-404-11241-2*) AMS Pr.

Stemming Middle-Class Decline: The Challenges to Economic Development Planning. Nancey G. Leigh. LC 94-18279. 236p. (C). 1994. pap. text ed. 14.95 (*0-88285-149-7*) Ctr Urban Pol Res.

Stemming the Tide: Controlling Introductions of Nonindigenous Species by Ships' Ballast Water. National Research Council Staff. 160p. (C). 1996. text ed. 39.95 (*0-309-05537-7*) Natl Acad Pr.

***Stemming the Tide of Juvenile Violence: A Legislator's Guide to Comprehensive Juvenile Justice.** 1996. 20.00 (*0-614-21758-X*, 9375) Natl Conf State Legis.

***Stemmons Family in America.** John D. Stemmons. 350p. 1996. lib. bdg. 54.95 (*0-9632139-1-1*) Stemmons.

Stemware Identification: Featuring Cordials with Values: 1920s-1960s. Gene Florence. (Illus.). 160p. 1996. 24.95 (*0-89145-738-0*, 4731) Collector Bks.

***Stemware in the 20th Century.** 1997. pap. 24.95 (*0-676-60084-0*) Random.

Sten. Allan Cole & Chris Bunch. (Military Science Fiction Promotion Ser.). 1984. mass mkt. 5.99 (*0-345-32460-9*, Del Rey) Ballantine.

Sten Screen: Making & Using a Low-Cost Printing Process. I. McLaren. 20p. (Orig.). 1983. pap. 9.50 (*1-85339-048-8*, Pub. by Intermed Tech UK) Women Ink.

***Stenberg Brothers: Constructing a Revolution in Soviet Design.** Christopher Mount. (Illus.). 96p. (Orig.). 1997. pap. 19.95 (*0-87070-051-0*, 0-8109-6173-3) Mus of Modern Art.

Stencil. (Five-Minute Art Ideas Ser.). (Illus.). 24p. (Orig.). (J). (ps up). 1995. pap. 6.95 (*1-57102-060-8*, Ideals Child) Hambleton-Hill.

Stencil Book. Louise Drayton & Jane Thomson. (Illus.). 1994. 14.95 (*1-56458-665-0*) DK Pub Inc.

Stencil Book. Amelia St. George & Penny David. (Illus.). 128p. 1989. pap. 25.95 (*0-525-48461-2*, Dutton) NAL-Dutton.

Stencil Collection. Jocasta Innes & Stewart Walton. (Illus.). 208p. 1995. pap. 29.95 (*1-85410-366-0*, Pub. by Aurum Pr UK) London Brdge.

Stencil Fun. Ray Gibson. (How to Make Ser.). (Illus.). 32p. (J). (gr. 2-6). 1996. pap. 5.95 (*0-7460-2075-9*, Usborne) EDC.

Stencil It! Sandra Buckingham. (Illus.). 64p. (J). 1993. pap. 9.95 (*0-921820-73-9*, Pub. by Camden Hse CN); lib. bdg. 17.95 (*0-921820-75-5*, Pub. by Camden Hse CN) Firefly Bks Ltd.

Stencil It! Book & Kit. 1993. 27.95 (*0-8069-0531-X*) Sterling.

Stencil It! Over 100 Step-by-Step Projects. Sally Walton & Stewart Walton. (Illus.). 80p. (Orig.). 1995. pap. 9.95 (*0-8069-0347-3*) Sterling.

Stencil Source Book: Over Two Hundred Designs to Make Stencils for All Around the House. Patricia Meehan. (Illus.). 144p. 1994. 22.95 (*0-89134-586-8*, North Lght Bks) F & W Pubns Inc.

Stencil Source Book 2, Vol. 2. Patricia Meehan. (Illus.). 144p. 1995. 22.99 (*0-89134-695-3*, North Lght Bks) F & W Pubns Inc.

Stencil Style: Ideas & Projects to Transform Your Home. Jocelyn K. Holding. (Illus.). 160p. 1996. pap. 16.95 (*0-7063-7434-7*, Pub. by Ward Lock UK) Sterling.

Stenciled House. Lynn Le Grice. (Illus.). 176p. 1995. pap. 14.95 (*0-7894-0014-6*) DK Pub Inc.

Stenciled Quilts: Techniques, Patterns & Projects. Marie M. Sturmer. 1992. 22.00 (*0-8446-6638-6*) Peter Smith.

Stenciled Quilts: Techniques, Patterns & Projects. Marie M. Sturmer. (Needlecraft Ser.). (Illus.). 168p. 1991. reprint ed. pap. 9.95 (*0-486-26717-2*) Dover.

Stenciled Strawberry Cookbook: Patterns for Fine Dining. Junior League of Albany, N. Y., Inc. Staff. (Illus.). 320p. 1985. spiral bd. 16.95 (*0-9614012-0-6*) Jr League Albany Pubns.

Stencilets. Christopher Jolly. (Illus.). (J). (ps-1). 1994. 14.95 (*1-870946-35-9*, Pub. by Jolly Lrning UK) Am Intl Dist.

***Stenciling.** Sacha Cohen & Isabel Stanley. (The Inspirations Ser.). (Illus.). 96p. 1997. 12.95 (*1-85967-429-1*, Lorenz Bks) Anness Pub.

Stenciling. Jamie Sapsford. (Start a Craft Ser.). 1994. 7.98 (*0-7858-0057-3*) Bk Sales Inc.

Stenciling Etc. Cy DeCosse Incorporated Staff. LC 96-15849. (Creative Touches Ser.). (Illus.). 64p. 1996. pap. 9.95 (*0-86573-995-1*) Cowles Creative.

Stenciling Made Easy. 1996. 12.99 (*0-517-14293-7*) Random Hse Value.

***Stenciling on a Grand Scale: Using Simple Stencils to Create Visual Magic.** Sandra Buckingham. 1997. 35.00 (*1-55209-143-0*) Firefly Bks Ltd.

An Asterisk (*) at the beginning of an entry indicates that the title is appearing in BIP for the first time.

Stenciling Techniques: A Complete Guide to Traditional & Contemporary Designs For the Home. Jane Gauss. (Illus.). 144p. 1995. pap. 24.95 (*0-8230-4992-2*) Watsn-Guptill.

Stencilled Ornament & Illustration. Compiled by Dorothy Abbe. pap. 15.00 (*0-89073-064-4*) Boston Public Lib.

***Stencilling.** Joanne Malone. 1997. write for info. (*0-8069-6139-2*) Sterling.

Stencilling. Gillie Spargo. (Illus.). 107p. 1995. pap. write for info. (*1-57215-188-9*) World Pubns.

Stencilling. James Ward. (Pleasures of Home Ser.). (Illus.). 128p. 1997. 21.95 (*0-304-34627-6*, Pub. by Cassell UK) Sterling.

Stencilling: A Harrowsmith Guide. Sandra Buckingham. Ed. by Merilyn S. Mohr. (Illus.). 156p. (Orig.). 1989. pap. 19.95 (*0-920656-09-9*, Pub. by Camden Hse CN) Firefly Bks Ltd.

Stencilling: A Practical & Inspirational Guide to Decorative Ideas for Interiors, Furnishings, Clothing, Stationery & More. Joanne Malone. LC 92-38336. (Illus.). 132p. 1993. pap. 14.95 (*0-8069-0360-0*) Sterling.

Stencilling: How to Create Clever Paint Effects on Wood, Ceramics, Paper, & Fabric - 12 Projects. Kathy F. Ritchie. 1995. pap. 15.95 (*0-8050-4267-9*) H Holt & Co.

Stencilling: Projects, Techniques Over 30 Stencil Designs. Lynne Robinson & Richard Lowther. (Illus.). 102p. 1995. pap. 22.95 (*1-57076-028-4*, Trafalgar Sq Pub) Trafalgar.

***Stencilling on Fabric.** Wren Loasby. Date not set. write for info. (*0-8069-3816-1*) Sterling.

Stencilling on Fabric: Patterns & Possibilities. Wren Loasby. LC 96-11968. (Illus.). 128p. 1996. 24.95 (*0-8069-3868-4*) Sterling.

Stencils. Frank Nichols. (J). 1989. pap. 3.99 (*0-85953-048-5*) Childs Play.

***Stendahl.** Jonathan Keates. LC 96-53977. 478p. 1997. 28.00 (*0-7867-0412-8*) Carroll & Graf.

Stendhal. Jonathan Keates. Date not set. pap. 10.99 (*0-7493-2475-9*) Heinemann.

Stendhal. Andrew Paton. 1972. 59.95 (*0-8490-1124-8*) Gordon Pr.

Stendhal: "The Red & the Black" Stirling Haig. (Landmarks of World Literature Ser.). (Illus.). 128p. (C). 1989. text ed. 29.95 (*0-521-34189-2*); pap. text ed. 11.95 (*0-521-34982-6*) Cambridge U Pr.

Stendhal: Concordances d'Armance. Ed. by Jean-Jaques Hamm & Gregory Lessard. vi, 576p. write for info. (*0-318-71993-2*) G Olms Pubs.

Stendhal: The Red & the Black & the Charterhouse of Parma. Intro. by Roger Pearson. LC 93-30285. (Modern Literatures in Perspective Ser.). (C). 1994. text ed. 56.50 (*0-582-09617-0*, 76705, Pub. by Longman UK) Longman.

Stendhal: The Red & the Black & the Charterhouse of Parma. Intro. by Roger Pearson. LC 93-30285. (Modern Literatures in Perspective Ser.). (C). 1995. pap. text ed. 25.50 (*0-582-09616-2*, 76704, Pub. by Longman UK) Longman.

Stendhal & Romantic Esthetics. Ed. by Emile J. Talbot. LC 85-80420. (French Forum Monographs: No. 61). 181p. (Orig.). 1985. pap. 12.95 (*0-917058-62-3*) French Forum.

Stendhal As Economist Vol. 7. Alfred Bornemann. LC 93-37343. (American University Studies: No. XVI). 156p. (C). 1994. text ed. 36.95 (*0-8204-1546-4*) P Lang Pubng.

Stendhal Bicentennial Papers. Ed. by Avriel H. Goldberger. LC 86-33607. (Contributions to the Study of World Literature Ser.: No. 19). 117p. 1987. text ed. 59.95 (*0-313-25875-9*, GST/, Greenwood Pr) Greenwood.

Stendhal Fichier. M. Francois. 1994. 365.00 (*0-7838-2306-1*, GK Hall) Thorndike Pr.

Stendhal's Italy: Themes of Political & Religious Satire. Greaves. 240p. 1995. text ed. 59.95 (*0-85989-446-0*, Pub. by Univ Exeter Pr UK) Northwestern U Pr.

Stendhal's The Red & the Black see Modern Critical Interpretations

Stengel: His Life & Times. Robert W. Creamer. LC 95-40143. 349p. 1996. pap. 15.00 (*0-8032-6367-8*, Bison Books) U of Nebr Pr.

Stengrow's Dad: A Novel. Elia Katz. 265p. (Orig.). 1995. pap. 11.00 (*1-881053-02-4*) Wavecrest Bks.

Steno on Muscles: Introduction, Texts & Translation. Troels Kardel et al. LC 93-73911. (Transactions Ser.: Vol. 84, Pt. 1). (Illus.). 252p. (C). 1994. pap. 30.00 (*0-87169-841-2*, T841-KAT) Am Philos.

Steno Tutorial User Manual. Beverly L. Ritter & George P. Andrews. (Realtime Machine Shorthand Ser.). (C). 1992. pap. text ed. 6.50 (*0-938643-43-6*) Stenotype Educ.

Stenographer. Jack Rudman. (Career Examination Ser.: C-766). 1994. pap. 19.95 (*0-8373-0766-X*) Nat Learn.

Stenographer (Law) Jack Rudman. (Career Examination Ser.: C-1036). 1994. pap. 23.95 (*0-8373-1036-9*) Nat Learn.

Stenographer-Secretary. Jack Rudman. (Career Examination Ser.: C-2559). 1994. pap. 23.95 (*0-8373-2559-5*) Nat Learn.

Stenographer-Typist. Jack Rudman. (Career Examination Ser.: C-1966). 1994. pap. 19.95 (*0-8373-1966-8*) Nat Learn.

Stenographer-Typist GS1-4. Jack Rudman. (Career Examination Ser.: C-767). 1994. pap. 19.95 (*0-8373-0767-8*) Nat Learn.

Stenographer-Typist GS5-7. Jack Rudman. (Career Examination Ser.: C-768). 1994. pap. 23.95 (*0-8373-0768-6*) Nat Learn.

Stenographer's Breakfast. Frances McCue. LC 91-41839. (Barnard New Women Poets Ser.). 96p. 1992. pap. 12.00 (*0-8070-6817-9*) Beacon Pr.

Stenographic Secretary. Jack Rudman. (Career Examination Ser.: C-1653). 1994. pap. 23.95 (*0-8373-1653-7*) Nat Learn.

Stenographic Specialist. Jack Rudman. (Career Examination Ser.: C-2453). 1994. pap. 23.95 (*0-8373-2453-X*) Nat Learn.

Stenographic/Secretarial Associate. Jack Rudman. (Career Examination Ser.: C-2452). 1994. pap. 23.95 (*0-8373-2452-1*) Nat Learn.

Stenographische Protokolle, 71 vols., Set. (GER.). 1992. write for info. incl. fiche (*0-318-70567-2*) G Olms Pubs.

Stenography & Typewriting (Gregg & Pitman), Sr. H. S. Jack Rudman. (Teachers License Examination Ser.: T-60). 1994. pap. 27.95 (*0-8373-8060-X*) Nat Learn.

Stenoscript ABC Shorthand. (C). 1989. teacher ed. 5.80 (*1-56118-450-0*) Paradigm MN.

Stenosis of the Cervical Spine: Causes, Diagnosis, & Treatment. V. Denaro. (Illus.). 225p. 1991. 225.00 (*0-387-53328-1*) Spr-Verlag.

Stenotype Text Entry. George P. Andrews. (Realtime Machine Shorthand Ser.). 15p. (C). 1993. student ed., pap. text ed. 8.00 incl. audio (*0-938643-61-4*) Stenotype Educ.

Stenotype Text Entry. George P. Andrews & Beverly L. Ritter. 15p. (C). 1993. pap. text ed. 4.00 (*0-938643-59-2*) Stenotype Educ.

Stenotype Text Entry: FasText Edition. George P. Andrews & Beverly L. Ritter. (Realtime Machine Shorthand Ser.). 196p. (Orig.). (C). 1992. pap. text ed. 29.00 (*0-938643-56-8*) Stenotype Educ.

Stenotype Text Entry: Rapidtext Edition. George P. Andrews & Beverly L. Ritter. 214p. (Orig.). (C). 1993. pap. text ed. 29.00 (*0-938643-57-6*) Stenotype Educ.

Stenotype Text Entry: RapidWrite Edition. George P. Andrews & Beverly L Ritter. 234p. (Orig.). (C). 1994. pap. text ed. 29.00 (*0-938643-58-4*) Stenotype Educ.

Stenotype Text Entry Package. George P. Andrews & Beverly L. Ritter. (Realtime Machine Shorthand Ser.). 234p. (Orig.). (C). 1993. pap. text ed. 33.00 incl. audio (*0-938643-62-2*) Stenotype Educ.

Stenotype Theory for the Professional Scopist. Jacqueline A. Nash & Joann Kinkaid. Ed. by Beverly L. Ritter & Patricia J. Rhyne. (Realtime Machine Shorthand Ser.). 218p. (Orig.). (C). 1995. pap. text ed. 25.00 (*0-938643-64-9*) Stenotype Educ.

Stenotype Theory for the Professional Scopist. Beverly L. Ritter & Patricia J. Rhyne. (Realtime Machine Shorthand Ser.). 88p. (Orig.). (C). 1995. teacher ed., pap. text ed. 15.00 (*0-938643-65-7*) Stenotype Educ.

Stenwick Days. R. T. Johnston. (C). 1986. 49.00 (*0-907618-09-X*, Pub. by Orkney Pr UK) St Mut.

***STEP: Towards Open Systems: STEP Fundamentals & Business Benefits.** Kais Al-Timimi & John MacKrell. (Illus.). 130p. (Orig.). 1996. pap. 79.95 (*1-889760-00-5*) CIMdata Inc.

Step Ahead Bk. 1. Michael Walker. 1984. student ed., text ed. 11.44 (*0-201-08223-3*) Addison-Wesley.

Step Ahead, an English Course, Vol. 4. Michael Walker. 1984. pap. 10.75 (*0-201-08233-0*) Addison-Wesley.

Step Ahead of Disaster: A Family Trapped in Divided Czechoslovakia. Eugene Von Teuber. Ed. by Basil Entwistle. (Illus.). 176p. 1993. pap. 7.95 (*1-85239-510-9*) Grosvenor USA.

Step Ahead Sesame Street Flash Cards Colors. Tom Cooke. (Illus.). (J). (ps-3). 1986. pap. 2.60 (*0-307-04982-5*, Golden Books) Western Pub.

Step Ahead Sesame Street Flash Cards Numbers. Tom Brannon. (Illus.). (J). (ps-3). 1986. pap. 3.25 (*0-307-04981-7*, Golden Books) Western Pub.

Step Away. B. J. James. (Desire Ser.: No. 692). 1992. pap. 2.79 (*0-373-05692-3*, 5-05692-4) Harlequin Bks.

Step Back from the Exit: Forty-Five Reasons to Say No to Suicide. Jillayne Arena. LC 95-94711. 1996. pap. text ed. 10.00 (*0-9647340-0-1*) Zebulon Pr.

***Step Back in Time.** Loretta Berner. (Illus.). 72p. 1990. pap. 11.00 (*0-9610250-4-2*) Hist Soc of Long Bch.

Step Beyond: Multi-Media Activities for Learning American History. Muriel M. Branch & Earlene G. Evans. LC 94-37766. 168p. (Orig.). 1995. pap. 34.95 (*1-55570-195-7*) Neal-Schuman.

Step Beyond Your Limits: Expanding Your MI Capaciataies Through the Interpersonal Intelligence. David G. Lazear. (Illus.). 50p. (Orig.). 1996. pap. 25.00 incl. digital audio (*1-56976-048-9*) Zephyr Pr AZ.

Step Beyond Your Limits: Expanding Your MI Capacities Through the Bodily-Kinesthetic Intelligence. David G. Lazear. (Illus.). 50p. (Orig.). 1996. pap. 25.00 incl. digital audio (*1-56976-046-2*) Zephyr Pr AZ.

Step Beyond Your Limits: Expanding Your MI Capacities Through the Intrapersonal Intelligence. David G. Lazear. (Illus.). 50p. (Orig.). 1996. pap. 25.00 incl. digital audio (*1-56976-049-7*) Zephyr Pr AZ.

Step Beyond Your Limits: Expanding Your MI Capacities Through the Logical-Mathematical Intelligence. David G. Lazear. (Illus.). 50p. (Orig.). 1996. pap. 25.00 incl. digital audio (*1-56976-051-9*) Zephyr Pr AZ.

Step Beyond Your Limits: Expanding Your MI Capacities Through the Musical-Rhythmic Intelligence. David G. Lazear. (Illus.). 50p. (Orig.). 1996. pap. 25.00 incl. digital audio (*1-56976-047-0*) Zephyr Pr AZ.

Step Beyond Your Limits: Expanding Your MI Capacities Through the Verbal-Linguistic Intelligence. David G. Lazear. (Illus.). 50p. (Orig.). 1996. pap. 25.00 incl. digital audio (*1-56976-050-0*) Zephyr Pr AZ.

Step Beyond Your Limits: Expanding Your MI Capacities Through the Visual-Spatial Intelligence. David G. Lazear. (Illus.). 50p. (Orig.). 1996. pap. 25.00 incl. digital audio (*1-56976-045-4*) Zephyr Pr AZ.

Step by Step. Sirkka-Liisa Konttinen. LC 89-51011. (Illus.). 144p. (Orig.). 8900. pap. 19.95 (*1-85224-059-8*, Pub. by Bloodaxe Bks UK) Dufour.

Step by Step. A. S. Larmour. 211p. 1986. 50.00 (*0-7212-0736-7*, Pub. by Regency Press UK) St Mut.

Step by Step. Bruce McMillan. LC 87-4195. (Illus.). 28p. (J). (ps-2). 1990. lib. bdg. 15.00 (*0-688-07234-8*) Apple Isl Bks.

***Step by Step.** Marilyn Turner. 256p. 1997. mass mkt. 4.99 (*0-7860-0406-1*, Pinncle Kensgtn) Kensgtn Pub Corp.

Step by Step. Diane Wolkstein. LC 93-14667. (Illus.). 40p. (J). (ps up). 1994. 15.00 (*0-688-10315-4*, Morrow Junior); lib. bdg. 14.93 (*0-688-10316-2*, Morrow Junior) Morrow.

Step by Step: A Complete Movement Education Curriculum from Pre-School to 6th Grade. Sheila Kogan. Ed. by Frank Alexander. (Illus.). 240p. 1982. pap. 17.00 (*0-915256-10-X*) Front Row.

Step-by-Step: A Financial Guide For Your Church. Kermit Braswell. 40p. (Orig.). 1995. pap. 7.95 (*0-687-01119-1*) Abingdon.

Step by Step: A Guide to "A Search for God Book 1" A. R. E. Research Staff. 94p. (Orig.). 1988. pap. 7.95 (*0-87604-229-9*, 339) ARE Pr.

Step by Step: A Guide to Stepfamily Living. Don Martin & Maggie Martin. LC 92-70822. 186p. (Orig.). 1992. pap. text ed. 9.95 (*0-932796-38-9*) Ed Media Corp.

***Step-by-Step: Card Play in No Trumps.** Robert Berthe & Norbert Lebely. 144p. 1997. pap. 16.95 (*0-7134-8051-3*, Pub. by Batsford UK) Trafalgar.

Step by Step: College Writing. 6th ed. Randy DeVillez. 26p. 1995. teacher ed., per. write for info. (*0-7872-0396-3*) Kendall-Hunt.

Step by Step: Container Gardening. Stephanie Donaldson. (Illus.). 96p. 1995. 9.98 (*0-8317-6548-8*) Smithmark.

Step-by-Step: Cooking for Christmas. Smithmark Staff. 1995. 9.98 (*0-8317-3079-X*) Smithmark.

Step-by-Step: Cushions, Covers, Curtains. Smithmark Staff. 1995. 9.98 (*0-8317-1034-9*) Smithmark.

Step by Step: Daily Meditations for Living the 12 Steps. Muriel Zink. 416p. (Orig.). 1991. pap. 10.00 (*0-345-36759-6*, Ballantine Trade) Ballantine.

***Step-by-Step: Deception in Defence.** Barry Rigal. 128p. 1997. pap. 16.95 (*0-7134-7841-1*, Pub. by Batsford UK) Trafalgar.

Step-by-Step: Deceptive Declarer Play. Barry Rigal. 128p. 1996. pap. 16.95 (*0-7134-8008-4*, Pub. by Batsford UK) Trafalgar.

Step by Step: Dried Flowers. Pamela Westland. (Illus.). 96p. 1995. 12.98 (*0-8317-2738-1*) Smithmark.

Step by Step: Eating to Lower Your High Blood Cholesterol. rev. ed. (Illus.). 97p. (C). 1994. pap. text ed. 20.00 (*0-7881-1576-6*) DIANE Pub.

Step-by-Step: Excel for Windows 5.0. Steve Harris. 350p. 1994. pap. 26.95 (*0-7506-1810-8*) Buttrwrth-Heinemann.

Step by Step: Fabulous Fish Dishes. Liz Trigg. (Illus.). 96p. 1995. 9.98 (*0-8317-6546-1*) Smithmark.

Step-by-Step: Fifty Great Party Snacks. Smithmark Staff. 1995. 9.98 (*0-8317-7921-7*) Smithmark.

Step by Step: For the Jewellery Crafts Person. Bud Knackstedt. (Illus.). 230p. 1996. spiral bd. 10.95 (*0-9644569-1-5*) Dane Pub.

Step-by-Step: Giftwrap, Cards, & Decorations. Smithmark Staff. 1995. 9.98 (*0-8317-1036-5*) Smithmark.

Step by Step: Hamburger Magic. Jennie Stacey. (Illus.). 96p. 1995. 9.98 (*0-8317-7699-4*) Smithmark.

Step by Step: How to Actively Ensure the Best Possible Care for Your Aging Relative. Ted Rossi. 192p. 1987. pap. 9.95 (*0-446-38427-5*) Warner Bks.

Step by Step: Irresistible Chocolate. Elizabeth Wolf-Cohen. (Illus.). 96p. 1995. 9.98 (*0-8317-7842-3*) Smithmark.

Step by Step: Low Fat Cookbook. Catherine Atkinson. (Illus.). 96p. 1995. 9.98 (*0-8317-6549-6*) Smithmark.

Step by Step: Low Maintenance Gardening. Peter McHoy. (Illus.). 96p. 1995. 9.98 (*0-8317-6547-X*) Smithmark.

Step by Step: Meditations on Wisdom & Compassion. Maha Ghosananda. LC 91-32829. 81p. (Orig.). 1991. pap. 9.00 (*0-938077-43-0*) Parallax Pr.

Step-by-Step: Nature Craft Projects for Kids. Cecilia Fitzsimons. (Illus.). 96p. (J). (gr. 3-6). 1995. 9.98 (*0-8317-7793-1*) Smithmark.

Step-by-Step: Overcalls. Sally Brock. 128p. 1995. pap. 16.95 (*0-7134-7769-5*, Pub. by Batsford UK) Trafalgar.

Step by Step: Pasta. Maxine Clark. (Illus.). 96p. 1995. 9.98 (*0-8317-6515-1*) Smithmark.

Step-by-Step: Planning the Defence. Raymond Brock. 112p. 1996. pap. 16.95 (*0-7134-7805-5*, Pub. by Batsford UK) Trafalgar.

Step by Step: Quick & Healthy Vegetarian. Annie Nichols. (Illus.). 96p. 1995. 9.98 (*0-8317-7847-4*) Smithmark.

Step by Step: Salads. Carole Handslip. (Illus.). 96p. 1995. 9.98 (*0-8317-6516-X*) Smithmark.

Step by Step: Sandwiches. Carole Handslip. (Illus.). 96p. 1995. 9.98 (*0-8317-6517-8*) Smithmark.

Step-by-Step: Sauces & Marinades. Smithmark Staff. 1995. 9.98 (*0-8317-7922-5*) Smithmark.

Step-by-Step: Signalling. Mark Horton. 144p. 1995. pap. 16.95 (*0-7134-7640-0*, Pub. by Batsford UK) Trafalgar.

Step by Step: Sixteen Steps Toward Legally Sound Sexual Abuse Investigations. Jan Hindman. 44p. 1987. pap. 5.95 (*0-9611034-3-4*) AlexAndria OR.

Step-by-Step: Slam Bidding. Alan Mould. 144p. 1995. 16.95 (*0-7134-7712-1*, Pub. by Batsford UK) Trafalgar.

***Step by Step: The Grilling Cookbook.** Random House Value Publishing Staff. 1997. pap. 8.99 (*0-517-18394-3*) Random Hse Value.

Step by Step: Twenty-Eight Devotionals for Christian Teens. Mark K. Gilroy. 36p. (Orig.). (YA). 1993. pap. 3.25 (*0-8341-1468-2*) Beacon Hill.

Step-by-Step: Victorian Embroidery Design. Smithmark Staff. 1995. 9.98 (*0-8317-7948-9*) Smithmark.

Step by Step: WiordPerfect 6.0, Lotus 1-2-3, dBASE IV, DOS 6.0. Lorraine J. Laby et al. LC 94-17416. (Increasing Your Productivity Ser.). 1994. 27.00 (*0-02-800958-4*) Glencoe.

Step by Step: 15 Energy Savings Projects. large type ed. Tom Tynan. Ed. by Pete Billac. LC 95-72894. (Illus.). 96p. (Orig.). 1996. pap. 9.95 (*0-943629-22-5*) Swan Pub.

Step-by-Step: 50 Low-Calorie Desserts. Smithmark Staff. 1995. 9.98 (*0-8317-7909-8*) Smithmark.

Step-by-Step: 50 Quick & Healthy Pizzas. Smithmark Staff. 1995. 9.98 (*0-8317-7911-X*) Smithmark.

Step-By-Step Across the Pond. Cordell Lindsey. 128p. 1996. pap. 11.00 (*0-8059-3848-6*) Dorrance.

***Step-by-Step Annuals.** Better Homes & Gardens Editors. (Illus.). 132p. 1997. pap. 12.95 (*0-696-20657-9*) Meredith Bks.

Step-by-Step Approach to Using the SAS System for Factor Analysis & Structural Equation Modeling. 588p. (C). 1996. pap. 38.95 (*1-55544-643-4*, BR55129) SAS Inst.

Step-by-Step Approach to Using the SAS System for Univariate & Multivariate Statistics. 568p. (C). 1994. pap. 38.95 (*1-55544-634-5*, BR55072) SAS Inst.

***Step by Step Art of Christmas Crafts.** Jan Eaton. (Art Ser.). (Illus.). 108p. 1996. 10.99 (*1-57215-152-8*, JG1152) World Pubns.

Step-by-Step Art of Christmas Crafts. Whitecap Books Staff. 1995. pap. text ed. 12.95 (*1-55110-214-5*, Pub. by Whitecap Bks CN) Gr Arts Ctr Pub.

Step by Step Art of Decoupage. 1995. pap. text ed. 12.95 (*1-55110-215-3*, Pub. by Whitecap Bks CN) Gr Arts Ctr Pub.

Step by Step Art of Decoupage: How to Use Paper Motifs to Create over 80 Designs. Cheryl Owen. 1995. 14.98 (*0-8317-4996-2*) Smithmark.

Step by Step Art of Dried Flowers. Book Sales, Inc. Staff. 1993. 12.98 (*1-55521-886-5*) Bk Sales Inc.

Step-by-Step Art of Dried Flowers. Ming Veevers-Carter. (Illus.). 124p. 1993. pap. text ed. 12.95 (*1-55110-074-6*, Pub. by Whitecap Bks CN) Gr Arts Ctr Pub.

Step By Step Art of Floral Paper Crafts. Cheryl Owen. 1994. 12.98 (*0-7858-0073-5*) Bk Sales Inc.

Step-by-Step Art of Floral Paper Crafts. Whitecap Books Staff. 1995. pap. text ed. 12.95 (*1-55110-213-7*, Pub. by Whitecap Bks CN) Gr Arts Ctr Pub.

Step-by-Step Art of Flower Arranging. Photos by Neil Sutherland. (Illus.). 124p. 1992. pap. text ed. 12.95 (*1-55110-042-8*, Pub. by Whitecap Bks CN) Gr Arts Ctr Pub.

Step-by-Step Art of Making Jewellery. 1995. pap. text ed. 12.95 (*1-55110-287-0*) Gr Arts Ctr Pub.

Step by Step Art of Making Jewellery. 1995. pap. text ed. 12.95 (*1-55110-227-7*, Pub. by Whitecap Bks CN) Gr Arts Ctr Pub.

Step-by-Step Art of Making Nature Crafts. Whitecap Books Staff. 1995. pap. text ed. 12.95 (*1-55110-210-2*, Pub. by Whitecap Bks CN) Gr Arts Ctr Pub.

Step By Step Art of Making Soft Toys. Cheryl Owen. 1994. 14.98 (*0-7858-0075-1*) Bk Sales Inc.

Step-by-Step Art of Making Soft Toys. Whitecap Books Staff. 1995. pap. text ed. 12.95 (*1-55110-212-9*, Pub. by Whitecap Bks CN) Gr Arts Ctr Pub.

Step By Step Art of Nature Crafts. Pamela Westland. 1994. 14.98 (*0-7858-0069-7*) Bk Sales Inc.

Step-by-Step Art of Origami. Whitecap Books Staff. 1995. pap. 12.95 (*1-55110-243-9*, Pub. by Whitecap Bks CN) Gr Arts Ctr Pub.

Step-By-Step Art of Origami. Whitecap Books Staff. 1995. pap. 12.95 (*1-55110-289-7*, Pub. by Whitecap Bks CN) Gr Arts Ctr Pub.

Step-by-Step Art of Paint Techniques. David Japp. (Illus.). 107p. 1995. write for info. (*1-57215-190-0*) World Pubns.

Step-by-Step Art of Paint Techniques. Whitecap Books Staff. 1995. pap. text ed. 12.95 (*1-55110-225-0*, Pub. by Whitecap Bks CN) Gr Arts Ctr Pub.

Step-By-Step Art of Paper Crafts. Whitecap Books Staff. 1995. pap. 12.95 (*1-55110-244-7*, Pub. by Whitecap Bks CN) Gr Arts Ctr Pub.

Step by Step Art of Papercrafts. Cheryl Owen. 1993. 12.98 (*1-55521-884-9*) Bk Sales Inc.

Step by Step Art of Papier Mache. Book Sales, Inc. Staff. 1993. 12.98 (*1-55521-885-7*) Bk Sales Inc.

Step-by-Step Art of Papier Mache. Whitecap Books Staff. 1995. pap. text ed. 12.95 (*1-55110-226-9*, Pub. by Whitecap Bks CN) Gr Arts Ctr Pub.

Step by Step Art of Ribbon Crafts. Anita Harrison. 1994. 14.98 (*0-7858-0068-9*) Bk Sales Inc.

Step-by-Step Art of Ribbon Crafts. Whitecap Books Staff. 1995. pap. text ed. 12.95 (*1-55110-209-9*, Pub. by Whitecap Bks CN) Gr Arts Ctr Pub.

Step-by-Step Art of Silk Painting. 1995. pap. text ed. 12.95 (*1-55110-229-3*, Pub. by Whitecap Bks CN) Gr Arts Ctr Pub.

Step-by-Step Art of Silk Painting. Whitecraft Books Staff. 1995. pap. 12.95 (*1-55110-293-5*, Pub. by Whitecap Bks CN) Gr Arts Ctr Pub.

Step-by-Step Art of Stencilling. 1995. pap. text ed. 12.95 (*1-55110-228-5*, Pub. by Whitecap Bks CN) Gr Arts Ctr Pub.

Step-by-Step Art of Table Decorating. Whitecap Books Staff. 1995. pap. text ed. 12.95 (*1-55110-211-0*, Pub. by Whitecap Bks CN) Gr Arts Ctr Pub.

Step-by-Step Art School. Patricia Monahan et al. LC 96-26488. 1996. write for info. (*1-57145-034-3*) Thunder Bay CA.

Step-by-Step Art School: Ceramics. Geraldine Christy. 1991. 14.98 (*1-55521-739-7*) Bk Sales Inc.

Step by Step Art School: Drawing. Jenny Rodwell. 1987. 12.98 (*0-671-08906-4*) S&S Trade.

S

Step by Step Art School: Watercolor. Patricia Monahan. 1987. 12.98 (*0-671-08907-2*) S&S Trade.

Step-by-Step Art School Landscape. Jack Buchan. 1993. 14.98 (*1-55521-828-8*) Bk Sales Inc.

Step-by-Step Art School Pastels. Geraldine Christy. 1992. 14.98 (*1-55521-759-1*) Bk Sales Inc.

Step-by-Step Art School Still Life. Jonathan Baker. 1993. 14.98 (*1-55521-829-6*) Bk Sales Inc.

Step by Step Ballet Class: The Official Illustrated Guide. Royal Academy of Dancing Staff. (Illus.). 144p. 1994. pap. 12.95 (*0-8092-3499-8*) Contemp Bks.

Step-by-Step Basketball Fundamentals for the Player & Coach. John Scott. (Illus.). 200p. 1988. pap. 17.00 (*0-13-846668-8*) P-H.

Step-by-Step Bead Stringing: A Complete Illustrated Professional Approach. Ruth F. Poris. (Illus.). 45p. 1985. pap. 7.99 (*0-9616422-1-1*) Golden Hands Pr.

Step-by-Step Book about Budgerigars. George A. Radtke. (Step-by-Step Ser.). (Illus.). 63p. (Orig.). 1987. pap. 5.95 (*0-86622-463-7*, SK-002) TFH Pubns.

Step by Step Book about Canaries. A. Barrie. (Step-by-Step Ser.). (Illus.). 64p. 1987. 5.95 (*0-86622-461-0*, SK-004) TFH Pubns.

Step-by-Step Book about Chameleons. Robert Anderson. (Illus.). 64p. 1989. pap. 5.95 (*0-86622-488-2*, SK-038) TFH Pubns.

S

Step-by-Step Book about Chinchillas. H. Kuhnder. (Step-by-Step Ser.). (Illus.). 64p. (Orig.). 1987. pap. 5.95 (*0-86622-452-1*, SK-006) TFH Pubns.

Step by Step Book about Cockatiels. A. Barrie. (Step-by-Step Ser.). (Illus.). 64p. (Orig.). 1987. pap. 5.95 (*0-86622-453-X*, SK-007) TFH Pubns.

Step-by-Step Book about Dwarf Hamsters. Chris Henwood. (Illus.). 50p. 1989. pap. 5.95 (*0-86622-479-3*, SK-040) TFH Pubns.

Step by Step Book about Ferrets. J. Field & Mary Field. (Step-by-Step Ser.). (Illus.). 64p. 1987. 5.95 (*0-86622-462-9*, SK-009) TFH Pubns.

Step-by-Step Book about Finches. Elaine Radford. (Illus.). 64p. 1989. pap. 5.95 (*0-86622-466-1*, SK-010) TFH Pubns.

Step-by-Step Book about Gerbils. Patrick Bradley & Heather Pence. (Step-by-Step Ser.). (Illus.). 64p. (Orig.). 1987. pap. 5.95 (*0-86622-467-X*, SK-011) TFH Pubns.

Step by Step Book about Goldfish. J. C. Harris. (Step-by-Step Ser.). (Illus.). 64p. (Orig.). 1987. pap. 5.95 (*0-86622-457-2*, SK-012) TFH Pubns.

Step-by-Step Book about Guinea Pigs. A. Barrie. (Step-by-Step Ser.). (Illus.). 64p. (Orig.). 1987. pap. 5.95 (*0-86622-450-5*, SK-013) TFH Pubns.

Step-by-Step Book about Guppies. Jack C. Harris. (Step-by-Step Ser.). (Illus.). 64p. (YA). (gr. 9-12). 1988. pap. 5.95 (*0-86622-464-5*, SK-035) TFH Pubns.

Step by Step Book about Hamsters. A. Barrie. (Step-by-Step Ser.). (Illus.). 64p. 1987. pap. 5.95 (*0-86622-458-0*, SK-014) TFH Pubns.

Step-by-Step Book about Housebreaking Your Puppy. Jack C. Harris. (Illus.). 64p. 1989. pap. 5.95 (*0-86622-974-4*, SK-025) TFH Pubns.

Step by Step Book about Iguanas. Jack C. Harris. (Step-by-Step Ser.). (Illus.). 64p. 1990. pap. 5.95 (*0-86622-459-9*, SK-015) TFH Pubns.

Step-by-Step Book about Lizards. (Illus.). 64p. 1989. pap. 5.95 (*0-86622-969-8*, SK-032) TFH Pubns.

Step-by-Step Book about Lovebirds. A. Weston. (Step-by-Step Ser.). (Illus.). 64p. (YA). (gr. 9-12). 1988. pap. 5.95 (*0-86622-456-4*, SK-016) TFH Pubns.

Step-by-Step Book about Marine Aquarium Set Up. Cliff W. Emmens. (Step-by-Step Ser.). 1989. pap. 5.95 (*0-86622-469-6*, SK-037) TFH Pubns.

Step-by-Step Book about Our First Aquarium. Anmarie Barrie. (Step-by-Step Ser.). (Illus.). 64p. (J). 1987. 5.95 (*0-86622-454-8*, SK003) TFH Pubns.

Step-by-Step Book about Parrots. Elaine Radford. (Step-by-Step Ser.). (Illus.). 64p. (YA). (gr. 9-12). 1988. pap. 5.95 (*0-8622-484-X*, SK-031) TFH Pubns.

Step-by-Step Book about Rabbits. A. Barrie. (Step-by-Step Ser.). (Illus.). 64p. 1987. pap. 5.95 (*0-86622-475-0*, SK-001) TFH Pubns.

Step-by Step Book about Rottweilers. Heinrich Von Beine. (Step-by-Step Ser.). (Illus.). 64p. 1987. 5.95 (*0-86622-455-6*, SK005) TFH Pubns.

Step by Step Book about Seahorses. Peter Giwojna. (Illus.). 64p. 1989. pap. 5.95 (*0-86622-485-8*, SK041) TFH Pubns.

Step-by-Step Book about Setting up Freshwater Aquarium. Cliff W. Emmens. (Step-by-Step Ser.). (Illus.). 64p. 1987. pap. 5.95 (*0-86622-961-2*, SK033) TFH Pubns.

Step-by-Step Book about Siamese Cats. Marge Naples. (Step-by-Step Ser.). (Illus.). 64p. (YA). (gr. 9-12). 1988. pap. 5.95 (*0-86622-473-4*, SK-021) TFH Pubns.

Step by Step Book about Snakes. R. Anderson. (Step-by-Step Ser.). (Illus.). 64p. 1987. pap. 5.95 (*0-86622-460-2*, SK-017) TFH Pubns.

Step-by-Step Book about Stick Insects. David Alderton. (Illus.). 64p. 1992. pap. 5.95 (*0-86622-349-5*, SK043) TFH Pubns.

Step-By-Step Book about Tortoises. Christine Adrian. (Step-by-Step Ser.). (Illus.). 63p. (Orig.). 1987. pap. 5.95 (*0-86622-487-4*, SK-034) TFH Pubns.

Step-by-Step Book about Training Cockatiels. Elaine Radford. (Step-by-Step Ser.). (Illus.). 64p. 1989. pap. 5.95 (*0-86622-964-7*, SK-026) TFH Pubns.

Step-by-Step Book about Tropical Fish. Cliff W. Emmens. (Step-by-Step Ser.). (Illus.). 64p. (YA). (gr. 9-12). 1988. pap. 5.95 (*0-86622-471-8*, SK-018) TFH Pubns.

Step-by-Step Book about Tropical Marine Fishes. Cliff W. Emmens. (Step-by-Step Ser.). (Illus.). 64p. 1989. pap. 5.95 (*0-86622-468-8*, SK036) TFH Pubns.

Step by Step Book about Turtles. J. Jahn. (Step-by-Step Ser.). (Illus.). 64p. (Orig.). 1987. pap. 5.95 (*0-86622-451-3*, SK-019) TFH Pubns.

Step-by-Step Bookkeeping. rev. ed. Robert C. Ragan. (Illus.). viii, 134p. 1994. lib. bdg. 25.00 (*0-8095-7625-2*) Borgo Pr.

Step-by-Step Bookkeeping: The Complete Handbook for the Small Business. rev. ed. Robert C. Ragan. LC 74-7814. (Illus.). 128p. (YA). (gr. 10-12). 1982. pap. 8.95 (*0-8069-8690-5*) Sterling.

***Step-by-Step Calligraphy: A Complete Guide with Creative Projects.** Susan Hufton. 1997. pap. text ed. 16.95 (*0-8069-3987-7*) Sterling.

Step-By-Step Candlewick Projects: A Creative Guide to Over 45 Patterns & Projects. Di Van Niekerk. (Illus.). 96p. 1996. 22.95 (*1-85368-547-X*, Pub. by New Holland Pubs UK) Sterling.

Step-by-Step Card Play in Suits. Brian Senior. 144p. 1995. pap. 16.95 (*0-7134-7641-9*, Pub. by Batsford UK) Trafalgar.

Step by Step Children's Guide to Dog Training. Denise Cherry. (Illus.). 64p. (J). 1993. pap. 5.95 (*0-86622-518-8*, SK044) TFH Pubns.

Step by Step Children's Party Cakes. Sue Maggs. 96p. 1994. 9.98 (*0-8317-7845-8*) Smithmark.

Step-by-Step Christmas Fun. Scholastic, Inc. Staff. (Illus.). 12p. (J). (gr. k-3). 1995. boxed 4.95 (*0-590-48051-0*, Cartwheel) Scholastic Inc.

Step by Step Christmas Treats. Janice Murfitt. 96p. 1994. 9.98 (*0-8317-7843-1*) Smithmark.

Step by Step College Writing. 7th ed. Randy Devillez. 548p. (C). 1996. per., pap. 26.19 (*0-7872-2203-8*) Kendall-Hunt.

Step-by-Step Competitive Bidding. Tony Sowter. 144p. 1996. pap. 16.95 (*0-7134-7705-9*, Pub. by Batsford UK) Trafalgar.

Step by Step Competitive Strategy. Dave Francis. LC 93-42359. (Self-Development for Managers Ser.). 1994. write for info. (*0-415-09690-1*, Routledge NY) Routledge.

Step-by-Step Compo & Mold Making. Robert F. Loeffler. LC 92-7144. (Illus.). 112p. 1992. 24.95 (*0-9632387-5-2*) LVI Pubns.

Step-by-Step Computer Guide. 1985. 159.20 (*0-13-846437-5*) P-H.

Step-by-Step Constructive Bidding. Tony Sowter. 144p. 1995. pap. 16.95 (*0-7134-7639-7*, Pub. by Batsford UK) Trafalgar.

Step-by-Step dBase IV. Toby Wraye. LC 94-12104. 1994. write for info. (*0-02-800952-5*) Glencoe.

***Step-by-Step Decorative Painting.** Meedith Press Staff. (Do-It-Yourself Ser.). (Illus.). 96p. 1997. pap. 12.95 (*0-696-20678-1*) Meredith Bks.

Step by Step Decoupage. Letty Oates. (Illus.). 80p. 1995. write for info. (*1-57215-098-X*) World Pubns.

Step-by-Step Desktop Publishing on the Macintosh. Waite Group Staff. 1989. pap. 22.95 (*0-452-25902-9*) NAL-Dutton.

Step-by-Step DOS 6. Robert Goldhamer. LC 94-8943. 1994. 23.00 (*0-02-800949-5*) Glencoe.

***Step-by-Step Exterior Painting.** Meredith Press Staff. (Do-It-Yourself Ser.). (Illus.). 96p. 1997. pap. 12.95 (*0-696-20677-3*) Meredith Bks.

Step by Step Fun for Kids. Marion Elliot. 96p. 1994. 9.98 (*0-8317-7844-X*) Smithmark.

Step-by-Step Gardening Techniques Illustrated. Oliver E. Allen & Nancy Bubel. LC 95-22047. (Illus.). 224p. (Orig.). 1996. 22.95 (*0-88266-912-5*, 912-5, Garden Way Pub) Storey Comm Inc.

Step by Step Gourmet. Meredith Press Staff. 1996. 29.95 (*0-696-20531-9*) Meredith Bks.

Step by Step Guide Book on Home Plumbing. Ray McReynolds. (Illus.). 56p. 1975. pap. text ed. write for info. (*0-9619201-1-4*) S by S Guide.

Step by Step Guide Book on Home Wiring. Ray McReynolds. (Illus.). 48p. 1982. pap. text ed. write for info. (*0-9619201-0-6*) S by S Guide.

Step by Step Guide Book on Room Finishing. (Illus.). 48p. pap. text ed. write for info. (*0-9619201-6-5*) S by S Guide.

Step by Step Guide Book on Sprinkling Systems. Ray McReynolds. (Illus.). 38p. (Orig.). (C). 1974. pap. text ed. write for info. (*0-9619201-2-2*) S by S Guide.

Step by Step Guide Books on Home Wiring Diagrams. Ray McReynolds. (Illus.). 48p. 1982. pap. text ed. write for info. (*0-9619201-4-9*) S by S Guide.

Step-by-Step Guide for Making Busts & Masks (Cold-Cast Bronze or Plaster/Hydrocal) 2nd ed. Donna Brice. LC 82-15703. (Illus.). 52p. 1982. 24.95 (*0-910733-00-7*); pap. 16.95 (*0-910733-01-5*) ICTL Pubns.

***Step-by-Step Guide to C Programming.** Jean Corriveau. (C). 1997. pap. text ed. 48.00 (*0-13-339946-X*) P-H.

Step-By-Step Guide to Caring for the Homebound. Gerri L. Cockburn. (Illus.). 96p. (Orig.). 1997. pap. 5.95 (*0-944214-12-6*) ABELexpress.

***Step-by-Step Guide to Complete Container Gardening.** Whitecap Books Staff. 1997. 24.95 (*1-55110-509-8*, Pub. by Whitecap Bks CN) Gr Arts Ctr Pub.

Step-by-Step Guide to Container Gardening. Sue Phillips. (Illus.). 108p. 1994. pap. text ed. 12.95 (*1-55110-153-X*, Pub. by Whitecap Bks CN) Gr Arts Ctr Pub.

Step by Step Guide to Correct English. 2nd ed. Mary Ann S. Pulaski. 160p. 1985. pap. 8.00 (*0-671-86955-8*, Arco) Macmillan Gen Ref.

***Step-by-Step Guide to Creative Garden Ideas.** Whitecap Books Staff. 1997. 24.95 (*1-55110-500-4*, Pub. by Whitecap Bks CN) Gr Arts Ctr Pub.

Step-by-Step Guide to Creative Patio & Container Gardening. Whitecap Books Staff. 1996. 24.95 (*1-55110-413-X*, Pub. by Whitecap Bks CN) Gr Arts Ctr Pub.

Step by Step Guide to Dealing with Your Breast Cancer. Rebecca Y. Robinson & Jeanne A. Petrek. LC 94-18102. (Illus.). 236p. 1994. 18.95 (*1-55972-257-6*, Birch Ln Pr) Carol Pub Group.

Step-by-Step Guide to Dealing with Your Breast Cancer. Rebecca Y. Robinson & Jeanne A. Petrek. 1996. pap. 12.95 (*0-8065-1763-8*, Citadel Pr) Carol Pub Group.

Step-by-Step Guide to Developing a Profitable Marketing Plan. Robert F. Stennholz & Lyn M. Stennholz. 80p. 1986. pap. 12.95 (*0-317-64326-6*) AgriData.

***Step-by-Step Guide to Drawing the Figure.** John Raynes. (Illus.). 1997. pap. text ed. 24.99 (*0-89134-794-1*, North Lght Bks) F & W Pubns Inc.

Step by Step Guide to Engine Blueprinting. R. Voeelin. (How to Ser.). (Illus.). 128p. 1985. pap. 18.95 (*0-931472-21-0*) Motorbooks Intl.

Step-by-Step Guide to Fruit & Vegetables. Peter Blackburne-Maze. (Illus.). 108p. 1995. pap. text ed. 12.95 (*1-55110-285-4*, Pub. by Whitecap Bks CN) Gr Arts Ctr Pub.

Step-by-Step Guide to Garden Design. Yvonne Reese. (Illus.). 108p. 1995. pap. text ed. 12.95 (*1-55110-177-7*, Pub. by Whitecap Bks CN) Gr Arts Ctr Pub.

Step-by-Step Guide to Growing & Displaying Bonsai. Colin Lewis. (Illus.). 124p. 1993. pap. 12.95 (*1-55110-080-0*, Pub. by Whitecap Bks CN) Gr Arts Ctr Pub.

Step-by-Step Guide to Growing & Displaying Orchids. Whitecap Books Staff. (Illus.). 1993. pap. text ed. 12.95 (*1-55110-078-9*, Pub. by Whitecap Bks CN) Gr Arts Ctr Pub.

Step-by-Step Guide to Growing & Displaying Roses. John Mattock & Jane Newdick. (Illus.). 124p. 1993. pap. 12.95 (*1-55110-076-2*, Pub. by Whitecap Bks CN) Gr Arts Ctr Pub.

Step-by-Step Guide to Growing Fuschias. Carol Gubler & Jane Newdick. (Illus.). 108p. 1995. pap. text ed. 12.95 (*1-55110-161-0*, Pub. by Whitecap Bks CN) Gr Arts Ctr Pub.

Step-by-Step Guide to Growing Herbs. Whitecap Books Staff. (Illus.). 124p. 1995. pap. 12.95 (*1-55110-155-6*, Pub. by Whitecap Bks CN) Gr Arts Ctr Pub.

Step-by-Step Guide to Hanging Baskets. (Illus.). 112p. 1996. pap. text ed. 12.95 (*1-55110-415-6*, Pub. by Whitecap Bks CN) Gr Arts Ctr Pub.

***Step-by-Step Guide to Houseplant Care.** Whitecap Books Staff. 1994. pap. text ed. 12.95 (*1-55110-043-6*, Pub. by Whitecap Bks CN) Gr Arts Ctr Pub.

***Step-by-Step Guide to Painting Realistic Watercolors.** Dawn M. Heim. LC 96-46687. (Illus.). 128p. 1997. 27.99 (*0-89134-714-3*, North Lght Bks) F & W Pubns Inc.

Step-by-Step Guide to Patio Gardening. Whitecap Books Staff. 1994. pap. text ed. 12.95 (*1-55110-157-2*) Gr Arts Ctr Pub.

Step-by-Step Guide to Personal Management for Blind Persons. 2nd ed. LC 74-76827. 136p. 1974. spiral bd. 19.95 (*0-89128-061-8*) Am Foun Blind.

Step-by-Step Guide to Photography. Michael J. Langford. LC 78-54894. (Illus.). 1978. 24.95 (*0-394-41604-X*) Knopf.

Step-by-Step Guide to Screen Process Printing. Robert M. Swerdlow. (Illus.). 192p. 1985. pap. 29.00 (*0-13-846956-3*) P-H.

Step by Step Guide to the Estimation of Child Mortality. 83p. 1989. 19.00 (*92-1-151183-6*, 89.XIII.9) UN.

Step-by-Step Guide to the Flower Garden. Whitecap Books Staff. 1995. pap. 12.95 (*1-55110-283-8*, Pub. by Whitecap Bks CN) Gr Arts Ctr Pub.

Step-by-Step Guide to Urban Gardens. Sue Phillips. 112p. 1995. pap. text ed. 12.95 (*1-55110-281-1*, Pub. by Whitecap Bks CN) Gr Arts Ctr Pub.

Step by Step Guide to Wills & Probate. Keith Biggs & Kevin Donnelly. 164p. 1991. 33.00 (*1-85190-119-1*, Pub. by Tolley Pubng UK) St Mut.

Step-by-Step Guide to Your Bernina. Jan Saunders. LC 90-55326. (Illus.). 288p. 1991. pap. 19.95 (*0-8019-8114-X*) Chilton.

Step-by-Step Guide to Your New Home. Jan Saunders. LC 90-55325. (Illus.). 256p. 1991. pap. 19.95 (*0-8019-8115-8*) Chilton.

Step-by-Step Guide to Your Sewing Machine. Jan Saunders. LC 89-45964. (Illus.). 196p. 1990. pap. 19.95 (*0-8019-8013-5*) Chilton.

Step-by-Step Guide Water Gardens. Yvonne Reese. 1994. pap. text ed. 12.95 (*1-55110-178-5*, Pub. by Whitecap Bks CN) Gr Arts Ctr Pub.

***Step-by-Step Herbs.** Better Homes & Gardens Editors. (Illus.). 132p. 1997. pap. 12.95 (*0-696-20658-7*) Meredith Bks.

Step by Step in Esperanto. 9th ed. Montagu C. Butler. 281p. 1991. text ed. 12.95 (*0-939785-01-3*, STE001) Esperanto League North Am.

Step by Step in the Jewish Religion. Isidore Epstein. lib. bdg. 7.95 (*0-685-00776-6*) Bloch.

Step by Step in the Jewish Religion. Isidore Epstein. 143p. 1993. pap. 8.95 (*0-900689-12-9*) Soncino Pr.

Step-by-Step Indian Cooking. Sharda Gopal. (Illus.). 192p. 1987. 24.95 (*0-8120-5829-1*) Barron.

***Step-by-Step Interior Painting.** Meredith Press Staff. (Do-It-Yourself Ser.). (Illus.). 96p. 1997. pap. 12.95 (*0-696-20676-5*) Meredith Bks.

***Step-by-Step ISDN: The Internet Connection Handbook.** Ben Catanzaro. 1997. pap. text ed. 34.95 (*0-13-890211-9*) P-H.

Step-by-Step Knifemaking. David Boye. LC 77-22383. 288p. 1977. pap. 16.95 (*0-87857-181-7*, 11-558-1) Rodale Pr Inc.

Step by Step Knitting Stitch Patterns. Kristina Bryszewski. (Illus.). 104p. (Orig.). 1989. pap. 9.95 (*0-88925-833-3*) Gordon Soules Bk.

Step-by-Step Landscaping. Better Homes & Gardens Editors. (Better Homes & Gardens Ser.). (Illus.). 312p. 1991. 29.95 (*0-696-01873-X*); pap. 15.95 (*0-696-02558-2*) Meredith Bks.

***Step-by Step Lawns, Ground Covers & Vines.** Better Homes & Gardens Editors. (Illus.). 132p. 1997. pap. 12.95 (*0-696-20654-4*) Meredith Bks.

Step-by-Step Learning Guide for Older Retarded Children. Vicki M. Johnson & Roberta A. Werner. (C). 1977. pap. 16.95 (*0-8156-2181-7*) Syracuse U Pr.

Step-by-Step Learning Guide for Retarded Infants & Children. Vicki M. Johnson & Roberta A. Werner. LC 75-22172. (Illus.). 208p. (C). 1975. pap. 16.95 (*0-8156-2174-4*) Syracuse U Pr.

Step-by-Step Legal Forms & Agreements. Charles B. Chernofsky & Griffith DeNoyelles, Jr. 446p. 1992. pap. 19.95 (*0-929543-10-6*) Round Lake Pub.

Step-by-Step Lotus 1-2-3. Miguel Pendas. LC 94-8944. 1994. write for info. (*0-02-800955-X*) Macmillan.

***Step-by-Step Low-Maintenance Gardens.** Better Homes & Gardens Editors. (Illus.). 132p. 1997. pap. 12.95 (*0-696-20656-0*) Meredith Bks.

Step-by-Step Massage: A Guide to Massage Techniques for Health, Relaxation & Vitality. Carole McGilvery. 1994. 10.98 (*0-8317-6514-3*) Smithmark.

Step by Step Math: Grade 5. unabridged ed. Marion Rochelle & Ruth Emmel. Ed. by Mary L. Muffoletto. (Illus.). 64p. 1996. teacher ed., pap. 6.95 (*1-889369-07-1*, TI0012) Teaching Ink.

Step by Step Math: Grade 6. unabridged ed. Marion Rochelle & Ruth Emmel. Ed. by Mary L. Muffoletto. (Illus.). 64p. 1996. teacher ed., pap. 6.95 (*1-889369-08-X*, TI0013) Teaching Ink.

Step by Step Math: Grades 3-4. unabridged ed. Marion Rochelle & Ruth Emmel. Ed. by Mary L. Muffoletto. (Illus.). 64p. 1996. teacher ed., pap. 6.95 (*1-889369-06-3*, TI0011) Teaching Ink.

Step by Step Math: K-2. unabridged ed. Lynne Backer & Debbie Cline. Ed. by Mary L. Muffoletto. (Illus.). 64p. 1996. teacher ed., pap. 6.95 (*1-889369-05-5*, TI0010) Teaching Ink.

Step-by-Step Meals: For People with Cognitive Challenges. Jennifer L. Nightingale & Nancy R. Nightingale. 248p. 1993. pap. text ed., ring bd. 66.00 (*0-88450-639-8*, 4287) Commun Skill.

***Step-by-Step Medical Coding.** Ed. by Carol J. Buck. (Illus.). 470p. 1996. pap. write for info. (*0-7216-5344-8*) Saunders.

***Step-by-Step Medical Coding.** Ed. by Carol J. Buck. (Illus.). 1996. teacher ed., pap. write for info. (*0-7216-5345-6*) Saunders.

***Step-by-Step Medical Coding.** 2nd ed. Buck. LC 97-20508. 1998. pap. text ed. write for info. (*0-7216-7536-0*) Saunders.

Step-by-Step Microsoft Works 3.0 for the Mac. Carolyn Taylor. LC 92-40134. 1993. write for info. (*0-02-800324-1*) Glencoe.

Step-by-Step Miracles: A Practical Guide to Achieving Your Dreams. Shira Block. 1995. pap. 11.00 (*0-8217-4990-0*, Zebra Kensgtn) Kensgtn Pub Corp.

***Step-by-Step Narratives: Illustrated Lessons for Telling & Writing Stories.** Nancy L. Coleman. LC 97-8516. 1997. write for info. (*1-888222-04-2*) Thinking Pubns.

Step-by-Step Needlecraft Encyclopedia. Judy Brittain. (Illus.). 512p. 1995. 24.99 (*0-517-14068-3*) Random Hse Value.

Step by Step, Nineteen Thirty-Six to Nineteen Thirty-Nine. Winston S. Churchill. LC 72-156631. (Essay Index Reprint Ser.). 1977. reprint ed. 21.95 (*0-8369-2310-3*) Ayer.

Step by Step Organic Vegetable Gardening. rev. ed. Shepherd Ogden. LC 91-55513. (Illus.). 320p. 1994. reprint ed. pap. 16.00 (*0-06-092225-7*, PL) HarpC.

Step-by-Step Origami. Paul Jackson. 1994. 12.98 (*0-8317-6265-9*) Smithmark.

Step-by-Step Origami & Papercraft. Paul Jackson. 1996. 6.98 (*0-7858-0545-1*) Bk Sales Inc.

***Step-by-Step Ornamental Grasses.** Better Homes & Gardens Editors. (Illus.). 132p. 1997. pap. 12.95 (*0-696-20659-5*) Meredith Bks.

Step-by-Step Outdoor Stonework: Over Twenty Easy-to-Build Projects for Your Patio & Garden. Ed. by Mike Lawrence. LC 94-23205. 1995. pap. 18.95 (*0-88266-891-9*, Garden Way Pub) Storey Comm Inc.

Step by Step Painting on Silk. Jane Wildgoose. 1994. 14.98 (*0-7858-0185-5*) Bk Sales Inc.

Step-by-Step Parenting: A Guide to Successful Living with a Blended Family. 2nd ed. James D. Eckler. 224p. (Orig.). 1993. pap. 12.99 (*1-55870-294-6*, Betrwy Bks) F & W Pubns Inc.

Step-by-Step Patchwork. Helen Fairfield. 1990. pap. 15.95 (*0-312-05278-2*) St Martin.

Step-by-Step Patios & Decks: Seventeen Easy-to-Build Projects for Your Outdoor Living Areas. Penny Swift & Janek Szymanowski. (Illus.). 96p. 1996. pap. 14.95 (*1-85368-338-8*, Pub. by New Holland Pubs UK) Sterling.

***Step-by-Step Perennials.** Better Homes & Gardens Editors. (Illus.). 132p. 1997. pap. 12.95 (*0-696-20660-9*) Meredith Bks.

Step by Step Phonics: Makes Reading & Writing Easy, Incl. 130p. study guide. rev. ed. Laurie L. Bell. LC 94-78951. 67p. 1994. teacher ed. 39.95 incl. audio (*0-9643274-0-6*) Back To The Basics.

***Step-by-Step Phonics Level 2: Makes Reading & Writing Easy.** Laurie L. Bell. 71p. (Orig.). 1997. teacher ed., pap. text ed. 29.95 (*0-9643274-3-0*) Back To The Basics.

***Step-by-Step Plumbing.** Ed. by Better Homes & Gardens Editors. (Better Homes & Gardens Ser.). (Illus.). 112p. 1997. pap. 12.95 (*0-696-20634-X*) Meredith Bks.

An Asterisk (*) at the beginning of an entry indicates that the title is appearing in BIP for the first time.

***Step-by-Step Ponds, Pools & Rockeries.** Penny Swift. 96p. 1997. pap. 15.95 (*1-85368-539-9*, Pub. by New Holland Pubs UK) Sterling.

Step-by-Step Problem Solving: A Practical Guide to Ensure Problems Get (& Stay) Solved. Richard Y. Chang & P. Keith Kelly. (Qualtiy Improvement Ser.). 100p. 1994. pap. 12.95 (*1-883553-11-3*) R Chang Assocs.

***Step-by-Step QFD: Customer Driven Product Design.** John Terninko. (Illus.). 240p. (Orig.). 1997. pap. 39.95 (*1-57444-110-8*) St Lucie Pr.

Step by Step QFD Vol. 1: Customer Driven Product Design. John Terninko. Ed. by Mary A. Kahl & Maggie Rogers. (QFD Ser.). (Illus.). 192p. (Orig.). 1995. pap. 45.00 (*1-882382-10-2*) Respons Mgmt.

***Step-by-Step Redecorating & Remodeling.** Time-Life Books Editors. LC 97-15615. (Illus.). 336p. 1997. write for info. (*0-7835-3917-7*) Time-Life.

Step-by-Step Reengineering: The Comprehensive Guide. Michael Mische. LC 96-67531. 450p. 1996. ring bd. write for info. (*0-88390-476-4*, Pfiffr & Co) Jossey-Bass.

Step by Step Series, 3 vols., Set. 641p. 1990. reprint ed. pap. 29.85 (*0-9619770-4-3*) Pearl Publishing.

***Step-by-Step Shade Gardens.** Better Homes & Gardens Editors. (Illus.). 132p. 1997. pap. 12.95 (*0-696-20661-7*) Meredith Bks.

Step-by-Step Skill Building Exercises for the Word Processor. 2nd ed. Iris Blanc. Ed. by Shirley Dembo & Elizabeth Lorton. 224p. 1989. 20.00 (*0-936862-54-8*, RWP-940); teacher ed. 10.00 (*0-936862-65-3*, RP-TM); student ed. 175.00 incl. trans. (*0-936862-58-0*, T-100E); disk 65.00 (*0-936862-21-1*, OF-12); disk 20.00 (*0-936862-67-X*, 10-TEWP) DDC Pub.

Step-by-Step Skill Building Exercises for the Word Processor Solutions Booklet. Iris Blanc. 100p. (YA). (gr. 9-12). 1989. pap. text ed. 1.00 (*1-56243-004-1*, RWP-SOL) DDC Pub.

***Step-by-Step Stenciling.** Meredith Press Staff. (Do-It-Yourself Ser.). (Illus.). 96p. 1997. pap. 12.95 (*0-696-20679-X*) Meredith Bks.

Step by Step Successful Gardening. Better Homes & Gardens Editors. (Better Homes & Gardens Ser.). 256p. 1992. pap. 14.95 (*0-696-00736-3*) Meredith Bks.

Step-by-Step Tai Chi: The Natural Way to Strength & Health. Lam Kam Chuen. LC 94-7581. 144p. 1994. pap. 14.00 (*0-671-89247-9*) S&S Trade.

Step by Step Tennis. Deutscher Tennis Bund Staff. 144p. 1990. pap. 14.95 (*0-8120-4473-8*) Barron.

Step by Step Theatre. Gregory Thompson. (J). (gr. 1-4). 1989. pap. 9.99 (*0-8224-6348-2*) Fearon Teach Aids.

Step-by-Step to a Classic Fireplace Mantel. Stephen Penberthy & Gary Jones. LC 94-65609. (Illus.). 64p. (Orig.). 1994. pap. 12.95 (*0-88740-653-X*) Schiffer.

Step by Step to Ballroom Dancing. Aurora S. Villacorta. (Ballroom Dance Ser.). 1986. lib. bdg. 79.95 (*0-8490-3376-4*) Gordon Pr.

Step by Step to Ballroom Dancing. Aurora S. Villacorta. (Ballroom Dance Ser.). 1985. lib. bdg. 79.00 (*0-87700-706-3*) Revisionist Pr.

Step by Step to Better Crochet. (Illus.). 144p. 1984. 14.95 (*0-668-06058-1*, 6058, Arco) Macmillan Gen Ref.

Step by Step to Better Knitting. (Illus.). 144p. 1984. lib. bdg. 14.95 (*0-668-06055-7*, Arco) Macmillan Gen Ref.

Step by Step to College Success. A. Jerome Jewler & John N. Gardner. 202p. (C). 1987. pap. 18.95 (*0-534-07998-9*) Wadsworth Pub.

Step by Step to Involving Parents in Health Education. David A. Birch. LC 95-24324. 1995. write for info. (*1-56071-474-3*) ETR Assocs.

Step by Step to Jerusalem. Hersh Goldman. 45p. 1978. pap. 3.95 (*0-88482-760-7*) Hebrew Pub.

Step-by-Step to Natural Food. Diane Campbell. LC 79-84548. 224p. 1979. spiral bd. 7.95 (*0-9603766-0-7*) C C Pubs.

***Step by Step to Peer Health Education Programs: A Planning Guide.** Malcolm Goldsmith & Sherri T. Reynolds. LC 96-32280. 1996. pap. write for info. (*1-56071-517-0*) ETR Assocs.

Step-by-Step to the Job You Want. Edward F. Hood. (Leverage Institute Ser.). 60p. (Orig.). 1996. pap. 14.95 (*1-886383-22-7*) Pride OH.

***Step-by-Step Trees & Shrubs.** Better Homes & Gardens Editors. (Illus.). 132p. 1997. pap. 12.95 (*0-696-20662-5*) Meredith Bks.

***Step-by-Step Vegetables.** Better Homes & Gardens Editors. (Illus.). 132p. 1997. pap. 12.95 (*0-696-20663-3*) Meredith Bks.

***Step-by-Step Watercolor Painting.** Gregory Alexander. 1997. pap. text ed. 16.95 (*0-8069-1333-9*) Sterling.

Step-by-Step Watercolor Painting: A Complete Guide to Mastering Techniques with the Alexander Brothers. Gregory Alexander & Matthew Alexander. LC 94-45006. (Illus.). 160p. 1995. 24.95 (*0-8069-1332-0*) Sterling.

Step by Step We Climb, Vol. 1. rev. ed. LC 88-18012. (Step by Step Ser.). (Illus.). 225p. 1990. reprint ed. pap. 9.95 (*0-9619770-2-7*) Pearl Publishing.

Step by Step We Climb to Freedom & Victory, Vol. 3. Pearl Dorris. LC 88-18013. (Step by Step Ser.). (Illus.). 216p. 1990. pap. 9.95 (*0-9619770-3-5*) Pearl Publishing.

Step-by-Step Wedding Flowers. Kally Ellis. 1994. 10.98 (*0-8317-6519-4*) Smithmark.

***Step-by-Step Wildflowers & Native Plants.** Better Homes & Gardens Editors. (Illus.). 132p. 1997. pap. 12.95 (*0-696-20655-2*) Meredith Bks.

***Step-by-Step Wiring.** Ed. by Better Homes & Gardens Editors. (Better Homes & Gardens Ser.). (Illus.). 112p. 1997. pap. 12.95 (*0-696-20453-3*) Meredith Bks.

Step-by-Step Wooden Toys: Over Twenty Easy-to-Make Toys. Roger Horwood. (Illus.). 96p. 1997. pap. 16.95 (*0-8117-2936-2*) Stackpole.

Step-by-Step Woodwork Projects: Over Twenty Practical Projects for Your Home. G. J. Engelbrecht. (Illus.). 96p. 1996. pap. 14.95 (*1-85368-341-8*, Pub. by New Holland Pubs UK) Sterling.

Step by Step Word for Windows 6.0. Steve Harris. 350p. 1994. pap. 26.95 (*0-7506-1813-2*) Buttrwrth-Heinemann.

***Step by Wicked Step.** Anne Fine. 1997. pap. 3.99 (*0-440-41329-X*) Dell.

Step by Wicked Step: A Novel. Anne Fine. LC 95-43251. 138p. (YA). (gr. 5 up). 1996. 15.95 (*0-316-28345-2*) Little.

Step Forward: Sexual Harassment in the Workplace: What You Need to Know. Susan L. Webb. 1991. pap. 9.95 (*0-942361-51-2*) MasterMedia Pub. STEP FORWARD: SEXUAL HARASSMENT IN THE WORKPLACE explains: What is Sexual Harassment? Why should I warn you about it? Don't women harass men too? Whose fault is it? How can I be sure it's sexual harassment? SMART COMPANIES will learn about limiting liability, training outlines & formats, & future trends. MANAGERS & SUPERVISORS will learn a 6-step program how to stop sexual harassment, the 10 factors for assessing an incident & pointers on how to conduct an investigation. EMPLOYEES will learn 25 things to do if sexual harassment happens to them. Ms. Webb's approach is direct & straightforward. This upbeat & positive book will be filled with interactive quizzes. ***Publisher Provided Annotation.***

Step Four for Young Adults. Paul E. Bjorklund. 44p. 1981. pap. 3.25 (*0-89486-118-2*, 1129B) Hazelden.

Step from Heaven. K. L. Bye. LC 96-90146. (Illus.). 88p. (Orig.). 1996. pap. 13.00 (*0-9641945-0-3*) Turtle Run.

Step Further. 2nd ed. Joni E. Tada & Steve Estes. (Illus.). 224p. 1980. pap. 9.99 (*0-310-23971-0*, 12007P) Zondervan.

Step-Growth Polymerizations. Ed. by David H. Solomon. LC 75-182216. (Kinetics & Mechanisms of Polymerization Ser.: Vol. 3). (Illus.). 407p. reprint ed. pap. 116.00 (*0-317-07874-7*, 2055002) Bks Demand.

Step-Growth Polymers for High-Performance Materials: New Synthetic Methods. Ed. by James L. Hedrick & Jeff W. Labadie. (ACS Symposium Ser.: No. 624). (Illus.). 469p. 1996. 125.95 (*0-8412-3394-2*) Am Chemical.

Step Human into This World: Travel Poems. Olav Munzberg. Tr. by Mitch Cohen from GER. LC 90-81862. (Illus.). 125p. (Orig.). 9100. pap. 21.00 (*0-948259-53-1*, Pub. by Forest Bks UK) Dufour.

Step I Have Taken. E. Dennett. Ed. by R. P. Daniel. 53p. pap. 3.95 (*0-88172-140-9*) Believers Bkshelf.

Step in the Dark. Stephen C. Behrendt. LC 96-25034. (Orig.). 1996. pap. 11.00 (*0-922811-27-X*) Mid-List.

Step in the Dark. large type ed. Marjorie Lewty. 1995. 21.50 (*0-263-14127-6*, Pub. by M & B UK) Ulverscroft.

Step In Time. Anne Barbour. 1996. pap. 4.99 (*0-451-18723-7*) NAL-Dutton.

Step Inside the Rain Forest. Meish Goldish. (Whole-Language Big Bks.). (Illus.). 16p. (Orig.). (J). (ps-2). 1994. pap. 14.95 (*1-56784-061-2*) Newbridge Comms.

Step into Africa. rev. ed. Jan White. (Illus.). 106p. 1994. pap. 26.95 (*0-943804-68-X*) U of Denver Teach.

***Step into Ancient Egypt.** Philip Steele. (Step into Ser.). (Illus.). 64p. (J). (gr. 3-7). 1997. 7.95 (*1-85967-525-5*, Lorenz Bks) Anness Pub.

***Step into Classics.** (Bullseye Step into Classics Ser.: No. 1). (J). 1996. boxed 19.95 (*0-679-88430-0*) Random.

***Step into Classics.** Step into Classics Staff. (Bullseye Step into Classics Ser.: No. 2). (J). 1996. boxed 19.95 (*0-679-88431-9*) Random.

Step into Fall: A New Season. Jane B. Moncure. LC 90-30637. (Discovery World Ser.). (Illus.). 32p. (J). (ps-2). 1990. lib. bdg. 21.36 (*0-89565-573-X*) Childs World.

Step into Heaven, Here & Now: The Acrobatics of Soul. Ron Kurz. 48p. (Orig.). 1986. pap. 4.95 (*0-939829-00-2*) R Kurz.

Step into Patchwork. Nancy Smith & Lynda S. Milligan. Ed. by Sharon Holmes. (Illus.). 72p. (J). (gr. 1-12). 1994. spiral bd. 15.95 (*1-880972-09-3*, DreamSpinners) Pssblts Denver.

Step into Reading Rack Base. Step into Reading Staff. 1993. pap. text ed. write for info. (*0-679-83749-3*) Random.

Step into Reading Signage. Step into Reading Staff. 1993. pap. write for info. (*0-679-67209-5*) McKay.

Step into Shape. Consumer Guide Editors. (Illus.). 64p. 1993. spiral bd. 5.98 (*1-56173-748-8*, 3210900) Pubns Intl Ltd.

Step into Shape. Consumers Guide Staff. 128p. 1992. 2.99 (*0-451-17451-8*, Sig) NAL-Dutton.

Step into Skiing Discoveries. Jul Kingery. LC 77-91906. (Skiing Your Way Ser.). (Illus.). 1978. pap. 7.97 (*0-9604574-0-2*) Alpine-Tahoe.

Step into Spring: A New Season. Jane B. Moncure. LC 90-30375. (Discovery World Ser.). (Illus.). 32p. (J). (ps-2). 1990. lib. bdg. 21.36 (*0-89565-571-3*) Childs World.

Step into Summer: A New Season. Jane B. Moncure. LC 90-30456. (Discovery World Ser.). (Illus.). 32p. (J). (ps-2). 1990. lib. bdg. 21.36 (*0-89565-572-1*) Childs World.

Step into the Light. Donna B. MacDonald. 233p. (Orig.). 1996. mass mkt. 4.99 (*1-55197-193-3*, Pub. by Comnwlth Pub CN) Partners Pubs Grp.

Step into the Light: Poems from Recovery. Ed. by Chuck Kramer. (Illus.). 64p. (Orig.). 1992. pap. 5.99 (*0-925037-16-8*) Great Lks Poetry.

***Step into the Roman Empire.** Philip Steele. (Step into Ser.). (Illus.). 64p. (J). (gr. 3-7). 1997. 7.95 (*1-85967-526-3*, Lorenz Bks) Anness Pub.

Step into Virtual Reality. John Iovine. LC 94-29300. 1995. text ed. 49.95 (*0-07-911905-0*, Windcrest) TAB Bks.

Step into Winter: A New Season. Jane B. Moncure. LC 90-30636. (Discovery World Ser.). (Illus.). 32p. (J). (ps-2). 1990. lib. bdg. 21.36 (*0-89565-574-8*) Childs World.

Step It Down: Games, Plays, Songs, & Stories from the Afro-American Heritage. Bessie Jones & Bess L. Hawes. LC 87-5945. (Brown Thrasher Bks.). 256p. 1987. reprint ed. pap. 12.95 (*0-8203-0960-5*) U of Ga Pr.

***STEP Key Stage 3 Teacher's Handbook.** 144p. 1996. teacher ed., spiral bd. 50.00 (*0-521-45583-9*) Cambridge U Pr.

Step Mother: A Chocolate Epistolary Novel. Carol J. Rose. LC 89-92530. 300p. (C). 1990. 39.00 (*1-878490-58-3*); lib. bdg. 49.00 (*1-878490-59-1*) Rosehips Ink.

Step Not Beyond. Maurice Blanchot. Tr. & Intro. by Lycette Nelson. LC 91-13269. (SUNY Series, Intersections: Philosophy & Critical Theory). 139p. 1992. text ed. 57.50 (*0-7914-0907-4*) State U NY Pr.

Step Not Beyond. Maurice Blanchot. Tr. by Lycette Nelson from FRE. LC 91-13269. (SUNY Series, Intersections: Philosophy & Critical Theory). 139p. 1992. pap. text ed. 18.95 (*0-7914-0908-2*) State U NY Pr.

***Step Not on Horseshoe! One Man's Discovery of God & Self...Through the Power of Memory, Time, & Respect.** unabridged ed. Kranin & Antonio Rodriguez. 384p. 1997. 24.50 (*0-9658816-0-1*) In Pace Lux.

Step on a Crack. M. T. Coffin. (Spinetinglers Ser.: No. 9). 160p. (Orig.). (J). 1996. pap. 3.50 (*0-380-78432-7*) Avon.

Step on a Crack. Ryan. LC 96-34184. (J). 1997. 16.00 (*0-689-80789-9*, S&S Bks Young Read) S&S Childrens.

Step on a Crack. Suzan L. Zeder. (J). (gr. 1-9). 1976. 5.00 (*0-87602-207-7*) Anchorage.

***Step One: Play Guitar Chords.** pap. 5.95 incl. cd-rom (*0-8256-1609-3*) Omnibus NY.

***Step One: Playing Bass Guitar.** Peter Pickow. pap. 5.95 incl. cd-rom (*0-8256-1592-5*) Omnibus NY.

***Step One: Playing Bass Scales.** Peter Pickow. pap. 5.95 incl. cd-rom (*0-8256-1593-3*) Omnibus NY.

***Step One: Playing Blues Guitar.** Darryl Winston. pap. 5.95 incl. cd-rom (*0-8256-1591-7*) Omnibus NY.

***Step One: Playing Guitar.** Artie Traum. pap. 5.95 incl. cd-rom (*0-8256-1589-5*) Omnibus NY.

***Step One: Playing Guitar Scales.** Peter Pickow. pap. 5.95 incl. cd-rom (*0-8256-1590-9*) Omnibus NY.

***Step One: Playing Harmonica.** Peter Pickow & Jason A. Shulman. pap. 5.95 incl. cd-rom (*0-8256-1594-1*) Omnibus NY.

Step One: The Foundation of Recovery. William Springborn. 24p. (Orig.). 1977. pap. 2.00 (*0-89486-017-8*, 1425B) Hazelden.

Step One for Young Adults. Della Van Dyke & Jane Nakken. (Step Pamphlets for Young Adults Ser.). 24p. (Orig.). 1985. pap. 3.25 (*0-89486-304-5*, 1362B) Hazelden.

Step out in Ministry! Carol Crook. LC 86-71831. 203p. (Orig.). 1986. pap. 9.95 (*0-939399-07-5*) Bks of Truth.

Step Out of the Crowd. J. J. Turner. 1988. pap. 5.75 (*0-89137-111-7*) Quality Pubns.

Step Outside: Community-Based Art Education. Peter London. LC 93-11569. (Illus.). 138p. (C). 1994. pap. text ed. 35.00 (*0-435-08794-0*, 08794) Heinemann.

Step Polymerization, Vol. 5. Ed. by Geoffrey Allen & J. C. Bevington. (Comprehensive Polymer Science Ser.: Vol. 5). (Illus.). 753p. 1990. 480.00 (*0-08-036209-5*, Pergamon Pr) Elsevier.

Step Right Up. Brooks McNamara. (Illus.). 264p. 1995. reprint ed. pap. 16.95 (*0-87805-832-X*); reprint ed. text ed. 40.00 (*0-87805-831-1*) U Pr of Miss.

Step Right Up: I'm Gonna Scare the Pants off America. William Castle. (Illus.). 256p. 1992. pap. 12.95 (*0-88687-657-5*, Pharos) Wrld Almnc.

Step Right Up! Math Problem Solving. Laurie Steding. (Great Beginnings Ser.: Level 1). (J). 1997. pap. 1.95 (*0-8167-3249-3*) Troll Communs.

Step Right Up see Memoirs of a Sword Swallower: Formerly Step Right Up

Step Spirit: The Twelve Steps As a Spiritual Program. Catherine Chapman. LC 92-19817. 112p. 1992. pap. 5.95 (*0-8091-3340-7*) Paulist Pr.

***Step-Spouse: Phantom Relationships with Real Impact.** Paul Nongard & Richard K. Nongard. 180p. (Orig.). 1997. pap. 15.95 (*0-9655979-3-8*, SS-03) Peachtree Prof.

STEP-Teen Parents Guide - Parenting Teenagers. rev. ed. Don Dinkmeyer, Sr. & Gary D. McKay. (Systematic Parenting for Effective Parenting of Teens Ser.). 1990. pap. 14.95 (*0-88671-404-4*, 5753) Am Guidance.

Step Ten: A Good Tenth Step. Mel B. 20p. (Orig.). 1982. pap. 2.00 (*0-89486-153-0*) Hazelden.

Step Three for Young Adults. Della Van Dyke. (Step Pamphlets for Young Adults Ser.). 20p. (Orig.). 1986. pap. 3.25 (*0-89486-352-5*, 5502B) Hazelden.

***Step Through Windows 3.1.** Elf. (C). 1995. write for info. (*0-15-504703-5*) HB Coll Pubs.

Step-Tongue: Children's English in Singapore. Anthea F. Gupta. LC 93-50650. (Multilingual Matters Ser.: No. 101). 264p. 1994. 89.95 (*1-85359-230-7*, Pub. by Multilingual Matters UK); pap. 29.95 (*1-85359-229-3*, Pub. by Multilingual Matters UK) Taylor & Francis.

Step Training Plus. Karen S. Mazzeo & Lauren Mangili. (Illus.). (Orig.). (C). 1993. pap. text ed. 15.95 (*0-89582-255-5*) Morton Pub.

Step Two for Young Adults. Jane Nakken. (Step Pamphlets for Young Adults Ser.). 20p. (Orig.). 1986. pap. 3.25 (*0-89486-351-7*) Hazelden.

Step-Up to Student Teaching: Guidelines for Student Teaching. 3rd ed. University of Central Oklahoma Staff. 64p. (C). 1995. 13.59 (*0-7872-1894-4*) Kendall-Hunt.

***Step Up to Wellness.** Bishop & Aldana. 1997. pap. text ed. 28.67 (*0-205-27970-8*) P-H.

Step Workbook for Adolescent Chemical Dependency Recovery: A Guide to the First Five Steps. Steven L. Jaffe. LC 90-30506. 72p. 1990. student ed., pap. 49.50 (*1-882103-00-9*, 0300) Am Psychiatric.

Step Zero: Getting to Recovery. Arnold M. Washton & Nannette Stone-Washton. 170p. (Orig.). 1991. pap. 11.00 (*0-89486-785-7*, 5042A) Hazelden.

Step 1 Simulated Exam. 8th ed. Ed. by John R. Thornborough. (Pretest Simulated Exam Ser.). 1996. pap. text ed. 32.00 (*0-07-052020-8*) McGraw-Hill HPD.

***Step 1 Success: Full Length Practice Test for the USMLE.** Stanley Zaslau. Ed. & Illus. by Paul McGrath. 240p. 1995. wbk. ed., spiral bd. 38.00 (*1-886468-07-9*) FMSG.

***Step 1 Update, Bk. A.** Stanley Zaslau. Ed. & Illus. by Paul L. McGrath. 65p. 1996. wbk. ed., spiral bd. 16.00 (*1-886468-13-3*) FMSG.

Step 2 Simulated Exam. 8th ed. Ed. by John R. Thornborough. LC 95-20546. (Pretest Simulated Exam Ser.). (Illus.). 192p. 1996. pap. text ed. 32.00 (*0-07-064525-6*) McGraw-Hill HPD.

***Step 2 Success: Full Length Practice Test for the USMLE.** Stanley Zaslau. Ed. & Illus. by Paul L. McGrath. 228p. 1995. wbk. ed., spiral bd. 38.00 (*1-886468-06-0*) FMSG.

***Step 2 Update, Bk. A.** Stanley Zaslau. Ed. & Illus. by Paul L. McGrath. 73p. 1996. wbk. ed., spiral bd. 16.00 (*1-886468-12-5*) FMSG.

Step 3 Simulated Exam. John R. Thornborough. Ed. by Gail Gavert. (Pretest Simulated Exam Ser.). (Illus.). 192p. 1996. pap. text ed. 32.00 (*0-07-052067-4*) McGraw-Hill HPD.

Step 3 Success: Full Length Practice Test. Stanley Zaslau. 248p. (C). 1995. pap. text ed. 38.00 (*1-886468-05-2*) FMSG.

***Step 3 Update, Bk. A.** Stanley Zaslau. Ed. by Paul L. McGrath. 80p. 1996. wbk. ed., spiral bd. 16.00 (*1-886468-14-1*) FMSG.

***Stepbrother.** R. L. Stine. (Fear Street Ser.: No. 52). (J). 1998. mass mkt. 3.99 (*0-671-01501-X*) PB.

Stepchildren of Music. Eric Blom. LC 67-28731. (Essay Index Reprint Ser.). 1977. 20.95 (*0-8369-0217-3*) Ayer.

Stepchildren of Progress: The Political Economy of Development in an Indonesian Mining Town. Kathryn M. Robinson. LC 86-5847. (SUNY Series in the Anthropology of Work). 315p. (Orig.). (C). 1986. text ed. 24.50 (*0-88706-119-2*) State U NY Pr.

Stepdaughter. Carol Ellis. 176p. (J). (gr. 7-9). 1993. pap. 3.25 (*0-590-46044-7*) Scholastic Inc.

Stepfamilies. Pete Sanders & Steve Myers. (What Do You Know About...Ser.). (Illus.). 32p. (J). (gr. 4-6). 1995. lib. bdg. 15.40 (*1-56294-940-3*, Copper Beech Bks) Millbrook Pr.

Stepfamilies: A Catholic Guide. Paul J. Cullen. LC 88-60925. 160p. 1988. pap. 4.95 (*0-87973-508-2*, 508) Our Sunday Visitor.

Stepfamilies: A Guide to Working with Stepparents & Stepchildren. Emily B. Visher & John S. Visher. LC 78-25857. 300p. 1984. text ed. 35.95 (*0-87630-190-1*) Brunner-Mazel.

Stepfamilies: Myths & Realities. Emily B. Visher & John S. Visher. 1980. pap. 10.95 (*0-8065-0743-8*, Citadel Pr) Carol Pub Group.

Stepfamilies: Personal Adjustment: Looking at Life. Center for Learning Network Staff. 12p. (YA). (gr. 7-12). 1992. pap. text ed. 0.80 (*1-56077-224-7*) Ctr Learning.

Stepfamilies: The Restructuring Process. Judy Osborne. 24p. (Orig.). 1983. pap. 5.00 (*0-9618303-3-6*) Emijo Pubns.

Stepfamilies: The Step by Step Model of Brief Therapy. Mala S. Burt & Roger B. Burt. 208p. 1996. 26.95 (*0-87630-832-9*) Brunner-Mazel.

Stepfamilies: Who Benefits? Who Does Not? Ed. by Alan Booth & Judith Dunn. 256p. 1994. text ed. 49.95 (*0-8058-1544-9*) L Erlbaum Assocs.

Stepfamilies & the Law. Margaret M. Mahoney. 350p. 1994. text ed. 47.50 (*0-472-10519-1*) U of Mich Pr.

***Stepfamilies from Various Perspectives.** Ed. by Irene Levin & Marvin B. Sussman. 415p. 1997. 79.95 (*0-7890-0337-6*) Haworth Pr.

***Stepfamilies from Various Perspectives.** Ed. by Irene Levin & Marvin B. Sussman. 415p. 1997. pap. 29.95 (*0-7890-0338-4*) Haworth Pr.

Stepfamilies I: Small Group Counseling Programs for Students in Grades Two Through Four. JoAnn Cooper & Arden Martenz. LC 93-79230. (Changing Family Ser.). 36p. 1993. 5.95 (*1-884063-09-8*) Mar Co Prods.

Stepfamilies II: Small Group Counseling Program for Students in Grades Five. JoAnn Cooper & Arden Martenz. LC 93-79230. (Changing Family Ser.). 36p. 1993. 5.95 (*1-884063-10-1*) Mar Co Prods.

Stepfamilies in Therapy: Understanding Systems, Assessment, & Intervention. Don Martin et al. LC 92-12519. (Social & Behavioral Science Ser.). 288p. 33.95 (*1-55542-453-8*) Jossey-Bass.

Stepfamilies Stepping Ahead: An Eight-Step Program for Successful Family Living. 2nd ed. Ed. by Mala Burt. LC 89-51436. Orig. Title: Stepping Ahead. 96p. (C). 1989. pap. 9.95 (*0-9624432-0-4*) Stepfamily Assn Amer.

Stepfamily: Living, Loving & Learning. Elizabeth A. Einstein. 214p. 1994. reprint ed. pap. 12.95 (*1-884944-00-0*) E Einstein. This award-winning book chronicles the

S

developmental passages of the stepfamily through interviews with over 50 stepfamilies, the author's experience as a stepchild & stepmother & discussions with many professionals who work with families. The highly readable book continues as a classic in stepfamily literature. THE STEPFAMILY has been reprinted many times & explores the challenges & potential of Stepfamily Living. Elizabeth Einstein is a Marriage & Family Therapist & national workshop leader. This professional consultant is one of America's leaders in stepfamily education. Her other educational materials are available. Send for brochure: Elizabeth Einstein, P.O. Box 6760, Ithaca, NY 14851. Please add $3.50 for postage & handling. ***Publisher Provided Annotation.***

S

*__Stepfamily Living, 4 vols.__ Elizabeth Einstein & Linda Albert. Incl. Vol. 1 Preparing for Remarriage. 28p. 1994. reprint ed. pap. Not sold separately (*1-884944-02-7*); Vol. 2 Pitfalls & Possibilities. 24p. 1994. pap. Not sold separately (*1-884944-03-5*); Vol. 3 Dealing with Discipline. 28p. 1994. pap. Not sold separately (*1-884944-04-3*); Vol. 4 Encourgement & Enrichment. 24p. 1994. pap. Not sold separately (*1-884944-05-1*); 11. 95 (*1-884944-01-9*) E Einstein.

*__Stepfamily Problems: How to Solve Them.__ Tom Frydenger & Adrienne Frydenger. 192p. 1997. mass mkt. 5.99 (*0-8007-8648-3*) Revell.

Stepfamily Puzzle: Intergenerational Influences. Intro. by Craig A. Everett. LC 93-11502. (Journal of Divorce & Remarriage: Vol. 19, Nos. 3-4). (Illus.). 251p. 1993. lib. bdg. 39.95 (*1-56024-518-2*) Haworth Pr.

Stepfamily Realities: How to Overcome Difficulties & Have a Happy Family. Margaret Newman. LC 93-86800. 264p. (Orig.). 1994. pap. 13.95 (*1-879237-70-9*) New Harbinger.

Stepfather. 2nd ed. Tony Gorman. LC 83-90199. (Orig.). 1985. reprint ed. pap. 11.95 (*0-9610894-0-7*) Gentle Touch.

Stepfathering. Michael Chandler. 1984. pap. 8.00 (*0-318-04449-8*) Pudding Hse Pubns.

Stepfathers Are People Too. D. L. Stewart. Ed. by Laura Dempsey & Karen Strider-Ilames. (Illus.). 195p. (Orig.). 1991. pap. 7.95 (*0-9616347-3-1*) Dayton Newspapers.

*__Stephan Balkenhol.__ (Illus.). 128p. 1997. pap. 23.50 (*2-906571-65-2*) Dist Art Pubs.

Stephan Balkenhol: Sculptures & Drawings. Neal Benezra. 116p. 1996. 55.00 (*3-89322-770-9*, Pub. by Edition Cantz GW) Dist Art Pubs.

*__Stephan Balkenhol: Sculptures, 1988-1996 in the Saatchi Collection.__ Stephen Balkenhol. 1996. 40.00 (*0-9527453-1-3*) D A Pub.

Stephan Problem. Richard K. Neumann. Ed. by Wells. (Expositions in Mathematics Ser.: No. 3). ix, 245p. (C). 1992. lib. bdg. 94.95 (*3-11-011479-8*) De Gruyter.

Stephan Schiffman's Telemarketing. Stephan Schiffman. 204p. 1992. pap. 9.95 (*1-55850-130-4*) Adams Media.

Stephane Mallarme Eighteen Forty-Two to Eighteen Ninety-Eight. Grange Woolley. LC 77-11499. (Illus.). 264p. reprint ed. 55.00 (*0-404-16358-0*) AMS Pr.

Stephane Mallarme, Twentieth-Century Criticism, 1972-1979. D. Hampton Morris. LC 89-34656. (Romance Monographs: No. 48). 1989. pap. 22.00 (*84-599-2717-2*) Romance.

Stephanie. Winston Graham. LC 92-42462. 304p. 1993. 19. 95 (*0-88184-939-1*) Carroll & Graf.

Stephanie. Debbie Macomber. 1992. pap. 2.89 (*0-373-03239-0*, 1-03239-0) Harlequin Bks.

Stephanie: A Love Story. Ed. by Clara M. Reida & David Brothers. LC 96-84148. (Illus.). 353p. (Orig.). 1996. pap. 12.95 (*1-881872-18-1*) Acclaim Pub.

*__Stephanie: A Previous Existence.__ Herbert Rosendorfer. Tr. by Mike Mitchell from GER. (Dedalus Europe 1992-97 Ser.). 153p. (Orig.). 1997. pap. 11.99 (*1-873982-17-8*, Pub. by Dedalus UK) Subterranean Co.

Stephanie: Phone Call from a Flamingo. Devra Newberger-Speregen. (Full House Ser.). 128p. (Orig.). (J). (gr. 3-6). mass mkt. 3.99 (*0-671-88004-7*, Minstrel Bks) PB.

Stephanie: The Boy-Oh-Boy Next Door. Ed. by Lisa Clancy. (Full House Ser.). (Orig.). (J). (gr. 3-6). mass mkt. 3.99 (*0-671-88121-3*, Minstrel Bks) PB.

Stephanie & the Coyote. 3rd rev. ed. Jack L. Crowder et al. Tr. by William Morgan. (Illus.). 32p. (ENG & NAV.). (J). (gr. 3 up). reprint ed. pap. 4.95 (*0-9616589-0-8*) Upper Strata.

Stephanie Brody Lederman: October 7-November 13, 1992. Pref. by Edward Albee. LC 92-36452. 1992. write for info. (*0-933699-27-1*) Hillwood Art.

Stephanie Culp's 12 Month Organizer & Project Planner. Stephanie Culp. 192p. (Orig.). 1995. pap. 12.99 (*1-55870-360-8*, Betrwy Bks) F & W Pubns Inc.

Stephanie Kaye. Ken Roberts. (Degrassi Book Ser.). (J). (gr. 6-9). 1995. pap. 4.95 (*1-55028-109-7*); bds. 16.95 (*1-55028-111-9*) Formac Dist Ltd.

Stephanie Winston's Best Organizing Tips: Quick, Simple Ways to Get Organized & Get on with Your Life. Stephanie Winston. LC 94-27012. 244p. 1995. 20.00 (*0-671-88643-6*) S&S Trade.

Stephanie Winston's Best Organizing Tips: Quick Ways to Organize & Get on Life. Stephanie Winston. 224p. 1996. pap. 11.00 (*0-684-81824-8*, Fireside) S&S Trade.

Stephanie's Feasts & Stories. Stephanie Alexander. 218p. 1993. pap. 24.95 (*1-86373-391-4*, Pub. by Allen & Unwin Aust Pty AT) IPG Chicago.

Stephanie's Ponytail. Robert Munsch. (Illus.). 24p. (Orig.). (J). (ps-3). 1996. 16.95 (*1-55037-485-0*, Pub. by Annick CN); pap. 5.95 (*1-55037-484-2*, Pub. by Annick CN) Firefly Bks Ltd.

Stephanie's Seasons. Stephanie Alexander. 1994. 39.95 (*1-86373-426-0*, Pub. by Allen & Unwin Aust Pty AT) IPG Chicago.

Stephanie's Seasons. Stephanie Alexander. 344p. 1995. pap. 19.95 (*1-86373-684-0*) IPG Chicago.

Stephanie's World. Jessica Stevens. 151p. 1991. pap. 12.95 (*0-9630361-0-6*) Saint Cecilia.

Stephans' Railroad Directory: ATSF. 9.00 (*0-9616890-5-6*) Tioga Pubns.

Stephans' Railroad Directory: Boston & Albany Railroad. Karen Stephans & Earl Stephans. (Orig.). 1990. pap. text ed. 9.00 (*1-56360-004-8*) Tioga Pubns.

Stephans' Railroad Directory: Boston & Maine Railroad. Karen Stephans & Earl Stephans. 1990. pap. text ed. 9.00 (*1-56360-005-6*) Tioga Pubns.

Stephans' Railroad Directory: C & O. 9.00 (*0-9616890-7-2*) Tioga Pubns.

Stephans' Railroad Directory: Canadian National Railroad. Karen Stephans & Earl Stephans. (Orig.). 1990. pap. text ed. 9.00 (*1-56360-007-2*) Tioga Pubns.

Stephans' Railroad Directory: Canadian Pacific Railroad. Karen Stephans & Earl Stephans. (Orig.). 1990. pap. text ed. 9.00 (*1-56360-008-0*) Tioga Pubns.

Stephans' Railroad Directory: Central Vermont Railroad. Karen Stephans & Earl Stephans. (Orig.). 1990. pap. text ed. 9.00 (*1-56360-006-4*) Tioga Pubns.

Stephans' Railroad Directory: East Tennessee & Western North Carolina Railroad. Karen Stephans & Earl Stephans. (Orig.). 1990. pap. text ed. 9.00 (*1-56360-009-9*) Tioga Pubns.

Stephans' Railroad Directory: Finelines, Vol. 4: All Issues Including Narrow Gauge Newsletter. 9.00 (*0-9616890-2-1*) Tioga Pubns.

Stephans' Railroad Directory: Flat Car Index. Karen Stephans & Earl Stephans. (Orig.). 1990. pap. text ed. 9.00 (*1-56360-016-1*) Tioga Pubns.

Stephans' Railroad Directory: Great Northern Advertisements. Karen Stephans & Earl Stephans. (Illus.). (Orig.). 1990. pap. text ed. 9.00 (*1-56360-019-6*) Tioga Pubns.

Stephans' Railroad Directory: Locomotive Plans. Karen Stephans & Earl Stephans. (Orig.). 1990. pap. text ed. 11.50 (*1-56360-017-X*) Tioga Pubns.

Stephans' Railroad Directory: Maine Central Railroad. Karen Stephans & Earl Stephans. (Orig.). 1990. pap. text ed. 9.00 (*1-56360-010-2*) Tioga Pubns.

Stephans' Railroad Directory: Model Railroader - Trains, Vol. 1. Earl Stephans. Ed. by Karen Stephans. (Stephans' Railroad Directory Ser.). (Illus.). 300p. 23.00 (*0-9616890-0-5*) Tioga Pubns.

Stephans' Railroad Directory: Model Railroading Index. Karen Stephans & Earl Stephans. (Orig.). 1990. pap. text ed. 16.50 (*1-56360-003-X*) Tioga Pubns.

Stephans' Railroad Directory: NH in Print. 9.00 (*0-9616890-3-X*) Tioga Pubns.

Stephans' Railroad Directory: Norfolk & Western Railroad. Karen Stephans & Earl Stephans. (Orig.). 1990. pap. text ed. 9.00 (*1-56360-011-0*) Tioga Pubns.

Stephans' Railroad Directory: PRR in Print. 11.50 (*0-9616890-4-8*) Tioga Pubns.

Stephans' Railroad Directory: Railroad - Railfan Index. Ed. by Karen Stephans & Earl Stephans. (Orig.). 1990. pap. text ed. 43.00 (*1-56360-000-5*) Tioga Pubns.

Stephans' Railroad Directory: Railroad Magazine, 1929-1927, Vol. 3. Railfan Magazine Staff. 600p. pap. 43.00 (*0-685-35153-X*) Tioga Pubns.

Stephans' Railroad Directory: Railway Quarterly, Vol. 5. 11.50 (*0-9616890-8-0*) Tioga Pubns.

Stephans' Railroad Directory: Railway Quarterly Index. Karen Stephans & Earl Stephans. (Orig.). 1990. pap. text ed. 11.50 (*1-56360-002-1*) Tioga Pubns.

Stephans' Railroad Directory: Rock Island Railroad. Karen Stephans & Earl Stephans. (Orig.). 1990. pap. text ed. 9.00 (*1-56360-014-5*) Tioga Pubns.

Stephans' Railroad Directory: Rutland Railroad. Karen Stephans & Earl Stephans. (Orig.). 1990. pap. text ed. 9.00 (*1-56360-012-9*) Tioga Pubns.

Stephans' Railroad Directory: Soo Railroad. Karen Stephans & Earl Stephans. (Orig.). 1990. pap. text ed. 9.00 (*1-56360-013-7*) Tioga Pubns.

Stephans' Railroad Directory: Structure Plans. Karen Stephans & Earl Stephans. (Orig.). 1990. pap. text ed. 11.50 (*1-56360-018-8*) Tioga Pubns.

Stephans' Railroad Directory: Tall Timber Short Lines. Karen Stephans & Earl Stephans. (Orig.). 1990. pap. text ed. 9.00 (*1-56360-001-3*) Tioga Pubns.

Stephans' Railroad Directory: Western Maryland Railroad. Karen Stephans & Earl Stephans. (Orig.). 1989. pap. text ed. 9.00 (*1-56360-015-3*) Tioga Pubns.

Stephans' Railroad Directory, Vol. 2: Railroad Model Craftsmans, 1932-1987. Earl Stephans. Ed. by Karen Stephans. (Stephans' Railroad Directory Ser.). (Illus.). 330p. 1988. pap. 27.00 (*0-9616890-1-3*) Tioga Pubns.

*__Stephen: Philosophical Works, 9 vols.__ 3812p. (C). 1991. text ed. 545.00 (*0-415-07775-3*) Routledge.

*__Stephen A. Douglas.__ LC 96-44592. 1997. pap. text ed. 24. 95 (*0-252-06635-9*) U of Ill Pr.

Stephen A. Douglas: A Study in American Politics. Allen Johnson. LC 77-98690. (American Scene Ser.). 1970. reprint ed. lib. bdg. 55.00 (*0-306-71836-7*) Da Capo.

Stephen A. Douglas & the American Union. Daniel Meyer. LC 94-2381. 48p. 1994. pap. 10.00 (*0-943056-21-7*) Univ Chi Lib.

Stephen & Bloom at Life's Feast: Alimentary Symbolism & the Creative Process in James Joyce's "Ulysses" Lindsey Tucker. LC 84-2342. 187p. 1984. 40.00 (*0-8142-0361-2*) Ohio St U Pr.

Stephen & Matilda. David Birt. (Resource Units: Middle Ages, 1066-1485 Ser.). (Illus.). 24p. 1974. teacher ed., pap. text ed. 12.95 (*0-582-39375-2*) Longman.

Stephen & Mr. Wilde. Bartley. 1994. per. 10.95 (*0-921368-36-4*, Pub. by Blizzard Pub CN) Genl Dist Srvs.

Stephen & Violet. large type ed. Susan Barrett. 1990. 25.99 (*0-7089-2116-7*) Ulverscroft.

Stephen Antonakos: Neon & Works on Paper. Sally Yard. LC 84-81111. (Illus.). 48p. (Orig.). 1984. pap. 15.00 (*0-934418-21-7*) Mus Contemp Art.

Stephen Archer & Other Tales. George MacDonald. (George MacDonald Original Works: Series IV). 354p. 1994. reprint ed. 16.00 (*1-881084-25-6*) Johannesen.

Stephen Archer, & Other Tales. George E. Macdonald. LC 79-152946. (Short Story Index Reprint Ser.). 1977. reprint ed. 23.95 (*0-8369-3805-4*) Ayer.

Stephen Arroyo's Chart Interpretation Handbook: Guidelines for Understanding the Essentials of the Birth Chart. Stephen Arroyo. Ed. by Jerilynn Marshall. 188p. (Orig.). 1989. pap. 10.95 (*0-916360-49-0*) CRCS Pubns CA.

Stephen Banks Leonard of Owego, Tioga Co., N. Y. W. A. Leonard. (Illus.). 342p. 1990. reprint ed. pap. 52.00 (*0-8328-1491-1*); reprint ed. lib. bdg. 60.00 (*0-8328-1490-3*) Higginson Bk Co.

Stephen Baron: De Regimine Principum: 1509. Ed. & Tr. by P. J. Mroczowski from LAT. LC 90-6126. (Illus.). 167p. (C). 1990. text ed. 54.95 (*0-8204-0648-1*) P Lang Pubng.

*__Stephen Biesty's Incredible Everything.__ Richard Platt. LC 97-15426. (Illus.). (J). 1997. 19.95 (*0-7894-2049-X*) DK Pub Inc.

Stephen Biesty's Incredible Explosions. Richard Platt. (Illus.). 32p. (J). 1996. 19.95 (*0-7894-1024-9*) DK Pub Inc.

*__Stephen Biesty's Incredible Explosions: Exploded Views of Astonishing Things.__ Stephen Biesty & Richard Platt. (Illus.). (J). 22.99 (*0-590-24893-6*) Scholastic Inc.

Stephen Biesty's Incredible Pop-Up Cross-Sections. Stephen Biesty. (Illus.). (J). 1995. 16.95 (*0-7894-0199-1*, 5-70612) DK Pub Inc.

Stephen Breyer. Paul L. Deegan. LC 96-3859. (United States Supreme Court Library). (J). 1996. lib. bdg. 14.98 (*1-56239-464-9*) Abdo & Dghtrs.

Stephen Cobb Advanced User's Guide to Excel: IBM Edition. Stephen Cobb. (Illus.). 400p. (Orig.). 1989. 34. 95 (*0-8306-9170-7*, Windcrest) TAB Bks.

Stephen Cobb Complete Book of PC & Lan Security. Stephen Cobb. (Illus.). 272p. 1991. 32.95 (*0-8306-9280-0*, Windcrest); pap. 24.95 (*0-8306-3280-8*, Windcrest) TAB Bks.

Stephen Cobb Complete Book of PC & LAN Security. Stephen Cobb. 1992. text ed. 36.95 (*0-07-157550-2*); pap. text ed. 24.95 (*0-07-157559-6*) McGraw.

Stephen Cobb User's Guide to FileMaker. Stephen Cobb & Chey Romfo. (Illus.). 400p. 1989. pap. 24.95 (*0-8306-3411-8*, Windcrest) TAB Bks.

Stephen Cobb User's Guide to FileMaker II. Stephen Cobb & Chey Romfo. 1991. pap. 24.95 (*0-07-156603-1*) McGraw.

Stephen Cobb User's Guide to WINGZ. Stephen Cobb. (Illus.). 400p. (Orig.). 1989. 31.95 (*0-8306-9150-2*, Windcrest); pap. 22.95 (*0-8306-3150-X*, Windcrest) TAB Bks.

Stephen Cobb User's Handbook to Lotus 1-2-3, Release 3.0. Stephen Cobb. 1990. pap. 24.95 (*0-07-156678-3*) McGraw.

Stephen Cobb User's Handbook to Lotus 1-2-3, Release 3.0. Stephen Cobb. (Illus.). 448p. 1989. pap. 24.95 (*0-8306-3417-7*, Windcrest) TAB Bks.

Stephen Collins Foster. H. V. Milligan. 1977. 250.00 (*0-87968-313-9*) Gordon Pr.

Stephen Crane. Michael Bettencourt. LC 93-17132. (Notebooks Ser.). (YA). (gr. 6 up). 1998. lib. bdg. 16.95 (*0-88682-621-7*) Creative Ed.

Stephen Crane. Intro. by Harold Bloom. (Modern Critical Views Series). 167p. 1987. 29.95 (*0-87754-694-0*) Chelsea Hse.

*__Stephen Crane.__ Ed. by Bonnie Szumski. LC 97-22100. (Literary Companion Ser.). (YA). (gr. 9-12). 1997. pap. 12.96 (*1-56510-642-3*) Greenhaven.

*__Stephen Crane.__ Ed. by Bonnie Szumski. LC 97-22100. (Literary Companion Ser.). (YA). (gr. 9-12). 1997. lib. bdg. 20.96 (*1-56510-643-1*) Greenhaven.

*__Stephen Crane.__ Ed. by Richard M. Weatherford. (Critical Heritage Ser.). 438p. (C). 1997. text ed. 15.00 (*0-415-15936-9*) Routledge.

Stephen Crane. Jean Cazemajou. LC 74-625287. (University of Minnesota Pamphlets on American Writers Ser.: No. 76). 47p. (Orig.). reprint ed. pap. 25.00 (*0-7837-2894-8*, 2057561) Bks Demand.

Stephen Crane: A Collection of Critical Essays. Ed. by M. Bassan. 1967. 12.95 (*0-13-188888-9*, Spectrum IN) Macmillan Gen Ref.

Stephen Crane: A Study in American Letters. Thomas Beer. (BCL1-PS American Literature Ser.). 248p. 1992. reprint ed. lib. bdg. 79.00 (*0-7812-6696-3*) Rprt Serv.

Stephen Crane: An Annotated Bibliography of Secondary Scholarship. Ed. by Patrick Dooley. (Reference Ser.). 300p. 1992. 45.00 (*0-8161-7265-X*, Hall Reference) Macmillan.

*__Stephen Crane: Great American Short Stories II.__ Ed. by Tony Napoli. LC 94-75023. (Classic Short Stories Ser.). (Illus.). 80p. 1994. pap. 5.95 (*0-7854-0583-6*) Am Guidance.

Stephen Crane see Modern Critical Views Series

Stephen Crane & Literary Impressionism. James Nagel. LC 80-16051. 200p. (C). 1980. 30.00 (*0-271-00267-0*) Pa St U Pr.

*__Stephen Crane Encyclopedia.__ Stanley Wertheim. LC 97-5859. 1997. text ed. write for info. (*0-313-29692-8*, Greenwood Pr) Greenwood.

Stephen Crane in Transition: Centenary Essays. Ed. & Intro. by Joseph Katz. LC 72-1390. (Illus.). 247p. 1972. 28.00 (*0-87580-032-7*) N Ill U Pr.

*__Stephen Crane, Journalism, & the Making of Modern American Literature.__ Michael Robertson. LC 97-15068. 1997. write for info. (*0-231-10968-7*); write for info. (*0-231-10969-5*) Col U Pr.

Stephen Crane's Artistry. Frank Bergon. LC 75-19159. 190p. reprint ed. pap. 54.20 (*0-685-20369-7*, 2029824) Bks Demand.

Stephen Crane's Love Letters to Nellie Crouse. Ed. by Edwin H. Cady & Lester G. Wells. 1954. 29.95 (*0-8156-2014-4*) Syracuse U Pr.

Stephen Crane's The Red Badge of Courage see Bloom's Notes

Stephen Crane's The Red Badge of Courage see Modern Critical Interpretations

Stephen Crane's The Red Badge of Courage see Bloom's Notes

Stephen D. adapted ed. James Joyce. 1968. pap. 5.25 (*0-8222-1079-7*) Dramatists Play.

Stephen Dodson Ramseur: Lee's Gallant General. Gary W. Gallagher. LC 84-13035. (Illus.). xiv, 232p. 1985. pap. 14.95 (*0-8078-4522-1*) U of NC Pr.

Stephen Dodson Ramseur: Lee's Gallant General. Gary W. Gallagher. LC 84-13035. (Illus.). 246p. 1995. 29.95 (*0-8078-1627-2*) U of NC Pr.

Stephen Donaldson. Melissa Barth. Ed. by Roger C. Schlobin. (Milford Ser.: Popular Writers of Today). pap. write for info. (*1-55742-028-9*); lib. bdg. write for info. (*1-55742-029-7*) Borgo Pr.

Stephen Douglas: The Last Years, 1857-1861. Damon Wells. (Illus.). 374p. 1990. reprint ed. pap. 14.95 (*0-292-77635-7*) U of Tex Pr.

Stephen E. Fabian's Women & Wonders. Stephen E. Fabian. 144p. 1995. 24.95 (*1-885611-08-0*); pap. 14.95 (*1-885611-09-9*) C F Miller.

Stephen E. Fabian's Women & Wonders. deluxe ed. Stephen E. Fabian. 144p. 1995. 60.00 (*1-885611-11-0*) C F Miller.

Stephen Elliott Welch of the Hampton Legion. John M. Priest. LC 94-10652. (Civil War Heritage Ser.: Vol. III). (Illus.). 101p. (Orig.). (C). 1994. pap. 12.00 (*0-942597-66-4*, Burd St Pr) White Mane Pub.

Stephen F. Austin: The Father of Texas. Jean Flynn. (Stories for Young Americans Ser.). (Illus.). 64p. (J). (gr. 4-7). 1981. 11.95 (*0-89015-285-3*) Sunbelt Media.

*__Stephen F. Austin: Wilderness Pioneer.__ Carol Hoff. LC 55-7501. (Illus.). 192p. (J). (gr. 4-8). 1987. reprint ed. pap. 10.95 (*1-885777-16-7*) Hendrick-Long.

*__Stephen F. Austin's Register of Families.__ Villamae Williams. 198p. 1996. reprint ed. 20.00 (*0-614-23481-6*, 6415) Clearfield Co.

Stephen Foster: American Troubadour. John Howard. 1993. reprint ed. lib. bdg. 89.00 (*0-7812-5470-1*) Rprt Serv.

*__Stephen Foster - Immortal Melodies.__ Ed. by Sy Feldman. 100p. (Orig.). (C). 1979. pap. text ed. 9.95 (*0-7692-0832-0*, TPF0076) Warner Brothers.

Stephen Foster Song Book. Stephen Foster & Richard Jackson. 224p. (Orig.). 1974. pap. 8.95 (*0-486-23048-1*) Dover.

Stephen Foster, Youth's Golden Gleam. Raymond Walters. 1993. reprint ed. lib. bdg. 89.00 (*0-7812-5412-4*) Rprt Serv.

Stephen Gates of Bingham & Lancaster, Massachusetts, & His Descendants. C. O. Gates. (Illus.). 370p. 1989. reprint ed. pap. 55.00 (*0-8328-0588-2*); reprint ed. lib. bdg. 63.00 (*0-8328-0587-4*) Higginson Bk Co.

Stephen Girard: The Life & Times of America's First Tycoon. George Wilson. (Illus.). 336p. 1995. 27.95 (*0-938289-56-X*) Combined Pub.

Stephen Girard, Founder. Cheesman A. Herrick. 1993. reprint ed. lib. bdg. 89.00 (*0-7812-5469-8*) Rprt Serv.

Stephen Hales: Scientist & Philanthropist. D. G. Allan & R. E. Schofield. 1980. 74.95 (*0-85967-482-7*, Pub. by Scolar Pr UK) Ashgate Pub Co.

Stephen Harris: Designer Craftsman. Hart Massey. (Illus.). 180p. 32.00 (*1-55046-124-9*, Pub. by Boston Mills Pr CN) Genl Dist Srvs.

Stephen Hawking. Harry Henderson. LC 93-49488. (Importance of... Biographies Ser.). (Illus.). 112p. (J). (gr. 5-8). 1995. lib. bdg. 17.96 (*1-56006-050-6*) Lucent Bks.

Stephen Hawking: A Life in Science. Michael White & John Gribbin. LC 92-36171. 320p. 1993. pap. 12.95 (*0-452-26988-1*, Plume) NAL-Dutton.

Stephen Hawking: Quest for a Theory of the Universe. Kitty Ferguson. LC 92-19542. 92p. 1992. mass mkt. 6.50 (*0-553-29895-X*) Bantam.

Stephen Hawking: Quest for a Theory of the Universe. Kitty Ferguson. (Non-Fiction Ser.). (Illus.). 160p. (YA). (gr. 9-12). 1991. lib. bdg. 22.70 (*0-531-11067-2*) Watts.

Stephen Hawking: The Physicist Who Has Lou Gehrig's Disease. Melissa McDaniel. (Great Achievers). (Illus.). 144p. (YA). (gr. 5 up). 1994. lib. bdg. 19.95 (*0-7910-2078-9*) Chelsea Hse.

Stephen Hawking: Understanding the Universe. Gail Sakurai. (Picture-Story Biographies Ser.). (Illus.). 32p. (J). (gr. 2-4). 1996. lib. bdg. 17.50 (*0-516-03394-8*) Childrens.

Stephen Hawking: Understanding the Universe. Gail Sakurai. (Picture-Story Biographies Ser.). 32p. (J). 1996. pap. 3.95 (*0-516-04195-9*); pap. 3.95 (*0-516-20055-0*) Childrens.

Stephen Hawking: Unlocking the Universe. Sheridan Simon. (People in Focus Ser.). (Illus.). 112p. (J). (gr. 5 up). 1991. lib. bdg. 13.95 (*0-87518-455-3*, Dillon Silver Burdett) Silver Burdett Pr.

An Asterisk (*) at the beginning of an entry indicates that the title is appearing in BIP for the first time.

Stephen Hawking's Universe: An Introduction to the Most Remarkable Scientist of Our Time. John Boslough. 168p. 1989. mass mkt. 5.99 (*0-380-70763-2*) Avon.

Stephen Hayes: Monotypes. Terri M. Hopkins. (Illus.). 4p. (Orig.). 1993. pap. text ed. 2.00 (*0-914435-21-3*) Marylhurst Art.

Stephen Hero. rev. ed. James Joyce. LC 63-14454. (Illus.). 1969. pap. 10.95 (*0-8112-0074-4*, NDP133) New Directions.

Stephen J. Field: Craftsman of the Law. Carl B. Swisher. (Brookings Institution Reprint Ser.). (Illus.). reprint ed. lib. bdg. 39.00 (*0-697-00171-7*) Irvington.

***Stephen Jenks: Complete Works.** Stephen Jenks. Ed. by David W. Steel. (Recent Researches in American Music Ser.: No. RRAM18). (Illus.). 404, lxxip. (Orig.). 1995. pap. 144.00 (*0-89579-316-4*) A-R Eds.

***Stephen King.** Ed. by Harold Bloom. (Modern Critical Views Ser.). (YA). 1997. text ed. 34.95 (*0-7910-4780-6*) Chelsea Hse.

Stephen King: A Critical Companion. Sharon A. Russell. LC 95-50460. (Critical Companions to Popular Contemporary Writers Ser.). 192p. 1996. text ed. 29.95 (*0-313-29417-8*, Greenwood Pr) Greenwood.

Stephen King: Master of Horror. Anne Saidman. (Achievers Ser.). (Illus.). 64p. (J). (gr. 4-9). 1992. lib. bdg. 17.50 (*0-8225-0545-2*, Lerner Publctns) Lerner Group.

Stephen King: Master of Horror. Anne Saidman. (J). (gr. 4-9). 1992. pap. 4.95 (*0-8225-9623-7*, Lerner Publctns) Lerner Group.

Stephen King: The Art of Darkness. Douglas E. Winter. 352p. 1986. pap. 5.99 (*0-451-16774-0*, Sig) NAL-Dutton.

Stephen King see Pop Culture Legends

Stephen King A to Z: A Dictionary of People, Places & Things in the Works of the King of Horror. Stephen J. Spignesi. LC 92-80347. 550p. 1995. lib. bdg. 85.00 (*1-56075-027-8*) Popular Culture.

Stephen King As Richard Bachman. Michael R. Collings. LC 85-2832. (Starmont Studies in Literary Criticism: No. 10). (Illus.). vi, 168p. 1985. pap. 21.00 (*0-930261-00-3*); lib. bdg. 31.00 (*0-930261-01-1*) Borgo Pr.

Stephen King Companion. George W. Beahm. 32.95 (*0-8488-1550-5*) Amereon Ltd.

Stephen King Companion. rev. ed. George W. Beahm. LC 95-23170. 332p. 1995. pap. 12.95 (*0-8362-0455-7*) Andrews & McMeel.

Stephen King: Man & Artist. rev. ed. Carroll F. Terrell. LC 89-64431. 160p. 1991. 50.00 (*0-9621570-9-0*); pap. 8.95 (*0-685-49334-2*) North Lights.

Stephen King Quiz Book. Stephen J. Spignesi. 1990. pap. 3.99 (*0-451-16708-2*, Sig) NAL-Dutton.

Stephen King Story. rev. ed. George W. Beahm. 340p. 1992. pap. 9.95 (*0-8362-8004-0*) Andrews & McMeel.

Stephen King's America. Jonathan P. Davis. LC 93-73797. (Illus.). 183p. 1994. 34.95 (*0-87972-647-4*); pap. 14.95 (*0-87972-648-2*) Bowling Green Univ Popular Press.

Stephen Korner: Philosophical Analysis & Reconstruction. Ed. by Jan T. Srzednicki. 184p. 1987. lib. bdg. 92.00 (*90-247-3543-2*, Pub. by M Nijhoff NE) Kluwer Ac.

Stephen Kroll Biography. (J). 1995. pap. write for info. (*0-590-39364-2*) Scholastic Inc.

Stephen le Heros. James Joyce. 288p. (FRE.). 1975. pap. 10.95 (*0-7859-2359-4*, 2070366707) Fr & Eur.

Stephen Leacock: Humour & Humanity. Gerald Lynch. 216p. (C). 1988. text ed. 44.95 (*0-7735-0652-7*, Pub. by McGill CN) U of Toronto Pr.

Stephen Leacock: The Sage of Orillia. James Doyle. (Illus.). 79p. (Orig.). 1993. pap. 9.95 (*1-55022-155-8*, Pub. by ECW Pr CN) LPC InBook.

***Stephen Leacock: The Sage of Orillia.** large type ed. James Doyle. (Illus.). 107p. 1995. pap. 15.95 (*1-55022-238-4*, Pub. by ECW Press CN) Genl Dist Srvs.

Stephen Lives! His Life, Suicide & Afterlife. Anne Puryear. Ed. by Pat Merrill. (Illus.). 400p. (Orig.). 1993. pap. 14.95 (*0-9634964-3-3*) N Paradigm.

***Stephen Lives! My Son Stephen: His Life, Suicide & Afterlife.** Anne Puryear. 1997. pap. 14.00 (*0-671-53664-8*) PB.

Stephen Long & America Frontier Expedition. Roger Nichols & Patrick L. Halley. LC 78-68878. (Illus.). 280p. 1980. 38.50 (*0-87413-149-9*) U Delaware Pr.

Stephen Long & American Frontier Exploration. Roger L. Nichols & Patrick L. Halley. LC 94-36696. (Illus.). 280p. 1995. pap. 14.95 (*0-8061-2724-4*) U of Okla Pr.

Stephen Mallory White. Kenneth M. Johnson. (Los Angeles Miscellany Ser.: No. 11). 33p. 1980. 15.00 (*0-87093-311-6*) Dawsons.

***Stephen Morris.** Nevil Shute. lib. bdg. 23.95 (*0-8488-2032-0*) Amereon Ltd.

Stephen of Lexington: Letters from Ireland, 1228-1229. Tr. by Barry W. O'Dwyer from LAT. (Cistercian Fathers Ser.: No. 28). Orig. Title: Registrum epistolarum Stephani de Lexinton abbatis de Stanniegia et de Saviagnaco. 1982. 24.95 (*0-87907-428-0*) Cistercian Pubns.

Stephen of Sawley: Treatises. Ed. by Bede K. Lackner. Tr. by Jeremiah F. O'Sullivan. 1984. 17.95 (*0-87907-636-4*) Cistercian Pubns.

Stephen Pollan's Fool Proof Guide to Selling Your Home. Stephen Pollan & Levine. (Illus.). 192p. 1996. pap. 11.00 (*0-684-80229-5*, Fireside) S&S Trade.

***Stephen Pollan's Guide to Buying a Home.** Stephen M. Pollan. LC 96-40870. 1997. pap. 11.00 (*0-684-80228-7*, Fireside) S&S Trade.

***Stephen Pollan's Guide to Renovating Your Kitchen.** Stephen M. Pollan. LC 96-48907. 1997. pap. 11.00 (*0-684-80227-9*, Fireside) S&S Trade.

Stephen Prina: "It Was the Best He Could Do at the Moment" Stephen Prina & Lynn Tillman. (Illus.). 104p. (Orig.). 1992. pap. 35.00 (*90-6918-094-4*, Pub. by Museum Boymans-van NE) Dist Art Pubs.

Stephen, Prophets Friend. Clarin D. Ashby. 436p. Date not set. 14.95 (*1-55517-210-5*) CFI Dist.

Stephen R. Deane: Early Maine Folk Calligrapher. Marius B. Peladeau. Ed. by Jean Howells. (Illus.). 128p. 1991. 24.95 (*0-933858-04-3*); pap. 19.95 (*0-933858-03-5*) Kennebec River.

Stephen R. Donaldson's Chronicles of Thomas Covenant: Variations on the Fantasy of Tradition. W. A. Senior. LC 95-1708. 280p. 1995. text ed. 35.00 (*0-87338-528-4*) Kent St U Pr.

Stephen Sayre: American Revolutionary Adventurer. John R. Alden. LC 88-771. 231p. 1983. pap. 65.90 (*0-7837-8526-7*, 2049335) Bks Demand.

Stephen Shore Photographs. Michael Auping. LC 81-83669. (Illus.). 20p. 1981. pap. 4.95 (*0-916758-07-9*) Ringling Mus Art.

***Stephen Sondheim.** Bloom. (Great Pop Songwriters Ser.). 1998. 45.00 (*0-02-864786-6*) S&S Trade.

Stephen Sondheim. Martin Gottfried. LC 93-6931. 1993. 49.50 (*0-8109-3844-8*) Abrams.

***Stephen Sondheim: A Casebook.** Joanne Gordon. Ed. by Kimball King. LC 97-25563. (Casebooks on Modern Dramatists: 23). 268p. 1997. text ed. 47.00 (*0-8153-2054-X*) Garland.

Stephen Spender. 35.00 (*0-8387-1370-X*) Bucknell U Pr.

***Stephen Spender: A Biography.** Leeming. 1996. 35.00 (*0-8050-4249-0*) St Martin.

Stephen Spender & the Thirties. A. Kingsley Weatherhead. LC 73-2891. 241p. 1975. 22.50 (*0-685-00935-1*) Bucknell U Pr.

Stephen the Black. Caroline H. Pemberton. LC 72-1520. (Black Heritage Library Collection). 1977. reprint ed. 28. 95 (*0-8369-9044-7*) Ayer.

Stephen Vincent Benet: The Life & Times of an American Man of Letters, 1898-1943. Charles A. Fenton. LC 77-19015. (Illus.). 436p. 1978. reprint ed. text ed. 37.50 (*0-313-20200-1*, FESB, Greenwood Pr) Greenwood.

Stephen Vincent Benet's Stories of America. adapted ed. Stephen Vincent Benet. 1971. pap. 5.25 (*0-8222-1080-0*) Dramatists Play.

Stephen Willats: Between Building & People. Stephen Willats. 144p. (Orig.). 1996. pap. 30.00 (*1-85490-436-1*) Academy Ed UK.

Stephens College. Photos by Dan White & Bob Krist. (Illus.). 112p. 1991. 39.00 (*0-916509-75-3*) Harmony Hse Pub.

Stephens Family with Collateral Branches. Edward S. Clark. (Illus.). 185p. 1994. reprint ed. pap. 29.50 (*0-8328-4385-7*) Higginson Bk Co.

Stephens Family with Collateral Branches. Edward S. Clark. (American Genealogical Record Ser.: Vol. I). (Illus.). 185p. 1994. reprint ed. lib. bdg. 39.50 (*0-8328-4384-9*) Higginson Bk Co.

Stephen's Frog. Barbara Feldman. (Illus.). 24p. (J). (ps-1). 1991. pap. 4.95 (*1-55037-201-7*, Pub. by Annick CN) Firefly Bks Ltd.

Stephen's Gift. Nancy Frederick. LC 92-91118. 64p. 1993. pap. 6.95 (*1-56002-263-9*, Univ Edtns) Aegina Pr.

Stephen's Green Dragon. Marie O. Hammond. (Illus.). 20p. (Orig.). (J). (gr. k-3). 1994. pap. text ed. 6.25 (*0-9642910-0-2*) Story Corner.

Stephen's Green Revisited. Richard Weber. LC 68-54471. 64p. 6800. 14.95 (*0-85105-140-5*) Dufour.

Stephen's Passion. 2nd ed. Roberta Kalechofsky. LC 75-30158. (Dover Pictorial Archives Ser.). (Illus.). 107p. (Orig.). 1975. reprint ed. pap. 10.00 (*0-916288-01-3*) Micah Pubns.

Stephen's Sermon & the Structure of Luke-Acts. Delbert L. Wiens. LC 96-13277. 1996. pap. 14.95 (*0-941037-39-8*) BIBAL Pr.

***Stephenson's Connecticut Civil Procedure.** Renee B. Bollier et al. 310p. 1997. text ed. 145.00 (*1-878698-38-9*) Atlantic Law.

Stepman. David Margolis. LC 95-22755. 192p. 1996. 22.00 (*1-877946-76-1*) Permanent Pr.

Stepmother in Fairy Tales. Jacqueline M. Schectman. 1991. 29.95 (*0-938434-78-0*); pap. 16.95 (*0-938434-77-2*) Sigo Pr.

Stepmotherhood: How to Survive Without Feeling Frustrated, Left Out, or Wicked. Cherie Burns. LC 86-45083. 240p. 1986. reprint ed. pap. 12.00 (*0-06-097064-2*, PL/7064, PL) HarpC.

Stepmothering. Donna Smith. LC 90-32771. 160p. 1990. text ed. 24.95 (*0-312-04792-4*) St Martin.

Stepmothers. Robin Lucas. 140p. 1996. pap. 16.95 (*0-7022-2644-0*, Pub. by Univ Queensland Pr AT) Intl Spec Bk.

Stepmothers: Keeping It Together with Your Husband & His Kids. Merry B. Jones & Jo A. Schiller. 256p. 1992. 18.95 (*1-55972-120-0*, Birch Ln Pr) Carol Pub Group.

Stepmothers Try Harder. Penny Humphrey. LC 87-30317. (Illus.). 64p. 1987. pap. 4.95 (*0-87131-525-4*) M Evans.

Stepparent Challenge: Making It Work. Stephen J. Williams. 1993. pap. 13.95 (*0-942361-72-5*) MasterMedia Pub.

Stepparenting. 1996. pap. 13.00 (*1-57566-113-6*) Kensgtn Pub Corp.

Stepparenting. Jeanette Lofas & Dawn E. Sova. 256p. 1987. mass mkt. 2.95 (*0-8217-1683-2*, Zebra Kensgtn) Kensgtn Pub Corp.

Stepparenting. Jeanette Lofas. 1990. pap. 3.95 (*0-8217-3192-0*) NAL-Dutton.

Stepparenting. Veryl Rosenbaum & Jean Rosenbaum. LC 77-22070. 160p. 1977. 12.95 (*0-88316-530-9*) Chandler & Sharp.

Stepparenting: Everything You Need to Know to Make It Work. Jeanette Lofas & Dawn B. Sova. 1995. pap. 12. 00 (*0-8217-4958-7*, Zebra Kensgtn) Kensgtn Pub Corp.

***Stepparenting: Everything You Need to Know to Make It Work!** Jeannette Lofas. pap. 13.00 (*0-8217-6113-7*) Kensgtn Pub Corp.

Stepparenting: Issues in Theory, Research, & Practice. Ed. by Kay Pasley & Marilyn Ihinger-Tallman. LC 93-25073. (Contributions in Sociology Ser.: No. 108). 304p. 1994. text ed. 65.00 (*0-313-28502-0*, PSO/, Greenwood Pr) Greenwood.

Stepparenting: Issues in Theory, Research, & Practice. Ed. by Kay Pasley & Marilyn Ihinger-Tallman. LC 93-25073. (Contributions in Sociology Ser.: 108). 304p. 1995. pap. text ed. 22.95 (*0-275-95381-5*, Greenwood Pr) Greenwood.

***Steppe.** Ilma Rakusa. Tr. by Solveig Emerson from GER. (Dichten Ser.: Vol. 3). 96p. (Orig.). 1997. pap. 10.00 (*1-886224-27-7*) Burning Deck.

Steppe. Piers Anthony. 256p. (Orig.). 1992. reprint ed. mass mkt. 3.99 (*0-8125-1922-1*) Tor Bks.

Steppe & Other Stories. Anton P. Chekhov. 400p. 1991. 17.00 (*0-679-40546-1*, Everymans Lib) Knopf.

Steppe & Other Stories. Anton P. Chekhov. Tr. by Adeline L. Kaye. LC 70-106263. (Short Story Index Reprint Ser.). 1977. 18.95 (*0-8369-3300-1*) Ayer.

Steppe & Other Stories. Anton P. Chekhov. Tr. & Intro. by Ronald Hingley. (World's Classics Ser.). 272p. 1991. pap. 5.95 (*0-19-282663-8*, 11921) OUP.

Steppelords of Mars. John A. Theisen. (Space: Eighteen Eighty-Nine Ser.). (Illus.). 64p. (Orig.). (YA). 1989. pap. 8.00 (*1-55878-025-4*) Game Designers.

Steppenwolf. Hermann Hesse. 1976. 21.95 (*0-8488-1050-3*) Amereon Ltd.

Steppenwolf. Hermann Hesse. LC 63-12171. 224p. 1990. pap. 7.95 (*0-8050-1247-8*, Owl) H Holt & Co.

***Steppenwolf.** Hermann Hesse. lib. bdg. 22.95 (*0-8488-2100-9*) Amereon Ltd.

Steppenwolf. Hermann Hesse. 190p. 1983. reprint ed. lib. bdg. 25.95 (*0-89966-448-2*) Buccaneer Bks.

Steppenwolf & Siddhartha. Hesse. (Book Notes Ser.). 1985. pap. 2.50 (*0-8120-3542-9*) Barron.

Steppenwolf & Siddhartha Notes. Carolyn R. Welch. 1973. pap. 3.95 (*0-8220-1224-3*) Cliffs.

Steppes to New Odessa: Germans from Russia Who Settled in Odessa Township, Dakota Territory. Cynthia A. Stupik. (Illus.). 87p. (Orig.). 1996. pap. 14.50 (*0-7884-0446-6*, S786) Heritage Bk.

Steppin' on the Blues: The Visible Rhythms of African American Dance. Jacqui Malone. LC 95-4413. (Illus.). 296p. 1996. 18.95 (*0-252-06508-5*); text ed. 44.95 (*0-252-02211-4*) U of Ill Pr.

Steppin' Out: New York Nightlife & the Transformation of American Culture, 1890-1930. Lewis A. Erenberg. LC 80-930. (Contributions in American Studies: No. 50). (Illus.). xix, 291p. 1981. text ed. 49.95 (*0-313-21342-9*, EUN/, Greenwood Pr) Greenwood.

Steppin' Out: New York Nightlife & the Transformation of American Culture, 1890-1930. Lewis A. Erenberg. LC 84-2770. (Illus.). xx, 312p. 1984. reprint ed. pap. text ed. 16.95 (*0-226-21515-6*) U Ch Pr.

Steppin' over the Glass: Life Journeys in Poetry & Prose. Johari Rashad. 80p. (Orig.). 1991. pap. 9.95 (*1-879260-05-0*) Evanston Pub.

Stepping -Stone Book Mar/April 96. Mark Sonnenfeld. 32p. Date not set. pap. 3.00 (*1-887379-06-1*) M Sonnenfeld.

Stepping Ahead see Stepfamilies Stepping Ahead: An Eight-Step Program for Successful Family Living

Stepping Away from Tradition - Children's Books of the Twenties & Thirties: Papers from a Symposium. Ed. by Sybille A. Jagusch. LC 88-600349. 139p. 1988. 25.00 (*0-8444-0620-1*) Lib Congress.

Stepping Back: Nuclear Arms Control & the End of the Cold War. William B. Vogele. LC 93-11861. 184p. 1994. text ed. 55.00 (*0-275-94644-4*, Praeger Pubs) Greenwood.

***Stepping Free of Limiting Patterns with Essence Repatterning.** Pat McCallum. 135p. 1992. pap. 16.00 (*0-9634488-0-3*) Source Unltd.

Stepping Heavenward. Elizabeth Prentiss. pap. 10.99 (*0-87377-078-1*) GAM Pubns.

Stepping Heavenward. rev. ed. Elizabeth Prentiss. 288p. 1992. pap. 11.95 (*1-879737-06-X*) Calvary Press.

Stepping Inside the Story: Sermons for Pentecost, Last Third - First Lesson. Thomas G. Rogers. LC 94-1001. (Orig.). 1994. pap. 9.00 (*0-7880-0045-4*) CSS OH.

Stepping into College English. 4th ed. Frederick C. Arnold. 264p. 1988. pap. 9.50 (*0-933704-63-1*) Dawn Pr.

Stepping Into Fantasy & Other Places. Carol McGinley. LC 90-70320. 1990. 5.95 (*1-55523-340-6*) Winston-Derek.

***Stepping into Freedom: Rules of Monastic Practice for Novices.** Thich Nhat Hanh. 220p. (Orig.). 1997. pap. 16.00 (*1-888375-02-7*) Parallax Pr.

Stepping into the Magic: A New Approach to Everyday Life. Gill Edwards. 240p. 1995. pap. 12.95 (*0-7499-1238-3*, Pub. by Piatkus Bks UK) London Brdge.

Stepping into Time. Jeannette M. Peek. 144p. 1994. pap. 19.95 (*1-56647-052-8*) Mutual Pub HI.

Stepping into Yourself, Grades Three to Six. Sindy Rosenbaum. (Illus.). 42p. (Orig.). 1988. pap. 7.95 (*0-673-38244-3*, GoodYrBooks) Addson-Wesley Educ.

***Stepping Left: Dance & Politics in New York City, 1928-1942.** Ellen Graff. LC 96-50908. (Illus.). 280p. 1997. pap. text ed. 17.95 (*0-8223-1948-9*); lib. bdg. 49.95 (*0-8223-1953-5*) Duke.

Stepping Lightly on Australia: A Traveller's Guide to Ecotourism. Photos & Text by Shirley LaPlanche. LC 95-43033. (Illus.). 1996. pap. 14.95 (*1-56440-904-X*) Globe Pequot.

Stepping Motors: A Guide to Modern Theory & Practice. rev. ed. P. P. Acarnley. (Control Engineering Ser.: No. 19). 160p. 1984. pap. 39.00 (*0-86341-027-8*, CEO19Z) Inst Elect Eng.

Stepping Motors & Their Microprocessor Controls. Takashi Kenjo & Akira Sugawara. (Monographs in Electrical & Electronic Engineering: No. 33). (Illus.). 288p. 1995. pap. 45.00 (*0-19-859385-6*) OUP.

***Stepping on Shadows.** Kay Thornton-Fitts. Ed. & Pref. by Don Thornton. (Illus.). 57p. (Orig.). 1996. write for info. (*1-882913-10-8*); pap. 10.00 (*1-882913-09-4*) Thornton LA.

Stepping on the Cracks. Mary D. Hahn. 224p. (J). 1992. pap. 4.50 (*0-380-71900-2*, Camelot) Avon.

Stepping on the Cracks. Mary D. Hahn. 240p. (J). (gr. 4-7). 1991. 16.00 (*0-395-58507-4*, Clarion Bks) HM.

Stepping on the Spiritual Scale. Larry Taylor. 146p. 1993. pap. 8.95 (*0-914936-58-1*) BT Pub.

Stepping Out. Rita Abrams. (J). 1991. audio 9.95 (*0-938971-75-1*) JTG Nashville.

Stepping Out. Bunn & Seymour. 1989. pap. 34.95 (*0-8384-3322-7*) Heinle & Heinle.

Stepping Out: A Guide to Short Term Missions. 212p. 1992. pap. 8.99 (*0-927545-29-2*) YWAM Pub.

Stepping Out: Nine Walks Through New York City's Gay & Lesbian History. Daniel Hurewitz. LC 97-1533. (Illus.). 240p. (Orig.). 1997. pap. 15.95 (*0-8050-4158-3*, Owl) H Holt & Co.

Stepping Out in Seattle: A Guide to Leisure Time Activities for Couples & Friends. Mandy Johnston. 1992. pap. 9.95 (*1-881409-03-1*) Jhnstn Assocs.

Stepping Out of Line: A Workbook on Lesbianism & Feminism. Hughes et al. 1984. pap. 12.95 (*0-88974-016-X*, Pub. by Press Gang CN) LPC InBook.

Stepping Out of the Plane under the Protection of the Army. Sal Salasin. LC 88-70975. 88p. (Orig.). 1988. pap. 9.50 (*0-9614644-6-1*) Another Chicago Pr.

Stepping Out of the Shadows: Alabama Women, 1819-1990. Ed. by Mary M. Thomas. LC 94-12230. 248p. 1995. pap. text ed. 19.95 (*0-8173-0756-7*) U of Ala Pr.

Stepping Out, Start Over. Montana. 1992. pap. text ed. write for info. (*0-07-042832-8*) McGraw.

Stepping Out Within: The Ennegram & Essence. Robert W. Olson. (Illus.). 276p. (Orig.). 1993. pap. 14.95 (*0-9634860-0-4*) Awakened Pr.

Stepping over Imaginary Lines. 112p. 1996. pap. 7.95 (*0-9650879-0-5*) Lemon Pie.

***Stepping over the Color Line: African-American Students in White Suburban Schools.** Amy S. Wells & Robert L. Crain. LC 96-43906. (Illus.). 384p. 1997. 35.00 (*0-300-06760-7*) Yale U Pr.

***Stepping Razor.** A. L. Nielsen. (Orig.). 1997. pap. 8.00 (*0-9619097-9-X*) Edge Bks.

Stepping Space. Ulli Freer. 1990. pap. 7.50 (*0-946904-12-X*) SPD-Small Pr Dist.

Stepping-Stone of God: Creation. Fintan Creven. 122p. 1994. pap. 35.00 (*0-85439-497-4*, Pub. by St Paul Pubns UK) St Mut.

Stepping-Stone to Architecture: Consisting of a Series of Questions & Answers Explaining in Simple Language the Principles & Progress of Architecture from the Earliest Times. Thomas Mitchell. 110p. 1995. reprint ed. pap. 12.95 (*1-56459-514-5*) Kessinger Pub.

Stepping Stone to the Supreme Court, Clarendon County, South Carolina. Benjamin F. Hornsby, Jr. Ed. by Judith M. Brimelow. (Topics in African American History Ser.). (Illus.). 28p. 1992. pap. text ed. 3.00 (*1-880067-12-9*) SC Dept of Arch & Hist.

Stepping-Stone Year: A Program for 8-10 Year Olds. 2nd ed. Margaret K. Gooding. Ed. by Judith Frediani. (Illus.). 176p. 1994. reprint ed. teacher ed., pap. 25.00 (*0-933840-54-3*) Unitarian Univ.

Stepping Stones. (Southern Exposure Ser.). (Illus.). (Orig.). (C). 1982. pap. 3.00 (*0-943810-72-8*) Inst Southern Studies.

Stepping-Stones. Ed. by Howard Booth. (C). 1990. pap. 24. 00 (*0-85305-297-2*, Pub. by J Arthur Ltd UK) St Mut.

Stepping Stones. Rose Fuller. 8p. 1979. 10.00 (*1-880220-01-6*) NW Family Srvs.

Stepping-Stones. Peter Jeffery. 144p. 1991. pap. text ed. 11. 99 (*0-85151-597-5*) Banner of Truth.

***Stepping Stones.** Alexander Karanikas. LC 93-86838. 178p. (Orig.). 1993. pap. text ed. 10.00 (*0-918618-60-6*) Pella Pub.

Stepping Stones. Dale V. Knowles. 120p. pap. 4.99 (*0-89900-344-3*) College Pr Pub.

Stepping Stones. Miriam Kosmon. 176p. 1992. write for info. (*1-56062-141-9*); pap. write for info. (*1-56062-142-7*) CIS Comm.

Stepping Stones. Dorothy E. Watts. Ed. by Raymond H. Woolsey. (Morning Watch Ser.). 384p. (J). (gr. 1 up). 1987. text ed. 9.99 (*0-8280-0384-X*) Review & Herald.

Stepping Stones: A Collection of Modern Poetry. Ed. by Louisa Persing. (Illus.). 1977. 5.95 (*0-686-20028-4*) Palomar.

Stepping Stones: Memoirs of Colonial Nigeria, 1907-1960. Sylvia Leith-Ross. 191p. 1983. 30.00 (*0-7206-0600-4*, Pub. by P Owen Ltd UK) Dufour.

Stepping Stones: The Pilgrims' Own Story. Illus. by Frank Hockaday. LC 86-72939. 232p. 1987. 19.95 (*0-8323-0453-0*) Binford Mort.

Stepping-Stones: The Reminiscences of a Woman Geologist in the Twentieth Century. Katharine Fowler-Billings. (Transactions Ser.: Vol. 53). (Illus.). 224p. 1996. text ed. 35.00 (*1-878508-11-3*) CT Acad Arts & Sciences.

S

Stepping Stones for Boys & Girls. Margaret M. Stevens. (Illus.). (J). (gr. 5 up). 1977. pap. 4.50 (*0-87516-248-7*) DeVorss.

Stepping Stones for Little Feet. Margaret M. Stevens. (Illus.). 31p. (J). (gr. 4-6). 1975. pap. 4.50 (*0-87516-202-9*) DeVorss.

Stepping Stones for Spiritual Success. Hua-Ching Ni. LC 89-64020. 160p. (Orig.). 1990. pap. 12.95 (*0-937064-25-4*) SevenStar Comm.

Stepping Stones of Faith. rev. ed. Donald R. Gilmore. LC 86-91881. 88p. 1987. write for info. (*0-9617810-0-9*) D R Gilmore.

***Stepping Stones of Love.** Ed. by Kelly O'Donnell. 1997. pap. 10.95 (*1-57532-043-6*) Press-Tige Pub.

Stepping Stones of the Steward: A Faith Journey Through Jesus' Parables. 2nd enl. rev. ed. Ronald E. Vallet. LC 94-34357. (Faith's Horizons Ser.: Vol. 1). 172p. 1994. pap. text ed. 11.00 (*0-8028-0834-4*) Eerdmans.

Stepping Stones to a Global Ethic. Ed. by Marcus Braybrooke. 160p. (Orig.). 1992. pap. 18.00 (*0-334-01574-X*, SCM Pr) TPI PA.

Stepping Stones to Bigger Faith for Little People. Joyce Herzog. (Illus.). 80p. (J). (gr. k-4). 1995. pap. 9.95 (*1-882514-16-5*) Greenleaf TN.

Stepping Stones to Further Jewish-Christian Relations. Helga B. Croner. LC 78-302169. (Studies in Judaism & Christianity: No. 1). 173p. reprint ed. pap. 49.40 (*0-8357-2703-3*, 2039815) Bks Demand.

Stepping Stones to Go. Shigemi Kishikawa. LC 65-13411. (Illus.). 160p. 1965. pap. 11.95 (*0-8048-0547-4*) C E Tuttle.

Stepping Stones to Hell: A Love Story. Jeanne Raffery. Ed. by Merit Group Staff. (Orig.). 1989. pap. text ed. 14.95 (*0-685-30397-7*) Merit Group.

Stepping Stones to Independence: National Insurance after 1990. Brandon R. Williams. Ed. by Hermione Parker. 76p. 1989. pap. text ed. 9.95 (*0-08-036594-9*, Pub. by Aberdeen U Pr) Macmillan.

***Stepping Stones to Praise & Worship.** Joyce Herzog. (Illus.). 128p. (J). (gr. k-4). 1997. pap. 14.95 (*1-882514-52-1*) Greenleaf TN.

Stepping Stones to Recovery. Bill Pittman. LC 87-73389. 308p. 1988. pap. 9.95 (*0-934125-04-X*) Hazelden.

Stepping Stones to Recovery: From Codependency. Ed. by Katie C et al. LC 91-42366. 240p. 1991. pap. 9.95 (*0-934125-24-4*) Hazelden.

Stepping Stones to Recovery for Men. Stephen Beal. LC 92-20195. 240p. (Orig.). 1992. pap. 9.95 (*0-934125-28-7*) Hazelden.

Stepping Stones to Recovery for Women. Ed. by B. Mary. LC 89-17751. 240p. (Orig.). 1990. pap. 9.95 (*0-934125-15-5*) Hazelden.

Stepping Stones to Recovery for Young People. Ed. by Lisa D. LC 91-8676. 240p. (Orig.). (YA). (gr. 9-12). 1991. pap. 10.95 (*0-934125-19-8*) Hazelden.

Stepping Stones to Recovery from Cocaine - Crack Addiction. Mark R & Mary L. LC 90-20336. 154p. (Orig.). 1990. pap. 7.95 (*0-934125-10-4*) Hazelden.

***Stepping Stones to Science: True Tales & Awesome Activities.** Kendall Haven. LC 97-7629. (Illus.). 165p. (Orig.). 1997. pap. 22.00 (*1-56308-516-X*) Libs Unl.

Stepping Stones to the Library. 1972. pap. 8.95 (*0-913308-04-8*) Fordham Pub.

Stepping Stones to Women's Liberty: Feminist Ideas in the Women's Suffrage Movement, 1900-1918. Les Garner. LC 83-25360. 144p. 1984. 29.50 (*0-8386-3223-8*) Fairleigh Dickinson.

***Stepping Stones 2 Coursebook.** Nelson U. K. Staff. 1991. pap. text ed. write for info. (*0-17-556492-2*) Addison-Wesley.

Stepping Through Excel 4.0 for Windows. Electronic Learning Facilitators, Inc. Staff. LC 92-72959. 264p. (C). 1993. pap. text ed. 17.50 (*0-03-096898-4*) Dryden Pr.

Stepping Through Excel 4.0 for Windows. Electronic Learning Facilitators, Inc. Staff. LC 92-72959. 264p. (C). 1993. teacher ed., pap. text ed. 28.00 (*0-03-097019-9*) Dryden Pr.

Stepping Through Windows. James Payne. LC 93-9770. 150p. 1993. pap. text ed. 25.20 (*0-13-014911-X*) P-H.

Stepping Through Windows 3.1. Electronic Learning Facilitators, Inc. Staff. LC 92-72957. 242p. (C). 1993. pap. text ed. 17.50 (*0-03-096901-8*) Dryden Pr.

Stepping Through Word 2.0 for Windows. Electronic Learning Facilitators, Inc. Staff. LC 92-72958. 307p. (C). 1993. pap. text ed. 17.50 (*0-03-096902-6*) Dryden Pr.

Stepping Through Word 2.0 for Windows. Electronic Learning Facilitators, Inc. Staff. LC 92-72958. 307p. (C). 1993. teacher ed., pap. text ed. 28.00 (*0-03-097017-2*) Dryden Pr.

***Stepping to the Dance: The Training of a Family Therapist.** Wells. LC 97-22912. (Social Work Ser.). 1998. pap. 29.95 (*0-534-34950-1*) Brooks-Cole.

Stepping Toward Control: A Book for People Who Live with Diabetes. Twila Okerlund. Ed. by Susan D. Allen & Colleen A. Holloran. (Illus.). 64p. pap. text ed. 3.75 (*0-916999-15-7*) HERC Inc.

Stepping Up to ISO 14000: Integrating Environmental Quality with ISO 9000 & TQM. Subash C. Puri. LC 96-13221. (Illus.). 280p. 1996. 39.00 (*1-56327-129-X*) Prod Press.

Stepping up to OS-2 Warp. R. Albrecht & M. Plura. 1995. 19.95 (*1-55755-269-X*) Abacus MI.

Stepping up to Supervisor. rev. ed. Marion E. Haynes. Ed. by Michael G. Crisp & Elaine Brett. LC 91-58108. 178p. 1991. pap. 16.95 (*1-56052-112-0*) Crisp Pubns.

Stepping Westward. Malcolm Bradbury. 352p. 1995. pap. 11.95 (*0-14-002865-X*, Penguin Bks) Viking Penguin.

Steppingstones. James A. Scarborough. 256p. 1987. 15.00 (*0-9618823-0-1*) Merigold Spirit Ctr.

Steppingstones: Ways to Better Reading. Patt McDermid. LC 92-33024. 379p. (C). 1993. pap. text ed. 29.95 (*1-55934-163-7*, 1163) Mayfield Pub.

Steppingstones, Instructor's Manual: Ways to Better Reading. Patt McDermid. LC 92-33024. (C). 1993. teacher ed., pap. text ed. write for info. (*1-55934-164-5*, 1164) Mayfield Pub.

Steppingstones One: Student Edition. J. Johnston. 1981. audio write for info. (*0-201-04656-3*) Addison-Wesley.

Steppingstones Toward an Ethics for Fellow Existers. Herbert Spiegelberg. 350p. 1986. lib. bdg. 118.50 (*90-247-2963-7*, Pub. by M Nijhoff NE) Kluwer Ac.

***Steps.** Jerzy N. Kosinski. LC 97-10183. 1997. write for info. (*0-8021-3517-X*, Grove) Grove-Atltic.

***Steps & Plateaus.** Zukowski. (C). 1995. pap. text ed. 17.00 (*0-15-599825-0*) HB Coll Pubs.

Steps for Better Reading Skills: Practice Test for the Georgia Regents' Reading Exam. Belita Gordon. 200p. (Orig.). (C). 1994. pap. text ed. 23.95 (*0-89892-128-7*) Contemp Pub Co of Raleigh.

***Steps for Launching a Capital Campaign.** Thomas W. Safranek. Ed. by Mary E. Tracy. (Development Ser.). 69p. (Orig.). 1996. pap. 6.00 (*1-55833-178-6*) Natl Cath Educ.

***Steps for Success in Starting & Operating a Business.** Ken Patchett. (Illus.). 90p. (ENG & SPA.). 1996. pap. 14.95 (*0-9654731-0-4*) K Patchett.

Steps Going Down. John McIntyre. 1993. reprint ed. lib. bdg. 89.00 (*0-685-62347-5*) Rprt Serv.

Steps Heavenward. R. L. Berry. 123p. pap. 1.00 (*0-686-29142-5*) Faith Pub Hse.

Steps in Classical Arthropod Biological Control. R. Van Driesche, pseud. (Thomas Say Monographs). 88p. 1993. 22.00 (*0-938522-46-9*, TSP3) Entomol Soc.

Steps in Clothing Skills. Draper & Bailey. (J). (gr. 7-9). 1978. teacher ed. 2.00 (*0-02-665720-1*); text ed. 20.80 (*0-02-665710-4*) Glencoe.

Steps in Commutative Algebra. R. Y. Sharp. (London Mathematical Society Student Texts Ser.: No. 19). 320p. (C). 1990. pap. text ed. 25.95 (*0-521-39732-4*) Cambridge U Pr.

Steps in Composition. 6th ed. Lynn Q. Troyka & Jerrold Nudelman. LC 93-29502. 512p. (C). 1993. pap. text ed. 37.00 (*0-13-042748-9*) P-H.

Steps in Composition: Alternate. 2nd ed. Lynn Q. Troyka & Jerrold Nudelman. (Illus.). 1979. pap. text ed. write for info. (*0-13-846550-9*) P-H.

Steps in Computing. R. Bateman & T. Hewitt. (C). 1986. 55.00 (*0-09-161311-6*, Pub. by S Thornes Pubs UK) St Mut.

Steps in Darkness. Krishna B. Vaid. 151p. 1972. pap. 2.75 (*0-88253-120-4*) Ind-US Inc.

Steps in Electronics. Ed. by J. Breithaupt et al. (C). 1989. 55.00 (*0-09-173093-7*, Pub. by S Thornes Pubs UK) St Mut.

Steps in Geography, Bk. 3. R. Bateman & F. Martin. (C). 1989. 50.00 (*0-7487-0185-0*, Pub. by S Thornes Pubs UK) St Mut.

Steps in History, Bk. 2: The Normans to the Birth of the U. S. A. L. F. Hobley. 96p. 8300. pap. 15.95 (*0-09-148991-1*) Dufour.

Steps in History, Bk. 3: The Modern World. Stanley Thornes. (C). 1983. 50.00 (*0-09-151991-8*, Pub. by S Thornes Pubs UK) St Mut.

Steps in Home Economics, Bk. 1. G. Hodge. (C). 1986. 50.00 (*0-09-163231-5*, Pub. by S Thornes Pubs UK) St Mut.

Steps in Home Economics, Bk. 2. Stanley Thornes. (C). 1987. 50.00 (*0-09-165831-4*, Pub. by S Thornes Pubs UK) St Mut.

Steps in Home Economics, Bk. 3. Stanley Thornes. (C). 1988. 50.00 (*0-09-165841-1*, Pub. by S Thornes Pubs UK) St Mut.

Steps in Home Living. Reiff & Ament. (gr. 7-9). 1984. text ed. 15.40 (*0-02-665750-3*) Glencoe.

Steps in Science, Bk. 1. B. Bateman & L. Lidston. (C). 1984. text ed. 55.00 (*0-7487-0192-3*, Pub. by S Thornes Pubs UK) St Mut.

Steps in Science, Bk. 2. B. Bateman & L. Lidston. (C). 1985. text ed. 50.00 (*0-7487-0193-1*, Pub. by S Thornes Pubs UK) St Mut.

Steps in Science, Bk. 3. B. Bateman & L. Lidston. (C). 1985. text ed. 50.00 (*0-09-159731-5*, Pub. by S Thornes Pubs UK) St Mut.

Steps in Technology. Ed. by R. Bateman & T. Hewitt. (C). 1989. 50.00 (*0-09-172984-X*, Pub. by S Thornes Pubs UK) St Mut.

Steps of Hope: A Recovery Guide for Sexual Addiction. Douglas Weiss. 110p. 1996. wbk. ed. 14.95 (*1-881292-21-5*) Discov TX.

Steps of Love: Single Adoptive Parenting. V. M. Cain. 133p. (Orig.). (YA). 1988. text ed. write for info. (*0-318-66287-6*) V M H Cain.

Steps of the Sun. Caroline Harvey. 1996. pap. 8.99 (*0-552-14407-X*) Bantam.

Steps of the Sun. Walter Tevis. LC 81-43899. 251p. 1983. 25.00 (*0-385-17037-8*) Ultramarine Pub.

***Steps of the Sun: A Novel.** Eva Thaddeus. LC 96-40210. 1997. 21.95 (*0-918056-09-8*) Ariadne Pr.

***Steps of Time.** Lou G. Cundiff. (Orig.). 1997. pap. write for info. (*1-57553-438-X*) Watermrk Pr.

Steps of Time. Thomas L. Fuller. 96p. (C). 1994. 19.99 (*0-9638966-0-1*) Decorum Pubng.

Steps to Better Health for Children. Ann R. Cox et al. 1985. pap. 13.95 (*0-8359-7110-4*, Reston) P-H.

Steps to Christ. Ellen G. White. (Devotional Ser.). (Illus.). 128p. 1995. pap. 7.95 (*1-886002-17-7*) Foy Inst Pr.

Steps to Christ. Ellen G. White. LC 56-7169. 134p. 1956. 8.99 (*0-8163-0045-3*, 19543-8); pap. 3.99 (*0-8163-0046-1*, 19547-9) Pacific Pr Pub Assn.

Steps to Christ for a Sanctified Life: How to Become & Remain a Christian. E. G. White. 134p. (Orig.). (C). 1993. pap. 6.95 (*1-883012-59-7*) Remnant Pubns.

***Steps to College Reading.** Seyler. LC 97-10323. 1997. pap. text ed. 30.00 (*0-205-26585-5*) P-H.

Steps to Common Entrance Mathematics One. W. Phillips. (C). 1989. text ed. 45.00 (*0-7487-0109-5*, Pub. by S Thornes Pubs UK) St Mut.

Steps to Composition: A Pre-Composition Workbook for Students of English As a Second Language. Ruth R. Alt & Mary L. Kirkland. 321p. 1973. pap. 7.95 (*0-87840-175-X*) Georgetown U Pr.

Steps to Consecutive Interpreting. David Bowen & Margareta Bowen. (Illus.). 160p. (C). 1997. pap. text ed. 9.50 (*0-9605686-4-6*) Pen & Booth.

Steps to Creating a School-to-Work Program: A General Guide for Program Design & Implementation. 27p. 1993. pap. 10.00 (*1-887410-59-7*) Jobs for Future.

Steps to End Illegal Immigration. 1996. lib. bdg. 250.75 (*0-8490-6912-2*) Gordon Pr.

Steps to English, Bk. 3. Doris Kernan. (Illus.). 288p. (gr. 5-6). 1975. text ed. 15.88 (*0-07-034163-X*) McGraw.

Steps to English, Bk. B. Doris Kernan. (gr. k-2). 1976. text ed. 8.28 (*0-07-034188-5*) McGraw.

***Steps to Follow: A Guide to the Treatment of Adult Hemiplegia.** 2nd expanded rev. ed. Patricia M. Davies. 300p. 1996. 59.00 (*3-540-60720-X*) Spr-Verlag.

Steps to Follow: A Guide to the Treatment of Adult Hemiplegia Based on the Concept of K. & B. Bobath. P. M. Davies. (Illus.). 335p. 1996. 46.00 (*0-387-13436-0*) Spr-Verlag.

***Steps to Freedom.** Reshad Field. 163p. 1996. pap. 9.00 (*0-614-21350-9*, 1163) Kazi Pubns.

Steps to Freedom: Discourses on the Alchemy of the Heart. Reshad Feild. LC 83-50115. 138p. (Orig.). 1983. pap. 9.00 (*0-939660-04-0*) Threshold VT.

***Steps to Handwriting.** Ashworth & Clark. Date not set. pap. text ed. write for info. (*0-17-556876-6*) Addison-Wesley.

***Steps to Handwriting Bk. 2.** Clark Ashworth. 1991. pap. text ed. write for info. (*0-00-370422-X*) Addison-Wesley.

Steps to Healthy Touching. Kee MacFarlane & Carolyn Cunningham. (Illus.). 144p. (Orig.). (J). (gr. k-7). 1988. student ed. 19.95 (*0-685-20041-8*, 1400) Kidsrights.

Steps to Help Your School Set up an AIDS Education Program. rev. ed. (Illus.). 23p. pap. 4.00 (*1-880002-04-3*) Natl Coal Advocates.

Steps to Hope. Joyce M. Shutt. LC 90-37806. 128p. (Orig.). 1990. pap. 7.99 (*0-8361-3524-5*) Herald Pr.

Steps to Improving Service Quality & Customer Satisfaction. 100p. 1991. pap. 194.00 (*0-89982-348-3*, 088700) Am Bankers.

Steps to Independence: A Skills Training Guide for Parents & Teachers of Children with Special Needs. 2nd ed. Bruce L. Baker et al. LC 88-22232. 336p. (C). 1989. pap. text ed. 24.00 (*1-55766-006-9*, 0069) P H Brookes.

Steps to Independence: A Skills Training Guide for Parents & Teachers of Children with Special Needs. 3rd ed. Bruce L. Baker et al. LC 96-26889. 1996. 26.00 (*1-55766-268-1*) P H Brookes.

Steps to Inner Freedom. Michiaki Horie & Hildegard Horie. Tr. by Dawn Huff from GER. (Illus.). 120p. (Orig.). (YA). (gr. 7 up). 1987. pap. 5.95 (*0-939925-06-0*) R C Law & Co.

Steps to Knowledge. 2nd rev. ed. Marshall V. Summers. LC 90-61253. 512p. 1995. reprint ed. pap. 25.00 (*0-9628028-7-5*) New Knowl Lib.

Steps to Language. I. M. Schlesinger. 448p. 1982. text ed. 79.95 (*0-89859-045-0*) L Erlbaum Assocs.

Steps to Learning: A Handbook of Developmental Activities. Mary S. Mank. LC 83-62303. 125p. (Orig.). (C). 1985. pap. text ed. 8.50 (*0-88247-723-4*) R & E Pubs.

Steps to Oratory: A School Speaker. F. Townsend Southwick. LC 72-167483. (Granger Index Reprint Ser.). 1977. reprint ed. 26.95 (*0-8369-6288-5*) Ayer.

Steps to Reading Proficiency. 3rd ed. Anne D. Phillips & Peter E. Sotiriou. 340p. (C). 1992. pap. 21.75 (*0-534-16518-4*) Wadsworth Pub.

Steps to Reading Proficiency. 4th ed. Anne D. Phillips & Peter E. Sotiriou. LC 95-23159. (C). 1996. pap. 31.95 (*0-534-26412-3*) Wadsworth Pub.

Steps to Self-Determination: A Curriculum to Help Adolescents Learn to Achieve Their Goals. Sharon Field & Alan Hoffman. (Orig.). 1996. pap. text ed. 25.00 (*0-89079-628-9*, 7800) PRO-ED.

Steps to Self-Mastery. S. R. Parchment. 223p. 1996. pap. 19.95 (*1-56459-627-3*) Kessinger Pub.

Steps to Self-Mastery. 3rd ed. S. R. Parchment. 242p. 1974. reprint ed. spiral bd. 11.00 (*0-7873-1095-6*) Hlth Research.

Steps to Singing for Voice Classes. 3rd ed. Royal Stanton. 291p. (C). 1983. Spiralbound. text ed. 36.95 (*0-534-01187-X*) Wadsworth Pub.

Steps to Small Business Start-Up: Everything You Need to Know to Turn Your Ideas into... 2nd ed. Linda Pinson & Jerry A. Jinnett. 256p. 1996. pap. 22.95 (*1-57410-038-6*, 61003602, Upstart) Dearborn Finan.

Steps to Stairs. 2nd ed. Nix Jacobsen. (Illus.). 175p. 1992. reprint ed. ring bd. 24.00 (*0-9634888-1-3*) N Jacobsen.

Steps to Success. James A. Meek. (Discover Life Ser.). 1994. pap. 19.05 (*1-56212-091-3*) CRC Pubns.

Steps to Success. Avi Rosen. 176p. 1995. pap. text ed. 19.95 (*0-7872-1624-0*) Kendall-Hunt.

Steps to the Abundant Life see Lay Counseling Series

***Steps to the Future: Fresh Thinking on the Managment of IT-Based Organizational Transformation.** Christopher Sauer & Philip W. Yetton. LC 96-51899. (The Jossey-Bass Business & Management Ser.). 1997. write for info. (*0-7879-0358-2*) Jossey-Bass.

Steps to the High Garden. Colin Duckworth. 350p. 1992. 26.95 (*0-7145-4155-9*); pap. 11.95 (*0-7145-4229-6*) Riverrun NY.

Steps to the Integrated Business System: A Comprehensive Guide to Business Concepts, Project Team Development, the Conference Room Pilot & Implementation Strategies. Max D. Fightmaster. (Illus.). 415p. (Orig.). 1993. pap. text ed. 88.00 (*0-9639003-0-7*) SIAM Intl.

Steps to the Sermon. Henry C. Brown, Jr. et al. LC 63-19068. 1963. 16.99 (*0-8054-2103-3*, 4221-03) Broadman.

Steps to the Sermon: An 8 Step Plan for Preaching with Confidence. rev. ed. H. Gordon Clinard et al. 240p. 1996. 24.99 (*0-8054-1238-7*, 4212-38) Broadman.

Steps to the Top. Zig Ziglar. LC 85-3428. 1985. 16.95 (*0-88289-460-9*) Pelican.

***Steps to Writing Well.** Jean Wyrick. (C). 1998. pap. text ed. 19.00 (*0-15-505453-8*) HB Coll Pubs.

Steps to Writing Well. 3rd ed. Jean Wyrick. (C). 1996. teacher ed., pap. text ed. 28.00 (*0-15-501990-2*) HB Coll Pubs.

Steps to Writing Well. 6th ed. Jean Wyrick. 467p. (C). 1996. pap. text ed. 33.75 (*0-15-501988-0*) HB Coll Pubs.

Steps to Writing Well: A Concise Guide to Composition. 4th ed. Jean Wyrick. 336p. (C). 1990. pap. text ed. 20.75 (*0-03-030807-0*) HB Coll Pubs.

Steps to Writing Well: A Concise Guide to Composition. 5th ed. Jean Wyrick. (Illus.). 400p. (C). 1993. pap. text ed. 20.75 (*0-03-076694-X*); Text with additional readings. pap. text ed. write for info. (*0-318-69514-6*); Instructor's manual. teacher ed. write for info. (*0-318-69515-4*) HB Coll Pubs.

Steps to Writing Well with Additional Reading. 3rd ed. Jean Wyrick. 624p. (C). 1996. pap. text ed. 36.75 (*0-15-501989-9*) HB Coll Pubs.

Steps to Writing Well with Additional Readings. 2nd ed. Jean Wyrick. (Illus.). 400p. (C). 1993. pap. text ed. 22.75 (*0-03-076696-6*) HB Coll Pubs.

Steps Toward Graduation: Access to Higher Education for People with Disabilities. Alan Hurst. 445p. 1993. 69.95 (*1-85628-379-8*, Pub. by Avebury Pub UK) Ashgate Pub Co.

Steps Toward Inner Peace. Peace Pilgrim. (Keepsake Editions Ser.). 64p. 1993. per. 8.00 (*0-943734-24-X*) Ocean Tree Bks.

Steps Toward Salvation: An Examination of Coinherence & Substitution in the Seven Novels of Charles Williams. Dennis L. Weeks. LC 90-28348. (American University Studies: English Language & Literature: Ser. IV, Vol. 125). 117p. (C). 1991. text ed. 35.95 (*0-8204-1438-7*) P Lang Pubng.

Steps Toward Wholeness: Coloring Book for Abuse Survivors. Paula A. Hurwitz. 180p. (Orig.). 1994. student ed., spiral bd. 14.95 (*1-56875-079-X*, 079-X) R & E Pubs.

Steps Towards European Nuclear Disarmament: Two Papers for the Rome Consultation on Nuclear Disarmament. K. Sorsa & Alva Myrdal. 79p. (Orig.). 1981. pap. 18.95 (*0-85124-304-5*, Pub. by Spokesman Bks UK) Coronet Bks.

Steps Towards Life: A Perspective on Evolution. Manfred Eigen & Ruthild Winkler-Oswatitsch. Tr. by Paul Woolley. (Illus.). 192p. 1996. reprint ed. pap. 24.95 (*0-19-854752-8*) OUP.

***Steps Towards Rembrandt: Selected Articles 1937-1972.** H. van de Waal. 292p. 1974. pap. text ed. 11.00 (*0-7204-8257-7*) Elsevier.

Steps under Water: A Novel. Alicia Kozameh. Tr. by David E. Davis from SPA. LC 96-13721. (Illus.). 161p. (C). 1996. pap. 12.95 (*0-520-20388-7*) U CA Pr.

Steps under Water: A Novel. Alicia Kozameh. Tr. by David E. Davis from SPA. LC 96-13721. (Illus.). 161p. (C). 1996. 35.00 (*0-520-20387-9*) U CA Pr.

Steps We Took. Joe McQ. (Illus.). 180p. (Orig.). 1990. pap. 11.95 (*0-87483-151-2*) August Hse.

Stepsister. R. L. Stine. Ed. by Patricia MacDonald. (Fear Street Ser.). 176p. (Orig.). (YA). (gr. 7 up). 1990. mass mkt. 3.99 (*0-671-70244-0*, Archway) PB.

***Stepsister from the Planet Weird.** Francess Lantz. (J). 1997. pap. 3.99 (*0-679-87330-9*, Bullseye Bks); lib. bdg. 11.99 (*0-679-97330-3*) Random Bks Yng Read.

Stepsister 2. R. L. Stine. (Fear Street Ser.: No. 33). (J). (gr. 7 up). 1995. mass mkt. 3.99 (*0-671-89426-9*) PB.

Stepsisters. Francine Pascal. (Sweet Valley High Ser.: No. 93). 160p. (YA). 1993. pap. 3.25 (*0-553-29850-X*) Bantam.

Stepson. Emmanuel Bove. 1994. 22.95 (*1-56897-004-8*) Marlboro Pr.

Stepson. Emmanuel Bove. Tr. by Nathalie Favre-Gilly from FRE. LC 93-80765. 330p. 1994. 22.95 (*1-56897-029-3*) Marlboro Pr.

Stepsons. Robert Liddell. 228p. 9200. 32.00 (*0-7206-0853-8*, Pub. by P Owen Ltd UK) Dufour.

Stepsons of France. Percival C. Wren. LC 74-169570. (Short Story Index Reprint Ser.). 1977. reprint ed. 21.95 (*0-8369-4033-4*) Ayer.

Stepwater: An Arbiter Tale. L. Warren Douglas. 288p. 1995. pap. 4.99 (*0-451-45468-5*, ROC) NAL-Dutton.

Stepwise Refinement of Distributed Systems: Models, Formalisms, Correctness; REX Workshop Mook, The Netherlands May 29-June 2, 1989 Proceedings. Ed. by J. W. De Bakker et al. (Lecture Notes in Computer Science Ser.: Vol. 430). x, 808p. 1990. 100.00 (*0-387-52559-9*) Spr-Verlag.

Stereo. (Illus.). 80p. 1990. 35.00 (*3-906700-31-3*, Pub. by Lars Muller SZ) Dist Art Pubs.

Stereo Book of Contours. Horace Macmahon. LC 74-188860. 32p. (J). (gr. 1 up). 1972. spiral bd. 6.95 (*0-8331-1705-X*, 456) Hubbard Sci.

Stereo Book of Fossils. Phillip Sandberg. (YA). (gr. 7 up). spiral bd. 12.95 (*0-8331-1702-5*, 585) Hubbard Sci.

An Asterisk (*) at the beginning of an entry indicates that the title is appearing in BIP for the first time.

Stereo Book of Rocks, Minerals & Gems. David Techter. 64p. (Orig.). (YA). (gr. 7-12). 1970. pap. text ed. 14.95 (*0-8331-1701-7*, 596) Hubbard Sci.

Stereo Boom Box, 4 vols., Set, Vols. 1-4. (J). (gr. 1-6). 1994. ring bd. 579.95 (*1-57405-047-8*) CharismaLife Pub.

Stereo Computer Graphics & Other True 3D Technologies. Ed. by David F. McAllister. LC 93-16642. (Computer Science Ser.). (Illus.). 328p. 1993. text ed. 85.00 (*0-691-08741-5*) Princeton U Pr.

Stereo Index: A Complete Catalogue of Every Recommended Stereo Disc. W. J. Wilson. LC 78-6968. 218p. 1978. reprint ed. text ed. 59.75 (*0-313-20512-4*, WITS, Greenwood Pr) Greenwood.

Stereo Infrared Landscapes. Steven Schwartzman. (Illus.). (Orig.). 1980. pap. 10.00 (*0-937710-01-6*) SunShine.

Stereo Installation Simplified. rev. ed. Donald R. Brann. LC 66-28495. Orig. Title: How to Build a Hi-Fi Music Wall. 1975. pap. 4.50 (*0-87733-612-1*); lib. bdg. 5.95 (*0-87733-120-0*) Easi-Bild.

Stereo Memories. Jim Sharp. 80p. 1996. pap. 11.95 (*0-9647155-0-3*) Bowman James.

Stereo Microphone Techniques. Bruce Bartlett. 192p. 1991. pap. 38.95 (*0-240-80076-1*, Focal) Buttrwrth-Heinemann.

***Stereo Nudes.** S. Narzarieff. 1994. pap. text ed. 8.99 (*3-8228-9440-0*) Taschen Amer.

Stereo Realist Camera Repair Manual: Repair & User's Manual. Edward H. Romney. 26p. 1992. pap. text ed. 20.00 (*1-886996-64-4*) Hillcrst Pub.

Stereo Views: An Illustrated History & Price Guide. John Waldsmith. LC 90-50638. (Illus.). 288p. 1991. pap. 22.95 (*0-87069-578-9*) Chilton.

Stereochemical Analysis of Alicyclic Compounds by C-13 NMR Spectroscopy. J. A. Whitesell & M. A. Minton. 240p. 1987. text ed. 65.00 (*0-412-29550-4*) Chapman & Hall.

***Stereochemical Applications of Gas-Phase Electron Diffraction, 2 pts.** Ed. by Istvan Hargittai & Magdolna Hargittai. Incl. Pt. A. . (Illus.). xviii, 563p. 1988. lib. bdg. 120.00 (*0-89573-337-4*, VCH); Pt. B. . (Illus.). xviii, 511p. 1988. Part B: Structural Information from Electron Diffraction for Selected Classes & Compounds, 511p. lib. bdg. 120.00 (*0-89573-292-0*, VCH); (Methods in Stereochemical Analysis Ser.). 220.00 (*0-89573-719-1*, VCH) Wiley.

***Stereochemical Applications of Gas-Phase Electron Diffraction: Part A.** Ed. by I. Hargittai & M. Hargittai. (Methods in Stereochemical Analysis Ser.). 1988. text ed. 120.00 (*0-471-18689-9*) Wiley.

Stereochemistry & Bonding. (Structure & Bonding Ser.: Vol. 71). (Illus.). 210p. 1989. 123.95 (*0-387-50775-2*) Spr-Verlag.

Stereochemistry & Mechanism Through Solved Problems. P. S. Kalsi. 1994. write for info. (*81-224-0655-6*, Pub. by Wiley Estrn II) Franklin.

Stereochemistry, Hydrocarbons, Halo Compounds & Oxygen Compounds see Comprehensive Organic Chemistry

Stereochemistry of Catalytic Reactions on Metals. M. Bartok et al. LC 84-13085. 632p. 1985. text ed. 565.00 (*0-471-90553-4*) Wiley.

Stereochemistry of Coordination Compounds. Alexander Von Zelewsky. LC 95-19754. (Inorganic Chemistry Ser.). 250p. 1996. text ed. 69.95 (*0-471-95057-2*); pap. text ed. 34.95 (*0-471-95599-X*) Wiley.

Stereochemistry of Heterogeneous Metal Catalysis. M. Bartok et al. LC 84-13085. (Illus.). 656p. reprint ed. pap. 180.00 (*0-7837-4393-9*, 2044133) Bks Demand.

Stereochemistry of Macromolecules, Vol. 1. A. D. Ketley. LC 67-19404. (Illus.). 424p. reprint ed. pap. 120.90 (*0-685-23656-0*, 2029000) Bks Demand.

Stereochemistry of Macromolecules, Vol. 2. Ed. by A. D. Ketley. LC 67-19404. 397p. reprint ed. pap. 113.20 (*0-685-16310-5*, 2027120) Bks Demand.

Stereochemistry of Macromolecules, Vol 3. Ed. by A. D. Ketley. LC 67-19404. 476p. reprint ed. pap. 135.70 (*0-317-08344-9*, 2055060) Bks Demand.

Stereochemistry of Optically Active Transition Metal Compounds. Ed. by Bodie Douglas & Yoshihiko Saito. LC 80-10816. (ACS Symposium Ser.: No. 119). 1980. 49.95 (*0-8412-0538-8*) Am Chemical.

***Stereochemistry of Optically Active Transition Metal Compounds.** Ed. by Bodie E. Douglas & Yoshihiko Saito. LC 80-10816. (ACS Symposium Ser.: Vol. 119). 456p. 1980. reprint ed. pap. 130.00 (*0-608-03057-0*, 2063510) Bks Demand.

Stereochemistry of Organic Compounds. Ernest L. Eliel & Samuel H. Wilen. LC 93-12476. 1267p. 1994. text ed. 79.95 (*0-471-01670-5*) Wiley.

***Stereochemistry of Organic Compounds.** Ernest L. Eliel & Samuel H. Wilen. LC 93-12476. 1994. pap. text ed. 51. 95 (*0-471-05446-1*) Wiley.

Stereochemistry of Organic Compounds: Principles & Applications. D. Nasipuri. (C). 1991. 55.00 (*0-685-51528-1*) S Asia.

Stereochemistry of Organic Compounds: Principles & Applications. 2nd ed. D. Nasipuri. 1994. write for info. (*81-224-0570-3*, Pub. by Wiley Estrn II) Franklin.

***Stereochemistry of Radical Reactions: Concepts, Guidelines, & Synthetic Applications.** Dennis P. Curran et al. (Illus.). xii, 280p. 1996. pap. 70.00 (*3-527-29409-0*, VCH) Wiley.

Stereocontrolled Organic Synthesis. Ed. by Barry M. Trost. LC 94-30353. 1994. 99.50 (*0-86542-833-6*) Blackwell Sci.

***Stereocopes: The First One Hundred Years.** Paul Wing. LC 96-61199. (Illus.). 272p. (Orig.). 1996. pap. 49.95 (*0-9654497-1-8*) Transit Pub.

Stereodirected Synthesis with Organoboranes. Paul V. Schleyer & R. Zahradnik. (Reactivity & Structure Ser.: Vol. 32). (Illus.). 400p. 1995. 174.95 (*3-540-59182-6*) Spr-Verlag.

Stereoelectronic Control in the Cleavage of Tetrahedral Intermediates in the Hydrolysis of Esters & Amides. Pierre Deslongchamps. Ed. by Barton et al. 1976. pap. 15.50 (*0-08-020480-5*, Pergamon Pr) Elsevier.

Stereoelectronic Effects. Antony J. Kirby. (Oxford Chemistry Primers Ser.: Vol. 36). (Illus.). 96p. (C). 1996. pap. text ed. 11.95 (*0-19-855893-7*) OUP.

Stereoencephalotomy Symposium, 5th, International, 1970. Stereoencephalotomy Symposium Staff. Ed. by F. Mundinger et al. (Advances in Stereoencephalotomy Ser.: Vol. 6). 1972. pap. 65.00 (*3-8055-1358-5*) S Karger.

Stereogram Programming Techniques. Christopher D. Watkins & Vincent P. Mallette. (Illus.). 250p. (Orig.). 1995. pap. 29.95 (*1-886801-00-2*) Chrles River Media.

Stereographic Projection Techniques in Structural Geology. Peter R. Leyshon & Richard J. Lisle. LC 95-14960. (Illus.). 112p. 1995. pap. 34.95 (*0-7506-2450-7*) Buttrwrth-Heinemann.

Stereolithography & Other RP&M Technologies: From Rapid Prototyping to Rapid Tooling. Paul F. Jacobs. LC 95-70369. (Illus.). 460p. 1995. 88.00 (*0-87263-467-1*, 2441) SME.

Stereological Methods, Vol. 2: Theoretical Foundations. Ewald Weibel. LC 78-75269. 1981. text ed. 179.00 (*0-12-742202-1*) Acad Pr.

Stereology & Morphometry in Election Microscopy: Some Problem & Their Solutions. Ed. by Albrecht Reith & Terry M. Mayhew. (Ultrastructural Pathology Publication). 215p. 1988. 104.00 (*0-89116-623-8*) Hemisp Pub.

Stereology & Quantitative Metallography - STP 504. 180p. 1972. 9.75 (*0-8031-0095-7*, 04-504000-28) ASTM.

***Stereophotogrammetrisch-Sedimentologische Aufnahme und 3-D-Modellierung von Schraeschichtungsgefuegen Am Biespiel Eines Pliozaenen Fluviaien Abfolge der Niederrheinischen Bucht.** Mario Valdivia-Manchego. (Bonner Geowissen Schaftliche Schriften Ser.: Band 21). 152p. pap. 55.00 (*3-931251-12-8*, Pub. by Martina Galunder GW) Balogh.

Stereophyllaceae. Robert R. Ireland & William R. Buck. (Flora Neotropica Monographs: Vol. 65). (Illus.). 50p. 1994. pap. text ed. 12.50 (*0-89327-388-0*) NY Botanical.

Stereoscope & Stereoscopic Photography. fac. ed. F. Drouin et al. Tr. by Matthew Surface from FRE. (Historical 3-D Reprint Ser.: No. 2). Orig. Title: Le Stereoscope et la Photographie Stereoscopique. (Illus.). 188p. 1995. reprint ed. pap. 14.95 (*0-939617-02-1*, 1050) Reel Three-D.

***Stereoscopes: The First One Hundred Years.** Paul Wing. LC 96-61199. (Illus.). 272p. 1996. 74.95 (*0-9654497-4-2*) Transit Pub.

Stereoscopic Acuity in Ocular Pursuit of Moving Objects: Dynamic Stereoscopy & Movement Parallax: Relevance to Road Safety & Occupational Medicine. Matthias Sachsenweger & Ulrich Sachsenweger. 136p. (C). 1992. pap. text ed. 104.50 (*0-7923-1486-7*) Kluwer Ac.

Stereoscopic Displays & Applications III. Ed. by S. S. Fisher & J. O. Merritt. 1992. 20.00 (*0-8194-0823-9*, 1669) SPIE.

Stereoscopic Perspective: Reflections on American Fine & Folk Art. Michael D. Hall. LC 87-30050. (Contemporary American Art Critics Ser.: No. 11). 282p. reprint ed. pap. 80.40 (*0-8357-1860-3*, 2070656) Bks Demand.

Stereoscopic Phenomena of Light & Sight: A Guide to the Practice of Steoscopic Photography & Its Relation to Binocular Vision. Theodore Brown. (Illus.). 144p. (C). 1994. reprint ed. pap. 14.95 (*0-939617-01-3*) Reel Three-D.

Stereoselective Chemical Technology. BCC Staff. 199p. 1990. 2,850.00 (*0-89336-724-9*, C079) BCC.

Stereoselective Reactions at the -Carbon Atom in Organosulfur Compounds, Vol. 3. J. Drabowicz. (Sulfur Reports). 439p. 1992. pap. text ed. write for info. (*3-7186-5316-8*, Harwood Acad Pubs) Gordon & Breach.

***Stereoselective Reactions of Metal-Activated Molecules: Proceedings of the 2nd Symposium Held in Wurzburg, September 21-23, 1994.** Helmut Werner & Jorg Sundermeyer. 236p. 1995. 91.00 (*3-528-06664-4*) Informatica.

Stereoselective Synthesis. (Studies in Natural Products Chemistry: Vol. 18, Pt. K). 1108p. 1996. text ed. 648.25 (*0-444-82458-8*) Elsevier.

Stereoselective Synthesis. Robert S. Atkinson. LC 94-20918. 300p. 1995. text ed. 149.00 (*0-471-95250-8*) Wiley.

Stereoselective Synthesis. Robert S. Atkinson. LC 94-20918. 300p. 1995. pap. text ed. 59.95 (*0-471-95419-5*) Wiley.

***Stereoselective Synthesis: A Practical Approach.** 2nd rev. ed. M. Nogradi. (Illus.). xviii, 368p. 1994. 90.00 (*3-527-29242-X*, VCH); pap. 45.00 (*3-527-29243-8*, VCH) Wiley.

Stereoselective Synthesis: Lectures Honouring Rudolf Wiechert. Ed. by E. Ottow et al. LC 93-34943. 160p. 1994. 123.95 (*0-387-57202-3*) Spr-Verlag.

Stereoselective Synthesis in Organic Chemistry. Atta-Ur-Rahman & Zahir Shah. LC 93-284. 1994. 95.95 (*0-387-94029-4*) Spr-Verlag.

***Stereoselective Synthesis-Workbench Edition: Houben-Weyl, Methods of Organic Chemistry.** G. Helmchen et al. (Methods in Organic Chemistry - Houben-Weyl Ser.). 6989p. 1996. pap. 2,400.00 (*0-86577-674-1*) Thieme Med Pubs.

Stereoselectivity of Pesticides: Biological & Chemical Problems. Ed. by E. J. Ariens et al. (Chemicals in Agriculture Ser.: Vol. 1). 544p. 1988. 258.75 (*0-444-42853-4*) Elsevier.

Stereotactic & Functional Neurosurgery. Philip L. Gildenberg & Ronald R. Tasker. (Illus.). 1968p. 1997. 325.00 (*0-07-023604-6*) McGraw-Hill HPD.

Stereotactic & Image Directed Surgery of Brain Tumours. Ed. by D. G. Thomas. LC 92-49428. 1993. 129.95 (*0-443-04445-7*) Churchill.

Stereotactic Neuro-Radio-Surgery: Proceedings of the International Symposium in Vienna, Austria, October 11-14, 1992. Ed. by Wolfgang T. Koos & B. Richling. LC 95-3226. (Acta Neurochirugica Ser.: Suppl. No. 63). (Illus.). 140p. 1995. 105.00 (*3-211-82657-2*) Spr-Verlag.

Stereotactic Radiosurgery. Ed. by Eben Alexander, 3rd et al. (Illus.). 254p. 1993. text ed. 110.00 (*0-07-001020-X*) McGraw-Hill HPD.

Stereotactic Radiosurgery: For Brain Tumors. (Illus.). 1996. write for info. (*0-944093-42-6*) Am Brain Tumor.

Stereotactic Radiosurgery Update. Dade L. Lunsford. (C). 1992. text ed. 128.00 (*0-13-050139-5*) P-H.

Stereotactic Techniques in Clinical Neurosurgery. D. A. Bosch. (Illus.). 288p. 1986. 112.00 (*0-387-81878-2*) Spr-Verlag.

Stereotaxic Atlas of the Brain of the Chick (Gallus Domesticus) Wayne J. Kuenzel & Manju Masson. LC 88-45396. (Illus.). 176p. 1988. text ed. 75.00 (*0-8018-3700-6*) Johns Hopkins.

Stereotaxic Atlas of the Cat Brain. Ray S. Snider & William T. Niemer. LC 60-7244. (Illus.). 136p. reprint ed. 38.80 (*0-8357-9656-6*, 2016990) Bks Demand.

Stereotaxic Atlas of the Developing Rat Brain. Nancy Sherwood & Paola S. Timiras. LC 70-103674. (Illus.). (FRE & GER.). 1970. 90.00 (*0-520-01656-4*) U CA Pr.

Stereotaxic Atlas of the Monkey Brain (Macaca Mulatta) Ray S. Snider & John C. Lee. LC 61-8079. 134p. reprint ed. pap. 38.20 (*0-317-29972-7*, 2051758) Bks Demand.

Stereotaxic Atlas of the New Zealand Rabbit's Brain. Ivan Urban & Philippe Richard. (Illus.). 92p. 1972. 21.95 (*0-398-02431-6*) C C Thomas.

Stereotaxic Atlas of the Rabbit Brain. Makram Girgis. (Illus.). 76p. 1981. 35.00 (*0-87527-297-5*) Green.

Stereotaxic Atlas of the Rat Brain. 2nd ed. L. J. Pellegrino et al. LC 79-9438. 280p. 1979. 52.50 (*0-306-40269-6*, Plenum Pr) Plenum.

Stereotaxy of the Human Brain: Anatomical, Physiological & Clinical Applications. Ed. by Georges Schaltenbrand & Earl A. Walker. (Illus.). 700p. 1982. 169.00 (*0-86577-055-7*) Thieme Med Pubs.

Stereotoceras & the Brevicoceratidae see Palaeontographica Americana: Vol. 3

Stereotype Accuracy: Toward Appreciating Group Differences. Ed. by Yueh-Ting Lee et al. LC 95-16845. 330p. 1995. text ed. 39.95 (*1-55798-307-0*) Am Psychol.

Stereotype & Status: Librarians in the U. S. Pauline Wilson. LC 82-6119. (Contributions in Librarianship & Information Science Ser.: No. 41). x, 225p. 1982. text ed. 55.00 (*0-313-23516-3*, WIL/, Greenwood Pr) Greenwood.

Stereotype Systems & Historical Changes. Gyorgy Hunyady. (International Series in Experimental Social Psychology: Vol. 33). 250p. 1995. write for info. (*0-08-042411-2*, Pergamon Pr) Elsevier.

Stereotyped Movement Disorders. Robert S. Jones et al. LC 94-43840. (Clinical Psychology Ser.). 240p. 1995. text ed. 50.00 (*0-471-93903-X*) Wiley.

Stereotyped Movements: Brain & Behavior Relationships. Ed. by Robert L. Sprague & Karl M. Newell. LC 95-4732. (APA Science Conference Ser.). (Illus.). 211p. 1996. 39.95 (*1-55798-301-1*) Am Psychol.

Stereotypes & Social Cognition. Jacques-Philippe Leyens et al. 256p. 1994. 69.95 (*0-8039-8583-5*); pap. 24.95 (*0-8039-8584-3*) Sage.

Stereotypes & Stereotyping. Ed. by C. Neil Macrae et al. LC 95-37283. 1996. lib. bdg. 55.00 (*1-57230-053-1*) Guilford Pr.

Stereotypes of Latin America, Press Images, & U. S. Foreign Policy, 1920-1933. Sarah E. Sharbach. LC 92-35098. (Modern American History: New Studies & Outstanding Dissertations). 256p. 1993. text ed. 67.00 (*0-8153-1102-8*) Garland.

Stereotypes of Women in Power: Historical Perspectives & Revisionist Views. Ed. by Barbara Garlick et al. LC 91-20042. (Contributions in Women's Studies: No. 125). 244p. 1992. text ed. 49.95 (*0-313-27731-1*, GSV, Greenwood Pr) Greenwood.

Stereotypic Animal Behaviour: Fundamentals & Applications to Welfare. Ed. by A. B. Lawrence & J. Rushen. 224p. 1993. 80.00 (*0-85198-824-5*) CAB Intl.

Stereotyping & Prejudice. Ed. by Daniel Bar-Tal et al. (Social Psychology Ser.). (Illus.). 275p. 1989. 44.00 (*0-387-96883-0*) Spr-Verlag.

Stereotyping & Social Reality. Penelope J. Oakes et al. (Illus.). 272p. 1994. pap. 25.95 (*0-631-18872-X*) Blackwell Pubs.

Stereoviews Illustrated: Fifty Early American, Vol. I. Russell Norton. LC 94-92191. (Illus.). 64p. (Orig.). 1994. pap. 18.95 (*0-9641653-0-9*) Stereoviews.

Steric Aspects of Biomolecular Interactions. Ed. by K. Simon & Gabor Naray-Szabo. 386p. 1987. 155.00 (*0-8493-6840-5*, QP517, CRC Reprint) Franklin.

Steric Exclusion Liquid Chromatography of Polymers. Janca. (Chromatographic Science Ser.: Vol. 25). 352p. 1984. 160.00 (*0-8247-7065-X*) Dekker.

Steric Factor in Medicinal Chemistry: Dissymmetric Probes of Pharmacological Receptors. Alan F. Casy. (Illus.). 590p. (C). 1994. 125.00 (*0-306-44289-2*, Plenum Pr) Plenum.

Steric Fit in Quantitative Structure-Activity Relations. Ed. by A. T. Balaban et al. (Lecture Notes in Chemistry Ser.: Vol. 15). (Illus.). 178p. 1980. 27.95 (*0-387-09755-4*) Spr-Verlag.

Sterile Cuckoo. John Nichols. 224p. 1996. reprint ed. pap. 12.00 (*0-393-31535-5*) Norton.

Sterile Dosage Forms, Their Preparations & Clinical Application. 4th ed. Salvatore J. Turco. (Illus.). 470p. 1993. pap. 45.00 (*0-8121-1617-8*) Williams & Wilkins.

Sterile-Male Technique for Control of Fruit Flies. (Panel Proceedings Ser.). (Illus.). (Orig.). 1970. pap. 25.00 (*92-0-111570-9*, ISP276, Pub. by IAEA AU) Bernan Associates.

Sterile-Male Technique for Eradication or Control of Harmful Insects. (Panel Proceedings Ser.). 1969. pap. 18.00 (*92-0-111369-2*, ISP224, Pub. by IAEA AU) Bernan Associates.

Sterile Pharmaceutical Manufacturing: Applications for the 1990s, Vol. I. Ed. by Michael Groves et al. 244p. 1991. 86.50 (*0-935184-21-X*) Interpharm.

Sterile Pharmaceutical Manufacturing: Applications for the 1990s, Vol. II. Ed. by Michael Groves et al. 243p. 1991. 89.50 (*0-935184-22-8*) Interpharm.

Sterile Pharmaceutical Packaging: Compatibility & Stability. No. 5. 125p. (*0-318-60095-1*) PDA.

Sterile Pharmaceutical Products: Process Engineering Applications I. Ed. by Kenneth Avis. LC 95-24999. (Drug Manufacturing Technology Ser.). (Illus.). 415p. 1995. 179.00 (*0-935184-81-3*) Interpharm.

***Sterile Product Facility Design & Project Management.** Jeffery N. Odum. (Illus.). 320p. 1996. ring bd. 179.00 (*1-57491-020-5*) Interpharm.

Sterilisation & Hygiene: A Practical Guide. W. Peberdy. 136p. (C). 1988. 75.00 (*0-85950-900-1*, Pub. by S Thornes Pubs UK) St Mut.

Sterilization: Changing Technologies, Products & Markets. 215p. 1993. 2,650.00 (*0-89336-997-7*, GA-056R) BCC.

Sterilization & Disinfection: Index of Modern Information for Medicine & Research with Bibliography. rev. ed. Stanley B. Gessler. 149p. 1994. 44.50 (*0-7883-0192-6*); pap. 39.50 (*0-7883-0193-4*) ABBE Pubs Assn.

Sterilization & Preservation of Biological Tissues by Ionizing Radiation. (Panel Proceedings Ser.). (Illus.). 127p. (Orig.). 1970. pap. 18.00 (*92-0-111370-6*, ISP247, Pub. by IAEA AU) Bernan Associates.

Sterilization for Human Betterment. E. S. Gosney & Paul Popenoe. Ed. by Gerald N. Grob. LC 78-22561. (Historical Issues in Mental Health Ser.). 1980. reprint ed. lib. bdg. 18.95 (*0-405-11915-1*) Ayer.

Sterilization (Involuntary) A Case Study. Intro. by Thomas J. Rundquist. (Illus.). 54p. (Orig.). (C). 1993. pap. 29.95 (*0-9618567-8-5*) Nova Media.

Sterilization (Involuntary) A Case Study. rev. ed. Ed. by Thomas J. Rundquist. (Illus.). 85p. (Orig.). (C). 1994. pap. text ed. 19.95 (*1-884239-00-5*) Nova Media.

Sterilization of Carrie Buck: Was She Feebleminded - Or Society's Pawn? J. David Smith & K. Ray Nelson. LC 89-61444. 268p. 1989. 22.95 (*0-88282-045-1*) New Horizon NJ.

Sterilization of Health Care Products: Requirements for Validation & Routine Control - Industrial Moist Heat Sterilization. (Illus.). 19p. (Orig.). 1993. pap. 74.00 (*1-57020-017-3*, ST1134-209) Assn Adv Med Instrn.

Sterilization of People with Mental Disabilities. LC 94-38499. 288p. 1995. text ed. 62.95 (*0-86569-225-4*) Greenwood.

Sterilization Option: A Guide for Christians. Ed. by David B. Biebel. LC 95-21486. 112p. (Orig.). (gr. 10). 1995. pap. 8.99 (*0-8010-5267-X*) Baker Bks.

Sterilization Systems. Kasinath Banerjee & Paul N. Cheremisinoff. 150p. 1985. pap. 24.95 (*0-87762-384-8*) Technomic.

Sterilization Technology: A Practical Guide for Manufacturers & Users of Health Care Products. R. Morrissey. Ed. by G. Briggs Phillips. LC 92-17950. 624p. (gr. 13). 1992. text ed. 114.95 (*0-442-23832-0*) Chapman & Hall.

Sterilization Technology for the Health Care Facility. Marimargaret Reichert & Jack H. Young. LC 93-18193. 320p. 1993. 139.00 (*0-8342-0373-1*, 20373) Aspen Pub.

***Sterilization Technology for the Health Care Facility.** 2nd ed. Ed. by Marimargaret Reichert & Jack H. Young. LC 97-8366. 400p. 1997. ring bd. 79.00 (*0-8342-0838-5*, 20838) Aspen Pub.

Sterling: Charles Sterling of Wilton, Connecticut, & His descendants. William G. Sterling. (Illus.). 71p. 1994. reprint ed. pap. 15.00 (*0-8328-4113-7*); reprint ed. lib. bdg. 25.00 (*0-8328-4112-9*) Higginson Bk Co.

Sterling: Its Meaning in World Finance. Judd Polk. Ed. by Mira Wilkins. LC 78-3945. (International Finance Ser.). (Illus.). 1979. reprint ed. lib. bdg. 29.95 (*0-405-11245-9*) Ayer.

Sterling A. Brown: Building the Black Aesthetic Tradition. Joanne V. Gabbin. LC 93-49520. 1994. pap. text ed. 16. 50 (*0-8139-1531-7*) U Pr of Va.

Sterling Advice. Sandy Steen. (Intimate Moments Ser.). 1994. mass mkt. 3.50 (*0-373-07545-6*, 5-07545-2) Silhouette.

***Sterling Advice.** Sandy Steen. 1997. 20.95 (*0-373-59763-0*) Thorndike Pr.

Sterling Book of Antonyms. Gratian Vas. (C). 1995. pap. 7.00 (*81-207-1781-3*, Pub. by Sterling Plns Pvt II) S Asia.

Sterling Book of Synonyms. Gratian Vas. (C). 1995. pap. text ed. 7.00 (*81-207-1766-X*, Pub. by Sterling Plns Pvt II) S Asia.

Sterling Book of Tongue Twisters. Gratian Vas. (C). 1995. pap. 6.50 (*81-207-1780-5*, Pub. by Sterling Plns Pvt II) S Asia.

S

Sterling Dialogues. Ed. by William M. Clark. LC 76-103086. (Granger Index Reprint Ser.). 1977. 19.95 (*0-8369-6101-3*) Ayer.

Sterling Flatware: An Identification & Value Guide. 2nd ed. Tere Hagan. (Illus.). 296p. 1991. pap. 29.95 (*0-9629105-0-3*) Tamm Pub.

Sterling Flatware: An Identification & Value Guide. 4th rev. ed. Tere Hagan. (Illus.). 1994. pap. 34.95 (*0-9629105-1-1*) Tamm Pub.

Sterling Genealogy, 2 vols. A. M. Sterling. (Illus.). 1418p. 1989. reprint ed. pap. 212.50 (*0-8328-1127-0*); reprint ed. lib. bdg. 220.50 (*0-8328-1126-2*) Higginson Bk Co.

Sterling Legend: Story of Lost Dutchman Mine. 2nd ed. Estee Conatser. (Illus.). 94p. 1987. pap. 7.95 (*0-935182-31-4*) Gem Guides Bk.

Sterling Partnership. Ed. by Doug Woolfolk & Ruth Newcomer. (Illus.). 112p. 1980. 12.50 (*0-86518-012-1*) Moran Pub Corp.

Sterling Performances: The Zest of Orange County. Guilds of the Orange County Performing Arts Center Staff. Ed. by Jane Biel. (Illus.). 288p. 1994. 19.95 (*0-9638430-0-1*) Guilds Orange Cnty PAC.

***Sterling Service.** Dothan Service League Members. (Illus.). 256p. 1996. 19.95 (*0-9653997-0-2*) Dothan Serv Leag.

Sterling Silver Flatware for Dining Elegance. Richard Osterberg. LC 94-65622. (Illus.). 256p. (Orig.). 1994. pap. 39.95 (*0-88740-630-0*) Schiffer.

***Sterling, Silverplate, & Souvenir Spoons.** 2nd rev. ed. (Illus.). 192p. 1996. pap. 12.95 (*0-89145-367-9*) L-W Inc.

Sterling Years. Bonnie S. Smith. LC 95-80495. 208p. (Orig.). 1995. pap. 9.95 (*0-9633919-4-1*) Hells Canyon.

Sterling's Relationship with the Dollar & the Deutschemark, 1976-89. A. G. Haldane & S. G. Hall. LC 91-37189. (Bank of England. Discussion Papers. Technical Ser.: No. 36). (Illus.). 14p. reprint ed. pap. 25.00 (*0-7837-3936-2*, 2043691) Bks Demand.

Stern. Bruce J. Friedman. 1994. lib. bdg. 24.95 (*1-56849-394-0*) Buccaneer Bks.

Stern. Bruce J. Friedman. LC 88-19357. 192p. 1990. pap. 8.95 (*0-87113-262-1*, Atlntc Mnthly) Grove-Atltic.

Stern der Erlosung. Rozenzweig. 553p. 1977. lib. bdg. 168.50 (*90-247-1766-3*, Pub. by M Nijhoff NE) Kluwer Ac.

Stern Gang: Ideology, Politics, & Terror, 1940-1949. Joseph Heller. LC 94-17641. 392p. (HEB.). (C). 1996. 47.50 (*0-7146-4558-3*, Pub. by F Cass Pubs UK); pap. 25.00 (*0-7146-4106-5*, Pub. by F Cass Pubs UK) Intl Spec Bk.

Stern Reckoning: The Story of Events Leading up to & Following the Partition of India. G. D. Khosla. 362p. 1990. pap. 10.95 (*0-19-562417-3*) OUP.

Stern Structured Programming: With Syntax Reference Guide-2nd Edition & Stern Getting Started with Ryan McFarland Dual Med. 7th ed. Robert A. Stern & Nancy B. Stern. 860p. 1994. pap. text ed. 43.50 (*0-471-04510-1*) Wiley.

Sternberg Family of Fossil-Hunters. Martin O. Riser. LC 94-48127. (Illus.). 520p. 1995. text ed. 119.95 (*0-7734-8985-1*) E Mellen.

Sternberg Fossil Hunters: A Dinosaur Dynasty. Katherine Rogers. (Illus.). 301p. 1991. pap. 12.00 (*0-87842-300-1*) Mountain Pr.

Sterne. H. D. Traill. Ed. by John Morley. LC 68-58403. (English Men of Letters Ser.). reprint ed. lib. bdg. 27.50 (*0-404-51734-X*) AMS Pr.

Sterne: "Tristram Shandy" Wolfgang Iser. (Landmarks of World Literature Ser.). 128p. 1988. text ed. 29.95 (*0-521-32807-1*); pap. text ed. 11.95 (*0-521-31263-9*) Cambridge U Pr.

Sterne: A Study. Walter S. Sichel. LC 78-163500. (English Literature Ser.: No. 33). 1971. reprint ed. lib. bdg. 67.95 (*0-8383-1310-8*) M S G Haskell Hse.

Sterne und Sternbilder Im Glauben Des Altertums und der Neuzeit. Wilhelm Gundel. vii, 353p. 1982. reprint ed. write for info. (*3-487-07017-0*) G Olms Pubs.

Sternenhimmel see Astro-Dome Book: 3-D Map of the Night Sky

Sterne's Fiction & the Double Principle. Jonathan Lamb. (Cambridge Studies in Eighteenth-Century English Literature & Thought: No. 3). 176p. (C). 1990. text ed. 54.95 (*0-521-37273-9*) Cambridge U Pr.

Sterns: Guide to Disney Collectibles. Michael Stern. 1992. pap. 14.95 (*0-89145-369-5*) Collector Bks.

Stern's Guide to Disney Collectibles. Michael Stern. 144p. 1995. pap. 18.95 (*0-89145-635-X*, 3975) Collector Bks.

Stern's Guide to Disney Collectibles II. Michael Stern. 1990. pap. 14.95 (*0-89145-437-3*) Collector Bks.

***Stern's Guide to the Cruise Vacation.** 7th ed. Steven B. Stern. LC 96-41342. 1997. pap. 18.95 (*1-56554-255-X*) Pelican.

Stern's Guide to the Greatest Resorts of the World. 5th ed. Steven B. Stern. (Illus.). 360p. 1995. pap. 18.99 (*1-886240-00-0*) Sterns Trvl.

Stern's Guide to the Greatest Resorts of the World. 5th ed. Steven B. Stern. (Illus.). 344p. 1995. pap. 18.99 (*1-56414-156-X*) Career Pr Inc.

***Stern's Guide to the Greatest Resorts of the World.** 6th ed. Steven B. Stern. LC 97-10173. Date not set. pap. 21.95 (*1-56554-297-5*) Pelican.

Stern's Guide to the World's Greatest Resorts: A Guide. Steven B. Stern. 1992. pap. 16.95 (*1-56171-047-4*) Sure Seller.

Stern's Performing Arts Directory, 1996. rev. ed. Dance Magazine Inc. Staff. Ed. by Allen E. McCormack. (Illus.). 300p. 1995. pap. 65.00 (*0-930036-25-5*) Dance Mag Inc.

***Stern's Performing Arts Directory 97.** Stern. 1996. 65.00 (*0-930036-27-1*) Dance Mag Inc.

***Stern's SourceFinder: Master Directory to Human Resource & Business Management Information, 1998-2000.** rev. ed. 620p. 1998. pap. 169.95 (*1-879162-21-0*) M Daniels Pubs.

Sternwheelers & Sidewheelers: The Romance of Steamdriven Paddleboats in Canada. Peter Charlebois. (Illus.). 144p. text ed. 21.95 (*0-919600-73-5*, Pub. by NC Press CN) U of Toronto Pr.

Sterochemistry of Radical Reactions: Concepts, Guidelines, & Synthetic Applications. Dennis P. Curran et al. (Illus.). xii, 280p. 1995. 95.00 (*3-527-29372-8*, VCH) Wiley.

Sterograms: Create Hidden 3D Illusions. Up Vision Computergraphik Staff. 1994. pap. 29.95 incl. cd-rom (*1-55755-273-8*) Abacus MI.

***Steroid Analysis.** Ed. by Kirk et al. (Illus.). 736p. 1995. text ed. 165.00 (*0-7514-0128-5*, Pub. by Blackie Acad & Prof UK) Routledge Chapman & Hall.

Steroid Analysis by HPLC: Recent Applications. Kautsky. (Chromatographic Science Ser.: Vol. 16). 424p. 1981. 210.00 (*0-8247-1324-9*) Dekker.

Steroid & Sterol Hormone Action. Ed. by T. C. Spelsberg & R. Kumar. (C). 1987. lib. bdg. 136.00 (*0-89838-894-5*) Kluwer Ac.

***Steroid Bible: Everything You Ever Wanted to Know about Anabolic, Tissue Building Steroids.** 3rd rev. ed. Steve Gallaway. LC 97-71977. (Illus.). 126p. 1997. pap. 24.95 (*1-890342-00-9*) Belle Intl.

Steroid Biochemistry, Vol. 1. R. Hobkirk. LC 79-11988. 176p. 1979. 104.00 (*0-8493-5193-6*) CRC Pr.

Steroid Biochemistry, Vol. 2. R. Hobkirk. LC 79-11988. 208p. 1979. 122.00 (*0-8493-5194-4*) CRC Pr.

Steroid Blues. Richard La Plante, pseud. 1996. pap. 6.99 (*0-614-98099-2*) Tor Bks.

Steroid Blues, Vol. 1. Richard La Plante. 1996. mass mkt. 6.99 (*0-8125-5073-0*) Tor Bks.

Steroid Contraceptives & Women's Responses: Regional Variability in Side-Effects & Steroid Pharmacokinetics. Ed. by R. Snow & P. Hall. (Reproductive Biology Ser.). (Illus.). 278p. (C). 1994. text ed. 85.00 (*0-306-44718-5*, Plenum Pr) Plenum.

Steroid Converting Enzymes & Diseases. Ed. by K. Fotherby & S. B. Pal. LC 84-17034. (Illus.). ix, 261p. 1984. 138.50 (*3-11-009556-4*) De Gruyter.

Steroid Hormone Action. Ed. by Malcolm G. Parker. LC 93-1165. 230p. 1993. pap. 42.00 (*0-19-963392-4*, IRL Pr) OUP.

Steroid Hormone Analysis, Vol. 1. Ed. by Hans Carstensen. LC 67-17002. 507p. reprint ed. pap. 144.50 (*0-685-16315-6*, 2027121) Bks Demand.

Steroid Hormone Receptors: Basic & Clinical Aspects. Ed. by Virinder K. Moudgil. LC 93-33850. (Hormones in Health & Disease Ser.). 1993. 87.00 (*0-8176-3694-3*) Birkhauser.

Steroid Hormone Receptors: Their Intracellular Localization. Ed. by C. R. Clark. (Ellis Horwood Series in Biomedicine: No. 3). 277p. 1987. 120.00 (*3-527-26471-X*, VCH) Wiley.

Steroid Hormone Resistance: Mechanisms & Clinical Aspects. Ed. by George P. Chrousos et al. LC 85-23250. (Advances in Experimental Medicine & Biology Ser.: Vol. 196). 454p. 1986. 95.00 (*0-306-42229-8*, Plenum Pr) Plenum.

***Steroid Hormones & the T-Cell Cytokine Profile.** G. A. Rook & Stafford L. Lightman. LC 97-15904. 1997. pap. write for info. (*3-540-76057-1*) Springer Pub.

Steroid Hormones & Uterine Bleeding. Ed. by Nancy J. Alexander & Catherine D'Arcangues. 350p. 1993. pap. 41.95 (*0-87168-508-6*, 92-43S) AAAS.

Steroid Hormones in Saliva. Ed. by D. B. Ferguson. (Frontiers of Oral Physiology Ser.: Vol. 5). (Illus.). x, 162p. 1984. 92.00 (*3-8055-3848-0*) S Karger.

Steroid Receptors & Antihormones. Ed. by M. K. Agarwal et al. LC 95-11022. (Annals Ser.: Vol. 761). 1995. write for info. (*0-89766-937-1*) NY Acad Sci.

Steroid Receptors & Antihormones: Proceedings. Ed. by David Henderson et al. LC 95-11022. (Annals of the New York Academy of Sciences Ser.: Vol. 761). 416p. 1995. pap. 120.00 (*0-89766-938-X*) NY Acad Sci.

Steroid Receptors & Disease: Cancer, Autoimmune, Bone & Circulatory Disorders. Sheridan et al. 672p. 1988. 195.00 (*0-8247-7954-1*) Dekker.

Steroid Receptors & the Management of Cancer, 2 vols., Vol. 1. E. Brad Thompson & Marc E. Lippman. 272p. 1979. 148.00 (*0-8493-5477-3*, RC271, CRC Reprint) Franklin.

Steroid Receptors & the Management of Cancer, 2 vols., Vol. 2. E. Brad Thompson & Marc E. Lippman. 176p. 1979. 94.00 (*0-8493-5478-1*, RC271, CRC Reprint) Franklin.

Steroid Receptors in Health & Disease. Ed. by Virinder K. Moudgil. LC 88-22477. (Serono Symposia U. S. A. Ser.). (Illus.). 346p. 1988. 95.00 (*0-306-42987-X*, Plenum Pr) Plenum.

Steroid-Thyroid Hormone Receptor Family & Gene Regulation. J. Carlstedt-Duke et al. (Congress Reports: No. 4). 400p. 1989. 87.50 (*0-8176-2275-6*) Birkhauser.

Steroids. Lawrence Clayton. LC 95-1464. (Drug Abuse Prevention Library). (Illus.). 64p. (YA). (gr. 7-12). 1996. lib. bdg. 15.95 (*0-8239-2063-1*) Rosen Group.

Steroids. Scott E. Lukas. LC 93-38524. (Drug Library Ser.). (Illus.). 112p. (YA). (gr. 6 up). 1994. lib. bdg. 18.95 (*0-89490-471-X*) Enslow Pubs.

Steroids: Big Muscles, Big Problems. Virginia B. Silverstein et al. LC 91-876. (Issues in Focus Ser.). (Illus.). 112p. (YA). (gr. 6 up). 1992. lib. bdg. 18.95 (*0-89490-318-7*) Enslow Pubs.

Steroids: Dangerous Game. Lisa Rogak. (Coping with Modern Issues Ser.). 64p. (J). (gr. 4 up). 1992. lib. bdg. 18.95 (*0-8225-0048-5*, Lerner Publctns) Lerner Group.

Steroids see Rodd's Chemistry of Carbon Compounds

Steroids & Neuronal Activity, No. 153. CIBA Foundation Staff. LC 90-12763. (CIBA Foundation Symposium Ser.: No. 153). 284p. 1990. text ed. 84.95 (*0-471-92689-2*) Wiley.

Steroids & Peptides: Selected Chemical Aspects for Biology, Biochemistry & Medicine. Joseph B. Dence. LC 79-21236. (Illus.). 430p. reprint ed. pap. 122.60 (*0-7837-3522-7*, 2057857) Bks Demand.

Steroids & Terpenoids see Methods in Enzymology

Steroids & Their Mechanism of Action in Nonmammalian Vertebrates. fac. ed. Ed. by G. Delrio & J. Brachet. LC 79-5399. (Illus.). 251p. pap. 71.60 (*0-7837-7531-8*, 2046973) Bks Demand.

Steroids in Diseases of the Central Nervous System. Ed. by Rudy E. Capildeo. 306p. 1989. text ed. 165.00 (*0-471-91959-4*) Wiley.

Steroids Made It Possible. Carl Djerassi. LC 90-906. (Illus.). 185p. 1990. 34.95 (*0-8412-1773-4*) Am Chemical.

Sterol Biosynthesis Inhibitors: Pharmaceutical & Agrochemical Aspects. D. Berg & M. Plempel. (Ellis Horwood Series in Biomedicine). 583p. 1988. 195.00 (*3-527-26744-1*, VCH) Wiley.

Sterol Biosynthesis Inhibitors & Anti-Feeding Compounds. (Chemistry of Plant Protection Ser.: Vol. 1). (Illus.). 160p. 1986. 108.95 (*0-387-13487-5*) Spr-Verlag.

Sterope: The Veiled Pleiad. William H. Acklan. LC 78-38637. (Black Heritage Library Collection). 1977. reprint ed. 22.95 (*0-8369-8963-5*) Ayer.

Steropticon's Biochemistry. Rawn. 1989. 4.67 (*0-13-015645-0*) P-H.

Sterrekinderen see Star Children

***Stet.** Jose Kozer. Tr. by Mark Weiss. 96p. (ENG & SPA.). 1998. pap. 11.00 (*1-881523-09-8*) Junction CA.

***Stet Again! More Tricks of the Trade for Publications People: Selections from the Editorial Eye.** LC 96-34410. 1996. write for info. (*0-935012-20-6*) Edit Experts.

Stethoscope Book & Kit. Linda Allison & Tom Ferguson. (J). (gr. 2-7). 1991. pap. 12.95 (*0-201-57096-3*) Addison-Wesley.

***Stetson Hats & the John B. Stetson Hat Company, 1865-1970.** Jeffrey B. Snyder. LC 97-5257. 1997. write for info. (*0-7643-0211-6*) Schiffer.

Stetson Kindred of America, Bks. 3 & 4. Ed. by N. M. Stetson. (Illus.). 147p. 1992. reprint ed. pap. 29.50 (*0-8328-2286-8*); reprint ed. lib. bdg. 39.50 (*0-8328-2285-X*) Higginson Bk Co.

Stetson Law Review: 1970-1995/96, 25 vols., Set. Bound set. 995.00 (*0-8377-9153-7*) Rothman.

Stetson University - Then & Now. Photos by Tommy Thompson. (First Edition Ser.). (Illus.). 112p. 1992. 39.95 (*0-916509-93-1*) Harmony Hse Pub.

Steuben Village & Mounds: A Multicomponent Late Hopewell Site in Illinois. Dan F. Morse. LC 64-7124. (Anthropological Papers: No. 21). (Illus.). 176p. reprint ed. 50.20 (*0-8357-9613-2*, 2011182) Bks Demand.

Steubenville: A Sequence of Poems. Julie H. White. 40p. (Orig.). 1992. pap. 6.00 (*0-9628094-3-8*) Pearl Edit.

***Steubenville Weekly Gazette by McFadden & Hunter, 1894.** Compiled by Leila S. Francy. LC 96-71482. 145p. (Orig.). 1997. pap. 12.95 (*1-55856-250-8*) Closson Pr.

***Steubenville Weekly Gazette 1893.** Leila S. Francy. LC 96-71398. 199p. (Orig.). 1997. pap. 18.95 (*1-55856-252-4*) Closson Pr.

Steuerliste aus Pheretnuis. P. J. Sijpesteijn & K. A. Worp. (Studia Amstelodamensia ad Epigraphicum, Ius Antiquum et Papyrologicam Pertinentia: No. 33). (Illus.). vi, 111p. (GER.). 1993. 94.00 (*90-5063-166-5*, Pub. by Gieben NE) Benjamins North Am.

Steuerrecht und Finanzrecht. 2nd ed. Franz Klein. 660p. (GER.). 1993. 225.00 (*0-7859-8393-7*, 3472001364) Fr & Eur.

Stevan. Elizabeth Howland. LC 90-83115. 1991. 14.95 (*0-8158-0461-X*) Chris Mass.

Steve: Remembrances of Stephen W. Kuffler. Ed. by U. J. McMahan. LC 90-10383. (Illus.). 142p. (Orig.). 1990. pap. 17.95 (*0-87893-516-9*) Sinauer Assocs.

Steve Allen Instrumental Collection. 14.95 (*0-7935-5606-6*, 00306055) H Leonard.

Steve Allen on the Bible, Bks. 1-2: Religion & Morality, 2 vols. Steve Allen. 1992. 47.95 (*0-87975-738-8*) Prometheus Bks.

Steve Allen on the Bible, Religion & Morality. Steve Allen. 428p. (C). 1990. 25.95 (*0-87975-638-1*) Prometheus Bks.

Steve Allen Songbook. 80p. 1994. otabind 9.95 (*0-7935-3049-0*, 00312495) H Leonard.

Steve Arrington's Hall of Fame: Master of Funk. Charles C. Carter. Ed. & Illus. by Dave Edwards. (Masters of Funk Ser.: Vol. 1). 80p. (Orig.). 1996. pap. 17.95 (*1-888885-00-9*, JPMC-1501) JPMC.

***Steve Bailey - Five-String Bass.** Ed. by Aaron Stang. 52p. (Orig.). (C). 1991. pap. text ed. 9.95 (*0-7692-0964-5*, F3110BGX) Warner Brothers.

Steve Caney's Toybook. Steven Caney. LC 75-8814. (Illus.). 176p. (J). (ps-5). 1972. pap. 8.95 (*0-911104-17-8*, 023) Workman Pub.

Steve Canyon, No. 21. Milton Ganiff. (Illus.). 6.95 (*0-614-13183-9*, 21-37910) EAA Aviation.

Steve Canyon: Taps for Shanty Town. Milton Caniff. Ed. by Peter Poplaski. (Steve Canyon Ser.: No. 24). (Illus.). 176p. 1989. pap. 13.95 (*0-87816-055-8*) Kitchen Sink.

***Steve Canyon Companion.** Milton Caniff & Carl Horak. Ed. by Rick Norwood. LC 96-42088. (Illus.). 120p. (Orig.). 1996. pap. 25.00 (*0-936414-10-3*) Manuscript Pr.

***Steve Claridge: Tales from the Boot Camps.** Ian Ridley. (Illus.). 256p. 1997. 40.00 (*0-575-06398-X*, Pub. by V Gollancz UK) Trafalgar.

Steve Colgate on Cruising. Steve Colgate. (Illus.). (Orig.). 1990. pap. 12.95 (*0-914747-01-0*) Offshore Sail Schl.

Steve Colgate on Sailing. Stephen Colgate. Ed. by Marcia Wiley. (Illus.). 1991. 29.95 (*0-393-02903-4*) Norton.

Steve Cropper: Soul Man. Ed. by Aaron Stang. 100p. (Orig.). (YA). 1995. pap. text ed. 19.95 (*0-89724-652-7*, PG9509) Warner Brothers.

***Steve Hart: A Bronx Family Album, the Impact of Aids.** 1997. spiral bd. 34.95 (*3-931141-54-3*) Dist Art Pubs.

Steve Howe Guitar Collection. Steve Howe & Tony Bacon. (Illus.). 88p. 1993. 29.95 (*0-87930-290-9*) Miller Freeman.

Steve Howe Guitar Pieces. Ed. by Aaron Stang. 48p. (Orig.). 1994. pap. 10.95 (*0-89724-346-3*, GF0213) Warner Brothers.

Steve Lyons: Psychoanalysis. Steve Lyons. LC 95-69132. (Illus.). 224p. 1995. 19.95 (*1-57167-013-0*) Sagamore Pub.

***Steve Mann's Fantasy Baseball Guide 1997: Let Major League Baseball's First Professional Analyst Help You Draft a Team That Puts You in the Money.** Steve Mann. 208p. (Orig.). 1997. pap. 13.00 (*0-06-273474-1*, Harper Ref) HarpC.

***Steve McCutcheon's Alaska.** Steve McCutcheon et al. Ed. by Penny Rennick. (Alaska Geographic Ser.: Vol. 25-1). (Illus.). 112p. 1998. pap. 21.95 (*1-56661-040-0*) Alaska Geog Soc.

Steve McQueen: Portrait of an American Rebel. Marshall Terrill. LC 94-71114. (Illus.). 480p. 1994. pap. 12.50 (*1-55611-414-1*, Primus) D I Fine.

Steve Miller Band, Greatest Hits. 19.95 (*0-7935-4451-3*, 00690040) H Leonard.

Steve Mizerak's Complete Book of Pool. Steve Mizerak & Michael E. Panozzo. (Illus.). 208p. (Orig.). 1990. pap. 14.95 (*0-8092-4255-9*) Contemp Bks.

Steve Mizerak's Play Better Pool. Steve Mizerak & Michael E. Panozzo. (Illus.). 160p. 1996. pap. 12.95 (*0-8092-3427-0*) Contemp Bks.

Steve Mizerak's Pocket Billiards Tips & Trick Shots. Steve Mizerak & Joel Cohen. (Illus.). 192p. 1982. 15.50 (*0-8092-5780-7*); pap. 10.95 (*0-8092-5779-3*) Contemp Bks.

Steve Mizerak's Winning Pool Tips. Steve Mizerak & Michael E. Panozzo. (Illus.). 112p. 1995. pap. 6.95 (*0-8092-3428-9*) Contemp Bks.

Steve Morse - Coast to Coast: Play-It-Like-It-Is-Guitar. pap. 19.95 (*0-89524-735-6*) Cherry Lane.

Steve Morse - High Tension Wires: Guitar - Vocal. Ed. by Jon Chappell & Jeff Jacobson. (Illus.). 86p. (Orig.). 1990. pap. text ed. 17.95 (*0-89524-523-X*) Cherry Lane.

***Steve Morse - Open Ears.** 125p. 14.95 (*0-614-20101-2*, 02503101, Cherry Ln) H Leonard.

Steve Morse - Songbook: Guitar. Ed. by Milton Okun. (Illus.). 103p. (Orig.). 1990. pap. text ed. 19.95 (*0-89524-323-7*) Cherry Lane.

Steve Morse Band - Southern Steel: Play-It-Like-It-Is-Guitar. pap. 19.95 (*0-89524-704-6*) Cherry Lane.

Steve Morse Band - Structural Damage. 102p. (YA). 1995. pap. 22.95 (*0-89524-908-1*) Cherry Lane.

Steve Morse Just the Riffs. 32p. 1995. pap. 9.95 (*0-89524-973-1*) Cherry Lane.

Steve Nelson, American Radical. Steve Nelson et al. LC 80-26528. 475p. 1981. 49.95 (*0-8229-3441-8*) U of Pittsburgh Pr.

Steve Nelson, American Radical. Steve Nelson et al. LC 80-26528. (Series in Social & Labor History). (Illus.). 475p. 1992. pap. 19.95 (*0-8229-5471-0*) U of Pittsburgh Pr.

Steve Romanoff Songbook: Songs Written for Schooner Fare. Steve Romanoff. 160p. 1993. spiral bd. 24.95 (*0-9638602-0-8*) Outer Green Recs.

Steve Rude Sketchbook. Steve Rude. Ed. by Eric Nesheim. (Illus.). 136p. 1989. 28.95 (*0-87816-046-9*); pap. 14.95 (*0-87816-047-7*) Kitchen Sink.

Steve Sint's Tips, Tricks & Hints: 101 Secrets of a Professional Photographer. Steve Sint. (Magic Lantern Guides Ser.). (Illus.). 160p. (Orig.). (C). 1995. pap. 19.95 (*1-883403-18-9*, H 155, Silver Pixel Pr) Saunders Photo.

Steve Star. Joanne Wall. (Christmas Ornaments Ser.). (Illus.). 34p. (Orig.). (J). (ps up). Date not set. pap. 12.95 (*0-9644283-1-8*) M J Wall.

Steve the Sure. Mary Towne. LC 90-584. 144p. (J). (gr. 4-7). 1990. lib. bdg. 13.95 (*0-689-31646-1*, Atheneum Bks Young) S&S Childrens.

Steve Tobin - Reconstructions. Karen Lodge & Lisa T. Barnes. (Illus.). 80p. 1995. 20.00 (*0-9624021-9-2*) Ursinus College.

Steve Vai: Alien Love Secrets. 19.95 (*0-7935-5092-0*, 00320032) H Leonard.

Steve Vai: Alien Love Secrets. 80p. otabind 24.95 (*0-7935-4449-1*, 00690039) H Leonard.

Steve Vai - Passion & Warfare: With Notes & Tablature. 224p. 1991. otabind 24.95 (*0-7935-0319-1*, 00660137) H Leonard.

Steve Vai Songbook: Play-It-Like-It-Is-Guitar. pap. 19.95 (*0-89524-572-8*) Cherry Lane.

Steve Weissman's Currents & Tides: Cedar Key to Tampa Bay. Steve Weissman. 186p. 1994. pap. text ed. 8.95 (*0-9643766-0-1*) Swamp Dog Pr.

Steve Weissman's Currents & Tides: Tampa Bay to the Everglades. Steve Weissman. 186p. 1994. pap. text ed. 8.95 (*0-9643766-2-8*) Swamp Dog Pr.

Steve Wozniak: A Wizard Called Woz. Rebecca Gold. LC 94-859. (Achievers Ser.). (Illus.). 72p. (YA). (gr. 4-9). 1994. lib. bdg. 19.95 (*0-8225-2881-9*, Lerner Publctns) Lerner Group.

Steve Wozniak: The Man Who Grew the Apple. Martha E. Kendall. (J). (gr. 4-7). 1995. 14.95 (*0-8027-8341-4*); 15.85 (*0-8027-8342-2*) Walker & Co.

Steve Young. Hal Bock. LC 95-18222. (Football Legends Ser.). (Illus.). 64p. (J). (gr. 3 up). 1996. lib. bdg. 15.95 (*0-7910-2499-7*) Chelsea Hse.

An Asterisk (*) at the beginning of an entry indicates that the title is appearing in BIP for the first time.

Steve Young. Richard Rambeck. (Sports Superstars Ser.). 24p. (J). (gr. 2-6). 1996. lib. bdg. 21.36 (*1-56766-264-1*) Childs World.

Steve Young. Chris W. Sehnert. LC 95-44793. (M. V. P. Ser.). (J). 1996. lib. bdg. 13.98 (*1-56239-543-2*) Abdo & Dghtrs.

Steve Young. Mark Stewart. LC 96-5108. (Grolier All-Pro Biographies Ser.). (Illus.). (J). 1996. pap. 3.95 (*0-516-26011-1*) Childrens.

Steve Young. Mark Stewart. LC 96-5108. (Grolier All-Pro Biographies Ser.). (Illus.). 48p. (J). 1996. lib. bdg. 20.00 (*0-516-20146-8*) Childrens.

Steve Young: Complete Quarterback. Terri Morgan & Shmuel Thaler. (Achievers Ser.). 1995. lib. bdg. 19.95 (*0-8225-2886-X*, Lerner Publctns) Lerner Group.

Steve Young: Complete Quarterback. Terri Morgan & Shmuel Thaler. (Achievers Ser.). 1996. pap. 5.95 (*0-8225-9716-0*, Lerner Publctns) Lerner Group.

Steve Young: NFL Passing Wizard. Bill Gutman. LC 96-6420. (Sports World Ser.). (Illus.). 48p. (J). (gr. 3-6). 1996. pap. 6.95 (*0-7613-0134-8*); lib. bdg. 14.90 (*1-56294-184-4*) Millbrook Pr.

Steve Young: Star Quarterback. Ron Knapp. LC 95-23282. (Sports Reports). (Illus.). 104p. (J). (gr. 4-10). 1996. lib. bdg. 18.95 (*0-89490-654-2*) Enslow Pubs.

Steve Young Story. Larry Livsey. LC 95-31504. 1995. 22.95 (*0-7615-0194-0*) Prima Pub.

Steve Young Story. Laury Livsey. 272p. 1996. per. 13.00 (*0-7615-0756-6*) Prima Pub.

Stevedores & Dockers: A Study of Trade Unionism in the Port of London, 1870-1914. John C. Lovell. LC 74-99263. (Illus.). 270p. 1969. 39.50 (*0-678-07003-2*) Kelley.

Steven & the Green Turtle. (J). Date not set. pap. 1.75 (*0-590-30904-8*) Scholastic Inc.

Steven & the Zombie. Francine Pascal. (Sweet Valley Twins Ser.: No. 78). 144p. (J). 1994. pap. 3.50 (*0-553-48104-5*) Bantam.

Steven Arnold: A Retrospective. Peter Weiermair. (Illus.). 144p. 1996. 49.95 (*3-905514-98-2*, Pub. by Edit Stemmle SZ) Dist Art Pubs.

Steven Caney's Invention Book. Steven Caney. LC 84-40679. (Illus.). 208p. (J). (gr. 3-8). 1985. pap. 9.95 (*0-89480-076-0*, 406) Workman Pub.

Steven Caney's Kids' America. Steven Caney. LC 77-27465. (Illus.). 416p. (J). (ps-9). 1978. pap. 13.95 (*0-911104-80-1*, 114) Workman Pub.

Steven Caney's Play Book. Steven Caney. LC 75-9816. (Illus.). 240p. (J). (ps-5). 1975. pap. 9.95 (*0-911104-38-0*, 050) Workman Pub.

Steven Curtis Chapman: 20 Favorites. 1992. 10.95 (*0-7935-3943-9*, 00308163) H Leonard.

Steven Gets Even. Francine Pascal. (Sweet Valley Twins Ser.: No. 88). 144p. (J). (gr. 4-7). 1995. pap. 3.50 (*0-553-48189-4*) Bantam.

Steven Hudson. (Contemporary Art Ser.: No. 5). (Illus.). 19p. 1995. pap. write for info. (*1-883015-11-1*) Krannert Art.

Steven Jobs. Laurie Rozakis. LC 92-43268. (Masters of Invention Ser.). (J). (gr. 5 up). 1993. 15.93 (*0-86592-001-X*); 11.95 (*0-685-66327-2*) Rourke Corp.

Steven Jobs & Stephen Wozniak: Creating the Apple Computer. Keith E. Greenberg. Ed. by Bruce Glassman. LC 94-20400. (Partners Ser.). (Illus.). 48p. (J). (gr. 2-5). 1994. lib. bdg. 13.95 (*1-56711-086-X*) Blackbirch.

Steven Kellog Connection. Will C. Howell. (J). (gr. 1-6). 1990. pap. 10.99 (*0-8224-6452-7*) Fearon Teach Aids.

Steven Meckler Photographs: Tucson Artists. Steven Meckler. LC 95-80565. 120p. 1996. 70.00 (*0-9647925-0-8*); pap. 30.00 (*0-9647925-1-6*) Black Spring.

Steven Otto Nevets. Carl Watts. LC 93-60236. (Illus.). 44p. (J). (gr. k-3). 1993. 7.95 (*1-55523-602-2*) Winston-Derek.

Steven Pippin, Photo, Videos, Sculpture, 1983-1995. Frederic Paul. (Illus.). 108p. 1996. pap. 25.00 (*2-908257-17-3*, Pub. by F R A C FR) Dist Art Pubs.

Steven Raichlen's High-Flavor, Low-Fat Chicken. Steven Raichlen. LC 95-32331. (Illus.). 96p. 1996. pap. 14.95 (*0-670-86580-X*, Viking) Viking Penguin.

Steven Raichlen's High-Flavor Low-Fat Cooking. Steven Raichlen. 180p. 1996. pap. 14.95 (*0-8118-0954-4*) Chronicle Bks.

Steven Schultz: Selected Works - 1988-1994. 32p. 1995. 8.95 (*1-886591-04-0*) Cabinet Crest Bks.

Steven Spielberg, Reading Level 2. McAllister. (Reaching Your Goal Bks.: Set II). (Illus.). 24p. (J). (gr. 1-4). 1989. 10.95 (*0-685-58803-3*); lib. bdg. 14.60 (*0-86592-427-9*) Rourke Corp.

Steven Spielberg: A Biography. Joseph McBride. LC 96-38053. 528p. 1997. 30.00 (*0-684-81167-7*) S&S Trade.

Steven Spielberg: Creator of E. T. Tom Collins. LC 83-21068. (Taking Part Ser.). (Illus.). 64p. (J). (gr. 3 up). 1983. lib. bdg. 13.95 (*0-87518-249-6*, Dillon Silver Burdett) Silver Burdett Pr.

Steven Spielberg: Hollywood Filmmaker. Virginia Meachum. LC 95-39022. (People to Know Ser.). 112p. (YA). (gr. 6 up). 1996. lib. bdg. 18.95 (*0-89490-697-6*) Enslow Pubs.

Steven Spielberg: Master Storyteller. Tom Powers. LC 96-22289. (J). 1996. lib. bdg. write for info. (*0-8225-4929-8*) Lerner Group.

Steven Spielberg: The Man, His Movies, & Their Meaning. enl. rev. ed. Philip M. Taylor. (Illus.). 176p. 1994. pap. text ed. 15.95 (*0-8264-0664-5*) Continuum.

***Steven Spielberg: The Unauthorized Biography.** John Baxter. (Illus.). 457p. 1997. 29.00 (*0-00-255587-5*) HarperColl Wrld.

Steven Spielberg see Pop Culture Legends

Steven Spielberg's Amazing Stories. Bauer. 21.95 (*0-8488-0732-4*) Amereon Ltd.

Stevenage: A Sociological Study of a New Town. Harold Orlans. LC 71-139142. 313p. (C). 1971. reprint ed. text ed. 55.00 (*0-8371-5758-7*, ORST, Greenwood Pr) Greenwood.

Stevenage: History & Guide. Margaret Ashby. (Illus.). 128p. 1994. pap. 14.00 (*0-7509-0426-7*, Pub. by Sutton Pubng UK) Bks Intl VA.

Stevenage, Nineteen Forty-Six to Nineteen Eighty-Six: Images of the First New Town. Ed. by Timothy Collings. 170p. (C). 1986. 65.00 (*0-907590-18-7*) St Mut.

Stevens & the Interpersonal. Mark Halliday. 208p. 1991. text ed. 35.00 (*0-691-06548-9*) Princeton U Pr.

Steven's Big Crush. Francine Pascal. (Sweet Valley Kids Ser.: Vol. 65). 96p. (J). 1996. pap. 3.50 (*0-553-48219-X*) Bantam.

Steven's Bride. large type ed. Francine Pascal. LC 93-1350. (Sweet Valley High Ser.). (J). 1993. pap. 15.95 (*1-56054-756-1*) Thorndike Pr.

Steven's Enemy. Francine Pascal. (Sweet Valley Twins & Friends Ser.: No. 82). 144p. (J). (gr. 4-7). 1994. pap. 3.50 (*0-553-48097-9*) Bantam.

Stevens Genealogy, Embracing Branches of the Family Descending from Puritan Ancestors, 1650 to the Present Time. E. Barney. (Illus.). 319p. 1989. reprint ed. pap. 48.00 (*0-8328-1129-7*); reprint ed. lib. bdg. 56.00 (*0-8328-1128-9*) Higginson Bk Co.

Stevens' Handbook of Experimental Psychology, 2 vols. 2nd ed. Ed. by Richard C. Atkinson et al. 1078p. 1988. text ed. 235.00 (*0-471-61625-7*) Wiley.

Stevens' Handbook of Experimental Psychology Vol. 1: Perception & Motivation. 2nd ed. Ed. by Richard C. Atkinson et al. LC 87-31637. 905p. 1988. text ed. 180.00 (*0-471-04203-X*) Wiley.

Stevens' Handbook of Experimental Psychology Vol. 2: Learning & Cognition, Vol. 2. 2nd ed. Ed. by Richard C. Atkinson et al. 1027p. 1988. text ed. 190.00 (*0-471-04207-2*) Wiley.

Steven's in Love. Francine Pascal. (Sweet Valley Twins Ser.: No. 57). 144p. (J). 1992. pap. 3.50 (*0-553-15943-7*) Bantam.

Stevens Pass: The Story of Railroading & Recreation in the North Cascades. JoAnn Roe. (Illus.). 180p. 1995. pap. 12.95 (*0-89886-371-6*) Mountaineers.

Steven's Twin. Francine Pascal. (Sweet Valley Kids Ser.: No. 50). 80p. (J). (ps-3). 1994. pap. 2.99 (*0-553-48095-2*) Bantam.

Stevenson & Edinburgh. M. McLaren. LC 73-21775. (English Biography Ser.: No. 31). 1974. lib. bdg. 48.95 (*0-8383-1831-2*) M S G Haskell Hse.

Stevenson Bibliography. J. Herbert Slater. LC 73-21753. (English Biography Ser.: No. 31). 1974. lib. bdg. 75.00 (*0-8383-1832-0*) M S G Haskell Hse.

Stevenson in Hawaii. Martha M. McGaw. LC 77-13757. (Illus.). 182p. 1978. reprint ed. text ed. 49.75 (*0-8371-9864-X*, MCSH, Greenwood Pr) Greenwood.

Stevensons: A Biography of an American Family. Jean H. Baker. LC 95-5823. 576p. 1996. 30.00 (*0-393-03874-2*) Norton.

***Stevensons: A Biography of an American Family.** Jean H. Baker. 592p. (C). 1997. pap. 16.95 (*0-393-31598-3*) Norton.

Stevenson's Germany: The Case Against Germany in the Pacific. C. Brunsdon Fletcher. LC 78-111755. (American Imperialism: Viewpoints of United States Foreign Policy, 1898-1941 Ser.). 1970. reprint ed. 19.95 (*0-405-02018-X*) Ayer.

Stevenson's Scottish Stories & Essays. Robert Louis Stevenson. 1994. pap. 14.50 (*0-7486-0463-4*, Pub. by Edinburgh U Pr UK) Col U Pr.

***Stevia: Miracle of No Calorie.** Donna Coates. 1997. pap. 10.00 (*0-609-80131-7*) Random Hse Value.

***Stevia Rebandiana No. 1: Nature's Sweet Secret.** David Richard. 60p. (Orig.). 1996. pap. 5.95 (*1-890612-00-6*, 58650) Vital Health.

Stevie. Garrett Christopher. Ed. by J. Friedland & R. Kessler. (Novel-Ties Ser.). 1993. student ed., pap. text ed. 14.95 (*0-88122-949-0*) Lrn Links.

Stevie. John L. Steptoe. LC 69-16700. (Illus.). 32p. (J). (ps-3). 1969. lib. bdg. 14.89 (*0-06-025764-4*) HarpC Child Bks.

Stevie. John L. Steptoe. LC 69-16700. (Trophy Picture Bk.). (Illus.). 32p. (J). (ps-3). 1986. pap. 4.95 (*0-06-443122-3*, Trophy) HarpC Child Bks.

Stevie. John L. Steptoe. Tr. by Teresa Mlawer from SPA. LC 95-17757. (Illus.). 32p. (SPA.). (J). (ps-3). 1996. 15.95 (*0-06-027038-1*, HpArco Iris); pap. 5.95 (*0-06-443442-7*, HpArco Iris) HarpC Child Bks.

Stevie. John L. Steptoe. (Illus.). (J). (gr. 1-4). 1987. 22.95 incl. audio (*0-87499-050-5*); pap. 15.95 incl. audio (*0-87499-049-1*) Live Oak Media.

Stevie, 4 bks., Set. John L. Steptoe. (Illus.). (J). (gr. 1-4). 1987. student ed., pap. 31.95 incl. audio (*0-87499-051-3*) Live Oak Media.

Stevie: A Biography of Stevie Smith. Jack Barbera & William McBrien. (Illus.). 384p. 1987. reprint ed. 35.00 (*0-19-520549-9*) OUP.

Stevie B. Sea Horse: A Tale of a Proud Papa. Suzanne Tate. LC 93-86779. (Suzanne Tate's Nature Ser.: No. 15). (Illus.). 28p. (Orig.). (J). (gr. k-4). 1993. pap. 3.95 (*1-878405-09-8*) Nags Head Art.

Stevie Has His Heart Examined. Sue Sauer et al. Ed. by Nancy Goldstein. (Illus.). (J). (ps-7). 1983. pap. text ed. 3.00 (*0-937423-00-9*) U M H & C.

Stevie Has His Heart Repaired. Sue Sauer et al. Ed. by Nancy Goldstein. (Illus.). (J). (ps-7). 1979. pap. text ed. 3.00 (*0-937423-01-7*) U M H & C.

Stevie Nicks: Rock's Mystical Lady. Edward Wincensten. Ed. by John Wooley. LC 93-91523. (Illus.). 103p. (Orig.). 1993. pap. 12.95 (*0-9628640-5-6*) Helion Pub.

Stevie Nicks - Rock's Mystical Lady. rev. ed. Edward Wincentsen. 122p. 1995. pap. 14.95 (*0-9642808-1-7*) Wynn Pubng.

Stevie Ray: Soul to Soul. Keri Leigh. LC 93-24011. (Illus.). 200p. 1993. pap. 18.95 (*0-87833-838-1*) Taylor Pub.

Stevie Ray Vaughan: Caught in the Crossfire. Joe N. Patoski. 1994. pap. 13.95 (*0-316-16069-5*) Little.

Stevie Ray Vaughan: Couldn't Stand Weather. 72p. 1995. otabind 19.95 (*0-7935-4203-0*, 00690024) H Leonard.

Stevie Ray Vaughan: Exploration Guitar Genius. 1991. pap. 17.95 incl. audio (*0-7935-0825-8*, 006993158) H Leonard.

Stevie Ray Vaughan: Lightnin' Blues 1983-1987, with Notes & Tablature. 208p. 1990. otabind 24.95 (*0-7935-2094-0*, 00660058) H Leonard.

Stevie Ray Vaughan: Lightnin' Blues 1983-1987, with Notes & Tablature. 192p. 1991. per. 19.95 (*0-7935-0739-1*, 00694778) H Leonard.

Stevie Ray Vaughan: Live Alive. 24.95 (*0-7935-4381-9*, 00690036) H Leonard.

***Stevie Ray Vaughan: Signature Guitar Licks.** Leonard, Hal, Corporation Staff. student ed., pap. 19.95 incl. audio compact disk (*0-7935-0824-X*) H Leonard.

Stevie Ray Vaughan: Soul to Soul. 96p. otabind 19.95 (*0-7935-4414-9*, 00690025) H Leonard.

Stevie Ray Vaughan & Double Trouble: The Sky Is Crying with Notes & Tablature. 80p. 1992. otabind 19.95 (*0-7935-1555-6*, 00694835) H Leonard.

***Stevie Ray Vaughan Anthology.** C. Lee Hopkins. (Illus.). vii, 196p. (Orig.). 1996. pap. 19.95 (*0-9654927-0-2*) S R Vaughan.

Stevie Smith: A Bibliography. Jack Barbera et al. (Twentieth Century Literary Bibliographies Ser.). 183p. 1987. text ed. 55.00 (*0-313-27666-8*) Greenwood.

***Stevie Smith's Resistant Antics.** Laura Severin. LC 96-43625. (Illus.). 174p. 1997. 47.95 (*0-299-15290-1*); pap. 18.95 (*0-299-15294-4*) U of Wis Pr.

Stevie Vaughan: In Step. 64p. 1991. pap. 14.95 (*0-7935-0740-5*, 00694777) H Leonard.

Stevie Wonder: Career of a Rock Legend. Martin E. Horn. 1996. pap. text ed. 16.95 (*0-935016-42-2*, Barclay House) Arrowood Pr.

Stevie Wonder: Conversation Peace. Ed. by Jeannette DeLisa. 104p. (YA). 1995. pap. text ed. 19.95 (*0-89724-831-7*, PF9523) Warner Brothers.

Stevie Wonder Greatest Hits, No. 292. 80p. 1992. pap. 8.95 (*0-7935-1476-2*, 00102233) H Leonard.

Stew Leonard's Customer Cookbook. Nita Howland et al. (Illus.). 129p. 1988. pap. 3.99 (*0-317-03330-1*) Stew Leonards.

Steward: A Biblical Symbol Come of Age. rev. ed. Douglas Hall. 1990. pap. 16.00 (*0-8028-0472-1*) Eerdmans.

Steward of Christendom. Sebastian Barry. 1996. pap. 11.95 (*0-413-70260-X*, Pub. by Methuen UK) Heinemann.

***Steward of Christendom.** Sebastian Barry. 1997. pap. 5.25 (*0-8222-1609-4*) Dramatists Play.

Steward's Life in the Royal Navy (1943-1961) Derek H. Warner. 106p. (C). 1989. pap. 29.00 (*0-7223-2439-1*, Pub. by A H S Ltd UK) St Mut.

Stewards, Lords & People: The Estate Steward & His World in Later Stuart England. D. R. Hainsworth. (Studies in Early Modern British History). 293p. (C). 1992. text ed. 69.95 (*0-521-36489-2*) Cambridge U Pr.

Stewards of Access/Custodians of Choice: A Philosophical Foundation for the Park & Recreation Profession. 2nd ed. Daniel L. Dustin et al. 112p. 1995. pap. text ed. 13.95 (*1-57167-009-2*) Sagamore Pub.

Stewards of Creation: On the Tamarack Trail Ecology. Lawrence H. Janssen. LC 88-71572. (Illus.). 56p. (Orig.). 1988. pap. 3.95 (*0-917575-05-9*) Cedars WI.

Stewards of Excellence: Studies in Modern English & American Poets. A. Alvarez. LC 70-159035. 191p. (C). 1971. reprint ed. 50.00 (*0-87752-152-2*) Gordian.

Stewards of God. Edward J. Higgins. 1984. 4.95 (*0-86544-022-0*) Salv Army Suppl South.

Stewards of God's Grace. Siegfried Grossman. 192p. (Orig.). 1981. pap. text ed. 14.95 (*0-85364-287-7*) Attic Pr.

Stewards of Life: Bioethics & Pastoral Care. Sondra E. Wheeler. LC 96-17677. 144p. (Orig.). 1996. pap. 12.95 (*0-687-02087-5*) Abingdon.

Stewards of the House: The Detective Fiction of Jonathan Latimer. Bill Brubaker. LC 92-75452. 128p. (C). 1993. 21.95 (*0-87972-610-5*); pap. 8.95 (*0-87972-611-3*) Bowling Green Univ Popular Press.

***Stewards of the State: Governors of Michigan.** George Weeks. Date not set. 21.95 (*0-88031-101-0*); pap. 17.95 (*0-88031-100-2*) Invisible-Red Hill.

Stewards of the State: The Governors of Michigan. George May. Ed. by Robert Kirk. (Illus.). 193p. 1987. 20.95 (*0-9614344-2-2*) Historical Soc MI.

Stewards of the Wisconsin, the Wisconsin Valley Improvement Company. Michael J. Goc. (Illus.). 152p. (YA). 1993. 29.95 (*0-938627-19-8*) New Past Pr.

Stewards Shaped by Grace: The Church's Gift to a Troubled World. Rhodes Thompson. 128p. (Orig.). 1990. pap. 9.99 (*0-8272-3431-7*) Chalice Pr.

Stewardship: Choosing Service over Self-Interest. Peter Block. LC 93-6597. (Illus.). 256p. 1993. 27.95 (*1-881052-28-1*) Berrett-Koehler.

Stewardship: Choosing Service over Self-Interest. Peter Block. LC 93-6597. 288p. 1996. pap. 16.95 (*1-881052-86-9*) Berrett-Koehler.

Stewardship: From Abraham to Zacchaeus with Some Contemporary Religious & Political Implications. Joseph Johnson. LC 95-90125. (Illus.). 60p. (Orig.). 1995. pap. 8.95 (*0-533-11463-2*) Vantage.

Stewardship: God's Plan for Living. Ben G. Gill. 1996. 22.95 (*1-56530-208-7*) Summit TX.

***Stewardship: Whole Life Discipleship.** James W. Lewis. Ed. by Arthur Kelly. (Bridges Ser.: Vol. 10). 50p. 1997. pap. 4.95 (*0-87162-713-2*, D5306) Warner Pr.

***Stewardship & Development in Catholic Dioceses & Parishes: Resource Manual.** Ad Hoc Committee on Stewardship National Conf. of Catholic Bishops Staff. 26p. (C). 1996. pap. 2.95 (*1-57455-132-9*) US Catholic.

Stewardship & Sacrificial Giving: A Way of Life. Francis N. Scholtz. 32p. pap. 2.50 (*0-8146-2118-X*) Liturgical Pr.

***Stewardship & Spiritual Maturity.** Leon Smith. 90p. (Orig.). 1995. pap. 6.95 (*1-56794-105-2*, C-2405) Star Bible.

Stewardship & the Catholic School Tuition Program. Robert J. Kealey & Kathleen C. Collins. (Illus.). 47p. (Orig.). 1993. pap. 9.30 (*1-55833-128-X*) Natl Cath Educ.

Stewardship & the Economy of God. fac. ed. John H. Reumann. LC 92-24696. (Library of Christian Stewardship). 171p. 1992. reprint ed. pap. 48.80 (*0-7837-7971-2*, 2047727) Bks Demand.

Stewardship & the Kingdom of God. Dennis J. Ireland. LC 92-15355. (Supplements to Novum Testamentum Ser.: Vol. 70). 1992. 107.00 (*90-04-09600-0*) E J Brill.

Stewardship Concepts & Practices. Ronald E. Romig & Anne L. Romig. LC 92-24180. (Studies in Restoration History). 35p. 1992. pap. 4.50 (*0-8309-0622-3*) Herald Hse.

Stewardship Is More Than Time, Talent, & Things: A New Agenda. C. Neil Strait. 80p. (Orig.). 1993. pap. 5.99 (*0-8341-1458-5*) Beacon Hill.

Stewardship Letters: Revitalizing Your Church's Fund-raising. Church Growth Institute Staff. Ed. by Cindy G. Spear. (Illus.). 84p. 1991. ring bd. 44.95 incl. disk (*0-941005-44-5*) Chrch Grwth VA.

Stewardship of Life in the Kingdom of Death. Douglas J. Hall. 160p. 1988. pap. 13.00 (*0-8028-0354-7*) Eerdmans.

***Stewardship of Private Wealth: Managing Personal & Family Assets.** Sally S. Kleberg. LC 96-29708. 312p. 1997. 35.00 (*0-7863-1032-4*) Irwin Prof Pubng.

Stewardship of the Heart. Linda Eyre & Richard Eyre. 1990. 12.95 (*0-916095-33-9*) Pubs Pr UT.

Stewardship of the Mystery vol. 1. T. A. Sparks. 246p. 1994. pap. text ed. 10.50 (*1-883137-15-2*) Christ Stewards.

Stewardship of the Mystery vol. 2. T. A. Sparks. 103p. 1994. pap. text ed. 5.70 (*1-883137-16-0*) Christ Stewards.

Stewardship of Wealth. Kingdon W. Swayne. LC 85-60034. 32p. (Orig.). 1985. pap. 3.00 (*0-87574-259-9*) Pendle Hill.

Stewardship Program Builder, No. 1. Compiled by Paul M. Miller. 1980. 5.50 (*0-8341-9173-3*, MP-617) Lillenas.

***Stewardship Starters.** 104p. 1996. 5.99 (*0-8341-1655-3*) Nazarene.

Stewardship, The Divine Order. Genevieve DeHoyos. LC 81-82055. 200p. 1982. 13.98 (*0-88290-191-5*, 1065) Horizon Utah.

***Stewart: Seattle's Skyscraper Falcon.** Linda Birman. 32p. (Orig.). (J). (gr. k-5). 1997. pap. 16.95 (*0-88839-389-X*) Hancock House.

Stewart: The Scottish Criminal Courts in Action. Alastair L. Stewart. 1990. pap. 55.00 (*0-406-17990-5*) MICHIE.

Stewart Agriculture-GATT. 1993. pap. text ed. 47.50 (*90-6544-749-0*) Kluwer Ac.

Stewart Edward White. Judy Alter. LC 75-7011. (Western Writers Ser.: No. 18). (Illus.). 48p. (Orig.). 1975. pap. 4.95 (*0-88430-017-X*) Boise St U W Writ Ser.

***Stewart GATT Uruguay Round.** 1993. lib. bdg. 198.50 (*90-6544-747-4*) Kluwer Law Tax Pubs.

Stewart Mason, the Art of Education. Jones. (C). 1982. text ed. 25.00 (*0-85315-699-9*, Pub. by Lawrence & Wishart UK) NYU Pr.

Stewart Overview. 1993. pap. text ed. 40.50 (*90-6544-748-2*) Kluwer Ac.

Stewart Stork. Ross M. Madsen. LC 92-30730. (Illus.). 40p. (J). (ps-3). 1993. lib. bdg. 11.89 (*0-8037-1326-6*) Dial Bks Young.

Stewart White Returns. Robert R. Leichtman. (From Heaven to Earth Ser.). (Illus.). 96p. (Orig.). 1980. pap. 3.50 (*0-89804-062-0*) Ariel GA.

Stewart's Bacterial Wilt of Corn. (Phytopathological Monographs). 1993. 15.00 (*0-89054-036-5*) Am Phytopathol Soc.

Stewart's Operative Urology, 2 vols., Set. 2nd ed. Andrew C. Novick et al. (Illus.). 908p. 1989. 225.00 (*0-683-06589-0*) Williams & Wilkins.

Stewed Screwed & Tattooed. Madame Chinchilla. Ed. by Chris H. Nibbrig & June Clark. LC 94-75673. (Illus.). 104p. (Orig.). 1997. pap. 20.00 (*0-9602600-1-3*) Isadore Pr.

Stews. Ed. by Chuck Williams. LC 94-48065. (Williams-Sonoma Kitchen Library). (Illus.). 108p. 1995. 17.95 (*0-7835-0307-5*) Time-Life.

Stews & Ragouts: Simple & Hearty One-Dish Meals. Kay S. Nelson. 1978. reprint ed. pap. 5.95 (*0-486-23662-5*) Dover.

***Stews, Ragouts & Burgoos: The Great American Stewpot.** James Villas. LC 96-50015. 1999. write for info. (*0-688-15253-8*) Morrow.

STI Review No. 17: Special Issue on Government Technology Foresight Exercises. 134p. 1995. pap. 28.00 (*92-64-14718-7*) OECD.

Stichus, Vol. V. Plautus. Bd. with Three Bob Day.; Truculentus.; Tale of a Traveling Bag.; Fragments. (Loeb Classical Library: No. 328). 15.50 (*0-674-99362-4*) HUP.

Stick. Elmore Leonard. 304p. 1984. mass mkt. 6.50 (*0-380-67652-4*) Avon.

Stick a Geranium in Your Hat & Be Happy! large type ed. Barbara Johnson. pap. 14.99 (*0-8499-3683-7*, 2436) Word Dist.

S

An Asterisk (*) at the beginning of an entry indicates that the title is appearing in BIP for the first time.

S

Stick a Geranium in Your Hat & Be Happy! Pain Is Inevitable but Misery Is Optional. Barbara Johnson. 179p. (C). pap. text ed. 9.99 (*0-8499-3201-7*) Omega Pubns OR.

Stick & Rudder: An Explanation of the Art of Flying. William Langewiesche. (Illus.). 384p. 1944. text ed. 22.95 (*0-07-036240-8*) McGraw.

Stick-Around Cloud. Marcia Vaughan. LC 93-28962. (Voyages Ser.). (Illus.). (J). 1994. 4.25 (*0-383-03777-8*) SRA McGraw.

Stick Boy. Joan T. Zeier. LC 92-23326. 144p. (J). (gr. 2-6). 1993. lib. bdg. 13.95 (*0-689-31835-9*, Atheneum Bks Young) S&S Childrens.

Stick 'em up! I've Got You Covered! Walter Swan. Ed. by Deloris Swan. (Illus.). 16p. (Orig.). (J). (ps-8). 1989. pap. 1.50 (*0-927176-03-3*) Swan Enterp.

Stick Exercises. Cherie Phillips. LC 86-62541. (Illus.). 281p. 1987. pap. write for info. (*0-9616287-0-7*) IntelSpectrum.

Stick Fighting. Masaaki Hatsumi & Q. Chambers. 15.00 (*0-685-38454-3*) Wehman.

Stick Fighting: Self-Defense. Bruce Tegner. LC 70-109225. (Illus.). 128p. 1972. pap. 7.00 (*0-87407-020-1*, T-20) Thor.

Stick-Fighting: Sport Forms. Bruce Tegner. (Illus.). 127p. 1973. pap. 7.00 (*0-87407-043-0*, T-21) Thor.

Stick Fighting: Techniques of Self-Defense. Masaaki Hatsumi & Quintin T. Chambers. LC 79-158643. (Illus.). 147p. 1981. pap. 15.00 (*0-87011-475-1*) Kodansha.

Stick Fighting for Combat. Michael D. Echanis. LC 78-65738. (Specialties Ser.). (Illus.). 1978. pap. 15.95 (*0-89750-059-8*, 130) Ohara Pubns.

***Stick Figure: A Memoir.** Lori Gottlieb. 192p. 1998. 19.95 (*0-7868-6308-0*) Hyperion.

Stick Figure: A Personal Journey Through Anorexia & Bulimia. Christine Fontana. 1996. pap. text ed. 17.95 (*0-85572-257-6*, Pub. by Hill Content Pubng AT) Seven Hills Bk.

Stick Like Glue. Colin Wells. Ed. by Liz Parker. (Take Ten Bks.). (Illus.). 45p. (Orig.). (J). (gr. 6-12). 1992. pap. text ed. 3.95 (*1-56254-058-0*) Saddleback Pubns.

Stick Out Your Tongue! Jokes about Doctors & Patients. Peter Roop & Connie Roop. (Make Me Laugh! Joke Bks.). (Illus.). 32p. (J). (gr. 1-4). 1986. pap. 2.95 (*0-8225-9546-X*, Lerner Publctns); lib. bdg. 6.95 (*0-8225-0990-3*, Lerner Publctns) Lerner Group.

Stick Stories. Margie Brown. LC 82-60030. (Illus.). 64p. (Orig.). 1982. pap. 7.95 (*0-89390-035-4*) Resource Pubns.

***Stick That Breaks & Breaks.** Marianne Boruch. LC 97-66614. (Field Poetry Ser.: Vol. 5). 80p. 1997. 22.95 (*0-932440-79-7*) Oberlin Coll Pr.

***Stick That Breaks & Breaks.** Marianne Boruch. LC 97-66614. (Field Poetry Ser.: Vol. 5). 80p. (Orig.). 1997. pap. 12.95 (*0-932440-80-0*) Oberlin Coll Pr.

Stick-tivity. Mona Rosenberg. (J). (gr. k-1). 1991. write for info. (*1-880056-07-0*) Play-Media.

Stick-tivity, Bk. 1: The Talking Drum & Trumpet. Mona Rosenberg. 16p. (J). (gr. k-1). 1991. write for info. (*1-880056-08-9*) Play-Media.

Stick-tivity, Bk. 2: Bob's Zoo. Mona Rosenberg. 16p. (J). (gr. k-1). 1991. write for info. (*1-880056-09-7*) Play-Media.

Stick-tivity, Bk. 3: On a Wet Day in Botswana. Mona Rosenberg. 16p. (J). (gr. k-1). 1991. write for info. (*1-880056-10-0*) Play-Media.

Stick-tivity, Bk. 4: Magical Thoughts on a Hot Day. Mona Rosenberg. 16p. (J). (gr. k-1). 1991. write for info. (*1-880056-11-9*) Play-Media.

Stick-tivity, Bk. 5: Planning to See the Whole World. Mona Rosenberg. 16p. (J). (gr. k-1). 1991. write for info. (*1-880056-12-7*) Play-Media.

Stick-tivity, Bk. 6: Mainly Math. Mona Rosenberg. 16p. (J). (gr. k-1). 1991. write for info. (*1-880056-13-5*) Play-Media.

Stick to It! The Power of Positive Persistence. rev. ed. C. Leslie Charles. LC 95-60861. 120p. 1995. pap. 11.95 (*0-9644621-0-9*) Yes Pr MI.

Stick up for Yourself! Every Kid's Guide to Personal Power & Positive Self-Esteem. Gershen Kaufman & Lev Raphael. LC 89-28642. (Illus.). 96p. (J). (gr. 2-7). 1990. pap. 9.95 (*0-915793-17-2*) Free Spirit Pub.

Stick Wife. Darrah Cloud. 66p. 1996. pap. 5.25 (*0-87129-618-7*, SB1) Dramatic Pub.

Stickball, Streetcars & Saturday Matinees. Ed. by Mike Martin. LC 95-69028. 1995. 14.95 (*0-89821-151-4*, 20106) Reiman Pubns.

Stickeen. John Muir. 74p. 1989. 8.95 (*1-55709-112-9*) Applewood.

Stickeen. John Muir. (Illus.). 96p. 1991. reprint ed. lib. bdg. 25.00 (*0-8095-4961-1*) Borgo Pr.

Stickeen. John Muir. LC 90-84443. (Illus.). 96p. 1990. reprint ed. pap. 6.95 (*0-930588-48-7*) Heyday Bks.

Stickeen: An Adventure with a Dog & a Glacier. John Muir. (Illus.). 1978. reprint ed. pap. 3.95 (*0-89646-032-0*) Vistabooks.

***Sticker Activity Atlas.** Nick Arnold et al. (Illus.). (J). pap. 9.99 (*0-590-24921-5*) Scholastic Inc.

Sticker Bugs: Colors & Shapes. David A. Carter. (Sticker Bugs Ser.). 12p. (J). 1996. 6.99 (*0-689-81042-3*) S&S Childrens.

Sticker Bugs: Numbers. David A. Carter. (Sticker Bugs Ser.). 12p. (J). 1996. 6.99 (*0-689-81041-5*) S&S Childrens.

Sticker Encyclopedia. Wishing Well Staff. (Illus.). 16p. (J). (ps-2). 1995. 3.99 (*0-88705-525-7*, Wshng Well Bks) Joshua Morris.

Sticker Fun. Barrie Henderson. (J). 1994. pap. 3.50 (*0-590-20843-8*) Scholastic Inc.

***Sticker Fun Book: Puzzle Fun.** DK Publishing, Inc. Staff. 1997. pap. text ed. 6.95 (*0-7894-1524-0*) DK Pub Inc.

Sticker Fun with Colors. (Early Learning Sticker Bks.). 32p. (J). 1991. pap. 5.99 (*0-517-03353-4*) Random Hse Value.

Sticker Fun with Dinosaur Bones. (Illus.). 16p. (J). (ps-3). 1994. pap. 3.95 (*1-56458-739-8*) DK Pub Inc.

Sticker Fun with Dinosaurs. (Illus.). 16p. (J). (ps-3). 1994. pap. 3.95 (*1-56458-740-1*) DK Pub Inc.

Sticker Fun with Farmyard Animals. (Illus.). 16p. (J). (ps-3). 1994. pap. 3.95 (*1-56458-741-X*) DK Pub Inc.

Sticker Fun with Numbers. (Early Learning Sticker Bks.). (Illus.). 32p. (J). (ps-1). 1991. pap. 5.99 (*0-517-03352-6*) Random Hse Value.

Sticker Fun with Teddy Bears. (Illus.). 16p. (J). (ps-3). 1994. pap. 3.95 (*1-56458-742-8*) DK Pub Inc.

Sticker Gingerbread House. Illus. by Scott McDougall. 16p. (Orig.). (J). (gr. 1-5). 1996. pap. 7.95 (*0-448-40955-0*, G&D) Putnam Pub Group.

Sticker Paper Dolls Bunny Rabbit Family. Elizabeth K. Brown. (Illus.). (J). (gr. k-3). 1990. pap. 3.95 (*0-486-26503-X*) Dover.

Sticker Tricks. Bill Colrus. (Uncle Louie Ser.). (Illus.). 6p. (Orig.). (J). (ps up). 1996. pap. 1.99 (*1-56293-837-1*) McClanahan Bk.

***Stickers - Action Hero Pictures.** Petrucc. (Illus.). (J). (ps-3). 1996. pap. 3.50 (*0-486-29342-4*, 312272Q) Dover.

***Stickers - Create Your Own Easter.** Anna Pomaska. (Illus.). (J). (ps-3). 1996. pap. 1.00 (*0-486-29399-8*, 256939Q) Dover.

***Stickers - Create Your Own Valentine.** Beylon. (Illus.). (J). (ps-4). 1996. pap. 1.00 (*0-486-29393-9*, 256769Q) Dover.

***Stickers - Desert Animals.** Petrucc. (Illus.). (J). (ps-4). 1996. pap. 1.00 (*0-486-29398-X*, 255860Q) Dover.

***Stickers - Make Your Own Cinderella.** Kilros. (J). (ps-3). 1996. pap. 1.00 (*0-486-29374-2*, 256408Q) Dover.

***Stickers - Make Your Own Little.** Kilros. (Illus.). (J). (ps-3). 1996. pap. 1.00 (*0-486-29367-X*, 256312Q) Dover.

***Stickers - Make Your Own Puss in Boots.** Anna Pomaska. (Illus.). (J). (ps-3). 1996. pap. 1.00 (*0-486-29391-2*, 256615Q) Dover.

***Stickers - Make Your Own Sleeping Beauty.** Beckett. (Illus.). (J). (ps-3). 1996. pap. 1.00 (*0-486-29392-0*, 256194Q) Dover.

***Stickers - Old Fashioned Seashells.** Maggie Kate. (Illus.). (J). (ps-3). 1996. pap. 1.00 (*0-486-29395-5*, 285699Q) Dover.

***Stickers - Peter Cottontail & Friends.** Stewart. (Illus.). (J). (ps-3). 1996. pap. 1.00 (*0-486-29403-X*, 255965Q) Dover.

Sticking It Out. Jim O'Connor. 96p. (J). (gr. 2-7). 1996. pap. 3.99 (*0-614-13973-2*, Bullseye Bks) Random Bks Yng Read.

***Sticking Things.** Dorling Kindersley Staff. (Play & Learn Ser.). (Illus.). 24p. (J). 1997. pap. 4.95 (*0-7894-1520-8*) DK Pub Inc.

Sticking to the Point: A Rational Method for the Step by Step Formulation of Administration of an Acupuncture Treatment. Bob Flaws. 150p. (Orig.). (C). 1990. pap. text ed. 17.95 (*0-936185-17-1*) Blue Poppy Pr.

Sticking Together: Friendships for Life. Sandy Larsen. (Bible Discovery Guide Ser.). 32p. (Orig.). 1987. student ed., pap. text ed. 1.50 (*0-87788-787-X*); teacher ed., pap. text ed. 3.50 (*0-87788-788-8*) Shaw Pubs.

Stickit Minister, & Some Common Men. 2nd ed. Samuel R. Crockett. LC 72-163023. (Short Story Index Reprint Ser.). 1977. reprint ed. 20.95 (*0-8369-3937-9*) Ayer.

Sticklewort & Feverfew. Robert D. Sutherland. LC 79-92898. (Illus.). 360p. (J). (gr. 2 up). 1980. 16.00 (*0-936044-00-4*); pap. 9.00 (*0-936044-01-2*) Pikestaff Pr.

Stickley Craftsman Furniture Catalogs. Gustav Stickley et al. 192p. 1979. reprint ed. pap. 9.95 (*0-486-23838-5*) Dover.

Stickley Craftsman Furniture Catalogs: Unabridged Reprints of Two Mission Furniture Catalogs-"Craftsman Furniture Made by Gustav Stickley" & "the Work of L. & J. G. Stickley" Gustav Stickley. (Illus.). 1990. 22.75 (*0-8446-5821-9*) Peter Smith.

Stickman. D. K. Jones. 33p. 1994. 5.95 (*0-9640186-0-8*) Ginabean Bks.

Stickman: John Trudell. John Trudell. (Illus.). 184p. (Orig.). 1994. bds., pap. 19.95 (*0-9625119-8-6*) Inanout Pr.

Stickney Family: A Genealogy of the Descendants of William & Elizabeth, 1637-1869. M. A. Stickney. (Illus.). 534p. 1989. reprint ed. pap. 80.00 (*0-8328-1131-9*); reprint ed. lib. bdg. 88.00 (*0-8328-1130-0*) Higginson Bk Co.

Sticks. Joan Bauer. 192p. (J). (gr. 3-7). 1996. 15.95 (*0-385-32165-1*) Delacorte.

***Sticks.** Joan Bauer. 1997. mass mkt. 3.99 (*0-440-41387-7*) Dell.

***Sticks & Stones.** (Illus.). (Orig.). Date not set. pap. write for info. (*1-881456-33-1*) B B K Natl Jew Mus.

Sticks & Stones. Jackie Calhoun. 224p. 1992. pap. 9.95 (*1-56280-020-5*) Naiad Pr.

Sticks & Stones. Carol Cummings. (Illus.). 24p. (Orig.). (J). (ps-3). 1992. pap. 4.99 (*0-9614574-8-1*) Teaching WA.

Sticks & Stones. Betty M. James. (Illus.). 96p. (Orig.). 1996. pap. 8.95 (*0-9651286-0-1*) Petrograph.

Sticks & Stones. rev. ed. Lewis Mumford. (Illus.). 1955. pap. 4.95 (*0-486-20202-X*) Dover.

Sticks & Stones. Lewis Mumford. 247p. 1993. reprint ed. lib. bdg. 79.00 (*0-7812-5301-2*) Rprt Serv.

***Sticks & Stones: Identifying & Avoiding All Forms of Abuse.** Miriam Adahan. LC 97-7351. 1997. write for info. (*0-87306-793-2*) Feldheim.

Sticks & Stones: Ten Artists Work with Nature. Barry Walker. (Illus.). 28p. 1991. 10.00 (*0-915171-21-X*) Katonah Gal.

Sticks & Stones: The Discipleship of Our Speech. William R. Baker. LC 96-8120. 180p. (Orig.). 1996. pap. 11.99 (*0-8308-1986-X*, 1986) InterVarsity.

Sticks & Stones & Ice Cream Cones. Phyllis Fiarotta. LC 74-160843. (Illus.). 322p. (J). (gr. 1-5). 1973. pap. 10.95 (*0-911104-30-5*, 011) Workman Pub.

Sticks & Stones & Other Poems. Marcia Muth. 32p. (Orig.). 1994. pap. 4.95 (*0-86534-214-8*) Sunstone Pr.

Sticks & Stones & Strawberries. Gwendolyn Jansma. LC 94-7541. 1994. pap. 11.95 (*0-87212-262-X*) Libra.

Sticks & Straw: Comparative house forms in Southern Sudan & Northern Kenya. Jonathan E. Arensen. LC 81-50907. (International Museum of Cultures Publications: No. 13). (Illus.). 140p. (Orig.). 1983. fiche 8.00 (*0-88312-249-9*) Summer Instit Ling.

Sticks 'n' Bones 'n' Chewing Gum: Creating Gifts from Finder's Art. Dar Pinson. 43p. 1993. spiral bd. 14.95 (*1-886724-00-8*) Pinson Pr.

Sticks that Kill: A Novel. Trevor Shearston. LC 83-10394. (Illus.). 592p. 1984. pap. 12.95 (*0-7022-1825-1*, Pub. by Univ Queensland Pr AT) Intl Spec Bk.

Sticky Beak. Morris Gleitzman. LC 94-33928. 160p. (J). (gr. 3-7). 1995. 11.00 (*0-15-200366-5*); pap. 5.00 (*0-15-200367-3*) HarBrace.

Sticky Fingers: A Close Look at America's Fastest-growing Crime. W. W. McCullough. LC 80-69696. 158p. reprint ed. pap. 45.10 (*0-317-26942-9*, 2023591) Bks Demand.

Sticky Mystery. Barbara Davoll. (Christopher Churchmouse Classics Ser.). (Illus.). 24p. (J). 1989. 8.99 (*0-89693-485-3*, 6-1485, Victor Bks) Chariot Victor.

Sticky Mystery. Barbara Davoll. (Illus.). 24p. (J). 1989. audio 11.99 (*0-89693-033-5*, 3-1205) SP Pubns.

Sticky Ricky. (J). (gr. k-3). 1994. pap. 3.50 (*0-9614746-9-6*) Berry Bks.

***Sticky Situations: 365 Devotions for Kids & Families.** Betsy Schmitt. LC 97-17526. 1997. write for info. (*0-8423-6550-8*) Tyndale.

***Sticky Trousers.** Groves. (J). Date not set. pap. text ed. write for info. (*0-582-18304-9*, Pub. by Longman UK) Longman.

Stickybeak. Hazel Edwards. Ed. by Rhoda Sherwood. LC 88-42915. (Illus.). 32p. (J). (gr. 2-3). 1988. lib. bdg. 18.60 (*1-55532-932-2*) Gareth Stevens Inc.

Stickybear Book of Weather. Richard Hefter. LC 83-2191. (Stickybear Bks.). (Illus.). 32p. (J). (ps-1). 1983. 5.95 (*0-911787-01-1*) Optimum Res Inc.

Stickybear's Scary Night. Richard Hefter. (Stickybear Bks.). (Illus.). 29p. (J). (ps-1). 1984. 1.95 (*0-911787-41-0*) Optimum Res Inc.

Stiefschwestern: Was Ost-Frauen und West-Fruen Voneinander Denken. Ed. by Katrin Rohnstock. 192p. (GER.). 1994. pap. 13.50 (*3-596-12221-X*, Pub. by Fischer Taschbch Verlag GW) Intl Bk Import.

Stieglitz: A Memoir-Biography. Sue D. Lowe. (Illus.). 419p. 1983. 25.50 (*0-374-26990-4*) FS&G.

Stiff Critique. Jaqueline Girdner. 272p. (Orig.). 1995. pap. text ed. 4.99 (*0-425-14719-3*, Prime Crime) Berkley Pub.

Stiff Drink & a Close Shave: The Lost Arts of Manliness. Robert Sloan & Steven Guarnaccia. 96p. 1995. 12.95 (*0-8118-0757-6*) Chronicle Bks.

Stiff Necked City. Malkah Raymist. 400p. 1992. pap. 15.95 (*965-229-038-6*, Pub. by Gefen Pub Hse IS) Gefen Bks.

Stiff-Necked People, Bottle-Necked System: The Evolution & Roots of Israeli Public Protest, 1949-1986. Sam N. Lehman-Wilzig. LC 89-45858. (Jewish Political & Social Studies). 224p. 1991. 27.50 (*0-253-33293-1*) Ind U Pr.

Stiff Upper Lip, Jeeves. P. G. Wodehouse. 20.95 (*0-8488-0682-4*) Amereon Ltd.

Stiffed. 5.98 (*0-8317-0045-9*) Smithmark.

Stiffed on Christmas Eve: A Simple & Practical Guide to Tipping. Charlie Nesbitt. LC 95-42644. 1996. pap. 9.95 (*1-56072-276-2*) Nova Sci Pubs.

Stiffness of Asphalt-Aggregate Mixes. A. Tayebali Akhtathusein et al. 101p. (Orig.). (C). 1994. pap. text ed. 15.00 (*0-309-05768-X*, SHRP-A-388) SHRP.

Stifled Laughter: One Woman's Story about Fighting Censorship. Claudia Johnson. 192p. 1994. 19.95 (*1-55591-200-1*) Fulcrum Pub.

Stifled Laughter: One Woman's Story about Fighting Censorship. Claudia Johnson. 192p. 1996. pap. 14.95 (*1-55591-337-7*) Fulcrum Pub.

Stifling Human Rights Advocacy in Mexico: The Censure of Brigadier General Jose Francisco Gallardo Rodriguez. MN. Advocates for Human Rights Staff. 11p. (Orig.). 1994. pap. 3.00 (*0-929293-19-3*) MN Advocates.

Stig. Mark Dunster. 1978. pap. 4.00 (*0-89642-042-6*) Linden Pubs.

Stiglitz Principles of Macro-Economics. Lawrence W. Martin. (C). 1993. student ed., pap. text ed. 15.95 (*0-393-96382-9*) Norton.

Stiglitz Principles of Micro-Economics. Martin. (C). Date not set. student ed., pap. text ed. 15.95 (*0-393-96383-7*) Norton.

Stigma. Charles Bernstein. 1981. pap. 3.00 (*0-930794-49-4*) Station Hill Pr.

Stigma: A Social Psychological Analysis. Irwin Katz. LC 80-20765. 160p. 1981. text ed. 39.95 (*0-89859-078-7*) L Erlbaum Assocs.

Stigma: Notes on the Management of Spoiled Identity. Erving Goffman. 168p. (Orig.). 1986. pap. 10.00 (*0-671-62244-7*, Touchstone Bks) S&S Trade.

Stigma: Notes on the Management of Spoiled Identity. Irving Goffman. (Orig.). 1963. pap. 5.95 (*0-13-846626-2*, Spectrum IN) Macmillan Gen Ref.

Stigma & Mental Illness. Ed. by Paul J. Fink & Allan Tasman. LC 91-26135. 236p. 1992. text ed. 36.00 (*0-88048-405-5*, 8405) Am Psychiatric.

***Stigma & Social Welfare: An International Comparative Study.** Matthew Colton et al. (Welfare & Society Ser.). 174p. 1997. text ed. 59.95 (*1-85972-525-2*, Pub. by Avebury Pub UK) Ashgate Pub Co.

Stigma of Genius: Einstein & Beyond Modern Education. Joe L. Kincheloe et al. LC 92-19359. 225p. (C). 1992. text ed. 37.50 (*0-89341-692-4*); pap. text ed. 17.50 (*0-89341-729-7*) Hollowbrook.

Stigma of Names: Antisemitism in German Daily Life, 1812-1933. Dietz Bering. Tr. by Neville Plaice. LC 92-19899. (Social History, Popular Culture, & Politics in Germany Ser.). 360p. (ENG & GER.). (C). 1993. text ed. 52.50 (*0-472-10407-1*) U of Mich Pr.

Stigma of Poverty: A Critique of Poverty Theories & Policies. 2nd ed. Chaim I. Waxman. LC 77-5760. 1983. text ed. 48.00 (*0-08-029408-1*, Pergamon Pr); pap. text ed. 20.95 (*0-08-029407-3*, Pergamon Pr) Elsevier.

Stigmata: A Medieval Mystery in a Modern Age. Ted Harrison. 176p. 1996. pap. 10.95 (*0-14-025205-3*) Viking Penguin.

Stigmata: A Medieval Phenomenon in a Modern Age. Ted Harrison. 160p. 1994. 16.95 (*0-312-11372-2*) St Martin.

Stigmata & Modern Science. Charles M. Carty. 31p. 1992. reprint ed. pap. 1.25 (*0-89555-104-7*) TAN Bks Pubs.

Stigmata of St. Francis of Assisi. Octavian Schmucki. (History Ser.). 393p. 1992. pap. 15.00 (*1-57659-085-2*) Franciscan Inst.

Stikhi: Nineteen Twenty-One to Nineteen Eighty-Three. Nina Berberova. LC 84-60081. (Russica Poetry Ser.: No. 4). 120p. (Orig.). (RUS.). 1984. pap. 18.50 (*0-89830-072-X*) Russica Pubs.

Stikhi I Liudi. Efim G. Etkind. LC 88-793. (Russian Ser.). 158p. (Orig.). 1988. pap. 9.00 (*0-938920-96-0*) Hermitage.

Stikhi o Terrore. Maksimilian A. Voloshin. 69p. (RUS.). 1983. reprint ed. pap. 5.00 (*0-933884-38-9*) Berkeley Slavic.

Stikhi, Poems, Poemes. Irina Ratushinskaya. Tr. by Meery Devergnas et al. LC 84-12974. 134p. (ENG, FRE & RUS.). 1984. pap. text ed. 8.50 (*0-938920-54-5*) Hermitage.

Stikhotvoreniia i Poemy. Vadim Andreyev. Ed. by Irina Shevelenko. (Modern Russian Literature & Culture, Studies & Text: Vol. 35). 326p. (Orig.). (RUS.). 1995. pap. 20.00 (*1-57201-015-0*) Berkeley Slavic.

Stikhotvoreniia i Poemy. Vadim Andreyev. Ed. by Irina Shevelenko. (Modern Russian Literature & Culture, Studies & Text: Vol. 36). 334p. (Orig.). (RUS.). 1995. pap. 20.00 (*1-57201-016-9*) Berkeley Slavic.

***Stikhotvoreniia; Stat'i o Russkoi Poezii.** Dimitry S. Mirsky. Ed. by G. S. Smith & Gareth K. Perkins. 299p. (Orig.). (RUS.). (C). 1997. pap. 20.00 (*1-57201-005-3*) Berkeley Slavic.

Stikhotvoreniya. Mikhail Eremin. Ed. & Afterword by Lev Losev. LC 86-14317. (RUS.). 1986. pap. 8.50 (*0-938920-46-4*) Hermitage.

Stikine River. Ed. by Alaska Geographic Staff. LC 79-20674. (Alaska Geographic Ser.: Vol. 6, No. 4). (Illus.). 1979. pap. 19.95 (*0-88240-133-5*) Alaska Geog Soc.

Stil & Epoche: Periodisierungsfragen, Herausgegeben von Friedrich Mobius & Helga Sciurie. Helga Sciurie. 420p. (GER.). 1990. pap. text ed. 8.00 (*3-364-00166-9*) Gordon & Breach.

Stil Des L. Apuleius. Heinrich Koziol. viii, 354p. 1988. reprint ed. write for info. (*3-487-07904-6*) G Olms Pubs.

***Stil in Fachsprachen.** Bernd Spillner. (Studien zur Allgemeinen und Romanischen Sprachwissenschaft Ser.: Bd.2). (Illus.). 181p. (GER.). 1996. 42.95 (*3-631-43055-8*) P Lang Pubng.

Stil Standing after All These Years: Eleven of Baseball's Longest Standing Records. Victor Debs, Jr. LC 96-31885. (Illus.). 0786403527p. 1998. pap. 29.95 (*0-7864-0230-X*) McFarland & Co.

***Stil und Stilwandel: Bernhard Sowinski zum 65. Gerburtstag Gewidmet.** Ulla Fix & Gotthard Lerchner. (Leipziger Arbeiten zur Sprach- und Kommunikationsgeschichte Ser.: Bd. 3). (Illus.). 409p. (GER.). 1996. 63.95 (*3-631-48931-5*) P Lang Pubng.

Stil und Text der Politeia Athenaion Des Aristoteles. Georg Kaibel. v, 277p. 1973. reprint ed. write for info. (*3-487-04576-1*) G Olms Pubs.

Stile Floreale: The Cult of Nature in Italian Design. Gabriel P. Weisberg. 1988. 45.00 (*0-295-96671-8*) U of Wash Pr.

Stiles Family in America: Genealogy of the Connecticut Family, Also the Connecticut-New Jersey Family, 1720-1894 with Contributions to the Genealogy of Some New York & Pennsylvania Families. H. R. Stiles. (Illus.). 794p. 1989. reprint ed. pap. 119.00 (*0-8328-1135-1*); reprint ed. lib. bdg. 127.00 (*0-8328-1134-3*) Higginson Bk Co.

Stiles Family in America: Genealogy of the Massachusetts Family & the Dover, N. H. Family. M. S. Guild. 689p. 1989. reprint ed. pap. 99.00 (*0-8328-1133-5*); reprint ed. lib. bdg. 107.00 (*0-8328-1132-7*) Higginson Bk Co.

***Stiles. From the Wyoming Valley of Penna. to the Platte Val. of Nebraska: History & Genealogy of the of the Family of Mary Elizabeth Stiles, 1630-1941.** Leopold H. Hoppe. (Illus.). 313p. 1996. reprint ed. pap. 47.50 (*0-8328-5318-6*); reprint ed. lib. bdg. 57.50 (*0-8328-5317-8*) Higginson Bk Co.

Stiletto. Roger Aplon. 1976. pap. 8.95 (*0-931848-14-8*) Dryad Pr.

***Stiletto.** Harold Robbins. LC 96-42517. 1997. pap. 19.95 (*1-55611-516-4*) D I Fine.

Stiletto. large type ed. Harold Robbins. 272p. 1983. 27.99 (*0-7089-8101-1*) Ulverscroft.

***Stiletto Talk: Poems by Sara Levy.** Sara Levy. Ed. by R. D. Baker. (Poetry Chapbook Ser.). (Illus.). 28p. (Orig.). 1995. pap. 4.00 (*1-887641-06-8*) Argonne Hotel Pr.

Stiletto2: The Disinherited. deluxe ed. Antler et al. Ed. & Des. by Michael Annis. 300p. 1992. per., pap. 21.50 (*1-882863-02-X*) Howling Dog.

An Asterisk (*) at the beginning of an entry indicates that the title is appearing in BIP for the first time.

Stilfragen. Ed. by Gerhard Stickel. (Institut fuer Deutsche Sprache-Jarhbuch 1994 Ser.). v, 455p. (GER.). (C). 1995. lib. bdg. 129.25 (*3-11-014748-3*) De Gruyter.

Stilistik: Sprachpragmatische Grundlegung der Stilbeschreibung. Barbara Sandig. (Grundlagen der Kommunikation De Gruyter Studienbuch Ser.). (C). 1978. 32.35 (*3-11-007374-9*) De Gruyter.

***Stilistik der Deutschen Gegenwartssprache: Auflage.** Wolfgang Fleischer et al. 341p. (GER.). 1996. 61.95 (*3-631-30640-7*) P Lang Pubng.

Stilistik III: Argumentationsstile. Ed. by Barbara Sandig & Ulrich Puschel. (Germanistische Linguistik Ser.: Heft 112-113/92). 292p. (GER.). 1993. write for info. (*3-487-09690-0*) G Olms Pubs.

Still. David Feintuch. LC 97-7059. 592p. (Orig.). 1997. pap. 12.99 (*0-446-67285-8*, Aspect) Warner Bks.

***Still.** David Feintuch. 1997. write for info. (*0-446-52223-6*, Aspect) Warner Bks.

***Still.** David Feintuch. 1998. mass mkt. write for info. (*0-446-60551-4*, Aspect) Warner Bks.

Still! The Only Investment Guide You'll Ever Need. Andrew Tobias. write for info. (*0-318-59624-5*) S&S Trade.

Still a Distant Drum. Garrison. Date not set. write for info. (*0-395-34401-8*) HM.

Still a Dream: The Changing Status of Blacks Since 1960. Sar A. Levitan et al. LC 74-16539. 398p. 1976. pap. 14. 95 (*0-674-83856-4*) HUP.

Still a Man's World: Men Who Do Women's Work. Christine L. Williams. LC 94-29009. (Men & Masculinity Ser.: No. 1). 1995. 40.00 (*0-520-08786-0*); pap. text ed. 15.00 (*0-520-08787-9*) U CA Pr.

Still a Nation of Immigrants. Brent Ashabranner. LC 92-44335. (Illus.). 144p. (J). (gr. 5 up). 1993. pap. 15.99 (*0-525-65130-6*, Cobblehill Bks) Dutton Child Bks.

***Still Ain't Satisfied: Canadian Feminism Today.** Ed. by Maureen FitzGerald et al. 320p. reprint ed. pap. 11.95 (*0-88961-074-6*, Pub. by Wmns Pr CN) LPC InBook.

Still Alive: An Autobiographical Essay. Jan Kott. Tr. by Jadwiga Kosicka. LC 93-29605. 304p. (POL.). 32.50 (*0-300-05276-6*) Yale U Pr.

Still an Open Door? U. S. Immigration Policy & the American Economy. Vernon M. Briggs, Jr. & Stephen Moore. 175p. (Orig.). 1994. pap. text ed. 16.95 (*1-879383-32-2*); lib. bdg. 49.50 (*1-879383-31-4*) Am Univ Pr.

Still & Icy Silence. Ronald C. Roat. (Stuart Mallory Mystery Ser.). 303p. 21.95 (*0-934257-94-9*) Story Line.

Still Another Day. Pablo Neruda. Tr. by William O'Daly. LC 84-70299. 80p. (ENG & SPA.). 1984. pap. 9.00 (*0-914742-77-9*) Copper Canyon.

Still Another Northwoods Reader. 4th ed. Cully Gage. LC 89-80866. 1990. pap. 10.95 (*0-932212-61-1*) Avery Color.

Still Another Pelican in the Breadbox. Kenneth Patchen. Ed. by Richard Morgan. LC 80-82905. 96p. 1981. pap. 5.95 (*0-917530-14-4*) Pig Iron Pr.

Still Artful Work: The Continuing Politics of Social Security Reform. 2nd ed. Paul C. Light. LC 94-17594. 1994. pap. text ed. write for info. (*0-07-037949-1*) McGraw.

Still As a Mountain, Powerful As Thunder: Simple Taoist Exercises for Healing, Vitality, & Peace of Mind. Y. P. Dong. LC 92-50442. (Illus.). 128p. (Orig.). 1993. pap. 15.00 (*0-87773-688-X*) Shambhala Pubns.

Still Black, Still Strong: Survivors of the War Against Black Revolutionaries. Dhoruba Bin Wahad et al. 270p. Date not set. 7.00 (*0-936756-74-8*, Semiotexte) Autonomedia.

Still By Your Side: A True Story of Love & Grief, Faith & Miracles. Marjorie Holmes. 168p. 1996. 17.95 (*0-8245-1631-1*) Crossroad NY.

***Still Can't Keep a Straight Face.** Ellen Orleans. (Illus.). 112p. (Orig.). 1996. pap. 8.95 (*1-889594-01-6*) Laugh Lines.

Still Catholic after All These Fears. Ed Stivender. (American Storytelling Ser.). 224p. 1995. 19.95 (*0-87483-403-1*) August Hse.

Still Catholic after All These Fears. Ed Stivender. 224p. 1996. pap. text ed. 11.95 (*0-87483-483-X*) August Hse.

***Still Close to Heaven, Vol. 1.** Kane. 1997. mass mkt. 5.99 (*0-312-96268-1*) St Martin.

Still Crazy about the Cats. Jamie H. Vaught. LC 95-80008. (Illus.). 256p. 1995. pap. 16.95 (*0-913383-41-4*) McClanahan Pub.

***Still Crazy after All These Quilts.** Charlotte Angotti. 36p. (Orig.). 1994. pap. 12.95 (*0-929950-15-1*, 118) ME Pubns.

Still Crazy after All These Years. Rachel Bowlby. LC 92-5061. 224p. (C). (gr. 13). 1992. text ed. 52.95 (*0-415-08639-6*, A7897) Routledge.

Still Crazy after All These Years. Rachel Bowlby. LC 92-5061. 224p. (C). 1992. pap. 17.95 (*0-415-08640-X*, Routledge NY) Routledge.

Still Cruising: Australia to Asia, Africa & America. Liza Copeland. (Illus.). 288p. (Orig.). 1995. pap. 16.95 (*0-9697690-1-6*) R Hale & Co.

Still Dancing with Love: More Stories of Life with Meher Baba. Margaret Craske. LC 89-78069. 104p. (Orig.). 1990. pap. 8.95 (*0-913078-64-6*) Sheriar Pr.

Still Dead. Ed. by John Skipp & Craig Spector. 29.95 (*0-929480-67-8*) Mark Ziesing.

Still Dead. limited ed. Ed. by John Skipp & Craig Spector. 85.00 (*0-929480-68-6*) Mark Ziesing.

***Still Dreaming of Jeannie: Behind the Scenes of the Wackiest Sitcom of All Time.** Mary Sheldon. 1997. pap. 12.95 (*0-7871-0699-2*, Dove Bks) Dove Audio.

Still Eatin' It: A Dana Crumb Cookbook. Dana Crumb. Ed. by Roger Williams. LC 96-32862. (Illus.). 176p. (Orig.). (YA). 1996. 15.00 (*0-943389-18-6*) Snow Lion-SLG Bks.

Still Explosion. Mary Logue. LC 92-43990. 248p. 1993. text ed. 18.95 (*1-878067-29-X*) Seal Pr WA.

Still Explosion. Mary Logue. LC 92-43990. 248p. 1994. pap. 9.95 (*1-878067-48-6*) Seal Pr WA.

Still Falls the Rain. large type ed. Chloe Gartner. 544p. 1986. 27.99 (*0-7089-8319-7*, Charnwood) Ulverscroft.

Still Following. Gary Sivewright. 32p. 1990. pap. 3.25 (*0-8341-1350-3*) Beacon Hill.

Still Following Percy. Lewis A. Lawson. LC 95-16820. 256p. 1995. 37.50 (*0-87805-826-5*) U Pr of Miss.

Still Forest Pool. Jack Kornfield & Paul Breiter. LC 85-40411. (Illus.). 225p. (Orig.). 1985. pap. 9.95 (*0-8356-0597-3*, Quest) Theos Pub Hse.

Still Forms on Foxfield. Joan Slonczewski. 224p. 1988. pap. 2.95 (*0-380-75328-6*) Avon.

Still Gathering: A Centennial Celebration. Auxiliary to the American Osteopathic Association Staff. (Illus.). 250p. 1992. text ed. 19.95 (*0-9633542-0-5*) Aux Am Osteopathic.

Still Glides the Stream. D. E. Stevenson. 278p. 1976. lib. bdg. 27.95 (*0-89966-158-0*) Buccaneer Bks.

Still Glides the Stream. Flora Thompson. (Illus.). 240p. 1976. reprint ed. pap. 10.95 (*0-19-281192-4*) OUP.

Still Going Against the Grain: Wheat-Free Cookery. Phyllis L. Potts. LC 94-94308. (Illus.). 260p. (Orig.). 1994. pap. 14.95 (*0-9630479-1-4*) Central Pt.

Still Hanging in There... Confessions of a Totaled Woman. Jan Marshall. (Illus.). 216p. 1996. reprint ed. pap. 20.00 incl. audio (*0-9645519-9-3*) Ult Mind Pub.

Still Harping on Daughters: Women & Drama in the Age of Shakespeare. Lisa Jardine. 216p. 1989. text ed. 49.50 (*0-231-07062-4*); pap. text ed. 15.50 (*0-231-07063-2*) Col U Pr.

Still Higher for His Highest: Now with NIV Text. Oswald Chambers & Glenn D. Black. 192p. 1989. 14.99 (*0-310-23600-2*) Zondervan.

***Still Home to Me.** F. Scott Fitzgerald. 1997. pap. text ed. 14.95 (*1-885061-19-6*) Adventure Pubns.

Still Hungry after All These Years: Food Assistance Policy from Kennedy to Reagan. Ardith L. Maney. LC 88-7711. (Studies in Social Welfare Policies & Programs). 203p. 1989. text ed. 49.95 (*0-313-26327-2*, MSY, Greenwood Pr) Greenwood.

***Still I Rise.** Laird, Jr. LC 97-8417. 1997. 21.95 (*0-393-04538-2*) Norton.

Still Image in Multimedia. Aaland Mikkel. 208p. 1996. 45. 00 (*1-56830-273-8*) Hayden.

Still Images - Moving Pictures: An Exhibition of Works by the Faculties of the Department of Visual Art & The Malcolm S. Forbes Center for Modern Culture & Media at Brown University. Diana L. Johnson et al. (Illus.). 52p. (Orig.). 1993. pap. 5.00 (*0-933519-27-3*) D W Bell Gallery.

Still in Love with You. rev. ed. Lycrecia Williams & Dale Vinicur. LC 89-37030. (Illus.). 224p. 1991. reprint ed. pap. 12.95 (*1-55853-105-X*) Rutledge Hill Pr.

Still in the Queue Bulgaria Waits for Democracy. Vallery Tchukov. (C). 1991. 35.00 (*0-907967-19-1*, Pub. by Inst Euro Def & Strat UK) St Mut.

Still Last in the American League: The St. Louis Browns Revisited. William Borst. (Illus.). 136p. 1992. 29.95 (*1-878005-53-7*); pap. 14.95 (*1-878005-54-5*) Northmont Pub.

***Still Lickin' the Spoon: And Other Confessions of a Grown-Up Kid.** Becky Freeman. LC 96-53396. 192p. 1997. pap. 11.99 (*0-8054-6279-1*) Broadman.

Still Life. Barron Staff. (Art Handbook Ser.). 1996. 9.95 (*0-8120-6618-9*) Barron.

Still Life. A. S. Byatt. LC 96-28801. 1997. pap. 12.00 (*0-684-83503-7*, Scribners PB Fict) S&S Trade.

***Still Life.** Rick Hansen. 1997. mass mkt. 5.50 (*0-614-27761-2*, Knsington) Kensgtn Pub Corp.

Still Life. Rick Hanson. 204p. 1996. 19.95 (*1-57566-041-5*) Kensgtn Pub Corp.

***Still Life.** Rick Hanson. 256p. 1997. mass mkt. 5.50 (*1-57566-200-0*, Knsington) Kensgtn Pub Corp.

Still Life. Catherine Harnett. LC 83-50967. (Series Eight). 60p. 1983. pap. 7.00 (*0-931846-25-0*) Wash Writers Pub.

***Still Life.** Mary Jenson. LC 97-20973. 144p. 1997. 12.99 (*1-57673-145-6*, Multnomah Bks) Multnomah Pubs.

Still Life. Diane Keaton & Marvin Heiferman. 1985. 14.95 (*0-671-60387-6*, Fireside) S&S Trade.

Still Life. Emily Mann. 1981. pap. 5.25 (*0-8222-1081-9*) Dramatists Play.

Still Life. Samuel F. Pickering, Jr. LC 89-28605. 240p. 1990. pap. 14.95 (*0-87451-561-0*); text ed. 30.00 (*0-87451-515-7*) U Pr of New Eng.

Still Life. James C. Schaap. 187p. (Orig.). 1994. pap. 8.50 (*0-932914-31-4*) Dordt Coll Pr.

***Still Life.** Norbert Schneider. 1994. pap. text ed. 19.99 (*3-8228-0296-4*) Taschen Amer.

Still Life. Donald Sultan. 1999. pap. write for info. (*0-14-011660-5*, Viking); pap. 25.00 (*0-670-82548-4*) Viking Penguin.

Still, Life: Clinical Portraits in Psychopathology. Christopher F. Monte. LC 92-49802. 240p. 1992. pap. text ed. 23.20 (*0-13-137217-3*) P-H.

Still Life: The Object in American Art, 1915-1995. Lowery Stokes-Sims & Sabine Rewald. LC 96-13235. (Illus.). 176p. 1996. 45.00 (*0-8478-1982-5*) Rizzoli Intl.

Still Life: The Object in American Art, 1915-1995: Selections from the Metropolitan Museum of Art. Lowery S. Sims & Sabine Rewald. LC 96-13235. 1996. pap. write for info. (*0-8478-1983-3*) Rizzoli Intl.

Still Life & Flowers Text & Prints. (Illus.). 16p. 1992. pap. text ed. 52.50 (*0-935493-68-9*) Modern Learn Pr.

Still Life & Other Stories. Junzo Shono. Tr. by Wayne P. Lammers from JPN. LC 92-28639. (Rock Spring Collection). 264p. (Orig.). 1992. pap. 11.95 (*1-880656-02-7*) Stone Bridge Pr.

Still Life in Acrylics. (Leisure Arts Ser.: No. 34). (Illus.). 32p. pap. 4.95 (*0-85532-633-6*, 633-6, Pub. by Search Pr UK) A Schwartz & Co.

***Still Life in Harlem.** Harris. 1997. pap. 12.00 (*0-8050-4852-9*) St Martin.

Still Life in Harlem. Eddy L. Harris. 224p. 1996. 20.00 (*0-8050-4851-0*) H Holt & Co.

Still Life in Pencil. Gene Franks. (How to Draw & Paint Ser.). (Illus.). 32p. (Orig.). 1989. pap. 6.95 (*0-929261-89-5*, HT215) W Foster Pub.

Still Life in Real Time: Theory after Television. Richard Dienst. LC 93-37942. (Post-Contemporary Interventions Ser.). 224p. (C). 1994. text ed. 49.95 (*0-8223-1451-7*); pap. text ed. 17.95 (*0-8223-1466-5*) Duke.

Still Life in Russian Art. I. Bolotina. (Illus.). (C). 1987. text ed. 130.00 (*0-685-40261-4*, Pub. by Collets) St Mut.

Still Life in the Physical World. Gayle Kaune. 96p. (Orig.). 1995. pap. 11.00 (*0-911287-17-5*) Blue Begonia.

Still Life of the Middle Temple with Some of Its Table Talk Preceded by Fifty Years' Reminiscences. William G. Thorpe. Ed. by Roy M. Mersky & J. Myron Jacobstein. LC 73-85733. (Classics in Legal History Reprint Ser.: Vol. 21). 392p. 1973. reprint ed. lib. bdg. 45.00 (*0-89941-020-0*, 301650) W S Hein.

Still Life with a Bridle: Essays & Apocryphas. Zbigniew Herbert. 1991. 19.95 (*0-88001-306-0*) Ecco Pr.

Still Life with a Bridle: Essays & Apocryphas. Zbigniew Herbert. Tr. by John Carpenter & Bogdana Carpenter. LC 92-38212. 1993. pap. 9.95 (*0-88001-320-6*) Ecco Pr.

Still Life with Books: A Novel. Simon Lane. LC 93-18948. 144p. 1993. 17.95 (*1-882593-02-2*) Bridge Wrks.

***Still Life with Bottle: Whiskey According to Ralph Steadman.** Ralph Steadman. LC 97-19469. 1997. 32.00 (*0-15-100310-6*) HarBrace.

***Still Life with Children, No. 76.** Rebecca Baggett. 28p. (Orig.). 1995. pap. 7.95 (*0-614-24058-1*) Pudding Hse Pubns.

Still Life with Insects. Brian Kiteley. LC 92-39956. (Discovery Ser.). 114p. 1993. 8.00 (*1-55597-189-X*) Graywolf.

Still Life with Menu Cookbook. Mollie Katzen. (Illus.). 304p. 1988. pap. 24.95 (*0-89815-236-4*) Ten Speed Pr.

Still Life with Menu Cookbook. rev. ed. Mollie Katzen. 256p. 1994. pap. 19.95 (*0-89815-669-6*) Ten Speed Pr.

***Still Life with Rice.** Lee. 1997. pap. 13.00 (*0-684-82711-5*, Touchstone Bks) S&S Trade.

Still Life with Rice: A Young American Woman Discovers the Life & Legacy of Her Korean Grandmother. Helie Lee. (Illus.). 320p. 1996. 24.00 (*0-684-80270-8*) S&S Trade.

Still Life with Volkswagens. Geoff Nicholson. 232p. 1995. 21.95 (*0-87951-616-X*) Overlook Pr.

Still Life with Volkswagens. Geoff Nicholson. 233p. 1996. pap. 12.95 (*0-87951-694-1*) Overlook Pr.

Still Life with Woodpecker. Tom Robbins. 288p. (Orig.). 1990. pap. 10.95 (*0-553-34897-3*) Bantam.

Still Life 1963-1993. Gayle Maxon. LC 93-85072. (Illus.). 79p. 1993. pap. 18.00 (*0-935037-51-9*) G Peters Gallery.

Still Lifes. 5p. 1994. 39.00 (*1-56290-100-1*, 6038) Crystal.

Still-Lifes & Nature Studies from the George J. McDonald Collection. J. J. White & G. J. McDonald. (Illus.). 20p. (Orig.). 1984. pap. 3.00 (*0-913196-45-2*) Hunt Inst Botanical.

***Still Lives with Whiskey Bottle.** Peter Markus. Ed. by Robert Bixby. 41p. 1996. pap. 6.00 (*0-614-30433-4*) March Street Pr.

***Still Looking: A Novel Concerning Single Men.** Larry Durstin. LC 90-70653. (Illus.). 249p. (Orig.). 1996. pap. 11.95 (*1-877978-14-0*, FLF Pr) Woldt.

Still Looking Forward. Elaine Winik. LC 95-71670. 272p. 1996. 19.95 (*1-887750-09-6*) Rutledge Bks.

Still Married after All These Years. Shoebox Greetings Staff. (Illus.). 72p. (Orig.). 1990. pap. 5.95 (*0-87529-645-9*) Hallmark.

Still Missing. Beth Gutcheon. LC 96-4316. 384p. 1996. pap. 13.00 (*0-06-097703-5*) HarpC.

Still Missing. Susan Ware. 304p. 1994. pap. 11.95 (*0-393-31255-0*) Norton.

Still Missing: Amelia Earhart & the Search for Modern Feminism. Susan Ware. LC 93-9468. (Illus.). 304p. 1993. 22.00 (*0-393-03551-4*) Norton.

Still Modern After All These Years. Thomas W. Styron. LC 82-83632. (Illus.). 48p. (Orig.). 1982. pap. 6.00 (*0-940744-40-6*) Chrysler Museum.

Still More Bone-Chilling Tales of Fright: A Collection of Scary Stories. Illus. by Eric Angeloch. LC 95-4895. 96p. (J). (gr. 5-7). 1995. pap. 5.95 (*1-56565-317-3*) Lowell Hse.

***Still More Church Chuckles.** Dick Hafer. LC 97-65163. 128p. (Orig.). 1997. pap. 8.95 (*0-89221-340-X*) New Leaf.

***Still More Distant Journeys: The Artistic Emigrations of Lasar Segall.** Reinhold Heller et al. Ed. by Sue Taylor. (Illus.). 256p. (Orig.). 1997. pap. text ed. 42.00 (*0-935573-19-4*) D & A Smart Museum.

***Still More Fright Night.** J. B. Stamper. (J). (gr. 3-7). Date not set. 3.99 (*0-614-19193-9*, Apple Paperbacks) Scholastic Inc.

Still More Games Trainers Play. John W. Newstrom & Edward E. Scannell. 320p. 1991. pap. text ed. 24.95 (*0-07-046427-8*) McGraw.

***Still More It Happened in Hockey.** Brian McFarlane. (Illus.). 176p. pap. 11.95 (*0-7737-5685-X*) ACCESS Pubs Network.

***Still More Management Ideas That Work!** 4th ed. Mark C. Zweig. 232p. 1997. pap. text ed. 39.00 (*1-885002-28-9*) Zweig White.

Still More Night Frights. J. B. Stamper. (J). (gr. 4-7). 1996. pap. text ed. 3.99 (*0-590-62406-7*) Scholastic Inc.

Still More of the World's Best Dirty Jokes. (Illus.). 144p. 1981. 8.95 (*0-8065-0780-2*, Citadel Pr); pap. 3.95 (*0-8065-0834-5*, Citadel Pr) Carol Pub Group.

Still More of the World's Best Dirty Jokes. Mr. J. 1985. mass mkt. 5.99 (*0-345-32622-9*) Ballantine.

Still More Poetry Hunter. Richard A. Spiegel. (Illus.). 36p. (Orig.). (J). (gr. k-6). 1981. pap. 2.00 (*0-934830-24-X*) Ten Penny.

Still More Prejudice. Arthur B. Walkley. LC 72-111870. (Essay Index Reprint Ser.). 1977. 20.95 (*0-8369-1633-6*) Ayer.

***Still More Scary Mysteries for Sleep-Overs.** Allen B. Ury. LC 96-31688. (Scary Mysteries Ser.: Vol. 3). (Illus.). 128p. (J). (gr. 1 up). 1997. pap. 5.95 (*0-8431-7955-4*) Price Stern Sloan.

Still More Scary Stories for Sleep-Overs. Querida L. Pearce. LC 93-12822. (Scary Stories Ser.). (Illus.). 128p. (Orig.). (J). (gr. 3-6). 1993. pap. 4.95 (*0-8431-3588-3*) Price Stern Sloan.

***Still More Scary Stories for Stormy Nights.** Don Wulffson. LC 97-5048. 1997. pap. text ed. 5.95 (*1-56565-606-7*) Lowell Hse.

***Still More Scary Stories for When You're Home Alone.** Allen B. Ury. (J). Date not set. pap. 5.95 (*1-56565-602-4*) Contemp Bks.

Still More Science Activities. 3rd ed. Megan Stine et al. (Science Activity Book Ser.). (Illus.). 100p. (J). (gr. 2-6). 1989. pap. text ed. 8.95 (*0-929648-01-3*) Galison.

Still More Single-Shot Rifles. James J. Grant. 1995. 27.50 (*0-913150-41-X*) Pioneer Pr.

Still More Small Poems. Valerie Worth. LC 78-11739. (Illus.). 48p. (J). (gr. 3 up). 1978. 11.00 (*0-374-37258-6*) FS&G.

Still More Solo Readings. Sonya Fogle. 1947. pap. 5.25 (*0-8222-1083-5*) Dramatists Play.

Still More Songs of the 30's. (Decade Ser.). 224p. 1995. otabind 14.95 (*0-7935-4654-0*, 00310027) H Leonard.

Still More Songs of the 30's, Vol. 387. (Thirties Ser.). 144p. 1995. otabind 12.95 (*0-7935-4718-0*, 00100009) H Leonard.

Still More Songs of the 40's. (Decade Ser.). 208p. 1995. otabind 14.95 (*0-7935-4430-0*, 00310028) H Leonard.

Still More Songs of the 40's, Vol. 388. (Forties Ser.). 144p. 1995. otabind 12.95 (*0-7935-4428-9*, 00100011) H Leonard.

Still More Songs of the 50's. (Decade Ser.). 176p. 1995. otabind 14.95 (*0-7935-4429-7*, 00310029) H Leonard.

Still More Songs of the 50's, Vol. 389. (Fifties Ser.). 144p. 1995. otabind 12.95 (*0-7935-4427-0*, 00100012) H Leonard.

Still More Songs of the 60's. Andrew Lloyd Webber. (Decade Ser.). 224p. 1995. otabind 14.95 (*0-7935-3588-3*, 00311680) H Leonard.

Still More Songs of the 60's, Vol. 390. (Sixties Ser.). 176p. 1995. otabind 12.95 (*0-7935-4284-7*, 00100006) H Leonard.

Still More Songs of the 70's. (Decade Ser.). 224p. 1995. otabind 14.95 (*0-7935-3635-9*, 00311683) H Leonard.

Still More Songs of the 70's, Vol. 391. 192p. Date not set. otabind 12.95 (*0-7935-5084-X*, 00100005) H Leonard.

Still More Stories from Grandma's Attic. Arleta Richardson. 128p. (J). (gr. 3-7). 1994. pap. 4.99 (*0-7814-0087-2*, Chariot Bks) Chariot Victor.

Still More Stories to Collect Stamps By. Herman Herst, Jr. 208p. 1992. pap. 12.95 (*0-9635526-0-0*) McKeels Weekly.

Still More Stories to Solve: Fourteen Folktales from Around the World. George Shannon. 64p. (J). (gr. 4-7). 1996. pap. 4.95 (*0-688-14743-7*) Morrow.

Still More Stories to Solve: Fourteen Folktales from Around the World. Illus. by Peter Sis. LC 93-26529. 64p. (J). 1994. 15.00 (*0-688-04619-3*) Greenwillow.

Still More Tales for the Midnight Hour. Judith B. Stamper. (J). 1992. pap. 2.95 (*0-685-53518-5*, Point) Scholastic Inc.

Still More Tales Mid. J. B. Stamper. 128p. (J). (gr. 7-9). 1992. pap. 2.95 (*0-590-45345-9*) Scholastic Inc.

Still More Two-Minute Mysteries. Donald J. Sobol. 128p. (J). (gr. 4-6). 1992. pap. 3.50 (*0-590-44786-6*) Scholastic Inc.

Still Mostly True: Collected Stories & Drawings. Brian Andreas. 80p. 1994. pap. 20.00 (*0-9642660-1-6*) StoryPeople.

Still Mr & Mrs. Pat Olney. (Loveswept Ser.: 789). 224p. 1996. mass mkt. 3.50 (*0-553-44554-5*, Loveswept) Bantam.

***Still Murder.** Finola Moorhead. 293p. 1997. pap. 14.95 (*0-7043-4397-5*, Pub. by Womens Press UK) Trafalgar.

Still My Aching Heart. Kay D. Rizzo. LC 92-43699. 1993. pap. 12.97 (*0-8163-1136-6*) Pacific Pr Pub Assn.

Still on the Cross: Meditations on the Suffering of Christ. Loretta Girzaitis & Richard L. Wood. LC 90-90306. 80p. (Orig.). 1990. pap. 5.95 (*0-89622-449-X*) Twenty-Third.

Still Performance: Writing, Self, & Interconnection in Five Postmodern American Poets. James McCorkle. LC 88-35305. 225p. 1989. text ed. 35.00 (*0-8139-1196-6*) U Pr of Va.

Still Performances: Rimma Gerlovina & Valeriy Gerlouin. John P. Jacob. (Illus.). 40p. (Orig.). 1989. pap. 6.00 (*0-938437-26-7*) MIT List Visual Arts.

Still Philadelphia: A Photographic History, 1890-1940. Fredric M. Miller et al. LC 82-19227. 312p. 1983. 24.95 (*0-87722-306-8*) Temple U Pr.

Still Pictures. LaMond F. Beatty. Ed. by James E. Duane. LC 80-21448. (Instructional Media Library: Vol. 14). (Illus.). 112p. 1981. 27.95 (*0-87778-174-5*) Educ Tech Pubns.

S

S

Still Pioneers: A Novel about Lindsborg, Kansas, & the Smoky Valley in Modern Times. Robert E. Segerhammar. (Saga of Smoky Hill Ser.: Vol. 3). (Illus.). 1995. write for info. (0-918331-05-6) Smoky Valley Hist.

Still Point. Laurence Gonzales. LC 89-4655. 336p. (Orig.). 1989. pap. 18.00 (1-55728-081-9) U of Ark Pr.

Still Point: Reflections on Zen & Christian Mysticism. William Johnston. LC 75-95713. xviii, 202p. 1986. pap. 15.00 (0-8232-0861-3) Fordham.

Still Proclaiming Your Wonders: Homilies for the Eighties. Walter J. Burghardt. 256p. (Orig.). 1984. pap. 9.95 (0-8091-2632-X) Paulist Pr.

Still Pumped from Using the Mouse. Scott Adams. (Dilbert Bk.). (Illus.). 128p. (Orig.). 1996. pap. 9.95 (0-8362-1026-3) Andrews & McMeel.

Still Rebels, Still Yankees, & Other Essays. fac. ed. Donald Davidson. LC 70-168395. (Library of Southern Civilization). 304p. 1972. reprint ed. pap. 86.70 (0-7837-7772-8, 2047528) Bks Demand.

Still Rhymin' on the Range. Mike Puhallo & Brian Brannon. (Illus.). 64p. (Orig.). (C). 1996. pap. 7.95 (0-88839-388-1) Hancock House.

Still Riding the Wind: Learning the Ways of the Spirit. rev. ed. George T. Montague. LC 94-66742. 112p. 1994. pap. 7.95 (1-878718-22-3) Resurrection.

Still Sane. Blackbridge & Gilhooly. 1985. pap. 12.95 (0-88974-028-3, Pub. by Press Gang CN) LPC InBook.

***Still Secrecies of Love: Poems L.D.S. & Other.** Michael R. Collings. 130p. (Orig.). pap. 15.00 (1-886405-54-9, Zarahemla Motets) White Crow Pr.

***Still Seeing Red.** John K. White. (Transforming American Politics Ser.). 1997. text ed. 29.95 (0-8133-1888-2) Westview.

***Still Sifting: Poems.** Monica Kaiser. LC 96-21183. (Illus.). 68p. 1996. pap. 12.95 (0-7734-2673-6, Mellen Poetry Pr) E Mellen.

Still Small Voice. Robert W. Crary. LC 92-82655. 210p. (Orig.). 1993. pap. 9.95 (0-914711-06-7) Rishis Inst.

Still, Small Voice: A Practical Guide on Reported Revelations. Benedict Groeschell. LC 92-74593. 180p. (Orig.). 1993. pap. 10.95 (0-89870-436-7) Ignatius Pr.

Still Small Voice: Women, Ordination, & the Church. Betty B. Schiess. 226p. 1995. 24.95 (0-8156-2683-5) Syracuse U Pr.

Still Small Voices. John Wallach. 1990. pap. 9.95 (0-8065-1171-0, Citadel Pr) Carol Pub Group.

Still Still. Manuel Pereiras. 57p. 1993. pap. text ed. 3.95 (1-885901-04-6) Presbyters Peartree.

Still Such. James Salter. (Illus.). 24p. 1992. pap. 12.00 (1-884381-03-0) W Drenttel NY.

Still Such Signed. James Salter. (Illus.). 24p. 1992. 60.00 (1-884381-02-2) W Drenttel NY.

***Still Sweet.** Debra Marshall. (Our Town Ser.). 288p. 1997. mass mkt. 5.99 (0-515-12130-4) Jove Pubns.

Still Sweet on Him: Premiere. Jodi O'Donnell. (Romance Ser.). 1993. pap. 2.75 (0-373-08969-4, 5-08969-3) Silhouette.

Still Talking. Joan Rivers. 328p. 1992. mass mkt. 5.99 (0-380-71992-4) Avon.

Still Teaching Ourselves. Agnes Leistico. LC 95-10137. 214p. 1995. pap. 10.75 (0-945097-27-1) Home Educ Pr.

Still Thankful: Arrangements for Piano Ministry. 1993. 8.99 (0-8341-9167-9, MB-651) Lillenas.

Still the Arms Debate. Robert A. Levine. 420p. 1990. text ed. 52.95 (1-85521-071-1, Pub. by Dartmth Pub UK) Ashgate Pub Co.

Still the Best Congress Money Can Buy. Phillip M. Stern. LC 92-8540. 356p. 1993. pap. 12.95 (0-89526-527-3) Regnery Pub.

Still the Best Fringe Benefit, Profit Sharing & Pension Plans. Andrew J. Bedsole et al. (Special Report Ser.: No. 3). 94p. 1988. pap. 25.00 (0-916181-02-2) Blackman Kallick Bartelstein.

Still the Frame Holds: Essays on Women Poets & Writers. Ed. by Sheila Roberts. LC 87-823. (I. O. Evans Studies in the Philosophy & Criticism of Literature: No. 10). 216p. 1993. pap. 23.00 (0-89370-404-0); lib. bdg. 33.00 (0-89370-304-4) Borgo Pr.

Still the Golden Door: The Third World Comes to America. David M. Reimers. LC 84-29273. 320p. 1985. text ed. 49.50 (0-231-05770-9) Col U Pr.

Still the Golden Door: The Third World Comes to America. David M. Reimers. LC 84-29273. 320p. 1987. pap. text ed. 19.00 (0-231-05771-7) Col U Pr.

Still the Golden Door: The Third World Comes to America. David M. Reimers. 350p. 1992. text ed. 52.50 (0-231-07680-0); pap. text ed. 17.00 (0-231-07681-9) Col U Pr.

Still the Law of the Land? Essays on Changing Interpretations of the Constitution. Edward J. Erler et al. 140p. 1989. pap. 5.00 (0-916308-92-8) Hillsdale Coll Pr.

Still the Moving World: Intolerance, Modernism, & Heart of Darkness. Jordan Leondopoulos. LC 90-35558. (Literature & the Visual Arts: Ser.: Vol. 7). 210p. (C). 1991. text ed. 40.95 (0-8204-1388-7) P Lang Pubng.

Still the One: Loving Thoughts from a Devoted Spouse. Jerry B. Jenkins. LC 94-23328. 1995. 14.99 (1-56179-339-6) Word Pub.

Still the Promised City? African-Americans & New Immigrants in Postindustrial New York. Roger Waldinger. LC 95-43335. (Illus.). 368p. 1996. text ed. 35.00 (0-674-83861-0) HUP.

Still the Sirens. Dennis Brutus. (Green Ser.). 6.00 (0-938631-09-8) Pennywhistle Pr.

Still Time. Sally Mann. (Illus.). 80p. 1994. pap. 29.95 (0-89381-593-4) Aperture.

Still Time to Die. Jack Belden. (China in the 20th Century Ser.). xi, 322p. 1975. reprint ed. lib. bdg. 32.50 (0-306-70735-7) Da Capo.

Still to Be Born. Pat Schwiebert & Paul Kirk. 112p. 1993. 5.25 (0-9615197-2-X) Perinatal Loss.

***Still to Be Determined: Collected Essays of Paul Fleischman.** 120p. (Orig.). Date not set. pap. write for info. (0-614-30217-X) Vipassana Res.

***Still Unborn about the Dead.** N. Stanescu. Date not set. pap. 14.95 (0-85646-010-9, Pub. by Anvil Press UK) Dufour.

Still Unequal. Lorraine Dusky. 1996. 27.50 (0-517-59389-0, Crown) Crown Pub Group.

Still Unsolved. Richard Glyn-Jones. 1990. 14.95 (0-8184-0536-8) Carol Pub Group.

Still Unsolved: Great True Murder Cases. Richard Glyn-Jones. 1990. pap. 9.95 (0-8184-0540-6) Carol Pub Group.

Still Unsolved: Great True Murder Cases. Intro. & Selected by Richard G. Jones. 320p. 1992. pap. 4.50 (0-8216-2511-X, Carol Paperbacks) Carol Pub Group.

Still War: Photographs from the North of Ireland. Mike Abrahams & Laurie Sparham. Ed. by Trisha Ziff. (Illus.). 128p. (Orig.). (C). 1990. pap. 20.00 (0-941533-86-7) New Amsterdam Bks.

Still Water. Sally Gunning. 1995. mass mkt. 5.50 (0-671-87138-2) PB.

Still Water Runs Deep. Marianne Gutteridge. Ed. by Liz Lake. LC 95-71986. 352p. (Orig.). 1996. pap. 14.95 (0-89716-610-8) P B Pubng.

Still Waters. Tami Hoag. 480p. 1992. mass mkt. 6.50 (0-553-29272-2) Bantam.

***Still Waters.** Donald Kirch. 1997. mass mkt. 5.99 (1-55197-373-1, Pub. by Comnwlth Pub CN) Partners Pubs Grp.

***Still Waters.** Saxton. Date not set. write for info. (0-312-18185-X) St Martin.

Still Waters. James A. Stewart. 1962. pap. 4.99 (1-56632-054-2) Revival Lit.

Still Waters. Pat Welch. (Helen Black Mystery Ser.). 176p. (Orig.). 1991. pap. 9.95 (0-941483-97-5) Naiad Pr.

Still Waters. Woodward. Date not set. pap. write for info. (0-8041-1400-5) Ivy Books.

Still Waters. large type ed. Marguerite Lees. 1977. 25.99 (0-7089-0045-3) Ulverscroft.

***Still Waters: A Crime Novel.** John Harvey. LC 97-12324. 1997. write for info. (0-8050-4149-4) H Holt & Co.

Still Waters By. Merilu Tiemich. 120p. (Orig.). 1986. pap. 10.00 (0-937953-01-6) Tiptoe Lit Serv.

Still Waters Run Deadly. large type ed. Isobel Lambot. 384p. 1989. 25.99 (0-7089-2040-3) Ulverscroft.

Still We Danced Forward: World War II & the Writer's Life. Rhonda Sonnenberg. LC 96-40039. 352p. 1997. 29.95 (1-57488-013-6) Brasseys Inc.

Still Weeps the Willow. large type ed. Mary Mackie. (Linford Romance Library). 336p. 1992. pap. 15.99 (0-7089-7242-X, Trailtree Bookshop) Ulverscroft.

Still Weird. Gahan Wilson. 288p. 1994. 24.95 (0-312-85290-8); pap. 13.95 (0-312-85779-9) Forge NYC.

Still Wild, Always Wild: A Journey into the Desert Wilderness of California. Susan Zwinger. LC 96-24201. 132p. 1997. 35.00 (0-87156-886-1); pap. 22.50 (0-87156-887-X) Sierra.

Still Working: Underknown Artists of Age in America. Stuart Shedletsky et al. (Parsons School of Design Ser.). (Illus.). 192p. 1994. pap. 30.00 (0-295-97385-4) U of Wash Pr.

Still Worlds Collide: Philip Wylie & the End of the American Dream. Clifford P. Bendau. LC 80-10756. (Milford Ser.: Popular Writers of Today: Vol. 30). 63p. 1980. pap. 13.00 (0-89370-244-7); lib. bdg. 23.00 (0-89370-144-0) Borgo Pr.

Stillborn. Z. Alkali. (Longman African Writers Ser.). (C). 1995. pap. text ed. 11.95 (0-582-26432-4) Addison-Wesley.

***Stillborn.** Drumbeat Publishing Staff. Date not set. pap. text ed. write for info. (0-582-78600-2, Pub. by Longman UK) Longman.

Stillborn: The Invisible Death. John D. DeFrain et al. LC 85-45340. 244p. pap. 10.95 (0-669-11354-9, Lexington) Jossey-Bass.

Stillborn Crusade: The Tragic Failure of Western Intervention in the Russian Civil War, 1918-1920. Ilya Somin. 178p. 1996. text ed. 32.95 (1-56000-274-3) Transaction Pubs.

Stillborn Education: A Critique of the American Research University. Paul Von Blum. (Illus.). 222p. (Orig.). (C). 1986. pap. text ed. 23.00 (0-8191-5510-1) U Pr of Amer.

Stillborn Revolution. Werner T. Angress. 529p. reprint ed. pap. 150.80 (0-317-09317-7, 2000030) Bks Demand.

Stille Zeile Sechs. Roman. Monika Maron. 224p. (GER.). 1993. pap. 13.50 (3-596-11804-2, Pub. by Fischer Taschbch Verlag GW) Intl Bk Import.

Stiller's Pond: New Fiction from the Upper Midwest. 2nd enl. ed. Ed. by Jonis Agee et al. 520p. 1991. pap. 18.95 (0-89823-106-X) New Rivers Pr.

Stilling, Stormy Stories. Ed. by Lawrence M. Ventline. 96p. 1994. pap. text ed. 4.95 (1-883520-06-1) Jeremiah Pr.

Stilling the Grumbling Hive: The Response to Social & Economic Problems in England, 1689-1750. Lee Davison et al. 224p. (C). 1992. text ed. 49.95 (0-312-08676-8) St Martin.

Still...Life. David Mibashan. 196p. 1995. lib. bdg. 35.00 (0-8095-4827-5) Borgo Pr.

Still...Life. David Mibashan. 196p. pap. 12.95 (0-88962-539-5) Mosaic.

Stillman: American Consul in a Cretan War. rev. ed. G. G. Arnakis. 146p. 1966. 10.00 (0-318-12222-7); pap. 8.00 (0-318-12223-5) Ad Council.

Stillman: Articles & Despatches from Crete. Ed. by G. G. Arnakis. LC 76-9149. 138p. 1976. 10.00 (0-317-34064-6); pap. 7.00 (0-317-34065-4) Ctr Neo Hellenic.

Stillmeadow Cook Book. Gladys Taber. 25.95 (0-8488-1198-4) Amereon Ltd.

Stillmeadow Cook Book. Gladys Taber. 336p. 1983. reprint ed. pap. 9.95 (0-940160-18-8) Parnassus Imprints.

Stillmeadow Daybook. Gladys Taber. LC 55-10455. (Illus.). 288p. 1989. reprint ed. pap. 8.95 (0-940160-42-0) Parnassus Imprints.

Stillmeadow Road. Gladys Taber. 23.95 (0-8488-0724-3) Amereon Ltd.

Stillmeadow Sampler. Gladys Taber. 288p. 1981. reprint ed. pap. 8.95 (0-940160-11-0) Parnassus Imprints.

Stillmeadow Seasons. Gladys Taber. reprint ed. lib. bdg. 23.95 (0-89190-594-4, Rivercity Pr) Amereon Ltd.

Stillness: Poems. Kalliope Constantaras. 83p. (Orig.). (ENG & GRE.). 1995. pap. 8.00 (0-9652259-0-9) Kalliope Constantaras.

Stillness at Appomattox. Bruce Catton. 1992. 23.00 (0-8446-6550-9) Peter Smith.

Stillness at Appomattox, Vol. III. Bruce Catton. 1953. pap. 12.95 (0-385-04451-8, Anchor NY) Doubleday.

Stillness Built of Motion: Living with Tourette's. 2nd ed. Emma Morgan. (Illus.). (Orig.). 1996. reprint ed. pap. 7.00 (0-9650733-4-3, ECHO-003) Echolalia Pr.

***Stillness, Gentleness: East Meets West: A Journey into the Internal Side of the Internal Arts.** Jay Wheeler & Cheng H. Yu. 103p. (Orig.). 1996. pap. 19.95 (1-877858-15-3, TC/SG) Amer Focus Pub.

Stillness in Bethlehem. Jane Haddam. 368p. 1993. 5.50 (0-553-29390-7) Bantam.

Stillness in the Pines: The Ecology of the Red-Cockaded Woodpecker. Robert W. McFarlane. 1994. pap. 10.95 (0-393-31167-8) Norton.

Stillness in the Storm: Quiet Encouragement from God's Heart to Yours. Anabel Gillham. LC 94-47487. (Orig.). 1995. pap. 9.99 (1-56507-287-1) Harvest Hse.

Stillness of the World Before Bach: New Selected Poems. Lars Gustafsson. Ed. & Tr. by Christopher Middleton from SWE. Tr. by Yvonne L. Sandstroem & Harriet Watts from SWE. LC 87-316690. 128p. 1988. 18.95 (0-8112-1057-X); pap. 9.95 (0-8112-1058-8, NDP656) New Directions.

Stillness, the Dancing. Linda Bierds. 1988. pap. 10.95 (0-8050-0766-0, Owl) H Holt & Co.

Stillness Without Shadows. Joseph J. Juknialis. LC 86-62620. 80p. 1986. pap. 7.95 (0-89390-081-8) Resource Pubns.

Stillpoint. Marilyn Kok. LC 96-25294. (Portraits Ser.: No. 2). 256p. 1996. pap. text ed. 8.99 (1-55661-821-2) Bethany Hse.

Stillpoint: The Dance of Selfcaring, Selfhealing: A Playbook for People Who Do Caring Work. Sheila K. Collins. LC 91-68151. (Illus.). (Orig.). 1992. pap. 14.95 (0-9631856-0-8) TLC Prods.

Stillroom Cookery: The Art of Preserving Foods Naturally, with Recipes, Menus & Metric Measures. Grace Firth. LC 76-28240. (Illus.). 279p. 1977. 4.95 (0-914440-13-6) EPM Pubns.

Stills. James Herbert. 104p. 1992. 45.00 (0-944092-19-5) Twin Palms Pub.

Stills from a Cinema: Poems, 1964-1968. 2nd ed. D. B. Axelrod. (Illus.). 62p. 1971. 20.00 (0-685-25235-3); pap. 15.00 (0-685-25236-1) Writers Ink Pr.

Stills from a Moving Picture. Lyle Glazier. (Paunch Ser.: No. 39). 1974. pap. 4.00 (0-9602478-3-1) Paunch.

Stillstand des Herzens see Heartstop

***Stillwatch.** Mary Higgins Clark. 1997. mass mkt. 7.50 (0-671-52820-3, Pocket Books) PB.

Stillwatch. Mary Higgins Clark. 1991. reprint ed. lib. bdg. 28.95 (1-56849-070-4) Buccaneer Bks.

Stillwater: Minnesota's Birthplace in Photographs by John Runk. rev. ed. Patricia C. Johnston. (Illus.). 112p. 1995. 45.00 (0-9639338-1-7); pap. 22.00 (0-9639338-2-5) Afton Hist Soc.

Stillwater, Minnesota: A Photographic History. Brent T. Peterson & Dean R. Thilgen. (Illus.). 128p. (Orig.). 1992. pap. 16.95 (0-9634842-0-6) Valley Hist Pr.

Stillwater, Minnesota's Birthplace. Patricia C. Johnston. LC 82-80726. (Illus.). 96p. 1982. 25.00 (0-942934-01-6); pap. 9.95 (0-942934-00-8) Johnston Pub.

***Stillwater Smith.** Frank Roderus. 192p. 1997. reprint ed. mass mkt. 3.99 (0-8439-4306-8, Leisure Bks) Dorchester Pub Co.

Stillwater Through the Years. Robert E. Cunningham. LC 79-89768. (Illus.). 1980. reprint ed. text ed. 14.95 (0-934188-05-X) Evans Pubns.

Stillwater Tragedy. Thomas B. Aldrich. LC 68-20001. (Americans in Fiction Ser.). 333p. reprint ed. pap. text ed. 5.95 (0-89197-949-2); reprint ed. lib. bdg. 29.00 (0-8398-0055-X) Irvington.

Stillwater Trout Fishing. John Bailey. (Illus.). 160p. 1996. 45.00 (1-85223-860-7, Pub. by Crowood Pr UK) Trafalgar.

Stillwater Where Oklahoma Began. Intro. by Robert E. Cunningham. LC 79-89767. (Illus.). 1979. reprint ed. text ed. 14.95 (0-934188-04-1) Evans Pubns.

Stilt Jack. John Thompson. 48p. pap. 6.95 (0-88784-055-8, Pub. by Hse of Anansi Pr CN) Genl Dist Srvs.

Stilwater Tragedy. Thomas B. Aldrich. (Works of Thomas Bailey Aldrich). 1989. reprint ed. lib. bdg. 79.00 (0-7812-1675-3) Rprt Serv.

***Stilwell: The First 100 Years.** Ed. by Betty Barker. (Illus.). 174p. (Orig.). 1997. pap. 15.00 (0-938041-29-0) Arc Pr AR.

Stilwell & the American Experience in China, 1911-1945. Barbara W. Tuchman. (Illus.). 600p. 1995. reprint ed. lib. bdg. 36.95 (1-56849-604-4) Buccaneer Bks.

Stilwell Papers. Joseph W. Stilwell. Ed. by Theodore H. White. LC 83-45889. reprint ed. 44.50 (0-404-20247-0, D811) AMS Pr.

Stilwell Papers. Joseph W. Stilwell. Ed. by Theodore H. White. (Quality Paperbacks Ser.). (Illus.). 357p. 1991. reprint ed. pap. 14.95 (0-306-80428-X) Da Capo.

***Stilwell's Britain: Cycleways 1998.** Tim Stilwell. (Stilwell's Bed & Breakfasts 1998 Ser.). (Illus.). 300p. 1998. pap. 17.95 (1-900861-06-2, Pub. by Stilwell Pubng UK) Seven Hills Bk.

***Stilwell's Independent Holiday Cottages 1998: 2,000 Cottages in England, Ireland, Scotland, Wales.** Tim Stilwell. (Illus.). 200p. 1998. pap. 12.95 (1-900861-07-0, Pub. by Stilwell Pubng UK) Seven Hills Bk.

Stimmen Eines Jahrhunderts, 1888-1990: Deutsche Autobiographien, Tagebucher, Bilder und Briefe. Andreas Lixl-Purcell. LC 89-77885. (Illus.). 304p. (C). 1991. pap. text ed. 22.00 (0-03-049182-7) HB Coll Pubs.

Stimson Legacy: Architecture in the Urban West. Lawrence M. Kreisman. LC 91-68426. (Illus.). 176p. 1992. 55.00 (0-9631630-0-0, U of Wash Pr); pap. 34.95 (0-9631630-1-9, U of Wash Pr) Willows WA.

Stimulants & Narcotics: Medically, Philosophically, & Morally Considered. George M. Beard. Ed. by Gerald N. Grob. LC 80-1213. (Addiction in America Ser.). 1981. reprint ed. lib. bdg. 18.95 (0-405-13569-6) Ayer.

Stimulants & Narcotics: Their Mutual Relations. Francis E. Anstie. Ed. by Gerald N. Grob. LC 80-1212. (Addiction in America Ser.). 1981. reprint ed. lib. bdg. 38.95 (0-405-13568-8) Ayer.

Stimulated Deposition Processes & Materials Aspects of Ion Beam Synthesis: Proceedings of Symposium C & Symposium G of the 1993 E-MRS Spring Conference, Strasbourg, France, May 4-7, 1993. Symposium C & Symposium G Staff. Ed. by H. Freller et al. (European Materials Research Society Symposia Proceedings Ser.: Vol. 41). 582p. 1994. text ed. 256.25 (0-444-82045-0, North Holland) Elsevier.

Stimulated Effects in Josephson Devices. Ed. by M. Russo. 332p. (C). 1990. text ed. 92.00 (981-02-0050-1) World Scientific Pub.

Stimulating Student Search: Library Media & Classroom Teacher Techniques. Hilda L. Jay. LC 82-22916. 176p. (C). 1983. pap. text ed. 24.00 (0-208-01926-X, Lib Prof Pubns) Shoe String.

Stimulating Technological Progress. (CED Statement on National Policy Ser.). 108p. 1980. pap. 5.00 (0-87186-070-8); lib. bdg. 6.50 (0-87186-770-2) Comm Econ Dev.

Stimulation Activities see Developmental Programming for Infants & Young Children

Stimulation & Control of Cardiac System, 3 vols., Set. Samuel Sideman. LC 87-9352. 1987. reprint ed. 363.00 (0-8493-6512-0, CRC Reprint) Franklin.

Stimulation & Control of Cardiac System, Vol. 1. Samuel Sideman. LC 87-9352. 185p. 1987. reprint ed. 104.00 (0-8493-6513-9, CRC Reprint) Franklin.

Stimulation & Control of Cardiac System, Vol. 2. Samuel Sideman. LC 87-9352. 224p. 1987. reprint ed. 126.00 (0-8493-6514-7, CRC Reprint) Franklin.

Stimulation & Control of Cardiac System, Vol. 3. Samuel Sideman. LC 87-9352. 240p. 1987. reprint ed. 134.00 (0-8493-6515-5, CRC Reprint) Franklin.

Stimulation Effect: Proceedings of a National Conference on the Uses of Government Procurement Leverage to Benefit Taxpayers, Consumers & the Environment. Ed. by Jessica Cowan & Steve Gold. 302p. (Orig.). 1990. pap. write for info. (0-936758-28-7) Ctr Responsive Law.

Stimulation Engineering Handbook. John W. Ely. LC 94-1886. 368p. 1994. 84.95 (0-87814-417-X, P4508) PennWell Bks.

Stimulation of Educational Undertakings: A Study of School Support in New York Cities & Villages Under Earmmarked & Non-Earmarked State Subsidy Plans. Jacob W. Wrightstone. LC 70-17762. (Columbia University. Teachers College. Contributions to Education Ser.: No. 562). reprint ed. 37.50 (0-404-55562-4) AMS Pr.

Stimulation of Fracture Healing with Ultrasound. H. G. Knoch & W. Klug. (Illus.). 104p. 1991. 75.00 (0-387-53674-4) Spr-Verlag.

Stimulation of Social Development in School. Ed. by C. F. Van Lieshout & D. J. Ingram. vi, 234p. 1977. pap. 48.50 (90-265-0258-3) Swets.

***Stimulus Class Formation in Humans & Animals, Vol. 117.** Thomas R. Zentall & Paul M. Smeets. LC 96-34862. (Advances in Psychology Ser.). 322p. 1996. 139.00 (0-444-82401-4) Elsevier.

Stimulus Drawings & Techniques: Therapy Development & Assessment. rev. ed. Rawley A. Silver. (Illus.). 97p. (C). 1991. pap. text ed. 20.00 (0-9621429-3-X) Ablin Pr.

Stimulus Generalization. Ed. by David I. Mostofsky. (Illus.). viii, 389p. 1965. 49.50 (0-8047-0221-7) Stanford U Pr.

Stimulus-Response Compatibility: An Integrated Perspective. Ed. by R. W. Proctor & T. G. Reeve. (Advances in Psychology Ser.: No. 65). 508p. 1989. 199.00 (0-444-88092-5, North Holland) Elsevier.

Stimulus Response Coupling. Smith & Dedman. 544p. 1990. 111.00 (0-8493-8805-8, QP552) CRC Pr.

Stimulus Response Coupling. Ed. by Vana L. Smith & John R. Dedman. 450p. 1989. 62.50 (0-936923-34-2) Telford Pr.

Stimulus Schedules. William N. Schoenfeld et al. LC 72-6647. 1972. reprint ed. pap. text ed. 6.95 (0-06-045789-9) Irvington.

Stimulus Secretion Coupling in Chromaffin Cells, 2 vols., Set. K. Rosenheck & P. I. Lelkes. LC 87-6378. 1987. 214.00 (0-8493-6534-1, CRC Reprint) Franklin.

An Asterisk (*) at the beginning of an entry indicates that the title is appearing in BIP for the first time.

Stimulus-Secretion Coupling in Chromaffin Cells, Vol. 2. K. Rosenheck & P. I. Lelkes. LC 87-6378. 1987. 100.00 (*0-8493-6537-6*, CRC Reprint) Franklin.
Stimulus/Sec Coup/Chrom Cells, Vol. I. K. Rosenheck. 200p. 1987. 115.00 (*0-8493-6536-8*) CRC Pr.
Stina. Lena Anderson. (Illus.). 40p. (J). (gr. k up). 1989. 13.95 (*0-688-08880-5*); lib. bdg. 13.88 (*0-688-08881-3*) Greenwillow.
Stine Babysitter Box. (YA). 1995. pap. 15.96 (*0-590-47844-3*) Scholastic Inc.
Stinehour Press: A Bibliographical Checklist of the First Thirty Years. Ed. by David Farrell. LC 88-80968. (Illus.). xxi, 300p. 1988. 60.00 (*0-87792-009-5*) Meriden-Stinehour Pr.
Sting. Adapted by David Rogers. 1985. pap. 5.95 (*0-87129-280-7*, S69) Dramatic Pub.
Sting: Fields of Gold. 19.95 (*0-7935-4282-0*, 00690021) H Leonard.
Sting: For Guitar with Tablature. 1994. 19.95 (*0-7935-3724-X*, 00694955) H Leonard.
Sting: Nothing Like the Sun. 48p. 1988. per. 12.95 (*0-7935-0267-5*, 00358203) H Leonard.
Sting: Nothing Like the Sun, Transcribed Scores. 136p. 1988. per. 19.95 (*0-7935-0274-8*, 00674655) H Leonard.
Sting: Piano Solo Selections from the Movie. (Illus.). 36p. 1985. pap. 7.95 (*0-88188-614-9*, 00129101) H Leonard.
Sting: Ten Summoner's Tales. 136p. 1994. otabind 19.95 (*0-7935-2460-1*, 00673230) H Leonard.
Sting: The Illustrated Lyrics. Roberto Gilgrov. 126p. 1991. pap. 19.95 (*1-879510-00-6*) IRS Bks.
Sting: The Illustrated Lyrics. Sting & Roberto Gligorov. (Illus.). 126p. pap. 19.95 (*1-879510-01-4*) IRS Bks.
Sting: The Secret Life of Gordon Sumner. Wensley Clarkson. 1996. 26.95 (*1-85782-125-4*, Pub. by Blake Publng UK) Seven Hills Bk.
Sting: The Soul Cages. (Piano-Vocal-Guitar Ser.). (Illus.). 72p. 1991. pap. 12.95 (*0-7935-0414-7*, 00308097) H Leonard.
Sting - Ten Summoner's Tales: Piano, Vocal, Guitar. (Illus.). 80p. (Orig.). 1993. pap. 14.95 (*0-7935-2199-8*, HL00308179) H Leonard.
Sting Book: A Guide to Setting up & Running a Clandestine Storefront Sting Operation. Steven K. Frazier. (Illus.). 266p. (C). 1994. pap. 56.95 (*0-398-05918-7*); pap. 37.95 (*0-398-06045-2*) C C Thomas.
Sting in the Tail. large type ed. Gerald Hammond. 368p. 1996. 25.99 (*0-7089-3517-6*) Ulverscroft.
Sting in the Wattle. Ed. by Philip Neilsen. 270p. 1994. pap. 16.95 (*0-7022-2565-7*, Pub. by Univ Queensland Pr AT) Intl Spec Bk.
Sting of Death & Other Stories. Shimao Toshio. Tr. by Kathryn Sparling from JPN. LC 83-26313. (Michigan Papers in Japanese Studies: No. 12). x, 190p. (Orig.). (C). 1985. pap. 11.95 (*0-939512-18-1*) U MI Japan.
Sting of the Scorpion. Franklin W. Dixon. LC 78-57930. (Hardy Boys Ser.: Vol. 58). (Illus.). 180p. (J). (gr. 3-7). 1978. 5.95 (*0-448-08958-0*, G&D) Putnam Pub Group.
Sting of the Scorpion. Ginna Gray. (Romance Ser.: No. 826). 1991. pap. 2.59 (*0-373-08826-4*) Silhouette.
Sting of the Scorpion. Marilyn Haddrill & Doris Holmes. 216p. (Orig.). 1994. pap. write for info. (*0-9623682-9-6*) Arroyo Pr.
Sting of the Scorpion. Robert Marcum. 1993. pap. 9.95 (*0-88494-889-7*) Bookcraft Inc.
Sting of the Wasp. Katharine Mortimer. 224p. 1987. 17.95 (*0-88191-047-3*) Freundlich.
***Sting of the Wasp: Memoirs of a Navy Fighter Pilot WWII.** unabridged ed. William A. Grant, Jr. LC 97-93107. 120p. (Orig.). 1997. pap. 12.95 (*0-9657726-0-8*) W Grant.
Sting Shift: The Street-Smart Cop's Handbook of Cons & Swindles. Lindsay E. Smith & Bruce A. Walstad. LC 88-92840. (Illus.). (Orig.). 1989. pap. 17.95 (*0-9621685-0-5*) Street-Smrt Comns.
Stingaree. Ernest W. Hornung. LC 71-110200. (Short Story Index Reprint Ser.). 1977. 26.95 (*0-8369-3351-6*) Ayer.
Stingaree. Max Brand. LC 81-38512. 224p. 1982. reprint ed. 16.00 (*0-8376-0461-3*) Bentley.
Stinger. Robert R. McCammon. Ed. by Sally Peters. 512p. 1988. pap. 6.50 (*0-671-73776-7*) PB.
Stinger Team Operations. 1995. lib. bdg. 250.95 (*0-8490-6665-4*) Gordon Pr.
***Stingiest Man in Town: Vocal Selections.** Ed. by Carol Cuellar. 148p. (Orig.). (C). Date not set. pap. text ed. 25.00 (*0-7692-0875-4*, OP0009) Warner Brothers.
***Stink Bomb.** Lynn Cullen. LC 97-16741. 1998. write for info. (*0-380-97647-1*) Avon.
Stink Bomb Mom. Martha Freeman. 128p. (J). 1996. 15.95 (*0-385-32219-4*) Delacorte.
***Stink Bomb Mom.** Martha Freeman. (Illus.). 112p. (J). (gr. 3-7). 1997. pap. 3.99 (*0-440-41189-0*) BDD Bks Young Read.
Stink Bugs of Ohio: Hemiptera: Pentatomidae. David G. Furth. (Bulletin New Ser.: Vol. 5, No. 1). 1974. 4.00 (*0-86727-069-1*) Ohio Bio Survey.
Stinker from Space. Pamela F. Service. 96p. (YA). (gr. 6 up). 1989. mass mkt. 4.50 (*0-449-70330-4*, Juniper) Fawcett.
***Stinkers.** Scholastic Inc., Staff. (J). 1997. pap. text ed. 3.99 (*0-590-30668-5*); pap. text ed. 3.50 (*0-590-30671-5*) Scholastic Inc.
Stinkers Ahoy! large type ed. Roger McGough. (Illus.). (J). 1995. 16.95 (*0-7451-2899-8*, Galaxy Child Lrg Print) Chivers N Amer.
Stinker's Return. Pamela F. Service. 96p. 1994. mass mkt. 3.99 (*0-449-70438-6*) Fawcett.
Stinker's Return. Pamela F. Service. LC 92-21800. 96p. (J). (gr. 4-6). 1993. lib. bdg. 12.95 (*0-684-19542-9*, C Scribner Sons Young) S&S Childrens.
Stinkin' Thinkin' Tape. Shirley Backels. (Self-Talk Unit Ser.). 22p. 1992. pap. text ed. 4.99 (*1-57156-027-0*) Wild Goose UT.
Stinking Cookbook: From the Stinking Rose, a Garlic Restaurant. Jerry Dal Bozzo. LC 94-41457. 76p. 1995. pap. 9.95 (*0-89087-730-0*) Celestial Arts.
Stinking Rose. Sujata Bhatt. 128p. 1995. pap. 16.95 (*1-85754-048-4*, Pub. by Carcanet Pr UK) Paul & Co Pubs.
Stinking Thinking. Gayle Rosellini. 24p. (Orig.). 1985. pap. 2.00 (*0-89486-326-6*, 5451B) Hazelden.
Stinky & Opie. Marie Richards. (Illus.). 1995. 7.95 (*0-533-11314-8*) Vantage.
Stinky Business. Page McBrier. (Treehouse Times Ser.: No. 9). 128p. (Orig.). (YA). 1991. pap. 2.95 (*0-380-76269-2*, Camelot) Avon.
Stinky Cheese Man. Jon Scieszka. (J). 1996. pap. write for info. (*0-14-054896-3*) NAL-Dutton.
Stinky Cheese Man: And Other Fairly Stupid Tales. Jon Scieszka. (Illus.). 56p. (J). (gr. 1). 1992. pap. 16.99 (*0-670-84487-X*) Viking Child Bks.
Stinky Cheese Man & Other Fairly Stupid Tales. Jon Scieszka. 1998. pap. 5.99 (*0-14-055878-0*) Viking Penguin.
Stinky, My Best Friend: Stinky the Skunk. Everett G. Uphoff. (Illus.). 20p. (J). (gr. k-7). Date not set. pap. 5.00 (*0-9633334-0-2*) Rainbow Artist.
***Stinky Science.** 1997. pap. 19.95 (*0-8069-9888-1*) Sterling.
Stinky Sneakers Contest. Julie A. Peters. (J). (ps-3). 1992. 13.95 (*0-316-70214-5*) Little.
Stinky Sneakers Contest. Julie A. Peters. 64p. (J). 1994. pap. 3.99 (*0-380-72278-X*, Camelot Young) Avon.
Stinky Sneakers Mystery. Beverly Lewis. (Cul-de-Sac Kids Ser.: Vol. 7). 80p. (J). (gr. 2-5). 1996. pap. 3.99 (*1-55661-727-5*) Bethany Hse.
Stinky Socks. Justine Korman. (J). (gr. 4-7). 1996. pap. 3.50 (*0-8167-3413-5*) Troll Communs.
Stinky Stanley. Ann Hodgman. Ed. by Patricia MacDonald. (Illus.). 128p. (Orig.). (J). (gr. 3-6). 1993. pap. 2.99 (*0-671-78548-6*, Minstrel Bks) PB.
Stinky Stanley Stinks Again. Ann Hodgman. Ed. by Patricia MacDonald. (Illus.). 128p. (Orig.). (J). 1993. pap. 2.99 (*0-671-78560-5*, Minstrel Bks) PB.

***Stinky the Skunk. John Lasne. 16p. (J). (gr. k-3). 1997. 7.95 (*0-9642815-5-4*, STSKY) Natl Fmly Prtnship.**
In STINKY THE SKUNK, the new classic by John Lasne, a lonely skunk uses his own special skill to come to the rescue of the other woodland animals, threatened by a hungry bobcat. They, in turn, creatively find a way around the obstacle in their relationship with Stinky. A tale about accepting others despite their differences, STINKY THE SKUNK illustrates the meaning of true friendship. Written in verse & illustrated in the manner of Richard Scarry, this engaging story will delight young children & the adults who read it to them. STINKY THE SKUNK follows THE RED RIBBON & ROBBIE RABBIT, other winning fables by John Lasne.
Publisher Provided Annotation.

Stinson Beach Salt Marsh: The Form of Its Growth. Bernard Poinssot. LC 77-70990. (Illus.). 1977. pap. 12.00 (*0-918540-01-1*) Stinson Beach.
Stint with the U.S. Air Force: Experiences of a 4-F Sergeant in World War II. Murrell R. Smith. (Illus.). 240p. 1995. text ed. 17.00 (*0-8059-3636-X*) Dorrance.
Stinz: Warhorse. Donna Barr. 112p. 1993. pap. 9.95 (*1-883847-02-8*) MU Press.
Stiquito (TM) Advanced Experiments with a Simple & Inexpensive Robot. James M. Conrad & Jonathan W. Mills. LC 96-29883. 250p. 1997. teacher ed. 35.00 (*0-8186-7408-3*) IEEE Comp Soc.
Stir-Fries & Sautes. Time-Life Books Editors. Ed. by Catherine Hackett. LC 96-17872. (Great Taste, Low Fat Ser.). (Illus.). 160p. Date not set. 16.99 (*0-614-16984-4*) Time-Life.
Stir Fry. Liz Trigg. (Step by Step Ser.). 96p. 1994. 9.98 (*0-8317-7794-X*) Smithmark.
Stir-Fry. Ed. by Chuck Williams. (Williams-Sonoma Kitchen Library). (Illus.). 108p. 17.95 (*0-7835-0300-8*) Time-Life.
Stir-Fry Etc. Cy DeCosse Incorporated Staff. LC 95-41576. (Meals for Life Ser.). (Illus.). 112p. 1996. 14.95 (*0-86573-977-3*) Cowles Creative.
Stir-Fry Meals: Healthy Ways with a Wok. rev. ed. Olivia Wu. LC 96-1171. 224p. 1996. pap. 14.95 (*0-8120-9714-9*) Barron.
Stir-Fry Recipes. Keith W. Strandberg & Carol A. Strandberg. 36p. (Orig.). 1986. pap. 3.25 (*0-940844-30-3*) Wellspring.
***Stir-Fry to Szechuan: 100 Classic Chinese Recipes.** Weight Watchers International Staff. LC 97-4298. 1997. write for info. (*0-02-861718-5*) Macmillan.
Stir Frying Beef & Book Combo. Wei-Chuan Staff. 1994. pap. 21.90 incl. vhs (*0-941676-52-8*) Wei-Chuan Pub.
Stir Frying Chicken & Book Combo. Wei-Chuan Staff. 1994. pap. 21.90 incl. vhs (*0-941676-53-6*) Wei-Chuan Pub.
Stir Frying Vegetables & Book Combo. Wei-Chuan Staff. 1994. pap. 21.90 incl. vhs (*0-941676-54-4*) Wei-Chuan Pub.
***Stir It Up: Musical Stews from Roots to Jazz.** Gene Santoro. 208p. 1997. 25.00 (*0-19-509869-2*) OUP.
Stir up a Story. Linda Polon. (Learning Works Creative Writing Ser.). 48p. (J). (gr. 3-6). 1981. 6.95 (*0-88160-037-7*, LW 222) Learning Wks.
Stir-Ups. Junior Welfare League of Enid, Ok., Inc. Staff. (Cookbook Ser.). 1982. pap. 14.95 (*0-9609340-0-6*) Starr-Toof.
***Stirling: The Royal Burgh.** Craig Mair. 220p. 1996. pap. 30.00 (*0-85976-420-6*, Pub. by J Donald UK) St Mut.
Stirling Alternative: Power Systems, Refrigerants, & Heat Pumps. G. Walker. LC 93-41262. 237p. 1994. text ed. 32.00 (*2-88124-600-1*) Gordon & Breach.
Stirling & the Trossachs. Charles McKean. 152p. (C). 1994. pap. 35.00 (*1-873190-21-2*, Pub. by Rutland Pr UK) St Mut.
***Stirling & the Trossachs.** Erl B. Wilkie. (Twenty-Five Cycle Routes Ser.). (Illus.). 128p. 1997. pap. 16.95 (*0-11-495821-1*, Pub. by Statnry Ofc UK) Seven Hills Bk.
Stirling & Vuilleumier Heat Pumps: Design & Applications. Jaroslav Wurm. 1991. text ed. 53.00 (*0-07-053567-1*) McGraw.
Stirling Castle: Historic Scotland. Richard Fawcett. (Illus.). 1996. pap. 35.00 (*0-7134-7623-0*, Pub. by Batsford UK) Trafalgar.
Stirling-Cycle Prime Movers Seminar, June 1978. (Research Bulletin Ser.). 183p. 1979. 25.00 (*0-910091-42-0*) Inst Gas Tech.
Stirling Wings: The Short Stirling Goes to War. Jonathan Falconer. (Illus.). 240p. 1996. 33.95 (*0-7509-1063-1*, Pub. by Sutton Pubng UK) Bks Intl VA.
***Stirling Wings: The Short Stirling Goes to War.** Jonathan Falconer. (Illus.). 256p. (Orig.). 1997. pap. 19.95 (*0-7509-1517-X*, Pub. by Sutton Pubng UK) Bks Intl VA.
Stirrin' the Pots on Daufuskie. Billie Burn. 212p. (Orig.). 1985. pap. 9.50 (*0-9614670-0-2*) Burn Books.
Stirring. Bob Moeller. LC 94-11476. (Jan Dennis Book). 1994. 10.99 (*0-7852-8136-3*) Nelson.
Stirring. Robert Moeller. 1996. mass mkt. 6.50 (*0-7852-7261-5*) Nelson.
Stirring It: Challenges for Feminism. Ed. by Gabriele Griffin et al. LC 94-16345. (Gender & Society Ser.). 1994. write for info. (*0-7484-0213-6*, Pub. by Tay Francis Ltd UK); pap. write for info. (*0-7484-0214-4*, Pub. by Tay Francis Ltd UK) Taylor & Francis.
Stirring of Soul in the Workplace. Alan Briskin. LC 96-9975. (Business & Management Ser.). 1996. 27.95 (*0-7879-0281-0*) Jossey-Bass.
Stirring the Chalkdust. Patricia Wasley. (Series on School Reform). 256p. (C). 1994. text ed. 45.00 (*0-8077-3421-7*); pap. text ed. 21.95 (*0-8077-3420-9*) Tchrs Coll.
Stirring the Deep: The Poetry of Mark Vinz. Thom Tammaro. (Midwest Writers & Their Work Ser.: No. 1). iv, 102p. (Orig.). 1989. 7.95 (*0-944024-18-1*) Spoon Riv Poetry.
Stirring the Dreamer. Oguchi H. Nkwocha. 52p. 1993. 8.95 (*0-533-07984-5*) Vantage.
Stirring the Head, Heart, & Soul: Redefining Curriculum & Instruction. H. Lynn Erickson. LC 94-31097. (Illus.). 224p. 1995. 49.95 (*0-8039-6153-7*) Corwin Pr.
Stirring the Head, Heart, & Soul: Redefining Curriculum & Instruction. H. Lynn Erickson. 224p. 1995. pap. 22.95 (*0-8039-6154-5*) Corwin Pr.
Stirring up Innovation: Environmental Improvements in Paints & Adhesives. John S. Young et al. 128p. 1994. pap. 25.00 (*0-918780-63-2*) INFORM NY.
Stirrings of Culture. Ed. by Robert J. Sardello & Gail Thomas. LC 86-24028. 250p. (Orig.). 1986. pap. 19.50 (*0-911005-07-2*) Dallas Inst Pubns.
Stirrings of My Soul. 2nd ed. Josephine A. Miller. 120p. 1995. pap. 10.95 (*1-57502-169-2*, PO284) Morris Pubng.
Stirrings of the Heart. William C. Kean. 25p. 1989. pap. 3.50 (*0-909991-29-4*) Bahai.
Stirrings Still. Samuel Beckett. 1991. pap. 5.95 (*1-56201-015-8*, North Star Line) Blue Moon Bks.
Stirrup Boss. large type ed. Peter Dawson. 278p. 1996. 18.95 (*0-7862-0582-2*, Thorndike Lrg Prnt) Thorndike Pr.
Stirrup Cup. John A. Tyson. 1993. reprint ed. lib. bdg. 89.00 (*0-7812-5847-2*) Rprt Serv.
***Stirrup High.** Walt Coburn. LC 96-47112. (Illus.). iv, 190p. 1997. pap. 9.95 (*0-8032-6377-5*, Bison Books) U of Nebr Pr.
Stitch by Stitch: A Guide to Equine Saddles. Diana R. Tuke. 109p. (C). 1990. 28.00 (*0-85131-049-4*, Pub. by J A Allen & Co UK) St Mut.
Stitch in Rhyme: A Nursery Rhymes Sampler with Embroidered Illustrations. Illus. by Belinda Downes. 48p. (J). 1996. 18.00 (*0-679-87679-0*) Knopf.
Stitch in Rhyme: A Nursery Rhymes Sampler with Embroidered Illustrations. Illus. by Belinda Downes. (J). 1996. lib. bdg. 19.99 (*0-679-97679-5*) Knopf.
Stitch in Time. John Gould. (Illus.). 1985. 12.95 (*0-393-01976-4*) Norton.
Stitch in Time. Ann Rinaldi. (Quilt Trilogy Ser.). 320p. (J). (gr. 7-9). 1994. 13.95 (*0-590-46055-2*, Scholastic Hardcover) Scholastic Inc.
Stitch in Time. Ann Rinaldi. LC 93-8964. (Quilt Trilogy Ser.: Vol. 1). 320p. (J). (gr. 7-9). 1995. 3.99 (*0-590-46056-0*) Scholastic Inc.
Stitch in Time. Alex A. Rowan. LC 96-19097. 55p. (Orig.). 1996. pap. 5.00 (*0-88734-361-9*) Players Pr.
Stitch in Time: A Complete Guide to Recycling Clothing & Odds-&-Ends Sewing. Shirley Thulin. LC 83-81178. 80p. 1983. pap. 8.98 (*0-88290-222-9*) Horizon Utah.
Stitch in Time: Helping Young Mothers Complete High School. Elizabeth A. McGee & Susan Blank. 70p. 1989. pap. 8.00 (*0-89492-068-5*) Acad Educ Dev.
Stitch-in-Time Guide to Growing Your Nest Egg. large type ed. Beardstown Ladies Staff. pap. 23.95 (*1-56895-353-4*) Wheeler Pub.
Stitch of Courage: A Woman's Fight for Freedom. Linda K. Hubalek. LC 96-83117. (Trail of Thread Ser.: Bk. 3). (Illus.). 120p. (Orig.). (J). (gr. 4-12). 1996. pap. 9.95 (*1-886652-08-2*) Butterfld Bks.
Stitcher's Christmas Album. Patti L. Bachelder. LC 92-33334. (Illus.). 66p. (Orig.). 1992. pap. 9.95 (*0-9622565-3-6*) Chitra Pubns.
Stitchery & Needlelace from Threads Magazine. Threads Editors. Ed. by Christine Timmons. LC 91-13242. (Illus.). 128p. 1991. pap. 17.95 (*1-56158-010-4*, 070157) Taunton.
Stitches. Harriet Ziefert. (Hello Reading! Ser.). (Illus.). 32p. (J). (ps-3). 1990. pap. 3.50 (*0-14-054224-8*, Puffin) Puffin Bks.
Stitches: Side-Splitting Humor from the Doctors Office, Hospital & Operating Room. W. John Cocker. 1994. pap. text ed. 10.95 (*0-7737-5605-1*) Genl Dist Srvs.
Stitches Level 1, Blue. Harriet Ziefert. (Easy-to-Read Ser.). (Illus.). (J). (ps-2). 1993. pap. 3.50 (*0-14-036553-2*, Puffin) Puffin Bks.
Stitches in Time. Barbara Michaels. 400p. 1996. mass mkt. 6.99 (*0-06-109253-3*, Harp PBks) HarpC.
Stitches in Time: A Legacy of Ozark Quilts. Ed. by E. B. Green. 70p. 1986. 16.00 (*0-9616640-1-0*); pap. 10.00 (*0-9616640-0-2*) Rogers Hist Mus.
***Stitches in Time: Doll Costumes & Accessories, 1850-1925.** Florence Theriault. (Illus.). 134p. 1996. pap. 39.00 (*0-614-23814-5*, N5177) Hobby Hse.
Stitches of Creative Embroidery. Jacqueline Enthoven. LC 87-61433. (Illus.). 238p. 1987. pap. 19.95 (*0-88740-111-2*) Schiffer.
Stitches with Variations. Jacqueline Enthoven. 40p. 1995. pap. text ed. 6.95 (*0-9629056-8-2*) Quilters Res.
Stitches with Variations. 2nd ed. Jacqueline Enthoven. (Illus.). 40p. 1985. reprint ed. pap. text ed. 4.95 (*0-933877-01-3*) Aardvark.
Stitchin' Time: Plastic Canvas & Cross-Stitch Projects. Workbasket Magazine Staff. 1995. pap. text ed. 9.95 (*0-86675-344-3*) KC Pub.
Stitching Porcelain: After Matteo Ricci in Sixteenth-Century China. Deborah Larsen. LC 90-21176. 80p. (Orig.). 1991. pap. 9.95 (*0-8112-1161-4*, NDP710) New Directions.
Stitching Stars: The Story Quilts of Harriet Powers. Mary E. Lyons. LC 92-38561. (African-American Artists & Artisans Ser.). (Illus.). 48p. (J). (gr. 3-6). 1993. lib. bdg. 17.00 (*0-684-19576-3*, C Scribner Sons Young) S&S Childrens.
Stitching the Wildflowers of Virginia: Brazilian Embroidery. Peggy Crawford. (Illus.). 118p. 1992. pap. 19.95 (*0-936015-28-4*) Pocahontas Pr.
Stix Picks: Strategies for Student-Centered Assessment. Andi Stix. Ed. by Janine Bartko. (Illus.). 95p. (Orig.). 1996. pap. text ed. 25.00 (*1-887015-07-8*) Interact Classroom.
Stix Picks: Teaching Strategies for Cooperative Learning. Andi Stix. 63p. 1994. teacher ed., pap. text ed. 25.00 (*1-887015-02-7*) Interact Classroom.
Stix Picks Vols. I-II: Active Strategies for Interdisciplinary Instruction. Andi Stix. 106p. 1993. teacher ed., pap. text ed. 25.00 (*1-887015-03-5*) Interact Classroom.
Stjordvik Domain Sourcebook. TSR Inc. Staff. 1996. 7.95 (*0-7869-0421-6*) TSR Inc.
***STL for C++ Programmers.** Leendert Ammeraal. LC 96-43517. 226p. 1996. pap. 49.95 (*0-471-97181-2*) Wiley.
STL Primer. Glass. 370p. (C). 1995. pap. text ed. 42.00 (*0-13-454976-7*) P-H.
STL Tutorial & Reference Guide: C++ Programming with Standard Template Library. David R. Musser. 400p. (C). 1996. text ed. 39.95 (*0-201-63398-1*) Addison-Wesley.
STM & SFM in Biology. Othmar Marti & Matthias Amrein. (Illus.). 331p. 1993. text ed. 49.95 (*0-12-474500-8*) Acad Pr.
Student Reader Two. Barbara A. Wilson. (Wilson Reading System Ser.). 78p. 1988. pap. text ed. 8.00 (*1-56778-013-X*) Wilson Lang Trning.
Stoa of Attalos II in Athens. rev. ed. Homer A. Thompson. (Excavations of the Athenian Agora Picture Bks.: No. 2). (Illus.). 32p. 1992. pap. 3.00 (*0-87661-634-1*) Am Sch Athens.
Stoats & Weasels, Polecats & Martens. Paddy Sleeman. (Illus.). 120p. text ed. 19.95 (*0-905483-75-8*, Pub. by Whittet Bks UK) Diamond Farm Bk.
Stobi: Results of the Joint American-Yugoslav Archaeological Investigations, 1970-1981. Virginia R. Anderson-Stojanovic. (Hellenistic & Roman Pottery Ser.: Vol. I). (Illus.). 400p. 1992. text ed. 210.00 (*0-691-03605-5*) Princeton U Pr.
Stochastic Adaptive Control Results & Simulation. A. Aloneftis. (Lecture Notes in Control & Information Sciences Ser.: Vol. 98). xii, 120p. 1987. 31.95 (*0-387-18055-9*) Spr-Verlag.
***Stochastic Analysis.** Paul Malliavin. LC 97-6419. (Grundlehren der Mathematischen Wissenschaften Ser.: Vol. 313). 370p. 1997. 125.00 (*3-540-57024-1*) Spr-Verlag.
Stochastic Analysis. Ed. by Michel Metivier & S. Watanabe. (Lecture Notes in Mathematics Ser.: Vol. 1322). 197p. 1988. 38.95 (*0-387-19352-9*) Spr-Verlag.
Stochastic Analysis, 57. Ed. by Michael C. Cranston et al. LC 94-27794. (Proceedings of Symposia in Pure Mathematics Ser.: Vol. 57). 1994. 129.00 (*0-8218-0289-5*, PSPUM/57) Am Math.
***Stochastic Analysis, Vol. XI.** P. Malliavin. (Grundlehren der Mathematischen Wissenschaften Ser.: Vol. 313). 370p. 1997. 125.00 (*0-387-57024-1*) Spr-Verlag.
Stochastic Analysis: A Tribute to the Memory of Rollo Davidson. Ed. by D. G. Kendall & E. F. Harding. LC 72-8605. 479p. reprint ed. pap. 136.60 (*0-317-08894-7*, 2013983) Bks Demand.

S

S

Stochastic Analysis & Application: Proceedings Oslo-Silivri, July 1992, Vol. 8. Ed. by Tom Lindstrm et al. LC 93-28190. (Stochastics Monographs: Vol. 8). 288p. 1993. text ed. 92.00 (*2-88124-948-5*) Gordon & Breach.

Stochastic Analysis & Applications. Pinsky. (Advances in Probability & Related Topics Ser.: Vol. 7). 472p. 1984. 155.00 (*0-8247-1906-9*) Dekker.

Stochastic Analysis & Applications. Ed. by A. Truman & D. Williams. (Lecture Notes in Mathematics Ser.: Vol. 1095). v, 199p. 1984. 37.95 (*0-387-13891-9*) Spr-Verlag.

***Stochastic Analysis & Applications: Proceedings of the Fifth Gregynog Symposium.** 520p. 1996. 76.00 (*981-02-2560-1*) World Scientific Pub.

Stochastic Analysis & Applications: Proceedings of the 1989 Lisbon Conference. Ed. by A. B. Cruzeiro & J. C. Zambrini. (Progress in Probability Ser.: Vol. 26). vii, 197p. 1991. 69.00 (*0-8176-3567-X*) Birkhauser.

Stochastic Analysis & Applications in Physics: Proceedings of the NATO Advanced Study Institute, Funchal, Madeira, Portugal, August 6-19, 1993. Ed. by Ana I. Cardoso. (NATO Advanced Science Institutes: Series C). 472p. (C). 1994. lib. bdg. 218.50 (*0-7923-3197-4*) Kluwer Ac.

Stochastic Analysis & Random Maps in Hilbert Space. A. A. Dorogovtsev. 114p. 1994. 122.50 (*90-6764-163-4*, Pub. by VSP NE) Coronet Bks.

Stochastic Analysis & Related Topics. Ed. by H. K. Korezlioglu. LC 92-30794. vii, 369p. 1992. 102.00 (*0-8176-3666-8*) Birkhauser.

Stochastic Analysis & Related Topics. Ali S. Ustunel. (Lecture Notes in Mathematics Ser.: Vol. 1316). 371p. 1988. 54.95 (*0-387-19315-4*) Spr-Verlag.

Stochastic Analysis & Related Topics V: The Silivri Workshop, 1994. Ali S. Ustunel et al. LC 95-49835. (Progress in Probability Ser.: No. 38). 294p. 1995. 82.00 (*0-8176-3887-3*); write for info. (*3-7643-3887-3*) Birkhauser.

Stochastic Analysis & Related Topics, Vol. II: Proceedings of a Second Workshop Held in Silivri, Turkey, July 18-30, 1988. Ali S. Ustunel. (Lecture Notes in Mathematics Ser.: Vol. 1444). v, 268p. 1990. 46.95 (*0-387-53064-9*) Spr-Verlag.

Stochastic Analysis of Computer & Communication Systems. Ed. by Hideaki Takagi. 800p. 1990. 167.50 (*0-444-88479-3*, North Holland) Elsevier.

Stochastic Analysis of Computer Storage. O. I. Aven et al. (C). 1987. lib. bdg. 171.00 (*90-277-2515-2*) Kluwer Ac.

***Stochastic Analysis of Structural & Mechanical Vibrations.** L. D. Lutes & Shahram Sarkani. LC 96-33323. 509p. 1996. 85.00 (*0-13-490533-4*) P-H.

Stochastic & Chaotic Oscillations. Yu. I. Neimark & P. S. Landa. (C). 1992. lib. bdg. 251.00 (*0-7923-1530-8*) Kluwer Ac.

Stochastic & Risk Analysis in Hydraulic Engineering. Ben C. Yen. 350p. 1986. text ed. 40.00 (*0-918334-57-8*) WRP.

***Stochastic & Spatial Structures of Dynamical Systems, Vol. 45.** S. J. Strien & Lunel Verduyn. 242p. pap. 47.00 (*0-444-85809-1*, North Holland) Elsevier.

Stochastic & Statistical Methods in Hydrology & Environmental Engineering. LC 94-27708. 1994. write for info. (*0-7923-2760-8*) Kluwer Ac.

Stochastic & Statistical Methods in Hydrology & Environmental Engineering Vol. 2: Stochastic & Statistical Modelling with Groundwater & Surface Water Applications. Ed. by Keith W. Hipel. (Water Science & Technology Library). 392p. (C). 1994. lib. bdg. 179.50 (*0-7923-2757-8*) Kluwer Ac.

Stochastic & Statistical Methods in Hydrology & Environmental Engineering Vol. 3: Time Series Analysis in Hydrology & Environmental Engineering. Ed. by Keith W. Hipel. (Water Science & Technology Library). 496p. (C). 1994. lib. bdg. 225.50 (*0-7923-2758-6*) Kluwer Ac.

Stochastic & Statistical Methods in Hydrology & Environmental Engineering Vol. 4: Effective Environmental Management for Sustainable Development. Ed. by Keith W. Hipel. (Water Science & Technology Library). 480p. (C). 1994. lib. bdg. 222.00 (*0-7923-2759-4*) Kluwer Ac.

Stochastic & Statistical Methods in Hydrology & Environmental Engineering Vol. I: Extreme Values: Floods & Droughts. Ed. by Keith W. Hipel. (Water Science & Technology Library). 416p. (C). 1994. lib. bdg. 190.50 (*0-7923-2756-X*) Kluwer Ac.

Stochastic Approach to Fatigue: Experiments, Modelling & Reliability Estimation. Ed. by Kazimierz Sobczyk. (CISM International Centre for Mechanical Sciences Ser.: No. 334). (Illus.). vi, 301p. 1993. 90.95 (*0-387-82452-9*) Spr-Verlag.

***Stochastic Approximation Algorithms & Applications.** Harold J. Kushner & George Yin. LC 96-48847. (Applications of Mathematics Ser.). 432p. 1997. 59.95 (*0-387-94916-X*) Spr-Verlag.

Stochastic Approximation & Optimization of Random Systems. Lennart Ljung et al. LC 92-10322. (DMV Seminar Ser.: No. Bd. 17). 120p. 1992. 24.50 (*3-7643-2733-2*, Pub. by Birkhauser Vlg SZ); 34.00 (*0-8176-2733-2*, Pub. by Birkhauser Vlg SZ) Birkhauser.

Stochastic Approximation & Recursive Estimation. M. B. Nevel'son & R. Z. Has'minskii. LC 76-48298. (Translations of Mathematical Monographs: Vol. 47). 244p. 1976. 75.00 (*0-8218-1597-0*, MMONO/47) Am Math.

Stochastic Approximation Methods for Constrained & Unconstrained Systems. Harold J. Kushner & D. S. Clark. LC 78-16855. (Applied Mathematical Sciences Ser.: Vol. 26). (Illus.). 1978. 52.95 (*0-387-90341-0*) Spr-Verlag.

Stochastic Approximations & Adaptive Algorithms. A. Benveniste et al. Ed. by A. V. Balakrishnan et al. Tr. by S. S. Wilson from FRE. (Applications of Mathematics Ser.: Vol. 22). (Illus.). xi, 365p. 1990. 98.95 (*0-387-52894-6*) Spr-Verlag.

Stochastic Aspects of Classical & Quantum Systems. Ed. by Sergio A. Albeverio et al. (Lecture Notes in Mathematics Ser.: Vol. 1109). ix, 227p. 1985. 37.95 (*0-387-13914-1*) Spr-Verlag.

Stochastic Automata: Stability, Nondeterminism, & Prediction. E. E. Doberkat. (Lecture Notes in Computer Science Ser.: Vol. 113). 135p. 1981. 20.00 (*0-387-10835-1*) Spr-Verlag.

Stochastic Calculus: A Practical Introduction. 2nd ed. Richard Durrett. LC 96-24642. (Probability & Stochastics Ser.). 341p. Date not set. 59.95 (*0-8493-8071-5*, QA274) CRC Pr.

Stochastic Calculus in Manifolds. M. Emery. (Universitext Ser.). (Illus.). 168p. 1989. 49.95 (*0-387-51664-6*) Spr-Verlag.

Stochastic Cellular Systems: Ergodicity, Memory, Morphogenesis. Ed. by R. L. Dobrushin et al. (Nonlinear Science: Theory & Applications Ser.). 565p. 1992. text ed. 399.00 (*0-471-93521-2*) Wiley.

Stochastic Complexity in Statistical Inquiry Theory. J. Rissanen. (Series in Computer Science: Vol. 15). 188p. (C). 1989. text ed. 55.00 (*9971-5-0859-1*); pap. text ed. 33.00 (*981-02-0311-X*) World Scientific Pub.

Stochastic Computational Methods for Complex Tasks: Methods for Dealing with Tasks of High Complexity. B. Ingelnik. 1996. write for info. (*0-614-17896-7*) Elsevier.

Stochastic Control & Nonlinear Filtering. Mark H. Davis. (Tata Institute Lectures on Mathematics). iv, 109p. 1984. 27.95 (*0-387-13343-7*) Spr-Verlag.

Stochastic Control, Chaos & Uncertainty Management. Chen et al. 1994. write for info. (*0-8493-7151-1*, QA) CRC Pr.

Stochastic Control of Partially Observable Systems. Alain Benoussan. 450p. (C). 1992. text ed. 85.00 (*0-521-35403-X*) Cambridge U Pr.

***Stochastic Differential & Difference Equations.** Imre Csiszar & Gyorgy Michaletzky. LC 97-20913. (Progress in Systems & Control Theory Ser.). 1997. write for info. (*0-8176-3971-3*); write for info. (*3-7643-3971-3*) Birkhauser.

Stochastic Differential Equations. Ed. by J. B. Keller & H. P. McKean. LC 72-13266. (SIAM-AMS Proceedings Ser.: No. 6). 209p. 1973. 55.00 (*0-8218-1325-0*, SIAMS/6) Am Math.

Stochastic Differential Equations. Bernt K. Oksendal. (Universitext Ser.). xiii, 205p. 1985. pap. 29.00 (*0-387-15292-X*) Spr-Verlag.

Stochastic Differential Equations. 2nd ed. Bernt K. Oksendal. (Universitext Ser.). 208p. 1989. pap. 29.95 (*0-387-51740-5*) Spr-Verlag.

Stochastic Differential Equations: An Introduction with Applications. 3rd ed. Bernt K. Oksendal. (Universitext Ser.). xiii, 224p. (C). 1993. pap. text ed. 32.00 (*0-387-53335-4*) Spr-Verlag.

Stochastic Differential Equations: An Introduction with Applications. 4th ed. Bernt K. Oksendal. 1995. pap. text ed. 36.00 (*0-387-60243-7*) Spr-Verlag.

Stochastic Differential Equations: An Introduction with Applications. 4th ed. Bernt Osendal. (Universitext Ser.). (Illus.). 240p. 1996. 36.00 (*3-540-60243-7*) Spr-Verlag.

Stochastic Differential Equations: Theory & Applications. Ludwig Arnold. LC 91-23724. 246p. (C). 1992. reprint ed. lib. bdg. 49.50 (*0-89464-635-4*) Krieger.

Stochastic Differential Equations in Infinite Dimensional Spaces, Vol. 26. Gopinath Kallianpur & Jie Xiong. LC 95-81176. (Lecture Notes-Monograph Ser.: Vol. 26). (Illus.). 348p. 1995. 40.00 (*0-940600-38-2*) Inst Math.

Stochastic Differential Systems. Ed. by N. Christopeit et al. (Lecture Notes in Control & Information Sciences Ser.: Vol. 78). (Illus.). v, 365p. 1986. 50.95 (*0-387-16228-3*) Spr-Verlag.

Stochastic Differential Systems. Ed. by H. Engelbert & W. Schmidt. (Lecture Notes in Control & Information Sciences Ser.: Vol. 96). 382p. 1987. 76.95 (*0-387-18010-9*) Spr-Verlag.

Stochastic Differential Systems. Ed. by Michel Metivier & E. Pardoux. (Lecture Notes in Control & Information Sciences Ser.: Vol. 69). ix, 310p. 1985. 47.95 (*0-387-15176-1*) Spr-Verlag.

Stochastic Differential Systems: Analysis & Filtering. V. S. Pugachev & I. N. Sinitsyn. LC 86-15952. 549p. 1987. text ed. 399.00 (*0-471-91243-3*) Wiley.

Stochastic Differential Systems, Bad Honnef, FRG 1982: Proceedings. Ed. by M. Kohlmann & N. Christopeit. (Lecture Notes in Control & Information Sciences Ser.: Vol. 43). 377p. 1982. 36.95 (*0-387-12061-0*) Spr-Verlag.

Stochastic Differential Systems, Stochastic Control Theory & Applications. Ed. by W. Fleming & P. L. Lions. (IMA Volumes in Mathematics & Its Applications Ser.: Vol. 10). (Illus.). xiii, 609p. 1987. 69.95 (*0-387-96641-2*) Spr-Verlag.

***Stochastic Dynamical Systems: Concepts, Numerical Methods, Data Analysis.** J. Honerkamp. 1993. text ed. 110.00 (*0-471-18834-4*) Wiley.

Stochastic Dynamical Systems: Concepts, Numerical Methods, Data Analysis. Josef Honerkamp. Tr. by Katja Lindenberg. LC 93-26666. xvi, 535p. 1994. 64.00 (*1-56081-563-9*, VCH) Wiley.

***Stochastic Dynamics.** Ed. by L. Schimansky-Geier & T. Poschel. LC 97-15161. (Lecture Notes in Physics Ser.: Vol. 484). xviii, 386p. 1997. 79.00 (*3-540-62893-2*) Spr-Verlag.

Stochastic Dynamics & Reliability of Nonlinear Ocean Systems: 1994 International Mechanical Engineering Congress & Exposition, Chicago, Illinois - November 6-11, 1994. Ed. by R. A. Ibrahim. LC 94-79145. (DE Ser.: Vol. 77). 128p. 1994. 54.00 (*0-7918-1436-X*, G00931) ASME.

Stochastic Equations & Differential Geometry. Y. I. Belopolskaya & Yu L. Dalecky. (C). 1990. lib. bdg. 167.00 (*90-277-2807-0*) Kluwer Ac.

Stochastic Equations for Complex Systems. A. V. Skorohod. (C). 1987. lib. bdg. 129.50 (*90-277-2408-3*) Kluwer Ac.

Stochastic Equations in Infinite Dimensions: Theory & Applications. Giuseppe Da Prato & J. W. Zabczyk. (Encyclopedia of Mathematics & Its Applications Ser.: No. 45). 450p. (C). 1993. text ed. 100.00 (*0-521-38529-6*) Cambridge U Pr.

Stochastic Evolution Equations: A Hilbert Space Approach. Wilfried Grecksch & Constantin Tudor. LC 95-20753. (Mathematical Research Ser.: Vol. 85). 1995. write for info. (*3-05-501697-1*, Pub. by Akademie Verlag GW) Wiley.

Stochastic Evolution of Quantum States in Open Systems. L. Diosi & B. Lukacs. 152p. 1994. text ed. 68.00 (*981-02-1694-7*) World Scientific Pub.

Stochastic Evolution Systems: Linear Theory & Applications to Non-Linear Filtering. B. L. Rozovskii. (Mathematics & Its Applications, Soviet Ser.). (C). 1990. lib. bdg. 180.50 (*0-7923-0037-8*) Kluwer Ac.

Stochastic Filtering Theory. Gopinath Kallianpur. (Applications of Mathematics Ser.: Vol. 13). 350p. 1980. 90.95 (*0-387-90445-X*) Spr-Verlag.

Stochastic Finite Element Method: Basic Perturbation Technique & Computer Implementation. Michael Kleiber & Tran D. Hien. LC 92-22814. 322p. 1993. text ed. 125.00 (*0-471-93626-X*) Wiley.

Stochastic Finite Elements: A Spectral Approach. R. E. Ghanem & P. D. Spanos. (Illus.). 224p. 1990. 74.95 (*0-387-97456-3*) Spr-Verlag.

Stochastic Flows & Stochastic Differential Equations. Hiroshi Kunita. (Cambridge Studies in Advanced Mathematics: No. 24). 300p. (C). 1990. text ed. 89.95 (*0-521-35050-6*) Cambridge U Pr.

***Stochastic Flows & Stochastic Differntial Equations.** H. Kunita. (Cambridge Studies in Advanced Mathematics: No. 24). 350p. 1997. pap. 29.95 (*0-521-59925-3*) Cambridge U Pr.

Stochastic Games & Related Topics: In Honor of Professor L. S. Shapley. Ed. by T. E. Raghavan. (Theory & Decision Library: Vol. C). (C). 1991. lib. bdg. 129.00 (*0-7923-1016-0*) Kluwer Ac.

Stochastic Geometry: A Tribute to the Memory of Rollo Davidson. Ed. by E. F. Harding & D. G. Kendall. LC 72-8603. (Wiley Series in Probability & Mathematical Statistics). (Illus.). 414p. reprint ed. pap. 118.00 (*0-685-23758-3*, 2032832) Bks Demand.

Stochastic Geometry & Its Applications. 2nd ed. Dietrich Stoyan. LC 95-4097. (Probability & Mathematical Statistics Ser.). 400p. 1996. text ed. 79.95 (*0-471-95099-8*) Wiley.

Stochastic Geometry & Its Applications. Dietrich Stoyan et al. LC 85-16865. 345p. reprint ed. pap. 98.40 (*0-7837-3415-8*, 2043382) Bks Demand.

***Stochastic Hydraulics '96: Proceedings of the 7th IAHR International Symnposium, MacKay, Queensland, Australia, 29-31 July 1996.** Ed. by Kevin S. Tickle et al. (Illus.). 674p. (C). 1996. text ed. 130.00 (*90-5410-817-7*, Pub. by A A Balkema NE) Ashgate Pub Co.

Stochastic Hydrology & its Use in Water Resources Systems Simulation & Optimization. Ed. by Juan B. Marco et al. LC 93-19300. (NATO Advanced Study Institutes Series E, Applied Sciences: Vol. 237). 1993. lib. bdg. 229.50 (*0-7923-2288-6*) Kluwer Ac.

Stochastic Inequalities. Ed. by Moshe Shaked & Y. L. Tong. (Lecture Notes - Monograph Ser.: Vol. 22). (Illus.). 411p. 1992. pap. 40.00 (*0-940600-29-3*) Inst Math.

Stochastic Integral Equations & Rainfall-Runoff Models. T. V. Hromadka, II & R. J. Whitley. (Illus.). 400p. 1989. 120.95 (*0-387-51086-9*) Spr-Verlag.

Stochastic Integration & Differential Equations. P. Protter. (Applications of Mathematics Ser.: Vol. 21). x, 302p. 1995. 69.00 (*0-387-50996-8*) Spr-Verlag.

Stochastic Integration & Stochastic Differential Equations. K. Bichteler. 1984. write for info. (*0-318-57812-3*, North Holland) Elsevier.

Stochastic Limit Theory. James Davidson. (Advanced Texts in Econometrics Ser.). (Illus.). 600p. 1994. 95.00 (*0-19-877402-8*); pap. 48.00 (*0-19-877403-6*) OUP.

***Stochastic Maximum Principle.** Haussmann. 1986. pap. text ed. write for info. (*0-582-98893-4*, Pub. by Longman UK) Longman.

Stochastic Mechanics & Stochastic Processes. Ed. by A. Truman & I. M. Davies. (Lecture Notes in Mathematics Ser.: Vol. 1325). v, 220p. 1988. pap. 35.00 (*0-387-50015-4*) Spr-Verlag.

Stochastic Mechanics of Discrete Media. D. R. Axelrad. LC 93-36464. 1993. 174.95 (*0-387-57070-5*) Spr-Verlag.

Stochastic Methods & Computer Techniques in Quantum Dynamics. Ed. by H. Mitter & Ludwig Pittner. (Acta Physica Austriaca Ser.: Supplementum 26). (Illus.). vi, 452p. 1984. 97.95 (*0-387-81835-9*) Spr-Verlag.

Stochastic Methods in Earthquake Engineering. Ed. by A. S. Cakmak. (Progress in Engineering Ser.). 170p. 1985. pap. 46.00 (*0-931215-08-0*) Computational Mech MA.

Stochastic Methods in Economics & Finance. T. G. Malliaris. (Advanced Textbooks in Economics Ser.: Vol. 17). 304p. 1982. 65.00 (*0-444-86201-3*, North Holland) Elsevier.

Stochastic Methods in Experimental Sciences: International Conference. W. Kasprzak & A. Weron. 488p. 1990. text ed. 130.00 (*981-02-0178-8*) World Scientific Pub.

Stochastic Methods in Mathematics & Physics: Proceedings of the Twenty-Fourth Karpacz Winter School, Karpacz, Poland, Jan 13-27, 1988. Ed. by R. Gielerak & Waldemar Karwowski. 412p. 1989. text ed. 109.00 (*9971-5-0648-3*) World Scientific Pub.

Stochastic Methods in Reliability Theory. N. Ravichandran. 201p. 1991. text ed. 49.95 (*0-470-21681-6*) Halsted Pr.

Stochastic Methods in Structural Dynamics. Ed. by G. I. Schueller & M. Shinozuke. (C). 1987. lib. bdg. 143.00 (*90-247-3611-0*) Kluwer Ac.

Stochastic Methods of Operations Research. Jurg Kohlas. LC 81-21574. 160p. 1982. text ed. 64.95 (*0-521-23899-4*); pap. text ed. 23.95 (*0-521-28292-6*) Cambridge U Pr.

Stochastic Modeling: Analysis & Simulation. Barry L. Nelson. (Industrial Engineering & Management Science Ser.). 1995. text ed. 46.00 (*0-07-046213-5*) McGraw.

Stochastic Modeling & Analysis of Manufacturing Systems. Ed. by David D. Yao. LC 94-19979. (Series in Operations Research). 1994. 59.95 (*0-387-94319-6*) Spr-Verlag.

Stochastic Modeling & Geostatistics Principles, Methods, & Case Studies. Ed. by Jeffrey M. Yarus & Richard L. Chambers. (AAPG Computer Applications in Geology Ser.: No. 3). (Illus.). x, 379p. 1995. 149.00 (*0-89181-702-6*, 322) AAPG.

Stochastic Modeling of Ocean Dynamics. I. E. Timchenko. 312p. 1984. text ed. 410.00 (*3-7186-0231-8*) Gordon & Breach.

***Stochastic Modeling of Scientific Data.** Guttorp. (Stochastic Modeling Ser.). (Illus.). 384p. 1995. text ed. 54.95 (*0-412-99281-7*, Chap & Hall NY) Chapman & Hall.

Stochastic Modelling & Analysis: A Computational Approach. Henk C. Tijms. LC 85-22696. 432p. reprint ed. pap. 123.20 (*0-7837-3416-6*, 2043383) Bks Demand.

Stochastic Modelling & Control. Mark H. Davis & Richard Vinter. (Monographs on Statistics & Applied Probability). 350p. (C). 1985. 42.50 (*0-412-16200-8*, 6874) Chapman & Hall.

Stochastic Modelling & Filtering: Proceedings of the IFIP-WG 7-1 Working Conference, Rome, Italy, December 10-14, 1984. Ed. by A. Germani. (Lecture Notes in Control & Information Sciences Ser.: Vol. 91). iv, 218p. 1987. 51.95 (*0-387-17575-X*) Spr-Verlag.

Stochastic Modelling in Biology: Relevant Mathematical Concepts & Recent Applications. Ed. by P. Tautu. 456p. (C). 1990. text ed. 113.00 (*981-02-0135-4*) World Scientific Pub.

***Stochastic Modelling in Innovative Manufacturing.** Anthony H. Christer et al. LC 96-43259. (Lecture Notes in Economics & Mathematical Systems: Vol. 445). (Illus.). 361p. 1996. 78.00 (*3-540-61768-X*) Spr-Verlag.

Stochastic Modelling in Physical Oceanography. Ed. by Robert J. Adler et al. LC 95-48417. (Progress in Probability Ser.: Vol. 39). xi, 467p. 1996. 84.50 (*0-8176-3798-2*) Birkhauser.

Stochastic Modelling in Physical Oceanography. Ed. by Robert J. Adler et al. LC 95-48417. (Progress in Probability Ser.: Vol. 39). 1996. write for info. (*3-7643-3798-2*) Birkhauser.

Stochastic Models. Ed. by D. P. Heyman & M. J. Sobel. (Handbooks in Operations Research & Management Science Ser.: No. 2). 726p. 1990. 165.00 (*0-444-87473-9*, HOR 2, North Holland) Elsevier.

Stochastic Models: An Algorithmic Approach. Henk C. Tijms. LC 94-1010. (Probability & Mathematical Statistics Ser.). 350p. 1995. text ed. 87.95 (*0-471-94380-0*); pap. text ed. 42.95 (*0-471-95123-4*) Wiley.

Stochastic Models & Option Values: Applications to Resources, Environment & Investment Problems. Ed. by Bernt K. Oksendal & D. Lund. (Contributions to Economic Analysis Ser.: No. 200). 302p. 1991. 131.50 (*0-444-88630-3*, North Holland) Elsevier.

Stochastic Models, Estimation & Control, Vol. 3. Peter S. Maybeck. (Mathematics in Science & Engineering Ser.). 270p. 1982. text ed. 83.00 (*0-12-480703-8*) Acad Pr.

Stochastic Models for Carcinogenesis. Tan. (Statistics: Textbooks & Monographs: Vol. 116). 264p. 1991. 145.00 (*0-8247-8427-8*) Dekker.

Stochastic Models for Laser Propagation in Atmospheric Turbulence. R. P. Leland. (Lecture Notes in Control & Information Sciences Ser.: Vol. 133). (Illus.). xii, 145p. 1989. pap. 35.00 (*0-387-51538-0*) Spr-Verlag.

Stochastic Models for Repairable Systems. E. Smeitink. (Tinbergen Institute Research Ser.). 140p. 1992. pap. 25.00 (*90-5170-135-7*, Pub. by Thesis Pubs NE) IBD Ltd.

Stochastic Models for Social Processes. 3rd ed. David J. Bartholomew. LC 82-117228. (Wiley Series in Probability & Mathematical Statistics). 377p. reprint ed. pap. 107.50 (*0-8357-3392-0*, 2039649) Bks Demand.

Stochastic Models in Engineering, Technology & Management: Proceeding of the 1st Australia-Japan Workshop. Shunji Osaki & D. N. Murth. 500p. 1993. text ed. 121.00 (*981-02-1452-9*) World Scientific Pub.

***Stochastic Models in Geosystems.** Ed. by S. A. Molchanov & Wojbor A. Woyczynski. LC 96-38280. (IMA Volumes in Mathematics & Its Applications). 460p. 1996. 69.95 (*0-387-94873-2*) Spr-Verlag.

Stochastic Models in Medicine & Biology: Proceedings of a Symposium Conducted by the Mathematics Research Center, 1963. John Gurland. LC 64-14509. (U. S. Army. Mathematics Research Center Publication Ser.: No. 10). 410p. reprint ed. pap. 116.90 (*0-317-12991-0*, 2021134) Bks Demand.

An Asterisk (*) at the beginning of an entry indicates that the title is appearing in BIP for the first time.

Stochastic Models in Reliability Theory. Ed. by S. Oskai & Y. Hatoyama. (Lecture Notes in Economics & Mathematical Systems Ser.: Vol. 235). vii, 212p. 1984. 36.00 (*0-387-13888-9*) Spr-Verlag.

Stochastic Models of Air Pollutant Concentration. J. Grandell. (Lecture Notes in Statistics Ser.: Vol. 30). v, 110p. 1985. 34.95 (*0-387-96197-6*) Spr-Verlag.

***Stochastic Models of Cancer.** (Monographs on Statistics & Applied Probability). 1996. text ed. 54.95 (*0-412-99481-X*, Chap & Hall NY) Chapman & Hall.

Stochastic Models of Manufacturing Systems. John A. Buzacott & J. George Shanthikumar. LC 92-11145. 544p. 1992. text ed. 92.00 (*0-13-847567-9*) P-H.

Stochastic Models of Migration. S. Ginsburg. write for info. (*0-318-56730-X*) Elsevier.

Stochastic Models of Tumor Latency & Their Applications. B. Asselain et al. (Series in Mathematical Biology & Medicine). 250p. 1996. text ed. 61.00 (*981-02-1831-1*) World Scientific Pub.

Stochastic Models Optimization Techniques & Computer Applications. Reddy G. Krishna & R. Nadarajan. 1994. write for info. (*81-224-0704-8*, Pub. by Wiley Estrn II) Franklin.

Stochastic Monotonicity & Queuing Applications of Birth-Death Processes. E. A. Van Doorn. (Lecture Notes in Statistics Ser.: Vol. 4). 118p. 1981. 38.95 (*0-387-90547-2*) Spr-Verlag.

Stochastic Networks. Ed. by Frank P. Kelly & Ruth J. Williams. LC 95-17145. (IMA Volumes in Mathematics & Its Applications Ser.: Vol. 71). (Illus.). 427p. 1995. 75.95 (*0-387-94531-8*) Spr-Verlag.

***Stochastic Networks: Stability & Rare Events.** Ed. by P. Glasserman et al. 312p. 1996. pap. 39.95 (*0-387-94828-7*) Spr-Verlag.

***Stochastic Networks: Theory & Applications.** F. P. Kelly et al. (Royal Statistical Society Lecture Notes Ser.: No. 4). (Illus.). 384p. 1996. 69.00 (*0-19-852399-8*) OUP.

***Stochastic Optimal Control: The Discrete-Time Case.** Dimitri P. Bertsekas & Steven E. Shreve. LC 96-80191. 325p. (C). 1996. pap. text ed. 49.50 (*1-886529-03-5*) Athena Scientific.

Stochastic Optimal Control: Theory & Application. Robert F. Stengel. LC 86-9096. 638p. 1986. text ed. 125.00 (*0-471-86462-5*) Wiley.

Stochastic Optimal Control see Optimal Control & Estimation

Stochastic Optimal Control Theory with Application in Self-Tuning Control. K. J. Hunt. (Lecture Notes in Control & Information Sciences Ser.: Vol. 117). (Illus.). 320p. 1989. 61.95 (*0-387-50532-6*) Spr-Verlag.

Stochastic Optimization. Roger J. Wets. (Lecture Notes in Control & Information Sciences Ser.: Vol. 81). (Illus.). 770p. 1986. 118.95 (*0-387-16659-9*) Spr-Verlag.

Stochastic Optimization: Numerical Methods & Technical Applications. Ed. by Kurt Marti. (Lecture Notes in Economics & Mathematical Systems Ser.: Vol. 379). (Illus.). vii, 182p. 1992. 50.95 (*0-387-55225-1*) Spr-Verlag.

Stochastic Optimization & Economic Models. Jati K. Sengupta. 1986. lib. bdg. 152.00 (*90-277-2301-X*) Kluwer Ac.

Stochastic Orders & Applications: A Classified Bibliography. Karl C. Mosler & Marco Scarsini. (Lecture Notes in Economics & Mathematical Systems Ser.: Vol. 401). vi, 379p. 1993. pap. write for info. (*3-540-56956-1*) Spr-Verlag.

Stochastic Orders & Applications: A Classified Biography. Karl C. Mosler & Marco Scarsini. LC 93-8817. (Lecture Notes in Economics & Mathematical Systems Ser.: Vol. 401). 1993. pap. 65.00 (*0-387-56956-1*) Spr-Verlag.

Stochastic Orders & Decision under Risk. Marco Scarsini. LC 91-77909. (IMS Lecture Notes - Monograph Ser.: Vol. 19). xiv, 392p. 1991. pap. 30.00 (*0-940600-26-9*) Inst Math.

Stochastic Orders & Their Applications. J. George Shanthikumar. (Probability & Mathematical Statistics Ser.). 545p. 1994. text ed. 84.00 (*0-12-638160-7*) Acad Pr.

Stochastic Parameter Regression Models. Paul Newbold & Theodore Bos. (Quantitative Applications in the Social Sciences Ser.: Vol. 51). 1985. 9.95 (*0-8039-2425-9*) Sage.

Stochastic Partial Differential Equations. Ed. by Alison Etheridge. (London Mathematical Society Lecture Note Ser.: No. 216). (Illus.). 350p. (C). 1995. pap. text ed. 42.95 (*0-521-48319-0*) Cambridge U Pr.

Stochastic Partial Differential Equations: A Modeling, White Noise Functional Analysis Approach. H. Holden. LC 96-22105. (Probability & Its Applications Ser.). 1996. write for info. (*3-7643-3928-4*) Birkhauser.

Stochastic Partial Differential Equations: A Modeling, White Noise Functional Analysis Approach. H. Holden et al. LC 96-22105. (Probability & Its Applications Ser.). 231p. 1996. 64.50 (*0-8176-3928-4*) Spr-Verlag.

Stochastic Partial Differential Equations & Applications. Ed. by Giuseppe Da Prato & L. Turvato. (Lecture Notes in Mathematics Ser.: Vol. 1236). v, 257p. 1987. 42.95 (*0-387-17211-4*) Spr-Verlag.

Stochastic Partial Differential Equations & Applications II. Ed. by Giuseppe Da Prato & Luciano Tubaro. (Lecture Notes in Mathematics Ser.: Vol. 1390). vi, 258p. 1989. 41.95 (*0-387-51510-0*) Spr-Verlag.

Stochastic Partial Differential Equations & Their Applications: Proceedings of IFIP WG 7-1 International Conference, June 6-8, 1991, University of North Carolina at Charlotte, NC. Ed. by B. L. Rozovskii & R. B. Sowers. (Lecture Notes in Control & Information Sciences Ser.: Vol. 176). (Illus.). iv, 251p. 1992. 90.95 (*0-387-55292-8*) Spr-Verlag.

Stochastic Phenomena & Chaotic Behavior im Complex Systems: Proceedings of the UNESCO, Working Group on Systems Analysis, 4th, Flattnitz, Karmten, Austria, June 6-10, 1983. UNESCO, Working Group on Systems Analysis Staff. Ed. by P. Schuster. (Synergetics Ser.: Vol. 21). (Illus.). 270p. 1984. 78.95 (*0-387-13194-9*) Spr-Verlag.

Stochastic Point Processes. S. K. Srinivasan. (Charles Griffin Series Griffins Statistical Monographs: No. 34). (Illus.). 186p. 1987. pap. 24.95 (*0-19-520587-1*) OUP.

Stochastic Population Theories. D. Ludwig. (Lecture Notes in Biomathematics Ser.: Vol. 3). 1978. reprint ed. pap. 22.00 (*0-387-07010-9*) Spr-Verlag.

Stochastic Problems in Control. American Society of Mechanical Engineers Staff. LC 68-8579. 124p. reprint ed. pap. 35.40 (*0-317-08716-9*, 2016484) Bks Demand.

Stochastic Process. Skalmierski. 1982. lib. bdg. 104.50 (*90-247-2686-7*, Pub. by M Nijhoff NE) Kluwer Ac.

Stochastic Process: Problems & Solutions. L. Takacs. 1966. pap. 16.95 (*0-412-20340-5*, 6284) Chapman & Hall.

Stochastic Processes. Joseph L. Doob. (Classics Library). 654p. 1990. pap. text ed. 54.95 (*0-471-52369-0*) Wiley.

Stochastic Processes. Emanuel Parzen. LC 62-9243. (Illus.). 1962. pap. 26.95 (*0-8162-6664-6*) Holden-Day.

Stochastic Processes. 2nd ed. Jyoti P. Medhi. 598p. 1994. text ed. 51.95 (*0-470-22053-8*) Halsted Pr.

Stochastic Processes. 2nd ed. Sheldon M. Ross. LC 95-38012. 384p. 1995. text ed. 54.50 (*0-471-12062-6*) Wiley.

Stochastic Processes: A Festschrift in Honor of Gopinath Kallianpur. Stamatis Cambanis et al. LC 92-31111. 392p. 1992. 65.95 (*0-387-97921-2*) Spr-Verlag.

Stochastic Processes: A Survey of the Mathematical Theory. J. Lamperti. LC 77-24321. (Applied Mathematical Sciences Ser.: Vol. 23). 1997. pap. 36.00 (*0-387-90275-9*) Spr-Verlag.

Stochastic Processes: General Theory. M. M. Rao. (Mathematics & Its Applications Ser.: Vol. 342). 1995. lib. bdg. 259.00 (*0-7923-3725-5*) Kluwer Ac.

Stochastic Processes: Mathematics & Physics. Sergio A. Albeverio et al. Ed. by P. Blanchard & Ludwig Streit. (Lecture Notes in Mathematics Ser.: Vol. 1158). vi, 257p. 1986. 48.95 (*0-387-15998-3*) Spr-Verlag.

Stochastic Processes: Mathematics & Physics. Sergio A. Albeverio. Ed. by P. Blanchard & Ludwig Streit. (Lecture Notes in Mathematics Ser.: Vol. 1250). vi, 359p. 1987. 52.95 (*0-387-17797-3*) Spr-Verlag.

Stochastic Processes: Physics & Geometry International Conference. Ed. by Sergio A. Albeverio et al. 760p. (C). 1990. text ed. 173.00 (*981-02-0019-6*) World Scientific Pub.

Stochastic Processes & Estimation Theory with Applications. Touraj Assefi. LC 79-17872. 304p. 1985. reprint ed. 41.50 (*0-471-06454-8*, (JW)) Krieger.

Stochastic Processes & Filtering Theory. A. H. Jazwinski. (Mathematics in Science & Engineering Ser.: Vol. 64). 1970. text ed. 79.95 (*0-12-381550-9*) Acad Pr.

***Stochastic Processes & Functional Analysis: In Celebration of M. M. Rao's 65th Birthday.** M. M. Rao et al. LC 96-48137. (Lecture Notes in Pure & Applied Mathematics Ser.: Vol. 186). 296p. 1997. pap. 140.00 (*0-8247-9801-5*) Dekker.

Stochastic Processes & Optimal Control, Vol. 7. Ed. by Hans J. Engelbert et al. LC 93-14592. (Stochastics Monographs: Vol. 7). 220p. 1993. text ed. 88.00 (*2-88124-927-2*) Gordon & Breach.

Stochastic Processes & Related Topics. Ed. by Marcus Dozzi et al. (Mathematical Research Ser.: Vol. 61). 168p. 1991. lib. bdg. 29.00 (*3-05-501262-3*, Pub. by Akademie Verlag GW) Wiley.

Stochastic Processes & Related Topics. J. Engelbert Hans. Ed. by Hans Follmer. (Stochastics Monographs). 1996. text ed. 78.00 (*2-88449-069-8*) Gordon & Breach.

Stochastic Processes & the Wiener Integral. LC 72-91439. (Pure & Applied Mathematics Ser.: No. 13). 574p. reprint ed. pap. 163.60 (*0-317-07837-2*, 2055026) Bks Demand.

Stochastic Processes & Their Applications: Proceedings of the Symposium Held in Honour of Professor S. K. Srinivasan at the Indian Institute of Technology Bombay, India, December 27-30, 1990. Ed. by Martin J. Beckmann et al. (Lecture Notes in Economics & Mathematical Systems Ser.: Vol. 370). (Illus.). xi, 292p. 1991. 65.00 (*0-387-54635-9*) Spr-Verlag.

Stochastic Processes & Their Applications in Mathematics & Physics. Ed. by Sergio A. Albeverio et al. (C). 1990. lib. bdg. 188.00 (*0-7923-0894-8*) Kluwer Ac.

Stochastic Processes Applied to Physics & Other Related Fields: Proceedings of the Conference in Cali, Colombia, June 21-July 9, 1982. Ed. by B. Gomez et al. (CIF Ser.: Vol. 1). 781p. 1983. 121.00 (*9971-950-56-1*) World Scientific Pub.

Stochastic Processes, Estimation, & Control: The Entropy Approach. George N. Saridis. LC 94-33109. 304p. 1995. text ed. 74.95 (*0-471-09756-X*) Wiley.

Stochastic Processes in Astrophysics. Ed. by J. Robert Buchler & Henry E. Kandrup. LC 93-41277. (Annals Ser.: Vol. 706). 203p. 1993. write for info. (*0-89766-802-2*); pap. 65.00 (*0-89766-801-4*) NY Acad Sci.

Stochastic Processes in Classical & Quantum Systems. Ed. by Sergio A. Albeverio et al. (Lecture Notes in Physics Ser.: Vol. 262). xi, 551p. 1986. 78.95 (*0-387-17166-5*) Spr-Verlag.

Stochastic Processes in Demography & Their Computer Implementation. C. J. Mode. (Biomathematics Ser.: Vol. 14). (Illus.). 430p. 1985. 121.95 (*0-387-13622-3*) Spr-Verlag.

Stochastic Processes in Dynamical Problems. American Society of Mechanical Engineers Staff. LC 71-105935. 121p. reprint ed. pap. 34.50 (*0-317-27786-3*, 2024180) Bks Demand.

Stochastic Processes in Engineering Systems. 2nd ed. E. Wong & B. Hajek. (Texts in Electrical Engineering Ser.). 240p. 1984. 69.95 (*0-387-96061-9*) Spr-Verlag.

Stochastic Processes in Epidemic Theory: Proceedings of a Conference Held in Luminy, France, 1988. Ed. by J-P. Gabriel et al. (Lecture Notes in Biomathematics Ser.: Vol. 86). vi, 197p. 1990. pap. 34.00 (*0-387-52571-8*) Spr-Verlag.

Stochastic Processes in Hydrology. Vujica Yevjevich. LC 78-168495. 1982. 40.00 (*0-918334-01-2*) WRP.

Stochastic Processes in Magnetic Resonance. Dan Gamliel & Haim Levanon. LC 95-16547. 300p. 1995. text ed. 64.00 (*981-02-2227-0*) World Scientific Pub.

Stochastic Processes in Mathematical Physics & Engineering: Proceedings. Ed. by R. Bellman. LC 64-18128. (Proceedings of Symposia in Applied Mathematics Ser.: Vol. 16). 318p. 1964. reprint ed. pap. 47.00 (*0-8218-1316-1*, PSAPM/16) Am Math.

Stochastic Processes in Physics & Chemistry. rev. ed. N. G. Van Kampen. LC 92-19518. 466p. 1992. pap. 80.25 (*0-444-89349-0*, North Holland) Elsevier.

Stochastic Processes in Physics & Engineering. Ed. by Sergio A. Albeverio et al. (C). 1988. lib. bdg. 162.50 (*90-277-2659-0*) Kluwer Ac.

Stochastic Processes in Polymeric Fluids. 1995. 82.95 (*3-540-58353-X*) Spr-Verlag.

Stochastic Processes in Polymeric Fluids: Tools & Examples for Developing Simulation Algorithms. H. C. Ottinger. LC 95-44913. 386p. 1995. 75.00 incl. 3.5 hd (*0-387-58353-X*) Spr-Verlag.

Stochastic Processes in the Neurosciences. Henry Tuckwell. LC 89-6115. (CBMS-NSF Regional Conference Series in Applied Mathematics: No. 56). v, 129p. 1989. pap. 31.00 (*0-89871-232-7*) Soc Indus-Appl Math.

Stochastic Processes in Underwater Acoustics. Ed. by C. R. Baker. (Lecture Notes in Control & Information Sciences Ser.: Vol. 85). v, 205p. 1986. pap. 32.00 (*0-387-16869-9*) Spr-Verlag.

Stochastic Processes on a Lattice & Gibbs Measures. Bernard Prum & Jean C. Fort. (Mathematical Physics Studies). (C). 1991. lib. bdg. 132.00 (*0-7923-1069-1*) Kluwer Ac.

Stochastic Processes, Physics & Geometry II. S. Albeverio et al. 756p. 1995. text ed. 162.00 (*981-02-2141-X*) World Scientific Pub.

Stochastic Processes with Applications. Rabi N. Bhattacharya & Edward C. Waymire. LC 89-28530. (Probability & Mathematical Statistics Ser.). 672p. 1990. text ed. 130.00 (*0-471-84272-9*) Wiley.

Stochastic Programming. 1995. 78.00 (*3-540-58996-1*) Spr-Verlag.

Stochastic Programming. Ed. by F. Archetti et al. (Lecture Notes in Control & Information Sciences Ser.: Vol. 76). v, 285p. 1985. 40.95 (*0-387-16044-2*) Spr-Verlag.

Stochastic Programming. Ed. by M. A. Dempster. LC 77-92826. (Institute of Mathematics & Its Applications Conference Series, New Ser.). 1980. text ed. 275.00 (*0-12-208250-8*) Acad Pr.

Stochastic Programming. Peter Kall & Stein W. Wallace. (Interscience Series in Systems). 300p. 1995. text ed. 84.95 (*0-471-95108-0*); pap. text ed. 42.95 (*0-471-95158-7*) Wiley.

Stochastic Programming. Vyacheslav V. Kolbin. Tr. by Igor P. Grigoryev. (Theory & Decision Library: No. 14). 1977. lib. bdg. 88.00 (*90-277-0750-2*) Kluwer Ac.

Stochastic Programming. Andras Prekopa. LC 95-10779. (Mathematics & Its Applications Ser.). 554p. (C). 1995. lib. bdg. 289.00 (*0-7923-3482-5*) Kluwer Ac.

Stochastic Programming - Numerical Techniques & Engineering Applications: Proceedings of the 2nd GAMM/IFIP-Workshop on "Stochastic Optimization: Numerical Methods & Technical Applications," Held at the Federal Armed Forces University, Munich, Neubiberg/Munchen, Germany, June 15-17, 1993. GAMM/IFIP-Workshop on "Stochastic Optimization: Numerical Techniques & Technical Applications" Staff. Ed. by Kurt Marti & Peter Kall. LC 95-1413. (Lecture Notes in Economics & Mathematical Systems: Vol. 423). 1995. write for info. (*0-387-58996-1*) Spr-Verlag.

Stochastic Programming Problems with Probability & Quantile Functions: Probability Guaranteed Risk Basic Theory & Application. Andrey I. Kibzun & Yuri S. Kan. 300p. 1996. text ed. 64.95 (*0-471-95815-8*) Wiley.

Stochastic Programming with Multiple Objective Functions. I. M. Stancu-Minasian. 1985. lib. bdg. 159.00 (*90-277-1714-1*) Kluwer Ac.

***Stochastic Programming '84, 2 vols.** Ed. by Roger J. Wets & A. Prekopa. Incl. Stochastic Programming '84. viii, 190p. 1986. text ed. (*0-444-87991-9*, North Holland); Vol. 2. Stochastic Programming '84. viii, 182p. 1986. pap. text ed. (*0-444-87992-7*, North Holland); 92.50 (*0-7204-1355-9*, North Holland) Elsevier.

Stochastic Programming '84 see Stochastic Programming '84

Stochastic Project Networks: Temporal Analysis, Scheduling & Cost Minimization. K. Neumann. (Lecture Notes in Economics & Mathematical Systems Ser.: Vol. 344). (Illus.). xii, 237p. 1990. 34.00 (*0-387-52664-1*) Spr-Verlag.

Stochastic Quantization. P. Damgaard & H. Huffel. 508p. (C). 1988. text ed. 99.00 (*9971-5-0254-2*); pap. text ed. 40.00 (*9971-5-0298-4*) World Scientific Pub.

Stochastic Quantization. Mikio Namiki et al. Ed. by W. Beiglbock et al. LC 92-17584. (Lecture Notes in Physics, New Series, Monographs: Vol. M9). (Illus.). x, 217p. 1992. 58.95 (*0-387-55563-3*) Spr-Verlag.

Stochastic Quantum Mechanics & Quantum Spacetime. Eduard Prugovecki. 1984. lib. bdg. 137.50 (*90-277-1617-X*) Kluwer Ac.

Stochastic Queue Location Problems. S. Zhang. (Tinbergen Institute Research Ser.). 147p. 1992. pap. 25.00 (*90-5170-070-9*, Pub. by Thesis Pubs NE) IBD Ltd.

Stochastic Simulation. Brian D. Ripley. LC 86-15728. (Probabilty & Mathematical Statistics Ser.). 237p. 1987. text ed. 84.95 (*0-471-81884-4*) Wiley.

***Stochastic Simulation in Physics.** P. K. MacKeown. LC 97-10647. 1997. write for info. (*981-3083-26-3*) Spr-Verlag.

Stochastic Space-Time Models & Limit Theories. Ed. by L. Arnold & P. Kotelenz. (Mathematics & Its Applications Ser.). 1985. lib. bdg. 129.50 (*90-277-2038-X*) Kluwer Ac.

Stochastic Spatial Processes. Ed. by P. Tautu. (Lecture Notes in Mathematics Ser.: Vol. 1212). viii, 311p. 1986. 53.95 (*0-387-16803-6*) Spr-Verlag.

Stochastic Stability of Differential Equations. 2nd ed. R. Z. Has'Minskii. 360p. 1980. lib. bdg. 135.00 (*90-286-0100-7*) Kluwer Ac.

Stochastic Storage Processes: Queues, Insurance Risk & Dams. N. U. Prabhu. (Applications of Mathematics Ser.: Vol. 15). 140p. 1980. 69.95 (*0-387-90522-7*) Spr-Verlag.

Stochastic Structural Dynamics Two: New Practical Applications. Ed. by I. Elishakoff & Y. K. Lin. xiii, 351p. 1991. 104.95 (*0-387-54168-3*) Spr-Verlag.

Stochastic Structural Dynamics 1: New Theoretical Developments. Ed. by Y. K. Lin & I. Elishakoff. xiii, 356p. 1991. 106.95 (*0-387-54167-5*) Spr-Verlag.

Stochastic Structural Mechanics. Ed. by Y. K. Lin & G. I. Schueller. (Lecture Notes in Engineering Ser.: Vol. 31). xi, 507p. 1987. pap. 79.00 (*0-387-18463-5*) Spr-Verlag.

Stochastic Subsurface Hydrology. Lynn W. Gelhar. LC 93-9519. 390p. (C). 1993. text ed. 84.00 (*0-13-846767-6*) P-H.

Stochastic System Reliability Modeling. Shunji Osaki. (Series in Modern Applied Mathematics: Vol. 5). 300p. 1985. text ed. 44.00 (*9971-978-56-3*) World Scientific Pub.

Stochastic Systems for Engineers: Modelling, Filtering & Control. John A. Borrie. 350p. 1992. pap. text ed. 53.00 (*0-13-847351-X*) P-H.

Stochastic Theory & Adaptive Control. Ed. by T. E. Duncan & B. Pasik-Duncan. LC 92-27045. (Lecture Notes in Control & Information Sciences Ser.: Vol. 184). 1992. 133.95 (*0-387-55962-0*) Spr-Verlag.

Stochastic Theory of Service Systems. L. Kosten. LC 72-10124. 180p. (C). 1973. 80.00 (*0-08-016948-1*, Pub. by Pergamon Repr UK) Franklin.

Stochastic Transport Processes in Discrete Biological Systems. E. Frehland. (Lecture Notes in Biomathematics Ser.: Vol. 47). 169p. 1982. pap. 25.40 (*0-387-11964-7*) Spr-Verlag.

Stochastic Two-Stage Programming. Karl Frauendorfer. LC 92-31170. (Lecture Notes in Economics & Mathematical Systems Ser.: Vol. 392). 1992. 48.00 (*0-387-56097-1*) Spr-Verlag.

Stochastic Visibility in Random Fields. S. Zacks. (Lecture Notes in Statistics Ser.: Vol. 95). xii, 178p. 1994. 48.95 (*0-387-94412-5*) Spr-Verlag.

Stochastic vs. Fuzzy Approaches to Multiobjective Mathematical Programming under Uncertainty. Ed. by Roman Slowinski & Jacques Teghem. (Theory & Decision Library: Pt. D). 440p. 1990. lib. bdg. 193.00 (*0-7923-0887-5*) Kluwer Ac.

Stochastic Wave Propagation. Kazimierz Sobczyk. (Fundamental Studies in Engineering: Vol. 6). 1985. 160.00 (*0-444-99614-1*) Elsevier.

Stochastically Dependent Equations. P. R. Fisk. (Griffin's Statistical Monographs: No. 21). 110p. 1967. pap. 22.95 (*0-85264-177-X*) Lubrecht & Cramer.

Stochasticity & Intramolecular Redistribution of Energy. Ed. by R. Lefebvre & S. Mukamel. (C). 1987. lib. bdg. 143.00 (*90-277-2462-8*) Kluwer Ac.

Stochasticity & Partial Order. Peter M. Alberti & Armin Uhlmann. 1982. lib. bdg. 78.00 (*90-277-1350-2*) Kluwer Ac.

Stochasticity & Quantum Chaos: Proceedings of the 3rd Max Born Symposium, Sobotka Castle, September 15-17, 1993. Third Max Born Symposium Staff. Ed. by Wojciech Cegla et al. LC 94-39755. (Mathematics & Its Applications Ser.: Vol. 317). 232p. (C). 1995. lib. bdg. 118.50 (*0-7923-3230-X*) Kluwer Ac.

Stochasticity Research in the U. S. S. R. The Novosibirsk Institute of Nuclear Physics. Samuel Heifets. Ed. by Maureen Young. 161p. (Orig.). 1984. pap. text ed. 75.00 (*1-55831-018-5*) Delphic Associates.

Stochastics, Algebra & Analysis in Classical & Quantum Dynamics. Ed. by Sergio A. Albeverio et al. (C). 1990. lib. bdg. 137.50 (*0-7923-0637-6*) Kluwer Ac.

Stochastics & Quantum Mechanics: Swansea, Summer 1990. Ed. by A. Truman & I. M. Davies. LC 92-10264. 300p. 1993. text ed. 95.00 (*981-02-1015-9*) World Scientific Pub.

Stochastics in Combinatorial Optimization. Ed. by G. Andretta et al. 272p. (C). 1988. text ed. 89.00 (*9971-5-0456-1*) World Scientific Pub.

Stock Assessment: Quantitative Methods & Applications for Small Scale Fisheries. Vincent F. Gallucci et al. 544p. 1995. 69.95 (*1-56670-151-1*, L1151) Lewis Pubs.

Stock Assessment in Inland Fisheries. Ian Cowx. LC 97-14109. 288p. (Orig.). 1996. pap. text ed. 110.00 (*0-85238-244-8*) Blackwell Sci.

Stock Assessment in Inland Fisheries. Ed. by Ian G. Cowx. 288p. 1996. 99.95 (*0-85238-224-3*) Blackwell Sci.

Stock Car Chassis Technology. Steve Smith. (Illus.). 144p. (Orig.). 1983. pap. text ed. 14.95 (*0-936834-39-0*) S S Autosports.

S

An Asterisk (*) at the beginning of an entry indicates that the title is appearing in BIP for the first time.

Stock Car Dirt Track Technology. Steve Smith. (Illus.). 144p. (Orig.). 1993. pap. text ed. 16.95 (*0-936834-96-X*) S S Autosports.

Stock Car Drivers & Tracks: Featuring NASCAR's Greatest Drivers! Ken Spooner. LC 96-68446. (Illus.). 128p. (Orig.). (J). (gr. 4 up). 1996. pap. 6.95 (*1-887654-05-4*) Premium Pr TN.

Stock Car Fun & Games: Puzzles, Word Games, & More! George C. Schnitzer, Jr. LC 96-68447. 128p. (Orig.). (J). (gr. 4 up). 1996. pap. 6.95 (*1-887654-07-0*) Premium Pr TN.

Stock Car Legends: The Laughs, Practical Jokes, & Fun Stories from Racing's Greats! Ronda J. Martin. LC 94-68978. 128p. 1994. reprint ed. pap. 6.95 (*0-9637733-5-6*) Premium Pr TN.

Stock Car Racing. Dick Berggren. (Illus.). 80p. 1995. 9.98 (*0-8317-7731-1*) Smithmark.

Stock Car Racing. Michael Dregni. LC 93-44568. (Motorsports Ser.). (J). 1994. 17.80 (*1-56065-206-3*) Capstone Pr.

***Stock Car Racing.** Michael Dregni. (Motorsports Ser.). (Illus.). 48p. (J). (gr. 3-6). 1994. 18.40 (*0-516-35206-7*) Childrens.

***Stock Car Racing Chassis: Design, Theory, Construction.** Steve Smith. (Illus.). 32p. (Orig.). 1975. pap. text ed. 8.95 (*0-936834-01-3*) S S Autosports.

***Stock Car Racing Collectibles: Fifty Years of NASCAR Memorabilia.** Ken Breslauer. (Illus.). 144p. (Orig.). 1997. pap. 24.95 (*0-9649722-5-5*, SCRC) D Bull.

Stock Car Racing Encyclopedia. Greg Fielden. LC 96-52887. 1997. 39.95 (*0-02-860859-3*) Macmillan.

Stock Car Spectacular. Michael Benson. (Illus.). 96p. 1995. 14.99 (*0-517-12236-7*) Random Hse Value.

Stock Car Trivia Encyclopedia: The ABC's of Racing! Keith Buchanan. LC 96-68427. 128p. (Orig.). (J). (gr. 4 up). 1996. pap. 6.95 (*1-887654-10-0*) Premium Pr TN.

Stock Cars. Jesse Young. (Cruisin' Ser.). 48p. (J). (gr. 3-4). 1994. lib. bdg. 17.80 (*1-56065-223-3*) Capstone Pr.

***Stock Cars.** Jesse Young. (Cruisin' Ser.). (Illus.). 48p. (J). (gr. 3-6). 1995. 18.40 (*0-516-35223-7*) Childrens.

Stock Clerk. Jack Rudman. (Career Examination Ser.: C-2617). 1994. pap. 23.95 (*0-8373-2617-6*) Nat Learn.

Stock Control Clerk see Gregg Office Job Training Program, Classroom Installation

Stock Control in Manufacturing Industries. A. B. Thomas. 221p. (C). 1980. 125.00 (*0-685-39890-0*, Pub. by Inst Pur & Supply UK) St Mut.

Stock Control in Manufacturing Industries. Adin B. Thomas. 221p. (C). 1989. 120.00 (*0-685-36162-4*) St Mut.

Stock Control Practice Set. Fred C. Archer et al. 1969. text ed. 12.96 (*0-07-002176-7*) McGraw.

Stock Control Systems & Records. B. Bailey & S. Storey. 132p. (C). 1984. 300.00 (*0-685-39888-9*, Pub. by Inst Pur & Supply UK) St Mut.

Stock de Coque. Herge. (Illus.). 62p. (SPA.). (J). 19.95 (*0-8288-5077-1*) Fr & Eur.

Stock Drive Products Handbook of Commercial Drive Components. Stock Drive Products Engineers Staff & Ferdinand Freudenstein. 520p. 1971. pap. 1.75 (*0-686-01078-7*) Stock Drive.

Stock Exchange & EEC Law: Commentary. Ed. by Martijn Van Empel. (Amsterdam Financial Ser.). 1991. ring bd. write for info. (*90-6544-949-3*) Kluwer Law Tax Pubs.

Stock Exchange Automation. Jamal Munshi. LC 94-483. (Financial Sector of the American Economy Ser.). 104p. 1994. text ed. 37.00 (*0-8153-1702-6*) Garland.

Stock Exchange Dictionary: Estonian - Finnish - English - German - Russian. U. Liivaku & U. Mereste. 217p. (EST, FIN & GER.). 1994. 125.50 (*951-640-664-5*) IBD Ltd.

Stock Exchange from Within. William C. Van Antwerp. LC 75-2679. (Wall Street & the Security Market Ser.). (Illus.). 1975. reprint ed. 40.95 (*0-405-07241-4*) Ayer.

Stock Exchange Practices: Proceedings of the Committee on Banking & Currency, U. S. Senate, 1934. Banking & Currency Committee. LC 75-2678. (Wall Street & the Security Market Ser.). 1975. reprint ed. 34.95 (*0-405-07240-6*) Ayer.

Stock Exchange Reporting. Dudley Hilton & Isobel Sharp. 202p. 1994. pap. text ed. 90.00 (*0-406-50214-5*, UK) MICHIE.

Stock Exchange Securities: An Essay on the General Causes of Fluctuation in Their Prices. Robert Giffen. LC 68-9574. (Reprints of Economic Classics Ser.). viii, 163p. 1968. reprint ed. 35.00 (*0-678-00423-4*) Kelley.

Stock Illustration Source: SIS. Ian Gunn. (Illus.). 272p. pap. 14.95 (*0-9635582-0-X*) Stock Illus.

Stock Illustration Source: SIS 1. 2nd ed. Ed. by Ian Gunn. (Illus.). 272p. 1994. pap. write for info. (*0-9635582-1-8*) Stock Illus.

Stock Illustration Source: SIS 2. Ed. by Ian Gunn. (Illus.). (Orig.). student ed. write for info. (*0-9635582-2-6*) Stock Illus.

Stock in Trade: A Guide to the World & Work of Wall Street. 235p. 1992. pap. 29.95 (*0-7931-0356-8*, 39010201) Dearborn Finan.

***Stock Index Futures.** 2nd ed. Charles Sutcliffe. 512p. 1997. 79.95 (*1-86152-092-1*, Pub. by Intl Thomson Busn UK) Inter Thomson.

Stock Index Futures: Theories & International Evidence. Charles M. Sutcliffe. LC 92-34660. 456p. 1993. pap. 45.00 (*0-412-40940-2*) Chapman & Hall.

Stock Index Futures & Options. Miller. 1992. text ed. 39.95 (*0-07-707686-9*) McGraw.

Stock Index Options: How to Use & Profit from Indexed Options in Volatile & Uncertain Markets. rev. ed. Scot G. Barenblat & Donald T. Mesler. 230p. 1991. 29.95 (*1-55738-181-X*) Irwin Prof Pubng.

Stock Life Insurance Company Profitability & Workable Competition. S. Travis Pritchett & Ronald P. Wilder. LC 85-61668. (S. S. Huebner Foundation Monographs: No. 14). (Illus.). 1986. pap. 20.95 (*0-918930-14-6*) Huebner Foun Insur.

Stock Market. R. J. Farrell & E. D. Brody. 1996. write for info. (*0-8129-2641-2*, Times Bks) Random.

Stock Market. Clifford F. Pratten. LC 93-2761. (Department of Applied Economics, Occasional Papers: No. 59). (Illus.). 220p. (C). 1993. text ed. 44.95 (*0-521-44065-3*) Cambridge U Pr.

Stock Market. 6th ed. Richard J. Teweles et al. LC 92-3778. 576p. 1992. text ed. 49.95 (*0-471-54019-6*) Wiley.

Stock Market: Theories & Evidence. 2nd ed. James H. Lorie et al. 192p. (C). 1984. pap. text ed. 36.95 (*0-256-01917-7*) Irwin.

***Stock Market Analysis Using the SAS System: Portfolio Selection & Evaluation.** 259p. (C). 1994. pap. 39.95 (*1-55544-623-X*) SAS Inst.

Stock Market Analysis Using the SAS System: Technical Analysis. 200p. (C). 1995. pap. 39.95 (*1-55544-222-6*, BR55217) SAS Inst.

Stock Market & Economic Efficiency. William J. Baumol. LC 65-24469. (Moorhouse I.X. Millar Lecture Ser.: No. 6). 109p. reprint ed. pap. 31.10 (*0-7837-5881-2*, 2045601) Bks Demand.

Stock Market & Finance from a Physicist's Viewpoint. M. F. Osborne. LC 95-69502. (Illus.). 381p. (Orig.). 1996. pap. 19.95 (*0-9646292-0-8*) Crossgar Pr.

Stock Market & Investment Business. 4th ed. Linner. 1995. pap. text ed. 30.60 (*0-13-367517-3*) P-H.

Stock Market & Me: An Independent Approach to Wall Street. Albert A. Spohler. LC 74-78226. 1974. 7.95 (*0-9606580-0-9*) A A Spohler.

Stock Market Barometer. William P. Hamilton. LC 93-72200. 349p. 1993. reprint ed. pap. 21.00 (*0-87034-111-1*) Fraser Pub Co.

Stock Market Barometer: A Study of Its Forecast Value Based on Charles H. Dow's Theory of the Price Movement, with an Analysis of the Market & Its History since 1897. William P. Hamilton. LC 89-60257. xiv, 354p. 1990. reprint ed. 45.00 (*1-55888-806-3*) Omnigraphics Inc.

Stock Market Crash of Nineteen Twenty-Nine. Nancy M. Davies. LC 92-23310. (American Events Ser.). (Illus.). 96p. (YA). (gr. 6 up). 1994. lib. bdg. 14.95 (*0-02-726221-9*, New Dscvry Bks) Silver Burdett Pr.

Stock Market Crash of October 1987: Federal Documents & Materials on the Stock Market & Stock Index Futures Markets, 2 vols. Bernard D. Reams, Jr. LC 88-81970. 2100p. 1988. lib. bdg. 180.00 (*0-89941-656-X*, 305650) W S Hein.

Stock Market Crash of October 1987: Federal Documents & Materials on the Volatility of the Stock Market & Stock Index Futures Markets, 6 vols., Set. Ed. by Bernard D. Reams, Jr. LC 88-81970. (Federal Legislative Histories of Law of Economics Ser.: Pt. 2). 1994. suppl. ed. 750.00 (*0-89941-909-7*, 308520) W S Hein.

Stock Market Crashes & Speculative Manias. Ed. by Eugene N. White. LC 96-5316. (International Library of Macroeconomic & Financial History: No. 13). 584p. 1996. 185.00 (*1-85278-559-4*) E Elgar.

Stock Market Explained for Young Investors: The Perfect Stock Market Start-up Kit for Any High School or College Student. Clayton P. Fisher. (Illus.). 180p. (YA). (gr. 9 up). 1995. 17.95 (*0-931133-02-5*, Busn Class) Pac Pub Grp.

Stock Market Forecasting for Alert Investors. John C. Touhey. LC 80-12878. (Illus.). 192p. reprint ed. pap. 54.80 (*0-317-09362-2*, 2051611) Bks Demand.

Stock Market Illusionology: Block-Volume Reversal, the Stock Specialist Theory. Anthony Campos. LC 87-62182. 75p. (Orig.). 1990. pap. 24.95 (*0-944527-00-0*) Wall St Inquirer.

Stock Market in India: Policy & Action Model for Making Money. D. R. Veena. 1988. 28.00 (*81-7024-181-2*, Pub. by Ashish II) S Asia.

Stock Market Logic: A Sophisticated Approach to Profits on Wall Street. Norman G. Fosback. LC 76-28826. (Illus.). 1986. 40.00 (*0-917604-48-2*) Inst Econometric.

***Stock Market Miracle.** Catskill Eagle Staff. (Illus.). 316p. 1997. text ed. 39.99 (*0-9657156-1-2*) Catskill Eagle.

***Stock Market Miracles.** Wade Cook. 1996. 24.95 (*0-910019-71-1*) Lghthse Pub Gp.

Stock Market Primer. rev. ed. Claude N. Rosenberg. 1991. pap. 14.99 (*0-446-38718-5*) Warner Bks.

Stock Market Probability: Using Statistics to Predict & Optimize Investment Outcomes. 2nd rev. ed. Joseph E. Murphy. 1994. text ed. 37.50 (*1-55738-564-5*) Irwin Prof Pubng.

Stock Market Profits. R. W. Schabacker. LC 67-18536. 1967. reprint ed. pap. 21.00 (*0-87034-022-0*) Fraser Pub Co.

Stock Market Quotations. Sophronia Tibbs. Ed. by Leonard Hatch. (Illus.). 72p. 1995. reprint ed. pap. 11.00 (*0-87034-122-7*) Fraser Pub Co.

Stock Market Rules: Fifty of the Most Widely Held Investment Axioms. Michael D. Sheimo. 1993. per. 18.95 (*1-55738-525-4*) Irwin Prof Pubng.

Stock Market Secrets: How Even a Rookie Can Make Big Money in the Market! Michelle Borzillo. 133p. (Orig.). 1995. pap. 12.95 (*0-9648582-0-7*) Old Twn Pr.

Stock Market Strategy. C. E. Anderson. 280p. (Orig.). 1993. pap. 17.95 (*0-9618383-3-7*) GN Inc.

Stock Market Structure, Volatility, & Volume. Hans R. Stoll & Robert E. Whaley. (Orig.). 1990. pap. 20.00 (*0-943205-08-5*) ICFARF.

Stock Market Technique, No. 1. Richard D. Wyckoff. LC 84-80545. 120p. 1984. reprint ed. pap. 12.00 (*0-87034-070-0*) Fraser Pub Co.

Stock Market Technique, No. 2. Richard D. Wyckoff. LC 84-80545. 210p. 1989. reprint ed. pap. 17.00 (*0-87034-093-X*) Fraser Pub Co.

Stock Market Trading Systems. Gerald Appel & Fred Hitschler. 208p. 1990. reprint ed. 29.00 (*0-934380-16-3*, 7) Traders Pr.

Stock Market Values & Yields, 1993. rev. ed. Research Institute of America, Inc. Staff. 192p. 1993. pap. text ed. 19.50 (*0-7811-0065-8*) Res Inst Am.

Stock Market Values, January 1, 1994. rev. ed. Research Institute of America Staff. 195p. 1994. pap. text ed. 19.50 (*0-7811-0083-6*) Res Inst Am.

Stock Market 101. Clark Holloway. LC 95-46384. 264p. (Orig.). 1996. pap. 14.95 (*0-87573-068-X*) Jain Pub Co.

Stock Markets & the Securities Industry: Law & Practice. 3rd ed. R. Baxt et al. 1988. Australia. pap. 61.00 (*0-409-49467-4*, A.T.) MICHIE.

Stock Markets of the Arab World. Ayman S. Abdul-Hadi. 208p. (C). 1988. lib. bdg. 52.50 (*0-415-00335-0*) Routledge.

Stock Movements & Speculation. 2nd ed. Frederic D. Bond. LC 75-871. (Wall Street & the Security Market Ser.). 1975. reprint ed. 25.95 (*0-405-07248-1*) Ayer.

Stock of Available Reality: R. P. Blackmur & John Berryman. James D. Bloom. LC 83-45489. 216p. 1984. 32.50 (*0-8387-5066-4*) Bucknell U Pr.

Stock Options. Jeffrey B. Little & Lucien Rhodes. 32p. 1977. pap. 2.95 (*0-89709-009-8*, 30009P) McGraw-Hill Prof.

***Stock Options: An Employee Primer.** James J. Pearce. 128p. (Orig.). 1997. pap. 24.95 (*0-9640133-7-1*) Rhapsody.

***Stock Options Book: How You Can Use Broad-Based Employee Stock Option Plans & Related Programs to Attract, Reward, Motivate, & Retain Employees.** Ed. by Scott S. Rodrick. 234p. (Orig.). Date not set. pap. text ed. 35.00 (*0-926902-34-2*) NCEO.

Stock Perqs Monitor: A Guide to Popular Benefits for Shareholders of America's Leading Businesses. Ed. by Michael Brooks. LC 94-79879. 400p. (Orig.). 1998. ring bd. 150.00 incl. disk (*0-9641544-3-9*, SPM-P1) Monitor Pubns.

Stock Perqs Monitor - a Guide to Popular Benefits: For Shareholders of America's Leading Businesses. rev. ed. Ed. by Michael Brooks. LC 94-79879. 400p. (Orig.). 1998. ring bd. 90.00 (*0-9641544-1-2*, SPM-B1) Monitor Pubns.

Stock Photo Deskbook. 5th ed. Ed. by Robert S. Persky. 360p. 1995. pap. 39.95 (*0-913069-43-4*) Consultant Pr.

Stock Photo Forms. Michal Heron. 32p. 1991. pap. 9.95 (*0-9607118-8-0*) Allworth Pr.

***Stock Photo Smart.** Joe Farace. (Illus.). 144p. 1997. 39.99 (*1-56496-381-0*) Rockport Pubs.

Stock Photographer's Marketing Guide. Richard J. Persson. (Illus.). (Orig.). 1984. pap. 2.50 (*0-9608486-0-6*) R J Persson Ent.

Stock Photographs: The Fort Worth Fat Stock Show & Rodeo. Garry Winogrand & Ron Tyler. (Illus.). 128p. 1980. 24.95 (*0-292-72433-0*) U of Tex Pr.

Stock Photography: The Complete Guide. Ann Purcell & Carl Purcell. 144p. 1993. pap. 19.95 (*0-89879-552-4*, Wrtrs Digest Bks) F & W Pubns Inc.

***Stock Photography Business Forms: Everything You Need to Succeed in Stock Photography.** Michal Heron. 128p. (Orig.). 1997. pap. 18.95 (*1-880559-70-6*) Allworth Pr.

Stock Pickers, Pocket Pickers: How to Invest in Wall Street. Lin Oh. Ed. by Charlotte St. John. 160p. (Orig.). Date not set. pap. 20.00 (*0-89896-201-3*, Better Life Bks) Larksdale.

Stock Picking: The Eleven Best Tactics for Beating the Market. Richard J. Maturi. LC 93-36. 1993. pap. text ed. 14.95 (*0-07-040938-2*) McGraw.

Stock Preparation Short Course, Chicago, April 13-15, 1988. Technical Association of the Pulp & Paper Industry Staff. (TAPPI Notes Ser.). (Illus.). 127p. reprint ed. pap. 36.20 (*0-685-44403-1*, 2032270) Bks Demand.

Stock Preparation Short Course, 1990: Westin Peachtree Plaza, Atlanta, GA, April 25-27. Technical Association of the Pulp & Paper Industry Staff. (TAPPI Notes Ser.). (Illus.). 133p. reprint ed. pap. 38.00 (*0-8357-4194-X*, 2036972) Bks Demand.

Stock Preparation Short Course, 1992: Opryland Hotel, Nashville, TN, April 8-10. Technical Association of the Pulp & Paper Industry Staff. (TAPPI Notes Ser.). 171p. 1992. reprint ed. pap. 48.80 (*0-7837-2448-9*, 2042597) Bks Demand.

***Stock Preparation Short Course, 1993: San Francisco Marriott, San Francisco, CA, April 27-29.** Technical Association of the Pulp & Paper Industry Staff. (TAPPI Course Notes Ser.). (Illus.). 281p. reprint ed. pap. 80.10 (*0-608-05358-9*, 2082406) Bks Demand.

***Stock Profits & Your Wealthbeing: A Simple, Successful Stock System.** Nanci A. Kelleher. Ed. by Gail Kearns. (Illus.). 144p. (Orig.). 1996. pap. 29.95 (*0-9653516-0-2*) Waterhse Pub.

***Stock Profits & Your Wealthbeing, The Workbook.** Nanci A. Kelleher. 64p. (Orig.). 1996. wbk. ed., spiral bd., pap. 19.95 (*0-9653516-1-0*) Waterhse Pub.

Stock Scenery Construction Handbook. Bill Raoul. 250p. 1991. pap. 12.95 (*0-911747-23-0*) Broadway Pr.

Stock Selector System: How to Build a Stock Portfolio for Profits in Any Market. Michael D. Sheimo. 288p. 1994. text ed. 27.95 (*0-471-57113-X*) Wiley.

***Stock Ships.** (Shatterzone Ser.). 18.00 (*0-87431-244-2*, 21013) West End Games.

Stock Tactics System. Peter Eliason. 72p. (Orig.). 1984. pap. 17.95 (*0-916777-99-5*) W P Allen.

Stock Values & Dividends for 1993 Tax Purposes: Pennsylvania Edition. 344p. 1993. pap. 21.00 (*0-685-67034-1*, 5853) Commerce.

Stock Values & Dividends for 1993 Tax Purposes: Regular Edition. 328p. 1993. pap. 21.00 (*0-685-67036-8*, 5913) Commerce.

Stock Values & Dividends for 1994 Tax Purposes: Pennsylvania Edition. 344p. 1994. pap. 23.00 (*0-685-67033-3*, 5854) Commerce.

Stock Values & Dividends for 1994 Tax Purposes: Regular Edition. 312p. 1994. pap. 23.00 (*0-685-67035-X*, 5914) Commerce.

***Stock Values & Dividends for 1997 Tax Purposes.** CCH Tax Law Editors. 344p. (Orig.). 1997. pap. 29.00 (*0-8080-0140-X*) Commerce.

***Stock Values & Dividends for 1997 Tax Purposes - Including Pennsylvania Tax Status of Bonds.** 336p. 1997. pap. 29.00 (*0-614-26817-6*, 13796BLS04) Commerce.

***Stock Workbook.** (Portfolio of Stock Photography Ser.: No. 10). 1996. 25.00 (*1-887528-13-X*) Scott & Daughters.

Stockbridge (Massachusetts) Sarah C. Sedgwick & Christina Marquand. 306p. 1993. reprint ed. lib. bdg. 35.00 (*0-8328-3538-2*) Higginson Bk Co.

Stockbridge, Past & Present: Or Records of an Old Mission Station. Electa F. Jones. 275p. 1994. reprint ed. lib. bdg. 29.50 (*0-8328-3958-2*) Higginson Bk Co.

Stockbridge Story: Seventeen Thirty-Nine to Nineteen Eighty-Nine. Residents of Stockbridge Staff. (Illus.). 1989. 25.00 (*0-685-27189-7*) Town Stockbridge.

Stockbroker Supervision: Managing Stockbrokers & Surviving Sanctions. Ralph C. Ferrara. 370p. 1990. boxed 79.50 (*0-614-05970-4*) MICHIE.

Stockbroker Supervision: Managing Stockbrokers & Surviving Sanctions. Ralph C. Ferrara et al. 370p. 1990. boxed 79.50 (*0-88063-288-7*) MICHIE.

Stockbroker's Exam Manual, Series No. 7. rev. ed. Jae K. Shim & Yojin Jung. Ed. by Norman Henteleff. 350p. (C). 1996. ring bd. 85.00 (*1-882312-06-6*) Delta Pub CA.

Stockdraw & Emergency Response Policies & Management. 320p. (Orig.). 1994. pap. 82.00 (*92-64-14209-6*, Pub. by Org for Econ FR) OECD.

Stocker on Drawing Wills. 11th ed. Jule E. Stocker & Jonathan J. Rikoon. 565p. 1993. ring bd. 115.00 (*0-614-17127-X*, D1-0162) PLI.

Stocker Probe for Fluency & Language. 3rd ed. Robert Goldfarb & Beatrice Stocker. 64p. 1995. pap. text ed. 75.00 (*0-937857-58-0*, 1370) Speech Bin.

Stockfootage. George LeGrady. (Illus.). 12p. 1984. pap. 10.00 (*0-939784-07-6*) CEPA Gall.

Stockhausen. Robin Maconie. LC 79-56837. (Illus.). 352p. 1981. pap. 20.00 (*0-7145-2706-8*) M Boyars Pubs.

Stockhausen: A Biography. Michael Kurtz. Tr. by Richard Toop. (Illus.). 270p. 1994. pap. 19.95 (*0-571-17146-X*) Faber & Faber.

Stockhausen: Life & Work. Karl H. Worner. Ed. & Tr. by Bill Hopkins. LC 76-174460. (Illus.). 1973. pap. 10.95 (*0-520-03272-1*) U CA Pr.

Stockhausen on Music. Karlheinz Stockhausen. 224p. 1989. 25.00 (*0-7145-2887-0*) M Boyars Pubs.

Stockhausen on Music: Lectures & Interviews. Karlheinz Stockhausen. 220p. 1991. reprint ed. pap. 16.95 (*0-7145-2918-4*) M Boyars Pubs.

Stockholm Pocket Guide: Stockholm. Berlitz Editors. (Pocket Guides Ser.). (Illus.). 136p. 1992. pap. 8.95 (*2-8315-1267-0*) Berlitz.

Stockholm School of Economics Revisited. Ed. by Lars Jonung. (Historical Perspectives on Modern Economics Ser.). (Illus.). 400p. (C). 1991. text ed. 89.95 (*0-521-39127-X*) Cambridge U Pr.

Stockholm Syndicate. Colin Forbes. 321p. (Orig.). 1982. pap. 15.95 (*0-330-26769-8*, Pub. by Pan Books UK) Trans-Atl Phila.

Stockholm Syndicate. large type ed. Colin Forbes. 608p. (Orig.). 1983. 25.99 (*0-7089-0985-X*) Ulverscroft.

Stockholm Syndrome. large type ed. Jonathan Havard. 640p. 1987. 27.99 (*0-7089-8429-0*, Charnwood) Ulverscroft.

Stockholm Township (Wright County Minnesota) Cemeteries. Compiled by Dassel Area Historical Society Staff. LC 94-48710. (Illus.). 32p. 1995. pap. 10.00 (*0-915709-18-X*) Pk Geneal Bk.

Stockholm, 1966 see Chemistry of Natural Products: Proceedings

***Stocking & Introduction of Fish.** I. G. Cowx. LC 97-12908. 1997. write for info. (*0-85238-239-1*) Blackwell Sci.

Stocking the Arsenal: A Guide to the Nation's Top Military Contractors. Linda S. Shaw et al. Ed. by Carolyn Mathiasen. 207p. (Orig.). 1985. pap. text ed. 10.00 (*0-931035-01-5*) IRRC Inc DC.

Stocking Up. 3rd ed. Carol Hupping. 1990. pap. 17.95 (*0-671-69395-6*) S&S Trade.

Stocking Up III. Carol Hupping. (Illus.). 1995. 10.98 (*1-56731-073-7*, MJF Bks) Fine Comms.

Stocking Up III: The All-New Edition of America's Classic Preserving Guide. Carol Hupping & Rodale Press Editors. LC 86-10225. (Illus.). 400p. 1986. 24.95 (*0-87857-613-4*, 09-091-0) Rodale Pr Inc.

***Stocking Your Garden Pond.** Herbert R. Axelrod. (Illus.). 64p. 1997. 12.95 (*0-7938-0221-0*, WW-055) TFH Pubns.

***Stockings of Buttermilk.** Philip. 1997. write for info. (*0-395-84980-2*) Ticknor & Fields.

Stockman. Jack Rudman. (Career Examination Ser.: C-769). 1994. pap. 23.95 (*0-8373-0769-4*) Nat Learn.

Stockman: The Man, the Myth, the Future. Owen Ullmann. 560p. 1987. mass mkt. 4.50 (*0-8217-2005-8*, Zebra Kensgtn) Kensgtn Pub Corp.

Stockman-Gallison Ancestral Lines: 114 Lines of Early New England Settlers & the Descendants, As of 1984 of John Gallison & Martha Moore. Katharine Dickson. LC 84-72376. (Illus.). xxii, 285p. 1985. 30.00 (*0-9613959-0-7*) Brown Katharine.

An Asterisk (*) at the beginning of an entry indicates that the title is appearing in BIP for the first time.

Stockman's Handbook. 7th ed. R. M. Ensminger. 1992. 83.95 (0-8134-2895-5) Interstate.

Stockman's Handbook Digest. M. E. Ensminger. (Illus.). 672p. 1992. 57.25 (0-8134-2896-3); teacher ed. 9.95 (0-8134-2897-1) Interstate.

Stockmanship: Improving the Care of the Pig & Other Livestock. P. R. English et al. (Illus.). 220p. 1992. text ed. 32.95 (0-85236-236-6, Pub. by Farming Pr UK) Diamond Farm Bk.

Stockmanship on the Farm. 1982. 35.00 (0-317-43804-2) St Mut.

Stockport Grammar School, 1487-1987: The Quincentenary History. James Ball & William Ball. 128p. (C). 1982. text ed. 60.00 (0-947818-06-5, Pub. by Old Vicarage UK); pap. text ed. 39.00 (0-947818-05-7, Pub. by Old Vicarage UK) St Mut.

Stockroom Worker. Jack Rudman. (Career Examination Ser.: C-770). 1994. pap. 23.95 (0-8373-0770-8) Nat Learn.

Stocks & Bonds. Abiud Ramos-Ramos. LC 80-20002. (Illus.). 30p. (C). 1980. pap. 2.80 (0-8477-2637-1) U of PR Pr.

***Stocks & Shares.** 2nd ed. Roger Hardman. (Finance & Taxation Ser.). 1989. pap. 10.95 (0-86367-173-X) Kogan Page Ltd.

Stocks, Bonds, Bills & Inflation. 1,988th ed. Roger G. Ibbotson & Rex A. Sinquefield. 224p. 1989. text ed. 45.00 (1-55623-140-7) Irwin Prof Pubng.

Stocks Bonds Bills & Inflation: Year-by-Year Historical Returns (1926-1974) see Stocks Bonds Bills & Inflation 1996 Yearbook: Market Results for 1926-1995

Stocks, Bonds, Bills & Inflation Yearbook, 1994: Market Results for 1926-1993. Ibbotson Associates Staff. (Illus.). 288p. 1994. 50.00 (1-882864-03-4) Ibbotson Assocs.

Stocks, Bonds, Bills & Inflation, 1993 Yearbook: Market Results for 1926 - 1992. Ibbotson Associates Staff. (Illus.). 207p. 1993. 50.00 (1-882864-01-8) Ibbotson Assocs.

Stocks, Bonds, Bills & Inflation 1995 Yearbook: Market Results for 1926-1994. Ibbotson Associates Staff. Ed. by Rita B. Brief. (Illus.). 230p. 1995. 50.00 (1-882864-04-2) Ibbotson Assocs.

***Stocks, Bonds, Bills & Inflation 1996 Yearbook.** Andrew F. Siegel & Skyline Technologies Staff. 1996. per. 92.00 (0-07-413246-6) Irwin.

Stocks Bonds Bills & Inflation 1996 Yearbook: Market Results for 1926-1995. annuals Roger G. Ibbotson et al. Orig. Title: Stocks Bonds Bills & Inflation: Year-by-Year Historical Returns (1926-1974). (Illus.). 320p. 1996. 50.00 (1-882864-05-0) Ibbotson Assocs.

***Stocks, Bonds Bills & Inflation 1997 Yearbook: Market Results for 1926-1996.** rev. ed. Ed. by Paul Kaplan et al. (Illus.). 320p. 1997. lib. bdg. 99.00 (1-882864-06-9) Ibbotson Assocs.

Stocks, Bonds, Options, Futures: Investments & Their Markets. New York Institute of Finance Staff. 1991. pap. 18.95 (0-13-847369-2, Busn) P-H.

Stocks, Bonds, Options, Futures: Investments & Their Markets. NYIF Staff. (Illus.). 320p. 1987. 27.95 (0-13-846718-8) NY Inst Finance.

Stocks for the Long Run: A Guide to Selecting Markets for Long-Term Growth. Jeremy J. Siegel. 336p. 1994. text ed. 29.95 (1-55623-804-5) Irwin Prof Pubng.

Stocktakings from an Apprenticeship. Pierre Boulez. Tr. by Stephen Walsh. (Illus.). 352p. 1991. 90.00 (0-19-311210-8, 7416) OUP.

Stockton: City of the Future. Carmen Spradley. (Illus.). 174p. 1996. 35.00 (1-885352-30-1) Community Comm.

Stockton Springs Vital Records 1859-1891. Ed. by Nancy S. Parsons. LC 79-55454. (Orig.). 1979. pap. 14.95 (0-918768-02-0) Cay-Bel.

Stockton Stock Exchange Yearbook 1995-1996. 1140p. 1996. 425.00 (1-56159-188-2, Stockton Pr) Groves Dictionaries.

***Stockton Stock Exchange Yearbook 1997.** 1200p. 1997. 425.00 (1-56159-217-X) Groves Dictionaries.

Stockton's Historic Public Schools. Robert Bonta & Horace A. Spencer. LC 81-52977. (Illus.). xii, 115p. (C). 1981. 15.00 (0-9607134-0-9) Stockton Unified Schl Dist.

Stockton's Stories, First Series. Frank R. Stockton. LC 74-98597. (Short Story Index Reprint Ser.). 1977. 19.95 (0-8369-3271-4) Ayer.

Stockton's Stories, Second Series. Frank R. Stockton. LC 74-98597. (Short Story Index Reprint Ser.). 1977. 20.95 (0-8369-3172-6) Ayer.

Stockwell Guide for Technical & Vocational Writing. 2nd ed. Richard E. Stockwell. LC 81-3675. (Engineering Technology Ser.). 354p. (C). 1982. student ed. write for info. (0-201-07155-X); pap. text ed. 25.75 (0-201-07154-1) Addison-Wesley.

Stockwell of Minneapolis: The Life & Times of S. A. Stockwell, 1857-1943, a Minnesota Politician. William P. Everts. LC 96-41286. (Illus.). 350p. (Orig.). 1996. pap. 14.95 (0-87839-103-7) North Star.

***Stockworth: American CEO.** Sarah E. Hutchinson & Stacey Sawyer. 240p. 1989. per. 15.00 (0-07-413142-7) Irwin.

Stockworth: An American CEO. Hinda Sterling. 240p. (Orig.). 1989. per. 15.00 (0-89011-600-8) Irwin Prof Pubng.

Stockworth: An American CEO. Hinda Sterling & Herb Selesnick. (Illus.). 240p. (Orig.). 1989. pap. 12.95 (0-9623786-0-7) Sterling & Selesnick.

Stoddard Family: Being Some Account of Some of the Descendants of John Stodder of Hingham, Massachusetts, Colony. F. R. Stoddard, Jr. 148p. 1993. reprint ed. pap. 23.00 (0-8328-3413-0); reprint ed. lib. bdg. 33.00 (0-8328-3412-2) Higginson Bk Co.

Stoddard-Sudduth Papers. M. S. Stoddard. 281p. 1991. reprint ed. pap. 45.00 (0-8328-1944-1); reprint ed. lib. bdg. 55.00 (0-8328-1943-3) Higginson Bk Co.

Stoff-und Motivgeschichte der Deutschen Literatur. 3rd ed. Franz A. Schmitt. (C). 1976. 130.80 (3-11-006506-1) De Gruyter.

***Stogies & Stilletos: A Woman's Guide to Cigar Smoking, Vol. 2.** Rhona Kasper. (Illus.). 72p. (Orig.). 1997. mass mkt. 6.95 (0-9652959-1-5) Cigar Savvy.

Stoic, Christian & Humanist. Gilbert Murray. LC 75-99712. (Essay Index Reprint Ser.). 1977. 19.95 (0-8369-1363-9) Ayer.

Stoic Comedians: Flaubert, Joyce & Beckett. Hugh Kenner. (Illus.). 1974. reprint ed. pap. 9.95 (0-520-02584-9) U CA Pr.

Stoic Creed. William L. Davidson. Ed. by Gregory Vlastos. LC 78-19341. (Morals & Law in Ancient Greece Ser.). 1979. reprint ed. lib. bdg. 33.95 (0-405-11535-0) Ayer.

Stoic Idea of the City. Malcolm Schofield. 170p. (C). 1991. 49.95 (0-521-39470-8) Cambridge U Pr.

Stoic Logic. Benson Mates. LC 53-9918. (California University Publications in Philosophy: Vol. 26). 156p. reprint ed. pap. 44.50 (0-317-10250-8, 2021174) Bks Demand.

Stoic Philosophy. John M. Rist. LC 79-85736. 1977. pap. 22.95 (0-521-29201-8) Cambridge U Pr.

Stoic Studies. A. A. Long. 326p. (C). 1996. text ed. 59.95 (0-521-48263-1) Cambridge U Pr.

Stoic Theory of Oikeiosis: Moral Development & Social Interaction in Early Stoic Philosophy. Troels Engberg-Pedersen. Ed. by Per Bilde et al. (Studies in Hellenistic Civilization: No. 2). 278p. (C). 1990. text ed. 27.00 (87-7288-323-5, Pub. by Aarhus Univ Pr DK) David Brown.

Stoic Tradition from Antiquity to the Early Middle Ages, Vol. 1: Stoicism in Classical Latin Literature. 2nd ed. Marcia L. Colish. LC 90-46844. xii, 459p. 1990. reprint ed. pap. 64.25 (90-04-09327-3) E J Brill.

Stoic Tradition from Antiquity to the Early Middle Ages, Vol. 2: Stoicism in Christian Latin Thought Through the Sixth Century. 2nd ed. Marcia L. Colish. LC 90-46844. xii, 342p. 1990. reprint ed. pap. 50.50 (90-04-09328-1) E J Brill.

Stoichedon Style in Greek Inscriptions. Reginald P. Austin. LC 72-7884. (Greek History Ser.). 1979. reprint ed. 18.95 (0-405-04778-9) Ayer.

Stoichiometry & Kinetics of Microbial Growth. S. John Pirt. (Pirtferm Papers). (C). 1994. 75.00 (1-874685-20-7, Pub. by Pirtferm Ltd UK) St Mut.

***Stoichiometry & Thermodynamics of Metallurgical Process.** Y. K. Rao. 976p. (C). 1996. reprint ed. text ed. 80.00 (1-878907-92-1, RAN) TechBooks.

Stoichiometry in Crystal Compounds & Its Influence on Their Physical Properties. Ed. by Yu M. Popov. (Proceedings of the Lebedev Physics Institute Ser.: Vol. 177). 303p. 1988. text ed. 130.00 (0-941743-21-7) Nova Sci Pubs.

Stoichiometry of the Reaction of Magnesium with Hydrochloric Acid. J. N. Spencer & H. Anthony Neidig. (Modular Laboratory Program in Chemistry Ser.). 12p. (C). 1989. pap. text ed. 1.35 (0-87540-369-7, STOI 369-7) Chem Educ Res.

Stoiciens: 1, Cleanthe; 2, Les Doctrines; 3, Les Directeurs de Conscience. 1512p. 45.00 (0-686-56575-4) Fr & Eur.

Stoicism. William W. Capes. 1976. lib. bdg. 59.95 (0-8490-2669-5) Gordon Pr.

Stoicism. S. George Stock. LC 75-38367. (Select Bibliographies Reprint Ser.). 1977. reprint ed. 16.95 (0-8369-6784-4) Ayer.

Stoicism in Major English Poets of the Nineteenth Century. Evelyn A. Hanley. LC 64-23596. 215p. (C). 1964. reprint ed. text ed. 75.00 (0-8383-0563-6) M S G Haskell Hse.

Stoicism in Renaissance English Literature: An Introduction. Audrey Chew. (American University Studies: English Language & Literature: Ser. IV, Vol. 82). 340p. (C). 1988. text ed. 41.25 (0-8204-0730-5) P Lang Pubng.

Stoicorum Veterum Fragmenta, 4 vols., Set. J. Von Arnim. (Classical Studies Ser.). 1054p. (GRE & LAT.). 1986. reprint ed. lib. bdg. 177.00 (0-89197-950-6) Irvington.

Stoicorum Veterum Fragmenta, 4 vols., Vols. 1 & 2. J. Von Arnim. (Classical Studies Ser.). 1054p. (GRE & LAT.). 1986. reprint ed. Vol. 1 & 2. lib. bdg. 88.50 (0-8290-1775-5) Irvington.

Stoicorum Veterum Fragmenta, 4 vols., Vols. 3 & 4. J. Von Arnim. (Classical Studies Ser.). 1054p. (GRE & LAT.). 1986. reprint ed. Vol. 3 & 4. lib. bdg. 88.50 (0-8290-1776-3) Irvington.

Stoics. F. H. Sandbach. 192p. (C). 1994. reprint ed. pap. text ed. 12.95 (0-87220-253-4); reprint ed. lib. bdg. 32.95 (0-87220-254-2) Hackett Pub.

Stoics & Neostoics: Rubens & the Circle of Lipsius. Mark Morford. (Illus.). 256p. 1991. text ed. 49.50 (0-691-04081-8) Princeton U Pr.

***Stoics & Saints.** James B. Brown. 296p. Date not set. 20.95 (0-8369-2936-5) Ayer.

Stoics & Sceptics. E. R. Bevan. 152p. 1980. reprint ed. pap. 15.00 (0-89005-364-2) Ares.

Stoics & Sceptics. Edwyn R. Bevan. Ed. by Gregory Vlastos. LC 78-15852. (Morals & Law in Ancient Greece Ser.). 1979. reprint ed. lib. bdg. 25.95 (0-405-11530-X) Ayer.

Stoics, Epicureans & Sceptics. R. W. Sharples. LC 95-26248. 176p. (C). 1996. pap. 16.95 (0-415-11035-1); text ed. 49.95 (0-415-11034-3) Routledge.

Stoics, Epicureans & Skeptics. Edward Zeller. 1973. 75.00 (0-8490-1125-6) Gordon Pr.

Stoics on Ambiguity. Catherine Atherton. LC 92-2469. (Classical Studies). 566p. (C). 1993. text ed. 90.00 (0-521-44139-0) Cambridge U Pr.

Stoke-by-Clare Cartulary I. Ed. by Christopher Harper-Bill & Richard Mortimer. (Suffolk Charters Ser.: No. IV). 160p. 1982. 39.00 (0-85115-165-5) Boydell & Brewer.

Stoke-by-Clare Cartulary II. Ed. by Christopher Harper-Bill & Richard Mortimer. (Suffolk Charters Ser.: No. V). 276p. 1983. 39.00 (0-85115-179-5) Boydell & Brewer.

Stoke-by-Clare Cartulary III. Christopher Harper-Bill & Richard Mortimer. 125p. 1984. 39.00 (0-85115-198-1) Boydell & Brewer.

Stoked. William Morris. 350p. 1994. pap. 19.95 (0-9639775-0-4) New Sun Pubns.

***Stoked: A History of Surf Culture.** Drew Kampion. 1997. 29.95 (1-57544-062-8) Genl Pub Grp.

Stokely Carmichael: The Story of Black Power. Jacqueline Johnson. Ed. by Richard Gallin. (History of the Civil Rights Movement Ser.). (Illus.). 128p. (J). (gr. 5 up). 1990. lib. bdg. 12.95 (0-382-09920-6) Silver Burdett Pr.

Stokely Carmichael: The Story of Black Power. Jacqueline Johnson. Ed. by Richard Gallin. (History of the Civil Rights Movement Ser.). (Illus.). 128p. (YA). (gr. 5 up). 1990. pap. 7.95 (0-382-24056-1) Silver Burdett Pr.

Stokely Carmichael & Black Power. Robert Cwiklik. LC 92-11560. (Gateway Civil Rights Ser.). (Illus.). 32p. (J). (gr. 2-4). 1993. pap. 4.95 (1-56294-839-3); lib. bdg. 15.40 (1-56294-276-X) Millbrook Pr.

Stokely Webster: Paintings Nineteen Twenty-Three to Nineteen Eighty-Four. Harry Rand. Ed. by Gary R. Libby. LC 85-60099. (Illus.). 104p. (Orig.). 1985. pap. 5.00 (0-933053-00-2) Museum Art Sciences.

Stoker. Franz Kafka. 1976. 18.95 (0-8488-1065-1) Amereon Ltd.

Stokers & Pokers: or The London & North-Western Railway, the Electronic Telegraph & the Railway Clearing House. Francis B. Head. 278p. 1968. 26.00 (0-7146-1440-8, Pub. by F Cass Pubs UK) Intl Spec Bk.

Stokes Beginner's Guide to Birds: Eastern Region. Donald W. Stokes. 144p. 1996. 7.95 (0-316-81811-9) Little.

Stokes Beginner's Guide to Birds: Western Region. Donald W. Stokes. 1996. 7.95 (0-316-81812-7) Little.

***Stokes Carson: Twentieth-Century Trading on the Navajo Reservation.** Willow Roberts. LC 86-19207. (Illus.). 246p. 1987. reprint ed. pap. 70.20 (0-608-04143-2, 2064876) Bks Demand.

Stokes County, N. C. Deeds, 1787-1797, Vols. 1-2. 200p. 1985. pap. 22.50 (0-89308-556-1) Southern Hist Pr.

Stokes County, N. C., Wills, 1790-1864, Vols. 1-4. W. D. Abster. 181p. 1985. pap. 21.50 (0-89308-557-X) Southern Hist Pr.

Stokes County, North Carolina Marriage Bonds & Certificates, 1783-1868, 2 vols., Set. Francis T. Ingmire. 232p. 1994. pap. 30.00 (0-8095-8697-5); lib. bdg. 60.00 (0-8095-8128-0) Borgo Pr.

Stokes Equations. Werner Varnhorn. LC 94-19799. (Mathematical Research Ser.: Vol. 76). 153p. 1994. pap. 40.00 (3-05-501634-3, Pub. by Akademie Verlag GW) Wiley.

Stokes Field Guides to Birds: Eastern Region. Donald W. Stokes & Lillian Q. Stokes. LC 95-6611. (Illus.). 496p. 1996. pap. 16.95 (0-316-81809-7) Little.

Stokes Field Guides to Birds: Western Region. Donald W. Stokes & Lillian Q. Stokes. LC 95-6610. (Illus.). 544p. 1994. pap. 16.95 (0-316-81810-0) Little.

***Stokes Phenomenon & Hilbert's 16th Problem.** 348p. 1996. 41.00 (981-02-2567-9) World Scientific Pub.

***Stokes Purple Martin Book: The Complete Guide to Attracting & Housing Purple Martins.** Donald Stokes et al. (Stokes Backyard Nature Book Ser.). 1997. pap. 11.95 (0-614-27430-3) Little.

***Stoke's Purple Martin Book: The Complete Guide to Attracting & Managing Purple Martins.** Donald W. Stokes et al. LC 96-46179. 1997. 11.95 (0-316-81702-3) Little.

Stokes System in an Infinite Cone. Paul Deuring. (Mathematical Research Ser.: Vol. 78). 267p. 1994. pap. 60.00 (3-05-501639-4, Pub. by Akademie Verlag GW) Wiley.

Stokey: The Story of a Playful Pig. Helen B. King. (Illus.). (J). (gr. 4-8). 1989. vinyl bd. 4.95 (0-9615366-1-6) King ME.

Stol Dolgoe Vozvrashchenie. Ester Markish. LC 84-60572. (Illus.). 320p. (Orig.). (RUS.). 1989. pap. 22.00 (0-89830-084-3) Russica Pubs.

Stole Patterns. Jeff Wedge. LC 85-61216. (Illus.). 82p. (Orig.). 1986. pap. 9.95 (0-8192-1398-5) Morehouse Pub.

Stolen Affections. Carolyn Keene. Ed. by Ruth Ashby. (Nancy Drew Files Ser.: No. 105). 160p. (Orig.). (YA). (gr. 6 up). 1995. mass mkt. 3.99 (0-671-88196-5, Archway) PB.

Stolen Air. Niall Quinn. LC 89-50973. (Illus.). 116p. 1989. 19.95 (0-86327-157-X); pap. 8.95 (0-86327-158-8) Dufour.

Stolen & Contaminated Poems. James Laughlin. 60p. 1985. text ed. 100.00 (0-918824-47-8) Turkey Pr.

Stolen Biography. 2nd ed. Szymon Szechter. Tr. by Frances L. Carroll & Nina Karsov. LC 84-70938. (Illus.). 174p. 8500. 16.95 (0-907652-16-6) Dufour.

Stolen Blessings. Lawrence Sanders. 320p. 1989. mass mkt. 6.99 (0-425-11872-X) Berkley Pub.

Stolen Bride. Jo Beverley. 224p. 1991. mass mkt. 3.99 (0-380-71439-6) Avon.

Stolen Bride. large type ed. Jo Beverley. 335p. 1991. reprint ed. lib. bdg. 18.95 (1-56054-115-6) Thorndike Pr.

Stolen Car: Poems. James Haug. LC 88-39928. 72p. 1989. 17.50 (0-87023-669-5); pap. 9.95 (0-87023-670-9) U of Mass Pr.

Stolen Child. Paul Cody. 233p. 1995. 20.00 (1-880909-30-8) Baskerville.

Stolen Childhood: In Search of the Rights of the Child. Anuradha Vittachi. 200p. 1990. 60.95 (0-7456-0714-4); pap. 24.95 (0-7456-0720-9) Blackwell Pubs.

Stolen Childhood: Slave Youth in Nineteenth-Century America. Wilma King. LC 94-49163. (Illus.). 384p. 1995. 27.95 (0-253-32904-3) Ind U Pr.

Stolen Continents: The Americas Through Indian Eyes Since 1492. Ronald Wright. (Illus.). 448p. 1993. pap. 14.95 (0-395-65975-2) HM.

Stolen Daughter: A Collection of Poems. Linda Anfuso. 25p. 1995. pap. 3.00 (1-57433-012-8) Interset Pr.

Stolen Dreams. Marilyn Campbell. (Innovation in International Law Ser.). 384p. (Orig.). 1994. pap. 4.99 (0-451-40500-5, Topaz) NAL-Dutton.

Stolen Dreams. Libby Sydes. 400p. 1995. mass mkt. 4.99 (0-440-21544-7) Dell.

***Stolen Dreams: Portraits of Working Children.** David L. Parker et al. LC 97-4939. 1997. write for info. (0-8225-2960-2) Lerner Group.

Stolen Ecstasy. Janelle Taylor. 1992. mass mkt. 4.99 (0-8217-3501-2, Zebra Kensgtn) Kensgtn Pub Corp.

Stolen Ecstasy. Janelle Taylor. 1996. pap. 5.99 (0-8217-5455-6) Kensgtn Pub Corp.

Stolen Faces. Michael Bishop. LC 76-26262. 176p. 1977. 25.00 (0-06-010362-0) Ultramarine Pub.

***Stolen Fire.** 1997. mass mkt. 1.00 (0-8217-5734-2) Kensgtn Pub Corp.

Stolen Fire: Selected Poems. Lyubomir Levchev. Tr. by Ewald Osers. LC 85-82112. (Illus.). 105p. 1986. pap. 13.95 (0-948259-04-3, Pub. by Forest Bks UK) Dufour.

Stolen Gods. Jake Page. (Southwest Mysteries Ser.). 272p. 1994. mass mkt. 4.99 (0-345-37929-2) Ballantine.

Stolen Goods. Susan Dworkin. LC 86-28615. 272p. 1991. pap. 3.95 (1-55704-020-6) Newmarket.

Stolen Heart. Kit Gardner. (Historical Ser.). 1993. mass mkt. 3.99 (0-373-28760-7, 1-28760-6) Harlequin Bks.

Stolen Heart. Barbara D. Smith. 1988. pap. 3.95 (0-380-75510-6) Avon.

Stolen Heart. large type ed. Margaret A. Carr. (Linford Romance Library). 1991. pap. 15.99 (0-7089-7105-9) Ulverscroft.

***Stolen Hearts.** Michelle Martin. 304p. 1997. mass mkt. 5.50 (0-553-57648-8, Fanfare) Bantam.

Stolen Hearts. Melinda McRae. (Historical Romance Ser.). 384p. 1995. mass mkt. 5.50 (0-451-40611-7, Topaz) NAL-Dutton.

***Stolen Heiress.** large type ed. Joanna Makepeace. (Mills & Boon Large Print Ser.). 350p. 1997. 22.50 (0-263-15092-5) Ulverscroft.

Stolen House. Bernard L. Herman. 240p. 1992. text ed. 35.00 (0-8139-1367-5); pap. text ed. 19.50 (0-8139-1400-0) U Pr of Va.

Stolen House. Jack Remick. LC 79-91912. (Fiction Ser.). 168p. (Orig.). 1980. pap. 4.95 (0-917530-13-6) Pig Iron Pr.

Stolen Identity. Brian Regrut. LC 93-20046. 300p. (Orig.). 1993. pap. 9.99 (0-8308-1371-3, 1371) InterVarsity.

Stolen Innocence: Preventing, Healing & Recovering from Child Molestation. Ivory L. Toldson. LC 95-83558. (Stories about Children Who Live the Blues Ser.). (Illus.). 152p. 1996. 24.95 (1-888764-00-7) CPHC Pr & Prods.

Stolen Joy: Healing after Infertility & Infant Loss. Anne Barney. LC 93-78192. 48p. (Orig.). 1993. pap. 5.95 (0-944806-06-6) Icarus Books.

Stolen Kingdom: An American Conspiracy. Rich Budnick. LC 92-72203. 204p. (Orig.). 1992. pap. 11.95 (0-944081-02-9) Aloha HI.

Stolen Kiss. Carolyn Keene. (Nancy Drew Files Ser.: No. 111). (J). (gr. 6 up). 1995. mass mkt. 3.99 (0-671-88202-3) PB.

***Stolen Kisses.** Suzanne Enoch. 1997. mass mkt. 5.99 (0-380-78813-6) Avon.

Stolen Kisses. Karen Lockwood. (Orig.). 1994. pap. 4.99 (0-515-11490-1) Jove Pubns.

Stolen Kisses. Michelle Mwansa. (Heartbeats Ser.). (YA). (gr. 7 up). 1995. pap. write for info. (0-7910-2929-8) Chelsea Hse.

Stolen Legacy. George G. James. Ed. by Al I. Obaba. 210p. 1954. pap. text ed. 18.00 (0-916157-79-2) African Islam Miss Pubns.

Stolen Legacy: Greek Philosophy Is Stolen Egyptian Philosophy. George G. James. 1992. 24.95 (0-86543-361-5); pap. 9.95 (0-86543-362-3) Africa World.

Stolen Legacy: Greek Philosophy Is Stolen Egyptian Philosophy. George G. James. 90p. (C). reprint ed. text ed. 22.95 (1-56411-004-4); reprint ed. pap. text ed. 13.95 (1-56411-003-6) Untd Bros & Sis.

Stolen Legacy: The Greeks Were Not the Authors of Greek Philosophy but the People of North Africa, Commonly Called the Egyptians. George G. James. 190p. 1988. reprint ed. pap. 13.95 (0-685-45609-9) J Richardson.

***Stolen Legacy of Anne Frank: Meyer Levin, Lillian Hellman, & the Dramatization of the Diary.** LC 96-46853. 1997. write for info. (0-300-06907-3) Yale U Pr.

Stolen Lives: Trading Women in Sex & Slavery. Sietske Altink. 1996. pap. text ed. 17.95 (1-56023-885-2) Haworth Pr.

Stolen Lives: Trading Women Into Sex & Slavery. Sietske Altink. 1995. pap. 19.95 (1-85727-097-5, Pub. by Scarlet Pr UK) LPC InBook.

Stolen Lives: Trading Women Into Sex & Slavery. Sietske Altink. 1996. 45.00 (1-85727-003-7, Pub. by Scarlet Pr UK) LPC InBook.

Stolen Memories. Susan A. Powell. 1995. 10.95 (0-533-11360-1) Vantage.

Stolen Memories. Kelsey Roberts. (Intrigue Ser.). 1994. mass mkt. 2.99 (0-373-22276-9) Harlequin Bks.

Stolen Mind: The Slow Disappearance of Ray Doernberg. Myrna Doernberg. (Illus.). 224p. 1986. 14.95 (0-912697-32-6) Algonquin Bks.

S

An Asterisk (*) at the beginning of an entry indicates that the title is appearing in BIP for the first time.

Stolen Mind: The Slow Disappearance of Ray Doernberg. Myrna Doernberg. LC 88-35066. 224p. 1989. pap. 8.95 (0-945575-11-4) Algonquin Bks.

***Stolen Moments.** Nellie Wong. LC 97-20630. 44p. (Orig.). 1997. pap. 10.00 (1-887344-03-9) Chicory Blue.

Stolen Moments. Sherryl Woods. 1990. mass mkt. 4.95 (0-445-21010-9, Mysterious Paperbk) Warner Bks.

Stolen Moments. limited ed. Michael Jones. (Illus.). 143p. 1984. write for info. (0-89904-015-2) Crumb Elbow Pub.

Stolen Moments. John Preston. (Mission of Alex Kane Ser.). (Orig.). 1993. reprint ed. mass mkt. 4.95 (1-56333-098-9, Badboy) Masquerade.

Stolen Moments: Conversations with Contemporary Musicians. Tom Schnabel. 1988. pap. 13.95 (0-918226-13-9) Acrobat.

Stolen Moments: Stories of Men, Women & Desire. Ed. by Michael Nagler & William Swanson. LC 95-69093. 325p. (Orig.). (C). 1997. pap. 14.50 (0-88739-112-5) Creat Arts Bk.

Stolen Necklace. Dave Gustaveson. (Reel Kids Adventures Ser.: Bk. 3). 152p. (J). (gr. 3-8). 1994. pap. 5.99 (0-927545-71-3) YWAM Pub.

Stolen Pay Train. Nicholas Carter. LC 74-15733. (Popular Culture in America Ser.). 128p. 1975. reprint ed. 16.95 (0-405-06368-7) Ayer.

Stolen Princess: A Northwest Indian Legend. Willard N. Morss & Janet M. Herren. LC 83-82920. (Illus.). 79p. (Orig.). (J). (gr. 4-8). 1983. pap. 8.95 (0-9613025-0-X) J M Herren.

Stolen Property Returned. rev. ed. John F. Avanzini. 116p. 1989. pap. 6.99 (0-89274-598-3) HIS Publish.

Stolen River. Paul J. Willis. 192p. (Orig.). 1993. mass mkt. 4.50 (0-380-72080-9, AvoNova) Avon.

Stolen Romney: Reading Level 3-4. (Stormy Night Stories Ser.). 16p. 1993. 2.50 (0-88336-072-1) New Readers.

Stolen Rose. Coral S. Saxe. 400p. (Orig.). 1995. mass mkt., pap. text ed. 4.99 (0-8439-3843-9) Dorchester Pub Co.

Stolen Splendor. Diana Haviland. 384p. 1994. mass mkt. 4.99 (1-55817-891-0, Pinncle Kensgtn) Kensgtn Pub Corp.

Stolen Splendor. Miriam Minger. 384p. (Orig.). 1989. pap. 3.95 (0-380-75862-8) Avon.

Stolen Spring. Hans Scherfig. Tr. by Frank Hugus from DAN. LC 82-82674. 196p. 1986. 15.95 (0-940242-20-6); pap. 7.95 (0-940242-00-1) Fjord Pr.

Stolen Steers: A Tale of the Big Thicket. Bill Brett. LC 76-51651. (Illus.). 120p. 1990. pap. 9.95 (0-89096-452-1) Tex A&M Univ Pr.

Stolen Stories. Steve Katz. LC 83-27410. 149p. 1984. 15.95 (0-914590-84-7); pap. 6.95 (0-914590-85-5) Fiction Coll.

Stolen Story & Other Newspaper Stories. Jesse L. Williams. LC 76-98604. (Short Story Index Reprint Ser.). 1977. 20.95 (0-8369-3178-5) Ayer.

Stolen Throne. Harry Turtledove. (Time of Troubles Ser.: Bk. 1). 1995. mass mkt. 5.99 (0-345-38047-9, Del Rey) Ballantine.

Stolen Thunder: A Norse Myth. Shirley Climo. LC 93-24627. (Illus.). (J). (gr. 1-5). 1994. 15.95 (0-395-64368-6, Clarion Bks) HM.

Stolen Thunder: The Cultural Roots of Political Communication, Vol. 4. Lisa S. Harvey. LC 93-30456. (American University Studies: Communications: Ser. XV, Vol. 4). 116p. (C). 1994. text ed. 32.95 (0-8204-2339-4) P Lang Pubng.

***Stolen Time: The History of Tempo Rubato.** Richard Hudson. LC 97-11322. (Illus.). 496p. 1997. pap. 22.00 (0-19-816667-2) OUP.

***Stolen Tongue.** Sheri Holman. 1997. 22.00 (0-614-19890-9) Atlantic.

***Stolen Tongue.** Sheri Holman. LC 96-42390. 320p. 1997. 23.00 (0-87113-669-4, Atlntc Mnthly) Grove-Atltic.

***Stolen Train.** Robert Ashley. (J). 1997. pap. text ed. 3.99 (0-590-92150-9) Scholastic Inc.

Stolen Treasure. Stewart Cowley. (Magical Mystery Bks.). (Illus.). 12p. (J). 1995. boxed 7.99 (0-88705-858-2, Wshng Well Bks) Joshua Morris.

***Stolen Unicorn.** Carolyn Keene. (Nancy Drew Notebooks Ser.). (Illus.). (J). (gr. k-3). 1997. pap. 3.99 (0-614-28888-6, Minstrel Bks) PB.

Stolen White Elephant. Mark Twain, pseud. (Works of Samuel Clemens). 1989. reprint ed. lib. bdg. 79.00 (0-685-28363-1) Rprt Serv.

***Stolen White Elephant & Other Detective Stories (1882, 1896, 1902)** Ed. by Shelley F. Fishkin. (Oxford Mark Twain). 720p. 1997. lib. bdg. 30.00 (0-19-511417-5) OUP.

Stolen White Elephant, Etc. Mark Twain, pseud. LC 70-121530. (Short Story Index Reprint Ser.). 1977. 19.95 (0-8369-3486-5) Ayer.

***Stolen Women: Reclaiming Our Sexuality, Taking Back Our Lives.** Gail E. Wyatt. LC 97-7409. 1997. text ed. 24.95 (0-471-12450-8) Wiley.

Stolen Writings: Blake's "Milton", Joyce's "Ulysses", & the Nature of Influence. Murray McArthur. Ed. by A. Walton Litz. LC 87-28566. (Studies in Modern Literature: No. 87). 188p. reprint ed. 53.60 (0-8357-1846-8, 2070742) Bks Demand.

Stolen Years. Gloria Repp. Ed. by Laurie Garner. (Light Line Ser.). 152p. (Orig.). (YA). (gr. 9-12). 1989. pap. 6.49 (0-89084-481-X, 044412) Bob Jones Univ Pr.

Stolen Years: In My Little Corner of the World. Maita Floyd. Ed. by Gerry Beninger. LC 92-82711. (Illus.). 248p. 1996. pap. 12.95 (0-9620599-4-3) Eskualdun Pubs Ltd.

Stolen Years: Memories of a Country Boyhood. Hugh Falkus. (Illus.). 216p. 1989. 24.95 (0-85493-130-9, Pub. by V Gollancz UK) Trafalgar.

Stolia. Wilfredo Garrido, Jr. 169p. (Orig.). 1984. pap. 12.50 (971-10-0109-8, Pub. by New Day Pub PH) Cellar.

***Stolpen.** Hans-Gunther Hartmann. 1996. pap. text ed. 15.00 (90-5705-006-4) Gordon & Breach.

Stolper-Samuelson Theorem: A Golden Jubilee. Ed. by Alan V. Deardorff & Robert M. Stern. (Studies In International Trade Policy). 376p. 1994. text ed. 52.50 (0-472-10533-7) U of Mich Pr.

Stoma: Selected Poems Nineteen Eighty-Five to Nineteen Eighty-Nine. Guy R. Beining. LC 90-579. (Illus.). 64p. (Orig.). 1990. pap. 10.50 (0-941749-14-2) Black Tie Pr.

***Stoma Care Nursing.** write for info. (0-340-59491-8, Pub. by E Arnold UK) Routledge Chapman & Hall.

Stoma Care Nursing: A Patient-Centered Approach. Celia Myers. 240p. 1995. pap. 38.25 (1-56593-597-7, 1222) Singular Publishing.

Stomach. Ed. by W. Domschke & S. J. Konturek. LC 93-21900. (Illus.). 1993. 137.00 (0-387-56613-9) Spr-Verlag.

Stomach. Ed. by W. Domschke & S. J. Konturek. (Illus.). 420p. 1993. pap. write for info. (3-540-56613-9) Spr-Verlag.

Stomach. Ed. by Sven Gustavsson et al. (Illus.). 444p. 1992. text ed. 139.95 (0-443-04417-1) Churchill.

Stomach. Leo Van Der Reis. (Frontiers of Gastrointestinal Research Ser.: Vol. 6). (Illus.). xii, 188p. 1980. 73.75 (3-8055-3071-4) S Karger.

Stomach Ailments & Digestive Disturbances - How You Can Benefit from Diet. Michael T. Murray. LC 97-10373. (Getting Well Naturally Ser.). 208p. 1997. per., pap. 11.00 (0-7615-0657-8) Prima Pub.

***Stomach & Digestive System.** Carol Ballard. LC 96-31769. (Human Body Ser.). (J). 1997. lib. bdg. 24.25 (0-8172-4801-3) Raintree Steck-V.

***Stomach Turners: Spew! & Other Tasteless Tales.** James Charbonneau. LC 97-4985. (Stomach Turners Ser.). 1997. pap. 5.95 (1-56565-610-5) Contemp Bks.

Stomach Virus & Other Forms of Family Bonding. Kathy Peel. 1993. pap. 9.99 (0-8499-3477-X) Word Pub.

Stomal Therapy. Bokey & Shell. 1985. pap. 20.00 (0-08-029862-1, Pergamon Pr) Elsevier.

Stomal Therapy. Bokey & Shell. 1985. 33.00 (0-08-029865-6) Elsevier.

***Stomata.** 2nd ed. Fricker & Colin M. Willmer. (Topics in Plant Functional Biology Ser.). (Illus.). 400p. 1995. pap. text ed. 45.95 (0-412-57430-6, Chap & Hall NY) Chapman & Hall.

Stomata. 2nd ed. Colin M. Willmer & Mark Fricker. 375p. (gr. 13). 1995. text ed. 99.95 (0-412-72500-2) Chapman & Hall.

Stomatal Function. Ed. by Eduardo Zeiger et al. (Illus.). 520p. 1987. 75.00 (0-8047-1347-2) Stanford U Pr.

***Stomp, Stomp!** Bob Kolar. LC 97-7537. (Illus.). (J). 1997. write for info. (1-55858-632-6); lib. bdg. write for info. (1-55858-633-4) North-South Bks NYC.

***Stompbox: A History of Guitar Fuzzes, Flangers, Phasers, Echoes, & Wahs.** Art Thompson. (Illus.). 160p. 1997. pap. 24.95 (0-87930-479-0) Miller Freeman.

Stomping the Blues. Albert Murray. (Quality Paperbacks Ser.). (Illus.). 272p. 1989. pap. 13.95 (0-306-80362-3) Da Capo.

Stone. Andy Goldsworthy. 1994. 49.50 (0-8109-3847-2) Abrams.

Stone. John Sallis. LC 93-45307. 160p. 1994. 25.95 (0-253-35062-X); pap. 12.95 (0-253-20888-2) Ind U Pr.

Stone: An Introduction. 2nd ed. Asher Shadmon. 176p. 1996. pap. 24.95 (1-85339-313-4, Pub. by Intermed Tech UK) Women Ink.

***Stone Age.** Patricia D. Netzley. (World History Ser.). (J). (gr. 4-12). 1997. lib. bdg. 17.96 (1-56006-316-5) Lucent Bks.

Stone Age. Ivan Shmelyov. Tr. & Pref. by Olga Sorokin. 146p. (Orig.). 1985. pap. 5.95 (0-936041-00-5) Barbary Coast Bks.

Stone Age Cave Site in Tangier. B. Howe & Hallam L. Movius. (Harvard University Peabody Museum of Archaeology & Ethnology Papers). 1974. reprint ed. 25.00 (0-527-01272-6) Periodicals Srv.

Stone Age Cultures of South Africa. Astly J. Goodwin & C. V. Lowe. LC 76-44725. reprint ed. 55.00 (0-404-15928-1) AMS Pr.

Stone Age Economics. Marshall D. Sahlins. LC 75-169506. 362p. 1972. pap. text ed. 25.95 (0-202-01099-6) Aldine de Gruyter.

Stone Age Farmers Beside the Sea: Scotland's Prehistoric Village of Skara Brae. Caroline Arnold. LC 96-20021. (J). 1997. 15.95 (0-395-77601-5, Clarion Bks) HM.

Stone Age in India. P. T. Ayyangar. 1988. reprint ed. 10.00 (81-206-0148-3, Pub. by Asian Educ Servs II) S Asia.

Stone Age in India. P. T. Iyengar. (Illus.). 60p. 1986. reprint ed. 16.00 (0-8364-1719-4, Pub. by Usha II) S Asia.

Stone Age in Malaya. Michael W. Tweedie. LC 77-87514. (Journal of the Royal Asiatic Society, Malayan Branch Ser.: Vol. 26). reprint ed. 32.50 (0-404-16872-8) AMS Pr.

Stone Age of Mount Carmel, 2 vols., Set. Incl. Vol. 1. Excavations at the Wady el-Mughara. D. A. Garrod & D. M. Bate. LC 77-86432. (0-404-16651-2); Vol. 2. Fossil Human Remains from the Levalloiso-Mousterian. T. D. McCown & Arthur Keith. LC 77-86432. (0-404-16652-0); LC 77-86432. reprint ed. 210.00 (0-404-16650-4) AMS Pr.

***Stone Age of the Upper Zambezi Valley.** Laurel Phillipson. 1978. pap. 12.00 (1-872566-07-3, Pub. by Brit Inst Estrn Africa UK) David Brown.

Stone Age Present. William F. Allman. 1995. pap. 12.00 (0-684-80455-7, Touchstone Bks) S&S Trade.

Stone Age Present: How Evolution Has Shaped Modern Life-From Sex, Violence, & Language to Emotions, Morals, & Communities. William F. Allman. 288p. 1994. 23.00 (0-671-89226-6) S&S Trade.

Stone Age Soccer. Plato Center Grade School Third Graders. (Wee Write Bks.: No. 8). (Illus.). 23p. (J). (ps-3). 1994. pap. 8.95 (1-884987-28-1) WeWrite.

Stone Age Spear & Arrow Points of the Midcontinental & Eastern United States: A Modern Survey & Reference. Noel D. Justice. LC 86-45399. (Illus.). 304p. 1988. text ed. 37.95 (0-253-35406-4) Ind U Pr.

Stone Age Spear & Arrow Points of the Midcontinental & Eastern United States: A Modern Survey & Reference. Noel D. Justice. (Illus.). 304p. 1995. pap. text ed. 22.95 (0-253-20985-4) Ind U Pr.

***Stone Alone: The Story of a Rock 'n' Roll Band.** Bill Wyman & Ray Coleman. LC 97-16406. (Illus.). 640p. 1997. reprint ed. pap. 17.95 (0-306-80783-1) Da Capo.

Stone & Man: A Photographic Exploration. Andreas Feininger. LC 78-73211. (Illus.). 1979. reprint ed. pap. 8.95 (0-486-23756-7) Dover.

Stone & Man: Nord 1995: 33. Ivars Silis. (Illus.). 80p. 1995. pap. 25.00 (92-9120-736-5, NC7365, Pub. by Nordic Coun Minsters DK) Bernan Associates.

***Stone & Plasterwork.** Yvonne Rees. (Practical Home Restoration Ser.). (Illus.). 96p. 1997. pap. 14.95 (0-7063-7469-X, Pub. by Ward Lock UK) Sterling.

***Stone & Silence.** Linde Waidhofer. (Illus.). 108p. 1997. pap. 29.95 (0-941283-15-1) Western Eye Pr.

***Stone & Silence.** Linde Waidhofer. (Illus.). 108p. 1997. 60.00 (0-941283-16-X) Western Eye Pr.

***Stone & Steel: Paintings of the Bridges of New York.** Bascove. (Illus.). 112p. 1997. 25.00 (1-56792-081-0) Godine.

Stone & the Flute. Ed. by Hans Bemmann. Tr. by Anthea Bell. 864p. 1988. pap. 12.95 (0-14-007445-7, Penguin Bks) Viking Penguin.

Stone and the Scorpion: The Female Subject of Desire in the Novels of Charlotte Bronte, George Eliot, & Thomas Hardy. Judith Mitchell. LC 93-43751. (Contributions in Women's Studies: Vol. 42). 240p. 1994. text ed. 55.00 (0-313-29043-1, Greenwood Pr) Greenwood.

Stone & the Thread: Andean Roots of Abstract Art. Cesar Paternosto. Tr. by Esther Allen. LC 95-22899. (Illus.). 296p. (ENG & SPA.). 1996. 35.00 (0-292-76565-7) U of Tex Pr.

Stone & Water. Ann Bardens. (Illus.). 96p. 1992. pap. 12.50 (0-945950-08-X) Canoe Pr MI.

Stone & Webster 1889-1989: A Century of Integrity & Service. David N. Keller. (Illus.). 375p. 1989. 20.00 (0-9623677-0-2) Stone & Webster Inc.

Stone Angel. Margaret Laurence. (Phoenix Fiction Ser.). 320p. (C). 1993. pap. 12.95 (0-226-46936-0) U Ch Pr.

***Stone Angel.** Carol O'Connell. LC 96-44504. 1997. 23.95 (0-399-14234-7) Putnam Pub Group.

Stone Angels. M. Jeffries. 320p. 1994. mass mkt. 4.50 (0-06-100679-3, Harp PBks) HarpC.

Stone Arbor, & Other Stories. Roger Angell. LC 79-121519. (Short Story Index Reprint Ser.). 1977. 20.95 (0-8369-3475-X) Ayer.

Stone Artifacts at & Near the Finley Site, Near Eden, Wyoming. Linton Satterthwaite. (University Museum Monographs: No. 14). (Illus.). iv, 22p. 1957. pap. 10.00 (0-934718-06-7) U PA Mus Pubns.

Stone Baby. Laura Chester. LC 89-39003. 228p. (Orig.). 1989. 20.00 (0-87685-776-4); pap. 12.50 (0-87685-775-6) Black Sparrow.

Stone Beloved. Dante Alighieri. Tr. by Harry Duncan from ITA. (Illus.). 40p. 1986. 475.00 (0-935072-08-X) W T Taylor.

Stone Boat. Andrew Solomon. 288p. 1994. 22.95 (0-571-17240-7) Faber & Faber.

Stone Boat. Andrew Solomon. LC 95-37579. 1996. 10.95 (0-452-27498-2) Faber & Faber.

Stone Boat. Andrew Solomon. Date not set. pap. 10.95 (0-614-14860-X, Plume) NAL-Dutton.

Stone, Bone, Antler & Shell: Artifacts of the Northwest Coast. Hilary Stewart. (Illus.). 160p. 1996. 29.95 (0-295-97536-9) U of Wash Pr.

***Stone Book.** Alan Garner. (J). Date not set. write for info. (0-688-05179-0); lib. bdg. write for info. (0-688-05180-4) Greenwillow.

Stone Boy. 3.98 (0-8317-5848-1) Smithmark.

Stone Boy & Other Stories. Thich Nhat Hanh. Tr. by Mobi Warren et al. from VIE. (Illus.). 175p. (Orig.). 1995. pap. 18.00 (0-938077-86-4) Parallax Pr.

***Stone Breakers & Other Novellas.** Ferdinand Von Saar et al. LC 97-24385. (Studies in Austrian Literature, Culture, & Thought Translation). 1997. write for info. (1-57241-055-8) Ariadne CA.

Stone Bruise. James C. McCormick. LC 93-70998. 442p. 1993. 23.00 (1-880909-11-1) Baskerville.

Stone Bull. Phyllis A. Whitney. 24.95 (0-89190-536-7) Amereon Ltd.

Stone Bull. Phyllis A. Whitney. 1983. mass mkt. 5.99 (0-449-20420-0, Crest) Fawcett.

Stone Butch Blues. Leslie Feinberg. LC 93-16092. 304p. (Orig.). 1993. pap. 12.95 (1-56341-029-X); lib. bdg. 26.95 (1-56341-030-3) Firebrand Bks.

Stone by Stone on the Oregon Trail. Bev Stone. (Illus.). 336p. 1993. write for info. (0-9619791-2-7) Stone Studios.

Stone-Campbell Movement. Leroy Garrett. LC 80-65965. 740p. 1981. 24.99 (0-89900-415-6) College Pr Pub.

Stone Canoe & Other Stories. John L. Peyton. LC 89-2294. (Illus.). 175p. (Orig.). 1989. 24.95 (0-939923-06-8); pap. 14.95 (0-939923-07-6) M & W Pub Co.

Stone Canyons of the Colorado Plateau. Photos by Jack W. Dykinga. LC 95-40455. (Illus.). 128p. 1996. 45.00 (0-8109-4468-5) Abrams.

Stone Cats. Yoshimi Nagata. LC 93-18223. (Illus.). 48p. 1993. 14.95 (0-8348-0279-1) Weatherhill.

Stone Cech Compactification. R. C. Walker. (Ergebnisse der Mathematik und Ihrer Grenzgebiete Ser.: Vol. 83). x, 332p. 1975. 103.95 (0-387-06699-3) Spr-Verlag.

***Stone Circle.** Gary Goshgarian. LC 97-23043. 1997. pap. 23.95 (1-55611-533-4) D I Fine.

Stone Circles: A Guide to the Megalithic Rings of Britain, Ireland & Brittany. Aubrey Burl. LC 94-23685. 1995. 14.00 (0-300-06331-8) Yale U Pr.

Stone Circles in Ireland. Sean O. Nuallain. (Irish Treasures Ser.). (Illus.). 48p. (Orig.). 1995. pap. 8.95 (0-946172-45-5, Pub. by Town Hse IE) R Rinehart.

Stone City. Mitchell Smith. 640p. 1991. pap. 5.99 (0-451-16930-1, Sig) NAL-Dutton.

Stone Cold. large type ed. John Francome. (Magna Mystery Ser.). 1992. 19.95 (0-7505-0416-1, Pub. by Magna Print Bks UK) Ulverscroft.

Stone Cold Dead. large type ed. Roger Ormerod. LC 96-19594. 344p. 1997. pap. 20.95 (0-7862-0787-6) Thorndike Pr.

Stone Cold Gothic. Helen Adam & Auste Adam. 1984. 7.00 (0-317-16221-7); pap. 3.50 (0-317-16222-5) Kulchur Foun.

Stone Cold Heart. 2nd ed. Stephen L. Hill. 52p. 1995. pap. 2.00 (0-9637090-1-1) Together Harvest.

Stone Connections (Updated Version) A More Complete Genealogy of the Stone Family. LC 95-69478. (Illus.). 450p. 1995. 49.95 (0-9609192-4-4) R H Stone.

Stone Conservation: An Overview of Current Research. C. A. Price. LC 95-51727. (Research in Conservation Ser.). 88p. (Orig.). 1996. pap. 25.00 (0-89236-389-4, Getty Conservation Inst) J P Getty Trust.

Stone Container Corp. A Report on the Company's Environmental Policies & Practices. (Illus.). 50p. (C). 1994. reprint ed. pap. text ed. 250.00 (0-7881-0968-5, Coun on Econ) DIANE Pub.

Stone Cottage: Pound, Yeats, & Modernism. James Longenbach. (Illus.). 352p. 1991. reprint ed. pap. 19.95 (0-19-506662-6) OUP.

***Stone Cowboy: A Novel.** Marks Jacobs. LC 97-20257. 1997. write for info. (1-56947-098-7) Soho Press.

Stone Cried Out. Shigeo Shimada. 208p. 1986. pap. 11.00 (0-8170-1111-0) Judson.

Stone Crop. Jody Gladding. LC 92-39605. (Younger Poets Ser.: No. 88). 54p. (C). 1993. pap. 10.00 (0-300-05544-7); text ed. 17.00 (0-300-05543-9) Yale U Pr.

Stone Crusade: A Historical Guide to Bouldering in America. John Sherman. (American Alpine Ser.). (Illus.). 452p. 1996. pap. text ed. 30.00 (0-930410-62-9) Amer Alpine Club.

Stone Cutter Who Wanted to Be Rich. Getzel. LC 90-82859. (Illus.). 48p. (J). (gr. 1-5). 1990. 9.95 (0-685-45648-X) CIS Comm.

Stone Dancer. Murray Smith. 1995. pap. 6.50 (0-671-78486-2) PB.

Stone Dancer. large type ed. Murray Smith. 601p. 1995. 24.95 (0-7838-1235-3, GK Hall) Thorndike Pr.

Stone Dancers. Nora Martin. (J). (ps-2). 1995. 15.00 (0-689-80312-5, S&S Bks Young Read) S&S Childrens.

Stone Dead. Ellen Jamison. 352p. 1993. mass mkt. 4.50 (0-8217-4265-5, Zebra Kensgtn) Kensgtn Pub Corp.

Stone Desert: A Naturalist's Explorations of Canyonlands. Craig L. Childs. 200p. 1995. pap. 12.95 (1-56579-122-3) Westcliffe Pubs.

Stone Desert see Novels by Hugo Wast

Stone Diaries. Carol Shields. LC 93-30239. (Illus.). 384p. 1994. pap. 21.95 (0-670-85309-7, Viking) Viking Penguin.

Stone Diaries. Carol Shields. (Illus.) 384p. 1995. pap. 11.95 (0-14-023313-X, Penguin Bks) Viking Penguin.

Stone Diaries. large type ed. Carol Shields. LC 95-21697. 418p. 1995. 25.95 (0-7838-1444-5, GK Hall) Thorndike Pr.

Stone Diseases. Ed. by D. Hauri & O. Schmucki. (Journal: Urologia Internationalis: Vol. 41, No. 5, 1986). 76p. 1987. pap. 61.75 (3-8055-4523-1) S Karger.

Stone Dogs. S. M. Stirling. (Orig.). 1990. mass mkt. 5.99 (0-671-72009-0) Baen Bks.

***Stone Dragon.** Rowena White. 195p. (Orig.). 1997. mass mkt. 4.99 (1-55197-681-1, Pub. by Comnwlth Pub CN) Partners Pubs Grp.

Stone Echoes: Original Prints by Francoise Gilot - a Catalogue Raisonne. Mel Yoakum. (Illus.). 92p. 1995. text ed. 30.00 (0-9624021-7-6) U of Pa Pr.

Stone Echoes: Original Prints by Francoise Gilot, a Catalogue Raisonne. Mei Yoakum. (Illus.). 92p. (C). 1995. text ed. 30.00 (0-614-07241-7) Ursinus College.

***Stone Edition of the Chumash, 5 vols., Set.** boxed 59.99 (0-89906-600-3) Mesorah Pubns.

Stone Edition of the Chumash: The Torah, Haftaros, & Five Megillos with a Commentary Anthologized from the Rabbinic Writings. Comment by Nosson Scherman. (ArtScroll Tanach Ser.). 1993. 41.99 (0-89906-014-5) Mesorah Pubns.

Stone Edition of the Chumash: The Torah, Haftaros, & Five Megillos with a Commentary Anthologized from the Rabbinic Writings, 5 vols., Set. Comment by Nosson Scherman. (ArtScroll Tanach Ser.). 1995. boxed 59.99 (0-89906-341-1) Mesorah Pubns.

***Stone Edition Tanach - Black: The Torch - Prophets - Writings: The Twenty-Four Books of the Bible Newly Translated & Annotated.** Nosson Scherman et al. (ArtScroll Ser.). 2108p. 1996. 59.99 (0-89906-269-5) Mesorah Pubns.

***Stone Edition Tanach - Hunter Green: The Torch - Prophets - Writings: The Twenty-Four Books of the Bible Newly Translated & Annotated.** Nosson Scherman et al. (ArtScroll Ser.). 2108p. 1996. 59.99 (0-89906-270-9) Mesorah Pubns.

***Stone Edition Tanach - Ivory: The Torch - Prophets - Writings: The Twenty-Four Books of the Bible Newly Translated & Annotated.** Nosson Scherman et al. (ArtScroll Ser.). 2108p. 1996. 59.99 (0-89906-271-7) Mesorah Pubns.

S

An Asterisk (*) at the beginning of an entry indicates that the title is appearing in BIP for the first time.

***Stone Edition Tanach - Maroon: The Torch - Prophets - Writings: The Twenty-Four Books of the Bible Newly Translated & Annotated.** Nosson Scherman et al. (ArtScroll Ser.). 2108p. 1996. lthr. 89.99 (0-89906-272-5) Mesorah Pubns.

Stone Face. William G. Smith. 213p. 1975. reprint ed. 15.95 (0-911860-48-7) Chatham Bkseller.

Stone-Faced Boy. Paula Fox. LC 68-9053. (Illus.). 112p. (J). (gr. 4-6). 1982. lib. bdg. 13.95 (0-02-735570-5, Bradbury S&S) S&S Childrens.

Stone-Faced Boy. Paula Fox. LC 86-22204. 112p. (J). (gr. 4-6). 1987. reprint ed. pap. 3.95 (0-689-71127-1, Aladdin Paperbacks) S&S Childrens.

Stone Fences: A Book from the Inner Townships from Childhood in the Fifties by Paal-Heige Haugen. Paal-Helge Haugen. Tr. by William Mishler & Roger Greenwald. LC 85-24613. 96p. 1986. pap. 12.95 (0-8262-0601-8) U of Mo Pr.

Stone Fey. Robin McKinley. LC 95-3915. (Illus.). 1996. write for info. (0-15-200017-8) HarBrace.

Stone Finishes Etc. Cy DeCosse Incorporated Staff. LC 96-15846. (Creative Touches Ser.). (Illus.). 64p. 1996. pap. 9.95 (0-86573-997-8) Cowles Creative.

Stone Flower. large type ed. Alan Scholefield. 1990. 27.99 (0-7089-8543-2) Ulverscroft.

Stone for a Pillow. Madeleine L'Engle. LC 86-6487. (Wheaton Literary Ser.). 240p. 1986. 14.99 (0-87788-789-6) Shaw Pubs.

Stone for Danny Fisher. Harold Robbins. 1994. pap. 6.99 (0-671-87497-7) PB.

Stone Fox. John R. Gardiner. LC 79-7895. (Illus.). 96p. (J). (gr. 2-6). 1980. 14.95 (0-690-03983-2, Crowell Jr Bks); lib. bdg. 14.89 (0-690-03984-0, Crowell Jr Bks) HarpC Child Bks.

Stone Fox. John R. Gardiner. LC 79-7895. (Trophy Bk.). (Illus.). 96p. (J). (gr. 2-6). 1992. pap. 3.95 (0-06-440132-4, Trophy) HarpC Child Bks.

***Stone Fox.** John R. Gardiner. (Illus.). (J). (gr. 4). 1995. 8.64 (0-395-73247-6) HM.

***Stone Fox.** large type ed. John R. Gardiner. (Illus.). 118p. (J). (gr. 4). 29.50 (0-614-20622-7, L-38187-00 APHB) Am Printing Hse.

Stone Fox: A Study Guide. Dina Claydon. Ed. by Joyce Friedland & Rikki Kessler. (Novel-Ties Ser.). 21p. (YA). (gr. 9-12). 1990. pap. text ed. 15.95 (0-88122-407-3) Lrn Links.

***Stone Fox y la Carrera de Trineos.** John R. Gardiner. 1996. pap. text ed. 7.95 (84-279-3232-4) Lectorum Pubns.

Stone Garden. Barbara E. Stanush. 75p. (Orig.). 1992. pap. 10.00 (1-877603-13-9) Pecan Grove.

Stone Gone Mad. 2nd ed. Jacquelyn H. Park. LC 91-52674. 320p. 1996. reprint ed. pap. text ed. 9.95 (1-55583-364-0) Alyson Pubns.

Stone Guide to Dog Grooming for All Breeds. Ben Stone & Pearl Stone. LC 81-7089. (Illus.). 302p. 1981. pap. 32.95 (0-87605-403-3) Howell Bk.

Stone Hill: The People & Their Stories. Guy T. Hollyday. (Illus.). 270p. 1994. 20.00 (0-9643487-0-5) G T Hollyday.

Stone Horse: A Study of the Function of the Minor Characters in Joseph Conrad's Nostromo. Jan A. Verleun. xvii, 318p. (Orig.). 1978. pap. 33.50 (0-685-10589-X, Pub. by Boumas Boekhuis NE) Benjamins North Am.

Stone Horses: A Novel. Sallie Gallegos. 280p. (Orig.). 1996. pap. 16.95 (0-8263-1666-2) U of NM Pr.

Stone Houses: How to Build Them at Low Cost. 1991. lib. bdg. 66.95 (0-8490-4673-4) Gordon Pr.

Stone Houses & Iron Bridges: Tradition & the Place of Women in Contemporary Japan. Marilyn F. Nefsky. LC 91-18444. (Toronto Studies in Religion: Vol. 12). 260p. (C). 1992. text ed. 47.95 (0-8204-1568-5) P Lang Pubng.

Stone Images of Esie, Nigeria. Phillips Stevens, Jr. 398p. 1979. 95.00 (0-8419-9850-7, Africana) Holmes & Meier.

Stone in Architecture: Properties, Durability. 3rd rev. ed. Erhard M. Winkler. LC 94-20332. Orig. Title: Stone: Properties, Durability in Man's Environment. 1994. 118.95 (0-387-57626-6) Spr-Verlag.

Stone in My Pocket & Other Poems. Emma S. Thornton. (Illus.). 82p. (Orig.). 1981. pap. 10.00 (0-9608802-1-6) Years Pr.

Stone in My Shoe: Teaching Literacy in Times of Change. Lorri Neilsen. (Illus.). 141p. (Orig.). 1994. pap. 12.00 (1-895411-73-4) Peguis Pubs Ltd.

Stone in the Hourglass. limited ed. Donald Windham. 1981. 35.00 (0-917366-05-0) S Campbell.

Stone in the Road. Leon Lukaszewski. 27p. 1956. pap. 3.00 (0-87129-673-X, S52) Dramatic Pub.

Stone Inheritance. Jacques-Yves Calvez. LC 92-61730. 140p. (Orig.). 1993. pap. 16.95 (0-9635239-0-2) Presse-Gauloise.

Stone Junction. Jim Dodge. LC 89-35587. 1991. pap. 10.95 (0-87113-454-3, Atlntc Mnthly) Grove-Atltic.

Stone Junk. 1993. pap. 5.25 (0-19-585266-4) OUP.

***Stone Killer.** J. Robert Janes. LC 96-48522. 265p. 1997. 22.00 (1-56947-083-9) Soho Press.

***Stone Laid Before the Lord.** Anselme Dimier. (Illus.). 1997. 38.95 (0-614-27494-X); pap. 18.95 (0-614-27495-8) Cistercian Pubns.

Stone Lake: The Poetry of Fan Chengda, 1126-1193. J. D. Schmidt. (Studies in Chinese History, Literature & Institutions). 208p. (C). 1992. text ed. 57.95 (0-521-41782-1) Cambridge U Pr.

Stone Lantern Essays: Services for the Collapse of the Living Room Carpet. Marlene Kamei. LC 79-91969. (Illus.). 75p. (Orig.). (C). 1980. pap. 4.95 (0-935684-02-6) Plumbers Ink Bks.

Stone Leopard. Colin Forbes. 252p. 1976. pap. 13.95 (0-330-24817-0, Pub. by Pan Books UK) Trans-Atl Phila.

Stone Leopard. large type ed. Colin Forbes. 481p. 1989. 24.95 (0-7089-1930-8) Ulverscroft.

Stone Lion. Alan Schroeder. LC 92-38257. (Illus.). 32p. (J). (gr. 1-3). 1994. lib. bdg. 14.95 (0-684-19578-X, C Scribner Sons Young) S&S Childrens.

Stone Lion. Bill Slavin. (Northern Lights Books for Children). (Illus.). 32p. (J). (gr. k-4). 1996. 15.95 (0-88995-154-3, Pub. by Red Deer CN) Orca Bk Pubs.

Stone Lion & Other Chinese Detective Stories: The Wisdom of Lord Bau. Tr. by Yin-lien C. Chin et al. from CHI. LC 91-46520. 200p. (YA). (gr. 8-12). 1992. 51.95 (0-87332-634-2, East Gate Bk); pap. 23.95 (0-87332-635-0, East Gate Bk) M E Sharpe.

Stone Made Flesh. Michael Niemoeller. Ed. by Terry Wolverton. LC 95-68980. 100p. (Orig.). 1995. pap. 9.95 (0-9629528-2-6) Silverton Bks.

***Stone Made Smooth.** Sue K. Hill. LC 96-90582. 88p. (Orig.). (YA). 1997. pap. 10.00 (1-56002-694-4, Univ Edtns) Aegina Pr.

Stone Made Smooth. 2nd ed. Wong Ming-Dao. 245p. (C). 1984. pap. 8.99 (0-907821-00-6) Revival Lit.

Stone Magic of the Ancients: The Petroglyphs & Shrine Sites of the Upper Little Colorado Region. James R. Cunkle & Markus Jacquemain. LC 95-22656. (Illus.). 1995. pap. 14.95 (1-885590-04-0) Golden West Pub.

Stone Maiden & Other Samoan Fables. Daniel Pouesi & Michael Igoe. Ed. by Michael Igoe. (Illus.). 56p. (Orig.). (YA). (gr. 6 up). 1995. pap. 10.00 (0-9644426-0-4) Kin Pub.

Stone Marmalade. Leslie Scalapino & Kevin Killian. 64p. (Orig.). 1996. pap. 9.50 (0-935162-16-X) Singing Horse.

Stone Masonry. John Ashurst & Nicola Ashurst. (Pratical Building Conservation Ser.: Vol. 1). 100p. 1988. text ed. 47.95 (0-470-21104-0) Wiley.

Stone Masonry. Kern et al. 200p. pap. 20.00 (0-686-31221-X) Owner-Builder.

Stone Men. Nicki Weiss. LC 92-3959. (Illus.). 32p. (J). (ps up). 1993. lib. bdg. 13.93 (0-688-11016-9) Greenwillow.

Stone Monuments of Southern Mexico. Matthew W. Stirling. (Bureau of American Ethnology Bulletins Ser.). 76p. 1995. lib. bdg. 79.00 (0-7812-4138-3) Rprt Serv.

Stone Mountain Mystery Gamebook. Carole Marsh. (Carole Marsh Bks.). (Illus.). (Orig.). (J). (gr. 3-9). 1994. pap. 19.95 (0-935326-80-4) Gallopade Pub Group.

Stone Mountain Mystery Set. Carole Marsh. (Carole Marsh Mysteries Ser.). 1994. 125.00 (0-7933-6957-6) Gallopade Pub Group.

Stone Movers. Patricia Mullen. 368p. (Orig.). 1995. mass mkt. 5.50 (0-446-60106-3, Aspect) Warner Bks.

Stone of Farewell. Tad Williams. (Memory, Sorrow & Thorn Ser.: Bk. 2). 768p. 1991. reprint ed. mass mkt. 6.99 (0-88677-480-2) DAW Bks.

Stone of Farewell, Bk. 2. Tad Williams. 1990. 21.95 (0-88677-435-7) DAW Bks.

Stone of Laughter: A Novel. Hoda Barakat. Tr. by Sophie Bennett. LC 95-14090. (Emerging Voices Ser.). 240p. 1995. 29.95 (1-56656-197-3); pap. 12.95 (1-56656-190-6) Interlink Pub.

Stone of Sisyphus: Critical Discourses on American Education Practices, 1947-1988. John E. Westburg. LC 89-28663. (Illus.). 1989. pap. 16.50 (0-87423-043-8) Westburg.

Stone of Tears. Terry Goodkind. (Sword of Truth Ser.: Bk. 2). (Illus.). 560p. 1995. 25.95 (0-312-85706-3) Tor Bks.

Stone of Tears. Terry Goodkind. 1996. pap. 6.99 (0-614-98104-2) Tor Bks.

Stone of Tears Bk. 2: The Sword of Truth. Terry Goodkind. 1996. mass mkt. 6.99 (0-8125-4809-4) Tor Bks.

Stone of the Heart. Tom Grimes. LC 89-49724. 131p. 1990. 15.95 (0-941423-40-9) FWEW.

Stone of the Heart. Eugene McEldowney. LC 95-21905. 1995. 20.95 (0-312-13609-9) St Martin.

***Stone of the Heart.** large type ed. Eugene McEldowney. (Magna Large Print Ser.). (Illus.). 356p. 1996. 25.99 (0-7505-0937-6) Ulverscroft.

***Stone of the Heart: A Novel.** Tom Grimes. LC 97-12881. 144p. 1997. reprint ed. pap. 12.95 (0-87074-418-6) SMU Press.

Stone of the Philosophers. Edward Kelly. 1990. pap. 7.95 (1-55818-174-1) Holmes Pub.

Stone of the Philosophers. Robert L. Peck & Thelma M. Peck. 1988. 14.95 (0-917828-02-X) Personal Dev Ctr.

***Stone of the Plough: The Search for the Secret of Giza.** Ann Walker. LC 96-29544. 352p. 1997. pap. 14.95 (1-85230-937-7) Element MA.

Stone of the Sun & the First Chapter of the History of Mexico. E. J. Palacios. 1977. lib. bdg. 59.95 (0-8490-2670-9) Gordon Pr.

Stone on Stone: Poems by Women of Diverse Heritages: Piedra Sobre Piedra: Poesia por Mujeres de Diversas Culturas. Ed. by Zoe Anglesey. Tr. by Rudolfo Dada from ENG. LC 93-35585. 132p. (Orig.). (SPA.). (YA). (gr. 10-12). 1993. pap. 12.95 (0-940880-48-2) Open Hand.

Stone Ornaments Used by Indians in the U. S. & Canada. Warren K. Moorehead et al. LC 76-43790. reprint ed. 55.00 (0-404-15645-2) AMS Pr.

Stone, Paper, Knife. Marge Piercy. LC 82-48050. 125p. 1983. pap. 12.00 (0-394-71219-6) Knopf.

***Stone People Medicine.** Manny Twofeathers. (Illus.). 165p. (Orig.). 1997. pap. 9.95 (1-886340-97-8) Wo-Pila Pub.

Stone Pony. Patricia Calvert. 160p. (J). (gr. 7-9). 1983. pap. 2.99 (0-451-13729-9, Sig) NAL-Dutton.

Stone Power. Dorothee L. Mella. 1988. pap. 12.99 (0-446-38696-0) Warner Bks.

Stone Prince. Fiona Patton. 1997. pap. 6.99 (0-88677-735-6) DAW Bks.

Stone Princess Year down Under. Robyn Donald. (Presents Ser.). 1993. mass mkt. 2.99 (0-373-11577-6, 1-11577-3) Harlequin Bks.

Stone Promise. Cara Reichel. Ed. by Nancy R. Thatch. LC 91-15059. (Books for Students by Students). (Illus.). 26p. (YA). (gr. 5 up). 1991. lib. bdg. 14.95 (0-933849-35-4) Landmark Edns.

Stone: Properties, Durability in Man's Environment see Stone in Architecture: Properties, Durability

Stone Psalter. Ed. by Andrew C. Kimmens. LC 78-23622. 339p. reprint ed. pap. 96.70 (0-7837-4290-8, 2043982) Bks Demand.

Stone Raft. Jose Saramago. Tr. by Helen Lane. 304p. 1996. pap. 13.00 (0-15-600401-1) HarBrace.

Stone Raft: A Novel. Jose Saramago. Tr. by Giovanni Pontiero. 304p. 1995. 23.00 (0-15-185198-0) HarBrace.

Stone Records of Groton, Ct. Frances M. Caulkins. Ed. by E. S. Gilman. 96p. 1994. reprint ed. pap. 18.00 (0-8328-4404-7) Higginson Bk Co.

Stone Remains in the Society Islands. K. P. Emory. (BMB Ser.). 1974. reprint ed. 30.00 (0-527-02222-5) Periodicals Srv.

Stone Roberts: Paintings & Drawings. Charles Michener. LC 93-6930. (Illus.). 64p. 1993. pap. 24.95 (0-8109-2550-8) Abrams.

Stone Roberts: Paintings & Drawings. Charles Michener. LC 93-6930. 1993. write for info. (0-8109-3773-5) Abrams.

Stone Roses: Poems from Transylvania. Keith Wilson. LC 83-10389. (Illus.). 88p. 1983. 12.95 (0-87421-120-4) Utah St U Pr.

Stone Roses: Poems from Transylvania. Keith Wilson. LC 83-10389. (Illus.). 98p. reprint ed. pap. 28.00 (0-7837-7069-3, 2046881) Bks Demand.

***Stone Roses: The Illustrated Story.** Dave Simpson. (Illus.). 1996. pap. text ed. 14.99 (1-886894-47-7) Mus Bk Servs.

Stone Run: Tidings. Cynthia Grenfell. LC 83-398. 96p. (Orig.). 1983. pap. 11.95 (0-86534-023-4) Sunstone Pr.

***Stone Sculpture in the Allahabad Museum, Vol. 2.** Krishna Deva & S. D. Trivedi. (C). 1996. 80.00 (81-7304-140-7, Pub. by Manohar II) S Asia.

Stone Sculpture of India: A Study of the Materials Used by Indian Sculptors from Ca. 2nd Century B. C. to the 16th Century. Richard Newman. (Illus.). 106p. 1984. pap. 14.00 (0-916724-57-3) Harvard Art Mus.

Stone Sculptures: The Greek, Roman, & Etruscan Collections of the Harvard University Art Museums. Cornelius C. Vermeule & Amy Brauer. (Illus.). 184p. 1990. pap. 15.00 (0-916724-70-0, 4-700) Harvard Art Mus.

Stone Shelters. Edward Allen. (Illus.). 222p. 1971. pap. 12.95 (0-262-51010-3) MIT Pr.

***Stone Skeleton: Structural Engineering of Masonry Architecture.** 170p. 1997. pap. text ed. 29.95 (0-521-62963-2) Cambridge U Pr.

Stone Skeleton: Structural Engineering of Masonry Architecture. Jacques Heyman. (Illus.). 172p. (C). 1995. text ed. 64.95 (0-521-47270-9) Cambridge U Pr.

Stone Song. Win Blevins. 400p. 1996. mass mkt. write for info. (0-614-05528-8); mass mkt. 6.99 (0-8125-3369-0) Forge NYC.

Stone Song. Win Blevins. 400p. 1995. 23.95 (0-312-85567-2) Tor Bks.

Stone Soup. (Read Along with Me Ser.: No. II). (Illus.). 24p. (J). (ps-3). 1989. 2.25 (1-56288-159-0) Checkerboard.

Stone Soup. Marcia Brown. (Illus.). (J). (gr. 1-4). 1987. 22.95 incl. audio (0-87499-053-X); pap. 15.95 incl. audio (0-87499-052-1) Live Oak Media.

Stone Soup. Marcia Brown. LC 47-11630. (Illus.). 48p. (J). (ps-4). 1947. lib. bdg. 16.00 (0-684-92296-7, C Scribner Sons Young) S&S Childrens.

Stone Soup. Ed. by Kathleen Cubley. (Cut & Tell Cutout Ser.). (Illus.). 8p. (J). (ps). 1995. pap. 2.95 (1-57029-065-2, WPH 2218, Totline Bks) Warren Pub Hse.

***Stone Soup.** Cathy Dubowski. LC 97-23590. (Domino Readers Ser.). (Illus.). 32p. (J). (ps-2). 1997. pap. 5.95 (1-887734-22-8) Star Brght Bks.

***Stone Soup.** Heather Forest. LC 97-10453. (Illus.). (J). 1997. 15.95 (0-87483-498-8) August Hse.

Stone Soup. Geof Hewitt. LC 75-303175. 61p. 1974. 3.45 (0-87886-045-2, Greenfld Rev Pr) Greenfld Rev Lit.

Stone Soup. Ann McGovern. (Illus.). 32p. (J). (gr. k-2). 1986. pap. text ed. 2.99 (0-590-41602-2) Scholastic Inc.

Stone Soup. Illus. by Diane Paterson. LC 80-27947. 32p. (J). (gr. 1-4). 1996. pap. 3.95 (0-89375-479-X) Troll Communs.

Stone Soup. Tony Ross. (J). (ps-3). 1990. pap. 3.95 (0-8037-0890-4, Puff Pied Piper) Puffin Bks.

Stone Soup. Tony Ross. 1992. pap. 5.99 (0-14-054708-8) NAL-Dutton.

Stone Soup. Marcia Brown. LC 86-10964. (Illus.). 48p. (J). (ps-2). 1986. reprint ed. pap. 5.99 (0-689-71103-4, Aladdin Paperbacks) S&S Childrens.

Stone Soup, 4 bks., Set. Marcia Brown. (Illus.). (J). (gr. 1-4). 1987. student ed., pap. 33.95 incl. audio (0-87499-054-8) Live Oak Media.

***Stone Soup: A Folktale Play for Children.** Martha Mutz. (Illus.). 65p. (Orig.). (J). (gr. 2-3). 1997. pap. 16.00 (1-889397-30-X, 030) Curiosity Canyon.

***Stone Soup: The First Collection of the Syndicated Strip, Vol. 2.** Jan Eliot. LC 96-79241. (Illus.). 128p. (Orig.). 1996. pap. 9.95 (0-8362-2893-6) Andrews & McMeel.

Stone Soup - Musical. Gary Peterson & Larry Nestor. 1983. 4.25 (0-87129-581-4, S68) Dramatic Pub.

Stone Soup (Brown) Garrett Christopher. Ed. by J. Friedland & R. Kessler. (Novel-Ties Ser.). 1995. student ed., pap. text ed. 14.95 (1-56982-239-5) Lrn Links.

Stone Soup Literature Mini-Unit. Janet Lovelady. (Illus.). 32p. (J). (gr. 2-4). 1989. student ed. 4.95 (1-56096-008-6) Mari.

Stone Soups & Support Groups: Your Guide to a Nurturing Grief Support Group. Patricia H. Zalaznik. (Illus.). 52p. (Orig.). 1996. pap. text ed. 11.95 (0-9642032-1-9) Abundant Res.

Stone Spaces. P. T. Johnstone. (Cambridge Studies in Advanced Mathematics: No. 3). 370p. 1986. pap. text ed. 37.95 (0-521-33779-8) Cambridge U Pr.

Stone Spirit Calling & Ancestral Memory Stones. Katherine Torres. (Illus.). 34p. (Orig.). 1994. 24.95 (1-885015-01-1); pap. 10.95 (0-685-75278-X) Metaphys Counsel Grp.

***Stone Spirits.** Susan Howe. (Redd Center Publications Ser.). 1997. pap. write for info. (1-56085-107-4) Brigham Young Mus.

Stone Surgery. Michael Marberger et al. (Practice of Surgery Ser.). (Illus.). 320p. 1991. text ed. 195.00 (0-443-03522-9) Churchill.

Stone Temple Pilots. Ian Gittins. (CD Bks.). (Illus.). 120p. 1995. pap. 7.99 (1-886894-04-3, MBS Paperbk) Mus Bk Servs.

Stone Temple Pilots. Mick Wall & Malcolm Dome. (Illus.). 64p. pap. 12.95 (0-7119-4822-4, OP 47755) Omnibus NY.

Stone Temple Pilots: Core. (Illus.). 96p. 1993. pap. 19.95 (0-8256-1371-X, AM91464) Music Sales.

Stone Temple Pilots: Purple. 1996. pap. 21.95 (0-8256-1420-1, AM 92217) Music Sales.

Stone Temple Pilots: Tiny Music: Songs from the Vatican Gift Shop. Music Sales Corporation Staff. pap. 17.95 (0-8256-1547-X) Omnibus NY.

Stone That Shines. large type ed. Brand. Date not set. 20.00 (0-7862-0757-4, Thorndike Lrg Prnt) Thorndike Pr.

Stone That Shines. large type ed. Max Brand. LC 96-36734. (Five Star Ser.). 276p. 1997. 17.95 (0-7862-0734-5, Five Star) Mac Lib Ref.

Stone the Poet. Elizabeth A. Petrochilos. 110p. (Orig.). (YA). 1991. pap. write for info. (0-9629730-0-9) E Petrochilos.

Stone Time, Southern Utah: A Portrait & a Meditation. T. H. Watkins. LC 94-17389. (Illus.). 120p. 1994. 34.95 (0-940666-53-7) Clear Light.

Stone Tool Procurement, Production, & Distribution in California Prehistory. Ed. by Jeanne E. Arnold. LC 92-5738. (Perspectives in California Archaeology Ser.: Vol. 2). (Illus.). 156p. 1992. pap. text ed. 20.00 (0-917956-76-1) UCLA Arch.

Stone Tool Use at Cerros: The Ethnoarchaeological & Use-Wear Evidence. Suzanne M. Lewenstein. LC 86-24910. (Illus.). 238p. 1987. text ed. 42.50 (0-292-77590-3) U of Tex Pr.

Stone Tools: Theoretical Insights into Human Prehistory. Ed. by George H. Odell. (Interdisciplinary Contributions to Archaeology Ser.). 400p. 1996. 59.50 (0-306-45198-0, Plenum Pr) Plenum.

Stone Tools & Mobility in the Illinois Valley: From Hunter-Gatherer Camps to Agricultural Villages. George H. Odell. LC 96-1824. (Archaeological Ser.: No. 10). (Illus.). xi, 418p. 1996. pap. 49.50 (1-879621-22-3); lib. bdg. 78.00 (1-879621-23-1) Intl Mono Prehstry.

Stone Trumpet: A Story of Practical School Reform, 1960-1990. Richard A. Gibboney. LC 93-42681. (Democracy & Education Ser.). 306p. (C). 1994. pap. text ed. 19.95 (0-7914-2010-8) State U NY Pr.

Stone Trumpet: A Story of Practical School Reform, 1960-1990. Richard A. Gibboney. LC 93-42681. (SUNY Series, Democracy & Education). 306p. (C). 1994. text ed. 59.50 (0-7914-2009-4) State U NY Pr.

Stone Vessels of the Cyclades in the Early Bronze Age. Pat Getz-Gentle. LC 95-9507. 504p. 1996. 75.00 (0-271-01535-7) Pa St U Pr.

Stone Virgin. Barry Unsworth. 320p. 1995. pap. 13.00 (0-393-31309-3, Norton Paperbks) Norton.

Stone Walk. Drew Gardner. 32p. 1991. pap. 4.00 (0-685-56983-7) St Lazaire.

Stone Wall: An Autobiography. Mary Casal. LC 75-12307. (Homosexuality Ser.). 1975. reprint ed. 19.95 (0-405-07404-2) Ayer.

Stone Walls & Deep Waters. Michael L. Resch. 32p. (Orig.). 1996. pap. 5.00 (1-886405-51-4) White Crow Pr.

Stone Warriors Rule! Paul Mantell. (Gargoyles Ser.: No. 1). (J). 1995. pap. 3.99 (0-590-59876-7) Scholastic Inc.

Stone Water. Barbara S. Gilbert. LC 95-50378. 176p. (YA). (gr. 5 up). 1996. 15.95 (1-886910-11-1, Front Street) Front Str.

Stone Within. David Wingrove. (Chung Kuo Ser.). 624p. 1994. pap. 5.99 (0-440-21755-5) Dell.

Stone, Wood, Oil & Water: Paintings & Sculpture by Sy Gresser, Leon Bibel, Paul Fox, & Chaim Naher. Ori Z. Soltes. (Orig.). pap. text ed. write for info. (1-881456-07-2) B B K Natl Jew Mus.

Stone Work: Reflections on Serious Play & Other Aspects of Country Life. John Jerome. LC 96-3938. 220p. 1996. reprint ed. pap. 11.95 (0-87451-762-1) U Pr of New Eng.

Stone 588. Gerald A. Browne. 448p. 1996. mass mkt. 6.50 (0-446-60170-5) Warner Bks.

Stonebearer. Bucky Montgomery. (Orig.). (YA). (gr. 6 up). 1995. pap. 5.00 (0-88092-258-3) Royal Fireworks.

Stoneboro: An Historical Sketch of a South Carolina Community. Andrea D. Van Landingham Steen. LC 92-43755. 1993. 25.00 (0-87152-462-7) Reprint.

Stonebridge. Linda Griffin. LC 92-85414. 315p. 1993. 11.95 (1-55523-549-2) Winston-Derek.

S

StoneBridge Art Guide: A Christian History Curriculum Guide for Teaching & Learning Art in the American Christian Principle Approach. StoneBridge Educational Foundation Staff. LC 93-247767. (FACE Curriculum Guides Ser.). (Illus.). 128p. (Orig.). 1992. pap. 18.00 (0-912498-12-9) F A C E.

Stonecarver's Rose. Robert Griffin. LC 96-90602. (Illus.). 64p. 1996. 20.00 (1-889314-23-4); pap. 10.00 (1-889314-24-2) Windhover Pub.

Stonecrop: The Country I Remember. Teo Savory. LC 75-43072. 180p. 1980. 20.00 (0-87775-105-6); pap. 9.95 (0-87775-106-4) Unicorn Pr.

Stonecutter. Hitz Demi. LC 93-42413. (J). 1995. 15.00 (0-517-59864-7) Crown Bks Yng Read.

Stonecutter. John Kuramoto. (Illus.). 1994. pap. 11.95 (1-880418-28-2) D M Grant.

Stonecutter. Gerald McDermott. (Illus.). (J). (gr. 1-3). 1978. pap. 5.99 (0-14-050289-0, Puffin) Puffin Bks.

***Stonecutter.** Regine Pernoud. LC 96-9519. (Day With Ser.). (Illus.). (J). 1997. lib. bdg. write for info. (0-8225-1913-5, Lerner Publctns) Lerner Group.

Stonecutter. deluxe ed. John Kuramoto. (Illus.). 1994. pap. 20.00 (1-880418-29-0) D M Grant.

Stonecutter: A Japanese Folk Tale. Illus. & Adapted by Gerald McDermott. LC 94-23302. (J). 1995. write for info. (0-15-200400-9); pap. write for info. (0-15-200399-1) HarBrace.

Stonecutter Who Wanted to Be Rich. (J). 1990. 10.95 (0-685-61053-5) CIS Comm.

Stonecutters at War with the Cliffdwellers: 9 Poems. S. R. Lavin. (Illus.). 1971. 95.00 (0-685-47825-4) Heron Pr.

Stonecutters at War with the Cliffdwellers: 9 Poems. deluxe ed. S. R. Lavin. (Illus.). 1971. boxed 200.00 (0-685-47826-2) Heron Pr.

Stonecutter's Hand. Richard Tillinghast. 96p. 1995. 19.95 (1-56792-011-X) Godine.

Stoned Apocalypse. Marco Vassi. 250p. 1993. pap. 16.95 (0-933256-81-7) Second Chance.

Stoned Apocalypse. Marco Vassi. 1993. reprint ed. pap. 12.95 (1-56333-132-2, Badboy) Masquerade.

Stoned Apocalypse. Marco Vassi. 1996. reprint ed. mass mkt. 5.95 (1-56333-401-1) Masquerade.

Stoned Free: How to Get High Without Drugs. Patrick Wells & Douglas Rushkoff. LC 95-76191. (Illus.). 168p. (Orig.). (C). 1995. pap. 14.95 (1-55950-126-X, 85203) Loompanics.

Stonedust. Justin Scott. 304p. 1996. pap. 5.95 (0-14-023456-X, Viking) Viking Penguin.

Stoneface. James Axler. (Deathlands Ser.: No. 34). 1996. mass mkt. 5.50 (0-373-62534-0, 1-62534-2, Wrldwide Lib) Harlequin Bks.

Stonefish. Charles West. Ed. by Janet Hutchings. 219p. 1991. 17.95 (0-8027-5795-2) Walker & Co.

Stoneflies for the Angler. Eric Leiser & Robert H. Boyle. LC 90-9576. (Illus.). 192p. 1990. reprint ed. pap. 14.95 (0-8117-2401-8) Stackpole.

Stoneflower Literary Journal. 118p. 1996. pap. text ed. write for info. (0-9631719-2-5) C R Shaddox.

***Stoneflower Literary Journal, Vol. 2.** Ed. by Brenda Davidson-Shaddox. (Illus.). 92p. (Orig.). 1997. per. 8.00 (0-9631719-3-3) C R Shaddox.

Stoneflowers. Sue Chance. LC 94-94172. 400p. 1994. 22.95 (0-9638398-4-5) Bonne Chance.

Stonehaven. Amanda MacLean. 1995. pap. 8.99 (0-88070-757-7, Multnomah Bks) Multnomah Pubs.

***Stoneheart: The Real Valentine's Day Story.** Gib O. Twyman. LC 96-80055. (Illus.). 32p. (J). (gr. k-3). 1997. 14.95 (1-886110-13-1) Addax Pubng.

Stonehenge. R. J. Atkinson. (Illus.). 256p. (Orig.). 1992. pap. 11.00 (0-14-013646-0, Penguin Bks) Viking Penguin.

Stonehenge. Harry Harrison & Leon Stover. 352p. 1992. mass mkt. 3.99 (0-8125-2068-8) Tor Bks.

Stonehenge. Catherine McMorrow. 1996. lib. bdg. write for info. (0-679-97499-7) Random Hse Value.

Stonehenge. Catherine McMorrow. (J). 1996. write for info. (0-679-87499-2) Random Bks Yng Read.

Stonehenge. NCCL Inquiry Staff. (C). 1988. 21.00 (0-946088-28-4, Pub. by NCCL UK) St Mut.

Stonehenge: A Doorway of Recall. Dianthus. LC 93-90485. (Illus.). 160p. (Orig.). 1994. pap. 12.95 (0-9622160-2-X) Dianthus.

Stonehenge: An Ancient Masonic Temple. enl. rev. ed. Russell A. Herner. LC 83-63526. (Illus.). xvi, 144p. 1984. text ed. 15.95 (0-88053-077-4, M-327) Macoy Pub.

***Stonehenge: Prehistoric Man & the Cosmos.** John North. 1997. 35.00 (0-684-84512-1) Free Pr.

Stonehenge: The Indo-European Heritage. Leon E. Stover & Bruce Kraig. LC 77-25255. 224p. 1978. 49.95 (0-88229-482-2) Nelson-Hall.

***Stonehenge: The Secret of the Solstice.** Terence Meaden. (Illus.). 176p. (Orig.). 1997. pap. 16.95 (0-285-63364-3, Pub. by Souvenir UK) IPG Chicago.

Stonehenge & Druidism. rev. ed. E. Raymond Capt. LC 79-54773. (Illus.). 96p. 1979. pap. 4.00 (0-934666-04-0) Artisan Sales.

Stonehenge & Its Environs. Royal Commission on Historical Monuments. (RCHM Inventory Vols Ser.). (Illus.). 50p. 1979. pap. 15.00 (0-85224-379-0, Pub. by Edinburgh U Pr UK) Col U Pr.

***Stonehenge & the Great Pyramid: Window on the Universe.** Bonnie Gaunt. LC 93-90098. (Illus.). 192p. (C). 1993. pap. 12.95 (0-932813-16-X) Adventures Unltd.

Stonehenge Complete. rev. ed. Christopher Chippindale. LC 93-61371. (Illus.). 296p. 1994. pap. 24.95 (0-500-27750-8) Thames Hudson.

Stonehenge People: An Exploration of Life in Neolithic Britain, 4700-2000 B.C. Rodney Castleden. (Illus.). 224p. 1987. text ed. 29.50 (0-7102-0968-1, RKP) Routledge.

Stonehenge People: An Exploration of Life in Neolithic Britain 4700-2000 BC. Rodney Castleden. LC 89-70136. 282p. (Orig.). (gr. 13). 1992. pap. 14.95 (0-415-04065-5, A4660) Routledge.

***Stonehenge Revealed.** David Souden. LC 97-24792. 1997. write for info. (0-8160-3720-5) Facts on File.

Stonehenge...A Closer Look. Bonnie Gaunt. LC 79-51777. (Illus.). 236p. 1980. pap. 10.00 (0-9602688-0-4) Adventures Unltd.

***Stonehook Schooner.** Judith C. Mills et al. 32p. (J). (gr. k-2). 1997. 14.95 (1-55013-653-4, Pub. by Key Porter Bks CN) Firefly Bks Ltd.

***Stonehook Schooner.** Judith C. Mills et al. 32p. (J). (gr. k-2). 1997. pap. 4.95 (1-55013-719-0, Pub. by Key Porter Bks CN) Firefly Bks Ltd.

Stonehurst. Barbara Johnson. 240p. 1992. pap. 9.95 (1-56280-024-8) Naiad Pr.

Stonekeep: The Official Strategy Guide. Rick Barba. 1995. pap. 19.95 (1-55958-733-4) Prima Pub.

***Stonekiller.** J. Robert Janes. 1997. pap. 12.00 (1-56947-107-X) Soho Press.

Stonemans: An Appalachian Family & the Music That Shaped Their Lives. Ivan M. Tribe. LC 92-22232. (Music in American Life Ser.). (Illus.). 352p. (C). 1993. 16.95 (0-252-06308-2); text ed. 44.95 (0-252-01978-4) U of Ill Pr.

Stonemason. Cormac McCarthy. 1995. pap. 12.00 (0-679-76280-9) Random Hse Value.

Stonemason: A Play in Five Acts. Cormac McCarthy. LC 93-41252. 1994. 19.95 (0-88001-359-1) Ecco Pr.

***Stonemill & Bhakti: From the Devotion of Peasant Women to the Philosophy of Swamis.** Guy Poitevin & Hema Rairkar. (C). 1996. 68.00 (81-246-0059-7, Pub. by DK Pubs Dist II) S Asia.

Stonemoor House. Kay Stephens. 288p. 1995. 20.00 (0-7278-4766-8) Severn Hse.

***Stonemoor House.** large type ed. Kay Stephens. (Magna Large Print Ser.). 400p. 1996. 25.99 (0-7505-0893-0, Pub. by Magna Print Bks UK) Ulverscroft.

Stoner. John E. Williams. LC 87-31948. (Reprint Ser.). 283p. 1988. reprint ed. pap. 18.00 (1-55728-029-0) U of Ark Pr.

Stoner McTavish. Sarah Dreher. LC 94-1758. (Stoner McTavish Mystery Ser.). 200p. 1985. pap. 9.95 (0-934678-06-5) New Victoria Pubs.

Stoner's Crossing. Judith Pella. (Lone Star Legacy Ser.: Bk. 2). 1994. pap. 10.99 (1-55661-294-X) Bethany Hse.

Stones. Catherine Chambers. (Would You Believe It! Ser.). (J). 1996. lib. bdg. 21.40 (0-8172-4105-1) Raintree Steck-V.

Stones. Pat Graversen. 288p. 1991. mass mkt. 3.95 (0-8217-3268-4, Zebra Kensgtn) Kensgtn Pub Corp.

Stones. Erica Pedretti. Tr. by Judith Black from GER. (Swiss Library). 220p. (Orig.). 1982. pap. 9.95 (0-7145-3942-2) Riverrun NY.

Stones. Philip Norman. 400p. 1994. reprint ed. pap. 10.95 (0-14-017411-7, Penguin Bks) Viking Penguin.

Stones: "Concepts about Print" Tests. Marie Clay. 20p. (Orig.). (J). 1980. pap. text ed. 4.00 (0-435-00556-1, 00556) Heinemann.

Stones: A Litnay. James Chichetto. (Illus.). 20p. 1980. pap. 4.00 (0-939622-06-8) Four Zoas Night Ltd.

Stones: Poems by Daisy Aldan. Daisy Aldan. (Illus.). 1973. 4.95 (0-913152-20-X) Folder Edns.

Stones about the Middle Sea & Other Poems - Yiddish - English. Isaac Imber. 96p. 1992. pap. 8.95 (965-229-061-0, Pub. by Gefen Pub Hse IS) Gefen Bks.

***Stones & Bones.** Carl Wieland. 40p. 1996. pap. 4.95 (0-89051-175-6, STOBON) Master Bks.

Stones & Bones. Lisa Yount. 82p. (Orig.). 1986. pap. 4.95 (0-9617366-0-7) Half Lump Pr.

Stones & Bones! How Archaeologists Trace Human Origins. Avraham Ronen. LC 93-2480. (Buried Worlds Ser.). (YA). (gr. 6 up). 1993. lib. bdg. 22.95 (0-8225-3207-7, Lerner Publctns) Lerner Group.

Stones & Poets: An Anthology of Poetry. 2nd ed. Ed. by Patricia C. Groth & Kitty Druck. LC 80-66853. (Illus.). 90p. (Orig.). 1981. pap. 7.00 (0-937158-01-1) Del Valley.

Stones & Roses. Erin C. Pitner. 80p. (Orig.). 1993. pap. 5.95 (0-9637559-0-0) Chamisa.

Stones & Switches. Lorne Simon. 156p. (Orig.). 1994. pap. 9.95 (0-919441-68-8, Pub. by Theytus Bks Ltd CN) Orca Bk Pubs.

Stones Bones & Ancient Cities. Lawrence H. Robbins. 1990. 18.95 (0-312-04431-3) St Martin.

Stones, Bones, & Ancient Cities: Great Discoveries in Archaeology & the Search for Human. Lawrence H. Robbins. 1992. pap. 10.95 (0-312-07848-X) St Martin.

Stones, Bones, & Ancient Cities: Great Discoveries in Archaeology & the Search for Human Origins. Lawrence H. Robbins. (Illus.). 304p. 1992. 10.95 (0-685-52431-0) St Martin.

Stones by Kruger. Sebastian Kruger. 96p. 1996. pap. text ed. 27.50 (1-883398-18-5) Morpheus Intl.

Stones Cry Out. William W. Francis. (Illus.). 138p. 1993. text ed. 19.95 (0-89216-097-7, 52892097) Salvation Army.

Stones Cry Out: God's Best Kept Secret Hidden in Stone. Bonnie Gaunt. (Illus.). 160p. (Orig.). 1991. pap. 10.00 (0-9602688-2-0) Adventures Unltd.

***Stones Cry Out: New Archaeological Discoveries of the Bible.** Randall Price. LC 97-16947. (Illus.). 250p. (Orig.). 1997. pap. 10.99 (1-56507-640-0) Harvest Hse.

Stones Cry Out: Sweden's Response to Persecution of Jews 1933-1945. Steven Koblik. 1988. 20.95 (0-89604-118-2, Holocaust Library); pap. 13.95 (0-89604-119-0, Holocaust Library) US Holocaust.

Stones Don't Float: Poems Selected & New. John Haag. LC 96-24145. 1996. write for info. (0-8142-0716-2); pap. 11.95 (0-8142-0717-0) Ohio St U Pr.

***Stone's Flower.** Miranda Fix. 231p. (Orig.). 1997. mass mkt. 4.99 (1-55197-835-0, Pub. by Comnwlth Pub CN) Partners Pubs Grp.

Stones for Ibarra. Harriet Doerr. 224p. 1985. pap. 10.95 (0-14-007562-3, Penguin Bks) Viking Penguin.

Stones For Ibarra. Harriet Doerr. 1988. mass mkt. 6.95 (0-14-011218-9, Penguin Bks) Viking Penguin.

***Stones from the Muse.** Jennifer R. Jacobson & Emily Herman. LC 97-3762. 1997. pap. 20.00 (0-684-83955-5) S&S Trade.

***Stones from the River.** Ursula Hegi. 1997. 26.00 (0-684-84472-9, Scribners PB Fict); pap. 13.00 (0-684-84477-X, Scribners PB Fict) S&S Trade.

***Stones from the River.** large type ed. Ursula Hegi. LC 97-12441. (Core Ser.). 846p. 1997. lib. bdg. 28.95 (0-7838-8202-5, GK Hall) Thorndike Pr.

Stones in the Brook. Gomer Press Staff. (C). 1978. pap. 20.00 (0-85088-790-9, Pub. by Gomer Pr UK) St Mut.

Stones in the Lake. John M. Bennett. (Illus.). 20p. (Orig.). 1987. pap. 3.00 (0-935350-14-4) Luna Bisonte.

***Stones in Water.** Donna J. Napoli. LC 97-14253. Orig. Title: WW II. (J). 1997. pap. 14.99 (0-525-45842-5) Dutton Child Bks.

Stones in Water. David Solway. 48p. 1995. lib. bdg. 25.00 (0-8095-4586-1) Borgo Pr.

Stones in Water. David Solway. 4p. pap. 7.95 (0-88962-211-6) Mosaic.

Stone's Justices' Manual, 1993, 3 vols., Set. Ed. by John Richman & A. T. Draycott. 7700p. 1993. 403.00 (0-406-38627-7, U.K.) MICHIE.

Stone's Justices' Manual 1994. 126th ed. Ed. by A. T. Draycott et al. 1994. write for info. (0-406-03501-6, U.K.) MICHIE.

Stone's Justices' Manual 1996, 3 vols., Set, incl. case. 128th ed. Ed. by A. T. Draycott et al. 7700p. 1996. write for info. (0-406-06463-6) MICHIE.

***Stones Laid Before the Lord.** Anselme Dimier. Tr. by Gilchrist Lavigne. (Cistercian Studies: No. 152). Date not set. write for info. (0-87907-552-X); pap. write for info. (0-87907-652-6) Cistercian Pubns.

Stones of Assyria. Cyril J. Gadd. LC 83-45767. reprint ed. 110.00 (0-404-20104-0) AMS Pr.

Stones of Athens. R. E. Wycherley. LC 77-72142. (Illus.). 312p. 1977. pap. text ed. 19.95 (0-691-10059-4) Princeton U Pr.

Stones of Chile. Pablo Neruda. Tr. by Dennis Maloney from SPA. 1987. pap. 10.00 (0-934834-01-6) White Pine.

Stones of Destiny. Eileen Dunlop. 142p. (J). (gr. 4-7). 1994. pap. 7.95 (1-85371-307-4, Pub. by Poolbeg Pr IE) Dufour.

Stones of Fire. Isobel Kuhn. 1951. pap. 5.95 (9971-972-00-X) OMF Bks.

Stones of Fire. Isobel Kuhn. 1996. pap. 6.99 (9971-972-76-X) OMF Bks.

Stones of Florence. Mary McCarthy. LC 64-49015. 230p. 1963. pap. 10.00 (0-15-685080-X, Harvest Bks) HarBrace.

Stones of Florence. Mary McCarthy. (Illus.). 1987. pap. 19.95 (0-15-685081-8, Harvest Bks); text ed. 49.95 (0-317-64159-X, Harvest Bks) HarBrace.

Stones of Muncaster Cathedral. Robert Westall. (J). (gr. 4-7). 1993. 11.00 (0-374-37263-2) FS&G.

Stones of Muncaster Cathedral. Robert Westall. (J). (gr. 4-7). 1994. pap. 3.95 (0-374-47119-3, Sunburst Bks) FS&G.

Stones of Muncaster Cathedral. large type ed. Robert Westall. LC 93-10871. (YA). 1993. pap. 14.95 (1-56054-766-9) Thorndike Pr.

Stones of Sanctity: Art & Architecture of the Jain Temples. M. A. Dhaki. (Illus.). 192p. 1996. 65.00 (0-944142-65-6, Pub. by Mapin Pubng II) Antique Collect.

Stones of Silence: Journeys in the Himalaya. George B. Schaller. (Illus.). xii, 304p. 1988. pap. 16.95 (0-226-73646-6) U Ch Pr.

Stones of the Dalai Lama. Ken Mitchell. LC 92-42445. 328p. 1993. 22.00 (0-939149-79-6) Soho Press.

***Stones of the Dalai Lama.** Ken Mitchell. 1997. pap. 13.00 (1-56947-100-2) Soho Press.

Stones of the Sky. Pablo Neruda. Tr. by James Nolan from SPA. LC 87-71140. 80p. (Orig.). 1987. 15.00 (1-55659-006-7); pap. 10.00 (1-55659-007-5) Copper Canyon.

Stones of the Temple. J. F. Voros, Jr. LC 93-9541. (Illus.). 1993. 12.95 (0-87579-735-0) Deseret Bk.

Stones of Time: Calendars, Sundials, & Stone Chambers of Ancient Ireland. Martin Brennan. (Illus.). 216p. 1994. pap. 19.95 (0-89281-509-4) Inner Tradit.

Stones of Venice. John Ruskin. Ed. by J. G. Links. (Quality Paperbacks Ser.). 256p. 1985. reprint ed. pap. 11.95 (0-306-80244-9) Da Capo.

Stones of Virtue: Chinese Jades from the Gerald Godfrey Collection. Clarence W. Kelley. (Illus.). 52p. 1989. pap. text ed. 12.00 (0-937809-06-3) Dayton Art.

Stones Remember. Ed. by Moshe Dor et al. LC 90-70198. 120p. (Orig.). 1991. pap. 15.00 (0-915380-25-0) Word Works.

Stones River: Bloody Winter in Tennessee. James L. McDonough. LC 80-11580. 286p. 1980. 31.95 (0-87049-301-9); pap. 16.95 (0-87049-373-6) U of Tenn Pr.

Stone's River: Turning Point of the Civil War. Wilson J. Vance. 1982. pap. text ed. 12.50 (0-87556-584-0) Saifer.

Stones River Ran Red. Richard J. Reid. LC 89-189682. (Illus.). 83p. (Orig.). 1986. reprint ed. pap. write for info. (1-877713-02-3) R J Reid.

Stones, the Dark Earth. Elizabeth Herron. 20p. 1995. pap. 5.00 (1-885141-04-1) Harlequin Ink.

Stones, Thrones & a Valley of Bones: Finding Your Way in the Old Testament. Dan Vander Ark. (Prime-Time Bible Studies). 1994. teacher ed. 8.45 (1-56212-059-X) CRC Pubns.

Stone's Throw: Selected Essays. Jennifer Stone. 200p. 1987. 25.00 (1-55643-032-9); pap. 12.95 (1-55643-031-0) North Atlantic.

Stone's Throw from Ellis Island: Economic Implications of Immigration to New Jersey. Ed. by Thomas J. Espenshade. LC 93-39234. 1994. 59.50 (0-8191-9416-6) U Pr of Amer.

***Stone's Throw from Paradise.** Linda O. High. LC 96-30694. 128p. (J). 1997. 15.00 (0-8028-5147-9); pap. 5.00 (0-8028-5142-8) Eerdmans.

Stones Unfolding from the Gardens of Time. Richard E. Raizman. 150p. (Orig.). 1994. pap. 7.95 (0-9642627-0-3) Mtn Meadow Pr.

Stones Unturned. Napoleon St. Cyr. LC 67-8221. 1967. 4.00 (0-910380-01-5) Cider Mill.

Stones Will Cry Out: Pastoral Reflections on the Shoah with Liturgical Resources. Douglas K. Huneke. LC 95-2094. 232p. 1995. text ed. 57.95 (0-313-29216-7, Greenwood Pr) Greenwood.

Stones with Fair Colors. Gary Bowell. pap. 7.99 (0-88019-111-2) Schmul Pub Co.

Stonescaping: A Guide to Using Stone in Your Garden. Jan K. Whitner. Ed. by Ben Watson. LC 91-55485. (Illus.). 168p. 1992. 27.95 (0-88266-756-4, Garden Way Pub); pap. 18.95 (0-88266-755-6, Garden Way Pub) Storey Comm Inc.

Stoneskin's Revenge. Tom Deitz. 320p. 1991. pap. 3.95 (0-380-76063-0) Avon.

Stonewall. Martin Duberman. LC 93-45838. (Illus.). 352p. 1994. pap. 13.95 (0-452-27206-8, Plume) NAL-Dutton.

Stonewall. Jean Fritz. (Illus.). (Orig.). (J). (gr. 3-7). 1979. 15.95 (0-399-20698-1, Putnam) Putnam Pub Group.

***Stonewall.** Jean Fritz. (Illus.). 160p. (Orig.). (YA). (gr. 5 up). 1997. pap. 5.95 (0-698-11552-X, Paperstar) Putnam Pub Group.

Stonewall: A Biography of General Thomas J. Jackson. Byron Farwell. 576p. 1993. pap. 16.95 (0-393-31086-8) Norton.

Stonewall Brigade. James I. Robertson, Jr. LC 63-9648. (Illus.). xiii, 272p. 1977. pap. 11.95 (0-8071-0396-9) La State U Pr.

Stonewall Experiment: A Gay Psychohistory. Ian Young. 1995. pap. 17.95 (0-304-33272-0, Pub. by Cassell Pubng UK) LPC InBook.

Stonewall in the Valley: Thomas J. "Stonewall" Jackson's Shenandoah Valley Campaign, Spring 1862. rev. ed. Robert G. Tanner. (Illus.). 624p. 1995. 34.95 (0-8117-1708-9) Stackpole.

Stonewall Jackson: Confederate General. Lynda Pflueger. LC 96-8827. (Historical American Biographies Ser.). 128p. (YA). (gr. 6 up). 1997. lib. bdg. 18.95 (0-89490-781-6) Enslow Pubs.

Stonewall Jackson: Lee's Greatest Lieutenant. Barbara J. Bennett. (History of the Civil War Ser.). (Illus.). 160p. (YA). (gr. 5 up). 1990. pap. 7.95 (0-382-24048-0) Silver Burdett Pr.

Stonewall Jackson: Loved in the South Admired in the North. Charles Ludwig. (Sower Ser.). (Illus.). (J). (gr. 3-6). 1989. pap. 7.99 (0-88062-157-5) Mott Media.

Stonewall Jackson: Portrait of a Soldier. John Bowers. 368p. 1990. reprint ed. pap. 12.00 (0-380-71164-8) Avon.

Stonewall Jackson: The Good Soldier. Allen Tate. LC 91-62455. (Southern Classics Ser.). (Illus.). 342p. (C). 1991. reprint ed. pap. 11.95 (1-879941-02-3) J S Sanders.

Stonewall Jackson: The Man, the Soldier, the Legend. James I. Robertson. LC 96-17042. 950p. 1997. 40.00 (0-02-864685-1) Mac Lib Ref.

Stonewall Jackson & the American Civil War. G. F. Henderson. (Quality Paperbacks Ser.). 740p. 1988. reprint ed. pap. 16.95 (0-306-80318-6) Da Capo.

Stonewall Jackson at Cedar Mountain. Robert K. Krick. LC 89-36158. (Illus.). xvi, 472p. (C). 1990. 32.50 (0-8078-1887-9) U of NC Pr.

Stonewall Jackson at Gettysburg. Douglas L. Gibboney. LC 96-6956. (Illus.). 118p. (Orig.). (YA). (gr. 10 up). 1996. pap. 9.95 (1-887901-04-3) Sergeant Kirk.

Stonewall Jackson, Robert E. Lee, & the Army of Northern Virginia, 1862. William Allan. (Illus.). 755p. 1995. reprint ed. pap. 19.95 (0-306-80656-8) Da Capo.

Stonewall Jackson's Romney Campaign, January 1 - February 20, 1862. Thomas M. Rankin. (Virginia Civil War Battles & Leaders Ser.). (Illus.). 192p. 1994. 25.00 (1-56190-070-2) H E Howard.

Stonewall Jackson's Surgeon Hunter Holmes McGuire: A Biography. Maurice F. Shaw. (Virginia Civil War Battles & Leaders Ser.). (Illus.). 114p. 1993. write for info. (1-56190-047-8) H E Howard.

Stonewall Jackson's Valley Campaign. William Allan. 1995. (0-8317-1432-8) Smithmark.

Stonewall Jackson's Verse. H. Rondel Rumburg. 147p. 1992. 16.95 (0-9639730-0-2) Soc Bibl & So Stud.

Stonewall Jackson's Way: Route, Method, Achievement. rev. unabridged ed. John W. Wayland. (Illus.). 244p. 1996. reprint ed. text ed. 45.00 (0-89029-083-0) Morningside Bkshop.

Stonewall Jim: A Biography of General James A. Walker, C. S. A. Lon K. Savage. (Illus.). 280p. (YA). (gr. 10-12). 1990. 24.95 (0-9617256-4-8); pap. 12.95 (0-9617256-5-6) Northcross Hse.

An Asterisk (*) at the beginning of an entry indicates that the title is appearing in BIP for the first time.

***Stonewall of the West: Patrick Cleburne & the Civil War.** Craig L. Symonds. LC 96-44624. (Modern War Studies). (Illus.). 340p. 1997. 34.95 (0-7006-0820-6) U Pr of KS.
Stonewall Riots. Andrea Natalie. (Stonewall Riots Cartoons Ser.). (Illus.). 74p. (Orig.). 1990. pap. 4.95 (0-9628027-0-0, VA 154-987) A Natalie Pub.
Stonewall Riots. Andrea Natalie. (Illus.). 76p. (Orig.). 1990. reprint ed. pap. 4.95 (0-9628027-1-9, VA154987) A Natalie Pub.
***Stonewall's Courier.** Virginia Hinkins. 192p. (YA). (gr. 9-12). 1997. 19.95 (0-9630797-4-3) Loft Pr.
Stoneware Creations. Duncan Staff Artists. 44p. 1992. pap. 7.95 (0-916809-57-9) Scott Pubns MI.
Stoneware in Southwestern Pennsylvania. Phil Schaltenbrand. LC 95-32171. (Illus.). 226p. (C). 1996. 49.95 (0-8229-3915-0); pap. 22.95 (0-8229-5578-4) U of Pittsburgh Pr.
Stoneware Monkey. R. Austin Freeman. (Mystery Classics Ser.). 224p. 1987. reprint ed. pap. 6.95 (0-486-25471-2) Dover.
Stonewares of Yixing: From the Ming Period to the Present Day. K. S. Lo. LC 85-50363. (Illus.). 288p. 1986. 125.00 (0-85667-181-9, Pub. by P Wilson Pubs) Sothebys Pubns.
***Stonewares of Yixing: From the Ming Period to the Present Day.** K. S. Lo. (Illus.). 287p. 1987. write for info. (962-209-112-1, Pub. by Hong Kong Univ Pr HK) Coronet Bks.
Stonewater Rapture. Doug Wright. 1990. pap. 3.25 (0-8222-1082-7) Dramatists Play.
Stonewords: A Ghost Story. Pam Conrad. LC 89-36382. 144p. (J). (gr. 5 up). 1990. lib. bdg. 14.89 (0-06-021316-7) HarpC Child Bks.
Stonewords: A Ghost Story. Pam Conrad. LC 89-36382. (Trophy Bk.). 144p. (YA). (gr. 5 up). 1991. pap. 4.50 (0-06-440354-8, Trophy) HarpC Child Bks.
***Stonework: A Weekend Retreat.** Jane M. Grant. 15p. 1992. pap. 6.50 (1-877871-39-7, 3318) Ed Ministries.
***Stonework: Techniques & Projects.** Charles McRaven. Ed. by Elizabeth McHale. 192p. 1997. pap. 18.95 (0-88266-976-1, Storey Pub) Storey Comm Inc.
Stonework of the Sky. Joseph A. Enzweiler. 69p. 1995. pap. 12.50 (1-55597-222-5) Graywolf.
***Stonewycke Legacy.** Michael Phillips. 1997. 12.99 (0-88486-169-4, Bristol Park Bks) Arrowood Pr.
Stonewycke Trilogy. Michael Phillips. 1996. 12.98 (0-88486-133-3) Arrowood Pr.
***Stonewycke Trilogy, Vol. 1-3.** Michael Phillips. 1987. pap. text ed. 26.99 (0-87123-971-X) Bethany Hse.
Stoney Creek Recipe Collection: A Treasury of Culinary Favorites & Historical Vignettes. (Illus.). 352p. 1994. 18.95 (1-881576-30-2) Providence Hse.
***Stoney Gaze: Archaic Head Carvings in West Yorkshire.** (Illus.). (Orig.). Date not set. pap. write for info. (1-898307-69-5, Pub. by Capall Bann Pubng UK) Holmes Pub.
Stoney Point Poems. Lorraine S. DeGennaro. Ed. by Alana Sherman. (Chapbooks Third Ser.). 16p. (Orig.). 1990. pap. 3.50 (0-939689-08-1) Alms Hse Pr.
***Stoneybatter: Dublin's Inner-Urban Village.** Kevin C. Kearns. (Illus.). 264p. 1996. pap. 25.95 (0-7171-2453-3, Pub. by Gill & MacMill IE) Irish Bks Media.
Stoning of Soraya M. Freidoune Sahebjam. Tr. by Richard Seaver from FRE. 160p. 1994. 15.95 (1-55970-233-8) Arcade Pub Inc.
Stoning of Soraya M. Freidoune Sahebjam. Tr. by Richard Seaver from FRE. 160p. 1995. pap. 9.95 (1-55970-270-2) Arcade Pub Inc.
Stonington Cook Book. Young People's Society of Christian Endeavor Staff. (Bicentennial Edition Ser.: 1776-1976). 102p. 1975. pap. 10.00 (0-910258-04-X) Book & Tackle.
Stonington Houses: A Panorama of New England Architecture, 1750-1900. John J. Trask. (Illus.). 120p. 1995. reprint ed. lib. bdg. 29.95 (0-8328-4648-1) Higginson Bk Co.
Stony Ground: One Teacher's Fight Against Juvenile Crime. Linda W. Post. LC 93-9095. 1994. 16.95 (0-89015-918-1) Sunbelt Media.
Stony Man, No. III. Don Pendleton. 1991. mass mkt. 4.99 (0-373-61887-5) Harlequin Bks.
Stony Man IV. (Stony Man Ser.: No. 888). 1992. mass mkt. 4.99 (0-373-61888-3, 1-61888-3) Harlequin Bks.
Stony Man Seven. 1993. mass mkt. 4.99 (0-373-61891-3, 1-61891-7) Harlequin Bks.
Stony Man Two. Don Pendleton. 1991. mass mkt. 4.50 (0-373-61886-7) Harlequin Bks.
Stony Man V. (Stony Man Ser.). 1992. mass mkt. 4.99 (0-373-61889-1, 1-61889-1) Harlequin Bks.
Stony Pass: The Tumbling & Impetuous Trail. Cathy E. Kindquist. (Illus.). 145p. (Orig.). (C). 1988. pap. 8.95 (0-9608000-5-0) San Juan County.
***Stony Point Illustrated: An Account of the Early Settlement on the Hudson, with Traditions & Relics of the Revolution & Some Genealogical Record of the Present (1888) Inhabitants.** Ed. by W. R. Kiefer. (Illus.). 166p. 1997. reprint ed. lib. bdg. 27.50 (0-8328-6251-7) Higginson Bk Co.
***Stony Point Illustrated: An Account of the Early Settlement on the Hudson, with Traditions & Relics of the Revolution & Some Genealogical Record of the Present (1888) Inhabitants.** Ed. by W. R. Kiefer. (Illus.). 166p. 1997. reprint ed. pap. 19.50 (0-8328-6252-5) Higginson Bk Co.
***Stony Point/Revolutionary War the Storming of Stony Point on the Hudson, Midnight, July 15, 1779.** Henry P. Johnston. (Illus.). 274p. 1997. reprint ed. lib. bdg. 35.00 (0-8328-6250-9) Higginson Bk Co.
Stony the Road We Trod: African American Biblical Interpretation. Ed. by Cain H. Felder. LC 91-19567. 272p. 1991. pap. 18.00 (0-8006-2501-3) Augsburg Fortress.
Stonyfield Farm Yogurt Cookbook. Susan E. Melrath. LC 94-12068. (Illus.). (Orig.). 1994. 17.95 (1-884943-04-7) Eat Well Bks.
Stonyfield Farm Yogurt Cookbook. 2nd ed. Meg C. Hirshberg. Ed. by Sharon Smith & Sandra Taylor. (Illus.). 224p. (Orig.). 1995. reprint ed. pap. 17.95 (0-9646695-0-1) Stonyfld Cultured Bks.
Stooge Fans IQ Test. Ronald L. Smith. 208p. 1993. reprint ed. pap. 5.50 (1-56171-217-5, S P I Bks) Sure Seller.
Stoogism Anthology. Ed. by Paul F. Fericano. LC 77-76619. (Illus.). 1977. pap. 50.00 (0-916296-01-6) Poor Souls Pr.
Stool Wives. William F. Van Wert. LC 95-50641. (Nivola Ser.). 190p. 1996. 20.00 (0-917635-20-5) Plover Pr.
Stools & Bottles. Gayle Rosellini. 160p. 1955. 10.00 (0-89486-027-5, 1040A) Hazelden.
Stop. David Appelbaum. LC 94-48098. (SUNY Series in Western Esoteric Traditions). 154p. 1995. text ed. 44.50 (0-7914-2381-6); pap. text ed. 16.95 (0-7914-2382-4) State U NY Pr.
***Stop! Just for Kids.** Terri Allred & Gary Burns. (Illus.). 168p. (Orig.). (J). (gr. 4). 1996. pap. 15.00 (1-884444-37-7) Safer Soc.
Stop a Moment: A Group Leader's Handbook of Energizing Experiences. Jim Ballard. LC 77-81459. (Mandala Series in Education). (Illus.). 73p. 1982. reprint ed. pap. 5.95 (0-8290-0981-7) Irvington.
Stop Aging Now! large type ed. Jean Carper. 435p. 1996. 26.95 (0-7838-1546-8) G K Hall.
Stop Aging Now! large type ed. Jean Carper. 1995. 24.00 (0-06-018355-1, HarpT) HarpC.
Stop Aging Now! The Ultimate Plan for Staying Young & Reversing the Aging Process. Jean Carper. 368p. 1996. pap. text ed. 14.00 (0-06-098500-3) HarpC.
Stop Aging or Slow the Process: Exercise with Oxygen Therapy. William C. Douglass. Ed. by Steven E. Kroening. (Illus.). 60p. (Orig.). 1994. pap. write for info. (1-885236-02-6) Second Opinion.
Stop & Find: Space Race Mazes. Anthony Tallarico. (Illus.). 12p. (Orig.). (J). 1991. pap. 1.95 (1-56156-030-8) Kidsbks.
Stop & Find Maze Madness. Anthony Tallarico. (Stop & Find Ser.). (Illus.). 14p. (Orig.). (J). 1991. pap. 1.95 (1-56156-108-8) Kidsbks.
Stop & Find Maze Madness. Anthony Tallarico. (Illus.). 12p. (Orig.). (J). (gr. 4-7). 1990. pap. 1.95 (1-878890-00-X) Palisades Prodns.
Stop & Go Potty. Judith Blau. LC 92-61706. (Illus.). 6p. (J). (ps). 1993. 6.99 (0-679-84021-4) Random Bks Yng Read.
Stop & Smell the Rosemary: Recipes & Traditions to Remember. Junior League of Houston Staff. LC 96-75924. (Illus.). 296p. 1996. 26.95 (0-9632421-2-1) Jr Leag Houston.
***Stop! & Think.** Joe E. Robinson. 32p. 1996. pap. 7.00 (0-8059-4030-8) Dorrance.
Stop & Think Parenting. Lindy Peterson. 83p. (Orig.). 1993. pap. 16.95 (0-86431-131-1, Pub. by Aust Coun Educ Res AT) Paul & Co Pubs.
Stop at Nothing. large type ed. Douglas Rutherford. 1989. 25.99 (0-7089-2109-4) Ulverscroft.
Stop Auto Repair Rip-Off. Mario Sasso & Michael Ross. (Life Line Ser.). 125p. (Orig.). 1995. pap. 11.95 (1-55059-094-4, Pub. by Detselig CN) Temeron Bks.
***Stop Being a Shnook & Protect Yourself! A Guide to Managing Your Creditor & Debtor Relationships.** Jared King. xii, 228p. 1997. 24.95 (0-9655624-0-9) White Knight.
Stop Being Manipulated. George H. Green & Carolyn Cotter. 192p. (Orig.). 1995. pap. text ed. 4.99 (0-425-14686-3) Berkley Pub.
***Stop Being Mean to Yourself.** Melody Beattie. LC 96-39644. 1997. write for info. (0-06-251119-X) Harper SF.
***Stop Being Mean to Yourself.** Melody Beattie. 1998. pap. 10.00 (0-06-251120-3) HarpC.
Stop Blaming, Start Loving: A Solution-Oriented Approach to Improving Your Relationship. Bill O'Hanlon & Pat Hudson. 192p. 1996. pap. 11.00 (0-393-31461-8, Norton Paperbks) Norton.
***Stop Committing Voice Suicide.** Martin Cooper. 1996. pap. text ed. 10.00 (0-87980-437-8) Wilshire.
Stop Dieting: Begin Losing with Gourmet Magic. rev. ed. Naomi Watson. LC 77-76948. 1978. 5.00 (0-918766-05-2) Butterfly Pr.
***Stop Dieting Before It Kills You!** William E. Straw. LC 96-71410. 70p. (Orig.). 1997. 12.95 (0-944183-21-2) PRC Pubng.
***Stop Domestic Domestic Violence.** Brown. LC 96-40417. 1997. pap. 11.95 (0-312-16611-7) St Martin.
Stop Doubting Yourself: How to Succeed & Prosper via the Process for Achievement. Darryl Webster. 200p. write for info. (0-9624825-7-9) Achivmnt USA.
Stop Drinking & Live. 3.00 (0-317-00672-X, SR10) Transitions.
Stop Drinking & Start Living. Stephen E. Schlesinger & John J. Gillick. (Illus.). 154p. 1985. 12.95 (0-8306-1937-2, 1937H) McGraw-Hill Prof.
Stop Drinking & Start Living. 2nd ed. Stephen E. Schlesinger. 1989. pap. 7.95 (0-8306-3227-1) McGraw-Hill Prof.
Stop Drunk Driving: An Illustration of a Peace Game. (Analysis Ser.: No. 14). 12.00 (0-686-45486-3) Inst Analysis.
Stop Female Genital Mutilation: Women Speak: Facts & Actions. Fran P. Hosken. 130p. (Orig.). 1995. pap. 15.00 (0-942096-10-X) WINNEWS.
***Stop Foreclosure Now: California Edition.** Lloyd Segal. LC 97-13533. (Illus.). 400p. (Orig.). 1997. pap. 39.95 (0-87337-383-9) Nolo Pr.
Stop Go. Jan Pienkowski. (Illus.). 24p. (J). (ps). 1992. pap. 2.95 (0-671-74519-0, Litl Simon S&S) S&S Childrens.
Stop-Go, Fast-Slow. Valjean McLenighan. LC 81-17080. (Rookie Reader Ser.). (Illus.). 32p. (J). (ps-2). 1982. pap. 3.50 (0-516-43617-1); lib. bdg. 15.00 (0-516-03617-3) Childrens.
***Stop, Go, Listen.** Marc Brown. 1997. lib. bdg. 11.99 (0-679-96735-4) Random Bks Yng Read.
Stop! Go! Word Bird. Jane B. Moncure. LC 80-16273. (Word Bird Library). (Illus.). 32p. (J). (ps-2). 1981. lib. bdg. 21.36 (0-89565-160-2) Childs World.
Stop Hair Loss. Paavo Airola. 32p. 1984. pap. 2.95 (0-932090-06-0) Health Plus.
***Stop Hurtful Words & Harmful Habits: A Life Therapy Guide to Personal Growth.** Kenneth L. Baldwin. LC 96-27982. 176p. (Orig.). 1997. pap. 14.95 (1-56825-034-7) Rainbow Books.
Stop Improving Yourself & Start Living. Roberta J. Bryant. LC 90-22422. 188p. 1991. pap. 10.95 (0-931432-69-3) New Wrld Lib.
Stop in the Name of Love. Nancy N. Rue. Ed. by Roger Rosen. (Flipside Fiction Ser.). (YA). (gr. 7-12). 1988. lib. bdg. 12.95 (0-8239-0794-5) Rosen Group.
Stop in the Name of Love: Ejaculation Control for Life. Michael Riskin. 103p. (Orig.). 1994. pap. 14.95 (0-9619609-1-4) Choice Fullerton.
Stop in the Name of the Law. Alex O'Kash. 1994. pap. 9.95 (1-886028-06-0) Savage Pr.
Stop It Now: How Targets & Managers Can End Sexual Harassment. Kenneth C. Cooper. LC 85-1280. (Illus.). 212p. (Orig.). 1985. pap. 9.95 (0-932801-00-5) Total Comm.
***Stop! It's Christmas.** Mary M. Simon. (J). 1997. write for info. (0-570-04972-5) Concordia.
Stop Junk Mail Forever. Marc Eisenson et al. 20p. (Orig.). 1994. pap. 3.00 (0-943973-11-2) Good Advice Pr.
Stop Justice Abuse. Eugene D. Wheeler & Robert E. Kallman. LC 85-72096. 256p. (Orig.). 1986. pap. 7.95 (0-934793-02-6) Pathfinder CA.
Stop Justice Abuse: Exposes the Unfair System & Proposes Action You Can Take. Eugene D. Wheeler & Robert Kallman. (Illus.). 256p. (C). 1993. reprint ed. lib. bdg. 31.00 (0-8095-5905-6) Borgo Pr.
***Stop, Look, & Listen! A Holistic Guide to More Effective Listening.** Michael Bruner & Lisa Polack. 130p. (Orig.). 1997. pap. 9.95 (0-9656937-0-8) Sagebrush Srvs.
Stop, Look, & Listen: Exploring the World Around You, Vol. 5. Sarah A. Williamson. Ed. by Susan Williamson. LC 95-49755. (Little Hands Book Ser.). (Illus.). 144p. (Orig.). (J). (ps up). 1996. pap. 12.95 (1-885593-03-1) Williamson Pub Co.
Stop, Look & Read. George H. Hamm. LC 88-51389. 44p. 1989. 5.95 (1-55523-202-7) Winston-Derek.
Stop, Look, Listen Up! And Other Dramas for Confronting Social Issues in Elementary Schools. R. William Pike. LC 93-1816. 128p. (Orig.). (C). 1993. teacher ed., pap. 14.95 (0-89390-267-5) Resource Pubns.
Stop, Look, Listen-Up! Teaching Tough Topics & Sensitive Personal Issues. (Illus.). 78p. (Orig.). (J). (gr. k-6). 1994. pap. text ed. 25.00 (0-7881-0801-8) DIANE Pub.
Stop Making Money, Start Getting Rich: Financial Awareness for a Secure Business & Personal Wealth. Lynn H. Fife. Ed. by Janet Lafferty & Lafferty & Assoc. Staff. (Illus.). 104p. (Orig.). (C). 1995. pap. text ed. 24.95 (1-882947-40-1) Evergreen Tech.
Stop Managing, Start Coaching! How Performance Coaching Can Enhance Commitment & Improve... Jerry W. Gilley. 208p. 1995. text ed. 25.00 (0-7863-0456-1) Irwin Prof Pubng.
Stop Managing Volunteers! New Competencies for Volunteer Administrators. Sue Vineyard. 184p. (Orig.). 1996. pap. 15.00 (0-911029-44-3) Heritage Arts.
Stop Marital Fights Before They Start. Norman M. Lobsenz & Fred P. Piercy. 224p. 1994. mass mkt. 4.99 (0-425-14402-X) Berkley Pub.
***Stop Me Before I Vote Again! Funny Minor Memos from the Wall Street Journal's Washington Wire Column.** Ed. by Ronald G. Shafer. LC 96-33999. 128p. (Orig.). 1997. pap. 8.95 (0-8362-2756-5) Andrews & McMeel.
Stop Me Before I Write More. Scott Gardner. (Illus.). 104p. (Orig.). 1984. 14.95 (0-9614112-1-X); pap. 6.95 (0-9614112-0-1) Draydel Pr.
***Stop Memory Loss: How to Fight Forgetfulness over Forty.** William Cone. 304p. (Orig.). 1997. pap. write for info. (0-9655563-9-5) Matteson Bks.
Stop Obsessing. Edna Foa. 272p. 1991. pap. 11.95 (0-553-35350-0) Bantam.
Stop Osteoarthritis Now. Harris H. McIlwain. LC 96-19453. 256p. 1996. pap. 12.00 (0-684-81439-0, S&S) S&S Trade.
Stop Paddling & Start Rocking the Boat: Business Lessons from the School of Hard Knocks. Lou Pritchett. 288p. 1996. pap. 13.50 (0-88730-822-8) Harper Busn.
Stop Paddling & Start Rocking the Boat: Business Lessons from the School of Hard Knocks. Lou Pritchett. LC 95-23213. 267p. 1995. 24.00 (0-88730-731-0, PL) HarpC.
Stop Postponing the Rest of Your Life. Paul Stevens. LC 92-23608. 156p. (Orig.). 1993. pap. 9.95 (0-89815-518-5) Ten Speed Pr.
Stop Procrastinating - Do It! 2nd ed. James R. Shermman. LC 80-82893. 1988. pap. 2.95 (0-935538-13-5) Pathway Bks.
Stop Procrastination & Do It Now. 3.00 (0-686-40901-9, SR6) Transitions.
Stop Renting Now: Here's How the New National Home Ownership Strategy Can Move You Out of a Rental & into Your Own Home. 2nd ed. Gary W. Eldred. 224p. 1996. pap. 15.95 (1-883745-03-9) Nat Init Home.
Stop Renting Now! (TM) Here's How to Develop a Financial Plan, Strategy, & Technique to Become a Homeowner. Gary W. Eldred. 224p. (Orig.). 1993. pap. 11.95 (1-883745-00-4) Nat Init Home.
***Stop Selling, Start Partnering.** Larry Wilson. pap. text ed. 5.99 (0-471-17688-5) Wiley.
Stop Selling, Start Partnering. Larry Wilson. 1996. pap. text ed. 14.95 (0-471-14741-9) Wiley.
Stop Selling Start Partnering: The New Thinking about Finding & Keeping Customers. Larry Wilson & Hersch Wilson. 200p. 1995. 22.00 (0-939246-74-0) Wiley.
Stop Selling, Start Partnering: The New Thinking About Finding & Keeping Customers. Larry Wilson. 288p. 1995. text ed. 22.95 (0-471-13363-9) Wiley.
***Stop Setting Goals If You Would.** Bob Diehl. 1996. pap. 9.99 (0-345-40778-4, Moorings) Ballantine.
***Stop Sign in Your Mind: Releasing Fear & Doubt.** Ed. by Gene Blythe et al. LC 96-93030. (Illus.). 64p. 1997. per. 11.95 (0-9656021-0-9) Rainbow Pub.
Stop Sleeping Through Your Dreams: A Guide to Awakening Consciousness During Dream Sleep. Charles McPhee. LC 95-22519. 304p. 1995. 22.50 (0-8050-2500-6) H Holt & Co.
Stop Sleeping Through Your Dreams: A Guide to Awakening Consciousness During Dream Sleep. Charles McPhee. LC 95-22519. 304p. 1996. pap. 12.95 (0-8050-2515-4) H Holt & Co.
Stop Smoking: Quit for Good! Rhoderick Elin. 31p. 1990. Incl. 3 audiocass. pap. 39.50 incl. audio (0-88432-287-4, S01670) Audio-Forum.
Stop Smoking for Good: With the NHA Stop-Smoking Program. Robert Brynin. 210p. 1996. pap. 8.95 (0-340-63240-2, Pub. by H & S UK) Trafalgar.
Stop Smoking Forever! The Easy Way. Arthur A. Hawkins, II. 24p. 1992. pap. 6.95 (1-881297-33-0); pap. text ed. 6.95 (1-881297-34-9) Info Res Lab.
Stop Smoking Program Guide. American Cancer Society Staff. 184p. (0-318-62025-1, 5003) Am Cancer NY.
Stop Smoking Soon. G-Jo Institute Staff. 1980. pap. 4.50 (0-916878-09-0) Falkyn Inc.
Stop Smoking Without Putting on Weight. Penny Ross. 1994. pap. 5.99 (0-7225-3015-3) Thorsons SF.
Stop Smoking Workbook. Anita Maximin & Lori Stevic-Rust. LC 95-61240. 171p. (Orig.). 1996. pap. 17.95 (1-57224-037-7) New Harbinger.
***Stop Smoking Workbook.** Anita Maximin & Lori Stevic-Rust. 1997. 9.98 (1-56731-207-1, MJF Bks) Fine Comms.
Stop Snowing on My Secretary. Charles M. Schulz. LC 77-71355. (Peanuts Parade Bks.: No. 20). 192p. 1977. pap. 5.95 (0-03-021391-6, Owl) H Holt & Co.
Stop Snowing on My Secretary. Charles M. Schulz. (Peanuts Classics Ser.). 128p. 1992. pap. 6.95 (0-8050-2399-2, Owl) H Holt & Co.
Stop Spitting at Your Brother! Life Lessons of a Rocky Mountain Llama. Diane White-Crane. LC 96-85123. (Illus.). 154p. (Orig.). (J). (gr. 2-6). 1996. pap. 9.95 (0-9631322-1-0) Aspentree Pr.
Stop, Start see **Learn-To-Read Series**
Stop Stealing Sheep & Find Out How Type Works. Erik Spiekermann & E. M. Ginger. LC 92-76016. (Illus.). 176p. (Orig.). 1993. pap. text ed. 19.95 (0-672-48543-5, Adobe) Hayden.
Stop Struggling with Your Child: Quick-Tip Parenting Solutions That Will Work for You - & Your Kids Ages 4-12. Evonne Weinhaus & Karen Friedman. LC 89-46493. (Illus.). 192p. 1991. pap. 11.00 (0-06-096481-2, PL) HarpC.
Stop Struggling with Your Teen. Evonne Weinhaus & Karen Friedman. 96p. (Orig.). 1988. pap. 9.95 (0-14-010604-9, Penguin Bks) Viking Penguin.
Stop Studying Start Learning: Or How to Jump-Start Your Brain. unabridged ed. Richard M. Fenker, Jr. & Reverdy Mullins. LC 81-8797. (Illus.). 161p. (Orig.). 1981. pap. text ed. 11.95 (0-940352-00-1, 4010) Mesa Hse.
Stop TB at the Source: WHO Report on the Tuberculosis Epidemic, 1995. 54p. 1995. pap. text ed. 9.00 (0-614-08054-1, 1930065) World Health.
***Stop Telling, Start Selling: How to Use Customer-Focused Dialogue to Close Sales.** Linda Richardson. LC 97-17550. 1997. pap. text ed. 16.95 (0-07-052558-7) McGraw.
Stop Telling, Start Selling: Using Customer-Focused Dialogue to Close Sales. Linda Richardson. 1993. pap. text ed. 16.95 (0-07-052368-1) McGraw.
Stop Telling Those Lies: Stories Based on Greek & Roman Myths That Have Been Urbanized & Blackenized. Henry Hardee. 23p. 1994. pap. 6.00 (1-884978-02-9) Black Boys Dream.
Stop That! Pet Peeves Between Men & Women. Blake Thomas & Jaclyn Caulfield. 144p. (Orig.). 1993. pap. 6.95 (0-9639170-4-8) Brycon.
Stop That Ball! Mike McClintock. LC 59-9741. (Illus.). (J). (gr. 1-2). 1959. 7.99 (0-394-80010-9) Beginner.
Stop That Eyeball! Gary Hogg. (Spencer's Adventures Ser.). (Illus.). 80p. 1995. pap. 3.99 (0-930771-16-8) Buckaroo UT.
***Stop That Eyeball!, Vol. 1.** Gary Hogg. (Spencer's Adventures Ser.). 1997. pap. 3.50 (0-590-93935-1, Little Apple) Scholastic Inc.
Stop That Garbage Truck! Linda Glaser. LC 92-22932. (Illus.). 32p. (J). (ps-2). 1993. lib. bdg. 14.95 (0-8075-7626-3) A Whitman.
Stop That Monkey! Monica Weiss. LC 93-85172. (Light-&-Sound Bks.). 12p. (J). (ps-3). 1994. 9.95 (0-89577-551-4, Rdrs Dig Kids) Rdrs Dgst Yng Fam.
Stop That Pickle! Peter Armour. LC 92-903544. (Illus.). (J). 1993. 14.95 (0-395-66375-X) HM.
Stop That Rabbit. Sharon Peters. (Illus.). 32p. (J). (gr. k-2). 1980. lib. bdg. 9.79 (0-89375-388-2) Troll Communs.
Stop That Rabbit. Sharon Peters. (Illus.). 32p. (J). (gr. k-2). 1997. pap. 2.50 (0-89375-288-6) Troll Communs.
Stop That Volcano. Cynthia Alvarez. (J). 1996. pap. 3.25 (0-679-87613-8) Random Bks Yng Read.

S

Stop That Woman! Sara H. Frommer. (Kaleidoscope Ser.: Set A). 1993. 2.95 (*0-88336-170-1*) New Readers.

Stop the Bad Service. Margo Chevers. 64p. 1994. per. 9.95 (*0-8403-9449-7*) Kendall-Hunt.

Stop the Balloon! Selected from Highlights for Children. LC 92-73625. (Illus.). 96p. (J). (gr. 2-5). 1993. pap. 2.95 (*1-56397-194-1*) Boyds Mills Pr.

***Stop the Blackman Now!** Ameenah R. Fuller. 49p. (Orig.). 1996. pap. 10.00 (*0-9653614-0-3*) Looking-In.

***Stop the Calls! A No-Nonsense Approach on How to Deal with Bill Collectors.** Robin Walker & Glenn L. Walker-Ver Wey. Ed. by Debbie Schiedel. LC 96-95372. (Illus.). 72p. (Orig.). 1997. pap. 9.95 (*1-890169-00-5*, Savvy Consumer) Leo Inc.

Stop the Heartburn. 2nd rev. ed. David S. Utley & Kathryn M. Utley. (Illus.). 96p. 1996. pap. 9.95 (*0-9650928-0-1*) Lagado Pub.

Stop the Insanity! Susan Powter. (Illus.). 320p. 1993. 22.00 (*0-671-79598-8*) S&S Trade.

Stop the Insanity. Susan Powter. Ed. by Bill Grose. 384p. 1995. pap. 7.50 (*0-671-52292-2*) PB.

Stop the Insanity. Susan Powter. 1996. pap. 9.95 (*0-684-82664-X*) S&S Trade.

Stop the Killing Train: Radical Visions for Radical Change. Michael Albert. 256p. (Orig.). 1993. 35.00 (*0-89608-471-X*); pap. 15.00 (*0-89608-470-1*) South End Pr.

Stop the Merry-Go-Round: Stories of Women Who Broke the Cycle of Abusive Relationships. Milton S. Trachtenburg. 196p. 1989. pap. 10.95 (*0-8306-8007-1*) McGraw-Hill Prof.

Stop the Nonsense: Health Without the Fads. Ezra Sohar. 268p. 1990. 16.95 (*1-56171-006-7*) Sure Seller.

Stop the Nonsense: Health Without the Fads. Ezra Sohar. 1992. pap. 10.99 (*1-56171-109-8*) Sure Seller.

***Stop the Presses, Ida Mae!** Mary E. Blakeslee. 116p. (J). (gr. 4-7). pap. 9.99 (*0-7710-1537-2*) McCland & Stewart.

Stop the Rollercoaster: How to Take Charge of Your Blood Sugars in Diabetes. John Walsh et al. (Illus.). 230p. (Orig.). 1996. pap. 21.95 (*1-884804-82-9*) Torrey PP.

***Stop the Snoring! At Last, End Your Mate's Nocturnal Noise.** Ralph Schoenstein. 128p. (Orig.). 1997. mass mkt. 5.99 (*0-446-60460-7*) Warner Bks.

Stop the Vacuum! I Want to Get Off. Toni Pighetti. 110p. 1987. pap. 6.95 (*0-913005-06-1*) TAM Assoc.

***Stop the Violence! Poetry for a Take Back the Night Ceremony of Remembrance.** Brainchild Writers Staff. 40p. (Orig.). 1996. pap. 5.00 (*0-9646037-7-2*) Rosehill Pr IL.

Stop the Violence on the Streets & the Corruption in DC by Teaching True Ethics in Elementary Schools. Edwin J. Szewc. 16p. 1995. pap. write for info. (*1-882969-19-7*) Pallas Pr.

Stop the Violence Please. Michele D. Clise. LC 94-9168. (Illus.). 64p. (J). 1994. pap. 9.95 (*0-295-97367-6*) U of Wash Pr.

Stop the Watch: A Book of Everyday, Ordinary, Anybody Olympics. Klutz Press Staff. (Illus.). 72p. 1993. per. 10.95 (*1-878257-52-8*) Klutz Pr.

***Stop the Wedding!** Trisha Alexander. 1997. mass mkt. 3.99 (*0-373-24097-X*, 1-24097-7) Silhouette.

Stop the Wedding! Maris Soule. 1994. pap. 2.75 (*0-373-19038-7*, 1-19038-8) Harlequin Bks.

Stop the Yeast Syndrome: Home Cooking That Prevents Yeast Infections Without Drugs. Morton Walker & Alice Burnsworth. 192p. (Orig.). 1995. pap. 12.95 (*1-882330-44-7*) Magni Co.

Stop, Thief! Robert Kalan. LC 92-30081. (Illus.). 24p. (J). (ps up). 1993. 14.00 (*0-688-11876-3*) Greenwillow.

Stop-Time. Frank Conroy. 288p. 1977. pap. 11.95 (*0-14-004446-9*, Penguin Bks) Viking Penguin.

Stop, Train, Stop! A Thomas the Tank Engine Story. Owain Bell. LC 94-15129. (J). (gr. 1 up). 1995. 7.99 (*0-679-85806-7*); lib. bdg. 11.99 (*0-679-95806-1*) Beginner.

Stop Treating Me Like a Child but First You Can Lend Me Some Money: Opening the Door to Healthy Relationships Between Parents & Adult Children. Phyllis Lieber et al. 224p. 1995. pap. 12.95 (*0-8065-1705-0*, Citadel Pr) Carol Pub Group.

Stop Treating Me Like a Kid: Everyday Parenting- the 10-13 Year Old. Robin Goldstein & Janet Gallant. LC 93-36032. 256p. 1994. pap. 9.95 (*0-14-017945-3*, Penguin Bks) Viking Penguin.

***Stop Violence in the Workplace a Guide to Understanding & Prevention.** Myers. 300p. 1995. pap. 39.00 (*0-8080-0059-4*, BLS-3393) Commerce.

Stop Watch & Bonus System in Government Work: Proceedings. U. S. House of Representatives, Congress, Committee on Labor. Ed. by Leon Stein. LC 77-70542. 1977. reprint ed. lib. bdg. 19.95 (*0-405-10211-9*) Ayer.

Stop Without Quitting. Joseph Danysh. LC 74-77668. 120p. 1974. pap. 10.00 (*0-918970-18-0*) Intl Gen Semantics.

***Stop Working & Start Thinking.** Cohen. (Illus.). 128p. 1997. text ed. 23.95 (*0-412-73010-3*, Chap & Hall NY) Chapman & Hall.

Stop Worrying about Backache. P. S. Ramani. 102p. 1983. 8.95 (*0-318-36400-X*) Asia Bk Corp.

***Stop Worrying about Money.** Mitch Gallow. 168p. 1997. pap. 11.95 (*1-886330-93-X*) Hatherleigh.

Stop Your Crowing, Kasimir! Ursel Scheffler. (Illus.). 32p. (J). (gr. k-3). 1988. lib. bdg. 19.95 (*0-87614-323-0*, Carolrhoda) Lerner Group.

Stop Your Herpes Now. Healthworks Medical Group Staff. 52p. (Orig.). 1981. pap. 4.50 (*0-938480-01-4*) Healthworks.

Stop Your Indigestion: Causes, Remedies, Recipes. Phyllis Avery. (Illus.). 228p. (Orig.). 1993. pap. 14.95 (*1-880598-36-1*) P Avery.

Stop Your Tinnitus: Causes, Preventatives, & Alternatives. Phyllis Avery. (Illus.). 192p. (Orig.). 1991. pap. 14.95 (*1-880598-22-1*) P Avery.

Stop, You're Killing Me. James L. Herlihy. 1969. pap. 5.25 (*0-8222-1084-3*) Dramatists Play.

Stopfkuchen. unabridged ed. Raabe. (World Classic Literature Ser.). (GER.). pap. 5.95 (*3-89507-021-1*, Pub. by Bookking Intl FR) Distribks Inc.

Stopford Brooke. Fred L. Stanley. LC 77-152017. (Twayne's English Authors Ser.). 158p. (C). 1972. lib. bdg. 17.95 (*0-8290-1731-3*) Irvington.

Stoplight Diet for Children: An Eight-Week Program for Parents & Children. Leonard H. Epstein & Sally Squires. 1988. 16.95 (*0-316-24575-5*) Little.

Stopover in Kansas. Ed. by Jon McAlpin. (Illus.). 156p. 1995. pap. text ed. 9.95 (*1-57166-014-3*) Quixote Pr IA.

Stoppard the Playwright. Michael Billington. 192p. 1988. 19.95 (*0-413-45850-4*, A0272, Pub. by Methuen UK) Heinemann.

Stopped Random Walks. Ed. by A. Gut. (Applied Probability Ser.: Vol. 5). 225p. 1987. 70.95 (*0-387-96590-4*) Spr-Verlag.

Stopped Rocking & Other Screenplays. Tennessee Williams. LC 84-6948. 352p. 1984. 24.95 (*0-8112-0901-6*); pap. 9.95 (*0-8112-0902-4*, NDP575) New Directions.

Stoppers: How to Put an End to Meetings, Monologues, Conferences, Discussions, Telephone Calls, Debates, Filibusters, Boring Parties, & Anything That Lasts Too Long. John Miles. LC 93-6277. 64p. (Orig.). 1994. pap. 3.98 (*0-687-39639-5*) Abingdon.

Stopping AIDS: HIV/AIDS Education & the Mass Media in Europe. Kaye Wellings. 224p. (C). 1996. pap. text ed. 21.95 (*0-582-29227-1*) Longman.

***Stopping Alcohol & Other Drug Use Before It Starts: The Future of Prevention.** Ed. by Robert L. DuPont. (Illus.). 99p. (C). 1996. reprint ed. pap. 30.00 (*0-7881-2965-1*) DIANE Pub.

***Stopping & Range of Ions in Matter.** J. F. Ziegler & J. P. Biersack. (Illus.). 683p. 1997. 178.00 (*0-9654207-1-X*) Ziegler Sci.

Stopping & Range of Ions in Matter, Volumes 1-4. Ed. by James F. Ziegler. 1985. 140.00 (*0-08-022053-3*, Pergamon Pr) Elsevier.

***Stopping & Seeing: A Comprehensive Course in Buddhist Meditation.** Thomas Cleary. 208p. 1997. pap. 12.00 (*1-57062-275-2*) Shambhala Pubns.

Stopping by: Portraits from Small Towns. Photos by Raymond Bial. LC 88-17407. (Visions of Illinois Ser.). (Illus.). 200p. 1988. 24.95 (*0-252-01587-8*) U of Ill Pr.

Stopping by Woods on a Snowy Evening. Robert Frost. LC 78-8134. (Illus.). (J). (ps up). 1978. pap. 14.99 (*0-525-40115-6*, 01063-320) Dutton Child Bks.

***Stopping Civil Conflict with Force.** Michael O'Hanlon. (Occasional Paper Ser.). 100p. 1996. pap. 12.95 (*0-8157-6447-2*) Brookings.

Stopping Family Violence: An Agenda of Research Priorities for the Coming Decade. David Finkelhor et al. 140p. (C). 1988. text ed. 28.95 (*0-8039-3215-4*) Sage.

Stopping Family Violence: Research Priorities for the Coming Decade. David Finkelhor et al. LC 87-27972. 127p. 1988. reprint ed. pap. 36.20 (*0-608-01534-2*, 2059578) Bks Demand.

Stopping for a Spell. Diana Wynne Jones. LC 92-12196. 160p. (J). (gr. 3 up). 1993. 14.00 (*0-688-11367-2*) Greenwillow.

Stopping for a Spell: Three Fantasies. Diana W. Jones. (Illus.). 160p. (J). (gr. 3-7). 1996. pap. 3.99 (*0-14-037937-1*, Puffin) Puffin Bks.

Stopping for Death: Poems of Death & Loss. Carol A. Duffy. (Illus.). 144p. (YA). (gr. 7 up). 1996. 14.95 (*0-8050-4717-4*) H Holt & Co.

Stopping for Time. Bonnie Jacobson. Ed. by Craig Goad & William Trowbridge. 60p. (Orig.). 1989. pap. 7.95 (*0-9616467-5-6*) GreenTower Pr.

Stopping on the Edge to Wave. James B. Hall. LC 87-33295. (Wesleyan Poetry Ser.). 80p. 1988. pap. 11.95 (*0-8195-1146-3*, Wesleyan Univ Pr); text ed. 25.00 (*0-8195-2145-0*, Wesleyan Univ Pr) U Pr of New Eng.

Stopping Power: Why Seventy Million Americans Own Guns. J. Neil Schulman. LC 94-65914. 288p. 1994. 22.95 (*1-882639-03-0*) Synapse Cent.

Stopping Powers & Ranges for Protons & Alpha Particles. Ed. by W. Roger Ney. (ICRU Report Ser.: No. 49). 260p. (Orig.). 1993. pap. text ed. 70.00 (*0-913394-47-5*) Intl Comm Rad Meas.

Stopping Powers for Electrons & Positrons. International Commission on Radiation Units & Measurements. LC 84-12780. (ICRU Report Ser.: No. 37). 268p. 1984. pap. text ed. 70.00 (*0-913394-31-9*) Intl Comm Rad Meas.

Stopping Powers for Use with Cavity Chambers. (Report Ser.: No. 27). 1961. pap. 20.00 (*0-913392-09-X*) NCRP Pubns.

Stopping Profit Leaks & Manufacturers Experience with New Plant Machinery, Equipment & Systems. 33p. 1978. 25.00 (*0-318-19694-8*) Clothing Mfrs.

Stopping Rape: A Challenge for Men. Rus E. Funk. 192p. 1993. pap. 12.95 (*0-86571-268-9*); lib. bdg. 39.95 (*0-86571-267-0*) New Soc Pubs.

Stopping Rape: Successful Survival Strategies. Pauline B. Bart & Patricia H. O'Brien. LC 85-6589. (Athene Ser.). 200p. 1985. 39.50 (*0-08-032814-8*, Pergamon Pr); pap. 15.95 (*0-08-032813-X*, Pergamon Pr) Elsevier.

Stopping Rape: Successful Survival Strategies. Pauline B. Bart & Patricia O'Brian. LC 93-16306. (Athene Ser.). 216p. (C). 1985. pap. text ed. 17.95 (*0-8077-6212-1*) Tchrs Coll.

Stopping Scoliosis: The Complete Guide to Diagnosis & Treatment. Nancy Schommer. LC 90-28147. (Illus.). 208p. (Orig.). pap. 9.95 (*0-89529-466-4*) Avery Pub.

Stopping Sexual Harassment: A Handbook. Camille Colatosti & Elissa Karg. 112p. (Orig.). 1992. pap. text ed. 9.00 (*0-914093-06-1*) Labor Notes.

Stopping Sexual Harassment: An Employer's Guide. rev. ed. Susan G. Kemp et al. (Illus.). 180p. (C). 1993. pap. text ed. 39.00 (*1-878630-58-X*) CA Chamber Commerce.

***Stopping Sexual Harassment Before It Starts: A Business & Legal Perspective.** Mike Deblieux. Ed. by Dave Kirchner. LC 97-70154. (How-to Book Ser.). 112p. (Orig.). 1997. pap. 12.95 (*1-884926-75-4*, HARAE) Amer Media.

***Stopping the Clock.** 1997. mass mkt. 6.50 (*0-553-57751-4*) Bantam.

Stopping the Clock. Ronald Klatz & Robert Goldman. Ed. by Don R. Bensen. 370p. 1996. 22.95 (*0-87983-717-9*) Keats.

Stopping the Clock: Why Many of Us Will Live Past 100 - & Enjoy Every Minute! rev. ed. Ronald Klatz & Robert Goldman. 400p. 1997. 29.98 (*0-941683-31-1*) Instant Improve.

Stopping the Indian Bomb. Brahma Chellaney. 240p. (C). 1997. text ed. 49.95 (*0-8133-2329-0*) Westview.

Stopping the Killing: How Civil Wars End. Ed. by Roy Licklider. (Illus.). 354p. (C). 1993. 50.00 (*0-8147-5070-2*) NYU Pr.

Stopping the Killing: How Civil Wars End. Ed. by Roy Licklider. (Illus.). 354p. (C). 1995. pap. 18.50 (*0-8147-5097-4*) NYU Pr.

Stopping the Spread of Nuclear Weapons: The Past & the Prospects. David Fischer. 368p. (C). (gr. 13). 1992. text ed. 99.95 (*0-415-00481-0*, A7077) Routledge.

Stopping Time: A Rephotographic Survey of Lake Tahoe. Peter Goin et al. LC 91-29145. 144p. 1992. pap. 32.50 (*0-8263-1285-3*) U of NM Pr.

Stopping Time: The Photographs of Harold Edgerton. Ed. by Gus Hayafus. LC 87-1064. (Illus.). 168p. 1987. 45.00 (*0-8109-1514-6*) Abrams.

Stopping Time Techniques for Analysts & Probabilists. L. Egghe. (London Mathematical Society Lecture Note Ser.: No. 100). 367p. 1985. pap. text ed. 49.95 (*0-521-31715-0*) Cambridge U Pr.

Stopping Times & Directed Processes. Gerald A. Edgar & Louis Sucheston. (Encyclopedia of Mathematics & Its Applications Ser.: No. 47). 400p. (C). 1992. text ed. 64.95 (*0-521-35023-9*) Cambridge U Pr.

***Stopping Wars: Defining Obstacles to Cease Fire.** James D. Smith. 2p. (C). 1997. pap. text ed. 28.00 (*0-8133-9980-7*) Westview.

***Stops.** Joel Sloman. LC 97-3165. 128p. (Orig.). 1997. 19.95 (*0-944072-82-8*) Zoland Bks.

Stops along the Country Road. Joseph Breighner. LC 96-15862. 232p. (Orig.). 1996. pap. 18.95 (*1-885938-03-9*) Cathdrl Fndtn Pr.

Stops along the Way. Jeffrey Sweet. 1981. pap. 3.25 (*0-8222-1085-1*) Dramatists Play.

***Stops along the Way, Your Career.** 11th ed. Miller & Ryan. (CA - Career Development Ser.). (C). 1994. wbk. ed., pap. 25.95 (*0-314-03562-1*) S-W Pub.

Stops of Various Quills: Poetry. William Dean Howells. (Notable American Authors Ser.). 1992. reprint ed. lib. bdg. 75.00 (*0-7812-3274-0*) Rprt Serv.

Stops on the Way to Eden & Beyond. Larry Turner. 69p. 1992. pap. 7.00 (*0-9637547-0-X*) Arbor Hill Pr.

Stopwatch Series, 18 vols., Set. LC 88-18344. (Illus.). (J). (gr. 1-5). 1991. pap. 71.10 (*0-382-09961-3*, Silver Pr NJ); lib. bdg. 179.10 (*0-382-09604-5*, Silver Pr NJ) Silver Burdett Pr.

***Stor Amhran.** Noirin N. Riain. 118p. write for info. (*1-900428-60-1*, OS 00122, Pub. by Ossian Publns IE) Music Sales.

Stor Norsk - Tysk Ordbok. Tom Hustad. 864p. (GER & NOR.). 195.00 (*0-7859-3670-X*, 8200072533) Fr & Eur.

Stora Synonymordboken. 4th ed. A. Stromberg. 725p. (SWE.). 1984. 125.00 (*0-8288-2073-2*, F64380) Fr & Eur.

***Storage.** Dinah Hall. LC 96-34441. (DK Home Design Workbks.). 96p. 1997. 18.95 (*0-7894-1450-3*) DK Pub Inc.

Storage: Food Cycle Technology Sourcebook. UNIFEM Staff. 35p. (Orig.). 1995. pap. 13.50 (*1-85339-309-6*, Pub. by Intermed Tech UK) Women Ink.

Storage & Commodity Markets. Jeffrey C. Williams & Brian D. Wright. 512p. (C). 1991. text ed. 89.95 (*0-521-32616-8*) Cambridge U Pr.

Storage & Control of Stock. David A. Jessop & Alex Morrison. 310p. (C). 1989. 110.00 (*0-685-36165-9*, Pub. by Inst Pur & Supply UK) St Mut.

Storage & Control of Stock. Ed. by J. Jessop & M. Morrison. 310p. (C). 1986. 130.00 (*0-685-39887-0*, Pub. by Inst Pur & Supply UK) St Mut.

Storage & Control of Stock see Storage & Supply of Materials

Storage & Handling of Liquefied Petroleum Gases. National Fire Protection Association Staff. 100p. 26.50 (*0-317-63204-3*, 58-92) Natl Fire Prot.

Storage & Handling of Petroleum Liquids. 3rd ed. John R. Hughes. 332p. 1988. text ed. 150.00 (*0-471-62966-9*) Wiley.

Storage & Recording Systems: Proceedings of the International Conference on Storage & Recording Systems (1994: U. of Keele, U. K.) (Conference Publication Ser.: No. 402). 143p. 1995. pap. 72.00 (*0-85296-630-X*, IC402) Inst Elect Eng.

Storage & Supply of Materials. 6th ed. David A. Jessop & Alex Morrison. Orig. Title: Storage & Control of Stock. 336p. (Orig.). 1994. pap. 49.50 (*0-273-60323-X*, Pub. by Pitman Pub Ltd UK) Trans-Atl Phila.

Storage & Treatment of Hazardous Wastes in Tank Systems. U. S. Environmental Protection Agency Office of Solid Waste. LC 87-12199. (Pollution Technology Review Ser.: No. 146). (Illus.). 428p. 1988. 54.00 (*0-8155-1138-8*) Noyes.

Storage & Use of Hazardous & Toxic Materials: Report of the Governor's Commission of Ohio. 200p. (Orig.). (C). 1992. pap. text ed. 40.00 (*1-56806-025-4*) DIANE Pub.

Storage Batteries Simplified. 1986. pap. 8.95 (*0-917914-47-3*) Lindsay Pubns.

Storage Battery Manufacturing Manual. 3rd ed. Joseph Orsino. 1985. 35.00 (*0-685-12355-3*) IBMA Pubns.

***Storage Book: Over 250 Ideas for Stylish Home Storage.** Cynthia Inions. (Illus.). 176p. 1997. 29.95 (*0-7892-0400-2*) Abbeville Pr.

Storage, Handling, & Processing of Magnesium. National Fire Protection Association Staff. 23p. 1993. 20.25 (*0-317-63445-3*, 480-87) Natl Fire Prot.

Storage, Handling & Use of Explosives License. (Career Examination Ser.: C-3769). pap. 23.95 (*0-8373-3769-0*) Nat Learn.

Storage Made Easy. Candace O. Manroe. LC 95-13633. 1995. write for info. (*1-56799-216-1*, Friedman-Fairfax); pap. 9.95 (*1-56799-211-0*, Friedman-Fairfax) M Friedman Pub Grp Inc.

Storage Made Easy: Great Ideas for Organizing Everything in Your Home. Candace O. Manroe. (Illus.). 128p. 1995. 14.95 (*1-56865-128-7*, GuildAmerica) Dblday Direct.

Storage of Ammonium Nitrate. National Fire Protection Association Staff. 1993. 16.75 (*0-317-63456-9*, 490-93) Natl Fire Prot.

Storage of Baled Cotton. National Fire Protection Association Staff. 1989. 16.75 (*0-317-63346-5*, 231E-89) Natl Fire Prot.

Storage of Cereal Grains & Their Products. 4th ed. Ed. by David B. Sauer. LC 91-78051. (Illus.). 615p. 1992. text ed. 145.00 (*0-913250-74-0*) Am Assn Cereal Chem.

Storage of Flammable & Combustible Liquids on Farms & Isolated Construction Projects. National Fire Protection Association Staff. 1993. 16.75 (*0-317-63420-8*, 395-88) Natl Fire Prot.

Storage of Flammable & Combustible Liquids Within Underground Metal & Non-Metal Mines (Other Than Coal) National Fire Protection Association Staff. 1994. 20.25 (*0-317-63319-8*, 122-90) Natl Fire Prot.

Storage of Forest Products. National Fire Protection Association Staff. 1990. 16.75 (*0-317-63080-6*, 46-90) Natl Fire Prot.

***Storage of Gases in Rock Caverns: Proceedings of the International Conference, Trondheim, 26-28 June 1989.** Ed. by B. Nilsen & J. Olsen. 480p. 1989. 155.00 (*90-6191-896-0*, Pub. by A A Balkema NE) Ashgate Pub Co.

Storage of Hazardous Materials: A Technical Guide for Safe Warehousing of Hazardous Materials. 80p. 1989. 19.00 (*92-807-1238-1*, 89.III.D.6) UN.

Storage of Natural Gas As Hydrate. Joseph D. Parent. (Research Bulletin Ser.: No. 1). iv, 40p. 1948. pap. 2.50 (*0-317-56708-X*) Inst Gas Tech.

Storage of Natural History Collections, Vol. 1. Carolyn L. Rose. 1995. write for info. (*0-9635476-1-5*) Soc Preser NHC.

Storage of Natural History Collections: Ideas & Practical Solutions. C. L. Rose & A. R. De Torres. 360p. (C). 1992. spiral bd. 30.00 (*0-9635476-0-7*) Soc Preser NHC.

Storage of Pesticides in Portable Containers. National Fire Protection Association Staff. 1994. 16.75 (*0-317-63078-4*, 43D-86) Natl Fire Prot.

Storage of Potatoes: Post Harvest Behaviour Store Design, Storage Practice, Handling. A. Rastovaski. 462p. 1989. pap. 425.00 (*81-7089-111-6*, Pub. by Intl Bk Distr II) St Mut.

Storage of Roll Paper. National Fire Protection Association Staff. 1987. 16.75 (*0-317-63351-1*, 231F-87) Natl Fire Prot.

Storage of Rubber Tires. National Fire Protection Association Staff. 1989. 16.75 (*0-317-63344-9*, 231D-89) Natl Fire Prot.

Storage, Processing, & Nutritional Quality of Fruits & Vegetables, 2 vols., Vol. 1. 2nd ed. D. K. Salunkhe et al. (Illus.). 312p. 1990. 153.00 (*0-8493-5623-7*, TX557) CRC Pr.

Storage, Processing, & Nutritional Quality of Fruits & Vegetables: Hemostasis, Set, Vol. 2. 2nd ed. D. K. Salunkhe et al. Ed. by Raymond Machovich. LC 87-24298. (Blood Vessel Wall & Thrombosis Ser.). (Illus.). 208p. 1990. Vol. 2, 208p. 257.00 (*0-8493-5624-5*, RC694, CRC Reprint) Franklin.

Storage Projects You Can Build. David Stiles & Jeanie Stiles. Ed. by Barry Estabrook. (Weekend Project Book Ser.). (Illus.). 152p. (Orig.). 1996. pap. 18.95 (*1-57630-017-X*) Chapters Pub.

Storage Solutions. LC 85-45449. (Conran Home Decorator Ser.). (Illus.). 80p. 1986. 6.95 (*0-394-74400-4*, Villard Bks) Random.

Storage Structures. K. Rajagopalan. (Illus.). 397p. (C). 1990. text ed. 95.00 (*90-6191-947-9*, Pub. by A A Balkema NE) Ashgate Pub Co.

***Storage Tank Emergencies: Guidelines & Procedures.** Michael S. Hildebrand et al. (Illus.). 170p. 1996. 20.00 (*0-614-29660-9*, 35941) IFSTA.

Storage Tanks, Vol. 1. Ed. by Paul N. Cheremisinoff. LC 95-51188. (Adavnces in Environmental Control Technology Ser.: Vol. 10). (Illus.). 304p. 1996. 89.00 (*0-87201-332-4*, No. 1332) Gulf Pub.

Storage Tanks for Liquid Radioactive Wastes: Their Design & Use. (Technical Reports: No. 135). (Illus.). 55p. (Orig.). 1972. pap. 14.00 (*92-0-125072-X*, IDC135, Pub. by IAEA AU) Bernan Associates.

An Asterisk (*) at the beginning of an entry indicates that the title is appearing in BIP for the first time.

Storage Tanks under the Military: Hazardous Materials in Underground Storage Tanks Owned by the Defense Department. 40p. (Orig.). (C). 1992. pap. text ed. 20.00 (*1-56806-034-3*) DIANE Pub.

Storage Vessels & Equipment. Ed. by James Beckman. (AIChеMI Modular Instruction Ser. G: Vol. 2). 86p. 1986. pap. 44.00 (*0-8169-0409-X*, J-33) Am Inst Chem Eng.

Storch Award, Conversion of FGD Residues & Utility Fly Ash to Marketable Products, Ash Chemistry: Phase Relationships in Ashes & Slags; General Papers. Preprints of Papers Presented at the 211th ACS National Meeting, Held in New Orleans, Louisiana, March 24-28, 1996. American Chemical Society, Division of Fuel Chemistry Staff. (American Chemical Society, Division of Fuel Chemistry, Preprints of Papers: Vol. 41, No. 2). 258p. 1996. reprint ed. pap. 73.60 (*0-608-01767-1*, 2062425) Bks Demand.

Storch Award, General Papers, Materials & Chemicals Synthesis from Fossil Fuels & Biomass, Advanced Power Generation, Ultrafine Particle Catalysis: Preprints of Papers Presented at the 209th ACS National Meeting, Anaheim, CA, April 2-7, 1995. American Chemical Society, Division of Fuel Chemistry Staff. (Preprints of Papers: Vol. 40, No. 2). 199p. 1995. reprint ed. pap. 56.80 (*0-7837-9209-3*, 2049959) Bks Demand.

Storch Award Symposium: Alternate Uses for Fossil Fuels; Coal Dissolution - Low Severity Liquefaction; Catalysts of Flue Gas Cleanup Processes: Preprints of Papers Presented at the 205th ACS National Meeting, Denver, CO, March 28-April 2, 1993. American Chemical Society, Division of Fuel Chemistry Staff. (Preprints of Papers: Vol. 38, No. 2). 423p. reprint ed. pap. 120.60 (*0-7837-4670-9*, 2044414) Bks Demand.

Store. Roberto Piumini. (J). (ps). 1993. Set of 3 bks. 13.50 (*1-56397-211-5*) Boyds Mills Pr.

Store. Roberto Piumini. LC 92-72120. (Illus.). 14p. (J). (ps). 1993. 4.50 (*1-56397-203-4*) Boyds Mills Pr.

Store. T. S. Stribling. 1991. lib. bdg. 21.95 (*1-56849-056-9*) Buccaneer Bks.

Store. T. S. Stribling. LC 85-1045. (Library of Alabama Classics). 592p. 1985. reprint ed. pap. 19.95 (*0-8173-0251-4*) U of Ala Pr.

Store Boy. Horatio Alger, Jr. (Works of Horatio Alger Jr.). 1989. reprint ed. lib. bdg. 79.00 (*0-685-27554-X*) Rprt Serv.

Store Choice, Store Location & Market Analysis. Ed. by Neil Wrigley. 388p. (C). 1988. lib. bdg. 79.95 (*0-415-00199-4*) Routledge.

Store Detective. Brassey. 1997. write for info. (*0-15-201409-8*) HarBrace.

***Store Fronts.** 5th ed. Retail Reporting Staff. 1994. 52.50 (*0-688-13844-6*) Morrow.

***Store Fronts & Facades.** 4th ed. Retail Reporting Staff. 1992. 52.50 (*0-688-11983-2*) Morrow.

***Store Fronts & Facades.** 6th ed. Retail Reporting Staff. 1996. 55.00 (*0-688-14805-0*) Morrow.

Store Fronts & Facades, No. 2. Ed. by Martin M. Pegler. (Illus.). 192p. 1988. 44.95 (*0-934590-26-5*) Retail Report.

Store Fronts & Facades, No. 3. Martin M. Pegler. (Illus.). 224p. 1990. 49.95 (*0-934590-38-9*) Retail Report.

Store Fronts & Facades - 4. Martin M. Pegler. (Illus.). 240p. 1992. 49.95 (*0-934590-48-6*) Retail Report.

Store It in Style. LC 96-15850. (Portable Workshop Ser.). 96p. 1996. 14.95 (*0-86573-683-9*) Cowles Creative.

Store Keeper-Stock Handler. 4th ed. Hammer. 224p. 1987. pap. 10.00 (*0-13-849696-X*, Arco) Macmillan Gen Ref.

Store Location & Assessment Research. Ed. by R. L. Davies & David S. Rogers. LC 83-21614. 375p. 1984. text ed. 175.00 (*0-471-90381-7*) Wiley.

***Store of Candles.** Frank Ormsby. 58p. 8600. pap. 12.95 (*0-904011-98-4*) Dufour.

Store of Common Sense: Gnomic Theme & Style in Old Icelandic & Old English Wisdom Poetry. Carolyne Larrington. LC 92-11139. (Oxford English Monographs). 256p. 1993. 55.00 (*0-19-811982-8*, Old Oregon Bk Store) OUP.

***Store of Joys: Writers Celebrate the NC Museum of Art's 50th Anniversary.** Compiled by NC Museum of Art Staff. LC 97-7004. (Orig.). 1997. pap. 22.00 (*0-89587-174-2*) Blair.

***Store of Joys: Writers Celebrate the North Carolina Museum of Art's Fiftieth Anniversary.** North Carolina Museum of Art Staff et al. LC 97-7004. 1997. write for info. (*0-89587-207-2*) Blair.

Store Operations in the Nineteen Ninety's: Control, Productivity & Profitability. Andrews. 224p. (C). 1990. 59.00 (*0-8403-5949-7*) Kendall-Hunt.

Store Planning - Design: History, Theory, Process. Lawrence J. Israel. 250p. 1994. text ed. 59.95 (*0-471-59488-1*) Wiley.

Store Planning & Design. Adolph Novak. LC 76-56649. (Illus.). 1977. pap. 28.95 (*0-86730-514-2*) Lebhar Friedman.

Store That Mama Built. Robert Lehrman. LC 91-39983. 128p. (J). (gr. 3-7). 1992. lib. bdg. 13.95 (*0-02-754632-2*, Mac Bks Young Read) S&S Childrens.

Store Wars: Shopkeepers & the Culture of Mass Marketing, 1890-1939. David Monod. (Illus.). 464p. 1996. 55.00 (*0-8020-0650-7*); pap. 22.95 (*0-8020-7604-1*) U of Toronto Pr.

Store Wars: The Battle for Mindspace & Shelfspace. Judith Corstjens & Marcel Corstjens. LC 94-22413. 303p. 1995. text ed. 65.00 (*0-471-95081-5*) Wiley.

***Store Windows.** 8th ed. Retail Reporting Staff. 1995. 55.00 (*0-688-14241-9*) Morrow.

***Store Windows.** 9th ed. Retail Reporting Staff. 1999. 55.00 (*0-688-14970-7*) Morrow.

***Store Windows That Sell.** 6th ed. Retail Reporting Staff. 1992. 52.50 (*0-688-11774-0*) Morrow.

***Store Windows That Sell.** 7th ed. Retail Reporting Staff. 1994. 52.50 (*0-688-13001-1*) Morrow.

Store Windows That Sell, No. 4. Ed. by Martin M. Pegler. (Illus.). 192p. 1988. 44.95 (*0-934590-27-3*) Retail Report.

Store Windows That Sell, No. 5. Martin M. Pegler. (Illus.). 1990. 49.95 (*0-934590-39-7*) Retail Report.

Store Windows that Sell, No. 6. Martin M. Pegler. (Illus.). 224p. 1992. 49.95 (*0-934590-47-8*) Retail Report.

Store Windows That Sell, No. 7. Ed. by Martin M. Pegler. (Illus.). 240p. 1994. 49.95 (*0-934590-57-5*) Retail Report.

Store Windows/8. Martin M. Pegler. 224p. 1995. 59.95 (*0-934590-72-9*) Retail Report.

Stored Data Description & Data Translation: A Model & Language. R. W. Taylor. 1977. pap. 25.00 (*0-08-021624-2*, Pergamon Pr) Elsevier.

Stored Energy Emergency & Standby Power Systems. 154p. 1993. 16.75 (*0-685-64958-X*, 111-93) Natl Fire Prot.

Stored Energy in Irradiated Salt Samples. A. G. Celma & H. Donker. 134p. 1994. pap. 20.00 (*92-826-7090-2*, CD-NA-14845-ENC, Pub. by Europ Com UK) Bernan Associates.

Stored-Grain Ecosystems. Ed. by Digvir S. Jayas et al. LC 94-22852. (Books in Soils, Plants & the Environment: Vol. 39). 776p. 1994. 195.00 (*0-8247-8983-0*) Dekker.

Stored-Grain Pests & Their Control. G. A. Zakladnoi & V. F. Ratanov. 279p. (C). 1987. text ed. 70.00 (*90-6191-494-9*, Pub. by A A Balkema NE) Ashgate Pub Co.

Stored-Grain Pests & Their Control. G. A. Zakladnoi & V. F. Ratanova. 1987. 35.00 (*0-8364-2270-8*, Pub. by Oxford IBH II) S Asia.

Stored-Product Protection: Proceedings of the 6th International Working Conference on Stored-product Protection, 2 vols., Set. Ed. by E. Highley et al. 1312p. 1994. 295.00 (*0-85198-932-2*) CAB Intl.

Storefront for Art & Architecture. Ed. by Kyong Park. (Illus.). 268p. (Orig.). pap. 29.95 (*1-56898-016-7*) Princeton Arch.

Storefront Revolution: Food Co-Ops & the Counterculture. Craig Cox. LC 93-45522. (Perspectives on the Sixties Ser.). 170p. (C). 1994. pap. 16.00 (*0-8135-2102-5*); text ed. 37.00 (*0-8135-2101-7*) Rutgers U Pr.

Storefronts & Facades. Martin M. Pegler. 1996. text ed. 59.95 (*0-07-049398-7*) McGraw.

Storefronts & Facades. 5th ed. Martin M. Pegler. 1995. text ed. 59.95 (*0-07-049385-5*) McGraw.

Storefronts & Facades, No. 6. Ed. by Martin M. Pegler. (Illus.). 208p. 1996. 59.95 (*0-934590-84-2*) Retail Report.

Storefronts & Facades No. 5. Martin M. Pegler. 240p. 1994. 59.95 (*0-934590-67-2*) Retail Report.

Storehouse & Stockyard Management. H. K. Compton. 530p. (C). 1989. 175.00 (*0-685-36164-0*, Pub. by Inst Pur & Supply UK) St Mut.

Storehouse of Sundry Valuables. Numata Center for Buddhist Translation & Research Staff. Tr. & Intro. by Charles Willemen. LC 92-82068. (BDK English Tripitaka Ser.: Vol. 10-I). 275p. (C). 1995. text ed. 35.00 (*0-9625618-3-5*) Numata Ctr.

Storekeeper. Jack Rudman. (Career Examination Ser.: C-771). 1994. pap. 23.95 (*0-8373-0771-6*) Nat Learn.

Storekeeper I. Jack Rudman. (Career Examination Ser.: C-2901). 1994. pap. 23.95 (*0-8373-2901-9*) Nat Learn.

Storekeeper II. Jack Rudman. (Career Examination Ser.: C-2902). 1994. pap. 27.95 (*0-8373-2902-7*) Nat Learn.

Storekeeper of Sleeman. large type ed. Lee F. Gregson. (Linford Western Library). 224p. 1993. pap. 15.99 (*0-7089-7370-1*, Linford) Ulverscroft.

***Storekeeper's Daughter: A Memoir.** Katie F. Wiebe. LC 96-49369. 216p. (Orig.). 1997. pap. 9.99 (*0-8361-9062-9*) Herald Pr.

***Storer Family, 1725-1965.** Mahlon A. Storer. (Illus.). 214p. 1996. reprint ed. pap. 34.00 (*0-8328-5426-3*); reprint ed. lib. bdg. 44.00 (*0-8328-5425-5*) Higginson Bk Co.

***Stores.** DK Publishing, Inc. Staff. 1997. 16.95 (*0-7894-2043-0*) DK Pub Inc.

S.T.O.R.E.S. Structured Teaching of Research & Experimentation Skills (Middle School) Mason, IV. 1991. pap. 15.00 (*0-89824-504-4*) Trillium Pr.

Stores Assistant. Jack Rudman. (Career Examination Ser.: C-3344). 1994. pap. 23.95 (*0-8373-3344-X*) Nat Learn.

Stores Clerk. Jack Rudman. (Career Examination Ser.: C-1494). 1994. pap. 23.95 (*0-8373-1494-1*) Nat Learn.

Stores Control. (Open Learning for Supervisory Management). 1986. pap. text ed. 19.50 (*0-08-034171-3*, Pergamon Pr) Elsevier.

Stores Control. (Open Learning for Supervisory Management Ser.). 1986. pap. text ed. 19.50 (*0-08-070055-1*, Pergamon Pr) Elsevier.

***Stores of the Year.** 6th ed. Retail Design Staff. 1991. 52.50 (*0-688-10714-1*) Morrow.

***Stores of the Year.** 8th ed. Retail Reporting Staff. 1994. 52.50 (*0-688-13530-7*) Morrow.

Stores of the Year. 9th ed. Martin M. Pegler. 1995. text ed. 59.95 (*0-07-049384-7*) McGraw.

***Stores of the Year.** 9th ed. Retail Reporting Staff. 1995. 55.00 (*0-688-14240-0*) Morrow.

Stores of the Year. 10th ed. Martin Pegleer. 1997. text ed. 59.95 (*0-07-049399-5*) McGraw.

***Stores of the Year.** 10th ed. Retail Reporting Staff. 1999. 55.00 (*0-688-14806-9*) Morrow.

***Stores of the Year, Bk. 4.** Retail Reporting Corporation Staff. 1987. 47.50 (*0-688-07828-1*) Morrow.

Stores of the Year, Bk. 7. Martin M. Pegler. 1993. 49.95 (*0-934590-53-2*) Retail Report.

Stores of the Year, No. 6. Martin M. Pegler. (Illus.). 224p. 1991. 49.95 (*0-934590-42-7*) Retail Report.

Stores of the Year, No. 8. Ed. by Martin M. Pegler. (Illus.). 240p. 1994. 49.95 (*0-934590-60-5*) Retail Report.

Stores of the Year, No. 9. Martin M. Pegler. 224p. 1995. 59.95 (*0-934590-71-0*) Retail Report.

Stores of the Year, No. 10. Ed. by Martin M. Pegler. (Illus.). 208p. 1996. 59.95 (*0-934590-85-0*) Retail Report.

Stores of the Year, Vol. II. Ed. by Martin M. Pegler. (Illus.). 176p. 1981. 39.95 (*0-934590-07-9*) Retail Report.

Stores of the Year, Vol. III. Ed. by Martin M. Pegler. (Illus.). 176p. 1984. 39.95 (*0-934590-11-7*) Retail Report.

Stores of the Year, Vol. IV. Intro. by Martin M. Pegler. (Illus.). 192p. 1987. 44.95 (*0-934590-22-2*) Retail Report.

Stores of the Year V. Martin M. Pegler. (Illus.). 256p. 1989. 34.98 (*0-934590-31-1*) Retail Report.

Store's Outing: A Tale of the 1960's. Ed. by Brynmill Pr. Ltd. Staff. 112p. (C). 1989. 70.00 (*0-9502723-5-3*, Pub. by Brynmill Pr Ltd UK) St Mut.

Stores to Gather All Those Lost. Ona Siporin. (Illus.). 124p. 1995. 10.00 (*0-87421-185-9*) Utah St U Pr.

Storey: Plays One. David Storey. 259p. (C). 1993. pap. 13.95 (*0-413-67350-2*, A0673, Pub. by Methuen UK) Heinemann.

Storey: Plays Two. David Storey. 256p. 1994. pap. 15.95 (*0-413-68610-8*, A0712, Pub. by Methuen UK) Heinemann.

Storeys from the Old Hotel. Gene Wolfe. 352p. 1995. pap. 14.95 (*0-312-89049-4*) Orb NYC.

Storia, Tome I. Elsa Morante. 1987. pap. 15.95 (*0-7859-4132-0*) Fr & Eur.

Storia: Five Centuries of the Italian American Experience. Jerre Mangione & Ben Morreale. LC 92-52553. (Illus.). 528p. 1993. reprint ed. pap. 17.00 (*0-06-092441-1*, PL) HarpC.

Storia del Coniglietto Pietro: Libro di Racconti in Colore - Di Beatrix Potter, con Disegni di Anna Pomaska. Beatrix Potter & Anna Pomaska. Tr. by Alessandra Vettori. (Illus.). 32p. (ITA.). (J). 1995. reprint ed. pap. text ed. 1.00 (*0-486-28558-8*) Dover.

Storia dell' eucaristia see Story of the Eucharist

Storia Della Musica Sacra, 2 vols. in 1. Francesco Caffi. 775p. 1982. reprint ed. 190.00 (*3-487-07174-6*) G Olms Pubs.

Storia dell'Arte Italiana: 1901-1940, 11. Vols. in 25 pts., Set. Incl. Vol. 1. Dai primordi dell'arte cristiana al tempo di Giustiniano. (*0-318-60667-4*); Vol. 2. Dell'arte barbarica all romanica. (*0-318-60668-2*); Vol. 3. Aret Romanica. (*0-318-60669-0*); Vol. 4. Scultura del Trecento e le Sue Origini. (*0-318-60670-4*); Vol. 5. Pittura del Trecento e le Sue Origini. (*0-318-60671-2*); Vol. 6. Scultura del Quattrocento. (*0-318-60672-0*); Vol. 7 (in 4 pts.). Pittura del Quattrocento. (*0-318-60673-9*); Vol 8 (in 2 pts.). Architetura del Quattrocento. (*0-318-60674-7*); Vol. 9 (in 7 pts.). Pittura del Cinquecento. (*0-318-60675-5*); Vol. 10 (in 3 pts.). Scultura del Cinquecento. (*0-318-60676-3*); Vol. 11 (in 3 pts.). Architetura del Cinquecento. (*0-318-60677-1*); 4, 150.00 (*0-8115-3505-3*) Periodicals Srv.

Storia Di Panini see Breadtime Story

Storia Di Sirio see Story of Sirio

Storia Di Una Capinera-The Sparrow. Giovanni Verga. Tr. by Christine Donougher from ITA. 160p. 1994. pap. 11.95 (*0-7818-0295-4*) Hippocrene Bks.

Storia Do Mogor, or Mogul India 1653-1708, 4 vols., Set. Niccolao Manucci. Tr. by William Irvine. reprint ed. text ed. 125.00 (*0-685-13412-1*) Coronet Bks.

Storia e Critica Di Testi Latini. Remigio Sabbadini. x, 458p. 1974. reprint ed. write for info. (*3-487-05395-0*) G Olms Pubs.

Storia E Interpretazione di Testi Bizantini. Antonio Garzya & Raffaele Contarella. (Collected Studies: No. CS28). 464p. (C). 1974. reprint ed. lib. bdg. 124.95 (*0-902089-63-3*, Pub. by Variorum UK) Ashgate Pub Co.

Storie, Tome II. Elsa Morante. 1987. pap. 13.95 (*0-7859-4133-9*) Fr & Eur.

Storied Cities: Literary Imaginings of Florence, Venice, & Rome. Michael L. Ross. LC 93-13011. (Contributions to the Study of World Literature Ser.: No. 51). 328p. 1993. text ed. 59.95 (*0-313-28717-1*, GM8717, Greenwood Pr) Greenwood.

Storied Lives: The Cultural Politics of Self-Understanding. Ed. by George C. Rosenwald & Richard L. Ochberg. 336p. (C). 1992. text ed. 40.00 (*0-300-05455-6*) Yale U Pr.

Stories. Ray Bradbury. Date not set. pap. write for info. (*0-679-44698-2*) Random.

Stories. Ida Fink. LC 97-6891. 1997. 23.00 (*0-8050-4557-0*) H Holt & Co.

Stories. Ida Fink. Date not set. pap. write for info. (*0-8050-4558-9*) H Holt & Co.

Stories. Gottfried Keller. Ed. by Frank G. Ryder. LC 81-22067. (German Library: Vol. 44). 348p. 1982. 29.50 (*0-8264-0256-9*); pap. text ed. 16.95 (*0-8264-0266-6*) Continuum.

Stories. Ram Kumar. 1976. 6.00 (*0-89253-267-X*); lib. bdg. 9.00 (*0-89253-085-5*) Ind-US Inc.

Stories. Doris Lessing. LC 79-22320. 1980. pap. 24.00 (*0-394-74249-4*, Vin) Random.

Stories. Leslie De Noronha. 8.00 (*0-89253-630-6*); text ed. 4.80 (*0-89253-631-4*) Ind-US Inc.

Stories. Cesare Pavese. Tr. & Intro. by A. E. Murch. 415p. 1987. pap. 12.95 (*0-88001-124-6*) Ecco Pr.

***Stories.** Rabkin. (C). 1994. teacher ed., text ed. 9.95 (*0-06-365306-0*) Addison-Wesley.

Stories. Eric S. Rabkin. (C). 1994. text ed. 39.50 (*0-06-045327-3*) Addson-Wesley Educ.

Stories. R. W. Schirmer. 194p. (Orig.). 1983. pap. 10.00 (*0-9611686-0-9*) R W Schirmer.

Stories, 4 vols., Set. Clare Roundhill & Penny King. Ed. by Bobbie Kalman. LC 95-50854. (Artists' Workshop Ser.). (Illus.). 32p. (J). (gr. 2-6). 1996. 19.96 (*0-86505-852-0*) Crabtree Pub Co.

Stories, 4 vols., Set. Clare Roundhill & Penny King. Ed. by Bobbie Kalman. LC 95-50854. (Artists' Workshop Ser.). (Illus.). 32p. (Orig.). (J). (gr. 2-6). 1996. pap. 8.95 (*0-86505-862-8*) Crabtree Pub Co.

Stories: A List of Stories to Tell & to Read Aloud. 3rd ed. Ed. by Marilyn B. Iarusso. LC 33-27120. 104p. 1990. reprint ed. pap. 6.00 (*0-87104-709-8*, Branch Libraries) NY Pub Lib.

Stories: Alchemy & Others. Andrew N. Lytle. 192p. 1984. pap. 9.95 (*0-918769-00-0*) Univ South Pr.

Stories: Children's Literature in Early Education. Shirley C. Raines & Rebecca T. Isbell. 31p. 1994. teacher ed. 14.95 (*0-8273-5510-6*) Delmar.

Stories: Children's Literature in the Early Childhood Classroom & Curriculum. Shirley C. Raines & Rebecca T. Isbell. LC 93-28119. 640p. 1994. text ed. 47.95 (*0-8273-5509-2*) Delmar.

Stories: Contemporary Southern Short Fiction. Ed. by Donald Hays. LC 88-20585. 470p. (Orig.). 1989. pap. 18.00 (*1-55728-039-8*) U of Ark Pr.

***Stories: Eleven Aboriginal Artists.** Craftsman House Staff. (Illus.). 176p. 1997. 55.00 (*90-5704-131-6*, Pub. by Craftsman Hse VB) IPG Chicago.

Stories: God's Hand in My Life. Kirk M. Dewey. Ed. by Jane D. Heald. LC 89-91377. 208p. (Orig.). 1990. pap. 10.95 (*0-9619558-2-1*) Support Source.

***Stories: Interior Designs.** Philip Graham. Date not set. write for info. (*0-688-11603-5*) Morrow.

Stories: Second Stories, Vol 1. Henry C. Bunner. LC 72-5900. (Short Story Index Reprint Ser.). 1977. reprint ed. 25.95 (*0-8369-4194-2*) Ayer.

Stories: The Family Legacy: A Guide for Recollection & Sharing. Richard Stone. 40p. 1994. pap. 6.95 (*0-9644168-0-8*) StoryWrk Inst.

Stories - A Little Book of Profitable Tales. Eugene Field. (Notable American Authors Ser.). 1992. reprint ed. lib. bdg. 75.00 (*0-7812-2647-3*) Rprt Serv.

Stories about Children from Many Lands. Jo E. Moore. (Illus.). 64p. (J). (gr. k-2). 1993. teacher ed., pap. 11.95 (*1-55799-248-7*, EMC 310) Evan-Moor Corp.

Stories about Incidents, 1915-1940. George A. Wildeboor. 150p. (Orig.). 1994. pap. write for info. (*1-885591-49-7*) Morris Pubng.

Stories about Jesus. Kenneth N. Taylor. LC 94-4083. (Illus.). 112p. (J). (ps-1). 1994. 8.99 (*0-8423-6093-X*) Tyndale.

Stories about Jesus for Young Readers. Illus. by Jenifer Schneider. 32p. (Orig.). (J). (gr. k-2). 1996. pap. 3.99 (*0-7847-0542-9*, 23942) Standard Pub.

Stories about Maxima & Minima. V. Tikhomirov. LC 90-21246. (Mathematical World Ser.: Vol. 1). 187p. 1992. pap. 19.00 (*0-8218-0165-1*, MAWRLD/1) Am Math.

Stories about Me. Linda G. Richman. (Illus.). 220p. 1989. spiral bd. 24.00 (*0-9609160-5-9*) Mayer-Johnson.

***Stories about My First Church.** Elmer L. Towns. LC 96-46206. 1997. 16.99 (*0-8307-1890-7*); write for info. (*0-8307-1920-2*) Gospel Lght.

Stories about the Partition of India. Alok Bhalla. (C). 1995. 24.00 (*81-7223-156-3*, Pub. by Indus Pub II) S Asia.

Stories about the Partition of India, Vol. I. Alok Bhalla. (C). 1994. 19.00 (*81-7223-119-9*, Pub. by Indus Pub II) S Asia.

Stories about the Partition of India, Vol. II. Alok Bhalla. (C). 1994. text ed. 9.00 (*81-7223-120-2*, Pub. by Indus Pub II) S Asia.

Stories & Activities for Articulation Reinforcement, No. 803118. Katherine T. McAvoy. 128p. (gr. k-6). 1990. student ed. 19.50 (*0-86703-216-2*) Opportunities Learn.

Stories & Early Novels: Pulp Stories; The Big Sleep; Farewell, My Lovely; The High Window. annot. deluxe ed. Raymond Chandler. Ed. by Frank McShane. LC 94-43705. 1200p. 1995. 35.00 (*1-883011-07-8*) Library of America.

Stories & Essays. Richard Wagner. 1973. 30.00 (*0-7206-9602-X*, Pub. by P Owen Ltd UK) Dufour.

Stories & Games for Easy Lipreading Practice. rev. ed. Rose F. Broberg. LC 77-70167. 1963. pap. 7.95 (*0-88200-080-2*, B0664) Alexander Graham.

Stories & Games for Easy Lipreading Practice. 2nd ed. Rose F. Broberg. LC 71-14203. 114p. reprint ed. pap. 32.50 (*0-7837-1253-7*, 2041390) Bks Demand.

***Stories & Legends Bible.** Mcleish. Date not set. pap. text ed. write for info. (*0-582-03406-X*, Pub. by Longman UK) Longman.

Stories & Legends of the Bering Strait Eskimos. Clark M. Garber. LC 74-5835. 260p. 1975. reprint ed. 45.00 (*0-404-11640-X*) AMS Pr.

Stories & Parables. Satguru S. Keshavadas. (Illus.). 100p. 1979. 8.00 (*0-533-03818-9*) Vishwa.

Stories & Parables for Preachers & Teachers. Paul J. Wharton. 1986. pap. 6.95 (*0-8091-2796-2*) Paulist Pr.

Stories & Pictures. Isaac L. Peretz. 1975. 250.00 (*0-87968-376-7*) Gordon Pr.

Stories & Pictures. Isaac L. Perez. Tr. by Helena Frank from YID. LC 75-152953. (Short Story Index Reprint Ser.). 1977. reprint ed. 25.95 (*0-8369-3868-2*) Ayer.

Stories & Plays for Children. Sunanda. 91p. (J). (gr. 3-8). 1984. pap. 3.00 (*0-89071-329-4*, Pub. by SAA II) Aurobindo Assn.

Stories & Poems by the Co-Op Kids. Susan O. Higgins & Co-Op Kids. (Co-Op Kids Ser.). (Illus.). 70p. (Orig.). (J). (ps-3). 1987. pap. 4.00 (*0-939973-04-9*) Pumpkin Pr Pub Hse.

S

Stories & Poems for Children. Celia L. Thaxter. LC 73-167486. (Granger Index Reprint Ser.). 1977. reprint ed. 20.95 (*0-8369-6291-5*) Ayer.

Stories & Poems from the Old North State. Ed. by Alga W. Leavitt. LC 71-163039. (Short Story Index Reprint Ser.). (Illus.). 1977. reprint ed. 23.95 (*0-8369-3953-0*) Ayer.

Stories & Prayers for Children. Illus. by Pamela Venus & Susie Adams. 80p. (J). (ps-2). 1995. 15.99 incl. audio (*0-88705-339-4*, Wshng Well Bks) Joshua Morris.

Stories & Readers: New Perspectives on Literature in the Elementary Classroom. Ed. by Charles Temple & Patrick Collins. 296p. (J). (gr. k-8). 1992. pap. text ed. 29.95 (*0-926842-10-2*) CG Pubs Inc.

***Stories & Recipes of the Great Depression.** Janet V. Paske & Rita C. Van Amber. 350p. 1997. pap. 15.00 (*0-9619663-3-5*) Van Amber Pubs.

Stories & Recipes of the Great Depression & Low Fat Pantry Cooking, Vol. II. Rita C. Van Amber & Janet V. Paske. 348p. (Orig.). 1993. pap. 15.00 (*0-9619663-2-7*) Van Amber Pubs.

Stories & Recipes of the Great Depression of the 1930's & More from Your Kitchen Today, Vol. I. rev. ed. Rita C. Van Amber & Janet V. Paske. 306p. 1986. pap. 15.00 (*0-9619663-1-9*) Van Amber Pubs.

Stories & Recollections of Umberto Saba. Umberto Saba. Tr. by Estelle Gilson from ITA. LC 92-39319. (Illus.). 245p. 1993. 22.50 (*1-878818-21-X*) Sheep Meadow.

Stories & Rhymes for under Fives. (Illus.). 80p. (J). (ps-1). 1990. 7.99 (*0-517-69420-4*) Random Hse Value.

Stories & Sketches. Saros Cowasjee & Khushwant Singh. (Writers Workshop Greenbird Ser.). 85p. 1975. 11.00 (*0-88253-646-X*) Ind-US Inc.

Stories & Songs. Claudia Vumakes. (Illus.). 128p. 1993. pap. 12.95 (*1-878279-58-0*) Monday Morning Bks.

Stories & Songs of Jesus. Christopher C. Walker. (Illus.). 64p. (J). 1994. text ed. 15.95 (*0-915531-27-5*) OR Catholic.

Stories & Songs of Jesus Activity/Coloring Book. Christopher C. Walker. (Illus.). 48p. (Orig.). (J). (gr. 1-7). 1994. pap. 1.50 (*0-915531-40-2*) OR Catholic.

Stories & Stone: An Anasazi Reader. Ed. by Reuben Ellis. LC 96-49918. (Illus.). 300p. (Orig.). 1996. pap. 18.95 (*0-87108-878-9*) Pruett.

Stories & Tales. Stephen Crane. Ed. by Robert W. Stallman. 1955. pap. 4.76 (*0-394-70010-4*, Vin) Random.

Stories & Tales, 7 Vols., Set. Sarah Orne Jewett. LC 83-45881. reprint ed. 185.00 (*0-404-20136-9*) AMS Pr.

Stories & Texts for Nothing. Samuel Beckett. Tr. by Richard Seaver from FRE. LC 67-20341. 142p. 1988. pap. 11.00 (*0-8021-5062-4*, Grove) Grove-Atltic.

***Stories & Their Limits: Narrative Approaches to Bioethics.** Ed. by Hilde L. Nelson. (Reflective Bioethics Ser.). 288p. (C). 1997. pap. 18.95 (*0-415-91910-X*, Routledge NY); text ed. 69.95 (*0-415-91909-6*, Routledge NY) Routledge.

Stories Animals Tell Me. Beatrice C. Lydecker. (Illus.). 160p. 1988. reprint ed. pap. 7.95 (*0-317-93280-2*) B Lydecker.

Stories As Continuing Education. (Illus.). 70p. 1993. ring bd. 31.00 (*1-56820-080-3*) Story Time.

Stories As Starting Points for Design & Technology. Design Council Staff. (C). 1991. pap. text ed. 50.00 (*0-85072-288-8*) St Mut.

Stories Based on Phonics, 34 bks., Set. Ellen L. Whitman. (Illus.). 24p. (J). (ps-3). 1996. 89.95 (*1-886410-50-X*) Lrning Pyramid.

Stories Behind Country Music's All Time Greatest 100 Songs. Ace Collins. 224p. (Orig.). 1996. pap. 10.00 (*1-57297-072-3*) Blvd Books.

Stories Behind New Orleans Street Names. Donald A. Gill. (Illus.). 280p. 1992. pap. 14.95 (*0-929387-41-4*) Bonus Books.

Stories Behind Popular Songs & Hymns. Lindsay Terry. 224p. (Orig.). (gr. 10). 1990. pap. 9.99 (*0-8010-8896-8*) Baker Bks.

Stories Behind Record Fish. Louis Bignami. LC 91-62283. (Complete Angler's Library). 218p. 1991. write for info. (*0-914697-41-2*) N Amer Outdoor Grp.

Stories Behind the Street Names of Albuquerque, Santa Fe & Taos. Donald A. Gill. (Illus.). 284p. 1994. pap. 14.95 (*1-56625-004-8*) Bonus Books.

Stories Behind the Street Names of Nashville & Memphis. Denise Strub. (Illus.). 175p. 1993. pap. 14.95 (*0-929387-83-X*) Bonus Books.

***Stories Behind the Testimonies: Why Ellen White Wrote the Letters in Testimonies for the Church.** Paul A. Gordon. LC 96-33565. 1997. write for info. (*0-8163-1369-5*) Pacific Pr Pub Assn.

Stories Bones Tell: From Body Basics to Mummy Mysteries. Craig Strasshofer. Ed. by Linda L. Yoshizawa. (Learn by Doing Library). (Illus.). 64p. (Orig.). (J). (gr. 4). 1995. pap. 19.95 (*1-886795-02-9*, Creat Pr) Creat for Kids.

Stories by American Authors, 10 vols in 5, Set. Ed. by Scibner Charles, & Sons Staff. 1972. reprint ed. lib. bdg. 150.00 (*0-685-36668-5*) Irvington.

Stories by American Authors, 10 vols in 5, Vols. 1-2. Ed. by Scribner Charles, & Sons Staff. 1972. reprint ed. 35.00 (*0-8422-8142-8*) Irvington.

Stories by American Authors, 10 vols in 5, Vols. 3-4. Ed. by Scribner Charles, & Sons Staff. 1972. reprint ed. 35.00 (*0-8422-8143-6*) Irvington.

Stories by American Authors, 10 vols in 5, Vols. 5-6. Ed. by Scribner charles, & Sons Staff. 1972. reprint ed. Vols 5-6. 35.00 (*0-8422-8144-4*) Irvington.

Stories by American Authors, 10 vols in 5, Vols. 7-8. Ed. by Scibner Charles, & Sons Staff. 1972. reprint ed. Vols 7-8. 35.00 (*0-8290-1658-9*) Irvington.

Stories by American Authors, 10 vols in 5, Vols. 9-10. Ed. by Scribner Charles, & Sons Staff. 1972. reprint ed. 35.00 (*0-8422-8146-0*) Irvington.

Stories by an Atheist. David Rogers. 267p. (Orig.). 1991. pap. 5.95 (*0-9618064-1-9*) D Rogers NY.

Stories by Contemporary Irish Women. Ed. by Linda M. Casey & Daniel J. Casey. LC 89-29523. (Irish Studies). 160p. 1990. pap. 14.95 (*0-8156-0249-9*); text ed. 39.95 (*0-8156-2489-1*) Syracuse U Pr.

Stories by Contemporary Japanese Women Writers. Kyoko I. Selden. LC 82-10270. 245p. 1982. reprint ed. pap. 69.90 (*0-7837-9924-1*, 2060651) Bks Demand.

Stories by Egyptian Women: My Grandmother's Cactus. Tr. & Intro. by Marilyn Booth. LC 92-43065. 175p. (C). 1993. pap. 10.95 (*0-292-70803-3*) U of Tex Pr.

Stories by English Authors, 10 vols in 5, Set. Ed. by Scribner Charles, & Sons Staff. 1972. reprint ed. lib. bdg. 150.00 (*0-8290-1414-4*) Irvington.

Stories by English Authors, 10 vols in 5, Vols. 1-2. Ed. by Scribner Charles, & Sons Staff. 1972. reprint ed. 35.00 (*0-8422-8147-9*) Irvington.

Stories by English Authors, 10 vols in 5, Vols. 3-4. Ed. by Scribner Charles, & Sons Staff. 1972. reprint ed. Vols 3-4. 35.00 (*0-8422-8148-7*) Irvington.

Stories by English Authors, 10 vols in 5, Vols. 5-6. Ed. by Scribner Charles, & Sons Staff. 1972. reprint ed. 35.00 (*0-8422-8149-5*) Irvington.

Stories by English Authors, 10 vols in 5, Vols. 7-8. Ed. by Scribner Charles, & Sons Staff. 1972. reprint ed. Vols.-7-8. 35.00 (*0-8422-8150-9*) Irvington.

Stories by English Authors, 10 vols in 5, Vols. 9-10. Ed. by Scribner Charles, & Sons Staff. 1972. reprint ed. 35.00 (*0-8422-8151-7*) Irvington.

Stories by Firelight. Shirley Hughes. LC 92-38207. (Illus.). 64p. (J). 1993. 16.00 (*0-688-04568-5*) Lothrop.

***Stories by Firelight.** Shirley Hughes. (Illus.). 64p. (J). 4.98 (*0-8317-2954-6*) Smithmark.

Stories by Foreign Authors, 10 vols in 5, Set. Ed. by Scribner Charles, & Sons Staff. 1972. reprint ed. lib. bdg. 175.00 (*0-685-36671-5*) Irvington.

Stories by Foreign Authors, 10 vols in 5, Vols. 1-2. Ed. by Scribner Charles, & Sons Staff. (FRE.). 1972. reprint ed. Vols 1-2, Fr. lib. bdg. 40.00 (*0-8422-8152-5*) Irvington.

Stories by Foreign Authors, Vols. 1 & 2. Ed. by Charles Scribners & Sons Staff. (C). 1988. pap. text ed. 10.95 (*0-8290-2143-4*) Irvington.

Stories by Foreign Authors, 10 vols in 5, Vols. 3-4. Ed. by Scribner Charles, & Sons Staff. (FRE & GER.). 1972. reprint ed. Vols 3-4, Fr. - Gr. lib. bdg. 40.00 (*0-8422-8153-3*) Irvington.

Stories by Foreign Authors, 10 vols in 5, Vols. 5-6. Ed. by Scribner Charles, & Sons Staff. (GER & ITA.). 1972. reprint ed. Vols 5-6, Gr. - It. lib. bdg. 40.00 (*0-8422-8154-1*) Irvington.

Stories by Foreign Authors, Vols. 5 & 6. Ed. by Scribner Charles, & Sons Staff. 1988. reprint ed. pap. text ed. 10.95 (*0-8290-2145-0*) Irvington.

Stories by Foreign Authors, 10 vols in 5, Vols. 7-8. Ed. by Scribner Charles, & Sons Staff. (RUS & SWE.). 1972. reprint ed. lib. bdg. 40.00 (*0-8422-8155-X*) Irvington.

Stories by Foreign Authors, 2 vols., Vols. 7 & 8. Ed. by Scribner Charles, & Sons Staff. (C). 1988. reprint ed. pap. text ed. 10.95 (*0-8290-2146-9*) Irvington.

Stories by Foreign Authors, 10 vols in 5, Vols. 9-10. Ed. by Scribner Charles, & Sons Staff. (POL & SPA.). 1972. reprint ed. lib. bdg. 40.00 (*0-8422-8156-8*) Irvington.

Stories by Foreign Authors, Vols. 9 & 10. Ed. by Charles Scribners & Sons Staff. (C). 1988. reprint ed. pap. text ed. 10.95 (*0-8290-2147-7*) Irvington.

Stories by Foreign Authors: German, 2 Vols. LC 72-110211. (Short Story Index Reprint Ser.). 1977. 30.95 (*0-8369-3363-X*) Ayer.

Stories by Foreign Authors: Italian. LC 72-110211. (Short Story Index Reprint Ser.). 1977. 17.95 (*0-8369-3364-8*) Ayer.

Stories by Foreign Authors: Polish, Greek, Belgian, Hungarian. LC 72-110211. (Short Story Index Reprint Ser.). 1977. 18.95 (*0-8369-3365-6*) Ayer.

Stories by Foreign Authors: Russian. LC 72-110211. (Short Story Index Reprint Ser.). 1977. 17.95 (*0-8369-3366-4*) Ayer.

Stories by Foreign Authors: Scandinavian. LC 72-110211. (Short Story Index Reprint Ser.). 1977. 17.95 (*0-8369-3367-2*) Ayer.

Stories by Foreign Authors: Spanish. LC 72-110211. (Short Story Index Reprint Ser.). 1977. 19.95 (*0-8369-3368-0*) Ayer.

Stories by Katherine Mansfield. Katherine Mansfield. LC 90-50474. 384p. 1991. pap. 13.00 (*0-679-73374-4*, Vin) Random.

Stories by Meir Blinkin. Meir Blinkin. Tr. by Max Rosenfeld from YID. LC 83-15564. (SUNY Series in Literature & Culture). 166p. 1984. 5.50 (*0-87395-818-7*) State U NY Pr.

Stories by the Sea. Betta Kym. LC 91-71172. (Living Stones Ser.). (Illus.). 83p. (J). (gr. 3-8). 1991. pap. 16.95 (*0-87303-059-1*) Faith & Life.

Stories Children Tell: Making Sense of the Narratives of Childhood. Susan Engel. 237p. (C). 1995. text ed. 22.95 (*0-7167-2382-4*) W H Freeman.

Stories Clouds Tell. 1993. 65.00 (*1-878220-12-8*) Am Meteorological.

Stories, Community, & Place: Narratives from Middle America. Barbara Johnstone. LC 89-46330. 192p. 1990. 10.95 (*0-253-33134-X*) Ind U Pr.

Stories Effie Told: The Crow, the Fawn, the Foxes. Effie Yeaw. (Stories Effie Told Ser.: Vol. 1). (Illus.). 28p. (Orig.). (J). (gr. k-6). 1995. pap. 4.95 (*1-887815-04-X*) Amer River Nat Hist.

Stories Et Cetera: A Country Lawyer. Gaylord. 1988. text ed. 19.00 (*0-442-01658-1*) Van Nos Reinhold.

Stories, Et Cetera: A Country Lawyer Looks at Life & the Law. C. Lester Gaylord. LC 87-82962. 1988. 19.00 (*0-318-37536-2*) Lawyers Cooperative.

Stories for Around the Campfire. 2nd ed. Ray Harriot. (Illus.). 176p. (Orig.). (J). (gr. 5-10). 1986. pap. 6.95 (*0-9617653-0-5*) Campfire Pub.

Stories for Bedtime. Illus. by Peter Stevenson. (Large Gift Bk.). 96p. (J). 1994. 11.95 (*0-7214-5458-5*, Ladybrd) Penguin.

Stories for Boys. Richard H. Davis. LC 73-150472. (Short Story Index Reprint Ser.). 1977. reprint ed. 20.95 (*0-8369-3812-7*) Ayer.

Stories for Children. Isaac B. Singer. LC 84-13612. 338p. (J). (gr. k up). 1984. 22.95 (*0-374-37266-7*) FS&G.

Stories for Children. Isaac B. Singer. LC 84-13612. 338p. (J). (gr. k up). 1985. pap. 13.00 (*0-374-46489-8*, Sunburst Bks) FS&G.

Stories for Children. Oscar Wilde. LC 90-38854. (Illus.). 96p. (J). (gr. 3 up). 1991. text ed. 15.00 (*0-02-792765-2*, Mac Bks Young Read) S&S Childrens.

Stories for Children with Problems & Wishes: A Therapeutic Workbook for Turning Problems into Gifts. Burt G. Wasserman. Ed. by Don L. Sorenson. (Illus.). 80p. (Orig.). 1994. pap. text ed. 9.95 (*0-932796-62-1*) Ed Media Corp.

Stories for Christian Initiation. Joseph J. Juknialis. LC 92-16485. (Illus.). 160p. (Orig.). (C). 1992. pap. text ed. 8.95 (*0-89390-235-7*) Resource Pubns.

Stories for Eight-Year-Olds. Ed. by Sara Corrin & Stephen Corrin. (Illus.). 192p. (J). (gr. 2-4). 1984. pap. 11.95 (*0-571-12969-2*) Faber & Faber.

Stories for Every Holiday. Carolyn S. Bailey. LC 89-43337. 277p. 1990. reprint ed. lib. bdg. 40.00 (*1-55888-880-2*) Omnigraphics Inc.

***Stories for Every Season.** Verna Martin. (Illus.). 268p. (Orig.). (YA). (gr. 4 up). 1996. pap. 7.95 (*0-87813-564-2*) Christian Light.

Stories for Five-Year-Olds. Sara Corrin. (J). (ps-3). 1989. pap. 10.95 (*0-571-12998-6*) Faber & Faber.

Stories for Home Schools. (Illus.). 65p. 1993. ring bd. 34.00 (*1-56820-078-1*) Story Time.

Stories for Jason. Mary L. Cromer. LC 93-37765. 110p. (J). 1993. pap. 8.95 (*0-944350-28-3*) Friends United.

Stories for Lesley. Robert Frost. Ed. by Roger D. Sell. LC 83-19756. 77p. reprint ed. pap. 25.00 (*0-7837-1245-6*, 2041382) Bks Demand.

Stories for Older Students, Bk. 1: Steps 1-3. Jay Brown. (Wilson Reading System Ser.). 40p. 1992. pap. text ed. 8.00 (*1-56778-039-3*) Wilson Lang Trning.

Stories for Older Students, Bk. 2: Steps 4-6. Jay Brown. (Wilson Reading System Ser.). 42p. 1992. pap. text ed. 8.00 (*1-56778-040-7*) Wilson Lang Trning.

Stories for Older Students, Bk. 3: Steps 7-9. Jay Brown. (Wilson Reading System Ser.). 40p. 1992. pap. text ed. 8.00 (*1-56778-041-5*) Wilson Lang Trning.

Stories for Our Children: A Book for African American Christian Families. Byron Douglas. 56p. (J). 1995. pap. 12.95 (*0-913543-45-4*) African Am Imag.

Stories for Parents, 6 bks. Feagin. 1990. pap. 21.65 (*0-8092-4137-4*) Contemp Bks.

Stories for Public Speakers. abr. rev. ed. Morris Mandel. LC 96-3750. Orig. Title: A Complete Treasury of Stories for Public Speakers. 1996. 19.95 (*0-8246-0389-3*) Jonathan David.

Stories for Ramu. Deepak Dubey. 10.00 (*0-89253-794-9*); text ed. 5.00 (*0-89253-795-7*) Ind-US Inc.

***Stories for Reflection.** Jack McArdle. 176p. (Orig.). 1996. pap. 14.95 (*1-85607-172-3*, Pub. by Columba Pr IE) Twenty-Third.

Stories for Seven-Year-Olds. Ed. by Sara Corrin & Stephen Corrin. (Illus.). 188p. (J). (gr. 1-3). 1982. pap. 11.95 (*0-571-12910-2*) Faber & Faber.

Stories for Sharing: With Themes & Discussion Starters for Teachers & Speakers. Charles Arcodia. 1991. pap. 8.95 (*0-85574-348-4*, Pub. by E J Dwyer AT) Morehouse Pub.

Stories for Six-Year-Olds. Ed. by Sara Corrin & Stephen Corrin. (Illus.). 198p. (J). (gr. k-2). 1984. pap. 11.95 (*0-571-12959-5*) Faber & Faber.

Stories for Speakers & Writers: A Compendium of Wit, Humor, & Inspiration from Everyday Life. E. L. McDonald. LC 91-126559. (Speakers & Toastmasters Library). 108p. (C). 1991. reprint ed. pap. 7.99 (*0-8010-5853-8*) Baker Bks.

Stories for Telling: A Treasury for Christian Storytellers. William R. White. LC 85-28980. 144p. (Orig.). 1986. pap. 11.99 (*0-8066-2192-3*, 10-6023, Augsburg) Augsburg Fortress.

Stories for the Campfire: A Collection of Tales with Morals, Memories, Magic, Beetles, Bugs, Bats, Cats & Tales. Robert Hanson. 38p. 1983. pap. 8.95 (*0-87603-120-3*) Am Camping.

Stories for the Children's Hour. 2nd ed. Kenneth N. Taylor. (J). (gr. 1-8). 1987. pap. 8.99 (*0-8024-2227-6*) Moody.

***Stories for the Gathering: A Treasury for Christian Storytellers.** William R. White. LC 97-13007. 1997. pap. 11.99 (*0-8066-3345-X*, Augsburg) Augsburg Fortress.

***Stories for the Heart: When Your Soul Needs More than Chicken Soup.** Alice Gray. 1996. pap. 10.99 (*1-57673-127-8*, Multnomah Bks) Multnomah Pubs.

Stories for the Journey: A Sourcebook for Christian Storytellers. William R. White. LC 88-47910. 128p. (Orig.). 1988. pap. 11.99 (*0-8066-2364-0*, 10-6026, Augsburg) Augsburg Fortress.

Stories for the Third Ear: Using Hypnotic Fables in Psychology. Lee Wallas. (Professional Bks.). 1985. 20.95 (*0-393-70019-4*) Norton.

Stories for Tight Places. Harry E. Randles. LC 89-91744. 156p. (Orig.). 1990. pap. 7.95 (*0-9623219-0-7*) H Randles.

Stories for Under-Fives. Ed. by Sara Corrin et al. (Illus.). 158p. (J). (ps-5). 1974. pap. 11.95 (*0-571-12920-X*) Faber & Faber.

***Stories for Youth, 3 vols.** Lass & Horwitz. (J). 30.00 (*0-614-30540-3*) NAVH.

Stories from a Ming Collection. Ed. & Tr. by Cyril Birch from CHI. LC 68-44187. 205p. 1968. pap. 10.95 (*0-8021-5031-4*, Grove) Grove-Atltic.

Stories from a Siberian Village. Vasily Shukshin. Tr. by John Givens & Laura Michael from RUS. LC 95-46643. 304p. (C). 1996. 35.00 (*0-87580-211-7*); pap. 16.00 (*0-87580-572-8*) N Ill U Pr.

***Stories from Africa: Tsie Na Atsie.** Rose E. Arkou-Tewia. (Illus.). 80p. (J). 1993. pap. write for info. (*0-904693-45-7*, Pub. by Temple Ldge Pub UK) Anthroposophic.

Stories from American Business. Patricia Costello. (Illus.). 112p. (C). 1986. pap. text ed. 9.00 (*0-13-849811-3*) P-H.

Stories from an Open Country: Essays on the Yellowstone Valley. Ed. by William L. Lang. (Illus.). 256p. 1995. pap. 19.95 (*0-9628215-1-9*) Westn Heritage Ctr.

Stories from Ancient Africa. Gloria T. Edwards. (Illus.). 66p. (Orig.). 1995. pap. write for info. (*1-57502-046-7*) Morris Pubng.

Stories from Ancient Canaan. Tr. by Michael D. Coogan. LC 77-20022. 120p. 1978. pap. 12.00 (*0-664-24184-0*, Westminster) Westminster John Knox.

***Stories from Asia, India, Pakistan & Bangladesh.** Bhinda. Date not set. pap. text ed. write for info. (*0-582-03922-3*, Pub. by Longman UK) Longman.

Stories from Asia Today: A Collection for Young Readers, Bk. I. Ed. by Asian Cultural Centre for UNESCO Staff. LC 74-82605. (Illus.). 144p. (J). (gr. 4-7). 1980. pap. 7.95 (*0-8348-1038-7*) Weatherhill.

Stories from Asia Today: A Collection for Young Readers, Bk. 2. Ed. by Asian Cultural Center for UNESCO Staff. LC 74-82605. (Illus.). 184p. (J). (gr. 4-7). 1980. pap. 8.95 (*0-8348-1040-9*) Weatherhill.

Stories from Bapu's Life. Uma Joshi. (Nehru Library for Children). (Illus.). (J). (gr. 1-9). 1979. pap. 2.50 (*0-89744-180-X*) Auromere.

Stories from Beyond the Double Rainbow. Elaine Hardt. (Orig.). (J). (gr. 1-8). 1982. pap. 10.95 (*0-932960-03-0*) Thinking Caps.

Stories from Black History Series II, 3 bks., Set. 2nd ed. Brenda A. Johnston et al. Ed. by John A. McCluskey. (Illus.). (J). (gr. 4-7). 1993. pap. 8.00 (*0-913678-24-4*) New Day Pr.

Stories from Central American Refugees & from Children Breaking the Cycle of Violence. Central American Refugees & Children Breaking the Cycle of Violence. (Common Ground Ser.: Vol. 1). (Illus.). 44p. (Orig.). 1985. pap. 5.00 (*1-884478-00-X*) Common Grnd.

Stories from Central & Southern Africa. Ed. by Paul Scanlon. (African Writers Ser.). 207p. (Orig.). (C). 1983. pap. 9.95 (*0-435-90254-7*, 90254) Heinemann.

Stories from China's Past: Han Dynasty Pictorial Tomb Reliefs & Archaeological Objects from Sichuan Province, People's Republic of China. Lucy Lim et al. LC 87-70422. (Illus.). 210p. 1988. reprint ed. pap. 35.00 (*0-295-96797-8*) U of Wash Pr.

Stories from Chocolate's Heart. Gwendolyn L. Williams. 100p. (Orig.). 1995. pap. write for info. (*1-885591-54-3*) Morris Pubng.

Stories from Eighty Years of Travel & Adventure. F. G. Shaw. 140p. (C). 1989. 75.00 (*0-7223-2273-9*, Pub. by A H S Ltd UK) St Mut.

Stories from el Barrio. Piri Thomas. LC 78-328. (J). (gr. 5-9). 1992. 15.00 (*0-394-83568-9*) Knopf Bks Yng Read.

Stories from Europe: Learning Center. rev. ed. Irene Handberg. (Multicultural Education Ser.). 90p. 1995. teacher ed. write for info. (*1-56831-611-9*) Lrning Connect.

Stories from Europe: Learning Center, Set. rev. ed. Irene Handberg. (Multicultural Education Ser.). 90p. 1995. write for info. (*1-56831-600-3*) Lrning Connect.

Stories from God's Son. (Bible Adventure Bks.). (J). (gr. 3-4). 1992. pap. 2.19 (*0-614-07610-2*) Accent CO.

Stories from Grandpa's Rocking Chair. Sarah Kaetler. (Kindred Press Sibling Ser.). 64p. (Orig.). (J). (gr. 1-5). 1983. pap. 3.95 (*0-919797-11-3*) Kindred Prods.

Stories from Greek Mythology. E. Constantopoulos. (Illus.). (GRE.). (gr. 3-4). 4.00 (*0-686-79632-2*) Divry.

Stories from Hans Christian Andersen. Illus. by Alan Snow. LC 92-45627. 96p. (J). (gr. 2-5). 1993. 18.95 (*0-531-05463-2*) Orchard Bks Watts.

Stories from Holy Writ. Helen Waddell. LC 74-25538. 280p. 1975. reprint ed. text ed. 59.75 (*0-8371-7872-X*, WAHW, Greenwood Pr) Greenwood.

Stories from Home. Date not set. 9.95 (*1-879669-06-4*) FMG Bks.

Stories from Home. Jerry Clower. LC 91-38118. 194p. 1993. 19.95 (*0-87805-547-9*); pap. 14.95 (*0-87805-642-4*) U Pr of Miss.

Stories from Indian Wigwams & Northern Campfires. E. R. Young. 1977. lib. bdg. 75.00 (*0-8490-2671-7*) Gordon Pr.

Stories from Iran 1921-1991: A Chicago Anthology. Bozorg Alavi et al. Ed. by Heshmat Moayyad. Tr. by John Perry et al. from PER. 576p. 1992. pap. 19.95 (*0-934211-33-7*) Mage Pubs Inc.

Stories from Iran 1921-1991: A Chicago Anthology. Bozorg Alavi et al. Ed. by Heshmat Moayyad. Tr. by John Perry et al. from PER. (Illus.). 576p. 1992. 35.00 (*0-934211-28-0*) Mage Pubs Inc.

Stories from Kenya. Tom Gates & Liz Gates. 1995. pap. 3.00 (*0-87574-319-6*) Pendle Hill.

An Asterisk (*) at the beginning of an entry indicates that the title is appearing in BIP for the first time.

Stories from Lakakh. Kusum Kapur. (C). 1994. text ed. 6.00 (*81-7223-115-6*, Pub. by Indus Pub II) S Asia.

Stories from Lake Wobegon: Advanced Listening & Conversation Skills. Frances Boyd & David Quinn. (YA). 1990. audio 37.95 (*0-8013-0492-X*, 78344) Longman.

Stories from Laos: Folktales & Cultures of the Lao, Hmong, Khammu, & Iu-Mien. Rosalie Giacchino-Baker. (Illus.). 104p. (Orig.). (ENG & LAO.). (YA). (gr. 7 up). 1995. pap. 14.95 (*1-879600-31-5*) Pac Asia Pr.

***Stories from Latin America: A Translator's Portfolio.** Ed. by Ilan Stavans. LC 97-16443. (Orig.). 1997. pap. 17.95 (*1-880684-49-7*) Curbstone.

Stories from Latin America: An ESL-EFL Reader. Larry T. Myers. (Illus.). 96p. (C). 1987. pap. text ed. write for info. (*0-318-61593-2*) P-H.

***Stories from Life: The Photography of Horace Bristol.** Horace Bristol. 187p. 1995. pap. text ed. 35.00 (*0-915977-20-6*, TR500) Georgia Museum of Art.

Stories from Many Lands. Ed. by G. C. Thornley. (Bridge Ser.). (Illus.). 133p. (Orig.). (YA). 1964. pap. text ed. 5.95 (*0-582-53025-3*) Longman.

Stories from Mesa Country. Jane C. Coleman. LC 91-4174. 160p. 1991. 24.95 (*0-8040-0949-X*) Swallow.

Stories from Mesa Country. large type ed. Jane C. Coleman. LC 96-11832. 210p. 1996. 19.95 (*0-7862-0710-8*) Thorndike Pr.

Stories from Mesa Country. Jane C. Coleman. LC 91-4174. 160p. 1992. reprint ed. pap. 10.95 (*0-8040-0957-0*) Swallow.

Stories From Mexico/Historias de Mexico. (BBC Phrase Books for Teenagers). 256p. 1995. pap. 11.95 (*0-8442-0811-6*, Passport Bks) NTC Pub Grp.

Stories from Mormon History. Alma P. Burton. 183p. 1995. pap. 10.95 (*1-55517-157-5*) CFI Dist.

***Stories from My Life: Cassandra Walker Talks to Teens about Growing Up.** Cassandra Walker. Ed. by Elizabeth Verdick. LC 96-46698. 152p. (Orig.). (YA). (gr. 5 up). 1997. pap. 6.95 (*1-57542-016-3*) Free Spirit Pub.

Stories from My Life with Other Animals. James McConkey. 160p. 1993. 19.95 (*0-87923-967-0*) Godine.

Stories from Nicaragua. Sergio Ramirez. Tr. by Nick Caistor from SPA. (Readers International Ser.). (Illus.). 130p. (Orig.). (C). 1987. pap. 7.95 (*0-930523-29-6*) Readers Intl.

Stories from Old-Fashioned Children's Books. Andrew W. Tuer. 1972. 35.00 (*0-8490-1126-4*) Gordon Pr.

Stories from Our Living Past. Francine Prose. Ed. by Jules Harlow. LC 74-8514. (Illus.). 128p. 1974. teacher ed., pap. 14.95 (*0-87441-082-7*) Behrman.

Stories from Our Living Past. Francine Prose. Ed. by Jules Harlow. LC 74-8514. (Illus.). 128p. (J). (gr. 3-4). 1974. pap. 8.95 (*0-87441-081-9*) Behrman.

Stories from Our Living Past, No. 1. Francine Prose. Ed. by Jules Harlow. LC 74-8514. (Illus.). 128p. (J). (gr. 3-4). 1974. wbk. ed., pap. 3.50 (*0-87441-083-5*) Behrman.

Stories from Our Living Past, No. 2. Francine Prose. Ed. by Jules Harlow. LC 74-8514. (Illus.). 128p. (J). (gr. 3-4). 1974. wbk. ed., pap. 3.50 (*0-87441-084-3*) Behrman.

Stories from Panchatantra. Bani R. Choudhary. (Illus.). (J). (gr. 3-10). 1979. 7.25 (*0-89744-136-2*) Auromere.

Stories from Panchatantra: Book I. Shivkumar. (Illus.). (J). (gr. 1-9). 1979. 4.50 (*0-89744-162-1*); pap. 3.00 (*0-685-57661-2*) Auromere.

Stories from Panchatantra: Book II. Shivkumar. (Illus.). (J). (gr. 1-9). 1979. 4.50 (*0-89744-163-X*); pap. 3.00 (*0-685-57662-0*) Auromere.

Stories from Panchatantra: Book III. Shivkumar. (Illus.). (J). (gr. 1-9). 1979. 4.50 (*0-89744-164-8*); pap. 3.00 (*0-685-57663-9*) Auromere.

Stories from Panchatantra: Book IV. Shivkumar. (Illus.). (J). (gr. 1-9). 1979. 4.50 (*0-89744-165-6*); pap. 3.00 (*0-685-57664-7*) Auromere.

Stories from Response-Centered Classrooms. Barbara S. Livdahl et al. 160p. (C). 1995. pap. text ed. 17.95 (*0-8077-3457-8*) Tchrs Coll.

Stories from Response-Centered Classrooms. Barbara S. Livdahl et al. 160p. (C). 1995. text ed. 38.00 (*0-8077-3458-6*) Tchrs Coll.

Stories from Sarala's Mahabharat. Prafulla K. Mohanty. 205p. 1990. text ed. 27.50 (*0-7069-4589-1*, Pub. by Vikas II) S Asia.

Stories from Shakespeare. Marchette Chute. 1959. pap. 3.95 (*0-452-00895-6*, Mer); pap. 9.95 (*0-452-01061-6*, Mer) NAL-Dutton.

Stories from Shakespeare. Illus. by Antony Maitland. (YA). (gr. 5 up). 1995. 19.95 (*0-689-80037-1*, McElderry) S&S Childrens.

Stories from Six Worlds. Ruth H. Whitehead. 1991. pap. 16.95 (*0-921054-14-9*, Pub. by Nimbus Publishing Ltd CN) Chelsea Green Pub.

Stories from Tagore. Rabindranath Tagore. 176p. 1983. 5.00 (*0-318-37007-7*) Asia Bk Corp.

Stories from Tennessee. Ed. by Linda Burton. LC 82-16016. 432p. 1983. pap. 16.95 (*0-87049-377-9*); text ed. 32.50 (*0-87049-376-0*) U of Tenn Pr.

Stories from the American Soul: A Reader in Ethics & American Policy in the 1990's. Robert F. Drinan. LC 90-35610. 154p. 1990. 3.00 (*0-8294-0696-4*) Loyola Pr.

Stories from the Arabian Nights. L. Housman. 144p. 1986. 80.00 (*1-85077-143-X*, Pub. by Darf Pubs Ltd UK) St Mut.

Stories from the Arabian Nights. Retold by Naomi Lewis. (Illus.). 224p. 1991. 9.99 (*0-517-05480-9*) Random Hse Value.

Stories from the Arabian Nights. Vernon Thomas. (Illus.). (YA). (gr. 8-12). 1979. 7.50 (*0-89744-142-7*) Auromere.

***Stories from the Bible.** Illus. by Sam Butcher. LC 78-97507. (Precious Moments Ser.). 288p. (J). 1995. pap. 12.99 (*0-8010-4085-X*) Baker Bks.

Stories from the Bible. Tony Morris. (J). (gr. k-3). 1995. 9.98 (*1-85854-365-7*) Brimax Bks.

Stories from the Bible--Newly Retold. Sipke Van Der Land. LC 79-10049. 205p. reprint ed. pap. 58.50 (*0-317-39654-4*, 2023224) Bks Demand.

Stories from the Big Black House. Jonathan Thomas. Ed. by Brian T. Gallagher et al. (Illus.). 128p. (Orig.). 1993. pap. 6.95 (*1-879484-01-3*) Radio Void.

Stories from The Catechist: Nine Hundred Seven Traditional Catholic Stories Illustrating the Truths of the Catholic Catechism. Canon & G. E. Howe. LC 82-50589. 387p. (YA). 1989. reprint ed. pap. 17.50 (*0-89555-184-5*) TAN Bks Pubs.

Stories from the Circle: Women's Leadership in Community. Ann Smith et al. LC 91-6754. 114p. (Orig.). 1991. pap. 8.95 (*0-8192-1536-8*) Morehouse Pub.

Stories from the Classical Ballet. Belinda Hollyer. (Illus.). 128p. (J). (gr. 3-7). 1995. pap. 15.99 (*0-670-86605-9*) Viking Child Bks.

Stories from the Country of Lost Borders. Mary Austin. Ed. by Marjorie Pryse. (American Women Writers Ser.). 267p. 1987. text ed. 40.00 (*0-8135-1217-4*); pap. text ed. 16.00 (*0-8135-1218-2*) Rutgers U Pr.

Stories from the Days of Columbus: A Multicultural Collection for Young Readers. Ed. by Richard Young. 160p. (YA). 1992. pap. 8.95 (*0-87483-198-9*) August Hse.

Stories from The Delight of Hearts: The Memoirs of Haji Mirza Haydar-'Ali. A. Q. Faizi. LC 79-91219. (Illus.). 176p. 1980. 13.95 (*0-933770-11-1*) Kalimat.

Stories from the Diary of a Doctor. L. T. Meade. LC 75-32767. (Literature of Mystery & Detection Ser.). (Illus.). 1976. reprint ed. 31.95 (*0-405-07886-2*) Ayer.

Stories from the English Saints. John Richardson. 96p. 1993. 22.00 (*0-85439-455-9*, Pub. by St Paul Pubns UK) St Mut.

Stories from the Front Lines: Power Evangelism in Today's World. Jane Rumph. LC 95-42595. 256p. (C). 1996. pap. 11.99 (*0-8007-9238-6*) Chosen Bks.

***Stories from the Front Porch: Coleslaw in My Pocket, Butter Beans under My Bed, Lessons I Learned in the Cat Patrol & Other Stories.** Elmer L. Towns. LC 96-2399. 1996. trans. write for info. (*0-8307-1899-0*) Regal.

Stories from the Greek Comedians. Alfred J. Church. 1994. pap. 20.00 (*0-8196-2081-5*) Biblo.

Stories from the Growing Years. Arleta Richardson. LC 90-20123. (Grandma's Attic Ser.). 160p. (J). (gr. 3-7). 1995. pap. 4.99 (*0-7814-0212-3*, 38190, Chariot Bks) Chariot Victor.

***Stories from the Heart: Case Studies of Emotional Abuse.** Ed. by M. T. Loring. 200p. 1997. 45.00 (*3-7186-0585-6*) Gordon & Breach.

***Stories from the Heart: Case Studies of Emotional Abuse.** Ed. by Marti T. Loring. (New Directions in Therapeutic Intervention Ser.). 1997. text ed. 45.00 (*90-5702-553-1*, Harwood Acad Pubs); pap. text ed. 19.00 (*90-5702-554-X*, Harwood Acad Pubs) Gordon & Breach.

Stories from the Heart: Teachers & Students Researching Their Literacy Lives. Richard Meyer. 176p. 1996. pap. 12.95 (*0-8058-8044-5*) L Erlbaum Assocs.

Stories from the Hearts of Two Grandmas. Ibbie Ledford & Johnnie Countess. LC 96-27456. 128p. 1996. pap. text ed. 10.95 (*1-56554-214-2*) Pelican.

Stories from the Life of Jesus. (Now You Can Read Bible Stories Ser.). 32p. (J). 1994. 3.98 (*0-86112-789-7*) Brimax Bks.

Stories from the Literary Review. Ed. by Charles Angoff. LC 68-21271. 312p. 1975. 35.00 (*0-8386-6899-2*) Fairleigh Dickinson.

Stories from the Microwave. Willie Smith. 28p. 1983. pap. text ed. 2.50 (*0-686-38441-5*) Skydog OR.

Stories from the New Testament. Lincoln. LC 96-46558. (J). 1997. 18.00 (*0-689-81297-3*) S&S Childrens.

Stories from the New Testament. G. Polyzoides. (Illus.). 112p. (GRE.). vinyl bd. 4.00 (*0-686-83966-8*) Divry.

Stories from the Old Squires Farm. Waugh & Waugh Staff. LC 95-5299. 288p. 1995. 18.95 (*1-55853-334-6*) Rutledge Hill Pr.

Stories from the Old Testament. G. Polyzoides. (Illus.). 71p. (GRE.). (J). (gr. 5 up). vinyl bd. 4.00 (*0-686-80434-1*) Divry.

***Stories From The Old Testament, No. 5.** Bear Run Publishing Staff. (J). 1996. 16.00 (*0-671-88665-7*) S&S Childrens.

Stories from the Old Testament, Vol 1. Bear. (J). 1998. 16.00 (*0-671-88661-4*, S&S Bks Young Read) S&S Childrens.

Stories from the Old Testament, Vol 2. Moser. (J). 1998. 16.00 (*0-671-88662-2*, S&S Bks Young Read) S&S Childrens.

Stories from the Old Testament, Vol 3. Moser. (J). 1998. 16.00 (*0-671-88663-0*, S&S Bks Young Read) S&S Childrens.

Stories from the Old Testament, Vol 4. Moser. (J). 1998. 16.00 (*0-671-88664-9*, S&S Bks Young Read) S&S Childrens.

Stories from the Old Testament: With Masterwork Paintings Inspired by Stories. Lincoln. (J). 1996. 18.00 (*0-689-80955-7*) S&S Childrens.

Stories from the Old Testament Coloring Book. (Illus.). 96p. (J). 1990. pap. 1.99 (*1-55748-604-2*) Barbour & Co.

Stories from the Pacific: The Island War 1942 - 1945. Lawrence F. Kirby. LC 94-74545. (Illus.). 218p. (Orig.). 1995. pap. 11.95 (*0-9645103-1-6*) Masconomo Pr.

Stories from the Rabbis. Abram S. Isaacs. LC 79-175868. 1972. reprint ed. 23.95 (*0-405-08661-X*, Pub. by Blom Pubns UK) Ayer.

Stories from the Sea. Illus. by Amanda Hall. 80p. (J). (ps-3). 1996. 19.95 (*0-7892-0282-4*, Abbeville Kids) Abbeville Pr.

Stories from the Stars: Greek Myths of the Zodiac. Illus. by Jackie Morris. 80p. (J). (ps-3). 1996. pap. 19.95 (*0-7892-0283-2*, Abbeville Kids) Abbeville Pr.

Stories from the Swedish Heritage. Arland O. Fiske. (Illus.). 224p. (Orig.). 1992. pap. 11.95 (*0-942323-17-3*) N Amer Heritage Pr.

Stories from Today's Russia. (BBC Phrase Books for Teenagers). 80p. 1994. pap. 7.95 (*0-8442-4252-7*, Passport Bks) NTC Pub Grp.

Stories from Ugadali: Cherokee Story Teller. Piper. 1981. pap. 3.95 (*0-89992-078-0*) Coun India Ed.

Stories from Under the Sky. John Madson. LC 87-34486. (Iowa Heritage Collection Ser.). (Illus.). 206p. 1988. reprint ed. pap. 12.95 (*0-8138-0077-3*) Iowa St U Pr.

Stories from Washington Heights & Other Corners of the World - Historias de Washington Heights y Otros Rincones del Mundo. Ed. by Daisy Cocco de Filippis & Franklin Gutierrez. 204p. (SPA.). 1994. pap. 10.00 (*1-884912-02-8*) Latino Pr.

Stories from Westport's Past, Bk. II. Foster. pap. 8.95 (*0-9615410-2-4*) Stories Westports Past.

Stories He Told, Vol. 1: The Dubno Maggid on the Weekly Parshah. Bereishis et al. 209p. 1991. 10.95 (*0-944070-70-1*); pap. 8.95 (*0-944070-71-X*) Targum Pr.

Stories Huey Tells. Ann Cameron. LC 94-6221. 112p. (J). 1995. 16.00 (*0-679-86732-5*); lib. bdg. 16.99 (*0-679-96732-X*) Knopf Bks Yng Read.

***Stories Huey Tells.** Ann Cameron. (J). 1997. pap. 4.99 (*0-679-88559-5*) Knopf Bks Yng Read.

Stories I Ain't Told Nobody Yet: Selections from the People Pieces. Jo Carson. LC 90-29030. 96p. 1991. pap. 10.95 (*1-55936-027-5*) Theatre Comm.

Stories I Couldn't Tell While I Was a Pastor. Bruce McIver. 1992. pap. 10.99 (*0-8499-3418-4*) Word Pub.

Stories I Like to Read. Edna K. Wenger. 1991. pap. 7.00 (*0-87813-913-3*) Christian Light.

Stories in an Almost Classical Mode. Harold Brodkey. LC 88-45299. 624p. 1988. 24.95 (*0-394-50699-5*) Knopf.

Stories in an Almost Classical Mode. Harold Brodkey. 1989. pap. 18.00 (*0-679-72431-1*, Vin) Random.

Stories in Art. Clare Gogerty. LC 94-8957. (Let's Investigate Art Ser.). (Illus.). (J). (gr. 3 up). 1994. 15.50 (*1-85435-770-0*) Marshall Cavendish.

Stories in Art. Helen Williams. (J). (gr. 4-7). 1992. pap. 7.64 (*0-395-64558-1*) HM.

Stories in Art. Helen Williams. LC 91-32185. (Millbrook Arts Library). (Illus.). 48p. (J). (gr. 2-6). 1992. pap. 8.95 (*1-56294-820-2*); lib. bdg. 17.40 (*1-56294-174-7*) Millbrook Pr.

Stories in Her Eyes. M. J. Pennington. Ed. by Dave Bakker. LC 95-70928. (Illus.). 302p. (Orig.). 1995. per. 14.00 (*0-9648049-0-5*) N Hrzns Publns.

Stories in Light & Shadow. Bret Harte. LC 78-116952. (Short Story Index Reprint Ser.). 1977. 19.95 (*0-8369-3455-5*) Ayer.

Stories in Manx with English Translations. (CEL & ENG.). pap. 7.50 (*0-89979-030-5*) British Am Bks.

Stories in My Pocket: Tales Kids Can Tell. Martha Hamilton & Mitch Weiss. LC 96-12750. (Illus.). 192p. (Orig.). (J). 1996. pap. 15.95 (*1-55591-957-X*) Fulcrum Pub.

Stories in Prose, Stories in Verse, Shorter Poems, Lectures & Essays. William Morris. Ed. by G. D. Cole. LC 75-41200. reprint ed. 94.50 (*0-404-14690-2*) AMS Pr.

***Stories in Scripture & Inscriptions: Comparative Studies in Biblical & Epigraphic Narratives.** Simon Parker. 208p. 1997. 35.00 (*0-19-511620-8*) OUP.

Stories in Stone. Kevin Cuff et al. Ed. by Lincoln Bergman et al. (Great Explorations in Math & Science (GEMS) Ser.). (Illus.). 164p. (Orig.). (J). (gr. 4-9). 1995. teacher ed., pap. 16.00 (*0-912511-93-1*) Lawrence Science.

Stories in Stone: Rock Art Pictures by Early Americans. Caroline Arnold. (Illus.). (J). 1996. 15.95 (*0-395-72092-3*) HM.

***Stories in Stone: Soapstone Sculptures from Northern Quebec & Kenya.** Thomas O. Eisemon et al. (Illus.). 84p. (ENG & FRE.). 1988. pap. 14.95 (*0-660-50288-7*, Pub. by Can Mus Civil CN) U of Wash Pr.

***Stories in Stone: The Medieval Roof Carvings of Norwich Cathedral.** Martial Rose. LC 96-61180. (Illus.). 194p. (Orig.). 1997. pap. 19.95 (*0-500-27937-3*) Thames Hudson.

Stories in the Classroom: A Directory of Stories for Teachers & Storytellers. (Illus.). 46p. 1993. ring bd. 26.95 (*1-56820-079-X*) Story Time.

Stories in the Classroom: Storytelling, Reading Aloud, & Roleplaying with Children. Bob Barton & David Booth. LC 89-77379. 194p. 1990. pap. text ed. 20.00 (*0-435-08527-1*, 08527) Heinemann.

Stories in the Worst Way. Gary Lutz. 160p. 1996. 21.00 (*0-679-42596-9*) Knopf.

Stories in Thread. Marsha MacDowell. Ed. by Ruth D. Fitzgerald & Sue Caltrider. (Illus.). (Orig.). 1989. spiral bd. 20.00 (*0-944311-02-4*) MSU Museum.

Stories Jesus Told. (Children's Bible Stories Ser.). (Illus.). 24p. (J). 1993. 4.98 (*0-7853-0265-4*) Pubns Intl Ltd.

Stories Jesus Told. (Now You Can Read Bible Stories Ser.). 24p. (J). 1994. 3.98 (*0-86112-788-9*) Brimax Bks.

Stories Jesus Told. Nick Butterworth & Mick Inkpen. 224p. (J). (ps-k). 1994. 10.99 (*0-88070-633-3*, Gold & Honey) Multnomah Pubs.

Stories Jesus Told. Bessie Dean. 72p. (J). 1979. pap. 6.98 (*0-88290-132-X*) Horizon Utah.

Stories Jesus Told. Illus. by Toni Goffe. LC 92-34973. (Life of Christ for Children Ser.). 24p. (J). 1992. 6.99 (*0-8423-5943-5*) Tyndale.

Stories Jesus Told. Maralene Wesner & Miles Wesner. LC 88-57869. (Parables for the Real World Ser.). 58p. (Orig.). 1988. pap. 3.95 (*0-936715-13-8*) Diversity Okla.

Stories Jesus Told Sticker Fun. (Little Lamb Mini Activity Bks.). (Illus.). 20p. (J). 1991. pap. 1.49 (*0-87403-900-2*, 01560) Standard Pub.

Stories Julian Tells. Ann Cameron. LC 80-18023. (Illus.). 96p. (J). (gr. k-5). 1981. 8.95 (*0-394-84301-0*) Pantheon.

Stories Julian Tells. Ann Cameron. LC 80-18023. (Illus.). 96p. (J). (gr. k-5). 1981. lib. bdg. 14.99 (*0-394-94301-5*) Pantheon.

***Stories Julian Tells.** HarBrace Staff. (J). 1995. pap. 11.00 (*0-15-305580-4*) HarBrace.

Stories Julian Tells. Pearl Neuman. Ed. by J. Friedland & R. Kessler. (Novel-Ties Ser.). 1994. pap. text ed. 15.95 (*1-56982-054-6*) Lrn Links.

Stories Julian Tells. Ann Cameron. LC 80-18023. (Illus.). 88p. (J). (gr. k-3). 1989. reprint ed. pap. 3.99 (*0-394-82892-5*) Knopf Bks Yng Read.

Stories Lives Tell: Narrative & Dialogue in Education. Ed. by Carol Witherell & Nel Noddings. 304p. (C). 1991. text ed. 49.00 (*0-8077-3071-8*); pap. text ed. 21.95 (*0-8077-3070-X*) Tchrs Coll.

Stories Made Easy for Spanish Speakers. Walker La Verne & Marta J. Planadeball. LC 86-6913. 75p. 1986. pap. 6.00 (*0-8477-3344-0*) U of PR Pr.

Stories My Mother Never Told Me. Ed. by Alfred Hitchcock. 1976. 21.95 (*0-8488-0532-1*) Amereon Ltd.

Stories of a Gold Miner: Trinity County, California 1848-1861. 2nd rev. ed. Patricia J. Hicks. LC 92-90248. (Illus.). 90p. 1992. pap. 7.25 (*0-9626392-3-0*) I Collect Facts.

Stories of a Salesman. Murli D. Melwani. 1976. 6.75 (*0-89253-268-8*); lib. bdg. 8.00 (*0-89253-084-7*) Ind-US Inc.

Stories of a Taxi Driver. Andrei Frolov. 1994. 10.95 (*0-533-10747-4*) Vantage.

Stories of a Twentieth-Century Life. William R. Sears. LC 93-87280. xii, 292p. (Orig.). 1994. 22.00 (*0-915760-05-3*); pap. 12.00 (*0-915760-04-5*) Parabolic Pr.

Stories of a Western Town. Alice French. 1972. reprint ed. pap. text ed. 8.50 (*0-8290-0673-7*); reprint ed. lib. bdg. 27.50 (*0-8422-8055-3*) Irvington.

Stories of Abdu'l-Baha. Jacqueline Mehrabi. 48p. 1984. pap. 8.95 (*0-900125-54-3*) Bahai.

Stories of Abdu'l-Baha. Jacqueline Mehrabi. 48p. 1996. 14.95 (*1-870989-66-X*) Bahai.

Stories of Abraham: Trusting the God Who Calls. Galen Meyer. (Revelation Ser.). 1993. teacher ed. 6.10 (*1-56212-088-3*) CRC Pubns.

Stories of Abraham: Trusting the God Who Calls. Marten Woudstra. LC 93-14320. (Revelation Series for Adults). 1993. student ed. 4.50 (*1-56212-042-5*) CRC Pubns.

Stories of Achievements: Narrative Features of Organizational Performance. Herve Corvellec. LC 96-49383. 154p. 1997. text ed. 29.95 (*1-56000-282-4*) Transaction Pubs.

Stories of Adoption: Loss & Reunion. Eric Blau. (Illus.). 132p. 1993. pap. 16.95 (*0-939165-17-1*) NewSage Press.

Stories of Aleutians & Kodiak. Kathleen Lynch. (Illus.). (Orig.). 1978. reprint ed. pap. 9.50 (*1-878051-33-4*, CP063) Circumpolar Pr.

Stories of American Life, 3 vols. 1972. reprint ed. lib. bdg. 42.00 (*0-318-53726-5*) Irvington.

Stories of American Life, 3 vols, Set. 1972. reprint ed. lib. bdg. 126.00 (*0-8422-8097-9*) Irvington.

Stories of an Imaginary Childhood. Melvin J. Bukiet. 197p. (Orig.). 1992. 29.95 (*0-8101-1006-7*); pap. 12.95 (*0-8101-1031-8*) Northwestern U Pr.

***Stories of Anton Chekhov.** unabridged ed. Anton P. Chekhov. 297p. 1997. reprint ed. pap. 14.95 (*1-57002-044-2*) Univ Publng Hse.

Stories of Australian Migration. Ed. by John Hardy. 1988. pap. 24.95 (*0-86840-155-2*, Pub. by New South Wales Univ Pr AT) Intl Spec Bk.

Stories of Authors, British & American. Edwin W. Chubb. LC 68-54338. (Essay Index Reprint Ser.). 1977. 23.95 (*0-8369-0305-6*) Ayer.

Stories of Awe & Abundance. Jose Hobday. 120p. (Orig.). 1995. pap. 9.95 (*1-55612-765-0*) Sheed & Ward MO.

Stories of Basel, Berne & Zurich. M. D. Hottinger. (Mediaeval Towns Ser.: Vol. 35). 1974. reprint ed. pap. 46.00 (*0-8115-0877-3*) Periodicals Srv.

Stories of Beatrix Potter, Vol. 1. Beatrix Potter. (Audio Gift Pack Ser.). (Illus.). 96p. (J). (ps-2). 1991. 16.98 incl. audio (*1-55886-063-0*) Smarty Pants.

Stories of Beatrix Potter, Vol. 2. Beatrix Potter. (Audio Gift Pack Ser.). (Illus.). 96p. (J). (ps-2). 1992. 16.98 incl. audio (*1-55886-067-3*) Smarty Pants.

Stories of Bernard Malamud. Bernard Malamud. LC 83-14100. 357p. 1983. 17.95 (*0-374-27037-6*) FS&G.

Stories of Bernard Malamud. Bernard Malamud. 370p. 1984. pap. 8.95 (*0-452-25911-8*, Plume) NAL-Dutton.

Stories of Bernard Malamud. limited ed. Bernard Malamud. LC 83-14100. 357p. 1983. 75.00 (*0-374-27038-4*) FS&G.

Stories of Bible Heroes: A Bible Story Coloring Book. Illus. by Laura Shepard. (Stories of...Bible Story Coloring Bks.). 72p. (Orig.). (J). (ps-3). 1996. pap. 3.95 (*1-57102-090-X*, Ideals Child) Hambleton-Hill.

***Stories of Broken Idol & the Jewish Rabbi.** Khurram Murad. 28p. (J). 1996. pap. 3.50 (*0-614-21041-0*, 1164) Kazi Pubns.

Stories of Charlemagne. Jennifer Westwood. LC 74-12435. (J). (gr. 6 up). 1976. 24.95 (*0-87599-213-7*) S G Phillips.

Stories of Childhood: Shifting Agendas of Child Concern. Rex Rogers & Wendy Rogers. 228p. 1992. 65.00 (*0-8020-2974-4*) U of Toronto Pr.

Stories of Childhood: Shifting Agendas of Child Concern. Rex S. Rogers. LC 93-136336. 228p. 1994. pap. 19.95 (*0-8020-6944-4*) U of Toronto Pr.

Stories of Christmas Carols. Earnest K. Emurian. LC 58-12415. 152p. (gr. 10). 1996. 12.99 (*0-8010-1136-1*) Baker Bks.

Stories of Composers for Young Musicians. large type ed. Catherine W. Kendall. (Illus.). 185p. (Orig.). (J). (gr. 1-12). 1982. pap. 13.75 (*0-9610878-0-3*) Toadwood Pubs.

*__Stories of Covenant.__ Ed. by June A. Gibble. 48p. 1993. reprint ed. pap. 25.00 (*0-608-04173-4*, 2064907) Bks Demand.

Stories of David Bergelson: Yiddish Short Fiction from Russia. David Bergelson. Ed. & Tr. by Golda Werman. LC 96-1795. (Judaic Traditions in Literature, Music, & Art Ser.). 160p. 1996. text ed. 34.95 (*0-8156-2712-2*, WESD); pap. text ed. 14.95 (*0-8156-0402-5*, WESDP) Syracuse U Pr.

*__Stories of Deliverance: Speaking with Men & Women Who Rescued Jews from the Holocaust.__ Marek Halter. Tr. by Michael Bernard from FRE. 256p. (C). 1996. pap. 17.95 (*0-8126-9364-7*) Open Court.

Stories of Detection & Mystery. (Fiction Ser.). (YA). 1993. pap. text ed. 7.50 (*0-582-08465-2*, 79828) Longman.

Stories of Divine Children: The Stories of Eight Famous Boys from the Mythology of India. 38p. pap. 4.95 (*81-7120-591-7*) Vedanta Ctr.

Stories of Dixie. James W. Nicholson. 1966. pap. 7.00 (*0-87511-153-X*) Claitors.

Stories of Don Bosco. 2nd ed. Peter Lappin. LC 78-72525. (Illus.). 272p. (J). (gr. 5-12). 1979. pap. 9.50 (*0-89944-036-3*) Salesiana Pubs.

Stories of Early Inns & Taverns of the East Tennessee Country. LaReine W. Clayton. LC 95-70153. (Illus.). 192p. 1995. lib. bdg. 19.95 (*0-9647748-0-1*) J G Buchanan.

Stories of Early Twentieth Century Life: An Oral History of Arlington, Massachusetts. Ed. by Oakes Plimpton. LC 92-61076. 192p. 1992. per. 12.00 (*0-89725-082-6*, 1388, Penobscot Pr) Picton Pr.

Stories of Eastern Religions. Denise L. Carmody & John T. Carmody. LC 91-18925. 242p. (C). 1992. pap. text ed. 28.95 (*1-55934-054-1*, 1054) Mayfield Pub.

*__Stories of Edith Wharton.__ Edith Wharton. 10.95 (*0-7867-0760-7*) Carroll & Graf.

Stories of Edith Wharton. Edith Wharton. 309p. 1990. 18.95 (*0-88184-620-1*) Carroll & Graf.

Stories of Edith Wharton. Edith Wharton. Ed. by Anita Brookner. 320p. 1991. pap. 10.95 (*0-88184-760-7*) Carroll & Graf.

Stories of Edith Wharton, Vol. 2. Intro. by Anita Brookner. 310p. 1990. 18.95 (*0-88184-637-6*) Carroll & Graf.

Stories of Edith Wharton, Vol. 2. Ed. by Anita Brookner. 320p. 1991. pap. 10.95 (*0-88184-707-0*) Carroll & Graf.

*__Stories of Edith Wharton, Vol. 2.__ Edith Wharton. 10.95 (*0-7867-0707-0*) Carroll & Graf.

Stories of Elijah, Elisha, & Daniel. (Bible Adventure Bks.). (J). (gr. 3-4). 1993. pap. 2.19 (*0-614-07611-0*) Accent CO.

Stories of Ernest Dowson. Ernest Dowson. Ed. by Mark Longaker. 1977. lib. bdg. 59.95 (*0-8490-2672-5*) Gordon Pr.

Stories of Erskine Caldwell. Erskine Caldwell. LC 96-18365. (Brown Thrasher Bks.). 680p. 1996. reprint ed. 55.00 (*0-8203-1693-8*); reprint ed. pap. 24.95 (*0-8203-1694-6*) U of Ga Pr.

Stories of Eva Luna. Isabel Allende. Tr. by Margaret S. Peden from SPA. 288p. 1991. text ed. 18.95 (*0-689-12102-4*) Macmillan.

Stories of Eva Luna. large type ed. Isabel Allende. 1991. lib. bdg. 20.95 (*0-8161-5253-5*, GK Hall) Thorndike Pr.

Stories of Eve Luna. Isabel Allende. 384p. 1992. mass mkt. 6.99 (*0-553-57535-X*) Bantam.

Stories of Excellence: Ten Case Studies from a Study of Exemplary Mathematics Programs. Mark Driscoll. LC 86-33193. 108p. 1987. pap. 10.00 (*0-87353-236-8*) NCTM.

Stories of F. Scott Fitzgerald. F. Scott Fitzgerald. 504p. 1977. 50.00 (*0-684-15366-1*, SL135) S&S Trade.

Stories of Faith. John Shea. (Rev. John Shea Library). (C). 1980. pap. 12.95 (*0-88347-112-4*, 7112) Res Christian Liv.

Stories of Falling Toward Grace. Carlton Allen. 136p. (Orig.). 1994. pap. 11.95 (*1-880837-81-1*) Smyth & Helwys.

Stories of Genesis. Hermann Gunkel. Ed. by William R. Scott. Tr. by John J. Scullion from GER. LC 93-41722. 192p. (ENG & GER.). 1994. pap. 15.95 (*0-941037-21-5*) BIBAL Pr.

Stories of Georgia. Joel C. Harris. 1998. reprint ed. 34.00 (*1-55888-228-6*) Omnigraphics Inc.

Stories of Ghosts, Witches, & Demons. Freya Littledale. 80p. (J). (gr. 4-7). 1992. pap. 2.95 (*0-590-45556-7*) Scholastic Inc.

Stories of God. Rainer M. Rilke. Tr. by M. D. Norton. 144p. 1992. pap. 8.95 (*0-393-30882-0*) Norton.

Stories of God: An Unauthorized Biography. John Shea. (Rev. John Shea Library). (C). 1978. pap. 12.95 (*0-88347-085-3*, 7085) Res Christian Liv.

Stories of God's Power: A Bible Story Coloring Book. Suzanne C. Smith. (Stories of...Bible Story Coloring Bks.). (Illus.). 72p. (Orig.). (J). (ps-3). 1996. pap. 3.95 (*1-57102-089-6*, Ideals Child) Hambleton-Hill.

*__Stories of Great Americans for Little Americans.__ Edward Eggleston. (J). (ps-4). 1996. 17.95 (*0-9652735-2-0*) Lost Classics.

Stories of Great Craftsmen. S. H. Glenister. LC 75-128247. (Essay Index Reprint Ser.). 1977. 15.95 (*0-8369-1831-2*) Ayer.

Stories of Great Muslims. A. Haye. 1985. 4.00 (*0-89259-020-3*) Am Trust Pubns.

Stories of Great Muslims. K. H. Hayes. (J). 6.50 (*0-933511-63-9*) Kazi Pubns.

Stories of Happy People. Lars Gustafsson. Tr. by Yvonne L. Sandstroem & John Weinstock from SWE. LC 85-31052. 160p. 1986. reprint ed. 16.95 (*0-8112-0977-6*); reprint ed. pap. 7.95 (*0-8112-0978-4*, NDP616) New Directions.

Stories of Hawaii. Jack London. Ed. by A. Grove Day. LC 65-11682. 282p. 1985. reprint ed. mass mkt. 4.95 (*0-935180-08-7*) Mutual Pub HI.

Stories of Heinrich Boll. Heinrich Boll. Tr. by Leila Vennewitz from GER. (European Classics Ser.). 690p. (C). 1995. pap. 19.95 (*0-8101-1207-8*) Northwestern U Pr.

Stories of Home Folks. Mabel Hale. 160p. pap. 1.50 (*0-686-29143-3*) Faith Pub Hse.

Stories of Hope & Healing: Six Women Confront Breast Cancer. Leslie E. Strong. 46p. 1993. pap. 14.95 (*1-881025-07-1*) Equinox Pr.

Stories of Hospital & Camp. C. E. McKay. LC 70-37312. (Black Heritage Library Collection). 1977. reprint ed. 25.95 (*0-8369-8949-X*) Ayer.

Stories of I. C. Eason, King of the Dog People. I. C. Eason. LC 95-26622. (Illus.). 129p. 1996. 24.95 (*1-57441-012-1*) UNTX Pr.

*__Stories of Indian Pacific.__ Dewi Anggraeni. 265p. 1992. pap. 14.95 (*0-9587718-3-9*, Pub. by Indra Pub AT) Intl Spec Bk.

Stories of Indian Saints. Justin E. Abbott & Narhar Godbole. 1988. reprint ed. 24.00 (*81-208-0469-4*, Pub. by Motilal Banarsidass II) S Asia.

Stories of Iowa: One Hundred Thirty Short Stories of Iowa's History. Ed. by O. J. Fargo. 136p. (Orig.). (YA). (gr. 5 up). 1991. pap. text ed. 4.50 (*0-924702-31-1*) Grn Valley Area.

Stories of Jerseys Ships. Jean. (Jersey Heritage Editions Ser.). 1991. write for info. (*0-86120-019-5*, Pub. by Aris & Phillips UK) David Brown.

Stories of Jesus, Bk. 1. Stanley Thornes. (C). 1985. text ed. 30.00 (*0-7175-1296-7*, Pub. by S Thornes Pubs UK) St Mut.

Stories of Jesus, Bk. 2. Stanley Thornes. (C). 1985. text ed. 30.00 (*0-7175-1297-5*, Pub. by S Thornes Pubs UK) St Mut.

Stories of Jesus, Bk. 3. Stanley Thornes. (C). 1985. text ed. 30.00 (*0-7175-1298-3*, Pub. by S Thornes Pubs UK) St Mut.

Stories of Jesus: Jesus' Parables Instant Ink. Laura Kelly. (Little Lamb Mini Activity Bks.). (Illus.). 16p. (J). 1994. pap. 1.49 (*0-7847-0192-X*, 01542) Standard Pub.

Stories of Jesus for Children: Lessons Jesus Taught, Let's Learn about Jesus, Stories Jesus Told, 3 bks., Set. Bessie Dean. (J). 1994. pap. 18.98 (*0-88290-491-4*) Horizon Utah.

Stories of Jesus, Tell Them to Me. P. Gwyn Filby. 200p. 1987. 60.00 (*0-317-62104-1*) St Mut.

Stories of Jewish Home Life. Salomon R. Von Mosenthal. LC 75-160945. (Short Story Index Reprint Ser.). 1977. reprint ed. 23.95 (*0-8369-3924-7*) Ayer.

Stories of Jibaro Juan. Raymond Watson & Evelyn De Jesus. 1995. 14.95 (*0-533-11576-0*) Vantage.

Stories of John Cheever. John Cheever. LC 78-106. 1978. 40.00 (*0-394-50087-3*) Knopf.

Stories of John Cheever. John Cheever. 704p. 1985. mass mkt. 7.99 (*0-345-33567-8*) Ballantine.

Stories of John Edgar Wideman. John Edgar Wideman. LC 91-50839. 448p. 1992. 25.00 (*0-679-40719-7*) Pantheon.

Stories of King David. Lillian S. Freehof. LC 95-20175. (Illus.). (J). 1995. 10.95 (*0-8276-0567-6*) JPS Phila.

Stories of King Solomon. Lilliam S. Freehof. (Illus.). 1995. 10.95 (*0-8276-0566-8*) JPS Phila.

Stories of Lake George: Fact & Fancy. Thomas R. Lord. 204p. 1986. pap. 19.95 (*0-9640267-1-6*) Pinelands Pr.

Stories of Little Brown Koko. Blanche S. Hunt. (Illus.). 96p. 1992. reprint ed. lib. bdg. 15.95 (*0-89968-309-6*, Lghtyr Pr) Buccaneer Bks.

Stories of Lost Israel in Folklore. James A. Haggart. LC 80-65735. 144p. 1981. pap. 5.00 (*0-934666-08-3*) Artisan Sales.

Stories of Love That Lasts. Don W. Hillis. 80p. (YA). (gr. 9-12). 1980. pap. 1.00 (*0-89323-015-4*) Bible Memory.

Stories of Maasaw: A Hopi God. Ekkehart Malotki & Michael Lomatuway'ma. LC 87-164. (American Tribal Religions Ser.: Vol. 10). (Illus.). 357p. 1987. reprint ed. pap. 101.80 (*0-7837-8895-9*, 2049606) Bks Demand.

*__Stories of Men.__ Anton P. Chekhov. LC 96-38096. 1997. pap. 13.95 (*1-57392-135-1*) Prometheus Bks.

Stories of Misbegotten Love, Angel on My Shoulder. Herbert Gold & Don Asher. (Capra Back-to-Back Ser.: No. 4). 138p. (C). 1988. reprint ed. lib. bdg. 27.00 (*0-8095-4103-3*) Borgo Pr.

Stories of Mummies & the Living Dead. Eric Kudalis. (Monsters & Their Stories Ser.). 48p. (J). (gr. 3-10). 1994. lib. bdg. 17.80 (*1-56065-214-4*) Capstone Pr.

*__Stories of Mummies & the Living Dead.__ Eric Kudalis. (Classic Monster Stories Ser.). (Illus.). 48p. (J). (gr. 3-7). 1994. 18.40 (*0-516-35214-8*) Childrens.

Stories of New Jersey. Frank R. Stockton. (Illus.). 263p. 1961. reprint ed. 15.95 (*0-8135-0369-8*) Rutgers U Pr.

Stories of Noah & Joseph. Dee Leone. (Bible-Time Puzzle Ser.). (Illus.). 48p. (J). (ps-1). 1992. 7.95 (*0-86653-645-0*, SS2811, Shining Star Pubns) Good Apple.

Stories of O. Henry. O. Henry. 224p. 1989. pap. 2.50 (*0-8125-0502-6*) Tor Bks.

Stories of Old Duck Hunters. Gordon Macquarrie. 1992. pap. 9.95 (*1-55971-051-9*) NorthWord.

Stories of Old Ireland for Children. Edmund Lenihan. (J). 1990. pap. 9.95 (*0-85342-777-1*) Dufour.

Stories of Old New Spain. Thomas A. Janvier. (C). 1972. reprint ed. lib. bdg. 26.50 (*0-8422-8081-2*) Irvington.

Stories of Old New Spain. Thomas A. Janvier. (C). 1986. reprint ed. pap. text ed. 6.95 (*0-8290-2031-4*) Irvington.

Stories of Old Upland: Early Years Picture Album, Pt. 5. 3rd ed. Esther B. Black. Orig. Title: Stories of Old Upland for Young Listeners. (Illus.). 124p. 1979. pap. text ed. 12.95 (*0-9603586-0-9*) Chaffey Commun Cult Ctr.

Stories of Old Upland for Young Listeners see Stories of Old Upland: Early Years Picture Album

Stories of Osaka Life. Oda Sakunosuke. Tr. by Burton Watson from JPN. 192p. 1994. pap. 12.95 (*0-8348-0308-9*) Weatherhill.

Stories of Our Blackfeet Grandmothers. Mary C. Boss-Ribs et al. (Indian Culture Ser.). (Orig.). (J). (gr. 1-6). 1984. pap. 4.95 (*0-89992-096-9*) Coun India Ed.

*__Stories of Padre Pio.__ M. K. Tangari. (Illus.). 218p. pap. 8.00 (*0-89555-536-0*) TAN Bks Pubs.

Stories of Paul for Children: Paul, God's Special Missionary, Paul's Letters of Love, 2 bks., Set. Bessie Dean. (J). 1994. pap. 12.98 (*0-88290-493-0*) Horizon Utah.

Stories of Peace & War. Frederic Remington. LC 75-125237. (Short Story Index Reprint Ser.). 1977. 15.95 (*0-8369-3604-3*) Ayer.

*__Stories of People: Native American.__ Smithsonian. 1997. 18.95 (*0-7893-0084-2*) St Martin.

Stories of Persian Heroes. E. M. Wilmot-Buxton. 1976. lib. bdg. 59.95 (*0-8490-2673-3*) Gordon Pr.

Stories of Ray Bradbury. Ray Bradbury. LC 80-7655. 928p. 1980. 40.00 (*0-394-51335-5*) Knopf.

Stories of Raymond Carver: A Critical Study. Kirk Nesset. 140p. (C). 1994. pap. text ed. 14.95 (*0-8214-1100-4*) Ohio U Pr.

Stories of Reading: Subjectivity & Literary Understanding. Michael Steig. LC 88-22599. 272p. 1989. text ed. 45.00 (*0-8018-3723-5*); pap. text ed. 14.95 (*0-8018-3804-5*) Johns Hopkins.

Stories of Remembrance & Restoration: 100 Years of the Western District of the General Conference Mennonite Church. Ed. by Loris A. Habegger. LC 92-62070. (Illus.). 184p. (Orig.). 1992. pap. 15.00 (*0-945530-08-0*) Wordsworth KS.

*__Stories of Resilience in Childhood: The Narratives of Maya Angelou, Maxine Hong Kingston, Richard Rodriguez, John Edgar Wideman, & Tobias Wolff.__ rev. ed. Daniel D. Challener. (Children of Poverty Ser.). 214p. 1997. 49.00 (*0-8153-2800-1*) Garland.

Stories of Rome. Livy. Tr. by Roger Nichols. LC 81-10227. (Translations from Greek & Roman Authors Ser.). (Illus.). 112p. 1982. pap. text ed. 12.95 (*0-521-22816-6*) Cambridge U Pr.

Stories of Saddleback Valley. Joe Osterman. LC 85-63697. (Illus.). 160p. (Orig.). 1992. pap. 7.95 (*1-881129-01-2*) Old El Toro Pr.

Stories of Scientific Discovery. D. B. Hammond. LC 74-76901. (Essay Index Reprint Ser.). 1977. 19.95 (*0-8369-0015-4*) Ayer.

Stories of Scottsboro. James E. Goodman. 1995. pap. 16.00 (*0-679-76159-4*, Vin) Random.

Stories of Scottsboro. James E. Goodman. Date not set. pap. write for info. (*0-679-46159-0*) Random.

Stories of Shao-Lin: Heroes of the Southern Shao-Lin School of Martial Arts. William C. Hu. LC 95-83951. (Illus.). 300p. 1996. write for info. (*0-614-96206-4*) Ars Ceramica.

Stories of Sickness. Howard Brody. LC 87-10657. 1988. 15.00 (*0-300-03977-8*) Yale U Pr.

Stories of Sickness. Howard Brody. 219p. (C). 1990. reprint ed. pap. 15.00 (*0-300-04692-8*) Yale U Pr.

Stories of Some of the Prophets, Vol. I. A. S. Hashim. (Islamic Books for Children: Bk. 8). (J). pap. 5.95 (*0-933511-61-2*) Kazi Pubns.

Stories of Some of the Prophets, Vol II. A. S. Hashim. (Islamic Books for Children: Bk. 9). (J). pap. 5.95 (*0-933511-64-7*) Kazi Pubns.

Stories of St. Nicholas. James K. Paulding. LC 95-8396. (New York Classics Ser.). Orig. Title: Book of Saint Nicholas. 152p. 1995. 19.95 (*0-8156-0325-8*) Syracuse U Pr.

Stories of Stephen Dixon. Stephen Dixon. 1994. 25.00 (*0-8050-2653-3*) H Holt & Co.

Stories of String. William Maranda. LC 93-93977. (Illus.). 184p. 1994. pap. 12.00 (*1-56002-359-7*, Univ Edtns) Aegina Pr.

*__Stories of Student Teaching: A Case Approach to the Student Teaching Experience.__ Debra E. Pitton. LC 96-49892. 1997. pap. 22.00 (*0-13-437310-3*, Merrill Coll) P-H.

Stories of Survival. Remmelt Hummelen & Kathleen Hummelen. 1985. pap. 5.95 (*0-377-00150-3*) Friendship Pr.

Stories of Suspense. Date not set. pap. 1.95 (*0-590-02971-1*) Scholastic Inc.

Stories of Teaching. 1993. pap. 12.95 (*0-590-73607-8*) Scholastic Inc.

Stories of the Ancestors: Clunn, Horan, Robinson & Mackintosh Families of New Jersey & Pennsylvania. Patricia C. Jones. (Illus.). 290p. (Orig.). 1995. pap. 15.95 (*0-939221-09-8*) Wellingham-Jones.

Stories of the Ants. Robert L. Merriam. (Illus.). 19p. (Orig.). 1981. pap. 2.00 (*0-686-32495-1*) R L Merriam.

Stories of the Army. Brander Matthews et al. LC 76-113683. (Short Story Index Reprint Ser.). 1977. reprint ed. 19.95 (*0-8369-3412-1*) Ayer.

Stories of the Beginning: A Bible Story Coloring Book. Illus. by Susan Harrison. (Stories of...Bible Story Coloring Bks.). 72p. (Orig.). (J). (ps-3). 1996. pap. 3.95 (*1-57102-091-8*, Ideals Child) Hambleton-Hill.

*__Stories of the Beginning: Genesis 1-11 & Other Creation Stories.__ Ellen Van Wolde. 285p. 1997. pap. 18.95 (*0-8192-1714-X*) Morehouse Pub.

Stories of the Buddha. Caroline A. Rhys-Davids. 288p. 1989. pap. 6.95 (*0-486-26149-2*) Dover.

Stories of the Buddha. Intro. by C. Rhys Davids. LC 78-72444. reprint ed. 30.00 (*0-404-17316-0*) AMS Pr.

*__Stories of the Caliphs: The Early Rulers of Islam.__ Denys Johnson-Davies. (Illus.). 48p. (Orig.). (J). (gr. 3-8). 1997. pap. 6.95 (*977-5325-41-2*, Pub. by Hoopoe Bks UA) AMIDEAST.

Stories of the Cherokee Hills. Maurice Thompson. LC 77-113686. (Short Story Index Reprint Ser.). 1977. 21.95 (*0-8369-3415-6*) Ayer.

Stories of the Christian Hymns. rev. ed. Narrated by Helen S. Rizk. (Ichthus Ser.). 1986. pap. 3.95 (*0-687-18300-6*) Abingdon.

Stories of the Countryside. Liao She. (CHI.). pap. 9.95 (*7-5321-0876-7*, Pub. by China Intl Bk CH) Distribks Inc.

Stories of the Dreamwalkers. Joyce C. Mills. (Illus.). 48p. 1989. 48.95 (*0-944082-01-7*) Santa Fe Fine Art.

Stories of the Dreamwalkers: Storyteller Edition. Joyce C. Mills. (Illus.). 48p. 1990. reprint ed. 48.00 (*0-944082-02-5*) Santa Fe Fine Art.

Stories of the Faith. Ruth A. Tucker. 384p. 1990. pap. 12.99 (*0-310-51621-8*) Zondervan.

Stories of the Faithful: A Bible Story Coloring Book. Illus. by Stacy Venturi-Pickett. (Stories of...Bible Story Coloring Bks.). 72p. (Orig.). (J). (ps-3). 1996. pap. 3.95 (*1-57102-088-8*, Ideals Child) Hambleton-Hill.

Stories of the Falls of French Creek. W. Edmunds Claussen. (Illus.). 75p. (Orig.). pap. text ed. 2.50 (*0-9616068-3-5*) Boyertown Hist.

Stories of the Fire: Personal Growth Through Firewalking. Michael McDermott. 179p. (Orig.). (C). 1994. 14.95 (*0-9640871-0-3*) Frog & Latte.

Stories of the Flood. Uma Krishnaswami. (Illus.). 41p. (J). (gr. 4-7). 1994. 15.95 (*1-57098-007-1*) R Rinehart.

Stories of the Foot Hills. Margaret Graham. LC 76-94727. (Short Story Index Reprint Ser.). 1977. 19.95 (*0-8369-3106-8*) Ayer.

Stories of the Great Lakes see Early Stories of the Great Lakes

Stories of the Great Operas & Their Composers, 3 vols. Ernest Newman. 1990. reprint ed. lib. bdg. 148.00 (*0-7812-9158-5*) Rprt Serv.

Stories of the Great Operas & Their Composers, 3 vols., Set. Ernest Newman. 1988. reprint ed. lib. bdg. 249.00 (*0-7812-0408-9*) Rprt Serv.

Stories of the Great Operas & Their Composers, 3 vols., Set. Ernest Newman. reprint ed. 195.00 (*0-403-01632-0*) Scholarly.

Stories of the Greeks & Romans: Introduction to Classical Mythology. Donald Richardson. (Illus.). (C). 1996. lib. bdg. 65.00 (*0-89241-515-0*) Caratzas.

Stories of the Greeks & Romans: Introduction to Classical Mythology, 2 vols., Set. 2nd rev. ed. Donald Richardson. (Illus.). (C). 1996. pap. text ed. 42.50 (*0-89241-549-5*) Caratzas.

Stories of the Greeks & Romans Vol. I: Introduction to Classical Mythology. 2nd rev. ed. Donald Richardson. (Illus.). (C). 1996. pap. text ed. 22.50 (*0-89241-575-4*) Caratzas.

Stories of the Greeks & Romans Vol. II: Introduction to Classical Mythology. 2nd rev. ed. Donald Richardson. (Illus.). (C). 1996. pap. text ed. 22.50 (*0-89241-576-2*) Caratzas.

*__Stories of the Heart.__ Keri A. Seitz & Evie E. VanVeen. 189p. (Orig.). 1996. pap. 4.95 (*0-9655340-0-6*) Neighbrhd Pr Pubng.

Stories of the Holy Fathers, 2 vols., Set. Anan Isho. Tr. by E. A. Budge. 1980. lib. bdg. 125.00 (*0-8490-3195-8*) Gordon Pr.

Stories of the Journey in the Circle of Life. Kathy S. Anderson. 1992. pap. 9.95 (*0-87839-075-8*) North Star.

Stories of the Jungle. Rudyard Kipling. (Rudyard Kipling Ser.). 1994. 16.95 incl. audio (*1-883049-10-5*); lib. bdg. 18.95 incl. audio (*1-883049-29-6*) Commuters Lib.

Stories of the Klamath National Forest: The First 50 Years, 1905-1955. Ed. by Gilbert W. Davies & Florice M. Frank. LC 92-73759. (Illus.). 436p. (Orig.). 1992. pap. 16.95 (*0-9634413-0-2*) HiSt Ink Bks.

Stories of the Modern South. Ed. by Ben Forkner & Patrick Samway. 1984. 22.00 (*0-8446-6171-6*) Peter Smith.

Stories of the Modern South. Ed. by Benjamin Forkner & Patrick Samway. 512p. 1986. pap. 12.95 (*0-14-009695-7*, Penguin Bks) Viking Penguin.

Stories of the Modern South. Ed. by Benjamin Forkner & Patrick Samway. 560p. 1991. pap. 8.95 (*0-14-099701-6*) Viking Penguin.

Stories of the Modern South. rev. ed. Ed. by Ben Forkner & Patrick Samway. LC 94-49529. 576p. 1995. pap. 13.95 (*0-14-024705-X*, Penguin Bks) Viking Penguin.

Stories of the Months & Days. Reginald C. Couzens. LC 89-43348. (Illus.). 160p. 1990. reprint ed. lib. bdg. 38.00 (*1-55888-881-0*) Omnigraphics Inc.

Stories of the Mutiny. Herbert Strang. 1990. reprint ed. 21.00 (*0-317-99723-8*, Pub. by Mittal II) S Asia.

Stories of the Neighborhood (Hekayat Haretna) (Novel in Arabic) Naguib Mahfouz. (ARA.). 1982. pap. 8.95 (*0-86685-156-9*) Intl Bk Ctr.

Stories of the Old Duck Hunters. Gordon M. Quarrie. Ed. by Zack Taylor. 228p. 1994. 19.50 (*1-57223-003-7*) Idyll Arbor.

Stories of the Old Duck Hunters & Other Drivel. Gordon MacQuarrie. Ed. by Zack Taylor. 228p. 1985. reprint ed. 17.50 (*0-932558-25-9*) Willow Creek Pr.

Stories of the Old Missions of California. Charles F. Carter. LC 71-116945. (Short Story Index Reprint Ser.). 1977. 17.95 (*0-8369-3447-4*) Ayer.

An Asterisk (*) at the beginning of an entry indicates that the title is appearing in BIP for the first time.

Stories of the Old South. Ed. by Ben Forkner & Patrick Samway. 544p. 1995. pap. 13.95 (*0-14-024707-6*, Penguin Bks) Viking Penguin.

Stories of the Old West. John Seelye. Date not set. pap. 22.95 (*0-670-83647-8*) Viking Penguin.

Stories of the Old West: Tales of the Mining Camp & Cattle Ranch. Ed. by John Seelye. LC 93-11941. 496p. 1994. pap. 13.95 (*0-14-014550-8*, Penguin Bks) Viking Penguin.

Stories of the Old World. Alfred J. Church. 1996. pap. 20.00 (*0-8196-1254-5*) Biblo.

***Stories of the Prophets: Qisas al-Anbiya: an Eastern Turkish Version, 2 vols.** Tr. by Hendrik Boeschoten. 832p. 1996. 322.75 (*0-614-21095-X*, 1415) Kazi Pubns.

Stories of the Prophets: Qisas al-Anbiya, in an Eastern Turkic Version, 2 vols., Set. Ali-Rabghuzi. Ed. by Hendrik Boeschoten et al. Tr. by J. O'Kane. 350p. 1995. text ed. 339.00 (*90-04-10222-1*) E J Brill.

Stories of the Prophets from the Earliest Sources, Vol. 1. Haji Amina. 256p. (Orig.). 1995. pap. 14.95 (*0-934905-35-5*) Kazi Pubns.

Stories of the Railway. George A. Hibbard et al. LC 70-113684. (Short Story Index Reprint Ser.). 1977. 19.95 (*0-8369-3413-X*) Ayer.

Stories of the Road Allowance People. Maria Campbell. (Illus.). 144p. (Orig.). (YA). (gr. 8-12). 1995. pap. 9.95 (*0-919441-53-X*, Pub. by Theytus Bks Ltd CN) Orca Bk Pubs.

***Stories of the Rose: The Making of the Rosary in the Middle Ages.** Anne Winston-Allen. LC 96-36239. 1997. 28.50 (*0-271-01631-0*) Pa St U Pr.

Stories of the Sea. John R. Spears et al. LC 73-113685. (Short Story Index Reprint Ser.). 1977. 19.95 (*0-8369-3414-8*) Ayer.

Stories of the Seen & the Unseen. Margaret O. Oliphant. LC 72-113682. (Short Story Index Reprint Ser.). 1977. 36.95 (*0-8369-3411-3*) Ayer.

Stories of the Seen & the Unseen. Oliphant. 316p. 1971. reprint ed. spiral bd. 10.50 (*0-7873-0643-6*) Hlth Research.

Stories of the Seven-Headed Sewing Machine. limited ed. Katalin Ladik. Tr. by Emoke B'Racz from HUN. 28p. 1992. pap. 4.50 (*0-685-64797-8*) New Native Pr.

Stories of the Sioux. Luther Standing Bear. LC 88-12221. (Illus.). x, 95p. 1988. reprint ed. pap. 5.95 (*0-8032-9187-6*, Bison Books) U of Nebr Pr.

***Stories of the Songs of Christmas.** L. E. McCullough. LC 97-2681. 1997. write for info. (*1-57525-116-7*) Smith & Kraus.

Stories of the South. Thomas N. Page et al. LC 74-110217. (Short Story Index Reprint Ser.). 1977. 24.95 (*0-8369-3369-9*) Ayer.

Stories of the Southern Mountains & Swamps. Cleitus O. Murray. (Illus.). 192p. (Orig.). (YA). 1992. pap. 9.95 (*0-9632132-0-2*) Murray Pubns.

Stories of the Spirit, Stories of the Heart: Parables of the Spiritual Path from Around the World. Ed. by Christina Feldman & Jack Kornfield. LC 90-55306. 304p. (Orig.). 1992. pap. 18.00 (*0-06-250300-6*) Harper SF.

Stories of the Spirit, Stories of the Heart see Soul Food: Stories to Nourish the Spirit & the Heart

Stories of the States Activity Book. Priscilla Lynch & Taryn Laraja. (Illus.). 72p. 1995. pap. 8.95 (*1-881889-83-1*) Silver Moon.

Stories of the States Series. (J). (gr. 4-6). 1994. text ed. 125.55 (*1-881889-77-7*) Silver Moon.

Stories of the Steppe. Maxim Gorky. LC 72-121552. (Short Story Index Reprint Ser.). 1977. 12.95 (*0-8369-3508-X*) Ayer.

Stories of the Victorian Writers. Janie R. Walker. LC 68-26484. (Essay Index Reprint Ser.). 1977. reprint ed. 18.95 (*0-8369-0964-X*) Ayer.

Stories of the Wagner Operas. H. A. Guerber. 1977. lib. bdg. 59.95 (*0-8490-2674-1*) Gordon Pr.

Stories of the World's Holidays. Grace Humphrey. LC 89-43336. vi, 335p. 1990. reprint ed. lib. bdg. 44.00 (*1-55888-882-9*) Omnigraphics Inc.

Stories of Three Decades. Thomas Mann. Tr. by Helen T. Lowe-Porter. LC 61-66696. 1979. 9.95 (*0-394-60483-0*, Modern Lib) Random.

***Stories of True Love: Shadows of a Dream, Heat of the Jungle, Unforgotten. Heike Hendler. LC 96-95190. (Illus.). 264p. 1997. 24.95 (*0-9655033-3-X*) H Design Pub.**

STORIES OF TRUE LOVE is a compilation of three sensual fiction novels portraying emotions that will carry you to tantalizing heights. Life's most intimate & fulfilling quest is revealed in "SHADOWS OF A DREAM," "HEAT OF THE JUNGLE," & "UNFORGOTTEN." The common thread that runs throughout these tales is passionate, overwhelming love. The contents of this 7" X 10" hardbound book is enhanced with meaningful poetry, illustrations & photographs. A red bow ribbon individually wrapped around each volume gives this item a personalized & intimate appeal. TRUE LOVE is a perfect gift for Birthdays, Special Occasions, Friends, Lovers, etc. "The three enchanting stories of this book touched me profoundly. A delicate thread of intimacy links the tales together like an exquisite necklace beautified with pearls of magical poetry. The author tantalizes the mind & senses with stimulating sensuality, yet the erotic flair of some scenes feels comfortable because it's set into a beautiful frame of pure & true love." --John Kennedy. Order from: H. Design Publishing, Tel: (714) 759-5565; FAX: (714) 759-1350; (800) 669-0773; E-mail: adlib100@aol.com. Available through Baker & Taylor & all major wholesalers.

Publisher Provided Annotation.

Stories of Virtue in Business. C. Edward Weber. LC 95-10749. 250p. (Orig.). (C). 1995. pap. text ed. 24.50 (*0-8191-9950-8*) U Pr of Amer.

Stories of Vladimir Nabokov. Vladimir Nabokov. Ed. by Dmitri Nabokov. 640p. 1995. 40.00 (*0-394-58615-8*) Random.

Stories of Vladimir Nabokov. Vladimir Nabokov. 1997. pap. 18.00 (*0-679-72997-6*) Random.

Stories of Willa Cather. Ed. by Sharon O'Brien. 1988. pap. 9.95 (*0-452-00874-3*, Mer) NAL-Dutton.

Stories of William Sansom. William Sansom. LC 77-144171. (Short Story Index Reprint Ser.). 1977. reprint ed. 26.95 (*0-8369-3786-4*) Ayer.

Stories of William Trevor. William Trevor. 799p. 1989. pap. 12.00 (*0-14-010921-8*, Penguin Bks) Viking Penguin.

Stories of Women. Anton Chekhov. Tr. by Paula P. Ross from RUS. 308p. (C). 1994. 29.95 (*0-87975-893-7*) Prometheus Bks.

Stories of Women. Anton P. Chekhov. Tr. by Paula P. Ross from RUS. 308p. 1994. pap. 16.95 (*0-87975-901-1*) Prometheus Bks.

***Stories of Women.** Shanta Rao. (Illus.). 136p. 1996. 45.00 (*1-899235-30-2*, 620353, Pub. by Dewi Lewis UK) Dist Art Pubs.

Stories of Women Composers for Young Musicians. large type ed. Catherine W. Kendall. (Illus.). 212p. (Orig.). (J). (gr. 1-12). 1993. pap. 13.75 (*0-9610878-2-X*) Toadwood Pubs.

Stories of Wonder. Bertha Naim. 1994. 12.95 (*0-533-10879-9*) Vantage.

Stories of Writers & Artists. Henry James. (BCL1-PS American Literature Ser.). 346p. 1993. reprint ed. lib. bdg. 89.00 (*0-7812-6974-1*) Rprt Serv.

Stories of Yesteryear: Horse & Buggy Days. Harry H. Brown. LC 82-90882. (Illus.). 74p. 1982. 6.95 (*0-9610806-0-4*) Kemah Pr.

Stories off the Wall. John Roskelley. LC 93-22667. (Illus.). 224p. 1993. 22.95 (*0-89886-349-X*) Mountaineers.

Stories on a String: The Brazilian Literatura De Cordel. Candace Slater. LC 80-29091. (Illus.). 360p. 1982. pap. 13.95 (*0-520-06802-5*) U CA Pr.

Stories on Rocks. Zilpha Both. Ed. by Jane Weinberger. LC 93-61627. (Illus.). 80p. (J). (gr. 4-8). 1994. pap. 8.00 (*1-883650-08-9*) Windswept Hse.

Stories on Stage: Scripts for Reader's Theater. Aaron Shepard. LC 91-42236. 162p. 1993. 40.00 (*0-8242-0851-X*) Wilson.

Stories on Stone: Rock Art: Images from the Ancient Ones. Jennifer O. Dewey. LC 94-3510. (Illus.). 32p. (J). (gr. 1-5). 1996. 16.95 (*0-316-18211-7*) Little.

Stories on the Orift. Bill Roberts. LC 87-63108. (Illus.). 220p. 1988. pap. 8.00 (*0-944100-02-3*) Pirogue Pub.

Stories Out of Omarie. Wendy Walker. (Sun & Moon Classics Ser.: No. 56). 322p. (Orig.). 1994. pap. 12.95 (*1-55713-172-4*) Sun & Moon CA.

***Stories, Poems, & Other Things, 4 vols.** Ashley Renkes. (Illus.). 48p. (Orig.). (J). (gr. k-8). 1997. boxed, pap. write for info. (*1-882792-40-8*) Proctor Pubns.

Stories, Poems, & Other Writings. Willa Cather. Ed. by Sharon O'Brien. 1039p. 1992. 35.00 (*0-940450-71-2*) Library of America.

Stories Revived; First Series. Henry James. LC 72-12605. (Short Story Index Reprint Ser.). 1977. reprint ed. 30.95 (*0-8369-4237-X*) Ayer.

Stories, Scripts, & Scenes: Aspects of Schema Theory. Jean M. Mandler. 144p. (C). 1984. text ed. 39.95 (*0-89859-446-4*) L Erlbaum Assocs.

Stories Selected from the Unexpected. Bennett Cerf. 1976. 20.95 (*0-8488-1277-8*) Amereon Ltd.

Stories, Sermons & Prayers of St. Nephon: An Ascetic Bishop. J. Gentithes & I. Apostolopoulos. 1989. pap. 10.95 (*0-937032-67-0*) Light&Life Pub Co MN.

Stories (So Far) of Deborah Eisenberg. Deborah Eisenberg. 496p. 1997. pap. 15.00 (*0-374-52492-0*) FS&G.

Stories, Songs, & Memories of Grace McKibben, Wintu. Alice Shepherd. 172p. 1996. 31.00 (*0-8095-4998-0*) Borgo Pr.

Stories, Songs, & Poetry for Teaching Reading & Writing: Literacy Through Language. Robert A. McCracken & Marlene J. McCracken. 176p. (C). 1986. pap. text ed. 16.95 (*0-8077-2856-X*) Tchrs Coll.

Stories, Songs & Poetry to Teach Reading & Writing. rev. ed. Marlene J. McCracken & Robert A. McCracken. (Illus.). 160p. (J). (gr. k-4). 1987. teacher ed. 15.00 (*0-920541-35-6*) Peguis Pubs Ltd.

Stories Subversive: Through the Field with Gloves Off. Nellie L. McCling. Ed. & Intro. by Marilyn I. Davis. 232p. 1996. pap. 21.00 (*0-7766-0424-4*, Pub. by Univ Ottawa Pr CN) Paul & Co Pubs.

Stories, Symbols, Songs & Skits for Lively Children's Liturgies. Anne M. Lee & Elaine Wisdom. LC 94-61925. 88p. (Orig.). 1995. pap. 9.95 (*0-89622-640-9*) Twenty-Third.

Stories That Educate, Inform, Entertain & Rhyme: Kids Workshop Workbook I. Story Time Stories That Rhyme Staff. (Illus.). 52p. (J). 1992. ring bd. 29.95 (*1-56820-040-4*) Story Time.

Stories That Educate, Inform, Entertain & Rhyme: Kids Workshop Workbook II. Story Time Stories That Rhyme Staff. (Illus.). 52p. (J). 1992. ring bd. 29.95 (*1-56820-041-2*) Story Time.

Stories That End with a Hug. Stephen Elkins. (Illus.). 32p. (J). (gr. k-8). 1993. 12.98 (*1-56919-002-X*) Wonder Wkshop.

Stories That End with a Prayer. Stephen Elkins. (Illus.). 32p. (J). (gr. k-8). 12.98 (*1-56919-003-8*) Wonder Wkshop.

Stories That End with a Song. Stephen Elkins. (Illus.). 32p. (J). (gr. k-8). 12.98 (*0-685-68095-9*) Wonder Wkshop.

Stories That Go Bump in the Night. Alfred Hitchcock. lib. bdg. 25.95 (*0-88411-707-3*, Aeonian Pr) Amereon Ltd.

Stories That Heal: Reparenting Adult Children of Dysfunctional Families Using Hypnotic Stories in Psychotherapy. Lee Wallas. 220p. (C). 1991. 22.95 (*0-393-70106-9*) Norton.

Stories That Jesus Told: The Parables Retold for Children. Patricia M. St. John. LC 95-7421. (Illus.). 56p. (J). (gr. 2-6). 1995. 16.95 (*0-8192-1644-5*) Morehouse Pub.

Stories That Live, 6 vols. Peter Enns & Glen Forsberg. (Stories That Live Ser.: No. I). (Illus.). 144p. (J). (ps-5). 1985. 29.70 incl. audio (*0-936215-00-3*) STL Intl.

Stories That Make the World: Oral Literature of the Indian Peoples of the Inland Northwest. Ed. by Rodney Frey. LC 94-39935. (Civilization of the American Indian Ser.: Vol. 218). (Illus.). 272p. 1995. 24.95 (*0-8061-2710-4*) U of Okla Pr.

Stories That Shape Us: Contemporary Women Write about the West. Ed. by Teresa Jordan & James R. Hepworth. 3242p. 1995. 23.00 (*0-393-03723-1*) Norton.

Stories that Shape Us: Contemporary Women Write about the West. Teresa Jordan & James R. Hepworth. 400p. 1996. pap. 14.00 (*0-393-31451-0*, Norton Paperbks) Norton.

Stories That Won't Go Away: Women in Vietnam 1959-1975. Betty Merrell & Priscilla Tunnel. Ed. by Susan Hansen. (Illus.). 205p. (Orig.). 1995. pap. text ed. 8.95 (*1-56309-112-7*, New Hope) Womans Mission Union.

Stories the Feet Can Tell Thru Reflexology. rev. ed. Eunice Ingham. (Illus.). 226p. 1984. pap. 11.50 (*0-9611804-3-9*) Ingham Pub.

Stories, Theories & Things. Christine Brooke-Rose. 320p. (C). 1991. text ed. 69.95 (*0-521-39181-4*) Cambridge U Pr.

Stories to Dramatize. Winifred Ward. 389p. 1952. pap. text ed. 21.00 (*0-87602-021-X*) Anchorage.

Stories to Dream On. Houghton Mifflin Company Staff. (Literature Experience 1993 Ser.). (J). (gr. 7). 1992. pap. 9.84 (*0-395-61848-7*) HM.

Stories to Grow on: Demonstrations of Language Learning in K-8 Classrooms. Ed. by Julie M. Jensen. LC 88-17601. (Illus.). 183p. (Orig.). (C). 1988. pap. text ed. 21.50 (*0-435-08482-8*, 08482) Heinemann.

Stories to Hold an Audience: For Speakers, Teachers, Preachers & Leaders, with a Wealth of Themes & Quotes to Inspire & Motivate. Catherine Hammond. 124p. (Orig.). pap. 9.95 (*1-86429-005-6*, Pub. by Millennium Bks AT) Morehouse Pub.

Stories to Invite Faith-Sharing: Experiencing the Lord Through the Seasons. Mary M. McGill. LC 92-37. (Illus.). 144p. (Orig.). 1992. pap. 8.95 (*0-89390-230-6*) Resource Pubns.

Stories to Live By: Continuity & Change in Three Generations of Puerto Rican Women. Rina Benmayor et al. 67p. 1987. lib. bdg. 7.00 (*1-878483-02-1*) Hunter Coll CEP.

Stories to Make You Feel Better. Bennett Cerf. (J). 1972. 12.95 (*0-394-47553-4*) Random Bks Yng Read.

***Stories to Play with Your Head.** Illus. by Neal Shusterman. (MindTwister Ser.). (J). (gr. 3-7). 1997. pap. 4.99 (*0-614-29125-9*) Tor Bks.

Stories to Remember: David, God's Champion. Peter Enns. (Illus.). 32p. (J). (ps-5). 1987. pap. 2.98 (*0-943593-04-2*); audio 5.98 (*0-943593-06-9*) Kids Intl Inc.

Stories to Remember: Here Comes Jesus. Peter Enns. (Illus.). 32p. (J). (ps-5). 1987. pap. 2.98 (*0-943593-12-3*); audio 5.98 (*0-943593-14-X*) Kids Intl Inc.

Stories to Remember: Look What God Made. Peter Enns & Terry Ligon. (Illus.). 32p. (J). (ps-5). 1987. pap. 2.98 (*0-943593-00-X*); audio 5.98 (*0-943593-02-6*) Kids Intl Inc.

Stories to Remember: Walking with Jesus. Peter Enns. (Illus.). 32p. (J). (ps-5). 1987. pap. 2.98 (*0-943593-08-5*) Kids Intl Inc.

Stories to See & Share, Vol. 3. Crockett. 1993. pap. 6.95 (*0-87579-677-X*) Deseret Bk.

***Stories to Share: A Family Treasury of Faith.** LC 97-21399. 1997. 15.99 (*0-87788-820-5*) Shaw Pubs.

Stories to Solve: Folktales from Around the World. George Shannon. LC 84-18656. (Illus.). 56p. (J). (gr. 3-5). 1985. 17.00 (*0-688-04303-8*); lib. bdg. 16.93 (*0-688-04304-6*) Greenwillow.

Stories to Solve: Folktales from Around the World. George Shannon. LC 84-18656. (Illus.). 56p. (J). (gr. 3 up). 1991. reprint ed. pap. 4.95 (*0-688-10496-7*) Morrow.

Stories to Start With: Interpersonal Relationships, Set. Judith Barnhart. LC 93-81085. (Illus.). 96p. (Orig.). (J). (gr. 4-8). 1993. pap. 15.95 (*1-884063-19-5*) Mar Co Prods.

Stories to Talk About: Helping Students Make Ethical Choices. Lillian R. Putnam. 1994. pap. 12.95 (*0-590-48922-4*) Scholastic Inc.

Stories to Tell a Five Year-Old. Alice Low. (Illus.). 160p. (J). (ps-1). 1996. pap. 8.95 (*0-316-53416-1*) Little.

Stories to Tell a Six-Year-Old. Illus. by Heather H. Maione. LC 96-5387. (J). (gr. 1). 1997. 8.95 (*0-316-53418-8*) Little.

Stories to Tell in Children's Church. Velma B. Kiefer. LC 66-18309. Orig. Title: Please Tell Me a Story. 160p. (gr. 10). 1977. pap. 7.99 (*0-8010-5371-4*) Baker Bks.

Stories to Tell Our Children. Weinstein-Shr. 1992. pap. 17.95 (*0-8384-2362-0*) Heinle & Heinle.

Stories to Treasure. Anna L. Carlson. (Illus.). 24p. (Orig.). (J). (ps-5). 1984. pap. 62.40 (*0-939938-06-5*) Karwyn Ent.

***Stories to Warm Your Heart.** Dorothy Pogats. LC 97-90006. (Illus.). 64p. (Orig.). (J). 1997. pap. 9.00 (*1-56002-732-0*, Univ Edtns) Aegina Pr.

Stories Told in the Kitchen. Kendall Morse. LC 81-8775. (Illus.). 95p. (Orig.). 1981. pap. 4.95 (*0-945980-19-1*) Nrth Country Pr.

Stories We Are: An Essay on Self-Creation. William L. Randall. 288p. 1995. 45.00 (*0-8020-0564-0*); pap. 19.95 (*0-8020-6986-X*) U of Toronto Pr.

Stories We Brought with Us. 2nd ed. Ann Silverman & Carol Kasser. 288p. 1994. pap. text ed. 15.25 (*0-13-122145-0*) P-H.

Stories We Brought with Us: Beginning Readings for ESL. Carol Kasser & Ann Silverman. (Illus.). 166p. (C). pap. 21.95 (*0-13-850124-6*) P-H.

Stories We Hold Secret: Tales of Women's Spiritual Development. Ed. by Carol Bruchac et al. LC 85-70536. 316p. (Orig.). 1987. pap. 12.95 (*0-912678-66-6*, Greenfld Rev Pr) Greenfld Rev Lit.

Stories We Listened To. John Haines. 16.00 (*0-930769-02-3*) Bench Pr SC.

Stories We Live: Cuentos Que Vivimos: Hispanic Women's Spirituality, 1996 Madeleva Lecture. Jeanette Rodriguez. (Madeleva Lectures). 64p. 1996. pap. 5.95 (*0-8091-3659-7*, 3659-7) Paulist Pr.

***Stories We Live By: Personal Myths & the Making of the Self.** LC 96-49264. 336p. 1997. pap. text ed. 17.95 (*1-57230-188-0*, 0188) Guilford Pr.

Stories We Tell: An Anthology of Oregon Folk Literature. Ed. by Jarold Ramsey. (Oregon Literature Ser.: Vol. 5). (Illus.). 352p. (Orig.). 1994. pap. 21.95 (*0-87071-380-9*); text ed. 35.95 (*0-87071-379-5*) Oreg St U Pr.

Stories We Tell Series, 6 bks., Set. Dora Peatman et al. 167p. 1993. pap. 24.00 (*1-884983-00-6*) Homegrown Bks.

Stories with Activities That Educate & Inform: Sea Shell Edition. Story Time Stories That Rhyme Staff. (Illus.). (Orig.). (J). 1992. ring bd. 19.95 (*1-56820-006-4*) Story Time.

Stories with Holes, Vol. II. Nathan Levy. (Orig.). (J). (gr. 3 up). 1996. pap. 7.50 (*1-87647-00-4*) NL Assocs.

Stories with Holes, Vol. III. Nathan Levy. (Orig.). (J). (gr. 3 up). 1996. pap. 7.50 (*1-878347-01-2*) NL Assocs.

Stories with Holes, Vol. IV. Nathan Levy. (Orig.). (J). (gr. 3 up). 1996. pap. 7.50 (*1-878347-02-0*) NL Assocs.

Stories with Holes, Vol. V. Nathan Levy. (Orig.). (J). (gr. 3 up). 1996. pap. 7.50 (*1-878347-03-9*) NL Assocs.

Stories with Holes, Vol. VI. Nathan Levy. (Orig.). (J). (gr. 3 up). 1996. pap. 7.50 (*1-878347-09-8*) NL Assocs.

Stories with Holes, Vol. VII. Nathan Levy. (Orig.). (J). (gr. 3 up). 1996. pap. 7.50 (*1-878347-10-1*) NL Assocs.

Stories with Holes, Vol. VIII. Nathan Levy. 20p. (Orig.). (J). (gr. 3 up). 1996. pap. 7.50 (*1-878347-11-X*) NL Assocs.

Stories with Holes, Vol. IX. Nathan Levy. (Orig.). (J). (gr. 3 up). 1996. pap. 7.50 (*1-878347-17-9*) NL Assocs.

Stories with Holes, Vol. X. Nathan Levy. (Orig.). (J). (gr. 3 up). 1996. pap. 7.50 (*1-878347-21-7*) NL Assocs.

Stories with Holes, Vol. XI. Nathan Levy. (Orig.). (J). (gr. 3 up). 1996. pap. 7.50 (*1-878347-22-5*) NL Assocs.

Stories with Holes, Vol. XII. Nathan Levy. (Orig.). (J). (gr. 3 up). 1996. pap. 7.50 (*1-878347-26-8*) NL Assocs.

Stories with Holes, Vol. XIII. Nathan Levy. (Orig.). (J). (gr. 3 up). 1996. pap. 7.50 (*1-878347-27-6*) NL Assocs.

Stories with Holes, Vol. XIV. Nathan Levy. (Orig.). (J). (gr. 3 up). 1996. 7.50 (*1-878347-28-4*) NL Assocs.

Stories with Holes, Vol. XV. Nathan Levy. (Orig.). (J). (gr. 3 up). 1996. pap. 7.50 (*1-878347-29-2*) NL Assocs.

Stories with Holes, Vol. XVI. Nathan Levy. (Orig.). (J). (gr. 3 up). 1996. 7.50 (*1-878347-30-6*) NL Assocs.

Stories with Holes, Vol. XVII. Nathan Levy. (Orig.). (J). (gr. 3 up). 1996. 7.50 (*1-878347-31-4*) NL Assocs.

Stories with Holes, Vol. XVIII. Nathan Levy. (Orig.). (J). (gr. 3 up). 1996. 7.50 (*1-878347-32-2*) NL Assocs.

Stories with Holes, Vol. XIX. Nathan Levy. 40p. (Orig.). 1996. pap. 7.50 (*1-878347-44-6*) NL Assocs.

Stories with Holes, Vol. 20. Nathan Levy. (Illus.). 40p. (Orig.). 1997. pap. 7.50 (*1-878347-46-2*) NL Assocs.

Stories with Holes: A Collection of Open-Ended Stories for Conducting Inquiry Training in the Classroom, Vol. 1. Jim Ballard. LC 75-25392. (Mandala Series in Education). 32p. (Orig.). (J). (gr. 3 up). 1996. 7.50 (*0-8290-0355-X*) NL Assocs.

Stories with Twists, Vol. 1. Thomas M. Kemnitz. 32p. (Orig.). (J). (gr. 3-12). 1994. pap. 2.50 (*0-88092-030-0*) Royal Fireworks.

Stories with Twists, Vol. 2. Thomas M. Kemnitz. 32p. (Orig.). (J). (gr. 3-12). 1994. pap. 2.50 (*0-88092-031-9*) Royal Fireworks.

Stories with Twists, Vol. 3. Thomas M. Kemnitz. 32p. (Orig.). (J). (gr. 3-12). 1994. pap. 2.50 (*0-88092-032-7*) Royal Fireworks.

Stories with Twists, Vol. 4. Thomas M. Kemnitz. 32p. (Orig.). (J). (gr. 3-12). 1994. pap. 2.50 (*0-88092-033-5*) Royal Fireworks.

Stories with Twists, Vol. 5. Thomas M. Kemnitz. 32p. (Orig.). (J). (gr. 3-12). 1994. pap. 2.50 (*0-88092-034-3*) Royal Fireworks.

Stories with Twists, Vol. 6. Thomas M. Kemnitz. 32p. (Orig.). (J). (gr. 3-12). 1994. pap. 2.50 (*0-88092-035-1*) Royal Fireworks.

Stories with Twists, Vol. 7. Thomas M. Kemnitz. 32p. (Orig.). (J). (gr. 3-12). 1994. pap. 2.50 (*0-88092-036-X*) Royal Fireworks.

Stories with Twists, Vol. 8. Thomas M. Kemnitz. 32p. (Orig.). (J). (gr. 3-12). 1994. pap. 2.50 (*0-88092-037-8*) Royal Fireworks.

S

Stories with Twists, Vol. 9. Thomas M. Kemnitz. 32p. (Orig.). (J). (gr. 3-12). 1994. pap. 2.50 (*0-88092-038-6*) Royal Fireworks.

Stories with Twists, Vol. 10. Thomas M. Kemnitz. 32p. (Orig.). (J). (gr. 3-12). 1994. pap. 2.50 (*0-88092-039-4*) Royal Fireworks.

Stories Within Stories: An Ecosystematic Theory of Metadiegetic Narrative. Dennis L. Seager. LC 90-24426. (American University Studies: General Literature: Ser. XIX, Vol. 27). 156p. (C). 1991. text ed. 30.95 (*0-8204-1494-8*) P Lang Pubng.

Stories Without Women & a Few with Women. Donn B. Byrne, pseud. LC 74-103502. (Short Story Index Reprint Ser.). 1977. 21.95 (*0-8369-3370-2*) Ayer.

Stories Worth Reading. Douglas H. Ball et al. (Triumph Ser.: Vol. I). (Illus.). 192p. (Orig.). (YA). (gr. 8-11). 1989. pap. text ed. write for info. (*0-9621844-0-3*) Printemps Bks.

Stories Worth Telling: Narratives, Poems, & Short Stories by New Writers of Broome & Tioga Counties. LC 95-80814. 100p. 1995. pap. 8.95 (*1-888024-01-1*) Ahead Desktop.

Stories You Can Sell. Laurence R. D'Orsay. LC 79-101280. (Short Story Index Reprint Ser.). 1977. 20.95 (*0-8369-3217-X*) Ayer.

Stories Your Mother Never Told You. Norman B. Colp. (Illus.). 8p. 1982. 10.00 (*0-685-70931-0*) Gal Assn NY.

Storing Your Goods see Designing & Applying Recognised Technologies

S

***Stork & Fox.** abr. large type ed. Kambiz-Azordegan. (Tootee's Magical Stories Ser.: Vol. 10). (Illus.). 36p. (J). (gr. 1-3). 1997. write for info. (*1-890571-34-2*) Parrot Prod.

***Stork & the Plow: The Equity Answer to the Human Dilemma.** Paul R. Ehrlich. 1997. pap. text ed. 16.00 (*0-300-07124-8*) Yale U Pr.

Stork & the Plow: The Equity Answer to the Human Dilemma. Paul R. Erlich et al. LC 95-5691. 400p. 1995. 30.00 (*0-399-14074-3*, Grosset-Putnam) Putnam Pub Group.

Stork & the Syringe: A Political History of Reproductive Medicine. Naomi Pfeffer. LC 93-32897. (Feminist Perspectives Ser.). 244p. 1993. pap. 22.95 (*0-7456-1187-7*) Blackwell Pubs.

***Stork Brought Three Vol. 1: Our Epic Journey As Parents of Triplets.** Jean P. Hall & Denny Hall. LC 97-60058. (Illus.). 82p. 1997. pap. 12.00 (*0-9655442-2-2*) Busn Word.

***Stork Club.** Iris R. Dart. 400p. 5.98 (*0-8317-6652-2*) Smithmark.

Stork Club. Iris Rainer Dart. 464p. 1994. mass mkt. 5.99 (*0-446-36481-9*, Warner Vision) Warner Bks.

Storkes: English Storkes in America. C. A. Storke. (Illus.). 224p. 1991. reprint ed. pap. 34.00 (*0-8328-2038-5*); reprint ed. lib. bdg. 44.00 (*0-8328-2037-7*) Higginson Bk Co.

Storks: Majestic Migrators. Eulalia Garcia. LC 96-8198. (Secrets of the Animal World Ser.). (Illus.). (J). 1996. lib. bdg. 18.60 (*0-8368-1587-4*) Gareth Stevens Inc.

Storks, Ibises & Spoonbills of the World. James A. Hancock et al. (Illus.). 385p. 1992. text ed. 99.95 (*0-12-322730-5*) Acad Pr.

Storkwood. rev. ed. Mark Dunster. (Rin Ser.: Pt. 8). 62p. (Orig.). 1980. pap. 4.00 (*0-89642-066-3*) Linden Pubs.

Storky Jones Is Back in Town. Anne Peters. (Romance Ser.: No. 850). 1992. pap. 2.69 (*0-373-08850-7*, 5-08850-5) Silhouette.

Storm. Meena Alexander. LC 88-92328. 28p. 1989. pap. 3.00 (*0-87376-062-X*) Red Dust.

Storm. David Drew. LC 92-30671. (Voyages Ser.). (Illus.). (J). 1993. write for info. (*0-383-03656-9*) SRA McGraw.

Storm. Marc Harshman. LC 94-4894. (J). 1995. pap. 14.99 (*0-525-65150-0*, Cobblehill Bks) Dutton Child Bks.

Storm. Norah Hess. 448p. (Orig.). 1994. mass mkt., pap. text ed. 4.99 (*0-8439-3672-X*) Dorchester Pub Co.

Storm. Brian Knapp. LC 89-11536. (World Disasters Ser.). (Illus.). 48p. (J). (gr. 5-9). 1990. lib. bdg. 24.26 (*0-8114-2372-7*) Raintree Steck-V.

Storm. W. Nikola-Lisa. LC 92-22775. (Illus.). 32p. (J). (ps-2). 1993. lib. bdg. 14.95 (*0-689-31704-2*, Atheneum Bks Young) S&S Childrens.

Storm. Alexander Ostrovsky. Tr. by David Magarshack from RUS. 120p. 1988. pap. 5.00 (*0-88233-551-0*) Ardis Pubs.

Storm. Robert G. Sauber. LC 93-40976. (Illus.). 32p. (J). (ps-3). 1994. 15.95 (*0-7868-0017-8*); lib. bdg. 15.89 (*0-7868-2013-6*) Hyprn Child.

Storm. Ian Slater. 384p. 1988. pap. 3.95 (*0-373-97073-0*) Harlequin Bks.

Storm! Blaine M. Yorgason & Brenton Yorgason. LC 95-72028. 160p. (Orig.). 1995. pap. text ed. 10.95 (*1-57636-004-0*) SunRise Pbl.

***Storm: A Novel.** George R. Stewart. LC 82-16098. 365p. pap. 104.10 (*0-608-04827-5*, 2065484) Bks Demand.

Storm: Aquis Submersus. Ed. by Patricia M. Boswell. (Bristol German Texts Ser.). 160p. (GER.). 1992. pap. 15.95 (*1-85399-289-5*, Pub. by Brstl Class Pr UK) Focus Pub-R Pullins.

Storm: Der Schimmelreiter. Ed. by P. Boswell. (Bristol German Texts Ser.). 165p. (GER.). 1994. pap. 17.95 (*1-85399-290-9*, Pub. by Brstl Class Pr UK) Focus Pub-R Pullins.

Storm: Personal Version 3.0 Quantitative Modeling for Decision Support. Storm Software, Inc. Staff. 512p. 1990. Incl. text & software (avail. on 5.25" & 3.25"). write for info. incl. disk (*0-8162-8522-5*) Holden-Day.

Storm: Stories & Prose Poems. Kahlil Gibran. Tr. by John Walbridge from ARA. (Illus.). 128p. 1993. 18.00 (*1-883991-01-3*) Whte Cloud Pr.

***Storm: Using RS for Improved Monitoring & Prediction of Heavy Rainfall & Related Events.** Ed. by Eric Barrett. (Remote Sensing Reviews Ser.). 1996. pap. text ed. 50.00 (*90-5702-101-3*, Harwood Acad Pubs) Gordon & Breach.

STORM - Personal Version 2.0: Quantitative Modeling for Decision Support. 470p. (Orig.). (C). 1989. pap. text ed. 89.95 (*0-8162-8514-4*); 34.95 (*0-8162-8507-1*) Holden-Day.

Storm & Cloud Dynamics. William R. Cotton & Richard A. Anthes. (International Geophysics Ser.). 900p. 1989. text ed. 202.00 (*0-12-192530-7*) Acad Pr.

Storm & Cloud Dynamics. William R. Cotton & Richard A. Anthes. (International Geophysics Ser.: Vol. 44). (Illus.). 883p. 1992. pap. text ed. 78.00 (*0-12-192531-5*) Acad Pr.

***Storm & Other Poems.** Eugenio Montale. Tr. by Charles Wright from ITA. (Field Translation Ser.: No. 1). (Orig.). 1978. pap. 8.95 (*0-932440-01-0*) Oberlin Coll Pr.

Storm & Other Stories. Sharat Kumar. 1976. 9.00 (*0-89253-815-5*); text ed. 6.75 (*0-89253-816-3*) Ind-US Inc.

Storm & Peace. John D. Beresford. LC 67-28744. (Essay Index Reprint Ser.). 1977. 19.95 (*0-8369-0201-7*) Ayer.

Storm & Stress of Language: Linguistic Catastrophe in the Early Works of Goethe, Lenz, Klinger, & Schiller. Bruce Kieffer. LC 86-9511. 160p. 1986. 28.50 (*0-271-00444-4*) Pa St U Pr.

Storm & the Splendor. Jennifer Blake. 1987. reprint ed. mass mkt. 4.95 (*0-449-13196-3*, GM) Fawcett.

Storm & the Splendor. Jennifer Blake. 1994. reprint ed. lib. bdg. 22.00 (*0-7278-4652-3*) Severn Hse.

Storm at Arberth. Sian James. 176p. 1997. pap. 14.95 (*1-85411-111-6*, Pub. by Seren Bks UK) Dufour.

Storm at Daybreak. B. J. Hoff. LC 96-12867. (Daybreak Mysteries Ser.: Vol. 1). 1996. pap. 8.99 (*0-8423-7192-3*) Tyndale.

Storm at the Edge of Time. Pamela F. Service. LC 93-50816. 1994. 16.95 (*0-8027-8306-6*) Walker & Co.

Storm at the Shore. Betsy Loredo. LC 93-16455. (Explorers Club Ser.). (Illus.). 64p. (Orig.). (J). (gr. 4-6). 1993. lib. bdg. 13.95 (*1-881889-10-6*) Silver Moon.

Storm at the Shore see Avalanche in the Alps; Storm at the Shore; Mystery on the Mississippi

Storm Bay. large type ed. Jessica Blair. 1996. 25.99 (*0-7505-0868-X*, Pub. by Magna Print Bks UK) Ulverscroft.

***Storm Book.** Charlotte Zolotow. (Illus.). (J). (ps-3). 1980. 7.66 (*0-06-027025-X*, 984482) HarpC.

Storm Book. Charlotte Zolotow. LC 52-7880. (Trophy Picture Bk.). (Illus.). 32p. (J). (ps-3). 1989. pap. 4.95 (*0-06-443194-0*, Trophy) HarpC Child Bks.

Storm Boy. Paul O. Lewis. LC 94-73364. (Illus.). 32p. (J). (gr. k-3). 14.95 (*1-885223-12-9*) Beyond Words Pub.

Storm Breaking. Mercedes Lackey. 448p. 1996. 21.95 (*0-88677-713-5*) DAW Bks.

***Storm Breaking.** Mercedes Lackey. 1997. mass mkt. 6.99 (*0-88677-755-0*) DAW Bks.

***Storm Captains.** Lamazares. 1999. write for info. (*0-395-86040-7*) HM.

Storm Center. Elizabeth V. Hamilton. LC 82-50861. (Illus.). 200p. 1983. 12.50 (*0-937684-16-3*) Tradd St Pr.

Storm Center: The Supreme Court in American Politics. David M. O'Brien. 404p. (C). 1992. pap. text ed. 15.95 (*0-393-96356-X*) Norton.

Storm Center: The Supreme Court in American Politics. 4th ed. David M. O'Brien. (C). 1996. pap. text ed. 16.95 (*0-393-96891-X*) Norton.

Storm Center: The USS Vincennes & Iran Air Flight 655. Will Rogers et al. LC 92-9202. (Illus.). 264p. 1992. 24.95 (*1-55750-727-9*) Naval Inst Pr.

Storm Centres of the Near East. Robert W. Graves. LC 76-180344. reprint ed. 56.50 (*0-404-56269-8*) AMS Pr.

Storm Chaser: In Pursuit of Untamed Skies. Warren Faidley. 192p. 1996. pap. text ed. 24.95 (*1-888763-00-0*) Weather Channel.

***Storm Chaser: Into the Eye of a Hurricane.** Keith E. Greenberg. LC 96-52455. (Risky Business Ser.). (Illus.). 32p. (J). (gr. 2-5). 1997. lib. bdg. 14.95 (*1-56711-161-0*) Blackbirch.

***Storm Chasers: Tracking Twisters.** Gail Herman. LC 96-52899. (All Aboard Reading Ser.: Level 3). (Illus.). 48p. (Orig.). (J). (gr. 1-4). 1997. 13.99 (*0-448-41638-7*, G&D); pap. 3.95 (*0-448-41624-7*, G&D) Putnam Pub Group.

***Storm Clouds, Vol. 5.** Lauraine Snelling. LC 97-21025. (High Hurdles Ser.). (J). Date not set. pap. text ed. 5.99 (*1-55661-509-4*) Bethany Hse.

Storm Clouds Clear over China: The Memoir of Ch'en Li-fu, 1900-1993. Ed. by Ramon H. Myers. LC 93-23214. (Studies in Economic, Social, & Political Change, the Republic of China Ser.: Vol. 419). (Illus.). 360p. 1993. pap. text ed. 24.95 (*0-8179-9272-3*) Hoover Inst Pr.

Storm Command: A Personal Account of the Gulf War. Peter De La Billiere. (Illus.). 346p. 1994. 34.95 (*1-873544-46-4*) Howell Pr VA.

Storm Damage. Lorna McKenzie. (Rainbow Romances Ser.: No. 907). 160p. 1994. 14.95 (*0-7090-4994-3*, Hale-Parkwest) Parkwest Pubns.

Storm Damage. large type ed. Lorna McKenzie. (Linford Romance Large Print Ser.). 240p. 1995. pap. 15.99 (*0-7089-7739-1*, Linford) Ulverscroft.

Storm Dancers. Allison Hayes. 384p. (Orig.). 1991. mass mkt. 4.50 (*0-380-76215-3*) Avon.

Storm Data for the United States, 1970 to 1974: A Quinquennial Compilation of the U. S. Environmental Data Service's Official Monthly Reports of Storm Activity Logged by the U. S. Weather Bureau. 74th ed. 888p. 1982. 210.00 (*0-8103-1140-2*) Gale.

Storm Data for the United States, 1975 to 1979: A Quinquennial Compilation of the U. S. Environmental Data Service's Official Monthly Reports of Storm Activity Logged by the U. S. Weather Bureau. 79th ed. 952p. 1982. 210.00 (*0-8103-1139-9*) Gale.

Storm Depositional Systems. T. Aigner. (Lecture Notes in Earth Sciences Ser.: Vol. 3). vii, 174p. 1985. 27.95 (*0-387-15231-8*) Spr-Verlag.

Storm Dreamer: The Making of a Shaman. Dean Braley. (Illus.). 171p. (Orig.). 1995. per., pap. 15.00 (*0-9638377-1-0*) D Braley.

Storm Flight. Berent. Date not set. 4.98 (*0-8317-6727-8*) Smithmark.

Storm Flight. Mark Berent. 512p. 1994. reprint ed. pap. text ed. 5.99 (*0-515-11432-4*) Jove Pubns.

***Storm Force from Navarone.** Sam Llewellyn. 1997. pap. 22.95 (*0-7862-1068-0*) Thorndike Pr.

Storm from Paradise: The Politics of Jewish Memory. Jonathan Boyarin. 192p. (C). 1992. text ed. 39.95 (*0-8166-2094-6*); pap. text ed. 14.95 (*0-8166-2095-4*) U of Minn Pr.

Storm from the East: From Ghengis Khan to Khubilai Khan. Robert Marshall. LC 92-36544. (C). 1993. 30.00 (*0-520-08300-8*) U CA Pr.

Storm from the Sea. Peter Young. 236p. 1989. 27.95 (*0-87021-991-X*) Naval Inst Pr.

Storm Front. Barbara Clark-Cross. 384p. 1992. mass mkt. 4.50 (*1-55817-668-3*, Pinnacle Kensgtn) Kensgtn Pub Corp.

Storm Front. Bill Knight. (Orig.). pap. write for info. (*0-9624613-0-X*) Mayfly Prodns.

Storm Gathering: The Penn Family & the American Revolution. Lorett Treese. LC 92-5573. (Keystone Bks.). (Illus.). 288p. 1992. 28.50 (*0-271-00858-X*) Pa St U Pr.

***Storm Glass.** Jane Urquhart. 128p. 1987. pap. 14.95 (*0-88984-106-3*, Pub. by Porcupines Quill CN) Genl Dist Srvs.

Storm Haven. Frank Slaughter. 23.95 (*0-89190-285-6*) Amereon Ltd.

Storm in Punjab. W. Kshitish. 264p. 1986. 120.00 (*0-317-61978-0*, Pub. by Archives Pubs II) St Mut.

Storm in the Mountains: A Case Study of Censorship, Conflict, & Consciousness. James Moffett. LC 87-20614. 280p. (C). 1989. pap. 15.95 (*0-8093-1584-X*) S Ill U Pr.

Storm in the Mountains: Thomas' Confederate Legion of Cherokee Indians & Mountaineers. Vernon H. Crow. LC 82-73852. (Illus.). 300p. 1982. pap. text ed. 7.95 (*0-685-47385-6*) Pr Mus Cherokee Indian.

Storm in the Night. Mary Stolz. LC 85-45838. (Illus.). 32p. (J). (gr. k-3). 1988. lib. bdg. 14.89 (*0-06-025913-2*) HarpC Child Bks.

Storm in the Night. Mary Stolz. LC 85-45838. (Trophy Picture Bk.). (Illus.). 32p. (J). (gr. k-3). 1990. pap. 4.95 (*0-06-443256-4*, Trophy) HarpC Child Bks.

***Storm in the Village.** Read. Date not set. lib. bdg. 22.95 (*0-8488-1691-9*) Amereon Ltd.

Storm in the Village. large type ed. Miss Read. (Illus.). 1996. 25.95 (*0-7838-1655-3*, GK Hall) Thorndike Pr.

Storm in the West. rev. ed. Sinclair Lewis & Dore Schary. LC 63-13228. (Illus.). 200p. (C). 1981. pap. 5.95 (*0-8128-6079-9*, Scrbrough Hse) Madison Bks UPA.

***Storm-Induced Geologic Hazards: Case Histories from the 1992-1993 Winter in Southern California & Arizona.** Ed. by Robert A. Larson & James E. Slosson. (Reviews in Engineering Geology Ser.: No. 11). (Illus.). 1997. write for info. (*0-8137-4111-4*) Geol Soc.

Storm Knight. large type ed. Frederick E. Smith. (Adventure Suspense Ser.). 416p. 1992. 25.99 (*0-7089-2649-5*) Ulverscroft.

Storm Knights. (Torg Ser.). 352p. 4.95 (*0-87431-301-5*, 20601) West End Games.

Storm Knights' Guide: Torg. (Torg Ser.). 15.00 (*0-87431-328-7*, 20569) West End Games.

Storm Lake Suite. (Illus.). 79p. (Orig.). (C). 1985. pap. text ed. 6.00 (*0-937131-01-6*) Barking Dog.

***Storm Landings: Epic Amphibious Battles in the Central Pacific.** Joseph H. Alexander. LC 96-53479. (Illus.). 216p. 1997. 28.95 (*1-55750-032-0*) Naval Inst Pr.

***Storm Maiden.** Mary Gillgannon. 384p. 1997. mass mkt. 5.50 (*0-7860-0414-2*, Pinnacle Kensgtn) Kensgtn Pub Corp.

Storm of Passion. Cartwright. 1994. pap. 2.99 (*0-373-17168-4*) Harlequin Bks.

Storm of Steel. Ernst Junger. Tr. by B. Creighton from GER. LC 75-22372. xiii, 319p. 1975. reprint ed. 45.00 (*0-86527-310-3*) Fertig.

Storm of Steel: From the Diary of a German Stormtroop Officer on the Western Front. Ernst Junger. Tr. by Basil Creighton from GER. LC 75-22372. xii, 319p. 1996. reprint ed. pap. 13.00 (*0-86527-423-1*) Fertig.

Storm of Wrath. large type ed. Alice Dwyer-Joyce. (Large Print Ser.). 416p. 1994. 25.99 (*0-7089-3015-8*) Ulverscroft.

Storm on the Desert. Carolyn Lesser. LC 95-44923. (Illus.). (J). 1997. 15.00 (*0-15-272198-3*) HarBrace.

Storm on the Lake. (Collect-a-Bible Story Bks.). (Illus.). 26p. (J). 1995. pap. text ed. 1.49 (*0-7847-0417-1*, 21507) Standard Pub.

Storm over a Mountain Island: Conservation Biology & the Mt. Graham Affair. Ed. by Conrad A. Istock & Robert S. Hoffmann. LC 95-13667. (Illus.). 291p. 1995. 42.00 (*0-8165-1551-4*); pap. 19.95 (*0-8165-1577-8*) U of Ariz Pr.

Storm over Biology: Essays on Science, Sentiment, & Public Policy. Bernard D. Davis. 324p. 1986. 29.95 (*0-87975-324-2*) Prometheus Bks.

***Storm over Boston.** Cameron Dokey. (J). 1997. write for info. (*0-614-29167-4*, Flare) Avon.

Storm over Chile: The Junta under Siege. rev. ed. Samuel Chavkin. LC 89-15510. 320p. 1989. reprint ed. pap. 12.95 (*1-55652-067-0*) L Hill Bks.

Storm over Cuba. Martin A. Sugarman. 148p. (Orig.). 1995. pap. text ed. 32.95 (*1-883071-02-X*) Sugarman Prods.

***Storm over Iraq: Air Power & the Gulf War.** Richard P. Hallion. (Illus.). 352p. 1997. pap. 16.95 (*1-56098-723-5*) Smithsonian.

Storm over Mono: The Mono Lake Battle & the California Water Future. John Hart. LC 95-32190. (Illus.). 253p. 1996. pap. 29.95 (*0-520-20368-2*) U CA Pr.

Storm over Mono: The Mono Lake Battle & the California Water Future. John Hart. LC 95-32190. (Illus.). 253p. (C). 1996. 50.00 (*0-520-20121-3*) U CA Pr.

Storm over Paradise. Robyn Donald. (Presents Ser.). 1992. pap. 2.89 (*0-373-11505-9*, 1-11505-4) Harlequin Bks.

Storm over Rangelands: Private Rights in Federal Lands. Wayne Hage. Ed. by Ron Arnold. 1989. 14.95 (*0-939571-06-4*); pap. 9.95 (*0-939571-07-2*) Free Enter Pr.

Storm over Rangelands: Private Rights in Federal Lands. 3rd ed. Wayne Hage. Ed. by Ron Arnold. xii, 265p. 1994. pap. 14.95 (*0-939571-15-3*) Free Enter Pr.

Storm over Sabah: A Novel. Ben Javier. 171p. (Orig.). 1993. pap. 10.75 (*971-10-0514-X*, Pub. by New Day Pub PH) Cellar.

Storm over the Constitution: Jaffa Answers Bork. Harry V. Jaffa. 67p. (Orig.). (C). 1994. pap. text ed. 5.00 (*0-930783-23-9*) Claremont Inst.

Storm over the Gilberts: War in the Central Pacific 1943. Edwin P. Hoyt. 200p. 1983. pap. 3.50 (*0-380-63651-4*) Avon.

Storm Over the Lake & To Love & Cherish. Diana Palmer. (Diana Palmer Duets Ser.: No. 2). 1990. mass mkt. 3.25 (*0-373-48223-X*) Harlequin Bks.

***Storm over the Land.** Carl Sandburg. (Civil War Library). (Illus.). 448p. 1996. reprint ed. 12.98 (*1-56852-042-5*, Konecky & Konecky) W S Konecky Assocs.

Storm over the Land: A Novel about War. Kalle Paatalo. Tr. & Frwd. by Richard A. Impola. 579p. (Orig.). 1993. pap. 15.00 (*1-880474-06-9*) FATA.

Storm over the Lightning L. Clifford Blair. 192p. 1993. 19.95 (*0-8027-1236-3*) Walker & Co.

Storm over the Lightning L. large type ed. Clifford Blair. LC 93-1387. 1993. lib. bdg. 17.95 (*1-56054-719-7*) Thorndike Pr.

Storm over the Multinationals: The Real Issues. Raymond Vernon. 208p. 1977. 32.00 (*0-674-83875-0*) HUP.

Storm over the South China Sea. Tzou-Chow Yang. 197p. (C). 1995. write for info. (*0-9648979-0-3*) SJU Ctr Asian.

Storm over the Sutlej: The Sikhs & Akali Politics. A. S. Narang. 1983. 24.00 (*0-8364-1079-3*) S Asia.

Storm Passage: Alone Around Cape Horn. Webb Chiles. LC 77-79025. (Illus.). 1977. write for info. (*0-8129-0703-5*, Times Bks) Random.

***Storm Passed By: Ireland, 1941-42.** Trevor Allen. 172p. 1996. 29.50 (*0-7165-2616-6*, Pub. by F Cass Pubs UK) Intl Spec Bk.

Storm Pattern. Greg Pape. LC 91-50873. (Poetry Ser.). 96p. 1992. 19.95 (*0-8229-3708-5*); pap. 10.95 (*0-8229-5472-9*) U of Pittsburgh Pr.

Storm Pattern: Poems from Two Navajo Women. Della Frank & Roberta D. Joe. 40p. 1993. pap. 12.00 (*0-912586-75-3*) Navajo Coll Pr.

Storm Personal Version 3.0 3.5 Quantitative Modeling for Decision Support. 3rd ed. Storm, Inc. Staff et al. (C). 1992. 61.00 (*0-13-847450-8*) P-H.

***Storm Prince.** Terri L. Wilhelm. 432p. 1997. mass mkt. 3.99 (*0-06-108384-4*) HarpC.

***Storm-Ready: A Boat Owner's Guide for Hurricane Preparation.** Richard Winer. 1996. pap. text ed. 15.95 (*0-07-070983-1*) McGraw.

Storm Riders. Roxanne Longstreet. Ed. by John Reummler. (Shadow World Ser.). (Illus.). 300p. (Orig.). (C). 1990. pap. 6.95 (*1-55806-138-X*, 6200) Iron Crown Ent Inc.

Storm Rising. Mercedes Lackey. 416p. 1996. mass mkt. 5.99 (*0-88677-712-7*) DAW Bks.

Storm Rising. Marilyn Singer. 224p. (J). (gr. 7-9). 1989. pap. 12.95 (*0-590-42173-5*) Scholastic Inc.

***Storm Run.** Libby Riddles. (Illus.). 40p. (J). (gr. 5-7). 1996. 13.95 (*0-934007-31-4*) Paws Four Pub.

Storm Runner. Tara K. Harper. (Tales of the Wolves Ser.: Bk. 3). 1993. mass mkt. 5.99 (*0-345-37162-3*, Del Rey) Ballantine.

Storm Shelter. Ron Blue. LC 94-27610. 1994. 18.99 (*0-7852-8276-9*) Nelson.

Storm Signals: Structural Adjustment & Development Alternatives in the Caribbean. Kathy McAfee. 240p. (Orig.). 1991. 30.00 (*0-89608-421-3*); pap. 15.00 (*0-89608-420-5*) South End Pr.

Storm Song. Adeline Foster. (Illus.). 100p. (Orig.). 1985. pap. 4.95 (*0-9609794-1-7*) A Foster.

Storm Surge. T. J. MacGregor. LC 92-42516. 336p. 1993. 19.95 (*1-56282-789-8*) Hyperion.

Storm Surge. William Sargent. 208p. (Orig.). 1995. pap. 12.50 (*0-940160-60-9*) Parnassus Imprints.

Storm Tactics Handbook: Modern Methods of Heaving-To for Survival in Extreme Conditions. Lin Pardey & Larry Pardey. (Illus.). 144p. (Orig.). 1995. pap. 19.95 (*0-9646036-6-7*) Paradise Cay Pubns.

Storm Testament: Porter Rockwell, Walkara, Butch Cassidy, Storm Testament, 4 bks., Set. Ed. by Lee Nelson. 1992. boxed 39.95 (*1-56684-009-0*, Council Pr) Pubs Dist Ctr Inc.

***Storm Tide.** Mel Keegan. 208p. 1996. pap. 12.95 (*0-85449-227-5*, Pub. by Gay Mens Pr UK) LPC InBook.

Storm Tide. Patricia Rae. 1983. mass mkt. 3.75 (*0-685-07867-1*, Zebra Kensgtn) Kensgtn Pub Corp.

An Asterisk (*) at the beginning of an entry indicates that the title is appearing in BIP for the first time.

Storm Tide. Elisabeth Ogilvie. LC 85-72648. (Tide Trilogy Ser.: Bk. 2). 368p. 1985. reprint ed. pap. 9.95 (*0-89272-217-7*) Down East.
Storm Track. Ron Terpening. 360p. 1989. 22.95 (*0-8027-1069-7*) Walker & Co.
Storm Treasure. James E. Sanford. 288p. 1995. mass mkt. 4.99 (*1-896329-54-3*, Pub. by Comnwlth Pub CN) Partners Pubs Grp.
Storm Warning. Billy Graham. 1995. mass mkt. 5.99 (*0-8499-3681-0*) Word Pub.
Storm Warning. Jack Higgins. 1991. mass mkt. 5.95 (*0-671-74629-4*) PB.
Storm Warning. Mercedes Lackey. (Mage Storms Ser.: Bk. 1). 432p. 1994. 21.95 (*0-88677-611-2*) DAW Bks.
Storm Warning. Mercedes Lackey. (Mage Storms Ser.: Bk. 1). 432p. 1995. pap. 6.99 (*0-88677-661-9*) DAW Bks.
Storm Warning. Nora Roberts. (NR Flowers Ser.: No. 4). 1992. mass mkt. 3.59 (*0-373-51004-7*, 5-51004-5) Harlequin Bks.
Storm Warning: The Power of Tornadoes & Hurricanes. Jonathan D. Kahl. LC 92-13627. (How's the Weather? Ser.). (J). (gr. 4 up). 1993. lib. bdg. 19.95 (*0-8225-2527-5*, Lerner Publctns) Lerner Group.
***Storm Warnings.** Judi Lind. 1997. mass mkt. 3.75 (*0-373-22433-8*, 1-22433-6) Harlequin Bks.
Storm Warnings: Science Fiction Confronts the Future. Ed. by George E. Slusser et al. LC 86-2611. (Alternatives Ser.). 296p. 1987. text ed. 29.95 (*0-8093-1376-6*) S Ill U Pr.
Storm Watch. Patrick S. Kelly et al. (Illus.). 52p. 1991. pap. 15.95 (*0-939251-60-4*) Accord CO.
Storm Water. large type ed. Peter Ling. 1996. 25.99 (*0-7505-0756-X*, Pub. by Magna Print Bks UK) Ulverscroft.
Storm Water: Guidance Manual for the Preparation of NPDES Permit Applications for Storm Water Discharges. EPA Staff. 180p. 1991. pap. text ed. 59.00 (*0-86587-258-9*) Gov Insts.
Storm Water Discharges: Regulatory Compliance & Best. Mark S. Dennison. 464p. 1995. 59.95 (*1-56670-198-8*, L1198) Lewis Pubs.
Storm Water Management & Technology. U. S. Environmental Protection Agency Staff. LC 92-45153. (Illus.). 375p. 1993. 48.00 (*0-8155-1327-5*) Noyes.
***Storm Water Management for Construction Activities: Developing Pollution Prevention Plans & Best Management Practices.** (Illus.). 33p. (Orig.). 1996. reprint ed. pap. text ed. 20.00 (*0-7881-2955-4*) DIANE Pub.
Storm Water Management for Industrial Activities: Developing Pollution Prevention Plans & Best Management Practices. U. S. Environmental Protection Agency Staff. 380p. 1992. pap. text ed. 69.00 (*0-86587-331-3*) Gov Insts.
***Storm Water Management for Industrial Activities: Developing Pollution Prevention Plans & Best Management Practices.** (Illus.). 350p. (Orig.). (C). 1996. reprint ed. pap. 50.00 (*0-7881-2956-2*) DIANE Pub.
Storm Water Pollution Control: Industry & Construction NPDES Compliance. Roy Dodson. 1995. text ed. 65.00 (*0-07-017334-6*) McGraw.
Storm Wife. Barton & Yudin. (J). Date not set. 12.95 (*1-55082-060-5*) LPC InBook.
Storm Wife. Barton & Yudin. 1993. per. 8.95 (*1-55082-061-3*, Pub. by Quarry Pr CN) LPC InBook.
Storm Wind. Cherith Baldry. Ed. by Sue Reck. (Saga of the Six Worlds Ser.). 160p. (YA). (gr. 8-12). 1994. pap. 4.99 (*0-7814-0095-3*, Chariot Bks) Chariot Victor.
Storm Winds. Iris Johansen. 544p. 1991. mass mkt. 5.99 (*0-553-29032-0*) Bantam.
Storm Within. David Hillier. 448p. 1996. 24.00 (*0-7278-4858-5*) Severn Hse.
Storm Within. Mark R. Littleton. LC 93-30564. 200p. 1994. pap. 7.99 (*0-8423-7207-5*) Tyndale.
Storm Within. Debra Robison. 1994. pap. 4.95 (*1-55673-934-6*) CSS OH.
Storm Without Rain. Jan Adkins. 1995. 18.00 (*0-8446-6809-5*) Peter Smith.
Storm Without Rain. Jan Adkins. LC 92-24601. 192p. (YA). (gr. 7 up). 1993. reprint ed. pap. 3.95 (*0-688-11852-6*) Morrow.
Storm 2.0 - Site License. Storm, Inc. Staff. 1991. write for info. (*0-13-847476-1*) P-H.
Stormalong. Alan Villiers. 20.95 (*0-8488-0655-7*) Amereon Ltd.
Stormalong: The Legendary Sea Captain. Eric Metaxas. LC 95-48132. (Illus.). (J). (gr. 1-4). 1995. 19.95 (*0-689-80194-7*, Rabbit) S&S Childrens.
Stormbound. Lynne Fairbridge. 176p. 1995. pap. 9.95 (*0-385-25519-5*) Doubleday.
Stormbringer. Michael Moorcock. 1987. pap. 4.99 (*0-441-78754-1*) Ace Bks.
Stormchaser. Rita C. Estrada. (Temptation Ser.). 1996. mass mkt. 3.50 (*0-373-25673-6*, 1-25673-4) Harlequin Bks.
Stormfire. Helen Bianchin. (Presents Ser.). 1993. mass mkt. 2.99 (*0-373-11561-X*, 1-11561-7) Harlequin Bks.
Stormfire. Christine Monson. 592p. 1984. pap. 3.95 (*0-380-87668-X*) Avon.
Stormhaven. Michael A. Stackpole. 1983. 7.95 (*0-940244-40-3*) Flying Buffalo.
Stormie. Stormie Omartian. (Orig.). 1995. mass mkt. 4.99 (*1-56507-400-9*) Harvest Hse.
Stormin' Back: Missouri Basketball Coach Norm Stewart's Battles on & off the Court. Norm Stewart & John Dewey. LC 91-161670. (Illus.). 279p. 1991. 19.95 (*0-915611-47-3*) Sagamore Pub.
Stormin' Norman: An American Hero. Jack Anderson. 1991. mass mkt. 4.50 (*0-8217-3562-4*, Zebra Kensgtn) Kensgtn Pub Corp.
Storming Gates. Dan Balz & Ronald Brownstein. 1996. 24.95 (*0-316-08038-1*) Little.
Storming Heaven. 1994. pap. 24.95 (*0-7871-0049-8*, Dove Bks) Dove Audio.
Storming Heaven. Dale Brown. 496p. 1995. mass mkt. 6.99 (*0-425-14723-1*) Berkley Pub.
Storming Heaven. Denise Giardina. 304p. 1988. mass mkt. 5.99 (*0-8041-0297-X*) Ivy Books.
Storming Heaven. large type ed. Dale Brown. LC 94-34298. 732p. 1994. lib. bdg. 25.95 (*0-7862-0334-X*) Thorndike Pr.
Storming Heaven's Gate: An Anthology of Spiritual Writings by Women. Ed. by Patrice Vecchione & Amber C. Sumrall. LC 97-1990. 1997. pap. 13.95 (*0-452-27621-7*, Plume) NAL-Dutton.
Storming Hell's Brazen Gates. Dick Bernal. 96p. 1988. pap. 4.95 (*0-88144-124-4*) Christian Pub.
Storming Hitler's Rhine. William B. Breuer. 1986. mass mkt. 4.95 (*0-312-90335-9*) St Martin.
Storming Intrepid. Payne Harrison. 400p. 1988. 19.95 (*0-517-57133-1*, Crown) Crown Pub Group.
Storming Intrepid. Payne Harrison. 512p. 1990. mass mkt. 5.95 (*0-8041-0553-7*) Ivy Books.
Storming of Stony Point on the Hudson, Midnight, July 15, 1779. Henry P. Johnston. LC 70-146150. (Era of the American Revolution Ser.). 1971. reprint ed. lib. bdg. 29.50 (*0-306-70141-3*) Da Capo.
Storming the Desert: A Marine Lieutenant's Day-by-Day Chronicle of the Persian Gulf War. Sean T. Coughlin. LC 96-27287. (Illus.). 168p. 1996. pap. 19.95 (*0-7864-0195-8*) McFarland & Co.
Storming the Gates: Protest Politics & the Republican Revival. Dan Balz & Ronald Brownstein. 424p. 1996. 24.95 (*0-614-12887-0*) Little.
***Storming the Gates of Hell.** Des Griffin. 200p. (Orig.). 1996. pap. 10.00 (*0-941380-07-6*) Emissary Pubns.
Storming the Reality Studio: A Casebook of Cyberpunk & Postmodern Science Fiction. Ed. by Larry McCaffery. LC 91-14316. (Illus.). 344p. 1992. text ed. 54.95 (*0-8223-1158-5*); pap. text ed. 19.95 (*0-8223-1168-2*) Duke.
Storming the Statehouse: Running for Governor with Ann Richards & Dianne Feinstein. Celia Morris. (Illus.). 352p. 1992. text ed. 25.00 (*0-684-19328-0*) S&S Trade.
Storming to Power. (Third Reich Ser.). (Illus.). 192p. 1989. 9.99 (*0-8094-6954-5*) Time-Life.
Storming Toward Armageddon. Ed. by W. T. James. LC 92-64450. (Essays in Apocalypse Ser.: Bk. 1). 336p. (Orig.). 1992. pap. 11.95 (*0-89221-228-4*) New Leaf.
Storming Washington: An Intern's Guide to National Government. 4th rev. ed. Stephen E. Frantzich. 63p. (C). 1994. pap. text ed. 6.00 (*1-878147-13-7*) Am Political.
Stormlands No. 1: The Islander. John M. Roberts. 1990. pap. 3.95 (*0-8125-0627-8*) Tor Bks.
Stormlight. Ed Greenwood. 1996. pap. 5.99 (*0-7869-0520-4*) TSR Inc.
Stormlight: Poems. Thomas R. McKague. LC 95-512. 64p. 1995. pap. 12.95 (*0-7734-2739-2*, Mellen Poetry Pr) E Mellen.
Stormont Crisis: A Memoir. Ken Bloomfield. 295p. 9500. pap. 25.00 (*0-85640-525-6*, Pub. by Blackstaff Pr IE) Dufour.
Stormqueen! Marion Zimmer Bradley. (Darkover Ser.). 368p. 1978. mass mkt. 5.99 (*0-88677-310-5*) DAW Bks.
Storms. Ray Broekel. LC 81-15455. (New True Bks.). (Illus.). 48p. (J). (gr. k-4). 1982. lib. bdg. 19.00 (*0-516-01654-7*) Childrens.
Storms. William R. Cotton. (Geophysical Science Ser.: Vol. 1). (Illus.). 158p. (Orig.). (C). 1990. pap. text ed. 25.00 (*0-9625986-0-7*) Aster Pr.
Storms. Ann Merk & Jim Merk. LC 94-13321. (Weather Report Ser.). (J). (gr. 3 up). 1994. write for info. (*0-86593-386-3*) Rourke Corp.
Storms. Seymour Simon. LC 88-22045. (Illus.). 32p. (J). (gr. k-3). 1989. 16.00 (*0-688-07413-8*, Morrow Junior); lib. bdg. 15.93 (*0-688-07414-6*, Morrow Junior) Morrow.
Storms. Seymour Simon. Ed. by ALC Staff. LC 88-22045. (Illus.). 32p. (J). (gr. k-3). 1992. pap. 4.95 (*0-688-11708-2*, Morrow Junior) Morrow.
Storms: Nature's Fury. Jenny Wood. LC 90-55461. (Wonderworks of Nature Ser.). (Illus.). 32p. (J). (gr. 3-4). 1991. lib. bdg. 19.93 (*0-8368-0471-6*) Gareth Stevens Inc.
***Storms above the Desert: Atmospheric Research in New Mexico, 1935-1985.** Joe Chew & Jim Corey. LC 87-6020. (Illus.). 179p. 1987. reprint ed. pap. 51.10 (*0-608-04144-0*, 2064877) Bks Demand.
Storms & Blizzards. Mary Micallef. (Natural Disaster Ser.). 48p. (J). (gr. 4-8). 1985. student ed. 7.95 (*0-86653-321-4*, GA 683) Good Apple.
Storms & Hurricanes. Stuart Atkinson. (Understanding Geography Ser.). (Illus.). 32p. (YA). (gr. 5-10). 1996. lib. bdg. 14.95 (*0-88110-827-8*, Usborne) EDC.
Storms & Hurricanes. Stuart Atkinson. (Understanding Geography Ser.). (Illus.). (J). (gr. 5-10). 1996. pap. 6.95 (*0-7460-2012-0*, Usborne) EDC.

***Storms & Illuminations 18 Years of Access Theatre. Cynthia Wisehart. (Illus.). 255p. (Orig.). 1997. pap. 19.95 (*0-9656894-0-9*) Emily Pubns CA.**
This is the story of an extraordinary adventure, told through the words & photographs of the people who were a part of it. During its 18-year history, Access Theatre created original musicals & plays that blended the talents of artists who are deaf, hearing, blind, sighted, physically disabled & non-disabled. The company grew from a grass-roots community theater to a professional, international touring company & paved the way for accessibility in the arts. This beautiful book, based on interviews with nearly 100 company members, explores the innovative theatre's life through stories about its plays & players - in rehearsal, on stage, & on tour. A readable, entertaining portrait of how a theater company - or any organization -- can find strength & magic in diversity. Sections on sign language interpretation, stagecraft, & funding offer a fascinating look behind the scenes & contain useful information for other cultural organizations seeking to be more accessible. STORMS & ILLUMINATIONS features a foreword by Michael Douglas who supported Access Theatre throughout its life. An introduction by actor Anthony Edwards (NBC's "ER") relates his own experiences as a member of the company. 150 photographs. Order through Emily Publications, 2428 Chapala Street, Santa Barbara, CA 93105. (805) 569-1064. $19.95.
Publisher Provided Annotation.

Storms & Rainbows: The Many Faces of Death. Intro. by Arnold Medvene. 200p. (Orig.). 1992. pap. 9.95 (*0-9630598-0-7*) Lilith Pr.
Storms Brewed in Other Men's Worlds: The Confrontation of Indians, Spanish, & French in the Southwest, 1540-1795. Elizabeth A. John. LC 96-16504. (Illus.). 836p. 1996. pap. 24.95 (*0-8061-2869-0*) U of Okla Pr.
Storm's Coming. Dave Saunders & Julie Saunders. (J). 1994. 14.95 (*0-02-778134-8*, Mac Bks Young Read) S&S Childrens.
Storm's Crossing: A Young Girl's Triumph over a Terrible Secret. Reanne S. Singer. 176p. 1993. 13.95 (*0-925190-62-4*) Fairview Press.
Storm's Fury: And Other Horse Stories. Highlights for Children Staff. LC 90-85910. (Illus.). 96p. (J). (gr. 3-7). 1992. pap. 2.95 (*1-878093-31-2*) Boyds Mills Pr.
Storms of a Soul. Joseph Delgado. 40p. (Orig.). 1995. pap. 5.49 (*0-9646866-0-0*) Enchanted Quill Pr.
Storms of Controversy: The Secret Avro Arrow Files Revealed. Palmiro Campagna. (Illus.). 176p. 1992. 26.95 (*0-7737-2649-7*) Genl Dist Srvs.
***Storms of Controversy: The Secret Avro Arrow Files Revealed.** Palmiro Campagna. (Illus.). 272p. 1997. pap. 16.95 (*0-7737-5861-5*, Pub. by Stoddart Pubng CN) Genl Dist Srvs.
Storms of Fate. Cynthia S. Roberts. 288p. 1992. lib. bdg. 19.00 (*0-7278-4337-0*) Severn Hse.
Storms of Life. Janet Anderson. 112p. write for info. (*0-8187-0139-0*) Harlo Press.
Storms of Love. Dencie Munns. LC 90-7513. 238p. 1990. 15.75 (*0-930950-23-2*); pap. 9.75 (*0-930950-24-0*) Nopoly Pr.
Storms of Perfection: In Their Own Words. Andy Andrews. 168p. 1991. pap. 12.95 (*0-9629620-1-5*) Lightning Crown Pub.
Storms of Perfection Vol. 2: Letters from the Heart. Andy Andrews. 171p. 1994. pap. 12.95 (*0-9629620-3-1*) Lightning Crown Pub.
Storms of Perfection Vol. 3: A Pathway to Personal Achievement. Andy Andrews. 176p. 1996. pap. 12.95 (*0-9629620-5-8*) Lightning Crown Pub.
***Storms of Silence.** Joe Simpson. (Illus.). 240p. (Orig.). 1997. pap. 19.95 (*0-89886-512-3*) Mountaineers.
Storms of Victory. Andre Norton & P. M. Griffin. (Witch World: The Turning Ser.: Vol. 1). 1992. mass mkt. 4.99 (*0-8125-1109-3*) Tor Bks.
***Storms over the Urban Forest: Planning, Responding, & Regreening - A Community Guide to Natural Disaster Relief.** 2nd ed. Lisa L. Burban & John W. Anderson. (Illus.). 152p. (Orig.). 1996. reprint ed. pap. text ed. 30.00 (*0-7881-2948-1*) DIANE Pub.
Storms Pass, So Hang On! Nancy Hoag. 136p. 1994. pap. 8.99 (*0-8341-1480-1*) Beacon Hill.
Stormsearch. Robert Westall. (J). (gr. 4-7). 1992. 14.00 (*0-374-37272-1*) FS&G.
***Stormshooters & Troubleknights.** (Paranoia Ser.). 6.95 (*0-87431-168-3*, 12304) West End Games.
Stormtide. large type ed. Bill Knox. 1975. 25.99 (*0-85456-334-2*) Ulverscroft.
Stormtroop Tactics: Innovation in the German Army, 1914-1918. Bruce I. Gudmundsson. LC 89-3882. 227p. 1995. pap. text ed. 19.95 (*0-275-95401-3*, Praeger Pubs) Greenwood.
Stormtroop Tactics: Innovation in the Germany Army,1914-1918. Bruce I. Gudmundsson. LC 89-3882. 227p. 1989. text ed. 55.00 (*0-275-93328-8*, C3328, Praeger Pubs) Greenwood.
Stormtroopers: A Social, Economic & Ideological Analysis: 1929-35. Conan Fischer. 240p. 1983. text ed. 55.00 (*0-04-943028-9*) Routledge Chapman & Hall.
Stormwalker. Dallas Schulze. (Men Made in America Ser.). 1993. mass mkt. 3.59 (*0-373-45156-3*, 1-45156-6) Harlequin Bks.
***Stormwalker.** Bronwyn Williams. 1998. mass mkt. 4.50 (*0-373-81062-8*, 1-81062-1) Harlequin Bks.
***Stormwatch: Change the World.** Warren Ellis. (Illus.). 112p. (Orig.). (YA). 1997. pap. write for info. (*1-887279-46-6*) Image Comics.
Stormwater: Pollution Prevention Manual for the Trucking Industry. 350p. 1994. pap. text ed. 47.95 (*0-88711-256-0*) Am Trucking Assns.
Stormwater Compliance Handbook. 1995. ring bd. 179.95 (*1-55645-310-8*, 170002) Busn Legal Reports.
Stormwater Detention Outlet Control Structures. 34p. 1985. 11.00 (*0-87262-480-3*) Am Soc Civil Eng.
Stormwater Infiltration. Bruce K. Ferguson. 288p. 1994. 69.95 (*0-87371-987-5*, L987) Lewis Pubs.
Stormwater Management. Richard K. Miller & Marcia E. Rupnow. (Survey on Technology & Markets Ser.: No. 225). 50p. 1993. pap. text ed. 200.00 (*1-55865-255-8*) Future Tech Surveys.
Stormwater Management. Martin P. Wanielista & Yousef A. Yousef. LC 92-6914. 579p. 1992. text ed. 84.95 (*0-471-57135-0*) Wiley.
Stormwater Management for Industrial Activities. Washington U. S. EPA Staff. 400p. 1993. 79.95 (*0-87371-959-X*, LS959) Lewis Pubs.
Stormwater Management in Urbanizing Areas. William Whipple et al. (Illus.). 240p. (C). 1983. 54.00 (*0-13-850214-5*) P-H.
Stormwater NPDES Related Monitoring Needs: Proceedings of an Engineering Foundation Conference. Engineering Foundation Conference Staff. Ed. by Harry C. Torno et al. LC 94-25292. (Illus.). 1994. 53.00 (*0-7844-0065-2*) Am Soc Civil Eng.
Stormwater Runoff & Receiving Systems: Impact, Monitoring, & Assessment. Ed. by Edwin E. Herricks & Jackie R. Jenkins. 480p. 1995. 69.95 (*1-56670-159-7*, L1159) Lewis Pubs.
Stormy. Jim Kjelgaard. 160p. (J). (gr. 4-8). 1983. pap. 4.50 (*0-553-15468-0*, Skylark BDD) BDD Bks Young Read.
Stormy. Jane Weinberger. LC 85-62021. (Illus.). 54p. (J). (gr. 1-6). 1985. pap. 5.95 (*0-932433-13-8*) Windswept Hse.
Stormy: Finds the New Forest. Tom Storm. (Illus.). 48p. (Orig.). (J). (gr. 1-6). 1994. pap. 8.95 (*0-9643019-0-3*) T Storm.
***Stormy: The Barrel Horse.** Ralph Galeano. Ed. by Ben V. Hess et al. (Illus.). 346p. (Orig.). 1996. pap. 16.95 (*1-57502-308-3*, PO1053) Morris Pubng.
Stormy Applause: Making Music in a Worker's State. Rostislav Dubinsky. 292p. 1992. reprint ed. pap. text ed. 15.95 (*1-55553-119-9*) NE U Pr.
***Stormy Bay.** Jo Grant. 460p. (Orig.). 1998. mass mkt. 9.99 (*1-58006-002-1*, Flirtation) Sovereign.
Stormy Courtship. Joann Ross. (Mira Bks.). 1995. mass mkt. 4.99 (*1-55166-072-5*, 1-66072-9, Mira Bks) Harlequin Bks.
Stormy Day. Claire Henley. LC 92-72025. (Illus.). 32p. (J). (ps). 1993. 11.95 (*1-56282-342-6*) Hyprn Child.
Stormy Escape: A Vietnamese Woman's Account of Her 1980 Flight Through Cambodia to Thailand. Kim Ha. LC 96-47893. (Illus.). 296p. 1996. lib. bdg. 32.50 (*0-7864-0244-X*) McFarland & Co.
***Stormy Hearts.** Norma F. Mars. 193p. (Orig.). 1997. mass mkt. 4.99 (*1-55237-289-8*, Pub. by Comnwlth Pub CN) Partners Pubs Grp.
Stormy Heritage. large type ed. Mary Williams. LC 94-19363. 298p. 1994. lib. bdg. 17.95 (*0-7862-0282-3*) Thorndike Pr.
Stormy Liaisons. Jaqueline Wallace. (Rainbow Romances Ser.). 160p. 1994. 14.95 (*0-7090-4845-9*, 911, Hale-Parkwest) Parkwest Pubns.
Stormy Liaisons. large type ed. Jacqueline Wallace. (Linford Romance Large Print Ser.). 272p. 1995. pap. 15.99 (*0-7089-7727-8*, Linford) Ulverscroft.
Stormy, Misty's Foal. Marguerite Henry. (J). 1996. 17.75 (*0-8446-6880-X*) Peter Smith.
Stormy, Misty's Foal. 2nd ed. Marguerite Henry. LC 90-27306. (Illus.). 224p. (J). (gr. 3-7). 1991. reprint ed. pap. 3.95 (*0-689-71487-4*, Aladdin Paperbacks) S&S Childrens.
Stormy Monday: The T-Bone Walker Story. Helen O. Dance. LC 86-21379. (Illus.). 264p. 1987. 24.95 (*0-8071-1355-7*) La State U Pr.
Stormy Monday: The T-Bone Walker Story. Helen O. Dance. (Quality Paperbacks Ser.). 302p. 1990. reprint ed. pap. 13.95 (*0-306-80413-1*) Da Capo.
***Stormy Night in Noahs Ark.** Patricia Hooper. (J). Date not set. 15.95 (*0-399-23188-9*, Putnam) Putnam Pub Group.
***Stormy of Major Wm. Gouverneur Morris in California & Alaska.** Albert Shumate. (Illus.). 137p. 1993. 21.00 (*0-614-29851-2*) A H Clark.
Stormy Patriot: The Life of Samuel Chase. James Haw et al. LC 80-83807. (Illus.). 305p. 1980. 16.95 (*0-938420-00-3*) MD Hist.
Stormy Petrel. Mary Stewart. 1994. mass mkt. 5.99 (*0-449-22085-0*, Expression) Fawcett.
Stormy Petrel. large type ed. Mary Stewart. LC 91-41834. 295p. 1992. reprint ed. lib. bdg. 20.95 (*1-56054-327-2*) Thorndike Pr.
Stormy Petrel: The Life & Times of General Benjamin F. Butler, 1818-1893. Howard P. Nash, Jr. LC 71-81498. 335p. 1975. 35.00 (*0-8386-7383-X*) Fairleigh Dickinson.
Stormy Relationship. Margaret Mayo. 1994. 2.99 (*0-373-11652-7*) Harlequin Bks.
***Stormy Science.** Sterling Publishing Company, Inc. Staff. 1997. pap. text ed. 19.95 (*0-8069-0537-9*) Sterling.
Stormy Search for the Self: A Guide to Personal Growth Through Transformational Crisis. Christina Grof & Stanislav Grof. 288p. 14.95 (*0-87477-649-X*, Tarcher Putnam) Putnam Pub Group.
Stormy Seas. 3rd ed. Wes Oleszowksi. LC 90-86206. 1991. pap. 11.95 (*0-932212-67-0*) Avery Color.
Stormy Surrender. large type ed. Patricia Wilson. 1991. reprint ed. lib. bdg. 18.95 (*0-263-12434-7*, Pub. by Mills & Boon UK) Thorndike Pr.
Stormy, the Brave Sponge Diver. Lillian Prichard & Alexander Key. 1955. pap. 0.75 (*0-614-05558-X*) Dietz.
Stormy Voyage. Sally Wentworth. (Presents Ser.). 1993. mass mkt. 2.99 (*0-373-11572-5*, 1-11572-4) Harlequin Bks.

An Asterisk (*) at the beginning of an entry indicates that the title is appearing in BIP for the first time.

***Stormy Voyage of Father's Day: Solo Across the North Atlantic in the Smallest Sailboat Ever.** Hugo Vihlen & Joanne Kimberlin. LC 96-47272. (Illus.). 272p. (Orig.). 1997. pap. 16.95 (0-943400-91-0) Marlor Pr.

Stormy Weather. Carl Hiaasen. 352p. 1995. 24.00 (0-679-41982-9) Knopf.

Stormy Weather. Carl Hiaasen. 400p. 1996. mass mkt. 6.99 (0-446-60342-2) Warner Bks.

Stormy Weather. large type ed. Carl Hiaasen. LC 95-47627. 1996. 25.95 (1-56895-276-7) Wheeler Pub.

Stormy Weather: The Music & Lives of a Century of Jazzwomen. Linda Dahl. LC 89-12352. (Illus.). 371p. 1989. reprint ed. pap. 18.95 (0-87910-128-8) Limelight Edns.

Storrs Meeting: Proceedings of the 1988 Division of Particles & Fields of the American Physical Society. Ed. by D. G. Caldi et al. 952p. (C). 1989. pap. 48.00 (9971-5-0797-8); text ed. 166.00 (9971-5-0777-3) World Scientific Pub.

Storrs. The Storrs Family: Genealogical & Other Memoranda. C. Storrs. xv, 552p. 1992. reprint ed. pap. 84.00 (0-8328-2326-0); reprint ed. lib. bdg. 94.00 (0-8328-2325-2) Higginson Bk Co.

***Story: A Guide to Screenwriting.** Robert Mckee. 1997. 25.00 (0-06-039168-5, ReganBooks) HarpC.

Story: Kansas State Football: The Greatest Turnaround in College Football History. David Smale & Mitch Holthus. (Illus.). 176p. 1994. 36.00 (1-885758-02-2) Quality Sports.

Story: Readers & Writers of Fiction. David Bergman. 640p. (C). 1988. Instr's manual. teacher ed. write for info. (0-318-62762-0) Macmillan.

Story: Turn. Ann Charters. Date not set. pap. text ed. 31.05 (0-312-13757-5) St Martin.

Story - Start Dinosaurs. Franco Pagnucci & Susan Pagnucci. 1991. 7.99 (0-86653-998-0) Fearon Teach Aids.

Story - Start Monsters. Franco Pagnucci & Susan Pagnucci. 1991. 7.99 (0-86653-999-9) Fearon Teach Aids.

Story a Day, Vol. I: Tishrei-Cheshvan. G. Sofer. Tr. by Shaindel Weinbach from HEB. (ArtScroll Youth Ser.). (Illus.). 206p. (YA). (gr. 7-12). 1989. 15.99 (0-89906-950-9); pap. 11.99 (0-89906-951-7) Mesorah Pubns.

Story a Day, Vol. II: Kislev-Teves. G. Sofer. Tr. by Shaindel Weinbach from HEB. (ArtScroll Youth Ser.). (Illus.). 232p. (YA). (gr. 7-12). 1988. 15.99 (0-89906-952-5); pap. 11.99 (0-89906-953-3) Mesorah Pubns.

Story a Day, Vol. III: Shevat-Adar. G. Sofer. Tr. by Shaindel Weinbach from HEB. (ArtScroll Youth Ser.). (Illus.). 224p. (YA). (gr. 7-12). 1989. 15.99 (0-89906-954-1); pap. 11.99 (0-89906-955-X) Mesorah Pubns.

Story a Day, Vol. IV: Nissan-Iyar. G. Sofer. Tr. by Shaindel Weinbach from HEB. (ArtScroll Youth Ser.). (Illus.). 210p. (YA). (gr. 7-12). 1989. 15.99 (0-89906-956-8); pap. 11.99 (0-89906-957-6) Mesorah Pubns.

Story a Day, Vol. V: Sivan-Tammuz. G. Sofer. Tr. by Shaindel Weinbach from HEB. (ArtScroll Youth Ser.). (Illus.). 210p. (YA). (gr. 7-12). 1989. 15.99 (0-89906-958-4); pap. 11.99 (0-89906-959-2) Mesorah Pubns.

Story a Day, Vol. VI: Ev-Elul. G. Sofer. Tr. by Shaindel Weinbach from HEB. (ArtScroll Youth Ser.). (Illus.). 210p. (YA). (gr. 7-12). 1989. 15.99 (0-89906-960-6); pap. 11.99 (0-89906-961-4) Mesorah Pubns.

Story, A Story. Gail E. Haley. LC 69-18961. (Illus.). 36p. (J). (ps-3). 1970. lib. bdg. 17.00 (0-689-20511-2, Atheneum Bks Young) S&S Childrens.

Story, a Story. Gail E. Haley. LC 87-17412. (Illus.). 36p. (J). (ps-3). 1988. reprint ed. pap. 4.95 (0-689-71201-4, Aladdin Paperbacks) S&S Childrens.

Story about a Real Man. Boris N. Polevoi. LC 79-98870. 558p. 1970. reprint ed. text ed. 65.00 (0-8371-3993-7, PORM, Greenwood Pr) Greenwood.

Story about Cat. Mo Yan. (CHI.). pap. 9.95 (7-80005-256-7, Pub. by China Intl Bk CH) Distribks Inc.

Story about Courage. Joel Vecere. (J). 1992. lib. bdg. 22.83 (0-8114-3579-2) Raintree Steck-V.

Story about Courage. Joel Vecere. (Publish-a-Book Ser.). (J). (gr. 4-7). 1993. pap. 4.95 (0-8114-4307-8) Raintree Steck-V.

Story About Feeling. Bill Neidjie. 180p. (C). 1990. 45.00 (0-9588101-0-9, Pub. by Pascoe Pub AT) St Mut.

Story about Learning to Tell Time see Elephant's Clock

Story about Mr. Silberstein. Erland Josephson. Tr. by Roger Greenwald. 150p. 1995. 24.95 (0-8101-1277-9) Northwestern U Pr.

Story about Ping. Marjorie Flack. (Illus.). (J). (gr. k-2). 1977. pap. 4.99 (0-14-050241-6, Puffin) Puffin Bks.

Story about Ping. Marjorie Flack & Kurt Wiese. (Illus.). (J). 1993. pap. 7.99 incl. audio (0-14-095117-2) Puffin Bks.

Story about Ping. Marjorie Flack. 1989. lib. bdg. 6.95 (0-14-095038-9, Puffin) Puffin Bks.

Story about Ping. Marjorie Flack. LC 33-29356. (Illus.). (J). (ps-2). 1933. pap. 14.99 (0-670-67223-8) Viking Child Bks.

***Story & Context.** Miller. 32.50 (0-687-39644-1) Abingdon.

Story & Discourse: Narrative Structure in Fiction & Film. Seymour B. Chatman. 288p. 1978. pap. 15.95 (0-8014-9186-X) Cornell U Pr.

Story & History: Narrative Authority & Social Identity in the Eighteenth-Century French & English Novel. William Ray. 400p. 1990. pap. 24.95 (0-631-17512-1) Blackwell Pubs.

Story & It Writer. 4th ed. Ann Charters. 1994. teacher ed., pap. text ed. 5.00 (0-312-10340-9) St Martin.

Story & Its Writer: An Introduction to Short Fiction. 4th ed. Ann Charters. 1666p. 1994. pap. text ed. 29.50 (0-312-10137-6) St Martin.

Story & Its Writers: An Introduction to Short Fiction. 4th ed. Ann Charters. 960p. 1994. pap. text ed. 23.50 (0-312-11170-3) St Martin.

Story & Promise: A Brief Theology of the Gospel about Jesus. Robert W. Jenson. 208p. (C). 1989. reprint ed. pap. 14.00 (0-9623642-0-7) Sigler Pr.

Story & Situation: Narrative Seduction & the Power of Fiction. Ross Chambers. LC 83-14787. (Theory & History of Literature Ser.: No. 12). 279p. (C). 1984. pap. text ed. 14.95 (0-8166-1298-6) U of Minn Pr.

Story & Space in Renaissance Art: The Rebirth of Continuous Narrative. Lew Andrews. (Illus.). 208p. (C). 1995. text ed. 49.95 (0-521-47356-X) Cambridge U Pr.

Story & Structure. 8th ed. Laurence Perrine & Thomas R. Arp. 663p. (C). 1993. text ed. 21.50 (0-15-583792-3) HB Coll Pubs.

Story & Structure. 8th ed. Laurence Perrine. (C). 1993. teacher ed., pap. text ed. 33.75 (0-15-500300-3) HB Coll Pubs.

Story & Structure. 9th ed. Laurence Perrine. (C). 1997. pap. text ed. 28.00 (0-15-503721-8); teacher ed., pap. text ed. 28.00 (0-15-503722-6) HB Coll Pubs.

***Story As a Way of Knowing.** Kevin Bradt. LC 96-53175. 192p. (Orig.). 1997. pap. 15.95 (1-55612-906-8, LL1906) Sheed & Ward MO.

Story As a Way to God: A Guide for Storytellers. H. Maxwell Butcher. LC 91-2835. 168p. (Orig.). (C). 1991. pap. 11.95 (0-89390-201-2) Resource Pubns.

Story As Vehicle. Edie Garvie. 200p. 1989. 69.00 (1-85359-050-9, Pub. by Multilingual Matters UK); pap. 24.95 (1-85359-049-5, Pub. by Multilingual Matters UK) Taylor & Francis.

Story Atlas of the Bible. Elrose Hunter. LC 94-40789. (Illus.). (J). (gr. 5-7). 1995. lib. bdg. 15.95 (0-382-39102-0) Silver Burdett Pr.

Story Atlas of the Bible. Elrose Hunter. 64p. (J). (gr. 5-7). 1995. pap. 8.95 (0-382-39103-9) Silver Burdett Pr.

Story Behind Medjugorje. Ronald S. Bourne. Ed. by Joi Bourne. 52p. (Orig.). 1992. pap. 2.50 (0-9630569-1-3) Follow Me Comm.

Story Behind the Success Vol. 1: What You Can Learn from Pittsburgh Professionals. Rhonda J. Elfstrand. 192p. 1996. pap. text ed. 12.95 (0-9650287-0-4) Steel Pubng.

***Story Behind the Touch of the Master's Hand: The Life of Myra Brooks Welch.** Photos by Phil Grout. (Illus.). 48p. (Orig.). 1997. pap. 9.95 (0-87178-010-0) Brethren.

Story Bible Series Set. Eve B. MacMasters. 1987. pap. text ed. 59.90 (0-8361-1009-9) Herald Pr.

Story Book. Review & Herald Publishing Editors. Date not set. pap. text ed. 5.99 (0-8280-0539-7) Review & Herald.

Story Book Afghans & Toys. Val Love. (Illus.). (Orig.). 1990. pap. 10.00 (1-886828-05-9) Dovetail Desgn.

Story Book of Embellishing: Great Ideas for Quilts & Garments. Mary Stori. 1995. pap. 16.95 (0-89145-843-3) Collector Bks.

Story Book Prince. Joanne F. Oppenheim. LC 85-31745. (Illus.). 32p. (J). (ps-3). 1987. 13.00 (0-15-200590-0, Gulliver Bks) HarBrace.

Story Book Sweaters: To Knit by Hand or Machine. Val Love. (Illus.). 16p. (Orig.). 1988. pap. 10.00 (1-886828-04-0) Dovetail Desgn.

Story Book Time. Hilda L. McMullins. LC 92-45560. 64p. 1995. pap. 12.95 (0-7734-2772-4, Mellen Poetry Pr) E Mellen.

Story Books for We Can Read. Incl. Eel, Ail, Ole. Illus. by Mary W. Walter. 5.40 (0-917186-03-6); Happenings. Illus. by Mary W. Walter. 5.40 (0-917186-04-4); We Learn at Play. Illus. by Mary W. Walter. 5.40 (0-917186-05-2); Things for All Seasons. Illus. by Mary W. Walter. 5.40 (0-917186-06-0); Tales & Tails. Mary W. Walter. 5.40 (0-917186-07-9); Just Like Me. Illus. by Mary W. Walter. 5.40 (0-917186-08-7); All Around Me. Illus. by Mary W. Walter. 5.40 (0-917186-09-5); Bridging the Summer. Illus. by Mary W. Walter. 5.40 (0-917186-10-9); (J). write for info. (0-318-54272-2) McQueen.

***Story Cards: Aesop's Fables.** Raymond C. Clark. (Illus.). 32p. (Orig.). 1995. pap. text ed. 14.50 (0-86647-086-7) Pro Lingua.

***Story Cards: North American Indian Tales.** Susannah J. Clark. Ed. by Raymond C. Clark. (Illus.). 32p. (Orig.). 1995. pap. text ed. 14.50 (0-86647-083-2) Pro Lingua.

Story Cards: The Tales of Nasreddin Hodja - Pairwork Conversation Activities. Raymond C. Clark. (Illus.). 44p. 1991. pap. text ed. 14.50 (0-86647-044-1) Pro Lingua.

***Story Carnival.** Marjorie Pratt & Mary Meighen. 10.00 (0-614-30541-1) NAVH.

Story Cartoons. Walter Foster. (How to Draw & Paint Ser.). (Illus.). 32p. (Orig.). 1989. pap. 6.95 (0-929261-54-2, HT23) W Foster Pub.

Story Catcher. Mari Sandoz. LC 85-31810. (Illus.). 175p. (J). (gr. 7-10). 1986. pap. 8.95 (0-8032-9163-9, Bison Books) U of Nebr Pr.

Story Clay. Lois Murphy. (Illus.). 8p. (J). (gr. 1-8). 1990. pap. write for info. (0-9620672-0-2) Dragon Studio.

Story Cloud. Cooper Edens. LC 91-13315. (Illus.). 48p. (J). (ps-1). 1991. lib. bdg. 16.00 (0-671-74823-8, Green Tiger S&S) S&S Childrens.

***Story Dance.** Barbara Satterfield. LC 96-38688. (Illus.). 32p. (J). (gr. k-4). 1997. 14.95 (1-57749-022-3) Fairview Press.

Story Dramas: A New Literature Experience for Young Children. Sarah Jossart & Gretchen Courtney. 96p. (J). (ps-2). 1996. pap. 9.95 (0-673-36325-2, GoodYrBooks) Addson-Wesley Educ.

Story Earth: Native Voices on the Environment. Ed. by Inter Press Service Staff. LC 92-43609. 224p. (Orig.). 1993. pap. 12.95 (1-56279-035-8) Mercury Hse Inc.

Story Experience. Jane B. Wilson. LC 79-13888. 177p. 1979. 20.00 (0-8108-1224-X) Scarecrow.

Story Fest: Story Rhymes for Schools, Camps, & Storytime. Story Time Stories That Rhyme Staff. (Illus.). 1992. ring bd. 19.95 (1-56820-004-8) Story Time.

Story First: The Writer As Insider. Kit Reed. Ed. by Joseph W. Reed. 150p. 1982. 19.95 (0-13-850487-3) P-H.

Story from Widg. Maddie St. John et al. LC 90-71987. (Illus.). 64p. (Orig.). (J). (gr. k-3). 1992. pap. 6.00 (1-56002-047-4) Aegina Pr.

***Story Gifts for Children.** Kathleen M. Fry-Miller. LC 90-21989. 72p. 1992. reprint ed. pap. 25.00 (0-608-04172-6, 2064906) Bks Demand.

Story Girl. Lucy Maud Montgomery. 1996. 8.99 (0-517-14818-8) Random.

Story Girl. Lucy Maud Montgomery. 272p. (J). 1987. mass mkt. 4.99 (0-7704-2285-3) Bantam.

Story Girl. Lucy Maud Montgomery. 272p. (J). 1989. mass mkt. 3.99 (0-553-21366-0, Bantam Classics) Bantam.

Story Girl. Lucy Maud Montgomery. (YA). 1991. pap. 3.95 (0-451-52532-9, Sig Classics) NAL-Dutton.

Story Habitat: Plant & Animal Stories. Story Time Stories That Rhyme Staff. (Illus.). 40p. (Orig.). (J). (gr. 4-7). 1992. 19.95 (1-56820-014-5) Story Time.

Story Handed Down: Introducing the Dutch School. Tony Barr. 88p. (Orig.). 1995. pap. 2.00 (0-915531-45-3) OR Catholic.

Story He Left Behind Him: Paddy the Cope. Lawrence Scanlon. LC 93-42112. 256p. 1994. lib. bdg. 38.50 (0-8191-9385-2) U Pr of Amer.

Story Hour: 55 Preschool Programs for Public Libraries. Jeri Kladder. LC 94-42093. 231p. (J). 1995. lib. bdg. 38.50 (0-7864-0065-X) McFarland & Co.

Story Hour Vol. 1: A Collection for Young Readers. Ed. by David S. Pape. (Illus.). 166p. (J). (gr. 3-8). 1994. 11.95 (0-922613-64-8) Hachai Pubns.

Story Hour Vol. 2: A Collection for Young Readers. Ed. by David S. Pape. LC 94-230830. (Illus.). 160p. (J). (gr. 3-9). 1995. 11.95 (0-922613-65-6) Hachai Pubns.

Story Hour see Child Horizons

Story Hungry: Roots, Relationships, Reflections. Lawrence M. Ventline. 84p. (Orig.). 1993. pap. text ed. 4.95 (1-883520-03-7) Jeremiah Pr.

***Story I Tell Myself: A Venture in Existentialist Autobiography.** LC 96-29600. 1996. 29.95 (0-226-03732-0) U Ch Pr.

Story in a Bottle. Dan Bellm. Ed. by Edward Mycue. (Took Modern Poetry in English Ser.: No. 19). (Illus.). 28p. (Orig.). 1991. pap. 3.00 (1-879457-22-9) Norton Coker Pr.

Story in History: Writing Your Way into the American Experience. Margot F. Galt. (Illus.). 280p. (Orig.). (J). 1992. 24.95 (0-915924-38-2); pap. 15.95 (0-915924-39-0) Tchrs & Writers Coll.

***Story in the Snow: Encounters with the Sasquatch.** Lunetta Woods. LC 96-18010. 196p. 1997. pap. 12.95 (1-880090-42-2) Galde Pr.

Story Jazz: A History of Chicago Jazz Styles. Robert Wolf. 168p. 1995. pap. 11.95 (1-878781-08-1) Free River Pr.

Story Journal for Middle Grades: Literature-Based Writing, Thinking & Curriculum Integration Activities, 5 pkgs. Sally D. Sharpe. (Illus.). 240p. (Orig.). (J). (gr. 2-6). 1990. Set. pap. text ed. 16.95 (0-86530-074-7, IP 190-4) Incentive Pubns.

***Story Journey.** Boomershine. 23.75 (0-687-39662-X) Abingdon.

***Story Knife: A Father Mark Townsend Mystery.** Brad Reynolds. 256p. 1996. mass mkt. 5.50 (0-380-78400-9) Avon.

Story Land: Walt Disney. Disney, Walt, Productions Staff. (Prestige Editions Ser.). (Illus.). 320p. (J). (gr. 1-5). 1987. 12.95 (0-307-16547-7, Golden Pr) Western Pub.

Story Like the Wind. Laurens Van Der Post. LC 78-5688. 370p. 1978. reprint ed. pap. 12.00 (0-15-685261-6, Harvest Bks) HarBrace.

Story-Lives of Master Musicians. Harriette M. Brower. LC 74-167316. (Essay Index Reprint Ser.). 1977. reprint ed. 26.95 (0-8369-2338-3) Ayer.

Story Making: Using Predictable Literature to Develop Communication. Robin E. Peura & Carolyn J. DeBoer. LC 94-43564. 1995. pap. 37.00 (0-930599-33-0) Thinking Pubns.

Story Menus for Schools & Educational Locations to Duplicate & Use. Story Time Stories That Rhyme Staff. (Illus.). (J). 1992. ring bd. 29.95 (1-56820-000-5) Story Time.

Story of a Bad Boy. Thomas B. Aldrich. LC 96-1905. (Hardscrabble Classics Ser.). (Illus.). 312p. 1996. pap. 13.95 (0-87451-794-X) U Pr of New Eng.

***Story of a Bad Boy.** Thomas B. Aldrich. 20.00 (0-614-30542-X) NAVH.

Story of a Bad Boy. Thomas B. Aldrich. (Works of Thomas Bailey Aldrich). 1989. reprint ed. lib. bdg. 79.00 (0-7812-1669-9) Rprt Serv.

Story of a Bill: Legalizing Homeschooling in Pennsylvania. Howard Richman. 152p. (Orig.). 1989. pap. 6.95 (0-929446-01-1) PA Homeschoolers.

***Story of a Blue Bird.** Tomasz Bogacki. LC 97-10875. (J). 1998. write for info. (0-374-37197-0) FS&G.

Story of a Bohemian. Jan Shuster. 134p. (C). 1988. 45.00 (1-85200-019-8, Pub. by United Writers Pubns UK) St Mut.

Story of a Bohemian-American Village: A Study of Social Persistence & Change. Robert I. Kutak. LC 70-129406. (American Immigration Collection. Series 2). 1970. reprint ed. 16.95 (0-405-00559-8) Ayer.

Story of a Cancer Cure: Book I. Thomas B. Caulfield. 224p. 1983. lib. bdg. 27.95 (0-9611788-0-9) Ctr Adv Psychic Res.

Story of a Cannoneer Under Stonewall Jackson. Edward A. Moore. LC 77-146866. (Select Bibliographies Reprint Ser.). 1977. reprint ed. 24.95 (0-8369-5633-8) Ayer.

Story of a Cavalry Regiment: The Career of the Fourth Iowa Veteran Volunteers from Kansas to Georgia, 1861-1865. William F. Scott. LC 92-73159. 630p. 1992. reprint ed. 40.00 (0-9628936-3-3) Pr Camp Pope.

Story of a Civil Suit: Dominguez v. Scott's Food Stores. 2nd ed. David Crump & Jeffrey B. Berman. 129p. 1985. pap. text ed. 18.00 (0-916081-03-6) J Marshall Pub Co.

Story of a Confederate Boy in the Civil War. David E. Johnston. 1980. reprint ed. 17.95 (0-89227-044-6) Commonwealth Pr.

Story of a Country Town. Edgar W. Howe. Ed. by Sylvia E. Bowman. (Masterworks of Literature Ser.). 1962. pap. 13.95 (0-8084-0287-0) NCUP.

Story of a Country Town. E. W. Howe. (Collected Works of E. W. Howe). 1988. reprint ed. lib. bdg. 59.00 (0-7812-1286-3) Rprt Serv.

Story of a Country Town see Collected Works of E. W. Howe

Story of a Cowhorse, Gotch. Luke D. Sweetman. LC 78-116053. (Illus.). 322p. reprint ed. pap. 91.80 (0-317-28813-X, 2020334) Bks Demand.

Story of a Criminal Case: The State v. Albert Delman Greene. David Crump & William J. Mertens. 154p. (Orig.). 1984. pap. text ed. 15.00 (0-916081-00-1) J Marshall Pub Co.

Story of a Desert Knight: The Legend of Slewih Al-Atawi & Other Utaybah Heroes. Marcel Kurpershoek. LC 95-4142. (Oral Poetry & Narratives from Central Arabia Ser.: Vol. 2). 1995. 129.00 (90-04-10102-0) E J Brill.

Story of a Dolphin. Katherine S. Orr. LC 92-28656. (Illus.). 32p. (J). (gr. k-4). 1993. lib. bdg. 14.96 (0-87614-777-5, Carolrhoda) Lerner Group.

Story of a Dolphin. Katherine S. Orr. (Illus.). (J). (gr. k-4). pap. 6.95 (0-87614-951-4, Carolrhoda) Lerner Group.

***Story of a Dynamic Community: York, Pennsylvania.** Betty Peckham. 257p. Date not set. 37.50 (0-8328-6550-8) Higginson Bk Co.

Story of a Fair Greek of Yesteryear: A Translation from the French of Antoine-Francois Prevost's "L'Histoire D'Une Grecque Moderne" Antoine-Francois Prevost. Tr. by James F. Jones, Jr. from FRE. 294p. 1984. 30.00 (0-916379-08-6) Scripta.

Story of a Family: History of the Family of Gorges. Raymond Gorges. 289p. 1944. 20.00 (0-934909-08-3) Mass Hist Soc.

Story of a Family: The Home of the Little Flower. Stephane-Joseph Piat. LC 93-61562. (Illus.). 421p. 1994. pap. 18.50 (0-89555-502-6) TAN Bks Pubs.

Story of a Farm. John S. Goodall. LC 88-3398. (Illus.). 72p. (J). (gr. 4 up). 1989. lib. bdg. 14.95 (0-689-50479-9, McElderry) S&S Childrens.

Story of a Fierce Bad Rabbit. Beatrix Potter. (Original Peter Rabbit Books: No. 20). (J). 1987. pap. 5.95 (0-7232-3479-5) Warne.

Story of a Forgotten Hero. Emerson Watkins, Jr. Ed. by Thelma Jackson. 240p. 1995. 22.50 (1-885618-00-X) Oxford Hse Pubs.

Story of a Grain of Wheat. William C. Edgar. LC 72-4158. (Select Bibliographies Reprint Ser.). 1977. reprint ed. 29.95 (0-8369-6877-8) Ayer.

Story of a Great Hospital. Logan Turner. 412p. (C). 1986. 65.00 (0-901824-59-3, Pub. by Mercat Pr Bks UK) St Mut.

Story of a Hedge School Master. Eugene Watters. 1974. pap. 7.95 (0-85342-436-5) Dufour.

Story of a Labor Agitator. Joseph R. Buchanan. LC 75-148873. (Select Bibliographies Reprint Ser.). 1977. reprint ed. 29.95 (0-8369-5644-3) Ayer.

Story of a Labor Agitator. Joseph R. Buchanan. (American Biography Ser.). 460p. 1991. reprint ed. lib. bdg. 89.00 (0-7812-8050-8) Rprt Serv.

Story of a Life. Claude Hartland. LC 85-12500. (Documents Ser.). 118p. 1985. reprint ed. 12.95 (0-912516-93-3); reprint ed. pap. 7.95 (0-912516-92-5) Grey Fox.

Story of a Life: St. Therese of Lisieux. Guy Gaucher. LC 92-56744. 224p. 1993. pap. 14.00 (0-06-063096-5) Harper SF.

Story of a Lifetime. John Skinner. LC 95-90992. 1996. 18.95 (0-533-11812-3) Vantage.

Story of a Lifetime: A Keepsake of Personal Memoirs. 2nd deluxe rev. ed. Pamela Pavuk. Ed. by Stephen Pavuk. (Illus.). 384p. 1996. 39.95 (0-9643032-8-0) Triangel Pubs.

***Story of a Lifetime: A Keepsake of Personal Memoirs.** 3rd deluxe rev. ed. Pamela Pavuk & Stephen Pavuk. (Illus.). 384p. 1996. 39.95 (0-9643032-4-8, TRIP01102396) Triangel Pubs.

Story of a Main Street. John S. Goodall. LC 87-60644. (Illus.). 60p. (J). 1987. lib. bdg. 14.95 (0-689-50436-5, McElderry) S&S Childrens.

Story of a Marriage Vol. I: The Letters of Bronislaw Malinowski & Elsie Masson. Ed. by Helena Wayne. (Illus.). 224p. (C). (gr. 13). 1995. pap. 17.95 (0-415-12076-4, C0596) Routledge.

Story of a Marriage Vol. II: The Letters of Bronislaw Malinowski & Elsie Masson. Ed. by Helena Wayne. (Illus.). 272p. (C). (gr. 13). 1995. text ed. 49.95 (0-415-11759-3, C0597) Routledge.

Story of a Marriage Vol. II: The Letters of Bronislaw Malinowski & Elsie Masson. Ed. by Helena Wayne. (Illus.). 272p. (C). (gr. 13). 1995. pap. 18.95 (0-415-12077-2, C0598) Routledge.

An Asterisk (*) at the beginning of an entry indicates that the title is appearing in BIP for the first time.

Story of a Marriage Vol. II: The Letters of Branislaw Malinowski & Elsie Masson, 2 vols., Set. Ed. by Helena Wayne. (Illus.). 496p. 1995. pap. 34.95 (*0-415-12937-0*, B4966) Routledge.

Story of a Meal. Regine Schindler. (Illus.). (C). 1989. 30.00 (*0-85439-302-1*, Pub. by St Paul Pubns UK) St Mut.

Story of a Modern Woman. Ella H. Dixon. (Radical Fiction Ser.). 288p. 1990. reprint ed. lib. bdg. 25.00 (*0-929587-40-5*) I R Dee.

Story of a Musical Life. George F. Root. LC 71-174964. reprint ed. 31.50 (*0-404-07205-4*) AMS Pr.

Story of a Musical Life: An Autobiography. George F. Root. LC 70-126072. (Music Ser.). 1970. reprint ed. lib. bdg. 35.00 (*0-306-70031-X*) Da Capo.

Story of a Musical Life: An Autobiography. George F. Root. (American Biography Ser.). 256p. 1991. reprint ed. lib. bdg. 69.00 (*0-7812-8329-9*) Rprt Serv.

Story of a Mustard Seed. Gabrielle L. Caffee. (Illus.). 184p. (Orig.). 1990. pap. 10.00 (*0-685-48817-9*) Coffeetable.

Story of a Page: Thirty Years in the Public Service in the Editorial Columns of the New York World Under the Editorship of J. Pulitzer. John L. Heaton. LC 75-125698. (American Journalists Ser.). 1971. reprint ed. 23.95 (*0-405-01677-8*) Ayer.

Story of a Pathfinder. Philander Deming. LC 77-128731. (Short Story Index Reprint Ser.). 1977. 19.95 (*0-8369-3622-1*) Ayer.

Story of a Play. William Dean Howells. (Notable American Authors Ser.). 1992. reprint ed. lib. bdg. 75.00 (*0-7812-3251-1*) Rprt Serv.

Story of a Poet: Madison Cawein. Otto A. Rothert. LC 76-146871. (Select Bibliographies Reprint Ser.). 1977. reprint ed. 42.95 (*0-8369-5640-0*) Ayer.

***Story of a Regiment.** Newell Chester. 256p. 1997. pap. write for info. (*0-87839-114-2*) North Star.

Story of a Rising Race. J. J. Pipkin. LC 70-173609. (Black Heritage Library Collection). 1977. reprint ed. 38.95 (*0-8369-8901-5*) Ayer.

Story of a Shipwrecked Sailor. Gabriel Garcia Marquez. Tr. by Randolph Hogan. (International Ser.). 1989. pap. 9.00 (*0-679-72205-X*, Vin) Random.

Story of a Single Woman. Uno Chiyo. Tr. & Intro. by Rebecca Copeland. 132p. 9300. pap. 19.95 (*0-7206-0878-3*, Pub. by P Owen Ltd UK) Dufour.

***Story of a Soul.** St. Therese of Lisieux. 220p. 1996. pap. 8.00 (*0-89555-548-4*) TAN Bks Pubs.

Story of a Soul. St. Therese of Lisieux. Tr. & Intro. by Michael Day. 169p. 1991. reprint ed. mass mkt. 6.95 (*0-940147-11-4*) Source Bks CA.

Story of a Soul: The Autobiography of Saint Therese of Lisieux. 3rd ed. Therese of Lisieux. LC 96-19517. 1996. pap. 11.95 (*0-935216-58-8*) ICS Pubns.

Story of a Story Across Cultures: The Case of the "Doncella Teodor" Margaret R. Parker. (Monografias A Ser.: Vol. 161). 166p. (C). 1996. 53.00 (*1-85566-038-5*, Pub. by Tamesis Bks Ltd UK) Boydell & Brewer.

Story of a Story & Other Stories. Brander Matthews. LC 70-98585. (Short Story Index Reprint Ser.). 1977. 20.95 (*0-8369-3159-9*) Ayer.

Story of a Street. Frederick T. Hill. LC 73-78824. 1969. reprint ed. pap. 13.00 (*0-87034-038-7*) Fraser Pub Co.

Story of a Throne: Catherine Second of Russia, 2 Vols., Set. Kazimierz Waliszewski. LC 79-157358. (Select Bibliographies Reprint Ser.). 1977. reprint ed. 44.95 (*0-8369-5819-5*) Ayer.

Story of a Tlingit Community: A Problem in the Relationship Between Archeological, Ethnological & Historical Methods. Ed. by Frederica De Laguna. (Bureau of American Ethnology Bulletins Ser.). 254p. 1995. lib. bdg. 89.00 (*0-7812-4172-3*) Rprt Serv.

Story of a Tlingit Community: A Problem in the Relationship between Archeological, Ethnological, & Historical Methods. Frederica De Laguna. (Illus.). vii, 254p. 1990. reprint ed. pap. 29.00 (*1-878592-04-1*); reprint ed. lib. bdg. 49.00 (*1-878592-05-X*) Native Amer Bk Pubs.

Story of a Varied Life. W. S. Rainsford. LC 70-126249. (Select Bibliographies Reprint Ser.). (Illus.). 1977. 25.95 (*0-8369-5476-9*) Ayer.

Story of a Victorian Maid. Nigel McParr. (Orig.). 1995. pap. text ed. 5.95 (*1-56333-241-8*) Masquerade.

Story of a Whim. Grace L. Hill. (Grace Livingston Hill Ser.: Vol. 68). 1993. pap. 3.99 (*0-8423-6584-2*) Tyndale.

Story of a Whim. Grace L. Hill. 1976. reprint ed. lib. bdg. 21.95 (*0-89190-023-3*, Rivercity Pr) Amereon Ltd.

Story of a Wonder Man: Being the Autobiography of Ring Lardner. Ring Lardner, Jr. LC 75-26216. (Illus.). 151p. 1975. reprint ed. text ed. 45.00 (*0-8371-8414-2*, LAWOM, Greenwood Pr) Greenwood.

Story of a Year see Works of Henry James Jr.: Collected Works

Story of a Year, 1865. Henry James. (Collected Works of Henry James). 1990. reprint ed. The Story of a Year, 1865. lib. bdg. 75.00 (*0-7812-3331-3*, 1577) Rprt Serv.

Story of Ab: A Tale of the Time of the Cave Man. Stanley Waterloo. LC 74-16524. (Science Fiction Ser.). (Illus.). 366p. 1975. reprint ed. 29.95 (*0-405-06316-4*) Ayer.

***Story of Abraham.** Jude Winkler. (Saint Joseph Bible Story Ser.). (Illus.). 1994. pap. 1.25 (*0-89942-940-8*, 940) Catholic Bk Pub.

***Story of Acadia.** 3rd ed. George B. Dorr. 127p. 1997. reprint ed. pap. 8.95 (*0-934745-21-8*) Acadia Pub Co.

***Story of Adam.** Talat M. Okby. (Illus.). 33p. (Orig.). (J). (gr. 1-5). 1997. mass mkt. 8.99 (*1-55197-998-5*, Pub. by Comnwlth Pub CN) Partners Pubs Grp.

Story of Adams County, Nebraska see Adams County

Story of Adamsville. Agnes Riedmann. 115p. (C). 1980. pap. 11.95 (*0-534-00823-2*) Wadsworth Pub.

Story of Admiral Peary at the North Pole. Zachary Kent. LC 88-11824. (Cornerstones of Freedom Ser.). (Illus.). 32p. (J). (gr. 3-6). 1988. pap. 4.95 (*0-516-44738-6*) Childrens.

Story of Africa. A. J. Wills. LC 72-86247. 1973. 24.50 (*0-8419-0128-7*, Africana) Holmes & Meier.

Story of Agricultural Economics in the United States, 1840-1932. Henry C. Taylor & Anne H. Taylor. LC 74-10646. (Illus.). 1121p. 1974. reprint ed. text ed. 59.50 (*0-8371-7653-0*, TAAE, Greenwood Pr) Greenwood.

Story of Aircraft. Robert J. Hoare. 1983. 14.95 (*0-7136-2249-0*) Dufour.

Story of Ajax. Alva Noyes. LC 67-6837. (Studies in European Literature: No. 56). (C). 1970. lib. bdg. 60.95 (*0-8383-1109-1*) M S G Haskell Hse.

Story of Alabama. 1986. write for info. (*0-932659-02-0*) Viewpoint Pubns.

Story of Alanis Morissette. Kalen Rogers. 48p. pap. 11.95 (*0-8256-1548-8*, OP47847) Omnibus NY.

Story of Alchemy & the Beginnings of Chemistry. M. M. Muir. 208p. 1992. reprint ed. pap. 18.95 (*1-56459-019-4*) Kessinger Pub.

Story of Alchemy & the Beginnings of Chemistry. Matthew M. Muir. LC 79-8618. reprint ed. 27.50 (*0-404-18482-0*) AMS Pr.

***Story of Alexander Graham Bell, Inventor of the Telephone.** Margaret Davidson. LC 97-586. (Famous Lives Ser.). (Illus.). (J). 1997. lib. bdg. write for info. (*0-8368-1483-5*) Gareth Stevens Inc.

Story of Algiers Seventeen Eighteen to Eighteen Ninety-Six. William H. Seymour. (Illus.). 143p. 1981. reprint ed. pap. 11.95 (*0-911116-33-8*) Pelican.

***Story of Alice Paul & the National Woman's Party.** Inez H. Irwin. 512p. 1977. reprint ed. pap. 16.95 (*0-614-26224-0*) Denlingers.

Story of Allen & Wheelock Firearms. H. H. Thomas. 1991. reprint ed. 10.00 (*0-913150-73-8*) Pioneer Pr.

Story of Aloha Bear. Dick Adair. (Illus.). 24p. (J). (ps). 1986. 10.95 (*0-89610-049-9*) Island Heritage.

Story of Aloha Bear. Dick Adair. 1987. 13.95 incl. audio (*0-89610-074-X*) Island Heritage.

Story of Aluminum Poisoning. Ed. by Health Research Staff. 53p. 1994. reprint ed. spiral bd. 6.50 (*0-7873-1110-3*) Hlth Research.

Story of America. Gerraty. 1991. text ed. 63.25 (*0-03-046994-5*) HR&W Schl Div.

Story of America. Ideals Editorial Staff. (Illus.). 80p. 1992. 6.95 (*0-8249-1105-9*) Ideals.

Story of America. abr. ed. Garraty. 1991. teacher ed., text ed. 97.75 (*0-03-046997-X*) HR&W Schl Div.

Story of America. rev. ed. John A. Scott. Ed. by Elizabeth L. Newhouse. LC 92-13800. (Illus.). 324p. (YA). 1992. lib. bdg. write for info. (*0-87044-888-9*) Natl Geog.

Story of America. rev. ed. John A. Scott. Ed. by Elizabeth L. Newhouse. LC 92-13800. (Illus.). 324p. (YA). 1993. 25.00 (*0-87044-887-0*) Natl Geog.

Story of America, vol. 2. Garraty. 1992. student ed., text ed. 57.00 (*0-03-072899-1*) H Holt & Co.

***Story of America, Vol. 2.** Garraty. 1992. 97.75 (*0-03-072901-7*) HR&W Schl Div.

Story of America: (Texas), vol. 1. Garraty. 1992. teacher ed., text ed. 90.50 (*0-03-072898-3*) H Holt & Co.

Story of America: Answer Key & Workbook. 1991. pap. text ed. 3.00 (*0-03-047327-6*) HR&W Schl Div.

Story of America: Workbook. 1991. pap. text ed. 10.00 (*0-03-047328-4*) HR&W Schl Div.

Story of America: 1992, vol. 1. Garraty. 1992. teacher ed., text ed. 90.50 (*0-03-072897-5*) H Holt & Co.

Story of America: 1994. Garraty. 1994. student ed., text ed. 58.50 (*0-03-097559-X*) H Holt & Co.

Story of America Beginnings to 1877, Vol. 1. John A. Garraty. 1992. text ed. 62.00 (*0-03-072896-7*) HR&W Schl Div.

Story of American Golf. 3rd rev. ed. Herbert W. Wind. (Illus.). 591p. 1994. reprint ed. 28.00 (*0-614-14882-0*) Classics Golf.

***Story of American Methodism.** Frederick A. Norwood. pap. 22.95 (*0-687-39641-7*) Abingdon.

Story of American Toys: From the Puritans to the Present. Richard O'Brien. (Illus.). 252p. 1993. 24.98 (*0-89660-029-7*, Artabras) Abbeville Pr.

Story of America's Air Transportation. Ray Spangenburg & Diane K. Moser. (Connecting a Continent Ser.). (Illus.). 96p. (YA). (gr. 6-12). 1992. lib. bdg. 18.95 (*0-8160-2260-7*) Facts on File.

Story of America's Bridges. Ray Spangenburg & Diane K. Moser. (Connecting a Continent Ser.). (Illus.). 96p. (YA). (gr. 6-9). 1991. lib. bdg. 18.95 (*0-8160-2259-3*) Facts on File.

Story of America's Canals. Ray Spangenburg & Diane K. Moser. (Connecting a Continent Ser.). (Illus.). 96p. (YA). (gr. 6-12). 1992. bds. 18.95 (*0-8160-2256-9*) Facts on File.

Story of America's Children's Books. Bader. (J). 20.00 (*0-06-020357-9*, HarpT); lib. bdg. 19.89 (*0-06-020358-7*, HarpT) HarpC.

Story of America's Railroads. Ray Spangenburg & Diane K. Moser. (Connecting a Continent Ser.). (Illus.). 96p. (YA). (gr. 6-9). 1991. lib. bdg. 18.95 (*0-8160-2257-7*) Facts on File.

Story of America's Roads. Ray Spangenburg & Diane K. Moser. (Connecting a Continent Ser.). (Illus.). 96p. (YA). (gr. 6-9). 1991. lib. bdg. 18.95 (*0-8160-2255-0*) Facts on File.

Story of America's Tunnels. Ray Spangenburg & Diane K. Moser. (Connecting a Continent Ser.). 96p. (J). (gr. 5 up). 1990. lib. bdg. 19.00 (*0-8160-2258-5*) Facts on File.

Story of an Abused Priest. Anthony Okaiye. LC 95-70228. 76p. (Orig.). (C). 1995. pap. text ed. 14.95 (*1-882792-16-5*) Proctor Pubns.

Story of an African Famine: Gender & Famine in Twentieth Century Malawi. Megan Vaughan. (Illus.). 176p. 1987. 69.95 (*0-521-32917-5*) Cambridge U Pr.

Story of an African Farm. Olive Schreiner. Ed. by Joseph Bristow. (World's Classics Ser.). 336p. 1993. pap. 7.95 (*0-19-282885-1*) OUP.

Story of an African Farm. Olive Schreiner & Dan Jacobson. 1990. 14.50 (*0-8446-0247-7*) Peter Smith.

Story of an African Farm. Olive Schreiner. 304p. 1983. pap. 11.95 (*0-14-043184-5*, Penguin Classics) Viking Penguin.

Story of an Amana Winemaker. George Kraus. (Illus.). 232p. 1984. pap. 9.95 (*0-941016-15-3*) Penfield.

Story of an American Tragedy: Survivors' Accounts of the Sinking of the Steamship Central America. Columbus-America Discovery Group, Inc. Staff. Ed. by Judy Conrad. (Illus.). 77p. 1988. pap. write for info. (*0-9621091-0-X*) Columbus-America.

Story of an Arabian Foal. Patricia Jesseau. (Illus.). 32p. (J). (ps-8). 1985. 6.95 (*0-920806-70-8*, Pub. by Penumbra Pr CN) U of Toronto Pr.

Story of an Epoch: Swami Virajananda & His Times. Swami Shraddhananda. 298p. 1982. pap. 4.95 (*0-87481-511-8*, Pub. by Ramakrishna Math II) Vedanta Pr.

Story of an Old Farm: Or Life in New Jersey in the 18th Century: With a Genealogical Appendix. Andrew D. Mellick, Jr. 742p. 1991. reprint ed. lib. bdg. 75.00 (*0-8328-2248-5*) Higginson Bk Co.

Story of an Old Town - Glen Ellyn, IL. Ada D. Harmon. Ed. by Audrie A. Chase. (Illus.). 208p. 1993. reprint ed. lib. bdg. 29.50 (*0-8328-3215-4*) Higginson Bk Co.

Story of an Orchestra. Boyd Neel. 1988. reprint ed. lib. bdg. 49.00 (*0-7812-0773-8*) Rprt Serv.

Story of an Orchestra. Boyd Neel. LC 71-181218. 133p. 1950. reprint ed. 19.00 (*0-403-01629-0*) Scholarly.

Story of an Ordinary Woman: The Extraordinary Life of Florence Cushman Milner. Ed. by Mary M. Oliver & Edward Surovell. (Illus.). 135p. 1989. 10.00 (*0-9614344-3-0*) Historical Soc MI.

Story of an Untold Love. Paul L. Ford. (Notable American Authors Ser.). 1992. reprint ed. lib. bdg. 75.00 (*0-7812-2874-3*) Rprt Serv.

Story of Ana: La Historia de Ana. Ely P. Vasquez et al. (Illus.). 28p. (Orig.). (ENG & SPA.). (J). (gr. 3-8). 1985. pap. 3.95 (*0-932727-01-8*); lib. bdg. 8.95 (*0-932727-15-8*) Hope Pub Hse.

***Story of Analytic Philosophy: Plot & Heroes.** Biletzki & Matar. LC 97-23396. 1998. write for info. (*0-415-16251-3*) Routledge.

Story of Andre. Lew Dietz. LC 78-73269. (Illus.). 88p. (J). (gr. 2-3). 1979. pap. 10.95 (*0-89272-052-2*) Down East.

Story of Anglican Ministry. Edward Echlin. (C). 1988. 50. 00 (*0-85439-102-9*, Pub. by St Paul Pubns UK) St Mut.

Story of Anna O: The Woman Who Led Freud to Psychoanalysis. Lucy Freeman. LC 94-70015. 282p. 1994. pap. 30.00 (*1-56821-226-7*) Aronson.

Story of Anthony Coombs & His Descendants. W. C. Coombs. (Illus.). 226p. 1993. reprint ed. pap. 38.00 (*0-8328-3028-3*); reprint ed. lib. bdg. 48.00 (*0-8328-3027-5*) Higginson Bk Co.

Story of Apollonius: The King of Tyre. Ed. by Zoya Pavloskis. 10.00 (*0-87291-095-4*) Coronado Pr.

Story of Aranka Ickovic Lowy: The Ugly Duckling (Non-Fiction Autobiography with Reference to WW II in Europe) 2nd ed. Aranka I. Lowy. LC 81-90799. (Illus.). 264p. (Orig.). 1988. pap. 8.25 (*0-317-99842-0*) Lowy Pub.

Story of Architecture. Patrick J. Nuttgens. (Illus.). 288p. (C). 1983. pap. text ed. 36.95 (*0-13-850131-9*) P-H.

***Story of Architecture.** 2nd ed. Patrick J. Nuttgens. (Illus.). 352p. 1997. pap. 24.95 (*0-7148-3616-8*, Pub. by Phaidon Press UK) Chronicle Bks.

***Story of Architecture.** 2nd ed. Patrick J. Nuttgenx. (Illus.). 200p. 1997. 39.95 (*0-7148-3615-X*, Pub. by Phaidon Press UK) Chronicle Bks.

Story of Art. 14th ed. Ernest H. Gombrich. (Illus.). 528p. (C). 1985. pap. text ed. 30.95 (*0-13-850066-5*) P-H.

Story of Art. 16th ed. Ernest H. Gombrich. 688p. 1995. pap. text ed. 56.00 (*0-13-440199-9*) P-H.

Story of Art. 16th rev. ed. Ernest H. Gombrich. (Illus.). 688p. 1995. 49.95 (*0-7148-3355-X*, Pub. by Phaidon Press UK); pap. 29.95 (*0-7148-3247-2*, Pub. by Phaidon Press UK) Chronicle Bks.

***Story of Ascendeara.** Nicky Ann. Ed. by Marion Wolsey. (Working Bks.: Vol. 1.2). (YA). 1996. wbk. ed. 17.75 (*0-9638312-1-6*) LWR Pubs.

Story of Ascension Parish. Sidney A. Marchand. (Illus.). 193p. 1995. reprint ed. lib. bdg. 29.50 (*0-8328-5034-9*) Higginson Bk Co.

***Story of Aspen: The History of Aspen As Told Through the Stories of Its People.** Mary E. Hayes. (Illus.). 352p. 1996. 50.00 (*0-9655202-0-X*) Aspen Three Pub.

Story of Assisi. Lina Gordon. 1977. lib. bdg. 59.95 (*0-8490-2675-X*) Gordon Pr.

Story of Astrology. Manly P. Hall. 14.50 (*0-89314-525-4*) Philos Res.

Story of Astronomy. Lloyd Motz & Jefferson H. Weaver. (Illus.). 397p. (C). 1995. 28.95 (*0-306-45090-9*, Plenum Pr) Plenum.

Story of Astronomy. Carole Scott. LC 91-36604. (Story of Ser.). (Illus.). 32p. (J). (gr. 1-4). 1993. lib. bdg. 13.95 (*0-8167-2703-1*) Troll Communs.

Story of Astronomy. Carole Scott. LC 91-36604. (Story of Ser.). (Illus.). 32p. (J). (gr. 1-4). 1996. pap. 4.95 (*0-8167-2704-X*) Troll Communs.

Story of Astronomy in Education: From Its Beginnings until 1975. H. A. Bruck. 151p. 1984. 25.00 (*0-85224-480-0*, Pub. by Edinburgh U Pr UK) Col U Pr.

Story of Athens. H. C. Butler. 1972. 59.95 (*0-8490-1127-2*) Gordon Pr.

Story of Augusta. 2nd ed. Edward J. Cashin. (Illus.). 334p. 1991. reprint ed. 35.00 (*0-87152-452-X*) Richmond Cty Hist Soc.

Story of "Aunt Nancy", Nancy Whitney French (1825-1927) A Pioneer from New York State to Illinois in 1837. Gary E. Swinson. 48p. 1987. pap. 7.50 (*0-9629573-0-5*) G E Swinson.

Story of Avignon. (Mediaeval Towns Ser.: Vol. 17). 1974. reprint ed. pap. 58.00 (*0-8115-0859-5*) Periodicals Srv.

Story of Avis. Elizabeth S. Ward. Ed. by Elizabeth Hardwick. LC 76-51681. (Rediscovered Fiction by American Women Ser.). 1977. reprint ed. lib. bdg. 29.95 (*0-405-10058-2*) Ayer.

Story of Avis, Elizabeth Stuart Phelps. Ed. by Carol F. Kessler. 312p. (C). 1985. 40.00 (*0-8135-1098-8*); pap. text ed. 15.00 (*0-8135-1099-6*) Rutgers U Pr.

Story of B: An Adventure of the Mind & Spirit. Daniel Quinn. 368p. 1996. 22.95 (*0-553-10053-X*, Loveswept) Bantam.

***Story of B: An Adventure of the Mind & Spirit.** Daniel Quinn. 336p. 1997. reprint ed. pap. 12.95 (*0-553-37901-1*) Bantam.

Story of Babar. Jean De Brunhoff. (J). pap. 2.25 (*0-590-10235-4*) Scholastic Inc.

Story of Babar. Jean De Brunhoff. (Illus.). (J). (ps). 1966. 13.00 (*0-394-80575-5*) Random Bks Yng Read.

Story of Babar. Jean De Brunhoff. (Illus.). (J). (ps). 1967. lib. bdg. 13.99 (*0-394-90575-X*) Random Bks Yng Read.

Story of Babar the Little Elephant. Jean De Brunhoff. (Illus.). 48p. (J). (ps up). 1995. 14.99 incl. audio (*0-9642066-1-7*) MK Prods.

***Story of Babe Ruth: Baseball's Greatest Legend.** Lisa Eisenberg. LC 97-689. (Famous Lives Ser.). (J). 1997. write for info. (*0-8368-1486-X*) Gareth Stevens Inc.

Story of Baby Jesus. Alice J. Davidson. (Alice in Bibleland Storybooks). (Illus.). 32p. (J). (gr. 3 up). 1985. 5.95 (*0-8378-5072-X*) Gibson.

Story of Baby Jesus. Marina Luzi. Tr. by Daughters of St. Paul Staff from ITA. (Illus.). 64p. (J). (ps). 1995. 12.95 (*0-8198-6972-4*) Pauline Bks.

Story of Baby Moses. Alice J. Davidson. (Alice in Bibleland Storybooks). (Illus.). 32p. (J). (gr. 3 up). 1985. 5.95 (*0-8378-5071-1*) Gibson.

Story of Baby Moses. Wedeven. (J). 1997. pap. 4.99 (*0-689-81056-3*) S&S Childrens.

***Story of Barbara.** Katherine H. Fryer. LC 96-37374. 250p. 1997. 18.75 (*0-944957-68-4*) Rivercross Pub.

Story of Barbie. Kitturah B. Westenhouser. 1994. pap. 19. 95 (*0-89145-595-7*) Collector Bks.

Story of Bardoli Satyagraha. Mahadev Desai. 257p. 1983. pap. 5.00 (*0-934676-46-1*) Greenlf Bks.

Story of Baseball. rev. ed. Lawrence S. Ritter. LC 89-48952. (Illus.). 224p. (J). (gr. 5 up). 1990. 17.95 (*0-688-09056-7*); pap. 9.95 (*0-688-09057-5*) Morrow.

Story of Baseball Coloring Book. E. Lisle Reedstrom. (Illus.). (J). (gr. k-3). 1991. pap. 2.95 (*0-486-26748-2*) Dover.

Story of Basingstoke. Anne Hawker. 96p. 1987. 45.00 (*0-86368-011-9*) St Mut.

***Story of Basketball.** Dave Anderson. LC 96-46147. (J). Date not set. 16.00 (*0-688-14316-4*) Morrow.

Story of Basketball. Dave Anderson. LC 88-6842. (Illus.). 192p. (YA). (gr. 5 up). 1988. 16.00 (*0-688-06748-4*, Morrow Junior); pap. 10.95 (*0-688-06749-2*, Morrow Junior) Morrow.

Story of Beatrix Potter. Sally G. Carr & Bronwen Hall. (Classics for Children Ser.). 48p. (J). (gr. k-3). 1995. 15. 00 (*1-888287-01-2*) Calvert Sch.

Story of Beautiful Puerto Rico: By Pen & Camera. C. H. Rector. 200p. 1974. lib. bdg. 250.00 (*0-8490-1128-0*) Gordon Pr.

***Story of Beijing.** Fan Liu. 128p. (Orig.). (CHI.). 1996. pap. 7.95 (*0-9644818-4-7*) Waymont Intl.

Story of Benjamin Banneker. Flossie E. Thompson-Peters. (African-American Heritage Ser.). (Illus.). 32p. (J). (gr. 1-8). 1986. pap. 5.00 (*1-880784-07-6*) Atlas Pr.

Story of Benjamin Banneker. Flossie E. Thompson-Peters. (Illus.). 32p. (Orig.). (J). (gr. 1-6). 1986. pap. text ed. 4.70 (*1-880784-02-5*) Atlas Pr.

Story of Benjamin Franklin: Amazing American. Margaret Davidson. 96p. (J). (gr. k-6). 1988. pap. 3.50 (*0-440-40021-X*, YB BDD) BDD Bks Young Read.

Story of Benjamin O. Davis, Jr. & Colin L. Powell: Two American Generals. Katherine Applegate. LC 95-16600. (Famous Lives Ser.). (J). 1995. lib. bdg. 19.93 (*0-8368-1380-4*) Gareth Stevens Inc.

***Story of Bernadette. Emile Pouvillon. Ed. by Henri Gautier. Tr. & Prologue by Diane P. Van Dien De Coeur. (Illus.). 70p. (J). (gr. 4-12). 1997. pap. 9.95 (*1-890857-00-9*) BVD Publ.**

St. Bernard looks below through cascades of mountains & valleys to see one sight alone which does not sadden him. It is Bernadette & he visits her & her guardian angel. The animals which accompany her lend further lyricism to a story which invites musical interpretation, dance & dramatic reading. It provides an excellent tool for study at a time that angels have become sensibly apparent. Diane de Coeur finds herself most naturally carried to the capture of Emile Pouvillon's tender sensible love for Bernadette & further writing on the saints through visiting sites of sanctity in Europe after a well rounded background in advertising & journalism. Larisa Ivakina who illustrated the book carries to it a realistic yet subjective view of Bernadette. She has a masters degree in art from Kuban

S

University & her artwork has been displayed in Europe & America. The still life of water & roses which decorates the front cover in its quietude evokes the highest form of haiku symbolism. She draws on the seriousness of Bernadette in her quiet valley, the flame that ignites her & the vision that will lead her. It is the contention of Ms. de Coeur that the statement of Immaculate Conception meant that this miracle in which Mary participated was the redemption of all mankind, now evident in the world, the message to Bernadette is foretelling. BVD Publishing, P.O. Box 30208, New Orleans, LA 70190-0208, Phone/FAX: 504-943-4594. Attn: Ellie. ***Publisher Provided Annotation.***

S

Story of Berwick. Compiled by Albert et al. (Illus.). 166p. 1995. reprint ed. lib. bdg. 29.50 (*0-8328-4688-0*) Higginson Bk Co.

Story of Bible Translation. William L. Ludlow. 1990. 14.95 (*0-533-08494-6*) Vantage.

Story of Big Bend. John R. Jameson. LC 96-1212. (Illus.). 208p. (Orig.). 1996. pap. 12.95 (*0-292-74042-5*); text ed. 35.00 (*0-292-74043-3*) U of Tex Pr.

Story of Bill Clinton & Al Gore: Our Nation's Leaders. Kate McMullan. LC 95-36841. (Famous Lives Ser.). 1996. lib. bdg. 19.93 (*0-8368-1463-0*) Gareth Stevens Inc.

Story of Bing & Grondahl Christmas Plates. Pat Owen. (Illus.). 1995. ring bd. 25.00 (*0-911576-02-9*) Viking Import.

Story of Birth. Viviane A. Prot. Tr. by Vicki Bogard from FRE. LC 90-50777. (Young Discovery Library). (Illus.). 38p. (J). (gr. k-5). 1991. 5.95 (*0-944589-34-0*, 340) Young Discovery Lib.

Story of Birthright: The Alternative to Abortion. Louise Summerhill. LC 72-96117. 126p. 1973. pap. 3.95 (*0-913382-06-X*, 101-4) Marytown Pr.

Story of Blindness. Gabriel Farrell. LC 56-7212. 280p. 1956. 29.00 (*0-674-83940-4*) HUP.

Story of Boats. Gillian Hutchinson. LC 91-39010. (Story of Ser.). (Illus.). 32p. (J). (gr. 1-4). 1993. lib. bdg. 13.95 (*0-8167-2705-8*) Troll Communs.

Story of Boats. Gillian Hutchinson. LC 91-39010. (Story of Ser.). (Illus.). 32p. (J). (gr. 1-4). 1997. pap. 4.95 (*0-8167-2706-6*) Troll Communs.

Story of Booker T. Washington. Patricia McKissack & Fredrick McKissack. LC 91-15895. (Cornerstones of Freedom Ser.). (Illus.). 32p. (J). (gr. 3-6). 1991. pap. 4.95 (*0-516-44758-0*) Childrens.

Story of Boon (Verse) Helen H. Jackson. (Notable American Authors Ser.). 1992. reprint ed. lib. bdg. 75.00 (*0-7812-3349-6*) Rprt Serv.

Story of Borge. H. C. Branner. Tr. by Kristi Planck from DAN. LC 73-1593. (Library of Scandinavian Literature). 1973. lib. bdg. 29.50 (*0-8057-3359-0*) Irvington.

Story of Bread. (Ladybird Stories Ser.). (Illus.). (ARA.). (J). (gr. 3-5). 1987. 4.50 (*0-86685-226-3*) Intl Bk Ctr.

Story of Brinkerhoff Home: On the Campus of Springfield College in Illinois - Springfield, Illinois. Alice R. Lacey. LC 95-72579. (Illus.). 128p. 1996. 21.95 (*0-9622491-2-2*); pap. 12.95 (*0-9622491-3-0*) Pheasant Pr.

***Story of Britain.** Roy Strong. (Illus.). 608p. 1997. 49.95 (*0-88064-178-9*) Fromm Intl Pub.

Story of Bruges. Ernest Gilliat-Smith. 1976. lib. bdg. 59.95 (*0-8490-2676-8*) Gordon Pr.

Story of Brussels. Ernest Gilliat-Smith. (Mediaeval Towns Ser.: Vol. 25). 1974. reprint ed. pap. 46.00 (*0-8115-0867-6*) Periodicals Srv.

Story of Buddha. Jonathan Landaw. (Illus.). (J). (gr. 3-10). 1979. 7.95 (*0-89744-140-0*) Auromere.

Story of Buddhism. K. J. Saunders. 1972. 69.95 (*0-8490-1129-9*) Gordon Pr.

Story of Buddy "L" Greenberg Publishing Staff. 24p. 1991. pap. 12.95 (*0-89778-276-3*, 10-7590, Greenberg Books) Kalmbach.

Story of Burma. Fryniwyd T. Jesse. LC 78-179210. reprint ed. 31.50 (*0-404-54838-5*) AMS Pr.

Story of Bush. Music Sales Corporation Staff. 1996. pap. text ed. 11.95 (*0-8256-1549-6*) Omnibus NY.

Story of Byfield, Mass., a New England Parish. Ed. by John L. Ewell. (Illus.). 344p. 1989. reprint ed. lib. bdg. 38.00 (*0-8328-0814-8*, MA0029) Higginson Bk Co.

Story of Cairo. Stanley Lane-Poole. (Mediaeval Towns Ser.: Vol. 11). 1974. reprint ed. pap. 46.00 (*0-8115-0853-6*) Periodicals Srv.

Story of California. Stewart E. White. 1992. reprint ed. lib. bdg. 75.00 (*0-7812-5102-8*) Rprt Serv.

Story of California, Bk. 1. Bellerophon Books Staff. 1996. pap. text ed. 4.95 (*0-88388-219-1*) Bellerophon Bks.

Story of California, Bk. 2. Bellerophon Books Staff. 1996. pap. text ed. 4.95 (*0-88388-220-5*) Bellerophon Bks.

Story of California, Bk. 3. Bellerophon Books Staff. 1996. pap. text ed. 4.95 (*0-88388-215-9*) Bellerophon Bks.

Story of California, Bk. 4. Bellerophon Books Staff. 1996. pap. text ed. 4.95 (*0-88388-217-5*) Bellerophon Bks.

Story of California: Gold, the Gray Dawn, the Rose Dawn. Stewart E. White. LC 75-126679. reprint ed. 64.50 (*0-404-06936-3*) AMS Pr.

Story of Calvin Caterpillar. Jennifer Lemmon. (Illus.). 12p. (J). (ps-2). 1994. pap. 4.95 (*0-909991-82-0*) Bahai.

Story of Cambridge. C. W. Stubbs. (Mediaeval Towns Ser.: Vol. 9). 1974. reprint ed. pap. 46.00 (*0-8115-0851-X*) Periodicals Srv.

Story of Camp Chase. William H. Knauss. (Illus.). 405p. (C). 1989. reprint ed. 30.00 (*0-685-26483-1*) Advance Wordsmithing.

Story of Camp Chase: A History of the Prison & Its Cemetery Where Confederate Prisoners Are Buried, Etc. William H. Knauss. (Illus.). 440p. 1994. reprint ed. 26.00 (*0-9626034-0-6*) Generals Bks.

Story of Canterbury. G. R. Taylor. (Mediaeval Towns Ser.: Vol. 8). 1974. reprint ed. pap. 46.00 (*0-8115-0850-1*) Periodicals Srv.

Story of Canterbury. George R. Taylor. LC 78-63479. (Illus.). reprint ed. 55.00 (*0-404-16545-1*) AMS Pr.

Story of Cape Cod. Kevin Shortsleeve. Ed. by Brian F. Shortsleeve. (Illus.). 64p. (J). (gr. k-3). 1993. pap. 9.95 (*0-9622782-1-1*) Cape Cod Life Mag.

***Story of Cape Cod.** 2nd rev. ed. Kevin Shortsleeve. (Illus.). 64p. (J). (gr. k-6). 1996. pap. 9.75 (*0-9622782-4-6*) Cape Cod Life Mag.

Story of Carbon. Mark D. Uehling. (First Bks.). (Illus.). 64p. (J). (gr. 4-6). 1995. lib. bdg. 21.00 (*0-531-20212-7*) Watts.

***Story of Carpets.** Essie Sakhai. LC 96-45980. (Illus.). 180p. 1997. 24.95 (*1-55921-203-9*) Moyer Bell.

Story of Cars. rev. ed. Howard W. Kanetzke. LC 87-23231. (Read about Science Ser.). (Illus.). 48p. (J). (gr. 2-6). 1987. pap. 4.95 (*0-8114-8217-0*) Raintree Steck-V.

Story of Carshalton House. A. E. Jones. 137p. (C). 1985. pap. 29.00 (*0-907335-01-2*, Pub. by Sutton Libs & Arts) St Mut.

Story of Casas Grandes Pottery. Rick Cahill. Ed. by Carrie Carson. Tr. by Julia Gates from ENG. (Illus.). (Orig.). (SPA.). 1991. pap. 14.95 (*0-9630853-0-1*) West Imports.

Story of Catherine Booth for Young People. Mildred Duff. 1979. pap. 4.99 (*0-88019-112-0*) Schmul Pub Co.

Story of Caux. Philippe Mottu. (Illus.). 1963. 8.95 (*0-901269-03-4*) Grosvenor USA.

Story of Cedar Rapids. Janette S. Murray & Frederick G. Murray. (Illus.). 284p. 1995. reprint ed. lib. bdg. 35.00 (*0-8328-4665-1*) Higginson Bk Co.

Story of Ceylon. E. F. Ludowyk. 1986. reprint ed. 28.50 (*81-7013-020-4*, Pub. by Navrang) S Asia.

Story of Chakapas. P. G. Downes. 32p. (J). (ps-8). 1987. 7.95 (*0-920806-91-0*, Pub. by Penumbra Pr CN) U of Toronto Pr.

Story of Champagne. Nicholas Faith. LC 89-32905. (Illus.). 262p. reprint ed. pap. 74.70 (*0-7837-6685-8*, 2046301) Bks Demand.

Story of Chanukah for Children. Beverly Charette. 24p. (J). (ps-2). 1981. pap. 3.95 (*0-8249-8020-4*, Ideals Child) Hambleton-Hill.

Story of Chartres. C. Headlam. (Mediaeval Towns Ser.: Vol. 28). 1974. reprint ed. pap. 46.00 (*0-8115-0870-6*) Periodicals Srv.

***Story of Chess.** Horacio Cardo. (Illus.). 48p. (YA). (gr. 3 up). 1997. 15.95 (*0-7892-0250-6*, Abbeville Kids) Abbeville Pr.

Story of China. Don-chean Chu. 156p. 1968. pap. write for info. (*0-913973-09-2*) Inst Sino-Amer.

Story of Chinaman's Hat. Dean Howell. (Illus.). 36p. (J). (ps-4). 1990. 10.95 (*0-89610-149-5*) Island Heritage.

Story of Chinese Philosophy. Chu Chai & Winberg Chai. LC 75-17196. (Illus.). 252p. 1975. reprint ed. text ed. 35.00 (*0-8371-8289-1*, CHSC, Greenwood Pr) Greenwood.

Story of Chinese Zen. Nan Huai-Chin. LC 95-23255. 1995. 16.95 (*0-8048-3050-9*) C E Tuttle.

Story of Ch'ing. John LaCrosse. 1979. pap. 3.00 (*0-932282-46-6*) Caledonia Pr.

Story of Christ in the Ethics of Paul: An Analysis of the Function of the Hymnic Material in the Pauline Corpus. Stephen E. Fowl. (Journal for the Study of the New Testament, Supplement Ser.: Vol. 36). 235p. 56.50 (*1-85075-220-6*) CUP Services.

***Story of Christian Music.** Andrew Wilson-Dickson. 1997. 35.00 (*0-8006-2987-6*) Augsburg Fortress.

Story of Christian Origins. Martin A. Larson. LC 76-40842. 711p. 1977. 15.00 (*0-88331-090-2*) Truth Seeker.

Story of Christian Origins: The Source & Establishment of Western Religion. Martin A. Larson. LC 76-40842. 712p. 1988. reprint ed. pap. 12.50 (*0-945027-00-1*) Sparrow Hawk Pr.

Story of Christianity. Justo L. Gonzalez. LC 83-49187. (Reformation to the Present Day Ser.: Vol. II). (Illus.). 448p. (Orig.). 1985. pap. 20.00 (*0-06-063316-6*, RD 511) Harper SF.

Story of Christianity, Volume 1: The Early Church to the Reformation. Justo L. Gonzalez. LC 83-48430. (Illus.). 448p. (Orig.). 1984. pap. 20.00 (*0-06-063315-8*, RD 510) Harper SF.

***Story of Christmas.** George Brundage. (St. Joseph Board Bks.). (Illus.). 16p. (J). (gr. 1-2). 1995. bds. 2.50 (*0-89942-847-9*, 847/22) Catholic Bk Pub.

Story of Christmas. R. J. Campbell. 1977. lib. bdg. 59.95 (*0-8490-2677-6*) Gordon Pr.

***Story of Christmas.** Anne Civardi. LC 97-2917. (Illus.). (J). 1997. 14.95 (*0-8118-1841-1*) Chronicle Bks.

Story of Christmas. Mary Engelbreit. (Illus.). 32p. 1994. 4.95 (*0-8362-3088-4*) Andrews & McMeel.

Story of Christmas. Paul Fehlner. (Golden Look-Look Bks.). (Illus.). 24p. (J). (ps-3). 1989. pap. write for info. (*0-307-11710-3*) Western Pub.

Story of Christmas. Retold by Anita Ganeri. LC 94-44796. (Illus.). 32p. (J). (ps-1). 1995. 12.95 (*0-7894-0146-0*, 5-70597) DK Pub Inc.

Story of Christmas. Illus. by Norma Garris. (Happy Day Ser.). 24p. (Orig.). (J). (ps-2). 1996. pap. 1.99 (*0-7847-0556-9*, 04246) Standard Pub.

Story of Christmas. Manly P. Hall. pap. 4.95 (*0-89314-379-0*) Philos Res.

Story of Christmas. Sally Owen. (Illus.). 12p. (J). (gr. 1 up). 1994. 12.99 (*0-8423-6027-1*) Tyndale.

***Story of Christmas.** Random House Value Publishing Staff. 1997. 4.99 (*0-517-18358-7*) Random Hse Value.

Story of Christmas. Illus. by Jane Ray. LC 91-11357. 32p. (J). (ps up). 1991. pap. 15.95 (*0-525-44768-7*) Dutton Child Bks.

Story of Christmas. rev. ed. Barbara Cooney. LC 94-18687. (Illus.). 32p. (J). (gr. 2-5). 1995. 14.95 (*0-06-023433-4*); lib. bdg. 14.89 (*0-06-023434-2*) HarpC Child Bks.

Story of Christmas: Story Book Set & Advent Calendar. Ed. by Sally Kovalchick. (Illus.). 96p. (Orig.). (J). 1994. pap. 17.95 (*1-56305-547-3*, 3547) Workman Pub.

Story of Christmas for Children. Beverly Charette. LC 89-11048. (Illus.). 24p. (J). (ps-2). 1989. pap. 3.95 (*0-8249-8254-1*, Ideals Child) Hambleton-Hill.

Story of Christmas Tree Lane. Rocco Rotunno & Betsy Rotunno. (Stamptime Stories Ser.). (Illus.). 12p. (Orig.). (J). (gr. 2-6). 1993. boxed 7.00 (*1-881980-04-9*) Noteworthy.

***Story of Christopher Columbus: Admiral of the Open Sea.** Mary O. Osborne. LC 97-3937. (Famous Lives Ser.). (Illus.). (J). 1997. lib. bdg. write for info. (*0-8368-1482-7*) Gareth Stevens Inc.

Story of Christopher Columbus & Our October 12th Holiday for Kindergarten Children. Eunice Cauper. (Kindergarten Holiday Bks.). (Illus.). 16p. (Orig.). (J). (gr. k-3). 1985. pap. 3.95 (*0-9617551-0-5*) E Cauper.

Story of Church Unity: The Lambeth Conference of Anglican Bishops & the Congregational-Episcopal Approaches. Norman Smyth. 1923. 49.50 (*0-686-83788-6*) Elliots Bks.

Story of Cinema: A Complete Narrative History from the Beginnings to the Present. David Shipman. (Illus.). 1248p. 1986. pap. 19.95 (*0-312-76280-1*) St Martin.

Story of Civil Liberties in the U. S. Leon Whipple. 1973. 69.95 (*0-8490-1130-2*) Gordon Pr.

Story of Civil Liberty in the United States. L. Whipple. LC 72-107419. (Civil Liberties in American History Ser.). 1970. reprint ed. lib. bdg. 45.00 (*0-306-71879-0*) Da Capo.

Story of Coal & Iron in Alabama. Ethel Armes. LC 73-1988. (Big Business; Economic Power in a Free Society Ser.). (Illus.). 1973. reprint ed. 44.95 (*0-405-05072-0*) Ayer.

Story of Colorado, 6 units, Set. Cynthia E. Schmidt. Incl. Unit 1. Colorado - Land & Animals. 75.00 (*0-913688-50-9*); Unit 2. Prehistoric People. 75.00 (*0-913688-51-7*); Unit 3. Tribes & Trailblazers. 75.00 (*0-913688-52-5*); Unit 4. Gold Fever. 75.00 (*0-913688-53-3*); Unit 5. Early Statehood. 75.00 (*0-913688-54-1*); Unit 6. Twentieth Century Colorado. 75.00 (*0-913688-55-X*); (Illus.). 400.00 (*0-913688-56-8*) Pawnee Pub.

Story of Commodore John Barry: Father of the American Navy. Martin I. Griffin. 1977. lib. bdg. 59.95 (*0-8490-2678-4*) Gordon Pr.

Story of Communications: From Fire to Fax. George D. Leon. (Illus.). 128p. (Orig.). 1993. pap. text ed. 6.95 (*0-486-27353-9*) Dover.

Story of Corfe Castle. Emmeline Hardy. 82p. 1984. 40.00 (*0-7212-0653-0*, Pub. by Regency Press UK) St Mut.

Story of Cornwall. S. Daniell. (C). 1989. pap. 40.00 (*0-85025-309-8*, Pub. by Tor Mark Pr UK) St Mut.

Story of Covent Garden. Mary C. Borer. (Illus.). 191p. 1984. 29.95 (*0-318-23283-9*) Trans-Atl Phila.

Story of Coventry. M. Harris. (Mediaeval Towns Ser.: Vol. 6). 1974. reprint ed. pap. 46.00 (*0-8115-0848-X*) Periodicals Srv.

Story of Craig County, Oklahoma: It's People & Places, Vol. II. Ed. by Craig County Heritage Association Staff. (Illus.). 325p. 1991. 65.00 (*0-88107-181-1*) Curtis Media.

Story of Crazy Horse. Jill Wheeler. Ed. by Paul Deegan. LC 89-84913. (Famous American Indian Leaders Ser.). (Illus.). 32p. (J). (gr. 4). 1989. lib. bdg. 12.98 (*0-939179-66-0*) Abdo & Dghtrs.

Story of Creation. Alice J. Davidson. (Alice in Bibleland Storybooks). (Illus.). 32p. (J). (gr. 3 up). 1984. 5.95 (*0-8378-5066-5*) Gibson.

***Story of Creation.** Illus. by Toni Goffe. 8p. (J). (ps). 1997. bds. 7.99 (*0-7847-0629-8*, 24-03799) Standard Pub.

Story of Creation. Standard Publishing Staff. (Illus.). 10p. (J). (ps). 1991. 7.99 (*0-87403-881-2*, 03791) Standard Pub.

Story of Creation. Tyndale. (J). 1992. pap. 12.99 (*0-8423-5923-0*) Tyndale.

***Story of Creation: Genesis 1-2.** (Arch Bks.). (J). (gr. k-4). 1996. 1.99 (*0-570-07523-8*, 59-1496) Concordia.

Story of Creation: Its Origin & Its Interpretation in Philosophy & the Fourth Gospel. Calum C. Carmichael. LC 96-6131. 144p. 1996. 24.95 (*0-8014-3261-8*) Cornell U Pr.

Story of Crofting. Douglas Willis. 180p. (C). 1996. pap. 30.00 (*0-85976-344-7*, Pub. by J Donald UK) St Mut.

Story of Crow. Pat Torres & Magdalene Williams. (C). 1990. 35.00 (*0-7316-1736-3*, Pub. by Pascoe Pub AT) St Mut.

Story of Crystal Hermitage. J. Donald Walters. LC 88-129746. (Illus.). 160p. (Orig.). 1987. pap. 9.95 (*0-916124-37-1*, CCP13) Crystal Clarity.

Story of Cupid & Psyche: As Related by Apuleius. Lucius Apuleius. Ed. by Louis C. Purser. (College Classical Ser.). cviii, 155p. (C). 1983. reprint ed. pap. text ed. 17.50 (*0-89241-111-2*); reprint ed. lib. bdg. 32.50 (*0-89241-359-X*) Caratzas.

Story of D-Day: June 6, 1944. Bruce Bliven, Jr. (Landmark Ser.: No. 94). (Illus.). (J). (gr. 6-8). 1963. lib. bdg. 8.99 (*0-394-90362-5*) Random Bks Yng Read.

Story of Dance Music. Paul Nettl. (Ballroom Dance Ser.). 1986. lib. bdg. 79.95 (*0-8490-3253-9*) Gordon Pr.

Story of Dance Music. Paul Nettl. (Ballroom Dance Ser.). 1985. lib. bdg. 79.95 (*0-87700-692-X*) Revisionist Pr.

Story of Dance Music. Paul Nettl. LC 77-88992. 370p. 1970. reprint ed. text ed. 35.00 (*0-8371-2114-0*, NEDM, Greenwood Pr) Greenwood.

Story of Daniel. (Bible Pop-Up Book Ser.). (Illus.). 12p. (J). (ps-3). Date not set. text ed. 7.95 (*1-56987-426-3*) Landoll.

Story of Daniel. (Little Landoll Bible Stories Ser.). 32p. (J). (ps-3). Date not set. text ed. 1.29 (*1-56987-369-0*) Landoll.

Story of Daniel & the Lion. Alice J. Davidson. (Alice in Bibleland Storybooks). 32p. (J). (gr. 3 up). 1986. 5.95 (*0-8378-5079-7*) Gibson.

Story of Daniel & the Lions. Patricia Pingry. (Story of... Ser.). (Illus.). 24p. (Orig.). (J). (ps-2). 1988. pap. 3.95 (*0-8249-8179-0*, Ideals Child) Hambleton-Hill.

Story of Daniel Boone. Walter Retan. (Illus.). 112p. (Orig.). (J). (gr. 2-5). 1992. pap. 3.50 (*0-440-40711-7*, YB BDD) BDD Bks Young Read.

Story of Daniel in the Lion's Den. Wedeven. (J). 1997. pap. 4.99 (*0-689-81058-X*) S&S Childrens.

Story of Daniel the Prophet. Stephen N. Haskell. LC 95-61929. (Illus.). 359p. (Orig.). 1993. per. 11.95 (*0-945383-60-6*) Teach Servs.

Story of Danny Three Times. Leibel Estrin. (Illus.). 32p. (J). (ps-1). 1989. 8.95 (*0-922613-10-9*); pap. 6.95 (*0-922613-11-7*) Hachai Pubns.

Story of Daphnis & Chloe. Longus. Ed. by W. R. Connor. LC 78-18586. (Greek Texts & Commentaries Ser.). (Illus.). 1979. reprint ed. lib. bdg. 19.00 (*0-405-11428-1*) Ayer.

Story of Darlington School. J. Daniel Hanks, Sr. 224p. 1991. 24.95 (*0-8187-0140-4*) Harlo Press.

***Story of David.** Petersham. (J). Date not set. mass mkt. 5.99 (*0-689-81400-3*) S&S Childrens.

***Story of David: How We Created a Family Through Open Adoption.** Dion Howells. 1997. 23.95 (*0-385-31886-3*) Doubleday.

Story of David & Goliath. Alice J. Davidson. (Alice in Bibleland Storybooks). (Illus.). 32p. (J). (gr. 3 up). 1985. 5.95 (*0-8378-5070-3*) Gibson.

Story of David & Goliath. Wedeven. (J). 1997. pap. 4.99 (*0-689-81057-1*) S&S Childrens.

Story of David & the Slingshot. Patricia Pingry. (Story of... Ser.). 24p. (J). (ps-2). 1988. pap. 3.95 (*0-8249-8180-4*, Ideals Child) Hambleton-Hill.

Story of David Grayson. Frank P. Rand. 160p. 1963. 9.95 (*0-686-31118-3*) Jones Lib.

Story of David Paint With Water. (Little Lamb Mini Activity Bks.). (Illus.). (J). 1995. pap. 1.49 (*0-7847-0368-X*, 01508) Standard Pub.

***Story of Davy Crockett, Frontier Hero.** Walter Retan. LC 97-3938. (Famous Lives Ser.). (Illus.). (J). 1997. lib. bdg. write for info. (*0-8368-1485-1*) Gareth Stevens Inc.

Story of Dentistry. Kenneth Wilson. 88p. 1986. pap. 30.00 (*0-7223-1989-4*, Pub. by A H S Ltd UK) St Mut.

Story of Detroit. George B. Catlin. (Illus.). 764p. 1998. reprint ed. lib. bdg. 35.00 (*0-7808-0251-9*) Omnigraphics Inc.

Story of Digby & Marie. Robert Shure. 104p. 1997. 16.95 (*0-312-15011-3*) St Martin.

Story of Dinosaurs. David Eastman. LC 81-11363. (J). 1997. pap. 2.95 (*0-89375-649-0*) Troll Communs.

Story of Dinosaurs. Steve Parker. LC 91-39007. (Story of Ser.). (Illus.). 32p. (J). (gr. 1-4). 1993. lib. bdg. 12.50 (*0-8167-2707-4*) Troll Communs.

Story of Dinosaurs. Steve Parker. LC 91-39007. (Story of Ser.). (Illus.). 32p. (J). (gr. 1-4). 1997. pap. 3.95 (*0-8167-2708-2*) Troll Communs.

Story of Discipleship: Christ, Humanity, & Church in Narrative Perspective. Elizabeth Barnes. 160p. (Orig.). 1995. pap. 14.95 (*0-687-39657-3*) Abingdon.

***Story of Doctor Dolittle.** Hugh Lofting. LC 96-51193. (Books of Wonder). (J). 1997. 20.00 (*0-688-14001-7*) Morrow.

***Story of Doctor Dolittle.** unabridged ed. Hugh Lofting. LC 96-51564. (Illus.). 96p. (J). 1996. reprint ed. pap. text ed. 2.00 (*0-486-29350-5*) Dover.

Story of Doctor Doolittle. Hugh Lofting. (Illus.). 128p. (J). 1997. pap. 3.99 (*0-440-41233-1*, YB BDD) BDD Bks Young Read.

Story of Don Miff. Viginius Dabney. (Notable American Authors Ser.). 1992. reprint ed. lib. bdg. 75.00 (*0-7812-2601-5*) Rprt Serv.

Story of Dona Gracia Mendes. Bea Stadtler. LC 70-83166. (Illus.). (J). (gr. 6-9). 1969. 4.50 (*0-8381-0734-6*) USCJE.

Story of Dorothy Jordan. Clare A. Jerrold. LC 70-82555. (Illus.). 429p. 1972. 26.95 (*0-405-08672-5*, Pub. by Blom Pubns UK) Ayer.

Story of Dr. Dolittle. Hugh Lofting. 176p. (J). (gr. 4-7). 1969. pap. 3.99 (*0-440-48307-7*) Dell.

Story of Dublin. (Mediaeval Towns Ser.: Vol. 32). 1974. reprint ed. 55.00 (*0-8115-0874-9*) Periodicals Srv.

Story of Dundas: Being a History of the County of Dundas, 1784 to 1904. J. Smyth Carter. (Illus.). 462p. 1996. reprint ed. lib. bdg. 49.00 (*0-8328-5154-X*) Higginson Bk Co.

Story of Dwight W. Morrow. M. M. McBride. 1972. 59.95 (*0-8490-1131-0*) Gordon Pr.

Story of E. B. White. Cynthia Rylant. (J). 1996. 16.00 (*0-689-80152-1*, S&S Bks Young Read) S&S Childrens.

***Story of Easter.** (Saint Joseph Picture Bks.). (Illus.). 1994. pap. 1.25 (*0-89942-492-9*, 492-00) Catholic Bk Pub.

***Story of Easter.** George Brundage. (St. Joseph Board Bks.). (Illus.). 16p. (J). (gr. 1-2). 1995. bds. 2.50 (*0-89942-848-7*, 848/22) Catholic Bk Pub.

***Story of Easter.** Robin Currier. (Eyewitness Animals Ser.). 64p. (J). (ps-2). 1997. 12.99 (*0-7847-0593-3*, 03813) Standard Pub.

An Asterisk (*) at the beginning of an entry indicates that the title is appearing in BIP for the first time.

Story of Easter. Alice J. Davidson. (Alice in Bibleland Storybooks). (Illus.). 32p. (J). (gr. 3 up). 1988. 5.95 (*0-8378-1839-7*) Gibson.

Story of Easter. Aileen Fisher. LC 96-17395. (Illus.). 32p. (J). (gr. 2-5). 1997. 14.95 (*0-06-027296-1*) HarpC Child Bks.

***Story of Easter.** Standard Publishing Staff. (Happy Day Coloring Bks.). 12p. 1996. pap. 0.99 (*0-7847-0438-4*, 22208) Standard Pub.

Story of Easter. Retold by Bill Yenne. LC 93-37475. (Children's Bible Classics Ser.). (Illus.). (J). 1993. 4.99 (*0-7852-8332-3*) Nelson.

Story of Easter. Retold by Bill Yenne. LC 93-37475. (Children's Bible Classics Ser.). (Illus.). (J). 1994. mass mkt. 4.99 (*0-7852-8328-5*) Nelson.

***Story of Easter: Eyewitness Animals.** Standard Publishing Staff. (J). 1997. pap. text ed. 1.49 (*0-7847-0604-2*) Standard Pub.

Story of Easter for Children. Beverly Charette. (Illus.). 24p. (Orig.). (J). (ps-3). 1987. pap. 3.95 (*0-8249-8183-9*, Ideals Child) Hambleton-Hill.

***Story of Edgar Cayce: There Is a River.** Thomas Sugrue. 376p. 1997. mass mkt. 6.95 (*0-87604-375-9*, 2002) ARE Pr.

Story of Edinburgh. William H. Smeaton. (Mediaeval Towns Ser.: Vol. 21). 1974. reprint ed. pap. 58.00 (*0-8115-0863-3*) Periodicals Srv.

Story of Effective Statesmanship see Strategy of St. Paul

Story of Elderhostel. Eugene S. Mills. LC 92-53864. (Illus.). 216p. 1993. pap. 14.95 (*0-87451-600-5*); text ed. 25.00 (*0-87451-599-8*) U Pr of New Eng.

Story of Electricity: With Twenty Easy-to-Perform Experiments. George D. Leon. (Illus.). 112p. 1988. reprint ed. pap. 4.95 (*0-486-25581-6*) Dover.

Story of Elijah. Rhonda Colburn. (Story of...Ser.). (Illus.). 24p. (J). (ps-2). 1990. pap. 3.95 (*0-8249-8419-6*, Ideals Child) Hambleton-Hill.

Story of Elizabethan Drama. George B. Harrison. (BCL1-PR English Literature Ser.). 134p. 1992. reprint ed. lib. bdg. 69.00 (*0-7812-7104-5*) Rprt Serv.

Story of England. Christopher Hibbert. (Illus.). 224p. (C). 1993. reprint ed. pap. 14.95 (*0-7148-2652-9*, Pub. by Phaidon Press UK) Chronicle Bks.

Story of England by Robert Manning of Brunne, from Manuscripts at Lambeth Palace & the Inner Temple, 2 vols., Set. Ed. by Frederick Furnivall. (Rolls Ser.: No. 87). 1974. reprint ed. 140.00 (*0-8115-1160-X*) Periodicals Srv.

Story of English. rev. ed. Robert McCrum et al. (Illus.). 384p. 1993. pap. 22.95 (*0-14-015405-1*, Penguin Bks) Viking Penguin.

Story of Ernie Pyle. Lee G. Miller. LC 78-100169. 439p. 1970. reprint ed. text ed. 65.00 (*0-8371-3743-8*, MIEP, Greenwood Pr) Greenwood.

Story of Esther. Alice J. Davidson. (Alice in Bibleland Storybooks). (Illus.). (J). (gr. 3 up). 1989. 5.95 (*0-8378-1851-6*) Gibson.

Story of Esther. Marilyn Hickey. 32p. (Orig.). pap. 1.00 (*1-56441-168-0*) M Hickey Min.

Story of Esther. Patricia Pingry. (Story of...Ser.). (Illus.). 24p. (J). (ps-2). 1990. pap. 3.95 (*0-8249-8420-X*, Ideals Child) Hambleton-Hill.

Story of Euclid. F. W. Frankland. 1972. 59.95 (*0-8490-1132-9*) Gordon Pr.

Story of Eugene. 2nd ed. Lucia W. Moore et al. (Illus.). 344p. 1995. reprint ed. pap. 12.95 (*0-9648434-0-4*) Lane Cnty Hist.

Story of Exodus. Alice J. Davidson. (Alice in Bibleland Storybooks). (Illus.). (J). (gr. 3 up). 1989. 5.95 (*0-8378-1849-4*) Gibson.

Story of Extinct Civilizations of the West. Robert Anderson. 1972. 59.95 (*0-8490-1133-7*) Gordon Pr.

Story of Fabian Socialism. Margaret Cole. LC 61-16949. (Illus.). xv, 366p. 1961. reprint ed. 52.50 (*0-8047-0091-5*); reprint ed. pap. 18.95 (*0-8047-0092-3*) Stanford U Pr.

Story of Fanny Burney. Muriel A. Masefield. LC 73-21629. (English Biography Ser.: No. 31). 1974. lib. bdg. 51.95 (*0-8383-1786-3*) M S G Haskell Hse.

Story of Ferdinand. (Illus.). (J). 1977. pap. 4.99 (*0-14-050234-3*, Puffin) Puffin Bks.

Story of Ferdinand. (Story Tapes Ser.). (Illus.). (J). (ps-3). 1988. pap. 6.95 (*0-14-095071-0*, Puffin) Puffin Bks.

Story of Ferdinand. Munro Leaf. (Illus.). (J). (ps-3). 1988. pap. 9.95 (*0-14-095075-3*, Puffin); 9.95 (*0-318-37105-7*, Puffin); audio 6.95 (*0-318-37106-5*, Puffin) Puffin Bks.

Story of Ferdinand. Munro Leaf. (Illus.). (J). 1993. pap. 7.99 incl. audio (*0-14-095115-6*, Puffin) Puffin Bks.

Story of Ferdinand. Munro Leaf. LC 36-19452. (Illus.). (J). (gr. k-3). 1936. pap. 14.99 (*0-670-67424-9*) Viking Child Bks.

Story of Ferdinand. Munro Leaf. (Illus.). 72p. 1989. reprint ed. lib. bdg. 17.95 (*0-89966-590-X*) Buccaneer Bks.

Story of Ferdinand: A Study Guide. Garrett Christopher. Ed. by Joyce Friedland & Rikki Kessler. (Little Novel-Ties Ser.). (J). (gr. k-3). 1991. pap. text ed. 14.95 (*0-88122-594-0*) Lrn Links.

Story of Firearm Ignition. Edsall James. 1974. 4.50 (*0-913150-27-4*) Pioneer Pr.

Story of Flight. Lizzy Pearl. LC 91-33412. (Story of Ser.). (Illus.). 32p. (J). (gr. 1-4). 1993. lib. bdg. 13.95 (*0-8167-2709-0*) Troll Communs.

Story of Flight. Lizzy Pearl. LC 91-33412. (Story of Ser.). (Illus.). 32p. (J). (gr. 1-4). 1997. pap. 4.95 (*0-8167-2710-4*) Troll Communs.

Story of Flight: Early Flying Machines, Balloons, Blimps, Gliders, Warplanes, & Jets. Scholastic Staff. (Voyages of Discovery Ser.). (Illus.). 45p. (J). (gr. 4-6). 1995. 19.95 (*0-590-47643-2*, Scholastic Voy Discov) Scholastic Inc.

Story of Florence. E. Gardner. 1976. lib. bdg. 59.95 (*0-8490-2679-2*) Gordon Pr.

Story of Folk Music. Melvin Berger. LC 76-18159. (Illus.). (J). (gr. 6 up). 1976. lib. bdg. 27.95 (*0-87599-215-3*) S G Phillips.

***Story of Football.** LC 96-46539. (J). Date not set. 16.00 (*0-688-14314-8*) Morrow.

Story of Football. Dave Anderson. LC 85-7195. (Illus.). 192p. (J). (gr. 5 up). 1985. 16.00 (*0-688-05634-2*); pap. 8.95 (*0-688-05635-0*) Morrow.

***Story of Football.** Dave Anderson. (J). 1999. pap. 9.95 (*0-688-14315-6*) Morrow.

Story of Fort Myers. Karl H. Grismer. LC 82-80620. (Illus.). 360p. 1982. reprint ed. pap. 17.95 (*0-87208-226-1*) Shoeless Pub.

Story of Fowey. John Keast. (C). 1989. 60.00 (*1-85022-035-2*, Pub. by Dyllansow Truran UK) St Mut.

Story of Frankie Frown. S. Myron Wright & Chris M. Wright. LC 94-90557. (Illus.). 32p. (Orig.). (J). (gr. k-6). 1994. pap. 5.95 (*0-9636377-1-1*) S L Wright.

Story of Frederick Douglass: Voice of Freedom. Eric Weiner. 112p. (J). (ps-3). 1992. pap. 3.25 (*0-440-40560-2*) Dell.

Story of Frederick Douglass, Voice of Freedom. Eric Weiner. LC 95-36844. (Famous Lives Ser.). (Illus.). 112p. (J). (gr. 3 up). lib. bdg. 19.93 (*0-8368-1464-9*) Gareth Stevens Inc.

Story of Free Enterprise. Joel R. Belknap. 1963. 9.95 (*0-8159-6825-6*) Devin.

Story of Freemasonry. W. G. Sibley. 114p. 1968. reprint ed. spiral bd. 5.50 (*0-7873-0791-2*) Hlth Research.

Story of Freemasonry (1913) W. G. Sibley. 114p. 1996. pap. 15.95 (*1-56459-822-5*) Kessinger Pub.

Story of Gandhi. R. Shankar. (Illus.). (J). (gr. 3-10). 1979. 5.00 (*0-89744-166-4*) Auromere.

Story of Gannon University: Education on the Square. Robert Barcio et al. LC 85-81770. 208p. (Orig.). 1985. 10.00 (*0-936063-00-9*); pap. text ed. 5.00 (*0-685-12412-6*) Gannon U Pr.

Story of Gardening. Martin Hoyles. (C). 1993. text ed. 48.00 (*0-85172-028-5*) Westview.

Story of Gardening: A Social. Martin Hoyles. (C). 53.00 (*1-85172-028-6*, Pub. by Pluto Pr UK) LPC InBook.

Story of Gardening: A Social History. Martin Hoyles. (Illus.). 313p. (C). 1993. pap. 19.95 (*1-85172-029-4*, Pub. by Pluto Pr UK) LPC InBook.

***Story of Genesis & Exodus.** Ed. by R. Morris. (EETS Original Ser.: Vol. 7). 1996. reprint ed. 54.00 (*0-85991-801-7*, Pub. by EETS UK) Boydell & Brewer.

Story of Genesis & Exodus an Early English Song. Ed. by R. Morris. (EETS, OS Ser.: No. 7). 1974. reprint ed. 54.00 (*0-527-00006-X*) Periodicals Srv.

Story of George Washington: Quiet Hero. Joyce Milton. (Famous Lives Ser.). (Illus.). (J). 1996. lib. bdg. 19.93 (*0-8368-1469-X*) Gareth Stevens Inc.

Story of George Washington Carver. Eva Moore. 96p. (J). 1990. pap. 3.99 (*0-590-42660-5*) Scholastic Inc.

Story of Georgia & the Georgia People, 1732 to 1860. 2nd ed. George G. Smith. (Illus.). 684p. 1968. reprint ed. 30.00 (*0-685-60371-7*, 5460) Clearfield Co.

Story of Geronimo. Zachary Kent. LC 88-37005. (Cornerstones of Freedom Ser.). (Illus.). 32p. (J). (gr. 3-6). 1989. pap. 4.95 (*0-516-44743-2*) Childrens.

Story of Geronimo. Jill Wheeler. Ed. by Paul Deegan. LC 89-84911. (Famous American Indian Leaders Ser.). (Illus.). 32p. (J). (gr. 4). 1989. lib. bdg. 12.98 (*0-939179-68-7*) Abdo & Dghtrs.

Story of Gilbert & Sullivan. Isaac Goldberg. 1972. 59.95 (*0-8490-1134-5*) Gordon Pr.

Story of Giuseppe Verdi. Gabriele Baldini. Tr. by Roger Parker from ITA. LC 79-41376. 330p. 1980. 59.95 (*0-521-22911-1*); pap. text ed. 24.95 (*0-521-29712-5*) Cambridge U Pr.

Story of Glass Coloring Book. Peter F. Copeland. (Illus.). (J). (gr. k-3). 1976. pap. 2.95 (*0-486-24199-8*) Dover.

Story of God: Wesleyan Theology & Biblical Narrative. Michael Lodahl. 256p. (C). 1994. kivar 21.99 (*0-8341-1479-8*) Beacon Hill.

Story of God's People. Clarence Y. Fretz. (Christian Day School Ser.). (J). (gr. 7). 1978. teacher ed. 7.00 (*0-87813-901-X*) Christian Light.

Story of God's People. Clarence Y. Fretz. (Christian Day School Ser.). (J). (gr. 7). 1978. pap. 4.75 (*0-87813-900-1*) Christian Light.

Story of Gold. Hal Hellman. (First Bks.). (Illus.). 64p. (J). (gr. 4-6). 1996. lib. bdg. 21.00 (*0-531-20224-0*) Watts.

Story of Gold Hill Colorado: Seventy-Odd Years in the Heart of the Rockies. rev. ed. Mabel G. Montgomery & Silvia Pettem. (Illus.). 37p. 1987. reprint ed. pap. 5.95 (*0-9617799-1-8*) Book Lode.

***Story of Golf.** Dave Anderson. Date not set. write for info. (*0-688-15796-3*); pap. write for info. (*0-688-15797-1*, Beech Tree Bks) Morrow.

Story of Gosport. Leonard White. (C). 1989. 39.00 (*1-85455-005-5*, Pub. by Ensign Pubns & Print UK) St Mut.

Story of Gotama Buddha. Tr. by N. A. Jayawickrama from PLI. 141p. (Orig.). (C). 1990. pap. 13.50 (*0-86013-293-5*, Pub. by Pali Text) Wisdom MA.

Story of Green Day: Omnibus Press Presents the Story Of... Kalen Rogers. (Illus.). 56p. (Orig.). pap. 11.95 (*0-8256-1504-6*, OP 47781) Omnibus NY.

Story of Gregg Shorthand. Louis A. Leslie. 1964. text ed. 16.65 (*0-07-037223-3*) McGraw.

Story of Griselda in Iceland. Griselda. Ed. by Halldor Hermannsson. (Islandica Ser.: Vol. 7). 1974. reprint ed. pap. 25.00 (*0-527-00337-9*) Periodicals Srv.

Story of Guru Nanak. Mala Singh. (Illus.). (J). (gr. 2-9). 1979. 7.25 (*0-89744-138-9*) Auromere.

Story of Gymnastics. Ellen Jacob. (Learn-by-Coloring Ser.). (Illus.). 48p. (J). (ps-7). 1991. pap. 4.95 (*0-937180-08-4*) Variety Arts.

Story of Hansel & Gretel. Illus. by Berta Hader & Elmer Hader. LC 94-1297. (J). 1994. write for info. (*0-486-28299-6*) Dover.

Story of Hanukkah. Amy Ehrlich. (Illus.). (J). (ps up). 1989. lib. bdg. 14.89 (*0-8037-0616-2*) Dial Bks Young.

Story of Hanukkah. Amy Ehrlich. (Illus.). 32p. (J). 1994. pap. 5.99 (*0-14-055285-5*, Puff Pied Piper) Puffin Bks.

***Story of Hanukkah.** Random House Value Publishing Staff. 1997. 4.99 (*0-517-18360-9*) Random Hse Value.

Story of Hanukkah. Norma Simon. LC 96-5141. (Illus.). (J). 1997. write for info. (*0-06-027127-2*) HarpC.

Story of Hanukkah. Norma Simon. LC 96-5141. (Illus.). (J). 1997. lib. bdg. write for info. (*0-06-027128-0*) HarpC.

Story of Hanukkah. Charles Wengrov. (Shulsinger Holiday Ser.). (Illus.). (J). (gr. k-7). 1965. pap. 2.99 (*0-914080-52-0*) Shulsinger Sales.

***Story of Hanukkah.** rev. ed. Norma Simon. LC 96-5141. (Illus.). 32p. (J). (gr. 2-5). 1997. 14.95 (*0-06-027419-0*); lib. bdg. 14.89 (*0-06-027420-4*) HarpC.

Story of Hanukkah: A Lift-the-Flap Rebus Book. Lisa Rojany. (Illus.). 16p. (J). (ps-3). 1993. 12.95 (*1-56282-420-1*) Hyprn Child.

Story of Hanumanji. K. D. Bharadwaj. (C). 1989. 30.00 (*81-209-0081-2*, Pub. by Pitambar Pub II) St Mut.

Story of Hardwood Plywood. 11p. 1987. 1.50 (*0-318-23061-5*) Hardwd Ply.

Story of Harriet Beecher Stowe. Maureen Ash. LC 89-25364. (Cornerstones of Freedom Ser.). (Illus.). 32p. (J). (gr. 3-6). 1990. pap. 4.95 (*0-516-44746-7*) Childrens.

Story of Harriet Tubman. Kate McMullan. 112p. (J). 1994. pap. 3.50 (*0-440-91003-X*) Dell.

Story of Haverhill in Massachusetts: With a Chronological Record of Historical Events with Notes. Albert L. Bartlett. 550p. 1990. text ed. 35.00 (*1-878651-12-9*) HPL Pr.

Story of Hay. Geoffrey Patterson. (Illus.). 32p. (Orig.). (J). (gr. 3). 1996. pap. 9.95 (*0-85236-324-9*, Pub. by Farming Pr UK) Diamond Farm Bk.

Story of Heart Disease. T. East. (Illus.). 148p. 1958. 19.95 (*0-8464-0886-4*) Beekman Pubs.

Story of Helen Duncan. Ed. by Alan E. Crossley. (C). 1990. 50.00 (*0-7223-0840-X*, Pub. by A H S Ltd UK) St Mut.

Story of Henri Tod. William F. Buckley, Jr. LC 96-32827. 320p. 1996. reprint ed. pap. 10.95 (*1-888952-12-1*) Cumberland Hse.

***Story of Hercules.** Robert Blaisdell. LC 97-11715. (Dover Children's Thrift Classics Ser.). (Illus.). (J). 1997. pap. write for info. (*0-486-29768-3*) Dover.

Story of Hercules. Marc Cerasini. LC 97-10010. (J). 1997. pap. 3.99 (*0-679-88393-2*) Random.

Story of Hercules. Moore. LC 96-42477. (J). 1997. 14.00 (*0-689-81228-0*) S&S Childrens.

Story of Hercules. Moore. LC 96-42477. (J). 1997. pap. 3.99 (*0-689-81229-9*) S&S Childrens.

Story of Hiawatha. Jill Wheeler. Ed. by Paul Deegan. LC 89-84908. (Famous American Indian Leaders Ser.). (Illus.). 32p. (J). (gr. 4). 1989. lib. bdg. 12.98 (*0-939179-71-7*) Abdo & Dghtrs.

Story of Hillary Rodham Clinton: First Lady of the United States. Joyce Milton. 112p. (J). 1994. pap. 3.50 (*0-440-40966-7*) Dell.

Story of Hillary Rodham Clinton: First Lady of the United States. Joyce Milton. LC 95-18325. (Famous Lives Ser.). (J). 1995. lib. bdg. 19.93 (*0-8368-1381-2*) Gareth Stevens Inc.

Story of Holland. James E. Rogers. 1977. lib. bdg. 59.95 (*0-8490-2680-6*) Gordon Pr.

Story of Holly & Ivy. Rumer Godden. LC 84-25799. (Illus.). 32p. (J). (ps-5). 1985. pap. 15.99 (*0-670-80622-6*) Viking Child Bks.

Story of Holly & Ivy. Rumer Godden. (Illus.). (J). (gr. k-5). 1987. reprint ed. pap. 5.99 (*0-14-050723-X*, Puffin) Puffin Bks.

Story of Hollywoodland. Gregory Williams & George Williams. Ed. by Alexa Williams & Dino Williams. LC 92-60611. (Illus.). 45p. (Orig.). 1992. pap. text ed. 15.95 (*0-9633086-0-2*) Papavasilopoulos.

Story of Hong Kong. Barbara Thomas. (Grace A. Tanner Lecture in Human Values Ser.). 17p. 1989. 7.50 (*0-910153-06-X*) E T Woolf.

***Story of Houlton: With Supplement.** Cora M. Putnam. (Illus.). 431p. 1997. reprint ed. lib. bdg. 47.00 (*0-8328-5861-7*) Higginson Bk Co.

***Story of Houlton, from the Public Records & from the Experience of Its Founders, Their Decendants, & Associates to the Present Time (1889)** Francis Barnes. (Illus.). 129p. 1997. reprint ed. pap. 17.50 (*0-8328-5859-5*) Higginson Bk Co.

Story of Hua Guan Suo. Gail O. King. LC 89-8242. (Monograph Ser.: No. 23). 279p. 1989. pap. 10.00 (*0-939252-20-1*) ASU Ctr Asian.

Story of Human Error. Ed. by Joseph Jastrow. LC 67-30219. (Essay Index Reprint Ser.). 1977. 21.95 (*0-8369-0568-7*) Ayer.

Story of Human Evolution. Geoffrey Barborka. 1979. 7.95 (*0-8356-7550-5*) Theos Pub Hse.

Story of Hydrogen. Mark D. Uehling. (First Bks.). (Illus.). 64p. (J). (gr. 4-6). 1995. lib. bdg. 21.00 (*0-531-20213-5*) Watts.

Story of Hymns & Tunes. Hezekiah Butterworth. 1988. reprint ed. lib. bdg. 89.00 (*0-685-55955-6*) Rprt Serv.

Story of Hymns & Tunes. Hezekiah Butterworth. 1981. reprint ed. lib. bdg. 95.00 (*0-403-00107-2*) Scholarly.

***Story of I. H. Schlezinger, Inc.** Edward Schlezinger. (Illus.). 24p. 1997. 20.00 (*0-929690-35-4*) Herit Pubs AZ.

Story of Idaho: Centennial Edition. Virgil M. Young. LC 89-36899. (Illus.). 304p. (J). (ps-4). 1990. teacher ed., spiral bd. 45.95 (*0-89301-159-2*) U of Idaho Pr.

Story of Idaho: Centennial Edition. 4th ed. Virgil M. Young. LC 89-36899. (Illus.). 304p. (J). (ps-4). 1990. text ed. 29.95 (*0-89301-131-2*) U of Idaho Pr.

Story of Illinois. 3rd ed. Theodore C. Pease. LC 65-17299. 383p. reprint ed. pap. 109.20 (*0-685-15637-0*, 2026738) Bks Demand.

Story of Illinois: Indian & Pioneer. rev. ed. Virginia S. Eifert. (Story of Illinois Ser.: No. 1). (Illus.). 24p. (J). (ps-12). 1979. pap. 1.00 (*0-89792-039-2*) Ill St Museum.

Story of Indian Music: Its Growth & Synthesis. O. Gosvami. 1988. reprint ed. lib. bdg. 79.00 (*0-7812-0761-4*) Rprt Serv.

Story of Indian Music: Its Growth & Synthesis. O. Gosvami. LC 79-181165. 332p. 1961. reprint ed. 75.00 (*0-403-01567-7*) Scholarly.

Story of Innovation: The Alexian Village Health Center, Milwaukee. Mark A. Proffitt & Chen-Jui Yang. (Illus.). xi, 75p. (C). 1995. 15.00 (*0-938744-86-0*, R94-5) U of Wis Ctr Arch-Urban.

Story of Instructional Excellence: Say "Yes" For Learning! Don Stewart. (Chance for Instructional Excellence Ser.: Bk. 5). (Illus.). 304p. (Orig.). 1988. 14.95 (*0-913448-22-2*); pap. 11.95 (*0-913448-23-0*) SLATE Servs.

Story of Integration: A New Interpretation of Princely States in India. Vanaja Rangaswami. 1982. 34.00 (*0-8364-0876-4*, Pub. by Manohar II) S Asia.

Story of Intermountain Health Care. Tom Vitelli. LC 95-76430. (Illus.). 365p. 1995. 25.00 (*0-9646476-0-5*); pap. 18.00 (*0-9646476-1-3*) Intermtn Hlth Care.

Story of Inyo. Willie A. Chalfant. 1992. reprint ed. lib. bdg. 75.00 (*0-7812-5011-0*) Rprt Serv.

Story of Inyo. Willie A. Chalfant. LC 33-19367. 1975. reprint ed. pap. 18.95 (*0-912494-35-2*) Commun Print.

Story of Ireland's National Theatre. Dawson Byrne. LC 70-119093. (Studies in Drama: No. 39). 1970. reprint ed. lib. bdg. 75.00 (*0-8383-1089-3*) M S G Haskell Hse.

***Story of Iron.** Karen Fitzgerald. LC 96-31541. (First Bk.). (J). 1997. lib. bdg. 21.00 (*0-531-20270-4*) Watts.

Story of Irving Berlin. Alexander Woollcott. LC 81-12535. (Music Ser.). (Illus.). 237p. 1982. reprint ed. lib. bdg. 32.50 (*0-306-76145-9*) Da Capo.

***Story of Isaac & Jacob.** Jude Winkler. (Saint Joseph Bible Story Ser.). (Illus.). 1994. pap. 1.25 (*0-89942-941-6*, 941) Catholic Bk Pub.

Story of Isaac & Rebeckah. Alice J. Davidson. (Alice in Bibleland Storybooks). (Illus.). (J). (gr. 3 up). 1989. 5.95 (*0-8378-1852-4*) Gibson.

***Story of Isaiah Shembe: History & Traditions Centered on Ekuphakameni & Mount Nhlangakazi.** Ed. by Irving Hexham & Gerhardus C. Oosthuizen. Tr. by Hans-Jurgen Becken. LC 96-48564. (Sacred History & Traditions of the Amanazaretha Ser.: Vol. 1). 280p. 1997. text ed. 89.95 (*0-7734-8775-1*) E Mellen.

***Story of Isaiah Shembe: History & Traditions Centered on Ekuphakameni & Mount Nhlangakazi.** Gerhardus C. Oosthuizen & Irving Hexham. LC 96-48564. (Sacred History & Traditions of the Amanazaretha Ser.). 1997. write for info. (*0-7734-8773-5*) E Mellen.

Story of Islamic Culture. A. Rauf. 1981. 3.00 (*0-933511-65-5*) Kazi Pubns.

Story of Israel in Coins. Jean Gould & Maurice Gould. 1978. pap. 2.00 (*0-87980-150-6*) Wilshire.

Story of Israel in Stamps. Maxim Shamir & Gabriel Shamir. 1975. pap. 1.00 (*0-87980-151-4*) Wilshire.

***Story of Jackie Robinson.** Barry Denenberg. (Stealing Home Ser.). 1997. pap. 3.99 (*0-590-04553-9*) Scholastic Inc.

Story of Jackie Robinson: Bravest Man in Baseball. Margaret Davidson. 96p. (Orig.). (J). (gr. k-6). 1988. pap. 3.50 (*0-440-40019-8*, YB BDD) BDD Bks Young Read.

Story of Jackie Robinson, Bravest Man in Baseball. Margaret Davidson. (Famous Lives Ser.). (Illus.). (J). 1996. lib. bdg. 19.93 (*0-8368-1470-3*) Gareth Stevens Inc.

Story of Jane: The Legendary Underground Feminist Abortion Service. Laura Kaplan. LC 95-30832. 336p. 1996. 25.00 (*0-679-42012-6*) Pantheon.

***Story of Jane: The Legendary Underground Feminist Abortion Service.** Laura Kaplan. LC 96-39768. 1997. pap. 14.95 (*0-226-42421-9*) U Ch Pr.

Story of Jazz. Rex Harris. Ed. by Thomas K. Scherman. LC 79-29696. (Little Music Library). 280p. 1980. reprint ed. text ed. 59.75 (*0-313-22350-5*, HASJ, Greenwood Pr) Greenwood.

Story of Jazz. Marshall W. Stearns. (Illus.). 380p. 1970. reprint ed. pap. 13.95 (*0-19-501269-0*) OUP.

***Story of Jazz: Bop & Beyond.** Franck Bergerot & Arnaud Merlin. Tr. by Marjolijn De Jager. (Discoveries Ser.). (Illus.). 160p. 1993. pap. 12.95 (*0-8109-2876-0*) Abrams.

Story of Jean Baptiste Du Sable. Robert Miller. (Illus.). 32p. (J). (gr. 4-8). 1994. pap. 12.95 (*0-382-24397-8*) Silver Burdett Pr.

Story of Jean Baptiste Du Sable. Robert H. Miller. (Stories of the Forgotten West Ser.). (Illus.). 32p. (J). (gr. k-3). 1994. 12.95 (*0-382-24402-8*); lib. bdg. 14.95 (*0-382-24392-7*) Silver Burdett Pr.

Story of Jean Baptiste DuSable: Father of Chicago. Flossie E. Thompson-Peters. (African-American Heritage Ser.). (Illus.). 32p. (Orig.). (J). (gr. 3-9). 1986. pap. 5.00 (*1-880784-03-3*) Atlas Pr.

Story of Jerusalem. C. M. Watson. (Mediaeval Towns Ser.: Vol. 26). 1974. reprint ed. 55.00 (*0-8115-0868-4*) Periodicals Srv.

Story of Jesus. (Little Landoll Bible Stories Ser.). 32p. (J). (ps-3). Date not set. text ed. 1.29 (*1-56987-368-2*) Landoll.

S

***Story of Jesus.** Lawrence G. Lovasik. (Illus.). (J). 1978. 4.95 (0-89942-535-6, 535/22) Catholic Bk Pub.

Story of Jesus. Mary McMillan. (Color, Cut & Paste Ser.). 48p. (J). (ps-1). 1988. 7.95 (0-86653-454-7, SS1804, Shining Star Pubns) Good Apple.

***Story of Jesus: Photographed As If You Were There.** Henry Wansbrough. (Illus.). (J). 1997. 9.95 (0-7641-5048-0) Barron.

Story of Jesus see Clothed with the Sun: The Mystery-Tale of Jesus the Avatara

Story of Jesus see Historia de Jesus

Story of Jesus & His Disciples. Alice J. Davidson. (Alice in Bibleland Storybooks). (Illus.). (J). (gr. 3 up). 1989. 5.95 (0-8378-1860-5) Gibson.

Story of Jesus Pop-Up Book. (Pop-Up Bks.). (Illus.). (J). (ps-1). 1.98 (0-517-43888-7) Random Hse Value.

Story of Jesus the Messiah: Acts & Letters. Julian G. Anderson. (New Testament Workbook Ser.). (Illus.). (gr. 7-12). 1979. pap. text ed. 4.95 (0-9602128-3-3) Anderson Bks.

Story of Jesus the Messiah, Four Gospels. Julian G. Anderson. LC 76-52054. (Life of Christ Workbook Ser.). (Illus.). (gr. 6-12). 1977. pap. 4.95 (0-9602128-1-7) Anderson Bks.

Story of Jesus the Messiah, Old Testament. Julian G. Anderson. (Old Testament Workbook Ser.). (Illus.). (gr. 6-12). 1977. pap. 4.95 (0-9602128-2-5) Anderson Bks.

Story of Jewish Philosophy. Joseph L. Blau. 11.95 (0-87068-174-5) Ktav.

***Story of Job.** Jessie Penn-Lewis. 240p. 1996. pap. 7.95 (0-87508-736-1, 736) Chr Lit.

Story of Job's Beginning: A Literary Analysis. Meir Weiss. 84p. (C). 1983. text ed. 12.00 (965-223-438-9, Pub. by Magnes Press IS) Eisenbrauns.

Story of Johann: The Boy Who Longed to Come to Amerika. Mela M. Lindsay. LC 90-85324. (Illus.). 190p. (YA). 1991. 14.50 (0-914222-18-X) Am Hist Soc Ger.

Story of John Fryxell. Fritiof M. Fryxell. LC 90-82055. 58p. 1990. pap. 10.00 (0-910184-38-0) Augustana.

Story of John Hope. Ridgely Torrence. LC 69-18568. (American Negro: His History & Literature. Series 3). 1970. reprint ed. 23.95 (0-405-01939-4) Ayer.

Story of John Wesley for Young People. Marianne Kirlew. pap. 5.99 (0-88019-158-9) Schmul Pub Co.

Story of John Wesley's Sisters: or Seven Sisters in Search of Love. Frederick E. Maser. LC 88-81533. (Illus.). 128p. (Orig.). 1988. 15.95 (0-914960-89-X); pap. 12.95 (0-914960-68-7) Academy Bks.

Story of Johnny Appleseed. Aliki. LC 88-3145. (J). (ps-3). 1971. pap. 5.95 (0-671-66746-7, S&S Bks Young Read) S&S Childrens.

Story of Jonah. LC 93-24837. (Children's Bible Classics Ser.). (J). 1993. mass mkt. 4.99 (0-8407-4909-0) Nelson.

Story of Jonah. (Bible Pop-Up Book Ser.). (Illus.). 12p. (J). (ps-3). Date not set. text ed. 7.95 (1-56987-425-5) Landoll.

Story of Jonah. (Little Landoll Bible Stories Ser.: No. I). 32p. (J). (ps-3). Date not set. text ed. 1.29 (1-56987-366-6) Landoll.

Story of Jonah. Alice J. Davidson. (Alice in Bibleland Storybooks). (Illus.). 32p. (J). (gr. 3 up). 1984. 5.95 (0-8378-5068-1) Gibson.

Story of Jonah. Illus. by Ying-Hwa Hu. (Read Along with Me Bible Stories Ser.). 24p. (J). (ps-3). 1992. 4.95 (1-56288-222-8) Checkerboard.

Story of Jonah. Retold by Bill Yenne & Timothy Jacobs. LC 93-24837. (Children's Bible Classics Ser.). (J). 1993. 4.99 (0-8407-4915-5) Nelson.

Story of Jonah: Paint with Water. Laura Kelly. (Little Lamb Mini Activity Bks.). (Illus.). 16p. (J). 1994. pap. 1.49 (0-7847-0195-4, 01545) Standard Pub.

Story of Jonah & the Big Fish. Patricia Pingry. (Story of... Ser.). (Illus.). 24p. (Orig.). (J). (ps-2). 1988. pap. 3.95 (0-8249-8181-2, Ideals Child) Hambleton-Hill.

Story of Jonah and the Whale. Wedeven. (J). 1997. pap. 4.99 (0-689-81059-8) S&S Childrens.

Story of Joseph. 79p. pap. 0.50 (0-686-29167-0) Faith Pub Hse.

Story of Joseph. Illus. by Tom Sperling. (Read Along with Me Bible Stories Ser.). 24p. (J). (ps-3). 1992. 4.95 (1-56288-224-4) Checkerboard.

Story of Joseph: From Shepherd Boy to a Ruler of Egypt. J. Edson White. (Pioneer Ser.). (Illus.). (J). (gr. 3 up). 1990. reprint ed. pap. 4.95 (0-945460-07-4) Upward Way.

***Story of Joseph: The Egyptian Elements in the Old Testament.** unabridged ed. Amin Sharif. 96p. (Orig.). 1995. pap. 7.95 (1-56411-117-2, 4BBG0094) Untd Bros & Sis.

Story of Joseph & a Dream Come True. Patricia Pingry. (Story of...Ser.). (Illus.). 24p. (Orig.). (J). (ps-2). 1988. pap. 3.95 (0-8249-8182-0, Ideals Child) Hambleton-Hill.

***Story of Joseph & His Brothers.** Jude Winkler. (Illus.). 1994. pap. 1.25 (0-89942-942-4, 942) Catholic Bk Pub.

Story of Joshua. Alice J. Davidson. (Alice in Bibleland Storybooks). (Illus.). (J). (gr. 3 up). 1989. 5.95 (0-8378-1850-8) Gibson.

***Story of Joshua.** Jude Winkler. (Saint Joseph Bible Story Ser.). (Illus.). 1994. pap. 1.25 (0-89942-944-0, 944) Catholic Bk Pub.

Story of Joshua & the Bugles of Jericho. Patricia Pingry. (Story of...Ser.). (Illus.). 24p. (Orig.). (J). (ps-2). 1988. pap. 3.95 (0-8249-8178-2, Ideals Child) Hambleton-Hill.

Story of Jumping Mouse. John L. Steptoe. LC 82-14848. (Illus.). 40p. (J). (gr. 1 up). 1989. pap. 4.95 (0-688-08740-X, Mulberry) Morrow.

Story of Jumping Mouse. John L. Steptoe. LC 82-14848. (Illus.). 40p. (J). (gr. k-3). 1984. 16.00 (0-688-01902-1); lib. bdg. 15.93 (0-688-01903-X) Lothrop.

Story of Junipero Serra: Brave Adventurer. Florence M. White. LC 95-36842. (Famous Lives Ser.). (Illus.). 112p. (J). (gr. 3 up). lib. bdg. 19.93 (0-8368-1460-6) Gareth Stevens Inc.

***Story of Junk: A Novel.** Linda Yablonsky. LC 96-48092. 325p. 1997. 23.00 (0-374-27024-4) FS&G.

Story of Karate: From Buddhism to Bruce Lee. Luana Metil & Jace Townsend. LC 93-32006. (Sports Legacy Ser.). (Illus.). 112p. (YA). (gr. 5 up). 1995. lib. bdg. 22.95 (0-8225-3325-1, Lerner Publctns) Lerner Group.

***Story of Karate: From Buddhism to Bruce Lee.** Luana Metil. (J). 1997. pap. text ed. 10.95 (0-8225-9770-5) Lerner Group.

Story of Kennett. Bayard Taylor. Ed. by C. W. La Salle, 2nd. (Masterworks of Literature Ser.). 1972. 19.95 (0-8084-0028-2); pap. 13.95 (0-8084-0029-0) NCUP.

Story of Kennett. Bayard Taylor. 1993. reprint ed. lib. bdg. 89.00 (0-7812-5842-1) Rprt Serv.

***Story of Kevin Ellis & the Rainbow Fish.** Nicky Ann. Ed. by Carol Magnuson. (Working Bks.: Vol. 1.1). (YA). (gr. 3 up). 1993. wbk. ed. 13.75 (0-9638312-6-7) LWR Pubs.

***Story of Kevin Ellis & the Rainbow Fish.** Nicky Ann. Ed. by Carol Magnuson. (Working Bks.: Vol. 1.1). 90p. (YA). (gr. 3 up). 1993. reprint ed. wbk. ed. 18.75 (1-889197-06-8) LWR Pubs.

Story of King Arthur. Tom Crawford. LC 94-3363. (Children's Thrift Classics Ser.). (Illus.). 96p. (Orig.). (J). (gr. 4 up). 1994. pap. text ed. 1.00 (0-486-28347-X) Dover.

***Story of King Arthur.** Robin Lister & Thomas Malory. LC 96-45022. (Kingfisher Classics Ser.). (Illus.). 96p. (J). (gr. 4 up). 1997. pap. 13.95 (0-7534-5101-8) LKC.

Story of King Arthur & His Knights. Howard Pyle. (Illus.). xviii, 313p. (J). (gr. 7 up). pap. 6.95 (0-486-21445-1) Dover.

Story of King Arthur & His Knights. Howard Pyle. (Illus.). 1986. pap. 5.95 (0-451-52488-8, Sig Classics) NAL-Dutton.

Story of King Arthur & His Knights. Howard Pyle. 25.95 (0-89190-662-2) Amereon Ltd.

Story of King Arthur & His Knights. Howard Pyle. (YA). (gr. 6-12). 1990. 21.00 (0-8446-2766-6) Peter Smith.

***Story of King Arthur & His Knights.** Howard Pyle. lib. bdg. 25.95 (0-8488-2107-6) Amereon Ltd.

Story of King Arthur & His Knights. deluxe ed. Howard Pyle. (Illus.). (YA). (gr. 7 up). 1978. reprint ed. lib. bdg. 12.00 (0-932106-01-3, Pub. by Marathon Press) S J Durst.

Story of King Arthur & His Knights. Howard Pyle. LC 84-50167. (Illus.). 344p. (J). 1984. reprint ed. lib. bdg. 21.00 (0-684-14814-5, C Scribner Sons Young) S&S Childrens.

Story of King Cotton. Harris Dickson. LC 79-107513. 309p. 1970. reprint ed. text ed. 52.50 (0-8371-3760-8, DKC&, Negro U Pr) Greenwood.

***Story of King Kabul the First & Gawain the Kitchen-Boy - Histoire du Roi Kaboul Ier & du Marmiton Gauwain: Followed by Vulcan's Crown - La Couronne de Vulcan.** Max Jacob. LC 93-5362. (Illus.). 87p. 1994. reprint ed. pap. 25.00 (0-608-03481-9, 2064193) Bks Demand.

Story of Kings County California. J. L. Brown. (Illus.). 123p. 1986. reprint ed. 8.75 (0-9612298-1-0) Forsan Bks.

Story of Krishna. Bani R. Choudhary. (Illus.). (J). (gr. 3-10). 1979. 7.25 (0-89744-134-6) Auromere.

Story of Krishna. Bhagat Singh. (Illus.). 20p. (Orig.). (J). (ps-5). 1976. pap. 2.50 (0-89744-135-4) Auromere.

Story of Kwanzaa. Donna L. Washington. LC 95-22356. (Illus.). 40p. (J). (gr. 1-5). 1996. 14.95 (0-06-024818-1) HarpC Child Bks.

Story of Kwanzaa. Donna L. Washington. LC 95-22356. (Illus.). 40p. (J). (gr. 1-5). 1996. lib. bdg. 14.89 (0-06-024819-X) HarpC Child Bks.

***Story of Kwanzaa.** Donna L. Washington. LC 95-22356. (Trophy Book Ser.). (Illus.). 40p. (J). (gr. 1-5). 1997. pap. 5.95 (0-06-446200-5, Trophy) HarpC Child Bks.

Story of Kwanzaa. Safisha Madhubuti. (J). (gr. 1). 1989. reprint ed. pap. 5.95 (0-88378-001-1) Third World.

Story of L. Frank Baum. Cynthia Rylant. (J). 1996. 16.00 (0-689-80153-X, S&S Bks Young Read) S&S Childrens.

Story of Land: A World History of Land Tenure & Agrarian Reform. John P. Powelson. LC 87-11247. 347p. (C). 1988. text ed. 30.00 (0-89946-218-9) Lincoln Inst Land.

***Story of Land Surveying.** Ray Connin & Betsy Murphy. (Illus.). 24p. (Orig.). (J). (gr. 4-6). 1996. pap. 3.95 (0-932514-32-4) Red Rose Studio.

Story of Land Warfare. Paul M. Kendall. LC 74-3764. (Illus.). x, 194p. 1981. reprint ed. text ed. 49.75 (0-8371-7463-5, KELW, Greenwood Pr) Greenwood.

Story of Laura Ingalls Wilder. Megan Stine. (Illus.). 112p. (Orig.). (J). (gr. 2-5). 1992. pap. 3.50 (0-440-40578-5, YB BDD) BDD Bks Young Read.

Story of Laura Ingalls Wilder: Pioneer Girl. Megan Stine. (Famous Lives Ser.). (Illus.). (J). 1996. lib. bdg. 19.93 (0-8368-1476-2) Gareth Stevens Inc.

Story of Lavender. Sally Festing. (C). 1985. pap. 35.00 (0-907335-18-7, Pub. by Sutton Libs & Arts) St Mut.

Story of Lavender. Sally Festing. 1987. pap. 40.00 (0-907335-05-5, Pub. by Sutton Libs & Arts) St Mut.

***Story of Law.** John M. Zane. xii, 486p. 1996. reprint ed. 99.00 (1-56169-229-8) Gaunt.

***Story of Layla & Majnun.** N. Nizami. Tr. by R. Gelpke. 192p. 1996. pap. 14.00 (0-614-21351-7, 1426) Kazi Pubns.

***Story of Layla & Majnun.** N. Nizami. Tr. by r. Gelpke. 192p. 1996. pap. 14.00 (0-614-21656-7, 1426) Kazi Pubns.

Story of Layla & Majnun. Ganjavi Nizami. Tr. by R. Gelpke from PER. 206p. 1996. reprint ed. pap. 14.00 (0-930872-52-5, 1204P) Omega Pubns NY.

Story of Lebanon & Other Poems & Stories. Alan Rickard. (Australian Collection). pap. 7.00 (0-936128-15-1) De Young Pr.

Story of Lee's Headquarters: Gettysburg, Pennsylvania. Timothy H. Smith. (Illus.). 88p. (C). 1995. pap. text ed. 7.95 (0-939631-85-7) Thomas Publications.

***Story of Leisure: Context, Concepts, & Current Controversies.** Jay S. Shivers & Lee J. Delislea. LC 96-48339. (Illus.). 256p. (C). 1997. text ed. 36.00 (0-87322-996-7, BSHI0996) Human Kinetics.

Story of Lem Ward As Told by Ida Ward to Glenn Lawson. Glenn Lawson. LC 84-72621. (Illus.). 128p. 1984. 35.00 (0-88740-028-0) Schiffer.

Story of Lettermaster: Part of the Scaredy Cat Reading System. Joyce Herzog. (Illus.). 29p. (Orig.). (J). 1997. pap. 4.95 (1-882514-30-0) Greenleaf TN.

Story of Lexington & Concord. R. Conrad Stein. LC 82-23518. (Cornerstones of Freedom Ser.). (Illus.). 32p. (J). (gr. 3-6). 1983. pap. 4.95 (0-516-44661-4) Childrens.

***Story of Liberty.** Charles C. Coffin. 14.95 (0-938558-20-X) Noble Pub Assocs.

Story of Lightning & Thunder. Ashley Bryan. LC 92-40509. (Illus.). 32p. (J). (ps-3). 1993. lib. bdg. 15.00 (0-689-31836-7, Atheneum Bks Young) S&S Childrens.

Story of Lina Holt. Gina V. Kaiper. LC 95-92564. 207p. (Orig.). 1996. pap. 12.95 (0-9645206-3-X) Days & Years Pr.

Story of Lincoln. I. E. Bell & J. D. Chambers. (Illus.). 1971. 22.95 (0-8464-0887-2) Beekman Pubs.

Story of Little Babaji. Helen Bannerman. LC 96-84139. (Michael di Capua Bks.). (Illus.). 72p. (J). (ps up). 1996. 14.95 (0-06-205064-8); lib. bdg. 14.89 (0-06-205065-6) HarpC Child Bks.

Story of Little Black Mingo. Helen Bannerman. (Illus.). 72p. (J). (ps-4). 1990. reprint ed. 12.95 (0-9616844-5-3) Greenhouse Pub.

***Story of Little Black Mingo.** Helen Bannerman. (Illus.). 72p. (J). (ps-4). 1990. reprint ed. 16.95 incl. audio (0-614-30301-X) Greenhouse Pub.

Story of Little Black Quasha. Helen Bannerman. (Illus.). 56p. (J). (ps-4). 1990. reprint ed. 12.95 (0-9616844-3-7) Greenhouse Pub.

Story of Little Black Quibba. Helen Bannerman. (Illus.). 68p. (J). (ps-4). 1990. reprint ed. 12.95 (0-9616844-4-5) Greenhouse Pub.

Story of Little Black Sambo. Helen Bannerman. LC 58-88. (Illus.). (J). (gr. k-3). 1923. 13.95 (0-397-30006-9, HarpT) HarpC.

Story of Little Black Sambo. Helen Bannerman. (Illus.). 24p. (J). (gr. k-4). 1994. 14.95 (0-87797-265-6) Cherokee.

***Story of Little Black Sambo.** Helen Bannerman. (Illus.). 58p. (J). 1996. 25.00 (0-9616844-8-8) Greenhouse Pub.

Story of Little Black Sambo. large type ed. Helen Bannerman. (Illus.). 58p. (J). 1986. pap. 12.95 (0-9616844-1-0) Greenhouse Pub.

***Story of Little Black Sambo.** large type ed. Helen Bannerman. (Illus.). 58p. (J). 1986. reprint ed. pap. 16.95 incl. audio (0-614-30302-8) Greenhouse Pub.

Story of Little Blue Hound: A Crystal Tale. Roger Neal. 56p. (J). (gr. 1-5). 1995. pap. 7.95 (1-55605-261-8, Cloverdale) Wyndham Hall.

Story of Little Christmas. abr. ed. George MacDonald. (Illus.). 32p. (J). (gr. 2-6). 1995. 14.99 (0-7814-0233-6, Chariot Bks) Chariot Victor.

Story of Little Woodcote & Woodcote Hall. Ed. by Margaret Cunningham. (C). 1985. pap. 35.00 (0-907335-20-9, Pub. by Sutton Libs & Arts) St Mut.

Story of Loganair. Iain Hutchinson. 1990. 60.00 (0-906437-14-8, Pub. by Kea Pubng UK) St Mut.

Story of London. H. B. Wheatley. (Mediaeval Towns Ser.: Vol. 29). 1974. reprint ed. 65.00 (0-8115-0871-4) Periodicals Srv.

Story of Louis Horst & the American Dance. Ernestine Stodelle. 15p. 1964. 6.00 (0-685-19180-X) Am Dance Guild.

Story of Louisa May Alcott, Determined Writer. Marci R. McGill. LC 95-36845. (Famous Lives Ser.). (Illus.). 112p. (J). (gr. 3 up). lib. bdg. 19.93 (0-8368-1461-4) Gareth Stevens Inc.

***Story of Louisiana, 4 vols.** Edward A. Davis. Incl. Vol. 1. Story of Louisiana. 45.00 (1-57980-033-5); Vol. 2. . 45.00 (1-57980-034-3); Vol. 3. . 55.00 (1-57980-035-1); Vol. 4. . 55.00 (1-57980-036-X); 170.00 (0-685-08217-2) Claitors.

Story of Louisiana see Story of Louisiana

***Story of Low German & Plautdietsch.** 1993. pap. write for info. (0-9638494-0-9) Readers Pr KS.

Story of Lucca. J. A. Ross & N. Erichsen. (Mediaeval Towns Ser.: Vol. 7). 1974. reprint ed. pap. 46.00 (0-8115-0849-8) Periodicals Srv.

Story of Lucy What's-Her-Name! And Your Name Too! Lucy D. Blount. (Illus.). 48p. (J). 1992. Spiral bdg. spiral bd. 12.00 (0-9630017-2-8) Light-Bearer.

Story of Lydia. Marty R. Figley. LC 96-21210. (Illus.). 32p. (J). (ps-2). 1996. 15.00 (0-8028-5114-2); pap. 7.50 (0-8028-5141-X) Eerdmans.

Story of Lynx. Claude Levi-Strauss. Tr. by Catherine Tihanyi from FRE. LC 94-34811. (Illus.). 294p. 1995. 24.95 (0-226-47471-2) U Ch Pr.

Story of Lynx. Claude Levi-Strauss. Tr. by Catherine Tihanyi. (Illus.). xviii, 276p. 1996. pap. 17.95 (0-226-47472-0) U Ch Pr.

***Story of Mah: A Hmong "Romeo & Juliet" Folktale.** Rosalie Giacchino-Baker. (Illus.). 31p. (YA). (gr. 6 up). 1997. 16.99 (1-879600-98-6) Pac Asia Pr.

***Story of Mah: A Hmong "Romeo & Juliet" Folktale.** Rosalie Giacchino-Baker. (Illus.). 32p. (YA). (gr. 6 up). 1997. 16.99 (1-879600-97-8) Pac Asia Pr.

Story of Mahabharata. Bani Choudhary. (Introduction to Classical Indian Lore for Children Ser.). (J). (ps up). 1988. 7.50 (0-318-37379-3) Auromere.

Story of Malcolm X, Civil Rights Leader. Megan Stine. 112p. (J). (gr. 4-7). 1994. pap. 3.50 (0-440-40900-4) Dell.

Story of Malcolm X, Civil Rights Leader. Megan Stine. LC 95-19273. (Famous Lives Ser.). (J). 1995. lib. bdg. 19.93 (0-8368-1383-9) Gareth Stevens Inc.

Story of Mankind. Hendrik W. Von Loon. 640p. 1994. pap. 12.00 (0-87140-156-8) Liveright.

Story of Manual Labor in All Lands & Ages. J. C. Simonds. 1972. 59.95 (0-8490-1135-3) Gordon Pr.

Story of Maps. Lloyd Brown. (Illus.). 1979. reprint ed. pap. 10.95 (0-486-23873-3) Dover.

Story of Maran BetYosef: R'Yosef Karo - Author of the Shulman Aruch. M. Pe'er. (ArtScroll Youth Ser.). (Illus.). 96p. 1986. 11.95 (0-89906-400-0) Mesorah Pubns.

Story of Margaret Wise Brown. Cynthia Rylant. LC 94-48812. (Illus.). (J). 1996. 16.00 (0-689-80151-3, S&S Bks Young Read) S&S Childrens.

***Story of Marilyn Manson.** Doug Small. (Illus.). 48p. (Orig.). (YA). 1997. pap. 11.95 (0-8256-1576-3, OP 47867) Omnibus NY.

***Story of Martha's Vineyard.** large type ed. Kevin Shortsleeve. (Illus.). 64p. (Orig.). (J). (ps-3). 1997. pap. 9.95 (0-9622782-6-2) Cape Cod Life Mag.

Story of Martin Luther King, Jr. Marching to Freedom. rev. ed. Joyce Milton. LC 95-19272. (Famous Lives Ser.). (J). 1995. lib. bdg. 19.93 (0-8368-1382-0) Gareth Stevens Inc.

Story of Mary & Jesus from the Quran: Reprinted from the Meaning of the Holy Quran. Tr. & Comment by Abdullah Y. Ali. LC 94-47660. 1995. pap. 3.00 (0-915957-24-8) amana pubns.

Story of Mary; by an American. William L. Spencer. LC 72-2124. (Black Heritage Library Collection). 1977. reprint ed. 38.95 (0-8369-9064-1) Ayer.

Story of Mary MacLane by Herself. Mary MacLane. (American Biography Ser.). 322p. 1991. reprint ed. lib. bdg. 79.00 (0-7812-8258-6) Rprt Serv.

Story of Mary Surratt. John Patrick. 1947. pap. 5.25 (0-8222-1086-X) Dramatists Play.

***Story of Masada: Discoveries from the Excavations.** Gilah Hurvits. LC 97-4655. (BYU Studies). 1997. pap. write for info. (0-8425-2342-1) Frnds of the Libry.

Story of Mathematics. Lloyd Motz & Jefferson H. Weaver. 366p. 1993. 25.95 (0-306-44508-5, Plenum Pr) Plenum.

Story of Mathematics. Lloyd Motz & Jefferson H. Weaver. 368p. 1995. pap. 14.00 (0-380-72458-8) Avon.

Story of Matt & Mary. Erica Frost. LC 85-14011. (Illus.). 48p. (Orig.). (J). (gr. 1-3). 1997. pap. 3.50 (0-8167-0603-4) Troll Communs.

Story of Me. Stan Jones & Brenna Jones. (God's Design for Sex Ser.: No. 1). (Illus.). 40p. (Orig.). (J). (ps up). 1995. pap. 9.00 (0-89109-843-7) NavPress.

Story of Meininger. Max Grube. Ed. by Wendell Cole. Tr. by Anne M. Koller. LC 63-23352. (Books of the Theatre: No. 4). (Illus.). 1963. 10.95 (0-87024-027-7) U of Miami Pr.

Story of Merwin, Hulbert & Co. Firearms. Arthur J. Phelps. LC 91-65703. 226p. 1993. 56.00 (1-882824-00-8) Graphic Pubs.

Story of Metals. (Illus.). (ARA.). (J). (gr. 5-12). 1987. 4.50 (0-86685-227-1) Intl Bk Ctr.

Story of Mexico. Susan Hale. 1976. lib. bdg. 59.95 (0-8490-2681-4) Gordon Pr.

Story of Mexico in Spanish & English. pap. 4.95 (0-88388-159-4) Bellerophon Bks.

***Story of Middletown, the Oldest Settlement in New Jersey.** Ernest W. Mandeville. (Illus.). 143p. 1997. reprint ed. pap. 21.00 (0-8328-6057-3) Higginson Bk Co.

Story of Milan. E. Noyes. (Mediaeval Towns Ser.: Vol. 20). 1974. reprint ed. 65.00 (0-8115-0862-5) Periodicals Srv.

Story of Mimmy & Simmy. Yaffa Ganz. (gr. k-2). 1985. 10.95 (0-87306-385-6) Feldheim.

Story of Minnesota's Past. Rhoda R. Gilman. LC 91-11189. (Illus.). ix, 231p. (J). 1991. pap. 22.50 (0-87351-267-7) Minn Hist.

Story of Mira's Love. Budhananda. 52p. (Orig.). 1987. pap. 2.00 (0-87481-546-0, Pub. by Ramakrishna Mission II) Vedanta Pr.

Story of Miss Moppet. Beatrix Potter. (Original Peter Rabbit Books: No. 21). (J). 1987. pap. 5.95 (0-7232-3480-9) Warne.

Story of Mississippi Steamboats. R. Conrad Stein. (Cornerstones of Freedom Ser.). (Illus.). 32p. (J). (gr. 3-6). 1987. pap. 4.95 (0-516-44726-2) Childrens.

Story of Mobile. rev. ed. Caldwell Delaney. (Illus.). 352p. 1981. reprint ed. 25.00 (0-940882-14-0) HB Pubns.

***Story of Modern Art.** 2nd ed. Norbert Lynton. (Illus.). 400p. Date not set. pap. 19.95 (0-7148-2422-4, Pub. by Phaidon Press UK) Chronicle Bks.

Story of Mohammad the Prophet. Bilzik Alladin. (Illus.). (J). (gr. 3-10). 1979. 7.25 (0-89744-139-7) Auromere.

Story of Money. Carolyn Kain. LC 91-38898. (Illus.). 32p. (J). (gr. 3-6). 1993. lib. bdg. 13.95 (0-8167-2711-2) Troll Communs.

Story of Money. Carolyn Kain. LC 91-38898. (Illus.). 32p. (J). (gr. 3-6). 1997. pap. 4.95 (0-8167-2712-0) Troll Communs.

Story of Money. Betsy C. Maestro. (Illus.). 48p. (J). (gr. 1 up). 1993. 15.95 (0-395-56242-2, Clarion Bks) HM.

Story of Money. Betsy C. Maestro. LC 94-26607. (Illus.). 48p. (J). (gr. 1 up). 1995. reprint ed. pap. 6.95 (0-688-13304-5, Mulberry) Morrow.

Story of Monique. 160p. (Orig.). 1990. mass mkt. 4.95 (1-878320-42-4) Masquerade.

Story of Mormonism. W. A. Linn. 637p. 1993. reprint ed. lib. bdg. 109.00 (0-7812-5311-X) Rprt Serv.

An Asterisk (*) at the beginning of an entry indicates that the title is appearing in BIP for the first time.

Story of Moscow. W. O. Gerrare. (Mediaeval Towns Ser.: Vol. 1). 1974. reprint ed. pap. 35.00 (*0-8115-0843-9*) Periodicals Srv.

Story of Moses. (Bible Pop-Up Book Ser.). (Illus.). 12p. (J). (ps-3). Date not set. text ed. 7.95 (*1-56987-428-X*) Landoll.

***Story of Moses.** Jude Winkler. (Illus.). 1994. pap. 1.25 (*0-89942-943-2*, 943) Catholic Bk Pub.

Story of Moses. Retold by Bill Yenne. LC 93-37476. (J). 1994. 4.99 (*0-7852-8329-3*); mass mkt. 4.99 (*0-7852-8325-0*) Nelson.

Story of Moses: Instant Ink. Laura Kelly. (Little Lamb Mini Activity Bks.). (Illus.). 16p. (J). 1994. pap. 1.49 (*0-7847-0191-1*, 01541) Standard Pub.

Story of Moses & the Ten Commandments. Patricia Pingry. (Story of...Ser.). (Illus.). 24p. (J). (ps-2). 1990. pap. 3.95 (*0-8249-8418-8*, Ideals Child) Hambleton-Hill.

***Story of Mother Tree.** Jane S. Bauld. Ed. by Thomas W. Petrick. (Illus.). 16p. (Orig.). (J). (gr. k-4). 1997. pap. 8.95 (*1-880384-12-4*) Coldwater Pr.

***Story of Mothers & Daughters.** Susan Wels. LC 96-37657. 1997. write for info. (*0-00-225113-2*) HarpC.

Story of Mrs. Lovewright & Purrless Her Cat. Lore Segal. 40p. (J). (ps-3). 1996. pap. 6.99 (*0-679-88085-2*) DK Pub Inc.

Story of Mrs. Lovewright & Purrless Her Cat. Lore Segal. LC 84-25011. (Illus.). 40p. (J). (ps up). 1985. 14.00 (*0-394-86817-X*) Knopf Bks Yng Read.

Story of Mrs. Lovewright & Purrless Her Cat. Lore Segal. (Illus.). (J). (ps-3). reprint ed. pap. 6.99 (*0-614-15734-X*) Random.

Story of Mrs. Tubbs. Christopher Lofting. (J). 1998. pap. 14.00 (*0-671-79694-1*, Litl Simon S&S) S&S Childrens.

Story of Muhammad Ali: Heavyweight Champion of the World. Barry Denenberg. LC 95-36797. (Famous Lives Ser.). 1996. lib. bdg. 19.93 (*0-8368-1462-2*) Gareth Stevens Inc.

Story of Mull & Iona. Nick Hesketh. 80p. (C). 1988. pap. 70.00 (*0-901824-89-5*, Pub. by Mercat Pr Bks UK) St Mut.

Story of Music. Mundy. (Fine Arts Ser.). (J). (gr. 6-9). 1980. lib. bdg. 14.95 (*0-88110-031-5*, Usborne) EDC.

Story of Music. Simon Mundy. (Fine Arts Ser.). (J). (gr. 6-9). 1980. pap. 6.95 (*0-86020-443-X*, Usborne) EDC.

Story of Music. rev. ed. Harriot B. Barbour & Warren S. Freeman. (Illus.). 312p. (J). (gr. 7-9). 1958. text ed. 13. 95 (*0-87487-033-X*) Summy-Birchard.

Story of Music: An Historical Sketch of the Changes in Musical Form. Paul Bekker. LC 74-124592. (BCL Ser. I). (Illus.). 1970. reprint ed. 34.50 (*0-404-00729-5*) AMS Pr.

Story of Music: An Historical Sketch of the Changes in Musical Form. Paul Bekker. 277p. 1990. reprint ed. lib. bdg. 69.00 (*0-7812-9020-1*) Rprt Serv.

Story of Musical Instruments: from Sheperd's Pipe to Symphony. Harry W. Schwartz. LC 70-114893. (Illus.). 377p. reprint ed. lib. bdg. 34.00 (*0-8290-0797-0*) Irvington.

Story of Musical Instruments, from Shepherd's Pipe to Symphony. Harry W. Schwartz. LC 70-114893. (Select Bibliographies Reprint Ser.). 1977. 39.95 (*0-8369-5297-9*) Ayer.

Story of My Boyhood & Youth. John Muir & Sierra Club Staff. LC 88-23988. (John Muir Library). (Illus.). 176p. 1989. pap. 10.00 (*0-87156-749-0*) Sierra.

Story of My Boyhood & Youth. John Muir. (Illus.). 246p. 1965. reprint ed. pap. 12.95 (*0-299-03654-5*) U of Wis Pr.

Story of My Childhood. Clara Barton. Ed. by Annette K. Baxter. LC 79-8773. (Signal Lives Ser.). (Illus.). 1980. reprint ed. lib. bdg. 18.95 (*0-405-12823-1*) Ayer.

Story of My Heart. Ali A. Furutan. (Illus.). 272p. 1984. 19. 95 (*0-85398-114-0*) G Ronald Pub.

Story of My Heart. Richard Jeffries. 3.95 (*0-7043-3257-4*, Pub. by Quartet UK) Charles River Bks.

Story of My Life. Clarence S. Darrow. LC 96-17195. 512p. 1996. pap. 16.95 (*0-306-80738-6*) Da Capo.

Story of My Life, 3 vols. Morarji Desai. LC 78-40613. 1979. 77.00 (*0-08-023566-2*, Pergamon Pr) Elsevier.

Story of My Life. Arnold Ehret. 1980. pap. 2.25 (*0-87904-048-3*) Lust.

Story of My Life. Helen A. Keller. 240p. 1990. pap. 4.50 (*0-553-21387-3*) Bantam.

Story of My Life. Helen A. Keller. (Classics Ser.). (YA). (gr. 8 up). 1965. mass mkt. 3.50 (*0-8049-0070-1*, CL-70) Airmont.

***Story of My Life.** Helen A. Keller. (Illustrated Classics Collection 2). 64p. 1994. pap. 4.95 (*0-7854-0723-5*, 40415) Am Guidance.

Story of My Life. Jay McInerney. (Contemporaries Ser.). 1989. pap. 11.00 (*0-679-72257-2*, Vin) Random.

Story of My Life. large type ed. Helen A. Keller. LC 93-10387. 350p. 1993. pap. 15.95 (*0-8161-5816-9*) G K Hall.

Story of My Life. unabridged ed. Helen A. Keller. LC 96-20637. (Thrift Editions Ser.). 96p. reprint ed. pap. text ed. 1.00 (*0-486-29249-5*) Dover.

Story of My Life. Clarence Darrow. 476p. 1992. reprint ed. lib. bdg. 28.95 (*0-89966-918-2*) Buccaneer Bks.

Story of My Life. Helen A. Keller. 301p. 1984. reprint ed. lib. bdg. 27.95 (*0-89966-509-8*) Buccaneer Bks.

Story of My Life. Mary A. Livermore. (American Biography Ser.). 730p. 1991. reprint ed. lib. bdg. 119.00 (*0-7812-8247-0*) Rprt Serv.

Story of My Life. James M. Sims. (American Biography Ser.). 471p. 1991. reprint ed. lib. bdg. 89.00 (*0-7812-8354-X*) Rprt Serv.

Story of My Life. Meadows Taylor. 400p. 1986. reprint ed. 22.00 (*0-685-14347-3*, Pub. by Usha II) S Asia.

Story of My Life, 2 Vols, Set. Marie - Queen of Roumania. LC 73-135820. (Eastern Europe Collection). 1971. reprint ed. 70.95 (*0-405-02793-1*) Ayer.

Story of My Life, 2 vols., Set. William Taylor. (American Biography Ser.). 1991. reprint ed. lib. bdg. 148.00 (*0-7812-8380-9*) Rprt Serv.

Story of My Life: An Account of What I Have Thought & Said & Done in My Ministry of More Than Fifty-Three Years in Christian Lands & Among the Heathen, 2 vols. William Taylor. Ed. by John C. Ridpath. LC 72-3999. (Black Heritage Library Collection). (Illus.). 1977. reprint ed. 82.95 (*0-8369-9107-9*) Ayer.

Story of My Life: Student Activity Book. Marcia Sohl & Gerald Dackerman. (Now Age Illustrated Ser.). (Illus.). (J). (gr. 4-10). 1976. student ed. 1.25 (*0-88301-195-6*) Pendulum Pr.

Story of My Life: The Autobiography of a Working Man. Frederick Booth. 120p. (C). 1988. 29.95 (*0-7212-0724-3*, Pub. by Regency Press UK) St Mut.

Story of My Life: The Autobiography of George Sand. George Sand, pseud. Ed. by Thelma Jurgrau. LC 90-35172. (SUNY Series, Women Writers in Translation). 1168p. 1991. pap. 24.95 (*0-7914-0581-8*); text ed. 74.50 (*0-7914-0580-X*) State U NY Pr.

Story of My Life: With Her Letters (1887-1901) & a Supplementary Account of Her Education, Including Passages from the Reports & Letters of Her Teacher, Anne Mansfield Sullivan. Helen A. Keller. (American Biography Ser.). 525p. 1991. reprint ed. lib. bdg. 99.00 (*0-7812-8230-6*) Rprt Serv.

Story of My Life & Work. Booker T. Washington. LC 70-82473. 423p. 1970. reprint ed. text ed. 35.00 (*0-8371-1647-3*, WAM&) Greenwood.

Story of My Life & Work. Booker T. Washington. (American Biography Ser.). 423p. 1991. reprint ed. lib. bdg. 89.00 (*0-7812-8402-3*) Rprt Serv.

Story of My Life: or The Sunshine & Shadow of Seventy Years...to Which Is Added Six of Her Most Popular Lectures. Mary A. Livermore. LC 74-3960. (Women in America Ser.). (Illus.). 760p. 1974. reprint ed. 57.95 (*0-405-06108-0*) Ayer.

***Story of My Life Readalong.** Helen Keller. (Illustrated Classics Collection 2). 64p. 1994. pap. 14.95 incl. audio (*0-7854-0689-1*, 40417) Am Guidance.

Story of My Wife. Milan Fust. Tr. by Ivan Sanders. (International Ser.). 1989. pap. 8.95 (*0-679-72217-3*, Vin) Random.

Story of Naples. C. Headlam. (Mediaeval Towns Ser.: Vol. 22). 1974. reprint ed. 55.00 (*0-8115-0864-1*) Periodicals Srv.

Story of Nat Love. Robert H. Miller. LC 93-46287. (Stories of the Forgotten West Ser.). (Illus.). 32p. (J). (gr. k-3). 1994. 12.95 (*0-382-24398-6*); pap. 5.95 (*0-382-24393-5*); lib. bdg. 14.95 (*0-382-24389-7*) Silver Burdett Pr.

Story of Nation Persia. S. G. Benjamin. 330p. 1987. 250.00 (*1-85077-149-9*, Pub. by Darf Pubs Ltd UK) St Mut.

Story of NationsBank: Changing the Face of American Banking. Howard E. Covington, Jr. & Marion A. Ellis. LC 92-50814. xviii, 328p. 1993. 27.50 (*0-8078-2093-8*) U of NC Pr.

Story of Negro League Baseball. William Brashler. LC 93-36547. 144p. (J). (gr. 3 up). 1994. 15.95 (*0-395-67169-8*) Ticknor & Flds Bks Yng Read.

Story of Negro League Baseball. William Brashler. LC 93-36547. 166p. (J). (gr. 3 up). 1994. pap. 10.95 (*0-395-69721-2*) Ticknor & Flds Bks Yng Read.

***Story of Nell Gwyn & the Sayings of Charles the Second.** Peter Cunnigham. Ed. by John Drinkwater. (Illus.). 176p. Date not set. write for info. (*0-405-18145-0*) Ayer.

Story of New Lanark. Robert Owen & David Dale. (C). 1989. 35.00 (*0-984473-02-9*) St Mut.

Story of New San Diego & of Its Founder Alonzo E. Horton. 2nd rev. ed. Elizabeth C. MacPhail. LC 79-63134. (Illus.). 63p. 1979. pap. 8.95 (*0-918740-01-0*) San Diego Hist.

***Story of New Sweden, As Told at the Quarter Centennial Celebration of the Founding of the Swedish Colony in the Woods of Maine.** (Illus.). 134p. 1997. reprint ed. pap. 17.50 (*0-8328-5878-1*) Higginson Bk Co.

Story of New York. E. S. Brooks. 1991. lib. bdg. 79.95 (*0-8490-4495-2*) Gordon Pr.

Story of Nicolet. Betty Brandt. Ed. by Jan Nestingen. (Illus.). 64p. (Orig.). (J). (gr. 3-5). 1991. pap. 6.95 (*0-9622014-3-X*) Beaver Valley.

Story of Nirvana: Omnibus Press Presents the Story Of. Suzi Black. (Illus.). 48p. (Orig.). pap. 11.95 (*0-8256-1539-9*, OP 47808) Omnibus NY.

Story of Nitrogen. Karen Fitzgerald. LC 96-25876. (First Bks.). (J). 1997. lib. bdg. 21.00 (*0-531-20248-8*) Watts.

Story of Noah. (Bible Pop-Up Book Ser.). (Illus.). 12p. (J). (ps-3). Date not set. text ed. 7.95 (*1-56987-427-1*); text ed. 1.29 (*1-56987-367-4*) Landoll.

Story of Noah. Alice J. Davidson. (Alice in Bibleland Storybooks). (Illus.). 32p. (J). (gr. 3 up). 1984. 5.95 (*0-8378-5067-3*) Gibson.

Story of Noah: Paint with Water. Laura Kelly. (Little Lamb Mini Activity Bks.). (Illus.). 16p. (J). 1994. pap. 1.49 (*0-7847-0196-2*, 01546) Standard Pub.

Story of Noah & His Ark. George Conklin. 1992. 10.00 (*0-533-10013-5*) Vantage.

***Story of Noah & the Flood.** Jude Winkler. (Saint Joseph Bible Story Ser.). (Illus.). 1989. 2.25 (*0-89942-961-0*, 961/22) Catholic Bk Pub.

Story of Noah & the Rainbow. Patricia Pingry. (Story of... Ser.). 24p. (J). (ps-2). 1988. pap. 3.95 (*0-8249-8176-6*, Ideals Child) Hambleton-Hill.

Story of Noah Stencil Fun. (Little Lamb Mini Activity Bks.). (Illus.). 12p. (J). 1991. pap. 1.49 (*0-87403-895-2*, 01555) Standard Pub.

Story of Noah's Ark: Genesis 6: 5-9: 17. Jane Latourette. (Arch Bks.). (J). (ps-3). 1993. pap. 1.99 (*0-570-06009-5*, 59-1110) Concordia.

Story of Notation. Charles F. Williams. LC 68-25306. (Studies in Music: No. 42). (Illus.). 1969. reprint ed. lib. bdg. 75.00 (*0-8383-0317-X*) M S G Haskell Hse.

Story of Notation. Charles F. Williams. 264p. 1990. reprint ed. lib. bdg. 69.00 (*0-7812-9108-9*) Rprt Serv.

Story of Nuclear Power. (Illus.). (ARA.). (J). (gr. 5-12). 1987. 4.50 (*0-86685-228-X*) Intl Bk Ctr.

Story of Numbers: How Mathematics Has Shaped Civilization. John McLeish. Orig. Title: Number. (Illus.). 272p. 1994. reprint ed. pap. 11.00 (*0-449-90938-7*, ExPress) Fawcett.

***Story of Numbers & Counting.** Anita Ganeri. (Signs of the Times Ser.). (Illus.). 32p. (J). 1996. lib. bdg. 14.95 (*0-19-521258-4*) OUP.

Story of Nuremberg. C. Headlam. 1972. 59.95 (*0-8490-2682-2*) Gordon Pr.

Story of O. Pauline Reage. 240p. 1981. mass mkt. 5.99 (*0-345-30111-0*) Ballantine.

Story of O. Pauline Reage. Tr. by John P. Hand. 186p. 1996. mass mkt. 5.95 (*1-56201-035-2*) Blue Moon Bks.

Story of O, Vol. 1. Guido Crepax. Tr. by Stefano Gaudiano from ITA. 96p. 1990. pap. 11.95 (*1-56163-002-0*, Eurotica) NBM.

Story of O, Vol. 2. Guido Crepax & Pauline Reage. Tr. by S. Gaudiano from ITA. 96p. 1991. pap. 11.95 (*1-56163-010-1*, Eurotica) NBM.

Story of O, Vol. 3. Guido Crepax & Pauline Reage. Tr. by S. Gaudiano from ITA. 96p. 1991. pap. 11.95 (*1-56163-011-X*, Eurotica) NBM.

Story of Odette. (Red Stripe Ser.). 1988. pap. 4.50 (*0-8216-5050-5*, Univ Books) Carol Pub Group.

Story of Og & Man, 3 vols., Set. Rikki. (Story of Og & Man Ser.). (Illus.). 662p. 1983. pap. 29.95 (*0-910149-06-2*) Msng Link AZ.

Story of Oklahoma. W. David Baird & Danney Goble. LC 93-47075. (Illus.). 528p. (J). 1994. text ed. 28.95 (*0-8061-2650-7*) U of Okla Pr.

Story of Old Abe Wisconsin's Civil War Hero. Malcolm Rosholt & Margaret Rosholt. (Illus.). 110p. (J). (gr. 4-12). 1987. 14.95 (*0-910417-09-1*) Rosholt Hse.

***Story of Old Falmouth.** James Otis. (Illus.). 127p. 1997. reprint ed. lib. bdg. 27.50 (*0-8328-5835-8*) Higginson Bk Co.

***Story of Old Falmouth.** James Otis. (Illus.). 127p. 1997. reprint ed. pap. 19.50 (*0-8328-5836-6*) Higginson Bk Co.

Story of Old Fort Johnson. W. Max Reid. 455p. 1993. reprint ed. lib. bdg. 99.00 (*0-7812-5132-X*) Rprt Serv.

Story of Old Fort Loudon. Mary N. Murfree. LC 73-104531. (Illus.). 409p. reprint ed. lib. bdg. 36.00 (*0-8398-1269-8*) Irvington.

Story of Old Fort Loudon. Mary N. Murfree. (C). 1986. reprint ed. pap. text ed. 10.95 (*0-8290-1941-3*) Irvington.

Story of Old Fort Plain & the Middle Mohawk Valley. Nelson Greene. (Illus.). 399p. 1993. reprint ed. lib. bdg. 42.50 (*0-8328-3522-6*) Higginson Bk Co.

Story of Old New York. H. C. Brown. 1977. lib. bdg. 59.95 (*0-8490-2683-0*) Gordon Pr.

***Story of Old Rensselaerville.** Mary F. Torrance. (Illus.). 72p. 1997. reprint ed. pap. 17.50 (*0-8328-6209-6*) Higginson Bk Co.

***Story of Old Saratoga & the Burgoyne Campaign.** John H. Brandow. (Illus.). 528p. 1997. reprint ed. lib. bdg. 55.00 (*0-8328-6221-5*) Higginson Bk Co.

Story of Old Ste. Genevieve. 5th ed. Gregory M. Franzwa. (Illus.). 169p. 1990. pap. 5.95 (*0-935284-86-9*) Patrice Pr.

Story of One Hundred Old Homes in Winchester. 238p. 1967. write for info. (*0-318-64329-4*) Winchester-Frederick Cty Hist Soc.

Story of One Soldier's Journey Through World War II. Nathan Handlin. 1992. 14.95 (*0-533-10241-3*) Vantage.

Story of Opera. Ernest M. Lee. 1972. 59.95 (*0-8490-1136-1*) Gordon Pr.

Story of Optometry. James R. Gregg. LC 65-12749. (Illus.). 315p. reprint ed. pap. 89.80 (*0-317-07936-0*, 2012411) Bks Demand.

Story of Orange. Vernise E. Pelzel. Ed. by Lenore Monk. (Illus.). 48p. (J). (gr. 3-12). 1987. pap. 6.95 (*0-944131-01-8*) HPL Pub.

Story of Organ Music. Charles F. Williams. LC 71-39643. (Select Bibliographies Reprint Ser.). 1977. reprint ed. 22. 95 (*0-8369-9948-7*) Ayer.

Story of Our Army: From Colonial Days to the Present. Willis J. Abbott. 1977. lib. bdg. 59.95 (*0-8490-2684-9*) Gordon Pr.

Story of Our Flag. 1988. pap. 3.95 (*0-88388-132-2*) Bellerophon Bks.

Story of Our Fruits & Vegetables. Dorothy Crispo. pap. 7.95 (*0-8159-6826-4*) Devin.

Story of Our Lady of Guadalupe. M.A.C.C. Team Staff. 11p. 1978. write for info. (*0-614-04888-5*) Mex Am Cult.

Story of Our Lady of Guadalupe: Three People, Four Days, Many Miracles. J. Janda. (Illus.). 48p. 1988. pap. 3.95 (*0-8091-6573-2*) Paulist Pr.

Story of Our Money. Olive C. Dwinell. 1979. lib. bdg. 59. 95 (*0-8490-3009-9*) Gordon Pr.

Story of Our Post Office, 2 vols. Marshall Cushing. 1976. lib. bdg. 200.00 (*0-8490-1137-X*) Gordon Pr.

Story of Our Regiment: A History of the 148th Pennsylvania Volunteers. Ed. by J. W. Muffley. (Army of the Potomac Ser.). (Illus.). 1200p. 1994. 55.00 (*0-935523-39-1*) Butternut & Blue.

Story of Our Rivers: Book II. Al Valiappa. (Nehru Library for Children). (Illus.). (J). (gr. 1-9). 1979. pap. 2.50 (*0-89744-184-2*) Auromere.

Story of Ourselves. A. F. Harper. 232p. 1962. pap. 10.99 (*0-8341-0119-X*) Beacon Hill.

Story of Ourselves: Teaching History Through Children's Literature. Ed. by Michael O. Tunnell & Richard Ammon. LC 92-30963. 196p. 1992. pap. text ed. 22.00 (*0-435-08725-8*, 08725) Heinemann.

Story of Oxford. 2nd rev. ed. Ed. by Museum of Oxford Staff. (Illus.). 48p. 1992. pap. 6.00 (*0-7509-0097-0*, Pub. by Sutton Pubng UK) Bks Intl VA.

Story of Oxford. C. Headlam. (Mediaeval Towns Ser.: Vol. 30). 1974. reprint ed. 55.00 (*0-8115-0872-2*) Periodicals Srv.

Story of Oxygen. Karen Fitzgerald. (First Bks.). (Illus.). 64p. (J). (gr. 4-6). 1996. lib. bdg. 21.00 (*0-531-20225-9*) Watts.

Story of P & O: The Peninsular & Oriental Steam Navigation Company. David Howarth & Stephen Howarth. (Illus.). 240p. 1996. pap. 35.00 (*0-297-83540-8*, Pub. by Orion Bks UK) Trafalgar.

Story of Padua. C. Foligno. (Mediaeval Towns Ser.: Vol. 4). 1974. reprint ed. pap. 46.00 (*0-8115-0846-3*) Periodicals Srv.

Story of Painting. Anthea Peppin. (Fine Arts Ser.). (Illus.). 32p. (J). 1980. pap. 6.95 (*0-86020-441-3*); lib. bdg. 14.95 (*0-88110-030-7*) EDC.

Story of Panama. Frank A. Gause & Charles C. Carr. LC 75-111714. (American Imperialism: Viewpoints of United States Foreign Policy, 1898-1941 Ser.). 1970. reprint ed. 20.95 (*0-405-02022-8*) Ayer.

Story of Paper. Odile Limousin. Tr. by Sarah Matthews from FRE. LC 87-31752. (Illus.). 38p. (J). (gr. k-5). 1988. 5.95 (*0-944589-16-2*, 162) Young Discovery Lib.

Story of Paris. T. Okey. (Mediaeval Towns Ser.: Vol. 15). 1974. reprint ed. 65.00 (*0-8115-0857-9*) Periodicals Srv.

Story of Passover. Bobbi Katz. (J). 1996. pap. 3.25 (*0-679-87038-5*) Random.

Story of Passover. Norma Simon. LC 95-41201. (Illus.). 32p. (J). (gr. 2-5). 1997. 14.95 (*0-06-027062-4*); lib. bdg. 14.89 (*0-06-027063-2*) HarpC Child Bks.

Story of Passover for Children. Francis B. Silberg. (Illus.). 24p. (J). (ps-3). 1989. pap. 3.95 (*0-8249-8309-2*, Ideals Child) Hambleton-Hill.

Story of "Patria" Erich G. Steiner. LC 81-85302. 224p. 1982. 11.95 (*0-89604-035-6*, Holocaust Library); pap. 10.95 (*0-89604-036-4*, Holocaust Library) US Holocaust.

Story of Paul. Alice J. Davidson. (Alice in Bibleland Storybooks). (Illus.). (J). (gr. 3 up). 1989. 50.95 (*0-8378-1853-2*) Gibson.

Story of Paul Bunyan. Barbara Emberley. LC 93-11791. (Illus.). (J). 1994. pap. 14.00 (*0-671-88557-X*, S&S Bks Young Read); pap. 5.95 (*0-671-88647-9*, Half Moon Paper) S&S Childrens.

Story of Paul J. Meyer. Susan Y. Snider. 1988. 14.95 (*0-8119-0720-1*) LIFETIME.

Story of Paul Revere: Messenger of Liberty. large type ed. Joyce Milton. 1991. 30.00 (*0-614-09884-X*, L-15920-00) Am Printing Hse.

***Story of Pearl Jam.** Brad Morrell. (Illus.). 64p. pap. 11.95 (*0-8256-1572-0*, OP 47858) Omnibus NY.

Story of Pears. Lesley-Anne Bourne. 72p. 1990. pap. 9.95 (*0-921254-21-0*, Pub. by Penumbra Pr CN) U of Toronto Pr.

***Story of Pemaquid.** James Otis. (Illus.). 181p. 1997. reprint ed. lib. bdg. 26.00 (*0-8328-5889-7*) Higginson Bk Co.

Story of Persia. S. G. Benjamin. 1977. lib. bdg. 59.95 (*0-8490-2685-7*) Gordon Pr.

Story of Perugia. Margaret Symonds & Lina D. Gordon. 1977. lib. bdg. 59.95 (*0-8490-2686-5*) Gordon Pr.

***Story of Peter Rabbit.** (Illus.). 24p. (J). (gr. 1-3). 1996. 3.98 (*1-890095-00-1*) Nesak Intl.

Story of Phallicism, with Other Essays on Related Subjects by Eminent Authorities. Lee A. Stone & Frederick Starr. LC 72-9682. reprint ed. 62.50 (*0-404-57500-5*) AMS Pr.

Story of Phillis Wheatley. Shirley Graham. 1995. pap. 9.95 (*0-86543-471-9*) Africa World.

***Story of Phillis Wheatley.** Shirley Graham. (Young Readers Ser.). (J). 1996. 29.95 (*0-86543-470-0*) Africa World.

Story of Philosophy. Will Durant. Date not set. mass mkt. 6.99 (*0-671-73916-6*) PB.

Story of Philosophy: The Lives & Opinions of the Great Philosophers. Will Durant. 432p. 1967. pap. 15.00 (*0-671-20159-X*) S&S Trade.

***Story of Photography.** 2nd ed. Michael Langford. (Illus.). 224p. 1997. pap. 35.95 (*0-240-51483-1*, Focal) Buttrwrth-Heinemann.

Story of Photography. Alfred T. Story. Ed. by Nathan Lyons. (Research & Reprint Ser.). (Illus.). 170p. 1974. reprint ed. 11.95 (*0-87992-003-3*); reprint ed. pap. 6.75 (*0-87992-002-5*) Visual Studies.

Story of Physics. Lloyd Motz & Jefferson H. Weaver. 432p. 1992. pap. 12.50 (*0-380-71725-5*) Avon.

Story of Physics. Lloyd Motz & Jefferson H. Weaver. LC 88-33655. (Illus.). 397p. 1989. 24.50 (*0-306-43076-2*, Plenum Pr) Plenum.

Story of Pisa. J. A. Ross & N. Erichsen. LC 85-47864. (Mediaeval Towns Ser.: Vol. 3). 1974. reprint ed. pap. 58.00 (*0-8115-0845-5*) Periodicals Srv.

Story of Pocahontas. Brian Doherty. (Illus.). 96p. (Orig.). (J). (gr. 3 up). 1994. pap. 1.00 (*0-486-28025-X*) Dover.

Story of Pocahontas, Indian Princess. Patricia Adams. (Famous Lives Ser.). (Illus.). 112p. (J). (gr. 3 up). lib. bdg. 19.93 (*0-8368-1471-1*) Gareth Stevens Inc.

***Story of Politics.** Milton Meltzer. (J). Date not set. lib. bdg. write for info. (*0-688-07495-2*, Morrow Junior) Morrow.

Story of Pontiac. Jill Wheeler. Ed. by Paul Deegan. LC 89-84910. (Famous American Indian Leaders Ser.). (Illus.). 32p. (J). (gr. 4). 1989. lib. bdg. 12.98 (*0-939179-69-5*) Abdo & Dghtrs.

Story of Pop see Heinemann Guided Readers

S

An Asterisk (*) at the beginning of an entry indicates that the title is appearing in BIP for the first time.

Story of Pope's Barrels. Ray M. Smith. 211p. 1993. 39.00 (*1-884849-07-5*) R&R Bks.

Story of Portugal. Henry M. Stephens. 1976. lib. bdg. 59.95 (*0-8490-2687-3*) Gordon Pr.

Story of Portugal. Henry M. Stephens. LC 78-137293. 1971. reprint ed. 49.50 (*0-404-06255-5*) AMS Pr.

Story of Prague. C. Lutzow. 1976. lib. bdg. 59.95 (*0-8490-2688-1*) Gordon Pr.

Story of Presidential Elections. Miles Harvey. LC 88-1021. (Cornerstones of Freedom Ser.). (Illus.). 32p. (J). (gr. 3-6). 1988. pap. 3.95 (*0-516-44737-8*) Childrens.

Story of Princess Nire. Carroll Smith. LC 95-79164. (Illus.). 30p. (Orig.). (J). (gr. k-3). pap. 4.95 (*0-9648351-0-X*) Adv Info Res.

Story of Prophecy. Henry J. Forman. 388p. 1981. pap. 32.00 (*0-89540-089-8*, SB-089) Sun Pub.

Story of Psychic Science (Psychical Research) Hereward Carrington. 400p. 1992. pap. 35.00 (*1-56459-259-6*) Kessinger Pub.

Story of Psychology. Morton Hunt. 784p. 1994. pap. 17.95 (*0-385-47149-1*, Anchor NY) Doubleday.

Story of Psychology: A Thematic History. Robert C. Bolles. (C). 1993. text ed. 66.95 (*0-534-19668-3*) Brooks-Cole.

Story of Public Utilities. Edward Hungerford. LC 72-5053. (Technology & Society Ser.). (Illus.). 384p. 1972. reprint ed. 38.95 (*0-405-04705-3*) Ayer.

***Story of Pumpkin.** Frank Fiorello. 40p. (J). (ps-6). Date not set. pap. 7.95 (*0-9646300-2-8*) Fiorellos Pumpkin Patch.

Story of Punishment: A Record of Man's Inhumanity to Man. 2nd rev. ed. Harry E. Barnes. LC 74-108229. (Criminology, Law Enforcement, & Social Problems Ser.: No. 112). (Illus.). (C). 1972. 30.00 (*0-87585-112-6*) Patterson Smith.

Story of Punxsutawney Phil, "The Fearless Forecaster" Julia S. Moutran. LC 86-82950. (Adventures of Punxsutawney Phil Ser.). (Illus.). 64p. (J). (ps-5). 1987. 14.95 (*0-9617819-2-0*); pap. 8.95 (*0-9617819-0-4*); audio 10.95 (*0-9617819-3-9*) Lit Pubns.

Story of Quailwood. Ethel H. Miller. (Illus.). 48p. 1952. 4.95 (*0-912142-07-3*); pap. 2.00 (*0-912142-04-9*) White S Bks.

Story of Rabbi Yisroel Salanter. Zalman F. Ury. 4.75 (*0-914131-60-5*, D540) Torah Umesorah.

Story of Rachel Carson & the Environmental Movement. Leila M. Foster. LC 90-2208. (Cornerstones of Freedom Ser.). (Illus.). 32p. (J). (gr. 3-6). 1990. pap. 4.95 (*0-516-44753-X*) Childrens.

Story of Ramakrishna. Swami Smaranananda. (Illus.). 31p. (Orig.). (J). (gr. k-5). 1976. pap. 2.00 (*0-87481-168-6*, Pub. by Advaita Ashrama II) Vedanta Pr.

Story of Ramayan. Bani R. Choudhary. (Illus.). (J). (gr. 3-10). 1979. 7.50 (*0-89744-133-8*) Auromere.

Story of Ramses. Richard Sullivan. LC 86-12713. (Illus.). 212p. 1986. lib. bdg. 89.95 (*0-88946-046-9*) E Mellen.

Story of Rauth & His Sons. Tr. by J. E. Turville-Petre. LC 77-90463. (Viking Society for Northern Research: Translation Ser.: Vol. 4). reprint ed. 32.50 (*0-404-60014-X*) AMS Pr.

Story of Ravena. E. Hutton. (Mediaeval Towns Ser.: Vol. 19). 1974. reprint ed. 55.00 (*0-8115-0861-7*) Periodicals Srv.

Story of Ray Davis: Gen, USMC, Ret (Medal of Honor) Ray Davis & W. J. Davis. 350p. 1994. 19.95 (*1-885541-00-7*) Marine Bks.

Story of Reb Baruch Ber Lebowitz: The Kamenitzer Rosh Yeshiba - Rabbi Baruch Ber Leibowitz & His Successor, Rabbi Reuven Grozovsky. Tzvi Z. Arem. (ArtScroll Youth Ser.). (Illus.). 128p. (YA). (gr. 6-12). pap. 8.99 (*0-89906-804-9*, RBBP) Mesorah Pubns.

Story of Reb Yosef Chaim: The Life & Times of Rabbi Yosef Chaim Sonnefield, the Guardian of Jerusalem. Shimon Finkelman. (ArtScroll Youth Ser.). (Illus.). 160p. (YA). (gr. 6-12). 11.99 (*0-89906-779-4*, CHFH) Mesorah Pubns.

Story of Reb Yosef Chaim: The Life & Times of Rabbi Yosef Chaim Sonnefield, the Guardian of Jerusalem. Shlomo Z. Sonnenfeld & Shimon Finkelman. (ArtScroll Youth Ser.). (Illus.). 160p. (YA). (gr. 6-12). pap. 11.99 (*0-89906-780-8*, JERP) Mesorah Pubns.

Story of Rebirthing. Leonard D. Orr. 1990. 5.00 (*0-945793-08-1*) Inspir Univ.

Story of Redemption. large type ed. 1980. pap. 6.99 (*0-8280-0058-1*, 19654-3) Review & Herald.

Story of Religion. Betsy C. Maestro. LC 92-38980. (Illus.). 48p. (J). (gr. 2-4). 1996. 15.00 (*0-395-62364-2*, Clarion Bks) HM.

Story of Roadless Traction. Stuart Gibbard. (Illus.). 192p. 1996. 49.90 (*0-85236-344-3*, Pub. by Farming Pr UK) Diamond Farm Bk.

Story of Roberto Clemente, All-Star Hero. Jim O'Connor. (Famous Lives Ser.). (Illus.). (J). 1995. lib. bdg. 19.93 (*0-8368-1384-7*) Gareth Stevens Inc.

***Story of Robin Hood.** Illus. by Nick Harris. LC 96-39117. (Eyewitness Classics Ser.). 64p. (J). 1997. 14.95 (*0-7894-1490-2*) DK Pub Inc.

Story of Robin Hood. Illus. by Barbara Loftheiser. 160p. (J). (gr. 4 up). 1995. pap. 6.95 (*0-7534-5021-6*, Kingfisher LKC) LKC.

Story of Rock. Carl Belz. 256p. reprint ed. lib. bdg. 39.00 (*0-685-14777-0*) Rprt Serv.

Story of Rock: Smash Hits & Superstars. Alain Dister. Tr. by Toula Ballas. (Discoveries Ser.). (Illus.). 176p. 1993. pap. 12.95 (*0-8109-2831-0*) Abrams.

Story of Rock 'n' Roll: The Year-by-Year Illustrated Chronicle. Ed. by Paul Du Noyer. (Illus.). 304p. (Orig.). 1995. pap. 19.99 (*1-886894-22-1*, MBS Paperbk) Mus Bk Servs.

Story of Rock 'n Roll: The Year-by-Year Illustrated Chronicle. Ed. by Paul Du Noyer. 3047p. 1995. 65.00 (*0-02-860284-6*) Schirmer Bks.

Story of Rolf & the Viking Bow. Allen French. LC 93-72606. 240p. (YA). (gr. 5 up). 1994. reprint ed. pap. 12.95 (*1-883937-01-9*, 01-9) Bethlehem ND.

Story of Rome. N. Young. (Mediaeval Towns Ser.: Vol. 38). 1974. reprint ed. 55.00 (*0-8115-0880-3*) Periodicals Srv.

***Story of Rose O'Neill: An Autobiography.** Ed. by Miriam Formanek-Brunell. LC 97-4477. (Illus.). 168p. 1997. pap. 24.95 (*0-8262-1106-2*) U of Mo Pr.

Story of Rosie Redbird. Jennifer Lemmon. (Illus.). 12p. (J). (ps-2). 1995. pap. 4.95 (*0-909991-74-X*) Bahai.

Story of Rosie's Rat: A True Story. Porter P. Swentzell & Rose Swentzell. (Illus.). 48p. (Orig.). (J). (gr. 1-4). 1995. pap. 10.00 (*0-9631909-5-4*) La Alameda Pr.

Story of Rosy Dock. Jeannie Baker. LC 94-4677. (Illus.). 32p. (J). (ps up). 1995. 15.00 (*0-688-11491-1*) Greenwillow.

Story of Rouen. T. A. Cook. (Mediaeval Towns Ser.: Vol. 24). 1974. reprint ed. pap. 58.00 (*0-8115-0866-8*) Periodicals Srv.

Story of Royal Copenhagen Christmas Plates. Pat Owen. (Illus.). 1995. ring bd. 25.00 (*0-911576-01-0*) Viking Import.

Story of Royal Worcester. (Illus.). 1973. pap. 5.00 (*0-685-57077-0*) Ars Ceramica.

Story of Ruby Bridges. Robert Coles. 1995. 13.95 (*0-590-57281-4*) Scholastic Inc.

Story of Rudy Bridges. Robert Coles. LC 92-33674. (Illus.). 32p. (J). (gr. k-4). 1995. 13.95 (*0-590-43967-7*) Scholastic Inc.

***Story of Ruth.** Jude Winkler. (Saint Joseph Bible Story Ser.). (Illus.). 1989. pap. 1.25 (*0-89942-945-9*, 945) Catholic Bk Pub.

Story of Ruth & Naomi. Alice J. Davidson. (Alice in Bibleland Storybooks). (Illus.). (J). (gr. 3 up). 1989. 5.95 (*0-8378-1855-9*) Gibson.

***Story of Ruth & the Story of David.** Petersham. (J). Date not set. mass mkt. 5.99 (*0-689-81399-6*) S&S Childrens.

Story of Sacajawea: Guide to Lewis & Clark. Della Rowland. 96p. (J). (gr. k-6). 1989. pap. 3.99 (*0-440-40215-8*, YB BDD) BDD Bks Young Read.

***Story of Sadhu Sundar Singh.** 96p. 1992. 5.99 (*0-8341-1435-6*) Nazarene.

Story of Saint Patrick. James A. Janda. LC 94-22992. (Illus.). 32p. (Orig.). (J). 1995. pap. 4.95 (*0-8091-6623-2*) Paulist Pr.

Story of Samson & His Great Strength. Patricia Pingry. (Story of...Ser.). (Illus.). 24p. (Orig.). (J). (ps-2). 1994. pap. 3.95 (*0-8249-8655-5*, Ideals Child) Hambleton-Hill.

Story of Samuel. Joan Kendall. (Very First Bible Stories Ser.). (J). (gr. k-4). 1984. 1.59 (*0-87162-271-8*, D8500) Warner Pr.

Story of San Michele. Axel Munthe. (Illus.). 351p. 1984. pap. 10.95 (*0-88184-109-9*) Carroll & Graf.

Story of San Michele. Axel Munthe. 425p. 1990. reprint ed. lib. bdg. 25.95 (*0-89966-676-0*) Buccaneer Bks.

Story of Santa Claus. Rick Bunsen. (Storytime Christmas Ser.). (Illus.). 24p. (J). (ps-2). 1994. pap. 1.29 (*1-56293-496-1*) McClanahan Bk.

Story of Santa Claus. Barbara S. Hazen. (Big Story Ser.). (Illus.). 32p. (J). (ps up). 1989. 4.50 (*0-307-12097-X*, Golden Pr) Western Pub.

***Story of Santa Claus.** Tom Paxton. (J). Date not set. pap. 5.95 (*0-688-15475-1*, Mulberry) Morrow.

Story of Santa Claus. Tom Paxton. LC 94-23919. (Illus.). 40p. (J). (gr. k up). 1995. 15.00 (*0-688-11364-8*, Morrow Junior) Morrow.

Story of Santa Claus. Scribbler Elf. 96p. (J). (ps-3). 1993. 19.95 (*1-878685-45-7*) Turner Pub GA.

Story of Santa Klaus: Told for Children of All Ages from Six to Sixty. William S. Walsh. (Illus.). 231p. 1991. reprint ed. lib. bdg. 40.00 (*1-55888-922-1*) Omnigraphics Inc.

Story of Santoshi Devi. Gayatri Rajan. (Illus.). 40p. (Orig.). (J). (gr. k-6). pap. write for info. (*0-9644226-0-3*) Buddhi Pubns.

Story of Sarada Devi. Swami Smaranananda. (Illus.). 31p. (Orig.). (J). (gr. k-4). 1987. pap. 2.00 (*0-87481-229-1*, Pub. by Advaita Ashrama II) Vedanta Pr.

Story of Science, Bk. 1. (Illus.). (ARA.). (J). (gr. 5-12). 1987. 4.50 (*0-86685-229-8*) Intl Bk Ctr.

Story of Scorpions. Gabriel Everett. LC 96-48588. 1997. 22.00 (*0-517-70665-2*) Crown Pub Group.

***Story of Scotia.** Harry M. Williams. Ed. by Betty F. Johnson. (Illus.). 128p. 1992. 30.00 (*1-887315-05-5*) Centre Cty Hist Soc.

***Story of Scotland Yard.** Nelson U. K. Staff. 1991. pap. text ed. write for info. (*0-00-370151-4*) Addison-Wesley.

Story of Scotland's Towns. Robert J. Naismith. (Illus.). 200p. (C). 1996. 45.00 (*0-85976-257-2*, Pub. by J Donald UK) St Mut.

Story of Scottish Philosophy: A Compendium of Selections from the Writings of Nine Pre-Eminent Scottish Philosophers, with Biobibliographical Essays. Ed. by Daniel S. Robinson. LC 78-12114. (Illus.). 290p. 1979. reprint ed. text ed. 38.50 (*0-313-21082-9*, ROST) Greenwood.

Story of Sculpture: From Prehistory to the Present. Francesca Romei. LC 95-7006. (Masters of Art Ser.). (Illus.). 64p. 1995. lib. bdg. 22.50 (*0-87226-316-9*) P Bedrick Bks.

Story of Sequoyah. Jill Wheeler. Ed. by Paul Deegan. LC 89-84909. (Famous American Indian Leaders Ser.). (Illus.). 32p. (J). (gr. 4). 1989. lib. bdg. 12.98 (*0-939179-70-9*) Abdo & Dghtrs.

***Story of Seven Sour Pickles.** Patricia T. Kienzle & Debbie Ruff. (Illus.). 28p. (J). (gr. 2-3). 1995. teacher ed., pap. 3.95 (*1-890798-05-3*) P T Kienzle.

Story of Seville: With Three Chapters on the Artists of Seville. Walter M. Gallichan & C. G. Hartley. (Mediaeval Towns Ser.: Vol. 14). 1974. reprint ed. pap. 35.00 (*0-8115-0856-0*) Periodicals Srv.

Story of Shadrach, Meshach & Abednego. Rhonda Colburn. (Story of...Ser.). (Illus.). 24p. (J). (ps-2). 1990. pap. 3.95 (*0-8249-8421-8*, Ideals Child) Hambleton-Hill.

Story of Shaw's Saint Joan. Brian Tyson. LC 84-166898. (Illus.). 152p. reprint ed. pap. 43.40 (*0-7837-6910-5*, 2046740) Bks Demand.

Story of Shirley. Shirley Inst. Staff. (C). 1988. 50.00 (*0-685-46366-4*, Pub. by British Textile Tech UK) St Mut.

***Story of Shirley Temple Black: Hollywood's Youngest Star.** Carlo Fiori. LC 97-1054. (Famous Lives Ser.). (J). 1997. write for info. (*0-8368-1481-9*) Gareth Stevens Inc.

Story of Shoes. Lucy Strauss. (Real Readers Ser.: Level Green). (Illus.). 32p. (J). (gr. 1-4). 1989. lib. bdg. 21.40 (*0-8172-3534-5*) Raintree Steck-V.

Story of Shoes. Lucy Strauss. (Real Reading Ser.). (Illus.). 32p. (J). (gr. 1-4). 1989. pap. 3.95 (*0-8114-6732-5*) Raintree Steck-V.

Story of Siddhartha's Release. Richard Bartholomew. (Writers Workshop Redbird Ser.). 1975. 8.00 (*0-88253-648-6*); pap. text ed. 4.00 (*0-88253-647-8*) Ind-US Inc.

Story of Sierra Leone. Francis A. Utting. LC 77-37357. (Select Bibliographies Reprint Ser.). 1977. reprint ed. 19.95 (*0-8369-6704-6*) Ayer.

Story of Simpson & Sampson. Munro Leaf. LC 88-39014. (Illus.). 64p. (J). (gr. 1-3). 1989. reprint ed. lib. bdg. 16.50 (*0-208-02244-9*, Linnet Bks) Shoe String.

Story of Sir Launcelot & His Companions. Howard Pyle. 1991. pap. 8.95 (*0-486-26701-6*) Dover.

Story of Sirio. Ferdinando Camon. Tr. by Cassandra Bertea from ITA. LC 84-63123. Orig. Title: Storia Di Sirio. 131p. (Orig.). 1985. pap. 9.95 (*0-910395-12-8*) Marlboro Pr.

Story of Sitting Bull. Lisa Eisenberg. 112p. (J). (gr. 4-7). 1991. pap. 3.99 (*0-440-40508-4*) Dell.

Story of Sitting Bull. Jill Wheeler. Ed. by Paul Deegan. LC 89-94912. (Famous American Indian Leaders Ser.). (Illus.). 32p. (J). (gr. 4). 1989. lib. bdg. 12.98 (*0-939179-67-9*) Abdo & Dghtrs.

Story of Sitting Bull: Great Sioux Chief. Lisa Eisenberg. LC 95-36799. (Dell Yearling Biography Ser.). (Illus.). (J). 1996. lib. bdg. 19.93 (*0-8368-1465-7*) Gareth Stevens Inc.

Story of Smokey the Bear. 32p. 1996. pap. 15.99 (*0-7214-5640-5*, Ladybrd) Penguin.

Story of Snow White. Ed. by Ogawa & Katayama. (Nihongo Folktales Ser.). (Illus.). 32p. (J). 1994. pap. 7.00 (*4-7700-1795-2*) Kodansha.

Story of Social Philosophy. Charles A. Ellwood. LC 79-152169. (Essay Index Reprint Ser.). 1977. 29.95 (*0-8369-2187-9*) Ayer.

Story of Some Famous Books. Frederick Saunders. LC 72-5752. (Essay Index Reprint Ser.). 1977. reprint ed. 20.95 (*0-8369-7290-2*) Ayer.

Story of Somerset. rev. ed. Ruth B. Porter. 70p. 1972. pap. 3.00 (*0-685-29128-6*) Niagara Cnty Hist Soc.

Story of South Africa: J. M. Coetzee's Fiction in Context. Susan V. Gallagher. 258p. (C). 1991. 36.00 (*0-674-83972-2*) HUP.

***Story of South African Painting.** Esme Berman. 272p. 1975. 105.00 (*0-86961-067-8*, Pub. by A A Balkema NE) Ashgate Pub Co.

Story of Southern Hymnology. Arthur L. Stevenson. LC 72-1676. reprint ed. 34.50 (*0-404-08334-X*) AMS Pr.

Story of Space & Rockets. Roger Arno. (Illus.). (J). (gr. 5). 1978. pap. 4.95 (*0-88388-063-6*) Bellerophon Bks.

Story of Spanish Painting. Charles H. Caffin. LC 72-100521. (BCL Ser. I). (Illus.). reprint ed. 37.50 (*0-404-01361-9*) AMS Pr.

Story of Sri Krishna for Children: Part I: Krishna as a Baby & Small Child. 60p. pap. 4.95 (*81-7120-140-7*) Vedanta Ctr.

Story of Sri Krishna for Children: Part II: His Adventures as a Youth & Adult. 42p. pap. 4.95 (*81-7120-278-0*) Vedanta Ctr.

Story of Sri Ramakrishna for Children. 30p. pap. 2.95 (*81-7120-217-9*) Vedanta Ctr.

Story of Sri Shankara for Children. 20p. pap. 2.95 (*81-7120-119-9*) Vedanta Ctr.

Story of St. Donat's Castle & Atlantic College. John B. Hilling et al. 128p. (C). 1989. 75.00 (*0-905928-26-1*, Pub. by D Brown & Sons Ltd UK) St Mut.

Story of St. Frideswide. Francis Goldie. 1992. pap. 2.95 (*0-89981-139-6*) Eastern Orthodox.

Story of St. Ives. Ann Pascoe. (C). 1990. pap. 24.95 (*0-85025-303-9*, Pub. by Tor Mark Pr UK) St Mut.

Story of "Stagecoach" Mary Fields. Robert H. Miller. (Stories of the Forgotten West Ser.). (Illus.). 32p. (J). (gr. k-3). 1994. 12.95 (*0-382-24399-4*); pap. 5.95 (*0-382-24394-3*); lib. bdg. 14.95 (*0-382-24390-0*) Silver Burdett Pr.

Story of Starlight Theatre: The History of Kansas City's Delightful Musical Theatre under the Stars. Kathleen H. Thorne. LC 09-73071. (Illus.). 168p. 1992. 29.95 (*0-9633565-0-X*) Generation Org.

Story of Stone: Intertexuality, Ancient Chinese Stone Lore, & the Stone Symbolism in the Dream of the Red Chamber, Water Margin, & Journey to the West. Jing Wang. LC 91-12211. (Post-Contemporary Interventions Ser.). 359p. 1992. text ed. 42.95 (*0-8223-1178-X*); pap. text ed. 21.95 (*0-8223-1195-X*) Duke.

Story of Stupidity: A History of Western Idiocy from the Days of Greece to the Present. 9th ed. James F. Welles. 270p. (Orig.). (C). 1997. pap. 8.95 (*0-9617729-1-3*) Mt Pleasant Pr.

***Story of Sunflower Island.** Carol Greene. LC 97-10703. (Illus.). (J). 1998. write for info. (*0-06-027326-7*) HarpC.

***Story of Sunflower Island.** Carol Greene. LC 97-10703. (Illus.). (J). 1999. lib. bdg. write for info. (*0-06-027327-5*) HarpC.

Story of Surnames. William D. Bowman. 1998. reprint ed. 40.00 (*1-55888-229-4*) Omnigraphics Inc.

***Story of Suzanne Aubert.** Jessie Munro. (Illus.). 472p. 1997. pap. 35.95 (*1-86940-155-7*, Pub. by Auckland Univ NZ) Paul & Co Pubs.

Story of Swarajya: Part I. Vishnu Prabhakar. (Nehru Library for Children). (Illus.). (J). (gr. 1-10). 1979. pap. 2.50 (*0-89744-185-0*) Auromere.

Story of Swarajya: Part II. Sumangal Prakash. (Nehru Library for Children). (Illus.). (J). (gr. 1-10). 1979. pap. 2.50 (*0-89744-186-9*) Auromere.

Story of Symphony. E. M. Lee. 1972. 59.95 (*0-8490-1138-8*) Gordon Pr.

Story of Tahoe Tessie: The Original Lake Tahoe Monster. 5th rev. ed. Bob McCormick. (Illus.). (J). (gr. 1-4). 1990. pap. 5.95 (*0-9626792-6-7*) Tahoe Tourist.

Story of Tatiana. Jacques Baynac. 1994. pap. 6.00 (*0-934868-31-X*) Black & Red.

***Story of Ted Corbitt.** John Chodes. 1974. 12.95 (*5-415-28717-5*) Cedarwinds.

***Story of Ted Corbitt.** John Chodes. 1974. pap. text ed. 12.95 (*0-915297-17-5*) Cedarwinds.

Story of Telecommunications. George P. Oslin. LC 92-38503. (C). 1992. 35.00 (*0-86554-418-2*, MUP-H322) Mercer Univ Pr.

Story of Television: The Life of Philo T. Farnsworth. George Everson. LC 74-4677. (Illus.). 270p. 1978. reprint ed. 26.95 (*0-405-06042-4*) Ayer.

Story of Texas. 2nd ed. John E. Weems. (Illus.). (Orig.). (J). (gr. 2-6). 1992. pap. 8.95 (*0-940672-35-9*) Shearer Pub.

Story of Texas: A History Picture Book. Betsy Warren. (Illus.). 46p. (J). (gr. 3 up). 1988. reprint ed. pap. 3.50 (*0-9618660-1-2*) Ranch Gate Bks.

Story of the Abbey Theatre. Peter Kavanagh. LC 84-60178. (Irish Art Ser.). (Illus.). 325p. 1984. reprint ed. 25.00 (*0-915032-29-5*); reprint ed. pap. 12.95 (*0-915032-30-9*) Natl Poet Foun.

Story of the Acadians. Amy Boudreau. (Illus.). 38p. 1971. pap. 2.95 (*0-911116-30-3*) Pelican.

Story of the Advent Wreath. 12p. (J). 1988. pap. 1.50 (*0-8066-2525-2*) Augsburg Fortress.

Story of the Alamo. Norman Richards. LC 70-100698. (Cornerstones of Freedom Ser.). (Illus.). 32p. (J). (gr. 3-6). 1970. pap. 4.95 (*0-516-44601-0*) Childrens.

***Story of the Alphabet: Ancient Languages.** 2nd ed. Eward Clodd. (Illus.). 375p. 1997. reprint ed. spiral bd. 15.00 (*1-57179-070-5*) Intern Guild ASRS.

Story of the American Board: An Account of the First Hundred Years of the American Board for Foreign Missions. William E. Strong. LC 79-83443. (Religion in America, Ser.). 1970. reprint ed. 29.95 (*0-405-00277-7*) Ayer.

Story of the American Flag. Diane Russomanno. (Ricky Rocket Ser.). 32p. (J). 1991. pap. text ed. write for info. (*1-880501-01-5*) Know Booster.

Story of the American Hymn. Edward S. Ninde. LC 72-1708. (Illus.). reprint ed. 57.45 (*0-404-09914-9*) AMS Pr.

Story of the American Merchant Marine. John R. Spears. 1977. lib. bdg. 250.00 (*0-8490-2689-X*) Gordon Pr.

Story of the America's Cup 1851-1995. Ranulf Rayner. (Illus.). 96p. 1996. 50.00 (*1-895629-65-9*, Pub. by Warwick Pub CN) Firefly Bks Ltd.

Story of the Amulet. Edith Nesbit. (J). 1996. pap. 3.99 (*0-14-036752-7*) Viking Penguin.

Story of the Amulet. Edith Nesbit. (J). pap. 4.95 (*0-8167-2901-8*) Troll Communs.

***Story of the Amulet.** Paul Zelinsky. Date not set. write for info. (*0-688-13547-1*, Morrow Junior) Morrow.

Story of the Atlantic Telegraph. Henry M. Field. LC 72-5049. (Technology & Society Ser.). (Illus.). 415p. 1972. reprint ed. 26.95 (*0-405-04701-0*) Ayer.

Story of the Baltimore & Ohio Railroad, 1827-1927, 2 vols, 1. Edward Hungerford. LC 72-5054. (Technology & Society Ser.). (Illus.). 600p. 1972. reprint ed. 38.95 (*0-405-04735-5*) Ayer.

Story of the Baltimore & Ohio Railroad, 1827-1927, 2 vols, Set. Edward Hungerford. LC 72-5054. (Technology & Society Ser.). (Illus.). 600p. 1972. reprint ed. 77.95 (*0-405-04706-1*) Ayer.

Story of the Baltimore & Ohio Railroad, 1827-1927, 2 vols, Vol. 2. Edward Hungerford. LC 72-5054. (Technology & Society Ser.). (Illus.). 600p. 1972. reprint ed. 38.95 (*0-405-04736-3*) Ayer.

***Story of the Baltimore & Ohio Railroad, 1875-1948.** Edward Hungerford. (Illus.). 1972. 70.95 (*0-8369-6829-8*) Ayer.

Story of the Barbary Corsairs. Stanley Lane-Poole. LC 73-97416. (Illus.). 316p. 1970. reprint ed. text ed. 38.50 (*0-8371-3231-2*, LBC&, Negro U Pr) Greenwood.

Story of the Battle Hymn of the Republic. Florence H. Hall. LC 71-178474. (Black Heritage Library Collection). 1977. reprint ed. 22.95 (*0-8369-8923-6*) Ayer.

Story of the Battle of Bull Run. Zachary Kent. LC 86-9642. (Cornerstones of Freedom Ser.). (Illus.). 32p. (J). (gr. 3-6). 1986. pap. 4.95 (*0-516-44703-3*) Childrens.

Story of the Battle of Shiloh. Zachary Kent. LC 90-21646. (Cornerstones of Freedom Ser.). (Illus.). 32p. (J). (gr. 3-6). 1991. pap. 4.95 (*0-516-44754-8*) Childrens.

Story of the Bible. Ed. by Johnny Ramsey. 1983. pap. 5.50 (*0-89137-543-0*) Quality Pubns.

Story of the Bible. Edgar J. Goodspeed. LC 36-21666. 374p. reprint ed. 106.60 (*0-8357-9657-4*, 2013612) Bks Demand.

An Asterisk (*) at the beginning of an entry indicates that the title is appearing in BIP for the first time.

Story of the Bible World see Fascinante Mundo de la Biblia

***Story of the Birth of Jesus.** Jude Winkler. (Saint Joseph Bible Story Ser.). (Illus.). 1989. 2.25 (*0-89942-960-2*, 960/22) Catholic Bk Pub.

***Story of the Blues.** Peter O. Bekker. LC 96-38465. (The Life, Times & Music Ser.). 1997. pap. write for info. (*1-56799-081-9*, Friedman-Fairfax) M Friedman Pub Grp Inc.

***Story of the Blues.** Peter O. Bekker. LC 96-38465. (The Life, Times & Music Ser.). 1997. write for info. (*1-56799-357-5*, Friedman-Fairfax) M Friedman Pub Grp Inc.

Story of the Blues. Friedman-Fairfax & Sony Music Staff. (Life, Times & Music Book/CD Ser.). 1995. pap. 16.98 incl. audio compact disk (*1-56799-075-4*, Friedman-Fairfax) M Friedman Pub Grp Inc.

Story of the Boston Tea Party. R. Conrad Stein. LC 83-27319. (Illus.). (J). (gr. 3-6). 1984. pap. 4.95 (*0-516-44666-5*) Childrens.

Story of the Calcutta Theatre, 1753-1980. Sushil K. Mukherjee. 1983. 32.00 (*0-8364-0994-9*, Pub. by KP Bagchi IA) S Asia.

Story of the California AHEC System: California Area Health Education Centers: 1972-1989. Malcolm S. Watts & Clark Jones. (Illus.). (Orig.). 1990. pap. text ed. 9.95 (*1-879107-00-7*) CA Area Hlth Educ Ctr Sys.

Story of the California Gold Rush Coloring Book. Peter Copeland. (Illus.). (J). (gr. k-3). 1991. pap. 2.95 (*0-486-25814-9*) Dover.

Story of the Canadian Pacific Railway. Keith Morris. Ed. by Stuart Bruchey. LC 80-1332. (Railroads Ser.). (Illus.). 1981. reprint ed. lib. bdg. 20.95 (*0-405-13806-7*) Ayer.

Story of the Carol. Edmondstoune Duncan. LC 89-49707. (Illus.). xii, 253p. 1992. reprint ed. lib. bdg. 40.00 (*1-55888-921-3*) Omnigraphics Inc.

***Story of the Catholic Church.** Matthew Bunson. 1997. pap. 14.00 (*0-609-80144-9*) Crown Pub Group.

Story of the Catholic Church. Matthew Bunson. 1997. write for info. (*0-517-70555-9*) Random.

Story of the Champions of the Round Table. Howard Pyle. (Illus.). xviii, 329p. (J). (ps-4). 1968. pap. 7.95 (*0-486-21883-X*) Dover.

Story of the Champions of the Round Table. Howard Pyle. LC 84-13881. (Illus.). 352p. (YA). (gr. 7 up). 1984. lib. bdg. 19.95 (*0-684-18171-1*, C Scribner Sons Young) S&S Childrens.

***Story of the Champions of the Round Table.** Howard Pyle. lib. bdg. 25.95 (*0-8488-2106-8*) Amereon Ltd.

Story of the Chasam Sofer. Shubert Spero. (Illus.). 80p. 2.25 (*0-914131-61-3*, D530) Torah Umesorah.

Story of the Cherokee People. Thomas B. Underwood. (Illus.). 48p. 1961. 3.50 (*0-935741-01-1*) Cherokee Pubns.

Story of the Chinese Zodiac: El Zodiaco Chino. Monica Chang. Tr. by Beatriz Zeller from CHI. (Illus.). 32p. (ENG & SPA.). (J). (gr. 2-4). 1994. 16.95 (*957-32-2143-8*) Pan Asian Pubns.

Story of the Chokoloskee Bay Country, with the Reminiscences of T. S. "Ted" Smallwood. Charlton W. Tebeau. LC 75-43288. (Illus.). 88p. 1976. pap. 4.95 (*0-916224-01-5*) Florida Flair Bks.

Story of the Christian Church. rev. ed. Jesse L. Hurlbut. 192p. 1967. 12.99 (*0-310-26510-X*, 6527) Zondervan.

Story of the Christian Year. Amy Boudreau. 1971. 6.50 (*0-685-27196-X*) Claitors.

Story of the Christian Year. Richard M. Nardone. 1991. pap. 9.95 (*0-8091-3277-X*) Paulist Pr.

Story of the Christian Year. George M. Gibson. LC 71-142635. (Essay Index Reprint Ser.). (Illus.). 1977. reprint ed. 27.95 (*0-8369-2770-2*) Ayer.

Story of the Christmas Bear. Donna Foreman. LC 91-77576. (Illus.). 40p. (J). (gr. k-3). 1992. 7.95 (*1-880851-02-4*) Greene Bark Pr.

Story of the Christmas Guest. Helen Steiner Rice. (Illus.). 34p. (J). 1991. reprint ed. pap. 9.95 (*0-89966-842-9*) Buccaneer Bks.

***Story of the Christmas Rose.** Alda Ellis. (Remembrance of Times Past Ser.). (Illus.). 16p. (Orig.). 1997. 6.99 (*1-56507-716-4*) Harvest Hse.

Story of the Christmas Rose. I. M. Richardson. LC 87-13817. (Illus.). 32p. (J). (gr. k-4). 1988. lib. bdg. 11.89 (*0-8167-1069-4*) Troll Communs.

Story of the Christmas Rose. I. M. Richardson. LC 87-13817. (Illus.). 32p. (J). (gr. k-4). 1996. pap. 3.95 (*0-8167-1070-8*) Troll Communs.

Story of the Church. Inez S. Davis. 1989. pap. 17.50 (*0-8309-0188-4*) Herald Hse.

Story of the Church. George Johnson et al. LC 80-51329. 521p. (J). (gr. 9). 1980. reprint ed. pap. 16.50 (*0-89555-156-X*) TAN Bks Pubs.

Story of the Church: Peak Moments from Pentecost to the Year 2000. rev. ed. Alfred A. McBride. (Illus.). 168p. (YA). (gr. 7-12). 1996. pap. text ed. 12.95 (*0-86716-246-5*) St Anthony Mess Pr.

Story of the Church of Egypt, 2 vols., Set. Edith L. Butcher. LC 75-41459. reprint ed. 175.00 (*0-404-56231-0*) AMS Pr.

Story of the CIO. Benjamin Stolberg. LC 77-156426. (American Labor Ser., No. 2). 1974. reprint ed. 23.95 (*0-405-02944-6*) Ayer.

Story of the Civilisation, 15 vols., Set. Prints India Staff. (C). 1988. 1,500.00 (*0-7855-0042-1*, Pub. by Print Hse II) St Mut.

Story of the Commonweal. Henry Vincent. LC 73-90194. (Mass Violence in America Ser.). (Illus.). 1969. reprint ed. 27.95 (*0-405-01339-6*) Ayer.

***Story of the Comstock.** unabridged ed. Silvia A. Sheafer. (Illus.). 68p. (Orig.). 1997. pap. text ed. 9.95 (*1-889971-00-6*, 201) Journal Pubns.

Story of the Confederacy. Robert S. Henry. (Quality Paperbacks Ser.). 526p. 1989. pap. 14.95 (*0-306-80370-4*) Da Capo.

Story of the Confederate States: or History of the War for Southern Independence Embracing the Early Settlement of the Country, Trouble with the Indians, the French, Revolutionary & Mexican Wars. Joseph T. Derry. 1980. 42.95 (*0-405-12295-0*) Ayer.

Story of the Congo Free State. Henry W. Wack. (Illus.). 1970. reprint ed. 27.50 (*0-87266-042-7*) Argosy.

Story of the Constitution. rev. ed. Marilyn Prolman. LC 69-14680. (Cornerstones of Freedom Bks.). (Illus.). 32p. (J). (gr. 3-6). 1995. pap. 3.95 (*0-516-44605-3*) Childrens.

Story of the Constitution. Sol Bloom. LC 86-12666. (Illus.). 192p. 1986. reprint ed. pap. text ed. 8.95 (*0-911333-45-2*, 200046) National Archives & Recs.

Story of the Creation: Words from Genesis. Illus. & Photos by Jane Ray. LC 92-20862. 32p. (J). (gr. 1 up). 1993. pap. 16.00 (*0-525-44946-9*) Dutton Child Bks.

Story of the Creation: Words from Genesis. Photos by Jane Ray. LC 92-20862. (Illus.). 32p. (SPA.). (J). (gr. 1 up). 1993. Spanish ed. pap. 16.00 (*0-525-45055-6*) Dutton Child Bks.

Story of the Crusaders: The Three Hundred Eighty-Sixth Bomb Group in World War Two. 2nd ed. Ed. by Barnett B. Young. LC 91-4456. (Illus.). 192p. 1991. 25.00 (*0-9621617-1-3*) Three Hundred Eighty-Sixth BGA.

Story of the Declaration of Independence. rev. ed. Norman Richards. LC 68-24379. (Cornerstones of Freedom Ser.). (Illus.). 32p. (J). (gr. 3-6). 1995. pap. 4.95 (*0-516-44606-1*) Childrens.

Story of the Dining Fork (Ohio) Joseph T. Harrison. (Illus.). 370p. 1993. reprint ed. lib. bdg. 41.00 (*0-8328-3224-3*) Higginson Bk Co.

Story of the Doors. John Tobler & Andrew Doe. (Illus.). 128p. (Orig.). pap. 14.95 (*0-8256-1550-X*, OP47850) Omnibus NY.

***Story of the Dream Catcher.** Illus. by Mona Woodard. LC 96-94598. 64p. (J). 1996. pap. 9.95 (*1-883821-11-8*) Mother Bird.

Story of the Dutch East Indies. Bernard H. Vlekke. LC 71-161775. reprint ed. 32.50 (*0-404-09043-5*) AMS Pr.

Story of the Earth. Peter Cattermole & Patrick Moore. (Illus.). 224p. 1985. text ed. 38.95 (*0-521-26292-5*) Cambridge U Pr.

Story of the Earth. Peter Cattermole & Patrick Moore. (Illus.). 224p. 1986. pap. text ed. 6.95 (*0-521-32413-0*) Cambridge U Pr.

Story of the Earth. Stuart Malin. LC 90-11019. (Exploring the Universe Ser.). (Illus.). 32p. (J). (gr. 4-6). 1991. lib. bdg. 13.95 (*0-8167-2134-3*) Troll Communs.

Story of the Earth. Stuart Malin. LC 90-11019. (Exploring the Universe Ser.). (Illus.). 32p. (J). (gr. 4-6). 1996. pap. 4.95 (*0-8167-2135-1*) Troll Communs.

Story of the Easter Bunny. Sheila Black. LC 87-81934. (Big Story Ser.). (Illus.). 32p. (J). (ps-1). 1988. 4.95 (*0-307-10415-X*, Golden Pr) Western Pub.

Story of the Eastern Province of Saudi Arabia. William Facey. 1993. 60.00 (*0-86685-564-5*) Intl Bk Ctr.

Story of the Eastern Province of Saudi Arabia. William Facey. (Illus.). 160p. 1995. boxed 60.00 (*0-905743-68-7*, Pub. by Stacey Intl UK) Intl Bk Ctr.

Story of the Empire see British Empire

Story of the Eucharist. Inos Biffi. Tr. by John Drury from ITA. LC 85-82173. (Illustrated History of Christian Culture Ser.). Orig. Title: Storia dell' eucaristia. (Illus.). 125p. (J). (gr. 5 up). 1986. 17.95 (*0-89870-089-2*) Ignatius Pr.

Story of the Eye. Georges Bataille. Tr. by Joachim Neugroschel from FRE. 72p. (Orig.). 1987. reprint ed. pap. 9.95 (*0-87286-209-7*) City Lights.

Story of the Falashas: "Black Jews" of Ethiopia. Simon D. Messing. (Illus.). 134p. 1982. pap. 10.00 (*0-9615946-9-1*) S D Messing.

Story of the Famous 34th Infantry Division. John H. Hougen. (Divisional Ser.: No. 10). (Illus.). 196p. 1979. reprint ed. 39.95 (*0-89839-024-9*) Battery Pr.

Story of the Fender Stratocaster: "Curves, Contours & Body Horns" a Celebration of the World's Greatest Guitar. Ray Minhinnett & Bob Young. LC 94-33586. (Illus.). 128p. 1995. 24.95 (*0-87930-349-2*) Miller Freeman.

Story of the Firm, 1864-1964. Ed. by Richard P. Brief. LC 89-23275. (Accounting History & Thought Ser.). 172p. 1990. text ed. 15.00 (*0-8240-3610-7*) Garland.

Story of the First Christmas. Ruth Sanderson. (J). (ps-3). 1994. 9.95 (*1-57036-039-1*) Turner Pub GA.

Story of the First Thanksgiving. Elaine Raphael & Don Bolognese. 32p. (J). 1992. pap. 3.95 (*0-590-44374-7*, Cartwheel) Scholastic Inc.

Story of the Flinders Ranges Mammals. Dorothy Tunbridge. (Illus.). 96p. (Orig.). 1993. pap. 16.95 (*0-86417-390-3*, Pub. by Kangaroo Pr AT) Seven Hills Bk.

Story of the Freeman. Francis Neilson. 1971. 250.00 (*0-87700-011-5*) Revisionist Pr.

Story of the Garden of Eden. Patricia Pingry. (Story of... Ser.). (Illus.). 24p. (Orig.). (J). (ps-2). 1994. pap. 3.95 (*0-8249-8654-7*, Ideals Child) Hambleton-Hill.

Story of the Gateway Arch: A Pictorial History. Ed. by David A. Grove. (Illus.). 31p. (Orig.). (C). 1992. pap. text ed. 3.95 (*0-931056-04-7*) Jefferson Natl.

Story of the General Crushed Stone Company. W. Julian Parton. (Illus.). 100p. 1992. text ed. 11.95 (*0-930973-13-5*) Canal Hist Tech.

Story of the Glittering Plain: Which Has Also Been Called the Land of the Living or the Acre of the Dying. Douglas A. Menville. LC 80-19460. (Forgotten Fantasy Library: Vol. 1). xvi, 174p. 1980. reprint ed. lib. bdg. 33.00 (*0-89370-500-4*) Borgo Pr.

Story of the Good Samaritan. Alice J. Davidson. (Alice in Bibleland Storybooks). (Illus.). (J). (gr. 3 up). 1989. 5.95 (*0-8378-1854-0*) Gibson.

Story of the Good Samaritan. Penny Frank. (Story Bible Ser.: No. 38). 24p. (J). (ps-3). 1994. pap. 1.99 (*0-7459-1783-6*) Lion USA.

Story of the Grail & the Passing of Arthur. unabridged ed. Howard Pyle. LC 92-29058. (Illus.). 272p. (J). 1992. reprint ed. pap. text ed. 7.95 (*0-486-27361-X*) Dover.

Story of the Great Armada. John R. Hale. 1972. lib. bdg. 59.95 (*0-8490-2690-3*) Gordon Pr.

Story of the Great Geologists. Carroll L. Fenton & Mildred A. Fenton. LC 73-84306. (Essay Index Reprint Ser.). 1977. 24.95 (*0-8369-1130-X*) Ayer.

Story of the Great March. George W. Nichols. (Illus.). 408p. 1996. pap. 29.00 (*0-7884-0455-5*, N313) Heritage Bk.

Story of the Great March. George W. Nichols. 394p. 1972. reprint ed. 26.95 (*0-87928-031-X*) Corner Hse.

Story of the Great Society. Leila M. Foster. LC 90-22445. (Cornerstones of Freedom Ser.). (Illus.). 32p. (J). (gr. 3-6). 1991. pap. 4.95 (*0-516-44755-6*) Childrens.

Story of the Greeks. Helene A. Guerber. 288p. 1996. 20.00 (*0-8196-2094-7*) Biblo.

Story of the Guard: A Chronicle of the War. Fremont. 1992. reprint ed. lib. bdg. 75.00 (*0-7812-5035-8*) Rprt Serv.

Story of the Hindus. Jacqueline S. Hirst. 32p. 1989. 12.95 (*0-521-26261-5*) Cambridge U Pr.

Story of the Hindus. Jacqueline S. Hirst. 32p. 1989. pap. text ed. 7.50 (*0-521-26900-8*) Cambridge U Pr.

Story of the Hoover Dam. (Illus.). 144p. 1986. 24.95 (*0-913814-80-6*); pap. 14.95 (*0-913814-79-2*) Nevada Pubns.

Story of the House of Witmark: From Ragtime to Swingtime. Isidore Witmark & Isaac Goldberg. LC 76-20707. (Roots of Jazz Ser.). 1975. reprint ed. lib. bdg. 45.00 (*0-306-70686-5*) Da Capo.

Story of the Human Aura. George S. White. 214p. 1969. reprint ed. spiral bd. 14.00 (*0-7873-0959-1*) Hlth Research.

Story of the Huna Work. E. Otha Wingo. 1981. pap. 3.00 (*0-910764-06-9*) Huna Res Inc.

Story of the Hutchinsons, 2 vols., Set. John Wallace Hutchinson. Ed. by Charles E. Mann. LC 76-58562. (Music Reprint Ser.). 1977. reprint ed. lib. bdg. 95.00 (*0-306-70864-7*) Da Capo.

Story of the Hymns. H. Butterworth. 1972. 59.95 (*0-8490-1139-6*) Gordon Pr.

Story of the Hymns. Hezekiah Butterworth. (Works of Hezekiah Butterworth). 1989. reprint ed. lib. bdg. 79.00 (*0-7812-0605-7*) Rprt Serv.

Story of the Iliad. E. T. Owen. Ed. by John H. Betts. 248p. (C). 1989. reprint ed. pap. 15.00 (*0-86516-235-2*) Bolchazy-Carducci.

Story of the Ingalls. William T. Anderson. (Laura Ingalls Wilder Family Ser.). (Illus.). 40p. (Orig.). 1971. pap. text ed. 3.95 (*0-9610088-0-6*) Anderson-Wade.

Story of the Inns of Court. D. Plunket Barton et al. (Illus.). 320p. 1986. reprint ed. lib. bdg. 32.50 (*0-8377-1936-4*) Rothman.

Story of the Integration of the Indian States. Vapal P. Menon. LC 72-4282. (World Affairs Ser.: National & International Viewpoints). (Illus.). 542p. 1972. reprint ed. 36.95 (*0-405-04575-1*) Ayer.

Story of the Irish Citizen Army. Sean O'Casey. (C). pap. 14.50 (*0-904526-50-X*, Pub. by Pluto Pr UK) LPC InBook.

Story of the Irish Race. Seumas Macmanus. 1990. 14.99 (*0-517-06408-1*) Random Hse Value.

Story of the Irish Race: A Popular History of Ireland. 41th rev. ed. Seumas MacManus. 740p. 1990. 24.95 (*0-8159-6827-2*) Devin.

***Story of the Jamaican People: The History of Jamaica & the World.** Philip M. Sherlock. LC 96-45648. (Illus.). 320p. 1997. 34.95 (*1-55876-145-4*); pap. 16.95 (*1-55876-146-2*) Wiener Pubs Inc.

Story of the Jesus People: A Factual Survey. Ronald M. Enroth et al. (Illus.). 256p. 1972. pap. 5.95 (*0-85364-131-5*) Attic Pr.

Story of the Jewish People: From Creation to the Second Temple, Vol. 1. Gilbert Klaperman & Libby Klaperman. (J). (gr. 4-5). 1995. pap. 6.95 (*0-87441-207-2*) Behrman.

Story of the Jewish People: From the Golden Age in Spain to the European Emancipation, Vol. 3. Gilbert Klaperman & Libby Klaperman. (J). (gr. 6-7). 1995. pap. 6.95 (*0-87441-209-9*) Behrman.

Story of the Jewish People: From the Second Temple to the Age of the Rabbis, Vol. 2. Gilbert Klaperman & Libby Klaperman. (J). (gr. 5-6). 1995. pap. 6.95 (*0-87441-208-0*) Behrman.

Story of the Jewish Way of Life. Meyer Levin & Toby Kurzband. LC 59-13487. (Jewish Heritage Ser.: Vol. 3). (J). (gr. 4-6). 1959. pap. 6.95 (*0-87441-003-7*) Behrman.

***Story of the Jews.** Stanley Mack. LC 97-24415. 1998. write for info. (*0-375-75032-0*) Random.

***Story of the Jews.** Mack Stanley. 1998. pap. write for info. (*0-679-77530-7*, Villard Bks) Random.

Story of the Jews. James K. Hosmer. (Notable American Authors Ser.). 1992. reprint ed. lib. bdg. 75.00 (*0-7812-3177-9*) Rprt Serv.

Story of the Jubilee Singers with Their Songs. rev. ed. J. B. Marsh. LC 72-165509. (Illus.). reprint ed. 31.50 (*0-404-04189-2*) AMS Pr.

Story of the Killing Dentist. Susan C. Bakas. 1989. pap. 4.95 (*1-55817-552-0*) Kensgtn Pub Corp.

Story of the Kilmarnock Burns. John D. Ross. LC 76-153519. reprint ed. 32.50 (*0-404-08978-X*) AMS Pr.

Story of the Kind Wolf. Peter Nickl. LC 82-670149. (Illus.). 32p. (J). (gr. k-3). Date not set. pap. 5.95 (*1-55858-058-1*) North-South Bks NYC.

Story of the Kind Wolf. Peter Nickl. 1994. mass mkt. 5.95 (*0-200-72929-2*) Criterion Bks.

Story of the Knights Templars (1118-1315) Ferris E. Lewis. 100p. 1994. pap. 14.95 (*1-56459-441-6*) Kessinger Pub.

Story of the Lafayette Escadrille. Georges Thenault. (Great War Ser.: No. 5). (Illus.). 235p. 1990. reprint ed. 29.95 (*0-89839-148-2*) Battery Pr.

Story of the Lake. Laura Chester. 380p. 1995. 24.95 (*0-571-19861-9*) Faber & Faber.

Story of the Latter-Day Saints. 2nd enl. rev. ed. James B. Allen & Glen M. Leonard. LC 92-33934. (Illus.). xiv, 802p. 1993. 25.00 (*0-87579-565-X*) Deseret Bk.

***Story of the Lesley Cup Matches.** William L. Quirin. LC 97-3176. 1997. write for info. (*0-89865-998-1*) Donning Co.

Story of the Lewis & Clark Expedition. R. Conrad Stein. LC 78-4648. (Cornerstones of Freedom Ser.). (Illus.). 32p. (J). (gr. 3-6). 1978. pap. 4.95 (*0-516-44620-7*) Childrens.

Story of the Life of John Anderson, the Fugitive Slave. John Anderson. Ed. by Harper Twelvetrees. LC 72-164378. (Black Heritage Library Collection). 1977. reprint ed. 26.95 (*0-8369-8837-X*) Ayer.

Story of the Life of the Lord Jesus Christ in Chronological Order. (Walk with Jesus Ser.). 27p. 1987. pap. 5.00 (*1-57277-401-0*) Script Rsch.

Story of the Little Big Horn. W. A. Graham. (Custer Library). (Illus.). 352p. 1994. 19.95 (*0-8117-0346-0*) Stackpole.

Story of the Little Big Horn: Custer's Last Fight. W. A. Graham. LC 87-30129. (Illus.). xl, 284p. 1988. pap. 9.95 (*0-8032-7026-7*, Bison Books) U of Nebr Pr.

Story of the Little Black Dog. J. B. Spooner. LC 93-34690. (Illus.). 32p. (J). (ps-3). 1994. 14.95 (*1-55970-239-7*) Arcade Pub Inc.

Story of the Little Mole who Went in Search of Whodunit. Werner Holzwarth & Wolf Erlbruch. LC 93-17676. 24p. (ENG.). (J). (gr. 3 up). 1993. 12.95 (*1-55670-348-1*) Stewart Tabori & Chang.

***Story of the Little Old Man.** Barbro Lindgren & Eva Eriksson. (Illus.). (J). (gr. k-5). 6.00 (*91-29-59942-3*, 575320, Pub. by R & S Bks) FS&G.

Story of the Little Round Barn. Velma Bright. LC 81-65540. (Illus.). 48p. (Orig.). (J). (gr. 2-3). 1981. 10.00 (*0-9605968-2-8*); pap. 5.00 (*0-9605968-3-6*) Bright Bks.

Story of the Loaves & Fishes. Alice J. Davidson. (Alice in Bibleland Storybooks). (Illus.). 32p. (J). (ps-3). 1985. 5.95 (*0-8378-5073-8*) Gibson.

Story of the Lost Reflection: The Alienation of the Image in Western & Polish Cinema. Paul Coates. (Orig.). 1985. text ed. 25.00 (*0-86091-100-4*, A0996, Pub. by Verso UK); pap. text ed. 14.95 (*0-86091-808-4*, A0361, Pub. by Verso UK) Routledge Chapman & Hall.

Story of the Lost Sheep. Alice J. Davidson. (Alice in Bibleland Storybooks). (Illus.). (J). (gr. 3 up). 1989. 5.95 (*0-8378-1865-6*) Gibson.

***Story of the Lost Son.** Illus. by Stacy Venturi-Pickett. (Story of...Ser.). 24p. (Orig.). (J). (ps-2). 1997. pap. 3.95 (*1-57102-110-8*, Ideals Child) Hambleton-Hill.

Story of the Lost Trail to Oregon. Ezra Meeker. 32p. 1984. pap. 4.95 (*0-87770-321-3*) Ye Galleon.

Story of the Lovat Scouts. Michael L. Melville. 118p. 1981. 90.00 (*0-7152-0474-2*) St Mut.

Story of the Lygon Arms. Alison Ridley & Curtis F. Garfield. (Illus.). 240p. 1992. pap. 17.50 (*0-9621976-1-0*) Porcupine Enter.

Story of the Lyric Theatre, Hammersmith. Nigel R. Playfair. LC 77-84524. (Illus.). 1972. 24.95 (*0-405-08858-2*) Ayer.

Story of the "Mary Celeste" Charles E. Fay. 320p. 1988. pap. 7.95 (*0-486-25730-4*) Dover.

Story of the Maumee Valley, Toledo & the Sandusky Region, 4 vols., Set. Charles S. Van Tassel. (Illus.). 1995. reprint ed. lib. bdg. 299.50 (*0-8328-4718-6*) Higginson Bk Co.

Story of the Mayflower Compact. Norman Richards. LC 67-22901. (Cornerstones of Freedom Ser.). (Illus.). 32p. (J). (gr. 3-6). 1967. pap. 4.95 (*0-516-44625-8*) Childrens.

Story of the Meadowlark. Scott B. Smith. (Illus.). 47p. 1986. 15.00 (*0-937594-12-1*) Stump Pub.

Story of the Mennonites. C. Henry Smith. Ed. by Cornelius Krahn. LC 81-65130. (Illus.). 589p. (C). 1981. pap. 17.95 (*0-87303-069-9*) Faith & Life.

Story of the Mexican War. Robert S. Henry. (Quality Paperbacks Ser.). (Illus.). 424p. 1989. reprint ed. pap. 14.95 (*0-306-80349-6*) Da Capo.

Story of the Milky Way: A Cherokee Tale. Joseph Bruchac & Gayle Ross. LC 94-20926. (Illus.). 32p. (J). (ps-3). 1995. pap. 14.99 (*0-8037-1737-7*); pap. 14.89 (*0-8037-1738-5*) Dial Bks Young.

Story of the Mine. Charles H. Shinn. LC 79-23102. (Vintage West Ser.). (Illus.). 296p. 1992. reprint ed. pap. 13.95 (*0-87417-059-1*) U of Nev Pr.

Story of the Mongols Whom We Call the Tartars. Giovanni Di Plan Carpini. Ed. by Adolph Caso. Tr. by Erik Hildinger. 1996. pap. text ed. 14.95 (*0-8283-2017-9*) Branden Pub Co.

Story of the Moors Vol. 1: Coloring & Activities Book. Robert L. Watt & Nijel L. Binns. (Illus.). 24p. (Orig.). (J). (gr. 5-8). 1995. 4.50 (*0-9647820-0-6*) Story of the Moors.

Story of the Moors in Spain. Stanley Lane-Poole. LC 90-81538. (Illus.). 274p. 1990. reprint ed. pap. 14.95 (*0-933121-19-9*) Black Classic.

Story of the Nativity. Priscilla Hunt. 1949. pap. 0.50 (*0-87517-011-0*) Dietz.

Story of the Nativity. Elizabeth Winthrop. (J). 1986. pap. 2.50 (*0-671-63019-9*, Litl Simon S&S) S&S Childrens.

Story of the New Testament. Ralph Earle. 128p. 1941. pap. 6.99 (*0-8341-0120-3*) Beacon Hill.

S

Story of the New York Times: The First Hundred Years, 1851-1951. Meyer Berger. LC 75-122933. (American Journalists Ser.). 1971. reprint ed. 21.95 (0-405-01652-2) Ayer.

*Story of the Night: A Novel. Colm Toibin. LC 96-49814. 1997. 23.00 (0-8050-5211-9) H Holt & Co.

Story of the NIH Grants Program. Stephen P. Strickland. LC 88-38887. 110p. (C). 1989. lib. bdg. 41.00 (0-8191-7322-3) U Pr of Amer.

Story of the Nonpartisan League: A Chapter in American Evolution. Charles E. Russell. Ed. by Dan C. McCurry & Richard E. Rubenstein. LC 74-30651. (American Farmers & the Rise of Agribusiness Ser.). (Illus.). 1975. reprint ed. 35.95 (0-405-06823-9) Ayer.

Story of the Normans. S. Jewett. 1972. 59.95 (0-8490-1140-X) Gordon Pr.

Story of the Northern Central Railway: From Baltimore to Lake Ontario. Robert L. Gunnarsson. Ed. by Herbert H. Harwood, Jr. (Illus.). 192p. 1991. 39.95 (0-89778-157-0, 10-7225, Greenberg Books) Kalmbach.

Story of the Nutcracker. abr. ed. E. T. A. Hoffmann. LC 96-16373. (Children's Thrift Classics Ser.). (Illus.). 96p. (Orig.). (J). pap. 1.00 (0-486-29153-7) Dover.

Story of the Nutcracker Ballet. Deborah Hautzig. (Illus.). 32p. (J). (ps-1). 1986. pap. 5.95 (0-394-88296-2); pap. 3.25 (0-394-88178-8) Random Bks Yng Read.

Story of the Nutcracker Coloring Book. E. T. A. Hoffman. (Illus.). (J). (gr. k-3). 1990. pap. 2.95 (0-486-26405-X) Dover.

Story of the Odyssey. Stephen V. Tracy. 176p. (C). 1990. pap. text ed. 14.95 (0-691-01494-9) Princeton U Pr.

Story of the Olympics. Dave Anderson. (Illus.). 1996. pap. 9.95 (0-688-12955-2, Morrow Junior) Morrow.

Story of the Olympics. Dave Anderson. (Illus.). (J). 1996. 16.00 (0-688-12954-4, Morrow Junior) Morrow.

Story of the One July Nineteen Thirty-One Cadet Class at Brooks, March & Randolph Fields: Forty-Four Years Later. Fred R. Freyer. (Illus.). 90p. 1977. pap. text ed. 27.00 (0-89126-052-8) MA-AH Pub.

Story of the Only Home Abraham Lincoln Ever Owned. Thomas J. Dyba. (Illus.). 16p. (Orig.). 1977. reprint ed. pap. 1.70 (0-931090-00-8) I B C Pubns.

Story of the Orchestra. Paul Bekker. (Music Book Index Ser.). 320p. 1992. reprint ed. lib. bdg. 89.00 (0-7812-9469-X) Rprt Serv.

Story of the Other Wise Man. Henry Van Dyke. 1985. mass mkt. 3.95 (0-345-31882-X, Ballantine Epiphany) Ballantine.

Story of the Other Wise Man. Henry Van Dyke. 128p. 1996. pap. 7.50 (0-345-40695-8) Ballantine.

Story of the Other Wise Man. Henry Van Dyke. 92p. 1992. reprint ed. lib. bdg. 15.95 (0-89968-316-9, Lghtyr Pr) Buccaneer Bks.

Story of the Other Wise Man & Other Xmas Stories. Henry Van Dyke. 80p. 1992. pap. 6.95 (0-89804-820-6, Enthea Pr) Ariel GA.

Story of the Palatines: An Episode in Colonial History. Sanford H. Cobb. 336p. 1988. reprint ed. pap. 25.50 (1-55613-144-5) Heritage Bk.

Story of the Pall Mall Gazette. John W. Robertson-Scott. LC 73-141266. (Illus.). ix, 470p. 1971. reprint ed. text ed. 79.50 (0-8371-5826-5, ROPM, Greenwood Pr) Greenwood.

Story of the People. E. Miriandra Rota. 209p. (Orig.). 1993. pap. 11.95 (0-929385-51-9) Light Tech Comns Servs.

Story of the Persian Gulf War. Leila M. Foster. LC 91-4037. (Cornerstones of Freedom Ser.). (Illus.). 32p. (J). (gr. 3-6). 1991. pap. 4.95 (0-516-44762-9); lib. bdg. 18.00 (0-516-04762-0) Childrens.

Story of the Phillipines. Amos Fiske. 1972. 59.95 (0-8490-1141-8) Gordon Pr.

Story of the Pilgrim Fathers. H. G. Tunnicliff. (J). pap. 5.99 (0-88019-095-7) Schmul Pub Co.

Story of the Pilgrims. Katharine Ross. (J). (ps-1). 1995. pap. 3.25 (0-679-85292-1) Random.

Story of the Pilgrims & Their Indian Friends: A Thanksgiving Story for Children. 5th ed. Eunice Cauper. (Illus.). 15p. (J). (gr. k). 1990. pap. 4.95 (0-9617551-1-3) E Cauper.

Story of the Political Philosophers, 2 vols, Set. George Catlin. 1976. 500.00 (0-87968-436-4) Gordon Pr.

Story of the Prayer Book. Azriel Eisenberg & Philip Arian. pap. 5.95 (0-87677-017-0) Hartmore.

Story of the Prodigal Son. Alice J. Davidson. (Alice in Bibleland Storybooks). (Illus.). (J). (gr. 3 up). 1989. 5.95 (0-8378-1848-6) Gibson.

Story of the Prussian Officer: Revisions: Littlewood among the Lawrence Scholars. Ed. by Brynmill Pr. Ltd. Staff. (C). 1989. 35.00 (0-907839-15-0, Pub. by Brynmill Pr Ltd UK) St Mut.

Story of the Psalters. Henry A. Glass. LC 72-1635. reprint ed. 37.50 (0-404-08308-0) AMS Pr.

Story of the Pullman Car. Joseph Husband. LC 72-5055. (Technology & Society Ser.). (Illus.). 238p. 1980. reprint ed. 21.95 (0-405-04707-X) Ayer.

*Story of the Real Prayer Book. 3rd expanded rev. ed. William Sydnor. 148p. 1997. pap. 8.95 (0-8192-1682-8) Morehouse Pub.

Story of the Red Man. Flora W. Seymour. LC 79-124257. (Select Bibliographies Reprint Ser.). 1977. 30.95 (0-8369-5445-9) Ayer.

*Story of the Renaissance. Suzanne Strauss. (Illus.). 232p. (YA). (gr. 7-12). 1997. pap. text ed. 12.95 (0-9656557-0-9) Pemblewick Pr.

Story of the Restoration. Bill J. Humble. 1969. pap. 2.75 (0-88027-040-3) Firm Foun Pub.

Story of the Riot: Persecution of Negroes by Roughs & Policemen, in the City of New York, August, Nineteen Hundred. Ed. by Frank Moss. LC 73-90186. (Mass Violence in America Ser.). 1976. reprint ed. 21.95 (0-405-01329-9) Ayer.

Story of the Rockefeller Foundation. Raymond B. Fosdick. 354p. 1989. 49.95 (0-88738-248-7) Transaction Pubs.

Story of the Root Children. Sibylle Von Olfers. (Illus.). 32p. (GER.). (J). (ps-3). 1992. reprint ed. 12.95 (0-86315-106-X, Pub. by Floris Bks UK) Gryphon Hse.

Story of the Rosary. Anne Vail. 1995. pap. 10.00 (0-00-627911-2) Harper SF.

Story of the Rough Riders. Zachary Kent. LC 90-22444. (Cornerstones of Freedom Ser.). (Illus.). 32p. (J). (gr. 3-6). 1991. pap. 4.95 (0-516-44756-4); lib. bdg. 18.00 (0-516-04756-6) Childrens.

*Story of the Salem Witch Trials. Lebeau. LC 97-5456. 1997. pap. text ed. 24.00 (0-13-442542-1) P-H.

*Story of the Sandman. Tom Paxton. (J). Date not set. write for info. (0-688-15335-6, Morrow Junior); lib. bdg. write for info. (0-688-15336-4) Morrow.

Story of the Savannah: An Episode in Maritime Labor-Management Relations. David Kuechle. LC 78-131466. (Wertheim Publications in Industrial Relations). (Illus.). 327p. 1971. 24.95 (0-674-83961-7) HUP.

Story of the Savoy Opera in Gilbert & Sullivan Days. S. J. Fitzgerald. (Music Reprint Ser.). 1979. reprint ed. lib. bdg. 35.00 (0-306-79543-4) Da Capo.

Story of the Scottish Rite of Freemasonry. Harold V. Voorhis. xiii, 56p. 1994. reprint ed. pap. 6.00 (0-88053-063-4, M342) Macoy Pub.

Story of the Scottish Soldier, 1600-1914: Bonny Fighters. Jenni Calder. (Illus.). 36p. 1992. pap. 2.95 (0-11-493386-3, 3863, Pub. by Natl Mus Scotland UK) A Schwartz & Co.

Story of the Second World War. Henry S. Commager. (Brassey's WWII Commemorative Ser.). 352p. 1991. 23.95 (0-08-041066-9) Brasseys Inc.

Story of the Seer of Patmos. Stephen N. Haskell. LC 95-61928. (Illus.). 424p. (Orig.). 1993. reprint ed. per. 12.95 (0-945383-50-9, 921-3275) Teach Servs.

*Story of the Sermon on the Mount. Illus. by Sherry Neidigh. (Story of...Ser.). 24p. (Orig.). (J). (ps-2). 1997. pap. 3.95 (1-57102-109-4, Ideals Child) Hambleton-Hill.

Story of the Seventh-Day Adventist Church. Eugene Durand. Ed. by Gerald Wheeler. (Better Living Ser.). 32p. (Orig.). 1986. pap. 0.89 (0-8280-0320-3) Review & Herald.

Story of the Shakers. Flo Morse. LC 85-31430. (Illus.). 128p. 1986. pap. 10.00 (0-88150-062-3) Countryman.

Story of the Smashing Pumpkins. Nick Wise. (Illus.). 56p. pap. 11.95 (0-7119-4166-1, OP 47664) Omnibus NY.

Story of the Smokey the Bear. Robin Bromley. 32p. (J). (ps-3). 1996. pap. 2.99 (0-7214-5632-4, Ladybrd) Penguin.

Story of the Spectator, Eighteen Twenty-Eight to Nineteen Twenty-Eight. William B. Thomas. LC 79-175711. (Select Bibliographies Reprint Ser.). 1977. reprint ed. 23.95 (0-8369-6626-0) Ayer.

Story of the Star Reusable Stickers. (Little Lamb Mini Activity Bks.). (Illus.). 16p. (J). 1992. pap. 1.49 (0-87403-946-0, 01569) Standard Pub.

Story of the Statue of Liberty. Betsy C. Maestro. LC 85-11324. (Illus.). 40p. (J). (ps-3). 1986. lib. bdg. 16.93 (0-688-05774-8) Lothrop.

Story of the Statue of Liberty. Betsy C. Maestro. LC 85-11324. (Illus.). 48p. (J). (gr. k up). 1989. pap. 5.95 (0-688-08746-9, Mulberry) Morrow.

Story of the Stewarts. Stewart Society Staff. (Illus.). 206p. 1993. reprint ed. pap. text ed. 17.50 (1-55613-866-0) Heritage Bk.

Story of the Stewartstown Railroad. Eric J. Bickleman. (Illus.). 80p. (Orig.). 1995. pap. 19.95 (0-9651235-0-2) Baltimore Chap.

Story of the Stick: Folklore & Anthropology. Antony Real. 1977. lib. bdg. 250.00 (0-8490-2691-1) Gordon Pr.

*Story of the Stone. Linda Ching. (Illus.). 138p. 1997. 40.00 (0-9619891-5-7) Hawaiian Goddesses.

Story of the Stone Vol. 1: The Golden Days. Cao Xueqin. Tr. by David Hawkes. (Classics Ser.). 544p. 1974. pap. 12.95 (0-14-044293-6, Penguin Classics) Viking Penguin.

Story of the Stone Vol. 2: The Crab-Flower Club. Cao Xueqin. Tr. by David Hawkes. (Classics Ser.). 606p. 1977. pap. 12.95 (0-14-044326-6, Penguin Classics) Viking Penguin.

Story of the Stone Vol. 3: The Warning Voice. Cao Xueqin. Tr. by David Hawkes. 640p. 1981. pap. 11.95 (0-14-044370-3, Penguin Classics) Viking Penguin.

Story of the Stone Vol. 4: The Debt of Tears. Cao Xueqin. Ed. by E. Gao. Tr. by John Minford. 400p. 1982. pap. 10.95 (0-14-044371-1, Penguin Classics) Viking Penguin.

Story of the Stone Vol. 5: The Dreamer Awakes. Cao Xueqin. Ed. by E. Gao. Tr. by John Minford from CHI. 384p. 1986. pap. 12.95 (0-14-044372-X, Penguin Classics) Viking Penguin.

Story of the Stone (Dream of the Red Chamber) Vol. 5: The Dreamer Wakes, Vol. 5. Cao Xueqin. Ed. by Gao E. Tr. by John Minford. LC 78-20279. (Chinese Literature in Translation Ser.). 384p. 1987. 35.00 (0-253-19265-X) Ind U Pr.

Story of the Stone (Dream of the Red Chamber), Vol. 2: The Crab-Flower Club. Xueqin Cao. Tr. by David Hawkes. LC 78-20279. (Chinese Literature in Translation Ser.). 608p. 1979. 29.50 (0-253-19262-5) Ind U Pr.

Story of the Stone (The Dream of the Red Chamber), Vol. 3: The Warning Voice. Cao Xueqin. Tr. by David Hawkes. LC 78-20279. (Chinese Literature in Translation Ser.). 640p. 1981. 35.00 (0-253-19263-3) Ind U Pr.

Story of the Stupa. A. H. Longhurst. (C). 1995. 18.00 (81-206-0160-2, Pub. by Asian Educ Servs II) S Asia.

Story of the Supreme Court. Earnest S. Bates. 377p. 1982. reprint ed. lib. bdg. 30.00 (0-8377-0322-0) Rothman.

Story of the Surrender at Appomattox Court House. Zachary Kent. LC 87-22468. (Cornerstones of Freedom Ser.). (Illus.). 32p. (J). (gr. 3-6). 1987. pap. 4.95 (0-516-44732-7) Childrens.

Story of the Surrender at Yorktown. Zachary Kent. LC 89-33784. (Cornerstones of Freedom Ser.). (Illus.). 32p. (J). (gr. 3-6). 1989. pap. 4.95 (0-516-44723-8) Childrens.

Story of the Texas Rangers. Walter P. Webb. (Illus.). 152p. 1971. reprint ed. 20.00 (0-88426-007-0) Encino Pr.

*Story of the Thimble: An Illustrated Guide for Collectors. Bridget McConnel. LC 97-23818. 1997. write for info. (0-7643-0311-2) Schiffer.

Story of the Three Bears. Ed. by W. U. Ober. LC 80-28325. 1981. 50.00 (0-8201-1362-X) Schol Facsimiles.

Story of the Three Kingdoms. Walter D. Myers. LC 94-2685. (Illus.). 32p. (J). (gr. 1-4). 1995. 14.95 (0-06-024286-8); lib. bdg. 14.89 (0-06-024287-6) HarpC Child Bks.

*Story of the Three Kingdoms. Walter D. Myers. LC 94-2685. (Illus.). 32p. (J). (gr. k-3). 1997. pap. 4.95 (0-06-443475-3, Trophy) HarpC Child Bks.

Story of the Three Little Pigs: A Story Clothes Book. Lilly Barnes. (J). 1994. 12.95 (0-8362-4237-8) Andrews & McMeel.

Story of the Three Whales. Giles Whittell. LC 88-35630. (True Adventures Ser.). (Illus.). 29p. (J). (gr. 2-4). 1988. lib. bdg. 18.60 (0-8368-0092-3) Gareth Stevens Inc.

*Story of the Titanic. Deborah Hubgiman. (J). 1998. pap. write for info. (0-679-88808-X) Random Bks Yng Read.

Story of the Titanic: As Told by Its Survivors. Ed. by Jack Winocour. 1990. 20.50 (0-8446-3194-9) Peter Smith.

Story of the Titanic As Told by Its Survivors. Ed. by Jack Winocour. (Illus.). 320p. (Orig.). 1960. pap. 6.95 (0-486-20610-6) Dover.

Story of the Tooth Fairy. Shelia Black. (Illus.). (J). (ps-3). 1990. 6.50 (0-307-14004-0) Western Pub.

Story of the Tooth Fairy. Robert G. Sauber. LC 95-13266. (Illus.). (C). 1996. lib. bdg. 15.93 (0-688-12988-9, Morrow Junior) Morrow.

Story of the Tooth Fairy. Robert G. Sauber. LC 95-13266. (Illus.). 32p. (J). (gr. k-3). 1996. 16.00 (0-688-12987-0, Morrow Junior) Morrow.

Story of the Tower of Babel. Alice J. Davidson. (Alice in Bibleland Storybooks). (Illus.). (J). (gr. 3 up). 1989. 5.95 (0-8378-1866-4) Gibson.

Story of the Trapp Family Singers. Maria A. Trapp. 320p. 1957. pap. 11.00 (0-385-02896-2, D46, Image Bks) Doubleday.

Story of the Trapp Family Singers. Maria A. Trapp. LC 87-16801. (Illus.). 336p. 1987. reprint ed. 29.95 (0-87797-164-1) Cherokee.

Story of the Treasure Seekers. Edith Nesbit. (Classics Ser.). (J). (gr. 4-6). 1987. pap. 2.25 (0-685-03990-0, Puffin) Puffin Bks.

Story of the Treasure Seekers. Edith Nesbit. 256p. (YA). (gr. 5 up). 1996. pap. 3.99 (0-14-036706-3) Puffin Bks.

Story of the Twenty-Sixth Louisiana. W. Hall. 1976. 34.00 (0-8488-1035-X) Amereon Ltd.

Story of the Twenty-Sixth Louisiana Infantry in the Service of the Confederate States. Winchester Hall. 250p. 1984. reprint ed. 28.00 (0-942211-90-1) Olde Soldier Bks.

Story of the U. S. Naval Academy. Clara A. Simmons. (Illus.). 128p. (J). 1995. 19.95 (1-55750-767-8) Naval Inst Pr.

Story of the Ugly Duckling. Illus. by Berta Hader & Elmer Hader. LC 94-1298. (J). (gr. 1 up). 1994. pap. write for info. (0-486-28300-3) Dover.

Story of the Underground Railroad. R. Conrad Stein. LC 82-3801. (Cornerstones of Freedom Ser.). (Illus.). 32p. (J). (gr. 3-6). 1981. pap. 4.95 (0-516-44643-6) Childrens.

Story of the Unification of Germany. Jim Hargrove. LC 91-12650. (Cornerstones of Freedom Ser.). (Illus.). 32p. (J). (gr. 3-6). 1991. pap. 4.95 (0-516-44761-0); lib. bdg. 18.00 (0-516-04761-2) Childrens.

Story of the Universe. David Hughes. LC 90-11025. (Exploring the Universe Ser.). (Illus.). 32p. (J). (gr. 4-6). 1991. pap. 4.95 (0-8167-2129-7); lib. bdg. 13.95 (0-8167-2128-9) Troll Communs.

Story of the Upper Canadian Rebellion: Largely Derived from Original Sources & Documents Upper Canadian Rebellion. John C. Dent. 1977. 57.95 (0-8369-7157-4, 7989) Ayer.

Story of the Vietnam Veterans Memorial. David K. Wright. LC 89-713. (Cornerstones of Freedom Ser.). (Illus.). 32p. (J). (gr. 3-6). 1989. pap. 4.95 (0-516-44745-9) Childrens.

Story of the Village of Intercourse. Joy Kraybill & Stephen E. Scott. (Illus.). 96p. 1996. pap. 6.95 (1-56148-206-4) Good Bks PA.

Story of the Village of Mumbles. Gerald Gabbs. 80p. (C). 1989. 75.00 (0-905928-61-X, Pub. by D Brown & Sons Ltd UK) St Mut.

Story of the Vilna Gaon. Leonard Oschry. 1.75 (0-914131-62-1, D520) Torah Umesorah.

Story of the Voyage: Sea-Narratives in Eighteenth-Century England. Philip Edwards. LC 93-48138. (Studies in Eighteenth-Century English Literature & Thought: No. 24). (Illus.). 276p. (C). 1995. text ed. 59.95 (0-521-41301-X) Cambridge U Pr.

Story of the West Florida Rebellion. S. Arthur. 1977. 30.00 (0-87511-148-3) Claitors.

Story of the West Highland. (Illus.). (C). 1987. 22.00 (0-317-90410-8, Pub. by Picton UK) St Mut.

Story of the Western Railroads: From 1852 Through the Reign of the Giants. Robert E. Riegel. LC 26-9772. xviii, 345p. 1964. pap. 11.95 (0-8032-5159-9, Bison Books) U of Nebr Pr.

Story of the Western Wing. Wang Shifu. Ed. by Stephen H. West & Wilt L. Idema. Tr. & Intro. by Wilt L. Idema. (Illus.). 300p. 1995. pap. 15.00 (0-520-20184-1) U CA Pr.

Story of the Wheel. Tim Healey. LC 91-40417. (Story of Ser.). (Illus.). 32p. (J). (gr. 1-4). 1993. lib. bdg. 12.50 (0-8167-2713-9) Troll Communs.

Story of the Wheel. Tim Healey. LC 91-40417. (Story of Ser.). (Illus.). 32p. (J). (gr. 1-4). 1997. pap. 3.95 (0-8167-2714-7) Troll Communs.

*Story of the White House. Esther Singleton. Date not set. write for info. (0-405-08974-0) Ayer.

Story of the White House. Kate Waters. 40p. (J). 1991. 12.95 (0-590-43335-0, Scholastic Hardcover) Scholastic Inc.

Story of the White House. Kate Waters. 40p. (J). 1992. 5.99 (0-590-43334-2, Blue Ribbon Bks) Scholastic Inc.

Story of the Widow's Son. Mary Lavin. (Short Stories Ser.). (J). (gr. 5 up). 1992. lib. bdg. 13.95 (0-88682-500-8) Creative Ed.

Story of the Wild West & Camp-Fire Chats: A Full & Complete History of the Renowned Pioneer Quartette, Boone, Crocket, Carson, & Buffalo Bill. William F. Cody. LC 75-109620. (Select Bibliographies Reprint Ser.). 1977. 51.95 (0-8369-5229-4) Ayer.

Story of the Wilders. William T. Anderson. (Laura Ingalls Wilder Family Ser.). (Illus.). 32p. 1983. pap. 3.95 (0-9610088-2-2) Anderson-Wade.

Story of the Winged-S. Igor Sikorsky. (American Autobiography Ser.). 314p. 1995. reprint ed. lib. bdg. 89.00 (0-7812-8639-5) Rprt Serv.

Story of the Women's Movement. Maureen Ash. LC 89-17325. (Cornerstones of Freedom Ser.). 32p. (J). (gr. 3-6). 1989. pap. 4.95 (0-516-44724-6) Childrens.

Story of the Wonder Man. Ring Lardner, Jr. 1976. 22.95 (0-8488-1073-2) Amereon Ltd.

Story of the World Cup. Brian Glanville. (Illus.). 384p. (Orig.). 1993. pap. 15.95 (0-571-16979-1) Faber & Faber.

Story of the Yiddish Theatre. Hershel Zohn. (Illus.). 256p. pap. 8.95 (1-881325-15-6) Yucca Tree Pr.

Story of the 116th Regiment: Pennsylvania Volunteers in the War of Rebellion. Clair Mullholland. Ed. by Lawrence F. Kohl. LC 95-39243. (Irish in the Civil War Ser.: 5). (Illus.). 512p. 1995. 27.50 (0-8232-1606-3) Fordham.

Story of the 116th Regiment Pennsylvania Infantry. St. Clair A. Mulholland. 422p. 35.00 (1-56013-005-9) Olde Soldier Bks.

Story of Things. Kate Morgan. (Illus.). 32p. (J). (gr. 3-7). 1991. 14.95 (0-8027-6918-7); lib. bdg. 15.85 (0-8027-6919-5) Walker & Co.

Story of Thomas Alva Edison. Margaret Cousins. LC 81-805. (Landmark Paperback Ser.: No. 8). (Illus.). 160p. (J). (gr. 5-9). 1981. pap. 5.99 (0-394-84883-7) Random Bks Yng Read.

Story of Thomas Alva Edison: The Wizard of Menlo Park. Margaret Davidson. 64p. (J). 1990. pap. 3.50 (0-590-42403-3) Scholastic Inc.

Story of Thomas Duncan & His Six Sons. Katherine D. Smith. (Illus.). 174p. 1988. reprint ed. lib. bdg. 29.00 (0-8328-0022-8) Higginson Bk Co.

Story of Thoracic Surgery: Milestones & Pioneers. A. P. Naef. LC 89-71619. 160p. 1990. 19.80 (0-920887-79-1) Hogrefe & Huber Pubs.

Story of Three Whales. (Illus.). 28p. 1989. 8.95 (1-55971-037-3) NorthWord.

Story of Thurgood Marshall: Justice for All. Joe Arthur. (Famous Lives Ser.). (J). 1996. lib. bdg. 19.93 (0-8368-1472-X) Gareth Stevens Inc.

*Story of Time & Clocks. Anita Ganeri. (Sign of the Times). (Illus.). 32p. (J). 1997. lib. bdg. 14.95 (0-19-521326-2) OUP.

Story of Tisha B'Av. Aryeh Kaplan. 160p. 1981. 5.00 (0-940118-32-7) Moznaim.

Story of Tisha B'av: Russian Edition. Arych Kaplan. Tr. by Alexander Slotkin. 138p. (RUS.). 1992. 5.00 (0-940118-86-6) Moznaim.

Story of Troilus. Ed. by R. K. Gordon. (Medieval Academy Reprints for Teaching Ser.). 1979. reprint ed. pap. 15.95 (0-8020-6368-3) U of Toronto Pr.

Story of Tuan Ngo. Kilborne. LC 97-15061. (J). 1998. 15.00 (0-689-80798-8); pap. 3.99 (0-689-80797-X, S&S Bks Young Read) S&S Childrens.

Story of "Twas the Night Before Christmas" The Life & Times of Clement Clarke Moore & His Best-Loved Poem of Yuletide. rev. ed. Gerard Del Re & Patricia Del Re. LC 91-11419. 128p. (gr. 10). 1994. reprint ed. 16.99 (0-922066-89-2) Wynwood.

Story of Two Kingdoms. Hua-Ching Ni. LC 88-93051. (Esoteric Teachings of the Tradition of Tao Ser.: Bk. 1). 122p. 1989. 14.95 (0-937064-24-6) SevenStar Comm.

Story of Two Souls. Dominga L. Reyes. 80p. 1984. pap. 5.50 (0-939375-02-8) World Univ Amer.

Story of Two Souls: The Correspondence of Jacques Maritain & Julien Green. Ed. by Henry Bars & Eric Jourdan. Tr. by Bernard Doering. LC 88-80056. (Illus.). viii, 276p. 1988. 50.00 (0-8232-1190-8) Fordham.

Story of Unity. rev. ed. James D. Freeman. (Illus.). 272p. 1978. 12.95 (0-87159-145-6) Unity Bks.

Story of Unity Theatre. Colin Chambers. LC 89-33030. 416p. 1989. text ed. 45.00 (0-312-03580-2) St Martin.

Story of Unity Theatre. Colin Chambers. (Illus.). 446p. 1990. 39.95 (0-685-31436-7) St Martin.

Story of Utopias. Lewis Mumford. 1990. 24.00 (0-8446-1319-3) Peter Smith.

Story of Venice. T. Okeay. (Mediaeval Towns Ser.: Vol. 31). 1974. reprint ed. 65.00 (0-8115-0873-0) Periodicals Srv.

Story of Venus & Tannhauser. Aubrey Beardsley & John Glassco. (Illus.). 150p. (Orig.). 1996. pap. 10.95 (1-56201-089-1, North Star Line) Blue Moon Bks.

S

An Asterisk (*) at the beginning of an entry indicates that the title is appearing in BIP for the first time.

Story of Verona. A. J. Wiel. (Mediaeval Towns Ser.: Vol. 13). 1974. reprint ed. pap. 35.00 (*0-8115-0855-2*) Periodicals Srv.

Story of Vivekananda. Irene R. Ray & Mallika C. Gupta. (Illus.). 72p. (J). (gr. 4-7). 1971. pap. 2.00 (*0-87481-125-2*, Pub. by Advaita Ashrama II) Vedanta Pr.

Story of Wagners "Ring" N. Kilburn. 50p. 1991. reprint ed. 59.00 (*0-7812-9311-1*) Rprt Serv.

***Story of Wake Island.** James Devereux. (Elite Unit Ser.: Vol. 33). (Illus.). 252p. 1997. reprint ed. 29.95 (*0-89839-264-0*) Battery Pr.

Story of Waldorf & Juli. Clifford Fazzorlari. 266p. (Orig.). 1996. mass mkt. 4.99 (*1-55197-087-2*, Pub. by Comnwlth Pub CN) Partners Pubs Grp.

***Story of Wali Dad.** Retold by Kristina Rodnas. (Illus.). 32p. (J). 3.98 (*0-8317-2955-4*) Smithmark.

Story of Walpole, Massachusetts, 1724-1924. Willard De Lue. 374p. 1993. reprint ed. lib. bdg. 41.00 (*0-8328-3141-7*) Higginson Bk Co.

Story of Walt Disney. (Yearling Biography Ser.: No. 12). 96p. (J). (gr. k-6). 1989. pap. 3.50 (*0-440-40240-9*, YB BDD) BDD Bks Young Read.

Story of Walt Disney: Maker of Magical Worlds. Bernice Selden. (Famous Lives Ser.). (J). 1996. lib. bdg. 19.93 (*0-8368-1468-1*) Gareth Stevens Inc.

Story of Watergate. Jim Hargrove. LC 88-11881. (Cornerstones of Freedom Ser.). (Illus.). 32p. (J). (gr. 3-6). 1988. lib. bdg. 18.00 (*0-516-04741-8*) Childrens.

Story of Weapons & Tactics. Thomas H. Wintringham. LC 79-128335. (Essay Index Reprint Ser.). 1977. 20.95 (*0-8369-2093-7*) Ayer.

Story of Webster's Third: Philip Gove's Controversial Dictionary & Its Critics. Herbert C. Morton. (Illus.). 368p. (C). 1994. text ed. 39.95 (*0-521-46146-4*) Cambridge U Pr.

Story of Webster's Third: Philip Gove's Controversial Dictionary & Its Critics. Herbert C. Morton. (Illus.). 360p. (C). 1995. pap. text ed. 18.95 (*0-521-55869-7*) Cambridge U Pr.

***Story of Weights & Measures.** Anita Ganeri. (Signs of the Times Ser.). (Illus.). 30p. (J). 1997. lib. bdg. 14.95 (*0-19-521328-9*) OUP.

***Story of Western Architecture.** rev. ed. Bill Risebero. (Illus.). 200p. 1997. pap. 20.00 (*0-262-68095-5*) MIT Pr.

Story of Western Furniture. (Illus.). 256p. 1994. pap. text ed. 22.00 (*1-871569-59-1*) New Amsterdam Bks.

Story of Western Philosophy. Francis H. Parker. LC 67-13033. 352p. reprint ed. pap. 100.40 (*0-317-08916-1*, 2050087) Bks Demand.

Story of Westminster Abbey. Violet Brooke-Hunt. 1977. lib. bdg. 59.95 (*0-8490-2692-X*) Gordon Pr.

Story of White Eagle Lodge. White Eagle Lodge Staff. Ed. by Colum Hayward & Joan Hodgson. (Illus.). 72p. (Orig.). 1986. pap. 6.95 (*0-85487-071-7*, Pub. by White Eagle UK) DeVorss.

Story of William Penn. Aliki. LC 93-26289. (Illus.). (Orig.). (J). 1994. pap. 14.00 (*0-671-88558-8*, S&S Bks Young Read) S&S Childrens.

Story of William Penn. Aliki. LC 93-26289. (J). 1994. pap. 5.95 (*0-671-88646-0*, Half Moon Paper) S&S Childrens.

Story of Winchester. W. L. Woodland. (Mediaeval Towns Ser.: Vol. 33). 1974. reprint ed. pap. 35.00 (*0-8115-0875-7*) Periodicals Srv.

***Story of Wine.** pap. 31.95 (*1-85732-997-X*, Pub. by M Beazley Pubs Ltd UK) Antique Collect.

Story of Wira. Wira Staff. (C). 1988. 135.00 (*0-900820-18-7*, Pub. by British Textile Tech UK) St Mut.

Story of Wise County (Virginia) Luther P. Addington. (Illus.). 306p. 1988. reprint ed. 24.95 (*0-932807-30-5*) Overmountain Pr.

Story of Women Who Shaped the West. Mary V. Fox. LC 90-21444. (Cornerstones of Freedom Ser.). (Illus.). 32p. (J). (gr. 3-6). 1991. pap. 4.95 (*0-516-44757-2*); lib. bdg. 18.00 (*0-516-04757-4*) Childrens.

Story of Wool. Geoffrey Patterson. (Illus.). 32p. (Orig.). (J). (gr. 3). 1996. pap. 9.95 (*0-85236-322-2*, Pub. by Farming Pr UK) Diamond Farm Bk.

Story of Worker Sport. Ed. by Arnd Kruger & James Riordan. LC 96-1281. 200p. 1996. text ed. 35.00 (*0-87322-874-X*, BKRU0874) Human Kinetics.

Story of World Religions. Denise Lardner Carmody & John Carmody. LC 87-24857. 503p. (C). 1988. text ed. 47.95 (*0-87484-756-7*, 756) Mayfield Pub.

Story of World Religions, Instructor's Manual. Denise Lardner Carmody & John Carmody. (C). 1988. teacher ed., pap. text ed. write for info. (*0-87484-874-1*, 874) Mayfield Pub.

Story of Wounded Knee. R. Conrad Stein. LC 83-6584. (Cornerstones of Freedom Ser.). (Illus.). 32p. (J). (gr. 3-6). 1983. pap. 4.95 (*0-516-44665-7*) Childrens.

Story of Writing: Alphabets, Hieroglyphs, & Pictographs. Andrew Robinson. LC 95-60276. (Illus.). 224p. 1995. 29.95 (*0-500-01665-8*) Thames Hudson.

***Story of Writing & Printing.** Anita Ganeri. (Signs of the Times Ser.). (Illus.). 32p. (J). 1996. lib. bdg. 14.95 (*0-19-521256-8*) OUP.

Story of Yellowstone Geysers. Clyde M. Bauer. LC 37-15316. 125p. 1986. reprint ed. lib. bdg. 29.00 (*0-8095-6100-X*) Borgo Pr.

Story of Yiddish Literature. Abraham A. Roback. 1972. 300.00 (*0-87968-084-9*) Gordon Pr.

Story of Your Bible. Harold G. Mackay. 1985. pap. 4.00 (*0-937396-65-6*) Walterick Pubs.

***Story of Your Life.** Aftel. 1997. pap. 11.00 (*0-684-82696-8*, Fireside) S&S Trade.

Story of Your Life: Becoming the Author of Your Experience. Mandy Aftel. 256p. 1996. 22.00 (*0-684-81557-5*) S&S Trade.

Story of Your Life: Writing a Spiritual Autobiography. Dan Wakefield. LC 90-52593. (Illus.). 256p. 1990. pap. 16.00 (*0-8070-2709-X*) Beacon Pr.

Story of Ypsilanti. Harvey C. Colburn. (Illus.). 327p. 1995. reprint ed. lib. bdg. 39.00 (*0-8328-5047-0*) Higginson Bk Co.

***Story of Yusuf: The Most Beautiful Story.** Tr. by Yahiya Emerick. (Illus.). 30p. (Orig.). (J). (gr. 5-10). 1996. mass mkt. 3.95 (*1-889720-09-7*) Amirah Pubng.

Story of Z. Jeanne Modesitt. LC 89-3923. (Illus.). 28p. (J). (ps up). 1991. pap. 14.95 (*0-88708-105-3*, Picture Book Studio) S&S Childrens.

Story of Zacchaeus. Marty R. Figley. LC 94-46174. (Illus.). 32p. (J). (ps-2). 1995. 15.00 (*0-8028-5092-8*) Eerdmans.

Story of Zahra. Hanan Al-Shaykh. Tr. by Peter Ford from ARA. LC 93-3678. 224p. 1995. pap. 11.00 (*0-385-47206-4*, Anchor NY) Doubleday.

***Story of Zahra.** Hanan Al-Shaykh. 192p. 1996. pap. 9.00 (*0-614-21395-9*, 1171) Kazi Pubns.

Story Only You Can Tell: Creating Your Family History with Ease & Expertise. Toni S. Brown. LC 95-72365. (Illus.). 150p. (Orig.). 1995. pap. text ed. 13.95 (*1-57636-006-7*) SunRise Pbl.

Story, Performance, & Event: Contextual Studies of Oral Narrative. Richard Bauman. (Cambridge Studies in Oral & Literate Culture: No. 10). 160p. 1986. pap. text ed. 17.95 (*0-521-31111-X*) Cambridge U Pr.

Story Picture Poem & Coloring Book for Children. Donald G. Taylor. (Illus.). 30p. (J). (ps-3). 1993. pap. 6.95 (*0-9638002-0-5*) D G Taylor.

Story Play: Costumes, Cooking, Music, & More for Young Children. Joyce Harlow. (Orig.). (ps-1). 1992. audio 10.00 (*0-685-59734-2*, X370) Teacher Ideas Pr.

Story Play: Costumes, Cooking, Music, & More for Young Children. Joyce Harlow. (Illus.). xii, 202p. (Orig.). (J). (ps-1). 1992. pap. text ed. 19.00 (*1-56308-037-0*) Teacher Ideas Pr.

Story Power: Compelling Illustrations for Preaching & Teaching. James A. Feehan. 160p. reprint ed. pap. 10.95 (*0-89390-304-3*) Resource Pubns.

***Story Problems: Combo ER 1.** J. Hoffman & B. Gregorich. Ed. by Lorie De Young. (Math Combo Bks.: No. 02201). (Illus.). 64p. (Orig.). (J). (gr. 1 up). 1997. wbk. ed., pap. 3.25 (*0-88743-137-2*, 02201) Sch Zone Pub Co.

***Story Problems: Grade 4.** Susan Loughrin et al. (Math Combo Bks.: No. 02204). (Illus.). 64p. (Orig.). (J). (gr. 3-4). 1997. wbk. ed., pap. 3.25 (*0-88743-140-2*) Sch Zone Pub Co.

Story Problems: Grades 1-2 Math. Barbara Gregorich. Ed. by Joan Hoffman. (I Know It! Bks.). (Illus.). 32p. (J). (gr. 1-2). 1982. student ed. 1.99 (*0-938256-45-9*) Sch Zone Pub Co.

Story Problems: Grades 3-4 Math. Barbara Gregorich. Ed. by Joan Hoffman. (I Know It! Bks.). (Illus.). 32p. (J). (gr. 3-4). 1982. student ed. 1.99 (*0-938256-46-7*) Sch Zone Pub Co.

Story Problems Made Easy see **Solving Math Word Problems, Bk. 1, Sums to 99 No Borrowing or Carrying**

Story Problems Made Easy see **Solving Math Word Problems, Bk. 2, Sums to 500 with Borrowing or Carrying**

***Story Programs: A Source Book of Materials.** 2nd rev. ed. Carolyn S. Peterson & Ann D. Fenton. (School Library Media Ser.: No. 10). (Illus.). 272p. 1997. pap. 29.50 (*0-8108-3207-0*) Scarecrow.

Story Puzzles: Tales in the Tangram Tradition. Valerie Marsh & Patrick K. Luzadder. LC 96-26676. 1996. pap. 11.95 (*0-917846-59-1*, Alleyside) Highsmith Pr.

Story Quilts & How to Make Them. Mary C. Clark. LC 95-34185. (Illus.). 128p. 1995. 27.95 (*0-8069-1316-9*) Sterling.

Story Re-Visions: Narrative Therapy in the Post Modern World. Alan Parry & Robert E. Doan. LC 94-18296. 216p. 1994. pap. text ed. 17.95 (*0-89862-570-X*) Guilford Pr.

Story Re-Visions: Narrative Therapy in the Postmodern World. Alan Parry & Robert E. Doan. LC 94-18296. 200p. 1994. lib. bdg. 39.95 (*0-89862-213-1*, 2213) Guilford Pr.

Story Rhyme Greetings: Directory of Story Letters for Birthdays, Celebrations, Holidays, Etcetera. Story Rhyme Staff. (Illus.). 60p. (J). (gr. 7-9). 1993. student ed., ring bd. 39.95 (*1-56820-106-0*) Story Time.

Story Rhyme Greetings for the Fax Machine: Correspondence, Etc. Bibliotheca Press Staff. (Illus.). 50p. 1991. ring bd. 26.95 (*0-939476-46-0*) Prosperity & Profits.

Story Rhyme Journal. A. C. Doyle. 60p. (Orig.). (J). (gr. 6-9). 1991. pap. text ed. 15.95 (*0-317-04222-X*, Biblio Pr) Prosperity & Profits.

Story S-t-r-e-t-c-h-e-r-s: Activities to Expand Children's Favorite Books. Shirley C. Raines & Robert J. Canady. Ed. by Kathleen Charner. 265p. 1989. pap. 19.95 (*0-87659-119-5*) Gryphon Hse.

Story S-t-r-e-t-c-h-e-r-s for the Primary Grades: Activities to Expand Children's Favorite Books. Shirley C. Raines & Robert J. Canady. 1992. pap. 19.95 (*0-87659-157-8*) Gryphon Hse.

***Story Samphlet of 5 Stories.** Story Time Staff. (Illus.). (Orig.). 1997. teacher ed., pap. 15.95 (*1-56820-192-3*) Story Time.

***Story Scorpions.** Gabriel Everett. 1997. mass mkt. 5.99 (*0-449-00173-3*, GM) Fawcett.

Story Sense. Gary Provost. 1999. pap. 12.95 (*0-452-27395-1*, Plume) NAL-Dutton.

Story Sense: Writing Story & Script for Feature Films & Television. Paul Lucey. 1996. pap. text ed. write for info. (*0-07-038996-9*) McGraw.

Story Sermons for Children. Luther S. Cross. (Object Lessons Ser.). 164p. (Orig.). (gr. 10). 1966. pap. 6.99 (*0-8010-2328-9*) Baker Bks.

Story-Shaped Christology: The Role of Narratives in Identifying Jesus Christ. Robert A. Krieg. 176p. 1988. pap. 8.95 (*0-8091-2941-8*) Paulist Pr.

Story Snail. Rockwell. LC 96-19215. (J). 1997. 15.00 (*0-689-81221-3*); pap. 3.99 (*0-689-81220-5*) S&S Childrens.

Story Spinner: The Easy Way to Write a Story Outline. Kate A. Rezvani. Ed. by Jay Lane. LC 94-96237. (Illus.). 64p. 1995. per. 19.95 (*0-9641318-4-6*) Lrning Circle.

Story Square Structure Verbs. Thomas Sheenan. pap. 12.00 (*0-685-65255-6*) P-H.

Story Start Animals. Franco Pagnucci & Susan Pagnucci. (J). (gr. 2-5). 1990. pap. 7.99 (*0-8224-6398-9*) Fearon Teach Aids.

Story-Start Set, 3 bks., Set. Franco Pagnucci & Susan Pagnucci. (J). (gr. 2-5). 20.99 (*1-56417-736-X*, FE0012) Fearon Teach Aids.

***Story Starters & Other Professional Writers' Techniques for Kids.** Date not set. write for info. (*0-614-21986-8*) Natl Lilac Pub.

Story-Teller. Saki. (Classic Short Stories Ser.). (J). 1991. lib. bdg. 13.95 (*0-88682-476-1*) Creative Ed.

Story Teller. Peter Vansittart. 285p. 6800. 28.00 (*0-7206-7602-9*) Dufour.

Story Teller: A Collection of Short Stories, Bk. 1. Radames Morales. LC 94-94610. 148p. (YA). (gr. 6 up). 1994. pap. 6.95 (*0-9642626-0-6*) R Morales.

Story-Teller's Holiday, 2 vols., Set. George Moore. (BCL1-PR English Literature Ser.). 1992. reprint ed. lib. bdg. 150.00 (*0-7812-7602-0*) Rprt Serv.

Story Telling: What to Tell & How to Tell It. Edna Lyman. 1971. reprint ed. 50.00 (*1-55888-230-8*) Omnigraphics Inc.

Story Telling for Fun & Profit. write for info. (*0-9640610-6-6*) Cheval Intl.

Story-Telling Poems. Compiled by Frances J. Olcott. LC 77-128155. (Granger Index Reprint Ser.). 1977. 21.95 (*0-8369-6182-X*) Ayer.

Story-Telling Techniques in the Arabian Nights. David Pinault. LC 91-28023. (Journal of Arabic Literature Supplements Ser.: No. 15). 292p. 1992. 83.00 (*90-04-09530-6*) E J Brill.

Story, Text, & Scripture: Literary Interests in Biblical Narrative. Wesley A. Kort. LC 87-42549. 180p. 1988. 29.50 (*0-271-00610-2*) Pa St U Pr.

Story That Stands Like a Dam: Glen Canyon & the Struggle for the Soul of the West. Russell Martin. 368p. 1991. pap. 12.95 (*0-8050-1551-5*, Owl) H Holt & Co.

***Story That the Sonnets Tell.** A. D. Wraight. 585p. 1995. 39.95 (*1-897763-01-8*, Pub. by Drake Intl Serv UK); pap. 19.95 (*1-897763-05-0*, Pub. by Drake Intl Serv UK) Intl Spec Bk.

Story the Soldiers Wouldn't Tell: Sex in the Civil War. Thomas P. Lowry. (Illus.). 240p. 1994. 19.95 (*0-8117-1515-9*) Stackpole.

Story Tide Collectus. Ed. by Bibliotheca Press Research Staff. 68p. (Orig.). 1982. pap. text ed. 17.95 (*0-939476-44-4*, Biblio Pr) Prosperity & Profits.

Story Time. Helen Bramos & Ann S. Bramos. (Illus.). 77p. (Orig.). (J). (ps-7). 1994. pap. 8.00 (*0-9635333-2-0*) A S Bramos.

***Story Time Sampler: Read Alouds, Booktalks, & Activities for Children.** Paula G. Sitarz. LC 96-3460. 275p. 1997. lib. bdg. 25.00 (*1-56308-464-3*) Libs Unl.

Story Time Stories That Rhyme, Vol. 1: Fish Convention, Rainbow, Miss Divine Sunshine & Others. Alpha Pyramis Research Division Staff. 106p. (J). (gr. 4-12). 1992. ring bd. 27.95 (*0-913597-99-6*) Prosperity & Profits.

Story Time with Grandma. Mary E. Yoder. 1979. pap. 3.95 (*0-87813-514-6*) Christian Light.

Story Time with Jesus: Activity, Story & Coloring Book for Children Ages 3 to 7. Suzanne Perdew. (Illus.). 32p. (J). 1995. pap. 2.99 (*0-945460-20-1*) Upward Way.

Story to Tell. Michael P. Novak. LC 90-39896. 72p. 1990. 9.50 (*0-933532-75-X*) BkMk.

***Story to Tell: Traditions of a Tlingit Community.** Richard Nichols. LC 97-9592. (We Are Still Here Ser.). (Illus.). (J). 1997. pap. write for info. (*0-8225-9807-8*, Lerner Publctns); lib. bdg. write for info. (*0-8225-2661-1*, Lerner Publctns) Lerner Group.

***Story Train.** Marjorie Pratt & Mary Meighen. 10.00 (*0-614-30543-8*) NAVH.

Story Tree. Tony Bradman. (Illus.). 32p. (J). (gr. 1-3). 1993. 17.95 (*0-460-88093-4*, Pub. by J M Dent & Sons UK) Trafalgar.

Story Tryme File - Notebook of 30 Stories. A. C. Doyle. 50p. 1996. 32.95 (*1-56820-182-6*) Story Time.

***Story T(R)yme File - Noteook of 30 Stories.** A. C. Doyle. 52p. 1996. 32.95 (*1-56820-183-4*) Story Time.

Story Uncle Minyard Told: A Family's 200-Year Migration Across the South. Davis B. Carter. LC 94-3416. 510p. 1994. 35.00 (*0-87152-484-8*) Reprint.

Story Vine: A Source Book of Unusual & Easy-to-Tell Stories from Around the World. Anne Pellowski. LC 83-26756. (Illus.). 128p. (J). 1984. lib. bdg. 15.95 (*0-02-770590-0*, Mac Bks Young Read) S&S Childrens.

Story Without an End. Mark Twain. LC 85-30885. (Creative's Classic Short Stories Ser.). 32p. (J). (gr. 4 up). 1986. lib. bdg. 13.95 (*0-88682-064-2*) Creative Ed.

Story Without Title. 244p. (ARA.). 1995. pap. write for info. (*0-9642938-5-4*) Ravenala Pubns.

Story Workshop Reader. 2nd rev. ed. Ed. by John Schultz. (Illus.). 498p. (C). pap. text ed. 10.95 (*0-932026-26-5*) Columbia College Chi.

Story Writing. Edith R. Mirrielees. LC 72-6277. 1988. pap. 10.00 (*0-87116-137-0*) Writer.

Story Writing in a Nursing Home: A Patchwork of Memories. Ed. by Martha T. John. LC 91-25476. (Activities, Adaptation & Aging Ser.: Vol. 16, No. 1). (Illus.). 137p. 1992. 24.95 (*1-56024-098-9*) Haworth Pr.

Story Writing in a Nursing Home: A Patchwork of Memories. Ed. by Martha T. John. LC 91-25476. (Activities, Adaptation & Aging Ser.: Vol. 16, No. 1). 137p. 1996. reprint ed. pap. 14.95 (*0-7890-6041-8*) Haworth Pr.

Storyboards: Drawing Movies. Ward Preston. 300p. Date not set. pap. text ed. 26.95 (*1-879505-32-0*) Silman James Pr.

Storyboards: Motion in Art. Mark Simon. Ed. by Jeanne P. Simon. (Illus.). 1994. pap. 24.95 (*1-887118-00-4*) Nomis Creat.

Storybook Bride. Pat Montana. 1996. mass mkt. 3.25 (*0-373-19190-1*, 1-19190-7) Silhouette.

Storybook Characters Writing Forms. Joy Evans & Jo E. Moore. (Illus.). 48p. (J). (gr. k-3). 1990. teacher ed., pap. text ed. 5.95 (*1-55799-175-8*, EMC 244) Evan-Moor Corp.

Storybook Classrooms: Using Children's Literature in the Classroom. Karla Wendelin & Jean Greenlaw. LC 83-81430. (Illus.). 224p. 1984. lib. bdg. 26.95 (*0-89334-180-0*, 180-0) Humanics Ltd.

Storybook Classrooms: Using Children's Literature in the Learning Center-Primary Grades. Karla H. Wendelin & M. Jean Greenlaw. LC 83-81430. 224p. (Orig.). (J). (ps-4). 1984. pap. 16.95 (*0-89334-043-X*) Humanics Ltd.

Storybook Connections. Mary Bannister. (Illus.). 320p. (Orig.). 1995. teacher ed., pap. 24.95 (*1-878279-78-5*, MM1999) Monday Morning Bks.

Storybook Cowboy. Pat Montana. 1995. mass mkt. 2.99 (*0-373-19111-1*, 1-19111-3) Silhouette.

Storybook Dictionary: Richard Scarry. Richard Scarry. LC 99-901821. (Prestige Editions Ser.). (Illus.). 126p. (J). (gr. k-2). 1966. 11.95 (*0-307-15548-X*, Golden Pr) Western Pub.

Storybook Dolls: Stuffed Dolls to Make & Treasure. Kyoko Yoneyama. (Illus.). 156p. 1994. pap. 19.95 (*0-87040-933-6*) Japan Pubns USA.

Storybook Dolls: Stuffed Dolls to Make & Treasure. Kyoto Yoneyama. (Illus.). 156p. 1994. pap. 19.95 (*0-685-75055-8*) Japan Pubns USA.

Storybook Favorites in Cross-Stitch. Gillian Souter. LC 95-45879. (Illus.). 128p. (J). 1996. pap. 19.95 (*0-525-45613-9*) Dutton Child Bks.

Storybook Hero. Shanna Swendson. 1993. 17.95 (*0-8034-8985-4*) Bouregy.

Storybook Journey: Pathways to Literature Through Story & Play. Sue McCord. LC 95-1304. 1995. pap. text ed. 24.67 (*0-13-183997-7*, Merrill Pub Co) Macmillan.

Storybook Knits. Amy Carroll & Denise Brown. (Illus.). 64p. 1991. text ed. 14.95 (*0-02-522111-6*) Macmillan.

Storybook Mazes. Dave Phillips. (Illus.). 62p. 1978. pap. 2.95 (*0-486-23628-5*) Dover.

Storybook Patterns. Marilynn Barr. (Illus.). 48p. 1995. teacher ed., pap. 6.95 (*1-878279-81-5*, MM2004) Monday Morning Bks.

Storybook Stew: Cooking with Books Kids Love. Suzanne I. Barchers & Peter J. Rauen. LC 96-13780. (Illus.). 128p. (J). 1996. pap. 15.95 (*1-55591-944-8*) Fulcrum Pub.

***Storybook Treasures of Early Childhood: Best-Loved Picture Books for Young Children Birth-7 Years.** Majorie R. Nelsen. LC 97-65780. (Illus.). (Orig.). 1997. pap. write for info. (*0-9630495-4-2*) Partners in Learn.

Storybooks. Francis H. Wise & Joyce M. Wise. (Dr. Wise Learn to Read Bk.: Bks. 16-20: Vol. 4). (Illus.). 105p. (J). (gr. k-1). 1979. pap. 7.50 (*0-685-05433-0*) Wise Pub.

Storybooks Teach about World Cultures. Tanya Lieberman. (Illus.). 48p. (Orig.). 1995. teacher ed., pap. 6.95 (*1-878279-77-7*, MM1998) Monday Morning Bks.

Storybuilding: A Guide to Structuring Oral Narratives. Peg Hutson-Nechkash. 128p. (Orig.). (J). (gr. 3-8). 1990. pap. text ed. 29.00 (*0-930599-63-2*) Thinking Pubns.

Storycases: Book Surprises to Take Home. Richard Tabor & Suzanne Ryan. LC 96-5020. (Illus.). xix, 161p. 1996. pap. text ed. 18.50 (*1-56308-199-7*) Teacher Ideas Pr.

Storyhood As We Know It & Other Tales. Jack Matthews. (Poetry & Fiction Ser.). 208p. 1993. pap. 12.95 (*0-8018-4623-4*); text ed. 32.50 (*0-8018-4622-6*) Johns Hopkins.

Storyhours with Puppets & Other Props. William M. Painter. LC 90-6554. vi, 187p. (C). 1990. lib. bdg. 29.50 (*0-208-02284-8*, Lib Prof Pubns) Shoe String.

***Storykeepers Vol. 8: Captured.** (J). (gr. 4-7). 1997. pap. 14.99 (*0-310-20639-1*, 700149T) Zondervan.

Storykeepers Activity Book, No. 1. Ed. by Lori Walburg. (Storykeepers Ser.). (Illus.). 80p. (J). (gr. k-5). 1996. pap. 1.99 (*0-310-20236-1*) Zondervan.

***Storylines.** Fletcher & Birt. Date not set. pap. text ed. write for info. (*0-582-79103-0*, Pub. by Longman UK) Longman.

StoryMaker: An Interactive Guide to Life Story Writing. Gayle Geurin. 1996. pap. 14.95 (*0-9648734-0-0*) Prema Commun.

***Storymaking & Creative Groupwork with Elderly People.** Paula Crimmens. LC 96-48680. 1997. pap. write for info. (*1-85302-440-6*, Pub. by J Kingsley Pubs UK) Taylor & Francis.

Storymaking & Drama: An Approach to Teaching Language & Literature at the Secondary & Postsecondary Levels. Nancy King. LC 93-29079. 262p. (C). 1993. pap. text ed. 22.00 (*0-435-08625-1*, 08625) Heinemann.

Storymaking in Bereavement. Alida Gersie. 208p. 1991. 66.00 (*1-85302-065-6*) Taylor & Francis.

Storymaking in Education & Therapy. Alida Gersie & Nancy King. 416p. 1990. 69.00 (*1-85302-519-4*); pap. 39.95 (*1-85302-520-8*) Taylor & Francis.

Storyology: Essays in Folklore, Sea-Lore, & Plant-Lore. Benjamin Taylor. 1976. lib. bdg. 59.95 (0-8490-2693-8) Gordon Pr.

Storypole Legends: Legends of the Indians of Puget Sound. 2nd ed. Emerson N. Matson. Orig. Title: Longhouse Legends. (Illus.). 132p. (Orig.). (J). (gr. 4-9). 1996. reprint ed. pap. 8.95 (0-89992-140-X) Coun India Ed.

Storyscaping: Holistic Approaches to Improving the Skills of Story Writing. Bob Stanish. (Illus.). 112p. (J). (gr. 4 up). 1994. 11.99 (0-86653-814-3, GA1506) Good Apple.

***Storyteller.** Binchy. 1990. pap. text ed. write for info. (0-582-05063-4, Pub. by Longman UK) Longman.

Storyteller. Elizabeth Koda-Callan. (Illus.). 40p. (J). (ps-4). 1996. 12.95 (0-7611-0535-2, 10535) Workman Pub.

***Storyteller.** Ted Lewin. LC 97-15744. 1998. write for info. (0-688-15178-7) Lothrop.

***Storyteller.** Ted Lewin. LC 97-15744. 1998. lib. bdg. write for info. (0-688-15179-5) Lothrop.

Storyteller. Ed. by Anthony Minghella. 144p. (C). 1990. 45.00 (1-85283-026-3, Pub. by Boxtree Ltd UK) St Mut.

Storyteller. Harold Robbins. 1994. mass mkt. 5.99 (0-671-87522-1) PB.

Storyteller. Smith. 1994. pap. 22.00 (0-02-612131-X) Macmillan.

Storyteller. Mario Vargas Llosa. Tr. by Helen Lane. 1989. 17.95 (0-374-27085-6) FS&G.

Storyteller. Mario Vargas Llosa. 256p. 1990. pap. 11.95 (0-14-014349-1, Penguin Bks) Viking Penguin.

Storyteller. Jane Yolen. LC 91-67894. (Illus.). 212p. 1992. 15.00 (0-915368-49-8) New Eng SF Assoc.

Storyteller. 3rd ed. Raymon R. Ross. LC 96-17345. 1996. pap. text ed. 23.95 (0-87483-451-1) August Hse.

Storyteller. V. Ben Kendrick. 145p. (Orig.). 1993. reprint ed. pap. 5.95 (0-941645-00-2) Bap Mid-Missions.

Storyteller. Leslie M. Silko. (Illus.). 288p. 1989. reprint ed. pap. 16.95 (1-55970-005-X) Arcade Pub Inc.

Storyteller, Vol. 1. Nissan Mindel. (Illus.). 318p. (YA). 1981. reprint ed. 12.00 (0-8266-0314-9, Merkos LInyonei Chinuch) Kehot Pubn Soc.

Storyteller, Vol. 2. Nissan Mindel. (Illus.). 268p. (YA). 1984. reprint ed. 12.00 (0-8266-0313-0, Merkos LInyonei Chinuch) Kehot Pubn Soc.

Storyteller, Vol. 3. Nissan Mindel. (Illus.). 368p. (YA). 1987. reprint ed. 12.00 (0-8266-0312-2, Merkos LInyonei Chinuch) Kehot Pubn Soc.

Storyteller, Vol. 4. Nissan Mindel. (Illus.). 346p. (YA). 1991. reprint ed. 12.00 (0-8266-1312-8, Merkos LInyonei Chinuch) Kehot Pubn Soc.

Storyteller & a City: Sherwood Anderson's Chicago. Kenny J. Williams. (Illus.). 322p. 1988. 30.00 (0-87580-135-8) N Ill U Pr.

Storyteller As Humanist: The Serees of Guillaume Bouchet. Hope H. Glidden. LC 80-70809. (French Forum Monographs: No. 25). 183p. (Orig.). 1981. pap. 13.95 (0-917058-24-0) French Forum.

Storyteller at Fault. Dan Yashinsky. (NFS Canada Ser.). (Illus.). 64p. (J). (gr. 4-9). 1992. pap. 9.95 (0-921556-29-2, Pub. by Gynergy-Ragweed CN) LPC InBook.

Storyteller Book. J. M. Barrie. (Anness Ser.). 48p. (J). (ps-1). 1994. pap. 7.98 (0-8317-0884-0) Smithmark.

Storyteller Book. Lesley Young. (Anness Ser.). 48p. (J). (ps-1). 1995. 7.98 (0-8317-0770-4) Smithmark.

Storyteller Book: Cinderella. Charles Perrault. 48p. (J). (ps-1). 1994. 7.98 (0-8317-0883-2) Smithmark.

Storyteller Guidebook Series. Barbara B. Griffin. 1991. write for info. (0-9623331-0-7) Strytller Guidebk.

Storyteller, Storyteacher: Discovering the Power of Storytelling for Teaching & Living. Marni Gillard. 232p. (Orig.). (C). 1995. pap. text ed. 19.50 (1-57110-014-8) Stenhse Pubs.

Storyteller with Nike Airs & Other Barrio Stories. Kleya Forte-Escamilla. LC 94-29817. 208p. (Orig.). 1994. pap. 8.95 (1-879960-34-6) Aunt Lute Bks.

StoryTellers. Karume Jumal. LC 94-96752. 460p. 1995. 19.75 (0-9644985-8-8) Griot Pub.

Storytellers: Folktales & Legends from the South. Ed. by John A. Burrison. LC 88-37143. (Illus.). 270p. 1989. 34.95 (0-8203-1099-9) U of Ga Pr.

Storytellers: Folktales & Legends from the South. Ed. by John A. Burrison. LC 88-37143. (Brown Thrasher Bks.). (Illus.). 384p. 1990. pap. 15.95 (0-8203-1267-3) U of Ga Pr.

***Storytellers: From Mel Allen to Bob Costas, Sixty Years of Baseball Tales from the Broadcast Booth.** Curt Smith. 1997. 14.00 (0-02-861510-7) Macmillan.

Storytellers: The Image of the Two-Year College in American Fiction & in Women's Journals. Nancy LaPaglia. LC 93-37645. 182p. 1994. pap. 15.95 (1-879528-07-X) LEPS Pr.

Storytellers & Other Figurative Pottery. Douglas Congdon-Martin. LC 90-61506. 144p. (Orig.). 1990. pap. 19.95 (0-88740-270-4) Schiffer.

Storyteller's Animal Stories. Adapted by Duane Hutchinson. LC 95-12819. 96p. (J). 1995. pap. 6.95 (0-934988-35-8) Foun Bks.

Storyteller's Bible Study for Internationals. Bill Perry. 160p. 1992. pap. 8.95 (0-9633645-0-2) Multi-Lang Media.

Storyteller's Companion to the Bible Vol. 1: Genesis. Ed. by Michael E. Williams. LC 90-26289. 208p. 1997. 19.95 (0-687-39670-0) Abingdon.

Storytellers Companion to the Bible Vol. 2: Exodus-Joshua. Michael Williams. LC 90-26289. 1992. 16.95 (0-687-39671-9) Abingdon.

Storyteller's Companion to the Bible Vol. 3: Judges-Kings. Ed. by Michael E. Williams. LC 90-26289. 208p. 1992. 16.95 (0-687-39672-7) Abingdon.

Storytellers Companion to the Bible Vol. 4: Old Testament Women. Ed. by Michael E. Williams. LC 90-26287. 208p. 1993. 16.95 (0-687-39674-3) Abingdon.

Storyteller's Companion to the Bible Vol. 5: Old Testament Wisdom. Ed. by Michael E. Williams. 208p. (Orig.). 1994. 16.95 (0-687-39675-1) Abingdon.

Storyteller's Companion to the Bible Vol. 6: The Prophets I. Mary D. Turner. Ed. by Michael E. Williams. 192p. 1996. 16.95 (0-687-00838-7) Abingdon.

Storyteller's Companion to the Bible Vol. 7: The Prophets II. Ed. by Michael E. Williams. 208p. 1995. 16.95 (0-687-00120-X) Abingdon.

***Storyteller's Companion to the Bible Vol. 8: Daniel & Revelation.** Ed. by Michael E. Williams. 208p. 1997. 16.95 (0-687-02652-0) Abingdon.

***Storyteller's Companion to the Bible Vol. 10: John.** Michael E. Williams & Dennis E. Smith. 208p. 1996. 16.95 (0-687-05585-7) Abingdon.

***Storyteller's Companion to the Bible Vol. 12: Acts of the Apostles.** Ed. by Michael E. Williams & Dennis E. Smith. (Storyteller's Companion to the Bible Ser.). 208p. 1997. 16.95 (0-687-08249-8) Abingdon.

Storyteller's Cornucopia. Cathie H. Cooper. (Illus.). 270p. (Orig.). (J). (ps-4). 1992. pap. text ed. 17.95 (0-913853-25-9, 32536, Alleyside) Highsmith Pr.

Storyteller's Daughter. Jean Thesman. LC 96-1756. (J). 1997. 16.00 (0-395-80978-9) HM.

Storyteller's Ghost Stories, Bk. 1. Duane Hutchinson. LC 89-23689. (Illus.). 112p. 1989. pap. 6.95 (0-934988-32-3) Foun Bks.

Storyteller's Ghost Stories, Bk. 2. Duane Hutchinson. LC 90-3122. 96p. (J). (gr. 4 up). 1990. pap. 6.95 (0-934988-18-8) Foun Bks.

Storyteller's Ghost Stories, Bk. 3. Duane Hutchinson. LC 89-23689. 104p. 1992. pap. 6.95 (0-934988-25-0) Foun Bks.

Storyteller's Goddess. Carolyn M. Edwards. LC 90-56445. 208p. (Orig.). 1991. pap. 13.00 (0-06-250263-8) Harper SF.

Storyteller's Guide: Storytellers Discuss Experiences in Classrooms, Boardrooms, Showrooms... Bill Mooney & David Holt. LC 96-9500. 224p. 1996. pap. text ed. 23.95 (0-87483-482-1) August Hse.

Storytellers Handbook. Ed. by Robert Hatch & Andrew Greenberg. (Vampire: the Masquerade Ser.). (Illus.). 152p. (Orig.). 1992. per. 18.00 (1-56504-024-4, 2222) White Wolf.

Storytellers Handbook to the Sabbat. Steven C. Brown. (Vampire: the Masquerade Ser.). 1993. 15.00 (1-56504-054-6, 2225) White Wolf.

Storytellers in Marguerite de Navare's Heptameron. Betty J. Davis. LC 77-93406. (French Forum Monographs: No. 9). 203p. (Orig.). 1978. pap. 10.95 (0-917058-08-9) French Forum.

Storyteller's Journal - A Guidebook for Story Research & Learning. Barbara B. Griffin. 88p. 1990. pap. 12.95 (0-9623331-3-1) Strytller Guidebk.

***Storytellers of God: Teacher's Toolbox.** Tony McCaffrey. 1996. pap. text ed. 19.95 (1-55612-920-3) Sheed Ward Ltd.

***Storytellers' Research Guide: Folktales, Myths & Legends.** Judy Sierra. LC 96-86625. 90p. (Orig.). 1996. pap. 14.95 (0-9636089-4-0) Folkprint.

Storytellers, Saints, & Scoundrels: Folk Narrative in Hindu Religious Teaching. Kirin Narayan. LC 89-31363. (Publications of the American Folklore Society, Bibliographical & Special Ser.). (Illus.). 296p. (C). 1989. pap. text ed. 16.50 (0-8122-1269-X) U of Pa Pr.

Storyteller's Sampler. Valerie Marsh. (Illus.). 88p. (Orig.). (J). (ps-5). 1996. teacher ed., pap. 11.95 (0-917846-58-3, 34006, Alleyside) Highsmith Pr.

Storyteller's Screen. 2nd ed. Graeme Davis. (Vampire Ser.). 1996. 10.00 (1-56504-055-4, 2003) White Wolf.

Storyteller's Sourcebook. Ed. by Margaret R. MacDonald. (Neal Schuman Bk.). 840p. 1995. 99.00 (0-8103-0471-6) Gale.

Storytellers Sourcebook. Clarence Trowbridge. 215p. (Orig.). 1996. pap. 9.95 (1-57502-233-8, P0902) Morris Pubng.

Storytellers Sourcebook. 2nd ed. Neal & Schuman. 1900. 99.00 (0-8103-5485-3) Gale.

Storyteller's Start-up Book: Finding, Learning, Performing, & Using Folktales. Margaret R. MacDonald. 215p. 1993. 26.95 (0-87483-304-3); pap. 16.95 (0-87483-305-1) August Hse.

Storyteller's Story. Rafe Martin. LC 92-7794. (Meet the Author Ser.). (Illus.). 32p. (J). (gr. 2-5). 1992. 13.95 (0-913461-03-2) R Owen Pubs.

Storyteller's Story. Sherwood Anderson. 250p. 1990. reprint ed. lib. bdg. 24.95 (0-89966-730-9) Buccaneer Bks.

Storytellers to the Nation: A History of American Television Writing. Tom Stempel. LC 95-40841. (Television Ser.). 316p. (C). 1996. pap. 16.95 (0-8156-0368-1, STSNP) Syracuse U Pr.

Storyteller's Worlds: Education of Shlomo Noble in Europe & America. Jonathan Boyarin. (New Perspectives: Jewish Life & Thought Ser.). 240p. 1994. text ed. 34.95 (0-8419-1343-9) Holmes & Meier.

Storytelling. 1991. pap. 9.95 (0-590-49139-3) Scholastic Inc.

Storytelling. David Oliveira. 12p. (Orig.). 1993. pap. 5.00 (0-9638843-0-1) Mille Grazie.

Storytelling: A Triad in the Arts. Gail N. Herman. 53p. 1986. pap. 8.95 (0-936386-36-3) Creative Learning.

Storytelling: Art & Technique. 2nd ed. Augusta Baker & Ellin Greene. LC 77-16481. 182p. 1987. 35.00 (0-8352-2336-1) Bowker.

Storytelling: Art & Technique. 3rd ed. Ellin Greene. 350p. 1996. 39.00 (0-8352-3458-4) Bowker.

Storytelling: Process & Practice. Norma J. Livo & Sandra A. Reitz. LC 85-23681. xvi, 462p. 1986. lib. bdg. 35.00 (0-87287-443-5) Libs Unl.

Storytelling - Folklore Series. rev. ed. (Illus.). (YA). 1992. pap. write for info. (0-938756-99-0) Yellow Moon.

Storytelling Activities. Norma J. Livo & Sandra A. Rietz. LC 86-33727. xiv, 140p. 1987. pap. text ed. 17.50 (0-87287-566-0) Libs Unl.

Storytelling Activities Kit: Ready-to-Use Techniques, Lessons, & Listening Cassettes for Early Childhood. Jerilynn Changar & Annette Harrison. 288p. 1992. pap. 37.95 incl. audio (0-87628-869-7) Ctr Appl Res.

Storytelling Adventures: Stories Kids Can Tell. Vivian Dubrovin. LC 96-92370. (Illus.). 80p. (Orig.). (J). (gr. 3-8). 1997. pap. 14.95 (0-9638339-2-8) Storycraft Pub.

Storytelling & Review Guide, Old Testament: Bible Story Cards Learning System. Ed. by Wendy Wagoner et al. (Illus.). 138p. (Orig.). (J). 1995. wbk. ed., pap. 9.95 (0-89827-150-9, GM411) Wesleyan Pub Hse.

Storytelling & Spirituality in Judaism. Yitzhak Buxbaum. LC 94-6122. 280p. 1994. pap. 25.00 (1-56821-173-2) Aronson.

Storytelling & the Art of Imagination. Nancy Mellon. 1992. pap. 13.95 (1-85230-339-5) Element MA.

Storytelling Coach. Doug Lipman. (American Storytelling Ser.). 1995. 24.95 (0-87483-435-X); pap. 14.95 (0-87483-434-1) August Hse.

***Storytelling Cottage.** Nora Mogielski. (Illus.). 32p. 1997. pap. write for info. (1-886094-55-1) Chicago Spectrum.

***Storytelling Encyclopedia: Historical, Cultural, & Multiethnic Approaches to Oral Traditions Around the World.** Book Builders, Inc. Staff. Ed. by David A. Leeming. (Illus.). 544p. 1997. boxed 69.95 (1-57356-025-1) Oryx Pr.

Storytelling Festivals, Fairs, Events, Etc. A Story Rhyme Resource. Story Time Stories That Rhyme Staff. (Illus.). 60p. (Orig.). 1992. ring bd. 25.95 (1-56820-068-4) Story Time.

Storytelling Folklore Sourcebook. Norma J. Livo & Sandra A. Rietz. xiv, 384p. 1991. pap. text ed. 34.00 (0-87287-601-2) Libs Unl.

***Storytelling for Literacy.** Sheila D. Carroll. 200p. 1998. lib. bdg. write for info. (0-208-02463-8) Shoe String.

Storytelling for the Fun of It: A Handbook for Children. Vivian Dubrovin. LC 93-93694. 160p. (J). (gr. 4-7). 1994. pap. 16.95 (0-9638339-0-1) Storycraft Pub.

Storytelling for Young Adults: Techniques & Treasury. Gail De Vos. x, 169p. 1991. lib. bdg. 24.50 (0-87287-832-5) Libs Unl.

Storytelling from the Bible: Make Scripture Live for All Ages Through the Art of Storytelling. Janet Litherland. Ed. by Arthur L. Zapel & Rhonda Wray. LC 91-29871. 192p. (Orig.). 1991. pap. 10.95 (0-916260-80-1, B145) Meriwether Pub.

Storytelling Games: Creative Activities for Language, Communication, & Composition across the Curriculum. Doug Lipman. LC 94-38939. (Illus.). 192p. 1994. pap. 26.50 (0-89774-848-4) Oryx Pr.

Storytelling Handbook: A Young People's Collection of Unusual Tales & Helpful Hints on How to Tell Them. Anne Pellowski. LC 95-2991. (Illus.). 122p. (YA). (gr. 3 up). 1995. 16.00 (0-689-80311-7, Aladdin Paperbacks) S&S Childrens.

Storytelling, Imagination & Faith. William J. Bausch. LC 83-51515. 232p. (Orig.). (C). 1984. pap. 9.95 (0-89622-199-7) Twenty-Third.

Storytelling in Animation, Vol. 2: The Art of the Animated Image. John Canemaker. pap. 9.95 (0-573-60697-8) French.

Storytelling in Mathematics & Science. Lipke. LC 96-22037. 1996. pap. text ed. 25.00 (0-435-07105-X) Heinemann.

Storytelling in Psychotherapy with Children. Richard Gardner. LC 93-14898. 296p. 1993. pap. 30.00 (1-56821-032-9) Aronson.

Storytelling in the Bible. 2nd ed. J. Licht. 154p. (C). 1986. text ed. 15.00 (965-223-542-3, Pub. by Magnes Press IS) Eisenbrauns.

Storytelling Made Easy with Puppets. Jan VanSchuyver. LC 92-45900. (Illus.). 160p. 1993. pap. 26.50 (0-89774-732-1) Oryx Pr.

***Storytelling Magic.** Susan Pagnucci & Franco Pagnucci. (Illus.). 32p. (Orig.). (J). (ps-3). 1997. pap. 4.99 (0-929326-08-3) Bur Oak Pr Inc.

Storytelling, Narrative & the Thematic Apperception Test. LC 96-5520. (Assessment of Personality & Psychopathology Ser.). 1996. lib. bdg. 42.00 (1-57230-094-9) Guilford Pr.

***Storytelling Patterns.** Susan Pagnucci. (Illus.). 32p. (Orig.). (J). (ps-3). 1991. pap. 4.99 (0-929326-06-7) Bur Oak Pr Inc.

***Storytelling Powerbook: Substance Abuse Prevention.** Annabelle Nelson. (Illus.). 1p. (YA). 1997. wbk. ed., pap. 29.95 (0-9656732-0-0) WHEEL Council.

Storytelling Professionally: The Nuts & Bolts of a Working Performer. Harlynne Geisler. LC 96-41964. 160p. (Orig.). 1997. pap. 22.50 (1-56308-370-1) Libs Unl.

Storytelling Rights: The Use of Oral & Written Texts by Urban Adolescents. Amy Shuman. (Cambridge Studies in Oral & Literate Culture: No. 11). (Illus.). 256p. 1986. text ed. 69.95 (0-521-32846-2) Cambridge U Pr.

Storytelling Step by Step. Marsh Cassady. LC 90-37986. 168p. (Orig.). (C). 1990. pap. 9.95 (0-89390-183-0) Resource Pubns.

Storytelling Stone: Traditional Native American Myths & Tales. Susan Feldman. 304p. 1991. mass mkt. 5.99 (0-440-38314-5, LE) Dell.

Storytelling the Word: Homilies & How to Write Them. William J. Bausch. LC 95-62067. 304p. (Orig.). 1996. pap. 14.95 (0-89622-687-5) Twenty-Third.

Storytelling Tips: How to Love, Learn, & Relate a Story. Duane Hutchinson. 96p. 1985. pap. 5.95 (0-934988-13-7) Foun Bks.

Storytelling with Children. 1995. pap. 12.95 (0-19-437202-2) OUP.

Storytelling with Music: Music Dramas. Robert B. Smith & John W. Flohr. 88p. (C). 1991. pap. text ed. 14.95 (0-914487-03-5) Troost Pr.

Storytelling with Music, Puppets, & Arts for Libraries & Classrooms. William M. Painter. LC 94-20096. (Illus.). vi, 164p. (C). 1994. pap. text ed. 27.50 (0-208-02372-0, Lib Prof Pubns) Shoe String.

***Storytelling with Puppets.** 2nd ed. Connie Champlin. LC 97-24810. 1997. write for info. (0-8389-0709-1) ALA.

Storytelling with the Computer. Connie Champlin & John DeVasure. (Illus.). 64p. (J). (gr. k-6). 1986. pap. 29.95 (0-938594-09-5); disk (0-318-59389-0) Spec Lit Pr.

Storytelling with the Flannel Board, 3 Bks., Bk. 1. Paul S. Anderson. LC 21-650. (Illus.). 270p. (J). (ps). 1963. 15.95 (0-513-00105-0) Denison.

Storytelling with the Flannel Board, 3 Bks., Bk. 2. Paul S. Anderson. LC 21-650. (Illus.). 260p. (J). (ps). 1970. 15.95 (0-513-00137-9) Denison.

Storytelling with the Flannel Board, Bk. 3. Idalee W. Vonk. LC 21-650. 313p. (J). (ps). 1983. 15.95 (0-513-01762-3) Denison.

Storytime. Arthur S. Maxwell. (J). 1989. 19.99 (1-877773-00-X) Review & Herald.

Storytime. Edna Menzies. (Illus.). 128p. (J). (gr. 1-3). 1993. pap. 5.95 (1-879224-15-1) Mailbox.

***Storytime Vol. I: Once upon a Time.** Peggy Friederich. (Illus.). 75p. (Orig.). (J). 1996. pap. write for info. (1-57579-020-3) Pine Hill Pr.

Storytime Around the Curriculum: A Comprehensive Early Childhood Curriculum Presented Through Literature. O'Berry, Little & Fields Staff. 1992. pap. 29.95 (0-933212-03-8) Partner Pr.

Storytime for Five Year Olds. Joan Stimson. (Illus.). 44p. (J). 1994. 3.50 (0-7214-1649-7, Ladybrd) Penguin.

Storytime for Four Year Olds. Joan Stimson. (Illus.). 44p. (J). 1994. 3.50 (0-7214-1648-9, Ladybrd) Penguin.

Storytime for One Year Olds. Joan Stimson. (Illus.). 28p. (J). 1994. 3.50 (0-7214-1645-4, Ladybrd) Penguin.

Storytime for Seven Year Olds. (Storytime Ser.: No. 887-5). (Illus.). (J). (gr. 2). 1990. 3.50 (0-7214-1347-1, Ladybrd) Penguin.

Storytime for Six Year Olds. Joan Stimson. (Illus.). 44p. (J). 1994. 3.50 (0-7214-1650-0, Ladybrd) Penguin.

Storytime for Three Year Olds. Joan Stimson. (Illus.). 44p. (J). 1994. 3.50 (0-7214-1647-0, Ladybrd) Penguin.

Storytime for Two Year Olds. Joan Stimson. (Illus.). 44p. (J). 1994. 3.50 (0-7214-1646-2, Ladybrd) Penguin.

Storytime Jamboree. Peter J. Dyck. LC 93-50209. (Illus.). 176p. (Orig.). (J). (gr. 1 up). 1994. pap. 6.99 (0-8361-3667-5) Herald Pr.

***Storytime Literacy Resource Guide.** KCET Television Station, Los Angeles, Calif. Staff. LC 97-577. (J). 1997. pap. write for info. (0-87207-178-2) Intl Reading.

Storytime Science: Have You Clanged Your Hanger Banger Today? Virginia V. Baeckler. Ed. by Kenneth G. Van Wynen. LC 86-61013. (Illus.). 100p. 1986. pap. text ed. 10.00 (0-9603232-2-8) Sources.

Storytime Sourcebook: A Compendium of Ideas & Resources for Storytellers. Carolyn M. Cullum. LC 90-49657. 177p. 1990. pap. text ed. 24.95 (1-55570-067-5) Neal-Schuman.

Storytime Theme-A-Saurus: The Great Big Book of Storytime Teaching Themes. Jean Warren. Ed. by Kathleen Cubley. LC 92-64377. (Illus.). 160p. (Orig.). (J). (ps-1). 1993. pap. 14.95 (0-911019-56-1, WPH 1006) Warren Pub Hse.

Storytime with the Millers. 2nd ed. Mildred A. Martin. (Miller Family Ser.). (Illus.). 110p. (Orig.). (J). (ps-3). 1994. pap. 5.00 (1-884377-00-9) Green Psturs Pr.

Storytown: Stories. Susan Daitch. LC 95-26578. (Illus.). 192p. (Orig.). 1996. pap. 12.95 (1-56478-094-5) Dalkey Arch.

***Storytracking: Texts, Stories & Histories in Central Australia.** Sam D. Gill. 304p. 1997. pap. 19.95 (0-19-511588-0) OUP.

***Storytracking: Texts, Stories & Histories in Central Australia.** Sam D. Gill. 304p. 1997. 45.00 (0-19-511587-2) OUP.

***Storyville.** Lois Battle. 1997. pap. 12.95 (0-14-026769-7) Viking Penguin.

Storyville. large type ed. Lois Battle. LC 93-12037. (Basic Ser.). 654p. 1993. reprint ed. lib. bdg. 23.95 (1-56054-659-X) Thorndike Pr.

Storyville: A Hidden Mirror. Brooke Bergan. LC 93-15235. (Illus.). 108p. (Orig.). 1993. pap. 12.95 (1-55921-094-X, Asphodel Pr) Moyer Bell.

Storyville, New Orleans: Being an Authentic, Illustrated Account of the Notorious Red Light District. Al Rose. 240p. 1974. pap. 19.95 (0-8173-4403-9) U of Ala Pr.

Storyville to Harlem: Fifty Years in the Jazz Scene. Stephen Longstreet. 211p. (C). 1986. 29.95 (0-8135-1174-7) Rutgers U Pr.

Storyweaving: You & Your Faith Journey. Wendell Brooker. 1990. student ed., pap. 5.50 (0-8170-1157-9) Judson.

Storyweaving: You & Your Faith Journey. Wendell Brooker. 1990. teacher ed., pap. 5.50 (0-8170-1167-6) Judson.

***Storyweaving: You & Your Faith Journey.** Wendell Brooker. Date not set. pap. 4.00 (0-8170-1158-7) Judson.

***Storyworlds.** 2nd ed. Brown. 1988. pap. text ed. write for info. (0-05-004201-7) Addison-Wesley.

Storyworlds: Linking Minds & Imagination Through Literature. Jon E. Shapiro et al. 72p. 1992. pap. text ed. 12.00 (0-88751-030-2, 00713) Heinemann.

Stotan! Chris Crutcher. 192p. (J). (gr. k-12). 1988. mass mkt. 3.99 (0-440-20080-6, LLL BDD) BDD Bks Young Read.

An Asterisk (*) at the beginning of an entry indicates that the title is appearing in BIP for the first time.

Stotan! Chris Crutcher. LC 85-12712. 192p. (YA). (gr. 7 up). 1986. 16.00 (0-688-05715-2) Greenwillow.

Stouffer Cookbook of Great American Food & Drink. Stouffer. 1974. 14.95 (0-394-48810-5) Random.

Stouffer Genealogical Memoranda, 1630-1903. K. S. Snively. (Illus.). 104p. 1994. reprint ed. pap. 19.00 (0-8328-4042-4); reprint ed. lib. bdg. 29.00 (0-8328-4041-6) Higginson Bk Co.

Stoughton Manuscript. Ed. by Peter Beal. (English Verse Miscellanies of the Seventeenth Century Ser.). 296p. 1991. 74.95 (0-85967-787-7, Pub. by Scolar Pr UK) Ashgate Pub Co.

Stoughton Musical Society's Centennial Collection of Sacred Music. Roger L. Hall. LC 80-11936. (Earlier American Music Ser.: No. 23). 304p. 1980. reprint ed. lib. bdg. 37.50 (0-306-79618-X) Da Capo.

Stout. Michael J. Lewis. (Classic Beer Style Ser.). (Illus.). 192p. 1996. pap. 11.95 (0-937381-44-6) Brewers Pubns.

Stout & Allied Families. H. F. Stout. (Illus.). xxii, 889p. 1992. reprint ed. pap. 129.50 (0-8328-2328-7); reprint ed. lib. bdg. 139.50 (0-8328-2327-9) Higginson Bk Co.

Stout-Hearted Seven. Neta L. Frazier. 174p. (J). (gr. 4-6). 1984. pap. text ed. 4.95 (0-914019-22-8) NW Interpretive.

Stout Hearts: Traditional Oak Basket Makers of the South Carolina Upcountry. 24p. 1993. pap. 5.95 (0-87249-955-3) U of SC Pr.

Stout Hearts: Traditional Oak Basket Makers of the South Carolina Upcountry. Gary Stanton & Tom Cowan. (Illus.). (Orig.). 1988. pap. 9.00 (0-318-35185-4) McKissick.

Stouthearted Men. R. C. House. Ed. by Doug Grad. 256p. (Orig.). 1995. mass mkt. 4.99 (0-671-87245-1) PB.

Stove. Jakov Lind. LC 82-10824. 77p. 1983. pap. 7.95 (0-935296-27-1) Sheep Meadow.

Stove by a Whale: Owen Chase & the "Essex" Thomas F. Heffernan. LC 90-38190. (Illus.). 288p. 1990. pap. 15.95 (0-8195-6244-0, Wesleyan Univ Pr) U Pr of New Eng.

Stove Maker, Stove User: Fuel-Efficient Stoves in Sri Lanka. Val Rea & Mike Martin. (Orig.). 1991. pap. 42.95 (1-85339-099-2, Pub. by Intermed Tech UK) Women Ink.

Stove-Up Cowboy's Story. James E. McCauley. LC 65-4439. (Illus.). 100p. 1965. reprint ed. 9.95 (0-87074-093-8) SMU Press.

Stovepiper. Greg Barbera et al. (Illus.). 144p. (Orig.). 1994. pap. 12.95 (0-9642339-0-8) Stovepiper Bks.

Stover Manufacturing & Engine Company. Charles H. Wendel. LC 82-80676. (Power in the Past Ser.: Vol. 3). (Illus.). 96p. 1982. pap. 12.50 (0-942804-00-7) Old Iron Bk Co.

Stow Church Restored. Mark Spurrell. (Lincoln Record Society Ser.: No. 75). (Illus.). 252p. 1984. 39.00 (0-901503-39-8) Boydell & Brewer.

***Stow, Mass. 1683-1933, Compiled in Honor of the 250th Anniversary of the Town.** Preston R. Crowell. (Illus.). 131p. 1997. reprint ed. lib. bdg. 27.50 (0-8328-5963-X) Higginson Bk Co.

***Stow, Mass. 1683-1933, Compiled in Honor of the 250th Anniversary of the Town.** Preston R. Crowell. (Illus.). 131p. 1997. reprint ed. pap. 17.50 (0-8328-5964-8) Higginson Bk Co.

Stow on the Wold. Joan Johnson. (Illus.). 96p. 1994. pap. 14.00 (0-7509-0590-5, Pub. by Sutton Pubng UK) Bks Intl VA.

Stow Wengenroth, Artist-Lithographer: A Retrospective Exhibition. Norton, R. W., Art Gallery Staff. LC 76-26456. (Contemporary Realists Ser.). (Illus.). 1976. pap. 3.00 (0-913060-10-0) Norton Art.

Stow Wengenroth's Lithographs: A Supplement. Ronald Stuckey & Joan Stuckey. LC 82-72164. (Illus.). 117p. (C). 1982. 35.00 (0-9608834-0-1) Black Oak NY.

Stowage of Heavy Goods in Containers & on Flats. ICHCA Staff. (C). 1988. 65.00 (0-685-46496-2, Pub. by ICHCA UK) St Mut.

Stowage of Heavy Goods in Containers & on Flats. Swedish Transport Research Commission Staff. (C). 1979. 120.00 (0-685-37338-X, Pub. by ICHCA UK) St Mut.

Stowaway. Carol Cordoba. LC 96-12335. 284p. 1996. 19.95 (1-55885-166-6) Arte Publico.

Stowaway. New International Version Of The Bible Staff. (Stories from the Great Book Ser.). (Illus.). (Orig.). (J). 1986. pap. 4.95 (0-918789-09-5) FreeMan Prods.

Stowaway. Nancy N. Rue. LC 94-41918. (Christian Heritage Ser.: No. 2). 1995. pap. 5.99 (1-56179-347-7) Focus Family.

Stowaway: A Tale of California Pirates. Kristiana Gregory. LC 94-42299. (Illus.). 144p. (YA). (gr. 4 up). 1995. 14.95 (0-590-48822-8, Scholastic Hardcover) Scholastic Inc.

Stowaway Fairy in Hawaii. Mary Koski. (Illus.). 36p. (J). (gr. k-5). 1991. 12.95 (0-89610-225-4) Island Heritage.

Stowaway Heart. Leona Karr. 416p. 1994. mass mkt. 4.50 (0-8217-4730-4, Zebra Kensgtn) Kensgtn Pub Corp.

Stowaway to California. Natalie N. Hernandez. (Illus.). 136p. (Orig.). (J). (gr. 3-6). 1994. pap. 9.95 (0-9644386-0-7) Santa Ines Pub.

Stowaway to Mars. John Wyndham. 1989. reprint ed. 18.00 (0-7278-1761-2) Severn Hse.

Stowaway to Texas. Ethel L. Evey. Ed. by Shelia S. Darst. 201p. (J). (gr. 4-7). 1986. 9.95 (0-89896-102-5, Post Oak Pr); pap. 6.95 (0-89896-101-7, Post Oak Pr) Larksdale.

Stowaway to the Mushroom Planet. Eleanor Cameron. (Illus.). (J). (gr. 3-7). 1956. 14.95 (0-316-12534-2, Joy St Bks) Little.

Stowaway to the Mushroom Planet. Eleanor Cameron. (J). (gr. 3-7). 1988. mass mkt. 6.95 (0-316-12541-5) Little.

Stowaways. Brad Strickland. (Star Trek: Deep Space Nine Ser.: No. 2). (J). (gr. 3-6). 1994. mass mkt. 3.99 (0-671-88000-4, Minstrel Bks) PB.

Stowe Debate: Rhetorical Strategies in "Uncle Tom's Cabin" Ed. by Mason I. Lowance et al. LC 94-12254. 328p. (C). 1994. pap. 18.95 (0-87023-952-X) U of Mass Pr.

Stowell C. Goding & France: A Festschrift in Honor of Stowell C. Goding. Ed. by Mel B. Yoken. LC 92-23625. 183p. (C). 1993. text ed. 47.95 (0-8204-2008-5) P Lang Pubng.

Stowe's Bible Astrology: The Bible Founded on Astrology. Lyman E. Stowe. 248p. 1965. reprint ed. spiral bd. 12.00 (0-7873-0850-1) Hlth Research.

Stowe's Bible Astrology (1907) Lyman E. Stowe. 250p. 1996. pap. 18.95 (1-56459-802-0) Kessinger Pub.

Stowing of Goods in Containers & on Flat. Swedish Transport Research Commission Staff. Tr. by ICHCA Staff from SWE. 94p. (C). 1973. 110.00 (0-685-37336-3, Pub. by ICHCA UK) St Mut.

Stowing of Goods in Containers & on Flats. ICHCA Staff. (C). 1988. 70.00 (0-685-36576-X, Pub. by ICHCA UK) St Mut.

Stoy Hayward: Company Car Taxation. Brian Friedman & Simon Garrett. 250p. 1993. pap. 46.00 (0-406-02654-8, U.K.) MICHIE.

Stoy Hayward Business Tax Guide 1989-90. Mavis Seymour & Stephen Say. 320p. 1989. 44.95 (0-8464-1380-9) Beekman Pubs.

***Stoy Hayward Guide to the Family Business.** 2nd ed. Peter Leach. (Business & Management Ser.). 1994. pap. 19.95 (0-7494-1258-5) Kogan Page Ltd.

ST(P) Caribbean Mathematics, Vol. I. C. E. Layne. (C). 1987. text ed. 40.00 (0-85950-762-9, Pub. by S Thornes Pubs UK) St Mut.

ST(P) Caribbean Mathematics, Vol. II. C. E. Layne. (C). 1987. text ed. 50.00 (0-85950-763-7, Pub. by S Thornes Pubs UK) St Mut.

ST(P) Caribbean Mathematics, Vol. III. C. E. Layne. (C). 1988. text ed. 55.00 (0-85950-764-5, Pub. by S Thornes Pubs UK) St Mut.

ST(P) Mathematics One-Half Supplementary Booklet. L. Bostock et al. (C). 1989. 50.00 (0-685-47485-2, Pub. by S Thornes Pubs UK) St Mut.

ST(P) Mathematics One Pupil's Book. Ed. by L. Bostock et al. (C). 1984. 55.00 (0-85950-149-3, Pub. by S Thornes Pubs UK) St Mut.

ST(P) Mathematics One Teacher's & Answer Book. Stanley Thornes. (C). 1984. 50.00 (0-85950-173-6, Pub. by S Thornes Pubs UK) St Mut.

ST(P) Mathematics Resource Book. Stanley Thornes. (C). 1989. 220.00 (0-85950-702-5, Pub. by S Thornes Pubs UK) St Mut.

ST(P) Mathematics Two Pupil's Book. L. Bostock & S. Chandler. Ed. by A. Shepherd & E. Smith. (C). 1984. 60.00 (0-85950-174-4, Pub. by S Thornes Pubs UK) St Mut.

ST(P) Mathematics Two Teacher's & Answer Book. Stanley Thornes. (C). 1985. 65.00 (0-85950-175-2, Pub. by S Thornes Pubs UK) St Mut.

ST(P) Mathematics Workbooks: Pupil Pack (1 of Each Title) L. Bostock & S. Chandler. Ed. by A. Shepherd & E. Smith. (C). 1988. 35.00 (0-7487-0407-8, Pub. by S Thornes Pubs UK) St Mut.

ST(P) Mathematics Workbooks - Measuring Instruments. Stanley Thornes. (C). 1988. text ed. 60.00 (0-85950-905-2, Pub. by S Thornes Pubs UK) St Mut.

ST(P) Mathematics Workbooks - Straight Line Graphs. Stanley Thornes. (C). 1988. text ed. 60.00 (0-85950-907-9, Pub. by S Thornes Pubs UK) St Mut.

ST(P) Mathematics Workbooks - Transformations & Symmetry. Stanley Thornes. (C). 1988. text ed. 55.00 (0-85950-906-0, Pub. by S Thornes Pubs UK) St Mut.

ST(P) Mathematics 1B Pupil's Book. Ed. by Stanley Thornes. (C). 1990. 50.00 (0-7487-0143-5, Pub. by Stanley Thornes UK) Trans-Atl Phila.

ST(P) Mathematics 1B Teacher's Book & Answers. L. Bostock & S. Chandler. Ed. by A. Shepherd & E. Smith. (C). 1990. 70.00 (0-7487-0170-2, Pub. by Stanley Thornes UK) Trans-Atl Phila.

ST(P) Mathematics 2B Pupil's Book. Stanley Thornes. (C). 1990. 60.00 (0-7487-0144-3, Pub. by Stanley Thornes UK) Trans-Atl Phila.

ST(P) Mathematics 2B Teacher's Book & Answers. Stanley Thornes. (C). 1990. 70.00 (0-7487-0171-0, Pub. by Stanley Thornes UK) Trans-Atl Phila.

ST(P) Mathematics 3A Pupil's Book. Stanley Thornes. (C). 1985. 70.00 (0-85950-207-4, Pub. by S Thornes Pubs UK) St Mut.

ST(P) Mathematics 3A Teacher's & Answer Book. Ed. by Stanley Thornes. (C). 1985. 50.00 (0-85950-208-2, Pub. by S Thornes Pubs UK) St Mut.

ST(P) Mathematics 3B Pupil's Book. Stanley Thornes. (C). 1985. 65.00 (0-85950-209-0, Pub. by S Thornes Pubs UK) St Mut.

ST(P) Mathematics 3B Teacher's & Answer Book. Stanley Thornes. (C). 1986. 50.00 (0-85950-210-4, Pub. by S Thornes Pubs UK) St Mut.

ST(P) Mathematics 4A Pupil's Book. Stanley Thornes. (C). 1986. 60.00 (0-85950-250-3, Pub. by S Thornes Pubs UK) St Mut.

ST(P) Mathematics 4A Teacher's & Answer Book. Stanley Thornes. (C). 1987. 60.00 (0-85950-251-1, Pub. by S Thornes Pubs UK) St Mut.

ST(P) Mathematics 4B Pupil's Book. Stanley Thornes. (C). 1986. 60.00 (0-85950-252-X, Pub. by S Thornes Pubs UK) St Mut.

ST(P) Mathematics 4B Teacher's & Answer Book. Ed. by Stanley Thornes. (C). 1987. 50.00 (0-85950-253-8, Pub. by S Thornes Pubs UK) St Mut.

ST(P) Mathematics 5A Pupil's Book (with Answers) Ed. by Stanley Thornes. (C). 1987. 70.00 (0-85950-254-6, Pub. by S Thornes Pubs UK) St Mut.

ST(P) Mathematics 5B Pupil's Book (with Answers) L. Bostock et al. (C). 1987. 65.00 (0-85950-256-2, Pub. by S Thornes Pubs UK) St Mut.

ST(P) Mathematics 5C: Teachers Notes & Answers. Stanley Thornes. (C). 1988. 75.00 (0-85950-930-3, Pub. by S Thornes Pubs UK) St Mut.

Strabismus. Brian Schorn. (Poetry Ser.). 64p. (Orig.). 1995. pap. 8.00 (0-930901-98-3) Burning Deck.

Strabismus. limited ed. Brian Schorn. (Poetry Ser.). 64p. (Orig.). 1995. pap. 15.00 (0-930901-99-1) Burning Deck.

Strabismus: A Decision Making Approach. Helveston Von Noorden. (Illus.). 224p. (C). (gr. 13). 1994. text ed. 79.95 (0-8151-4048-7, 23669) Mosby Yr Bk.

Strabismus: A Neurodevelopmental Approach. J. T. Flynn. (Nature's Experiment Ser.). (Illus.). 144p. 1990. 96.00 (0-387-97409-1) Spr-Verlag.

***Strabismus & Ambliopy.** Borislav Vukov. 330p. 1997. pap. write for info. (0-9657106-9-6) Zona Incerta.

Strabismus & Amblyopia: Experimental Basis for Advances in Clinical Management. Ed. by G. Lennerstrand et al. (Wenner-Gren International Symposia Ser.: Vol. 49). (Illus.). 452p. 1988. 110.00 (0-306-42943-8, Plenum Pr) Plenum.

Strabismus & Amblyopia: Visual Training. rev. ed. Donald J. Getz. (Introduction to Behavioral Optometry Ser.). (Illus.). 105p. 1990. reprint ed. pap. text ed. 140.00 (0-943599-08-3) OEPF.

Strabismus & the Sensorimotor Reflex. Y. Mitsui. 228p. 1986. 100.00 (4-900392-74-X) Elsevier.

Strabismus & Tumors of the Uvea. Ed. by H. Saraux. (Journal: Ophthalmologica: Vol. 182, No. 2). (Illus.). 84p. 1981. pap. 35.25 (3-8055-3418-3) S Karger.

Strabismus Management. William V. Good et al. (Illus.). 379p. 1995. 95.00 (0-7506-9075-5) Buttrwrth-Heinemann.

Strabismus Symposium, Amsterdam, September Third-Fourth, 1981. A. T. Van Balen & W. A. Houtman. 1982. lib. bdg. 165.00 (90-6193-728-0) Kluwer Ac.

Strachey Boy. Richard Strachey. Ed. & Frwd. by Simonette Strachey. 154p. 8000. 21.00 (0-7206-0571-7, Pub. by P Owen Ltd UK) Dufour.

Strad Model 'Cello, Plans. rev. ed. Harry S. Wake. 1994. pap. 24.00 (0-9607048-4-1) H S Wake.

Strada. Ed. by Peter Bondanella et al. (Films in Print Ser.). (Illus.). 200p. 1987. text ed. 35.00 (0-8135-1236-0); pap. text ed. 17.00 (0-8135-1237-9) Rutgers U Pr.

Strada. deluxe ed. Louise O. Neaderland. (Illus.). 1986. boxed 12.00 (0-942561-06-6) Bone Hollow.

Stradivari Memorial. William D. Orcutt. LC 76-58561. (Music Reprint Ser.). 1977. reprint ed. lib. bdg. 21.50 (0-306-70865-5) Da Capo.

Stradivari's Singing Violin. Catherine Deverell. (J). (gr. k-3). 1992. lib. bdg. 13.13 (0-87614-732-5, Carolrhoda) Lerner Group.

Stradivari's Singing Violin. Catherine Deverell. (J). (gr. k-3). 1992. pap. 5.95 (0-87614-583-7, Carolrhoda) Lerner Group.

Stradivarius. Donald P. Ladew. 304p. 1995. 21.95 (0-7867-0136-6) Carroll & Graf.

Stradtrecht von Gortyn & Seine Beziehungen zum Gemeingriechischen Rechte. Josef Kohler. (GER.). 1979. 15.95 (0-405-11558-X) Ayer.

Straf in Suid-Afrika. E. Du Toit. 600p. 1981. write for info. (0-7021-1215-1, Pub. by Juta SA) Gaunt.

Strafford in Ireland, 1633-1641: A Study in Absolutism. Hugh F. Kearney. 304p. (C). 1989. 69.95 (0-521-37189-9); pap. text ed. 22.95 (0-521-37822-2) Cambridge U Pr.

Strafford, New Hampshire, U. S. Census & Town Tax Records, People, Land, Livestock, Crops, 1790-1880. Delmar W. Goodwin. 473p. (Orig.). 1993. pap. text ed. 55.00 (1-55613-833-4) Heritage Bk.

Strafprosesreg. J. Snyman & D. W. Morkel. 625p. 1988. pap. write for info. (0-7021-1963-6, Pub. by Juta SA) Gaunt.

Strafproseswet Fifty-One van 1977: Criminal Procedure Act 51 of 1977. ring bd. write for info. (0-7021-1633-5, Pub. by Juta SA) Gaunt.

Strafproseswet 51 van 1977. 5th ed. Owen J. Barrow. 315p. 1993. pap. write for info. (0-7021-2958-5, Pub. by Juta SA) Gaunt.

Strafrecht Allgemeiner Teil: Die Grundiagen und die Zurechnungslehre lehrbuch. Gunther Jakobs. 787p. 1983. 144.65 (3-11-009700-1) De Gruyter.

Strafreg en Jeugregspleging. D. J. McQuoid-Mason et al. Bk. 2. 1993. student ed. write for info. (0-318-72249-6, Pub. by Juta SA); teacher ed. write for info. (0-318-72250-X, Pub. by Juta SA) Gaunt.

Strafreg-Vonnisbundel - Criminal Law Case Book. rev. ed. C. R. Snyman. 243p. 1992. reprint ed. pap. write for info. (0-7021-2519-9, Pub. by Juta SA) Gaunt.

Strafvollzug Im Europeaischen Vergleich see Prison Systems & Correctional Laws: Europe, the United States & Japan, a Comparative Analysis

Stragegic Service Management - Beyond the Moment of Truth. Ed. by Denis Boyle. (Best of Long Range Planning Ser.). 144p. 1990. text ed. 86.50 (0-08-037752-1, Pergamon Pr); pap. text ed. 41.50 (0-08-037751-3, Pergamon Pr) Elsevier.

Straight. Dick Francis. 320p. 1991. mass mkt. 5.99 (0-449-21720-5) Fawcett.

Straight-A Teacher. Beverly Lewis. (Holly's Heart Ser.: Vol. 8). 160p. (J). 1994. pap. 6.99 (0-310-46111-1) Zondervan.

***Straight Acting: Popular Gay Drama from Wilde to Rattigan.** Sean O'Connor. LC 97-13548. 1997. write for info. (0-304-32866-9, Pub. by Cassell UK); pap. write for info. (0-304-32864-2, Pub. by Cassell UK) Sterling.

Straight Ahead: Essays on the Struggle of Blacks in America 1934-1994. William H. McClendon. Ed. & Pref. by Robert Chrisman. (Illus.). 227p. (Orig.). 1995. pap. 19.95 (0-933296-16-9) Black Scholar Pr.

Straight Ahead: The Story of Stan Kenton. Carol Easton. LC 81-7863. (Quality Paperbacks Ser.). (Illus.). 252p. 1981. reprint ed. pap. 7.95 (0-306-80152-3) Da Capo.

Straight Ahead: Twenty-Eight Devotionals for Teen Disciples. Susie Shellenberger. 32p. (YA). 1987. pap. 3.25 (0-8341-1199-3) Beacon Hill.

Straight Ahead Jazz Fakebook. Ed. by Charley Gerard. 192p. 1994. pap. 25.00 (0-9628467-4-0) Gerard Sarzin Pub.

Straight & Devious Pathways from Childhood to Adulthood. Ed. by Lee N. Robins & Michael Rutter. (Illus.). 416p. (C). 1990. text ed. 80.00 (0-521-36408-6) Cambridge U Pr.

Straight & Devious Pathways from Childhood to Adulthood. Ed. by Lee N. Robins & Michael Rutter. (Illus.). 389p. (C). 1992. pap. text ed. 25.95 (0-521-42739-8) Cambridge U Pr.

***Straight & Level: Growing up in the '40s.** Jack Botts. (Illus.). 1996. pap. 14.95 (0-9654527-0-0) Twin Pines Pub.

***Straight & Level: Practical Airline Economics.** Stephen Holloway. 300p. 1997. 59.95 (0-291-39848-0, Pub. by Avebury Technical UK) Ashgate Pub Co.

Straight & Level: The Autobiography of Air Chief Marshal Sir Kenneth "Bing" Cross, KCB, CBE, DSO, DFC, 1911-1945. Marshal Sir Kenneth Bing Cross & Vincent Orange. 288p. 1993. 29.95 (0-948817-72-0, Pub. by Grub St Pubns UK) Seven Hills Bk.

Straight & Narrow. Anton P. Sohn. 233p. 1992. write for info. (0-9649759-4-7) Greasewood.

Straight & Narrow? Compassion & Clarity in the Homosexuality Debate. Thomas E. Schmidt. 240p. (Orig.). 1995. pap. 10.99 (0-8308-1858-8, 1858) InterVarsity.

Straight Answers on the New Age. Bob Larson. 1989. pap. 12.99 (0-8407-3032-2) Nelson.

Straight Answers to People Problems. Fred E. Jandt. 180p. 1993. text ed. 19.95 (1-55623-849-5) Irwin Prof Pubng.

Straight Answers to People Problems: International Edition. Fred E. Jandt. (Briefcase Bks.). 180p. 1993. per. 13.95 (0-7863-0201-1) Irwin Prof Pubng.

Straight Answers to Tough Questions about Sex. Rich Wilkerson. 224p. 1987. mass mkt. 3.99 (0-88368-191-9) Whitaker Hse.

Straight Arrow: The Art Schlichter Story. Ritter Collett. (Illus.). 160p. 1981. 10.95 (0-913428-33-7) Landfall Pr.

Straight A's: How to Help Your Child Improve School Grades. Sal Di Francesca. Ed. by Ric Solano. LC 84-82154. (Illus.). 150p. 1985. 24.95 (0-931657-00-8) Learning Proc Ctr.

Straight A's: If I Can Do It, So Can You. John C. Stowers, Jr. LC 95-784. 1995. pap. write for info. (0-07-061824-0) McGraw.

Straight A's: If I Can Do It, So Can You. John C. Stowers, Jr. LC 95-784. 1996. pap. text ed. write for info. (0-07-061823-2) McGraw.

***Straight A's Never Made Anybody Rich.** Wess Roberts. mass mkt. write for info. (0-06-109152-9, Harp PBks) HarpC.

Straight Back Home: To the Young Person Leaving Treatment. Jane Nakken. 16p. (Orig.). 1984. pap. 1.75 (0-89486-250-2, 1401B) Hazelden.

Straight Baselines in International Maritime Boundary Delimitation. W. Michael Reisman & Gayl L. Westerman. 210p. 1992. text ed. 59.95 (0-312-06034-3) St Martin.

Straight Cut. Madison Smartt Bell. 240p. 1987. pap. 3.95 (0-14-010471-2, Penguin Bks) Viking Penguin.

Straight Cut. Madison Smartt Bell. (Contemporary American Fiction Ser.). 240p. 1991. pap. 11.95 (0-14-015386-1, Penguin Bks) Viking Penguin.

Straight Cut Ditch. Richard Andersen. Ed. by Debbie Hammond. LC 79-7034. 1979. 22.95 (0-87949-139-6) Ashley Bks.

Straight Dope. Cecil Adams. (Orig.). 1986. mass mkt. 5.95 (0-345-33315-2) Ballantine.

Straight Dope. Cecil Adams. Ed. by Ed Zotti. LC 84-17060. (Illus.). 324p. (Orig.). 1991. pap. 9.95 (0-914091-54-9) Chicago Review.

Straight Dope on Hormones. Delia Van Maris. Ed. by JoAnn Roberts. 24p. (Orig.). (C). pap. text ed. 4.00 (1-880715-11-2) Creat Des Srvs.

Straight Egyptian Index, Vol. 2. Hansi Heck-Melnyk. write for info. (0-942407-14-8) Father & Son.

Straight Egyptian Index, Vol. 3. Hansi Heck-Melnyk. write for info. (0-942407-15-6) Father & Son.

Straight Egyptian Index, Vol. 4. Hansi Heck-Melnyk. 1338p. write for info. (0-942407-20-2) Father & Son.

Straight Egyptian Index, Vol. 5. Hansi Heck-Melnyk. 912p. write for info. (0-942407-21-0) Father & Son.

Straight for the Heart. Marsha Canham. 448p. 1995. mass mkt. 5.50 (0-440-21786-5) Dell.

Straight from a Dad's Heart. Robert Hamrin. LC 93-4504. 1993. pap. 9.99 (0-8407-9670-6) Nelson.

Straight from the Bear's Mouth: The Story of Photosynthesis. Bill Ross. (Illus.). 32p. (J). (gr. 5-9). 1995. 16.00 (0-689-31726-3, Atheneum Bks Young) S&S Childrens.

Straight from the Heart. Mike Bowen. (C). 1990. 30.00 (0-7316-7410-3, Pub. by Pascoe Pub AT) St Mut.

Straight from the Heart. Rod Jackson-Paris & Bob Jackson-Paris. (Illus.). 336p. 1994. 21.95 (0-446-51748-8) Warner Bks.

Straight from the Heart. Rod Jackson-Paris & Bob Jackson-Paris. 336p. 1995. pap. 11.99 (0-446-67066-9) Warner Bks.

S

An Asterisk (*) at the beginning of an entry indicates that the title is appearing in BIP for the first time.

***Straight from the Heart.** Doreen Reynolds. LC 96-61378. 80p. 1997. pap. 9.95 (1-887798-05-6) WriteMore Pubns.
Straight from the Heart. Pamela Wallace. 304p. 1996. mass mkt. 5.50 (0-06-108289-9) HarpC.
Straight from the Heart. Ina L. Yalof. 192p. 1996. 20.00 (1-57566-094-6, Knsington) Kensgtn Pub Corp.
***Straight from the Heart.** Ina L. Yalof. 224p. 1997. pap. 12.50 (1-57566-217-5, Knsington) Kensgtn Pub Corp.
Straight from the Heart: A Torah Perspective on Mothering Through Nursing. Tehilla Abramov. 156p. 1990. 15.95 (0-944070-18-3) Targum Pr.
Straight from the Heart: An Essential Guide for Developing, Deepening, & Renewing Your Relationships. Layne Cutright & Paul Cutright. 144p. (Orig.). 1996. pap. 14.95 (0-9651371-0-4) Hrt To Hrt.
Straight from the Heart: Authors, Celebrities & Others Share Their Philosophies on Making a Difference in the World. Danielle Marie. LC 92-70221. (Illus.). 160p. 1992. pap. 10.95 (1-880741-09-1) Dickens Pr.
Straight from the Heart: Poems of Love, Logic & Lunacy. Vernon Harris. (We Write Bks.: Vol. 1). (Illus.). 75p. 1994. pap. 8.95 (1-884987-71-0) WeWrite.
Straight from the Heart for Christmas. Richard Exley. Date not set. 10.99 (1-56292-113-4) Honor Bks OK.
Straight from the Heart for Couples. Richard Exley. (Straight from the Heart Ser.). 80p. Date not set. 9.99 (1-56292-094-4) Honor Bks OK.
Straight from the Heart for Dad. Richard Exley. (Straight from the Heart Ser.). 80p. Date not set. 9.99 (1-56292-093-6) Honor Bks OK.
Straight from the Heart for Graduates. Richard Exley. (Straight from the Heart Ser.). 80p. Date not set. 9.99 (1-56292-095-2) Honor Bks OK.
Straight from the Heart for Mom. Richard Exley. (Straight from the Heart Ser.). 80p. Date not set. 9.99 (1-56292-092-8) Honor Bks OK.
Straight from the Horse's Mouth. Jayne Bremyer. (Illus.). 124p. (Orig.). 1991. pap. 13.95 (0-944996-06-X) Carlsons.
Straight from the Horse's Mouth. Ed. by Richard A. Spears. 544p. 1996. pap. 12.95 (0-8442-0901-5) NTC Pub Grp.
Straight from the Horse's Mouth: Firsthand Accounts of the Erie Canal. Erie Canal Museum Staff. 64p. 1988. pap. 6.95 (1-883582-03-2) Erie Canal Mus.
Straight Girls Have More Fun! Sallie Cochren. 310p. (Orig.). 1995. pap. 12.99 (1-57502-081-5) Morris Pubng.
Straight Hearts' Delight: Love Poems & Selected Letters. Allen Ginsberg & Peter Orlovsky. Ed. by Winston Leyland. (Illus.). 240p. 1980. pap. 8.95 (0-917342-65-8, Gay Sunshine); lib. bdg. 25.00 (0-917342-64-X, Gay Sunshine) Gay Sunshine.
Straight Impressions. Lloyd J. Reynolds. LC 78-60187. (Illus.). 1979. 12.50 (0-931474-06-X) TBW Bks.
Straight Impressions. Lloyd J. Reynolds. LC 78-60187. (Illus.). 1984. pap. 5.95 (0-931474-07-8) TBW Bks.
Straight Jacket. Greg Schwartz. LC 92-61972. 144p. 1994. pap. 10.00 (1-56002-221-3, Univ Edtns) Aegina Pr.
Straight Jobs, Gay Lives. Annette Friskopp. 1996. pap. 16.00 (0-684-82413-2) S&S Trade.
Straight Jobs, Gay Lives: Gay & Lesbian MBA's, the Harvard Business School, & the American Workplace. Annette Friskopp & Sharon Silverstein. 528p. 1995. 32.50 (0-684-80424-7) S&S Trade.
Straight Left: An Autobiography. Paddy Devlin. 312p. 9400. pap. 17.95 (0-85640-514-0, Pub. by Blackstaff Pr IE) Dufour.
Straight Life: The Story of Art Pepper. 2nd rev. ed. Art Pepper & Laurie Pepper. (Illus.). 610p. 1994. reprint ed. pap. 17.95 (0-306-80558-8) Da Capo.
Straight Line & the Conic Section. P. H. Francis. (Mathematics Ser.: Vol. 2). (Illus.). 1975. pap. 13.50 (0-902675-76-1) Oleander Pr.
Straight Line Wonder. Mem Fox. LC 96-3708. (Illus.). 1996. write for info. (1-57255-206-9) Mondo Pubng.
Straight Line Wonder. Mem Fox. LC 96-3708. (Illus.). (J). 1996. pap. write for info. (1-57255-205-0) Mondo Pubng.
***Straight Line Wonder.** Mem Fox. (Illus.). (J). 1997. write for info. (0-614-29269-7) Mondo Pubng.
Straight Lines. William Neill. 98p. (Orig.). 9200. pap. 12.95 (0-85640-475-6, Pub. by Blackstaff Pr IE) Dufour.
Straight Look at the Third Reich. Austin J. App. 1984. lib. bdg. 79.95 (0-87700-521-4) Revisionist Pr.
Straight, Male, Modern: A Cultural Critique of Psychoanalysis. John Brenkman. LC 93-14035. 320p. (C). 1993. pap. 17.95 (0-415-90218-5, A3974, Routledge NY) Routledge.
Straight Man. Sallie Bingham. LC 96-16398. 244p. 1996. 22.95 (0-944072-65-8) Zoland Bks.
***Straight Man.** Richard Russo. LC 96-48578. 1997. 25.00 (0-679-43246-9) Random.
Straight Mind: And Other Essays. Monique Wittig. LC 91-18409. 128p. 1992. pap. 14.00 (0-8070-7917-0) Beacon Pr.
Straight News: Gays, Lesbians, & the News Media. Edward Alwood. LC 96-526. (Between Men - Between Women Ser.). (Illus.). 386p. 1996. 29.95 (0-231-08436-6) Col U Pr.
Straight No Chaser. Al Young. (Loveletter Editions Ser.). 32p. (Orig.). (C). 1994. pap. text ed. 5.95 (0-88739-106-0) Creat Arts Bk.
***Straight, No Chaser: How I Became a Grown-Up Black Woman.** Jill Nelson. LC 97-14596. 224p. 1997. 23.95 (0-399-14262-2) Putnam Pub Group.
Straight on Till Morning: The Biography of Beryl Markham. Mary S. Lovell. (Illus.). 432p. 1988. pap. 10.95 (0-312-01895-9) St Martin.
Straight-out Man: F. W. Albrecht & Central Australian Aborigines. Barbara Henson. 348p. 1994. pap. 24.95 (0-522-84632-7, Pub. by Melbourne Univ Pr AT) Paul & Co Pubs.
Straight Out of View. Joyce Sutphen. LC 94-24509. (Barnard New Women Poets Ser.). 128p. 1995. pap. 12.95 (0-8070-6825-X) Beacon Pr.
Straight Outta Compton. Ricardo C. Cruz. 121p. 1992. 18.95 (0-932511-60-0); pap. 8.95 (0-932511-61-9) Fiction Coll.
Straight Parents/Gay Children: Keeping Families Together. Robert Bernstein. 1994. pap. 12.95 (1-56025-086-0) Thunders Mouth.
Straight Path: A Story of Healing & Transformation in Fiji. Richard Katz. (Illus.). 336p. 1993. 27.95 (0-201-60867-7) Addison-Wesley.
Straight Path: A Story of Healing & Transformation in Fiji. Richard Katz. 1994. pap. 15.00 (0-201-40831-7) Addison-Wesley.
Straight Path: Studies in Medieval Philosophy & Culture. Ed. by Ruth Link-Salinger et al. LC 87-18403. (Essays in Honor of Arthur Hyman Ser.). 309p. 1988. 35.00 (0-8132-0648-0) Cath U Pr.
Straight Razor. Harold Jaffe. 132p. (Orig.). 1995. pap. 7.00 (1-57366-001-9) Fiction Coll.
***Straight Science? Homosexuality Evolution & Adaptation.** Jim McKnight. 240p. (C). 1997. pap. 18.95 (0-415-15773-0, Routledge NY); text ed. 69.95 (0-415-15772-2, Routledge NY) Routledge.
Straight Scoop: An Expert Guide to Great Community Journalism. Hartford Courant Staff. Ed. by Bruce DeSilva & John Mura. 250p. 1996. pap. text ed. 13.95 (0-9646638-1-3) Hartford Courant.
Straight Sex: Rethinking the Politics of Pleasure. Lynne Segal. LC 94-20214. 1994. 35.00 (0-520-20000-4) U CA Pr.
Straight Sex: Rethinking the Politics of Pleasure. Lynne Segal. LC 94-20214. 1994. pap. 15.00 (0-520-20001-2) U CA Pr.
Straight Shooter (Playscript) Nellie McCaslin. LC 93-5252. 16p. (J). 1993. pap. 5.00 (0-88734-429-1) Players Pr.
Straight Speaking from a Pacifist to a Militarist. Duke of Bedford. 1982. lib. bdg. 59.95 (0-87700-337-8) Revisionist Pr.
Straight Speech. Jane Folk. (Illus.). 80p. 1992. 14.95 (0-937857-32-7, 1525) Speech Bin.
Straight Stitch Machine Applique: Patterns & Instructions for This Easy Technique. Letty Martin. LC 94-38946. (Illus.). 158p. 1995. pap. 16.95 (0-89145-839-5, Am Quilters Soc) Collector Bks.
***Straight Studies Modified: Lesbian Interventions in the Academy.** Gabriele Griffin & Sonya Andermahr. LC 97-1949. (Lesbian & Gay Studies). 256p. 1997. 89.50 (0-304-33633-5); pap. 29.95 (0-304-33630-0) Cassell.
Straight Talk. 64p. 1992. pap. 12.95 (0-7935-1601-3, 00312475) H Leonard.
Straight Talk. David Bennefield. 1995. pap. text ed. 5.95 (0-9645743-0-6) Franklin Pub.
Straight Talk: A Fresh Look at One Timothy. Remkes Kooistra. LC 96-18162. (Fresh Look Ser.). 1996. 11.30 (1-56212-179-0) CRC Pubns.
***Straight Talk: A Fresh Look at 1 Timothy.** Robert DeMoor. (Fresh Look Ser.). 80p. (Orig.). 1996. pap. 11.10 (1-56212-180-4) CRC Pubns.
Straight Talk: A Guide to Saying More with Less. Robert Maidment. LC 82-12211. 112p. (Orig.). 1983. pap. 5.95 (0-88289-340-8) Pelican.
Straight Talk: A New Way to Get Close to Others by Saying What You Really Mean. Elam Nunnally et al. 1982. pap. 4.95 (0-451-15907-1, Sig) NAL-Dutton.
Straight Talk: Answers to Questions Young People Ask about Alcohol. Ralph E. Jones. Ed. by Lee M. Joiner. 64p. (Orig.). (YA). (gr. 10 up). 1988. pap. 4.95 (0-943519-08-X, B1908) Sulzburger & Graham Pub.
Straight Talk: Answers to Questions Young People Ask about Alcohol, 70005. Ralph E. Jones. (Orig.). (J). 1989. pap. 4.95 (0-8306-9005-0) McGraw-Hill Prof.
Straight Talk: Sexuality Education for Parents & Kids. Marilyn Ratner & Susan Chamlin. 48p. (gr. 4-7). 1987. pap. 7.95 (0-14-009413-X, Penguin Bks) Viking Penguin.
Straight Talk: What Men Need to Know, What Women Should Understand. rev. ed. James Dobson. 222p. 1995. pap. 12.99 (0-8499-3858-9) Word Pub.
Straight Talk about Anger. Christine Dentemaro & Rachel Kranz. LC 94-34591. 156p. (J). 1995. 16.95 (0-8160-3079-0) Facts on File.
***Straight Talk about Anger.** Christine Dentemaro & Rachel Kranz. (Straight Talk Ser.). 128p. (YA). 1996. pap. 9.95 (0-8160-3551-2) Facts on File.
Straight Talk about Anxiety & Depression. Michael Maloney & Rachel Kranz. (Straight Talk Ser.). 128p. (YA). (gr. 5-12). 1991. lib. bdg. 16.95 (0-8160-2434-0) Facts on File.
Straight Talk about Bonds & Bond Funds. Hildy Richelson & Stan Richelson. (Straight Talk Ser.). (Illus.). 265p. 1996. pap. text ed. 14.95 (0-07-052303-7) McGraw.
Straight Talk about Breast Cancer: From Diagnosis to Recovery. Suzanne Braddock et al. Ed. by Melanie M. Clark. LC 94-72529. 144p. (Orig.). 1994. pap. 9.95 (1-886039-21-6) Addicus Bks.
Straight Talk about Child Abuse. Susan Mufson & Rachel Kranz. (Straight Talk Ser.). 112p. (YA). 1991. 16.95 (0-8160-2376-X) Facts on File.
Straight Talk about Cults. Kay M. Porterfield. LC 94-37296. 144p. (J). 1995. 16.95 (0-8160-3115-0) Facts on File.
***Straight Talk about Cults.** Kay M. Porterfield. 1997. pap. text ed. 9.95 (0-8160-3750-7) Facts on File.
Straight Talk about Date Rape. Susan Mufson & Rachel Kranz. Ed. by Elizabeth A. Ryan. (Straight Talk Ser.). 128p. (YA). (gr. 9-12). 1993. 16.95 (0-8160-2863-X) Facts on File.
***Straight Talk about Date Rape.** Susan Mufson. 1997. pap. text ed. 9.95 (0-8160-3752-3) Facts on File.
Straight Talk about Death & Dying. Robert DiGiulio & Rachel Kranz. LC 95-2488. (Straight Talk Ser.). 144p. (YA). (gr. 5 up). 1995. 16.95 (0-8160-3078-2) Facts on File.
***Straight Talk about Death & Dying.** Robert DiGiulio & Rachel Kranz. (Straight Talk Ser.). 128p. (YA). 1996. pap. 9.95 (0-8160-3553-9) Facts on File.
Straight Talk about Death for Teenagers: How to Cope with Losing Someone You Love. Earl A. Grollman. LC 92-34540. 144p. (YA). 1993. pap. 9.95 (0-8070-2501-1) Beacon Pr.
Straight Talk about Drugs & Alcohol. rev. ed. Elizabeth A. Ryan. 160p. (J). 1995. 16.95 (0-8160-3249-1) Facts on File.
***Straight Talk about Drugs & Alcohol.** rev. ed. Elizabeth A. Ryan. (Straight Talk Ser.). 144p. (YA). 1996. pap. 9.95 (0-8160-3549-0) Facts on File.
Straight Talk about Eating Disorders. Michael Maloney & Rachel Kranz. (Straight Talk Ser.). 128p. (YA). (gr. 7-12). 1991. 16.95 (0-8160-2414-6) Facts on File.
Straight Talk about Gays in the Workplace: Creating an Inclusive, Productive Environment for Everyone in Your Organization. Liz Winfeld & Susan Spielman. LC 95-23800. 208p. 1995. 21.95 (0-8144-0305-0) AMACOM.
Straight Talk about Gospel Principles. Allan K. Burgess & Max H. Molgard. 1994. 10.95 (0-88494-953-2) Bookcraft Inc.
Straight Talk about Money. Marion B. Rendon & Rachel Kranz. Ed. by Elizabeth A. Ryan. (Straight Talk Ser.). 128p. (YA). (gr. 7-12). 1992. lib. bdg. 16.95 (0-8160-2612-2) Facts on File.
Straight Talk About Mutual Funds. rev. ed. Dian Vujovich. (Straight Talk Ser.). 224p. 1996. pap. text ed. 12.95 (0-07-067025-0) McGraw.
Straight Talk about Parents. Elizabeth A. Ryan. (Straight Talk Ser.). 144p. (YA). 1989. 16.95 (0-8160-1526-0) Facts on File.
Straight Talk about Post-Trauma Stress. (Straight Talk Ser.). 144p. (YA). (gr. 5 up). 1996. 16.95 (0-8160-3258-0) Facts on File.
***Straight Talk about Post-Traumatic Stress Disorder.** Kay M. Porterfield. (Straight Talk Ser.). 144p. (YA). 1996. pap. 9.95 (0-8160-3552-0) Facts on File.
Straight Talk about Prejudice. Elizabeth A. Ryan. (Straight Talk Ser.). 128p. (YA). (gr. 5-12). 1992. lib. bdg. 16.95 (0-8160-2488-X) Facts on File.
Straight Talk about School Administrators. 2nd rev. ed. Association of School Administrators Staff. 16p. (Orig.). 1996. 5.00 (0-943397-36-7) Assn Calif Sch Admin.
Straight Talk about Sex. Barry Chant. 176p. 1978. mass mkt. 2.99 (0-88368-078-5) Whitaker Hse.
Straight Talk about Sex. Henry W. Spaulding, II. (Christian Living Ser.). 44p. 1990. pap. 3.25 (0-8341-1367-8) Beacon Hill.
Straight Talk about Sexually Transmitted Diseases. John Thacker & Rachel Kranz. Ed. by Elizabeth A. Ryan. (Straight Talk Ser.). 144p. (YA). (gr. 9-12). 16.95 (0-8160-2864-8) Facts on File.
Straight Talk About Stock Investing. John Slatter. LC 94-32872. 1995. pap. text ed. 14.95 (0-07-058142-8) McGraw.
Straight Talk About Stock Investing. John Slatter. LC 94-32872. 1996. text ed. 19.95 (0-07-058141-X) McGraw.
Straight Talk about Student Life. Christine Dentemaro & Rachel Kranz. LC 92-31488. 144p. (YA). 1993. 16.95 (0-8160-2735-8) Facts on File.
Straight Talk about Surgical Penis Enlargement. Gary Griffin. (Illus.). 96p. (Orig.). 1993. pap. 9.95 (1-879967-12-X) Added Dimensns.
Straight Talk about Teenage Suicide. Bernard Frankel & Rachel Kranz. Ed. by Elizabeth A. Ryan. LC 93-38381. (Straight Talk Ser.). 144p. (YA). (gr. 7-12). 1994. 16.95 (0-8160-2987-3) Facts on File.
***Straight Talk about Teenage Suicide.** Bernard Frankel. 1997. pap. text ed. 9.95 (0-8160-3751-5) Facts on File.
***Straight Talk about Therapy.** Jacob Stone & Margaretta Stone. vi, 46p. (Orig.). 1997. pap. 7.95 (1-890361-00-3) Paradigm Press.
Straight Talk about Violence. (Straight Talk Ser.). (YA). (gr. 5 up). 1995. 16.95 (0-8160-3179-7) Facts on File.
Straight Talk for Girls. Bill Sanders. LC 95-34251. (Illus.). 160p. (Orig.). (YA). (gr. 8-11). 1995. pap. 7.99 (0-8007-5577-4) Revell.
Straight Talk for Growing Your Small Business: Savvy Strategies to Go with Your Guts & Borrowed Money. Tom S. Gillis. 416p. 1996. 29.95 (1-885167-08-3) Bard Press.
Straight Talk for Growing Your Small Business: Savvy Strategies to Go with Your Guts & Borrowed Money. Tom S. Gillis. 416p. 1996. pap. 19.95 (1-885167-09-1) Bard Press.
Straight Talk for Guys. Bill Sanders. LC 95-31724. (Illus.). 144p. (Orig.). (YA). (gr. 8-11). 1995. pap. 7.99 (0-8007-5578-2) Revell.
Straight Talk for Parents: What Teenagers Wish They Could Tell You. Barbara B. Jones & Brad Wilcox. LC 93-39919. xvi, 317p. 1994. pap. 12.95 (0-87579-819-5) Deseret Bk.
Straight Talk for Teens: What the Bible Says to Teens about Today's Moral Issues. Randy Simmons. 1987. pap. 5.99 (0-89225-299-5) Gospel Advocate.
Straight Talk from Prison: A Convict Reflects on Youth, Crime, & Society. Lou Torok. LC 74-1074. (Illus.). 142p. 1974. 30.95 (0-87705-136-4) Human Sci Pr.
Straight Talk Is More Than Words: Persuasive Communications: The Key to Achieving Your Goals. Patricia A. Ball. Ed. by Sue Politella. (Illus.). (Orig.). 1996. pap. 20.00 (1-887373-00-4) T Knox Pub.
Straight Talk on Designing Experiments. Robert G. Launsby & Daniel L. Weese. 150p. 1993. text ed. 39.95 (0-9636093-3-5) Launsby Cnslting.
Straight Talk on Money: Ken & Daria Dolan's Guide to Family Money Management. Ken Dolan & Daria Dolan. 288p. 1993. 22.00 (0-671-79808-1) S&S Trade.
Straight Talk on Money: Ken & Daria Dolan's Guide to Family Money Management. Ken Dolan. 336p. 1995. pap. 12.00 (0-684-80049-7, Fireside) S&S Trade.
Straight Talk on Raising Kids: Help for Concerned Parents of School Age Children, Set 4. Curt Shreiner & Douglas Powell. 76p. 1988. pap. text ed. 49.95 incl. audio (1-55678-007-9) Learn Inc.
Straight Talk on Raising Young Children: Understanding & Guiding Your 1 to 6 Year Old. Lendon H. Smith & Curt Shreiner. 114p. 1989. pap. text ed. 49.95 incl. audio (1-55678-011-7) Learn Inc.
Straight Talk on Spondylitis. 2nd ed. Rodney Bluestone et al. Ed. by Robert L. Swezey et al. LC 92-36216. 1993. write for info. (1-881941-01-9) Spondylitis Assn.
Straight Talk on Stuttering: Information, Encouragement, & Counsel for Stutterers, Caregivers, & Speech-Language Clinicians. Lloyd M. Hulit. 278p. 1996. 54.95 (0-398-06591-8); pap. 35.95 (0-398-06592-6) C C Thomas.
Straight Talk on Tough Topics: A Discussion Guidebook for Today's Afrikan-American Youth. Chris Jackson. LC 96-22617. 112p. 1996. pap. 8.99 (0-310-20819-X) Zondervan.
Straight Talk on Women's Health: How to Get the Health Care You Deserve. Janice Teal. 1993. pap. 14.95 (0-942361-68-7) MasterMedia Pub.
Straight Talk to Parents: Cognitive Restructuring Training for Families. Rian E. McMullin et al. (Illus.). 63p. (Orig.). 1978. pap. 4.00 (0-935205-03-9) Counseling Res.
Straight Talk with Your Gynecologist: How to Get Answers That Will Save Your Life. Eddie C. Sollie. Ed. by Julie Livingston. 240p. (Orig.). 1993. pap. 12.95 (0-941831-83-3) Beyond Words Pub.
Straight Teeth: Orthodontics for Everyone. Robert L. Holt. LC 80-10562. (Illus.). 283p. 1980. pap. 12.95 (0-930926-72-2) Calif Fin Pubns.
Straight Texas. Ed. by J. Frank Dobie et al. LC 77-8134. (Texas Folklore Society Publications: No. 13). 348p. 1984. reprint ed. 16.95 (0-87074-164-0) UNTX Pr.
Straight Through the Night. Edward Allen. LC 88-26707. 270p. 1990. 17.95 (0-939149-19-2); pap. 9.95 (0-939149-36-2) Soho Press.
Straight to the Heart: Children of the World. Ethan Hubbard. (Illus.). 84p. (Orig.). 1992. pap. 8.95 (0-9604992-1-0) Craftsbury.
***Straight to the Heart: Political Cantos.** Angela Alioto. LC 97-65290. (Illus.). 272p. 1997. 22.95 (0-9653524-2-0) Russn Hill Pr.
Straight to the Point: Angles on Giving up Crime. Julie Lebrich. 310p. 1993. pap. 34.95 (0-908569-78-5, Pub. by U Otago Pr NZ) Intl Spec Bk.
Straight to the Top & Beyond: Nine Keys for Meeting the Challenge of Changing Times. John Amatt. LC 95-48869. 192p. 1996. reprint ed. write for info. (0-89384-296-6, Pfffr & Co) Jossey-Bass.
Straight Twigs: A KidGrower's Guide Book. Susan Henry. LC 92-70567. (Illus.). 192p. (Orig.). 1993. pap. 11.95 (0-943149-12-6) Alpha Bks OR.
Straight Up! A Teenager's Guide to Taking Charge of Your Life. Elizabeth Taylor-Gerdes. Ed. by Jane Crouse. (Illus.). 105p. (YA). (gr. 7-12). 1994. pap. 12.95 (1-885242-00-X) Lindsey Pubng.
Straight up to See the Sky: An Illustrated Guide to the Great Trans-Allegheny Adventurers. Timothy Truman. 1992. pap. 14.95 (1-56060-136-1) Eclipse Bks.
Straight White American Male: A Politically Incorrect Illustrated Survival Guide. James Overbey & Taylor Overbey. LC 96-75032. (Illus.). 21.95 (0-9651198-0-7) Marina Pubs.
***Straight White Male: Performance Art Monologues.** LC 96-30086. (Performance Studies: Expressive Behavior in Culture). 1997. write for info. (0-87805-977-6) U Pr of Miss.
***Straight White Male: Performance Monologues.** LC 96-30086. (Performance Studies: Expressive Behavior in Culture). 1997. pap. write for info. (0-87805-978-4) U Pr of Miss.
Straight White Male Handbook. Tim Tuttle. 92p. 1994. pap. 9.95 (0-87012-525-7) McClain.
Straight Wire. Lawrence F. Andrews. Ed. by John Valleau & Julie T. Olfe. (Illus.). 448p. (C). 1990. text ed. 125.00 (0-9616256-0-0) L A Wells.
Straight with the Medicine: Narrative of Washoe Followers of the Tipi Way. Warren L. D'Azevedo. 64p. 1991. reprint ed. lib. bdg. 25.00 (0-8095-4959-X) Borgo Pr.
Straight Woman's Guide to Lesbianism. Mikaya Heart. (Illus.). 72p. 1994. pap. 5.95 (0-9615129-4-6) Tough Dove.
Straighten up & Fly Right: A Chronology & Discography of Nat "King" Cole. Compiled by Klaus Teubig. LC 93-44459. (Discographies Ser.: No. 56). 320p. 1994. text ed. 65.00 (0-313-29251-5, Greenwood Pr) Greenwood.
Straightened Out: From Mobster to Government Agent. George Fresolone. 1994. 23.00 (0-671-77905-2) S&S Trade.
Straightforward Statistics for Behavoiral Science. Evans. (Psychology Ser.). 1996. student ed., pap. 19.95 (0-534-33864-X) Brooks-Cole.
Straightforward Statistics for the Behavioral Sciences. James D. Evans. LC 95-18736. 634p. 1996. text ed. 64.95 (0-534-23100-4) Brooks-Cole.

Straightforward Statistics for the Behavioral Sciences: Instructor's Manual. James D. Evans. Date not set. teacher ed. write for info. (*0-534-33863-1*) Brooks-Cole.

Straights: Raw Materials for Animal Feed Compounders & Farmers. Chris Lonsdale. 92p. (Orig.). 1988. pap. text ed. 25.00 (*0-948617-15-2*) Scholium Intl.

Straightway Dangerous: Collections of Poems by Writers in Delaware, Maryland, Pennsylvania, Virginia, & the District of Columbia. Ed. & Photos by Joseph D. Adams. (Poet's Domain Ser.: Vol. 13). (Illus.). 144p. (Orig.). 1996. pap. 8.00 (*1-880016-23-0*) Road Pubs.

Strain & Counterstrain. Lawrence H. Jones. LC 81-67256. (Illus.). 112p. (Orig.). 1981. text ed. 40.00 (*0-940668-00-9*); pap. text ed. 30.00 (*0-940668-01-7*) Am Acad Osteopathy.

Strain & Its Implications in Organic Chemistry: Organic Stress & Reactivity. Armin De Meijere. Ed. by Siegfried Blechert. (C). 1989. lib. bdg. 216.00 (*0-7923-0176-5*) Kluwer Ac.

Strain & Stress Analysis by Holographic & Speckle Interferometry. Valery Shchepinov et al. LC 95-22521. 483p. 1996. text ed. 145.00 (*0-471-96077-2*) Wiley.

***Strain & Temperature Measurement with Fiber Optic Sensors.** Regis J. Van Steenkiste & George S. Springer. LC 96-61097. 326p. 1996. text ed. 199.95 (*1-56676-480-7*) Technomic.

Strain Gage Based Transducers: Their Design & Construction. Measurements Group, Inc. Technical Staff. (Illus.). 74p. (Orig.). (C). 1988. pap. 10.00 (*0-9619057-0-0*) Measure Grp.

Strain Measurement in Biomechanics. Ed. by A. W. Miles & K. E. Tanner. (Illus.). 212p. (C). (gr. 13). 1992. text ed. 84.95 (*0-412-43270-6*, A6906) Chapman & Hall.

Strain of Meeting. Meng Wang. Tr. by Denis C. Mair. (Selected Works of Wang Meng: No. 1). (Illus.). 382p. (Orig.). 1989. pap. 14.95 (*0-8351-2263-8*) China Bks.

Strain Patterns in Rocks. Ed. by S. H. Treagus. 250p. 1984. 48.00 (*0-08-030273-4*, 2302, Pergamon Pr) Elsevier.

Strain Patterns in Rocks. S. H. Treagus. (Journal of Structural Geology Ser.). 1985. pap. 48.00 (*0-08-032619-6*, Pergamon Pr) Elsevier.

Strain Vegetation & Environment. (Havs Ser.). 1974. lib. bdg. 104.50 (*90-6193-187-8*) Kluwer Ac.

Strain Your Brain. Becky Daniel & Charlie Daniel. (Enrichment & Gifted Ser.). 48p. (J). (gr. 4-6). 1980. 6.95 (*0-88160-032-6*, LW 217) Learning Wks.

Strained Layer Epitaxy - Materials, Processing, & Device Applications. Ed. by J. C. Bean et al. (Symposium Proceedings Ser.: Vol. 379). 521p. 1995. text ed. 76.00 (*1-55899-282-0*) Materials Res.

***Strained-Layer Quantum Wells & Their Applications.** Ed. by M. O. Manasreh. (Optoelectronic Properties of Semiconducter Ser.: No. 4). 611p. 1997. text ed. 125.00 (*90-5699-567-7*) Gordon & Breach.

Strained Organic Molecules. Ed. by Edward Lee-Ruff et al. 128p. 1991. pap. 35.00 (*1-56081-509-4*, VCH) Wiley.

Strained Relations: Ireland at Peace & the U. S. A. at War 1941-1945. T. Ryle Dwyer. 1988. 52.50 (*0-389-20774-8*, N8333) B&N Imports.

Strained Sisterhood: Gender & Class in the Boston Female Anti-Slavery Society. Debra G. Hansen. LC 92-40310. 248p. (C). 1993. lib. bdg. 30.00 (*0-87023-848-5*) U of Mass Pr.

Strains of Change: The Impact of Tourism on Hawaiian Music. Elizabeth Tatar. (Illus.). 29p. 1987. pap. 5.95 (*0-930897-23-4*, SP78) Bishop Mus.

Strains of Discord. Robert M. Adams. LC 75-142601. (Essay Index Reprint Ser.). 1977. 18.95 (*0-8369-1917-3*) Ayer.

***Strains of Economic Growth: Labor Unrest & Social Dissatisfaction in Korea.** David L. Lindauer & Harvard Institute for International Development Staff. LC 97-5513. (Harvard Studies in International Development Ser.). 1997. write for info. (*0-674-83981-1*) HUP.

Strains of Eloquence: Emerson & His Sermons. Wesley T. Mott. LC 88-28123. 288p. 1989. lib. bdg. 32.50 (*0-271-00660-9*) Pa St U Pr.

Strains of Human Viruses. Ed. by M. Majer & S. A. Plotkin. 160p. 1972. 78.50 (*3-8055-1401-8*) S Karger.

Strains of Utopia: Gender, Nostalgia, & Hollywood Film Music. Caryl Flinn. 192p. 1992. text ed. 49.50 (*0-691-04801-0*); pap. text ed. 15.95 (*0-691-00619-9*) Princeton U Pr.

Strait: Book of Obenabi, His Songs. Fredy Perlman. 1988. pap. 5.00 (*0-934868-29-8*) Black & Red.

Strait Crossing Ninety Four: Proceedings of the Third Symposium, Alesund, Norway, June 1994. Ed. by Jon Krokeborg. (Illus.). 886p. (C). 1994. text ed. 125.00 (*90-5410-388-4*, Pub. by A A Balkema NE) Ashgate Pub Co.

Strait Crossings: Proceedings of the Second Symposium, Trondheim, 10 - 13 June 1990. Ed. by Jon Krokeborg. (Illus.). 668p. (C). 1990. text ed. 135.00 (*90-6191-118-4*, Pub. by A A Balkema NE) Ashgate Pub Co.

Strait Is the Gate. Andre Gide. Tr. by Dorothy Bussy from FRE. LC 79-23999. Orig. Title: La Porte Etroite. 1980. reprint ed. lib. bdg. 18.00 (*0-8376-0453-2*) Bentley.

Strait of Dover. Luc Cuyvers. 1986. lib. bdg. 96.50 (*90-247-3252-2*) Kluwer Ac.

Strait of Gibraltar & the Mediterranean. Scott G. Truver. (International Straits of the World Ser.: No. 4). 280p. 1980. lib. bdg. 93.50 (*90-286-0709-9*) Kluwer Ac.

Strait of Magellan. Michael A. Morris. (C). 1989. lib. bdg. 111.00 (*0-7923-0181-1*) Kluwer Ac.

Strait Way, Vol. 1. Jack Rowe. (Illus.). 128p. (Orig.). 1988. spiral bd. 4.95 (*0-9621384-0-1*) Rowe Evangelistic Minist.

Straitened Stage: A Study of the Theatre of J. Saunders Lewis. Ioan Williams. 212p. 1991. 35.00 (*1-85411-043-8*, Pub. by Seren Bks UK) Dufour.

Straitjacket. Louise O. Neaderland. (Illus.). 1987. 5.00 (*0-942561-00-7*) Bone Hollow.

Straitjacket & Tie. Eugene Stein. LC 96-14617. 278p. 1996. reprint ed. pap. text ed. 9.95 (*1-55583-358-6*) Alyson Pubns.

Straitjacket Society: A Rebel Bureaucrat Tells All. Masao Miyamoto. Tr. by Juliet W. Carpenter. 208p. 1995. 22.00 (*4-7700-1848-7*) Kodansha.

Straits. Michael Daley. 68p. 1989. pap. 5.00 (*0-912887-04-4*) Empty Bowl.

***Straits: British Policy Towards the Ottoman Empire & the Origins of the Dardanelles Campaign.** Geoffrey Miller. (Illus.). 300p. 1997. 27.95 (*0-85958-655-3*, Pub. by Univ of Hull Pr UK) Paul & Co Pubs.

Straits of Mackinac & Mackinac Island. rev. ed. John S. Penrod. (YA). (gr. 7 up). 1989. pap. 5.00 (*0-942618-20-3*) Penrod-Hiawatha.

Straits of Messina. Samuel R. Delany. 170p. 1989. 19.95 (*0-934933-02-2*) Serconia Pr.

Straits of Messina. William P. Mack. LC 94-22931. (Destroyer Ser.). 1994. 22.95 (*1-877853-34-8*) Nautical & Aviation.

Straits Used for International Navigation: A Spanish Perspective. Jose Antonio de Yturriaga. 388p. (C). 1991. lib. bdg. 143.50 (*0-7923-1141-8*) Kluwer Ac.

Straits Used for International Navigation Vol. 1: Legislative History of Part 3 of the United Nations Convention on the Law of the Sea. (Law of the Sea Ser.). 152p. 1991. 20.00 (*92-1-133420-9*) UN.

Straits Used for International Navigation Vol. 2: Legislative History of Part 3 of the United Nations Convention on the Law of the Sea. (Law of the Sea Ser.). 176p. 1992. 25.00 (*92-1-133437-3*) UN.

Straley's Guide to CA-Visual Objects for Clipper & xBASE Programmers. Stephen J. Straley. LC 95-35179. 608p. 1995. pap. 49.95 incl. disk (*0-201-40943-7*) Addison-Wesley.

Straley's Guide to Object-Oriented Programming with CA-Visual Objects. Stephen J. Straley. LC 95-37109. 896p. 1996. pap. 49.95 incl. disk (*0-201-40945-3*) Addison-Wesley.

Straley's Guide to Programming with CA-Realizer. Stephen J. Straley. LC 95-3960. 416p. 1995. pap. 34.95 (*0-201-40944-5*) Addison-Wesley.

***Stramonium: With an Introduction to Analysis Using Cycles & Segments.** Paul Herscu. LC 96-70061. (Illus.). 239p. (Orig.). 1996. pap. 28.00 (*0-9654004-0-9*) New Engld Schl Homeopthy.

Stran 1.4: Strength Analyzer of Multilayered Hybrid Composites. Petr A. Zinoviev et al. 72p. 1995. ring bd. 349.95 incl. disk (*1-56676-277-4*, 762774) Technomic.

Strand. Violet V. Englund. LC 77-76176. (Illus.). 1977. pap. 6.95 (*0-9601258-0-9*) Golden Owl Pub.

***Strand.** Ellen S. Vaughn. LC 97-1769. 384p. 1997. 16.99 (*0-8499-1328-4*) Word Pub.

Strand. large type ed. Claire Rayner. (General Fiction Ser.). 576p. 1992. 25.99 (*0-7089-2669-X*) Ulverscroft.

***Strand of Dreams.** Audrey Howard. 448p. 1997. 27.00 (*0-340-66604-8*, Pub. by H & S UK) Trafalgar.

***Strand of Dreams.** Audrey Howard. 448p. 1997. pap. 10.95 (*0-340-66605-6*, Pub. by H & S UK) Trafalgar.

Stranded! Idella F. Bodie. LC 84-14098. (Illus.). 132p. (Orig.). (J). (gr. 5-7). 1984. pap. 6.95 (*0-87844-060-7*) Sandlapper Pub Co.

Stranded. Sara Compton. (Choose Your Own Adventure Ser.: No. 50). 64p. (J). 1989. pap. 3.50 (*0-553-15762-0*) Bantam.

Stranded. Camarin Grae. 304p. (Orig.). 1991. pap. 9.95 (*0-941483-99-1*) Naiad Pr.

Stranded. Ben Mikaelsen. LC 94-27069. 288p. (J). (gr. 4-8). 1995. 15.95 (*0-7868-0072-0*); lib. bdg. 15.89 (*0-7868-2059-4*) Hyprn Child.

Stranded. Ben Mikaelsen. LC 94-27069. 288p. (J). (gr. 4-8). 1996. pap. 4.95 (*0-7868-1109-9*) Hyprn Child.

Stranded. Esther Tusquets. Tr. by Susan E. Clark from SPA. LC 91-15357. 230p. 1991. 19.95 (*0-916583-83-X*) Dalkey Arch.

Stranded. Esther Tusquets. Tr. by Susan E. Clark from SPA. LC 91-15357. 230p. 1992. reprint ed. pap. 9.95 (*0-916583-91-0*) Dalkey Arch.

Stranded: Rock & Roll for a Desert Island. rev. ed. Ed. by Greil Marcus. 320p. 1996. pap. 14.95 (*0-306-80682-7*) Da Capo.

Stranded at Plimoth Plantation 1626. Gary Bowen. LC 93-31016. (Illus.). 88p. (J). (gr. 3-7). 1994. 19.95 (*0-06-022541-6*); lib. bdg. 19.89 (*0-06-022542-4*) HarpC Child Bks.

***Stranded Benefits.** Ed. by Dianna Gordon. (Restructure? What Then? Ser.). 51p. 1996. 15.00 (*1-55516-809-4*, 4118) Natl Conf State Legis.

***Stranded in Harmony.** LC 96-44976. 192p. (YA). (gr. 7 up). 1997. lib. bdg. 17.89 (*0-7868-2284-8*) Hyprn Child.

Stranded in Harmony. Barbara Shoup. LC 96-44976. 192p. (YA). (gr. 7 up). 1997. 17.95 (*0-7868-0287-1*) Hyprn Child.

***Stranded in Moscow: An American's Story of Life in the New Russia.** Rick Furmanek. LC 96-71741. 288p. 1997. 19.95 (*0-9655703-5-5*) Square Peg Pr.

Stranded in the Philippines: Missionary Professor Organizes Resistance to the Japanese. Scott A. Mills. (Illus.). 137p. (Orig.). 1994. pap. 12.50 (*971-10-0519-0*, Pub. by New Day Pub PH) Cellar.

Stranded Objects: Mourning, Memory, & Film in Postwar Germany. Eric Santner. LC 89-38522. (Illus.). 216p. 1993. 35.00 (*0-8014-2344-9*); pap. 12.95 (*0-8014-8162-7*) Cornell U Pr.

Stranded on Terror Island, No. 14. Lee Roddy. (Ladd Family Adventure Ser.). (J). 1996. pap. text ed. 5.99 (*1-56179-482-1*) Focus Family.

Stranded on the Information Highway. John Levesque. 200p. (Orig.). 1996. pap. 16.95 (*0-88962-608-1*) Mosaic.

Strandia. Susan L. Reynolds. (Illus.). 240p. (YA). (gr. 9-12). 1991. 14.95 (*0-374-37274-8*) FS&G.

***Strandloper.** Alan Garner. 208p. 1997. 24.00 (*1-86046-160-3*) HarperColl Wrld.

Strands. Eric Wilson. 1994. 5.00 (*0-87129-410-9*, SA3) Dramatic Pub.

Strands Afar Remote. LC 97-19193. 1997. write for info. (*0-87413-597-4*) U Delaware Pr.

***Strands of Gold.** Kathleen Morgan. 400p. (Orig.). 1997. mass mkt. 5.99 (*0-505-52239-X*, Love Spell) Dorchester Pub Co.

Strands of Life. Robert L. Sinsheimer. LC 93-13122. 320p. 1994. 30.00 (*0-520-08248-6*) U CA Pr.

Strands of Love. Markis L. Gardner. LC 92-90467. 82p. (Orig.). 1992. pap. 6.50 (*0-9634058-0-2*) M L Gardner.

Strands of Media Criticism: Study Guide 1A. Deakin University Press Staff. 102p. (C). 1988. 70.00 (*0-7300-0539-9*, Pub. by Deakin Univ AT) St Mut.

***Strands of My Life.** Robert L. Sinsheimer. Date not set. 22.95 (*0-465-08225-4*); pap. write for info. (*0-465-08252-1*) Basic.

Strands of Organic Chemistry: A Series of Lectures. Claude E. Wintner. LC 78-60358. 1978. pap. text ed. 13.95 (*0-8162-9661-8*) Holden-Day.

Strands of Starlight. Gael Baudino. 384p. 1989. mass mkt. 4.99 (*0-451-45316-6*, ROC) NAL-Dutton.

Strands of Starlight. Gael Baudino. 352p. 1990. pap. 4.50 (*0-451-16371-0*, 015, Sig) NAL-Dutton.

Strands of Strands. Date not set. pap. 5.99 (*0-451-45573-8*, ROC) NAL-Dutton.

Strands of Sunlight. Gael Baudino. 400p. (Orig.). 1994. pap. 4.99 (*0-451-45408-1*, ROC) NAL-Dutton.

Strands of System: The Philosophy of Charles Peirce. Douglas R. Anderson. LC 94-3571. (Series in the History of Philosophy). 218p. (C). 1995. 24.95 (*1-55753-058-0*); pap. 13.95 (*1-55753-059-9*) Purdue U Pr.

Strands of the Cable: The Place of the Past in Jewish American Women's Writing. Ellen S. Uffen. LC 91-28481. (Twentieth Century American Jewish Writers Ser.: Vol. 4). 200p. (C). 1992. text ed. 30.95 (*0-8204-1701-7*) P Lang Pubng.

***Strang Anticancer.** Strang Cancer Center Staff. 1998. pap. 24.95 (*0-525-94313-7*) NAL-Dutton.

Strange: Biographical & Historical Sketches of the Stranges of America & Across the Seas. A. T. Strange. 137p. 1993. reprint ed. pap. 22.50 (*0-8328-3415-7*); reprint ed. lib. bdg. 32.50 (*0-8328-3414-9*) Higginson Bk Co.

Strange: The Alloway Strange (Family) 2nd ed. John R. Mayer. (Illus.). 285p. 1995. reprint ed. pap. 42.00 (*0-8328-4736-4*); reprint ed. lib. bdg. 52.00 (*0-8328-4735-6*) Higginson Bk Co.

Strange Abstraction: Robert Gober, Cady Noland, Philip Taaffe, Christopher Wool. (Illus.). 92p. 1992. pap. 19.95 (*1-56466-017-6*) Archer Fields.

Strange Adventures of Andrew Battell in Angola. Ed. by E. G. Ravenstein. (Hakluyt Society Second Ser.: Vol. 6). 1996. 45.00 (*0-85115-955-9*, Pub. by Hakluyt Soc UK) Boydell & Brewer.

Strange Adventures of the Great Lakes. Dwight Boyer. 248p. 1960. pap. 12.75 (*0-912514-52-3*) Freshwater.

Strange Aeons: New Adventures for Call of Cthulhu. Ed. by Lynn Willis. (Call of Cthulhu Roleplaying Game Ser.). (Illus.). 96p. (Orig.). (YA). 1995. pap. 14.95 (*1-56882-031-3*, 2353) Chaosium.

Strange Affinity. Paul Bennett. 1975. pap. 6.00 (*0-318-04215-0*) Orchard.

Strange Allies: The United States & Poland, 1941-1945. Richard C. Lukas. LC 77-8585. 240p. reprint ed. 68.40 (*0-685-16069-6*, 2027566) Bks Demand.

***Strange, Amazing & Mysterious Places.** Intro. by William S. Burroughs. (Illus.). 160p. 19.98 (*0-8317-8039-8*) Smithmark.

Strange, Amazing True Tales of Alaska. Ronald R. Wendt. (Illus.). 60p. (Orig.). 1995. pap. text ed. 9.95 (*1-886574-10-3*) Goldstream Pubns.

Strange & Amazing Facts about Star Trek. Cohen. 1990. pap. 2.95 (*0-671-72956-X*) PB.

Strange & Ancient Name. Josepha Sherman. 1993. mass mkt. 5.99 (*0-671-72151-8*) Baen Bks.

Strange & Blighted Land: Gettysburg: The Aftermath of a Battle. Gregory A. Coco. (Illus.). 448p. (C). 1995. text ed. 39.95 (*0-939631-82-2*) Thomas Publications.

Strange & Dangerous Voyage of Capt. Thomas James. W. A. Kenyon. 1994. pap. 10.95 (*0-88854-171-6*, Pub. by Royal Ont Mus CN) U of Toronto Pr.

Strange & Dangerous Voyage of Captaine T. James. Thomas James. LC 68-54650. (English Experience Ser.: No. 58). 1968. reprint ed. 45.00 (*90-221-0058-8*) Walter J Johnson.

Strange & Distant Shore: Indians of the Great Plains in Exile. Brent Ashabranner. (Illus.). 64p. (YA). (gr. 6 up). 1996. pap. 16.99 (*0-525-65201-9*, Cobblehill Bks) Dutton Child Bks.

Strange & Eerie Stories. Pat Hancock. LC 94-12225. (Illus.). (J). 1994. pap. 11.95 (*0-590-20258-8*) Scholastic Inc.

Strange & Exciting Adventures of Jeramiah Hush. Uri Shulevitz. (Illus.). 96p. (J). (gr. 2-5). 1986. 14.00 (*0-374-33656-3*) FS&G.

***Strange & Spooky Stories.** Andrew F. Peters. LC 97-3270. (Illus.). 80p. (J). (gr. 3-6). 1997. lib. bdg. 17.90 (*0-7613-0321-9*) Millbrook Pr.

Strange & Unexplained Happenings, Vol. 1. Nancy Pear. 1995. write for info. (*0-8103-9781-1*) Gale.

Strange & Unexplained Happenings, Vol. 2. Nancy Pear. 1995. write for info. (*0-8103-9782-X*) Gale.

Strange & Unexplained Happenings, Vol. 3. Nancy Pear. 1995. write for info. (*0-8103-9889-3*) Gale.

Strange & Unexplained Happenings: When Nature Breaks the Rules of Science, 3 vols., Set. Ed. by Jerome Clark & Nancy Pear. (Illus.). 538p. (YA). (gr. 5 up). 1995. 62.00 (*0-8103-9780-3*, UXL) Gale.

Strange & Unexplained Mysteries of the 20th Century. Jenny Randles. LC 93-45608. Orig. Title: The Unexplained. (Illus.). 144p. 1994. pap. 14.95 (*0-8069-0768-1*) Sterling.

Strange & Unusual Creatures: Natures Unlovables. Consumer Guide Editors. 1990. 12.99 (*0-517-02738-0*) Random Hse Value.

Strange & Wonderful Aircraft. Harvey Weiss. LC 94-3788. 64p. (J). (gr. 5-9). 1995. 15.95 (*0-395-68716-0*) HM.

Strange & Wonderful Tale of Robert McDoodle. Bauer. LC 96-35360. (J). 1998. 16.00 (*0-689-80619-1*) S&S Childrens.

Strange Angel: The Gospel According to Benny Joe. Ben Davis. LC 91-73968. 237p. 1991. 15.95 (*0-931722-89-6*) Corona Pub.

Strange Angel: The Gospel According to Benny Joe. Ben Davis. LC 91-73968. 237p. 1993. pap. 7.95 (*0-931722-94-2*) Corona Pub.

Strange Angels. J. Agee. LC 94-12374. 416p. 1994. pap. 12.50 (*0-06-097589-X*) HarpC.

Strange Angels. Kathe Koja. 368p. 1995. mass mkt. 5.50 (*0-440-21498-X*) Dell.

Strange Animals of the Sea. National Geographic Society Staff. (Books for World Explorers). (Illus.). 1994. 16.00 (*0-87044-686-X*) Natl Geog.

***Strange Are the Ways.** Teresa Crane. 570p. 4.98 (*0-8317-4637-8*) Smithmark.

Strange Attachment & Other Stories. Bibhutibhusan Bandyopadhyay. Tr. by Phyllis Granoff. 300p. 1995. lib. bdg. 35.00 (*0-8095-4871-2*) Borgo Pr.

Strange Attachment & Other Stories. Bibhutibhushan Bandyopadhyay. Tr. by Phyllis Granoff. 277p. pap. 12.95 (*0-88962-222-1*) Mosaic.

Strange Attraction: The Best of Ten Years of Zyzzyva. Ed. by Howard Junker. LC 95-21119. (Western Literature Ser.). 352p. (Orig.). 1995. pap. 18.00 (*0-87417-275-6*) U of Nev Pr.

Strange Attractors. Jeffrey A. Carver. 352p. 1996. pap. write for info. (*0-614-05544-X*) Tor Bks.

Strange Attractors. Jeffrey A. Carver. 352p. mass mkt. 5.99 (*0-8125-3516-2*) Tor Bks.

Strange Attractors. Rebecca Goldstein. 288p. 1994. pap. 11.95 (*0-14-017246-7*, Penguin Bks) Viking Penguin.

Strange Attractors. William Sleator. LC 89-33840. 176p. (YA). (gr. 5-11). 1990. pap. 13.95 (*0-525-44530-7*) Dutton Child Bks.

Strange Attractors. William Sleator. (Illus.). 144p. (YA). (gr. 7 up). 1991. pap. 4.99 (*0-14-034582-5*, Puffin) Puffin Bks.

Strange Attractors: Chaos, Complexity, & the Art of Family Therapy. Michael R. Butz et al. LC 96-1600. (Couples & Family Dynamics & Treatment Ser.). 304p. 1996. text ed. 39.95 (*0-471-07951-0*) Wiley.

Strange Attractors: Literature, Culture & Chaos Theory. Hawkins. 1995. pap. text ed. 21.50 (*0-13-355355-8*) P-H.

Strange Attractors: Literature, Culture & Chaos Theory. Harriet Hawkins. LC 94-35486. 1995. 22.00 (*0-7450-1141-1*) P-H.

Strange Attractors: Signs of Chaos. Laura Trippi et al. Ed. by Alice Yang. (Illus.). 69p. 1989. pap. text ed. 16.00 (*0-915557-66-5*) New Mus Contemp Art.

Strange Bedfellow. Janet Dailey. 1992. mass mkt. 3.59 (*0-373-89889-4*, 1-89889-9) Harlequin Bks.

***Strange Bedfellows.** Pat Boran. 116p. 9100. pap. 13.95 (*0-948339-65-9*, Pub. by Poolbeg Pr IE) Dufour.

***Strange Bedfellows.** Kasey Michaels. (36 Hours Ser.: Vol. 2). 1997. mass mkt. 4.50 (*0-373-65007-8*) Harlequin Bks.

Strange Bedfellows: The First American Avant-Garde. Steven Watson. (Illus.). 440p. 1991. 19.98 (*0-89659-934-5*) Abbeville Pr.

Strange Bedfellows: The First American Avant-Garde. Steven Watson. 440p. 1993. pap. 9.98 (*1-55859-655-0*) Abbeville Pr.

Strange Bedpersons. Jennifer Crusie. (Temptation Ser.). 1994. mass mkt. 2.99 (*0-373-25598-5*, 1-25598-3) Harlequin Bks.

Strange Bedpersons. Jennifer Crusie. (Temptation Ser.). 1994. mass mkt. 2.99 (*0-373-25620-5*, 1-25620-5) Harlequin Bks.

Strange Bird on the Lagoon. Margaret Reeves. 224p. (C). 1990. pap. 39.00 (*0-908175-95-7*, Pub. by Boolarong Pubns AT) St Mut.

***Strange Birds.** Bobbie Kalman. (Birds up Close Ser.). (Illus.). 32p. (J). 1997. lib. bdg. 18.64 (*0-86505-755-9*) Crabtree Pub Co.

***Strange Birds.** Bobbie Kalman. (Birds up Close Ser.). (Illus.). 32p. (J). 1997. pap. 5.95 (*0-86505-769-9*) Crabtree Pub Co.

Strange Birthday, Vol. 6. Hilda Stahl. (Elizabeth Gail Ser.: Vol. 6). 128p. (J). 1989. pap. 5.99 (*0-8423-0803-2*) Tyndale.

Strange Boarders. George Batson & Jack Kirkland. 1947. pap. 5.25 (*0-8222-1087-8*) Dramatists Play.

Strange Bod Fellows: Did the Littlest Witch, Robbed of Her Childhood Come Back to Salem to Recover the Lost Years? Hilda Terry. (Illus.). 200p. (Orig.). 1992. pap. text ed. 8.88 (*0-9627043-1-8*) Art Ltd.

Strange Bodies on a Stranger Shore. Ann Copeland. 236p. 1994. pap. 12.95 (*0-86492-143-8*) LPC InBook.

Strange Breed of Cat: An Encounter in Human Sexuality. B. Mark Schoenberg. LC 74-5281. 336p. 1975. 19.95 (*0-88280-015-9*) ETC Pubns.

Strange Brew. Betsy Haynes. (Bone Chillers Ser.: No. 5). 144p. 1995. mass mkt. 3.99 (*0-06-106299-5*, Harp PBks) HarpC.

S

***Strange Brew.** Kathy H. Trocheck. LC 97-23515. (Callahan Garrity Mystery Ser.). 1997. 22.50 (0-06-017542-7) HarpC.

Strange Brother. Blair Niles. LC 75-12341. (Homosexuality Ser.). 1975. reprint ed. 17.95 (0-405-07390-9) Ayer.

Strange Business. Rilla Askew. 208p. 1993. pap. 10.95 (0-14-016595-9, Penguin Bks) Viking Penguin.

***Strange But True.** Jenny Randles & Peter Hough. (Illus.). 192p. (Orig.). 1996. pap. 16.95 (0-7499-1459-9, Pub. by Piatkus Bks UK) London Brdge.

Strange but True. Patrick M. Reynolds. 1978. pap. 3.95 (0-932514-00-6) Red Rose Studio.

***Strange but True: A True-Life Japanese Reader.** Tom Gally. 1997. pap. text ed. 13.00 (4-7700-2057-0, Pub. by Kodansha Int JA) OUP.

***Strange but True: From the Files of Fate Magazine.** Corrine Kenner. 1997. pap. text ed. 9.95 (1-56718-298-4) Llewellyn Pubns.

Strange but True Mysteries. Tony Tallarico. (I Didn't Know That about Ser.). (Illus.). 24p. (J). 1992. 4.98 (0-8317-4980-6) Smithmark.

Strange But True Stories of World War II. George Sullivan. 128p. (J). (gr. 5 up). 1983. 14.95 (0-8027-6489-4) Walker & Co.

Strange Career of Bishop Sterling. Walter A. Roberts. LC 73-18603. reprint ed. 42.50 (0-404-11413-X) AMS Pr.

Strange Career of Jim Crow. 3rd rev. ed. C. Vann Woodward. 256p. 1974. pap. 10.95 (0-19-501805-2) OUP.

Strange Career of Legal Liberalism. Laura Kalman. 1996. write for info. (0-300-06369-5) Yale U Pr.

Strange Career of Marihuana: Politics & Ideology of Drug Control in America. Jerome L. Himmelstein. LC 82-12181. (Contributions in Political Science Ser.: No. 94). (Illus.). xii, 179p. 1983. text ed. 45.00 (0-313-23517-1, HSC/, Greenwood Pr) Greenwood.

***Strange Case of Dr. Jeckyll & Mr. Hyde.** Robert Louis Stevenson. 272p. 1996. reprint ed. pap. text ed. 6.95 (0-460-87792-5, Everyman's Classic Lib) C E Tuttle.

Strange Case of Dr. Jekyll & Mr. Hyde. (Fiction Ser.). (YA). 1993. pap. text ed. 6.50 (0-582-08484-9, 79829) Longman.

Strange Case of Dr. Jekyll & Mr. Hyde. (J). (gr. 4-7). 1997. pap. 2.95 (0-89375-357-2) Troll Communs.

Strange Case of Dr. Jekyll & Mr. Hyde. David Edgar. 112p. Date not set. pap. 13.95 (1-85459-121-5, Pub. by N Hern Bks UK) Theatre Comm.

Strange Case of Dr. Jekyll & Mr. Hyde. Robert Louis Stevenson. Ed. by Raymond Harris. (Classics Ser.). (Illus.). 48p. (YA). (gr. 6-12). 1982. teacher ed. 7.32 (0-89061-254-4, 453); pap. text ed. 5.99 (0-89061-253-6, 451); audio 13.00 (0-89061-255-2, 452) Jamestown Pubs.

***Strange Case of Dr. Jekyll & Mr. Hyde.** Robert Louis Stevenson. (Young Collector's Illustrated Classics Ser.). (Illus.). 192p. (J). (gr. 3-7). write for info. (1-56156-460-5) Kidsbks.

Strange Case of Dr. Jekyll & Mr. Hyde. Robert Louis Stevenson. 1991. pap. 1.00 (0-486-26688-5) Dover.

Strange Case of Dr. Jekyll & Mr. Hyde. Robert Louis Stevenson. 1993. pap. 5.25 (0-19-585429-2) OUP.

Strange Case of Dr. Jekyll & Mr. Hyde. Robert Louis Stevenson. LC 90-30544. (Illus.). xxii, 164p. 1990. reprint ed. 25.00 (0-8032-4212-3) U of Nebr Pr.

Strange Case of Dr. Kappler: The Doctor Who Became a Killer. Keith R. Ablow. 1994. 19.95 (0-02-900161-7, Free Press) Free Pr.

Strange Case of Rudi Schneider. Anita Gregory. LC 84-10591. 464p. 1985. 37.50 (0-8108-1711-X) Scarecrow.

Strange Case of the Disapparing Antiproton. Ian McCrimmon. (C). 1992. text ed. 19.00 (0-9514698-9-4, Pub. by Cosmatom UK) St Mut.

Strange Case of the Ghosts of the Robert Louis Stevenson House. Randall A. Reinstedt. Ed. by John Bergez. LC 88-81933. (History & Happenings of California Ser.). (Illus.). 70p. (J). (gr. 3-6). 1988. pap. 8.95 (0-933818-78-5); boxed 12.95 (0-933818-22-X) Ghost Town.

Strange Case of the Lost Elvis Diaries. Barry Willis. LC 94-60408. (Illus.). 96p. (Orig.). 1995. pap. 8.95 (1-885197-00-4) Waynoka Pr.

Strange Case of the Spotted Mice & Other Classic Essays on Science. Peter B. Medawar. 256p. (C). 1996. pap. 12.95 (0-19-286193-X) OUP.

Strange Case of T.L. Art by Tony Labat & Fiction by Carlo McCormick. Carlo McCormick. 56p. 1995. 15.00 (0-9631095-4-5) Artspace Bks.

Strange Change. unabridged ed. Nicholas Ifkovits. 213p. (Orig.). 1998. pap. 11.95 (0-9651700-1-2) Counter-Force Pr.

Strange Child. E. T. A. Hoffmann. LC 84-8404. (Illus.). 28p. (J). (gr. 3 up). 1991. pap. 16.95 (0-907234-60-7, Picture Book Studio) S&S Childrens.

Strange Conflict. Dennis Wheatley. 1996. mass mkt. 6.99 (0-7493-2486-4, Reed Trade) Buttrwrth-Heinemann.

Strange Connection: U. S. Intervention in China 1944-72. Bevin Alexander. LC 91-27239. (Contributions to the Study of World History Ser.: No. 34). 264p. 1992. text ed. 52.95 (0-313-28008-8, AXS/, Greenwood Pr) Greenwood.

Strange Contrarieties: Pascal in England During the Age of Reason. John C. Barker. LC 74-81661. (Illus.). 352p. reprint ed. pap. 100.40 (0-7837-1163-8, 2041692) Bks Demand.

Strange Country. Anthony J. Hassall. 1990. pap. 14.95 (0-7022-2273-9, Pub. by Univ Queensland Pr AT) Intl Spec Bk.

***Strange Country: Modernity & Nationhood in Irish Writing since 1790.** Seamus Deane. (Clarendon Lectures in English Literature). 280p. 1997. text ed. 45.00 (0-19-818337-2) OUP.

Strange Courage. Max Brand. 213p. 1975. reprint ed. lib. bdg. 20.95 (0-89190-211-2, Rivercity Pr) Amereon Ltd.

Strange Creatures of the Sea Coloring Book. Llyn Hunter. (Illus.). (J). (gr. k-3). 1991. pap. 2.95 (0-486-26836-5) Dover.

Strange Creatures That Really Lived. Selsam. (J). 1989. pap. 3.95 (0-590-40493-8) Scholastic Inc.

Strange Customs, Manners & Beliefs. Alpheus H. Verrill. LC 75-86791. (Essay Index Reprint Ser.). 1977. 20.95 (0-8369-1199-7) Ayer.

***Strange Customs of the World.** Ed. by Fred L. Israel & Arthur M. Schlesinger, Jr. (Looking into the Past). (Illus.). 64p. (YA). (gr. 5 up). 1997. lib. bdg. 16.95 (0-7910-4679-6) Chelsea Hse.

Strange Days. James Cameron. (Illus.). 192p. 1995. pap. 12.95 (0-452-27581-4, Plume) NAL-Dutton.

***Strange Days.** Dave Riddle. (Illus.). 1995. pap. 8.95 (0-940696-41-X) Monroe County Lib.

Strange Days: My Life with & Without Jim Morrison. Patricia Kennealy. (Illus.). 456p. 1993. pap. 14.95 (0-452-26981-4, Plume) NAL-Dutton.

Strange Days: The Official Movie Adaptation. Dan Chichester. 1996. pap. text ed. 4.95 (0-7851-0183-7) Marvel Entmnt.

Strange Days No. 1: The Year in Weirdness. Fortean Times Editors. (Illus.). 160p. 1996. pap. 9.95 (0-8362-1499-4) Andrews & McMeel.

***Strange Days No. 2: The Year in Wierdness.** Ed. by Fortean Times Staff. LC 97-6688. 168p. (Orig.). 1997. pap. 9.95 (0-8362-2767-0, Cader Bks) Andrews & McMeel.

Strange Days Ahead. Michael Brownstein. LC 75-26450. (Illus.). 98p. (Orig.). 1976. pap. 5.00 (0-915990-01-6) Z Pr.

Strange Death of American Life. Schulman. 1996. 23.00 (0-02-928115-6, Free Press) Free Pr.

Strange Death of American Life. Schulman. 1998. 23.00 (0-684-82814-6) Free Pr.

Strange Death of Capitalist Individualism. J. A. Banks. LC 93-22659. 132p. 1993. 57.95 (1-85521-407-5, Pub. by Dartmth Pub UK) Ashgate Pub Co.

Strange Death of Franklin Delano Roosevelt. Emanuel M. Josephson. 1979. 250.00 (0-685-96469-8) Revisionist Pr.

Strange Death of Franklin Delano Roosevelt: A History of the Roosevelt-Delano Dynasty. Emanuel M. Josephson. 288p. 1976. 75.00 (0-685-66413-9) Chedney.

Strange Death of Liberal America. Siegel. 1997. 22.50 (0-02-874084-X) Free Pr.

Strange Death of Liberal America. Siegel. LC 97-23050. 1997. 23.00 (0-684-82747-6) Free Pr.

Strange Death of Marilyn Monroe. 1991. lib. bdg. 63.95 (0-8490-4438-3) Gordon Pr.

Strange Death of Mistress Coffin. Robert J. Begiebing. 252p. 1991. 17.95 (0-945575-56-4) Algonquin Bks.

Strange Death of Mistress Coffin. Robert J. Begiebing. LC 90-19528. 240p. 1996. pap. 9.95 (1-56512-145-7, 72145) Algonquin Bks.

Strange Death of Perestroika: Causes & Consequences of the Soviet Coup. John Gray. (C). 1991. 35.00 (0-907967-27-2, Pub. by Inst Euro Def & Strat UK) St Mut.

Strange Death of the Liberal Empire: Lord Selbourne in South Africa. David E. Torrance. 286p. 1996. 55.00 (0-7735-1319-1, Pub. by McGill CN) U of Toronto Pr.

***Strange Death of the Soviet Empire.** Pryce-Jones. Date not set. write for info. (0-8050-4155-9) St Martin.

Strange Death of the Soviet Empire. David Pryce-Jones. 456p. 1995. 30.00 (0-8050-4154-0) H Holt & Co.

Strange Deaths of President Harding. Robert H. Ferrell. (Illus.). 208p. (C). 1996. 24.95 (0-8262-1093-7) U of Mo Pr.

***Strange Deliverance.** Mary Brown. 384p. 1997. mass mkt. 5.99 (0-671-87795-X) Baen Bks.

Strange Desire. large type ed. Kay Mitchell. 432p. 1995. 25.99 (0-7089-3244-4) Ulverscroft.

Strange Disappearance of Uncle Dudley: A Child's Story of Los Alamos. Inez Ross. (Illus.). 40p. (Orig.). (J). (ps-2). 1996. pap. 6.98 (0-9645703-2-7) Otowi Crossing Pr.

Strange Disappearances. Elliot O'Donnell. 1990. pap. 9.95 (0-8065-1140-0, Citadel Pr) Carol Pub Group.

Strange Dislocations: Childhood & the Idea of Human Interiority, 1780-1930. Carolyn Steedman. LC 95-7257. 272p. (C). 1995. text ed. 29.95 (0-674-83978-1) HUP.

Strange Dreams: The Writings & Poetry of Derek Welsh. Derek Welsh. 160p. 1996. 17.95 (0-9649895-0-6) Miami Intl.

Strange Eating Habits of Sea Creatures. Jean H. Sibbald. LC 85-11621. (Ocean World Library). (Illus.). 112p. (J). (gr. 4 up). 1987. lib. bdg. 13.95 (0-87518-349-2, Dillon Silver Burdett) Silver Burdett Pr.

Strange Empire. Joseph K. Howard. LC 94-27626. (Illus.). xxxv, 601p. 1994. reprint ed. pap. 16.95 (0-87351-298-7, Borealis Book) Minn Hist.

Strange Encounter. Page Smith. Date not set. pap. write for info. (0-14-017504-0, Viking) Viking Penguin.

Strange Encounters: A Graphic Novel. Fred Hull. Ed. by Joan Harryman. (Illus.). (Orig.). 1987. pap. 5.95 (0-944099-05-X) Comic Art.

Strange Encounters: UFOs, Aliens, & Monsters among Us. Curt Sutherly. LC 96-16994. (Fate Presents Ser.). 272p. (Orig.). 1996. mass mkt. 5.99 (1-56718-699-8) Llewellyn Pubns.

Strange Enthusiasm: A Life of Thomas Wentworth Higginson. Tilden G. Edelstein. LC 68-27752. 437p. reprint ed. pap. 124.60 (0-8357-8765-6, 2033714) Bks Demand.

Strange Eons. Robert Bloch. LC 78-66962. (Illus.). 1979. 15.00 (0-918372-30-5) Whispers.

Strange Experience: How to Become the World's Second Greatest Lover. Strange de Jim. LC 80-69868. (Illus.). 192p. (Orig.). 1980. per. 29.95 (0-9605308-1-9) Ash-Kar Pr.

Strange. "Extraneus" Strange (Family) of Eastern America. 2nd ed. John R. Mayer. (Illus.). 398p. 1995. reprint ed. pap. 59.50 (0-8328-4734-8); reprint ed. lib. bdg. 69.50 (0-8328-4733-X) Higginson Bk Co.

Strange Files of F. Jones. Diane Day. 272p. 1996. mass mkt. 4.99 (0-553-56921-X, Crimeline) Bantam.

Strange Files of Fremont Jones. large type ed. Dianne Day. (Niagara Large Print Ser.). 341p. 1996. 27.99 (0-7089-5824-9) Ulverscroft.

***Strange Fire.** B. Harker. 206p. (Orig.). 1996. pap. 11.95 (0-614-30875-5) Hartland Pubns.

***Strange Fire.** Indigo Girls. pap. 14.95 (0-7935-6536-7) H Leonard.

Strange Fits of Passion. Anita Shreve. 384p. 1992. pap. 5.99 (0-451-40300-2, Onyx) NAL-Dutton.

Strange Fits of Passion: Epistemologies of Emotion, Hume to Austen. Adela Pinch. LC 95-52593. (C). 1996. pap. write for info. (0-8047-2549-7); text ed. write for info. (0-8047-2548-9) Stanford U Pr.

Strange Folks along the Mississippi. Pat Wallace. Ed. & Illus. by Bruce Carlson. 173p. (Orig.). 1990. pap. 9.95 (1-878488-31-7) Quixote Pr IA.

***Strange Forces, No. 3.** Marty Engle & Johnny R. Barnes, Jr. 280p. (Orig.). (YA). (gr. 4 up). 1997. pap. 5.50 (1-56714-086-6) Montage Bks.

***Strange Forces, No. 4.** Marty Engle & Johnny R. Barnes, Jr. 280p. (Orig.). (YA). (gr. 4 up). 1997. pap. 5.50 (1-56714-087-4) Montage Bks.

***Strange Forces, Vol. 5.** Marty Engle & Johnny R. Barnes, Jr. 288p. (Orig.). (YA). (gr. 4 up). 1997. pap. 5.50 (1-56714-089-0) Montage Bks.

***Strange Forces, Vol. 6.** Marty Engle & Johnny R. Barnes, Jr. 288p. (Orig.). (YA). (gr. 4 up). 1997. pap. 5.50 (1-56714-093-9) Montage Bks.

Strange Forces 1. Marty Engle & Barnes. (Strange Forces Ser.: No. 1). 280p. (YA). (gr. 5 up). 1996. pap. 5.50 (1-56714-057-2) Montage Bks.

Strange Forces 2. Engle & Barnes. (Strange Forces Ser.: Vol. 2). 280p. (Orig.). (YA). (gr. 5 up). 1996. pap. 5.50 (1-56714-060-2) Montage Bks.

Strange Friends: A Learning Guide for Students of Intermediate Chinese. 2nd ed. Jing-heng Ma. 224p. (C). 1991. pap. text ed. 25.00 (0-89264-102-9) Ctr Chinese Studies.

Strange Fruit. Lillian Smith. 1994. lib. bdg. 24.95 (1-56849-420-3) Buccaneer Bks.

Strange Fruit. Lillian E. Smith. 1992. pap. 11.95 (0-15-685636-0, Harvest Bks) HarBrace.

Strange Genius: The Life of Ferdinand Vandeveer Hayden. Mike Foster. LC 94-66097. (Illus.). 460p. 1994. 29.95 (1-57098-004-7) R Rinehart.

***Strange Gourmets: Sophistication, Theory, & the Novel.** Joseph Litvak. LC 96-54812. 208p. 1997. text ed. 49.95 (0-8223-2007-X); pap. text ed. 16.95 (0-8223-2016-9) Duke.

Strange Gravity: Songs Physical & Metaphysical. Paul Petrie. LC 84-50796. (Illus.). 77p. (Orig.). 1984. 10.00 (0-930954-21-1) Tidal Pr.

Strange Gravity: Songs Physical & Metaphysical. Paul Petrie. LC 84-50796. (Illus.). 77p. (Orig.). 1984. pap. 5.00 (0-930954-22-X) Tidal Pr.

Strange Ground: Americans in Vietnam, 1945-1975. Harry Maurer. 656p. 1990. reprint ed. pap. 12.95 (0-380-70931-7) Avon.

Strange Heart: Poems. Jane O. Wayne. LC 96-8435. 1996. pap. 9.95 (1-884235-18-2) Helicon Nine Eds.

Strange Highways. Dean R. Koontz. 624p. 1996. mass mkt. 6.99 (0-446-60339-2, Warner Vision) Warner Bks.

Strange Highways. large type ed. Dean R. Koontz. 1995. 26.95 (1-56895-255-4, Compass) Wheeler Pub.

***Strange History of Buckingham Palace: People, Places & Legend.** Patricia Wright. LC 96-42548. (Illus.). 224p. 1996. 36.95 (0-7509-1001-1, Pub. by Sutton Pubng UK) Bks Intl VA.

Strange Holiday. large type ed. Clare B. Smith. (Romance Ser.). 352p. 1993. 25.99 (0-7089-2974-5) Ulverscroft.

Strange Illness: A Commedia Dell 'Arte. Rita Crump. 12p. 1995. pap. 6.00 (0-88734-346-5) Players Pr.

Strange Illusions: Strange Beliefs, Rituals & Ceremonies of Primitive Peoples. Lloyd K. Ulery. 96p. 1986. 6.95 (0-930984-05-6) Psychic Bks.

Strange Intimacy. Anne Mather. 1994. mass mkt. 2.99 (0-373-11697-7, 1-11697-9) Harlequin Bks.

***Strange Invaders, Bk. I.** Rodman Philbrick & Lynn Harnett. (Visitors Ser.). (J). (gr. 4-7). 1997. mass mkt. 3.99 (0-590-97213-8) Scholastic Inc.

Strange Journey. large type ed. Marjorie Harte. (Linford Romance Library). 288p. 1994. pap. 15.99 (0-7089-7525-9, Linford) Ulverscroft.

Strange Journey: The Vision Life of a Psychic Indian Woman. Louise Lone Dog. Ed. by Patricia Powell. LC 89-13484. (Illus.). 105p. 1990. reprint ed. pap. 8.95 (0-87961-207-X) Naturegraph.

Strange Journey Back. Paul McCusker. (Adventures in Odyssey Ser.: No. 1). (J). (gr. 4-7). 1991. pap. 5.99 (1-56179-101-6) Focus Family.

***Strange Journey of Byron & Cyros: Exploratory Guide.** Sandy Meyer. LC 96-90385. (Woods in the Round Ser.). (Illus.). 20p. (J). (ps-6). 1997. wbk. ed., pap. 4.75 (1-889928-01-1) Wood-in-the-Round Pub.

***Strange Journey of Byron & Cyrus, Incls. Parent-Teacher Exploratory Guide.** Sandy Meyer. LC 96-90385. (Woods-in-the-Round Ser.: Vol. 1). (Illus.). 48p. (J). (ps-6). 1997. lib. bdg. 17.95 (1-889928-00-3) Wood-in-the-Round Pub.

Strange Justice: The Selling of Clarence Thomas. Jane Mayer. 1994. 24.95 (0-395-63318-4) HM.

Strange Justice: The Selling of Clarence Thomas. Jane Mayer & Jill Abramson. LC 95-13311. 1995. pap. 12.95 (0-452-27499-0, Plume) NAL-Dutton.

***Strange Juxtaposition of Parts: Poems by Richard Pflum.** Richard Pflum. 80p. (Orig.). 1995. per. 8.95 (1-880649-33-0) Writ Ctr Pr.

Strange Kind of Loving. Sheila Mooney. 192p. 1990. pap. 11.95 (1-85371-076-8, Pub. by Poolbeg Pr IE) Dufour.

Strange Land. large type ed. Hammond Innes. 1969. 25.99 (0-85456-852-2) Ulverscroft.

Strange Land Songs. Etta M. Ladson. (Illus.). 146p. (YA). (gr. 7-12). 1992. text ed. 14.95 (0-9630574-0-5) Jewelgate.

Strange Lands. Michel Russell. 118p. 1986. 39.00 (0-7212-0756-1, Pub. by Regency Press UK) St Mut.

***Strange Landscape.** Christopher Frayling. Date not set. pap. 11.95 (0-14-026124-9) Penguin.

Strange Last Voyage of Donald Crowhurst. Ron Hall & Nicholas Tomalin. LC 95-766. 1995. pap. text ed. 15.95 (0-07-065084-5) Intl Marine.

Strange Liberalism of Alexis de Tocqueville. Roger Boesche. LC 86-29141. 288p. 1987. 39.95 (0-8014-1964-6) Cornell U Pr.

Strange Liberation: Tibetan Lives in Chinese Hands. David Patt. LC 92-44590. 228p. 1992. pap. 12.95 (1-55939-013-1) Snow Lion Pubns.

Strange Life of Ivan Osokin. P. D. Ouspensky. 1988. pap. 11.95 (0-14-019058-9, Penguin Bks) Viking Penguin.

Strange Loops. David Evett. (Cleveland Poets Ser.: No. 38). 63p. (Orig.). 1985. pap. 5.00 (0-914946-47-1) Cleveland St Univ Poetry Ctr.

Strange Loops. David Evett. (Orig.). 5.00 (0-317-01116-2) League Bks.

Strange Loyalties. William McIlvanney. 1993. pap. 9.95 (0-15-685644-1) HarBrace.

Strange Man. Amu Djoleto. (African Writers Ser.). 279p. (C). 1968. pap. 9.95 (0-435-90041-2, 90041) Heinemann.

Strange Manuscript Found in a Copper Cylinder. James De Mille. LC 74-15964. (Science Fiction Ser.). (Illus.). 291p. 1975. reprint ed. 23.95 (0-405-06285-0) Ayer.

Strange Market. Robert Kelly. LC 92-15230. 217p. (Orig.). 1992. 25.00 (0-87685-876-0); pap. 12.50 (0-87685-875-2) Black Sparrow.

Strange Market, signed ed. deluxe ed. Robert Kelly. LC 92-15230. 217p. (Orig.). 1992. 30.00 (0-87685-877-9) Black Sparrow.

Strange Masonic Stories. Alec Mellor. (Illus.). xii, 184p. 1985. pap. 11.95 (0-88053-082-0, M-313) Macoy Pub.

Strange Meat, Poems Nineteen Sixty-Eight to Nineteen Seventy-Four. Gloria Bosque. LC 74-23345. 1974. 2.00 (0-914134-03-5) Konocti Bks.

Strange Meeting. Susan Hill. LC 89-46187. 1992. pap. 10.95 (0-87923-830-5) Godine.

***Strange Memories.** Keene. (YA). 1997. mass mkt. 3.99 (0-671-56880-9) PB.

Strange Message in the Parchment. Carolyn Keene. (Nancy Drew Ser.: Vol. 54). 180p. (J). (gr. 4-7). 1976. 5.95 (0-448-09554-8, G&D) Putnam Pub Group.

Strange Multiplicity: Constitutionalism in an Age of Diversity. James Tully. (Seeley Lectures: Vol. 1). (Illus.). 296p. (C). 1995. text ed. 54.95 (0-521-47117-6); pap. text ed. 17.95 (0-521-47694-1) Cambridge U Pr.

Strange Mysteries from Around the World. Seymour Simon. LC 96-2693. (J). 1997. 16.00 (0-688-14636-8, Morrow Junior) Morrow.

Strange Mysteries from Around the World. Seymour Simon. (J). 1997. pap. 6.95 (0-688-14637-6, Morrow Junior) Morrow.

Strange Nature. (Curious Creatures Ser.). (Illus.). 48p. (J). (gr. 3-4). 1992. lib. bdg. 24.26 (0-8114-3157-6) Raintree Steck-V.

Strange Nature. Joyce Pope. (Curious Creatures Ser.). (J). (gr. 4-7). 1993. pap. 4.95 (0-8114-6259-5) Raintree Steck-V.

Strange Necessity: Essays. Rebecca West. (BCL1-PR English Literature Ser.). 380p. 1992. reprint ed. lib. bdg. 89.00 (0-7812-7062-6) Rprt Serv.

Strange Negro Stories of the Old Deep South. Harry D. Howell, Sr. LC 78-122722. (Short Story Index Reprint Ser.). 1977. 28.95 (0-8369-3555-1) Ayer.

Strange Neighbours: The Australia-Indonesia Relationship. Ed. by Desmond Ball & Helen Wilson. 288p. 1991. pap. 24.95 (0-04-442233-4, Pub. by Allen & Unwin Aust Pty AT) Paul & Co Pubs.

Strange Neutrality: Soviet - Japanese Relations During the Second World War, 1941-1945. George A. Lensen. LC 72-178091. (Illus.). 332p. 1972. 15.00 (0-910512-14-0) Diplomatic IN.

Strange New Gospels. Edgar J. Goodspeed. LC 70-156652. (Essay Index Reprint Ser.). 1977. reprint ed. 15.95 (0-8369-2364-2) Ayer.

Strange New Land: African Americans 1617-1776 see Young Oxford History of African Americans

Strange Night Writing of Jessamine Colter. Cynthia DeFelice. LC 88-4325. 56p. (YA). (gr. 5 up). 1988. 13.95 (0-02-726451-3, Mac Bks Young Read) S&S Childrens.

Strange Night Writings of Jessamine Colter. Cynthia C. Defelice. (J). 1996. pap. 3.99 (0-380-72663-7) Avon.

Strange Northwest: Weird Encounters in Alaska, British Columbia, Idaho, Oregon, & Washington. Chris Bader. 1995. pap. 11.95 (0-88839-359-8) Hancock House.

Strange Objects. Gary Crew. LC 92-30519. 224p. (J). (gr. 5-9). 1993. pap. 15.00 (0-671-79759-X, S&S Bks Young Read) S&S Childrens.

Strange Occupation. Georgiana Melrose. 128p. 1989. 30.00 (0-7223-2200-3, Pub. by A H S Ltd UK) St Mut.

Strange of Balcaskie: Strangus de Caledonia. 2nd ed. Ed. by John D. Mayer. (Extraneus Ser.: Vol. IV, Bk. IX). xxxvi, 542p. 1996. pap. 84.00 (0-9638665-5-9, B09BA) Arapacana Pr.

An Asterisk (*) at the beginning of an entry indicates that the title is appearing in BIP for the first time.

Strange of Blisland: Extraneus De Terra Felicitas. 2nd rev. ed. Ed. by John R. Mayer. LC 90-148997. (Extranus Ser.: Vol. IV, Bk. XI). xl, 708p. (C). 1995. pap. 84.00 (*0-9638665-6-7*) Arapacana Pr.

Strange of Eastern America: Extraneus De America Orientalis. 2nd rev. ed. Ed. by John R. Mayer. LC 90-148977. (Extraneus Ser.: Vol. I, Bk. V). (Illus.). xviii, 380p. (Orig.). (C). 1993. pap. 36.00 (*0-9638665-0-8*) Arapacana Pr.

Strange of the Carolinas: Extraneus de Carolina. 2nd ed. Ed. by John R. Mayer. (Extraneus Ser.: Vol. IV, Bk. XII). (Illus.). xxvi, 548p. (C). 1993. pap. 58.00 (*0-9638665-2-4*) Arapacana Pr.

Strange Orbit. Margaret Simpson. LC 94-43347. 221p. 1995. 12.50 (*0-7914-2629-7*) State U NY Pr.

Strange Orbit. Margaret Simpson. LC 94-43347. 221p. 1995. pap. 9.95 (*0-7914-2630-0*) State U NY Pr.

Strange Orchid. H. G. Wells. 1994. lib. bdg. 18.95 incl. audio (*1-883049-27-X*) Commuters Lib.

Strange Orchid. H. G. Wells. (H. G. Wells Ser.). 1994. 16. 95 incl. audio (*1-883049-08-3*) Commuters Lib.

Strange Orchid. rev. ed. H. G. Wells. (Read-Along Radio Dramas Ser.). (J). (gr. 6-10). 1983. reprint ed. boxed 35. 00 (*1-878298-12-7*) Balance Pub.

Strange Ordeal of Edwin Banquo & Other Stories. Ruth Jespersen. 85p. (Orig.). 1986. pap. 6.95 (*0-9617134-0-2*) Biblia Candida.

***Strange, Outlandish, Crude & Sometimes Funny Jokes.** Dean Livelsberger. LC 96-48097. 1997. pap. 9.95 (*1-56980-097-9*) Barricade Bks.

Strange Papers of Dr. Blayre. Douglas A. Menville. LC 76-14332. (Supernatural & Occult Fiction Ser.). 1976. reprint ed. lib. bdg. 23.95 (*0-405-08418-8*) Ayer.

Strange Parallel: Zebulun a Tribe of Israel. rev. ed. Helene Koppejan. LC 83-73689. (Illus.). 96p. 1984. reprint ed. pap. 4.00 (*0-934666-13-X*) Artisan Sales.

Strange Partnership of George Alexander McGuire & Marcus Garvey. Bishop K. Pruter. LC 86-17628. 50p. 1986. pap. 13.00 (*0-912134-08-9*); lib. bdg. 23.00 (*0-89370-529-2*) Borgo Pr.

Strange People with Books: A Twenty-Year Followup of Students from a Summer Enrichment Program for Low-Income Rural Black Youth from South Carolina. Nancy Gall-Clayton. Ed. by Vernell Lee. (Illus.). 95p. (Orig.). (C). 1990. pap. text ed. 9.00 (*0-9627064-0-X*) Advocado Pr.

Strange Phenomena in Convex & Discrete Geometry. C. Zong & J. J. Dudziak. LC 96-11737. (Universitext Ser.). (Illus.). 160p. 1996. pap. 29.00 (*0-387-94734-5*) Spr-Verlag.

Strange Philadelphia: Stories from the City of Brotherly Love. Lou Harry. LC 95-4796. 192p. (Orig.). (C). 1995. pap. 9.95 (*1-56639-375-2*) Temple U Pr.

Strange Piece of Paper. (Junior African Writers Ser.). (Illus.). 128p. (J). (gr. 4-5). 1995. pap. 3.98 (*0-7910-3022-9*) Chelsea Hse.

Strange Pilgrims. Gabriel Garcia Marquez. Tr. by Edith Grossman. 1993. 21.00 (*0-679-42566-7*) Knopf.

Strange Pilgrims. Gabriel Garcia Marquez. 208p. 1994. pap. 10.95 (*0-14-023940-5*, Penguin Bks) Viking Penguin.

***Strange Place to Sing.** Standard Publishing Staff. (Happy Day Coloring Bks.). 12p. (J). 1996. pap. 0.99 (*0-7847-0433-3*, 22203) Standard Pub.

Strange Place to Sing. Terry Whalin. LC 94-7171. (Happy Day Bks.). (J). (ps). 1994. 1.99 (*0-7847-0273-X*, 04223) Standard Pub.

Strange Planet: A Sourcebook of Unusual Geological Facts, Vol. E1. William R. Corliss. LC 74-26226. (Illus.). 283p. 1975. ring bd. 9.95 (*0-9600712-3-7*) Sourcebook.

Strange Plants. J. Cooper. (Earth's Garden Ser.). (J). 1991. 8.95 (*0-86592-625-5*) Rourke Enter.

Strange Plays. Francesco Bivona. 80p. (Orig.). 1993. pap. 10.00 (*0-88734-808-4*) Players Pr.

Strange Power of Pets. Brad Steiger & Sherry H. Steiger. 256p. (Orig.). 1993. mass mkt. 4.99 (*0-425-13712-0*) Berkley Pub.

Strange Power of Speech: Wordsworth, Coleridge, & Literary Possession. Susan Eilenberg. 296p. 1992. 49.95 (*0-19-506856-4*) OUP.

Strange Proposal, Vol. 31. Grace L. Hill. (Grace Livingston Hill Ser.: Vol. 31). 320p. 1994. pap. 4.99 (*0-8423-5944-3*) Tyndale.

Strange Relation. Daniel Hall. LC 95-43875. (Penguin Poets Ser.). 69p. 1996. pap. 13.95 (*0-14-058771-3*, Penguin Bks) Viking Penguin.

***Strange Reward for a Friend.** P. H. McMillan. 596p. (Orig.). 1997. mass mkt. 5.99 (*1-55237-003-8*, Pub. by Comnwlth Pub CN) Partners Pubs Grp.

Strange Ritual. Photos by David Byrne. LC 94-39514. (Illus.). 176p. 1995. 24.95 (*0-8118-1046-1*) Chronicle Bks.

Strange Road. Leland W. Starkey. 300p. (Orig.). 1994. pap. write for info. (*1-885591-12-8*) Morris Pubng.

Strange Routine. Tony Flynn. 56p. 8000. pap. 10.95 (*0-906427-20-7*, Pub. by Bloodaxe Bks UK) Dufour.

***Strange Sad War Revolving: Walt Whitman, Reconstruction, & the Emergence of Black Citizenship.** Luke Mancuso. (ENG Ser.). x, 160p. 1997. 55.00 (*1-57113-125-6*) Camden Hse.

"Strange Sapience" The Creative Imagination of D. H. Lawrence. Daniel Dervin. LC 84-2681. (Illus.). 256p. 1984. lib. bdg. 30.00 (*0-87023-455-2*) U of Mass Pr.

Strange Schemes of Randolph Mason. Melville D. Post. 15. 95 (*0-8488-1451-7*) Amereon Ltd.

Strange Schemes of Randolph Mason. Melville D. Post. LC 75-32776. (Literature of Mystery & Detection Ser.). 1976. reprint ed. 24.95 (*0-405-07895-1*) Ayer.

Strange Schemes of Randolph Mason. Melville D. Post. 280p. 1980. reprint ed. lib. bdg. 14.25 (*0-89968-200-6*, Lghtyr Pr) Buccaneer Bks.

Strange Science: Outer Space. Querida L. Pearce. 64p. (Orig.). 1994. pap. 3.50 (*0-8125-2364-4*) Tor Bks.

Strange Science: Planet Earth. Querida L. Pearce. 64p. (Orig.). (YA). 1993. pap. 3.50 (*0-8125-2365-2*) Tor Bks.

Strange Scottish Stories. (Ghost Ser.). (Illus.). 144p. 1993. pap. 7.95 (*0-7117-0530-5*) Seven Hills Bk.

Strange Scriptures That Perplex the Western Mind. Barbara M. Bowen. 1943. pap. 7.00 (*0-8028-1511-1*) Eerdmans.

Strange Seas & Shores. Avram Davidson. 1993. reprint ed. lib. bdg. 18.95 (*0-89968-337-1*, Lghtyr Pr) Buccaneer Bks.

Strange Seas of Thought: Studies in William Wordsworth's Philosophy of Man & Nature. Newton P. Stallknecht. LC 77-22222. 290p. 1977. reprint ed. text ed. 35.00 (*0-8371-9774-0*, STSS, Greenwood Pr) Greenwood.

Strange Sensation. Higginson. 1996. 29.95 (*0-226-33330-2*) U Ch Pr.

Strange Shadows: The Uncollected Fiction & Essays of Clark Ashton Smith. Ed. by Steve Behrends et al. LC 88-24632. (Contributions to the Study of Science Fiction & Fantasy Ser.: No. 36). 295p. 1989. text ed. 55.00 (*0-313-26611-5*, BEQ) Greenwood.

Strange Shadows of Love. large type ed. Peggy Gaddis. (General Ser.). 272p. 1993. 25.99 (*0-7089-2804-8*) Ulverscroft.

Strange Silence: Emergence of Democracy in Nicaragua. Stephen Schwartz. LC 91-39299. 175p. 1992. 19.95 (*1-55815-071-4*) ICS Pr.

Strange Sins. Robert Rand. 1995. 22.00 (*0-671-78689-X*) S&S Trade.

***Strange Soldiers.** Edmond De Rubeis. 224p. (Orig.). 1997. mass mkt. 4.99 (*1-55197-800-8*, Pub. by Comnwlth Pub CN) Partners Pubs Grp.

Strange Stains & Mysterious Smells: Based on the Cottington Journal Faery Research. Terry Jones. LC 96-8891. (Illus.). 1996. 23.00 (*0-684-83206-2*) S&S Trade.

Strange Stories. Douglas A. Menville. LC 75-46255. (Supernatural & Occult Fiction Ser.). 1976. reprint ed. lib. bdg. 60.95 (*0-405-08114-6*) Ayer.

Strange Stories, Amazing Facts: Stories that are Bizarre, Unusual, Odd, Astonishing, & Often Incredible. Reader's Digest Editors. LC 76-2966. (Illus.). 608p. 1976. 25.95 (*0-89577-028-8*) RD Assn.

Strange Stories, Amazing Facts of America's Past. Reader's Digest Editors. LC 88-11515. (Illus.). 416p. 1989. 32.95 (*0-89577-307-4*, Random) RD Assn.

Strange Stories from a Chinese Studio. rev. ed. Linda Hsia & Roger Yue. 1977. 10.95 (*0-88710-114-3*); audio 17.95 (*0-88710-115-1*) Yale Far Eastern Pubns.

Strange Stories from History. George C. Eggleston. (Notable American Authors Ser.). 1992. reprint ed. lib. bdg. 75.00 (*0-7812-2781-X*) Rprt Serv.

Strange Stories of Alaska & the Yukon. Ed Ferrell. (Illus.). 160p. (Orig.). 1996. pap. 13.95 (*0-945397-51-8*) Epicenter Pr.

Strange Stories of the Supernatural. (J). (gr. 4-7). 1993. pap. 2.95 (*0-89375-403-X*) Troll Communs.

Strange Story. Edward B. Lytton. 499p. 1971. reprint ed. spiral bd. 16.50 (*0-7873-1094-8*) Hlth Research.

Strange Story & the Haunted & the Haunters: Or the House & the Brain. Edward B. Lytton. 500p. 1992. reprint ed. pap. text ed. 35.00 (*1-56459-000-3*) Kessinger Pub.

Strange Story of Ahrinziman. 2nd ed. Anita Silvani. 284p. 1968. reprint ed. spiral bd. 13.50 (*0-7873-0793-9*) Hlth Research.

Strange Story of the Quantum. Banesh Hoffmann. 1959. pap. text ed. 7.95 (*0-486-20518-5*) Dover.

Strange Survivals: Some Chapters in the History of Man. Sabine Baring-Gould. 1972. 59.95 (*0-8490-1142-6*) Gordon Pr.

Strange Tactics of Extremism. Harry A. Overstreet & Bonaro W. Overstreet. 1964. 5.95 (*0-393-05268-0*) Norton.

Strange Tactics of Extremism. Harry A. Overstreet & Bonaro W. Overstreet. (C). 1965. pap. text ed. 4.95 (*0-393-09749-8*) Norton.

Strange Tales. Mildred Sproxton. 1987. 35.00 (*0-7223-2131-7*, Pub. by A H S Ltd UK) St Mut.

Strange Tales from Ancient China. Pu Sung-Ling. 144p. 1987. pap. 9.95 (*9971-4-9064-1*) Heian Intl.

Strange Tales from Make-Do Studio. Songling Pu. Tr. by Denis C. Mair & Victor H. Mair from CHI. 446p. (Orig.). 1989. pap. 9.95 (*0-8351-2256-5*) China Bks.

Strange Tales from Old Quabbin. J. R. Greene. (Illus.). 136p. (Orig.). 1993. pap. 9.95 (*1-884132-00-6*) J R Greene.

Strange Tales from Strange Lands: Stories by Zheng Wanlong. Intro. by Kam Louie. (Cornell East Asia Ser.: No. 66). 147p. (Orig.). (C). 1993. 18.00 (*0-939657-85-6*); pap. 12.00 (*0-939657-66-X*) Cornell East Asia Pgm.

Strange Tales from the Nile Empire. (Torg Ser.). 352p. 4.95 (*0-87431-343-0*, 20604) West End Games.

Strange Texts but Grand Truths. Clarence E. Macartney. 192p. 1994. pap. 9.99 (*0-8254-3272-3*) Kregel.

Strange Things: The Malevolent North in Canadian Literature. Margaret Atwood. (Clarendon Lectures in Economics). 160p. 1996. 25.00 (*0-19-811976-3*) OUP.

Strange Things & Stranger Places. Ramsey Campbell. 256p. 1994. pap. 4.99 (*0-8125-2479-9*) Tor Bks.

Strange Things Sometimes Still Happen: Fairy Tales from Around the World. Ed. by Angela Carter. (Illus.). 233p. 1994. pap. 13.95 (*0-571-19838-4*) Faber & Faber.

Strange to Relate. Allan Barham. 191p. 8400. 19.95 (*0-86140-186-7*, Pub. by Colin Smythe Ltd UK) Dufour.

Strange to Say. Edith Harrison. (American Autobiography Ser.). 188p. 1995. reprint ed. lib. bdg. 69.00 (*0-7812-8552-6*) Rprt Serv.

Strange Traffic: Stories. Irene Dische. LC 95-7635. 243p. 1995. 22.50 (*0-8050-4172-9*) H Holt & Co.

***Strange Traffic: Stories.** Irene Dische. 1997. pap. text ed. 12.00 (*0-8050-4173-7*, Owl) H Holt & Co.

Strange Triangle. large type ed. Florence Stuart. (Linford Romance Library). 272p. 1993. pap. 15.99 (*0-7089-7415-5*, Linford) Ulverscroft.

Strange True Stories of Louisiana. George W. Cable. LC 78-116944. (Short Story Index Reprint Ser.). 1977. 27. 95 (*0-8369-3446-6*) Ayer.

Strange True Stories of Louisiana. George W. Cable. LC 93-41973. 368p. 1994. pap. 4.95 (*1-56554-038-7*) Pelican.

Strange True Stories of Louisiana see Collected Works of George W. Cable

Strange Vagabond of God: The Story of John Bradburne. John Dove. 302p. 1990. pap. 12.95 (*1-85371-082-2*, Pub. by Poolbeg Pr IE) Dufour.

Strange Valentine. Meredith. 168p. pap. 5.99 (*1-886820-00-7*) Meredith WA.

***Strange Vanishings: Unexplained Disappearances.** Colin Wilson. (Strange but True Ser.). 1997. pap. text ed. 5.95 (*0-8069-0585-9*) Sterling.

Strange Virtues: Ethics in Multicultural Perspective. Bernard T. Adeney. 281p. (Orig.). 1995. pap. 19.99 (*0-8308-1855-3*, 1855, Pub. by IVP UK) InterVarsity.

Strange Visitation. Marie Corelli. 190p. 1996. pap. 17.95 (*1-56459-783-0*) Kessinger Pub.

Strange Visitation. Marie Corelli. 188p. 1970. reprint ed. spiral bd. 12.50 (*0-7873-0214-7*) Hlth Research.

Strange Visitation of Josiah McNason: A Christmas Ghost Story. Douglas A. Menville. LC 75-46262. 1976. reprint ed. lib. bdg. 17.95 (*0-405-08120-0*) Ayer.

Strange Visitor - Una Extrana Visita. Alma F. Ada. (Libros para Contar Ser.). (Illus.). 26p. (Orig.). (J). (gr. k-2). 1989. English ed. 3.95 (*0-88272-802-4*); Spanish Ed. 3.95 (*0-88272-793-1*) Santillana.

Strange Visitors: A Clairvoyant. 249p. 1975. reprint ed. spiral bd. 12.00 (*0-7873-0009-8*) Hlth Research.

Strange Voyage of the Malayan Princess. Frank F. Farrar. (Illus.). (Orig.). 1995. pap. write for info. (*0-9637291-0-1*) Sextant Pr.

Strange Ways & Sweet Dreams: Afro-American Folklore from the Hampton Institute. Donald J. Waters. 1983. lib. bdg. 52.00 (*0-8161-9022-4*, Univ Bks) Macmillan.

Strange Weather: Culture, Science & Technology in the Age of Limits. Andrew Ross. LC 91-22782. 240p. (C). 1991. pap. text ed. 18.00 (*0-86091-567-0*, A6401, Pub. by Vrso UK) Norton.

Strange Witness. large type ed. Day Keene. (Linford Mystery Library). 1991. pap. 15.99 (*0-7089-7078-8*) Ulverscroft.

***Strange Woman: Power & Sex in the Bible.** Gail Streete. LC 97-23140. 1997. pap. text ed. 19.00 (*0-664-25622-8*) Westminster John Knox.

Strange Women: Essays on Art & Gender. Ed. by Jeanette Hoorn. 192p. 1994. pap. 29.95 (*0-522-84567-3*, Pub. by Melbourne Univ Pr AT) Paul & Co Pubs.

Strange World. Frank Edwards. 1963. 4.95 (*0-8184-0087-0*) Carol Pub Group.

Strange World. Frank Edwards. 288p. 1992. pap. 4.50 (*0-8216-2515-2*, Univ Books) Carol Pub Group.

Strange World. Frank Edwards. 208p. 1985. reprint ed. pap. 6.95 (*0-8065-0978-3*, Citadel Pr) Carol Pub Group.

***Strange World: Baboon.** Melvin Berger. (J). 1997. mass mkt. 2.99 (*0-590-93779-0*) Scholastic Inc.

***Strange World: Frogs.** Melvin Berger. (J). 1997. mass mkt. 2.99 (*0-590-93778-2*) Scholastic Inc.

Strange World of Deep-Sea Vents. R. V. Fodor. LC 89-71442. (Illus.). 64p. (YA). (gr. 6 up). 1991. lib. bdg. 15. 95 (*0-89490-249-0*) Enslow Pubs.

Strange World of Frank Edwards. Frank Edwards. Ed. by Rory Stuart. 1977. 8.95 (*0-8184-0252-0*) Carol Pub Group.

Strange World of Frank Edwards. Frank Edwards. 1987. 19.85 (*0-8065-1071-4*, Citadel Pr) Carol Pub Group.

Strange World of Prison. Lou Torok. LC 72-88761. 1973. 6.50 (*0-672-51711-6*, Bobbs) Macmillan.

Strange Writing: Anomaly Accounts in Early Medieval China. Robert F. Campany. LC 94-45736. (SUNY Series in Chinese Philosophy & Culture). 524p. (C). 1996. text ed. 74.50 (*0-7914-2659-9*); pap. text ed. 24.95 (*0-7914-2660-2*) State U NY Pr.

Strangehold on Africa. Rene Dumont & Marie-France Mottin. 272p. 1984. 56.00 (*0-389-20466-8*, 08027) B&N Imports.

Strangely Familiar: Narratives of Architecture in the City. Ed. by Iain Borden et al. LC 95-50629. 96p. 1996. pap. 17.00 (*0-415-14418-3*) Routledge.

Strangeness & Quark Matter. G. Vassiliadis et al. 350p. 1995. text ed. 99.00 (*981-02-2269-6*) World Scientific Pub.

Strangeness in Hadronic Matter, Proceedings: Conference on Strangeness in Hadronic Matter, 1995, Tucson, AZ. Ed. by Johann Rafelski. LC 95-77477. (AIP Conference Proceedings Ser.: Vol. 340). 500p. 1995. 135.00 (*1-56396-489-9*) Am Inst Physics.

Strangeness in Nuclei. S. T. Kistryn & O. W. Schult. 420p. 1993. text ed. 109.00 (*981-02-1267-4*) World Scientific Pub.

Strangeness of God. Ed. by Elizabeth Templeton. (C). 1993. pap. text ed. 24.00 (*0-85305-296-4*, Pub. by J Arthur Ltd UK) St Mut.

Stranger. Albert Camus. LC 92-54290. 1993. 15.00 (*0-679-42026-6*, Everymans Lib) Knopf.

Stranger. Albert Camus. Tr. by Joseph Laredo. LC 83-48885. 1988. 24.00 (*0-394-53305-4*) Knopf.

Stranger. Albert Camus. 20.95 (*0-89190-220-1*) Amereon Ltd.

Stranger. Albert Camus. (International Ser.). 144p. 1989. pap. 9.00 (*0-679-72020-0*, Vin) Random.

Stranger. Albert Camus. (Book Notes Ser.). 1985. pap. 2.50 (*0-8120-3543-7*) Barron.

Stranger. Caroline B. Cooney. 176p. (YA). (gr. 7-9). 1993. pap. 3.50 (*0-590-45680-6*) Scholastic Inc.

***Stranger.** Portia Da Costa. (Orig.). 1997. mass mkt. 5.95 (*0-352-33211-5*, Pub. by Black Lace UK) London Brdge.

***Stranger.** Eric J. Fullilove. 1997. mass mkt. 5.99 (*0-553-57576-7*, Spectra) Bantam.

***Stranger.** Ed. by Michele B. Slung. 1997. write for info. (*0-06-105245-0*, HarperPrism) HarpC.

Stranger. Chris Van Allsburg. LC 86-15235. (Illus.). 32p. (J). (gr. 2-4). 1986. 17.95 (*0-395-42331-7*) HM.

Stranger. Albert Camus. 156p. 1988. reprint ed. lib. bdg. 24.95 (*0-89966-623-X*) Buccaneer Bks.

***Stranger, Vol. 7.** K. A. Applegate. (Animorphs Ser.). 1997. pap. 3.99 (*0-590-99726-2*) Scholastic Inc.

Stranger among Friends. David Mixner. 320p. 1996. 22.95 (*0-553-10073-4*) Bantam.

***Stranger Among Friends.** David Mixner. 384p. 1997. pap. 13.95 (*0-553-37554-7*) Bantam.

Stranger & Alone. J. Saunders Redding. (Northeastern Library of Black Literature). 320p. 1989. reprint ed. text ed. 42.50 (*1-55553-055-9*); reprint ed. pap. text ed. 15.95 (*1-55553-053-2*) NE U Pr.

Stranger & Friend. Hortense Powdermaker. 1967. pap. 11. 95 (*0-393-00410-4*) Norton.

Stranger at Green Knowe. Lucy M. Boston. LC 78-71150. (Illus.). 208p. (J). (gr. 5-9). 1989. pap. 6.00 (*0-15-281755-7*, Odyssey) HarBrace.

Stranger at Stonewycke. Michael Phillips. (Stonewycke Legacy Ser.). 1995. mass mkt. 6.99 (*1-55661-581-7*) Bethany Hse.

Stranger at Stonewycke. Mike Phillips & Judith Pella. LC 87-6605. (Stonewycke Legacy Ser.). 352p. (Orig.). 1987. pap. 9.99 (*0-87123-900-0*) Bethany Hse.

Stranger at the Gate. Mel White. 1994. 23.00 (*0-671-88407-7*) S&S Trade.

Stranger at the Gate: To Be Gay & Christian in America. Mel White. (Illus.). 336p. 1995. pap. 12.95 (*0-452-27381-1*, Plume) NAL-Dutton.

Stranger at the Wedding. Barbara Hambly. 1994. mass mkt. 5.99 (*0-345-38097-5*, Del Rey) Ballantine.

***Stranger at the Window.** Vivien Alcock. LC 97-14195. (J). 1998. write for info. (*0-395-81661-0*) HM.

Stranger Beside Me. Ann Rule. (Illus.). 432p. 1981. pap. 6.99 (*0-451-16493-8*, Sig) NAL-Dutton.

Stranger Beside Me: Short Stories from Kashmir. Neerga Mattoo. (C). pap. 8.50 (*81-86112-14-6*, Pub. by UBS Pubs Dist II) S Asia.

***Stranger by Her Side.** Sizemore. 1997. mass mkt. 3.99 (*0-373-07826-9*) Harlequin Bks.

Stranger by Night. Jeff Gelb. (Hot Blood Ser.). 1995. mass mkt. 5.99 (*0-671-53754-7*) PB.

Stranger by the Lake. Jennifer Wilde. 224p. 1993. lib. bdg. 20.00 (*0-7278-4526-8*) Severn Hse.

Stranger by the River. Paul Twitchell. 198p. 1998. pap. 11. 00 (*1-57043-038-1*) ECKANKAR.

Stranger Calls Me Home. Deborah Savage. 240p. (J). (gr. 5-9). 1992. 14.95 (*0-395-59424-3*) HM.

Stranger Came Ashore. Mollie Hunter. LC 75-10814. 176p. (J). (gr. 5-8). 1975. lib. bdg. 14.89 (*0-06-022652-8*) HarpC Child Bks.

Stranger Came Ashore. Mollie Hunter. LC 75-10814. (Trophy Bk.). 176p. (J). (gr. 4-8). 1977. pap. 4.50 (*0-06-440082-4*, Trophy) HarpC Child Bks.

Stranger Came By. large type ed. Alanna Knight. 1989. 25. 99 (*0-7089-2090-X*) Ulverscroft.

Stranger Danger. Ellen Jackson. 24p. 1991. pap. 5.98 (*0-88290-426-4*) Horizon Utah.

***Stranger Danger: What to Tell Your Child.** Carol S. Cope. LC 96-53644. 128p. (Orig.). 1997. pap. 7.95 (*0-8362-2758-1*, Cader Bks) Andrews & McMeel.

Stranger for Christmas. Carol L. Pearson. 1994. pap. 3.50 (*1-57514-176-0*, 11086) Encore Perform Pub.

Stranger for Christmas. Carol L. Pearson. LC 96-19004. 1996. 13.95 (*0-312-14680-9*) St Martin.

***Stranger for Christmas.** large type ed. Carol L. Pearson. LC 96-27255. 1996. 20.95 (*0-7838-1914-5*, GK Hall) Thorndike Pr.

Stranger from Arizona. Norman A. Fox. 176p. 1987. pap. 2.75 (*0-380-70296-7*) Avon.

Stranger from Home. Elizabeth L. Simpson. LC 78-59770. (Illus.). 174p. (Orig.). 1979. pap. 8.00 (*0-912292-51-2*) Smith.

Stranger from Nowhere. Jim Miller. Ed. by Doug Grad. (Ex-Rangers Ser.: No. 10). 224p. (Orig.). 1993. mass mkt. 3.99 (*0-671-74828-9*) PB.

Stranger from Shanghai. large type ed. Rosaline Redwood. (Linford Mystery Library). 384p. 1992. pap. 15.99 (*0-7089-7218-7*, Trailtree Bookshop) Ulverscroft.

Stranger from the Past. Penny Jordan. (Presents Plus Ser.). 1993. mass mkt. 2.99 (*0-373-11599-7*, 1-11599-7) Harlequin Bks.

Stranger from the Sea. Winston Graham. 22.95 (*0-8488-1017-1*) Amereon Ltd.

Stranger from the Sea. large type ed. Ivy Preston. (Linford Romance Library). 240p. 1992. pap. 15.99 (*0-7089-7294-2*, Trailtree Bookshop) Ulverscroft.

Stranger from the Tonto. Zane Grey. 272p. 1992. mass mkt. 3.99 (*0-06-100174-0*, Harp PBks) HarpC.

Stranger Here. Thelma H. Wyss. LC 92-15307. 144p. (YA). (gr. 7 up). 1993. lib. bdg. 13.89 (*0-06-021439-2*) HarpC Child Bks.

Stranger Here. Thelma H. Wyss. LC 92-15307. (Trophy Bk.). 144p. (YA). (gr. 7 up). 1996. pap. 4.50 (*0-06-447098-9*, Trophy) HarpC Child Bks.

***Stranger Here Myself.** Ed. by Kim H. Kowalke & Horst Edler. 384p. (GER.). 1993. write for info. (*3-487-09722-2*) G Olms Pubs.

S

Stranger Here, Myself. Thelma C. Nason. Ed. by Constance Hunting. 1980. pap. 3.50 (0-913006-11-4) Puckerbrush.

*__Stranger I Left Behind.__ George E. Lyon. LC 96-31631. (J). 1997. pap. 3.95 (0-8167-4026-7) Troll Communs.

Stranger in a Strange Land. Robert A. Heinlein. 416p. 1987. mass mkt. 6.99 (0-441-79034-8) Ace Bks.

Stranger in a Strange Land. Robert A. Heinlein. 1991. pap. 15.00 (0-441-78838-6) Ace Bks.

Stranger in a Strange Land. Robert A. Heinlein. 1976. 16.95 (0-8488-0522-4) Amereon Ltd.

Stranger in a Strange Land. Leonora R. Scholte. 120p. (Orig.). 1987. pap. 6.90 (0-921100-01-9) Inhtce Pubns.

Stranger in a Strange Land. Robert A. Heinlein. 1994. reprint ed. lib. bdg. 39.95 (1-56849-290-1) Buccaneer Bks.

Stranger in Big Sur. Lillian B. Ross. 282p. 1985. pap. 9.95 (0-88496-233-4) Coast Pub.

Stranger in Her Arms. Elizabeth Sites. (Romance Ser.). 1995. mass mkt. 2.99 (0-373-19094-8, 1-19094-1) Silhouette.

*__Stranger in Her Bed.__ Bonnie Gardner. (Intimate Moments Ser.: No. 798). 1997. mass mkt. 3.99 (0-373-07798-X, 1-07798-1) Silhouette.

Stranger in Her House. Sharon Chmielarz. Ed. by Patrick McKinnon. 34p. (Orig.). 1994. pap. 3.95 (0-9641986-4-9) Poetry Harbor.

Stranger in Her Native Land: Alice Fletcher & the American Indians. Joan Mark. LC 87-30201. (Women in the West Ser.). (Illus.). xx, 428p. 1988. pap. 16.95 (0-8032-8156-0, Bison Books); text ed. 40.00 (0-8032-3128-8) U of Nebr Pr.

*__Stranger in Medieval Society.__ F. R. Akehurst & Stephanie C. Van D'Elden. LC 97-21249. (Medieval Cultures Ser.). 1998. write for info. (0-8166-3031-3); pap. write for info. (0-8166-3032-1) U of Minn Pr.

Stranger in My Arms (Secret Fantasies) Madeline Harper. 1995. mass mkt. 3.25 (0-373-25654-X) Harlequin Bks.

Stranger in My Grave. Margaret Millar. 308p. 1990. reprint ed. pap. 7.95 (1-55882-066-3) Intl Polygonics.

Stranger in My Heart. large type ed. Sarah Devon. 1990. 25.99 (0-7089-2168-X) Ulverscroft.

Stranger in My House. Elfman. Date not set. write for info. (0-395-32202-2) HM.

Stranger in New Mexico: A Doctor's Journey, 1951-1986. J. Peter Voute. LC 86-27268. (Historical Society of New Mexico Ser.). 235p. reprint ed. pap. 67.00 (0-7837-5853-7, 2045572) Bks Demand.

Stranger in Our Midst: Images of the Jew in Polish Literature. Ed. by Harold B. Segel. (Illus.). 432p. 1996. 49.50 (0-8014-2865-3); pap. 17.95 (0-8014-8104-X) Cornell U Pr.

Stranger in Paradise. Marilyn Kaye. 224p. (Orig.). (YA). (gr. 5 up). 1996. pap. 3.95 (0-8167-3973-0) Troll Communs.

Stranger in Paradise. Amanda Stevens. (Intrigue Ser.). 1996. mass mkt. 3.75 (0-373-22373-0, 1-22373-4) Harlequin Bks.

*__Stranger in Right Field: A Peach Street Mudders Story.__ LC 96-49014. (J). 1997. 13.95 (0-316-14111-9) Little.

Stranger in Savannah. Eugenia Price. 1990. pap. 6.99 (0-515-10344-6) Jove Pubns.

Stranger in Texas. Lass Small. (Desire Ser.). 1996. mass mkt. 3.50 (0-373-05994-9, 1-05994-8) Silhouette.

Stranger in the Family. Claire Burch. LC 76-173211. 1972. 6.95 (0-672-51566-0, Bobbs) Macmillan.

Stranger in the Family. Steven W. Naifeh. 1996. pap. 6.99 (0-451-40622-2, Onyx) NAL-Dutton.

Stranger in the Family: (The Family Way) Patricia McLinn. (Special Edition Ser.). 1995. pap. 3.75 (0-373-09959-2, 1-09959-7) Silhouette.

Stranger in the Family: A Guide to Living with the Emotionally Disturbed. Claire Burch. 214p. Date not set. 34.95 (0-916147-70-3); pap. 19.95 (0-916147-25-8) Regent Pr.

Stranger in the Family: Culture, Families & Therapy. Di Nicola. LC 96-40310. 384p. 1997. 45.00 (0-393-70228-6) Norton.

Stranger in the Forest: On Foot Across Borneo. Eric Hansen. (Illus.). 1989. pap. 8.95 (0-14-011726-1, Penguin Bks) Viking Penguin.

Stranger in the Hague: The Letters of Queen Sophie of the Netherlands to Lady Malet, 1842-1877. Ed. by Sidney W. Jackman & Hella Haasse. LC 88-26749. 338p. 1989. text ed. 69.95 (0-8223-0875-4) Duke.

Stranger in the House. Gloria Murphy. 416p. 1995. pap. 5.99 (0-451-18586-2, Sig) NAL-Dutton.

Stranger in the House. Francine Pascal. (Sweet Valley High Thriller Ser.). 224p. (YA). (gr. 7-12). 1995. mass mkt. 4.50 (0-553-56711-X) Bantam.

Stranger in the House (Visible & Invisible) Willa J. Smith. 114p. (Orig.). 1993. pap. text ed. 14.00 (0-9636226-0-9) W J Smith.

Stranger in the Kingdom. Howard F. Mosher. 432p. 1990. pap. 11.95 (0-385-31263-6, Delta) Dell.

Stranger in the Land. large type ed. Helen Cannam. 1995. 25.99 (0-7505-0696-2, Pub. by Magna Print Bks UK) Ulverscroft.

*__Stranger in the Midst: A Memoir of Spiritual Discovery.__ Nan Fink. 256p. 1997. 23.00 (0-465-08200-9) Basic.

Stranger in the Mirror. Lynn Beach. Ed. by Patricia MacDonald. (Phanton Valley Ser.: No. 4). 128p. (Orig.). 1992. pap. 2.99 (0-671-75922-1, Minstrel Bks) PB.

Stranger in the Mirror. JoAnn Sands. 1993. 17.95 (0-8034-8996-X) Bouregy.

Stranger in the Mirror. Allen Say. LC 95-2296. (Illus.). (J). 1995. 16.95 (0-395-61590-9) HM.

Stranger in the Mirror. Sidney Sheldon. 320p. 1988. mass mkt. 6.99 (0-446-35657-3) Warner Bks.

Stranger in the Mirror. Sidney Sheldon. (Sheldon Continuity Ser.). 300p. 1994. 12.95 (1-56865-093-0, GuildAmerica) Dbldy Direct.

Stranger in the Mist. Lee Karr. 1993. mass mkt. 3.50 (0-373-27003-8, 5-27003-8) Silhouette.

Stranger in the Mist. Paul McCusker. (Time Twists Ser.: No. 2). 144p. (YA). 1996. pap. text ed. 5.99 (0-7459-3612-1) Lion USA.

Stranger in the Night. Roseanne Williams. (Temptation Ser.). 1996. mass mkt. 3.50 (0-373-25688-4, 1-25688-2) Harlequin Bks.

Stranger in the Shadows. Carolyn Keene. Ed. by Anne Greenberg. (Nancy Drew Ser.: No. 103). 160p. (Orig.). (J). (gr. 3-6). 1991. pap. 3.99 (0-671-73049-5, Minstrel Bks) PB.

Stranger in the Valley of Kings: The Idenfification of Yuya As the Patriarch Joseph. Ahmed Osman. (Illus.). 190p. (Orig.). 1994. pap. 11.00 (0-586-08784-2, IntlDept) HarpC.

Stranger in the Village. large type ed. Margaret Lovell. (Linford Romance Library). 272p. 1994. pap. 15.99 (0-7089-7526-7, Linford) Ulverscroft.

Stranger in the Wind. Jan Renfrow. 28p. (Orig.). 1983. pap. 6.00 (0-9613072-0-X) Jan Renfrow.

Stranger in Their Midst. Pierre L. Van den Berghe. LC 89-14732. (Illus.). 300p. 1989. 24.95 (0-87081-202-5) Univ Pr Colo.

Stranger in This Town. 112p. 1992. otabind 19.95 (0-7935-1554-8, 00694836) H Leonard.

Stranger in This World. Kevin Canty. LC 95-6780. 1995. pap. 10.00 (0-679-76394-5, Vin) Random.

Stranger in Tibet: The Adventures of a Wandering Zen Monk. Scott Berry. (Illus.). 324p. 1990. pap. 6.95 (0-87011-858-7) Kodansha.

Stranger in Tomorrow's Land. Doreen Kirban & Diane Kirban. 1970. 4.95 (0-912582-40-5) Kirban.

Stranger in Town. Laura Parker. (Intimate Moments Ser.). 1994. mass mkt. 3.50 (0-373-07562-6, 5-07562-7) Silhouette.

*__Stranger in Town: A Play for Students of English.__ Lou Spaventa. (Illus.). 48p. (Orig.). 1992. pap. text ed. 8.50 (0-86647-039-5); pap. text ed. 19.00 incl. audio (0-86647-096-4); audio 16.00 (0-86647-059-X) Pro Lingua.

Stranger in Two Worlds. Jean Harris. 1993. mass mkt. 4.99 (0-8217-4313-9, Zebra Kensgtn) Kensgtn Pub Corp.

Stranger in Vienna. large type ed. Harriet La Barre. 640p. 1995. 25.99 (0-7089-3332-7) Ulverscroft.

Stranger in Williamsburg. Wanda Luttrell. LC 94-20574. 196p. (YA). 1995. 12.99 (0-7814-0235-2, Chariot Bks) Chariot Victor.

Stranger in Williamsburg. Wanda Luttrell. LC 94-20574. (Sarah's Journey Ser.: Vol. 2). 196p. (J). 1995. pap. 5.99 (0-7814-0902-0, Chariot Bks) Chariot Victor.

Stranger in You. Mary Di Michele. 92p. Date not set. pap. write for info. (0-19-541158-7) OUP.

Stranger in Your Bed: A Guide to Emotional Intimacy. Dean C. Dauw. LC 78-23444. 120p. 1979. 21.95 (0-88229-472-5) Nelson-Hall.

*__Stranger Is Our Own: Reflections on the Journey of Puerto Rican Migrants.__ Joseph P. Fitzpatrick. LC 96-46596. 1996. write for info. (1-55612-905-X) Sheed & Ward MO.

Stranger Is Watching. Mary Higgins Clark. Ed. by Julie Rubenstein. 288p. 1991. pap. 6.99 (0-671-74120-9) PB.

Stranger Is Watching. Mary Higgins Clark. 1991. reprint ed. lib. bdg. 25.95 (1-56849-071-2) Buccaneer Bks.

Stranger Music. Leonard Cohen. pap. write for info. (0-679-43333-3) Random.

Stranger Music: Selected Poems & Songs. Leonard Cohen. 1994. pap. 15.00 (0-679-75541-1, Publishers Media) Random.

Stranger Next Door. Amelie Nothomb. 1996. 19.00 (0-8050-4841-3) H Holt & Co.

Stranger Notes. Gary Carey. (Orig.). 1979. pap. 3.75 (0-8220-1229-4) Cliffs.

*__Stranger of Galilee: The Sermon on the Mount & the Universal Spiritual Tradition.__ Russell Perkins. LC 94-74917. 508p. (Orig.). 1994. pap. 15.00 (0-89142-047-9) Sant Bani Ash.

Stranger on the Earth: A Psychological Biography of Vincent Van Gogh. Albert J. Lubin. LC 96-14082. (Illus.). 304p. 1996. reprint ed. pap. 14.95 (0-306-80726-2) Da Capo.

*__Stranger on the Line.__ unabridged ed. Marilyn Halvorson. 216p. (YA). (gr. 7 up). 1997. mass mkt. 5.95 (0-7736-7457-8, Pub. by Stoddart Kids CN) Genl Dist Srvs.

Stranger on the Planet: The Small Book of Laurie. Claire Burch. 175p. 1997. pap. 10.00 (0-916147-67-3) Regent Pr.

Stranger on the Run. Marilyn Halvorson. 224p. (Orig.). (YA). (gr. 7-12). 1992. pap. 7.95 (0-7737-5532-2, Pub. by Stoddart Pubng CN) Genl Dist Srvs.

Stranger on Trust. large type ed. Malcolm Williams. (Linford Romance Library). 1990. pap. 15.99 (0-7089-6835-X) Ulverscroft.

Stranger Passing By. Lilian Peake. (Presents Ser.). 1994. mass mkt. 2.99 (0-373-11629-2, 1-11629-2) Harlequin Bks.

Stranger Passing By. large type ed. Lilian Peake. 1993. 19.95 (0-263-13320-6) Thorndike Pr.

Stranger Returns. Michael R. Perry. Ed. by Linda Marrow. 432p. (Orig.). 1992. mass mkt. 5.50 (0-671-73495-4, Pocket Star Bks) PB.

Stranger Riding. large type ed. Peggy L. Jones. (Linford Romance Library). 1991. pap. 15.99 (0-7089-7112-1) Ulverscroft.

Stranger Safety. Pati Gross. Ed. by Deborah Kenly. LC 96-92306. (Adventures in the Roo World - Young Roo Ser.). (Illus.). 24p. (Orig.). (J). (ps-1). 1996. pap. 4.95 (0-9652579-0-8) Roo Publns.

*__Stranger Souls.__ Jak Koke. (Shadowrun Ser.: No. 26). 1997. pap. 5.99 (0-451-45610-6, ROC) NAL-Dutton.

Stranger Still. Anna Kavan. 320p. 9600. 30.00 (0-7206-0955-0, Pub. by P Owen Ltd UK) Dufour.

*__Stranger Than Fact: Tales of Legal Perplexity, Political Correctness, & Cultural Mayhem.__ Judith S. Weizner. 185p. 1996. pap. write for info. (1-886442-05-3) Ctr Study Popular.

Stranger Than Fiction. Jim Stone. (Illus.). 66p. 1993. text ed. write for info. (0-935445-02-1); pap. text ed. write for info. (0-935445-03-X) Light Work.

Stranger Than Fiction. Jeanne M. Walker. (QRL Poetry Bks.: Vol. XXXI). 1992. 20.00 (0-614-06442-2) Quarterly Rev.

Stranger Than Fiction: Killer Bugs. Melvin Berger. 128p. (Orig.). (J). 1990. pap. 3.50 (0-380-76036-3, Camelot) Avon.

Stranger Than Fiction: Sea Monsters. Melvin Berger. 96p. (J). 1991. pap. 2.95 (0-380-76054-1, Camelot) Avon.

Stranger Than Fiction: Vignettes of San Diego History. Richard W. Crawford. (Illus.). vii, 72p. (Orig.). 1995. mass mkt., pap. 9.95 (0-918740-19-3) San Diego Hist.

*__Stranger Than Fiction: When Our Minds Betray Us.__ Marc D. Feldman et al. LC 97-5481. 1998. write for info. (0-88048-930-8) Am Psychiatric.

Stranger Than Science. Frank Edwards. 312p. 1992. pap. 4.50 (0-8216-2513-6, Carol Paperbacks) Carol Pub Group.

Stranger Than Science. Frank Edwards. 256p. 1983. reprint ed. pap. 6.95 (0-8065-0850-7, Citadel Pr) Carol Pub Group.

Stranger Than Truth! John Tynes et al. (Pandemonium! Ser.). 96p. 1994. pap. 13.95 (1-887801-30-8, Atlas Games) Trident MN.

Stranger Things. Mildred Cram. LC 78-121532. (Short Story Index Reprint Ser.). 1977. 19.95 (0-8369-3488-1) Ayer.

*__Stranger to Love.__ Patricia McLinn. 1997. mass mkt. 3.99 (0-373-24098-8, 1-24098-5) Silhouette.

Stranger to Myself: An Adult Guide to Higher Self-Esteem & Creative Living. J. Graham Reaves. 120p. 1991. pap. text ed. 8.95 (0-9630046-0-3) Lydian Comm.

Stranger to Self-Hatred. Brennan Manning. 1981. pap. 11.95 (0-87193-156-7) Dimension Bks.

Stranger to the Game: The Autobiography of Bob Gibson. Bob Gibson & Lonnie Wheeler. (Illus.). 304p. 1996. pap. 12.95 (0-14-017528-8, Viking) Viking Penguin.

Stranger to the Ground. Richard Bach. 192p. 1990. mass mkt. 5.99 (0-440-20658-8) Dell.

Stranger to the Ground. Richard Bach. (Illus.). 192p. 1983. 17.95 (0-02-504520-2) Macmillan.

Stranger to These Briefs. Parillo. 1996. pap. text ed. write for info. (0-205-17332-2) Allyn.

Stranger Violence: A Theoretical Inquiry. Marc Riedel. LC 92-432. (Current Issues in Criminal Justice Ser.: Vol. 1). 208p. 1993. text ed. 35.00 (0-8153-0094-8, SS753) Garland.

Stranger Who Bore Me: Adoptee-Birth Mother Interactions. Karen March. 192p. 1995. pap. 17.95 (0-8020-7235-6) U of Toronto Pr.

Stranger Who Bore Me: Adoptee-Birth Mother Interactions. Karen March. 160p. 1995. 45.00 (0-8020-0447-4) U of Toronto Pr.

Stranger Wilde: Interpreting Oscar. Gary Schmidgall. 512p. 1995. pap. 14.95 (0-452-27157-6, Plume) NAL-Dutton.

Stranger with My Face. Lois Duncan. 176p. (J). (gr. 7 up). 1990. mass mkt. 4.50 (0-440-98356-8, LLL BDD) BDD Bks Young Read.

Stranger with My Face. Lois Duncan. (J). (gr. 8 up). 1981. 15.95 (0-316-19551-0) Little.

Stranger Within. Will Hochman. LC 92-45267. 64p. 1993. pap. 12.95 (0-7734-2780-5, Mellen Poetry Pr) E Mellen.

Stranger Within. Marvin Kistler. LC 94-92397. (Illus.). 348p. (Orig.). 1995. pap. 19.95 (0-9644784-1-2) Synergy Press.

Stranger Within the Gates. large type ed. Mira Stables. 1995. 25.99 (0-7089-3301-7) Ulverscroft.

Stranger Within the Gates, Vol. 14. Grace L. Hill. (Grace Livingston Hill Ser.: Vol. 14). 1990. pap. 3.95 (0-8423-6441-2, 076441-2) Tyndale.

Stranger Within Your Gates: Converts & Conversion in Rabbinic Literature. Gary G. Porton. 424p. 1994. 29.95 (0-226-67586-6) U Ch Pr.

Stranger, You & I. Patricia Calvert. 160p. (YA). (gr. 7 up). 1988. pap. 2.50 (0-380-70600-8, Flare) Avon.

Strangers. Dean R. Koontz. 688p. 1989. mass mkt. 7.50 (0-425-11992-0) Berkley Pub.

Strangers. Matthew Manning. 176p. 9600. pap. 13.95 (0-86140-387-8, Pub. by Colin Smythe Ltd UK) Dufour.

Strangers: A Book of Poems. David K. Ferry. LC 83-1163. (Phoenix Poets Ser.). 64p. 1983. pap. 7.95 (0-226-24470-9) U Ch Pr.

Strangers: The Tragic World of Tristan l'Hermite. Claude K. Abraham. LC 66-64916. (University of Florida Humanities Monographs: No. 23). 83p. reprint ed. pap. 25.00 (0-7837-5029-3, 2044698) Bks Demand.

Strangers, All Strangers. Robert A. Yereance. LC 79-27016. 1981. 21.95 (0-87949-151-5) Ashley Bks.

Strangers Always: A Jewish Family in Wartime Shanghai. Rena Krasno. LC 92-61320. (Illus.). 218p. 1992. 24.95 (1-881896-02-1) Pacific View Pr.

Strangers Among Us. Ruth Montgomery. 256p. 1984. mass mkt. 5.99 (0-449-20801-X, Crest) Fawcett.

Strangers among Us. David C. Woodman. 1995. pap. 29.95 (0-7735-1348-5, Pub. by McGill CN) U of Toronto Pr.

Strangers among Us. Laurali R. Wright. 256p. 1996. 21.00 (0-684-81382-3, Scribners PB Fict) S&S Trade.

Strangers among Us. Laurali R. Wright. 320p. 1996. 26.95 (0-385-25532-2) Doubleday.

Strangers & Brothers. C. P. Snow. LC 60-12605. 320p. 1977. 35.00 (0-684-15367-X) S&S Trade.

Strangers & Friends: The Franco-German Security Relationship. Ed. by Robbin F. Laird. 220p. 1989. text ed. 45.00 (0-312-03242-0) St Martin.

Strangers & Pilgrims. David B. Boone, Jr. 1996. 22.95 (0-9652676-0-1) Curberry Pubs.

Strangers & Pilgrims: A Study of Genesis. V. Paul Flint. LC 88-781. 147p. 1988. 16.99 (0-87213-177-7) Loizeaux.

Strangers & Secrets: Communication in the Nineteenth-Century Novel. R. A. York. LC 92-55125. (C). 1994. 32.50 (0-8386-3533-4) Fairleigh Dickinson.

Strangers & Sojourners: A History of Michigan's Keweenaw Peninsula. Arthur W. Thurner. LC 93-49673. 408p. 1994. text ed. 44.95 (0-8143-2395-2, Great Lks Bks); pap. text ed. 17.95 (0-8143-2396-0, Great Lks Bks) Wayne St U Pr.

*__Strangers & Sojourners: A Novel.__ Michael O'Brien. 573p. 1997. 24.95 (0-89870-609-2) Ignatius Pr.

Strangers & Traders: Yoruba Migrants, Markets, & the State in Northern Ghana. J. S. Eades. LC 93-43842. 240p. 1994. 45.95 (0-86543-419-0); pap. 16.95 (0-86543-420-4) Africa World.

*__Strangers & Wayfarers.__ Sarah Orne Jewett. (Collected Works of Sarah Orne Jewett). 1988. reprint ed. lib. bdg. 59.00 (0-7812-1310-X) Rprt Serv.

Strangers & Wayfarers see Collected Works of Sarah Orne Jewett

*__Strangers at Home: Essays on the Long-Term Impact of Living Overseas & Coming "Home" to a Strange Land.__ Ed. by Carolyn D. Smith. LC 96-85760. 230p. (Orig.). 1996. pap. 15.95 (0-9639260-4-7) Aletheia.

Strangers at Home: Jews in the Italian Literary Imagination. Lynn M. Gunzberg. 326p. (C). 1992. 45.00 (0-520-07840-3) U CA Pr.

Strangers at Home: Vietnam Veterans since the War. Ed. by Charles R. Figley & Seymour Leventman. LC 90-1310. (Brunner-Mazel Psychosocial Stress Ser.: No. 19). 416p. 1990. pap. text ed. 34.95 (0-87630-575-3) Brunner-Mazel.

Strangers at Ithaca: The Story of the Spongers of Tarpon Springs. George Frantzis. 240p. reprint ed. pap. 68.40 (0-8357-3250-9, AU00412) Bks Demand.

Strangers at Lisconnel: A Second Series of Irish Idylls. Jane Barlow. LC 73-150535. (Short Story Index Reprint Ser.). 1977. reprint ed. 18.95 (0-8369-3832-1) Ayer.

*__Strangers at the Gate: Social Disorder in South China, 1839-1861.__ Frederic Wakeman. 1997. pap. text ed. 19.95 (0-520-21239-8) U CA Pr.

Strangers at the Gates Again: Asian American Immigration after 1965. Ronald Takaki. LC 94-21105. (Asian American Experience Ser.). (Illus.). (YA). (gr. 5 up). 1995. lib. bdg. 19.95 (0-7910-2190-4) Chelsea Hse.

*__Strangers at the Stables.__ Michelle Bates. (Sandy Lane Stables Ser.). (Illus.). 96p. (Orig.). (J). (gr. 4-8). 1997. pap. 3.95 (0-7460-2488-6, Usborne) EDC.

*__Strangers at the Stables.__ Michelle Bates. (Sandy Lane Stables Ser.). (Illus.). 96p. (J). (gr. 4-8). 1997. lib. bdg. 11.95 (0-88110-944-4, Usborne) EDC.

Strangers at Your Door: How to Respond to Jehovah's Witnesses, the Mormons, Televangelists, Cults, & More. Albert J. Nevins. LC 88-61111. 160p. (Orig.). 1988. pap. 7.95 (0-87973-496-5, 496) Our Sunday Visitor.

Stranger's Baby. Judith Arnold. (Weddings by DeWilde Ser.). 1996. mass mkt. 4.50 (0-373-82543-9, 1-82543-9) Harlequin Bks.

Strangers Become Neighbors. Calvin W. Redekop. LC 80-13887. (Studies in Anabaptist & Mennonite History: Vol. 22). (Illus.). 312p. 1980. 24.99 (0-8361-1228-8) Herald Pr.

Strangers from a Different Shore: A History of Asian Americans. Ronald T. Takaki. 584p. 1990. pap. 13.95 (0-14-013885-4, Penguin Bks) Viking Penguin.

Strangers from a Secret Land. Peter Thomas. 319p. (C). 1986. 30.00 (0-86383-278-4, Pub. by Gomer Pr UK) St Mut.

Strangers from a Secret Land: The Voyages of the Brig Albion & the Founding of the First Welsh Settlement in Canada. Peter Thomas. 1986. 35.00 (0-8020-5694-6); pap. 18.95 (0-8020-6620-8) U of Toronto Pr.

Strangers from a Secret Land: The Voyages of the Brig Albion & the Founding of the First Welsh Settlement in Canada. Peter Thomas. LC 87-206771. (Illus.). 335p. reprint ed. pap. 95.50 (0-8357-3654-7, 2036382) Bks Demand.

Strangers from the Sky. Margaret W. Bonanno. (Star Trek Ser.). 1990. mass mkt. 5.99 (0-671-73481-4) PB.

Strangers' Hall. large type ed. Elizabeth Jeffrey. 1990. 25.99 (0-7089-2253-8) Ulverscroft.

Stranger's House. Bret Lott. 272p. 1990. pap. 7.95 (0-671-68328-4, WSP) PB.

Strangers in a Stolen Land: American Indians in San Diego. Richard L Carrico. LC 86-63076. (Illus.). 130p. (C). 1987. reprint ed. pap. 10.95 (0-940113-03-1) Sierra Oaks Pub.

Strangers in a Strange Land: Escape to Neutrality, Vol. 2. Hans-Heiri Stapfer. (Specials Ser.). (Illus.). 64p. 1992. pap. 12.95 (0-89747-278-0, 6056) Squad Sig Pubns.

Strangers in African Society. Ed. by William A. Shack & Elliott P. Skinner. LC 77-73501. 1979. pap. 16.95 (0-520-03812-6) U CA Pr.

Strangers in Blood: Fur Trade Company Families in Indian Country. Jennifer S. Brown. LC 95-36771. (Illus.). 292p. 1996. pap. 16.95 (0-8061-2813-5) U of Okla Pr.

An Asterisk (*) at the beginning of an entry indicates that the title is appearing in BIP for the first time.

Strangers in Buckhorn. large type ed. John Hunt. (Linford Western Library). 288p. 1993. pap. 15.99 (*0-7089-7371-X*, Linford) Ulverscroft.

Strangers in Company. large type ed. Jane A. Hodge. 432p. 1988. 25.99 (*0-7089-1788-7*) Ulverscroft.

Strangers in Eden. large type ed. E. G. Bartlett. (Linford Romance Library). 1991. pap. 15.99 (*0-7089-7109-1*) Ulverscroft.

Strangers in High Places: The Story of the Great Smoky Mountains. expanded ed. Michael Frome. LC 93-7122. (Illus.). 496p. (C). 1993. pap. 17.50 (*0-87049-806-1*) U of Tenn Pr.

Strangers in Hollywood: A History of Scandinavian Actors in American Films from 1910 to World War II. Hans J. Wollstein. LC 94-17605. (Filmmakers Ser.: No. 43). (Illus.). 420p. 1994. 49.50 (*0-8108-2938-X*) Scarecrow.

***Strangers in Our Midst: The Startling World of Sonoran Desert Arthropods.** Peter Friederici. (Illus.). 24p. (Orig.). 1996. pap. 4.95 (*1-886679-06-1*) Ariz-Sonora Des Mus.

Strangers in Paradise. Heather G. Pozzessere. 1995. mass mkt. 4.99 (*1-55166-038-5*, 1-66038-0, Mira Bks) Harlequin Bks.

Strangers in Paradise: Academics from the Working Class. 2nd ed. Jake Ryan & Charles Sackrey. 328p. (Orig.). (C). 1995. pap. text ed. 34.00 (*0-7618-0142-1*); lib. bdg. 59.00 (*0-7618-0141-3*) U Pr of Amer.

***Strangers in Paradise: Impact & Management of Nonindigenous Species in Florida.** Ed. by Daniel Simberloff et al. (Illus.). 480p. 1997. 50.00 (*1-55963-429-4*, Shearwater Bks); pap. 29.95 (*1-55963-430-8*, Shearwater Bks) Island Pr.

Strangers in Paradise: Stories. Lee K. Abbott. LC 96-15038. 256p. 1996. pap. 14.95 (*0-8142-0712-X*) Ohio St U Pr.

Strangers in Paradise: The Israel Kibbutz Experience. David Mittelberg. 308p. 1988. 39.95 (*0-88738-183-9*) Transaction Pubs.

Strangers in Paradise: Transnational Corporations in the Caribbean. Tom Barry et al. 44p. (Orig.). 1984. pap. 5.00 (*0-911213-04-X*) Interhemisp Res Ctr.

Strangers in Paradise, Aliens in the Promised Land: How to Recover the Joyful Experience of Having It All. Paul L. Garlington. LC 92-74164. 192p. 1993. 24.95 (*0-9634473-1-9*); pap. 19.95 (*0-9634473-2-7*) Heartsight.

Strangers in Paradox: Explorations in Mormon Theology. Paul J. Toscano & Margaret M. Toscano. LC 89-27210. xiii, 301p. 1990. pap. 12.95 (*0-941214-98-2*) Signature Bks.

Strangers in the Forest. Carol R. Brink. LC 93-12731. (Washington State University Press Reprint Ser.). 314p. 1993. reprint ed. pap. 17.95 (*0-87422-096-3*) Wash St U Pr.

Strangers in the House: The World of Stepsiblings & Half-Siblings. Ed. by William R. Beer. 276p. 1989. 34.95 (*0-88738-262-2*) Transaction Pubs.

Strangers in the Land: Patterns of American Nativism, 1860-1925. John Higham. 431p. (C). 1988. pap. text ed. 16.95 (*0-8135-1308-1*) Rutgers U Pr.

***Strangers in the Lands.** Loughery. 1997. 35.00 (*0-8050-3896-5*) St Martin.

Strangers in the Night. Peg Tyre. 352p. 1995. mass mkt. 5.99 (*0-380-72394-8*) Avon.

***Strangers in the Night.** Peg Tyre. 1996. 3.99 (*0-517-17220-8*) Random Hse Value.

Strangers in the Senate: Politics & the New Revolution of Women in America. Barbara Boxer & Nicole Boxer. (Illus.). 288p. 1993. 23.95 (*1-882605-06-3*) Natl Pr Bks.

Strangers in the Senate: Politics & the New Revolution of Women in America. Barbara Boxer. 1994. pap. 12.95 (*1-882605-16-0*) Natl Pr Bks.

Strangers in Their Land: CBI Bombardier, 1939-1945. Thurzal Q. Terry. (Illus.). 264p. 1992. pap. 21.95 (*0-89745-147-3*) Sunflower U Pr.

Strangers in Their Midst: Small-Town Jews & Their Neighbors. Peter I. Rose. 1977. lib. bdg. 12.95 (*0-915172-32-1*) Richwood Pub.

Strangers in Their Midst: The Free Black Population of Amherst County, Virginia. Sherrie S. McLeRoy & William R. McLeRoy. iv, 237p. (Orig.). 1993. pap. text ed. 23.00 (*1-55613-786-9*) Heritage Bk.

Strangers in Their Own Country: A Curriculum Guide on South Africa. William Bigelow. LC 85-71369. (Illus.). 104p. (Orig.). (YA). (gr. 8 up). 1987. pap. 12.95 (*0-86543-010-1*) Africa World.

Strangers in Their Own Land: A Century of Colonial Rule in the Caroline & Marshall Islands. Francis X. Hezel. LC 94-34834. (Pacific Islands Monographs: No. 13). (Illus.). 496p. (C). 1995. text ed. 40.00 (*0-8248-1642-0*) UH Pr.

Strangers in Their Own Land: A Choctaw Portfolio. Intro. by Carole Thompson. (State Historical Museum Catalog Ser.). (Illus.). 38p. 1983. pap. 3.00 (*0-938896-34-2*) Mississippi Archives.

Strangers in Their Own Land: An American Indian History Guide. Sandra Sheffield & Jude Urich. 55p. (C). 1988. pap. 6.95 (*0-317-93046-X*) Open Bk Pubs.

Strangers into Friends: The Evolution of Friendship Networks Using an Individual Oriented Modeling Approach. Evelien Zeggelink. 206p. 1993. pap. 23.50 (*90-5170-243-4*, Pub. by Thesis Pubs NE) IBD Ltd.

Stranger's Kiss. Liz Fielding. (Romance Ser.). 1995. pap. 2.99 (*0-373-17217-6*, 1-17217-0) Harlequin Bks.

Stranger's Kiss. Shelly Thacker. 384p. (Orig.). 1994. mass mkt. 4.99 (*0-380-77036-9*) Avon.

Stranger's Kiss. large type ed. Sondra Stanford. 1991. 25.99 (*0-7089-2487-5*) Ulverscroft.

***Stranger's Message.** Paul McCusker. (Adventures in Odyssey Ser.: Bk. 11). (J). (gr. 3-7). 1997. pap. 5.99 (*1-56179-537-2*) Focus Family.

***Stranger's Neighborhood.** Donald Morrill. (Emerging Writers in Creative Nonfiction Ser.). 220p. 1997. pap. 16.95 (*0-8207-0281-1*); text ed. 29.95 (*0-8207-0280-3*) Duquesne.

Strangers No More. William Gellin. LC 85-63442. 192p. 1986. 11.95 (*0-88400-121-0*) Shengold.

Strangers on Earth. Mark O'Donnell. (Illus.). 96p. 1993. 5.99 (*1-56865-067-1*, GuildAmerica) Dblday Direct.

Strangers on Earth. Mark O'Donnell. 1993. pap. 5.25 (*0-8222-1350-8*) Dramatists Play.

Strangers or Friends: Principles for a New Alien Admission Policy. Mark Gibney. LC 86-7572. (Contributions in Political Science Ser.: No. 157). 184p. 1986. text ed. 49.95 (*0-313-25344-7*, GSG/, Greenwood Pr) Greenwood.

"Strangers Settled Here Amongst Us" Policies, Perceptions, & the Presence of Aliens in Elizabethan England. Laura H. Yungblut. LC 95-39757. 192p. (C). 1996. text ed. 55.00 (*0-415-02144-8*) Routledge.

Stranger's Supper: An Oral History of Centenarian Women in Montenegro. Zorka Milich. 192p. 1995. pap. 15.95 (*0-8057-9132-9*, Twayne) Scribnrs Ref.

Stranger's Supper: An Oral History of Centenarian Women in Montenegro. Zorka Milich. 192p. 1996. 26.95 (*0-8057-9131-0*, Twayne) Scribnrs Ref.

***Stranger's Surprise.** Laura Anthony. 1997. mass mkt. 3.25 (*0-373-19260-6*, 1-19260-8) Silhouette.

Strangers to Failure. Benson Idahosa. 128p. 1993. pap. 6.99 (*0-89274-761-7*, HH-761) Harrison Hse.

Strangers to Ourselves. Julia Kristeva. Tr. by Leon S. Roudiez. 240p. 1991. text ed. 32.50 (*0-231-07156-6*) Col U Pr.

Strangers to Ourselves. Julia Kristeva. 1994. pap. 14.50 (*0-231-07157-4*) Col U Pr.

Strangers to That Land: British Perspectives of Ireland from the Reformation to the Famine. Ed. by Andrew Hadfield & John McVeagh. 315p. (C). 1994. lib. bdg. 72.50 (*0-86140-350-9*, Pub. by C Smythe Ltd UK) B&N Imports.

Strangers to the City: Urban Man in Jos, Nigeria. Leonard Plotnicov. LC 67-13928. (Illus.). 333p. (C). 1967. pap. 14.95 (*0-8229-5135-5*) U of Pittsburgh Pr.

Strangers to the Constitution: Immigrants, Borders, & Fundamental Law. Gerald L. Neuman. LC 95-39587. 296p. (C). 1996. text ed. 39.50 (*0-691-04360-4*) Princeton U Pr.

***Strangers to the Tribe.** Glaser. LC 97-18827. 1997. 24.00 (*0-395-72776-6*) HM.

Strangers to Themselves: Encounters with Retarded & Insane People. Nita Lindenberg. 110p. 1990. pap. 12.95 (*0-86315-087-X*, 1421, Pub. by Floris Books UK) Anthroposophic.

Strangers to these Shores. 5th ed. Vincent N. Parrillo. 640p. 1996. 59.00 (*0-205-19171-1*) Allyn.

Strangers to This Ground: Cultural Diversity in Contemporary American Writing. Wilbur M. Frohock. LC 61-17183. 192p. reprint ed. pap. 54.80 (*0-8357-7039-7*, 2033417) Bks Demand.

Stranger's Trust. Emma Richmond. (Presents Ser.). 1993. mass mkt. 2.99 (*0-373-11582-2*, 1-11582-3) Harlequin Bks.

Stranger's Welcome: Oral Theory & the Aesthetics of the Homeric Hospitality Scene. Steve Reece. (Monographs in Classical Antiquity). 240p. (C). 1992. text ed. 42.50 (*0-472-10386-5*) U of Mich Pr.

Strangers When We Meet. Suzanne Carey. (Intimate Moments Ser.: No. 392). 1991. mass mkt. 3.25 (*0-373-07392-5*) Silhouette.

***Strangers When We Meet.** Rebecca Winters. 1997. mass mkt. 3.99 (*0-373-70737-1*, 1-70737-1) Harlequin Bks.

Strangers When We Meet. large type ed. Alex Stuart. 400p. 1988. 25.99 (*0-7089-1888-3*) Ulverscroft.

Strangers Who Molest: Protecting Children from Sexual Predators. Trudy K. Dana. 49p. 1991. pap. 4.50 (*0-9632692-0-8*) Snohomish Cnty CC.

Stranger's Wife. Hilda Stahl. (Prairie Ser.: Vol. 2). 201p. pap. 6.99 (*0-934998-44-2*) Bethel Pub.

Strangers Within the Realm: Cultural Margins of the First British Empire. Ed. by Bernard Bailyn & Philip D. Morgan. LC 90-40278. xii, 456p. (C). 1991. 49.95 (*0-8078-1952-2*); pap. 17.95 (*0-8078-4311-3*) U of NC Pr.

Strangest Animals in the World. S. Talalaj & Janusz Talalaj. (Illus.). 221p. (Orig.). 1994. pap. 16.95 (*0-85572-231-2*, Pub. by Hill Content Pubng AT) Seven Hills Bk.

Strangest Cat & Dog Stories. Janusz Talalaj. 1996. pap. text ed. 10.95 (*0-85572-268-1*, Pub. by Hill Content Pubng AT) Seven Hills Bk.

***Strangest Christmas.** Bob Todd. LC 96-78187. (Illus.). 64p. (Orig.). 1996. pap. 9.95 (*0-913383-49-X*) McClanahan Pub.

Strangest Dream: Canadian Communists, the Spy Trials, & the Cold War. 2nd ed. Merrily Weisbord. (Illus.). 270p. 1994. reprint ed. pap. 17.95 (*1-55065-053-X*, Pub. by Vehicule Pr CN) Genl Dist Srvs.

Strangest Friendship in History. George S. Viereck. LC 75-26222. 375p. 1976. reprint ed. text ed. 59.75 (*0-8371-8413-4*, VISF, Greenwood Pr) Greenwood.

Strangest Halloween, No. 1. 24p. (J). 1996. 3.99 (*0-689-80928-X*) S&S Childrens.

Strangest Human Sex, Ceremonies & Customs. Janusz Talalaj & Stan Talalaj. (Strangest Ser.). (Illus.). 300p. (Orig.). 1995. pap. 16.95 (*0-85572-247-9*) Seven Hills Bk.

Strangest of All. Frank Edwards. 224p. 1987. pap. 5.95 (*0-8065-1023-4*, Citadel Pr) Carol Pub Group.

Strangest of All. Frank Edwards. 206p. 1991. pap. 4.50 (*0-8216-2504-7*, Carol Paperbacks) Carol Pub Group.

***Strangest People Know God.** Hugh Hewitt. 292p. 1997. pap. 14.99 (*0-8499-1419-1*) Word Pub.

Strangest Plants in the World. S. Talalaj. (Illus.). 165p. (Orig.). 1994. pap. 20.95 (*0-85572-205-3*, Pub. by Hill Content Pubng AT) Seven Hills Bk.

***Strangest Secret.** Earl Nightingale & Diana Nightingale. (Earl Nightingale's Library of Little Gems). 72p. (Orig.). 1996. pap. write for info. incl. audio (*0-9655760-4-3*) Keys Co Inc.

***Strangest Secret.** unabridged ed. Earl Nightingale & Diana Nightingale. (Earl Nightingale's Library of Little Gems: Vol. 1). 72p. (Orig.). 1996. pap. 7.95 (*0-9655760-1-9*) Keys Co Inc.

Strangest Thing about Frankie Castle. Carol Casatelli-Vivenzio. 54p. (Orig.). (J). (gr. 4-5). 1994. pap. write for info. (*0-9641300-0-9*) Casatelli-Vivenzio.

Strangled Cries. Julius Balbin. Ed. by Stanley H. Barkan. Tr. by Charlz Rizzuto. (Cross-Cultural Review Chapbook Ser.: No. 8: Esperanto Poetry 1). 24p. (ENG & ESP.). 1980. 15.00 (*0-89304-848-8*, CCC134); pap. 5.00 (*0-89304-807-0*) Cross-Cultrl NY.

Strangled Prose. Joan Hess. 1987. mass mkt. 5.99 (*0-345-34059-0*) Ballantine.

Strangled Roots. Isaac Quiring. 186p. (Orig.). 1982. pap. 8.95 (*0-920490-26-3*) Temeron Bks.

***Strangled Waters.** Dorothy Ainslie. LC 96-61790. 192p. (Orig.). 1997. pap. 15.00 (*1-883893-90-9*) WinePress Pub.

Stranglehold. Edward Hess. 320p. (Orig.). 1994. pap. 4.99 (*0-451-17984-6*, Sig) NAL-Dutton.

Stranglehold. Jack Ketchum. 256p. (Orig.). 1995. mass mkt. 5.50 (*0-425-14946-3*) Berkley Pub.

Stranglehold. large type ed. Jennifer Rowe. LC 94-49410. 338p. 1995. lib. bdg. 19.95 (*0-7838-1247-7*, GK Hall) Thorndike Pr.

Stranglehold. Jerome Doolittle. Ed. by Bill Grose. 304p. 1992. reprint ed. mass mkt. 4.99 (*0-671-74571-9*) PB.

Stranglers. Ed. by Rose G. Mandelsberg. 448p. 1994. mass mkt. 4.99 (*0-7860-0015-5*, Pinncle Kensgtn) Kensgtn Pub Corp.

Strangling Figs in Sanskrit Literature. Murray B. Emeneau. LC 49-2733. (University of California Publications in Social Welfare: Vol. 13, No. 10). 30p. reprint ed. pap. 25.00 (*0-317-09833-0*, 2021166) Bks Demand.

Strangling of Persia. W. M. Shuster. LC 86-31244. (Illus.). 496p. 1987. reprint ed. 24.95 (*0-934211-06-X*) Mage Pubs Inc.

Strap on Your Spurs: Technology & Change Cowboy Style. Annette Lamb & Larry Johnson. (Illus.). 173p. (C). 1994. pap. text ed. 23.95 (*0-9641581-0-8*) Vision to Action.

Straregic Board Recruitment, the Not-for-Profit Model. Kile & Losvacio. 160p. 1996. 160.00 (*0-8342-0797-4*) Aspen Pub.

Strasberg at the Actors Studio: Tape-Recorded Sessions. Robert H. Hethmon. LC 90-29039. 446p. 1991. pap. 12.95 (*1-55936-022-4*) Theatre Comm.

Strasberg's Method: As Taught by Lorrie Hull. S. Loraine Hull. LC 85-2968. (C). 1985. 32.00 (*0-918024-38-2*); pap. 17.95 (*0-918024-39-0*) Ox Bow.

***Strasbourg City Plan.** (Grafocarte Maps Ser.). 1995. 8.95 (*2-7416-0038-4*, 80038) Michelin.

Strasburg Tapes. Henry Madden. write for info. (*0-318-62725-6*) Daedalus Act.

Strassburg Alexander & the Munich Oswald. J. W. Thomas. LC 89-38834. (GERM Ser.: Vol. 44). 180p. (C). 1989. 38.00 (*0-938100-69-6*) Camden Hse.

Strassburger Family & Allied Families of Penna., Being the Ancestry of Jacob Andrew Strassburger, Esquire, of Montgomery Co. PA. R. B. Strassburger. (Illus.). 520p. 1993. reprint ed. pap. 76.50 (*0-8328-3785-7*); reprint ed. lib. bdg. 86.50 (*0-8328-3784-9*) Higginson Bk Co.

Strastnaja Sedmitsa see Tserkovno-Pjevcheskiji Sbornik

Strata. Roger Jones. (Texas Review Southern & Southwestern Poets Breakthrough Ser.). 64p. 1993. pap. 6.95 (*1-881515-03-6*) TX Review Pr.

Strata Chart to Zyskind-Martin see Encyclopedia of Statistical Sciences

Strata Control in Deep Mines: Proceedings of the 11th Plenary Scientific Session of the International Bureau of Strata Mechanics, World Mining Congress, Novosibirsk, 5-9 June 1989. Ed. by A. Kidybinski & J. Dubinski. (Illus.). 208p. (C). 1990. text ed. 135.00 (*90-6191-124-9*, Pub. by A A Balkema NE) Ashgate Pub Co.

Strata Control in Mineral Engineering. Z. T. Bieniawski. 223p. (C). 1987. student ed., pap. 70.00 (*90-6191-608-9*, Pub. by A A Balkema NE) Ashgate Pub Co.

***Strata Control in Mineral Engineering.** Z. T. Bieniawski. 223p. 1987. 130.00 (*90-6191-607-0*, Pub. by A A Balkema NE) Ashgate Pub Co.

Strata Mechanics in Coal Mining. Ed. by M. L. Jeremic. 576p. (C). 1985. text ed. 125.00 (*90-6191-508-2*, Pub. by A A Balkema NE); pap. text ed. 70.00 (*90-6191-556-2*, Pub. by A A Balkema NE) Ashgate Pub Co.

***Strata Title & Community Title Management & the Law.** 2nd ed. Alex Ilkin. 770p. 1996. pap. 59.00 (*0-455-21367-4*, Pub. by Law Bk Co AT) Gaunt.

Strata Title Management & the Law. Alex Ilkin. xxxiii, 504p. 1989. pap. 29.95 (*0-455-20909-X*, Pub. by Law Bk Co AT) Gaunt.

Strata Title Units in New South Wales. 4th ed. L. Robinson. 230p. 1989. Australia. pap. 44.00 (*0-409-30248-1*, A.T.) MICHIE.

Strata Titles in Malaysia: Law & Practice. Teo Keang Sood. 164p. 1987. 64.00 (*0-409-99538-X*) MICHIE.

Stratabound Ore Deposits in the Andes. Ed. by G. C. Amstutz et al. (Special Publications of the Society for General Microbiology: Vol. 8). (Illus.). 800p. 1990. 238.95 (*0-387-52181-X*) Spr-Verlag.

Stratadesign. Sue Hu. LC 90-90199. (Illus.). 99p. (Orig.). 1991. pap. 19.95 (*0-9623736-2-1*) WE Enterprises.

Stratadesign II. Sue Hu. LC 92-80921. (Illus.). 52p. (Orig.). 1992. 550.00 (*0-9623736-5-6*) WE Enterprises.

Stratagem & Other Stories. Aleister Crowley. 1973. lib. bdg. 250.00 (*0-87968-117-9*) Krishna Pr.

Stratagem & Other Stories. Aleister Crowley. LC 74-167446. (Short Story Index Reprint Ser.). 1977. reprint ed. 13.95 (*0-8369-3972-7*) Ayer.

Stratagem, Strategy. abr. ed. Intro. by Luanna C. Blagrove. (Illus.). 275p. 1988. 24.95 (*0-685-17760-2*) Blagrove Pubns.

Stratagems. Julia Lorusso & Joel Glick. 108p. (Orig.). 1985. pap. 7.95 (*0-914732-15-3*) Bro Life Inc.

Stratagems & Aqueducts. Sextus J. Frontinus. (Loeb Classical Library: No. 174). 524p. 1925. 18.95 (*0-674-99192-3*) HUP.

Stratagems & Spoils: Stories of Love & Politics. William A. White. (C). 1972. reprint ed. lib. bdg. 17.50 (*0-8422-8125-8*) Irvington.

Stratagems & Spoils: Stories of Love & Politics. William A. White. (C). 1986. reprint ed. pap. text ed. 8.95 (*0-8290-2033-0*) Irvington.

Strategic Acquisitions: A Guide to Growing & Enhancing the Value of Your Business. Bruce R. Robinson & Walter Peterson. LC 94-21386. 264p. 1994. text ed. 65.00 (*1-55623-853-3*) Irwin Prof Pubng.

Strategic Adaptation in the Health Professions: Meeting the Challenges of Change. James W. Begun & Ronald C. Lippincott. LC 93-13377. (Health-Management Ser.). 270p. text ed. 37.95 (*1-55542-582-8*) Jossey-Bass.

Strategic Advantage & the Exploitability of Information Technology: An Empirical Study of the Effects of IT on Supplier-Distributor Relationships in the U. S. Airline Industry. Ellen Christiaanse. 209p. 1994. pap. 25.00 (*90-5170-283-3*, Pub. by Thesis Pubs NE) IBD Ltd.

Strategic Advertising Campaigns. 4th ed. Don E. Schultz & Beth Barnes. LC 93-42796. 1994. 47.95 (*0-8442-3015-4*, NTC Busn Bks) NTC Pub Grp.

Strategic Air Attack in the United States Air Force: A Case Study. Thomas A. Fabyanic. 216p. 1977. pap. text ed. 35.95 (*0-89126-029-3*) MA-AH Pub.

Strategic Air Command: Evolution & Consolidation of Nuclear Forces, 1945-1955. William S. Borgiasz. LC 95-22014. 176p. 1996. text ed. 55.00 (*0-275-94861-7*, Praeger Pubs) Greenwood.

Strategic Air Command: People, Aircraft, & Missiles. Norman Polmar & John T. Bohn. 1980. 22.95 (*0-405-13275-1*) Ayer.

Strategic Air Defense. Ed. by Stephen J. Cimbala. LC 88-26079. 275p. 1989. 40.00 (*0-8420-2285-6*) Scholarly Res Inc.

Strategic Air Offensive Against Germany 1939-1945 Vol. III: Victory. Charles W. Franklin. (Official History Ser.: No. 9). (Illus.). 416p. (Orig.). 1994. reprint ed. 42.50 (*0-89839-205-5*) Battery Pr.

Strategic Air Warfare: An Interview with Generals Curtis E. LeMay, Leon W. Johnson, David A. Burchinal, & Jack J. Catton. Ed. by Richard H. Kohn & Joseph P. Harahan. 1988. 11.00 (*0-912799-56-0*) Off Air Force.

Strategic Airport Planning. Caves. 300p. 1997. text ed. write for info. (*0-08-042764-2*, Pergamon Pr) Elsevier.

Strategic Alignment. Russell D. Kimbaall & David P. Reinhardt. (Illus.). 122p. 1993. pap. 39.95 (*0-9635900-0-6*) Operat Align Spec.

Strategic Alignment: Managing Integrated Health Systems. Ed. by Douglas A. Conrad & Geoffrey A. Hoare. LC 93-34353. 303p. (Orig.). (C). 1993. pap. text ed. 34.00 (*1-56793-003-4*, 0937) Health Admin Pr.

Strategic Alliances. (Best Practices Ser.). 1994. 175.00 (*0-85058-770-0*) Economist Intell.

Strategic Alliances: An Entrepreneurial Approach to Globalization. Michael Y. Yoshino & U. Srinivasa Rangan. LC 94-39669. 272p. 1995. 29.95 (*0-87584-584-3*) Harvard Busn.

Strategic Alliances: An Entrepreneurial Approach to Globalization. Michael Y. Yoshino & U. Srinivasa Rangan. 1995. text ed. 29.95 (*0-07-103621-0*) McGraw.

***Strategic Alliances: Building Network Relationships for Mutual Gain.** S. Shiva Ramu. LC 96-3336. (Response Bks.). 192p. 1997. 33.50 (*0-8039-9343-9*) Sage.

***Strategic Alliances: Cooperation & Competition.** Ravinder Kumar. 1997. pap. text ed. 19.95 (*981-00-7083-7*) Buttrwrth-Heinemann.

***Strategic Alliances: Managing the Supply Chain.** Tim Underhill. 300p. 1996. 69.95 (*0-87814-615-6*) PennWell Bks.

Strategic Alliances & Process Redesign: Effective Management & Restructuring of Cooperative Projects & Networks. Alexander Gerybadze. LC 94-28393. (De Gruyter Studies in Organization: No. 59). 326p. (C). 1994. lib. bdg. 69.95 (*3-11-013989-8*) De Gruyter.

Strategic Alliances Deskbook, No. 149. 1995. 125.00 (*1-56789-021-0*) Busn Laws Inc.

Strategic Analysis & the Management of Power: Johan Jorgen Holst, the cold War, & the New Europe. Ed. by Olav F. Knudsen. LC 95-30966. 256p. 1996. text ed. 59.95 (*0-312-12885-1*) St Martin.

Strategic Analysis for Hospital Management. Roger Kropf & James A. Greenberg. 330p. (C). 1984. 81.00 (*0-89443-855-7*) Aspen Pub.

Strategic Analysis of AT&T. Gartner Group, Inc. Staff. 1987. pap. 995.00 (*0-9614408-1-3*) Gartner Group.

Strategic Analysis of Science & Technology Policy. Harvey A. Averch. LC 84-47961. 232p. 1985. text ed. 37.50 (*0-8018-2467-2*) Johns Hopkins.

Strategic Analysis of System Integration & Outstanding Markets. Market Intelligence Staff. 420p. 1993. 1,495.00 (*1-56753-464-3*) Frost & Sullivan.

Strategic Analysis of the United States Banking Industry. rev. ed. Ajay K. Mehra. LC 95-16134. (Financial Sector of the American Economy Ser.). (Illus.). 160p. 1995. text ed. 52.00 (*0-8153-2007-8*) Garland.

S

Strategic Analysis, Selection, & Management of R & D Projects. D. Bruce Merrifield. LC 77-14599. (AMA Management Briefing Ser.). 54p. reprint ed. pap. 25.00 (0-317-29944-1, 2051699) Bks Demand.

Strategic Anatomy of the IBM PS-2: Product Opportunities(& Pitfalls) in Hardware Software & Systems. 130p. 495.00 (0-317-65582-5) TBC Inc.

Strategic & Interpersonal Skill Building. Herbert S. Kindler & Marilyn Ginsburg. 160p. (C). 1994. pap. text ed. 14.00 (0-03-009603-0) Dryden Pr.

Strategic & Operational Deception in the Second World War. Michael I. Handel. 1987. 39.50 (0-7146-3316-X, Pub. by F Cass Pubs UK); pap. 19.50 (0-7146-4056-5, Pub. by F Cass Pubs UK) Intl Spec Bk.

Strategic & Operational Issues in Production Economics: Proceedings of the Seventh International Working Seminar on Production Economics, Igls, Austria, February 17-21, 1992. Ed. by R. W. Grubbstrom & H. H. Hinterhuber. LC 93-30181. 612p. 1993. 307.00 (0-444-81689-5) Elsevier.

Strategic & Tactical Decisions. 2nd ed. K. J. Radford. (Illus.). 215p. 1988. 85.95 (0-387-96819-9) Spr-Verlag.

Strategic Antisubmarine Warfare & Naval Strategy. Tom Stefaneck. LC 86-45596. 411p. 63.95 (0-609-14015-9) Peninsula CA.

Strategic Appraisal 1996. Ed. by Zalmay M. Khalilzad. LC 95-52612. 300p. 1996. pap. 20.00 (0-8330-2343-8, MR-543-AF) Rand Corp.

***Strategic Appraisal 1997: Strategy & Defense Planning for the 21st Century.** Ed. by Zalmay M. Khalilzad & David A. Ochmanek. LC 97-6497. xviii, 351p. 1997. pap. 20.00 (0-8330-2456-6, MR-826-AF) Rand Corp.

Strategic Approach to Business Marketing. Robert E. Spekman. LC 84-18537. (American Marketing Association, Proceedings Ser.). (Illus.). 201p. (Orig.). 1985. reprint ed. pap. 57.30 (0-7837-9760-5, 2060488) Bks Demand.

Strategic Approach to Quality Service in Health Care. Kristine Peterson. (Health Care Administration Ser.). 332p. 71.00 (0-87189-764-4) Aspen Pub.

Strategic Approaches in Coronary Intervention. Stephen G. Ellis & David R. Holmes, Jr. 763p. 1995. 95.00 (0-683-02797-2) Williams & Wilkins.

Strategic Approaches to the International Economy: Selected Essays of Koichi Hamada. Koichi Hamada. LC 96-601. (Economists of the Twentieth Century Ser.). 784p. 1996. 120.00 (1-85898-330-4) E Elgar.

Strategic Arms Control after SALT. Ed. by Stephen J. Cimbala. LC 88-35254. 233p. 1989. 40.00 (0-8420-2290-2) Scholarly Res Inc.

Strategic Arms Reductions. Michael M. May et al. 73p. 1988. pap. 8.95 (0-8157-5525-2) Brookings.

Strategic Aspects of Oligopolistic Vertical Integration. Changqi Wu. LC 92-29630. (Studies in Mathematical & Managerial Economics: Vol. 36). 228p. 1992. 125.50 (0-444-89451-9, North Holland) Elsevier.

***Strategic Assessment in War.** Scott S. Gartner. LC 96-39931. 1997. write for info. (0-300-06034-3) Yale U Pr.

***Strategic Assessment 1997: Flashpoints & Force Structure.** Hans A. Binnendijk et al. LC 96-52237. 1997. write for info. (1-57906-029-3) Natl Defense.

Strategic Bankruptcy: How Corporations & Creditors Use Chapter 11 to Their Advantage. Kevin J. Delaney. 1992. 34.95 (0-520-07358-4) U CA Pr.

Strategic Behavior & the United States Unfair Trade Statues. rev. ed. Jeffrey W. Steagall. LC 94-24359. (Foreign Economic Policy of the United States Ser.). (Illus.). 248p. 1995. text ed. 66.00 (0-8153-1913-4) Garland.

Strategic Behavior in Economics & Business. H. Scott Bierman & Luis Fernandez. (Illus.). 448p. (C). 1993. pap. text ed. 36.75 (0-201-56298-7) Addison-Wesley.

Strategic Benchmarking: How to Rate Your Company's Performance Against the World's Best. Gregory H. Watson. LC 92-41907. 288p. 1993. text ed. 37.50 (0-471-58600-5) Wiley.

Strategic Bombers: How Many Are Enough? Jeffrey Record. LC 86-6. (National Security Papers: No. 3). 26p. 1986. 7.50 (0-89549-069-2) Inst Foreign Policy Anal.

Strategic Bombing. Coldfelter. 1997. 22.95 (0-02-905585-7, Free Press) Free Pr.

Strategic Bombing: The American Experience. Herman S. Wolk. 43p. 1981. pap. 21.95 (0-89126-101-X) MA-AH Pub.

Strategic Bombing of Germany, 1940-1945. Alan J. Levine. LC 91-45610. 248p. 1992. text ed. 49.95 (0-275-94319-4, C4319, Praeger Pubs) Greenwood.

***Strategic Brand Management.** 2nd ed. Jean-Noel Kapferer. 1997. pap. text ed. 30.00 (0-7494-2089-8) Kogan Page Ltd.

***Strategic Brand Management: Building & Managing Brand Equity.** Kevin L. Keller. LC 97-23327. 1998. write for info. (0-13-120115-8) P-H.

Strategic Brand Management: New Approaches to Creating & Evaluating Brand Equity. Jean-Noel Kapferer. 340p. 1994. 29.95 (0-02-917045-1, Free Press) Free Pr.

Strategic Budgeting. Roy T. Meyers. LC 94-3056. 250p. (C). 1994. text ed. 47.50 (0-472-10362-8) U of Mich Pr.

Strategic Budgeting. Roy T. Meyers. LC 94-3056. (C). 1996. pap. 22.95 (0-472-08414-3) U of Mich Pr.

Strategic Budgeting: A Comparison Between U. S. & Japanese Companies. Akira Ishikawa. LC 84-18037. 240p. 1985. text ed. 37.95 (0-275-90120-3, C0120, Praeger Pubs) Greenwood.

Strategic Business Engineering: A Synergy of Software Engineering & Information Engineering. Brian Dickinson. LC 91-60471. (Illus.). 236p. (Orig.). 1992. pap. text ed. 27.95 (0-9629276-0-0) LCI Pr.

***Strategic Business Finance.** Keith Ward. 1997. pap. text ed. 24.95 (0-7494-1937-7, Kogan Pg Educ) Stylus Pub VA.

Strategic Business Forecasting: The Complete Guide to Forecasting Real-World Company Performance. Jae K. Shim et al. 1994. text ed. 47.50 (1-55738-569-6) Irwin Prof Pubng.

***Strategic Business Foundations: Building Concepts & Skills.** Ed. by Whetten. (C). 1996. text ed. 58.50 (0-321-01237-2) Addison-Wesley.

***Strategic Business Planning.** Clive Reading. (Business & Management Ser.). 1995. pap. 24.95 (0-7494-1639-4) Kogan Page Ltd.

Strategic Business Planning: An Action Program for Forward-Looking Businesses. Clive Reading. 400p. 1993. text ed. 47.95 (0-89397-391-2) Nichols Pub.

Strategic Business Planning: The Pursuit of Competitive Advantage. George S. Day. (Strategic Marketing Ser.). (Illus.). 237p. (C). 1984. pap. text ed. 37.00 (0-314-77884-5) West Pub.

Strategic Business Transformation: Achieving Strategic Objectives Through Business Re-Engineering. Warren Winslow. (Quality in Action Ser.). 1996. pap. write for info. (0-07-707955-8) McGraw.

Strategic Buying for the Future: Opportunities for Innovation in Government Electronics System Acquisition. Barry M. Horowitz. LC 92-40304. (Libey Business Library). 182p. 1993. 19.95 (1-882222-04-0) Libey Pub.

Strategic Calling: The Center for Strategic & International Studies, 1962-1992. James A. Smith. LC 93-29993. (CSIS Book Ser.). 303p. (gr. 13). 1993. text ed. 21.95 (0-89206-237-1) CSI Studies.

Strategic Capital Budgeting: Developing & Implementing the Corporate Capital Allocation. Hazel J. Johnson. 1994. text ed. 42.50 (1-55738-426-6) Irwin Prof Pubng.

Strategic Capitalism: Private Business & Public Purpose in Japanese Industrial Finance. Kent E. Calder. 395p. (C). 1993. pap. text ed. 18.95 (0-691-04475-9) Princeton U Pr.

Strategic Change: Building a High Performance Organization. Philip Sadler. LC 95-15781. (Best of Long Range Planning Ser.). 250p. 1995. text ed. 57.50 (0-08-042571-2) Elsevier.

***Strategic Change in Colleges & Universities: Planning to Survive & Prosper.** Daniel J. Rowley et al. LC 96-25370. (Higher & Adult Education Ser.). 1997. write for info. (0-7879-0348-5) Jossey-Bass.

Strategic Changes & Organizational Reorientations in Local Government: A Cross-National Perspective. Ed. by Nahum Ben-Elia. LC 95-19327. 1996. text ed. 59.95 (0-312-12856-8) St Martin.

Strategic Chess: Mastering the Closed Game. Edmar Mednis. 236p. 1993. pap. 14.95 (0-945806-11-6) Summit CA.

Strategic Choice & Path-Dependency in Post-Socialism: Institutional Dynamics in the Transformation Process. Ed. by Jerzy Hausner et al. LC 95-7199. 352p. 1995. 80.00 (1-85898-045-3) E Elgar.

Strategic Choices: Supremacy, Survival or Sayonara. Edward Primozic et al. 256p. 1991. text ed. 24.95 (0-07-051036-9) McGraw.

Strategic Choices for a Changing Health Care System. Ed. by Stuart H. Altman & Uwe E. Reinhardt. LC 96-2630. (Baxter Health Policy Review Ser.: Vol. 2). 413p. 1996. 49.00 (1-56793-040-9, 0975) Health Admin Pr.

Strategic Choices for America's Hospitals: Managing Change in Turbulent Times. Stephen M. Shortell & Ellen M. Morrison. LC 89-45605. (Health-Management Ser.). 427p. pap. text ed. 22.95 (1-55542-438-4) Jossey-Bass.

Strategic Choices for America's Hospitals: Managing Change in Turbulent Times. Stephen M. Shortell et al. LC 89-45605. (Health-Management Ser.). 427p. text ed. 41.95 (1-55542-188-1) Jossey-Bass.

Strategic Command & Control: Redefining the Nuclear Threat. Bruce G. Blair. LC 84-73164. 341p. 1985. 42.95 (0-8157-0982-X); pap. 18.95 (0-8157-0981-1) Brookings.

***Strategic Communication in Business & the Professions, 2 Vols.** 2nd ed. Dan O'Hair et al. 512p. (C). 1994. pap. text ed. 37.16 (0-395-70889-3) HM.

***Strategic Communication in Business & the Professions, 2 Vols.** 2nd ed. Dan O'Hair et al. (C). 1995. teacher ed., text ed. 11.96 (0-395-70890-7) HM.

***Strategic Compensation: Human Resource Management Approach.** Joseph J. Martocchio. LC 96-50312. 1997. 65.33 (0-13-440983-3) P-H.

Strategic Compromise. William Nixon. 400p. 1990. 19.95 (1-55972-026-3, Birch Ln Pr) Carol Pub Group.

Strategic Concepts in Fire Fighting. Edward McAniff. (Illus.). 1994. 18.95 (0-912212-02-0) Fire Eng.

Strategic Concepts of Go. Yoshiaki S. Nagahara. 1972. pap. 13.95 (4-87187-006-5, G6) Ishi Pr Intl.

Strategic Consequences of Nuclear Proliferation in South Asia. Ed. by Neil Joeck. 120p. 1986. 35.00 (0-7146-3300-3, Pub. by F Cass Pubs UK) Intl Spec Bk.

Strategic Control. Peter Lorange et al. 1986p. (C). 1986. pap. text ed. 38.25 (0-314-85258-1) West Pub.

Strategic Control: Establishing Milestones for Long-Term Performance. Michael Goold & John J. Quinn. LC 93-4023. (Illus.). 240p. 1993. 29.95 (0-201-60899-5) Addison-Wesley.

Strategic Control: Milestone for Long Term Performance. Michael Gould & John J. Quinn. 240p. 1990. 75.00 (0-273-60536-4, Pub. by Pitman Pubng UK) St Mut.

Strategic Control of Marketing Finance. David Haigh. (Financial Times Management Ser.). 224p. 1994. 77.50 (0-273-60231-4, Pub. by Pitman Pub Ltd UK) Trans-Atl Phila.

Strategic Cooperation & Competition in the Pacific Islands. Fedor Mediansky. 391p. (Orig.). 1995. pap. write for info. (1-884296-02-5) Austlia-NZ Studies.

Strategic Corporate Alliances: A Study of the Present, a Model for the Future. Louis E. Nevaer & Steven A. Deck. LC 90-30010. 240p. 1990. text ed. 55.00 (0-89930-361-7, Quorum Bks) Greenwood.

Strategic Corporate Facilities Management. Stephen Binder. 1992. text ed. 43.00 (0-07-005306-5) McGraw.

Strategic Cost Analysis: The Evolution from Managerial to Strategic Accounting. John K. Shank & Vijay Govindarajan. 180p. (C). 1989. per. 33.25 (0-256-07042-3) Irwin.

***Strategic Cost Management.** Ed. by Richard M. Wilson. LC 97-17262. (International Library of Management). 350p. 1997. text ed. 112.95 (1-85521-581-0, Pub. by Ashgate UK) Ashgate Pub Co.

Strategic Cost Management: The New Tool for Competitive Advantage. John K. Shank & Vijay Govindarajan. LC 93-3370. 320p. 1993. 35.00 (0-02-912651-7, Free Press) Free Pr.

Strategic Credit Management: Strategic Approach. Harold L. Rolfes. LC 95-19597. 256p. 1995. text ed. 69.95 (0-471-58343-X) Wiley.

Strategic Credit Risk Management. John McKinley & John Barrickman. LC 93-35888. (Illus.). 120p. (Orig.). 1994. pap. text ed. 60.00 (0-936742-98-4, 31176) Robt Morris Assocs.

Strategic Customer Alliances: How to Win, Manage & Develop Key Account Business in the 1990s. Ken Burnett. 1994. 35.00 (0-7863-0144-9) Irwin Prof Pubng.

Strategic Customer Alliances: How to Win, Manage & Develop Key Account Business in the 1990s. Ken Burnett. 224p. 1992. 111.00 (0-273-03873-7, Pub. by Pitman Pubng UK) St Mut.

Strategic Cycle Investing: The Investor's Survival Guide for All Markets. Richard Coghlan. LC 93-16272. 1993. text ed. 34.95 (0-07-707596-X) McGraw.

Strategic Database Marketing. Robert R. Jackson et al. 256p. 1995. 39.95 (0-8442-3232-7, NTC Busn Bks) NTC Pub Grp.

Strategic Database Marketing: The Masterplan for Starting & Managing a Profitable Customer. Arthur M. Hughes. 1994. text ed. 35.00 (1-55738-551-3) Irwin Prof Pubng.

Strategic Database Technology: Management for the Year 2000. Alan Simon. 1995. pap. 34.95 (1-55860-264-X) Morgan Kaufmann.

Strategic Deception in the Second World War. Michael Howard. 320p. 1995. pap. 13.95 (0-393-31293-3, Norton Paperbks) Norton.

***Strategic Decision Challenge.** D. E. Hussey. LC 97-25694. (The Wiley Series in Contemporary Strategic Concerns). 1997. write for info. (0-471-97480-3) Wiley.

Strategic Decision Making. Chris Gore et al. 256p. 1992. text ed. 70.00 (0-304-32559-7); pap. text ed. 24.95 (0-304-31965-1); teacher ed. write for info. (0-304-32547-3) Cassell.

Strategic Decision Making. Kirkwood. (Business Statistics Ser.). 300p. 1996. pap. 30.95 (0-534-51693-9) Wadsworth Pub.

Strategic Decision Making: Multiobjective Decision Analysis with Spreadsheets. Craig W. Kirkwood. LC 96-20271. (Business Statistics Ser.). (C). 1997. pap. text ed. 36.95 (0-534-51692-0) Wadsworth Pub.

Strategic Decisions from Behavioral Research: 1st Annual Behavioral Research Conference, January 24-26, 1990, Axioms under Review: Challenging the Conventional Wisdom of Marketing & Attitude Research. Behavioral Research Conference Staff. LC 90-1051. (Illus.). 238p. 1990. reprint ed. pap. 67.90 (0-7837-9764-8, 2060492) Bks Demand.

Strategic Defence Initiative: Some Implications for Europe. Werner Kaltefleiter. (C). 1990. 45.00 (0-907967-45-0, Pub. by Inst Euro Def & Strat UK) St Mut.

Strategic Defences in the Nineteen Nineties: Criteria for Deployment. Ivo H. Daalder. LC 91-12417. 256p. 1991. text ed. 69.95 (0-312-06544-2) St Martin.

Strategic Defense & Extended Deterrence. Jacquelyn K. Davis & Robert L. Pfaltzgraff. LC 86-69. (National Security Papers: No. 4). 56p. 1986. 8.00 (0-89549-070-6) Inst Foreign Policy Anal.

Strategic Defense & the Future of the Arms Race: A Pugwash Symposium. Ed. by John P. Holdren & Joseph Rotblat. 256p. 1987. pap. 14.95 (0-312-00790-6); text ed. 45.00 (0-312-00789-2) St Martin.

Strategic Defense Debate: Can "Star Wars" Make Us Safe? Ed. by Craig Snyder. LC 86-25057. (Illus.). 268p. 1986. pap. text ed. 22.95 (0-8122-1233-9) U of Pa Pr.

Strategic Defense Initiative. Business Communications Co., Inc. Staff. (Illus.). 300p. 1986. pap. 1,750.00 (0-89336-477-0, GB-088) BCC.

Strategic Defense Initiative. Edward Reiss. (Studies in International Relations: No. 23). (Illus.). 280p. (C). 1992. text ed. 64.95 (0-521-41097-5) Cambridge U Pr.

Strategic Defense Initiative: An International Perspective. Ed. by C. James Haug. 1987. text ed. 46.00 (0-88033-979-9) East Eur Monographs.

Strategic Defense Initiative: Its Effect on the Economy & Arms Control. David Z. Robinson. (Joseph I. Lubin Memorial Lectures: No. 4). 88p. (C). 1988. text ed. 12.00 (0-8147-7404-0) NYU Pr.

Strategic Defense Initiative: Progress & Challenge. Douglas C. Waller et al. (Guides to Contemporary Issues Ser.: No. 7). (Illus.). xii, 174p. (Orig.). 1987. pap. 11.95 (0-941690-25-3); lib. bdg. 19.95 (0-941690-24-5) Regina Bks.

Strategic Defense Initiative: Some Claims Overstated for Early Flight Tests of Interceptors. (Illus.). 42p. (Orig.). (C). 1993. pap. text ed. 20.00 (1-56806-677-5) DIANE Pub.

Strategic Defense Initiative: Splendid Defense or Pipe Dream? Scott Armstrong & Peter Grier. LC 86-80312. (Headline Ser.: No. 275). (Illus.). 64p. (Orig.). 1985. pap. 5.95 (0-87124-103-X) Foreign Policy.

Strategic Defense Initiative: Survivability & Software: A Report from the Office of Technology Assessment. (Illus.). 275p. 1988. pap. text ed. 17.95 (0-691-02270-4) Princeton U Pr.

Strategic Defense Initiative: Symbolic Containment of the Nuclear Threat. Rebecca S. Bjork. LC 91-34487. (SUNY Series in the Making of Foreign Policy). 182p. 1992. text ed. 64.50 (0-7914-1161-3); pap. text ed. 21.95 (0-7914-1162-1) State U NY Pr.

Strategic Defenses & Arms Control. Ed. by Jack N. Barkenbus & Alvin M. Weinberg. LC 87-2280. 263p. 1987. 24.95 (0-88702-218-9); pap. 12.95 (0-88702-219-7) Washington Inst Pr.

Strategic Derivatives: Successful Corporate Practices for Today's Global Marketplace. 1995. 295.00 (0-614-12670-3) Economist Intell.

Strategic Design & Organizational Change: Pacific Rim Seaports in Transition. Herman L. Boschken. LC 86-14673. (Illus.). 256p. 1988. text ed. 34.95 (0-8173-0339-1) U of Ala Pr.

***Strategic Development of Credit Union.** Charles Ferguson & Donald McKillop. text ed. 90.00 (0-471-96912-5) Wiley.

Strategic Dimensions of Economic Behavior. Ed. by Gordon H. McCormick & Michael E. Bissell. LC 84-13292. 288p. 1984. text ed. 45.00 (0-275-91225-6, C1225, Praeger Pubs) Greenwood.

Strategic Direction for Information Technology in California State Government, 1993-1999. Thomas W. Hayes & Steve E. Kolodney. 51p. (Orig.). (C). 1994. pap. text ed. 20.00 (0-7881-1258-9) DIANE Pub.

Strategic Directions in Supermarket Deli-Prepared Foods. John W. Allen et al. (Illus.). 98p. (Orig.). (C). 1992. pap. text ed. 25.00 (1-56806-001-7) DIANE Pub.

Strategic Disagreement: Stalemate in American Politics. John B. Gilmour. (Policy & Institutional Studies). (Illus.). 184p. (C). 1995. 49.95 (0-8229-3907-X); pap. 14.95 (0-8229-5575-X) U of Pittsburgh Pr.

Strategic Disarmament, Verification & National Security. 174p. 1977. 21.00 (0-85066-127-7) Taylor & Francis.

***Strategic Discovery: Competing in New Arenas.** Howard Thomas & Don O'Neal. LC 97-9431. 1997. write for info. (0-471-97632-6) Wiley.

Strategic Divestment. Leonard Vignola. LC 73-85193. 157p. reprint ed. pap. 44.80 (0-317-39711-7, 2055937) Bks Demand.

Strategic Doctrines & Their Alternatives. Y. Sakamoto. x, 300p. 1987. pap. text ed. 53.00 (0-677-21990-3) Gordon & Breach.

Strategic Dynamics of the Insurance Industry: Asset & Liability Management Issues. Edward I. Altman & Irwin T. Vanderhoof. 416p. 1996. text ed. 75.00 (0-7863-0463-4) Irwin Prof Pubng.

Strategic Economics. Norman A. Bailey. (Special Issue of Comparative Strategy Ser.: Vol. 7, No. 2). 75p. 1988. pap. 18.00 (0-8448-1553-5) Taylor & Francis.

Strategic Emotional Involvement. Lawrence E. Hedges. LC 94-11703. 1996. 40.00 (1-56821-065-5) Aronson.

Strategic Energy Supply & National Security. Carl Vansant. LC 78-139882. (Special Studies in International Politics & Government). 1971. 39.50 (0-89197-951-4) Irvington.

***Strategic Enrollment Management: A Primer for Campus Administrators.** Michael G. Dolence. 1996. write for info. (0-614-23452-2, 1244) Am Assn Coll Registrars.

***Strategic Enrollment Management: Cases from the Field.** Ed. by Michael G. Dolence. 96p. 1996. 20.00 (0-614-23453-0, 9914) Am Assn Coll Registrars.

Strategic Environment Assessment. Riki Therivel. 1992. 24.95 (1-85383-147-6, Pub. by Erthscan Pubns UK) Island Pr.

Strategic Environmental Management: Using TQEM & ISO 14000 for Competitive Advantage. Grace H. Wever. LC 95-52787. (Illus.). 256p. 1996. text ed. 54.95 (0-471-14746-X) Wiley.

Strategic Evaluation & Management of Capital Expenditures. Robert E. Pritchard & Thomas J. Hindelang. LC 80-69702. 336p. reprint ed. pap. 95.80 (0-317-27193-8, 2023925) Bks Demand.

Strategic Executive Decisions: An Analysis of the Difference Between Theory & Practice. Michael J. Stahl. LC 88-18666. 197p. 1989. text ed. 55.00 (0-89930-316-1, SLL/, Quorum Bks) Greenwood.

Strategic Exposure: Proliferation Around the Mediterranean. Ian O. Lesser et al. LC 96-3054. 125p. 1996. pap. 15.00 (0-8330-2373-X, MR-742-A) Rand Corp.

Strategic Extension Campaign: Participation in Dry-Oriented Method of Agricultural Extension. Ronny Adhikarya. (Illus.). 210p. 1995. pap. text ed. 50.00 (92-5-103570-9, F35709, Pub. by FAO IT) Bernan Associates.

Strategic Factors in Business Cycles. John M. Clark. 234p. 1963. reprint ed. 35.00 (0-678-00016-6) Kelley.

Strategic Factors in Business Cycles. John M. Clark. (General Ser.: No. 24). 256p. 1934. reprint ed. 66.60 (0-87014-023-X) Natl Bur Econ Res.

Strategic Factors in Nineteenth Century American Economic History: A Volume to Honor Robert W. Fogel. Ed. by Claudia D. Goldin & Hugh Rockoff. (National Bureau of Economic Research Conference Report Ser.). (Illus.). 502p. 1992. 69.00 (0-226-30112-5) U Ch Pr.

***Strategic Failures in the Modern Presidency.** Mary E. Stuckey. LC 96-44486. (Hampton Press Communication Ser.). 240p. 1997. pap. 21.50 (1-57273-101-X) Hampton Pr NJ.

An Asterisk (*) at the beginning of an entry indicates that the title is appearing in BIP for the first time.

***Strategic Failures in the Modern Presidency.** Mary E. Stuckey. 240p. 1997. 45.00 (*1-57273-100-1*) Hampton Pr NJ.

Strategic Family Play Therapy. S. Ariel. (Series on Psychotherapy & Counselling). 256p. 1992. text ed. 52.95 (*0-471-92401-6*) Wiley.

Strategic Family Therapy. Cloe Madanes. LC 80-26286. (Social & Behavioral Science Ser.). 270p. 30.95 (*0-87589-487-9*) Jossey-Bass.

Strategic Family Therapy. Cloe Madanes. LC 80-26286. (Social & Behavioral Science Ser.). 272p. 1991. pap. 17.95 (*1-55542-363-9*) Jossey-Bass.

Strategic Finance Workout: Test & Build Your Financial Performance. David Parker. (Illus.). 250p. (Orig.). 1997. pap. 25.00 (*0-273-62565-9*, Fincl Times) Pitman Publng.

Strategic Financial Analyzer (St Fan) Version 2.0: Spreadsheet Templates For Strategic Management & Business Policy. 4th ed. Wheelen. (C). 1992. pap. 14.95 (*0-201-52623-9*) Addison-Wesley.

***Strategic Financial Decisions.** David Allen. (CIMA Financial Skills Ser.). 1994. pap. 24.95 (*0-7494-1147-3*) Kogan Page Ltd.

Strategic Financial Management for Conferences, Workshops, & Meetings. Robert G. Simerly. LC 92-30631. (Higher & Adult Education Ser.). 150p. text ed. 27.95 (*1-55542-518-6*) Jossey-Bass.

Strategic Financial Planning for Healthcare Organizations: An Executive Guide to Capital Debt. Christopher T. Payne. (C). 1994. text ed. 60.00 (*1-55738-615-3*) Irwin Prof Pubng.

Strategic Financial Planning with Simulation. Dennis E. Grawoig & Charles L. Hubbard. (Illus.). 1982. text ed. 42.95 (*0-89433-115-9*) Petrocelli.

Strategic Flexibility: A Management Guide for Changing Times. Kathryn R. Harrigan. LC 84-40815. 224p. 1985. 29.95 (*0-669-10222-9*) Free Pr.

Strategic Focus: A Game Plan for Developing Your Competitive Advantage. Stephen C. Tweed. 1993. 12.95 (*0-8119-0651-5*) LIFETIME.

Strategic Focus: A Gameplan for Developing Your Competitive Advantage. Stephen C. Tweed. LC 94-30012. 1994. 12.95 (*0-8119-0800-3*) LIFETIME.

Strategic Focus: How Corporate Managers Gain the Competitive Advantage in Today's Marketplace. rev. ed. Stephen C. Tweed. LC 96-5053. 240p. 1999. pap. 14.95 (*0-8119-0834-8*) LIFETIME.

Strategic Force Modernization & Arms Control. Edward L. Rowny et al. LC 85-10579. (National Security Papers: No. 6). 1986. 7.50 (*0-89549-075-7*) Inst Foreign Policy Anal.

Strategic Forces: Issues for the Mid-Seventies. Alton H. Quanbeck. LC 73-1088. (Brookings Institution Staff Paper Ser.). 104p. reprint ed. pap. 29.70 (*0-317-26347-1*, 2025400) Bks Demand.

Strategic Forces & Deterrence. Harold Brown. (CISA Working Papers: No. 42). 48p. (Orig.). 1983. pap. 15.00 (*0-86682-054-X*) Ctr Intl Relations.

***Strategic Fund Development: Building Profitable Relationships That Last.** Simone P. Joyaux. LC 96-48500. (Aspen's Fund Raising Series for the 21st Century). 1997. pap. write for info. (*0-8342-0796-6*) Aspen Pub.

Strategic Futures: Evolving Missions for Traditional Strategic Delivery Vehicles. Richard Mesic et al. LC 94-16172. (Illus.). xxv, 100p. (Orig.). 1995. pap. text ed. 15.00 (*0-8330-1617-2*, MR-375-DAG) Rand Corp.

Strategic Gas Marketing Symposium. vi, 286p. 1983. pap. 40.00 (*0-910091-49-8*) Inst Gas Tech.

Strategic Geography: NATO, the Warsaw Pact, & the Superpowers. 2nd ed. Hugh Faringdon. 384p. (C). 1989. text ed. 55.00 (*0-415-00980-4*, A3226) Routledge.

Strategic Geography & the New Middle East. Geoffrey T. Kemp & Robert Harkavy. LC 97-12997. 232p. 1993. pap. 14.95 (*0-87003-023-X*) Carnegie Endow.

Strategic Governance: How to Make Big Decisions Better. Jack H. Schuster. LC 94-28927. (American Council on Education-Oryx Press Series on Higher Education). 240p. 1994. 29.95 (*0-89774-847-6*) Oryx Pr.

Strategic Grasp of the Bible: Studies in the Structural & Dispensational Characteristics of the Bible. J. Sidlow Baxter. LC 91-24389. 352p. 1991. reprint ed. 13.99 (*0-8254-2198-5*) Kregel.

Strategic Groups, Strategic Moves & Performance. Herman Daems & Howard Thomas. LC 94-3388. 364p. 1994. text ed. 66.25 (*0-08-037768-8*, Pergamon Pr) Elsevier.

Strategic Guide to International Trade. Ed. by Jonathan Reuvid. 350p. 1996. pap. 60.00 (*0-7494-1621-1*, Pub. by Kogan Pg UK) Cassell.

Strategic Hamlets in South Vietnam: A Survey & Comparison. Milton E. Osborne. LC 65-64732. (Cornell University, Southeast Asia Program, Data Paper Ser.: No. 55). 88p. reprint ed. pap. 25.10 (*0-8357-3668-7*, 2036394) Bks Demand.

Strategic Health Care Manager: Mastering Essential Leadership Skills. George H. Stevens. LC 90-15634. (Health-Management Ser.). 295p. text ed. 37.95 (*1-55542-324-8*) Jossey-Bass.

Strategic Health Management: A Guide for Employers, Employees, & Policymakers. Jeffrey S. Harris. LC 93-47964. (Health-Management Ser.). 413p. text ed. 40.95 (*1-55542-655-7*) Jossey-Bass.

Strategic Health Planning: Methods - Techniques Applied to Marketing - Management. Allen D. Spiegel & Herbert H. Hyman. Ed. by Glenn R. Caddy. (Developments in Clinical Psychology Ser.). 544p. (C). 1991. pap. 49.50 (*0-89391-892-X*); text ed. 125.00 (*0-89391-742-7*) Ablex Pub.

Strategic Heart: Using the New Science To Lead Growing Organizations. Michael H. Shenkman. LC 96-587. 208p. 1996. pap. text ed. 19.95 (*0-275-95620-2*, Praeger Pubs) Greenwood.

Strategic Heart: Using the New Science to Lead Growing Organizations. Michael H. Shenkman. LC 96-587. 208p. 1996. text ed. 59.95 (*1-56720-078-8*, Quorum Bks) Greenwood.

Strategic Highways of Africa. Guy Arnold & Ruth Weiss. LC 76-53953. (Illus.). 1977. text ed. 29.95 (*0-312-76431-6*) St Martin.

Strategic Hospitality Management. Ed. by Richard Teare & Andrew Boer. 256p. 1991. text ed. 55.00 (*0-304-32535-X*); pap. text ed. 24.95 (*0-304-32285-7*) Cassell.

Strategic Hotel-Motel Marketing. rev. ed. Christopher W. Hart & David A. Troy. LC 86-19926. (Illus.). 420p. 1996. pap. write for info. (*0-86612-111-0*) Educ Inst Am Hotel.

Strategic Human Resource Management. Charles J. Fombrun et al. LC 84-15223. 499p. 1984. text ed. 72.50 (*0-471-81079-7*) Wiley.

Strategic Human Resource Management. Chris Hendry. (Illus.). 300p. 1995. pap. 34.95 (*0-7506-0994-X*) Buttrwrth-Heinemann.

Strategic Human Resource Management. Kenneth A. Kovach. 374p. 1996. pap. text ed. 34.50 (*0-7618-0331-9*) U Pr of Amer.

***Strategic Human Resource Management.** Olive Lundy & Alan Cowling. 416p. 1995. 69.00 (*0-415-13603-2*) Routledge.

Strategic Human Resource Management. A. J. Romiszowski et al. 172p. 1990. 34.75 (*90-265-1092-6*) Swets.

Strategic Human Resource Management. 2nd ed. Anthony. (C). 1995. text ed. 63.25 (*0-03-012887-0*) HB Coll Pubs.

Strategic Human Resource Management: Ford & the Search for Competitive Advantage. Ken Starkey & Alan McKinlay. LC 92-43004. (Human Resource Management in Action Ser.). 256p. 1993. pap. 44.95 (*0-631-18674-3*) Blackwell Pubs.

Strategic Human Resource Management & Total Compensation: Canadian DEBS Course VIII Study Manual. Dalhousie University Staff. (CEBS Canadian Course Ser.: 8). 614p. 1994. student ed., ring bd. write for info. (*0-89154-481-X*) Intl Found Employ.

Strategic Human Resource Management Sourcebook. Lloyd S. Baird et al. 400p. 1988. pap. 39.95 (*0-87425-068-4*) HRD Press.

Strategic Human Resource Planning Applications. Richard J. Niehaus. 248p. 1987. 75.00 (*0-306-42561-0*, Plenum Pr) Plenum.

Strategic Human Resources Management. Christopher Mabey et al. LC 93-9495. (Illus.). 450p. (C). 1995. pap. 37.95 (*0-631-18505-4*) Blackwell Pubs.

Strategic Human Resources Planning & Management. William J. Rothwell & Hercules C. Kazanas. (Illus.). 416p. (C). 1988. text ed. 85.00 (*0-13-851643-X*) P-H.

Strategic Illusion: The Singapore Strategy & the Defence of Australia & New Zealand, 1919-1942. Ian Hamill. 406p. 1981. 57.50 (*9971-69-008-X*, Pub. by Sgapore Univ SI) Coronet Bks.

Strategic Impasse: Offense, Defense, & Deterrence Theory & Practice. Stephen J. Cimbala. LC 89-2166. (Contributions in Military Studies: No. 89). 287p. 1989. text ed. 65.00 (*0-313-26516-X*, CSI/, Greenwood Pr) Greenwood.

Strategic Imperatives & Western Responses in the South & Southwest Pacific. Ed. by Henry S. Albinski. 462p. (C). 1986. vinyl bd. 18.00 (*0-317-91351-4*) Pac Forum.

Strategic Implications of the All-Volunteer Force: The Conventional Defense of Central Europe. Kenneth J. Coffey. LC 79-19110. (Studies on Armed Forces & Society). 220p. reprint ed. pap. 62.70 (*0-8357-4405-1*, 2037225) Bks Demand.

Strategic Indicators for Higher Education. 2nd ed. Barbara E. Taylor et al. 168p. 1996. reprint ed. 49.95 (*1-56079-522-0*) Petersons.

Strategic Industrial Marketing. 3rd ed. Peter Chisnall. 380p. 1995. pap. text ed. 52.00 (*0-13-203365-8*) P-H.

Strategic Industrial Sourcing: The Japanese Advantage. Toshihiro Nishiguchi. LC 92-13254. (Illus.). 384p. 1994. 48.00 (*0-19-507109-3*) OUP.

Strategic Industries in a Global Economy: Policy Issues for the 1990s. OECD Staff. 106p. (Orig.). 1991. pap. 20.00 (*92-64-13559-6*) OECD.

Strategic Industry at Risk: Semiconductors. (Illus.). 50p. (Orig.). (C). 1993. pap. text ed. 20.00 (*1-56806-891-3*) DIANE Pub.

Strategic Information Management: Challenges & Strategies in Managing Information Systems. Robert Galliers & Bernadette Baker. 280p. 1994. pap. 45.95 (*0-7506-1731-4*) Buttrwrth-Heinemann.

Strategic Information Planning Methodologies. 2nd ed. James Martin. 1989. text ed. 86.00 (*0-13-850538-1*) P-H.

Strategic Information Systems. Charles Wiseman. 320p. (C). 1988. pap. text ed. 31.95 (*0-256-06030-4*) Irwin.

Strategic Information Systems: A European Perspective. Ed. by Claudia Ciborra & Tawfik Jelassi. LC 93-8851. (Series in Information Systems). 242p. 1994. text ed. 65.00 (*0-471-94107-7*) Wiley.

Strategic Information Systems: Forging the Business & Technology Alliance. Henry E. Firdman. 1991. text ed. 44.95 (*0-07-157695-9*) McGraw.

Strategic Information Systems: Forging the Business & Technology Alliance. Henry E. Firdman. (Illus.). 456p. 1991. 44.95 (*0-8306-7723-2*, 3723, TAB/TPR) TAB Bks.

Strategic Information Systems for Strategic, Manufacturing, Operations, Marketing, Sales, Financial & Human Resources Management, Vol. 16. Robert P. Cerveny. Ed. by C. Carl Pegels et al. LC 93-33185. (Monographs in Organizational Behavior & Industrial Relations: Vol. 16). 307p. 1993. 73.25 (*1-55938-716-5*) Jai Pr.

Strategic Information Technology Management: Perspectives on Organizational Growth & Competitive Advantage. Ed. by Rajiv Banker et al. LC 91-76952. 704p. 1993. text ed. 84.95 (*1-878289-16-0*) Idea Group Pub.

Strategic Information Warfare: A New Face of War. Roger C. Molander et al. LC 95-53673. 105p. (Orig.). 1996. pap. 15.00 (*0-8330-2352-7*, MR-661) Rand Corp.

Strategic Intelligence & National Decisions. Roger Hilsman. LC 80-29549. 187p. 1981. reprint ed. text ed. 49.75 (*0-313-22717-9*, HISI, Greenwood Pr) Greenwood.

Strategic Intelligence & Statecraft: Selected Essays. Adda B. Bozeman. 269p. 1992. 21.95 (*0-02-881009-0*) Brasseys Inc.

Strategic Intelligence for American National Security. Bruce D. Berkowitz. 264p. 1989. pap. text ed. 16.95 (*0-691-02339-5*) Princeton U Pr.

***Strategic Interaction.** Erving Goffman. LC 74-92857. (University of Pennsylvania Series in Conduct & Communication Monograph: Vol. 1). 155p. pap. 44.20 (*0-608-04812-7*, 2065469) Bks Demand.

Strategic Interaction: Learning Languages Through Scenarios. Robert J. DiPietro. (New Directions in Language Teaching Ser.). (Illus.). 160p. 1987. pap. text ed. 18.95 (*0-521-31197-7*) Cambridge U Pr.

Strategic Interaction: Learning Languages Through Scenarios. Robert J. DiPietro. (New Directions in Language Teaching Ser.). (Illus.). 160p. 1987. text ed. 44.95 (*0-521-32425-4*) Cambridge U Pr.

Strategic Interaction & Language Acquisition: Theory, Practice, & Research. Georgetown University Round Table on Languages & Linguistics Staff. Ed. by James E. Alatis. LC 58-31607. 620p. 1993. reprint ed. pap. 176.70 (*0-7837-9498-3*, 2060242) Bks Demand.

Strategic International Marketing. H. G. Meissner. (Illus.). 260p. 1990. 71.95 (*0-387-52254-9*) Spr-Verlag.

Strategic Internet Marketing. Tom Vassos. 400p. 1996. pap. text ed. 24.99 (*0-7897-0827-2*) Que.

***Strategic Internet Marketing.** 2nd ed. Tom Vassos. Date not set. 24.99 (*0-7897-1276-8*) Macmillan.

Strategic Interpersonal Communication. Ed. by John A. Daly & John M. Wiemann. LC 92-45190. (Interpersonal Communication Ser.). 320p. 1994. text ed. 69.95 (*0-89859-957-1*) L Erlbaum Assocs.

Strategic Intervention in Organizations: Resolving Ethical Dilemmas. M. Cash Mathews. (Library of Social Research: Vol. 169). 160p. (C). 1988. 54.00 (*0-8039-3303-7*); pap. 24.95 (*0-8039-3304-5*) Sage.

Strategic Interventions for Hyperactive Children. Ed. by Martin Gittelman. LC 81-14407. 223p. reprint ed. pap. 63.60 (*0-685-44443-0*, 2032780) Bks Demand.

***Strategic Intuition for the 21st Century: Tarot for Business.** James Wanless. 206p. 1997. 2.95 (*1-886708-01-0*) Merrill-West Pub.

Strategic Investment Decision: Evaluating Investment Opportunities. Roger Oldcorn & David Parker. (Financial Times Management Ser.). (Illus.). 256p. 1996. 39.95 (*0-273-61779-6*) Pitman Publng.

Strategic Investment Decisions: A Comparative Study of Companies in the Motor Industry in the U. K. & West Germany. Chris Carr et al. (Avebury Business Research Library). 407p. 1994. 76.95 (*1-85628-975-3*, Pub. by Avebury Pub UK) Ashgate Pub Co.

Strategic Investment Planning & Technology Choice in Manufacturing Systems. rev. ed. Shan L. Li. LC 93-38434. (Studies on Industrial Productivity). 176p. 1994. text ed. 52.00 (*0-8153-1594-5*) Garland.

Strategic Investment Timing: How to Pinpoint & Profit from Short & Long Term Changes. Richard A. Stoken. 1993. pap. 18.95 (*1-55738-491-6*) Irwin Prof Pubng.

Strategic IS/IT Planning. Ed Tozer. LC 95-21570. (Datamation Bk. Ser.). 530p. 1996. pap. 51.95 (*0-7506-9666-4*, Digital DEC) Buttrwrth-Heinemann.

Strategic Issues for Electronic Records Management: Towards Open Systems Interconnection. 126p. 1992. 32.00 (*92-1-100374-1*) UN.

Strategic Issues in Finance. Keith Ward. (Management Reader Ser.). 250p. 1994. pap. 41.95 (*0-7506-0996-6*) Buttrwrth-Heinemann.

Strategic Issues in Health Care Management. Ed. by Mo Malek et al. 279p. 1993. text ed. 87.95 (*0-471-93964-1*) Wiley.

Strategic Issues in Public Sector Productivity: The Best of Public Productivity Review 1975-1985. Ed. by Marc Holzer & Arie Halachmi. LC 94-69117. 235p. 1995. pap. text ed. 29.95 (*0-9639874-6-1*) Chatelaine.

Strategic Issues in Public Sector Productivity: The Best of Public Productivity Review, 1975-1985. Ed. by Marc Holzer & Arie Halachmi. LC 86-27793. (Jossey-Bass Management Ser.). 245p. reprint ed. pap. 69.90 (*0-7837-2505-1*, 2042664) Bks Demand.

Strategic Issues in State-Owned Organizations. Ed. by Taieb Hafsi. LC 89-19389. (Strategic Management, Policy & Planning Ser.). 339p. 1989. 73.25 (*0-89232-803-7*) Jai Pr.

Strategic Issues Management: Guide to Environmental Scanning. John D. Stoffels. 274p. 1994. text ed. 65.00 (*0-08-042394-9*, Ed Skills Dallas) Elsevier.

Strategic Issues Management: How Organizations Influence & Respond to Public Interests & Policies. Heath, Robert L., & Associates. LC 87-46335. (Management Ser.). 436p. 42.95 (*1-55542-083-4*) Jossey-Bass.

***Strategic Issues Management: Organizations & Public Policy Challenges.** Robert L. Heath. LC 97-4749. 392p. 1997. text ed. 58.00 (*0-8039-7034-X*); pap. text ed. 26.95 (*0-8039-7035-8*) Sage.

***Strategic Job-Jumping: How to Get from Where You Are.** Julia Hartman. 176p. 1997. per. 13.00 (*0-7615-1023-0*) Prima Pub.

Strategic Justification of Flexible Automation. Automated Systems, NEMA Staff. 10.00 (*0-318-18040-5*) Natl Elec Mfrs.

***Strategic Labor Relations.** Kenneth A. Kovach. 332p. 1996. pap. 39.00 (*0-7618-0581-8*) U Pr of Amer.

Strategic Leadership. (C). 1995. write for info. (*0-615-00556-X*) West Pub.

Strategic Leadership: A Multiorganizational-Level Perspective. Ed. by Robert L. Phillips & James G. Hunt. LC 92-8383. 352p. 1992. text ed. 55.00 (*0-89930-756-6*, PSJ, Quorum Bks) Greenwood.

Strategic Leadership: Achieving Your Preferred Future. Glen Hiemstra & Bill Hainer. 64p. (Orig.). 1993. pap. 19.95 (*0-929656-00-8*) Lincoln Global Prodns.

Strategic Leadership: Managing the Missing Links. 2nd enl. ed. Richard S. Handscombe & Philip A. Norman. LC 92-43218. 1993. write for info. (*0-07-707763-6*) McGraw.

Strategic Leadership: Top Executives & Their Effect on Organizations. Sydney Finkelstein & Donald C. Hambrick. LC 95-45380. (Strategic Management Ser.). 200p. (C). 1996. pap. text ed. 26.00 (*0-314-04605-4*) West Pub.

Strategic Leadership for Schools: Creating & Sustaining Productive Change. John J. Mauriel. LC 89-45592. (Education-Higher Education Ser.). 373p. text ed. 34.95 (*1-55542-184-9*) Jossey-Bass.

Strategic Leadership Process. Glen Hiemstra & Bill Hainer. (Illus.). 180p. (Orig.). 1990. student ed. 9.95 (*0-317-91196-1*); pap. 18.95 (*0-317-91195-3*); audio 65.00 (*0-317-91197-X*); vhs 149.00 (*0-317-91198-8*); disk 79.95 (*0-317-91199-6*) Lincoln Global Prodns.

Strategic Learning. Ian Cunningham. 1994. pap. text ed. 24.95 (*0-07-707894-2*) McGraw.

Strategic Learning & Knowledge Management. Ron Sanchez & Aime Heene. LC 96-27866. (Strategic Management Ser.). 1996. text ed. 66.00 (*0-471-96881-1*) Wiley.

Strategic Learning in Action: How to Accelerate & Sustain Business Change. Tony Grundy. LC 94-10894. (Henley Management Ser.). 1994. write for info. (*0-07-707825-X*) McGraw.

Strategic Learning in the Content Areas. Doris M. Cook. 203p. (C). 1989. pap. text ed. 30.00 (*1-57337-015-0*) WI Dept Pub Instruct.

Strategic Logistics Management. 3rd ed. Douglas M. Lambert & James R. Stock. 820p. (C). 1992. text ed. 68.95 (*0-256-08838-1*) Irwin.

Strategic Management. Bourgeois. (C). 1995. text ed. 67.25 (*0-03-055789-5*) HB Coll Pubs.

Strategic Management. Bourgeois. (C). 1996. teacher ed., pap. text ed. 28.00 (*0-03-072254-3*) HarBrace.

Strategic Management. Paulette Bourgeois. (C). 1994. write for info. (*0-201-10717-1*) Addison-Wesley.

Strategic Management. Lloyd L. Byars et al. LC 95-38589. (Illus.). 1072p. (C). 1995. per. 72.75 (*0-256-13619-X*) Irwin.

Strategic Management. G. A. Cole. 284p. 1994. pap. 59.95 (*1-85805-099-5*, Pub. by DP Publns UK) St Mut.

Strategic Management. Robert M. Grant & James Craig. 160p. (Orig.). 1993. pap. text ed. 25.95 (*0-7494-1063-9*, Pub. by Kogan Page UK) Nichols Pub.

Strategic Management. Harrison. Date not set. pap. text ed. 27.25 incl. disk (*0-314-03808-6*) West Pub.

Strategic Management. Harvard Business Review Staff. LC 83-1336. (Harvard Business Review Executive Book Ser.). 560p. 1983. text ed. 34.95 (*0-471-87596-1*) Wiley.

Strategic Management, 3 Vols. Hill. (C). Date not set. suppl. ed., teacher ed., text ed. write for info. (*0-395-71675-6*) HM.

Strategic Management, 3 Vols. Hill. (C). 1995. teacher ed., pap. 11.96 (*0-395-70942-3*) HM.

***Strategic Management.** Katsioloud. (C). 1996. teacher ed., pap. text ed. 66.50 (*0-03-018852-0*) HB Coll Pubs.

Strategic Management. Pitts. Date not set. teacher ed., pap. text ed. write for info. (*0-314-08285-9*) West Pub.

Strategic Management. 2nd ed. Alex Miller & Gregory G. Dess. LC 95-36996. (Management Ser.). 1996. text ed. write for info. (*0-07-042791-7*) McGraw.

Strategic Management. 2nd ed. Thomas L. Wheelen & J. David Hunger. LC 86-17227. 329p. (C). 1986. pap. text ed. write for info. (*0-201-09038-4*) Addison-Wesley.

Strategic Management. 3rd ed. Byars. (C). 1991. text ed. 62.50 (*0-06-500049-8*) Addson-Wesley Educ.

***Strategic Management.** 3rd ed. Alex Miller. LC 97-22814. 1997. text ed. write for info. (*0-07-043014-4*) McGraw.

Strategic Management. 4th ed. J. David Hunger & Thomas L. Wheelen. LC 92-10211. (Illus.). 434p. (C). 1993. pap. text ed. 36.75 (*0-201-55838-6*) Addison-Wesley.

Strategic Management. 4th ed. Rowe. (C). 1994. pap. text ed. write for info. (*0-201-60082-X*) Addison-Wesley.

***Strategic Management.** 4th ed. Wright & Knoll. 1997. pap. text ed. 74.67 (*0-13-628801-4*) P-H.

Strategic Management. 5th ed. J. David Hunger. (C). 1996. pap. text ed. write for info. (*0-201-88040-7*) Addison-Wesley.

Strategic Management. 5th ed. J. David Hunger & Wheelen. Ed. by Michael Payne. LC 95-6673. (C). 1996. pap. text ed. 42.50 (*0-201-53740-0*) Addison-Wesley.

***Strategic Management.** 6th ed. Fred David. LC 96-36834. (Illus.). 1000p. (C). 1996. text ed. 75.00 (*0-13-486011-X*) P-H.

Strategic Management: A Choice Approch. Richard Montanari et al. 1216p. (C). 1990. text ed. 54.00 (*0-03-008857-7*) Dryden Pr.

Strategic Management: A Focus on Process. 2nd ed. Samuel C. Certo & J. Paul Peter. LC 92-36103. 384p. (C). 1993. per. 47.95 (*0-256-14120-7*) Irwin.

Strategic Management: A Framework for Decision Making & Problem Solving. A. J. Almaney. 370p. (Orig.). (C). 1992. pap. text ed. 29.95 (*1-879215-04-7*) Sheffield WI.

S

An Asterisk (*) at the beginning of an entry indicates that the title is appearing in BIP for the first time.

Strategic Management: A Methodological Approach. 2nd ed. Alan J. Rowe et al. 396p. (C). 1986. teacher ed. write for info. (*0-318-59831-0*); pap. text ed. write for info. (*0-201-16898-7*) Addison-Wesley.

Strategic Management: A Methodological Approach. 4th ed. Alan J. Rowe. LC 93-6599. (Illus.). 992p. (C). 1994. pap. text ed. 58.25 (*0-201-58638-X*) Addison-Wesley.

Strategic Management: A Resource-Based Approach for the Hospitality & Tourism Industries. Richard Teare. (Hotel & Catering Ser.). 64p. 1993. pap. 9.95 (*0-304-32867-7*) Cassell.

Strategic Management: An Analytical Introduction. 3rd ed. George Luffman et al. 550p. 1996. text ed. 62.95 (*0-631-20103-3*) Blackwell Pubs.

Strategic Management: An Integrative Context Specific Process. Robert J. Mockler. 928p. 1993. 84.95 (*1-878289-19-5*) Idea Group Pub.

***Strategic Management: An Introduction.** Ronald Rosen. (Illus.). 197p. (Orig.). 1995. pap. 39.50 (*0-273-61250-6*, Pub. by Pitman Pub Ltd UK) Trans-Atl Phila.

Strategic Management: Awareness & Change. 2nd ed. John L. Thompson. LC 92-44936. 784p. 1993. pap. 29.95 (*0-412-46340-7*) Chapman & Hall.

***Strategic Management: Awareness & Change.** 3rd ed. John Thompson. 784p. 1997. pap. 31.95 (*1-86152-100-6*) Inter Thomson.

Strategic Management: Building & Sustaining Competitive Advantage. Robert A. Pitts & David Lei. LC 95-32131. 450p. (C). 1996. pap. text ed. 36.50 (*0-314-06113-4*) West Pub.

Strategic Management: Canadian Cases. 2nd ed. Mark C. Baetz & Paul W. Beamis. (C). 1990. 54.95 (*0-256-08340-1*) Irwin.

Strategic Management: Casebook in Policy & Planning. 2nd ed. Charles W. Hofer et al. (Illus.). 766p. (C). 1984. text ed. 60.25 (*0-314-77915-9*) West Pub.

***Strategic Management: Cases.** 3rd ed. Hitt & Ireland. (GC - Principles of Management Ser.). Date not set. pap. 44.95 (*0-538-88189-5*) S-W Pub.

Strategic Management: Cases. 3rd ed. Peter Wright et al. LC 95-34268. 709p. 1995. pap. text ed. 49.00 (*0-13-234014-3*) P-H.

Strategic Management: Competitiveness & Globalization. Michael A. Hitt et al. LC 94-34793. 1136p. (C). 1995. text ed. 68.50 (*0-314-04340-3*) West Pub.

Strategic Management: Competitiveness & Globalization: Cases. Michael A. Hitt et al. LC 94-34795. 650p. (C). 1995. pap. text ed. 45.25 (*0-314-04338-1*) West Pub.

***Strategic Management: Competitiveness & Globalization: Cases.** 2nd ed. Michael A. Hitt et al. LC 96-48464. 1996. pap. write for info. (*0-314-20076-2*) West Pub.

***Strategic Management: Competitiveness & Globalization: Cases.** 2nd ed. Michael A. Hitt et al. LC 96-43209. 1996. pap. write for info. (*0-314-20073-8*) West Pub.

Strategic Management: Competitiveness & Globalization: Concepts. Michael A. Hitt et al. LC 94-34794. 432p. (C). 1995. pap. text ed. 45.25 (*0-314-04339-X*) West Pub.

***Strategic Management: Competitiveness & Globalization: Theory & Cases.** 2nd ed. Michael A. Hitt et al. LC 96-40947. 1100p. 1997. write for info. (*0-314-20112-2*); teacher ed. write for info. (*0-314-20113-0*) West Pub.

***Strategic Management: Concepts.** 3rd ed. Hitt & Ireland. (GC - Principles of Management Ser.). (C). Date not set. text ed. 43.95 (*0-538-88188-7*) S-W Pub.

Strategic Management: Concepts. 3rd ed. Peter Wright et al. LC 95-31720. 304p. 1995. pap. text ed. 44.00 (*0-13-439340-6*) P-H.

***Strategic Management: Concepts.** 4th ed. Wright & Mark Knoll. (C). 1997. pap. text ed. 74.67 (*0-13-631623-9*) P-H.

Strategic Management: Concepts & Applications. 3rd ed. Samuel C. Certo & J. Paul Peter. (C). 1995. 72.75 (*0-256-15158-X*) Irwin.

Strategic Management: Concepts & Cases. John H. Barnett & William D. Wilsted. 992p. (C). 1988. text ed. 78.95 (*0-534-87176-3*) S-W Pub.

Strategic Management: Concepts & Cases. 3rd ed. Peter Wright et al. LC 95-34267. 1995. text ed. 80.00 (*0-13-362815-9*) P-H.

Strategic Management: Concepts & Cases. 6th ed. Arthur A. Thompson, Jr. & A. J. Strickland, III. 1008p. (C). 1992. text ed. 66.95 (*0-256-09698-8*, 11-1284-06) Irwin.

Strategic Management: Concepts & Cases. 7th ed. Gregory J. Stappenbeck et al. (C). 1994. 72.95 (*0-256-18623-5*) Irwin.

Strategic Management: Concepts & Cases. 7th ed. Arthur A. Thompson, Jr. & A. J. Strickland, III. LC 92-37023. 960p. (C). 1993. text ed. 17.95 (*0-256-12707-7*) Irwin.

Strategic Management: Concepts & Cases. 8th ed. Ed. by Arthur A. Thompson, Jr. et al. LC 94-22560. 1024p. (C). 1994. text ed. 72.75 (*0-256-14055-3*) Irwin.

Strategic Management: Concepts & Cases. 8th ed. Arthur A. Thompson & J. A. Strickland. (C). 1994. ring bd. 88.75 (*0-256-18362-7*) Irwin.

Strategic Management: Concepts & Cases. 9th ed. Arthur A. Thompson. 960p. (C). 1996. text ed. 72.45 (*0-256-16205-0*) Irwin.

Strategic Management: Concepts, Decisions & Cases. 2nd ed. Lester A. Digman. 928p. (C). 1989. text ed. 59.95 (*0-256-06673-6*) Irwin.

Strategic Management: Creating Your Credit Union's Future. Allan M. Crecelius & Sandra M. Comrie. 257p. (Orig.). 1994. pap. 99.00 (*1-889394-22-X*) Credit Union Execs.

Strategic Management: Formulation & Implementation. Michael J. Stahl & David W. Grigsby. 271p. (C). 1992. pap. 42.95 (*0-534-93102-2*) S-W Pub.

Strategic Management: Formulation, Implementation & Control. 4th ed. John A. Pearce, II & Richard B. Robinson, Jr. 1056p. (C). 1990. 34.95 (*0-256-08324-X*) Irwin.

Strategic Management: Formulation, Implementation & Control. 4th ed. Richard Robinson & John A. Pearce. (C). 1990. text ed. 60.95 (*0-256-08323-1*) Irwin.

Strategic Management: Formulation, Implementation, & Control. 5th ed. John A. Pearce, II & Richard B. Robinson, Jr. LC 94-41400. 976p. (C). 1994. 68.95 (*0-256-17067-3*) Irwin.

***Strategic Management: Formulation, Implementation, & Control.** 6th ed. John A. Pearce & Richard B. Robinson. LC 96-9674. 960p. (C). 1996. 72.75 (*0-256-15478-3*) Irwin.

Strategic Management: Methods & Studies. Ed. by B. V. Dean & J. C. Cassidy. (Studies in Management Science & Systems: No. 18). 362p. 1990. 150.75 (*0-444-88047-X*, North Holland) Elsevier.

Strategic Management: Public Planning at the Local Level. Leonard C. Moffitt. LC 84-47775. (Contemporary Studies in Economic & Financial Analysis: Vol. 45). 160p. 1984. 73.25 (*0-89232-428-7*) Jai Pr.

Strategic Management: Selected Cases. 7th ed. Arthur A. Thompson & A. J. Strickland. (C). 1994. pap. text ed. 23.95 (*0-256-18096-2*) Irwin.

Strategic Management: Selected Chapters. 7th ed. Arthur A. Thompson & A. J. Strickland. (C). 1994. text ed. 31.95 (*0-256-18211-6*) Irwin.

Strategic Management: Selected Text. 7th ed. Richard Robinson et al. (C). 1994. text ed. 33.95 (*0-256-17210-2*) Irwin.

Strategic Management: Selected Text & Cases. 5th ed. Richard Robinson & John A. Pearce. (C). 1994. text ed. 36.50 (*0-256-16524-6*) Irwin.

Strategic Management: Selected Text & Cases. 6th rev. ed. Arthur A. Thompson & A. J. Strickland. (C). 1994. text ed. 40.95 (*0-256-17887-9*) Irwin.

Strategic Management: Test Bank. Bourgeois. (C). 1996. suppl. ed., pap. text ed. 28.00 (*0-03-072257-8*) HB Coll Pubs.

Strategic Management: Text & Cases. 4th ed. James M. Higgins & Julian W. Vincze. LC 88-430. (Illus.). 1173p. (C). 1989. text ed. 55.25 (*0-03-021613-3*) Dryden Pr.

Strategic Management: Text & Cases. 5th ed. James M. Higgins & Julian W. Vincze. LC 92-81291. 1175p. (C). 1993. IBM 3 1/2". disk 17.50 (*0-03-092839-7*) Dryden Pr.

Strategic Management: Text & Cases. 5th ed. James M. Higgins & Julian W. Vincze. LC 92-81291. 1175p. (C). 1993. text ed. 57.75 (*0-03-054757-1*); teacher ed., pap. text ed. 6.00 (*0-03-054759-8*) Dryden Pr.

Strategic Management: Text & Cases on Business Policy. LaRue T. Hosmer. (Illus.). 736p. (C). 1982. write for info. (*0-13-851063-6*) P-H.

Strategic Management: The Process of Gaining a Competitive Advantage. 2nd ed. A. J. Almaney. (Illus.). 429p. 1995. pap. 29.80 (*0-87563-520-2*) Stipes.

***Strategic Management: Theory & Cases 3.** 3rd ed. Hitt & Ireland. (GC - Principles of Management). (C). Date not set. text ed. 68.95 (*0-538-88182-8*) S-W Pub.

Strategic Management: Theory & Practice. 3rd ed. Hussey. 250p. 1995. text ed. 95.00 (*0-08-041394-3*, Prgamon Press) Buttrwrth-Heinemann.

Strategic Management: Theory & Practice. 3rd ed. David E. Hussey. 686p. 1994. pap. 37.95 (*0-08-042562-3*, Prgamon Press) Buttrwrth-Heinemann.

***Strategic Management: Total Quality & Global Competition.** Michael J. Stahl & David W. Grisby. (Illus.). 350p. 1997. pap. 34.95 (*1-55786-650-3*) Blackwell Pubs.

Strategic Management Accounting. Keith Ward & Sri Srikanthan. 307p. 1992. pap. 47.95 (*0-7506-0110-8*) Buttrwrth-Heinemann.

***Strategic Management Accounting: Text & Cases.** Malcom Smith. LC 96-36315. 1996. pap. write for info. (*0-7506-3097-3*) Buttrwrth-Heinemann.

Strategic Management & Business Planning: A Methodological Approach. Alan J. Rowe et al. 1982. text ed. write for info. (*0-201-06387-5*) Addison-Wesley.

Strategic Management & Business Policy. Thomas L. Wheelen & J. David Hunger. LC 82-13886. 400p. 1983. teacher ed. write for info. (*0-201-09012-0*) Addison-Wesley.

Strategic Management & Business Policy. 3rd ed. Lawrence R. Jauch & William F. Glueck. 448p. 1988. pap. text ed. write for info. (*0-07-032339-9*) McGraw.

Strategic Management & Business Policy. 3rd ed. Thomas L. Wheelen & J. David Hunger. LC 82-13886. (Illus.). 1096p. (C). 1989. text ed. 38.36 (*0-201-60000-5*) Addison-Wesley.

Strategic Management & Business Policy. 4th ed. Thomas L. Wheelen & J. David Hunger. LC 82-13886. (Illus.). 1120p. (C). 1992. text ed. 60.25 (*0-201-53281-6*) Addison-Wesley.

Strategic Management & Business Policy. 5th ed. Wheelan. (C). 1993. pap. text ed. write for info. (*0-201-84555-5*) Addison-Wesley.

Strategic Management & Business Policy. 5th ed. Thomas L. Wheelen & Hunger. Ed. by Michael Payne. LC 82-13886. (Illus.). (C). 1995. text ed. 60.25 (*0-201-56388-6*) Addison-Wesley.

***Strategic Management & Business Policy.** 6th ed. Thomas L. Wheelen. (C). 1998. text ed. write for info. (*0-201-09581-5*) Addison-Wesley.

***Strategic Management & Business Policy.** 6th ed. Thomas L. Wheelen & J. David Hunger. LC 97-20401. 992p. (C). 1998. text ed. write for info. (*0-201-84657-8*) Addison-Wesley.

Strategic Management & Business Policy: A Methodological Approach. 2nd ed. Alan J. Rowe & Richard O. Mason. Ed. by Karl E. Dickel. 700p. 1985. teacher ed. write for info. (*0-201-06088-4*); pap. text ed. write for info. (*0-201-06087-6*) Addison-Wesley.

Strategic Management & Business Policy: A Methodological Approach. 3rd ed. Alan J. Rowe. (C). 1989. pap. text ed. 54.95 (*0-201-15736-5*) Addison-Wesley.

Strategic Management & Information Systems: An Integrated Approach. 2nd ed. Wendy Robson. (Illus.). 400p. (Orig.). 1997. pap. 57.50 (*0-273-61591-2*, Pub. by Pitman Pub Ltd UK) Trans-Atl Phila.

Strategic Management & Organisational Dynamics. 2nd ed. Ralph Stacey. (Illus.). 592p. (Orig.). 1996. pap. 62.50 (*0-273-61375-8*, Pub. by Pitman Pub Ltd UK) Trans-Atl Phila.

Strategic Management & Strategic Management MBA Strategy Case Book: University of Hawaii-Manoa, Hawaii Edition. 7th ed. John A. Pearce et al. (C). 1995. 26.00 (*0-256-18891-2*) Irwin.

Strategic Management Blueprint. Paul Dobson & Ken Starkey. LC 92-31273. 176p. 1993. pap. 33.95 (*0-631-18624-7*) Blackwell Pubs.

Strategic Management Casebook & Skill Builder. Alan N. Hoffman & Hugh M. O'Neill. Ed. by Fenton. LC 92-18133. 500p. (C). 1993. pap. text ed. 43.75 (*0-314-01216-8*) West Pub.

Strategic Management Cases. David W. Grigsby & Michael J. Stahl. LC 92-30048. 565p. 1993. pap. 48.95 (*0-534-93134-0*) S-W Pub.

Strategic Management Cases. Ed. by Robert J. Mockler. 1993. 30.00 (*0-536-58303-X*) Ginn Pr.

Strategic Management Cases. Neil H. Snyder et al. (Illus.). 704p. (C). 1991. pap. text ed. 35.50 (*0-201-54616-7*) Addison-Wesley.

Strategic Management Concepts. James M. Higgins & Julian W. Vincze. LC 92-81290. 488p. (C). 1993. pap. text ed. 34.25 (*0-03-096586-1*) Dryden Pr.

Strategic Management for Academic Libraries: A Handbook. Robert M. Hayes. LC 92-40775. (Library Management Collection). 240p. 1993. text ed. 59.95 (*0-313-28111-4*, HYS, Greenwood Pr) Greenwood.

Strategic Management for Bankers. Richard W. Sapp & Roger W. Smith. 221p. 1984. pap. 23.00 (*0-912841-19-2*) Planning Forum.

Strategic Management for Business: Concepts & Cases. Hale C. Bartlett. (Illus.). 786p. (C). 1988. text ed. 45.25 (*0-03-007183-6*) Dryden Pr.

Strategic Management for Decision Making. Michael J. Stahl & David W. Grigsby. 999p. (C). 1992. text ed. 75.95 (*0-534-92681-9*) S-W Pub.

Strategic Management for Insurers: Selected Readings, 2 vols. Ed. by Christine L. Lewis. LC 92-74543. 610p. (C). 1992. 26.00 (*0-89462-073-8*, ARP102) IIA.

Strategic Management for Nonprofit Organizations: Theory & Cases. Sharon M. Oster. (Illus.). 288p. 1995. 38.00 (*0-19-508503-5*) OUP.

Strategic Management for Physicians. Linda E. Swayne & Peter M. Ginter. 304p. 1996. text ed. 45.00 (*0-7863-1027-8*) Irwin Prof Pubng.

Strategic Management for Public Libraries: A Handbook. Robert M. Hayes & Virginia A. Walter. LC 96-2548. (Greenwood Library Management Collection). 248p. 1996. text ed. 59.95 (*0-313-28954-9*, Greenwood Pr) Greenwood.

Strategic Management Frontiers, Vol. 10. Ed. by John H. Grant & Samuel B. Bacharach. LC 88-8839. (Monographs in Organizational Behavior & Industrial Relations: Vol. 10). 483p. 1988. 73.25 (*0-89232-775-8*) Jai Pr.

***Strategic Management in a Hostile Environment: Lessons from the Tobacco Industry.** Raymond M. Jones. LC 97-5884. 1997. text ed. write for info. (*1-56720-158-X*, Quorum Bks) Greenwood.

Strategic Management in Construction. David Langford & Steven Male. 144p. 1991. text ed. 64.95 (*0-566-09015-5*, Pub. by Gower UK) Ashgate Pub Co.

Strategic Management in Developing Countries: Case Studies. James E. Austin & Thomas O. Kohn. 624p. 1990. 45.00 (*0-02-901105-1*, Free Press) Free Pr.

Strategic Management in Education: A Focus on Strategic Planning. Evelyn P. Valentine. 200p. 1990. ring bd. 38.95 (*0-205-12579-4*, H25794) Allyn.

Strategic Management in High Technology Firms, Vol. 12. Ed. by Michael W. Lawless et al. LC 90-33863. (Monographs in Organizational Behavior & Industrial Relations: Vol. 12). 245p. 1990. 73.25 (*1-55938-105-1*) Jai Pr.

Strategic Management in Information Technology. David B. Yoffie. LC 93-5827. 380p. (C). 1993. text ed. 56.20 (*0-13-098559-7*) P-H.

Strategic Management in Japanese Companies. Ed. by Toyohiro Kono. (Best of Long Range Planning Ser.: No. 11). (Illus.). 178p. 1992. text ed. 95.75 (*0-08-040670-X*, Pergamon Pr) Elsevier.

Strategic Management in Major Multinational Companies. Ed. by Nigel J. Freedman. (Best of Long Range Planning Ser.: No. 8). (Illus.). 140p. 1991. text ed. 86.50 (*0-08-037754-8*, Pergamon Pr) Elsevier.

Strategic Management in Multinational Companies. Yves Doz. (Illus.). 155p. 1986. pap. text ed. 34.95 (*0-08-031807-X*, Prgamon Press) Buttrwrth-Heinemann.

Strategic Management in Non-Profit Organizations: An Administrator's Handbook. Robert D. Hay. LC 89-24368. 416p. 1990. text ed. 69.50 (*0-89930-551-2*, HSJ/, Greenwood Pr) Greenwood.

***Strategic Management in Public & Nonprofit Organizations: Managing Public Concerns in an Era of Limits.** 2nd ed. Jack Koteen. LC 96-44678. 376p. 1997. text ed. 75.00 (*0-275-95531-1*, Praeger Pubs); pap. text ed. 29.95 (*0-275-95532-X*, Praeger Pubs) Greenwood.

Strategic Management in the Asian Context: A Casebook in Business Policy & Strategy. Luis M. Calingo. LC 95-52959. 1996. pap. text ed. 30.00 (*0-471-19003-9*) Wiley.

Strategic Management in the Global Economy. 3rd ed. Heidi Vernon-Wortzel & Lawrence H. Wortzel. LC 96-8695. 582p. 1996. pap. text ed. 56.95 (*0-471-15873-9*) Wiley.

Strategic Management in the Hospitality Industry. Michael D. Olsen. 392p. 1992. text ed. 49.95 (*0-442-00246-7*) Van Nos Reinhold.

Strategic Management International: Concepts & Cases. 7th ed. Arthur A. Thompson & A. J. Strickland. 960p. (C). 1993. student ed., per. 34.50 (*0-256-13930-X*) Irwin.

***Strategic Management of Agricultural Research: Proceedings, 39th Annual Meeting of the Agricultural Research Institute, October 16-18, 1990.** 137p. pap. 25.00 (*0-614-24233-9*) Agri Research Inst.

Strategic Management of Behavioral Problems. 3rd ed. Kerr. LC 97-15169. 1997. 53.00 (*0-02-363527-4*, Macmillan Coll) P-H.

Strategic Management of College Enrollments. Don Hossler et al. LC 90-40146. (Higher & Adult Education Ser.). 354p. text ed. 38.95 (*1-55542-292-6*) Jossey-Bass.

Strategic Management of Development Programmes: Guidelines for Action. Samuel Paul. (Management Development Ser.: No. 19). vii, 137p. 1990. pap. 18.00 (*92-2-103252-3*) Intl Labour Office.

Strategic Management of Health Care Organizations. 2nd ed. Peter M. Ginter et al. LC 94-27573. (Illus.). 600p. (C). 1994. text ed. 75.95 (*1-55786-534-5*) Blackwell Pubs.

***Strategic Management of Health Care Organizations.** 3rd ed. W. Jack Duncan et al. LC 97-12153. (Illus.). 960p. 1997. text ed. 84.95 (*1-55786-968-5*) Blackwell Pubs.

Strategic Management of Human Knowledge, Skills, & Abilities: Workforce Decision Making in the Postindustrial Era. Eugene B. McGregor, Jr. LC 90-20738. (Public Administration - Management Ser.). 376p. 42.95 (*1-55542-307-8*) Jossey-Bass.

Strategic Management of Human Resources: A Portfolio Approach. George S. Odiorne. LC 84-47993. (Management Ser.). 376p. text ed. 36.95 (*0-87589-625-1*) Jossey-Bass.

Strategic Management of Human Resources in Health Services Organizations. Myron D. Fottler et al. LC 87-34059. (Health Services Ser.). 454p. 1989. text ed. 47.50 (*0-8273-4240-3*) Delmar.

Strategic Management of Human Resources in Health Services Organizations. 2nd ed. Ed. by Myron D. Fottler et al. LC 93-27232. (Delmar Series in Health Services Administration). 547p. 1994. pap. 44.00 (*0-8273-5676-5*) Delmar.

Strategic Management of Organizations & Stakeholders: Cases. Jeffrey S. Harrison & Caron H. St. John. Ed. by Leyh. LC 93-30589. 640p. (C). 1993. pap. text ed. 45.25 (*0-314-02624-X*) West Pub.

Strategic Management of Organizations & Stakeholders: Concepts. Jeffrey S. Harrison & Caron H. St. John. Ed. by Leyh. LC 93-30590. 350p. (C). 1993. pap. text ed. 45.25 (*0-314-02625-8*) West Pub.

Strategic Management of Organizations & Stakeholders: Theory & Cases. Jeffrey S. Harrison & Caron H. St. John. Ed. by Leyh. LC 93-30591. 980p. (C). 1993. text ed. 68.50 (*0-314-02626-6*) West Pub.

Strategic Management of Public & Third Sector Organizations: A Handbook for Leaders. Paul C. Nutt & Robert W. Backoff. LC 91-16608. (Public Administration Ser.). 510p. 39.95 (*1-55542-386-8*) Jossey-Bass.

***Strategic Management of Science & Technology.** Bernard Taylor. 1997. 40.00 (*0-13-485160-9*) P-H.

***Strategic Management of Services: Framework & Cases.** Ranjan Das. (Illus.). 384p. 1997. 29.95 (*0-19-564170-1*) OUP.

Strategic Management of Services in the Arab Gulf States: Company & Industry Cases. M. Sami Kassem & Ghazi M. Habib. xii, 480p. (C). 1989. pap. text ed. 77.90 (*3-11-011449-6*) De Gruyter.

Strategic Management of Teams. David I. Cleland. LC 95-35708. (Illus.). 320p. 1996. text ed. 39.95 (*0-471-12058-8*) Wiley.

Strategic Management of Technological Innovation. Ed. by Raymond Loveridge & Martin Pitt. 404p. 1990. text ed. 104.50 (*0-471-92499-7*) Wiley.

Strategic Management of Technological Innovation. Ed. by Raymond Loveridge & Martyn Pitt. LC 89-70548. 404p. 1992. pap. text ed. 55.00 (*0-471-93465-8*) Wiley.

Strategic Management of Technology. 2nd ed. Robert A. Burgelman & Modesto A. Maidique. 944p. (C). 1995. 72.75 (*0-256-09128-5*) Irwin.

Strategic Management of Technology & Innovation. Robert Burgelman & Modesto Maidique. 672p. (C). 1996. pap. text ed. 37.50 (*0-256-22814-0*) Irwin.

Strategic Management of Technology & Innovation. Robert A. Burgelman & Modesto A. Maidique. 624p. (C). 1987. text ed. 72.75 (*0-256-03481-8*) Irwin.

Strategic Management of Technology in the Chemical & Petrochemical Industries. Rogerio H. Quintella. LC 93-21542. 1994. 69.00 (*1-85567-146-8*) St Martin.

Strategic Management of the China Venture. Paul Steidlmeier. LC 95-6920. 264p. 1995. text ed. 65.00 (*1-56720-001-X*, Quorum Bks) Greenwood.

Strategic Management Practice. John A. Pearce, II & Richard B. Robinson, Jr. 420p. (C). 1990. pap. text ed. 29.50 (*0-256-09452-7*, 11-3384-01) Irwin.

An Asterisk (*) at the beginning of an entry indicates that the title is appearing in BIP for the first time.

Strategic Management Process. 3rd ed. Samuel C. Certo et al. LC 94-24725. (C). 1994. 57.25 (*0-256-18149-7*) Irwin Prof Pubng.

Strategic Management Process: Integrating the OD Perspective. David Hitchin & Walter Ross. (Organization Development Ser.). (Illus.). 200p. (C). 1995. pap. text ed. 22.75 (*0-201-52429-5*) Addison-Wesley.

Strategic Management Readings. Michael A. Hitt. Date not set. pap. text ed. 13.75 (*0-314-06464-8*) West Pub.

Strategic Management Select Text & Cases. 6th ed. Arthur A. Thompson & J. A. Strickland. 600p. (C). 1995. text ed. 46.95 (*0-256-19776-8*) Irwin.

Strategic Management Selected Cases: Northern Kentucky University Edition. 7th ed. J. A. Strickland & Arthur A. Thompson. (C). 1994. 20.95 (*0-256-18910-2*) Irwin.

Strategic Management Skills. Daniel J. Power et al. 300p. (C). 1986. pap. text ed. 31.25 (*0-201-13978-2*) Addison-Wesley.

Strategic Management Support Systems. Christine Fidler & Simon. (Illus.). 352p. (Orig.). 1996. pap. 52.50 (*0-273-61418-5*, Pub. by Pitman Pub Ltd UK) Trans-Atl Phila.

Strategic Management Theory. Harrison. Date not set. teacher ed., pap. text ed. write for info. (*0-314-03285-1*) West Pub.

Strategic Management Theory, 3 Vols. Hill. (C). 1994. text ed. 70.76 (*0-395-70943-1*); text ed. 44.76 (*0-395-71995-X*) HM.

Strategic Management Theory: Testbank. Harrison. Date not set. suppl. ed., pap. text ed. write for info. (*0-314-03286-X*) West Pub.

Strategic Managment. Hoffman. Date not set. suppl. ed., pap. text ed. 13.75 (*0-314-01671-6*) West Pub.

Strategic Mangement of Intellectual Capital. David A. Klein. 240p. 1996. pap. 17.95 (*0-7506-9850-0*) Buttrwrth-Heinemann.

Strategic Manufacturing: Directech Special Edition, Dynamic New Directions for the 1990s. Patricia E. Moody. 1992. text ed. write for info. (*1-55623-992-0*) Irwin Prof Pubng.

Strategic Manufacturing: Dynamic New Directions for the 1990s. Patricia E. Moody. 350p. 1989. text ed. 45.00 (*1-55623-193-8*) Irwin Prof Pubng.

Strategic Manufacturing for Competitive Advantage: Transforming Operations from Shop Floor to Strategy. Steve Brown. LC 95-25503. 1996. 48.00 (*0-13-184508-X*) P-H.

Strategic Market Management. 4th ed. David A. Aaker. 400p. 1994. pap. text ed. 52.95 (*0-471-30956-7*) Wiley.

Strategic Market Planning. Robert J. Hamper & L. Sue Baugh. 256p. 1994. pap. 27.95 (*0-8442-3216-5*, NTC Busn Bks) NTC Pub Grp.

Strategic Market Planning. Robert J. Hamper. 256p. 1995. 39.95 (*0-8442-3215-7*, NTC Busn Bks) NTC Pub Grp.

Strategic Market Planning: An Aid to the Evaluation of an Athletic Recreation Program. Earle F. Zeigler & John Cambell. (Monograph Series on Sport & Physical Education Management). 35p. (Orig.). 1984. pap. text ed. 4.80 (*0-87563-245-9*) Stipes.

Strategic Market Timing. Robert M. Bowker. 1989. 29.95 (*0-13-504754-4*) NY Inst Finance.

***Strategic Marketing.** Adikibi. (Illus.). 368p. 1997. write for info. (*0-412-63710-3*, Chap & Hall NY) Chapman & Hall.

Strategic Marketing. Associated Equipment Distributors Staff. 48p. 1984. 25.00 (*0-318-19175-X*) Assn Equip Distrs.

Strategic Marketing. John Cady & Robert D. Buzzell. (C). 1987. pap. text ed. 57.00 (*0-673-39047-0*) Addison-Wesley Educ.

Strategic Marketing. Paisley College Staff. (Marketing for Manufacturing Managers Ser.). 1989. 105.00 (*0-08-037128-0*) Elsevier.

Strategic Marketing. 3rd ed. David W. Cravens. 832p. (C). 1990. text ed. 61.95 (*0-256-08793-8*, 09-1481-03) Irwin.

Strategic Marketing. 4th ed. David W. Cravens. LC 93-15608. (Series in Marketing). 848p. (C). 1993. text ed. 70.95 (*0-256-12212-1*) Irwin.

Strategic Marketing. 5th ed. David W. Cravens. (Irwin Series in Marketing). 704p. (C). 1996. per. 70.95 (*0-256-21438-7*) Irwin Prof Pubng.

Strategic Marketing: A Handbook for Entrepreneurs & Managers. B. M. Bradway et al. LC 81-3638. 1982. text ed. write for info. (*0-201-00079-2*) Addison-Wesley.

Strategic Marketing: Selected Material. 4th ed. David Cravens. (C). 1994. text ed. 37.95 (*0-256-18263-9*) Irwin.

Strategic Marketing see Marketing for Manufacturing Managers

Strategic Marketing & Management. Ed. by Howard Thomas & David Gardner. LC 83-25902. 519p. reprint ed. pap. 148.00 (*0-7837-0198-5*, 2040494) Bks Demand.

Strategic Marketing Channel Management. Donald J. Bowersox & M. Bixby-Cooper. 1992. text ed. write for info. (*0-07-006757-0*) McGraw.

Strategic Marketing for Educational Institutions. 2nd ed. Philip Kotler & Karen F. Fox. LC 94-24025. (C). 1995. text ed. 80.00 (*0-13-668989-2*) P-H.

Strategic Marketing for Electric Utilities. Clark W. Gellings & Dilip R. Limaye. LC 86-46138. 250p. 1987. text ed. 79.00 (*0-88173-037-8*) Fairmont Pr.

Strategic Marketing For Libraries: A Handbook. Elizabeth J. Wood & Victoria L. Young. LC 87-15022. (Library Management Collection). 240p. 1988. text ed. 45.00 (*0-313-24405-7*, WMK/, Greenwood Pr) Greenwood.

Strategic Marketing for Nonprofit Organizations. 5th rev. ed. Alan R. Andreasen & Philip Kotler. LC 95-40725. Orig. Title: Strategic Marketing for Nonprofit Organizations. 1995. text ed. 71.33 (*0-13-232547-0*) P-H.

Strategic Marketing for Nonprofit Organizations see Strategic Marketing for Nonprofit Organizations

Strategic Marketing for Not-for-Profit Organizations: Program & Resource Development. Armand Lauffer. LC 83-49509. 384p. (C). 1984. 40.00 (*0-02-918260-3*, Free Press) Free Pr.

***Strategic Marketing for OTC Pharmaceuticals.** J. Dudley. (Chapman & Hall Pharmaceutical Industry Ser.). (Illus.). 256p. 1997. text ed. 112.00 (*0-412-48550-8*, Chap & Hall NY) Chapman & Hall.

Strategic Marketing in Central America. Lawrence W. Tuller. LC 94-90585. (LA-C Market Strategies Ser.). 260p. (Orig.). 1996. pap. 26.95 (*1-886188-26-2*) Fomalhaut Pr.

Strategic Marketing in South America. Lawrence W. Tuller. LC 94-90584. (LA-C Market Strategies Ser.). 280p. (Orig.). 1995. pap. 22.95 (*1-886188-24-6*) Fomalhaut Pr.

Strategic Marketing in the Caribbean. Lawrence W. Tuller. LC 94-90583. (LA-C Market Strategies Ser.). 304p. (Orig.). 1995. pap. 26.95 (*1-886188-25-4*) Fomalhaut Pr.

Strategic Marketing, International. 3rd ed. David Cravens. (C). 1991. student ed., per. 30.95 (*0-256-11405-6*) Irwin.

Strategic Marketing Management. Selected by Robert J. Dolan. (Practice of Management Ser.). 640p. 1992. pap. 29.95 (*0-87584-310-7*) Harvard Busn.

Strategic Marketing Management. Robert J. Dolan. 1993. pap. 33.50 (*0-07-017810-0*) McGraw.

Strategic Marketing Management. Robert J. Dolan. 1996. pap. text ed. 29.95 (*0-07-103361-0*) McGraw.

***Strategic Marketing Management.** Jean-Jacques Lambin. LC 96-27234. 1996. pap. write for info. (*0-07-709227-9*) McGraw.

Strategic Marketing Management: Planning & Control, Analysis, & Decision. Paul Fifield & Colin Gilligan. (CIM Workbook Ser.). 320p. 1995. wbk. ed., pap. 31.95 (*0-7506-1990-2*) Buttrwrth-Heinemann.

Strategic Marketing Management: Planning, Implementation & Control. R. M. Wilson et al. 720p. 1992. pap. 50.95 (*0-7506-0329-1*) Buttrwrth-Heinemann.

Strategic Marketing Management & Cases in Marketing Management: "Marketing Management Strategy University of Minnesota Edition. 4th ed. Kenneth Bernhardt. (C). 1994. 30.95 (*0-256-18860-2*) Irwin.

Strategic Marketing Management Cases. 4th ed. David W. Cravens & Charles W. Lamb, Jr. 928p. (C). 1992. text ed. 51.95 (*0-256-10531-6*) Irwin.

Strategic Marketing Management Cases. 5th ed. David W. Cravens et al. LC 95-12120. (Series in Marketing). 608p. (C). 1995. per. 53.50 (*0-256-13689-0*) Irwin.

Strategic Marketing of Electrical Utilities. Gellings & Limaye. 1988. text ed. 79.00 (*0-13-851585-9*) P-H.

***Strategic Marketing Planning.** 2nd ed. Malcolm McDonald. (Cranfield Management Research Ser.). 1996. pap. 24.95 (*0-7494-2096-0*) Kogan Page Ltd.

***Strategic Marketing, Planning & Evaluation.** Geoff Lancaster & Lester Massingham. (Marketing in Action Ser.). 1996. pap. 22.95 (*0-7494-1784-6*) Kogan Page Ltd.

***Strategic Marketing Problems.** 8th ed. Kerin & Peterson. 1997. text ed. 71.33 (*0-13-632860-1*) P-H.

Strategic Marketing Problems: Cases & Comments. 5th ed. Roger A. Kerin & Robert A. Peterson. 750p. 1990. text ed. 55.00 (*0-205-12129-2*, H21298) Allyn.

Strategic Marketing Problems: Cases & Comments. 5th ed. Roger A. Kerin & Robert A. Peterson. 750p. 1990. teacher ed. write for info. (*0-318-66370-8*, H21306); write for info. (*0-318-66371-6*, H24649); disk 20.00 (*0-685-29835-3*, H21280); disk write for info. (*0-318-66372-4*, H22247) P-H.

Strategic Marketing Problems: Cases & Comments. 7th annot. ed. Roger A. Kerin & Robert A. Peterson. 738p. 1995. teacher ed. 68.00 (*0-13-181942-9*) P-H.

Strategic Marketing Problems: Cases & Comments. 7th ed. Roger A. Kerin & Robert A. Peterson. LC 94-12524. 784p. 1994. text ed. 78.00 (*0-205-16170-7*) P-H.

Strategic Materials: A World Survey. Rae Weston. LC 84-3358. 198p. (C). 1984. 60.50 (*0-86598-165-5*) Rowman.

Strategic Media Planning. Kent Lancaster & Helen T. Katz. 320p. 1993. pap. 39.95 incl. disk (*0-8442-3475-3*, NTC Busn Bks) NTC Pub Grp.

Strategic Media Planning. 2nd ed. Kent Lancaster & Helen T. Katz. Ed. by Anne Knudsen. 1995. 79.95 (*0-8442-3537-7*, NTC Busn Bks) NTC Pub Grp.

Strategic Middle Manager: How to Create & Sustain Competitive Advantage. Steven W. Floyd & Bill Woolridge. LC 95-25970. (Management Ser.). 195p. 1996. 26.95 (*0-7879-0208-X*) Jossey-Bass.

Strategic Military Surprise: Incentives & Opportunities. Klaus Knorr & Patrick M. Morgan. LC 82-2784. 265p. (Orig.). 1982. pap. 21.95 (*0-87855-912-4*) Transaction Pubs.

Strategic Minerals: A Resource Crisis. Economics & National Security Council Staff. (Illus.). 105p. (C). 1980. pap. text ed. 16.95 (*0-87855-913-2*) Transaction Pubs.

Strategic Minerals: The Geopolitical Problems for the United States. Ewan W. Anderson. LC 88-12028. 172p. 1988. text ed. 55.00 (*0-275-93062-9*, C3062, Praeger Pubs) Greenwood.

Strategic Minerals: U. S. Alternatives. 1991. lib. bdg. 79.95 (*0-8490-4576-2*) Gordon Pr.

Strategic Minerals: U. S. Alternatives. Kenneth A. Kessel. (Illus.). 293p. (Orig.). (C). 1994. pap. text ed. 45.00 (*0-7881-1113-2*) DIANE Pub.

Strategic Missile Defense: Necessities, Prospects, & Dangers in the Near Term. (Special Report of the Center for International Security & Arms Control, Stanford University Ser.). 26p. (Orig.). 1985. pap. 5.00 (*0-935371-13-3*) CFISAC.

Strategic Model of Chinese Checkers: Power & Exchange in Beijing's Interactions with Washington & Moscow. Peter Kein-hong Yu. LC 84-47538. (American University Studies: Political Science: Ser. X, Vol. 4). (Illus.). 233p. (Orig.). (C). 1984. text ed. 27.25 (*0-8204-0123-4*) P Lang Pubng.

Strategic Negotiations: A Theory of Change in Labor-Management Relations. Richard E. Walton et al. LC 93-50838. 400p. 1994. 35.00 (*0-87584-551-7*) Harvard Busn.

Strategic Negotiations: A Theory of Change in Labor-Management Relations. Richard E. Walton et al. 1994. text ed. 39.95 (*0-07-103608-3*) McGraw.

Strategic Networking: From LAN & WAN to Information Superhighways. Paul D. Henry & Gene De Libero. (Illus.). 400p. 1995. pap. 36.95 (*1-85032-203-1*) ITCP.

Strategic Networks: Creating the Borderless Organization. J. Carlos Jarillo. 208p. 1993. 66.95 (*0-7506-1572-9*) Buttrwrth-Heinemann.

Strategic Networks: Creating the Borderless Organization. J. Carlos Jarillo. (Illus.). 178p. 1995. pap. 34.95 (*0-7506-2327-6*) Buttrwrth-Heinemann.

Strategic Newspaper Management. Conrad C. Fink. 1988. pap. text ed. write for info. (*0-07-554619-1*) McGraw.

Strategic Newspaper Management. Conrad C. Fink. 464p. (C). 1988. pap. text ed. 26.00 (*0-317-58322-0*) Random.

Strategic Newspaper Management. Conrad C. Fink. LC 87-26617. 416p. 1988. text ed. 34.95 (*0-8093-1333-2*) S Ill U Pr.

Strategic Newspaper Management. 2nd ed. Conrad C. Fink. LC 95-7144. 1995. pap. text ed. 48.00 (*0-02-337731-3*, Macmillan Coll) P-H.

Strategic Nonfuel Minerals & Western Security. Rocco M. Paone. 242p. (C). 1992. lib. bdg. 47.50 (*0-8191-8469-1*) U Pr of Amer.

Strategic Nonviolent Conflict. Peter Ackerman & Christopher Kruegler. LC 93-2870. 392p. 1993. text ed. 59.95 (*0-275-93915-4*, C3915, Praeger Pubs); pap. text ed. 24.95 (*0-275-93916-2*, B3916, Praeger Pubs) Greenwood.

Strategic Nuclear Arms Control Verification: An Annotated Bibliography 1977-1984. Ed. by Richard A. Scribner & Robert T. Scott. 90p. (Orig.). (C). 1995. pap. text ed. 25.00 (*0-7881-2205-3*) DIANE Pub.

Strategic Nuclear Balance, Vol. 1: And Why It Matters. Peter V. Pry. 340p. (C). 1990. text ed. 63.00 (*0-8448-1642-6*, Crane Russak); pap. text ed. 36.00 (*0-8448-1643-4*, Crane Russak) Taylor & Francis.

Strategic Nuclear Balance, Vol. 2: Nuclear War: Exchanges & Outcomes. Peter V. Pry. 450p. (C). 1990. text ed. 70.00 (*0-8448-1644-2*, Crane Russak); pap. text ed. 47.00 (*0-8448-1645-0*, Crane Russak) Taylor & Francis.

Strategic Nuclear Targeting. Ed. by Jeffrey T. Richelson & Desmond Ball. LC 85-48195. (Cornell Studies in Security Affairs). (Illus.). 367p. 1986. 45.00 (*0-8014-1898-4*); pap. 16.95 (*0-8014-9507-5*) Cornell U Pr.

Strategic Nuclear War: What the Superpowers Target & Why. William C. Martel & Paul L. Savage. LC 85-9869. (Contributions in Military Studies: No. 43). (Illus.). 280p. 1986. text ed. 55.00 (*0-313-24192-9*, SNU/, Greenwood Pr) Greenwood.

Strategic Nursing Management: Power & Responsibility in a New Era. Howard L. Smith et al. 306p. (C). 1990. 60.00 (*0-8342-0147-X*, 20147) Aspen Pub.

Strategic Offensive Air Operations. Michael Knight. Ed. by R. A. Mason. (Air Power Ser.: Vol. 8). (Illus.). 262p. 1989. 40.00 (*0-08-035806-3*, Pub. by Brasseys UK) Brasseys Inc.

Strategic Operations: Competing Through Capabilities. Robert H. Hayes et al. (Illus.). 912p. 1996. 50.00 (*0-684-82305-5*) Free Pr.

Strategic Opportunities in Serving Low to Moderate Income Members. Albert E. Burger & Mary Zellmer. 42p. 1995. pap. 40.00 (*1-880572-19-2*) Filene Res.

Strategic Options for Latin America in the 1990s. Ed. by Colin Bradford, Jr. 288p. (Orig.). 1992. pap. 42.00 (*92-64-13634-7*) OECD.

Strategic Options for the Early 1980s. Ed. by William R. Van Cleave & Scott W. Thompson. 200p. 1979. pap. 21.95 (*0-87855-798-9*) Transaction Pubs.

Strategic Options for Urban Infrastructure Management. William F. Fox. (Urban Management Programme Paper: No. 17). 98p. 1994. 8.95 (*0-8213-2826-3*, 12826) World Bank.

Strategic Organization Planning: Downsizing for Survival. David C. Dougherty. LC 88-11355. 271p. 1989. text ed. 59.95 (*0-89930-339-0*, DYS/, Quorum Bks) Greenwood.

Strategic Organizational. 3rd ed. Conrad. (C). 1993. teacher ed., pap. text ed. 34.00 (*0-15-501595-8*) HB Coll Pubs.

Strategic Organizational Communication: An Integrated Perspective. Charles Conrad. Ed. by Michael D. Hinshaw. LC 89-24527. (Illus.). 384p. (C). 1990. text ed. 32.00 (*0-03-030423-7*) HB Coll Pubs.

Strategic Organizational Communication: Toward the 21st Century. 3rd ed. Charles Conrad. LC 92-75766. 480p. 1994. 34.75 (*0-15-500786-6*) HarBrace.

Strategic Organizational Diagnosis & Design: Developing Theory for Application. Richard M. Burton & Borge Obel. LC 95-22948. 480p. (C). 1995. lib. bdg. 89.95 (*0-7923-9628-6*) Kluwer Ac.

Strategic Orientations of Small European Businesses. Stratos Group Staff. 125p. 1990. text ed. 68.95 (*1-85628-015-2*, Pub. by Avebury Pub UK) Ashgate Pub Co.

Strategic Outlook & Alliances. Incl. Support Every Outbreak of Protest & Rebellion. 28p. 1981. 1.00 (*0-89851-052-X*); Charting the Uncharted Course: Proletarian Revolution in the U. S. 18p. 1982. 0.50 (*0-89851-054-6*); Coming From Behind to Make Revolution & Crucial Questions in Coming From Behind. 80p. 1981. 1.25 (*0-89851-048-1*); You Can't Beat the Enemy While Raising His Flag. 15p. 1981. 0.50 (*0-89851-050-3*); Bob Avakian Replies to a Letter from Black Nationalist with Communistic Inclinations. Bob Avakian. 18p. 1981. 1.00 (*0-89851-046-5*); Break the Chains! Unleash the Fury of Women As a Mighty Force for Revolution. 1979. 1.00 (*0-89851-031-7*); 32p. 5.00 (*0-685-06181-7*) RCP Pubns.

Strategic Partnering: How to Join Forces with Other Companies to Get Capital, Research & Development, Marketing, Product Testing, & Sales Support. A. David Silver. 324p. 1993. text ed. 29.95 (*0-07-057612-2*) McGraw.

Strategic Partnerships: States, Firms & International Competition. Ed. by Lynn K. Mytelka. LC 90-49475. 1991. 45.00 (*0-8386-3445-1*) Fairleigh Dickinson.

Strategic Pastoral Counseling: A Short-Term Structured Model. David G. Benner. LC 92-17613. 144p. (Orig.). (C). 1992. pap. 9.99 (*0-8010-1027-6*) Baker Bks.

Strategic Pay: Aligning Organizational Strategies & Pay Systems. Edward E. Lawler, III. LC 90-37168. (Management Ser.). 328p. text ed. 30.95 (*1-55542-262-4*) Jossey-Bass.

Strategic Petroleum Reserve: Planning, Implementation, & Analysis. David L. Weimer. LC 82-6184. (Contributions in Economics & Economic History Ser.: No. 48). (Illus.). xvii, 229p. 1982. text ed. 55.00 (*0-313-23404-3*, WPO/, Greenwood Pr) Greenwood.

Strategic Plan to Combat HIV & AIDS in the U. S. (Illus.). 52p. (Orig.). (C). 1993. pap. text ed. 20.00 (*1-56806-188-9*) DIANE Pub.

Strategic Planning. Clark Holloway. LC 85-25837. 382p. 1986. 39.95 (*0-8304-1070-8*) Nelson-Hall.

***Strategic Planning.** Steiner. 1997. pap. 16.00 (*0-684-83245-3*, Free Press) Free Pr.

Strategic Planning. Taylor. (Best of Long Range Planning Ser.). 122p. 1989. text ed. 82.25 (*0-08-037404-2*, Pergamon Pr) Elsevier.

Strategic Planning: A How-to-Do-It Manual for Librarians. M. E. Jacob. (How-to-Do-It Ser.). 125p. 1990. pap. text ed. 39.95 (*1-55570-074-8*) Neal-Schuman.

Strategic Planning: A Human Resource Tool for Higher Education. Ed. by Kathleen M. Alvino. LC 95-70889. 121p. (Orig.). 1995. pap. 30.00 (*1-878240-46-3*) Coll & U Personnel.

Strategic Planning: A Human Resource Tool for Higher Education. Ed. by Kathleen M. Alvino. (Orig.). 1996. 30.00 (*0-614-96413-X*) Coll & U Personnel.

***Strategic Planning: A Law Library Management Tool for the 90's & Beyond.** 2nd ed. Richard A. Danner. LC 96-29606. (Law Library Information Reports: Vol. 11). 67p. 1996. pap. text ed. 100.00 (*0-87802-110-8*) Glanville.

Strategic Planning: A Practical Guide. Peter Rea & Harold Kerzner. (Industrial Engineering Ser.). 500p. 1997. text ed. 39.95 (*0-442-02271-9*) Van Nos Reinhold.

Strategic Planning: A Step-by-Step Guide to Building a Successful CPA Firm. Sheryl L. Barbich. LC 93-31677. 1993. 41.25 (*0-87051-140-8*) Am Inst CPA.

Strategic Planning: Developing Strategies for Economic Stability & Growth. M. Ross Boyle. Ed. by Jenny Murphy. 62p. (Orig.). 1987. pap. 20.00 (*0-317-04869-4*) Natl Coun Econ Dev.

Strategic Planning: Tax Minimization & Investment Strategy. 6th ed. Richard R. Sylvester. 1990. 69.00 (*0-932010-59-8*) PhD Pub.

Strategic Planning: The Chief Executive & the Board. Ed. by Bernard Taylor. LC 88-19506. (Best of Long Range Planning Ser.: Vol. 1, No. 1). 122p. 1988. pap. text ed. 39.50 (*0-08-036566-3*, Pergamon Pr) Elsevier.

***Strategic Planning: The Nine Step Plan.** Simon Wootton & Terry Horne. (Business & Management Ser.). 1997. pap. 19.95 (*0-7494-2060-X*) Kogan Page Ltd.

Strategic Planning: Theory & Application. William D. Trotter. (Education Ser.). 88p. (Orig.). 1984. pap. 12.00 (*0-912841-18-4*) Planning Forum.

Strategic Planning: Threats & Opportunities for Planners. Ed. by John M. Bryson & Robert C. Einsweiler. LC 87-73537. (Illus.). 230p. (Orig.). 1988. pap. 29.95 (*0-918286-54-9*) Planners Pr.

Strategic Planning: What Every Manager Must Know. George A. Steiner. LC 78-20647. (Illus.). 383p. 1979. 32.95 (*0-02-931110-1*, Free Press) Free Pr.

Strategic Planning & Control: Issues in the Strategy Process. Ed. by Peter Lorange. (Corporate Strategy, Organization, & Change Ser.). 256p. 1993. 44.95 (*1-55786-103-X*) Blackwell Pubs.

Strategic Planning & Leadership in Continuing Education: Enhancing Organizational Vitality, Responsiveness, & Identity. Simerly, Robert G. & Associates Staff. LC 86-27382. (Higher & Adult Education Ser.). 268p. text ed. 32.95 (*1-55542-034-6*) Jossey-Bass.

Strategic Planning & Management: The Key to Corporate Success. Delmar W. Karger. 368p. 1991. 115.00 (*0-8247-8490-1*) Dekker.

Strategic Planning & Management Control Systems for Survival & Success. John C. Camillus. LC 85-40001. 331p. 27.95 (*0-669-10315-2*, Lexington) Jossey-Bass.

Strategic Planning & Modeling in Property-Liability Insurance. J. David Cummins. (S. S. Huebner International Ser.). 1985. lib. bdg. 82.00 (*0-89838-159-2*) Huebner Foun Insur.

Strategic Planning & Needs Assessment for Schools & Communities. Valerie A. Romney. 96p. (Orig.). 1996. pap. 14.95 (*0-930388-14-3*) Comm Collaborators.

S

An Asterisk (*) at the beginning of an entry indicates that the title is appearing in BIP for the first time.

Strategic Planning & Policy. W. King. 1986. text ed. write for info. (*0-442-24835-0*) Van Nos Reinhold.

Strategic Planning & the Nonprofit Board. Dabney G. Park, Jr. (Nonprofit Governance Ser.: No. 06). 12p. (Orig.). (C). 1992. reprint ed. pap. text ed. 11.00 (*0-925299-06-5*) Natl Ctr Nonprofit.

Strategic Planning Basics for Special Libraries. Doris Asantewa. LC 92-13276. 57p. 1992. 16.00 (*0-87111-399-6*) SLA.

Strategic Planning for America's Schools. 2nd ed. William J. Cook, Jr. 131p. 1995. 23.95 (*0-87652-132-4*, 021-0295) Am Assn Sch Admin.

***Strategic Planning for Association Executives.** Gerald L. Gordon. LC 97-5285. 1997. write for info. (*0-88034-115-7*) Am Soc Assn Execs.

Strategic Planning for Banks. Douglas Austin. 1990. text ed. 50.00 (*1-55520-171-7*) Irwin Prof Pubng.

Strategic Planning for Catholic Schools: A Diocesan Model of Consultation. John J. Convey & Maria J. Ciriello. 239p. (Orig.). (C). 1996. pap. 44.95 (*1-57455-055-1*) US Catholic.

Strategic Planning for Cogenteration & Energy Management. Association of Energy Engineers Staff. Ed. by F. William Payne. LC 85-80321. 600p. 1985. text ed. 62.95 (*0-88173-008-4*); pap. text ed. 38.00 (*0-88173-009-2*) Fairmont Pr.

Strategic Planning for Competitive Advantage. Eben G. Fetters. (Illus.). 145p. (C). 1996. 49.00 (*0-923680-02-0*, 4103) Amer ComVision Inc.

Strategic Planning for Computer Integrated Manufacturing. 459p. 495.00 (*0-317-65604-X*) TBC Inc.

Strategic Planning for Correctional Emergencies. Robert M. Freeman. LC 96-24867. 1996. pap. 39.95 (*1-56991-052-9*, 249) Am Correctional.

Strategic Planning for Economic Development. David R. Kolzow. (Illus.). (Orig.). 1992. pap. 30.00 (*0-9616567-2-7*) Amer Econ Dev Council.

Strategic Planning for Electronic Banking. Dimitris N. Chorafas. 260p. 1987. boxed 60.00 (*0-88063-204-6*); boxed 60.00 (*0-614-05971-2*) MICHIE.

Strategic Planning for Enterprise Information Systems. Computer Technology Research Corp. Staff. (Illus.). 182p. (Orig.). 1996. 270.00 (*1-56607-965-9*) Comput Tech Res.

Strategic Planning for Exploration Management. Susan J. Buck & Allen N. Quick. 161p. 1988. text ed. 56.00 (*0-13-851809-2*) P-H.

Strategic Planning for Exploration Management. Allen N. Quick & Neal A. Buck. LC 83-12710. (Illus.). 161p. 1984. 184.00 (*0-934634-66-1*) Intl Human Res.

Strategic Planning for Fund Raising: How to Bring in More Money Using Strategic Resource Allocation. Wesley E. Lindahl. LC 92-25900. (Nonprofit Sector-Public Administration Ser.). 152p. text ed. 37.95 (*1-55542-495-3*) Jossey-Bass.

Strategic Planning for Human Resources. Steven M. Director. (Studies in Productivity: No. 42). 46p. 1985. pap. 55.00 (*0-08-029516-9*) Work in Amer.

Strategic Planning for Human Resources. Ed. by Sheila Rothwell. (Best of Long Range Planning Ser.: No. 6). 158p. 1990. text ed. 86.50 (*0-08-037272-4*, Pergamon Pr); pap. text ed. 41.50 (*0-08-037770-X*, Pergamon Pr) Elsevier.

Strategic Planning for Independent Schools. Susan C. Stone. 1987. pap. 16.00 (*0-934338-58-2*) NAIS.

Strategic Planning for Information Resource Management. 60p. (Orig.). 1996. pap. text ed. 10.00 (*1-887464-16-6*) Intl Fed Accts.

Strategic Planning for Information Resource Management: A Multinational Perspective. Gad J. Selig. LC 83-4997. (Management Information Systems Ser.: No. 4). 271p. reprint ed. pap. 77.30 (*0-685-20448-0*, 2070311) Bks Demand.

Strategic Planning for Information Systems. John M. Ward et al. (Information Systems Ser.). 450p. 1990. text ed. 65.95 (*0-471-92002-9*) Wiley.

Strategic Planning for Information Systems. rev. ed. Robert V. Head. LC 82-80713. (Illus.). 192p. reprint ed. pap. 54.80 (*0-685-27068-8*, 2034610) Bks Demand.

Strategic Planning for Information Systems. 2nd ed. John Ward & Pat Griffiths. LC 95-44206. (Information Systems Ser.). 450p. 1996. text ed. 50.00 (*0-471-96183-3*) Wiley.

***Strategic Planning for Information Systems.** John Ward et al. LC 89-29726. (John Wiley Information Systems Ser.). (Illus.). 466p. 1990. reprint ed. pap. 132.90 (*0-608-04001-0*, 2064738) Bks Demand.

Strategic Planning for Local Government. Gerald L. Gordon. LC 93-401. (Practical Management Ser.). 119p. 1993. 23.95 (*0-87326-065-1*) Intl City-Cnty Mgt.

Strategic Planning for Local Government: A Handbook for Officials & Citizens. Roger L. Kemp. LC 92-50949. 320p. 1993. lib. bdg. 47.50 (*0-89950-832-4*) McFarland & Co.

Strategic Planning for Magazine Executives. 2nd ed. Richard Koff. 1987. 59.95 (*0-918110-16-5*) Cowles Busn Media.

Strategic Planning for Mortgage Lenders: Positioning Your Company for Success. James D. Jones. (Illus.). 178p. (Orig.). 1995. pap. text ed. 50.00 (*0-945359-45-4*) Mortgage Bankers.

***Strategic Planning for Nonprofit Organizations: A Practical Guide & Workbook.** Michael Allison et al. LC 97-9145. 1997. pap. 39.95 incl. disk (*0-471-17832-2*) Wiley.

Strategic Planning for Not-for-Profit Organizations. R. Henry Migliore et al. LC 93-17360. (Illus.). 209p. 1994. lib. bdg. 29.95 (*1-56024-919-6*) Haworth Pr.

Strategic Planning for Pastoral Ministry. Michael J. Balhoff. (Illus.). 136p. 1992. student ed. 19.95 (*0-912405-87-2*) Pastoral Pr.

Strategic Planning for Positive CAD-CAM Results. John Stark. LC 87-6859. (Series of Special Reports: No. 18). 131p. reprint ed. pap. 37.40 (*0-7837-3372-0*, 2043330) Bks Demand.

***Strategic Planning for Private Higher Education.** Carle M. Hunt et al. LC 96-40976. (Illus.). 298p. (C). 1997. 49.95 (*0-7890-0098-9*) Haworth Pr.

***Strategic Planning for Private Higher Education.** Carle M. Hunt et al. LC 96-40976. (Illus.). 292p. (C). 1997. pap. text ed. 24.95 (*0-7890-0191-8*) Haworth Pr.

Strategic Planning for Public & Nonprofit Organizations: A Guide to Strengthening & Sustaining Organizational Achievement. 2nd ed. John M. Bryson. (Public Administration, Nonprofit Sector Ser.). 347p. 27.95 (*0-7879-0141-5*) Jossey-Bass.

Strategic Planning for Public Managers. James L. Mercer. LC 90-47590. 240p. 1991. text ed. 55.00 (*0-89930-355-2*, MSZ/, Quorum Bks) Greenwood.

Strategic Planning for Public Service & Non-Profit Organizations. Ed. by John M. Bryson. LC 92-35238. (Best of Long Range Planning Ser.: No. 12). 1993. 77.00 (*0-685-62558-3*, Pergamon Pr) Elsevier.

Strategic Planning for Public Service & Non-Profit Organizations, Vol. 12. J. M. Bryson & B. Taylor. LC 92-35238. (Best of Long Range Planning Ser.). 1993. 72.00 (*0-08-040672-6*, Pub. by Pergamon Repr UK) Franklin.

***Strategic Planning for School Improvement.** Brian Fidler et al. 268p. (Orig.). 1996. pap. 47.50 (*0-273-61645-5*, Pub. by Pitman Pub Ltd UK) Trans-Atl Phila.

Strategic Planning for Sponsored Projects Administration: The Role of Information Management. Keith Harman & Charles M. McClure. LC 85-9881. (Emerging Patterns of Work & Communications in an Information Age Ser.: No. 1). (Illus.). xiii, 279p. 1985. text ed. 59.95 (*0-313-24931-8*, MST/) Greenwood.

Strategic Planning for the Entrepreneur. Ronald D. Kraft. 240p. (C). 1991. pap. text ed. 22.50 (*0-9630618-0-1*) Center CA.

Strategic Planning for the Entrepreneur (Custom Publication) 2nd ed. Kraft. 1993. pap. text ed. write for info. (*0-07-035870-2*) McGraw.

Strategic Planning for the New & Small Business. Fred L. Fry & Charles R. Stoner. 225p. 1995. pap. 47.95 (*0-936894-85-7*) Upstart Pub.

Strategic Planning for the Non-Profit Sector. Katsioloudes. 1993. pap. text ed. write for info. (*0-07-034051-X*) McGraw.

Strategic Planning for the Real Estate Manager. 2nd rev. ed. Kenneth Reyhons. Ed. by Christopher Bettin. (Illus.). 125p. 1989. reprint ed. pap. 22.00 (*0-913652-68-7*) Realtors Natl.

Strategic Planning for the Real Estate Manager. 3rd ed. Kenneth Reyhons. Ed. by Christopher Bettin. LC 93-4861. 1993. 22.00 (*0-913652-78-4*) Realtors Natl.

Strategic Planning for the Small Business: Situations, Weapons, Objectives & Tactics. Craig S. Rice. 300p. 1990. pap. 10.95 (*1-55850-858-9*) Adams Media.

Strategic Planning for the 1990's (Yearbooks) 171p. 1990. write for info. (*0-933964-31-5*) Natl Busn Ed Assoc.

Strategic Planning for University Research. Ed. by Oliver D. Hensley. LC 92-18227. (SRA Monographs: No. 4). 1992. 40.00 (*0-89672-239-2*) Tex Tech Univ Pr.

Strategic Planning for Workplace Drug Abuse Programs: A Guide for Employers. 1991. lib. bdg. 79.75 (*0-8490-4369-7*) Gordon Pr.

***Strategic Planning Guide for Community Banks & Thrifts.** Douglas V. Austin. 1997. 55.00 (*0-7863-1183-5*) Irwin Prof Pubng.

Strategic Planning in Emerging Companies. Steven C. Brandt. (Illus.). 192p. 1981. 23.95 (*0-201-00942-0*) Addison-Wesley.

Strategic Planning in Emerging Companies see Focus Your Business: Strategic Planning in Emerging Companies

Strategic Planning in Energy & Natural Resources: Proceedings of the 2nd Symposium in Analytic Techniques for Energy, Natural Resources, & Environmental Planning, Philadelphia PA, 3-4 April, 1986. Ed. by Baruch Lev et al. (Studies in Management Science & Systems: No. 15). 340p. 1987. 167.50 (*0-444-70230-X*, North Holland) Elsevier.

Strategic Planning in Health Care: A Guide for Board Members. Jonathan G. Weaver. LC 94-33244. 124p. 1994. pap. 35.00 (*1-55648-127-6*, 196130) AHPI.

Strategic Planning in Health Care Management. William Flexner et al. LC 81-2488. 408p. 1981. text ed. 95.00 (*0-89443-298-2*) Aspen Pub.

***Strategic Planning in Healthcare: Building a Quality-Based Plan Step by Step.** Bernard J. Horak. 1997. write for info. (*0-527-76314-4*) Qual Resc.

Strategic Planning in Higher Education: Implementing New Roles for the Academic Library. Ed. by James F. Williams, II. LC 90-26627. (Journal of Library Administration: Vol. 13, Nos. 3-4). 221p. 1991. text ed. 49.95 (*1-56024-091-1*) Haworth Pr.

Strategic Planning in Local Government. Roger L. Kemp. LC 91-77424. 188p. (Orig.). 1992. pap. 34.95 (*0-918286-77-8*) Planners Pr.

Strategic Planning in South East England 1968-78: A Case Study. B. E. Linders. (Illus.). 83p. 1985. pap. 22.00 (*0-08-032720-6*, Pergamon Pr) Elsevier.

Strategic Planning in Technology Transfer to Less Developed Countries. Christian N. Madu. LC 91-22020. 224p. 1992. text ed. 52.95 (*0-89930-629-2*, MTY, Quorum Bks) Greenwood.

Strategic Planning Management Reader. Liam Fahey. 448p. 1989. boxed 30.00 (*0-13-851759-2*) P-H.

Strategic Planning, Marketing & Evaluation for Nursing Education & Service. Carolyn F. Waltz et al. 224p. 1989. 34.95 (*0-88737-444-1*) Natl League Nurse.

Strategic Planning, Marketing & Public Relations, & Fund-raising in Higher Education: Perspectives, Reading, & Annotated Bibliography. Cynthia C. Ryans & William L. Shanklin. LC 86-3871. 280p. 1986. 25.00 (*0-8108-1891-4*) Scarecrow.

Strategic Planning Plus: An Organizational Guide. Roger Kaufman. 1992. 48.00 (*0-8039-4804-2*); pap. 23.50 (*0-8039-4805-0*) Sage.

Strategic Planning Process. Ed. by Peter Lorange. (International Library Management). 400p. 1994. 127.95 (*1-85521-350-8*, Pub. by Dartmth Pub UK) Ashgate Pub Co.

Strategic Planning Review: Oxfam Research Discussion Papers. Tina Wallace. (Oxfam Research Discussion Papers). 70p. (C). 1994. pap. 15.95 (*0-85598-272-1*, Pub. by Oxfam UK) Humanities.

Strategic Planning Simulation: Leader's Guide. Cresencio Torres. (Consensus Decision-Making Simulations Ser.). (Orig.). 1995. pap. write for info. (*0-87425-283-0*) HRD Press.

Strategic Planning System for Businesses. John L. Green, Jr. 1986. pap. 49.95 (*0-9617567-0-5*) Strategic Plan Mgmt Assocs.

Strategic Planning System for Higher Education. John L. Green, Jr. Ed. by Barbara Burgess & William McFarlane. 500p. (C). 1987. pap. 75.00 (*0-9617567-1-3*) Strategic Plan Mgmt Assocs.

Strategic Planning Technology Workbook. William C. Bean. 1993. ring bd. 150.00 (*0-87425-205-9*) HRD Press.

Strategic Planning That Makes Things Happen. William C. Bean. 300p. 1993. pap. 24.95 (*0-87425-212-1*) HRD Press.

Strategic Planning Workbook. American Hospital Association Staff. (Illus.). 114p. 1989. 60.00 (*0-87258-520-4*, 184205) Am Hospital.

Strategic Planning Workbook. 2nd ed. Joseph C. Krallinger & Karsten G. Hellebust. LC 92-22589. 380p. 1993. text ed. 115.00 incl. disk (*0-471-58256-5*) Wiley.

Strategic Planning Workbook for Nonprofit Organizations. Bryan W. Barry. 88p. (Orig.). 1986. pap. 25.00 (*0-940069-00-8*) A H Wilder.

Strategic Planning Workbook for Nonprofit Organizations. 2nd rev. ed. Bryan W. Barry. Ed. by Vincent Hyman. (Illus.). 144p. (Orig.). 1997. pap. text ed. 25.00 (*0-940069-07-5*) A H Wilder.

Strategic Planning Workshop. William J. Rothwell. 179p. 1989. ring bd. 139.95 (*0-87425-079-X*) HRD Press.

Strategic Policy Changes at Private Colleges. Richard E. Anderson. LC 77-13257. 112p. reprint ed. 32.00 (*0-685-07756-X*, 2013172) Bks Demand.

Strategic Power: U.S.A. - U.S.S.R. Ed. by Carl G. Jacobsen. LC 89-28848. 384p. 1990. text ed. 49.95 (*0-312-04086-5*) St Martin.

Strategic Pragmatism: Japanese Lessons in the Use of Economic Theory. Michele Schmiegelow & Henrik Schmiegelow. LC 88-34251. 224p. 1989. text ed. 55.00 (*0-275-93182-X*, C3182, Praeger Pubs) Greenwood.

Strategic Pragmatism: The Culture of Singapore's Economic Development Board. Edgar H. Schein. (Illus.). 310p. 1996. 27.50 (*0-262-19367-1*) MIT Pr.

Strategic Precision: Improving Performance Through Organizational Efficiency. Bengt Karlof. LC 93-7364. 227p. 1994. text ed. 60.00 (*0-471-93989-7*) Wiley.

Strategic Presidency: Hitting the Ground Running. 2nd rev. ed. James P. Pfiffner. (Studies in Government & Public Policy). 264p. 1996. 35.00 (*0-7006-0768-4*); pap. 14.95 (*0-7006-0769-2*) U Pr of KS.

Strategic Processes in Monsoon Asia's Economic Development. Harry T. Oshima. LC 92-33545. (Studies in Development). 352p. (C). 1993. text ed. 55.00 (*0-8018-4479-7*) Johns Hopkins.

Strategic Program Planning. Laurie Wilson. 176p. (C). 1996. pap. text ed. 35.64 (*0-7872-1598-8*) Kendall-Hunt.

***Strategic Prospects for HRM.** Shaun Tyson. 304p. 1995. pap. 60.00 (*0-85292-578-6*, Pub. by IPM UK) St Mut.

Strategic Psychological Operations & American Foreign Policy. Robert T. Holt & Robert W. Van de Velde. LC 60-14238. 254p. reprint ed. pap. 72.40 (*0-317-09684-2*, 2020083) Bks Demand.

***Strategic Public Relations.** Ed. by Carol Friend. 1996. pap. 16.95 (*0-7494-1854-0*) Kogan Page Ltd.

Strategic Public Relations Counseling: Models from the Counselors Academy. Norman R. Nager & Richard H. Truitt. 392p. (C). 1991. reprint ed. pap. 34.50 (*0-8191-8331-8*) U Pr of Amer.

***Strategic Purchasing & Supply Chain Management.** 2nd ed. Malcolm Saunders. xiii, 354p. 1997. pap. 52.50 (*0-273-62382-6*, Pub. by Pitman Pub Ltd UK) Trans-Atl Phila.

Strategic Purchasing Manager: How to Unlock Buying Power. Peter Trim. (Financial Times Management Ser.). 224p. 1994. 72.50 (*0-273-60972-6*, Pub. by Pitman Pub Ltd UK) Trans-Atl Phila.

Strategic Quadrangle: Japan, China, Russia, & the United States in East Asia. Mike M. Mochizuki et al. Ed. by Michael Mandelbaum. 215p. 1994. pap. text ed. 16.95 (*0-87609-168-0*) Coun Foreign.

Strategic Questioning. Ronald T. Hyman. LC 79-783. (Illus.). 1979. pap. text ed. 15.95 (*0-685-03909-9*) P-H.

Strategic Readiness: The Making of A Learning Organization. John C. Redding & Ralph F. Catalanello. LC 93-48673. (Business-Management Ser.). 200p. text ed. 27.95 (*1-55542-633-6*) Jossey-Bass.

***Strategic Reading & Writing for HSPT Competency, Vol. 1.** Mary A. Reilly. 182p. (Orig.). (YA). (gr. 9-12). 1997. wbk. ed., pap. 19.95 (*1-886292-22-1*) CEO Sftware.

***Strategic Recycling: Necessary Revolutions in Local Government Policy.** Kay Martin. (Illus.). xx, 250p. (Orig.). (C). 1996. pap. text ed. 29.99 (*0-9653545-0-4*) Drkhorse Pr.

Strategic Renaissance & Business Transformation. Ed. by Howard Thomas et al. LC 95-5190. (Strategic Management Ser.). 484p. 1995. text ed. 60.00 (*0-471-95751-8*) Wiley.

Strategic Resource Management: Allocation, Deployment, & Productive Use of Resources for Improved Performance Results. Paul R. Cone et al. LC 85-73592. (Illus.). 420p. (C). 1986. text ed. 32.99 (*0-943872-52-9*) Andrews Univ Pr.

Strategic Resources for the Operating Room Nurse Manager. Ed. by Diane I. Howery. (Illus.). (Orig.). 1989. ring bd. 43.75 (*0-939583-56-9*) Assn Oper Rm Nurses.

Strategic Restraint: Ethical Perspectives & Political Intitiatives. Alton Frye. (CISA Working Papers: No. 39). 20p. (Orig.). 1983. pap. 15.00 (*0-86682-051-5*) Ctr Intl Relations.

Strategic Resumes: Writing for Results. Marci Mahoney. Ed. by Beverly Manber. LC 91-76255. (Fifty-Minute Ser.). (Illus.). 151p. (Orig.). 1993. pap. 10.95 (*1-56052-129-5*) Crisp Pubns.

Strategic Retail Management. Danny R. Arnold et al. LC 82-8852. 752p. 1983. teacher ed. write for info. (*0-201-10086-X*); text ed. write for info. (*0-201-10085-1*) Addison-Wesley.

Strategic Retail Management: A Lotus 1-2-3 Based Simulation. John Gifford. (C). 1988. disk (*0-318-63235-7*, SF60A8) S-W Pub.

Strategic Retailing Management: Text & Cases. David E. Bell & Walter J. Salmon. 1996. pap. 75.95 (*0-538-84908-8*) S-W Pub.

Strategic Revitalization: Managing the Challenges of Change. 2nd ed. Douglas B. Gutknecht. LC 88-24839. 242p. (C). 1989. pap. text ed. 25.00 (*0-8191-7197-2*) U Pr of Amer.

Strategic Revolution. Neville Brown. 245p. 1992. 37.00 (*0-08-040721-8*, Pub. by Brasseys UK) Brasseys Inc.

Strategic Rhetoric: Campaigning for the American Constitution. William H. Riker. Ed. by Randall L. Calvert et al. LC 96-12669. 1996. 30.00 (*0-300-06169-2*) Yale U Pr.

Strategic Risk: A State-Defined Approach. James M. Collins & Timothy W. Ruefli. LC 95-44243. 240p. (C). 1995. lib. bdg. 82.50 (*0-7923-9661-8*) Kluwer Ac.

Strategic Risk Management: How Global Corporations Manage Financial Risk for Competitive Advantage. William D. Falloon & Mark J. Ahn. (Institutional Investor Publication Ser.). 300p. 1991. text ed. 50.00 (*1-55738-199-2*) Irwin Prof Pubng.

Strategic Rocket Forces: A Military Historical work. Ed. by Yu P. Maksimov. (Illus.). 246p. (Orig.). Date not set. pap. write for info. (*0-614-14022-6*) East View Pubns.

Strategic Role of Indian Ocean in World Politics: A Case Study of Diego Garcita. Anita Bhatta. (C). 1992. 21.00 (*0-8364-2809-9*, Pub. by Ajanta II) S Asia.

Strategic Role of Marketing: Understanding Why Marketing Should Be Central to Your Business Strategy. Adrian Davies. LC 95-7927. 1995. write for info. (*0-07-707854-3*) McGraw.

Strategic Sales Development: A Consultative Selling Process, 2 vols. Malcolm E. Bernstein et al. 1986. write for info. (*0-318-59344-0*) Human Equat.

Strategic Sales Management. C. David Hughes & Charles H. Singler. 352p. 1983. teacher ed. write for info. (*0-318-56809-8*); pap. write for info. (*0-201-10261-7*); text ed. write for info. (*0-201-10260-9*) Addison-Wesley.

Strategic Sales Promotion see Promotional Marketing: Ideas & Techniques for Success in Sales Promotion

***Strategic Sealift: Summary of Workshop.** (Illus.). 94p. 1994. pap. text ed. 45.00 (*1-57979-089-5*) BPI Info Servs.

Strategic Sealift: Summary of Workshop on Crewing the Ready Reserve Force. (Illus.). 55p. (Orig.). (C). 1994. pap. text ed. 25.00 (*0-7881-1234-1*) DIANE Pub.

Strategic Sectors in Mexican - U.S. Free Trade. Alan Stoga et al. (Significant Issues Ser.). (Orig.). 1991. pap. text ed. 9.95 (*0-89206-172-3*) CSI Studies.

***Strategic Segmentation & Target Marketing.** Dennis J. Cahill. LC 96-41430. (Illus.). 154p. (C). 1997. pap. text ed. 19.95 (*0-7890-0184-5*) Haworth Pr.

***Strategic Segmentation & Target Marketing: How To Pick a Hotel.** Dennis J. Cahill. LC 96-41430. (Illus.). 154p. (C). 1997. lib. bdg. 39.95 (*0-7890-0139-X*) Haworth Pr.

Strategic Selling. Miller. 1988. pap. 10.95 (*0-446-38922-6*) Warner Bks.

Strategic Selling. Robert B. Miller et al. 320p. 1988. pap. 14.99 (*0-446-38627-8*) Warner Bks.

Strategic Selling: The Unique Sales System Proven Successful by America's Best Companies. Robert B. Miller et al. LC 84-25463. (Illus.). 352p. 1985. 19.95 (*0-688-04313-5*) Morrow.

Strategic Significance of the West Bank. Aryeh Shalev. LC 84-26305. 236p. 1985. text ed. 55.00 (*0-275-90162-9*, C0162, Praeger Pubs) Greenwood.

Strategic Silence: Gender & Economic Policy. Ed. by Isabel Bakker. LC 94-35309. 170p. (C). 1994. pap. 17.50 (*1-85649-262-1*, Pub. by Zed Bks Ltd UK) Humanities.

Strategic Silence: Gender & Economic Policy. Ed. by Isabella Bakker. LC 94-35309. 256p. (C). 1994. text ed. 55.00 (*1-85649-261-3*, Pub. by Zed Bks Ltd UK) Humanities.

Strategic Stability in the Post-Cold War World & the Future of Nuclear Disarmament: Proceedings of the NATO Advanced Research Workshop, Washington, D.C., U. S. A., April 6-10, 1995. Ed. by Melvin L. Best, Jr. et al. (Partnership Sub-Series 1: Disarmament Technologies: Vol. 3, No. 1). 352p. (C). 1995. lib. bdg. 169.00 (*0-7923-3805-7*) Kluwer Ac.

An Asterisk (*) at the beginning of an entry indicates that the title is appearing in BIP for the first time.

Strategic Studies: A Critical Assessment. Colin S. Gray. LC 81-6820. (Contributions in Political Science Ser.: No. 70). x, 213p. 1982. text ed. 55.00 (*0-313-22862-0*, GSS/, Greenwood Pr) Greenwood.

Strategic Studies & Public Policy: The American Experience. fac. ed. Colin S. Gray. LC 80-5175. 238p. 1982. pap. 67.90 (*0-7837-7591-1*, 2047344) Bks Demand.

Strategic Studies & World Order: The Global Politics of Deterrance. Bradley S. Klein. LC 93-36182. (Studies in International Relations: No. 34). 224p. (C). 1994. text ed. 54.95 (*0-521-37034-5*); pap. text ed. 17.95 (*0-521-46644-X*) Cambridge U Pr.

Strategic Studies Reference Guide: Indexes & Document Descriptions, Vol. 1- 1975. Strategic Studies Reference Guide Staff. LC 79-644393. 242p. reprint ed. pap. 69.00 (*0-317-29755-4*, 2017381) Bks Demand.

Strategic Styles: Coping in the Inner City. Janet K. Mancini. LC 79-56773. 349p. reprint ed. pap. 99.50 (*0-8357-6519-9*, 2035890) Bks Demand.

Strategic Supplier Partnering: An International Study. Thomas Hendrick & Lisa Ellram. LC 92-75604. 113p. (Orig.). (C). 1993. pap. text ed. 20.00 (*0-945968-11-6*) Ctr Advanced Purchasing.

Strategic Supply Management: A Blueprint for Revitalizing the Manufacturer-Supplier Partnership. Keki R. Bhote. LC 88-48029. 448p. 1989. 65.00 (*0-8144-5925-0*) AMACOM.

Strategic Supply Management: An Implementation Toolkit. Tom Chadwick & Shan Rajogopal. (Illus.). 288p. 1995. 50.95 (*0-7506-2253-9*) Buttrwrth-Heinemann.

Strategic Surprise in the Age of Glasnost. David T. Twining. 376p. (C). 1991. 49.95 (*0-88738-433-1*) Transaction Pubs.

Strategic Surrender: The Politics of Victory & Defeat. Paul Kecskemeti. LC 58-7840. ix, 287p. 1958. 39.50 (*0-8047-0549-6*) Stanford U Pr.

Strategic Survey 1988-89. 1989. pap. 21.00 (*0-08-037556-1*, Pergamon Pr) Elsevier.

Strategic Survey 1994-95. International Institute for Stragegic Studies Staff. 256p. 1995. pap. 29.95 (*0-19-878136-9*) OUP.

Strategic Survey 1995-1996. International Institute for Strategic Studies Staff. (Illus.). 268p. 1996. pap. 35.00 (*0-19-828091-2*) OUP.

***Strategic Survey 1996-1997.** International Institute for Strategic Studies Staff. (Illus.). 266p. 1997. pap. 35.00 (*0-19-829296-1*) OUP.

Strategic Symposium: SALT & United States Defense Policy. Richard Burt. 144p. 1979. pap. 21.95 (*0-87855-767-9*) Transaction Pubs.

Strategic Synergy. Andrew Campbell & Kathleen S. Luchs. 250p. 1992. pap. 45.95 (*0-7506-0521-9*) Buttrwrth-Heinemann.

Strategic Systems Planning for Financial Institutions: Using Automated Solutions & Technology for Competitive Advantage. Geoffrey H. Wold & Robert F. Schriver. 300p. 1992. text ed. 60.00 (*1-55738-339-1*) Irwin Prof Pubng.

***Strategic Tax Planning for Managers.** Swenson. (AG - Income Tax Ser.). (C). Date not set. text ed. 74.95 (*0-538-87951-3*) S-W Pub.

Strategic Tax Update: 1996. 96th ed. Johnson. 1995. pap. text ed. 79.00 (*0-15-602182-X*) HarBrace.

Strategic Teaching & Learning: Cognitive Instruction in the Content Areas. Donna Alvermann et al. Ed. by Richard Beach et al. LC 87-71387. 167p. 1987. pap. text ed. 12.00 (*0-87120-147-X*, 611-87030) Assn Supervision.

Strategic Technology Management. Frederick Betz. 1993. text ed. 53.00 (*0-07-005137-2*) McGraw.

Strategic Technology Management. Pierre Dussauge et al. LC 91-39732. 218p. 1992. text ed. 60.00 (*0-471-93418-6*) Wiley.

Strategic Telemarketing: How to Fit This New Medium into Your Marketing Plans. Richard L. Bencin. LC 86-30057. 200p. 1987. 37.50 (*0-915601-02-8*) Swansea Press.

Strategic Themes in Endgames. Edmar Mednis. 124p. (Orig.). 1990. pap. 8.95 (*0-931462-94-0*) Chess Ent.

Strategic Theories. Raoul Castex. Tr. & Intro. by Eugenia C. Kiesling. LC 93-1840. (Classics of Sea Power Ser.). 479p. 1993. 39.95 (*1-55750-100-9*) Naval Inst Pr.

***Strategic Thinking & Reading.** Debbie G. Longman et al. LC 96-21078. 500p. 1997. write for info. (*0-314-20181-5*) West Pub.

Strategic Thinking for Information Technology. Bernard H. Boar. LC 96-27114. 320p. 1996. pap. text ed. 49.95 (*0-471-15881-X*) Wiley.

Strategic Thinking, Leadership & the Management of Change. Ed. by Gerry Johnson et al. 350p. 1994. text ed. 65.00 (*0-471-93990-0*) Wiley.

Strategic Thrusts for the Future: Report of the Strategic Planning Committee. fac. ed. American Inst. of Certified Public Accountants Staff. 174p. 1988. reprint ed. pap. 49.60 (*0-7837-8213-6*, 2047972) Bks Demand.

Strategic Total Quality Mangement: Corporate Performance & Product Quality. Christian N. Madu & Chu-Hua Kuei. LC 94-32082. 224p. 1995. text ed. 55.00 (*0-89930-817-1*, Quorum Bks) Greenwood.

Strategic Trade Policy: A Survey of Issues & Early Analysis. Gene M. Grossman & J. David Richardson. LC 85-196. (Special Papers in International Economics: No. 15). 38p. 1985. pap. text ed. 11.00 (*0-88165-304-7*) Princeton U Int Finan Econ.

Strategic Trade Policy & Multinational Enterprises: Essays on Trade & Investment by Japanese Electronics Firms. Rene Belderbos. (Tinbergen Institute Research Ser.: No. 68, Series A). 282p. 1994. pap. 27.00 (*90-5170-274-4*, Pub. by Thesis Pubs NE) IBD Ltd.

Strategic Trade Policy & the New International Economics. Ed. by Paul R. Krugman. 296p. (Orig.). (C). 1986. pap. 22.00 (*0-262-61045-0*) MIT Pr.

Strategic Transformation & Information Technology: Paradigms for Performing While Transforming. Marilyn M. Parker. LC 95-18153. (William R. King Series in Information Management). 1995. text ed. 87.00 (*0-13-190794-8*) P-H.

***Strategic Transformations in Nigerian Writing: Orality & History in the Work of Rev. Samuel Johnson, Amos Tutuola, Wole Soyinka & Ben Okri.** Ato Quayson. LC 97-10960. 1997. write for info. (*0-253-33343-1*); pap. write for info. (*0-253-21148-4*) Ind U Pr.

Strategic Triangle & Regional Conflicts: Lessons from the Indochina Wars. Min Chen. LC 91-20699. 230p. 1992. lib. bdg. 40.00 (*1-55587-287-5*) Lynne Rienner.

Strategic Use of Circumstantial Evidence. 2nd ed. John F. Romano & Michael J. McHale. 773p. 1991. 80.00 (*0-87473-774-5*) MICHIE.

Strategic Use of Information Technology. Ed. by Stuart E. Madnick. (Executive Bookshelf-Sloan Management Review Ser.). (Illus.). 220p. 1987. 25.00 (*0-19-505048-7*) OUP.

***Strategic Value of Fossil Fuels: Challenges & Responses.** 700p. 1996. 152.00 (*92-64-14706-3*, Pub. by Org for Econ FR) OECD.

Strategic Views from the Second Tier: The Nuclear Weapons Policies of France, Britain, & China. Ed. by John C. Hopkins & Weixing Hu. 282p. (C). 1995. pap. 24.95 (*1-56000-790-7*) Transaction Pubs.

Strategic Vision & Planning: Keys to Educational Improvement. Willard R. Daggett. 26p. 1984. 3.00 (*0-318-22203-5*, OC100); vhs 100.00 (*0-317-01419-6*, VS103VHS, VS103UM) Ctr Educ Trng Employ.

***Strategic War Against Germany: The British Bombing Survey Unit.** British Bombing Survey Unit Staff. Ed. by Sebastian Cox. LC 97-22017. (Studies in Air Power: Vol. 4). (Illus.). 240p. 1997. text ed. 47.50 (*0-7146-4722-5*, Pub. by F Cass Pubs UK) Intl Spec Bk.

Strategic War Termination. Ed. by Stephen J. Cimbala. LC 86-91508. 244p. 1986. text ed. 55.00 (*0-275-92239-1*, C2239, Praeger Pubs) Greenwood.

Strategic Women: How Do They Manage in Scotland? Elizabeth Gerver & Lesley Hart. (SWSS Ser.). 192p. 1991. pap. text ed. 19.90 (*0-08-037741-6*, Pub. by Aberdeen U Pr) Macmillan.

Strategical Management. 2nd ed. Hofer. Date not set. teacher ed., pap. text ed. write for info. (*0-314-77916-7*) West Pub.

Strategical Themes. Tom Unger. Ed. by Robert B. Long. (Illus.). 101p. 1989. pap. 12.95 (*0-938650-45-9*) Thinkers Pr.

Strategics: The Logistics - Strategy Link. Kenneth N. Brown. 75p. (C). 1995. pap. text ed. 20.00 (*0-7881-2147-2*) DIANE Pub.

Strategie de Developpement Agricole en Afrique Subsaharienne et Role Particulier de la Banque Mondiale. Kevin M. Cleaver. (Technical Paper Ser.: No. 203F). 178p. 1993. 9.95 (*0-8213-2679-1*, 12679) World Bank.

Strategie de la lecture. Rene Galand. Ed. by Mary A. Caws. (Reading Plus Ser.: Vol. 7). 216p. (FRE.). 1990. 51.00 (*0-8204-1196-5*) P Lang Pubng.

Strategie de Marketing: Activities de Formation Pour Entrepreneurs. Suzanne Kindervatter & Maggie Range. LC 87-61358. (Formation Commerciale Appropriee pour la Femme du Tiers Monde Ser.). 96p. (Orig.). (FRE.). 1986. reprint ed. pap. 15.50 (*0-912917-14-8*) UNIFEM.

Strategie Operationnelle du Fonds Pour l'Environnement Mondial. (Orig.). (SPA.). (C). 1996. pap. write for info. (*1-884122-18-3*) Global Environ.

Strategien zur Finanzierung der Altlastensanierung. Carsten Kuhl. write for info. (*3-631-47370-2*) P Lang Pubng.

Strategies: A Rhetoric & Reader. Arnold M. Tibbetts. (C). 1991. text ed. 27.50 (*0-673-46268-4*) Addson-Wesley Educ.

Strategies: A Rhetoric & Reader, with Handbook. 5th ed. Charlene Tibbetts & Arn Tibbetts. LC 95-47739. (C). 1997. text ed. 33.50 (*0-673-98035-9*) Addson-Wesley Educ.

Strategies: College, Career, Life, West Virginia State College Edition. 4th ed. Janet Amos & Barbara Henry. 304p. (C). 1995. 41.95 (*0-256-12587-2*) Irwin.

***Strategies: Studies in Modern Cultural Policy.** Ed. by Jorn Langsted. 88p. (Orig.). (C). 1990. pap. 11.95 (*87-7288-321-9*, Pub. by Aarhus Univ Pr DK) David Brown.

Strategies Against Poverty in America. John B. Williamson. 256p. 1974. 18.95 (*0-87073-214-5*); pap. 11.95 (*0-87073-215-3*) Schenkman Bks Inc.

Strategies & Activities. 80p. 1993. pap. 9.95 (*0-590-49353-1*) Scholastic Inc.

Strategies & Activities for Reinforcement & Enrichment. Terri Breeden & Emalie Egan. Ed. by Leslie Britt & Janet Noble. (Illus.). 128p. (Orig.). 1995. pap. text ed. 10.95 (*0-86530-315-0*, 1P315-0) Incentive Pubns.

Strategies & Alternatives for Transforming Federal Human Resources Management. Center for Human Resources Management Staff. (Implementing Real Change in Human Resources Management Ser.). 115p. (Orig.). 1995. pap. 15.00 (*0-9646874-3-7*) Nat Acad Public Admin.

Strategies & Applications in Quantum Chemistry: From Molecular Astrophysics to Molecular Engineering. Ed. by Y. Ellinger & M. Defranceschi. LC 95-45654. (Topics in Molecular Organization & Engineering Ser.: No. 14). 476p. (C). 1996. lib. bdg. 207.00 (*0-7923-3837-5*) Kluwer Ac.

Strategies & Consequences: Managing the Costs in Higher Education. John S. Waggaman. Ed. by Jonathan D. Fife. LC 92-81698. (ASHE-ERIC Higher Education Reports: No. 8, 1991). 113p. (Orig.). 1992. pap. text ed. 17.00 (*1-878380-13-3*) GWU Grad Schl E&HD.

Strategies & Design for Afforestation, & Reforestation & Tree Planting. K. E. Wiersum. 432p. (C). 1987. pap. 375.00 (*81-7089-053-5*, Pub. by Intl Bk Distr II) St Mut.

Strategies & Design for Afforestation, Reforestation & Tree Planting. K. F. Wilrsum. (C). 1987. reprint ed. 32.00 (*0-685-21829-5*, Pub. by Intl Bk Distr II) St Mut.

Strategies & Environments of America's Small, Rural Hospitals: A Report on a Study Funded by the Pew Charitable Trusts. John W. Seavey et al. LC 92-7079. (Illus.). 336p. (Orig.). 1992. pap. text ed. 29.95 (*0-87258-623-5*, 184160) Am Hospital.

Strategies & Leadership: Impact on Organizational Performance. Fred J. McLimore. 512p. (C). 1996. per., pap. text ed. 45.09 (*0-7872-1784-0*) Kendall-Hunt.

Strategies & Norms in a Changing Matrilineal Society: Descent, Succession & Inheritance among the Toka of Zambia. Ladislav Holy. (Cambridge Studies in Social & Cultural Anthropology: No. 58). 200p. 1986. text ed. 59.95 (*0-521-30300-1*) Cambridge U Pr.

Strategies & Policies for Air Pollution Abatement. 56p. 1991. 15.00 (*92-1-116517-2*) UN.

Strategies & Saints: Fighting Drugs in Subsidized Housing. Langley C. Keyes. 300p. (Orig.). (C). 1992. pap. text ed. 24.00 (*0-87766-560-5*); lib. bdg. 57.00 (*0-87766-559-1*) Urban Inst.

Strategies & Skills for Managerial Women. 2nd ed. Joanna S. Hunsaker & Phillip L. Hunsaker. 304p. (C). 1991. text ed. 43.95 (*0-538-80573-0*, GM85BA) S-W Pub.

Strategies & Skills of Technical Presentations: A Guide for Professionals in Business & Industry. James G. Gray, Jr. LC 85-23252. 160p. 1986. text ed. 49.95 (*0-89930-123-1*, GTH/, Quorum Bks) Greenwood.

Strategies & Structure of Real Estate Development Firms. Arvind Bhambri et al. LC 91-66063. 63p. 1991. 30.95 (*0-87420-723-1*, S42) Urban Land.

Strategies & Structures: The Processing of Relative Clauses. Gary D. Prideaux & William J. Baker. LC 86-26863. (Current Issues in Linguistic Theory Ser.: Vol. 46). vii, 195p. 1987. 52.00 (*90-272-3540-6*) Benjamins North Am.

Strategies & Structures of Presenting World History: With Islam & Muslim History As a Case Study. Susan Douglass. LC 94-42643. (Illus.). 238p. (Orig.). (ARA & ENG.). 1994. pap. text ed. 18.95 (*0-915957-23-X*) amana pubns.

Strategies & Styles: The Role of the Centre in Managing Diversified Corporations. Michael Goold & Andrew Campbell. 384p. 1989. pap. text ed. 38.95 (*0-631-16846-X*) Blackwell Pubs.

Strategies & Tactics. Tony Scott & Clive Miller. 1984. 45.00 (*0-317-40617-5*, Pub. by Natl Inst Soc Work) St Mut.

Strategies & Tactics: Planning & Decision Making in Social Services Fieldwork Teams. Clive Miller & Tony Scott. (C). 1984. 55.00 (*0-685-28591-X*, Pub. by Natl Inst Soc Work); 59.00 (*0-685-40352-1*, Pub. by Natl Inst Soc Work); 75.00 (*0-7855-0073-1*, Pub. by Natl Inst Soc Work); pap. 35.00 (*0-902789-32-5*, Pub. by Natl Inst Soc Work) St Mut.

***Strategies & Tactics for Effective Instruction.** 2nd ed. Bob Algozzine & Jim Ysseldyke. (Illus.). 280p. 1997. pap. text ed. 29.50 (*1-57035-119-8*, C31STE1) Sopris.

***Strategies & Tactics for First Year Law.** 2nd rev. ed. (Strategies & Tactics Ser.). (C). 1997. pap. text ed. 12.95 (*1-56542-577-4*) E Pub Corp.

Strategies & Tactics for Management of Fertilized Hatchery Ponds. Ed. by Richard O. Anderson. LC 93-44926. (Journal of Applied Aquaculture). (Illus.). 290p. 1993. pap. text ed. 24.95 (*1-56022-049-X*); lib. bdg. 49.95 (*1-56022-048-1*) Haworth Pr.

Strategies & Tactics for Successful Retail Recruitment Downtown. 68p. 1988. 43.50 (*0-317-05046-X*) Natl Coun Econ Dev.

Strategies & Tactics for Successful Retail Recruitment Downtown. Ed. by Laurence A. Alexander. LC 88-51534. 68p. 1988. pap. text ed. 44.00 (*0-915910-28-4*) Downtown Res.

***Strategies & Tactics for the MBE.** 2nd rev. ed. (Strategies & Tactics Ser.). 760p. (C). 1997. pap. text ed. 34.95 (*1-56542-579-0*) E Pub Corp.

***Strategies & Tactics for the MPRE.** (Strategies & Tactics Ser.). 272p. (C). reprint ed. pap. text ed. 19.95 (*1-56542-576-6*) E Pub Corp.

Strategies & Tactics for the Multistate Bar Exam. Kimm A. Walton. 770p. (Orig.). (C). 1989. pap. 34.95 (*0-929479-05-X*) Prof Flash Cards.

Strategies & Tactics in Fashion Marketing: Selected Readings. Sidney Packard. LC 82-70063. (Illus.). 143p. reprint ed. pap. 40.80 (*0-8357-3714-4*, 2036436) Bks Demand.

Strategies & Tactics in Management by Objectives. Richard Babcock & Peter Sorensen. (Illus.). 273p. (C). 1980. pap. text ed. 7.40 (*0-87563-119-3*) Stipes.

Strategies & Tactics in Organic Synthesis, Vol. 1. Ed. by Thomas Lindberg. (Illus.). 370p. 1993. reprint ed. pap. text ed. 45.00 (*0-12-450275-X*) Acad Pr.

Strategies & Tactics in Organic Synthesis, Vol. 2. Ed. by Thomas Lindberg. 507p. 1988. text ed. 139.00 (*0-12-450281-4*) Acad Pr.

Strategies & Tactics in Organic Synthesis, Vol. 3. Ed. by Thomas Lindberg. (Illus.). 544p. 1991. text ed. 153.00 (*0-12-450282-2*) Acad Pr.

Strategies & Techniques for Successful Teaching. Frank Paoni. 148p. (C). 1994. per. 26.19 (*0-8403-9276-1*) Kendall-Hunt.

Strategies & Techniques for Teaching: With Lesson Design & Micro-Teaching Guidelines. Sharon K. Zenger. 1991. spiral bd. 21.95 (*0-88247-846-X*) R & E Pubs.

Strategies & Technologies for Meeting SDWA Requirements. Ed. by Robert Clark & R. Scott Summers. LC 92-56465. 400p. 1992. pap. text ed. 79.95 (*0-87762-957-9*) Technomic.

***Strategies de Gestion pour Ameliorer les Services de Planification Familiale: Un Compendium du Mangement de la Planification Familiale.** Janice Miller et al. Ed. by Hannorde Bellamine. (Illus.). 434p. (Orig.). (FRE.). 1997. pap. 25.00 (*0-913723-39-8*) Mgmt Sci Health.

Strategies et Choix dans la Recherche. Gerard Lemaine et al. (Maison des Sciences de l'Homme, Paris, Publications: No. 5). 1977. pap. 33.85 (*90-279-7674-0*) Mouton.

Strategies Fatales. Jean Baudrillard. (FRE.). 1986. pap. 16.95 (*0-7859-3129-5*) Fr & Eur.

Strategies for a Successful Marriage: A Study Guide for Men. E. Glenn Wagner & Dietrich Gruen. 96p. (Orig.). 1994. pap. 6.00 (*0-89109-857-7*) NavPress.

Strategies for Academic Communication. Steer. (College ESL Ser.). 1994. student ed., suppl. ed. 36.95 incl. audio (*0-8384-4284-6*) Heinle & Heinle.

Strategies for Academic Communication. Steer. (College ESL Ser.). 1995. teacher ed., pap. 21.95 (*0-8384-4257-9*) Heinle & Heinle.

Strategies for Academic Writing: A Guide for College Students. Irvin Y. Hashimoto et al. (C). 1982. pap. text ed. 18.95 (*0-472-08020-2*) U of Mich Pr.

Strategies for Active Learning. James E. Twining. 350p. 1991. pap. text ed. 32.00 (*0-205-13070-4*, H30704) Allyn.

Strategies for African Development. Ed. by Robert J. Berg & Jennifer S. Whitaker. (Illus.). 280p. 1986. pap. 22.50 (*0-520-05782-1*) U CA Pr.

Strategies for Analyzing Neuropeptide Systems. Ed. by R. M. Dores & T. C. Stevenson. (Journal: Cellular Physiology & Biochemistry: Vol. 3, No. 3-4, 1993). (Illus.). 88p. 1993. pap. 75.75 (*3-8055-5803-1*) S Karger.

Strategies for Antibiotic Usage & Utilization Review: A Comprehensive Sourcebook. Timothy R. Franson & William M. Valenti. (Illus.). 225p. 1987. pap. 59.95 (*0-9603332-8-2*) Am Health Consults.

Strategies for Argument: A Reader & Sourcebook. Sally D. Spurgin. 512p. (C). 1991. pap. text ed. 34.00 (*0-13-853268-0*) P-H.

Strategies for Asia Pacific. Philippe Lasserre & Hellmut Schutte. 400p. 1996. 59.95 (*0-7329-3664-0*, Pub. by Macmill Educ AT) Paul & Co Pubs.

Strategies for Asia Pacific. Philippe Lasserre & Hellmut Schutte. 400p. (C). 1995. 29.95 (*0-8147-5109-1*) NYU Pr.

Strategies for Assessing the Safety of Foods Produced by Biotechnology: Report of a Joint FAO-WHO Consultation. iv, 59p. (ENG, FRE & SPA.). 1991. pap. text ed. 11.00 (*92-4-156145-9*, 1150369) World Health.

***Strategies for Assessment in Teaching History.** White. 1992. pap. text ed. write for info. (*0-582-05933-X*, Pub. by Longman UK) Longman.

***Strategies for Board Leadership.** John Carver. (Carverguide Ser.: No. 10). 1997. pap. 10.95 (*0-7879-1082-1*) Jossey-Bass.

Strategies for Building a Customer-Focused Organization. Mary S. Gober. (Illus.). 38p. 1997. pap. 15.00 (*0-9624563-2-2*) Gober & Assocs.

Strategies for Business & Technical Writing. 3rd ed. Kevin J. Harty. 306p. (C). 1989. pap. text ed. 22.50 (*0-15-583926-8*) Dryden Pr.

Strategies for Business in Mexico: Free Trade & the Emergence of North America, Inc. Louis E. Nevaer. LC 95-6921. 240p. 1995. text ed. 59.95 (*0-89930-882-1*, Quorum Bks) Greenwood.

Strategies for Business Peak Performance: How to Start, Build, Manage Your Business for Peak Performance. A. D. Jeary. 1993. student ed. write for info. (*1-883454-02-6*) TPG Inc.

Strategies for Change. (Trainer Development Programme Management & Design Ser.). 1994. pap. text ed. 38.00 (*0-08-042460-0*, Pergamon Pr) Elsevier.

Strategies for Change. IPM Staff. (Training Design & Management Ser.: No. 6). (C). 1994. pap. 93.00 (*0-08-042169-5*, Pub. by IPM Hse UK) St Mut.

Strategies for Change. Lyle E. Schaller. LC 92-33159. 160p. (Orig.). 1993. pap. 12.95 (*0-687-39673-5*) Abingdon.

Strategies for Change: New Directions in Drug Policy. Ed. by Kevin B. Zeese et al. 392p. (Orig.). (C). 1992. pap. text ed. 25.00 (*1-879189-06-2*) Drug Policy.

Strategies for Change: The Future of French Society. Michel Crozier. Tr. by William Beer from FRE. (Organization Studies). 1982. 27.50 (*0-262-03082-9*) MIT Pr.

Strategies for Cities & Counties: A Strategic Planning Guide. 76p. 1984. 35.00 (*0-685-30547-3*) Pub Tech Inc.

Strategies for Classroom Discipline. Meryl E. Englander. LC 85-28287. 380p. 1986. text ed. 55.00 (*0-275-92093-3*, C2093, Praeger Pubs) Greenwood.

Strategies for College Reading & Thinking. Nancy V. Wood. 1991. pap. text ed. write for info. (*0-07-071707-9*) McGraw.

Strategies for College Reading & Thinking. Instructor's Manual. Nancy V. Wood. 1991. pap. text ed. write for info. (*0-07-071708-7*) McGraw.

Strategies for College Success: Student Planner. 2nd ed. Mary C. Starke. 1993. 37.80 (*0-13-855529-X*) P-H.

S

An Asterisk (*) at the beginning of an entry indicates that the title is appearing in BIP for the first time.

***Strategies for Communication Research.** Ed. by Paul W. Hirsch et al. LC 77-88630. (Sage Annual Reviews of Communication Research Ser.: Vol. 6). 288p. 1977. reprint ed. pap. 82.10 (*0-608-02994-7*, 2059634) Bks Demand.

Strategies for Community Empowerment: Direct Action & Transformative Approaches to Social Change Practice. Mark G. Hanna & Buddy Robinson. LC 93-51033. 1994. write for info. (*0-7734-2297-8*, Mellen Univ Pr) E Mellen.

***Strategies for Community Policing.** Elizabeth M. Watson et al. LC 97-25534. 1998. write for info. (*0-13-441197-8*) P-H.

Strategies for Competitive Success. Robert A. Pitts & Charles C. Snow. LC 85-10483. 76p. 1986. Net. pap. text ed. 17.00 (*0-471-81656-6*) Wiley.

Strategies for Competitive Volleyball. Stephen D. Fraser. LC 87-31853. (Illus.). 208p. 1988. text ed. 22.00 (*0-88011-304-9*, PFRA0304) Human Kinetics.

Strategies for Confronting Domestic Violence: A Resource Manual. 122p. 1994. 19.95 (*92-1-130158-0*) UN.

Strategies for Counseling with Children & Their Parents. Geraldine L. Orton. (Counseling Ser.). 390p. (C). 1997. text ed. 54.95 (*0-534-23280-9*) Brooks-Cole.

Strategies for Creative Problem-Solving. H. Folger & Steven LeBlanc. 200p. 1994. pap. text ed. 32.00 (*0-13-179318-7*) P-H.

Strategies for Creditors in Bankruptcy Proceedings. 2nd ed. Lynn M. LoPucki. 1991. 155.00 (*0-316-53228-2*) Little.

***Strategies for Crop Insurance Planning.** 167p. 1990. 17.00 (*92-5-102980-6*, F9806, Pub. by FAO IT) Bernan Associates.

Strategies for Cultural Change. Paul Bate. (Illus.). 320p. 1996. pap. 32.95 (*0-7506-2328-4*) Buttrwrth-Heinemann.

Strategies for Culture Change. Paul Bate. LC 93-34325. 308p. 1994. 50.95 (*0-7506-0519-7*) Buttrwrth-Heinemann.

Strategies for Currency Unification: The Economics of Currency Competition & Case for a European Parallel Currency. Roland Vaubel. 486p. 1978. pap. text ed. 52.00 (*3-16-340571-1*, Pub. by J C B Mohr GW) Coronet Bks.

Strategies for Defining the Army's Objective Vision of Command & Control for the 21st Century. Edison M. Cesar. LC 95-8471. xxiv, 56p. 1995. pap. text ed. 9.00 (*0-8330-1643-1*, MR-487-A) Rand Corp.

Strategies for Developing New Reactions, Vol. 7. Alexander Senning et al. (Sulfer Reports: Vol. 7, No. 2). 108p. 1986. pap. text ed. 158.00 (*3-7186-0376-4*) Gordon & Breach.

Strategies for Development of Foreign Language & Literature Programs. Claire Gaudiani et al. LC 83-17370. xxviii, 338p. 1984. pap. 25.00 (*0-87352-124-2*, D3110) Modern Lang.

Strategies for Effective Classroom Management: Creating a Collaborative Climate. Barbara Larrivee. (C). 1992. teacher ed., pap. text ed. 34.95 (*0-205-13941-8*, H39415) Allyn.

Strategies for Effective Customer Education. Peter C. Honebein. LC 96-20664. 176p. 1996. 37.95 (*0-8442-3582-2*, NTC Busn Bks) NTC Pub Grp.

Strategies for Effective Enrollment Management. Frank R. Kemerer et al. 198p. 1982. lib. bdg. 23.50 (*0-88044-062-7*) AASCU Press.

Strategies for Effective Teaching. Allan C. Ornstein. 508p. (C). 1990. text ed. 57.95 (*0-06-044927-6*) Addson-Wesley Educ.

Strategies for Effective Teaching. 2nd ed. Allan C. Ornstein. 512p. (C). 1994. per. write for info. (*0-697-24415-6*) Brown & Benchmark.

Strategies for Effective Workers' Compensation Cost Control. William English. 97p. 1988. 25.00 (*0-939874-83-0*) ASSE.

Strategies for Employee Assistance Programs: The Crucial Balance. 2nd rev. ed. William M. Sonnenstuhl & Harrison M. Trice. (Key Issues Ser.: No. 30). 88p. (Orig.). 1990. pap. 10.00 (*0-87546-167-0*, ILR Press) Cornell U Pr.

Strategies for Enabling Readers. Jerry L. Johns. 416p. (C). 1996. per., pap. text ed. 31.44 (*0-8403-8984-1*) Kendall-Hunt.

Strategies for Energy Efficient Plants & Intelligent Buildings. Association of Energy Engineers Staff. LC 86-82315. 500p. (Orig.). 1986. pap. 38.00 (*0-88173-021-1*); text ed. 62.00 (*0-88173-020-3*) Fairmont Pr.

Strategies for Energy-Efficient Plants 7 Intelligent Buildings. Fairmont Press Staff. 1987. text ed. 62.00 (*0-13-850686-8*) P-H.

Strategies for Engineering Organisms. 300p. 1993. pap. 46.95 (*0-7506-0559-6*) Buttrwrth-Heinemann.

Strategies for Environmental Enforcement. 350p. (Orig.). 1995. pap. text ed. 19.50 (*0-942007-41-7*) Stanford Enviro.

***Strategies for Exploitation of Mineral Resources in Developing Countries: Proceedings of the International Symposium, Dhanbad, 6-8 November 1986.** Ed. by A. K. Ghose. (Indian Edition Ser.: No. 16). 286p. 1987. 130.00 (*90-6191-498-1*, Pub. by A A Balkema NE) Ashgate Pub Co.

***Strategies for Fast-Changing Times: The Art of Using Change to Your Advantage.** Nate Booth. 256p. 1997. boxed 23.00 (*0-7615-1134-2*) Prima Pub.

Strategies for Fitness see Leisure Wellness Series

Strategies for Getting Charge Card Merchant Status at Your Bank: Even If You're Running a Home-Based or Mail Order Business. rev. ed. John Cali. 64p. 1990. pap. 27.95 (*0-924033-22-3*) Great West Pub.

Strategies for Growth in Religious Life. Gerald A. Arbuckle. LC 86-17359. 240p. (Orig.). 1986. pap. 11.95 (*0-8189-0505-0*) Alba.

Strategies for Growth in Religious Life. Gerald A. Arbuckle. (Orig.). (C). 1988. 39.00 (*0-85439-160-6*, Pub. by St Paul Pubns UK) St Mut.

Strategies for Guiding Content Reading. 2nd ed. Sharon J. Crawley & Lee Mountain. LC 94-42835. 331p. 1995. text ed. 39.95 (*0-205-14886-7*) Allyn.

Strategies for Health Care Finance in Developing Countries with a Focus on Community Financing in Sub-Saharan Africa. Ed. by Guy Carrin & Marc Vereecke. LC 92-17151. (Economic Issues in Health Care Ser.). 1992. text ed. 39.95 (*0-312-08402-1*) St Martin.

Strategies for Helping Victims of Elder Mistreatment. Risa S. Breckman & Ronald D. Adelman. (Human Services Guides Ser.: Vol. 53). 160p. (C). 1988. pap. text ed. 17.95 (*0-8039-3094-1*) Sage.

Strategies for High Performance Work & Learning in Small & Medium-Sized Firms. Erin Flynn. 54p. 1993. pap. 10.00 (*1-887410-62-7*) Jobs for Future.

Strategies for Higher Education - the Alternative White Paper. J. Barnes & N. Barr. (David Hume Papers). 66p. 1988. pap. text ed. 14.00 (*0-08-036589-2*, Pergamon Pr) Elsevier.

Strategies for Housing & Social Integration in Cities. 310p. (Orig.). (ENG & FRE.). 1996. pap. 57.00 (*92-64-14663-6*, Pub. by Org for Econ FR) OECD.

***Strategies for Human Resource Management.** Ed. by Michael Armstrong. (Human Resource Management Ser.). 1992. 40.00 (*0-7494-0537-6*) Kogan Page Ltd.

Strategies for Identity: The Fiction of Margaret Atwood. Eleonora Rao. LC 93-14218. (Writing about Women Ser.: Vol. 9). 204p. (Orig.). 1994. pap. text ed. 31.95 (*0-8204-2216-9*) P Lang Pubng.

Strategies for Immigration Control: An International Comparison. Ed. by Mark J. Miller. LC 93-85877. (Annals of the American Academy of Political & Social Science Ser.: Vol. 534). 1994. 28.00 (*0-8039-5590-1*); pap. 18.00 (*0-8039-5591-X*) Am Acad Pol Soc Sci.

***Strategies for Immunointerventions in Dermatology.** Ed. by G. Burg & R. G. Dummer. LC 97-8062. (Illus.). 340p. 1997. 129.00 (*3-540-62680-8*) Spr-Verlag.

Strategies for Impasse Resolution. Ed. by Harry Kershen & Claire Meirowitz. (Public Sector Contemporary Issues Ser.). 356p. (C). 1992. text ed. 38.95 (*0-89503-085-3*); pap. text ed. 29.21 (*0-89503-086-1*) Baywood Pub.

Strategies for Implementing Integrated Marketing Communications. Larry Percy. 272p. 1997. 39.95 (*0-8442-3583-0*, NTC Busn Bks) NTC Pub Grp.

***Strategies for Improvement of Salt Tolerance in Higher Plants.** Ed. by P. K. Jaiwal. (Illus.). 450p. 1997. text ed. 95.00 (*1-886106-97-5*) Science Pubs.

Strategies for Improving Environmental Quality & Increasing Economic Growth. 122p. 1995. pap. text ed. 25.00 (*1-884032-04-4*) Am Coun Capital.

Strategies for Increasing Access & Performance in Higher Education. J. K. Koppen & W. Webler. 1993. pap. 23.00 (*90-5170-208-6*, Pub. by Thesis Pubs NE) IBD Ltd.

Strategies for Innovation: Creating Successful Products, Systems, & Organizations. William B. Rouse. LC 91-42515. (Series in Systems Engineering). 272p. 1992. text ed. 84.95 (*0-471-55904-0*) Wiley.

Strategies for Interactive Reading. Maxine B. Zinn. (C). 1996. teacher ed., pap. text ed. 28.00 (*0-15-503243-7*) HB Coll Pubs.

Strategies for International Industrial Marketing: The Management of Customer Relationships in European Industrial Markets. Ed. by Peter W. Turnbull & Jean-Paul Valla. LC 85-29047. 336p. 1987. 59.95 (*0-7099-2494-1*, Pub. by Croom Helm UK) Routledge Chapman & Hall.

Strategies for Interpreting Qualitative Data: Four Techniques. Martha S. Feldman. (Qualitative Research Methods Ser.: Vol. 33). 96p. 1994. 22.95 (*0-8039-5915-X*) Sage.

Strategies for Interpreting Qualitative Data: Four Techniques. Martha S. Feldman. (Qualitative Research Methods Ser.: Vol. 33). 1994. pap. 9.95 (*0-8039-5916-8*) Sage.

Strategies for Involving Parents in Their Children's Education. Linda T. Jones. LC 91-60204. (Fastback Ser.: No. 315). (Orig.). 1991. pap. 3.00 (*0-87367-315-8*) Phi Delta Kappa.

Strategies for Joint Ventures in the People's Republic of China. Ike Mathur & Chen Jai-Sheng. LC 87-7033. 208p. 1987. text ed. 55.00 (*0-275-92354-1*, C2354, Praeger Pubs) Greenwood.

***Strategies for Keeping Kids in School: Evaluation of Dropout Prevention & Reentry Projects in Vocational Education.** 1997. lib. bdg. 250.75 (*0-8490-8236-6*) Gordon Pr.

***Strategies for Learning.** Phyllis J. Read et al. 132p. (C). 1996. pap. text ed., spiral bd. 20.94 (*0-7872-3030-8*) Kendall-Hunt.

Strategies for Learning: Small-Group Activities in American, Japanese, & Swedish Industry. Robert E. Cole. (Illus.). 364p. 1991. pap. 16.00 (*0-520-07398-3*) U CA Pr.

Strategies for Learning & Remembering: Study Skills Across the Curriculum. Mary A. Rafoth et al. LC 93-589. (Analysis & Action Ser.). 152p. 1993. pap. 14.95 (*0-8106-3048-6*) NEA.

Strategies for Learning Spanish. Sara M. Saz. LC 95-8442. 240p. (C). 1995. pap. text ed. 21.00 (*0-13-107160-2*) P-H.

Strategies for Lifelong Learning. Ed. by Per Himmelstrup et al. 1981. 7.95 (*0-87060-025-7*, DAG 1) Syracuse U Cont Ed.

Strategies for Litigating Contaminated Property Disputes. (Litigation & Administrative Practice Ser.). 560p. 1991. pap. text ed. 70.00 (*0-685-56920-9*, H4-5121) PLI.

Strategies for Long-Term Care. 528p. 1988. pap. 32.95 (*0-88737-413-1*, 20-2231) Natl League Nurse.

Strategies for Managing Behavior Problems in the Classroom. 2nd ed. Mary M. Kerr & C. Michael Nelson. 464p. (C). 1990. pap. text ed. 63.00 (*0-675-21033-X*, Merrill Coll) P-H.

Strategies for Managing Change: Practical Tools to Help You Make the Right Decisions. Allan L. Austin. (Financial Times Management Ser.). 256p. 1995. 105.00 (*0-273-60194-6*, Pub. by Pitman Pubng UK) St Mut.

Strategies for Managing Intergovernmental Policies & Networks. Ed. by Robert W. Gage & Myrna P. Mandell. LC 89-27561. 208p. 1990. text ed. 47.95 (*0-275-93247-8*, C3247, Praeger Pubs) Greenwood.

***Strategies for Managing Macroeconomic Risk: Corporate Performance & Exposure Assessments.** Lars Oxelheim & Clas Wihlborg. LC 97-1101. 1997. write for info. (*0-471-97474-9*) Wiley.

Strategies for Managing Ozone-Depleting Refrigerants: Confronting the Future. Katherine B. Miller et al. LC 94-32043. 134p. 1995. pap. 34.95 (*0-935470-84-0*) Battelle.

Strategies for Marketing Cosmetics & Toiletries in Europe: Competitive Positioning in a 33 Billion Dollar Marketplace. Market Intelligence Staff. 469p. 1993. 3,800.00 (*1-56753-565-8*) Frost & Sullivan.

Strategies for Mars: A Guide to Human Exploration. Ed. by Carol R. Stoker & Carter Emmart. (Science & Technology Ser.: Vol. 86). 619p. Date not set. pap. 45.00 (*0-87703-406-0*, TL794) Am Astronaut.

***Strategies for Mars: A Guide to Human Exploration.** Ed. by Carol R. Stoker & Carter Emmart. (Science & Technology Ser.: Vol. 86). (Illus.). 644p. 1996. 70.00 (*0-87703-405-2*) Am Astronaut.

Strategies for Measuring Industrial Structure & Growth. (Studies in Methods). 95p. 1994. 24.00 (*92-1-161369-8*) UN.

Strategies for Medical Record Management. Leslie A. Fox et al. 262p. 1986. 35.00 (*0-317-05440-6*) Am Hlth Info.

Strategies for Modern Living. Alfred Bloom. LC 91-61704. 188p. (C). 1993. pap. 11.95 (*0-9625618-1-9*) Numata Ctr.

Strategies for Motivation. (Study Units Ser.). 1977. pap. 9.00 (*0-89401-116-2*) Didactic Syst.

Strategies for Natural Language Processing. Ed. by Wendy G. Lehnert & Martin H. Ringle. (Illus.). 560p. 1982. pap. text ed. 69.95 (*0-89859-266-6*) L Erlbaum Assocs.

Strategies for Needs Assessment in Prevention. Ed. by Alex Zautra et al. LC 83-10861. (Prevention in Human Services Ser.: Vol. 2, No. 4). 133p. 1983. text ed. 32.95 (*0-86656-187-0*) Haworth Pr.

Strategies for Nintendo Games. Ed. by Consumer Guide Staff. (Illus.). 128p. (YA). 1991. spiral bd. 5.99 (*0-517-03208-2*) Random Hse Value.

***Strategies for Organic Drug Synthesis & Design.** Daniel Lednicer. LC 97-11813. 300p. 1997. 69.95 (*0-471-19657-6*) Wiley.

Strategies for Passing the Essay Portion of the Georgia Regents' Exam. Joan M. Elifson & Mary P. Deming. (Illus.). 200p. (Orig.). (C). 1996. pap. text ed. 23.95 (*0-89892-138-4*) Contemp Pub Co of Raleigh.

Strategies for Passing the Georgia Regents' Exam. 4th ed. Joan Elifson & Belita Gordon. 249p. (C). 1989. pap. text ed. 28.95 (*0-89892-035-3*) Contemp Pub Co of Raleigh.

Strategies for Personality Research. Donald W. Fiske. LC 78-1150. (Jossey-Bass Social & Behavioral Science Ser.). 472p. reprint ed. pap. 134.60 (*0-8357-4883-9*, 2037815) Bks Demand.

Strategies for Physical Mapping. Ed. by Kay E. Davies & Shirley M. Tilghman. LC 92-70761. (Genome Analysis Ser.: Vol. 4). 165p. 1992. 16.00 (*0-87969-412-2*, QH445) Cold Spring Harbor.

Strategies for Players in a Larger World: The Effect of Regulatory & Information Changes. Ed. by Richard M. Burton et al. LC 92-26722. viii, 190p. 1992. 134.50 (*0-444-89290-7*) Elsevier.

Strategies for Political Participation. 3rd ed. Frank Kendrick et al. 208p. (C). reprint ed. pap. text ed. 22.00 (*0-8191-3319-1*) U Pr of Amer.

Strategies for Primary Health Care: Technologies Appropriate for the Control of Disease in the Developing World. Ed. by Julia A. Walsh & Kenneth S. Warren. xii, 344p. 1986. lib. bdg. 42.00 (*0-226-87207-6*) U Ch Pr.

Strategies for Private Sector Participation in the Provision of Transportation Facilities. Edward Beimborn et al. (Publications in Architecture & Urban Planning: No. R85-4). v, 18p. 1985. 5.00 (*0-938744-40-2*) U of Wis Ctr Arch-Urban.

Strategies for Productive Motor Carrier Sales Management. Paul Preston. 237p. 1987. pap. 10.80 (*0-88711-108-4*) Am Trucking Assns.

Strategies for Promoting Health & Assuring Access to Health Care in Child Care Settings. Karen N. Bell. 28p. (Orig.). 1995. pap. 8.00 (*0-926582-14-3*) NCCP.

***Strategies for Promoting Pluralism in Education & the Workplace.** Lynne B. Welch et al. LC 96-37691. 1997. text ed. 55.00 (*0-275-95675-X*, Praeger Pubs) Greenwood.

Strategies for Protein Purification & Characterization: A Laboratory Course Manual. Daniel Marshak et al. (Illus.). 304p. (C). 1996. pap. 85.00 (*0-87969-385-1*) Cold Spring Harbor.

Strategies for Readers: A Reading Communication Text for Students of ESL, Bk. 1. Christine P. Casanave. (Illus.). 192p. (C). 1985. pap. text ed. 16.95 (*0-13-850728-7*) P-H.

Strategies for Reading Japanese: A Structural Analysis Approach. Setsuko Aihara. 352p. (Orig.). 1992. pap. 43.00 (*0-87040-894-1*) Japan Pubns USA.

Strategies for Reading Nonfiction: Comprehension & Study Activities. Sandra M. Simons. 128p. (Orig.). 1991. pap. text ed. 15.95 (*0-9627689-1-X*) Spring St OR.

Strategies for Real-Time System Specification. Derek J. Hatley & Imtiaz A. Pirbhai. LC 87-50801. (Illus.). 408p. 1988. 49.50 (*0-932633-11-0*) Dorset Hse Pub Co.

Strategies for Reducing Natural Gas. Fairmont Press Staff. 1989. pap. text ed. 75.00 (*0-13-850595-0*) P-H.

Strategies for Reducing Natural Gas, Electric & Oil Costs. Association of Energy Engineers Staff. Ed. by Mary J. Winer. LC 89-45581. 540p. 1989. pap. text ed. 75.00 (*0-88173-094-7*) Fairmont Pr.

Strategies for Research & Development in Higher Education. Ed. by Noel Entwistle. vi, 282p. 1976. pap. 50.00 (*90-265-0242-7*) Swets.

Strategies for Resolving Individual & Family Problems. Fred W. Vondracek & Sherry Corneal. LC 94-21195. 512p. 1995. text ed. 62.95 (*0-534-25470-5*) Brooks-Cole.

Strategies for Retaining Minority Students in Higher Education. Ed. by Marvel Lang & Clinita A. Ford. (Illus.). 180p. (C). 1992. text ed. 39.95 (*0-398-05820-2*) C C Thomas.

Strategies for Retaining Minority Students in Higher Education. Ed. by Marvel Lang & Clinita A. Ford. (Illus.). 180p. 1992. pap. 26.95 (*0-398-06222-6*) C C Thomas.

Strategies for Retrenchment & Turnaround: The Politics of Survival. Cynthia Hardy. (Studies in Organization: No. 18). xii, 222p. (C). 1990. lib. bdg. 52.95 (*3-11-011612-X*) De Gruyter.

Strategies for River Basin Management: Environmental Integration of Land & Water in a River Basin. Ed. by Jan Lundqvist et al. LC 85-18293. 1985. lib. bdg. 162.50 (*90-277-2111-4*) Kluwer Ac.

Strategies for Rural Competitiveness: Policy Options for State Governments. Thomas W. Bonnett. LC 93-11723. 1993. 19.95 (*0-934842-71-X*) CSPA.

Strategies for Saving the Next Generation. David Burrows. 1995. pap. 5.95 (*1-56229-403-2*) Pneuma Life Pub.

Strategies for Selecting & Verifying Hearing Aid Fittings. Ed. by Michael Valente. LC 93-33542. 1993. 49.00 (*0-86577-500-1*) Thieme Med Pubs.

Strategies for Sequential Search & Selection in Real Time. F. Bruss et al. LC 91-38281. (Contemporary Mathematics Ser.: Vol. 125). 248p. 1992. pap. 47.00 (*0-8218-5133-0*, CONM/125) Am Math.

Strategies for Short-Term Testing for Mutagens-Carcinogens. Byron E. Butterworth. 160p. 1979. 87.00 (*0-8493-5661-X*, QH465, CRC Reprint) Franklin.

***Strategies for Showing: Women, Possession, & Representation in English Visual Culture 1665-1800.** Marcia Pointon. (Illus.). 456p. 1997. 85.00 (*0-19-817411-X*) OUP.

Strategies for Side Impact Protection: Two Papers. 78p. 1993. 18.00 (*1-56091-359-2*, SP-974) Soc Auto Engineers.

Strategies for Social Mobility: Family, Kinship & Ethnicity Within Jewish Families in Pittsburgh. Myrna Silverman. LC 88-84004. (Immigrant Communities & Ethnic Minorities in the U. S. & Canada Ser.: No. 57). 1989. 49.50 (*0-404-19467-2*) AMS Pr.

Strategies for Software Engineer: The Management of Risk & Quality. Martyn A. Ould. 243p. 1990. text ed. 65.00 (*0-471-92628-0*) Wiley.

***Strategies for Solving Problems.** Carole Greenes et al. (Spotlight on Understanding Ser.). 1996. text ed. 13.95 (*0-614-19585-3*, G172) Janson Pubns.

Strategies for State Reciprocity in Asbestos Accreditation. Doug Farquhar. (State Legislative Reports: Vol. 17, No. 15). 8p. 1992. pap. text ed. 5.00 (*1-55516-287-8*, 7302-1715) Natl Conf State Legis.

Strategies for Stillwater: Tackle, Techniques, & Flies for Taking Trout in Lakes & Ponds. Dave Hughes. LC 91-8427. (Illus.). 256p. 1991. 19.95 (*0-8117-1916-2*) Stackpole.

Strategies for Stroke Prevention: Sanofi Wintrop Symposium to the Third European Stroke Conference, Stockholm, May 1994. Ed. by J. Bogousslavsky & H. P. Adams. (Journal: Chemotherapy: Vol. 4, Suppl. 4, 1994). (Illus.). iv, 38p. 1995. pap. 21.75 (*3-8055-6073-7*) S Karger.

Strategies for Structural Adjustment: The Experience of Southeast Asia. Ed. by Ungku A. Aziz. LC 90-5296. x, 202p. 1990. pap. 18.50 (*1-55775-147-1*) Intl Monetary.

***Strategies for Struggling Learners: A Guide for the Teaching Parent.** 2nd ed. Joe P. Sutton & Connie J. Sutton. 212p. 1997. pap. text ed. 17.00 (*0-9645684-1-1*) Except Diag.

Strategies for Student Writers: Guide to Writing Essays, Tutorial Papers, Exam Papers & Reports. Pamela Peters. 141p. 1987. text ed. 9.95 (*0-471-33406-5*) Wiley.

***Strategies for Studying: A Handbook of Study Skills.** Orca Staff. 160p. 1996. pap. 12.95 (*1-55143-063-0*) Orca Bk Pubs.

Strategies for Studying Suicide & Suicidal Behavior. Ed. by Irma S. Lann et al. 164p. 1989. lib. bdg. 20.95 (*0-89862-383-9*) Guilford Pr.

Strategies for Success. Wilson Grant. 200p. (Orig.). 1996. pap. 15.00 (*1-57502-183-8*, P0807) Morris Pubng.

Strategies for Success: Amerasian Resettlement - 1989 Conference Proceedings. 100p. (Orig.). (C). 1994. pap. text ed. 25.00 (*1-56806-156-0*) DIANE Pub.

Strategies for Success: An Effective Guide for Teachers of Secondary-Level Slow Learners. Gloria Wilkins & Susanne Miller. LC 82-5438. 380p. reprint ed. pap. 108.30 (*0-8357-2581-2*, 2040275) Bks Demand.

An Asterisk (*) at the beginning of an entry indicates that the title is appearing in BIP for the first time.

Strategies for Success: Teaching Techniques for Students with Learning Problems. rev. ed. Lynn J. Meltzer et al. LC 95-18217. (Illus.). (C). 1996. pap. text ed. 28.00 (*0-89079-673-4*, 7313) PRO-ED.

Strategies for Success: Using Type to Do Better in High School & College. Judith A. Provost. 13p. 1992. 4.50 (*0-935652-15-9*) Ctr Applications Psych.

Strategies for Success in Real Estate. Sam Young. 1983. 18.00 (*0-8359-7080-9*, Reston) P-H.

Strategies for Success in Small Business. Donald R. Armstrong. (Illus.). 1977. text ed. 10.00 (*0-918464-15-3*) D Armstrong.

Strategies for Success in the Band & Orchestra. 52p. (Orig.). (C). 1994. pap. 11.00 (*1-56545-038-8*, 1624) Music Ed Natl.

Strategies for Successful Enforcement of Rules & Deed Restrictions. F. Scott Jackson & David G. Baratti. 1994. pap. 15.95 (*0-941301-20-6*) CAI.

Strategies for Successful Writing: A Rhetoric, Research Guide & Reader. 4th ed. James A. Reinking et al. LC 95-8295. 1995. pap. text ed. 33.33 (*0-13-439860-2*); pap. text ed. 38.40 (*0-13-190802-2*) P-H.

***Strategies for Successfully Buying or Selling a Business: Laws of the Jungle, Proven Techniques, Insiders Secrets, & Fundamentals for Business Buyers & Sellers.** Russell L. Brown. LC 97-66714. 176p. 1997. pap. 29.95 (*0-9657400-0-5*, B101, Busn Bk Pr) RDS Assocs.

***Strategies for Supporting Classroom Success: Focus on Communication - an Audio Workshop, 6 cass.** Ed. by Nickola W. Nelson & Barbara Hoskins. (School-Age Children Ser.). (Illus.). 100p. (Orig.). 1997. pap. 125.00 incl. audio (*1-56593-810-0*, 1586) Singular Publishing.

Strategies for Supporting Local Institutional Development. Gerard Finin et al. (Special Series on Local Institutional Development: No. 7). 99p. (Orig.). (C). 1985. pap. text ed. 7.50 (*0-86731-114-2*) Cornell CIS RDC.

Strategies for Survival: A Gay Men's Health Manual for the Age of AIDS. Martin Delaney & Peter Goldblum. 190p. 1987. pap. 10.95 (*0-312-00558-X*) St Martin.

Strategies for Survival: American Indians in the Eastern United States. Ed. by Frank W. Porter, III. LC 85-30189. (Contributions in Ethnic Studies: No. 15). 248p. 1986. text ed. 55.00 (*0-313-25253-X*, PST/, Greenwood Pr) Greenwood.

Strategies for Survival: Cultural Behavior in an Ecological Context. Michael Jochim. LC 81-7887. 1981. text ed. 52.00 (*0-12-385460-1*) Acad Pr.

Strategies for Survival: The Psychology of Cultural Resilience in Ethnic Minorities. Peter Elsass. (Illus.). 228p. (C). 1992. text ed. 32.00 (*0-8147-2188-5*) NYU Pr.

Strategies for Survival: The Psychology of Cultural Resilience in Ethnic Minorities. Peter Elsass. 228p. (C). 1995. pap. 19.00 (*0-8147-2196-6*) NYU Pr.

Strategies for Sustainable Development: Local Agendas for the Southern Hemisphere. Ed. by Michael Redclift & Colin Sage. LC 93-3272. 195p. 1994. text ed. 95.00 (*0-471-94278-2*) Wiley.

Strategies for Sustaining Religious Commitment: The Art of the Religious Life. Theodore Weinberger. LC 91-27149. (Studies in Religion & Society: Vol. 28). 228p. 1991. lib. bdg. 89.95 (*0-7734-9678-5*) E Mellen.

Strategies for Teachers: Information Processing Models in the Classroom. Paul D. Eggen et al. (Curriculum & Teaching Ser.). (Illus.). 1979. write for info. (*0-13-851162-4*) P-H.

Strategies for Teachers: Teaching Content & Thinking Skills. 3rd ed. Paul D. Eggen & Donald P. Kauchak. 1995. text ed. 54.00 (*0-205-15011-X*) Allyn.

Strategies for Teaching. Anthony S. Jones et al. LC 79-20596. 249p. 1979. 27.50 (*0-8108-1257-6*) Scarecrow.

Strategies for Teaching American History, Vol. No. 1. HRW Staff. 1992. pap. 17.00 (*0-03-073599-8*) H Holt & Co.

Strategies for Teaching American History, Vol. No. 2. HRW Staff. 1992. pap. 17.00 (*0-03-073601-3*) H Holt & Co.

Strategies for Teaching At-Risk & Handicapped Infants & Toddlers. Sharon A. Raver. 460p. (C). 1991. text ed. 69.00 (*0-675-21202-2*, Merrill Coll) P-H.

***Strategies for Teaching Beginning & Intermediate Band.** Ed. by Edward J. Kvet & Janet M. Tweed. (Strategies for Teaching Ser.). 72p. (Orig.). 1996. pap. 18.25 (*1-56545-088-4*, 1650) Music Ed Natl.

***Strategies for Teaching Elementary & Middle-Level Chorus.** Ed. by Ann R. Small & Judy K. Bowers. (Strategies for Teaching Ser.). 133p. (Orig.). 1997. pap. 18.25 (*1-56545-086-8*, 1648) Music Ed Natl.

Strategies for Teaching Exceptional Children in Inclusive Settings. Ed. by Edward L. Meyen et al. 528p. (Orig.). (C). 1996. pap. text ed. 39.95 (*0-89108-244-1*, 9603) Love Pub Co.

***Strategies for Teaching High School General Music.** Ed. by Keith P. Thompson & Gloria J. Kiester. 110p. (Orig.). 1997. pap. 18.25 (*1-56545-085-X*, 1647) Music Ed Natl.

***Strategies for Teaching in a Diverse Society: Instructional Models.** Thomas J. Lasley & Thomas J. Matczynski. LC 96-41180. (C). 1997. text ed. 55.95 (*0-534-51645-9*) Wadsworth Pub.

***Strategies for Teaching K-4 General Music.** Sandra Stauffer & Jennifer Davidson. (Strategies for Teaching Ser.). 72p. (Orig.). 1995. pap. 18.25 (*1-56545-081-7*, 1645) Music Ed Natl.

Strategies for Teaching Learners with Special Needs. 6th ed. Edward A. Polloway & James R. Patton. LC 96-23937. (C). 1996. 58.00 (*0-13-466666-6*) P-H.

***Strategies for Teaching Middle Level & High School Keyboard.** Martha F. Hilley & Tommie Pardue. (Strategies for Teaching Ser.). (Orig.). 1996. pap. 18.25 (*1-56545-092-2*, 1655) Music Ed Natl.

***Strategies for Teaching Middle-Level General Music.** Ed. by June M. Hinckley & Suzanne M. Shull. (Strategies for Teaching Ser.). 64p. (Orig.). 1996. pap. 18.25 (*1-56545-084-1*, 1646) Music Ed Natl.

Strategies for Teaching Nursing. 3rd ed. Rheba De Tornyay & Martha A. Thompson. LC 86-19060. 353p. 1989. pap. text ed. 33.50 (*0-8273-4228-4*) Delmar.

***Strategies for Teaching Prekindergarten Music.** Wendy L. Sims. (Strategies for Teaching Ser.). 96p. (Orig.). 1995. pap. 18.25 (*1-56545-083-3*, 1644) Music Ed Natl.

***Strategies for Teaching Strings & Orchestra.** Dorothy Straub et al. (Strategies for Teaching Ser.). 108p. (Orig.). 1996. pap. 18.25 (*1-56545-082-5*, 1652) Music Ed Natl.

Strategies for Teaching Students with Disorders Emotional & Behavioral. Reese L. Meese. LC 95-42261. (Special Education Ser.). 448p. 1996. pap. 53.95 (*0-534-24288-X*) Brooks-Cole.

Strategies for Teaching Students with Learning & Behavior Problems. 3rd ed. Candace S. Bos & Sharon Vaughn. LC 93-6050. 521p. 1993. pap. text ed. 64.00 (*0-205-14885-9*) Allyn.

***Strategies for Teaching Students with Learning & Behavior Problems.** 4th ed. Candace S. Bos & Sharon Vaughn. LC 97-10906. 1997. 57.00 (*0-205-27228-2*) Allyn.

Strategies for Teaching Students with Mild to Severe Mental Retardation. Ed. by Robert A. Gable & Steven F. Warren. LC 92-26139. 336p. 1993. pap. text ed. 35.00 (*1-55766-118-9*, STK-1189) P H Brookes.

Strategies for Teaching Universal Design. Ed. by Polly Welch. 1995. pap. 29.95 (*0-944661-23-8*) MIG Comns.

Strategies for Teaching Writing. Ed. by Mary L. Kuhns & Robert H. Weiss. 104p. Date not set. pap. 6.50 (*1-887732-00-4*) West Chester Univ.

Strategies for Technical Communication. fac. ed. Nancy R. Blyler. LC 84-26134. (Illus.). 441p. 1985. reprint ed. pap. 125.70 (*0-7837-8215-2*, 2047915) Bks Demand.

Strategies for Technical Communication: A Collection of Teaching Tips. Meg P. Morgan et al. 112p. pap. text ed. 30.00 (*0-914548-76-X*, 152-94) Soc Tech Comm.

Strategies for the European Construction Sector: A Programme for Change. 170p. 1994. pap. 70.00 (*92-826-7833-4*, CO-83-94-264ENC, Pub. by Europ Com UK) Bernan Associates.

Strategies for the Future. Ed. by Sajjad A. Hashmi. 244p. (Orig.). (C). 1989. pap. 15.00 (*0-685-29121-9*) ESU RRCIB&ED.

Strategies for the Nineteen Eighties: Lessons of Cuba, Vietnam & Afghanistan. Philip Van Slyck. LC 81-4627. (Studies in Freedom: No. 1). 104p. 1981. text ed. 45.00 (*0-313-22975-9*, VAS/); text ed. 19.95 (*0-317-43257-5*) Greenwood.

Strategies for the Options Trader. Claud E. Cleeton. LC 78-11230. 184p. reprint ed. pap. 52.50 (*0-7837-2832-8*, 2057640) Bks Demand.

Strategies for the Practice of Institutional Research: Concepts, Resources, & Applications. Michael F. Middaugh et al. 124p. (C). 1994. pap. text ed. 14.95 (*1-882393-04-X*) Assn Instl Res.

Strategies for the Single Market, 1992. J. Dudley. 400p. (C). 1989. 225.00 (*0-685-39852-8*, Pub. by Inst Pur & Supply UK) St Mut.

Strategies for the Treatment of Hepatobiliary Disease. Ed. by G. Paumgartner et al. (Falk Symposium Ser.). (C). 1990. lib. bdg. 114.00 (*0-7923-8903-4*) Kluwer Ac.

Strategies for Theory Construction in Nursing. 3rd ed. Lorraine W. Walker & Kay C. Avant. LC 94-7951. 1994. pap. text ed. 39.95 (*0-8385-8688-0*, A8680-2) Appleton & Lange.

Strategies for Therapy with the Elderly: Living with Hope & Meaning. Claire M. Brody & Vicki G. Semel. LC 93-3273. 200p. 1993. 32.95 (*0-8261-8010-8*) Springer Pub.

Strategies for Third World Development. Ed. by John S. Augustine. 156p. (C). 1989. text ed. 24.00 (*0-8039-9612-8*) Sage.

Strategies for Women's Studies in the Eighties. G. Bowles. 100p. 1984. pap. 19.25 (*0-08-031320-5*, Pergamon Pr) Elsevier.

Strategies for Word Identification: Phonics from a New Perspective. Barbara J. Fox. LC 95-15688. 1995. pap. text ed. 23.00 (*0-02-339191-X*, Macmillan Coll) P-H.

Strategies for Work with Involuntary Clients. Ronald H. Rooney. (Illus.). 392p. 1992. text ed. 65.00 (*0-231-06768-2*); pap. text ed. 24.50 (*0-231-06769-0*) Col U Pr.

Strategies for Working with Families of Young Children with Disabilities. Ed. by Paula Beckman. 304p. (Orig.). 1996. pap. text ed. 30.00 (*1-55766-257-6*, 2576) P H Brookes.

Strategies for World-Class Products. Mike Farish. LC 95-1550. 1995. 48.95 (*0-566-07535-0*, Pub. by Gower UK) Ashgate Pub Co.

***Strategies for Writing: A Basic Approach.** Ann E. Healy & Martha Walusayi. LC 96-30726. 1996. pap. write for info. (*0-8442-5922-5*) NTC Pub Grp.

***Strategies for Writing Successful Essays.** Nell Meriwether. LC 97-18518. 272p. 1997. pap. 16.95 (*0-8442-5992-6*) NTC Pub Grp.

Strategies in Electric & Hybrid Vehicle Design: 1996 International Congress & Exposition. (Special Publications). 144p. 1996. pap. 61.00 (*1-56091-786-5*, SP-1156) Soc Auto Engineers.

Strategies in Genetic Counseling: The Challenge of the Future. Ed. by Susie Ball. (National Society of Genetic Counselors Ser.: Vol. 1). 216p. 1988. 35.95 (*0-89885-388-5*) Human Sci Pr.

Strategies in Genetic Counseling - Tools for Professional Advancement, Vol. 2. Ed. by N. J. Zellers. (National Society of Genetic Counselors Ser.). (Illus.). 236p. 1989. 38.00 (*0-89885-450-4*) Human Sci Pr.

Strategies in Global Competition. Ed. by Neil Hood & Jan-Erik Vahlne. 432p. 1988. lib. bdg. 75.00 (*0-7099-3796-2*, Pub. by Croom Helm UK) Routledge Chapman & Hall.

Strategies in Global Industries: How U. S. Businesses Compete. Allen J. Morrison. LC 89-24370. 216p. 1990. text ed. 59.95 (*0-89930-528-8*, MBG/, Greenwood Pr) Greenwood.

Strategies in Gynecologic Surgery. Ed. by Herbert J. Buchsbaum & L. A. Walton. (Clinical Perspectives in Obstetrics & Gynecology Ser.). (Illus.). 256p. 1986. 120.00 (*0-387-96278-6*) Spr-Verlag.

Strategies in Humanistic Education, 3 vols., 1. Tim Timmermann & Jim Ballard. LC 75-25394. (Mandala Series in Education). 592p. 1976. reprint ed. pap. 9.95 (*0-916250-03-2*) Irvington.

Strategies in Humanistic Education, 3 vols., 2. Tim Timmermann & Jim Ballard. LC 75-25394. (Mandala Series in Education). 592p. 1976. reprint ed. pap. 9.95 (*0-8290-0434-3*) Irvington.

Strategies in Humanistic Education, 3 vols., 3. Tim Timmermann & Jim Ballard. LC 75-25394. (Mandala Series in Education). 592p. 1976. reprint ed. pap. 9.95 (*0-916250-25-3*) Irvington.

Strategies in Interlanguage Communication. Ed. by Claus Faerch & Gabriele Kasper. (Applied Linguistics & Language Ser.). 240p. (Orig.). 1983. pap. text ed. 14.95 (*0-582-55373-3*) Longman.

Strategies in Listening: Tasks for Listening Development. Michael A. Rost. 80p. 1986. teacher ed. 10.95 (*0-8013-0521-7*, 78367); audio 55.00 (*0-8013-0522-5*, 78368) Longman.

Strategies in Listening: Tasks for Listening Development. Michael A. Rost. 80p. 1987. pap. text ed. 14.85 (*0-8013-0520-9*, 78366) Longman.

Strategies in Primary & Secondary Prevention of Coronary Artery Disease. Ed. by T. Ischinger & H. Gohlke. (Illus.). 304p. 1992. text ed. 75.00 (*3-88603-440-2*, Pub. by W Zuckschwerdt GW) Scholium Intl.

***Strategies in Reading.** Motai. Date not set. pap. text ed. write for info. (*1-85294-065-4*) Addison-Wesley.

Strategies in Reading: Developing Essential Reading Skills. L. Motai & Edgar J. Boone. 112p. 1988. teacher ed. 14.95 (*0-8013-0516-0*, 78362); pap. text ed. 13.95 (*0-8013-0515-2*, 78361) Longman.

Strategies in Reading: Level A. Romm. 1984. pap. text ed. 16.00 (*0-15-337118-8*); teacher ed., pap. text ed. 22.75 (*0-15-337124-2*) HR&W Schl Div.

Strategies in Reading: Level B. Romm. 1984. pap. text ed. 16.00 (*0-15-337119-6*); teacher ed., pap. text ed. 22.75 (*0-15-337125-0*) HR&W Schl Div.

Strategies in Reading: Level C. Romm. 1984. pap. text ed. 16.00 (*0-15-337120-X*); teacher ed., pap. text ed. 22.75 (*0-15-337126-9*) HR&W Schl Div.

Strategies in Rural Economic Development: A Case Study in Five Philippine Villages. Orlando J. Sacay et al. 109p. 1971. pap. text ed. 3.00 (*0-942717-15-5*) Intl Inst Rural.

Strategies in Size Exclusion Chromatography. Ed. by Martin Potschka & Paul L. Dubin. LC 96-13254. (ACS Symposium Ser.: No. 635). (Illus.). 432p. 1996. 109.95 (*0-8412-3414-0*) Am Chemical.

Strategies in Social Work Consultation: From Theory to Practice in the Mental Health Field. Dwight W. Rieman. 208p. (C). 1992. pap. text ed. 39.95 (*0-8013-0394-X*, 78173) Longman.

Strategies in Teaching Greek & Latin: Two Decades of Experimentation. Ed. by Floyd L. Moreland. LC 81-18428. (American Philological Association Pamphlet Ser.). 145p. 1981. pap. 11.50 (*0-89130-556-4*, 40 06 07) Scholars Pr GA.

Strategies in Tenant Representation, 1990. Society Of Industrial Realtors Staff. 190p. 1990. per. 35.00 (*0-939623-24-2*) Soc Industrial Realtors.

Strategies in the Middle Game. Hodgson. 1995. pap. 14.95 (*1-85744-046-3*) S&S Trade.

Strategies in Transgenic Animal Science. Ed. by Glenn M. Monastersky & James M. Robl. LC 95-2396. 1995. write for info. (*1-55581-096-9*) Am Soc Microbio.

Strategies in Vaccine Design. Ed. by Gordon L. Ada. LC 93-46422. (Medical Intelligence Unit Ser.). 232p. 1994. 94.00 (*1-57059-094-X*, LN9094) R G Landes.

Strategies in Vaccine Development. Ed. by Stefan H. Kaufmann. 184p. 1992. pap. 60.00 (*1-56081-352-0*, Pub. by G Fischer Verlag GW) Lubrecht & Cramer.

***Strategies Interact Reading.** Zinn. (C). 1996. pap. write for info. (*0-15-502083-8*) HB Coll Pubs.

Strategies National Sustaining Development. IIED & IUCN Staff. 1995. 22.00 (*1-85383-193-X*, Pub. by Erthscan Pubns UK) Island Pr.

Strategies Novels, 6 bks. (J). (gr. 4-6). 1991. Mice in Centre Field. text ed. 7.72 (*0-8123-6926-2*); Project Egg. text ed. 7.72 (*0-8123-6927-0*); Face-off in Moscow. text ed. 7.72 (*0-8123-6928-9*); The Tiger Catcher's Kid. text ed. 7.72 (*0-8123-6929-7*); The Muffled Man. text ed. 7.72 (*0-8123-6930-0*) McDougal-Littell.

Strategies of Argument. 2nd ed. Stuart Hirschberg. 1996. pap. text ed. 33.00 (*0-205-17425-6*) Allyn.

Strategies of Arms Control. Croft. LC 96-8349. 1997. text ed. 24.95 (*0-7190-4878-8*) St Martin.

Strategies of Arms Control: A History & Typology. Stuart Croft. LC 96-8349. 1996. text ed. 59.95 (*0-7190-4877-X*, Pub. by Manchester Univ Pr UK) St Martin.

Strategies of Community Intervention: Macro Practice. 5th ed. Ed. by Jack Rothman et al. LC 94-66869. 464p. (C). 1995. pap. text ed. 40.00 (*0-87581-390-9*) Peacock Pubs.

Strategies of Containment: A Critical Appraisal of Postwar American National Security Policy. John L. Gaddis. LC 81-772. 416p. 1982. pap. 14.95 (*0-19-503097-4*) OUP.

Strategies of Deconstruction: Derrida & the Myth of the Voice. J. Claude Evans. 228p. (Orig.). 1991. pap. text ed. 14.95 (*0-8166-1926-3*) U of Minn Pr.

Strategies of Democratization. Tatu Vanhanen. 230p. 1992. 45.00 (*0-8448-1719-8*, Crane Russak); pap. 24.50 (*0-8448-1720-1*, Crane Russak) Taylor & Francis.

Strategies of Deviance: Studies in Gay Male Representation. Earl Jackson. (Theories of Representation & Difference Ser.). 344p. 1995. 39.95 (*0-253-33115-3*); pap. 15.95 (*0-253-20950-1*) Ind U Pr.

***Strategies of Distinction: The Construction of Ethnic Communities, 300-800.** Ed. by Walter Pohl. (Transformation of the Roman World Ser.: Vol. 2). (Illus.). (ENG & FRE.). 1997. 97.00 (*90-04-10846-7*) E J Brill.

Strategies of Drama: The Experience of Form. Oscar L. Brownstein. LC 91-10431. (Contributions in Drama & Theatre Studies: No. 39). 216p. 1991. text ed. 49.95 (*0-313-27754-0*, BEY, Greenwood Pr) Greenwood.

Strategies of Economic Development: Readings in the Political Economy of Industrialization. Ed. by Kurt Martin. LC 91-23306. 340p. 1991. text ed. 69.95 (*0-312-06800-X*) St Martin.

Strategies of Economic Order: German Economic Discourse, 1750-1950. Keith Tribe. (Ideas in Context Ser.: No. 33). 308p. (C). 1995. text ed. 54.95 (*0-521-46291-6*) Cambridge U Pr.

Strategies of Educational Research: Qualitative Methods. Ed. by Robert G. Burgess. 336p. 1985. pap. text ed. 35.00 (*1-85000-034-4*, Falmer Pr) Taylor & Francis.

Strategies of Expertise in Technical Controversies: A Study of Wood Energy Development. Frederick Frankena. LC 89-64068. 280p. 1992. 42.50 (*0-934223-14-9*) Lehigh Univ Pr.

Strategies of Fantasy. Brian Attebery. LC 91-15884. 180p. 1992. text ed. 29.95 (*0-253-31070-9*) Ind U Pr.

Strategies of Genius, Vol. II. Robert Dilts. LC 94-7813. 1994. 21.95 (*0-916990-33-8*) META Pubns.

Strategies of Genius, Vol. III. Robert Dilts. LC 94-7813. 1995. 29.95 (*0-916990-34-6*) META Pubns.

Strategies of Genius Vol. I. Robert Dilts. LC 94-77813. 1994. 24.95 (*0-916990-32-X*) META Pubns.

Strategies of Industrial & Hazardous Waste Disposal. Nemerown. 1998. text ed. 99.95 (*0-442-02445-2*) Van Nos Reinhold.

Strategies of International Mass Retailers. Charles Waldman. LC 78-19467. (Praeger Special Studies). 176p. 1978. text ed. 55.00 (*0-275-90319-2*, C0319, Praeger Pubs) Greenwood.

Strategies of Intervention with Public Offenders. Ed. by Sol Chaneles. LC 82-15383. (Journal of Offender Counseling, Services & Rehabilitation: Vol. 6, Nos. 1-2). 137p. 1982. pap. text ed. 19.95 (*0-86656-171-4*) Haworth Pr.

Strategies of Knowledge Acquisition. Deanna Kuhn et al. (Monographs of the Society for Research in Child Development: No. 245, Vol. 60: 4). 166p. 1995. pap. text ed. 15.00 (*0-226-45809-1*) U Ch Pr.

Strategies of Living in Different Societies. Gordon Burnand. 177p. 1985. 75.00 (*0-907774-02-4*, Pub. by Ldrship Ltd UK) St Mut.

Strategies of Love. Mose Durst. LC 87-12389. 184p. 1987. lib. bdg. 79.95 (*0-88946-209-7*) E Mellen.

***Strategies of Microsurgery in Problematic Brain Areas: With Special Reference to NMR.** Wolfgang Seeger. 398p. 1990. 195.00 (*3-211-82189-9*) Spr-Verlag.

Strategies of Microsurgery in Problematic Brain Areas with Special Reference to NMR. Wolfgang Seeger. 400p. 1990. 214.00 (*0-387-82189-9*) Spr-Verlag.

Strategies of Plant Reproduction. Ed. by Werner J. Meudt. LC 82-11594. (Beltsville Symposia in Agricultural Research Ser.: No. 6). (Illus.). 400p. 1983. text ed. 66.50 (*0-86598-054-3*) Rowman.

Strategies of Poetic Narrative: Chaucer, Spenser, Milton, Eliot. Clare R. Kinney. 266p. (C). 1992. text ed. 65.00 (*0-521-40542-4*) Cambridge U Pr.

Strategies of Politeness in the Chinese Language. Kaidi Zhan. LC 92-82737. 1992. pap. 10.00 (*1-55729-037-7*) IEAS.

Strategies of Political Inquiry. Ed. by Elinor Ostrom. LC 82-852. (Sage Focus Editions Ser.: No. 48). 224p. 1982. reprint ed. pap. 63.90 (*0-608-01483-4*, 2059527) Bks Demand.

Strategies of Resistance in "Les Liaisons Dangereuses" Heroines in Search of "Authority" Ann-Marie Brinsmead. LC 88-32603. (Studies in French Civilization). 194p. 1989. lib. bdg. 79.95 (*0-88946-639-4*) E Mellen.

Strategies of Reticence: Silence & Meaning in the Works of Jane Austen, Willa Cather, Katherine Ann Porter & Joan Didion. Janis P. Stout. 224p. 1990. text ed. 32.50 (*0-8139-1262-8*) U Pr of Va.

Strategies of Rhetoric with Handbook. 6th ed. Arnold M. Tibbetts. (C). 1991. pap. text ed. 40.50 (*0-673-38987-1*) Addison-Wesley Educ.

Strategies of Slaves & Women. Marcia Wright. LC 91-32722. 238p. 1993. text ed. 24.95 (*0-936508-27-2*); pap. text ed. 12.95 (*0-936508-28-0*) Barber Pr.

Strategies of Social Research: The Methodological Imagination. Herman W. Smith. (C). 1991. text ed. 46.00 (*0-03-023077-2*) HB Coll Pubs.

Strategies of the Major Oil Companies. William N. Greene. LC 84-24076. (Research for Business Decisions Ser.: No. 70). 361p. reprint ed. pap. 102.90 (*0-8357-1606-6*, 2070383) Bks Demand.

S

Strategies of Transformation Toward a Multicultural Society: Fulfilling the Story of Democracy. David T. Abalos. LC 95-37649. (Praeger Series in Transformational Politics & Political Science). 208p. 1996. text ed. 57.95 (*0-275-95270-3*, Praeger Pubs); pap. text ed. 16.95 (*0-275-95271-1*, Praeger Pubs) Greenwood.

Strategies of Zeus. Gary Hart. 448p. 1988. mass mkt. 4.50 (*0-373-97060-9*) Harlequin Bks.

Strategies Requiring the Use of Criminal History Record Information. (Illus.). 63p. (Orig.). (C). 1993. pap. text ed. 20.00 (*1-56806-807-7*) DIANE Pub.

Strategies Search. Michael Papagiannis. (Astrophysics & Space Science Library). 1980. pap. text ed. 58.00 (*90-277-1226-3*); lib. bdg. 100.50 (*90-277-1181-X*) Kluwer Ac.

Strategies Success. 2nd ed. USU (Call-Saunders) Staff. 228p. (C). 1996. pap. text ed., ring bd. 23.62 (*0-7872-0986-4*) Kendall-Hunt.

Strategies, Tactics, Techniques & Tricks, Guaranteed to Increase Your No-Till Profits, Vol. III. 1995. 79.95 (*0-944079-23-7*) Lessiter Pubns.

Strategies That Work in Secondary Schools. Steve G. Contos. Ed. by Diane Parker. LC 92-50862. 125p. 1993. spiral bd. 11.95 (*0-88247-988-1*) R & E Pubs.

Strategies to College Success. 3rd ed. Starke. 1996. pap. text ed. 29.33 (*0-13-449570-5*) P-H.

Strategies to Combat Poverty in Latin America. Dagmar Raczynski. 225p. (Orig.). 1995. pap. text ed. 18.50 (*0-940602-95-4*) IADB.

Strategies to Control Tobacco Use in the U. S. A Blueprint for Public Health Action in the 1990's. (Illus.). 307p. (Orig.). (C). 1994. pap. text ed. 40.00 (*0-7881-0293-1*) DIANE Pub.

Strategies to Implement Benefit-Sharing for Fixed-Rate Transit Facilities. (National Cooperative Transit Research Program Synthesis Ser.: No. 12). 214p. 1985. 14.00 (*0-309-03857-X*) Transport Res Bd.

Strategies to Improve Community Energy Use Practices. 66p. 1982. 10.00 (*0-318-17716-1*, DG 82-307) Pub Tech Inc.

***Strategies to Pinpoint Trading Ranges, Trends & Trading Reversals.** Brendan Moynihan. LC 97-9276. (Wiley Finance Edition Ser.). 256p. 1997. 59.95 (*0-471-17782-2*) Wiley.

Strategies to Reduce Urban Proverty: Integrating Human Development & Economic Opportunity. Susan V. Smith. 53p. (Orig.). (C). 1994. pap. text ed. 20.00 (*0-7881-1547-2*) DIANE Pub.

***Strategies Towards Self-Government.** James Mitchell. (Determinations Ser.). 1996. pap. 24.00 (*0-7486-6113-1*, Pub. by Polygon UK) Subterranean Co.

***Strategies, 1995.** (Telecom Power-2000 Ser.: Vol. 3). 1995. 2,495.00 (*0-614-18334-0*, IGIC-89) Info Gatekeepers.

***Strategische Allianzen & Ihre Herausforderungen an das Wettbewerbsrecht der Europaischen Union.** Andre Fiebig. xix, 237p. (GER.). 1996. 51.95 (*3-631-30684-9*) P Lang Pubng.

***Strategische Analyse: Empfehlungen zum Vorgehen & zu Sinnvollen Methodenkombinationen.** Kurt Aeberhard. 351p. (GER.). 1996. 55.95 (*3-906756-80-7*) P Lang Pubng.

***Strategische Fuhrung Europaischer Mittelstandischer Unternehmen: Am Beispiel der Werkzeugmaschinenbranche.** Christoph A. Muller. (Illus.). 476p. (GER.). 1995. 68.95 (*3-906755-43-6*) P Lang Pubng.

***Strategische Koordination von Beschaffung und Absatz Vol. XXI: Entwicklung Einer Konzeption zur Analyse und Gestaltung eines Koordinationssystems zur Abstimmung Beschaffungs- und Absatzwirtschaftlicher Ziel-, Strategie- und Marktorientierter Instrumententenscheidungen.** Frank Reintjes. (Marktorientierte Unternehmensfuhrung Ser.: Bd. 20). (Illus.). 345p. (GER.). 1995. pap. 55.95 (*3-631-48728-2*) P Lang Pubng.

***Strategische Planung als Komponente Eines Controllingsystems im Krankenhaus: Eine Untersuchung fur das Deutsche Krankenhauswesen.** Claudia Patt. (Illus.). 262p. (GER.). 1996. 51.95 (*3-631-30087-5*) P Lang Pubng.

***Strategische Unternehmensentwicklung durch Mergers & Acquisitions: Konzeption und Leitlinien fur Einen Strategisch Orientierten Mergers & Acquisitions-Prozeb.** Stefan Hagemann. (Schriften zur Unternehmensplanung Ser.: Bd. 39). (Illus.). 232p. (GER.). 1996. pap. 44.95 (*3-631-30675-X*) P Lang Pubng.

***Strategisches Controlling in Ortlichen Gasversorgungsunternehmen.** Gerhard Konig. (Illus.). xxi, 302p. (GER.). 1996. 57.95 (*3-631-30335-1*) P Lang Pubng.

Strategist. Hadi Salavitabar & Peter Fairweather. 350p. (C). 1993. pap. text ed. 22.00 (*0-256-10813-7*) Irwin.

Strategist CEO: How Visionary Executives Build Organizations. Michel Robert. LC 87-10945. 160p. 1988. text ed. 45.00 (*0-89930-268-8*, RST/, Quorum Bks) Greenwood.

Strategos Upatos: Etude Sur la Traduction En Grec Du Titre Consulaire. Maurice Holleaux. LC 75-7325. (Roman History Ser.). (FRE.). 1975. reprint ed. 17.95 (*0-405-07088-8*) Ayer.

Strategy. Aleksandr A. Svechin. Tr. by Kent D. Lee from RUS. 374p. 1991. 44.95 (*1-879944-00-6*) East View Pubns.

Strategy. Aleksandra Svechin. Ed. by Kent D. Lee. 374p. 1993. pap. 19.95 (*1-879944-33-2*) East View Pubns.

Strategy. 2nd rev. ed. Basil H. Liddell-Hart. (Illus.). 432p. 1991. pap. 14.95 (*0-452-01071-3*, Mer) NAL-Dutton.

Strategy: A Business Unit Simulation. 2nd ed. H. Richard Priesmeyer. (C). 1992. text ed. write for info. (*0-538-80776-8*, GH72B8H81) S-W Pub.

Strategy: A Computer Assisted Program. 2nd ed. Patton & Tangedahl. (BE-Accounting Advanced Ser.). 1992. pap. 12.95 (*0-538-60394-1*) S-W Pub.

Strategy: A Guide to Marketing for Senior Executives. Simon Majaro et al. (Gower Business Enterprise Ser.). 191p. 1989. text ed. 25.95 (*0-7045-0618-1*, Pub. by Gower UK) Ashgate Pub Co.

Strategy: Form, Implementation, & Control. James M. Higgins. 307p. (C). 1985. pap. text ed. 40.00 (*0-03-070639-4*) Dryden Pr.

Strategy: Its Theory & Application: The War for German Unification, 1866-1871. Helmuth J. Von Moltke. LC 77-84279. 229p. 1971. reprint ed. text ed. 65.00 (*0-8371-5020-5*, MOST, Greenwood Pr) Greenwood.

Strategy: Seeking & Securing Competitive Advantage. Ed. by Cynthia A. Montgomery & Michael E. Porter. (Harvard Business Review Book Ser.). 512p. 1991. 35.00 (*0-87584-243-7*) Harvard Busn.

Strategy: Seeking & Securing Competitive Advantage. Ed. by Cynthia A. Montgomery & Michael E. Porter. 1991. text ed. 35.00 (*0-07-103295-9*) McGraw.

Strategy: The Logic of War & Peace. Edward N. Luttwak. 296p. 1990. pap. text ed. 10.95 (*0-674-83996-X*) HUP.

Strategy after Deterrence. Stephen J. Cimbala. LC 90-39027. 288p. 1991. text ed. 59.95 (*0-275-93741-0*, C3741, Praeger Pubs) Greenwood.

Strategy & Architecture of Health Care Information Systems. Michael K. Bourke. LC 93-27727. 1996. 54.00 (*0-387-97982-4*) Spr-Verlag.

Strategy & Business Policy: Cases. Garry D. Smith et al. LC 85-80860. 650p. (C). 1986. teacher ed. 3.16 (*0-685-12005-8*) HM.

Strategy & Choice. Richard Zeckhauser. (Illus.). 400p. 1991. 45.00 (*0-262-24033-5*) MIT Pr.

Strategy & Choice in Congressional Elections. Gary G. Jacobson & Samuel Kernell. LC 81-40439. 125p. reprint ed. pap. 35.70 (*0-8357-8334-0*, 2033768) Bks Demand.

Strategy & Collective Bargaining Negotiation. Carl M. Stevens. LC 78-5304. (Publications of the Wertheim Committee). (Illus.). 192p. 1978. reprint ed. text ed. 35.00 (*0-313-20377-6*, STST, Greenwood Pr) Greenwood.

Strategy & Computers: Information Systems As Competitive Weapons. Charles Wiseman. LC 85-70567. 246p. 1985. text ed. 45.00 (*0-87094-590-4*) Irwin Prof Pubng.

Strategy & Consistency of Federal Reserve Monetary Policy, 1924-1933. David C. Wheelock. (Studies in Monetary & Financial History). (Illus.). 176p. (C). 1991. text ed. 59.95 (*0-521-39155-5*) Cambridge U Pr.

Strategy & Diplomacy: Eighteen Seventy to Nineteen Forty-Five. Paul M. Kennedy. 256p. (C). 1984. text ed. 29.95 (*0-04-902007-2*); pap. text ed. 12.95 (*0-04-902008-0*) Routledge Chapman & Hall.

Strategy & Finance in Higher Education. Ed. by William F. Massy & Joel W. Meyerson. LC 92-12863. 109p. 1992. 29.95 (*1-56079-178-0*) Petersons.

Strategy & Force Planning. Richmond M. Lloyd et al. LC 95-2794. 1995. write for info. (*0-615-00487-3*) Naval War Coll.

***Strategy & Force Planning.** 2nd ed. Ed. by Richmond M. Lloyd et al. (Illus.). 676p. (Orig.). (C). 1997. pap. text ed. write for info. (*1-884733-08-5*) Naval War Coll.

Strategy & Force Planning: The Case of the Persian Gulf. Joshua M. Epstein. LC 87-73160. 169p. 1987. 31.95 (*0-8157-2454-3*); pap. 12.95 (*0-8157-2453-5*) Brookings.

Strategy & Governmental Organization. Carnes Lord. (Special Issue of Comparative Strategy Ser.: Vol. 6, No. 3). 127p. 1987. pap. 18.00 (*0-8448-1532-2*) Taylor & Francis.

Strategy & History: Collected Essays. Edward N. Luttwak. 225p. (C). 1985. 39.95 (*0-88738-065-4*) Transaction Pubs.

Strategy & Human Resources: A General Managerial Perspective. Charles R. Greer. 304p. 1994. pap. text ed. 36.67 (*0-13-192238-6*) P-H.

Strategy & Intelligence: British Policy During the First World War. Ed. by Michael Dockril & David French. LC 95-47677. 1996. boxed 60.00 (*1-85285-099-X*) Hambledon Press.

Strategy & Management Accounting. Shahid L. Ansari et al. 16p. (C). 1996. 5.60 (*0-256-23788-3*) Irwin.

Strategy & Nuclear Deterrence: An International Security Reader. Ed. by Steven E. Miller. LC 84-42549. 312p. 1984. pap. text ed. 15.95 (*0-691-00597-4*) Princeton U Pr.

Strategy & Performance of British Industry, 1970-80. George A. Luffman & Richard Reed. LC 84-17716. 360p. 1985. text ed. 39.95 (*0-312-76469-3*) St Martin.

Strategy & Performance of Foreign Companies in Japan. Sikander Khan & Hideki Yoshihara. LC 93-49034. 328p. 1994. text ed. 59.95 (*0-89930-899-6*, Quorum Bks) Greenwood.

Strategy & Politics: Collected Essays. Edward N. Luttwak. LC 79-65224. 328p. 1980. pap. 24.95 (*0-87855-904-3*) Transaction Pubs.

Strategy and Power in Russia 1600-1914. William C. Fuller, Jr. (Illus.). 576p. 1992. 40.00 (*0-02-910977-9*, Free Press) Free Pr.

Strategy & Process in Marketing. John A. Murray & Aidan O'Driscoll. LC 95-38852. 320p. (C). 1996. pap. text ed. 40.00 (*0-13-182163-6*) P-H.

Strategy & Prospects in Neuroscience. Ed. by Osamu Hayaishi. (Taniguchi Symposia on Brain Sciences Ser.: No. 10). 260p. 1987. lib. bdg. 132.50 (*90-6764-111-1*, Pub. by VSP NE) Coronet Bks.

Strategy & Security in the Caribbean. Ed. by Ivelaw L. Griffith. LC 91-7208. 224p. 1991. text ed. 55.00 (*0-275-93830-1*, C3830, Praeger Pubs) Greenwood.

Strategy & Security in U. S.-Mexican Relations Beyond the Cold War. Ed. by John Bailey & Sergio Aquauo-Quezada. (Contemporary Perspectives Ser.: Vol. 9). (Orig.). 1996. pap. 21.95 (*1-878367-32-3*) UCSD Ctr US-Mex.

Strategy & Skill in Learning a Foreign Language. Steven M. McDonough. LC 95-5125. 1995. text ed. 49.95 (*0-340-62532-5*); text ed. 17.95 (*0-340-59109-9*) St Martin.

Strategy & Structure: Chapters in the History of the American Industrial Enterprise. Alfred D. Chandler, Jr. 1969. pap. 17.50 (*0-262-53009-0*) MIT Pr.

Strategy & Structure: Short Readings for Composition. Ed. by William J. Kelly. LC 94-26644. 1995. pap. text ed. 25.00 (*0-205-13786-5*) Allyn.

Strategy & Structure of Enterprise in a Developing Country. Chi B. Anyansi-Archibong. 220p. 1988. text ed. 68.95 (*0-566-05471-X*, Pub. by Avebury Pub UK) Ashgate Pub Co.

Strategy & Structure of Japanese Enterprises. Toyohiro Kono. LC 84-5382. 350p. (gr. 13). 1984. pap. text ed. 22.95 (*0-87332-288-6*) M E Sharpe.

Strategy & Supply: The Anglo-Russian Alliance, 1914-17. Keith Neilson. 240p. 1984. text ed. 55.00 (*0-04-940072-X*) Routledge Chapman & Hall.

Strategy & Tactics. Hoang N. Lung. 1994. pap. text ed. 15.00 (*0-923135-27-8*) Dalley Bk Service.

Strategy & Tactics of Dynamic Functionalism. Michael A. Faia. (American Sociological Assn. Rose Monograph Ser.). (Illus.). 208p. 1986. text ed. 49.95 (*0-521-32657-5*) Cambridge U Pr.

Strategy & Tactics of India's Agricultural Development. G. N. Seetharam. 1984. 12.00 (*0-8364-1134-X*, Pub. by Ajanta II) S Asia.

Strategy & Tactics of Pricing: A Guide to Profitable Decision Making. 2nd ed. Thomas T. Nagle. 400p. (C). 1994. pap. text ed. 55.00 (*0-13-669060-2*) P-H.

Strategy & Tactics of the Salvadoran FMLN Guerrillas: Last Battle of the Cold War, Blueprint for Future Conflicts. Jose A. Bracamonte & David E. Spencer. LC 94-42844. 216p. 1995. text ed. 59.95 (*0-275-95018-2*, Praeger Pubs) Greenwood.

Strategy & the Social Sciences: Issues in Defense Policy. Ed. by Amos Perlmutter & John Gooch. 102p. 1981. 32.50 (*0-7146-3157-4*, Pub. by F Cass Pubs UK) Intl Spec Bk.

Strategy & Uncertainty: A Guide to Practical Systems Thinking, Vol. 17. T. Clementson. 214, xivp. 1988. text ed. 122.00 (*2-88124-654-0*) Gordon & Breach.

***Strategy As Action: Industry Rivalry & Coordination.** Curtis M. Grimm & Ken G. Smith. LC 96-49179. 1997. pap. write for info. (*0-314-21650-2*) West Pub.

Strategy As Rationality: Redirecting Strategic Thought & Action. Alan E. Singer. (Avebury Series in Philosophy). 144p. 1996. 58.95 (*1-85972-270-9*, Pub. by Avebury Pub UK) Ashgate Pub Co.

Strategy Assessment & Instruction for Students with Learning Disabilities: From Theory to Practice. Ed. by Lynn J. Meltzer. LC 91-48272. 424p. 1993. text ed. 41.00 (*0-89079-540-1*, 5194) PRO-ED.

Strategy Concept & Process: A Pragmatic Approach. 2nd ed. Arnoldo C. Hax & Nicholas S. Majluf. LC 95-25156. 1995. text ed. 70.00 (*0-13-458894-0*) P-H.

Strategy Development & Implementation for Banks. John L. Green, Jr. (Illus.). 500p. (C). 1988. pap. 49.95 (*0-9617567-2-1*) Strategic Plan Mgmt Assocs.

Strategy Development Workshop for Public Education on Weight & Obesity: Summary Report. 139p. (Orig.). (C). 1995. pap. text ed. 30.00 (*0-7881-2467-6*) DIANE Pub.

Strategy for a Black Agenda: A Critique of New Theories of Liberation in the United States & Africa. Henry Winston. LC 73-80570. 323p. reprint ed. pap. 92.10 (*0-317-28797-4*, 2020637) Bks Demand.

Strategy for a Loss of Faith: Jung's Proposal. John P. Dourley. 1995. pap. 16.00 (*0-919123-57-0*, Pub. by Inner City CN) BookWorld Dist.

Strategy for a Metaphorical Reading of the Epistle of James. S. H. Ong. 194p. (Orig.). (C). 1995. pap. text ed. 26.00 (*0-7618-0150-2*); lib. bdg. 51.00 (*0-7618-0149-9*) U Pr of Amer.

Strategy for African Mining. John E. Strongman et al. LC 92-24426. (Technical Paper, Africa Technical Department Ser.: No. 181). 95p. 1992. 7.95 (*0-8213-2192-7*, 12192) World Bank.

Strategy for British Sport. Don Anthony. 1980. 44.95 (*0-7735-0531-8*, Pub. by McGill CN) U of Toronto Pr.

Strategy for Change. Ed. by Phyllis Marcuccio & Sheila Marshall. (Illus.). 176p. 1993. pap. text ed. 17.50 (*0-87355-118-4*) Natl Sci Tchrs.

Strategy for Conquest: Communist Documents on Guerrilla Warfare. Ed. by Jay Mallin. LC 71-102688. 1970. 19.95 (*0-87024-144-3*) U of Miami Pr.

Strategy for Creation. T. Murakami et al. 224p. 1991. 65.00 (*1-85573-061-8*, Pub. by Woodhead Pubng UK) Am Educ Systs.

***Strategy for Daily Living.** Ari Kiev. 1997. 12.95 (*0-684-83432-4*, Free Press) Free Pr.

Strategy for Data Modelling: Application & Enterprise-Wide. fac. ed. Max Vetter. LC 87-10449. (Illus.). 344p. 1987. pap. 98.10 (*0-7837-7653-5*, 2047406) Bks Demand.

Strategy for Defeat: Vietnam in Retrospect. Sharp. LC 78-17607. (Illus.). 348p. 1986. reprint ed. pap. 15.95 (*0-89141-272-7*) Presidio Pr.

Strategy for Energy Conservation Through Tribology, Bk. No. H00109. 2nd ed. Ed. by O. Pinkus & D. F. Wilcock. 1982. 20.00 (*0-685-37585-4*) ASME.

***Strategy for Evaluating the Effectiveness & Longevity of In-Lake Treatment.** 52p. 1992. pap. 10.00 (*0-614-30381-8*, G1) Terrene Inst.

Strategy for Financial Mobility. Gordon Donaldson. 1986. pap. text ed. 14.95 (*0-07-103229-0*) McGraw.

Strategy for Growth. Aldona Robbins & Gary Robbins. (Illus.). 21p. (C). 1992. pap. 10.00 (*0-943802-73-3*, 170) Natl Ctr Pol.

Strategy for Indian Defence. Satinder Singh. 168p. (C). 1987. 22.50 (*81-7062-006-6*, Pub. by Lancer II) S Asia.

Strategy for Integrated Area Development: Case Study of North Kanara District (Karnataka) L. S. Bhat. (C). 1988. 17.00 (*81-7022-198-6*, Pub. by Concept II) S Asia.

Strategy for Leadership: Planning, Activating, Motivating, Elevating. Edward Dayton & Ted Engstrom. LC 79-11180. 240p. 1988. pap. 9.99 (*0-8007-1590-X*) Revell.

Strategy for Life for Singles & Young Adults. Ed. by R. M. Davis & P. D. Buford. 160p. 1986. pap. 5.99 (*1-56722-062-2*) Word Aflame.

Strategy for Managing Water in the Middle East & North Africa. Jeremy Berkoff. LC 93-23728. (Technical Paper Ser.: Vol. 239). 72p. 1994. 6.95 (*0-8213-2709-7*, 12709) World Bank.

Strategy for Managing Water in the Middle East & North Africa. Jeremy Berkoff. 108p. (FRE.). 1995. 6.95 (*0-8213-3128-0*, 13128) World Bank.

Strategy for Managing Water in the Middle East & North Africa. Jeremy Berkoff. 72p. (ARA.). 1995. 6.95 (*0-8213-3160-4*, 13160) World Bank.

Strategy for Minority Businesses. abr. rev. ed. Intro. by Luanna C. Blagrove. (Illus.). 235p. 1988. pap. 10.95 (*0-685-17761-0*) Blagrove Pubns.

Strategy for Mobility. Wilfred Owen. LC 78-17067. 249p. 1978. reprint ed. text ed. 59.75 (*0-313-20571-X*, OWSM, Greenwood Pr) Greenwood.

Strategy for Occupational Exposure Assessment. Ed. by N. Hawkins et al. 195p. 1991. 50.00 (*0-932627-46-3*) Am Indus Hygiene.

Strategy for Operating Success. H. C. Howlett, 2nd. (Illus.). 16p. 1994. pap. 8.00 (*1-57614-015-6*) TECHSTAR.

Strategy for Personal Finance. 4th ed. Larry R. Lang. 640p. 1988. text ed. write for info. (*0-07-036317-X*) McGraw.

Strategy for Personal Finance. 5th ed. Larry R. Lang. LC 92-37247. (Series in Finance). 1993. text ed. write for info. (*0-07-036400-1*) McGraw.

Strategy for Personal Finance. 5th ed. Larry R. Lang. LC 92-37247. (Series in Finance). 1993. Wkbk. student ed., pap. text ed. write for info. (*0-07-036402-8*) McGraw.

Strategy for Promoting Sustainability in Narcotics Awareness & Education Projects. Development Associates, Inc. Staff. 43p. 1993. pap. 15.00 (*1-879839-04-0*) Develop Assocs.

Strategy for R & D: Studies in the Microeconomics of Development. Thomas Marschak et al. LC 67-28248. (Econometrics & Operations Research Ser.: Vol. 8). (Illus.). 1967. 105.95 (*0-387-03945-7*) Spr-Verlag.

Strategy for Real Estate Companies: Marketing, Finance, Organization. Christopher B. Leinberger. LC 93-61041. 136p. 1993. pap. text ed. 41.95 (*0-87420-742-8*, S43) Urban Land.

Strategy for Rural Development: Dairy Cooperatives in India. R. C. Mascarenhas. 288p. (C). 1988. text ed. 27.50 (*0-8039-9548-2*) Sage.

Strategy for Rural Development: Saemaeul Undong in Korea. Young-Pyoung Kim. 1980. pap. 3.50 (*0-89249-032-2*) Intl Development.

Strategy for Sales Growth of the Precast & Prestressed Concrete Industry. 42p. 1988. 24.00 (*0-318-35236-2*, R&D9) P-PCI.

Strategy for Success: An Outline for Personal Growth. Sujantra G. McKeever. 104p. 1994. pap. text ed. 10.00 (*1-885479-00-X*) McKeever Pubng.

Strategy for Survival. Thomas L. Martin, Jr. & Donald C. Latham. LC 63-17720. (Illus.). 399p. reprint ed. 113.80 (*0-8357-9624-8*, 2011564) Bks Demand.

Strategy for Sustainable Business: Environmental Opportunity & Strategic Choice. Liz Crosbie & Ken Knight. LC 95-23580. 320p. 1996. text ed. 29.95 (*0-07-709133-7*) McGraw.

Strategy for the Detection & Study of Other Planetary Systems & Extrasolar Planetary Materials: 1990-2000. National Research Council Staff. 96p. 1990. pap. text ed. 15.00 (*0-309-04193-7*) Natl Acad Pr.

Strategy for the Forest Sector in Sub-Saharan Africa. Narendra P. Sharma et al. LC 94-25509. (Technical Papers, Africa Technical Department Ser.: 251). 100p. 1994. 7.95 (*0-8213-2880-8*, 12880) World Bank.

Strategy for the Forest Sector in Sub-Saharan Africa. Narendra P. Sharma. 100p. (FRE.). 1995. 7.95 (*0-8213-3146-9*, 13146) World Bank.

Strategy for the Technological Transformation of Developing Countries. 23p. 1985. 5.00 (*92-1-112193-0*, E.84.11.D.19) UN.

Strategy for U. S. Industrial Competitiveness: Committee for Economic Development. (CED Statement on National Policy Ser.). 160p. 1984. pap. 9.50 (*0-87186-078-3*); lib. bdg. 11.50 (*0-87186-778-8*) Comm Econ Dev.

Strategy for Victory Without War. Ed. by Herbert I. London. LC 89-5731. 126p. (Orig.). (C). 1989. pap. text ed. 17.50 (*0-8191-7438-6*, Hudson Instit IN); lib. bdg. 35.50 (*0-8191-7437-8*, Pub. by Hudson Inst) U Pr of Amer.

Strategy for Winning: Winning...in Business, in Sports, in Family, in Life. Carl Mays. LC 90-62803. (Illus.). 272p. 1991. 21.95 (*1-879111-75-6*) Lincoln-Bradley.

Strategy Formulation: Analytical Concepts. Charles W. Hofer & Dan E. Schendel. (Business Policy & Planning Ser.). (Illus.). 219p. 1978. pap. text ed. 41.00 (*0-8299-0213-9*) West Pub.

An Asterisk (*) at the beginning of an entry indicates that the title is appearing in BIP for the first time.

Strategy Formulation: Power & Politics. 2nd ed. Ian C. MacMillan & Patricia E. Jones. LC 85-20389. (Strategic Management Ser.). (Illus.). 160p. (C). 1986. pap. text ed. 37.00 (*0-314-85260-3*) West Pub.

Strategy Formulation & Implementation. 4th ed. Arthur A. Thompson & A. J. Strickland, III. 384p. (C). 1989. pap. text ed. 38.95 (*0-256-06901-8*) Irwin.

Strategy Formulation & Implementation & Strategic Management Selected Cases: University of Cincinnati. 5th ed. A. J. Strickland & Arthur A. Thompson. (C). 1994. 54.95 (*0-256-18530-1*) Irwin.

Strategy Formulation for General Managers. Henry H. Beam. 128p. (C). 1992. per. 17.79 (*0-8403-8203-0*) Kendall-Hunt.

Strategy Game: An Interactive Business Game Where You Make or Break the Company. Craig R. Hickman. 1994. pap. text ed. 14.95 (*0-07-028725-2*) McGraw.

***Strategy Games: A Collection of 50 Games & Puzzles to Stimulate Mathematical Thinking.** Reg Sheppard & John Wilkinson. 50p. teacher ed., pap. 9.95 (*0-906212-70-7*, Pub. by Tarquin UK) Parkwest Pubns.

Strategy in a Changing Environment. Lloyd L. Byars & Leslie W. Rue. 384p. (C). 1995. per. 43.75 (*0-256-22052-2*) Irwin.

***Strategy in Action.** J. L. Thompson. 264p. 1995. pap. 19.95 (*0-412-62340-4*) Chapman & Hall.

Strategy in Action, 5 vols., Set. Harvard Business Review Staff. Five vol. set. pap. 99.75 (*0-87584-353-0*) Harvard Busn.

***Strategy in Action: Lecturers' Resource Manual.** Thompson. (Illus.). 320p. (Orig.). 1995. pap. text ed. 52.00 (*0-412-63690-5*, Chap & Hall NY) Chapman & Hall.

Strategy in Action: The Execution, Politics & Payoff of Business Planning. Boris Yavitz & William H. Newman. LC 81-71956. 1984. 22.95 (*0-02-935970-8*, Free Press); pap. 16.95 (*0-02-934670-3*, Free Press) Free Pr.

Strategy in Advertising: Matching Media & Messages to Markets & Motivations. Leo Bogart. 444p. 1994. 29.95 (*0-8442-3094-4*, NTC Busn Bks) NTC Pub Grp.

Strategy in Advertising: Matching Media & Messages to Markets & Motivations. Leo Bogart. 444p. 1995. pap. 17.95 (*0-8442-3098-7*, NTC Busn Bks) NTC Pub Grp.

Strategy in Advertising: Matching Media & Messages to Markets & Motivations. 3rd ed. Leo Bogart. 420p. 1995. 37.95 (*0-8442-3014-6*, NTC Busn Bks) NTC Pub Grp.

Strategy in Head Injury Management. Richard H. Simon & James T. Sayre. 214p. 1987. text ed. 60.00 (*0-8385-8682-1*, A8682-5) Appleton & Lange.

Strategy in Poker, Business & War. rev. ed. John McDonald. (Illus.). 128p. 1996. pap. 11.00 (*0-393-31457-X*, Norton Paperbks) Norton.

Strategy in the Missile Age. Bernard Brodie. LC 58-6102. (Rand Corporation Research Studies). 436p. 1959. pap. text ed. 21.95 (*0-691-01852-9*) Princeton U Pr.

Strategy in the Missile Age. Bernard Brodie. LC 58-6102. 439p. 1965. reprint ed. pap. 125.20 (*0-7837-8163-6*, 2047868) Bks Demand.

Strategy in the Southern Oceans: A South American View. Virginia Gamba-Stonehouse. 256p. 1989. text ed. 55.00 (*0-312-03733-3*) St Martin.

Strategy in Unarmed Combat. Paul Maslak. LC 80-130558. (Illus.). 136p. 1980. pap. 7.50 (*0-86568-000-0*, 101) Unique Pubns.

***Strategy in Vietnam: The Marines & Revolutionary Warfare in I Corps, 1965-1971.** Michael A. Hennessy. LC 96-33989. (Studies in Diplomacy & Strategic Thought). 224p. 1997. text ed. 59.95 (*0-275-95667-9*, Praeger Pubs) Greenwood.

Strategy-Led Business. rev. ed. Kerry Napuk. LC 96-12410. 1996. pap. write for info. (*0-07-709285-6*) McGraw.

Strategy-Led Business: Step by Step Planning for Your Company's Future. Kerry Napuk. LC 93-982. 1994. pap. text ed. 34.95 (*0-07-707775-X*) McGraw.

Strategy of a Megamerger: An Insider's Account of the Baxter Travenol-American Hospital Supply Combination. Thomas G. Cody. LC 90-8482. 328p. 1990. text ed. 59.95 (*0-89930-345-5*, CYS, Quorum Bks) Greenwood.

Strategy of a Megamerger: An Insider's Account of the Baxter Travenol-American Hospital Supply Combination. Thomas G. Cody. LC 92-30382. 1992. pap. text ed. 21.95 (*0-275-94518-9*, B4518, Praeger Pubs) Greenwood.

Strategy of Cash: A Liquidity Approach to Maximizing the Company's Profits. S. D. Slater. LC 74-9811. (Wiley Series on Systems & Controls for Financial Management). (Illus.). 414p. reprint ed. pap. 118.00 (*0-317-09008-9*, 2022494) Bks Demand.

Strategy of Composition: A Rhetoric with Readings. Clarence A. Brown & Ronald Zoellner. LC 68-13470. 704p. reprint ed. pap. 180.00 (*0-317-09507-2*, 2012470) Bks Demand.

Strategy of Conflict. Thomas C. Schelling. LC 60-11560. (Illus.). 1990. pap. 15.95 (*0-674-84031-3*) HUP.

Strategy of Decision: Policy Evaluation As a Social Process. David Braybrooke & Charles E. Lindblom. LC 63-13537. 1970. reprint ed. pap. 18.95 (*0-02-904610-6*, Free Press) Free Pr.

Strategy of Distribution Management. Martin Christopher. LC 84-18214. (Illus.). x, 192p. 1985. text ed. 42.95 (*0-89930-114-2*, CSD/, Quorum Bks) Greenwood.

***Strategy of Dominance: The History of an American Concentration Camp, Pomona, California.** Francis Feeley. (Illus.). 128p. (Orig.). 1995. pap. text ed. 9.96 (*1-881089-55-X*) Brandywine Press.

Strategy of Drug Design: A Guide to Biological Activity. William P. Purcell et al. LC 72-13240. 200p. reprint ed. pap. 57.00 (*0-8357-9983-2*, 2055156) Bks Demand.

Strategy of Economic Policy. Raymond J. Saulnier. LC 63-14408. (Moorhouse I.X. Millar Lecture Ser.: No. 5). 95p. reprint ed. pap. 27.10 (*0-7837-0471-2*, 2040794) Bks Demand.

Strategy of Electromagnetic Conflict. Ed. by Richard E. Fitts. LC 80-81837. 1979. reprint ed. 29.95 (*0-932146-02-3*) Peninsula CA.

Strategy of Export-Led Growth. James K. Galbraith. (Working Paper Ser.: No. 43). 20p. 1988. pap. 5.00 (*0-89940-524-X*) LBJ Sch Pub Aff.

Strategy of Ignorance: From Decision Logic to Evolutionary Epistemology. Soren Hallden. (Library Theoria: No. 17). 191p. (Orig.). 1986. pap. 62.50 (*91-87172-02-X*) Coronet Bks.

Strategy of International Business. Maunuhal Singh. 240p. 1986. 19.00 (*81-7003-069-2*, Pub. by S Asia Pubs II) S Asia.

Strategy of International Development: Essays in the Economics of Backwardness. Hans W. Singer. Ed. by Alec Cairncross & Mohinder Puri. LC 74-21810. 264p. reprint ed. pap. 75.30 (*0-685-16348-2*, 2027624) Bks Demand.

Strategy of Involvement: A Diplomatic Biography of Sumner Welles. Frank W. Graff. LC 88-10271. (Modern American History Ser.). 472p. 1988. 25.00 (*0-8240-4329-4*) Garland.

Strategy of Letters. Mette Hjort. LC 92-41460. 279p. 1993. text ed. 39.95 (*0-674-84052-6*) HUP.

Strategy of Life. Timothy Lenoir. 326p. 1982. lib. bdg. 158.50 (*90-277-1363-4*, D Reidel) Kluwer Ac.

Strategy of Life: Teleology & Mechanics in Nineteenth Century German Biology. Timothy Lenoir. (Illus.). 328p. 1989. pap. text ed. 18.00 (*0-226-47183-7*) U Ch Pr.

Strategy of Marketing Research. Chester R. Wasson. LC 64-15387. (Illus.). 1964. 36.50 (*0-89197-426-1*) Irvington.

Strategy of Meetings. George D. Kieffer. 1988. 17.45 (*0-671-61197-6*) S&S Trade.

Strategy of Nonviolent Defense: A Gandhian Approach. Robert J. Burrowes. LC 95-2223. 367p. 1995. text ed. 49.50 (*0-7914-2587-8*); pap. text ed. 16.95 (*0-7914-2588-6*) State U NY Pr.

Strategy of Peace in a Changing World. Arthur N. Holcombe. LC 67-27085. 340p. 1967. 29.95 (*0-674-84075-5*) HUP.

Strategy of Preventive Medicine. Geoffrey Rose. (Illus.). 160p. 1994. reprint ed. pap. 21.95 (*0-19-262486-5*) OUP.

Strategy of Satan. Warren W. Wiersbe. 157p. 1979. mass mkt. 5.99 (*0-8423-6665-2*) Tyndale.

Strategy of Sea Power: Its Development & Application. Stephen W. Roskill. LC 80-27028. (Lees-Knowles Lecture Ser., Cambridge, 1961). 287p. 1981. reprint ed. text ed. 52.50 (*0-313-22801-9*, ROSSP, Greenwood Pr) Greenwood.

Strategy of Social Regulation: Decision Frameworks for Policy. Lester B. Lave. LC 81-7685. (Studies in the Regulation of Economic Activity). 166p. 1981. 31.95 (*0-8157-5162-1*); pap. 12.95 (*0-8157-5161-3*) Brookings.

Strategy of Soviet Imperialism: Expansion in Eurasia. Martin Sicker. LC 87-25882. 172p. 1988. text ed. 49.95 (*0-275-92932-9*, C2932, Praeger Pubs) Greenwood.

Strategy of St. Paul. Paul Campbell & Peter Howard. Orig. Title: A Story of Effective Statesmanship. 85p. (Orig.). 1985. reprint ed. pap. 2.95 (*0-901269-69-7*) Grosvenor USA.

Strategy of the Dolphin: Scoring a Win in a Chaotic World. Dudley Lynch & Paul L. Kordis. 288p. 1990. pap. 12.00 (*0-449-90529-2*, ExPress) Fawcett.

Strategy of the Lloyd George Coalition, 1916-1918. David French. 460p. 1995. 59.00 (*0-19-820559-7*) OUP.

Strategy of Treaty Termination: Lawful Breaches & Retaliations. Arie E. David. LC 74-82748. 342p. reprint ed. pap. 97.50 (*0-7837-4556-7*, 2080493) Bks Demand.

Strategy of Truth: A Study of Sir Thomas Browne. Leonard Nathanson. LC 67-18216. 253p. reprint ed. pap. 72.20 (*0-317-08080-6*, 2020135) Bks Demand.

Strategy of World Order, 4 vols. Incl. Vol. 2. International Law. Frwd. by Wolfgang Friedmann. 1966. pap. 29.95 (*0-87855-770-9*); Vol. 3. United Nations. Frwd. by Oscar Schacter. 1966. pap. 24.95 (*0-87855-771-7*); Vol. 4. Disarmament & Economic Development. Frwd. by David Singer. 1966. pap. 24.95 (*0-87855-772-5*); 1966. write for info. (*0-318-53550-5*) Transaction Pubs.

Strategy, Opportunity Identification & Entrepreneurship: A Study of the Entrepreneurial Opportunity Identification Process. Peder S. Christensen. 194p. (C). 1990. pap. 16.95 (*87-7288-292-1*, Pub. by Aarhus Univ Pr DK) David Brown.

Strategy Options to Strengthen the European Programme Industry in the Context of the Audiovisual Policy of the European Union. 54p. (Orig.). (C). 1994. pap. text ed. 50.00 (*0-7881-1131-0*) DIANE Pub.

Strategy, Organization Design, & Human Resource Management. Ed. by Charles C. Snow. LC 88-8549. (Strategic Management, Policy & Planning Ser.). 367p. 1989. 73.25 (*0-89232-807-X*) Jai Pr.

***Strategy Planning in Logistics & Transportation.** Ed. by James Cooper. (Cranfield Management Research Ser.). 1993. pap. 24.95 (*0-7494-1137-6*) Kogan Page Ltd.

Strategy Process. Henry Mintzberg et al. LC 94-19998. 595p. 1994. text ed. 79.00 (*0-13-556557-X*) P-H.

Strategy Process: Concepts, Contexts & Cases. 3rd ed. Henry Mintzberg & James B. Quinn. LC 95-32626. 1120p. (C). 1995. text ed. 81.00 (*0-13-234030-5*) P-H.

Strategy Process: European Edition. Henry Mintzberg et al. LC 95-1818. 1995. write for info. (*0-13-149626-3*) P-H.

***Strategy Pure & Simple: How to Out Think & Outsmart Your Competition.** Michel Robert. 1997. text ed. 24.95 (*0-07-053133-1*) McGraw.

Strategy Pure & Simple: How Winning CEOs Outthink Their Competition. Michel Robert. 1992. text ed. 22.95 (*0-07-053131-5*) McGraw.

Strategy Quest: Releasing the Energy of Manufacturing Within a Market Driven Strategy. Terry Hill. (Financial Times Management Ser.). 275p. 1995. 62.50 (*0-273-03949-0*, Pub. by Pitman Pub Ltd UK) Trans-Atl Phila.

Strategy, Risk, & Personality in Coalition Politics: The Case of India. Bruce Bueno de Mesquita. LC 75-3853. 208p. reprint ed. pap. 59.30 (*0-317-20837-3*, 2024439) Bks Demand.

***Strategy, Security, & Spies.** Maria E. Paz. LC 96-31047. 1997. pap. 19.95 (*0-271-01666-3*) Pa St U Pr.

***Strategy, Security, & Spies: Mexico.** Maria E. Paz. LC 96-31047. 1997. 55.00 (*0-271-01665-5*) Pa St U Pr.

Strategy, Structure, & Antitrust in the Carbonated Soft Drink Industry. Timothy J. Muris et al. LC 92-34944. 272p. 1993. text ed. 65.00 (*0-89930-788-4*, MYJ, Quorum Bks) Greenwood.

***Strategy, Structure & Style.** Howard Thomas et al. LC 96-36291. (Strategic Management Ser.). 1997. write for info. (*0-471-96882-X*) Wiley.

Strategy, Systems, & Integration: Handbook for Information Managers. George M. Hall. (Illus.). 500p. 1990. 39.95 (*0-8306-3614-5*, 3614) McGraw-Hill Prof.

Strategy to Develop Agriculture in Sub-Saharan Africa & a Focus for the World Bank. Kevin M. Cleaver. LC 93-3624. (Technical Paper, Africa Department Ser.: No. 203). 178p. 1993. 9.95 (*0-8213-2420-9*, 12420) World Bank.

Strategy to Maximize Your Tax Gains. Jimmy L. Kum & David J. Kum. 382p. 1993. 49.95 (*0-9626817-6-8*) J L Kum.

Strategy to Revitalize the American Dream: Justice in Jeopardy. Albert B. Logan & William R. Cheney. (Illus.). 260p. 1973. 8.95 (*0-317-01152-9*); pap. 5.95 (*0-317-01153-7*) NIJD Colorado.

Strategy Traps: And How to Avoid Them. Robert A. Stringer, Jr. & Joel Uchenick. LC 84-48444. 224p. 29.95 (*0-669-09362-9*, Lexington) Jossey-Bass.

Strategy Two Thousand: The World Market for White Goods. Euromonitor Staff. (C). 1990. write for info. (*0-318-67342-8*, Pub. by Euromonitor Pubns UK) Gale.

Strategy Two Thousand Biscuits & Snacks: A Global Analysis. Euromonitor Staff. (C). 1990. write for info. (*0-318-67344-4*, Pub. by Euromonitor Pubns UK) Gale.

Strategy Two Thousand Car Leasing & Rental. Euromonitor Staff. (C). 1990. write for info. (*0-318-67343-6*, Pub. by Euromonitor Pubns UK) Gale.

Strategy Two Thousand European Retail Banking. Euromonitor Staff. (C). 1990. write for info. (*0-318-67341-X*, Pub. by Euromonitor Pubns UK) Gale.

***Strategy 2000: Churches Making Disciples for the Next Millennium.** Aubrey Malphurs. LC 96-30480. 240p. 1996. pap. 11.99 (*0-8254-3196-4*) Kregel.

Stratemeyer Pseudonyms & Series Books: An Annotated Checklist of Stratemeyer & Stratemeyer Syndicate Publications. Ed. by Deidre Johnson. LC 81-23750. (Illus.). 343p. 1982. text ed. 55.00 (*0-313-22632-6*, JST/, Greenwood Pr) Greenwood.

Stratenomic Forecast 1996. Alden Solove. (Illus.). 120p. 1995. spiral bd. 295.00 (*0-9650725-0-9*) Stratenomics.

Stratford Festival Story: A Catalogue-Index to the Stratford, Ontario, Festival 1953-1990. J. Alan Somerset. LC 91-11238. (Bibliographies & Indexes in the Performing Arts Ser.: No. 8). 360p. 1991. text ed. 59.95 (*0-313-27804-0*, SZB/, Greenwood Pr) Greenwood.

Stratford-On-Avon from the Earliest Times to the Death of Shakespeare. Sidney Lee. LC 71-109654. (Select Bibliographies Reprint Ser.). 1977. 26.95 (*0-8369-5263-4*) Ayer.

Stratford-on-Avon from the Earliest Times to the Death of Shakespeare. Sidney Lee. (BCL1-PR English Literature Ser.). 327p. 1992. reprint ed. lib. bdg. 89.00 (*0-7812-7286-6*) Rprt Serv.

Stratford to Dogberry: Studies in Shakespeare's Earlier Plays. John W. Draper. (Select Bibliographies Reprint Ser.). 1977. 31.95 (*0-8369-5255-3*) Ayer.

Stratford-upon-Avon. Ed. by Levi Fox. (Shakespeare Travel Ser.). (Illus.). 32p. (Orig.). 1994. pap. 3.50 (*0-7117-0311-6*) Seven Hills Bk.

Stratford Upon-Avon & Shakespeare Country. William Caldecott. (C). 1989. 30.00 (*1-85368-029-X*, Pub. by New Holland Pubs UK) St Mut.

Stratford-upon-Avon & the Shakespeare Country. Ed. by Levi Fox. (Shakespeare Travel Ser.). (Illus.). 32p. (Orig.). 1994. pap. 3.95 (*0-7117-0258-6*) Seven Hills Bk.

Stratford-upon-Avon, Shakespeare's Town. Ed. by Levi Fox. (Shakespeare Travel Ser.). (Illus.). 32p. (Orig.). 1994. pap. 3.95 (*0-7117-0314-0*) Seven Hills Bk.

Stratgey Workout: Build & Implement a Robust Strategic Plan. Cyril Levicki. (Illus.). 250p. (Orig.). 1997. pap. 25.00 (*0-273-62442-3*, Fincl Times) Pitman Publng.

Stratgies-Deferring & Shifting Taxes. 96th ed. Fowler. 1996. pap. text ed. 35.00 (*0-15-601953-1*) HarBrace.

Strathblair: The Novel. Alanna Knight. 311p. 1994. pap. 7.95 (*0-563-36778-4*, Pub. by BBC UK) Parkwest Pubns.

Strathcairn: A Novel, 2 vols. in 1. Charles A. Collins. LC 79-8257. reprint ed. 44.50 (*0-404-61832-4*) AMS Pr.

***Strathmore's Who's Who Vol. 3.** 3rd rev. ed. 675p. 1996. write for info. (*1-890347-00-0*) Strathmore Dir.

Strathspey Players: Past & Present. William C. Honeyman. 1989. pap. 49.00 (*0-946868-01-8*, Pub. by Hardie Pr UK) St Mut.

Stratification: Leader Manual & Instructional Guide. rev. ed. Donald L. Dewar. (Illus.). 42p. (Orig.). 1993. pap. 14.00 (*0-937670-18-9*) QCI Intl.

Stratification: Socioeconomic & Sexual Inequality. Rae Blumberg. 136p. 1978. pap. text ed. write for info. (*0-697-07521-4*) Brown & Benchmark.

Stratification & Organization: Selected Papers. Arthur L. Stinchcombe. (Studies in Rationality & Social Change). 350p. 1986. text ed. 85.00 (*0-521-32588-9*) Cambridge U Pr.

Stratification, Hierarchy & Ethnicity in Northeast India. Ed. by R. K. Bhadra & Sekh R. Mondal. (C). 1991. 30.00 (*81-7035-086-7*, Pub. by Daya Pub Hse II) S Asia.

Stratification of a Tropical Forest As Seen in Dispersal Types. I. Roth. (Tasks for Vegetation Science Ser.). 1987. lib. bdg. 263.00 (*90-6193-613-6*) Kluwer Ac.

Stratification of Tropical Forests as seen in Leaf Structure. I. Roth. (Tasks for Vegetation Science Ser.). 1984. lib. bdg. 320.00 (*90-6193-946-1*) Kluwer Ac.

Stratification of Tropical Forests as Seen in Leaf Structure, Pt. 2. B. Rollet et al. (Tasks for Vegetation Science Ser.). (C). 1990. lib. bdg. 236.00 (*0-7923-0397-0*) Kluwer Ac.

Stratificational Grammar: A Definition & an Example. Geoffrey Sampson. LC 74-118282. (Janua Linguarum, Ser. Minor: No. 88). (Illus.). (Orig.). 1970. pap. text ed. 42.35 (*90-279-0712-9*) Mouton.

Stratificational View of Linguistic Change. William M. Christie, Jr. LC 79-115787. (Edward Sapir Monograph Ser. in Language, Culture & Cognition: No. 4). viii, 71p. (Orig.). (C). 1977. pap. 18.00 (*0-933104-04-9*) Jupiter Pr.

Stratifiction & Power: Structures of Class, Status, & Command. John Scott. LC 96-18282. 278p. (C). 1996. text ed. 57.95 (*0-7456-1041-2*); pap. text ed. 23.95 (*0-7456-1042-0*) Blackwell Pubs.

S

Stratified Flows. Ed. by E. John List & Gerhard H. Jirka. LC 90-41159. 1120p. 1990. pap. text ed. 97.00 (*0-87262-775-6*) Am Soc Civil Eng.

Stratified Mappings: Structure & Triangulability. A. Verona. (Lecture Notes in Mathematics Ser.: Vol. 1102). ix, 160p. 1984. 34.95 (*0-387-13898-6*) Spr-Verlag.

Stratified Morse Theory. M. Goresky & R. Macpherson. (Ergebnisse der Mathematik und Ihrer Grenzgebiete Ser.: Vol. 14). 290p. 1988. 150.95 (*0-387-17300-5*) Spr-Verlag.

Stratified State: Radical Institutionalist Theories of Participation & Duality. Ed. by William M. Dugger & William T. Waller. LC 92-27890. (Studies in Institutional Economics). 280p. (gr. 13). 1993. text ed. 67.95 (*1-56324-020-3*) M E Sharpe.

***Stratifying Endomorphism Algebras.** L. L. Scott & Edward Cline. LC 96-29325. (Memoirs of the American Mathematical Society Ser.: Vol. 124/591). 1996. 37.00 (*0-8218-0488-X*, MEMO/124/591) Am Math.

Stratigraphic Correlation Between Sedimentary Basins of the ESCAP Region: ESCAP Atlas of Stratigraphy Four. Peoples Republic of China, Vol. X. (Mineral Resources Development Ser.: No.52). 83p. 1985. 25.00 (*92-1-119272-2*, E.85.II.F.13) UN.

Stratigraphic Correlation Between Sedimentary Basins of the Escap Region: Escap Atlas of Stratigraphy IX. (Mineral Resources Development Ser.: No. 59). 96p. 1991. 25.00 (*92-1-119560-8*, E.90.II.F.9) UN.

Stratigraphic Correlation Between Sedimentary Basins of the ESCAP Region: ESCAP Atlas of Stratigraphy V - Republic of Korea, Vol. XI. (Mineral Resources Development Ser.: No. 53). 34p. 1986. 25.00 (*92-1-119406-7*, E.86.II.F.5) UN.

Stratigraphic Correlation Between Sedimentary Basins of the ESCAP Region No. VIII: ESCAP Atlas of Stratigraphy: Afghanistan & Australia. (Mineral Resources Development Ser.: No. 58). 32p. 1990. 25.00 (*92-1-119558-6*, 90.II.F.5) UN.

Stratigraphic Correlation Between Sedimentary Basins of the ESCAP Region, Vol. XII: ESCAP Atlas of Stratigraphy VI, Socialist Republic of Viet Nam. (Mineral Resources Development Ser.: No. 54). 211p. 1986. 25.00 (*92-1-119429-6*, E.86.II.F.21) UN.

Stratigraphic Correlation Between Sedimentary Basins of the ESCAP Region, Vol. XIII: ESCAP Atlas of Stratigraphy VII; Triassic of Asia, Australia & the Pacific. 25p. 1988. 25.00 (*92-1-119450-4*, 88.II.F.3) UN.

Stratigraphic Correlation by Microfacies of the Cenomanian-Coniacian of the Sergipe Basin, Brazil. Pierre-Yves Berthou & Peter Bengtson. (Fossils & Strata: No. 21). 88p. 1988. pap. 33.50 (*82-00-37413-0*) Scandnvan Univ Pr.

Stratigraphic Evolution of Clastic Depositional Sequences. Gordon S. Fraser. 416p. 1989. boxed 52.00 (*0-318-37860-4*) P-H.

Stratigraphic Evolution of Foreland Basins. G. M. Ross. (SEPM Special Publications: No. 52). (Illus.). 320p. 1995. text ed. 97.00 (*1-56576-016-6*) SEPM.

Stratigraphic Framework of the Alaska Peninsula. Robert L. Detterman. Vol. 1969. 1994. write for info. (*0-318-72571-1*) US Geol Survey.

Stratigraphic Index of Dinoflagellate Cysts. Ed. by A. J. Powell. (British Micropalaeontological Society Publications). (Illus.). 296p. (C). (gr. 13). 1992. text ed. 199.95 (*0-412-36280-5*, A6924) Chapman & Hall.

***Stratigraphic Modeling & Interpretation: Geophysical Principles & Techniques.** Norman S. Neidell. (Education Course Note Ser.: No. 13). (Illus.). 145p. 1979. reprint ed. pap. 41.40 (*0-608-04226-9*, 2064983) Bks Demand.

Stratigraphic, Paleontologic, & Paleoenvironmental Analysis of the Upper Cretaceous Rocks of Cimarron County, Northwestern Oklahoma. Erle G. Kauffman et al. LC 76-47800. (Geological Society of America, Memoir Ser.: No. 149). 160p. reprint ed. pap. 45.60 (*0-7837-2684-8*, 2043061) Bks Demand.

Stratigraphic Record of Global Change, 1993 SEPM Meeting, Abstracts with Program, Penn State University Campus, State College, PA, August 8-12, 1993. fac. ed. Society for Sedimentary Geology Staff. 70p. 1993. pap. 25.00 (*0-7837-7683-7*, 2047436) Bks Demand.

Stratigraphic Record of the Neogene Globorotalidradiation (Planktonic Foraminiferida) Richard Cifelli & George Scott. LC 84-600360. (Smithsonian Contributions to Paleobiology Ser.: No. 58). 105p. reprint ed. pap. 30.00 (*0-685-16386-5*, 2027135) Bks Demand.

Stratigraphic Sections & Records of Spring in the Glen Canyon Region of Utah & Arizona. M. E. Cooley. (Technical Ser.). 140p. 1965. pap. 2.25 (*0-685-14715-0*, TS-6) Mus Northern Ariz.

Stratigraphic, Tectonic, Thermal, & Diagenetic Histories of the Monterry Formation, Pismo & Huasna Basin, California. (Guidebook Ser.: No. 2). 96p. 1984. pap. 15.50 (*0-918985-44-7*) SEPM.

Stratigraphic Traps I. Ed. by Edward A. Beaumont & Norman H. Foster. (Treatise of Petroleum Geology Atlas of Oil & Gas Fields Ser.: No. 3). (Illus.). 295p. 1990. 10.00 (*0-89181-582-1*, 018) AAPG.

Stratigraphic Traps II. Ed. by Norman H. Foster & Edward A. Beaumont. (Treatise of Petroleum Geology Atlas of Oil & Gas Fields Ser.: No. 6). (Illus.). 360p. 1991. 10.00 (*0-89181-585-6*, 021) AAPG.

Stratigraphic Traps III. Ed. by Norman H. Foster & Edward A. Beaumont. (Treatise of Petroleum Geology Atlas of Oil & Gas Fields Ser.: No. 8). (Illus.). xiii, 445p. 1992. 10.00 (*0-89181-587-2*, 023) AAPG.

Stratigraphic Traps in Sandstones: Exploration Techniques. Daniel A. Busch. LC 74-83506. (American Association of Petroleum Geologists. Memoir Ser.: No. 21). (Illus.). 186p. reprint ed. pap. 53.10 (*0-7837-1652-4*, 2041950) Bks Demand.

Stratigraphic Type Oil Fields, 2 vols. Arville I. Levorsen. 1976. lib. bdg. 250.00 (*0-8490-2694-6*) Gordon Pr.

Stratigraphical Index of British Ostracoda: Geological Journal Special Issue, Vol. 8. Ed. by Raymond H. Bate & Eric Robinson. (Liverpool Geological Society & the Manchester Geological Association Ser). 552p. 1980. text ed. 300.00 (*0-471-27755-X*) Wiley.

Stratigraphy. Pierre Cotillon. Tr. by James P. Noble. LC 92-19762. (Illus.). 200p. (ENG & FRE.). 1992. 54.95 (*0-387-54675-8*) Spr-Verlag.

Stratigraphy: Proceedings of the 27th International Geological Congress, Vol. 1. International Geological Congress Staff. 388p. 1984. lib. bdg. 112.00 (*90-6764-010-7*, Pub. by VSP NE) Coronet Bks.

Stratigraphy & Archaeology of Ventana Cave. Emil W. Haury. LC 51-802. (Illus.). xxvii, 599p. 1975. 56.00 (*0-8165-0536-5*) U of Ariz Pr.

Stratigraphy & Depositional History of the Star Peak Group (Triassic), Northwestern Nevada. Kathryn M. Nichols & N. J. Silberling. LC 77-89753. (Geological Society of America, Special Paper Ser.: No. 178). (Illus.). 79p. reprint ed. pap. 25.00 (*0-8357-3146-4*, 2039409) Bks Demand.

Stratigraphy & Genera of Clacerous Foraminifera of the Fraileys Facies of Central Kentucky, No. 280 see Bulletins of American Paleontology: Vol. 64

Stratigraphy & Glacial-Marine Sediments of the Amerasian Basin, Central Arctic Ocean. David L. Clark. LC 80-65270. (Geological Society of America, Special Paper Ser.: No. 181). 95p. (Orig.). reprint ed. pap. 27.10 (*0-317-27883-5*, 2025453) Bks Demand.

Stratigraphy & Life History. Marshall Kay & Edwin H. Colbert. LC 64-20072. 748p. reprint ed. pap. 180.00 (*0-317-28755-9*, 2055486) Bks Demand.

Stratigraphy & Paleobotany of the Golden Valley Formation, Early Tertiary, of Western North Dakota. Leo J. Hickey. LC 76-50970. (Geological Society of America, Memoir Ser.: No. 150). 336p. reprint ed. pap. 95.80 (*0-7837-1256-1*, 2041393) Bks Demand.

Stratigraphy & Paleoenvironments of Late Quaternary Valley Fills on the Southern High Plains. Vance T. Holliday. (Memoir Ser.: No. 186). (Illus.). 1996. 54.00 (*0-8137-1186-X*) Geol Soc.

Stratigraphy & Sedimentation. 2nd ed. William C. Krumbein & L. L. Sloss. LC 61-11422. (Illus.). 660p. (C). 1995. text ed. write for info. (*0-7167-0219-3*) W H Freeman.

Stratigraphy & Uranium Deposits, Lisbon Valley District, San Juan County, Utah. G. C. Huber. Ed. by Jon W. Raese. LC 80-18873. (Colorado School of Mines Quarterly Ser.: Vol. 75, No. 2). (Illus.). 45p. (Orig.). 1980. pap. 8.00 (*0-686-63163-3*) Colo Sch Mines.

Stratigraphy, Depositional Environments & Sedimentary Tectonics of the Western Margin, Cretaceous Western Seaway. Ed. by J. D. Nation & J. G. Eaton. (Special Papers: No. 260). (Illus.). 240p. 1991. pap. 21.00 (*0-8137-2260-8*) Geol Soc.

Stratigraphy of the Late Proterozoic Murdama Group, Saudi Arabia. Robert C. Greene. Vol. 1976. 1993. write for info. (*0-318-70178-2*) US Geol Survey.

Stratigraphy of the Pre-Simpson Paleozoic Subsurface Rocks of Texas & Southeast New Mexico, 2 Vols. V. E. Barnes et al. (Publication Ser.: PUB 5924). (Illus.). 836p. 1959. pap. 7.75 (*0-318-03311-9*) Bur Econ Geology.

Stratigraphy, Petrology, & Depositional Environments of the Jarvis Creek Coalfield, Alaska. Michael Belowich. (MIRL Reports: No. 85). 82p. 1988. 8.00 (*0-911043-09-8*) UAKF Min Ind Res Lab.

Stratigraphy, Sedimentology & Provenance of the Raging River Formation (Early? & Middle Eocene), King County, Washington. Samuel Y. Johnson & Joseph T. Connor. 0132085. 1995. write for info. (*0-615-00096-7*) US Geol Survey.

Stratigraphy, Structure, & Graptolites of an Ordovician & Silurian Sequence in The Terra Cotta Mountains, Alaska Range, Alaska. Michael Churkin, Jr. & Claire Carter. (Professional Papers). 1995. write for info. (*0-615-00129-7*) US Geol Survey.

Stratiomyoidea (Diptera) of Fennoscandia & Denmark. R. Rozkosny. (Fauna Entomologica Scandinavica Ser.: No. 1). (Illus.). 151p. 1973. pap. 25.50 (*87-87491-00-1*) Lubrecht & Cramer.

Stratonice. Edward Bartlet. (Fropse Ser.: No. 10, Vol. LXX11B). 1997. 92.00 (*0-918728-95-9*) Pendragon NY.

Stratonice. Quinault. Ed. by Dubois. (Exeter French Texts Ser.: Vol. 63). 117p. (FRE.). Date not set. pap. text ed. 19.95 (*0-85989-203-4*, Pub. by Univ Exeter Pr UK) Northwestern U Pr.

Stratonikeia in Caria. M. Cetin Sahin. (Illus.). 53p. 1980. pap. 6.00 (*0-89005-266-2*) Ares.

Stratospheric Canticles. Will Alexander. (Illus.). 80p. (Orig.). 1995. pap. 8.95 (*1-880766-08-6*) Pantograph Pr.

Stratospheric Ozone & Man, Vol. I: Stratospheric Ozone. Ed. by Frank A. Bower & Richard B. Ward. 232p. 1982. 131.00 (*0-8493-5753-5*, QC879, CRC Reprint) Franklin.

Stratospheric Ozone & Man, Vol. II: Man's Interactions & Concerns. Ed. by Frank A. Bower & Richard B. Ward. 280p. 1981. 129.95 (*0-8493-5755-1*, QC879) CRC Pr.

Stratospheric Ozone Depletion - UV-B Radiation in the Biosphere. Ed. by R. Hilton Biggs & Margaret E. Joyner. LC 94-5044. (NATO ASI Series I: Global Environmental Change). xv, 358p. 1994. 202.95 (*0-387-57810-2*) Spr-Verlag.

Stratospheric Ozone Reduction, Solar Ultraviolet Radiation & Plant Life. Ed. by R. C. Worrest & M. M. Caldwell. (NATO ASI Series G: Ecological Sciences: Vol. 8). ix, 374p. 1986. 149.95 (*0-387-13875-7*) Spr-Verlag.

StratSim: The Business Strategy Simulation. Stuart W. James et al. 140p. (Orig.). (C). 1996. pap. text ed. 95.00 (*1-885837-21-6*) Interpret Sftware.

Stratsim: The Corporate Strategy Simulation Game. Roger Evered & Richard A. Craig. (Illus.). 105p. 1981. reprint ed. pap. text ed. 6.80 (*0-87563-410-9*) Stipes.

Stratton's Islands of Saco Bay: An Interwoven History, 1605-1993. Georgiana P. Chase. LC 93-78914. (Illus.). 126p. 1994. pap. 16.98 (*0-9637490-1-3*) Mendocino Lith.

Stratum Corneum. Ed. by R. M. Marks & Gerd Plewig. (Illus.). 300p. 1983. 68.95 (*0-387-11704-0*) Spr-Verlag.

Strauss: "Also Sprach Zarathustra" John Williamson. LC 92-20457. (Cambridge Music Handbooks Ser.). 128p. (C). 1993. text ed. 34.95 (*0-521-40076-7*); pap. text ed. 11.95 (*0-521-40935-7*) Cambridge U Pr.

Strauss' & Sayles' Behavioral Strategies for Managers. Leonard R. Sayles & George Strauss. 304p. 1980. text ed. write for info. (*0-13-791459-8*) P-H.

Strauss Family. Peter Kemp. (Illustrated Lives of the Great Composers Ser.). (Illus.). 272p. 1996. 14.95 (*0-7119-1726-4*, OP 45194) Omnibus NY.

Strauss' Life of Jesus Volume One from George Eliot: From George Eliot. David F. Strauss. Ed. by Yoesh Gloger. Tr. by George Eliot from GER. LC 92-75332. (Illus.). 224p. (Orig.). 1993. pap. 20.00 (*1-878632-53-1*, SAN 297-2182) Gloger Family Bks.

Strauss-Rolland Correspondence. Ed. by Rollo H. Myers. 1987. pap. 11.95 (*0-7145-0503-X*) Riverrun NY.

***Strauss Tone Poems.** Michael Kennedy. (BBC Music Guides Ser.). 68p. 1996. 5.95 (*0-563-20275-0*, BB 11132, Pub. by BBC UK) Parkwest Pubns.

Strauss Waltz Album, EFS8. (Illus.). 128p. pap. 11.95 (*0-8256-2008-2*, AM40072) Music Sales.

Strauss's Federal Drug Laws & Examination Review. Steven Strauss. LC 96-60692. 440p. 1996. pap. text ed. 39.95 (*1-56676-465-3*) Technomic.

Strauss's Pharmacy Law Examination Review. 3rd rev. ed. Steven Strauss. LC 94-62189. 454p. 1995. pap. text ed. 29.95 (*1-56676-285-5*) Technomic.

Stravinsky. Andre Boucourechliev. Tr. by Martin Cooper from FRE. LC 86-33488. 336p. 1987. 45.00 (*0-8419-1058-8*); pap. 24.50 (*0-8419-1162-2*) Holmes & Meier.

Stravinsky. Paul Griffiths. (Master Musicians Ser.). (Illus.). 253p. 1993. 30.00 (*0-02-871483-0*) Schirmer Bks.

Stravinsky: "Oedipus Rex" Stephen Walsh. LC 92-30088. (Cambridge Music Handbooks Ser.). 120p. (C). 1993. text ed. 34.95 (*0-521-40431-2*); pap. text ed. 11.95 (*0-521-40778-8*) Cambridge U Pr.

***Stravinsky: A Critical Survey, 1882-1946.** Eric W. White. LC 97-21924. 1997. pap. write for info. (*0-486-29755-1*) Dover.

***Stravinsky: Chronicle of a Friendship.** Robert Craft. LC 94-12666. (Illus.). 608p. 1996. pap. 24.95 (*0-8265-1285-2*) Vanderbilt U Pr.

Stravinsky: Chronicle of a Friendship. rev. ed. Robert Craft. LC 94-12666. (Illus.). 608p. (C). 1994. 39.95 (*0-8265-1258-5*) Vanderbilt U Pr.

Stravinsky: Chronicle of a Friendship, 1948-1971. Robert Craft. 424p. reprint ed. lib. bdg. 59.00 (*0-685-14852-1*) Rprt Serv.

Stravinsky: Classic Humanist. Heinrich Strobel. LC 73-4338. 186p. 1973. reprint ed. lib. bdg. 27.50 (*0-306-70580-X*) Da Capo.

Stravinsky: Seen & Heard. Hans Keller & Milein Cosman. LC 84-17648. (Music Ser.). 128p. 1985. reprint ed. 21.50 (*0-306-76264-1*) Da Capo.

Stravinsky: The Composer & His Works. 2nd ed. Eric W. White. LC 66-27667. (Illus.). 656p. 1980. pap. 22.00 (*0-520-03985-8*) U CA Pr.

Stravinsky: The Music Box & the Nightingale. Daniel Albright. (Monographs on Musicology: Vol. 9). 88p. 1989. pap. text ed. 26.00 (*2-88124-295-2*) Gordon & Breach.

Stravinsky, a Critical Survey. Eric W. White. LC 79-9863. 192p. 1979. reprint ed. text ed. 35.00 (*0-313-21463-8*, WHST, Greenwood Pr) Greenwood.

Stravinsky, a Critical Survey: Music Book Index. Eric W. White. 192p. 1993. reprint ed. lib. bdg. 69.00 (*0-7812-9625-0*) Rprt Serv.

Stravinsky & the Piano. Charles M. Joseph. LC 83-9206. (Russian Music Studies: No. 8). (Illus.). 322p. reprint ed. pap. 91.80 (*0-685-20447-2*, 2070310) Bks Demand.

Stravinsky & the "Rite of Spring" Pieter C. Van den Toorn. LC 86-31778. 200p. 1987. 50.00 (*0-520-05958-1*) U CA Pr.

Stravinsky & the Russian Traditions: A Biography of the Works Through "Mavra", 2 vols., Set. Richard F. Taruskin. LC 93-28500. 1800p. 1995. boxed 125.00 (*0-520-07099-2*) U CA Pr.

Stravinsky Festival of the New York City Ballet. Nancy Goldner. LC 73-84996. (Illus.). 304p. 1973. 22.50 (*0-87130-037-0*) Eakins.

Stravinsky in Modern Music. Ed. by Carol J. Oja. LC 82-1473. (Music Reprint Ser.). 1982. reprint ed. 39.50 (*0-306-76108-4*) Da Capo.

***Stravinsky Retrospectives.** Ed. by Ethan Haimo & Paul Johnson. LC 86-1262. (Illus.). 216p. 1997. pap. text ed. 20.00 (*0-8032-7301-0*) U of Nebr Pr.

Stravinsky's Dream. Conger Beasley, Jr. Ed. by Gloria V. Hickok. 10p. (Orig.). 1994. pap. 3.00 (*1-884235-06-9*) Helicon Nine Eds.

Straw: Some Genealogies & Family Records. A. Y. Straw. (Illus.). 292p. 1994. reprint ed. pap. 46.00 (*0-8328-4242-7*); reprint ed. lib. bdg. 56.00 (*0-8328-4241-9*) Higginson Bk Co.

Straw see Six Short Plays of Eugene O'Neill

Straw - Some Genealogies & Family Records. A. Y. Straw. (Illus.). 292p. 1994. reprint ed. pap. 46.00 (*0-8328-4512-4*); reprint ed. lib. bdg. 56.00 (*0-8328-4511-6*) Higginson Bk Co.

Straw & Straw Craftsmen. Arthur R. Staniforth. 1989. pap. 25.00 (*0-7478-0103-7*, Pub. by Shire UK) St Mut.

Straw Bale House. Athena S. Steen et al. (Real Goods Independent Living Bks.). (Illus.). 336p. (Orig.). 1994. pap. 30.00 (*0-930031-71-7*) Chelsea Green Pub.

Straw Damsel. large type ed. Emily Wynn. 1990. pap. 15.99 (*0-7089-6925-9*, Trailtree Bookshop) Ulverscroft.

Straw Decay & Its Effect on Disposal & Utilization: Proceedings of a Symposium...Held at Hatfield Polytechnic, April 10-11th, 1979. Symposium on Straw Decay (1979: Hatfield Polytechnic) Staff. Ed. by E. Grossbard. LC 79-42841. (Illus.). 359p. reprint ed. pap. 102.40 (*0-685-20759-5*, 2030402) Bks Demand.

Straw Giant: America's Armed Forces-Triumphs & Failures. Arthur T. Hadley. 336p. 1987. pap. 10.95 (*0-380-70391-2*) Avon.

Straw in the Wind. large type ed. Mary Mackie. LC 94-33451. (Nightingale Ser.). 216p. 1995. pap. 16.95 (*0-8161-7453-9*, GK Hall) Thorndike Pr.

Straw into Gold. Bruce Bennett. (CSU Poetry Ser.: No. XVI). 52p. (Orig.). 1984. pap. 4.50 (*0-914946-45-5*) Cleveland St Univ Poetry Ctr.

Straw into Gold: Books & Activities about Folktales. Jan Irving & Robin Currie. LC 93-30271. (Peddler's Pack Ser.: No. 2). (Illus.). xii, 109p. 1993. pap. text ed. 18.00 (*1-56308-074-5*) Teacher Ideas Pr.

***Straw into Gold: Peoms New & Selected.** C. K. Stead. 176p. 1997. pap. 18.95 (*1-86940-161-1*, Pub. by Auckland Univ NZ) Paul & Co Pubs.

Straw Obelisk. Adolph Caso. (Illus.). 390p. 1995. 24.95 (*0-8283-2005-5*) Branden Pub Co.

Straw on the Wind. Elizabeth Power. 1995. mass mkt. 3.25 (*0-373-11768-X*, 1-11768-8) Harlequin Bks.

***Straw Polyhedra.** Mary Laycock. (Illus.). 39p. (Orig.). (YA). (gr. 4-12). Date not set. pap. 6.50 (*0-918932-99-8*) Activity Resources.

Straw Sense. Rona Rupert. LC 92-8775. (Illus.). (J). 1993. pap. 14.00 (*0-671-77047-0*, S&S Bks Young Read) S&S Childrens.

***Straw Sense.** Rone Rupert. (Illus.). 32p. (J). 3.98 (*0-7651-0099-1*) Smithmark.

***Straw Structures: Exploring Students' Learning in Hands-On Science.** (Sense Making in Science Ser.). 26p. 1996. pap. text ed. 6.00 (*0-435-07120-3*, 07120) Heinemann.

Straw Votes, a Study of Political Prediction. Claude E. Robinson. LC 75-41231. reprint ed. 29.50 (*0-404-14697-X*) AMS Pr.

***Strawbeater's Thanksgiving.** Irene S. Hector. LC 97-11711. (Illus.). (J). 1998. write for info. (*0-316-79866-5*) Little.

Strawberries: Recipes for America's Favorite Fruit. Ed. by Nana Whalen. LC 83-60022. (Illus.). 64p. (Orig.). 1983. pap. 3.95 (*0-942320-05-0*) Am Cooking.

Strawberries & Rhymes. Gertrude E. Rawson. Ed. by Rayma B. Kreider & Jane B. Irwin. (Illus.). 180p. (Orig.). 1996. pap. write for info. (*0-9652212-0-2*) R & J Beebe.

Strawberries in November: A Guide to Year-Round Gardening in the East Bay. Judith Goldsmith. (Illus.). 112p. (Orig.). 1991. reprint ed. lib. bdg. 35.00 (*0-8095-4968-9*) Borgo Pr.

Strawberry. Jennifer Coldrey. (Stopwatch Ser.). (Illus.). 25p. (J). (gr. k-4). 1990. pap. 3.95 (*0-382-24340-4*, Silver Pr NJ); lib. bdg. 9.95 (*0-382-09801-3*, Silver Pr NJ) Silver Burdett Pr.

Strawberry: Cultivars to Marketing. Ed. by Norman F. Childers. (Illus.). 400p. 1981. 15.00 (*0-317-03715-3*) Horticult Pubns.

Strawberry Connection. Beatrice R. Buszek. 1991. pap. 12.95 (*0-920852-31-9*, Pub. by Nimbus Publishing Ltd CN) Chelsea Green Pub.

Strawberry Deficiency Symptoms: A Visual & Plant Analysis Guide to Fertilization. Albert Ulrich et al. LC 79-67379. (Illus.). 60p. 1980. pap. text ed. 15.00 (*0-931876-37-0*, 1917) ANR Pubns CA.

Strawberry Diseases. Antonios G. Plakides. LC 64-21596. (Louisiana State University Studies Biological Science Ser.: No. 5). 207p. reprint ed. pap. 59.00 (*0-317-29858-5*, 2019566) Bks Demand.

***Strawberry Eats & Treats: The Guide to Enjoying Strawberries.** Association Members. LC 96-71975. (Illus.). 112p. (Orig.). 1997. pap. 12.95 (*0-942495-62-4*) Amherst Pr.

Strawberry Fair. Illus. by Chris Rothero. 96p. (J). (gr. 1-6). 14.95 (*0-7136-2676-3*, Pub. by A&C Black UK) Talman.

Strawberry Fields: Politics, Class, & Work in California Agriculture. Miriam J. Wells. (Anthropology of Contemporary Issues Ser.). (Illus.). 360p. 1996. 45.00 (*0-8014-3172-7*); pap. 18.95 (*0-8014-8279-8*) Cornell U Pr.

Strawberry Girl. Lois Lenski. 1976. 20.95 (*0-8488-1410-X*) Amereon Ltd.

Strawberry Girl. Lois Lenski. LC 45-7609. (Illus.). 192p. (J). (gr. 4-6). 1945. 16.00 (*0-397-30109-X*, Lipp Jr Bks); lib. bdg. 15.89 (*0-397-30110-3*, Lipp Jr Bks) HarpC Child Bks.

Strawberry Girl. large type ed. Helen A. Upshall. 597p. 1994. 25.99 (*0-7505-0591-5*) Ulverscroft.

Strawberry Girl. Lois Lenski. 250p. 1991. reprint ed. lib. bdg. 19.95 (*0-89966-851-8*) Buccaneer Bks.

Strawberry Harvest. Sally Buckner. 84p. (Orig.). 1986. pap. 10.00 (*0-932662-61-7*) St Andrews NC.

Strawberry into the 21st Century. Ed. by Adam Dale & James J. Luby. LC 91-2306. (Illus.). 292p. 1991. text ed. 49.95 (*0-88192-197-1*) Timber.

Strawberry Junction. Mark Verderame. (Illus.). 16p. (J). (gr. 1-3). 1996. pap. 7.00 (*0-8059-3959-8*) Dorrance.

Strawberry Lace Vol. 1. Amy B. Brown. 1994. mass mkt. 4.50 (*0-312-95327-5*) St Martin.

Strawberry Man & 27 Love Poems. Eugenia Macer-Story. 1992. 12.95 (*1-879980-01-0*) Magick Mirror.

Strawberry Patchwork. Susan A. McCreary. (Illus.). 104p. 1977. reprint ed. pap. 5.00 (*0-9608428-1-0*) Straw Patchwork.

Strawberry Road: A Japanese Immigrant Discovers America. Yoshimi Ishikawa. Tr. by Eve Zimmerman from JPN. 256p. 1991. 19.95 (*4-7700-1551-8*) Kodansha.

Strawberry Sampler. Jan Siegrist. (Illus.). 48p. (Orig.). 1985. pap. 3.95 (*0-933050-29-1*) New Eng Pr VT.

Strawberry Serendipity: Unexpected Discoveries. Susan A. McCreary. Ed. by Mallory McCreary. LC 95-68715. (Illus.). 160p. (Orig.). 1995. pap. 14.95 (*0-9608428-6-1*) Straw Patchwork.

***Strawberry Sky.** T. R. Wilson. 368p. 1997. pap. 11.95 (*0-7472-4964-4*, Pub. by Headline UK) Trafalgar.

Strawberry Statement: Notes of a College Revolutionary. James S. Kunen. 168p. (Orig.). (C). 1995. reprint ed. pap. text ed. 14.50 (*1-881089-52-5*) Brandywine Press.

Strawberry Verses. Dorene Paradiso. 160p. 1992. 8.95 (*0-9632050-0-5*) Paradise CA.

Strawbery Banke, a Historic Waterfront Neighborhood in Portsmouth, New Hampshire: Official Guidebook. 90p. 1982. pap. 5.00 (*0-9603896-0-1*) Strawbery Banke Mus.

Straws Blowing in the Air see My Theory of Life A to Z

Straws in the Wind. R. Rabindranath Menon. (Writers Workshop Redbird Ser.). 1975. 12.00 (*0-88253-650-8*); pap. text ed. 4.80 (*0-88253-649-4*) Ind-US Inc.

Straws in the Wind: Medieval Urban Environmental Law. Ronald E. Zupko. (C). 1996. pap. text ed. 18.95 (*0-8133-2972-8*) Westview.

Stray. Dick King-Smith. LC 96-4230. (Illus.). (J). 1996. 16.00 (*0-517-70934-1*) Crown Pub Group.

Stray. Dick King-Smith. LC 96-4230. (Illus.). (J). 1996. lib. bdg. 17.99 (*0-517-70935-X*) Crown Pub Group.

Stray. Ed. by George Le Pera. (Illus.). 66p. (Orig.). 1989. pap. text ed. 7.95 (*0-9624466-0-2*) United Action.

Stray Birds. Rabindranath Tagore. 62p. 1985. 3.95 (*0-318-37012-3*) Asia Bk Corp.

***Stray Cat.** Linda R. Apolzon. Ed. by Myrna Kemnitz. 110p. (Orig.). (YA). (gr. 7-8). 1996. pap. 6.99 (*0-88092-329-6*) Royal Fireworks.

Stray Cat. Don Matheson. 1988. pap. 3.50 (*0-671-66508-1*) PB.

***Stray Cat Handbook.** Tamara Kreuz. 1998. 12.95 (*0-87605-146-8*) Howell Bk.

***Stray Cats.** Warren Leight. 1997. pap. 5.25 (*0-8222-1614-0*) Dramatists Play.

Stray Current Corrosion: The Past, Present, & Future of Rail Transit Systems. Ed. by Michael J. Szeliga. (Illus.). 300p. 1994. 93.00 (*1-877914-57-6*) NACE Intl.

Stray Dog Story: An Adventure in Ten Scenes. Robert Chesley. LC 84-776. (Gay Play Script Ser.). (Illus.). 97p. 1984. 7.95 (*0-935672-11-7*) T n T Class.

Stray Dogs. Julie Jensen. 1987. pap. 5.25 (*0-8222-1088-6*) Dramatists Play.

***Stray Dogs.** John Ridley. LC 97-1414. 1997. 19.95 (*0-345-41345-8*) Ballantine.

***Stray Dogs.** John Ridley. 1997. pap. write for info. (*0-345-41346-6*) Ballantine.

***Stray Hearts.** Annie Kimberlin. 320p. (Orig.). 1997. mass mkt. 4.99 (*0-505-52221-7*, Leisure Bks) Dorchester Pub Co.

Stray Leaves from an Arctic Journal: Or, Eighteen Months in the Polar Regions in Search of Sir John Franklin's Expedition in the Years 1850-1851. Sherard Osborn. LC 74-5861. 1852. 27.50 (*0-404-11667-1*) AMS Pr.

Stray Leaves from Strange Literatures. Lafcadio Hearn. (Notable American Authors Ser.). 1992. reprint ed. lib. bdg. 75.00 (*0-7812-3068-3*) Rprt Serv.

Stray Shot. large type ed. Gerald Hammond. 1990. 25.99 (*0-7089-2211-2*) Ulverscroft.

Stray Studies: Second Series. John R. Green. LC 72-3362. (Essay Index Reprint Ser.). 1977. reprint ed. 20.95 (*0-8369-2904-7*) Ayer.

Stray Tales of the Big Bend. Elton Miles. LC 92-39729. (Centennial Series of the Association of Former Students: No. 47). (Illus.). 160p. 1993. 25.00 (*0-89096-534-X*); pap. 12.50 (*0-89096-542-0*) Tex A&M Univ Pr.

Stray Toasters. Bill Sienkiewicz. (Spiderman Ser.). (Illus.). 192p. 1991. pap. 16.95 (*0-87135-713-5*) Marvel Entmnt.

Stray Voltage: The Proceedings of the National Stray Voltage Symposium. LC 85-70628. 225p. 1985. pap. 23.00 (*0-916150-70-4*, P0585) Am Soc Ag Eng.

Strayer Root's. Frances E. Hanson. Ed. by Elizabeth Strayer. LC 86-9991. (Illus.). 432p. 1986. lib. bdg. 24.95 (*0-938015-25-7*) Avaln Wrtng Ctr.

StrayngeBook. Bob Grumman. (Illus.). 38p. (Orig.). 1987. pap. 3.00 (*0-926935-00-3*) Runaway Spoon.

StrayngeCatalogue. Bob Grumman. (Illus.). 34p. (Orig.). 1989. pap. 1.00 (*0-926935-13-5*) Runaway Spoon.

***Strays Like Us.** Richard Peck. LC 97-18575. 1998. write for info. (*0-8037-2291-5*) Dial Bks Young.

Streak of Chalk. Miguelanxo Prado. 88p. 1994. pap. 16.95 (*1-56163-108-6*, Comics Lit) NBM.

***Streak of Fire Balls.** Myungkark Park. 1996. pap. write for info. (*1-877974-29-3*) Prompter Pubns.

Streak of Gold. large type ed. Daphne Clair. (Linford Romance Library). 336p. 1984. pap. 15.99 (*0-7089-6039-1*) Ulverscroft.

Streaks of Squatter Life & Far-West Scenes. John S. Robb. LC 62-7018. 1978. reprint ed. 50.00 (*0-8201-1038-8*) Schol Facsimiles.

Stream. Barbara Beveridge. LC 92-33738. (Voyages Ser.). (Illus.). (J). 1993. 3.75 (*0-383-03657-7*) SRA McGraw.

Stream. Robert Herz. LC 82-14903. 53p. 1983. 9.95 (*0-934332-30-4*); pap. 4.95 (*0-934332-26-6*) LEpervier Pr.

Stream Analysis. 2nd ed. Jerry I. Porras & R. Kass. (Organization Development Ser.). (Illus.). 163p. (C). 1995. pap. text ed. write for info. (*0-201-53971-3*) Addison-Wesley.

Stream Analysis: Diagnosis & Planning for Managing Organization Development. Jerry I. Porras. LC 86-22183. (Organization Development Ser.). (Illus.). 180p. (C). 1987. pap. text ed. 26.95 (*0-201-05693-3*) Addison-Wesley.

***Stream & the Sapphire: Selected Poems on Religious Themes.** Denise Levertov. LC 96-30012. 80p. 1997. 19.95 (*0-8112-1353-6*); pap. 8.95 (*0-8112-1354-4*, NDP844) New Directions.

Stream Channel Enlargement Due to Urbanization. Thomas R. Hammer. (Discussion Paper Ser.: No. 55). 1972. pap. 10.00 (*1-55869-123-5*) Regional Sci Res Inst.

Stream Ecology: Application & Testing of General Ecological Theory. Ed. by James R. Barnes et al. LC 83-11145. 412p. 1983. 105.00 (*0-306-41460-0*, Plenum Pr) Plenum.

Stream Ecology: Structure & Function of Running Waters. Allan. 400p. (gr. 13). 1994. pap. text ed. 47.95 (*0-412-35530-2*) Chapman & Hall.

***Stream Ecology: Structure & Function of Running Waters.** D. Allan. (Illus.). 400p. (C). (gr. 13 up). 1994. text ed. 99.95 (*0-412-29430-3*) Chapman & Hall.

Stream Ecology & Self-Purification: An Introduction for Wastewater & Water Specialists. Frank R. Spellman. LC 95-62015. 143p. 1996. pap. text ed. 49.95 (*1-56676-377-0*) Technomic.

Stream Garden: Create & Plant Your Own Natural-Looking Water Feature. Archie Skinner & David Arscott. (Illus.). 128p. (Orig.). 1996. pap. 14.95 (*0-7063-7477-0*, Pub. by Ward Lock UK) Sterling.

Stream Hydrology: An Introduction for Ecologists. N. Gordon et al. 526p. 1992. text ed. 65.00 (*0-471-93084-9*) Wiley.

Stream in the Desert see Manantiales en el Desierto

Stream, Lake, Estuary & Ocean Pollution. 2nd rev. ed. Nelson L. Nemerow. (Environmental Engineering Ser.). (Illus.). 464p. 1991. text ed. 72.95 (*0-442-00767-1*) Van Nos Reinhold.

Stream Magazine, Bks. 1 & 2. Witness Lee. 816p. per. 42.00 (*0-87083-036-8*, 20004001) Living Stream Ministry.

Stream of Becoming: A Study of Martha Rogers's Theory. Barbara Sarter. 136p. 1989. 19.95 (*0-685-45119-4*) Natl League Nurse.

Stream of Consciousness: Scientific Investigations into the Flow of Human Experience. Ed. by Kenneth S. Pope & Jerome L. Singer. LC 78-2003. (Emotions, Personality, & Psychotherapy Ser.). reprint ed. pap. 74.10 (*0-317-08026-1*, 2-17802) Bks Demand.

***Stream of Consciousness: 8 Los Angeles Artists.** Elizabeth A. Brown. (Illus.). 84p. (Orig.). 1996. pap. 6.00 (*0-942006-31-3*) U of CA Art.

Stream of Life. Clarice Lispector. Tr. by Elizabeth Lowe & Earl Fitz from POR. (Emergent Literatures Ser.). Orig. Title: Agua Viva. 128p. (Orig.). 1989. pap. 10.95 (*0-8166-1782-1*) U of Minn Pr.

Stream of Light. Conrad Wright. 1989. pap. 12.00 (*1-55896-155-0*, Skinner Hse Bks) Unitarian Univ.

Stream of Living Souls, Vol. I: Thirty-Six Stories for Home & Worship. Denise D. Tracy. Ed. by Diane Miller. (Illus.). 118p. 1986. pap. 15.00 (*0-685-24734-1*) Delphi Resources.

Stream of Living Souls, Vol. II: Stories for Home & Worship. Denise D. Tracy. Ed. by Barbara Boockmeier. (Illus.). 93p. 1987. pap. 15.00 (*0-685-24735-X*) Delphi Resources.

Stream of Living Souls, Vol. III: Living in the Wind. Denise D. Tracy. Ed. by Nancy Fasano. (Illus.). 1988. pap. 15.99 (*0-685-24736-8*) Delphi Resources.

Stream of Living Water: Elements of Holy Tradition. 100p. (Orig.). 1988. pap. text ed. 7.00 (*1-887158-04-9*) God With Us.

Stream of Music: Music Book Index. Richard A. Leonard. 454p. 1993. reprint ed. lib. bdg. 99.00 (*0-7812-9581-5*) Rprt Serv.

Stream Protection Approach: Guidance for Developing Effective Local Nonpoint Source Control Programs in the Great Lakes Region. Thomas R. Schueler. 1994. reprint ed. pap. 16.95 (*0-614-14308-X*) Terrene Inst.

***Stream Reconnaissance Handbook.** Colin R. Thorne. pap. text ed. 45.00 (*0-471-96856-0*) Wiley.

Stream, Sea, Cloud. Adams. 1991. 30.00 (*0-8212-1863-8*) Bulfinch Pr.

Stream Smallmouth Fishing. Tim Holschlag. LC 90-31614. (Illus.). 224p. (Orig.). 1990. pap. 16.95 (*0-8117-2384-4*) Stackpole.

Stream Team on Patrol. John G. Shepherd. LC 93-15386. (Target Earth Ser.). (J). (gr. 4 up). 1993. lib. bdg. 15.98 (*1-56239-207-7*) Abdo & Dghtrs.

Streamer Fly Tying & Fishing. Joseph D. Bates. LC 94-44618. (Illus.). 384p. 1995. 34.95 (*0-8117-1702-X*) Stackpole.

Streamers. Sandra McPherson. 175p. (C). 1988. 13.95 (*0-88001-213-7*) Ecco Pr.

Streamers. Sandra McPherson. LC 88-4253. 1989. pap. 7.95 (*0-88001-214-5*) Ecco Pr.

Streamers. David Rabe. 1995. reprint ed. lib. bdg. 24.95 (*1-56849-633-8*) Buccaneer Bks.

Streamers Level 6: HBJ Reading 1987. Early. (J). 1987. teacher ed., pap. 108.00 (*0-15-330521-5*) HB Schl Dept.

Streamers Level 6: HBJ Reading 1987. Early. (J). 1987. student ed., pap. 30.00 (*0-15-330506-1*) HB Schl Dept.

***Streamflow Measurement.** 2nd ed. Herschy. (Illus.). 544p. 1995. text ed. 159.95 (*0-419-19490-8*, E & FN Spon) Routledge Chapman & Hall.

Streamflow Synthesis. Myron B. Fiering. LC 67-29625. 159p. reprint ed. pap. 45.40 (*0-317-10931-6*, 2001560) Bks Demand.

Streaming. Larry Kearney. 96p. 1988. 8.00 (*0-917588-20-7*) Trike.

Streamkeeper's Field Guide: Watershed Inventory & Stream Monitoring Methods. 5th rev. ed. Tom Murdoch et al. (Illus.). 315p. 1996. per. 29.95 (*0-9652109-0-1*) Adopt-A-Stream.

Streamline: American Art Deco Graphic Design. Steven Heller & Louise Fili. LC 94-13128. 144p. 1995. pap. 16.95 (*0-8118-0662-6*) Chronicle Bks.

Streamline Your Dancing. H. Ware. (Ballroom Dance Ser.). 1986. lib. bdg. 79.95 (*0-8490-3385-3*) Gordon Pr.

Streamline Your Dancing. H. Ware. (Ballroom Dance Ser.). 1985. lib. bdg. 65.00 (*0-87700-720-9*) Revisionist Pr.

Streamlined: A Metaphor for Progress. Claude Lichtens. 320p. 1996. pap. 29.95 (*1-56898-065-5*) Princeton Arch.

Streamlined Bookkeeping for Multi-Level Marketing. Audrey A. Scannell. (Illus.). 58p. 1985. pap. 7.95 (*0-9615341-0-9*) Advantage Pr.

Streamlined Briefing Technique: For All States Except California, Florida, Illinois, Indiana, Maryland, New York, Ohio, Pennsylvania, Texas, Virginia, & West Virginia. 38p. 1970. pap. 2.75 (*0-685-29723-3*, 527-0009-01) Amer Bar Assn.

Streamlined Briefing Technique: For the States of California, Florida, Illinois, Indiana, Maryland, New York, Ohio, Pennsylvania, Texas, Virginia, & West Virginia. 45p. 1970. pap. 2.75 (*0-685-29724-1*, 527-0010-01) Amer Bar Assn.

Streamlined Cooking for a Healthy Lifestyle. Mary H. Carroll. (Cole Group Ser.). 240p. (Orig.). 1995. pap. 18.95 (*1-56426-067-4*) Cole Group.

Streamlined Decade: Design in the Nineteen Thirties. Donald J. Bush. LC 75-10868. (Illus.). 192p. 1975. pap. 17.95 (*0-8076-0793-2*) Braziller.

***Streamlined Double Decker Bus.** Brownie Macintosh. (Illus.). 16p. (Orig.). (J). (gr. 2-5). 1995. pap. 9.95 (*0-924771-57-7*, Covered Brdge Pr) D C Press.

Streamlined Elementary Education. Stanley D. Porteus. LC 64-23745. (Illus.). 32p. (Orig.). 1964. pap. text ed. 3.95 (*0-87015-125-8*) Pacific Bks.

Streamlined Waltz. (Ballroom Dance Ser.). 1986. lib. bdg. 79.95 (*0-8490-3442-6*) Gordon Pr.

Streamlined Waltz. (Ballroom Dance Ser.). 1985. lib. bdg. 50.00 (*0-87700-841-8*) Revisionist Pr.

Streamliner Diner Cookbook. Irene Clark et al. 192p. (Orig.). 1995. pap. 16.95 (*0-89815-694-7*) Ten Speed Pr.

Streamlining & Integrating Human Resource Development for Adults. Shirley Downs. Ed. by Gerry Feinstein & Karen Glass. 51p. (Orig.). 1991. pap. text ed. 15.00 (*1-55877-134-4*) Natl Governor.

***Streamlining Defense Acquisition Laws: Report of the DOD Acquisition Law Advisory Panel.** 90p. 1996. reprint ed. pap. 30.00 (*0-7881-3306-3*) DIANE Pub.

Streamlining Government & Other Corporations: A Reality Check: Why Re-Inventing Fails & What to Do about It. Francis A. Zampiello & Jeff Salvage. LC 96-90138. 1996. 16.95 (*0-533-11900-6*) Vantage.

Streamlining Internal Control Processes: Strengthening Management Controls with Less Effort. 125p. (Orig.). (C). 1994. pap. text ed. 30.00 (*1-56806-956-1*) DIANE Pub.

Streamlining Local Government? Ed. by A. Rodriguez-Bachiller. (C). 1984. 35.00 (*0-685-30265-2*, Pub. by Oxford Polytechnic UK) St Mut.

Streamlining the Business of Government: Toward a State Human Investment System Conference Proceedings November 20-22, 1991, Washington, D. C. Ed. by Gerry Feinstein & Mark Miller. 102p. (Orig.). 1991. pap. text ed. 15.00 (*1-55877-137-9*) Natl Governor.

Streamlining the United Nations, Pt. A: Wanted: A U. N. Personnel System That Works. Estelle S. Perry. (Monograph in CURE Ser.: No. 12A). 68p. 1993. pap. text ed. 5.00 (*1-881520-02-1*) Ctr U N Reform Educ.

Streamlining Your Life. Stephanie Culp. 142p. 1991. pap. 11.99 (*0-89879-462-5*, Wrtrs Digest Bks) F & W Pubns Inc.

Streams. Joseph P. Kent. LC 95-70499. 88p. (Orig.). 1996. pap. 12.95 (*0-9623751-3-6*) Sunlight SF.

Streams, No. 1. Richard A. Spiegel. (Illus.). 138p. (YA). (gr. 9-12). 1987. pap. 5.00 (*0-934830-39-8*) Ten Penny.

Streams, No. 2. Richard A. Spiegel. (Illus.). 142p. (YA). (gr. 9-12). 1988. pap. 5.00 (*0-934830-42-8*) Ten Penny.

Streams, No. 3. Richard A. Spiegel. (Illus.). (YA). (gr. 9-12). 1989. pap. 5.00 (*0-934830-43-6*) Ten Penny.

Streams, No. V. Ed. by Richard A. Spiegel & Barbara Fisher. (Illus.). 150p. (Orig.). (YA). (gr. 8-12). 1991. pap. 5.00 (*0-934830-47-9*) Ten Penny.

Streams, No. 8. Richard A. Spiegel. (Illus.). 144p. (Orig.). (YA). (gr. 7-12). 1994. pap. 5.00 (*0-934830-56-8*) Ten Penny.

Streams: Catalogue for the Exhibition. Truman Lowe. (Illus.). 24p. (Orig.). 1991. pap. 5.00 (*0-9621886-1-1*) Univ WI Art Gal.

Streams & Rivers of Minnesota. Thomas F. Waters. LC 77-84166. (Illus.). 1977. pap. 14.95 (*0-8166-0960-8*) U of Minn Pr.

Streams Four. Richard A. Spiegel. (Illus.). 150p. (Orig.). (YA). (gr. 9-12). 1990. pap. 5.00 (*0-934830-44-4*) Ten Penny.

***Streams in the Desert.** Lettie B. Cowman. (Daybreaks Ser.). 1996. 9.99 (*0-310-96769-4*) Zondervan.

Streams in the Desert. Ajaib Singh. Ed. by Russell Perkins & Judith Perkins. LC 81-85843. (Illus.). 468p. (Orig.). 1991. pap. 12.00 (*0-89142-038-X*) Sant Bani Ash.

Streams in the Desert. anniversary ed. Lettie B. Cowman. (Zondervan Classics Ser.). 384p. 1996. 15.99 (*0-310-48400-6*) Zondervan.

Streams in the Desert. 3rd large type ed. Lettie B. Cowman. 370p. 1974. 12.99 (*0-310-22527-2*, 12555L) Zondervan.

Streams in the Desert, Vol. 1. Lettie B. Cowman. 384p. 1984. 14.99 (*0-310-22420-9*, 6901) Zondervan.

Streams in the Desert, Vol. 2. Lettie B. Cowman. 384p. 1984. 14.99 (*0-310-22430-6*, 6902) Zondervan.

***Streams in the Desert: An Updated Version in Today's Language.** rev. ed. L. B. Cowman. Ed. by James Reimann. LC 96-48454. 464p. 1997. 14.99 (*0-310-21006-2*) Zondervan.

Streams in the Desert & Springs in the Valley. Lettie B. Cowman. 752p. 1996. 24.99 (*0-310-21038-0*) Zondervan.

Streams of Change: The Fertility of Guestworker Populations in the Federal Republic of Germany. Thomas T. Kane. (Studies in Historical Demography). 225p. 1990. reprint ed. text ed. 15.00 (*0-8240-5093-2*) Garland.

Streams of Consciousness. T. Nadine Tucker. 57p. pap. text ed. 6.95 (*0-9646814-0-4*) Streetwize Pub.

Streams of Idealism & Health Care Innovation: An Assessment of Service-Learning & Community Mobilization. Richard A. Couto. LC 82-10240. 189p. reprint ed. pap. 53.90 (*0-8357-3030-1*, 2039277) Bks Demand.

Streams of Living Water: Celebrating the Great Traditions of Christian Faith. Richard J. Foster. 256p. 1997. 19.00 (*0-06-066743-5*) Harper SF.

Streams of Nectar: Lives, Poetry & Teachings of Saints & Mystics. Darshan Singh. LC 92-85401. (Illus.). 423p. 1993. 20.00 (*0-918224-25-X*) S K Pubns.

Streams of Nector: Lives, Poetry, & Teachings of Mystics. Darshan Singh. (C). 1993. text ed. 32.00 (*0-685-72784-X*) S Asia.

Streams of Renewal. Peter Hocken. 288p. (Orig.). 1986. pap. 11.95 (*0-932085-03-2*) Word Among Us.

Streams of Silver. R. A. Salvatore. LC 88-51721. (Forgotten Realms Icewind Dale Trilogy Ser.: Bk. 2). 1989. pap. 5.99 (*0-88038-672-X*) TSR Inc.

Streams of Silver: Six Contemporary Women Writers from Argentina. Monica R. Flori. LC 94-34079. 1995. 42.50 (*0-8387-5283-7*) Bucknell U Pr.

Streams Primer. 1989. pap. 14.95 (*0-13-944928-0*) P-H.

Streams Programmer's Guide. 1989. pap. text ed. 41.00 (*0-13-944810-1*) P-H.

Streams Seven. Richard A. Spiegel. 150p. (Orig.). (YA). (gr. 7-12). 1993. pap. 5.00 (*0-934830-53-3*) Ten Penny.

Streams to the River, River to the Sea. Scott O'Dell. 176p. 1988. mass mkt. 4.50 (*0-449-70244-8*, Juniper) Fawcett.

Streams to the River, River to the Sea: A Novel of Sacagawea. Scott O'Dell. (YA). 1986. 16.00 (*0-395-40430-4*) HM.

Streams to the River, River to the Sea: A Novel of Sacagawea. large type ed. Scott O'Dell. 312p. (J). (gr. 7 up). 1989. lib. bdg. 14.95 (*0-8161-4811-2*, GK Hall) Thorndike Pr.

Streams VI. Richard A. Spiegel. (Illus.). 152p. (Orig.). (YA). (gr. 7-12). 1992. pap. 5.00 (*0-934830-50-9*) Ten Penny.

***Streams 10.** Richard A. Spiegel. 131p. (Orig.). (YA). (gr. 8-12). 1996. pap. 5.00 (*0-934830-63-0*) Ten Penny.

***Streams 11.** Richard A. Spiegel. 140p. (Orig.). (YA). (gr. 8-12). 1997. pap. 5.00 (*0-934830-64-9*) Ten Penny.

Streams 9. Richard A. Spiegel. (Illus.). 150p. (Orig.). (YA). (gr. 7-12). 1995. pap. 5.00 (*0-934830-59-2*) Ten Penny.

Streamside Reflections: 30 Postcards from an Angler's Paradise. (Postcard Bks.). (Illus.). pap. 7.95 (*1-55859-706-9*) Abbeville Pr.

Streamside Trails: Day Hiking Central Arizona's Lakes, Rivers, & Creeks. Steve Krause. 160p. 1994. pap. 8.95 (*0-910973-09-1*) Arrowhead AZ.

***Streans in the Desert: 366 Daily Devotional Readings.** L.B. Cowman. Ed. by James Reimann. 512p. 1997. lib. bdg. 23.99 (*0-310-21737-7*) Zondervan.

Street. Ann Petry. 448p. 1992. pap. 12.00 (*0-395-57380-7*) HM.

Street. Israel Rabon. Tr. by Leonard Wolf. LC 90-14113. 192p. 1990. pap. 9.95 (*0-941423-45-X*) FWEW.

Street! A Two-Act Drama to Be Produced on the Stage or Read. Helen Smith. Ed. by Catherine Snyder. LC 93-81239. (Illus.). 144p. (Orig.). 1993. pap. 17.95 (*0-945437-14-5*) MacDonald-Sward.

Street: An Autobiographical Novel. Aram Saroyan. 100p. 1974. pap. 10.00 (*0-912846-07-0*) Bookstore Pr.

Street Addict Role: A Theory of Heroin Addiction. Richard C. Stephens. LC 90-39205. (SUNY Series, the New Inequalities). 223p. 1991. text ed. 64.50 (*0-7914-0619-9*); pap. text ed. 21.95 (*0-7914-0620-2*) State U NY Pr.

Street Addicts in the Political Economy. Alisse Waterston. 264p. (C). 1993. 34.95 (*0-87722-992-9*) Temple U Pr.

Street & Electric Railways. U. S. Census Office Staff. LC 75-22867. (America in Two Centuries Ser.). 1976. reprint ed. 18.95 (*0-405-07732-7*) Ayer.

Street & Highway Maintenance Manual. Gary Byrd & George Briggs. (Illus.). 698p. 1985. ring bd. 65.00 (*0-917084-33-0*) Am Public Works.

Street & Other Stories. Gerry Adams. LC 93-12328. (Orig.). 1993. 11.95 (*1-879823-02-0*, Natl Bk Netwk); pap. 7.95 (*1-879823-03-9*, Natl Bk Netwk) Sheridan Sq Pr.

***Street & Other Stories.** 2nd ed. Gerry Adams. 160p. (Orig.). 1997. pap. 12.95 (*1-57098-132-9*) R Rinehart.

***Street & Smith's Guide to Baseball.** Street & Smith. 1997. mass mkt. 5.99 (*0-345-40852-7*) Ballantine.

***Street & Smith's Guide to Football.** Street & Smith. 1997. mass mkt. 5.99 (*0-345-40850-0*) Ballantine.

Street & Smith's Guide to Pro Basketball 1996-97. Street & Smith's Magazines Editors. 1996. mass mkt. 6.99 (*0-345-40441-6*) Ballantine.

***Street & Smith's Guide to Pro Basketball 1997-98.** Street & Smith's Magazine Editors. 1997. pap. 6.99 (*0-345-40851-9*) Ballantine.

Street & Smith's Guide to Pro Football, 1994. Street & Smith's Magazines Editors. (Orig.). 1994. mass mkt. 5.99 (*0-345-38618-3*) Ballantine.

Street Art. Donald J. Davenport. (Illus.). 56p. 1989. Trade manual, saddle stitched. 22.50 (*0-9606640-0-9*) Video Educ Art.

Street Art: Punk Poster in San Francisco. Peter Belsito. 128p. 1982. 9.95 (*0-86719-300-X*) Last Gasp.

Street Atlas of Volusia & Flagler Counties. (Illus.). 274p. (Orig.). 1995. pap. 28.95 (*1-882829-03-4*) Map & Globe.

***Street Atlas Oklahoma City, Oklahoma: 1997-1998.** (Illus.). vii, 153p. (Orig.). 1997. mass mkt. 21.95 (*1-886395-01-2*) Mosher-Adams.

***Street Atlas U. S. A.** 1995. 84.95 (*0-89933-953-0*, 00153185, Gale Res Intl) Gale.

Street Ballads. George Barker. 96p. (Orig.). 1992. pap. 8.95 (*0-571-16609-1*) Faber & Faber.

Street Bikes. Jesse Young. (Motorcycles Ser.). 48p. (J). (gr. 3-4). 1994. lib. bdg. 17.80 (*1-56065-227-6*) Capstone Pr.

***Street Bikes.** Jesse Young. (Motorcycles Ser.). (Illus.). 48p. (J). (gr. 3-6). 1995. 18.40 (*0-516-35227-X*) Childrens.

Street Birth. Diana Bickston. (Prison Writing Ser.). 36p. 1982. pap. 2.00 (*0-912678-52-6*, Greenfld Rev Pr) Greenfld Rev Lit.

Street Book: An Encyclopedia of Manhattan's Street Names & Their Origins. Henry Moscow. LC 78-66990. (Illus.). 119p. 1990. pap. 14.95 (*0-8232-1275-0*) Fordham.

Street Called Home. Robinson. 1997. write for info. (*0-15-201465-9*) HarBrace.

Street Cars to Old Orchard Beach: The Biddeford & Saco Railroad & Connecting Lines. O. R. Cummings & Edward D. Leavitt. (Illus.). 64p. (Orig.). 1989. pap. 9.00 (*0-911940-46-4*) Cox.

Street Child. Berlie Doherty. LC 94-5020. 160p. (J). (gr. 3-7). 1994. 15.95 (*0-531-06864-1*); lib. bdg. 16.99 (*0-531-08714-X*) Orchard Bks Watts.

Street Child. Berlie Doherty. 160p. (J). (gr. 5-9). 1996. pap. 4.99 (*0-14-037936-3*, Puffin) Puffin Bks.

Street Children in Global Perspective. large type ed. Hraf. 1996. 15.95 (*0-8161-1637-7*, GK Hall); lib. bdg. 26.95 (*0-8161-1636-9*, GK Hall) Thorndike Pr.

Street Children in India. W. S. Phillips. (C). 1994. 22.50 (*81-7033-188-9*, Pub. by Rawat II) S Asia.

Street Children of Cali. Lewis Aptekar. LC 87-34234. (Illus.). xxi, 272p. 1988. text ed. 44.95 (*0-8223-0834-7*) Duke.

Street Children of India. Rajendra Pandey. (C). 1991. 42.50 (*81-85613-37-0*, Pub. by Chugh Pubns II) S Asia.

Street Cleaner. Annie Kubler. LC 90-25105. (Pride Ser.). (J). 1991. 3.99 (*0-85953-530-4*) Childs Play.

***Street Cleaner.** Annie Kubler. (GRE.). (J). 1991. 3.99 (*0-85953-866-4*); 3.99 (*0-85953-632-7*) Childs Play.

Street Cleaning Practice. 2nd ed. American Public Works Association, Street Sanitation Committee. (American Public Works Association Research Foundation Projects Ser.: No. 105). 440p. reprint ed. pap. 125.40 (*0-317-09892-6*, 2015936) Bks Demand.

Street Cleaning Practice. 3rd ed. American Public Works Association Staff. (Illus.). (C). 1978. text ed. 28.00 (*0-917084-27-6*) Am Public Works.

Street Club Worker. Jack Rudman. (Career Examination Ser.: C-1038). 1994. pap. 27.95 (*0-8373-1038-5*) Nat Learn.

Street Cop: Innovative Tactics for Taking Back the Streets. Donovan Jacobs. (Illus.). 216p. 1993. pap. 20.00 (*0-87364-731-9*) Paladin Pr.

S

Street Corner Boys. Romen Basu. Tr. by Veronica Hauge. 154p. (YA). (gr. 9-10). 1992. 14.95 (0-932377-40-8) Facet Bks.

Street Corner Society: The Social Structure of an Italian Slum. 3rd ed. William F. Whyte. LC 81-10337. 1981. pap. text ed. 9.95 (0-226-89543-2) U Ch Pr.

Street Corner Society: The Social Structure of an Italian Slum. 4th ed. William F. Whyte. LC 92-42262. 418p. 1993. pap. text ed. 14.95 (0-226-89545-9); lib. bdg. 40.00 (0-226-89544-0) U Ch Pr.

Street Corner Theology: Indigenous Reflections on the Reality of God in the African-American Experience. Carlyle F. Stewart. LC 94-60449. 171p. 1995. pap. 9.95 (1-55523-687-1) Winston-Derek.

Street Crime. Ed. by Mike Maguire. (International Library of Criminology, Criminal Justice & Penology). 608p. 1996. text ed. 149.95 (1-85521-416-4, Pub. by Dartmth Pub UK) Ashgate Pub Co.

Street Crime Investigations: A Street Cop's Guide to Solving Felony Crimes. Donovan Jacobs. (Illus.). 192p. 1995. pap. 20.00 (0-87364-818-8) Paladin Pr.

Street Dancer. Keith R. Neely. Ed. by David B. Forman. LC 90-91640. 265p. (Orig.). 1990. pap. 8.95 (0-936174-06-4) Jems Comm.

Street Drugs: A Reference Guide to Controlled Substances. Carl L. Vidano. Ed. by Kenneth M. Goddard. (Illus.). 100p. (Orig.). 1986. pap. text ed. 10.95 (0-9616606-0-0) C L Vidano Pub.

Street Drugs: The Facts Explained, the Myths Exploded. Andrew Tyler. 518p. 1996. pap. 11.95 (0-340-60975-3, Pub. by H & S UK) Trafalgar.

Street E&E: Evading, Escaping, & Other Ways to Save Your Ass When Things Get Ugly. Marc A. MacYoung. (Illus.). 192p. 1993. pap. 16.00 (0-87364-743-2) Paladin Pr.

Street Economics. Rufus Shaw, Jr. 130p. (Orig.). 1984. pap. 10.50 (0-936436-02-6) R S Publishing.

Street Fashion. Miriam Moss. LC 90-48913. (Fashion World Ser.). (Illus.). 32p. (J). (gr. 5-6). 1991. lib. bdg. 13.95 (0-89686-611-4, Crstwood Hse) Silver Burdett Pr.

Street Fight in Tombstone, near the O.K. Corral. Michael M. Hickey. LC 91-37748. (Illus.). 130p. 1991. pap. 21.95 (0-9631772-0-6) Talei Pubs.

*__Street Fighter.__ Red J. Arobateau. (Orig.). 1997. mass mkt. 6.95 (1-56333-583-2, Rosebud) Masquerade.

Street Fighter. Todd Strasser & Steven E. De Souza. (Illus.). 160p. (J). 1994. pap. 4.50 (1-55704-224-1) Newmarket.

Street Fighter: The Graphic Novel. Len Strazewski. 1994. pap. 12.95 (1-56398-049-5) Malibu Comics Ent.

Street Fighter Alpha Warriors' Dreams Unauthorized Game Secrets. Erik Suzuki. 96p. 1996. per., pap. 12.99 (0-7615-0610-1) Prima Pub.

*__Street Fighter II: Cammy.__ Masahiko Nakahira. 1997. pap. text ed. 15.95 (1-56931-212-5, Viz Comics) Viz Commns Inc.

Street Fighter II Turbo Hyper Fighting Strategy Guide. Tien Hung-mao. (Illus.). 164p. (YA). (gr. 7-12). 1995. 9.95 (1-882455-02-9) Gamepro Pub.

Street Fighter Two Turbo Hyper Fighting Strategy Guide. GamePro Magazine Editors. (Illus.). 164p. (YA). (gr. 7-12). 1993. 9.95 (0-685-70290-1) Infotainment.

Street Fighting Tactics From Karate-Do. Michael Rosenbaum. 96p. (Orig.). 1985. pap. 5.95 (0-89826-015-9) Natl Paperback.

Street Fighting Years: An Autobiography of the Sixties. Tariq Ali. (Citadel Underground Ser.). 288p. (Orig.). 1991. pap. 10.95 (0-8065-1282-2, Citadel Pr) Carol Pub Group.

Street Fights. Joe Martori. Ed. by Toby Stein. 1987. 17.95 (0-915643-24-3) Santa Barb Pr.

*__Street Foods: Urban Food & Employment in Developing Countries.__ Irene Tinker. LC 96-23909. (Illus.). 256p. 1997. 35.00 (0-19-510435-8); pap. 24.95 (0-19-511711-5) OUP.

Street French I: How to Speak & Understand French Slang. David Burke. LC 96-4202. 256p. 1996. pap. text ed. 15.95 (0-471-13898-3) Wiley.

Street French 2: The Best of French Idioms. David Burke. LC 96-15950. 256p. 1996. pap. text ed. 15.95 (0-471-13899-1) Wiley.

*__Street French 3: The Best of Naughty French.__ David Burke. LC 97-5827. 1997. pap. text ed. 15.95 (0-471-13900-9) Wiley.

Street Furniture. Henry Aaron. 1989. pap. 25.00 (0-85263-864-7, Pub. by Shire UK) St Mut.

Street Gallery: A Guide to One Thousand Murals of Los Angeles County. Robin J. Dunitz. LC 92-97162. (Illus.). 469p. 1993. pap. 24.95 (0-9632862-1-8) RJD Ent.

*__Street Games.__ Kathryn Dahlstrom. (Good News Club Ser.). Date not set. pap. 4.99 (1-55976-830-4) CEF Press.

Street Games: A Neighborhood. Rosellen Brown. LC 91-13695. (Alive Again Ser.). 188p. 1991. reprint ed. pap. 9.95 (0-915943-68-9) Milkweed Ed.

*__Street Gang Awareness: A Resource Guide for Parents & Professionals.__ Steven L. Sachs. (Illus.). 224p. (Orig.). 1997. pap. 12.95 (1-57749-035-5) Fairview Press.

Street Gangs. Paul Almonte & Theresa Desmond. LC 93-25330. (Update Ser.). (J). 1994. pap. 4.95 (0-382-24758-2, Crstwood Hse) Silver Burdett Pr.

Street Gangs. Daniel A. Carrie. LC 93-86917. (Illus.). 112p. (Orig.). 1993. pap. 5.25 (1-884493-00-9) Pocket Pr.

Street Gangs: Bringing Back the Home Boys. rev. ed. Jim Parker. 1995. pap. 0.50 (0-89230-249-6) Do It Now.

Street Gangs: Current Knowledge & Strategies. Catherine H. Conly. 115p. (Orig.). (C). 1994. pap. text ed. 30.00 (0-7881-0880-8) DIANE Pub.

Street Gangs: Gaining Turf, Losing Ground. LC 91-22204. (Icarus World Issues Ser.: Vol. 3). (Illus.). (YA). (gr. 7-12). 1991. lib. bdg. 16.95 (0-8239-1332-5) Rosen Group.

Street Gangs & the Schools: A Blueprint for Intervention. Kevin W. Riley. LC 91-60198. (Fastback Ser.: No. 321). (Orig.). 1991. pap. 3.00 (0-87367-321-2) Phi Delta Kappa.

Street Gangs in America. Sandra Gardner. LC 92-16618. (Illus.). 112p. (YA). (gr. 9-12). 1992. lib. bdg. 22.70 (0-531-11037-0) Watts.

Street Genealogy Begun by H. A. Street. M. A. Street. (Illus.). 551p. 1989. reprint ed. pap. 82.50 (0-8328-1141-6); reprint ed. lib. bdg. 90.50 (0-8328-1140-8) Higginson Bk Co.

Street German: The Best of German Idioms, No. 1. David Burke. Ed. by Robert Graul. (Illus.). 320p. (Orig.). 1996. pap. 16.95 (1-879440-21-0) Optima CA.

Street Girl. Muriel Cerf. Tr. by Dominic Di Bernardi from FRE. LC 88-23694. 200p. 1988. 19.95 (0-916583-33-3) Dalkey Arch.

Street Graphics. William Ewald & Daniel R. Mandelker. 175p. 1977. reprint ed. 15.00 (0-318-14686-X, Landscape Architecture); reprint ed. 10.50 (0-318-14687-8, Landscape Architecture) Am Landscape Arch.

Street Graphics & the Law. 3rd ed. Daniel R. Mandelker & William R. Ewald, Jr. LC 87-71118. (Illus.). 207p. 1988. pap. 35.95 (0-918286-50-6) Planners Pr.

Street Guide to Seattle Area Restaurants. Ed. by D. Craig Erken. 1985. 9.95 (0-938047-00-0) Cedar River Pub.

*__Street Hydraulics & Inlet Sizing, Using the Computer Model UDINLET.__ James C. Guo. LC 96-60664. 102p. 1997. pap. 85.00 (1-887201-00-9) WRP.

Street in Marrakech: A Personal View of Urban Women in Morocco. Elizabeth W. Fernea. (Illus.). 382p. (C). 1988. reprint ed. pap. text ed. 13.95 (0-88133-404-9) Waveland Pr.

Street, Interurban & Rapid Transit Railways of the United States: A Selective Historical Bibliography. Thomas R. Bullard. (Illus.). 96p. (Orig.). 1984. pap. 11.00 (0-911940-38-3) Cox.

Street Is Not a Home: Solving America's Homeless Dilemma. Robert C. Coates. (Illus.). 356p. (Orig.). (C). 1990. pap. 18.95 (0-87975-621-7) Prometheus Bks.

*__Street Jewellery.__ Christopher Baglee & Andrew Morley. (Illus.). 104p. 1996. 35.00 (0-904568-16-4, Pub. by New Cavendish UK) Pincushion Pr.

Street Jewellery: A History of Enamel Advertising Signs. Christopher Baglee & Andrew Morley. (Illus.). 104p. 1996. pap. 35.00 (0-904568-21-0, Pub. by New Cavendish UK) Pincushion Pr.

Street Journal: Finding God in the Homeless. Gary N. Smith. 160p. (Orig.). 1993. pap. 10.95 (1-55612-656-5) Sheed & Ward MO.

Street Kids: The Tragedy of Canada's Runaways. Marlene Webber. 265p. 1991. 45.00 (0-8020-5789-6); pap. 17.95 (0-8020-6705-0) U of Toronto Pr.

Street Kids & Other Plays. Brio Burgess. Ed. by Daryl F. Mallett. LC 94-47230. 168p. 1995. pap. 21.00 (0-913960-27-6); lib. bdg. 31.00 (0-913960-26-8) Borgo Pr.

Street Kids, Street Drugs, Street Crime: An Examination of Drug Use & Serious Delinquency in Miami. James A. Inciardi et al. LC 92-5753. 234p. (C). 1993. pap. 20.95 (0-534-19242-4) Wadsworth Pub.

Street Law: A Course in Practical Law. 2nd ed. Lee P. Arbetman et al. 365p. 1980. pap. text ed. 41.75 (0-8299-1031-X) West Pub.

Street Law: A Course in Practical Law. 3rd ed. Edward T. McMahon et al. LC 85-26560. (Illus.). 446p. 1986. pap. text ed. 41.75 (0-314-89283-4) West Pub.

Street Law: A Course in Practical Law. 4th ed. Lee P. Arbetman et al. 1990. text ed. 46.50 (0-314-68198-1) West Pub.

Street Law - Allemansreg, Bk. 1: Introduction to South African Law & the Legal System. D. J. McQuoid-Mason et al. (Human Rights for All Ser.). 70p. 1987. student ed., pap. write for info. (0-7021-2461-3, Pub. by Juta SA) Gaunt.

Street Law - Allemansreg, Bk. 1: Introduction to South African Law & the Legal System. D. J. McQuoid-Mason et al. (Human Rights for All Ser.). 93p. 1990. teacher ed., pap. write for info. (0-7021-2462-1, Pub. by Juta SA) Gaunt.

Street Law, Natural Law & Constitution. Date not set. teacher ed., pap. text ed. 13.95 (0-314-67870-0) West Pub.

*__Street-League.__ Peter Regan. (Riverside Ser.). 112p. Date not set. pap. 6.95 (0-947962-46-8) Dufour.

Street Legal: The Betrayal. William Deverell. 356p. 1996. 22.95 (0-7710-2669-2) McCland & Stewart.

Street Lethal: Unarmed Urban Combat. Sammy Franco. (Illus.). 192p. 1989. pap. 15.95 (0-87364-517-0) Paladin Pr.

Street Level. Patrick Carey. 1989. boxed 10.00 (0-685-29147-2) Cottage Wordsmiths.

Street-Level Bureaucracy: Dilemmas of the Individual in Public Services. Michael Lipsky. LC 79-7350. 275p. 1983. pap. 12.95 (0-87154-526-8) Russell Sage.

Street-Level Drug Enforcement: Examining the Issues. Mark A. Kleiman et al. Ed. by Marcia R. Chaiken. (Illus.). 55p. (Orig.). (C). 1993. pap. text ed. 20.00 (0-7881-0013-0) DIANE Pub.

Street Life in London. Adolphe Smith & John Thompson. LC 68-28169. (Illus.). 1972. reprint ed. 23.95 (0-405-08982-1) Ayer.

Street Life in London see Victorian London Street Life in Historic Photographs

Street Light Inspections Foreman. Jack Rudman. (Career Examination Ser.: C-2961). 1994. pap. 29.95 (0-8373-2961-2) Nat Learn.

Street Lighting Installation Worker. Jack Rudman. (Career Examination Ser.: C-3108). 1994. pap. 27.95 (0-8373-3108-0) Nat Learn.

Street Lighting Manual. 2nd ed. 186p. 1969. 7.50 (0-317-34111-1, 046832) Edison Electric.

Street Lives: An Oral History of Homeless Americans. Ed. by Steven Vander Staay. (Illus.). 224p. (Orig.). 1992. pap. 14.95 (0-86571-237-9); lib. bdg. 39.95 (0-86571-236-0) New Soc Pubs.

*__Street Luge Racing.__ Pat Ryan. LC 97-11338. (Extreme Sports Ser.). (J). 1998. write for info. (1-56065-538-0) Capstone Pr.

Street Markets of London. Laszlo Moholy-Nagy. LC 72-84542. (Illus.). 1972. reprint ed. 19.95 (0-405-08792-6, Pub. by Blom Pubns UK) Ayer.

Street Mathematics & School Mathematics. Terezhina Nunes et al. LC 92-23183. (Learning in Doing: Social, Cognitive & Computational Perspectives Ser.). (Illus.). 160p. (C). 1993. text ed. 54.95 (0-521-38116-9); pap. text ed. 16.95 (0-521-38813-9) Cambridge U Pr.

Street Mime. James W. Gousseff. 1993. pap. 9.95 (0-87129-175-4, S55) Dramatic Pub.

Street Music: City Poems. Arnold Adoff. LC 92-28539. (Illus.). 32p. (J). (gr. k-4). 1995. 16.00 (0-06-021522-4); lib. bdg. 15.89 (0-06-021523-2) HarpC Child Bks.

Street Ninja: Ancient Secrets for Today's Mean Streets. Dirk Skinner. LC 94-44560. 272p. 1995. pap. 16.00 (1-56980-029-4) Barricade Bks.

Street Noises: Studies in Parisian Pleasure, 1900-1940. Adrian Rifkin. LC 92-29425. (Illus.). 272p. (C). 1993. text ed. 49.95 (0-7190-3835-9, Pub. by Manchester Univ Pr UK) St Martin.

Street Noises: Studies in Parisian Pleasure, 1900-1940. Adrian Rifkin. (Illus.). 272p. 1995. text ed. 22.50 (0-7190-4589-4, Pub. by Manchester Univ Pr UK) St Martin.

Street of a Thousand Delights. Jay Gelzer. LC 75-167449. (Short Story Index Reprint Ser.). 1977. reprint ed. 20.95 (0-8369-3975-1) Ayer.

Street of Ankh Morpork. Terry Pratchett. 16p. 1994. pap. 10.95 (0-552-14161-5) Bantam.

Street of Crocodiles. Bruno Schulz. (Writers from the Other Europe Ser.). 1977. mass mkt. 6.95 (0-14-004227-X, Penguin Bks) Viking Penguin.

Street of Crocodiles. Bruno Schulz. Tr. by Celina Wieniewski. 160p. 1992. pap. 11.95 (0-14-018625-5, Penguin Classics) Viking Penguin.

Street of Dreams: The Nature & Legacy of the 1960s. Douglas M. Knight. LC 88-36420. xv, 213p. 1989. text ed. 25.95 (0-8223-0902-5) Duke.

Street of Ho's. Leo Guild. 224p. (Orig.). 1986. mass mkt. 2.50 (0-87067-285-1, BH285) Holloway.

Street of Knives. Rick Kearns. 49p. (Orig.). 1993. pap. 9.00 (1-879294-03-6) Warm Spring Pr.

Street of Lost Brothers. Arnost Lustig. 207p. (Orig.). 1990. 39.95 (0-8101-0959-X); pap. 13.95 (0-8101-0960-3) Northwestern U Pr.

Street of Mansions, No. 12. Dick Ferry. Ed. by Kerr Spooner. 23p. 1983. pap. 3.00 (0-932884-11-3) Red Herring.

Street of No Return. David Goodis. LC 90-50597. 176p. 1991. pap. 8.00 (0-679-73473-2, Vin) Random.

Street of Queer Houses & Other Tales. Douglas A. Menville. LC 75-46285. (Supernatural & Occult Fiction Ser.). 1976. reprint ed. lib. bdg. 20.95 (0-405-08146-4) Ayer.

*__Street of Riches.__ Roy Gabrielle. 1996. pap. text ed. 6.95 (0-7710-9878-2) McCland & Stewart.

Street of Riches. Gabrielle Roy. Tr. by Harry Binsse. LC 93-8661. viii, 247p. 1993. pap. 8.95 (0-8032-8947-2, Bison Books) U of Nebr Pr.

Street of the City. Grace L. Hill. 21.95 (0-8488-0082-6) Amereon Ltd.

Street of the City. Grace L. Hill. (Grace Livingston Hill Ser.: Vol. 47). 1995. mass mkt., pap. 4.99 (0-8423-5940-0) Tyndale.

Street of the Dead. large type ed. Lee F. Gregson. (Dales Large Print Ser.). 203p. 1996. pap. 17.99 (1-85389-618-7, Dales) Ulverscroft.

Street of the Eye, & Nine Other Tales. Gerald W. Bullett. LC 77-167444. (Short Story Index Reprint Ser.). 1977. reprint ed. 20.95 (0-8369-3970-0) Ayer.

Street of the Five Moons. Elizabeth Peters. 256p. 1990. mass mkt. 5.99 (0-8125-1244-8) Tor Bks.

Street on Torts. 9th ed. Margaret Brazier. 632p. 1993. pap. 52.00 (0-406-00591-5, U.K.) MICHIE.

Street People Speak. Ruth Morris & Colleen Heffren. (Illus.). 96p. 1995. lib. bdg. 29.00 (0-8095-4931-X) Borgo Pr.

Street People Speak. Ruth Morris & Colleen Heffren. (Illus.). 96p. pap. 9.95 (0-88962-364-3) Mosaic.

Street Photographs: Manchester & Salford. Shirley Baker. (Illus.). 1989. pap. 21.00 (1-85224-058-X, Pub. by Bloodaxe Bks UK) Dufour.

*__Street Pizza.__ D. B. Petit. Ed. by Carolyn S. Zagury. LC 96-60787. 288p. (Orig.). 1996. pap. 14.95 (1-880254-38-7) Vista.

Street Players. Donald Goines. (Orig.). 1996. mass mkt. 4.95 (0-87067-960-0, BH960-0) Holloway.

*__Street Politics: Poor People's Movements in Iran.__ Assef Bayat. LC 97-18986. 1997. write for info. (0-231-10858-3); pap. write for info. (0-231-10859-1) Col U Pr.

Street Preachers, Faith Healers & Herb Doctors in Jamaica, 1890-1925. W. F. Elkins. (Caribbean Studies Ser.). 1976. lib. bdg. 250.00 (0-87700-241-X) Revisionist Pr.

Street Railway & the Growth of Los Angeles. Robert C. Post. LC 89-23777. (Illus.). 188p. 1989. 48.95 (0-87095-104-1) Gldn West Bks.

Street Railways of Birmingham. Alvin W. Hudson & Harold E. Cox. (Illus.). 216p. (Orig.). 1976. pap. 18.00 (0-911940-25-1) Cox.

Street Railways of Harrisburg. Richard H. Steinmetz & Harold E. Cox. (Illus.). 96p. (Orig.). 1988. pap. 13.00 (0-911940-44-8) Cox.

Street Railways of Louisiana. Louis G. Hennick & E. Harper Charlton. LC 76-30481. (Illus.). 143p. 1979. 25.00 (0-88289-065-4) Pelican.

Street Railways of St. Petersburg, Florida. James Buckley. (Illus.). 48p. (Orig.). 1983. pap. 8.00 (0-911940-37-5) Cox.

Street Railways of Trenton. Barker Gummere. (Illus.). 88p. (Orig.). 1986. pap. 11.00 (0-911940-42-1) Cox.

Street Rhymes Around the World. Ed. by Jane Yolen. LC 91-66058. (Illus.). 40p. (J). (ps-5). 1992. 16.95 (1-878093-53-3, Wordsong) Boyds Mills Pr.

Street Rod Building Skills. John Thawley. (Illus.). 96p. (Orig.). 1980. pap. text ed. 11.95 (0-936834-32-3) S S Autosports.

Street Samurai. Julia Vinograd. (Illus.). 60p. (Orig.). 1989. pap. 4.95 (0-929730-10-0) Zeitgeist Pr.

Street Samurai Catalog: A Shadowrun Sourcebook. FASA Staff. (Shadowrun Ser.). (Illus.). 128p. 1990. pap. 12.00 (1-55560-122-7, 7104) FASA Corp.

Street Scenarios for the EMT & Paramedic. Brent Braunworth & Albert L. Howe. Ed. by Laurence W. Schlanger. LC 93-14345. 256p. 1993. pap. 24.25 (0-89303-976-4) P-H.

Street Scene. (Vocal Score Ser.). 280p. 1981. pap. 40.00 (0-88188-052-3, 00312405) H Leonard.

Street Scenes: Afro-American Culture in Urban Trinidad. Michael Lieber. 120p. 1981. pap. 11.95 (0-87073-874-7) Schenkman Bks Inc.

Street Scenes: Leonard Bramer's Drawings of 17th-Century Dutch Daily Life. Donna R. Barnes. (Illus.). 80p. 1991. pap. 14.95 (0-8122-1368-8) U of Pa Pr.

Street Self-Defense. Don Sewalson. (Martial Arts Ser.: Vol. 1). (Illus.). 81p. (YA). (gr. 6-12). 1986. pap. 6.75 (0-938419-01-3) DM Pub.

Street Self-Defense. Don Sewalson. (Martial Arts Ser.: Vol. 2). (Illus.). 58p. (YA). (gr. 6-12). 1986. pap. 6.75 (0-938419-02-1) DM Pub.

Street Self-Defense. Don Sewalson. (Martial Arts Ser.: Vol. 3). (Illus.). 63p. (YA). (gr. 6-12). 1986. pap. 6.75 (0-938419-03-X) DM Pub.

Street Self-Defense: Complete Edition. Don Sewalson. (Martial Arts Ser.). (Illus.). 193p. (YA). (gr. 6-12). 1986. 27.00 (0-938419-04-8); pap. 16.95 (0-938419-00-5) DM Pub.

Street Sense for Parents. Louis R. Mizell, Jr. 176p. (Orig.). 1995. mass mkt. 4.99 (0-425-14947-1, Berkley Trade) Berkley Pub.

*__Street Sense for Seniors.__ 1994. 4.99 (0-425-14378-3) Berkley Pub.

Street Sense for Seniors. Louis R. Mizell, Jr. 224p. 1994. mass mkt. 4.99 (0-425-14364-3, Berkley Trade) Berkley Pub.

Street Sense for Students. Louis R. Mizell. 1996. mass mkt. 4.99 (0-425-14986-2) Berkley Pub.

*__Street Sense for Students.__ Louis R. Mizell, Jr. 1996. 4.99 (0-425-15535-8) Berkley Pub.

Street Sense for Women. Louis R. Mizell, Jr. 160p. (Orig.). 1993. mass mkt. 4.99 (0-425-13971-9, Berkley Trade) Berkley Pub.

*__Street Sense Parent.__ Louis R. Mizell, Jr. 1995. pap. 4.99 (0-425-14950-1) Berkley Pub.

Street Shadows: Best of Year One. Kyle Garrett et al. (Illus.). 128p. 1995. 12.95 (0-941613-68-2) Stabur Pr.

Street Sharks: Genetic Meltdown. Cynthia Alvarez. 1995. pap. 5.99 (0-679-87713-4) Fodors Travel.

Street Sharks: Moby Lick's Revenge. Illus. by Miro Sinovcic. (Street Sharks Storybooks Ser.). (J). (ps-2). 1996. pap. 4.99 (0-614-15727-7) Random.

Street Sharks: Mutant Mania! Cynthia Alvarez. (Street Sharks Storybooks Ser.). (J). (ps-2). 1996. pap. 4.99 (0-614-15725-0) Random.

Street Signs: An Identification Guide of Symbols of Crime & Violence. Mark S. Dunston. LC 91-66378. (Illus.). 256p. (Orig.). 1992. pap. 14.95 (1-879411-13-X); vhs 29.95 (1-879411-14-8) Perf Dimensions Pub.

Street Smart! Cities in Ancient Times. Geography Department. LC 94-632. (Buried Worlds Ser.). (YA). (gr. 6 up). 1994. lib. bdg. 22.95 (0-8225-3208-5, Lerner Publctns) Lerner Group.

Street Smart: Home, Business Resource Guide. Fordson Wilder. 1995. 39.95 (0-615-00909-3) Lifecraft.

Street Smart Business Resource Guide - The Entrepreneur's Inside Edge: Property Seller's Guide. Fordson Wilder. 1996. 29.95 (0-911505-29-6) Lifecraft.

Street Smart Design. Ed. by Diana Martin & Lynn Haller. LC 95-53170. (Illus.). 144p. 1996. 29.99 (0-89134-686-4, North Lght Bks) F & W Pubns Inc.

Street Smart Estate Planning: A Complete Family Guide to Understanding Living Trusts, Probate, & How to Reduce or Eliminate Estate Taxes. Vincent DiLeo. Ed. by Paula Church. (Illus.). 120p. (Orig.). 1993. pap. 19.95 (1-880037-49-1) Info Plus CA.

Street Smart Guide to Blue Collar Secrets for Finding & Getting a Good Job. Bobby Bodega. (Illus.). 150p. (Orig.). 1992. pap. 11.95 (0-9632079-0-3) Cisco Pr.

Street Smart Gun Book. John Farnum. 1986. pap. 11.95 (0-936279-06-0) Police Bkshelf.

*__Street-Smart Network Marketing.__ Robert Butwin. 288p. 1997. per. 14.00 (0-7615-1000-1) Prima Pub.

Street Smart Public Relations: A Top Pro Tells How to Get Things Done. John F. Budd, Jr. 218p. 1992. pap. 19.95 (0-9633947-0-3) Turtle Pub.

Street Smart Real Estate Investing: Allen Cymrot's Strategies for Increasing Your Net Worth. Allen Cymrot. (Illus.). 288p. 1993. reprint ed. 21.95 (0-9633472-2-5); reprint ed. pap. 19.95 (0-9633472-1-7) C R Pub.

An Asterisk (*) at the beginning of an entry indicates that the title is appearing in BIP for the first time.

Street Smart Salesman: Making Opportunities Happen. Arthur Rogen. LC 91-19025. (Illus.). 224p. (Orig.). pap. 9.95 (0-89529-487-7) Avery Pub.

Street-Smart Survival: A Nineties Guide to Staying Alive & Living Well. Victor Santoro. 168p. 1991. pap. 15.00 (0-87364-641-X) Paladin Pr.

Street-Smart Ways to Generate Income. Arthur A. Hawkins, II. 28p. 1992. pap. 7.99 (1-881297-23-3); pap. text ed. 7.99 (1-881297-24-1) Info Res Lab.

Street Smarts. Devorah Major. 64p. (Orig.). 1996. pap. 10.95 (1-880684-27-6) Curbstone.

***Street Smarts: A Personal Safety Guide for Women.** Louise Rafkin. pap. write for info. (0-06-251383-4) HarpC.

Street Smarts: A Personal Safety Guide for Women. Louise Rafkin. 144p. 1996. mass mkt. 5.99 (0-06-101134-7, Harp PBks) HarpC.

Street Smarts: Activities That Help Teenagers Take Care of Themselves. Michael Kirby. LC 95-11212. 128p. 1995. teacher ed., pap. 29.95 (0-89390-331-0) Resource Pubns.

***Street Smarts: High Probability Short Term Trading Strategies.** Laurence A. Connors & Linda B. Raschke. (Illus.). 240p. 1996. 175.00 (0-9650461-0-9) M Gordon Pubng.

***Street Smarts: Linking Professional Conduct with Shareholder Value in the Securities Industry.** Roy C. Smith & Ingo Walter. LC 96-48383. 352p. 1997. 27.50 (0-87584-653-X) Harvard Busn.

***Street Smarts: Linking Professional Conduct with Shareholder Value in the Securities Industry.** Roy C. Smith & Ingo Walter. 1997. text ed. 27.50 (0-07-103881-7) McGraw.

Street Smarts: New Ideas for Small Companies. William H. Franklin. 239p. 1990. 34.95 (0-88406-212-0) GA St U Busn Pr.

Street Smarts: Real Life Lessons from a Successful Entrepreneur. John Fernandez. 80p. (Orig.). 1994. pap. 14.95 (1-879260-30-1) Evanston Pub.

Street Smarts! The Rewards of a Good Education. Peter Enns. (Illus.). 40p. (Orig.). (J). (ps-6). 1992. pap. 5.98 incl. audio (0-943593-75-1) Kids Intl Inc.

Street Smarts & Critical Theory: Listening to the Vernacular. Thomas A. McLaughlin. LC 96-15117. (Wisconsin Project on American Writers Ser.). 190p. 1996. 45.00 (0-299-15170-0) U of Wis Pr.

Street Smarts & Critical Theory: Listening to the Vernacular. Thomas A. McLaughlin. LC 96-15117. (Wisconsin Project on American Writers Ser.). 190p. (Orig.). 1996. pap. 17.95 (0-299-15174-3) U of Wis Pr.

Street Smarts for Business Reengineers. Dorine C. Andrews. 320p. 1994. 33.00 (0-13-014853-9) P-H.

***Street Smarts for the New Millennium.** Jack Luger. LC 96-77088. (Orig.). 1996. pap. 15.00 (1-55950-149-9, 19197) Loompanics.

***Street Smarts in Corporate Corridors: A Survival & Success Manual for Employees, Middle Managers, & Professionals.** Ernie Stech. 145p. (Orig.). 1997. pap. 7.95 (0-614-29618-8) Chief Mtn Pub.

***Street Soldier.** E. Joseph. 1997. mass mkt. 12.95 (0-385-31706-9) Doubleday.

Street Soldier: One Man's Struggle to Save a Generation - One Life at a Time. Joseph Marshall, Jr. & Lonnie Wheeler. 336p. 1996. 22.95 (0-385-31430-2) Delacorte.

Street Song Brass Quintet. 16.95 (0-7935-4597-8, 50482404) H Leonard.

Street Spanish: How to Speak & Understand Spanish Slang. David Burke. LC 90-43297. 242p. 1991. pap. text ed. 15.95 (0-471-52846-3) Wiley.

***Street Spanish 1: The Best of Spanish Slang.** David Burke. LC 97-21377. 256p. (SPA.). 1997. pap. 15.95 (0-471-17970-1) Wiley.

Street Steel: Choosing & Carrying Self-Defense Knives. Michael Janich. (Illus.). 112p. 1996. pap. 23.00 (0-87364-886-2) Paladin Pr.

Street Stock Chassis Technology. Steve Smith. (Illus.). 160p. (Orig.). 1994. pap. text ed. 16.95 (0-936834-92-7) S S Autosports.

Street Stoppers: The Latest Handgun Stopping Power Street Results. Evan P. Marshall & Edwin J. Sanow. 392p. 1996. pap. 39.95 (0-87364-872-2) Paladin Pr.

Street Supercharging. Pat Ganahl. (Illus.). 128p. 1984. 18.95 (0-931472-17-2) Motorbooks Intl.

Street Surface Railway Franchises of New York City. Harry J. Carman. LC 76-77998. (Columbia University. Studies in the Social Sciences: No. 200). reprint ed. 37.50 (0-404-51200-3) AMS Pr.

Street Survival: Tactics for Armed Encounters. Ronald J. Adams et al. LC 79-57196. (Illus.). 416p. 1980. text ed. 31.95 (0-935878-00-9) Calibre Pr.

Street Talk. Ann Turner. (J). (gr. 4-7). 1992. pap. 3.95 (0-395-61625-5) HM.

Street Talk: Character Monologues for Actors. Glenn Alterman. (Monologue Audition Ser.). 112p. 1991. pap. 8.95 (0-9622722-5-6) Smith & Kraus.

Street Talk: Notes from a Rescuer. Thom Dick. Ed. by Valla Howell & Gary R. Williams. LC 88-80335. (Illus.). 192p. 1988. text ed. 15.95 (0-936174-05-6) Jems Comm.

Street Talk in Real Estate. Bill W. West & Richard L. Dickinson. LC 86-50605. (Illus.). 217p. (Orig.). 1987. pap. 9.95 (0-934189-01-3); pap. text ed. 9.95 (0-934189-04-8) Unique Pub CA.

Street Talk 1: How to Speak & Understand American Slang. David Burke. LC 92-149368. (Illus.). 256p. 1992. pap. 16.95 (1-879440-00-8) Optima CA.

Street Talk 2: Slang Used in Popular American Television Shows (plus slang used by teens, rappers & surfers) David Burke. LC 92-81410. (Illus.). 286p. (Orig.). (C). 1992. pap. 14.95 (1-879440-06-7) Optima CA.

Street Talk 3: The Best of American Idioms. David Burke. (Illus.). 336p. (C). 1994. pap. 16.95 (1-879440-12-1) Optima CA.

Street Theater: The Side Splitting Comedy about the Night Gay History Exploded. Doric Wilson. LC 82-7760. (Gay Play Script Ser.). (Illus.). 151p. (Orig.). 1983. 7.95 (0-935672-07-9) T n T Class.

Street Theatre & Other Outdoor Performance. Bim Mason. LC 91-43615. (Illus.). 176p. (C). (gr. 13). 1992. pap. 18.95 (0-415-07050-3, A7103); text ed. 65.00 (0-415-07049-X, A7099) Routledge.

Street Tree Factsheets. rev. ed. Ed. by Henry D. Gerhold et al. LC 93-72203. (AGRS Ser.: No. 56). (Illus.). 394p. 1993. 20.00 (1-883956-00-5) PSU Coll Agricult.

Street Trees: A Manual for Municipalities. Richard D. Schein. LC 93-93844. (Illus.). 428p. (Orig.). 1993. pap. text ed. 44.50 (0-9636359-0-5) TreeWorks.

Street Trees of Egypt. rev. ed. Loufty Boulos et al. (Illus.). 138p. 1989. pap. 15.00 (977-424-173-8, Pub. by Am Univ Cairo Pr UA) Col U Pr.

***Street Trends: How Today's Alternative Youth Cultures Are Creating Tomorrow's Mainstream.** Janine L. Misdom. 1997. 25.00 (0-88730-875-9) Harper Busn.

Street Vending in Washington, D. C. Vol. O3: Reassessing the Regulation of a Public Nuisance. Roberta M. Spalter-Roth & Eileen Zeitz. 1985. 4.00 (1-888028-16-5) GWU Ctr WAS.

Street Violence in the Nineteenth Century. Rob Sindall. 176p. 1993. pap. 17.95 (0-7185-1490-4) St Martin.

Street Violence in the Nineteenth Century: Media Panic or Real Danger? Robin Sindall. (Illus.). 208p. 1990: text ed. 45.00 (0-7185-1345-2) St Martin.

Street Wars. Joseph Nazel. 224p. (Orig.). 1987. mass mkt. 2.50 (0-87067-284-3) Holloway.

Street Weapons: An Identification Manual for Improvised, Unconventional, Unusual, Homemade, Disguised & Exotic Personal Weapons. Edward J. Nowicki & Dennis A. Ramsey. LC 90-92207. (Illus.). 272p. (Orig.). 1991. pap. 19.95 (1-879411-11-3) Perf Dimensions Pub.

Street Where I Live. Alan J. Lerner. (Illus.). 333p. 1994. reprint ed. pap. 13.95 (0-306-80602-9) Da Capo.

Street Where the Heart Lies. Illus. by Ludwig Bemelmans. 240p. 1995. 24.95 (0-87008-143-8) JAS Heineman.

Street Where Your Heart Lies. Ludwig Bemelmans. (Illus.). 1993. write for info. (0-318-69578-2) JAS Heineman.

Street Wise: A Colorful Look at the Avenues in Syracuse. rev. ed. Jack Carpenter. (Illus.). 70p. 1996. 7.95 (0-9648622-1-2) Pine Grve Pr.

Street-Wise Drug Prevention: A Realistic Approach to Prevent & Intervene in Adolescent Drug Use. Guillermo D. Jalil. (Illus.). 132p. (Orig.). 1995. pap. 19.95 (0-9649533-5-8) No More Drugs.

Street Without Joy. Bernard Fall. (Illus.). 416p. 1994. 22.95 (0-8117-1700-3) Stackpole.

Street Woman. Eleanor M. Miller. (Women in the Political Economy Ser.). 216p. 1987. pap. 16.95 (0-87722-509-5) Temple U Pr.

Street Zen: The Life & Work of Issan Dorsey. David I. Schneider. LC 93-22186. (Illus.). 208p. (Orig.). 1993. pap. 13.00 (0-87773-914-5) Shambhala Pubns.

***Streetbird.** Janwillem Van de Wetering. LC 96-37388. (Soho Crime Ser.). 1997. pap. 12.00 (1-56947-093-6) Soho Press.

Streetcar Named Desire. Tennessee Williams. LC 48-5556. 1980. pap. 8.95 (0-8112-0765-X, NDP501) New Directions.

Streetcar Named Desire. Tennessee Williams. 1986. mass mkt. 4.99 (0-451-16778-3) NAL-Dutton.

Streetcar Named Desire. Tennessee Williams. 1952. pap. 5.25 (0-8222-1089-4) Dramatists Play.

Streetcar Named Desire. Tennessee Williams. 1995. reprint ed. lib. bdg. 21.95 (1-56849-639-7) Buccaneer Bks.

Streetcar Named Desire: A Screen Adaptation Directed by Elia Kazan. Tennessee Williams. Ed. by George P. Garrett et al. LC 71-135273. (Film Scripts Ser.). 1989. pap. text ed. 19.95 (0-89197-954-9) Irvington.

Streetcar Named Desire see Best American Plays: Third Series, 1945-51

Streetcar Suburbs: The Process of Growth in Boston, 1870-1900. 2nd ed. Sam B. Warner, Jr. LC 62-17228. (Joint Center for Urban Studies). (Illus.). 229p. 1962. 24.00 (0-674-84210-3) HUP.

Streetcar Suburbs: The Process of Growth in Boston, 1870-1900. 2nd ed. Sam B. Warner, Jr. LC 62-17228. (Joint Center for Urban Studies). (Illus.). 229p. 1978. pap. 13.95 (0-674-84211-1) HUP.

Streetcar to Subduction & Other Plate Tectonic Trips by Public Transport in San Francisco. Clyde Wahrhafting. (Illus.). 80p. 1984. 13.60 (0-87590-225-1) Am Geophysical.

Streetcars & Interurbans of Old Sandusky. Glenn D. Everett. LC 88-72364. (Illus.). 100p. (Orig.). 1988. pap. 12.95 (0-914960-80-6) Academy Bks.

Streetcleaner: The Yorkshire Ripper Case on Trial. Nicole Ward-Jouve. (Illus.). 224p. 1988. 19.95 (0-7145-2847-1); pap. 12.00 (0-7145-2884-6) M Boyars Pubs.

***Streetcorner Strategy for Winning Local Markets.** Sarah E. Hutchinson & Stacey Sawyer. 1996. text ed. 24.95 (0-07-413227-X) Irwin.

Streetcorner Strategy for Winning Local Markets: Right Sales, Right Service, Right Customers. Robert E. Hall. 1994. 24.95 (0-9639485-0-4) Perf Press.

Streeter. Scott I. Barry. 288p. (Orig.). 1994. mass mkt. 4.99 (0-8125-0000-8) Tor Bks.

Streetfighter Marketing. Jeff Slutsky. 244p. 24.95 (0-02-929231-X, Free Press) Free Pr.

Streetfighting: An Official Cyberpunk 2020 Adventure Anthology. Andrew Borelli et al. (Cyberpunk Ser.). 64p. 1993. pap. 10.00 (1-887801-36-7, Atlas Games) Trident MN.

Streetlamps & Distant Stars: A Collection of Poems (1986-89) Richard Panchyk. 36p. (Orig.). 1989. pap. 2.25 (0-9622473-0-8) No Ink.

Streetlethal. Steven Barnes. 320p. 1991. mass mkt. 4.99 (0-8125-1034-8) Tor Bks.

***Streetlife.** Karl Francis. 86p. 1996. pap. 12.95 (0-9521558-4-2) Dufour.

Streetlights: Illuminating Tales of the Urban Black Experience. John A. Williams. LC 94-24868. 512p. (Orig.). 1996. pap. 14.95 (0-14-017471-0, Penguin Bks) Viking Penguin.

Streetmedic's Handbook. Owen T. Traynor et al. LC 95-13932. (Illus.). 503p. (C). 1995. pap. text ed. 19.95 (0-8036-0012-7) Davis Co.

Streets: A Memoir of the Lower East Side. Bella Spewack. LC 95-13874. (Helen Rose Schever Jewish Women Ser.). (Illus.). 180p. 1995. 19.95 (1-55861-115-0) Feminist Pr.

Streets: A Memoir of the Lower East Side. Bella Spewack. LC 95-13874. (Helen Rose Scheuer Jewish Women's Ser.). (Illus.). 195p. 1996. reprint ed. pap. 10.95 (1-55861-153-3) Feminist Pr.

Streets: Critical Perspectives on Public Space. Ed. by Zeynep Celik et al. LC 93-42658. 1994. 40.00 (0-520-08550-7) U CA Pr.

Streets: Critical Perspectives on Public Space. Ed. by Zeynep Celik et al. (Illus.). 300p. 1996. pap. 19.95 (0-520-20528-6) U CA Pr.

Streets after Rain. Elizabeth Knies. LC 80-66181. 64p. 1980. pap. 3.95 (0-914086-31-6) Alicejamesbooks.

Streets & Alleys: Stories with a Chicago Accent. Syd Lieberman. (American Storytelling Ser.). 1995. 19.95 (0-87483-424-4) August Hse.

Streets & Seasons. Tom Neale. 16p. 1981. pap. 2.00 (0-941160-00-9) Ghost Pony Pr.

***Streets & Squares, Vol. 1.** Arco Editorial Staff. (Urban Spaces Ser.). 1997. 80.00 (84-8185-005-5) Watsn-Guptill.

Streets & the Shaping of Towns & Cities. Michael Southworth & Eran Ben-Joseph. LC 96-14939. (Illus.). 256p. 1996. text ed. 39.95 (0-07-059808-8) McGraw.

Streets Are Free. Kurusa. (Illus.). 50p. (J). (gr. k-5). 1995. per., pap. 7.95 (1-55037-370-6, Pub. by Annick CN) Firefly Bks Ltd.

Streets Are Paved with Gold. Fran Weissenberg. LC 89-24413. (Illus.). 160p. (Orig.). (YA). (gr. 5 up). 1990. pap. 6.95 (0-943173-51-5, Harbinger CO) R Rinehart.

Street's Cruising Guide to the Eastern Caribbean: Anguilla to Dominica. rev. ed. Donald M. Street, Jr. (Illus.). 192p. 1994. 39.95 (0-393-03525-5) Norton.

Street's Cruising Guide to the Eastern Caribbean: Martinique to Trinidad, Vol. 4. rev. ed. Donald M. Street, Jr. (Illus.). 224p. (Orig.). 1993. pap. 39.95 (0-393-03523-9) Norton.

Street's Cruising Guide to the Eastern Caribbean: Puerto Rico, the Passage Islands, the U. S. & the British Virgin Islands, Vol. 2. rev. ed. Donald M. Street, Jr. (Illus.). 256p. 1995. 39.95 (0-393-03896-3) Norton.

Street's Cruising Guide to the Eastern Caribbean: Venezuela. rev. ed. Donald M. Street, Jr. 1991. 32.95 (0-393-03345-7) Norton.

Street's Cruising Guide to the Eastern Caribbean, Vol. II. D. M. Street, Jr. (C). 1989. 175.00 (0-685-40367-X, Pub. by Imray Laurie Norie & Wilson UK) St Mut.

Street's Cruising Guide to the Eastern Caribbean, Vol. II: Anguilla to Dominica, Pt. 2. D. M. Street, Jr. (C). 1989. write for info. (0-318-68268-0, Pub. by Imray Laurie Norie & Wilson UK) St Mut.

Street's Cruising Guide to the Eastern Caribbean, Vol. II: Puerto Rico, Passage & Virgin Islands, Pt. 1. D. M. Street, Jr. (C). 1989. write for info. (0-318-68267-2, Pub. by Imray Laurie Norie & Wilson UK) St Mut.

Street's Cruising Guide to the Eastern Caribbean, Vol. IV: Venezuela. (C). 1989. 175.00 (0-685-40365-3, Pub. by Imray Laurie Norie & Wilson UK) St Mut.

Streets Enough to Welcome Snow. Rosmarie Waldrop. LC 85-27825. 88p. (Orig.). 1986. pap. 5.95 (0-88268-034-X) Station Hill Pr.

Streets of Blood. Carl Sargent. (Shadowrun Ser.: No. 8). 288p. (Orig.). 1992. pap. 4.99 (0-451-45199-6, ROC) NAL-Dutton.

Streets of East London. William J. Fishman & N. Breach. 140p. 1979. pap. 18.95 (0-7156-1416-9, Pub. by Duckworth UK) Focus Pub-R Pullins.

Streets of Fire. Soledad Santiago. 342p. 1996. pap. 23.95 (0-525-94078-2) NAL-Dutton.

***Streets of Fire.** Soledad Santiago. 1997. pap. 5.99 (0-451-18855-1, Sig) NAL-Dutton.

Streets of Hedon. John Markham. (C). 1989. text ed. 40.00 (0-948929-24-3) St Mut.

Streets of Hope: The Fall & Rise of an Urban Neighborhood. Peter Medoff & Holly Sklar. LC 94-4613. 320p. (Orig.). (C). 1994. pap. 16.00 (0-89608-482-5); lib. bdg. 40.00 (0-89608-483-3) South End Pr.

Streets of Hull. John Markham. (C). 1989. text ed. 35.00 (0-948929-43-X) St Mut.

Streets of Hull: A History of Their Names. John Markham. (C). 1989. text ed. 35.00 (0-948929-07-3) St Mut.

Streets of Laredo: A Novel. large type ed. Larry McMurtry. LC 93-47082. 1994. lib. bdg. 19.95 (0-8161-5956-4, GK Hall) Thorndike Pr.

Streets of Loredo. Larry McMurtry. 1995. pap. 7.99 (0-671-53746-6) PB.

Streets of Mexico. L. Obregon. 1976. lib. bdg. 59.95 (0-8490-2695-4) Gordon Pr.

Streets of Night. John R. Dos Passos. Ed. by Michael Clark. LC 88-43406. 224p. 1990. 39.50 (0-945636-02-4) Susquehanna U Pr.

Streets of San Francisco. 3rd ed. Louis Loewenstein. LC 96-3537. 1996. pap. 9.95 (0-89997-192-X) Wilderness Pr.

Streets of St. Louis. William B. Magnan. 260p. (Orig.). 1994. pap. 14.95 (0-9638816-1-2) Right Press.

***Streets of the Near West Side.** William S. Bike. 128p. (Orig.). 1996. pap. 8.95 (0-87946-153-5) ACTA Pubns.

Streets of Winchester, Virginia, the Origin & Significance of Their Names. 47p. 1988. pap. write for info. (0-318-64328-6) Winchester-Frederick Cty Hist Soc.

***Streets Tell Stories.** Mayfair Games Staff. 1993. 25.00 (0-923763-89-9) Mayfair Games.

Street's Transatlantic Crossing Guide. Donald M. Street, Jr. (Illus.). 1989. 39.95 (0-393-03329-5) Norton.

Streets Were Paved with Gold: A Pictorial History of the Klondike Gold Rush 1896-99. Stan B. Cohen. LC 77-80011. (Illus.). 192p. 1977. pap. 9.95 (0-933126-03-4) Pictorial Hist.

Streetscape Equipment Sourcebook 2: Lighting; Paving & Fixtures; Traffic Safety & Control; Housekeeping & Amenity; Signage; Communications & Safety Devices; Shelters; Recreation & Play; Miscellaneous. Center for Design Planning Staff. LC 79-56221. 244p. reprint ed. pap. 69.60 (0-317-39655-2, 2023241) Bks Demand.

***Streetsense: Communication, Safety & Control. 3rd rev. ed. Kate B. Dernocoeur. LC 96-31540. (Illus.). 330p. 1996. pap. 22.95 (0-938106-21-X) Laing Res Servs.**
Dernocoeur's STREETSENSE: COMMUNICATION, SAFETY & CONTROL, is one of only three books named as "must read" material for every emergency medical services professional. This expanded & revised third edition of STREETSENSE provides key information about important non-clinical elements of emergency medical care, including interpersonal communication strategies, safety issues on the "streets", death & dying, driving hazards, lifting & back safety, gangs, the elderly & other "special" populations, legal risk management, stress & wellness, service orientation, weaponry, self awareness... & more. STREETSENSE is for all EMS providers, including first responders, veteran or not - plus their educators & administrators. Dr. Norm Dinerman: STREETSENSE starts where your textbooks stop...You're never too smart for more STREETSENSE." Dwayne Clayden, Paramedic Educator/Administrator: "I own nearly every EMS text in print, yet STREETSENSE is the only text I have read cover to cover, both editions. I recommend it to all my students - in fact, to everyone in EMS. Now available for only $22.95 (plus shipping & handling) - a bargain over previous editions!! A great gift for graduation, a birthday, or the holidays for the rescuers in your life. To order STREETSENSE, call 1-800-367-0382 (Emergency Training Associates) or 1-800-240-0703 (Jems Lifeline Bookstore). ***Publisher Provided Annotation.***

StreetSmart. Quincy Howe. LC 93-1397. 106p. (YA). (gr. 7-12). 1993. pap. 6.95 (0-932765-42-4, 1325-93) Close Up Fnd.

StreetSmart. Quincy Howe & Close Up Staff. LC 93-1397. 40p. 1993. teacher ed., pap. 5.95 (0-685-70875-6, 1414-94) Close Up Fnd.

Streetsmart Financial Basics for Nonprofit Managers. Thomas A. McLaughlin. LC 94-37588. (Nonprofit Law, Finance & Management Set). 265p. 1995. text ed. 54.95 (0-471-04226-9) Wiley.

Streetsmart Financial Basics for Nonprofit Managers. Thomas A. McLaughlin. LC 94-37588. (Nonprofit Law, Finance & Management Ser.). 265p. 1995. pap. text ed. 24.95 (0-471-11457-X) Wiley.

***Streetsmart Homebuyer: Investor Secrets Anyone Can Use to Buy a Home.** Charles Steed. 224p. 1997. 24.95 (0-9654396-0-7) Gold Standard.

Streetsmart Marketing. Jeff Slutsky. 241p. 1989. text ed. 39.95 (0-471-61883-7) Wiley.

Streetsmart Teleselling: The 33 Secrets. Jeff Slutsky. 1990. pap. text ed. 10.95 (0-13-851858-0) P-H.

Streetsmarts: A Teenager's Safety Guide. Jane Goldman. (YA). 1996. pap. 4.95 (0-8120-9762-9) Barron.

Streetstyle. Ted Polhemus. LC 94-60281. (Illus.). 144p. 1994. pap. 19.95 (0-500-27794-X) Thames Hudson.

Streetsweepers: The Complete Book of Combat Shotguns. Duncan Long. (Illus.). 160p. 1987. pap. 17.95 (0-87364-424-7) Paladin Pr.

Streetwalking in San Diego County. William Carroll. LC 92-70341. (Explore San Diego County Ser.). (Illus.). 132p. (Orig.). 1992. pap. 10.00 (0-910390-35-5, Coda Pubns) Auto Bk.

Streetwalking on a Ruined Map: Cultural Theory & the City Films of Elvira Notari. Giuliana Bruno. (Illus.). 424p. 1993. text ed. 70.00 (0-691-08628-1); pap. text ed. 24.95 (0-691-02533-9) Princeton U Pr.

Streetwise. Mohamed Choukri. Tr. by Ed Emery from ARA. 220p. 1996. 39.95 (0-86356-093-8, Pub. by Saqi Bks UK); pap. 12.95 (0-86356-045-8, Pub. by Saqi Bks UK) Interlink Pub.

Streetwise. Mary E. Mark. (Illus.). 78p. (Orig.). 1991. pap. 24.95 (0-89381-487-3) Aperture.

Streetwise: He Thought He Was Free, but His Lifestyle Had Taken Him Prisoner. John Goodfellow. 240p. 1991. pap. 7.99 (0-927545-12-8) YWAM Pub.

Streetwise! Practical Risk Management for Practicing Physicians. Rosemary Gafner. 101p. 1992. student ed. 45.00 (1-884269-00-1) Med Risk Mgmt.

Streetwise: Race, Class, & Change in An Urban Community. Elijah Anderson. LC 90-34048. (Illus.). 288p. 1990. 23.95 (*0-226-01815-6*) U Ch Pr.

Streetwise: Race, Class, & Change in an Urban Community. Elijah Anderson. LC 90-18646. 288p. 1992. pap. 12.95 (*0-226-01816-4*) U Ch Pr.

***Streetwise: The Best of the Journal of Portfolio Management.** Peter L. Bernstein & Frank J. Fabozzi. LC 97-15849. 1997. write for info. (*0-691-01129-X*); pap. write for info. (*0-691-01128-1*) Princeton U Pr.

***Streetwise Amsterdam.** Michael E. Brown. (Illus.). 5.95 (*0-935039-82-1*) Stwise Maps.

Streetwise Baltimore: The Stories Behind Baltimore Street Names. Carleton Jones. (Illus.). 223p. (Orig.). 1991. pap. 14.95 (*0-929387-27-9*) Bonus Books.

Streetwise Barcelona. Michael E. Brown. pap. 5.95 (*1-886705-11-9*) Stwise Maps.

***Streetwise Budapest.** Michael E. Brown. (Illus.). 5.95 (*1-886705-22-4*) Stwise Maps.

***Streetwise California.** Michael E. Brown. 6.95 (*1-886705-29-1*) Stwise Maps.

Streetwise Chicago: A History of Chicago Street Names. Don Hayner & Tom McNamee. LC 88-12922. (Illus.). 153p. 1988. 22.50 (*0-8294-0597-6*); pap. 14.95 (*0-8294-0596-8*) Loyola Pr.

Streetwise Criminology. Duane Denfield. 1986. 15.95 (*0-87073-663-9*) Schenkman Bks Inc.

***Streetwise Dublin.** Michael E. Brown. (Illus.). 5.95 (*1-886705-04-6*) Stwise Maps.

***Streetwise East Hampton.** Michael E. Brown. (Illus.). 5.95 (*0-935039-83-X*) Stwise Maps.

***Streetwise Florence.** Michael E. Brown. (Illus.). 5.95 (*0-935039-65-1*) Stwise Maps.

Streetwise German: Speaking & Understanding Colliquial German. Paul G. Graves. 144p. 1994. pap. 12.95 (*0-8442-2514-2*, Natl Textbk) NTC Pub Grp.

***Streetwise Greenwich Village, Chinatown, Little Italy, East Village, Soho, TriBeCa.** Michael E. Brown. (Illus.). 5.95 (*0-935039-28-7*) Stwise Maps.

Streetwise Guide to Chinese Herbal Medicine. Martha Dahlen. 1996. pap. 11.95 (*0-614-97831-9*) China Bks.

***Streetwise Hawaii.** Michael E. Brown. (Illus.). 5.95 (*0-935039-79-1*) Stwise Maps.

***Streetwise Houston.** Michael Braun. (Illus.). 4.95 (*0-935039-89-9*) Stwise Maps.

Streetwise Investing in Rental Properties: A Detailed Strategy for Financial Independence. H. Roger Neal. LC 93-32874. 1994. 15.95 (*1-882877-03-9*) Panoply Pr.

StreetWise Investor: Steering Clear of Investment Traps, Pitfalls & Other Dangerous Lures. Charles L. Fahy & Sydney LeBlanc. 225p. 1993. text ed. 24.95 (*1-55738-445-2*) Irwin Prof Pubng.

***Streetwise Jerusalem.** Michael E. Brown. (Illus.). 5.95 (*1-886705-23-2*) Stwise Maps.

***Streetwise Las Vegas.** Michael E. Brown. (Illus.). 5.95 (*1-886705-07-0*) Stwise Maps.

Streetwise Lifetime Encyclopedia. Meyer. 1996. pap. text ed. 4.28 (*0-13-461906-4*) P-H.

***Streetwise Los Angeles.** Michael E. Brown. (Illus.). 5.95 (*0-935039-17-1*) Stwise Maps.

***Streetwise Manhattan.** Michael E. Brown. (Illus.). 5.95 (*0-935039-03-1*) Stwise Maps.

***Streetwise Miami.** Michael E. Brown. (Illus.). 5.95 (*0-935039-51-1*) Stwise Maps.

***Streetwise Monterey.** Michael E. Brown. (Illus.). 5.95 (*1-886705-28-3*) Stwise Maps.

***Streetwise Montreal.** Michael E. Brown. (Illus.). 5.95 (*1-886705-09-7*) Stwise Maps.

***Streetwise New Orleans.** Michael E. Brown. (Illus.). 5.95 (*0-935039-10-4*) Stwise Maps.

***Streetwise New York, New Jersey.** Michael E. Brown. (Illus.). 5.95 (*1-886705-21-6*) Stwise Maps.

Streetwise Parents, & Foolproof Kids. 2nd rev. ed. Dan Korem. (Illus.). 302p. (Orig.). 1996. 19.95 (*0-9639103-2-9*) Intl Focus Pr.

***Streetwise Parents, & Foolproof Kids. 3rd ed. Dan Korem. (Illus.). 302p. (Orig.). 1998. 19.95 (*0-9639103-0-2*) Intl Focus Pr.**
"Today's youths are the EASIEST to deceive in U.S. history, says Dan Korem, investigative journalist & internationally recognized expert on deception. In this vastly expanded & updated edition, Dan Korem, a father of three who has lectured for the FBI & has spoken to tens of thousands of kids in live presentations, has produced the first hard-hitting guide that shows parents, educators, cops, & youth workers how to teach kids (5-18) how to spot & respond to deception. Without reliable thought armor kids are defenseless. Invaluable lessons for kids & adults include: 1) The profile of the person who is the easiest to deceive & how NOT to become that person; 2) How to detect if someone is lying; 3) Why gangs are forming in upscale communities & how to talk a friend out of joining one; 4) How to recognize if someone is dangerously violent & what to do. From the author of the critically acclaimed books, SUBURBAN GANGS--THE AFFLUENT REBELS & THE ART OF PROFILING--READING PEOPLE RIGHT THE FIRST TIME, STREETWISE PARENTS, & FOOLPROOF KIDS is the only easy-to-read guide that cuts to the core of how deception works in the mind & can affect kids. Only field-tested ideas here--no pop-psychology. Critical areas addressed in the 20 chapters laced with photos include: resisting harmful media & how to check out a news story; how to stop a gang from forming; do's & dont's on the Internet; the tell-tale signs of drug use; & identifying & resisting cults. Distributed by Ingram, Baker & Taylor, Brodart & Spring Arbor. Or order direct from International Focus Press: P.O. Box 1857, Richardson, TX 75083. phone: 972-234-4003; FAX: 972-234-2396. ***Publisher Provided Annotation.***

***Streetwise Philadelphia.** Michael E. Brown. (Illus.). 4.95 (*0-935039-07-4*) Stwise Maps.

***Streetwise Phoenix.** Michael E. Brown. (Illus.). 5.95 (*0-935039-94-5*) Stwise Maps.

***Streetwise San Antonio.** Michael E. Brown. (Illus.). 4.95 (*0-935039-91-0*) Stwise Maps.

***Streetwise San Diego.** Michael E. Brown. (Illus.). 5.95 (*0-935039-53-8*) Stwise Maps.

***Streetwise San Francisco.** Michael E. Brown. (Illus.). 5.95 (*0-935039-20-1*) Stwise Maps.

***Streetwise Seattle.** Michael E. Brown. (Illus.). 5.95 (*0-935039-55-4*) Stwise Maps.

Streetwise Self-Defense. Edwin Deser. (Illus.). 96p. (Orig.). 1989. pap. 17.95 (*0-572-01467-8*, Pub. by W Foulsham UK) Trans-Atl Phila.

***Streetwise Southampton.** Michael E. Brown. (Illus.). 1997. 5.95 (*1-886705-31-3*) Stwise Maps.

***Streetwise Sydney.** Michael E. Brown. (Illus.). 5.95 (*0-935039-92-9*) Stwise Maps.

***Streetwise Toronto.** Michael E. Brown. (Illus.). 5.95 (*1-886705-08-9*) Stwise Maps.

***Streetwise Vancouver.** Michael E. Brown. (Illus.). 5.95 (*1-886705-10-0*) Stwise Maps.

***Streetwise Washington, D. C.** Michael E. Brown. (Illus.). 5.95 (*0-935039-06-6*) Stwise Maps.

Streetwork: The Way to Police Officer Safety & Survival. Steve Albrecht. 256p. 1992. pap. 19.95 (*0-87364-650-9*) Paladin Pr.

Streex: A Coloring Book. Cynthia Alvarez. (Happy House Coloring Ser.). (J). 1996. pap. 0.55 (*0-679-87999-4*, Bullseye Bks) Random Bks Yng Read.

Strega. Andrew Vachss. 1994. lib. bdg. 24.95 (*1-56849-466-1*) Buccaneer Bks.

Strega. Andrew Vachss. 304p. 1996. pap. 11.00 (*0-679-76409-7*) Random.

Strega - Other Stories. Louise De La Ramee. LC 72-101797. (Short Story Index Reprint Ser.). 1977. 18.95 (*0-8369-3185-8*) Ayer.

Strega Nona. Garrett Christopher. Ed. by J. Friedland & R. Kessler. (Novel-Ties Ser.). 1995. student ed., pap. text ed. 14.95 (*1-56982-240-9*) Lrn Links.

Strega Nona. Tomie De Paola. (Big Bks.). (J). (ps-3). 1992. 19.95 (*0-590-72625-0*) Scholastic Inc.

Strega Nona. Tomie De Paola. LC 75-11565. (Illus.). 32p. (J). (ps-4). 1975. pap. 15.00 (*0-671-66283-X*, S&S Bks Young Read) S&S Childrens.

Strega Nona. Tomie De Paola. LC 75-11565. (Illus.). 32p. (J). (ps-4). 1979. pap. 6.95 (*0-671-66606-1*, S&S Bks Young Read) S&S Childrens.

Strega Nona. Tomie De Paolo. 1996. 11.95 (*84-241-3349-8*) Lectorum Pubns.

***Strega Nona.** Tomie Depaola. (J). 1997. 7.99 (*0-689-81764-9*, Litl Simon S&S) S&S Childrens.

Strega Nona: A Literature Unit. Patsy Carey & Susan Kilpatrick. (Literature Units Ser.). (Illus.). 48p. (Orig.). (J). (gr. k-3). 1993. student ed., pap. 7.95 (*1-55734-436-1*) Tchr Create Mat.

Strega Nona: Her Story. Tomie DePaola. (Illus.). 32p. (J). (ps-3). 1996. 15.95 (*0-399-22818-7*, Putnam) Putnam Pub Group.

Strega Nona Doll. Tomie De Paola. (J). 1995. 10.95 (*0-689-80615-9*) S&S Childrens.

Strega Nona Literature Mini-Unit. Janet Lovelady. (Illus.). 32p. (J). (gr. 2-4). 1989. student ed. 4.95 (*1-56096-009-4*) Mari.

Strega Nona Meets Her Match. Tomie DePaola. LC 92-8199. (Illus.). 32p. (J). (ps-3). 1993. 15.95 (*0-399-22421-1*, Putnam) Putnam Pub Group.

Strega Nona Meets Her Match. Tomie DePaola. (Illus.). 32p. (J). (ps-3). 1996. pap. 5.95 (*0-698-11411-6*, Paperstar) Putnam Pub Group.

Strega Nona's Magic Lessons. Tomie De Paola. LC 80-28260. (Illus.). 32p. (J). (ps up). 1982. 14.00 (*0-15-281785-9*, HB Juv Bks) HarBrace.

Strega Nona's Magic Lessons. Tomie De Paola. LC 80-28260. (Illus.). 32p. (J). (gr. k up). 1984. pap. 4.95 (*0-15-281786-7*, Voyager Bks) HarBrace.

Streifzuge Eines Bucherfreundes. Gustav A. Bogeng et al. (Buchkundliche Arbeiten Ser.: Vol. VIII). 452p. 1985. reprint ed. 75.00 (*3-487-07519-9*) G Olms Pubs.

Streifzuge Um Den Persischen Golf. Hans-Erich Tzschirner. 196p. reprint ed. write for info. (*0-318-71569-4*) G Olms Pubs.

***Streisand.** Anne Edwards. 1997. write for info. (*0-316-21577-5*) Little.

Streisand: Her Life. James Spada. 560p. 1995. 25.00 (*0-517-59753-5*) Random Hse Value.

Streisand: Her Life. James Spada. 1996. mass mkt. 6.99 (*0-8041-1119-7*) Ivy Books.

***Streisand: It Only Happens Once.** Anne Edwards. LC 96-41091. (Illus.). 600p. 1997. 24.95 (*0-316-21138-9*) Little.

***Streisand: The Pictorial Biography.** Diana K. Harvey & Jackson Harvey. (Illus.). 120p. 1997. 19.98 (*0-7624-0069-2*) Courage Bks.

Streit der Fakultaten. Immanuel Kant. Tr. by Mary J. Gregor. LC 77-86235. (Janus Ser.). 221p. 1979. 25.00 (*0-913870-34-X*) Abaris Bks.

Streit Um Asterix. Rene De Goscinny & M. Uderzo. (Illus.). (GER.). (J). 19.95 (*0-8288-4906-4*) Fr & Eur.

Streit um "Nietzsches Geburt der Tragodie" Friedrich Wilhelm Nietzsche. (Olms Paperbacks Ser.: Bd. 40). 136p. 1989. pap. write for info. (*3-487-02599-X*) G Olms Pubs.

***Streiten und Bewahren: Die Religionspadagogische Rezeption und Kritik der Dialektischen Theologie.** Frank Fruhling. (Europaische Hochschulschriften Ser.: Reihe 33, Bd. 16). 304p. (GER.). 1997. 57.95 (*3-631-30820-5*) P Lang Pubng.

***Stremmel House.** Mark Mack. 1997. pap. 19.95 (*1-885254-49-0*) Monacelli Pr.

Strenghening Health Management in Districts & Provinces. Andrew Cassels & Katja Janovsky. vi, 75p. (FRE & SPA.). (C). 1995. pap. text ed. 20.00 (*92-4-154483-X*, 1150428) World Health.

Strenghtening Policy Analysis: Econometric Tests Using SPSS/PC+, SAS PC, & GAUSS-386. Daniel Driscoll. LC 95-5179. (Microcomputers in Policy Research Ser.: Vol. 2). 1995. write for info. (*0-89629-330-0*) Intl Food Policy.

Strength. 1980. 34.50 (*0-8176-0596-7*) Spr-Verlag.

Strength-A-Lyzer. Joseph S. Renzulli & Linda H. Smith. 1978. pap. 22.95 (*0-936386-24-X*) Creative Learning.

Strength & Durability of Residential Concretes Containing Fly Ash. D. Whiting. 43p. 1991. 15.00 (*0-89312-191-6*, RD099T) Portland Cement.

Strength & Elongation Testing of Single & Ply Yarns (MOTT-QCAS) R. Furter. 123p. (C). 1985. pap. text ed. 36.00 (*0-900739-78-9*, Pub. by Textile Inst UK) St Mut.

Strength & Fracture of Engineering Solids. David K. Felbeck & Anthony G. Atkins. (Illus.). 608p. 1983. text ed. 82.00 (*0-13-851709-6*) P-H.

Strength & Fracture of Engineering Solids. 2nd ed. David K. Felbeck & Anthony G. Atkins. LC 95-34197. 1995. text ed. 90.00 (*0-13-856113-3*) P-H.

Strength & Fracture of Glass & Ceramics. Jaroslav Mencik. (Glass & Science Technology Ser.: Vol. 12). 358p. 1992. 153.75 (*0-444-98685-5*) Elsevier.

Strength & Stiffness of Polymers. Ed. by Anagnostis E. Zachariades & Roger S. Porter. LC 83-5196. (Plastics Engineering Ser.: No. 4). 396p. 1983. reprint ed. pap. 112.90 (*0-608-01326-9*, 2062069) Bks Demand.

Strength & Structure of Engineering Materials. N. H. Polakowski & E. Ripling. 1965. text ed. 54.00 (*0-13-851790-8*) P-H.

Strength & Sympathy: Essays & Epigrams. David D. Horowitz. LC 96-92067. 96p. (Orig.). 1996. pap. 8.95 (*0-9651210-1-1*) Rose Alley Pr.

Strength & Water Resistance of Adhesive-Bonded Copper Metals. Battelle Memorial Institute Staff. 96p. 1970. 14.40 (*0-317-34548-6*, 108) Intl Copper.

Strength & Weakness: The Authoritarian Personality Today. Ed. by William F. Stone et al. 264p. 1994. 87.95 (*0-387-97698-1*) Spr-Verlag.

Strength & Weight Training for Young Athletes: A Safe, Scientific Approach to Weight Training That Puts Young Athletes Ahead of the Game. Scott Roberts et al. (Illus.). 192p. 1994. pap. 14.95 (*0-8092-3697-4*) Contemp Bks.

Strength Basics: Your Guide to Resistance Training for Health & Optimal Performance. Gordon W. Stewart. LC 96-15785. (Illus.). 200p. 1996. pap. 14.95 (*0-87322-843-X*, PCOO0843) Human Kinetics.

Strength Calculations. Ed. by N. B. Tarabasov. (Illus.). xii, 406p. 1988. 72.50 (*0-89864-037-7*) Allerton Pr.

Strength Calculations for Oil Country Tubular Goods. Alexandre Madrelle. 1956. pap. 60.00 (*2-7108-0003-9*, Pub. by Edits Technip FR) St Mut.

Strength Connection: How to Build Strength & Improve the Quality of Your Life. Institute for Aerobics Research Staff. LC 90-83129. (Illus.). 192p. (Orig.). 1990. pap. write for info. (*0-9622206-0-4*) Inst Aerobics.

Strength Design for Reinforced-Concrete Hydraulic Structures. LC 93-6335. (Technical Engineering & Design Guides as Adapted from the U. S. Army Corps of Engineers Ser.: No. 2). 1993. 18.00 (*0-87262-969-4*, ASCE Press) Am Soc Civil Eng.

Strength Design of Reinforced Concrete Columns. rev. ed. 48p. 1969. pap. 10.00 (*0-89312-124-X*, EB009D) Portland Cement.

Strength Enough. Photos by Robert E. Dorksen. (Illus.). 110p. 1980. pap. 10.95 (*0-911704-25-6*) Western Res.

Strength Evaluation of Existing Concrete Bridges. 1985. 42.50 (*0-317-39825-3*, SP-88BOW6) ACI.

Strength Evaluation of Existing Reinforced Concrete Bridges. (National Cooperative Highway Research Program Report Ser.: No. 292). 133p. 1987. 14.00 (*0-309-04415-4*) Transport Res Bd.

***Strength Fitness.** 5th ed. Westcott. 1998. pap. text ed. 17.00 (*0-697-29580-X*) McGraw.

Strength Fitness: Physiological Principles & Training Techniques. 3rd ed. Wayne L. Westcott. 256p. (C). 1990. pap. write for info. (*0-697-10629-2*) Brown & Benchmark.

Strength Fitness: Physiological Principles & Training Techniques. 4th ed. Wayne L. Westcott. 224p. (C). 1994. per. write for info. (*0-697-15270-7*) Brown & Benchmark.

***Strength for a Man's Heart.** Paul Brownlow. 1997. 9.99 (*1-57051-140-3*) Brownlow Pub Co.

Strength for Suffering. John M. Drescher. 1989. pap. 1.99 (*0-8361-1599-6*) Herald Pr.

Strength for the Fight: A History of Black Americans in the Military. Bernard C. Nalty. 1989. pap. 16.95 (*0-02-922411-X*, Free Press) Free Pr.

***Strength for the Journey.** Ann B. Reynolds. 96p. (Orig.). 1996. pap. 9.95 (*1-888257-02-4*, 257) Cameron Press.

Strength for the Storm: Spiritual Lessons from Chinese Preachers. Reynolds. 1988. pap. 4.95 (*9971-972-62-X*) OMF Bks.

Strength for Today. Frances Hunter. 1990. pap. 6.95 (*0-917726-98-7*) Hunter Bks.

***Strength for Today: Daily Readings for a Deeper Faith.** John F. MacArthur, Jr. 1997. 19.99 (*0-89107-969-6*) Crossway Bks.

Strength for Today: Devotions for Those Who Are Ill. large type ed. Vincent Gallagher & Amy Gallagher. LC 95-44368. 144p. (Orig.). 1996. pap. 7.99 (*0-8007-5583-9*) Revell.

***Strength for Today & Bright Hope for Tomorrow: Let God Guide You Through Your Pain & Grief.** Steve Brock. LC 97-2907. 224p. (Orig.). 1997. pap. 12.99 (*0-7852-7557-6*, J Thoma Bks) Nelson.

Strength from Movement: Mastering Chi. Hua-Ching Ni. LC 93-40503. (Illus.). 256p. (Orig.). 1994. pap. 16.95 (*0-937064-73-4*) SevenStar Comm.

Strength from the Hills: The Story of Mick Stuart, My Father. rev. ed. Jesse H. Stuart. LC 92-3995. (Illus.). 175p. (J). (gr. 3 up). 1992. reprint ed. 12.00 (*0-945084-29-3*) J Stuart Found.

Strength from the Psalms: Verses to Comfort, Uplift, & Challenge. Ed. by Elizabeth C. Newenhuyse. (Pocketpac Bks.). 80p. (Orig.). 1993. mass mkt. 2.99 (*0-87788-799-3*) Shaw Pubs.

Strength in Numbers: A Gay, Lesbian, & Bisexual Resource Guide. Visible Ink Staff. LC 96-8233. (Illus.). 416p. 1996. 16.95 (*0-7876-0881-5*) Visible Ink Pr.

Strength in Numbers: Discovering the Joy & Power of Mathematics in Everyday Life. Sherman K. Stein. LC 95-48056. 240p. 1996. text ed. 24.95 (*0-471-15252-8*) Wiley.

***Strength in the Struggle: Leadership Development for Women.** Vashti M. McKenzie. 112p. (Orig.). 1997. pap. 9.95 (*0-8298-1212-1*) Pilgrim OH.

Strength in Times of Trouble. Lea Fowler. 1989. pap. 6.25 (*0-89137-455-8*) Quality Pubns.

Strength in Weakness. Hilary Hinds. 336p. 1996. text ed. 24.95 (*0-7190-4887-7*, Pub. by Manchester Univ Pr UK) St Martin.

Strength in Weakness: Renaissance Sectarian Women & Feminist Criticism. Hilary Hinds. 336p. 1996. text ed. 74.95 (*0-7190-4886-9*, Pub. by Manchester Univ Pr UK) St Martin.

Strength Interaction Surfaces for Tall Buildings. Bruno Zimmerli & Bruno Thurlimann. (IBA Ser.: No 91). 12p. 1980. 7.50 (*0-8176-1124-X*) Birkhauser.

Strength of a Man: Encouragement for Today. David Roper. LC 89-1180. 160p. 1989. pap. 9.99 (*0-929239-07-5*) Discovery Hse Pubs.

***Strength of a People: The Idea of an Informed Citizenry in America, 1650-1870.** Richard D. Brown. 272p. 1997. pap. text ed. 16.95 (*0-8078-4663-5*) U of NC Pr.

Strength of a People: The Idea of an Informed Citizenry in America, 1650-1870. Richard D. Brown. LC 95-35013. (Illus.). 272p. (C). (gr. 13). 1997. text ed. 29.95 (*0-8078-2261-2*) U of NC Pr.

***Strength of a Woman.** Roger Schwab. (Illus.). 175p. 1997. write for info. (*0-9656490-0-8*) Main Line Pubns.

Strength of a Woman: Activating the 12 Dynamic Qualities Every Woman Possesses. Linda R. McGinn. LC 92-35746. (Orig.). 1993. pap. 9.99 (*0-8054-5353-9*, 4253-53) Broadman.

Strength of an Exacting Passion: Acts 18-28. (Swindoll Bible Study Guide Ser.). 1993. pap. 5.99 (*0-8499-8437-8*) Word Pub.

Strength of Being Clean: The Philosophy of Hope. David S. Jordan. LC 86-120984. 90p. 1983. reprint ed. pap. 4.95 (*0-9616281-0-3*) J Thompson Pub.

Strength of Brick Walls Under Enforced End Rotation. Bruno Thurlimann & Rene Furler. (IBA Ser.: No. 89). 14p. 1979. pap. text ed. 5.95 (*3-7643-1108-8*) Birkhauser.

Strength of Desire. Alison Fraser. (Presents Ser.). 1996. mass mkt. 3.50 (*0-373-11836-8*, 1-11836-3) Harlequin Bks.

Strength of Desire. large type ed. Alison Fraser. (Harlequin Romance Ser.). 1996. 19.95 (*0-263-14384-8*, Pub. by Mills & Boon UK) Thorndike Pr.

Strength of Dilating Soil & Load-Holding Capacity of Deep Foundations: Introduction to Theory & Practical Application. D. Yu Sobolevsky. (Illus.). 350p. (C). 1994. 75.00 (*90-5410-164-4*, Pub. by A A Balkema NE) Ashgate Pub Co.

Strength of Gideon. Paul L. Dunbar. LC 69-18589. 1991. reprint ed. pap. write for info. (*0-88143-137-0*) Ayer.

Strength of Gideon & Other Stories. Paul L. Dunbar. LC 69-18589. (American Negro: His History & Literature. Series 2). (Illus.). (C). 1974. reprint ed. 30.95 (*0-405-01860-6*) Ayer.

Strength of Government. McGeorge Bundy. LC 68-54016. (Godkin Lectures: 1968). 125p. 1968. 17.00 (*0-674-84300-2*) HUP.

Strength of Inorganic Glass. Ed. by Charles R. Kurkjian. (NATO Conference Series VI, Materials Science: Vol. 11). 632p. 1986. 135.00 (*0-306-42096-1*, Plenum Pr) Plenum.

Strength of Lovers see Novels by Hugo Wast

Strength of Materials. J. M. Alexander & J. S. Gunasekera. (Mechanical Engineering Ser.). 450p. 1991. 99.95 (*0-13-853722-4*, 520701) P-H.

Strength of Materials. Jacob P. Den Hartog. 1949. pap. 7.50 (*0-486-60755-0*) Dover.

Strength of Materials. Kane. (Miscellaneous/Catalogs Ser.). 1997. text ed. 82.95 (*0-534-95150-3*) Wadsworth Pub.

Strength of Materials. Logan. (C). 1991. text ed. 82.00 (*0-06-044108-9*) Addson-Wesley Educ.

Strength of Materials. 3rd ed. John W. Breneman. 1965. text ed. 39.95 (*0-07-007536-0*) McGraw.

Strength of Materials. 3rd rev. ed. Surendra Singh. 736p. 1990. text ed. 45.00 (*81-220-0066-5*, Pub. by Konark Pubs Pvt Ltd II) Advent Bks Div.

An Asterisk (*) at the beginning of an entry indicates that the title is appearing in BIP for the first time.

Strength of Materials. 4th ed. Andrew Pytel & Ferdinand L. Singer. 592p. (C). 1987. text ed. 84.68 (*0-06-045313-3*) Addson-Wesley Educ.

***Strength of Materials: Solutions Manual.** Bicrford. (C). 1997. teacher ed., pap. text ed. write for info. (*0-673-97505-3*) Addison-Wesley.

***Strength of Materials: Solutions Manual.** 5th ed. Pytel. (C). 1996. teacher ed., pap. text ed. write for info. (*0-673-55580-1*) Addison-Wesley.

Strength of Materials & Mechanics of Solids Problem Solver. rev. ed. Research & Education Association Staff. LC 80-83305. (Illus.). 1152p. (Orig.). (C). 1996. pap. text ed. 29.95 (*0-87891-522-2*) Res & Educ.

Strength of Materials & Structures. 3rd ed. Case. (Civil Engineering Ser.). 1994. 46.50 (*0-340-56829-1*, Pub. by E Arnold UK) Routledge Chapman & Hall.

Strength of Materials for Engineering Technology. 2nd ed. Irving Granet. (Illus.). 448p. 1980. teacher ed. write for info. (*0-8359-7075-2*, Reston) P-H.

***Strength of Materials in Orthotic & Prosthetic Design.** AAOP (Striker) Staff. 112p. 1996. 49.95 (*0-7872-1913-4*) Kendall-Hunt.

Strength of Materials Problems Solved in BASIC. 1988. 39.50 (*0-685-24854-2*, 83-2-B); disk 24.00 (*0-685-24855-0*, 83-2-ID) Kern Intl.

Strength of Members with Dapped Ends. 224p. 1988. 34.00 (*0-318-35234-6*, R&D6) P-PCI.

Strength of Metals & Alloys: Proceedings of the International Conference, 8th, Tampere, Finland, 22-26 August 1988, 3 vols., Set. P. O. Kettunen et al. (International Series on the Strength & Fracture of Materials & Structures). (Illus.). 1800p. 1989. 325.00 (*0-08-034806-8*, Pergamon Pr) Elsevier.

Strength of Our Mothers: African & African American Women & Families - Essays & Speeches. Niara Sudarkasa. 360p. 1995. pap. text ed. 18.95 (*0-86543-497-2*) Africa World.

Strength of Our Mothers: African & African American Women & Families: Essays & Speeches. Niara Sudarkasa. 360p. 1996. 59.95 (*0-86543-496-4*) Africa World.

Strength of Sampson. Michael H. Brown. 112p. 1988. pap. 6.00 (*0-939482-11-8*, Noontide Pr) Legion Survival.

Strength of Soul: The Sacred Use of Time. W. Phillip Keller. LC 92-43992. 192p. 1993. 12.99 (*0-8254-2997-8*) Kregel.

Strength of Structural Elements. Ed. by Michal Zyczkowski. (Studies in Applied Mechanics: No. 26). 786p. 1991. 278.75 (*0-444-98763-0*) Elsevier.

Strength of Structural Materials: Understanding Basic Structural Design. Ginseppe De Campoli. LC 84-3569. 478p. 1988. reprint ed. lib. bdg. 44.50 (*0-471-89082-0*) Krieger.

Strength of the Hills: A Portrait of a Family Farm, Vol. 1. Nancy P. Graff. (J). 1989. 14.95 (*0-316-32277-6*) Little.

Strength of the Hills: Middlebury College, 1915-1990. David M. Stameshkin. LC 95-4799. (Illus.). 468p. 1996. 24.95 (*0-87451-732-X*) U Pr of New Eng.

Strength of the Strong. Jack London. 1976. 21.95 (*0-8488-1083-X*) Amereon Ltd.

Strength of the Weak: Towards a Christian Feminist Identity. Dorothee Soelle. Tr. by Rita Kimber & Robert Kimber. LC 83-27348. 184p. (Orig.). 1984. pap. 11.00 (*0-664-24623-0*, Westminster) Westminster John Knox.

***Strength of These Arms: Life in the Slave Quarters.** Raymond Bial. LC 96-39860. (J). 1997. 15.00 (*0-395-77394-6*) HM.

***Strength of Weakness.** Roy Clements. 240p. Date not set. write for info. (*1-85792-073-2*, Pub. by Christian Focus UK) Spring Arbor Dist.

Strength of Weakness: How God Uses Flaws to Achieve His Goals. Roy Clements. LC 95-2577. 224p. (gr. 10). 1995. reprint ed. pap. 14.99 (*0-8010-5091-X*) Baker Bks.

Strength Perspective in Social Work Practice. 2nd ed. Dennis Saleeby. (C). 1997. pap. text ed. 30.50 (*0-8013-1745-2*) Addison-Wesley.

***Strength Rating of Helical Gears - Derivations, Factors & Examples.** E. J. Wellauer. (Technical Papers). 1960. pap. text ed. 30.00 (*1-55589-272-8*) AGMA.

Strength Testing of Marine Sediments: Laboratory & in-Situ STP 883. Ed. by Ronald C. Chaney & Kenneth R. Demars. LC 85-15838. (Illus.). 557p. 1985. text ed. 69.00 (*0-8031-0431-6*, 04-883000-38) ASTM.

Strength to Climb: A Collection of the Writing of Twelve Senior Citizens. Ed. by Sarah Emery & Josie H. Cloud. LC 84-70421. (Illus.). x, 277p. 1984. pap. 10.00 (*0-9606146-1-3*) Denton Senior Ctr.

Strength to Love. large type ed. Martin Luther King, Jr. 304p. 1985. pap. 14.95 (*0-8027-2472-8*) Walker & Co.

Strength to Love. Martin Luther King, Jr. LC 80-2374. 160p. 1981. reprint ed. pap. 10.00 (*0-8006-1441-0*, 1-1441, Fortress Pr) Augsburg Fortress.

Strength to Strive. David Pease. 1992. pap. 12.95 (*0-8119-0770-8*) LIFETIME.

Strength to Your Sword Arm: Selected Writings. Brenda Ueland. LC 92-54181. (Illus.). 280p. (Orig.). 1992. pap. 14.95 (*0-930100-50-6*) Holy Cow.

Strength Training: Beginners, Body Builders & Athletes. Philip E. Allsen. 192p. (C). 1996. per. 15.69 (*0-7872-1837-5*) Kendall-Hunt.

Strength Training Book. Edwin J. Sobey. (Runner's World Ser.). 1981. pap. 16.95 (*0-02-499600-9*, Macmillan Coll) P-H.

Strength Training Book. Edwin J. Sobey. (Runner's World Ser.). 1982. pap. 9.95 (*0-02-499590-8*, Macmillan Coll) P-H.

Strength Training by the Experts. 2nd ed. Ed. by Daniel P. Riley. LC 81-85627. (Illus.). 256p. (Orig.). 1982. pap. 15.95 (*0-88011-041-4*, PRIL0041) Human Kinetics.

Strength Training for Basketball. Bruno Pauletto. LC 93-17540. (Illus.). 144p. 1994. pap. 14.95 (*0-87322-433-7*, PPAU0433) Human Kinetics.

Strength Training for Beauty. Leen. 1983. 7.95 (*0-02-499810-9*, Macmillan Coll) P-H.

Strength Training for Coaches. Bruno Pauletto. LC 90-13122. (Illus.). 192p. (Orig.). 1991. pap. text ed. 19.00 (*0-88011-371-5*, PPAU0371) Human Kinetics.

Strength Training for Football. Bruno Pauletto. LC 92-12982. (Illus.). 141p. 1992. pap. 14.95 (*0-87322-398-5*, PPAU0398) Human Kinetics.

Strength Training for Performance Driving. Mark Martin et al. LC 93-21106. (Illus.). 128p. 1994. pap. 17.95 (*0-87938-843-9*) Motorbooks Intl.

Strength Training for Preventive Medicine. Denton Smith & E. Leslie Knight. write for info. (*0-929736-16-8*) ISC Div Wellness.

Strength Training for Rugby. Bruce Walsh. (Illus.). 136p. 1992. reprint ed. pap. 13.95 (*0-86417-293-1*, Pub. by Kangaroo Pr AT) Seven Hills Bk.

Strength Training for Runners & Hurdlers. rev. ed. John Jesse. LC 73-131245. (gr. 10-12). 1981. pap. 7.95 (*0-87095-036-3*, Athletic) Gldn West Bks.

Strength Training for Sport. Rex Hazeldine. (Illus.). 167p. 1990. pap. 19.95 (*1-85223-217-X*, Pub. by Crowood Pr UK) Trafalgar.

Strength Training for the Martial Arts. Tony Gummerson. pap. 16.95 (*0-7136-3263-1*, 92256, Pub. by A&C Black UK) Talman.

Strength Training for Women. James A. Peterson et al. LC 94-47646. (Illus.). 392p. (Orig.). 1995. pap. 15.95 (*0-87322-752-2*, PPET0752) Human Kinetics.

Strength Training for Women Only: Using Nautilus Equipment. Joe Mullen. 115p. 1986. 19.95 (*0-935783-05-9*) Fitness Ctr Info.

Strength Training for Young Athletes. William J. Kraemer & Steven J. Fleck. LC 92-22624. (Illus.). 224p. 1993. pap. 17.95 (*0-87322-396-9*, PKRA0396) Human Kinetics.

***Strength Training Past 50.** Wyane L. Westcott et al. LC 97-24819. (Ageless Athlete Ser.). (Illus.). 216p. (Orig.). 1997. pap. 16.95 (*0-88011-716-8*, PWES0716) Human Kinetics.

***Strength Within.** Barbara Guyhto. (Illus.). 91p. (Orig.). (J). (gr. 1-6). 1997. pap. 8.99 (*1-55237-361-4*, Pub. by Comnwlth Pub CN) Partners Pubs Grp.

Strengthen Anti-Imperialist Solidarity. 1969. pap. 0.35 (*0-87898-041-5*) New Outlook.

Strengthen School-Based Management by Chartering All Schools. Ray Budde. 130p. (Orig.). (C). 1995. pap. text ed. write for info. (*1-878234-09-9*) Reg Lab Educ IOT NE Isls.

Strengthen the Country & Enrich the People: The Reform Writings of Ma Jianzhong. Ma Jianzhong. Tr. by Paul Bailey. (Durham East Asia Ser.). 240p. (C). 1997. text ed. 45.00 (*0-7007-0468-X*, Pub. by Curzon Press UK) UH Pr.

Strengthen Your Immune System! Gun Agell. 180p. 1994. pap. write for info. (*0-9640299-0-1*) G Agell.

Strengthen Your Performance in Psychological Tests. Cecile Cesari. 1996. pap. text ed. 15.95 (*0-572-02208-5*, Pub. by W Foulsham UK) Trans-Atl Phila.

Strengthened Glass Technology. Frank L. Bouquet. (Illus.). 60p. (Orig.). 1991. 79.00 (*1-56216-009-5*) Systems Co.

Strengthened Glass Technology. abr. ed. Frank L. Bouquet. (Illus.). 60p. (Orig.). 1991. pap. 49.00 (*1-56216-010-9*) Systems Co.

Strengthened Glass Technology for Solar Applications. Frank L. Bouquet. (Illus.). 65p. (C). 1991. 69.00 (*1-56216-021-4*); pap. 39.00 (*1-56216-022-2*) Systems Co.

Strengthened to Serve: 2 Corinthians. Jim Plueddemann & Carol Plueddemann. (Fisherman Bible Studyguide Ser.). 64p. 1991. pap. text ed. 4.99 (*0-87788-783-7*) Shaw Pubs.

Strengthening Adult & Continuing Education: A Global Perspective on Synergistic Leadership. Alan B. Knox. LC 92-41687. (Higher & Adult Education Ser.). 620p. text ed. 55.00 (*1-55542-537-2*) Jossey-Bass.

Strengthening Aging Families: Toward Diversity in Practice & Policy. Paul W. Power et al. 280p. 1995. pap. text ed. 22.50 (*0-8039-5425-5*) Sage.

Strengthening Aging Families: Toward Diversity in Practice & Policy. Paul W. Power et al. 280p. 1995. text ed. 46.00 (*0-8039-5424-7*) Sage.

Strengthening Basic Academic Skills Through Home Economics. Cecelia Thompson & Linda Floyd. 1990. 8.00 (*0-911365-30-3*, A261-80476) Family & Consumer Sci Educ.

Strengthening Capacities in Trade Investment & the Environment for the Comprehensive Development of Indo-China. 123p. 1995. 15.00 (*92-1-127034-0*, E.95.II.F.97) UN.

Strengthening Collegiate Education in Community Colleges. Judith S. Eaton. LC 93-46056. (Higher Education Ser.). 222p. text ed. 32.95 (*1-55542-615-8*) Jossey-Bass.

Strengthening Computer Technology Programs: Examples from Developing Institutions. Compiled by Floyd L. McKinney. 120p. 1984. 10.50 (*0-318-22204-3*, SN49) Ctr Educ Trng Employ.

Strengthening Conventional Deterrence in Europe: Proposals for the 1980s. European Security Study Staff. LC 83-42831. 260p. 1983. pap. 9.95 (*0-685-06977-X*); text ed. 39.95 (*0-312-76600-9*) St Martin.

***Strengthening Cooperation in the 21st Century: Advances in the Astronautical Sciences, Vol. 91.** Ed. by Peter M. Bainum et al. 1136p. 1996. 145.00 (*0-87703-409-5*) Am Astronaut.

Strengthening Democracy: A Parliamentary Perspective. Ron Gould et al. 172p. 1995. text ed. 59.95 (*1-85521-775-9*, Pub. by Dartmth Pub UK) Ashgate Pub Co.

Strengthening Democratic Process in Nepal General Elections Monitoring Program, 1991. S. Search. (C). 1991. text ed. 60.00 (*0-7855-0158-4*, Pub. by Ratna Pustak Bhandar) St Mut.

Strengthening Democratic Processes in Nepal-Voter Education Program, 1991. S. Search. (C). 1991. text ed. 65.00 (*0-7855-0159-2*, Pub. by Ratna Pustak Bhandar) St Mut.

Strengthening Departmental Leadership: A Team-Building Guide for Chairs in Colleges & Universities. Ann F. Lucas. LC 94-21302. (Higher & Adult Education Ser.). 319p. text ed. 30.95 (*0-7879-0012-5*) Jossey-Bass.

***Strengthening Development: The Interplay of Macro- & Microeconomics.** Economic Commission for Latin America & the Caribbean Staff. 116p. 1996. pap. 17.50 (*92-1-121207-3*, HB172) UN.

Strengthening EIA Capacity in Asia: Environmental Impact Assessment in the Philippines, Indonesia & Sri Lanka. Ed. by Mieke Van der Wansem & David Smith. 96p. 1995. pap. write for info. (*1-56973-001-6*) World Resources Inst.

Strengthening Experiential Education Within Your Institution. LC 86-60472. 154p. 1986. 25.00 (*0-937883-00-X*) NSEE.

Strengthening Families. Nicholas Hobbs et al. LC 83-49263. (Jossey-Bass Social & Behavioral Science Ser.). 368p. reprint ed. pap. 104.90 (*0-8357-4889-8*, 2037821) Bks Demand.

***Strengthening Family & Self.** Leona Johnson. LC 97-11491. (J). 1997. write for info. (*1-56637-396-4*) Goodheart.

Strengthening Family & Self. Leona Johnson. LC 93-26392. 688p. 1998. 46.60 (*0-87006-075-9*) Goodheart.

***Strengthening Family Life.** Catherine Martin. (Impact Ser.). 16p. 1996. pap. text ed. 1.95 (*1-55612-866-5*, LL1866) Sheed & Ward MO.

Strengthening Geography in the Social Studies. Ed. by Salvatore J. Natoli. LC 88-61299. (Bulletin Ser.: No. 8). (Illus.). 127p. 1989. reprint ed. pap. 9.95 (*0-87986-056-1*, BU810088) Nat Coun Soc Studies.

Strengthening Geriatric Nursing Education. Ed. by Terry Fulmer & Marianne Matzo. LC 95-2116. (Illus.). 200p. 1995. 33.95 (*0-8261-8940-7*) Springer Pub.

***Strengthening Health Care Organizations: Successful Approaches to Redesign.** Mickey L. Parsons et al. LC 97-21500. (Strategies for Improving Patient Care Ser.). 1997. write for info. (*0-8342-0970-5*) Aspen Pub.

Strengthening Health Management in Districts & Provinces: Handbook for Facilitators. A. Cassels & Katja Janovsky. 121p. 1991. pap. text ed. 18.00 (*0-614-08047-9*, 1930027) World Health.

Strengthening High-Risk Families: A Handbook for Practitioners. Lisa Kaplan & Judith L. Girard. LC 94-4759. 166p. 35.00 (*0-02-916915-1*, Free Press) Free Pr.

Strengthening Humanities in Community Colleges: National Assembly Report. Ed. by Roger Yarrington. LC 80-107493. (Illus.). 128p. reprint ed. pap. 36.50 (*0-7837-2485-3*, 2042642) Bks Demand.

Strengthening IAEA Safeguards: Lessons from Iraq. Anthony Fainberg. 64p. (Orig.). 1993. pap. 6.00 (*0-935371-27-3*) CFISAC.

Strengthening K-Twelve School Counseling Programs: A Support System Approach. Donald R. Rye & Rozanne Sparks. LC 90-82965. vii, 168p. (Orig.). (C). 1991. pap. text ed. 19.95 (*1-55959-018-1*) Accel Devel.

Strengthening Local Flood Protection Programs: Proceedings of the 10th Annual Conference of the Association of State Floodplain Managers, Pittsburgh, Pennsylvania, June 17-19, 1986. (Special Publications: No. 15). 308p. (Orig.). (C). 1987. pap. 10.00 (*0-685-28096-9*) Natural Hazards.

Strengthening Maternal & Child Health Programmes Through Primary Health Care: Guidelines for Countries of the Eastern Mediterranean Region. (WHO EMRO Technical Publication Ser.: No. 18). 75p. 1991. pap. text ed. 3.00 (*92-9021-131-8*, 1450018) World Health.

***Strengthening Ministries of Health for Primary Health Care.** WHO Staff. (WHO Offset Publications: No. 82). 58p. 1984. 8.00 (*92-4-170082-3*) World Health.

***Strengthening Ministries of Health for Primary Health Care: Report of a WHO Expert Committee.** (Technical Report Ser.: No. 766). 110p. 1988. pap. text ed. 12.00 (*92-4-120766-3*, 1100766) World Health.

Strengthening National Agricultural Research Systems in Eastern & Central Africa: A Framework for Action. Jan Weijenberg et al. (World Bank Technical Paper Ser.: Vol. 290). 164p. 1995. 10.95 (*0-8213-3322-4*, 13322) World Bank.

Strengthening National Agricultural Research Systems in the Humid & Sub-Humid Zones of West & Central Africa: A Framework for Action. Ajibola Taylor et al. (Technical Paper Ser.: No. 318). 120p. 1996. 8.95 (*0-8213-3566-9*, 13566) World Bank.

Strengthening Nutrition Through Primary Health Care: The Experience of JNSP in Myanmar. (SEARO Regional Health Paper Ser.: No. 20). 35p. 1991. pap. text ed. 5.00 (*92-9022-189-5*, 1580020) World Health.

Strengthening of Ceramics: Treatment, Tests, & Design Applications. Kirchner. (Manufacturing Engineering & Materials Processing Ser.: Vol. 3). 256p. 1979. 145.00 (*0-8247-6851-5*) Dekker.

Strengthening of Regional Cooperation in Human Resources Development in Asia & the Pacific. 156p. Date not set. 25.00 (*92-1-127036-7*, E.95.II.F.99) UN.

Strengthening of Skills: Advanced Teacher's Manual. Lynn O'Brien. 206p. 1991. teacher ed. 199.00 (*1-56602-044-1*); student ed. 69.95 (*1-56602-045-X*) Research Better.

Strengthening of Skills: Basic Teacher's Manual. 3rd ed. Lynn O'Brien. 221p. 1991. teacher ed. 199.00 (*1-56602-042-5*); student ed. 69.95 (*1-56602-043-3*) Research Better.

Strengthening of the U. S. - Japan Partnership in the 1990s: Ensuring the Alliance in an Unsure World. Shoichi Akazawa et al. Ed. by Richard Grant. (Significant Issues Ser.). 1992. pap. text ed. 7.95 (*0-89206-188-X*) CSI Studies.

Strengthening Parents & Families During the Early Childhood Years. Kevin J. Swick. 485p. (Orig.). (C). 1993. pap. text ed. 24.80 (*0-87563-475-3*) Stipes.

Strengthening Programs for Writing Across the Curriculum. Ed. by Susan H. McLeod. LC 85-644763. (New Directions for Teaching & Learning Ser.: No. TL 36). 1988. 19.00 (*1-55542-899-1*) Jossey-Bass.

Strengthening Radiation & Nuclear Safety Infrastructures in Countries of Former U. S. S. R. 143p. 1993. pap. 30.00 (*92-0-102793-1*, STI/PUB/939, Pub. by IAEA AU) Bernan Associates.

***Strengthening Refugee Families: Designing Programs for Refugees & Other Families in Need.** Daniel Scheinfeld & Lorraine Wallach. LC 97-8947. (Illus.). 192p. 1997. pap. 25.95 (*0-925065-13-7*) Lyceum IL.

Strengthening Research in Academic OB-GYN Departments. Institute of Medicine Staff. Ed. by Jessica Townsend. LC 92-70987. 320p. 1992. pap. text ed. 30.00 (*0-309-04697-1*, RG648) Natl Acad Pr.

Strengthening State Departments of Education. Gerald E. Sroufe & Donald H. Layton. Ed. by Roald F. Campbell. LC 67-25738. 1967. pap. 6.00 (*0-931080-02-9*) U Chicago Midwest Admin.

Strengthening State Legislatures. 40p. 1994. 5.00 (*1-55516-993-7*, 9361) Natl Conf State Legis.

Strengthening Stepfamilies. Elizabeth Einstein & Linda Albert. 1986. 149.95 (*0-88671-216-5*, 6470); teacher ed., pap. 45.95 (*0-88671-218-1*, 6471) Am Guidance.

Strengthening Support & Recruitment of Women & Minorities to Positions in Education Administration: A Resource Manual. (Illus.). 186p. (Orig.). (C). 1993. pap. text ed. 40.00 (*0-7881-0075-0*) DIANE Pub.

Strengthening Support & Recruitment of Women & Minorities to Positions in Education Administration: A Resourse Manual. 1995. lib. bdg. 250.00 (*0-8490-6550-X*) Gordon Pr.

Strengthening Teacher Education: The Challenges to College & University Leaders. C. Peter Magrath et al. LC 86-46336. (Jossey-Bass Higher Education Ser.). 206p. reprint ed. pap. 58.80 (*0-7837-2524-8*, 2042683) Bks Demand.

Strengthening Teamwork: Trade Version. Mescon Group Staff. (GC - Principles of Management Ser.). 1995. text ed. 16.95 (*0-538-84364-0*); teacher ed., text ed. 25.95 (*0-538-85041-8*) S-W Pub.

Strengthening Technological Capabilities: A Challenge for the Nineties: A Review of ILO Activities on Technology. 3rd rev. ed. v, 116p. 1992. pap. 13.50 (*92-2-108165-6*) Intl Labour Office.

Strengthening the Biological Weapons Convention by Confidence-Building Measures. Ed. by Erhard Geissler. (SIPRI Chemical & Biological Warfare Studies: No. 10). 224p. 1990. pap. 42.00 (*0-19-829139-6*) OUP.

***Strengthening the Bonds of Peace: Parish Resource Packet.** National Conference of Catholic Bishops. 52p. (Orig.). 1996. pap. text ed. 9.95 (*1-57455-018-7*) US Catholic.

Strengthening the College Major. Ed. by Carol G. Schneider & William S. Green. LC 85-644752. (New Directions for Higher Education Ser.: No. 84). 115p. (Orig.). 1993. pap. 16.95 (*1-55542-723-5*) Jossey-Bass.

Strengthening the Effectiveness of Aid: Lessons for Donors. LC 95-10662. (Development in Practice Ser.). 56p. 1995. 6.95 (*0-8213-3222-8*, 13222) World Bank.

Strengthening the Family: Guidelines for the Design of Relevant Programmes. (The Family Ser.). 44p. pap. 10.00 (*92-1-130124-6*, E.87.IV.4) UN.

Strengthening the Family: Implications for International Development. M. Zeitlin et al. 276p. 1995. pap. text ed. 35.00 (*92-808-0890-7*) Bernan Associates.

Strengthening the Federal Budget Process: A Requirement for Effective Fiscal Control. (CED Statement on National Policy Ser.). 106p. (Orig.). 1983. pap. 8.50 (*0-87186-077-5*) Comm Econ Dev.

Strengthening the Financial Sector in the Adjustment Process. Ed. by Roberto Frenkel. 246p. (Orig.). 1994. pap. text ed. 18.50 (*0-940602-78-4*) IADB.

Strengthening the International Monetary System: Exchange Rates, Surveillance & Objective Indicators. International Monetary Fund Staff et al. (Occasional Paper Ser.: No. 50). 84p. 1987. pap. 7.50 (*0-939934-76-0*) Intl Monetary.

Strengthening the New Nation see **U. S. History - One**

***Strengthening the Performance of Community Health Workers in Primary Health Care: Report of a WHO Study Group, 1987.** WHO Staff. (Technical Report Ser.: No. 780). 46p. 1989. 6.00 (*92-4-120780-9*) World Health.

Strengthening the Poor: What Have We Learned? John P. Lewis. Ed. by Richard E. Feinberg & Valeriana Kallab. (U. S. Third World Policy Perspectives Ser.: No. 10). 1988. 39.95 (*0-88738-267-3*); pap. 21.95 (*0-88738-768-3*) Transaction Pubs.

Strengthening the Progressive Income Tax: The Responsible Answer to America's Budget Problem. Richard A. Musgrave. 1989. 10.00 (*0-944826-07-5*) Economic Policy Inst.

S

Strengthening the Roots of Your Family Tree: A Teaching Syllabus. Rod Parsley. 110p. (Orig.). 1991. pap. 10.00 (*1-880244-03-9*) Wrld Harvest Church.

Strengthening the Spiritual Man. Lex W. Adams & Lynn M. Adams. 125p. 1982. pap. write for info. (*0-9643206-1-4*) Spirit of Truth.

Strengthening the U. S. - Japan Library Partnership in the Global Information Flow: Fourth U. S. - Japan Conference on Library & Information Science in Higher Education. Theodore F. Welch et al. LC 89-18141. (C). 1991. text ed. 20.00 (*0-8389-3378-5*, 3378-5) ALA.

Strengthening the United Nations. Organization of Peace Commission & Arthur N. Holcombe. LC 74-7536. 276p. 1976. reprint ed. text ed. 65.00 (*0-8371-7579-8*, HOUN, Greenwood Pr) Greenwood.

Strengthening the United Nations: A Bibliography on U. N. Reform & World Federalism. Compiled by Joseph P. Baratta. LC 87-134. (Bibliographies & Indexes in World History Ser.: No. 7). 361p. 1987. text ed. 65.00 (*0-313-25840-6*, BSU/) Greenwood.

Strengthening the World Monetary System. Intro. by Philip M. Klutznick. LC 73-84800. 87p. 1973. pap. 1.50 (*0-87186-051-1*) Comm Econ Dev.

Strengthening U. S. - Korean Relations in the Coming Years: A Blueprint for Policy: The Final Report of the CSIS U. S. - Korea Task Force. Ed. by Scott Boller et al. LC 94-14111. (CSIS Panel Report Ser.). 48p. (Orig.). 1994. pap. 16.00 (*0-89206-263-0*) CSI Studies.

Strengthening Urban Management: International Perspectives. Ed. by Thomas L. Blair. (Urban Innovation Abroad Ser.). 368p. 1985. 75.00 (*0-306-42081-3*, Plenum Pr) Plenum.

Strengthening Vocational Education's Role in Decreasing the Dropout Rate. James Weber. 28p. 1987. 4.75 (*0-318-23417-3*, RD 267) Ctr Educ Trng Employ.

Strengthening Voluntary Action in India: Health-Family Planning, the Environment & Women's Development. Ravi Gulhati et al. (C). 1995. 30.00 (*81-220-0399-0*, Pub. by Konark Pubs II) S Asia.

Strengthening Work-Related Education & Training Through Improved Guidance Programs in the 1990s. Center on Education & Training for Employment Staff. 1989. 3.00 (*0-317-04617-9*, SN58) Ctr Educ Trng Employ.

Strengthening Your Grip. Charles R. Swindoll. 1990. pap. 10.99 (*0-8499-3215-7*) Bantam.

Strengthening Your Grip. rev. ed. Charles R. Swindoll. 160p. 1995. pap. 5.99 (*0-8499-8643-5*) Word Pub.

Strengthening Your Marriage. Wayne A. Mack. (Christian Growth Ser.). 1977. pap. 6.99 (*0-87552-333-1*, Pub. by Evangelical Pr) Presby & Reformed.

Strengthening Your Marriage see Fortaleciendo el Matrimonio

***Strengthening Your Marriage & Family.** Douglas A. Brinley. 1997. pap. 7.95 (*1-57008-308-8*) Bookcraft Inc.

Strengthening Your Stepfamily. Elizabeth Einstein & Linda Albert. 1986. pap. 14.95 (*0-88671-217-3*, 6472) Am Guidance.

Strengthening Your Stepfamily. Elizabeth Einstein & Linda Albert. 1987. pap. 14.95 (*0-394-75283-X*) Random.

Strengths: African-American Children & Families. Asa G. Hilliard, III. 20p. (Orig.). (C). 1982. pap. 3.00 (*0-317-45081-6*) City Coll Wk.

***Strengths Model: Case Management with People Suffering from Severe & Persistent Mental Illness.** Charles A. Rapp. (Illus.). 288p. (C). 1997. text ed. 35.00 (*0-19-511444-2*) OUP.

Strengths Perspective in Social Work Practice. Dennis Saleebey. 198p. (Orig.). (C). 1992. pap. text ed. 33.50 (*0-8013-0549-7*, 78464) Longman.

Strenna Teatrale Europea. Ed. by H. Robert Cohen. (Repertoire International de la Presse Musicale Ser.). 182p. (ITA.). 1989. 120.00 (*0-8357-0871-3*) Univ Microfilms.

Strensall, Near York, in the Mid-Nineteenth Century. Theresa Mitchell. (C). 1988. 80.00 (*1-85072-055-X*, Pub. by W Sessions UK) St Mut.

Strenuous Age in American Literature. Grant C. Knight. LC 75-129461. 1970. reprint ed. 53.00 (*0-8154-0351-8*) Cooper Sq.

Strenuous Commands: The Ethic of Jesus. Anthony Harvey. LC 90-42290. 256p. (Orig.). (C). 1990. pap. 17.95 (*0-334-02471-4*) TPI PA.

Strenuous Life. Theodore Roosevelt. 30p. 1991. 8.95 (*1-55709-142-0*) Applewood.

Strenuous Life: Essays & Addresses. Theodore Roosevelt. 1902. 39.00 (*0-403-00311-3*) Scholarly.

Streptococcal & Staphylococcal Infections: Proceedings of the WHO Expert Committee, Geneva, 1967. WHO Staff. (Technical Report Ser.: No. 394). 56p. 1968. pap. text ed. 5.00 (*92-4-120394-3*, 1100394) World Health.

Streptococci. Ed. by Fredrick A. Skinner & Louis B. Quesnel. (Society for Applied Bacteriology Symposium Ser.). 1978. text ed. 179.00 (*0-12-648035-4*) Acad Pr.

***Streptococci & the Host.** Ed. by T. Horaud & A. Bouvet. (Experimental Medicine & Biology Ser.: Vol. 418). (C). 1997. write for info. (*0-306-45603-6*, Plenum Pr) Plenum.

Streptokinase Treatment in Chronic Arterial Occlusions & Stenoses. Ed. by Michael Martin. 208p. 1982. 120.00 (*0-8493-5046-8*, RC694, CRC Reprint) Franklin.

Stresemann & the Revision of Versailles. Henry L. Bretton. xii, 199p. 1953. 35.00 (*0-8047-0444-9*) Stanford U Pr.

Stress. Laurie Beckelman. LC 94-2735. (J). 1994. text ed. 13.95 (*0-89686-848-6*, Crstwood Hse) Silver Burdett Pr.

Stress. Laurie Beckelman. 1994. pap. 5.95 (*0-382-24746-9*, Crstwood Hse) Silver Burdett Pr.

Stress. Charles G. Edwards. (Outreach Ser.). 32p. 1982. pap. 1.49 (*0-8163-0468-8*) Pacific Pr Pub Assn.

Stress. Loren D. Estelman. 256p. 1997. mass mkt. 5.99 (*0-446-40367-9*, Mysterious Paperbk) Warner Bks.

Stress. Loren D. Estleman. 288p. 1996. 21.95 (*0-89296-553-3*) Mysterious Pr.

***Stress.** Loren D. Estleman. 1997. mass mkt. 5.99 (*0-614-27762-0*) Mysterious Pr.

Stress. Mary D. Miles. (Lifesearch Ser.). 64p. (Orig.). 1994. pap. 4.95 (*0-687-77876-X*) Abingdon.

Stress. Alan H. Rosenstein. Ed. by Margaret A. Chesney & Nancy Wiltsek. (Illus.). 23p. 1986. pap. 2.50 (*0-933161-06-9*) Better H Prog.

Stress. Charles R. Swindoll. (Swindoll Booklets Ser.). 32p. 1995. pap. 3.99 (*0-310-20092-X*) Zondervan.

Stress: A Mind-Body Approach to Understanding & Overcoming Stress. Harold J. Margolis. (Frontiers of Consciousness Ser.). 750p. 1990. text ed. 69.50 (*0-685-26542-0*) Irvington.

Stress: A New Positive Approach. Jenni Adams. 176p. (Orig.). (C). 1990. reprint ed. lib. bdg. 29.00 (*0-8095-7591-4*) Borgo Pr.

Stress: A Novel of Detroit. large type ed. Loren D. Estleman. LC 96-10419. 407p. 1996. 24.95 (*0-7862-0695-0*, Thorndike Lrg Prnt) Thorndike Pr.

Stress: A Nutritional Approach. Louise Tenney. (Todays Health Ser.: No. 5). pap. 3.95 (*0-913923-32-X*) Woodland UT.

Stress: Causes & Symptoms & the Use of Herbs, Vitamins & Minerals & Diet to Fight Stress. 1991. lib. bdg. 79.95 (*0-8490-5107-X*) Gordon Pr.

Stress: Conceptual & Biological Aspects. Fredrick Toates & Milton Keynes. 400p. 1996. text ed. 75.00 (*0-471-96021-7*) Wiley.

Stress: Facilitator's Manual. Kathy A. Miller et al. (Well Aware About Health Risk Reduction Ser.). (Illus.). (Orig.). 1983. 35.00 (*0-943562-53-8*) Well Aware.

Stress: From Synapse to Syndrome. Ed. by S. Clare Stanford et al. (Illus.). 376p. 1993. text ed. 95.00 (*0-12-663370-3*) Acad Pr.

Stress: Handbook of Psychology & Health, Vol. 5. Ed. by Andrew Baum & Jerome E. Singer. 352p. 1987. text ed. 79.95 (*0-89859-209-7*) L Erlbaum Assocs.

***Stress: Just Chill Out!** Joeanne Adler. LC 96-32678. (Teen Issues Ser.). 104p. (YA). (gr. 6 up). 1997. lib. bdg. 18.95 (*0-89490-918-5*) Enslow Pubs.

Stress: Letting Go & Letting God. Melanie Jongsma. (Friendship Ser.). (Illus.). 48p. (Orig.). 1993. pap. write for info. (*1-882536-20-7*, A100-0059) Bible League.

***Stress: Molecular Genetic & Neurobiological Advances, 2 vols.** Ed. by Richard McCarty et al. 992p. 1996. text ed. 250.00 (*90-5702-520-5*, ECU208, Harwood Acad Pubs) Gordon & Breach.

Stress: Neurobiology & Neuroendocrinology. Ed. by Marvin Brown et al. 728p. 1990. 225.00 (*0-8247-8325-5*) Dekker.

Stress: Neurochemical & Humoral Mechanisms: Proceedings of the 4th Symposium on Catecholamines & Other Neurotransmitters in Stress, Czechoslovakia, June 1987, 2 vols., Set. Ed. by Glen R. Van Loon. 1074p. 1989. text ed. 432.00 (*2-88124-339-8*) Gordon & Breach.

Stress: Neuroendocrine & Molecular Approaches, 2 vols., Vols. 1 & 2. LC 91-46587. 1044p. 1992. text ed. 273.00 (*2-88124-506-4*) Gordon & Breach.

Stress: Participant Workbook. Kathy A. Miller et al. (Well Aware About Health Risk Reduction Ser.). (Illus.). 120p. (Orig.). 1982. student ed. 8.75 (*0-943562-54-6*) Well Aware.

Stress: Physiological & Psychological Aspects: A Source Guide. 1991. lib. bdg. 76.00 (*0-8490-4902-4*) Gordon Pr.

Stress: Proven Stress-Coping Strategies for Better Health. Leon Chaitow. 208p. 1996. pap. 11.00 (*0-7225-3192-3*) Harper SF.

Stress: Psychological & Physiological Interactions. Ed. by Susan R. Burchfield. LC 83-12971. (Clinical & Community Psychology Ser.). 399p. 1985. text ed. 79.95 (*0-89116-267-4*) Hemisp Pub.

Stress: Taming the Tyrant. Richard Neil. LC 94-60991. 118p. 1994. per. 8.95 (*1-57258-001-1*) Teach Servs.

Stress: The Agony Within. Jose B. Viloria, Jr. Ed. by Josie Eswagen. (Illus.). (Orig.). 1996. pap. 5.95 (*0-9623298-5-1*) SGV Pub Co.

Stress: The Nature & History of Engineered Grief. Robert Kugelmann. LC 92-8381. 224p. 1992. text ed. 55.00 (*0-275-94271-6*, C4271, Praeger Pubs) Greenwood.

Stress: The Role of Catecholamines & Other Neurotransmitters, 2 vols., Set. Earl Usdin et al. 1100p. 1984. text ed. 483.00 (*2-88124-102-6*) Gordon & Breach.

Stress: Theory & Practice. King. 1985. text ed. 33.95 (*0-8089-1874-5*, Grune) Saunders.

Stress: What It Is, What It Can Do to Your Health, How to Handle It. rev. ed. Walter McQuade & Ann Aikman. 288p. 1993. pap. 5.99 (*0-451-17651-0*, Sig) NAL-Dutton.

Stress: 63 Ways to Relieve Tension & Stay Healthy. Charles B. Inlander & Cynthia K. Moran. 96p. (Orig.). 1996. pap. 8.95 (*0-8027-7505-5*) Walker & Co.

***Stress: 63 Ways to Relieve Tension & Stay Healthy.** Charles B. Inlander & Cynthia K. Moran. LC 96-9901. Date not set. write for info. (*0-8027-1324-6*) Walker & Co.

Stress Vol. I: The Cause of Disease. 5th ed. Ingrid Naiman. (Astrology of Healing Ser.). (Illus.). 274p. 1997. reprint ed. 35.00 (*1-882834-01-1*) Seventh Ray.

Stress see From Stress to Balance

***Stress - An Owners Manual: Positive Techniques for Taking Charge of Your Life.** Arthur Rowshan. 1997. pap. 10.95 (*1-85168-140-X*) Onewrld Pubns.

Stress - Basis Mechanism & Clinical Implications: Proceedings of the First World Congress on Stress, Held October 2-7, 1994. Ed. by George P. Chrousos et al. 755p. 1995. 165.00 (*0-89766-943-6*) NY Acad Sci.

Stress - Basis Mechanisms & Clinical Implications: Proceedings of the First World Congress on Stress, Held October 2-7, 1994. Ed. by George P. Chrousos et al. 1995. pap. write for info. (*0-89766-944-4*) NY Acad Sci.

Stress - the Only Disease: Basics of Wellness. Jonathon D. Miller. (Orig.). 1996. pap. 3.95 (*0-935815-06-6*) Lifecircle.

Stress among Older Adults: Understanding & Coping. James H. Humphrey. 172p. 1992. pap. 24.95 (*0-398-06169-6*) C C Thomas.

Stress among Older Adults: Understanding & Coping. James H. Humphrey. 172p. (C). 1992. text ed. 35.95 (*0-398-05790-7*) C C Thomas.

Stress among Women in Modern Society. James H. Humphrey. 176p. 1992. pap. 27.95 (*0-398-06170-X*) C C Thomas.

Stress among Women in Modern Society. James H. Humphrey. 176p. (C). 1992. text ed. 38.95 (*0-398-05824-5*) C C Thomas.

Stress Analysis. Ed. by Carlos A. Brebbia. (Boundary Elements X Ser.: Vol. 3). 480p. 1988. 199.95 (*0-387-50093-6*) Spr-Verlag.

Stress Analysis see Advances in Boundary Elements

Stress Analysis by Boundary Element Methods. J. Balas et al. (Studies in Applied Mechanics: Vol. 23). 1989. 342.50 (*0-444-98830-0*) Elsevier.

***Stress Analysis of Spiral Bevel Gear: A Novel Approach to Tooth Modelling.** C. Rama & M. Rao. (1993 Fall Technical Meeting). 1993. pap. text ed. 30.00 (*1-55589-597-2*) AGMA.

Stress & Accidents in the Offshore Oil & Gas Industry. Valerie J. Sutherland & Cary L. Cooper. 227p. 1991. 55.00 (*0-87201-802-4*) Gulf Pub.

Stress & Adaptation. Elemer Endroczi. 189p. (C). 1991. 90.00 (*963-05-5834-3*, Pub. by Akad Kiado HU) St Mut.

Stress & Adaptation in the Context of Culture: Depression in a Southern Black Community. William W. Dressler. LC 89-26307. 354p. 1991. text ed. 74.50 (*0-7914-0413-7*); pap. text ed. 24.95 (*0-7914-0414-5*) State U NY Pr.

Stress & Addiction. Edward Gottheil et al. LC 87-7987. (Psychosocial Stress Ser.: No. 9). 352p. 1987. text ed. 49.95 (*0-87630-463-3*) Brunner-Mazel.

***Stress & Adversity over the Life Course: Trajectories & Turning Points.** Ed. by Ian H. Gotlib & Blair Wheaton. (Illus.). 275p. (C). 1997. text ed. 49.95 (*0-521-55075-0*) Cambridge U Pr.

Stress & Anger Management. Cheryl S. Johnson & Richard L. Johnson. (Living Skills Ser.). 108p. 1993. teacher ed. 8.95 (*1-884245-19-6*); pap. text ed. 7.95 (*1-884245-18-8*) Life Choices.

Stress & Animal Welfare. D. Broom & K. G. Johnson. LC 93-32185. (Animal Behaviour Ser.). 224p. (gr. 13). 1993. pap. text ed. 33.95 (*0-412-39580-0*, Chap & Hall NY) Chapman & Hall.

Stress & Anxiety, Vol. 8. Charles D. Spielberger et al. 1981. text ed. 34.95 (*0-07-060239-5*) McGraw.

Stress & Anxiety, Vol. 9. Ed. by Charles D. Spielberger et al. LC 74-28292. (Clinical & Community Psychology Ser.). (Illus.). 283p. 1985. text ed. 68.95 (*0-89116-310-7*) Hemisp Pub.

Stress & Anxiety, Vol. 11. Ed. by Charles D. Spielberger et al. (Clinical & Community Psychology Ser.). 258p. 1988. 78.95 (*0-89116-312-3*) Hemisp Pub.

Stress & Anxiety, Vol. 12. Ed. by Charles D. Spielberger & Irwin G. Sarason. (Clinical & Community Psychology Ser.). 360p. 1989. 78.95 (*0-89116-890-7*) Hemisp Pub.

Stress & Anxiety, Vol. 13. Ed. by Charles D. Spielberger et al. (Clinical & Community Psychology Ser.). 336p. 1990. 80.95 (*1-56032-139-3*) Hemisp Pub.

Stress & Anxiety, Vol. 10: A Sourcebook of Theory & Research. Ed. by Charles D. Spielberger & Irwin G. Sarason. (Clinical & Community Psychology Ser.). (Illus.). 450p. 1986. pap. 36.95 (*0-89116-460-X*) Hemisp Pub.

Stress & Burnout among Providers Caring for the Terminally Ill & Their Families. Ed. & Intro. by Lenora F. Paridis. LC 87-25949. (Hospice Journal: Vol. 3, Nos. 2-3). 276p. 1988. text ed. 39.95 (*0-86656-674-0*) Haworth Pr.

Stress & Burnout in Library Service. Janette S. Caputo. LC 90-41637. 184p. 1991. pap. 24.95 (*0-89774-602-3*) Oryx Pr.

Stress & Campus Response. Ed. by G. Kerry Smith. LC 68-57441. (Jossey-Bass Higher Education Ser.). 316p. reprint ed. pap. 90.10 (*0-317-08577-8*, 2013869) Bks Demand.

Stress & Common Gastrointestinal Disorders: A Comprehensive Approach. Gerhard Dotevall. LC 85-6565. (Gastroenterology Ser.: Vol. 3). 192p. 1985. text ed. 59.95 (*0-275-91310-4*, C1310, Praeger Pubs) Greenwood.

Stress & Coping. Ed. by Neil Schneiderman et al. 376p. (C). 1985. text ed. 69.95 (*0-89859-564-9*) L Erlbaum Assocs.

Stress & Coping. 3rd ed. Alan Monat & Richard S. Lazarus. 1991. pap. text ed. 25.00 (*0-231-07457-3*) Col U Pr.

Stress & Coping: An Anthology. 2nd ed. Alan Monat & Richard S. Lazarus. LC 77-3264. 560p. 1985. text ed. 65.00 (*0-231-05820-9*); pap. text ed. 21.00 (*0-231-05821-7*) Col U Pr.

Stress & Coping: The Indian Experience. D. M. Pestonjee. 224p. (C). 1992. 32.00 (*0-8039-9400-1*) Sage.

Stress & Coping Across Development. Tiffany M. Field et al. 288p. 1988. 59.95 (*0-89859-960-1*) L Erlbaum Assocs.

Stress & Coping in Child Health. Ed. by Annette M. La Greca et al. LC 91-38224. (Advances in Pediatric Psychology Ser.). 413p. 1991. lib. bdg. 45.00 (*0-89862-112-7*) Guilford Pr.

Stress & Coping in Infancy & Childhood. Ed. by Tiffany Field et al. 272p. 1991. text ed. 59.95 (*0-8058-0944-9*) L Erlbaum Assocs.

Stress & Coping in Later-Life Families. Mary A. Stephens et al. (Series in Applied Psychology: Social Issues & Questions). 304p. 1990. 66.95 (*0-89116-928-8*) Hemisp Pub.

Stress & Coping in Mental Health. Carson. 221p. 1994. pap. 41.50 (*1-56593-330-3*, 0660) Singular Publishing.

Stress & Coping in Nursing. Roy Bailey & Margaret Clarke. 352p. 1990. pap. 32.50 (*0-412-33830-0*, A4441) Chapman & Hall.

Stress & Deflection Reduction in 2x4 Studs Spaced 24 Inches on Center Resulting from the Addition of Interior & Exterior Surfaces, Vol. 3. NAHB Research Foundation Staff. (Research Report Ser.). 46p. 1981. pap. 6.50 (*0-86718-117-6*) Home Builder.

Stress & Deformation: A Handbook on Tensors in Geology. Oertel. (Illus.). 304p. 1996. 65.00 (*0-19-509503-0*) OUP.

Stress & Disease Processes: Perspectives in Behavioral Medicine. Ed. by Andrew Baum et al. (Advances in Behavioral Medicine Ser.). 328p. 1992. text ed. 69.95 (*0-8058-1161-3*) L Erlbaum Assocs.

Stress & Emotion, Vol. 14. Ed. by Charles D. Spielberger et al. (Series in Stress & Emotion: Anxiety, Anger, & Curiosity). 340p. 1991. 87.95 (*1-56032-187-3*) Hemisp Pub.

Stress & Emotion, Vol. 15. Charles D. Spielberger et al. 1995. 73.95 (*1-56032-284-5*) Hemisp Pub.

Stress & Emotion: Anxiety, Anger, & Curiosity, Vol. 16. Ed. by Charles D. Spielberger & Irwin G. Sarason. 300p. 1996. 69.95 (*1-56032-449-X*) Hemisp Pub.

***Stress & Employer Liability.** Jill Earnshaw & Cary Cooper. (Law & Employment Ser.). 200p. 1996. pap. 51.00 (*0-85292-615-4*, Pub. by IPM UK) St Mut.

Stress & Error in Aviation. Eric Farmer. (Proceedings of the Eighteenth WEAAP Conference Ser.: Vol. 2). 176p. 1991. text ed. 49.95 (*1-85628-169-8*, Pub. by Avebury Pub UK) Ashgate Pub Co.

Stress & Fatigue in Human Performance. fac. ed. Robert V. Hockey. LC 82-13490. (Wiley Series on Studies in Human Performance: No. 1-507). 412p. 1983. reprint ed. pap. 117.50 (*0-7837-8290-X*, 2049072) Bks Demand.

Stress & Fish. Ed. by A. D. Pickering. LC 81-67907. 1981. text ed. 99.00 (*0-12-554550-9*) Acad Pr.

Stress & Health. 2nd ed. Phillip L. Rice. LC 91-36428. 436p. (C). 1992. pap. 34.95 (*0-534-17280-6*) Brooks-Cole.

***Stress & Health: A Reversal Theory Perspective.** Sven Svebak & Michael J. Apter. LC 96-28946. (Health Psychology & Behavioral Medicine Ser.). 1997. write for info. (*1-56032-473-2*) Taylor & Francis.

***Stress & Health: A Reversal Theory Perspective.** Sven Svebek & Michael J. Apter. LC 96-28946. (Health Psychology & Behavioral Medicine Ser.). 1997. pap. write for info. (*1-56032-474-0*) Taylor & Francis.

***Stress & Health: Biological & Psychological Interactions.** William R. Lovallo. (Behavioral Medicine & Health Psychology Ser.: Vol. 1). 240p. 1997. 46.00 (*0-8039-7000-5*); pap. 21.95 (*0-8039-7001-3*) Sage.

Stress & Health among the Elderly. Ed. by May L. Wykle et al. LC 91-4873. 280p. 1992. 36.95 (*0-8261-7320-9*) Springer Pub.

Stress & Heart Disease. Ed. by R. E. Beamish et al. (Developments in Cardiovascular Medicine Ser.). 1985. lib. bdg. 121.00 (*0-89838-709-4*) Kluwer Ac.

Stress & Human Performance. Ed. by James E. Driskell & Eduardo Salas. (Applied Psychology Ser.). 360p. 1996. text ed. 65.00 (*0-8058-1182-6*) L Erlbaum Assocs.

Stress & Hypertension. Ed. by J. Bahlmann & H. Liebau. (Contributions to Nephrology Ser.: Vol. 30). (Illus.). xiv, 206p. 1982. pap. 72.00 (*3-8055-3450-7*) S Karger.

Stress & Immunity. Nicholas P. Plotnikoff et al. (Illus.). 528p. 1991. 121.95 (*0-8493-8845-7*, QP82) CRC Pr.

Stress & Its Management by Yoga. K. N. Udupa. 1986. 19.95 (*0-685-44106-7*) Asia Bk Corp.

Stress & Its Management by Yoga. K. N. Udupa. Ed. by R. C. Prasad. 395p. 1996. reprint ed. 29.00 (*81-208-0000-1*, Pub. by Motilal Banarsidass II) S Asia.

Stress & Marriage: The Conflict-Reducing, Intimacy-Enhancing, Problem-Solving Guide to a Better Marriage. Lyle H. Miller & Alma D. Smith. 1996. pap. 14.00 (*0-671-87246-X*) PB.

Stress & Medical Procedures. Ed. by Marie Johnston & Louise Wallace. 200p. 1990. 55.00 (*0-19-261673-0*) OUP.

Stress & Mental Health: Contemporary Issues & Prospects for the Future. Ed. by W. R. Avison & I. Gotlib. (Stress & Coping Ser.). (Illus.). 332p. (C). 1994. 49.50 (*0-306-44687-1*, Plenum Pr) Plenum.

Stress & Motor Performance: Understanding & Coping. David Pargman. (Illus.). 204p. 1986. pap. 15.95 (*0-685-17375-5*) Mouvement Pubns.

***Stress & Natural Healing: Herbal Medicines & Natural Therapies.** Christopher Hobbs. LC 97-14001. 1997. write for info. (*1-883010-38-1*) Interweave.

Stress & Old Age. Wilbur Watson. LC 79-65127. 144p. 1980. 32.95 (*0-87855-296-0*) Transaction Pubs.

Stress & Organizational Problems in Hospitals. Ed. by Don Wallis & Charles J. De Wolff. 256p. 1988. 49.95 (*0-7099-5255-4*) Routledge Chapman & Hall.

Stress & Performance Effectiveness Vol. 3: Stress & Performance Effectiveness. Ed. by Earl A. Alluisi & Edwin A. Fleishman. (Human Performance & Productivity Ser.). 288p. 1982. text ed. 59.95 (*0-89859-091-4*) L Erlbaum Assocs.

Stress & Performance in Diving. Arthur J. Bachrach & Glen H. Egstrom. 183p. (C). 1987. text ed. 42.00 (*0-941332-06-3*, D235) Best Pub Co.

Stress & Performance in Sport. Ed. by J. Graham Jones & Lew Hardy. (Studies in Human Performance). 301p. 1990. text ed. 71.95 (*0-471-92084-3*) Wiley.

Stress & Policing: Sources & Strategies. Jennifer M. Brown & Elizabeth A. Campbell. 204p. 1994. text ed. 60.00 (*0-471-94138-7*) Wiley.

Stress & Pregnancy. John J. Sullivan & Joyce C Foster. LC 86-82022. (Stress in Modern Society Ser.: No. 8). 1990. 32.50 (*0-404-63261-0*) AMS Pr.

Stress & Productivity. Ed. by Leonard W. Krinsky et al. LC 83-22606. (Problems of Industrial Psychiatric Medicine Ser.: Vol. 9). 176p. 1984. 35.95 (*0-89885-137-8*) Human Sci Pr.

Stress & Reading Difficulties: Research, Assessment, Intervention. Lance M. Gentile & Merna M. McMillan. LC 87-2643. 54p. reprint ed. pap. 25.00 (*0-7837-0589-1*, 2040933) Bks Demand.

Stress & Recovery. Patricia Hoolihan. 24p. (Orig.). (C). 1984. pap. 2.00 (*0-89486-236-7*, 1414B) Hazelden.

Stress & Related Disorders. Ed. by A. R. Genazzani et al. (Illus.). 490p. (C). 1991. 85.00 (*1-85070-358-2*) Prthnon Pub.

Stress & Satisfaction on the Job: Work Meanings & Coping of Mid-Career Men. Patricia E. Benner. LC 84-3252. 176p. 1984. text ed. 49.95 (*0-275-91127-6*, C1127, Praeger Pubs) Greenwood.

Stress & Self Awareness: A Guide for Nurses. Meg Bond. 256p. 1986. pap. 27.50 (*0-7506-0125-6*) Buttrwrth-Heinemann.

Stress & Sexuality. Jerrold S. Greenberg. (Stress in Modern Society Ser.: No. 6). 1987. 32.50 (*0-404-63257-2*) AMS Pr.

Stress & Strain: Basic Concepts of Continuum Mechanics for Geologists. W. D. Means. (Illus.). 336p. (C). 1991. 49.95 (*0-387-07556-9*) Spr-Verlag.

Stress & Strain Concentration Factors of Welded Multiplanar Tubular Joints. A. Romeijn. 170p. 1994. pap. 57.50 (*90-407-1057-0*, Pub. by Delft U Pr NE) Coronet Bks.

Stress & Strategies for Lifestyle Management. Kenneth B. Matheny & Richard J. Riordan. 250p. 1992. pap. 29.95 (*0-88406-250-3*) GA St U Busn Pr.

Stress & Stress Coping in Cultivated Plants. Bryan D. Mckersie. 260p. (C). 1994. lib. bdg. 155.00 (*0-7923-2827-2*) Kluwer Ac.

Stress & Tension Control, Vol. 2. Ed. by Frank J. McGuigan et al. 420p. 1985. 85.00 (*0-306-41815-0*, Plenum Pr) Plenum.

Stress & Tension Control, Vol. 3: Stress Management. Ed. by Frank J. McGuigan et al. (Illus.). 298p. 1989. 85.00 (*0-306-43327-3*, Plenum Pr) Plenum.

Stress & Tension Relief. rev. ed. Linda R. Page. (Healthy Healing Library Ser.). (Illus.). 32p. 1994. pap. 3.50 (*1-884334-33-4*) Hlthy Healing.

***Stress & the Aging Brain: Integrative Mechanisms.** Ed. by Giuseppe Nappi et al. LC 90-8692. (Aging Ser.: Vol. 37). 239p. 1990. reprint ed. pap. 68.20 (*0-608-03434-7*, 2064135) Bks Demand.

Stress & the Blood System. P. D. Gorizontov et al. LC 88-13625. 250p. 1989. 30.00 (*0-8236-6162-8*) Intl Univs Pr.

Stress & the Family: Vol. II Coping with Catastrophe. Ed. by Charles R. Figley & Hamilton I. McCubbin. LC 83-6048. (Psychosocial Stress Ser.: No. 2). 272p. 1983. text ed. 35.95 (*0-87630-332-7*) Brunner-Mazel.

Stress & the Family Vol. I: Coping with Normative Transitions. Ed. by Hamilton I. McCubbin & Charles R. Figley. LC 83-6048. (Psychosocial Stress Ser.: No. 2). 296p. 1983. text ed. 35.95 (*0-87630-321-1*) Brunner-Mazel.

Stress & the Healthy Family: How Healthy Families Handle the 10 Most Common Stresses. Dolores Curran. 1987. pap. 14.00 (*0-06-254833-6*, PL) HarpC.

Stress & the Heart: Interactions of the Cardiovascular System, Behavioral State, & Psychotropic Drugs. 2nd ed. Ed. by David Wheatley. LC 80-28999. (Illus.). 434p. 1981. reprint ed. pap. 123.70 (*0-7837-9554-8*, 2060303) Bks Demand.

Stress & the Heart: Storm in a Bottle. Sander Orent. LC 87-7540. 256p. 1989. text ed. 24.95 (*0-89876-139-5*) Gardner Pr.

Stress & the Manager: Making It Work for You. Karl Albrecht. (Illus.). 1979. pap. 8.95 (*0-13-852673-7*) P-H.

Stress & the Military Family. Carol B. Richardson. (Family Forum Library Ser.). 16p. 1993. 1.95 (*1-56688-070-X*) Bur For At-Risk.

Stress & the Nurse Manager. Peter Hingley & Cary L. Cooper. LC 84-4090. (Wiley-Medical Publication Ser.). 239p. reprint ed. pap. 68.20 (*0-7837-1874-8*, 2042075) Bks Demand.

Stress & the Police Officer. Katherine W. Ellison & John L. Genz. (Illus.). 224p. 1983. 31.95 (*0-398-04829-0*); pap. 19.95 (*0-398-06106-8*) C C Thomas.

Stress & the Power Nap. Dennis Shea & Kristen Barber. (Illus.). 102p. (Orig.). 1993. pap. 9.95 (*0-87411-600-7*) Copley Pub.

***Stress & the Risk of Psychobiological Disorder in College Women.** Alfred B. Heilbrun. LC 97-13317. 1997. write for info. (*0-7618-0845-0*); pap. write for info. (*0-7618-0846-9*) U Pr of Amer.

Stress & the Search for Happiness. Susan A. Muto & Adrian Van Kaam. (Spirit Life Ser.). 64p. (Orig.). 1993. pap. 3.95 (*1-878718-17-7*) Resurrection.

Stress & the Woman's Body. W. David Hager & Linda C. Hager. LC 95-36883. 224p. (gr. 10). 1996. 14.99 (*0-8007-1717-1*) Revell.

***Stress & Time.** (YouthSearch: Small-Group Resources Ser.). 64p. 1995. pap. 4.95 (*0-687-00589-2*) Abingdon.

Stress & Vision. Elliott B. Forrest. Ed. by Frances Conkey & Sally M. Corngold. (Illus.). 325p. 1988. 30.00 (*0-943599-00-8*) OEPF.

Stress & Well-Being at Work: Assessments & Interventions for Occupational Mental Health. Ed. by James C. Quick et al. 372p. 1992. pap. text ed. 34.95 (*1-55798-175-2*) Am Psychol.

Stress & Wellness Reference Guide: A Comprehensive Index to the Chalktalks, Processes, & Activities in the Whole Person Structured Exercises Series. Ed. by Nancy L. Tubesing. LC 95-33567. (Structured Exercises Ser.). 192p. (Orig.). 1995. otabind 29.95 (*1-57025-080-4*) Whole Person.

Stress & Women Physicians. Marjorie A. Bowman & Deborah I. Allen. (Illus.). 160p. 1988. 30.00 (*0-387-96117-8*) Spr-Verlag.

Stress & Women Physicians. 2nd ed. Marjorie A. Bowman & Deborah I. Allen. (Illus.). xi, 216p. 1990. pap. 19.50 (*0-387-97319-2*) Spr-Verlag.

Stress & Your Child: Helping Kids Cope with the Strains & Pressures of Life. Bettie B. Youngs. 336p. (Orig.). 1995. pap. 10.00 (*0-449-90902-6*) Fawcett.

Stress & Your Child: Know the Signs & Prevent Harm. Archibald Hart. 272p. 1994. mass mkt. 5.99 (*0-8499-3571-7*) Word Pub.

Stress, Anxiety, & Depression: The Natural Way of Healing. Natural. 304p. 1995. mass mkt. 4.99 (*0-440-21659-1*) Dell.

Stress, Anxiety & Insomnia. Michael T. Murray. 1994. pap. 11.00 (*1-55958-489-0*) Prima Pub.

Stress, Appraisal, & Coping. Richard S. Lazarus & Susan Folkman. 464p. (C). 1984. pap. 42.95 (*0-8261-4191-9*) Springer Pub.

Stress at Work. Ed. by Cary L. Cooper & Roy Payne. LC 77-9626. (Wiley Series on Studies in Occupational Stress). (Illus.). 305p. reprint ed. pap. 87.00 (*0-685-23755-9*, 2032829) Bks Demand.

***Stress at Work in the Social Services.** Ed. by Naomi Connelly. 1995. pap. 40.00 (*1-899942-04-1*, Pub. by Natl Inst Soc Work) St Mut.

Stress, Attitudes & Decisions: Selected Papers. Irving L. Janis. LC 82-9007. 366p. 1982. text ed. 69.50 (*0-275-90826-7*, C0826, Praeger Pubs) Greenwood.

Stress Awareness & Management Lesson Plan. Gary F. Cornelius. Ed. by Rosalie Rosetti & Katherine Scott. 225p. 1991. 215.00 (*0-929310-66-7*, 143) Am Correctional.

Stress Between Work & Family. Ed. by J. Eckenrode & S. Gore. (Stress & Coping Ser.). (Illus.). 242p. 1989. 37.50 (*0-306-43318-4*, Plenum Insight) Plenum.

***Stress Blaster.** D. G. Chichester. LC 96-27694. 1997. pap. 14.95 (*0-87596-358-7*) St Martin.

Stress Breakers. Roberta Elins et al. LC 84-17506. (Illus.). 110p. 1985. pap. 10.95 (*0-89638-074-2*) Hazelden.

Stress Burnout: An Annotated Bibliography. T. F. Riggar. LC 84-5447. 319p. 1985. 19.95 (*0-8093-1186-0*) S Ill U Pr.

Stress Busters: Bust the Stress Before It Busts You. Jack Hofer. LC 85-62946. 100p. 1986. 11.95 (*0-9615743-0-5*) SunShine CO.

Stress Busters: Twenty-One Thoughts for Your Emotional Wellness. Jack O'Neill. 160p. 1993. pap. 9.95 (*1-883000-00-9*) Derrymore West.

Stress Busters for Kids: A Parent's Guide to Helping Kids Cope with Stress. Bonnie M. Brown. LC 89-91558. (Illus.). 74p. (Orig.). 1990. pap. 8.95 (*0-9624705-0-3*) B M Brown.

Stress-Busters for Moms. Deborah S. Lewis & Charmaine C. Yoest. LC 95-48932. 112p. 1996. pap. 7.99 (*0-310-20566-2*) Zondervan.

Stress Busting Through Personal Empowerment. Thomas F. Holcomb et al. LC 94-19539. vi, 90p. 1994. pap. 15.95 (*1-55959-075-0*) Accel Devel.

Stress, Catecholamines, & Cardiovascular Disease. David S. Goldstein. (Illus.). 528p. 1995. 79.50 (*0-19-506538-7*) OUP.

***Stress Claims in Michigan: Worker's Compensation Entitlement for Mental Disability.** Jurgen Skoppek. (Illus.). 36p. (Orig.). 1995. pap. 5.00 (*0-9647703-2-6*, S95-07) Mackinac Ctr Public Pol.

Stress Concentration Factors. Rudolph E. Peterson. 336p. 1974. text ed. 99.95 (*0-471-68329-9*) Wiley.

Stress Concentrations in Laminated Composites. Seng C. Tan. LC 94-60852. 470p. 1994. pap. text ed. 99.95 (*1-56676-077-1*) Technomic.

***Stress Control.** Steve Bell. Ed. by Kelly Scanlon. LC 96-68882. (Self-Study Sourcebook Ser.). (Illus.). 149p. 1996. pap. 15.95 (*1-57294-052-2*, 13-0020) SkillPath Pubns.

Stress Control. Vernon Coleman. 214p. 1979. 20.00 (*0-85117-167-2*) Transatl Arts.

Stress Control. Darrell Franken. 48p. 1986. pap. 5.95 (*0-934957-14-2*) Wellness Pubns.

Stress, Coping & Development: A Lifespan Perspective. Carolyn M. Aldwin. LC 94-18295. 331p. 1994. lib. bdg. 36.00 (*0-89862-261-1*, 2261) Guilford Pr.

Stress, Coping & Development in Children. Norman Garmezy & Michael Rutter. 384p. (C). 1984. reprint ed. pap. text ed. 17.95 (*0-8018-3651-4*) Johns Hopkins.

Stress, Coping & Disease. N. Schneiderman & Phillip M. McCabe. Ed. by Tiffany M. Field & Jay S. Skyler. 264p. 1991. 39.95 (*0-8058-0408-0*) L Erlbaum Assocs.

Stress, Coping, & Health: A Situation-Behavior Approach - Theory, Methods, Applications. Meinrad Perrez & Michael Reicherts. LC 91-35352. (Illus.). 233p. 1992. pap. text ed. 24.00 (*0-88937-065-6*) Hogrefe & Huber Pubs.

Stress, Coping & Relationships in Adolescence. Inge Seiffge-Krenke. (Research Monographs in Adolescence). 296p. 1995. text ed. 59.95 (*0-8058-1235-0*) L Erlbaum Assocs.

Stress, Coping, & Resiliency in Children & Families. Ed. by E. Mavis Hetherington & Elaine A. Blechman. (Advances in Family Research Ser.). 256p. 1996. text ed. 55.00 (*0-8058-1710-7*) L Erlbaum Assocs.

Stress Corrosion - New Approaches - STP 610. Ed. by H. L. Craig. 429p. 1976. 43.00 (*0-8031-0580-0*, 04-610000-27) ASTM.

Stress-Corrosion Cracking: Materials Performance & Evaluation. Ed. by Russell H. Jones. (Illus.). 448p. 1992. text ed. 149.00 (*0-87170-441-2*, 6355) ASM.

Stress Corrosion Cracking Control Measures. LC 76-608306. (Illus.). 71p. 1977. 42.00 (*0-915567-74-1*) NACE Intl.

Stress Corrosion Cracking of Metals: A State of the Art - STP 518. 172p. 1983. 15.00 (*0-8031-0096-5*, 04-518000-27) ASTM.

Stress Corrosion Cracking-The Slow Strain-Rate Technique: A Symposium. American Society for Testing & Materials Staff. Ed. by Gilbert M. Ugiansky & J. H. Payer. LC 78-68418. (ASTM Special Technical Publication Ser.: No. 665). (Illus.). 452p. pap. 117.50 (*0-685-20423-5*, 2056403) Bks Demand.

Stress Corrosion Research, No. 30. H. Arup & R. N. Parkins. (NATO Advanced Study Institute Ser.). 279p. 1979. lib. bdg. 82.50 (*90-286-0647-5*) Kluwer Ac.

Stress Corrosion Testing. American Society for Testing & Materials Staff. LC 67-20038. (American Society for Testing & Materials Special Technical Publication Ser.: Special Technical Publication, No. 425). 388p. reprint ed. pap. 110.60 (*0-317-11257-0*, 2001144) Bks Demand.

Stress, Crowding & Blood Pressure in Prison. Adrian M. Ostfeld et al. (Health Environment Ser.). 256p. 1987. text ed. 49.95 (*0-89859-574-6*) L Erlbaum Assocs.

Stress, Culture, & Aggression. Arnold S. Linsky et al. LC 94-48643. 1995. 25.00 (*0-300-05706-7*) Yale U Pr.

Stress Determination for Fatigue Analysis of Welded Components. Ed. by Erkki Niemi. 76p. 1995. pap. 99.00 (*1-85573-213-0*, Pub. by Woodhead Pubng UK) Am Educ Systs.

Stress, Diet, & Your Heart. Dean Ornish. 384p. 1984. pap. 4.99 (*0-451-15853-9*, Sig) NAL-Dutton.

Stress, Diet & Your Heart. Dean Ornish. 1984. 5.99 (*0-451-17113-6*, ROC) NAL-Dutton.

Stress Disorders. Douglas M. Baker. 1977. pap. 12.50 (*0-906006-11-2*, Pub. by Baker Pubns UK) New Leaf Dist.

Stress Disorders Among Vietnam Veterans: Theory, Research, & Treatment. Ed. by Charles R. Figley. LC 77-94734. (Psychosocial Stress Ser.: No. 1). 356p. 1978. text ed. 34.95 (*0-87630-164-2*) Brunner-Mazel.

Stress, Distress & Illness. Ian Hislop. (Illus.). 224p. 1991. pap. text ed. 27.00 (*0-07-452809-2*) McGraw-Hill HPD.

Stress Doppler Echocardiograpy. Ed. by Steve M. Teague. (Developments in Cardiovascular Medicine Ser.). (C). 1990. lib. bdg. 206.00 (*0-7923-0499-3*) Kluwer Ac.

Stress Echocardiography. 2nd ed. Eugenio Picano. LC 94-29136. 1996. 79.50 (*0-387-58137-5*) Spr-Verlag.

***Stress Echocardiography.** 3rd ed. Eugenio Picano. LC 97-4381. 1997. write for info. (*3-540-62620-4*) Springer Pub.

Stress Echocardiography: Its Role in the Diagnosis & Evaluation of Coronary Artery Disease. Thomas H. Marwick. LC 93-41121. (Developments in Cardiovascular Medicine Ser.: No. 149). 192p. (C). 1994. lib. bdg. 102.00 (*0-7923-2579-6*) Kluwer Ac.

Stress Effects on Family Caregivers of Alzheimer's & Related Dementias: Research & Interventions. Ed. by Enid Light et al. 440p. 1994. 64.95 (*0-8261-7890-1*) Springer Pub.

Stress Effects on Natural Ecosystems. Ed. by Gary W. Barrett & Rutger Rosenberg. LC 80-40851. (Environmental Monographs & Symposia). 323p. reprint ed. pap. 92.10 (*0-7837-3222-8*, 2043239) Bks Demand.

***Stress Evaluation Profile.** 4p. 1992. pap. 6.00 (*1-58034-020-2*, C008S) IML Pubns.

Stress Factor: Thriving Emotionally & Spiritually in the Turbulant 90's. Frank Minirth et al. 1992. pap. 10.99 (*1-881273-02-4*) Northfield Pub.

Stress Factors As Identified by Research in Prisons. Debra M. Hydge & Donald Conway. 1977. 2.00 (*0-686-19102-1*, 1244, Sage Prdcls Pr) Sage.

Stress? Find Your Balance. rev. ed. Lynn Osterkamp & Allan N. Press. 160p. 1988. reprint ed. pap. 6.95 (*0-9620725-0-8*) Preventive Measures.

Stress First Aid for the Working Woman: How to Keep Cool When You're under Fire. Bee Epstein. 64p. (Orig.). 1985. pap. 7.95 (*0-9616204-0-4*) Becoming Pr.

Stress First Aid for the Working Woman: How to Keep Cool When You're under Fire! Bee J. Epstein. 96p. (Orig.). 1991. pap. 7.95 (*0-9616204-1-2*) Becoming Pr.

***Stress for Success.** David Lewis. 10.95 (*0-7867-0872-7*) Carroll & Graf.

Stress for Success: The Proven Program for Transforming Stress into Positive Energy. Loehr et al. LC 96-38020. 1997. 25.00 (*0-8129-2675-7*, Times Bks) Random.

Stress for Success: Using Your Hidden Creative Energy for Health, Achievement & Happiness. David Lewis. 208p. 1992. pap. 10.95 (*0-88184-872-7*) Carroll & Graf.

Stress Fractures: Advice & Encouragement for Handling Your Fast-Paced Life. Charles R. Swindoll. 1995. audio 9.99 (*0-310-42178-0*) Zondervan.

Stress Fractures: Advice & Encouragement for Handling Your Fast-Paced Life. Charles R. Swindoll. 272p. 1995. pap. 11.99 (*0-310-49741-8*) Zondervan.

Stress-Free, Anti-Aging Diet. D. R. Morse & R. L. Pollack. (Stress in Modern Society Ser.: No. 19). 1989. 32.50 (*0-404-63270-X*) AMS Pr.

Stress Free at Your Computer. Scott Donkin. (Illus.). 12p. 1996. 9.95 incl. audio (*1-55961-347-5*, BP7507) Relaxtn Co.

Stress-Free Habit: Powerful Techniques for Health & Longevity from the Andes, Yucatan, & Far East. John M. Perkins. 128p. 1989. pap. 8.95 (*0-89281-292-3*, Heal Arts VT) Inner Tradit.

Stress-Free Living. Lilburn S. Barksdale. LC 93-44360. 1994. pap. 5.95 (*0-918588-27-8*, 210) Barksdale Foun.

***Stress Free Living, 3 cass.** Mike George. (Illus.). 31p. 1996. wbk. ed. write for info. incl. audio (*1-886872-07-4*) Brahma Kumaris.

Stress-Free Living Kit, Incl. Handbook for Achieving Stress-Free Living. Lilburn S. Barksdale. 1980. pap., vinyl bd. 43.95 (*0-918588-24-3*, 207) Barksdale Foun.

***Stress Free Living: 222 Ways to Stress Free Living: Reduce Stress & Make Love with Life.** Ken Vegotsky. Ed. by D. Christie. (Love Living & Live Loving Ser.). (Illus.). 101p. 1998. pap. 7.95 (*1-886508-04-6*) Adi Gaia Esalen.

***Stress-Free Success: How to Really Achieve All Your Goals Without Giving up Your Life.** Jeffrey D. Smith. LC 97-91453. 236p. (Orig.). 1997. pap. 12.95 (*1-890190-19-5*) Ctr for Persnl Excell.

Stress, Gender, & Alcohol-Seeking Behavior. Ed. by Walter A. Hunt & Sam Zakhari. (Illus.). 364p. (Orig.). (C). 1996. pap. text ed. 45.00 (*0-7881-2675-X*) DIANE Pub.

Stress, Immunity & Aging. Cooper. (Immunology Ser.: Vol. 24). 336p. 1984. 145.00 (*0-8247-7114-1*) Dekker.

Stress in Academic Life. Shirley Fisher. LC 93-19667. 100p. (C). 1994. 75.00 (*0-335-15721-1*, Open Univ Pr); pap. 26.00 (*0-335-15720-3*, Open Univ Pr) Taylor & Francis.

Stress in Childhood. Ed. by James H. Humphrey. LC 83-45028. (Studies in Modern Society: Political & Social Issues: No. 17). 1984. 32.50 (*0-404-61624-0*) AMS Pr.

Stress in Childhood: An Intervention Model for Teachers & Other Professionals. Gaston E. Blom et al. LC 85-14825. (Special Education Ser.). 219p. reprint ed. pap. 62.50 (*0-7837-4627-X*, 2044350) Bks Demand.

Stress in Children. 171p. 1985. 14.95 (*0-940221-06-3*) Lrng Tools-Bilicki Pubns.

Stress in Children. Bettie B. Youngs. 192p. 1986. mass mkt. 4.50 (*0-380-70161-8*) Avon.

Stress in Health Professionals. Roy Payne & Jenny Firth-Cozens. LC 87-8122. (Studies in Occupational Stress). 288p. 1987. text ed. 175.00 (*0-471-91254-9*) Wiley.

***Stress in Health Professionals.** Ed. by Roy Payne & Jenny Firth-Cozens. LC 87-8122. (Illus.). 312p. 1987. reprint ed. pap. 89.00 (*0-608-02605-0*, 2063263) Bks Demand.

Stress in Industry: Cause, Effects, & Prevention. L. Levi. (Occupational Safety & Health Ser.: No. 51). vi, 70p. (Orig.). 1984. pap. 11.25 (*92-2-103539-5*) Intl Labour Office.

Stress in Modern Society, 19 vols., Set. Ed. by James H. Humphrey. 1987. write for info. (*0-404-63250-5*) AMS Pr.

Stress in Organizations: Toward a Phase Model of Burnout. Robert T. Golembiewski et al. LC 85-16744. 286p. 1985. text ed. 59.95 (*0-275-90024-X*, C0024, Praeger Pubs) Greenwood.

Stress in Psychiatric Disorders. Ed. by Robert P. Liberman & Joel Yager. LC 93-41244. 208p. 1994. 34.95 (*0-8261-8310-7*) Springer Pub.

Stress in Psychotherapists. Ed. by Ved P. Varma. LC 96-4647. 256p. (C). 1997. pap. 18.95 (*0-415-12175-2*); text ed. 69.95 (*0-415-12174-4*) Routledge.

***Stress in Teachers of Children with Special Educational Needs.** Graham Upton & Ved P. Varma. 300p. 1996. text ed. 56.95 (*1-85742-272-4*, Pub. by Arena UK) Ashgate Pub Co.

Stress in Teaching. 2nd ed. Jack Dunham. LC 91-44817. 224p. (C). (gr. 13). 1992. text ed. 85.00 (*0-415-06634-4*, A7511) Routledge.

Stress in the American Workplace: Alternatives for the Working Wounded. Donald T. De Carlo & Deborah H. Gruenfeld. LC 89-13187. 188p. (Orig.). 1989. pap. 19.95 (*0-934753-34-2*) LRP Pubns.

Stress in the Speech Stream: The Rhythm of Spoken English. Wayne B. Dickerson. 312p. 1989. teacher ed., pap. text ed. 19.95 (*0-252-06096-2*); student ed., pap. text ed. 24.95 (*0-252-06097-0*); digital audio 39.95 (*0-252-06098-9*) U of Ill Pr.

Stress in the Workplace: Costs, Liability, & Prevention. (BNA Special Reports). 128p. 1987. 55.00 (*0-87179-938-3*) BNA Plus.

Stress Indices & Stress Intensification Factors of Pressure Vessel & Piping Components. Ed. by R. W. Schneider & E. C. Rodabaugh. (PVP Ser.: Vol. 50). 1164p. 1981. 15.00 (*0-686-34508-8*, H00186) ASME.

Stress-Induced Analgesia, Vol. 467. Ed. by Dennis D. Kelly. 112.00 (*0-89766-330-6*); pap. 112.00 (*0-317-47638-6*) NY Acad Sci.

Stress-Induced Gene Expression in Plants. Ed. by Amarjit S. Basra. LC 93-6159. 1994. text ed. 125.00 (*3-7186-5466-0*) Gordon & Breach.

Stress-Induced Phenomena in Metallization. Ed. by Paul S. Ho et al. (AIP Conference Proceedings Ser.: No. 305). 320p. 1994. text ed. 301.00 (*1-56396-251-9*) Am Inst Physics.

Stress-Induced Phenomena in Metallization. Paul S. Ho et al. (AIP Press Conference Proceedings Ser.: No. 373). (Illus.). 320p. 1996. 140.00 (*1-56396-439-2*, CP 373, AIP) Am Inst Physics.

Stress Induced Phenomena in Metallization. C. Y. Li et al. (Conference Proceeding Ser.: No. 263). 288p. 1992. 95.00 (*1-56396-082-6*) Am Inst Physics.

Stress-Inducible Cellular Responses. U. Feige. LC 96-22168. (Experientia Supplementum Ser.). 1996. 180.00 (*0-8176-5205-1*); 180.00 (*3-7643-5205-1*) Birkhauser.

Stress Inoculation Training. Miechenbau. (Practitioner Guidebook Ser.). (C). 1992. pap. text ed. 31.50 (*0-205-14418-7*, H4418, Longwood Div) Allyn.

***Stress Intensity Factors & Weight Functions.** T. Tett & D. Munz. LC 96-72298. (Advances in Fracture Ser.). 390p. 1997. text ed. 169.00 (*1-85312-497-4*, 4974) Computational Mech MA.

S

An Asterisk (*) at the beginning of an entry indicates that the title is appearing in BIP for the first time.

S

***Stress-Life-Reliability Rating System for Gear & Rolling-Element Bearing Compressive Stress & Gear Root Bending Stress.** E. J. Bodensieck. (Technical Papers). 1974. pap. text ed. 30.00 (*1-55589-286-8*) AGMA.

Stress Management. Karen Albert. 1979. pap. write for info. (*1-879715-15-5*) Albert & Co.

***Stress Management.** Auerbach & Gramling. 1997. pap. text ed. 35.00 (*0-13-722281-5*) P-H.

Stress Management. Bosworth et al. (Body Awareness Resource Network Ser.). (YA). (gr. 7-12). 120.00 incl. disk (*0-912899-57-3*) Lrning Multi-Systs.

***Stress Management.** Chris Fife. 10p. (Orig.). 1996. pap. 4.00 (*1-890143-05-7*) Kinetic Aesthetics.

Stress Management. Great Performance Staff. 1987. write for info. (*1-56066-386-3*, 36354) Great Performance.

Stress Management. Leebov. (gr. 13). 1995. 5.95 (*0-8151-5314-7*) Mosby Yr Bk.

Stress Management. National Safety Council Staff. LC 94-16818. 1994. pap. 15.00 (*0-86720-980-1*) Jones & Bartlett.

Stress Management. 3rd ed. Walt Schafer. (C). 1996. teacher ed., pap. text ed. 42.00 (*0-15-503150-3*) HB Coll Pubs.

Stress Management: A Comprehensive Guide to Wellness. Edward A. Charlesworth. 1985. mass mkt. 5.99 (*0-345-32734-9*) Ballantine.

Stress Management: A Conceptual & Procedural Guide. Ronald G. Nathan & Edward A. Charlesworth. LC 80-70400. (Illus.). 119p. (Orig.). 1980. pap. text ed. 19.95 (*0-938176-01-3*) Biobehavioral Pr.

Stress Management: A Manual for Nurses. Vicki D. Lachman. 227p. 1983. pap. 19.50 (*0-685-06533-2*, 792424, Grune) Saunders.

Stress Management: An Integrated Approach. Dorothy H. Cotton. LC 89-38991. (Psychosocial Stress Ser.: No. 17). 288p. 1990. text ed. 38.95 (*0-87630-557-5*) Brunner-Mazel.

Stress Management: Does Anyone in Chicago Know about It? David N. Nelson. LC 92-93554. 96p. (Orig.). 1992. pap. 12.95 (*0-88100-078-7*) Natl Writ Pr.

Stress Management: HP 630. California College for Health Sciences Staff. 23p. (C). 1990. student ed. write for info. (*0-933195-30-3*) CA College Health Sci.

***Stress Management: Increasing Your Stress Resistance.** Ed. by Brehm. LC 97-17767. (C). 1998. text ed. write for info. (*0-321-01068-X*) Addson-Wesley Educ.

***Stress Management: Increasing Your Stress Resistance.** Barbara A. Brehm. LC 97-17767. 1998. write for info. (*0-321-00226-1*) Addson-Wesley Educ.

Stress Management: The Quest for Zest. Aina O. Nucho. (Illus.). 194p. 1988. pap. text ed. 22.95 (*0-398-06645-0*) C C Thomas.

Stress Management: The Quest for Zest. Aina O. Nucho. (Illus.). 194p. (C). 1988. text ed. 36.95 (*0-398-05478-9*) C C Thomas.

Stress Management & Counselling: Theory, Practice, Research & Methodology. Ed. by Stephen Palmer & Windy Dryden. LC 96-5302. (Stress Counselling Ser.). (Illus.). 160p. 1996. pap. 24.95 (*0-304-33565-7*); text ed. 75.00 (*0-304-33564-9*) Cassell.

Stress Management & Me: Participation Activities to Brighten Each Student's Day. Maria Pertik & Sandra Senter. Ed. by Dianna Richey. (Illus.). 64p. (Orig.). 1990. pap. text ed. 8.95 (*0-86530-144-1*, IP 191-1) Incentive Pubns.

***Stress-Management & Relaxation Activities for Trainers.** Robert Epstein. 275p. 1997. pap. text ed. 34.95 (*0-07-021762-9*); ring bd. 89.95 (*0-07-021763-7*) McGraw.

Stress-Management & Self-Esteem Activities. Patricia R. Toner. LC 93-14841. (Just for the Health of It Ser.: Unit 5). 1993. pap. 18.95 (*0-87628-874-3*) Ctr Appl Res.

***Stress Management for Busy People.** Carol Turkington. 1998. pap. text ed. 16.95 (*0-07-065535-9*) McGraw.

Stress Management for Educators: A Guide to Manage Our Response to Stress (Staff) Bettie B. Youngs. 112p. 1992. pap. 12.95 (*0-915190-77-X*, JP 9077-X) Jalmar Pr.

Stress Management for Elementary Schools. James H. Humphrey. 198p. (C). 1993. pap. 28.95 (*0-398-06171-8*); text ed. 41.95 (*0-398-05843-1*) C C Thomas.

Stress Management for Health Care Professionals. Steven Appelbaum. LC 80-25213. 487p. 1981. text ed. 80.00 (*0-89443-332-6*) Aspen Pub.

Stress Management for HIV: Clinical Validation & Intervention Manual. Antoni et al. Ed. by Jean Kristeller. LC 97-9633. (Behavioral Medicine - from Research to Practice). 300p. 1996. pap. write for info. (*0-8058-2246-1*) L Erlbaum Assocs.

Stress Management for Human Services. Richard E. Farmer et al. LC 84-3350. (Sage Human Services Guides Ser.: No. 37). 96p. (Orig.). 1984. reprint ed. pap. 27.40 (*0-608-01484-2*, 2059528) Bks Demand.

Stress Management for Law Enforcement Officers. Wayne Anderson et al. LC 94-36883. 384p. 1994. pap. text ed. 39.20 (*0-13-146945-2*) P-H Gen Ref & Trav.

***Stress Management for Lawyers: How to Increase Personal & Professional Satisfaction in the Law.** 2nd ed. Amiram Elwork. LC 96-61265. (Illus.). 175p. 1997. pap. 19.95 (*0-9644727-1-6*) Vorkell Grp.

Stress Management for the Dental Team. James M. George et al. LC 85-23824. 293p. reprint ed. pap. 83.60 (*0-7837-2707-0*, 2043087) Bks Demand.

Stress Management for the Healthy Type A: A Skills-Training Program. Ethel Roskies. LC 86-31856. 224p. 1987. pap. text ed. 20.95 (*0-89862-692-7*) Guilford Pr.

Stress Management for the Healthy Type A: Theory & Practice. Ethel Roskies. LC 86-31856. 252p. 1987. lib. bdg. 32.50 (*0-89862-689-7*) Guilford Pr.

***Stress Management for the Veterinary Practice Team.** A. D. Elkins & Sandra Brackenridge. 42p. (Orig.). (C). 1996. pap. 25.00 (*0-9603534-9-6*) Vet Practice.

Stress Management for Wellness. Walt Schafer. 408p. (C). 1987. pap. text ed. 20.00 (*0-03-011474-8*) HB Coll Pubs.

Stress Management for Wellness. 2nd ed. Walt Schafer. 544p. (C). 1992. pap. text ed. 20.00 (*0-03-052774-0*) HB Coll Pubs.

Stress Management for Wellness. 3rd ed. Walt Schafer. (Illus.). 615p. (C). 1995. pap. text ed. 28.50 (*0-15-502301-2*) HB Coll Pubs.

Stress Management for Women. Nancy J. Sullivan. x, 72p. 1993. 10.95 (*1-878542-36-2*) SkillPath Pubns.

Stress Management Guide. 3.00 (*0-318-37761-6*) Transitions.

Stress Management Guide for Administrators. 96p. 1989. pap. 10.00 (*0-940221-02-0*) Lrng Tools-Bilicki Pubns.

Stress Management Guide for Administrators. Bettie B. Youngs. 112p. 1993. pap. 12.95 (*0-915190-90-7*, JP 9090-7) Jalmar Pr.

Stress Management Guide for Educators. 92p. 1989. pap. 9.95 (*0-940221-03-9*) Lrng Tools-Bilicki Pubns.

Stress Management Guide for Young People. 6th ed. Bettie B. Youngs. (Illus.). 88p. (J). (gr. 6-12). 1986. reprint ed. pap. text ed. 9.95 (*0-940221-00-4*) Lrng Tools-Bilicki Pubns.

Stress Management Handbook. (Lifestyle Ser.). 64p. (Orig.). 1989. pap. 9.95 (*1-55852-024-4*) Natl Pr Pubns.

***Stress Management in Primary Care.** Kenneth Hambly & Alice J. Muir. LC 96-40480. 201p. 1997. pap. 35.00 (*0-7506-2737-9*) Buttrwrth-Heinemann.

Stress Management in Work Settings. (Illus.). 190p. (Orig.). (C). 1993. pap. text ed. 40.00 (*0-7881-0165-X*) DIANE Pub.

Stress Management in Work Settings. 1995. lib. bdg. 251.95 (*0-8490-6680-8*) Gordon Pr.

Stress Management in Work Settings. Ed. by Lawrence R. Murphy & Theodore F. Schoenborn. LC 88-32439. 183p. 1989. text ed. 55.00 (*0-275-93271-0*, C3271, Praeger Pubs) Greenwood.

***Stress Management Kit.** Alix Needham. 1997. pap. text ed. 24.95 (*1-885203-39-X*) C E Tuttle.

Stress Management Manual. Yvon Morris. 55p. 1995. pap. 9.98 (*1-888139-03-X*) Y Morris Carib.

Stress Management Skillbook. Educational Foundation of the National Restaurant Association Staff. (Management Skills Program Ser.). 28p. (Orig.). 1993. pap. 10.95 (*0-915452-40-5*) Educ Found.

***Stress Management Sourcebook.** Bart Cunningham. 288p. 1997. 25.00 (*1-56565-792-6*, Anodyne) Lowell Hse.

Stress Management Strategies. 3rd ed. Glenn R. Schiraldi. 64p. (C). 1996. 12.54 (*0-7872-1369-1*) Kendall-Hunt.

Stress Management through Yoga & Meditation. Pandit S. Nath. 1993. pap. 7.95 (*81-207-1514-4*, Pub. by Sterling Pubs II) Apt Bks.

Stress Management Training: A Group Leader's Guide. Nancy Norvell & Dale Belles. LC 89-62711. 96p. 1990. pap. 16.20 (*0-943158-33-8*, SM-GBP) Pro Resource.

Stress Management Workbook for Law Enforcement Officers. Dale Belles & Nancy Norvell. 50p. 1990. pap. 12.20 (*0-943158-32-X*, SM-WBP) Pro Resource.

***Stress Manager's Manual with Cassette Trainer: Your Guide to Better Health & Quality of Life.** Jordan Friedman. Ed. by Melissa C. Burns et al. (Illus.). 114p. (Orig.). 1996. pap. 21.95 incl. audio (*0-9656213-0-8*) StressHelp Pr.

Stress Manual: Recognize & Resolve the Processes & Results of Stress in the Professional Teacher. Dean Juniper. 160p. 1990. 75.00 (*1-870167-25-2*, Pub. by P Francis UK) St Mut.

Stress Mess Solution. George S. Everly & Daniel A. Girdano. LC 79-14652. 174p. 1981. 11.50 (*0-13-852616-8*) P-H.

Stress-Models. 1980. 45.00 (*0-8176-0745-5*) Spr-Verlag.

Stress Monitoring for Improved Worker Performance. Kaare Rodahl. 176p. 1993. 66.95 (*0-87371-655-8*, L655) Lewis Pubs.

Stress of Her Regard. Tim Powers. 1991. pap. 4.95 (*0-441-79097-6*) Ace Bks.

Stress of Her Regard. limited ed. Tim Powers. (Illus.). 544p. 1989. 125.00 (*0-927389-01-0*); 400.00 (*0-927389-00-2*) Charnel Hse.

Stress of Hot Environments. D. M. Kerslake. LC 74-168896. (Monographs of the Physiological Society: No. 29). 326p. reprint ed. pap. 93.00 (*0-685-16001-7*, 2027228) Bks Demand.

Stress of Life. 2nd ed. Hans Selye. (McGraw-Hill Paperbacks Ser.). 1978. reprint ed. pap. text ed. 9.95 (*0-07-056212-1*) McGraw.

***Stress of Parenting Infants.** David C. Rainham. (Illus.). 24p. (Orig.). 1996. pap. 3.50 (*1-884241-48-4*, EHO5TO) Energeia Pub.

Stress of Sea Power, 1915-1916 see Naval History of the World War

***Stress of Teaching.** David C. Rainham. 36p. (Orig.). 1997. pap. 5.00 (*1-884241-37-9*, ETMO020) Energeia Pub.

***Stress of Unemployment.** David C. Rainham. (Illus.). 24p. (Orig.). 1996. pap. 3.50 (*1-884241-46-8*, CEO010) Energeia Pub.

Stress or Sanity: Coping with Life in the 90's. Sherrie Weaver. Ed. by Patrick Caton. LC 96-76130. 168p. (Orig.). 1996. pap. 5.95 (*1-56245-263-0*) Great Quotations.

Stress Owner's Manual: Meaning, Balance & Health in Your Life. Edmond W. Boenisch & Michele Haney. LC 96-26977. 208p. (Orig.). 1996. pap. 12.95 (*0-915166-84-4*) Impact Pubs CA.

Stress Passages: Surviving Life's Transitions Gracefully. John Mason. LC 86-26904. (Illus.). 269p. (Orig.). 1988. pap. 11.95 (*0-89087-489-1*) Celestial Arts.

Stress, Personal Control & Health. Ed. by Andrew Steptoe & A. D. Appels. LC 89-14696. 323p. 1992. pap. text ed. 60.00 (*0-471-93105-5*) Wiley.

Stress Personalities: A Look Inside Our Selves. 2nd ed. Mary H. Dempcy & Rene Tihista. (Illus.). 232p. 1991. reprint ed. pap. 15.00 (*0-9631277-4-8*) Focal Pt Pr.

Stress Physiology & Forest Productivity. Ed. by T. C. Hennssey et al. (Forestry Sciences Ser.). 1986. lib. bdg. 128.00 (*90-247-3359-6*) Kluwer Ac.

Stress Physiology in Crop Plants. Ed. by Harry Mussell & Richard C. Staples. 526p. (C). 1990. reprint ed. lib. bdg. 67.50 (*0-471-03809-1*) Krieger.

Stress Physiology in Livestock, Vol. I: Principles. Ed. by M. K. Yousef. 240p. 1985. 131.00 (*0-8493-5667-9*, SF768, CRC Reprint) Franklin.

Stress Physiology in Livestock, Vol. II: Ungulates. Ed. by M. K. Yousef. 272p. 1985. 155.00 (*0-8493-5668-7*, CRC Reprint) Franklin.

Stress Physiology in Livestock, Vol. III: Avians. Ed. by M. K. Yousef. 168p. 1985. 101.00 (*0-8493-5669-5*, CRC Reprint) Franklin.

***Stress Point.** Dixon. (Hardy Boys Case Files Ser.: No. 125). (J). 1997. mass mkt. 3.99 (*0-671-56241-X*) PB.

Stress Points. Dom Minasi. Ed. by Thomas Gambino. (Illus.). (Orig.). 1986. pap. 11.95 (*0-936519-00-2*) Sunrise Artistries.

Stress, Power & Ministry. John C. Harris. 160p. (Orig.). 1977. pap. 9.95 (*1-56699-002-5*, AL27) Alban Inst.

***Stress Prevention in the Workplace: Assessing the Costs & Benefits to Organizations.** 120p. 1996. pap. 18.00 (*92-827-6503-2*, SY94-96-574-ENC, Pub. by Europ Com UK) Bernan Associates.

STRESS Proofing Your Child: Mind-Body Exercise to Enhance Your Child's Growth. Sheldon Lewis & Sheila Lewis. 256p. (Orig.). 1996. pap. 10.95 (*0-553-35319-5*, Bantam Trade Bks) Bantam.

Stress Protection Plan. Leon Chaitow. 1992. pap. 11.00 (*0-7225-2501-X*) Thorsons SF.

Stress Proteins: Induction & Function. Ed. by M. J. Schlesinger et al. (Illus.). 136p. 1991. 79.95 (*0-387-52776-1*) Spr-Verlag.

Stress Proteins in Biology & Medicine. Ed. by Richard I. Morimoto et al. LC 89-23926. (Cold Spring Harbor Monograph Ser.: No. 19). (Illus.). 460p. 1990. reprint ed. pap. 131.10 (*0-608-00930-X*, 2061724) Bks Demand.

Stress Proteins in Medicine. Ed. by Van Eden & Young. 592p. 1995. 195.00 (*0-8247-9623-3*) Dekker.

Stress Recess: The ABC's. Richard D. Erickson. 83p. 1994. pap. 8.00 (*0-9649922-0-5*) Deforest Pr.

***Stress Reducing Attitudes.** David C. Rainham. (Illus.). (Orig.). 1996. pap. 3.00 (*1-884241-63-8*, EHO520) Energeia Pub.

***Stress Reducing Habits.** David C. Rainham. (Illus.). 8p. (Orig.). 1996. pap. 2.50 (*1-884241-65-4*, EHO580) Energeia Pub.

Stress Reduction. 2nd rev. ed. David H. Barber. (Winning in Law School Ser.: Bk. 1). (Illus.). 52p. 1986. pap. text ed. 12.95 (*0-915667-06-1*) Spectra Pub Co.

Stress Reduction & Prevention. Ed. by Donald Meichenbaum & Matt Jaremko. 512p. 1983. 49.50 (*0-306-41066-4*, Plenum Pr) Plenum.

Stress Reduction for Mormons. John C. Turpin. 56p. 1983. 5.50 (*0-939506-01-7*); pap. 5.95 (*0-685-09892-3*) Turpin & Assocs.

Stress Regimes in the Lithosphere. Terry Engelder. 351p. 1992. text ed. 75.00 (*0-691-08555-2*) Princeton U Pr.

Stress Relaxation in Copper-Base Alloys. Polytechnic Institute of New York Staff. 18p. 1974. 28.20 (*0-317-34549-4*, 207) Intl Copper.

Stress Relaxation Testing - STP 676. Ed. by A. Fox. 224p. 1979. 23.75 (*0-8031-0581-9*, 04-676000-23) ASTM.

Stress Release. rev. ed. Wayne W. Topping. (Illus.). 163p. (Orig.). 1985. pap. 10.95 (*0-935299-03-3*) Topping Inst.

***Stress Releaser Stretchcloth: The Gentle Way to Physical Fitness.** Lilian Jarvis. (Illus.). 72p. spiral bd. 16.95 (*0-9697079-2-4*, Pub. by Moulin Pub CN) Genl Dist Srvs.

Stress Relief for the Childcare Professional. Ann P. Wildemann. 67p. 1994. pap. text ed. 19.95 (*1-885477-17-1*) Fut Horizons.

***Stress Relief for Women.** Janet Wright. (Practical Health Ser.). 1997. 12.98 (*0-7651-9537-2*) Smithmark.

Stress Relieving Heat Treatments of Welded Steel Constructions: Proceedings of the International Conference, Sofia, Bulgaria, 6-7 July 1987. Ed. by International Institute of Welding Staff. (Illus.). 420p. 1987. 168.00 (*0-08-035900-0*) Franklin.

***Stress Remedies.** Sherman. LC 97-4299. 1997. 27.95 (*0-87596-308-0*) Rodale Pr Inc.

Stress Research: Issues for the Eighties. Ed. by Cary L. Cooper. LC 82-11049. (Illus.). 159p. reprint ed. pap. 45.40 (*0-8357-3105-7*, 2039361) Bks Demand.

Stress Resources: An Annotated Guide to Essential Books, Periodicals, A-V Materials, & Teaching Tools for Trainers, Consultants, Counselors, Educators, & Health Professionals. Selected by Jim Polidora. LC 94-43752. 1995. 34.95 (*1-57025-064-2*) Whole Person.

Stress Response Syndromes. 2nd ed. Mardi J. Horowitz. LC 85-71507. 384p. 1992. reprint ed. pap. 30.00 (*0-87668-298-0*) Aronson.

Stress Response Syndromes. 3rd ed. Mardi J. Horowitz. 1997. pap. 40.00 (*0-7657-0025-5*) Aronson.

Stress Responses in Plants: Adaptation Mechanisms. Ed. by Ruth G. Alscher & Jonathan R. Cumming. LC 90-35151. 426p. 1990. text ed. 219.95 (*0-471-56810-4*) Wiley.

Stress Revisited, 2 vols., Set, Vols. 1 & 2. Ed. by G. Jasmin & M. Cantin. (Methods & Achievements in Experimental Pathology Ser.: Vols. 14-15). (Illus.). xxviii, 400p. 1991. Set, Vol. 1: Neuroendocrinology of Stress, Vol. 2: Systemic Effects of Stress. 347.00 (*3-8055-5404-4*) S Karger.

Stress Revisited: Neuroendocrinology of Stress. Ed. by M. Cantin & G. Jasmin. (Methods & Achievements in Experimental Pathology Ser.: Vol. 14). (Illus.). xii, 176p. 1991. 169.75 (*3-8055-5374-9*) S Karger.

Stress Revisited, Vol. 2: Systemic Effects of Stress. Ed. by G. Jasmin & M. Cantin. (Methods & Achievements in Experimental Pathology Ser.: Vol. 15). (Illus.). xvi, 224p. 1991. 215.75 (*3-8055-5403-6*) S Karger.

Stress, Risk, & Resilience in Children & Adolescents: Processes, Mechanisms, & Interventions. Ed. by Robert J. Haggerty et al. LC 93-42814. (Illus.). 432p. (C). 1994. text ed. 52.95 (*0-521-44146-3*) Cambridge U Pr.

Stress, Risk, & Resilience in Children & Adolescents: Processes, Mechanisms, & Interventions. Ed. by Robert J. Haggerty et al. 432p. 1996. pap. text ed. 19.95 (*0-521-57662-8*) Cambridge U Pr.

Stress, Salespeople, Serial Killers, & Seminars: Not Your Ordinary Day at the Office. Laura DeChaine et al. (Business Playground Ser.). (Illus.). 194p. (Orig.). 1995. pap. 10.95 (*0-9648485-0-3*) Baird Commun.

Stress, Sanity & Survival. Robert I. Woolfolk & Frank C. Richardson. 1979. pap. 3.95 (*0-451-14848-7*, Sig) NAL-Dutton.

Stress Scripting: A Guide to Stress Management. Jonathan C. Smith. LC 90-38840. 280p. 1990. text ed. 49.95 (*0-275-93639-2*, C3639, Praeger Pubs) Greenwood.

Stress, Self-Concept, & Violence. John A. Corson. Ed. by James H. Humphrey. LC 86-82026. (Stress in Modern Society Ser.: No. 11). 1989. 32.50 (*0-404-63271-8*); pap. 14.95 (*0-404-63263-7*) AMS Pr.

Stress Skills Workbook. Donald A. Tubesing. 75p. 1979. student ed. 10.00 (*0-938586-15-7*) Whole Person.

Stress, Social Support & Women. Ed. by Stevan E. Hobfoll. (Clinical & Community Psychology Ser.). 225p. (C). 1986. text ed. 68.95 (*0-89116-404-9*) Hemisp Pub.

Stress Solution. Lyle Miller. 1994. mass mkt. 5.99 (*0-671-75311-8*) PB.

Stress, Spasm & You. large type ed. Harold A. Serebro. Ed. by Digby Ricci & Earl Moorhouse. (Illus.). 1996. 49.75 (*0-9650604-0-3*, 0115); pap. 14.50 (*0-9650604-1-1*) Petiolate Pubns.

Stress Stoppers for Children & Adolescents. 2nd ed. Miriam J. Wilson. Ed. by Gerald Wheeler. (Illus.). 111p. (YA). (gr. 9 up). 1988. pap. 6.95 (*0-944576-01-X*) Rocky River Pubs.

Stress, Strain, & Vietnam: An Annotated Bibliography of Two Decades of Psychiatric & Social Sciences Literature Reflecting the Effect of the War on the American Soldier. Norman M. Camp et al. LC 88-30138. (Bibliographies & Indexes in Military Studies). 334p. 1988. text ed. 79.50 (*0-313-26272-1*, CSN) Greenwood.

Stress Strategies for Parents. Kimberly Barrett. 208p. (Orig.). 1993. mass mkt. 4.99 (*0-425-13626-4*) Berkley Pub.

***Stress Strategy For Parents.** Kim Barrett. 1993. 4.99 (*0-425-13631-0*) Berkley Pub.

***Stress, Stress Hormones & the Immune System.** J. C. Buckingham et al. LC 97-5380. 1997. text ed. write for info. (*0-471-95886-7*) Wiley.

Stress Survival Kit: Fifty Two Stress Management Tools. 2nd ed. Bob Czimbal & Maggie Zadikov. Ed. by L. Tobin. (Illus.). 160p. 1993. pap. 18.00 (*1-878793-03-9*) Open Bk OR.

Stress Test: Cartoons on Medicine. Sidney Harris. LC 93-31590. (Illus.). 150p. (Orig.). 1994. pap. 10.95 (*0-8135-2065-7*) Rutgers U Pr.

Stress Test Biofeedback Card & Booklet. Alfred A. Barrios. 1985. pap. 3.95 (*0-9601926-3-8*) Self-Prog Control.

Stress Test for Children. Jerome Vogel & Richard Walsh. Ed. by Richard A. Passwater & Earl R. Mindell. (Good Health Guide Ser.). 32p. (Orig.). 1983. pap. 1.45 (*0-87983-299-1*) Keats.

Stress Testing: Principles & Practice. 4th ed. Myrvin H. Ellestad et al. LC 95-20317. (Illus.). 593p. (C). 1995. 69.95 (*0-8036-0055-0*) Davis Co.

Stress That Motivates: Self-Talk Secrets for Success. Dru Scott. Ed. by Beverly Manber. LC 91-77750. (Fifty-Minute Ser.). (Illus.). 114p. (Orig.). 1992. pap. 10.95 (*1-56052-150-3*) Crisp Pubns.

Stress, the Aging Brain, & the Mechanisms of Neuron Death. Robert M. Sapolsky. (Illus.). 448p. 1992. 55.00 (*0-262-19320-5*, Bradford Bks) MIT Pr.

Stress, the Immune System & Psychiatry. Ed. by Brian E. Leonard & Klara Miller. LC 94-30641. 250p. 1995. text ed. 59.95 (*0-471-95258-3*) Wiley.

***Stress Therapy.** Tom McGrath. LC 96-79961. (Illus.). 96p. 1997. pap. 4.95 (*0-87029-301-X*, 20153) Abbey.

Stress Tolerance of Fungi. D. H. Jennings. LC 93-1187. (Mycology Ser.: Vol. 10). 368p. 1993. 155.00 (*0-8247-9061-8*) Dekker.

Stress Training for Life. Herbert Kindler & Marilyn Ginsburg. 160p. 1990. 14.95 (*0-89397-335-1*) Nichols Pub.

Stress Transients in Solids. John S. Rinehart. 240p. (C). 1975. pap. 8.95 (*0-913270-48-2*) HyperDynamics.

Stress-Unstress: How You Can Control Stress at Home & on the Job. Keith W. Sehnert. LC 81-65647. 224p. (Orig.). 1981. pap. 5.99 (*0-8066-1883-3*, 10-6065, Augsburg) Augsburg Fortress.

Stress Walk. Richard L. Harding. (Illus.). 40p. (Orig.). 1988. pap. 4.95 (*0-929494-00-8*); audio 9.95 (*0-929494-01-6*) Internet Bks.

Stress Walk: The Walking Cure. Richard L. Harding. (Illus.). 40p. (Orig.). 1988. pap. 4.95 (*0-317-90356-X*); audio 9.95 (*0-317-90357-8*) Internet Bks.

Stress Wave Propagation in Solids: An Introduction. Richard J. Wasley. LC 73-78561. (Monographs & Textbooks in Material Science: No. 7). 316p. reprint ed. pap. 90.10 (*0-7837-0772-X*, 2041086) Bks Demand.

An Asterisk (*) at the beginning of an entry indicates that the title is appearing in BIP for the first time.

Stress Waves in Solids. 2nd ed. H. Kolsky. (Illus.). 1963. pap. text ed. 8.95 (*0-486-61098-5*) Dover.

Stress Without Distress: Rx for Burnout. George Manning & Kent Curtis. (Human Side of Work Ser.). 273p. (C). 1988. pap. text ed. 172.95 (*0-538-21250-0*, U251) S-W Pub.

Stress Without Distress: Rx for Burnout. George Manning. (GC - Principles of Management Ser.). 1988. pap. 25.95 (*0-538-21251-9*) S-W Pub.

Stress Without Tears. Tom Rhodes. (Illus.). 130p. (Orig.). 1990. 22.50 (*0-9615234-1-7*) Jacobs Pub.

Stress Without Tears: A Primer on Aircraft-Stress Analysis Requiring No Advanced Mathematics. Tom Rhodes. (Illus.). 123p. (Orig.). (C). 1994. pap. 40.00 (*0-7881-1343-7*) DIANE Pub.

***Stress Work Book: How Individuals, Teams & Organisations Can Balance Pressure & Performance.** 2nd rev. ed. Eve Warren & Caroline Toll. (Illus.). 200p. 1996. pap. 19.95 (*1-85788-171-0*) Nicholas Brealey.

Stress, Work Design, & Productivity. Ed. by E. N. Corlett & J. Richardson. LC 81-13075. (Wiley Series on Studies in Occupational Stress). (Illus.). 287p. reprint ed. pap. 81.80 (*0-8357-3049-2*, 2039305) Bks Demand.

Stress Workbook. Kathleen G. Santor. (Illus.). (C). 1994. 5.95 (*0-9643078-0-4*) Free Flowing Stars.

***Stress, You Can't Live With It & You Can't Live Without It: Changing Stress into Success. James P. Cima. 150p. (Orig.). 1997. pap. 19.95 (*0-9659476-2-9*) JPC Pubng.**
This book is a must if you want to change your life, by changing the stresses you now face into tomorrow's successes. After seventeen years of careful research & by applying & orchestrating the necessary principles of success to his life, Dr. Cima now shares with you how to take your minuses & change them into pluses by creating lemonade from lemons. Dr. Cima explains & provides the necessary principles that are to be followed whether your stress comes from family, finance, friends, business or your profession. Dr. Cima helps you focus on the task at hand so that "you" create your own blueprint for success by solving your own particular set of problems. When this is achieved you become more powerful, caring & serving human being, & by doing so have a positive impact on those around you as well as any set of circumstances you may now be facing. "Stress kills," don't let it control & ruin your life. Take action today by not only purchasing this book, but by reading it many times & mastering the principles within. To order write: Dr. Cima, 3300 PGA Suite 600, Palm Beach Gardens, FL 33410. ***Publisher Provided Annotation.***

Stress/An Owner's Manual: Positive Techniques for Taking Charge of Your Life. Arthur Rowshan. 1994. pap. 8.95 (*1-85168-068-3*) Onewrld Pubns.

Stressbusters Five Minute Massage see 5 Minute Massage: Quick & Simple Exercises to Reduce Tension & Stress

***Stressed??? Miniature Editions Pop-Up.** Bonnie Mathews. (Illus.). 14p. 1997. 4.95 (*0-7624-0108-7*, Running Pr Mini Edtns) Running Pr.

Stressed Ecosystems & Sustainable Agriculture. Ed. by S. M. Virmani et al. (Illus.). 454p. 1995. text ed. 80.00 (*1-886106-14-2*) Science Pubs.

Stressed Heart. Ed. by Marianne J. Legato. (Developments in Cardiovascular Medicine Ser.). 1987. lib. bdg. 143.50 (*0-89838-849-X*) Kluwer Ac.

Stressed Out! Strategies for Working with Stress in Corrections. Gary F. Cornelius. (Illus.). 132p. 1994. pap. 21.95 (*1-56991-010-3*, 257) Am Correctional.

***Stressed Out? A Special Unit, Foundation.** 11th ed. Rainey. (HA - Social Studies). (C). 1996. pap. 16.95 (*0-314-22523-4*) S-W Pub.

Stresses & Displacements for Shallow Foundations. D. Milovic. LC 92-10556. (Developments in Geotechnical Engineering Ser.: Vol. 70). 620p. 1992. 255.00 (*0-444-88349-5*) Elsevier.

Stresses in Concrete Armor Units. Ed. by D. D. Davidson & Orville T. Magoon. LC 90-698. 421p. 1990. pap. text ed. 37.00 (*0-87262-760-8*) Am Soc Civil Eng.

Stresses in Layed Shells of Revolution. V. Kovarik. (Developments in Civil Engineering Ser.: No. 24). 442p. 1989. 250.75 (*0-444-98893-9*) Elsevier.

Stresses in Plates & Shells. Ansel C. Ugural. (Illus.). 352p. 1981. text ed. write for info. (*0-07-065730-0*) McGraw.

Stresses in Rock. G. Herget. 200p. (C). 1987. text ed. 85.00 (*90-6191-685-2*, Pub. by A A Balkema NE) Ashgate Pub Co.

Stresses in Shells. 2nd ed. W. Fluegge. LC 74-183604. (Illus.). 525p. 1990. 108.95 (*0-387-05322-0*) Spr-Verlag.

***Stresses in the Webs of Helical Gears.** J. M. Rodarte & R. Zab. (Technical Papers). 33p. 1983. pap. text ed. 30.00 (*1-55589-076-8*) AGMA.

Stresses in U. S.-Japanese Security Relations. Fred Greene. (Studies in Defense Policy). 110p. 1975. pap. 7.95 (*0-8157-3271-6*) Brookings.

Stresses of Counselling in Action. Windy Dryden & Ved P. Varma. (Counselling in Action Ser.). 208p. 1995. text ed. 49.95 (*0-8039-8995-4*); pap. text ed. 21.50 (*0-8039-8996-2*) Sage.

***Stresses of Parenting Teenagers.** David C. Rainham. (Illus.). 24p. (Orig.). 1996. pap. 3.50 (*1-884241-47-6*, EHO500) Energeia Pub.

Stressfire. Massad F. Ayoob. (Gunfighting for Police: Advanced Tactics & Techniques Ser.: Vol. 1). (Illus.). 149p. 1986. pap. 9.95 (*0-936279-03-6*) Police Bkshelf.

Stressful Life Events. Ed. by Thomas W. Miller. (Stress & Health Ser.: No. 4). 838p. 1989. 75.00 (*0-8236-6165-2*, BN#00165) Intl Univs Pr.

Stressful Life Events & Their Contexts. Ed. by Barbara S. Dohrenwend & Bruce P. Dohrenwend. (Monographs in Psychosocial Epidemiology). 287p. 1984. pap. text ed. 15.00 (*0-8135-1004-X*) Rutgers U Pr.

Stressing & Unstressing in a Tent: A Narrative Reminiscence. Stuart L. Burns. LC 87-4211. (Illus.). 207p. 1987. reprint ed. pap. 59.00 (*0-608-00110-4*, 2060875) Bks Demand.

Stressmap: Personal Diary Edition. rev. ed. Essi Systems Staff. LC 90-48965. 1991. pap. 15.95 (*1-55704-081-8*) Newmarket.

Stressmaster: The Thirty Minute Stress Reducer. Carol R. Barbeito & David Linke. Ed. by Domain Inc., Information Division Managers Staff. (Illus.). 57p. (Orig.). 1988. 9.95 (*0-685-26066-6*) Domain Inc Info.

StressMaster: The Thirty-Minute Stress Reducer. rev. ed. Carol R. Barbeito. (Illus.). 57p. 1988. pap. 7.95 (*1-877805-00-9*); pap. 8.95 (*1-877805-01-7*); pap. 9.95 (*1-877805-02-5*) Domain Inc Info.

Stressors & the Adjustment Disorders. Joseph D. Noshpitz & R. Dean Coddington. (Series on Personality Processes). 693p. 1990. text ed. 90.00 (*0-471-62186-2*) Wiley.

***Stretch.** Wells. 1997. pap. text ed. 34.67 (*0-13-617903-7*) P-H.

Stretch & Sew Guide to Sewing Knits. Ann Person. 144p. 1994. pap. 19.95 (*0-8019-8593-5*) Chilton.

Stretch & Strengthen. Judy Alter. 1986. pap. 9.95 (*0-685-11807-X*) HM.

Stretch & Strengthen: A Safe, Comprehensive Exercise Program to Balance Your Muscle Strength. Judy Alter. 1992. pap. 14.95 (*0-395-52808-9*) HM.

***Stretch & Strengthen: The New York City Ballet Workout.** Peter Martins. Date not set. 40.00 (*0-614-20666-9*) Morrow.

Stretch & Strengthen for Rehabilitation & Development. Bob Anderson & Donald G. Bornell. (Illus.). 91p. (Orig.). 1984. spiral bd. 6.95 (*0-9601066-2-6*) Stretching Inc.

Stretch & Strengthen Your Way to Great Golf. Greg Comeaux & Larry Cano. 1996. pap. text ed. 6.95 (*1-57028-088-6*) Masters Pr IN.

Stretch & Surrender: A Guide to Yoga, Health, & Relaxation for People in Recovery. Annalisa Cunningham. LC 92-17806. 150p. 1992. pap. 14.95 (*0-915801-31-0*) Rudra Pr.

Stretch My Faith, Lord. Juanita Purcell. (Women's Ser.). 104p. (Orig.). 1992. pap. text ed. 5.95 (*0-87227-174-9*, RBP5207) Reg Baptist.

Stretch on the River. Richard Bissell. LC 87-20390. 252p. 1987. reprint ed. pap. 8.95 (*0-87351-220-0*, Borealis Book) Minn Hist.

Stretch Quick Pascal. Porter. 1990. pap. 24.95 (*0-13-851890-4*) P-H.

Stretch Think Program 1. Sydney Tyler-Parker. (Stretch Think Program Ser.). 144p. (J). (gr. k-2). 1984. pap. 35.00 (*0-912781-12-2*) Thomas Geale.

Stretch Think Program 2. Sydney Tyler-Parker. (Stretch Think Program Ser.). 140p. (gr. 2-4). 1984. pap. 35.00 (*0-912781-10-6*) Thomas Geale.

Stretch Think Program 3. Sydney B. Tyler. (Stretch Think Program Ser.). 138p. (gr. 5-8). 1984. pap. 35.00 (*0-912781-11-4*) Thomas Geale.

Stretch, Twist, Fold: The Fast Dynamo, Vol. XI. Stephen Childress & A. D. Gilbert. Ed. by W. Beiglbock et al. LC 95-38008. (Lecture Notes in Physics Ser.: No. M37). 410p. 1995. 69.95 (*3-540-60258-5*) Spr-Verlag.

Stretch Your Gas Dollars. P. Ross Aletto. LC 79-54982. (Illus.). 72p. (Orig.). 1979. pap. 2.95 (*0-935126-00-7*) E & C Bks.

Stretch Yourself for Health & Fitness. Bob Anderson. (C). 1993. 8.00 (*81-85674-96-5*, Pub. by UBS Pubs Dist II) S Asia.

Stretched Out AASHO-PCI Beams Types III & IV for Longer Span Highway Bridges. Prestressed Concrete Institute Staff. (PCI Journal Reprints Ser.). 19p. 1973. pap. 12.00 (*0-318-19840-1*, JR134) P-PCI.

Stretcher: Allied Families of Delaware: Stretcher, Fenwick, Davis, Draper, Kipshaven, Stidham. E. E. Sellers. 171p. 1992. reprint ed. pap. 23.00 (*0-8328-2330-9*); reprint ed. lib. bdg. 38.00 (*0-8328-2329-5*) Higginson Bk Co.

Stretchercize: Is Your Limber Lost? Mary Long. (Illus.). 75p. (Orig.). 1985. pap. 3.95 (*0-916005-03-8*) Silver Sea.

Stretching. Bob Anderson. LC 79-5567. (Illus.). 192p. (Orig.). 1980. pap. 13.00 (*0-394-73874-8*) Shelter Pubns.

***Stretching.** Godin, Seth, Productions Staff. (Cader Flip Ser.). 1997. pap. text ed. 3.95 (*0-8362-2558-9*, Cader Bks) Andrews & McMeel.

***Stretching: Simple Exercises to Make You Limber.** Manine Golden & Mark Hofer. Ed. by Marquand Bks. Staff. 72p. (Orig.). 1997. pap. 8.95 (*0-8362-2892-8*) Andrews & McMeel.

Stretching & Massage for Hikers & Backpackers. Frank Logue. (Nuts-N-Bolts Guides Ser.). (Illus.). 32p. (Orig.). 1994. pap. 4.95 (*0-89732-167-7*) Menasha Ridge.

***Stretching & Shrinking: Similarity.** Glenda Lapan et al. Ed. by Catherine Anderson et al. (Connected Mathematics Ser.). (Illus.). 84p. (Orig.). 1996. wbk. ed., pap. 5.95 (*1-57232-164-4*, 21459) Seymour Pubns.

***Stretching & Shrinking: Similarity.** Glenda Lapan et al. Ed. by Catherine Anderson et al. (Connected Mathematics Ser.). (Illus.). 168p. (Orig.). 1996. teacher ed., pap. 16.50 (*1-57232-165-2*, 21460) Seymour Pubns.

***Stretching & Shrinking: Similarity.** rev. ed. Glenda Lappan et al. Ed. by Catherine Anderson et al. (Connected Mathematics Ser.). (Illus.). 90p. (YA). (gr. 7 up). 1997. student ed., pap. text ed. 5.95 (*1-57232-643-3*, 45838) Seymour Pubns.

***Stretching & Shrinking: Similarity.** rev. ed. Glenda Lappan et al. Ed. by Catherine Anderson et al. (Connected Mathematics Ser.). (Illus.). 189p. (YA). (gr. 7 up). 1997. teacher ed., pap. text ed. 16.50 (*1-57232-644-1*, 45839) Seymour Pubns.

Stretching & Strengthening Exercises. Hans Spring et al. (Flexibook Ser.). (Illus.). 156p. 1990. text ed. 10.00 (*0-86577-366-1*) Thieme Med Pubs.

Stretching at Your Computer or Desk. Bob Anderson & Jean Anderson. Ed. by Lloyd Kahn. (Illus.). 128p. (Orig.). 1997. pap. 9.95 (*0-679-77084-4*) Random.

***Stretching at Your Computer or Desk.** Bob Anderson & Jean Anderson. Ed. by Lloyd Kahn. LC 96-34996. (Illus.). 128p. (Orig.). 1997. pap. 9.95 (*0-936070-19-6*) Shelter Pubns.

Stretching Book. Runner's World Editors. (Runner's World Ser.). 1982. pap. 9.95 (*0-02-499610-6*, Macmillan Coll) P-H.

Stretching for All Sports. John E. Beaulieu. LC 80-12695. (Illus.). 214p. 1980. pap. 8.95 (*0-87095-079-7*, Athletic) Gldn West Bks.

***Stretching for Flexibility & Health.** Francine St. George. LC 97-24476. (Illus.). 192p. (Orig.). 1997. pap. 14.95 (*0-89594-882-6*) Crossing Pr.

Stretching for Strings. Jack S. Winberg & Merle F. Salus. LC 90-86191. (Illus.). 126p. (Orig.). (C). 1990. pap. 17.95 (*0-89917-772-7*) Am String Tchrs.

Stretching for Working America. Bob Anderson & Sally Carlson. (Illus.). 72p. (Orig.). 1988. spiral bd. 7.95 (*0-9601066-4-2*) Stretching Inc.

Stretching Scientifically: A Guide to Flexibility Training. 3rd ed. Thomas Kurz. LC 92-85420. (Illus.). 152p. 1994. pap. 18.95 (*0-940149-30-3*); lib. bdg. 25.95 (*0-940149-29-X*) Stadion Pub.

Stretching the Eyes' Distance Reflections on the Chesapeake Bay. Barclay Sheaks. Ed. & Intro. by Nancy G. Harris. (Illus.). 72p. 1981. 25.00 (*0-941376-00-1*) Bleecker St Pub.

Stretching the Imagination: Representation & Transformation in Mental Imagery. Ed. by Cesare Cornoldi & Robert Logie. (Counterpoints Ser.). (Illus.). 208p. (C). 1996. 45.00 (*0-19-509947-8*); pap. text ed. 18.95 (*0-19-509948-6*) OUP.

Stretching the Soul: Learning the Art of Watching God Work. Ronald E. Wilson. LC 94-39930. (Spiritual Biography Ser.). 208p. (Orig.). (gr. 10). 1995. pap. 9.99 (*0-8007-5554-5*) Revell.

Stretching the Truth. Created by Francine Pascal. (Sweet Valley Twins Ser.: No. 13). 112p. (J). (gr. 3-7). 1987. pap. 3.25 (*0-553-15654-3*, Skylark BDD) BDD Bks Young Read.

Stretching Tradition: New Images for Traditional Quilts. Lynn G. Kough. Ed. by Mary C. Penders. (Illus.). 160p. 1995. pap. 27.95 (*1-881588-13-0*) EZ Quilting.

Stretching Your Dollars: A Daily Guide to Smart Spending. Great Quotations Staff. (Day Riser Ser.). 366p. 1995. 6.50 (*1-56245-219-3*) Great Quotations.

Stretto House: Steven Holl Architects. Steven Holl. LC 96-5621. (One House Ser.). (Illus.). 80p. (Orig.). 1996. pap. 19.95 (*1-885254-29-6*) Monacelli Pr.

Stricken Deer: The Life of Cowper. David Cecil. 303p. 1988. reprint ed. pap. 23.50 (*0-09-468430-8*, Pub. by Constable Pubs UK) Trans-Atl Phila.

Stricken Field. Dave Duncan. 368p. 1994. mass mkt. 5.99 (*0-345-38874-7*) Ballantine.

Stricken Land, the Story of Puerto Rico. Rexford G. Tugwell. LC 68-23335. 704p. 1968. reprint ed. text ed. 48.50 (*0-8371-0252-9*, TUSL, Greenwood Pr) Greenwood.

Stricker: Daniel of the Blossoming Valley (Daniel von dem Bluhenden Tal) Der Stricker. Tr. by Michael Resler. LC 89-28774. (Library of Medieval Literature). 228p. 1990. text ed. 20.00 (*0-8240-1515-0*) Garland.

Stricker & Wernher: A View of Chivalry & Peasantry in Germany in the Late Middle Ages. Marion L. Huffines. 1978. lib. bdg. 250.00 (*0-685-01974-8*) Gordon Pr.

Strickers Daniel Von Dem Bluehenden Tal: Werkstruktur und Interpretation. Ingeborg Henderson. (German Language & Literature Monographs: No. 1). viii, 206p. 1976. 48.00 (*90-272-0961-8*) Benjamins North Am.

Strickland. Hilary Masters. 1991. reprint ed. 10.00 (*0-941038-03-3*) Coyne & Chenoweth.

Strickland, the Stricklands of Sizergh Castle: Records of Twenty-Five Generations of a Westmoreland, England Family. Daniel Scott. (Illus.). 293p. 1993. reprint ed. pap. 46.50 (*0-8328-3751-2*); reprint ed. lib. bdg. 56.50 (*0-8328-3750-4*) Higginson Bk Co.

Strict Convexity & Complex Strict Convexity: Theory & Applications. Ioana Istratescu. (Lecture Notes in Pure & Applied Mathematics Ser.: Vol. 89). 328p. 1983. 140.00 (*0-8247-1796-1*) Dekker.

Strict Liability: Legal & Economic Analysis. Frank J. Vandall. LC 89-3868. 200p. 1989. text ed. 59.95 (*0-89930-396-X*, VSL/, Greenwood Pr) Greenwood.

Strictly Ballroom. Baz Luhrmann & Craig Pearce. 86p. (C). 1992. pap. 17.95 (*0-86819-359-3*) Aubrey Bks.

Strictly Business: Walter Carpenter at Du Pont & General Motors. Charles W. Cheape. LC 94-22652. (Studies in Industry & Society: No. 6). (Illus.). 328p. 1995. text ed. 48.50 (*0-8018-4941-1*) Johns Hopkins.

Strictly Dishonorable & Other Lost American Plays. Ed. by Richard Nelson. LC 86-5782. (Illus.). 260p. (Orig.). (C). 1986. pap. 10.95 (*0-930452-55-0*) Theatre Comm.

Strictly for Beginners CP-M Book or, How to Talk with Your New Personal Computer. Joseph T. Finnell, Jr. LC 83-51318. (Illus.). 304p. (Orig.). 1984. spiral bd. 9.95 (*0-915767-00-7*) Topaz Pr.

Strictly for the Birds! Ruth Seeley-Scheel. (Illus.). 1990. pap. 6.95 (*0-9619815-5-5*) Laugh Goose.

***Strictly Personal.** Mary A. Wilson. (Yours Truly Ser.). 1997. mass mkt. 3.50 (*0-373-52048-4*, 1-52048-5) Silhouette.

Strictly Personal. W. Somerset Maugham. LC 75-25376. (Works of W. Somerset Maugham). 1977. reprint ed. 23.95 (*0-405-07829-3*) Ayer.

Strictly Speaking: Will America Be the Death of English? Edwin Newman. LC 74-6525. 224p. 1974. 9.95 (*0-672-51990-9*, Bobbs) Macmillan.

Strictly Strings: A Comprehensive String Method, Bk. 1: Bass. Jacquelyn Dillon et al. (Illus.). 40p. (Orig.). (J). (gr. 4-6). 1992. pap. 5.50 (*0-88284-533-0*, 5296) Alfred Pub.

Strictly Strings: A Comprehensive String Method, Bk. 1: Cello. Jacquelyn Dillon et al. (Illus.). 40p. (Orig.). (J). (gr. 4-6). 1992. pap. 5.50 (*0-88284-532-2*, 5295) Alfred Pub.

Strictly Strings: A Comprehensive String Method, Bk. 1: Score. Jacquelyn Dillon et al. (Illus.). 216p. (Orig.). (J). (gr. 4-6). 1992. pap. 24.95 (*0-88284-534-9*, 5297) Alfred Pub.

Strictly Strings: A Comprehensive String Method, Bk. 1: Viola. Jacquelyn Dillon et al. (Illus.). 40p. (Orig.). (J). (gr. 4-6). 1992. pap. 5.50 (*0-88284-531-4*, 5294) Alfred Pub.

Strictly Strings: A Comprehensive String Method, Bk. 1: Violin. Jacquelyn Dillon et al. (Illus.). 40p. (Orig.). (J). (gr. 4-6). 1992. pap. 5.50 (*0-88284-530-6*, 5293) Alfred Pub.

Strictly Strings - Piano, Bk. 1: A Comprehensive String Method. Jacquelyn Dillon et al. (Illus.). 64p. (Orig.). (J). (gr. 4-6). 1992. pap. 11.95 (*0-88284-535-7*, 5298) Alfred Pub.

Strictly Structured BASIC. Eli Berlinger. LC 85-21489. (Illus.). 372p. (C). 1986. pap. text ed. 48.00 (*0-314-93152-X*) West Pub.

Strictly Structured VAX BASIC. Eli Berlinger. 451p. 1988. pap. text ed. 48.00 (*0-314-64977-8*) West Pub.

Stricture in Feature Geometry: Dissertations in Linguistics. Jaye Padgett. 230p. (Orig.). 1995. text ed. 49.95 (*1-881526-67-4*); pap. text ed. 22.95 (*1-881526-66-6*) CSLI.

Strictures on a Life of William Wilberforce. William Wilberforce & Samuel Wilberforce. Ed. by Thomas Clarkson. LC 77-164398. (Black Heritage Library Collection). 1977. reprint ed. 18.95 (*0-8369-8857-4*) Ayer.

Strictures on Female Education. Hannah More. LC 94-35575. (Revolution & Romanticism, 1789-1834 Ser.). 1995. 95.00 (*1-85477-186-8*, Pub. by Woodstock Bks UK) Cassell.

Strictures on Mr. Colliers New Edition of Shakespeare, 1858. Alexander Dyce. LC 72-164816. reprint ed. 42.50 (*0-404-02231-6*) AMS Pr.

***Strictures on the Modern System of Female Education: 1799 Edition, 2 vols.** Hannah More. Ed. & Intro. by Jeffrey Stern. (Classics in Education Ser.). 648p. 1996. reprint ed. write for info. (*1-85506-297-6*) Bks Intl VA.

Strictures upon the Declaration of the Congress at Philadelphia. Thomas Hutchinson. (Notable American Authors Ser.). 1992. reprint ed. lib. bdg. 75.00 (*0-7812-3300-3*) Rprt Serv.

Stride & Glide: A Guide to Wisconsin's Best Cross-Country Ski Trails. William C. McGrath. LC 94-71147. (Illus.). 112p. 1994. pap. 12.95 (*0-9640613-0-9*) Amherst Pr.

Stride Guitar. Guy Van Duser. 1993. 8.95 (*1-56222-540-5*, 93939); audio 9.98 (*1-56222-610-X*, 93939C) Mel Bay.

***Stride Guitar.** Guy Van Duser. 1993. 17.95 incl. audio (*0-7866-0951-6*, 93939P) Mel Bay.

***Strident Whisper.** Mary Minton. 288p. 1996. 22.00 (*0-7278-4933-6*) Severn Hse.

Strider. Beverly Cleary. 160p. (J). 1992. pap. 4.50 (*0-380-71236-9*, Camelot) Avon.

***Strider.** Beverly Cleary. (Illus.). (J). (gr. 6). 1995. 9.00 (*0-395-73264-6*) HM.

Strider. Beverly Cleary. LC 90-6608. (Illus.). 192p. (J). (gr. 3 up). 1991. 16.00 (*0-688-09900-9*, Morrow Junior); lib. bdg. 15.93 (*0-688-09901-7*, Morrow Junior) Morrow.

Strider. Beverly Cleary. (J). 1996. mass mkt. 4.50 (*0-380-72802-8*) Avon.

***Strider.** large type ed. Beverly Cleary. (Illus.). 182p. (J). (gr. 6). 45.50 (*0-614-20623-5*, L-38202-00 APHB) Am Printing Hse.

Strider. large type ed. Beverly Cleary. 176p. (J). (gr. 4-8). 1995. lib. bdg. 16.95 (*1-885885-13-X*, Cornerstone FL) Pages Inc FL.

***Striders to Beboppers & Beyond.** Leslie Gourse. LC 96-31530. (Art of Jazz Ser.). (J). 1997. lib. bdg. 22.00 (*0-531-11320-5*) Watts.

***Striders to Beboppers & Beyond: The Art of Jazz Piano.** Leslie Gourse. (The Art of Jazz Ser.). 1997. pap. text ed. 6.95 (*0-531-15836-5*) Watts.

Striding Out: Aspects of Contemporary & New Dance in Britain. Stephanie Jordan. 224p. 1992. pap. 23.95 (*1-85273-032-3*, Pub. by Dance Bks UK) Princeton Bk Co.

Strife. John Galsworthy. (Methuen Student Editions Ser.). 61p. (C). 1988. pap. 9.95 (*0-413-54270-X*, A0276, Pub. by Methuen UK) Heinemann.

Strife. Shirley Greenslade. 59p. 1996. pap. write for info. (*1-886799-03-2*) Agape Word.

Strife Before Dawn. Mary Schumann. 1993. reprint ed. lib. bdg. 89.00 (*0-7812-5829-4*) Rprt Serv.

S

S

Strife Beyond Tamar. large type ed. Oliver. (Dales Large Print Ser.). 1995. pap. 17.99 (*1-85389-573-3*, Dales) Ulverscroft.

Strife of Systems: An Essay on the Grounds & Implications of Philosophical Diversity. Nicholas Rescher. LC 84-21958. 295p. 1985. reprint ed. pap. 84.10 (*0-608-02053-2*, 2062706) Bks Demand.

Strife of the Sea. Thornton J. Hains. LC 72-103515. (Short Story Index Reprint Ser.). 1977. 22.95 (*0-8369-3257-9*) Ayer.

Strife of the Spirit. Adin Steinsaltz. LC 87-32173. 280p. 1991. 30.00 (*0-87668-986-1*) Aronson.

Strife of the Spirit. Adin Steinsaltz. LC 87-32173. 280p. 1996. pap. 25.00 (*1-56821-981-4*) Aronson.

Strife of Tongues: Fray Luis de Leon & the Golden Age of Spain. Colin P. Thompson. (Cambridge Iberian & Latin American Studies). 320p. (C). 1988. text ed. 80.00 (*0-521-35388-2*) Cambridge U Pr.

Strigat (Scream) Silvia Cinca. Silvia Cinca. (Orig.). (RUM.). 1990. pap. text ed. 14.99 (*0-9623183-1-0*) Moonfall Pr VA.

Strike! Maureen Bayless. (Illus.). 24p. (J). (ps-3). 1994. pap. 5.95 (*0-921556-41-1*, Pub. by Gynergy-Ragweed CN) LPC InBook.

Strike. Hermann Huppen. Ed. by Bernd Metz. Tr. by Dwight Decker from FRE. (Jeremiah Ser.). (Illus.). 49p. (Orig.). 1990. pap. text ed. 9.95 (*0-87416-106-1*) Catalan Communs.

Strike! David D. Saltzman. 305p. 1992. pap. write for info. (*0-9634833-0-7*) Rocking Bridge.

Strike! Mary H. Vorse. 264p. 1991. 15.95 (*0-252-06217-5*) U of Ill Pr.

*__Strike!__ 4th rev. ed. Jeremy Brecher. (Classics Ser.). (Illus.). 420p. 1997. 40.00 (*0-89608-570-8*); pap. 20.00 (*0-89608-569-4*) South End Pr.

Strike: A Study in Collective Action. Ernest T. Hiller. LC 70-89738. (American Labor, from Conspiracy to Collective Bargaining Ser., No. 1). 304p. 1976. reprint ed. 19.95 (*0-405-02127-5*) Ayer.

Strike! The Bitter Struggle of American Workers from Colonial Times to the Present. Penny Colman. LC 94-29706. (Illus.). 80p. (J). (gr. 4-6). 1995. lib. bdg. 17.40 (*1-56294-459-2*) Millbrook Pr.

Strike: The Daily News War & the Future of American Labor. Richard Vigilante. 1994. 23.00 (*0-671-79631-3*) S&S Trade.

Strike Able-Peter: The Stranding & Salvage of the USS Missouri. John A. Butler. LC 95-18391. (Illus.). 246p. 1995. 31.95 (*1-55750-094-0*) Naval Inst Pr.

Strike Aces. Lindsay Peacock. (Illus.). 160p. 1989. 14.99 (*0-517-68847-6*) Random Hse Value.

Strike Anywhere. Dean Young. 1995. pap. 14.95 (*0-87081-423-0*) Univ Pr Colo.

Strike at Tivoli Mills. Timothy S. Arthur. (Works of Timothy Shay Arthur). 1989. reprint ed. lib. bdg. 79.00 (*0-7812-1807-1*) Rprt Serv.

Strike Commander: The Ultimate Strategy Guide. Bruce Shelley. 1993. pap. 19.95 (*1-55958-203-0*) Prima Pub.

Strike Commander Playtesters' Guide. Carolyn Cutler. (Illus.). 96p. (Orig.). 1993. pap. 14.95 (*0-929373-14-6*) Origin Syst.

Strike Defense Manual. fac. ed. Walter G. Mullins. LC 80-14961. 152p. pap. 43.40 (*0-7837-7418-4*, 2047213) Bks Demand.

Strike Eagle: Flying the F-15E in the Gulf War. William L. Smallwood. (Illus.). 240p. 1994. 23.95 (*0-02-881058-9*) Brasseys Inc.

*__Strike Eagle: Flying the F-15E in the Gulf War.__ William L. Smallwood. (Illus.). 240p. 1997. reprint ed. pap. 18.95 (*1-57488-122-1*) Brasseys Inc.

*__Strike Father Dead.__ Wain. 1978. pap. text ed. write for info. (*0-582-53793-2*, Pub. by Longman UK) Longman.

Strike for Union. Heber Blankenhorn. LC 75-89718. (American Labor, from Conspiracy to Collective Bargaining Ser., No. 1). 259p. 1974. reprint ed. 21.95 (*0-405-02104-6*) Ayer.

Strike Force: U. S. Marine Corps Special Operations. Kathleen D. Valenzi. 1993. pap. 19.95 (*0-943231-49-3*) Howell Pr VA.

Strike Four! Harriet Ziefert & Mavis Smith. (Easy-to-Read Ser.: Level 1, Blue). (Illus.). (J). (ps-2). 1995. pap. 3.50 (*0-14-036999-6*) Puffin Bks.

Strike Four: Adventures in European Baseball. Milton A. Simms. (Illus.). 250p. (Orig.). 1995. pap. 12.50 (*0-9625006-7-4*) White-Boucke.

Strike From Mariel. Carey Matthews. LC 83-81519. 254p. (Orig.). 1983. 14.95 (*0-912709-00-6*); pap. 7.95 (*0-912709-01-4*) First Commonwealth.

Strike from Space. Phyllis Schlafly & Chester Ward. LC 66-16734. 1965. 1.00 (*0-934640-07-6*) Pere Marquette.

Strike from the Sky: Israeli Airborne Troops. LC 85-40985. (Villard Military Ser.: The Elite Forces). (Illus.). 96p. 1986. 4.95 (*0-394-74404-7*, Villard Bks) Random.

Strike from the Sky: The History of Battlefield Air Attack, 1911-1945. Richard P. Hallion. (Smithsonian History of Aviation Ser.). (Illus.). 336p. 1989. 34.95 (*0-87474-452-0*) Smithsonian.

Strike from the Sky: The Story of the Battle of Britain. Alexander McKee. LC 72-169429. (Literature & History of Aviation Ser.). 1972. reprint ed. 29.95 (*0-405-03772-4*) Ayer.

*__Strike Hard: A Bomber Airfield at War, RAF Downham Market & Its Squadrons 1942-46.__ John B. Hilling. (Illus.). 160p. (Orig.). 1997. pap. 22.95 (*0-7509-1600-1*, Pub. by Sutton Pubng UK) Bks Intl VA.

Strike Manual: Related to Potential School Employees Strike Action. 135p. (Orig.). 1995. ring bd. 36.00 (*0-943397-33-2*, 119) Assn Calif Sch Admin.

Strike Midnight: Is This Their Final Hour, the Last Desperate Drama of Human History. D. M. Matera. 278p. 1994. pap. 10.99 (*0-89283-859-0*, Vine Bks) Servant.

Strike of a Sex & Zugassent's Discovery: After the Sex Struck. George N. Miller. LC 73-20636. (Sex, Marriage & Society Ser.). 124p. 1974. reprint ed. 19.95 (*0-405-05812-8*) Ayer.

Strike of the China Falcon. Stephen Cassell. 1992. mass mkt. 4.50 (*1-55817-584-9*, Pinncle Kensgtn) Kensgtn Pub Corp.

Strike of the Cobra. Timothy Rizzi. 480p. 1994. reprint ed. mass mkt., pap. text ed. 5.99 (*0-8439-3630-4*) Dorchester Pub Co.

Strike of 'Twenty Eight. Daniel Georgianna. (Illus.). 160p. 1993. pap. 15.95 (*0-932027-17-2*) Spinner Pubns.

Strike Out! Elise Howard. (Leftovers Ser.: No. 1). (J). (gr. 1-4). 1996. pap. 2.99 (*0-590-56923-6*) Scholastic Inc.

Strike Prevention & Control Handbook. Robert W. Mulcahy & Marion C. Smith. 1983. pap. 29.95 (*0-88057-065-2*) Exec Ent Pubns.

Strike-Slip Deformation, Basin Formation, & Sedimentation. Ed. by Kevin T. Biddle & Nicholas Christie-Blick. (Special Publications: No. 37). 386p. 1985. 49.00 (*0-918985-58-7*) SEPM.

*__Strike-Slip Deformation, Basin Formation, & Sedimentation Based on a Symposium Sponsored by the Society of Economic Paleontologists & Mineralogists.__ Ed. by Kevin T. Biddle & Nicholas Christie-Blick. LC 87-160028. (Society of Economic Paleontologists & Mineralogists Ser.: No. 37). (Illus.). 395p. pap. 112.60 (*0-608-05189-6*, 2065726) Bks Demand.

*__Strike Swiftly! The 70th Battalion: From North Africa to Normandy to Germany.__ Marvin G. Jensen. LC 96-50273. 352p. 1997. 24.95 (*0-89141-610-2*) Presidio Pr.

Strike the Bell. Roy Palmer. LC 78-1282. (Resources of Music Ser.: No. 18). (Illus.). 1978. pap. 10.95 (*0-521-21921-3*) Cambridge U Pr.

Strike the Original Match. Charles R. Swindoll. 251p. 1990. mass mkt. 5.99 (*0-8423-6445-5*, 076445-5) Tyndale.

Strike the Original Match. Charles R. Swindoll. LC 93-26368. 368p. 1993. pap. 10.99 (*0-310-41351-6*) Zondervan.

Strike Three. Clair Bee. 17.95 (*0-8488-1248-4*) Amereon Ltd.

Strike Three! Clair Bee. (Illus.). 208p. 1990. reprint ed. lib. bdg. 25.95 (*0-89966-742-2*) Buccaneer Bks.

Strike Three, You're Dead. Richard D. Rosen. 1986. pap. 2.95 (*0-451-14233-0*, Sig) NAL-Dutton.

*__Strike Three, You're Out!__ Linda L. Maifair. LC 96-45170. (Winners! Ser.). 64p. (Orig.). (J). (gr. 2-5). 1997. pap. 3.99 (*0-310-20705-3*) Zondervan.

Strike Through the Mask: Herman Melville & the Scene of Writing. Elizabeth Renker. (Illus.). 200p. (C). 1996. text ed. 35.00 (*0-8018-5230-7*) Johns Hopkins.

Strike Up the Orchestra: A Child's Guide to Classical Music. Friedman-Fairfax & Sony Music Staff. (Life, Times & Music Book/CD Ser.). 1995. pap. 16.98 incl. audio compact disk (*1-56799-226-9*, Friedman-Fairfax) M Friedman Pub Grp Inc.

Strike Zone. Jim Bouton & Eliot Asinof. 416p. 1995. pap. 5.99 (*0-451-18334-7*, Sig) NAL-Dutton.

Strike Zone. Peter David. (Star Trek: The Next Generation Ser.: No. 5). 1991. mass mkt. 5.50 (*0-671-74647-2*) PB.

Strikeout. 1996. pap. write for info. (*0-517-88605-7*) Random Hse Value.

Strikeout: The Celebration of the Art of Pitching. William Curran. LC 94-3605. 1995. 23.00 (*0-517-58841-2*) Crown Pub Group.

Striker Hits Pay-Dirt. large type ed. Amy Sadler. (Dales Large Print Ser.). 219p. 1995. pap. 17.99 (*1-85389-549-0*, Dales) Ulverscroft.

Striker II: Miniature Warfare in the Far Future. Frank Chadwick & David Nilsen. (Travellers the New Era Ser.). (Illus.). 196p. (Orig.). 1994. pap. 20.00 (*1-55878-173-0*) Game Designers.

Striker, Vol. 1: The Armored Warrior. Ryoji Minagawa & Hiroshi Takashige. Ed. by Seiji Horibuchi. Tr. by Satoru Fujii from JPN. (Illus.). 128p. (Orig.). 1993. pap. 14.95 (*0-929279-84-0*) Viz Commns Inc.

Strikers & Subsidies: The Influence of Government Transfer Programs on Strike Activity. Robert M. Hutchens et al. LC 89-16693. 210p. 1989. text ed. 23.00 (*0-88099-080-5*); pap. text ed. 13.00 (*0-88099-079-1*) W E Upjohn.

Strikers, Communists, Tramps & Detectives. Allan Pinkerton. LC 79-90190. (Mass Violence in America Ser.). 1977. reprint ed. 32.95 (*0-405-01332-9*) Ayer.

Strikes. Norman McCord. 1980. text ed. 29.95 (*0-312-76640-8*) St Martin.

Strikes: Causes, Conduct & Consequences. Douglas Blackmur. 216p. 1993. pap. 39.00 (*1-86287-114-0*, Pub. by Federation Pr AU) Gaunt.

*__Strikes & Lock Outs.__ Roger Blanpain. 1994. pap. text ed. 93.00 (*90-6544-841-1*) Kluwer Ac.

Strikes & Revolution in Russia, 1917. Diane P. Koenker & William G. Rosenberg. (Illus.). 456p. (C). 1990. text ed. 55.00 (*0-691-05578-5*) Princeton U Pr.

Strikes & Social Problems. Joseph S. Nicholson. LC 72-4517. (Essay Index Reprint Ser.). 1977. reprint ed. 20.95 (*0-8369-2964-0*) Ayer.

Strikes, Dispute Procedures, & Arbitration: Essays on Labor Law. William B. Gould, IV. LC 85-944. (Contributions in American Studies: No. 82). xi, 313p. 1985. text ed. 59.95 (*0-313-24468-5*, GSD/, Greenwood Pr) Greenwood.

Strikes Have Followed Me All My Life: A South African Autobiography. Emma Mashinini. (Illus.). 142p. (gr. 13). 1991. pap. 15.95 (*0-415-90415-3*, A5583, Routledge NY) Routledge.

Strikes in Essential Services. G. S. Morris. Ed. by Bob Hepple & Paul O'Higgins. (Studies in Labour & Social Law). 232p. 1986. pap. text ed. 50.00 (*0-7201-1869-7*, Mansell Pub) Cassell.

Strikes in the United States. Florence Peterson. 1988. reprint ed. lib. bdg. 25.00 (*0-7812-0546-8*) Rprt Serv.

Strikes in the United States, 1880-1936. Florence Peterson. LC 70-145232. 190p. 1972. reprint ed. 25.00 (*0-403-01148-5*) Scholarly.

Strikes, Wars, & Revolutions in an International Perspective: Strike Waves in the Late Nineteenth & Early Twentieth Centuries. Ed. by Leopold Haimson & Charles Tilly. 576p. (C). 1989. text ed. 80.00 (*0-521-35285-1*) Cambridge U Pr.

Striking a Balance: Dancers Talk about Dancing. rev. ed. Barbara Newman. LC 91-44442. (Illus.). 402p. 1992. reprint ed. pap. 17.95 (*0-87910-154-7*) Limelight Edns.

*__Striking a Balance: Improving Stewardship of Marine Areas.__ 200p. 1997. 39.95 (*0-309-06369-8*) Natl Acad Pr.

Striking a Balance: Making National Economic Policy. Albert E. Rees. LC 83-17881. (Illus.). x, 128p. 1984. 15.00 (*0-226-70707-5*) U Ch Pr.

Striking a Balance: Making National Economic Policy. Albert E. Rees. LC 83-17881. (Illus.). x, 128p. 1986. pap. text ed. 8.50 (*0-226-70708-3*) U Ch Pr.

Striking a Balance: The Environmental Challenge of Development. 52p. 1989. 6.95 (*0-8213-1271-5*, 11271) World Bank.

Striking & Chiming Clocks: Their Working & Repair. Eric Smith. (Illus.). 192p. 1996. 24.95 (*0-7153-0370-8*, Pub. by D & C Pub UK) Sterling.

Striking at the Joints: Contemporary Psychology & Literary Criticism. John V. Knapp. 316p. 1996. pap. text ed. 32.00 (*0-7618-0257-6*); lib. bdg. 52.00 (*0-7618-0256-8*) U Pr of Amer.

*__Striking Back: A Jewish Commando's War Against the Nazis.__ Peter Masters. LC 97-24416. (Illus.). 320p. 1997. 24.95 (*0-89141-629-3*) Presidio Pr.

Striking Chords: Multicultural Literary Interpretations. Sneja Gunew & Kateryna Longley. 224p. 1992. pap. 19.95 (*1-86373-089-3*, Pub. by Allen Unwin AT) Paul & Co Pubs.

Striking Clock Repair Guide. Steven G. Conover. (Illus.). 90p. 1995. pap. 22.95 (*0-9624766-4-1*, 115) Clockmakers.

Striking Flint: Genora (Johnson) Dollinger Remembers the 1936-37 G. M. Sit-Down Strike. Susan Rosenthal. 41p. (Orig.). 1996. pap. 3.50 (*0-9652359-0-4*) L J Page.

Striking for Life: Labor's Side of the Labor Question. John Swinton et al. 1972. 59.95 (*0-8490-1143-4*) Gordon Pr.

Striking for Life: Labor's Side of the Labor Question; the Right of the Workingman to a Fair Living. John Swinton. LC 76-88492. (Illus.). 498p. 1971. reprint ed. text ed. 75.00 (*0-8371-4963-0*, SWSL) Greenwood.

Striking Impressions: A Visual Guide to Collecting U. S. Coins. Robert R. Van Ryzin. LC 91-75366. (Illus.). 208p. 1992. pap. 9.95 (*0-87341-176-5*, SI01) Krause Pubns.

Striking In: The Early Notebooks of James Dickey. Ed. & Intro. by Gordan Van Ness. 304p. (C). 1996. 39.95 (*0-8262-1056-2*) U of Mo Pr.

Striking It Rich: The Story of the California Gold Rush. Stephen Krensky. (J). 1996. 15.00 (*0-689-80804-6*) S&S Childrens.

Striking It Rich: The Story of the California Gold Rush. Stephen Krensky. (J). 1996. pap. 3.99 (*0-689-80803-8*, S&S Bks Young Read) S&S Childrens.

Striking New Images: Studies on Roman Imperial Coinage & the New Testament World. Larry J. Kreitzer. (HSNT Supplement Ser.: No. 134). 226p. 1996. 37.50 (*1-85075-623-6*, Pub. by Sheffield Acad UK) CUP Services.

*__Striking Out.__ Gail Bowen. 1997. mass mkt. 5.99 (*0-7710-3415-6*) McCland & Stewart.

Striking Out! Michael B. Dixon et al. (Orig.). (J). (gr. k up). 1984. pap. 5.00 (*0-87602-252-2*) Anchorage.

Striking Out. Robert Lamb. LC 90-53327. 264p. 1991. 22.00 (*1-877946-06-0*) Permanent Pr.

Striking Out. Will Weaver. LC 93-565. 288p. (J). (gr. 5 up). 1993. lib. bdg. 14.89 (*0-06-023347-8*) HarpC Child Bks.

Striking Out. Will Weaver. LC 93-565. 288p. (YA). (gr. 5 up). 1995. pap. 3.95 (*0-06-447113-6*, Trophy) HarpC Child Bks.

Striking Out: A Kate Henry Mystery. Alison Gordon. 272p. 1995. 19.95 (*0-7710-3423-7*) McCland & Stewart.

*__Striking Out & Winning! A Music-Maker's Guide for the Hammered Dulcimer.__ 2nd ed. Lucille Reilly. LC 84-199357. (Illus.). 170p. 1984. pap. 35.00 (*0-9613356-4-5*) Shadrach.

Striking Performances/Performing Strikes. Kirk W. Fuoss. LC 96-41266. (Performance Studies). 1997. text ed. 45.00 (*0-87805-913-X*); pap. text ed. 18.00 (*0-87805-914-8*) U Pr of Miss.

Striking Resemblance. Tina Darragh. (Burning Deck Poetry Ser.). 64p. (Orig.). 1989. pap. 7.00 (*0-930901-64-9*) Burning Deck.

Striking Resemblance. deluxe ed. Tina Darragh. (Burning Deck Poetry Ser.). 64p. (Orig.). 1989. pap. 15.00 (*0-930901-65-7*) Burning Deck.

Striking Roots: Reflections on Five Decades of Jewish Life. Aron Horowitz. 412p. 1995. lib. bdg. 29.00 (*0-8095-4932-8*) Borgo Pr.

Striking Roots: Reflections on Five Decades of Jewish Life. Aron Horowitz. 412p. pap. 9.95 (*0-88962-099-7*) Mosaic.

Striking Success. Tricia Szirom. (Australian Women Talk about Success Ser.). 184p. (Orig.). 1992. pap. text ed. 16.95 (*1-86373-037-0*, Pub. by Allen Unwin AT) Paul & Co Pubs.

*__Striking Terror No More: The Church Responds to Domestic Violence.__ Beth Basham & Sra Lisherness. LC 97-10417. 1997. write for info. (*1-57895-014-7*) Bridge Resources.

Striking the Balance: A History of the Oppenheim Bank. Michael Sturmer et al. (Illus.). 544p. 1994. 85.00 (*0-297-81399-4*) Trafalgar.

Striking Water. Paul Genega. 74p. 1989. pap. 7.00 (*0-948339-22-5*) Story Line.

Strindberg. George A. Campbell. LC 71-163501. (Studies in Drama: No. 39). 1971. reprint ed. lib. bdg. 49.95 (*0-8383-1320-5*) M S G Haskell Hse.

Strindberg: An Introduction to His Life & Work. Brita M. Mortensen & Brian W. Downs. 246p. reprint ed. pap. 70.20 (*0-317-09198-0*, 2051420) Bks Demand.

Strindberg: Five Plays. August Strindberg. Tr. by Harry G. Carlson. 1984. pap. 6.95 (*0-451-51862-4*, Sig Classics) NAL-Dutton.

Strindberg: Five Plays. August Strindberg. Tr. by Harry G. Carlson from SWE. 297p. (C). 1996. pap. 14.95 (*0-520-04698-6*) U CA Pr.

Strindberg: Plays One. August Strindberg. Tr. & Intro. by Michael Meyer. (Methuen World Dramatists Ser.). 191p. (C). 1990. reprint ed. pap. 8.95 (*0-413-52160-5*, A0447, Pub. by Methuen UK) Heinemann.

Strindberg: Plays Three. August Strindberg. Tr. by Michael Meyer. (Methuen World Dramatists Ser.). 276p. (Orig.). (C). 1991. pap. 7.95 (*0-413-64840-0*, AO618, Pub. by Methuen UK) Heinemann.

Strindberg: Plays Two. August Strindberg. Tr. & Intro. by Michael Meyer. (Methuen World Dramatists Ser.). 254p. (C). 1990. reprint ed. pap. 10.95 (*0-413-49750-X*, A0448, Pub. by Methuen UK) Heinemann.

Strindberg: Three Experimental Plays. August Strindberg. Tr. by F. R. Southerington. LC 74-19142. 138p. reprint ed. pap. 39.40 (*0-317-09273-1*, 2015043) Bks Demand.

Strindberg & Autobiography. Michael Robinson. LC 87-62756. 192p. (Orig.). 8600. pap. 23.00 (*1-870041-00-3*, Pub. by Norvik Pr UK) Dufour.

Strindberg & Genre. Ed. by Michael Robinson. (Norvik Press Series A: No. 9). 297p. 9100. 45.00 (*1-870041-18-6*, Pub. by Norvik Pr UK) Dufour.

Strindberg & Shakespeare: Shakespeare's Influence on Strindberg's Historical Drama. Joan Bulman. LC 73-153482. (Studies in Comparative Literature: No. 35). 1971. reprint ed. lib. bdg. 75.00 (*0-8383-1239-X*) M S G Haskell Hse.

Strindberg & the Historical Drama. Walter Johnson. LC 63-9937. 336p. 1963. 25.00 (*0-295-73942-8*) U of Wash Pr.

Strindberg & the Poetry of Myth. Harry G. Carlson. LC 81-12989. 252p. 1982. 45.00 (*0-520-04442-8*) U CA Pr.

Strindberg & Van Gogh: An Attempt of a Pathographic Analysis with Reference to Parallel Cases of Swedenborg & Holderlin. Karl Jaspers. LC 77-9394. 234p. reprint ed. pap. 66.70 (*0-317-51983-2*, 2027382) Bks Demand.

Strindberg As a Modern Poet: A Critical & Comparative Study. John E. Bellquist. LC 86-4293. (University of California Publications in Modern Philology: No. 117). 201p. 1986. pap. 57.30 (*0-7837-7471-0*, 2049193) Bks Demand.

Strindberg As a Modern Poet: A Critical & Comparative Study. John E. Bellquist. LC 86-4293. (Publications in Modern Philology: Vol. 117). 1986. pap. 28.00 (*0-520-09710-6*) U CA Pr.

Strindberg in Inferno. Gunnar Brandell. Tr. by Barry Jacobs. LC 73-90851. 358p. reprint ed. pap. 102.10 (*0-7837-3831-5*, 2043652) Bks Demand.

Strindberg the Man. Gustaf Uddgren. LC 74-39416. (Studies in European Literature: No. 56). 165p. 1972. reprint ed. lib. bdg. 49.95 (*0-8383-1401-5*) M S G Haskell Hse.

Strindberg's Conception of History. Harry V. Palmblad. 1972. 250.00 (*0-8490-1144-2*) Gordon Pr.

Strindberg's Dramatic Expressionism. Carl E. Dahlstrom. LC 64-14697. 264p. 1972. reprint ed. 29.95 (*0-405-08426-9*, Pub. by Blom Pubns UK) Ayer.

Strindberg's Influence on Eugene O'Neill. I. Haywood. 1972. 59.95 (*0-8490-1145-0*) Gordon Pr.

Strindberg's Letters, 2 vols., I. August Strindberg. Ed. & Tr. by Michael Robinson. LC 91-36244. (Illus.). 462p. 1992. 55.00 (*0-226-77727-8*) U Ch Pr.

Strindberg's Letters, 2 vols., Set. August Strindberg. Ed. & Tr. by Michael Robinson. LC 91-36244. (Illus.). 968p. 1992. 110.00 (*0-226-77725-1*) U Ch Pr.

Strindberg's Letters, 2 vols., Vol. II: 1892-1912. August Strindberg. Ed. & Tr. by Michael Robinson. LC 91-36244. (Illus.). 506p. 1992. Vol II: 1892-1912. 55.00 (*0-226-77728-6*) U Ch Pr.

Strindberg's Master Olof & Shakespeare. Hans Andersson. (Essays & Studies on English Language & Literature: Vol. 11). 1974. reprint ed. 25.00 (*0-8115-0209-0*) Periodicals Srv.

Strindberg's Miss Julie: A Play & Its Transpositions. Egil Tornqvist & Barry Jacobs. LC 88-63188. (Illus.). 302p. (Orig.). 8800. pap. 24.00 (*1-870041-08-9*, Pub. by Norvik Pr UK) Dufour.

String. Guy De Maupassant. (Classic Short Stories Ser.). 32p. (J). (gr. 6). 1990. lib. bdg. 13.95 (*0-88682-297-1*) Creative Ed.

String: Tying It up, Tying It Down. Jan Adkins. LC 91-25786. (Illus.). 48p. (YA). (gr. 5 up). 1992. lib. bdg. 13.95 (*0-684-18875-9*, C Scribner Sons Young) S&S Childrens.

String along Numbers. John Speirs. (J). (ps-3). 1996. 6.95 (*0-307-17680-0*, Golden Pr) Western Pub.

An Asterisk (*) at the beginning of an entry indicates that the title is appearing in BIP for the first time.

String & Sticky Tape Experiments. Ed. by Ronald Edge. (Occasional Publications). (Illus.). 448p. (Orig.). 1987. pap. text ed. 31.00 (*0-917853-28-8*, OP58) Am Assn Physics.

String Around Autumn: Selected Poems 1952-1980. Ooka Makoto. Ed. & Tr. by Thomas Fitzsimmons from JPN. LC 82-80672. (Asian Poetry in Translation: Japan Ser.: No. 3). 94p. (Orig.). 1982. pap. 9.50 (*0-942668-01-4*) Katydid Bks.

String Around Autumn: Selected Poems 1952-1980. Makoto Ooka. Ed. by Thomas Fitzsimmons. Tr. by Makoto Ooka & Thomas Fitzsimmons from JPN. LC 82-80672. (Asian Poetry in Translation: Japan Ser.: No. 3). 94p. (Orig.). 1982. text ed. 14.50 (*0-942668-13-8*) Katydid Bks.

***String Creek Saga 1990-1997.** Robin Rule. 31p. 1997. pap. 5.00 (*0-614-30307-9*) Rainy Day CA.

String (Double) Bass. David H. Stanton. 8.00 (*0-686-15896-2*) Instrumental.

String Figure Bibliography: A Publication of the International String Figure Association. 2nd rev. ed. Thomas F. Storer. LC 96-76197. vi, 110p. (Orig.). 1996. pap. 13.95 (*0-9651467-1-5*) ISFA Pr.

String Figures. A. Johnston Abraham. Ed. by Keith Irvine. LC 86-15518. (Folk Games Ser.). (Illus.). 1987. 14.95 (*0-917256-37-9*); pap. 8.95 (*0-917256-23-9*) Ref Pubns.

String Figures & How to Make Them. Caroline F. Jayne. (Illus.). 407p. (J). (gr. 7 up). 1906. pap. 5.95 (*0-486-20152-X*) Dover.

String Figures from Around the World. Sorena Dewitt. (Illus.). 32p. (J). (gr. 2-6). 1992. pap. 9.95 (*0-89346-356-6*) Heian Intl.

String Figures from Around the World, Vol. 2. Sorena De Witt. (Illus.). 32p. (Orig.). (J). (gr. 1-7). 1995. pap. text ed. 4.95 (*0-89346-827-4*) Heian Intl.

String Figures from Fiji & Western Polynesia. J. Hornell. (BMB Ser.). 1974. reprint ed. 25.00 (*0-527-02142-3*) Periodicals Srv.

String Figures from Hawaii, Including Some from New Hebrides & Gilbert Islands. L. A. Dickey. (BMB Ser.: No. 54). 1974. reprint ed. 35.00 (*0-527-02160-1*) Periodicals Srv.

String Figures from the Marquesas & Society Islands. Willowdean C. Handy. (BMB Ser.). 1974. reprint ed. 25.00 (*0-527-02121-0*) Periodicals Srv.

String Games from Around the World. Anne A. Johnson. (Illus.). 80p. (J). (gr. 2 up). 1996. spiral bd. 12.95 (*1-57054-040-3*) Klutz Pr.

String in the Harp. Nancy Bond. LC 75-28181. 384p. (J). (gr. 4-8). 1976. lib. bdg. 19.00 (*0-689-50036-X*, McElderry) S&S Childrens.

String in the Harp. Nancy Bond. LC 75-28181. (J). (gr. 5-9). 1996. pap. 4.95 (*0-689-80445-8*, Aladdin Paperbacks) S&S Childrens.

String Instruments of North India, No. II. Sharmistha Sen. (C). 1992. 30.00 (*0-8364-2821-8*, Pub. by Eastern Bk Linkers II) S Asia.

String Light: Poems by C. D. Wright. C. D. Wright. LC 90-45957. 80p. 1991. 14.95 (*0-8203-1297-5*) U of Ga Pr.

String Music in Print: 1984 Supplement. Ed. by Margaret K. Farish. LC 84-3478. (Music in Print Ser.: Vol. 6S). 269p. 1984. lib. bdg. 95.00 (*0-88478-016-3*) Musicdata.

String Music of Black Composers: A Bibliography. Aaron Horne. LC 91-26742. (Music Reference Collection: No. 33). 352p. 1991. text ed. 65.00 (*0-313-27938-1*, HSX/, Greenwood Pr) Greenwood.

***String of Beads.** Lucy Kincaid. (You Can Make It Ser.). (Illus.). 24p. (J). 1997. 3.49 (*1-85854-540-4*) Brimax Bks.

***String of Beads.** Margarette S. Reid. LC 97-10686. 1997. pap. 14.99 (*0-525-45721-6*) NAL-Dutton.

String of Beads: Complete Poems of Princess Shikishi. Princess Shikishi. Tr. by Hiroaki Sato. LC 93-29024. (SHAPS Library of Translations). (Illus.). 192p. (C). 1993. text ed. 34.00 (*0-8248-1483-5*) UH Pr.

String of Blue Beads. large type ed. Pamela Oldfield. LC 94-45926. 509p. 1995. reprint ed. lib. bdg. 21.95 (*0-7838-1240-X*, GK Hall) Thorndike Pr.

String of Chinese Pearls: Ten Tales of Chinese Girls Ancient & Modern. W. Fisher. 1972. lib. bdg. 79.95 (*0-87968-518-2*) Krishna Pr.

***String of Lights.** Terry Earp. 1992. pap. 2.50 (*1-57514-196-5*) Encore Perform Pub.

String of Monarchs. Florence Miller & Alexis K. Rotella. 25p. 1995. pap. 13.00 (*0-614-07899-7*) Jade Mtn.

String of Pearls. Richard Brooks. 1990. pap. 8.99 (*0-85234-280-2*, Pub. by Evangelical Pr) Presby & Reformed.

String on a Roast Won't Catch Fire in the Oven: An A-Z Encyclopedia of Common Sense for the Newly Independent Young Adult. Candice Kohl. LC 93-3961. (Illus.). 188p. 1993. pap. 12.95 (*1-880197-07-3*) Gylantic Pub.

String on the Harp. Nancy Bond. (YA). (gr. 5-9). 1987. reprint ed. pap. 5.99 (*0-14-032376-7*, Puffin) Puffin Bks.

String Orchestra Accompaniments: Bass. Ed. by Kendall. 10p. 1974. pap. text ed. 3.95 (*0-87487-323-1*) Summy-Birchard.

String Orchestra Accompaniments: Cello. Ed. by Kendall. 10p. 1974. pap. text ed. 3.95 (*0-87487-322-3*) Summy-Birchard.

String Orchestra Accompaniments: Score. Ed. by Kendall. 32p. 1974. pap. text ed. 6.95 (*0-87487-318-5*) Summy-Birchard.

String Orchestra Accompaniments: Viola. Ed. by Kendall. 10p. 1974. pap. text ed. 3.95 (*0-87487-321-5*) Summy-Birchard.

String Orchestra Accompaniments: Violin I. Ed. by Kendall. 10p. 1974. pap. text ed. 3.95 (*0-87487-319-3*) Summy-Birchard.

String Orchestra Accompaniments: Violin II. Ed. by Kendall. 10p. 1974. pap. text ed. 3.95 (*0-87487-320-7*) Summy-Birchard.

***String Orchestra Super List.** Ed. by Frederick R. Mayer. 96p. (C). 1993. pap. 16.50 (*1-56545-023-X*, 1616) Music Ed Natl.

String Path Integral Realization of Vertex Operator Algebras. H. Tsukada. LC 91-2228. (Memoirs Ser.: Vol. 91/444). 138p. 1991. pap. 23.00 (*0-8218-2510-0*, MEMO 91/444) Am Math.

String Play: The Drama of Playing & Teaching Strings. Phyllis Young. (Illus.). 150p. (C). 1986. 25.00 (*0-292-77606-3*); pap. 14.95 (*0-292-77607-1*) U of Tex Pr.

String Potpourri Pattern & Other Ideas: A Poem Book. Scentouri Staff. 1984. pap. text ed. 5.95 (*0-318-04424-2*, Scentouri) Prosperity & Profits.

String Processing & Text Manipulation in C: Selected Data Structures & Tech. Bernice Lipkin. 464p. 1994. pap. text ed. 43.00 (*0-13-121443-8*) P-H.

String Quantum Gravity & Physics at the Planck Energy Scale: International Workshop on Theoretical Physics. Antonio L. Zichichi. (Science & Culture Series - Physics). 500p. 1993. text ed. 121.00 (*981-02-1168-6*) World Scientific Pub.

String Quartet at the Oettingen-Wallerstein Court: Iganaz von Beecks & His Contemporaries. Fiona Little. (British Music Theses Ser.: Vol. 32). 640p. 1989. reprint ed. text ed. 20.00 (*0-8240-2343-9*) Garland.

String Quartet No. 1. E. Carter. 236p. 1986. pap. text ed. 35.00 (*0-7935-3785-1*) H Leonard.

String Quartet No. 1 1951: Score. E. Carter. 124p. 1987. per. 20.00 (*0-7935-3734-7*) H Leonard.

String Quartet No. 4: Score. Villa Lobos. 116p. 1994. pap. 15.00 (*0-7935-1923-3*) H Leonard.

String Quartet Opus 11: Study Score, No. 28. S. Barber. 20p. 1986. pap. 15.00 (*0-7935-5560-4*, 50338950) H Leonard.

String Quartets for Beginning Ensembles: Score & Parts, Vol. 2. Des. by Joseph Knaus. (Suzuki Method Ser.). 1991. pap. text ed. 19.95 (*0-87487-282-0*) Summy-Birchard.

String Quartets for Beginning Ensembles: Scores & Parts, Vol. 1. Ed. by Joseph Knaus. (Suzuki Method Ser.). 1990. pap. text ed. 19.95 (*0-87487-281-2*) Summy-Birchard.

String Quartets for Beginning Ensembles, Vol. 3: Score & Parts. Joseph Knaus. (Suzuki Method Ser.). 1992. pap. text ed. 19.95 (*0-87487-283-9*) Summy-Birchard.

***String Quartets Nos. 06-10.** Shostakovich. 12.95 (*0-486-29300-9*) Dover.

String Quartets of Haydn, Mozart, & Beethoven: Studies of the Autograph Manuscripts. Christoph Wolff. (Isham Library Papers: No. 3). (Illus.). 368p. (C). 1981. 37.50 (*0-674-84331-2*) HUP.

String Quartets Opus 18 No. 1-6. Ludwig van Beethoven. 1986. pap. text ed. 40.00 (*0-7935-3888-2*, 50261890) H Leonard.

String-Rewriting Systems. Ronald V. Book & Friedrich Otto. LC 92-37370. (Texts & Monographs in Computer Science). 1993. 52.95 (*0-387-97965-4*) Spr-Verlag.

String Searching Algorithms. A. Stephen Graham. (Lecture Notes on Computing Ser.). 260p. 1994. text ed. 43.00 (*981-02-1829-X*) World Scientific Pub.

String Teaching Guide, Bk. 1: Sequenced Lesson Plans for the Beginning String Class. Edward Krebs & Susan Krebs. (Illus.). 200p. 1989. 74.95 (*0-685-35172-6*); ring bd. 94.95 (*0-9623341-9-7*) K Pub.

String Theory - Quantum Cosmology & Quantum Gravity Integrable & Conformal Variant Theories: Proceedings of the Paris-Meudon Colloquium, Meudon, France, September 22-26, 1986. Ed. by H. J. De Vega & N. Sanchez. 524p. 1987. pap. 58.00 (*9971-5-0299-2*); text ed. 137.00 (*9971-5-0286-0*) World Scientific Pub.

String Theory & Grand Unification: Proceedings of the Conference. M. Bianchi et al. 450p. 1993. text ed. 109.00 (*981-02-1161-9*) World Scientific Pub.

String Theory & Quantum Gravity: Proceedings of the Trieste Spring School, Trieste, Italy, April 23 to May 1, 1990. Ed. by Michael B. Green et al. 184p. 1991. pap. 28.00 (*981-02-0373-X*); text ed. 74.00 (*981-02-0372-1*) World Scientific Pub.

String Theory & Quantum Gravity: Spring School & Workshop. J. A. Harvey et al. 500p. 1993. text ed. 121.00 (*981-02-1342-5*) World Scientific Pub.

String Theory & Quantum Gravity '91. Ed. by J. A. Harvey et al. 400p. (C). 1992. text ed. 114.00 (*981-02-0774-3*) World Scientific Pub.

String Theory, Gauge Theory & Quantum Gravity, '93: Proceedings of the Spring School & Workshop. R. Dijkgraff et al. 352p. 1994. text ed. 99.00 (*981-02-1806-0*) World Scientific Pub.

String Too Short to Be Saved: Recollections of Summers on a New England Farm. Donald Hall. LC 78-74249. (Illus.). 176p. 1979. pap. 12.95 (*0-87923-282-X*) Godine.

String Trimmer & Blower Service Manual. 1992. pap. 24.95 (*0-87288-508-9*, STR-2) Intertec Pub.

Stringalong. John Pearse & John Warde. (Illus.). 96p. 1986. pap. 10.95 (*0-9617175-0-5*) J Pearse Mus Pub.

Stringbean's Trip to the Shining Sea. Jennifer Williams. 48p. (J). 1990. pap. 5.99 (*0-590-44851-X*) Scholastic Inc.

Stringbean's Trip to The Shining Sea. Vera B. Williams. LC 86-29502. (Illus.). 48p. (J). (gr. k-3). 1988. 16.00 (*0-688-07161-9*); lib. bdg. 15.93 (*0-688-07162-7*) Greenwillow.

Stringed Instruments of Ancient Greece. Martha Maas & Jane M. Snyder. LC 87-2103. 288p. (C). 1989. text ed. 50.00 (*0-300-03686-8*) Yale U Pr.

Stringed Instruments of the Middle Ages. Hortense Panum. LC 73-127279. (Music Ser.). (Illus.). 1971. reprint ed. lib. bdg. 55.00 (*0-306-70039-5*) Da Capo.

Stringed Keyboard Instruments. Franz J. Hirt. Tr. by M. Boehme-Brown from GER. (Music Ser.). (Illus.). 235p. 1983. 95.00 (*0-685-05858-1*) Da Capo.

Stringer. Don Pendleton. (Stony Man Ser.: Vol. 18). 1995. mass mkt. 4.99 (*0-373-61902-2*) Harlequin Bks.

Stringin' up Sandy: A Christmas Story for Little Buckaroos. Randy Grochoske. (Illus.). (Orig.). (J). (gr. 1-6). 1995. mass mkt., pap. 8.95 (*0-9649909-0-3*) Peckerwood.

***Stringing Along.** Trice Boerens. (Illus.). 96p. pap. text ed. 7.95 (*0-486-29467-6*) Dover.

Stringmusic: Full Score String Orchestra Parts. M. Gould. 56p. 1995. pap. 29.95 (*0-7935-5086-6*, 50482481) H Leonard.

Strings. Dave Duncan. 224p. 1990. mass mkt. 3.95 (*0-345-36191-1*, Del Rey) Ballantine.

Strings. Alyn Shipton. LC 93-15278. (Exploring Music Ser.). (Illus.). 32p. (J). (gr. 5-8). 1993. lib. bdg. 22.83 (*0-8114-2320-4*) Raintree Steck-V.

Strings: A Comparative View, Vol. I. Phyllis Skoldberg. LC 81-70184. 244p. (C). 1988. pap. text ed. 19.95 (*0-88284-380-X*, 2941) Alfred Pub.

Strings: A Comparative View, Vol. II. Phyllis Skoldberg. 187p. 1988. pap. text ed. 19.95 (*0-88284-381-8*, 2942) Alfred Pub.

***Strings: An Oddesy of Mind, Medicine, Transplant & Healing.** John Robbins. 1998. 23.95 (*1-880823-17-9*) N Star Pubns.

Strings & Superstrings: Proceedings of the XVIII International Gift Seminar on Theoretical Physics. Ed. by Juan R. Mittelbrunn et al. 300p. (C). 1988. pap. 46.00 (*9971-5-0524-X*); text ed. 90.00 (*9971-5-0523-1*) World Scientific Pub.

Strings & Superstrings: Proceedings on the Third Jerusalem. Ed. by S. Weinberg & T. Piran. 232p. (C). 1988. text ed. 58.00 (*9971-5-0374-3*); pap. text ed. 36.00 (*9971-5-0375-1*) World Scientific Pub.

Strings & Symmetries: Proceedings of the Gursey Memorial Conference I, Held at Istanbul, Turkey, 6-10 June 1994. Ed. by Gulen Aktas et al. LC 95-12986. (Lecture Notes in Physics Ser.: Vol. 447). xii, 398p. 1995. 101.95 (*3-540-59163-X*) Spr-Verlag.

Strings & Symmetries, 1991: SUNY, Stony Brook, 20-25 May 1991. Ed. by Peter Van Nieuwenhuizen. LC 92-10269. 400p. (C). 1992. pap. 36.00 (*981-02-0743-3*); text ed. 130.00 (*981-02-0742-5*) World Scientific Pub.

Strings, Conformal Fields, & Topology: An Introduction. Michio Kaku. (Graduate Texts in Contemporary Physics Ser.). (Illus.). 480p. 1992. 59.95 (*0-387-97496-2*) Spr-Verlag.

Strings, Lattice Gauge Theory & High Energy Phenomenology: Proceedings of the Winter School of Theoretical Physics, Panchgani, India, January 25-February 5, 1986. Ed. by V. Singh & S. R. Wadia. 612p. 1987. text ed. 144.00 (*9971-5-0157-0*) World Scientific Pub.

Strings of Fortune. Karen Rhodes. (Lucky in Love Ser.: No. 25). 320p. 1993. mass mkt. 3.50 (*0-8217-4111-X*, Zebra Kensgtn) Kensgtn Pub Corp.

Strings '88. Ed. by S. James Gates, Jr. et al. 528p. (C). 1989. pap. 53.00 (*9971-5-0829-X*); text ed. 135.00 (*9971-5-0766-8*) World Scientific Pub.

Strings '89: Proceedings. Michael J. Duff & R. Arnowitt. 1990. pap. 32.00 (*981-02-0006-4*); text ed. 98.00 (*981-02-0005-6*) World Scientific Pub.

Strings '90. Ed. by R. Arnowitt et al. 548p. (C). 1991. pap. 35.00 (*981-02-0313-6*); text ed. 98.00 (*981-02-0312-8*) World Scientific Pub.

Strings '93. M. B. Halpern et al. 504p. 1995. text ed. 99.00 (*981-02-2187-8*) World Scientific Pub.

***Stringwork.** Deena Beverley. (New Crafts Ser.). (Illus.). 96p. 1997. 14.95 (*1-85967-377-5*, Lorenz Bks) Anness Pub.

Strip. Phyllis Nagy. 96p. 1995. pap. 12.95 (*1-85459-223-8*, Pub. by N Hern Bks UK) Theatre Comm.

Strip AIDS U. S. A. A Collection of Cartoon Art to Benefit People with AIDS. Trina Robbins. (Illus.). 1988. pap. text ed. 9.95 (*0-86719-373-5*) Last Gasp.

***Strip-Built Sea Kayak: Three Rugged, Beautiful Boats You Can Build.** Nick Schade. LC 97-19039. 1997. write for info. (*0-07-057989-X*) McGraw.

Strip Mining. Susan Osterman. (Cambric Poetry Ser.). 72p. (Orig.). 1987. pap. 7.00 (*0-918342-26-0*) Cambric.

Strip Mining: An Annotated Bibliography. Robert F. Munn. LC 72-96636. 110p. 1973. 15.00 (*0-937058-09-2*) West Va U Pr.

***Strip Patchwork.** Valerie Campbell-Harding. (Illus.). pap. 8.95 (*0-486-25729-0*) Dover.

Strip-Pieced Watercolor Magic: A Faster, New Approach to Creating 30 Watercolor Quilts. Deanna Spingola. LC 95-49071. (Illus.). 108p. (Orig.). 1996. pap. 24.95 (*1-56477-134-2*, B251) That Patchwork.

Strip Quilting. Diane Wold. (Illus.). 160p. (Orig.). 1987. 21.95 (*0-8306-2522-4*); pap. 14.95 (*0-8306-2822-3*) McGraw-Hill Prof.

Strip Quilting Projects, Vol. 3. Kaye Wood. (Illus.). 40p. (Orig.). 1989. pap. 9.00 (*0-944588-13-1*) K Wood.

***Strip Quilting Projects, Vol. 5.** Kaye Wood. (Illus.). 43p. (Orig.). 1990. pap. 12.00 (*0-944588-17-4*) K Wood.

***Strip Quilting Projects, Vol. 7.** Kaye Wood. (Illus.). 40p. (Orig.). 1992. pap. 11.00 (*0-944588-24-7*) K Wood.

Strip Quilting Projects: Quick Strip Quilting from the PBS-TV Series "Strip Quilting" by Kaye Wood. Kaye Wood. (Illus.). 48p. 1988. pap. 8.00 (*0-944588-11-5*) K Wood.

Strip Quilting Projects Eight: Landscapes & Seascapes. Kaye Wood. (Illus.). 52p. 1992. pap. text ed. 11.00 (*0-944588-26-3*) K Wood.

Strip Quilting Projects, No. 9: A Victorian Sampler. Kaye Wood. (Illus.). (Orig.). 1993. pap. text ed. 12.00 (*0-944588-27-1*) K Wood.

Strip Quilting Projects, Vol. 2: Quick Strip Quilting from the PBS-TV Series "Strip Quilting 2" Kaye Wood. (Illus.). 40p. 1989. pap. 10.98 (*0-944588-12-3*) K Wood.

Strip Quilting Projects, Vol. 4: Quick Strip Quilting from the PBS-TV Series "Strip Quilting" Kaye Wood. (Illus.). 40p. (Orig.). 1990. pap. 10.98 (*0-944588-16-6*) K Wood.

Strip Quilting Projects, Vol. 6: Quick Strip Quilting from the PBS-TV Series 6 Strip Quilting by Kaye Wood. Kaye Wood. (Illus.). 32p. (Orig.). 1991. pap. 11.00 (*0-944588-19-0*, KWB11) K Wood.

Strip Quilting Projects 10: Easy Strip Piecing with Design Shapes. Kaye Wood. (Illus.). 56p. 1994. pap. 12.00 (*0-944588-29-8*, KWB15) K Wood.

Strip Replacement Pack. Dorothee Baker. (CrossWord Sticklers Ser.). (J). (gr. 1-12). 1993. 17.50 (*1-883459-03-6*) Adv Methodologies.

***Strip Search: Poems.** W. R. Wilkins. 80p. (Orig.). 1997. pap. 10.00 (*1-56474-216-4*) Fithian Pr.

Strip-Search Procedures. Johns Enterprises Staff. 9p. 1994. pap. 20.00 (*0-930179-25-0*) Johns Enter.

Strip Searches - Constitutional Issues. FBI Staff. 9p. 1994. pap. 10.00 (*0-930179-31-5*) Johns Enter.

Strip Searching: Women Remand Prisoners at Armagh Prison, 1982-85. NCCL Staff. (C). 1988. 40.00 (*0-946088-20-9*, Pub. by NCCL UK) St Mut.

Strip Spring Making & Forming. 1988. 60.00 (*0-685-05780-1*) St Mut.

Strip Steel. LC 88-81559. 88p. 1995. 25.00 (*0-932897-34-7*) Iron & Steel.

Strip Steel Pocketbook. 52p. 1988. 12.00 (*1-886362-13-0*) Iron & Steel.

Strip Tease. Carl Hiaasen. LC 93-12358. 1993. 21.00 (*0-679-41981-0*) Knopf.

Strip Tease. Carl Hiaasen. 432p. 1994. mass mkt. 6.50 (*0-446-60066-0*, Warner Vision) Warner Bks.

Strip-Tease. Georges Simenon. (FRE.). 1993. pap. 11.95 (*0-7859-3259-3*, 2266052691) Fr & Eur.

Strip Tease. large type ed. Carl Hiaasen. LC 93-43828. 1993. 25.95 (*1-56895-049-7*) Wheeler Pub.

Strip Tease: Movie Cover Version. Carl Hiaasen. 1996. mass mkt. 6.50 (*0-446-78496-6*) Warner Bks.

Strip the Experts. Brian Martin. (Anarchist Discussion Ser.). 69p. 1991. pap. 4.00 (*0-900384-63-8*) Left Bank.

Striped Bass. rev. ed. Nick Karas. LC 93-41437. 492p. 1993. 35.00 (*1-55821-259-0*) Lyons & Burford.

***Striped Bass & Other Morone Culture.** LC 96-29983. (Developments in Aquaculture & Fisheries Science Ser.). 1997. write for info. (*0-444-82547-9*) Elsevier.

Striped Bass & Other Sport Fish. 2nd ed. Phil Schwind. LC 77-172355. (Illus.). 224p. 1991. pap. 12.50 (*0-940160-48-X*) Parnassus Imprints.

***Striped Bass Chronicles.** George Reiger. LC 97-1925. (Illus.). 192p. 1997. 22.95 (*1-55821-478-X*) Lyons & Burford.

Striped Bass Fishing. Frank Woolner & Henry Lyman. LC 82-20300. (Illus.). 192p. 1996. pap. 16.95 (*0-8329-0281-0*) Lyons & Burford.

Striped Holes. Damien Broderick. 1988. pap. 2.95 (*0-380-75377-4*) Avon.

Striped Ice Cream. Joan M. Lexau. LC 68-10774. (Illus.). 96p. (J). (gr. k-3). 1968. lib. bdg. 14.89 (*0-397-31047-1*, Lipp Jr Bks) HarpC Child Bks.

Striped Ice Cream. Joan M. Lexau. 128p. (J). 1992. 2.99 (*0-590-45729-2*, Little Apple) Scholastic Inc.

Striper: A Story of Fish & Man. John Cole. 272p. 1989. pap. 15.95 (*1-55821-040-7*) Lyons & Burford.

Striper Hot Spots. 2nd rev. ed. Frank Daignault. LC 96-23060. (Illus.). 288p. 1996. pap. 14.95 (*1-56440-994-5*) Globe Pequot.

Striper Moon. J. Kenney Abrames. (Illus.). 48p. 1994. pap. 15.95 (*1-878175-67-X*) F Amato Pubns.

Striper Surf. Frank Daignault. LC 91-30129. (Illus.). 272p. (Orig.). 1996. pap. 16.95 (*1-56440-278-9*) Globe Pequot.

***Stripers: An Angler's Anthology.** John R. Waldman. LC 97-19656. 1997. write for info. (*0-07-067810-3*) McGraw.

***Stripers & Streamers.** Ray Bondorew. (Illus.). 120p. 1996. pap. 19.95 (*1-57188-072-0*) F Amato Pubns.

Stripes: Active Graphic Design. 80p. 1991. pap. 18.95 (*88-7070-162-X*) Belvedere USA.

Stripes in Quilts. Mary Mashuta. Ed. by Barbara K. Kuhn. (Illus.). 96p. (Orig.). 1996. pap. 21.95 (*1-57120-008-8*, 10231) C & T Pub.

Stripes in the Sky: A Wartime Memoir. Gerhard Durlacher. Tr. by Susan Massotty from DUT. 108p. (Orig.). 1992. pap. 13.95 (*1-85242-202-5*) Serpents Tail.

Striplate Piecing: Piecing Circle Designs with Speed & Accuracy. Debra Wagner. 1995. 24.95 (*0-89145-821-2*) Collector Bks.

Stripline Circuit Design. Harlan H. Howe. LC 73-81242. (Artech House Microwave Library). (Illus.). 352p. reprint ed. pap. 100.40 (*0-7837-5039-0*, 2044715) Bks Demand.

Stripline-Like Transmission Lines for Microwave Integrated Circuits. Bherathi Bhat & Shiban K. Koul. LC 86-24530. 697p. 1990. text ed. 112.00 (*0-470-20700-0*) Halsted Pr.

Stripling Thames: From the Source to Oxford with Mollie Harris. Mollie Harris. (Illus.). 160p. 1994. 34.00 (*0-7509-0403-8*, Pub. by Sutton Pubng UK) Bks Intl VA.

Stripmall Bohemia. Jethro Paris. 202p. (Orig.). 1996. pap. 10.95 (*0-9650966-2-9*) LandMine Bks.

Stripped. E. A. Guldenzopf. 175p. (Orig.). 1996. pap. 6.99 (*0-9646170-1-3*, ES Bks) ES Communs.

***Stripped.** Peter Kuper. 96p. 1995. pap. 9.95 (*1-56097-177-0*) Fantagraph Bks.

***Stripped down, Do It Now, I Want a Job, Complete Job Search Workbook.** Greg Tzinberg. 1996. 27.50 (*0-938609-06-8*) Graduate Group.

Stripped Naked. Lauren Stratford. LC 93-16878. 336p. 1993. pap. 10.95 (*0-88289-967-8*) Pelican.

Stripped Tales. Barbara Guest & Anne Dunn. LC 95-25399. (Illus.). 53p. (Orig.). (C). 1995. 14.00 (*0-932716-36-9*) Kelsey St Pr.

Stripped Tales. limited ed. Barbara Guest & Anne Dunn. LC 95-25399. (Illus.). 53p. (Orig.). 1995. 50.00 (*0-932716-38-5*) Kelsey St Pr.

***Stripper Lessons.** John O'Brien. LC 96-44137. 1997. 12.00 (*0-8021-1606-X*, Grove); pap. 12.00 (*0-8021-3507-2*, Grove) Grove-Atltic.

Stripper's Guide to Canoe-Building. David Hazen. LC 76-19972. 1982. 17.95 (*0-917436-00-8*) Tamal Vista.

Stripping. Laura Boss. LC 82-4192. (Illus.). 52p. (Orig.). 1982. pap. 5.00 (*0-941608-01-8*) Chantry Pr.

Stripping: The Assembly of Film Images. 2nd ed. Harold L. Peck. Ed. by Thomas M. Destree. LC 88-82939. (Illus.). 300p. (C). 1988. pap. text ed. 40.00 (*0-88362-117-7*) Graphic Arts Tech Found.

Stripping & Other Stories. Pagan Kennedy. 160p. (Orig.). 1994. pap. 10.99 (*1-85242-322-6*, High Risk Bks) Serpents Tail.

Stripping & Polishing Furniture. David Lawrence. 1985. 39.00 (*0-685-12460-6*, Pub. by Bishopsgate Pr Ltd UK); pap. 21.00 (*0-685-12461-4*, Pub. by Bishopsgte Pr UK) St Mut.

Stripping & Polishing Furniture: A Practical Guide. David Lawrence. (Illus.). 95p. 1987. pap. 11.95 (*0-900873-55-8*, Pub. by Bishopsgte Pr UK) Intl Spec Bk.

Stripping of the Altars: Traditional Religion in England, 1400-1580. Eamon Duffy. (Illus.). 608p. 1994. pap. 18.00 (*0-300-06076-9*) Yale U Pr.

Stripping Sulla Sponda dell'Hudson: English & Italian Poetry. Laura Boss. Tr. by Nina Scammacca & Nat Scammacca. (ITA.). 1988. 15.00 (*0-89304-523-3*); pap. 7.50 (*0-89304-522-5*) Cross-Cultrl NY.

***Stripping the Adult Century Bare: New & Selected Writings.** M. L. Liebler. (White Noise Poetry Ser.: No. 6). 88p. (Orig.). 1995. pap. 12.00 (*1-885215-09-6*, Viet Nam Gnrtn) Burning Cities Pr.

Stripples. Donna L. Thomas. 1995. pap. 22.95 (*1-56477-124-5*, B241) That Patchwork.

***Stripples Strikes Again! More Quilts to Make with the Bias Stripper Ruler.** Donna L. Thomas. Ed. by Ursula Reikes. (Illus.). 112p. (Orig.). 1997. pap. 19.95 (*1-56477-195-4*, B309) That Patchwork.

Striptease. Elliot Fried. 36p. (Orig.). 1979. pap. 2.00 (*0-930090-09-8*) Applezaba.

***Stripy Whiskers.** Sue Inman. (Illus.). 24p. (J). (gr. k-3). 1997. 8.00 (*1-85854-575-7*) Brimax Bks.

Strive & Succeed. Horatio Alger, Jr. (Works of Horatio Alger Jr.). 1989. reprint ed. lib. bdg. 79.00 (*0-685-27553-1*) Rprt Serv.

Strive for the Truth, Vol. 1: The World of Rav Dessler. E. E. Dessler. Tr. by Aryeh Carmell from HEB. 1978. 16.95 (*0-87306-139-X*) Feldheim.

Strive for Truth, Vol. 2. Eliyahu Dessler. 1985. 16.95 (*0-87306-395-3*); pap. 9.95 (*0-87306-396-1*) Feldheim.

Strive for Truth, Vol. 3. Rabbi E. Dessler. Tr. by Aryeh Carmel from HEB. 1989. 16.95 (*0-87306-519-0*); pap. 11.95 (*0-87306-520-4*) Feldheim.

Strive to Attain God. Swami Virajananda. 246p. 1996. 5.95 (*81-85301-99-9*) Vedanta Pr.

***Strive to Excel: The Will & Wisdom of Vince Lombardi.** Compiled by Jennifer Briggs. 160p. 1997. 12.95 (*1-55853-550-0*) Rutledge Hill Pr.

Strive to Thrive: An Innovative Profit Strategy for Business Owners & Professionals. Charles E. Stuart. 150p. 1991. Wkbk. student ed. write for info. (*0-9632767-1-9*) Charles E Stuart.

Strive to Thrive: An Innovative Profit Strategy for Business Owners & Professionals, Set. Charles E. Stuart. 150p. 1991. pap. 69.95 (*0-9632767-0-0*) Charles E Stuart.

Striving: Keene State College, 1909-1984: The History of a Small Public Institution. James G. Smart. LC 84-5906. (Illus.). 400p. 1984. 25.00 (*0-914659-04-9*) Phoenix Pub.

Striving & Feeling: Interactions among Goals, Affect, & Self-Regulation. Ed. by Leonard L. Martin & Abraham Tesser. 424p. 1996. text ed. 79.95 (*0-8058-1629-1*) L Erlbaum Assocs.

Striving for a Closer Walk. Fredell D. McCord. 24p. 1996. pap. 7.00 (*0-8059-3947-4*) Dorrance.

Striving for Excellence in College. M. Neil Browne & Keeley. LC 96-31843. 80p. (C). 1996. pap. text ed. 12.60 (*0-13-458878-9*) P-H.

Striving for Growth after Adjustment: The Role of Capital Formation. Ed. by Luis Serven & Andres Solimano. 298p. 1993. 17.95 (*0-8213-2484-5*, 12484) World Bank.

Striving for Holiness. Bobbie C. Jobe. 1982. 4.25 (*0-89137-423-X*) Quality Pubns.

***Striving for Jewish Virtues: A Contemporary Guide for Ethical Behavior.** Kerry M. Olitzky. 1996. 23.00 (*0-614-19812-7*) Ktav.

Striving for Law in a Lawless Land: Memoirs of a Russian Reformer. Alexander M. Yakovlev. LC 95-9030. 256p. (C). (gr. 13). 1995. text ed. 75.00 (*1-56324-639-2*) M E Sharpe.

Striving for Peace, Security & Development in the World: Annals of Pugwash 1991. Joseph Rotblat. 296p. 1993. text ed. 55.00 (*981-02-1249-6*) World Scientific Pub.

Striving for the Wind. Meja Mwangi. (African Writers Ser.). 199p. (C). 1992. pap. 8.95 (*0-435-90979-7*, 90979) Heinemann.

***Striving Together.** Charles Kimball. 132p. 1996. pap. 11.95 (*0-614-21682-6*, 1172) Kazi Pubns.

Striving Together: A Way Forward in Christian-Muslim Relations. Charles Kimball. LC 90-46565. 1990. pap. 12.50 (*0-88344-691-X*) Orbis Bks.

Striving Toward Improvement. Joint Commission on Accreditation of Healthcare Staff. 1992. 55.00 (*0-86688-255-3*) Joint Comm Hlthcare.

***Striving Toward Virtue: A Contemporary Guide for Jewish Ethical Behavior.** Kerry M. Olitzky & Rachel T. Sabath. 204p. Date not set. 23.00 (*0-614-19885-2*) Ktav.

Striving Towards Being: The Letters of Thomas Merton & Czeslaw Milosz. Ed. by Robert Faggen. LC 96-23827. 160p. 1996. 21.00 (*0-374-27100-3*) FS&G.

Striving Towards Wholeness. Barbara Hannah. 316p. 1987. 32.00 (*0-938434-31-4*); pap. 16.95 (*0-938434-32-2*) Sigo Pr.

Striving Upward: An Autobiography. Jimmy Lowe. 1996. write for info. (*0-87483-463-5*) August Hse.

***Strivings: Poems, 1972-1976.** William Radice. 56p. 1980. pap. 14.95 (*0-85646-056-7*, Pub. by Anvil Press UK) Dufour.

Strobridge Genealogy: Strobridge Morrison or Morison Strawbridge. M. S. Guild. (Illus.). 318p. 1989. reprint ed. pap. 47.50 (*0-8328-1145-9*); reprint ed. lib. bdg. 55.50 (*0-8328-1144-0*) Higginson Bk Co.

Stroebel's View Camera Basics. Leslie Stroebel. LC 95-17394. (Illus.). 112p. 1995. pap. 24.95 (*0-240-80220-9*, Focal) Buttrwrth-Heinemann.

Stroka Prospekt. Richard Lupoff. Ed. by Thomas M. Disch. LC 82-19269. (Singularities Ser.). (Illus.). 45p. (Orig.). 1982. pap. 10.00 (*0-915124-73-4*, Toothpaste) Coffee Hse.

***Stroke.** write for info. (*0-340-57719-3*, Pub. by E Arnold UK) Routledge Chapman & Hall.

Stroke. Derick T. Wade. (Practical Guides for General Practice Ser.: No. 4). (Illus.). 110p. 1988. pap. 12.95 (*0-19-261760-5*) OUP.

Stroke: A Clinical Approach. 2nd ed. Louis R. Caplan. LC 92-49251. (Illus.). 562p. 1993. text ed. 95.00 (*0-7506-9181-6*) Buttrwrth-Heinemann.

Stroke: A Guide for Patient & Family. Janice Frye-Pierson & James F. Toole. (Illus.). 224p. 1987. text ed. 37.00 (*0-88167-279-3*); pap. text ed. 21.00 (*0-89004-637-9*) Lppncott-Raven.

Stroke: A Guide for Patients & Their Families. John E. Sarno. 1991. pap. 9.95 (*0-13-853730-5*) P-H.

Stroke: A Practical Guide to Management. Charles P. Warlow et al. Ed. by Martin Dennis et al. (Illus.). 900p. 1996. 199.95 (*0-86542-874-3*) Blackwell Sci.

Stroke: An Epidemiological Overview. 72p. 1994. pap. 25.00 (*0-11-321668-8*, HM16688, Pub. by Stationery Ofc UK) Bernan Associates.

Stroke: An Owner's Manual: The Invaluable Guide to Life after Stroke. Arthur Josephs. LC 91-77440. 160p. (Orig.). 1992. pap. 14.95 (*0-9631493-9-3*) Amadeus CA.

Stroke: Animal Models: Proceedings of an International Symposium Held at Wiesbaden, Germany, 16 November 1981. Ed. by Hoechst Stefanovich. (Illus.). 196p. 1982. 79.00 (*0-08-029799-4*, Pergamon Pr) Elsevier.

Stroke: Pathophysiology, Diagnosis & Management. 2nd ed. Ed. by Henry J. Barnett et al. LC 92-17477. (Illus.). 1270p. 1992. text ed. 235.00 (*0-443-08732-6*) Churchill.

Stroke: Pathophysiology, Diagnosis, & Management, Vol. 1. Ed. by Henry J. Barnett et al. LC 85-19553. (Illus.). 681p. reprint ed. pap. 180.00 (*0-7837-3060-8*, 2042754) Bks Demand.

Stroke: Pathophysiology, Diagnosis, & Management, Vol. 2. Ed. by Henry J. Barnett et al. LC 85-19553. (Illus.). 671p. reprint ed. pap. 180.00 (*0-7837-3061-6*) Bks Demand.

Stroke: Populations, Cohorts & Clinical Trials. J. P. Whisnant. (International Medical Review Series - Neurology: Vol. 12). (Illus.). 262p. 1993. pap. 75.00 (*0-7506-0574-X*) Buttrwrth-Heinemann.

Stroke: Questions You Have - Answers You Need. Jennifer Hay. LC 95-21858. 192p. 1995. pap. 10.95 (*1-882606-22-1*) Peoples Med Soc.

Stroke: The Facts. Clifford F. Rose & Rudy E. Capildeo. (Facts Ser.). (Illus.). 160p. 1981. text ed. 19.95 (*0-19-261170-4*) OUP.

Stroke: The Road Back. Doris W. Braley. LC 94-19807. 1994. 24.95 (*1-879560-29-1*) Harbor Hse West.

Stroke: Your Complete Exercise Guide. Neil F. Gordon. LC 92-39742. 144p. 1993. pap. 11.95 (*0-87322-428-0*, PGOR0428) Human Kinetics.

***Stroke: Your Complete Exercise Guide.** Neil F. Gordon. LC 97-19898. (Cooper Clinic & Research Institute Fitness Ser.). 1997. write for info. (*0-88011-825-3*) Human Kinetics.

Stroke & Heart Disease. Anne Galperin. (Encyclopedia of Health Ser.). (Illus.). 112p. (YA). (gr. 7 up). 1991. lib. bdg. 19.95 (*0-7910-0077-X*) Chelsea Hse.

Stroke & Microcirculation. Ed. by J. Cervos-Navarro & Ron Ferszt. LC 86-45980. 609p. 1987. reprint ed. pap. 173.60 (*0-608-00327-1*, 2061044) Bks Demand.

Stroke & the Extracranial Vessels. Ed. by Robert R. Smith. LC 83-24635. (Illus.). 389p. 1984. reprint ed. pap. 110.90 (*0-7837-9533-5*, 2060282) Bks Demand.

Stroke Book: One on One Advice about Stroke Prevention, Management & Rehabilitation. large type ed. Arthur Ancowitz. LC 93-40726. 1994. 24.95 (*0-7862-0115-0*) Thorndike Pr.

Stroke Book: One on One Advice about Stroke Prevention, Management & Rehabilitation. large type ed. Arthur Ancowitz. LC 93-40726. 1994. pap. 17.95 (*0-7862-0116-9*) Thorndike Pr.

Stroke Data Banks: Challenges for Research. Ed. by M. Brainin & M. A. Foulkes. (Journal: Neuroepidemiology Ser.: Vol. 13, No. 6, 1994). (Illus.). iv, 104p. 1994. pap. 47.00 (*3-8055-6016-8*) S Karger.

Stroke Diagnosis & Management: Current Procedures & Equipment. William S. Fields et al. LC 72-13847. (Illus.). 298p. 1973. 15.70 (*0-87527-101-4*) Green.

Stroke-Head Injury - A Guide to Functional Outcomes in Physical Therapy: Rehabilitation Institute of Chicago Procedure Manual. Ann L. Charness. (Illus.). 330p. (C). 1986. 69.00 (*0-87189-226-X*) Aspen Pub.

Stroke in Children & Young Adults. Ed. by Jose Biller et al. LC 93-49468. 280p. 1994. text ed. 80.00 (*0-7506-9203-0*) Buttrwrth-Heinemann.

Stroke Manual for Families. Tampa General Rehabilitation Center Staff. 60p. (Orig.). 1989. pap. 9.50 (*1-882855-05-1*) HDI Pubs.

Stroke of Fortune: The Adventures of a Motion Picture Showman. William C. Cline. LC 95-61162. (Illus.). 260p. (Orig.). 1995. pap. 15.00 (*0-944019-18-8*) Empire NC.

Stroke of Genius. Paul West. Date not set. pap. 9.95 (*0-14-023442-X*) Viking Penguin.

Stroke of Luck & Dream of Destiny. Arnold Bennett. LC 74-17075. (Collected Works of Arnold Bennett: Vol. 76). 1977. reprint ed. 24.95 (*0-518-19157-5*) Ayer.

Stroke of Midnight. Kathy Clark. (American Romance Ser.). 1995. pap. 3.50 (*0-373-16571-4*, 1-16571-1) Harlequin Bks.

Stroke Patient: A Team Approach. 3rd ed. Margaret Johnstone. LC 86-17584. (Illus.). 114p. (Orig.). 1987. pap. text ed. 19.95 (*0-443-03397-8*) Churchill.

Stroke Prevention. Ed. by W. Dorndorf & P. Marx. (Illus.). viii, 200p. 1994. 64.50 (*3-8055-5882-1*) S Karger.

***Stroke Rehabilitation: A Function-Based Approach.** Ed. by Gillen. 672p. (gr. 13). 1997. text ed. 68.00 (*0-8151-3460-6*, 29193, Yr Bk Med Pubs) Mosby Yr Bk.

Stroke Rehabilitation: Basic Concepts & Research Trends. William S. Fields & William A. Spencer. LC 67-19383. (Illus.). 184p. 1967. 10.60 (*0-87527-034-4*) Green.

Stroke Rehabilitation: Structure & Strategy. P. Laidler. 336p. 1994. 44.95 (*1-56593-208-0*, 0522) Singular Publishing.

Stroke Rehabilitation: The Recovery of Motor Control. Pamela Duncan. (Illus.). 226p. (gr. 13). 1987. text ed. 28.95 (*0-8151-2936-X*, Yr Bk Med Pubs) Mosby Yr Bk.

Stroke Rehabilitation Patient Education Manual. Aspen Reference Group Staff. Ed. by Sara N. De Lima. LC 95-35240. 454p. Date not set. ring bd. 159.00 (*0-8342-0675-7*) Aspen Pub.

Stroke Survivors. William H. Bergquist et al. LC 94-11647. (Health-Management Ser.). 279p. pap. 25.00 (*1-55542-669-7*) Jossey-Bass.

Stroke Syndromes. Ed. by Julien Bogousslavsky & Louis Caplan. (Illus.). 500p. (C). 1995. text ed. 130.00 (*0-521-45397-6*) Cambridge U Pr.

Stroke Therapy. Ed. by Marc Fisher. LC 95-13079. 490p. 1995. text ed. 90.00 (*0-7506-9575-7*) Buttrwrth-Heinemann.

Stroke...Now What? Neub Petschulat & Joyce Corinna. 240p. (Orig.). 1991. 17.95 (*0-9631426-0-7*) CAM Pub.

Strokes: Essays & Reviews, 1966-1986. John Clute. 178p. 1988. 16.95 (*0-934933-03-0*) Serconia Pr.

Strokes: What Families Should Know. Elaine F. Shimberg. (Family Health Ser.). 256p. (Orig.). 1990. mass mkt. 5.99 (*0-345-36209-8*) Ballantine.

Strokes & Head Injuries: A Guide for Patients, Families, Friends, & Carers. Mary Lynch & Vivian Grisogono. (Illus.). 160p. 1992. pap. 19.95 (*0-7195-4697-4*, Pub. by John Murray UK) Trafalgar.

Strokes & Strokes: An Instructor's Manual for Developing Swim Programs for Stroke Victims. Jill Heckathorn. LC 83-190770. 79p. reprint ed. pap. 25.00 (*0-317-55560-X*, 2029560) Bks Demand.

Strokes of Genius. Thomas Boswell. 272p. 1989. pap. 11.00 (*0-14-011368-1*, Penguin Bks) Viking Penguin.

***Strokes of Genius: Imagination & Englishness in Early Nineteenth-Century Landscape Painting.** Kay D. Kriz. LC 96-43187. 1997. write for info. (*0-300-06833-6*) Yale U Pr.

Stroll: Inner City Subcultures. John Davidson. (Illus.). 165p. pap. 12.95 (*0-920053-65-3*, Pub. by NC Press CN) U of Toronto Pr.

Stroll down Cobb Lane: In the Kitchen with a Southern Lady. Mikki Bond. Ed. by Lynn Edge. (Illus.). 159p. 1995. pap. 15.00 (*0-9650888-0-4*) Dar-Dar Pr.

Stroll down Millenium Alleys. Dokia Humenna. LC 87-60430. (Mini Short Stories Ser.). 170p. 1987. 7.50 (*0-914834-76-2*) Smoloskyp.

***Stroll in the Vatican Gardens.** Eva M. Inglessis. (Illus.). 72p. 1996. pap. 25.00 (*0-614-24668-7*) Sheed & Ward MO.

***Stroll in the Vatican Gardens.** Eva M. J. Inglessis. (Illus.). 72p. 1995. pap. 25.00 (*88-86921-06-3*, Pub. by Musei Vaticani IT) Treasures Inc.

Stroll Through Life. Nelson A. Ossorio. (Orig.). 1995. pap. 11.95 (*1-56721-111-9*) Twnty-Fifth Cent Pr.

Stroll with William James. Jacques Barzun. LC 84-2612. viii, 352p. 1983. reprint ed. lib. bdg. 30.00 (*0-226-03865-3*) U Ch Pr.

Strollercize. Trindade. 1996. pap. write for info. (*0-8092-3208-1*) Contemp Bks.

Strolling Down Country Roads: Okeechobee County, a Pictorial History. Twila Valentine & Betty C. Williamson. LC 93-7436. 1993. write for info. (*0-89865-866-7*) Donning Co.

Strolling Through Barcelona. Charles Teetor. (Illus.). 238p. (Orig.). 1992. pap. 11.95 (*0-9628651-3-3*) Teetor Twn Pr.

Strolling Through Istanbul: A Guide to the City. Hilary Sumner-Boyd & John Freely. 210p. 1987. pap. 19.95 (*0-7103-0214-2*, 02142) Routledge Chapman & Hall.

Strolling Through Seville. Charles Teetor. (Illus.). 272p. (Orig.). 1992. pap. 11.95 (*0-9628651-2-5*) Teetor Twn Pr.

Strolls with Pushkin. Abram Tertz, pseud. Tr. by Catharine T. Nepomnyashchy & Slava I. Yastremski. (Russian Literature & Thought Ser.). 184p. 1994. 30.00 (*0-300-05279-0*) Yale U Pr.

Strom Thurmond: And the Politics of Southern Change. Nadine Cohodas. (Illus.). 608p. 1993. 27.50 (*0-671-68935-5*) S&S Trade.

Strom Thurmond & the Politics of Southern Change. Nadine Cohodas. LC 94-15867. 1994. 18.95 (*0-86554-446-8*, MUP/P108) Mercer Univ Pr.

Strom Toys: Classic Toys in Wood. rev. ed. Richard H. Strombeck & Janet A. Strombeck. (Illus.). 100p. (Orig.). 1984. pap. 9.95 (*0-912355-01-8*) Sun Designs.

Stromata. David Miller. (Poetry Ser.). 64p. (Orig.). 1994. pap. 8.00 (*0-930901-96-7*, PR9619.3.M47S77) Burning Deck.

Stromata. limited ed. David Miller. (Poetry Ser.). 64p. (Orig.). 1994. pap. 15.00 (*0-930901-97-5*) Burning Deck.

Stromateis, Bks. 1-3. Clement Of Alexandria. Tr. by John Ferguson from LAT. LC 90-21352. (Fathers of the Church Ser.: Vol. 85). 354p. 1992. text ed. 36.95 (*0-8132-0085-7*) Cath U Pr.

Strombeck's Small Animal Gastroenterology. 3rd rev. ed. W. Grant Guilford et al. LC 95-22527. 1072p. 1996. text ed. 145.00 (*0-7216-3760-4*) Saunders.

Stroneys: A Novella. Dan Ford. 1990. pap. 4.95 (*0-9625951-0-1*) Hensley-Murray Pubns.

Strong & Courageous. Ellen W. Caughey. 64p. 1996. 5.97 (*1-55748-783-9*) Barbour & Co.

Strong & Free. Amy Hagstrom. LC 87-3942. (Books for Students by Students). (Illus.). 24p. (J). (gr. 1 up). 1987. lib. bdg. 14.95 (*0-933849-15-X*) Landmark Edns.

Strong & Safe: A Children's Guide to Self Protection. Susan C. Elias. (Illus.). 60p. (Orig.). (J). (gr. 1-3). 1989. pap. 8.95 (*0-317-93904-1*) Womansource.

Strong & Steady. Horatio Alger, Jr. (Works of Horatio Alger Jr.). 1989. reprint ed. lib. bdg. 79.00 (*0-685-44740-5*) Rprt Serv.

Strong & Ultrastrong Magnetic Fields. Ed. by F. Herlach. (Topics in Applied Physics Ser.: Vol. 57). (Illus.). 375p. 1985. 106.95 (*0-387-13504-9*) Spr-Verlag.

Strong Approximation by Fourier Series. Laszlo Leindler. 210p. (C). 1985. 157.00 (*0-685-46648-5*, Pub. by Collets); 75.00 (*963-05-4044-4*, Pub. by Akad Kiado HU) St Mut.

Strong-Arm. large type ed. Basil Copper. (Linford Mystery Library). 319p. 1989. pap. 15.99 (*0-7089-6629-2*, Linford) Ulverscroft.

Strong Arms of the Law. Dallas Schulze. (American Romance Ser.). 1993. mass mkt. 3.39 (*0-373-16486-6*, 1-16486-2) Harlequin Bks.

Strong Arts, Strong Schools: The Promising Potential & Shortsighted Disregard of the Arts in American Schooling. Charles Fowler. (Illus.). 272p. 1996. 27.50 (*0-19-510089-1*) OUP.

Strong As Death. Sharan Newman. 384p. 1996. 23.95 (*0-312-86179-6*) Forge NYC.

***Strong as Death.** Sharan Newman. 1997. mass mkt. 5.99 (*0-8125-3935-4*) Forge NYC.

Strong As Death: A Love Story. Michael Lister. (Orig.). 1996. pap. 9.95 (*1-888146-03-6*) St Matthews.

Strong Asymptotics for Extremal Polynomials Associated with Weights on IR. D. S. Lubinsky & Edward B. Saff. (Lecture Notes in Mathematics Ser.: Vol. 1305). vii, 153p. 1988. 35.95 (*0-387-18958-0*) Spr-Verlag.

Strong at the Broken Places. Max Cleland. LC 86-26814. (Illus.). 168p. 1989. reprint ed. pap. 8.95 (*0-87797-172-2*) Cherokee.

Strong at the Broken Places: Overcoming the Trauma of Childhood Abuse. Linda T. Sanford. 240p. 1992. mass mkt. 4.99 (*0-380-71535-X*) Avon.

Strong at the Broken Places: Overcoming the Trauma of Childhood Abuse. Linda T. Sanford. 191p. 1990. 18.95 (*0-394-56563-0*) Random.

Strong at the Broken Places: Persons with Disabilities & the Church. Stewart D. Govig. LC 88-13848. 156p. 1989. pap. 11.00 (*0-8042-1153-1*) Westminster John Knox.

***Strong Bones Healthy Exchanges Cookbook.** JoAnna M. Lund. LC 97-3466. 320p. 1997. pap. 14.00 (*0-399-52337-5*, Perigee Bks) Berkley Pub.

Strong Brew: A Man's Prelude to Change. Claude Saks. 278p. (Orig.). 1996. pap. 13.98 (*1-57174-050-3*, Heartsfire) Hampton Roads Pub Co.

Strong Cigars & Lovely Women. John Lardner. 21.95 (*0-8488-0124-5*) Amereon Ltd.

Strong Correlation & Superconductivity. Ed. by H. Fukuyama et al. (Solid-State Sciences Ser.: Vol. 89). (Illus.). xii, 396p. 1989. 86.95 (*0-387-51320-5*) Spr-Verlag.

Strong Coupling Gauge Theories & Beyond: The 2nd International Workshop. T. Muta & K. Yamawaki. 500p. 1991. text ed. 118.00 (*981-02-0424-8*) World Scientific Pub.

Strong Delusion: Confronting the Gay Christian Movement. Joe Dallas. 300p. (Orig.). 1996. pap. 10.99 (*1-56507-431-9*) Harvest Hse.

Strong Democracy: Participatory Politics for a New Age. Benjamin R. Barber. LC 83-4842. 320p. (C). 1984. pap. 16.00 (*0-520-05616-7*) U CA Pr.

Strong Discontinuities in Magnetohydrodynamics. A. M. Blokhin. Tr. by A. V. Zakharov. 167p. 1994. lib. bdg. 95.00 (*1-56072-144-8*) Nova Sci Pubs.

Strong Drink, Strong Language. John Espey. LC 90-2791. 160p. 1990. 17.95 (*0-936784-80-6*) J Daniel.

Strong Enough for Two. James L. Mastrich & William J. Birnes. 256p. 1989. pap. 10.95 (*0-02-040581-2*) Macmillan.

Strong Enough for Two. James L. Mastrich & William J. Birnes. 256p. 1991. pap. 9.95 (*0-02-034520-8*) Macmillan.

Strong Faith. Charles H. Spurgeon. 95p. 1995. mass mkt. 4.99 (*0-88368-341-5*) Whitaker Hse.

Strong Faith for the Last Days. Jack Hartman. 234p. 1992. pap. 7.95 (*0-915445-15-8*) Lamplight FL.

Strong Families, Strong Schools: Building Community Partnerships for Learning. (Illus.). 50p. (Orig.). (C). 1995. pap. text ed. 25.00 (*0-7881-1980-X*) DIANE Pub.

An Asterisk (*) at the beginning of an entry indicates that the title is appearing in BIP for the first time.

Strong Family. Charles R. Swindoll. Orig. Title: Growing Wise in Family Life. 320p. 1994. pap. 11.99 (*0-310-42191-8*) Zondervan.

Strong Family: Growing Wise in Family Life. Charles R. Swindoll. 1994. pap. 7.99 (*0-310-96226-9*) Zondervan.

***Strong for Potatoes.** Thayer. Date not set. write for info. (*0-312-18187-6*) St Martin.

Strong Ground Motion Seismology. Ed. by Mustafa O. Erdik & M. Nafi Toksoz. (C). 1987. lib. bdg. 222.00 (*90-277-2532-2*) Kluwer Ac.

***Strong Heart.** large type ed. Denise Robins. (Ulverscroft Large Print Ser.). 432p. 1997. 27.50 (*0-7089-3727-6*) Ulverscroft.

Strong Heart Society. Susan Power. 304p. 1997. 23.95 (*0-399-14212-6*, Putnam) Putnam Pub Group.

***Strong Heart Song: Lines from a Revolutionary Text.** Lance Henson. 72p. (Orig.). 1997. pap. 8.95 (*0-931122-86-4*) West End.

Strong Hearts. George W. Cable. LC 76-106254. (Short Story Index Reprint Ser.). 1977. 19.95 (*0-8369-3291-9*) Ayer.

Strong Hearts. George W. Cable. 1972. reprint ed. lib. bdg. 16.00 (*0-8422-8020-0*) Irvington.

Strong Hearts. George W. Cable. (C). 1986. reprint ed. pap. text ed. 8.95 (*0-8290-1865-4*) Irvington.

Strong Hearts. George W. Cable. (Works of George Washington Cable). 1990. reprint ed. lib. bdg. 79.00 (*0-7812-1142-5*) Rprt Serv.

Strong Hearts: Native American Visions & Voices. 128p. 1995. 35.00 (*0-89381-637-X*) Aperture.

Strong Hearts see Collected Works of George W. Cable

***Strong Hearts, Inspired Minds: 21 Artists Who Are Mothers Tell Their Stories.** Anne Mavor. (Illus.). 256p. (Orig.). (C). 1996. pap. 24.95 (*0-9653724-0-5*) Rowanberry Bks.

Strong Hearts, Wounded Souls: The Native American Veterans of the Vietnam War. Tom Holm. LC 95-4380. (Illus.). 248p. (C). 1995. pap. 14.95 (*0-292-73098-5*); text ed. 35.00 (*0-292-73095-0*) U of Tex Pr.

***Strong Hermeneutics: Contingency & Moral Identity.** LC 96-51763. 208p. (C). 1997. text ed. write for info. (*0-415-16431-1*) Routledge.

***Strong Hermeneutics: Contingency & Moral Identity.** LC 96-51763. 208p. (C). 1997. pap. write for info. (*0-415-16432-X*) Routledge.

Strong, Hot Winds. large type ed. Iris Johansen. (Nightingale Series Large Print Bks.). 220p. 1991. pap. 14.95 (*0-8161-5175-X*, GK Hall) Thorndike Pr.

Strong in the Broken Places: A Theological Reverie on the Ministry of George Everett Ross. Leonard I. Sweet. LC 95-31452. 272p. (Orig.). (C). 1995. 29.95 (*1-884836-09-7*); pap. 14.95 (*1-884836-10-0*) U Akron Pr.

Strong in the Time of Testing. 93p. 1993. 2.95 (*1-897647-03-4*) Evang Sisterhood Mary.

Strong Interaction. Thomas S. Smith. LC 92-16211. (Illus.). 330p. 1992. 42.50 (*0-226-76413-3*) U Ch Pr.

Strong Interaction. Thomas S. Smith. 330p. 1995. pap. text ed. 16.95 (*0-226-76414-1*) U Ch Pr.

Strong Interaction Physics. International Summer Institute in Theoretical Physics Staff. (Tracts in Modern Physics Ser.: Vol. 57). 1971. 65.00 (*0-387-05252-6*) Spr-Verlag.

Strong Interactions at Long Distances. Ed. by Lazslo L. Jenkovszky. (Illus.). 443p. (Orig.). (C). 1995. pap. 85.00 (*0-911767-99-1*) Hadronic Pr Inc.

Strong Interest Inventory Manual. Edward K. Strong, Jr. 1985. write for info. (*0-8047-1068-6*) Stanford U Pr.

***Strong is the Peace: The Other Half of the Gospel.** Albert N. Wells. LC 97-13668. 1997. write for info. (*1-56825-061-4*) Rainbow Books.

Strong Kids Life Skills Program: Level K, 25 vols., Set. Linda P. Silbert & Alvin J. Silbert. 1991. 69.95 (*0-89544-400-3*) Silbert Bress.

Strong Kids Life Skills Program: Level 1, 25 vols., Set. Linda P. Silbert & Alvin J. Silbert. 1991. 69.95 (*0-89544-401-1*) Silbert Bress.

Strong Kids Life Skills Program: Level 2, 25 vols., Set. Linda P. Silbert & Alvin J. Silbert. 1991. 69.95 (*0-89544-402-X*) Silbert Bress.

Strong Kids Life Skills Program: Level 3, 25 vols., Set. Linda P. Silbert & Alvin J. Silbert. 1991. 69.95 (*0-89544-403-8*) Silbert Bress.

Strong Kids Life Skills Program: Level 4, 25 vols., Set. Linda P. Silbert & Alvin J. Silbert. 1991. 69.95 (*0-89544-404-6*) Silbert Bress.

Strong Kids Life Skills Program: Level 5, 25 vols., Set. Linda P. Silbert & Alvin J. Silbert. 1991. 69.95 (*0-89544-405-4*) Silbert Bress.

Strong Limit Theorems. Lin Zhengyan. (Mathematics & Its Applications Ser.). 200p. (CHI.). 1992. lib. bdg. 126.00 (*0-7923-1798-X*) Kluwer Ac.

Strong Limit Theorems in Non-Commutative Probability. R. Jajte. (Lecture Notes in Mathematics Ser.: Vol. 1110). vi, 152p. 1985. 34.95 (*0-387-13915-X*) Spr-Verlag.

Strong Limit Theorems in Noncommutative L2-Spaces. Ed. by R. Jajte et al. (Lecture Notes in Mathematics Ser.: Vol. 1477). x, 113p. 1991. 31.95 (*0-387-54214-0*) Spr-Verlag.

Strong, Loving & Wise: Presiding in Liturgy. Robert W. Hovda. (Illus.). 96p. 1981. pap. 7.95 (*0-8146-1253-9*) Liturgical Pr.

Strong Man of Berkeley. Jonathan Berman. 300p. (Orig.). 1989. pap. write for info. (*0-318-64796-6*) JMPS Pubs.

Strong Man of China. Robert Berkov. LC 70-124225. (Select Bibliographies Reprint Ser.). (Illus.). 1977. 21.95 (*0-8369-5413-0*) Ayer.

Strong Managers, Weak Owners: The Political Roots of American Corporate Finance. Mark J. Roe. LC 94-12179. 336p. 1994. text ed. 39.50 (*0-691-03683-7*) Princeton U Pr.

Strong Managers, Weak Owners: The Political Roots of American Corporate Finance. Mark J. Roe. 342p. 1994. pap. text ed. 18.95 (*0-691-02631-9*) Princeton U Pr.

***Strong Marriage & Family Experiences.** 51th ed. Strong. Date not set. pap. write for info. (*0-314-00114-X*) Wadsworth Pub.

Strong Materials. J. W. Martin. (Wykeham Science Ser.: No. 21). 124p. 1972. pap. 18.00 (*0-85109-260-8*) Taylor & Francis.

Strong Materials. J. W. Martin & R. A. Hull. LC 72-189452. (Wykeham Science Ser.: No. 21). 124p. (C). 1972. 18.00 (*0-8448-1123-8*, Crane Russak) Taylor & Francis.

Strong Measures: Contemporary American Poetry in Traditional Forms. Philip Dacey & David Jauss. 432p. (C). 1985. pap. text ed. 31.50 (*0-06-041471-5*) Addson-Wesley Educ.

Strong Medicine. Arthur Hailey. 448p. 1986. mass mkt. 5.99 (*0-440-18366-9*) Dell.

Strong Medicine: Health Politics in the 21st Century. Iliffe. (C). 1988. pap. 15.00 (*0-85315-694-8*, Pub. by Lawrence & Wishart UK) NYU Pr.

Strong Medicine: The Ethical Rationing of Health Care. Paul T. Menzel. 256p. 1990. 37.95 (*0-19-505710-4*) OUP.

Strong Medicine: What's Wrong with America's Healthcare System & How We Can Fix It. George Halvorson. 1993. 19.00 (*0-679-42980-8*) Random.

Strong Medicine: Chemistry at the Pharmacy see Science in Our World

Strong Medicine for a Sick Society. Mark Finley & Steven R. Mosley. LC 95-7341. 1995. pap. 1.99 (*0-8163-1262-1*) Pacific Pr Pub Assn.

***Strong Men Armed: The United States Marines vs. Japan.** Robert Leckie. LC 97-11830. (Illus.). 600p. 1997. reprint ed. pap. 17.95 (*0-306-80785-8*) Da Capo.

Strong Men in Tough Times: Developing Strong Character in an Age of Compromise. Edwin L. Cole. 1994. pap. 10.99 (*0-88419-376-4*) Creation House.

Strong Men, Weak Men: Godly Strength & the Male Identity. Leonard E. LeSourd. LC 90-35761. 256p. (gr. 10). 1994. reprint ed. pap. 8.99 (*0-8007-9211-4*) Chosen Bks.

***Strong Metal-Support Interactions.** Ed. by R. T. Baker et al. LC 85-30708. (ACS Symposium Ser.: Vol. 298). 248p. 1986. reprint ed. pap. 70.70 (*0-608-03844-X*, 2064291) Bks Demand.

Strong-Minded Women: The Emergence of the Woman-Suffrage Movement in Iowa. Louise R. Noun. LC 86-18597. (Iowa Heritage Collection Ser.). (Illus.). 322p. 1986. reprint ed. pap. 9.95 (*0-8138-1724-2*) Iowa St U Pr.

Strong Mothers, Strong Sons: Raising the Next Generation of Men. Ann F. Caron. LC 94-40537. 336p. 1995. pap. 14.00 (*0-06-097648-9*, PL) HarpC.

Strong Mothers, Weak Wives: The Search for Gender Equality. Miriam M. Johnson. 325p. (C). 1988. 38.00 (*0-520-06161-6*); pap. 15.95 (*0-520-06162-4*) U CA Pr.

Strong Motion. Jonathan Franzen. 508p. 1992. 22.95 (*0-374-27105-4*) FS&G.

Strong Motion. Jonathan Franzen. LC 92-46234. 512p. 1993. pap. 10.95 (*0-393-30996-7*) Norton.

Strong Necessity of Time: The Philosophy of Time in Shakespeare & Elizabethan Literature. G. F. Waller. (De Proprietatibus Litterarum, Ser. Practica: No. 90). 1976. pap. text ed. 46.15 (*90-279-3254-9*) Mouton.

Strong Night Wind. Donald R. Wilson. Ed. by Jack Wright. (Illus.). 280p. 1995. 100.00 (*0-9646254-0-7*) Wright Pub FL.

Strong Night Wind. limited ed. Donald R. Wilson. Ed. by Jack Wright. 280p. 1995. 800.00 (*0-9646254-1-5*) Wright Pub FL.

Strong on Defense: Simple Strategies to Protect You & Your Family from Crime. Sanford Strong. 256p. 1996. 22.00 (*0-671-52293-0*, PB Hardcover) PB.

***Strong on Defense: Survival Rules to Protect You & Your Family from Crime.** Sanford Strong. 1997. pap. 14.00 (*0-671-53511-0*) PB.

Strong on Music: The New York Music Scene in the Days of George Templeton Strong. Vera B. Lawrence. (Illus.). xxii, 864p. 1995. pap. text ed. 27.50 (*0-226-47011-3*); lib. bdg. 90.00 (*0-226-47010-5*) U Ch Pr.

Strong on Music - The New York Music Scene in the Days of George Templeton Strong, 1836-1850 Vol. 1: Resonances, 1836-1850. Vera B. Lawrence. LC 94-205956. (Illus.). lvi, 686p. 1995. pap. text ed. 27.50 (*0-226-47009-1*) U Ch Pr.

Strong Opinions. Vladimir Nabokov. (Vintage International Ser.). 1990. pap. 15.00 (*0-679-72609-8*, Vin) Random.

Strong Pagans & Other Stories. Mary O'Donnell. 258p. 1991. pap. 12.95 (*1-85371-123-3*, Pub. by Poolbeg Pr IE) Dufour.

***Strong Parties & Lame Ducks: Presidential & Factionalism in Venezuela.** Michael Coppedge. 1997. pap. text ed. 16.95 (*0-8047-2961-1*) Stanford U Pr.

Strong Parties & Lame Ducks: Presidential Patriarchy & Factionalism in Venezuela. Michael Coppedge. LC 93-36656. 264p. 1994. 45.00 (*0-8047-2278-1*) Stanford U Pr.

Strong Poison. Dorothy L. Sayers. 20.95 (*0-8488-1154-2*) Amereon Ltd.

Strong Poison. Dorothy L. Sayers. 272p. 1995. mass mkt. 4.99 (*0-06-104350-8*, Harp PBks) HarpC.

Strong Presidents: A Theory of Leadership. Philip Abbott. LC 95-41758. 296p. 1996. pap. text ed. 20.00 (*0-87049-932-7*); lib. bdg. 40.00 (*0-87049-931-9*) U of Tenn Pr.

Strong, Proud, & above All, Free: A Collection of Cowboy Poetry. unabridged ed. Dwight E. Burgess. LC 96-17594. (Illus.). 80p. (J). 1996. pap. 11.95 (*1-879984-25-3*) Premier KS.

Strong Representations: Narrative & Circumstantial Evidence in England. Alexander Welsh. LC 91-30039. 320p. 1992. text ed. 44.00 (*0-8018-4271-9*) Johns Hopkins.

Strong Representations: Narrative & Circumstantial Evidence in England. Alexander Welsh. LC 91-30039. 280p. 1995. pap. text ed. 15.95 (*0-8018-5119-X*) Johns Hopkins.

Strong Reproofs: 1 Corinthians. (Swindoll Bible Study Guide Ser.). 1988. pap. 5.99 (*0-8499-8298-7*) Word Pub.

***Strong Republicans & Anxious Liberals.** Ronald J. Terchek. 320p. 1996. 67.50 (*0-8476-8373-7*); pap. 24.95 (*0-8476-8374-5*) Rowman.

Strong Shadows: Scenes from an Inner City AIDS Clinic. Abigail Zuger. LC 95-7587. 243p. 1995. text ed. 22.95 (*0-7167-2916-4*) W H Freeman.

***Strong Shadows: Scenes from an Inner City AIDS Clinic.** Abigail Zuger. 264p. 1997. pap. 11.95 (*0-7167-3100-2*) W H Freeman.

Strong Shall Live. Louis L'Amour. 176p. 1985. 3.99 (*0-553-25200-3*) Bantam.

Strong Shall Live. large type ed. Louis L'Amour. (Special Ser.). 242p. 1993. reprint ed. 18.95 (*1-56054-647-6*) Thorndike Pr.

Strong Silent Cowboy. Leanna Wilson. (Romance Ser.). 1996. mass mkt. 3.25 (*0-373-19179-0*, 1-19179-0) Silhouette.

Strong, Silent Type: (Bachelor Arms) Kate Hoffmann. (Temptation Ser.). 1995. pap. 3.25 (*0-373-25629-9*, 1-25629-6) Harlequin Bks.

Strong Societies & Weak States: State-Society Relations & State Capabilities in the Third World. Joel S. Migdal. (Illus.). 344p. 1988. pap. text ed. 16.95 (*0-691-01073-0*) Princeton U Pr.

Strong Solids. 3rd ed. A. Kelly & N. H. MacMillan. (Monographs on the Physics & Chemistry of Materials). (Illus.). 420p. 1987. 98.00 (*0-19-851362-3*) OUP.

Strong Spirits. Elisa DeCarlo. 160p. (Orig.). 1994. mass mkt. 4.50 (*0-380-77405-4*, AvoNova) Avon.

***Strong Stable Markov Chains.** N. V. Kartashov. (Illus.). 144p. 1996. 122.00 (*90-6764-205-3*, Pub. by VSP NE) Coronet Bks.

Strong Start in Language: Grades K-3. Ruth Beechick. (Three-R's Ser.). 32p. (Orig.). 1986. pap. 4.00 (*0-940319-02-0*) Arrow Press.

Strong State & Economic Interest Groups: The Post-1980 Turkish Experience. Ed. by Martin Heper. x, 198p. (C). 1991. lib. bdg. 87.15 (*3-11-012924-8*) De Gruyter.

Strong Supporting Cast: The Shaw Lefevres 1789-1936. F. M. Willson. LC 93-8413. 280p. (C). 1993. text ed. 70.00 (*0-485-11435-6*, Pub. by Athlone Pr UK) Humanities.

***Strong. The Strongs of Strongville: Descendants of John Stoughton Strong & Eliphalet Strong, Suppl. to "Hist. of the Strong Family," by Benj. W. Dwight.** Albert Strong. (Illus.). 91p. 1996. reprint ed. pap. 18.00 (*0-8328-5452-2*); reprint ed. lib. bdg. 28.00 (*0-8328-5451-4*) Higginson Bk Co.

Strong, Typical, & Weak College Writers Vol. 5: Twenty-Two Case Studies. Hildy Miller & Mary E. Ashcroft. Ed. by Lillian Bridwell-Bowles & Mark Olson. (Monographs: Vol. 5). 211p. (Orig.). 1996. pap. 16.00 (*1-881221-11-3*) U Minn Ctr Interdis.

Strong Vocational Interest Blanks. Edward K. Strong, Jr. 1985. write for info. (*0-8047-1069-4*) Stanford U Pr.

Strong, Weak, & Electromagnetic Interactions in Nuclei, Atoms, & Astrophysics: A Workshop in Honor of Stewart D. Bloom's Retirement. Ed. by Grant J. Matthews. LC 91-76876. (AIP Conference Proceedings Ser.: No. 242). 248p. 1992. 88.00 (*0-88318-943-7*) Am Inst Physics.

Strong-Willed Child. James Dobson. 335p. 1992. mass mkt. 6.99 (*0-8423-5924-9*) Tyndale.

***Strong-Willed Child.** James Dobson. 240p. 1978. pap. 11.99 (*0-8423-6661-X*) Tyndale.

Strong-Willed Child or Dreamer? Dana S. Spears & Ron L. Braund. 252p. 1996. pap. 12.99 (*0-7852-7700-5*) Nelson.

Strong Winds below the Canyons. Larry Kramer. (QRL Poetry Bks.: Vol. XXV). 1984. 20.00 (*0-614-06411-2*) Quarterly Rev.

***Strong Wits & Spider Webs: A Study in Hobbes's Philosophy of Language.** Deborah H. Soles. (Avebury Series in Philosophy). 184p. 1996. text ed. 59.95 (*1-85972-411-6*, Pub. by Avebury Pub UK) Ashgate Pub Co.

***Strong Women Stay Young.** Miriam E. Nelson & Sarah Wernick. LC 96-41541. 288p. 1997. 23.95 (*0-553-10347-4*) Bantam.

Strongbow. Morgan Llywelyn. LC 95-53841. 1996. 15.95 (*0-312-86150-8*) Tor Bks.

***Strongbow: The Story of Richard & Aoife.** Morgan Llywelyn. 1997. mass mkt. 4.99 (*0-8125-4462-5*) Tor Bks.

Stronger see Three Plays

***Stronger Abs & Back.** Dean Brittenham. LC 96-48346. (Illus.). 248p. (Orig.). 1997. pap. 16.95 (*0-88011-558-0*, PBRI0558) Human Kinetics.

Stronger Competitive Bidding. Marshall Miles. LC 92-70047. 324p. (Orig.). 1992. pap. 14.95 (*1-877908-03-7*) Lawrence & Leong Pub.

***Stronger Faster: Workday Workouts That Build Maximum Muscle in Minimum Time.** Brian Kaufman et al. LC 96-48687. (Men's Health Life Improvement Guides Ser.). 1997. pap. write for info. (*0-87596-359-5*) Rodale Pr Inc.

Stronger Pump. rev. ed. Julia A. Purcell & Barbara J. Fletcher. Ed. by Nancy R. Hull. LC 80-10191. (Illus.). 40p. (Orig.). 1994. pap. text ed. 6.50 (*0-939838-05-2*) Pritchett & Hull.

Stronger Soul Within a Finer Frame: Portraying Afro-Americans in the Black Renaissance. John S. Wright & Tracy E. Smith. Ed. by Susan Brown. LC 89-52012. (Illus.). 64p. (Orig.). 1990. 6.50 (*0-938713-06-X*) Univ MN Art Mus.

***Stronger Than a Hundred Men: A History of the Vertical Water Wheel.** Terry S. Reynolds. LC 82-15346. (Johns Hopkins Studies in the History of Technology; New Ser.: Vol. 7). 472p. 1983. reprint ed. pap. 134.60 (*0-608-03744-3*, 2064569) Bks Demand.

Stronger Than Death: When Suicide Touches Your Life--a Mother's Story. Sue Chance. 192p. 1994. mass mkt. 4.99 (*0-380-72110-4*) Avon.

Stronger Than Magic. Heather Cullman. 1997. pap. 5.99 (*0-451-40732-6*) NAL-Dutton.

Stronger than Power. (Mongolia Society Occasional Papers: No. 14). 1989. pap. 12.00 (*0-910980-54-3*) Mongolia.

Stronger Than Steel: The Wayne Alderson Story. R. C. Sproul. LC 80-7746. 244p. 1980. 15.00 (*0-06-067502-0*) Value of the Person.

Stronger Than Steel: The Wayne Alderson Story. Robert C. Sproul. LC 80-7746. 208p. 1980. 15.00 (*0-318-23249-9*) W T Alderson.

Stronger Women Get, the More Men Love Football. Mariah B. Nelson. 320p. 1995. reprint ed. pap. 11.00 (*0-380-72527-4*) Avon.

Stronger Women Get, the More Men Love Football: Sex & Sports in America. Mariah B. Nelson. LC 93-44358. 1994. 22.95 (*0-15-181393-0*) HarBrace.

Strongest Animal. Janice Boland. (Books for Young Learners). (Illus.). 12p. (Orig.). (J). (gr. k-2). 1996. pap. 5.00 (*1-57274-024-8*) R Owen Pubs.

Strongest Man in the World. Ed. by Dmitry Ivanov. LC 79-9425. (Illus.). 289p. 1979. 30.00 (*0-943071-09-7*) Sphinx Pr.

Strongest Part of the Family: A Study of Lao Refugee Women in Columbus, Ohio. Karen L. Muir. LC 87-45782. (Immigrant Communities & Ethnic Minorities in the U. S. & Canada Ser.: No. 17). 1988. 38.50 (*0-404-19427-3*) AMS Pr.

Strongest Weapon. Notburga Tilt. (C). 1991. 45.00 (*0-7223-0344-0*, Pub. by A H S Ltd UK) St Mut.

Strongheart Jack & the Beanstalk. Illus. by Joe Shlichta. LC 94-45815. (J). (gr. k-3). 1995. 15.95 (*0-87483-414-7*) August Hse.

Stronghold. Phillips Kloss. LC 86-14557. 128p. 1987. 10.95 (*0-86534-093-5*) Sunstone Pr.

Stronghold. Melanie Rawn. (Dragon Star Ser.: Bk. 1). 488p. 1990. 21.95 (*0-88677-440-3*) DAW Bks.

Stronghold. Melanie Rawn. (Dragon Star Ser.: Bk. 1). 592p. 1991. mass mkt. 6.99 (*0-88677-482-9*) DAW Bks.

Stronghold: A Novel of Suspense. Stanley Ellin. 322p. 1996. pap. 11.00 (*0-88150-380-0*, Foul Play) Countryman.

Stronghold: A Story of Historic Northern Neck of Virginia & Its People. Miriam Haynie. 1959. 8.50 (*0-87517-042-0*) Dietz.

Strongholds & Sanctuaries: The Borderland of England & Wales. Ellis Peters & Roy Morgan. LC 93-17979. (Illus.). 192p. 1993. 33.99 (*0-7509-0200-0*, Pub. by Sutton Pubng UK) Bks Intl VA.

Strongholds of the 10/40 Window: Intercessor's Guide to the World's Least Evangelized Nations. Ed. by George Otis, Jr. 274p. 1995. pap. 12.99 (*0-927545-86-1*) YWAM Pub.

Strongly Correlated Election Systems. Ed. by M. P. Das & D. Neilson. 255p. (C). 1992. text ed. 125.00 (*1-56072-090-5*) Nova Sci Pubs.

Strongly Correlated Electron Systems: Proceedings of Adriatico Research Conference & Workshop. G. Baskaran et al. (Progress in High Temperature Super Conductivity Ser.: Vol. 23). 506p. 1990. text ed. 151.00 (*981-02-0066-8*) World Scientific Pub.

Strongly Correlated Electron Systems & High-Tc Superconductivity: Proceedings of the 14th International School of Theoretical Physics. Ed. by E. Zipper et al. 200p. (C). 1991. text ed. 63.00 (*981-02-0767-0*) World Scientific Pub.

Strongly Correlated Electron Systems II: Prog in Hts, Vol. 29. G. Baskaran et al. 444p. 1991. pap. 38.00 (*981-02-0510-4*); text ed. 118.00 (*981-02-0509-0*) World Scientific Pub.

Strongly Correlated Electron Systems III: Proceedings of the Adriatico Research Conference & Miniworkshop. G. Baskaran et al. (Series on Progress in High Temperature Superconductivity: No. 33). 400p. 1992. text ed. 95.00 (*981-02-0903-7*) World Scientific Pub.

Strongly Correlated Electronic Materials: The Los Alamos Symposium, 1993. Ed. by Kevin S. Bedell. LC 94-28602. (C). 1994. 49.95 (*0-201-40930-5*) Addison-Wesley.

***Strongly Correlated Magnetic & Superconducting Systems: Proceedings of the El Escorial Summer School, Held at Madrid, Spain, 15-19, July, 1996.** German Sierra & Miguel A. Indelgado. LC 97-17892. (Lecture Notes in Physics Ser.: Vol. 478). 1997. write for info. (*3-540-62476-7*) Spr-Verlag.

Strongly Coupled Plasma Physics. Ed. by Forrest J. Rogers & Hugh E. Dewitt. (NATO ASI Series B, Physics: Vol. 154). (Illus.). 610p. 1987. 135.00 (*0-306-42581-5*, Plenum Pr) Plenum.

Strongly Coupled Plasma Physics. Ed. by H. M. Van Horn & S. Ichimaru. (Illus.). 580p. (C). 1993. 90.00 (*1-878822-27-6*) Univ Rochester Pr.

Strongly Interacting Electrons & Quantum Magnetism. Assa Auerbach. LC 94-6510. (Graduate Texts in Contemporary Physics Ser.). (Illus.). 256p. 1994. 39.95 (*0-387-94286-6*) Spr-Verlag.

Strongly Interacting Fermions & High Tc Superconductivity, 56. Ed. by B. Doucot & J. Zinn-Justin. 624p. 1995. 256.25 (*0-444-82190-2*) Elsevier.

An Asterisk (*) at the beginning of an entry indicates that the title is appearing in BIP for the first time.

Strongly Interacting Particles. Riccardo Levi-Setti & Thomas Lasinski. LC 73-83750. (Chicago Lectures in Physics). 328p. reprint ed. pap. 93.50 (*0-685-23872-5*, 2056656) Bks Demand.

***Strongman.** Jack Barron. 260p. (Orig.). 1997. mass mkt. 4.99 (*1-55237-394-0*, Pub. by Comnwlth Pub CN) Partners Pubs Grp.

Strongput Workout System. Strongput, Inc. Staff. 96p. 1995. ring bd. 15.95 (*0-8403-9753-4*) Kendall-Hunt.

Strong's Book of Designs. 92p. 1982. reprint ed. 15.00 (*0-911380-61-2*) ST Pubns.

Strong's Comprehensive Concordance of the Bible. Ed. by James Strong. 1425p. 1986. pap. 19.99 (*0-529-06334-4*, SC1); Thumb-indexed edition. text ed. 26.99 (*0-529-06335-2*, SC1-I) World Publng.

***Strongs' Concise Concordance.** James Strong. 1996. 19.99 (*0-7852-6003-X*) Nelson.

Strong's Concordance: Comprehensive Edition. 2nd abr. ed. James Strong. 1425p. 1995. pap. 17.99 (*0-529-10456-3*, 5C1P) World Publng.

Strong's Exhaustive Concordance. James Strong. 1552p. 1977. pap. 19.99 (*0-8010-8108-4*) Baker Bks.

Strong's Exhaustive Concordance. James Strong. 1994. 24. 95 (*0-932453-08-2*) Dugan Pubs Inc.

Strong's Exhaustive Concordance of the Bible. Ed. by James Strong. 1552p. 1982. 22.99 (*0-87981-626-0*) Broadman.

Strong's Exhaustive Concordance of the Bible. James Strong. 1552p. 1988. 24.95 (*0-917006-01-1*) Hendrickson MA.

Strong's Greek & Hebrew Dictionaries: Plus Literal English Translation with Strong's Numbers. (Ellis' Bible Study Ser.). 190p. (C). 1993. 59.95 (*0-933186-58-4*) IBM Corp Pub.

***Strong's Math Dictionary - Solution Guide.** unabridged ed. (Illus.). 500p. (Orig.). 1996. pap. 39.99 (*0-9653033-0-6*) Strongs.

Strong's New Exhaustive Concordance of the Bible. James Strong. 1992. text ed. 31.99 (*0-529-07248-3*, SC4-I) World Publng.

Strong's New Exhaustive Concordance of the Bible: Handi-Size. James Strong. 1992. 24.99 (*0-529-07235-1*, SC4) World Publng.

Strong's North Carolina Index, 26 vols., Set, Suppl. 1991. 4th ed. LC 89-85552. 1991. Set, suppl. 1991. 3,682.00 (*0-318-57156-0*) Lawyers Cooperative.

Strongyloidiasis: A Major Roundworm Infection of Man. Ed. by D. I. Grove. 220p. 1989. 99.00 (*0-85066-732-1*, Pub. by Tay Francis Ltd UK) Taylor & Francis.

Strontium. (Metals & Minerals Ser.). 1993. lib. bdg. 248.95 (*0-8490-8954-9*) Gordon Pr.

Strontium. 1931. 240.00 (*0-387-93256-9*) Spr-Verlag.

Strontium Isotope Geology. G. Faure & J. L. Powell. Ed. by W. Von Engelhurdt. LC 72-75720. (Minerals, Rocks & Inorganic Materials Ser.: Vol. 5). (Illus.). 200p. 1972. 38.95 (*0-387-05784-6*) Spr-Verlag.

Sr 90 from Worldwide Fallout in Teeth & Bones. Florence T. Cua. 175p. 1992. 40.00 (*0-9645418-0-7*) F T Cua.

Strophariaceae & Coprinaceae Pt. 5: Strophariaceae & Coprinaceae p.p., Hypholoma, Melanotus, Psilocybe, Stropharia, Lacrymaria & Panaeolus. R. Watling & N. M. Gregory. (British Fungus Flora (Agarics & Boleti) Ser.: Pt. 5). (Illus.). ii, 122p. 1987. pap. 20.00 (*0-9504270-7-1*, Pub. by Royal Botanic Edinburgh UK) Balogh.

***Stross Graphical Programming with Tic Perg.** Charles Stross. (C). 1998. pap. text ed. write for info. (*0-201-17516-9*) Addison-Wesley.

Stroud Valley Childhood. Terry Jones. LC 92-34322. 1992. 14.00 (*0-7509-0257-4*, Pub. by Sutton Pubng UK) Bks Intl VA.

***Struck by Lighting.** Deborah Morris. (Real Kids Real Adventures Ser.: No. 5). 112p. 1997. mass mkt. 3.99 (*0-425-16117-X*) Berkley Pub.

Struck Copies of Early American Coins. E. Kenny. (Illus.). 1982. reprint ed. pap. 6.00 (*0-915262-91-6*) S J Durst.

Struck down but Not Destroyed: A Christian Response to Chronic Illness & Pain. Doug Wiegand. (Illus.). 144p. (Orig.). 1996. pap. 9.95 (*1-880451-20-4*) Rainbows End.

Struck Eagle: Micah Jenkins of the 5th South Carolina Volunteers & the "Palmetto Sharpshooters" James J. Baldwin, 3rd. LC 96-14115. (Illus.). 448p. 1996. 34.95 (*1-57249-017-9*) White Mane Pub.

***Structronic Systems: Active Structures, Devices & Systems, 2 vols.** 900p. 1997. lib. bdg. write for info. (*981-02-2652-7*); lib. bdg. 74.00 (*981-02-2955-0*); lib. bdg. 74.00 (*981-02-2956-9*) World Scientific Pub.

Structual Equations with Latent Variables. William Bollen. LC 88-27272. (Probability & Mathematical Statistics Ser.). 528p. 1989. text ed. 79.95 (*0-471-01171-1*) Wiley.

Structual Steel Design: LRFD Approach. 2nd ed. J. C. Smith. LC 95-36503. 608p. 1996. text ed. write for info. (*0-471-10693-3*) Wiley.

Structural Adhesives: Chemistry & Technology. Ed. by S. R. Hartshorn. (Topics in Applied Chemistry Ser.). 524p. 1986. 115.00 (*0-306-42121-6*, Plenum Pr) Plenum.

Structural Adhesives: Developments in Resins & Primers. Ed. by Anthony J. Kinloch. 322p. 1986. 128.50 (*1-85166-002-X*, Pub. by Elsevier Applied Sci UK) Elsevier.

Structural Adhesives & Bonding: Proceedings of a Special Conference, March 1979, El Segundo, California. rev. ed. (Illus.). 442p. 1989. reprint ed. 49.00 (*0-938648-07-1*, 0111) T-C Pr CA.

Structural Adhesives with Emphasis on Aerospace Applications: A Report of the Ad Hoc Committee on Structural Adhesives for Aerospace Use, National Materials Advisory Board, National Research Council. National Research Council, Committee on Vision Staff. LC 75-17033. (Treatise on Adhesion & Adhesives Ser.: Vol. 4). 264p. reprint ed. pap. 75.30 (*0-685-16321-0*, 2027122) Bks Demand.

Structural Adjustment: Retrospect & Prospect. Daniel Schydlowsky. LC 94-32920. 256p. 1995. text ed. 62.95 (*0-275-94433-6*, Praeger Pubs) Greenwood.

Structural Adjustment & African Women Farmers. Ed. by Christina H. Gladwin. (Carter Lecture Series, Center for African Studies). 424p. (C). 1991. lib. bdg. 23.95 (*0-8130-1063-2*) U Press Fla.

***Structural Adjustment & Agriculture: African & Asian Experiences.** 159p. 1994. 17.00 (*92-5-103487-7*, F34877, Pub. by FAO IT) Bernan Associates.

Structural Adjustment & Agriculture: Theory & Practice in Africa & Latin America. Ed. by Simon Commander. LC 89-1968. 250p. (C). 1989. pap. text ed. 27.50 (*0-435-08037-7*, 08037) Heinemann.

Structural Adjustment & Beyond in Sub-Sahara Africa: Research & Policy Issues. Ralph V. Hoeven & Fred V. Kraaij. LC 94-28091. 270p. (Orig.). 1994. 60.00 (*0-435-08962-5*, 08962) Heinemann.

Structural Adjustment & Beyond in Sub-Sahara Africa: Research & Policy Issues. Ralph V. Hoeven. Ed. by Fred V. Kraaij. LC 94-28091. 270p. (Orig.). 1994. pap. 30.00 (*0-435-08964-1*, 08964) Heinemann.

***Structural Adjustment & Employment Policy: Issues & Experience.** John Toye. ix, 88p. 1995. pap. 13.50 (*92-2-109445-6*) Intl Labour Office.

***Structural Adjustment & Household Welfare in Rural Areas: A Micro-Economic Perspective.** 64p. 1991. 9.00 (*92-5-102858-3*, F8583, Pub. by FAO IT) Bernan Associates.

Structural Adjustment & Income Distribution: Issues & Experience. Azizur R. Kahn. xi, 80p. 1993. pap. 18.00 (*92-2-108742-5*) Intl Labour Office.

Structural Adjustment & Macroeconomic Policy Issues: Papers Presented at a Seminar Held in Lahore, Pakistan, October 26-28, 1991. Contrib. by V. A. Jafarey. LC 92-22648. x, 137p. 1992. pap. 17.50 (*1-55775-302-4*) Intl Monetary.

***Structural Adjustment & Mass Poverty in Ghana.** Kwabena Donkor. (Making of Modern Africa Ser.). (Illus.). 2810p. 1997. text ed. 59.95 (*1-84014-122-0*, Pub. by Ashgate UK) Ashgate Pub Co.

Structural Adjustment & Policy Reform. Bruce M. Koppel. 258p. 1991. pap. 15.00 (*92-833-2103-0*) Qual Resc.

Structural Adjustment & Rural Labour Markets in Africa. Ed. by Vali Jamal. LC 94-31706. (International Political Economy Ser.). 1995. text ed. 75.00 (*0-312-12432-5*) St Martin.

Structural Adjustment & Rural Smallholder Welfare: A Comparative Analysis from Sub-Saharan Africa. David E. Sahn. (Working Papers). (C). 1991. pap. text ed. 7.00 (*1-56401-103-8*) Cornell Food.

Structural Adjustment & Stabilization in Niger: Macroeconomic Consequences & Social Adjustment. Cathy L. Jabara. (Monographs). (Illus.). 120p. (C). 1991. pap. text ed. 12.00 (*1-56401-011-2*) Cornell Food.

Structural Adjustment & the African Farmer. Ed. by Alex Duncan & John Howell. LC 92-11274. 214p. (C). 1992. pap. 25.00 (*0-435-08073-3*, 08073) Heinemann.

Structural Adjustment & the Crisis in Africa: Economic & Political Perspectives. Ed. by David Kennett & Tukumbi Lumumba-Kasongo. LC 92-30301. 164p. 1992. text ed. 79.95 (*0-7734-9184-8*) E Mellen.

***Structural Adjustment & the Nigerian State.** Pita O. Agbese & Julius O. Ihonvbere. LC 97-2790. 1997. write for info. (*0-88258-196-1*) Howard U Pr.

Structural Adjustment in a Newly Industrialized Country: The Korean Experience. Vittorio Corbo & Sang-Mok Suh. 376p. 1992. text ed. 39.95 (*0-8018-4328-6*, 44328) Johns Hopkins.

Structural Adjustment in Africa. Ed. by Bonnie K. Campbell & John Loxley. LC 89-34361. (International Political Economy Ser.). 290p. 1990. text ed. 55.00 (*0-312-03553-5*) St Martin.

Structural Adjustment in Africa. R. Lensink. LC 95-21944. 160p. (C). 1996. pap. text ed. 24.50 (*0-582-24886-8*, Pub. by Longman UK) Longman.

Structural Adjustment in Developed Open Economies: Proceedings of a Conference of the International Economic Association Held at Yxtaholm, Sweden. Ed. by Karl Jungenfelt & Douglas C. Hague. LC 83-22966. 448p. 1985. text ed. 39.95 (*0-312-76662-9*) St Martin.

Structural Adjustment in Europe. Pauline Creasey. 280p. 1988. 35.00 (*0-86187-902-3*) St Martin.

Structural Adjustment in Sub-Saharan Africa: Ajustement Structurel en Afrique Subsaharienne. Cadman M. Mills. (EDI Policy Seminar Report Ser.). 56p. 1989. 6.95 (*0-8213-1336-3*, 11336) World Bank.

Structural Adjustment in the Federal Republic of Germany. Klaus W. Schatz et al. (Employment, Adjustment & Industrialisation Ser.: No. 4). xi, 141p. (Orig.). 1987. pap. 24.75 (*92-2-106114-0*) Intl Labour Office.

Structural Adjustment of Economies: Transatlantic Investment & Economic Interdependence. Intro. by Jacqueline Grapin. (Conclusions from an International Round Table Seminar Ser.). 39p. (Orig.). 1993. pap. 7.00 (*0-9628287-5-0*) European Inst.

***Structural Adjustment Policy Sequencing in Sub-Saharan Africa.** 137p. 1992. 12.00 (*92-5-102868-0*, Pub. by FAO IT) Bernan Associates.

Structural Adjustment Programme & Food Security: Hunger & Poverty in India. Amitabha Mukherjee. 373p. 1994. 72.95 (*1-85628-595-2*, Pub. by Avebury Pub UK) Ashgate Pub Co.

***Structural Adjustment Reconsidered: Economic Policy & Poverty in Africa.** David E. Sahn et al. (Illus.). 312p. (C). 1997. text ed. 64.95 (*0-521-58451-5*) Cambridge U Pr.

***Structural Adjustment, Reconstruction & Development in Africa.** Ed. by Kempe R. Hope, Sr. (Contemporary Perspectives on Developing Societies Ser.). 224p. 1997. text ed. 63.95 (*1-84014-127-1*, Pub. by Ashgate UK) Ashgate Pub Co.

Structural Allegory: Reconstructive Encounters with the New French Thought. Ed. by John Fekete. LC 83-19878. (Theory & History of Literature Ser.: No. 11). 293p. reprint ed. pap. 83.60 (*0-7837-2957-X*, 2057497) Bks Demand.

Structural Ambiguity in Brahms: Analytical Approaches to Four Works. Jonathan Dunsby. LC 81-24. (Studies in British Musicology). 128p. reprint ed. pap. 36.50 (*0-685-20819-2*, 2070033) Bks Demand.

Structural Analysis. Aslam Kassimali. 768p. 1993. text ed. 69.95 (*0-534-93070-0*) PWS Pubs.

Structural Analysis. Ronald Sack. 1984. teacher ed., pap. text ed. write for info. (*0-07-054393-3*) McGraw.

Structural Analysis. Steven M. Sack. 1984. text ed. write for info. (*0-07-054392-5*) McGraw.

Structural Analysis. G. B. Vine. LC 80-42209. (Constructions & Civil Engineering Sector: Technician Ser.). (Illus.). 288p. (Orig.). (C). 1982. pap. text ed. 10. 95 (*0-582-41618-3*) Longman.

Structural Analysis. rev. ed. Aslam Kassimali. (Civil Engineering Ser.). 1995. text ed. 82.95 (*0-534-95046-9*) PWS Pubs.

***Structural Analysis.** 3rd ed. Coates et al. (Illus.). 624p. (Orig.). (C). (gr. 13 up). 1990. pap. text ed. 43.95 (*0-412-37980-5*, Chap & Hall NY) Chapman & Hall.

Structural Analysis. 3rd ed. Russell C. Hibbeler. LC 93-41397. (Illus.). 752p. (C). 1994. text ed. 90.00 (*0-02-354041-9*, Macmillan Coll) P-H.

Structural Analysis. 3rd ed. Harold I. Laursen. 512p. (C). 1988. text ed. write for info. (*0-07-036645-4*) McGraw.

***Structural Analysis.** 3rd rev. ed. Russell C. Hibbeler. 729p. 1996. text ed. 89.33 (*0-13-493370-2*) P-H.

Structural Analysis. 4th ed. Jack C. McCormac. 640p. (C). 1983. text ed. 83.75 (*0-06-044342-1*) Addson-Wesley Educ.

Structural Analysis. G. B. Vine. LC 80-42209. (Longman Technician Series, Construction & Civil Engineering). (Illus.). 261p. (Orig.). reprint ed. pap. 74.40 (*0-8357-3552-4*, 2034470) Bks Demand.

Structural Analysis: A Classical & Matrix Approach. 2nd ed. Jack C. McCormac & James K. Nelson. LC 96-23304. (C). 1997. text ed. 69.95 (*0-673-99753-7*) Addison-Wesley.

Structural Analysis: A Classical & Matrix Approach. 5th ed. Jack C. McCormac & Rudolph E. Elling. 608p. (C). 1989. text ed. 87.50 (*0-06-044341-3*) Addson-Wesley Educ.

***Structural Analysis: A Unified Classical & Matrix Approach.** 3rd ed. Wagdy R. Ghali & Neville. (Illus.). 896p. (C). (gr. 13 up). 1990. pap. text ed. 57.95 (*0-412-29040-5*) Chapman & Hall.

***Structural Analysis: A Unified Classical & Matrix Approach.** 3rd ed. Wagdy R. Ghali & Neville. 896p. 1989. pap. text ed. write for info. (*0-419-16070-1*, E & FN Spon) Routledge Chapman & Hall.

Structural Analysis: The Solution of Statically Indeterminate Structures. 3rd ed. W. F. Cassie. LC 67-72611. 295p. reprint ed. pap. 84.10 (*0-317-11039-X*, 2004914) Bks Demand.

Structural Analysis & Behavior. Freydoon Arbabi. 592p. 1991. text ed. write for info. (*0-07-002143-0*); teacher ed. write for info. (*0-07-002146-5*) McGraw.

Structural Analysis & Design. Conrad P. Heins, Jr. & Kenneth N. Derucher. LC 80-16139. (Civil Engineering Ser.: No. 2). (Illus.). 464p. reprint ed. pap. 132.30 (*0-7837-0601-4*, 2040949) Bks Demand.

Structural Analysis & Design: Some Microcomputer Applications, 2 vols. 2nd ed. H. B. Harrison. LC 89-8694. (Illus.). 860p. 1990. pap. text ed. 65.00 (*0-08-037521-9*, Pergamon Pr) Elsevier.

Structural Analysis & Design: Some Microcomputer Applications, 2 vols., Set. 2nd ed. H. B. Harrison. LC 89-8694. (Illus.). 827p. 1990. text ed. 210.00 (*0-08-037520-0*, 1104; 1303; 1307, Pergamon Pr) Elsevier.

Structural Analysis & Design: Some Minicomputer Applications, 2 pts. H. B. Harrison. (Illus.). 1980. pap. text ed. 44.00 (*0-08-023240-X*, Pergamon Pr) Elsevier.

Structural Analysis & Design: Some Minicomputer Applications, 2 pts., Set. H. B. Harrison. (Illus.). 1980. text ed. 130.00 (*0-08-023239-6*, Pergamon Pr) Elsevier.

Structural Analysis & Design of Multivariable Control Systems. Y. T. Tsay et al. (Lecture Notes in Control & Information Sciences Ser.: Vol. 107). vi, 208p. 1988. 45. 95 (*0-387-18916-5*) Spr-Verlag.

Structural Analysis & Design of Process Equipment. 2nd ed. Maan H. Jawad & James R. Farr. LC 88-2796. 722p. 1989. text ed. 165.00 (*0-471-62471-3*) Wiley.

Structural Analysis & Synthesis: A Laboratory Course in Structural Geology. 2nd ed. Stephen M. Rowland & Ernest M. Duebendorfer. LC 93-28089. 304p. 1994. pap. 36.95 (*0-86542-366-0*) Blackwell Sci.

Structural Analysis & Synthesis: Answer Book. Stephen M. Rowland & Ernest M. Duebendorfer. LC 93-28089. 1994. write for info. (*0-86542-436-5*) Blackwell Sci.

Structural Analysis, Design & Control by the Virtual Distortion Method. Jan Holnicki-Szulc & Jacek T. Gierlinski. 304p. 1995. text ed. 98.00 (*0-471-95656-2*) Wiley.

Structural Analysis in Microelectronic & Fiber Optic Systems Vol. 12. Ephraim Suhir. (1995 ASME International Mechanical Engineering Congress & Exposition Ser.: EEP-Vol. 12). 204p. 1995. 88.00 (*0-7918-1737-7*, H01019) ASME.

Structural Analysis in Microelectronics & Fiber Optics. Ephraim Suhir. LC 93-73614. 163p. pap. 52.50 (*0-7918-1258-8*) ASME.

***Structural Analysis in Microelectronics & Fiber Optics: Proceedings, ASME International Mechanical Engineering Congress & Exposition, Atlanta, GA, 1996.** Ed. by E. Suhir. LC 96-78681. (EEP Ser.: Vol. 16). 225p. 1996. pap. 84.00 (*0-7918-1539-0*, TK7874) ASME.

Structural Analysis in Microelectronics & Fiber Optics: 1994 International Mechanical Engineering Congress & Exposition, Chicago, Illinois - November 6-11, 1994. Ephraim Suhir. (Electrical & Electronics Packaging Ser.: Vol. 8). 88p. 1994. 40.00 (*0-7918-1448-3*, G00943) ASME.

Structural Analysis of Complex Aerial Photographs. Ed. by Makoto Nagao & Takashi Matsuyama. (Advanced Applications in Pattern Recognition Ser.). 224p. 1980. 75.00 (*0-306-40571-7*, Plenum Pr) Plenum.

Structural Analysis of Composite Beam Systems. A. Skudra et al. LC 91-58004. 300p. 1991. text ed. 89.95 (*0-87762-837-8*) Technomic.

Structural Analysis of Expectation Formation: Based on Business Surveys of French Manufacturing Industry. M. Ivaldi. (Lecture Notes in Economics & Mathematical Systems Ser.: Vol. 354). (Illus.). xii, 230p. 1991. 38.95 (*0-387-53665-5*) Spr-Verlag.

Structural Analysis of Kinship: Prolegomena to the Sociology of Kinship. Kingsley Davis. Ed. by Harriet Zuckerman & Robert K. Merton. LC 79-8990. (Dissertations on Sociology Ser.). 1980. lib. bdg. 41.95 (*0-405-12962-9*) Ayer.

Structural Analysis of Laminated Anisotropic Plates. James M. Whitney. LC 87-50430. 200p. 1987. 49.95 (*0-87762-518-2*) Technomic.

Structural Analysis of Mozart's Piano Concertos. Hans Tischler. (Wissenschaftliche Abhandlungen-Musicological Studies: Vol. 10). 140p. (ENG, FRE & GER.). 1968. lib. bdg. 48.00 (*0-912024-80-1*) Inst Mediaeval Mus.

Structural Analysis of Narrative Texts, Conference Papers. Ed. by Andrej Kodjak et al. (New York University Slavic Papers: Vol. II). (Illus.). 203p. (Orig.). 1980. pap. 19.95 (*0-89357-071-0*) Slavica.

Structural Analysis of Pound's Usura Canto: Jakobson's Method Extended & Applied to Free Verse. Christine Brooke-Rose. (De Proprietatibus Litterarum Ser.: No. 26). 76p. 1976. pap. text ed. 36.15 (*90-279-3361-8*) Mouton.

Structural Analysis of Printed Circuit Board Systems. Peter Engel. LC 92-21531. (Mechanical Engineering Ser.). 280p. 1993. 79.95 (*0-387-97939-5*) Spr-Verlag.

Structural Analysis of Shells. E. H. Baker et al. LC 79-27250. 364p. 1981. reprint ed. lib. bdg. 49.95 (*0-89874-118-1*) Krieger.

Structural Analysis of the Sermon on the Mount. Andrej Kodjak. (Religion & Reason Ser.: No. 34). (Illus.). x, 234p. 1986. lib. bdg. 89.25 (*0-89925-159-5*) Mouton.

Structural Analysis of Thermoplastic Components. Gerry Trantina & Ron Nimmer. Ed. by Peggy Malnati. LC 93-35994. 1994. text ed. 54.00 (*0-07-065202-3*) McGraw.

Structural Analysis Software for Micros. 2nd ed. Bernard J. Korites. Orig. Title: Sturctural Analysis for Micros. (Illus.). 222p. (Orig.). 1987. pap. 48.00 (*0-940254-07-7*, 07-7) Kern Intl.

Structural Analysis Systems. A. Niku-Lari. 1986. 120.00 (*0-08-032581-5*, Pergamon Pr) Elsevier.

Structural Analysis Systems, 3 vols., Vol. 2. A. Niku-Lari. 1986. 40.00 (*0-08-033436-9*, Pergamon Pr) Elsevier.

Structural Analysis Systems, 3 vols., Vol. 3. A. Niku-Lari. 1986. 40.00 (*0-08-033437-7*, Pergamon Pr) Elsevier.

Structural Analysis Systems, 3 vols., Vol. 1. A. Niku-Lari. 1986. 40.00 (*0-08-033435-0*, Pergamon Pr) Elsevier.

Structural Analysis Systems I: Software, Hardware, Capability, Compatibility, Applications. Ed. by A. Niku-Lari. (Structural Analysis Systems Ser.: Vol. 1). (Illus.). 250p. 1986. 142.00 (*0-08-032577-7*, Pub. by PPL UK) Franklin.

Structural Analysis Systems III: Software, Hardward, Capability, Compatibility, Applications. Ed. by A. Niku-Lari. (Structural Analysis Systems Ser.: Vol. 3). (Illus.). 250p. 1986. 127.00 (*0-08-032582-3*, Pub. by PPL UK) Franklin.

Structural Analysis (with Software) Louis C. Tartaglione. 560p. 1991. text ed. write for info. (*0-07-909703-0*) McGraw.

Structural & cis-trans Isomerism in Carbon Compounds. Conrad L. Stanitski. (Modular Laboratory Program in Chemistry Ser.). 12p. (C). 1995. pap. text ed. 1.35 (*0-87540-467-7*, STRC 467-7) Chem Educ Res.

Structural & Dynamic Properties of Lipids & Membranes. Ed. by P. J. Quinn & R. J. Cherry. (Portland Press Research Monographs: Vol. 3). 250p. (C). 1992. text ed. 85.00 (*1-85578-014-3*, Pub. by Portland Pr Ltd UK) Ashgate Pub Co.

Structural & Dynamic Vibrations 1993. Ed. by A. Ertas et al. LC 92-55137. 281p. 1993. pap. 50.00 (*0-7918-0948-X*, H00780) ASME.

***Structural & Electronic Paradigms in Cluster Chemistry.** D. M. Mingos. LC 97-22417. (Structure & Bonding Ser.). 1997. write for info. (*3-540-62791-X*); write for info. (*0-387-62791-X*) Spr-Verlag.

Structural & Functional Abnormalities in Subclinical Diabetic Angiopathy. Ed. by B. Weber et al. (Pediatric & Adolescent Endocrinology Ser.: Vol. 22). (Illus.). x, 242p. 1992. 213.25 (*3-8055-5606-3*) S Karger.

An Asterisk (*) at the beginning of an entry indicates that the title is appearing in BIP for the first time.

Structural & Functional Aspects of Enzyme Catalysis. Ed. by H. Eggerer & R. Hiber. (Colloquium Mosbach Ser.: Vol. 32). (Illus.). 280p. 1982. 45.00 (*0-387-11110-7*) Spr-Verlag.

Structural & Functional Aspects of Transport in Roots. B. C. Loughman et al. (Developments in Plant & Soil Sciences Ser.). (C). 1900. pap. text ed. 79.00 (*0-7923-0061-0*) Kluwer Ac.

Structural & Functional Changes in the Joint Family System: A Study Based on D.O.M. Workers. J. L. Raina. (C). 1989. 25.00 (*81-7022-237-0*, Pub. by Concept II) S Asia.

Structural & Functional Organization of the Neocortex: Proceedings of a Symposium in the Memory of Otto D. Creutzfeldt, May 1993. Ed. by B. Albowitz et al. LC 94-16023. 1994. 135.00 (*0-387-57205-8*) Spr-Verlag.

Structural & Functional Organization of the Placenta. Ed. by P. Kaufmann & B. F. King. (Bibliotheca Anatomica Ser.: No. 22). (Illus.). viii, 164p. 1982. 122.50 (*3-8055-3520-1*) S Karger.

***Structural & Functional Responses to Environmental Stresses: Water Shortage.** K. H. Kreeb. 308p. 1989. 75.00 (*90-5103-027-4*, Pub. by SPB Acad Pub NE) Balogh.

Structural & Lexical Comparison of the Tunica, Chitimacha & Atakapa Languages. Ed. by John R. Swanton. (Bureau of American Ethnology Bulletins Ser.). 99p. 1995. lib. bdg. 79.00 (*0-7812-4068-9*) Rprt Serv.

Structural & Lexical Comparison of the Tunica, Chitimacha & Atakapa Languages. John R. Swanton. reprint ed. 19.00 (*0-403-03699-2*) Scholarly.

***Structural & Magnetic Phase.** 1988. 131.95 (*0-387-96710-9*) Spr-Verlag.

***Structural & Mechanical Properties of Glassy Polymers.** Ed. by M. S. Arzhakov et al. 295p. (C). 1997. lib. bdg. 79.00 (*1-56072-434-X*) Nova Sci Pubs.

Structural & Multidisciplinary Optimization: Proceedings of the First World Congress of Multidisciplinary Optimization, Goslar, Germany, Held May 28-June 2, 1995. Ed. by Niels Olhoff & George I. Rozvany. 960p. 1996. 188.50 (*0-08-042267-5*, Pergamon Pr) Elsevier.

Structural & Other Alternatives for the Federal Courts of Appeals: Report to the U. S. Congress & the Judicial Conference of the U. S. Ed. by Judith A. McKenna. (Illus.). 179p. (Orig.). (C). 1994. pap. text ed. 35.00 (*0-7881-1575-8*) DIANE Pub.

Structural & Phase Stability of Alloys. Ed. by J. L. Moran-Lopez et al. LC 92-8513. (Illus.). 278p. (C). 1992. 79.50 (*0-306-44211-6*, Plenum Pr) Plenum.

Structural & Residual Stress Analysis by Nondestructive Methods: Evaluation & Application. V. Hauk & W. Reimers. 1996. write for info. (*0-614-17897-5*, North Holland) Elsevier.

Structural & Sectoral Adjustment: World Bank Experience, 1980 - 1992. Carl A. Jayarajah et al. LC 94-23671. (Operations Evaluation Studies). 377p. 1995. 21.95 (*0-8213-3122-1*, 13122) World Bank.

Structural & Specialty Adhesives: Update, No. C-009X. Business Communications Co., Inc. Staff. 197p. 1991. 1,950.00 (*0-89336-797-4*) BCC.

Structural & Stress Analysis. T. H. Megson. 592p. 1996. pap. text ed. 39.95 (*0-470-23597-7*) Wiley.

Structural & Stress Analysis. T. H. Megson. 1996. pap. text ed. 39.95 (*0-470-23563-2*) Halsted Pr.

Structural & Tectonic Modelling Had Its Application to Petroleum Geology. Ed. by R. M. Larsen et al. 550p. 1992. 219.75 (*0-444-88607-9*) Elsevier.

Structural Anthropology, Vol. 1. Claude Levi-Strauss. LC 63-17344. 432p. 1974. pap. 22.00 (*0-465-09516-X*) Basic.

Structural Anthropology, Vol. 2. Claude Levi-Strauss. Tr. by Monique Layton. LC 82-16115. xvi, 400p. 1983. pap. text ed. 21.00 (*0-226-47491-7*) U Ch Pr.

***Structural Applications of Mechanical Alloying: Proceedings of an ASM International Conference, Myrtle Beach, South Carolina, March 27-29, 1990.** ASM International Staff. Ed. by F. H. Froes et al. LC 90-62191. (Illus.). 302p. 1990. reprint ed. pap. 86.10 (*0-608-02615-8*, 2063273) Bks Demand.

Structural Appraisal of Traditional Buildings. Patrick Robson. 200p. 1990. text ed. 69.95 (*0-566-09081-3*, Pub. by Gower UK) Ashgate Pub Co.

Structural Approach to Direct Practice in Social Work. Gale G. Wood & Ruth R. Middleman. 277p. 1989. text ed. 32.50 (*0-231-05506-4*) Col U Pr.

Structural Approach to the Analysis of Drama. Paul M. Levitt. LC 79-159466. (De Proprietatibus Litterarum, Ser. Major: No. 15). 119p. 1971. text ed. 25.40 (*90-279-1841-4*) Mouton.

Structural Aspects of Homogeneous, Heterogeneous & Biological Catalysis. Ed. by L. J. Guggenberger et al. (Transactions of the American Crystallographic Association Ser.: Vol. 14). 141p. 1978. pap. 25.00 (*0-686-60384-2*) Polycrystal Bk Serv.

***Structural Aspects of Manufacturing.** pap. 7.95 (*0-8213-3807-2*, 13807) World Bank.

Structural Assessment: The Use of Large & Full Scale Testing. F. K. Garas et al. (Illus.). 391p. 1988. 140.00 (*0-408-00356-1*) Buttrwrth-Heinemann.

Structural Basis of Architecture. Bjorn N. Sandaker & Arne P. Eggen. LC 92-19153. (Illus.). 224p. 1992. 35.00 (*0-8230-4936-1*, Whitney Lib) Watsn-Guptill.

Structural Basis of Muscular Contraction. John M. Squire. LC 81-2321. 716p. 1981. 120.00 (*0-306-40582-2*, Plenum Pr) Plenum.

Structural Behaviour of Concrete with Coarse Lightweight Aggregates. Centre for Civil Engineering Research & Codes Staff. (CUR Report Ser.: No. 173). (Illus.). 76p. (C). 1995. text ed. 85.00 (*90-5410-625-5*, Pub. by A A Balkema NE) Ashgate Pub Co.

Structural Behaviour of Timber. Borg Madsen. 456p. 1992. 72.00 (*0-614-16836-8*, TEL01-1) Am Soc Civil Eng.

Structural Biology: The State of the Art, 2 vols., Set. Ed. by Sarma et al. (Illus.). 1994. lib. bdg. 250.00 (*0-940030-42-X*) Adenine Pr.

Structural Biology: The State of the Art, Vol. 1. Ed. by Sarma et al. (Illus.). 338p. 1994. lib. bdg. 125.00 (*0-940030-43-8*) Adenine Pr.

Structural Biology: The State of the Art, Vol. 2. Ed. by Sarma et al. (Illus.). 380p. 1994. lib. bdg. 125.00 (*0-940030-44-6*) Adenine Pr.

Structural Biology of Palms. P. B. Tomlinson. (Illus.). 492p. 1990. 125.00 (*0-19-854572-X*) OUP.

***Structural Biology of Viruses.** Ed. by Wah Chiu et al. LC 95-26844. (Illus.). 464p. 1997. 90.00 (*0-19-508627-9*) OUP.

***Structural Biology of Viruses.** Robert Garcea. Ed. by Wah Chiu & Roger M. Burnett. (Illus.). 464p. 1997. pap. 55.00 (*0-19-511850-2*) OUP.

Structural Biomaterials. Julian F. Vincent. (Illus.). 256p. 1990. text ed. 49.50 (*0-691-08558-7*); pap. text ed. 24.95 (*0-691-02513-4*) Princeton U Pr.

Structural Botany, Physiology, Genetics, Taxomony & Geobotany. Ed. by H. D. Behnke & K. Esser. (Progress in Botany Ser.: Vol. 56). 400p. 1995. 235.95 (*3-540-58407-2*) Spr-Verlag.

Structural Botany, Physiology, Genetics, Taxonomy, Geobotany. Ed. by H. D. Behnke et al. (Progress in Botany Ser.: Vol. 54). (Illus.). 576p. 1993. 262.95 (*0-387-56358-X*) Spr-Verlag.

***Structural Botany, Physiology, Genetics, Taxonomy, Geobotany.** Ed. by H. D. Behnke et al. (Progress in Botany Ser.: Vol. 58). (Illus.). 616p. 1996. 269.00 (*3-540-61329-3*) Spr-Verlag.

Structural Budget Deficits in the Federal Government: Causes, Consequences, & Remedies. Khi V. Thai. LC 86-33961. (Illus.). 304p. (Orig.). 1987. pap. text ed. 27.00 (*0-8191-6139-X*) U Pr of Amer.

Structural Carbohydrates in the Liver: Falk Symposium, No 34. Ed. by Werner Reutter et al. 600p. 1983. lib. bdg. 225.50 (*0-85200-711-6*) Kluwer Ac.

Structural Carbon. 197p. 1989. 2,450.00 (*0-89336-701-X*, GB-120) BCC.

Structural Ceramics Joining II. Ed. by A. J. Moorhead et al. (Ceramic Transactions Ser.: Vol. 35). 334p. 1993. 69.00 (*0-944904-65-3*, TRANS035) Am Ceramic.

Structural Ceramics/Fracture Mechanics: Materials Research Society International Symposium Proceedings-IMAM. Ed. by Y. Hamano et al. 566p. 1989. text ed. 75.00 (*1-55899-034-8*, IMAM-5) Materials Res.

Structural Change & Economic Development: The Role of the Service Sector. Norman Gemmell. LC 85-24996. 214p. 1986. text ed. 39.95 (*0-312-76669-6*) St Martin.

Structural Change & Economic Growth: A Theoretical Essay on the Dynamics of the Wealth of Nations. Luigi L. Pasinetti. LC 80-41496. 296p. 1983. pap. 22.95 (*0-521-27410-9*) Cambridge U Pr.

Structural Change & Small-Farm Agriculture in Northwest Portugal. Eric Monke et al. LC 92-54973. (Food Systems & Agrarian Change Ser.). 240p. (C). 1993. 42.50 (*0-8014-2640-5*) Cornell U Pr.

Structural Change, Economic Interdependence & World Development: Proceedings of the Seventh World Congress of the International Economic Association, Madrid, Spain, Vol. 1. Ed. by Victor L. Urquidi. LC 86-31371. 220p. 1987. Basic & Issues. text ed. 49.95 (*0-312-00415-X*) St Martin.

Structural Change, Employment & Unemployment in Market & Transition Economies. (UN/ECE Discussion Papers: Vol.3, No. 1). 23p. 1994. pap. 23.00 (*92-1-100675-9*, E.GV.94.0.2) UN.

Structural Change in a Developing Economy: Colombia's Problems & Prospects. Richard R. Nelson et al. LC 72-146645. (Rand Corporation Research Study Ser.). (Illus.). 336p. reprint ed. pap. 95.80 (*0-685-44421-X*, 2032642) Bks Demand.

Structural Change in African Agriculture. large type ed. 56p. 1990. 10.00 (*0-685-53326-3*) Intl Food Policy.

Structural Change in an Urban Industrial Region: The Northeastern Ohio Case. Ed. by David L. McKee & Richard E. Bennett. LC 86-30652. 268p. 1987. text ed. 59.95 (*0-275-92353-3*, C2353, Praeger Pubs) Greenwood.

Structural Change in Banking. Ed. by Michael Klausner & Lawrence J. White. LC 92-41872. 372p. 1992. text ed. 60.00 (*1-55623-600-X*) Irwin Prof Pubng.

Structural Change in Macroeconomic Models. M. J. Vilares. 1986. lib. bdg. 146.00 (*90-247-3277-8*) Kluwer Ac.

Structural Change in the American Economy. Anne P. Carter. LC 73-95516. (Studies in Technology & Society). 310p. 1970. 37.00 (*0-674-84370-3*) HUP.

Structural Change in the U. K. Economy. Ed. by Ciaran Driver & Paul Dunne. LC 92-16216. (Illus.). 300p. (C). 1993. text ed. 59.95 (*0-521-41569-1*) Cambridge U Pr.

Structural Change in the World Economy. Ed. by Allan Webster & John H. Dunning. 208p. (C). (gr. 13). 1990. text ed. 79.95 (*0-415-02420-X*, A3962) Routledge.

Structural Change in Turkish Society. (Turkish Studies Book Ser.). 14.95 (*1-878318-02-0*) IN Univ Turkish.

Structural Changes in Consumption & Trade in Steel: 1994. (ECE Steel Ser.). 209p. 1994. 32.00 (*92-1-116619-5*) UN.

Structural Changes in Foreign Exchange Markets. Hiroya Akiba. (Illus.). xi, 318p. 1994. 39.00 (*81-7024-602-4*, Pub. by Ashish Pub Hse II) Nataraj Bks.

Structural Changes in Ports & the Competitiveness of Latin American & Caribbean Foreign Trade. (Cuadernos de la CEPAL Ser.: No. 65). 125p. 1990. 17.50 (*92-1-121161-1*, 90.II.G.10) UN.

Structural Changes in Puerto Rico's Economy 1947-1976. Robert J. Tata. LC 80-19080. (Papers in International Studies: Latin America Ser.: No. 9). (Illus.). 104p. (Orig.). (C). 1981. pap. 12.00 (*0-89680-107-1*, Ohio U Ctr Intl) Ohio U Pr.

Structural Changes in Tanzanian Poverty over the Last 15 Years: A Comparison Using Survey Data. Alexander H. Sarris. (Working Papers: No. 59). 35p. (C). 1994. pap. 7.00 (*1-56401-159-3*) Cornell Food.

Structural Changes in the World Economy. Bela Kadar. LC 83-10954. 250p. 1984. text ed. 29.95 (*0-312-76671-8*) St Martin.

Structural Changes in U. S. Labor Markets: Causes & Consequences. Ed. by Randall W. Eberts & Erica L. Groshen. LC 91-11478. 248p. (gr. 13). 1992. text ed. 67.95 (*0-87332-825-6*) M E Sharpe.

***Structural Changes Within the Global Forestry Sector.** 110p. (Orig.). 1997. pap. 40.00 (*0-935018-84-0*, 7290) Forest Prod.

Structural Chemistry of Silicates. Ed. by Adrian C. Wright. (Transactions of the American Crystallographic Association Ser.: Vol. 27). 349p. (Orig.). (C). 1993. pap. text ed. 25.00 (*0-937140-36-8*) Am Crystallographic.

Structural Clay Products. W. E. Brownell. LC 76-40216. (Applied Mineralogy Ser: Vol. 9). 1977. 91.95 (*0-387-81382-9*) Spr-Verlag.

Structural COBOL Programming: Interactive & Batch Processing. 602p. 1995. pap. 50.95 (*0-87709-892-1*) Course Tech.

Structural Communications & the Teacher of English. Charles L. Thompson et al. 139p. 1975. pap. text ed. 4.95 (*0-8422-0527-6*) Irvington.

Structural Competitiveness in the Pacific: Corporate & State Rivalries. Ed. by Gavin Boyd. LC 95-49729. (New Horizons in International Business Ser.). (Illus.). 328p. 1996. 80.00 (*1-85898-233-2*) E Elgar.

Structural Complexity, No. II. Jose L. Balcazar et al. (EATCS Monographs on Theoretical Computer Science: Vol. 22). (Illus.). 296p. 1990. 55.95 (*0-387-52079-1*) Spr-Verlag.

Structural Complexity I. Jose L. Balcazar et al. (EATCS Monographs on Theoretical Computer Science: Vol. 11). (Illus.). ix, 191p. 1988. 39.00 (*0-387-18622-0*) Spr-Verlag.

Structural Complexity I. Jose L. Balcazar et al. LC 94-36688. (Texts in Theoretical Computer Science Ser.). 1995. 39.00 (*3-540-58384-X*) Spr-Verlag.

Structural Concepts & Techniques I: Basic Concepts, Folding, & Structural Techniques. Ed. by Norman H. Foster & Edward A. Beaumont. (AAPG Treatise of Petroleum Geology Reprint Ser.: No. 9). (Illus.). 723p. 1988. pap. 10.00 (*0-89181-408-6*, 733) AAPG.

Structural Concepts & Techniques II: Basement-Involved Deformation. Ed. by Edward A. Beaumont. (Treatise of Petroleum Geology Reprint Ser.: No. 10). (Illus.). 479p. 1989. pap. 10.00 (*0-89181-409-4*, 735) AAPG.

Structural Concepts & Techniques III: Detached Deformation. Ed. by Edward A. Beaumont. (Treatise of Petroleum Geology Reprint Ser.: No. 11). (Illus.). 651p. 1989. pap. 10.00 (*0-89181-410-8*, 737) AAPG.

Structural Concrete: Theory & Its Application. A. S. Bruggeling. (Illus.). 504p. (C). 1991. text ed. 120.00 (*90-6191-182-6*, Pub. by A A Balkema NE) Ashgate Pub Co.

Structural Conflict: The Third World Against Global Liberalism. Stephen D. Krasner. (Studies in International Political Economy: Vol. 12). 1985. pap. 15.95 (*0-520-05478-4*) U CA Pr.

Structural Conflict: The Third World Against Global Liberalism. Stephen D. Krasner. LC 84-16332. (Studies in International Political Economy). 374p. reprint ed. pap. 106.60 (*0-7837-4812-4*, 2044459) Bks Demand.

Structural Considerations & Findings from Testing of Nuclear Components: Presented at the Joint Conference of the Pressure Vessels & Piping, Materials, Nuclear Engineering, Solar Energy Divisions, Denver, Colorado, June 21-25, 1981. Joint Conference of the Pressure Vessels & Piping, Materials, Nuclear Engineering, Solar Energy Divisions Staff. Ed. by L. K. Severud et al. LC 81-65369. (PVP Ser.: Vol. 49). (Illus.). 106p. reprint ed. pap. 30.30 (*0-8357-2901-X*, 2039137) Bks Demand.

Structural Contexts of Opportunities. Peter M. Blau. LC 94-10313. 244p. 1994. 32.50 (*0-226-05729-1*) U Ch Pr.

***Structural Control First European Conference.** 600p. 1997. 97.00 (*981-02-3019-2*) World Scientific Pub.

Structural Crashworthiness: Proceedings of the Structural Crashworthiness Conference, Liverpool University, 14-16 September 1983. Ed. by Norman Jones. 100p. 1983. pap. 46.00 (*0-08-031136-9*, Pergamon Pr) Elsevier.

Structural Criminology. John Hagan. LC 88-42887. (Crime, Law & Deviance Ser.). 294p. (C). 1989. text ed. 45.00 (*0-8135-1375-8*) Rutgers U Pr.

Structural Cybernetics: An Overview. N. Dean Meyer. (Orig.). 1995. pap. 8.95 (*0-9641635-1-9*) NDMA Pubng.

Structural Depths of Indian Thought. P. T. Raju. (SUNY Series in Philosophy). 599p. 1985. text ed. 64.50 (*0-88706-139-7*) State U NY Pr.

Structural Depths of Indian Thought. P. T. Raju. (SUNY Series in Philosophy). 599p. 1989. pap. text ed. 21.95 (*0-88706-140-0*) State U NY Pr.

Structural Description of the Macedonian Dialect of Dihovo: Phonology, Morphology, Texts, Lexicon. B. M. Groen. viii, 307p. 1977. pap. 35.00 (*90-316-0143-8*, Pub. by B R Gruener NE) Benjamins North Am.

Structural Design. B. Currie & R. Sharp. (Illus.). 208p. (Orig.). (C). 1990. 70.00 (*0-7487-0417-5*, Pub. by Stanley Thornes UK) Trans-Atl Phila.

Structural Design, Analysis & Testing. Ed. by A. H-S. Ang. LC 89-6766. 1086p. 1989. pap. text ed. 84.00 (*0-87262-700-4*, 700) Am Soc Civil Eng.

Structural Design & Crashworthiness of Automobiles. Ed. by T. K. Murthy & C. A. Brebbia. 1987. 72.00 (*0-931215-21-8*) Computational Mech MA.

Structural Design & Crashworthiness of Automobiles. Ed. by T. K. Murthy & Carlos A. Brebbia. 240p. 1987. 81.95 (*0-387-17504-0*) Spr-Verlag.

Structural Design & Drawing: Reinforced Concrete & Steel. N. Krishna Raju. 1993. 37.50 (*0-86311-189-0*, Pub. by Universities Pr II) Apt Bks.

Structural Design, Cementitious Products, & Case Histories: Proceedings of Three Sessions Sponsored by the Structural Division & the Michigan Section of ASCE. Ed. by Yogindra N. Anand. 129p. 1985. 17.00 (*0-87262-502-8*) Am Soc Civil Eng.

***Structural Design, Codes, & Special Building Projects.** Ed. by Council on Tall Buildings & Urban Habitats Staff. (Illus.). 119p. 1997. text ed. 25.00 (*0-939493-16-0*) Coun Tall Bldg.

***Structural Design for Architecture.** Angus J. MacDonald. 1997. pap. text ed. 37.95 (*0-7506-3090-6*) Buttrwrth-Heinemann.

***Structural Design for Hazardous Loads: The Role of Physical Testing.** Ed. by Clarke & Garas. (Illus.). 488p. 1992. text ed. 140.50 (*0-419-17250-5*, E & FN Spon) Routledge Chapman & Hall.

Structural Design Guide for Hardwood Plywood, HP-SG-86. 25p. 1986. 8.00 (*0-318-18928-3*) Hardwd Ply.

S

Structural Design Guide to AISC (LRFD) Specifications for Structural Steel Buildings. 2nd ed. Edward S. Hoffman et al. LC 95-14942. 312p. (gr. 13). 1995. text ed. 64.95 (*0-412-06871-0*, Chap & Hall NY) Chapman & Hall.

Structural Design Guide to AISC Specifications for Buildings. Paul F. Rice & Edward S. Hoffman. LC 75-40491. (Illus.). 368p. reprint ed. pap. 104.90 (*0-317-11089-6*, 2007877) Bks Demand.

***Structural Design Guide to the ACI Building Code.** 4th rev. ed. Edward S. Hoffmann et al. LC 97-6021. (Illus.). 528p. 1997. 79.95 (*0-412-12981-7*) Chapman & Hall.

Structural Design in Metals. 2nd ed. Clifford D. Williams & Ernest C. Harris. LC 57-6824. 673p. reprint ed. pap. 180.00 (*0-317-08682-0*, 2012442) Bks Demand.

Structural Design in Wood. Judith J. Stalnaker & Ernest C. Harris. (Illus.). 448p. (gr. 13). 1989. text ed. 68.95 (*0-442-23300-0*) Chapman & Hall.

Structural Design in Wood. 2nd ed. Judith J. Stalnaker & Ernest C. Harris. 450p. (gr. 13). 1996. text ed. 68.95 (*0-412-10631-0*, Chap & Hall NY) Chapman & Hall.

Structural Design of Air & Gas Ducts for Power Stations & Industrial Boiler Applications: Air & Gas Duct Structural Design Committee of the Civil Engineers. Contrib. by Air & Gas Structural Design Committee. LC 95-24709. 312p. 1995. 28.00 (*0-7844-0112-8*) Am Soc Civil Eng.

Structural Design of Asphalt Concrete Pavement Systems. (Special Reports: No. 126). 207p. 1971. 6.00 (*0-309-01972-9*) Transport Res Bd.

Structural Design of Asphalt Concrete Pavements to Prevent Fatigue Cracking. (Special Reports: No. 140). 201p. 1973. 6.00 (*0-309-02160-X*) Transport Res Bd.

***Structural Design of Closure Structures for Local Flood Protection Projects.** American Society of Civil Engineers Staff. LC 96-45930. (Technical Engineering & Design Guides As Adapted from the U. S. Army Corps of Engineers). 1996. write for info. (*0-7844-0211-6*) Am Soc Civil Eng.

***Structural Design of Masonry.** 2nd ed. Andrew Orton. (C). 1992. pap. text ed. 57.95 (*0-582-09101-2*, Pub. by Longman UK) Longman.

Structural Design of Nuclear Plant Facilities, 3 vols. 1263p. 1973. pap. 58.00 (*0-87262-155-3*) Am Soc Civil Eng.

Structural Design of Nuclear Plant Facilities, 3 vols. 2118p. 1975. pap. 80.00 (*0-87262-172-3*) Am Soc Civil Eng.

Structural Design of Steel Joist Roofs to Resist Ponding Loads. (Technical Digest Ser.: No. 3). 1971. 10.00 (*0-318-04227-4*) Steel Joist Inst.

Structural Design of Steel Joist Roofs to Resist Uplift Loads. (Technical Digest Ser.: No. 6). 1994. 10.00 (*0-318-04230-4*) Steel Joist Inst.

Structural Design Via Optimality Criteria: The Prager Approach to Structural Optimization. George I. Rozvany. (C). 1989. lib. bdg. 220.50 (*90-247-3613-7*) Kluwer Ac.

Structural Detailing for Technicians. Gerald L. Weaver. (Illus.). 256p. (C). 1974. text ed. 41.50 (*0-07-068712-9*) McGraw.

Structural Details for Masonry Construction. Morton Newman. 1988. pap. text ed. 32.95 (*0-07-046361-1*) McGraw.

Structural Drafting. David L. Goetsch. (Drafting Ser.). (Illus.). 355p. (Orig.). (C). 1982. pap. 34.95 (*0-8273-1930-4*); teacher ed., pap. 16.00 (*0-8273-1931-2*) Delmar.

Structural Drafting. fac. ed. Rip B. Weaver. LC 76-15454. (Illus.). 207p. pap. 59.00 (*0-7837-7432-X*, 2047227) Bks Demand.

Structural Drafting. 2nd ed. David L. Goetsch. LC 93-32937. 365p. (Orig.). 1994. pap. 36.95 (*0-8273-6302-8*) Delmar.

Structural Drafting. 2nd ed. David L. Goetsch. 39p. (Orig.). 1994. teacher ed. 16.00 (*0-8273-6303-6*) Delmar.

Structural Drafting Workbook. fac. ed. Rip B. Weaver. LC 76-15454. (Illus.). 112p. pap. 32.00 (*0-7837-7410-9*, 2047204) Bks Demand.

Structural Dynamic Aspects of Bladed Disk Assemblies: Presented at the Winter Annual Meeting of ASME, NY Dec. 5-10, 1976 (Sponsored by Structures & Materials Comm., Aerospace Div., Structures & Dynamics Comm., Gas Turbine Division) Ed. by A. V. Srinivasan. LC 76-28856. 120p. reprint ed. pap. 34.20 (*0-317-11231-7*, 2016850) Bks Demand.

*__Structural Dynamics.__ Tedesco. (C). 1998. text ed. write for info. (*0-673-98052-9*) Addison-Wesley.

Structural Dynamics: Proceedings of the First European Conference, Bochum, 5-7 June 1990, 2 vols. Ed. by W. B. Kratzig et al. (Illus.). 1248p. (C). 1991. Set. text ed. 205.00 (*90-6191-168-0*, Pub. by A A Balkema NE) Ashgate Pub Co.

*__Structural Dynamics: Proceedings of the 3rd European Conference on Structural Dynamics, EURODYN '96, Florence, Italy, 5-8 June 1996, 2 vols., Set.__ Ed. by G. Augusti et al. (Illus.). 1178p. (C). 1996. text ed. 170.00 (*90-5410-813-4*, Pub. by A A Balkema NE) Ashgate Pub Co.

Structural Dynamics: Proceedings, 2nd European Conference, Eurodyn 93, Trondheim, Norway, June 1993. Anthony N. Kounadis et al. (Illus.). 1300p. 1993. text ed. 170.00 (*90-5410-336-1*, Pub. by A A Balkema NE) Ashgate Pub Co.

Structural Dynamics: Recent Advances. Ed. by G. I. Schueller. (Illus.). x, 475p. 1991. 146.95 (*0-387-53593-4*) Spr-Verlag.

*__Structural Dynamics: Solutions Manual.__ Tedesco. (C). 1998. teacher ed., pap. text ed. write for info. (*0-673-97411-1*) Addison-Wesley.

*__Structural Dynamics: Theory & Computation.__ 3rd ed. Mario Paz. 600p. (C). (gr. 13 up). 1990. text ed. 69.95 (*0-412-07141-X*) Chapman & Hall.

*__Structural Dynamics: Theory & Computation.__ 4th ed. Mario Paz. LC 96-37415. 1997. write for info. (*0-412-07461-3*) Chapman & Hall.

Structural Dynamics & Soil Structure Interaction, 3 vols., Vol. 1: Structural Dynamics & Soil Structure Inter. Ed. by A. S. Cakmak. LC 89-85630. (SDEE Ser.: Vol. 4). 498p. 1989. 152.00 (*0-945824-36-X*) Computational Mech MA.

Structural Dynamics & Vibration 1994, Vol. 63. Ed. by B. A. Ovunc et al. LC 93-74684. 168p. 1994. pap. 42.50 (*0-7918-1191-3*) ASME.

Structural Dynamics & Vibration, 1995: Proceedings: The Energy & Environmental EXPO '95 - the Energy-Sources Technology Conference & Exhibition (1995: Houston, TX) Ed. by B. A. Ovunc et al. LC 93-74684. (PD Ser.: Vol. 70). 245p. 1995. pap. 94.00 (*0-7918-1293-6*, H00925) ASME.

Structural Dynamics & Vibrations. Vol. 7. 360p. 1994. write for info. (*0-318-72843-5*, H0912G) ASME.

*__Structural Dynamics for the Practising Engineer.__ Irvine. (Illus.). 224p. (Orig.). 1986. pap. text ed. 33.00 (*0-419-15930-4*, E & FN Spon) Routledge Chapman & Hall.

Structural Dynamics for the Practising Engineer. H. M. Irvine. 192p. (C). 1986. text ed. 55.00 (*0-04-624007-1*) Routledge Chapman & Hall.

Structural Dynamics for the Practising Engineer. H. M. Irvine. (Illus.). 224p. 1992. pap. 39.95 (*0-04-446003-1*, A7499) Routledge Chapman & Hall.

Structural Dynamics in Practice: Guide for Professional Engineers. Arthur Bolton. LC 93-1511. (International Series in Civil Engineering). 1994. text ed. 49.00 (*0-07-707813-6*) McGraw.

Structural Dynamics of Industrial Policy. Ed. by Bodo B Gemper. 208p. 1985. pap. 24.95 (*3-87895-284-8*) Transaction Pubs.

Structural Dynamics of Large Scale & Complex Systems. Ed. by C. Pierre & N. C. Perkins. LC 93-72635. (DE Ser.: Vol. 59). 160p. 1993. 55.00 (*0-7918-1176-X*, G00820) ASME.

Structural Economic Change & the Powers of State Government: The Viability of Regional Development Strategies. Robert Wilson. (Working Paper Ser.: No. 45). 38p. 1988. pap. 5.00 (*0-89940-526-6*) LBJ Sch Pub Aff.

Structural Economic Dynamics: A Theory of the Economic Consequences of Human Learning. Luigi L. Pasinetti. LC 92-13438. (Illus.). 216p. (C). 1993. text ed. 49.95 (*0-521-43282-0*) Cambridge U Pr.

Structural Effects in Electrolysis & Oxygen Electrochemistry. Ed. by D. Scherson et al. LC 92-71312. (Proceedings Ser.: Vol. 92-11). 288p. 1992. 38.00 (*1-56677-011-4*) Electrochem Soc.

Structural Effects on Equilibria in Organic Chemistry. Jack Hine. LC 80-11714. 362p. 1980. reprint ed. lib. bdg. 31.50 (*0-89874-144-0*) Krieger.

Structural Electron Crystallography. Douglas L. Dorset. LC 95-34721. 452p. (C). 1995. 69.50 (*0-306-45049-6*, Plenum Pr) Plenum.

Structural Elements: Biology of Nervous Tissue see Central Nervous System of Vertebrates: A General Survey of Its Comparative Anatomy with an Introduction to Pertinent Fundamental Biologic & Logical Concepts

Structural Elements Design Manual. Trevor Draycott. (Illus.). 235p. 1990. pap. 44.95 (*0-7506-0313-5*) Buttrwrth-Heinemann.

*__Structural Elements of the German Novella from Goethe to Thomas Mann.__ Henry H. Remak. (North American Studies in Nineteenth-Century German Literature: Vol. 14). 344p. (C). 1996. text ed. 54.95 (*0-8204-3451-5*) P Lang Pubng.

Structural Elucidation & Chemical Transformation of Natural Products & Physical Methods for Investigation of Natural Products see Eleventh IUPAC International Symposium on Chemistry: Bulgarian Academy of Sciences

Structural Engineer. Jack Rudman. (Career Examination Ser.: C-3335). 1994. pap. 39.95 (*0-8373-3335-0*) Nat Learn.

*__Structural Engineer License Review.__ 2nd rev. ed. Alan Williams. (Illus.). 565p. 1996. 69.50 (*1-57645-016-3*) Engineering.

Structural Engineering Analysis by Finite Elements. Robert J. Melosh. 384p. 1990. boxed 53.00 (*0-13-855701-2*) P-H.

Structural Engineering Analysis on Personal Computers. J. F. Fleming. 224p. 1986. write for info. (*0-07-021300-3*) McGraw.

*__Structural Engineering & Applied Mechanics Data Handbook, Vol. 1.__ Teng H. Hsu. LC 88-7227. (Illus.). 296p. pap. 84.40 (*0-608-05004-0*, 2065556) Bks Demand.

*__Structural Engineering & Applied Mechanics Data Handbook, Vol. 4.__ Teng H. Hsu. LC 88-7227. (Illus.). 400p. pap. 114.00 (*0-608-05005-9*, 2065556) Bks Demand.

Structural Engineering & Applied Mechanics Data Handbook Vol. 2: Frames. Teng H. Hsu. LC 88-7227. 544p. 1991. reprint ed. pap. 155.10 (*0-608-01334-X*, 2062078) Bks Demand.

Structural Engineering & Applied Mechanics Data Handbook Vol. 3: Plates. Teng H. Hsu. 358p. 1990. 59.00 (*0-87201-335-9*) Gulf Pub.

Structural Engineering & Construction, 3 vols., Vol. 1-3. Kanok-Nukulchai. 1986. pap. 165.00 (*0-08-034082-2*, Pergamon Pr) Elsevier.

Structural Engineering & Microcomputers. Ed. by Joseph J. Rencis & Robert L. Mullens. 80p. 1987. 13.00 (*0-87262-585-0*) Am Soc Civil Eng.

Structural Engineering Design in Practice. 3rd ed. R. K. Westbrook. (C). 1996. pap. text ed. 51.95 (*0-582-23630-4*) Addison-Wesley.

Structural Engineering Fracture Mechanics. A. Carpinteri. 1994. 121.00 (*0-419-17950-X*, E & FN Spon) Routledge Chapman & Hall.

Structural Engineering Handbook. 4th ed. Ed. by Edwin H. Gaylord et al. (Illus.). 1184p. 1996. text ed. 115.00 (*0-07-023724-7*) McGraw.

Structural Engineering in Natural Hazards Mitigation: Proceedings of Papers Presented at the Structures Congress '93, Held at the Hyatt Regency, Irvine, California, April 19-21, 1933. Ed. by A. H. Sang & R. Villaverde. LC 93-7114. 864p. 1993. 138.00 (*0-87262-910-4*) Am Soc Civil Eng.

Structural Engineering in Nuclear Facilities: Proceedings of a Conference Sponsored by the Committee on Nuclear Structures & Materials of the Structural Division, 2 vols. Ed. by Joseph J. Ucciferro. 1362p. 1984. 120.00 (*0-87262-412-9*) Am Soc Civil Eng.

Structural Engineering Materials. 4th ed. Ed. by N. Jackson & R. K. Dhir. 430p. (C). 1989. 68.95 (*0-89116-947-4*) Hemisp Pub.

Structural Engineering of Microwave Antennas: For Electrical, Mechanical, & Civil Engineers. Roy Levy. LC 95-45351. 376p. 1996. 149.95 (*0-7803-1020-9*, PC3681) Inst Electrical.

Structural Engineering, Vol. 1: Introduction to Design Concepts & Analysis. 2nd ed. Richard N. White et al. LC 75-174772. 336p. (C). reprint ed. 95.80 (*0-8357-9984-0*, 2019294) Bks Demand.

Structural Equation Modeling: Issues & Applications. Rick H. Hoyle. 336p. 1995. text ed. 52.00 (*0-8039-5317-8*); pap. text ed. 25.00 (*0-8039-5318-6*) Sage.

Structural Equation Modeling with EQS and EQS-Windows: Basic Concepts, Applications, and Programming. Barbara M. Byrne. LC 93-38513. 288p. (C). 1994. text ed. 46.00 (*0-8039-5091-8*); pap. text ed. 21.00 (*0-8039-5092-6*) Sage.

Structural Equation Modeling with Lisrel: Essentials & Advances. Leslie A. Hayduk. LC 87-2844. 464p. (C). 1988. text ed. 39.95 (*0-8018-3478-3*) Johns Hopkins.

*__Structural Equation Modeling with Lisrel, Prelis, & Simplis: Basic Concepts, Applications, & Programming.__ Barbara Byrne. 400p. 1998. write for info. (*0-8058-2924-5*) L Erlbaum Assocs.

Structural Evolution: An Illustrated History. B. S. Benjamin. (Illus.). 206p. (C). 1990. 50.00 (*0-942387-05-8*) AB Lit Hse.

Structural Evolution of the Western Transverse Ranges. Ed. by Thomas L. Davis & Jay S. Namson. (Illus.). 156p. (Orig.). 1987. pap. 8.00 (*1-878861-23-9*) Pac Section SEPM.

*__Structural Exegesis for New Testament Critics.__ Daniel Patte. LC 96-42565. 144p. 1996. reprint ed. pap. 16.00 (*1-56338-178-8*) TPI PA.

Structural Fabrics in Deep Sea Drilling Project Cores from Forearcs. Ed. by J. Casey Moore. (Memoir Ser.: No. 166). (Illus.). 168p. 1987. 4.00 (*0-8137-1166-5*) Geol Soc.

Structural Fabulation: An Essay on Fiction of the Future. Robert E. Scholes. LC 74-30167. (Ward-Phillips Lectures in English Language & Literature Ser: No. 7). 123p. reprint ed. pap. 35.10 (*0-318-34708-3*, 2031908) Bks Demand.

Structural Failure. Tomasz Wierzbick & Norman Jones. LC 88-18571. 551p. 1989. text ed. 125.00 (*0-471-63733-5*) Wiley.

*__Structural Failure: Technical, Legal & Insurance Aspects.__ Hans P. Rossmanith. (Illus.). 224p. 1995. text ed. 86.00 (*0-419-20710-4*, E & FN Spon) Routledge Chapman & Hall.

Structural Failure, Product Liability & Technical Insurance: Proceedings of the 4th International Conference on Structural Safety, Product Safety, Product Liability & Technical Insurance, Vienna, Austria, 6-9 July 1992. Ed. by H. P. Rossmanith. LC 92-38099. 1992. 213.25 (*0-444-89600-7*) Elsevier.

Structural Failures: Modes, Causes, Responsibilities. American Society of Civil Engineers Staff. (Illus.). 111p. reprint ed. pap. 31.70 (*0-317-08323-6*, 2019539) Bks Demand.

Structural Fatigue in Aircraft. American Society for Testing & Materials Staff. LC 66-28344. (American Society for Testing & Materials: No. 404). 207p. reprint ed. pap. 59.00 (*0-317-09263-4*, 2001130) Bks Demand.

Structural Fetal Abnormalities: The Total Picture. Ed. by Roger C. Sanders et al. LC 95-23082. 272p. (C). (gr. 13). 1995. pap. text ed. 62.95 (*0-8151-7838-7*) Mosby Yr Bk.

Structural Fire Protection: Manual of Practice. Ed. by T. T. Lie. 250p. 1992. text ed. 56.00 (*0-87262-888-4*) Am Soc Civil Eng.

Structural Foam: A Purchasing & Design Guide. Bruce C. Wendle. (Plastics Engineering Ser.: Vol. 9). 184p. 1985. 115.00 (*0-8247-7398-5*) Dekker.

Structural Form & Utterance Context in Lhasa Tibetan: Grammar & Indexicality in a Nonconfigurational Language. Asif Agha. LC 93-21593. (Monographs in Linguistics & the Philosophy of Language: Vol. 2). 270p. (C). 1993. text ed. 60.95 (*0-8204-2091-3*) P Lang Pubng.

Structural Fortran 77 for Engineers & Scientists. 5th ed. Delores Etter. LC 96-38608. (C). 1997. text ed. 42.95 (*0-201-49854-5*) Addison-Wesley.

*__Structural Foundation Designer's Manual.__ W. G. Curtin et al. LC 93-12682. 377p. 1997. pap. 79.95 (*0-632-04215-X*, TA775) Blackwell Sci.

Structural Foundations Manual for Low-Rise Buildings. M. F. Atkinson. LC 93-3334. 1993. write for info. (*0-419-17940-2*, E & FN Spon) Routledge Chapman & Hall.

Structural Foundations on Rock: Proceedings of the International Conference, Sydney, 7-9th May 1980, 2 vols., Set. Ed. by P. J. Pells. 494p. (C). 1981. text ed. 210.00 (*90-6191-072-2*, Pub. by A A Balkema NE) Ashgate Pub Co.

Structural Functions in Music. Wallace Berry. 480p. 1987. reprint ed. pap. 11.95 (*0-486-25384-8*) Dover.

Structural Funding & Employment in the European Union: Financing the Path to Integration. Jeffrey Harrop. LC 95-21331. (Illus.). 192p. (C). 1996. text ed. 80.00 (*1-85898-219-7*) E Elgar.

*__Structural Funds in 1995 - Seventh Annual Report.__ European Communities Staff. 340p. 1996. pap. 40.00 (*92-827-8941-1*, CX98-96-405-ENC, Pub. by Europ Com UK) Bernan Associates.

Structural Geology. Hatcher. 1990. lab manual ed., pap. text ed. 42.00 (*0-675-20627-8*, Merrill Coll) P-H.

Structural Geology. Robert J. Twiss & Eldridge M. Moores. LC 92-4058. (Illus.). 532p. (C). 1995. text ed. write for info. (*0-7167-2252-6*) W H Freeman.

Structural Geology. Ben A. Van Der Pluijm & Stephen Marshak. 448p. (C). 1997. per. write for info. (*0-697-17234-1*) Wm C Brown Pubs.

Structural Geology: An Introduction to Geometrical Techniques. 3rd ed. Donal M. Ragan. LC 84-19658. 405p. 1985. Net. pap. text ed. 34.50 (*0-471-08043-8*) Wiley.

Structural Geology: An Introduction to Geometrical Techniques. 4th ed. Donal M. Ragan. 400p. 1997. pap. text ed. write for info. (*0-471-62413-6*) Wiley.

Structural Geology: Fundamentals & Modern Developments. Sanjib K. Ghosh. LC 92-31294. 548p. 1993. text ed. 36.75 (*0-08-041879-1*, Prgamon Press); pap. text ed. 36.95 (*0-08-041878-3*, Prgamon Press) Buttrwrth-Heinemann.

Structural Geology: Principles, Concepts, & Problems. 2nd ed. Robert D. Hatcher. 528p. (C). 1994. text ed. 75.00 (*0-02-355713-3*, Macmillan Coll) P-H.

Structural Geology & Personal Computers. De Paor. LC 96-42328. (Computer Methods in the Geosciences Ser.). 546p. 1996. 154.00 (*0-08-042430-9*, Pergamon Pr) Elsevier.

*__Structural Geology & Personal Computers.__ De Paor. (Computer Methods in the Geosciences Ser.). 546p. 1996. pap. 48.00 (*0-08-043110-0*, Pergamon Pr) Elsevier.

Structural Geology & Petroleum Potential of Southwest Elko County, Nevada. Ed. by James H. Trexler et al. (NPS Fieldtrip Guidebooks Ser.). (Illus.). 100p. 1992. pap. text ed. write for info. (*1-881308-04-9*) NV Petroleum.

Structural Geology & Physiography of the Northern End of the Teton Range, Wyoming. Rudolph W. Edmund. LC 52-3353. (Augustana College Library Publications: No. 23). 82p. 1951. pap. 7.00 (*0-910182-18-3*) Augustana Coll.

Structural Geology & Physiography of the Teton Pass Area, Wyoming. Leland Horberg. LC 39-7044. (Augustana College Library Publications: No. 16). 86p. 1938. pap. 10.00 (*0-910182-11-6*) Augustana Coll.

Structural Geology Exercises with Glaciotectonic Examples. Aber. 140p. 1988. teacher ed., pap. text ed. 24.95 (*0-88725-087-4*) Hunter Textbks.

Structural Geology of Fold & Thrust Belts. Ed. by Shankar Mitra & George W. Fisher. (Studies in Earth & Space Sciences). (Illus.). 296p. 1992. text ed. 55.00 (*0-8018-4350-2*) Johns Hopkins.

Structural Geology of Rocks & Regions. 2nd ed. George H. Davis & Steven Reynolds. LC 95-40790. 512p. 1996. text ed. 45.00 (*0-471-52621-5*) Wiley.

Structural Geology of Silurian & Devonian Strata in the Mid-Hudson Valley, New York: Fold-Thrust Belt Tectonics in Miniature. Stephen Marshak. (New York State Museum Map & Chart Ser.: No. 41). (Illus.). 66p. (Orig.). 1990. pap. 15.00 (*1-55557-200-6*) NYS Museum.

Structural Geology of the Cache Creek Area, Gros Ventre Mountains, Wyoming. Vincent E. Nelson. LC 43-15519. (Augustana College Library Publications: No. 18). 46p. 1942. pap. 6.00 (*0-910182-13-2*) Augustana Coll.

*__Structural Glass.__ Rice & Dutton. (Illus.). 144p. 1995. pap. text ed. 59.95 (*0-419-19940-3*, E & FN Spon) Routledge Chapman & Hall.

Structural Glycoproteins in Cell-Matrix Interactions. Ed. by L. Robert et al. (Frontiers of Matrix Biology Ser.: Vol. 11). (Illus.). viii, 184p. 1986. 113.75 (*3-8055-4318-2*) S Karger.

*__Structural Grouts.__ Ed. by Domone & Jefferis. (Illus.). 240p. 1993. text ed. 110.95 (*0-7514-0097-1*, Pub. by Blackie Acad & Prof UK) Routledge Chapman & Hall.

*__Structural Hearing.__ Felix Salzer. pap. 14.95 (*0-486-22275-6*) Dover.

Structural Holes: The Social Structure of Competition. Ronald S. Burt. (Illus.). 313p. 1992. text ed. 49.95 (*0-674-84372-X*) HUP.

Structural Holes: The Social Structure of Competition. Ronald S. Burt. (Illus.). 328p. (C). 1995. pap. text ed. 16.95 (*0-674-84371-1*) HUP.

Structural Hypothesis: An Evolutionary Hypothesis. Arnold Rothstein. LC 83-18490. vii, 194p. 1984. 31.50 (*0-8236-6175-X*) Intl Univs Pr.

*__Structural Impact.__ 591p. 1998. pap. text ed. 49.95 (*0-521-62890-3*) Cambridge U Pr.

Structural Impact. Norman Jones. (Illus.). 591p. (C). 1990. text ed. 185.00 (*0-521-30180-7*) Cambridge U Pr.

Structural Induction on Partial Algebras. Horst Reichel. 206p. (C). 1984. 85.00 (*0-685-36876-9*, Pub. by Collets) St Mut.

Structural Inorganic Chemistry. 5th ed. A. F. Wells. (Illus.). 1382p. 1984. text ed. 245.00 (*0-19-855370-6*) OUP.

Structural Inquiry into the Symbolic Representation of Ideas. Ed. by Arnold Grava. LC 69-10555. (Studies in Philosophy: No. 18). (Orig.). 1969. pap. text ed. 20.80 (*0-686-22464-7*) Mouton.

Structural Integrity - Theory & Experiment. Ed. by E. S. Folias. (C). 1989. lib. bdg. 145.00 (*0-7923-0174-9*) Kluwer Ac.

Structural Integrity in Aging Aircraft: Proceedings of the ASME International Mechanical Engineering Congress & Exposition, 1995, San Francisco, CA. Ed. by C. I. Chang & C. T. Sun. (1995 ASME International Mechanical Engineering Congress & Exposition Ser.: AD-Vol. 47). 332p. 1995. 96.00 (*0-7918-1724-5*, H01006) ASME.

Structural Integrity Monitoring. Raoph A. Collacott. 450p. 1986. text ed. 69.95 (*0-412-21920-4*, 9640) Chapman & Hall.

*__Structural Integrity NDE Risk & Material Performance for Petroleum Process & Power.__ Ed. by M. Prager. 373p. 1996. pap. text ed. 120.00 (*0-7918-1783-0*, TS283) ASME Pr.

Structural Integrity of Aging Airplanes. Ed. by S. N. Atluri et al. (Computational Mechanics Ser.). (Illus.). 512p. 1991. 139.95 (*0-387-53461-X*) Spr-Verlag.

Structural Integrity of Fastners, STP 1236. Ed. by Pir M. Toor. LC 95-12078. (Special Technical Publication Ser.: Vol. 1236). (Illus.). 195p. 1995. text ed. 69.00 (*0-8031-2017-6*, 04-012360-30) ASTM.

Structural Integrity of Pressure Vessels, Piping, & Components. Ed. by H. H. Chung et al. (Proceedings of the 1995 ASME/JSME Pressure Vessels & Piping Conference Ser.: PVP-Vol. 318). 384p. 1995. 120.00 (*0-7918-1349-5*, H00981) ASME.

Structural Integrity Technology. Conference on Structural Integrity Technology, 1979 Washington D.C. Staff. Ed. by J. P. Gallagher & T. W. Crooker. LC 79-50210. (Illus.). 233p. reprint ed. pap. 66.50 (*0-8357-3553-2*, 2056816) Bks Demand.

Structural Intermetallics: Proceedings. Ed. by R. Darolia et al. LC 93-79895. (Illus.). 900p. 1993. 20.00 (*0-87339-253-1*, 2531) Minerals Metals.

Structural Interpretation. Schmoll & Helbig. (Handbook of Geophysical Exploration Ser.). Date not set. write for info. (*0-08-037220-1*, Pergamon Pr) Elsevier.

Structural Investigation of Polymers. Geza Bodor. 477p. 1991. 125.00 (*963-05-5606-5*, Pub. by Akad Kiado HU) St Mut.

Structural Knowledge: Techniques for Representing, Conveying, & Acquiring Structural Knowledge. Ed. by David Jonassen et al. 280p. 1993. pap. 32.50 (*0-8058-1360-8*); text ed. 59.95 (*0-8058-1009-9*) L Erlbaum Assocs.

Structural Lightweight Aggregate Concrete. Ed. by John L. Clarke. LC 93-12642. 1993. write for info. (*0-7514-0006-8*, Pub. by Blackie Acad & Prof UK) Routledge Chapman & Hall.

Structural Lightweight Aggregate Concrete Performance. 424p. 1992. 80.95 (*0-685-72539-1*, SP-136BOW6) ACI.

Structural Load Modeling & Combination for Performance & Safety Evaluation. Y. K. Wen. (Developments in Civil Engineering Ser.: No. 31). 220p. 1990. 127.00 (*0-444-88148-4*) Elsevier.

Structural Materials. Ed. by James F. Orofino. LC 89-6764. 592p. 1989. pap. text ed. 49.00 (*0-87262-699-7*, 699) Am Soc Civil Eng.

*__Structural Materials.__ George W. Weidmann et al. (Materials in Action Ser.). 430p. pap. write for info. (*0-7506-1901-5*) Buttrwrth-Heinemann.

Structural Materials: Engineering Application Through Scientific Insight. Ed. by E. D. Hondros & M. McLean. 325p. 1996. text ed. 90.00 (*0-901716-82-0*, Pub. by Inst Materials UK) Ashgate Pub Co.

Structural Materials for Harbor & Coastal Construction. Lawrence L. Whiteneck & Lester A. Hockney. 496p. 1988. text ed. 64.00 (*0-07-068153-8*) McGraw.

Structural Materials for Service at Elevated Temperatures in Nuclear Power Generation: Symposium November 30-December 3, 1975, Houston, TX: Held as Part of the ASME, Winter Annual Meeting. Adolph O. Schaefer. LC 75-32494. 396p. reprint ed. pap. 112.90 (*0-317-08139-X*, 2016880) Bks Demand.

Structural Materials in Nuclear Power Systems. Ed. by J. T. Roberts. LC 81-1883. (Modern Perspectives in Energy Ser.). 500p. 1981. 89.50 (*0-306-40669-1*, Plenum Pr) Plenum.

Structural Materials Technology: An NDT Conference. Ed. by Robert J. Scandella. LC 94-60025. 355p. 1994. text ed. 199.95 (*1-56676-141-7*) Technomic.

Structural Materials Technology, 1996: An NDT Conference. Ed. by Phil Stolarski. LC 95-62454. 420p. 1996. text ed. 199.95 (*1-56676-424-6*) Technomic.

***Structural Mechanics.** Date not set. 23.95 (*0-8464-4422-4*) Beekman Pubs.

***Structural Mechanics.** Cain. Date not set. pap. 24.95 (*0-333-48078-3*, Pub. by Macm UK) St Martin.

***Structural Mechanics.** Durka. Date not set. pap. text ed. write for info. (*0-582-25199-0*, Pub. by Longman UK) Longman.

***Structural Mechanics.** 4th ed. Durka. 1989. pap. text ed. write for info. (*0-582-01851-X*, Pub. by Longman UK) Longman.

Structural Mechanics: Graph & Matrix Methods. 2nd ed. A. Kaveh. LC 95-26020. (Applied & Engineering Mathematical Ser.: Vol. 9). 1995. write for info. (*0-86380-186-2*) Wiley.

Structural Mechanics: Graph & Matrix Methods. 2nd ed. A. Kaveh. (Applied & Engineering Mathematical Ser.). 430p. 1996. text ed. 95.00 (*0-471-96028-4*) Wiley.

Structural Mechanics Computer Programs: Surveys, Assessments, & Availability. Ed. by W. Pilkey et al. LC 74-8300. 1118p. reprint ed. pap. 180.00 (*0-317-28094-5*, 2055728) Bks Demand.

Structural Mechanics in Reactor Technology. Ed. by K. Kussmaul. 4928p. 1993. pap. 859.50 (*0-444-81515-5*, North Holland) Elsevier.

Structural Mechanics in Reactor Technology: Advances 1987. Ed. by Folker H. Wittman. 216p. (C). 1987. text ed. 130.00 (*90-6191-738-7*, Pub. by A A Balkema NE) Ashgate Pub Co.

Structural Mechanics in Reactor Technology: Transaction of the International Conference on Structural Mechanics in Reactor Technology, Lausanne, 9th, 17-21 August 1987, 14 vols., Set. Ed. by Folker H. Wittmann. 6800p. 1987. text ed. 910.00 (*90-6191-762-X*, Pub. by A A Balkema NE) Ashgate Pub Co.

Structural Mechanics Software Series, 5 vols., Vol. 1. Ed. by Nicholas Perrone & W. Pilkey. LC 77-641779. 640p. 1977. reprint ed. pap. 172.80 (*0-8357-2719-X*, 2039833) Bks Demand.

Structural Mechanics Software Series, 5 vols., Vol. 2. Ed. by Nicholas Perrone & W. Pilkey. LC 77-641779. 466p. 1978. reprint ed. pap. 132.90 (*0-8357-2720-3*) Bks Demand.

Structural Mechanics Software Series, 5 vols., Vol. 3. Ed. by Nicholas Perrone & W. Pilkey. LC 77-641779. 352p. 1980. reprint ed. pap. 100.40 (*0-8357-2721-1*) Bks Demand.

Structural Mechanics Software Series, 5 vols., Vol. 4. Ed. by Nicholas Perrone & W. Pilkey. LC 77-641779. 476p. 1982. reprint ed. pap. 135.70 (*0-8357-2722-X*) Bks Demand.

Structural Mechanics Software Series, 5 vols., Vol. 5. Ed. by Nicholas Perrone & W. Pilkey. LC 77-641779. 350p. 1984. reprint ed. pap. 99.80 (*0-8357-2723-8*) Bks Demand.

Structural Methods of Inorganic Chemistry. 2nd ed. Ebsworth. 1991. 66.00 (*0-8493-7732-3*, QA) CRC Pr.

Structural Minerology: An Introduction. J. Lima-de-Faria. LC 94-10374. (Solid Earth Sciences Library: Vol. 7). 1994. lib. bdg. 176.50 (*0-7923-2821-3*) Kluwer Ac.

Structural Model for Malaysian Balance of Payment, 1963-1982. M. Zainudin Saleh. LC 91-31757. (Developing Economies of the Third World Ser.). 176p. 1991. text ed. 15.00 (*0-8153-0661-X*) Garland.

Structural Modeling & Experimental Techniques. 2nd ed. Harry G. Harris et al. 600p. 1995. write for info. (*0-8493-2469-6*, 2469) CRC Pr.

Structural Modelling by Example: Applications in Educational, Sociological & Behavioural Research. Ed. by Peter Cuttance & Russell Ecob. (Illus.). 285p. 1988. text ed. 69.95 (*0-521-26195-3*) Cambridge U Pr.

Structural Models in Anthropology. Per Hage & Frank Harary. LC 83-7552. (Cambridge Studies in Social & Cultural Anthropology: No. 46). (Illus.). 240p. 1984. pap. 21.95 (*0-521-27311-0*) Cambridge U Pr.

Structural Models in Folklore & Transformational Essays. E. Kongas-Maranda & P. Kongas-Maranda. (Approaches to Semiotics Ser.). (Illus.). 145p. 1971. text ed. 35.40 (*90-279-1705-1*) Mouton.

Structural Notes & Corpus. William E. Welmers et al. (English As a Foreign Language Ser.). 119p. (Orig.). 1980. pap. 2.50 (*0-87950-290-8*) Spoken Lang Serv.

Structural Optimization. Ed. by S. Hernandez et al. LC 95-68887. (OPTI Ser.: Vol. 4). 344p. 1995. 181.00 (*1-56252-249-3*, 3250) Computational Mech MA.

Structural Optimization. Ed. by George I. Rozvany & Bhushan L. Karihaloo. (C). 1988. lib. bdg. 203.00 (*90-247-3771-0*) Kluwer Ac.

Structural Optimization: Fundamentals & Applications. Uri Kirsch. LC 93-18581. 1993. 114.95 (*0-387-55919-1*) Spr-Verlag.

Structural Optimization: Recent Developments & Applications. Ed. by Ovadia E. Lev. LC 81-69232. 220p. 1981. pap. 20.00 (*0-87262-281-9*) Am Soc Civil Eng.

Structural Optimization Vol. 1: Optimality Criteria. Ed. by M. Save & W. Prager. (Mathematical Concepts & Methods in Science & Engineering Ser.: Vol. 34). 1985. 85.00 (*0-306-41861-4*, Plenum Pr) Plenum.

Structural Optimization Vol. 2: Mathematical Programming. Ed. by M. Save et al. LC 85-22590. (Mathematical Concepts & Methods in Science & Engineering Ser.: Vol. 40). (Illus.). 408p. 1990. 95.00 (*0-306-41862-2*, Plenum Pr) Plenum.

Structural Optimization Symposium: Presented at the Winter Annual Meeting of the American Society of Mechanical Engineers, New York, November 17-21, 1974. Structural Optimization Symposium Staff. Ed. by L. A. Schmit, Jr. LC 74-81162. (AMD Ser: Vol. 7). 170p. reprint ed. pap. 48.50 (*0-685-15813-6*, 2026786) Bks Demand.

Structural Optimization under Stability & Vibration Contraints. Ed. by Michal Zyczkowski. (CISM Courses & Lectures: Vol. 308). (Illus.). vi, 329p. 1990. 82.95 (*0-387-82173-2*) Spr-Verlag.

Structural Order in Polymers: International Symposium on Macromolecules, Florence, Italy, 7-12 September 1980. F. Ciardelli & P. Giusti. (IUPAC Symposium Ser.). (Illus.). 260p. 1981. 113.00 (*0-08-025296-6*, Pub. by Pergamon Repr UK) Franklin.

Structural Pattern Analysis. R. Mohr et al. (Series in Computer Science: Vol. 19). 268p. (C). 1990. pap. 18.00 (*981-02-0147-8*); text ed. 74.00 (*981-02-0097-8*) World Scientific Pub.

Structural Pattern Recognition. T. Pavlidis. LC 77-21105. (Electrophysics Ser.: Vol. 1). (Illus.). 1977. 51.95 (*0-387-08463-0*) Spr-Verlag.

Structural Patterns of Pirandello's Work. Jorn Moestrup. (Etudes Romanes Ser.: No. 2). 294p. (Orig.). 1972. pap. 32.50 (*87-7492-056-1*, Pub. by Odense Universitets Forlag DK) Coronet Bks.

Structural Patterns of Tropical Barks. Ingrid Roth. (Encyclopedia of Plant Anatomy: Special Part Ser.: Vol. 9, Pt. 3). (Illus.). 609p. 1981. 196.00 (*3-443-14012-2*) Lubrecht & Cramer.

Structural Performance of Flexible Pipes: Proceedings of the First National Conference on Flexible Pipes, Columbus, Ohio, 21-23 October 1990. Ed. by Shad M. Sargand & Gayle F. Mitchell. 176p. (C). 1990. text ed. 70.00 (*90-6191-165-6*, Pub. by A A Balkema NE) Ashgate Pub Co.

Structural Performance of Pipes: Proceedings of the Second National Conference on Structural Performance of Pipes, Columbus, Ohio, 14-17 March 1993. Ed. by G. F. Mitchell et al. (Illus.). 174p. (C). 1993. text ed. 85.00 (*90-5410-308-6*, Pub. by A A Balkema NE) Ashgate Pub Co.

Structural Phase in Transitions in Layered Transition Metal Compounds. Ed. by Kazuko Motizuki. 1986. lib. bdg. 180.50 (*90-277-2171-8*) Kluwer Ac.

Structural Phase Transitions, Vol. I. Ed. by K. A. Mueller & H. Thomas. (Topics in Current Physics Ser.: Vol. 23). (Illus.). 190p. 1981. 44.95 (*0-387-10329-5*) Spr-Verlag.

Structural Phase Transitions Data Base. A. M. Glaxer. 104p. 1992. text ed. 212.00 (*2-88124-867-5*) Gordon & Breach.

Structural Phase Transitions Two. Ed. by K. A. Muller & H. Thomas. (Topics in Current Physics Ser.: Vol. 45). (Illus.). 192p. 1991. 49.95 (*0-387-52238-7*) Spr-Verlag.

Structural Plasticity: Theory, Problems & CAE Software. Wai-Fah Chen & H. Zhang. (Illus.). x, 250p. 1990. 59.95 (*0-387-96789-3*) Spr-Verlag.

Structural Plastics: Proceedings of the Structural Plastics Symposium on Properties & Possibilities, 1st, Louisville, Ky., 1969. Structural Plastics Symposium Staff. LC 72-16688. (Illus.). 246p. reprint ed. pap. 70.20 (*0-317-08600-6*, 2020824) Bks Demand.

Structural Plastics Design Manual: ASCE Manuals & Reports on Engineering Practice No. 63. Task Committee on Design of the Structural Plastics Research Council. 1176p. 1984. 95.00 (*0-87262-391-2*) Am Soc Civil Eng.

Structural Plastics Selection Manual: ASCE Manuals & Reports on Engineering Practice, No. 66. Task Committee on Properties of Selected Plastics Systems of the Structural Plastics Research Council. 584p. 1985. 64.00 (*0-87262-475-7*) Am Soc Civil Eng.

Structural Principles. Irving Engel. (Illus.). 384p. (C). 1984. text ed. 66.80 (*0-13-854019-5*) P-H.

Structural Principles in Inorganic Compounds. W. E. Addison. 200p. reprint ed. pap. 57.00 (*0-317-08948-X*, 2006383) Bks Demand.

Structural Principles of the Chinese Language, 3 vols. Sozef L. Mullie. 1976. lib. bdg. 300.00 (*0-8490-2698-9*) Gordon Pr.

Structural-Process Models of Complex Human Behavior, No. 26. M. N. Scandura. (NAT0 Advanced Study Applied Science Ser.). 620p. 1978. lib. bdg. 135.00 (*90-286-0578-9*) Kluwer Ac.

Structural Properties of Polylogarithms. L. Lewin. LC 91-18172. (Mathematical Surveys & Monographs: No. 37). 412p. 1991. 133.00 (*0-8218-1634-9*, SURV/37) Am Math.

***Structural Reform in Education.** Jane Hannaway. 1997. 41.95 (*0-8133-1782-7*); pap. 15.95 (*0-8133-1783-5*) Westview.

Structural Reform, Stabilization, & Growth in Turkey. George F. Kopits. (Occasional Paper Ser.: No. 52). 46p. 1987. pap. 7.50 (*0-939934-84-1*) Intl Monetary.

Structural Reliability--Probabilistic Safety Assessment. Ed. by Folker H. Wittmann. (Structural Mechanics in Reactor Technology Ser.: Vol. M). 498p. (C). 1987. text ed. 130.00 (*90-6191-774-3*, Pub. by A A Balkema NE) Ashgate Pub Co.

Structural Reliability Methods. Ove Ditlevsen & Henrick O. Madsen. LC 95-19753. 1996. text ed. 150.00 (*0-471-96086-1*) Wiley.

Structural Repair & Maintenance of Historical Buildings. Carlos A. Brebbia. 632p. 1989. 295.00 (*0-8176-2302-7*) Birkhauser.

Structural Repair & Maintenance of Historical Buildings II, Vol. 2: Dynamics, Stabilisation & Restoration. Ed. by C. A. Brebbia et al. LC 89-60103. (Stremah Ser.). 353p. 1991. 126.00 (*1-56252-079-2*) Computational Mech MA.

Structural Repair & Maintenance of Historical Buildings III. Ed. by C. A. Brebbia & R. J. Frewer. LC 93-71023. (Stremah Ser.). 664p. 1993. 221.00 (*1-56252-167-5*, 2440) Computational Mech MA.

Structural Revolution. Jean-Marie Benoist. LC 78-5298. 1978. text ed. 29.95 (*0-312-76698-X*) St Martin.

Structural Safety & Reliability, 3 vols. Ed. by A. H-S. Ang et al. 2389p. 1990. text ed. 240.00 (*0-87262-743-8*) Am Soc Civil Eng.

Structural Safety & Reliability: International Conference on Structural Safety & Reliability, Innsbruck, Austria, 1993, 3 vol. 6th ed. Ed. by G. I. Schueller et al. LC 89-18539. 2296p. 1994. 210.00 (*90-5410-357-4*, Pub. by A A Balkema NE) Ashgate Pub Co.

Structural Safety Evaluation Based on System Identification Approaches: Proceedings of the Workshop at Lambrecht-Pfalz. James T. Yao & Hans G. Natke. x, 502p. (C). 1988. pap. 94.00 (*3-528-06313-0*, Pub. by Vieweg & Sohn GW) Informatica.

Structural Safety Studies: Proceedings of a Symposium Sponsored by the Structural Division. Ed. by James T. Yao. 205p. 1985. 26.00 (*0-87262-451-X*) Am Soc Civil Eng.

Structural Semantics: An Attempt at a Method. A. J. Greimas. Tr. by Daniele McDowell et al. from FRE. LC 83-5864. lvi, 325p. 1983. text ed. 40.00 (*0-8032-2112-6*) U of Nebr Pr.

Structural Shielding Design & Evaluation for Medical Use of X-Rays & Gamma-Rays of Energies up to Ten MeV. LC 76-22969. (Report Ser.: No. 49). 134p. 1976. pap. text ed. 40.00 (*0-913392-31-6*) NCRP Pubns.

Structural Slumps: The Modern Equilibrium Theory of Unemployment, Interest, & Assets. Edmund S. Phelps. LC 93-15775. 436p. 1994. Acid-free paper. 49.95 (*0-674-84373-8*) HUP.

Structural Sociology. Ed. by Ino Rossi. LC 81-12246. (Illus.). 416p. 1982. text ed. 67.00 (*0-231-04846-7*) Col U Pr.

Structural Sociology. Ed. by Ino Rossi. LC 81-12246. (Illus.). 416p. 1984. pap. text ed. 22.00 (*0-231-04847-5*) Col U Pr.

Structural Solvability & Controllability. K. Murota. (Algorithms & Combinatorics Ser.: Vol. 3). (Illus.). 295p. 1987. 71.95 (*0-387-17659-4*) Spr-Verlag.

Structural Stability: Theory & Implementation. Wai-Fah Chen & E. M. Lui. LC 86-19931. 534p. 1987. 56.75 (*0-444-01119-6*); text ed. 64.60 (*0-13-500539-6*) P-H.

Structural Stability & Culture Change in a Mexican-American Community. Barbara J. Macklin. Ed. by Carlos E. Cortes. LC 76-1249. (Chicano Heritage Ser.). 1977. 25.95 (*0-405-09513-9*) Ayer.

Structural Stability & Design: Proceedings: International Conference (1995: Sydney, Australia) Ed. by S. Kitipornchai et al. (Illus.). 516p. (C). 1995. text ed. 120.00 (*90-5410-582-8*, TA658, Pub. by A A Balkema NE) Ashgate Pub Co.

Structural Stability & Morphogenesis. Rene Thom. (C). 1993. pap. 36.95 (*0-201-40685-3*) Addison-Wesley.

Structural Stability & Morphogenesis: An Outline of a General Theory of Models. Rene Thom. Tr. by D. H. Fowler from FRE. reprint ed. pap. write for info. (*0-8053-9279-3*) Addison-Wesley.

Structural Stability Design. Yuhshi Fukumato. 450p. 1997. 105.00 (*0-08-042263-2*, Pergamon Pr) Elsevier.

Structural Stability of Deposits & Welded Joints in Power Engineering. V. Pilous & K. Stransky. 200p. 1995. pap. 74.00 (*1-898326-08-8*, Pub. by Cambdge Intl UK) Am Educ Systs.

Structural Steel: PSSC '95: 4th Pacific Structural Steel Conference, 3 Vol. Set. Ed. by N. E. Shanmugam & Y. S. Choo. 1500p. 1995. 231.00 (*0-08-042265-9*, Pergamon Pr) Elsevier.

Structural Steel Design. 4th ed. Jack C. McCormac. (C). 1992. text ed. 84.68 (*0-06-500060-9*) Addson-Wesley Educ.

***Structural Steel Design.** 5th ed. McCormac. (C). 1997. text ed. write for info. (*0-673-98235-1*) Addison-Wesley.

Structural Steel Design: LRFD Approach. J. C. Smith. LC 90-44495. 570p. 1991. Net. text ed. 51.00 (*0-471-62142-0*) Wiley.

Structural Steel Design: LRFD Method. 2nd ed. Jack C. McCormac. LC 94-29972. (C). 1995. 48.00 (*0-06-501627-0*) HarpC.

Structural Steel Designer's Handbook. 2nd ed. Roger L. Brockenbrough. 1994. text ed. 95.00 (*0-07-008776-8*) McGraw.

Structural Steel Design/Fabric Drawing. MacLaughlin. LC 97-10389. (Construction & Building Trades Ser.). 1997. text ed. 46.95 (*0-8273-7313-9*) Delmar.

Structural Steel Design/Fabric Drawing. McLaughlin. (Construction & Building Trades Ser.). 1997. teacher ed. 16.95 (*0-8273-7314-7*) Delmar.

***Structural Steel Fabrication Practices.** John W. Shuster. (Illus.). 448p. 1997. text ed. 49.95 (*0-07-057770-6*) McGraw.

Structural Steel Shop Inspector Training Guide. 58p. 1985. 16.20 (*1-56424-026-6*, F504) Am Inst Steel Construct.

Structural Steels. Earl Kent. 1977. pap. text ed. 10.00 (*0-918782-02-3*) E Kent.

Structural Steelwork: Design to Limit State Theory. T. J. MacGinley & T. C. Ang. (Illus.). 224p. (C). 1987. pap. 59.95 (*0-408-03020-8*) Buttrwrth-Heinemann.

Structural Steelwork: Design to Limit State Theory. 2nd ed. T. J. MacGinley & T. C. Ang. 400p. 1992. pap. 49.95 (*0-7506-0440-9*) Buttrwrth-Heinemann.

Structural Steelwork: Limit State Design to BS 5950. Antony B. Clarke & Sidney H. Coverman. 300p. (gr. 13). 1987. text ed. 92.50 (*0-412-29660-8*) Chapman & Hall.

Structural Steelwork Connections. Graham W. Owens & Brian Cheal. (Illus.). 330p. 1989. 145.00 (*0-408-01214-5*) Buttrwrth-Heinemann.

Structural Studies of Historical Buildings IV Vol. 1: Architectural Studies, Materials & Analysis. Ed. by C. A. Brebbia & B. Leftheris. LC 95-67477. (STREMAH Ser.: No. 4). 464p. 1995. 196.00 (*1-56252-343-0*, 4257) Computational Mech MA.

Structural Studies of Historical Buildings IV Vol. 2: Dynamics, Repairs & Restoration. Ed. by C. A. Brebbia & B. Leftheris. LC 95-67477. (STREMAH Ser.: No. 4). 384p. 1995. 163.00 (*1-56252-344-9*, 4265) Computational Mech MA.

Structural Studies of Historical Buildings V. Ed. by C. A. Brebbia & S. Sanchez-Beitia. (Stremah Ser.: Vol. 5). 800p. 1997. 329.00 (*1-85312-466-4*, 4664) Computational Mech MA.

Structural Studies of Macromolecules by Spectroscopic Methods. Ed. by Kenneth J. Ivin. LC 75-19355. 353p. reprint ed. pap. 100.70 (*0-685-20765-X*, 2030409) Bks Demand.

Structural Studies of Protein-Nucleic Acid Interaction: The Sources of Sequence-Specific Binding. Thomas A. Steitz. LC 92-41805. (Illus.). 104p. (C). 1993. pap. text ed. 22.95 (*0-521-41489-X*) Cambridge U Pr.

Structural Studies on Molecules of Biological Interest: A Volume in Honour of Professor Dorothy Hodgkin. David A. Sayre. (Illus.). 400p. 1981. 45.00 (*0-19-855362-5*) OUP.

Structural Studies, Repair & Maintenance of Historical Buildings IV: Proceedings of the Fourth International Conference, Set, 2 vols., Set. Ed. by C. A. Brebbia & B. Leftheris. LC 95-67477. (STREMAH Ser.: Vol. 4). 848p. 1995. 322.00 (*1-56252-238-8*, 3145) Computational Mech MA.

Structural Study of Myth & Totemism. Ed. by Edmund R. Leach. (Orig.). 1968. pap. 13.95 (*0-422-72530-7*, NO. 2287, Pub. by Tavistock UK) Routledge Chapman & Hall.

Structural Styles in Petroleum Exploration. James D. Lowell. LC 84-62622. 487p. 1985. 56.00 (*0-930972-08-2*) Oil & Gas.

Structural Stylistic Analysis of La Princesse De Cleves. Susan Tiefenbrun. (De Proprietatibus Litterarum, Ser. Practica: No. 25). 185p. (Orig.). 1976. pap. text ed. 43.10 (*90-279-3263-8*) Mouton.

Structural Theory of the Emotions. Joseph De Rivera. LC 76-53916. (Psychological Issues Monograph: No. 40). 178p. 1977. 32.50 (*0-8236-6171-7*); pap. 27.50 (*0-8236-6170-9*) Intl Univs Pr.

Structural Thermodynamics of Alloys. J. Manenc. Tr. by N. Corcoran from FRE. LC 73-83564. Orig. Title: Thermodynamique Structurale Des Alliages. (Illus.). 1973. lib. bdg. 80.00 (*90-277-0346-9*) Kluwer Ac.

Structural Tools for the Analysis of Protein-Nucleic Acid Complexes. Ed. by David M. Lilley et al. LC 92-30658. (Advances in Life Sciences Ser.). ix, 469p. 1992. 117.50 (*0-8176-2776-6*) Birkhauser.

Structural Transformation of the Public Sphere: An Inquiry into a Category of Bourgeois Society. Jurgen Habermas. (Studies in Contemporary German Social Thought). 323p. 1991. pap. 18.00 (*0-262-58108-6*) MIT Pr.

Structural Transformations in Liquid Crystals. S. A. Pikin. Tr. by Michael Alferieff from RUS. 423p. 1991. text ed. 372.00 (*2-88124-296-0*) Gordon & Breach.

Structural Traps I: Tectonic Fold Traps, No. 1. Ed. by Edward A. Beaumont & Norman H. Foster. (Treatise of Petroleum Geology Atlas of Oil & Gas Fields Ser.). (Illus.). 150p. 1990. 10.00 (*0-89181-580-5*, 016) AAPG.

Structural Traps II: Traps Associated with Tectonic Faulting, No. 2. Ed. by Edward A. Beaumont & Norman H. Foster. (Treatise of Petroleum Geology Atlas of Oil & Gas Fields Ser.). (Illus.). 267p. 1990. 10.00 (*0-89181-581-3*, 017) AAPG.

Structural Traps III: Tectonic Fold & Fault Traps, Vol. 3. Ed. by Edward A. Beaumont & Norman H. Foster. (Treatise of Petroleum Geology Atlas of Oil & Gas Fields Ser.). (Illus.). 355p. 1990. 10.00 (*0-89181-583-X*, 019) AAPG.

Structural Traps IV: Tectonic & Nontectonic Fold Traps, No. 4. Ed. by Edward A. Beaumont & Norman H. Foster. (Treatise of Petroleum Geology Atlas of Oil & Gas Fields Ser.). (Illus.). 382p. 1990. 10.00 (*0-89181-584-8*, 020) AAPG.

Structural Traps V, No. 5. Ed. by Norman H. Foster & Edward A. Beaumont. (Treatise of Petroleum Geology Atlas of Oil & Gas Fields Ser.). (Illus.). 305p. 1991. 10.00 (*0-89181-586-4*, 022) AAPG.

Structural Traps VI. Ed. by Norman H. Foster & Edward A. Beaumont. (Treatise of Petroleum Geology Atlas of Oil & Gas Fields Ser.: No. 9). (Illus.). 304p. 1992. 10.00 (*0-89181-588-0*, 024-28) AAPG.

Structural Traps VII. Ed. by Norman H. Foster & Edward A. Beaumont. (Treatise of Petroleum Geology Atlas of Oil & Gas Fields Ser.: No. 10). (Illus.). 347p. 1992. 10.00 (*0-89181-589-9*, 025) AAPG.

Structural Traps VIII. Ed. by Norman H. Foster & Edward A. Beaumont. (Treatise of Petroleum Geology Atlas of Oil & Gas Fields Ser.). (Illus.). 328p. 1993. 10.00 (*0-89181-590-2*, 026) AAPG.

S

Structural Unemployment. Ed. by W. Franz et al. (Studies in Contemporary Economics). (Illus.). x, 132p. 1992. pap. 39.00 (*0-387-91417-X*) Spr-Verlag.

***Structural Vibration.** write for info. (*0-340-64580-6*, Pub. by E Arnold UK) Routledge Chapman & Hall.

Structural Welder. Jack Rudman. (Career Examination Ser.: C-773). 1994. pap. 23.95 (*0-8373-0773-2*) Nat Learn.

Structural Welding Code - Aluminum (D1.2-90) 226p. 1990. 66.00 (*0-685-60549-3*) Am Welding.

Structural Welding Code - Reinforcing Steel (D1.4-92) 1992. 39.00 (*0-87171-378-0*) Am Welding.

Structural Welding Code - Sheet Steel (D1.3-89) 64p. 1989. 48.00 (*0-87171-308-X*) Am Welding.

Structural Welding Code - Steel (AWS D1.1-96) 450p. 1996. 180.00 (*0-87171-465-5*) Am Welding.

Structural Welding Code Study Guide. Henry L. Jackson. 75p. (C). 1996. pap. text ed. 28.00 (*1-881870-02-2*) BJ Pubns.

Structural Wood Composites: Meeting Today's Needs & Tomorrow's Challenges. 178p. (Orig.). 1985. pap. 55.00 (*0-935018-24-7*, 7339) Forest Prod.

Structural Wood Composites: New Technologies for Expanding Markets. 148p. 1988. 55.00 (*0-935018-40-9*, 7359) Forest Prod.

Structural Wood Design. Shan Somayaji. (West - Engineering Ser.). 1990. text ed. 77.95 (*0-534-93845-0*) PWS Pubs.

Structural Wood Design. Shan Somayaji. (West - Engineering Ser.). 1990. student ed., pap. 8.75 (*0-534-93850-7*) PWS Pubs.

Structural Wood Detailing in CAD Format. Kamal A. Zayat. LC 92-33267. 1993. text ed. 49.95 (*0-442-01442-2*) Chapman & Hall.

Structural Wood Research: State-of-the-Art & Research Needs: Proceedings of a Workshop Sponsored by the ASCE Committee on Wood, the National Science Foundation, & Washington State University. Ed. by Rafik Y. Itani & Keith F. Faherty. 214p. 1984. 26.00 (*0-87262-411-0*) Am Soc Civil Eng.

Structuralism. Kellner. 1997. 24.95 (*0-8057-8600-7*, Twayne) Scribnrs Ref.

***Structuralism: A Philosophy for the Human Science.** LC 96-52015. (Contemporary Sudies in Philosophy & the Human Science Ser.). 1997. pap. 19.95 (*0-391-04044-8*) Humanities.

Structuralism: An Interdisciplinary Study. Ed. by Susan Wittig. LC 76-899. (Pittsburgh Reprint Ser.: No. 3). 1976. pap. 4.75 (*0-915138-16-6*) Pickwick.

Structuralism: Theory & Practice: Laclos, Critical Monographs in English. Jean Duffy. 104p. 1993. pap. 40.00 (*0-85261-319-9*, Pub. by Univ of Glasgow UK) St Mut.

Structuralism & Biblical Hermeneutics. Ed. & Tr. by Alfred M. Johnson, Jr. LC 79-9411. (Pittsburgh Theological Monographs: No. 22). 1979. pap. 12.95 (*0-915138-18-2*) Pickwick.

Structuralism & Myth: Levi-Strauss, Barthes, Dumezil, & Propp. Robert A. Segal. LC 95-41491. (Theories of Myth Ser.: Vol. 6). 352p. 1996. text ed. 70.00 (*0-8153-2260-7*) Garland.

Structuralism & Semiotics. Terence Hawkes. LC 76-55560. 1977. pap. 13.95 (*0-520-03422-8*) U CA Pr.

Structuralism & Since: From Levi-Strauss to Derrida. Ed. by John Sturrock. 196p. (C). 1981. pap. 9.95 (*0-19-289105-7*) OUP.

Structuralism & Structures. Charles E. Rickart. LC 94-28563. (Series in Pure Mathematics: Vol. 21). 236p. 1995. text ed. 48.00 (*981-02-1860-5*) World Scientific Pub.

Structuralism & the Biblical Text. David C. Greenwood. (Religion & Reason Ser.: No. 32). xi, 155p. 1985. 61.55 (*0-89925-103-X*) Mouton.

Structuralism & the Logic of Dissent: Barthes, Derrida, Foucault, Lacan. Eve Tavor-Bannet. LC 88-14220. 312p. 1989. pap. text ed. 14.95 (*0-252-06045-8*) U of Ill Pr.

Structuralism for Beginners. Illus. & Text by Donald D. Palmer. 160p. 1995. pap. 11.00 (*0-86316-193-6*) Writers & Readers.

Structuralism in Literature: An Introduction. Robert Scholes. LC 73-90578. 250p. 1975. pap. 14.00 (*0-300-01850-9*) Yale U Pr.

Structuralism, Moscow, Prague, Paris. Jan M. Broekman. Tr. by J. F. Beekman & B. Helm from GER. LC 74-79570. (Synthese Library: No. 67). Orig. Title: Strukturalismus. 125p. 1974. lib. bdg. 70.50 (*90-277-0478-3*, D Reidel) Kluwer Ac.

Structuralism or Criticism? Thoughts on How We Read. Geoffrey Strickland. LC 80-40721. 209p. 1983. pap. 22.95 (*0-521-27657-8*) Cambridge U Pr.

Structuralist Controversy: The Languages of Criticism & the Sciences of Man. Ed. by Richard Macksey & Eugenio Donato. LC 78-95789. 365p. reprint ed. pap. 104.10 (*0-7837-3390-9*, 2043348) Bks Demand.

Structuralist Poetics: Structuralism, Linguistics & the Study of Literature. Jonathan Culler. LC 74-11608. 316p. 1976. pap. 13.95 (*0-8014-9155-X*) Cornell U Pr.

Structuralist Program in Psychology: Foundations & Applications. Ed. by Hans Westmeyer. LC 92-48722. (Illus.). 290p. 1992. text ed. 35.90 (*0-88937-100-8*) Hogrefe & Huber Pubs.

***Structuralist Studies in Arabic Linguistics: Charles A. Ferguson's Papers, 1954-1994.** R. Kirk Belnap & Niloofar Haeri. LC 97-9136. (Studies in Semitic Languages & Linguistics: No. 24). 336p. 1997. 85.75 (*90-04-10511-5*, NLG119) E J Brill.

Structuralist Theory of Logic. Arnold Koslow. (Illus.). 450p. (C). 1992. text ed. 89.95 (*0-521-41267-6*) Cambridge U Pr.

Structuralist Theory of Science: Focal Issues, New Results. Ed. by Wolfgang Balzer & C. Ulises Moulines. LC 95-45839. (Perspektiven der Analytischen Philosophie - Perspectives in Analytical Philosophy Ser.: Vol. 6). xi, 295p. (C). 1996. lib. bdg. 155.60 (*3-11-014075-6*) De Gruyter.

Structurally Adjusted Africa: Poverty, Debt, & Basic Needs. Ed. by David Simon et al. LC 94-49045. (C). 69.95 (*0-7453-0972-0*, Pub. by Pluto Pr UK); pap. 17.95 (*0-7453-0973-9*, Pub. by Pluto Pr UK) LPC InBook.

***Structuration des Grands Ensembles Bibliques et Intertextualite a l'Epoque Perse: De la Redaction Sacerdotale di Livre d'Lsaie a la Contestation de la Sagesse.** Bernard Gosse. (Beihefte zur Zeitschrift fuer die Alttestamentliche Wissenschaft Ser.: Vol. 246). 220p. (FRE & GER.). (C). 1997. lib. bdg. 107.00 (*3-11-015395-5*) De Gruyter.

Structuration Theory: Anthony Giddens & the Constitution of Social Life. Ira J. Cohen. LC 89-31803. 318p. 1989. pap. 15.95 (*0-312-00394-3*); text ed. 45.00 (*0-312-00392-7*) St Martin.

Structure: From Physics to General Systems - Festschrift Volume in Honor of Caianiello's 70th Birthday. M. Marinaro & G. Scarpetta. 832p. 1993. text ed. 162.00 (*981-02-1291-7*) World Scientific Pub.

Structure: The Complete Toolkit for Structuring Assembly Language Programs. Kurt M. Schindler. (Illus.). 256p. (Orig.). 1989. Incl. disk. 29.95 incl. disk (*0-685-26945-0*); disk 19.95 (*0-685-26946-9*) Logical Soltns.

Structure see Introduction to the Theory of AUTOMATA

Structure Across a Mesozoic Ocean-Continent Suture Zone in the Northern Sierra Nevada, California. S. H. Edelman et al. (Special Papers: No. 224). (Illus.). 64p. 1989. pap. 4.50 (*0-8137-2224-1*) Geol Soc.

Structure-Activity & Selectivity Relationships in Heterogeneous Catalysis: Proceedings of the ACS Symposium, Boston, MA, April 22-27 1990. Ed. by R. K. Grasselli & A. W. Sleight. (Studies in Surface Science & Catalysis: No. 67). 364p. 1991. 243.25 (*0-444-88942-6*) Elsevier.

Structure Activity Correlation as a Predictive Tool in Toxicology: Fundamentals, Methods, & Applications. Ed. by Leon Golberg. LC 82-3007. (Chemical Industry Institute of Toxicology Ser.). (Illus.). 330p. 1983. text ed. 120.00 (*0-89116-276-3*) Hemisp Pub.

***Structure-Activity Relationships.** Nendza. (Ecotoxicology Ser.). 288p. 1997. text ed. 92.00 (*0-412-56430-0*) Chapman & Hall.

Structure-Activity Relationships in Human Chemoreception. M. G. Beets. (Illus.). 408p. 1978. 106.25 (*0-85334-746-8*, Pub. by Elsevier Applied Sci UK) Elsevier.

Structure-Activity Relationships of Thiophene Derivatives of Biological Interest, Vol. 3. G. Drehsen & J. Engel. 46p. 1983. pap. text ed. 70.00 (*3-7186-0181-8*) Gordon & Breach.

Structure Analysis by Small-Angle X-Ray & Neutron Scattering. L. A. Feigin & D. I. Svergun. LC 87-25489. 350p. 1987. 95.00 (*0-306-42629-3*, Plenum Pr) Plenum.

Structure Analysis of Point Defects in Solids: An Introduction to Multiple Magnetic Resonance Spectroscopy. Johann-Martin Spaeth et al. Ed. by M. Cardona et al. LC 92-21884. (Solid-State Sciences Ser.: Vol. 43). (Illus.). xi, 371p. 1992. 75.95 (*0-387-53615-9*) Spr-Verlag.

Structure & Activity of Anti-Tumour Agents. D. N. Reinhoudt. 1982. lib. bdg. 129.50 (*90-247-2783-9*) Kluwer Ac.

Structure & Agency in Explaining Democratization: Insights from the Colombian Case. John Dugas. LC 93-655022. (MacArthur Scholar Ser.: No. 23). 111p. (Orig.). 1994. pap. 4.00 (*1-881157-25-3*) In Ctr Global.

Structure & Agency in the Formation of National Urban Policy in the U. S. A., 1976-1980. D. Wilmoth. 48p. 1986. pap. 22.00 (*0-08-034147-0*, Pub. by PPL UK) Elsevier.

Structure & Analysis of the Modern Improvised Line: Theory, Vol. 1. D. Zinn. 264p. 1981. pap. text ed. 60.00 (*0-935016-03-1*) Gordon & Breach.

Structure & Architecture. Angus J. MacDonald. LC 94-1101. (Illus.). 144p. 1994. pap. 34.95 (*0-7506-1798-5*) Buttrwrth-Heinemann.

Structure & Bifurcations of Dynamical Systems: Proceedings of the RIMS Conference on Dynamical Systems. S. Ushiki. (Advanced Series in Dynamical Systems). 216p. 1992. text ed. 92.00 (*981-02-1102-3*) World Scientific Pub.

***Structure & Bonding: Atoms & Molecules in Intense Fields, Vol. 86.** N. H. Marsh et al. (Illus.). 256p. 1996. 149.50 (*3-540-61015-4*) Spr-Verlag.

Structure & Bonding: Complexes, Clusters & Crystal Chemistry, Vol. 79. (Illus.). 416p. 1992. 238.95 (*0-387-55095-X*) Spr-Verlag.

***Structure & Bonding: Optical & Electronic Phenomena in Sol-Gel Glasses & Modern Application, Vol. 85.** Ed. by C. K. Jorgensen & R. Reisfeld. (Illus.). 256p. 1996. 159.00 (*3-540-60982-2*) Spr-Verlag.

Structure & Bonding: Relationships Between Quantum Chemistry & Crystallography. Ed. by T. F. Koetzle. (Transactions of the American Crystallographic Association Ser.: Vol. 16). 95p. 1980. pap. 25.00 (*0-937140-25-2*) Polycrystal Bk Serv.

Structure & Bonding Vol. 84: Metal Complexes with Tetrapyrrole Ligands III. Ed. & Contrib. by J. W. Buchler. (Illus.). 215p. 1995. 174.95 (*3-540-59281-4*) Spr-Verlag.

Structure & Bonding in Condensed Matter. Carol S. Nichols. (Illus.). 312p. (C). 1995. 59.95 (*0-521-46283-5*); pap. 24.95 (*0-521-46822-1*) Cambridge U Pr.

Structure & Bonding in Noncrystalline Solids. Ed. by George E. Walrafen & Akos G. Revesz. 442p. 1986. 120.00 (*0-306-42396-0*, Plenum Pr) Plenum.

Structure & Bonding, Vol. 74: Metal Complexes with Tetrapyrrole Ligands II. Ed. by J. W. Buchler. (Illus.). 160p. 1991. 103.95 (*0-387-52899-7*) Spr-Verlag.

Structure & Bonding, Vol. 75: Long-Range Electron Transfer in Biology. G. Palmer. (Illus.). 240p. 1991. 118.95 (*0-387-53260-9*) Spr-Verlag.

Structure & Bonding, Vol. 78: Bioinorganic Chemistry. Ed. by P. J. Sadler. (Illus.). vii, 199p. 1991. 118.95 (*0-387-54261-2*) Spr-Verlag.

Structure & Change in Economic History. Douglass C. North. (C). 1982. pap. text ed. 9.95 (*0-393-95241-X*) Norton.

Structure & Change in Indian Society. Ed. by Bernard S. Cohn & Milton B. Singer. LC 67-17609. (Viking Fund Publications in Anthropology: No. 47). 523p. reprint ed. pap. 149.10 (*0-317-26248-3*, 2052137) Bks Demand.

Structure & Change in the Space Economy: Festschrift in Honor of Martin H. Beckmann. Ed. by T. R. Lakshmanan & Peter Nijkamp. LC 93-16821. 1993. 119.95 (*0-387-56490-X*) Spr-Verlag.

Structure & Change of Castilian Peasant Community: A Sociological Inquiry into Rural Castile, 1550-1990. Victor Perez-Diaz. LC 91-22825. (Harvard Studies in Sociology). 266p. 1992. text ed. 22.00 (*0-8240-8473-X*) Garland.

Structure & Chaos in Modernist Works, Vol. 27. Bruce E. Fleming. (New Studies in Aesthetics). 152p. (C). 1995. text ed. 42.95 (*0-8204-2786-1*) P Lang Pubng.

Structure & Chemistry. (Studies in Natural Products Chemistry: Vol. 17. Pt. D). 680p. 1995. 425.50 (*0-444-82265-8*) Elsevier.

Structure & Chemistry. (Studies in Natural Products Chemistry: Vol. 15, Pt. C). 594p. 1995. text ed. 369.75 (*0-444-82083-3*) Elsevier.

Structure & Chemistry of the Apatites & Other Calcium Orthophosphates. J. C. Elliott. LC 94-8066. (Studies in Inorganic Chemistry: Vol. 18). 404p. 1994. 245.75 (*0-444-81582-1*) Elsevier.

Structure & Coherence: Measuring the Undergraduate Curriculum. Robert Zemsky. (Illus.). vi, 41p. 1989. 10.00 (*0-911696-45-8*) Assn Am Coll.

Structure & Composition of Jeremiah 50: 2 - 51: 58. Alice O. Bellis. LC 94-13279. (Biblical Press Ser.: Vol. 24). 248p. 1995. 89.95 (*0-7734-2353-2*, Mellen Biblical Pr) E Mellen.

Structure & Confirmation of Evolutionary Theory. Elisabeth Lloyd. 247p. 1993. pap. text ed. 15.95 (*0-691-00046-8*) Princeton U Pr.

Structure & Confirmation of Evolutionary Theory. Elisabeth A. Lloyd. LC 88-3123. (Contributions in Philosophy Ser.: No. 37). 243p. 1988. text ed. 49.95 (*0-313-25563-6*, LVY/, Greenwood Pr) Greenwood.

Structure & Conflict in Nigeria Nineteen Sixty to Nineteen Sixty-Five. Kenneth Post & Michael Vickers. 256p. 1974. 29.50 (*0-299-06470-0*) U of Wis Pr.

Structure & Conformation of Amphiphilic Membranes: Proceedings of the International Workshop on Amphiphilic Membranes, Julich, Germany, September 16-18, 1991. Ed. by D. Richter et al. LC 92-14296. (Proceedings in Physics Ser.: Vol. 66). (Illus.). xi, 298p. 1992. 90.95 (*0-387-55452-1*) Spr-Verlag.

Structure & Content of Molecular Clouds - 25 Years of Molecular Radioastronomy: Proceedings of a Conference Held at Schloss Ringberg, Tegernsee, Germany, 14-16 April 1993. Ed. by T. L. Wilson & K. J. Johnston. LC 94-23577. (Lecture Notes in Physics: Vol. 439). 1994. 72.95 (*3-540-58621-0*) Spr-Verlag.

***Structure & Contingency: In the Evolution of Life, Human Evolution & Human History.** Ed. & Contrib. by John Bintliff. (Illus.). 224p. 1997. 69.95 (*0-7185-0025-3*, Pub. by Leicester Univ Pr) Bks Intl VA.

Structure & Creativity in Religion. Douglas Allen. (Religion & Reason Ser.: No. 14). 1978. 53.85 (*90-279-7594-9*) Mouton.

Structure & Crystallization of Glasses. W. Vogel. 1971. 112.00 (*0-08-006998-3*, Pub. by Pergamon Repr UK) Franklin.

Structure & Deformation of Boundries: Proceedings of a Symposium "Phase Boundary Effects on Deformation" Sponsored by the Physical Metallurgy, Structural Materials & Mechanical Metallurgy Committees of the Metallurgical Society of AIME & the Flow & Fracture Activity of American Society for Metals Held at the 1985 TMS-AIME Fall Meeting, Toronto, Canada, October 13-17, 1985. fac. ed. Metallurgical Society of AIME Staff. Ed. by K. N. Subramanian & M. A. Imam. LC 86-16420. 355p. 1986. reprint ed. pap. 101.20 (*0-7837-8304-3*, 2049090) Bks Demand.

Structure & Design of Programming Languages. John E. Nicholls. LC 74-12801. (IBM Systems Programming Ser.). (Illus.). 592p. (C). 1975. text ed. write for info. (*0-201-14454-9*) Addison-Wesley.

Structure & Development of Meat Animals & Poultry. Howard J. Swatland. LC 94-60385. 610p. 1994. 129.95 (*1-56676-120-4*) Technomic.

Structure & Development of Russian. William K. Matthews. LC 77-90152. 224p. 1969. reprint ed. text ed. 55.00 (*0-8371-2246-5*, MARU, Greenwood Pr) Greenwood.

Structure & Development of Science. Ed. by Gerard Radnitzky & Gunnar Anderson. (Boston Studies in the Philosophy of Science: No. 136). 291p. 1979. lib. bdg. 104.50 (*90-277-0994-7*, D Reidel) Kluwer Ac.

Structure & Development of Solar Active Regions: Proceedings of the I.A.U. Symposium, No. 35, Budapest, Hungary, Sept. 1967. International Astronomical Union Staff. Ed. by Karl O. Kiepenheuer. (I.A.U. Symposia Ser.). 608p. 1968. lib. bdg. 152.00 (*90-277-0122-9*) Kluwer Ac.

Structure & Development of the Greenland-Scotland Ridge: New Methods & Concepts. Ed. by Martin H. Bott et al. (NATO Conference Series IV, Marine Sciences: Vol. 8). 696p. 1982. 135.00 (*0-306-41019-2*, Plenum Pr) Plenum.

Structure & Dimensions of European Community Policy/ Structures et Dimensions des Politiques Communautaires. Ed. by Jurgen Schwarze & Harry G. Schermers. 238p. (ENG & FRE.). 1988. 90.00 (*3-7890-1521-0*, Pub. by Nomos Verlags GW) Intl Bk Import.

***Structure & Diversity: Studies in the Phenomenological Philosophy of Max Scheler.** Eugene Kelly. LC 97-2848. (Phaenomenologica Ser.: Vol. 141). 1997. lib. bdg. 110.00 (*0-7923-4492-8*) Kluwer Ac.

Structure & Dynamics of Atoms & Molecules: Conceptual Trends. Ed. by J. L. Calais & Eugene S. Kryachko. 288p. (C). 1995. lib. bdg. 120.00 (*0-7923-3388-8*) Kluwer Ac.

Structure & Dynamics of Biopolymers. C. Nicolini. (C). 1987. lib. bdg. 138.00 (*90-247-3527-0*) Kluwer Ac.

Structure & Dynamics of Bulk Polymers by NMR-Methods. V. D. Fedotov & H. Schneider. (NMR-Basic Principles & Progress Ser.). (Illus.). 190p. 1989. 119.95 (*0-387-50151-7*) Spr-Verlag.

Structure & Dynamics of Earth's Deep Interior, Vol. 46, IUGG 1. Ed. by D. E. Smylie & R. Hide. 134p. 1989. 25.00 (*0-87590-450-5*) Am Geophysical.

Structure & Dynamics of Elliptical Galaxies. Ed. by Tim De Zeeuw. (C). 1987. pap. text ed. 83.00 (*90-277-2586-1*); lib. bdg. 206.00 (*90-277-2585-3*) Kluwer Ac.

***Structure & Dynamics of Glasses & Glass Formers.** Ed. by C. A. Angell et al. LC 97-20773. (Materials Research Society Symposium Proceedings Ser.: No. 455). 1997. text ed. 75.00 (*1-55899-359-2*) Materials Res.

Structure & Dynamics of Globular Clusters. Ed. by S. G. Djorgovski & G. Meylan. (ASP Conference Series Proceedings: Vol. 50). 416p. 1993. 28.00 (*0-937707-69-4*) Astron Soc Pacific.

Structure & Dynamics of Health Research & Public Funding: An International Institution Comparison. Dietmar Braun. Tr. by Neil Solomon. LC 94-7725. 216p. (C). 1994. lib. bdg. 106.00 (*0-7923-2777-2*) Kluwer Ac.

Structure & Dynamics of Membranes - Generic & Specific Interactions: From Cells to Visicles. Ed. by Reinhard Lipowsky & Erich Sackmann. LC 95-8846. (Handbook of Biological Physics Ser.: Vol. 1A). 1036p. 1995. 353.25 (*0-444-81975-4*) Elsevier.

Structure & Dynamics of Molecular Systems, No. I. Ed. by D. Daudel et al. 1985. lib. bdg. 116.50 (*90-277-1977-2*) Kluwer Ac.

Structure & Dynamics of Molecular Systems, No. II. Ed. by Raymond Daudel et al. 1986. lib. bdg. 131.00 (*90-277-2246-3*) Kluwer Ac.

Structure & Dynamics of Nonlinear Waves in Fluids: Proceedings of the Iutam-Isimm Symposium. K. Kirchgassner & A. Mielke. (Advanced Series in Nonlinear Dynamics). 300p. 1995. text ed. 91.00 (*981-02-2124-X*) World Scientific Pub.

Structure & Dynamics of Nucleic Acids & Proteins. M. H. Sarma & Ramaswamy H. Sarma. (Illus.). 500p. (C). 1983. lib. bdg. 80.00 (*0-940030-04-7*) Adenine Pr.

Structure & Dynamics of Nucleic Acids, Proteins & Membranes. Ed. by E. Clementi & S. Chin. LC 87-2366. 468p. 1987. 95.00 (*0-306-42553-X*, Plenum Pr) Plenum.

Structure & Dynamics of Partially Solidified Systems. Ed. by David E. Loper. (C). 1987. lib. bdg. 230.50 (*90-247-3500-9*) Kluwer Ac.

Structure & Dynamics of RNA. Ed. by P. H. Van Knippenberg & C. W. Hilbers. LC 86-15111. (NATO ASI Series A, Life Sciences: Vol. 110). 348p. 1986. 85.00 (*0-306-42365-0*, Plenum Pr) Plenum.

Structure & Dynamics of Solutions. Ed. by H. Ohtaki & H. Yamatera. LC 92-16273. (Studies in Physical & Theoretical Chemistry: Vol. 79). 344p. 1992. 228.50 (*0-444-89651-1*) Elsevier.

Structure & Dynamics of Strongly Interacting Colloids & Supramolecular Aggregates in Solution: Proceedings of the NATO Advanced Study Institute, Acquafredda di Maratea, Italy, June 11-21, 1991. Ed. by Sow-Hsin Chen et al. LC 92-8532. (NATO Advanced Science Institutes Series C: Mathematical & Physical Sciences). 872p. (C). 1992. lib. bdg. 328.50 (*0-7923-1729-7*) Kluwer Ac.

Structure & Dynamics of Surfaces I. Ed. by W. Schommers & P. V. Blanckenhagen. (Topics in Current Physics Ser.: Vol. 41). (Illus.). 290p. 1986. 66.95 (*0-387-16252-6*) Spr-Verlag.

Structure & Dynamics of Surfaces II. Ed. by W. Schommers & P. Von Blanckenhagen. (Topics in Current Physics Ser.: Vol. 43). (Illus.). 480p. 1987. 80.95 (*0-387-17338-2*) Spr-Verlag.

Structure & Dynamics of the Interstellar Medium. Guillermo Tenorio-Tagle. (Lecture Notes in Physics Ser.: Vol. 350). xxi, 537p. 1989. 93.95 (*0-387-51956-4*) Spr-Verlag.

Structure & Dynamics of U. S. Government Policymaking: The Case of Strategic Minerals. Ewan W. Anderson. LC 88-11757. 239p. 1988. text ed. 59.95 (*0-275-93061-0*, C3061, Praeger Pubs) Greenwood.

Structure & Dynamics of Weakly Bound Molecular Complexes. Ed. by Alfons Weber. (C). 1987. lib. bdg. 226.50 (*90-277-2584-5*) Kluwer Ac.

An Asterisk (*) at the beginning of an entry indicates that the title is appearing in BIP for the first time.

Structure & Ethos of the Wisdom Admonitions in Proverbs. Philip J. Nel. (Beiheft zur Zeitschrift fuer die Alttestamentliche Wissenschaft Ser.: Vol. 158). xii, 142p. 1982. 66.95 (*3-11-008750-2*) De Gruyter.

Structure & Evolution of Active Galactic Nuclei. Ed. by G. Giuricin et al. 1986. lib. bdg. 252.00 (*90-277-2155-6*) Kluwer Ac.

Structure & Evolution of Close Binary Systems. Ed. by P. P. Eggleton et al. LC 76-21688. (Symposia of the International Astronomical Union Ser.: No. 73). 1976. pap. text ed. 117.50 (*90-277-0683-2*); lib. bdg. 141.50 (*90-277-0682-4*) Kluwer Ac.

Structure & Evolution of Galaxies. James Lequeux. (Documents on Modern Physics Ser.). 220p. 1969. text ed. 226.00 (*0-677-30110-3*) Gordon & Breach.

Structure & Evolution of Galaxies. Roger J. Tayler. LC 92-19071. (Illus.). 224p. (C). 1993. text ed. 59.95 (*0-521-36431-0*); pap. text ed. 24.95 (*0-521-36710-7*) Cambridge U Pr.

Structure & Evolution of Galaxies: Proceedings of the International School of Astrophysics, 2nd, Italy, June-July, 1974. International School of Astrophysics Staff & Giancarlo Setti. LC 75-22261. (NATO Advanced Study Institute Ser: No. C-21). viii, 334p. 1975. lib. bdg. 112.00 (*90-277-0325-6*) Kluwer Ac.

Structure & Evolution of Neutron Stars: Proceedings. R. Tamagaki et al. 450p. (C). 1992. 54.95 (*0-201-56293-6*, Adv Bk Prog) Addison-Wesley.

Structure & Evolution of Recent U. S. Trade Policy. Ed. by Robert E. Baldwin & Anne O. Krueger. LC 84-2560. (National Bureau of Economic Research Conference Report Ser.). 448p. 1985. lib. bdg. 60.00 (*0-226-03604-9*) U Ch Pr.

Structure & Evolution of Single & Binary Stars. Camiel W. De Loore. (Astrophysics & Space Science Library). 480p. (C). 1992. pap. text ed. 94.00 (*0-7923-1844-7*) Kluwer Ac.

Structure & Evolution of Single & Binary Stars. Camiel W. De Loore & C. Doom. LC 92-10276. (Astrophysics & Space Science Library). 480p. (C). 1992. lib. bdg. 188.00 (*0-7923-1768-8*) Kluwer Ac.

***Structure & Evolution of Surfaces.** Ed. by R. C. Cammarata et al. (Materials Research Society Symposium Proceedings Ser.: No. 440). 1997. text ed. 68.00 (*1-55899-344-4*) Materials Res.

Structure & Evolution of the Continental Lithosphere. Ed. by H. N. Pollack & V. Rama Murthy. (Illus.). 210p. 1984. 83.00 (*0-08-030023-5*, Pergamon Pr) Elsevier.

Structure & Evolution of the Stars. Schwarzschild. 1962. pap. 8.95 (*0-486-61479-4*) Dover.

Structure & Evolution of Vertebrates: A Laboratory Text for Comparative Vertebrate Anatomy. Alan Feduccia. 275p. (C). 1974. pap. text ed. 11.95 (*0-393-09291-7*) Norton.

Structure & Evolutionary History of the Solar System. Hannes Alfven & Gustaf Arrhenius. LC 75-29444. (Geophysics & Astrophysics Monographs: No. 5). xvi, 280p. 1975. pap. text ed. 82.50 (*90-277-0660-3*); lib. bdg. 104.50 (*90-277-0611-5*) Kluwer Ac.

Structure & Excitation of Amorphous Solids: Proceedings of the AIP International Conference, Williamsburg, 1976. American Institute of Physics. Ed. by G. Lucovsky & F. L. Galeener. LC 76-22279. (AIP Conference Proceedings Ser.: No. 31). 1976. 19.50 (*0-88318-130-4*) Am Inst Physics.

Structure & Expression: DNA & Its Drug Complexes, Vol. 2. M. H. Sarma & Ramaswamy H. Sarma. (Structure & Expression Ser.). (Illus.). 342p. 1988. lib. bdg. 100.00 (*0-940030-22-5*) Adenine Pr.

Structure & Expression: DNA Bending & Curvature, Vol. 3. M. H. Sarma & Ramaswamy H. Sarma. (Structure & Expression Ser.). (Illus.). 280p. 1988. lib. bdg. 100.00 (*0-940030-23-3*) Adenine Pr.

Structure & Expression: From Proteins to Ribosomes, Vol. 1. M. H. Sarma & Ramaswamy H. Sarma. (Structure & Expression Ser.). (Illus.). 288p. 1988. lib. bdg. 100.00 (*0-940030-21-7*) Adenine Pr.

Structure & Expression: From Proteins to Ribosomes; DNA & Its Drug Complexes; DNA Bending & Curvature, 3 vols., Set. Ed. by W. K. Olson et al. (Illus.). 1988. lib. bdg. 300.00 (*0-940030-24-1*) Adenine Pr.

Structure & Fabric, Vol. 1. 5th ed. Jack S. Foster. (Illus.). 260p. 1994. pap. 52.50 (*0-582-21605-2*, Pub. by Longman Group UK) Trans-Atl Phila.

Structure & Fabric, Vol. 2. 5th ed. Jack S. Foster & Raymond Harington. (Illus.). 432p. 1994. pap. 67.50 (*0-582-21865-9*, Pub. by Longman Group UK) Trans-Atl Phila.

***Structure & Fate of Subducting Slabs.** Ed. by Thorne Lay. Orig. Title: Advances in Geophysics, Vol. 35. (Illus.). 185p. 1996. reprint ed. pap. 34.95 (*0-12-439860-X*, AP Prof) Acad Pr.

Structure & Fiber Connections of the Hippocampus. Walter K. Schwerdtfeger. (Advances in Anatomy, Embryology & Cell Biology Ser.: Vol. 83). (Illus.). 90p. 1984. 40.95 (*0-387-13092-6*) Spr-Verlag.

Structure & Flow. David A. Fryxell. (Elements of Article Writing Ser.). 176p. 1996. 15.99 (*0-89879-705-5*, Wrtrs Digest Bks) F & W Pubns Inc.

Structure & Flow in Surfactant Solutions. Ed. by Craig A. Herb & Robert K. Prud'homme. LC 94-38931. (Symposium Ser.: No. 578). (Illus.). 424p. 1994. 99.95 (*0-8412-3054-4*) Am Chemical.

Structure & Form in the Babylonian Talmud. Louis Jacobs. 176p. (C). 1992. text ed. 65.00 (*0-521-40345-6*) Cambridge U Pr.

***Structure & Form of the French Enlightenment Vol. 2: Esprit Revolutionnaire.** Ira O. Wade. LC 77-72139. 467p. 1977. reprint ed. pap. 133.10 (*0-608-03333-2*, 2064045) Bks Demand.

Structure & Function. 8th ed. Gary A. Thibodeau. (Illus.). 512p. (C). (gr. 13). 1987. text ed. 30.95 (*0-8016-5036-4*) Mosby Yr Bk.

Structure & Function: Nucleic Acids; Proteins, 2 vols., Set. Ed. by Sarma et al. (Illus.). 1992. lib. bdg. 190.00 (*0-940030-36-5*) Adenine Pr.

Structure & Function - Special Edition. 9th ed. Thibodeau & Kevin T. Patton. 492p. (C). (gr. 13). 1991. text ed. 30.95 (*0-8016-6403-9*) Mosby Yr Bk.

***Structure & Function in Criminal Law.** Paul Robinson. (Oxford Monographs on Criminal Law & Justice). 288p. 1997. 75.00 (*0-19-825886-0*) OUP.

Structure & Function in Normal & Abnormal Hips: How to Rescue Mechanically Jeopardized Hips. 3rd enl. rev. ed. Renato Bombelli. LC 93-18576. 1993. 298.00 (*0-387-56266-4*) Spr-Verlag.

Structure & Function in Normal & Abnormal Hips: How to Rescue Mechanically Jeopardized Hips. 3rd rev. ed. Renato Bombelli. (Illus.). 235p. 1993. write for info. (*3-540-56266-4*) Spr-Verlag.

Structure & Function in Primitive Society. Alfred R. Radcliffe-Brown. 1965. pap. 17.95 (*0-02-925620-8*, Free Press) Free Pr.

Structure & Function Nine Ancillary Binder. Gary A. Thibodeau. 1992. 25.00 (*0-8016-6845-X*) Mosby Yr Bk.

Structure & Function of Alzheimer's Amyloid Beta Proteins. Schubert. (Molecular Biology Intelligence Unit Ser.). 100p. 1994. 89.95 (*1-57059-216-0*) R G Landes.

Structure & Function of Antibodies. Ed. by Leonard E. Glynn & M. W. Steward. LC 80-41379. (Illus.). 316p. reprint ed. pap. 48.80 (*0-685-20714-5*, 2030502) Bks Demand.

Structure & Function of Apolipoproteins. Ed. by Maryvonne Rosseneu. 437p. 1992. 153.00 (*0-8493-6906-1*, QP99) CRC Pr.

Structure & Function of Biofilms. Ed. by William G. Characklis & P. A. Wildrer. (Dahlem Workshop Reports - Life Sciences). 387p. 1989. text ed. 237.00 (*0-471-92480-6*) Wiley.

Structure & Function of Chromatin. CIBA Foundation Staff. LC 76-357416. (CIBA Foundation Symposium: New Ser.: No. 28). 378p. reprint ed. pap. 107.80 (*0-317-29182-3*, 2022156) Bks Demand.

Structure & Function of Domestic Animals. Bruce W. Currie. 464p. 1992. 51.95 (*0-8493-8766-3*) CRC Pr.

Structure & Function of Endothelial Cells. F. Hammersen. Ed. by K. Messmer. (Mikrozirkulation in Forschung und Klinik; Progress in Applied Microcirculation Ser.: Vol. 1). (Illus.). x, 138p. 1983. pap. 37.00 (*3-8055-3635-6*) S Karger.

Structure & Function of Eukaryotic Chromosomes. Ed. by W. Hennig. (Results & Problems in Cell Differentiation Ser.: Vol. 14). (Illus.). 320p. 1987. 158.95 (*0-387-17717-5*) Spr-Verlag.

Structure & Function of Excitable Cells. Ed. by Donald C. Chang et al. 516p. 1983. 120.00 (*0-306-41338-8*, Plenum Pr) Plenum.

Structure & Function of Fc Receptors. Ed. by Arnold Froese & Frixos Paraskevas. LC 83-5297. (Receptors & Ligands in Intercellular Communications Ser.: No. 2). (Illus.). 312p. reprint ed. pap. 89.00 (*0-7837-0947-1*, 2041251) Bks Demand.

Structure & Function of Fresh-Water Microbial Communities. Ed. by John Cairns. LC 75-30823. (Research Division Monographs: No. 3). 309p. reprint ed. pap. 88.10 (*0-8357-3278-9*, 2039501) Bks Demand.

Structure & Function of Invertebrate Oxygen Carriers. Ed. by S. N. Vinogradov & O. H. Kapp. (Illus.). 384p. 1991. 79.95 (*0-387-97585-3*) Spr-Verlag.

Structure & Function of Invertebrate Respiratory Proteins. Ed. by E. J. Wood. (Life Chemistry Reports). 416p. 1983. text ed. 182.00 (*3-7186-0155-9*) Gordon & Breach.

Structure & Function of Invertebrate Respiratory Proteins: EMBO Workshop 1982. Ed. by E. J. Wood. 432p. 1983. 79.00 (*3-7186-0136-2*) Gordon & Breach.

Structure & Function of Lamellar Bodies. Gerd Schmitz. 115p. 1993. 89.95 (*1-879702-61-4*, R) CRC Pr.

Structure & Function of Living Organisms. Deborah Ross. 84p. (C). 1995. student ed., pap. text ed., spiral bd. 20.94 (*0-7872-1857-X*) Kendall-Hunt.

Structure & Function of Monoamine Enzymes: Proceedings of a Conference Held in Steamboat Springs, Colorado, March 10-13, 1977. Conference on Structure & Function of Monoamine Enzymes Staff. Ed. by Earl Usdin et al. LC 77-14089. (Modern Pharmacology-Toxicology Ser.: No. 10). 1025p. reprint ed. pap. 180.00 (*0-7837-0611-1*, 2040959) Bks Demand.

***Structure & Function of Nucleic Acids & Proteins.** Ed. by Felicia Y. Wu & Cheng-Wen Wu. LC 90-8484. 352p. 1990. reprint ed. pap. 100.40 (*0-608-03460-6*, 2064161) Bks Demand.

Structure & Function of Peptidergic & Aminergic Neurons. Ed. by Y. Sano et al. (Taniguchi Symposia on Brain Sciences Ser.: No. 5). 363p. 1983. lib. bdg. 147.50 (*90-6764-001-8*, Pub. by VSP NE) Coronet Bks.

Structure & Function of Primary Messengers in Invertebrates: Insect Diuretic & Antidiuretic Peptides. Ed. by K. W. Beyenbach. (Molecular Comparative Physiology Ser.: Vol. 12). (Illus.). viii, 180p. 1993. 213.25 (*3-8055-5704-3*) S Karger.

Structure & Function of Roots: Proceedings of the 4th International Symposium on Structure & Function of Roots, Stara, Lesna, Slovakia, June 20-26, 1993. International Symposium on Structure & Function of Roots Staff. Ed. by F. Baluska et al. LC 95-8174. (Development in Plant & Soil Sciences Ser.: Vol. 58). 368p. (C). 1995. lib. bdg. 195.00 (*0-7923-2832-9*) Kluwer Ac.

Structure & Function of the Aspartic Proteinases: Genetics, Structure, & Mechanisms. Ed. by B. M. Dunn. (Advances in Experimental Medicine & Biology Ser.: Vol. 306). (Illus.). 580p. 1991. 149.50 (*0-306-44052-0*, Plenum Pr) Plenum.

Structure & Function of the Body. 10th ed. Gary A. Thibodeau & Kevin T. Patton. LC 96-17642. 000512p. (C). (gr. 13). 1996. text ed. 33.95 (*0-8151-8714-9*) Mosby Yr Bk.

Structure & Function of the Body. 10th ed. Gary A. Thibodeau & Kevin T. Patton. LC 96-17642. 000512p. (C). (gr. 13). 1996. pap. text ed. 31.95 (*0-8151-8713-0*) Mosby Yr Bk.

Structure & Function of the Circulation, Vol. 3. Ed. by Colin J. Schwartz et al. 554p. 1981. 95.00 (*0-306-40751-5*, Plenum Pr) Plenum.

Structure & Function of the Glutathione Transferases. Ed. by Kenneth D. Tew et al. LC 93-8303. 336p. 1993. 206.95 (*0-8493-4582-0*, QP606) CRC Pr.

Structure & Function of the Human Body. 6th ed. Ruth L. Memmler et al. (Illus.). 368p. 1996. pap. 57.50 (*0-397-55172-X*, Pub. by Stanley Thornes UK) Trans-Atl Phila.

Structure & Function of the Human Body. 6th ed. Ruth L. Memmler. 368p. 1995. text ed. 31.95 (*0-397-55173-8*); pap. text ed. 15.95 (*0-397-55190-8*) Lppncott-Raven.

Structure & Function of the Kidney. Ed. by R. K. Kinne. (Comparative Physiology Ser.: Vol. 1). viii, 198p. 1989. 132.00 (*3-8055-4886-9*) S Karger.

Structure & Function of the Skin. 3rd ed. William Montagna & P. F. Parakkal. 1974. text ed. 149.00 (*0-12-505263-4*) Acad Pr.

Structure & Function, Vol. 1: Nucleic Acids. Ed. by Sarma et al. (Illus.). 276p. 1992. lib. bdg. 95.00 (*0-940030-37-3*) Adenine Pr.

Structure & Function, Vol. 2: Proteins. Ed. by Sarma et al. (Illus.). 192p. 1992. lib. bdg. 95.00 (*0-940030-38-1*) Adenine Pr.

***Structure & Functioning of Plant Populations.** Ed. by A. H. J. Freysen & J. W. Woldendorp. (Verhandelingen der Koninklijke Nederlandse Akademie van Wetenschappen, Afd. Natuurkunde Ser.: No. 70). 336p. 1978. pap. text ed. 37.50 (*0-7204-8444-8*) Elsevier.

***Structure & Functioning of Plant Populations 2: Phenotypic & Genotypic Variation in Plant Populations.** Ed. by J. Haeck & J. W. Woldendorp. vii, 408p. 1985. pap. text ed. 59.50 (*0-444-85624-2*) Elsevier.

Structure & Functioning of Seminatural Meadows. Ed. by Milena Rychnovska. LC 92-11732. (Developments in Agricultural & Managed-Forest Ecology Ser.). 386p. 1993. 224.75 (*0-444-98669-3*) Elsevier.

Structure & Functions of Amine Oxidases. Ed. by Bruno Mondovi. 304p. 1986. 167.00 (*0-8493-5869-8*, QP603, CRC Reprint) Franklin.

Structure & Functions of Governance: Its National & International Setting. Ed. by Kenneth W. Thompson. LC 92-10044. 1992. 49.50 (*0-8191-8544-2*); pap. 24.50 (*0-8191-8545-0*) U Pr of Amer.

Structure & Functions of the Human Prefrontal Cortex. Ed. by Jordan Grafman et al. (Annals of the New York Academy of Sciences Ser.: Vol. 769). 411p. 1995. 95.00 (*0-89766-991-6*); pap. write for info. (*0-89766-992-4*) NY Acad Sci.

Structure & Gestalt: Philosophy & Literature in Austria-Hungary & Her Successor States. Ed. by Barry Smith. (Linguistic & Literary Studies in Eastern Europe: Vol. 7). x, 349p. 1981. 78.00 (*90-272-1510-3*) Benjamins North Am.

Structure & Governance of Library Networks. Ed. by Kent & Galvin. (Books in Library & Information Science: Vol. 27). 376p. 1979. 140.00 (*0-8247-6866-3*) Dekker.

Structure & Growth of Residential Neighborhoods in American Cities. U. S. Federal Housing Administration Staff. 1988. reprint ed. lib. bdg. 49.00 (*0-7812-0997-8*) Rprt Serv.

Structure & Growth of Residential Neighborhoods in American Cities. U. S. Federal Housing Administration Staff. Ed. by Homer Hoyt. LC 75-115283. (Illus.). 190p. 1972. reprint ed. 39.00 (*0-403-00266-4*) Scholarly.

Structure & Growth of the Italian Economy. U. S. Mutual Security Agency Staff. LC 78-109870. (Illus.). v, 165p. 1972. reprint ed. text ed. 52.50 (*0-8371-4361-6*, SGIE, Greenwood Pr) Greenwood.

Structure & History in Greek Mythology & Ritual. Walter Burkert. LC 78-62856. (Sather Classical Lectures: No. 47). 1980. pap. 16.00 (*0-520-04770-2*) U CA Pr.

Structure & History in Greek Mythology & Ritual. Walter Burkert. LC 78-62856. (Sather Classical Lectures: No. 47). (Illus.). 246p. reprint ed. pap. 70.20 (*0-7837-4755-1*, 2044502) Bks Demand.

Structure & History in John Eleven: A Methodological Study Comparing Structuralist & Historical Critical Approaches. James J. Bridges. LC 90-28591. (Distinguished Dissertations Ser.: Vol. 4). 332p. 1991. lib. bdg. 99.95 (*0-7734-9942-3*) E Mellen.

Structure & Ideology in an Association of Deviants. Edward Sagarin. LC 75-12346. (Homosexuality Ser.). 1975. reprint ed. 26.95 (*0-405-07402-6*) Ayer.

Structure & Imagery in Ancrene Wisse. Janet Grayson. LC 73-77480. 251p. reprint ed. pap. 71.60 (*0-317-55642-8*, 2029252) Bks Demand.

Structure & Impact of Population Redistribution in New England. Ed. by Thomas E. Steahr & A. E. Luloff. 197p. (Orig.). 1986. pap. 7.00 (*0-9609010-1-9*) NE Regional Ctr.

Structure & Influence: Statistical Models for the Dynamics of Actor Attributes, Network Structure & Their Interdependence. Roger T. Leenders. (ICS (Dissertations of the Interuniversity Center for Social Science Theory & Methodology - The Netherlands) Ser.). 253p. 1995. pap. 26.50 (*90-5170-329-5*, Pub. by Thesis Pubs NE) IBD Ltd.

Structure & Insight. Pierree M. Van Hiele. (Developmental Psychology Ser.). 1985. pap. text ed. 50.00 (*0-12-714161-8*) Acad Pr.

Structure & Interpretation of Computer Programs. Harold Abelson et al. (Electrical Engineering & Computer Science Ser.). 1989. pap. text ed. 19.95 (*0-262-51046-4*); disk 24.95 (*0-262-51044-8*); disk 25.00 (*0-262-51045-6*) MIT Pr.

Structure & Interpretation of Computer Programs. 2nd ed. Harold Abelson et al. LC 96-17756. 1985. pap. 28.50 (*0-262-51087-1*) MIT Pr.

Structure & Interpretation of Computer Programs. 2nd ed. Harold Abelson & Gerald J. Sussman. (Illus.). 648p. 1996. 60.00 (*0-262-01153-0*) MIT Pr.

***Structure & Interpretation of Computer Programs.** 2nd ed. Harold Abelson et al. 1996. text ed. write for info. (*0-07-000484-6*) McGraw.

Structure & Interpretation of Quantum Mechanics. R. I. Hughes. LC 88-16551. (Illus.). 384p. 1989. 49.95 (*0-674-84391-6*) HUP.

Structure & Interpretation of Quantum Mechanics. R. I. Hughes. (Illus.). 384p. (C). 1992. pap. 22.00 (*0-674-84392-4*) HUP.

Structure & Kinship in Tribal India. Bhabananda Mukherjee. 1981. 10.00 (*0-8364-0769-5*, Pub. by Minerva II) S Asia.

Structure & Meaning: Relinking Classical Sociology. Jeffrey C. Alexander. 300p. 1989. text ed. 49.50 (*0-231-06688-0*) Col U Pr.

Structure & Meaning in Old Norse Literature: New Approaches to Textual Analysis & Literary Criticism. Ed. by John Lindow et al. (Studies in Northern Civilization: No.3). 454p. 1986. pap. text ed. 67.50 (*87-7492-607-1*, Pub. by Odense Universitets Forlag DK) Coronet Bks.

Structure & Meaning in the Fourth Gospel: A Text-Linguistic Analysis of John. Birgur Olsson. (New Testament Ser.: No. 6). 328p. 1974. pap. 53.00 (*91-40-03344-9*, Pub. by LiberUtbildning SW) Coronet Bks.

Structure & Meaning in the Prehistoric Art of Zimbabwe. Peter S. Garlake. (Orig.). 1987. pap. 5.00 (*0-941934-51-9*) Indiana Africa.

Structure & Meaning of Badarayana's Brahma Sutras: A Translation & Analysis of Adhyaya 1. George C. Adams, Jr. (C). 1993. text ed. 14.00 (*81-208-0931-9*, Pub. by Motilal Banarsidass II) S Asia.

Structure & Meaning of Second Baruch. Frederick J. Murphy. 148p. (C). 1985. pap. 15.95 (*0-89130-845-8*, 06 01 78) Scholars Pr GA.

Structure & Mechanism in Vinyl Polymerization. Ed. by Teiji Tsuruta & Kenneth F. O'Driscoll. LC 68-25345. 552p. reprint ed. pap. 157.40 (*0-317-08383-X*, 2055022) Bks Demand.

Structure & Mesomorphism of Cholesteric Liquid Crystals. A. I. Galatina et al. 86p. 1986. text ed. 67.00 (*2-88124-178-6*) Gordon & Breach.

Structure & Methods: Human Genome Initiative & DNA Recombination; DNA Protein Complexes & Proteins; DNA & RNA, 3 vols., Set. Ed. by Sarma et al. (Illus.). 1990. lib. bdg. 290.00 (*0-940030-32-2*) Adenine Pr.

Structure & Methods, Vol. One: Human Genome Initiative & DNA Recombination. Ed. by Sarma et al. (Structure & Methods Ser.). (Illus.). 252p. 1990. lib. bdg. 90.00 (*0-940030-29-2*) Adenine Pr.

Structure & Methods, Vol. Two: DNA Protein Complexes & Proteins. Ed. by Sarma et al. (Structure & Methods Ser.). (Illus.). 236p. 1990. lib. bdg. 90.00 (*0-940030-30-6*) Adenine Pr.

Structure & Methods, Vol. 3: DNA & RNA. Ed. by Sarma et al. (Structure & Methods Ser.). (Illus.). 358p. 1990. lib. bdg. 110.00 (*0-940030-31-4*) Adenine Pr.

Structure & Mobility: The Men & Women of Marseille, 1820-1870. William H. Sewell, Jr. (Illus.). 410p. 1985. text ed. 80.00 (*0-521-26237-2*) Cambridge U Pr.

Structure & Mobility in Molecular & Atomic Glasses, Vol. 371. Ed. by James M. O'Reilly. LC 81-14226. 354p. 1981. pap. 76.00 (*0-89766-132-X*) NY Acad Sci.

Structure & Models Used in Profiles 2.0 with Application to Bangladesh. Barton R. Burkhalter et al. 80p. (Orig.). 1994. pap. text ed. write for info. (*0-89492-106-1*) Acad Educ Dev.

Structure & Motion: Membranes, Nucleic Acids & Proteins. Ed. by E. Clementi et al. (Illus.). 582p. 1985. lib. bdg. 130.00 (*0-940030-12-8*) Adenine Pr.

Structure & Operation of the World Gold Market. Gary O'Callaghan. LC 93-22746. (Occasional Paper Ser.: No. 105). 60p. 1993. 15.00 (*1-55775-281-8*) Intl Monetary.

Structure & Organic Matter Storage in Agricultural Soils. Ed. by Martin R. Carter & B. A. Stewart. LC 95-38348. (Advances in Soil Science Ser.). 496p. 1995. 85.00 (*1-56670-033-7*, L1033) Lewis Pubs.

Structure & Performance in Adult Education. Graham Mee & Harold Wiltshire. LC 77-7051. 1978. pap. text ed. 9.50 (*0-582-48944-X*) Longman.

Structure & Persuasive Power of Mark: A Linguistic Approach. John G. Cook. LC 95-8489. (Society of Biblical Literature Semeia Studies). 402p. (C). 1995. 44.95 (*0-7885-0027-9*, 060628); pap. 29.95 (*0-7885-0028-7*, 060628) Scholars Pr GA.

Structure & Physical Properties of Paper. H. F. Rance. (Handbook of Paper Science Ser.: Vol. 2). 288p. 1982. 188.25 (*0-444-41974-8*) Elsevier.

S

Structure & Policy in Japan & the United States. Ed. by Peter F. Cowhey & Mathew D. McCubbins. (Political Economy of Institutions & Decisions Ser.). (Illus.). 319p. (C). 1995. 59.95 (*0-521-46151-0*) Cambridge U Pr.

Structure & Policy in Japan & the United States. Ed. by Peter F. Cowhey & Mathew D. McCubbins. (Political Economy of Institutions & Decisions Ser.). (Illus.). 219p. (C). 1995. pap. 18.95 (*0-521-46710-1*) Cambridge U Pr.

Structure & Process in a Melanesian Society: Ponam's Progress in the Twentieth Century. A. H. Carrier. (Studies in Anthropology & History). 261, xxiip. 1991. text ed. 64.00 (*3-7186-5149-1*, Harwood Acad Pubs) Gordon & Breach.

Structure & Process in Secondary Schools: The Academic Impact of Educational Climates. Edward L. McDill & Leo C. Rigsby. LC 73-8123. 224p. reprint ed. pap. 63.90 (*0-317-41751-7*, 2025861) Bks Demand.

Structure & Process in Southeastern Archaeology. Ed. by Roy S. Dickens, Jr. & H. Trawick Ward. LC 84-23. (A Dan Josselyn Memorial Publication). (Illus.). 365p. 1985. pap. 104.10 (*0-7837-8369-8*, 2059179) Bks Demand.

Structure & Process in Superpower Arms Control: Lessons from INF. Thomas Risse-Kappen. (CISA Working Papers: No. 69). 41p. (Orig.). 1989. pap. 15.00 (*0-86682-085-X*) Ctr Intl Relations.

S

Structure & Process of International Law. Ed. by Ronald S. Macdonald & Douglas M. Johnston. 1983. lib. bdg. 317.00 (*90-247-2882-7*) Kluwer Ac.

Structure & Process of International Law. Ed. by Ronald S. Macdonald & Douglas M. Johnston. 1986. lib. bdg. 147.50 (*90-247-3273-5*) Kluwer Ac.

Structure & Processes of Organization. H. C. Ganguli. 1984. 14.00 (*0-8364-1163-3*, Pub. by Allied II) S Asia.

Structure & Profitability of the Antebellum Rice Industry: 1859. Dale E. Swan. LC 75-2598. (Dissertations in American Economic History Ser.). (Illus.). 1975. 34.95 (*0-405-07219-8*) Ayer.

Structure & Properties of Cell Membranes: Molecular Basis of Selected Transport Systems, Vol. II: Molecular Basis of Selected Transport Sys. Gheorghe Benga. LC 84-19942. 304p. 1985. 149.00 (*0-8493-5765-9*, QH509, CRC Reprint) Franklin.

Structure & Properties of Cell Membranes: Survey of Molecular Aspects of Membrane Structure & Function, Vol. I. Ed. by Gheorghe Benga. LC 84-19943. 240p. 1985. 138.00 (*0-8493-5764-0*, QH601, CRC Reprint) Franklin.

Structure & Properties of Cell Membranes: Survey of Molecular Aspects of Membrane Structure & Function, 3 vols., Vol. III: Methodology & Propertiese of Membrane. Ed. by Gheorghe Benga. LC 84-19943. 304p. 1985. Vol. III: Methodology & Properties of Membranes, 304p. 170.00 (*0-8493-5766-7*, QH601, CRC Reprint) Franklin.

Structure & Properties of Ceramics. Ed. by Alex Koller. LC 93-38986. 588p. 1994. 243.25 (*0-444-98719-3*) Elsevier.

Structure & Properties of Ceramics see Materials Science & Technology: A Comprehensive Treatment

Structure & Properties of Composites see Materials Science & Technology: A Comprehensive Treatment

Structure & Properties of Conducting Polymer Composites. Ed. by V. E. Gul'. 218p. 1996. 215.00 (*90-6764-204-5*, Pub. by VSP NE) Coronet Bks.

Structure & Properties of Energetic Materials. Ed. by R. W. Armstrong & J. J. Gilman. (Materials Research Society Symposium Proceedings Ser.: Vol. 296). 387p. 1993. text ed. 30.00 (*1-55899-191-3*) Materials Res.

Structure & Properties of Engineering Alloys. 2nd ed. William F. Smith. (Materials Science & Engineering Ser.). 1992. text ed. write for info. (*0-07-059172-5*) McGraw.

Structure & Properties of Engineering Materials. 4th ed. R. M. Brick et al. (McGraw-Hill Series in Materials Science & Engineering). (Illus.). (C). 1977. text ed. write for info. (*0-07-007721-5*) McGraw.

Structure & Properties of Engineering Materials. Bryan Harris & A. R. Bunsell. LC 76-41771. (Introductory Engineering Ser.). (Illus.). 363p. reprint ed. pap. 103.50 (*0-317-08294-9*, 2019608) Bks Demand.

Structure & Properties of Ferromagnetic Materials. Ed. by R. A. McCurrie. (Illus.). 320p. 1994. text ed. 74.00 (*0-12-482495-1*) Acad Pr.

Structure & Properties of Interfaces in Ceramics: 1994 MRS Fall Meeting, Boston, MA. Ed. by Dawn A. Bonnell et al. (MRS Symposium Proceedings Ser.: Vol. 357). 468p. 1995. 67.00 (*1-55899-258-8*) Materials Res.

Structure & Properties of Interfaces in Materials. Ed. by W. A. Clark et al. (Symposium Proceedings Ser.: Vol. 238). 889p. 1992. text ed. 17.50 (*1-55899-132-8*) Materials Res.

Structure & Properties of Ionomers. Ed. by Michel Pineri & Adi Eisenberg. 1987. lib. bdg. 230.50 (*90-277-2458-X*) Kluwer Ac.

Structure & Properties of Materials, Vol. 2: Thermodynamics of Structure. Jere Brophy et al. 228p. 1964. reprint ed. pap. 65.00 (*0-317-28066-X*, 2055769) Bks Demand.

Structure & Properties of Matter. Ed. by T. Matsubara. (Solid-State Sciences Ser.: Vol. 28). (Illus.). 450p. 1982. 89.95 (*0-387-11098-4*) Spr-Verlag.

Structure & Properties of Metals. Welding Institute Staff. 76p. 1995. pap. 49.95 (*1-85573-171-1*, Pub. by Woodhead Pubng UK) Am Educ Systs.

Structure & Properties of Molecular Crystals. Ed. by M. Pierrot. (Studies in Physical & Theoretical Chemistry: Vol. 69). 354p. 1990. 208.25 (*0-444-88177-8*) Elsevier.

Structure & Properties of Multilayered Thin Films. S. C. Shin. (Symposium Proceedings Ser.: Vol. 382). 496p. 1995. text ed. 85.00 (*1-55899-285-5*) Materials Res.

Structure & Properties of Nearby Galaxies: Proceedings of the International Astronomical Union Symposium, No. 77. International Astronomical Union Staff. Ed. by Elly M. Berkhuijsen & Richard Wielebinski. 1978. pap. text ed. 70.50 (*90-277-0875-4*); lib. bdg. 88.00 (*90-277-0874-6*) Kluwer Ac.

Structure & Properties of Nonferrous Alloys see Materials Science & Technology: A Comprehensive Treatment

Structure & Properties of Polymeric Materials. D. W. Clegg & A. A. Collyer. 300p. 1993. 70.00 (*0-901716-39-1*, Pub. by Inst Materials UK) Ashgate Pub Co.

Structure & Properties of Polymers see Materials Science & Technology: A Comprehensive Treatment

Structure & Properties of Silicate Melts. B. O. Mysen. (Developments in Geochemistry Ser.: Vol. 4). 354p. 1988. 150.00 (*0-444-42959-X*) Elsevier.

Structure & Properties of Solid Solutions. J. Sivertsen & M. Nicholson. LC 49-50107. (Progress in Materials Science Ser.: Vol. 9, Pt. 5). 1961. 43.00 (*0-08-009473-2*, Pub. by Pergamon Repr UK) Franklin.

Structure & Properties of Thin Films: Proceedings of the International Conference, Bolton Landing, New York, 1959. International Conference on Structure & Properties of Thin Films Staff. Ed. by C. A. Neugebauer & J. B. Newkirk. LC 59-15871. 575p. reprint ed. pap. 163.90 (*0-317-42403-3*, 2056076) Bks Demand.

Structure & Properties of Ultrahigh-Strength Steels. American Society for Testing & Materials Staff. LC 65-19686. (American Society for Testing & Materials Special Technical Publication Ser.: Special Technical Publication, No. 370). 227p. reprint ed. pap. 64.70 (*0-317-11239-2*, 2000741) Bks Demand.

Structure & Property Relationships for Interfaces. Ed. by J. L. Walter et al. 811p. 1991. 97.00 (*0-87170-426-9*, 6271) ASM.

***Structure & Property Relationships for Interfaces.** Ed. by John L. Walter et al. LC 91-73858. (Illus.). 431p. 1991. reprint ed. pap. 122.90 (*0-608-02651-4*, 2063311) Bks Demand.

Structure & Reaction Processes of Coal. Kenneth L. Smith et al. LC 94-4702. (Chemical Engineering Ser.). (Illus.). 415p. (C). 1994. 110.00 (*0-306-44602-2*, Plenum Pr) Plenum.

Structure & Reactions of Unstable Nuclei. Ed. by K. Ikeda et al. 350p. (C). 1992. text ed. 114.00 (*981-02-0769-7*) World Scientific Pub.

Structure & Reactivity in Aqueous Solution: Characterization of Chemical & Biological Systems. Ed. by Christopher J. Cramer & Donald G. Truhlar. LC 94-29430. (Symposium Ser.: No. 568). (Illus.). 448p. 1994. 99.95 (*0-8412-2980-5*) Am Chemical.

***Structure & Reactivity in Reverse Micelles.** M. P. Pileni. (Studies in Physical & Theoretical Chemistry: Vol. 65). 388p. 1989. 231.00 (*0-444-88166-2*) Elsevier.

Structure & Reactivity of Cycloimmonium Ylides. J. P. Surpateanu et al. 1977. pap. 14.00 (*0-08-021585-8*, Pergamon Pr) Elsevier.

Structure & Reform of Centrally Planned Economic Systems. Paul Jonas. (East European Monographs). 256p. 1990. text ed. 44.00 (*0-88033-172-0*) Col U Pr.

Structure & Reform of the U. S. Tax System. Albert Ando et al. 184p. 1985. 22.50 (*0-262-01086-0*) MIT Pr.

Structure & Regulation of Type-1 Protein Phosphataese Involved in Hepatic Glycogen Metabolism. M. Bollen. No. 49. 79p. (Orig.). 1991. pap. 28.00 (*90-6186-481-X*, Pub. by Leuven Univ BE) Coronet Bks.

Structure & Relationship in Constitutional Law. Charles L. Black. LC 69-17621. (Edward Douglass White Lectures: 1968). 107p. reprint ed. pap. 30.50 (*0-317-28671-4*, 2055300) Bks Demand.

Structure & Relationship in Constitutional Law. Charles L. Black, Jr. LC 85-13904. 98p. (C). 1986. reprint ed. 24.00 (*0-918024-42-0*); reprint ed. pap. 14.00 (*0-918024-44-7*) Ox Bow.

Structure & Representations of Jordan Algebras. Nathan Jacobson. LC 67-21813. (Colloquium Publications: Vol. 39). 453p. 1969. 52.00 (*0-8218-1039-1*, COLL/39) Am Math.

Structure & Representations of Q-Groups. Dennis Kletzing. (Lecture Notes in Mathematics Ser.: Vol. 1084). vi, 290p. 1984. 42.95 (*0-387-13865-X*) Spr-Verlag.

Structure & Reproduction of Corn. Theodore A. Kiesselbach. LC 79-19648. (Illus.). 104p. reprint ed. pap. 29.70 (*0-7837-5313-6*, 2044390) Bks Demand.

Structure & Reproduction of the Algae: Introduction, Chlorophyceae, Xanthophyceae, Chrysophyseae, Bacillariophyceae, Vol. I. Felix E. Fritsch. LC 35-8014. 809p. reprint ed. Vol. 1: Introduction, Chlorophyceae, Xanthophyceae, Chrysophyseae, Bacillariophyceae, Cryptophyceae. pap. 180.00 (*0-317-41818-1*, 2025582) Bks Demand.

***Structure & Retention in Chromatography: A Chemometric Approach.** R. Kaliszan. (Chromatography: Principles & Practice Ser.: Vol. 1). 224p. 1997. text ed. 95.00 (*90-5702-028-9*, Harwood Acad Pubs) Gordon & Breach.

Structure & Sacring: The Systematic Kingdom in Chretien's Erec et Enide. Donald Maddox. LC 77-93405. (French Forum Monographs: No. 8). 221p. (Orig.). 1978. pap. 10.95 (*0-917058-07-0*) French Forum.

Structure & Scale in the Roman Economy. Robert Duncan-Jones. (Illus.). 264p. (C). 1990. text ed. 69.95 (*0-521-35477-3*) Cambridge U Pr.

Structure & Sentiment: A Test Case in Social Anthropology. Ed. by Rodney Needham. LC 62-9738. xii, 148p. 1984. pap. text ed. 14.50 (*0-226-56989-6*, Midway Reprint) U Ch Pr.

Structure & Size of the Corporate Tax Department: An Empirical Analysis. Tax Executives Institute, Inc. Staff. 356p. (Orig.). 1993. pap. 35.00 (*0-915128-01-2*) Tax Exec Inst.

Structure & Society in Literary History: Studies in the History & Theory of Historical Criticism. Robert Weimann. LC 75-17719. 285p. reprint ed. pap. 81.30 (*0-7837-4372-6*, 2044082) Bks Demand.

Structure & Society in Literary History: Studies in the History & Theory of Historical Criticism. Robert Weimann. LC 84-9706. (C). 1984. reprint ed. pap. text ed. 15.95 (*0-8018-3122-9*) Johns Hopkins.

Structure & Spectroscopy see Pentacoordinated Phosphorus

Structure & Stability of Biological Macromolecules. Ed. by Serge N. Timasheff & Gerald D. Fasman. LC 70-76084. (Biological Macromolecules Ser.: No. 2). (Illus.). 704p. reprint ed. pap. 180.00 (*0-7837-0899-8*, 2041204) Bks Demand.

Structure & Stability of Salts of Halogen Oxyacids in the Solid Phase. F. Solymosi. LC 75-19287. 467p. 133.10 (*0-8357-9985-9*, 2016157) Bks Demand.

Structure & Stability of Salts of Halogen Oxycadis in the Solid Phase. F. Solymosi. 468p. (C). 1977. 90.00 (*963-05-1030-8*, Pub. by Akad Kiado HU) St Mut.

Structure & Statistics in Crystallography. Ed. by A. J. Wilson. 234p. 1985. lib. bdg. 90.00 (*0-940030-10-1*) Adenine Pr.

***Structure & Status of Pidgins & Creoles: Including Selected Papers from the Society for Pidgin & Creole Linguistics.** Ed. by Arthur K. Spears & Donald Winford. LC 97-6149. (Creole Language Library: Vol. 19). 1997. lib. bdg. 99.00 (*1-55619-174-X*) Benjamins North Am.

Structure & Strategy in Sikh Society. Harry Izmirlian, Jr. 221p. 1979. 18.95 (*0-318-36783-1*) Asia Bk Corp.

Structure & Stratigraphy of Trans-Pecos Texas. Ed. by Muehlberger. (IGC Field Trip Guidebooks Ser.). 216p. 1989. 35.00 (*0-87590-574-9*, T317) Am Geophysical.

***Structure & Structure Development of Al-Zn Alloys.** H. Loffler. 1995. text ed. 115.00 (*3-05-501506-1*) Wiley.

Structure & Style. enl. rev. ed. Leon Stein. LC 78-15541. (Illus.). xx, 297p. (Orig.). (gr. 9 up). 1979. pap. text ed. 17.95 (*0-87487-164-6*) Summy-Birchard.

***Structure & Style in Javanese: A Semiotic View of Linguistic Etiquette.** James J. Errington. LC 87-31672. (University of Pennsylvania Press Conduct & Communication Ser.). 309p. pap. 88.10 (*0-608-04817-8*, 2065474) Bks Demand.

Structure & Subject Interaction: Toward a Sociology of Knowledge in the Social Sciences. Stephen Bulick. (Books in Library & Information Science: Vol. 41). (Illus.). 256p. 1982. 99.75 (*0-8247-1847-X*) Dekker.

Structure & Surface: Beads in Contemporary American Art. Contrib. by Mark R. Leach. (Illus.). 48p. 1990. pap. 15.95 (*0-932718-28-0*) Kohler Arts.

Structure & Tectonics of Precambrian Rocks of India. S. Sinha-Roy. 252p. 1983. 59.95 (*0-318-37337-8*) Asia Bk Corp.

Structure & Texture: Selected Essays in Cheremis Verbal Art. Thomas A. Sebeok. LC 72-94505. (De Proprietatibus Litterarum, Ser. Practica: No. 44). (Illus.). 158p. (Orig.). 1974. pap. text ed. 67.70 (*90-279-2695-6*) Mouton.

Structure & the Book of Zechariah. Mike Butterworth. (JSOT Supplement Ser.: No. 130). 330p. (C). 1992. 60.00 (*1-85075-293-1*, Pub. by Sheffield Acad UK) CUP Services.

Structure & Theme: Don Quixote to James Joyce. Margaret Church. LC 83-2292. 219p. 1983. 42.00 (*0-8142-0348-5*) Ohio St U Pr.

Structure & Transformation: Developmental & Historical Aspects. Ed. by Klaus F. Riegel & George C. Rosenwald. LC 75-15659. (Origins of Behavior Ser.: Vol. 3). 268p. reprint ed. pap. 76.40 (*0-317-08075-X*, 2016470) Bks Demand.

Structure & Transport Properties. Emo Chiellini et al. 500p. 1997. text ed. 162.00 (*981-02-1894-X*) World Scientific Pub.

Structure & Variability of Antarctic Circumpolar Current. E. I. Sarukhanyan. Tr. by M. N. Pillai from RUS. 110p. (C). 1986. text ed. 55.00 (*90-6191-467-1*, Pub. by A A Balkema NE) Ashgate Pub Co.

***Structure-Based Drug Design.** Ed. by Veerapandian. LC 97-20396. 647p. 1997. 175.00 (*0-8247-9869-4*) Dekker.

***Structure-Based Drug Design: Thermodynamics, Modeling & Strategy.** John E. Ladbury & Pat R. Connelly. LC 97-21929. (Biotechnology Intelligence Unit Ser.). 1997. write for info. (*1-57059-469-4*) R G Landes.

***Structure-Based Edge Detection: Delineation of Boundaries in Aerial & Space Images.** M. J. Lemmens. x, 142p. (Orig.). 1996. pap. 44.50 (*90-407-1366-9*, Pub. by Delft U Pr NE) Coronet Bks.

Structure-Based Editors & Environments. Ed. by Gerd Szwillus & Lisa Neal. (Computers & People Ser.). (Illus.). 384p. 1996. boxed 75.00 (*0-12-681890-8*) Acad Pr.

Structure-Based Ligand Design. Ed. by Gubernator. (Methods in Medicinal Chemistry Ser.). 400p. 1996. 140.00 (*3-527-29343-4*, VCH) Wiley.

Structure-Borne Sound. L. Cremer & M. A. Heckl. (Illus.). 550p. 1988. 142.95 (*0-387-18241-1*) Spr-Verlag.

Structure, Cellular Synthesis, & Assembly of Biopolymers. Ed. by Steven T. Case. LC 92-36490. (Results & Problems in Cell Differentiation Ser.: Vol. 19). 1992. 238.95 (*0-387-55549-8*) Spr-Verlag.

Structure Charts for Program Design. Lang. 1994. pap. text ed. write for info. (*0-07-036328-5*) McGraw.

Structure, Conduct, & Performance: A Resurgent Paradigm. Leonard W. Weiss. Ed. by David B. Audretsch & Hideki Yamawaki. 456p. (C). 1992. 45.00 (*0-8147-9244-8*) NYU Pr.

Structure, Constitution, & General Characteristics of Wrought Ferritic Stainless Steels-STP 619. J. J. Demo. 72p. 1977. 7.50 (*0-8031-0793-5*, 04-619000-02) ASTM.

Structure, Context, Complexity & Organization: Physical Aspects of Information & Value. Karl E. Eriksson. 256p. 1987. text ed. 58.00 (*9971-5-0023-X*) World Scientific Pub.

Structure Correlation, 2 vols. Ed. by H. B. Burgi & J. D. Dunitz. 888p. 1994. 235.00 (*3-527-29042-7*, VCH) Wiley.

Structure Data of Elements & Intermetallic Phases see Nuclear Particles & Physics: Group I

Structure Data of Free Polyatomic Molecules see Atomic & Molecular Physics: Group II

Structure Data of Inorganic Compounds, Subvol. A see Crystal & Solid State Physics: Group III

Structure Data of Organic Compounds see Crystal & Solid State Physics: Group III

Structure Data of Organic Crystals see Nuclear Particles & Physics: Group I

***Structure de Dedoublement: Objectivite et Mythe Dans "Les Thibaultde" Roger Martin du Gard.** W. Donald Wilson. 238p. (FRE.). 1997. lib. bdg. 37.95 (*1-883479-18-5*) Summa Pubns.

Structure Des Exportations Du Quebec. Carmine Nappi. LC 79-1097. (Accent Quebec Ser.). 74p. 1978. reprint ed. pap. 25.00 (*0-608-01369-2*, 2062109) Bks Demand.

Structure Determination by X-Ray Crystallography. 3rd ed. M. F. Ladd & R. A. Palmer. (Illus.). 600p. (C). 1993. 59.50 (*0-306-44290-6*, Plenum Pr) Plenum.

Structure Determination by X-Ray Crystallography. 3rd ed. M. F. Ladd & R. A. Palmer. LC 94-6538. 1994. pap. 34.50 (*0-306-44751-7*) Plenum.

Structure, Development, & Phykogeny of Cranial Nerves. Ed. by R. L. Boord. (Journal: Acta Anatomica: Vol. 148, Nos. 2-3, 1993). (Illus.). 104p. 1993. pap. 214.00 (*3-8055-5909-7*) S Karger.

Structure du Comportement. Maurice Merleau-Ponty. (FRE.). 1990. pap. 21.95 (*0-7859-3015-9*) Fr & Eur.

Structure d'un Mythe Vedique: Le Mythe Cosmogonique dans le Rgveda. B. L. Ogibenin. (Approaches to Semiotics Ser.: No. 30). 1973. 56.95 (*90-279-2404-X*) Mouton.

Structure, Dynamics, & Biogenesis of Biomembranes. Ed. by Ryo Sato & Shun-Ichi Ohnishi. LC 83-51051. 188p. 1982. 65.00 (*0-306-41283-7*, Plenum Pr) Plenum.

Structure, Dynamics & Equilibrium Properties of Colloidal Systems. Ed. by D. M. Bloor & E. Wyn-Jones. (NATO Advanced Science Institutes Series C: Mathematical & Physical Sciences). 900p. 1990. lib. bdg. 308.50 (*0-7923-0993-6*) Kluwer Ac.

Structure, Dynamics & Properties of Silicate Melts. Ed. by J. F. Stebbins et al. (Reviews in Mineralogy Ser.: Vol. 32). (Illus.). 616p. (Orig.). (C). 1995. pap. text ed. 28.00 (*0-939950-39-1*) Mineralogical Soc.

Structure, Dynamics, Interactions & Evolution of Biological Macromolecules. Helene. 1983. lib. bdg. 175.00 (*90-277-1531-9*) Kluwer Ac.

Structure Elucidation by NMR in Organic Chemistry: A Pratical Guide. Eberhard Breitmaier. LC 92-18531. 265p. 1993. pap. text ed. 42.95 (*0-471-93381-3*) Wiley.

Structure Elucidation of Modern NMR: A Workbook. 2nd enl. rev. ed. W. Dietrich & H. Duddeck. x, 274p. 1992. 44.00 (*0-387-91425-0*) Spr-Verlag.

Structure, Energetics & Dynamics of Organic Ions. LC 95-54157. (Series in Ion Chemistry & Physics: Vol. 5). 1996. text ed. 175.00 (*0-471-96241-4*) Wiley.

Structure et Evolution su Capitalisme Europeen, XVIE-XVIIE Siecles. Andre E. Sayous. Ed. by Mark Steele. (Collected Studies: No. CS293). 318p. (C). 1989. lib. bdg. 98.95 (*0-86078-241-7*, Pub. by Variorum UK) Ashgate Pub Co.

Structure, Fluctuation, & Relaxation in Solutions. Ed. by H. Nomura et al. 452p. 1996. 324.25 (*0-444-82384-0*) Elsevier.

Structure for Intercommunity Governance of North Central Victoria, Vol. 5. Nancy Chamberlain & John Power. 1993. pap. 60.00 (*0-7300-2011-8*, PTSSSO, Pub. by Deakin Univ AT) St Mut.

Structure for Population Education: Goals, Generalizations, & Behavioral Objectives. 2nd ed. Mary T. Lane & Ralph E. Wileman. LC 74-77985. 1978. pap. 4.00 (*0-89055-128-6*) Carolina Pop Ctr.

Structure Formation in the Universe. T. Padmanabhan. (Illus.). 400p. (C). 1994. pap. text ed. 39.95 (*0-521-42486-0*) Cambridge U Pr.

Structure Formation in the Universe. T. Padmanabhan. (Illus.). 400p. (C). 1994. text ed. 110.00 (*0-521-41448-2*) Cambridge U Pr.

Structure Foundations. (Research Record Ser.: No. 1105). 58p. 1986. 9.00 (*0-309-04451-0*) Transport Res Bd.

Structure, Function & Genetics of Ribosomes. G. W. Kramer. (Molecular Biology Ser.). (Illus.). 815p. 1986. 288.00 (*0-387-96233-6*) Spr-Verlag.

Structure, Function & Modulation of Striated Muscle Calcium Channels. D. J. Pelzer. (Molecular Biology Intelligence Unit Ser.). 115p. 1994. 89.95 (*1-57059-057-5*) CRC Pr.

Structure, Function, & Regulation of Molecules Involved in Leukocyte Adhesion: Proceedings of the Second International Conferences on "Structure & Function of Molecules Involved in Leukocyte Adhesion II" Held in Titisee, Germany, October 2-6, 1991. Ed. by Peter E. Lipsky et al. LC 92-2337. (Illus.). 567p. 1992. 130.95 (*0-387-97870-4*) Spr-Verlag.

Structure, Function, Energy, & Information Laboratory Manual: General Biology for Science Majors. 3rd ed. GBG Staff. 320p. (C). 1994. spiral bd. 19.89 (*0-8403-9437-3*) Kendall-Hunt.

An Asterisk (*) at the beginning of an entry indicates that the title is appearing in BIP for the first time.

Structure-Function Properties of Food Proteins. Ed. by Lance G. Phillips & Dana M. Whitehead. (Food Science & Technology International Ser.). (Illus.). 271p. 1994. text ed. 69.00 (*0-12-554360-3*) Acad Pr.

Structure-Function Relations of Warm Desert Plants. Arthur C. Gibson. LC 96-18699. (Adaptations of Desert Organisms Ser.). 313p. 1996. 149.00 (*3-540-59267-9*) Spr-Verlag.

Structure Functions. R. Voss. 200p. 1998. text ed. 36.00 (*981-02-2435-4*, Ph-B2907) World Scientific Pub.

Structure in Complexity Theory. Alan L. Selman. (Lecture Notes in Computer Science Ser.: Vol. 223). vi, 401p. 1986. 45.00 (*0-387-16486-3*) Spr-Verlag.

Structure in Complexity Theory, 10th Annual Conference On. LC 10-636870. 344p. 1995. pap. 80.00 (*0-8186-7052-5*, PR07052) IEEE Comp Soc.

Structure in Complexity Theory, 9th Annual Conference. LC 10-636870. 408p. 1994. pap. 80.00 (*0-8186-5670-0*, 5670) IEEE Comp Soc.

Structure in Dynamics: Finite Dimensional Deterministic Studies. H. W. Broer et al. (Studies in Mathematical Physics: Vol. 2). 1991. 131.25 (*0-444-89257-5*, STU 2); pap. 80.25 (*0-444-89258-3*) Elsevier.

Structure in Fives: Designing Effective Organizations. 2nd ed. Henry Mintzberg. 320p. 1992. pap. text ed. 38.40 (*0-13-855479-X*) P-H.

Structure in Medieval Narrative. William W. Ryding. LC 72-154531. (De Proprietatibus Litterarum, Ser. Major: No. 12). 177p. 1971. text ed. 34.65 (*90-279-1795-7*) Mouton.

Structure in Polymers with Special Properties. Ed. by H. G. Zachmann. (Advances in Polymer Science Ser.: Vol. 108). (Illus.). 144p. 1993. 100.95 (*0-387-56579-5*) Spr-Verlag.

Structure in Process Control. Jens G. Balchen & Mumme. 640p. (gr. 13). 1987. text ed. 102.95 (*0-442-21155-4*) Chapman & Hall.

Structure in Protein Chemistry Vol. 1. Jack Kyte. LC 94-23417. 616p. 1995. text ed. 68.00 (*0-8153-1701-8*) Garland.

Structure in Sculpture. Daniel L. Schodek. LC 92-16904. (Illus.). 328p. (C). 1993. 75.00 (*0-262-19313-2*) MIT Pr.

Structure Level Adaptation for Artificial Neural Networks. Tsu-Chang Lee. (C). 1991. lib. bdg. 75.00 (*0-7923-9151-9*) Kluwer Ac.

Structure, Logic, & Program Design. Alan Cohen. LC 83-10207. (Illus.). 301p. reprint ed. pap. 85.80 (*0-8357-4610-0*, 2037543) Bks Demand.

Structure Maintainer. Jack Rudman. (Career Examination Ser.: C-772). 1994. pap. 23.95 (*0-8373-0772-4*) Nat Learn.

Structure Maintainer, Group A (Carpentry) Jack Rudman. (Career Examination Ser.: C-1495). 1994. pap. 23.95 (*0-8373-1495-X*) Nat Learn.

Structure Maintainer, Group B (Masonry) Jack Rudman. (Career Examination Ser.: C-1730). 1994. pap. 23.95 (*0-8373-1730-4*) Nat Learn.

Structure Maintainer, Group C (Iron Work) Jack Rudman. (Career Examination Ser.: C-1731). 1994. pap. 23.95 (*0-8373-1731-2*) Nat Learn.

Structure Maintainer, Group D (Sheet Metal) Jack Rudman. (Career Examination Ser.: C-1732). 1994. pap. 23.95 (*0-8373-1732-0*) Nat Learn.

Structure Maintainer, Group E (Plumbing) Jack Rudman. (Career Examination Ser.: C-1733). 1994. pap. 23.95 (*0-8373-1733-9*) Nat Learn.

Structure Maintainer, Group F (Sign Painting) Jack Rudman. (Career Examination Ser.: C-1776). 1994. reprint ed. pap. 23.95 (*0-8373-1776-2*) Nat Learn.

Structure Maintainer, Group G (Painting) Jack Rudman. (Career Examination Ser.: C-3528). 1994. pap. 23.95 (*0-8373-3528-0*) Nat Learn.

Structure Maintainer, Group H (Air Conditioning & Heating) Jack Rudman. (Career Examination Ser.: C-1422). 1994. pap. 23.95 (*0-8373-1422-4*) Nat Learn.

Structure Maintainer-Groups A, B, C, D & E. Jack Rudman. (Career Examination Ser.: C-2064). 1994. reprint ed. pap. 23.95 (*0-8373-2064-X*) Nat Learn.

Structure Maintainer Trainee, Group A (Carpentry) Jack Rudman. (Career Examination Ser.: C-1670). 1994. pap. 23.95 (*0-8373-1670-7*) Nat Learn.

Structure Maintainer Trainee, Group B (Masonry) Jack Rudman. (Career Examination Ser.: C-1671). 1994. pap. 23.95 (*0-8373-1671-5*) Nat Learn.

Structure Maintainer Trainee, Group C (Iron Work) Jack Rudman. (Career Examination Ser.: C-1672). 1994. pap. 23.95 (*0-8373-1672-3*) Nat Learn.

Structure Maintainer Trainee, Group D (Sheet Metal) Jack Rudman. (Career Examination Ser.: C-1673). 1994. pap. 23.95 (*0-8373-1673-1*) Nat Learn.

Structure Maintainer Trainee, Group E (Plumbing) Jack Rudman. (Career Examination Ser.: C-1674). 1994. pap. 23.95 (*0-8373-1674-X*) Nat Learn.

Structure Maintainer Trainee, Group G (Painting) Jack Rudman. (Career Examination Ser.: C-3529). 1994. pap. 23.95 (*0-8373-3529-9*) Nat Learn.

Structure Maintainer Trainee, Group H (Air Conditioning & Heating) Jack Rudman. (Career Examination Ser.: C-1491). 1994. pap. 23.95 (*0-8373-1491-7*) Nat Learn.

Structure, Movements & Reproduction in Three Costa Rican Bat Communities. Richard K. LaVal & Henry S. Fitch. (Occasional Papers: No. 69). 28p. 1977. pap. 1.00 (*0-317-04875-9*) U KS Nat Hist Mus.

Structure Mythique de "La Modification" de Michel Butor, Vol. 95. Patricia A. Struebig. LC 92-27672. (American University Studies: Vol. II). 126p. (C). 1994. text ed. 39.95 (*0-8204-0770-4*) P Lang Pubng.

Structure of a Modern Economy: The United States, 1929-89, As a Case Study. Kenneth E. Boulding & Meng Chi. LC 92-29613. 215p. (C). 1993. 65.00 (*0-8147-1203-7*) NYU Pr.

Structure of Accounting Theory. Ananias C. Littleton. (Monograph No. 5). 234p. 1953. 12.00 (*0-86539-026-6*) Am Accounting.

Structure of Accounting Theory. Shih C. Yu. LC 76-10355. 327p. reprint ed. pap. 93.20 (*0-7837-5063-3*, 2044753) Bks Demand.

***Structure of Aikido Vol. 1: Kenjutsu & Taijutsu Movement Relationships.** Gaku Homma. Tr. by Emily Busch from JPN. LC 96-36202. (Illus.). 200p. (Orig.). 1997. pap. 18.95 (*1-883319-55-2*) Frog Ltd CA.

Structure of Algebras. Abraham A. Albert. LC 41-9. (Colloquium Publications: Vol. 24). 210p. 1939. reprint ed. pap. 45.00 (*0-8218-1024-3*, COLL/24) Am Math.

Structure of American Economy, Nineteen Nineteen to Nineteen Thirty-Nine: An Empirical Application of Equilibrium Analysis. 2nd enl. ed. Wassily W. Leontief. LC 76-17415. 264p. (gr. 13). 1977. reprint ed. text ed. 77.95 (*0-87332-087-5*) M E Sharpe.

Structure of American English: Workbook. Raven I. McDavid & Donald C. Green. 147p. reprint ed. pap. 41.90 (*0-317-09501-3*, 2012513) Bks Demand.

Structure of American Industry. 9th ed. Ed. by Walter Adams. LC 94-6773. 336p. (C). 1994. text ed. 39.00 (*0-02-300833-4*, Macmillan Coll) P-H.

Structure of an African Pastoralist Community: Demography, History, & Ecology of the Ngamiland Herero. Renee Pennington & Henry Harpending. (Research Monographs on Human Population Biology: No. 11). (Illus.). 288p. 1993. 69.00 (*0-19-852286-X*) OUP.

Structure of an Ice Age: Abstracts. 206p. 1980. 10.00 (*0-318-13128-5*) Am Quaternary Assn.

Structure of Antigens, Vol. II. Marc H. Van Regenmortel. 400p. 1992. 163.95 (*0-8493-8867-8*, QR186) CRC Pr.

Structure of Antigens, Vol. 3. Ed. by Mare H. Van Regenmortel. 480p. 1995. 179.95 (*0-8493-9225-X*, 9225) CRC Pr.

***Structure of Applied General Equilibrium Models.** Victor Ginsburgh & Michiel Keyzer. LC 96-47835. 1997. 65.00 (*0-262-07179-7*) MIT Pr.

Structure of Arabic: From Sound to Sentence. Raja T. Nasr. 251p. (ARA.). 18.95 (*0-86685-045-7*, LDL0457, Pub. by Librairie du Liban FR) Intl Bk Ctr.

Structure of Argument. 5th ed. Annette T. Rottenberg. 1996. pap. text ed. 5.00 (*0-312-15035-0*) St Martin.

Structure of Associations in Language & Thought. James E. Deese. LC 65-26181. 232p. reprint ed. pap. 66.20 (*0-317-10518-3*, 2003839) Bks Demand.

Structure of Atonal Music. Allen Forte. LC 72-91295. 1977. pap. 18.00 (*0-300-02120-8*) Yale U Pr.

Structure of Behavior. Maurice Merleau-Ponty. 288p. 1983. reprint ed. pap. 19.50 (*0-8207-0163-7*) Duquesne.

Structure of Being: A Neoplatonic Interpretation. Ed. by R. Baine Harris. LC 81-5627. 187p. 1981. text ed. 64.50 (*0-87395-532-3*); pap. text ed. 21.95 (*0-87395-533-1*) State U NY Pr.

Structure of Big History: From the Big Bang until Today. Fred Spier. (Orig.). 1996. pap. 24.95 (*90-5356-220-6*, Pub. by Amsterdam U Pr NE) U of Mich Pr.

Structure of Biological Membranes. Philip L. Yeagle. 1248p. 1991. 119.95 (*0-8493-8837-6*, QH601) CRC Pr.

Structure of Biological Science. Alexander Rosenberg. (Illus.). 352p. 1985. text ed. 80.00 (*0-521-25566-X*); pap. text ed. 22.95 (*0-521-27561-X*) Cambridge U Pr.

Structure of Biological Theories. Paul Thompson. LC 88-15376. (Philosophy & Biology Ser.). 148p. (C). 1989. pap. text ed. 21.95 (*0-88706-934-7*) State U NY Pr.

Structure of Biological Theories. Paul Thompson. LC 88-15376. (Philosophy & Biology Ser.). 148p. (C). 1989. text ed. 64.50 (*0-88706-933-9*) State U NY Pr.

Structure of Biopolymers. O. L. Horer. (Abacus Bks.). 294p. 1973. text ed. 64.00 (*0-85626-000-2*) Gordon & Breach.

Structure of Brazilian Development. Ed. by Neuma Aguiar. LC 78-55936. 258p. 1979. 39.95 (*0-87855-138-7*) Transaction Pubs.

Structure of British Industry. 2nd ed. Peter Johnson. 400p. 1988. text ed. 60.00 (*0-04-338146-4*) Routledge Chapman & Hall.

Structure of Business. M. Maguire & M. P. Lawton. Ed. by J. R. Aslett. 224p. (C). 1986. 75.00 (*0-7175-1243-6*, Pub. by S Thornes Pubs UK) St Mut.

***Structure of Central Authority in Qajar Iran: 1871-1896.** A. Reza Sheikholeslami. LC 96-44954. (Studies in Near Eastern Culture & Society). 1997. pap. write for info. (*0-7885-0323-5*) Scholars Pr GA.

Structure of Certain Quasisymmetric Groups. A. Hinkkanen. LC 89-18137. (Memoirs Ser.: Vol. 83/422). 87p. 1990. pap. 18.00 (*0-8218-2485-6*, MEMO/83/422) Am Math.

***Structure of Christian Ethics.** Joseph Sittler. 1997. pap. text ed. write for info. (*0-664-25763-1*) Westminster John Knox.

***Structure of Classical Diffeomorphism Groups.** Augustin Banyaga. LC 97-3534. 1997. lib. bdg. 112.00 (*0-7923-4475-8*) Kluwer Ac.

Structure of Complex Nuclei. Ed. by Nikolai N. Bogolyubov. LC 69-12510. 225p. reprint ed. pap. 64.20 (*0-317-09191-3*, 2020679) Bks Demand.

Structure of Complex Predicates in Urdu. Miriam J. Butt. (Dissertations in Linguistics Ser.). 1995. text ed. 45.00 (*1-881526-59-3*); pap. text ed. 22.95 (*1-881526-58-5*) CSLI.

Structure of Complex Turbulent Shear Flow: Marseille, France, 1982, Proceedings. Ed. by R. Dumas & L. Fulachier. (International Union of Theoretical & Applied Mechanics Symposia Ser.). (Illus.). 444p. 1983. 76.95 (*0-387-12156-0*) Spr-Verlag.

Structure of Complex Words. William Empson & Jonathan Culler. LC 88-28701. 456p. 1989. reprint ed. pap. 17.50 (*0-674-84375-4*) HUP.

Structure of Conflict. Clyde H. Coombs & George S. Avrunin. 264p. 1988. text ed. 55.00 (*0-8058-0011-5*) L Erlbaum Assocs.

Structure of Consumption Decisions: A Disaggregated Analysis. Vani K. Borooah. (Illus.). 128p. 1989. text ed. 68.95 (*0-566-05772-7*, Pub. by Avebury Pub UK) Ashgate Pub Co.

Structure of Corporate Political Action: Interfirm Relations & Their Consequences. Mizruchi. (Illus.). 299p. 1992. 42.50 (*0-674-84377-0*) HUP.

Structure of Criminal Procedure: Laws & Practice of France, the Soviet Union, China & the United States. Barton L. Ingraham. LC 86-27139. (Contributions in Criminology & Penology Ser.: No. 16). 212p. 1987. text ed. 55.00 (*0-313-25431-1*, INS/) Greenwood.

Structure of Crystalline Polymers. Hiroyuki Tadokoro. LC 89-11220. 486p. (C). 1990. reprint ed. lib. bdg. 73.00 (*0-89464-349-5*) Krieger.

***Structure of Dagaare.** Adams Bodomo. LC 96-37999. (Stanford Monographs in African Languages). 168p. (C). 1997. text ed. 34.95 (*1-57586-077-5*) CSLI.

Structure of Daily Hydrologic Series. Vujica Yevjevich. (Illus.). 264p. (Orig.). 1984. pap. 32.00 (*0-918334-55-1*) WRP.

Structure of Decidable Locally Finite Varieties. R. McKenzie & M. Valeriote. (Progress in Mathematics Ser.: No. 79). 224p. 1989. 51.50 (*0-8176-3439-8*) Birkhauser.

Structure of Decision: The Cognitive Maps of Political Elites; Written under the Auspices of the Institute of International Studies, University of California (Berkeley) & the Institute of Public Policy Studies, the University of Michigan. Ed. by Robert M. Axelrod. LC 76-3242. (Illus.). 421p. reprint ed. pap. 120.00 (*0-8357-3852-3*, 2036585) Bks Demand.

Structure of Delight. Nelson Zink. 264p. (Orig.). pap. 14.95 (*0-9629621-0-4*) Metamorphous Pr.

***Structure of Delight.** Nelson Zink. 264p. 1997. pap. 16.95 (*1-55552-072-3*) Metamorphous Pr.

Structure of Desire. Warren W. Werner. 1983. pap. 4.00 (*0-936600-03-9*) Riverstone Foothills.

***Structure of Dynamical Systems.** J. M. Souriau. Ed. by R. H. Cushman & G. M. Tuynman. Tr. by C. H. Cushman-de Vries from FRE. LC 97-300. 400p. 74.50 (*0-8176-3695-1*) Birkhauser.

***Structure of Dynamical Systems: A Symplectic View of Physics.** J. M. Souriau. LC 97-300. 1997. write for info. (*3-7643-3695-1*) Birkhauser.

Structure of Earnings & the Measurement of Income Inequality in the U. S. D. J. Slottje. (Contributions to Economic Analysis Ser.: No. 184). 206p. 1989. 125.75 (*0-444-88320-7*, North Holland) Elsevier.

Structure of Economic Plants. Herman E. Hayward. (Illus.). 1967. reprint ed. 56.00 (*3-7682-0503-7*) Lubrecht & Cramer.

Structure of Economic Systems. John M. Montias. LC 75-43327. 336p. reprint ed. pap. 95.80 (*0-8357-8335-9*, 2033830) Bks Demand.

Structure of Economics: A Mathematical Analysis. 2nd ed. Eugene Silberberg. 1990. text ed. write for info. (*0-07-057550-9*) McGraw.

Structure of Electrified Interfaces. Ed. by Jacek Lipowski & Philip N. Ross. LC 92-44292. (Frontiers of Electrochemistry Ser.). 406p. 1993. 125.00 (*0-89573-787-6*, VCH) Wiley.

Structure of Emotion: Psychophysiological, Cognitive, & Clinical Aspects. Ed. by N. Birbaumer & A. Ohman. LC 91-20856. (Illus.). 312p. 1993. text ed. 65.00 (*0-88937-055-9*) Hogrefe & Huber Pubs.

Structure of Emotions: Investigations in Cognitive Philosophy. Robert M. Gordon. (Studies in Philosophy). (Illus.). 180p. (C). 1990. pap. text ed. 18.95 (*0-521-39568-2*) Cambridge U Pr.

Structure of Empirical Knowledge. Laurence Bonjour. 312p. (C). 1988. pap. 14.50 (*0-674-84381-9*) HUP.

Structure of Energy Markets. Ed. by Robert S. Pindyke. (Advances in the Economics of Energy & Resources Ser.: Vol. 1). 310p. 1979. 73.25 (*0-89232-078-8*) Jai Pr.

Structure of English. F. L. Sack. 1978. 20.00 (*0-87556-306-6*) Saifer.

Structure of English: A Handbook of English Grammar. Richard Newby. 112p. 1987. pap. text ed. 9.95 (*0-521-34996-6*) Cambridge U Pr.

Structure of English: Phonetics, Phonology, Morphology. Thomas E. Murray. LC 94-188. 1994. pap. text ed. 27.00 (*0-205-16053-0*) Allyn.

Structure of English Orthography. Richard L. Venezky. (Janua Linguarum, Ser. Minor: No. 82). 1970. pap. text ed. 21.55 (*90-279-0707-2*) Mouton.

Structure of English Words. 4th ed. Clarence Sloat & Sharon Taylor. 188p. (C). 1996. spiral bd. 25.14 (*0-7872-2248-8*) Kendall-Hunt.

Structure of European Industry. Ed. by Henry W. De Jong. (C). 1988. lib. bdg. 153.00 (*90-247-3689-7*) Kluwer Ac.

Structure of European Industry. Ed. by Henry W. De Jong. LC 92-47383. (Studies in Industrial Organization: Vol. 18). 440p. (C). 1993. lib. bdg. 134.00 (*0-7923-2160-X*) Kluwer Ac.

Structure of Factors & Automorphism Groups. Masamichi Takesaki. LC 83-6435. (CBMS Regional Conference Series in Mathematics: No. 51). 107p. 1983. pap. text ed. 26.00 (*0-8218-0701-3*, CBMS/51) Am Math.

Structure of Fields. D. J. Winter. LC 73-21824. (Graduate Texts in Mathematics Ser.: Vol. 16). (Illus.). 320p. 1974. 44.00 (*0-387-90074-8*) Spr-Verlag.

Structure of Finite Algebras. D. Hobby & R. McKenzie. LC 88-16712. (Contemporary Mathematics Ser.: No. 76). 203p. 1988. pap. text ed. 35.00 (*0-8218-5073-3*, CONM/76) Am Math.

Structure of Folk Models. Ed. by Ladislav Holy & M. Stuchlik. LC 80-41359. (Monograph: No. 20). 1981. text ed. 130.00 (*0-12-353750-9*) Acad Pr.

Structure of Freedom. rev. ed. Christian Bay. LC 58-10475. xii, 419p. 1970. reprint ed. 57.50 (*0-8047-0539-9*); reprint ed. pap. 17.95 (*0-8047-0540-2*) Stanford U Pr.

Structure of French: A Programmed Course on the Linguistic Structure of French. Edgar N. Mayer. (C). 1969. pap. text ed. 9.75 (*0-89197-429-6*) Irvington.

Structure of Freudian Thought: The Problem of Immutability & Discontinuity in Developmental Theory. Melvin Feffer. LC 81-23610. 298p. 1981. 45.00 (*0-8236-6185-7*) Intl Univs Pr.

Structure of Geology. David B. Kitts. LC 77-7395. 200p. reprint ed. pap. 57.00 (*0-8357-7040-0*, 2033444) Bks Demand.

Structure of German. Anthony Fox. 336p. 1990. pap. 35.00 (*0-19-815821-1*) OUP.

Structure of Hadrons & Hadronic Matter. Ed. by Olaf Scholten & J. H. Koch. 372p. (C). 1991. text ed. 118.00 (*981-02-0590-2*) World Scientific Pub.

Structure of Hebrews: A Text-Linguistic Analysis. George H. Guthrie. LC 93-36640. (Supplements to Novum Testamentum Ser.: No. 73). 1993. 90.00 (*90-04-09866-6*) E J Brill.

Structure of Households in Tanzania in 1991: Results from a National Household Survey. Alexander H. Sarris et al. (Working Papers: No. 58). (C). Date not set. pap. 7.00 (*1-56401-158-5*) Cornell Food.

Structure of Human Abilities. 2nd ed. Philip E. Vernon. LC 79-9751. 208p. 1979. reprint ed. text ed. 35.00 (*0-313-20804-2*, VEST, Greenwood Pr) Greenwood.

Structure of Human Decisions. David W. Miller & Martin K. Starr. (Orig.). 1967. pap. text ed. write for info. (*0-13-854687-8*) P-H.

Structure of Human Reflexion: The Reflexional Psychology of Vladimir Lefebvre. Harvey Wheeler. LC 89-14537. (American University Studies: Psychology: Ser. VIII, Vol. 17). 216p. 1990. text ed. 39.95 (*0-8204-0933-2*) P Lang Pubng.

Structure of Idealization: Towards a Systematic Interpretation of the Marxian Idea of Science. Leszek Nowak. (Synthese Library: No. 139). 288p. 1979. lib. bdg. 88.00 (*90-277-1014-7*, D Reidel) Kluwer Ac.

Structure of Indecomposable Modules. Hagen Metlzer. 96p. (C). 1986. 60.00 (*0-685-46647-7*, Pub. by Collets) St Mut.

Structure of Individual Psychotherapy. Bernard D. Beitman. LC 86-3160. 330p. 1986. lib. bdg. 47.50 (*0-89862-682-X*) Guilford Pr.

Structure of Individual Psychotherapy. Bernard D. Beitman. LC 86-3160. 330p. 1990. reprint ed. pap. text ed. 20.95 (*0-89862-461-4*) Guilford Pr.

Structure of Industry in Britain: A Study in Economic Change. 3rd ed. George C. Allen. LC 66-70817. 281p. reprint ed. pap. 80.10 (*0-317-20851-9*, 2025263) Bks Demand.

Structure of Industry in the EEC. Kenneth D. George & T. S. Ward. LC 75-319762. (University of Cambridge, Dept. of Applied Economics, Occasional Papers: 43). 83p. reprint ed. pap. 25.00 (*0-317-26403-6*, 2024460) Bks Demand.

Structure of Intelligence: A New Mathematical Theory of Mind. Ben Goertzel. LC 92-44224. 1993. 52.95 (*0-387-94004-9*) Spr-Verlag.

Structure of Intelligent Justice. John Richcreek. LC 87-71747. (Illus.). 650p. (Orig.). 1988. pap. 21.50 (*0-9600434-1-1*) Camda.

Structure of International Conflict. C. R. Mitchell. LC 79-25423. 368p. 1989. text ed. 12.95 (*0-312-02414-2*) St Martin.

Structure of International Publishing in the 1990s. Ed. by Fred Kobrak & Beth Luey. (Concordance Ser.: No. 37). 350p. (C). 1991. pap. text ed. 22.95 (*1-56000-568-8*) Transaction Pubs.

Structure of International Society: A Conceptual Analysis. Michael Nicholson. 256p. 1996. pap. 18.95 (*1-85567-243-X*, Pub. by Pntr Pubs UK) Bks Intl VA.

Structure of International Society: A Conceptual Analysis. Geoffrey Stern. 320p. 1995. 59.95 (*1-85567-275-8*); pap. 18.95 (*1-85567-276-6*) St Martin.

Structure of Intonational Meaning: Evidence from English. D. Robert Ladd. LC 79-3093. 250p. reprint ed. pap. 71.30 (*0-685-16319-9*, 2056235) Bks Demand.

Structure of Jacaltec. Colette G. Craig. LC 76-27109. 444p. reprint ed. pap. 126.60 (*0-8357-7734-0*, 2036091) Bks Demand.

Structure of Jewish History & Other Essays. Heinrich Graetz. Tr. by Schorsch. 25.00 (*0-87068-466-3*) Ktav.

Structure of Justification. Robert Audi. LC 92-37498. 592p. (C). 1993. pap. text ed. 24.95 (*0-521-44612-0*) Cambridge U Pr.

Structure of Justification. Robert Audi. LC 92-37498. 592p. (C). 1993. text ed. 69.95 (*0-521-44064-5*) Cambridge U Pr.

***Structure of K-Cs: Transitive Cycle-Free Partial Orders.** Richard Warren. LC 97-21322. (Memoirs of the American Mathematical Society Ser.). 1997. write for info. (*0-8218-0622-X*) Am Math.

Structure of Language. Owen Thomas. LC 67-18657. (Orig.). (C). 1967. pap. write for info. (*0-672-60889-8*, CR1, Bobbs) Macmillan.

Structure of Language: A New Approach. Petr Beckmann. LC 72-77116. (Illus.). 320p. 1972. 25.00 (*0-911762-13-2*) Golem.

Structure of Language & Its Mathematical Aspects: Proceedings. Ed. by R. Jakobson. LC 50-1183. (Proceedings of Symposia in Applied Mathematics Ser.: Vol. 12). 279p. 1983. reprint ed. pap. 36.00 (*0-8218-1312-9*, PSAPM/12) Am Math.

Structure of Lasting Peace. Horace M. Kallen. LC 74-1944. (World History Ser.: No. 48). 1974. lib. bdg. 75.00 (*0-8383-2030-9*) M S G Haskell Hse.

Structure of Latin: An Introductory Text Based on Caesar & Cicero. Ed. by Valdis Leinieks. 423p. (LAT.). 1975. text ed. 39.50 (*0-8422-5236-3*); pap. text ed. 19.95 (*0-8290-0461-0*) Irvington.

Structure of Laws As Represented by Symbolic Methods. Ward Waddell, Jr. 1961. pap. 2.75 (*0-9600130-0-8*) Waddell.

Structure of Learning Processes. Jaan Valsiner et al. (Illus.). 350p. 1996. pap. 39.50 (*1-56750-253-9*); text ed. 73.25 (*0-89391-981-0*) Ablex Pub.

Structure of Legal Argument & Proof: Cases, Materials & Analyses. J. S. Covington, Jr. LC 93-79684. 415p. 1993. pap. 36.60 (*0-916081-09-5*) J Marshall Pub Co.

Structure of Lexical Variation: Meaning, Naming, & Context. Dirk Geeraerts et al. LC 94-12628. (Cognitive Linguistics Research Ser.: No. 5). vii, 221p. (C). 1994. lib. bdg. 98.50 (*3-11-014387-9*, 112-94) Mouton.

Structure of Liquid Crystal Phases. P. S. Pershan. (Lecture Notes in Physics Ser.: Vol. 23). 440p. 1988. text ed. 93.00 (*9971-5-0668-8*); pap. text ed. 55.00 (*9971-5-0705-6*) World Scientific Pub.

Structure of Liquids see Encyclopedia of Physics

Structure of Local Government in England & Wales. 4th ed. William E. Jackson. LC 74-29792. 253p. 1976. reprint ed. text ed. 59.75 (*0-8371-8001-5*, JASL, Greenwood Pr) Greenwood.

Structure of Long-Term Memory: A Connectivity Model of Semantic Processing. Wolfgang Klimesch. 256p. 1994. text ed. 49.95 (*0-8058-1354-3*) L Erlbaum Assocs.

Structure of Love. Alan Soble. LC 89-16571. 392p. (C). 1990. text ed. 42.00 (*0-300-04566-2*) Yale U Pr.

Structure of Magic, Vol. 1. Richard Bandler & John Grinder. LC 75-12452. 1975. pap. 16.95 (*0-8314-0044-7*) Sci & Behavior.

Structure of Magic, Vol. 2. John Grinder & Richard Bandler. LC 75-12452. 1976. pap. 16.95 (*0-8314-0049-8*) Sci & Behavior.

Structure of Manufacturing Production: A Cross-Section View. Charles A. Bliss. (General Ser.: No. 36). 252p. 1939. reprint ed. 65.60 (*0-87014-035-3*); reprint ed. mic. film 32.80 (*0-685-61194-9*) Natl Bur Econ Res.

Structure of Marx's World-View. John M. McMurtry. LC 77-85552. 283p. reprint ed. pap. 80.70 (*0-8357-4047-1*, 2036737) Bks Demand.

Structure of Material Systems: Ethnoarchaeology in the Maya Highlands. Brian Hayden & Aubrey Cannon. (SAA Papers: No. 3). 246p. 1984. pap. 25.00 (*0-932839-06-1*) Soc Am Arch.

Structure of Matter. C. Suits & H. Way. LC 60-7068. (Collected Works of Irving Langmuir: Vol. 6). 1961. 148.00 (*0-08-009358-2*, Pub. by Pergamon Repr UK) Franklin.

Structure of Matter. Time-Life Books Editors. (Understanding Science & Nature Ser.). 176p. (J). 1992. 17.95 (*0-8094-9662-3*) Time-Life.

Structure of Matter. Karl Schuster. (Siemens Programmed Instruction Ser.: No. 8). 63p. reprint ed. pap. 25.00 (*0-317-27769-3*, 2052085) Bks Demand.

Structure of Matter: A Survey of Modern Physics. Stephen Gasiorowicz. LC 78-18645. (Physics Ser.). (Illus.). 1979. text ed. write for info. (*0-201-02511-6*) Addison-Wesley.

Structure of Matthew's Gospel: A Study in Literary Design. David R. Bauer. (JSNT Supplement/Bible & Literature Ser.: Nos. 31/15). 182p. 1996. reprint ed. pap. 14.95 (*1-85075-104-8*, Pub. by Sheffield Acad UK) CUP Services.

Structure of Meaning: A Semiotic Approach to the Play Text. Thomas J. Donahue. LC 91-58955. 184p. 1993. 35.00 (*0-8386-3476-1*) Fairleigh Dickinson.

Structure of Metals: Crystallographic Methods, Principles & Data. 3rd rev. ed. C. S. Barrett & T. B. Massalski. LC 80-49878. (International Series on Materials Science & Technology: Vol. 14). (Illus.). 654p. 1980. pap. text ed. 62.95 (*0-08-026172-8*, Prgamon Press) Buttrwrth-Heinemann.

Structure of Metals Through Optical Microscopy. A. Tomer. 284p. 1990. 75.00 (*0-87170-410-2*, 6082) ASM.

Structure of Metaphor: The Way the Language of Metaphor Works. Roger M. White. (Philosophical Theory Ser.). 400p. (C). 1996. text ed. 62.95 (*0-631-16811-7*) Blackwell Pubs.

Structure of Mind. Reinhardt S. Grossman. LC 65-13505. 256p. reprint ed. pap. 73.00 (*0-317-08118-7*, 2002041) Bks Demand.

Structure of Mind in History: Five Major Figures in Psychohistory. Philip Pomper. LC 84-22988. 192p. 1985. text ed. 34.50 (*0-231-06064-5*) Col U Pr.

Structure of Modern Ideology: Critical Perspectives on Social & Political Theory. Ed. by Noel O'Sullivan. 232p. 1989. text ed. 80.00 (*1-85278-036-3*) E Elgar.

Structure of Modular Lattices of Width Four with Applications to Varieties of Lattices. R. S. Freese. LC 76-49468. (Memoirs Ser.: No. 9/181). 91p. 1977. pap. 21.00 (*0-8218-2181-4*, MEMO/9/181) Am Math.

Structure of Moral Action: A Hermeneutic Study of Moral Conflict. Martin J. Packer. (Contributions to Human Development Ser.: Vol. 13). (Illus.). xii, 164p. 1985. 77.75 (*3-8055-3999-1*) S Karger.

Structure of Multimodal Dialogue. Ed. by M. M. Taylor et al. (Human Factors in Information Technology Ser.: No. 4). 540p. 1989. 230.25 (*0-444-87421-6*, North Holland) Elsevier.

Structure of Music. Percy Goetschius. LC 72-109736. 170p. 1971. reprint ed. text ed. 42.50 (*0-8371-4226-1*, GOSM, Greenwood Pr) Greenwood.

Structure of Nations & Empires: A Study of the Recurring Patterns & Problems of the Political Order in Relation to the Unique Problems of the Nuclear Age. Reinhold Niebuhr. LC 72-128064. xi, 306p. 1977. reprint ed. 39.50 (*0-678-02755-2*) Kelley.

Structure of Nematodes. 2nd ed. Alan F. Bird & Jean Bird. (Illus.). 316p. 1991. text ed. 85.00 (*0-12-099651-0*) Acad Pr.

Structure of Non-Crystalline Materials, 1976. Ed. by P. H. Gaskell. 272p. 1977. 55.00 (*0-85066-120-X*) Taylor & Francis.

Structure of Non-Crystalline Materials, 1982. Ed. by P. H. Gaskell et al. 610p. 1983. 115.00 (*0-85066-241-9*) Taylor & Francis.

Structure of Nonprofit Management: A Casebook. Ed. by Pranab Chatterjee & Albert J. Abramovitz. LC 93-2206. 296p. (Orig.). (C). 1993. pap. text ed. 34.00 (*0-8191-9148-5*); lib. bdg. 59.50 (*0-8191-9147-7*) U Pr of Amer.

Structure of Obscurity: Gertrude Stein, Language, & Cubism. Randa Dubnick. LC 83-3603. (Illus.). 184p. 1984. 24.95 (*0-252-00909-6*) U of Ill Pr.

Structure of Ocean Transport Costs. Robert E. Lipsey & Merle Y. Weiss. (Explorations in Economic Research One Ser.: No. 1). 42p. 1974. reprint ed. 35.00 (*0-685-61371-2*) Natl Bur Econ Res.

Structure of Old Norse "Drottkvaett" Poetry. Kari E. Gade. (Islandica Ser.). 312p. 1994. 45.00 (*0-8014-3023-2*) Cornell U Pr.

Structure of Partially Ordered Sets with Transitive Automorphism Groups. Manfred Droste. LC 85-15625. (Memoirs of the AMS Ser.: No. 57/334). 100p. 1985. pap. 18.00 (*0-8218-2335-3*, MEMO/57/334) Am Math.

Structure of Paul's Theology: The Truth Which Is the Gospel. Christopher A. Davis. LC 94-48472. (Biblical Press Ser.: Vol. 36). 452p. 1995. text ed. 109.95 (*0-7734-2422-9*, Mellen Biblical Pr) E Mellen.

Structure of Peace: The Arab-Israeli Conflict. John Stebbing. 1993. pap. text ed. 14.95 (*0-9517695-2-9*, Pub. by New Cherwell UK) Intl Spec Bk.

Structure of Personal Characteristics. David M. Romney & John M. Bynner. LC 92-18845. 160p. 1992. text ed. 47.95 (*0-275-93995-2*, C3995, Praeger Pubs) Greenwood.

Structure of Petrarch's Canzoniere: A Chronological, Psychological & Stylistic Analysis. Frederic J. Jones. (Illus.). 340p. (C). 1995. 71.00 (*0-85991-410-0*) Boydell & Brewer.

Structure of Phototrophic Prokaryotes. Stolz. 144p. 1990. 129.00 (*0-8493-4814-5*, QP372) CRC Pr.

Structure of Pindar's Epinician Odes. C. Greengard. viii, 135p. 1980. pap. text ed. 47.50 (*0-317-54496-9*, Pub. by AM Hakkert NE) Coronet Bks.

Structure of Pindar's Epinician Odes. Carola Greengard. viii, 135p. 1980. pap. 54.00 (*90-256-0872-8*, Pub. by A M Hakkert NE) Benjamins North Am.

Structure of Planets. G. H. Cole. (Wykeham Science Ser.: No. 45). 232p. 1977. 32.00 (*0-85109-610-7*); pap. 18.00 (*0-85109-600-X*) Taylor & Francis.

Structure of Plato's Philosophy. Jerry S. Clegg. LC 75-31467. 207p. 1978. 32.50 (*0-8387-1878-7*) Bucknell U Pr.

Structure of Police Organizations. Robert H. Langworthy. LC 86-21173. 176p. 1986. text ed. 49.95 (*0-275-92328-2*, C2328, Praeger Pubs) Greenwood.

Structure of Political Thought: A Study in the History of Political Ideas. Charles N. McCoy. LC 74-25996. 323p. 1978. reprint ed. text ed. 52.50 (*0-8371-7880-0*, MCPT, Greenwood Pr) Greenwood.

Structure of Portuguese Society: The Failure of Fascism. Diamantino P. Machado. LC 91-9646. 240p. 1991. text ed. 59.95 (*0-275-93784-4*, C3784, Praeger Pubs) Greenwood.

Structure of Postwar Prices. Frederick C. Mills. (Occasional Papers: No. 27). 72p. 1948. reprint ed. 20.00 (*0-87014-342-5*); reprint ed. mic. film 20.00 (*0-685-61275-9*) Natl Bur Econ Res.

Structure of Power in America: The Corporate Elite as a Ruling Class. Ed. by Michael Schwartz. LC 87-14849. 288p. 1987. pap. 22.50 (*0-8419-0765-X*) Holmes & Meier.

Structure of Power in North China During the Five Dynasties. Wang Gungwu. viii, 257p. 1963. reprint ed. 42.50 (*0-8047-0786-3*) Stanford U Pr.

Structure of Procedure. Robert M. Couer & Owen M. Fiss. (University Textbook Ser.). 560p. (C). 1992. reprint ed. pap. text ed. 21.00 (*0-88277-499-9*) Foundation Pr.

Structure of Production. Mark Skousen. (C). 1990. text ed. 36.00 (*0-8147-7895-X*) NYU Pr.

Structure of Protection in Developing Countries. Bela A. Balassa. LC 77-147366. 395p. reprint ed. pap. 112.60 (*0-7837-5380-2*, 2045144) Bks Demand.

Structure of Psalms 93-100. David M. Howard, Jr. LC 96-49913. (Biblical & Judaic Studies from UCSD: Vol. 5). 1997. 35.00 (*1-57506-009-4*) Eisenbrauns.

Structure of Psychiatry in the U. S. S. R. Edward A. Babayan. LC 85-18100. 350p. 1986. 50.00 (*0-8236-6169-5*) Intl Univs Pr.

Structure of Psychoanalytic Theory: A Systematizing Attempt. David Rapaport. (Psychological Issues Monograph: No. 6, Vol. 2, No. 2). 158p. (Orig.). 1967. 27.50 (*0-8236-6180-6*) Intl Univs Pr.

Structure of Psychological Well-Being. Norman M. Bradburn. LC 67-27388. (Monographs in Social Research: No. 15). (Illus.). 1969. 12.95 (*0-202-25029-6*) Natl Opinion Res.

Structure of Recognizable Diatonic Tunings. Easley Blackwood. LC 85-42972. (Illus.). 360p. 1985. text ed. 70.00 (*0-691-09129-3*) Princeton U Pr.

Structure of Regular Semigroups, No. 1. K. S. Nambooripad. LC 79-21160. (Memoirs of the American Mathematical Society Ser.: No. 224). 132p. reprint ed. pap. 37.70 (*0-7837-7001-4*, 2046814) Bks Demand.

Structure of Regular Semigroups - I. K. S. Nambooripad. K. S. Nambooripad. LC 79-21160. (Memoirs Ser.: No. 22/224). 117p. 1985. reprint ed. pap. 18.00 (*0-8218-2224-1*, MEMO/22/224) Am Math.

Structure of Relation Algebras Generated by Relativizations. Steven R. Givant. LC 93-36607. (Contemporary Mathematics Ser.: Vol. 156). 156p. 1994. pap. 25.00 (*0-8218-5177-2*, CONM/156) Am Math.

Structure of Resurrection Belief. Peter Carnley. (Illus.). 408p. (C). 1993. reprint ed. pap. 26.00 (*0-19-826756-8*, 14554) OUP.

Structure of Retail Trade by Size of Store. Paul A. Vatter. Ed. by Stuart Bruchey & Vincent P. Carosso. LC 78-18151. (Small Business Enterprise in America Ser.). (Illus.). 1979. lib. bdg. 17.95 (*0-405-11509-1*) Ayer.

Structure of Rings. Nathan Jacobson. LC 63-21795. (Colloquium Publications: Vol. 37). 299p. 1956. reprint ed. 24.00 (*0-8218-1037-5*, COLL/37) Am Math.

Structure of Science. Ernest Nagel. LC 60-15504. 640p. (C). 1979. reprint ed. pap. text ed. 19.95 (*0-915144-71-9*); reprint ed. lib. bdg. 39.95 (*0-915144-72-7*) Hackett Pub.

Structure of Scientific Revolutions. Thomas S. Kuhn. LC 70-107472. (Foundations of the Unity of Science Ser.: Vol. 2, No. 2). xii, 222p. 1970. pap. 10.95 (*0-226-45804-0*) U Ch Pr.

Structure of Scientific Revolutions. 2nd ed. Thomas S. Kuhn. (Foundations of the Unity of Science Ser.: Vol. 2, No. 2). xii, 222p. 1970. lib. bdg. 25.00 (*0-226-45803-2*) U Ch Pr.

Structure of Scientific Revolutions. 3rd ed. Thomas S. Kuhn. 240p. 1996. pap. 10.95 (*0-226-45808-3*); lib. bdg. 25.00 (*0-226-45807-5*) U Ch Pr.

Structure of Scientific Theories. 2nd ed. Ed. by Frederick Suppe. LC 72-89604. (Illus.). 832p. 1977. reprint ed. text ed. 49.95 (*0-252-00655-0*); reprint ed. pap. text ed. 22.50 (*0-252-00634-8*) U of Ill Pr.

Structure of Shakespearean Scenes. James E. Hirsh. LC 81-2473. 224p. (C). 1981. 42.00 (*0-300-02650-1*) Yale U Pr.

Structure of Shakespeare's Sonnets. Eugene P. Wright. LC 93-30484. 428p. 1993. 109.95 (*0-7734-9370-0*) E Mellen.

Structure of Shock Waves in Magnetohydrodynamics. Mahmud Hesaaraki. LC 84-3085. (Memoirs Ser.: No. 49/302). 96p. 1984. pap. 17.00 (*0-8218-2303-5*, MEMO/49/302) Am Math.

Structure of Singing: System & Art in Vocal Technique. Richard Miller. (Illus.). 372p. 1986. 39.00 (*0-02-872660-X*) Schirmer Bks.

Structure of Small Molecules & Ions. Ed. by R. Naaman & Z. Vager. (Illus.). 354p. 1988. 95.00 (*0-306-43016-9*, Plenum Pr) Plenum.

Structure of Social Action, 1. 2nd ed. Talcott Parsons. LC 49-49353. 1967. pap. 14.95 (*0-02-924240-1*, Free Press) Free Pr.

Structure of Social Action, 2. 2nd ed. Talcott Parsons. LC 49-49353. 1967. pap. 21.95 (*0-02-924250-9*, Free Press) Free Pr.

Structure of Social Interaction: A Systemic Approach to the Semiotics of Service Encounters. Eija Ventola. (Open Linguistics Ser.). 289p. 1992. 59.00 (*0-86187-626-1*) St Martin.

Structure of Social Stratification in the United States. 2nd ed. Leonard Beeghley. LC 95-15287. 1995. text ed. 57.00 (*0-205-16805-1*) Allyn.

Structure of Social Systems. Frederick L. Bates & Clyde C. Harvey. LC 85-10009. 432p. 1986. reprint ed. lib. bdg. 46.50 (*0-89874-874-7*) Krieger.

Structure of Social Theory: Strategies, Dilemmas & Projects. Terry Johnson et al. LC 84-13285. 262p. 1985. text ed. 35.00 (*0-312-76833-8*) St Martin.

Structure of Social Welfare. David Macarov. 344p. 1995. text ed. 52.00 (*0-8039-4939-1*); pap. text ed. 25.50 (*0-8039-4940-5*) Sage.

Structure of Society. Julian Marias. Tr. by Harold C. Raley from SPA. LC 84-185. 248p. 1987. text ed. 26.50 (*0-8173-0181-X*) U of Ala Pr.

***Structure of Society.** Julian Marias. Tr. by Harold C. Raley. LC 84-185. 246p. pap. 70.20 (*0-608-05145-4*, 2065706) Bks Demand.

Structure of Sociological Theory. 5th ed. Jonathan H. Turner. 661p. (C). 1991. text ed. 59.95 (*0-534-13842-X*) Wadsworth Pub.

***Structure of Sociological Theory.** 6th ed. Jonathan H. Turner. (Sociology Ser.). (C). 1997. text ed. 59.95 (*0-534-51353-0*) Wadsworth Pub.

Structure of Solids see Materials Science & Technology: A Comprehensive Treatment

Structure of Solutions in the Iterated Prisoner's Dilemma. Bjorn Lomborg. (CISA Working Papers, New: No. 4). 25p. (Orig.). (C). 1993. pap. 15.00 (*0-86682-095-7*) Ctr Intl Relations.

Structure of Solutions of Differential Equations. M. Morimoto & T. Kawai. 550p. 1996. text ed. 128.00 (*981-02-2321-8*) World Scientific Pub.

Structure of Soviet Wages: A Study in Socialist Economics. Abram Bergson. LC 44-1242. (Economic Studies: No. 76). 271p. 1944. 20.00 (*0-674-84480-7*) HUP.

Structure of Surfaces. Ed. by M. A. Van Hove & S. Y. Tong. (Surface Sciences Ser.: Vol. 2). (Illus.). 470p. 1985. 110.95 (*0-387-15410-8*) Spr-Verlag.

Structure of Surfaces II. Ed. by J. F. Van der Veen & M. A. Van Hove. (Surface Sciences Ser.: Vol. 11). (Illus.). 600p. 1988. 88.95 (*0-387-18784-7*) Spr-Verlag.

Structure of Surfaces IV: Proceedings of the International Conference. Xide D. Xie et al. 656p. 1994. text ed. 137.00 (*981-02-1551-7*) World Scientific Pub.

Structure of Surfaces Three: Proceedings of the 3rd International Conference on the Structure of Surfaces (ICSOS III) Milwaukee, Wisconsin, U. S. A., July 9-12, 1990. Ed. by S. Y. Tong et al. (Surface Sciences Ser.: Vol. 24). (Illus.). xviii, 683p. 1991. 111.95 (*0-387-54171-3*) Spr-Verlag.

Structure of Texts & Semiotics of Culture. Ed. by Jan Van Der Eng & Mojmir Grygar. (Slavistic Printings & Reprintings Ser.: No. 294). 1973. 115.40 (*90-279-2514-3*) Mouton.

Structure of Thai Narrative. Somsonge Burusphat. LC 90-72069. (Publications in Linguistics: No. 98). xiv, 231p. (Orig.). 1991. pap. 18.00 (*0-88312-805-5*); fiche 20.00 (*0-88312-494-7*) Summer Instit Ling.

Structure of the American Economy, 2 vols. in 1. United States National Resources Committee. LC 78-173418. (FDR & the Era of the New Deal Ser.). 1972. reprint ed. lib. bdg. 55.00 (*0-306-70388-2*) Da Capo.

Structure of the Arabic Language. N. V. Yushmanov. Tr. by Moshe Perlmann from RUS. LC 78-269168. 92p. reprint ed. pap. 26.30 (*0-8357-3382-3*, 2039635) Bks Demand.

Structure of the Book of Job: A Form-Critical Analysis. Claus Westermann. LC 80-2379. 160p. reprint ed. pap. 45.60 (*0-317-55777-7*, 2029297) Bks Demand.

Structure of the Christian Science Textbook: Our Way of Life. Max Kappeler. LC 58-26857. 206p. 1954. 16.00 (*0-85241-071-9*) Kappeler Inst Pub.

Structure of the Corporation. Melvin A. Eisenberg. 1976. pap. 22.00 (*0-316-22542-8*) Little.

Structure of the Defense Market, 1955-1964. William L. Baldwin. LC 67-23730. 257p. reprint ed. 73.30 (*0-685-07745-4*, 2017880) Bks Demand.

Structure of the Earth. Sydney P. Clark. (Foundations of Earth Science Ser.). 1971. pap. text ed. write for info. (*0-13-854646-0*) P-H.

Structure of the Human Brain: A Photographic Atlas. 3rd ed. Stephen J. DeArmond et al. (Illus.). 208p. 1989. spiral bd. 26.50 (*0-19-504357-X*) OUP.

Structure of the Japanese Auto Parts Industry. 3rd ed. 450p. 1986. 600.00 (*0-8002-4202-5*) Taylor & Francis.

Structure of the Japanese Auto Parts Industry. 5th ed. 600p. 1993. pap. 890.00 (*0-8002-4316-1*) Intl Pubns Serv.

Structure of the Japanese Economy: Changes in the Domestic & International Character. LC 94-17219. (Studies in the Modern Japanese Economy). 1994. text ed. 55.00 (*0-312-12219-5*) St Martin.

Structure of the Japanese Language. Susumu Kuno. 384p. (C). 1973. 50.00 (*0-262-11049-0*) MIT Pr.

Structure of the Legal Environment: Law, Ethics & Business. 2nd ed. Bill M. Shaw. 832p. (C). 1991. text ed. 55.00 (*0-534-92497-2*) PWS Pubs.

Structure of the Legal Environment of Business. 3rd ed. Bill M. Shaw et al. LC 95-31396. 1996. 74.95 (*0-538-84428-0*) S-W Pub.

Structure of the Lexicon: Human vs. Machine. Juergen Handke. (Natural Language Processing Ser.: No. 5). xi, 388p. (C). 1995. lib. bdg. 88.50 (*3-11-014732-7*) Mouton.

Structure of the Lexicon: Human vs. Machine, Vol. 5. Juergen Handke. LC 95-35380. (Natural Language Processing Ser.: No. 5). xi, 388p. (C). 1995. pap. text ed. 38.00 (*3-11-014786-6*) Mouton.

Structure of the Literary Process: Studies Dedicated to the Memory of Felix Vodicka. Ed. by P. Steiner et al. (Linguistic & Literary Studies in Eastern Europe: No. 8). viii, 613p. 1982. 127.00 (*90-272-1512-X*) Benjamins North Am.

Structure of the Missionary Call to the Sandwich Islands, 1790-1830: Sojourners among Strangers. Sandra Wagner-Wright. LC 90-45926. (Distinguished Dissertations Ser.: Vol. 2). 248p. 1990. lib. bdg. 89.95 (*0-7734-9938-5*) E Mellen.

Structure of the Netherlands Indian Economy. Julius H. Boeke. LC 75-30047. (Institute of Pacific Relations Ser.). 1983. reprint ed. 39.50 (*0-404-59509-X*) AMS Pr.

***Structure of the Nu Meson: New Mexico State University, 8-9 March 1996.** Ed. by Matthias Burkardt et al. 150p. 1997. 34.00 (*981-02-3159-8*) World Scientific Pub.

Structure of the Nucleus. M. A. Preston. (C). 1993. pap. 54.95 (*0-201-62729-9*) Addison-Wesley.

***Structure of the Ordinary: Form & Control in the Built Environment.** N. J. Habraken & Jonathan Teicher. LC 97-24601. 1998. write for info. (*0-262-08260-8*) MIT Pr.

Structure of the Ottoman Dynasty. Anthony D. Alderson. LC 81-23751. xvi, 186p. 1982. reprint ed. text ed. 75.00 (*0-313-22522-2*, ALSO, Greenwood Pr) Greenwood.

Structure of the Planets. John W. Elder. (Academic Press Geology Ser.). 226p. 1987. text ed. 102.00 (*0-12-236452-X*) Acad Pr.

Structure of the Proton: Deep Inelastic Scattering. R. G. Roberts. (Monographs on Mathematical Physics). 192p. (C). 1993. pap. text ed. 28.95 (*0-521-44944-8*) Cambridge U Pr.

Structure of the Relational Database Model. J. Psaedaens et al. (EATCS Monographs on Theoretical Computer Science: Vol. 17). (Illus.). 231p. 1989. 58.95 (*0-387-13714-9*) Spr-Verlag.

Structure of the Roman De Thebes. Mary Paschal. LC 80-66540. 96p. 1980. pap. 9.95 (*0-89729-261-8*) Ediciones.

***Structure of the Samson Cycle.** Jichan Kim. 464p. 1993. pap. 42.00 (*90-390-0016-6*, Pub. by KOK Pharos NE) Eisenbrauns.

***Structure of the Seraglio.** Alain Grosrichard. Date not set. pap. 19.00 (*1-85984-122-8*) Routledge Chapman & Hall.

An Asterisk (*) at the beginning of an entry indicates that the title is appearing in BIP for the first time.

***Structure of the Seraglio.** Alain Grosrichard. (C). Date not set. text ed. 60.00 (*1-85984-816-8*) Routledge Chapman & Hall.

Structure of the Siddur. Stephen R. Schach. LC 96-37005. 312p. 1997. 30.00 (*1-56821-974-1*) Aronson.

Structure of the Slovenian Economy, Eighteen Forty-Eight to Nineteen Sixty-Three. Toussaint Hocevar. LC 65-22710. 277p. 1965. 15.00 (*0-686-28378-3*) Studia Slovenica.

Structure of the Southern Canadian Cordillera. John P. Wheeler. LC 71-567025. (Geological Association of Canada. Special Paper Ser.: No. 6). 210p. reprint ed. pap. 59.90 (*0-685-17106-X*, 2027841) Bks Demand.

Structure of the Standard Modules for the Affine Lie Algebra A - Sub 1. James Lepowsky & M. Primc. LC 85-15639. (Contemporary Mathematics Ser.: Vol. 46). 84p. 1985. pap. text ed. 21.00 (*0-8218-5048-2*, CONM/46) Am Math.

Structure of the Sun. Ed. by T. Roca Cortes & F. Sanchez. (Illus.). 350p. (C). 1996. text ed. 69.95 (*0-521-56307-0*) Cambridge U Pr.

Structure of the Transition Zone. Ed. by Shuzo Asano. (Advances in Earth & Planetary Sciences Ser.: No. 8). 184p. 1980. lib. bdg. 89.00 (*90-277-1149-6*) Kluwer Ac.

Structure of the Universe. Paul Halpern. LC 96-40993. 1997. 22.50 (*0-8050-4028-5*, Owl) H Holt & Co.

Structure of the Universe. Paul Halpern. LC 96-40993. (Scientific American Focus Bks.). (Illus.). 128p. 1997. pap. 10.95 (*0-8050-4029-3*, Owl) H Holt & Co.

***Structure of the Visual Book.** Keith A. Smith. (Illus.). 124p. (Orig.). pap. 25.00 (*0-614-18196-8*) Visual Studies.

Structure of the Visual Book Bk. 95, Bk. 95. 3rd ed. Keith A. Smith. LC 92-81370. 240p. (Orig.). 1994. pap. 25.00 (*0-9637682-1-2*) K A Smith Bks.

Structure of the World Economy & Prospects for a New International Economic Order. Ed. by Ervin Laszlo & Joel Kurtzman. LC 79-23350. (Policy Studies on the New International Economic Order). 120p. 1980. 44.00 (*0-08-025119-6*, Pergamon Pr) Elsevier.

Structure of the World in Udayana's Realism. Musashi Tachikawa. 194p. 1982. lib. bdg. 104.50 (*90-277-1291-3*, D Reidel) Kluwer Ac.

Structure of Thucydides' History. Hunter R. Rawlings. LC 80-8572. 293p. reprint ed. pap. 83.60 (*0-8357-7898-3*, 2036317) Bks Demand.

Structure of Time. W. H. Newton-Smith. 274p. 1984. pap. 14.95 (*0-7102-0389-6*, RKP) Routledge.

Structure of Traditional Moroccan Rural Society. Bernard G. Hoffman. (Studies in Social Anthropology: No. 2). 1967. text ed. 60.00 (*0-686-22465-5*) Mouton.

Structure of Turbulence in Heat & Mass Transfer. Zoran P. Zaric. 1982. text ed. 90.00 (*0-07-072731-7*) McGraw.

Structure of Turbulent Shear Flow. 2nd ed. A. A. Townsend. LC 79-8526. (Cambridge Monographs on Mechanics & Applied Mathematics). (Illus.). 441p. 1980. pap. text ed. 47.95 (*0-521-29819-9*) Cambridge U Pr.

Structure of Twana Culture: With Comparative Notes on the Structure of Yurok Culture. William W. Elmendorf & A. L. Kroeber. LC 92-20697. (Washington State University Press Reprint Ser.). (Illus.). 576p. (C). 1992. reprint ed. pap. text ed. 25.00 (*0-87422-087-4*) Wash St U Pr.

Structure of Typed Programming Languages. David Schmidt. LC 93-39912. (Foundations of Computing Ser.). 367p. 1994. pap. 24.00 (*0-262-69171-X*) MIT Pr.

Structure of Typed Programming Languages. David A. Schmidt. LC 93-39912. (Foundations of Computing Ser.). 352p. (C). 1994. 42.00 (*0-262-19349-3*) MIT Pr.

***Structure of Universe.** Nicastro. Date not set. text ed. 41.00 (*0-697-11296-9*) McGraw.

Structure of Urban Poverty: The Case of Bombay Slums. S. S. Jha. 1986. 22.50 (*0-86132-134-0*, Pub. by Popular Prakashan II) S Asia.

Structure of Urban Systems. John Marshall. 394p. 1989. text ed. 50.00 (*0-8020-5756-X*); pap. text ed. 24.95 (*0-8020-6735-2*) U of Toronto Pr.

***Structure of Vacuum & Elementary Matter.** 600p. 1997. lib. bdg. 83.00 (*981-02-2789-2*) World Scientific Pub.

Structure of Value. R. T. Allen. (Avebury Series in Philosophy). 170p. 1993. 58.95 (*1-85628-458-1*, Pub. by Avebury Pub UK) Ashgate Pub Co.

Structure of Vasko Popa's Poetry. Ronelle Alexander. (UCLA Slavic Studies: Vol. 14). (Illus.). 196p. 1987. 24.95 (*0-89357-149-0*) Slavica.

Structure of Verse. rev. ed. Harvey Gross. LC 78-6781. 320p. 1979. reprint ed. pap. 9.95 (*0-912946-59-8*) Ecco Pr.

Structure of Verse: English Versification. A. Everett. 200p. 1995. pap. 25.00 (*0-87556-784-3*) Saifer.

Structure of Volatile Sulphur Compounds. Istvan Hargittai. 1985. lib. bdg. 138.00 (*90-277-1395-2*) Kluwer Ac.

Structure of Wages in Latin American Manufacturing Industries. Jorge Salazar-Carrillo et al. LC 80-25072. (Illus.). 184p. reprint ed. pap. 52.50 (*0-7837-4953-8*, 2044619) Bks Demand.

Structure of Weaving. Ann Sutton. LC 82-24941. (Illus.). 192p. 1982. 29.95 (*0-934026-38-6*) Interweave.

***Structure of Women's Nonprofit Organizations.** Rebecca L. Bordt. LC 97-5225. (IU Center on Philanthropy Series in Governance). 1997. write for info. (*0-253-33347-4*) Ind U Pr.

Structure of World Energy Demand. Robert S. Pindyck. (Illus.). 1979. 32.50 (*0-262-16074-9*) MIT Pr.

Structure of Written Communication: Studies in Reciprocity Between Writers & Readers. Martin Nystrand. 1986. text ed. 59.00 (*0-12-523482-1*) Acad Pr.

***Structure-Performance Relationships in Surfactants.** Ed. by Esumi & Ueno. (Surfactant Science Ser.: Vol. 70). 608p. 1997. 195.00 (*0-8247-0068-6*) Dekker.

Structure-Performance Relationships in Surfactants. Milton J. Rosen. LC 84-6384. (ACS Symposium Ser.: No. 253). 356p. 1984. lib. bdg. 60.95 (*0-8412-0839-5*) Am Chemical.

Structure, Policies & Growth Prospects of Nigeria. Pyare L. Arya. LC 92-46730. (African Studies: Vol. 29). 164p. 1993. text ed. 79.95 (*0-7734-9252-6*) E Mellen.

Structure Practice in Context: Workbooks 1-3, No. 1. Penny LaPorte & Jay Maurer. 106p. (Orig.). 1985. Wkbk. 1. student ed., pap. text ed. 12.95 (*0-582-79858-2*, 12.95 WKBK. 3) Longman.

Structure Practice in Context: Workbooks 1-3, No. 2. Penny LaPorte & Jay Maurer. 106p. (Orig.). 1985. Wkbk. 2. student ed., pap. text ed. 12.95 (*0-582-79859-0*, 75105) Longman.

Structure Practice in Context: Workbooks 1-3, No. 3. Penny LaPorte & Jay Maurer. 106p. (Orig.). 1985. Wkbk. 3. student ed., pap. text ed. 12.95 (*0-582-79860-4*, 75106) Longman.

Structure, Process, & Party: Essays in American Political History. Peter H. Argersinger. LC 91-9567. 240p. (gr. 13). 1991. text ed. 59.95 (*0-87332-798-5*) M E Sharpe.

Structure-Property Correlations in Drug Research. Ed. by Han Van de Waterbeemd. LC 96-3247. (Biotechnology Intelligence Unit Ser.). 210p. 1996. 69.95 (*0-12-711650-8*) R G Landes.

Structure-Property Relations in Polymers: Spectroscopy & Performance. Ed. by Marek W. Urban & Clara D. Craver. LC 93-15964. (Advances in Chemistry Ser.: No. 236). (Illus.). 850p. 1994. 139.95 (*0-8412-2525-7*) Am Chemical.

Structure-Property Relationships & Correlations with the Environmental Degradation of Engineering Materials. Ed. by D. A. Wheeler et al. (Microstructural Science Ser.: Vol. 19). 811p. 1992. 81.00 (*0-87170-463-3*, 6445) ASM.

***Structure-Property Relationships & Correlations with the Environmental Degradation of Engineering Materials: Proceedings of the Twenty-Fourth Annual Technical Meeting of the International Metallographic Society.** Ed. by D. A. Wheeler et al. LC 92-82801. (Microstructural Science Ser.: No. 19). (Illus.). 827p. 1992. reprint ed. pap. 180.00 (*0-608-02632-8*, 2063290) Bks Demand.

Structure-Property Relationships in Polymers. Raymond B. Seymour, Jr. & Charles E. Carraher. 246p. 1984. 69.50 (*0-306-41650-6*, Plenum Pr) Plenum.

Structure-Property Relationships in Surface-Modified Ceramics. Ed. by Carl J. McHargue et al. (C). 1989. lib. bdg. 211.50 (*0-7923-0310-5*) Kluwer Ac.

Structure Reports for Nineteen Eighty-Five, Vol. 52B: Organic Compounds. Ed. by G. Ferguson. vi, 2143p. 1993. lib. bdg. write for info. (*0-7923-2405-6*) Kluwer Ac.

Structure, Role, & Ideology in the Hebrew & Greek Texts of Genesis 1:1-2:3. William P. Brown. LC 93-17786. (Society of Biblical Literature Dissertation Ser.: Vol. 132). 284p. 1993. 44.95 (*1-55540-759-5*, 062132); pap. 29.95 (*1-55540-760-9*, 062132) Scholars Pr GA.

Structure Selection of Stochastic Dynamic Systems: The Information Criterion Approach, Vol. 4. S. M. Veres. (Stochastics Monographs). 342p. 1991. text ed. 132.00 (*2-88124-715-6*) Gordon & Breach.

Structure, Sign, & Function: Selected Essays. Jan Mukarovsky. Ed. by John Burbank & Peter Steiner. Tr. by Peter Steiner. LC 77-76310. (Yale Russian & East European Studies: No. 14). 309p. reprint ed. pap. 88.10 (*0-8357-8336-7*, 2033836) Bks Demand.

Structure, Solid Mechanics & Engineering Design, the Proceedings of the Southampton 1969 Civil Engineering Materials Conference, Pt. 1. Ed. by M. Teeni. LC 71-149573. reprint ed. pap. 160.00 (*0-317-29877-1*, 2016150) Bks Demand.

Structure, Solid Mechanics & Engineering Design, the Proceedings of the Southampton 1969 Civil Engineering Materials Conference, Pt. 2. Ed. by M. Teeni. LC 71-149573. xp. reprint ed. pap. 147.00 (*0-317-29878-X*) Bks Demand.

Structure, Space & Skin: The Work of Nicholas Grimshaw & Partners. Kenneth Powell. Ed. by Rowan Moore. (Illus.). 256p. 1996. pap. text ed. 39.95 (*0-7148-3457-2*, Pub. by Phaidon Press UK) Chronicle Bks.

Structure, Stratigraphy & Hydrocarbon Occurrences of the San Joaquin Basin, California. Ed. by Jonathon G. Kuespert & Stephen A. Reid. (Illus.). 366p. (Orig.). 1990. pap. 24.00 (*1-878861-05-0*) Pac Section SEPM.

***Structure, Strength & Radiation Damage of Corrosion-Resistant Steels & Alloys.** A. M. Parshin. LC 96-36371. (Russian Materials Monographs). 361p. 1996. 45.00 (*0-89448-563-6*) Am Nuclear Soc.

Structure, Style & Interpretation in the Russian Short Story. L. M. O'Toole. LC 81-11650. 288p. 1982. 40.00 (*0-300-02730-3*) Yale U Pr.

Structure, Support & Style. Michael Zeitsoff. 320p. (C). 1994. per. 34.59 (*0-8403-9429-2*) Kendall-Hunt.

Structure Theory - Language, Science, & Aesthetics. Eugene H. Hussey. LC 78-73684. (Illus.). 1978. text ed. 14.00 (*0-943700-00-0*) Demecon.

Structure Underlying Measure Phrase Sentences. W. G. Klooster. LC 76-188003. (Foundations of Language Supplementary Ser.: No. 17). 247p. 1972. lib. bdg. 104.50 (*90-277-0229-2*) Kluwer Ac.

Structure vs. Special Properties. Ed. by M. J. Clarke et al. (Structure & Bonding Ser.: Vol. 52). (Illus.). 204p. 1982. 86.95 (*0-387-11781-4*) Spr-Verlag.

Structure Worksheets for Contemporary English. Ralph B. Long. 253p. reprint ed. pap. 72.20 (*0-317-26521-0*, 2024056) Bks Demand.

Structured Activities for Dynamic Counseling. James L. Lee et al. LC 94-72560. 248p. (Orig.). (C). 1994. pap. text ed. 21.95 (*0-932796-67-2*) Ed Media Corp.

Structured Adolescent Psychotherapy Groups. Billie F. Corder. LC 93-44822. 164p. (Orig.). 1994. pap. 23.70 (*0-943158-74-5*, SAPGBP, Prof Resc Pr) Pro Resource.

Structured Alternative: Programming Style, Debugging & Verification. Don Cassel. (C). 1983. teacher ed. write for info. (*0-8359-7085-X*, Reston) P-H.

Structured Analysis. Victor Weinberg. (Illus.). 1979. text ed. 65.00 (*0-13-854414-X*) P-H.

Structured Analysis & System Specification. Tom DeMarco. 1979. text ed. 74.00 (*0-13-854380-1*) P-H.

Structured & Object-Oriented Techniques: An Introduction Using C++ 2nd ed. Andrew C. Staugaard. 770p. 1996. pap. text ed. 49.00 (*0-13-488736-0*) P-H.

Structured ANS COBOL, Pt. 1: A Course for Novices Using 1974 or 1985 ANS COBOL, Pt. 1. 2nd ed. Mike Murach & Paul Noll. LC 86-61654. 438p. (C). 1986. pap. 32.50 (*0-911625-37-2*) M Murach & Assoc.

Structured ANS COBOL, Pt. 2: An Advanced Course Using 1974 or 1985 ANS COBOL. 2nd ed. Mike Murach & Paul Noll. LC 86-61654. 498p. (C). 1987. pap. 32.50 (*0-911625-38-0*) M Murach & Assoc.

Structured Approach to Building Programs. Timothy D. Wells. 384p. (C). 1987. pap. text ed. 19.95 (*0-317-52260-4*) P-H.

Structured Approach to Building Programs: BASIC. Timothy D. Wells. LC 85-51511. 330p. (Orig.). (C). 1986. pap. text ed. 34.00 (*0-13-854076-4*, Yourdon) P-H.

Structured Approach to Building Programs: Pascal. Timothy D. Wells. LC 85-52003. 300p. (Orig.). (C). 1986. pap. 23.00 (*0-917072-46-4*, Yourdon) P-H.

Structured Approach to FORTRAN 77 Programming. T. M. Ellis. 1982. pap. text ed. write for info. (*0-201-13790-9*) Addison-Wesley.

Structured Approach to Learning the Basic Inflections of the Cherokee Verb. Durbin Feeling. 190p. (Orig.). 1994. pap. text ed. 25.00 (*0-940392-26-7*) Indian U Pr OK.

***Structured Approach to Low Vision Care, Vol. 3, No. 3.** 30.00 (*1-888504-16-1*, P235) Lighthouse NYC.

Structured Approach to Programming. 2nd ed. Joan K. Hughes et al. (Illus.). 320p. 1987. text ed. 37.00 (*0-13-854159-0*) P-H.

Structured Assembler Language for IBM Computers. Alton R. Kindred. 576p. (C). 1995. text ed. 38.00 (*0-15-584070-3*) OUP.

Structured Assembler Language for IBM Microcomputers. Alton R. Kindred. (Illus.). 473p. (C). 1995. text ed. 57.00 (*0-15-584072-X*) OUP.

Structured Assembler Language for IBM Microcomputers: Instructor's Manual & Test Bank. Alton R. Kindred. (Illus.). (C). 1995. pap. text ed. write for info. (*0-15-584073-8*) OUP.

Structured Assembly Language. Len Dorfman. 1990. text ed. 34.95 (*0-07-157360-7*) McGraw.

Structured Assembly Language. Len Dorfman. (Illus.). 464p. 1990. 34.95 (*0-8306-9484-6*); pap. 24.95 (*0-8306-3484-3*) McGraw-Hill Prof.

Structured Assembly Language. Len Dorfman. 1991. 24.95 (*0-8306-6745-8*); 24.95 (*0-8306-7744-5*) McGraw-Hill Prof.

Structured Assembly Language Programming for the VAX II. Robert W. Sebesta. 1984. teacher ed. 6.50 (*0-8053-7004-8*); text ed. 48.50 (*0-8053-7001-3*) Benjamin-Cummings.

Structured Basic. 2nd ed. Clark. (DG - Computer Programming Ser.). 1989. wbk. ed., pap. 18.95 (*0-538-10841-X*) S-W Pub.

Structured Basic. 2nd ed. Clark. (DG - Computer Programming Ser.). 1989. teacher ed. 31.95 (*0-538-28727-6*) S-W Pub.

Structured Basic: Apple. 2nd ed. Clark. (DG - Computer Programming Ser.). 1989. wbk. ed., pap. 18.95 (*0-538-10813-4*) S-W Pub.

Structured BASIC: Apple Version. 3rd ed. James F. Clark & William O. Drum. LC 93-4720. 1994. text ed. 48.95 (*0-538-61801-9*) S-W Pub.

Structured Basic: Apple Version Textbook. 2nd ed. Clark. (DG - Computer Programming Ser.). 1989. text ed. 45.95 (*0-538-10812-6*) S-W Pub.

Structured BASIC: DOS Version. 3rd ed. James F. Clark & William O. Drum. LC 93-1153. 1994. text ed. 48.95 (*0-538-61800-0*) S-W Pub.

Structured BASIC: IBM PC, TRS 80. 2nd ed. Clark. 1989. text ed. 45.95 (*0-538-10840-1*) S-W Pub.

Structured Basic: IBM Version. 3rd ed. Clark. (DG - Computer Programming Ser.). 1994. wbk. ed., pap. 15.95 (*0-538-61802-7*) S-W Pub.

Structured BASIC & Program Design. Margaret McRitchie. 416p. (C). 1989. pap. text ed. 40.00 (*0-03-921892-9*) SCP.

Structured Basic Apple Version. 3rd ed. Clark. (DG - Computer Programming Ser.). 1994. wbk. ed., pap. 15.95 (*0-538-61803-5*) S-W Pub.

Structured Basic Applied to Technology. 3rd ed. Thomas Adamson & Kenneth Mansfield. LC 96-33453. 480p. (C). 1996. pap. text ed. 61.33 (*0-13-442351-8*) P-H.

Structured Basic Programming. Clark. (DG - Computer Education Ser.). 1983. wbk. ed., pap. 18.95 (*0-538-10801-0*) S-W Pub.

Structured BASIC Programming. 2nd ed. Harry Moriber. 480p. (C). 1989. pap. write for info. (*0-675-20715-0*, Merrill Coll) P-H.

Structured BASIC Texas Manual. 2nd ed. Clark. (DG - Computer Programming Ser.). 1989. 39.95 (*0-538-28246-0*) S-W Pub.

Structured Biological Modelling: A New Approach to Biophysical Cell Biology. Michael Kraus & Bernhard H. Wolf. LC 94-48033. 288p. 1995. 160.00 (*0-8493-4772-6*, 4772) CRC Pr.

Structured C for Engineering & Technology. 2nd ed. Tom Adamson et al. LC 94-21783. Orig. Title: Structured C for Technology. 713p. 1994. pap. text ed. 63.00 (*0-02-300812-1*, Macmillan Coll) P-H.

***Structured C for Engineering & Technology.** 3rd ed. Adamson & James L. Antonakos. LC 97-20691. (C). 1997. pap. text ed. 64.00 (*0-13-625229-X*) P-H.

Structured C for Technology see Structured C for Engineering & Technology

***Structured Clinical Interview for DSM-IV Axis I Disorders (SCID-I), Clinician Version: Administration Booklet.** Michael B. First et al. 96p. (Orig.). 1997. teacher ed., spiral bd. 24.00 (*0-88048-932-4*, 8932) Am Psychiatric.

***Structured Clinical Interview for DSM-IV Axis I Disorders (SCID-I), Clinician Version: Score Sheets.** Michael B. First et al. 64p. (Orig.). 1997. teacher ed., pap. text ed. 21.95 (*0-88048-933-2*, 8933) Am Psychiatric.

***Structured Clinical Interview for DSM-IV Axis I Disorders (SCID-I), Clinician Version: User's Guide.** Michael B. First et al. 160p. (Orig.). 1997. student ed., pap. text ed. 27.50 (*0-88048-931-6*, 8931) Am Psychiatric.

***Structured Clinical Interview for DSM-IV Axis II Personality Disorders (SCID-II) User's Guide.** Michael B. First et al. 80p. (Orig.). 1997. pap. text ed. 29.95 (*0-88048-810-7*, 8810) Am Psychiatric.

Structured Clinical Interview for DSM-IV Dissociative Disorders (SCID-D) rev. ed. Marlene Steinberg. 86p. 1994. pap. text ed. 21.95 (*0-88048-860-3*, 8860) Am Psychiatric.

Structured Clinical Interview for DSM-IV Dissociative Disorders (SCID-D) Marlene Steinberg. LC 92-49449. 89p. 1993. reprint ed. pap. 25.40 (*0-608-02022-2*, 2062678) Bks Demand.

***Structured Clinical Interview for DSM-IV Personality Disorders (SCID-II) Interview & Questionnaire.** Michael B. First et al. 64p. (Orig.). 1997. pap. text ed. 21.95 (*0-88048-811-5*, 8811) Am Psychiatric.

***Structured Clinical Interview for DSM-IX Axis II Personality Disorders (SCID-II) Set of User's Guide, Interview, & Questionnaire.** Michael B. First et al. (Orig.). 1997. pap. text ed. 46.00 (*0-88048-812-3*, 8812) Am Psychiatric.

Structured COBOL. 2nd ed. Gerard A. Paquette. 848p. (C). 1990. per. 59.08 (*0-697-07763-2*) Bus & Educ Tech.

Structured COBOL. 3rd ed. Gerard A. Paquette. 864p. (C). 1994. per. 59.08 (*0-697-12394-4*) Bus & Educ Tech.

Structured COBOL. 3rd ed. Andreas S. Philippakis & Leonard J. Kazmier. 440p. (C). 1986. pap. text ed. write for info. (*0-07-049809-1*) McGraw.

Structured COBOL. 3rd ed. Tyler Welburn. 1990. text ed. write for info. (*0-07-069166-5*) McGraw.

Structured COBOL: A Direct Approach. Rina Varmish & Gerald Wohl. LC 92-24833. 752p. 1992. pap. text ed. 75.00 (*0-13-855362-9*) P-H.

Structured COBOL: American National Standard. 2nd ed. V. Thomas Dock. (Illus.). 240p. 1984. pap. text ed. 49.25 (*0-314-77896-9*); pap. text ed. write for info. (*0-314-77897-7*) West Pub.

Structured Cobol: First Course. M. B. Khan. (Machine Language Programming Ser.). 600p. 1996. pap. 48.95 (*0-7895-0098-1*) Course Tech.

Structured COBOL: Flowchart Edition. Gary B. Shelly & Thomas J. Cashman. 540p. (C). 1986. teacher ed. write for info. (*0-87835-201-5*) Course Tech.

Structured COBOL: Flowchart Edition. Gary B. Shelly & Thomas J. Cashman. 540p. (C). 1986. pap. 38.00 (*0-87835-197-3*) Course Tech.

Structured COBOL: Pseudocode Edition. Gary B. Shelly & Thomas J. Cashman. 540p. (C). 1986. teacher ed. write for info. (*0-318-60366-7*) Course Tech.

Structured COBOL: Pseudocode Edition. Gary B. Shelly & Thomas J. Cashman. 540p. (C). 1986. pap. 38.00 (*0-87835-196-5*) Course Tech.

***Structured COBOL for Technical Students.** Watt. (C). 1997. pap. text ed. 63.67 (*0-13-446733-7*) P-H.

***Structured COBOL Methods: How to Design, Code, & Test Your Programs So They're Easier to Debug, Document, & Maintain.** Paul Noll. LC 97-4306. (Illus.). 208p. 1997. pap. 25.00 (*0-911625-94-1*) M Murach & Assoc.

Structured COBOL Programming. Robert T. Grauer. (Illus.). 496p. 1985. pap. text ed. 51.00 (*0-13-854217-1*) P-H.

Structured Cobol Programming. Gary B. Shelly. 1996. pap. 41.00 (*0-87835-486-7*) Course Tech.

Structured COBOL Programming. 6th ed. Nancy B. Stern. 800p. 1990. Net. pap. text ed. 36.00 (*0-471-52421-2*) Wiley.

Structured COBOL Programming. 7th ed. Nancy B. Stern. 1060p. 1994. pap. text ed. 39.50 (*0-471-00838-9*) Wiley.

Structured COBOL Programming. 7th ed. Nancy B. Stern & Robert A. Stern. 1994. Net. pap. text ed. write for info. (*0-471-59747-3*) Wiley.

***Structured COBOL Programming.** 8th ed. Nancy B. Stern & Robert A. Stern. pap. text ed. write for info. (*0-471-18384-9*) Wiley.

Structured COBOL Programming. 8th ed. Robert A. Stern & Nancy B. Stern. LC 96-9924. 816p. 1996. pap. text ed. 70.95 (*0-471-13886-X*) Wiley.

***Structured COBOL Programming, Incl. MicroFocus Compiler & instr. manual.** Gary B. Shelly et al. (Illus.). 544p. 1996. text ed. write for info. incl. 3.5 ld (*0-7895-1022-7*) Course Tech.

***Structured COBOL Programming, MicroFocus Compiler.** Gary B. Shelly et al. (Illus.). 1996. text ed. write for info. (*0-7895-1164-9*) Course Tech.

S

Structured COBOL Programming: Interactive & Batch Processing. Bernard L. Levite. 1994. write for info. (0-615-00038-X) Course Tech.
Structured COBOL Programming: Syntax Guide. 6th ed. Nancy B. Stern & Robert A. Stern. 80p. 1991. Net. pap. text ed. write for info. (0-471-54028-5) Wiley.
Structured Cobol Programming: With Syntax Reference Guide & Micro Focus Personal Cobol Compiler & MF Cobol Student Manual, Set. Robert A. Stern & Nancy B. Stern. 1066p. 1994. pap. text ed. write for info. (0-471-03448-7) Wiley.
Structured Cobol Programming with Business Applications. N. L. Sarda. 388p. 1990. 60.00 (81-209-0016-2, Pub. by Pitambar Pub II) St Mut.
Structured COBOL, Solutions. 3rd ed. Tyler Welburn & Wilson Price. 1990. write for info. (0-07-069164-9) McGraw.
Structured COBOL with Compiler. 2nd ed. Gerard A. Paquette. 848p. (C). 1991. pap. text ed. 69.60 incl. 3.5 ld (0-697-14305-8) Irwin.
Structured COBOL with Micro Focus Personal COBOL 2.0. 4th ed. Tyler Welburn & Wilson Price. 1994. pap. text ed. write for info. (0-07-912044-X) McGraw.
Structured COBOL/Wolff's RM COBOL-85. 3rd ed. Gerard A. Paquette et al. 864p. (C). 1994. pap. text ed. 69.60 incl. disk (0-697-25984-6) Irwin.
Structured Computer Organization. 2nd ed. Andrew S. Tanenbaum. (Illus.). 480p. 1984. teacher ed. write for info. (0-13-854423-9) P-H.
Structured Computer Organization. 3rd ed. Andrew S. Tanenbaum. 386p. 1989. text ed. 79.00 (0-13-854662-2) P-H.
Structured Concurrent Programming with Operating Systems Applications. Richard C. Holt et al. 1978. pap. text ed. 23.16 (0-201-02937-5) Addison-Wesley.
Structured Crowd: Essays in English Social History. Harold Perkin. 250p. 1981. 44.00 (0-389-20116-2, N6890) B&N Imports.
Structured Data Processing Design. Harry H. Ort. LC 84-14506. 224p. 1985. teacher ed. write for info. (0-201-05426-4); pap. text ed. 17.56 (0-201-05425-6) Addison-Wesley.
Structured Derivatives: New Tools for Investment Management. 300p. 1997. 75.00 (0-273-61120-8) Pitman Publng.
Structured Design: Fundamentals of a Discipline of Computer Program & System Design. 2nd ed. Edward Yourdon & Larry L. Constantine. 1979. text ed. 88.00 (0-13-854471-9) P-H.
Structured Design Using HIPO II. William H. Roetzheim. 240p. 1990. text ed. 36.00 (0-13-853599-X) P-H.
Structured Development & Evolution of Reptiles. Mark W. Ferguson. (Symposium Zoological Society Ser.: No. 52). 1984. text ed. 164.00 (0-12-613352-2) Acad Pr.
Structured Development for Real Time Systems: Essential Modeling Techniques, Vol. 2. Paul T. Ward & Stephen J. Mellor. 144p. (Orig.). (C). 1986. pap. text ed. 47.00 (0-13-854795-5, Yourdon) P-H.
Structured Development for Real-Time Systems: Implementation Modeling Techniques, Vol. 3. Paul T. Ward & Stephen J. Mellor. LC 85-50815. 168p. (Orig.). (C). 1986. pap. 33.00 (0-685-10761-2, Yourdon) P-H.
Structured Digital Design Including MSI-LSI Components & Microprocessors. Raymond M. Kline. (Illus.). 544p. (C). 1983. text ed. 39.95 (0-685-06110-8) P-H.
Structured Document Image Analysis. Ed. by H. S. Baird et al. LC 92-27386. ix, 584p. 1992. 100.95 (0-387-55141-7) Spr-Verlag.
Structured Documents. Ed. by J. Andre et al. (Cambridge Series on Electronic Publishing). (Illus.). 232p. (C). 1989. text ed. 74.95 (0-521-36554-6) Cambridge U Pr.
Structured Essay: A Formula for Writing. 2nd ed. Mary Spangler & Rita Werner. 416p. (C). 1996. per., pap. text ed. 42.99 (0-8403-3813-9) Kendall-Hunt.
Structured Exercises for Promoting Family & Group Strengths: A Handbook for Group Leaders, Trainers, Educators, Counselors, & Therapists. Ed. by Ron McManus & Glen H. Jennings. LC 95-4829. (Illus.). 303p. (C). 1996. 39.95 (1-56024-978-1) Haworth Pr.
***Structured Exercises for Promoting Family & Group Strengths: A Handbook for Group Leaders, Trainers, Educators, Counselors, & Therapists.** Ed. by Ron McManus & Glen H. Jennings. LC 95-4829. 303p. (C). 1996. pap. 19.95 (0-7890-0224-8) Haworth Pr.
Structured Exercises in Stress Management. Ed. by Nancy L. Tubesing & Sandy S. Christian. LC 83-61073. 192p. 1995. 54.95 (1-57025-076-6) Whole Person.
Structured Exercises in Stress Management, Vol. I. Ed. by Nancy L. Tubesing & Donald A. Tubesing. LC 83-61073. (Stress Management Handbook Ser.). 144p. 1983. pap. 29.95 (0-938586-01-7) Whole Person.
Structured Exercises in Stress Management, Vol. 1. Nancy L. Tubesing & Donald A. Tubesing. LC 83-61073. 1990. ring bd. 54.95 (0-938586-34-3) Whole Person.
Structured Exercises in Stress Management, Vol. 2. Nancy L. Tubesing & Donald A. Tubesing. LC 83-61073. 1990. ring bd. 54.95 (0-938586-35-1) Whole Person.
Structured Exercises in Stress Management, Vol. 2. Ed. by Nancy L. Tubesing & Donald A. Tubesing. (Stress Management Handbook Ser.). 192p. 1994. pap. text ed. 29.95 (1-57025-015-4) Whole Person.
Structured Exercises in Stress Management, Vol. 3. Nancy L. Tubesing & Donald A. Tubesing. LC 83-61073. 1990. ring bd. 54.95 (0-938586-36-X) Whole Person.
Structured Exercises in Stress Management, Vol. 4. Nancy L. Tubesing & Donald A. Tubesing. LC 83-61073. 1990. ring bd. 54.95 (0-938586-37-8) Whole Person.
Structured Exercises in Stress Management, Vol. 4. Ed. by Nancy L. Tubesing & Donald A. Tubesing. (Stress Management Handbook Ser.). 192p. 1994. pap. text ed. 29.95 (1-57025-017-0) Whole Person.
Structured Exercises in Stress Management, Vol. 5. Ed. by Nancy L. Tubesing & Sandy S. Christian. LC 83-61073. (Stress Management Handbook Ser.). 192p. 1995. otabind 29.95 (1-57025-016-2) Whole Person.
Structured Exercises in Wellness Promotion. Ed. by Nancy L. Tubesing & Sandy S. Christian. LC 83-61074. 164p. 1995. 54.95 (1-57025-077-4) Whole Person.
Structured Exercises in Wellness Promotion, Vol. 1. Ed. by Nancy L. Tubesing & Donald A. Tubesing. (Wellness Promotion Handbook Ser.). 192p. 1994. pap. text ed. 29.95 (1-57025-018-9) Whole Person.
Structured Exercises in Wellness Promotion, Vol. 2. Ed. by Nancy L. Tubesing & Donald A. Tubesing. (Wellness Promotion Handbook Ser.). 192p. 1994. pap. text ed. 29.95 (1-57025-019-7) Whole Person.
Structured Exercises in Wellness Promotion, Vol. 3. Ed. by Nancy L. Tubesing & Donald A. Tubesing. (Wellness Promotion Handbook Ser.). 192p. 1994. pap. text ed. 29.95 (1-57025-020-0) Whole Person.
Structured Exercises in Wellness Promotion, Vol. 4. Ed. by Nancy L. Tubesing & Donald A. Tubesing. (Wellness Promotion Handbook Ser.). 192p. 1994. pap. text ed. 29.95 (1-57025-021-9) Whole Person.
Structured Exercises in Wellness Promotion, Vol. 5. Ed. by Nancy L. Tubesing & Sandy S. Christian. LC 83-61074. (Wellness Promotion Handbook Ser.). 192p. (Orig.). 1995. otabind 29.95 (1-57025-075-8) Whole Person.
Structured Exercises in Wellness Promotion: Loose-Leaf Edition, Vol. 1. Ed. by Nancy L. Tubesing & Donald A. Tubesing. (Wellness Promotion Handbook Ser.). 192p. (Orig.). 1994. ring bd. 54.95 (0-938586-38-6) Whole Person.
Structured Exercises in Wellness Promotion: Loose-Leaf Edition, Vol. 2. Ed. by Nancy L. Tubesing & Donald A. Tubesing. (Wellness Promotion Handbook Ser.). 192p. (Orig.). 1994. ring bd. 54.95 (0-938586-39-4) Whole Person.
Structured Exercises in Wellness Promotion: Loose-Leaf Edition, Vol. 3. Ed. by Nancy L. Tubesing & Donald A. Tubesing. (Wellness Promotion Handbook Ser.). 192p. (Orig.). 1994. ring bd. 54.95 (0-938586-40-8) Whole Person.
Structured Exercises in Wellness Promotion: Loose-Leaf Edition, Vol. 4. Ed. by Nancy L. Tubesing & Donald A. Tubesing. (Wellness Promotion Handbook Ser.). 192p. (Orig.). 1994. ring bd. 54.95 (0-938586-41-6) Whole Person.
Structured Finance: A Guide to the Fundamentals of Asset Securitization. Steven L. Schwarcz. LC 90-63381. 70p. 1990. pap. 19.95 (0-87224-019-3) PLI.
Structured Financing: A Guide to the Principles of Asset Securitization. 2nd ed. Steven L. Schwarcz. 70p. (C). 1993. pap. text ed. 29.95 (0-87224-056-8) PLI.
Structured Formula Translation. Lester Klein. 250p. (Orig.). (C). 1986. pap. text ed. write for info. (0-89894-037-0) Advocate Pub Group.
Structured FORTRAN for Business. Charles E. Paddock. LC 84-18377. (Illus.). 272p. (C). 1985. pap. text ed. 32.00 (0-13-854233-3) P-H.
Structured FORTRAN 77 for Engineers & Scientists. 3rd ed. D. M. Etter. 520p. 1990. teacher ed. 10.75 (0-8053-0052-X); pap. text ed. 44.25 (0-8053-0051-1); 10.75 (0-8053-0053-8); disk 11.95 (0-8053-0054-6) Benjamin-Cummings.
Structured FORTRAN 77 for Engineers & Scientists. 4th ed. D. M. Etter. LC 92-35063. (C). 1993. pap. text ed. 46.25 (0-8053-1775-9) Benjamin-Cummings.
Structured Fortran '77 with Numerical Methods for Scientist & Engineers. Delores M. Etter. (C). 1992. text ed. 55.95 (0-8053-1781-3) Addison-Wesley.
Structured FORTRAN 77 with Numerical Methods for Scientists & Engineers. D. M. Etter. (C). 1992. write for info. (0-8053-1771-6) Benjamin-Cummings.
Structured Group Psychotherapy for Bipolar Disorder: The Life Goals Program. Mark S. Bauer & Linda McBride. (Illus.). 312p. (Orig.). 1996. 48.95 (0-8261-9300-5) Springer Pub.
Structured Hereditary Systems. Reneke et al. (Pure & Applied Mathematics Ser.: Vol. 107). 232p. 1987. 125.00 (0-8247-7772-7) Dekker.
Structured Induction in Expert Systems. Alen Shapiro. 256p. (C). 1987. text ed. 31.25 (0-201-17813-3) Addison-Wesley.
***Structured Interview for DSM-IV Personality (SIDP-IV)** Bruce Pfohl et al. 48p. (Orig.). 1997. pap. text ed. write for info. (0-88048-937-5, 8937) Am Psychiatric.
Structured Introduction to Numerical Mathematics. P. J. Hartley & A. Wynn-Evans. 464p. (C). 1979. 89.00 (0-85950-426-3, Pub. by S Thornes Pubs UK) St Mut.
Structured Logic Design with VHDL. James Armstrong & Gail Gray. 400p. 1993. text ed. 63.00 (0-13-855206-1) P-H.
Structured Meanings: The Semantics of Propositional Attitudes. Maxwell J. Cresswell. 1985. 27.50 (0-262-03108-6) MIT Pr.
Structured Microprocessor Programming. Morris Krieger et al. LC 79-67229. (Illus.). 240p. (Orig.). 1979. pap. 12.95 (0-917072-18-9, Yourdon) P-H.
Structured Note Market: The Definitive Guide for Investors, Traders & Issuers. Ravi E. Dattatreya. 1995. per. 65.00 (1-55738-826-1) Irwin Prof Pubng.
Structured On-the-Job Training: Unleashing Employee Expertise in the Workplace. Ronald L. Jacobs & Michael J. Jones. LC 94-37973. (Illus.). 194p. 1995. 29.95 (1-881052-20-6) Berrett-Koehler.
Structured PC Cobol for the '90s. Raphael E. Serebreny. 640p. 1993. pap. 40.00 (0-13-855859-0) P-H.
Structured Personality Learning Theory: A Holistic Multivariate Research Approach. Raymond B. Cattell. LC 83-16103. (Centennial Psychology Ser.). 480p. 1983. text ed. 69.50 (0-275-90958-1, C0958, Praeger Pubs) Greenwood.
Structured PL-Zero PL-One. Michael Kennedy & Martin B. Solomon. (Illus.). 1977. pap. write for info. (0-13-854901-X) P-H.
Structured Polymer Properties. Robert J. Samuels. LC 73-21781. 265p. reprint ed. 75.60 (0-8357-9986-7, 2015851) Bks Demand.
***Structured Population Models.** Ed. by Shripad Tuljapurkar & Hal Caswell. LC 96-2940. 496p. (gr. 13). 1996. pap. 38.95 (0-412-07271-8) Chapman & Hall.
***Structured-Population Models in Marine, Terrestrial, & Freshwater Systems.** Shripad Tuljapurkar & Hal Caswell. LC 96-2940. 496p. (gr. 13). 1996. text ed. 85.00 (0-412-07261-0) Chapman & Hall.
Structured Program Design: A Designer's Handbook. David Nicol. (Illus.). 256p. 1994. pap. 32.95 (0-7506-1759-4) Buttrwrth-Heinemann.
Structured Program Design Using JSP (ELBS) B. Burgess. (C). 1989. 50.00 (0-09-173206-9, Pub. by S Thornes Pubs UK) St Mut.
Structured Programming: PL-1 with PL-C. Cathy H. Davis & Lyle Domina. LC 87-12473. 704p. (C). 1995. pap. text ed. 45.50 (0-03-003723-9) OUP.
Structured Programming Applications. Dahl. 1972. text ed. 61.00 (0-12-200550-3) Acad Pr.
Structured Programming Design Using JSP. B. Burgess. (C). 1989. 100.00 (0-09-173151-8, Pub. by S Thornes Pubs UK) St Mut.
Structured Programming in Assembly Language for the IBM PC. William C. Runnion. 690p. (C). 1988. text ed. 56.95 incl. disk (0-534-91480-2) PWS Pubs.
Structured Programming in Assembly Language for the IBM PC. 2nd ed. William C. Runnion. LC 94-286. 1995. text ed. 69.95 (0-534-93268-1) PWS Pubs.
Structured Programming in COBOL. Robert B. Boettcher. 620p. (C). 1987. text ed. 35.00 (0-03-070559-2) Dryden Pr.
Structured Programming in Cobol. B. J. Holmes. 400p. (C). 1991. 55.00 (1-870941-82-9) St Mut.
Structured Programming in dBASE IV. Robert L. Buchanan. 426p. (C). 1991. pap. 43.95 (0-534-14400-4) Course Tech.
Structured Programming in dBASE IV: Version 2.0. 2nd ed. Robert L. Buchanan. LC 94-5015. 440p. 1995. pap. 40.95 (0-534-23808-4) Course Tech.
Structured Programming in PL - 1 & PL - C. Bernhard Fischer & Herman Fischer. LC 76-1592. (Computer Science Ser.: No. 1). (Illus.). 416p. reprint ed. pap. 118.60 (0-7837-0869-6, 2041177) Bks Demand.
Structured Programming in QBasic Text. Larry J. Goldstein. LC 92-40006. (C). 1993. text ed. write for info. incl. 5.25 hd (0-06-501838-9) Addison-Wesley Educ.
Structured Programming in QBasic Text. Larry J. Goldstein. LC 92-40007. (C). 1993. text ed. 32.00 incl. 3.5 hd (0-06-501839-7) Addison-Wesley Educ.
Structured Programming in Turbo Pascal. 2nd ed. Wayne Horn. LC 94-35625. 891p. (C). 1995. pap. text ed. 61.33 (0-13-311721-9) P-H.
Structured Programming Logic: A Flowcharting Approach. Jerry L. Jones. (Illus.). 144p. 1986. pap. text ed. 17.95 (0-318-11865-3) P-H.
Structured Programming Using FORTRAN 77. Patrick G. McKeown. 482p. (C). 1985. pap. text ed. 35.00 (0-15-584411-3) Dryden Pr.
Structured Programming Using True BASIC: An Introduction. Wade Ellis, Jr. & Ed Lodi. 356p. (C). 1988. pap. text ed. 32.00 (0-15-584076-2) Dryden Pr.
Structured Programming Using Turbo BASIC. Wade Ellis, Jr. & Ed Lodi. 337p. 1988. pap. text ed. 52.00 (0-12-237460-6) Acad Pr.
Structured Programming Using Turbo Pascal: A Brief Introduction. 2nd ed. Margaret Anderson. 200p. (C). 1990. pap. text ed. 16.50 (0-15-584081-9) Dryden Pr.
Structured Programming Using WATFIV. Patrick G. McKeown. 405p. (C). 1985. pap. text ed. 33.25 (0-15-584414-8) Dryden Pr.
Structured Programming with Lotus 1-2-3. Nancy Woodard Cain & Thomas Cain. (Illus.). 352p. 1989. pap. 29.95 (0-13-853540-X) Brady Pub.
Structured Programming with Microsoft BASIC. Robert D. Brown & Patrick G. McKeown. 350p. (C). 1992. Instructor's manual with IBM 5.25 inch disk. teacher ed. write for info. incl. disk (0-15-500561-8); Instructor's manual with IBM 3.5 inch disk. teacher ed. write for info. incl. disk (0-15-500560-X); pap. text ed. 29.50 (0-15-500018-7) Dryden Pr.
Structured Programming with QuickBASIC. James Payne. 363p. (C). 1991. pap. 64.95 (0-534-92563-4) PWS Pubs.
Structured Programming with QuickBASIC. James Payne. 363p. (C). 1991. pap. 52.95 (0-534-93060-3) PWS Pubs.
Structured Publishing from the Desktop: Frame Technology's FrameMaker. Michael Fraase. Ed. by Susan Glinert. 350p. 1992. 30.00 (1-55623-616-6) Irwin Prof Pubng.
Structured Reading. 3rd ed. Lynn Q. Troyka. 384p. (C). 1989. pap. text ed. 39.00 (0-13-855016-6) P-H.
Structured Reading. 4th ed. Lynn Q. Troyka. LC 94-19881. (C). 1995. pap. text ed. 35.40 (0-13-030842-0) P-H.
Structured Receivables Financing: Managing Risks More Efficiently in Security Form. Edward F. Green & Walter G. McNeill. 270p. write for info. (0-318-60935-5) HarBrace.
Structured Settlements. 2nd ed. Paul Lesti et al. LC 86-80969. 1993. 135.00 (0-685-59909-4) Clark Boardman Callaghan.
Structured Settlements: A Practical Guide. Iain S. Goldrein et al. 217p. 1993. pap. text ed. 60.00 (0-406-02056-6, UK) MICHIE.
Structured Settlements & Interim & Provisional Damages. (Law Commission Consultation Papers: No. 125). 102p. 1992. pap. 16.00 (0-11-730208-2, HM02082, Pub. by Stationery Ofc UK) Bernan Associates.
Structured Settlements & Periodic Payment Judgments. Daniel W. Hindert et al. 1050p. 1986. ring bd. 98.00 (0-318-21441-5, 00598) NY Law Pub.
Structured Stochastic Matrices of M-G-1 Type & Their Applications. Marcel F. Neuts. (Probability Ser.: Vol. 5). 512p. 1989. 170.00 (0-8247-8283-6) Dekker.
Structured Strategic Planning: A Practical Guide to Formulating & Implementing Corporate, Business Unit & Cost Center Strategies. Alan S. Michaels. LC 94-96085. (Illus.). 324p. (Orig.). 1994. pap. 85.00 (0-9641122-0-5) A S Michaels.
Structured System Analysis: A New Technique. Barbara F. Medina. 82p. 1981. text ed. 132.00 (0-677-05570-6) Gordon & Breach.
Structured Systems Analysis: Tools & Techniques. Chris Gane & Trish Sarson. 373p. (C). 1977. 22.50 (0-930196-00-7); pap. 15.00 (0-686-37676-5) McDonnell Douglas.
Structured Systems Analysis: Tools & Techniques. Chris Gane & Trish Sarson. 1979. text ed. 90.00 (0-13-854547-2) P-H.
***Structured Systems Analysis & Design: A Team Oriented Approach.** Leon R. Price & Wayne R. Headrick. text ed. 16.95 (0-471-07678-3) Wiley.
Structured Systems Analysis & Design Methods. 2nd ed. Ed Downs et al. 300p. 1991. pap. text ed. 61.00 (0-13-853698-8) P-H.
Structured Systems Development. Kenneth T. Orr. LC 77-88593. (Illus.). 192p. (Orig.). 1986. pap. 19.95 (0-917072-06-5, Yourdon) P-H.
Structured Techniques: A Basis for CASE. rev. ed. James Martin & Carma L. McClure. (Illus.). 816p. (C). 1987. text ed. 96.00 (0-13-854936-2) P-H.
Structured Tutoring. Grant Von Harrison & Ronald E. Guymon. Ed. by Danny G. Langdon. LC 79-23035. (Instructional Design Library). 108p. 1980. 27.95 (0-87778-154-0) Educ Tech Pubns.
Structured VAX Assembly Language Programming. Robert W. Sebesta. 1991. teacher ed. 10.75 (0-8053-7123-0) Benjamin-Cummings.
Structured VAX Assembly Language Programming. 2nd ed. Robert W. Sebesta. 550p. (C). 1991. text ed. 51.75 (0-8053-7122-2) Benjamin-Cummings.
Structured VAX BASIC. R. Hirschfelder et al. 643p. (C). 1987. teacher ed. 17.25 (0-8053-3691-5); pap. text ed. 40.95 (0-8053-3690-7) Benjamin-Cummings.
Structured VAX BASIC: A GOTO-less Approach. Wilson T. Price & Richard Spitzer. 581p. (C). 1988. pap. write for info. (0-02-396620-3, Macmillan Coll) P-H.
Structured Walkthroughs. 4th ed. Edward Yourdon. 192p. 1988. text ed. 61.00 (0-13-855289-4) P-H.
***Structure/Performance Relationships in Surfactants.** Ed. by Milton J. Rosen. LC 84-6384. (ACS Symposium Ser.: No. 253). (Illus.). 368p. 1984. reprint ed. pap. 104.90 (0-608-03131-3, 2063584) Bks Demand.
Structure/Property Relationships for Metal/Metal Interfaces Vol. 229: Materials Research Society Symposium Proceedings. Ed. by A. D. Romig et al. 357p. 1991. text ed. 74.00 (1-55899-123-9) Materials Res.
Structures. 1980. 10.50 (0-8176-0592-4) Spr-Verlag.
Structures. Sally Morgan & Adrian Morgan. LC 93-20164. (Illus.). 48p. (J). 1993. 14.95 (0-8160-2983-0) Facts on File.
Structures. Brendan Tripp. 28p. 1980. pap. 5.00 (1-57353-003-4) Eschaton Prods.
Structures. Bernie Zubrowski. 64p. (J). (gr. 5-8). 1993. pap. text ed. 11.50 (0-938587-34-X) Cuisenaire.
Structures. 2nd ed. Daniel L. Schodek. 576p. 1991. text ed. 86.00 (0-13-855313-0) P-H.
***Structures.** 3rd ed. Schodek. 1997. text ed. 66.67 (0-13-619693-4) P-H.
Structures: A Textbook for Technician. Samuel E. French. (Construction & Building Trades Ser.). 896p. 1995. 64.95 (0-8273-6000-2) Delmar.
Structures: Business, Entrepreneurs, the Free Market. Robert E. Sonntag. (Illus.). 288p. (Orig.). 1986. pap. 14.95 (0-938545-00-0) Philomod Corp.
Structures: Matrix & Finite Element. 3rd ed. M. Mukhopadhyay. 423p. 1993. 70.00 (90-5410-234-9, Pub. by A A Balkema NE) Ashgate Pub Co.
Structures: Or Why Things Don't Fall Down. Ed. by J. E. Gordon. LC 81-9755. 396p. 1978. 25.00 (0-306-40025-1); pap. 15.95 (0-306-80151-5) Da Capo.
Structures: The Way Things Are Built. Nigel Hawkes. (Illus.). 240p. 1990. text ed. 39.95 (0-02-549105-9) Macmillan.
Structures: The Way Things are Built. Nigel Hawkes. LC 93-16736. (Illus.). 240p. 1993. pap. 20.00 (0-02-000510-5) Macmillan.
Structures & Abstractions: A Brief Introduction to Turbo Pascal (5.x, 6.x, 7.0. William I. Salmon & Edward L. Salmon. LC 93-42642. (C). 1993. text ed. 41.95 (0-256-15966-1) Irwin Prof Pubng.
Structures & Abstractions: An Introduction to Computer Science with Pascal. William I. Salmon. (Illus.). 800p. (C). 1991. pap. text ed. 41.95 (0-256-08273-1) Irwin.
Structures & Abstractions: An Introduction to Computer Science with Turbo Pascal. William I. Salmon. 992p. (C). 1991. per. 43.00 (0-256-10211-2, 07-3506-01) Irwin.
Structures & Abstractions: An Introduction to Computer Science with Turbo Pascal. 2nd ed. William I. Salmon. LC 93-21441. 880p. (C). 1993. per. 47.75 (0-256-12666-6) Irwin.

An Asterisk (*) at the beginning of an entry indicates that the title is appearing in BIP for the first time.

Structures & Abstractions Labs: Experiments in Pascal & Turbo Pascal. 2nd ed. William I. Salmon. LC 93-45333. (C). 1994. text ed. 28.00 (*0-256-15303-5*) Irwin.

Structures & Abstractions Labs: Experiments with Pascal & Turbo Pascal. William I. Salmon. 300p. (C). 1992. 23.00 (*0-256-10352-6*, 30-3158-01) Irwin.

Structures & Biological Effects. R. E. Benfield et al. LC 93-15374. (Structure & Bonding Ser.: Vol. 81). 1993. 119.00 (*0-387-56481-0*) Spr-Verlag.

Structures & Buildings. Nigel Hawkes. (New Technology Ser.). (Illus.). 32p. (J). (gr. 5-8). 1994. lib. bdg. 13.98 (*0-8050-3418-8*) TFC Bks NY.

Structures & Categories for the Representation of Meaning. Timothy C. Potts. (Illus.). 314p. (C). 1994. text ed. 59.95 (*0-521-43481-5*) Cambridge U Pr.

Structures & Conformations of Non-Rigid Molecules: Proceedings of the NATO Advanced Research Workshop, Reisenburg, Germany, September 6-10, 1992. Ed. by Jaan Laane. (NATO Advanced Science Institutes Series C: Mathematical & Physical Sciences). 656p. (C). 1993. lib. bdg. 292.50 (*0-7923-2415-3*) Kluwer Ac.

Structures & Controls Optimization. Ed. by N. S. Khot & R. T. Haftka. LC 93-73610. 119p. pap. 100.00 (*0-7918-1253-7*) ASME.

Structures & Dynamics of Agricultural Exploitations: Ownership, Occupation, Investment, Credit, & Markets: Proceedings of the Tenth International Economic History Congress, Leuven, Belgium, August 1990. Ed. by E. Aerts et al. (Studies in Social & Economic History: No. 5). 143p. (Orig.). 1990. pap. 32.50 (*90-6186-377-5*, Pub. by Leuven Univ BE) Coronet Bks.

Structures & Function of Low Affinity Fc Receptors. Ed. by W. H. Fridman. (Chemical Immunology Ser.: Vol. 47). (Illus.). xii, 260p. 1989. 172.00 (*3-8055-4959-8*) S Karger.

***Structures & Machines.** Snape & Rowlands. (Science at Work Ser.). 1992. pap. text ed. write for info. (*0-582-07830-X*, Pub. by Longman UK) Longman.

Structures & Materials: A Programmed Approach. P. C. Croxton et al. (Illus.). 300p. 1974. 27.95 (*0-8464-0890-2*) Beekman Pubs.

Structures & Materials: Collection of Technical Papers, 10th Conference, New Orleans, Louisiana, April 14-16, 1969. AIAA-ASME Structures, Structural Dynamics & Material Conference Staff. (Illus.). 481p. reprint ed. pap. 137.10 (*0-317-08388-0*, 2016452) Bks Demand.

Structures & Procedures of Implicit Knowledge. Arthur C. Graesser & Leslie F. Clark. LC 85-7336. (Advances in Discourse Processes Ser.: Vol. 17). 336p. 1985. pap. 42.50 (*0-89391-362-6*); text ed. 78.50 (*0-89391-192-5*) Ablex Pub.

Structures & Processes of Urban Life. 2nd ed. Raymond E. Pahl et al. LC 82-13093. (Aspects of Modern Sociology: the Social Structure of Modern Britain Ser.). 170p. reprint ed. pap. 48.50 (*0-7837-1581-1*, 2041873) Bks Demand.

Structures & Properties of Fibres. R. Meredith. 85p. 1975. 70.00 (*0-686-63798-4*) St Mut.

***Structures & Properties of Rubberlike Networks.** Burak Erman & James E. Mark. LC 96-48699. (Illus.). 352p. 1997. 70.00 (*0-19-508237-0*) OUP.

Structures & Reactions of the Aromatic Compounds. Geoffrey M. Badger. LC 54-3317. 470p. reprint ed. pap. 134.00 (*0-317-08966-8*, 2051390) Bks Demand.

Structures & Reactivity of Surfaces: Proceedings of a European Conference, Trieste, Italy, September 13-16. Ed. by C. Morterra et al. (Studies in Surface Science & Catalysis: Vol. 48). 970p. 1989. 268.25 (*0-444-87465-8*) Elsevier.

Structures & Spatiotemporal Chaos in Nonequilibrium Media, Vol. 10. A. V. Gaponov-Grekhov & M. I. Rabinovich. (Physics Reviews Ser.: SSR Sec. A, Vol. 10, Pt. 3). 108p. 1989. pap. text ed. 94.00 (*3-7186-4862-8*) Gordon & Breach.

Structures & Stochastic Methods. Ed. by A. S. Cakmak. LC 87-70781. (SDEE Ser.: Vol. 3). 500p. 1987. 134.00 (*0-931215-88-9*) Computational Mech MA.

Structures & Strategies: An Introduction to Academic Writing. Lloyd Davis & Susan McKay. 237p. 1996. 59.95 (*0-7329-2929-6*, Pub. by Macmill Educ AT) pap. 29.95 (*0-7329-2930-X*, Pub. by Macmill Educ AT) Paul & Co Pubs.

Structures & Strategies: Women, Work & Family. Ed. by Leela Dube & Rajni Palrewala. (Women & the Household in Asia Ser.: Vol. 3). (Illus.). 284p. (C). 1990. text ed. 26.00 (*0-8039-9621-7*) Sage.

Structures & Their Functions in Usan: A Papuan Language of Papua New Guinea. Ger P. Reesink. LC 86-17518. (Studies in Language Companion: Vol. 13). xviii, 369p. 1987. 97.00 (*90-272-3015-3*) Benjamins North Am.

Structures & Transformations: The Romance Verb. Christopher J. Pountain. LC 83-12287. (Illus.). 272p. 1983. 44.00 (*0-389-20436-6*, N7322) B&N Imports.

Structures Approach to Software Systems Development. Gary Heap. 1992. text ed. 40.00 (*0-07-707483-1*) McGraw.

***Structures Assisting the Migrations of Non-Salmonid Fish: U. S. S. R.** 104p. 1989. 14.00 (*92-5-102857-5*, Pub. by FAO IT) Bernan Associates.

Structures Congress XII: Proceedings of Papers Presented at the Structures Congress '94, Held in Atlanta, GA, April 24-28, 1994. Structural Division Staff of the American Society of Civil Engineers. Ed. by N. C. Baker & B. J. Goodno. LC 94-7101. 1994. 140.00 (*0-87262-952-X*) Am Soc Civil Eng.

Structures De la Pensee: Modes - Temps - Aspects - Modes De Proces En Anglais et En Francais. Edouard J. Matte. LC 92-15123. (American University Studies: Linguistics: Ser. XIII, Vol. 27). 420p. (FRE.). 1993. 62.95 (*0-8204-1880-3*) P Lang Pubng.

***Structures for Architects.** Gauld. 1984. pap. text ed. write for info. (*0-7114-5753-0*) Addison-Wesley.

Structures for Architects. 3rd ed. Bryan J. Gauld. (Illus.). 176p. 1994. pap. 39.50 (*0-582-23658-4*, Pub. by Longman Group UK) Trans-Atl Phila.

***Structures for Buildings.** Malcolm Millais. (Illus.). 384p. 1996. pap. 49.95 (*0-419-21970-6*, E & FN Spon) Routledge Chapman & Hall.

Structures for Enhanced Safety & Physical Security. Ed. by Theodor Krauthammer. 438p. 1989. 40.00 (*0-87262-686-5*) Am Soc Civil Eng.

Structures for Growth. Oswill E. Williams. (Equipped to Serve Ser.). (Illus.). 77p. (Orig.). 1996. pap. text ed. 4.95 (*0-934942-90-0*) White Wing Pub.

***Structures for Living.** Otto Steidle. 1996. pap. text ed. 56.00 (*3-7643-5545-X*) Birkhauser.

***Structures for Mission.** Hoff. 1985. pap. 12.00 (*0-8028-0081-5*) Eerdmans.

Structures for Semantics. Fred Landman. 384p. (C). 1991. lib. bdg. 154.00 (*0-7923-1239-2*, Pub. by Klwr Acad Pubs NE) Kluwer Ac.

Structures for Semantics. Fred Landman. (Studies in Linguistics & Philosophy: No. 45). 384p. 1994. pap. text ed. 39.00 (*0-7923-1240-6*) Kluwer Ac.

Structures for Water Control Training Manual. B. E. Van den Bosch. (Irrigation Water Management Training Manual Ser.: Vol. 8). 1993. pap. 10.00 (*92-5-103418-4*, F34184, Pub. by FAO IT) Bernan Associates.

Structures from the Trivium in the "Cantar de Mio Cid" James F. Burke. (Romance Ser.: No. 66). 256p. 1992. 55.00 (*0-8020-5947-3*) U of Toronto Pr.

Structures in Concurrency Theory: Proceedings of the International Workshop on Structures in Concurrency Theory (STRICT), Berlin, 11-13 May 1995. Ed. by Jorg Desel. LC 95-32279. (Workshops in Computing Ser.). 364p. 1995. 74.00 (*3-540-19982-9*) Spr-Verlag.

Structures in Spelling: Words with Prefixes, Roots, & Suffixes. 1993. 12.00 (*0-88336-151-5*); teacher ed. 14.00 (*0-88336-134-5*) New Readers.

Structures in the Stream: Water, Science, & the Rise of the U. S. Army Corps of Engineers. Todd Shallat. Ed. by William H. Goetzmann. LC 93-42972. (American Studies). (Illus.). 288p. (C). 1994. text ed. 34.95 (*0-292-77679-9*) U of Tex Pr.

Structures in Topology. Douglas Harris. LC 52-42839. (Memoirs Ser.: No. 1/115). 96p. 1971. pap. 16.00 (*0-8218-1815-5*, MEMO/1/115) Am Math.

Structures Maintenance. (Transportation Research Record Ser.: No. 1184). 55p. 1988. 7.50 (*0-309-04724-2*) Transport Res Bd.

Structures, Mecanismes et Spectroscope: 120, 60 Solutions. B. Waegell & J. C. Maire. (Cours & Documents de Chimie Ser.). 300p. (FRE.). 1969. text ed. 321.00 (*0-677-50160-9*) Gordon & Breach.

Structures of Antigens, Vol. I. Regenmortel. 432p. 1992. 164.00 (*0-8493-8865-1*, QR186) CRC Pr.

Structures of Binary Compounds. Ed. by F. R. De Boer & D. G. Pettifor. (Cohesion & Structure Ser.: Vol. 2). 382p. 1990. 208.75 (*0-444-87478-X*, North Holland) Elsevier.

Structures of Capital: The Social Organization of the Economy. Ed. by Sharon Zukin & Paul DiMaggio. (Illus.). 448p. (C). 1990. pap. text ed. 17.95 (*0-521-37678-5*) Cambridge U Pr.

***Structures of Cellulose: Characterization of the Solid State.** Ed. by Rajai H. Atalia. LC 87-11537. (ACS Symposium Ser.: Vol. 340). 328p. 1987. reprint ed. pap. 93.50 (*0-608-03533-5*, 2064252) Bks Demand.

Structures of Consciousness: The Genius of Jean Gebser - an Introduction & Critique. Georg Feuerstein. LC 86-83184. (Illus.). 240p. (Orig.). 1987. pap. 14.95 (*0-941255-20-4*) Integral Pub.

Structures of Control in Health Management. Rob Flynn. (International Library of Sociology). 208p. (C). 1991. text ed. 74.95 (*0-415-04855-9*, Routledge NY) Routledge.

Structures of Disintegration: Narrative Strategies in Elias Canetti's "Die Blendung" David Darby. (Studies in Austrian Literature, Culture, & Thought). 240p. 1992. 33.00 (*0-929497-50-3*) Ariadne CA.

Structures of DNA, Pt. 1. Cold Spring Harbor Symposia on Quantitative Biology Staff. LC 34-8174. (Cold Spring Harbor Symposia on Quantitative Biology Ser.: Vol. 47). (Illus.). 599p. 1983. pap. 170.80 (*0-7837-8986-6*, 2049765) Bks Demand.

Structures of DNA, Pt. 2. Cold Spring Harbor Symposia on Quantitative Biology Staff. LC 34-8174. (Cold Spring Harbor Symposia on Quantitative Biology Ser.: Vol. 47). (Illus.). 675p. 1983. pap. 180.00 (*0-7837-8987-4*, 2049765) Bks Demand.

Structures of Everyday Life in Japan in the Last Decade of the Twentieth Century. Kazuo Mizuta. LC 93-1751. 400p. 1993. text ed. 99.95 (*0-7734-9320-4*) E Mellen.

Structures of Experience: History, Society, & Personal Life in the Eighteenth-Century British Novel. W. Austin Flanders. (Illus.). 308p. 1984. text ed. 25.95 (*0-87249-419-5*) U of SC Pr.

Structures of History. Christopher Lloyd. LC 92-32022. (Studies in Social Discontinuity). 272p. 1993. 56.95 (*0-631-18464-3*); pap. 26.95 (*0-631-18465-1*) Blackwell Pubs.

Structures of Influence: A Comparative Approach to August Strindberg. Ed. by Marilyn J. Blackwell. LC 80-29545. (University of North Carolina Studies in Comparative Literature: No. 98). 323p. reprint ed. pap. 92.10 (*0-7837-3771-8*, 2043588) Bks Demand.

Structures of Knowing. Katherine Arens. 440p. (C). 1989. lib. bdg. 145.00 (*0-7923-0009-2*, Pub. by Klwr Acad Pubs NE) Kluwer Ac.

Structures of Life: To Accompany an Exhibit by the Beckman Center for the History of Chemistry. Basil Achilladelis & Mary E. Bowden. (BCHOC Publication: No. 8). (Illus.). 36p. (Orig.). 1989. pap. 6.00 (*0-941901-07-6*) Chem Heritage Fnd.

***Structures of Materials.** Adams. (C). 1998. text ed. write for info. (*0-06-501215-1*) Addison-Wesley.

***Structures of Materials.** Adams. (C). 1998. text ed. write for info. (*0-321-01058-2*) Addison-Wesley Educ.

Structures of Matter & Patterns of Science. Ed. by Marjorie Senechal. 200p. 1980. pap. text ed. 16.95 (*0-87073-909-3*) Schenkman Bks Inc.

Structures of Negation: The Writings of Zulfikar Ghose. Chelva Kanaganayakam. LC 93-93561. 226p. 1993. 50.00 (*0-8020-0542-X*) U of Toronto Pr.

Structures of Patriarchy: The State, the Community & the Household. Ed. by Bina Agarwal. LC 88-706. (C). 1988. pap. 17.50 (*0-86232-773-3*, Pub. by Zed Bks Ltd UK) Humanities.

Structures of Permanent Magnets: Generation of Uniform Fields. Manlio G. Abele. LC 92-35449. 416p. 1993. text ed. 89.95 (*0-471-59112-2*) Wiley.

Structures of Power: Essays on Twentieth-Century Spanish-American Fiction. Ed. by Terry J. Peavler & Peter Standish. LC 95-20009. (SUNY Series in Latin American & Iberian Thought & Culture). 193p. 1996. text ed. 49.50 (*0-7914-2839-7*); pap. text ed. 16.95 (*0-7914-2840-0*) State U NY Pr.

Structures of Power & Constraint: Essays in Honor of Peter M. Blau. Ed. by Craig Calhoun et al. (Illus.). 496p. (C). 1990. text ed. 89.95 (*0-521-36598-8*) Cambridge U Pr.

Structures of Social Action: Studies in Conversation Analysis. Ed. by J. Maxwell Atkinson & John Heritage. 480p. 1985. pap. text ed. 32.95 (*0-521-31862-9*) Cambridge U Pr.

Structures of Social Life: The Four Elementary Forms of Human Relations. Alan P. Fiske. 1993. pap. 19.95 (*0-02-906687-5*, Free Press) Free Pr.

Structures of Society: Imperial Russia's "People of Various Ranks" Elise K. Wirtschafter. LC 94-14632. 232p. 1994. lib. bdg. 30.00 (*0-87580-190-0*) N Ill U Pr.

Structures of Subjectivity: Explorations in Psychoanalytic Phenomenology, Vol. 4. George E. Atwood & Robert D. Stolorow. (Psychoanalytic Inquiry Bk.: Vol. 4). 144p. (C). 1993. pap. 22.50 (*0-88163-166-3*) Analytic Pr.

Structures of the Appalachian Foreland Fold-Thrust Belt. Ed. by Engelder. (IGC Field Trip Guidebooks Ser.). 96p. 1989. 21.00 (*0-87590-586-2*, T166) Am Geophysical.

Structures of the Education & Initial Training Systems in the European Union. 2nd ed. Eurydice Staff & Cedefop Staff. 200p. 1995. pap. text ed. 30.00 (*92-826-9319-8*, CY-86-94-828ENC, Pub. by Commiss Europ Commun BE) Bernan Associates.

Structures of the Elements. Jerry Donohue. LC 80-15363. 448p. 1982. reprint ed. lib. bdg. 47.50 (*0-89874-230-7*) Krieger.

Structures of the Level One Standard Modules for the Affine Lie Algebra. M. Mandia. LC 86-28797. (Memoirs of the American Mathematical Society Ser.: Vol. 66/362). 146p. 1987. pap. text ed. 25.00 (*0-8218-2423-6*, MEMO/66/362) Am Math.

Structures of the Life-World, Vol. 2. Alfred Schutz & Thomas Luckmann. Tr. by Richard Zaner & David J. Parent from GER. (Studies in Phenomenology & Existential Philosophy). 339p. (Orig.). 1989. 49.95 (*0-8101-0832-1*); pap. 22.95 (*0-8101-0833-X*) Northwestern U Pr.

Structures of the Life-World, Vol. 1. Alfred Schutz & Thomas Luckmann. Tr. by Richard Zaner & Tristram Engelhardt, Jr. from GER. (Studies in Phenomenology & Existential Philosophy). 335p. 1973. pap. 29.95 (*0-8101-0622-1*) Northwestern U Pr.

Structures of Thinking. Karl Mannheim. Ed. by David Kettler et al. (International Library of Sociology). 240p. 1985. pap. 15.95 (*0-7102-0730-1*, RKP) Routledge.

***Structures of Thinking (1982)** Intro. by Bryan Turner. (Karl Mannheim Ser.: Vol. 10). 1997. 105.00 (*0-415-13675-X*) Routledge.

Structures on Manifolds. K. Yano & Masahiro Kon. (Series in Pure Mathematics: Vol. 3). 520p. 1985. text ed. 86.00 (*9971-966-15-8*); pap. text ed. 41.00 (*9971-966-16-6*) World Scientific Pub.

Structures That Changed the Way the World Looked. Donna Singer. (Twenty Events Ser.). (Illus.). 48p. (J). (gr. 4-8). 1994. lib. bdg. 24.26 (*0-8114-4937-8*) Raintree Steck-V.

Structures (TRR 1393) Ed. by Luanne Crayton. (Transportation Research Record Ser.). (Illus.). 208p. 1993. pap. text ed. 41.00 (*0-309-05466-4*) Transport Res Bd.

Structures under Extreme Loading Conditions. Ed. by Y. S. Shin. (Proceedings of the 1995 ASME/JSME Pressure Vessels & Piping Conference Ser.: PVP-Vol. 299). 140p. 1995. 90.00 (*0-7918-1330-4*, H00962) ASME.

***Structures under Extreme Loading Conditions.** Jonas A. Zukas. 265p. 1996. pap. text ed. 110.00 (*0-7918-1772-5*, TS283) ASME Pr.

Structures under Shock & Impact. Ed. by P. S. Bulson. LC 89-61081. (SUSI Ser.: Vol. 1). 541p. 1989. 149.00 (*0-945824-21-1*) Computational Mech MA.

Structures Under Shock & Impact: Proceedings of the First International Conference (SUSI '89), Cambridge, MA, 11-13 July, 1989. Ed. by P. S. Bulson. 534p. 1989. 235.75 (*0-444-88024-0*) Elsevier.

Structures under Shock & Impact III. Ed. by P. S. Bulson. LC 94-70410. (SUSI Ser.: Vol. 3). 520p. 1994. 219.00 (*1-56252-185-3*, 2610) Computational Mech MA.

Structures under Shock & Impact IV. Ed. by N. Jones et al. (SUSI Ser.: Vol. 4). 576p. 1996. text ed. 238.00 (*1-85312-400-1*, 4001) Computational Mech MA.

Structuring a Learner-Centered School. Linda Schrenko. LC 94-75255. 192p. 1994. pap. 25.95 (*0-932935-74-5*) IRI-SkyLght.

***Structuring & Managing Successful Joint Ventures in India.** 1996. 595.00 (*0-614-25473-6*) Econ Intel.

Structuring Biological Systems: A Computer Modeling Approach. B. K. Iyengar. 288p. 1992. 91.00 (*0-8493-7961-X*, Q) CRC Pr.

Structuring Buy-Sell Agreements: Tax & Legal Analysis with Forms. Howard M. Zaritsky. 1993. ring bd. 160.00 (*0-685-69549-2*, SBSA) Warren Gorham & Lamont.

Structuring Change: Doing Effective Clinical Social Work. Ed. by Kevin J. Corcoran. LC 91-43836. 460p. (Orig.). (C). 1992. pap. text ed. 31.95 (*0-925065-14-5*) Lyceum IL.

Structuring Child Behavior Through Visual Art: A Therapeutic, Individualized Art Program to Develop Positive Behavior Attitudes in Children. Florence Singer. (Illus.). 144p. 1980. 25.95 (*0-389-04114-9*); pap. 15.95 (*0-398-06432-6*) C C Thomas.

Structuring Commercial Loan Agreements. 2nd ed. Sandra S. Stern. 1990. ring bd. 135.00 (*0-685-70155-7*, SCLA) Warren Gorham & Lamont.

Structuring Committees for a Board of Directors. Prentice Hall Editorial Staff. 22p. 1984. 2.75 (*0-317-07503-9*, 85526-2) P-H.

Structuring Complex Real Estate Transactions: Law, Procedure, Forms. James L. Lipscomb. LC 88-198. 471p. 1988. text ed. 130.00 (*0-471-84713-5*) Wiley.

Structuring Complex Real Estate Transactions: Law, Procedures & Forms. James L. Lipscomb. 246p. 1994. suppl. ed., pap. text ed. 60.00 (*0-471-03327-8*) Wiley.

Structuring Cooperative Learning: Lesson Plans for Teachers, 1987. Ed. by Roger T. Johnson et al. 339p. (Orig.). 1987. pap. write for info. (*0-939603-00-4*) Interaction Bk Co.

Structuring Diversity: Ethnographic Perspectives on the New Immigration. Ed. by Louise Lamphere. LC 91-41183. (Illus.). 268p. 1992. pap. text ed. 16.95 (*0-226-46819-4*) U Ch Pr.

Structuring Drama Work: A Handbook of Available Forms in Theatre & Drama. Jonothan Neelands. Ed. by Tony Goode. (Illus.). 87p. (C). 1990. pap. text ed. 20.95 (*0-521-37635-1*) Cambridge U Pr.

Structuring Estate Freezes under Chapter 14: Final Regulations. 2nd ed. Howard M. Zaritsky. 1992. pap. 130.00 incl. disk (*0-685-69554-9*, SEF3) Warren Gorham & Lamont.

Structuring Forces of Detection: The Cases of C. P. Snow & John Fowles. Bo H. Eriksson. (Studia Anglistica Upsaliensia Ser.: No. 93). 254p. (Orig.). 1995. pap. 46.50 (*91-554-3646-3*) Coronet Bks.

Structuring Foreign Investment in U. S. Real Estate (1989) rev. ed. W. Donald Knight, Jr. & Richard L. Doernberg. 1990. ring bd. 189.00 (*90-6544-975-2*) Kluwer Law Tax Pubs.

Structuring IDBs: A Guide to Conventional & Innovative IDB Financing. Eric Anderson. Ed. by Jenny Murphy & Andrea Kailo. 24p. (Orig.). 1985. pap. 16.00 (*0-317-04903-8*) Natl Coun Econ Dev.

Structuring in Organizations Vol. 7: Ecosystem Theory Evaluated. Charles E. Bidwell et al. Ed. by Samuel B. Bacharach. LC 87-2749. (Monographs in Organizational Behavior & Industrial Relations: Vol. 7). 397p. 1987. 73.25 (*0-89232-732-4*) Jai Pr.

Structuring International Co-Operation Between Companies. K. Byttebier & A. Verroken. LC 94-38628. 1995. lib. bdg. 105.00 (*1-85966-106-8*) G & T Inc.

Structuring International Economic Cooperation. Gavin Boyd. LC 90-19782. 250p. 1991. text ed. 49.95 (*0-312-05802-0*) St Martin.

***Structuring International Transactions.** Dennis Campbell et al. LC 97-14653. 1997. pap. write for info. (*90-411-0404-6*) Kluwer Law Tax Pubs.

Structuring Loan Participations. Sandra S. Stern. 1992. ring bd. 135.00 (*0-685-69628-6*, SLP) Warren Gorham & Lamont.

Structuring Mortgage Banking Transactions. Dominick A. Mazzagetti. 620p. 1996. 155.00 (*0-7913-2596-2*) Warren Gorham & Lamont.

Structuring of a State: The History of Illinois, 1899-1928. Donald F. Tingley. LC 79-14964. (Sesquicentennial History of Illinois Ser.: Vol. 5). (Illus.). 446p. 1980. text ed. 29.95 (*0-252-00736-0*) U of Ill Pr.

Structuring of Organizations. Henry Mintzberg. (Theory of Management Policy Ser.). (Illus.). 1978. text ed. 89.00 (*0-13-855270-3*) P-H.

Structuring Paragraphs. 4th ed. Parks et al. 1995. teacher ed., pap. text ed. 1.31 (*0-312-11514-8*) St Martin.

Structuring Paragraphs. 4th ed. Parks et al. 1995. teacher ed., pap. text ed. 0.44 (*0-312-11516-4*) St Martin.

Structuring Paragraphs: A Guide to Effective Writing. Parks et al. 1995. pap. text ed. 25.50 (*0-312-11513-X*) St Martin.

Structuring Partnership Agreements: Forms, Analytical Text, State-by-State Requirements, 3 vols. Supplements avail. suppl. ed. 210.00 (*0-317-29402-4*, #H43910) HarBrace.

Structuring Politics: Historical Institutionalism in Comparative Analysis. Ed. by Sven Steinmo et al. (Illus.). 304p. (C). 1992. text ed. 65.00 (*0-521-41780-5*); pap. text ed. 19.95 (*0-521-42830-0*) Cambridge U Pr.

Structuring Real Estate Investments in the Mid-Eighties. Ed. by Raymond J. Werner. LC 85-72126. 928p. 1985. 55.00 (*0-89707-188-3*, PC: 5430070) Amer Bar Assn.

Structuring Real Estate Joint Ventures. Robert Bell. LC 91-19857. (Real Estate Practice Library). 432p. 1991. text ed. 135.00 (*0-471-54771-9*) Wiley.

S

An Asterisk (*) at the beginning of an entry indicates that the title is appearing in BIP for the first time.

S

***Structuring Role of Submerged Macrophytes in Lakes.** Erik Jeppesen. LC 97-22884. (Ecological Studies). 1997. write for info. (0-387-98284-1) Spr-Verlag.

Structuring Schools for Success: A View from the Inside. Mary Scheetz & Tracy Benson. LC 93-44471. (Total Quality Education for the World's Best Schools Ser.: Vol. 11). 112p. 1994. pap. 18.00 (0-8039-6130-8) Corwin Pr.

Structuring Secured Commercial Loan Documents. James J. Cunningham et al. 1991. ring bd. 135.00 (0-685-69629-4, SSL) Warren Gorham & Lamont.

Structuring Security: Technology Against Terrorism. 1996. lib. bdg. 252.99 (0-8490-5976-3) Gordon Pr.

Structuring State & Local Tax Reform Commissions. William R. Dodge. (Lincoln Institute Monograph Ser.: No. 86-2). 75p. (Orig.). reprint ed. pap. 25.00 (0-7837-5775-1, 2045440) Bks Demand.

Structuring Techniques: An Introduction Using C B Plus Plus S. Andrew C. Staugaard, Jr. LC 93-34289. (Alan R. Apt Book Ser.). 768p. 1994. pap. text ed. 55.00 (0-13-012576-8) P-H.

Structuring Techniques: An Introduction Using Turbo C. Andrew C. Staugaard, Jr. (C). 1995. pap. text ed. 53.00 (0-13-188020-9) P-H.

Structuring Techniques: An Introduction Using Turbo Pascal. Andrew C. Staugaard, Jr. 304p. 1988. pap. 63.00 incl. disk (0-13-853425-X) P-H.

Structuring the Therapeutic Process: Compromise with Chaos - a Therapist's Response to the Individual & the Group. Murray Cox. 1978. pap. 34.00 (1-85302-028-1) Taylor & Francis.

Structuring the Void: The Struggle for Subject in Contemporary American Fiction. Jerome Klinkowitz. LC 91-24113. 192p. 1992. text ed. 34.95 (0-8223-1205-0) Duke.

Structuring U. S. Forces after the Cold War: Costs & Effects of Increased Reliance on the Reserves. (Illus.). 83p. (Orig.). (C). 1992. pap. text ed. 25.00 (1-56806-141-2) DIANE Pub.

Structuring Uncertainties in Long-Range Power Planning. Cyrus K. Motlagh. LC 76-620019. (MSU Public Utilities Papers: No. 1976). 183p. reprint ed. pap. 52.20 (0-7837-6267-4, 2045979) Bks Demand.

Structuring Your Business for Success. Ira S. Kalb. (Illus.). 437p. 1992. 55.95 (0-924050-02-0) K & A Pr.

Structuring Your Classroom for Academic Success. Stan C. Paine et al. LC 83-61812. (Illus.). 188p. 1983. pap. 14.95 (0-87822-228-6, 2286) Res Press.

Structuring Your Classroom Successfully for Cooperative Team Learning. Teresa L. Cantlon. (Orig.). 1989. teacher ed. 22.00 (0-9622312-0-7) Prestige Portland.

Structuring Your Novel: From Basic Idea to Finished Manuscript. Robert C. Meredith & John D. Fitzgerald. LC 70-170126. 240p. 1993. reprint ed. pap. 12.00 (0-06-273170-X, Harper Ref) HarpC.

Strudel, Strudel, Strudel. Steve Sanfield. LC 94-24858. (Illus.). 32p. (J). (ps-2). 1995. 15.95 (0-531-06879-X); lib. bdg. 16.99 (0-531-08729-8) Orchard Bks Watts.

Strudwick: A Sheep in Wolf's Clothing. Robert Kraus. LC 94-31911. (Illus.). 32p. (YA). (gr. 5 up). 1995. pap. 14.99 (0-670-85887-0) Viking Child Bks.

Struggle. Jerry Ahern. (Survivalist Ser.: No. 18). 224p. 1989. mass mkt. 2.95 (0-8217-2581-5, Zebra Kensgtn) Kensgtn Pub Corp.

Struggle. Shelomi, pseud. (Illus.). 61p. (Orig.). 1991. pap. 5.95 (1-56411-010-9) Untd Bros & Sis.

Struggle: A History of the African National Congress. Heidi Holland. LC 89-70782. (Illus.). 256p. 1990. pap. 10.95 (0-8076-1255-3) Braziller.

Struggle a Hard Battle: Essays on Working-Class Immigrants. Ed. by Dirk Hoerder. LC 85-25894. 384p. 1986. 32.00 (0-87580-112-9); pap. 15.00 (0-87580-533-7) N Ill U Pr.

Struggle Against Fascism in Germany. Leon Trotsky. Ed. by George Breitman & Merry Maisel. LC 73-119532. 479p. 1971. reprint ed. pap. 28.95 (0-87348-136-4); reprint ed. lib. bdg. 70.00 (0-87348-135-6) Pathfinder NY.

Struggle Against the Bomb Vol. I: One World or None: A History of the World Nuclear..., Vol. I. Lawrence S. Wittner. (Stanford Nuclear Age Ser.). (Illus.). 488p. (C). 1995. pap. 16.95 (0-8047-2528-4) Stanford U Pr.

Struggle Against the Bomb Vol. No. 1: One World or None: A History of the Nuclear Disarmament Movement Through 1953, Vol. 1. Lawrence S. Wittner. LC 92-28026. (Nuclear Age Ser.). 420p. 1993. 55.00 (0-8047-2141-6) Stanford U Pr.

Struggle Against the Historical Blackout. Harry E. Barnes. 1971. 250.00 (0-87700-195-2) Revisionist Pr.

Struggle Against the State & Other Essays. Nestor Makhno. Tr. by Alexandre Skirda from RUS. 128p. (Orig.). 1996. pap. 9.95 (1-873176-78-3, AK Pr San Fran) AK Pr Dist.

Struggle Against Tyranny, & the Beginning of a New Era: Virginia, 1677-1699. Richard L. Morton. (Jamestown 350th Anniversary Historical Booklet Ser.: No. 9). 90p. reprint ed. pap. 25.70 (0-7837-2023-8, 2042298) Bks Demand.

***Struggle & Hope: Essays on Stabilization & Reform in a Postsocialist Economy.** Janos Kornai. LC 97-25017. 1997. write for info. (1-85898-606-0) E Elgar.

***Struggle & Love: From the Gary Convention to the Present (1972-)** Ed. by Darlene C. Hine et al. (Milestones in Black American History Ser.). (Illus.). 144p. (YA). (gr. 5 up). 1996. pap. 8.95 (0-7910-2688-4) Chelsea Hse.

Struggle & Love: From the Gary Convention to the Present (1972-) Ed. by Darlene C. Hine et al. (Milestones in Black American History Ser.). (Illus.). 144p. (YA). (gr. 5 up). 1997. lib. bdg. 19.95 (0-7910-2262-5) Chelsea Hse.

Struggle & Success: An Anthology of the Italian Immigrant Experience in California. Paola A. Sensi-Isolani & Phylis C. Martinelli. (Illus.). 284p. (C). 1993. 19.50 (0-934733-65-1); pap. 14.50 (0-934733-66-X) CMS.

Struggle & Survival in Colonial America. Ed. by David G. Sweet & Gary B. Nash. 1981. pap. 16.95 (0-520-04501-7) U CA Pr.

***Struggle & Survival in the Modern Middle East.** Ed. by Edmund Burke, III. 395p. 1996. pap. 16.00 (0-614-21631-1, 1173) Kazi Pubns.

Struggle & Survival in the Modern Middle East. Ed. by Edmund E. Burke. 395p. 1994. 55.00 (0-520-07566-8); pap. 17.00 (0-520-07988-4) U CA Pr.

Struggle & Survival on Wall Street: The Economics of Competition Among Securities Firms. John O. Matthews. LC 93-98. 288p. 1994. Alk. paper. 39.95 (0-19-505063-0) OUP.

Struggle & the Triumph. Lech Walesa. Ed. by Franklin Phillip & Helen Mahut. (Illus.). 336p. 1994. reprint ed. pap. 12.95 (1-55970-221-4) Arcade Pub Inc.

Struggle & the Triumph: An Autobiography. Lech Walesa. Tr. by Franklin Philip from POL. 464p. 1992. 24.95 (1-55970-149-8) Arcade Pub Inc.

Struggle Between President Johnson & Congress over Reconstruction. Charles E. Chadsey. LC 79-181926. (Columbia University. Studies in the Social Sciences: No. 19). reprint ed. 24.50 (0-404-51019-1) AMS Pr.

Struggle Between President Johnson & Congress over Reconstruction. Charles E. Chadsey. (History - United States Ser.). 142p. 1992. reprint ed. lib. bdg. 69.00 (0-7812-6202-X) Rprt Serv.

Struggle Between Religion & Science. Marshall J. Gauvin. 76p. 1965. reprint ed. spiral bd. 6.50 (0-7873-0345-3) Hlth Research.

Struggle Between Religion & Science (1923) Marshall J. Gauvin. 76p. 1996. pap. 12.95 (1-56459-966-3) Kessinger Pub.

Struggle Between the Civilization of Slavery & That of Freedom. Edward C. Billings. LC 76-164379. (Black Heritage Library Collection). 1977. reprint ed. 13.95 (0-8369-8838-8) Ayer.

Struggle Continues. Eula M. Glenn. (Illus.). 20p. (Orig.). (YA). (gr. 5 up). 1991. pap. text ed. 4.95 (1-877860-11-5) Eula Intl Pub.

Struggle, Defeat or Rebirth: Eugene O'Neill's Vision of Humanity. Thierry Dubost. Tr. by Rosalind Dilys & Christin McGarry. LC 96-32268. 280p. 1996. lib. bdg. 36.50 (0-7864-0265-2) McFarland & Co.

***Struggle for a Continent.** Betsy C. Maestro. Date not set. write for info. (0-688-13450-5); lib. bdg. write for info. (0-688-13451-3) Lothrop.

Struggle for a Continent: The French & Indian Wars: 1690-1760. Albert Marrin. LC 86-26508. (Illus.). 232p. (YA). (gr. 5 up). 1987. lib. bdg. 15.95 (0-689-31313-6, Atheneum Bks Young) S&S Childrens.

Struggle for a Continent: The Wars of Early America. John E. Ferling. Ed. by John H. Franklin & A. S. Eisenstadt. LC 92-32469. (American History Ser.). 256p. (C). 1993. pap. text ed. write for info. (0-88295-896-8) Harlan Davidson.

Struggle for a Free Stage in London. Watson Nicholson. LC 65-27915. 487p. 1972. reprint ed. 24.95 (0-405-08816-7, Pub. by Blom Pubns UK) Ayer.

Struggle for a Just World Order: An Agenda of Inquiry & Praxis for the 1980's. Saul H. Mendlovitz. 23p. 1982. pap. 12.95 (0-911646-26-4) Transaction Pubs.

Struggle for a Proletarian Party. 2nd rev. ed. James P. Cannon. Ed. by John G. Wright. LC 73-133396. 302p. 1972. reprint ed. pap. 19.95 (0-87348-260-3) Pathfinder NY.

Struggle for a State System of Public Schools in Tennessee, 1903-1936. A. D. Holt. LC 70-176876. (Columbia University. Teachers College. Contributions to Education Ser.: No. 753). reprint ed. 37.50 (0-404-55753-8) AMS Pr.

Struggle for Academic Democracy: Lessons from the 1938 Revolution in New York's City Colleges. Abraham Edel. 240p. 1990. 29.95 (0-87722-691-1) Temple U Pr.

Struggle for Africa: Politics of the Great Powers. Gerard Chaliand. LC 82-5967. 1982. text ed. 39.95 (0-312-76868-0) St Martin.

Struggle for Airways in Latin America. William A. M. Burden. Ed. by Mira Wilkins. LC 76-29797. (European Business Ser.). (Illus.). 1977. reprint ed. lib. bdg. 35.95 (0-405-09716-6) Ayer.

***Struggle for "Amazon Town" Gurupa Revisited.** Richard Pace. LC 97-242. 1997. write for info. (1-55587-339-1); pap. write for info. (1-55587-352-9) Lynne Rienner.

Struggle for American Independence, 2 vols, Set. Sidney G. Fisher. LC 78-37341. (Select Bibliographies Reprint Ser.). 1977. reprint ed. 70.95 (0-8369-6688-0) Ayer.

Struggle for American Independence, Vol. 1. Sydney G. Fisher. (Illus.). 1988. reprint ed. lib. bdg. 30.00 (0-8290-2149-3) Irvington.

Struggle for American Independence, Vol. II. Sydney G. Fisher. LC 78-37341. (Illus.). 585p. reprint ed. lib. bdg. 30.00 (0-8290-0499-8) Irvington.

Struggle for Animal Rights. Tom Regan & Colman McCarthy. 208p. (Orig.). 1987. pap. 5.95 (0-9602632-1-7) ISAR Inc.

Struggle for Arab Independence. 2nd ed. Zeine N. Zeine. LC 77-5149. 280p. 1977. lib. bdg. 50.00 (0-88206-002-3) Caravan Bks.

Struggle for Asia. Francis Low. LC 79-167379. (Essay Index Reprint Ser.). 1977. reprint ed. 20.95 (0-8369-2699-4) Ayer.

Struggle for Australian Industrial Relations. Braham Dabscheck. (oup). 208p. (C). 1996. pap. 35.00 (0-19-553486-7) OUP.

Struggle for Auto Safety. Jerry L. Mashaw & David L. Harfst. 285p. 1990. 37.00 (0-674-84530-7) HUP.

Struggle for Being: An Interpretation of the Poetry of Ana Maria Fagundo. Zelda I. Brooks. LC 93-84477. (Coleccion Polymita). (Illus.). 215p. (Orig.). 1994. pap. 19.00 (0-89729-725-3) Ediciones.

Struggle for Black Empowerment in New York City: Beyond the Politics of Pigmentation. Green & Wilson. 1992. pap. text ed. write for info. (0-07-024411-1) McGraw.

Struggle for Black Equality, 1954-1992. Harvard Sitkoff. Ed. by Eric Foner. LC 92-20244. (American Century Ser.). 270p. 1993. 10.95 (0-374-52356-8) Hill & Wang.

Struggle for Black Political Empowerment in Three Georgia Counties. Lawrence J. Hanks. LC 86-24987. 248p. 1987. 35.00 (0-87049-521-6); pap. 16.00 (0-87049-644-1) U of Tenn Pr.

Struggle for Change: (International Economic Relations) K. B. Lall. 327p. 1983. 34.95 (0-318-37215-0) Asia Bk Corp.

Struggle for Change: International Economic Relations. K. B. Lal. 1984. 22.50 (0-8364-1226-5, Pub. by Allied II) S Asia.

Struggle for Change: The Story of One School. Marvin F. Wideen. 176p. 1994. 80.00 (0-7507-0168-4, Falmer Pr); pap. 27.00 (0-7507-0169-2, Falmer Pr) Taylor & Francis.

Struggle for Choice: Students with Special Needs in Transition to Adulthood. Jenny Corbett & Len Barton. 135p. (C). 1993. pap. 17.95 (0-415-08001-0, B0291) Routledge.

***Struggle for Constitutionalism.** Brzezinski. LC 97-15100. 1997. text ed. 49.95 (0-312-17612-0) St Martin.

Struggle for Control: A Study of Law, Disputes, & Deviance. Pat Lauderdale & Michael Cruit. LC 91-47942. (SUNY Series in Deviance & Social Control). 256p. 1993. text ed. 64.50 (0-7914-1311-X); pap. text ed. 21.95 (0-7914-1312-8) State U NY Pr.

Struggle for Crete, 10 May-1 June 1941: A Story of Lost Opportunity. Ian M. Stewart. 528p. reprint ed. pap. 150.50 (0-317-28731-1, 2051318) Bks Demand.

Struggle for Democracy. Benjamin R. Barber & Patrick Watson. 1989. 29.95 (0-316-08058-6) Little.

Struggle for Democracy. abr. ed. Edward S. Greenberg & Benjamin I. Page. (C). 1995. teacher ed. write for info. (0-06-502568-7) Addson-Wesley Educ.

Struggle for Democracy. abr. ed. Edward S. Greenberg & Benjamin I. Page. 560p. (C). 1996. text ed. 39.95 (0-06-501290-9); student ed., pap. text ed. 17.95 (0-06-502566-0) Addson-Wesley Educ.

Struggle for Democracy. 2nd ed. Carns. (C). 1995. teacher ed. write for info. (0-673-55667-0) Addson-Wesley Educ.

Struggle for Democracy. 2nd ed. Carns. (C). 1995. student ed., text ed. 13.75 (0-673-99303-5) Addson-Wesley Educ.

Struggle for Democracy. 2nd ed. England. Date not set. teacher ed. write for info. (0-673-55668-9) Addson-Wesley Educ.

Struggle for Democracy. 2nd ed. Edward S. Greenberg & Benjamin I. Page. LC 94-18791. 735p. (C). 1995. text ed. 42.00 (0-673-99302-7) Addson-Wesley Educ.

***Struggle for Democracy.** 3rd ed. Greenberg. (C). 1997. student ed., pap. text ed. 17.95 (0-673-98530-X) Addison-Wesley.

***Struggle for Democracy.** 3rd ed. Edward S. Greenberg & Benjamin I. Page. LC 96-41899. (C). 1997. text ed. 53.95 (0-673-98089-8) Addison-Wesley.

***Struggle for Democracy: Brief Version.** Ed. by Greenberg. (C). 1995. text ed. 39.95 (0-673-67500-9) Addison-Wesley.

Struggle for Democracy: Guide to Interp. Media. David L. Paletz. 1995. 3.00 (0-673-97038-8) Addson-Wesley Educ.

***Struggle for Democracy: Second Custom Edition.** Ed. by Greenberg. (C). 1995. text ed. 47.50 (0-673-67533-5) Addison-Wesley.

***Struggle for Democracy: Special Edition.** Ed. by Greenberg. (C). 1994. text ed. 42.50 (0-06-502497-4) Addison-Wesley.

Struggle for Democracy Brief. England. Date not set. teacher ed., pap. write for info. (0-06-502569-5) Addson-Wesley Educ.

Struggle for Democracy East Europe. Schwartz. 1995. 32.00 (0-226-74195-8) U Ch Pr.

Struggle for Democracy in Chile. Ed. by Paul E. Drake & Ivan Jaksic. LC 95-1353. xiv, 358p. 1995. text ed. 22.50 (0-8032-6600-6, Bison Books) U of Nebr Pr.

***Struggle for Democracy with Lecture Notes.** Ed. by Greenberg. (C). 1996. text ed. write for info. (0-673-67614-5) Addison-Wesley.

Struggle for Democratic Education: Equality & Participation in Sweden. Ed. by Stephen J. Ball & Staffan Larsson. 240p. 1989. 65.00 (1-85000-385-8, Falmer Pr); pap. 33.00 (1-85000-386-6, Falmer Pr) Taylor & Francis.

Struggle for Development: National Strategies in an International Context. Ed. by Manfred Bienefeld & Martin Godfrey. LC 81-19821. 386p. reprint ed. pap. 110.10 (0-7837-6368-9, 2046080) Bks Demand.

Struggle for Dominance in the Persian Gulf: Past, Present & Future Prospects. Nozar Alaolmolki. LC 91-7327. (American University Studies: Political Science: Ser. X, Vol. 31). 320p. 1991. 49.95 (0-8204-1590-1) P Lang Pubng.

Struggle for Domination in the Middle East: The Ottoman-Mamluk War, 1485-91. Shai Har-El. LC 94-40784. (Ottoman Empire & Its Heritage Ser.: Vol. 4). 1995. 78.00 (90-04-10180-2) E J Brill.

Struggle for Economic Democracy in Sweden. Gregg M. Olsen. 159p. 1992. 68.95 (1-85628-298-8, Pub. by Avebury Pub UK) Ashgate Pub Co.

Struggle for Educational Justice: Bicultural Studies in Education. Ed. by Antonia Darder. 208p. (Orig.). (C). 1993. pap. text ed. 15.00 (0-941742-12-1) Claremont Grad.

Struggle for Equal Education. Clarence Lusane. (African-American Experience Ser.). (Illus.). 144p. (YA). (gr. 7-12). 1992. lib. bdg. 22.70 (0-531-11121-0) Watts.

Struggle for Equality: Abolitionists & the Negro in the Civil War & Reconstruction. James M. McPherson. (Illus.). 486p. 1964. pap. text ed. 16.95 (0-691-00555-9) Princeton U Pr.

Struggle for Equality: Blacks in Texas. James M. Smallwood. (Texas History Ser.). (Illus.). 46p. (C). 1983. pap. text ed. 8.95 (0-89641-120-6) American Pr.

Struggle for Equality: Urban Women Workers in Prestate Israeli Society. Deborah Bernstein. LC 86-8203. 219p. 1986. text ed. 55.00 (0-275-92139-5, C2139, Praeger Pubs) Greenwood.

Struggle for Europe. Chester Wilmot. LC 75-138138. (Illus.). 766p. 1972. reprint ed. text ed. 43.00 (0-8371-5711-0, WISE, Greenwood Pr) Greenwood.

Struggle for Fame: Victorian Women Artists & Authors. Susan P. Casteras & Linda H. Peterson. LC 94-60143. (Illus.). 104p. (Orig.). 1994. pap. 14.95 (0-930606-72-8) Yale Ctr Brit Art.

Struggle for Federal Aid, First Phase: A History of the Attempts to Obtain Federal Aid for the Common Schools. Gordon C. Lee. LC 79-176979. (Columbia University. Teachers College. Contributions to Education Ser.: No. 957). reprint ed. 37.50 (0-404-55957-3) AMS Pr.

Struggle for Freedom: African-American Slave Resistance. Dennis Wepman. LC 95-34557. (Library of African-American History). 128p. (J). 1996. 17.95 (0-8160-3270-X) Facts on File.

Struggle for Freedom: Plays on the American Revolution, 1762-1788. Charles F. Baker, III. Ed. by Carolyn P. Yoder. (Illus.). 144p. (Orig.). (J). (gr. 4-9). 1990. pap. 15.95 (0-942389-05-0) Cobblestone Pub.

Struggle for Freedom & Henry Box Brown. Brenda A. Johnston & Pamela Pruitt. Ed. by John A. McCluskey. (Read-Along Bk.). (Illus.). 22p. (J). (gr. 2-4). 1987. reprint ed. pap. 4.00 incl. audio (0-913678-16-3) New Day Pr.

Struggle for Georgia Coast: An Eighteenth-Century Spanish Retrospective on Guale & Mocama. John E. Worth. 1995. pap. text ed. 26.95 (0-8203-1745-4) U of Ga Pr.

Struggle for Greece 1941-1949. C. M. Woodhouse. (Illus.). 1979. 34.95 (0-8464-0042-1) Beekman Pubs.

Struggle for Grenada. 5th rev. ed. Richard Krooth. 1997. pap. 8.95 (0-939074-12-5) Harvest Pubns.

Struggle for Guadalcanal, August 1942-February 1943 see History of the United States Naval Operations in World War Two

Struggle for Health: A Case Study of Malnutrition & Ill-Health among South Indian Tribals. Stuart Gillespie. 1993. 20.00 (81-7022-463-2, Pub. by Concept II) S Asia.

Struggle for Hegemony in India, 1920-41: The Colonial State, the Left, & the National Movement, Vol II: 1934-1941. Bhagwan Josh. (Struggle for Hegemony Ser.). 320p. (C). 1992. 38.95 (0-8039-9439-7) Sage.

Struggle for Hegemony in India 1920-47 Vol. III: The Colonial State, the Left & the National Movement, 1941-47: Culture, Community, & Power. Shashi Joshi & Bhagwan Josh. 356p. (C). 1994. text ed. 38.95 (0-8039-9141-X) Sage.

Struggle for Hegemony in South America: Argentina, Brazil, & the United States During the Second World War. Gary Frank. 116p. (C). 1979. pap. text ed. 24.95 (1-56000-658-7, LA202) Transaction Pubs.

Struggle for Hegomony in India, Vol. 1: The Colonial State, the Left & the National Movement. Shashi Joshi. 400p. (C). 1991. text ed. 38.00 (0-8039-9405-2) Sage.

Struggle for Human Rights: An International South African Perspective. Lorenzo Togni. 295p. (Orig.). (C). 1994. pap. text ed. 37.00 (0-7021-3072-9, Pub. by Juta & Co SA) Intl Spec Bk.

***Struggle for Human Rights in Latin America.** Edward L. Cleary. LC 97-5580. 1997. text ed. write for info. (0-275-95980-5, Praeger Pubs); pap. text ed. write for info. (0-275-95981-3, Praeger Pubs) Greenwood.

Struggle for Humanity: Agents of Nonviolent Change in a Violent World. Marjorie Hope & James Young. LC 77-5573. 318p. (Orig.). reprint ed. pap. 90.70 (0-8357-4073-0, 2036763) Bks Demand.

Struggle for Indochina, 1940-1955. Ellen J. Hammer. x, 374p. 1955. 49.50 (0-8047-0458-9) Stanford U Pr.

Struggle for Intimacy. Janet G. Woititz. 100p. 1985. pap. text ed. 6.95 (0-932194-25-7, 22H103) Health Comm.

Struggle for Kenya: The Loss & Reassertion of Imperial Initiative, 1912-1923. Robert M. Maxon. LC 91-58952. (Illus.). 352p. 1993. 47.50 (0-8386-3486-9) Fairleigh Dickinson.

Struggle for Land & the Fate of the Forests. Ed. by Marcus Colchester & Larry Lohmann. 208p. (C). 1993. pap. 17.50 (1-85649-140-4, Pub. by Zed Bks Ltd UK) Humanities.

Struggle for Land in Brazil: Rural Violence Continues. Ed. by Human Rights Watch Staff. 120p. (Orig.). 1992. pap. 10.00 (1-56432-070-7) Hum Rts Watch.

Struggle for Law. Rudolph Von Jhering. Tr. by John J. Lalor from GER. LC 97-6826. lii, 138p. 1997. reprint ed. lib. bdg. 60.00 (1-886363-25-0) Lawbk Exchange.

Struggle for Legitimacy: Latin American Labor & the United States 1930-1960. Jon V. Kofas. LC 90-25503. 448p. 1992. pap. 28.00 (0-87918-075-7); text ed. 36.00 (0-87918-071-4) ASU Lat Am St.

Struggle for Liberation: From Du Bois to Nyerere. Bert Thomas. LC 81-84242. 208p. 1982. pap. 8.95 (0-912444-23-1) DARE Bks.

An Asterisk (*) at the beginning of an entry indicates that the title is appearing in BIP for the first time.

***Struggle for Life No. 9: A Companion to William James's the Varieties of Religious Experience.** Ed. by Donald Capps & Janet L. Jacobs. 320p. Date not set. 18.00 (*1-882380-02-9*) Soc Sci Stud Rel.

Struggle for Market Power: Industrial Relations in the Northern British Coal Industry, 1800-1840. James A. Jaffe. (Illus.). 320p. (C). 1991. text ed. 80.00 (*0-521-39146-6*) Cambridge U Pr.

Struggle for Mastery in Europe: 1848-1918. Alan J. Taylor. (Oxford History of Modern Europe Ser.). 674p. 1955. 65.00 (*0-19-822101-0*) OUP.

Struggle for Mastery in Europe: 1848-1918. Alan J. Taylor. (Oxford History of Modern Europe Ser.). 674p. 1980. pap. 22.00 (*0-19-881270-1*) OUP.

Struggle for Modern Tibet: The Autobiography of Tashi Tsering. Tashi Tsering et al. LC 97-4968. 220p. (C). (gr. 13). 1997. 27.95 (*1-56324-950-2*, East Gate Bk) M E Sharpe.

Struggle for National & Constitutional Rights in the Last Years of Tsarism: The Life of Bogdan A. Kistiakovsky. Susan Heuman. (Illus.). 300p. 1996. 35.00 (*0-916458-61-X*); pap. 17.00 (*0-916458-65-2*) Harvard Ukrainian.

Struggle for Neutrality: Franco-American Diplomacy. Albert H. Bowman. LC 73-21917. 480p. reprint ed. pap. 136.80 (*0-8357-6912-7*, 2037970) Bks Demand.

Struggle for North China. George E. Taylor. LC 75-30100. (Institute of Pacific Relations Ser.). reprint ed. 39.50 (*0-404-59566-9*) AMS Pr.

Struggle for Pakistan. Lal Bahadur & J. C. Johari. 380p. 1988. text ed. 45.00 (*81-207-0802-4*, Pub. by Sterling Pubs II) Apt Bks.

Struggle for Peace. Oscar Arias. Ed. by David H. Darst. (International Albert Schweitzer Lecture Ser. at Yale University). (Illus.). 12p. (Orig.). (C). pap. text ed. 3.50 (*1-885007-01-9*) A Schweitzer.

Struggle for Peace: An Inaugural Lecture. Oscar Arias. (Lecture Ser.). (Illus.). 49p. (Orig.). 1990. pap. 3.25 (*1-881157-00-8*) In Ctr Global.

Struggle for Peace: Israelis & Palestinians. Ed. by Elizabeth W. Fernea & Mary E. Hocking. LC 91-43509. (Illus.). 351p. (Orig.). (C). 1992. pap. 16.95 (*0-292-73071-3*); text ed. 35.00 (*0-292-76541-X*) U of Tex Pr.

Struggle for Peace - Chinese Edition. Henry R. Brandt. Tr. by Molica Hsu. 120p. (CHI.). 1993. pap. 4.50 (*1-56582-042-8*) Christ Renew Min.

Struggle for Peace in Central America. Dario Moreno. LC 93-36885. 264p. (C). 1994. pap. text ed. 19.95 (*0-8130-1275-9*); lib. bdg. 49.95 (*0-8130-1274-0*) U Press Fla.

Struggle for Pedagogies: Critical & Feminist Discourses as Regimes of Truth. Jennifer Gore. 224p. (C). 1992. pap. 16.95 (*0-415-90564-8*, A6915, Routledge NY) Routledge.

Struggle for Power: Russia in 1923. Valentina Vilkova. 320p. 1996. 32.95 (*1-57392-026-6*) Prometheus Bks.

Struggle for Power: The American Revolution. Theodore Draper. 608p. 1996. 35.00 (*0-8129-2575-0*, Times Bks) Random.

Struggle for Power: The American Revolution. Theodore Draper. 1997. pap. 17.00 (*0-679-77642-7*, Vin) Random.

***Struggle for Power: The American Revolution.** Theodore Draper. Date not set. 35.00 (*0-685-23291-3*, Times Bks) Random.

Struggle for Power in Europe: Competition & Regulation in the EC Electricity Industry. Francis McGowan. 1993. pap. text ed. 22.25 (*0-905031-67-9*, Pub. by Royal Inst Intl Affairs UK) Brookings.

Struggle for Recognition: The Moral Grammar of Social Conflicts. Axel Honneth. Tr. by Joel Anderson. 220p. (C). 1995. 66.95 (*0-7456-1160-5*, Pub. by Polity Pr UK) Blackwell Pubs.

Struggle for Recognition: The Moral Grammar of Social Conflicts. Axel Honneth. LC 96-21276. (Studies in Contemporary German Social Thought). (Illus.). 240p. 1996. pap. 18.00 (*0-262-58147-7*) MIT Pr.

Struggle for Religious Freedom in Virginia. William T. Thom. LC 78-63877. (Johns Hopkins University. Studies in the Social Sciences. Thirtieth Ser. 1912: 10-12). reprint ed. 29.50 (*0-404-61133-8*) AMS Pr.

Struggle for Religious Survival in the Soviet Union. Ed. by Ann Gillen. LC 86-72630. 76p. 1986. pap. 5.00 (*0-87495-085-6*) Am Jewish Comm.

Struggle for Rescue Action. Ed. by David S. Wyman. LC 88-27102. (America & the Holocaust Ser.: Vol. 2). 320p. 1990. text ed. 60.00 (*0-8240-4534-3*) Garland.

Struggle for Responsible Government in Marwar. Mathur Sobhag. 208p. 1982. 95.00 (*0-317-62317-6*, Pub. by Scientific UK) St Mut.

Struggle for Rural Mexico. Gustavo Esteva. LC 82-24447. Orig. Title: La Batalla En el Mexico Rural. (Illus.). 320p. (C). 1983. text ed. 38.50 (*0-89789-025-6*, Bergin & Garvey) Greenwood.

Struggle for Russia. Boris Yeltsin. 1995. pap. 14.00 (*0-8129-2533-5*, Times Bks) Random.

Struggle for Russia: Power & Change in the Democratic Revolution. Ruslan Khasbulatov. Ed. by Richard Sakwa. LC 93-9490. 240p. (ENG.). (C). (gr. 13). 1993. 35.00 (*0-415-09292-2*, B0669) Routledge.

Struggle for Scripture & Covenant: The Purpose of the Epistle of Barnabas & Jewish-Christian Competition in the Second Century. Reidar Hvalvik. (WissUNT Zum Neuen Testament: No. 2). 428p. (Orig.). 1996. pap. 95.00 (*3-16-146534-2*, Pub. by J C B Mohr GW) Coronet Bks.

Struggle for Sobriety: Protestants & Prohibition in Texas, 1919-1935. Jeanne B. McCarty. (Southwestern Studies: No. 62). 1980. pap. 5.00 (*0-87404-121-X*) Tex Western.

Struggle for Social Change in Southern Africa: Visions of Liberty. Dickson A. Mungazi. (Illus.). 180p. (C). 1989. text ed. 58.00 (*0-8448-1594-2*); pap. text ed. 32.00 (*0-8448-1595-0*) Taylor & Francis.

***Struggle for Social Justice in British Columbia: Helena Gutteridge, the Unknown Reformer.** Irene Howard. 1992. 59.95 (*0-7748-0425-4*, Pub. by U BC Pr) U of Wash Pr.

Struggle for Social Security, 1900-1935. Roy Lubove. LC 85-40854. (Series in Policy & Institutional Studies). 304p. 1986. reprint ed. pap. 14.95 (*0-8229-5379-X*) U of Pittsburgh Pr.

Struggle for Socialism in the "American Century" Writings & Speeches, 1945-1947. James P. Cannon. Ed. by Les Evans. LC 75-20719. 480p. 1977. 60.00 (*0-87348-550-5*); pap. 22.95 (*0-87348-551-3*) Pathfinder NY.

Struggle for South America: Economy & Ideology. J. F. Normano. 1977. lib. bdg. 59.95 (*0-8490-3067-6*) Gordon Pr.

Struggle for Sovereignty: Relations Between Great Britain & Jordan, 1946-1951. Ron Pundik. 384p. 1994. 71.95 (*0-631-19295-6*) Blackwell Pubs.

Struggle for Soviet Jewish Emigration, 1948-1967. Yaacov Ro'i. (Cambridge Russian, Soviet & Post-Soviet Studies: No. 75). (Illus.). 512p. (C). 1991. text ed. 69.95 (*0-521-39084-2*) Cambridge U Pr.

Struggle for Stability in Early Modern Europe. Theodore K. Rabb. (Illus.). 186p. 1976. pap. 16.95 (*0-19-501956-3*) OUP.

Struggle for Statehood: Focus on the United Nations. Ed. by Aaron Klieman. LC 90-45876. (American Zionism Ser.: Vol. 12). 632p. 1991. reprint ed. text ed. 60.00 (*0-8240-7360-6*) Garland.

Struggle for Status: A History of Accounting Education. Glen Van Wyhe. LC 93-39293. (New Works in Accounting History). 288p. 1994. text ed. 55.00 (*0-8153-1654-2*) Garland.

***Struggle for Student Rights: Tinker vs. Des Moines & the 1960s.** John W. Johnson. LC 97-19621. (Landmark Law Cases & American Society Ser.). (Illus.). 240p. 1997. 35.00 (*0-7006-0866-4*) U Pr of KS.

***Struggle for Student Rights: Tinker vs. Des Moines & the 1960s.** John W. Johnson. LC 97-19621. (Landmark Law Cases & American Society Ser.). (Illus.). 240p. 1997. pap. 12.95 (*0-7006-0867-2*) U Pr of KS.

Struggle for Succession, 1966-1970: Personal Account of the Nigerian Civil War. Ntieyong U. Akpan. 220p. 1972. pap. 22.50 (*0-7146-2949-9*, BHA-02949, Pub. by F Cass Pubs UK) Intl Spec Bk.

Struggle for Survival. Eula M. Glenn. 42p. (Orig.). (YA). (gr. 5 up). 1989. pap. text ed. 10.00 (*1-877860-02-6*) Eula Intl Pub.

Struggle for Survival: Indian Cultures & the Protestant Ethic in British Columbia. rev. ed. Forrest E. LaViolette. LC 73-84433. 215p. reprint ed. pap. 61.30 (*0-317-27022-2*, 2023643) Bks Demand.

Struggle for Survival: The History of the Second World War. R. A. Parker. (Illus.). 370p. 1990. 27.50 (*0-19-219126-8*) OUP.

Struggle for Survival: The History of the Second World War. R. A. Parker. (Illus.). 370p. 1991. pap. 12.95 (*0-19-289112-X*) OUP.

Struggle for Swazi Labour, 1890-1920. Jonathan Crush. 304p. 1987. 55.00 (*0-7735-0569-5*, Pub. by McGill CN) U of Toronto Pr.

Struggle for Syria: A Study in Post-War Arab Politics. Patrick Seale. LC 87-8265. 384p. 1987. text ed. 50.00 (*0-300-03944-1*); pap. text ed. 23.00 (*0-300-03970-0*) Yale U Pr.

Struggle for Tennessee. (Civil War Ser.). (Illus.). 176p. 1985. 18.95 (*0-8094-4760-6*); lib. bdg. 25.93 (*0-8094-4761-4*) Time-Life.

Struggle for the American Curriculum, 1893-1958. Herbert M. Kliebard. 293p. 1987. pap. 13.95 (*0-7102-1363-8*, RKP) Routledge.

Struggle for the American Curriculum, 1893-1958. 2nd ed. Herbert M. Kliebard. LC 94-21419. 320p. (C). 1994. pap. 17.95 (*0-415-91013-7*, B3841, Routledge NY) Routledge.

Struggle for the American Curriculum, 1893-1958. 2nd ed. Herbert M. Kliebard. LC 94-21419. 320p. (C). (gr. 13). 1994. text ed. 59.95 (*0-415-90896-5*, B4790, Routledge NY) Routledge.

Struggle for the Arab World: Egypt's Nasser & the Arab League. Tawfig Y. Hasou. 300p. 1985. 65.00 (*0-7103-0080-8*) Routledge Chapman & Hall.

Struggle for the Balkans. Svetozar Vukmanovic. (Illus.). 364p. 1990. 39.95 (*0-85036-347-0*, Pub. by Merlin Pr UK) Humanities.

Struggle for the Bliss Farm of Gettysburg: "Over a Wide Hot...Crimson Plain" 2nd ed. Elwood Christ. (Illus.). 220p. (C). 1994. 25.00 (*0-935523-31-6*) Butternut & Blue.

Struggle for the Border. Bruce Hutchinson. LC 70-140358. (Select Bibliographies Reprint Ser.). 1977. reprint ed. 27.95 (*0-8369-5601-X*) Ayer.

Struggle for the Breeches: Gender & the Making of the British Working Class. Anna Clark. LC 93-50835. (Studies on the History of Society & Culture: No. 23). 1995. 35.00 (*0-520-08624-4*) U CA Pr.

***Struggle for the Breeches: Gender & the Making of the British Working Class.** Anna Clark. LC 93-50835. (Studies on the History of Society & Culture: Vol. 23). (Illus.). 1997. pap. 15.95 (*0-520-20883-8*) U CA Pr.

Struggle for the City: Migrant Labor, Capital, & the State in Urban Africa. Ed. by Frederick Cooper. LC 83-11196. (Sage Series on African Modernization & Development: No. 8). (Illus.). 319p. reprint ed. pap. 91.00 (*0-8357-4778-6*, 2037715) Bks Demand.

Struggle for the Falkland Islands: A Study in Legal & Diplomatic History. John C. Metford. 512p. (C). 1982. text ed. 55.00 (*0-300-02943-8*); pap. text ed. 22.00 (*0-300-02945-4*, Y-445) Yale U Pr.

Struggle for the Good, 2 pts., Pt. I. Ilija Poplasen. (Illus.). 61p. 1981. reprint ed. 20.00 (*0-935352-03-1*) MIR PA.

Struggle for the Good, 2 pts., Pt. II. Ilija Poplasen. (Illus.). 128p. 1981. reprint ed. 25.00 (*0-935352-04-X*) MIR PA.

Struggle for the Gulf Borderlands: The Creek War & the Battle of New Orleans, 1812-1815. Frank L. Owsley, Jr. LC 80-11109. (Illus.). vii, 255p. 1981. 34.95 (*0-8130-0662-7*) U Press Fla.

Struggle for the Holy Land: Arabs, Jews, & the Emergence of Israel. William Hare. 380p. 1996. 29.95 (*1-56833-040-5*) Madison Bks UPA.

***Struggle for the Holy Land: Arabs, Jews, & the Emergence of Israel.** rev. ed. William Hare. 380p. 1996. pap. 18.95 (*1-56833-082-0*) Madison Bks UPA.

Struggle for the Jewish Mind: Debates & Disputes on Judaism Then & Now. Jacob Neusner. (Studies in Judaism). 200p. (Orig.). (C). 1988. lib. bdg. 32.00 (*0-8191-6689-8*) U Pr of Amer.

Struggle for the Land: Indigenous Insight & Industrial Empire in the Semiarid World. Ed. by Paul A. Olson. LC 89-22422. (Illus.). x, 317p. 1990. text ed. 42.50 (*0-8032-3555-0*) U of Nebr Pr.

Struggle for the Land: Indigenous Resistance to Genocide, Ecocide & Expropriation in Contemporary North America. Ward Churchill. (Genocide & Resistance Ser.). (Illus.). 480p. (Orig.). 1993. pap. 17.95 (*1-56751-000-0*) Common Courage.

Struggle for the Mediterranean, 1939-1945. Raymond De Belot. Tr. by James A. Field, Jr. LC 51-12459. 306p. reprint ed. pap. 87.30 (*0-317-26671-3*, 2055993) Bks Demand.

Struggle for the Mind of German Youth, 1890-1914. Sterling Fishman. 1974. lib. bdg. 250.00 (*0-87700-229-0*) Revisionist Pr.

Struggle for the Soul of the French Novel: French Catholic & Realist Novelists, 1850-1970. Malcolm Scott. LC 89-27785. 294p. 1990. 49.95 (*0-8132-0720-7*) Cath U Pr.

Struggle for the Soul of the SBC: Moderate Responses to the Fundamentalist Movement. Ed. by Walter B. Shurden. LC 93-14799. 1993. pap. 18.95 (*0-86554-424-7*, MUP-P101) Mercer Univ Pr.

***Struggle for the Spirit: Religious Transformation & Popular Culture in Brazil & Latin America.** David Lehmann. LC 96-26914. 1996. 59.95 (*0-7456-1784-0*, Pub. by Polity Pr UK) Blackwell Pubs.

Struggle for the Third World. Brian Crozier. LC 66-18563. 6600. 18.95 (*0-8023-1035-4*) Dufour.

Struggle for the Victory of Good, Pt. I. Ilija Poplasen. (Illus.). 61p. 1984. 20.00 (*0-935352-18-X*) MIR PA.

Struggle for the Victory of Good, Pt. II. Ilija Poplasen. (Illus.). 128p. 1984. 20.00 (*0-935352-19-8*) MIR PA.

Struggle for Theology's Soul. William Thompson. 360p. 1996. 35.00 (*0-8245-1543-9*) Crossroad NY.

Struggle for Tiananmen: Anatomy of the 1989 Mass Movement. Nan Lin. LC 92-15780. 232p. 1992. text ed. 49.95 (*0-275-93656-2*, C3656, Praeger Pubs) Greenwood.

Struggle for Utopia: Essays on Rodchenko, Lissitzky, and Moholy-Nagy 1917-1946. Victor Margolin. LC 96-3409. 1997. 39.95 (*0-226-50515-4*) U Ch Pr.

***Struggle for Utopia: Rodchenko, Lissitzky, Moholy-Nagy: 1917-1946.** Victor Margolin. LC 96-3409. 1997. pap. write for info. (*0-226-50516-2*) U Ch Pr.

Struggle for Wholeness: Daily Briefings for the Spiritual Journey. Martti Simojoki. Tr. & Intro. by Walter J. Kukkonen. 320p. (Orig.). 1989. pap. text ed. 9.95 (*0-9622985-0-6*) Polaris AZ.

Struggle for Workers' Health. Ed. by Ray H. Elling. 500p. (C). 1986. text ed. 39.95 (*0-89503-047-0*) Baywood Pub.

Struggle for Zimbabwe. David Martin & Phyllis Johnson. LC 81-84556. 400p. (Orig.). 1982. pap. 10.00 (*0-85345-599-6*) Monthly Rev.

Struggle for Zimbabwe: Battle in the Bush. Lewis H. Gann & Thomas H. Henriksen. LC 81-5190. 172p. 1981. text ed. 45.00 (*0-275-90630-2*, C0630, Praeger Pubs) Greenwood.

Struggle in the Andes: Peasant Political Mobilization in Peru. Howard Handelman. LC 74-10796. (Latin American Monographs: No. 35). 321p. reprint ed. pap. 91.50 (*0-8357-7743-X*, 2036100) Bks Demand.

Struggle Is My Life. 2nd ed. Nelson Mandela. LC 90-63060. (Illus.). 281p. 1990. pap. 15.95 (*0-87348-593-9*); lib. bdg. 50.00 (*0-87348-594-7*) Pathfinder NY.

Struggle Is One: Voices & Visions of Liberation. Mev Puleo. LC 93-37873. 251p. (C). 1994. pap. 19.95 (*0-7914-2014-0*); text ed. 59.50 (*0-7914-2013-2*) State U NY Pr.

Struggle of Blind People for Self-Determination: The Dependency-Rehabilitation Conflict: Empowerment in the Blindness Community. C. Edwin Vaughan. LC 93-20088. (Illus.). 256p. 1993. pap. 28.95 (*0-398-06472-5*) C C Thomas.

Struggle of Blind People for Self-Determination: The Dependency-Rehabilitation Conflict: Empowerment in the Blindness Community. C. Edwin Vaughan. LC 93-20088. (Illus.). 256p. (C). 1993. text ed. 43.95 (*0-398-05854-7*) C C Thomas.

Struggle of Jewish Youth for Productivization. Israel Oppenheim. 240p. 1989. text ed. 52.50 (*0-88033-170-4*) East Eur Monographs.

***Struggle of Latino/Latina University Students: In Search of a Liberating Education.** Felix M. Padilla. LC 96-50207. 256p. (C). 1997. pap. write for info. (*0-415-91294-6*); text ed. write for info. (*0-415-91293-8*) Routledge.

Struggle of Memory. Joan Dugdale. (Orig.). 1991. pap. 16.95 (*0-7022-2315-8*, Pub. by Univ Queensland Pr AT) Intl Spec Bk.

Struggle of Muslim Women. Kaukab Siddique. LC 86-70641. 152p. (Orig.). 1986. reprint ed. pap. 9.95 (*0-942978-10-2*) Am Soc Ed & Rel.

Struggle of Prayer. Donald G. Bloesch. LC 87-23764. 192p. (C). 1988. pap. 17.95 (*0-939443-04-X*) Helmers Howard Pub.

Struggle of Protestant Dissenters for Religious Toleration in Virginia. Henry R. McIlwaine. LC 78-63830. (Johns Hopkins University. Studies in the Social Sciences. Thirtieth Ser. 1912: 4). reprint ed. 11.50 (*0-404-61090-0*) AMS Pr.

Struggle of the Cattleman, Sheepman & Settler for Control of Lands in Wyoming, 1867-1910. George W. Rollins. Ed. by Stuart Bruchey. LC 78-56671. (Management of Public Lands in the U. S. Ser.). (Illus.). 1979. lib. bdg. 35.95 (*0-405-11353-6*) Ayer.

Struggle of the Magicians: Why Uspenski Left Gurdjieff/ Exploring the Student-Teacher Relationship. William P. Patterson. Ed. by Barbara C. Allen. 274p. (Orig.). 1996. pap. 16.95 (*1-879514-80-X*) Arete Commns.

Struggle over Lebanon. Tabitha Petran. LC 86-18284. 320p. 1987. 27.50 (*0-85345-651-8*) Monthly Rev.

Struggle over North Sea Oil & Gas: Government Strategies in Denmark, Britain, & Norway. Svein S. Andersen. (Scandinavian University Press Publication). 204p. (C). 1993. 37.00 (*82-00-21815-5*, 14493) Scandnvan Univ Pr.

Struggle over Singapore's Soul: Western Modernization & Asian Culture. Joseph B. Tamney. (De Gruyter Studies in Organization: No. 70). xii, 241p. (C). 1996. text ed. 49.95 (*3-11-014699-1*); pap. text ed. 24.95 (*3-11-014698-3*) De Gruyter.

Struggle over the Past: Fundamentalism in the Modern World. Ed. by William M. Shea. (College Theology Society Publications: No. 35). 384p. (Orig.). (C). 1993. pap. 37.50 (*0-8191-7920-5*); lib. bdg. 66.00 (*0-8191-7919-1*) U Pr of Amer.

Struggle Stops Here: When You Believe in You. Michael R. Clark. LC 92-97390. 82p. 1993. pap. 8.95 (*0-9636042-0-1*) Clark Assoc Busn.

***Struggle Through the 20th Century.** E. V. Holding. 346p. (Orig.). 1997. mass mkt. 4.99 (*1-55197-940-3*, Pub. by Commwlth Pub CN) Partners Pubs Grp.

Struggle to Adore. Alane Rollings. 105p. pap. 12.95 (*0-934257-97-3*) Story Line.

Struggle to Be the Sun Again: Introducing Asian Women's Theology. Hyun K. Chung. LC 90-42683. 1990. pap. 15.00 (*0-88344-684-7*) Orbis Bks.

Struggle to Believe: Rethinking Faith for the 21st Century. William L. Turner. LC 93-713. 129p. 1993. pap. 10.95 (*1-880837-28-5*) Smyth & Helwys.

Struggle to Continue: Progressive Reading Instruction in the United States. Patrick Shannon. LC 90-34029. 220p. (Orig.). (C). 1990. pap. text ed. 23.00 (*0-435-08534-4*, 08534) Heinemann.

Struggle to Grow: Expansionism & Industrialization (1880-1913) Gene Brown. LC 93-24992. (First Person America Ser.). (Illus.). 64p. (J). (gr. 5-8). 1993. lib. bdg. 15.98 (*0-8050-2584-7*) TFC Bks NY.

Struggle to Serve: The Ordination of Women in the Roman Catholic Church. Simone M. St. Pierre. LC 93-41758. 215p. 1994. lib. bdg. 27.50 (*0-89950-901-0*) McFarland & Co.

Struggle to Survive: Funding Higher Education in the Next Century. Ed. by David S. Honeyman et al. LC 96-25275. (Yearbook of the American Education Finance Association Ser.). (Illus.). 208p. 1996. 49.95 (*0-8039-6530-3*) Corwin Pr.

Struggle to Understand: A History of Human Wonder & Discovery. Herbert C. Corben. 398p. 1991. 32.95 (*0-87975-683-7*) Prometheus Bks.

***Struggle Within Islam: The Conflict Between Religion & Politics.** Rafiq Zakaria. 350p. 1996. pap. 9.95 (*0-614-21170-0*, 1174) Kazi Pubns.

Struggle Worthy of Note: The Engineering & Technological Education of Black Americans. David E. Wharton. LC 92-12524. (Contributions in Afro-American & African Studies: No. 155). 170p. 1992. text ed. 45.00 (*0-313-28207-2*, WTJ/, Greenwood Pr) Greenwood.

Strugglers. August. 112p. (C). 1995. pap. 9.95 (*0-413-65690-X*, A0619) Heinemann.

Strugglers: Working with Children Who Fail to Learn to Read. Tony Martin. 160p. 1989. 75.00 (*0-335-09512-7*, Open Univ Pr); pap. 24.00 (*0-335-09511-9*, Open Univ Pr) Taylor & Francis.

Struggles. 220p. (Orig.). 1995. pap. 8.95 (*0-942341-11-2*) Dawn Pubns TX.

Struggles & Triumphs. Phineas T. Barnum. LC 77-125677. (American Journalists Ser.). 1971. reprint ed. 53.95 (*0-405-01651-4*) Ayer.

Struggles for Freedom: An Anthology of Multicultural Experiences. Donna L. Clovis. Ed. by Gwendolynne A. Blakeley. LC 94-78465. (Illus.). 144p. (Orig.). (YA). 1994. pap. 11.95 (*0-9638672-2-9*) Bryant & Dillon.

***Struggles for Inclusive Education: An Ethnographic Study.** Anastasia D. Vlachou. LC 96-45150. 1997. write for info. (*0-335-19764-7*, Open Univ Pr); pap. write for info. (*0-335-19763-9*, Open Univ Pr) Taylor & Francis.

Struggles for Justice: Social Responsibility & the Liberal State. Alan Dawley. (Illus.). 538p. 1991. text ed. 32.00 (*0-674-84580-3*) Belknap Pr.

Struggles for Justice: Social Responsibility & the Liberal State. Alan Dawley. (C). 1991. text ed. 27.95 (*0-685-48479-3*) HUP.

Struggles for Justice: Social Responsibility & the Liberal State. Alan Dawley. (Illus.). 538p. (C). 1993. pap. text ed. 16.95 (*0-674-84581-1*) HUP.

S

An Asterisk (*) at the beginning of an entry indicates that the title is appearing in BIP for the first time.

Struggles from Both Shores. Greg S. Castilla. (Illus.). 267p. (Orig.). 1995. pap. text ed. 11.95 (0-9636557-1-X) Paperworks.

Struggles in South Africa for Survival & Equality. H. J. Simons. 1997. text ed. 65.00 (0-312-16260-X) St Martin.

*__Struggles in the Promised Land: Towards a History of Black-Jewish Relations in the United States.__ Ed. by Jack Salzman & Cornel West. 448p. 1997. 35.00 (0-19-508828-X) OUP.

Struggles of Brown, Jones, & Robinson. Anthony Trollope. Ed. by N. John Hall. LC 80-1889. (Selected Works of Anthony Trollope). 1981. reprint ed. lib. bdg. 31.95 (0-405-14156-4) Ayer.

Struggles of Brown, Jones, & Robinson: By One of the Firm. Anthony Trollope. (World's Classics Ser.). 208p. 1993. pap. 7.95 (0-19-282860-6) OUP.

Struggles of Brown, Jones & Robinson: By One of the Firm (1862) Anthony Trollope. 272p. 1993. pap. 7.95 (0-14-043813-0, Penguin Classics) Viking Penguin.

Struggles of Gods. Ed. by Hans G. Kippenberg. LC 84-11501. (Religion & Reason Ser.: No. 31). vii, 296p. 1984. 60.00 (90-279-3460-6) Mouton.

Struggles of the Italian Film Industry During Fascism, 1930-1935. Elaine Mancini. LC 85-1069. (Studies in Cinema: No. 34). (Illus.). 310p. reprint ed. pap. 88.40 (0-8357-1655-4, 2070506) Bks Demand.

Struggletown: Public & Private Life in Richmond 1900-1965. Janet McCalman. 154p. (Orig.). 1994. pap. 24.95 (0-522-84303-4, Pub. by Melbourne Univ Pr AT) Paul & Co Pubs.

Strugglin' 2B Free. Markhum Who. (Orig.). 1996. pap. 10.95 (0-9647391-9-4) Veracity CA.

Struggling & Ruling: The Indian National Congress, 1885-1985. Ed. by Jim Masselos. (South Asian Publications: No. 2). 224p. 1987. text ed. 35.00 (81-207-0691-9, Pub. by Sterling Pubs II) Apt Bks.

Struggling Sexes. C. G. Tomson. (Orig.). 1996. pap. 14.95 (0-533-11648-1) Vantage.

Struggling Through Tight Times: Introductory Handbook for Women's & Other Non-Profit Organizations on Fiscal Management. Sara Gould. 125p. 1984. pap. 4.75 (0-9605828-5-1) Womens Action.

Struggling to Be 'Good Enough' Administrative Practices & School District Ethos. Ed. by Peter Coleman et al. 240p. 1990. 75.00 (1-85000-860-4, Falmer Pr); pap. 33.00 (1-85000-861-2, Falmer Pr) Taylor & Francis.

Struggling to Be Prophets: The Mill Hill Missionaries in North America, 1871-1985. John Rooney. 188p. 1991. pap. 10.00 (0-317-04686-1) Mill Hill Fthrs.

Struggling to Implement Developmentally Appropriate Practices: Learning from Five Teacher's Stories. Carol A. Wien. (Early Childhood Education Ser.). 192p. (C). 1995. text ed. 37.00 (0-8077-3443-8); pap. text ed. 17.95 (0-8077-3442-X) Tchrs Coll.

Struggling to Shake of Old Shackles: 20th Century Georgia. Ed. by William F. Holmes. (A Documentary History Ser.). 288p. 1995. 35.00 (0-88322-019-9) Beehive GA.

*__Struggling to Surrender: Some Impressions of an American Convert to Islam.__ Jeffery B. Lang. 246p. 1996. pap. 11.75 (0-614-21683-4, 1379) Kazi Pubns.

*__Struggling to Surrender: Some Impressions of an American Convert to Islam.__ 2nd ed. Jeffrey B. Lang. LC 94-29827. 1995. pap. 11.75 (0-915957-29-9) amana pubns.

Struggling to Survive in A Welfare Hotel. John H. Simpson et al. LC 85-105459. 47p. (Orig.). 1984. pap. 6.00 (0-88156-037-5) Comm Serv Soc NY.

Struggling to Swim on Concrete. Vassar Miller. Ed. by Maxine Cassin. LC 84-60413. (Journal Press Bks.). (Illus.). 80p. (Orig.). 1984. pap. 12.00 (0-938498-05-3) New Orleans Poetry.

Struggling Toward Civil Rights. Judith Lechner. Ed. by J. Friedland & R. Kessler. (Novel-Ties Ser.). 1993. student ed., pap. text ed. 20.95 (1-56982-024-4) Lrn Links.

Struggling Under the Destructive Glance: Androgyny in the Novels of Guy de Maupassant. Rachel M. Hartig. LC 90-19207. (American University Studies: Romance Languages & Literature: Ser. II, Vol. 113). 135p. (C). 1991. text ed. 31.95 (0-8204-1075-6) P Lang Pubng.

Struggling Upward. fac. ed. Horatio Alger, Jr. (J). 1971. Fasc. 6.95 (0-87874-005-8) Galloway.

Struggling Upward. Horatio Alger, Jr. (Works of Horatio Alger Jr.). 1989. reprint ed. lib. bdg. 79.00 (0-685-27564-7) Rprt Serv.

Struggling Upward or Luke Larkin's Luck. Horatio Alger, Jr. 160p. 1984. reprint ed. pap. 4.95 (0-486-24737-6) Dover.

Struggling with Destiny in Karimpur, 1925-1984. Susan S. Wadley. LC 93-48297. (Illus.). 319p. (C). 1994. 45.00 (0-520-08406-3); pap. 14.00 (0-520-08407-1) U CA Pr.

*__Struggling with Selfishness.__ Woodrow M. Kroll. 1996. 7.99 (0-8474-1470-1) Back to Bible.

*__Struggling with Their Histories: Economic Decline & School Improvement in Four Rural Southeastern School Districts.__ 1991. text ed. 73.25 (0-89391-817-2) Ablex Pub.

Struktur der Reden in der Odyssee 1-8. Carlos J. Larrain. (Spudasmata Ser.: Bd. 41). xi, 497p. (GER.). 1987. write for info. (3-487-07831-7) G Olms Pubs.

Struktur der Vegetation auf Periglazialen Basaltblockhalden des Hessischen Berglandes: Bryophytenvegetation & Waldgesellschaften. J. Halfmann. (Dissertationes Botanicae Ser.: Vol. 168). (Illus.). 228p. (GER.). 1991. pap. 84.00 (3-443-64080-X, Pub. by Cramer-Borntraeger GW) Lubrecht & Cramer.

Struktur des Verhaltens. Maurice Merleau-Ponty. (Phaenomenologisch-Psychologische Forschungen Ser.: Vol. 13). xxvi, 278p. (C). 1976. text ed. 75.40 (3-11-004469-2) De Gruyter.

*__Struktur des Zaubermarchens II Transformation und Narrative Formen.__ Kurt Derungs. (Germanistische Texte und Studien: Vol. 47). 314p. (GER.). 1994. write for info. (3-487-09898-9) G Olms Pubs.

Struktur, Spleissprozesse und Funktionen Mitrochondrialer Introne: Das "Mobile Intron" des Ascomyceter Podospora Anserina. Udo Schmidt. (Bibliotheca Mycologica Ser.: Vol. 127). (Illus.). 128p. (GER.). 1989. pap. text ed. 45.00 (3-443-59028-4, Pub. by Cramer GW) Lubrecht & Cramer.

Struktur und Bezeichnung des Scheltworts. Ludwig Markert. (Beiheft 40 zur Zeitschrift fuer die Alttestamentliche Wissenschaft Ser.). (C). 1977. text ed. 134.60 (3-11-005813-8) De Gruyter.

Struktur und Dynamik von Waeldern: Rinteln, April 1981, Berichte der Internationalen Symposien der Intern'len Vereinigung fuer Vegetationskunde. Ed. by Hartmut Dierschke. (Illus.). 736p. (Orig.). (GER.). 1983. lib. bdg. 120.00 (3-7682-1334-X) Lubrecht & Cramer.

Struktur und Funktion Endothelialer Zellen. Ed. by K. Messmer & F. Hammersen. (Illus.). x, 150p. 1983. pap. 39.25 (3-8055-3712-3) S Karger.

Struktur und Funktion Linearer Plasmide bei dem Phytopatogenen Ascomyceten Claviceps Purpurea. Andrea Duvell. (Bibliotheca Mycologica Ser.: Vol. 126). (Illus.). 108p. (GER.). 1989. pap. 40.00 (0-318-41530-5, Pub. by Cramer GW) Lubrecht & Cramer.

Struktur und Funktionen Mitochondrialer dna Bei Pilzen. H. U. Kueck. (Bibliotheca Mycologica Ser.: No. 84). (Illus.). 148p. (GER.). 1981. pap. text ed. 24.00 (3-7682-1323-4) Lubrecht & Cramer.

Struktur, Verbreitung und Oekologie der Fliesswasserflora Oberschwabens Un der Schwaebischen Alb. W. Schuetz. (Dissertationes Botanicae Ser.: Vol. 192). (Illus.). 203p. (GER.). 1992. pap. text ed. 63.00 (3-443-64104-0, Pub. by Cramer-Borntraeger GW) Lubrecht & Cramer.

Strukturale Beobachtungen zum Neuen Testament. Werner Stenger. LC 89-49295. (New Testament Tools & Studies: Vol. XII). (Illus.). vii, 321p. (GER.). 1989. 96.50 (90-04-09113-0) E J Brill.

Strukturalismus see Structuralism, Moscow, Prague, Paris

Strukturanalyse und zeigerwert der Auen und-Ufervegetation im Hamburger Hafen und-Hafenrandgebiet. Helmut Freisinger. (Dissertationes Botanicae Ser.: Vol. 174). (Illus.). 298p. (GER.). 1991. pap. 81.90 (3-443-64086-9, Pub. by Cramer-Borntraeger GW) Lubrecht & Cramer.

Strukturelle Textanalyse - Analyse Du Recit - Discourse Analysis. Walter A. Koch. (Studia Semiotica, Collecta Semiotica Ser.: Vol. I). ix, 486p. (Orig.). 1972. pap. write for info. (3-487-04291-6) G Olms Pubs.

Strukturelle und instrumentalphonetische Untersuchungen zur gesprochenen Sprache. Joachim Goeschel. LC 72-76054. (Studia Linguistica Germanica: Vol. 9). (Illus.). 1973. 101.55 (3-11-003624-X) De Gruyter.

*__Strukturen des Musiklebens in Wien: Zum Musikalischen Vereinsleben in der Ersten Republik - Unter Mitarbeit von Gertraud Pressler, Gottfried Weinfurter-Kinsky, Christian Bohm und Astrid Schramek.__ Paulus Ebner. Ed. by Friedrich C. Heller. (Musikleben - Studien zur Musikgeschichte Osterreichs: Bd. 5). 286p. (GER.). 1996. 51.95 (3-631-30375-0) P Lang Pubng.

Strukturen in Shakespeares King Henry the Sixth. Regina Dombrowa. (BAS Ser.: No. 18). x, 320p. (Orig.). 1985. pap. 77.00 (90-6032-267-3, Pub. by Gruner NE) Benjamins North Am.

Strukturen Lokaler Nachrichten: Eine Empirische Untersuchung von Text - & Bildberichterstattung. Thomas Wilking. (Dortmunder Beitrage Zur Zeitungsforschung Ser.: Vol. 47). 263p. (GER.). 1990. pap. 29.00 (3-598-21308-5) K G Saur.

Strum Along Songs. Patricia A. Welsh. (Illus.). 60p. (Orig.). 1995. spiral bd. 12.95 (1-884620-14-0) PAW Prods.

Strum-Liouville & Dirac Operators. B. M. Levitan & I. S. Sargsjan. (C). 1990. lib. bdg. 206.00 (0-7923-0992-8) Kluwer Ac.

Strumpet Muse: Art & Morals in Chaucer's Poetry. Alfred David. LC 76-11939. 280p. reprint ed. pap. 82.70 (0-7837-1747-4, 2057281) Bks Demand.

Strumpet Wind. Gordon Merrick. 256p. 1992. reprint ed. lib. bdg. 18.95 (0-89966-892-5) Buccaneer Bks.

Strums for Guitar with Tablature. 16p. 1987. pap. 6.95 (0-7935-3439-9, 00699135) H Leonard.

Strung with Care: Timeless. Hanna Manson-Perry. 77p. 1996. pap. 17.50 (0-9643885-3-7) Personal Profiles.

Strut. Bruce Hart & Carole Hart. 240p. (Orig.). 1992. mass mkt. 3.99 (0-380-75962-4, Flare) Avon.

Struthers Burt. Raymond C. Phillips, Jr. LC 82-74090. (Western Writers Ser.: No. 56). (Illus.). 48p. (Orig.). 1983. pap. 4.95 (0-88430-030-7) Boise St U W Writ Ser.

Struthiomimus. Swann. (Dinosaur Library: Set V). (Illus.). 24p. (J). 1984. lib. bdg. 14.00 (0-86592-525-9) Rourke Enter.

Strutter's Complete Guide to Clown Makeup. Jim Roberts. LC 90-52814. (Illus.). 96p. (Orig.). 1991. pap. 24.00 (0-941599-10-8, Empire Pub Srvs) Players Pr.

Strutter's Complete Guide to Clown Makeup. Jim Roberts. LC 90-52814. (Illus.). 1991. 30.00 (0-88734-607-3) Players Pr.

Strutting & Fretting: Standards for Self-Esteem. Jann Benson & Dan Lyons. 240p. (Orig.). (C). 1991. pap. text ed. 19.95 (0-87081-193-2) Univ Pr Colo.

Strutts & the Arkwrights, 1758-1830: A Study of the Early Factory System. R. S. Fitton & Alfred P. Wadsworth. LC 72-375. 1968. reprint ed. 45.00 (0-678-06758-9) Kelley.

Struttura Del Sistema Bancario Toscano Dal 1815 Al 1859, 2 Vols. Anna Cecchi. Ed. by Stuart Bruchey. LC 80-2804. (Dissertations in European Economic History Ser.). (Illus.). 1981. lib. bdg. 39.95 (0-405-13988-8) Ayer.

Struve: Liberal on the Left, 1870-1905. Richard E. Pipes. (Russian Research Center Studies: No. 64). 429p. 1970. 39.95 (0-674-84595-1) HUP.

Struve: Liberal on the Right, 1905-1944. Richard E. Pipes. LC 79-16145. (Russian Research Center Studies: No. 80). 536p. 1980. 47.50 (0-674-84600-1) HUP.

Struwwelpeter in English Translation. Heinrich Hoffmann. LC 94-38306. (Illus.). 32p. (GER.). (J). 1995. pap. text ed. 5.95 (0-486-28469-7) Dover.

Struwwelpeter Tales of Hoffmann. Seanair. (Illus.). 64p. (Orig.). (J). (ps-5). 1996. pap. 14.95 (0-9641804-1-3) Iolair Pubng.

Stryker's Wife. Dixie Browning. 1996. mass mkt. 3.50 (0-373-76033-7, 1-76033-9) Silhouette.

STS Education: International Perspectives on Reform. Ed. by Joan Solomon & Glen Aikenhead. LC 94-10822. (Ways of Knowing in Science Ser.). 272p. (C). 1994. text ed. 46.00 (0-8077-3366-0); pap. text ed. 21.95 (0-8077-3365-2) Tchrs Coll.

*__STS Version 2.0: Synthesis Tree Search in 2.5 Million Chemical Reactions, 2 disks.__ Ed. by InfoChem GmbH Staff. 20p. 1997. 10,400.00 incl. cd-rom (3-540-14600-8) Spr-Verlag.

*__STS Version 2.0 (for ChemReact41 Users: Synthesis Tree Search in 2.5 Million Chemical Reactions.__ Ed. by InfoChem GmbH Staff. 20p. 1996. 680.00 incl. cd-rom (3-540-14601-6) Spr-Verlag.

STT 366: Deutungsbersuch 1982 & other articles. Karlheinz Deller & Kazuke Watanabe. (Assur Ser.: Vol. 3, Issue 4). 40p. (GER.). 1983. pap. 7.50 (0-685-07468-4) Undena Pubns.

Stu Apte's Fishing in the Florida Keys & Flamingo. 6th ed. Stuart C. Apte. (Illus.). 80p. 1995. pap. 6.95 (0-89317-062-3) Windward Pub.

Stuart: Some Account of the Stuarts of Aubigny, in France, 1422-1672. Elizabeth Cust. (Illus.). 130p. 1992. reprint ed. pap. 24.00 (0-8328-2593-X); reprint ed. lib. bdg. 34.00 (0-8328-2592-1) Higginson Bk Co.

Stuart - History of the American Light Tank, Vol. 1. R. P. Hunnicutt. LC 92-19623. 1992. 95.00 (0-89141-462-2) Presidio Pr.

Stuart Age. Barry Coward. LC 79-42887. (History of England Ser.). (Illus.). 493p. (C). 1980. pap. text ed. 28.50 (0-582-48833-8, 73385) Longman.

Stuart Age: A History of England, 1603-1714. 2nd ed. Barry Coward. LC 93-26405. (History of England Ser.). 496p. (C). 1995. pap. text ed. 34.95 (0-582-06722-7, 76265, Pub. by Longman UK) Longman.

Stuart & Georgian Moments: Clark Library Seminar Papers on Seventeenth & Eighteenth Century Literature. Ed. by Earl R. Miner. LC 78-100020. (Publications of the 17th & 18th Centuries Studies Group, UCLA: No. 3). 325p. reprint ed. pap. 92.70 (0-685-44492-9, 2031507) Bks Demand.

*__Stuart & Sundeen's Pocket Guide to Psychiatric Nursing.__ 4th ed. Stuart. (C). (gr. 13). 1997. pap. text ed. 22.95 (0-8151-2602-6, 31072, Yr Bk Med Pubs) Mosby Yr Bk.

*__Stuart & Sundeen's Principles & Practice of Psychiatric Nursing.__ 6th ed. Stuart. (C). (gr. 13). 1997. text ed. 53.00 (0-8151-2603-4, 31073, Yr Bk Med Pubs) Mosby Yr Bk.

Stuart Constitution: Documents & Commentary. 2nd ed. J. P. Kenyon. 550p. 1986. pap. text ed. 29.95 (0-521-31327-9) Cambridge U Pr.

Stuart Constitution: Documents & Commentary. 2nd ed. J. P. Kenyon. 550p. 1986. text ed. 80.00 (0-521-30810-0) Cambridge U Pr.

Stuart Court & Europe: Essays in Politics & Political Culture. Ed. by R. Malcolm Smuts. (Illus.). 290p. (C). 1996. text ed. 54.95 (0-521-55439-X) Cambridge U Pr.

Stuart Court in Exile & the Jacobites. Ed. by Eveline Cruickshanks & Edward Corp. Staff. LC 95-49130. 1995. 55.00 (1-85285-119-8) Hambledon Press.

Stuart Davis. Patricia Hills. LC 95-22046. (Library of American Art). (Illus.). 160p. 1996. 45.00 (0-8109-3219-9) Abrams.

Stuart Davis: Graphic Work & Related Paintings with a Catalogue Raisonne of the Prints. Jane E. Myers et al. LC 86-70931. (Illus.). 100p. 1986. 5.00 (0-88360-054-4); pap. 2.50 (0-88360-055-2) Amon Carter.

*__Stuart Davis: Sketchbooks.__ (Illus.). 1996. 65.00 (0-8008-7483-8) Taplinger.

Stuart Davis see Three American Modernist Painters

Stuart Davis' New York. Bruce Weber. LC 85-72521. (Illus.). 96p. 1985. pap. 12.95 (0-943411-13-0) Norton Gal Art.

Stuart Davis's Abstract Argot. William Wilson. LC 93-4338. (Essential Paintings Ser.). (Illus.). 88p. 1993. 24.95 (1-56640-316-2) Pomegranate Calif.

Stuart England. J. P. Kenyon. 384p. 1986. mass mkt. 5.95 (0-14-022552-8, Penguin Bks) Viking Penguin.

Stuart England. J. P. Kenyon. 1990. pap. 7.95 (0-14-013768-8, Viking) Viking Penguin.

Stuart Hall: Critical Dialogues in Cultural Studies. Ed. by David Morley & Kuan-Hsing Chen. LC 95-16455. 544p. 1996. pap. 19.95 (0-415-08804-6) Routledge.

Stuart Hall: Critical Dialogues in Cultural Studies. Ed. by David Morley & Kuan-Hsing Chen. LC 95-16455. (Comedia Ser.). 544p. (C). 1996. text ed. 74.95 (0-415-08803-8) Routledge.

Stuart Hamm: Bass Book. 112p. 1993. 19.95 (0-7935-1421-5, 00694823) H Leonard.

Stuart Little. E. B. White. LC 45-9585. (Illus.). 132p. (J). (gr. 3-6). 1945. lib. bdg. 12.89 (0-06-026396-2) HarpC Child Bks.

Stuart Little. E. B. White. LC 45-9585. (Illus.). 132p. (J). (gr. 3-6). 1945. 13.00 (0-06-026395-4) HarpC Child Bks.

Stuart Little. E. B. White. LC 45-9585. (Trophy Bk.). (Illus.). 132p. (J). (gr. 3-7). 1974. pap. 3.95 (0-06-440056-5, Trophy) HarpC Child Bks.

Stuart Little. E. B. White. (J). 1990. mass mkt. 3.50 (0-06-107009-2, Harp PBks) HarpC.

Stuart Little. E. B. White. 1995. pap. text ed. 7.95 (84-204-4669-6) Santillana.

Stuart Little: Musical. E. B. White & Joseph Robinette. 1993. pap. 5.25 (0-87129-239-4, SA1) Dramatic Pub.

Stuart Little see E. B. White Boxed Set: Charlotte's Web, Stuart Little, & The Trumpet of the Swan

Stuart Little - Str. Joseph Robinette. 52p. 1991. pap. 5.25 (0-87129-155-X, S99) Dramatic Pub.

Stuart Masques & the Renaissance Stage. Allardyce Nicoll. LC 63-23186. (Illus.). 224p. 1972. 30.95 (0-405-08817-5, Pub. by Blom Pubns UK) Ayer.

Stuart Politics in Chapman's Tragedy of Chabot. Norma D. Solve. LC 74-1304. (English Literature Ser.: No. 33). 1974. lib. bdg. 48.95 (0-8383-2037-6) M S G Haskell Hse.

*__Stuart Princesses.__ Alison Plowden. (Illus.). 240p. 1997. pap. 17.95 (0-7509-1611-7, Pub. by Sutton Pubng UK) Bks Intl VA.

Stuart Tracts, Sixteen Hundred Three to Sixteen Ninety-Three. Ed. by Gerald M. Straka. LC 72-83161. (English Studies). 1972. reprint ed. lib. bdg. 43.00 (0-8420-1419-5) Scholarly Res Inc.

Stuart Wales. W. S. Thomas. 216p. (C). 1989. pap. 33.00 (0-86383-439-6, Pub. by Gomer Pr UK) St Mut.

*__Stuart Women of Letters.__ Maureen E. Mulvihill. (Literature Reference Ser.). 450p. Date not set. text ed. 65.00 (0-8240-6316-3) Garland.

Stuarts. (History of Britain Ser.: No. F895-5). (Illus.). (YA). (gr. 5 up). 1990. pap. 3.95 (1-85543-010-X, Ladybrd) Penguin.

Stuarts. Jennifer Ruby. (Costume in Context Ser.). (Illus.). 72p. (YA). (gr. 7-9). 1988. 24.95 (0-7134-5604-3, Pub. by Batsford UK) Trafalgar.

Stuart's Cavalry in the Gettysburg Campaign. John S. Mosby. 228p. 1987. reprint ed. 25.00 (0-942211-28-6) Olde Soldier Bks.

*__Stuart's Tarheels: James B. Gordon & His North Carolina Cavalry.__ Chris J. Hartley. (Army of Northern Virginia Ser.). (Illus.). 453p. 1996. 35.00 (0-935523-57-X) Butternut & Blue.

Stubble Field. Mary Nichols. 432p. 1993. 25.95 (1-85797-177-9) Trafalgar.

Stubblefield, Inventor of Radio, 1892. Troy Stubblefield-Cory. 1994. write for info. (0-318-72987-3) TV Int Pubs.

Stubborn As a Mule Back to the Ranch. Roz Denny. (Romance Ser.). 1993. mass mkt. 2.99 (0-373-03276-5, 1-03276-2) Harlequin Bks.

Stubborn Children: Controlling Delinquency in the United States, 1640-1981. John R. Sutton. (Medicine & Society Ser.: Vol. 2). 1988. 50.00 (0-520-06093-8); pap. 13.00 (0-520-08452-7) U CA Pr.

Stubborn Earth: American Agriculturalists on Chinese Soil, 1898-1937. Randall E. Stross. 272p. 1986. pap. 16.95 (0-520-06620-0) U CA Pr.

Stubborn Fact & Creative Advance: An Introduction to the Metaphysics of Alfred North Whitehead. Thomas E. Hosinki. 300p. (Orig.). (C). 1993. pap. text ed. 24.95 (0-8476-7828-8); lib. bdg. 62.50 (0-8476-7827-X) Rowman.

Stubborn Fisherman. 2nd ed. Elda M. Roberts. LC 86-71820. (Illus.). 234p. 1997. pap. 16.95 (0-9617139-0-9) Creighton Pub.

Stubborn for Liberty: The Dutch in New York. Alice P. Kenney. LC 75-16403. (New York State Bks.). (Illus.). 320p. 1989. pap. text ed. 15.95 (0-8156-2482-4) Syracuse U Pr.

Stubborn Forest. Paul Hyland. 8400. pap. 11.95 (0-906427-59-2, Pub. by Bloodaxe Bks UK) Dufour.

Stubborn Hope: Religion, Politics, & Revolution in Central America. Phillip Berryman. 288p. 1994. 22.95 (1-56584-136-0) New Press NY.

Stubborn Hope: Religion, Politics, & Revolution in Central America. Phillip Berryman. 288p. 1995. pap. 13.95 (1-56584-137-9) New Press NY.

Stubborn Hope: Religion, Politics, & Revolution in Central America. Phillip Berryman. LC 94-2253. 276p. (Orig.). 1995. pap. 13.95 (1-57075-025-4) Orbis Bks.

Stubborn Hope: Selected Poems of South Africa & a Wider World. Dennis Brutus. LC 91-9327. (African Writers Ser.). 98p. (C). 1991. pap. 9.95 (0-435-90208-3, 90208) Heinemann.

Stubborn Hope: The Churches, Politics, & Revolution in Central America. Phillip Berryman. LC 94-2253. 225p. (Orig.). 1994. 22.95 (0-88344-962-5) Orbis Bks.

*__Stubborn Hope: Without Disappointment.__ Jeanne DeTellis & Renee Meloche. 244p. (Orig.). 1996. pap. write for info. (0-9653234-0-4) New Missions.

Stubborn March. Gerard Chaliand. Tr. by Andre Demir. LC 92-28719. 112p. (Orig.). (ENG & FRE.). 1992. pap. 15.95 (0-9628715-3-2) Blue Crane Bks.

Stubborn Ounces - Just Scales. Donovan Roberts. 1992. pap. 14.95 (1-55673-417-4, 7900) CSS OH.

Stubborn Particulars of Social Psychology: Essays on the Research Process. Frances E. Cherry. LC 94-10637. (Critical Psychology Ser.). 144p. (C). (gr. 13). 1994. text ed. 49.95 (0-415-06666-2, A7782) Routledge.

Stubborn Particulars of Social Psychology: Essays on the Research Process. Frances E. Cherry. LC 94-10637. (Critical Psychology Ser.). 144p. (C). 1995. pap. 17.95 (0-415-06667-0, A7786) Routledge.

Stubborn Poems. Roland Flint. (National Poetry Ser.). 80p. 1990. 11.95 (0-252-06132-2) U of Ill Pr.

An Asterisk (*) at the beginning of an entry indicates that the title is appearing in BIP for the first time.

Stubborn Porridge & Other Stories. Wang Meng. Tr. & Intro. by Zhu Hong. LC 93-47466. 180p. 1994. 18.50 (*0-8076-1353-3*) Braziller.

Stubborn Tide. large type ed. Anne Durham. 1990. 25.99 (*0-7089-2299-6*) Ulverscroft.

Stubborn Twig: Three Generations in the Life of a Japanese American Family. Lauren Kessler. (Illus.). 368p. 1994. pap. 12.95 (*0-452-27301-3*, Plume) NAL-Dutton.

Stubborn Weeds: Popular & Controversial Chinese Literature after the Cultural Revolution. Ed. by Eugene P. Link. LC 82-48268. (Chinese Literature in Translation Ser.). 302p. 1983. reprint ed. pap. 86.10 (*0-7837-9658-7*, 2059291) Bks Demand.

Stubbornness: A Field Guide. John Hildebidle. (Illus.). 194p. (Orig.). 1986. pap. 6.95 (*0-938621-00-9*) MSS-New Myths.

Stubbs: Descendants of John Stubbs of Cappahosic, Gloucester County, Virginia, 1652. W. C. Stubbs. 116p. 1993. reprint ed. pap. 19.50 (*0-8328-3417-3*); reprint ed. lib. bdg. 29.50 (*0-8328-3416-5*) Higginson Bk Co.

Stubs: The Seating Plan Guide for New York Theaters, Music Halls & Sports Stadia, 1986 Edition. Ed. by Ronald S. Lee & Patricia Lee. (Illus.). 1986. pap. 6.95 (*0-911458-06-9*, MNYE9) Stubs.

Stucco Decoration & Architectural Assemblage of Structure 1-Sub Dzibilchaltun, Yucatan, Mexico. Clemency C. Coggins. LC 83-61021. (Publications: No. 49). 70p. 1983. pap. 20.00 (*0-939238-78-0*) Tulane MARI.

Stuck for Words: What to Say to Someone Who Is Grieving. Doris Zagdanski. 140p. (Orig.). 1994. pap. 12.95 (*0-85572-237-1*, Pub. by Hill Content Pubng AT) Seven Hills Bk.

Stuck in a Sticky World: Learning to See God's Best in Life's Worst. Jon Johnston. LC 96-1631. 246p. 1996. 19.99 (*0-89900-752-X*) College Pr Pub.

Stuck in the Big Bang Quagmire: Sixty Years Is Enough. unabridged ed. Billy L. Farmer. 63p. (Orig.). 1993. pap. 8.00 (*0-9649983-2-7*) B L Farmer.

***Stuck in the Middle - the Misunderstood Age: A Handbook for Christian Educators & Especially Parents.** James DiVirgilio & Anne Adams. (Orig.). 1997. pap. 10.95 (*0-533-12336-4*) Vantage.

Stuck in the Mud, Vol. 1. George C. Peterson. (Illus.). 208p. (Orig.). (YA). (gr. 9-12). 1988. pap. write for info. (*0-9621320-0-4*) G Peterson.

Stuck in the Mud - Tall Book. J. Croser & J. Vassillou. 8p. (J). 1987. 19.95 (*0-88679-542-7*) Educ Insights.

Stuck in the Mud-Small Book. J. Croser & J. Vassillou. 8p. (J). 1987. 3.95 (*0-88679-543-5*) Educ Insights.

Stuck in the Seventies: One Hundred Thirteen Things That Screwed up the Twentysomething Generation. 2nd ed. Scott Matthews et al. (Illus.). 228p. 1995. pap. 12.95 (*1-56625-051-X*) Bonus Books.

Stuck in Traffic: Coping with Peak-Hour Traffic Congestion. Anthony Downs. 210p. (C). 1992. 38.95 (*0-8157-1924-8*); pap. 16.95 (*0-8157-1923-X*) Brookings.

Stuck Like Glue: Sticker Studies. Paula Rinehart. (Sticker Studies: No. 1). (Illus.). (Orig.). (J). (gr. 3-7). 1996. pap. 5.99 (*1-57673-006-9*, Multnomah Bks) Multnomah Pubs.

***Stuck on Cactus: A Growing Guide for Beginners.** David Wright. (Illus.). 128p. (Orig.). 1996. pap. 9.95 (*1-57427-056-7*) Howell Pr VA.

Stuck on Magnets. Kate Mason. (J). 1995. pap. 6.95 (*0-8167-3670-7*) Troll Communs.

Stuck on Magnets: An Integrated Activity Unit. Ed Catherall & Bev McKay. (Illus.). 32p. 1993. pap. text ed. 4.95 (*0-86530-234-0*) Incentive Pubns.

Stuck on the Cubs. Rick Schwab. 192p. (Orig.). 1977. pap. 1.95 (*0-930528-01-8*) Sassafras Pr.

Stuck on the Presidents. Lara Bergen et al. (Books & Stuff). (Illus.). 48p. (Orig.). (J). (gr. 2 up). 1997. pap. 7.95 (*0-448-41284-5*, G&D) Putnam Pub Group.

Stuck on the Sox. Rick Lindberg. 192p. (Orig.). 1978. pap. 1.95 (*0-930528-02-6*) Sassafras Pr.

Stuck on the U. S. A. (Books & Stuff). (Illus.). 64p. (J). (gr. 1-7). 1994. pap. 7.95 (*0-448-40179-7*, G&D) Putnam Pub Group.

Stuck Rubber Baby. Cruse. Ed. by B. Taggart. (Illus.). 224p. 1995. 24.95 (*1-56389-216-2*, Paradox) DC Comics.

Stuck Rubber Baby. Cruse. Ed. by B. Taggart. (Illus.). 224p. 1996. pap. 14.95 (*1-56389-255-3*, Paradox) DC Comics.

Stuck Rubber Baby. Howard Cruse. (Illus.). 224p. 1996. pap. 14.00 (*0-06-097713-2*) HarpC.

Stuck Up. John Dolan. 72p. 1995. pap. 12.95 (*1-86940-120-4*, Pub. by Auckland Univ NZ) Paul & Co Pubs.

***Stuck Up!** Jennifer Ericsson. Date not set. write for info. (*0-688-13556-0*, Tambourine Bks); lib. bdg. write for info. (*0-688-13557-9*, Tambourine Bks) Morrow.

Stuck with Baby. Geoff Kelly. 32p. (J). (gr. 1-5). 1996. 14.95 (*1-86373-941-6*); pap. text ed. 6.95 (*1-86373-942-4*) IPG Chicago.

Stuck with You. Vicki L. Thompson. (Love & Laughter Ser.). 1996. mass mkt. 3.50 (*0-373-44005-7*, 1-44005-6) Harlequin Bks.

Stucky Points for Weight Control see Calorie Points for Weight Control

Stucture & Dynamics of Non-Rigid Molecular Systems. Ed. by Yves G. Smeyers. LC 94-7726. (Topics in Molecular Organization & Engineering Ser.: Vol. 12). 1995. lib. bdg. 146.50 (*0-7923-2774-8*) Kluwer Ac.

***Stuctures & Strategies.** Ed. by Young. (C). 1982. text ed. write for info. (*0-321-01591-6*) Addson-Wesley Educ.

Stud. Jackie Collins. 304p. 1971. pap. 5.99 (*0-451-16391-5*, Sig) NAL-Dutton.

Stud. Barbara Delinsky. (Temptation Ser.: No. 357). 1991. pap. 2.95 (*0-373-25457-1*) Harlequin Bks.

Stud. abr. rev. ed. Phil Andros, pseud. 216p. 1982. pap. 7.95 (*0-932870-02-3*) Alyson Pubns.

Stud: Architectures of Masculinity. Ed. by Joel Sanders. (Illus.). 304p. (Orig.). 1996. pap. 19.95 (*1-56898-076-0*) Princeton Arch.

Stud Poker. John Francome. 320p. 1995. mass mkt. 4.99 (*0-06-104289-7*, Harp PBks) HarpC.

***Stud Rites.** Susan Conant. 256p. 1997. mass mkt. 5.99 (*0-553-57300-4*, Crimeline) Bantam.

Stud Rites: A Dog Lover's Mystery. Susan Conant. LC 95-44439. 288p. 1996. 21.00 (*0-385-47724-4*) Doubleday.

Stud Shorts. Clay Caldwell. (Orig.). 1995. mass mkt. 5.95 (*1-56333-320-1*, Badboy) Masquerade.

Studebaker: Less Than They Promised. Michael Beatty et al. LC 84-81548. (Illus.). 94p. (Orig.). 1984. 24.95 (*0-89708-150-1*); pap. 9.95 (*0-89708-129-3*) And Bks.

Studebaker Cars. James H. Maloney. (Crestline Ser.). (Illus.). 320p. 1994. 44.95 (*0-87938-884-6*, Crestline Pub) Motorbooks Intl.

Studebaker Trucks 1927-1940 Photo Archive. Ed. by Howard L. Applegate. LC 95-77494. (Photo Archive Ser.). (Illus.). 128p. 1995. pap. 29.95 (*1-882256-40-9*) Iconografix.

Studebaker Trucks 1941-1964 Photo Archive. Ed. by Howard L. Applegate. LC 95-77493. (Photo Archive Ser.). (Illus.). 128p. 1995. pap. 29.95 (*1-882256-41-7*) Iconografix.

Studebaker 1926-1938 Photo Archive. Ed. by Howard Applegate. LC 94-79319. (Photo Archive Ser.). (Illus.). 144p. 1995. pap. 29.95 (*1-882256-24-7*) Iconografix.

Studebaker 1939-1958 Photo Archive. Ed. by Howard Applegate. LC 94-79320. (Photo Archive Ser.). (Illus.). 144p. 1995. pap. 29.95 (*1-882256-25-5*) Iconografix.

Student: A Statistical Biography of William Sealy Gosset. E. S. Pearson. Ed. by Robert L. Plackett & G. A. Barnard. (Illus.). 152p. 1990. 35.00 (*0-19-852227-4*) OUP.

Student: At Chicago in Hutchins' Hey-day. Alfred De Grazia. 364p. 1992. pap. 21.00 (*0-940268-25-6*) Metron Pubns.

Student Access Guide for Paying for College: 1996 Edition. Geoffrey Martz & Kalman A. Chany. (Princeton Review Ser.). 1995. pap. 18.00 (*0-679-76469-0*, Villard Bks) Random.

Student Access Handbook for College Bound Students with Learning Disabilities. Eric L. Lewis. (Princeton Review Ser.). 1996. pap. 20.00 (*0-679-76461-5*, Villard Bks) Random.

Student Achievement & The Changing American Family. David W. Grissmer et al. LC 94-41953. 174p. 1994. pap. 15.00 (*0-8330-1616-4*, MR-488-LE) Rand Corp.

Student Achievement Through Staff Development: Fundamentals of School Renewal. 2nd ed. Bruce Joyce & Beverly Showers. LC 94-26678. 304p. (C). 1995. pap. text ed. 32.95 (*0-8013-0782-1*) Longman.

Student Activism. Irving Howe. LC 67-18658. (Orig.). 1967. pap. 2.05 (*0-672-60899-5*, CR13, Bobbs) Macmillan.

Student Activism & Protest: Alternatives for Social Change. Edward E. Sampson et al. LC 77-92898. (Jossey-Bass Higher Education Ser.). 284p. reprint ed. 81.00 (*0-8357-9349-4*, 2013868) Bks Demand.

Student Activities Assistant. 2nd ed. Kushner. (PB - Keyboarding Ser.). (J). (gr. k-8). 1990. pap. 10.95 (*0-538-60103-5*) S-W Pub.

Student Activities for Taking Charge of Your Career Direction & Job Search: Career Planning Guide, Bk. 3. 2nd ed. Robert D. Lock. 136p. (YA). 1992. pap. 13.20 (*0-534-13659-1*) Brooks-Cole.

Student Activities in the Secondary Schools: A Handbook & Guide. Ward Sybouts & Wayne J. Krepel. LC 83-18535. (Illus.). x, 428p. 1984. text ed. 47.95 (*0-313-23379-9*, SYS/, Greenwood Pr) Greenwood.

Student Activity Manual to Accompany the Text: A Clinical Management of Articulatory & Phonological Disorders. Kathryn O. Falconer. (Illus.). 79p. (Orig.). 1991. pap. 15.00 (*1-878276-35-2*) Educ Systs Assocs Inc.

Student Advancement Programs: Shaping Tomorrow's Alumni Leaders Today. Ed. by Barbara T. Todd. 167p. 1993. pap. 41.50 (*0-89964-298-5*, 28602) Coun Adv & Supp Ed.

***Student Advantage Guide to America's Top Internships, 1998.** Mark Oldman. 1997. pap. 21.00 (*0-679-78394-6*) Random.

Student Advantage Guide to Paying for College, 1997. Kalman A. Chany. 1996. pap. 18.00 (*0-679-77363-0*) Random.

Student Advantage Guide to Summer: 1996 Edition. Michael Freedman. (Princeton Review Ser.). 1996. pap. 18.00 (*0-679-76470-4*, Villard Bks) Random.

Student Advantage Guide To Summer, 1997 Edition. Michael Freedman. 1996. pap. 18.00 (*0-679-77362-2*) Random.

Student Advantage Guide to the Best Graduate Programs: Humanities & Social Sciences. Nell Goddin. (Princeton Review Ser.). 300p. 1997. pap. 24.00 (*0-679-76911-0*) Random.

***Student Advantage Guide to the Best Graduate Programs, 1997-1998.** Jonathan Spaihts. (Princeton Review Ser.). 1997. pap. 24.00 (*0-679-77888-8*, Villard Bks) Random.

Student Advantage Guide to the Best Graduate Schools: Health Professions: 1997 Edition. Joe Sampson. (Princeton Review Ser.). 300p. 1997. pap. 20.00 (*0-679-77107-7*, Villard Bks) Random.

***Student Advantage Guide to the Best 311 Colleges, 1998.** Princeton Review Publishing Staff. 1997. pap. 20.00 (*0-679-78397-0*) Random.

***Student Advantage Guide to the Complete Book of Colleges, 1998.** Princeton Review Publishing Staff. 1997. pap. 26.95 (*0-679-78398-9*) Random.

Student Advantage Guide to Visiting College Campuses: 1996 Edition. Janet Spencer & Sandra Maleson. (Princeton Review Ser.). 1996. pap. 19.95 (*0-679-76988-9*, Villard Bks) Random.

Student Affairs: A Profession's Heritage. 2nd ed. Ed. by Audrey L. Rentz. LC 94-19521. 782p. (C). 1995. pap. text ed. 44.50 (*1-883485-06-1*) Am Coll Personnel.

Student Affairs: A Profession's Heritage. 28th ed. Ed. by Audrey L. Rentz. LC 94-19521. 782p. (C). 1994. lib. bdg. 75.00 (*1-883485-05-3*) Am Coll Personnel.

Student Affairs & the Law. Ed. by Margaret J. Barr. LC 82-84204. (New Directions for Student Services Ser.: No. 22). 105p. 1983. 19.00 (*0-87589-970-6*) Jossey-Bass.

Student Affairs Decisions & the Law. Kent M. Weeks. 65p. (C). 1991. pap. text ed. write for info. (*1-881434-02-8*) Coll Legal Info.

Student Affairs Decisions & the Law. Kent M. Weeks. 72p. (C). 1992. pap. text ed. write for info. (*1-881434-01-X*) Coll Legal Info.

Student Affairs Functions in Higher Education see Student Affairs Practice in Higher Education

***Student Affairs Practice in Higher Education.** 2nd ed. Audrey L. Rentz. (Illus.). 426p. 1996. pap. 54.95 (*0-398-06675-2*) C C Thomas.

Student Affairs Practice in Higher Education. 2nd rev. ed. Ed. by Audrey L. Rentz. LC 96-12918. Orig. Title: Student Affairs Functions in Higher Education. (Illus.). 426p. 1996. 69.95 (*0-398-06658-2*) C C Thomas.

***Student Affairs Reconsidered: A Christian View of the Profession & Its Contexts.** David S. Guthrie. LC 97-17068. 1997. write for info. (*0-7618-0794-2*); pap. write for info. (*0-7618-0795-0*) U Pr of Amer.

Student Aggression: Prevention, Management, & Replacement Training. Arnold P. Goldstein et al. LC 93-34735. 280p. 1994. lib. bdg. 31.50 (*0-89862-246-8*) Guilford Pr.

Student Aid: Bases of Selection of Students to Whom Loans, Scholarships & Fellowships Are Awarded in a Graduate School of Education. Margaret R. Smith. LC 75-177766. (Columbia University. Teachers College. Contributions to Education Ser.: No. 704). reprint ed. 37.50 (*0-404-55704-X*) AMS Pr.

***Student Aid Game: Meeting Need & Rewarding Talent in American Higher Education.** Michael S. McPherson & Morton O. Schapiro. LC 97-14999. 1997. write for info. (*0-691-05783-4*) Princeton U Pr.

Student Aid in the Secondary Schools of the United States. V. A. Carley. LC 77-176626. (Columbia University. Teachers College. Contributions to Education Ser.: No. 594). reprint ed. 37.50 (*0-404-55594-2*) AMS Pr.

Student Aide. Jack Rudman. (Career Examination Ser.: C-1496). 1994. pap. 23.95 (*0-8373-1496-8*) Nat Learn.

Student & Singer. Charles Santley. LC 80-2756. reprint ed. 39.50 (*0-404-18866-4*) AMS Pr.

Student & Teacher Commitment: A Study & Recommendations. William A. Firestone et al. 94p. 1990. pap. 21.95 (*1-56602-032-8*) Research Better.

Student Anthologies. (C). 1993. pap. 58.84 (*0-395-63541-1*) HM.

Student Applications Guide to Accompany Wolford-Vanneman, Business Communication. Robert J. Motley. 378p. (C). 1993. student ed., pap. text ed. 23.00 (*0-15-500252-X*) Dryden Pr.

Student Applications in Databases. Linda Hazelip & Frances Roberson. 15p. 1989. student ed. 3.50 (*1-880967-02-2*) LHR Assocs.

Student Applications in Spreadsheets. Linda Hazelip & Frances Roberson. 15p. 1989. student ed. 3.50 (*1-880967-01-4*) LHR Assocs.

Student Applications in Word Processing. Linda Hazelip & Frances Roberson. 42p. 1989. student ed. 5.00 (*1-880967-00-6*) LHR Assocs.

Student Aptitude Test: Barber. Milady Publishing Company Staff. (Cosmetology Ser.). 1983. pap. 6.50 (*0-87350-867-X*) Van Nos Reinhold.

Student Aptitude Test: Cosmetology. Milady Publishing Company Staff. (Cosmetology Ser.). 1973. pap. 6.50 (*0-87350-878-5*) Van Nos Reinhold.

Student As Commuter: Developing a Comprehensive Institutional Response. Ed. by Barbara C. Jacoby. LC 89-63438. (ASHE-ERIC Higher Education Reports: No. 7, 1989). 101p. (Orig.). (C). 1989. pap. text ed. 15.00 (*0-9623882-6-2*) GWU Grad Schl E&HD.

***Student Assessment in Calculus: A Report of the NSF Working Group on Assessment in Calculus.** Ed. by Alan Schoenfeld. LC 97-70507. (MAA Notes Ser.: No. 43). 136p. (Orig.). 1997. pap. text ed. 29.95 (*0-88385-152-0*, NTE-43/PMDS97) Math Assn.

Student Assistance Program: How it Works. rev. ed. Tom Griffin & Roger Svendsen. 68p. 1986. pap. 10.00 (*0-89486-350-9*) Hazelden.

Student Assistance Programs: Guidelines for Planning, Implementation & Evaluation. 1995. 10.75 (*0-917160-30-4*) Am Sch Health.

Student Assistants in Archival Repositories: A Handbook for Managers. SAA College & University Archives Section Staff. 56p. 1992. 15.00 (*0-931828-87-2*) Soc Am Archivists.

Student Athletes: Shattering the Myths & Sharing the Realities. Ed. by Sarah V. Kirk & Wyatt D. Kirk. LC 92-18721. 173p. (C). 1993. pap. text ed. 19.95 (*1-55620-098-6*, 72058) Am Coun Assn.

Student Athlete's Guide to Colleges & Universities. Jo Ann M. Arrietta. LC 96-68052. 780p. (YA). (gr. 11-12). 1996. pap. 24.95 (*0-9649252-0-6*) J Nick Pubns.

***Student Athlete's Guide to Colleges & Universities.** 2nd ed. Joey Arrietta. 1997. pap. 28.95 (*0-9649252-1-4*) J Nick Pubns.

***Student Athlete's Handbook: The Complete Guide for Success.** Perry Bromwell & Howard Gensler. LC 97-19049. 256p. (YA). (gr. 12). 1997. pap. 14.95 (*0-471-14975-6*) Wiley.

Student Atlas. Michael Dempsey. Ed. by John C. Miles & Constance Novis. LC 90-675152. (Illus.). 128p. (J). (gr. 3-7). 1996. pap. 9.95 (*0-8167-2254-4*) Troll Communs.

Student Atlas of California. 4th annot. rev. ed. Rice D. Oliver. (Illus.). 74p. (J). (gr. 4-8). 1993. teacher ed., pap. 14.00 (*0-936778-64-4*) Calif Weekly.

Student Atlas of California. 4th rev. ed. Rice D. Oliver. (Illus.). 66p. (J). (gr. 4-8). 1993. pap. text ed. 11.00 (*0-936778-63-6*) Calif Weekly.

Student Atlas of the Bible. American Map Corp. Staff. (Series 9500). (Illus.). 1994. 6.95 (*0-8416-9559-8*) Am Map.

Student Atlas of the World. rev. ed. Hammond, Inc. Staff. (YA). (gr. 8-12). 1995. pap. text ed. 6.75 (*0-8437-7926-8*) Hammond Inc.

***Student Atlas Study Book.** Moroz. 1990. pap. text ed. write for info. (*0-582-87067-4*, Pub. by Longman UK) Longman.

Student Bass Method. William Bay. 1993. 5.95 (*0-87166-883-1*, 94097) Mel Bay.

Student Bass Method - Metodado Para el Estudiante de Bajo. William Bay. (SPA.). 1993. 5.95 (*1-56222-184-1*, 94563SP) Mel Bay.

Student Behavior in Art Classrooms: The Dynamics of Discipline. Frank Susi. 41p. (Orig.). 1995. pap. text ed. 20.00 (*0-937652-75-X*, 219) Natl Art Ed.

Student Behavior Management & School-to-Work: A Practitioner's Guide. Carl Sargent & Larry Spier. 28p. 1996. spiral bd. 4.95 (*1-884362-11-7*) Butte Pubns.

Student Behavior Problems: Widening Horizons, New Challenges, Directions & Achievements. Mark Tainsh & John Izard. 1995. pap. 70.00 (*0-86431-165-6*, Pub. by Aust Council Educ Res AT) St Mut.

Student Behaviour: Theory & Practice for Teachers. Louise Porter. 352p. 1996. pap. 34.95 (*1-86373-956-4*, Pub. by Allen Unwin AT) Paul & Co Pubs.

Student Behaviour Problems: Context, Initiatives & Programs. John Elkins & John Izard. (C). 1992. 80.00 (*0-86431-126-5*, Pub. by Aust Council Educ Res AT) St Mut.

Student Behaviour Problems: Directions, Perspectives & Expectations. Bill Willis & John Izard. (C). 1992. 80.00 (*0-86431-134-6*, Pub. by Aust Council Educ Res AT) St Mut.

Student Behaviour Problems: Positive Iritiatives & New Frontiers. David Evans. 1994. 70.00 (*0-86431-146-X*, Pub. by Aust Council Educ Res AT) St Mut.

Student Bible Atlas. Tim Dowley. LC 95-43345. (Illus.). 32p. (J). 1996. pap. 4.99 (*0-8066-2038-2*, 9-2038, Augsburg) Augsburg Fortress.

Student Bible Guide. Tim Dowley. LC 95-47644. (Illus.). 32p. (J). 1996. pap. 4.99 (*0-8066-2040-4*, 9-2040, Augsburg) Augsburg Fortress.

***Student Bible Guide to Jerusalem.** Robert Backhouse. LC 97-1657. (J). 1997. write for info. (*0-8066-3340-9*) Augsburg Fortress.

Student Bible Timeline see Cronologia Biblica Portavoz

Student Body. J. S. Borthwick. 304p. 1991. mass mkt. 4.50 (*0-312-92605-7*) St Martin.

Student Body. Diane Hoh. (Nightmare Hall Ser.: No. 21). 176p. (YA). (gr. 7-9). 1995. pap. 3.50 (*0-590-20299-5*) Scholastic Inc.

Student Body. Nicholas Pine. (Terror Academy Ser.: No. 6). (YA). 1993. mass mkt. 3.99 (*0-425-13983-2*) Berkley Pub.

Student Body: A Survival Guide to College Eating & Weight Control. Jane E. Myers & Jill Brown. 90p. (C). 1993. pap. 11.95 (*0-9635449-1-8*) Two-J Bks.

Student Book Classroom Library. Melvin Berger. Ed. by Susan Evento. (Macmillan Early Science Big Bks.). (Illus.). (J). (ps-2). 1995. pap. write for info. (*1-56784-190-2*) Newbridge Comms.

Student Book Starter Set. Melvin Berger. Ed. by Susan Evento. (Macmillan Early Science Big Bks.). (Illus.). (J). (ps-2). 1995. pap. write for info. (*1-56784-191-0*) Newbridge Comms.

Student C Set: Organic Chemistry Model. Benjamin Maruzen. (C). 1995. pap. text ed. write for info. (*0-7167-1972-X*) W H Freeman.

Student Calculator. Linda Hazelip & Frances Roberson. 92p. 1991. pap. text ed. 10.00 (*1-880967-08-1*) LHR Assocs.

Student Case Book on Business Entities. Ed. by J. T. Pretorius. 256p. 1994. pap. 20.00 (*0-7021-3337-X*, Pub. by Juta SA) Gaunt.

Student Cassette Series, Set C. rev. ed. Beverly L. Ritter. (Realtime Machine Shorthand Ser.). 29p. (C). 1993. pap. text ed. 30.00 incl. audio (*0-938643-19-3*, 703) Stenotype Educ.

Student Cassette Series, Set D. rev. ed. Beverly L. Ritter. (Realtime Machine Shorthand Ser.). 40p. (C). 1993. pap. text ed. 31.25 incl. audio (*0-938643-20-7*, 704) Stenotype Educ.

Student Cassette Series, Set A. rev. ed. Beverly L. Ritter. (Realtime Machine Shorthand Ser.). 6p. (C). 1993. pap. text ed. 27.50 incl. audio (*0-938643-17-7*, 701) Stenotype Educ.

Student Cassette Series, Set B. rev. ed. Beverly L. Ritter. (Realtime Machine Shorthand Ser.). 24p. (C). 1993. pap. text ed. 28.75 incl. audio (*0-938643-18-5*, 702) Stenotype Educ.

Student Cassette Series, Set E. rev. ed. Beverly L. Ritter. (Realtime Machine Shorthand Ser.). 70p. (C). 1993. pap. text ed. 32.50 incl. audio (*0-938643-21-5*, 705) Stenotype Educ.

Student Cassette Series, Set F. Beverly L. Ritter. (Realtime Machine Shorthand Ser.). 63p. (C). 1993. pap. text ed. 35.00 incl. digital audio (0-938643-22-3) Stenotype Educ.

Student Cassette Series, Set G. Beverly L. Ritter. (Realtime Machine Shorthand Ser.). 73p. (C). 1993. pap. text ed. 35.00 incl. digital audio (0-938643-23-1) Stenotype Educ.

Student-Centered Classroom Management. Beatrice Fennimore. (Teaching Methods Ser.). 256p. 1996. teacher ed., pap. 24.50 (0-8273-6692-2) Delmar.

Student-Centered Language Arts, K-12. 4th ed. James Moffett & Betty J. Wagner. LC 91-29010. 437p. 1991. pap. text ed. 32.50 (0-86709-292-0, 0292) Boynton Cook Pubs.

Student Chord Writing Book. 1.95 (0-87166-657-X, 93691) Mel Bay.

Student Clarinetist: A Method for Class Instruction, 3 bks. rev. ed. Benjamin D. Spieler. (Illus.). (J). (gr. 4-9). 1989. pap. write for info. (0-318-65497-0) Player Pr.

Student Clarinetist: A Method for Class Instruction, 3 bks., Bk. I. rev. ed. Benjamin D. Spieler. (Illus.). 56p. (J). (gr. 4-9). 1989. pap. 2.80 (0-685-74121-4) Player Pr.

Student Clarinetist: A Method for Class Instruction, 3 bks., Bk. II. rev. ed. Benjamin D. Spieler. (Illus.). 64p. (J). (gr. 4-9). 1989. pap. 2.80 (0-685-74122-2) Player Pr.

Student Clarinetist: A Method for Class Instruction, 3 bks., Bk. III. rev. ed. Benjamin D. Spieler. (Illus.). 36p. (J). (gr. 4-9). 1989. pap. 2.80 (0-685-74123-0) Player Pr.

Student Community at Aberdeen, 1860-1939. R. D. Anderson. (Quincentennial Studies in the History of the University of Aberdeen). 146p. 1988. pap. 17.00 (0-08-036588-4, Pub. by Aberdeen U Pr) Macmillan.

***Student Companion.** 2nd ed. Best. 1991. pap. text ed. write for info. (0-582-07517-3, Pub. by Longman UK) Longman.

Student Concerto No. 2 in G Major for Violin & Piano, Op. 13. F. Seitz. (Carl Fischer Music Library: No. 591). 1904. pap. 7.00 (0-8258-0078-1, L591) Fischer Inc NY.

Student Concerto No. 3 in G Minor, for Violin & Piano, Op. 12. Seitz. (Carl Fischer Music Library: No. 592). 1906. pap. 6.95 (0-8258-0079-X, L592) Fischer Inc NY.

Student Conference Follow-Up Manual. Dawson McAllister. (Illus.). (J). (gr. 5-12). 1989. pap. 2.95 (0-923417-10-9) Shepherd Minst.

***Student Connections.** Carolyn J. Brown. (Illus.). 22p. 1995. teacher ed., spiral bd. 25.00 (1-890891-05-3) Breakthrough Inc.

***Student Contact Book.** 2nd ed. 1998. 35.00 (0-8103-9086-8, 00009237, Gale Res Intl) Gale.

Student Contact Book: A Guide to Organizations & People that Provide Free & Low-Cost Information on Current Topics & Issues. 525p. 1992. 35.00 (0-8103-8876-6, 101525) Gale.

Student Contracts. Thorwald Esbensen. Ed. by Danny G. Langdon. LC 77-25411. (Instructional Design Library). (Illus.). 100p. 1978. 27.95 (0-87778-121-4) Educ Tech Pubns.

Student Council Handbook. rev. ed. 1990. 15.00 (0-685-34752-4, 6207523) Natl Assn Student.

Student Culture: Social Structure & Continuity in a Liberal Arts College. Walter L. Wallace. LC 66-15212. (Monographs in Social Research: No. 9). 1966. 9.50 (0-202-09006-X) Natl Opinion Res.

Student Culture & Activism in Black South African Universities: The Roots of Resistance. Mokubung Nkomo. LC 84-3819. (Contributions in Afro-American & African Studies: No. 78). (Illus.). xiii, 209p. 1984. text ed. 55.00 (0-313-24357-3, NSC/) Greenwood.

Student Day Planner. Contrib. by Joellyn Cicciarelli. (Daily Planners Ser.). 112p. (Orig.). (J). (gr. 4-8). 1995. spiral bd., pap. 7.98 (0-916119-94-7) Creat Teach Pr.

Student Developing Choir: Essential Repertoire Treble. 12.95 (0-7935-4341-X, 08740095) H Leonard.

***Student Development.** (Contemporary Higher Education Ser.). 400p. 1997. text ed. 75.00 (0-8153-2663-7) Garland.

Student Development & College Teaching. Ronda Beaman. 140p. (Orig.). (C). 1995. pap. text ed. 18.95 (0-943025-67-2) Cummngs & Hath.

***Student Development in Student Activities.** Nancy D. Metz. 141p. 1996. pap. 55.00 (0-923276-06-8) Assn Coll Unions Intl.

Student Diagnosis, Placement, & Prescription: A Criterion-Referenced Approach. Roger B. Worner. LC 76-26432. (Illus.). 251p. reprint ed. 71.60 (0-8357-9243-9, 2015839) Bks Demand.

***Student Dictionary of Compound Words of the Russian Language.** P. N. Denisova & V. V. Morkovkina. 688p. (C). 1978. 25.95 (0-8285-5190-1) Firebird NY.

Student Dictionary of Music Terms. 1993. pap. 1.95 (0-933224-21-4, T/44) Bold Strummer Ltd.

Student Dictionary with Merriam-Webster Phonetic Key. 1976. pap. 6.25 (0-87738-021-X) Youth Ed.

Student-Directed Learning: Teaching Self-Determination Skills. Martin Agran. (C). 1997. teacher ed., pap. text ed. write for info. (0-534-34069-5) Brooks-Cole.

Student-Directed Learning: Teaching Self-Determination Skills. Martin Agran. LC 96-34861. (Special Educations Ser.). (Illus.). 449p. 1997. pap. 45.95 (0-534-15942-7) Brooks-Cole.

***Student Discipline in American Higher Education.** Michael Dannells. Ed. by Jonathan D. Fife. (ASHE-ERIC Higher Education Reports). 100p. (Orig.). 1997. pap. 21.75 (1-878380-74-5) GWU Grad Schl E&HD.

Student Discipline Strategies: Research & Practice. Oliver C. Moles. LC 89-4578. (SUNY Series, Educational Leadership). 331p. 1990. text ed. 64.50 (0-7914-0192-8); pap. text ed. 23.95 (0-7914-0193-6) State U NY Pr.

Student Edition of Lotus 1-2-3 Release 2.4. Timothy J. O'Leary & Linda L. O'Leary. 524p. (C). student ed., pap. text ed. 44.99 incl. 3.5 hd (0-8053-1353-2); student ed. 44.99 incl. 3.5 hd (0-685-73067-0) Benjamin-Cummings.

Student Edition of Lotus 1-2-3 Release 2.4. Timothy J. O'Leary. (C). 1994. pap. 35.00 incl. disk (0-8053-1354-0) Benjamin-Cummings.

***Student Employment: Linking College & the Workplace, No. 23.** Ed. by Rick Kincaid. 137p. 1997. 30.00 (1-889271-22-5) Nat Res Ctr.

Student Employment Directory. 2nd ed. Ed. by Carolyn Schulze & Richard Schulze. 1977. 4.95 (0-686-18796-2) Shaker Prairie.

Student Encyclopedia. Michael W. Dempsey & Keith Lye. LC 90-11116. (Illus.). 128p. (J). (gr. 3-7). 1991. lib. bdg. 15.50 (0-8167-2257-9) Troll Communs.

Student Encyclopedia. Michael W. Dempsey & Keith Lye. LC 90-11116. (Illus.). 128p. (J). (gr. 3-7). 1996. pap. 9.95 (0-8167-2258-7) Troll Communs.

Student Encyclopedia 1981, Vol. 1. 1981. 18.00 (0-02-945450-6) Mac Lib Ref.

Student Encyclopedia 1981, Vol. 4. 1981. 18.00 (0-02-945480-8) Mac Lib Ref.

Student Encyclopedia 1981, Vol. 6. 1981. 18.00 (0-02-945500-6) Mac Lib Ref.

Student Encyclopedia 1982, Vol. 1. 1982. 20.00 (0-02-945670-3) Mac Lib Ref.

Student Encyclopedia 1982, Vol. 2. 1982. 20.00 (0-02-945680-0) Mac Lib Ref.

Student Encyclopedia 1982, Vol. 3. 1982. 20.00 (0-02-945690-8) Mac Lib Ref.

Student Encyclopedia 1982, Vol. 7. 1982. 20.00 (0-02-945730-0) Mac Lib Ref.

Student Encyclopedia 1982, Vol. 8. 1982. 20.00 (0-02-945740-8) Mac Lib Ref.

Student Encyclopedia 1982, Vol. 9. 1982. 20.00 (0-02-945750-5) Mac Lib Ref.

Student Encyclopedia 1982, Vol. 11. 1982. 20.00 (0-02-945770-X) Mac Lib Ref.

Student Encyclopedia 1982, Vol. 12. 1982. 20.00 (0-02-945780-7) Mac Lib Ref.

Student Encyclopedia 1982, Vol. 13. 1982. 20.00 (0-02-945790-4) Mac Lib Ref.

Student Encyclopedia 1982, Vol. 14. 1982. 20.00 (0-02-945800-5) Mac Lib Ref.

Student Encyclopedia 1982, Vol. 15. 1982. 20.00 (0-02-945810-2) Mac Lib Ref.

Student Encyclopedia 1982, Vol. 16. 1982. 20.00 (0-02-945820-X) Mac Lib Ref.

Student Encyclopedia 1982, Vol. 18. 1982. 20.00 (0-02-945840-4) Mac Lib Ref.

Student Encyclopedia 1982, Vol. 20. 1982. 20.00 (0-02-945860-9) Mac Lib Ref.

Student Encyclopedia 1984, Vol. 1. 1984. 22.00 (0-02-944870-0) Mac Lib Ref.

Student Encyclopedia 1984, Vol. 2. 1984. 22.00 (0-02-944860-3) Mac Lib Ref.

Student Encyclopedia 1984, Vol. 3. 1984. 22.00 (0-02-944850-6) Mac Lib Ref.

Student Encyclopedia 1984, Vol. 4. 1984. 22.00 (0-02-944840-9) Mac Lib Ref.

Student Encyclopedia 1984, Vol. 5. 1984. 22.00 (0-02-944830-1) Mac Lib Ref.

Student Encyclopedia 1984, Vol. 6. 1984. 22.00 (0-02-944820-4) Mac Lib Ref.

Student Encyclopedia 1984, Vol. 7. 1984. 22.00 (0-02-944810-7) Mac Lib Ref.

Student Encyclopedia 1984, Vol. 8. 1984. 22.00 (0-02-944800-X) Mac Lib Ref.

Student Encyclopedia 1984, Vol. 9. 1984. 22.00 (0-02-944790-9) Mac Lib Ref.

Student Encyclopedia 1984, Vol. 10. 1984. 22.00 (0-02-944780-1) Mac Lib Ref.

Student Encyclopedia 1984, Vol. 11. 1984. 22.00 (0-02-944770-4) Mac Lib Ref.

Student Encyclopedia 1984, Vol. 12. 1984. 22.00 (0-02-944760-7) Mac Lib Ref.

Student Encyclopedia 1984, Vol. 13. 1984. 22.00 (0-02-944750-X) Mac Lib Ref.

Student Encyclopedia 1984, Vol. 14. 1984. 22.00 (0-02-944740-2) Mac Lib Ref.

Student Encyclopedia 1984, Vol. 15. 1984. 22.00 (0-02-944730-5) Mac Lib Ref.

Student Encyclopedia 1984, Vol. 16. 1984. 22.00 (0-02-944720-8) Mac Lib Ref.

Student Encyclopedia 1984, Vol. 17. 1984. 22.00 (0-02-944710-0) Mac Lib Ref.

Student Encyclopedia 1984, Vol. 18. 1984. 22.00 (0-02-944700-3) Mac Lib Ref.

Student Encyclopedia 1984, Vol. 19. 1984. 22.00 (0-02-944690-2) Mac Lib Ref.

Student Encyclopedia 1984, Vol. 20. 1984. 22.00 (0-02-944680-5) Mac Lib Ref.

Student Encyclopedia, 1985, 20 vols. Incl. Vol. 1. . 1985. 25.00 (0-02-943530-7); Vol. 2. . 1985. 25.00 (0-02-943540-4); Vol. 3. . 1985. 25.00 (0-02-943550-1); Vol. 4. . 1985. 25.00 (0-02-943560-9); Vol. 5. . 1985. 25.00 (0-02-943570-6); Vol. 6. . 1985. 25.00 (0-02-943580-3); Vol. 7. . 1985. 25.00 (0-02-943590-0); Vol. 8. . 1985. 25.00 (0-02-943600-1); Vol. 9. . 1985. 25.00 (0-02-943610-9); Vol. 10. . 1985. 25.00 (0-02-943620-6); Vol. 11. . 1985. 25.00 (0-02-943630-3); Vol. 12. . 1985. 25.00 (0-02-943640-0); Vol. 13. . 1985. 25.00 (0-02-943650-8); Vol. 14. . 1985. 25.00 (0-02-943660-5); Vol. 15. . 1985. 25.00 (0-02-943670-2); Vol. 16. . 1985. 25.00 (0-02-943680-X); Vol. 17. . 1985. 25.00 (0-02-943690-7); Vol. 18. . 1985. 25.00 (0-02-943700-8); Vol. 19. . 1985. 25.00 (0-02-943710-5); Vol. 20. . 1985. 25.00 (0-02-943720-2); 399.00 (0-02-943520-X) Mac Lib Ref.

Student Energy Awareness Journal: Project Energy '93. Ed. by Beverley Billings & Steve R. Merkley. (Illus.). 450p. 1993. 20.00 (0-9631634-3-4) Intl Acad Science.

Student Engagement & Achievement in American Secondary Schools. Ed. by Fred M. Newmann. LC 92-15727. 240p. (C). 1992. 38.00 (0-8077-3183-8); pap. 17.95 (0-8077-3182-X) Tchrs Coll.

Student English Arabic Dictionary (Al-Mughni Plus) Hasan S. Karmi. (Al-Muhni Plus Ser.). 720p. (ARA & ENG.). 1994. student ed. 25.00 (0-86685-644-7, LDL6447, Pub. by Librairie du Liban FR) Intl Bk Ctr.

Student Environment Action Guide. HarperCollins Staff & Earth Works Group Staff. (C). 1991. text ed. 6.95 (0-06-500432-9) Addson-Wesley Educ.

Student Environmental Action Guide. Student Environmental Action Co. Staff. 96p. 1991. pap. 4.95 (1-879682-04-4) Earth Works.

Student Essential Musicianship, Bk. 1. 192p. 1995. 9.95 (0-7935-4329-0, 08740069) H Leonard.

Student Evaluation Package. Donald R. Byrd. 176p. 1994. pap. text ed. 21.00 (0-13-832593-6); audio 10.50 (0-13-826629-8) P-H.

Student Evaluation Portfolio: Level ABC. Read. 1991. pap. write for info. (0-395-55914-6) HM.

Student Evaluation Portfolio: Level 1. Read. 1991. pap. write for info. (0-395-55915-4) HM.

Student Evaluation Portfolio: Level 1. Read. 1993. pap. write for info. (0-395-64854-8) HM.

Student Evaluation Portfolio: Level 1+ Read. 1991. pap. write for info. (0-395-55916-2) HM.

Student Evaluation Portfolio: Level 1+ Read. 1993. pap. write for info. (0-395-64855-6) HM.

Student Evaluation Portfolio: Level 2. Read. 1991. pap. write for info. (0-395-55917-0) HM.

Student Evaluation Portfolio: Level 2. Read. 1993. pap. write for info. (0-395-64856-4) HM.

Student Evaluation Portfolio: Level 2+ Read. 1991. pap. write for info. (0-395-55918-9) HM.

Student Evaluation Portfolio: Level 2+ Read. 1993. pap. write for info. (0-395-64857-2) HM.

Student Evaluation Portfolio: Level 3. Read. 1991. pap. write for info. (0-395-55919-7) HM.

Student Evaluation Portfolio: Level 3. Read. 1993. pap. write for info. (0-395-64858-0) HM.

Student Evaluation Portfolio: Level 3+ Read. 1991. pap. write for info. (0-395-55920-0) HM.

Student Evaluation Portfolio: Level 3+ Read. 1993. pap. write for info. (0-395-64859-9) HM.

Student Evaluation Portfolio: Level 4. Read. 1991. pap. write for info. (0-395-55921-9) HM.

Student Evaluation Portfolio: Level 4. Read. 1993. pap. write for info. (0-395-64860-2) HM.

Student Evaluation Portfolio: Level 5. Read. 1991. pap. write for info. (0-395-55922-7) HM.

Student Evaluation Portfolio: Level 5. Read. 1993. pap. write for info. (0-395-64861-0) HM.

Student Evaluation Portfolio: Level 6. Read. 1991. pap. write for info. (0-395-55923-5) HM.

Student Evaluation Portfolio: Level 6. Read. 1993. pap. write for info. (0-395-64862-9) HM.

Student Evaluation Portfolio: Level 7. Read. 1991. pap. write for info. (0-395-55924-3) HM.

Student Evaluation Portfolio: Level 8. Read. 1991. pap. write for info. (0-395-55925-1) HM.

***Student Exchange.** M. T. Coffin. (Spinetinglers Ser.: No. 22). (J). (gr. 3-7). 1997. pap. 3.99 (0-380-78804-7, Camelot) Avon.

Student Execustat 3.0: Miniguide. S. Christian Albright. 152p. 1994. pap. 20.95 (0-534-22014-2) Wadsworth Pub.

Student Experience. Ed. by Susan Haselgrove. LC 94-25732. 192p. 1994. 85.00 (0-335-19335-8, Open Univ Pr); pap. 32.00 (0-335-19358-7) Taylor & Francis.

Student-Faculty Relations in Medical School: A Study of Professional Socialization. David Caplovitz. Ed. by Harriet Zuckerman & Robert K. Merton. LC 79-8980. (Dissertations on Sociology Ser.). 1980. lib. bdg. 29.95 (0-405-12956-4) Ayer.

Student Financial Aid & Women: Equity Dilemma? Mary Moran. LC 86-72856. (ASHE-ERIC Higher Education Reports: No. 5, 1986). 153p. (Orig.). 1987. pap. 10.00 (0-913317-32-2) GWU Grad Schl E&HD.

Student Folkways & Spending at Indiana University, 1940-1941. Mary M. Crawford. LC 68-58563. (Columbia University. Studies in the Social Sciences: No. 499). reprint ed. 34.50 (0-404-51499-5) AMS Pr.

Student Generations. Stephen I. Brown. (Hi Map Ser.: No. 7). (Illus.). 60p. pap. text ed. 9.99 (0-614-05320-X, HM 5607) COMAP Inc.

Student Goals for College & Courses: A Missing Link in Assessing & Improving Academic Achievement. Kathleen M. Shaw & Malcolm A. Lowther. Ed. by Joan S. Stark et al. LC 89-63442. (ASHE-ERIC Higher Education Reports: No. 6, 1989). 110p. (Orig.). (C). 1989. pap. text ed. 15.00 (0-9623882-4-6) GWU Grad Schl E&HD.

Student Grub Guide. Alastair Williams. (Illus.). 160p. 1996. pap. 9.95 (1-873475-24-1) Howell Pr VA.

Student Guide & Resource Manual to Accompany Human Development, 2nd ed. Lawrence B. Schiamberg & Gale S. Schiamberg. 179p. (C). 1985. pap. text ed. 29.40 (0-02-406900-0, Macmillan Coll) P-H.

Student Guide Biosphere. 2nd ed. Donald D. Kaufman & Cecilia Franz. 320p. (C). 1995. per., pap. text ed. 29.53 (0-7872-0461-7) Kendall-Hunt.

Student Guide for Course 6/Course 340. Jennifer Herrod et al. (FLMI Insurance Education Program Ser.). 1995. student ed., pap. text ed. 10.00 (0-939921-71-5) Life Office.

Student Guide Health Occupation Clinical Experience. Thomson. (Health Occupations Ser.). 1996. teacher ed. 12.00 (0-8273-6291-9) Delmar.

Student Guide Health Occupation Clinical Experience. Thomson. (Health Occupations Ser.). 272p. 1997. 19.95 (0-8273-6290-0) Delmar.

Student Guide Prentice Hall 1988 Federal Tax Course. Dale D. Bandy. (Illus.). 304p. (C). 1987. pap. text ed. write for info. (0-13-313065-7) P-H.

***Student Guide to America's 100 Best College Buys: 1997-1998.** Lewis T. Lindsey. 1997. pap. text ed. 17.95 (1-887269-26-6) J Culler & Sons.

Student Guide to Bible People. Robert Backhouse. LC 95-47645. (Illus.). 32p. (J). 1996. pap. 4.99 (0-8066-2039-0, 9-2039, Augsburg) Augsburg Fortress.

Student Guide to Boston. Andrea Brox. pap. 9.95 (0-924771-21-6) Brick Hse Pub.

Student Guide to Buildability. Neale. Date not set. pap. write for info. (0-7506-1055-7) Buttrwrth-Heinemann.

Student Guide to Engineering Report Writing see **Engineering Report Writing**

Student Guide to Helicopter Flight Maneuvers. Knight. 98p. 1987. pap. 19.95 (0-685-24702-3) Aviation.

Student Guide to Japanese Sources in the Humanities. Yasuko Makino & Masaei Saito. LC 93-34031. (Michigan Papers in Japanese Studies: No. 24). ix, 155p. (C). 1994. pap. 17.95 (0-939512-64-5) U MI Japan.

Student Guide to Language Skills. rev. ed. Keith D. Holmes. (Illus.). 95p. (Orig.). (C). 1983. reprint ed. 7.75 (0-9608250-2-9) Educ Serv Pub.

Student Guide to Relapse Prevention. Thomas J. Shiltz. (Illus.). 82p. (Orig.). 1991. student ed. 6.95 (0-9618023-3-2) Community Rec Pr.

Student Guide to Research-Doctorate Programs in the United States. National Research Council Committee on the Study of Research-Doctorate Programs in the U. S. 250p. (Orig.). 1997. pap. 19.95 (0-309-05444-3) Natl Acad Pr.

Student Guide to Research in Social Science. Renate Howe & Ros Lewis. LC 92-39527. 1994. pap. 15.95 (0-521-40888-1) Cambridge U Pr.

Student Guide to Structural Design. S. A. Lavan & B. G. Fletcher. (Illus.). 105p. 1989. pap. 39.95 (0-408-02171-3) Buttrwrth-Heinemann.

Student Guide to the Bible see **Guia Biblica Portavoz**

***Studen't Guide to the Cohens of Tzefat.** Yitzchak Kasnett. (J). pap. 3.99 (0-89906-849-9, SGCO) Mesorah Pubns.

Student Guide to the Genitive of Agent in Indo-European Languages. William R. Schmalstieg. (Journal of Indo-European Studies Monograph: No. 14). 54p. 1995. pap. text ed. 18.00 (0-941694-47-X) Inst Study Man.

Student Guide to the Internet. Carol L. Clark. LC 95-35805. 184p. 1995. pap. text ed. 19.20 (0-13-442310-0) P-H.

Student Guide to the Registered Nurse (R.N.) Examination. Maryanne C. Glynn. Ed. by David M. Tarlow. (Illus.). 1981. pap. 12.95 (0-931572-03-7) Datar Pub.

Student Guide to the World's Medical Schools Where the Language of Instruction Is in English. David M. Tarlow. 1993. pap. 12.95 (0-931572-02-9) Datar Pub.

Student Handbook: How to Succeed in School & College. Charles A Heidenreich. 1973. 3.00 (0-9600428-2-2) Heidenreich.

Student Handbook Education 164. Dennis Nord. 68p. (C). 1994. per. 8.34 (0-8403-9335-0) Kendall-Hunt.

Student Handbook for Concepts of Genetics. 4th ed. Harry Nickla. (Illus.). 283p. (C). 1994. pap. text ed. 25.00 (0-02-386722-1, Macmillan Coll) P-H.

Student Handbook on the Basics of Elementary Harmony. Darrell R. Douglas. LC 93-4189. (Illus.). 208p. 1993. 89.95 (0-7734-9308-5) E Mellen.

Student Handbook to Essentials of Genetics. Harry Nickla. (Illus.). 208p. (Orig.). (C). 1993. pap. text ed. 26.40 (0-02-387483-X, Macmillan Coll) P-H.

Student Health Problems: An Educator's Reference. Wilma W. Tompkins & Theodore P. Shannon. LC 92-35114. 261p. 1993. text ed. 27.95 (0-8273-4989-0) Delmar.

Student Housing: Architectural & Social Aspects. William Mullins & Phyllis Allen. LC 76-159965. (Illus.). 1971. 94.50 (0-89197-955-7) Irvington.

Student Housing: The German Experience. Ed. by A. Von Mutius & J. Nussberger. 216p. (ENG.). 1994. 79.50 (0-8176-5018-0) Birkhauser.

***Student Housing: The German Experience.** A. Von Mutius. 1996. 89.00 (3-7643-5018-0) Birkhauser.

Student Housing & Residential Life: A Handbook for Professionals Committed to Student Development Goals. Roger B. Winston, Jr. & Scott Anchors. LC 92-37735. (Higher & Adult Education Ser.). 664p. text ed. 52.00 (1-55542-507-0) Jossey-Bass.

***Student Identity & Popular Music in the Context of School.** Chris Richards et al. Ed. by Joe Kincheloe & Shirley R. Steinberg. (Critical Education Practice Ser.). 250p. 1997. text ed. 37.50 (0-8153-1725-5); pap. text ed. 18.95 (0-8153-2317-4) Garland.

Student Impact - Complete Camps & Retreats for High School: Complete Summer Camps, Weekend Retreats, & Small-Group Retreats. Student Impact Team Staff & Bo Boshers. (Student Impact Ser.). (Illus.). 128p. 1997. pap. 14.99 (0-310-20123-3) Zondervan.

Student Impact/Small Group Resources Vol. 1: High Participation & Experiential Discipleship for High School Students. Student Impact Team Staff & Bo Boshers. (Student Impact Ser.). (Illus.). 112p. (Orig.). 1997. pap. 14.99 (0-310-20124-1) Zondervan.

Student in Central America, 1914-1916. Dana G. Munro. LC 83-60479. (Publications: No. 51). 75p. 1983. pap. 15.00 (0-939238-77-2) Tulane MARI.

Student Inventors Workbook. Melvin L. Fuller & Maggie Weisberg. (Illus.). 50p. 1989. pap. 5.00 (1-877782-02-5) M&M Assocs.

Student Lab Notebook. Chemistry Study Staff. (C). 1995. pap. text ed. write for info. (0-7167-1876-6) W H Freeman.

An Asterisk (*) at the beginning of an entry indicates that the title is appearing in BIP for the first time.

Student Lamps of the Victorian Era. Richard C. Miller & John F. Solverson. (Illus.). 176p. (Orig.). 1992. pap. 34.95 (*0-915410-86-9*, 4012) Antique Pubns.
Student Lamps of the Victorian Era. limited ed. Richard C. Miller & John F. Solverson. (Illus.). 176p. (Orig.). 1992. 49.95 (*0-915410-87-7*, 4013) Antique Pubns.
Student Law Review: 1996 Yearbook. 198p. (C). Date not set. pap. 26.00 (*1-85941-234-3*, Pub. by Cavendish UK) Gaunt.
Student Law Review 1991 Yearbook. 204p. (C). 1992. pap. write for info. (*1-874241-05-8*, Pub. by Cavendish UK) Gaunt.
Student Law Review 1992 Yearbook. 180p. (C). 1993. pap. write for info. (*1-874241-06-6*, Pub. by Cavendish UK) Gaunt.
Student Law Review 1993 Yearbook. 174p. (C). 1994. pap. write for info. (*1-874241-07-4*, Pub. by Cavendish UK) Gaunt.
Student Law Review 1994 Yearbook. 180p. (C). 1995. pap. write for info. (*1-85941-007-3*, Pub. by Cavendish UK) Gaunt.
Student Law Review 1995 Yearbook. 202p. (C). 1996. pap. write for info. (*1-85941-226-2*, Pub. by Cavendish UK) Gaunt.
Student Lawyer. 4th ed. Date not set. teacher ed., pap. text ed. 21.95 (*0-314-24873-0*) West Pub.
Student Lawyer: A Guide to Minnesota's Legal System. Minnesota State Bar Association Staff & Joseph L. Daly. 217p. 1987. reprint ed. pap. text ed. 26.00 (*0-314-23039-4*) West Pub.
***Student Leader's Starter Kit.** (Nineteen Ninety-Seven 50-Day Spiritual Adventure Ser.). 1996. 39.00 (*1-57849-015-4*) Chapel of Air.
Student Learning: Research on Education & Cognitive Psychology. John T. Richardson et al. 240p. 1987. 95.00 (*0-335-15601-0*, Open Univ Pr); pap. 39.00 (*0-335-15600-2*, Open Univ Pr) Taylor & Francis.
Student Learning Guide - Exploring Accounting. Wilson. (AB - Accounting Principles Ser.). 1997. text ed. 19.95 (*0-538-85118-X*) S-W Pub.
***Student Learning Guide-Effective Market.** Zikmund. (SS - Marketing Management Ser.). (C). 1995. pap. 17.95 (*0-314-05256-9*) S-W Pub.
Student Learning Guide to Accompany Basic Nursing. 3rd ed. Potter. 224p. 1994. 12.95 (*0-8016-8024-7*) Mosby Yr Bk.
***Student Learning Guide to Accompany Mar.** 4th ed. Zikmunddamico. (C). 1993. pap. 14.56 (*0-314-01780-1*) West Pub.
Student Learning Guide to Accompany Maternity & Gynecologic Care. 5th ed. Irene M. Bobak. 118p. 1992. pap. 12.95 (*0-8016-7284-8*) Mosby Yr Bk.
Student Learning Guide to Accompany Pharmacologic Basis. 4th ed. Clark. 55p. 1992. 12.95 (*0-8016-7404-2*) Mosby Yr Bk.
Student Learning in Physical Education: Applying Research to Enhance Instruction. Stephen Silverman & Catherine D. Ennis. LC 95-42629. (Illus.). 416p. (C). 1996. text ed. 39.00 (*0-87322-714-X*, BSIL0714) Human Kinetics.
***Student Learning in the Information Age.** 2nd ed. Patricia S. Breivik. (Ace/Oryx Series on Higher Education). 240p. 1997. text ed. 34.95 (*1-57356-000-6*) Oryx Pr.
***Student Learning Outside the Classroom: Transcending Artificial Boundaries.** George D. Kuh. LC 96-75972. (ASHE-ERIC Higher Education Reports). (Illus.). 147p. (Orig.). 1996. pap. 21.75 (*1-878380-64-8*) GWU Grad Schl E&HD.
Student Learning Styles & Brain Behavior: Programs, Instrumentation, Research. National Association of Secondary School Principals Staff. LC 83-110391. (Illus.). 240p. reprint ed. pap. 68.40 (*0-8357-5551-7*, 2035170) Bks Demand.
***Student-Led Parent Conferences.** Linda Pierce-Picciotto. 1997. pap. text ed. 10.95 (*0-590-89649-0*) Scholastic Inc.
Student Life & Customs. Henry D. Sheldon. LC 70-89233. (American Education: Its Men, Institutions, & Ideas. Series 1). 1975. reprint ed. 30.95 (*0-405-01470-8*) Ayer.
Student Life, & Other Essays. William Osler. LC 67-23256. (Essay Index Reprint Ser.). 1977. 18.95 (*0-8369-0756-6*) Ayer.
***Student Loan Default Remedies.** Susan Ryan. (Illus.). 16p. (Orig.). 1996. pap. 3.00 (*1-884241-62-X*, PO317) Energeia Pub.
Student Loans: Risks & Realities. Ed. by Joseph M. Cronin & Sylvia Q. Simmons. LC 87-1275. 207p. 1987. text ed. 49.95 (*0-86569-165-7*, Auburn Hse) Greenwood.
Student Loans: The Next Stop. Nicholas Barr. (David Hume Papers). 104p. 1989. pap. text ed. 14.00 (*0-08-037966-4*, Pergamon Pr) Elsevier.
Student Lovers. Kristina Lindell. Ed. by John DeFrancis. LC 70-189615. (PALI Language Texts, Chinese Ser.). (Illus.). 68p. (Orig.). (C). 1975. pap. text ed. 8.00 (*0-8248-0225-X*) UH Pr.
Student Management Forms for Writing Guides. 2nd ed. Sandra Panman & Richard Panman. 1990. 1.95 (*0-912813-11-3*) Active Lrn.
Student Manual for Computers: Inside & Out. 5th ed. Pamela Moore et al. Ed. by Joan L. Witte. (Illus.). 272p. 1996. pap. 12.00 (*1-880066-14-9*) Pippin Publishing.
Student Manual for Counseling Families. David L. Fenell & Barry K. Weinhold. 144p. (Orig.). (C). 1996. pap. text ed. 14.95 (*0-89108-246-8*, 9605) Love Pub Co.
Student Manual for Essential Mathematics. 2nd ed. Rudolf A. Zimmer. 128p. 1994. per. 11.49 (*0-8403-8479-3*) Kendall-Hunt.
Student Manual for Radiation Protection Technology. 3rd ed. Daniel A. Gollnick. 183p. 1994. student ed., ring bd. 230.00 (*0-916339-06-8*, 302) Pacific Rad.
Student Manual for the Donut Franchise: A Microcomputer Simulation. P. C. Lewis & C. Lewis. 32p. 1985. pap. text ed. 9.15 (*0-07-037604-2*) McGraw.
Student Manual for Theory & Practice of Counseling & Psychotherapy see Theory & Practice of Group Counseling
Student Manual for WordPerfect Includes Horizontal & Vertical Template. Eleanor Davidson. 192p. (C). 1992. wbk. ed., per. 11.95 (*0-256-11236-3*) Irwin.
Student Manual to Accompany Computer-Based Information Systems: A Management Approach. Marianne M. Kroeber et al. 160p. 1984. pap. write for info. (*0-02-365390-6*, Macmillan Coll) P-H.
Student Manual to Accompany Reporter's Notebook - MAC. John Frair & Lloyd Chiasson. 52p. (C). 1992. spiral bd. write for info. (*0-697-16756-9*) Brown & Benchmark.
Student Manuscript Book. 1.95 (*0-87166-739-8*, 93412) Mel Bay.
Student Ministry for the 21st Century: Transforming Your Youth Group into a Vital Student Ministry. Bo Boshers & Kim Anderson. LC 97-4240. (Student Impact Ser.). (Illus.). 256p. 1997. boxed 19.99 (*0-310-20122-5*) Zondervan.
Student Mission Power: Report of the First International Convention of the Student Volunteer Movement for Foreign Missions, 1891. John R. Mott et al. LC 79-92013. 235p. 1979. reprint ed. pap. 7.95 (*0-87808-736-2*) William Carey Lib.
Student Modelling: The Key to Individualized Knowledge-Based Instruction. Ed. by Gord McCalla & Jim Greer. LC 94-2917. (NATO ASI Series F: Computer & Systems Sciences, Special Programme AET: Vol. 125). 1994. 107.05 (*0-387-57510-3*) Spr-Verlag.
Student Moral Development in the Catholic School. Mary P. Traviss. 96p. 1986. 6.00 (*0-318-20565-3*) Natl Cath Educ.
Student Motivation. Paul R. Pintrich & Dale H. Schunk. 1995. pap. text ed. 38.00 (*0-02-395621-6*, Macmillan Coll) P-H.
Student Motivation, Cognition, & Learning: Essays in Honor of Wilbert J. McKeachie. Ed. by Paul R. Pintrich et al. 400p. 1994. text ed. 79.95 (*0-8058-1376-4*) L Erlbaum Assocs.
***Student Movements in Assam.** Meeta Deka. (C). 1996. 28.00 (*0-7069-9882-0*, Pub. by Vikas II) S Asia.
Student Nationalism in China, 1924-1949. Lincoln Li. LC 93-6639. (SUNY Series in Chinese Philosophy & Culture). 209p. (C). 1994. text ed. 59.50 (*0-7914-1749-2*); pap. text ed. 19.95 (*0-7914-1750-6*) State U NY Pr.
Student Nationalism in China, 1927-1937. John Israel. ix, 253p. 1966. 39.50 (*0-8047-0280-2*) Stanford U Pr.
Student, News Watcher & Couch Potato Guide to the Constitution. Pete Bohaczyk. 174p. (Orig.). (C). 1991. pap. text ed. 21.50 (*0-8191-8313-X*) U Pr of Amer.
Student Nonviolent Coordinating Committee: The Growth of Radicalism in a Civil Rights Organization. Emily Stoper. LC 89-22265. (Martin Luther King, Jr., & the Civil Rights Movement Ser.: Vol. 17). 351p. 1989. 70.00 (*0-926019-11-2*) Carlson Pub.
***Student Notetaking Guide-Effective Mark.** Zikmund. (SS - Marketing Management Ser.). (C). 1995. pap. 12.95 (*0-314-05658-0*) S-W Pub.
***Student Notetaking Guide to Biology.** Cummings. 1996. pap. 12.25 (*0-314-21310-4*) Wadsworth Pub.
Student Nurse. large type ed. Peggy Gaddis. (Linford Romance Library). 1995. pap. 15.99 (*0-7089-7744-8*, Linford) Ulverscroft.
Student Obesity: What Can the Schools Do? Phillip M. Wishon. LC 90-60211. (Fastback Ser.: No. 305). 40p. (Orig.). (C). 1990. pap. 3.00 (*0-87367-305-0*) Phi Delta Kappa.
Student of Salamanca: El Estudiante de Salamanca. Jose De Espronceda. Ed. by R. A. Cardwell. Tr. by C. K. Davis from SPA. (Hispanic Classics Ser.). (C). 1991. 49.95 (*0-85668-501-1*, Pub. by Aris & Phillips UK); pap. text ed. 22.00 (*0-85668-502-X*, Pub. by Aris & Phillips UK) David Brown.
***Student of the Word Notetaker.** spiral bd. 4.99 (*0-89274-828-1*) Harrison Hse.
Student Organization & Academic Strategies: A Student Survival Text. 2nd ed. Franklin O. Sutton. 168p. (C). 1996. per., pap. text ed. 33.54 (*0-7872-2364-6*) Kendall-Hunt.
Student Organization Software. Advantage International, Inc. Staff. (C). 1992. teacher ed. 25.00 (*1-56756-017-2*); 299.00 (*1-56756-025-3*, OD270I); disk 69.00 (*1-56756-012-1*, OD250I); mac hd 69.00 (*1-56756-013-X*, OD260M) Advant Intl.
Student Organizational Planbook. Cathy A. Doerr. 112p. (J). (gr. 3-12). 1992. pap. 3.95 (*0-9632893-0-6*) Skills For Lrn.
Student Outcomes Assessment: A Historical Review & Guide to Program Development. Serbrenia J. Sims. LC 91-27811. (Contributions to the Study of Education Ser.: No. 52). 168p. 1992. text ed. 42.95 (*0-313-27591-2*, SYG/, Greenwood Pr) Greenwood.
Student Outcomes Assessment: What Institutions Stand to Gain. Ed. by Diane F. Halpern. LC 85-644752. (New Directions for Higher Education Ser.: No. HE 59). 1987. 19.00 (*1-55542-949-1*) Jossey-Bass.
Student-Parent Socialization Study, 1965. M. Kent Jennings. 1971. write for info. (*0-89138-023-X*) ICPSR.
Student Participation in Administration. R. C. Srivastava. LC 75-905820. 1975. 7.75 (*0-88386-657-9*) S Asia.
Student Peer Counseling Training Curriculum. Ed. by Larry Burns & Jan Osborne. 1985. teacher ed. 95.00 (*1-56117-029-1*); student ed. 3.50 (*1-56117-004-6*); Span., Laotian, Cambodian & Vietnamese. student ed. 3.95 (*1-56117-003-8*) Telesis CA.
Student Perceptions in the Classroom. Ed. by Dale H. Schunk & Judith L. Meece. 376p. 1992. text ed. 79.95 (*0-8058-0981-3*); pap. text ed. 39.95 (*0-8058-0982-1*) L Erlbaum Assocs.
Student Personnel Work: A Program of Developmental Relationships. Edmund G. Williamson & Donald A. Biggs. LC 74-28492. 400p. reprint ed. pap. 114.00 (*0-317-09835-7*, 2022501) Bks Demand.
Student-Physician: Introductory Studies in the Sociology of Medical Education. Ed. by Robert K. Merton et al. LC 57-12526. (Commonwealth Fund Publications Ser). (Illus.). 372p. reprint ed. 106.10 (*0-8357-9179-3*, 2011023) Bks Demand.
Student Physician As Psycho-therapist. Ed. by Ralph W. Heine. LC 62-19624. 255p. reprint ed. pap. 72.70 (*0-317-26509-1*, 2024047) Bks Demand.
Student Pilot Guide. 1996. lib. bdg. 250.95 (*0-8490-5970-4*) Gordon Pr.
***Student Pilot Guide.** 1997. lib. bdg. 250.95 (*0-8490-8129-7*) Gordon Pr.
Student Pilot Guide. rev. ed. Federal Aviation Administration Staff. 36p. 1979. reprint ed. pap. text ed. 3.25 (*0-685-05989-8*) Flightshops.
Student Pilot Handbook. Art Parma. (Illus.). 84p. (Orig.). 1992. reprint ed. pap. 10.95 (*0-9631973-3-9*) Flight Time.
Student Pilot's Flight Manual. 7th ed. William K. Kershner. LC 92-36448. (Illus.). 494p. 1993. pap. 34.95 (*0-8138-1612-2*) Iowa St U Pr.
***Student Pilot's Flight Manual Syllabus.** William K. Kershner. 1997. pap. text ed. 14.95 (*0-8138-2928-3*) Iowa St U Pr.
Student Planned Acquisition of Required Knowledge. Margaret Norton et al. Ed. by Danny G. Langdon. LC 79-23442. (Instructional Design Library). 104p. 1980. 27.95 (*0-87778-155-9*) Educ Tech Pubns.
Student Planner & Assignment Book. 2nd ed. V. Nichols. (Illus.). 120p. (YA). (gr. 5-12). 1993. reprint ed. pap. 3.95 (*1-879424-20-7*) Nickel Pr.
Student Political Activism: An International Reference Handbook. Philip G. Altbach. LC 88-34719. 519p. 1989. text ed. 95.00 (*0-313-26016-8*, ASQ, Greenwood Pr) Greenwood.
***Student Politics in America: A Historical Analysis.** Philip G. Altbach. LC 97-597. (Foundations of Higher Education Ser.). 1997. pap. 24.95 (*1-56000-944-6*) Transaction Pubs.
Student Politics in India. Subas C. Hazary. (C). 1987. 34.00 (*81-7024-086-7*, Pub. by Ashish II) S Asia.
Student Portfolios. Laura Grosvenor et al. LC 93-13849. (Teacher to Teacher Ser.). 96p. 1993. pap. 12.95 (*0-8106-2901-1*, Tchr-to-Tchr Bks) NEA.
Student Portfolios: A Collection of Articles. Ed. by Robin Fogarty. LC 95-81913. (Illus.). 240p. (Orig.). 1996. pap. 22.95 (*1-57517-011-6*, 1422) IRI-SkyLght.
Student Prince. pap. 9.95 (*0-943351-69-3*, XW1629) Astor Bks.
***Student Prince: Vocal Score.** Ed. by Carol Cuellar. 170p. (Orig.). (C). 1995. pap. text ed. 45.00 (*0-7692-0870-3*, VP0016) Warner Brothers.
***Student Prince: Vocal Selections.** Ed. by Carol Cuellar. 32p. (Orig.). (C). 1984. pap. text ed. 9.95 (*0-7692-0850-9*, SF0126) Warner Brothers.
Student Privacy in the Classroom. Edward B. Jenkinson. LC 90-60221. (Fastback Ser.: No. 298). 40p. (Orig.). (C). 1990. pap. 3.00 (*0-87367-298-4*) Phi Delta Kappa.
Student Projects: Ideas & Plans. Lois F. Roets. 272p. (YA). (gr. 3 up). 1994. pap. text ed. 30.00 (*0-911943-39-0*) Leadership Pub.
Student Promise Pocketbook. (Pocketpac Bks.). 96p. 1982. mass mkt. 2.99 (*0-87788-912-0*) Shaw Pubs.
***Student Protest & the Technocratic Society: The Case of ROTC.** Jack N. Porter. (Illus.). 146p. 1997. reprint ed. pap. 8.95 (*0-614-29568-8*) Spencer Pr.
Student Protests in Twentieth-Century China: The View from Shanghai. Jeffrey N. Wasserstrom. LC 90-22307. (Illus.). 464p. 1991. 49.50 (*0-8047-1881-4*) Stanford U Pr.
Student Psychiatry Today. Cohen. 1988. 55.00 (*0-7506-0322-4*) Buttrwrth-Heinemann.
Student Psychiatry Today: A Comprehensive Textbook. 2nd ed. Robert I. Cohen & Jerome J. Hart. LC 95-4192. 448p. 1995. pap. 55.00 (*0-7506-1586-9*) Buttrwrth-Heinemann.
Student Publications: Legalities, Governance, & Operation. Louis E. Inglehart. LC 90-27874. 196p. (C). 1993. pap. text ed. 24.95 (*0-8138-1478-2*) Iowa St U Pr.
Student Ratings of Instruction: Issues for Improving Practice. Ed. by Michael Theall & Jennifer Franklin. LC 85-644763. (New Directions for Teaching & Learning Ser.: No. 43). 1990. 19.00 (*1-55542-817-7*) Jossey-Bass.
Student Reader Eight. Barbara A. Wilson. (Wilson Reading System Ser.). 56p. 1988. pap. text ed. 8.00 (*1-56778-019-9*) Wilson Lang Trning.
Student Reader Eleven. Barbara A. Wilson. (Wilson Reading System Ser.). 58p. 1988. pap. text ed. 8.00 (*1-56778-022-9*) Wilson Lang Trning.
Student Reader Five. Barbara A. Wilson. (Wilson Reading System Ser.). 60p. 1988. pap. text ed. 8.00 (*1-56778-016-4*) Wilson Lang Trning.
Student Reader Four. Barbara A. Wilson. (Wilson Reading System Ser.). 58p. 1988. pap. text ed. 8.00 (*1-56778-015-6*) Wilson Lang Trning.
Student Reader Nine. Barbara A. Wilson. (Wilson Reading System Ser.). 77p. 1988. pap. text ed. 8.00 (*1-56778-020-2*) Wilson Lang Trning.
Student Reader One. Barbara A. Wilson. (Wilson Reading System Ser.). 80p. 1988. pap. text ed. 8.00 (*1-56778-012-1*) Wilson Lang Trning.
Student Reader Seven. Barbara A. Wilson. (Wilson Reading System Ser.). 54p. 1988. pap. text ed. 8.00 (*1-56778-018-0*) Wilson Lang Trning.
Student Reader Six. Barbara A. Wilson. (Wilson Reading System Ser.). 50p. 1988. pap. text ed. 8.00 (*1-56778-017-2*) Wilson Lang Trning.
Student Reader Ten. Barbara A. Wilson. (Wilson Reading System Ser.). 46p. 1988. pap. text ed. 8.00 (*1-56778-021-0*) Wilson Lang Trning.
Student Reader Three. Barbara A. Wilson. (Wilson Reading System Ser.). 60p. 1988. pap. text ed. 8.00 (*1-56778-014-8*) Wilson Lang Trning.
Student Reader Twelve. Barbara A. Wilson. (Wilson Reading System Ser.). 46p. 1988. pap. text ed. 8.00 (*1-56778-023-7*) Wilson Lang Trning.
Student Readers One-Six. Barbara A. Wilson. (Wilson Reading System Ser.). 386p. 1988. pap. text ed. 36.00 (*1-56778-010-5*) Wilson Lang Trning.
Student Readers One-Twelve. Barbara A. Wilson. (Wilson Reading System Ser.). 723p. 1988. pap. text ed. 78.00 (*1-56778-009-1*) Wilson Lang Trning.
Student Readers Seven-Twelve. Barbara A. Wilson. (Wilson Reading System Ser.). 337p. 1988. pap. text ed. 36.00 (*1-56778-011-3*) Wilson Lang Trning.
Student Recruitment in Psychosocial Occupational Therapy: Intergenerational Approaches. Susan Haiman. LC 90-4541. (Occupational Therapy in Mental Health Ser.: Vol. 10, No. 1). 84p. 1990. text ed. 24.95 (*0-86656-993-6*) Haworth Pr.
Student Recruitment/Retention Pocket Guide. Milady Publishing Company Staff. (Cosmetology Ser.). 1988. pap. 9.95 (*0-87350-448-8*) Van Nos Reinhold.
Student Reference Manual for Electronic Instrumentation Laboratories. Stanley Wolf & Frank Smith. 560p. 1989. pap. text ed. 45.00 (*0-13-855776-4*) P-H.
Student Relationships, Vol. 1. Dawson McAllister. (J). (gr. 5-12). 1981. teacher ed., pap. 6.95 (*0-923417-18-4*) Shepherd Minst.
Student Relationships, Vol. 2. Dawson McAllister & Tim Kimmel. (J). (gr. 5-12). 1981. teacher ed., pap. 6.95 (*0-923417-04-4*) Shepherd Minst.
Student Relationships, Vol. 3. Dawson MacAllister & Tim Kimmel. (J). (gr. 5-12). 1981. teacher ed., pap. 6.95 (*0-923417-19-2*) Shepherd Minst.
Student Repertoire Series. Lawrence Ferrara. 89p. (Orig.). (C). 1995. pap. text ed. 19.95 (*0-9627832-5-0*) Guitar Solo.
Student Research Papers in Calculus. Marcus Cohen et al. LC 91-62052. (Spectrum Ser.). 232p. (C). 1992. pap. 29.50 (*0-88385-503-8*, SRPC) Math Assn.
Student Resource Book: Grade 5 Mathematics Unlimited. Fennell. 1988. 32.50 (*0-03-021912-4*) HB Schl Dept.
Student Resource Book 1988: Grade 3. Fennell. 1988. 32.50 (*0-03-021907-8*) HB Schl Dept.
Student Resource Book 1988: Grade 4. Fennell. 1988. 32.50 (*0-03-021719-9*) HB Schl Dept.
Student Resource Book 1988: Grade 4 Mathematics Unlimited. Fennell. 1988. 32.50 (*0-03-021909-4*) HB Schl Dept.
Student Resource Book 1988: Grade 7 Mathematics Unlimited. Fennell. 1996. 32.50 (*0-03-021913-2*) HB Schl Dept.
***Student Resource Guide to the Internet.** Leshin. LC 97-22922. 1997. pap. text ed. 25.33 (*0-13-621079-1*) P-H.
Student Resource Manual to Accompany Management. 6th ed. Hellriegel. (C). 1992. pap. text ed. 17.95 (*0-201-52605-0*) Addison-Wesley.

S

Student Retention Success Models in Higher Education. Ed. by Clinita A. Ford. 361p. 1996. pap. 49.50 (*0-9649919-0-X*) CNJ Assocs. STUDENT RETENTION SUCCESS MODELS IN HIGHER EDUCATION is a resource book of "success-proven" approaches & solutions to the increasing problem of minority retention & graduation. Over two dozen university & higher education systems/agency administrators, faculty & staff from across the nation come together & share successful retention programs. The authors bring the results of their hands-on experiences. Planning, implementation & evaluation; problems, pitfalls & failures; solutions & recommendations are all there for you. It is a "how-to" book with procedures that can be easily adapted to other institutional settings; in the areas of pre-college & orientation retention programs, classroom retention strategies, undergraduate & graduate recruitment & retention programs, national & system-wide retention models, providing conducive campus climate & creating a model retention program on campus. Detailed descriptions, & in many instances step-by-step descriptions are included for models of AHANA programs, outreach & bridge programs, academic advisement, extended orientation, mentoring, tutorials, collaborative initiatives, faculty development, organizational structures & special emphasis programs in athletics, engineering, music & nursing. Additionally, the book provides a good review of literature & an extensive bibliography. To order contact: CNJ Assoc., Inc., P.O. Box 10042, Tallahassee, FL 32302-2042, (904) 385-1747. ***Publisher Provided Annotation.***

***Student Review Book for AP United States History.** Michael Henry. 48p. 1997. pap. 8.00 (0-8059-4093-6) Dorrance.

Student Review for Clinical Medicine. Woods. 1993. pap. text ed. 12.00 (0-7216-5238-7) HarBrace.

Student Revolution: A Global Confrontation. Joseph A. Califano, Jr. (C). 1970. pap. text ed. 1.50 (0-393-00519-4) Norton.

Student Revolution in Assam. S. Bora. (C). 1992. 28.00 (81-7099-332-6, Pub. by Mittal II) S Asia.

Student Rights & Responsibilities. 2nd ed. Baum. (LA - Business Law Ser.). 1988. wbk. ed., pap. 16.95 (0-538-12540-3) S-W Pub.

Student Rights under the Constitution: Selected Federal Decisions Affecting the Public School Community. J. Devereux Weeks. 50p. 1992. pap. 11.95 (0-89854-157-3) U of GA Inst Govt.

***Student Satisfaction Manual.** Lee Harvey. LC 96-32768. 352p. 1996. 299.00 (0-335-19779-5, Open Univ Pr) Taylor & Francis.

Student Science Opportunities: Your Guide to over Three Hundred Exciting National Programs, Competitions, Internships, & Scholarships. Gail L. Grand. 292p. 1994. pap. text ed. 14.95 (0-471-31088-3) Wiley.

Student Self-Esteem: Integrating the Self. Ed. by Gail McEachron-Hirsch. LC 93-60638. 440p. 1993. text ed. 39.95 (1-56676-031-3) Technomic.

Student Self-Evaluation: Fostering Reflective Learning. Ed. by Jean MacGregor. LC 85-644763. (New Directions for Teaching & Learning Ser.: No. 56). 123p. (Orig.). 1993. pap. 19.00 (1-55542-683-2) Jossey-Bass.

Student Service: The New Carnegie Unit. Charles H. Harrison. LC 86-34304. 70p. 1987. pap. text ed. 6.50 (0-931050-30-8) Carnegie Fnd Advan Teach.

Student Services: A Handbook for the Profession. 2nd ed. Ursula Delworth et al. LC 88-46086. (Higher Education Ser.). 680p. text ed. 40.00 (1-55542-148-2) Jossey-Bass.

Student Services: A Handbook for the Profession. 3rd ed. Ed. by Susan R. Komives et al. LC 95-25768. (Higher & Adult Education Ser.). 608p. Date not set. 45.00 (0-7879-0210-1) Jossey-Bass.

Student Services: A Handbook for the Profession. Ed. by Ursula Delworth et al. LC 80-8008. (Jossey-Bass Series in Higher Education). 527p. reprint ed. pap. 150.20 (0-8357-4877-4, 2037809) Bks Demand.

Student Services & the Law: A Handbook for Practitioners. Barr, Margaret J., & Associates. LC 87-46330. (Higher Education Ser.). 430p. text ed. 42.00 (1-55542-079-6) Jossey-Bass.

Student Services in a Changing Federal Climate. Ed. by Michael D. Coomes & Donald D. Gehring. LC 85-644751. (New Directions for Student Services Ser.: No. 68). 110p. (Orig.). 1994. pap. 19.00 (0-7879-9997-0) Jossey-Bass.

***Student Skills Guide.** Sue Drew & Rosie Bingham. (Student Skills Project Ser.). 350p. 1996. pap. text ed. 20.95 (0-566-07847-3, Pub. by Gower UK) Ashgate Pub Co.

***Student Skills Tutor's Handbook.** Sue Drew & Rosie Bingham. (Student Skills Project Ser.). 350p. 1996. pap. text ed. 39.95 (0-566-07846-5, Pub. by Gower UK) Ashgate Pub Co.

Student Sociologist's Handbook. 4th ed. Pauline Bart & Linda Frankel. 228p. 1986. pap. text ed. write for info. (0-07-554884-4) McGraw.

Student Solution Manual: Differential Equations. Andrews. (C). 1991. 18.00 (0-06-500002-1) Addson-Wesley Educ.

Student Solutions Guide to Accompany Chemistry: The Molecule. Peck. 200p. 1993. pap. 14.95 (0-8016-5071-2) Mosby Yr Bk.

Student Solutions Manual to Accompany Kolman-Shapiro: Algebra for College Students. 3rd ed. Jorge Cossio. 119p. (C). 1991. pap. text ed. 20.75 (0-15-502164-8) SCP.

Student Space Simulation. L. Jerry Bernhardt, Jr. & Larry J. McHaney. 256p. 1990. pap. 19.95 (0-8273-4191-1) Delmar.

Student Spiral Manuscript Book. 2.50 (0-87166-911-0, 93965) Mel Bay.

Student Storyfest: How to Organize a Storytelling Festival. Barbara B. Griffin. 112p. (Orig.). 1989. pap. 12.95 (0-9623331-2-3) Strytller Guidebk.

Student Stress: A Classroom Management System. Kevin J. Swick. 96p. 1987. pap. 9.95 (0-8106-1696-3) NEA.

Student Stress: Effects & Solutions. Neal A. Whitman et al. Ed. & Frwd. by Jonathan D. Fife. LC 84-223037. (ASHE-ERIC Higher Education Reports: No. 2, 1984). (Illus.). 115p. (Orig.). 1984. pap. 7.50 (0-913317-11-X) GWU Grad Schl E&HD.

***Student Study Guide & Solution Manual to Introductory Chemistry.** Jerry Driscoll. 180p. (C). 1996. student ed., pap. text ed. 28.35 (0-7872-2912-1) Kendall-Hunt.

Student Study Guide for Calculus. Gilbert Strang & Jennifer Carmody. (Illus.). 200p. (C). 1992. pap. text ed. 12.50 (0-9614088-4-7) Wellesley-Cambridge Pr.

Student Study Guide for Military History. Hugh G. Earnhart. 126p. (Orig.). 1985. reprint ed. pap. 36.00 (0-608-00065-5, 2060831) Bks Demand.

***Student Study Guide for Social Work Research & Evaluation.** 5th ed. R. Grinnell et al. 150p. (C). 1997. pap. text ed. 18.00 (0-87581-408-5) Peacock Pubs.

Student Study Guide for Soil Science Simplified. 2nd ed. Milo I. Harpstead et al. LC 87-22754. (Illus.). 58p. 1988. reprint ed. pap. 25.00 (0-608-00063-9, 2060829) Bks Demand.

Student Study Guide for Sorensen & Luckmann's Basic Nursing: A Psychophysiologic Approach. 3rd ed. Verolyn B. Bolander. (Illus.). 380p. 1994. pap. text ed. 17.95 (0-7216-4327-2) Saunders.

Student Study Guide to a Basic Course in American Sign Language. Frances De Capite. 1986. spiral bd. 9.95 (0-932666-33-7) T J Pubs.

Student Study Guide to Accompany Biology & Human Concerns. 4th ed. E. Peter Volpe & Peter A. Rosenbaum. 256p. (C). 1993. spiral bd. write for info. (0-697-10227-0) Wm C Brown Pubs.

Student Study Guide to Accompany Environmental Geology. 4th ed. Carla W. Montgomery. 160p. (C). 1994. spiral bd. write for info. (0-697-15813-6) Wm C Brown Pubs.

Student Study Guide to Accompany Environmental Science: Managing Biological & Physical Resources. Michael D. Morgan & Joseph M. Moran. 136p. (C). 1992. spiral bd. write for info. (0-697-10834-1) Wm C Brown Pubs.

Student Study Guide to Accompany Hegarty Decisions. Spaide. 352p. 1988. pap. 16.95 (0-8016-2366-9) Mosby Yr Bk.

Student Study Guide to Accompany Zoology. 3rd ed. Stephen A. Miller & Jay M. Templin. 256p. (C). 1995. spiral bd. write for info. (0-697-26068-2) Wm C Brown Pubs.

Student Study Guide/Workbook to Accompany Justice, Crime & Ethics. 2nd ed. Michael C. Braswell et al. 188p. (C). 1995. wbk. ed. write for info. (0-87084-098-3) Anderson Pub Co.

Student Success. 7th ed. Walter. (C). 1996. teacher ed., pap. text ed. 28.00 (0-15-502679-8) HB Coll Pubs.

***Student Success.** 8th ed. Walter. (C). pap. text ed. write for info. (0-15-508278-7) HB Coll Pubs.

Student Success: How to Succeed in College & Still Have Time for Your Friends. 6th ed. Timothy L. Walter. 200p. 1993. text ed. write for info. (0-15-500588-X) HB Coll Pubs.

Student Success: How to Succeed in College & Still Have Time for Your Friends. 6th ed. Timothy L. Walter. 200p. (C). 1993. Instructor's manual. teacher ed., pap. text ed. 7.00 (0-15-500772-6) HB Coll Pubs.

Student Success: How to Succeed in College & Still Have Time for Your Friends. 7th ed. Timothy L. Walter & Al Siebert. 272p. (C). 1995. pap. text ed. 17.00 (0-15-502674-7) HarBrace.

Student Success Handbook. 2nd ed. Vivian Sathre. 80p. (C). 1995. 6.77 (0-8403-7164-0) Kendall-Hunt.

Student Success Secrets. 4th ed. Eric P. Jensen. LC 96-13826. (Illus.). 1996. pap. 8.95 (0-8120-9488-3) Barron.

Student Success Strategies. Hatch. (C). 1996. pap. text ed. 13.50 (0-15-501008-5) HB Coll Pubs.

Student Success Strategies. Walter. (C). 1996. teacher ed., pap. write for info. (0-15-503242-9) HB Coll Pubs.

Student Success Through Collaboration: Summer Institute Papers & Recommendations, 1992. 140p. 1993. pap. write for info. (1-884037-01-1) Coun Chief St Schl Offs.

Student Suicide: A Guide for Intervention. John A. Vidal. 56p. 1989. pap. 7.95 (0-8106-0244-X) NEA.

Student Survival: Succeeding in School: A Quick Guide & Reference of Study Skills & Procedures. Deane H. Howard. 250p. (YA). (gr. 6 up). 1991. pap. 24.95 (0-9629207-0-3) Ed Res Pub Co.

Student Survival Guide. Joe Cammarata. Ed. by Gary Tunmore. (Illus.). 108p. (YA). (gr. 6-12). 1991. student ed. 9.95 (0-924649-03-8) Scribblers Pub.

Student Survival Guide. rev. ed. Gregory F. Kishel. Ed. by Patricia G. Kishel. LC 79-90414. (Illus.). 96p. (Orig.). (C). 1982. pap. 8.95 (0-935346-00-7) K & K Enter.

Student Survival Handbook. 2nd ed. Eula M. Glenn. (Illus.). 30p. (J). (gr. 1-12). 1990. pap. text ed. 3.95 (1-877860-06-9) Eula Intl Pub.

Student Syllabus: The SUM Program Beginning Medical Transcription Course. Susan M. Turley & Linda C. Campbell. 1992. pap. 35.00 (0-934385-52-1) Hlth Prof Inst.

Student Teacher Handbook: For Reflective Student Teaching. Wittmeyer & Moulton. 1994. pap. text ed. write for info. (0-07-071236-0) McGraw.

***Student Teacher to Master Teacher: A Guide for Preservice & Beginning Teachers of Students with Mild to Moderate Disabilities.** 2nd ed. Michael S. Rosenberg et al. LC 97-13532. 1997. 43.00 (0-13-632514-9, Merrill Coll) P-H.

Student Teacher to Master Teacher: A Handbook for Preservice & Beginning Teachers of Students with Mild & Moderate Handicaps. Michael S. Rosenberg et al. 352p. (C). 1990. pap. text ed. 32.20 (0-02-403650-1, Macmillan Coll) P-H.

Student Teacher's Guide: Intervention Strategies for the Most Common Learning & Behavior Problems Encountered by Student Teachers in Our Schools. Stephen B. McCarney. 470p. (Orig.). 1989. pap. 20.00 (1-878372-12-2) Hawthorne Educ Servs.

Student Teacher's Handbook. 3rd ed. Milton Schwebel et al. 280p. (C). 1996. text ed. 59.95 (0-8058-2129-5); pap. text ed. 24.95 (0-8058-2130-9) L Erlbaum Assocs.

Student Teacher's Handbook for Physical Education. Lynda E. Randall. LC 92-19454. 160p. 1992. spiral bd. 13.00 (0-87322-365-9, BRAN0365) Human Kinetics.

Student Teacher's Troubled Teaching Experience in Rural Alaska. Ed. by Judith Kleinfeld. (Teaching Cases in Cross-Cultural Education Ser.). 60p. (Orig.). (C). 1989. pap. text ed. 7.50 (1-877962-05-8) Univ AK Ctr CCS.

Student Teaching: Early Childhood Practicum. 3rd ed. Jeanne M. Machado & Botnaerescue. (Early Childhood Education Ser.). 464p. 1996. text ed. 35.95 (0-8273-7619-7) Delmar.

Student Teaching: Early Childhood Practicum Guide. 2nd ed. Jeanne M. Machado & Helen M. Botnarescue. LC 92-10647. 456p. 1993. pap. 27.95 (0-8273-5242-5) Delmar.

Student Teaching: Early Childhood Practicum Guide. 3rd ed. Jeanne M. Machado. (Early Childhood Education Ser.). 1997. teacher ed. 10.50 (0-8273-7620-0) Delmar.

Student Teaching & Field Experience Handbook. 3rd ed. Betty D. Roe & Elinor P. Ross. (Illus.). 321p. (C). 1993. pap. text ed. 45.00 (0-02-402661-1, Macmillan Coll) P-H.

***Student Teaching & Field Experiences Handbook.** 4th ed. Betty D. Roe & Elinor P. Ross. LC 96-40022. 1997. 38.00 (0-13-490780-9) P-H.

Student Teaching Casebook for Supervising Teachers & Teaching Interns. Patricia Wentz & James R. Yarling. 160p. (C). 1993. pap. text ed. 23.00 (0-02-425491-6, Macmillan Coll) P-H.

Student Teaching, Classroom Management & Professionalism. W. Heitzman et al. 1974. text ed. 29.50 (0-8422-5143-X); pap. text ed. 9.95 (0-8422-0367-2) Irvington.

Student Teaching Guide for Blind & Visually Impaired University Students: Adapted Methods & Procedures. braille ed. Lou Alonso. LC 86-7979. 52p. 1987. 12.95 (0-89128-183-5) Am Foun Blind.

Student Teaching Guide for Blind & Visually Impaired University Students: Adapted Methods & Procedures. large type ed. Lou Alonso. LC 86-7979. 52p. 1987. pap. 12.95 (0-89128-142-8) Am Foun Blind.

Student Teaching Guidebook. Janet T. Bercik. 131p. (C). 1990. ring bd. 24.90 (0-89420-269-3, 343550) Natl Book.

***Student Teaching Handbook.** Blair & Jones. 1997. pap. text ed. 30.00 (0-205-26761-0) P-H.

***Student Teaching Handbook.** Martha Fletcher. 64p. (C). 1997. text ed. write for info. (0-7872-3386-2) Kendall-Hunt.

Student Teaching Handbook. Teresa Nichols. 80p. (C). 1994. 6.67 (0-8403-8508-0) Kendall-Hunt.

***Student Teaching Handbook.** Teresa Nichols. 74p. (C). 1996. 9.95 (0-7872-3317-X) Kendall-Hunt.

Student Teaching Handbook. Penn State College of Education Staff. 176p. 1993. spiral bd. 25.14 (0-8403-7308-2) Kendall-Hunt.

***Student Teaching Handbook.** 2nd ed. Penn State, College of Education Staff. 192p. (C). 1996. spiral bd. write for info. (0-7872-2930-X) Kendall-Hunt.

Student Teaching Handbook. 6th ed. Gerald H. Krockover. 64p. 1996. 7.29 (0-8403-7836-X) Kendall-Hunt.

***Student Teaching Manual.** 3rd ed. John M. Carlevale. 230p. 1997. pap. text ed. 19.95 (0-940139-36-7) Consortium RI.

Student Team Learning: A Practical Guide to Cooperative Learning. 3rd ed. Robert E. Slavin. 128p. 1991. pap. 18.95 (0-8106-1845-1) NEA.

Student Test Lesson Books, Pt. 1 (Lessons 1-15) Raymond E. Laurita. 55p. (Orig.). (J). (ps-8). 1980. Stages 1-15. student ed., pap. 8.50 (0-914051-05-9) Leonardo Pr.

Student Test Lesson Books, Pt. 1 (Lessons 16-30) Raymond E. Laurita. 52p. (Orig.). (J). (ps-8). 1980. Stages 16-30. student ed., pap. 8.50 (0-914051-14-8) Leonardo Pr.

Student Test Lesson Books, Pt. 2 (Lessons 1-15) Raymond E. Laurita. 66p. (Orig.). (YA). (gr. 6 up). 1989. Stages 1-15. student ed., pap. 8.50 (0-914051-07-5) Leonardo Pr.

Student Test Lesson Books, Pt. 2 (Lessons 16-30) Raymond E. Laurita. 43p. (Orig.). (YA). (gr. 6 up). 1989. Stages 16-30. student ed., pap. 8.50 (0-914051-17-2) Leonardo Pr.

Student Text-Voila! 3rd ed. Heinlenman & Kaplan. (College French Ser.). 1997. pap. 55.75 (0-8384-7133-1) Heinle & Heinle.

Student, the College, the Law. William T. O'Hara & John T. Hill, Jr. LC 72-87116. 234p. 1972. reprint ed. pap. 66.70 (0-608-02105-9, 2026049) Bks Demand.

Student Theory Package. Beverly L. Ritter. (Realtime Machine Shorthand Ser.). 458p. (C). 1991. pap. text ed. 90.00 incl. digital audio (0-938643-36-3) Stenotype Educ.

Student Thesaurus. Elizabeth A. Ryan. LC 89-20305. (Illus.). 160p. (J). (gr. 2-8). 1990. pap. 7.95 (0-8167-1856-3); lib. bdg. 15.50 (0-8167-1914-4) Troll Communs.

Student to Student Guide to Medical School. Betcher. 278p. 1985. pap. 19.95 (0-316-09246-0, Little Med Div) Little.

Student Trainee. Jack Rudman. (Career Examination Ser.: C-1039). 1994. pap. 23.95 (0-8373-1039-3) Nat Learn.

Student Transfers from White to Black Colleges. Narendra H. Patel. (National Association for Equal Opportunity in Higher Education Ser.: No. 3). 40p. (Orig.). (C). 1988. pap. text ed. 10.00 (0-8191-6952-8, NAEOHE) U Pr of Amer.

Student Version of PC: Solve. Ed. by PCS Associates Staff. (C). 1990. pap. 67.00 incl. 3.5 hd (1-878437-03-8) Pac Crest Soft.

Student Viewer's Handbook to Accompany Destinos: An Introduction to Spanish. Bill VanPatten et al. LC 92-12110. 1992. pap. text ed. write for info. (0-07-067209-1) McGraw.

Student Vision. Visual Solutions Inc. Staff. (General Engineering Ser.). 1996. 69.95 (0-534-95485-5) PWS Pubs.

Student Voice, 1960-1965: Periodical of the Student Nonviolent Coordinating Committee. Ed. by Clayborne Carson. LC 89-49690. 264p. 1990. text ed. 135.00 (0-313-28050-9, CSY/, Greenwood Pr) Greenwood.

Student Voices: The Writer's Range. Hans P. Guth. 209p. (C). 1989. pap. 18.95 (0-534-11724-4) Wadsworth Pub.

Student with a Genetic Disorder: Educational Implications for Special Education Teachers & for Physical Therapists, Occupational Therapists, & Speech Pathologists. Diane M. Plumridge et al. LC 92-39088. (Illus.). 382p. 1993. pap. 44.95 (0-398-06327-3); text ed. 75.95 (0-398-05839-3) C C Thomas.

Student Work Manual for Introductory Clinical Pharmacology. 4th ed. Jeanne C. Scherer. 160p. 1992. text ed. 14.95 (0-397-54844-3) Lppncott-Raven.

Student Workbook: Adolescent Coping with Depression Course. Peter M. Lewinsohn et al. 196p. (YA). 1990. spiral bd., pap. 9.95 (0-916154-21-1) Castalia Pub.

Student Workbook see Hazardous Materials: Managing the Incident

Student Workbook Eight. Barbara A. Wilson. (Wilson Reading System Ser.). 35p. 1990. 4.00 (1-56778-034-2) Wilson Lang Trning.

Student Workbook Eleven. Barbara A. Wilson. (Wilson Reading System Ser.). 31p. 1990. 4.00 (1-56778-037-7) Wilson Lang Trning.

Student Workbook Five. Barbara A. Wilson. (Wilson Reading System Ser.). 38p. 1990. 4.00 (1-56778-031-8) Wilson Lang Trning.

Student Workbook for Clinical Pharmacology & Nursing. 4th ed. Roberta T. Spencer. 368p. 1992. pap. text ed. 17.95 (0-397-54936-9) Lppncott-Raven.

Student Workbook for Comprehensive Maternity Nursing: Nursing Process & the Childbearing Family. 2nd ed. May & Mehlmeister. 272p. 1990. text ed. 15.95 (0-397-54754-4) Lppncott-Raven.

Student Workbook for Essentials of Anatomy & Physiology. 2nd ed. Valerie C. Scanlon. 417p. 1994. pap. 18.95 (0-8036-7736-7) Davis Co.

Student Workbook for Health Careers Today. Gerdin. 368p. (gr. 13). 1990. pap. text ed. 14.95 (0-8016-2470-3) Mosby Yr Bk.

Student Workbook for History of the United States with Topics, Vol. II. Contrib. by Jerry R. Baydo et al. 206p. 1995. 12.00 (0-911541-38-1) Gregory Pub.

Student Workbook for Interactive Differential Equations Version 1.0. Beverly West. (C). 1997. pap. text ed. 12.95 (0-201-57132-3) Addison-Wesley.

Student Workbook for Introduction to Communication Sciences & Disorders. Fred D. Minifie et al. (Illus.). 128p. (Orig.). (C). 1994. spiral bd. 24.95 (1-56593-361-3, 0690) Singular Publishing.

Student Workbook for the Oklahoma Story by Arrell M. Gibson. Barbara Schindler. (Illus.). 49p. (gr. 6-12). 1982. pap. 4.95 (0-8061-1766-4) U of Okla Pr.

***Student Workbook for Understanding Human Structure & Function.** Valerie C. Scanlon & Tina Sanders. (Illus.). 356p. 1997. pap. 15.95 (0-8036-0242-1) Davis Co.

Student Workbook Four. Barbara A. Wilson. (Wilson Reading System Ser.). 36p. 1990. 4.00 (1-56778-030-X) Wilson Lang Trning.

Student Workbook Lesson 1-6. Christensen. (gr. 13). 1985. spiral bd. 16.95 (0-8016-1383-3) Mosby Yr Bk.

Student Workbook Nine. Barbara A. Wilson. (Wilson Reading System Ser.). 42p. 1990. 4.00 (1-56778-035-0) Wilson Lang Trning.

Student Workbook One. Barbara A. Wilson. (Wilson Reading System Ser.). 52p. 1990. 4.00 (1-56778-027-X) Wilson Lang Trning.

Student Workbook Seven. Barbara A. Wilson. (Wilson Reading System Ser.). 34p. 1990. 4.00 (1-56778-033-4) Wilson Lang Trning.

Student Workbook Six. Barbara A. Wilson. (Wilson Reading System Ser.). 32p. 1990. 4.00 (1-56778-032-6) Wilson Lang Trning.

Student Workbook Ten. Barbara A. Wilson. (Wilson Reading System Ser.). 28p. 1990. 4.00 (1-56778-036-9) Wilson Lang Trning.

Student Workbook Three. Barbara A. Wilson. (Wilson Reading System Ser.). 34p. 1990. 4.00 (1-56778-029-6) Wilson Lang Trning.

***Student Workbook to Accompany Clinical Pharmacology & Nursing Management.** 5th ed. Laurel Eisenhauer et al. 368p. 1997. pap. text ed. 17.95 (0-397-55332-3) Lppncott-Raven.

Student Workbook to Accompany Criminology: Explaining Crime & Its Context. 2nd ed. Randy C. Hass et al. 213p. (C). 1995. write for info. (0-87084-114-9) Anderson Pub Co.

Student Workbook to Accompany Introduction to Criminal Justice Research & Statistics. Larry S. Miller et al. 221p. (C). 1995. wbk. ed. write for info. (0-87084-566-7) Anderson Pub Co.

Student Workbook Twelve. Barbara A. Wilson. (Wilson Reading System Ser.). 30p. 1990. 4.00 (1-56778-038-5) Wilson Lang Trning.

Student Workbook Two. Barbara A. Wilson. (Wilson Reading System Ser.). 36p. 1990. 4.00 (1-56778-028-8) Wilson Lang Trning.

Student Workbooks One-Six. Barbara A. Wilson. (Wilson Reading System Ser.). 228p. 1990. 18.00 (1-56778-025-3) Wilson Lang Trning.

Student Workbooks One-Twelve. Barbara A. Wilson. (Wilson Reading System Ser.). 428p. 1990. 36.00 (1-56778-024-5) Wilson Lang Trning.

Student Workbooks Seven-Twelve. Barbara A. Wilson. (Wilson Reading System Ser.). 200p. 1990. 18.00 (1-56778-026-1) Wilson Lang Trning.

Student World Atlas. Julia Gorton. (Illus.). 48p. (J). (gr. 3-6). 1994. pap. 12.99 (0-525-67491-8, Lodestar Bks) Dutton Child Bks.

Student Worlds, Student Words: Teaching Writing Through Folklore. Elizabeth R. Simons. LC 89-71286. 232p. 1990. pap. text ed. 19.50 (0-86709-256-4, 0256) Boynton Cook Pubs.

Student Writer. Smith. (C). 1991. pap. text ed. 38.50 (0-06-046323-6) Addson-Wesley Educ.

Student Writer: Editor & Critic. 3rd ed. Barbara F. Clouse. LC 91-23061. 1992. text ed. write for info. (0-07-011414-5) McGraw.

Student Writer: Editor & Critic. 4th ed. Barbara F. Clouse. LC 95-14357. 1995. pap. text ed. write for info. (0-07-011448-X) McGraw.

An Asterisk (*) at the beginning of an entry indicates that the title is appearing in BIP for the first time.

Student Writer's Guide: An A-Z of Writing & Language. 2nd ed. Ed. by Nigel Kent. 1990. pap. 36.50 (*0-7487-0499-X*, Pub. by Stanley Thornes UK) Trans-Atl Phila.

Student Writing in Philosophy: A Companion to Cover & Garns (Custom Publication) Oja. 1989. pap. text ed. write for info. (*0-07-013274-7*) McGraw.

Student Young Choir: Essential Repertoire in Tenor Bass Level One. 184p. 1995. 12.95 (*0-7935-4224-3*, 08740096) H Leonard.

Student Young Choir: Essential Repertoire Level One Treble. 168p. 1995. 12.95 (*0-7935-4336-3*, 08740071) H Leonard.

Studenten der Universitat zu Rinteln. Compiled by August Woringer. (Alumni of German Universities Ser.). 1990. reprint ed. 30.00 (*0-8115-3821-4*) Periodicals Srv.

Studenthood New Age Reader: Educational Collection of Essays with Supplements. Ed. by Sdiane A. Bogus. 213p. (Orig.). 1996. pap. 40.00 (*0-536-58729-9*) WIM Pubns.

Students: Changing Roles, Changing Lives. Harold Silver & Pamela Silver. LC 96-25916. 208p. 1996. 89.00 (*0-335-19559-8*); pap. 29.95 (*0-335-19558-X*, Open Univ Pr) Taylor & Francis.

Student's A to Z Guide to Bible Application. LC 95-40482. 1996. pap. 10.99 (*0-8423-5938-9*) Tyndale.

Students Abroad - Strangers at Home: Education for a Global Society. Norman L. Kauffmann et al. LC 91-38527. 208p. (Orig.). 1992. pap. 19.95 (*0-933662-94-7*) Intercult Pr.

***Students Against Violence.** Gerri Holden. (Illus.). 48p. (J). (gr. 1-5). 1995. 7.95 (*1-55734-518-X*) Tchr Create Mat.

Students & Drugs: College & High School Observations. Richard H. Blum et al. LC 73-75936. (Jossey-Bass Behavioral Science Ser. & Series in Higher Education). 419p. reprint ed. pap. 119.50 (*0-8357-4968-1*, 2037901) Bks Demand.

***Students & National Socialism in Germany.** Geoffrey J. Giles. LC 85-42686. 377p. 1985. reprint ed. pap. 107.50 (*0-608-03298-0*, 2063816) Bks Demand.

Students & Politics: A Case Study of Benares Hindu University, India. Anil Ray. 1978. 14.00 (*0-88386-789-3*) S Asia.

Students & Politics in India. A. B. Ray. 232p. 1977. 15.95 (*0-318-36618-5*) Asia Bk Corp.

Students & Research: Practical Strategies for Science Classrooms & Competitions. 2nd ed. Julia H. Cothron. 304p. 1995. per. 25.14 (*0-8403-7766-5*) Kendall-Hunt.

Students & Science Learning: Papers from the 1987 National Forum for School Science. National Forum for School Science Staff. Ed. by Audrey B. Champagne & Leslie E. Hornig. (AAAS Publication Ser.: No. 87-29). 181p. reprint ed. pap. 51.60 (*0-8357-2824-2*, 2039060) Bks Demand.

Students & Society in Early Modern Spain. Richard L. Kagan. LC 74-6828. (Illus.). 304p. reprint ed. pap. 86.70 (*0-8357-6616-0*, 2035261) Bks Demand.

Students & Teachers Writing Together: Perspectives on Journal Writing. Ed. by Joy K. Peyton. LC 89-51728. 138p. (Orig.). 1990. pap. 11.95 (*0-939791-36-6*) Tchrs Eng Spkrs.

Students & the Cold War. Joel Kotek. Tr. by Ralph Blumenau. 296p. 1996. text ed. 65.00 (*0-312-15877-7*) St Martin.

Students & the Law. Lawrence F. Rossow & Janice A. Hininger. LC 91-60202. (Fastback Ser.: No. 317). (Orig.). 1991. pap. 3.00 (*0-87367-317-4*) Phi Delta Kappa.

Students & University in Twentieth Century Egyptian Politics. Haggai Erlich. (Illus.). 268p. 1989. text ed. 45.00 (*0-7146-3333-X*, Pub. by F Cass Pubs UK) Intl Spec Bk.

Students As Researchers of Culture & Language. Ed. by Ann Egan-Robertson & David Bloome. (Language & Social Processes Ser.). 320p. (C). 1997. text ed. 65.00 (*1-57273-044-7*); pap. text ed. 27.50 (*1-57273-045-5*) Hampton Pr NJ.

Students As Storytellers: The Long & the Short of Learning a Story. Barbara B. Griffin. 130p. (Orig.). 1989. pap. 12.95 (*0-9623331-1-5*) Strytller Guidebk.

Students at Risk. M. Lee Manning & Leroy G. Baruth. LC 93-50125. 1994. pap. text ed. 40.00 (*0-205-15464-6*) Allyn.

Students at Risk: A Study of Three Minnesota Counties. Harold L. Hodgkinson. 13p. 1990. 7.00 (*0-937846-59-7*) Inst Educ Lead.

***Students At-Risk: The Teachers Call to Action.** Carlos A. Bonilla et al. LC 97-71123. (Illus.). 100p. (Orig.). 1997. teacher ed., pap. 19.95 (*1-879774-09-7*) ICA Pub Co.

Students at Risk: Winning Colors Power Pack. (Personality Language Ser.). 87p. (YA). (gr. 6-12). 1990. teacher ed., spiral bd. 30.00 (*1-880830-10-8*); student ed., spiral bd. 20.00 (*1-880830-11-6*) AEON-Hierophant.

Students at Risk in At-Risk Schools: Improving Environments for Learning. Ed. by Hersholt C. Waxman et al. LC 91-38882. 296p. 1992. 44.95 (*0-8039-4003-3*, D1478) Corwin Pr.

Students at the Center: Feminist Assessment. Ed. by Caryn M. Musil. 80p. 1992. 12.00 (*0-911696-56-3*) Assn Am Coll.

***Student's Atlas of American Presidential Elections 1789-1996.** Fred L. Israel. LC 97-10233. 1997. write for info. (*1-56802-377-4*) Congr Quarterly.

Student's Atlas of Nueroanatomy. Walter J. Hendelman. LC 93-41702. 1994. pap. text ed. 32.50 (*0-7216-5428-2*) Saunders.

***Students Autosketch.** Yarwood. (C). 1992. pap. text ed. 12.95 (*0-582-08383-4*, Pub. by Longman UK) Longman.

Student's Basic Exercises for Piano, Vol. 1. John F. Loth. 1993. 5.95 (*1-56222-268-6*, 94587) Mel Bay.

Student's Basic Exercises for Piano, Vol. 2. John F. Loth. 1993. 5.95 (*1-56222-269-4*, 94634) Mel Bay.

Students Being Disciplined: Getting Confused, Getting by, Getting Rewarded, Getting Smart, Getting Real. Charles Bazerman. Ed. by Lillian Bridwell-Bowles & Kim Donethower. (Technical Reports: Vol. 12). 9p. (Orig.). 1996. pap. 2.00 (*1-881221-20-2*) U Minn Ctr Interdis.

Student's Bible Atlas. Ed. by H. H. Rowley. 40p. 1984. pap. 5.50 (*0-8170-1022-X*) Judson.

Student's Book of College English: Rhetoric, Readings, Handbook. 6th ed. David Skwire & Harvey S. Wiener. (Illus.). 656p. (C). 1992. teacher ed. write for info. (*0-318-69284-8*) Macmillan.

Student's Book of College English: Rhetoric, Readings, Handbook. 7th ed. David Skwire & Harvey S. Wiener. 1995. student ed., pap. text ed. 38.00 (*0-205-18025-6*) Allyn.

Student's Catullus. annuals 2nd ed. Ed. by Daniel H. Garrison. LC 95-1280. (Oklahoma Series in Classical Culture: Vol. 5). (Illus.). 248p. (LAT.). 1995. pap. text ed. 14.95 (*0-8061-2763-5*) U of Okla Pr.

Student's Choice Professional Set, Set. 1988. 49.50 (*0-318-40015-4*, SP700SC) Ctr Educ Trng Employ.

Student's Choice Student Workbook, Dropout Prevention. National Center for Research in Vocational Education Staff. 1988. write for info. (*0-318-67189-1*, SP700SC01) Ctr Educ Trng Employ.

***Student's Companion to Social Policy.** Ed. by Pete Alcock et al. (Illus.). 320p. (C). 1997. text ed. 69.00 (*0-631-20239-0*) Blackwell Pubs.

***Student's Companion to Social Policy.** Ed. by Pete Alcock et al. (Illus.). 320p. (C). 1997. pap. text ed. 29.95 (*0-631-20240-4*) Blackwell Pubs.

***Student's Companion to Sociology.** Ed. by Chet Ballard et al. LC 96-33056. (Illus.). 320p. 1997. text ed. 59.95 (*0-631-19947-0*); pap. text ed. 21.95 (*0-631-19948-9*) Blackwell Pubs.

Student's Complete Music Handbook. L. Dean Bye. 1993. 7.95 (*0-87166-988-9*, 94407) Mel Bay.

Student's Complete Vocabulary Guide to the Greek New Testament. Warren C. Trenchard. 350p. 1992. pap. 12.99 (*0-310-53341-4*) Zondervan.

Student's Concerto for Violin & Piano, No. 5. (Carl Fischer Music Library: No. 594). 1904. pap. 6.95 (*0-8258-0081-1*, L594) Fischer Inc NY.

Student's Concerto No. 1 in D Major for Violin & Piano, Op. 7. F. Seitz. (Carl Fischer Music Library: No. 590). 1904. pap. 6.95 (*0-8258-0077-3*, L590) Fischer Inc NY.

Students Cookbook. Lodge. (Quick & Easy Ser.). 1995. pap. 7.95 (*0-572-01804-5*, Pub. by Foulsham UK) Assoc Pubs Grp.

Student's Cookbook. 2nd ed. Jenny Baker. (Illus.). 176p. 1996. reprint ed. pap. 10.95 (*0-571-17646-1*) Faber & Faber.

Student's Coursebook for Introduction to Communicative Disorders. 2nd ed. M. N. Hegde. 1995. pap. 19.00 (*0-89079-614-9*, 6871) PRO-ED.

Students, Courses & Jobs: The Relationship Between Higher Education & the Labour Market. J. L. Brennan. (Higher Education Policy Ser.: No. 21). 204p. 1993. 55.00 (*1-85302-538-0*) Taylor & Francis.

***Student's Dictionary of Language & Linguistics.** pap. write for info. (*0-340-65266-7*, Pub. by E Arnold UK) Routledge Chapman & Hall.

***Student's Dictionary of Language & Linguistics.** write for info. (*0-340-65267-5*, Pub. by E Arnold UK) Routledge Chapman & Hall.

Student's Dictionary of Psychology. Peter Stratton & Nicky Hayes. 224p. 1989. 49.50 (*0-7131-6500-6*, Pub. by E Arnold UK); pap. 13.95 (*0-7131-6501-4*, Pub. by E Arnold UK) Routledge Chapman & Hall.

Student's Dictionary of Psychology. 2nd ed. Peter Stratton & Nicky Hayes. LC 92-30214. 256p. 1995. text ed. 16.95 (*0-340-56926-3*, Pub. by E Arnld UK) St Martin.

Students' Discourse: Comprehensive Examples & Explanations of All Expository Modes & Argument, Precis, Narrative, Examination Writing & MLA Reccomendations for Research Paper Documentation Writing Exposition. 2nd ed. Valerie H. Weisberg. 126p. (YA). 1990. pap. 9.95 (*0-685-49571-X*) V H Pub.

Student's Effective Writer's Kit. Jim Evers. 1994. 21.95 (*0-9628230-4-X*) J L Evers Assocs.

Students Encyclopedia 1978. 1978. 15.00 (*0-02-945390-9*) Mac Lib Ref.

Students Encyclopedia 1983 see Students Encylopedia 1983

Students Encyclopedia 1986, Vol. 1. 1986. 30.00 (*0-02-943760-1*) Mac Lib Ref.

Students Encyclopedia 1986, Vol. 2. 1986. 30.00 (*0-02-943770-9*) Mac Lib Ref.

Students Encyclopedia 1986, Vol. 3. 1986. 30.00 (*0-02-943780-6*) Mac Lib Ref.

Students Encyclopedia 1986, Vol. 4. 1986. 30.00 (*0-02-943790-3*) Mac Lib Ref.

Students Encyclopedia 1986, Vol. 5. 1986. 30.00 (*0-02-943800-4*) Mac Lib Ref.

Students Encyclopedia 1986, Vol. 6. 1986. 30.00 (*0-02-943810-1*) Mac Lib Ref.

Students Encyclopedia 1986, Vol. 7. 1986. 30.00 (*0-02-943820-9*) Mac Lib Ref.

Students Encyclopedia 1986, Vol. 8. 1986. 30.00 (*0-02-943830-6*) Mac Lib Ref.

Students Encyclopedia 1986, Vol. 9. 1986. 30.00 (*0-02-943840-3*) Mac Lib Ref.

Students Encyclopedia 1986, Vol. 10. 1986. 30.00 (*0-02-943850-0*) Mac Lib Ref.

Students Encyclopedia 1986, Vol. 11. 1986. 30.00 (*0-02-943860-8*) Mac Lib Ref.

Students Encyclopedia 1986, Vol. 12. 1986. 30.00 (*0-02-943870-5*) Mac Lib Ref.

Students Encyclopedia 1986, Vol. 13. 1986. 30.00 (*0-02-943880-2*) Mac Lib Ref.

Students Encyclopedia 1986, Vol. 14. 1986. 30.00 (*0-02-943890-X*) Mac Lib Ref.

Students Encyclopedia 1986, Vol. 15. 1986. 30.00 (*0-02-943900-0*) Mac Lib Ref.

Students Encyclopedia 1986, Vol. 16. 1986. 30.00 (*0-02-943910-8*) Mac Lib Ref.

Students Encyclopedia 1986, Vol. 17. 1986. 30.00 (*0-02-943920-5*) Mac Lib Ref.

Students Encyclopedia 1986, Vol. 18. 1986. 30.00 (*0-02-943930-2*) Mac Lib Ref.

Students Encyclopedia 1986, Vol. 19. 1986. 30.00 (*0-02-943940-X*) Mac Lib Ref.

Students Encyclopedia 1986, Vol. 20. 1986. 30.00 (*0-02-943950-7*) Mac Lib Ref.

Students Encylopedia 1983, 20 vols. Incl. Vol. 1. Students Encyclopedia 1983. 1983. 22.00 (*0-02-945020-9*); Vol. 2. Students Encyclopedia 1983. , 20 vols. 1983. 22.00 (*0-02-945030-6*); Vol. 3. Students Encyclopedia 1983. 1983. 22.00 (*0-02-945040-3*); Vol. 5. Students Encyclopedia 1983. , 20 vols. 1983. 22.00 (*0-02-945070-5*); Vol. 6. Students Encyclopedia 1983. , 20 vols. 1983. 22.00 (*0-02-945090-X*); Vol. 7. Students Encyclopedia 1983. , 20 vols. 1983. 22.00 (*0-02-945100-0*); Vol. 8. Students Encyclopedia 1983. , 20 vols. 1983. 22.00 (*0-02-945110-8*); Vol. 9. Students Encyclopedia 1983. , 20 vols. 1983. 22.00 (*0-02-945120-5*); Vol. 10. Students Encyclopedia 1983. , 20 vols. 1983. 22.00 (*0-02-945130-2*); Vol. 11. Students Encyclopedia 1983. , 20 vols. 1983. 22.00 (*0-02-945140-X*); Vol. 12. Students Encyclopedia 1983. , 20 vols. 1983. 22.00 (*0-02-945150-7*); Vol. 13. Students Encyclopedia 1983. , 20 vols. 1983. 22.00 (*0-02-945160-4*); Vol. 14. Students Encyclopedia 1983. , 20 vols. 1983. 22.00 (*0-02-945170-1*); Vol. 15. Students Encyclopedia 1983. , 20 vols. 1983. 22.00 (*0-02-945190-6*); Vol. 16. Students Encyclopedia 1983. , 20 vols. 1983. 22.00 (*0-02-945200-7*); Vol. 18. Students Encyclopedia 1983. , 20 vols. 1983. 22.00 (*0-02-945220-1*); Vol. 19 . Students Encyclopedia 1983. , 20 vols. 1983. 22.00 (*0-02-945230-9*); 349.00 (*0-02-945010-1*) Mac Lib Ref.

Students for a Democratic Society Papers, 1958-1970: A Guide to the Microfilm Edition of the Original Records in the State Historical Society of Wisconsin. Ed. by Jack T. Ericson. 82p. 1986. pap. 55.00 (*0-667-00542-0*) Chadwyck-Healey.

Students! Get Ready for the Mathematics SAT I: Problem-Solving Strategies & Practice Tests. Alfred S. Posamentier. LC 95-49784. (Illus.). 216p. 1996. pap. 17.95 (*0-8039-6415-3*) Corwin Pr.

Student's Glossary of Finnish. M. Branch. 378p. (ENG, FRE, GER, HUN, RUS & SWE.). 1980. 59.95 (*0-8288-1449-X*, F47180) Fr & Eur.

Student's Gold: A Treasury of Wisdom & Inspiration for Today's Student. 1994. 14.99 (*1-56292-007-3*) Honor Bks OK.

Student's Grammar of English Language. Sylvia Chalker. 300p. (C). 1992. student ed., pap. text ed. 20.50 (*0-582-08819-4*) Longman.

Student's Grammar of the English Language. Sidney Greenbaum & Randolph Quirk. 490p. (C). 1990. pap. text ed. 33.95 (*0-582-05971-2*, 78821) Longman.

Student's Guide for Projects, Field Studies & Research. enl. rev. ed. Arthur Adamson. 96p. (C). 1986. 33.00 (*0-685-34647-1*) St Mut.

Students Guide for Writing College Papers. 3rd rev. ed. Kate L. Turabian. LC 76-435. 268p. 1977. pap. 8.95 (*0-226-81623-0*) U Ch Pr.

Students' Guide to Accounting, Vols. I & II. 4th ed. C. Edward Cavert et al. 467p. (C). 1982. text ed. 25.95 (*0-931920-43-4*) Dame Pubns.

Students Guide to Accounting & Financial Reporting Standards 1995-96. Geoff Black. 270p. 1995. pap. 59.95 (*1-85805-125-8*, Pub. by DP Publns UK) St Mut.

***Student's Guide to African American Genealogy.** Anne E. Johnson & Adam M. Cooper. (Our American Family Tree Ser.). (Illus.). 200p. (J). (gr. 7-12). 1996. 24.95 (*0-8239-2587-0*, D2587-0) Rosen Group.

Student's Guide to African American Genealogy see Oryx American Family Tree

Student's Guide to American Government. Carl M. Dibble. 96p. 1993. spiral bd. 12.54 (*0-8403-8973-6*) Kendall-Hunt.

Student's Guide to Archaeological Illustrating. 2nd rev. ed. Ed. by Brian D. Dillon. LC 85-24066. (UCLA Institute of Archaeology Publications: No. 1). (Illus.). 185p. (C). 1985. pap. 20.00 (*0-917956-38-9*) UCLA Arch.

Student's Guide to Basic French. 2nd ed. Arnold. 1980. pap. text ed. 23.28 (*0-88334-021-6*, 76043) Longman.

Student's Guide to Better Grades. J. A. Richard. 1976. pap. 3.00 (*0-87980-152-2*) Wilshire.

Student's Guide to British American Genealogy see Oryx American Family Tree

***Student's Guide to British American Genealogy (England, Scotland, & Wales)** Anne E. Johnson. (Our American Family Tree Ser.). (Illus.). 200p. (J). (gr. 7-12). 1996. 24.95 (*0-8239-2588-9*, D2588-9) Rosen Group.

Student's Guide to Brown & Lemay--Chemistry--the Central Science. 4th ed. James C. Hill. (Illus.). 316p. (C). 1988. pap. text ed. write for info. (*0-13-129859-3*) P-H.

Student's Guide to Calculus, Vol. 3. F. H. Soon. (Illus.). 312p. 1992. 28.95 (*0-387-96348-0*) Spr-Verlag.

Student's Guide to "Calculus" by J. Marsden & A. Weinstein, Vol. 1. F. H. Soon. xiv, 312p. 1985. 27.95 (*0-387-96207-7*) Spr-Verlag.

Student's Guide to Calculus by J. Marsden & A. Weinstein, Vol. 2. F. H. Soon. (Illus.). xiv, 281p. 1985. 27.95 (*0-387-96234-4*) Spr-Verlag.

***Student's Guide to Chinese American Genealogy.** Colleen She. (Our American Family Tree Ser.). (Illus.). 200p. (J). (gr. 7-12). 1996. 24.95 (*0-8239-2589-7*, D2589-7) Rosen Group.

Student's Guide to Chinese American Genealogy see Oryx American Family Tree

Student's Guide to College Admissions: Everything Your Guidance Counselor Has No Time to Tell You. 3rd ed. Harlow G. Unger. LC 94-42395. 192p. 1995. 22.95 (*0-8160-3198-3*); pap. write for info. (*0-8160-3199-1*) Facts on File.

Student's Guide to Conducting Social Science Research. Barbara Bunker et al. LC 74-11814. 120p. (C). 1975. pap. 16.95 (*0-87705-238-7*) Human Sci Pr.

Student's Guide to Creative Writing. Naomi L. Madgett. LC 79-93055. 134p. (C). 1980. pap. 11.00 (*0-916418-24-3*, Penway Bks) Lotus.

Student's Guide to Doing Research on the Internet. Dave Campbell & Mary Campbell. LC 95-13498. (C). 1995. pap. text ed. 14.95 (*0-201-48916-3*) Addison-Wesley.

***Students Guide to Easements, Real Covenants & Equitable Servitudes.** 2nd ed. Siegel. 1996. student ed., text ed. 20.76 (*0-256-22165-0*) McGraw.

Student's Guide to Estates in Land & Future Interests: Text, Examples, Problems, & Answers. 2nd ed. Robert Laurence & Pamela B. Minzner. (Student Guide Ser.). 1981. write for info. (*0-8205-0351-7*, 635); teacher ed. write for info. (*0-8205-0352-5*) Bender.

Student's Guide to Estates in Land & Future Interests: Text, Examples, Problems, & Answers. 2nd ed. Robert Laurence & Pamela B. Minzner. LC 93-14440. (Student Guide Ser.). 1993. write for info. (*0-8205-0353-3*) Bender.

Student's Guide to Finding a Superior Job. 2nd ed. William A. Cohen. Ed. by JoAnn Padgett. LC 87-4487. 108p. 1993. pap. 9.95 (*0-89384-200-1*, Pfffr & Co) Jossey-Bass.

***Student's Guide to First-Year English & Advanced Writing.** Beth Daniell. (Illus.). 50p. (C). Date not set. pap. text ed. 5.00 (*1-886855-55-2*) Tavenner Pub.

Student's Guide to Fourier Transforms: With Applications in Physics & Engineering. J. F. James. (Illus.). 128p. (C). 1995. text ed. 39.95 (*0-521-46298-3*) Cambridge U Pr.

Student's Guide to Fourier Transforms: With Applications in Physics & Engineering. J. F. James. (Illus.). 128p. (C). 1995. pap. text ed. 16.95 (*0-521-46829-9*) Cambridge U Pr.

***Student's Guide to German American Genealogy.** Gregory Robl. (Our American Family Tree Ser.). (Illus.). 200p. (J). (gr. 7-12). 1996. 24.95 (*0-8239-2590-0*, D2590-0) Rosen Group.

Student's Guide to German American Genealogy see Oryx American Family Tree

Student's Guide to Good Writing. Rick Dalton & Marianne Dalton. 166p. 1990. pap. 9.95 (*0-87447-353-5*) College Bd.

Student's Guide to History. 6th ed. Jules R. Benjamin. 176p. 1994. pap. text ed. 11.00 (*0-312-08432-3*) St Martin.

Student's Guide to Hong Kong Conveyancing. Judith E. Sihombing. 710p. (C). 1994. pap. write for info. (*0-409-99681-5*, ASIA) MICHIE.

Students' Guide to Information Technology. 2nd ed. Roger Carter. LC 92-39699. 255p. 1993. pap. 31.95 (*0-7506-0941-9*) Buttrwrth-Heinemann.

***Student's Guide to Irish American Genealogy.** Erin McKenna. (Our American Family Tree Ser.). (Illus.). 200p. (J). (gr. 7-12). 1996. 24.95 (*0-8239-2591-9*, D2591-9) Rosen Group.

Student's Guide to Irish American Genealogy see Oryx American Family Tree

***Student's Guide to Italian American Genealogy.** Terra C. Brockman. (Our American Family Tree Ser.). (Illus.). 200p. (J). (gr. 7-12). 1996. 24.95 (*0-8239-2592-7*, D2592-7) Rosen Group.

Student's Guide to Italian American Genealogy see Oryx American Family Tree

***Student's Guide to Japanese American Genealogy.** Yoji Yamaguchi. (Our American Family Tree Ser.). (Illus.). 200p. (J). (gr. 7-12). 1996. 24.95 (*0-8239-2593-5*, D2593-5) Rosen Group.

Student's Guide to Japanese American Genealogy see Oryx American Family Tree

***Student's Guide to Jewish American Genealogy.** Jay Schleifer. (Our American Family Tree Ser.). (Illus.). 200p. (J). (gr. 7-12). 1996. 24.95 (*0-8239-2594-3*, D2594-3) Rosen Group.

Student's Guide to Jewish American Genealogy see Oryx American Family Tree

Student's Guide to Mediation & the Law. Rogers & Salem. 1987. teacher ed. write for info. (*0-8205-0402-5*) Bender.

***Student's Guide to Mexican American Genealogy.** George R. Ryskamp & Peggy Ryskamp. (Our American Family Tree Ser.). (Illus.). 200p. (J). (gr. 7-12). 1996. 24.95 (*0-8239-2595-1*, D2595-1) Rosen Group.

Student's Guide to Mexican American Genealogy see Oryx American Family Tree

Student's Guide to Music Theory. L. Dean Bye. 1993. 3.95 (*0-87166-312-0*, 94086) Mel Bay.

***Student's Guide to Native American Genealogy.** E. Barrie Kavasch. (Our American Family Tree Ser.). (Illus.). 200p. (J). (gr. 7-12). 1996. 24.95 (*0-8239-2596-X*, D2596-X) Rosen Group.

Student's Guide to Native American Genealogy see Oryx American Family Tree

Student's Guide to Ontario Universities. Dyanne Gibson. 286p. 1990. pap. 15.95 (*0-8020-6759-X*) U of Toronto Pr.

Students' Guide to Operations Research. Paul A. Jensen. LC 86-80839. 502p. 1986. 16.95 (*0-317-59480-X*) Holden-Day.

S

S

Student's Guide to Philosophy. Peter A. Facione. LC 87-24864. 162p. (C). 1988. pap. text ed. 18.95 (*0-87484-832-6*, 832) Mayfield Pub.

Student's Guide to Playwriting Opportunities. Ed. by Michael Wright. 136p. 1995. spiral bd. 14.95 (*0-933919-33-6*) Theatre Directories.

***Student's Guide to Polish American Genealogy.** Carl S. Rollyson & Lisa O. Paddock. (Our American Family Tree Ser.). (Illus.). 200p. (J). (gr. 7-12). 1996. 24.95 (*0-8239-2597-8*, D2597-8) Rosen Group.

Student's Guide to Polish American Genealogy see Oryx American Family Tree

Student's Guide to Racine. Philip Butler. (Student's Guides to European Literature Ser.). 106p. (C). 1978. pap. text ed. 7.50 (*0-435-37582-2*, 37582) Heinemann.

Student's Guide to Roman Law (Justinian & Gaius) Dalzell Chalmers & L. H. Barnes. LC 93-79704. 367p. 1994. reprint ed. 80.00 (*1-56169-062-7*) Gaunt.

Student's Guide to Sales, Letters of Credit & Documents of Title. Hart & Laurence. 1987. write for info. (*0-8205-0417-3*, 677) Bender.

Student's Guide to Sales of Goods, Letters of Credit & Documents of Title. Frederick Hart & Robert Lawrence. (Student Guides Ser.). (C). 1993. pap. text ed. 25.00 (*0-256-14693-4*) Irwin.

Student's Guide to Sanskrit Composition: Being a Treatise on Sanskrit Syntax. Vaman S. Apte. 404p. 1995. 12.00 (*81-86339-20-5*, Pub. by Estrn Bk Linkers II) Nataraj Bks.

***Student's Guide to Scandinavian American Genealogy.** Lisa O. Paddock & Carl S. Rollyson. (Our American Family Tree Ser.). (Illus.). 200p. (J). (gr. 7-12). 1996. 24.95 (*0-8239-2598-6*, D2598-6) Rosen Group.

Student's Guide to Scandinavian American Genealogy see Oryx American Family Tree

***Student's Guide to Success in the Real World: Method to the Madness.** John R. Jell. LC 97-60294. 190p. 1997. pap. text ed. 24.95 (*1-56676-532-3*) Technomic.

Student's Guide to the Art of Teaching the Pianoforte. Cyril R. Horrocks. 245p. 1991. reprint ed. lib. bdg. 79.00 (*0-7812-9337-5*) Rprt Serv.

Student's Guide to the Best Study Abroad. Charley Winkler & Greg Tannen. LC 95-49169. (Illus.). 320p. 1996. pap. 12.00 (*0-671-55027-6*) PB.

Student's Guide to the Bible. Philip Yancey & Tim Stafford. 96p. 1988. pap. 5.99 (*0-310-58961-4*, 10290P) Zondervan.

Students Guide to the Doctrine & Covenants. F. Henry Edwards. 1980. pap. 12.50 (*0-8309-0267-8*) Herald Hse.

Student's Guide to the Gospels. James M. Reese. (Good News Studies: Vol. 24). 150p. (Orig.). 1992. pap. text ed. 11.95 (*0-8146-5689-7*) Liturgical Pr.

Student's Guide to the Great Composers. L. Dean Bye. 1993. 3.95 (*0-87166-314-7*, 94230) Mel Bay.

Student's Guide to the Insolvency Law of South Africa. 5th ed. Robert Sharrock. 277p. 1990. pap. write for info. (*0-7021-2518-0*, Pub. by Juta SA) Gaunt.

Student's Guide to the Internet. David Clark. (Illus.). 350p. (Orig.). 1995. student ed. 14.99 (*1-56761-545-7*, Alpha Ref) Macmillan Gen Ref.

***Students' Guide to the Internet.** Ian Winship & Alison McNab. 96p. 1996. pap. 14.00 (*1-85604-207-3*, LAP2073, Pub. by Library Association UK) Bernan Associates.

Students Guide to the Internet. 2nd ed. David Clark. 352p. 1996. 14.99 (*0-7897-0881-7*) Que.

***Student's Guide to the Internet.** 2nd ed. Carol C. Powell. (C). 1997. pap. text ed. 15.00 (*0-13-649112-X*) P-H.

Student's Guide to the Internet: Exploring the World Wide Web, Gopherspace, Electronic Mail, & More! Elizabeth L. Marshall. LC 96-5163. (Illus.). 160p. (YA). (gr. 5 up). 1996. lib. bdg. 17.90 (*1-56294-923-3*) Millbrook Pr.

Student's Guide to the Job Market of Tomorrow. Linda Hewitt. (Lenox Publishing Company Career Materials Ser.). (Illus.). 240p. (Orig.). 1985. pap. 11.95 (*0-917421-03-5*) Lenox Pub.

Student's Guide to the MELAB. Mary C. Spaan. 146p. 1992. pap. text ed. 14.95 (*0-472-08146-2*); pap. text ed. 25.00 incl. audio (*0-472-08165-9*); audio 15.00 (*0-472-00232-5*) U of Mich Pr.

Student's Guide to the Sea Shore. John Fish & Stanley Fish. 400p. 1990. text ed. 60.00 (*0-04-574043-7*) Routledge Chapman & Hall.

Student's Guide to the Seashore. 2nd ed. J. D. Fish & S. Fish. (Illus.). 512p. (C). 1996. student ed., text ed. 105.00 (*0-521-46279-7*); student ed., pap. text ed. 39.95 (*0-521-46819-1*) Cambridge U Pr.

Student's Guide to the Selected Poems of T. S. Eliot. B. C. Southam. (Student Guides Ser.). 206p. (Orig.). 1990. pap. 8.95 (*0-571-14292-3*) Faber & Faber.

Student's Guide to UNIX. Harley Hahn. 1993. pap. text ed. 30.25 (*0-07-025511-3*) McGraw.

Student's Guide to Unix. 2nd ed. Harley Hahn. 1996. pap. text ed. write for info. (*0-07-025492-3*) McGraw.

Student's Guide to Volunteering: Do the Right Thing. Theresa DeGeronimo. 192p. (Orig.). (YA). 1995. pap. 10.99 (*1-56414-170-5*) Career Pr Inc.

Student's Guide to Will Drafting. Levin. 1987. teacher ed. write for info. (*0-8205-0442-4*) Bender.

Student's Guide to Writing a Sceintific Paper: How to Survive the Laboratory Research Report. 2nd ed. Alan Gubanich. 48p. (C). 1994. per. 7.45 (*0-8403-9412-8*) Kendall-Hunt.

Student's Gujarati Grammar. 2nd ed. G. P. Taylor. 264p. 1985. 33.75 (*0-8431-568-1*) IBD Ltd.

Student's Handbook for the Fourth R: Relating. rev. ed. Richard D. Solomon & Elaine C. Solomon. (Illus.). 181p. 1987. pap. text ed. 14.95 (*0-9617198-2-6*) NIRT Inc.

Student's Handbook of Figure Symmetry. Helen Fraser. 20p. 1970. reprint ed. spiral bd. 3.50 (*0-7873-0335-6*) Hlth Research.

Student's Handbook of Modern English. W. A. Gatherer. (C). 1988. 60.00 (*0-7157-2352-9*) St Mut.

Student's Hindi-Urdu Reference Manual. Franklin C. Southworth. LC 71-164367. 249p. 1971. reprint ed. pap. 71.00 (*0-608-02101-6*, 2055354) Bks Demand.

Student's History of Education. rev. ed. Frank P. Graves. LC 75-106716. (Illus.). xix, 567p. 1970. reprint ed. text ed. 85.00 (*0-8371-3541-9*, GRSH, Greenwood Pr) Greenwood.

Students in Trouble: A Casebook. Graham Hurlburt et al. 96p. (Orig.). 1996. pap. text ed. 13.95 (*1-55059-134-7*, Pub. by Detselig CN) Temeron Bks.

Students in Urban Settings: Achieving the Baccalaureate Degree. Richard C. Richardson, Jr. & Louis W. Bender. Ed. by Jonathan D. Fife. LC 85-73509. (ASHE-ERIC Higher Education Reports: No. 6, 1985). 90p. (Orig.). (C). 1985. pap. 10.00 (*0-913317-25-X*) GWU Grad Schl E&HD.

Students Indexed World Atlas, No. 695512. American Map Corp. Staff. (Illus.). (gr. 7-12). 1983. pap. 2.95 (*0-8416-9551-2*) Am Map.

Student's Introduction to History. 2nd ed. Donald W. Whisenhunt. 64p. 1993. pap. text ed. 8.95 (*0-89641-258-X*) American Pr.

Student's Latin Grammar: Cambridge Latin Course, North American Edition. M. R. Griffin & Ed Phinney. 96p. (C). 1992. pap. text ed. 13.95 (*0-521-38587-3*) Cambridge U Pr.

***Student's Law Lexicon: A Dictionary of Legal Words & Phrases with Appendices...** William C. Cochran. LC 97-25771. vii, 332p. 1997. reprint ed. lib. bdg. 47.50 (*0-8377-2060-5*) Rothman.

Student's Legal Rights on a Public School Campus. 119p. (YA). (gr. 9-12). Date not set. pap. 10.00 (*0-9648148-2-X*) Roever Commun.

Student's Manual for Balancing Body Chemistry with Nutrition. Robert J. Peshek. 1977. 20.00 (*0-9605902-1-8*) Color Coded Charting.

Students Manual of Auditing. 3rd ed. V. Cooper. 1985. pap. 55.95 (*0-85258-237-4*) Chapman & Hall.

Student's Marathi Grammar. R. Navlkar Ganpatrao. 392p. (ENG & MAR.). 1992. 49.95 (*0-8288-8443-9*) Fr & Eur.

Student's Musical Dictionary. L. Dean Bye. 1993. 3.95 (*0-87166-313-9*, 94057) Mel Bay.

Students Must Write: A Guide to Better Coursework & Examinations. 2nd ed. Robert Barrass. LC 95-14275. 208p. (C). 1995. pap. 14.95 (*0-415-13222-3*) Routledge.

Student's New Testament: The Greek Text & the American Translation. Edgar J. Goodspeed. 1065p. 1954. reprint ed. pap. 180.00 (*0-608-02102-4*, 2024115) Bks Demand.

Student's New Testament: The Greek Text & the American Translation, 2 vols., 1. Edgar J. Goodspeed. (Midway Reprint Ser.). 487p. 1975. reprint ed. pap. 138.80 (*0-608-02103-2*, 2026775) Bks Demand.

Student's New Testament: The Greek Text & the American Translation, 2 vols., 2. Edgar J. Goodspeed. (Midway Reprint Ser.). 584p. 1975. reprint ed. pap. 166.50 (*0-608-02104-0*, 2026775) Bks Demand.

Student's Obligation: Advice from the Rebbe of the Warsaw Ghetto. Kalonymus K. Shapira. Tr. by Micha Odenheimer. LC 90-28118. 264p. 1992. 29.95 (*0-87668-653-6*) Aronson.

Student's Obligation: Advice from the Rebbe of the Warsaw Ghetto. Kalonymus K. Shapira. Tr. by Micha Odenheimer. LC 90-28118. 268p. 1995. reprint ed. pap. 25.00 (*1-56821-517-7*) Aronson.

***Students Occupational Outlook Handbook, Vol. 1.** 2nd rev. ed. CFKR Staff. Ed. by Francis Ferry. (Illus.). 296p. (J). (gr. 6-9). 1994. pap. 16.95 (*0-934783-74-8*, SK94) CFKR Career.

Students of Color in the Writing Classroom: An Annotated Bibliography. Carolyn Evans & Carol Miller. Ed. by Lillian Bridwell-Bowles & Susan Batchelder. (Technical Reports: No. 2). 15p. (Orig.). 1992. pap. 2.50 (*1-881221-05-9*) U Minn Ctr Interdis.

Students of English. Robert Protherough. 200p. 1989. 59.95 (*0-415-01637-1*) Routledge.

Students of Snow. Jane Flanders. LC 82-8461. 68p. 1982. pap. 9.95 (*0-87023-379-3*); lib. bdg. 15.00 (*0-87023-378-5*) U of Mass Pr.

Students of the Covenant: A History of Jewish Biblical Scholarship in North America. S. David Sperling. (Society of Biblical Literature Confessional Perspectives Ser.). 228p. (C). 1992. 54.95 (*1-55540-655-6*, 061404); pap. 34.95 (*1-55540-656-4*, 06 14 04) Scholars Pr GA.

Students of the Third Age: University - College Programs for Retired Adults. Henry Lipman & Mark Blazey. Ed. by Richard B. Fischer et al. (ACE-Oryx Series on Higher Education). (Illus.). 192p. 1992. 29.95 (*0-02-897143-4*, ACE-Oryx) Oryx Pr.

Students of Thought: Personal Journeys. Ed. by R. Wayne Shute & Sharon Gibb. (Illus.). 139p. (C). 1993. pap. text ed. 17.95 (*1-55059-070-7*) Temeron Bks.

Students on Autocad. Alfred J. Yarwood. (C). 1991. pap. text ed. 28.95 (*0-582-07490-8*) Longman.

Student's Only Survival Guide to Essay Writing. Steve Good & Bill Jensen. 224p. (Orig.). (YA). (gr. 12 up). 1995. pap. 14.95 (*1-55143-038-X*) Orca Bk Pubs.

Student's Partial Solutions Manual T-A Applied Regression Analysis. 2nd ed. Hafner & Carr. 112p. (C). 1988. pap. 20.95 (*0-534-91513-2*) PWS Pubs.

Students Political Scientists Handbook. Richard L. Merritt & Gloria L. Pyszka. 192p. 1975. pap. 13.95 (*0-87073-251-X*) Schenkman Bks Inc.

Students, Professors, & the State in Tsarist Russia. Samuel D. Kassow. (California Studies on the History of Society & Culture: No. 5). 480p. 1988. 55.00 (*0-520-05760-0*) U CA Pr.

Students Reports & Articles by "Outside" Authors As Published in "The White Light" (Vols. 1-10) Ed. by Nelson White & Anne White. LC 83-91007. (Illus.). 50p. (Orig.). 1983. pap. 18.00 (*0-939856-36-0*) Tech Group.

Students Resolving Conflict: Peer Mediation in Schools. Richard Cohen. 400p. (Orig.). 1995. pap. text ed. 14.95 (*0-673-36096-2*, GoodYrBooks) Addson-Wesley Educ.

Student's Rorschach Manual: An Introduction to Administering, Scoring & Interpreting Researcher's Psychodiagnostic Inkblot Test. rev. ed. Robert M. Allen. LC 77-14710. 361p. 1978. 49.50 (*0-8236-6201-2*) Intl Univs Pr.

Student's Russian & Serbocroatian Pocket Dictionary: Ruso-Hrvatski Ili Srpski I Hrvatsko Ili Srpskoruski Dzepni Rjecnik Za Osnovn. Tajana Miljkovic. 496p. (RUS & SER.). 1984. pap. 19.95 (*0-8288-1641-7*, F114890) Fr & Eur.

Student's Sanskrit-English Dictionary. Vaman S. Apte. 1987. 59.95 (*0-8288-1778-2*, M7830); 59.95 (*0-8288-4022-9*, F43360) Fr & Eur.

Student's Sanskrit-English Dictionary: Containing Appendices on Sanskrit Prosody & Important Literary & Geographical Names in the Ancient History of India. Shivram A. Vaman. (ENG & SAN.). (C). 1993. reprint ed. text ed. 22.50 (*0-685-68099-1*, Pub. by Motilal Banarsidass II) S Asia.

Students Shop Reference Handbook. Compiled by Edward G. Hoffman. LC 85-8200. (Illus.). 530p. 1986. text ed. 16.95 (*0-8311-1161-5*) Indus Pr.

Students Shopping for a Better World. Alice T. Marlin et al. 262p. 1993. 7.49 (*0-685-64983-0*) CEP.

Students, Society, & Politics in Imperial Germany: The Rise of Academic Illiberalism. Konrad H. Jarausch. LC 81-47926. 464p. 1982. reprint ed. pap. 132.30 (*0-7837-9353-7*, 2060095) Bks Demand.

***Students Solutions Manual to Accompany Elementary Algebra: Concepts & Applications.** 5th ed. Marvin L. Bittinger. (C). 1998. pap. text ed. write for info. (*0-201-30497-X*) Addison-Wesley.

***Student's Solutions Manual to Accompany Elementary &d Intermediate Algebra, Concepts & Applications: A Combined Approach.** 2nd ed. Marvin L. Bittinger. (C). 1998. pap. text ed. write for info. (*0-201-31225-5*) Addison-Wesley.

Student's Solutions Manual to Accompany Functional Calculus & Applied Calculus. William C. Ramaley & Pat Foard. 128p. (C). 1995. spiral bd. write for info. (*0-697-21629-2*) Wm C Brown Pubs.

Students Solutions Manual to Accompany Functioning in The Real World: A Precalculus Experience, Preliminary Edition. Gordon. Ed. by Bill Poole. (C). 1996. pap. text ed. write for info. (*0-201-87786-4*) Addison-Wesley.

***Students Solutions Manual to Accompany Intermediate Algebra Concepts & Applications.** 5th ed. Martin L. Bittinger. (C). 1998. pap. text ed. write for info. (*0-201-30502-X*) Addison-Wesley.

Students Solutions Manual to Accompany Technical Mathematics & Technical Mathematics with Calculus. John C. Peterson & Alan Herweyer. 208p. 1994. pap. 17.00 (*0-8273-6506-3*) Delmar.

Student's Solutions Manual to John Scott's Intermediate Algebra. 5th ed. William Echols & Ernest Lowrey. 248p. (Orig.). (C). 1990. pap. text ed. 18.95 (*0-89641-195-8*) American Pr.

Students Speak: A Survey of Health Interests & Concerns: Kindergarten Through Twelfth Grade. Lucille Trucano. 208p. (Orig.). 1984. pap. 6.50 (*0-935529-02-0*) Comprehen Health Educ.

***Student's Statistical Software Library.** Prins & Statlib. 1996. pap. text ed. write for info. (*0-07-912913-7*) McGraw.

Students Teaching, Teachers Learning. Ed. by N. Amanda Branscombe et al. 343p. 1992. pap. text ed. 27.50 (*0-86709-299-8*, 0299) Boynton Cook Pubs.

Students Technology of Breadma. W. J. Fance. 1986. pap. 17.95 (*0-7100-9046-3*, RKP) Routledge.

Students' Text-Book of Astrology. Vivian E. Robson. 243p. 1981. pap. 18.50 (*0-89540-117-7*, SB-117, Sun Bks) Sun Pub.

Student's Textbook of Surgery. William M. Rambo. (Illus.). 400p. 1995. pap. 39.95 (*0-86542-485-3*) Blackwell Sci.

Student's Textbook of Surgery. William M. Rambo. LC 95-12316. (Medical Bks.). 1995. pap. write for info. (*0-393-71032-7*) Norton.

Students Themselves: Assembly on University Goals & Governance. Robert Coles. 320p. 1974. text ed. 18.95 (*0-87073-432-6*) Schenkman Bks Inc.

Student's Theory & Practice Workbook for Competency in Cosmetology: A Professional Text. Anthony B. Colletti. (Illus.). 528p. (Orig.). 1987. pap. text ed. 12.75 (*0-912126-76-0*) Keystone Pubns.

Students under Stress: A Study in the Social Psychology of Adaptation. David Mechanic. LC 77-91058. 268p. 1978. reprint ed. 20.00 (*0-299-07470-6*); reprint ed. pap. text ed. 10.95 (*0-299-07474-9*) U of Wis Pr.

***Student's Vegetarian Cookbook: Quick, Easy, Economical, & Great Tasting.** Carole Raymond. LC 97-8932. 256p. 1997. per. 12.00 (*0-7615-0854-6*) Prima Pub.

Student's View of the College of St. James on the Eve of the Civil War: The Letters of W. Wilkins Davis (1842-1866) David Hein. LC 88-12716. (Studies in American Religion: Vol. 30). 175p. 1988. lib. bdg. 79.95 (*0-88946-674-2*) E Mellen.

Student's Vision Guide. Henry Draughon. (Illus.). 160p. (J). (gr. 6-12). 1995. student ed., pap. 9.95 (*1-885147-03-1*) FamilyTalk.

Student's Vision Guide: Parent's & Mentor's Supplement. Henry Draughon. (Illus.). 1995. student ed., pap. 2.95 (*1-885147-04-X*) FamilyTalk.

Students Vocabulary Bible Hebrew. George M. Landes. (C). 1985. pap. text ed. 5.50 (*0-684-41323-X*) S&S Trade.

Student's Vocabulary for Biblical Hebrew & Aramaic. Larry A. Mitchel. 128p. 1984. pap. 12.99 (*0-310-45461-1*, 11607P) Zondervan.

Student's Vocabulary of Biblical Hebrew. George M. Landes. 56p. (Orig.). (C). 1961. pap. text ed. 23.00 (*0-02-367410-5*, Macmillan Coll) P-H.

***Students with Acquired Brain Injury: The School's Response.** Glang. LC 97-2177. 1997. pap. text ed. 29.95 (*1-55766-285-1*) P H Brookes.

***Students with Autism: Characteristics & Instructional Programming.** Jack Scott & Claudia Clark. 450p. 1997. 45.00 (*1-56593-630-2*, 1306) Singular Publishing.

***Students with Disabilities & Special Education.** 13th ed. 1983. pap. 119.25 (*0-939675-58-7*) Data Res MN.

Students with Mild Disabilities. Tom E. Smith et al. LC 92-70786. (Illus.). 450p. (C). 1993. text ed. 38.75 (*0-03-047519-8*) HB Coll Pubs.

Students with Seizures: A Manual for School Nurses. Nancy Santilli et al. LC 91-72641. (Illus.). (Orig.). 1991. spiral bd. write for info. (*0-941932-25-7*) HealthScan.

Students Without Teachers: The Crisis in the University. Harold Taylor. LC 70-79499. 348p. 1975. text ed. 12.95 (*0-8093-0750-2*) S Ill U Pr.

Student's Workbook - Self Esteem. Shaun Hains. Ed. by Diane Parker. LC 92-50907. 60p. 1993. spiral bd. 7.95 (*0-88247-972-5*) R & E Pubs.

Student's World Atlas. rev. ed. LC 93-41312. (J). 1994. 7.95 (*0-528-83699-4*) Rand McNally.

Students Writing Across the Curriculum. Clegg. (C). 1991. teacher ed., pap. text ed. 3.00 (*0-03-028763-4*) HB Coll Pubs.

Students Writing Across the Curriculum. Cyndia S. Clegg & Michael M. Wheeler. (Illus.). 500p. (C). 1991. pap. text ed. 19.50 (*0-03-028762-6*) HB Coll Pubs.

Student's Writing Guide for the Arts & Social Sciences. Gordon Taylor. (Illus.). 250p. 1989. pap. text ed. 19.95 (*0-521-36905-3*) Cambridge U Pr.

Students' Yoman. Shimon Grama. 112p. (ENG & HEB.). (J). (gr. 4-12). 1993. pap. text ed. 10.00 (*0-9635739-0-X*) Innovat NY.

Student/Staff Support Teams: SST Program Kit, 3 vols., Set. Vicki Phillips & Laura McCullough. (Illus.). 390p. 1993. pap. text ed. 145.00 (*0-944584-74-8*, 42KIT) Sopris.

Student/Staff Support Teams (SST) Administrator Handbook. Vicki Phillips & Laura McCullough. (Illus.). 78p. 1993. pap. text ed. 16.50 (*0-944584-61-6*, 42AH) Sopris.

Student/Staff Support Teams (SST) Team Member Implementation Guide. Vicki Phillips & Laura McCullough. (Illus.). 86p. 1993. pap. text ed. 16.50 (*0-944584-60-8*, 42TG) Sopris.

Student/Staff Support Teams (SST) Trainer Manual. Vicki Phillips & Laura McCullough. (Illus.). 226p. 1993. teacher ed., pap. text ed. 125.00 (*0-944584-68-3*, 42TM) Sopris.

Studflesh, Vol. 8: True Gay Encounters. Ed. by Winston Leyland. 160p. (Orig.). 1989. pap. 10.00 (*0-943595-25-8*) Leyland Pubns.

Studia Arabica et Islamia: Festschrift for Ihsan Abbas. Ed. by Wadad Al-Qadi. 1981. 175.00 (*0-8156-6058-8*, Am U Beirut) Syracuse U Pr.

Studia Aramaica: New Sources & New Approaches. Ed. by Markham Geller et al. (Journal of Semitic Studies Supplement: No. 4). (Illus.). 350p. 1995. text ed. 65.00 (*0-19-922194-4*) OUP.

Studia Biblica 1978 III: Papers on Paul & Other New Testament Authors. Ed. by E. Livingstone. (Journal for the Study of the New Testament, Supplement Ser.: Vol. 3). 468p. 70.00 (*0-905774-27-2*) CUP Services.

Studia Byzantina: Studies in English, French, German, Italian, Russian & Neo-Greek. G. Moravcsik. 438p. (C). 1967. 60.00 (*963-05-2222-5*, Pub. by Akad Kiado HU) St Mut.

Studia Hispanica I in Honor of Rodolfo Cardona. Ed. by Luis A. Ramos-Garcia & Nestor Lugones. 1982. 12.95 (*0-934840-01-6*) Studia Hispanica.

Studia Historica: Chapters on the Hungarian Political Emigration (1849-1867) Lajos Lukacs. (Studia Historica Academiae Scientarium Hungaricae Ser.: No. 196). 188p. 1996. 29.00 (*963-05-6838-1*, Pub. by A K HU) Intl Spec Bk.

Studia Linguistica Alexandro Vasilii Filio Issatschenko: A Collegis Amicusque Oblata. Ed. by H. Birnbaum et al. xxvi, 517p. (Orig.). (ENG, FRE, GER & RUS.). 1978. pap. 85.00 (*0-686-32343-2*) Benjamins North Am.

Studia Linguistica Diachronica et Synchronica. Ursula Pieper & Gerhard Stickel. 988p. 1985. text ed. 292.30 (*3-11-009664-1*) Mouton.

Studia Mystica, Vol. XVI. Ed. by Robert Boenig et al. (Illus.). 260p. 1995. text ed. 89.95 (*0-7734-9045-0*) E Mellen.

Studia nad Muzyka Polskiego Sredniowiecza. Hieronim Feicht. Ed. by Zofia Lissa. LC 75-543338. (Opera Musicologica Hieronymi Feicht Ser.: No. 1). (Illus.). 400p. (ENG, GER & POL.). 1975. 10.00 (*0-934082-16-2*) Theodore Front.

Studia Occitanica in Memoriam Paul Remy, Vol. II: The Narrative-Philology. Ed. by Hans-Erich Keller. 1986. pap. 17.95 (*0-918720-75-3*); boxed 37.95 (*0-918720-72-9*) Medieval Inst.

Studia Occitanica in Memoriam Paul Remy, Vol. 1: The Troubadours. Ed. by Hans-Erich Keller. 1986. pap. 15.95 (*0-918720-74-5*); boxed 32.95 (*0-918720-71-0*) Medieval Inst.

Studia Orientalia: Memoriae D. H. Baneth Dedicata. Ed. by S. Shaked et al. (Illus.). 604p. 1979. text ed. 30.00 (*965-223-325-0*, Pub. by Magnes Press IS) Eisenbrauns.

An Asterisk (*) at the beginning of an entry indicates that the title is appearing in BIP for the first time.

Studia Otiosa. Richard W. Bond. LC 71-99683. (Essay Index Reprint Ser.). 1977. 20.95 (*0-8369-1341-8*) Ayer.

Studia Patristica Nineteen-Three, Vol. 3: Second Century-Tertullian to Nicaea in the West- Clement & Origen-The Cappadocian Fathers. Papers of the 1983 Oxford Patristics Conference. Ed. by E. A. Livingston. (Cistercian Studies). 584p. 1989. pap. 55.00 (*0-87907-352-7*) Cistercian Pubns.

Studia Patristica Nineteen-Two, Vol. 2: Critica-Classica-Ascetica-Liturgica Papers of the 1983 Oxford Patristics Conference. E. A. Livingston. (Cistercian Studies). 416p. (Orig.). 1989. pap. 55.00 (*0-87907-351-9*) Cistercian Pubns.

Studia Patristica XVII, 3 vols., Set. Ed. by Elizabeth A. Livingstone. 1520p. 1982. 642.00 (*0-08-025779-8*, Pub. by Pergamon Repr UK) Franklin.

Studia Patristica XVIII: Papers of the 1983 Oxford International Patristics Conference, Vol. 1. 1986. pap. 40.00 (*0-87907-350-0*) Cistercian Pubns.

***Studia Philonica Annual Vol. I: Studies in Hellenistic Judaism: 1989.** Ed. by David T. Runia. 187p. 1991. 44.95 (*1-55540-399-9*, 140226) Scholars Pr GA.

Studia Philonica Annual: Studies in Hellenistic Judaism, Vol. VI. Ed. by David T. Runia. (Brown Judaic Studies). 248p. 1994. 44.95 (*0-7885-0030-9*, 140299) Scholars Pr GA.

Studia Philonica Annual: Studies in Hellenistic Judaism, 1995, Vol. VII. Ed. by David T. Runia. (Brown Judaic Studies). 268p. (C). 1995. 34.95 (*0-7885-0171-2*, 140305) Scholars Pr GA.

***Studia Philonica Annual Vol. II: Studies in Hellenistic Judaism: 1990.** Ed. by David T. Runia. 252p. 1991. 59.95 (*1-55540-590-8*, 140226) Scholars Pr GA.

***Studia Philonica Annual Vol. VIII: Studies in Hellenistic Judaism: 1996.** Ed. by David T. Runia. 236p. 1996. 34.95 (*0-7885-0311-1*, 140309) Scholars Pr GA.

Studia Philonica Annual, Vol. Four, 1992: Studies in Hellenistic Judaism. David T. Runia. 195p. 1992. 59.95 (*1-55540-771-4*, 140264) Scholars Pr GA.

Studia Philonica Annual, Vol. V: Studies in Hellenistic Judaism. Ed. by David T. Runia. (Brown Judaic Studies). 271p. 1993. 44.95 (*1-55540-917-2*, 140287) Scholars Pr GA.

Studia Philonica Annual 1991 Vol. III: Studies in Hellenistic Judaism. Ed. by David T. Runia et al. (Studies in Hellenistic Judaism). 405p. 1991. 74.95 (*1-55540-625-4*, 140230) Scholars Pr GA.

Studia Phycologica: Festschrift. J. Gerloff. (Nova Hedwigia Ser.: No. 33). (Illus.). 1004p. 1980. pap. 130.00 (*0-686-33174-5*) Lubrecht & Cramer.

Studia Pindarica. Elroy L. Bundy. LC 83-40482. 150p. (C). 1987. pap. 18.00 (*0-520-05111-4*) U CA Pr.

Studia Pomeiana et Classica in Honor of Wilhelmina F. Jashemski: Vol. I: Pompeiana; Vol. II: Classica, 2 vols., Set. Ed. by Robert I. Curtis. (Illus.). 1989. 160.00 (*0-89241-425-1*) Caratzas.

Studia Pompeiana et Classica in Honor of Wilhelmina F. Jashemski, Vol. I: Pompeiana. Ed. by Robert I. Curtis. (Illus.). xxii, 330p. 1988. lib. bdg. 90.00 (*0-89241-423-5*) Caratzas.

Studia Pompeiana et Classica in Honor of Wilhelmina F. Jashemski, Vol. II: Classica. Ed. by Robert I. Curtis. (Illus.). xxii, 271p. 1989. lib. bdg. 80.00 (*0-89241-424-3*) Caratzas.

Studia Semitica, 2 vols. Erwin I. Rosenthal. Incl. Vol. 1. Jewish Themes. 384p. 1971. text ed. 69.95 (*0-521-07958-6*); Vol. 2. Islamic Themes. 240p. 1971. text ed. 64.95 (*0-521-07959-4*); (University of Cambridge Oriental Publications: Nos. 16 & 17). 1971. write for info. (*0-318-51296-3*) Cambridge U Pr.

Studia Serica Bernhard Karlgren Dedicata: Sinological Studies Dedicated to Bernhard Kalgren on His Seventieth Birthday. Ed. by Soren Egerod & Else Glabn. 282p. 1959. pap. 89.50 (*0-614-01829-3*) Elliots Bks.

Studia Varia from the J. Paul Getty Museum, No. 1. Ed. by Marion True & Kenneth Hamma. LC 93-16382. (Occasional Papers on Antiquities: No. 8). (Illus.). 140p. 1993. pap. 40.00 (*0-89236-203-0*, J P Getty Museum) J P Getty Trust.

StudiAct: Leader's Guide. Marti Solomon. Ed. by Jan Turrentine. 23p. (Orig.). 1991. pap. text ed. 1.95 (*1-56309-007-4*) Womans Mission Union.

StudiAct: Queen. Marti Solomon. Ed. by Cathy Butler. 31p. (Orig.). (J). 1991. pap. text ed. 2.25 (*1-56309-006-6*) Womans Mission Union.

StudiAct: Queen Regent. Marti Solomon. Ed. by Jan Turrentine. 32p. (Orig.). (YA). (gr. 7-12). 1991. pap. text ed. 2.25 (*1-56309-003-1*) Womans Mission Union.

StudiAct: Queen Regent in Service. Marti Solomon. Ed. by Jan Turrentine. 31p. (Orig.). (YA). (gr. 7-12). 1991. pap. text ed. 2.25 (*1-56309-004-X*) Womans Mission Union.

StudiAct: Queen with Scepter. Marti Solomon. Ed. by Jan Turrentine. 31p. (Orig.). (YA). (gr. 7-12). pap. text ed. 2.25 (*1-56309-005-8*) Womans Mission Union.

StudiAct: Service Aide. Marti Solomon. Ed. by Jan Turrentine. 16p. (Orig.). (YA). (gr. 7-12). 1991. pap. text ed. 2.25 (*1-56309-002-3*) Womans Mission Union.

Studied Madness. Heywood H. Broun. LC 79-84436. 298p. 1979. reprint ed. 22.00 (*0-933256-00-0*) Second Chance.

Studied Madness. Heywood H. Broun. LC 79-84436. 298p. 1983. reprint ed. pap. 5.95 (*0-933256-40-X*) Second Chance.

***Studien.** Karl Rosenkranz. (GER.). 1975. reprint ed. write for info. (*3-487-05686-0*) G Olms Pubs.

Studien an eingebuergerten Arten der Gattung Solidago L. M. L. Voser-Huber. (Dissertationes Botanicae Ser.: No. 68). (Illus.). 158p. (GER.). 1983. pap. text ed. 30.00 (*3-7682-1359-5*) Lubrecht & Cramer.

Studien Auf Dem Gebiete Des Archaischen Lateins, 2 vols. Wilhelm Studemund. 182p. 1972. reprint ed. Zusatzlich Lieferbar: Register, 182p. write for info. (*3-487-04517-6*) G Olms Pubs.

Studien Auf Dem Gebiete Des Archaischen Lateins, 2 vols., Set. Wilhelm Studemund. xviii, 1080p. 1972. reprint ed. write for info. (*3-487-04328-9*) G Olms Pubs.

Studien fur Tonkunstler und Musikfreunde, eine Historisch-Kritiscshe Zeitschrift, 2 vols. in 1. Ed. by Friedrich L. Kunzen & Johann F. Reichardt. 364p. (GER.). 1992. write for info. (*3-487-09669-2*) G Olms Pubs.

Studien Uber Den Eleatismus. Guido Calogero. viii, 327p. 1970. reprint ed. 70.00 (*0-318-70888-4*) G Olms Pubs.

***Studien Uber die Inneren Zustande, Das Volksleben und Insbesondere die Landlichen Einrichtungen Rublands.** A. Freiherr Von Haxthausen. xxxvi, 1716p. (GER.). 1973. reprint ed. write for info. (*3-487-04535-4*) G Olms Pubs.

Studien uber Salomon Ibn Gabirol. David Kaufmann. Ed. by Steven Katz. LC 79-7144. (Jewish Phhilosophy, Mysticism & History of Ideas Ser.). (GER & HEB.). 1980. reprint ed. lib. bdg. 17.95 (*0-405-12272-1*) Ayer.

Studien ueber die saxicolen Arten der Flechtengattung Lecania II. Lecania s. Str. Michaela Mayrhofer. (Bibliotheca Lichenologica Ser.: Vol. 28). (Illus.). 134p. (GER.). 1988. pap. text ed. 48.00 (*3-443-58007-6*) Lubrecht & Cramer.

***Studien und Materialien Zum Rechtswesen des Pharaonenreiches der Dynastien XVIII-XXI.** Wilhelm Spiegelberg. vi, 134p. (GER.). 1994. reprint ed. write for info. (*3-487-09845-8*) G Olms Pubs.

Studien zu Gregor von Nyssa und der Christlichen Spatantike. Ed. by Hubertus R. Drobner & Christoph Klock. (Supplements to Vigiliae Christianae Ser.: Vol. 12). xii, 418p. (ENG, FRE, GER, ITA & SPA.). 1989. 128.50 (*90-04-09222-6*) E J Brill.

Studien zu Italienischen Memorialzeugnissen des XI & XII: Jahrunderts. Thomas Frank. (Arbeitem zur Fruehmittelalterforschung Ser.: Band 21). xii, 296p. (GER.). 1991. lib. bdg. 113.85 (*3-11-012588-9*) De Gruyter.

***Studien Zu Romanischen Fachtexten Aus Mittelalter und Fruher Neuzeit.** Herausgegeben V. Mensching & Karl-Heinz Rottgen. (Romanistische Texte und Studien: Bd. 6). (GER.). 1995. write for info. (*3-487-09944-6*) G Olms Pubs.

Studien Zu Tritojesaja. Odil H. Steck. (Beihefte zur Zeitschrift fuer die Alttestamentliche Wissenschaft Ser.: Bd. 203). xii, 294p. (GER.). (C). 1991. lib. bdg. 93.85 (*3-11-013434-9*) De Gruyter.

Studien zum Alten Testament (1966-1988) Mitsamt Bibliographie Georg Fohrer (1990) Georg Fohrer. (Beiheft zur Zeitschrift fuer die Alttestamentliche Wissenschaft Ser.: Vol. 196). vii, 186p. (GER.). (C). 1991. lib. bdg. 80.00 (*3-11-012819-5*) De Gruyter.

Studien zum Altgermanischen: Festschrift fuer Heinrich Beck. Ed. by Heiko Uecker. (Ergaenzungsbaende Zum Reallexikon der Germanischen Altertumskunde Ser.: Bd. 11). xv, 760p. (GER.). (C). 1994. lib. bdg. 232.25 (*3-11-012978-7*, 128-94) De Gruyter.

Studien zum aristotelischen Materie-Begriff. Heinz H. Happ. 953p. (C). 1971. 273.10 (*3-11-001796-2*) De Gruyter.

Studien Zum Buch Tobit. Merten Rabenau. (Beihefte zur Zeitschrift fuer die Alttestamentliche Wissenschaft Ser.). viii, 249p. (GER.). (C). 1994. lib. bdg. 106.15 (*3-11-014125-6*) De Gruyter.

Studien Zum Deuteronomistischen Geschichtswerk. Ernst Wuerthwein. (Beiheft zur Zeitschrift fuer die Alttestamentliche Wissenschaft Ser.: Bd. 227). vi, 222p. (GER.). (C). 1994. lib. bdg. 106.15 (*3-11-014269-4*, 13-94) De Gruyter.

***Studien Zum Deutschen Prozessionsspiel.** Elizabeth Wainwright. (Muncher Beitrage zur Mediavistik und Renaissance Forschung Ser.: Bd. 16). viii, 292p. (GER.). 1974. 38.00 (*3-615-00153-2*, Pub. by Weidmann GW) Lubrecht & Cramer.

Studien zum juedischen Neuplatonismus: Die Religionsphilosophie des Abraham Ibn Ezra. Hermann Greive. (Studia Judaica: Vol. 7). 225p. 1973. 89.25 (*3-11-004116-2*) De Gruyter.

Studien zum Mykenischen Kasussystem. Ivo Hajnal. (Untersuchungen zur indogermanischen Sprachund Kulturwissenschaft Ser.: No. 7). xvii, 377p. (GER.). 1995. lib. bdg. 213.85 (*3-11-013986-3*) De Gruyter.

Studien Zum Verstandnis Herodots. Hartmut Erbse. (Untersuchungen zur Antiken Literatur und Geschichte Ser.: Vol. 38). xiv, 199p. (GER.). (C). 1992. lib. bdg. 92.35 (*3-11-013621-X*) De Gruyter.

Studien Zur Alten Geschichte, Band 1 & 2. Renate Zoepffel. (Collectanea Ser.: Bd. XLII). xlix, 1143p. (GER.). 1982. write for info. (*3-487-07083-9*) G Olms Pubs.

Studien Zur Alten Geschichte, Band 3. Hermann Strasburger. Ed. by Walter Schmitthenner & Renate Zoepffel. (Collectanea Ser.: Bd. XLII). xi, 529p. (GER.). 1990. write for info. (*3-487-09363-4*) G Olms Pubs.

Studien Zur Alteren Athenischen Verfassungsgeschichte. Arthur Ledl. LC 72-7898. (Greek History Ser.). (GER.). 1973. reprint ed. 31.95 (*0-405-04797-5*) Ayer.

Studien zur antiken Literatur und Kunst. Paul Friedlaender. (C). 1969. 150.00 (*3-11-000139-X*) De Gruyter.

Studien zur antiken Philosophie. Olof Gigon. Ed. by Andreas Graeser. 1972. 146.15 (*3-11-003928-1*) De Gruyter.

Studien zur Arithmetik und Geometrie. Edmund Husserl. 528p. 1983. lib. bdg. 245.50 (*90-247-2497-X*, Pub. by M Nijhoff NE) Kluwer Ac.

Studien Zur Ars Poetica Des Horaz. Wolf Steidle. 147p. (GER.). 1967. reprint ed. write for info. (*0-318-70463-3*) G Olms Pubs.

Studien zur Epikur und den Epikureern. Robert Philippson. Ed. by C. Joachim Classen. (Olms GW Studien: Bd. 17). vi, 354p. (GER.). 1983. write for info. (*3-487-07380-3*) G Olms Pubs.

***Studien Zur Ethik.** Jurgen-Eckardt Pleines. (Philosophische Texte und Studien: Vol. 27). iv, 431p. (GER.). 1992. write for info. (*3-487-09452-5*) G Olms Pubs.

Studien Zur Geschichte der Begriffe. Gustav Teichmuller. xi, 667p. 1966. reprint ed. write for info. (*0-318-71051-X*) G Olms Pubs.

Studien zur Geschichte des griechischen Alphabets. A. Kirchhoff. (Illus.). vi, 179p. (GER.). (C). 1970. reprint ed. pap. 40.00 (*90-70265-12-5*, Pub. by Gieben NE) Benjamins North Am.

Studien Zur Geschichte Des Griechischen Alphabets. Adolf Kirchhoff. vi, 180p. 1973. reprint ed. write for info. (*3-487-05011-0*) G Olms Pubs.

Studien Zur Gliederung der Flechtengattung Lecanora. G. Eigler. (Illus.). 1969. 18.00 (*3-7682-0628-9*) Lubrecht & Cramer.

Studien Zur Griechischen und Lateinischen Grammatik, 10 vols. in 5, Set. Ed. by Georg Curtius & Karl Brugmann. xvi, 4667p. 1972. reprint ed. 1,185.00 (*3-487-04284-3*) G Olms Pubs.

Studien zur humanistischen Jurisprudenz. Guido Kisch. (C). 1972. 123.10 (*3-11-003600-2*) De Gruyter.

Studien Zur Hydronymie des Savesystems: Woerterbuch der Gewaessernamen, Auswertung. 2nd ed. (GER.). 1966. pap. 110.00 (*0-8288-6727-5*, M-7629) Fr & Eur.

***Studien Zur Judischen Folklore.** Immanuel Low. (Collectanea Ser.: No. XVI). x, 150p. (GER.). 1975. write for info. (*3-487-04327-0*) G Olms Pubs.

Studien zur Komposition des Pentateuch. Erhard Blum. (Beiheft zur Zeitschrift fuer die Alttestamentliche Wissenschaft Ser.: Band 189). x, 433p. (C). 1990. lib. bdg. 113.85 (*3-11-012027-5*) De Gruyter.

Studien Zur Lateinischen und Romanischen Lyrik Des Mittelalters. Hans Spanke. Ed. by Ulrich Molk. (Collectanea Ser.: Bd. XXXI). viii, 472p. 1984. write for info. (*3-487-07426-5*) G Olms Pubs.

Studien Zur Literarkritischen Methode: Gericht und Heil in Jesaja 7, 1-17 und 29, 1-8. Jurgen Werlitz. (Beihefte zur Zeitschrift fuer die Alttestamentliche Wissenschaft Ser.: No. 204). x, 351p. (GER.). (C). 1992. lib. bdg. 106.15 (*3-11-013488-8*) De Gruyter.

Studien Zur Literaturgeschichte des 18. Jahrhunderts: Moralische Zeitschriften. Max Kawczynski. 171p. 1969. reprint ed. write for info. (*0-318-71462-0*) G Olms Pubs.

Studien Zur Literaturgeschichte des 18 Jahrhunderts: Moralische Zeitschriften. Max Kawczynski. 171p. 1969. reprint ed. write for info. (*0-318-71831-6*) G Olms Pubs.

Studien zur Minne und Ehe in Wolframs Parzival und Hartmanns Artusepik. Herbert E. Wiegand. (Quellen und Forschungen zur Sprach und Kulturgeschichte der Germanischen Voelker Ser.: No. 49). 352p. (GER.). (C). 1972. 142.35 (*3-11-003672-X*) De Gruyter.

Studien Zur Modernen Deutschen Lexikographie. Ruth Klappenbach. (Linguistik Aktuell Ser.: No. 1). xxiii, 313p. 1980. 59.00 (*90-272-2721-7*) Benjamins North Am.

***Studien zur Musikgeschichte Rastatts im 18. Jahrhundert.** Rudiger Thomsen-Furst. (Stadtgeschichtliche Reihe: Bd. 2). 281p. (GER.). 1996. 57.95 (*3-631-49644-3*) P Lang Pubng.

Studien zur Priesterschrift. Ludwig Schmidt. (Beihefte zur Zeitschrift fuer die Alttestamentliche Wissenschaft Ser.: Bd. 214). viii, 281p. (GER.). (C). 1993. lib. bdg. 103.10 (*3-11-013867-0*) De Gruyter.

***Studien zur Redaktion und Komposition des Amosbuchs.** Dirk U. Rottzoll. (Beihefte zur Zeitschrift fuer die Alttestamentliche Wissenschaft Ser.: Vol. 243). x, 319p. (GER.). (C). 1996. lib. bdg. 124.45 (*3-11-015240-1*, 114/96) De Gruyter.

***Studien zur Regionalen und Chronologischen Gliederung der Noerdlichen Aunjetitzer Kultur.** Bernd Zich. (Vorgeschichtliche Forschungen Ser.: Vol. 20). (Illus.). ix, 738p. (GER.). (C). 1996. lib. bdg. 474.10 (*3-11-014327-5*) De Gruyter.

***Studien Zur Sichem - Area.** Karl Jaros & Brigitte Deckert. (Orbis Biblicus et Orientalis Ser.: Vol. 11a). (Orig.). 1977. pap. 18.75 (*3-7278-0180-8*) Eisenbrauns.

***Studien zur Wiener Schule 1: Johannes Kretz: Erwin Ratz - Leben und Wirken; Olaf Winnecke: Das Geheime Programm in Alban Bergs Oper "Lulu"** Johannes Kretz & Olaf Winnecke. Ed. by Friedrich C. Heller. (Musikleben - Studien zur Musikgeschichte Osterreichs: Bd. 4). 264p. (GER.). 1996. 51.95 (*3-631-49520-X*) P Lang Pubng.

Studien Zur Zweisprachigen Lexikographie Mit Deutsch, Bd. 1: Pia Virtanen, Zur Geschichte der Finnisch-Deutschen Lexikographie 1888-1991. Ed. by Herbert E. Wiegand. (Germanistische Linguistik Ser.: Heft 114/92). 176p. (GER.). 1993. write for info. (*3-487-09691-9*) G Olms Pubs.

Studies: Military & Diplomatic. Charles F. Adams, Jr. (Works of Charles Francis Adams Jr. (1835-1915)). 1989. reprint ed. lib. bdg. 79.00 (*0-7812-1416-5*) Rprt Serv.

Studies about Kamose & Ahmose. Hans Goedicke. vi,p. (Orig.). 1995. pap. 36.00 (*0-9613805-8-6*) Halgo Inc.

Studies & Appreciations. Lewis E. Gates. LC 76-134079. (Essay Index Reprint Ser.). 1977. 20.95 (*0-8369-1927-0*) Ayer.

Studies & Appreciations. William Sharp. Ed. by W. Sharp. LC 67-26783. (Essay Index Reprint Ser.). 1977. 21.95 (*0-8369-0871-6*) Ayer.

Studies & Documents Relating to the History of the Greek Church & People Under Turkish Domination. Theodore H. Papadopoullos. LC 78-38759. reprint ed. 39.50 (*0-404-56314-7*) AMS Pr.

Studies & Essays in Honor of Abraham A. Neuman. Ed. by Meir Ben-Horin et al. xiii, 650p. 1962. 28.50 (*0-685-70558-7*, Ctr Judaic Studies) Eisenbrauns.

Studies & Essays in the History of Science & Learning. Ed. by Ashley Montagu. LC 74-26275. (History, Philosophy & Sociology of Science Ser.). (Illus.). 1975. reprint ed. 52.95 (*0-405-06603-1*) Ayer.

Studies & Essays on International Humanitarian Law & Red Cross Principles. Ed. by Christophe Swinarski. 1984. lib. bdg. 50.00 (*90-247-3078-3*) Kluwer Ac.

Studies & Further Studies in a Dying Culture. Christopher Caudwell. LC 77-142989. 544p. 1972. reprint ed. pap. 11.00 (*0-85345-218-0*) Monthly Rev.

Studies & Games. Jan Timman. 1996. pap. 19.95 (*1-85744-126-5*) Macmillan.

Studies & Issues in Smoking Behavior. National Research Conference on Smoking Behavior (2nd: 1966: University of Arizona) Staff. Ed. by Salvatore V. Zagona. LC 67-28650. 277p. reprint ed. pap. 79.00 (*0-685-20953-9*, 2031489) Bks Demand.

Studies & Records, Vol. 1: 1926. Norwegian-American Historical Association Staff. LC 87-657087. (Illus.). 195p. reprint ed. pap. 55.60 (*0-7837-1650-8*, 2041948) Bks Demand.

Studies & Sketches. Oxford Staff & Herbert H. Asquith. LC 68-54366. (Essay Index Reprint Ser.). 1977. 18.95 (*0-8369-0759-0*) Ayer.

Studies & the Structure of National Elite Groups, Vol. 1. Ed. by Gwen Moore & J. Allen Whitt. (Research in Politics & Society Ser.: Vol. 1). 283p. 1985. 73.25 (*0-89232-335-3*) Jai Pr.

Studies by Einar Haugen Presented on the Occasion of His 65th Birthday, April 19, 1971. Ed. by Evelyn S. Firchow et al. (Janua Linguarum, Ser.: No. 49). 1972. 147.70 (*0-89925-061-0*) Mouton.

Studies by Members of the English Department, University of Illinois, in Memory of John Jay Parry. University of Illinois - Department of English Staff. LC 68-58798. (Essay Index Reprint Ser.). 1977. 20.95 (*0-8369-0120-7*) Ayer.

Studies by Samuel Horodezky: An Original Anthology. Ed. by Steven Katz. LC 79-51391. (Jewish Philosophy, Mysticism & History of Ideas Ser.). 1980. lib. bdg. 19.95 (*0-405-12233-0*) Ayer.

Studies Concerning Organisms Occurring in Water Supplies. L. B. Walton. (Bulletin Ser.: No. 24). 1930. 2.00 (*0-86727-023-3*) Ohio Bio Survey.

Studies Concerning the Origins of Milton's Paradise Lost. Heinrich Mutschmann. LC 79-163459. (Studies in Milton: No. 22). 1971. reprint ed. lib. bdg. 49.95 (*0-8383-1324-8*) M S G Haskell Hse.

Studies for a Byron Bibliography. Francis L. Randolph. LC 79-13752. 144p. 1979. 25.00 (*0-915010-26-7*) Sutter House.

Studies for Violin, Op. 32, 2 pts., Pt. 1. Hans Sitt. Ed. by Gustav Saenger. (Carl Fischer Music Library: Nos. 110 & 111). 1899. pap. 7.95 (*0-8258-0017-X*, L-110) Fischer Inc NY.

Studies for Violin, Op. 32, 2 pts., Pt. 2. Hans Sitt. Ed. by Gustav Saenger. (Carl Fischer Music Library: Nos. 110 & 111). 19p. 1899. pap. 7.75 (*0-8258-0018-8*, 111) Fischer Inc NY.

Studies for William A. Read: A Miscellany Presented by Some of His Colleagues & Friends. LC 68-22116. (Essay Index Reprint Ser.). 1977. 21.95 (*0-8369-0912-7*) Ayer.

Studies French & English. Frank L. Lucas. LC 69-17583. (Essay Index Reprint Ser.). 1977. 21.95 (*0-8369-0084-7*) Ayer.

Studies from Ten Literatures. Ernest A. Boyd. LC 68-20287. (Essay Index Reprint Ser.). 1977. 23.95 (*0-8369-0236-X*) Ayer.

Studies from the Psychological Laboratory of Oberlin College see Memory Defects in Organic Psychoses

Studies, Green & Gray. Henry J. Newbolt. LC 68-8485. (Essay Index Reprint Ser.). 1977. reprint ed. 20.95 (*0-8369-0740-X*) Ayer.

Studies, Historical & Critical. Pasquale Villari. Tr. by Luigi Villari. LC 68-16983. (Essay Index Reprint Ser.). 1977. reprint ed. 23.95 (*0-8369-0960-7*) Ayer.

Studies Honoring Ignatius Charles Brady, Friar Minor. Romano S. Almagno & Conrad L. Harkins. (Theology Ser.). 496p. 1976. pap. 25.00 (*1-57659-029-1*) Franciscan Inst.

Studies in a Folk-Play-Li-Ching-Chi. Wu Shou-Li. (Asian Folklore & Social Life Monographs: No. 7). (CHI.). 1970. 14.00 (*0-89986-010-9*) Oriental Bk Store.

Studies in a Hawaiian Community: Na Makamaka o Nanakuli. Ed. by Ronald Gallimore & Alan Howard. LC 79-17014. (Bernice P. Bishop Museum, Pacific Anthropological Records Ser.: No. 1). 154p. reprint ed. pap. 43.90 (*0-317-28837-7*, 2020786) Bks Demand.

Studies in a Mosque, Vol. 1. Stanley Lane-Poole. Ed. by Al I. Obaba. 184p. 1990. pap. text ed. 18.00 (*0-916157-22-9*) African Islam Miss Pubns.

Studies in a Mosque, Vol. II. Stanley Lane-Poole. 136p. 1990. pap. text ed. 18.00 (*0-916157-58-X*) African Islam Miss Pubns.

Studies in a Song Book - Pang Xie Duan Er. Taro Hatano. (Asian Folklore & Social Life Monographs: No. 9). (CHI & JPN.). 1970. 14.00 (*0-89986-012-5*) Oriental Bk Store.

S

Studies in Abhidharma Literature & the Origins of Buddhist Philosophical Systems. Erich Frauwallner. Ed. by Ernst Steinkellner. Tr. by Sophie F. Kidd. LC 95-36. (Indian Thoughts Ser.). 247p. 1996. pap. 14.95 (*0-7914-2700-5*); text ed. 44.50 (*0-7914-2699-8*) State U NY Pr.

Studies in Abnormal Pressures. Ed. by Walter H. Fertl et al. LC 93-34171. (Developments in Petroleum Science Ser.: No. 38). 472p. 1994. 215.00 (*0-444-89999-5*) Elsevier.

Studies in Abstract Families of Languages. Seymour Ginsburg & J. Hopcroft. LC 52-42839. (Memoirs Ser.: No. 1/87). 51p. 1983. reprint ed. pap. 16.00 (*0-8218-1287-4*, MEMO/1/87) Am Math.

Studies in Abstract Families of Languages. Seymour Ginsburg et al. (American Mathematical Society, Memoirs Ser.: No. 87). 57p. reprint ed. pap. 25.00 (*0-7837-6752-8*, 2046381) Bks Demand.

Studies in Abstract Phonology. Edmund Gussmann. (Linguistic Inquiry Monographs). 176p. (Orig.). 1980. pap. 15.95 (*0-262-57057-2*) MIT Pr.

Studies in Accounting History: Traditions & Innovation for the Twenty-First Century. Ed. by Atsuo Tsuji & Paul Garner. LC 94-47429. (Contributions in Economics & Economic History Ser.: No. 163). 240p. 1995. text ed. 79.50 (*0-313-29489-5*, Greenwood Pr) Greenwood.

Studies in Acts. T. C. Smith. (Kerygma & Church Ser.). 84p. (Orig.). 1990. pap. 6.95 (*0-9628455-0-7*) Smyth & Helwys.

Studies in Acts, Vol. II. Frances Easter. (Bible Study Ser.). 1986. pap. 4.50 (*0-8309-0442-5*) Herald Hse.

Studies in Ada Style. 2nd ed. Peter Hibbard et al. (Illus.). 111p. 1983. pap. 30.00 (*0-387-90816-1*) Spr-Verlag.

Studies in Administration & Finance, 1558-1825: With Special Reference to the History of Salt Taxation in England. Edward Hughes. LC 79-12656. xii, 528p. 1980. reprint ed. lib. bdg. 57.50 (*0-87991-856-X*) Porcupine Pr.

Studies in Administrative Theory. Robert L. Hefner & Edward H. Seifert. Ed. by Edward H. Seifert. 466p. 1980. pap. text ed. 29.95 (*0-89641-046-3*) American Pr.

Studies in Adult Education 1969, Vol. 1, Nos. 1-2. Ed. by T. Kelly. LC 73-110939. (Illus.). 1970. 24.95 (*0-678-05687-0*) Kelley.

Studies in African Native Law. Julius Lewin. 173p. reprint ed. 35.95 (*0-933121-90-3*) Black Classic.

Studies in American Church History, 25 vols. Catholic University of America Staff. reprint ed. 958.00 (*0-404-57750-4*) AMS Pr.

Studies in American Indian Literature: Critical Essays & Course Designs. Ed. by Paula G. Allen. LC 82-12516. (MLA Commission on the Literatures & Languages of America Ser.). xiv, 384p. 1983. pap. 19.75 (*0-87352-355-5*, B104P) Modern Lang.

Studies in American Literature. Ed. by Waldo F. McNeir & Leo B. Levy. (Essay Index Reprint Ser.). 1977. reprint ed. 17.95 (*0-518-10152-5*) Ayer.

Studies in American Political Development: An Annual, Vol. 3. Karen Orren & Stephen Skowronek. 352p. (C). 1989. pap. 18.00 (*0-300-04487-9*); text ed. 38.00 (*0-300-04486-0*) Yale U Pr.

Studies in American Political Development, Vol. 4: An Annual. Ed. by Karen Orren & Stephen Skowronck. 320p. (C). 1990. pap. 20.00 (*0-300-04679-0*) Yale U Pr.

Studies in American Tort Law. Vincent R. Johnson & Alan Gunn. LC 94-70136. 1058p. (C). 1994. boxed 75.00 (*0-89089-579-1*) Carolina Acad Pr.

Studies in American Trade Unionism. Ed. by Jacob H. Hollander & George E. Barnett. LC 77-120106. (Library of American Labor History). v, 380p. 1970. reprint ed. 45.00 (*0-678-00677-6*) Kelley.

Studies in American Trade Unionism. Jacob H. Hollander & George E. Barnett. LC 73-89739. (American Labor, from Conspiracy to Collective Bargaining Ser., No. 1). 380p. 1974. reprint ed. 24.95 (*0-405-02128-3*) Ayer.

Studies in Analytical Geochemistry. Ed. by Denis M. Shaw. LC 64-6495. (Royal Society of Canada, Special Publications: No. 6). 151p. reprint ed. pap. 43.10 (*0-317-28231-X*, 2014408) Bks Demand.

Studies in Analytical Psychology. Gerhard Adler. LC 67-10652. (Illus.). 1967. 10.00 (*0-913430-14-5*) C G Jung Foun.

Studies in Anaphora. Ed. by Barbara Fox. LC 96-21121. (Typological Studies in Language: Vol. 33). xii, 518p. 1996. pap. 115.00 (*1-55619-641-5*); lib. bdg. 34.95 (*1-55619-642-3*) Benjamins North Am.

***Studies in Ancient Coinage from Turkey.** Ed. by R. Ashton. (Monographs: Vol. 17). (Illus.). 168p. 1996. 75.00 (*0-901405-33-7*, Pub. by Brit Inst Arch UK) David Brown.

Studies in Ancient Egypt, the Aegean, & the Sudan: Essays in Honor of Dows Dunham. Ed. by William K. Simpson & W. Davis. (Illus.). 218p. 1981. 50.00 (*0-87846-197-3*) Mus Fine Arts Boston.

Studies in Ancient Greek Epistolography. M. Luther Stirewalt, Jr. LC 93-32706. (Society of Biblical Literature Resources for Biblical Study: No. 27). 95p. 1993. 29.95 (*1-55540-908-3*, 060327); pap. 19.95 (*1-55540-909-1*, 06 03 27) Scholars Pr GA.

Studies in Ancient Greek Topography, Pt. V. William K. Pritchett. (UC Publications in Classical Studies: Vol. 31). 1986. pap. 48.00 (*0-520-09698-3*) U CA Pr.

Studies in Ancient Greek Topography, Pt. VII. W. Kendrick Pritchett. x, 224p. 1991. pap. 97.00 (*90-5063-071-5*, Pub. by Gieben NE) Benjamins North Am.

Studies in Ancient Greek Topography, Pt. VIII. W. Kendrick Pritchett. (Illus.). xxi, 159p. 1993. pap. 97.00 (*90-5063-087-1*, Pub. by Gieben NE) Benjamins North Am.

Studies in Ancient Greek Topography: Battlefields, Part 2. William K. Pritchett. LC 65-65210. (University of California Publications: Classical Studies: Vol. 4). 292p. reprint ed. pap. 83.30 (*0-317-29555-1*, 2021261) Bks Demand.

Studies in Ancient Greek Topography: Part III (Roads) William K. Pritchett. (UC Publications in Classical Studies: Vol. 22). 436p. 1981. pap. 45.00 (*0-520-09635-5*) U CA Pr.

Studies in Ancient Greek Topography, Pt. 4: Passes. William K. Pritchett. LC 65-65210. (University of California Publications, Classical Studies: No. 28). (Illus.). 374p. reprint ed. pap. 106.60 (*0-8357-6855-4*, 2035553) Bks Demand.

Studies in Ancient History. J. H. Thiel. Ed. by H. T. Wallinga. Tr. by A. M. De Bruin-Cousins. xii, 175p. 1994. lib. bdg. 50.00 (*90-5063-092-8*, Pub. by Gieben NE) Benjamins North Am.

Studies in Ancient History & Numismatics: Presented to Rudi Thomsen. Ed. by Aksel Damsgaard-Madsen et al. (Illus.). 270p. (C). 1988. 48.00 (*87-7288-161-5*, Pub. by Aarhus Univ Pr DK) David Brown.

Studies in Ancient Indian History: (D. C. Sircar Commemoration Volume) Ed. by K. K. Dasgupta et al. (C). 1988. 110.00 (*81-85067-10-4*, Pub. by Sundeep II) S Asia.

Studies in Ancient Technology, Vol. 1: Bitumen & Petroleum in Antiquity; The Origin of Alchemy; Water Supply. 3rd ed. R. J. Forbes. LC 92-39555. (Illus.). 199p. 1993. reprint ed. 85.50 (*90-04-00621-4*) E J Brill.

Studies in Ancient Technology, Vol. 2: Irrigation & Drainage; Power; Water & Windmills; Land Transport & Road Building; The Coming of the Camel. 3rd ed. R. J. Forbes. LC 92-39555. (Illus.). 220p. 1993. reprint ed. 92.75 (*90-04-00622-2*) E J Brill.

Studies in Ancient Technology, Vol. 3: Cosmetics & Perfumes in Antiquity; Food, Alcoholic Beverages, Vinegar; Fermented Beverages 500 B.C.-500 A.D.; Crushing; Salts, Preservation Processes, Mummification; Paints, Pigments, Inks & Varnishes. 2nd rev. ed. R. J. Forbes. LC 92-39555. (Illus.). 276p. 1993. reprint ed. 103.25 (*90-04-00623-0*) E J Brill.

Studies in Ancient Yahwistic Poetry. Frank M. Cross, Jr. & David N. Freedman. LC 96-19207. (Biblical Resource Ser.). 208p. 1997. pap. 27.50 (*0-8028-4159-7*) Eerdmans.

Studies in Anglo-French History During the Eighteenth, Nineteenth & Twentieth Centuries. Ed. by Alfred Coville et al. LC 67-23197. (Essay Index Reprint Ser.). 1977. 19.95 (*0-8369-0343-9*) Ayer.

Studies in Antarctic Meteorology. Ed. by M. J. Rubin. LC 66-6578. (Antarctic Research Ser.: Vol. 9). (Illus.). 231p. 1966. 18.00 (*0-87590-109-3*) Am Geophysical.

Studies in Antisemitism Series. Studies in Antisemitism Series Staff. Date not set. text ed. write for info. (*0-08-044430-X*, Pergamon Pr) Elsevier.

Studies in Apollonius Rhodius Argonautica, Bk. III. Malcolm Campbell. (Altertumswissenschaftliche Texte und Studien: Vol. 9). viii, 131p. (GER.). 1983. 25.00 (*3-487-07436-2*) G Olms Pubs.

Studies in Applied Demography: Proceedings of the International Conference on Applied Demography. Jerry W. Wicks & K. Vaninadha Rao. 476p. 1994. pap. text ed. write for info. (*0-944244-02-5*) PSRC.

Studies in Applied Econometrics. Ed. by H. Schneeweib & K. F. Zimmermann. (Contributions to Economics Ser.). (Illus.). vi, 238p. 1993. 61.95 (*0-387-91460-9*); pap. 61.95 (*3-7908-0716-8*) Spr-Verlag.

Studies in Applied Probability & Management Science. Ed. by Kenneth J. Arrow et al. 287p. 1962. 45.00 (*0-8047-0099-0*) Stanford U Pr.

Studies in Arab History: The Antonius Lectures, 1976-87. Ed. by Derek Hopwood. (Illus.). 189p. 1990. text ed. 49.95 (*0-312-04623-5*) St Martin.

Studies in Arabian Architecture. Paolo M. Costa. (Collected Studies: No. CS 455). (Illus.). 336p. 1994. 140.00 (*0-86078-436-3*, Pub. by Variorum UK) Ashgate Pub Co.

Studies in Arabian History & Civilisation. R. B. Serjeant. (Collected Studies: No. CS145). (Illus.). 350p. (C). 1981. reprint ed. lib. bdg. 98.95 (*0-86078-092-9*, Pub. by Variorum UK) Ashgate Pub Co.

Studies in Arabic Literary Papyri: Language & Literature, Vol. 3. Nabia Abbott. LC 56-5027. (Oriental Institute Publications: No. 77). (Illus.). xvi, 216p. 1974. lib. bdg. 48.00 (*0-226-62178-2*) U Ch Pr.

Studies in Arabic Versions of Greek Texts & in Mediaeval Science. Shlomo Pines. (Collected Works of Shlomo Pines: Vol. 2). ix, 468p. 1986. 91.50 (*965-223-626-8*) E J Brill.

Studies in Arcady & Other Essays for a Country Parsonage. Richard L. Gales. LC 70-107701. (Essay Index Reprint Ser.: No. 1). 1977. 26.95 (*0-8369-1502-X*) Ayer.

Studies in Arcady & Other Essays from a Country Parsonage. Richard L. Gales. LC 70-107701. (Essay Index Reprint Ser.: No. 2). 1977. 28.95 (*0-8369-1589-5*) Ayer.

Studies in Archaeology. Ed. by Asok Datta. (C). 1991. 100.00 (*81-85016-29-1*, Pub. by Bks & Bks IA) S Asia.

***Studies in Archaic Corinthian Vase Painting.** D. A. Amyx & Patricia Lawrence. (Hesperia Supplement Ser.: No. 29). xi, 161p. 1996. pap. 65.00 (*0-87661-528-0*) Am Sch Athens.

Studies in Arid Land Management. T. S. Chouhan & K. N. Joshi. 432p. 1993. pap. 250.00 (*81-7233-064-2*, Pub. by Scientific Pubs II) St Mut.

Studies in Aristotle. Ed. by Dominic J. O'Meara. LC 81-4381. (Studies in Philosophy & the History of Philosophy: No. 9). 321p. reprint ed. pap. 91.50 (*0-7837-1000-3*, 2041307) Bks Demand.

Studies in Armenian Literature & Christianity. R. W. Thompson. (Collected Studies: No. CS 451). 1994. 89.95 (*0-86078-411-8*, Pub. by Variorum UK) Ashgate Pub Co.

Studies in Art History I: Studies in Italian Art & Architecture. Henry A. Millon. (Fifteenth - Eighteenth Centuries Ser.). (Illus.). 344p. 1980. 56.00 (*0-271-00457-6*) Am Acad Rome.

Studies in Arthur Schnitzler. Ed. by Herbert W. Reichert & Herman Salinger. LC 63-62703. (North Carolina. University. Studies in the Germanic Languages & Literatures: No. 42). reprint ed. 31.50 (*0-404-50942-8*) AMS Pr.

Studies in Athenian Architecture, Sculpture & Topography, No. 20. American School of Classical Studies at Athens Staff. LC 81-14994. (Hesperia Supplement Ser.: No. 20). (Illus.). xii, 191p. 1982. pap. 15.00 (*0-87661-520-5*) Am Sch Athens.

Studies in Attic Epigraphy, History & Topography, No. 19. American School of Classical Studies at Athens Staff. LC 81-12876. (Hesperia Supplement Ser.: No. 19). (Illus.). xii, 207p. 1982. pap. 15.00 (*0-87661-519-1*) Am Sch Athens.

Studies in Augustine & Eriugena. John O'Meara. Ed. by Thomas P. Halton. LC 92-7188. 362p. 1993. text ed. 59.95 (*0-8132-0768-1*) Cath U Pr.

Studies in Aulus Gellius. Barry Baldwin. 130p. 1975. 10.00 (*0-87291-071-7*) Coronado Pr.

Studies in Australian Totemism. Adolphus P. Elkin. LC 76-44712. reprint ed. 34.50 (*0-404-15857-9*) AMS Pr.

Studies in Austrian Capital Theory, Investment & Time. Ed. by M. Faber. (Lecture Notes in Economics & Mathematical Systems Ser.: Vol. 277). vi, 317p. 1986. 39.95 (*0-387-16804-4*) Spr-Verlag.

Studies in Austronesian Linguistics. Richard McGinn. LC 87-11242. (Monographs in International Studies, Southeast Asia Ser.: No. 76). 650p. 1986. pap. text ed. 20.00 (*0-89680-137-3*, Ohio U Ctr Intl) Ohio U Pr.

Studies in Babi & Baha'i History, Vol. 1. Ed. by Moojan Momen. (Illus.). 337p. (C). 1982. text ed. 32.50 (*0-933770-16-2*) Kalimat.

Studies in Babi & Baha'i History: Vol. 2: From Iran East & West. Ed. by Juan R. Cole & Moojan Momen. (Illus.). 205p. (C). 1984. 32.50 (*0-933770-40-5*) Kalimat.

Studies in Babi & Baha'i History, Vol. 4: Music, Devotions, & Mashriq'l-Adhkhar. R. Jackson Armstrong-Ingram. (Illus.). 1988. 32.50 (*0-933770-62-6*); pap. 22.50 (*0-933770-77-4*) Kalimat.

Studies in Babi & Baha'i History Volume 3: In Iran. Ed. & Intro. by Peter Smith. (Illus.). 1986. 32.50 (*0-933770-46-4*) Kalimat.

Studies in Banking Theory, Financial Theory & Vertical Control. Meyer L. Burstein. LC 87-30406. 1988. text ed. 49.95 (*0-312-01576-3*) St Martin.

***Studies in Begoniaceae, Vol. I.** J. J. De Wilde. (Wageningen Agricultural University Papers: No. 83-9). 70p. 1983. pap. 25.00 (*90-6754-053-6*, Pub. by Backhuys Pubs NE) Balogh.

***Studies in Begoniaceae, Vol. II.** J. F. De Wilde. (Wageningen Agricultural University Papers: No. 84-3). 129p. 1985. pap. 46.00 (*90-6754-060-9*, Pub. by Backhuys Pubs NE) Balogh.

***Studies in Begoniaceae, Vol. V.** M. S. Sosef. (Wageningen Agricultural University Papers: No. 94-1). (Illus.). 306p. 1994. pap. 125.00 (*90-6754-336-5*, Pub. by Backhuys Pubs NE) Balogh.

Studies in Biblical & Jewish Folklore. Raphael Patai et al. LC 72-6871. (Studies in Comparative Literature: No. 35). 1972. reprint ed. lib. bdg. 75.00 (*0-8383-1665-4*) M S G Haskell Hse.

Studies in Biblical & Semitic Symbolism. Maurice H. Fairbridge. 1977. lib. bdg. 59.95 (*0-8490-2700-4*) Gordon Pr.

Studies in Biblical Holiness. Donald Metz. 292p. 1971. 21.99 (*0-8341-0117-3*) Beacon Hill.

Studies in Biblical Law: From the Hebrew Bible to the Dead Sea Scrolls. G. Brin. (Journal for the Study of the Old Testament Supplement Ser.: Vol. 176). 309p. 67.00 (*1-85075-484-5*, Pub. by Sheffield Acad UK) CUP Services.

Studies in Bibliography, Vol. 36. Fredson Bowers. LC 49-3353. 271p. 1983. text ed. 35.00 (*0-8139-0987-2*) U Pr of Va.

Studies in Bibliography, Vol. 43. Ed. by Fredson Bowers. LC 49-3353. 292p. 1990. lib. bdg. 35.00 (*0-8139-1263-6*) U Pr of Va.

Studies in Bibliography, Vol. 44. Ed. by Fredson Bowers. LC 49-3353. 300p. 1991. text ed. 35.00 (*0-8139-1316-0*) U Pr of Va.

Studies in Bibliography, Vol. 45. Ed. by Fredson Bowers & David L. Vander Meulen. LC 49-3353. 338p. (C). 1992. text ed. 35.00 (*0-8139-1384-5*) U Pr of Va.

Studies in Bibliography, Vol. 46. Ed. by Fredson Bowers & David L. Vander Meulen. LC 49-3353. 388p. (C). 1993. text ed. 35.00 (*0-8139-1452-3*) U Pr of Va.

Studies in Bibliography, Vol. XLVII. Ed. by Fredson Bowers & David L. Vander Meulen. LC 49-3353. 300p. (C). 1994. text ed. 35.00 (*0-8139-1523-6*) U Pr of Va.

***Studies in Bibliography, Vol. L.** Ed. by David L. Vander Meulen. 300p. (C). 1997. 40.00 (*0-8139-1731-X*) U Pr of Va.

Studies in Bibliography: Papers of the Bibliographical Society of the University of Virginia, Vol. 1, 1948-1949. Incl. Vol. 2. Vol. 2 1949-50. Fredson Bowers. LC 49-3353. 211p. 1950. (*0-8139-0033-6*); Vol. 3. Vol. 3 1950-51. Fredson Bowers. LC 49-3353. 306p. 1951. (*0-8139-0034-4*); Vol. 4. Vol. 4 1951-52. Fredson Bowers. LC 49-3353. 237p. 1952. (*0-8139-0035-2*); Vol. 5. Vol. 5 1952-53. Fredson Bowers. LC 49-3353. 230p. 1953. (*0-8139-0036-0*); Vol. 6. Vol. 6 1953-54. Fredson Bowers. 288p. 1954. (*0-8139-0037-9*); Vol. 7. Vol. 7 1955. 240p. 1955. (*0-8139-0038-7*); Vol. 8. Vol. 8 1956. 272p. 1956. (*0-8139-0039-5*); Vol. 11. Vol. 11 1958. 295p. (*0-8139-0042-5*); Vol. 12. Vol. 12 1959. 259p. (*0-8139-0043-3*); Vol. 13. Vol. 13 1960. (*0-8139-0044-1*); Vol. 14. Vol. 14 1961. 290p. (*0-8139-0045-X*); Vol. 15. Vol. 15 1962. 311p. (*0-8139-0046-8*); Vol. 16. 1963. LC 49-3353. 276p. (*0-8139-0047-6*); Vol. 17. . LC 49-3353. 258p. (*0-8139-0048-4*); Vol. 18. 1965. LC 49-3353. 312p. (*0-8139-0049-2*); Vol. 19. . LC 49-3353. 282p. (*0-8139-0050-6*); Vol. 20. . LC 49-3353. 298p. (*0-8139-0051-4*); Vol. 21. . LC 49-3353. 290p. (*0-8139-0052-2*); Vol. 22. . LC 49-3353. 341p. (*0-8139-0053-0*); Vol. 23. . LC 49-3353. 280p. (*0-8139-0309-2*); Vol. 24. . LC 49-3353. 240p. (*0-8139-0331-9*); Vol. 25. . Fredson Bowers. LC 49-3353. 1972. (*0-8139-0404-8*); Vol. 26. . Fredson Bowers. LC 49-3353. 1973. (*0-8139-0468-4*); Vol. 27. . Fredson Bowers. LC 49-3353. 1974. (*0-8139-0580-X*); Vol. 28. . Fredson Bowers. LC 49-3353. 1975. (*0-8139-0636-9*); Vol. 29. . Fredson Bowers. LC 49-3353. 1976. (*0-8139-0687-3*); Vol. 30. . Fredson Bowers. LC 49-3353. 1977. (*0-8139-0717-9*); Vol. 31. 1980. Ed. by Fredson Bowers. LC 49-3353. 1977. (*0-8139-0777-2*); Vol. 32. Vol. 32 1979. (Illus.). 285p. 35.00 (*0-8139-0817-5*); Vol. 33. Vol. 33 1980. 282p. 35.00 (*0-8139-0860-4*); Vol. 34. Vol. 34 1981. 276p. (*0-8139-0898-1*); Vol. 35. Vol. 35 1982. 338p. (*0-8139-0948-1*); Vol. 36. Vol. 36 1983. 271p. (*0-318-65014-2*); Vol. 37. Vol. 37 1984. 312p. (*0-8139-1029-3*); Vol. 38. Vol. 38 1985. LC 49-3353. 380p. (*0-8139-1065-X*); Vol. 39. Vol. 39 1986. 375p. (Orig.). (*0-8139-1095-1*); Vol. 40. Vol. 40 1987. LC 49-3353. 265p. (*0-8139-1133-8*); Vol. 41. Vol. 41 1988. LC 49-3353. 325p. (*0-8139-1175-3*); Vol. 42. Vol. 42 1989. LC 49-3353. 336p. (*0-8139-1190-7*); 1948-49. 1949. (*0-8139-0032-8*); LC 49-3353. 1964. reprint ed. pap. 59.30 (*0-7837-9997-7*, 2060724) Bks Demand.

Studies in Bibliography: Papers of the Bibliographical Society of the University of Virginia, Vols. 1-31. Incl. Vol. 2. Vol. 2 1949-50. Fredson Bowers. LC 49-3353. 211p. 1950. (*0-8139-0033-6*); Vol. 3. Vol. 3 1950-51. Fredson Bowers. LC 49-3353. 306p. 1951. (*0-8139-0034-4*); Vol. 4. Vol. 4 1951-52. Fredson Bowers. LC 49-3353. 237p. 1952. (*0-8139-0035-2*); Vol. 5. Vol. 5 1952-53. Fredson Bowers. LC 49-3353. 230p. 1953. (*0-8139-0036-0*); Vol. 6. Vol. 6 1953-54. Fredson Bowers. 288p. 1954. (*0-8139-0037-9*); Vol. 7. Vol. 7 1955. 240p. 1955. (*0-8139-0038-7*); Vol. 8. Vol. 8 1956. 272p. 1956. (*0-8139-0039-5*); Vol. 11. Vol. 11 1958. 295p. (*0-8139-0042-5*); Vol. 12. Vol. 12 1959. 259p. (*0-8139-0043-3*); Vol. 13. Vol. 13 1960. (*0-8139-0044-1*); Vol. 14. Vol. 14 1961. 290p. (*0-8139-0045-X*); Vol. 15. Vol. 15 1962. 311p. (*0-8139-0046-8*); Vol. 16. 1963. LC 49-3353. 276p. (*0-8139-0047-6*); Vol. 17. . LC 49-3353. 258p. (*0-8139-0048-4*); Vol. 18. 1965. LC 49-3353. 312p. (*0-8139-0049-2*); Vol. 19. . LC 49-3353. 282p. (*0-8139-0050-6*); Vol. 20. . LC 49-3353. 298p. (*0-8139-0051-4*); Vol. 21. . 290p. (*0-8139-0052-2*); Vol. 22. . LC 49-3353. 341p. (*0-8139-0053-0*); Vol. 23. . LC 49-3353. 280p. (*0-8139-0309-2*); Vol. 24. . LC 49-3353. 240p. (*0-8139-0331-9*); Vol. 25. . Fredson Bowers. LC 49-3353. 1972. (*0-8139-0404-8*); Vol. 26. . Fredson Bowers. LC 49-3353. 1973. (*0-8139-0468-4*); Vol. 27. . Fredson Bowers. LC 49-3353. 1974. (*0-8139-0580-X*); Vol. 28. . Fredson Bowers. LC 49-3353. 1975. (*0-8139-0636-9*); Vol. 29. . Fredson Bowers. LC 49-3353. 1976. (*0-8139-0687-3*); Vol. 30. . Fredson Bowers. LC 49-3353. 1977. (*0-8139-0717-9*); Vol. 31. 1980. Ed. by Fredson Bowers. LC 49-3353. 1977. (*0-8139-0777-2*); Vol. 32. Vol. 32 1979. (Illus.). 285p. 35.00 (*0-8139-0817-5*); Vol. 33. Vol. 33 1980. 282p. 35.00 (*0-8139-0860-4*); Vol. 34. Vol. 34 1981. 276p. (*0-8139-0898-1*); Vol. 35. Vol. 35 1982. 338p. (*0-8139-0948-1*); Vol. 36. Vol. 36 1983. 271p. (*0-318-65014-2*); Vol. 37. Vol. 37 1984. 312p. (*0-8139-1029-3*); Vol. 38. Vol. 38 1985. LC 49-3353. 380p. (*0-8139-1065-X*); Vol. 39. Vol. 39 1986. 375p. (Orig.). (*0-8139-1095-1*); Vol. 40. Vol. 40 1987. LC 49-3353. 265p. (*0-8139-1133-8*); Vol. 41. Vol. 41 1988. LC 49-3353. 325p. (*0-8139-1175-3*); Vol. 42. Vol. 42 1989. LC 49-3353. 336p. (*0-8139-1190-7*); 1948-49. 1949. (*0-8139-0032-8*); LC 49-3353. write for info. (*0-318-56227-8*) U Pr of Va.

An Asterisk (*) at the beginning of an entry indicates that the title is appearing in BIP for the first time.

Studies in Bibliography: Papers of the Bibliographical Society of the University of Virginia, Vols. 32-42. Incl. Vol. 2. Vol. 2 1949-50. Fredson Bowers. LC 49-3353. 211p. 1950. (0-8139-0033-6); Vol. 3. Vol. 3 1950-51. Fredson Bowers. LC 49-3353. 306p. 1951. (0-8139-0034-4); Vol. 4. Vol. 4 1951-52. Fredson Bowers. LC 49-3353. 237p. 1952. (0-8139-0035-2); Vol. 5. Vol. 5 1952-53. Fredson Bowers. LC 49-3353. 230p. 1953. (0-8139-0036-0); Vol. 6. Vol. 6 1953-54. Fredson Bowers. 288p. 1954. (0-8139-0037-9); Vol. 7. Vol. 7 1955. 240p. 1955. (0-8139-0038-7); Vol. 8. Vol. 8 1956. 272p. 1956. (0-8139-0039-5); Vol. 11. Vol. 11 1958. 295p. (0-8139-0042-5); Vol. 12. Vol. 12 1959. 259p. (0-8139-0043-3); Vol. 13. Vol. 13 1960. (0-8139-0044-1); Vol. 14. Vol. 14 1961. 290p. (0-8139-0045-X); Vol. 15. Vol. 15 1962. 311p. (0-8139-0046-8); Vol. 16. 1963. LC 49-3353. 276p. (0-8139-0047-6); Vol. 17. . LC 49-3353. 258p. (0-8139-0048-4); Vol. 18. 1965. LC 49-3353. 312p. (0-8139-0049-2); Vol. 19. . LC 49-3353. 282p. (0-8139-0050-6); Vol. 20. . LC 49-3353. 298p. (0-8139-0051-4); Vol. 21. . LC 49-3353. 290p. (0-8139-0052-2); Vol. 22. . LC 49-3353. 341p. (0-8139-0053-0); Vol. 23. . LC 49-3353. 280p. (0-8139-0309-2); Vol. 24. . LC 49-3353. 240p. (0-8139-0331-9); Vol. 25. . Fredson Bowers. LC 49-3353. 1972. (0-8139-0404-8); Vol. 26. . Fredson Bowers. LC 49-3353. 1973. (0-8139-0468-4); Vol. 27. . Fredson Bowers. LC 49-3353. 1974. (0-8139-0580-X); Vol. 28. . Fredson Bowers. LC 49-3353. 1975. (0-8139-0636-9); Vol. 29. . Fredson Bowers. LC 49-3353. 1976. (0-8139-0687-3); Vol. 30. . Fredson Bowers. LC 49-3353. 1977. (0-8139-0717-9); Vol. 31. 1980. Ed. by Fredson Bowers. LC 49-3353. 1977. (0-8139-0777-2); Vol. 32. Vol. 32 1979. (Illus.). 285p. 35.00 (0-8139-0817-5); Vol. 33. Vol. 33 1980. 282p. 35.00 (0-8139-0860-4); Vol. 34. Vol. 34 1981. 276p. (0-8139-0898-1); Vol. 35. Vol. 35 1982. 338p. (0-8139-0948-1); Vol. 36. Vol. 36 1983. 271p. (0-318-65014-2); Vol. 37. Vol. 37 1984. 312p. (0-8139-1029-3); Vol. 38. Vol. 38 1985. LC 49-3353. 380p. (0-8139-1065-X); Vol. 39. Vol. 39 1986. 375p. (Orig.). (0-8139-1095-1); Vol. 40. Vol. 40 1987. LC 49-3353. (0-8139-1133-8); Vol. 41. Vol. 41 1988. LC 49-3353. 325p. (0-8139-1175-3); Vol. 42. Vol. 42 1989. LC 49-3353. 336p. (0-8139-1190-7); 1948-49. 1949. (0-8139-0032-8); LC 49-3353. write for info. (0-318-65013-4) U Pr of Va.

Studies in Bibliography Vol. 48. Ed. by David L. Vander Meulen. (Illus.). 300p. (C). 1995. text ed. 35.00 (0-8139-1617-8) U Pr of Va.

Studies in Bibliography Series, Vol. 49. Ed. by David L. Vander Meulen. 300p. (C). 1996. text ed. 35.00 (0-8139-1669-0) U Pr of Va.

Studies in Biography. Ed. by Daniel Aaron. (English Studies: No. 8). 200p. (C). 1978. 16.00 (0-674-84651-6); pap. 5.95 (0-674-84652-4) HUP.

Studies in Biological Control. Ed. by Vittorio L. Delucchi. LC 75-16867. (International Biological Programme Ser.: No. 9). 320p. reprint ed. pap. 91.20 (0-317-29377-X, 2024479) Bks Demand.

Studies in Black & White. Jerome Bruce. 1977. 21.95 (0-8369-9160-5, 9035) Ayer.

Studies in Boiotian Inscriptions. John M. Fossey. (Epigraphica Boeotica Ser.: Vol. 1). (Illus.). xv, 304p. 1991. 94.00 (90-5063-061-8, Pub. by Gieben NE) Benjamins North Am.

Studies in British Imperial History: Essays in Honor of A. P. Thornton. Ed. by Gordon Martel. LC 85-8110. 256p. 1986. text ed. 29.95 (0-312-77080-4) St Martin.

Studies in British Overseas Trade, 1870-1914. S. B. Saul. LC 88-14686. 256p. 1990. reprint ed. text ed. 59.75 (0-313-26469-4, SBOT, Greenwood Pr) Greenwood.

Studies in Brown Humanity Being Scrawls & Smudges in Sepia, White & Yellow. Hugh C. Clifford. 1977. text ed. 18.95 (0-8369-9240-7, 9094) Ayer.

Studies in Browning. Josiah Flew. LC 74-115859. (Studies in Browning: No. 4). 1970. reprint ed. lib. bdg. 59.95 (0-8383-1071-0) M S G Haskell Hse.

Studies in Brythonic Word Order. Ed. by James Fife & Erich Poppe. LC 91-34225. (Current Issues in Linguistic Theory Ser.: No. 83). x, 360p. 1991. 100.00 (1-55619-138-3) Benjamins North Am.

Studies in Buddhist Art of South Asia. A. K. Narain. (Illus.). 140p. 1986. 48.00 (0-8364-1852-2, Pub. by Usha II) S Asia.

Studies in Buddhist Iconography. Dipak C. Bhattacharya. 1978. 22.50 (0-8364-0016-X) S Asia.

Studies in Business-Cycle Theory. Robert E. Lucas, Jr. 312p. (C). 1983. pap. 21.00 (0-262-62044-8) MIT Pr.

Studies in Byzantine History & Modern Greek Folklore, Vol. I. Constantine N. Tsirpanlis. 180p. 1980. pap. 21.95 (0-317-36319-0) EO Pr.

Studies in Byzantine Institutions, Society & Culture, 2 vols., Set. Speros Vryonis, Jr. (Hellenism: Ancient, Mediaeval, Modern Ser.). (C). 1996. text ed. 125.00 (0-89241-542-8) Caratzas.

Studies in Byzantine Institutions, Society & Culture, Vol. 1: Institutions & Society. Speros Vryonis, Jr. (Hellenism: Ancient, Mediaeval, Modern Ser.: No. 14). 288p. (C). 1996. text ed. 60.00 (0-89241-528-2) Caratzas.

Studies in Byzantine Institutions, Society & Culture, Vol. 2: Provinces, Foreigners & the Twilight of the Empire. Speros Vryonis, Jr. (Hellenism: Ancient, Mediaeval, Modern Ser.: No. 15). 384p. (C). 1996. text ed. 70.00 (0-89241-530-4) Caratzas.

Studies in Byzantine Political History Sources & Controversies. Patricia Karlin-Hayter. (Collected Studies: No. CS141). 336p. (C). 1981. reprint ed. lib. bdg. 98.95 (0-86078-088-0, Pub. by Variorum UK) Ashgate Pub Co.

Studies in Byzantine Sigillography. Ed. by Nicolas Oikonomides. LC 87-22266. 128p. 1988. pap. 18.00 (0-88402-171-8) Dumbarton Oaks.

Studies in Byzantine Sigillography, No. 2. Ed. by Nicolas Oikonomides. LC 90-33600. (Illus.). 328p. 1990. pap. 45.00 (0-88402-188-2, OBS2P, Dumbarton Rsch Lib) Dumbarton Oaks.

Studies in Byzantine Sigillography, No. 3. Ed. by Nicolas Oikonomides. (Illus.). 244p. 1993. pap. 25.00 (0-88402-218-8) Dumbarton Oaks.

Studies in Cahuilla Culture: Ethnography of the Cahuilla Indians. A. L. Kroeber & Lucile Hooper. (Classics in California Anthropology Ser.: Vol. 4). (Illus.). 106p. (C). 1993. reprint ed. lib. bdg. 41.00 (0-8095-6212-X) Borgo Pr.

Studies in Canon Law: Presented to P. J. M. Huizing. Ed. by J. Provost & Knut Walf. (Annua Nuntia Lovaniensia Ser.: No. 32). 270p. (Orig.). 1991. pap. 57.50 (90-6186-439-9, Pub. by Leuven Univ BE) Coronet Bks.

Studies in Caribbean Spanish Dialectology. Ed. by Melvyn C. Resnick. LC 88-4340. 156p. 1988. pap. 14.95 (0-87840-098-2) Georgetown U Pr.

Studies in Cash Flow Accounting & Analysis: Aspects of Interface Between Managerial Planning, Reporting & Control & External Performance Measurement. Ed. by G. H. Lawson. LC 92-5927. (New Works in Accounting History). 328p. 1992. text ed. 20.00 (0-8153-0687-3) Garland.

Studies in Cassius Dio & Herodian. H. A. Andersen & E. Hohl. LC 75-7342. (Roman History Ser.). (Illus.). (GER.). 1975. reprint ed. 19.95 (0-405-07063-2) Ayer.

Studies in Castles & Castle-Building. A. J. Taylor. (Illus.). 350p. (C). 1986. text ed. 65.00 (0-907628-51-6) Hambledon Press.

Studies in Celtic Literature & the Early Irish Church. Doris Edel. 320p. 1997. 65.00 (1-85182-269-0, Pub. by Four Cts Pr IE) Intl Spec Bk.

Studies in Cephaloziellaceae. R. M. Schuster. (Illus.). 1977. 32.00 (3-7682-0823-0) Lubrecht & Cramer.

Studies in Ch'an & Hua-Yen. Ed. by Robert M. Gimello & Peter N. Gregory. (Studies in East Asian Buddhism: No. 1). 406p. 1984. pap. text ed. 18.00 (0-8248-0835-5) UH Pr.

Studies in Character Analysis. Manly P. Hall. pap. 6.95 (0-89314-804-0) Philos Res.

Studies in Chaucer's House of Fame. Wilbur O. Sypherd. LC 65-26459. (Studies in Chaucer: No. 6). 1969. reprint ed. lib. bdg. 44.95 (0-8383-0631-4) M S G Haskell Hse.

Studies in Cherokee Basketry: Including a Reprint of Decorative Art & Basketry of the Cherokee by Frank G. Speck. Ed. by Betty J. Duggan & Brett H. Riggs. (Museum Occasional Paper Ser.: No. 9). 60p. 1991. pap. 10.00 (1-880174-01-4) U TN F H McClung.

Studies in Child Development. Arnold L. Gesell. LC 76-138114. (Illus.). 224p. 1971. reprint ed. text ed. 38.50 (0-8371-5690-4, GECD, Greenwood Pr) Greenwood.

Studies in Child Guidance. Jean W. Macfarlane. (SRCD M Ser.: Vol. 3, No. 6). 1938. 25.00 (0-527-01506-7) Periodicals Srv.

Studies in Child Language & Multilingualism. Ed. by Virginia Teller & Sheila J. White. LC 80-16810. (Annals Ser.: Vol. 345). 187p. 1980. 30.00 (0-89766-078-1); pap. 30.00 (0-89766-079-X) NY Acad Sci.

Studies in Child Psychoanalysis, Pure & Applied: The Scientific Proceedings of the 20th Anniversary Celebrations of the Hampstead Child-Therapy Course & Clinic. Anna Freud. LC 74-20082. (Monograph Series of the Psychoanalytic Study of the Child: No. 5). 189p. 1975. reprint ed. pap. 53.90 (0-7837-3297-X, 2057699) Bks Demand.

Studies in Childhood, Vol. 3. James Sully. LC 77-72191. (Contributions to the History of Psychology Ser.: Psychometrics & Educational Psychology). 486p. 1977. reprint ed. text ed. 85.00 (0-313-26938-6, U6938, Greenwood Pr) Greenwood.

Studies in Chinese Art. J. Hackin. 1972. lib. bdg. 79.95 (0-87968-522-0) Krishna Pr.

Studies in Chinese Art & Some Indian Influences. J. Hackin. 1976. lib. bdg. 59.95 (0-8490-2701-2) Gordon Pr.

Studies in Chinese Buddhism. Arthur F. Wright. 224p. (C). 1990. text ed. 30.00 (0-300-04717-7) Yale U Pr.

Studies in Chinese Diplomatic History. Ching-Lin Hsia. LC 75-32333. 226p. 1976. reprint ed. text ed. 59.95 (0-313-26953-X, U6953, Greenwood Pr) Greenwood.

Studies in Chinese Institutional History. Yang Lieu-Shengyang. LC 61-8844. (Harvard-Yenching Institute Studies: No. 20). 233p. 1961. pap. 6.95 (0-674-84660-5) HUP.

Studies in Chinese Literary Genres. Ed. by Cyril Birch. LC 77-157825. 408p. reprint ed. pap. 116.30 (0-685-44410-4, 2032282) Bks Demand.

Studies in Chinese Literature. Ed. by John L. Bishop. LC 65-13836. (Harvard-Yenching Institute Studies: No. 21). 253p. (Orig.). 1965. pap. 8.50 (0-674-84705-9) HUP.

Studies in Chinese Philosophy & Philosophical Literature. Angus C. Graham. LC 90-30958. (SUNY Series in Chinese Philosophy & Culture). 435p. (C). 1990. text ed. 64.50 (0-7914-0449-8); pap. text ed. 21.95 (0-7914-0450-1) State U NY Pr.

Studies in Chinese Proverbs. Chu Chien-Fan. (Asian Folklore & Social Life Monographs: No. 5). (CHI.). 1972. 14.00 (0-89986-008-7) Oriental Bk Store.

Studies in Chinese Society. Ed. by Arthur P. Wolf. LC 78-62272. xii, 372p. 1978. 52.50 (0-8047-1006-6); pap. 14.95 (0-8047-1007-4, SP-149) Stanford U Pr.

Studies in Chinese Society. Ed. by Arthur P. Wolf. LC 78-62272. 1978. reprint ed. pap. 30.00 (0-608-00732-3, 2061508) Bks Demand.

Studies in "Christ & Satan" Charles Sleeth. (McMaster Old English Studies & Texts). 160p. 1981. 35.00 (0-8020-5484-6) U of Toronto Pr.

Studies in Christian Antiquity. Richard Hanson. 408p. 1986. 49.95 (0-567-09363-8, Pub. by T & T Clark UK) Bks Intl VA.

Studies in Christian Education: Christ's Education Was Gained from Heaven-Appointed Sources, from Useful Work, from the Study of the Scriptures, from Nature, & from the Experiences of Life - God's Lesson Books. E. A. Sutherland. (Pioneer Classics Ser.). 160p. (YA). (gr. 9 up). 1989. pap. 6.95 (0-945460-04-X) Upward Way.

Studies in Christian Enthusiasm. Geoffrey F. Nuttall. (C). 1948. pap. 7.00 (0-87574-041-3) Pendle Hill.

Studies in Christian Ethics. Steve Williams. 1990. pap. 5.50 (0-89137-850-2) Quality Pubns.

Studies in Christian Mysticism. W. H. Dyson. 1977. lib. bdg. 69.95 (0-8490-2702-0) Gordon Pr.

Studies in Christianity. Borden P. Bowne. LC 75-3074. reprint ed. 28.50 (0-404-59075-6) AMS Pr.

Studies in Chronic Mental Illness: New Horizons for Social Work Researchers. Ed. by Joan P. Bowker & Allen Rubin. 1986. 6.50 (0-87293-015-7) Coun Soc Wk Ed.

Studies in Church History. Henry C. Lea. LC 83-48780. 1988. reprint ed. 57.50 (0-404-19154-1) AMS Pr.

Studies in Church History Vol. 1: Papers Read at the First Winter & Summer Meetings of the Ecclesiastical History Society. C. W. Dugmore & C. Duggan. 1964. 69.50 (0-614-01797-1) Elliots Bks.

Studies in Chuvash Etymology I. Ed. by A. Rona-Tas. (Studia Oralo-Altaica Ser.: No. 17). 240p. 1982. 48.00 (0-686-36268-3) Benjamins North Am.

Studies in Cistercian Art & Architecture, Vol. IV. Ed. by Meredith P. Lillich. (Cistercian Studies: No. 134). (Illus.). 300p. (Orig.). 1993. 49.95 (0-87907-534-1); pap. 22.95 (0-87907-634-8) Cistercian Pubns.

Studies in Cistercian Art & Architecture, I. Ed. by Meredith P. Lillich et al. (Cistercian Studies: No. 66). (Illus.). (Orig.). 1982. pap. 12.95 (0-87907-866-9) Cistercian Pubns.

Studies in Cistercian Art & Architecture, II. Ed. by Meredith P. Lillich. (Cistercian Studies: No. 69). (Illus.). pap. 14.95 (0-87907-869-3) Cistercian Pubns.

Studies in Cistercian Art & Architecture, III. Ed. by Meredith P. Lillich. (Cistercian Studies: No. 89). (Orig.). 1987. 49.95 (0-87907-789-1); pap. 22.95 (0-87907-889-8) Cistercian Pubns.

Studies in Class Structure. George D. Cole. LC 76-2503. 195p. 1976. reprint ed. text ed. 35.00 (0-8371-8779-6, COSS, Greenwood Pr) Greenwood.

Studies in Classic American Literature. D. H. Lawrence. 1976. 24.95 (0-8488-1075-9) Amereon Ltd.

Studies in Classic American Literature. D. H. Lawrence. 1977. mass mkt. 6.95 (0-14-003300-9, Penguin Bks) Viking Penguin.

Studies in Classic American Literature. D. H. Lawrence. 190p. 1990. pap. 11.95 (0-14-018377-9, Penguin Classics) Viking Penguin.

Studies in Classic Maya Iconography. George Kubler. (Connecticut Academy of Arts & Sciences Ser., Trans.: Vol. 18). 1969. 100.00 (0-685-22853-3) Elliots Bks.

Studies in Classical & Quantum Nonlinear Optics. Ed. by Ole Keller. (Illus.). 359p. (C). 1994. lib. bdg. 98.00 (1-56072-168-5) Nova Sci Pubs.

Studies in Classical Armenian Literature. Ed. by John A. Greppin. LC 94-6123. (Classical Armenian Texts Ser.). 1994. 50.00 (0-88206-080-5); pap. 25.00 (0-88206-512-2) Caravan Bks.

Studies in Classical Chinese Thought: Papers Presented at the Workshop on Classical Chinese Thought Held at Harvard University, August 1976. Workshop on Classical Chinese Thought Staff. Ed. by Henry Rosemont, Jr. & Benjamin I. Schwartz. (Journal of the American Academy of Religion. Thematic Issue Ser.: Vol. 47, No. 3S). 259p. reprint ed. pap. 73.90 (0-7837-5414-0, 2045178) Bks Demand.

Studies in Classical Philolgy, Vol. 1. Giuseppe Giangrande. 110p. 1992. pap. 38.00 (90-256-0966-X, Pub. by A M Hakkert NE) Benjamins North Am.

***Studies in Classical Pietism: The Flowering of the Ecclesiola.** Harry E. Yeide. (Studies in Church History: Vol. 6). 208p. (C). 1997. text ed. 44.95 (0-8204-2854-X) P Lang Pubng.

Studies in Classics & Jewish Hellenism. Ed. by Richard Koebner. (Scripts Hierosolymitana Ser.: Vol. 1). 156p. reprint ed. pap. 44.50 (0-317-28711-7, 2051594) Bks Demand.

Studies in Clinical Psychodiagnostics & Psychotherapy. L. Kardos et al. 191p. (C). 1987. pap. 51.00 (963-05-4068-1, Pub. by Akad Kiado HU) St Mut.

Studies in Clinical Psychology, Vol. 3. Ed. by Lee E. Travis. Bd. with Dynamic of Binocular Depth Perception. H. Werner. ; Plateaus & the Curve of Learning in Motor Skill. Dji-Lih Kao. ; Reminiscence & Rote Learning. L. B. Ward. (Psychology Monographs General & Applied: Vol. 49). 1974. reprint ed. 55.00 (0-8115-1448-X) Periodicals Srv.

Studies in Colossians. John Kachelman, Jr. 1986. pap. 6.95 (0-89137-562-7) Quality Pubns.

Studies in Colossians & Philemon. Handley C. Moule. LC 77-79185. (Kregel Popular Commentary Ser.). 196p. 1977. kivar 6.99 (0-8254-3217-0) Kregel.

Studies in Colossians & Philemon. W. H. Thomas. LC 86-7178. 192p. 1986. reprint ed. pap. 8.99 (0-8254-3834-9) Kregel.

Studies in Combinatorics. Ed. by Gian-Carlo Rota. LC 78-60730. (Studies in Mathematics: No. 17). 273p. 1978. 33.95 (0-88385-117-2, MAS-17) Math Assn.

Studies in Communication Vol. 1: Studies in Mass Communication & Technology. Ed. by Sari Thomas. LC 83-25746. 272p. (C). 1984. text ed. 73.25 (0-89391-133-X) Ablex Pub.

Studies in Communication Vol. 2: Communication Theory & Interpersonal Interaction. Ed. by Sari Thomas. LC 83-25650. 208p. 1984. text ed. 73.25 (0-89391-134-8) Ablex Pub.

Studies in Communication Vol. 3: Culture & Communication. Sari Thomas. 320p. 1986. text ed. 82.50 (0-89391-253-0) Ablex Pub.

Studies in Communication Vol. 4: Communication & Culture: Language, Performance Technology & Media. Ed. by Sari Thomas & William Evans. LC 89-17536. 392p. (C). 1990. text ed. 82.50 (0-89391-497-5) Ablex Pub.

Studies in Communications, Vol. 2: Culture, Code & Content Analysis. Ed. by Thelma McCormick. 192p. 1982. 73.25 (0-89232-305-1) Jai Pr.

Studies in Communications, Vol. 4: Censorship & Libel: The Chilling Effect. Ed. by Thelma McCormick. 166p. 1990. 73.25 (0-89232-761-8) Jai Pr.

Studies in Communications, Vol. 5. Ed. by Thelma McCormick. 171p. 1995. 73.25 (1-55938-235-X) Jai Pr.

Studies in Communications, Vol. 6. Ed. by Thelma McCormick. 1996. 73.25 (0-7623-0052-3) Jai Pr.

Studies in Communications: Impact of the Sixties, Vol. 1: The Decade of Dissent: Impact of the Sixti. Ed. by Thelma McCormick. (Studies in Communications Ser.: Vol. 1). 1985p. 1980. 73.25 (0-89232-146-6) Jai Pr.

Studies in Communications: News & Knowledge, Vol. 3: News & Knowledge. Ed. by Thelma McCormick. 232p. 1986. 73.25 (0-89232-363-9) Jai Pr.

Studies in Comparative Germanic Syntax. Hubert Hiader. Ed. by Susan Olsen et al. LC 94-45109. (Studies in Natural Language & Linguistic Theory: Vol. 30). 340p. (C). 1995. lib. bdg. 96.00 (0-7923-3280-6) Kluwer Ac.

***Studies in Comparative Germanic Syntax, Vol. 2.** Ed. by Hoskuldur Thrainsson. (Studies in Natural Language & Linguistic Theory). 344p. (C). 1996. lib. bdg. 126.00 (0-7923-4215-1) Kluwer Ac.

Studies in Comparative Jurisprudence & the Conflict of Laws. George Merrill. xii, 247p. 1985. reprint ed. lib. bdg. 30.00 (0-8377-0850-8) Rothman.

Studies in Comparative Jurisprudence & the Conflict of Laws. George Merrill. LC 33-33040. (Historical Reprints in Jurisprudence & Classical Legal Literature Ser.). xii, 247p. 1984. reprint ed. lib. bdg. 45.00 (0-89941-340-4, 303440) W S Hein.

Studies in Comparison. Ulrich K. Goldsmith. Ed. by Hugo Schmidt et al. LC 89-2253. (Utah Studies in Literature & Linguistics: Vol. 28). 501p. (C). 1989. text ed. 72.95 (0-8204-0886-7) P Lang Pubng.

Studies in Compensatory Lengthening. Ed. by L. Wetzels & E. Sezer. (Publications in Language Sciences). viii, 353p. 1986. pap. 75.40 (90-6765-247-4) Mouton.

Studies in Complexity Theory. Ed. by Ronald V. Book. 240p. (C). 1986. pap. text ed. 210.00 (0-273-08755-X, Pub. by Pitman Pubng UK) St Mut.

Studies in Computational Science: Parallel Programming Paradigms. Per Brinch Hansen. LC 94-47128. (C). 1995. text ed. 69.00 (0-13-439324-4) P-H.

Studies in Computer-Aided Modelling, Design & Operation. Tr. & Rev. by Gy Jalsovszky. LC 92-11530. 1992. 295.00 (0-444-98673-1); 295.00 (0-444-98672-3) Elsevier.

Studies in Computer Algebra in Industry: Problem Solving in Practice - Proceedings of the 1991 SCAFI Seminar at Cwi, Amsterdam. Ed. by Arjeh M. Cohen. 252p. 1993. text ed. 69.95 (0-471-93829-7) Wiley.

Studies in Computer Science: In Honor of Samuel D. Conte. Ed. by J. Rice & R. A. DeMillo. (Software Science & Engineering Ser.). (Illus.). 170p. 1994. 69.50 (0-306-44697-9) Plenum.

Studies in Computer Supported Cooperative Work: Theory, Practice & Design. Ed. by J. Bowers & S. Benford. (Human Factors in Information Technology Ser.: No. 8). 356p. 1991. 173.50 (0-444-88811-X, North Holland) Elsevier.

Studies in Conservation of Natural Terrestrial Ecosystems in Japan, Pt. 1. Makoto Numata. LC 77-360040. (JIBP Synthesis Ser.: No. 8-9). 167p. 1975. reprint ed. pap. 47.60 (0-608-01588-1, 2062008) Bks Demand.

Studies in Conservation of Natural Terrestrial Ecosystems in Japan, Pt. 2. Ed. by M. M. Kato et al. LC 77-360040. (JIBP Synthesis Ser.: No. 8-9). 99p. 1975. reprint ed. pap. 28.30 (0-608-01589-X, 2062008) Bks Demand.

Studies in Constitutional Law. Colin R. Munro. 1987. pap. 28.00 (0-406-26145-8) MICHIE.

Studies in Constitutional Law: France-England-United States. 2nd ed. Emile Boutmy. Tr. by E. M. Dicey. xiv, 183p. 1982. reprint ed. lib. bdg. 22.50 (0-8377-0332-8) Rothman.

Studies in Constructive Mathematics & Mathematical Logic. Ed. by A. O. Slisenko. LC 69-12507. (Seminars in Mathematics Ser.: Vol. 4, Pt. 1). 96p. reprint ed. pap. 27.40 (0-317-08580-8, 2020696) Bks Demand.

Studies in Contemporary Biography. James B. Bryce. LC 77-156619. (Essay Index Reprint Ser.). 1977. reprint ed. 28.95 (0-8369-2271-9) Ayer.

Studies in Contemporary Indian-English Short Story: A Collection of Critical Essays. A. N. Dwivedi. (New World Ser.: No. 38). (C). 1991. 15.00 (81-7018-658-7, Pub. by BR Pub II) S Asia.

Studies in Contemporary Jewry, Vol. II. Institute of Contemporary Jewry of The Hebrew University of Jerusalem. 512p. 1986. 27.50 (0-253-39512-7) Ind U Pr.

Studies in Contemporary Jewry: A New Jewry? America since the Second World War, Vol. VIII. Ed. by Peter Y. Medding. (Illus.). 448p. 1992. 49.95 (0-19-507449-1) OUP.

S

S

***Studies in Contemporary Jewry: Literary Strategies: Jewish Texts & Contexts, Vol. XII.** Ed. by Ezra Mendelsohn. 496p. 1997. 55.00 (*0-19-511203-2*) OUP.

Studies in Contemporary Jewry Vol. 6: Art & Its Uses: The Visual Image & Modern Jewish Society. Ed. by Ezra Mendelsohn & Richard I. Cohen. (Illus.). 416p. 1990. 49.95 (*0-19-506188-8*) OUP.

Studies in Contemporary Jewry, Values, Interests, & Identity Vol. 11: Jews & Politics in a Changing World, Vol. 11. Ed. by Peter Y. Medding. (Illus.). 384p. (C). 1996. 49.95 (*0-19-510331-9*) OUP.

Studies in Contemporary Jewry, Vol. III: Jews & Other Ethnic Groups in a Multi-Ethnic World. Ed. by Ezra Mendelsohn. (Illus.). 360p. 1987. 42.00 (*0-19-504896-2*) OUP.

Studies in Contemporary Jewry, Vol. IV: The Jews & the European Crisis, 1914-1921. Ed. by Jonathan Frankel. 448p. 1988. 45.00 (*0-19-505113-0*) OUP.

Studies in Contemporary Jewry, Vol. IX: Modern Jews & Their Musical Agendas. Ed. by Ezra Mendelsohn. (Illus.). 352p. 1994. 49.95 (*0-19-508617-1*) OUP.

Studies in Contemporary Jewry, Vol. V: Israel: State & Society, 1948-1988. Ed. by Peter Y. Medding. 448p. 1989. 45.00 (*0-19-505827-5*) OUP.

Studies in Contemporary Jewry, Vol. VII: Jews & Messianism in the Modern Era: Metaphor & Meaning. Ed. by Jonathan Frankel. 464p. 1991. 45.00 (*0-19-506690-1*) OUP.

***Studies in Continental Margin Geology.** Ed. by J. S. Watkins & C. L. Drake. LC 83-70685. (AAPG Memoir Ser.: Vol. 34). 879p. 1982. reprint ed. pap. 180.00 (*0-608-02774-X*, 2063840) Bks Demand.

Studies in Contract Law. 4th ed. Edward J. Murphy & Richard E. Speidel. (University Casebook Ser.). 1401p. 1991. text ed. 46.50 (*0-88277-875-7*) Foundation Pr.

***Studies in Contract Law.** 5th ed. Edward J. Murphy et al. LC 97-9348. (University Casebook Ser.). 1083p. 1997. text ed. write for info. (*1-56662-468-1*) Foundation Pr.

Studies in Contract Law, Teaching Notes. 4th ed. Edward J. Murphy & Richard E. Speidel. (University Casebook Ser.). 150p. (C). 1991. pap. text ed. write for info. (*0-88277-938-9*) Foundation Pr.

Studies in Creation: A General Introduction to the Creation-Evolution Debate. John Klotz. 224p. (Orig.). (C). 1985. pap. 10.95 (*0-570-03969-X*, 12-3004) Concordia.

Studies in Creativity. L. Kardos et al. 162p. (C). 1987. pap. 42.00 (*963-05-4382-6*, Pub. by Akad Kiado HU) St Mut.

***Studies in Crime: Introduction to Forensic Archaeology.** John Hunter. 176p. (C). 1997. pap. 34.95 (*0-415-16612-8*, Routledge NY) Routledge.

Studies in Crisis Behavior. Ed. by Michael Brecher. 384p. (C). 1979. text ed. 44.95 (*0-87855-292-8*) Transaction Pubs.

Studies in Cross-Cultural Psychology, Vol. 2. Ed. by Neil Warren. LC 76-48386. (Serial Publication Ser.). 1981. text ed. 158.00 (*0-12-609202-8*) Acad Pr.

Studies in Cultural Development of India. Ed. by N. R. Ray & P. N. Chakrabarti. (C). 1991. 44.00 (*81-85094-43-8*, Pub. by Punthi Pus II) S Asia.

***Studies in Culture Contact: Interaction, Culture Change, & Archaeology.** Ed. by James G. Cusick. LC 96-83282. (Center for Archaeological Investigations Research Paper Ser.: Vol. 25). 350p. (Orig.). (C). 1997. pap. write for info. (*0-88104-082-7*) Center Archaeol.

Studies in Currency Eighteen Ninety-Eight: Or Inquiries into Certain Modern Problems Connected with the Standard Value & the Media of Exchange. Thomas H. Farrer. LC 67-19961. (Library of Money & Banking History). xxiii, 415p. 1968. reprint ed. 49.50 (*0-678-00397-1*) Kelley.

Studies in Cypriote Archaeology. Ed. by Jane C. Biers & David Soren. (Monographs: No. 18). 189p. (C). 1981. pap. 16.50 (*0-917956-23-0*) UCLA Arch.

Studies in Daniel & Revelation. LC 88-50303. 245p. (Orig.). 1988. per. 4.95 (*0-945383-02-9*) Teach Servs.

Studies in Dante, First Series. E. Moore. LC 68-24955. (Studies in Dante: No. 9). 1969. reprint ed. lib. bdg. 75.00 (*0-8383-0217-3*) M S G Haskell Hse.

Studies in Dante, Fourth Series: A Textual Criticism of the Convivo & Miscellaneous Essays. E. Moore. LC 68-29737. (Studies in Dante: No. 9). 1968. reprint ed. lib. bdg. 75.00 (*0-8383-0220-3*) M S G Haskell Hse.

Studies in Dante, Second Series. E. Moore. LC 68-24956. (Studies in Dante: No. 9). 1969. reprint ed. lib. bdg. 75.00 (*0-8383-0218-1*) M S G Haskell Hse.

Studies in Dante, Second Series: Miscellaneous Essays. Edward Moore. LC 68-57628. (Illus.). 386p. 1970. reprint ed. text ed. 65.00 (*0-8371-0908-6*, MOSD, Greenwood Pr) Greenwood.

Studies in Dante, Third Series. E. Moore. LC 68-24957. (Studies in Dante: No. 9). (Illus.). 1969. reprint ed. lib. bdg. 75.00 (*0-8383-0219-X*) M S G Haskell Hse.

Studies in Decision Making. Ed. by Martin Irle & Lawrence B. Katz. 917p. 1982. 157.70 (*3-11-008087-7*) De Gruyter.

Studies in Demetrius on Style. D. M. Schenkeveld. 186p. 1964. lib. bdg. 48.50 (*0-685-13817-8*, Pub. by AM Hakkert NE) Coronet Bks.

Studies in Dependency Syntax. Igor A. Mel'cuk. Ed. by Paul T. Roberge. Tr. by Lev Stern from RUS. (Linguistica Extranea: Studia Ser.: Studia 2). 172p. 1979. pap. 5.50 (*0-89720-001-2*) Karoma.

Studies in Deuteronomy: In Honour of C. J. Labuschagne on the Occasion of His 65th Birthday. Ed. by F. Garcia Martinez. LC 94-4098. (Supplements to Vetus Testamentum Ser.: Vol. 53). 1994. 108.75 (*90-04-10052-0*) E J Brill.

Studies in Developmental Planning. Hollis B. Chenery. LC 70-143227. (Economic Studies: No. 136). 436p. 1971. 30.00 (*0-674-84725-3*) HUP.

Studies in Diachronic, Synchronic & Typological Linguistics: Festschrift for Oswald Szemerenyi on the Occasion of His 65th Birthday, 2 vols., Set. Ed. by Bela Brogyanyi. (Current Issues in Linguistic Theory Ser.: No. 11). 1979. 177.00 (*90-272-3504-X*) Benjamins North Am.

Studies in Dickens. Mabel S. Smith. LC 72-3291. (Studies in Dickens: No. 52). 1972. reprint ed. lib. bdg. 59.95 (*0-8383-1499-6*) M S G Haskell Hse.

Studies in Differential Equations. Harold T. Davis. Ed. by Walter Scott. LC 56-14277. (Northwestern University Series in Mathematical & Physical Sciences: No. 3). 120p. reprint ed. pap. 34.20 (*0-317-08636-7*, 2006876) Bks Demand.

Studies in Discourse Analysis. Ed. by Martin Montgomery & Malcolm Coulthard. 1981. pap. 15.95 (*0-7100-0510-5*, RKP) Routledge.

Studies in Discourse Representation Theory & the Theory of Generalized Quantifiers. Martin Stokhof. (Groningen-Amsterdam Studies in Semantics). 200p. 1986. pap. 50.00 (*90-6765-267-9*) Mouton.

Studies in Divergent Series & Summability & the Asymptotic Development of Functions. Walter B. Ford. LC 60-16836. 371p. 1985. text ed. 22.50 (*0-8284-0143-8*) Chelsea Pub.

***Studies in Doctrine.** Alister E. McGrath. LC 96-53076. 480p. 1997. boxed 24.99 (*0-310-21326-6*) Zondervan.

***Studies in Drug Utilization: Methods & Applications.** U. Bergman et al. (WHO Regional Publications, European Ser.: No. 8). 185p. 1979. 20.00 (*92-9020-108-8*, 1310008) World Health.

Studies in Ear Training. Jerry A. Dapdap. (Illus.). 48p. (Orig.). (C). 1990. pap. 6.50 (*971-10-0417-8*, Pub. by New Day Pub PH) Cellar.

Studies in Earlier Old English Prose. Ed. by Paul E. Szarmach. LC 84-8849. 420p. 1985. text ed. 49.50 (*0-87395-947-7*); pap. text ed. 19.95 (*0-87395-948-5*) State U NY Pr.

Studies in Early Buddhist Architecture of India. H. C. Sarkar. (Illus.). 128p. 1993. 43.50 (*81-215-0599-2*, Pub. by M Manoharial II) Coronet Bks.

Studies in Early Christology. Martin Hengel. Tr. by Rollin Kearns. 424p. 1996. 54.95 (*0-567-09705-6*, Pub. by T & T Clark UK) Bks Intl VA.

Studies in Early Egyptian Glass. Christine Lilyquist et al. LC 93-24451. (Illus.). 77p. 1993. pap. 20.00 (*0-87099-683-5*, 0-8109-6457-0) Metro Mus Art.

Studies in Early French Poetry. Walter Besant. LC 72-13206. (Essay Index Reprint Ser.). 1977. reprint ed. 23.95 (*0-8369-8147-2*) Ayer.

Studies in Early French Poetry. Walter Besant. LC 72-13206. (Essay Index Reprint Ser.). 319p. reprint ed. lib. bdg. 19.00 (*0-8290-0522-6*) Irvington.

Studies in Early German Comedy 1500-1650: 1500-1650. Richard E. Schade. LC 86-71135. (GERM Ser.: Vol. 24). (Illus.). 256p. (C). 1988. 36.50 (*0-938100-41-6*) Camden Hse.

Studies in Early Graduate Education. W. Carson Ryan. LC 73-165729. (American Education Ser, No. 2). 1972. reprint ed. 12.95 (*0-405-03718-X*) Ayer.

***Studies in Early Hadith.** M. Azami. 510p. 1996. pap. 15.50 (*0-614-21096-8*, 1175) Kazi Pubns.

Studies in Early Hadith Literature. M. M. Azami. LC 77-90341. 1978. pap. 12.75 (*0-89259-125-0*) Am Trust Pubns.

Studies in Early Impressionism. Kermit S. Champa. LC 84-81040. (Illus.). 106p. 1985. reprint ed. lib. bdg. 75.00 (*0-87817-299-8*) Hacker.

Studies in Early Islamic History. Martin Hinds. Ed. by Jere L. Bacharach et al. LC 95-6228. (Studies in Late Antiquity & Early Islam: No. 4). (Illus.). 262p. 1996. 39.95 (*0-87850-109-6*) Darwin Pr.

Studies in Early Jainism: Selected Research Article. Jagdish C. Jain. (C). 1992. 27.00 (*81-7013-076-X*, Pub. by Navrang) S Asia.

Studies in Early Jewish Epigraphy. Pieter W. Van der Horst. Ed. by Jan Willem van Henten. LC 93-41725. 1993. 92.00 (*90-04-09916-6*) E J Brill.

Studies in Early Medieval Latin Glossaries. Wallace M. Lindsay. Ed. by Michael Lapidge. LC 95-30954. (Collected Studies: Vol. 467). 416p. 1996. 116.95 (*0-86078-353-7*, Pub. by Variorum UK) Ashgate Pub Co.

Studies in Early Modern English. Ed. by Dieter Kastrovsky. (Topics in English Linguistics Ser.: 13). 507p. (C). 1994. lib. bdg. 190.80 (*3-11-014127-2*) Mouton.

Studies in Early Muslim Jurisprudence. Norman Calder. LC 92-27068. (Illus.). 272p. 1993. 65.00 (*0-19-825813-5*, Old Oregon Bk Store) OUP.

***Studies in Early Mysticism in the Near & Middle East.** Margaret Smith. 286p. 1996. pap. 14.95 (*0-614-21352-5*, 1460); pap. 14.95 (*0-614-21684-2*, 1460) Kazi Pubns.

Studies in Early Mysticism in the Near & Middle East. Margaret Smith. 286p. 1995. pap. 14.95 (*1-85168-098-5*) Onewrld Pubns.

Studies in Earth & Space Sciences: A Memoir in Honor of Harry Hammond Hess. Ed. by R. Shagam et al. LC 76-190172. (Geological Society of America, Memoir Ser.: No. 132). 719p. reprint ed. pap. 180.00 (*0-317-29124-6*, 2025026) Bks Demand.

Studies in Earth Sciences. T. V. Murty. 614p. 1971. 25.00 (*0-88065-164-4*, Messers Today & Tomorrow) Scholarly Pubns.

Studies in East African History. Norman R. Bennett. LC 63-11193. Date not set. 12.50 (*0-8419-8701-7*, Boston Univ) Holmes & Meier.

Studies in East European Jewish Mysticism. Joseph Weiss. Ed. by David Goldstein. (Littman Library of Jewish Civilization). 288p. (C). 1986. 22.50 (*0-19-710034-1*) Bnai Brith Bk.

Studies in Eastern Chant, Vol. IV. Ed. by Milos Velimirovic. 248p. 1979. pap. text ed. 10.95 (*0-913836-57-5*) St Vladimirs.

Studies in Eastern Chant, Vol. 5. Ed. by Dimitri Conomos. 186p. (Orig.). 1991. pap. 15.95 (*0-913836-79-6*) St Vladimirs.

Studies in Eco-Development: Himalayas Mountains & Men. Tej V. Singh. 509p. (C). 1983. 350.00 (*81-85009-03-1*, Pub. by Print Hse II) St Mut.

***Studies in Ecological Psychology: Proceedings of the Fourth European Workshop on Ecological Psychology, Zeist, the Netherlands, July 2-5, 1996.** A. M. Kappers et al. (Illus.). 151p. (Orig.). 1996. pap. 39.50 (*90-407-1352-9*, Pub. by Delft U Pr NE) Coronet Bks.

Studies in Ecology: A Laboratory Manual for Biology 307. 3rd ed. Mark R. Walbridge & Luther P. Brown. 230p. (C). 1996. pap. text ed., spiral bd. 16.80 (*0-8403-8092-5*) Kendall-Hunt.

Studies in Econometric Theory: The Collected Essays of Takeshi Amemiya. Takeshi Amemiya. (Economists of the Twentieth Century Ser.). 496p. 1994. 90.00 (*1-85278-797-X*) E Elgar.

Studies in Economic Appraisal in Health Care, 2 vols., 1. Michael F. Drummond. 224p. 1981. text ed. 39.95 (*0-19-261274-3*) OUP.

Studies in Economic Appraisal in Health Care, 2 vols., 2. Michael F. Drummond. 304p. 1986. text ed. 49.00 (*0-19-261398-7*) OUP.

Studies in Economic Policy of Frederick the Great. W. O. Henderson. 205p. 1963. 35.00 (*0-7146-1321-5*, Pub. by F Cass Pubs UK) Intl Spec Bk.

Studies in Economics & Russia. Alec Nove. LC 89-70362. 270p. 1991. text ed. 49.95 (*0-312-04509-3*) St Martin.

Studies in Ecstatic Kabbalah. Moshe Idel. LC 87-6522. (SUNY Series in Judaica: Hermeneutics, Mysticism, & Religion). 160p. 1988. text ed. 64.50 (*0-88706-604-6*); pap. text ed. 21.95 (*0-88706-605-4*) State U NY Pr.

Studies in Educational Evaluation. Arieh Lewy. (Reviews in Educational Evaluation Ser.: Vol. 6, No. 2). (Illus.). 116p. 1980. pap. 21.00 (*0-08-026760-2*, Pergamon Pr) Elsevier.

Studies in Educational Evaluation, ser. vol. 6. Arieh Lewy. (Studies in Educational Evaluation). 1980. pap. 21.00 (*0-08-026116-7*, 1, Pergamon Pr) Elsevier.

Studies in Egyptology Presented to Miriam Lichtheim, 2 vols. Ed. by Sarah Israelit-Groll. xi, 1128p. 1990. text ed. 45.00 (*965-223-733-7*, Pub. by Magnes Press IS) Eisenbrauns.

Studies in Eighteenth Century British Art & Aesthetics. Ed. by Ralph Cohen. LC 84-2693. (Clark Library Professorship, UCLA: No. 9). 1985. 50.00 (*0-520-05258-7*) U CA Pr.

Studies in Eighteenth-Century Culture, Vol. 17. Ed. by John W. Yolton & Leslie E. Brown. 384p. 1987. 35.00 (*0-937191-04-3*) Colleagues Pr Inc.

Studies in Eighteenth-Century Culture, Vol. 18. Ed. by John W. Yolton & Leslie E. Brown. 515p. 1988. 35.00 (*0-937191-09-4*) Colleagues Pr Inc.

Studies in Eighteenth-Century Culture, Vol. 19. Ed. by Leslie E. Brown & Patricia B. Craddock. 452p. 1989. 35.00 (*0-937191-14-0*) Colleagues Pr Inc.

Studies in Eighteenth-Century Culture, Vol. 20. Ed. by Leslie E. Brown & Patricia B. Craddock. LC 75-648277. 353p. 1990. 35.00 (*0-937191-24-8*) Colleagues Pr Inc.

Studies in Eighteenth-Century Culture, Vol. 21. Ed. by Patricia B. Craddock & Carla H. Hay. 320p. 1991. 35.00 (*0-937191-42-6*) Colleagues Pr Inc.

Studies in Eighteenth-Century Culture, Vol. 22. Ed. by Patricia B. Craddock & Carla H. Hay. 360p. 1992. 35.00 (*0-937191-46-9*) Colleagues Pr Inc.

Studies in Eighteenth-Century Culture, Vol. 23. Ed. by Carla H. Hay & Syndy Conger. 450p. 1994. 35.00 (*0-937191-54-X*) Colleagues Pr Inc.

***Studies in Eighteenth Century Culture, Vol. 25.** Ed. by Syndy M. Conger & Julie C. Hayes. (Illus.). 336p. 1997. text ed. 40.00 (*0-8018-5462-8*) Johns Hopkins.

***Studies in Eighteenth Century Culture, Vol. 26.** Ed. by Syndy M. Conger & Julie C. Hayes. (Illus.). 352p. 1997. text ed. 40.00 (*0-8018-5627-2*) Johns Hopkins.

Studies in Eighteenth-Century Culture Vol. 24. Ed. by Carla H. Hay & Syndy M. Conger. (Illus.). 362p. 1995. text ed. 40.00 (*0-8018-5136-X*) Johns Hopkins.

Studies in Eighteenth-Century Diplomacy, 1740-1748. Richard Lodge. LC 73-109771. 421p. 1970. reprint ed. text ed. 65.00 (*0-8371-4261-X*, LODI, Greenwood Pr) Greenwood.

Studies in Eighteenth Century Music: A Tribute to Karl Geiringer on His 70th Birthday. Robbins H. Landon & Roger Chapman. (Music Reprint Ser.). 1979. reprint ed. lib. bdg. 49.50 (*0-306-79519-1*) Da Capo.

***Studies in Elizabethan Audience Response to the Theatre Pt. 2: As I Am Man - Aspects of the Presentation & Audience Perception of the Elizabethan Female Page.** Henk Gras. (European University Studies, Series 30: Vol. 49). (Illus.). 387p. 1993. 54.80 (*3-631-45804-5*) P Lang Pubng.

Studies in Elizabethan Foreign Trade. Thomas S. Willan. LC 74-878. ix, 349p. 1959. 45.00 (*0-678-06772-4*) Kelley.

Studies in Empowerment: Steps Toward Understanding & Action. Ed. by Julian Rappaport & Robert Hess. LC 84-4461. (Prevention in Human Services Ser.: Vol. 3, Nos. 2-3). 230p. 1984. text ed. 49.95 (*0-86656-283-4*) Haworth Pr.

Studies in English Adverbial Usage. Sidney Greenbaum. LC 70-90047. (Miami Linguistics Ser.: No. 5). 1969. 14.95 (*0-87024-137-0*) U of Miami Pr.

Studies in English & Hungarian Contrastive Linguistics. Ed. by L. Dezso & W. Nemser. 589p. (C). 1980. 170.00 (*963-05-1376-5*, Pub. by Akad Kiado HU) St Mut.

Studies in English in Honor of Raphael Dorman O'Leary & Seldon Lincoln Whitcomb. Kansas Univ. Humanistic Studies, Vol. 6. University of Kansas - Department of English Staff. LC 68-20340. (Essay Index Reprint Ser.). 1977. 18.95 (*0-8369-0913-5*) Ayer.

Studies in English Language & Literature: Doubt Wisely: Papers in Honour of E. G. Stanley. Ed. by M. J. Toswell & E. M. Tyler. 560p. (C). 1996. text ed. 125.00 (*0-415-13848-5*) Routledge.

Studies in English Legal History. Theodore F. Plucknett. 350p. (C). 1983. text ed. 55.00 (*0-907628-11-7*) Hambledon Press.

Studies in English Renaissance Literature. Waldo F. McNeir. (Essay Index Reprint Ser.). 1977. reprint ed. 22.95 (*0-518-10153-3*) Ayer.

Studies in Entertainment: Critical Approaches to Mass Culture. Ed. by Tania Modleski. LC 85-45980. (Theories of Contemporary Culture Ser.). (Illus.). 228p. 1986. 31.50 (*0-253-35566-4*); pap. 10.95 (*0-253-20395-3*, MB-395) Ind U Pr.

Studies in Ephesians. Jerry W. Nieft. (Bible Study Ser.). 36p. 1991. pap. 4.50 (*0-8309-0590-1*) Herald Hse.

Studies in Epistemology. Ed. by Peter A. French. LC 79-26706. (Midwest Studies in Philosophy: No. 5). 576p. reprint ed. pap. 164.20 (*0-7837-2958-8*, 2057496) Bks Demand.

Studies in Equality. Richard Norman. LC 96-14677. 288p. 1996. 76.95 (*1-85972-220-2*, Pub. by Avebury Pub UK) Ashgate Pub Co.

Studies in Ethnomethodology. Harold Garfinkel. 1967. text ed. write for info. (*0-13-858381-1*) P-H.

Studies in Etymology. Charles W. Dunmore. (Texts Ser.). 402p. 1993. pap. 19.95 (*0-941051-29-3*) Focus Pub-R Pullins.

Studies in Euripides' Orestes. John R. Porter. LC 94-16657. (Mnemosyne, Bibliotheca Classica Batava. Supplementum). 1994. 115.00 (*90-04-09662-0*) E J Brill.

Studies in European Arms & Armor: The C. Otto von Kienbusch Collection in the Philadelphia Museum of Art. Claude Blair et al. LC 91-47037. (Illus.). 208p. 1992. pap. 30.00 (*0-87633-088-X*) Phila Mus Art.

Studies in European Arms & Armor: The C. Otto von Kienbusch Collection in the Philadelphia Museum of Art. Helmut Nickel et al. LC 95-47037. (Illus.). 208p. (C). 1992. 49.95 (*0-8122-7963-8*) Phila Mus Art.

Studies in European Literature, Being the Taylorian Lectures 1920-1930. Oxford University. Taylor Institution Staff. LC 76-90673. (Essay Index Reprint Ser.). 1977. 26.95 (*0-8369-1232-2*) Ayer.

Studies in European Realism. Georg Lukacs. 267p. 1997. reprint ed. lib. bdg. 35.00 (*0-86527-421-5*) Fertig.

Studies in European Realism: A Sociological Survey of the Writings of Balzac, Stendhal, Tolstoy, Gorky, & Others. Georg Lukacs. Tr. by Edith Bone from HUN. 267p. 1997. reprint ed. pap. text ed. 12.00 (*0-86527-427-4*) Fertig.

Studies in Evolution. Charles E. Beecher. Ed. by Stephen J. Gould. LC 79-8324. (History of Paleontology Ser.). (Illus.). 1980. reprint ed. lib. bdg. 61.95 (*0-405-12704-9*) Ayer.

Studies in Exodus, Vol. 2. Clifford A. Cole. (Bible Study Ser.). 1986. pap. 4.50 (*0-8309-0462-X*) Herald Hse.

Studies in Fascism: Ideology & Practice, 101 titles in 113 vols., Set. (AMS Press Reprint Ser.). reprint ed. write for info. (*0-404-56100-4*) AMS Pr.

Studies in Faulkner. Carnegie Institute of Technology, Department of English Staff et al. LC 72-1325. (Essay Index Reprint Ser.). 1977. reprint ed. 17.95 (*0-8369-2839-3*) Ayer.

Studies in Fifteenth-Century Stagecraft. J. W. Robinson. (Early Drama, Art & Music Monograph: No. 14). 1992. pap. 16.95 (*0-918720-39-7*); boxed 26.95 (*0-918720-38-9*) Medieval Inst.

Studies in Financial Institutions: Commercial Banks. Ed. by Christopher M. James & Clifford W. Smith. LC 93-40434. (Series in Advanced Topics in Finance & Accounting). 1994. pap. text ed. write for info. (*0-07-032397-6*) McGraw.

Studies in Finnic Folklore. Felix J. Oinas. LC 84-80930. (Uralic & Altaic Ser.: Vol. 147). 219p. (Orig.). (C). 1985. pap. 30.00 (*0-933070-15-2*) Res Inst Inner Asian Studies.

Studies in Finno-Ugric Linguistics: In Honor of Alo Raun. Ed. by Denis Sinor. LC 81-622858. (Uralic & Altaic Ser.: Vol. 131). 440p. 1977. 70.00 (*0-933070-00-4*) Res Inst Inner Asian Studies.

Studies in First Corinthians. Paul T. Butler. LC 84-72347. (Bible Study Textbook Ser.). 406p. (C). 1985. text ed. 14.99 (*0-89900-063-0*) College Pr Pub.

Studies in First Corinthians. Don Compier. (Bible Study Ser.). 1987. pap. 4.50 (*0-8309-0448-4*) Herald Hse.

Studies in First Corinthians: Messages on Practical Christian Living. M. R. DeHaan. LC 95-37636. 192p. 1995. pap. 9.99 (*0-8254-2478-X*) Kregel.

Studies in First Corinthians 15: Life in a Risen Savior. Robert S. Candlish. LC 89-2564. 440p. 1989. reprint ed. pap. 15.99 (*0-8254-2331-7*, Kregel Class) Kregel.

Studies in First Thessalonians. Michael Penny. 40p. 1992. pap. text ed. 3.00 (*1-880573-02-4*) Grace WI.

Studies in Fiscal Federalism. Wallace E. Oates. (Economists of the Twentieth Century Ser.). 480p. 1991. text ed. 90.00 (*1-85278-520-9*) E Elgar.

Studies in Folk Life: Essays in Honor of Iorwerth C. Peate, John G. Jenkins. Ed. by Richard M. Dorson. LC 77-70603. (International Folklore Ser.). 1977. lib. bdg. 33.95 (*0-405-10102-3*) Ayer.

Studies in Folklore: In Honor of Distinguished Service Professor Stith Thompson. Ed. by Winthrop E. Richmond. LC 72-163547. (Illus.). 270p. 1972. reprint ed. lib. bdg. 15.00 (*0-8371-6208-4*, RISF, Greenwood Pr) Greenwood.

An Asterisk (*) at the beginning of an entry indicates that the title is appearing in BIP for the first time.

Studies in Foraminifera. A. B. Loeblich et al. 1970. 42.00 (*0-934454-75-2*) Lubrecht & Cramer.

***Studies in Frank Waters Vol. 18: Afterwords.** Shawn McKenzie et al. 1990. pap. 10.00 (*1-878277-13-8*) Frank Waters Soc.

Studies in Frank Waters, Vol. IX: Flight from Fiesta. Intro. by Charles L. Adams. 79p. (Orig.). (C). 1987. pap. 5.00 (*1-878277-03-0*) Frank Waters Soc.

Studies in Frank Waters, Vol. Thirteen: "Frank Waters & the Land" Intro. by Charles L. Adams. 100p. (Orig.). 1991. pap. 10.00 (*1-878277-07-3*) Frank Waters Soc.

Studies in Frank Waters, Vol. VI: The Papers from "Dialogues" Intro. by Charles L. Adams. 85p. (Orig.). (C). 1984. pap. 5.00 (*1-878277-00-6*) Frank Waters Soc.

Studies in Frank Waters, Vol. VII: An Appreciation. Intro. by Charles L. Adams. 113p. (Orig.). (C). 1985. pap. 5.00 (*1-878277-01-4*) Frank Waters Soc.

Studies in Frank Waters, Vol. VIII: Emergences. Intro. by Charles L. Adams. 98p. (Orig.). (C). 1986. pap. 5.00 (*1-878277-02-2*) Frank Waters Soc.

Studies in Frank Waters, Vol. X: Connections. Intro. by Charles L. Adams. (Illus.). 200p. (C). 1988. pap. 10.00 (*1-878277-04-9*) Frank Waters Soc.

Studies in Frank Waters, Vol. XVI: Environmental Concerns. Intro. by Charles L. Adams. 100p. (Orig.). 1994. pap. 10.00 (*1-878277-11-1*) Frank Waters Soc.

Studies in Frank Waters, Vol. 12: The Form of the Novel. Intro. by Charles L. Adams. 100p. (Orig.). (C). 1990. pap. 10.00 (*1-878277-06-5*) Frank Waters Soc.

Studies in French & Comparative Phonetics. Pierre Delattre. (Janua Linguarum, Series Major: No. 18). (ENG & FRE.). 1966. text ed. 80.00 (*90-279-0610-6*) Mouton.

Studies in French-Classical Tragedy. Lacy Lockert. LC 59-298. 1959. 29.95 (*0-8265-1049-3*) Vanderbilt U Pr.

Studies in French Language & Mediaeval Literature. LC 70-84340. (Essay Index Reprint Ser.). 1977. 31.95 (*0-8369-1109-1*) Ayer.

Studies in French Language, Literature & History. LC 76-80400. (Essay Index Reprint Ser.). 1977. 21.95 (*0-8369-1067-2*) Ayer.

Studies in Functional Logical Semiotics of Natural Languages. Jerzy Pelc. (Janua Linguarum, Ser. Minor: No. 90). 1971. text ed. 52.35 (*90-279-1599-7*) Mouton.

Studies in Functional Stylistics. Ed. by Jan Chloupek & Jiri Nevkapil. LC 93-18296. (Linguistic & Literary Studies in Eastern Europe: No. 36). 286p. 1993. 100.00 (*1-55619-261-4*) Benjamins North Am.

Studies in Galatians: Twenty-Two Simple Studies in Paul's Teaching of Law & Grace. Martin R. DeHaan. 184p. 1996. pap. 9.99 (*0-8254-2477-1*) Kregel.

Studies in Galations. Charles E. Crouch. 1992. pap. 6.95 (*0-89137-137-0*) Quality Pubns.

Studies in GDR Culture & Society: Selected Papers from the Twelfth New Hampshire Symposium on the German Democratic Republic, No. 7. Ed. by Margy Gerber. (Illus.). 246p. (Orig.). (C). 1987. pap. text ed. 25.50 (*0-8191-6486-0*, Intl Symposium on the German Democratic Republic) U Pr of Amer.

Studies in GDR Culture & Society Eight: Selected Papers from the Thirteenth New Hampshire Symposium on the German Democratic Republic. Ed. by Margy Gerber. (Illus.). 214p. (Orig.). (C). 1988. pap. text ed. 22.50 (*0-8191-7047-X*, Intl Symposium on the German Democratic Republic) U Pr of Amer.

Studies in GDR Culture & Society Four: Selected Papers from the Ninth New Hampshire Symposium on the German Democratic Republic. Ed. by Margy Gerber et al. Tr. by Volker Gransow et al. (Illus.). 316p. (Orig.). 1984. pap. text ed. 37.00 (*0-8191-4016-3*); lib. bdg. 60.50 (*0-8191-4015-5*) U Pr of Amer.

Studies in GDR Culture & Society, No. 10: Selected Papers from the Fifteenth New Hampshire Symposium on the German Democratic Republic. Ed. by Margy Gerber. 224p. (C). 1991. lib. bdg. 49.50 (*0-8191-8094-7*, Intl Symposium on the German Democratic Republic) U Pr of Amer.

Studies in GDR Culture & Society, No. 9: Selected Papers from the Fourteenth New Hampshire Symposium on German Democratic Republic. Ed. by Margy Gerber. LC 89-9193. 218p. 1990. lib. bdg. 41.00 (*0-8191-7508-0*) U Pr of Amer.

Studies in GDR Culture & Society 6: Selected Papers from the Eleventh New Hampshire Symposium on the German Democratic Republic. W. Christoph Schmauch. 214p. (Orig.). (C). 1986. pap. text ed. 24.00 (*0-8191-5469-5*, Intl Symposium on the German Democratic Republic); lib. bdg. 44.00 (*0-8191-5468-7*, Intl Symposium on the German Democratic Republic) U Pr of Amer.

Studies in General & English Phonetics: Essays in Honour of Professor J. D. O'Connor. Ed. by Jack W. Lewis. LC 94-4050. (Illus.). 504p. (C). (gr. 13). 1994. text ed. 135.00 (*0-415-08068-1*, C0285) Routledge.

Studies in General Psychology see Studies in the Psychology of Art

Studies in Genesis. John B. Burke. 1979. pap. 5.99 (*0-88469-048-2*) BMH Bks.

Studies in Genesis, 2 vols. in one. Robert S. Candlish. LC 79-14084. (Kregel Bible Study Classics Ser.). 854p. 1979. 24.99 (*0-8254-2315-5*, Kregel Class) Kregel.

Studies in Genesis, Vol. 1. Wayne Ham. 1987. pap. 4.50 (*0-8309-0482-4*) Herald Hse.

Studies in Geriatric Psychiatry. Ed. by Anthony D. Isaacs & F. Post. LC 77-9990. 280p. reprint ed. pap. 79.80 (*0-317-07821-6*, 2022402) Bks Demand.

Studies in German & Scandinavian Literature after 1500: A Festschrift in Honor of George C. Schoolfield. Ed. by James A. Parente & Richard E. Schade. (GERM Ser.). xiv, 322p. 1993. 65.00 (*1-879751-23-2*) Camden Hse.

Studies in German Colonial History. W. O. Henderson. 150p. 1962. 39.50 (*0-7146-1674-5*, Pub. by F Cass Pubs UK) Intl Spec Bk.

Studies in German Literature. Ed. by Carl Hammer. LC 82-15862. (Louisiana State University Studies: Humanities Ser.: No. 13). xviii, 172p. 1982. reprint ed. text ed. 55.00 (*0-313-23735-2*, HASGL, Greenwood Pr) Greenwood.

Studies in German Literature. Bayard Taylor. LC 72-1145. (Essay Index Reprint Ser.). 1977. reprint ed. 25.95 (*0-8369-2865-2*) Ayer.

Studies in Global Differential Geometry. Ed. by Shiing-Shen Chern. (MAA Studies in Mathematics: Vol. 27). 320p. 1989. 36.50 (*0-88385-129-6*, MAS-27) Math Assn.

Studies in Global Econometrics. Henri Theil. (Advanced Studies in Theoretical & Applied Econometrics: Vol. 30). 124p. (C). 1996. lib. bdg. 59.00 (*0-7923-3660-7*) Kluwer Ac.

Studies in Globalization & Economic Transitions. Keith Griffin. LC 96-17558. 1996. text ed. 59.95 (*0-312-16224-3*) St Martin.

Studies in Gnosticism & Alexandrian Christianity. R. Van Den Broek & Johannes Van Oort. LC 96-20947. (Nag Hammadi & Manichawan Studies). 312p. 1996. 106.50 (*90-04-10654-5*) E J Brill.

Studies in Gnosticism & in the Philosophy of Religion: Gnostic Trends in Contemporary Thought. Gerald Hanratty. 200p. 1997. boxed 55.00 (*1-85182-202-X*, Pub. by Four Cts Pr IE) Intl Spec Bk.

Studies in Graeco-Roman Religions & Gnosticism. Miroslav Marcorich. 194p. (C). 1988. text ed. 50.00 (*90-04-08624-2*) E J Brill.

Studies in Greek Culture & Roman Policy. Erich S. Gruen. LC 89-9722. (Cincinnati Classical Studies: Vol. VII). 209p. 1989. 53.75 (*90-04-09051-7*) E J Brill.

Studies in Greek Culture & Roman Policy. Erich S. Gruen. LC 95-40099. 209p. (C). 1996. pap. 14.95 (*0-520-20483-2*) U CA Pr.

Studies in Greek Elegy & Iambus. Martin West. LC 73-93168. (Untersuchungen zur Antiken Literatur und Geschichte Ser.: Vol. 14). ix, 198p. (C). 1974. 87.70 (*3-11-004585-0*) De Gruyter.

***Studies in Greek History & Thought.** P. A. Brunt. 424p. 1997. reprint ed. pap. 45.00 (*0-19-815242-6*) OUP.

Studies in Greek Philosophy, 2 Vols., Set. Gregory Vlastos. Incl. Vol. 1. Presocratics. LC 94-3112. 384p. 1995. text ed. 59.50 (*0-691-03310-2*); Vol. 1. Presocratics. LC 94-3112. 424p. 1995. pap. text ed. 19.95 (*0-691-01937-1*); Vol. 2. Socrates, Plato & Their Tradition. LC 94-3112. 344p. 1995. text ed. 59.50 (*0-691-03311-0*); Vol. 2. Socrates, Plato & Their Tradition. LC 94-3112. 376p. 1995. pap. text ed. 19.95 (*0-691-01938-X*); LC 94-3112. 800p. 1995. Set pap. text ed. 37.50 (*0-691-01939-8*) Princeton U Pr.

Studies in Greek Philosophy, 2 Vols., Set. Gregory Vlastos. Incl. Vol. 1. Presocratics. LC 94-3112. 384p. 1995. text ed. 59.50 (*0-691-03310-2*); Vol. 1. Presocratics. LC 94-3112. 424p. 1995. pap. text ed. 19.95 (*0-691-01937-1*); Vol. 2. Socrates, Plato & Their Tradition. LC 94-3112. 344p. 1995. text ed. 59.50 (*0-691-03311-0*); Vol. 2. Socrates, Plato & Their Tradition. LC 94-3112. 376p. 1995. pap. text ed. 19.95 (*0-691-01938-X*); LC 94-3112. 728p. 1995. Set text ed. 119.00 (*0-691-03312-9*) Princeton U Pr.

Studies in Greek Poetry. Miroslav Marcovich. (Illinois Classical Studies). 249p. 1991. pap. 39.95 (*1-55540-603-3*, 33 00 01) Scholars Pr GA.

***Studies in Hadith: Methodology & Literature.** M. Azami. 124p. 1996. pap. 6.95 (*0-614-21072-0*, 1177) Kazi Pubns.

Studies in Hadith Methodology & Literature. Mustafa Azami. Ed. by Anwer Beg. LC 77-90335. 1978. pap. 5.25 (*0-89259-011-4*) Am Trust Pubns.

Studies in Hausa Language & Linguistics. Graham Furniss & Philip J. Jagger. 320p. 1988. lib. bdg. 57.50 (*0-7103-0282-7*) Routledge Chapman & Hall.

Studies in Health. pap. text ed. write for info. (*0-86663-651-X*); lib. bdg. write for info. (*0-86663-650-1*) Ide Hse.

Studies in Hebrew & Aramaic Orthography. Ed. by David N. Freedman et al. LC 91-32408. (Biblical & Judaic Studies from the University of California, San Diego: No. 2). xii, 328p. 1992. 37.50 (*0-931464-63-3*) Eisenbrauns.

Studies in Hebrew & Aramaic Syntax: Presented to Professor J. Hoftijzer on the Occasion of His Sixty-Fifth Birthday. Ed. by K. Jongeling et al. LC 91-29240. (Studies in Semitic Languages & Linguistics: No. 17). xvi, 219p. 1991. 86.00 (*90-04-09520-9*) E J Brill.

Studies in Hebrew & Ugaritic Psalms. Yitzhak Avishur. 388p. 1994. 35.00 (*965-223-864-3*, Pub. by Magnes Press IS) Eisenbrauns.

Studies in Hebrews. M. R. De Haan. 216p. 1996. pap. 9.99 (*0-8254-2479-8*) Kregel.

Studies in Hebrews. Handley C. Moule. LC 77-79181. (Kregel Popular Commentary Ser.). 120p. 1977. kivar 5.99 (*0-8254-3223-5*) Kregel.

Studies in Hegel. 192p. 1969. pap. text ed. 41.50 (*90-247-0283-6*, Pub. by M Nijhoff NE) Kluwer Ac.

Studies in Hegelian Cosmology. 2nd ed. John M. McTaggart. (C). 1986. reprint ed. pap. text ed. 11.95 (*0-935005-60-9*); reprint ed. lib. bdg. 21.95 (*0-935005-59-5*) Lincoln-Rembrandt.

Studies in Hellenistic Judaism. Louis H. Feldman. LC 95-50001. (Arbeiten zur Geschichte des Antiken Judentums und des Urchristentums Ser.: No. 30). 1996. 202.50 (*90-04-10418-6*) E J Brill.

Studies in Henry James. R. P. Blackmur. Ed. by Veronica A. Makowsky. LC 82-18911. 256p. 1983. 19.50 (*0-8112-0863-X*); pap. 9.25 (*0-8112-0864-8*, NDP552) New Directions.

***Studies in Heraclitus.** Roman Dilcher. (Spudasmata Ser.: Vol. 56). 206p. (GER.). 1995. write for info. (*3-487-09986-1*) G Olms Pubs.

Studies in Herodotus. Joseph Wells. LC 77-137388. (Select Bibliographies Reprint Ser.). 1977. 24.95 (*0-8369-5589-7*) Ayer.

Studies in Himalayan Ecology. Ed. by Tej V. Singh & Jagdish Kaur. 312p. (C). 1990. 300.00 (*81-7002-036-0*, Pub. by Himalayan Bks II) St Mut.

Studies in Hinduism. Rene Guenon. 1986. 18.50 (*0-8364-1548-5*, Pub. by Navrang) S Asia.

Studies in Historical Change. Ed. by Ralph Cohen. 312p. 1992. text ed. 42.50 (*0-8139-1374-8*); pap. text ed. 20.00 (*0-8139-1375-6*) U Pr of Va.

Studies in History. Henry C. Lodge. LC 70-39132. (Essay Index Reprint Ser.). 1977. reprint ed. 28.95 (*0-8369-2698-6*) Ayer.

Studies in History & Jurisprudence, 2 Vols, Set. James B. Bryce. LC 68-8444. (Essay Index Reprint Ser.). 1977. reprint ed. 48.95 (*0-8369-0261-0*) Ayer.

Studies in History & Museums. Ed. by Peter E. Rider. (Mercury Ser.: No. 47). (Illus.). 178p. 1994. pap. 24.95 (*0-660-14022-5*, Pub. by Can Mus Civil CN) U of Wash Pr.

Studies in History & Politics. Herbert A. Fisher. LC 67-26740. (Essay Index Reprint Ser.). 1977. 20.95 (*0-8369-0441-9*) Ayer.

***Studies in History of Biology, Vol. 1, 1977.** Ed. by William Coleman & Camille Limoges. LC 78-647138. (Illus.). 229p. 1977. reprint ed. pap. 65.30 (*0-608-04063-0*, 2064799) Bks Demand.

***Studies in History of Biology, Vol. 2, 1978.** Ed. by William Coleman & Camille Limoges. LC 78-647138. (Illus.). 217p. 1978. reprint ed. pap. 61.90 (*0-608-04064-9*, 2064799) Bks Demand.

Studies in History of Biology, Vol. 3. Ed. by William R. Coleman & Camille Limoges. LC 76-47139. (Illus.). 297p. reprint ed. pap. 84.70 (*0-685-24142-4*, 2033014) Bks Demand.

Studies in History of Biology, Vol. 4. Ed. by William R. Coleman & Camille Limoges. LC 76-47139. 206p. reprint ed. pap. 58.80 (*0-8357-8337-5*, 2034133) Bks Demand.

***Studies in History of Biology, Vol. 5, 1981.** Ed. by William Coleman & Camille Limoges. LC 78-647138. (Illus.). 213p. 1981. reprint ed. pap. 60.80 (*0-608-04065-7*, 2064799) Bks Demand.

***Studies in History of Biology, Vol. 6, 1983.** Ed. by William Coleman & Camille Limoges. LC 78-647138. (Illus.). 227p. 1983. reprint ed. pap. 64.70 (*0-608-04066-5*, 2064799) Bks Demand.

***Studies in History of Biology, Vol. 7, 1984.** Ed. by William Coleman & Camille Limoges. LC 78-647138. (Illus.). 155p. 1984. reprint ed. pap. 44.20 (*0-608-04067-3*, 2064799) Bks Demand.

Studies in History of Buddhism: Papers Presented at the International Conference on the History of Buddhism at the University of Wisconsin, Madison, WIS, USA, August, 19-21, 1976. (C). 1980. text ed. 26.00 (*0-8364-2839-0*, Pub. by Agam II) S Asia.

Studies in Homosexuality: Anthology of Scholarly Articles, 13 vols., Set. Ed. by Stephen Donaldson. 1992. 990.00 (*0-8153-0545-1*) Garland.

Studies in Honor of Dewitt T. Starnes. Ed. by Thomas P. Harrison et al. LC 66-64359. (Illus.). 1967. 15.00 (*0-87959-058-0*) U of Tex H Ransom Ctr.

***Studies in Honor of Donald W. Bleznick.** Ed. by Delia V. Galvan et al. (Homenajes Ser.: Vol. 11). 218p. 1995. 22.50 (*0-936388-71-4*) Juan de la Cuesta.

Studies in Honor of Dr. Paul Z. Bedoukian, Armenian Numismatic Journal, 1989, Vol. 15: Essays Dedicated in Honor of Dr. Paul Z. Bedoukian on the Fortieth Year of His Contributions. Ed. by Y. T. Nercessian. (Illus.). 192p. (ARM & ENG.). 1989. 30.00 (*0-9606842-6-3*) ANS.

Studies in Honor of Elias Rivers. Ed. by Bruno M. Damiani & Ruth El Saffar. 200p. 30.00 (*0-916379-32-9*) Scripta.

Studies in Honor of Everett W. Hesse. William C. McCrary & Jose A. Madrigal. LC 80-53824. 208p. (Orig.). reprint ed. pap. 59.30 (*0-685-15879-9*, 2027062) Bks Demand.

***Studies in Honor of Frank Dauster.** Ed. by Kirsten F. Nigro & Sandra M. Cypress. (Homenajes Ser.: Vol. 9). 220p. 1995. 22.50 (*0-936388-66-8*) Juan de la Cuesta.

Studies in Honor of Frederick W. Shipley, by His Colleagues. Washington Univ. Studies NS No. 14. Washington University, St. Louis Staff. LC 68-20341. (Essay Index Reprint Ser.). 1977. 23.95 (*0-8369-0914-3*) Ayer.

Studies in Honor of George R. Hughes. Edward F. Wente. Ed. by Janet H. Johnson. LC 76-47851. (Studies in Ancient Oriental Civilization: No. 39). (Illus.). 1977. pap. 15.00 (*0-918986-01-X*) Orient Inst.

Studies in Honor of Gertrude Rosenthal: Annual III, Pt. I. 1970. pap. 7.50 (*0-912298-27-8*) Baltimore Mus.

Studies in Honor of Gertrude Rosenthal: Annual IV, Pt. II. (Illus.). 1972. pap. 7.50 (*0-912298-31-6*) Baltimore Mus.

***Studies in Honor of Gilberto Paolini.** Ed. by Mercedes V. Tibbits & Tom Lathrop. (Homenajes Ser.: No. 12). 496p. 1997. 26.00 (*0-936388-78-1*) Juan de la Cuesta.

Studies in Honor of Hans-Erich Keller: Medieval French & Occitan Literature & Romance Linguistics. Ed. by Rupert T. Pickens. LC 93-12695. (Studies in Medieval Culture). 1993. pap. 25.00 (*1-879288-22-2*); boxed 45.00 (*1-879288-21-4*) Medieval Inst.

Studies in Honor of Hermann Collitz. LC 76-84339. (Essay Index Reprint Ser.). 1977. 21.95 (*0-8369-1196-2*) Ayer.

***Studies in Honor of Jaan Puhvel.** Ed. by Dorothy Disterheft et al. (Journal of Indo-European Monograph Ser.: No. 20). 240p. (Orig.). (C). 1997. pap. 48.00 (*0-941694-54-2*) Inst Study Man.

***Studies in Honor of Jaan Puhvel: Part Two Mythology & Religion.** Ed. by John Greppin & Edgar C. Polome. (Journal of Indo-European Studies Monograph Ser.: No. 21). (Illus.). 280p. (Orig.). (C). 1997. pap. 48.00 (*0-941694-55-0*) Inst Study Man.

Studies in Honor of John A. Wilson. Oriental Institute Staff. LC 76-81081. 124p. 1969. pap. text ed. 11.00 (*0-226-62408-0*, SAOC35) U Ch Pr.

Studies in Honor of John Albrecht Walz. LC 68-29249. (Essay Index Reprint Ser.). 1977. reprint ed. 23.95 (*0-8369-0915-1*) Ayer.

Studies in Honor of Jose Rubia Barcia. Ed. by Roberta Johnson & Paul C. Smith. LC 81-86349. (Illus.). 204p. (Orig.). 1982. pap. 30.00 (*0-89295-020-X*) Society Sp & Sp-Am.

***Studies in Honor of Maria A. Salgado.** Ed. by Millicent A. Bolden & Luis A. Jimenez. (Homenjas Ser.: Vol. 10). 181p. 1995. 22.50 (*0-936388-67-6*) Juan de la Cuesta.

Studies in Honor of Sumner M. Greenfield. Ed. by H. L. Boudreau & Luis T. Gonzalez-del-Valle. LC 83-51006. 236p. 1985. pap. 25.00 (*0-89295-030-7*) Society Sp & Sp-Am.

Studies in Honor of Tatiana Fotitch. Josep M. Sola-Sole. LC 78-339493. 371p. reprint ed. pap. 105.80 (*0-317-55472-7*, 2029526) Bks Demand.

Studies in Honor of William C. McCrary. Ed. by Robert L. Fiore et al. LC 83-51007. (Illus.). 248p. (ENG & SPA.). reprint ed. pap. 70.70 (*0-7837-5170-2*, 2044899) Bks Demand.

Studies in Honor of Xenia Gasiorowska. Ed. by Lauren G. Leighton. (Illus.). 191p. (Orig.). 1983. pap. 19.95 (*0-89357-102-4*) Slavica.

Studies in Honour of T. B. L. Webster, Vol. 1. Ed. by J. H. Betts et al. 264p. 1987. 45.00 (*0-8453-4515-X*, Pub. by Brstl Class Pr UK) Assoc Univ Prs.

Studies in Honour of T. B. L. Webster, Vol. 2. Ed. by J. H. Betts et al. (Illus.). 208p. 1988. 48.00 (*0-8453-4523-0*, Pub. by Brstl Class Pr UK) Assoc Univ Prs.

Studies in Human Capital, Vol. 1: The Collected Essays of Jacob Mincer. Jacob Mincer. (Economists of the Twentieth Century Ser.). 448p. 1993. 110.00 (*1-85278-579-9*) E Elgar.

Studies in Human Development: Selections from the Publications & Addresses of Harold Ellis Jones. Ed. by Herbert S. Conrad. (Century Psychology Ser.). (Illus.). 1966. 64.50 (*0-89197-581-0*) Irvington.

Studies in Human Sexuality: A Selected Guide. 2nd ed. Suzanne G. Frayser & Thomas J. Whitby. xx, 737p. 1995. lib. bdg. 85.00 (*1-56308-131-8*) Libs Unl.

Studies in Human Time. Georges Poulet. Tr. by Elliot Coleman. LC 78-13572. 363p. 1979. reprint ed. text ed. 65.00 (*0-8371-9348-6*, POSH, Greenwood Pr) Greenwood.

Studies in Humanism. John W. Mackail. LC 73-84322. (Essay Index Reprint Ser.). 1977. 20.95 (*0-8369-1092-3*) Ayer.

Studies in Humanism. Ferdinand C. Schiller. LC 76-102255. (Select Bibliographies Reprint Ser.). 1977. 36.95 (*0-8369-5140-9*) Ayer.

Studies in Humanism, 2 vols., Set. Ferdinand C. Schiller. (Select Bibliographies Reprint Ser.). 492p. lib. bdg. 32.00 (*0-8290-0518-8*) Irvington.

Studies in I Nephi. Steven L. Shields. (Book of Mormon Study). 40p. 1987. pap. 4.50 (*0-8309-0489-1*) Herald Hse.

Studies in Iconography: Journal - Annual - Volumes 15 & Beyond. 1994. pap. 15.00 (*1-879288-44-3*) Medieval Inst.

Studies in Iconology: Humanistic Themes in the Art of the Renaissance. Erwin Panofsky. 1992. 31.00 (*0-8446-6619-X*) Peter Smith.

Studies in Iconology: Humanistic Themes in the Art of the Renaissance. Erwin Panofsky. (Icon Editions Ser.). (Illus.). 306p. 1972. reprint ed. pap. text ed. 21.00 (*0-06-430025-0*, IN-25, Icon Edns) HarpC.

Studies in III Nephi. Steven L. Shields. (Book of Mormon Study). 1987. pap. 4.50 (*0-8309-0485-9*) Herald Hse.

Studies in Illinois Poetry. Ed. by John E. Hallwas. 160p. 1989. pap. 7.00 (*0-935153-13-6*) Stormline Pr.

Studies in Immersion Education. Elaine M. Day & Stan M. Shapson. LC 95-49679. (Language & Education Library: Vol. 11). 160p. 1996. 89.00 (*1-85359-356-7*, Pub. by Multilingual Matters UK); pap. 24.95 (*1-85359-355-9*, Pub. by Multilingual Matters UK) Taylor & Francis.

Studies in Impressionism. John Rewald. Ed. by Irene Gordon & Frances Weitzenhoffer. (Illus.). 232p. 1986. 39.95 (*0-8109-1617-7*) Abrams.

Studies in Income & Wealth. Conference on Research in National Income & Wealth. LC 75-19704. (National Bureau of Economic Research Ser.). (Illus.). 1975. reprint ed. 29.95 (*0-405-07589-8*) Ayer.

Studies in Income & Wealth, No. 1. 369p. 1937. reprint ed. 96.00 (*0-87014-156-2*); reprint ed. mic. film 48.00 (*0-685-61181-7*) Natl Bur Econ Res.

Studies in Income & Wealth, No. 2. 357p. 1938. reprint ed. 92.90 (*0-87014-157-0*); reprint ed. mic. film 46.50 (*0-685-61189-2*) Natl Bur Econ Res.

Studies in Income & Wealth, No. 3. 507p. 1939. reprint ed. 131.90 (*0-87014-158-9*); reprint ed. mic. film 66.00 (*0-685-61195-7*) Natl Bur Econ Res.

Studies in Income & Wealth, No. 6. 302p. 1943. reprint ed. 78.60 (*0-87014-161-9*); reprint ed. mic. film 39.30 (*0-685-61239-2*) Natl Bur Econ Res.

Studies in Income & Wealth, No. 8. 319p. 1946. reprint ed. 83.00 (*0-87014-163-5*); reprint ed. mic. film 41.50 (*0-685-61266-X*) Natl Bur Econ Res.

S

An Asterisk (*) at the beginning of an entry indicates that the title is appearing in BIP for the first time.

S

Studies in Income & Wealth, No. 10. 352p. 1947. reprint ed. 91.60 (0-87014-165-1); reprint ed. mic. film 45.80 (0-685-61269-4) Natl Bur Econ Res.

Studies in Income & Wealth, No. 11. 464p. 1949. reprint ed. 120.70 (0-87014-166-X); reprint ed. mic. film 60.40 (0-685-61277-5) Natl Bur Econ Res.

Studies in Income & Wealth, No. 12. 608p. 1950. reprint ed. 158.10 (0-87014-167-8) Natl Bur Econ Res.

Studies in Income & Wealth, No. 13. 608p. 1951. reprint ed. 158.10 (0-87014-168-6); reprint ed. mic. film 79.10 (0-685-61285-6) Natl Bur Econ Res.

Studies in Income & Wealth, No. 14. 286p. 1951. reprint ed. 74.40 (0-87014-169-4); reprint ed. mic. film 37.20 (0-685-61286-4) Natl Bur Econ Res.

Studies in Income & Wealth, No. 15. 240p. 1952. reprint ed. 62.40 (0-87014-170-8); reprint ed. mic. film 31.20 (0-685-61289-9) Natl Bur Econ Res.

Studies in Indian Agricultural Economics. Ed. by J. P. Bhattacharjee. LC 75-26296. (World Food Supply Ser.). (Illus.). 1976. reprint ed. 30.95 (0-405-07769-6) Ayer.

Studies in Indian & Anglo-Indian Fiction. Saros Cowasjee. (C). 1993. 18.00 (81-7223-072-9, Pub. by Indus Pub II) S Asia.

Studies in Indian Folk Traditions. Ved P. Vatuk. 221p. 1979. 17.95 (0-318-36324-0) Asia Bk Corp.

Studies in Indian History: Historical Records at GOA. Nath S. Surendra. (C). 1994. 26.00 (81-206-0773-2, Pub. by Asian Educ Servs II) S Asia.

Studies in Indian History & Culture. Narendra N. Law. 1990. reprint ed. 17.50 (0-8364-2516-2, Pub. by Low Price II) S Asia.

Studies in Indian Literature & Philosophy: Collected Articles. JAB VanBuitenen. 1988. 26.00 (81-208-0458-9, Pub. by Motilal Banarsidass II) S Asia.

Studies in Indian Metal Sculptures. Bholanath Bandyopadhyay. 250p. (C). 1987. 44.00 (0-8364-2180-9, Pub. by Sundeep II) S Asia.

Studies in Indian Music & Applied Arts. Leela Omchery. 1990. 180.00 (0-317-99586-3, Pub. by Sundeep II) S Asia.

Studies in Indian Society, Culture & Religion. Charles Sandford. (C). 1988. 44.00 (81-85066-10-8) S Asia.

Studies in Indian Thought: The Collected Papers of Professor TRV Murti. T. R. Murty. Ed. by Harold Coward. 1983. 25.00 (0-8364-0866-7); text ed. 17.00 (0-8364-0984-1) S Asia.

Studies in Indian Urban Development. Edwin S. Mills & Charles M. Becker. (World Bank Publication). 224p. 1986. 29.95 (0-19-520507-3) OUP.

Studies in Indian Writing in English. Bayapa Reddy. 128p. 1990. text ed. 20.00 (81-85218-26-9, Pub. by Prestige II) Advent Bks Div.

Studies in India's Economic Problems. N. C. Saha. 1985. 79.00 (0-317-38796-0, Pub. by Current Dist II) St Mut.

Studies in Inductive Probability & Rational Expectation. Theo A. Kuipers. (Synthese Library: No. 123). 157p. 1978. lib. bdg. 70.50 (90-277-0882-7, D Reidel) Kluwer Ac.

Studies in Inflationary Dynamics: Financial Repression & Financial Liberalisation in Less Developed Countries. Basant K. Kapur. 164p. (Orig.). 1986. pap. 32.50 (9971-69-099-3, Pub. by Sgapore Univ SI) Coronet Bks.

Studies in Inherited Metabolic Disease: Lipoproteins; Ethical Issues. Ed. by R. J. Pollitt et al. (C). 1988. lib. bdg. 153.00 (0-7462-0101-X) Kluwer Ac.

Studies in Inherited Metabolic Diseases: Prenatal & Perinatal Diagnosis. Ed. by G. M. Addison et al. (C). 1989. lib. bdg. 188.00 (0-7923-8916-6) Kluwer Ac.

Studies in Innovation in the Steel & Chemical Industries. James A. Allen. LC 68-583. x, 246p. 1967. lib. bdg. 39.50 (0-678-06790-2) Kelley.

Studies in Insular Art & Archaeology. Catherine Karkov & Robert Farrell. (American Early Medieval Studies). 161p. (C). 1991. pap. 27.00 (1-879836-00-9) Am Erly Medieval.

Studies in International Business. Peter J. Buckley. LC 91-44083. 179p. 1992. text ed. 69.95 (0-312-07601-0) St Martin.

***Studies in International Corporate Finance & Governance Systems: A Comparison of the U.S., Japan, & Europe.** Donald H. Chew. (Illus.). 384p. (C). 1997. text ed. 26.95 (0-19-510795-0) OUP.

Studies in International Finance: Private Interest & Public Policy in the International Political Economy. Jeffry A. Frieden. LC 92-33882. (Foreign Economic Policy of the United States Ser.). 480p. 1993. text ed. 40.00 (0-8153-1106-0) Garland.

Studies in International History: Essays Presented to W. Norton Medicott. Ed. by K. Bourne & D. C. Watt. 460p. (C). 1967. 45.00 (0-208-00406-8, Archon Bks) Shoe String.

Studies in International Law. Thomas E. Holland. LC 04-14210. viii, 314p. 1984. reprint ed. lib. bdg. 45.00 (0-89941-342-0, 303460) W S Hein.

Studies in International Macroeconomics. Jagdeep S. Bhandari. LC 86-8095. 279p. 1986. text ed. 69.50 (0-275-92087-9, C2087, Praeger Pubs) Greenwood.

Studies in International Taxation. Ed. by Alberto Giovanni et al. (National Bureau of Economic Research Project Reports Ser.). (Illus.). x, 342p. 1995. pap. text ed. 22.50 (0-226-29702-0) U Ch Pr.

Studies in International Taxation. Ed. by Alberto Giovannini et al. LC 93-9797. (National Bureau of Economic Research Project Report Ser.). (Illus.). 336p. 1993. 55.00 (0-226-29701-2) U Ch Pr.

Studies in Interpersonal Relationships. lib. bdg. write for info. (0-86663-968-3) Ide Hse.

Studies in Invalid Occupation: A Manual for Nurses & Attendants. Susan R. Tracy. Ed. by William R. Phillips & Janet Rosenberg. LC 79-6926. (Physically Handicapped in Society Ser.). (Illus.). 1980. reprint ed. lib. bdg. 19.95 (0-405-13133-X) Ayer.

Studies in Iqbal. Syed Abdul Vahid. 350p. 1985. 19.50 (1-56744-394-X) Kazi Pubns.

Studies in Irish & Scandinavian Folktales. Reider T. Christiansen. Ed. by Richard M. Dorson. LC 80-741. (Folklore of the World Ser.). 1981. reprint ed. lib. bdg. 29.95 (0-405-13307-3) Ayer.

Studies in Irrigation & Water Management. B. D. Dhawan. 1989. 38.00 (81-7169-027-0, Pub. by Commonwealth II) S Asia.

Studies in Isaiah. Allan A. MacRae. LC 95-80673. vi, 358p. (Orig.). 1995. pap. 12.95 (0-944788-88-2) IBRI.

Studies in Ishhali Documents. S. Greengus. (Bibliotheca Mesopotamica Ser.: Vol. 19). 1986. 48.00 (0-89003-166-5); pap. 37.50 (0-89003-167-3) Undena Pubns.

Studies in Islamic & Judaic Traditions, Vol. I. Ed. by William M. Brinner & Stephen D. Ricks. LC 86-15552. (Brown Judaic Studies). 263p. (C). 1986. 31.95 (1-55540-047-7, 14-01-10); pap. 25.95 (1-55540-048-5, 14 01 10) Scholars Pr GA.

Studies in Islamic & Judaic Traditions, Vol. II. Ed. by William M. Brinner & Stephen D. Ricks. LC 86-15552. (Brown Judaic Studies). 247p. 1989. 56.95 (1-55540-373-5, 14 01 78) Scholars Pr GA.

Studies in Islamic Economics. Ed. by Khurshid Ahmad. 390p. (Orig.). 1980. 31.50 (0-86037-066-6, Pub. by Islamic Fnd UK); pap. 15.95 (0-86037-067-4, Pub. by Islamic Fnd UK) New Era Publns MI.

Studies in Islamic History & Civilization. Ed. by Uriel Heyd. (Scripta Hierosolymitana Ser.: Vol. 9). 240p. reprint ed. pap. 68.40 (0-317-08597-2, 2051596) Bks Demand.

Studies in Islamic History & Civilization in Honour of Professor David Ayalon. M. Sharon. (Illus.). 611p. 1986. 103.50 (965-264-014-X) E J Brill.

Studies in Islamic Law, Religion & Society. H. S. Bhatia. (C). 1989. 315.00 (0-685-27909-X) St Mut.

Studies in Islamic Law, Religion & Society. Ed. by H. S. Bhatia. (C). 1990. 160.00 (0-89771-146-7) St Mut.

Studies in Islamic Mysticism. Reynold A. Nicholson. 288p. (C). 1994. pap. 25.00 (0-7007-0278-4) Paul & Co Pubs.

***Studies in Islamic Science & Polity.** Masudul A. Choudhury. LC 97-22307. 1998. write for info. (0-312-17740-2) St Martin.

***Studies in Islamic Social Sciences.** Masudul A. Choudhury. LC 97-3011. 1997. write for info. (0-312-17516-7) St Martin.

Studies in Israel Law. G. Tedeschi. (Hebrew University Legal Studies: No. 7). vi, 302p. 1960. 10.00 (0-8377-1200-9) Rothman.

Studies in Israeli Ethnicity: After the Ingathering. Ed. by Alex Weingrod. xx, 362p. 1985. text ed. 98.00 (2-88124-007-0) Gordon & Breach.

Studies in Israelite Poetry & Wisdom. Patrick W. Skehan. Ed. by Joseph A. Fitzmyer. LC 77-153511. (Catholic Biblical Quarterly Monographs: I). xii, 265p. 1971. pap. 9.00 (0-915170-00-0) Catholic Bibl Assn.

Studies in Italian American Folklore. Intro. by Luisa Del Giudice. LC 93-21459. (Publications of the American Folklore Society, Bibliographical & Special Ser.). (Illus.). 288p. (C). 1994. pap. text ed. 19.95 (0-87421-171-9) Utah St U Pr.

Studies in Italian American Social History: Essays in Honor of Leonard Covello. Ed. by Francesco Cordasco. 264p. 1975. 32.50 (0-87471-705-1) St Aedans Pr & Bk.

Studies in Italian Applied Linguistics. Leonard G. Sbrocchi. (Biblioteca di Quaderni d'Italianistica Ser.: Vol. 1). 236p. (Orig.). (C). 1984. pap. 15.00 (0-9691979-0-X, Pub. by Can Soc Ital Stu CN) Speedimpex.

Studies in Italian Renaissance Architecture. Wolfgang Lotz. LC 76-44833. (Illus.). 256p. 1981. pap. 15.00 (0-262-62036-7) MIT Pr.

Studies in Italian Renaissance Diplomatic History. Vincent Ilardi. (Collected Studies: No. CS239). 332p. (ENG & ITA.). (C). 1986. reprint ed. text ed. 98.95 (0-86078-187-9, Pub. by Variorum UK) Ashgate Pub Co.

Studies in Item Analysis & Prediction. Ed. by Herbert Solomon. xii, 310p. 1961. 49.50 (0-8047-0590-9) Stanford U Pr.

Studies in Jacob Boehme. A. J. Penny. 503p. 1992. pap. 30.00 (1-56459-290-1) Kessinger Pub.

Studies in Jagannatha-Cult. Bidyut L. Ray. (C). 1993. text ed. 19.50 (81-7054-176-X, Pub. by Classical Pub II) S Asia.

Studies in Jahiliyya & Early Islam. M. J. Kister. (Collected Studies: No. CS123). 360p. (C). 1980. reprint ed. lib. bdg. 109.95 (0-86078-068-6, Pub. by Variorum UK) Ashgate Pub Co.

***Studies in Jaimini Astrology.** Bangalore V. Raman. 1996. reprint ed. 6.00 (81-208-1397-9, Pub. by Motilal Banarsidass II) S Asia.

Studies in Jaina Art & Iconography & Allied Subjects in Honour of UP Shah. Ed. by R. T. Vyas. (C). 1995. 115.00 (81-7017-316-7, Pub. by Abhinav II) S Asia.

Studies in Jaina Sanskrit Literature. Satya Vrat. 8, 205p. 1994. 20.00 (81-85133-60-3, Pub. by Estrn Bk Linkers II) Nataraj Bks.

Studies in Jainism. Ed. by M. P. Marathe et al. 267p. 1986. pap. 9.50 (0-8364-1665-1, Pub. by Abhinav II) S Asia.

***Studies in Jainism: Primer.** Ed. by Duli C. Jain. 64p. (Orig.). 1997. pap. text ed. 4.00 (0-9626105-1-8) Jain Study Cir.

Studies in Jainism: Reader 1. Ed. by Duli C. Jain. (Illus.). 90p. (Orig.). 1990. pap. text ed. 2.00 (0-9626105-0-X) Jain Study Cir.

***Studies in Jainism: Reader 2.** Ed. by Duli C. Jain. 160p. (Orig.). 1997. pap. text ed. 2.00 (0-9626105-2-6) Jain Study Cir.

Studies in Japanese Buddhism. August K. Reischauer. 1973. 250.00 (0-8490-1147-7) Gordon Pr.

Studies in Japanese Buddhism. August K. Reischauer. LC 73-107769. reprint ed. 37.50 (0-404-05237-1) AMS Pr.

Studies in Japanese Folklore. Ed. by Richard M. Dorson. LC 80-744. (Folklore of the World Ser.). (Illus.). 1981. reprint ed. lib. bdg. 37.95 (0-405-13310-3) Ayer.

Studies in Jazz Discography, I. LC 78-5037. 122p. reprint ed. pap. 34.80 (0-317-27281-0, 2024161) Bks Demand.

Studies in Jeremiah & Lamentations, 1. Robert Taylor, Jr. 1992. pap. 8.50 (0-89137-139-7) Quality Pubns.

Studies in Jeremiah & Lamentations, 2. Robert Taylor, Jr. 1992. pap. 8.50 (0-89137-140-0) Quality Pubns.

Studies in Jewish & Christian History, Pt. 3. Elias Bickerman. (Arbeiten zur Geschichte des Antiken Judentums & des Urchristentums Ser.: Band 9-3). xvi, 392p. 1986. 156.75 (90-04-07480-5) E J Brill.

Studies in Jewish & World Folklore. Haim Schwarzbaum. (Fabula Supplement Ser.: No. B 3). (C). 1968. 192.35 (3-11-000393-7) De Gruyter.

Studies in Jewish Bibliography, History & Literature: In Honor of I. Edward Kiev. Charles Berlin. (C). 1971. 50.00 (0-87068-143-5) Ktav.

Studies in Jewish Demography. U. O. Schmelz. 1983. 25.00 (0-88125-013-9) Ktav.

Studies in Jewish Dream Interpretation. Monford Harris. LC 93-38060. 176p. 1994. 30.00 (1-56821-126-0) Aronson.

Studies in Jewish Education & Judaica in Honor of Louis Newman. Alexander M. Shapiro & Burton I. Cohen. 1984. 20.00 (0-317-13172-9) Ktav.

Studies in Jewish Folklore. Dov Noy. 1981. 25.00 (0-87068-802-2) Ktav.

Studies in Jewish Folklore: Proceedings of a Regional Conference Held at the Spertus College of Judaica in May, 1977. Ed. by Frank Talmage. 408p. 1980. 25.00 (0-685-18407-2, Ktav) Assn for Jewish Studies.

Studies in Jewish Literature Issued in Honor of Professor Kaufmann Kohler, Ph.D. David Philipson et al. Ed. by Steven Katz. LC 79-7167. (Jewish Philosophy, Mysticism & History of Ideas Ser.). 1980. reprint ed. lib. bdg. 29.95 (0-405-12283-7) Ayer.

Studies in Jewish Mysticism. Ed. by Joseph Dan. 220p. 1981. 25.00 (0-685-11699-9) Assn for Jewish Studies.

Studies in Jewish Mysticism. Ed. by Joseph Dan & Frank Talmage. 25.00 (0-87068-803-0) Ktav.

Studies in Jewish Mysticism, Esotericism, & Hasidism. Ed. by Elliot Woltson. 187p. 1993. pap. text ed. 73.00 (3-7186-5502-0, Harwood Acad Pubs) Gordon & Breach.

Studies in Jewish Myth & Messianism. Yehuda Liebes. Tr. by Batya Stein from HEB. LC 91-36470. (SUNY Series in Judaica: Hermeneutics, Mysticism, & Religion). 226p. (C). 1992. pap. text ed. 19.95 (0-7914-1194-X) State U NY Pr.

Studies in Jewish Myth & Messianism. Yehuda Liebes. Tr. by Batya Stein from HEB. LC 91-36470. (SUNY Series in Judaica: Hermeneutics, Mysticism, & Religion). 226p. (C). 1992. text ed. 59.50 (0-7914-1193-1) State U NY Pr.

Studies in Jewish Philosophy: Collected Essays of the Academy for Jewish Philosophy, 1980-1985. Ed. by Norbert M. Samuelson. LC 87-14691. (Studies in Judaism). (Illus.). 600p. (Orig.). 1987. pap. text ed. 44.50 (0-8191-6509-3, Studies in Judaism); lib. bdg. 74.50 (0-8191-6508-5, Studies in Judaism) U Pr of Amer.

Studies in Jewish Theology: The Arthur Marmorstein Memorial Volume. Arthur Marmorstein. Ed. by Joseph Rabbinowitz & Meyer S. Lew. LC 76-39174. (Essay Index Reprint Ser.). 1977. reprint ed. 23.95 (0-8369-2702-8) Ayer.

Studies in Jewish Thought: An Anthology of German Jewish Scholarship. Alfred Jospe. LC 80-29338. 434p. reprint ed. pap. 123.70 (0-685-20907-5, 2032035) Bks Demand.

Studies in Jocular Literature. William C. Hazlitt. 1973. 59.95 (0-8490-1148-5) Gordon Pr.

***Studies in John the Scot (Erigena) A Philosopher of the Dark Ages (1900 Edition)** Alice Gardner. 160p. 1996. reprint ed. write for info. (1-85506-192-9) Bks Intl VA.

Studies in John's Epistles: Fellowship in the Life Eternal. George G. Findlay. LC 89-2562. 448p. 1989. reprint ed. pap. 14.99 (0-8254-2629-4, Kregel Class) Kregel.

Studies in John's Epistles: Fellowship in the Life Eternal. George G. Findlay. LC 89-2562. 448p. 1989. reprint ed. lib. bdg. 19.99 (0-8254-2632-4, Kregel Class) Kregel.

Studies in Jonah. John L. Kachelman. 5p. 1983. pap. 6.95 (0-89137-319-5) Quality Pubns.

Studies in Jonson's Comedies. Elizabeth M. Woodbridge. LC 66-29470. 101p. 1966. reprint ed. 40.00 (0-87752-123-9) Gordian.

Studies in Joyce. Nathan Halper. LC 83-1360. (Studies in Modern Literature: No. 5). 177p. reprint ed. pap. 50.50 (0-685-20451-0, 2070316) Bks Demand.

Studies in Judaism. Solomon Schechter. LC 78-38775. (Essay Index Reprint Ser.). 1977. reprint ed. 22.95 (0-8369-2670-6) Ayer.

Studies in Jude. Michael Penny. 32p. (Orig.). 1995. pap. 3.00 (1-880573-26-1) Grace WI.

Studies in Judges. John Kachelman, Jr. 1986. pap. 6.95 (0-89137-564-3) Quality Pubns.

Studies in Kabuki: Its Acting, Music, & Historical Context. James R. Brandon et al. LC 77-5336. 202p. 1978. pap. text ed. 16.00 (0-8248-0452-X) EW Ctr HI.

Studies in Keats. John M. Murry. LC 78-185023. (Studies in Keats: No. 19). 1969. reprint ed. lib. bdg. 75.00 (0-8383-0671-3) M S G Haskell Hse.

Studies in Labor Markets. Ed. by Sherwin Rosen. LC 81-7488. (National Bureau of Economic Research Ser.: Universities-Nat'l Conference Series No. 31). (Illus.). 406p. (C). 1981. lib. bdg. 56.50 (0-226-72628-2) U Ch Pr.

Studies in Labor Markets & Institutions. Ed. by Kenneth L. Sokoloff. (Monograph & Research Ser.: No. 56). 151p. (Orig.). 1992. pap. 12.00 (0-89215-167-6) U Cal LA Indus Rel.

Studies in Labor Supply, Vol. 2: The Collected Essays of Jacob Mincer. Jacob Mincer. (Economists of the Twentieth Century Ser.). 352p. 1993. 95.00 (1-85278-578-0) E Elgar.

Studies in Labor Theory & Practice. Ed. by William L. Rowe. LC 81-82455. (Studies in Marxism: Vol. 12). 107p. 1982. 16.25 (0-930656-23-7); pap. 6.50 (0-930656-24-5) MEP Pubns.

Studies in Labour Economics. Ed. by Erkin I. Bairam. 159p. 1993. 59.95 (1-85628-476-X, Pub. by Avebury Pub UK) Ashgate Pub Co.

Studies in Lake Nantua (France) A Eutrophic Lake on the Way to Rehabilitation. Ed. by Jacques Feuillade. (Advances in Limnology Ser.: No. 41). (Illus.). 144p. 1994. pap. text ed. 80.00 (3-510-47042-7, Pub. by Schweitzerbartsche GW) Lubrecht & Cramer.

Studies in Land & Credit in Ancient Athens, 500-200 B. C. The Horos Inscriptions. Moses I. Finley. LC 72-7890. (Greek History Ser.). 1978. reprint ed. 41.95 (0-405-04786-X) Ayer.

Studies in Land & Credit in Ancient Athens, 500-200 B.C. The Horos Inscriptions. Moses I. Finley. 340p. 1986. text ed. 49.95 (0-88738-066-2) Transaction Pubs.

Studies in Language & Linguistics Vol. I: Literacy. R. N. Srivastava. Ed. by Bina Srivastava. xiv, 243p. 1993. 23.00 (81-85163-45-6, Pub. by Kalinga Pubns) Nataraj Bks.

Studies in Language & Linguistics Vol. II: Stylistics. R. N. Srivastava. Ed. by Bina Srivastava. xiv, 200p. 1994. 20.00 (81-85163-46-4, Pub. by Kalinga Pubns) Nataraj Bks.

Studies in Language & Linguistics Vol. III: Bi/ Multilingualism. R. N. Srivastava. Ed. by Bina Srivastava. 14, 325p. 1994. 30.00 (81-85163-44-8, Pub. by Kalinga Pubns) Nataraj Bks.

Studies in Language & Reason. Ilham Dilman. LC 79-55527. 228p. 1981. text ed. 53.00 (0-389-20229-0, N6436) B&N Imports.

Studies in Language Origins, Vol. 1. Edward G. Pulleysblank et al. Ed. by Jan Wind et al. LC 88-7542. xxii, 332p. (C). 1989. 94.00 (1-55619-054-9) Benjamins North Am.

Studies in Language Origins, Vol. 2. Ed. by Walburga Raffler-Engel et al. LC 88-7542. xxi, 348p. 1991. 112.00 (1-55619-077-8) Benjamins North Am.

Studies in Language Origins Vol. 3. Ed. by Jan Wind et al. xvi, 344p. 1994. lib. bdg. 79.00 (1-55619-497-8) Benjamins North Am.

***Studies in Language Testing 1: An Investigation into the Comparability of Two Tests of English as a Foreign Language.** 228p. 1995. text ed. 49.95 (0-521-48167-8) Cambridge U Pr.

***Studies in Language Testing 1: An Investigation into the Comparability of Two Tests of English as a Foreign Language.** 256p. 1995. pap. text ed. 26.95 (0-521-48467-7) Cambridge U Pr.

Studies in Language Testing 2. 180p. 1996. pap. text ed. 26.95 (0-521-48466-9) Cambridge U Pr.

Studies in Language Testing 2: Test-Taker Characteristics & Performance: Structural Modeling Approach. Antony J. Kunnan. (Studies in Language Testing). 156p. 1996. text ed. 47.95 (0-521-48168-6) Cambridge U Pr.

***Studies in Language Testing 3: Performance Testing, Cognition & Assessment.** 313p. 1995. pap. text ed. 26.95 (0-521-48465-0) Cambridge U Pr.

***Studies in Language Testing 3: Performance Testing, Cognition & Assessment.** Michael Milanovic. (Studies in Language Testing). 313p. 1996. text ed. 49.95 (0-521-48169-4) Cambridge U Pr.

***Studies in Language Testing 4: The Development of IELTS: A Study of the Effect of Background Knowledge on Reading Comprehension.** Caroline Clapham. (Illus.). 316p. (C). 1997. 52.95 (0-521-56199-X) Cambridge U Pr.

***Studies in Language Testing 4: The Development of IELTS: A Study of the Effect of Background Knowledge on Reading Comprehension.** Caroline Clapham. (Illus.). 316p. (C). 1997. pap. write for info. (0-521-56708-4) Cambridge U Pr.

Studies in Late Byzantine History & Prosopography. Donald M. Nicol. (Collected Studies: No. CS242). (Illus.). 330p. (C). 1986. reprint ed. lib. bdg. 92.95 (0-86078-190-9, Pub. by Variorum UK) Ashgate Pub Co.

Studies in Late Greek Epic Poetry. Heather White. (London Studies in Classical Philology: Vol. 18). (Illus.). 153p. 1987. 47.00 (90-70265-39-7, Pub. by Gieben NE) Benjamins North Am.

Studies in Late Medieval & Renaissance Painting in Honor of Millard Meiss. Ed. by Irving Lavin & John Plummer. LC 75-27118. 550p. (C). 1977. Set. text ed. 200.00 (0-8147-4963-1) NYU Pr.

Studies in Later Greek Comedy. Thomas B. Webster. LC 81-5016. (Illus.). xiv, 282p. 1981. reprint ed. text ed. 59.75 (0-313-23050-1, WESL, Greenwood Pr) Greenwood.

Studies in Later Greek Philosophy & Gnosticism. Jaap Mansfeld. (Collected Studies: No. CS292). 334p. (C). 1989. lib. bdg. 94.95 (0-86078-240-9, Pub. by Variorum UK) Ashgate Pub Co.

Studies in Latin American Popular Culture, Vol. I. Ed. by Harold E. Hinds, Jr. & Charles M. Tatum. (C). 1982. pap. 30.00 (0-9608664-0-X) Studies Lat Am.

Studies in Latin American Popular Culture, Vol. 2. Ed. by Harold E. Hinds, Jr. & Charles M. Tatum. 1983. pap. 30.00 (0-9608664-1-8) Studies Lat Am.

An Asterisk (*) at the beginning of an entry indicates that the title is appearing in BIP for the first time.

Studies in Latin American Popular Culture, Vol. 4. Ed. by Harold E. Hinds, Jr. & Charles M. Tatum. 1985. pap. 30.00 (*0-9608664-3-4*) Studies Lat Am.

Studies in Latin American Popular Culture, Vol. 5. Ed. by Harold E. Hinds, Jr. & Charles M. Tatum. 1986. pap. 30.00 (*0-9608664-4-2*) Studies Lat Am.

Studies in Latin American Popular Culture, Vol. 6. Ed. by Harold E. Hinds, Jr. & Charles M. Tatum. 1987. pap. text ed. 30.00 (*0-9608664-5-0*) Studies Lat Am.

Studies in Latin American Popular Culture, Vol. 7. Ed. by Harold E. Hinds, Jr. & Charles M. Tatum. 1988. pap. text ed. 40.00 (*0-318-32874-7*) Studies Lat Am.

Studies in Latin American Popular Culture, Vol. 8. Ed. by Harold E. Hinds, Jr. & Charles M. Tatum. 1989. pap. text ed. 40.00 (*0-9608664-6-9*) Studies Lat Am.

Studies in Latin American Popular Culture, Vol. 9. Ed. by Harold E. Hinds, Jr. & Charles M. Tatum. 1990. pap. text ed. 40.00 (*0-9608664-7-7*) Studies Lat Am.

Studies in Law & Politics. Harold J. Laski. LC 68-22106. (Essay Index Reprint Ser.). 1977. 20.95 (*0-8369-0608-X*) Ayer.

Studies in Law & Practice for Health Service Management. Ed. by W. A. Farndale. (C). 1987. 145.00 (*0-685-28606-1*); pap. 89.00 (*0-685-28607-X*) St Mut.

Studies in Law, Politics & Society, Vol. 5. Ed. by Susan S. Silbey & Austin Sarat. 222p. 1984. 73.25 (*0-89232-334-5*) Jai Pr.

Studies in Law, Politics & Society, Vol. 10. Ed. by Susan S. Silbey & Austin Sarat. 260p. 1990. 73.25 (*0-89232-992-0*) Jai Pr.

Studies in Law, Politics & Society, Vol. 11. Ed. by Susan S. Silbey & Austin Sarat. 293p. 1991. 73.25 (*1-55938-375-5*) Jai Pr.

Studies in Law, Politics & Society, 2 pts., Vol. 12: Trends & Opportunities in Disputing Resea. Ed. by Susan S. Silbey & Austin Sarat. 445p. 1992. 146.50 (*1-55938-393-3*) Jai Pr.

Studies in Law, Politics & Society, Vol. 13. Ed. by Susan S. Silbey & Austin Sarat. 271p. 1993. 73.25 (*1-55938-623-1*) Jai Pr.

Studies in Law, Politics & Society, Vol. 14. Ed. by Susan S. Silbey & Austin Sarat. 397p. 1994. 73.25 (*1-55938-571-5*) Jai Pr.

Studies in Law, Politics & Society, Vol. 15. Ed. by Susan S. Silbey & Austin Sarat. 1995. 73.25 (*1-55938-901-X*) Jai Pr.

***Studies in Law, Politics & Society, Vol. 16.** Ed. by Susan S. Silbey & Austin Sarat. 325p. 1997. 73.25 (*0-7623-0232-1*) Jai Pr.

Studies in Law, Politics & Society: An Annual Compilation of Research, Vol. 1. Ed. by Susan S. Silbey & Austin Sarat. 318p. 1978. 73.25 (*0-89232-024-9*) Jai Pr.

Studies in Learning & Memory: Selected Papers. Benton J. Underwood. Ed. by Charles D. Spielberger. LC 81-22694. (Centennial Psychology Ser.). 346p. 1982. text ed. 59.95 (*0-275-90917-4*, C0917, Praeger Pubs) Greenwood.

Studies in Legal Systems: Mixed & Mixing. Ed. by Esin Orucu et al. LC 95-51331. 1996. write for info. (*90-411-0906-4*) Kluwer Law Tax Pubs.

Studies in Legal Terminology. Erwin Hexner. vi, 150p. 1981. reprint ed. lib. bdg. 20.00 (*0-8377-0635-1*) Rothman.

Studies in Legato for Trombone. Reginald H. Fink. 1967. pap. 10.95 (*0-8258-0245-8*, 04767) Fischer Inc NY.

Studies in Levitical Terminology: Vol. 1, The Encroacher & the Levite. The Term Aboda. Jacob Milgrom. LC 76-626141. (Univeraity of California Publications. Near Eastern Studies: Vol. 14). 120p. reprint ed. pap. 34.20 (*0-317-10194-3*, 2021380) Bks Demand.

Studies in Leviticus. Samuel H. Kellogg. LC 88-12062. 574p. reprint ed. pap. 18.99 (*0-8254-3041-0*) Kregel.

Studies in Linear & Non-linear Programming. Kenneth J. Arrow et al. 229p. 1958. pap. 29.95 (*0-8047-0562-3*) Stanford U Pr.

Studies in Linguistic Geography: The Dialects of English in Britain & Ireland. Ed. by John M. Kirk et al. LC 84-23118. (Illus.). 208p. 1986. 72.50 (*0-7099-1502-0*, Pub. by Croom Helm UK) Routledge Chapman & Hall.

Studies in Linguistic Semantics. Ed. by Charles J. Fillmore & D. Terence Langendoen. LC 74-140383. 307p. reprint ed. write for info. (*0-8290-0982-5*) Irvington.

Studies in Linguistics in Honor of George L. Trager. Ed. by M. E. Smith. (Janua Linguarum, Series Major: No. 52). 1972. 124.65 (*90-279-2309-4*) Mouton.

Studies in Literary Types in Seventeenth Century America. Josephine Piercy. (BCL1-PS American Literature Ser.). 360p. 1993. reprint ed. lib. bdg. 89.00 (*0-7812-6573-8*) Rprt Serv.

Studies in Literature. Arthur T. Quiller-Couch. (BCL1-PR English Literature Ser.). 324p. 1992. reprint ed. lib. bdg. 89.00 (*0-7812-7018-9*) Rprt Serv.

Studies in Literature - Second Series. Arthur T. Quiller-Couch. (BCL1-PR English Literature Ser.). 301p. 1992. reprint ed. lib. bdg. 89.00 (*0-7812-7019-7*) Rprt Serv.

Studies in Literature & Belief. Martin Jarrett-Kerr. LC 74-134101. (Essay Index Reprint Ser.). 1977. reprint ed. 20.95 (*0-8369-1978-5*) Ayer.

Studies in Literature & History. Alfred C. Lyall. LC 68-29227. (Essay Index Reprint Ser.). 1977. reprint ed. 23.95 (*0-8369-0637-3*) Ayer.

Studies in Literature from the Ancient Near East: Dedicated to Samuel Noah Kramer. Ed. by Jack M. Sasson. (American Oriental Ser.: Vol. 65). 369p. 1984. 35.00 (*0-940490-65-X*) Am Orient Soc.

Studies in Loess. Marton Pecsi. 556p. (C). 1981. 120.00 (*963-05-2871-1*, 41212, Pub. by Akad Kiado HU) St Mut.

Studies in Logic: By Members of the Johns Hopkins University (1883) Ed. by Charles S. Peirce. (Foundations of Semiotics Ser.: No. 1). xl, 203p. (C). 1983. reprint ed. 65.00 (*90-272-3271-7*) Benjamins North Am.

Studies in Logical Theory. John Dewey. LC 75-3128. reprint ed. 34.50 (*0-404-59129-9*) AMS Pr.

Studies in Long Term Memory. Ed. by Alan Kennedy & Alan Wilkes. LC 74-13149. 378p. reprint ed. pap. 107.80 (*0-317-30318-X*, 2024801) Bks Demand.

Studies in Love & in Terror. Marie A. Lowndes. LC 74-167462. (Short Story Index Reprint Ser.). 1977. reprint ed. 21.95 (*0-8369-3988-3*) Ayer.

Studies in Lucian's De Syria Dea. R. A. Oden. LC 76-54988. (Harvard Semitic Monographs: No. 15). (Illus.). 189p. reprint ed. pap. 53.90 (*0-7837-5412-4*, 2045176) Bks Demand.

Studies in Lutheran Doctrine. Paul F. Keller. LC 60-15574. (J). (gr. 7-8). 1968. student ed. 1.00 (*0-570-03525-2*, 14-1266) Concordia.

Studies in Lutheran Doctrine. Paul F. Keller. LC 60-15574. (YA). (gr. 7-8). 1968. pap. 7.95 (*0-570-03517-1*, 14-1265); 0.85 (*0-570-03526-0*, 14-1267) Concordia.

Studies in Macedonian Language, Literature, & Culture: Proceedings of the First North American-Macedonian Conference, Ann Arbor, 1991. Benjamin A. Stolz. LC 95-14378. (Michigan Slavic Materials Ser.: Vol. 37). 1995. write for info. (*0-930042-76-X*) Mich Slavic Pubns.

Studies in Macromolecular Biosynthesis. Ed. by Richard B. Roberts. (Illus.). 702p. 1964. 29.00 (*0-87279-635-3*, 624) Carnegie Inst.

Studies in Magic from Latin Literature. Eugene Tavenner. LC 16-25151. reprint ed. 32.50 (*0-404-06350-0*) AMS Pr.

Studies in Maimonides. Ed. by Isadore Twersky. (Harvard Judaic Texts & Studies: Vol. 7). 214p. 1992. 14.95 (*0-674-85175-7*); pap. 14.95 (*0-674-85176-5*) HUP.

Studies in Malory. Ed. by James W. Spisak. LC 84-16542. 1986. pap. 13.95 (*0-918720-55-9*); boxed 22.95 (*0-918720-54-0*) Medieval Inst.

Studies in Management Education. John B. Miner. LC 65-16849. (Illus.). 1965. text ed. 25.00 (*0-317-99717-3*) Organizat Meas.

Studies in Mark, Vol. 1. Kees Compier. (Bible Study Ser.). (Illus.). 34p. 1989. pap. 4.50 (*0-8309-0532-4*) Herald Hse.

Studies in Mark, Vol. 2. Kees Compier. (Bible Study Ser.). (Illus.). 1989. pap. 4.50 (*0-8309-0537-5*) Herald Hse.

Studies in Mathematical Analysis & Related Topics: Essays in Honor of George Polya. Ed. by Gabor Szego et al. xxi, 447p. 1962. 57.50 (*0-8047-0140-7*) Stanford U Pr.

Studies in Mathematical Analysis & Related Topics: Essays in Honor of George Polya. fac. ed. Ed. by Gabor Szego et al. LC 62-15265. (Stanford Studies in Mathematics & Statistics: No. 4). 111p. 1962. reprint ed. pap. 30.00 (*0-7837-7914-3*, 2047670) Bks Demand.

Studies in Mathematical Economics. Ed. by Stanley Reiter. LC 85-63770. (Studies in Mathematics: Vol. 25). 422p. 1987. 12.00 (*0-88385-127-X*, MAS-25) Math Assn.

Studies in Mathematical Economics & Econometrics in Memory of Henry Schultz. Ed. by Oskar Lange et al. LC 68-8498. (Essay Index Reprint Ser.). 1977. 23.95 (*0-8369-0916-X*) Ayer.

Studies in Mathematical Geology. Andrei B. Vistelius. LC 65-25266. 310p. reprint ed. pap. 88.40 (*0-317-28726-5*, 2020676) Bks Demand.

Studies in Mathematical Learning Theory. Ed. by Robert R. Bush & William K. Estes. viii, 432p. 1959. 55.00 (*0-8047-0563-1*) Stanford U Pr.

Studies in Mathematical Psychology. Ed. by Richard C. Atkinson. viii, 414p. 1964. 55.00 (*0-8047-0181-4*) Stanford U Pr.

Studies in Mathematical Statistics: Proceedings. Ed. by Juril V. Linnik. (Proceedings of the Steklov Institute of Mathematics Ser.: No. 104). 260p. 1971. pap. 58.00 (*0-8218-3004-X*, STEKLO/104) Am Math.

Studies in Mathematics Education, Vol. 8: Moving into the 21st Century. 135p. 1992. pap. 17.00 (*92-3-102780-8*, U7808, Pub. by UNESCO FR) Bernan Associates.

Studies in Matthew, Vol. 1. Frances Easter. (Illus.). 35p. 1990. 4.50 (*0-8309-0575-8*) Herald Hse.

Studies in Medical Anthropology. Ed. by P. C. Joshi & Anil Mahajan. 210p. 1990. text ed. 30.00 (*81-85047-66-9*, Pub. by Reliance Pub Hse II) Apt Bks.

Studies in Medieval & Renaissance Culture, Vol. 20: Boundaries. Ed. by Paul M. Clogan. (Medievalia et Humanistica Ser.). 256p. (C). 1993. text ed. 65.00 (*0-8476-7882-2*) Rowman.

Studies in Medieval & Renaissance History, 4 vols., 2. Studies in Medieval & Renaissance History Staff. LC 63-22098. reprint ed. pap. 79.50 (*0-685-15835-7*, 2056180) Bks Demand.

Studies in Medieval & Renaissance History, 4 vols., 3. Studies in Medieval & Renaissance History Staff. LC 63-22098. reprint ed. pap. 80.30 (*0-685-15836-5*) Bks Demand.

Studies in Medieval & Renaissance History, 4 vols., 9. Studies in Medieval & Renaissance History Staff. LC 63-22098. reprint ed. pap. 55.80 (*0-685-15837-3*) Bks Demand.

Studies in Medieval & Renaissance History, 4 vols., 10. Studies in Medieval & Renaissance History Staff. LC 63-22098. reprint ed. pap. 51.00 (*0-685-15838-1*) Bks Demand.

Studies in Medieval & Renaissance History, Vol. 1. LC 63-22098. 1964. pap. 75.00 (*0-317-27624-7*, 2023489) Bks Demand.

Studies in Medieval & Renaissance History, Vol. 4. LC 63-22098. 1967. pap. 63.00 (*0-317-27625-5*) Bks Demand.

Studies in Medieval & Renaissance History, Vol. 5. LC 63-22098. 1968. pap. 71.30 (*0-317-27626-3*) Bks Demand.

Studies in Medieval & Renaissance History, Vol. 6. LC 63-22098. 1969. pap. 88.00 (*0-317-27627-1*) Bks Demand.

Studies in Medieval & Renaissance History, Vol. 7. LC 63-22098. 1970. pap. 63.80 (*0-317-27628-X*) Bks Demand.

Studies in Medieval & Renaissance History, Vol. 8. LC 63-22098. 1971. pap. 54.30 (*0-317-27629-8*) Bks Demand.

Studies in Medieval & Renaissance History, Vol. 14. rev. ed. Ed. by J. A. Evans & R. W. Unger. (Illus.). 270p. 1994. 55.00 (*0-404-62864-8*) AMS Pr.

Studies in Medieval & Renaissance History, 1978-1993, Set, Vols. 1-14. Ed. by J. A. Evans & R. W. Unger. LC 63-22098. Set. write for info. (*0-404-62850-8*) AMS Pr.

Studies in Medieval & Renaissance Literature. C. S. Lewis. 206p. 1980. pap. text ed. 19.95 (*0-521-29701-X*) Cambridge U Pr.

Studies in Medieval Art & Architecture. Ed. by David Buckton & T. A. Heslop. (Illus.). 224p. (C). 1994. text ed. 90.00 (*0-7509-0619-7*, Pub. by Sutton Pubng UK) Bks Intl VA.

Studies in Medieval Cistercian History, Vol. 2. John R. Sommerfeldt. (Studies: No. 24). 1977. pap. 2.00 (*0-87907-824-3*) Cistercian Pubns.

Studies in Medieval English Romances: Some New Approaches. Ed. by Derek S. Brewer. 208p. (Orig.). (C). 1991. pap. 25.00 (*0-85991-324-4*) Boydell & Brewer.

Studies in Medieval English Romances: Some New Approaches. Ed. by Derek S. Brewer. 205p. (C). 1991. reprint ed. 70.00 (*0-85991-247-7*) Boydell & Brewer.

Studies in Medieval Eurasian History. Omeljan Pritsak. (Collected Studies: No. CS132). 376p. (C). 1981. reprint ed. lib. bdg. 116.95 (*0-86078-078-3*, Pub. by Variorum UK) Ashgate Pub Co.

Studies in Medieval History. Ed. by Henry Mayr-Harting & R. I. Moore. (Illus.). 330p. 1985. text ed. 60.00 (*0-907628-68-0*) Hambledon Press.

Studies in Medieval History Presented to Frederick Maurice Powicke. Ed. by Richard W. Hunt et al. LC 79-14227. 504p. 1979. reprint ed. text ed. 85.00 (*0-313-21484-0*, SMFM, Greenwood Pr) Greenwood.

Studies in Medieval Indian Architecture. R. Nath. 172p. 1995. pap. 375.00 (*81-85880-56-5*, Pub. by Print Hse II) St Mut.

***Studies in Medieval Inner Asia.** Denis Sinor. LC 97-25253. (Collected Studies: Vol. 583). 360p. 1997. text ed. 98.95 (*0-86078-632-3*, DS329.4.S56, Pub. by Variorum UK) Ashgate Pub Co.

Studies in Medieval Jewish History & Literature. Ed. by Isadore Twersky. LC 79-11588. (Judaic Monographs: No. 2). 381p. 1979. 25.00 (*0-674-85192-7*) HUP.

Studies in Medieval Jewish History & Literature, Vol. 2. Ed. by Isadore Twersky. (Harvard Judaic Monographs: No. V). 460p. 1985. text ed. 25.00 (*0-674-85193-5*) Harvard U Ctr Jewish.

Studies in Medieval Jewish Philosophy. Israel I. Efros. LC 73-12512. 279p. reprint ed. pap. 79.60 (*0-685-20371-9*, 2029826) Bks Demand.

Studies in Medieval Language & Culture. Michael Richter. 250p. 1995. 49.50 (*1-85182-171-6*, Pub. by Four Cts Pr IE) Intl Spec Bk.

Studies in Medieval Life & Literature. Edward T. McLaughlin. LC 74-39101. (Essay Index Reprint Ser.). 1977. reprint ed. 18.95 (*0-8369-2701-X*) Ayer.

***Studies in Medieval Music Theory & the Early Sequence.** Richard L. Crocker. (Variorum Collected Studies Ser.: Vol. 580). (Illus.). 352p. 1997. text ed. 98.95 (*0-86078-643-9*, Pub. by Ashgate UK) Ashgate Pub Co.

Studies in Medieval Painting. Bernard Berenson. LC 73-153884. (Graphic Art Ser.). (Illus.). 148p. 1975. reprint ed. pap. 5.95 (*0-306-80010-1*); reprint ed. lib. bdg. 39.50 (*0-306-70292-4*) Da Capo.

Studies in Medieval Philosophy. Ed. by John F. Wippel. LC 86-23282. (Studies in Philosophy & the History of Philosophy: Vol. 17). 310p. 1987. reprint ed. pap. 88.40 (*0-7837-9116-X*, 2049917) Bks Demand.

***Studies in Medieval Sculpture.** Ed. by F. H. Thompson. (Illus.). 232p. 1983. pap. 17.98 (*0-614-21818-7*, Pub. by Soc Antiquaries UK) David Brown.

Studies in Medieval Spanish Frontier History. Charles J. Bishko. (Collected Studies: No. CS124). 336p. (C). 1980. reprint ed. lib. bdg. 97.95 (*0-86078-069-4*, Pub. by Variorum UK) Ashgate Pub Co.

Studies in Medieval Thought & Learning from Abelard to Wyclif. Beryl Smalley. (Illus.). 455p. (C). 1982. text ed. 65.00 (*0-9506882-6-6*) Hambledon Press.

Studies in Medieval Trade & Finance. E. B. Fryde. 430p. (C). 1983. text ed. 60.00 (*0-907628-10-9*) Hambledon Press.

Studies in Medievalism, Vol. III, Nos. 3-4. Ed. by Leslie J. Workman et al. 328p. (Orig.). (C). 1991. 50.00 (*0-85991-320-1*) Boydell & Brewer.

***Studies in Medievalism: Architecture & Design, Vol. 3, No. 2.** Ed. by Leslie Workman & John R. Zukowsky. 30.00 (*0-85991-377-5*) Boydell & Brewer.

Studies in Medievalism Vol. IV: Medievalism in England. Ed. by Leslie J. Workman. (Studies in Medievalism: Vol. IV). (Illus.). 336p. (C). 1992. 59.00 (*0-85991-348-1*, DS Brewer) Boydell & Brewer.

Studies in Medievalism Vol. V: Medievalism in Europe. Ed. by Leslie J. Workman. (Studies in Medievalism: Vol. V). (Illus.). 272p. (C). 1994. 63.00 (*0-85991-400-3*, DS Brewer) Boydell & Brewer.

Studies in Medievalism Vol. VI: Medievalism in North America. Ed. by Kathleen Verduin. LC 94-19099. (Illus.). 256p. (C). 1994. 53.00 (*0-85991-417-8*, DS Brewer) Boydell & Brewer.

Studies in Medievalsim Vol. VII: Medievalism in England II. Ed. by Leslie J. Workman & Kathleen Verduin. (Illus.). 262p. (C). 1996. 53.00 (*0-85991-487-9*) Boydell & Brewer.

Studies in Melody: Studies in Melody see Study of Sensory Control in the Rat

Studies in Memory of Ramon Menendez Pidal: Hispanic Review Special Issue, November 1970. Hispanic Review Editors. (Illus.). 114p. 1970. pap. 5.00 (*0-87535-117-4*) Hispanic Soc.

Studies in Memory of Warren Cowgill (1929-1985) Ed. by Calvert Watkins. (Studies in Indo-European Language & Culture NF: Vol. 3). 327p. (C). 1987. lib. bdg. 161.75 (*3-11-011127-6*) De Gruyter.

Studies in Mental Health Policy. Ed. by Kenneth Whittemore. 152p. (Orig.). 1994. pap. 15.00 (*0-944285-39-2*) Pol Studies.

Studies in Metaphysics. Ed. by Peter A. French et al. LC 79-10221. (Midwest Studies in Philosophy: No. 4). 451p. 1979. reprint ed. pap. 128.60 (*0-7837-2963-4*, 2057491) Bks Demand.

Studies in Mexican Compositae I see Memoirs of the New York Botanical Garden: No. 12(3)

Studies in Middle America, Set. Incl. Maya Skull from Uloa Valley, Honduras. Frans Blom. (Illus.). 1934. 5.00 (*0-685-19922-3*); Dermatoglyphics & Functional Lateral Dominance in Mexican Indians (Mayas & Tarahumaras). Stella M. Leche. 1934. 5.00 (*0-685-19923-1*); Manuscripts in the Department of Middle American Research. Arthur e. Gropp. 81p. 1934. 5.00 (*0-685-19924-X*); Relation of the Synodical Month & Eclipses to the Maya Correlation Problem. Hermann Beyer. 1934. 4.00 (*0-685-19925-8*); Mexican Bone Rattles. Hermann Beyer. (Illus.). 1934. 5.00 (*0-685-19926-6*); (Publications: No. 5). (Illus.). 401p. 1934. 40.00 (*0-939238-06-3*) Tulane MARI.

S

Studies in Middle American Anthropology. Incl. Extent of Dominance of Tenochtitlan During the Reign of Mocteczoma Ilhuicamina. H. Barry Holt. (Illus.). 1975. 2.00 (*0-685-19982-7*); Critical Analysis of Yuri Knoeozov's Decipherment of the Maya Hieroglyphics. Arthur A. Demarest. (Illus.). 1976. 2.00 (*0-685-19983-5*); Re-Evaluation of the Archaeological Sequences of Preclassic Chaipas. Arthur A. Demarest. (Illus.). 1976. 5.00 (*0-685-19984-3*); (Publications: No. 22). 107p. 1976. 12.00 (*0-939238-24-1*) Tulane MARI.

Studies in Middle American Economics. Incl. Impact of the United Fruit Company on the Economic Development of Guatemala, 1946-1954. Richard A. La Barge. (Illus.). 72p. 1960. 7.00 (*0-685-74054-4*); Maudslay's Central America: A Strategic View in 1887. Wayne M. Clegern. (Illus.). 21p. 1962. 3.00 (*0-685-74055-2*); Zamora: A Regional Economy in Mexico. Oriol Pi-Sunyer. 85p. 1967. 9.00 (*0-685-74056-0*); (Publications: No. 29). 180p. 1968. 18.00 (*0-939238-32-2*) Tulane MARI.

***Studies in Middle English Linguistics.** Ed. by Jacek Fisiak. LC 97-11738. (Trends in Linguistics Ser.). 560p. (C). 1997. lib. bdg. 206.00 (*3-11-015242-8*) Mouton.

Studies in Migration: Internal & International Migration in India. M. S. Rao. 410p. 1986. 34.00 (*81-85054-08-8*, Pub. by Manohar II) S Asia.

Studies in Milton. Sten Liljegren. LC 67-30816. (Studies in Milton: No. 22). 1969. reprint ed. lib. bdg. 75.00 (*0-8383-0718-3*) M S G Haskell Hse.

Studies in Milton & an Essay on Poetry. Alden Sampson. LC 71-126686. 1970. reprint ed. 45.00 (*0-404-05555-9*) AMS Pr.

Studies in Mimamsa. Ed. by R. C. Dwivedi. (C). 1994. text ed. 34.00 (*81-208-1109-7*, Pub. by Motilal Banarsidass II) S Asia.

Studies in Mineralogy & Precambrian Geology: A Volume in Honor of John W. Gruner. Ed. by B. R. Doe & D. K. Smith. LC 70-190173. (Geological Society of America, Memoir Ser.: No. 135). 372p. reprint ed. pap. 106.10 (*0-317-30052-0*, 2025029) Bks Demand.

Studies in Minor Irrigation with Special Reference to Ground Water. B. D. Dhawan. 1990. 29.00 (*81-7169-061-0*, Commonwealth) S Asia.

Studies in Minority Aging: An Annotated Bibliography. Tai S. Kang. (Council on International Studies & Programs Special Studies: No. 153). 92p. 1986. pap. text ed. 10.00 (*0-924197-04-8*, 153) SUNYB Coun Intl Studies.

Studies in Miscue Analysis: An Annotated Bibliography. Kenneth S. Goodman et al. (Orig.). 1996. pap. 20.95 (*0-87207-238-X*) Intl Reading.

Studies in Modeltheoretic Semantics. Ed. by A. Ter Meulen. (Groningen-Amsterdam Studies in Semantics). x, 206p. 1983. pap. 36.95 (*90-70176-80-7*) Mouton.

Studies in Modern Albanian Literature & Culture. Robert Elsie. 200p. 1996. 28.00 (*0-88033-352-9*) East Eur Monographs.

Studies in Modern Arabic Poetry: Thought & Criticism. Mounah A. Khouri. (Middle Eastern Ser.: No. 16). 120p. (Orig.). 1986. pap. 9.00 (*0-936665-02-5*) Jahan Bk Co.

Studies in Modern Choice-of-Law: Torts, Insurance, Land Titles. Moffatt Hancock. LC 84-80150. xviii, 446p. 1984. lib. bdg. 52.00 (*0-89941-320-X*, 303120) W S Hein.

***Studies in Modern Demitic Languages.** Ed. by Shlomo Izre'el & Shlomo Raz. 250p. Date not set. 90.50 (*90-04-10646-4*) E J Brill.

Studies in Modern German Literature. Otto Heller. LC 67-26748. (Essay Index Reprint Ser.). 1977. 20.95 (*0-8369-0531-8*) Ayer.

Studies in Modern History. George P. Gooch. LC 68-16934. (Essay Index Reprint Ser.). 1977. 23.95 (*0-8369-0482-6*) Ayer.

Studies in Modern Indian Art. R. Paramoo. (Illus.). 246p. 1975. pap. 16.95 (*0-318-36267-8*) Asia Bk Corp.

Studies in Modern Indian Fiction in English, 2 vols., Set. Haydn M. Williams. (Greybird Ser.). 182p. (C). 1975. text ed. 24.00 (*0-88253-652-4*); pap. text ed. 15.00 (*0-88253-651-6*) Ind-US Inc.

S

Studies in Modern Italian History: From the 'Risorgimento' to the Republic. Ed. by Frank J. Coppa. 299p. 1986. text ed. 48.00 (*0-8204-0180-3*) P Lang Pubng.

***Studies in Modern Jewish & Hindu Thought.** Margaret Chatterjee. LC 96-43150. 1997. text ed. 59.95 (*0-312-16594-3*) St Martin.

***Studies in Modern Overseas Chinese History.** Ed. by Yen Ching-Hwang. 272p. 1995. pap. write for info. (*981-210-065-2*, Pub. by Times Academic SI) Intl Spec Bk.

Studies in Modern Portuguese Literature, Vol. 4. 104p. 1971. pap. 7.00 (*0-912788-03-8*) Tulane Romance Lang.

***Studies in Modern Theology & Prayer.** Jakob J. Petuchowski. LC 96-45217. 376p. 1997. 39.95 (*0-8276-0577-3*) JPS Phila.

Studies in Moldovan: The History, Culture, Language, & Contemporary Politics of the People of Moldova. Ed. by Donald L. Dyer. 250p. 1996. 35.00 (*0-88033-351-0*) East Eur Monographs.

Studies in Monastic Theology. Odo Brooke. (Cistercian Studies: No. 37). 1980. 8.95 (*0-87907-837-5*) Cistercian Pubns.

Studies in Mother Infant Interaction. H. Rudolph Schaffer. 1977. text ed. 152.00 (*0-12-622560-5*) Acad Pr.

Studies in Mulk Raj Anand. P. K. Rajan. viii, 122p. 1986. 11.00 (*81-7017-207-1*, Pub. by Abhinav II) S Asia.

Studies in Multilevel Planning, Vol. I: Researches in Decentralisation with Special Reference to District Planning in India. Amitava Mukherjee. Ed. by B. N. Yugandhar. 1990. 48.50 (*81-7026-158-9*, Pub. by Heritage IA) S Asia.

Studies in Multimedia: State-of-the-Art Solutions in Multimedia & Hypertext. Ed. by Susan Stone & Michael Buckland. 263p. 1992. 39.50 (*0-938734-59-8*) Info Today Inc.

Studies in Music. Robin Grey. LC 74-24092. reprint ed. 40.00 (*0-404-12937-4*) AMS Pr.

Studies in Music History: Essays for Oliver Strunk. Ed. by Harold Powers. LC 80-14086. (Illus.). x, 527p. 1980. reprint ed. text ed. 85.00 (*0-313-22501-X*, POSM, Greenwood Pr) Greenwood.

Studies in Music History: Presented to H. C. Robbins Landon. Ed. by Otto Biba & David W. Jones. LC 95-62054. (Illus.). 272p. 1996. 34.95 (*0-500-01696-8*) Thames Hudson.

Studies in Musical Interpretation. Alfred Cortot. (Music Reprint Ser.). 1989. 37.50 (*0-306-79715-1*) Da Capo.

Studies in Musical Sources & Style: Essays in Honor of Jan LaRue. Ed. by Eugene K. Wolf & Edward H. Roesner. LC 90-48347. 555p. 1990. 49.95 (*0-89579-253-2*) A-R Eds.

Studies in Musicology: Essays in History, Style & Bibliography of Music in Memory of Glenn Haydon. Compiled by James W. Pruett. LC 76-7574. (Illus.). 286p. 1976. reprint ed. text ed. 59.75 (*0-8371-8883-0*, PRSM, Greenwood Pr) Greenwood.

Studies in Musicology Two, 1929-1979. Charles Seeger. LC 93-20928. 1994. 75.00 (*0-520-07791-1*) U CA Pr.

Studies in Muslim-Jewish Relations, Vol. 1. Ed. by Ronald L. Nettler. 204p. 1993. text ed. 51.00 (*3-7186-5283-8*, Harwood Acad Pubs) Gordon & Breach.

Studies in Muslim Philosophy. Mahmud S. Saeed. 18.50 (*0-933511-66-3*) Kazi Pubns.

Studies in Muslim Political Thought & Administration. H. K. Sherwani. 14.95 (*0-933511-67-1*) Kazi Pubns.

***Studies in Mycenaean Inscriptions & Dialect 1980-81.** Ed. by Elizabeth Sikkenga. (Orig.). Date not set. pap. text ed. 30.00 (*0-9649410-1-5*) UnivTex Dept Classics.

Studies in Mysticism & Certain Aspects of the Secret Tradition. Arthur E. Waite. 348p. 1970. reprint ed. spiral bd. 17.50 (*0-7873-0919-2*) Hlth Research.

Studies in Mysticism & Certain Aspects of the Secret Tradition (1906) Arthur E. Waite. 360p. 1996. pap. 29.95 (*1-56459-670-2*) Kessinger Pub.

Studies in Napoleonic Statesmanship: Germany. Herbert A. Fisher. LC 68-25230. (World History Ser.: No. 48). 1969. reprint ed. lib. bdg. 54.95 (*0-8383-0939-9*) M S G Haskell Hse.

Studies in Natural Products Chemistry: Stereoselective Synthesis, Pt. E. A. Rahman. (Studies in Natural Products Chemistry: Vol. 8). 500p. 1991. 270.50 (*0-444-88967-1*) Elsevier.

Studies in Natural Products Chemistry: Stereoselective Synthesis, Part J, 16. Ed. by A. U. Rahman. 772p. 1995. 484.00 (*0-444-82264-X*) Elsevier.

Studies in Natural Products Chemistry: Structure & Chemistry. Ed. by A. Rahman. (Studies & Natural Products Chemistry: Vol. 7). 528p. 1990. 284.00 (*0-444-88829-2*) Elsevier.

Studies in Natural Products Chemistry: Structure Elucidation, Vol. 5 No. 2. A. Rahman. 1990. 383.75 (*0-444-88336-3*) Elsevier.

***Studies in Natural Products Chemistry Vol. 9: Structure & Chemistry, Pt. B.** A. U. Rahman. 632p. 1991. 332.25 (*0-444-89165-X*) Elsevier.

***Studies in Natural Products Chemistry Vol. 10: Stereoselective Synthesis, Pt. F.** A. U. Rahman. 718p. 1992. 382.25 (*0-444-89558-2*) Elsevier.

***Studies in Natural Products Chemistry Vol. 11: Stereoselective Selective, Pt. G.** A. U. Rahman. 504p. 1992. 294.00 (*0-444-89744-5*) Elsevier.

***Studies in Natural Products Chemistry Vol. 12: Stereoselective Synthesis, Pt. H.** A. U. Rahman. 528p. 1993. 312.50 (*0-444-89366-0*) Elsevier.

***Studies in Natural Products Chemistry Vol. 13: Bioactive Natural Products, Pt. A.** A. U. Rahman & F. Z. Basha. 694p. 1993. 395.25 (*0-444-89937-5*) Elsevier.

Studies in Natural Products Chemistry, Vol. 14: Stereoselective Synthesis, Pt. 1. Ed. by A. U. Rahman. 938p. 1994. 507.50 (*0-444-81780-8*) Elsevier.

Studies in Natural Products Chemistry, Vol. 4: Stereoselective Synthesis, Part C. Ed. by A. Rahman. 760p. 1989. 345.75 (*0-444-88033-X*) Elsevier.

Studies in Natural Products Chemistry, Volume Three: Stereoselective Synthesis (Part B) A. Rahman. 540p. 1989. 201.25 (*0-444-87298-1*) Elsevier.

Studies in Natural Products Chemistry, Volume 2: Structure Elucidation (Part A) Ed. by A. Rahman. 470p. 1988. 238.25 (*0-444-43038-5*) Elsevier.

Studies in Near Eastern Culture & History. Ed. by James A. Bellamy. (Michigan Series on the Middle East: No. 2). 225p. (Orig.). 1990. pap. 17.95 (*0-932098-22-3*) UM Ctr MENAS.

Studies in Neo-Aramaic. Ed. by Wolfhart Heinrichs. (Harvard Semitic Studies). 225p. 1990. 20.95 (*1-55540-430-8*, 04 04 36) Scholars Pr GA.

Studies in Netherlandic Culture & Literature. Ed. by Martinus A. Bakker & Beverly H. Morrison. (Publications of the American Association for Netherlandic Studies). (Illus.). 260p. 1994. lib. bdg. 49.50 (*0-8191-9466-2*) U Pr of Amer.

Studies in Neurophysiology: Presented to A. K. McIntyre. Ed. by Robert Porter. LC 78-1695. (Illus.). 470p. reprint ed. pap. 134.00 (*0-685-20565-7*, 2030614) Bks Demand.

Studies in Neuropsychology: Selected Papers of Arthur Benton. Arthur L. Benton. Ed. by Otfried Spreen & Louis Costa. (Illus.). 320p. 1985. 45.00 (*0-19-503636-0*) OUP.

Studies in New Age Prediction. John Soric. 70p. 1985. 7.95 (*0-86690-323-2*, S2471-014) Am Fed Astrologers.

Studies in New England Geology: A Memoir in Honor of C. Wroe Wolfe. Ed. by Paul C. Lyons & Arthur H. Brownlow. LC 75-30494. (Geological Society of America, Memoir Ser.: No. 146). (Illus.). 410p. reprint ed. pap. 116.90 (*0-8357-3149-9*, 2039412) Bks Demand.

Studies in Newspaper & Periodical History: 1994 Annual. Ed. by Michael Harris & Tom O'Malley. (Newspaper & Periodical History Ser.). 240p. 1996. text ed. 85.00 (*0-313-29051-2*, Greenwood Pr) Greenwood.

***Studies in Newspaper & Periodical History: 1995 Annual.** Ed. by Michael Harris & Tom O'Malley. (Newspaper & Periodical History Ser.). 272p. 1997. text ed. 89.50 (*0-313-29052-0*, Greenwood Pr) Greenwood.

Studies in Newspaper & Periodical History, 1993. Ed. by Michael Harris. 240p. 1994. text ed. 79.50 (*0-313-29050-4*, Greenwood Pr) Greenwood.

Studies in Nietzsche & the Judaeo-Christian Tradition. Ed. by James C. O'Flaherty et al. LC 84-11963. (Germanic Languages & Literatures Ser.: No. 103). 424p. (C). 1985. lib. bdg. 45.00 (*0-8078-8104-X*) U of NC Pr.

Studies in Nineteenth-Century Literature & Culture, 2 vols., Set. Ed. by Fred Kaplan et al. (Numbered Monographic Series, 1992). 1992. write for info. (*0-404-64350-7*) AMS Pr.

Studies in Non-Determining Psychology. Ed. by Gerald N. Epstein. 294p. 1992. pap. 18.00 (*1-883148-02-2*) ACMI Pr.

Studies in Nonlinear Aeroslasticity. E. H. Dowell & M. Ilgamov. (Illus.). 475p. 1988. 85.00 (*0-387-96791-5*) Spr-Verlag.

Studies in Occult Philosophy. G. De Purucker. LC 73-81739. 762p. 1973. reprint ed. 24.00 (*0-911500-52-9*); reprint ed. pap. 16.00 (*0-911500-53-7*) Theos U Pr.

Studies in Occultism. Helena P. Blavatsky. LC 67-18822. 218p. (C). 1980. 13.00 (*0-911500-08-1*) Theos U Pr.

Studies in Occultism. Helena P. Blavatsky. LC 67-18822. 218p. (C). 1987. pap. 8.00 (*0-911500-09-X*) Theos U Pr.

Studies in Occultism Vol. 1, 2 & 3: (1910) H. P. Blavatsky. 200p. 1996. pap. 18.95 (*1-56459-781-4*) Kessinger Pub.

Studies in Occultism No. Two. H. P. Blavatsky. 68p. 1976. reprint ed. spiral bd. 5.50 (*0-7873-0113-2*) Hlth Research.

Studies in Ohio Archaeology. rev. ed. Ed. by Olaf H. Prufer & Douglas H. McKenzie. LC 75-45380. 400p. reprint ed. pap. 114.00 (*0-317-28372-3*, 2025452) Bks Demand.

Studies in Old Babylonian History. Marten Stol. x, 114p. 1976. pap. text ed. 42.00 (*90-6258-040-8*, Pub. by Netherlands Inst NE) Eisenbrauns.

Studies in Old English Fractured "EA" H. Hallovist. (Lund Studies in English: Vol. 14). 1974. reprint ed. pap. 30.00 (*0-8115-0557-X*) Periodicals Srv.

Studies in Old Testament Theology: Historical & Contemporary Images of God & God's People. Ed. by Robert L. Hubbard et al. 1992. 18.99 (*0-8499-0865-5*) Word Pub.

Studies in Operating Systems. R. M. McKeag & R. Wilson. (APIC Ser.). 1976. text ed. 149.00 (*0-12-484350-6*) Acad Pr.

Studies in Optics. unabridged ed. A. A. Michelson. LC 95-10180. (Illus.). 208p. 1995. reprint ed. pap. text ed. 8.95 (*0-486-68700-7*) Dover.

Studies in Organizational Sociology Vol. 10: Essays in Honor of Charles K. Warriner. Ed. by Gale Miller. LC 91-28828. (Contemporary Studies in Sociology: Vol. 10). 239p. 1984. 73.25 (*1-55938-372-0*) Jai Pr.

Studies in Osteoarthrosis: Pathogenesis, Intervention, Assessment. Ed. by D. J. Lott et al. LC 86-23428. 136p. 1987. text ed. 195.00 (*0-471-91336-7*) Wiley.

Studies in Ottoman Social & Economic History. Halil Inalcik. (Collected Studies: No. CS214). 348p. (C). 1985. reprint ed. lib. bdg. 97.95 (*0-86078-162-3*, Pub. by Variorum UK) Ashgate Pub Co.

Studies in Outdoor Recreation. Robert E. Manning. LC 85-15447. (Illus.). 184p. 1986. pap. text ed. 19.95 (*0-87071-345-0*) Oreg St U Pr.

Studies in Overseas Settlement & Population. Anthony Lemon & Norman C. Pollock. LC 79-42738. 133p. reprint ed. pap. 38.00 (*0-317-30106-3*, 2025274) Bks Demand.

Studies in Paleo-Oceanography: Based on a Symposium Sponsored by the Society of Economic Paleontologists & Mineralogists. Ed. by William W. Hay. LC 74-193155. (Society of Economic Paleontologists & Mineralogists, Special Publication Ser.: No. 2). (Illus.). 222p. reprint ed. pap. 63.30 (*0-685-23794-X*, 2032891) Bks Demand.

Studies in Paleoecology: Report 1979-1981. A. Adolf Seilacher. (Neues Jahrgb. f. Geologie und Palaeontologie Ser.: Vol. 164 1/2). (Illus.). (ENG & GER.). 1982. pap. text ed. 110.00 (*0-945345-33-X*, Pub. by Schweitzerbartsche GW) Lubrecht & Cramer.

Studies in Pascal's Ethics. A. W. Baird. (Archives Internationales D'Histoire des Idees Ser.: No. 16). 108p. 1975. pap. text ed. 47.00 (*90-247-1677-2*, Pub. by M Nijhoff NE) Kluwer Ac.

Studies in Pathogenesis of Brain Lesions in Alzheimer's Disease & Related Disorders. D. Van Gool. No. 94. 136p. (Orig.). 1994. pap. 33.50 (*90-6186-638-3*, Pub. by Leuven Univ BE) Coronet Bks.

***Studies in Pattern Recognition: A Memorial to the Late Professor K. S. Fu.** 200p. 1997. lib. bdg. 42.00 (*981-02-2823-6*) World Scientific Pub.

Studies in Paul's Epistles. Frederic L. Godet. LC 84-7138. 352p. 1984. 15.99 (*0-8254-2723-1*, Kregel Class) Kregel.

Studies in Peace History. Peter Brock. 112p. 1992. pap. text ed. 14.95 (*1-85072-090-8*) Syracuse U Pr.

***Studies in Peerage & Family History.** J. Horace Round. 496p. 1996. reprint ed. pap. 39.95 (*0-614-23502-2*, 5015) Clearfield Co.

Studies in Perception. Ed. by Gerald M. Murch. LC 74-8398. (C). 1976. pap. text ed. write for info. (*0-672-61189-9*, Bobbs) Macmillan.

Studies in Perception: Interrelations in the History of Philosophy & Science. Ed. by Peter K. Machamer & Robert G. Turnbull. LC 77-10857. (Illus.). 577p. 1978. 58.50 (*0-8142-0244-6*) Ohio St U Pr.

***Studies in Perception & Action, Vol. IV.** Ed. by Mark Schmuckler & John M. Kennedy. LC 97-17261. 350p. 1997. pap. write for info. (*0-8058-2872-9*) L Erlbaum Assocs.

Studies in Perception & Action II: Posters Presented at the VIIth International Conference on Event Perception & Action. Ed. by S. Stavros Valenti & John Pittenger. 416p. 1993. pap. 99.95 (*0-8058-1405-1*) L Erlbaum Assocs.

Studies in Perception & Action III, Vol. III. Ed. by Benoit Bardy et al. 464p. 1995. text ed. 99.95 (*0-8058-1867-7*) L Erlbaum Assocs.

Studies in Perfectionism. Benjamin B. Warfield. LC 58-11208. 1958. 19.99 (*0-87552-528-8*, Pub. by Evangelical Pr) Presby & Reformed.

Studies in Persian Art & Architecture. Bernard O'Kane. (Illus.). 334p. 1996. 39.00 (*977-424-370-6*, Pub. by Am Univ Cairo Pr UA) Col U Pr.

Studies in Persian Painting. Ed. by Robert Hillenbrand. (Pembroke Persian Papers). (Illus.). 224p. 1993. text ed. 59.95 (*1-85043-659-2*, Pub. by I B Tauris UK) St Martin.

Studies in Personality, Social & Clinical Psychology: Nonobvious Findings. Russell Eisenman. 106p. (C). 1994. pap. text ed. 19.50 (*0-8191-9674-6*) U Pr of Amer.

Studies in Pessimism. Arthur Schopenhauer. 1988. reprint ed. lib. bdg. 49.00 (*0-7812-0489-5*) Rprt Serv.

Studies in Pessimism. Arthur Schopenhauer. 1903. reprint ed. 49.00 (*0-403-00044-0*) Scholarly.

Studies in Pharmaceutical Economics. Ed. by Mickey C. Smith. LC 96-4736. (Illus.). 682p. 1996. lib. bdg. 79.95 (*0-7890-0062-8*, Pharmctl Prods) Haworth Pr.

Studies in Phenomenology & Psychology. Aron Gurwitsch. (Studies in Phenomenology & Existential Philosophy). 452p. 1966. pap. 19.95 (*0-8101-0592-6*) Northwestern U Pr.

Studies in Philosophical Psychology. (Tulane Studies in Philosophy: No. 13). 147p. 1964. pap. text ed. 41.50 (*90-247-0287-9*, Pub. by M Nijhoff NE) Kluwer Ac.

Studies in Philosophy. Reinhold F. Hoernle. Ed. by Daniel S. Robinson. LC 72-5614. (Essay Index Reprint Ser.). 1977. reprint ed. 24.95 (*0-8369-2992-6*) Ayer.

Studies in Philosophy & in the History of Science. Richard A. Tursman. 220p. 1970. 10.00 (*0-87291-007-5*) Coronado Pr.

Studies in Philosophy & Psychology. Ed. by James H. Tufts et al. LC 75-3153. 1976. reprint ed. 34.50 (*0-404-59159-0*) AMS Pr.

Studies in Philosophy & the History of Philosophy, Vol. 2. Ed. by John K. Ryan. LC 61-66336. 266p. reprint ed. pap. 75.90 (*0-685-17845-5*, 2029505) Bks Demand.

Studies in Philosophy & the History of Philosophy, Vol. 4. Ed. by John K. Ryan. LC 61-66336. 238p. reprint ed. 67.90 (*0-8357-9057-6*, 2017279) Bks Demand.

Studies in Philosophy & the History of Philosophy: Ancients & Moderns, Vol.5. Ed. by John K. Ryan. LC 61-66336. 374p. reprint ed. pap. 106.60 (*0-317-12990-2*, 2017280) Bks Demand.

Studies in Philosophy & Theology. Ed. by Emil C. Wilm. LC 75-3078. reprint ed. 37.50 (*0-404-59079-9*) AMS Pr.

Studies in Philosophy for Children: Harry Stottlemeier's Discovery. Ed. by Ann M. Sharp & Ronald F. Reed. (C). 1991. 59.95 (*0-87722-872-8*); pap. 24.95 (*0-87722-873-6*) Temple U Pr.

Studies in Phonetics. Milan Romportle. (Janua Linguarum, Ser. Major: No. 61). 217p. (C). 1973. text ed. 46.15 (*90-279-2667-0*) Mouton.

Studies in Physical Oceanography, 2 vols., Vol. 2. A. Gordon. 232p. (C). 1972. text ed. 279.00 (*0-677-15170-5*) Gordon & Breach.

Studies in Plant Survival: An Ecophysiological Examination of Plant Distribution. R. M. Crawford. (Illus.). 300p. (C). 1988. pap. text ed. 49.95 (*0-632-01477-6*) Blackwell Sci.

Studies in Platonic Political Philosophy. Leo Strauss et al. Ed. by Thomas L. Pangle. LC 83-5064. 272p. 1984. lib. bdg. 36.00 (*0-226-77703-0*) U Ch Pr.

Studies in Platonic Political Philosophy. Leo Strauss et al. Ed. by Thomas L. Pangle. LC 83-5064. 268p. 1985. pap. text ed. 16.95 (*0-226-77700-6*) U Ch Pr.

Studies in Platonism & Patristic Thought. John Whittaker. (Collected Studies: No. CS201). 354p. (C). 1984. reprint ed. lib. bdg. 97.95 (*0-86078-149-6*, Pub. by Variorum UK) Ashgate Pub Co.

Studies in Play & Games, 21 Vols., Set. Ed. by Brian Sutton-Smith. 1976. 536.00 (*0-405-07912-5*) Ayer.

Studies in Poetic Discourse: Mallarme, Baudelaire, Rimbaud, Holderin. Hans-Jost Frey. Tr. by William Whobrey. (Meridian: Crossing Aesthetics Ser.). 216p. 1996. 39.50 (*0-8047-2469-5*) Stanford U Pr.

Studies in Poetic Discourse: Mallarme, Baudelaire, Rimbaud, Holderlin. Hans-Jost Frey. Tr. by William Whobrey. (Meridian: Crossing Aesthetics Ser.). 216p. (Orig.). 1996. pap. 14.95 (*0-8047-2600-0*) Stanford U Pr.

Studies in Poetics Commemorative Volume, Krystyna Pomorska (1928-1986) Ed. by Elena Semeka-Pankratov. xix, 588p. (RUS.). 1995. 34.95 (*0-89357-256-X*) Slavica.

Studies in Polish Civilization: Selected Papers of the Polish Institute of Arts & Sciences in America, N. Y., 1966. Polish Institute of Arts & Sciences in America Staff. Ed. by Damian Wandycz. 1971. 9.00 (*0-940962-43-8*) Polish Inst Art & Sci.

Studies in Polish Life & History. A. E. Tennant. 1977. lib. bdg. 59.95 (*0-8490-2703-9*) Gordon Pr.

Studies in Political Economy. Anthony Musgrave. LC 67-18581. (Reprints of Economic Classics Ser.). viii, 185p. 1968. reprint ed. 35.00 (*0-678-00337-8*) Kelley.

Studies in Population & Economic Development, 2 vols. B. N. Ghosh. (C). 1987. write for info. (*81-7100-024-X*, Pub. by Deep II) S Asia.

Studies in Population & Economic Development, 2 vols., Set. B. N. Ghosh. (C). 1987. 80.00 (*81-7100-025-8*, Pub. by Deep II) S Asia.

Studies in Portuguese Literature. A. F. Bell. 1972. 250.00 (*0-87968-243-4*) Gordon Pr.

Studies in Portuguese Literature & History in Honour of Luis de Sousa Rebelo. Ed. by Helder Macedo. (Monografias A Ser.: No. 147). (Illus.). 208p. (POR.). (C). 1993. 63.00 (*1-85566-012-1*) Boydell & Brewer.

Studies in Positive & Normative Economics. Martin J. Bailey. (Economists of the Twentieth Century Ser.). 320p. 1992. 85.00 (*1-85278-604-3*) E Elgar.

Studies in Post-Impressionism. John Rewald. (Illus.). 296p. 1986. 39.95 (*0-8109-1632-0*) Abrams.

Studies in Post-Medieval Semantics. E. J. Ashworth. (Collected Studies: No. CS227). 342p. (C). 1985. reprint ed. text ed. 98.95 (*0-86078-175-5*, Pub. by Variorum UK) Ashgate Pub Co.

Studies in Power & Class in Africa. Ed. by Irving L. Markovitz. (Illus.). 415p. (C). 1987. pap. text ed. 19.95 (*0-19-504130-5*) OUP.

Studies in Pragma - Dialectics. Ed. by Frans H. Van Eemeren & Rob Grootendorst. (Sic Sat Series in Argumentation & Communication: Vol. 4). 291p. 1994. 24.95 (*90-800777-5-5*, Pub. by SICSAT Pubns NE) Vale Pr.

Studies in Probability Theory. Ed. by Murray Rosenblatt. LC 78-71935. (MAA Studies in Mathematics: Vol. 18). 268p. 1978. 12.00 (*0-88385-118-0*, MAS-18) Math Assn.

Studies in Process Philosophy I. Ed. by R. C. Whittemore. (Tulane Studies in Philosophy: No. 23). 112p. 1974. pap. 33.00 (*0-614-15019-1*, Pub. by M Nijhoff NE) Kluwer Ac.

Studies in Products Chemistry, Vol. 6: Stereoselective Synthesis (Part D) Ed. by A. Rahman. 606p. 1990. 299.50 (*0-444-88566-8*) Elsevier.

Studies in Prose & Poetry. Algernon C. Swinburne. 1977. 17.95 (*0-8369-7331-3*, 8124) Ayer.

Studies in Prose & Verse. Arthur Symons. LC 78-148315. reprint ed. 27.50 (*0-404-07827-3*) AMS Pr.

Studies in Proverbs. William Arnot. LC 78-6014. (Reprint Library). Orig. Title: Laws From Heaven for Life on Earth. 584p. 1986. reprint ed. pap. 16.99 (*0-8254-2123-3*, Kregel Class) Kregel.

Studies in Psalms. Robert R. Taylor, Jr. 1985. pap. 7.50 (*0-89137-560-0*) Quality Pubns.

Studies in Pseudocyphellaria (Lichens) Three: The South American Species. David J. Galloway. (Bibliotheca Lichenologica Ser.: Vol. 46). (Illus.). 319p. 1992. pap. text ed. 112.00 (*3-443-58025-4*) Lubrecht & Cramer.

Studies in Psychical Research. Frank Podmore. LC 75-7393. (Perspectives in Psychical Research Ser.). 1975. reprint ed. 39.95 (*0-405-07042-X*) Ayer.

Studies in Psychology. 2nd ed. William Reich. 1991. pap. 14.00 (*0-536-58075-8*) Ginn Pr.

Studies in Psychology from Smith College see Serial Reactions Considered As Conditioned Reactions

Studies in Psychology from the University of Illinois see On the Melodic Relativity of Tones

Studies in Psychology of Reading. William C. Morse et al. LC 68-54427. (Michigan University Monographs in Education: No. 4). 188p. 1968. reprint ed. text ed. 38.50 (*0-8371-0176-X*, MOPR, Greenwood Pr) Greenwood.

Studies in Psychology of Reading see Studies in the Psychology of Art

Studies in Psychopathology: The Descriptive Psychology Approach. Ed. by Raymond M. Bergner. 256p. (C). 1993. pap. 19.95 (*0-9625661-3-6*) Descriptive Psych Pr.

Studies in Public Administration: The Berkeley-Hong Kong Project, 1988-1989. Ed. by Claudia Phillips. (C). 1992. pap. text ed. 20.00 (*1-880963-00-0*) U of Cal HK Proj.

An Asterisk (*) at the beginning of an entry indicates that the title is appearing in BIP for the first time.

Studies in Public Administration: The Berkeley-Hong Kong Project, 1989-1990. Ed. by Claudia Phillips et al. LC 93-24207. 1993. write for info. (*1-880963-01-9*) U of Cal HK Proj.

Studies in Public Enterprise. V. V. Ramanadham. 275p. 1986. 42.00 (*0-7146-3267-8*, Pub. by F Cass Pubs UK) Intl Spec Bk.

Studies in Public Finance. Edwin R. Seligman. LC 68-58013. (Reprints of Economic Classics Ser.). ix, 302p. 1969. reprint ed. 45.00 (*0-678-00490-0*) Kelley.

Studies in Public Regulation. Ed. by Gary Fromm & Richard Schmalensee. (Regulation of Economic Activity Ser. (REA)). (Illus.). 368p. 1983. pap. 19.95 (*0-262-56028-3*) MIT Pr.

Studies in Punjab Economy. R. S. Johar & J. S. Khanna. 1983. 14.50 (*0-8364-1602-3*, Pub. by Nanak Dev Univ IA) S Asia.

Studies in Pure Mathematics: To the Memory of Paul Turan. Ed. by Paul Erdoes. 400p. 1983. 106.50 (*0-8176-1288-2*) Birkhauser.

Studies in Puritan American Spirituality Vol. V: Early Protestantism & American Culture. Ed. by Michael Schuldiner. 184p. 1996. text ed. 79.95 (*0-7734-8801-4*) E Mellen.

Studies in Puritan American Spirituality, 1993, Vol. IV. Michael Schuldiner. 258p. 1993. text ed. 49.95 (*0-7734-9403-0*) E Mellen.

Studies in Qualitative Methodology, Vol. 4: Issues in Qualitative Research. Ed. by Robert G. Burgess. 296p. Date not set. 73.25 (*0-614-10221-9*) Jai Pr.

Studies in Qualitative Methodology, Vol. 5. Ed. by Robert G. Burgess. 216p. 1984. 73.25 (*1-55938-902-8*) Jai Pr.

Studies in Qualitative Methodology, Vol. 6. Ed. by Robert G. Burgess. 1996. 73.25 (*0-7623-0053-1*) Jai Pr.

Studies in Qualitative Methodology: Issues in Qualitative Research, Vol. 4. Ed. by Robert G. Burgess. 1994. 73.25 (*1-55938-569-3*) Jai Pr.

Studies in Qualitative Methodology: Learning about Fieldwork, Vol. 3. Ed. by Robert G. Burgess. 237p. 1981. 73.25 (*1-55938-246-5*) Jai Pr.

Studies in Qualitative Methodology Vol. 1: Conducting Qualitative Research. Ed. by Robert G. Burgess. 257p. 1988. 73.25 (*0-89232-762-6*) Jai Pr.

Studies in Qualitative Methodology Vol. 2: Reflections on Field Experience. Ed. by Robert G. Burgess. 238p. 1990. 73.25 (*1-55938-023-3*) Jai Pr.

Studies in Qur'an & Tafsir. Ed. by Alford T. Welch. (Journal of the American Academy of Religion. Thematic Issue Ser.: Vol. 47, No. 4S). 143p. reprint ed. pap. 40.80 (*0-7837-5428-0*, 2045193) Bks Demand.

Studies in Radiotherapeutics. Joseph S. Mitchell. LC 60-3368. (Illus.). 281p. 1960. 23.95 (*0-674-84930-2*) HUP.

Studies in Railway Expansion & the Capital Market in England: 1825-73. Seymour Broadbridge. 216p. 1970. 45.00 incl. sl. (*0-7146-1287-1*, Pub. by F Cass Pubs UK) Intl Spec Bk.

Studies in Regional Consciousness & Environment: Essays Presented to H. J. Fleure. Ed. by I. C. Peate. LC 68-26478. (Essay Index Reprint Ser.). (Illus.). 1977. reprint ed. 23.95 (*0-8369-0917-8*) Ayer.

***Studies in Regulation.** Yarrow. Date not set. text ed. 65.00 (*0-312-10647-5*) St Martin.

Studies in Relational Grammar, No. 3. Ed. by Paul M. Postal & Brian D. Joseph. LC 82-6945. (Illus.). 402p. 1990. pap. text ed. 39.00 (*0-226-67573-4*) U Ch Pr.

Studies in Relational Grammar 1. Ed. by David M. Perlmutter. LC 82-6945. xvi, 428p. 1983. lib. bdg. 41.00 (*0-226-66050-8*) U Ch Pr.

Studies in Relational Grammar 1. Ed. by David M. Perlmutter. LC 82-6945. xvi, 428p. 1986. pap. text ed. 19.50 (*0-226-66052-4*) U Ch Pr.

Studies in Relational Grammar 2, No. 2. David M. Perlmutter et al. LC 82-6945. 404p. 1984. 42.00 (*0-226-66051-6*) U Ch Pr.

Studies in Religion. Glyn Richards. LC 95-5584. 1995. text ed. 65.00 (*0-312-12676-X*) St Martin.

Studies in Religious Dualism, 1909 see Shelburne Essays

Studies in Religious Fundamentalism. Ed. by Lionel Caplan. LC 86-30026. 216p. 1988. text ed. 24.50 (*0-88706-518-X*) State U NY Pr.

Studies in Religious Philosophy & Mysticism. Alexander Altmann. (New Reprints in Essay & General Literature Index Ser.). 1977. reprint ed. 26.95 (*0-518-10194-0*) Ayer.

Studies in Remembering: The Reproduction of Connected & Extended Verbal Material. I. H. Paul. (Psychological Issues Monograph: No. 2, Vol. 1, No. 2). 152p. (Orig.). 1959. 27.50 (*0-8236-6240-3*) Intl Univs Pr.

Studies in Renaissance Philosophy & Science. Charles B. Schmitt. (Collected Studies: No. CS146). 342p. (ENG, FRE & ITA.). (C). 1981. reprint ed. text ed. 98.95 (*0-86078-093-7*, Pub. by Variorum UK) Ashgate Pub Co.

Studies in Resource Allocation Process. Ed. by Kenneth J. Arrow & Leonid Hurwicz. LC 76-9171. (Illus.). 576p. 1977. text ed. 99.95 (*0-521-21522-6*) Cambridge U Pr.

Studies in Revelation. Herman A. Hoyt. pap. 7.99 (*0-88469-118-7*) BMH Bks.

Studies in Roman Economic & Social History in Honor of Allan Chester Johnson. Ed. by Paul R. Coleman-Norton. LC 70-80384. (Essay Index Reprint Ser.). 1977. 35.95 (*0-8369-1027-3*) Ayer.

Studies in Roman Law with Comparative View of the Laws of France, England & Scotland. 7th ed. Lord Mackenzie. Ed. by John Kirkpatrick. LC 90-56337. 524p. 1991. reprint ed. 83.00 (*0-912004-88-6*) Gaunt.

Studies in Roman Private Law. Alan Watson. 384p. 1991. boxed 60.00 (*1-85285-047-7*) Hambledon Press.

Studies in Roman Property. Ed. by M. I. Finley. (Cambridge Classical Studies). (Illus.). 192p. 1976. text ed. 29.95 (*0-521-21115-8*) Cambridge U Pr.

Studies in Romance Linguistics: Selected Proceedings from the Linguistic Symposium on Romance Languages, No. XVII. Janet Decasaris. Ed. by Carl Kirschner. LC 89-15585. (Current Issues in Linguistic Theory Ser.: No. 60). xii, 494p. 1989. 130.00 (*90-272-3554-6*) Benjamins North Am.

Studies in Romans. R. C. Bell. 1957. pap. 2.75 (*0-88027-025-X*) Firm Foun Pub.

Studies in Romans. W. Leon Tucker. LC 83-6114. 112p. 1983. reprint ed. pap. 5.99 (*0-8254-3827-6*) Kregel.

Studies in Romans, Vol. 2. Richard A. Brown. (Bible Study Ser.). 1986. pap. 4.50 (*0-8309-0454-9*) Herald Hse.

Studies in Romans 12: The Christian's Sacrifice & Service of Praise. Robert S. Candlish. LC 89-2660. 368p. 1989. reprint ed. pap. 12.99 (*0-8254-2332-5*, Kregel Class) Kregel.

Studies in Russian Literature in Honor of Vsevolod Setchkarev. Ed. by Julian W. Connolly & Sonia I. Ketchian. (Illus.). 288p. (Orig.). 1987. pap. 22.95 (*0-89357-174-1*) Slavica.

Studies in Russian Music. Gerald E. Abraham. LC 68-20285. (Essay Index Reprint Ser.). 1980. 20.95 (*0-8369-0133-9*) Ayer.

Studies in Russian Music. Gerald E. Abraham. 1988. reprint ed. lib. bdg. 49.00 (*0-7812-0107-1*) Rprt Serv.

Studies in Russian Music. Gerald E. Abraham. 1976. reprint ed. lib. bdg. 59.00 (*0-403-03700-X*) Scholarly.

Studies in Ruth. Brenda Robertson. (Bible Study Ser.). (Illus.). 32p. 1988. pap. 4.50 (*0-8309-0523-5*) Herald Hse.

Studies in Sanskrit Syntax. Tr. by Hans H. Hock. (C). 1991. 22.00 (*81-208-0837-1*, Pub. by Motilal Banarsidass II) S Asia.

Studies in Sardinian Archaeology, Vol. II: Sardinia in the Mediterranean. Ed. by Miriam S. Balmuth. (Illus.). 320p. 1986. text ed. 47.50 (*0-472-10081-5*) U of Mich Pr.

Studies in Scarlet. Michael Hardwick et al. (Illus.). 199p. 1989. pap. 19.95 (*0-938501-07-0*) Wessex.

Studies in School Self-Evaluation. Phillip S. Clift et al. 180p. 1987. 55.00 (*1-85000-242-8*, Falmer Pr); pap. 29.00 (*1-85000-241-X*, Falmer Pr) Taylor & Francis.

Studies in Science. Ed. by William C. Coker. LC 77-39098. (Essay Index Reprint Ser.). 1977. reprint ed. 44.95 (*0-8369-2683-8*) Ayer.

Studies in Scottish Business History. Ed. by P. L. Payne. 435p. 1967. 37.50 (*0-7146-1349-5*, Pub. by F Cass Pubs UK) Intl Spec Bk.

Studies in Scottish Business History. Ed. by Peter L. Payne. LC 67-20815. (Illus.). xviii, 435p. 1967. 49.50 (*0-678-05076-7*) Kelley.

***Studies in Scottish Fiction: 1945 to the Present.** Ed. by Susanne Hagemann. LC 96-7279. (Scottish Studies: Vol. 19). 281p. 1996. pap. 54.95 (*0-8204-3160-5*, PR8603) P Lang Pubng.

Studies in Scripture: Acts to Revelation, Vol. 6. Ed. by Robert L. Millet. LC 87-70686. 303p. 1987. 14.95 (*0-87579-084-4*) Deseret Bk.

Studies in Scripture: The Gospels, Vol. 5. Compiled by Kent P. Jackson & Robert L. Millet. LC 86-23981. 492p. 1986. text ed. 15.95 (*0-87579-064-X*) Deseret Bk.

Studies in Scripture, Vol. 1: The Doctrine & Covenants. Ed. by Robert L. Millet & Kent P. Jackson. 615p. 1989. reprint ed. 17.95 (*0-87579-274-X*) Deseret Bk.

Studies in Scripture, Vol. 3: The Old Testament, Genesis to 2 Samuel. Ed. by Kent P. Jackson & Robert L. Millet. 345p. 1989. reprint ed. 15.95 (*0-87579-284-7*) Deseret Bk.

Studies in Scripture, Vol. 4: First Kings to Malachi. Ed. by Kent P. Jackson. LC 93-36633. x, 533p. 1993. 18.95 (*0-87579-789-X*) Deseret Bk.

Studies in Second Corinthians. Don Compier. (Bible Study Ser.). 1987. pap. 4.50 (*0-8309-0479-4*) Herald Hse.

Studies in Second Timothy. Handley C. Moule. LC 77-79182. (Kregel Popular Commentary Ser.). 180p. 1977. kivar 6.99 (*0-8254-3219-7*) Kregel.

Studies in Seicento Art & Theory. Denis Mahon. LC 73-114544. (Illus.). 351p. 1971. reprint ed. text ed. 35.00 (*0-8371-4743-3*, MAST, Greenwood Pr) Greenwood.

***Studies in Seventeenth-Century European Philosophy.** Ed. by M. A. Stewart. (Oxford Studies in the History of Philosophy: No. 2). 272p. 1997. 65.00 (*0-19-823940-8*) OUP.

Studies in Seventeenth Century Imagery, 2 vols. in 1. Manrio Praz. LC 40-3654. reprint ed. 79.00 (*0-403-07208-5*) Somerset Pub.

Studies in Seventeenth-Century Poetic. Ruth C. Wallerstein. (Illus.). 432p. 1964. pap. 7.50 (*0-299-00654-9*) U of Wis Pr.

Studies in Several Literatures. Harry T. Peck. LC 68-16967. (Essay Index Reprint Ser.). 1977. 20.95 (*0-8369-0781-7*) Ayer.

Studies in Sexual Inversion. John A. Symonds. LC 72-9683. reprint ed. 32.50 (*0-404-57503-X*) AMS Pr.

Studies in Shakespeare. 3rd ed. Richard G. White. LC 74-177834. reprint ed. 34.50 (*0-404-06935-5*) AMS Pr.

Studies in Shakespeare. John C. Collins. LC 72-944. reprint ed. 34.50 (*0-404-01637-5*) AMS Pr.

Studies in Shakespeare. Ed. by Arthur D. Matthews & Clark M. Emery. LC 79-144658. reprint ed. 20.00 (*0-404-04267-8*) AMS Pr.

Studies in Shakespeare. Allardyce Nicoll. (BCL1-PR English Literature Ser.). 164p. 1992. reprint ed. lib. bdg. 69.00 (*0-7812-7300-5*) Rprt Serv.

Studies in Shakespeare, Bibliography, & Theatre. James G. McManaway. Ed. by Richard Hosley et al. (Illus.). 417p. 1990. 50.00 (*0-918016-48-7*) Folger Bks.

Studies in Shakespeare, Milton & Donne. Oscar J. Campbell et al. Ed. by Eugene S. McCartney. LC 78-93244. (University of Michigan Publications: Vol. 1). 235p. 1970. reprint ed. 50.00 (*0-87753-020-3*) Phaeton.

Studies in Shakespeare, Milton & Donne. Michigan University, Department of English Staff. LC 65-15881. (Studies in English Literature: No. 33). 1972. reprint ed. lib. bdg. 75.00 (*0-8383-0638-1*) M S G Haskell Hse.

Studies in Shinto Thought, 10 vols., Set. Tsunetsugu Muraoka. Tr. by Delmer M. Brown & James T. Araki. (Documentary Reference Collections). 293p. 1988. 395.00 (*0-318-35981-2*, CMJ05, Greenwood Pr) Greenwood.

Studies in Shinto Thought, 10 vols., Vol. 5. Tsunetsugu Muraoka. Tr. by Delmer M. Brown & James T. Araki. LC 88-21311. (Documentary Reference Collections). 243p. 1988. text ed. 49.95 (*0-313-26555-0*, CNJ05, Greenwood Pr) Greenwood.

Studies in Siberian Ethnogenesis. LC 67-53579. (Arctic Institute of North America-Anthropology of the North; Translation from Russian Sources Ser.: No. 2). 321p. reprint ed. pap. 91.50 (*0-317-10879-4*, 2019172) Bks Demand.

Studies in Sinological Sex: Religion, Racism, & Nationalism, Vol. I: The Patriotism Thesis & Argument in Tokugawa, Japan. Saffa A. Prasad. 71p. 1975. pap. text ed. 21.95 (*0-9597151-0-X*) Transaction Pubs.

Studies in Skanda Purana, Pt. 1: Thesis Accepted for the Ph.D. Degree of the Lucknow University. Abl Awasthi. (C). 1965. 28.00 (*0-8364-2867-6*, Pub. by Manohar II) S Asia.

Studies in Social & General Psychology from the University of Illinois see Mental Measurements of the Blind

Studies in Social & Legal Theories: An Historical Account of the Social, Ethical, Political & Legal Doctrines of the Foremost Ancient & Medieval Philosophers. Meyer B. Barr. 148p. 1982. reprint ed. lib. bdg. 20.00 (*0-8377-0327-1*) Rothman.

Studies in Social Change Since 1948, Vol. 1: Methodological. James A. Davis. (Report Ser.: No. 127-A). 1976. 4.50 (*0-932132-19-7*) Natl Opinion Res.

Studies in Social Change Since 1948, Vol. 2: Substantive. James A. Davis. (Report Ser.: No. 127-B). 1976. 7.00 (*0-932132-20-0*) Natl Opinion Res.

Studies in Social History. Ed. by John H. Plumb. LC 71-80395. (Essay Index Reprint Ser.). 1977. 24.95 (*0-8369-1063-X*) Ayer.

Studies in Social Identity. Theodore R. Sarbin & Karl E. Scheibe. LC 82-16580. 410p. 1983. text ed. 75.00 (*0-275-91073-3*, C1073, Praeger Pubs) Greenwood.

Studies in Social Power. Ed. by Dorwin P. Cartwright. LC 59-63036. 225p. 1959. 12.00 (*0-87944-230-1*) Inst Soc Res.

Studies in Social Psychology in World War II, Prepared & Edited under the Auspices of a Special Committee of the Social Science Research Council: Volume 3 - Experiences on Mass Communication. Carl I. Hovland et al. 355p. reprint ed. pap. 101.20 (*0-317-10520-5*, 2000439) Bks Demand.

Studies in Social Psychology in World War 2, 3 vols. Ed. by Robert K. Merton. LC 73-14180. (Perspectives in Social Inquiry Ser.). 1662p. 1974. reprint ed. 106.95 (*0-405-05523-4*) Ayer.

Studies in South Asian Devotional Literature. Ed. by Alan W. Entwistle & Francoise Mallison. (C). 1994. text ed. 50.00 (*81-7304-095-8*, Pub. by Manohar II) S Asia.

***Studies in South Asian Linguistics: Sinhala & Other South Asian Languages.** James W. Gair. (Illus.). 448p. 1997. 65.00 (*0-19-509521-9*) OUP.

Studies in South Indian Customs, Vol. 2. Ed. by A. V. Murthy. (C). 1992. 19.50 (*0-8364-2765-3*, Pub. by New Era Pubns) S Asia.

Studies in South Indian History & Epigraphy. K. C. Krishnan. (C). 1981. 12.50 (*0-685-48885-3*, Pub. by New Era) S Asia.

Studies in Southern Nigerian History. Ed. by Boniface I. Obichere. 278p. 1982. 45.00 (*0-7146-3106-X*, Pub. by F Cass Pubs UK) Intl Spec Bk.

Studies in Southern Presbyterian Theology. Morton H. Smith. LC 87-7368. 367p. 1987. reprint ed. 11.99 (*0-87552-449-4*, Pub. by Evangelical Pr) Presby & Reformed.

Studies in Soviet Economic Planning. Aron I. Katsenelinboigen. Tr. by Arlo Schultz. LC 77-90277. 245p. reprint ed. pap. 69.90 (*0-317-41954-4*, 2026133) Bks Demand.

Studies in Soviet Thought. Ed. by J. M. Bochenski & Thomas J. Blakeley. (Sovietica Ser.: No. 7). 141p. 1970. lib. bdg. 67.00 (*90-277-0051-6*) Kluwer Ac.

Studies in Spanish-American Literature. Isaac Goldberg. 1972. 59.95 (*0-8490-1149-3*) Gordon Pr.

Studies in Spanish Literature of the Golden Age Presented to Edward M. Wilson. Ed. by R. O. Jones. (Monografias A Ser.: Vol. XXX). 372p. (Orig.). (C). 1973. pap. 46.00 (*0-900411-68-6*, Pub. by Tamesis Bks Ltd UK) Boydell & Brewer.

Studies in Spanish Phonology. Tomas Navarro. Tr. by Richard D. Abraham. LC 68-31043. (Miami Linguistics Ser.: No. 4). 1968. 9.95 (*0-87024-096-X*) U of Miami Pr.

Studies in Spanish Renaissance Thought. Carlos G. Norena. (International Archives of the History of Ideas Ser.: No. 82). 286p. 1975. lib. bdg. 123.50 (*90-247-1727-2*, Pub. by M Nijhoff NE) Kluwer Ac.

Studies in Spinoza: Critical & Interpretative Essays. Ed. by S. Paul Kashap. LC 71-174459. 360p. 1973. pap. 14.00 (*0-520-02590-3*) U CA Pr.

Studies in Spiritism. Amy E. Tanner. LC 93-14161. (Skeptic's Bookshelf Ser.). 408p. 1994. reprint ed. pap. 18.95 (*0-87975-864-3*) Prometheus Bks.

Studies in St. Augustine. John J. O'Meara. 200p. 1996. 65.00 (*1-85182-272-0*, Pub. by Four Cts Pr IE) Intl Spec Bk.

Studies in Starlight: Understanding Our Universe. Charles J. Caes. LC 87-33515. (Illus.). 256p. 1988. pap. 12.95 (*0-8306-2946-7*) McGraw-Hill Prof.

Studies in State & Local Public Finance. Ed. by Harvey S. Rosen. (National Bureau of Economic Research Project Report Ser.). x, 248p. 1986. lib. bdg. 40.00 (*0-226-72621-5*) U Ch Pr.

Studies in Stemmatology. Ed. by Pieter T. Van Reenen & Margot Van Mulken. LC 96-665. xvi, 311p. 1996. 79.00 (*1-55619-507-9*) Benjamins North Am.

Studies in Stock Speculation, 2 vols., 1. H. J. Wolf. LC 65-29150. 1966. reprint ed. pap. 17.00 (*0-87034-017-4*) Fraser Pub Co.

Studies in Stock Speculation, 2 vols., 2. H. J. Wolf. LC 65-29150. 1967. reprint ed. pap. 15.00 (*0-87034-018-2*) Fraser Pub Co.

***Studies in Stomatology & Craniofacial Biology.** Ed. by M. Cohen & B. Baum. LC 96-77470. 500p. (gr. 12). Date not set. 125.00 (*90-5199-283-1*, 283-1) IOS Press.

Studies in Stratigraphy & Paleontology in Honor of Donald W. Fisher. Ed. by Ed Landing. (Bulletin Ser.: No. 481). (Illus.). 380p. 1994. 25.00 (*1-55557-196-4*) NYS Museum.

Studies in Structure of American Economy: Theoretical & Empirical Explorations in Input-Output Analysis. Wassily W. Leontief. LC 76-16433. 562p. (C). (gr. 13). 1977. reprint ed. text ed. 77.95 (*0-87332-086-7*) M E Sharpe.

Studies in Subjective Probability. 2nd ed. Henry E. Kyburg & Howard E. Smokler. LC 79-16294. 272p. 1980. reprint ed. pap. 21.00 (*0-88275-296-0*) Krieger.

Studies in Sublime Failure. Shane Leslie. LC 70-117817. (Essay Index Reprint Ser.). 1977. 23.95 (*0-8369-1670-0*) Ayer.

Studies in Substantive Tax Reform. Ed. by Arthur B. Willis. xv, 183p. Date not set. pap. 20.00 (*0-910058-40-7*, 305040) W S Hein.

Studies in Symbolic Interaction, Vol. 2. Ed. by Norman K. Denzin. 456p. 1979. 73.25 (*0-89232-105-9*) Jai Pr.

Studies in Symbolic Interaction, Vol. 3. Ed. by Norman K. Denzin. 304p. 1981. 73.25 (*0-89232-153-9*) Jai Pr.

Studies in Symbolic Interaction, Vol. 4. Ed. by Norman K. Denzin. 269p. 1982. 73.25 (*0-89232-232-2*) Jai Pr.

Studies in Symbolic Interaction, Vol. 5. Ed. by Norman K. Denzin. 289p. 1984. 73.25 (*0-89232-362-0*) Jai Pr.

Studies in Symbolic Interaction, Vol. 6. Ed. by Norman K. Denzin. 432p. 1986. 73.25 (*0-89232-625-5*) Jai Pr.

Studies in Symbolic Interaction, 2 pts., Vol. 7. Ed. by Norman K. Denzin. 521p. 1987. 5.25 hd 146.50 (*0-89232-743-X*) Jai Pr.

Studies in Symbolic Interaction, Vol. 8. Ed. by Norman K. Denzin. 233p. 1988. 73.25 (*0-89232-719-7*) Jai Pr.

Studies in Symbolic Interaction, Vol. 9. Ed. by Norman K. Denzin. 243p. 1988. 73.25 (*0-89232-934-3*) Jai Pr.

Studies in Symbolic Interaction, 2 pts., Vol. 10. Ed. by Norman K. Denzin. 544p. 1989. Set: Pt. A, 235p.; Pt. B, 309p. 146.50 (*0-89232-974-2*) Jai Pr.

Studies in Symbolic Interaction, Vol. 11. Ed. by Norman K. Denzin. 439p. 1990. 73.25 (*1-55938-100-0*) Jai Pr.

Studies in Symbolic Interaction, Vol. 12. Ed. by Norman K. Denzin. 299p. 1991. 73.25 (*1-55938-395-X*) Jai Pr.

Studies in Symbolic Interaction, Vol. 13. Ed. by Norman K. Denzin. 303p. 1992. 73.25 (*1-55938-479-4*) Jai Pr.

Studies in Symbolic Interaction, Vol. 14. Ed. by Norman K. Denzin. 288p. 1993. 73.25 (*1-55938-579-0*) Jai Pr.

Studies in Symbolic Interaction, Vol. 15. Ed. by Norman K. Denzin. 289p. 1994. 73.25 (*1-55938-764-5*) Jai Pr.

Studies in Symbolic Interaction, Vol. 16. Ed. by Norman K. Denzin. 1994. 73.25 (*1-55938-862-5*) Jai Pr.

Studies in Symbolic Interaction, Vol. 17. Ed. by Norman K. Denzin. 1995. 73.25 (*1-55938-863-3*) Jai Pr.

Studies in Symbolic Interaction, Vol. 18. Ed. by Norman K. Denzin. 282p. 1995. 73.25 (*1-55938-985-0*) Jai Pr.

***Studies in Symbolic Interaction, Vol. 20.** Ed. by Norman K. Denzin. 238p. 1996. 73.25 (*0-7623-0224-0*) Jai Pr.

Studies in Symbolic Interaction: An Annual Compilation of Research, Vol. 1. Norman K. Denzin. 1978. lib. bdg. 73.25 (*0-89232-065-6*) Jai Pr.

Studies in Symbolic Interaction: Original Essays in Symbolic Interaction, Supp. 1: Foundations of Interpretive Sociology: Or. Ed. by Norman K. Denzin. (Studies in Symbolic Interaction: Suppl. 1). 357p. 1985. 73.25 (*0-89232-550-X*) Jai Pr.

Studies in Symbolic Interaction: The Iowa School, Supp. 2. Ed. by Norman K. Denzin. 484p. 1986. 146.50 (*0-89232-552-6*) Jai Pr.

Studies in Symbology. Ronald A. Lidstone. 93p. 1961. reprint ed. spiral bd. 5.50 (*0-7873-0559-6*) Hlth Research.

Studies in Symbology: Astrology, the Tarot, Numerology, the Bible. Ronald A. Lidstone. 1991. lib. bdg. 69.95 (*0-8490-4517-7*) Gordon Pr.

Studies in Symbology: The Tarot, Astrology, the Bible, Numerology. Ronald A. Lidstone. 1991. lib. bdg. 79.95 (*0-8490-4990-3*) Gordon Pr.

Studies in Symbology (1926) Ronald A. Lidstone. 94p. 1996. pap. 14.95 (*1-56459-861-6*) Kessinger Pub.

Studies in Syntactic Typology. Ed. by Michael Hammond et al. LC 88-18632. (Topical Studies in Language: Vol. 17). xiv, 380p. 1988. 103.00 (*1-55619-020-4*) Benjamins North Am.

Studies in Syntax of Mixtecan Languages. Ed. by C. Henry Bradley & Barbara E. Hollenbach. LC 88-60931. (Publications in Linguistics: No. 83). 525p. 1988. fiche 28.00 (*0-88312-473-4*) Summer Instit Ling.

Studies in Syriac Christianity: History, Literature & Theology. Sebastian Brock. (Collected Studies: No. CS357). 350p. 1992. text ed. 89.95 (*0-86078-305-7*, Pub. by Variorum UK) Ashgate Pub Co.

Studies in Systemic Phonology. Ed. by Paul Tench. 256p. 1992. text ed. 75.00 (*0-86187-784-5*) St Martin.

Studies in Tape Reading. Rollo Tape. LC 82-71246. 1982. reprint ed. pap. 15.00 (*0-87034-064-6*) Fraser Pub Co.

S

An Asterisk (*) at the beginning of an entry indicates that the title is appearing in BIP for the first time.

Studies in Targum Jonathan to the Prophets. Pinchas Churgin et al. 59.50 (0-87068-109-5) Ktav.

***Studies in Tasawwuf.** Khaja Khan. 260p. 1996. 12.00 (0-614-21353-3, 1574) Kazi Pubns.

Studies in Teacher Appraisal. Glenn Turner & Phillip S. Clift. 200p. 1988. 65.00 (1-85000-267-3, Falmer Pr); pap. 33.00 (1-85000-268-1, Falmer Pr) Taylor & Francis.

Studies in Tectonic Culture: The Poetics of Construction in Nineteenth & Twentieth Century Architecture. Ed. by Kenneth Frampton & John Cava. LC 95-9812. (Illus.). 608p. 1995. 50.00 (0-262-06173-2) MIT Pr.

Studies in Tertullian & Augustine. Benjamin B. Warfield. LC 73-109980. 412p. 1970. reprint ed. text ed. 35.00 (0-8371-4490-6, WATT, Greenwood Pr) Greenwood.

***Studies in Texan Folklore - Rio Grande Valley: Twelve Folklore Studies with Introductions, Commentaries, & Notes, Lore 1.** Thomas M. Harwell. LC 97-947. 180p. 1997. text ed. 79.95 (0-7734-4208-1) E Mellen.

Studies in Text Grammar. Ed. by J. S. Petoefi & H. Rieser. LC 73-75766. (Foundations of Language Supplementary Ser.: No. 19). 370p. 1973. lib. bdg. 135.00 (90-277-0368-X) Kluwer Ac.

Studies in the Acoustic Characteristics of Hungarian Speech Sounds. Klara Magdics. LC 68-65314. (Uralic & Altaic Ser.: Vol. 97). (Illus.). 141p. 1969. pap. text ed. 12.00 (0-87750-041-X) Res Inst Inner Asian Studies.

Studies in the Acquisition of Anaphora. Ed. by Barbara Lust. 1986. pap. text ed. 57.00 (90-277-2122-X) Kluwer Ac.

Studies in the Acquisition of Anaphora. Ed. by Barbara Lust. (C). 1987. lib. bdg. 146.00 (1-55608-022-0) Kluwer Ac.

Studies in the Acquisition of Anaphoria. Ed. by Barbara Lust. 1986. lib. bdg. 154.50 (90-277-2121-1) Kluwer Ac.

Studies in the African Diaspora: A Memorial to James R. Hooker (1929-1976) Ed. by John P. Henderson & Harry A. Reed. (Illus.). xiv, 162p. (C). 1989. text ed. 39.95 (0-912469-25-0) Majority Pr.

Studies in the Age of Chaucer, Vol. 1. Roy D. Pearcy. 1979. 40.00 (0-933784-00-7) New Chaucer Soc.

Studies in the Age of Chaucer, Vol. 2. Roy J. Pearcy. 1980. 40.00 (0-933784-01-5) New Chaucer Soc.

Studies in the Age of Chaucer, Vol. 3. Roy J. Pearcy. 1981. 40.00 (0-933784-02-3) New Chaucer Soc.

Studies in the Age of Chaucer, Vol. 4. Roy J. Pearcy. 1982. 40.00 (0-933784-03-1) New Chaucer Soc.

Studies in the Age of Chaucer, Vol. 5. Thomas J. Heffernan. 1983. 40.00 (0-937664-64-2) New Chaucer Soc.

Studies in the Age of Chaucer, Vol. 6. T. J. Heffernan. 1984. 40.00 (0-933784-05-8) New Chaucer Soc.

Studies in the Age of Chaucer, Vol. 7. Thomas J. Heffernan. 1985. 40.00 (0-933784-06-6) New Chaucer Soc.

Studies in the Age of Chaucer, Vol. 8. Thomas J. Heffernan. 353p. 1986. 30.00 (0-933784-09-0) New Chaucer Soc.

Studies in the Age of Chaucer, Vol. 9. Thomas J. Heffernan. 1987. 30.00 (0-933784-10-4) New Chaucer Soc.

Studies in the Age of Chaucer, Vol. 10. Thomas J. Heffernan. 1988. 30.00 (0-933784-12-0) New Chaucer Soc.

Studies in the Age of Chaucer, Vol. 11. Thomas J. Heffernan. 1989. 30.00 (0-933784-13-9) New Chaucer Soc.

Studies in the Age of Chaucer, Vol. 12. Thomas J. Heffernan. 1990. 30.00 (0-933784-14-7) New Chaucer Soc.

Studies in the Age of Chaucer, Vol. 13. Ed. by Thomas J. Heffernan. 392p. 1991. 30.00 (0-933784-15-5) New Chaucer Soc.

Studies in the Age of Chaucer, Vol. 14. Ed. by Lisa J. Kiser. 327p. 1992. 30.00 (0-933784-16-3) New Chaucer Soc.

Studies in the Age of Chaucer, Vol. 15. Ed. by Lisa J. Kiser. 413p. 1993. 30.00 (0-933784-17-1) New Chaucer Soc.

Studies in the Age of Chaucer, Vol. 16. Ed. by Lisa J. Kiser. 1994. 30.00 (0-933784-18-X) New Chaucer Soc.

Studies in the Age of Chaucer, Vol. 17. Ed. by Lisa J. Kiser. 390p. 1995. 30.00 (0-933784-19-8) New Chaucer Soc.

***Studies in the Age of Chaucer, Vol. 18.** Ed. by Lisa J. Kiser. 407p. 1996. write for info. (0-933784-20-1) New Chaucer Soc.

Studies in the Age of Chaucer, Proceedings I: York Proceedings. 1985. 30.00 (0-933784-07-4) New Chaucer Soc.

Studies in the Age of Chaucer, Proceedings II: Philadelphia Proceedings. 1987. 30.00 (0-933784-11-2) New Chaucer Soc.

Studies in the Ajanta Paintings. D. Schlingloff. 500p. (C). 1987. 70.00 (81-202-0173-6, Pub. by Ajanta II) S Asia.

Studies in the American Renaissance, 1983. Ed. by Joel Myerson. (Illus.). x, 417p. 1983. text ed. 50.00 (0-8139-0997-X) U Pr of Va.

Studies in the American Renaissance, 1984. Ed. by Joel Myerson. (Illus.). vii, 458p. (C). 1984. text ed. 50.00 (0-8139-1021-8) U Pr of Va.

Studies in the American Renaissance, 1985. Ed. by Joel Myerson. (Illus.). x, 410p. 1985. text ed. 50.00 (0-8139-1060-9) U Pr of Va.

Studies in the American Renaissance 1986. Ed. by Joel Myerson. (Illus.). x, 450p. 1986. text ed. 50.00 (0-8139-1106-0) U Pr of Va.

Studies in the American Renaissance, 1987. Ed. by Joel Myerson. (Illus.). x, 416p. 1987. text ed. 50.00 (0-8139-1114-1) U Pr of Va.

Studies in the American Renaissance, 1988. Ed. by Joel Myerson. (Illus.). 475p. 1989. text ed. 50.00 (0-8139-1164-8) U Pr of Va.

Studies in the American Renaissance, 1989. Ed. by Joel Myerson. (Illus.). 400p. 1990. text ed. 50.00 (0-8139-1230-X) U Pr of Va.

Studies in the American Renaissance, 1991. 15th ed. Ed. by Joel Myerson. (Illus.). 436p. (C). 1992. text ed. 50.00 (0-8139-1337-3) U Pr of Va.

Studies in the American Renaissance, 1992. Ed. by Joel Myerson. (Illus.). 350p. (C). 1992. text ed. 50.00 (0-8139-1389-6) U Pr of Va.

Studies in the American Renaissance, 1993. Ed. by Joel Myerson. 400p. 1993. text ed. 50.00 (0-8139-1453-1) U Pr of Va.

Studies in the American Renaissance 1994. Ed. by Joel Myerson. (Illus.). 370p. (C). 1994. text ed. 50.00 (0-8139-1292-X) U Pr of Va.

Studies in the American Renaissance 1994. Joel Myerson. 1994. text ed. 50.00 (0-8139-1534-1) U Pr of Va.

Studies in the American Renaissance 1995. Joel Myerson. (Illus.). 400p. (C). 1995. text ed. 50.00 (0-8139-1631-3) U Pr of Va.

Studies in the American Renaissance 1996. Ed. by Joel Myerson. (Illus.). 400p. 1996. text ed. 50.00 (0-8139-1663-1) U Pr of Va.

Studies in the Anthropology of Bougainville, Solomon Islands. D. L. Oliver. (HU PMP Ser.). 1974. reprint ed. 30.00 (0-527-01274-2) Periodicals Srv.

***Studies in the Apocalypse.** R. H. Charles. 199p. 1997. pap. 15.00 (0-9653517-9-3) Wipf & Stock.

Studies in the Archaeological History of the Deh Luran Plain: The Excavation of Chagha Sefid. Frank Hole. (Memoirs Ser.: No. 9). (Illus.). 1977. pap. 5.00 (0-932206-71-9) U Mich Mus Anthro.

Studies in the Archaeology of Coastal Yucatan & Campeche, Mexico. (Publications: No. 46). (Illus.). x, 146p. 1978. 25.00 (0-939238-51-9) Tulane MARI.

Studies in the Archaeology of India & Pakistan. Ed. by Jerome Jacobson. 335p. 1986. 45.00 (81-204-0085-2, Pub. by Oxford IBH II) S Asia.

Studies in the Atonement. rev. ed. Robert A. Morey. 320p. reprint ed. pap. write for info. (0-925703-07-9) Crown MA.

Studies in the Augsburg Confession. John Meyer. 1995. 23.99 (0-8100-0571-9, 15N0572) Northwest Pub.

Studies in the Babi & Baha'i Religions Vol. 7: Symbol & Secret: Qur'an Commentary in Baha'u'llah's Kitab-i Iqan. Christopher Buck. LC 62-18891. 1995. pap. 32.50 (0-933770-80-4) Kalimat.

Studies in the Babi & Baha'i Religions Vol. 9: Baha'is in the West. Ed. by Peter Smith. (Illus.). 1996. 32.50 (0-933770-64-2) Kalimat.

Studies in the Babi & Baha'i Religions, Vol. 5: Essays in Honor of the late H. M. Balyuzi. Moojan Mamen. 1989. 32.50 (0-933770-72-3); pap. 24.95 (0-933770-44-8) Kalimat.

Studies in the Babi & Baha'i Religions, Vol. 6: Community Histories. Ed. by Richard V. Hollinger. (Illus.). 1992. 35.00 (0-933770-76-6) Kalimat.

Studies in the Babi & Baha'i Religions, Vol. 7: Symbol & Secret: Qur'an Commentary in Baha'u'llah's Kitab-i Iqan. Christopher Buck. 1995. 42.50 (0-933770-78-2) Kalimat.

Studies in the Bible & Jewish Thought. Moshe Greenberg. LC 93-47361. (JPS Scholar of Distinction Ser.). 1995. 39.95 (0-8276-0504-8) JPS Phila.

Studies in the Biblical Sea-Storm Type-Scene: Convention & Invention. Pamela L. Thimmes. LC 92-27795. 244p. 1992. lib. bdg. 89.95 (0-7734-9939-3) E Mellen.

Studies in the Book of Daniel. Leslie G. Thomas. 1987. pap. 5.95 (0-89137-333-0) Quality Pubns.

Studies in the Book of Esther. Carey A. Moore. 1982. 79.50 (0-87068-718-2) Ktav.

Studies in the Book of Jonah. Karin Almbladh. (Studia Semitica Upsaliensia: No. 7). 54p. (Orig.). 1986. pap. text ed. 25.00 (91-554-1535-0, Pub. by Uppsala Univ Acta Univ Uppsaliensis SW) Coronet Bks.

Studies in the Book of Revelation. John L. Kachelman, Jr. 1989. pap. 7.95 (0-89137-114-1) Quality Pubns.

Studies in the Buddhistic Culture of India. Lalmani Joshi. 500p. (C). 1987. reprint ed. 28.00 (81-208-0281-0, Pub. by Motilal Banarsidass II) S Asia.

Studies in the Byzantine Monetary Economy: 300-1450. Michael Hendy. (Illus.). 596p. 1985. 195.00 (0-521-24715-2) Cambridge U Pr.

Studies in the Calcite Group. William E. Ford. (Connecticut Academy of Arts & Sciences Ser., Trans.: Vol. 22). 1917. pap. 49.50 (0-685-22838-X) Elliots Bks.

Studies in the Chinese Drama. K. Buss. 1977. lib. bdg. 59.95 (0-8490-2704-7) Gordon Pr.

Studies in the Chronology & Regional Style of Old Babylonian Cylinder Seals. Lamia W. Al-Gailani. (Bibliotheca Mesopotamica Ser.: Vol. 23). 166p. 1988. 27.50 (0-685-13464-4); pap. 19.50 (0-685-43552-0) Undena Pubns.

Studies in the Chronology of the Divided Monarchy of Israel. William H. Barnes. 186p. 1991. 29.95 (1-55540-527-4, 04 00 48) Scholars Pr GA.

Studies in the Civil Law & Its Relations to the Law of England & America. William W. Howe. xv, 340p. 1980. reprint ed. lib. bdg. 27.50 (0-8377-0631-9) Rothman.

Studies in the Classical Theories of Money. Karl H. Niebyl. LC 70-173795. reprint ed. 20.00 (0-404-04709-2) AMS Pr.

Studies in the Colonial History of Spanish America. Mario Gongora. LC 74-19524. (Cambridge Latin American Studies: vol. 20). 305p. reprint ed. pap. 87.00 (0-317-28400-2, 2022450) Bks Demand.

Studies in the Comic. B. H. Bronson et al. LC 76-29415. reprint ed. 23.50 (0-404-15324-0) AMS Pr.

Studies in the Contemporary Theatre. John L. Palmer. LC 70-97716. (Essay Index Reprint Ser.). 1977. 20.95 (0-8369-1369-8) Ayer.

Studies in the Control of Radio, Nos. 1-6. Radio Broadcasting Research Project Staff. LC 79-161174. (History of Broadcasting: Radio to Television Ser.). 1977. reprint ed. 31.95 (0-405-03581-0) Ayer.

Studies in the Cult of Yahweh, 2 vols., Set. Morton Smith. Ed. by S. J. Cohen. (Religions in the Graeco-Roman World Ser.: No. 130). 650p. 1995. 135.00 (90-04-10372-4) E J Brill.

Studies in the Cult of Yahweh, Vol. I. Morton Smith. Ed. by Shaye J. Cohen. LC 95-39979. (Religions in the Graeco-Roman World Ser.: No. 130-1). 1995. 79.00 (90-04-10477-1) E J Brill.

Studies in the Cult of Yahweh, Vol. II. Morton Smith. Ed. by Shaye J. Cohen. LC 95-39979. (Religions in the Graeco-Roman World Ser.: No. 130-1). 1996. 84.00 (90-04-10479-8) E J Brill.

Studies in the Culture of Science in France & Britian Since the Enlightment. (Collected Studies: Vol. 501). 320p. 1995. 77.50 (0-86078-498-3, Pub. by Variorum UK) Ashgate Pub Co.

Studies in the Distribution of Income. (Illus.). 79p. (Orig.). (C). 1994. pap. text ed. 25.00 (1-56806-263-X) DIANE Pub.

Studies in the Early History of Judaism, 2 vols., 1. Solomon Zeitlin. 1973. 59.50 (0-87068-208-3) Ktav.

Studies in the Early History of Judaism, 2 vols., 2. Solomon Zeitlin. 1973. 59.50 (0-87068-209-1) Ktav.

Studies in the Early History of Judaism, 3. Solomon Zeitlin. 59.50 (0-87068-278-4) Ktav.

Studies in the Early History of Judaism, 4. Solomon Zeitlin. 59.50 (0-87068-454-X) Ktav.

Studies in the Economic & Social History of Palestine in the 19th & 20th Centuries. Ed. by Roger Owen. LC 82-80662. 271p. 1982. 29.95 (0-8093-1089-9) S Ill U Pr.

Studies in the Economic History of Late Imperial China: Handicraft, Modern Industry, & the State, Vol. 41. Albert Feuerwerker. LC 95-23351. (Michigan Monographs in Chinese Studies: 71). 323p. 1996. text ed. 50.00 (0-89264-117-7) Ctr Chinese Studies.

Studies in the Economic History of Orissa from Ancient Times to 1833. Binod S. Das. 1978. 11.50 (0-8364-0200-6) S Asia.

Studies in the Economic History of Southern Africa, Vol. 1: The Front-Line States. Ed. by Zbigniew A. Konczacki et al. 228p. 1990. text ed. 39.50 (0-7146-3379-8, Pub. by F Cass Pubs UK); pap. text ed. 25.00 (0-7146-4071-9, Pub. by F Cass Pubs UK) Intl Spec Bk.

Studies in the Economic History of Southern Africa, Vol. 2: South Africa, Lesotho & Swaziland. Ed. by Zbigniew A. Konczacki et al. 228p. 1991. text ed. 45.00 (0-7146-3380-1, Pub. by F Cass Pubs UK); pap. text ed. 25.00 (0-7146-4072-7, Pub. by F Cass Pubs UK) Intl Spec Bk.

Studies in the Economic History of the Ohio Valley. Louis C. Hunter. LC 72-98689. (American Scene Ser.). 1973. reprint ed. lib. bdg. 24.50 (0-306-71837-5) Da Capo.

***Studies in the Economic History of the Pacific Rim.** Sally M. Miller & A. J. Latham. LC 96-50306. 280p. (C). 1998. text ed. write for info. (0-415-14819-7) Routledge.

Studies in the Economic Policy of Frederick the Great. William O. Henderson. LC 64-39262. 1963. 35.00 (0-678-05176-3) Kelley.

Studies in the Economics of Aging. Ed. by David A. Wise. (Illus.). 468p. 1994. 65.00 (0-226-90294-3) U Ch Pr.

Studies in the Economics of Central America. Victor Bulmer-Thomas. LC 88-15822. 272p. 1988. text ed. 59.95 (0-312-02395-2) St Martin.

Studies in the Economics of Income Maintenance. Ed. by Otto Eckstein. LC 91-23671. (Brookings Institution, Studies of Government Finance Ser.). 254p. 1977. reprint ed. text ed. 59.75 (0-8371-9488-1, ECTE, Greenwood Pr) Greenwood.

Studies in the Economics of Uncertainty. Ed. by T. B. Fomby & T. K. Seo. (Illus.). 240p. 1989. 65.95 (0-387-97047-9) Spr-Verlag.

Studies in the Elizabethan Drama. Arthur Symons. LC 75-155222. reprint ed. 27.50 (0-404-06331-4) AMS Pr.

Studies in the English Mystery Plays. Charles Davidson. LC 68-752. (Studies in Drama: No. 39). 1969. reprint ed. lib. bdg. 49.95 (0-8383-0536-9) M S G Haskell Hse.

Studies in the Exact Islamic Sciences. E. S. Kennedy. 790p. 1983. text ed. 80.00 (0-8156-6067-7, Am U Beirut) Syracuse U Pr.

***Studies in the Exact Sciences in Medieval Islam.** Ali A. Daffa & John J. Stroyls. LC 83-21847. (Illus.). 253p. reprint ed. pap. 72.20 (0-608-05290-6, 2065828) Bks Demand.

Studies in the Fairy Mythology of Arthurian Romance. L. A. Paton. 1972. 69.95 (0-8490-1150-7) Gordon Pr.

Studies in the First Six Upanisads, & the Isa & Kena Upanisads with the Commentary of Sankara. Srisa C. Vasu. Tr. by Srisa C. Vidyarnava. LC 73-3814. (Sacred Books of the Hindus: No. 22, Pt. 1). reprint ed. 18.00 (0-404-57822-5) AMS Pr.

Studies in the Form of Sirach 44-50. Thomas R. Lee. LC 85-26179. (Society of Biblical Literature Dissertation Ser.). 284p. (C). 1986. 25.95 (0-89130-834-2, 06-01-75); pap. 16.95 (0-89130-835-0, 06 01 75) Scholars Pr GA.

Studies in the Foundations, Methodology & Philosophy of Science, 4 vols. Mario Bunge. Incl. Vol. 3, Pt. 2. Search for Truth. LC 71-163433. (Illus.). viii, 374p. 1967. 77.95 (0-387-03995-3); LC 71-163433. write for info. (0-318-55829-7) Spr-Verlag.

Studies in the Gospel of Thomas. Robert M. Wilson. LC 82-45827. (Orthodoxies & Heresies in the Early Church Ser.). reprint ed. 23.00 (0-404-62374-3) AMS Pr.

Studies in the Grammatical Tradition in Tibet. Roy A. Miller. (Studies in the History of Linguistics: No. 6). xix, 142p. 1976. 39.00 (90-272-0897-2) Benjamins North Am.

Studies in the Greek Negatives. A. C. Moorhouse. xi, 163p. 1959. 9.95 (0-317-06158-5) Bks Intl VA.

Studies in the Greek New Testament: Theory & Practice, Vol. 6. Stanley E. Porter. (Studies in Biblical Greek). 304p. (C). 1995. pap. 32.95 (0-8204-2858-2) P Lang Pubng.

Studies in the Hekanakhte Papers. Hans Goedicke. (Illus.). 154p. (Orig.). 1984. pap. text ed. 24.00 (0-9613805-0-0) Halgo Inc.

Studies in the Himalayan Communities. A. C. Sinha. xxvi, 113p. 1984. 17.00 (1-55528-054-4, Pub. by Today & Tomorrows P & P II) Scholarly Pubns.

Studies in the Historical Geography of Ancient India. O. P. Bharadwaj. (Illus.). xii, 290p. 1986. 27.00 (81-85055-89-0, Pub. by Sundeep Prak II) Nataraj Bks.

Studies in the Historical Phonology of Asian Languages. Ed. by William G. Boltz & Michael C. Joseph. LC 91-34227. (Current Issues in Linguistic Theory Ser.: No. 77). viii, 249p. 1991. 65.00 (1-55619-132-4) Benjamins North Am.

Studies in the History & Archaeology of Jordan, 2 vols., Vol. I. Ed. by Adnan Hadidi. 400p. (C). 1986. lib. bdg. 69.50 (0-7102-0735-2, RKP) Routledge.

Studies in the History & Archaeology of Jordan, 2 vols., Vol. II. Ed. by Adnan Hadidi. 358p. (C). 1986. lib. bdg. 69.50 (0-7102-0734-4, RKP) Routledge.

Studies in the History & Archaeology of Jordan, Vol. III. Ed. by Adnan Hadidi. 300p. 1988. text ed. 99.00 (0-7102-1372-7, RKP) Routledge.

Studies in the History & Method of Science, 2 Vols. Ed. by Charles Singer. LC 74-26291. (History, Philosophy & Sociology of Science Ser.). (Illus.). 1979. reprint ed. 70.95 (0-405-06617-1) Ayer.

***Studies in the History & Topography of Lycia in Memoriam A. S. Hall.** Alan Hall et al. (Illus.). 120p. 1994. 45.00 (1-898249-03-2, Pub. by Brit Inst Arch UK) David Brown.

Studies in the History of Accounting. Ed. by Ananias C. Littleton et al. LC 77-87275. (Development of Contemporary Accounting Thought Ser.). 1978. reprint ed. lib. bdg. 34.95 (0-405-10903-2) Ayer.

Studies in the History of Arabic Grammar II: Proceedings of the Second Symposium on the History of Arabic Grammar, Nijmegen, 27 April-1 May 1987. Ed. by Kees Versteegh & Michael G. Carter. LC 90-457. (Studies in the History of the Language Sciences: Vol. 56). x, 320p. 1990. 74.00 (1-55619-351-3) Benjamins North Am.

Studies in the History of Arabic Logic. Nicholas Rescher. LC 63-17521. 108p. reprint ed. pap. 30.80 (0-317-08256-6, 2010499) Bks Demand.

Studies in the History of Art, Vol. 8. LC 72-600309. (Illus.). 93p. 1978. pap. 8.95 (0-89468-050-1, U Pr of New Eng) Natl Gallery Art.

Studies in the History of Art, Vol. 9. Anne M. Schulz et al. LC 72-600309. (Illus.). 91p. 1980. pap. 8.95 (0-89468-051-X, U Pr of New Eng) Natl Gallery Art.

Studies in the History of Art, Vol. 12. LC 72-600309. (Illus.). 109p. 1982. pap. 8.95 (0-89468-063-3, U Pr of New Eng) Natl Gallery Art.

Studies in the History of Art, Vol. 18. LC 72-600309. (Illus.). 129p. 1985. pap. 8.95 (0-89468-109-5) Natl Gallery Art.

Studies in the History of Art, Vol. 24. LC 72-600309. (Illus.). 180p. 1990. pap. 20.00 (0-89468-115-X, U Pr of New Eng) Natl Gallery Art.

Studies in the History of Art: American Art Around 1900: Lectures in Memory of Daniel Fraad. Linda S. Ferber et al. (Symposium Papers XXI: Vol. 37). (Illus.). 136p. 1990. 15.00 (0-89468-143-5) Natl Gallery Art.

Studies in the History of Art: Claude Lorrain, 1600-1682: A Symposium. Ed. by Pamela Askew. LC 72-600309. (Symposium Papers III: Vol. 14). (Illus.). 91p. 1984. pap. 8.95 (0-89468-153-2, U Pr of New Eng) Natl Gallery Art.

Studies in the History of Art: Cultural Differentiation & Cultural Identity in the Visual Arts. Ed. by Susan J. Barnes & Walter S. Melion. LC 72-600309. (Symposium Papers XII: Vol. 27). (Illus.). 149p. (Orig.). 1989. pap. 18.00 (0-89468-133-8, U Pr of New Eng) Natl Gallery Art.

Studies in the History of Art: El Greco: Italy & Spain. Ed. by Jonathan Brown & Jose M. Andrade. LC 72-600309. (Symposium Papers II: Vol. 13). (Illus.). 188p. 1984. pap. 8.95 (0-89468-068-4) Natl Gallery Art.

Studies in the History of Art: Figures of Thought: El Greco as Interpreter of History, Tradition & Ideas, Vol. 11. Ed. by Jonathan Brown. LC 82-6317. (Illus.). 101p. (Orig.). 1982. pap. 8.95 (0-89468-058-7, U Pr of New Eng) Natl Gallery Art.

Studies in the History of Art: Italian Medals. Ed. by J. Graham Pollard. LC 72-600309. (Symposium Papers VIII: Vol. 21). (Illus.). 299p. 1987. pap. 20.00 (0-89468-106-0, U Pr of New Eng) Natl Gallery Art.

Studies in the History of Art: Italian Plaquettes, Vol. 22. Ed. by Alison Luchs. LC 72-600309. (Illus.). 310p. (Orig.). 1989. pap. 20.00 (0-89468-114-1, U Pr of New Eng) Natl Gallery Art.

Studies in the History of Art: James McNeil Whistler: A Reexamination. Ed. by Ruth E. Fine. LC 72-600309. (Symposium Papers VIII: Vol. 19). (Illus.). 103p. (Orig.). 1987. 10.00 (0-89468-108-7, U Pr of New Eng) Natl Gallery Art.

Studies in the History of Art: Macedonia & Greece in Late Classical & Early Hellenistic Times. Ed. by Beryl Barr-Sharrar & Eugene N. Borza. LC 72-600309. (Symposium Papers I: Vol. 10). (Illus.). 268p. (Orig.). 1982. pap. 8.95 (0-89468-005-6, U Pr of New Eng) Natl Gallery Art.

Studies in the History of Art: Pictorial Narrative in Antiquity & the Middle Ages. Ed. by Herbert L. Kessler & Marianna S. Simpson. LC 72-600309. (Symposium Papers IV: Vol. 116). (Illus.). 181p. (Orig.). 1985. pap. 8.95 (*0-89468-079-X*, U Pr of New Eng) Natl Gallery Art.

Studies in the History of Art: Raphael Before Rome. Ed. by James Beck. LC 72-600309. (Symposium Papers V: Vol. 17). (Illus.). 214p. (Orig.). 1986. pap. 8.95 (*0-89468-080-3*) Natl Gallery Art.

Studies in the History of Art: Retaining the Original: Multiple Originals, Copies, & Reproductions. LC 72-600309. (Symposium Papers VII: Vol. 20). (Illus.). 180p. (Orig.). 1989. pap. 20.00 (*0-89468-113-3*, U Pr of New Eng) Natl Gallery Art.

Studies in the History of Art: Stained Glass Before 1700 in American Collections I, New England & New York. Ed. by Madeline H. Caviness et al. LC 72-600309. (Monograph Series I: Vol. 15). (Illus.). 219p. (Orig.). 1985. pap. 8.95 (*0-89468-078-1*, U Pr of New Eng) Natl Gallery Art.

Studies in the History of Art: Stained Glass Before 1700 in American Collections I, New England & New York. Ed. by Madeline H. Caviness et al. LC 84-22794. (Monograph Series I: Vol. 23). (Illus.). 202p. (Orig.). 1987. pap. 16.95 (*0-89468-110-9*, U Pr of New Eng) Natl Gallery Art.

Studies in the History of Art: Stained Glass Before 1700 in American Collections I, New England & New York. Ed. by Madeline H. Caviness et al. (Monograph Series I: Vol. 28). (Illus.). 250p. (Orig.). 1989. pap. 16.95 (*0-89468-131-1*, U Pr of New Eng) Natl Gallery Art.

Studies in the History of Art: The Architectural Historian in America. Ed. by Elisabeth B. MacDougall. (Symposium Papers XIX: Vol. 35). (Illus.). 316p. 1990. pap. 20.00 (*0-89468-139-7*) Natl Gallery Art.

Studies in the History of Art: The Fashioning & Functioning of the British Country House. Ed. by Gervase Jackson-Stops et al. LC 72-600309. (Symposium Papers XX: Vol. 25). (Illus.). 417p. (Orig.). 1989. pap. 24.95 (*0-89468-128-1*, U Pr of New Eng) Natl Gallery Art.

Studies in the History of Art: The Mall in Washington, 1791-1991. Ed. by Richard Longstreth. (Symposium Papers XIV: Vol. 30). (Illus.). 1991. pap. 39.95 (*0-89468-138-9*, U Pr of New Eng) Natl Gallery Art.

Studies in the History of Art: Winslow Homer: A Symposium. Ed. by Nicolai Cikovsky, Jr. LC 72-600309. (Symposium Papers XI: Vol. 26). (Illus.). 140p. (Orig.). 1989. pap. 25.00 (*0-89468-132-X*, U Pr of New Eng) Natl Gallery Art.

Studies in the History of Art, Vol. 6: 1974. (Illus.). 214p. 1975. pap. 8.95 (*0-89468-024-2*, U Pr of New Eng) Natl Gallery Art.

Studies in the History of Art, Vol. 7: 1975. LC 72-600309. (Illus.). 94p. 1977. pap. 8.95 (*0-89468-049-8*, U Pr of New Eng) Natl Gallery Art.

Studies in the History of Bookbinding. Miriam Foot. 483p. 1993. 109.95 (*0-85967-935-7*, Pub. by Scolar Pr UK) Ashgate Pub Co.

Studies in the History of Business Writing. Ed. by George H. Douglas & Herbert W. Hildebrandt. 224p. (Orig.). 1985. pap. text ed. 12.95 (*0-931874-16-5*) Assn Busn Comm.

Studies in the History of Culture. American Council of Learned Societies. LC 70-86728. (Essay Index Reprint Ser.). 1977. 28.95 (*0-8369-1170-9*) Ayer.

Studies in the History of Educational Opinion from the Renaissance. S. S. Laurie. 261p. 1968. reprint ed. 30.00 (*0-7146-1447-5*, Pub. by F Cass Pubs UK) Intl Spec Bk.

Studies in the History of Educational Opinion from the Renaissance. Simon S. Laurie. LC 72-93272. vi, 261p. 1969. reprint ed. 39.50 (*0-678-05086-4*) Kelley.

Studies in the History of Educational Theory: Artifice & Nature, 1350-1765, Vol. 1. G. A. Bantock. 1980. text ed. 55.00 (*0-04-370092-6*) Routledge Chapman & Hall.

Studies in the History of Educational Theory: The Minds & Masses, 1760-1980, Vol. 2. G. H. Bantock. (Illus.). 368p. 1984. text ed. 55.00 (*0-04-370119-1*) Routledge Chapman & Hall.

Studies in the History of General Relativity: Proceedings of the Second International Conference on the History of General Relativity, Luminy (Marseille), France, 6-9 September 1988. J. Eisenstaedt & A. J. Kox. (Einstein Studies: Vol. 3). (Illus.). 625p. 1991. 161.50 (*0-8176-3479-7*) Birkhauser.

Studies in the History of Ideas, 3 Vols, Set. Ed. by Columbia University, Department of Philosophy Staff. LC 79-130993. reprint ed. 125.00 (*0-404-19510-5*) AMS Pr.

Studies in the History of Indian Philosophy, 3 vols., Set. Ed. by Debiprasad Chattopadhyaya. 1990. 82.00 (*81-7074-063-0*, Pub. by KP Bagchi IA) S Asia.

Studies in the History of Italian Music & Music Theory. Claude V. Palisca. (Illus.). 528p. 1994. 59.00 (*0-19-816167-0*) OUP.

***Studies in the History of Latin American Economic Thought.** Oreste Popescu. LC 96-33540. 360p. (C). 1997. text ed. write for info. (*0-415-14901-0*) Routledge.

Studies in the History of Linguistics: Traditions & Paradigms. Ed. by Dell Hymes. LC 72-88630. (Indiana University Studies in the History & Theory of Linguistics). 530p. 1974. reprint ed. pap. 151.10 (*0-7837-5648-8*, 2059073) Bks Demand.

Studies in the History of Mathematics. Ed. by Esther R. Phillips. LC 87-60581. (Studies in Mathematics: Vol. 26). 320p. 1987. 15.00 (*0-88385-128-8*, MAS-26) Math Assn.

Studies in the History of Medieval Canon Law. Stephan Kuttner. (Collected Studies). 368p. 1990. text ed. 103.95 (*0-86078-274-3*, Pub. by Variorum UK) Ashgate Pub Co.

Studies in the History of Musical Pitch. Alexander J. Ellis. (Music Ser.). 238p. 1981. lib. bdg. 32.50 (*0-306-76020-7*) Da Capo.

Studies in the History of Philosophy & Religion, 2 vols., Vol. 1. Harry A. Wolfson. Ed. by Isadore Twersky & George H. Williams. LC 72-86385. 646p. reprint ed. pap. 180.00 (*0-7837-3929-X*, 2043657) Bks Demand.

Studies in the History of Philosophy & Religion, 2 vols., Vol. 2. Harry A. Wolfson. Ed. by Isadore Twersky & George H. Williams. LC 72-86385. 655p. reprint ed. pap. 180.00 (*0-7837-3930-3*, 2043657) Bks Demand.

Studies in the History of Statistical Method: Special Reference to Certain Educational Problems. Helen M. Walker. LC 74-26304. (History, Philosophy & Sociology of Science Ser.). (Illus.). 1975. reprint ed. 21.95 (*0-405-06628-7*) Ayer.

Studies in the History of the Common Law. S. F. Milsom. 368p. 1985. text ed. 60.00 (*0-907628-61-3*) Hambledon Press.

Studies in the History of the English Feudal Barony. Sidney Painter. LC 78-64191. (Johns Hopkins University. Studies in the Social Sciences. Thirtieth Ser. 1912: 3). reprint ed. 37.50 (*0-404-61298-9*) AMS Pr.

Studies in the History of the Greek Civil War 1945-1949. Ed. by Lars Baerentzen et al. (Modern Greek & Balkin Studies: Suppl. Vol. 2). 324p. (Orig.). 1987. pap. 99.50 (*87-7289-004-5*) Coronet Bks.

Studies in the History of the Near East. P. M. Holt. (Illus.). 261p. 1973. 39.50 (*0-7146-2984-7*, Pub. by F Cass Pubs UK) Intl Spec Bk.

Studies in the History of the Sanhedrin. Hugo Mantel. LC 61-7391. (Harvard Semitic Studies: No. 17). 392p. 1961. reprint ed. pap. 110.90 (*0-7837-4121-9*, 2057944) Bks Demand.

Studies in the History of the Third Dynasty of Vijayanagara. N. Venkata Ramamyya. 568p. 1986. 30.00 (*81-212-0066-0*, Pub. by Gian Publng Hse II) S Asia.

Studies in the History of Worship in Scotland. Ed. by Duncan B. Forrester & Douglas M. Murray. 190p. 1984. pap. 24.95 (*0-567-29349-1*, Pub. by T & T Clark UK) Bks Intl VA.

Studies in the History of Worship in Scotland. 2nd ed. Duncan Forrester & Douglas Murray. 224p. 1996. pap. 24.95 (*0-567-08504-X*, Pub. by T & T Clark UK) Bks Intl VA.

Studies in the Idylls. Henry Elsdale. LC 70-148774. reprint ed. 31.50 (*0-404-08748-5*) AMS Pr.

Studies in the Inner Life of Jesus. A. E. Garvie. 1977. lib. bdg. 69.95 (*0-8490-2705-5*) Gordon Pr.

Studies in the Institutional History of Early Modern Japan. Ed. by John W. Hall & Marius B. Jansen. LC 68-15766. (Illus.). 408p. reprint ed. pap. 116.30 (*0-8357-7891-6*, 2036310) Bks Demand.

Studies in the Instructions of King Amenemhet the First for His Son. Hans Goedicke. (Varia Aegyptiaca Supplement Ser.: No. 2). (Illus.). iv, 78p. (Orig.). 1988. pap. 20.00 (*0-933175-15-9*) Van Siclen Bks.

Studies in the Intellectual History of Tokugawa Japan. Masao Maruyama. Tr. by Mikiso Hane. 424p. (C). 1989. pap. text ed. 24.50 (*0-691-00832-9*) Princeton U Pr.

Studies in the Intellectual History of Tokugawa Japan. Masao Maruyama. Tr. by Mikiso Hane. 422p. 1994. pap. 34.50 (*0-86008-444-2*) Col U Pr.

Studies in the Interrelationship Between Miracles & Laws of Nature. Albert W. Harper. LC 93-19169. 136p. 1993. text ed. 69.95 (*0-7734-9875-3*, Mellen Univ Pr) E Mellen.

***Studies in the Interwar European Economy.** Derek H. Aldcroft. LC 96-40442. 192p. 1997. text ed. 68.95 (*1-85928-360-8*, Pub. by Scolar Pr UK) Ashgate Pub Co.

Studies in the Jewish Background of Christianity. Daniel R. Schwartz. (WissUNT Neuen Testament Ser.: No. 60). 311p. 1992. 137.50 (*3-16-145798-6*, Pub. by J C B Mohr GW) Coronet Bks.

Studies in the Language & Poetics of Anglo-Saxon England. Sherman M. Kuhn. 250p. 1984. pap. 15.50 (*0-89720-067-5*) Karoma.

Studies in the Lankavatara Sutra. D. T. Suzuki. 464p. 1977. reprint ed. 30.00 (*957-638-032-4*) Oriental Bk Store.

Studies in the Late Romances of William Morris. 139p. 1976. pap. 5.00 (*0-931332-00-1*) Wm Morris Soc.

Studies in the Law of Corporation Finance. Adolf A. Berle, Jr. LC 95-77926. (Business Enterprises Reprint Ser.). xvii, 199p. 1995. reprint ed. 55.00 (*0-89941-975-5*, 308840) W S Hein.

Studies in the Law of Landlord & Tenant: The Adams Memorial Essays. Ernest C. Adams & G. W. Hinde. 473p. 1976. boxed 55.00 (*0-409-60640-5*, NZ) MICHIE.

Studies in the Lesser Mysteries. Montagu Powell. 124p. 1971. reprint ed. spiral bd. 7.00 (*0-7873-0675-4*) Hlth Research.

Studies in the Lesser Mysteries (1913) F. G. Powell. 124p. 1996. pap. 16.95 (*1-56459-787-3*) Kessinger Pub.

Studies in the Life & Ministry of the Early Paul & Related Issues. Raymond A. Martin. LC 93-20603. (Biblical Press Ser.: Vol. 11). 264p. 1993. text ed. 89.95 (*0-7734-2368-0*, Mellen Biblical Pr) E Mellen.

Studies in the Life & Ministry of the Historical Jesus. Raymond A. Martin. (Illus.). 172p. (C). 1995. pap. text ed. 23.50 (*0-8191-9773-4*); lib. bdg. 48.00 (*0-8191-9772-6*) U Pr of Amer.

Studies in the Life of Christ: Introduction, the Early Period, the Middle Period, the Final Week. R. C. Foster. LC 94-43411. Orig. Title: Introduction to the Life of Christ. 1995. 34.99 (*0-89900-644-2*) College Pr Pub.

Studies in the Life of Jesus: A Liberal Approach. Rolland E. Wolfe. LC 90-37713. 120p. 1990. pap. text ed. 39.95 (*0-88946-504-5*) E Mellen.

Studies in the Life of John Wesley. E. B. Chappell. 1991. reprint ed. pap. 12.99 (*0-88019-284-4*) Schmul Pub Co.

Studies in the Literary Backgrounds of English Radicalism, with Special Reference to the French Revolution. Martin R. Adams. LC 68-28591. (Illus.). 330p. 1968. reprint ed. text ed. 59.75 (*0-8371-0000-3*, ADSL, Greenwood Pr) Greenwood.

Studies in the Literature of the Great Vehicle: Three Mahayana Buddhist Texts. Ed. by Luis O. Gomez & Jonathan A. Silk. LC 89-60438. (Michigan Studies in Buddhist Literature: No. 1). 240p. 1989. 37.95 (*0-89148-054-4*); pap. 19.95 (*0-89148-055-2*) Ctr S&SE Asian.

Studies in the Logic of Charles Sanders Peirce. Don D. Roberts et al. Ed. by Nathan Houser. LC 96-3853. (Illus.). 704p. 1997. text ed. 49.95 (*0-253-33020-3*) Ind U Pr.

Studies in the Lyric Poems of Friedrich Hebbel. Albert E. Gubelmann. 1912. 69.50 (*0-685-89788-5*) Elliots Bks.

***Studies in the Macroeconomics of Developing Countries.** Mihir Rakshit. (Illus.). 200p. 1997. pap. 9.95 (*0-19-564275-9*) OUP.

Studies in the Management of Government Enterprise. Ed. by Richard J. Horn. (Social Dimensions of Economics Ser.: Vol. 1). 1981. lib. bdg. 50.00 (*0-89838-052-9*) Kluwer Ac.

Studies in the Marvellous. Benjamin P. Kurtz. LC 77-164580. (Studies in Comparative Literature: No. 35). 1972. reprint ed. lib. bdg. 59.95 (*0-8383-1326-4*) M S G Haskell Hse.

Studies in the Massachusetts Franchise, 1631-1691. Richard C. Simmons. (Outstanding Studies in Early American History). 131p. 1989. reprint ed. 15.00 (*0-8240-6178-0*) Garland.

Studies in the Mathematical Theory of Inventory & Production. Kenneth J. Arrow et al. x, 340p. 1958. 49.50 (*0-8047-0541-0*) Stanford U Pr.

Studies in the Meaning of Art. LC 71-138693. (Contemporary Art Ser.). (Illus.). 1972. reprint ed. 18.95 (*0-405-00773-6*) Ayer.

Studies in the Medicine of Ancient India. August F. Hoernle. (C). 1994. reprint ed. 16.00 (*81-7022-137-4*, Pub. by Concept II) S Asia.

Studies in the Medicine of Ancient India, Pt. 1: Osteology, or the Bones of the Human Body. August F. Hoernle. LC 75-23723. reprint ed. 45.00 (*0-404-13281-2*) AMS Pr.

***Studies in the Medieval History of the Yemen & South Arabia.** G. Rex Smith. (Variorum Collected Studies: Vol. 574). 320p. 1997. 94.95 (*0-86078-641-2*, Pub. by Ashgate UK) Ashgate Pub Co.

Studies in the Mesha Inscription & Moab. Ed. by John A. Dearman. LC 89-36493. (Archaeology & Biblical Studies). 324p. 1989. 20.95 (*1-55540-356-5*, 06 17 02) Scholars Pr GA.

Studies in the Mesha Inscription & Moab. Ed. by John A. Dearman. LC 89-36493. (Archaeology & Biblical Studies: No. 2). 324p. 1989. reprint ed. pap. 13.95 (*1-55540-357-3*, 06 17 02) Scholars Pr GA.

Studies in the Metabolism of Vitamin B12. Alfred Doscherholmen. LC 65-12097. 279p. reprint ed. pap. 79.60 (*0-317-27930-0*, 2055856) Bks Demand.

Studies in the Methodology & Foundations of Science: Selected Papers, 1951-1969. Patrick C. Suppes. (Synthese Library: No. 22). 485p. 1969. lib. bdg. 183.00 (*90-277-0020-6*, D Reidel) Kluwer Ac.

Studies in the Middle Way. Christmas Humphreys. 170p. 1984. reprint ed. pap. 6.75 (*0-8356-0307-5*, Quest) Theos Pub Hse.

Studies in the Middle Way: Being Thoughts on Buddhism Applied. Christmas Humphreys. 176p. (C). 1984. pap. text ed. 16.00 (*0-7007-0171-0*, Pub. by Curzon Press UK) UH Pr.

Studies in the Milton Tradition. John W. Good. LC 73-144619. (Catholic University of America. Studies in Romance Languages & Literature: No. 7). reprint ed. 37.50 (*0-404-02862-4*) AMS Pr.

Studies in the Mind & Art of Robert Browning. J. Fotheringham. LC 72-756. (Studies in Browning: No. 4). 1972. reprint ed. lib. bdg. 75.00 (*0-8383-1416-3*) M S G Haskell Hse.

Studies in the Narrative Method of Defoe. Arthur W. Secord. (BCL1-PR English Literature Ser.). 248p. 1992. reprint ed. lib. bdg. 79.00 (*0-7812-7342-0*) Rprt Serv.

Studies in the National Balance Sheet of the United States, 2 Vols, 1. Raymond W. Goldsmith et al. (Studies in Capital Formation & Financing: No. 11). 1963. 38.50 (*0-686-66494-9*, Princeton U Pr) NAL-Dutton.

Studies in the National Balance Sheet of the United States, 2 Vols, 2. Raymond W. Goldsmith et al. (Studies in Capital Formation & Financing: No. 11). 1963. 38.50 (*0-686-66495-7*, Princeton U Pr) NAL-Dutton.

Studies in the National Balance Sheet of the United States, 2 Vols, Set. Raymond W. Goldsmith et al. (Studies in Capital Formation & Financing: No. 11). 1963. 70.00 (*0-317-00254-6*) NAL-Dutton.

Studies in the National Balance Sheet of the United States, Vol. 1. Raymond W. Goldsmith. LC 63-7520. 459p. reprint ed. pap. 130.90 (*0-7837-5209-1*, 2044940) Bks Demand.

***Studies in the National Balance Sheet of the United States Vol. 2: Basic Data on Balance Sheets & Fund Flows.** Raymond W. Goldsmith et al. LC 63-7520. 553p. 1963. reprint ed. pap. 157.70 (*0-608-02880-0*, 2063944) Bks Demand.

Studies in the Nature of Character: Studies in Deceit. Hugh Hartshorne & Mark May. LC 74-21415. (Classics in Child Development Ser.: Vol. 1). 440p. 1975. reprint ed. 36.95 (*0-405-06465-9*) Ayer.

Studies in the Natyasastra. G. H. Tarlekar. 1991. reprint ed. text ed. 20.00 (*81-208-0660-3*, Pub. by Motilal Banarsidass II) S Asia.

Studies in the Neurosciences Series. Studies in the Neurosciences Series Staff. Date not set. write for info. (*0-08-044444-X*, Pergamon Pr) Elsevier.

Studies in the New Experimental Aesthetics. Ed. by D. E. Berlyne. LC 74-13600. 348p. reprint ed. 99.20 (*0-8357-9148-3*, 2050704) Bks Demand.

Studies in the New Testament. Frederic L. Godet. LC 84-7137. 408p. 1984. 15.99 (*0-8254-2722-3*, Kregel Class) Kregel.

Studies in the New Testament. Robert G. Hoerber. (Illus.). 144p. (Orig.). (C). 1991. pap. 11.95 (*0-9620063-5-1*) Gods Word.

Studies in the New Testament see Estudios en el Nuevo Testamento

Studies in the Nominal Sentence in Egyptian & Coptic. fac. ed. John B. Callender. LC 83-17961. (University of California Publications: No. 24). 231p. 1984. reprint ed. pap. 65.90 (*0-7837-8134-2*, 2047941) Bks Demand.

Studies in the Old Testament. Frederic L. Godet. LC 84-7143. 352p. 1984. 15.99 (*0-8254-2721-5*, Kregel Class) Kregel.

Studies in the Old Testament Syllabus. Christine J. Dillon. 14p. (YA). 1993. pap. 3.50 (*0-7137-1771-8*, 1903) Hewitt Res Fnd.

Studies in the Paleopathology of Egypt. Marc A. Ruffer. Ed. by Roy L. Moodie. LC 75-23758. reprint ed. 135.00 (*0-404-13364-9*) AMS Pr.

Studies in the Pathology of Radiation Disease. N. Krayevskii & A. Lieberman. LC 64-21692. 1965. 108.00 (*0-08-010772-9*, Pub. by Pergamon Repr UK) Franklin.

Studies in the Pentateuch. Ed. by J. A. Emerton. LC 90-38605. (Supplements to Vetus Testamentum Ser.: Supplement 41). vii, 253p. 1990. 78.50 (*90-04-09195-5*) E J Brill.

Studies in the Perception of Language. Ed. by Willem J. Levelt & G. B. Flores d'Arcais. LC 78-2548. 353p. reprint ed. pap. 100.70 (*0-685-20462-6*, 2029858) Bks Demand.

Studies in the Period of David & Solomon & Other Essays: Papers Read at the International Symposium for Biblical Studies, 6-7 December 1979. Ed. by Tomoo Ishida. LC 82-11183. xvi, 409p. 1982. text ed. 47.50 (*0-931464-16-1*) Eisenbrauns.

Studies in the Philosophy of Kant. Lewis W. Beck. LC 81-7247. (Essay & Monograph Series of the Liberal Arts Press). viii, 242p. 1981. reprint ed. text ed. 55.00 (*0-313-23183-4*, BESK, Greenwood Pr) Greenwood.

Studies in the Philosophy of Religion. Andrew Pringle-Pattison Seth. LC 77-27204. (Gifford Lectures: 1923). reprint ed. 39.00 (*0-404-60474-9*) AMS Pr.

Studies in the Philosophy of the Scottish Enlightenment. Ed. by M. A. Stewart. (Oxford Studies in the History of Philosophy: No. 1). 336p. 1991. pap. 29.95 (*0-19-824966-7*) OUP.

Studies in the Phonology of Asian Languages, Nine: Word Accent in Japanese. Raymond S. Weitzman. LC 73-141215. 128p. 1970. 19.00 (*0-403-04545-2*) Scholarly.

Studies in the Poetry of Nicander. Heather White. viii, 123p. 1987. pap. 46.00 (*90-256-0899-X*, Pub. by A M Hakkert NE) Benjamins North Am.

Studies in the Political & Administrative Systems in Ancient & Medieval India. D. C. Sircar. (C). 1974. text ed. 15.00 (*0-8426-0579-7*, Pub. by Motilal Banarsidass II) S Asia.

Studies in the Pollen Morphology of Indian Heteromerae. P. K. Nair & Sushma Kothari. (Advances in Pollen Spore Research Ser.: Vol. 13). xii, 90p. 1985. 15.00 (*1-55528-055-2*, Messers Today & Tomorrow) Scholarly Pubns.

Studies in the Pollen Morphology of Rosales. Kamlesh Katiyar. Ed. by P. K. Nair. (Advances in Pollen Spore Research Ser.: Vol. 8). (Illus.). 150p. (C). 1982. 15.00 (*0-88065-226-8*, Messers Today & Tomorrow) Scholarly Pubns.

Studies in the Pollen Morphology of South Indian Rubiaceae. P. M. Mathew & Omana Philip. (Advances in Pollen Spore Research Ser.: Vol. 10). viii, 80p. 1983. 20.00 (*1-55528-056-0*, Pub. by Today & Tomorrows P & P II) Scholarly Pubns.

Studies in the Pragmatics of Discourse. Teun A. van Dijk. (Janua Linguarum, Series Major: No. 101). 332p. 1981. 65.40 (*90-279-3249-2*) Mouton.

Studies in the Processing, Marketing & Distribution of Commodities: The Marketing of Bovine Meat & Products: Areas for International Co-Operation. 76p. 1989. 15.00 (*92-1-112272-4*, E.89.II.D.6) UN.

Studies in the Prophecy of Jeremiah. G. Campbell & Morgan. 288p. 1982. 15.99 (*0-8007-0298-0*) Revell.

Studies in the Prose Style of Joseph Addison. J. Lannering. (Essays & Studies on English Language & Literature: Vol. 9). 1974. reprint ed. pap. 25.00 (*0-8115-0207-4*) Periodicals Srv.

Studies in the Psychology of Art. Ed. by Christian A. Ruckwick. Bd. with Experimental Study of Factors Influencing Consonance Judgements. E. G. Bugg. ; Binocular & Monocular Relation in Foveal Dark Adaptations. T. W. Cook. ; Brain Fields & Learning Process. J. A. Gengerelli. ; Practice & Variability: A Study in Psychological Method. Anne Anastasi. (Psychology Monographs General & Applied: Vol. 45). 1974. reprint ed. 55.00 (*0-8115-1444-7*) Periodicals Srv.

Studies in the Psychology of Art, Vol. 2. Ed. by Norman C. Meier. Bd. with Vol. 2. Studies in General Psychology. Ed. by Christian A. Ruckwick. ; Vol. 1. Studies in Psychology of Reading. Ed. by J. Tiffin. ; Etiology of Mental Deficiency. A. J. Rosanoff. (Psychological Monographs General & Applied: Vol. 48). 1974. reprint ed. 55.00 (*0-8115-1447-1*) Periodicals Srv.

S

Studies in the Psychology of Art, Vol. 3. Ed. by Norman C. Meier. LC 73-2977. (Classics in Psychology Ser.). 1976. reprint ed. 15.95 (*0-405-05149-2*) Ayer.

Studies in the Psychology of Art see Differential Forecasts of Achievement & Their Use in Educational Counseling

Studies in the Psychology of Intemperance. G. E. Partridge. Ed. by Gerald N. Grob. LC 80-1244. (Addiction in America Ser.). 1981. reprint ed. lib. bdg. 27.95 (*0-405-13614-5*) Ayer.

Studies in the Puranic Records on Hindu Rites & Customs. R. C. Hazra. (C). 1987. 24.00 (*81-208-0422-8*, Pub. by Motilal Banarsidass II) S Asia.

Studies in the Reign of Tiberius. Robert S. Rogers. LC 77-152601. 181p. 1972. reprint ed. text ed. 52.50 (*0-8371-6036-7*, RORT, Greenwood Pr) Greenwood.

Studies in the Religious Tradition of the Old Testament. Peter Ackroyd. 320p. (C). 1987. 22.95 (*0-334-01560-X*, SCM Pr) TPI PA.

Studies in the Romano-British Villa. Malcolm Todd. LC 79-315069. (Illus.). 244p. reprint ed. pap. 69.60 (*0-317-10627-9*, 2017340) Bks Demand.

Studies in the Schoenbergian Movement in Vienna & the United States: Essays in Honor of Marcel Dick. Ed. by Anne Trenkamp & John G. Suess. LC 89-13821. (Studies in History & Interpretation of Music: Vol. 24). 344p. 1990. lib. bdg. 99.95 (*0-88946-449-9*) E Mellen.

Studies in the Science of Society Presented to Albert Galloway Keller. LC 68-55860. (Essay Index Reprint Ser.). 1977. 39.95 (*0-8369-1157-1*) Ayer.

Studies in the Scientific & Mathematical Philosophy of Charles S. Pierce: Essays by Carolyn Eisele. Ed. by Carolyn Eisele & Richard M. Martin. (Studies in Philosophy). 1979. text ed. 73.85 (*90-279-7808-5*) Mouton.

Studies in the Scriptures, 1947. Arthur W. Pink. 298p. 1982. pap. 13.99 (*0-85151-347-6*) Banner of Truth.

Studies in the Semantic Structure of Hindi, Two. Kali C. Bahl. 1979. 17.50 (*0-8364-0513-7*) S Asia.

Studies in the Sermon on the Great War: Investigations of a Manichaean-Coptic Text from the Fourth Century. Nils A. Pedersen. 512p. 1996. 40.00 (*87-7288-559-9*, Pub. by Aarhus Univ Pr DK) David Brown.

***Studies in the Sermon on the Mount.** Oswald Chambers. 96p. 1995. pap. 7.95 (*0-87508-310-2*, 310) Chr Lit.

Studies in the Sermon on the Mount. D. Martyn Lloyd-Jones. 1971. pap. 25.00 (*0-8028-0036-X*) Eerdmans.

Studies in the Sermon on the Mount: God's Character & the Believer's Conduct. Oswald Chambers. LC 95-46704. 96p. 1996. reprint ed. pap. 7.99 (*1-57293-009-8*) Discovery Hse Pubs.

Studies in the Short Story. 6th ed. Ed. by David Madden & Virgil Scott. LC 83-8590. 540p. (C). 1984. pap. text ed. 22.00 (*0-03-063644-2*) HB Coll Pubs.

Studies in the Social & Economic Development of the Netherlands East Indies, 3 vols. in 1. John S. Furnivall. LC 77-87488. reprint ed. 21.50 (*0-404-16713-6*) AMS Pr.

Studies in the Social & Religious History of the Mediaeval Greek World, 3 vols., Set. Demetrios J. Constantelos. Date not set. 165.00 (*0-89241-511-8*) Caratzas.

Studies in the Social Aspects of the Depression: Social Science Research Council, 13 Vols, Set. Ed. by Alex Baskin. 1972. reprint ed. 219.00 (*0-405-00840-6*) Ayer.

Studies in the Social War: Kiene, Marcks, Haug, Voirol: An Original Anthology. Adolf Kiene. LC 75-7343. (Roman History Ser.). (Illus.). (GER.). 1975. 50.95 (*0-405-07064-0*) Ayer.

Studies in the Sociology of Music. Louis Wildman. (Orig.). (C). 1981. pap. text ed. 8.00 (*0-939630-08-7*) Inst Qual Hum Life.

Studies in the Sociology of Social Problems. Ed. by Joseph Schneider et al. LC 84-14549. (Modern Sociology Ser.). 240p. 1984. pap. 39.50 (*0-89391-450-9*); text ed. 73.25 (*0-89391-053-8*) Ablex Pub.

Studies in the Sociology of Sport. Ed. by Aidan O. Dunleavy et al. LC 82-16807. 402p. (C). 1982. pap. 15.00 (*0-912646-78-0*) Tex Christian.

Studies in the Sources on the History of Pre-Islamic Central Asia. A. J. Harmatta. (Collection of the Sources for the History of Pre-Islamic Central Asia: Vols. 1 & 2). 162p. (ENG, FRE & GER.). (C). 1979. 45.00 (*963-05-2236-5*, Pub. by Akad Kiado HU) St Mut.

Studies in the Structure of the Urban Economy. Edwin S. Mills. LC 71-179873. (Resources for the Future Ser.). (Illus.). 162p. 1972. 15.95 (*0-8018-1367-0*); pap. 9.95 (*0-8018-1595-9*) Johns Hopkins.

Studies in the Syntax of Mixetecan Languages, Vol. 4. Ed. by C. Henry Bradley & Barbara E. Hollenbach. LC 88-60931. x, 438p. 1992. fiche 32.00 (*0-88312-860-8*) Summer Instit Ling.

Studies in the Syntax of Mixtecan Languages, Vol. 2. Ed. by Barbara E. Hollenbach. (Publications in Linguistics: No. 90). 449p. 1990. fiche 36.00 (*0-88312-475-0*) Summer Instit Ling.

Studies in the Syntax of Mixtecan Languages 3. Ed. by Barbara E. Hollenbach & C. Henry Bradley. LC 88-60931. (Publications in Linguistics: No. 105). ix, 502p. (Orig.). 1992. fiche 36.00 (*0-88312-267-7*) Summer Instit Ling.

Studies in the Syntax of the Old English Passive. Louise G. Frary. (LD Ser.: No. 5). 1929. pap. 25.00 (*0-527-00751-X*) Periodicals Srv.

Studies in the Tantras & the Veda. M. P. Pandit. 176p. 1988. text ed. 25.00 (*81-207-0883-0*, Pub. by Sterling Pubs II) Apt Bks.

Studies in the Technological Development of the American Economy During the First Half of the Nineteenth Century. Paul J. Uselding. LC 75-2600. (Dissertations in American Economic History Ser.). (Illus.). 1975. 23.95 (*0-405-07221-X*) Ayer.

Studies in the Text History of the Life & Fables of Aesop. Ben E. Perry. LC 81-13575. (American Philological Association Philological Monographs). 240p. 1981. reprint ed. pap. 23.50 (*0-89130-534-3*, 40 00 07) Scholars Pr GA.

Studies in the Text of Jeremiah. John G. Janzen. LC 73-81265. (Harvard Semitic Monographs: Vol. 6). 256p. reprint ed. pap. 73.00 (*0-317-09145-X*, 2021591) Bks Demand.

Studies in the Text of Matthew Arnold's Prose Works. Edward K. Brown. 1972. 59.95 (*0-8490-1151-5*) Gordon Pr.

Studies in the Textual Tradition of Terence. John N. Grant. (Phoenix Supplementary Volumes Ser.). 272p. 1986. 40.00 (*0-8020-2574-9*) U of Toronto Pr.

Studies in the Theological Ethics of Ernst Troeltsch. Ed. by Max A. Myers & Michael R. LaChat. LC 90-33012. (Toronto Studies in Theology: Vol. 49). 264p. 1991. lib. bdg. 89.95 (*0-88946-923-7*) E Mellen.

Studies in the Theory & Method of New Testament Textual Criticism. Eldon J. Epp & Gordon D. Fee. (Studies & Documents). 336p. 1993. 40.00 (*0-8028-2430-7*) Eerdmans.

Studies in the Theory of Descent, 2 vols. in 1. August Weismann. LC 72-1661. reprint ed. 97.50 (*0-404-08192-4*) AMS Pr.

Studies in the Theory of International Trade. Jacob Viner. LC 65-20928. (Reprints of Economic Classics Ser.). xv, 650p. 1965. reprint ed. 57.50 (*0-678-00122-7*) Kelley.

Studies in the Theory of Money & Capital. Erik R. Lindahl. LC 70-117915. (Reprints of Economic Classics Ser.). (Illus.). 391p. 1970. reprint ed. 45.00 (*0-678-00655-5*) Kelley.

Studies in the Theory of Money, 1690-1776. Douglas Vickers. LC 59-9191. 313p. 1959. 45.00 (*0-678-08048-8*) Kelley.

Studies in the Theory of Welfare Economics. Melvin W. Reder. LC 68-54288. (Columbia University. Studies in the Social Sciences: No. 534). reprint ed. 20.00 (*0-404-51534-7*) AMS Pr.

***Studies in the Use of Fire in Ancient Greek Religion.** William D. Furley. Date not set. write for info. (*0-88143-026-9*) Ayer.

Studies in the Use of Fire in the Ancient Greek Religion. rev. ed. William D. Furley. Ed. by W. R. Connor. LC 80-2650. (Monographs in Classical Studies). (Illus.). 1981. lib. bdg. 29.00 (*0-405-14037-1*) Ayer.

Studies in the Variety of Rabbinic Cultures. Gerson D. Cohen. LC 90-20704. (Scholar of Distinction Ser.). 344p. 1990. text ed. 39.95 (*0-8276-0383-5*) JPS Phila.

Studies in the Vedanta Sutras of Badarayana. Chandra Vasu Srisa. LC 73-3815. (Sacred Books of the Hindus: Vol. 22, Part 2). reprint ed. 18.00 (*0-404-57843-8*) AMS Pr.

Studies in the Vernon Manuscript. Ed. by Derek Pearsall. (Illus.). 249p. 1990. 79.00 (*0-85991-310-4*) Boydell & Brewer.

Studies in the Wagnerian Drama. Henry Krehbiel. LC 76-56860. (Studies in Music: No. 42). 1977. lib. bdg. 52.95 (*0-8383-2137-2*) M S G Haskell Hse.

Studies in the Way of Words. Paul Grice. LC 88-21400. 408p. 1989. 47.50 (*0-674-85270-2*) HUP.

Studies in the Way of Words. Paul Grice. 408p. 1991. pap. 16.95 (*0-674-85271-0*, GRISTX) HUP.

Studies in the Weekly Parashah, Vol. I: Bereishis. Yehuda Nachshoni. Tr. by Shmuel Himelstein from HEB. (ArtScroll Judaica Classics Ser.). 320p. 1988. 22.99 (*0-89906-933-9*); pap. 19.99 (*0-89906-934-7*) Mesorah Pubns.

Studies in the Weekly Parashah, Vol. II: Sh'mos. Yehuda Nachshoni. Tr. by Shmuel Himelstein from HEB. (ArtScroll Judaica Classics Ser.). 296p. 1988. 22.99 (*0-89906-935-5*); pap. 19.99 (*0-89906-936-3*) Mesorah Pubns.

Studies in the Weekly Parashah, Vol. III: Vayikra. Yehuda Nachshoni. Tr. by Shmuel Himelstein from HEB. (ArtScroll Judaica Classics Ser.). 278p. 1989. 22.99 (*0-89906-937-1*); pap. 19.99 (*0-89906-938-X*) Mesorah Pubns.

Studies in the Weekly Parashah, Vol. IV: Bamidbar. Yehuda Nachshoni. Tr. by Raphael Blumberg from HEB. (ArtScroll Judaica Classics Ser.). 296p. 1989. 22.99 (*0-89906-939-8*); pap. 19.99 (*0-89906-940-1*) Mesorah Pubns.

Studies in the Weekly Parashah, Vol. V: Devarim. Yehuda Nachshoni. Tr. by Shmuel Himelstein from HEB. (ArtScroll Judaica Classics Ser.). 256p. 1989. 22.99 (*0-89906-941-X*); pap. 19.99 (*0-89906-942-8*) Mesorah Pubns.

Studies in the Work of Colley Cibber. DeWitt C. Croissant. (English Literature Ser.: No. 33). 1970. reprint ed. pap. 27.95 (*0-8383-0088-X*) M S G Haskell Hse.

Studies in the Yorkshire Coal Industry. Ed. by John Benson & Robert G. Neville. LC 76-11778. xii, 180p. 1976. lib. bdg. 35.00 (*0-678-06793-7*) Kelley.

Studies in the Zohar. Yehuda Liebes. Tr. by Arnold Schwartz & Stephanie Nakache. LC 91-36469. (SUNY Series in Judaica Hermeneutics, Mysticism, & Religion). 262p. 1993. pap. text ed. 19.95 (*0-7914-1190-7*) State U NY Pr.

Studies in the Zohar. Yehuda Liebes. Tr. by Arnold Schwartz & Stephanie Nakache. LC 91-36469. (SUNY Series in Judaica: Hermeneutics, Mysticism, & Religion). 262p. 1993. text ed. 59.50 (*0-7914-1189-3*) State U NY Pr.

Studies in Theatre & Drama. Ed. & Frwd. by Oscar G. Brockett. (De Proprietatibus Litterarum, Ser. Major: No. 23). 217p. 1972. text ed. 56.95 (*90-279-2112-1*) Mouton.

Studies in Theocritus & Other Hellenistic Poets. Heather White. (London Studies in Classical Philology: Vol. 3). (Illus.). 89p. (C). 1979. 24.00 (*90-70265-81-8*, Pub. by Gieben NE) Benjamins North Am.

Studies in Theology. Loraine Boettner. 1947. 8.99 (*0-87552-115-0*, Pub. by Evangelical Pr) Presby & Reformed.

Studies in Theology. Benjamin B. Warfield. 690p. 1988. reprint ed. 27.99 (*0-85151-533-9*) Banner of Truth.

Studies in Theology & Education. John L. Elias. LC 85-9887. 240p. 1986. lib. bdg. 26.50 (*0-89874-841-0*) Krieger.

Studies in Theosophy - Historical & Practical: A Manual for the People (1890) W. J. Colville. 503p. 1996. pap. 33.00 (*1-56459-644-3*) Kessinger Pub.

Studies in Thirteenth Century Justice & Administration. C. A. Meekings. 342p. (C). 1982. text ed. 60.00 (*0-9506882-3-1*) Hambledon Press.

Studies in Thomistic Theology. Ed. by Paul Lockey. 365p. (C). 1996. 32.00 (*0-268-01755-7*); pap. 19.95 (*0-268-01756-5*) Ctr Thomistic.

Studies in Thought & Language. Ed. by Joseph L. Cowan. LC 75-89620. 232p. reprint ed. pap. 66.20 (*0-317-08180-2*, 2022755) Bks Demand.

Studies in Three Literatures: English, Latin & Greek Contrasts & Comparisons. Maurice R. Ridley. LC 78-42. 1977p. 1978. reprint ed. text ed. 49.75 (*0-313-20189-7*, RISTL, Greenwood Pr) Greenwood.

Studies in Tibetan Medicine. Elisabeth Finckh. LC 88-39158. (Illus.). 95p. 1988. pap. 9.95 (*0-937938-61-0*) Snow Lion Pubns.

Studies in Timothy. Noah W. Hutchings. 250p. (Orig.). (C). 1991. pap. 8.95 (*0-9624517-2-X*) Hearthstone OK.

Studies in Titus. Glen Burch. 36p. (Orig.). 1995. pap. 3.00 (*1-880573-25-3*) Grace WI.

Studies in Trade Liberalization: Problems & Prospects for the Industrial Countries. Bela A. Balassa & M. E. Kreinin. LC 67-22889. 362p. reprint ed. pap. 103.20 (*0-317-19827-0*, 2023080) Bks Demand.

Studies in Training & Development, No. 1. Ed. by Richard D. Peterson. (ASTD Research Ser.). 196p. pap. 9.50 (*0-318-13283-4*, &ESTP) Am Soc Train & Devel.

Studies in Troilus: Chaucer's Text, Meter & Diction. Stephen A. Barney. (Medieval Texts & Studies: No. 14). 167p. 1993. 28.00 (*0-937191-45-0*) Colleagues Pr Inc.

Studies in Tropical American Mollusks. Ed. by Frederick M. Bayer & Gilbert L. Voss. LC 70-170142. 1971. 12.00 (*0-87024-230-X*) U of Miami Pr.

Studies in Truth: Explorations in Metaphysics. rev. ed. Roy E. Davis. 128p. 1987. pap. 3.95 (*0-87707-227-2*) CSA Pr.

Studies in Tudor & Stuart Politics & Government, Vol. 4: Papers & Reviews, 1983-1990. Geoffrey R. Elton. 336p. (C). 1992. text ed. 59.95 (*0-521-41832-1*) Cambridge U Pr.

Studies in Turbulence: In Recognition of Contributions by John Lumley. Ed. by T. B. Gatski et al. (Illus.). xvii, 602p. 1991. 144.95 (*0-387-97613-2*) Spr-Verlag.

Studies in Turkish Folklore. Ed. by Ilhan Basgoz & Mark Glazer. (Turkish Studies Ser.: Vol. 1). 232p. (C). 1978. 12.95 (*0-685-29320-3*) IN Univ Turkish.

Studies in Turkish Linguistics. Karl E. Zimmer. LC 86-11777. (Typological Studies in Language: Vol. 8). vi, 294p. 1986. 91.00 (*0-915027-35-6*); pap. 34.95 (*0-915027-36-4*) Benjamins North Am.

Studies in Twentieth-Century Diaries: The Concealed Self. Alex Aronson. LC 90-21050. (Studies in Comparative Literature: Vol. 12). 135p. 1991. lib. bdg. 69.95 (*0-88946-385-9*) E Mellen.

Studies in Typology & Diachrony: Papers Presented to Joseph H. Greenberg on His 75th Birthday. Ed. by William Croft et al. LC 90-356. (Typological Studies in Language: Vol. 20). xxxiv, 243p. 1990. 74.00 (*1-55619-098-0*); pap. 24.95 (*1-55619-099-9*) Benjamins North Am.

Studies in U. S.-Asia Economic Relations. Ed. by Manoranjan Dutta. LC 83-70889. (Acorn Economic Communication Ser.: No. 2). xvi, 578p. 1985. 48.50 (*0-89386-010-7*) Acorn NC.

Studies in Ukrainian History. Jaroslaw Pelenski. 300p. 1993. 42.00 (*0-88033-275-1*, 378) East Eur Monographs.

Studies in Urban Public Sector, India. N. Nageswara Rao. 1985. 30.00 (*0-8364-1386-5*, Pub. by Ashish II) S Asia.

Studies in Utilitarianism. Thomas K. Hearn, Jr. LC 79-151031. (Century Philosophy Ser.). (Orig.). (C). 1971. 29.50 (*0-89197-431-8*); pap. text ed. 10.95 (*0-89197-432-6*) Irvington.

Studies in Uto-Aztecan Grammar: Modern Aztec Grammatical Sketches, Vol. 2. Patricia Beller et al. Ed. by Ronald W. Langacker. LC 78-56488. (Publications in Linguistics: No. 56). 380p. 1979. fiche 16.00 (*0-88312-405-X*) Summer Instit Ling.

Studies in Venetian Social & Economic History. Frederic C. Lane. Ed. by Benjamin G. Kohl & Reinhold C. Mueller. (Collected Studies: No. CS254). (Illus.). 346p. (ENG, FRE & ITA.). (C). 1987. reprint ed. lib. bdg. 97.95 (*0-86078-202-6*, Pub. by Variorum UK) Ashgate Pub Co.

Studies in Viable Cell Immobilization. Colin Webb & George A. Dervakos. (Biotechnology Intelligence Unit Ser.). 170p. 1995. 69.95 (*1-57059-314-0*) R G Landes.

Studies in Victorian Literature. Stanley T. Williams. (BCL1-PR English Literature Ser.). 299p. 1992. reprint ed. lib. bdg. 79.00 (*0-7812-7058-8*) Rprt Serv.

Studies in Village India: Issues in Rural Development. B. N. Yugandhar. (C). 1991. 17.50 (*81-7022-361-X*, Pub. by Concept II) S Asia.

Studies in Walt Whitman's Leaves of Grass. Ed. by Harry R. Warfel. LC 54-8472. 1978. reprint ed. 50.00 (*0-8201-1226-7*) Schol Facsimiles.

Studies in War & Peace. Michael Howard. (Modern Revivals in Military History Ser.). 262p. 1992. 49.95 (*0-7512-0030-1*, Pub. by Gregg Revivals UK) Ashgate Pub Co.

Studies in Weather & Climate. 3rd ed. P. W. Suckling & R. R. Doyon. 220p. (C). 1991. pap. text ed. 29.95 (*0-89892-093-0*) Contemp Pub Co of Raleigh.

Studies in West African Islamic History: The Cultivators of Islam, Vol. 1. Ed. by John R. Willis. (Illus.). 325p. 1979. 45.00 (*0-7146-1737-7*, Pub. by F Cass Pubs UK) Intl Spec Bk.

***Studies in Western Australian History, Vol. I.** Andrew Gill et al. pap. 5.95 (*0-614-25199-0*) Intl Spec Bk.

***Studies in Western Australian History, Vol. II.** Su-Jane Hunt et al. pap. 5.95 (*0-614-25200-8*) Intl Spec Bk.

***Studies in Western Australian History Sheet 2: Great Sandy Desert.** J. S. Beard & M. J. Webb. pap. 14.95 (*0-85564-045-6*, Pub. by Univ of West Aust Pr AT) Intl Spec Bk.

***Studies in Western Australian History Sheet 3: Great Victoria Desert.** J. S. Beard. pap. 14.95 (*0-85564-085-5*, Pub. by Univ of West Aust Pr AT) Intl Spec Bk.

***Studies in Western Australian History Sheet 4: Nullarbor.** J. S. Beard. pap. 14.95 (*0-85564-089-8*, Pub. by Univ of West Aust Pr AT) Intl Spec Bk.

Studies in Words. C. S. Lewis. (Canto Book Ser.). 352p. (C). 1990. pap. text ed. 11.95 (*0-521-39831-2*) Cambridge U Pr.

Studies in World Economics. George D. Cole. LC 67-23195. (Essay Index Reprint Ser.). 1977. 20.95 (*0-8369-0324-2*) Ayer.

Studies in World Public Order. McDougal, Myers S., & Associates Staff et al. 1986. lib. bdg. 280.00 (*0-89838-900-3*) Kluwer Ac.

Studies in 18th Century Literature. L. Ferenczi & M. J. Szenczi. 388p. (ENG & FRE.). (C). 1974. 66.00 (*963-05-0243-7*, Pub. by Akad Kiado HU) St Mut.

Studies, Military & Diplomatic, 1775-1865. Charles F. Adams, Jr. LC 73-150168. (Select Bibliographies Reprint Ser.). 1977. 25.95 (*0-8369-5681-8*) Ayer.

Studies, Military & Diplomatic, 1775-1865. Charles F. Adams. LC 73-150168. (Select Bibliographies Reprint Ser.). 424p. 1982. reprint ed. 22.50 (*0-8290-0474-2*) Irvington.

Studies of a Biographer, 4 vols. in 3, Set. Leslie Stephen. (Anglistica & Americana Ser.: No. 97). 1987. reprint ed. 161.20 (*3-487-07599-7*) G Olms Pubs.

Studies of a Biographer, 4 vols., Set. Leslie Stephen. (BCL1-PR English Literature Ser.). 1992. reprint ed. lib. bdg. 300.00 (*0-7812-7021-9*) Rprt Serv.

Studies of a Biographer, Vol. 3. Leslie Stephen. 1977. 16.95 (*0-8369-7236-8*, 8035) Ayer.

Studies of a Biographer, Vol. 4. Leslie Stephen. 1977. text ed. 16.95 (*0-8369-7346-1*, 8139) Ayer.

Studies of a Booklover. Thomas M. Parrott. LC 67-28763. (Essay Index Reprint Ser.). 1977. 20.95 (*0-8369-0771-X*) Ayer.

Studies of A. J. Wensinck: An Original Arno Press Anthology. Ed. by Kees W. Bolle. LC 77-82275. (Mythology Ser.). 1978. lib. bdg. 19.95 (*0-405-10567-3*) Ayer.

Studies of a Litterateur. George E. Woodberry. (Essay Index Reprint Ser.). 1977. reprint ed. 20.95 (*0-8369-1009-5*) Rprt Serv.

Studies of a Litterateur. George E. Woodberry. (BCL1-PR English Literature Ser.). 328p. 1992. reprint ed. lib. bdg. 89.00 (*0-7812-7022-7*) Rprt Serv.

***Studies of American Plants, Pt. 10.** Paul C. Standley. LC 30-7147. (Field Museum of Natural History, Publication 184, Anthropological Ser.: Vol. 22, No. 2). 66p. 1940. reprint ed. pap. 25.00 (*0-608-03771-0*, 2064594) Bks Demand.

Studies of Arianism: Chiefly Referring to the Character & Chronology of the Reaction Which Followed the Council of Nicaea. 2nd ed. Henry M. Gwatkin. LC 77-84703. reprint ed. 49.50 (*0-404-16110-3*) AMS Pr.

Studies of Azorin: In Memoriam of L. D. Joiner. Lawrence D. Joiner. Ed. by Joseph W. Zdenek. LC 82-60058. 88p. 1982. pap. 7.00 (*0-938972-03-0*) Spanish Lit Pubns.

Studies of Biosynthesis in Escherichia Coli. Richard B. Roberts et al. (Illus.). 521p. 1958. pap. 22.00 (*0-87279-618-3*, 607) Carnegie Inst.

Studies of Birds Killed in Nocturnal Migration. Harrison B. Tordoff & Robert M. Mengel. (Museum Ser.: Vol. 10, No. 1). 44p. 1956. pap. 2.50 (*0-317-04637-3*) U KS Nat Hist Mus.

Studies of Brain Metabolism in Psychiatric Patients: Can Standards Be Drawn? Ed. by H. Agren et al. (Journal of Neural Transmission: Suppl. 37). (Illus.). 100p. 1992. 63.95 (*0-387-82346-8*) Spr-Verlag.

Studies of Carboniferous Crinoids: Oklahoma & Nebraska see Palaeontographica Americana: Vol. 3

Studies of Cellular Function Using Radiotracers. Ed. by Mervyn W. Billinghurst. 272p. 1982. 149.00 (*0-8493-6025-0*, QP519, CRC Reprint) Franklin.

Studies of Congress. Ed. by Glenn R. Parker. LC 84-16993. (Illus.). 586p. reprint ed. pap. 167.10 (*0-8357-8536-X*, 2034839) Bks Demand.

Studies of Contemporary Superstition. William H. Mallock. LC 72-333. (Essay Index Reprint Ser.). 1977. reprint ed. 23.95 (*0-8369-2804-0*) Ayer.

Studies of Development & Change in the Modern World. Ed. by Michael T. Martin & Terry R. Kandal. (Illus.). 480p. (C). 1989. pap. text ed. 23.95 (*0-19-505647-7*) OUP.

Studies of Electron Distributions in Molecules & Crystals. M. Hall et al. (Transactions of the American Crystallographic Association Ser.: Vol. 26). (Illus.). 150p. (Orig.). (C). 1993. pap. text ed. 25.00 (*0-937140-34-1*) Am Crystallographic.

An Asterisk (*) at the beginning of an entry indicates that the title is appearing in BIP for the first time.

Studies of English Mystics. William R. Inge. LC 69-17578. (Essay Index Reprint Ser.). 1977. 18.95 (*0-8369-0081-2*) Ayer.

Studies of English Poets. John W. Mackail. LC 68-25604. (Essay Index Reprint Ser.). 1977. reprint ed. 20.95 (*0-8369-0651-9*) Ayer.

Studies of Food Microstructure. Ed. by O. N. Holcomb & M. Kalab. LC 81-84080. (Illus.). x, 342p. 1981. 49.00 (*0-931288-22-3*) Scanning Microscopy.

Studies of German Prose Fiction in the Age of European Realism. Martin Swales. LC 94-47096. 264p. 1995. text ed. 89.95 (*0-7734-8924-X*) E Mellen.

Studies of Governmental Institutions in Chinese History. Ed. by John L. Bishop. LC 68-17622. (Harvard-Yenching Institute Studies: No. 23). 280p. 1968. pap. 8.50 (*0-674-85110-2*) HUP.

***Studies of Great Composers.** C. Hubert Parry. 376p. Date not set. 26.95 (*0-8369-2852-0*) Ayer.

Studies of Gymnomyzinae: Diptera: Ephydridae, IV: A Revision of the Shore-Fly Genus Hecamede Haliday. Wayne N. Mathis. LC 91-14038. (Smithsonian Contributions to Zoology Ser.: No. 541). (Illus.). 50p. reprint ed. pap. 25.00 (*0-7837-5896-0*, 2045687) Bks Demand.

Studies of Gymnomyzinae Pt. 6: Diptera: Ephydridae: A Revision of the Genus Glenanthe Haliday from the New World. Wayne N. Mathis. LC 94-28014. (Smithsonian Contributions to Zoology Ser.: Vol. 567). 30p. 1994. reprint ed. pap. 25.00 (*0-7837-8868-1*, 2049579) Bks Demand.

Studies of Gymnomyzinae, Diptera, Ephydridae, Pt. 5: A Revision of the Shore-Fly Genus Mosillus Latreille. Wayne N. Mathis et al. LC 93-24454. (Smithsonian Contributions to Zoology Ser.: No. 548). 42p. reprint ed. pap. 25.00 (*0-7837-6416-2*, 2046396) Bks Demand.

Studies of High Temperature Superconductors, Vol. 1. Ed. by A. V. Narlikar. (Illus.). 382p. 1989. text ed. 135.00 (*0-941743-54-3*) Nova Sci Pubs.

Studies of High Temperature Superconductors, Vol. 5. Ed. by A. V. Narlikar. (Illus.). 413p. (C). 1990. text ed. 140.00 (*0-941743-87-X*) Nova Sci Pubs.

Studies of High Temperature Superconductors, Vol. 6. Ed. by A. V. Narlikar. (Illus.). 413p. (C). 1990. text ed. 140.00 (*0-941743-88-8*) Nova Sci Pubs.

Studies of High Temperature Superconductors, Vol. 7. Ed. by A. V. Narlikar. 398p. (C). 1991. text ed. 135.00 (*1-56072-007-7*) Nova Sci Pubs.

Studies of High Temperature Superconductors, Vol. 8. Ed. by A. V. Narlikar. 414p. (C). 1991. text ed. 140.00 (*1-56072-019-0*) Nova Sci Pubs.

Studies of High Temperature Superconductors, Vol. 9. Ed. by A. V. Narlikar. 331p. 1992. 135.00 (*1-56072-061-1*) Nova Sci Pubs.

Studies of High Temperature Superconductors, Vol. 11. Ed. by A. V. Narlikar. (Illus.). 467p. 1993. lib. bdg. 125.00 (*1-56072-132-4*) Nova Sci Pubs.

Studies of High Temperature Superconductors Vol. 12: High Tc Squids & Related Studies. Ed. by A. V. Narlikar. (Illus.). 212p. (C). 1994. lib. bdg. 115.00 (*1-56072-184-7*) Nova Sci Pubs.

Studies of High Temperature Superconductors Vol. 13: HTSC Thin Films. Ed. by A. V. Narlikar. (Illus.). 323p. (C). 1994. lib. bdg. 115.00 (*1-56072-183-9*) Nova Sci Pubs.

Studies of High Temperature Superconductors Vol. 14: Field Penetration & Magnetization of High Temperature Superconductors. Ed. by A. V. Narlikar. (Illus.). 445p. (C). 1994. lib. bdg. 115.00 (*1-56072-182-0*) Nova Sci Pubs.

***Studies of High Temperature Superconductors Vol. 18: Microwave Studies of High Temperature Superconductors, Pt. 2.** Ed. by Anant Narlikar. 265p. 1996. 89.00 (*1-56072-381-5*, QC611) Nova Sci Pubs.

***Studies of High Temperature Superconductors Vol. 23, Pt. I: Hg-Based High Tc Superconductors.** Ed. by Anant Narlikar. 287p. 1997. lib. bdg. 87.00 (*1-56072-472-2*) Nova Sci Pubs.

Studies of High Temperature Superconductors, Vol. 10 Vol. 10: Advances in Research & Applications. Ed. by A. V. Narlikar. 345p. (C). 1992. lib. bdg. 135.00 (*1-56072-087-5*) Nova Sci Pubs.

Studies of High Temperature Superconductors, Vol. 2 Vol. 2: Advances in Research & Applications. Ed. by A. V. Narlikar. (Illus.). 370p. 1989. text ed. 135.00 (*0-941743-55-1*) Nova Sci Pubs.

Studies of High Temperature Superconductors, Vol. 3 Vol. 3: Advances in Research & Applications. Ed. by A. V. Narlikar. (Illus.). 413p. 1989. text ed. 135.00 (*0-941743-56-X*) Nova Sci Pubs.

Studies of High Temperature Superconductors, Vol. 4 Vol. 4: Advances in Research & Applications. Ed. by A. V. Narlikar. (Illus.). 402p. 1989. text ed. 135.00 (*0-941743-57-8*) Nova Sci Pubs.

Studies of Illnesses of Children Followed from Birth to Eighteen Years. Isabelle Valadian et al. (SRCD M Ser.: Vol. 26, No. 3). 1961. 25.00 (*0-527-01590-3*) Periodicals Srv.

Studies of Imitation in Some Latin Authors. Robert E. Colton. xii, 396p. 1995. pap. 80.00 (*90-256-1005-6*, Pub. by A M Hakkert NE) Benjamins North Am.

Studies of Indian Jewish Identity. Ed. by Nathan Katz. (C). 1995. 30.00 (*81-7304-071-0*, Pub. by Manohar II) S Asia.

Studies of Israeli Society: Politics & Society in Israel, Vol. III. Ed. by Ernest Krausz. 400p. 1984. pap. 24.95 (*0-685-43044-8*) Transaction Pubs.

Studies of Land & Agricultural Problems in Taiwan: An Annotated Bibliography. 24p. (Orig.). (C). 1993. pap. text ed. 20.00 (*1-56806-727-5*) DIANE Pub.

Studies of Law in Social Change & Development: Law & Social Enquiry-Case Studies of Research. Ed. by R. Luckham. 1981. 20.00 (*91-7106-181-9*); pap. 12.00 (*91-7106-178-9*) Intl Ctr Law.

Studies of Law in Social Change & Development: Law in the Political Economy of Public Enterprise - African Perspectives. Ed. by Y. Ghai. 1977. 15.00 (*91-7106-117-7*); pap. 10.00 (*91-7106-116-9*) Intl Ctr Law.

Studies of Law in Social Change & Development: Lawyers in the Third World-Comparative & Developmental Perspectives. Ed. by C. J. Dias et al. 1981. 25.00 (*91-7106-179-7*); pap. 12.00 (*91-7106-176-2*) Intl Ctr Law.

Studies of Law in Social Change & Development: Legal Roles in Columbia, No. 4. Ed. by D. O. Lynch. 1981. 14.00 (*91-7106-180-0*); pap. 7.00 (*91-7106-177-0*) Intl Ctr Law.

Studies of Law in Social Change & Development: Urban Legal Problems in Eastern Africa. Ed. by G. W. Kanyeihamba & J. P. McAuslan. 1978. 15.00 (*91-7106-136-3*); pap. 10.00 (*91-7106-135-5*) Intl Ctr Law.

Studies of Magnetic Properties of Fine Particles & Their Relevance to Materials Science: Proceedings of the International Workshop on Studies of Magnetic Properties of Fine Particles & Their Relevance to Materials Science, Rome, Italy, 4-8 November, 1991. Ed. by J. L. Dormann & D. Fiorani. LC 92-20648. (Delta Ser.). 430p. 1992. 215.00 (*0-444-89552-3*, North Holland) Elsevier.

Studies of Mascarene Island Birds. A. W. Diamond. 450p. 1987. 150.00 (*0-521-25808-1*) Cambridge U Pr.

Studies of Mind & Brain. Stephen Grossberg. 660p. 1982. pap. text ed. 65.50 (*90-277-1360-X*, D Reidel); lib. bdg. 165.00 (*90-277-1359-6*, D Reidel) Kluwer Ac.

Studies of Narcosis. Charles E. Overton. Ed. by Robert L. Lipnick. xi, 203p. (C). 1990. 65.00 (*0-412-35240-0*) Wood Lib-Mus.

Studies of Neotropical Caddisflies, XLV: The Taxonomy, Phenology, & Faunistics of the Trichoptera of Antioquia, Columbia. Oliver S. Flint. LC 91-1985. (Smithsonian Contributions to Zoology Ser.: No. 520). (Illus.). 121p. reprint ed. pap. 34.50 (*0-7837-1178-6*, 2041706) Bks Demand.

Studies of Opisthobranchiate Mollusks of the Pacific Coast of North America. Frank MacFarland. Ed. by Howard L. Kessell. (Memoirs of the California Academy of Sciences Ser.: No. 6). (Illus.). 546p. 1966. 25.00 (*0-940228-10-6*) Calif Acad Sci.

Studies of Paris. Edmondo De Amicis. LC 72-3348. (Essay Index Reprint Ser.). 1977. reprint ed. 21.95 (*0-8369-2888-1*) Ayer.

Studies of Parydrinae: Diptera: Ephydridae: A Review of the Genus Brachydeutere Loew from the Oriental, Australian & Oceanian Regions, Pt. 1. Wayne N. Mathis & Kumar D. Ghorpade. LC 84-600345. (Smithsonian Contributions to Zoology Ser.: No. 406). 29p. reprint ed. pap. 25.00 (*0-317-30040-7*, 2025043) Bks Demand.

Studies of Parydrinae: Diptera: Ephydridae: Revision of the Shore Fly Genus Pelinoides Cresson, Pt. 2. Wayne N. Mathis. LC 84-600299. (Smithsonian Contributions to Zoology Ser.: No. 410). 51p. reprint ed. pap. 25.00 (*0-317-30174-8*, 2025356) Bks Demand.

Studies of Passive Clauses. Paul M. Postal. LC 84-26850. (SUNY Series in Linguistics). 271p. 1985. text ed. 29.50 (*0-88706-083-8*) State U NY Pr.

Studies of Play: An Original Anthology. Judith K. Gardner & Howard Gardner. LC 74-21429. (Classics in Child Development Ser.). 198p. 1977. reprint ed. 21.95 (*0-405-06478-0*) Ayer.

Studies of Political Thought from Gerson to Grotius, 1414-1625. John N. Figgis. LC 75-41092. 1976. reprint ed. 37.50 (*0-404-14540-X*) AMS Pr.

Studies of Psychosocial Risk: The Power of Longitudinal Data. Ed. by Michael Rutter. (Illus.). 440p. 1989. 85.00 (*0-521-35330-0*) Cambridge U Pr.

Studies of Reading & Arithmetic in Mentally Retarded Boys. L. Dunn & R. J. Capobianco. (SRCD M Ser.: Vol. 19, No. 1). 1954. pap. 25.00 (*0-527-01560-1*) Periodicals Srv.

Studies of Savages & Sex. Ernest Crawley. Ed. by Theodore Besterman. LC 77-102231. (Select Bibliographies Reprint Ser.). 1977. 29.95 (*0-8369-5116-6*) Ayer.

Studies of Schizophrenia: Papers Read at the World Psychiatric Association Symposium, "Current Concepts of Schizophrenia", London, November, 1972. Ed. by Malcolm H. Lader. LC 76-382728. (British Journal of Psychiatry. Special Publication Ser.: No. 10). 170p. reprint ed. pap. 48.50 (*0-318-34928-0*, 2031465) Bks Demand.

Studies of Shakespeare. Charles Knight. LC 72-171547. reprint ed. 49.50 (*0-404-03733-X*) AMS Pr.

Studies of Small Mammal Populations at Three Sites on the Northern Great Plains. Jaime E. Pefaur & Robert S. Hoffmann. (Occasional Papers: No. 37). 27p. 1975. pap. 1.00 (*0-317-04897-X*) U KS Nat Hist Mus.

Studies of Software Design: ICSE '93 Workshop, Baltimore Maryland, U. S. A., May 17-18, 1993, Selected Papers, Vol. 107. Davd A Lamb. LC 96-8638. (Lecture Notes in Computer Science Ser.). 188p. 1996. pap. 36.00 (*3-540-61285-8*) Spr-Verlag.

Studies of Some of Robert Browning's Poems. F. Walters. LC 79-184648. (Studies in Browning: No. 4). 180p. 1972. reprint ed. lib. bdg. 49.95 (*0-8383-1380-9*) M S G Haskell Hse.

Studies of Sonoran Geology. Ed. by E. Perez-Segura & Cesar Jacques-Ayala. (Special Papers: No. 254). (Illus.). 136p. 1991. pap. 15.00 (*0-8137-2254-3*) Geol Soc.

Studies of South India: An Anthology of Recent Research & Scholarship. Ed. by Robert E. Frykenberg & Pauline Kolenda. 464p. 1986. 32.00 (*0-8364-1675-9*, Pub. by Manohar II) S Asia.

Studies of Suburbanization in Connecticut, 3 vols. Ed. by Richard C. Wade. LC 73-11933. (Illus.). 402p. 1974. reprint ed. 26.95 (*0-405-05427-0*) Ayer.

Studies of Supply & Demand in Higher Education. Ed. by Charles T. Colfelter & Michael Rothschild. LC 92-37932. (National Bureau of Economic Research Project Report Ser.). (Illus.). 304p. (C). 1993. 45.00 (*0-226-11054-0*) U Ch Pr.

Studies of Terelliinae: Diptera: Tephritidae: A Revision of the Genus Neaspilota Osten Sacken. Amnon Freidberg & Wayne N. Mathis. LC 85-600290. (Smithsonian Contribution to Zoology Ser.: No. 439). 79p. reprint ed. pap. 25.00 (*0-317-55745-9*, 2029360) Bks Demand.

Studies of the Book of Mormon. 2nd ed. B. H. Roberts. Ed. by Brigham D. Madsen. LC 92-22758. (Illus.). xxxi, 377p. 1992. pap. 14.95 (*1-56085-027-2*) Signature Bks.

Studies of the Church in History: Essays Honoring Robert S. Paul on His Sixty-Fifth Birthday. Ed. by Horton Davies. LC 83-9715. (Pittsburgh Theological Monographs, New Ser.: No. 5). 276p. (Orig.). 1983. pap. 10.00 (*0-915138-55-7*) Pickwick.

Studies of the Design of Steel Castings & Steel Weldments As Related to Methods of Their Manufacture: Castings vs. Weldments. 1959. 20.00 (*0-686-44993-2*) Steel Founders.

Studies of the Environmental Costs of Electricity. (Illus.). 178p. (Orig.). (C). 1995. pap. text ed. 35.00 (*0-7881-2059-X*) DIANE Pub.

Studies of the Environmental Costs of Electricity. 1996. lib. bdg. 250.95 (*0-8490-6003-6*) Gordon Pr.

Studies of the French Dog Sports "Championship of France" (1982-1988) & the Belgian Shepherd Dog Breeds (Malinois, Teruren Groenendael, Laenenois) in Schutzhund Competition in the U. S. A. (1979-1988) John A. Jons. (Illus.). 87p. 1989. pap. text ed. 15.00 (*0-9623099-0-7*) J Jons LA.

Studies of the Geology of the San Joaquin Basin. Ed. by Stephan A. Graham & Hilary C. Olson. (Illus.). 351p. (Orig.). 1988. pap. 20.00 (*1-878861-09-3*) Pac Section SEPM.

Studies of the History of Papermaking in Britain. Alfred H. Shorter. Ed. by Richard L. Hills. (Collected Studies: No. CS 425). (Illus.). 336p. 1993. 89.95 (*0-86078-386-3*, Pub. by Variorum UK) Ashgate Pub Co.

Studies of the Identification of Timbers with a Note on the Seasoning of Wood. A. L. Howard. 110p. 1986. 85.00 (*0-685-54023-5*, Pub. by Intl Bk Distr II); 60.00 (*81-7089-078-0*, Pub. by Intl Bk Distr II) St Mut.

Studies of the Location, Planning, Zoning & Development of Civil Airports in the U. S. A Selected Bibliography of Sources for the Period 1920-1974, No. 830. Ed. by Eugene C. Kirchherr. 1975. 5.00 (*0-686-20360-7*, Sage Prdcls Pr) Sage.

***Studies of the Middle Atmosphere.** 198p. 1988. text ed. 74.95 (*0-521-36343-8*) Cambridge U Pr.

Studies of the Normal & Abnormal Development of the Nervous System. Ed. by W. Lierse & F. Beck. (Bibliotheca Anatomica Ser.: No. 19). (Illus.). 1981. pap. 149.75 (*3-8055-1039-X*) S Karger.

Studies of the Northern Campus Martius in Ancient Rome. Robert E. Palmer. LC 90-55217. (Transactions Ser.: Vol. 80, Pt. 2). (Illus.). 64p. (C). 1990. pap. 12.00 (*0-87169-802-1*, T802-PAR) Am Philos.

Studies of the Pollution of the Tennessee River System. G. R. Scott. LC 77-125764. (American Environmental Studies). 1974. reprint ed. 23.95 (*0-405-02690-0*) Ayer.

Studies of the Spanish & Portuguese Ballad. Ed. by N. D. Shergold. (Monagrafias A Ser.: Vol. XXVI). 176p. (Orig.). (ENG, POR & SPA.). (C). 1972. pap. 36.00 (*0-900411-39-2*, Pub. by Tamesis Bks Ltd UK) Boydell & Brewer.

Studies of the Spanish Mystics, 3 vols. E. Allison Peers. 1977. lib. bdg. 300.00 (*0-8490-2706-3*) Gordon Pr.

Studies of the Stage. Brander Matthews. LC 72-294. (Essay Index Reprint Ser.). 1977. reprint ed. 20.95 (*0-8369-2806-7*) Ayer.

Studies of the Wild Turkey in Florida. Lovett E. Williams, Jr. & David H. Austin. LC 87-14730. (Illus.). 250p. 1988. 39.95 (*0-8130-0874-3*) U Press Fla.

Studies of the Yaqui Indians of Sonora, Mexico. William C. Holden et al. LC 76-43747. (Texas Tech. College, Bulletin Ser.: 12). reprint ed. 42.50 (*0-404-15586-3*) AMS Pr.

Studies of Thermal Convection in a Rotating Cylinder with Some Implications for Large-Scale Atmospheric Motions. Dave Fultz et al. (Meteorological Monograph Ser.: Vol. 4, No. 21). (Illus.). 104p. (Orig.). 1959. pap. 17.00 (*0-933876-09-2*) Am Meteorological.

Studies of Tropical American Birds. Alexander F. Skutch. (Publications of the Nuttall Ornithological Club: No. 10). (Illus.). 228p. 1972. 12.00 (*1-877973-20-3*) Nuttall Ornith.

Studies of Vacuum Ultraviolet & X-Ray Processes, 3 vols., Set, Vols. 1-3. Ed. by Uwe Becker. 1993. Set. write for info. (*0-404-69950-2*) AMS Pr.

Studies of Vortex Dominated Flows. Ed. by M. Yousuff Hussaini & M. D. Salas. (Illus.). xii, 364p. 1986. 65.95 (*0-387-96430-4*) Spr-Verlag.

Studies of War. Henk Houweling & Jan G. Siccama. (C). 1988. lib. bdg. 112.50 (*0-89838-932-1*) Kluwer Ac.

Studies of War: Nuclear & Conventional. Patrick M. Blackett. LC 78-16364. (Illus.). 242p. 1978. reprint ed. text ed. 35.00 (*0-313-20575-2*, BLSW, Greenwood Pr) Greenwood.

Studies of War & Peace. Ed. by Oyvind Osterud. (Scandinavian University Press Publication). 281p. 1986. 39.50 (*82-00-07749-7*) Scandnvan Univ Pr.

Studies on Abraham Ibn Ezra. Abe Lipshitz. 118p. (C). 1969. 7.95 (*0-935982-43-4*, AL-01) Spertus Coll.

Studies on Amanita (Amanitaceae from Andean Colombia) Rodham E. Tulloss et al. (Memoirs Ser.: No. 66). (Illus.). 46p. 1992. pap. text ed. 11.25 (*0-89327-371-6*) NY Botanical.

Studies on Amphipoda: Proceedings of the VIth International Colloquium on Amphipod Crustaceans, Ambleteuse, France 28 June-3 July 1985. (Crustaceana Supplements Ser.: No. 13). (Illus.). vi, 285p. (Orig.). 1988. pap. 105.50 (*90-04-08779-6*) E J Brill.

Studies on Archaeology of Michoacan Mexico. Leon & Holmes. 33p. reprint ed. pap. 3.95 (*0-8466-4012-0*, I12) Shorey.

Studies on Art & Archeology in Honor of Ernst Kitzinger. Ed. by William Tronzo et al. LC 42-6499. (Dumbarton Oaks Papers: No. 41). (Illus.). 528p. 1987. 65.00 (*0-88402-169-6*) Dumbarton Oaks.

Studies on Asia, Vol. 1. LC 60-15432. 1960. pap. 26.80 (*0-317-27609-3*, 2023481) Bks Demand.

Studies on Asia, Vol. 2. LC 60-15432. 1961. pap. 23.80 (*0-317-27610-7*) Bks Demand.

Studies on Asia, Vol. 3. LC 60-15432. 1962. pap. 24.30 (*0-317-27611-5*) Bks Demand.

Studies on Asia, Vol. 4. LC 60-15432. 1963. pap. 51.50 (*0-317-27612-3*) Bks Demand.

Studies on Asia, Vol. 5. LC 60-15432. 1964. pap. 49.50 (*0-317-27613-1*) Bks Demand.

Studies on Asia, Vol. 6. LC 60-15432. 1965. pap. 54.80 (*0-317-27614-X*) Bks Demand.

Studies on Asia, Vol. 7. LC 60-15432. 1966. pap. 48.80 (*0-317-27615-8*) Bks Demand.

Studies on Asia, Vol. 8. LC 60-15432. 1967. pap. 50.50 (*0-317-27616-6*) Bks Demand.

Studies on Buddhism: In Honour of Professor A. K. Warder. Ed. by N. K. Wagle. (South Asian Studies Papers: No. 5). (C). 1993. 44.00 (*1-895214-06-8*, Pub. by Ctre South Asian CN) S Asia.

Studies on Byzantine Literature of the Eleventh & Twelfth Centuries. Alexander P. Kazhdan. LC 83-7442. (Past & Present Publications). 320p. 1984. text ed. 80.00 (*0-521-24656-3*) Cambridge U Pr.

Studies on Byzantium, Seljuks & Ottomans: Reprinted Studies. Speros Vryonis, Jr. LC 81-51168. (Byzantina Kai Metabyzantina Ser.: Vol. 2). x, 343p. 1981. pap. 24.25 (*0-89003-071-5*) Undena Pubns.

Studies on Camille Pissaro. Ed. by Christopher Lloyd. (Illus.). 192p. 1986. pap. 37.50 (*0-7102-0928-2*, 09882, RKP) Routledge.

Studies on Canadian Literature: Introductory & Critical Essays. Ed. by Arnold E. Davidson. LC 90-6529. v, 371p. 1991. pap. 19.75 (*0-87352-380-6*, T125P); lib. bdg. 37.50 (*0-87352-199-4*, T125C) Modern Lang.

Studies on Carbohydrate Metabolism in Fish. Sadao Shimeno. 136p. (C). 1982. text ed. 55.00 (*90-6191-215-6*, Pub. by A A Balkema NE) Ashgate Pub Co.

***Studies on Causes & Consequences of the 1989-92 Credit Slowdown.** 1996. lib. bdg. 359.95 (*0-8490-6945-9*) Gordon Pr.

Studies on Child Language & Aphasia. Roman Jakobson. (Janua Linguarum, Ser. Minor: No. 114). (Orig.). 1971. pap. text ed. 23.10 (*90-279-1640-3*) Mouton.

Studies on Chinese & Islamic Inner Asia. Joseph F. Fletcher, Jr. Ed. by Beatrice F. Manz. (Collected Studies: No. CS480). 256p. 1995. 84.95 (*0-86078-469-X*, Pub. by Variorum UK) Ashgate Pub Co.

Studies on Chinese Salamanders. Zhao. LC 88-60508. 1988. write for info. (*0-916984-18-4*) SSAR.

Studies on Christiaan Huygens: Invited Papers of the Symposium, Amsterdam, August 22-25, 1979. Life & Work of Christiaan Huygens Symposium Staff. Ed. by H. J. Bos et al. vi, 321p. 1980. text ed. 69.25 (*90-265-0333-4*) Swets.

Studies on Clarin: An Annotated Bibliographies. David Torres. LC 87-4362. (Author Bibliographies Ser.: No. 79). 224p. 1987. 20.00 (*0-8108-1993-7*) Scarecrow.

Studies on Co-Ordinate Expressions in Middle English. U. Ohlander. (Lund Studies in English: Vol. 5). 1974. reprint ed. pap. 30.00 (*0-8115-0548-0*) Periodicals Srv.

Studies on Constantinople. Cyril A. Mango. (Collected Studies: No. 394). 288p. 1993. 98.95 (*0-86078-372-3*, Pub. by Variorum UK) Ashgate Pub Co.

Studies on Copular Sentences, Clefts & Pseudo-Clefts. R. Declerck. 270p. (Orig.). 1988. pap. 49.50 (*90-6186-289-2*, Pub. by Leuven Univ BE) Coronet Bks.

Studies on Copular Sentences, Clefts & Pseudo-Clefts. Renaat DeClerck. (Orig.). (C). 1988. pap. 57.70 (*90-6765-124-9*) Mouton.

Studies on Don Quijote & Other Cervantine Works. Donald W. Bleznick. LC 83-51090. 79p. 1984. 12.00 (*0-938972-07-3*) Spanish Lit Pubns.

Studies on Early Byzantine Gold Coinage. Ed. by Wolfgang Hahn & William E. Metcalf. 144p. 1988. 75.00 (*0-89722-225-3*, ANSNS 17) Am Numismatic.

Studies on Economic Growth Theory: The Role of Imperfections & Externalities. Jos Verbeek. (Tinbergen Institute Ser.). 160p. 1993. pap. 25.00 (*90-5170-194-2*, Pub. by Thesis Pubs NE) IBD Ltd.

Studies on Economic Reforms & Development in the People's Republic of China. Ed. by Hsueh Tien-Tung et al. LC 92-37439. 384p. 1993. pap. text ed. 45.00 (*0-312-09165-6*) St Martin.

Studies on Ethnicity: The East European Experience in America. Ed. by Charles A. Ward et al. (East European Monographs: No. 73). 254p. 1980. text ed. 68.50 (*0-914710-67-2*) East Eur Monographs.

Studies on Excitation & Inhibition in the Retina. Ed. by Floyd Ratliff. LC 73-89539. (Illus.). 688p. 1974. 17.50 (*0-87470-019-1*) Rockefeller.

S

Studies on Fronting. Ed. by Frank Jansen. v, 112p. (Orig.). (C). 1978. pap. text ed. 26.95 (*3-11-013349-0*) Mouton.

Studies on Gandhi. Ed. by V. T. Patil. viii, 296p. 1984. text ed. 30.00 (*0-86590-520-7*, Pub. by Sterling Pubs II) Apt Bks.

Studies on German Grammar. Ed. by Jindrich Toman. (Studies in Generative Grammar: No. 21). x, 452p. (Orig.). 1985. pap. 100.00 (*90-6765-113-3*) Mouton.

Studies on Gersonides: A Fourteenth-Century Jewish Philosopher-Scientist. Ed. by Gad Freudenthal. LC 92-31896. (Collection de Travaux de l'Academie Internationale d'Histoire des Sciences: Vol. 36). 1992. 119.50 (*90-04-09641-8*) E J Brill.

Studies on Governments & Non-Dominant Ethnic Groups in Europe (1850-1940), 8 vols., Set. Ed. by Paul Smith. (C). 1993. 650.00 (*0-8147-2179-6*) NYU Pr.

Studies on Governments & Non-Dominant Ethnic Groups in Europe (1850-1940), Vol. 3. Ed. by Paul Smith. 466p. (C). 1992. 80.00 (*0-8147-2178-8*) NYU Pr.

Studies on Governments & Non-Dominant Ethnic Groups in Europe (1850-1940), Vol. 7. Ed. by D. A. Howell. 400p. (C). 1993. 80.00 (*0-8147-8764-9*) NYU Pr.

Studies on Governments & Non-Dominant Ethnic Groups in Europe (1850-1940), Vol. 8. Ed. by J. J. Tomiak. 432p. (C). 1990. 80.00 (*0-8147-8193-4*) NYU Pr.

S

Studies on Governments & Non-Dominant Ethnic Groups in Europe (1850-1940) Ethnic Groups in International Relations, Vol. 5. Ed. by Paul Smith. 374p. (C). 1990. 80.00 (*0-8147-7914-X*) NYU Pr.

Studies on Greek & Roman History & Literature. Barry Baldwin. (London Studies in Classical Philology: Vol. 15). xiv, 588p. (C). 1985. lib. bdg. 94.00 (*90-70265-09-5*, Pub. by Gieben NE) Benjamins North Am.

Studies on Hysteria. Josef Breuer & Sigmund Freud. LC 57-12310. 320p. 1982. pap. 21.00 (*0-465-08276-9*) Basic.

Studies on Immersion Education: A Collection for U. S. Educators. California Department of Education Staff. 192p. 1984. pap. 5.50 (*0-8011-0234-0*) Calif Education.

Studies on India & Vietnam. Helen B. Lamb. Ed. by Corliss Lamont. LC 76-1668. 267p. reprint ed. pap. 76.10 (*0-7837-3922-2*, 2043770) Bks Demand.

Studies on Indian Agromyzidae (Diptera) M. Ipe et al. (Oriental Insects Monographs: No. 1). 1971. pap. 30.00 (*1-877711-11-X*) Assoc Pubs FL.

Studies on Indian Chelonethi. V. A. Murthy & T. N. Ananthakrishnan. (Oriental Insects Monographs: No. 4). 1977. pap. 55.00 (*1-877711-10-1*) Assoc Pubs FL.

Studies on Indian Medical History: Papers Presented at the International Workshop on the Study of Indian Medicine Held at the Wellcome Institute for the History of Medicine, Sept. 2-4, 1985. Ed. by G. Jan Meulenbeld & Dominik Wujastyk. (Groningen Oriental Studies: Vol. II). 247p. (Orig.). (C). 1987. pap. 46.00 (*90-6980-015-2*, Pub. by Egbert Forsten NE) Benjamins North Am.

Studies on Indiana: A Bibliography of Theses & Dissertations, 1902-1977. Betty M. Jarboe. 377p. 1980. pap. 6.25 (*1-885323-33-6*) IN Hist Bureau.

***Studies on Indology.** Ed. by Ashok K. Goswmi & Dharmeswar Chutia. 1996. 82.00 (*81-7030-488-1*, Pub. by Sri Satguru Pubns II) S Asia.

Studies on Industrial Productivity, Set. Ed. by Stephen Orgel. LC 94-484. 192p. 1993. 783.00 (*0-8153-1529-5*) Garland.

Studies on Industrial Relations (I. L. O.) Studies & Reports, Vol. II. (Series A: No. 35, vol. 6). 1974. reprint ed. 40.00 (*0-8115-3238-0*) Periodicals Srv.

Studies on Iroquoian Culture. Nancy Bonvillain. (Occasional Publications in Northeastern Anthropology: No. 6). 1980. 6.00 (*0-318-19885-1*) Fund Anthrop.

Studies on Iroquoian Culture. Ed. by Nancy Sonvillain. (Occasional Publications in Northeastern Anthropology: No. 6). (Illus.). 148p. 6.00 (*0-318-22326-0*) F Pierce College.

Studies on Italian-American Literature. Francesco Mulas. LC 95-496. 88p. 1995. pap. 14.50 (*0-934733-87-2*) CMS.

Studies on Japanese Ostracoda. Tetsuro Hanai. (Illus.). 300p. 1982. 99.50 (*0-86008-314-4*, Pub. by U of Tokyo JA) Col U Pr.

Studies on Jorge de Sena. Ed. by Harvey L. Sharrer & Frederick G. Williams. LC 81-85956. 280p. (Orig.). 1981. pap. 20.00 (*0-942208-20-X*) Bandanna Bks.

Studies on Kosova. Ed. by Arshi Pippa & Sami Repishti. 279p. 1984. text ed. 61.00 (*0-88033-047-3*) East Eur Monographs.

Studies on Lake Vechten & Tjeukemeer: The Netherlands. Ramesh D. Gulati & S. Parma. 1982. lib. bdg. 234.00 (*90-6193-762-0*) Kluwer Ac.

Studies on Large Branchiopod Biology & Aquaculture. Ed. by D. Belk et al. (Developments in Hydrobiology Ser.). 320p. 1991. lib. bdg. 222.00 (*0-7923-1169-8*) Kluwer Ac.

Studies on Large Branchiopod Biology & Aquaculture II. Ed. by D. Belk et al. LC 94-43529. (Developments in Hydrobiology Ser.: Vol. 103). 1995. lib. bdg. 231.00 (*0-7923-3292-X*) Kluwer Ac.

Studies on Late Roman & Byzantine History, Literature & Language. Barry Baldwin. (London Studies in Classical Philology: Vol. 12). xii, 502p. (C). 1984. 94.00 (*90-70265-56-7*, Pub. by Gieben NE) Benjamins North Am.

Studies on Levantine Trade in the Middle Ages. Eliyahu Ashtor. (Collected Studies: No. CS74). 372p. (FRE & ITA.). (C). 1978. reprint ed. lib. bdg. 107.95 (*0-86078-020-1*, Pub. by Variorum UK) Ashgate Pub Co.

Studies on Mathematical Programming. A. Prekopa. (Mathematical Methods of Operations Research Ser.: Vol. 1). 200p. (C). 1980. 53.00 (*963-05-1854-6*, Pub. by Akad Kiado HU) St Mut.

***Studies on Medieval Spanish Literature in Honor of Charles F. Fraker.** Ed. by Mercedes Vaquero & Alan Deyermond. xviii, 287p. 1995. 50.00 (*1-56954-035-7*) Hispanic Seminary.

Studies on Methods of Estimating Population Density, Biomass, & Productivity in Terrestrial Animals. Ed. by Masaaki Morisita. LC 78-322192. (JIBP Synthesis Ser.: No. 17). 247p. 1977. reprint ed. pap. 70.40 (*0-608-01249-1*, 2061937) Bks Demand.

Studies on Middle English Local Surnames. M. T. Lofvenberg. (Lund Studies in English: Vol. 11). 1974. reprint ed. pap. 45.00 (*0-8115-0554-5*) Periodicals Srv.

Studies on Middle Welsh Literature. Brynley F. Roberts. LC 91-36558. (Welsh Studies: Vol. 5). 160p. 1992. lib. bdg. 69.95 (*0-7734-9641-6*) E Mellen.

Studies on Modern Painters. Arthur Symons. LC 67-30233. (Essay Index Reprint Ser.). 1925. 7.00 (*0-8369-0920-8*) Ayer.

Studies on Money in Early America. Ed. by Eric P. Newman. LC 76-6790. (Illus.). 222p. reprint ed. pap. 63. 30 (*0-7837-6359-X*, 2046071) Bks Demand.

Studies on Nehru. Ed. by V. T. Patil. 421p. 1987. text ed. 45.00 (*81-207-0624-2*, Pub. by Sterling Pubs II) Apt Bks.

Studies on Neotropical Water Mites. David Cook. (Memoir Ser.: No. 31). (Illus.). 644p. 1980. 75.00 (*1-56665-029-1*) Assoc Pubs FL.

Studies on Nepali Language & Linguistics: A Bibliography. A. Agrawal. (C). 1991. text ed. 60.00 (*0-7855-0157-6*, Pub. by Ratna Pustak Bhandar) St Mut.

Studies on Neuromuscular Diseases: Proceedings of the Quantitative Methods of Investigations in the Clinics of Neuromuscular Diseases International Symposium, Giessen, April 1974. Quantitative Methods of Investigations in the Clinics of Neuromuscular Diseases International Symposium Staff. Ed. by K. Kunze & J. E. Desmedt. 250p. 1975. 152.00 (*3-8055-1749-1*) S Karger.

Studies on Normal Pressure Glaucoma. H. Caroline Geijssen. (Illus.). 240p. 1991. lib. bdg. 62.50 (*90-6299-068-1*, Pub. by Kugler NE) Kugler Pubns.

Studies on Ohio Diatoms: Diatoms of the Scioto River Basin & Referenced Checklist from Ohio Exclusive of Lake Erie & the Ohio River. Gary B. Collins & Robert G. Kalinsky. (Bulletin New Ser.: Vol. 5, No. 3). 1977. 7.00 (*0-86727-080-2*) Ohio Bio Survey.

Studies on Oriental Pipunculidae (Diptera) D. Elmo Hardy. (Oriental Insects Monographs: No. 2). 1972. pap. 30.00 (*1-877711-12-8*) Assoc Pubs FL.

Studies on Palestine During the Ottoman Period. Ed. by Moshe Ma'Oz. 224p. 1979. text ed. 35.00 (*965-223-589-X*, Pub. by Magnes Press IS) Eisenbrauns.

Studies on Pali Commentaries. Kanai L. Hazra. 1991. 36.00 (*81-7018-608-0*, Pub. by BR Pub II) S Asia.

Studies on Plant Demography: A Festschrift for John L. Harper. Ed. by James White. 1986. text ed. 149.00 (*0-12-746630-4*); pap. text ed. 65.00 (*0-12-746631-2*) Acad Pr.

Studies on Q: Aspects of the History of Early Christianity As Reflected in the Sayings Source Q. Christopher Tuckett. 448p. 1996. 49.95 (*0-567-09742-0*, Pub. by T & T Clark UK) Bks Intl VA.

Studies on Receptors Involved in Liver Glycogenolysis in Rabbit, Guinea Pig & Man. A. Vandekerckhove. No. 24. 111p. (Orig.). 1990. pap. 27.50 (*90-6186-369-4*, Pub. by Leuven Univ BE) Coronet Bks.

Studies on Religion & Politics. Ed. by Jerome J. Hanus & James V. Schall. LC 86-9166. 120p. (Orig.). (C). 1986. pap. text ed. 22.50 (*0-8191-5392-3*) U Pr of Amer.

Studies on Research in Reading & Libraries: Approaches & Results from Several Countries. Ed. by Paul Kaegbein et al. (Contributions to Library Theory & Library History Ser.). 300p. 1991. lib. bdg. 46.00 (*3-598-22171-1*) K G Saur.

Studies on Scarab Seals, Vol. II, Pt. 2. Tufnell. 1984. pap. write for info. (*0-85668-279-9*, Pub. by Aris & Phillips UK) David Brown.

Studies on Scarab Seals, Vol. 1: Pre 12th Dynasty Scarab Studies on Scarab Seals. Ward. 1979. 75.00 (*0-85668-124-5*, Pub. by Aris & Phillips UK) David Brown.

Studies on Scarab Seals, Vol. 2: Two Parts Scarab Seals & Their Contribution to History in the Early Second Millennium BC, Set. 1984. pap. 90.00 (*0-85668-130-X*, Pub. by Aris & Phillips UK) David Brown.

Studies on Scipio Africanus. Richard M. Haywood. LC 78-64148. (Johns Hopkins University. Studies in the Social Sciences. Thirtieth Ser. 1912: 1). reprint ed. 29.50 (*0-404-61259-8*) AMS Pr.

Studies on Scrambling: Movement & Non-Movement Approaches to Free Word-Order Phenomena. Ed. by Norbert Corver & Henk Van Riemsdijk. LC 94-14409. (Studies in Generative Grammar: No. 41). vi, 531p. (C). 1994. lib. bdg. 152.35 (*3-11-013572-8*) Mouton.

Studies on Semantics in Generative Grammar. Noam Chomsky. LC 74-189711. (Janua Linguarum, Ser. Minor: No. 107). 207p. (Orig.). 1972. pap. text ed. 24.65 (*90-279-7964-2*) Mouton.

Studies on Slavery, in Easy Lessons. John Fletcher. LC 70-83962. (Black Heritage Library Collection). 1977. 36.95 (*0-8369-8572-9*) Ayer.

Studies on Slavic Derivation. Kristine Heltberg. 160p. (Orig.). 1970. pap. 23.50 (*87-7492-001-4*, Pub. by Odense Universitets Forlag DK) Coronet Bks.

Studies on Spanish Theatre. Enrique G. Jardiel. (C). 1993. 14.50 (*81-7018-758-3*, Pub. by BR Pub II) S Asia.

Studies on Stewardship. Aaron M. Wilson. 160p. 1988. pap. 5.95 (*1-882449-20-7*) Messenger Pub.

Studies on Syntactic Topology & Contrastive Grammar. Laslo Dezsoe. (Janua Linguarum, Series Major). 307p. 1982. pap. text ed. 64.65 (*90-279-3108-9*) Mouton.

Studies on the Ancient Palestinian World: Presented to Professor F. V. Winnett on the Occasion of His Retirement, July 1971. John W. Wevers. LC 79-151397. (Toronto Semitic Texts & Studies: No. 2). (Illus.). 191p. reprint ed. pap. 54.50 (*0-685-23657-9*, 2026479) Bks Demand.

Studies on the Animal Ecology of the Hocking River Basin: The Bottom Invertebrates of the Hocking River & the Plankton of the Hocking River. William B. Ludwig & Lee S. Roach. (Bulletin Ser.: No. 26). 1932. 2.00 (*0-86727-025-X*) Ohio Bio Survey.

Studies on the Biology & Pathology of the Skin. Ed. by L. Robert. (Frontiers of Matrix Biology Ser.: Vol. 4). (Illus.). 220p. 1977. 109.00 (*3-8055-2666-0*) S Karger.

Studies on the Blood Serum of the Euryhaline Cyprinodont Fish, Fundulus Heteroclitus, Adapted to Fresh or to Salt Water. Grace E. Pickford et al. (Connecticut Academy of Arts & Sciences Ser., Trans.: Vol. 43). 1969. pap. 39.50 (*0-685-22887-8*) Elliots Bks.

Studies on the Ceramiaceous Algae (Rhodophyta) from Southern Parts of Japan. H. Itono. (Bibliotheca Phycologica Ser.: No. 35). 1977. lib. bdg. 98.00 (*3-7682-1148-7*) Lubrecht & Cramer.

Studies on the Chemical Analysis of Archaeological Sites, Vol. 2. S. F. Cook & R. F. Heizer. (University of California Publications in American Archaeology & Ethnology: Vol. 2). (Illus.). 107p. 1964. reprint ed. pap. text ed. 9.65 (*1-55567-479-8*) Coyote Press.

Studies on the Crusader States & on Venetian Expansion. David Jacoby. (Collected Studies: No. CS301). 348p. (ENG & FRE.). (C). 1989. reprint ed. text ed. 98.95 (*0-86078-249-2*, Pub. by Variorum UK) Ashgate Pub Co.

***Studies on the Derveni Papyrus.** Ed. by Andre Laks & Glenn W. Most. 208p. 1997. 55.00 (*0-19-815032-6*) OUP.

Studies on the Development of Anther & Palynology of Indian Cucurbitaceae. S. Sharma. 150p. 1991. 65.00 (*0-685-59968-X*, Messers Today & Tomorrow) Scholarly Pubns.

Studies on the Development of Consciousness. Yves Chesni. Tr. by Joseph Zenk. 153p. 1994. text ed. 37.50 (*0-931095-02-6*) Live Oak.

Studies on the Development of Economical Drainage Systems for Multi-Storeyed Buildings. Chakrabarti. (C). 1986. 15.00 (*0-317-68062-5*, Pub. by Oxford IBH II) S Asia.

Studies on the Development of Economical Drainage Systems for Multi-Storeyed Buildings. S. P. Chakrabarti. 114p. (C). 1987. text ed. 70.00 (*90-6191-474-4*, Pub. by A A Balkema NE) Ashgate Pub Co.

Studies on the Digestive Enzymes of Spiders. Grace E. Pickford. (Connecticut Academy of Arts & Sciences Ser., Trans.: Vol. 35). 1942. pap. 49.50 (*0-685-22911-4*) Elliots Bks.

Studies on the Dorset Dialect. B. Widen. (Lund Studies in English: Vol. 16). 1974. reprint ed. pap. 30.00 (*0-8115-0559-6*) Periodicals Srv.

Studies on the Earliest Farm Settlement & Other Studies. Ed. by Asbjorn E. Heiteig. (The Bryggen Papers Supplementary Ser.: No. 1). 100p. (Orig.). 1984. pap. 26. 00 (*82-00-07119-7*) Scandnvan Univ Pr.

Studies on the Ecology of Tropical Zooplankton. Ed. by H. J. Dumont et al. LC 93-43395. (Developments in Hydrobiology Ser.: Vol. 92). 304p. (C). 1994. lib. bdg. 211.50 (*0-7923-2639-3*) Kluwer Ac.

***Studies on the Ethnology of Yemen.** Ed. by Lucine Taminian & Abdul K. Al-Aug. (Translations of Western-Language Articles into Arabic for Use in Yemeni Universities Ser.: Vol. 2). Date not set. write for info. (*1-882557-04-2*) Am Inst Yemeni.

Studies on the Genus Scenedesmus Meyen (Chlorophyceae, Chlorococcales) from Southern India, with Special Reference to the Cell Wall Structure. E. Hegewald et al. (Nova Hedwigia Beiheft Ser.: No. 99). (Illus.). 210p. 1990. pap. text ed. 85.00 (*0-685-37773-3*, Pub. by Cramer-Borntraeger GW) Lubrecht & Cramer.

Studies on the Gynaikothrips-Liophleaothrips-Liothrips Complex from India. T. N. Ananthakrishnan & N. Muraleedharan. (Oriental Insects Monographs: No. 4). 1974. pap. 30.00 (*1-877711-14-4*) Assoc Pubs FL.

Studies on the Hasmonean Period. J. Efron. (Studies in Judaism in Late Antiquity: Vol. 39). 1987. 103.00 (*90-04-07609-3*) E J Brill.

Studies on the History of Behavior: Ape, Primitive Man, & Child. L. S. Vygotsky & A. R. Luria. Ed. by Victor I. Golod & Jane E. Knox. Tr. by Jane E. Knox from RUS. 264p. 1993. text ed. 59.95 (*0-8058-1014-5*) L Erlbaum Assocs.

Studies on the History of Logic: Proceedings of the III Sympoisum on the History of Logic. Ed. by Igancio Angelelli & Maria Cerezo. LC 96-5201. (Perspektiven der Analytischen Philosophie - Perspectives in Analytical Philosophy Ser.: Vol. 8). xii, 413p. (C). 1996. lib. bdg. 189.65 (*3-11-014829-3*, 112/96) De Gruyter.

Studies on the History of Logic & Semantics, 12th-17th Centuries. Gabriel Nuchelmans. Ed. by E. P. Bos. LC 96-9296. (Collected Studies: No. CS560). 352p. 1996. 98.95 (*0-86078-618-8*, Pub. by Variorum UK) Ashgate Pub Co.

Studies on the History of Musical Style. Arnold Salop. LC 78-155673. 345p. reprint ed. 98.40 (*0-685-16221-4*, 2027599) Bks Demand.

Studies on the History of Safawid Iran. Roger M. Savory. (Collected Studies: No. CS256). 316p. (C). 1987. reprint ed. lib. bdg. 94.95 (*0-86078-204-2*, Pub. by Variorum UK) Ashgate Pub Co.

Studies on the History of the Church of Cyprus, 4th-20th Centuries. Benedict Englezakis. Ed. by Silouan Ioannou & Misael Ioannou. 487p. 1995. 110.00 (*0-86078-486-X*, Pub. by Variorum UK) Ashgate Pub Co.

Studies on the History of the Theory of Atomic Structure. Ed. by John L. Heibron & I. Bernard Cohen. LC 80-2090. (Development of Science Ser.). (Illus.). 1981. lib. bdg. 38.95 (*0-405-13962-4*) Ayer.

Studies on the Holocaust in Hungary. Ed. by Randolph L. Braham. 1990. text ed. 44.00 (*0-88033-198-4*) Col U Pr.

Studies on the Iconography of Cosmic Kingship in the Ancient World. H. P. L'Orange. (Illus.). 206p. 1982. reprint ed. lib. bdg. 55.00 (*0-89241-150-3*) Caratzas.

***Studies on the Internal Diaspora of the Byzantine Empire.** Ed. by Helene G. Ahrweiler & Angeliki E. Laiou. LC 96-53525. 1997. write for info. (*0-88402-247-1*, ALBD) Dumbarton Oaks.

***Studies on the Jurchens & the Chin Dynasty.** Herbert Franke & Hok-Lam Chan. LC 97-15877. (Variorum Collected Studies Ser.: Vol. 591). 400p. 1997. text ed. 116.95 (*0-86078-645-5*, Pub. by Ashgate UK) Ashgate Pub Co.

Studies on the Left, Set, Vols. 1-7. reprint ed. Set. lib. bdg. 425.00 (*0-404-19559-8*) AMS Pr.

Studies on the Life & Legend of St. Patrick. Ludwig Bieler. Ed. by Richard Sharpe. (Collected Studies: No. CS244). 342p. (ENG & GER.). (C). 1986. reprint ed. lib. bdg. 95.00 (*0-86078-192-5*, Pub. by Variorum UK) Ashgate Pub Co.

Studies on the Literary Tradition of Medieval Orthodox Slavdom. Riccardo Picchio. Ed. by Harvey Goldblatt. (Renovatio Ser.: No. 2). (Illus.). 480p. 1996. 35.00 (*0-916458-33-4*) Harvard Ukrainian.

Studies on the Local Sense of the Prepositions "in", "at", "on", "to" in Modern English. K. G. Lindkvist. (Lund Studies in English: Vol. 20). 1974. reprint ed. pap. 50.00 (*0-8115-0563-4*) Periodicals Srv.

Studies on the Mesozoic of Sonora & Adjacent Areas. Ed. by Cesar Jacques-Ayala et al. (Special Papers: No. 301). (Illus.). 1996. pap. 75.00 (*0-8137-2301-9*) Geol Soc.

Studies on the Natural Killer Mediated Cytotoxicity in Women with Endometriosis. D. Oosterlynck. No. 70. 187p. (Orig.). 1993. pap. 33.50 (*90-6186-572-7*, Pub. by Leuven Univ BE) Coronet Bks.

Studies on the Optimal Search Plan. K. Iida & Stephen E. Fienberg. Ed. by J. O. Berger et al. (Lecture Notes in Statistics Ser.: Vol. 70). viii, 130p. 1992. 38.95 (*0-387-97739-2*) Spr-Verlag.

Studies on the Origin & Early Tradition of English Utopian Fiction. S. B. Liljegren. (Essays & Studies on English Language & Literature: Vol. 23). (Orig.). 1961. pap. 25. 00 (*0-8115-0221-X*) Periodicals Srv.

Studies on the Origin of Harmonic Tonality. Carl Dahlhaus. Tr. by Robert O. Gjerdingen. 310p. 1990. text ed. 65.00 (*0-691-09135-8*) Princeton U Pr.

Studies on the Origins & Uses of Islamic Hadith. G. H. Juynboll. (Collected Studies: No. CS550). 350p. 1996. 89.95 (*0-86078-604-8*, Pub. by Variorum UK) Ashgate Pub Co.

Studies on the Ottoman Architecture of the Balkans: A Legacy in Stone. Machiel Kiel. (Collected Studies: No. CS326). 368p. 1990. text ed. 145.00 (*0-86078-276-X*, Pub. by Variorum UK) Ashgate Pub Co.

Studies on the Person of Chirst. James Stalker. Ed. by Zodhiates. (Bible Study Ser.:Pulpit Legends Collection: Vol. 483). 496p. 1995. 19.99 (*0-89957-205-7*) AMG Pubs.

Studies on the Piriform Lobe. Facundo Valverde-Garcia. LC 65-16689. (Illus.). 138p. 1965. 18.00 (*0-674-85200-1*) HUP.

Studies on the Pollen Biology of Certain Cultivated Malvaceae. D. Srivastava. Ed. by P. K. Nair. (Advances in Pollen Spore Research Ser.: Vol. 9). (Illus.). 175p. (C). 1982. 15.00 (*0-88065-227-6*, Messers Today & Tomorrow) Scholarly Pubns.

Studies on the Population of China, 1368-1953. Ping-Ti Ho. LC 59-12970. (East Asian Ser.: No. 4). 391p. 1959. 39. 95 (*0-674-85245-1*) HUP.

Studies on the Self & Social Cognition. M. F. Pichevin et al. 344p. 1993. text ed. 109.00 (*981-02-1237-2*) World Scientific Pub.

***Studies on the Spanish Sentimental Romance (1440-1550) Redefining a Genre, Vol. 168.** Joseph J. Gwara & E. Michael Gerli. LC 97-20992. 1997. write for info. (*1-85566-028-8*, Pub. by Tamesis Bks Ltd UK) Boydell & Brewer.

Studies on the Structure & Development of Vertebrates. Edwin S. Goodrich. (Illus.). xxxiv, 872p. (C). 1986. pap. text ed. 37.95 (*0-226-30354-3*) U Ch Pr.

Studies on the Structure & Development of Vertebrates, 2 vols., Set. Edwin S. Goodrich. 837p. 1984. pap. 350.00 (*0-7855-0393-5*, Pub. by Intl Bks & Periodicals II) St Mut.

Studies on the Synthesis of Corrins & Related Ligands. Robert V. Stevens. 14p. 1976. pap. 12.75 (*0-08-021333-2*, Pergamon Pr) Elsevier.

Studies on the Tea in Modern Taiwan. Wu Chen-Tau. (Asian Folklore & Social Life Monographs: No. 94). 481p. (CHI.). 1977. 18.00 (*0-89986-385-X*) Oriental Bk Store.

Studies on the Testament of Abraham. Ed. by George W. Nickelsburg, Jr. LC 76-44205. (Society of Biblical Literature. Septuagint & Cognate Studies: No. 6). 350p. reprint ed. pap. 99.80 (*0-7837-5436-1*, 2045201) Bks Demand.

Studies on the Testament of Job. Ed. by Michael A. Knibb & Pieter W. Van Der Horst. (Society for New Testament Studies Monographs: No. 66). 192p. (C). 1990. text ed. 65.00 (*0-521-37216-X*) Cambridge U Pr.

Studies on the Text of Shakespeare. John Bulloch. LC 75-39557. reprint ed. 41.50 (*0-404-01227-2*) AMS Pr.

An Asterisk (*) at the beginning of an entry indicates that the title is appearing in BIP for the first time.

Studies on the Text of Suetonius De Grammaticis & Rhetoribus. Robert A. Kaster. LC 92-5797. (American Philological Association, American Classical Studies: No. 28). 174p. 1992. 29.95 (*1-55540-720-X*, 400428); pap. 19.95 (*1-55540-721-8*) Scholars Pr GA.

Studies on the Theory of General Dynamic Economic Equilibrium. Giulio La Volpe. (Classics in the History & Development of Economics Ser.). 90p. (C). 1993. text ed. 69.95 (*0-312-08104-9*) St Martin.

***Studies on the Volume & Yield of Tropical Forest Stands: Dry Forest Formations.** 112p. 1989. 14.00 (*92-5-102184-8*, Pub. by FAO IT) Bernan Associates.

Studies on the Works of Jose Donoso: An Anthology of Critical Essays. Ed. by Miriam Adelstein. LC 89-13564. (Hispanic Literature Ser.: Vol. 5). 208p. 1990. lib. bdg. 89.95 (*0-88946-390-5*) E Mellen.

Studies on Tick-Borne Encephalitis. D. Blaskovic et al. (Bulletin of WHO Ser.: Suppl. No. 1 to Vol. 36). 94p. 1967. pap. 9.00 (*92-4-068361-5*, 1033601) World Health.

Studies on Trophoblastic Disease in China. Hongzhao Song & Baozhen Wu. (International Academic Publishers Ser.). (Illus.). 300p. 1989. 105.00 (*0-08-036144-7*, Pergamon Pr) Elsevier.

Studies on Tropical Andean Ecosystems: La Cordillera Central Colombiana Transecto parque los Nevados, Vol. 1. (Illus.). 346p. 1984. lib. bdg. 120.00 (*3-7682-1371-4*) Lubrecht & Cramer.

Studies on Tropical Andean Ecosystems, Estudios de Ecosistemas Tropandinos: La Sierra Nevada de Santa Marta (Columbia) Transecto Buritaca-La Cumbre, Vol. 2. (Illus.). 603p. (ENG & SPA.). 1986. lib. bdg. 154.00 (*3-443-65001-5*) Lubrecht & Cramer.

Studies on Tropical Andean Ecosystems (Estudios de Ecosistemas Tropandinos), Vol. 3: La Cordillera Central Colombiana Transecto Parque los Nevados. Ed. by Thomas Van Der Hammen et al. (Illus.). 600p. (ENG & SPA.). 1989. lib. bdg. 154.00 (*3-443-65002-3*) Lubrecht & Cramer.

Studies on Tumor Formation. Gilbert W. Nicholson. LC 51-3965. (Illus.). 649p. reprint ed. pap. 180.00 (*0-317-41707-X*, 2025720) Bks Demand.

Studies on Turkish-Jewish History: Political & Social Relations, Literature & Linguistics: The Quincentennial Papers. David F. Altabe et al. LC 96-12191. 1996. 29.95 (*0-87203-146-2*) Hermon.

***Studies on Universal Grammar & Typological Variation.** Ed. by Artemis Alexiadou & T. Allen Hall. LC 96-37873. (Linguistik Actuel - Linguistics Today Ser.: Vol. 13). viii, 252p. 1997. lib. bdg. 78.00 (*1-55619-232-0*) Benjamins North Am.

Studies on Vietnamese Language & Literature: A Preliminary Bibliography. Nguyen Dinh Tham. (Southeast Asia Program Ser.: No. 10). 227p. (Orig.). 1992. pap. text ed. 18.00 (*0-87727-127-5*) Cornell SE Asia.

Studies on William Harvey. Ed. by I. Bernard Cohen. LC 80-2101. (Development of Science Ser.). (Illus.). 1981. lib. bdg. 71.95 (*0-405-13866-0*) Ayer.

***Studies on Women in Yemen.** Ed. by Lucine Taminian. (Translations of Western-Language Articles into Arabic for Use in Yemeni Universities Ser.: Vol. 3). Date not set. write for info. (*1-882557-05-0*) Am Inst Yemeni.

***Studies on Yemen, 1975-1990: A Bibliography of European Language Sources for Social Scientists.** Compiled by Thomas B. Stevenson. (Yemen Bibliography Ser.). xx, 197p. 1994. 15.00 (*1-882557-01-8*) Am Inst Yemeni.

Studies on Zone. Alice G. Brand. LC 89-13344. 72p. 1989. 8.95 (*0-933532-71-7*) BkMk.

Studies Out in Left Field: Defamatory Essays Presented to James D. McCawley on His 33rd or 34th Birthday. Ed. by Arnold M. Zwicky et al. LC 92-8095. xvi, 200p. 1992. reprint ed. pap. 12.95 (*1-55619-460-9*) Benjamins North Am.

Studies Presented to Professor Roman Jakobson by His Students. Ed. by Charles E. Gribble. 333p. 1968. 19.95 (*0-89357-001-X*); pap. 22.95 (*0-89357-000-1*) Slavica.

Studies Presented to the International Commission for the History of Representative & Parliamentary Institutions. 68p. 1982. 11.55 (*0-685-42548-7*) P Lang Pubng.

Studies Relating Automobile Design & Vehicle Safety: An Annotated Bibliography. Margaret E. Shepard. (CPL Bibliographies Ser.: No. 93). 93p. 1982. 10.00 (*0-86602-093-4*, Sage Prdcls Pr) Sage.

***Studies Show: A Popular Guide to Understanding Scientific Studies.** John H. Fennick. LC 97-3486. 1997. pap. 17.95 (*1-57392-136-X*) Prometheus Bks.

Studies to Enhance the Evaluation of Family Planning Programs, No. 87. 246p. 1998. 25.00 (*92-1-151106-2*, E.84.XIII.9) UN.

Studies to Evaluate the Potential for Improvements in Biological & Chemical Characteristics of Potable Water Transported in Copper Pipe. Midwest Research Institute Staff. 26p. 1984. write for info. (*0-318-60414-0*) Intl Copper.

***Studies Toward ISDN - The CCITT Organization & U. S.** (Satellites in an ISDN World Ser.). 50.00 (*0-614-18396-0*, 126P90) Info Gatekeepers.

Studies with Economic Rationality. Ed. by Klaus Weiermair & Mark Perlman. LC 89-77534. 450p. (C). 1990. reprint ed. text ed. 57.50 (*0-472-10154-4*) U of Mich Pr.

***Studio.** John G. Dunne. 1998. pap. write for info. (*0-375-70008-0*, Vin) Random.

Studio: And What to Do in It. Henry P. Robinson. LC 72-9231. (Literature of Photography Ser.). 1973. reprint ed. 18.95 (*0-405-04937-4*) Ayer.

STUDIO: Structured User-Interface Design for Interaction Optimisation. Dermot P. Browne. LC 93-12402. 350p. 1993. pap. text ed. 52.00 (*0-13-014721-4*) P-H.

Studio - Jazz Drum Cookbook. John Pickering. 1993. 8.95 (*0-87166-682-0*, 93625) Mel Bay.

Studio Affairs: My Life As a Film Director. Vincent Sherman. LC 96-14263. (Illus.). 360p. 1996. 24.95 (*0-8131-1975-8*) U Pr of Ky.

Studio & Stage. Joseph Harker. LC 70-174413. 283p. 1972. reprint ed. 26.95 (*0-405-08599-0*, Pub. by Blom Pubns UK) Ayer.

Studio Art: Praxis, Symbol, Presence. Marilyn Zurmuehlen. 68p. 1990. pap. 18.00 (*0-937652-51-2*) Natl Art Ed.

Studio Business Book. Jim Mandell. Ed. by Andy Jewett. (Illus.). 274p. (Orig.). 1994. pap. 34.95 (*0-918371-04-X*, MixBooks) Cardinal Busn Media.

Studio Calculus. Ecker. (C). 1995. teacher ed. write for info. (*0-673-97303-4*) Addson-Wesley Educ.

Studio Calculus. alternate ed. Ecker. 576p. (C). 1996. text ed. 47.95 (*0-673-99947-5*) Addson-Wesley Educ.

Studio Ceramic Dictionary. John W. Conrad. 90p. (Orig.). 1990. pap. 13.66 (*0-935921-12-5*) Falcon Co.

Studio Collotype: Continuous Tone Printing for the Artist, Printmaker & Photographer. Kent B. Kirby. (Illus.). 240p. (C). 1988. pap. text ed. 39.95 (*0-9620699-1-4*); lib. bdg. 56.00 (*0-9620699-0-6*) Heliochrome Pr.

Studio Drama Processes & Procedures. Robert J. Schihl. (Multiple Camera Video Ser.). 126p. 1991. pap. 32.95 (*0-240-80096-6*, Focal) Buttrwrth-Heinemann.

Studio Historiae Ardens: Ancient Near Eastern Studies: Presented to Philo H. J. Houwink Ten Cate on the Occasion of His 65th Birthday. Ed. by Theo P. Van Den Hout & Johan De Roos. xxviii, 344p. 1995. pap. 84.00 (*90-6258-075-0*, Pub. by Netherlands Inst NE) Eisenbrauns.

Studio Image 1. Sydney J. Mead. (Portfolio Ser.). (Illus.). (Orig.). 1988. 17.00 (*0-929463-00-5*) Oblagon.

Studio Image 2. Sydney J. Mead. (Portfolio Ser.). (Illus.). (Orig.). 1989. 19.00 (*0-929463-01-3*) Oblagon.

Studio Image 3. Sydney J. Mead. Ed. by Roger Servick. (Portfolio Ser.). (Illus.). 36p. (Orig.). 1994. 21.00 (*0-929463-02-1*) Oblagon.

Studio Monitoring Design: A Personal View. Philip R. Newell. LC 95-35572. (Illus.). 400p. 1995. 99.95 (*0-240-51407-6*, Focal) Buttrwrth-Heinemann.

Studio Nudes: Selected Photographs 1989-1992. Craig Morey. (Illus.). 80p. 1992. 25.00 (*0-9632813-0-5*) C Morey Photo.

Studio Portrait Photography. Rotovision S. A. Staff. (Pro-Photo Ser.). (Illus.). 160p. 1995. pap. 29.95 (*0-8230-6468-9*, Amphoto) Watsn-Guptill.

Studio Potter's Ceramic Extruder. John W. Conrad. (Illus.). 110p. (Orig.). (C). 1997. pap. 30.00 (*0-935921-16-8*) Falcon Co.

Studio Pottery. Oliver Watson. (Illus.). 288p. (C). 1993. pap. 35.00 (*0-7148-2948-X*, Pub. by Phaidon Press UK) Chronicle Bks.

Studio Recording for Musicians. Fred Miller. (Illus.). 144p. pap. 17.95 (*0-8256-4204-3*, AM32681) Music Sales.

Studio System. Ed. by Janet Staiger. LC 94-14489. (Depth of Field Ser.). (Illus.). 275p. (C). 1994. text ed. 48.00 (*0-8135-2130-0*); pap. text ed. 16.00 (*0-8135-2131-9*) Rutgers U Pr.

Studio Works No. 3: Student Work from the Harvard University Graduate School of Design. (Studio Works Ser.: Vol. 3). (Illus.). 144p. (Orig.). 1996. pap. 24.95 (*1-56898-071-X*) Princeton Arch.

Studio Works Vol. 4: Student Work from the Harvard University Graduate School of Design. (Illus.). 144p. (Orig.). 1997. pap. 24.95 (*1-56898-100-7*) Princeton Arch.

Studio 16A. Inner London Education Authority Staff. (C). 1986. student ed. 60.00 (*0-85950-599-5*, Pub. by S Thornes Pubs UK); teacher ed. 65.00 (*0-85950-600-2*, Pub. by S Thornes Pubs UK); audio 170.00 (*0-85950-601-0*, Pub. by S Thornes Pubs UK); Bulk cassette pack (minimum order 10 sets). audio 40.00 (*0-85950-633-9*, Pub. by S Thornes Pubs UK) St Mut.

Studio 16B. Inner London Education Authority Staff. (C). 1987. 70.00 (*0-85950-636-3*, Pub. by S Thornes Pubs UK); teacher ed. 65.00 (*0-85950-637-1*, Pub. by S Thornes Pubs UK); audio 195.00 (*0-85950-638-X*, Pub. by S Thornes Pubs UK); Bulk cassette pack (minimum order 10 sets). audio 45.00 (*0-85950-639-8*, Pub. by S Thornes Pubs UK) St Mut.

Studio 16C. Inner London Education Authority Staff. (C). 1987. student ed. 50.00 (*0-85950-640-1*, Pub. by S Thornes Pubs UK); teacher ed. 65.00 (*0-85950-641-X*, Pub. by S Thornes Pubs UK); audio 110.00 (*0-85950-642-8*, Pub. by S Thornes Pubs UK); Bulk cassette pack (minimum order 10 sets). audio 35.00 (*0-85950-643-6*, Pub. by S Thornes Pubs UK) St Mut.

Studiolo of Urbino: An Iconographic Investigation. Luciano Cheles. LC 85-25984. (Illus.). 195p. 1986. 50.00 (*0-271-00423-1*) Pa St U Pr.

Studios of Frances & Margaret MacDonald. Janice Helland. 1996. text ed. 69.95 (*0-7190-4783-8*, Pub. by Manchester Univ Pr UK) St Martin.

Studios of Paris: The Capital of Art in the Late Nineteenth Century. John Milner. 256p. (C). 1990. reprint ed. pap. 28.00 (*0-300-04749-5*) Yale U Pr.

Studios of Paris: The Capital of Art in the Nineteenth Century. John Milner. (C). 1988. 50.00 (*0-300-03990-5*) Yale U Pr.

Studiosorum Speculum Essays in Honor of Louis J. Lekai, O. Cist. Ed. by John R. Sommerfeldt & Francis R. Swietek. (Cistercian Studies: No. 141). 1993. 45.95 (*0-87907-641-0*) Cistercian Pubns.

***Studs.** William Boniface. 356p. 1996. 18.95 (*0-9654573-0-3*) W Boniface.

Studs Kirby: The Voice of America. Peter Bagge. (Illus.). 112p. (Orig.). 1989. pap. 13.95 (*1-56097-010-3*) Fantagraph Bks.

***Studs Lonigan.** James T. Farrell. Date not set. lib. bdg. 38.95 (*0-8488-1974-8*) Amereon Ltd.

Studs Lonigan: A Trilogy Comprising Young Lonigan, the Manhood of Studs Lonigan, & Judgment Day. James T. Farrell. LC 93-13851. (Prairie State Bks.). 912p. 1993. 17.95 (*0-252-06282-5*); text ed. 49.95 (*0-252-02062-6*) U of Ill Pr.

Studs Lonigan's Neighborhood: And the Making of James T. Farrell. Edgar M. Branch. LC 95-48322. (Illus.). 104p. (Orig.). 1996. pap. 20.00 (*0-933292-22-8*) Arts End.

Studs Terkel: A Life in Words. Tony Parker. 384p. 1996. 27.50 (*0-8050-3483-8*) H Holt & Co.

Study: A Guide to Effective Study, Revision & Examination Techniques. Robert Barrass. 200p. (gr. 13). 1984. pap. text ed. 26.00 (*0-412-25690-8*, NO. 9186) Chapman & Hall.

Study Abroad: The Experience of American Undergraduates. Jerry S. Carlson et al. LC 89-49243. (Contributions to the Study of Education Ser.: No. 37). (Illus.). 272p. 1990. text ed. 59.95 (*0-313-27385-5*, CSH/, Greenwood Pr) Greenwood.

Study Abroad see Foreign Language Teaching: Challenges to the Profession

Study Abroad & Early Careers: Experience of Former ERASMUS Students. Friedhelm Maiworm & Ulrich Teichler. 112p. 1996. pap. 34.95 (*1-85302-378-7*, Pub. by J Kingsley Pubs UK) Taylor & Francis.

Study Abroad Programmes, Vol. 1. Ed. by Barbara B. Burn et al. (Higher Education Policy Ser.: No. 11). 280p. 1990. 45.00 (*1-85302-522-4*) Taylor & Francis.

Study Abroad 1995: A Guide to Semester & Year Abroad Academic Programs. 2nd ed. 1071p. 1994. pap. 19.95 (*1-56079-430-5*) Petersons.

***Study Abroad 1998-1999.** UNESCO Staff. 1150p. 1997. pap. 29.95 (*92-3-003401-0*, U3401, Pub. by UNESCO-Bangkok TH) Bernan Associates.

Study Adventure in Trial by Fire. Anne S. White & Don Vanzant. 56p. (Orig.). 1985. pap. 1.95 (*0-89228-102-2*) Impact Christian.

Study-Aids & Review Notes for Student & Parents. 1968. pap. 3.50 (*0-87738-022-8*) Youth Ed.

***Study American Folklore.** 4th ed. Jan Brunvand. (C). Date not set. teacher ed., pap. text ed. write for info. (*0-393-97224-0*) Norton.

***Study American Folklore.** 4th ed. Jan Brunvand. LC 97-26188. (C). 1997. pap. text ed. write for info. (*0-393-97223-2*) Norton.

Study & Analysis of the Conditional Reflex. Ignatius A. Hamel. Bd. with Image & Meaning in Memory & Perception. T. V. Moore. ; Correlation Between Memory & Perception. T. V. Moore. ; Clinical & Psychoanalytical Studies. P. H. Furfey. ; Development of Meaning. A. R. McDonough. (Psychology Monographs General & Applied: Vol. 27). 1974. reprint ed. Set pap. 55.00 (*0-8115-1426-9*) Periodicals Srv.

Study & Critical Thinking Skills in College. 3rd ed. Kathleen T. McWhorter. LC 95-3935. (Illus.). 448p. (C). 1996. text ed. 32.50 (*0-673-99496-1*) Addson-Wesley Educ.

Study & Criticism of Italian Sculpture. John W. Pope-Hennessy. LC 80-20651. (Illus.). 271p. 1981. 45.00 (*0-87099-239-2*) Metro Mus Art.

Study & Criticism of Italian Sculpture. John W. Pope-Hennessy. LC 80-8589. (Illus.). 256p. (C). 1981. text ed. 85.00 (*0-691-03967-4*) Princeton U Pr.

Study & Exam-taking Made Easy. 3.00 (*0-686-40902-7*, SR7) Transitions.

Study & Interpretation of the Chemical Characrteristics of Natural Water. D. Usdi Hem. (C). 1991. text ed. 250.00 (*0-685-63520-1*, Pub. by Scientific Pubs II) St Mut.

Study & Interpretation of the Chemical Characteristics of Natural Water. 1996. lib. bdg. 252.99 (*0-8490-5980-1*) Gordon Pr.

***Study & Interpretation of the Chemical Characteristics of Natural Water.** 1997. lib. bdg. 251.95 (*0-8490-7699-4*) Gordon Pr.

Study & Interpretation of the Chemical Characteristics of Natural Water. D. Hem. (C). 1991. text ed. 250.00 (*81-7233-012-X*, Pub. by Scientific Pubs II) St Mut.

Study & Interpretation of the Chemical Characteristics of Natural Water. John D. Hem. (C). 1990. 400.00 (*0-685-54210-6*, Pub. by Scientific UK) St Mut.

Study & Learning. 2nd ed. Wayne R. Herlin. 298p. (C). 1996. per., pap. text ed. 19.42 (*0-7872-0320-3*) Kendall-Hunt.

Study & Love: Aristotle's Fall. Ed. by Ayers Bagley. (SPE Monographs). 1986. 3.00 (*0-933669-39-9*) Soc Profs Ed.

Study & Practice of Astral Projection. Robert Crookall. 1977. pap. 5.95 (*0-8065-0547-8*, Citadel Pr) Carol Pub Group.

Study & Practice of Astral Projection. Robert Crookall. 1966. 7.50 (*0-8216-0154-7*, Univ Bks) Carol Pub Group.

Study & Practice of Military Law. G. K. Sharma. (C). 1988. 250.00 (*0-685-27898-0*) St Mut.

Study & Reading Skills. (Basic Academics Ser.: Module 1). (Illus.). 80p. 1982. spiral bd. 27.50 (*0-87683-225-7*) GP Courseware.

Study & Research Guide Computer Science: Profiles of the Top 40 Universities in the U. S. A. W. Tolle et al. LC 92-39481. 1993. write for info. (*3-540-55319-3*); 19.95 (*0-387-55319-3*) Spr-Verlag.

Study & Writing of Poetry by American Women Poets. 2nd rev. ed. Wauneta A. Hackleman. Ed. by Amy J. Zook. LC 82-50773. 375p. 1996. pap. 18.50 (*0-87875-464-4*) Whitston Pub.

Study & Writing Skills Manual. Barbara A. Wilson. (Wilson Reading System Ser.). 34p. (J). 1992. teacher ed. 8.00 (*1-56778-042-3*) Wilson Lang Trning.

Study Atlas of Electron Micrographs. 3rd rev. ed. Judy M. Strum. LC 86-80327. (Illus.). 208p. (C). 1992. text ed. 28.00 (*0-9608786-2-9*) Univ Maryland.

Study Buddies: Parent Tutoring Tactics. Julie Bowen et al. (Homework Partners Ser.). (Illus.). 126p. (Orig.). 1996. pap. 16.50 (*1-57035-014-0*, 44STUDY) Sopris.

Study Cards for Kinesiology & Anatomy. rev. ed. Barbara Gench & Marilyn M. Hinson. 132p. 1995. 22.95 (*0-912855-33-9*) E Bowers Pub.

Study Circles: Coming Together for Personal Growth and Social Change. Leonard P. Oliver. LC 87-12874. (Illus.). 165p. (Orig.). 1987. pap. 9.95 (*0-932020-47-X*) Seven Locks Pr.

Study Companion & Index to the Recorded Teachings of J. Krishnamurti (1979-1986) Krishnamurti Foundation of America Staff. Ed. by John Van der Struijf & Cathy Van der Struijf. 672p. 1997. per. write for info. (*1-888004-09-6*) Krishnamurti.

Study Companion to Old Testament Literature: An Approach to the Writing of Pre-Exilic & Exilic Israel. Anthony F. Campbell. LC 86-45319. (Old Testament Message Ser.). 504p. (Orig.). 1989. pap. 24.95 (*0-8146-5586-6*) Liturgical Pr.

Study Course in Christian Evidences. Bert Thompson & Wayne Jackson. 162p. 1991. reprint ed. pap. 4.00 (*0-932859-19-4*) Apologetic Pr.

Study Course in Homoeopathy. Phyllis Speight. 111p. 1991. pap. 15.95 (*0-85207-250-3*, Pub. by C W Daniel UK) Natl Bk Netwk.

Study Design, Procedures & Available Data for 1968-1972 Interviewing Years see Panel Study of Income Dynamics: Complete Documentation for Interviewing Years 1968-1981

Study English-Korean - Korean-English Dictionary. (Illus.). (ENG & KOR.). 1987. 19.50 (*0-89346-300-0*) Heian Intl.

Study for Applying Computer-Generated Images to Visual Stimulation. Robert A. Schumaker et al. LC 74-131394. 142p. 1969. 19.00 (*0-403-04536-3*) Scholarly.

Study Group Readings. Compiled by Associations for Research & Enlightenment, Readings Research Department Staff. (Library: Vol. 7). 545p. 1977. lib. bdg. 19.95 (*0-87604-094-6*, 1107) ARE Pr.

Study Guide: Advanced Placement French Literature - Le Cid. Stephen C. Clem. 60p. (Orig.). (FRE.). (YA). (gr. 11-12). 1996. pap. text ed. 6.67 (*1-877653-40-3*, 36) Wayside Pub.

Study Guide: Advanced Placement French Literature - L'Ecole des Femmes. Stephen C. Clem. 52p. (Orig.). (FRE.). (YA). (gr. 11-12). 1996. pap. text ed. 6.67 (*1-877653-41-1*, 37) Wayside Pub.

Study Guide: Advanced Placement French Literature - Pierre et Jean. Stephen C. Clem. 76p. (Orig.). (YA). (gr. 11-12). 1996. pap. text ed. 6.67 (*1-877653-33-0*, 33) Wayside Pub.

Study Guide: The Once & Future Church, Transforming Congregations. Gilbert R. Rendle. (Once & Future Church Ser.). pap. text ed. 11.95 (*1-56699-159-5*) Alban Inst.

Study Guide - Self Test for Physiological Chemistry I. Joann M. Coppola & Michael Frechette. 112p. 1995. spiral bd. 15.69 (*0-8403-8942-6*) Kendall-Hunt.

Study Guide & Creativity Exercises to Accompany Creativity Is Forever. Gary Davis. 76p. (C). 1995. write for info. (*0-8403-9875-1*) Kendall-Hunt.

Study Guide & Exam Review for Comprehensive Dent. Finkbeiner. 1993. text ed. write for info. (*0-397-54924-5*) Lppncott-Raven.

Study Guide & Manual for the National Certification Examinations for Nurse Practitioners & Other Primary Health Care Providers. Patricia Martinell et al. 125p. 1989. pap. text ed. 19.95 (*0-8290-1279-6*) Irvington.

***Study Guide & Personal Growth Exercise.** Jewell. 1989. pap. 20.95 (*0-314-52486-X*) Wadsworth Pub.

***Study Guide & Readings to Accompany the Journey Vol. 1: Pak.** Dorothy Salem. 352p. (C). 1997. 39.95 (*0-7872-3922-4*) Kendall-Hunt.

***Study Guide & Readings to Accompany the Journey Vol. 2: Pak.** Dorothy Salem. 304p. (C). 1997. 39.95 (*0-7872-3912-7*) Kendall-Hunt.

Study Guide & Self-Assessment for the American Psychiatric Press Textbook of Neuropsychiatry. Michael D. Franzen & Mark R. Lovell. LC 87-1057. 231p. 1987. reprint ed. pap. 65.90 (*0-7837-2092-0*, 2042368) Bks Demand.

Study Guide & Self-Assessment for the American Psychiatric Press Textbook of Psychiatry. Mark R. Lovell & Michael D. Franzen. 406p. 1988. reprint ed. pap. 115.80 (*0-608-02025-7*, 2062681) Bks Demand.

Study Guide & Self-Examination Review for Kaplan & Sadock's Synopsis of Psychiatry. 5th ed. Harold I. Kaplan & Benjamin J. Sadock. Ed. by Caroly Pataki & Rebecca Jones. LC 94-13269. Orig. Title: Study Guide & Self-Examination Review for Synopsis of Psychiatry & Comprehensive Textbook of Psychiatry. (Illus.). 480p. 1994. 45.00 (*0-683-04541-5*) Williams & Wilkins.

Study Guide & Self-Examination Review for Synopsis of Psychiatry & Comprehensive Textbook of Psychiatry see Study Guide & Self-Examination Review for Kaplan & Sadock's Synopsis of Psychiatry

Study Guide & Self-Examination Review for Understanding Human Behavior in Health & Illness. 3rd ed. Richard C. Simons. 348p. write for info. (*0-683-04571-7*) Williams & Wilkins.

Study Guide & Solutions Manual to Accompany Stuart J. Baum & John W. Hill Introduction to Organic & Biological Chemistry. Marvin L. Hackert & Robert K. Sandwick. (Illus.). 256p. (C). 1993. pap. text ed. 27.40 (*0-02-348605-8*, Macmillan Coll) P-H.

S

An Asterisk (*) at the beginning of an entry indicates that the title is appearing in BIP for the first time.

S

Study Guide & Work-book to Accompany Financial Institutions, Investments, & Management: An Introduction. 5th ed. Herbert B. Mayo. 240p. (C). 1994. student ed., pap. text ed. 25.75 (*0-03-098652-4*) Dryden Pr.

Study Guide Book. ACCESS Staff. (Mathematics for Modern Living Ser.). 1980. pap. text ed. 25.00 (*1-55740-000-8*) Magna Systems.

Study Guide College Physics. Davis. (C). 1912. teacher ed., pap. text ed. 16.75 (*0-03-097157-8*) HarBrace.

***Study Guide "Discipleship" Living for Christ in the Daily Grind.** Bruderhof Communities Staff. 94p. (Orig.). 1997. pap. 3.50 (*0-87486-088-1*) Plough.

***Study Guide Electrical General: Electrical Inspector Certification Program.** 6th ed. Ed. by Ed Lawry. (Illus.). iv, 174p. 1996. spiral bd., pap. 22.50 (*1-890659-09-6*, 360016) Intl Assn Elec Inspect.

***Study Guide Electrical Plan Review: Electrical Inspector Certification Program.** 6th ed. Ed. by Ed Lawry. (Illus.). iv, 156p. 1996. spiral bd., pap. 22.50 (*1-890659-10-X*, 360018) Intl Assn Elec Inspect.

***Study Guide Electrical 1- & 2-Family: Electrical Inspector Certification Program.** 6th ed. Ed. by Ed Lawry. (Illus.). iv, 142p. 1996. spiral bd., pap. 22.50 (*1-890659-08-8*, 360014) Intl Assn Elec Inspect.

Study Guide for ACSW Certification. Ruth R. Middleman. 1995. pap. 15.95 (*0-87101-264-2*) Natl Assn Soc Wkrs.

Study Guide for Building Self-Esteem. 2nd ed. Lilburn S. Barksdale. LC 88-7661. 54p. 1989. pap. 6.95 (*0-918588-12-X*, 113) Barksdale Foun.

Study Guide for CCH Federal Taxation, 1992: Advanced Topics. Foth. 320p. pap. 19.50 (*0-318-33416-X*, 4908) Commerce.

Study Guide for Communication & Human Behavior. Brent D. Ruben. 96p. (C). 1996. spiral bd. 14.43 (*0-8403-9050-5*) Kendall-Hunt.

***Study Guide for Contemporary Non-Western Cultures.** Dorothy Bruner. 150p. (C). 1996. pap. text ed. 12.54 (*0-7872-2775-7*) Kendall-Hunt.

Study Guide for Credit Life & Disability Insurance. Gary Fagg. 198p. (Orig.). 1990. text ed. 20.00 (*0-9627820-1-7*) CreditRe.

Study Guide for Criminal Justice. James A. Inciardi. 1983. 7.00i (*0-12-370751-X*) HarBrace.

Study Guide for Criminal Justice. James A. Inciardi. 1984. teacher ed. 5.00i (*0-12-370752-8*) HarBrace.

***Study Guide for Digital Image Processing.** Mark J. Smith & Alen Docef. (Illus.). (C). 1997. text ed. 66.00 (*0-9657311-0-3*) Sci Pub GA.

***Study Guide for Discovering Psychology Telecourse to Accompany Psychology.** 5th ed. David G. Myers. (C). 1997. pap. text ed. 14.95 (*1-57259-546-9*) Worth.

Study Guide for Economics: Dealing with Scarcity. 2nd ed. Dale M. Sievert. 169p. 1991. pap. 9.95 (*0-9621796-4-7*) Glengarry Pub.

Study Guide for Efficient Reading: Alternate Edition. James I. Brown & Karyn S. Prois. Ed. by W. W. Kemmerer. 52p. (C). pap. text ed. 4.95 (*0-943000-05-X*) Telstar Inc.

Study Guide for Efficient Reading: Form B. James I. Brown & Karyn S. Prois. 52p. (C). 1982. reprint ed. pap. text ed. 4.95 (*0-943000-06-8*) Telstar Inc.

Study Guide for Electrical Examinations: Based on 1996 NEC. 5th ed. Michael G. Owen. 137p. 1996. student ed., pap. text ed. 39.95 (*1-888512-04-0*) Elect Trnging.

Study Guide for Electrical Examinations: Instructor's Solution Manual. Michael G. Owen. 42p. 1996. teacher ed., pap. 19.95 (*1-888512-05-9*) Elect Trnging.

Study Guide for Emergency Care in the Streets. 5th ed. Nancy L. Caroline. (Illus.). 259p. 1995. pap. text ed. 24.95 (*0-316-12893-7*) Lppncott-Raven.

Study Guide for Engineering & the Physical Sciences. William A. Levinson. (Illus.). 101p. (Orig.). 1988. pap. text ed. 7.00 (*0-913811-04-1*) Northeast A S.

Study Guide for Essentials of Critical Care Nursing. Varrassi. 156p. 1990. pap. text ed. 16.95 (*0-397-54846-X*) Lppncott-Raven.

Study Guide for Essentials of Fire Fighting: Study Guide for Third Edition. Marsha Sneed. LC 92-73546. (Illus.). 322p. (Orig.). 1992. pap. text ed. 16.50 (*0-87939-102-2*) IFSTA.

Study Guide for Evangelism Praying: For Evangelism Praying. Evelyn Christenson. 72p. (Orig.). 1996. student ed., pap. 5.99 (*1-56507-527-7*) Harvest Hse.

Study Guide for Ezekiel. Kieth B. Kuschel. (People's Bible Ser.). 56p. (Orig.). 1987. pap. text ed. 4.00 (*0-938272-58-6*, 22-2199) WELS Board.

Study Guide for Ezra, Nehemiah, Esther. John F. Brug. (Study Guide for People's Bible Ser.). 60p. (Orig.). 1985. pap. 4.00 (*0-938272-53-5*, 22-2178) WELS Board.

Study Guide for Family & Child Development-200. Ed. by Catherine Solheim. (Illus.). 120p. (C). 1994. student ed. 16.95 (*0-89892-111-2*) Contemp Pub Co of Raleigh.

Study Guide for Federal Tax Course, 1994. Foth. 416p. 1993. pap. 21.50 (*0-685-67037-6*, 5409) Commerce.

Study Guide for Fire Department Pumping Apparatus. Robert Fleischner. Ed. by Gene P. Carlson. LC 89-82378. (Illus.). 100p. (Orig.). 1990. pap. text ed. 16.50 (*0-87939-085-9*) IFSTA.

Study Guide for First Corinthians. Carleton A. Toppe. (People's Bible Ser.). 70p. (Orig.). 1988. pap. text ed. 4.00 (*0-938272-65-9*, 22-2207) WELS Board.

Study Guide for First Edition of Awareness Level Training for Hazardous Materials. Susan S. Walker. (Illus.). 152p. (Orig.). 1995. pap. text ed. 18.50 (*0-87939-118-9*) IFSTA.

***Study Guide for First Edition of Principles of Foam Fire Fighting.** Pam Griffith. Ed. by Susan Walker & Barbara Adams. (Illus.). 174p. (Orig.). 1996. pap. 14.50 (*0-87939-134-0*, 36001) IFSTA.

Study Guide for General Biology I. Eddie C. McNack. 156p. (C). 1989. pap. text ed. 15.95 (*0-89641-179-6*) American Pr.

Study Guide for Handbook of Speech-Language Pathology & Audiology. Northern. 446p. (gr. 13). 1988. pap. text ed. 38.95 (*1-55664-036-6*) Mosby Yr Bk.

Study Guide for Hazardous Materials for First Responders. Susan Walker. LC 89-60946. (Illus.). 196p. (Orig.). 1989. pap. text ed. 15.00 (*0-87939-081-6*) IFSTA.

Study Guide for Health, Safety & Nutrition for the Young Child. 3rd ed. Lynn R. Marotz et al. 169p. 1993. student ed. 14.95 (*0-8273-6060-6*) Delmar.

Study Guide for Hebrews. Richard E. Lauersdorf. Ed. by William E. Fischer. (Study Guide for People's Bible Ser.). 48p. (Orig.). 1986. pap. 4.00 (*0-938272-56-X*, 22-2189) WELS Board.

Study Guide for Human Embryology. William J. Larsen. (Illus.). 272p. 1993. 21.95 (*0-443-08944-2*) Churchill.

Study Guide for IFSTA Fire Department Aerial Apparatus. Susan S. Walker. Ed. by Gene P. Carlson. LC 91-70082. (Illus.). 140p. (Orig.). 1991. pap. text ed. 16.50 (*0-87939-091-3*) IFSTA.

Study Guide for IFSTA Fire Department Company Officer. Susan S. Walker. LC 89-82071. 243p. (Orig.). 1991. pap. text ed. 16.50 (*0-87939-096-4*) IFSTA.

Study Guide for IFSTA Fire Inspection & Code Enforcement. Robert Fleischner. Ed. by Gene P. Carlson. LC 87-82661. (Illus.). 266p. 1989. pap. text ed. 16.50 (*0-87939-080-8*) IFSTA.

Study Guide for IFSTA Self-Contained Breathing Apparatus. Susan S. Walker. LC 91-71902. (Illus.). 131p. (Orig.). 1991. pap. text ed. 14.50 (*0-87939-094-8*) IFSTA.

Study Guide for Intermediate Labanotation. 2nd rev. ed. Jane Marriet & Muriel Topaz. (Illus.). 110p. (C). 1970. pap. text ed. 22.95 (*0-932582-58-3*, Pub. by Dance Bks UK) Princeton Bk Co.

***Study Guide for Introductory Genetics.** 2nd ed. David Peebles. 324p. (C). 1997. spiral bd. 36.95 (*0-7872-3669-1*) Kendall-Hunt.

Study Guide for Language & Deafness. 2nd ed. Peter V. Paul & Stephen P. Quigley. 192p. (C). 1994. pap. text ed. 24.50 (*1-56593-363-X*, 0700) Singular Publishing.

***Study Guide for Learning Sequences in Music: Skill, Content & Patterns : A Music Learning Theory : 1997.** Edwin Gordon. LC 97-21941. 1997. write for info. (*1-57999-005-3*) GIA Pubns.

Study Guide for Leviticus. Mark J. Lenz. (People's Bible Ser.). 62p. (Orig.). 1989. pap. text ed. 4.00 (*0-938272-68-3*, 22-2214) WELS Board.

Study Guide for Microbiology: An Introduction. 5th ed. Berdell R. Funke. Ed. by Gerard J. Tortora. (C). 1995. pap. text ed. 19.50 (*0-8053-8508-8*) Benjamin-Cummings.

Study Guide for Ministry & Counsel. rev. ed. 30p. (Orig.). 1985. pap. 1.50 (*0-942727-11-8*) NC Yrly Pubns Bd.

Study Guide for Modern Real Estate Practice. 14th ed. 1996. pap. 14.95 (*0-7931-2303-8*, 15100214, Real Estate Ed) Dearborn Finan.

Study Guide for National Certification in Therapeutic Recreation. Gerald O'Morrow & Ron Reynolds. LC 90-71335. 89p. 1990. 11.95 (*0-910251-38-X*) Venture Pub PA.

***Study Guide for Ninth Edition of Fire Service Ground Ladders.** Pam Griffith. Ed. by Susan Walker & Barbara Adams. (Illus.). 64p. (Orig.). 1996. pap. text ed. 14.50 (*0-87939-132-4*, 35940) IFSTA.

Study Guide for Obadiah, Jonah, Micah. Cyril W. Spaude. (People's Bible Ser.). 60p. (Orig.). 1988. pap. text ed. 4.00 (*0-938272-67-5*, 22-2211) WELS Board.

Study Guide for Obstetrics. 2nd ed. Steven G. Gabbe et al. 170p. 1992. 29.95 (*0-443-08846-2*) Churchill.

Study Guide for Obstetrics: Normal & Problem Pregnancies. Steven G. Gabbe et al. (Illus.). 147p. reprint ed. pap. 41.90 (*0-7837-1610-9*, 2041902) Bks Demand.

Study Guide for Operating Systems: A Systematic View. 4th ed. William Davis. (C). 1992. pap. text ed. 12.95 (*0-201-56703-2*) Addison-Wesley.

Study Guide for Oregon Real Estate Law. 2nd ed. John Jeddeloh. (C). 1990. text ed. write for info. (*1-878572-01-6*) Metro Brokers.

Study Guide for Oregon Real Estate Practices. 2nd ed. John Jeddeloh. (C). 1990. pap. 25.00 (*1-878572-03-2*) Metro Brokers.

Study Guide for Out of Many, Vol. 1. Neumeyer. 1994. student ed., pap. text ed. 19.40 (*0-13-564485-2*) P-H.

Study Guide for Paul's Letters to the Thessalonians. David P. Kuske. 41p. (Orig.). 1984. pap. 3.00 (*0-938272-51-9*, 22N2167) WELS Board.

Study Guide for Philippians-Colossians & Philemon. Harlyn J. Kuschel. Ed. by William E. Fischer. (Study Guide for People's Bible Ser.). 48p. (Orig.). 1987. pap. text ed. 4.00 (*0-938272-57-8*, 22-2198) WELS Board.

***Study Guide for Photo/Imaging.** 4th ed. Kim Mosley. 44p. (C). 1997. pap. text ed. 6.00 (*0-88196-010-1*) Oak Woods Media.

Study Guide for Planet Earth: A Telecourse. S. Carl Opper. 80p. (C). 1992. spiral bd. 7.60 (*1-880847-01-9*) DEWMAR Hse.

Study Guide for Preventive Medicine Certification, 1990: A Manual for Specialists in Occupational Medicine, Aerospace Medicine & General Preventive Medicine. Nick A. Vlachos et al. 247p. 1990. pap. text ed. 55.00 (*0-9623864-1-3*) OEM Health.

Study Guide for Principles of Accounting. Shubiak & Hibbitts. (Illus.). 85p. (C). 1988. student ed. write for info. (*0-944324-15-0*) Am Artist Pub.

Study Guide for Principles of Statistics. Herzberg & Elke U. Weber. 350p. (C). 1989. reprint ed. pap. 21.00 (*0-89464-409-2*) Krieger.

Study Guide for Psalms, Vol. 1. John F. Brug. (People's Bible Ser.). 64p. (Orig.). 1989. pap. text ed. 4.00 (*0-938272-61-6*, 22-2204) WELS Board.

Study Guide For Real Estate License Examinations. R. Ripley. (Orig.). pap. 3.95 (*0-13-858753-1*, Reward) P-H.

Study Guide for Second Edition of Materials for First Responders. Susan S. Walker. (Illus.). 260p. (Orig.). 1994. pap. text ed. 16.50 (*0-87939-113-8*) IFSTA.

***Study Guide for Sixth Edition of Fire Service Rescue.** 1997. 14.50 (*0-87939-138-3*, 35003) IFSTA.

***Study Guide for the Actuarial Exam 100: Calculus & Linear Algebra.** Thomas McGannon. 276p. (C). 1996. ring bd. 18.95 (*0-87563-670-5*) Stipes.

***Study Guide for the Actuarial Exam 110: Probability & Statistics.** Thomas McGannon. 200p. (C). 1996. ring bd. 13.95 (*0-87563-671-3*) Stipes.

Study Guide for the Associate CET Test. 4th ed. Ed. by Joseph A. Risse. 72p. 1989. pap. 10.00 (*0-317-04954-2*) Intl Soc Cert Elect.

Study Guide for the Associate Level CET Test. 4th ed. 1989. reprint ed. 10.00 (*0-317-05557-7*) Intl Soc Cert Elect.

Study Guide for the Book of St. John: Knowing & Understanding Jesus Christ. Avaneda D. Hobbs. (Illus.). (Orig.). 1993. pap. 3.95 (*1-878898-07-8*) Christian Star.

Study Guide for the Bull's-Eye of Life. Leon J. LeBorgne. LC 94-96684. 76p. (YA). 1995. pap. text ed. 4.95 (*1-886707-02-2*) L & L Enter.

Study Guide for the CET Test-Computer Option. 4th ed. Ed. by Elmer Poe. 31p. 1993. pap. 10.00 (*0-318-17467-7*) Intl Soc Cert Elect.

Study Guide for "The Chinese" Thomas M. Buoye. 109p. 1992. pap. text ed. 10.00 (*0-89264-104-5*) Ctr Chinese Studies.

Study Guide for the Developing Person Through the Life Span Telecourse. 2nd ed. Richard O. Straub. 367p. 1993. Season of Life study guide (telecourse). student ed., pap. text ed. 12.95 (*0-87901-467-9*) Worth.

Study Guide for the Discovering Psychology Telecourse, Myers, Psychology. 4th ed. Richard O. Straub. 468p. 1995. pap. text ed. 14.95 (*0-87901-777-5*) Worth.

Study Guide for the Florida Law Enforcement Officer's Certification Examination. William G. Doerner & Charles W. Rushing. LC 96-23269. 320p. (Orig.). 1996. pap. 16.95 (*1-56164-109-X*) Pineapple Pr.

Study Guide for the Nata Board of Certification, Inc. Entry-Level Athletic Trainer Certification Examination. 2nd ed. NATA Board of Certification Staff. (Illus.). 146p. (C). 1993. pap. text ed. 32.95 (*0-8036-6501-6*) Davis Co.

Study Guide for the National Counselor Examination. 3rd ed. Andrew A. Helwig. 270p. 1996. pap. text ed. 40.00 (*0-9648377-0-6*) A A Helwig.

Study Guide for the NCTRC Therapeutic Recreation Specialist Certification Examination. Norma Stumbo & Jean Folkerth. LC 90-70830. 108p. 1990. pap. text ed. 14.95 (*0-915611-28-7*) Sagamore Pub.

Study Guide for the New Birth. Neil Stegall & David K. Bernard. LC 87-10491. 120p. (Orig.). 1987. spiral bd. 7.99 (*0-932581-15-3*) Word Aflame.

Study Guide for The Oneness of God. David K. Bernard & Neil Stegall. 114p. (Orig.). (C). 1989. pap. 7.99 (*0-932581-59-5*) Word Aflame.

Study Guide for the Registration Examination for Dietitians. 5th ed. Commission on Dietetic Registration Staff. 50p. 1991. ring bd. 25.00 (*0-88091-086-0*, 0608) Am Dietetic Assn.

Study Guide for "The Return" by Sonia Levitin. Brenda Custodio. (Ethnic Explorations Ser.). 32p. (YA). 1994. teacher ed., wbk. ed. 11.95 (*1-882628-11-X*) Lotus Hse.

Study Guide for the Telecourse to Accompany Marketing to Accompany Contemporary Marketing Plus. 8th ed. Louis E. Boone et al. 448p. (C). 1995. student ed., pap. text ed. 25.00 (*0-03-003983-5*) Dryden Pr.

Study Guide for the Textbook of Gynecology. Larry J. Copeland. 304p. 1993. pap. text ed. 37.95 (*0-7216-3383-8*) Saunders.

***Study Guide for the Therapeutic Recreation Certification Examination.** 2nd ed. Norma Stumbo & Jean Folkerth. 1997. pap. 21.95 (*1-57167-034-3*) Sagamore Pub.

Study Guide for We Americans, Vol. I. 3rd ed. Leonard Pitt. 112p. 1989. per. 28.29 (*0-8403-5628-5*) Kendall-Hunt.

Study Guide for We Americans, Vol. II. 3rd ed. Leonard Pitt. 160p. 1989. per. 31.44 (*0-8403-5629-3*) Kendall-Hunt.

Study Guide Head & Neck Surgery. Byron J. Bailey. 352p. 1993. pap. text ed. 49.50 (*0-397-51345-3*) Lppncott-Raven.

Study Guide in Alternating Current Circuits: A Personalized System of Instruction. Irving L. Kosow. LC 77-22152. (Electronic Technology Ser.). 515p. reprint ed. pap. 146.80 (*0-317-10110-2*, 2015180) Bks Demand.

Study Guide in Direct Current Circuits: A Personalized System of Instruction. Irving L. Kosow. LC 77-1739. (Series in Electronic Technology). 399p. reprint ed. 113.80 (*0-8357-9873-9*, 2015181) Bks Demand.

Study Guide Mathematical Thinking. Jimmy Solomon & Glenn Hopkins. 208p. (C). 1994. per., pap. text ed. 14.64 (*0-7872-0047-6*) Kendall-Hunt.

Study Guide of Clinical Hematology: Theory & Practice. Janice Hudson & Robert F. Bunting, Jr. LC 93-41166. (Illus.). 259p. (C). 1994. pap. text ed. 23.95 (*0-8036-4604-6*) Davis Co.

Study Guide, Physical Chemistry. Clyde R. Metz. (C). Date not set. pap. text ed. 13.25 (*0-03-097866-1*) HarBrace.

Study Guide Program Evaluation. 2nd ed. Blaine Worthen. (C). 1997. teacher ed., pap. text ed. 15.95 (*0-8013-1985-4*) Addison-Wesley.

Study Guide-Solutions Manual to Accompany General CChemistry. 3rd ed. Donald A. McQuarrie. (C). 1995. pap. text ed. write for info. (*0-7167-2179-1*) W H Freeman.

Study Guide Some Fundamental Spiritual Verities: A Study Guide to the Revelation of Baha'u'llah. R. T. Anderson. 1988. pap. 4.95 (*0-85398-282-1*) G Ronald Pub.

Study Guide to Accompany Anthony Textbook. 11th ed. Prezbindowski. 370p. 1993. pap. 15.95 (*0-8016-4011-3*) Mosby Yr Bk.

Study Guide to Accompany Bedeian, "Management," Third Edition. 3rd ed. Sally A. Coltrin et al. 360p. (C). 1993. pap. text ed. 24.00 (*0-03-074688-4*) Dryden Pr.

Study Guide to Accompany Bloomfield-Fairley: Business Communication: A Process Approach. Thomas Lochhaas. 257p. (C). 1991. pap. text ed. 18.75 (*0-15-505670-0*) HB Coll Pubs.

Study Guide to Accompany Chemistry: The Molecular Science. Tikkanen. 400p. 1993. pap. 16.95 (*0-8016-5070-4*) Mosby Yr Bk.

***Study Guide to Accompany Clinical Drug Therapy.** 5th ed. Ropelewski & Ryan. 256p. 1997. pap. text ed. 15.95 (*0-397-55373-0*) Lppncott-Raven.

Study Guide to Accompany College Physics. 7th ed. Francis W. Sears. (C). 1991. pap. text ed. 25.50 (*0-201-51246-7*) Addison-Wesley.

Study Guide to Accompany Computed Tomography. Euclid Seeram. Ed. by Lisa Biello. LC 96-41148. 416p. 1996. student ed., pap. text ed. 35.00 (*0-7216-6103-3*) Saunders.

Study Guide to Accompany Economics. 4th ed. Stephen L. Slavin. 160p. (C). 1996. per. 14.36 (*0-256-21919-2*) Irwin.

Study Guide to Accompany Economics Theory & Practice. 5th ed. Patrick Welch & Gerry F. Welch. 384p. (C). 1995. student ed., pap. text ed. 24.00 (*0-03-006652-2*) Dryden Pr.

***Study Guide to Accompany Edwards, Wattenberg, Lineberry's Government in America.** 8th ed. Matzke. (C). 1998. pap. text ed. write for info. (*0-321-01898-2*) Addison-Wesley.

Study Guide to Accompany Effective Police Supervision. 2nd ed. Contrib. by Bonnie Wilbanks. 129p. 1995. pap. 16.95 (*0-87084-580-2*) Anderson Pub Co.

Study Guide to Accompany Ekelund-Tollison Microeconomics. Robert Ekelund. (C). 1997. pap. text ed. 21.50 (*0-201-92016-6*) Addison-Wesley.

Study Guide to Accompany Elements of Economics. John Egger. 316p. (C). 1994. student ed., per., pap. text ed. 19.89 (*0-8403-9727-5*) Kendall-Hunt.

Study Guide to Accompany Essentials of Pediatric Nursing. 4th ed. Murphy. 230p. 1992. pap. 17.95 (*0-8016-7415-8*) Mosby Yr Bk.

***Study Guide to Accompany Fundamentals of Nursing.** 3rd ed. Lillis & LeMone. (Illus.). 384p. 1996. pap. text ed. 17.95 (*0-397-55279-3*) Lppncott-Raven.

***Study Guide to Accompany Health in the New Millennium.** Jeffrey Nevid et al. (C). 1997. pap. text ed. 15.95 (*1-57259-502-7*) Worth.

Study Guide to Accompany Human Anatomy & Physiology. 3rd ed. LC 94-39756. (C). 1995. pap. text ed. 23.75 (*0-8053-4283-4*) Benjamin-Cummings.

Study Guide to Accompany Human Physiology. Schauf & Kevin T. Patton. 320p. 1989. pap. 16.95 (*0-8016-4279-5*) Mosby Yr Bk.

Study Guide to Accompany Human Sexuality. 2nd ed. Carole Wade & Sarah Cirese. 245p. (C). 1991. pap. text ed. 12.00 (*0-685-49593-0*) HB Coll Pubs.

Study Guide to Accompany Jacob & Francone's Elements of Anatomy & Physiology. 2nd ed. Terry Bristol. (Illus.). 183p. 1992. pap. text ed. 16.95 (*0-7216-3644-6*) Saunders.

***Study Guide to Accompany Lippincott's Textbook for Medical Assistants.** Herschfelt & Brill. 512p. 1997. pap. text ed. 19.95 (*0-397-55107-X*) Lppncott-Raven.

Study Guide to Accompany Lloyd Saxton's The Individual, Marriage, & the Family. 8th ed. M. Betsy Bergen. 253p. (C). 1993. student ed., pap. 12.00 (*0-534-19730-2*) Wadsworth Pub.

Study Guide to Accompany Macroeconomics: Private Markets & Public Choice. Robert Ekelund. (C). 1997. pap. text ed. 21.50 (*0-201-87430-X*) Addison-Wesley.

Study Guide to Accompany Maternal & Neonatal Care: Family-Centered Care. 3rd ed. Tiller. 336p. (C). 1994. pap. text ed. 16.95 (*0-397-55124-X*, Lippncott) Lppncott-Raven.

Study Guide to Accompany Maternity Nursing: An Introductory Text. 6th ed. Arlene Burroughs. (Illus.). 224p. 1992. pap. text ed. 19.95 (*0-7216-3314-5*) Saunders.

Study Guide to Accompany Medical-Surgical Nursing. Priscilla Lemone. (C). 1997. pap. text ed. 17.95 (*0-8053-4078-5*) Addison-Wesley.

Study Guide to Accompany Microbiology. Raul J. Cano & Jaime S. Colome. 1989. pap. text ed. 22.75 (*0-314-87261-2*) West Pub.

Study Guide to Accompany Nursing: A Human Needs Approach. 5th ed. Barbara R. Stright. 356p. (C). 1994. pap. text ed. 15.95 (*0-397-55119-3*, Lippncott) Lppncott-Raven.

***Study Guide to Accompany Nursing Pharmacology & Clinical Management.** Venable. 368p. 1998. pap. text ed. write for info. (*0-397-55245-9*) Lppncott-Raven.

Study Guide to Accompany Our Global Environment: A Health Perspective. 4th rev. ed. Anne Nadakavukaren. 196p. (C). 1995. pap. text ed. 10.95 (*0-88133-832-X*) Waveland Pr.

***Study Guide to Accompany Practicing American Politics.** David Edwards & Alessandra Lippucci. (C). 1997. pap. text ed. write for info. (*1-57259-529-9*) Worth.

An Asterisk (*) at the beginning of an entry indicates that the title is appearing in BIP for the first time.

***Study Guide to Accompany Psychiatric Mental Health Nursing.** Mary Ann Boyd & Mary Ann Nihart. 200p. 1998. pap. text ed. 17.95 (*0-397-55179-7*) Lppncott-Raven.

***Study Guide to Accompany Psychology.** 5th ed. David G. Myers. (C). 1997. pap. text ed. 14.95 (*1-57259-208-7*) Worth.

Study Guide to Accompany Psychology: A Concise Introduction. 3rd ed. Terry F. Pettijohn. LC 92-71288. (Illus.). 254p. (Orig.). (C). 1992. per. 10.95 (*1-56134-064-2*) Dushkin Pub.

***Study Guide to Accompany Psychology: A Concise Version.** Don H. Hockenbury & Sandra E. Hockenbury. (C). 1997. pap. text ed. write for info. (*1-57259-557-4*) Worth.

Study Guide to Accompany Rittenberg - Schweiger Auditing. William Kelting. 258p. (C). 1993. pap. text ed. 22.75 (*0-03-029923-3*) Dryden Pr.

Study Guide to Accompany Robert D. Pursley Introduction to Criminal Justice. 6th ed. Ellen F. Van Valkenburgh. (Illus.). 176p. (C). 1994. pap. text ed. 24.80 (*0-02-422723-4*, Macmillan Coll) P-H.

Study Guide to Accompany Survey of Historic Costume. 2nd ed. Lynda A. Snyder. 368p. per., pap. 25.00 (*1-56367-023-2*) Fairchild.

***Study Guide to Accompany the Bible: Genesis.** Rose A. Scott-Lusk. 130p. (C). 1997. pap. text ed. 15.95 (*1-883866-13-8*) Clarion Pub.

Study Guide to Accompany The Human Brain: Introduction to Its Functional Anatomy. 3rd ed. John Nolte. 192p. (C). (gr. 13). 1992. pap. text ed. 20.95 (*0-8016-6332-6*) Mosby Yr Bk.

Study Guide to Accompany the Psychology of Women: Ongoing Debates. Mary R. Walsh. 1987. pap. text ed. 4.00 (*0-300-04455-0*) Yale U Pr.

Study Guide to Accompany Visual Merchandising & Display: The Business of Presentation. 3rd ed. Laura C. Bliss. 210p. 1995. pap. 25.00 (*1-56367-045-3*) Fairchild.

Study Guide to Activities Therapy. fac. ed. Diana P. Burnell. LC 75-28928. 189p. pap. 53.90 (*0-7837-7439-7*, 2047233) Bks Demand.

***Study Guide to American Defense Policy.** 3rd ed. Richard G. Head. Ed. by Ervin J. Rokke. 224p. 1973. reprint ed. pap. 63.90 (*0-608-03702-8*, 2064527) Bks Demand.

Study Guide to Biblical Eldership: Twelve Lessons for Mentoring Men to Eldership. Alexander Strauch. 168p. (Orig.). 1996. student ed., ring bd. 23.99 (*0-936083-13-1*) Lewis-Roth.

***Study Guide to Building Codes for Interior Designers.** Robert A. King. xii, 203p. (Orig.). 1996. pap. 49.00 (*0-9654127-0-9*) R A King.

Study Guide to Caddie Woodlawn: A Comprehensive Reading Program Using Real Books. Debbie Ward. (Reading Skills Discovery Ser.). 77p. 1993. pap. 9.00 (*1-880892-61-8*) Com Sense FL.

Study Guide to Child Health Care: Process & Practice. Sharla Feldscher. 250p. 1992. pap. text ed. 16.95 (*0-397-54760-9*) Lppncott-Raven.

Study Guide to Color Atlas & Textbook of Diagnosis Microbiology. 4th ed. Elmer W. Koneman & Neuburger. 256p. 1993. spiral bd. 21.95 (*0-397-51212-0*) Lppncott-Raven.

Study Guide to DSM-IV. Michael A. Fauman. 420p. 1994. pap. text ed. 32.00 (*0-88048-696-1*) Am Psychiatric.

***Study Guide to "Educating Young Children"** Mary Hohmann. (Illus.). 400p. 1997. write for info. (*1-57379-065-6*, P1117) High-Scope.

Study Guide to Epidemiology & Biostatistics. 4th rev. ed. Richard F. Morton et al. 224p. 1995. student ed., pap. 33.00 (*0-8342-0740-0*) Aspen Pub.

Study Guide to Gary North's Liberating Planet Earth. Charles W. Armstrong, Jr. 84p. 1991. pap. 5.95 (*0-930464-42-7*) Inst Christian.

Study Guide to General Chemistry. Atkins. (C). 1995. pap. text ed. write for info. (*0-7167-2274-7*) W H Freeman.

Study Guide to Greater Bible Knowledge. Wayne Jackson. 156p. (Orig.). 1986. pap. 6.00 (*0-932859-12-7*) Apologetic Pr.

Study Guide to Hearing & Hearing Aids. 4th ed. Wayne J. Staab. LC 92-93349. (Illus.). 205p. (C). 1994. pap. text ed. 27.50 (*1-881148-09-2*) W J Staab.

Study Guide to Jacques Ferron's Tales from the Uncertain Country. Mary Ziroff. 28p. 1977. 1.00 (*0-88784-053-1*, Pub. by Hse of Anansi Pr CN) Genl Dist Srvs.

Study Guide to John E. H. Sherry, "The Laws of Innkeepers, Third Edition" Gwen Seaquist. LC 92-56783. 256p. 1993. pap. 16.95 (*0-8014-9923-2*) Cornell U Pr.

***Study Guide to Mark's Gospel.** Scott G. Sinclair. LC 96-35882. (Orig.). 1996. pap. 12.95 (*0-941037-44-4*) BIBAL Pr.

Study Guide to Operations Management Strategy & Analysis: Strategy & Analysis. 4th ed. Lee J. Krajewski & Larry P. Ritzman. (C). 1996. student ed., pap. text ed. 19.50 (*0-201-60723-9*) Addison-Wesley.

Study Guide to Out of Many, Vol. 2. Neumeyer. 1994. student ed., pap. text ed. 20.40 (*0-13-564501-8*) P-H.

Study Guide to Pharmacology Essentials. Judy M. Fair. 176p. 1996. pap. text ed. 16.95 (*0-7216-6487-3*) Saunders.

Study Guide to Psychology. Schultz & Hailstorks. 1995. pap. text ed. 23.00 (*0-205-17418-3*) Allyn.

Study Guide to Sarah, Plain & Tall: A Comprehensive Reading Program Using Real Books. Susan Thurlow. (Reading Skills Discovery Ser.). 33p. 1994. 9.00 (*1-880892-64-2*) Com Sense FL.

Study Guide to Steinbeck, Pt. II. Tetsumaro Hayashi. LC 74-735. 252p. 1979. 27.50 (*0-8108-1220-7*) Scarecrow.

Study Guide to Steinbeck: A Handbook to His Major Works. Tetsumaro Hayashi. LC 74-735. 332p. 1974. 29.50 (*0-8108-0706-8*) Scarecrow.

Study Guide to Steinbeck's The Long Valley. Ed. by Tetsumaro Hayashi. LC 76-42125. 1976. 19.50 (*0-87650-074-2*) Pierian.

***Study Guide to the American Psychiatric Press Textbook of Neuropsychiatry.** Jude Berman et al. 256p. (Orig.). 1997. pap. text ed. 25.00 (*0-88048-804-2*, 8804) Am Psychiatric.

Study Guide to the American Psychiatric Press Textbook of Psychiatry. 2nd ed. Jude Berman et al. 176p. (Orig.). 1996. student ed., pap. text ed. 25.00 (*0-88048-890-5*, 8890) Am Psychiatric.

Study Guide to the ARI-GAMA Competency in HVACR, 1987-1988. ARI Staff & PES Staff. 80p. 1987. student ed., pap. text ed. 8.60 (*0-13-855636-9*) P-H.

Study Guide to the Caribbean: Culture of Resistance, Spirit of Hope. Nancy Carter. 1993. pap. 5.95 (*0-377-00255-0*) Friendship Pr.

Study Guide to the Christian History of the Constitution of the United States of America, Vol. II: Christian Self-Government with Union. Mary-Elaine Swanson. 116p. (Orig.). (YA). (gr. 7-12). 1988. pap. text ed. 10.00 (*0-9616201-0-2*) Am Christ Hist.

Study Guide to the United Nations. Mia Adjali & Deborah Storms. 48p. (Orig.). 1995. teacher ed., pap. text ed. 5.95 (*0-377-00293-3*) Friendship Pr.

Study Guide to the Wheel on the School: A Comprehensive Reading Program Using Real Books. Susan Thurlow. (Reading Skills Discovery Ser.). 53p. 1993. pap. 9.00 (*1-880892-62-6*) Com Sense FL.

Study Guide to Treatments of Psychiatric Disorders. 2nd ed. Sarah D. Atkinson & Glen O. Gabbard. 525p. 1996. pap. text ed. 39.95 (*0-88048-858-1*, 8858) Am Psychiatric.

Study Guide to Understanding Radiography. 3rd ed. Stephen S. Hiss. LC 93-8612. (Illus.). 206p. (C). 1993. text ed. 35.95 (*0-398-05880-6*) C C Thomas.

Study Guide to Westminster Confession. W. Gary Crampton. (Trinity Papers: Vol. 48). 80p. (Orig.). 1996. student ed., wbk. ed., pap. text ed. 11.95 (*0-940931-48-6*) Trinity Found.

Study Guide to Wilbur & Orville Wright Young Fliers: A Comprehensive Reading Program Using Real Books. Debbie Ward. (Reading Skills Discovery Ser.). 49p. 1994. 9.00 (*1-880892-63-4*) Com Sense FL.

Study Guide to Young Children in Action. Mary Hohmann et al. Ed. by Charles Silverman. LC 83-13030. (Illus.). 292p. (Orig.). 1979. student ed. 10.95 (*0-931114-21-7*) High-Scope.

Study Guide Vector Calculus. 3rd ed. Jerrold E. Marsden. 1995. student ed. write for info. (*0-7167-1980-0*) W H Freeman.

Study Guide-Workbook to Accompany Speech & Hearing Science Anatomy & Physiology. Eileen Zemlin & W. R. Zemlin. (Illus.). 300p. (C). 1988. spiral bd. 17.80 (*0-87563-314-5*) Stipes.

Study Guide 1: People...Politics. 4th ed. DCCCD Staff. 320p. (C). 1996. per. 20.94 (*0-7872-1763-8*) Kendall-Hunt.

Study Guide 2: Executive...Judicial. 4th ed. DCCCD Staff. 320p. (C). 1995. per. 20.94 (*0-7872-1764-6*) Kendall-Hunt.

Study Guides for Solving Algebraic Word. Hensley. (MA - Academic Math Ser.). 1987. pap. 21.95 (*0-538-13381-3*) S-W Pub.

Study-Habits Inventory. rev. ed. C. Gilbert Wrenn. 1941. pap. 0.12 (*0-8047-1070-8*) Stanford U Pr.

Study Helps in Point & Figure Technique. Alexander H. Wheelan. LC 89-85655. 73p. 1989. reprint ed. pap. 17.00 (*0-87034-091-3*) Fraser Pub Co.

Study Helps in Point & Figure Technique. Alexander H. Wheelan. 74p. 1990. reprint ed. pap. 19.95 (*0-934380-19-8*, 302) Traders Pr.

Study in Aesthetics. Louis A. Reid. LC 70-114546. 415p. 1973. reprint ed. text ed. 65.00 (*0-8371-4794-8*, RESA, Greenwood Pr) Greenwood.

Study in Association Reaction & Reaction Time see Mental & Physical Measurements of Working Children

Study in Bohairic Coptic. Nabil Mattar. LC 90-33325. (Illus.). 641p. (Orig.). (ARA, COP & ENG.). (C). 1990. pap. text ed. 34.95 (*0-932727-41-7*); lib. bdg. 44.95 (*0-932727-42-5*) Hope Pub Hse.

Study in Consciousness. 6th ed. Annie Besant. 1994. 12.25 (*81-7059-080-9*) Theos Pub Hse.

Study in Corneille. Lee D. Lodge. 1976. lib. bdg. 59.95 (*0-8490-2707-1*) Gordon Pr.

Study in Courage: The Story of Jan & Catharina Wubbena & Their Ten Children. Catherine Wubbgna et al. (Illus.). 550p. 1996. lib. bdg. write for info. (*0-9650662-0-7*) B&D Press.

Study in Creative History: The Interaction of the Eastern & Western Peoples to 500 B. C. O. E. Burton. 1977. lib. bdg. 59.95 (*0-8490-2708-X*) Gordon Pr.

Study in Culture Contact & Culture Change: The Whiterock Utes in Transition. Gottfried O. Lang. (Utah Anthropological Papers: No. 15). reprint ed. 10.50 (*0-404-60615-6*) AMS Pr.

Study in Daniel. Howard B. Rand. 1948. 12.00 (*0-685-08814-6*) Destiny.

Study in Disguised Intelligence Tests: Interview Form. Donald S. Snedden. LC 71-177765. (Columbia University. Teachers College. Contributions to Education Ser.: No. 291). reprint ed. 37.50 (*0-404-55291-9*) AMS Pr.

Study in Educational Prognosis. Elbert K. Fretwell. LC 72-177603. (Columbia University. Teachers College. Contributions to Education Ser.: No. 99). reprint ed. 37.50 (*0-404-55099-1*) AMS Pr.

Study in Eighteenth-Century Advertising Methods: The Anodyne Necklace. Francis Doherty. LC 92-34967. 476p. 1992. text ed. 109.95 (*0-7734-9177-5*) E Mellen.

Study in Friendship: St. Robert Southwell & Henry Garnet. Philip Caraman. (Studies on Jesuit Topics: Series IV, Vol. 16). xii, 124p. (Orig.). 1995. pap. 14.95 (*1-880810-15-8*) Inst Jesuit.

Study in Hosea. Howard B. Rand. 1955. 5.00 (*0-685-08815-4*) Destiny.

Study in Jeremiah. Howard B. Rand. 1947. 12.00 (*0-685-08816-2*) Destiny.

Study in Kant's Metaphysics of Aesthetic Experience: Reason & Feeling. Lewis Baldacchino. LC 91-44832. (Studies in the History of Philosophy: Vol. 25). 156p. 1992. lib. bdg. 69.95 (*0-7734-9468-5*) E Mellen.

Study in Karma. Annie Besant. 1987. 5.95 (*81-7059-046-9*) Theos Pub Hse.

Study in Latin Prognosis. William S. Allen. LC 70-176513. (Columbia University. Teachers College. Contributions to Education Ser.: No. 135). reprint ed. 37.50 (*0-404-55135-1*) AMS Pr.

Study in Law of Evidence. M. S. Prasad. 292p. 1982. 45.00 (*0-317-54676-7*) St Mut.

Study in Memorizing Various Materials by the Reconstruction Method see Johns Hopkins University Psychology Laboratories: Studies

Study in Milton's Christian Doctrine. Arthur Sewell. 1967. 69.50 (*0-614-00046-7*) Elliots Bks.

Study in Milton's Christian Doctrine. Arthur Sewell. 1967. 69.50 (*0-614-00152-8*) Elliots Bks.

Study in Nativism: The American Red Scare of 1919-20. Stanley Coben. (Irvington Reprint Series in American History). (C). 1991. reprint ed. pap. 2.30 (*0-8290-2611-8*, H-373) Irvington.

***Study in Plato: 1936 Edition.** F. R. Hardie. 192p. 1996. reprint ed. write for info. (*1-85506-239-9*) Bks Intl VA.

Study in Public Finance. 3rd rev. ed. Arthur C. Pigou. xviii, 285p. 1975. reprint ed. lib. bdg. 39.50 (*0-678-07009-1*) Kelley.

Study in Pyramidology. E. Raymond Capt. LC 86-70103. (Illus.). 264p. (Orig.). 1986. 15.00 (*0-934666-20-2*); pap. 10.00 (*0-934666-21-0*) Artisan Sales.

***Study in Quran & Hadith.** David S. Powers. 265p. 1996. 39.95 (*0-614-21073-9*, 1182) Kazi Pubns.

Study in Racism: U. S. A. (White, Black & Angry) Bert Underwood. LC 96-83622. (Illus.). 150p. 1996. pap. write for info. (*0-935763-05-8*) Chester Hse Pubs.

Study in Racism: U. S. A. (White, Black & Angry) Bert Underwood. LC 96-83622. (Illus.). 150p. 1996. write for info. (*0-935763-04-X*) Chester Hse Pubs.

Study in Radicalism & Dissent. William S. Fowler. LC 72-11684. (Illus.). 192p. 1973. reprint ed. text ed. 69.50 (*0-8371-6673-X*, FOSR, Greenwood Pr) Greenwood.

Study in Reaction Time & Movement. T. V. Moore. Bd. with Individual & His Relation to Society. J. H. Tufts. ; Time & Reality. J. E. Boddin. ; Differentiation of the Religious Consciousness. Irving King. ; No. 4. Iowa University Studies in Psychology. Ed. by Carl E. Seashore. (Psychology Monographs General & Applied: Vol. 6). 1974. reprint ed. Set pap. 55.00 (*0-8115-1405-6*) Periodicals Srv.

Study in Realism. John Laird. LC 77-152991. (Select Bibliographies Reprint Ser.). 1977. reprint ed. 20.95 (*0-8369-5743-1*) Ayer.

Study in Revelation. Howard B. Rand. 1941. 12.00 (*0-685-08817-0*) Destiny.

Study in Scarlet. Arthur Conan Doyle. 1989. lib. bdg. 15.95 (*0-89966-231-5*) Buccaneer Bks.

Study in Scarlet. Arthur Conan Doyle. Ed. by S. A. Bennett. (Adventures of Sherlock Holmes Ser.). (Illus.). 64p. 1992. pap. write for info. (*0-944099-18-1*) Comic Art.

Study in Scarlet. Arthur Conan Doyle. Ed. by Owen D. Edwards. (Oxford Sherlock Holmes Ser.). 208p. (C). 1993. 11.00 (*0-19-212313-0*, 14615) OUP.

Study in Scarlet. Arthur Conan Doyle. (J). 1997. pap. 1.95 (*0-8167-0850-9*) Troll Communs.

Study in Scarlet. Arthur Conan Doyle. 144p. 1982. pap. 5.95 (*0-14-005707-2*, Penguin Bks) Viking Penguin.

***Study in Scarlet.** Simon Goodenough. Date not set. write for info. (*0-688-04766-1*) Morrow.

Study in Scarlet. Arthur Conan Doyle. Ed. & Intro. by Dudley Edwards. (World's Classics Ser.). 256p. 1995. reprint ed. pap. 5.95 (*0-19-282380-9*) OUP.

Study in Scarlet see Sign of Four

Study in Scarlet & the Sign of the Four. Arthur Conan Doyle. 256p. (J). (gr. 10 up). 1986. pap. 4.50 (*0-425-10240-8*) Berkley Pub.

Study in Smollett Chiefly "Peregrine Pickle" Howard S. Buck. 228p. reprint ed. 12.50 (*0-911858-09-1*) Appel.

Study in String Processing Languages. P. Klint. (Lecture Notes in Computer Science Ser.: Vol. 205). vii, 165p. 1985. 27.00 (*0-387-16041-8*) Spr-Verlag.

Study in Symbolism: An Empirical Foundation of Graphology. Ralph V. Gologie. LC 73-86368. 256p. 1973. pap. 5.95 (*0-915286-00-9*) Landrum & Assocs.

***Study in the Book of First Peter.** Ernest L. Walker. 96p. (Orig.). 1996. pap. 4.95 (*1-56794-124-9*, C-2446) Star Bible.

***Study in the Book of Revelation.** Ernest L. Walker. 1995. pap. 14.95 (*1-56794-080-3*, C-2375) Star Bible.

Study in the Concept of Transcendence in Contemporary German Theology. Lorant Hegedus. LC 92-7710. (Rutherford Studies in Contemporary Theology). 124p. 1992. reprint ed. 59.95 (*0-7734-1637-4*) E Mellen.

Study in the Determination of Quality/Value Relationships in Rice. Ed. by J. A. Conway et al. 1992. pap. 25.00 (*0-85954-314-5*, Pub. by Nat Res Inst UK) St Mut.

Study in the Etymology of the Indian Place Name. G. McAleer. 1977. 59.95 (*0-8490-2709-8*) Gordon Pr.

Study in the Evolution of Sy Agnon's Style. Joseph Kaspi. 168p. (Orig.). (C). 1969. pap. 2.95 (*0-935982-06-X*, JK-01) Spertus Coll.

Study in the History & Politics of the Morning Post, 1905-1926. Keith M. Wilson. LC 90-20317. (Studies in British History: Vol. 23). (Illus.). 316p. 1991. lib. bdg. 99.95 (*0-88946-503-7*) E Mellen.

Study in the Theory & Practice of German Liberalism: Eduard Lasker, 1829-1884. James F. Harris. (Illus.). 194p. (Orig.). 1984. pap. text ed. 20.50 (*0-8191-4175-5*); lib. bdg. 47.50 (*0-8191-4174-7*) U Pr of Amer.

Study in the Theory of Economic Evolution. Trygve Haavelmo. LC 90-43174. (Reprints of Economic Classics Ser.). viii, 114p. 1991. reprint ed. lib. bdg. 29.50 (*0-678-01462-0*) Kelley.

Study in the Theory of Economic Expansion. Erik Lundberg. (Reprints of Economic Classics Ser.). x, 265p. 1964. reprint ed. 39.50 (*0-678-00046-8*) Kelley.

Study in the Warwickshire Dialect. 3rd ed. Ed. by James A. Morgan. LC 76-169927. (Shakespeare Society of New York. Publications: No. 10). reprint ed. 45.00 (*0-404-54210-7*) AMS Pr.

Study in Tolerance as Practiced by Muhammed & His Immediate Successors. Adolph L. Wismar. LC 27-24455. (Columbia University. Contributions to Oriental History & Philology Ser.: No. 13). reprint ed. 29.50 (*0-404-50543-0*) AMS Pr.

Study in Trans-Ethnicity in Modern South Africa: The Writings of Alex La Guma (1925-1985) Balasubramanyam Chandramohan. LC 92-30300. 292p. 1993. text ed. 89.95 (*0-7734-9186-4*) E Mellen.

Study in Wisdom. Dale Simpson. (Illus.). 22p. (J). (gr. k-5). 1993. pap. 6.00 (*1-880892-48-0*) Com Sense FL.

***Study in Wittgenstein's Tractatus.** Alexander Maslow. (Wittgenstein Studies). 184p. 1997. pap. 14.95 (*1-85506-538-X*) Thoemmes Pr.

Study in Zodiacal Symbology. J. Henry Van Stone. 110p. 1973. pap. 2.95 (*0-912504-19-6*) Sym & Sign.

Study Is Hard Work: The Most Eclectic & Lucid Text Available on Acquiring, Maintaining & Improving Study Skills Throughout a Lifetime. William H. Armstrong. 144p. (YA). (gr. 8-12). 1995. 10.95 (*1-56792-025-X*) Godine.

Study Manual for E.I.T. Examination. 2nd rev. ed. Young C. Kim. LC 82-82593. (Illus.). 480p. (C). 1987. 35.00 (*0-944999-01-8*) EPDS.

Study Materials for Clarinet, 3 vols., 1. Phillip Rehfeldt. (Clarinet Ser.). 1985. 11.00 (*0-933251-05-X*) Mill Creek Pubns.

Study Materials for Clarinet, 3 vols., 2. Phillip Rehfeldt. (Clarinet Ser.). 1985. 14.00 (*0-933251-18-1*) Mill Creek Pubns.

Study Materials for Clarinet, 3 vols., 3. Phillip Rehfeldt. (Clarinet Ser.). 1985. 17.50 (*0-933251-19-X*) Mill Creek Pubns.

Study Methods. Longman. Date not set. teacher ed., pap. text ed. write for info. (*0-314-03382-3*) West Pub.

Study Methods & Reading Techniques (SMART) Debbie G. Longman & Rhonda H. Atkinson. Ed. by Baxter. LC 93-23612. 400p. (C). 1993. pap. text ed. 32.75 (*0-314-02804-8*) West Pub.

Study Notes from My Bible, 1. Dale M. Yocum. 1990. pap. 10.99 (*0-88019-262-3*) Schmul Pub Co.

Study Notes from My Bible, 2. Dale M. Yocum. 1990. pap. 10.99 (*0-88019-274-7*) Schmul Pub Co.

***Study Notes in System Dynamics.** Michael R. Goodman. LC 74-84407. (Illus.). 388p. (C). 1974. pap. text ed. 25.00 (*1-56327-162-1*) Prod Press.

Study of a Child. Louise E. Hogan. LC 74-21416. (Classics in Child Development Ser.). (Illus.). 1975. reprint ed. 31.95 (*0-405-06466-7*) Ayer.

Study of a Static Screen, Jig, Spiral, & a Compound Water Cyclone in a Placer Gold Recovery Plant. Daniel E. Walsh & Donald J. Cook. LC 87-62002. (MIRL Reports: No. 73). (Illus.). 78p. (C). 1987. pap. text ed. 10.00 (*0-911043-01-2*) UAKF Min Ind Res Lab.

Study of Abhinavabharati on Bharata's -Natyasastra & Avalok on Dhananjaya's Dasearupaka: Dramaturgical Principles. Manjul Gupta. 342p. 1987. text ed. 25.00 (*81-212-0086-5*, Pub. by Gian Publng Hse II) S Asia.

Study of Abortion in Primitive Societies. rev. ed. George Devereux. LC 75-10572. 390p. 1976. 52.50 (*0-8236-6245-4*); pap. 24.95 (*0-8236-8311-7*, 26245) Intl Univs Pr.

Study of Action-Adventure Fiction: The Executioner & Mack Bolan. William H. Young. LC 95-11000. (Studies in American Literature: Vol. 18). 552p. 1996. 119.95 (*0-7734-8918-5*) E Mellen.

Study of Aggregate Consumption Functions. Robert Ferber. 7.00 (*0-405-18755-6*, 16467) Ayer.

Study of Aggregate Consumption Functions. Robert Ferber. (Technical Papers: No. 8). 82p. 1953. reprint ed. 21.40 (*0-87014-453-7*) Natl Bur Econ Res.

Study of Alcohol Prevention Grants in the State of Nebraska, 1973-1979. CAUR Staff. 40p. (Orig.). 1980. pap. 3.00 (*1-55719-090-9*) U NE CPAR.

Study of Allegory in Its Historical Context & Relationship to Contemporary Theory. Ralph Flores. LC 95-49118. 264p. 1996. text ed. 89.95 (*0-7734-8792-1*) E Mellen.

Study of Alternative Education in Virginia. (Illus.). 47p. (Orig.). (C). 1995. pap. text ed. 20.00 (*0-7881-2335-1*) DIANE Pub.

Study of Amber Spiders. Alexander Petrunkevitch. (CT Academy of Arts & Science Transactions Ser.: Vol. 34). 1942. pap. 100.00 (*0-686-51318-5*) Elliots Bks.

Study of American & Korean Attitudes & Values Through Associative Group Analysis. Lorand B. Szalay et al. LC 71-135080. 107p. 1970. 19.00 (*0-403-04541-X*) Scholarly.

Study of American Folklore. Jan H. Brunvand. (C). 1986. Instr's. manual. teacher ed., pap. text ed. write for info. (*0-393-95580-X*) Norton.

Study of American Folklore. 3rd ed. Jan H. Brunvand. (C). 1986. text ed. 31.95 (*0-393-95495-1*) Norton.

Study of American History: Being the Inaugural Lecture of Literature, & Institutions; with an Appendix Relating to the Foundation. James B. Bryce. (BCL1 - U. S. History Ser.). 118p. 1991. reprint ed. lib. bdg. 69.00 (*0-7812-6036-1*) Rprt Serv.

Study of American Indian Religions. Ake Hultkrantz. Ed. by Christopher Vecsey. LC 82-10533. (American Academy of Religion & Studies in Religion). 142p. 1983. 31.95 (*0-89130-587-4*, 01 00 29) Scholars Pr GA.

***Study of American Indian Religions.** Ake Hultkrantz & Christopher Vecsey. LC 82-10533. (American Academy of Religion Studies in Religion: Vol. 29). 142p. 1983. reprint ed. pap. 40.50 (*0-608-02840-1*, 2063907) Bks Demand.

Study of Americanization in Carneta. Clement L. Valletta. LC 74-17958. (Italian American Experience Ser.). (Illus.). 522p. 1975. 37.95 (*0-405-06427-6*) Ayer.

Study of Americans' Awareness & Attitudes Toward Vacation Timesharing. 1985. 65.00 (*0-318-03349-6*) ARDA.

Study of an Interest Test & Affectivity Test in Forecasting Freshman Success in College. Charles A. Drake. LC 76-176729. (Columbia University. Teachers College. Contributions to Education Ser.: No. 504). reprint ed. 37.50 (*0-404-55504-7*) AMS Pr.

Study of an Italian Village. A. L. Maraspini. 1968. pap. text ed. 41.55 (*90-279-6039-9*) Mouton.

Study of Ancient Greek Prosopography. J. M. Fossey. (Illus.). xi, 79p. (Orig.). (C). 1991. pap. 12.50 (*0-89005-449-5*) Ares.

***Study of Ancient Judaism: The Palestinian & Babylonian Talmuds, Vol. II.** Jacob Neusner. 336p. 1992. 69.95 (*1-55540-742-0*, 240050) Scholars Pr GA.

Study of Ancient Judaism, Vol. 1: Mishnah, Midrash, Siddur. Ed. by Jacob Neusner. LC 92-19867. 194p. 1992. 69.95 (*1-55540-741-2*, 240049) Scholars Pr GA.

Study of Andean Social Institutions. Philip A. Means. (Connecticut Academy of Arts & Sciences Ser., Trans.: Vol. 27). 1925. pap. 69.50 (*0-685-22815-0*) Elliots Bks.

Study of Angels: Systematic Bible Doctrines. rev. ed. Edward P. Myers. 97p. (Orig.). 1993. pap. 8.99 (*1-878990-00-4*) Howard Pub LA.

Study of Anglicanism. Ed. by Stephen Sykes & John Booty. LC 87-45906. 490p. 1988. pap. 32.00 (*0-8006-2087-9*, 1-2087, Fortress Pr) Augsburg Fortress.

Study of Animal Behavior. Felicity A. Huntingford. (Illus.). 411p. (gr. 13). 1984. pap. text ed. 36.95 (*0-412-22330-9*, NO. 6885) Chapman & Hall.

Study of Anthroposophy As an Aspect of the Free Spiritual Life. Alan Howard. 1985. pap. 2.50 (*0-916786-80-3*, Saint George Pubns) R Steiner Col Pubns.

Study of Archeology. Walter W. Taylor. LC 83-71270. xvi, 263p. 1983. reprint ed. pap. 15.00 (*0-88104-009-6*) Center Archaeol.

Study of Argumentation. F. H. Van Eemeren et al. 333p. 1986. text ed. 37.50 (*0-8290-0978-7*) Irvington.

***Study of Aspect, Tense, & Action: Towards a Theory of the Semantics of Grammatical Categories.** Carl Bache. LC 95-49056. 350p. 1996. pap. 63.95 (*0-8204-2969-4*, 68724) P Lang Pubng.

***Study of Aspect, Tense & Action: Towards a Theory of the Semantics of Grammatical Categories.** Carl Bache. (Illus.). 350p. 1995. 63.95 (*3-631-49510-2*) P Lang Pubng.

Study of Assimilation Among the Roumanians in the United States. Christine A. Galitzi. LC 72-76634. (Columbia University. Studies in the Social Sciences: No. 315). 1969. reprint ed. 34.50 (*0-404-51315-8*) AMS Pr.

Study of Astrology, Vol. II. Henry Weingarten. pap. 12.95 (*0-88231-030-5*) ASI Pubs Inc.

Study of Astrology: Vol. I. Henry Weingarten. LC 77-314. 1977. 14.95 (*0-88231-029-1*) ASI Pubs Inc.

Study of B. Traven's Fiction: The Journey to Solipaz. Richard E. Mezo. LC 92-46178. 212p. 1993. text ed. 89.95 (*0-7734-9838-9*, Mellen Univ Pr) E Mellen.

Study of Ballad Rhythm with Special Reference to Ballad Music. Joseph W. Hendren. LC 66-29463. (Princeton Studies in English: No. 14). 1966. reprint ed. 50.00 (*0-87752-052-6*) Gordian.

Study of Basketmaker Two Settlement on Northern Black Mesa, Arizona: Excavations 1973-1979. Susan E. Bearden. LC 84-72847. (Center for Archaeological Investigations Research Paper Ser.: No. 44). (Illus.). xii, 194p. 1984. pap. 12.00 (*0-88104-021-5*) Center Archaeol.

Study of Ben Jonson. Algernon Swinburne. (BCL1-PR English Literature Ser.). 181p. 1992. reprint ed. lib. bdg. 69.00 (*0-7812-7267-X*) Rprt Serv.

Study of Ben Jonson. Algernon C. Swinburne. LC 68-24922. (Studies in Drama: No. 39). (C). 1969. reprint ed. lib. bdg. 75.00 (*0-8383-0245-9*) M S G Haskell Hse.

Study of Ben Jonson. Algernon C. Swinburne. Ed. by Howard B. Norland. LC 69-12400. 244p. reprint ed. pap. 69.60 (*0-7837-6180-5*, 2045902) Bks Demand.

Study of Ben Jonson. Algernon C. Swinburne. (BCL1-PR English Literature Ser.). 181p. 1992. reprint ed. lib. bdg. 69.00 (*0-7812-7248-3*) Rprt Serv.

Study of Biology. 4th ed. Jeffrey J. Baker & Garland A. Allen. LC 81-17550. (Illus.). 1040p. 1982. text ed. write for info. (*0-201-10180-7*); student ed. write for info. (*0-201-10182-3*) Addison-Wesley.

Study of Black Self Help. William L. Pollard. LC 78-62225. 1978. pap. 16.00 (*0-88247-532-0*) R & E Pubs.

Study of Boat Ownership in the Omaha-Council Bluffs Metropolitan Area. Paul S. Lee & Yeshen Chen. 26p. (Orig.). 1978. pap. 2.50 (*1-55719-079-8*) U NE CPAR.

Study of Bohairic Coptic. Nabil Mattar. (Illus.). 725p. (Orig.). (ARA & ENG.). (C). 1989. pap. write for info. (*0-318-65809-7*) Holy Virgin Mary.

Study of Bows & Arrows. fac. ed. Saxton Pope. (University of California Publications in American Archaeology & Ethnology: Vol. 13: 9). 85p. (C). 1923. reprint ed. pap. text ed. 7.75 (*1-55567-216-7*) Coyote Press.

Study of Brief Psychotherapy. D. H. Malan. LC 75-30916. 326p. 1976. pap. 27.50 (*0-306-20019-8*, Plenum Pr) Plenum.

Study of Browning's Ring & the Book. James A. Cassidy. LC 74-117581. (Studies in Browning: No. 4). 1970. reprint ed. lib. bdg. 49.95 (*0-8383-1014-1*) M S G Haskell Hse.

Study of Capital Mobilization: The Life Insurance Industry of the 19th Century. Bruce M. Pritchett. Ed. by Stuart Bruchey. LC 76-45109. (Nineteen Seventy-Seven Dissertations Ser.). (Illus.). 1977. lib. bdg. 41.95 (*0-405-09921-5*) Ayer.

Study of Cardboard Voids for Prestressed Concrete Box Slabs. 56p. 1964. 22.00 (*0-318-17394-8*, JR284) P-PCI.

Study of Cases: A Course of Instruction in Reading & Stating Reported Cases, Composing Head-notes & Briefs, Criticising & Comparing Authorities, & Compiling Digests. Eugene Wambaugh. xi, 306p. 1981. reprint ed. lib. bdg. 28.50 (*0-8377-1310-2*) Rothman.

Study of Caste. P. Lakshmi Narasu. (C). 1988. reprint ed. 15.00 (*81-206-0411-3*, Pub. by Asian Educ Servs II) S Asia.

Study of Change: Chemistry in China, 1840-1949. James Reardon-Anderson. (Illus.). 464p. (C). 1991. text ed. 80.00 (*0-521-39150-4*) Cambridge U Pr.

Study of Change in Mexican Folk Medicine see Contemporary Latin American Culture

Study of Child Welfare in a Rural New York County. Abd-El-Hamid Zaki. LC 72-177611. (Columbia University. Teachers College. Contributions to Education Ser.: No. 927). reprint ed. 37.50 (*0-404-55927-1*) AMS Pr.

***Study of Children in Family Child Care & Relative Care: Highlights of Findings.** Ellen Galinsky et al. 133p. 1994. pap. 18.00 (*0-614-22674-0*, C94-01) Families & Work.

Study of Chinese Alchemy. Obed S. Johnson. LC 74-352. (Gold Ser.: Vol. 12). 156p. 1974. reprint ed. 20.95 (*0-405-05914-0*) Ayer.

Study of Chinese Boycotts, with Special References to Their Economic Effectiveness. Charles F. Remer. 1979. 28.95 (*0-405-10620-3*) Ayer.

Study of Chinese Society: Essays by Maurice Freedman. Maurice Freedman. LC 78-65395. xxiv, 497p. 1979. 59.50 (*0-8047-0964-5*) Stanford U Pr.

Study of Chiriquian Antiquities. George G. MacCurdy. (Connecticut Academy of Arts & Sciences Ser., Trans.: Vol. 3). 1911. pap. 300.00 (*0-685-22870-3*) Elliots Bks.

Study of Chivalry: Resources & Approaches. Ed. by Howell Chickering & Thomas H. Seiler. 1989. pap. 19.95 (*0-918720-94-X*); boxed 39.95 (*0-918720-93-1*) Medieval Inst.

Study of Chord Frequencies Based on the Music of the Eighteenth & Nineteenth Centuries. Helen Budge. LC 75-176604. (Columbia University. Teachers College. Contributions to Education Ser.: No. 882). reprint ed. 37.00 (*0-404-55882-8*) AMS Pr.

Study of Circulation Control Systems: Public Libraries, College & University Libraries, Special Libraries. George Fry. LC 61-16167. (American Library Association - Library Technology Project Ser.: No. 1). 146p. reprint ed. pap. 41.70 (*0-317-26364-1*, 2024222) Bks Demand.

Study of Classic Maya Sculpture. Tatiana A. Proskouriakoff. LC 77-11515. (Carnegie Institution of Washington. Publications: No. 593). reprint ed. 62.50 (*0-404-16275-4*) AMS Pr.

***Study of Colt Conversions & Other Percussion Revolvers.** R. Bruce McDowell. 1997. 39.95 (*0-87341-446-2*, FCOL) Krause Pubns.

Study of Concepts. Christopher Peacocke. (Bradford Representation & Mind Ser.). (Illus.). 260p. 1992. 35.00 (*0-262-16133-8*, Bradford Bks) MIT Pr.

Study of Concepts. Christopher Peacocke. (Representation & Mind Ser.). (Illus.). 288p. 1995. reprint ed. pap. 15.00 (*0-262-66097-0*, Bradford Bks) MIT Pr.

Study of Contemporary Law School Curricula. ABA, Legal Education & Admissions to the Bar Section Staff. 174p. 1987. pap. 4.00 (*0-318-36446-8*, 529-0033) Amer Bar Assn.

Study of Cranial & Skeletal Material Excavated at Nippur. D. R. Swindler. (University Museum Monographs: No. 12). (Illus.). v, 40p. 1956. pap. 10.00 (*0-934718-04-0*) U PA Mus Pubns.

***Study of Crisis.** Michael Brecher & Jonathan Wilkenfeld. LC 97-6067. (C). 1997. 97.50 (*0-472-10806-9*) U of Mich Pr.

Study of Cultural Centres & Margins in British Poetry since 1950: Poets & Publishers. Rob Jackaman. LC 94-48126. 344p. 1995. text ed. 99.95 (*0-7734-2275-7*, Mellen Univ Pr) E Mellen.

Study of Culture. rev. ed. L. L. Langness. LC 86-32716. (Publications in Anthropology & Related Fields). (Illus.). 288p. 1987. pap. 16.95 (*0-88316-556-2*) Chandler & Sharp.

Study of Current In-School Suspension Programs in New York State. Herbert L. Foster & Howard R. Kight. LC 88-21527. 135p. 1988. 12.95 (*0-929720-00-8*) SUNYB Inst Class Mgmt.

Study of Damage to a Residential Structure from Blast Vibrations. Harry R. Nicholls. 71p. 1974. pap. 6.00 (*0-87262-074-3*) Am Soc Civil Eng.

Study of Daniel. John A. Copeland. 1973. pap. 5.50 (*0-89137-703-4*) Quality Pubns.

Study of "Daphnis & Chloe" Richard L. Hunter. LC 83-3929. (Cambridge Classical Studies). 144p. 1984. text ed. 44.95 (*0-521-25452-3*) Cambridge U Pr.

Study of Data Base Processor Technology. Laura A. Gregory. LC 79-119010. (QED Monograph Series. Data Base Management: No. 8). 82p. (Orig.). reprint ed. pap. 25.00 (*0-318-34680-X*, 2031752) Bks Demand.

Study of Day Calendars. Herman Oliphant & Theodore S. Hope. 1979. 15.95 (*0-405-10618-1*) Ayer.

Study of Death: Works of Henry Mills Alden. Henry M. Alden. (Works of Henry Mills Alden). vii, 335p. 1985. reprint ed. 49.00 (*0-685-10448-6*) Rprt Serv.

Study of Delaware Indian Medicine Practice & Folk Beliefs. Gladys Tantaquidgeon. LC 76-43864. (Pennsylvania Historical & Musuem Commission Anthroplogical Ser.). reprint ed. 35.50 (*0-404-15724-6*) AMS Pr.

Study of Deviates in Versatility & Sociability of Play Interest. Paul A. Witty. LC 73-177630. (Columbia University. Teachers College. Contributions to Education Ser.: No. 470). reprint ed. 37.50 (*0-404-55470-9*) AMS Pr.

Study of Dogen: His Philosophy & Religion. Masao Abe. Ed. by Steven Heine. LC 90-93566. 224p. (C). 1991. text ed. 59.50 (*0-7914-0837-X*); pap. text ed. 19.95 (*0-7914-0838-8*) State U NY Pr.

Study of Dragons, East & West. Qiguang Zhao. LC 92-1392. (Asian Thought & Culture Ser.: Vol. 2). 256p. 1993. 56.95 (*0-8204-1758-0*) P Lang Pubng.

Study of Dynamical Systems. Ed. by N. Aoki. (Advanced Series in Dynamical Systems: Vol. 7). 244p. (C). 1989. text ed. 74.00 (*981-02-0040-4*) World Scientific Pub.

Study of Economic History: Collected Inaugural Lectures, 1893-1970. Ed. by N. B. Harte. 385p. 1971. 37.50 (*0-7146-2905-7*, Pub. by F Cass Pubs UK); pap. 17.50 (*0-7146-4013-1*, Pub. by F Cass Pubs UK) Intl Spec Bk.

Study of Economics: Principles, Concepts, & Applications. 5th ed. Mings Prof Turley & Turley Mings. 576p. (C). 1996. text ed. 41.76 (*0-256-23048-X*) Irwin.

Study of Economics: Principles, Concepts & Applications. 5th ed. Turley Mings. (Illus.). 526p. (C). 1995. text ed. 41.76 (*1-56134-303-X*) Dushkin Pub.

Study of Education: A Collection of Inaugural Lectures, Vol. 1: Early & Modern. Ed. by Peter Gordon. (A Collection of Inaugural Lectures). 340p. 1980. text ed. 37.50 (*0-7130-0170-4*, Pub. by Woburn Pr UK); pap. text ed. 19.50 (*0-7130-4005-X*, Pub. by Woburn Pr UK) Intl Spec Bk.

Study of Education: A Collection of Inaugural Lectures, Vol. II: The Last Decade. Ed. by Peter Gordon. 325p. 1980. text ed. 37.50 (*0-7130-0171-2*, Pub. by Woburn Pr UK); pap. text ed. 19.50 (*0-7130-4006-8*, Pub. by Woburn Pr UK); pap. text ed. 19.50 (*0-7130-4004-1*, Pub. by Woburn Pr UK) Intl Spec Bk.

Study of Education: A Collection of Inaugural Lectures, Vol. III: The Changing Scene. Ed. by Peter Gordon. (A Collection of Inaugural Lectures). 1988. text ed. 35.00 (*0-7130-0176-3*, Pub. by Woburn Pr UK) Intl Spec Bk.

Study of Education: A Collection of Inaugural Lectures, Vol. IV: End of an Era? Ed. by Peter Gordon. (A Collection of Inaugural Lectures). 320p. (C). 1995. 45.00 (*0-7130-0196-8*, Pub. by F Cass Pubs UK) Intl Spec Bk.

Study of Educational Achievement of Problem Children. Richard H. Paynter & Phyllis Blanchard. LC 74-160985. (Select Bibliographies Reprint Ser.). 1977. reprint ed. 16.95 (*0-8369-5853-5*) Ayer.

Study of Educational Politics: The 1994 Commemorative Yearbook of the Politics of Education Association (1969-1994) Ed. by Jay D. Scribner & Donald H. Layton. 224p. 1995. 75.00 (*0-7507-0418-7*, Falmer Pr) Taylor & Francis.

Study of Educational Politics: The 1994 Commemorative Yearbook of the Politics of Education Association (1969-1994) Ed. by Jay D. Scribner & Donald H. Layton. 224p. 1995. pap. 24.95 (*0-7507-0419-5*, Falmer Pr) Taylor & Francis.

***Study of Effect of Machining Parameters on Performance of Worm Gears.** Anand Narayan & Donald R. Houser. (1995 Fall Technical Meeting). 1995. pap. text ed. 30.00 (*1-55589-663-4*) AGMA.

Study of Eighty-One Principal American Markets. Leslie M. Barton. LC 75-22800. (America in Two Centuries Ser.). (Illus.). 1976. reprint ed. 37.95 (*0-405-07672-X*) Ayer.

Study of Elizabeth Barrett Browning. Lilian Whiting. LC 71-148332. reprint ed. 24.50 (*0-404-08924-0*) AMS Pr.

Study of English & American Writers: A Laboratory Method. John S. Clark & John P. Odell. LC 72-1070. reprint ed. 74.50 (*0-404-01559-X*) AMS Pr.

Study of Epistemology in Legal History. Michael D. Roumeliotis. LC 94-594. (Avebury Series in Philosophy). 1994. 59.95 (*1-85628-697-5*, Pub. by Avebury Pub UK) Ashgate Pub Co.

Study of Ethics: A Syllabus. John Dewey. 1976. lib. bdg. 59.95 (*0-8490-2710-1*) Gordon Pr.

Study of Ethnomusicology: Twenty-Nine Issues & Concepts. Bruno Nettl. LC 82-7065. 424p. 1983. pap. text ed. 14.95 (*0-252-01039-6*) U of Ill Pr.

Study of Ethnomusicology: Twenty-Nine Issues & Concepts. Bruno Nettl. LC 82-7065. 422p. reprint ed. pap. 120.30 (*0-8357-3554-0*, 2034454) Bks Demand.

Study of Exhaust Emissions from Natural Gas Pipeline Compressor Engines. Southwest Research Institute Staff et al. 100p. 1975. pap. 5.00 (*0-318-12705-9*, L22276) Am Gas Assn.

Study of Factors Suspected of Influencing the Settling Velocity of Fine Gold Particles. Daniel E. Walsh & P. Dharma Rao. (MIRL Reports: No. 76). (Illus.). 52p. (Orig.). (C). 1988. pap. 5.00 (*0-911043-05-5*) UAKF Min Ind Res Lab.

Study of Fashion Interest & Clothing Selection Motives. Donna L. Bernett. Ed. by Don Y. Lee. 180p. 1992. 39.00 (*0-939758-24-5*); lib. bdg. 39.00 (*0-685-60787-9*) Eastern Pr.

Study of Fast Processes & Transient Species by Electron Pulse Radiolysis. J. Baxendale & F. Busi. 1982. lib. bdg. 206.50 (*90-277-1431-2*) Kluwer Ac.

Study of Feasibility of Basing Natural Gas Pipeline Operating Pressure on Hydrostatic Test Pressure. Batelle Columbus Labs. Staff & A. R. Duffy. 100p. 1968. pap. 10.00 (*0-318-12706-7*, L30050) Am Gas Assn.

Study of Federal Tax Law: Taxation of Business Enterprises (STDB) 1992-1993. 992p. 1991. 56.50 (*0-318-37888-4*, 4905) Commerce.

Study of Federal Tax Law: Taxation of Estates, Gifts & Trusts (STDE) 1991-1993. 1072p. 1991. 56.50 (*0-318-37890-6*, 4907) Commerce.

***Study of Federal Tax Law Series Taxation of Income (STDI)** 19th ed. 1136p. 1994. 57.50 (*0-8080-0026-8*, BLS-3349) Commerce.

***Study of Federal Tax Law, Taxation Law, Taxation of Business Enterprises (STDE)** 17th ed. 1056p. 1995. 64.00 (*0-614-26818-4*, BLS-3419) Commerce.

***Study of Federal Tax Law, Taxation of International Transactions.** 100p. 1995. suppl. ed., pap. 15.00 (*0-614-26819-2*, 12295BLS01) Commerce.

Study of Federal Tax Law 1991-1993 Edition: Taxation of International Transactions (STDT) 904p. 1991. 60.00 (*0-317-44574-X*, 4903) Commerce.

Study of Federal Tax Law, 1992-93: Taxation of Income (STDI) 1104p. 1992. 57.50 (*0-685-67038-4*, 4754) Commerce.

***Study of Federal Tax Law, 1992-93 Edition - Taxation of Partnerships & S Corporations (STDP)** 368p. 1992. pap. 37.50 (*0-614-26820-6*, BLS-3030) Commerce.

Study of Film As an Art Form in American Secondary Schools. S. A. Selby. LC 77-22913. 1978. lib. bdg. 23.95 (*0-405-10755-2*) Ayer.

Study of Fluid Milk Prices. John M. Cassels. LC 75-39237. (Getting & Spending: Tthe Consumer's Dilemma Ser.). (Illus.). 1976. reprint ed. 28.95 (*0-405-08014-X*) Ayer.

Study of Folk Music in the Modern World. Philip V. Bohlman. LC 87-45401. 182p. 1988. 35.00 (*0-253-35555-9*); pap. 15.95 (*0-253-20464-X*, MB 464) Ind U Pr.

Study of Folklore. Alan Dundes. (Illus.). 1965. text ed. 66.00 (*0-13-858944-5*) P-H.

Study of Fossil Vertebrate Types in the Academy of Natural Sciences of Philadelphia: Taxonomic, Systematic, & Historical Perspectives. Earle E. Spamer et al. (Special Publication Ser.: No. 16). (Illus.). 434p. (Orig.). 1995. pap. 38.00 (*0-910006-51-2*) Acad Nat Sci Phila.

Study of Fugue. Alfred Mann. 352p. 1987. reprint ed. pap. 9.95 (*0-486-25439-9*) Dover.

Study of Fugue. Alfred Mann. LC 81-4183. (Illus.). x, 341p. 1981. reprint ed. text ed. 65.00 (*0-313-22623-7*, MASF, Greenwood Pr) Greenwood.

Study of Games. Elliott M. Avedon & Brian Sutton-Smith. LC 79-21194. 544p. 1979. reprint ed. lib. bdg. 59.50 (*0-89874-045-2*) Krieger.

***Study of Gene Action.** Bruce Wallace & Joseph O. Falkinham, 3rd. LC 96-52356. (Illus.). 264p. 1996. 45.00 (*0-8014-3265-0*); pap. 16.95 (*0-8014-8340-9*) Cornell U Pr.

Study of Gersonides in His Proper Perspective. Nima H. Adlerblum. LC 73-158229. reprint ed. 27.50 (*0-404-00296-X*) AMS Pr.

Study of God, 10 vols., Set. Kitaro Nishida. Tr. by V. H. Viglielmo. (Documentary Reference Collections). 1988. 395.00 (*0-318-35982-0*, CMJ/, Greenwood Pr) Greenwood.

Study of God, 10 vols., Vol. 2. Kitaro Nishida. Tr. by V. H. Viglielmo. (Documentary Reference Collections). 217p. 1988. lib. bdg. 45.00 (*0-313-26560-7*, CMJ02, Greenwood Pr) Greenwood.

Study of Goethe. Barker Fairley. LC 76-56253. 280p. 1977. reprint ed. text ed. 35.00 (*0-8371-9330-3*, FASG, Greenwood Pr) Greenwood.

Study of Greatness in Men. Josephus N. Larned. LC 73-156677. (Essay Index Reprint Ser.). 1977. reprint ed. 23.95 (*0-8369-2557-2*) Ayer.

Study of Greek Inscriptions. 2nd ed. Pref. by A. G. Woodhead. LC 92-54148. (Oklahoma Series in Classical Culture: Vol. 16). (Illus.). 164p. 1992. pap. 15.95 (*0-8061-2431-8*) U of Okla Pr.

***Study of Hadith: Ilm Al-Haidth, Methodology, Literature, & Anthology.** unabridged ed. Khalid M. Shaikh. Ed. by Shaista Ali & Mahlaqa Patel. LC 96-75423. 156p. (J). (gr. 6-8). 1996. pap. text ed. 6.00 (*1-56316-202-4*) Iqra Intl Ed Fdtn.

Study of Hamlet. John Conolly. LC 72-942. reprint ed. 32.50 (*0-404-01695-2*) AMS Pr.

Study of Handedness. Wallace F. Jones. LC 78-72804. (Brainedness, Handedness, & Mental Abilities Ser.). reprint ed. 32.50 (*0-404-60867-1*) AMS Pr.

Study of Handwriting Movement: Peripheral Models & Signal Processing Techniques. F. J. Maarse. 160p. 1987. pap. 26.75 (*90-265-0812-3*) Swets.

Study of Harmony: An Historical Perspective. Jeffrey Prater. 384p. (C). 1991. text ed. write for info. (*0-697-11966-1*) Brown & Benchmark.

Study of Hawthorne. George P. Lathrop. LC 78-107178. 1970. reprint ed. 16.00 (*0-403-00237-0*) Scholarly.

Study of Hawthorne. George P. Lathrop. (BCL1-PS American Literature Ser.). 350p. 1992. reprint ed. lib. bdg. 89.00 (*0-7812-6728-5*) Rprt Serv.

Study of Hegel's Logic. Geoffrey R. Mure. LC 83-26391. viii, 375p. 1984. reprint ed. text ed. 69.50 (*0-313-24397-2*, MUSH, Greenwood Pr) Greenwood.

An Asterisk (*) at the beginning of an entry indicates that the title is appearing in BIP for the first time.

Study of Heinrich Ott's Theological Development: His Hermeneutical & Ontological Programme. Colin B. O'Connell. LC 91-16572. (American University Studies: Theology & Religion: Ser. VII, Vol. 107). 262p. (C). 1992. text ed. 45.95 (*0-8204-1569-3*) P Lang Pubng.

Study of Heliocentric Science. Swami Abhedananda. 1968. 5.95 (*0-87481-619-X*) Vedanta Pr.

Study of Henry D. Thoreau. Helena Dickinson. 1972. 59.95 (*0-8490-1152-3*) Gordon Pr.

***Study of Heroes: A Program That Inspires & Educates Through the Example of Heroes.** 2nd ed. Wallenberg, Raoul, Committee of the United States Staff. (Illus.). 1000p. 1996. boxed 290.00 (*1-57035-072-8*, C83 HERO) Sopris.

Study of High Altitude Obsidian Distribution in the Southern Sierra Nevada, California. C. Kristina Roper-Wickstrom. 178p. (C). 1992. pap. text ed. 17.00 (*1-55567-112-8*) Coyote Press.

Study of Hindu Criminology. V. Upadhyaya. 504p. 1978. 28.95 (*0-318-36843-9*) Asia Bk Corp.

***Study of History, Vol. 1-6.** Arnold J. Toynbee. (Royal Institute of International Affairs). 630p. 1947. 30.00 (*0-19-500198-2*) OUP.

***Study of History, Vol. 7-10.** Arnold J. Toynbee. 428p. 1957. 30.00 (*0-19-500199-0*) OUP.

Study of History: A Bibliographical Guide. R. C. Richardson. 112p. 1988. text ed. 79.95 (*0-7190-1881-1*, Pub. by Manchester Univ Pr UK) St Martin.

Study of History: A Collection of Inaugural Lectures, 2 vols., Set. Arthur J. Taylor. 1980. write for info. (*0-7146-3125-6*, Pub. by F Cass Pubs UK) Intl Spec Bk.

Study of History: Abridgement of Volumes I-VI, Part I of II. David C. Somervell. 640p. 1987. pap. 16.95 (*0-19-505080-0*) OUP.

Study of History: Abridgement of Volumes VII-X, Part II of II. David C. Somervell. 432p. 1987. pap. 16.95 (*0-19-505081-9*) OUP.

Study of Human Abilities. Shao Liu. (American Oriental Ser.: Vol. 11). 1937. 25.00 (*0-527-02685-9*) Periodicals Srv.

Study of Human Nature. Ed. by Leslie Stevenson. 320p. (C). 1981. pap. text ed. 17.95 (*0-19-502827-9*) OUP.

Study of Human Values. Richard W. Kilby. 272p. (C). lib. bdg. 47.00 (*0-8191-8944-8*) U Pr of Amer.

Study of Humor in Greek Tragedy. A. Reardon. 1972. 59.95 (*0-8490-1153-1*) Gordon Pr.

Study of Husband-Wife Interaction in Three Cultures. Fred L. Strodtback. Ed. by Harriet Zuckerman & Robert K. Merton. LC 79-9032. (Dissertation on Sociology Ser.). 1980. lib. bdg. 58.95 (*0-405-12998-X*) Ayer.

Study of Husserl's Formal & Transcendental Logic. Suzanne Bachelard. Tr. by Lester Embree from FRE. (Studies in Phenomenology & Existential Philosophy). 227p. 1990. reprint ed. pap. 19.95 (*0-8101-0859-3*) Northwestern U Pr.

Study of Hymn-Writing & Hymn-Singing in the Christian Church. Randle Manwaring. LC 90-47020. (Texts & Studies in Religion: Vol. 50). 188p. 1990. lib. bdg. 79.95 (*0-88946-798-6*) E Mellen.

Study of Ignatius of Antioch in Syria & Asia. Christine Trevett. LC 92-13316. (Studies in the Bible & Early Christianity: Vol. 29). 264p. 1992. lib. bdg. 89.95 (*0-7734-9495-2*) E Mellen.

Study of Imagination in Early Childhood & Its Function in Mental Development: Imaginary Playmates & Other Mental Phenomena of Children. Ruth Griffiths & Nathan A. Harvey. LC 74-21411. (Classics in Child Development Ser.). 390p. 1975. reprint ed. 37.95 (*0-405-06463-2*) Ayer.

Study of Infra-Red Energy Generated by Radiant Gas Burners. D. W. DeWerth. 61p. 1962. 2.00 (*0-318-12707-5*, U71141) Am Gas Assn.

Study of Institutional Children with Particular Reference to the Caloric Value As Well As Other Factors of the Dietary. Pauline B. Mack & C. Urbach. (SRCD M Ser.: Vol. 13, No. 1). 1948. pap. 25.00 (*0-527-01543-1*) Periodicals Srv.

Study of Intelligence Test Elements. Elizabeth L. Vincent. (Columbia University. Teachers College. Contributions to Education Ser.: No. 152). reprint ed. 37.50 (*0-404-55152-1*) AMS Pr.

Study of Intercultural Communiciation. John C. Condon, Jr. 384p. (C). 1996. pap. write for info. (*0-02-324211-6*, Macmillan Coll) P-H.

Study of International Attitudes of High School Students with Special Reference to Those Nearing Completion of Their High School Courses. George B. Neumann. LC 77-177118. (Columbia University. Teachers College. Contributions to Education Ser.: No. 239). reprint ed. 37.50 (*0-404-55239-0*) AMS Pr.

Study of International Fisheries Research. World Bank Staff et al. (Policy & Research Ser.: No. 19). 115p. 1992. 7.95 (*0-8213-1987-6*, 11987) World Bank.

Study of International Relations: A Guide to Information Sources. Ed. by Robert L. Pfaltzgraff, Jr. LC 73-17511. (International Relations Information Guide Ser.: Vol. 5). 168p. 1977. 68.00 (*0-8103-1331-6*) Gale.

Study of Introvert-Extrovert Responses to Certain Test Situations. Raymond A. Schwegler. LC 76-177805. (Columbia University. Teachers College. Contributions to Education Ser.: No. 361). reprint ed. 37.50 (*0-404-55361-3*) AMS Pr.

***Study of Investment Income Vol. II: Proceedings Supplement, 1984.** 875p. 1984. 150.00 (*0-89382-163-2*, INV-PB) Nat Assn Insurance.

Study of Ionic Equilibria: An Introduction. Hazel Rossotti. LC 77-26048. (Illus.). 208p. reprint ed. pap. 59.30 (*0-8357-3555-9*, 2034442) Bks Demand.

Study of Isaiah: Holiness & Wholeness-Welcoming the Saving Reign of God. Ed. by Jack W. Hayford. 160p. 1996. pap. 6.99 (*0-7852-1167-5*) Nelson.

Study of Japanese Clause Linkage: The Connective - TE in Japanese. Yoko Hasegawa. 256p. (Orig.). (C). 1995. 64.95 (*1-57586-027-9*); pap. text ed. 22.95 (*1-57586-026-0*) CSLI.

Study of Japanese Syntax. Kazuko Inoue. LC 68-17883. (Janua Linguarum, Ser. Practica: No. 41). (Orig.). 1969. pap. text ed. 46.15 (*90-279-0692-0*) Mouton.

Study of Jazz. 6th ed. Paul O. Tanner et al. 280p. (C). 1987. per. write for info. (*0-697-03663-4*) Wm C Brown Pubs.

Study of Jean-Jacques Bernard's Theatre De L'inexprime. Kester A. Branford. LC 76-58424. (Romance Monographs: No. 24). 1977. 30.00 (*84-399-6422-6*) Romance.

Study of Job 4-5 in the Light of Contemporary Literary Theory. David W. Cotter. (Society of Biblical Literature Dissertation Ser.). 272p. (C). 1992. 44.95 (*1-55540-464-2*, 062124); pap. 29.95 (*1-55540-465-0*, 06 21 24) Scholars Pr GA.

Study of Judaism: Essays in Medieval Judaism. Ed. by Lawrence V. Berman et al. 35.00 (*0-87068-486-8*) Ktav.

Study of Judicial Review in Virginia, 1789-1928. Margaret V. Nelson. LC 47-31482. (Columbia University. Studies in the Social Sciences: No. 532). reprint ed. 27.50 (*0-404-51532-0*) AMS Pr.

Study of Kant's Psychology see On Sensations from Pressure & Impact

Study of Karl Barth's Doctrine of Man & Woman. JoAnn F. Watson. 1995. pap. 10.00 (*0-533-11126-9*) Vantage.

Study of Labor Market Information in Virginia. 1988. (*0-318-69550-2*) U VA Ctr Pub Serv.

Study of Land Reforms in Uttar Pradesh. Baljit Singh & Shridhar Misra. LC 65-17358. (Illus.). 287p. reprint ed. pap. 81.80 (*0-7837-3980-X*, 2043810) Bks Demand.

Study of Landforms. 2nd ed. R. J. Small. LC 77-71427. 512p. 1978. pap. text ed. 45.95 (*0-521-29238-7*) Cambridge U Pr.

Study of Language. 2nd ed. George Yule. (Illus.). 272p. (C). 1996. text ed. 49.95 (*0-521-56053-5*); pap. text ed. 17.95 (*0-521-56851-X*) Cambridge U Pr.

Study of Language: An Introduction. George Yule. 250p. 1985. pap. 17.95 (*0-521-31877-7*) Cambridge U Pr.

Study of Language in England: Seventeen Eighty to Eighteen Sixty. Hans Aarsleff. LC 78-13573. 279p. 1979. reprint ed. text ed. 55.00 (*0-313-21046-2*, AASL, Greenwood Pr) Greenwood.

Study of Language in Seventeenth-Century England. 2nd rev. ed. Vivian Salmon. LC 88-34350. (Studies in the History of the Language Sciences: Vol. 17). xix, 220p. 1988. 59.00 (*90-272-4535-5*) Benjamins North Am.

Study of Lapses see On Inhibition

Study of Law Enforcement: A Comprehensive Study of the World's Greatest, Yet Most Difficult Profession. Neal E. Trautman. (Illus.). 210p. (C). 1990. pap. text ed. 34.95 (*0-398-05639-0*) C C Thomas.

Study of Learning & Retention in Young Children. Lois H. Stolz. LC 71-177067. (Columbia University. Teachers College. Contributions to Education Ser.: No. 164). reprint ed. 37.50 (*0-404-55164-5*) AMS Pr.

Study of Learning Environments. Ed. by Barry J. Fraser. 85p. 1986. pap. text ed. 15.00 (*0-937987-00-X*) Assessment Res.

Study of Learning Environments, Vol. 4. Ed. by Hersholt C. Waxman & Chad D. Ellett. 110p. (C). 1989. pap. text ed. write for info. (*0-318-65871-2*) U Houston ERS Ctr.

Study of Legislation & Regulation of Internal Auditing in Selected Governments. Mortimer A. Dittenhofer. LC 88-1126. (McQueen Accounting Monographs: Vol. 4). xvii, 67p. (Orig.). 1988. pap. text ed. 10.00 (*0-935951-03-2*) U AR Acc Dept.

Study of Leisure: An Introduction. Jarmila L. Horna. (Illus.). 320p. (C). Date not set. pap. 26.95 (*0-19-540921-3*) OUP.

Study of Liberty. Horace M. Kallen. LC 72-7964. 151p. 1973. reprint ed. text ed. 52.50 (*0-8371-6554-7*, KASL, Greenwood Pr) Greenwood.

Study of Life: A Naturalist's View. R. D. Lawrence. (Illus.). 43p. (gr. 7-12). 1980. pap. 1.50 (*0-913098-37-X*) Myrin Institute.

Study of Literature for Readers & Critics. David Daiches. LC 71-152593. 240p. 1972. reprint ed. text ed. 35.00 (*0-8371-6026-X*, DARC, Greenwood Pr) Greenwood.

Study of Liturgy. 2nd ed. Cheslyn Jones. 646p. 1992. pap. 24.95 (*0-19-520922-2*) OUP.

Study of Llewelyn Powys: His Literary Achievement & Personal Philosophy. Peter J. Foss. LC 91-26422. (Illus.). 416p. 1992. lib. bdg. 109.95 (*0-7734-9700-5*) E Mellen.

Study of Logics. John P. Cleave. (Oxford Logic Guides Ser.: No. 18). 384p. 1992. 135.00 (*0-19-853211-3*) OUP.

Study of Macbeth for the Stage. Francis Neilson. 1981. lib. bdg. 250.00 (*0-686-72851-3*) Revisionist Pr.

Study of Mammalia & Geology Across the Cretaceous-Tertiary Boundary in Garfield County, Montana. J. David Archibald. (Publications in Geological Sciences: Vol. 122). 1982. pap. 40.00 (*0-520-09639-8*) U CA Pr.

Study of Man. Alfred C. Haddon. LC 76-44729. reprint ed. 55.00 (*0-404-15930-3*) AMS Pr.

Study of Man & the Way to Health. J. D. Buck. 260p. 1994. pap. 17.95 (*1-56459-421-1*) Kessinger Pub.

Study of Mary Wollstonecraft & the Rights of Woman. E. R. Clough. 1972. 59.95 (*0-8490-1154-X*) Gordon Pr.

Study of Maya Art. Herbert J. Spinden. 1976. lib. bdg. 39.95 (*0-8490-2711-X*) Gordon Pr.

Study of Maya Art: Its Subject Matter & Historical Development. Herbert J. Spinden. LC 74-20300. (Illus.). 352p. 1975. reprint ed. pap. text ed. 14.95 (*0-486-21235-1*) Dover.

Study of Medical Sciences (Theodor Billroth & Abraham Flexner) An Analysis from Past to Present. Karel B. Absolon. (Illus.). 170p. 1986. pap. 39.50 (*0-930329-10-4*) Kabel Pubs.

Study of Memory see Sociality & Sympathy

Study of Merlin in English Literature from the Middle Ages to the Present Day. Christopher Dean. LC 92-12081. 388p. 1992. lib. bdg. 99.95 (*0-7734-9532-0*) E Mellen.

Study of Methods of Preparation & Properties of Synthetic Inorganic Coatings on Copper: The Corrosion of Copper in Acidic Chlorate Solution. University of Utah Staff. 178p. 1971. 26.70 (*0-317-34550-8*, 94) Intl Copper.

Study of Modern Manuscripts: Public, Confidential & Private. Donald H. Reiman. LC 92-43641. 224p. (C). 1993. text ed. 29.95 (*0-8018-4590-4*) Johns Hopkins.

Study of "Monarchical" Tendencies in the United States: From 1776 to 1801. Louise B. Dunbar. (BCL1 - U. S. History Ser.). 164p. 1991. reprint ed. lib. bdg. 69.00 (*0-7812-6112-0*) Rprt Serv.

Study of Moneyflows in the United States. Morris A. Copeland. 1976. 33.95 (*0-405-07586-3*, 16432) Ayer.

Study of Moneyflows in the United States. Morris A. Copeland. (General Ser.: No. 54). 620p. 1952. reprint ed. 160.00 (*0-87014-053-1*) Natl Bur Econ Res.

Study of Monopoly Power, 12 vols., Set. Ed. by Bernard D. Reams, Jr. LC 90-83671. 1990. 1,020.00 (*0-89941-748-5*, 306750) W S Hein.

Study of Mozart's Last Three Symphonies. Alan E. Dickinson. 58p. 1990. reprint ed. lib. bdg. 59.00 (*0-7812-0231-0*, 10,163) Rprt Serv.

Study of Mozart's Last Three Symphonies. Alan E. Dickinson. LC 73-181142. 1927. reprint ed. 49.00 (*0-403-01543-X*) Scholarly.

***Study of Music in the Elementary School: A Conceptual Approach.** Ed. by Charles L. Gary. LC 67-31352. 190p. pap. 54.20 (*0-608-04836-4*, 2065493) Bks Demand.

Study of Mutual Funds: Report of the Committee on Interstate & Foreign Commerce, 87th Congress, 2nd Session, House Report No. 2274. Wharton School of Finance & Commerce Staff. LC 62-62400. xxxiii, 595p. 1982. reprint ed. lib. bdg. 55.00 (*0-89941-181-9*, 302450) W S Hein.

Study of Names: A Guide to the Principles & Topics. Frank Nuessel. LC 92-5424. 176p. 1992. text ed. 49.95 (*0-313-28356-7*, NSM, Greenwood Pr) Greenwood.

Study of Nationwide Costs to Implement Municipal Stormwater Best Management Practices: Final Report. American Public Works Association, Water Resources Committee Staff. (Illus.). 105p. (Orig.). 1992. pap. text ed. 20.00 (*0-917084-19-5*) Am Public Works.

Study of Navajo Symbolism, 3 pts. in 1, Set. Incl. Pt. 1. Navajo Symbols in Sandpaintings & Ritual Objects. Franc J. Newcomb. 1956. (*0-318-54043-6*); Pt. 2. Navajo Picture Writing. S. A. Fishler. 1956. (*0-318-54044-4*); Pt. 3. Notes on Corresponding Symbols in Various Parts of the World. Mary C. Wheelwright. 1956. (*0-318-54045-2*); 1956. 28.00 (*0-527-01284-X*, HU.PMP) Periodicals Srv.

Study of Nehru. 2nd rev. ed. Ed. by Rafig Zakaria. (Illus.). 478p. 1964. reprint ed. 25.00 (*0-7146-1574-9*, Pub. by F Cass Pubs UK) Intl Spec Bk.

Study of Neurosis. John S. Duryee. LC 84-18699. 300p. (C). 1984. text ed. 29.95 (*0-940524-02-3*); pap. text ed. 19.95 (*0-940524-03-1*) G Handwerk.

Study of Nickel Complexation with Fluvic Acid in Groundwater Using High Water. P. Warwick et al. 57p. 1994. pap. 12.00 (*92-826-7385-5*, CD-NA-15163-ENC, Pub. by Europ Com UK) Bernan Associates.

Study of Nine & Eighty-Five Widows Known to Certain Charity Organization Societies in 1910. Mary E. Richmond & Fred S. Hall. LC 74-3971. (Women in America Ser.). (Illus.). 84p. 1974. reprint ed. 16.95 (*0-405-06119-6*) Ayer.

Study of Numbers. R. A. Schwaller De Lubicz. 1986. pap. 9.95 (*0-89281-112-9*) Inner Tradit.

Study of Numbers. J. Adrian Verkouteren. 355p. (J). (gr. 5-8). 1981. pap. text ed. 12.95 (*0-685-32862-7*) Longman.

Study of Numbers see Mathematics Textbooks

Study of Numbers up to 1,000 see Mathematics Textbooks

Study of Numbers up to 20 see Mathematics Textbooks

Study of Nutrition Label Formats: Performance & Preference. Alan S. Levy et al. 55p. (Orig.). (C). 1992. pap. text ed. 20.00 (*1-56806-050-5*) DIANE Pub.

Study of Obituaries As a Source for Polish Genealogical Research. Thomas E. Golembiewski. (Illus.). 63p. 1985. pap. 10.95 (*0-318-17020-5*) Polish Genealog.

Study of Olmec Sculptural Chronology. Susan Milbrath. LC 79-89248. (Studies in Pre-Columbian Art & Archaeology: No. 23). (Illus.). 75p. 1979. pap. 10.00 (*0-88402-093-2*) Dumbarton Oaks.

Study of Omaha Indian Music. Alice C. Fletcher & Francis La Flesche. LC 94-26951. xxx, 152p. 1994. pap. 5.95 (*0-8032-6887-4*, Bison Books) U of Nebr Pr.

Study of Omaha Indian Music with a Report of the Structural Peculiarities of the Music by J. C. Fillmore. Alice C. Fletcher & Francis LaFlesche. (HU PMP Ser.). 1893. 25.00 (*0-527-01187-8*) Periodicals Srv.

Study of Orchestration. Samuel Adler. 400p. (C). 1989. Instr's. manual. teacher ed., pap. text ed. write for info. (*0-393-95809-4*) Norton.

Study of Orchestration. Samuel Adler. 400p. (C). 1989. Recordings (5 compact disks). 85.00 (*0-393-99390-6*) Norton.

Study of Orchestration. 2nd ed. Samuel Adler. 400p. (C). 1989. text ed. 45.95 (*0-393-95807-8*) Norton.

Study of Orchestration. 2nd ed. Samuel Adler. (C). 1989. wbk. ed., pap. text ed. 19.95 (*0-393-95808-6*) Norton.

Study of Organization & Method of the Course of Study in Agriculture in Secondary Schools. Theodore H. Eaton. LC 78-176740. (Columbia University. Teachers College. Contributions to Education Ser.: No. 86). reprint ed. 37.50 (*0-404-55086-X*) AMS Pr.

Study of Organizations: Findings from Field & Laboratory. Ed. by Daniel Katz et al. LC 80-15488. (Jossey-Bass Social & Behavioral Science Ser.). 589p. reprint ed. pap. 167.90 (*0-8357-4897-9*, 2037827) Bks Demand.

Study of Organizations: Patterns, Positions, Persons. Larry C. Ingram. LC 94-42826. 192p. 1995. text ed. 59.95 (*0-275-95026-3*, Praeger Pubs) Greenwood.

Study of Organizations: Positions, Persons and Patterns. Larry C. Ingram. LC 94-42826. 192p. 1995. pap. text ed. 16.95 (*0-275-95162-6*, Praeger Pubs) Greenwood.

Study of Oscar Wilde. Walter W. Kenilworth. LC 72-3091. (English Literature Ser.: No. 33). 1972. reprint ed. lib. bdg. 75.00 (*0-8383-1524-0*) M S G Haskell Hse.

Study of Ovulation & Early Pregnancy, Vol. 2. Ed. by Y. Boutaleb & A. Gzouli. (Recent Developments in Fertility & Sterility Ser.). (Illus.). 250p. (C). 1991. 85.00 (*1-85070-285-3*) Prthnon Pub.

Study of Palaeozoic Arachnida. Alexander Petrunkevitch. (Connecticut Academy of Arts & Sciences Ser., Trans.: Vol. 37). 1949. pap. 100.00 (*0-685-22904-1*) Elliots Bks.

Study of Palmistry. Comte C. Saint-Germain. (Illus.). 416p. 1987. reprint ed. pap. 19.95 (*1-871948-03-7*) Heian Intl.

Study of Palmistry for Professional Purposes. Comte C. De Saint-Germain. 416p. 1973. reprint ed. spiral bd. 27.50 (*0-7873-0267-8*) Hlth Research.

Study of Palmistry for Professional Purposes. Comte C. De Saint-Germain. (Illus.). 415p. 1994. reprint ed. pap. 39.95 (*1-56459-447-5*) Kessinger Pub.

Study of Parallelism in the Classifier System & Its Application to Classification in KL-One Semantic Networks. Ed. by Stephanie Forrest. 240p. (C). 1990. pap. text ed. 180.00 (*0-273-08825-4*, Pub. by Pitman Pubng UK) St Mut.

Study of Patanjali. 2nd ed. Surendranath Dasgupta. (C). 1989. 18.00 (*81-208-0452-X*, Pub. by Motilal Banarsidass II) S Asia.

Study of Patriotism in the Elizabethan Drama. Richard V. Lindabury. LC 68-54170. (Studies in Drama: No. 39). 1969. reprint ed. lib. bdg. 75.00 (*0-8383-0584-9*) M S G Haskell Hse.

Study of Peter Pan. unabridged ed. James M. Barrie. LC 92-18641. (Children's Thrift Classics Ser.). (Illus.). 96p. (J). 1992. reprint ed. 1.00 (*0-486-27294-X*) Dover.

Study of Philosophy. 3rd ed. S. Morris Engel. (Illus.). 415p. (C). 1990. pap. text ed. 34.90 (*0-939693-11-9*) Collegiate Pr.

***Study of Philosophy.** 4th ed. S. Morris Engel. (Illus.). 413p. (C). 1996. pap. text ed. 34.90 (*0-939693-38-0*) Collegiate Pr.

Study of Play Selection in Women's Colleges. Mary P. Doyle. LC 72-176728. (Columbia University. Teachers College. Contributions to Education Ser.: No. 648). reprint ed. 37.50 (*0-404-55648-5*) AMS Pr.

Study of Policy see Pan-Africanism & the Black Diaspora: A Study of Policy & Practice

Study of Policy, Organisation & Provision in Community Education & Leisure & Recreation in Three Scottish Regions. D. J. Alexander et al. 538p. (C). 1984. 60.00 (*0-317-94041-4*, Pub. by Univ Nottingham UK) St Mut.

Study of Politics: Inaugural Lectures. Ed. by Preston King. 341p. 1977. 37.50 (*0-7146-3084-5*, Pub. by F Cass Pubs UK) Intl Spec Bk.

Study of Politics: The Present State of American Political Science. Charles S. Hyneman. LC 59-10554. 243p. 1959. text ed. 24.95 (*0-252-72671-5*) U of Ill Pr.

Study of Popular Fiction: A Source Book. Ed. by Bob Ashley. LC 89-50131. 252p. (C). 1989. pap. text ed. 17.95 (*0-8122-1295-9*) U of Pa Pr.

Study of Population. Ed. by Philip M. Hauser & Otis D. Duncan. (Illus.). 878p. 1959. lib. bdg. 36.00 (*0-226-31951-2*) U Ch Pr.

Study of Populations. Ed. by Harry Messel. (Illus.). 266p. 1986. pap. text ed. 26.00 (*0-08-029877-X*, PPA) Elsevier.

Study of Porous Plate Flameholders. S. A. Weil. (Research Bulletin Ser.: No. 35). iv, 30p. 1964. pap. 3.50 (*0-317-56887-6*) Inst Gas Tech.

Study of Possible Societies. Walter Firey. LC 76-55578. (Illus.). (C). 1977. 10.00 (*0-9603066-0-9*) Firey.

Study of Practice see Pan-Africanism & the Black Diaspora: A Study of Policy & Practice

Study of Prehistory in the Tuolumne River Valley, California. fac. ed. Michael J. Moratto. (San Francisco State College - Treganza Anthropology Museum Papers: No. 9). (Illus.). 186p. 1971. reprint ed. pap. text ed. 16.85 (*1-55567-580-8*) Coyote Press.

Study of Primary Education: A Source Book: Classroom & Teaching Studies, Vol. 4. Ed. by Brenda Lofthouse. 285p. 1990. 75.00 (*1-85000-737-3*, Falmer Pr); pap. 31.00 (*1-85000-738-1*, Falmer Pr) Taylor & Francis.

Study of Primary Education: A Source Book: Perspectives, Vol. 1. 2nd ed. Ed. by Brenda Lofthouse. 285p. 1990. 95.00 (*1-85000-734-9*, Falmer Pr); pap. 31.00 (*1-85000-779-9*, Falmer Pr) Taylor & Francis.

Study of Primary Education: A Source Book: School Organization & Management, Vol. 3. Compiled by Geoff Southworth & Brenda Lofthouse. 285p. 1990. 90.00 (*1-85000-735-7*, Falmer Pr); pap. 31.00 (*1-85000-736-5*, Falmer Pr) Taylor & Francis.

Study of Primary Education: A Source Book: The Curriculum, Vol. 2. Compiled by Brenda Lofthouse. 285p. 1990. 90.00 (*1-85000-718-7*, Falmer Pr); pap. 31.00 (*1-85000-719-5*, Falmer Pr) Taylor & Francis.

Study of Primitive Christianity. Lewis G. Janes. (Notable American Authors Ser.). 1992. reprint ed. lib. bdg. 75.00 (*0-7812-3486-7*) Rprt Serv.

S

S

Study of Problem Material in High School Algebra. Jesse J. Powell. LC 71-177162. (Columbia University. Teachers College. Contributions to Education Ser.: No. 405). reprint ed. 37.50 (*0-404-55405-9*) AMS Pr.

Study of Professional Training & Development Roles & Competencies. Patrick R. Pinto & James W. Walker. 124p. pap. 9.00 (*0-318-13285-0*, PWBCP) Am Soc Train & Devel.

Study of Programming Languages. Ryan Stansifer. LC 94-14862. 352p. 1994. text ed. 71.00 (*0-13-726936-6*) P-H.

Study of Proverbs: Learn & Live-Everyday Wisdom for Everlasting Life. Ed. by Jack W. Hayford. 160p. 1996. pap. 6.99 (*0-7852-1168-3*) Nelson.

Study of Psychology & Mind As a Function of the Organism see Problems of Life & Mind

Study of Public Administration. Keith M. Henderson. LC 83-16648. 122p. (C). 1984. pap. text ed. 15.00 (*0-8191-3542-9*) U Pr of Amer.

***Study of Public Employees Retirement Systems.** (SOA Monographs: No. M-RS96-1). 1996. pap. 125.00 (*0-938959-42-5*) Soc Actuaries.

***Study of Public Financial Guarantee Programs.** (SOA Monographs: No. M-FI96-2). 1996. pap. 75.00 (*0-938959-43-3*) Soc Actuaries.

Study of Public Policy. Richard I. Hofferbert. LC 73-9826. (Policy Analysis Ser.). (C). 1974. write for info. (*0-672-51475-3*, Bobbs); pap. text ed. write for info. (*0-672-61062-0*, Bobbs) Macmillan.

***Study of Public Policy Influences upon the Development of China's Rural Enterprises 1978-1992.** Zhonghui Wang. 176p. 1997. text ed. 55.95 (*1-85972-543-0*, Pub. by Avebury Pub UK) Ashgate Pub Co.

Study of Pueblo Architecture in Tusayan & Cibola. Victor Mindeleff. LC 88-43115. (Illus.). 653p. (C). 1989. pap. text ed. 24.95 (*0-87474-619-1*) Smithsonian.

Study of Quantity Surveying & Client Demand. RICS Staff & Building Design Partnership Staff. (C). 1984. text ed. 90.00 (*0-685-40842-6*, Pub. by Surveyors Pubns) St Mut.

Study of Reality: A Supradisciplinary Approach. Marion Brady. (Illus.). 185p. (Orig.). 1994. teacher ed., pap. 21.95 (*0-9624475-4-4*) Bks Educators.

Study of Reality: A Supradisciplinary Approach. Marion Brady. (Illus.). 134p. (Orig.). (YA). (gr. 7-12). 1994. student ed., pap. 13.95 (*0-9624475-5-2*) Bks Educators.

Study of Religion. Morris Jastrow, Jr. Ed. by William A. Clebsch. LC 81-9184. (American Academy of Religion Classics in Religious Studies Ser.). 483p. (C). 1981. text ed. 16.95 (*0-89130-519-X*, 01-05-01) Scholars Pr GA.

Study of Religion: Where Are We Going. Ninian Smart. (C). 1987. 35.00 (*0-7300-0490-2*, Pub. by Deakin Univ AT) St Mut.

Study of Religion & Its Meaning. J. E. Barnhart. 1977. 51.55 (*90-279-7762-3*) Mouton.

Study of Religion in British Columbia: A State-of-the-Art Review. Brian J. Fraser. (Study of Religion in Canada Ser.: No. 5). x, 127p. (C). 1996. pap. 21.95 (*0-88920-261-3*) Wilfrid Laurier.

Study of Religion in Colleges & Universities. Ed. by Paul Ramsey & John F. Wilson. LC 70-90957. 365p. 1970. reprint ed. pap. 104.10 (*0-7837-9429-0*, 2060170) Bks Demand.

Study of Religion in Two-Year Colleges. Ed. by C. Freeman Sleeper & Robert A. Spivey. LC 75-28158. 114p. reprint ed. pap. 32.50 (*0-7837-5407-8*, 2045171) Bks Demand.

***Study of Religions in Africa: Past, Present & Prospects.** Ed. by Jacob Olupona et al. (Religions of Africa Ser.: No. 1). 366p. (Orig.). 1996. pap. 54.50 (*0-9525772-2-4*, Pub. by Almqvist & Wiksell SW) Coronet Bks.

Study of Religious Fanaticism & Responses to It: Adversary Identity. Hal W. French. LC 90-44857. (Studies in Religion & Society: Vol. 26). 180p. 1990. 79.95 (*0-88946-238-0*) E Mellen.

Study of Retroactive Inhibition see On the Function of the Cerebrum

Study of Rhythmic Structure in the Verse of William Butler Yeats. Adelyn Dougherty. (De Proprietatibus Litterarum, Ser. Practica: No. 38). (Illus.). 135p. 1973. pap. text ed. 40.00 (*90-279-2506-2*) Mouton.

Study of Roles in the Arashiyama West Troop of Japanese Monkeys (Macaca Fuscata) Linda M. Fedigan. Ed. by F. S. Szalay. (Contributions to Primatology Ser.: Vol. 9). (Illus.). 116p. 1976. 39.25 (*3-8055-2334-3*) S Karger.

Study of Romans 6:51: "United to a Death Like Christ's" Florence M. Gillman. LC 92-34446. 420p. 1992. 109.95 (*0-7734-9946-6*, Mellen Univ Pr) E Mellen.

Study of Russian Folklore. Felix J. Oinas & Stephen Soudakoff. (Indian Univ. Folklore Ser.: No. 25). 341p. 1975. text ed. 73.85 (*90-279-3147-X*) Mouton.

Study of Samurai Income & Entrepreneurship: Quantitative Analyses of Economic & Social Aspects of the Samurai in Tokugawa & Meiji, Japan. Kozo Yamamura. LC 73-87378. (Harvard East Asian Ser.: No. 76). 278p. reprint ed. pap. 79.30 (*0-7837-3862-5*, 2043684) Bks Demand.

Study of Saving in the United States, 3 Vols, 1. Raymond W. Goldsmith. LC 69-13910. 1971. reprint ed. lib. bdg. 41.80 (*0-685-02010-X*, GOST) Greenwood.

Study of Saving in the United States, 3 Vols, Set. Raymond W. Goldsmith. LC 69-13910. 1971. reprint ed. text ed. 195.00 (*0-8371-0998-1*, GOSS) Greenwood.

Study of Saving in the United States, 3 Vols, Vol. 2. Raymond W. Goldsmith. LC 69-13910. 1969. reprint ed. text ed. 75.00 (*0-8371-0999-X*, GOSU) Greenwood.

Study of Saving in the United States, 3 Vols, Vol. 3. Raymond W. Goldsmith. LC 69-13910. 1969. reprint ed. text ed. 75.00 (*0-8371-1000-9*, GOSV) Greenwood.

Study of Schooling: Field-Based Methodologies in Educational Research & Evaluation. Thomas S. Popkewitz & B. Robert Tabachnick. LC 81-1416. 316p. 1981. text ed. 55.00 (*0-275-90705-8*, C0705, Praeger Pubs) Greenwood.

Study of Selected Concepts for Government Financial Accounting & Reporting. William W. Holder. LC 85-50315. 69p. 1980. pap. 5.00 (*0-686-84264-2*) Municipal.

Study of Selected English Critical Terms from 1650 to 1800. Edward A. Watson. (American University Studies: English Language & Literature: Ser. IV, Vol. 55). 686p. (C). 1987. text ed. 78.95 (*0-8204-0518-3*) P Lang Pubng.

Study of Sensory Control in the Rat. Florence Richardson. Bd. with On the Influence of Complexity & Dissimilarity on Memory. H. A. Peterson. ; Studies in Melody: Studies in Melody. W. Van Dyke Bingham. ; Report Presented 1909. American Psychology Association Committee on Teaching of Psychology. ; Some Mental Processes of the Rhesus Monkey. W. T. Shepherd. (Psychology Monographs General & Applied: Vol. 12). 1974. reprint ed. Set pap. 55.00 (*0-8115-1411-0*) Periodicals Srv.

Study of Shakespeare. Algernon C. Swinburne. LC 09-30432. reprint ed. 34.50 (*0-404-06315-2*) AMS Pr.

Study of Shakespeare's Versification, with an Inquiry into the Trustworthiness of the Early Texts. Matthew A. Bayfield. LC 77-130616. reprint ed. 39.50 (*0-404-00695-7*) AMS Pr.

Study of Shamanism & Alternate Modes of Healing: The Proceedings of the Fifth International. Ruth-Inge Heinze. 1992. pap. 18.95 (*0-8290-2471-9*) Irvington.

Study of Shelley. P. Edgar. LC 70-116792. (Studies in Shelley: No. 25). 1970. reprint ed. lib. bdg. 49.95 (*0-8383-1034-6*) M S G Haskell Hse.

Study of Shelley's Defense of Poetry. L. Verkoren. LC 72-95451. (Studies in Shelley: No. 25). (C). 1970. reprint ed. lib. bdg. 39.95 (*0-8383-1208-X*) M S G Haskell Hse.

Study of Shelley's Poetry. Seymour Reiter. LC 67-22735. 1967. 20.00 (*0-8263-0085-5*) Lib Soc Sci.

***Study of Short Circuiting Arc Welding.** M. Hermans. viii, 168p. (Orig.). 1997. pap. 44.50 (*90-407-1430-4*, Pub. by Delft U Pr NE) Coronet Bks.

Study of Simon Willard's Clocks. R. W. Husher & W. W. Welch. LC 80-65021. (Illus.). 292p. 1980. 49.50 (*0-9603944-0-0*) Husher & Welch.

Study of Sir Thomas Wyatt's Poems. Agnes K. Foxwell. (BCL1-PR English Literature Ser.). 160p. 1992. reprint ed. lib. bdg. 69.00 (*0-7812-7233-5*) Rprt Serv.

Study of Skanda Cult. S. S. Rana. 1995. 28.00 (*81-7081-303-4*, Pub. by Nag Pubs II) S Asia.

Study of Slavery in New Jersey. Henry S. Cooley. LC 78-63853. (Johns Hopkins University. Studies in the Social Sciences. Thirtieth Ser. 1912: 9-10). reprint ed. 32.50 (*0-404-61109-5*) AMS Pr.

Study of Social & Constitutional Tendencies in the Early Years of Edward Three. Dorothy Hughes. LC 78-14508. (Perspectives in European History Ser.: No. 16). viii, 245p. 1978. reprint ed. lib. bdg. 37.50 (*0-87991-623-0*) Porcupine Pr.

Study of Social Change in Six American Institutions During the Twentieth Century. Gerhard Falk. LC 93-6002. (Illus.). 492p. 1993. 109.95 (*0-7734-9358-1*) E Mellen.

Study of Social Effects. Jacques Vallee et al. (Group Communication Through Computers Ser.: Vol. 2). 160p. 1974. 10.50 (*0-318-14424-7*, R33) Inst Future.

Study of Social Problems: Seven Perspectives. 5th ed. Earl Rubington & Martin S. Weinberg. 352p. (C). 1995. pap. text ed. 24.50 (*0-19-508367-9*) OUP.

Study of Some Aspects of Satisfaction in the Vocation of Stenography. Margaret S. Quayle. LC 76-177174. (Columbia University. Teachers College. Contributions to Education Ser.: No. 659). reprint ed. 37.50 (*0-404-55659-0*) AMS Pr.

Study of Some Negro-White Families in the U. S. Caroline Day. LC 76-106857. (Illus.). 126p. 1971. reprint ed. text ed. 38.50 (*0-8371-3479-X*, DNF&, Negro U Pr) Greenwood.

Study of Some of the Influences of Regents Requirements & Examinations in French. Arnold L. Frizzle. LC 70-176789. (Columbia University. Teachers College. Contributions to Education Ser.: No. 964). reprint ed. 37.50 (*0-404-55964-6*) AMS Pr.

Study of Some Problems Arising in the Admission of Students As Candidates for Professional Degrees in Education. Clarence Linton. LC 73-176999. (Columbia University. Teachers College. Contributions to Education Ser.: No. 285). reprint ed. 37.50 (*0-404-55285-4*) AMS Pr.

Study of Sophoclean Drama. enl. ed. G. M. Kirkwood. (Studies in Classical Philology). 328p. 1994. pap. 16.95 (*0-8014-8241-0*) Cornell U Pr.

Study of Spinoza. 3rd ed. James Martineau. LC 78-152994. (Select Bibliographies Reprint Ser.). 1977. reprint ed. 25.95 (*0-8369-5746-6*) Ayer.

Study of Spinoza's Ethics. Jonathan Bennett. LC 83-18568. 406p. (C). 1984. pap. text ed. 16.95 (*0-915145-83-9*); lib. bdg. 34.95 (*0-915145-82-0*) Hackett Pub.

Study of Spirituality. Cheslyn Jones et al. (Illus.). 664p. (C). 1986. pap. text ed. 24.95 (*0-19-504170-4*) OUP.

Study of St. Paul: His Character & Opinions. S. Baring-Gould. 1977. lib. bdg. 59.95 (*0-8490-2712-8*) Gordon Pr.

Study of St. Paul's Letter to the Galatians: The Christian Emancipation Proclamation. Robert D. Noble. 83p. (Orig.). 1993. pap. 10.00 (*0-944687-14-8*) Gather Family Inst.

***Study of Stolen Love.** Iranar Nakk. Tr. by David C. Buck & K. Paramasivam from TAM. LC 96-6539. (Texts & Translations Ser.). 1997. write for info. (*0-7885-0331-6*, 010218); pap. write for info. (*0-7885-0332-4*, 010218) Scholars Pr GA.

***Study of Story.** Trachey. 242p. 1996. pap. text ed. 26.95 (*0-88725-233-8*) Hunter Textbks.

Study of Stravinsky's Sonate Pour Piano (1924) & Serenade en La: A Performer's Analysis & Comparison. Bonna J. Boettcher. LC 91-45208. 104p. 1992. lib. bdg. 59.95 (*0-7734-9806-0*) E Mellen.

Study of Subject Bibliography with Special Reference to the Social Sciences. Ed. by Christopher D. Needham & Esther Herman. LC 75-630095. (Student Contribution Ser.: No. 3). 1970. pap. 5.00 (*0-911808-05-1*) U of Md Lib Serv.

Study of Surgery. Glenn W. Geelhoed. LC 94-79793. (Illus.). 392p. 1994. pap. 40.00 (*0-9632873-6-2*) J & S Pub VA.

Study of Svatantrika. Donald S. Lopez, Jr. LC 86-14636. 450p. (Orig.). (C). 1987. pap. 19.95 (*0-937938-19-X*); lib. bdg. 35.00 (*0-937938-20-3*) Snow Lion Pubns.

Study of Swinburne. Thomas E. Welby. (BCL1-PR English Literature Ser.). 289p. 1992. reprint ed. lib. bdg. 79.00 (*0-7812-7681-0*) Rprt Serv.

Study of Talmud: Understanding the Halachic Mind. Abraham H. Rabinowitz. LC 96-13496. 240p. 1996. 30.00 (*1-56821-946-6*) Aronson.

Study of Teacher Training in Vermont. Robert M. Steele. LC 70-177743. (Columbia University. Teachers College. Contributions to Education Ser.: No. 243). reprint ed. 37.50 (*0-404-55243-9*) AMS Pr.

Study of Telephone Records: How to Trace Them. 1991. lib. bdg. 69.75 (*0-8490-4503-7*) Gordon Pr.

Study of Temperament: Changes, Continuities & Challenges. Ed. by Robert Plomin & Judy Dunn. 192p. 1986. text ed. 39.95 (*0-89859-670-X*) L Erlbaum Assocs.

Study of Textile Mill Closings in Selected New England Communities. W. Stanley Devino et al. 1986. pap. 8.95 (*0-89101-014-9*) U Maine Pr.

Study of the Absorption Spectra of Solutions of Certain Salts of Potassium, Cobalt, Nickel, Copper, Chromium, Erbium, Praseodymium, Neodymium & Uranium. Harry C. Jones. LC 11-670. (Carnegie Institution of Washington Publication Ser.: No. 130). 363p. reprint ed. pap. 103.50 (*0-317-29734-1*, 2015701) Bks Demand.

Study of the Achievement of College Students in Beginning Courses in Food Preparation & Serving & Related Factors. Mary K. Wilson. LC 75-177628. (Columbia University. Teachers College. Contributions to Education Ser.: No. 958). reprint ed. 37.50 (*0-404-55958-1*) AMS Pr.

Study of the Acooli Language: Grammar & Vocabulary. rev. ed. J. Pasquale Crazzolara. LC 39-14126. 455p. reprint ed. pap. 129.70 (*0-8357-6948-8*, 2039007) Bks Demand.

Study of the American School Superintendency, 1992: America's Education Leaders in a Time of Reform. American Association of School Administrators Staff & Tom Glass. 103p. 1992. pap. 25.00 (*0-87652-177-4*, 21-00189) Am Assn Sch Admin.

Study of the Ancient Near East in the Twenty-First Century: The William Foxwell Albright Centennial Conference. Ed. by Jerrold S. Cooper & Glenn Schwartz. 432p. 1996. 39.50 (*0-931464-96-X*) Eisenbrauns.

Study of the Application of an Educational Theory to Science Instruction. Eugene A. Waters. LC 76-177663. (Columbia University. Teachers College. Contributions to Education Ser.: No. 864). reprint ed. 37.50 (*0-404-55864-X*) AMS Pr.

***Study of the Bayeux Tapestry.** Ed. by Richard Gameson. LC 96-46931. (Illus.). 252p. 1997. 71.10 (*0-85115-664-9*) Boydell & Brewer.

Study of the Bible. rev. ed. Ernest C. Colwell. LC 64-23411. (Midway Reprint Ser.). 218p. reprint ed. pap. 62.20 (*0-685-15681-8*, 2026769) Bks Demand.

Study of the Bible in the Middle Ages. Beryl Smalley. 1964. pap. 18.50 (*0-268-00267-3*) U of Notre Dame Pr.

Study of the Bronze Drums of South China. Princeton S. Hsu. (Asian Folklore & Social Life Monographs: No. 95). (CHI.). 1977. 14.00 (*0-89986-327-2*) Oriental Bk Store.

Study of the Business Fortunes of William Cotesworth, 1668-1726. Joyce Ellis. Ed. by Stuart Bruchey. LC 80-2805. (Dissertations in European Economic History Ser.: No. 2). (Illus.). 1981. lib. bdg. 24.95 (*0-405-13989-6*) Ayer.

Study of the Capital Market in Britain from 1919-1936. 2nd ed. Alexander T. Grant. 320p. 1967. 37.50 (*0-7146-1224-3*, Pub. by F Cass Pubs UK) Intl Spec Bk.

Study of the Cat. 5th ed. Walker. (C). 1993. pap. text ed. 45.00 (*0-03-047433-7*) HB Coll Pubs.

Study of the Characteristics, Costs & Magnitude of Interlibrary Loans in Academic Libraries. Compiled by Vernon E. Palmour et al. LC 70-39344. 1972. pap. 8.50 (*0-685-02011-8*); text ed. 42.95 (*0-8371-6340-4*, PIL/) Greenwood.

Study of the Child Support Collection Business. Ralph D. Thomas. 45p. (C). pap. text ed. 29.95 (*0-918487-68-4*) Thomas Pubns TX.

Study of the 'Clock' Reaction on Copper Surfaces. Lehigh University Staff. 87p. 1983. write for info. (*0-318-60086-2*, 333A) Intl Copper.

***Study of the Colt Single Action Army Revolver.** 4th ed. Graham et al. (Illus.). 520p. 79.95 (*0-614-28374-4*) Kopec Pubns.

Study of the Colt Single Action Army Revolver. Ron Graham et al. LC 75-42934. (Illus.). 550p. 1985. reprint ed. lthr. 169.95 (*0-9615236-1-0*) Kopec Pubns.

Study of the Colt Single Action Army Revolver. Ron Graham et al. LC 75-42934. (Illus.). 550p. 1992. reprint ed. 79.95 (*0-9615236-0-3*) Kopec Pubns.

Study of the Comedies of Richard Brome, Especially as Representative of Dramatic Decadence. Herbert F. Allen. (BCL1-PR English Literature Ser.). 61p. 1992. reprint ed. lib. bdg. 59.00 (*0-7812-7238-6*) Rprt Serv.

Study of the Concept of Transfer & Closure under Industrial Disputes Act, 1947. H. A. Panlwala. (C). 1990. 45.00 (*0-89771-306-0*) St Mut.

***Study of the Dawn of Religion.** LeMoyne Brown. LC 96-62045. 272p. 1997. pap. 12.95 (*1-55523-860-2*) Winston-Derek.

Study of the De Potentia of Thomas Aquinas in Light of the Dogmatik of Paul Tillich: Creation As Discipleship. Robert E. Barron. LC 93-1354. 516p. 1993. text ed. 119.95 (*0-7734-2238-2*, Mellen Univ Pr) E Mellen.

Study of the Delaware Indian Big House Ceremony: In Native Text Dictated by Witapanoxwe. Frank G. Speck. LC 76-43846. (Publications of the Pennsylvania Historical Commission: Vol. 2). reprint ed. 47.50 (*0-404-15698-3*) AMS Pr.

Study of the Dialectic of Hegel. B. Nirmala Devi. vi, 168p. 1995. 15.00 (*81-86339-17-5*, Pub. by Estrn Bk Linkers II) Nataraj Bks.

Study of the Division of Jurisdiction Between State & Federal Courts: Official Draft. xix, 587p. 1969. 35.00 (*0-8318-5045-0*, 5045) Am Law Inst.

Study of the Dramatic Works of Cristobal De Virues. Cecilia V. Sargent. 168p. 1930. 2.25 (*0-318-14307-0*) Hispanic Inst.

***Study of the Economic History of Pre-Modern Sri Lanka.** W. I. Siriweera. 1994. 22.00 (*0-7069-7621-5*, Pub. by Vikas II) S Asia.

Study of the Effect of the Interest of a Passage of Learning Vocabulary. Harriet E. O'Shea. LC 71-177138. reprint ed. 37.50 (*0-404-55351-6*) AMS Pr.

Study of the Effects of the Teacher Tenure Law in New Jersey. Raleigh W. Holmstedt. LC 76-176875. (Columbia University. Teachers College. Contributions to Education Ser.: No. 526). reprint ed. 37.50 (*0-404-55526-8*) AMS Pr.

Study of the Elementary Teaching Personnel of Hunterdon, Morris, Sussex & Warren Counties, New Jersey, with Particular Reference to the State Program of Teacher Training. Mary H. McLees. LC 79-177034. (Columbia University. Teachers College. Contributions to Education Ser.: No. 512). reprint ed. 37.50 (*0-404-55512-8*) AMS Pr.

Study of the Ethics of Bertrand Russell. D. D. Bandishte. 160p. 1984. 12.95 (*0-318-37010-7*) Asia Bk Corp.

Study of the Evolution, Effectiveness & Financing of Public & Private Drug Treatment Services. 1994. lib. bdg. 250.95 (*0-8490-6424-4*) Gordon Pr.

Study of the Evolution of the Malay Language: Social Change & Cognitive Development. Tham S. Chee. 182p. (Orig.). 1990. pap. 29.50 (*9971-69-136-1*, Pub. by Sgapore Univ SI) Coronet Bks.

Study of the Fashion Dolls of France. rev. ed. Mildred Seeley & Colleen Seeley. Orig. Title: How to Collect French Fashion Dolls. 176p. Date not set. pap. 29.95 (*0-916809-85-4*) Scott Pubns MI.

Study of the Feasibility of No-Fault Automobile Insurance for Texas. Ed. by Lynn Anderson. (Policy Research Project Report: No. 10). 85p. 1975. pap. 3.00 (*0-89940-606-8*) LBJ Sch Pub Aff.

Study of the Fe'i Banana & Its Distribution with Reference to Polynesian Migrations. L. H. MacDaniels. (BMB Ser.: No. 190). 1947. 25.00 (*0-527-02298-5*) Periodicals Srv.

Study of the Fishes of the Southern Piedmont & Coastal Plain. Henry W. Fowler. (Monograph: No. 7). (Illus.). 408p. (Orig.). 1945. pap. 20.00 (*0-910006-16-4*) Acad Nat Sci Phila.

Study of the Five Zarathushtrian (Zoroastrian) Gathas, 4 pts. in 1 vol., Pts. I-IV. Ed. by Lawrence H. Mills. LC 74-21252. reprint ed. 110.00 (*0-404-12803-3*) AMS Pr.

Study of the Future. Edward Cornish. 310p. 1977. pap. 15.95 (*0-930242-03-3*) Transaction Pubs.

Study of the Greek Love Names. David M. Robinson & Edward J. Fluck. Ed. by Gregory Vlastos. LC 78-19375. (Morals & Law in Ancient Greece Ser.). 1979. reprint ed. lib. bdg. 23.95 (*0-405-11569-5*) Ayer.

Study of the History of Music. Edward Dickinson. 1972. 59.95 (*0-8490-1155-8*) Gordon Pr.

***Study of the Holy Ghost.** Ernest L. Walker. 160p. (Orig.). 1996. pap. 5.95 (*1-56794-123-0*, C-2445) Star Bible.

Study of the Holy Spirit. William E. Biederwolf. LC 84-25099. 128p. (C). 1985. reprint ed. pap. 5.99 (*0-8254-2244-2*) Kregel.

Study of the Imagery in the Gothic Romances of Ann Radcliffe. Ford H. Swigart. Ed. by Devendra P. Varma. LC 79-8484. (Gothic Studies & Dissertations). 1980. lib. bdg. 23.95 (*0-405-12663-8*) Ayer.

Study of the Impact of Buddhism Upon Japanese Life As Revealed in the Order of Kokin-Shu. Toyozo W. Nakarai. 1972. 59.95 (*0-8490-1156-6*) Gordon Pr.

Study of the International Press & Other Media in the Shaping of Public Opinion: The Sarah Churchill Cause. 5th ed. Burton R. Landes. 80p. 1985. pap. 25.00 (*0-915568-08-X*) B R Landes.

Study of the International Press & Other Media in the Shaping of Public Opinion: The Sarah Churchill Clause. Date not set. write for info. (*0-614-13004-2*) B R Landes.

Study of the Kanuri Language, Grammar & Vocabulary. Johannes Lukas. LC 38-24176. 271p. 1937. reprint ed. pap. 77.60 (*0-8357-3017-4*, 2057103) Bks Demand.

Study of the Knowledge & Use of Hospice by Health Care Professionals in Omaha. Carole M. Davis et al. 48p. (Orig.). 1984. pap. 3.50 (*1-55719-093-3*) U NE CPAR.

Study of the Languages of Torres Straits. Sidney H. Ray & Alfred C. Haddon. LC 75-35153. reprint ed. 31.50 (*0-404-14168-4*) AMS Pr.

An Asterisk (*) at the beginning of an entry indicates that the title is appearing in BIP for the first time.

Study of the Leisure Activities of Certain Elementary School Teachers of Long Island. Lucile E. Allard. LC 70-176510. (Columbia University. Teachers College. Contributions to Education Ser.: No. 779). reprint ed. 37.50 (*0-404-55779-1*) AMS Pr.

Study of the Local Literature of the Upper Ohio Valley: With Especial Reference to the Early Pioneer & Indian Tales, 1820-1840. Mary Atkeson. LC 74-7917. (Ohio State University, Columbus Contributions to English Ser.: No. 2). reprint ed. 31.50 (*0-404-11800-3*) AMS Pr.

Study of the Logbara (Ma'di) Language: Grammar & Vocabulary. J. Pasquale Crazzolara. LC 60-2046. 392p. reprint ed. pap. 111.80 (*0-8357-6949-6*, 2039008) Bks Demand.

Study of the Louisiana Court System. 339p. 1972. 6.00 (*0-318-14445-X*) IJA NYU.

Study of the Mahavastu. Ed. by Bimala C. Law. LC 78-72469. reprint ed. 32.50 (*0-404-17339-X*) AMS Pr.

***Study of the Management, Deployment & Utilization of Crime Labs in Texas.** Max Courtney & Edward E. Hueske. 92p. 1984. 7.50 (*0-936440-58-9*) U TX SUPA.

Study of the Markets for Natural Gas Engines. 85p. 1970. pap. 4.00 (*0-318-12708-3*, X60100) Am Gas Assn.

Study of the Master Universe. William S. Sadler, Jr. LC 68-58958. (Illus.). 150p. 1968. 16.00 (*0-686-05760-0*); pap. write for info. (*0-686-05761-9*) Second Soc Foun.

***Study of the Mexican Tax Reform for 1996 by Paras, S. C.** 144p. 1996. pap. 29.50 (*0-614-26859-1*, 34995BLS01) Commerce.

Study of the Middle East: Research & Scholarship in the Humanities & the Social Sciences. Ed. by Leonard Binder. LC 76-7408. 655p. reprint ed. pap. 180.00 (*0-317-11061-6*, 2055412) Bks Demand.

Study of the Mill Schools of North Carolina. John H. Cook. LC 73-176668. (Columbia University. Teachers College. Contributions to Education Ser.: No. 178). reprint ed. 37.50 (*0-404-55178-5*) AMS Pr.

Study of the Money Question. Hugo Bilgram. 1973. 59.95 (*0-8490-1157-4*) Gordon Pr.

Study of the Moral Development of Children see Memory Defects in Organic Psychoses

Study of the Nature, Incidence & Consequences of Elementary School Playground Related Injuries: Final Report. (Illus.). 100p. (Orig.). (C). 1996. pap. text ed. 30.00 (*0-7881-2700-4*) DIANE Pub.

Study of the Nature of Difficulty. Jacob S. Orleans. LC 74-177136. (Columbia University. Teachers College. Contributions to Education Ser.: No. 206). reprint ed. 37.50 (*0-404-55206-4*) AMS Pr.

Study of the Neuronal Characteristics of Pattern Reversal Visual Evoked Cortical Potentials. W. Spileers. No. 48. 165p. (Orig.). 1991. pap. 42.50 (*90-6186-480-1*, Pub. by Leuven Univ BE) Coronet Bks.

Study of the New Metamorphosis. John H. Lyon. LC 20-3786. reprint ed. 27.50 (*0-404-04087-X*) AMS Pr.

Study of the "New Science" 2nd ed. Vico Giambattista. Ed. by Leon Pompa. 208p. (C). 1990. pap. text ed. 17.95 (*0-521-38871-6*) Cambridge U Pr.

Study of the "New Science" 2nd ed. Vico Giambattista. Ed. by Leon Pompa. 208p. (C). 1990. 59.95 (*0-521-38217-3*) Cambridge U Pr.

Study of the Notched Effect & of the Specimen Design & Loading see Fatigue of Cast Steels

Study of the Novels of George Moore. Richard A Cave. (Irish Literary Studies: Vol. # 3). 272p. 7800. 40.00 (*0-901072-58-3*, Pub. by Colin Smythe Ltd UK) Dufour.

Study of the Oboe. William D. Fitch. 1984. pap. 15.00 (*0-911586-09-1*) Wahr.

Study of the Omaha Area Delivery System for Social Welfare, Health, Education, Employment, Courts, Law, & Recreation. David W. Hinton & Ralph H. Todd. 208p. (Orig.). 1973. pap. 15.00 (*1-55719-082-8*) U NE CPAR.

Study of the Opinions of Certain Professional & Non-Professional Groups Regarding Homogeneous or Ability Grouping. Walter H. Sauvain. LC 74-177231. (Columbia University. Teachers College. Contributions to Education Ser.: No. 596). reprint ed. 37.50 (*0-404-55596-9*) AMS Pr.

***Study of the Past in the Victorian Age.** Ed. by Vanessa Brand. (Oxbow Monographs in Archaeology: No. 73). (Illus.). 176p. 1997. pap. 35.00 (*1-900188-28-7*, Pub. by Oxbow Bks UK) David Brown.

Study of the Population of Manhattanville. Howard B. Woolston. LC 79-76684. (Columbia University. Studies in the Social Sciences: No. 93). reprint ed. 27.50 (*0-404-51093-0*) AMS Pr.

Study of the Possibilities of Graphs As a Means of Instruction in the First Four Grades of the Elementary School. Ruth G. Strickland. LC 73-177736. (Columbia University. Teachers College. Contributions to Education Ser.: No. 745). reprint ed. 37.50 (*0-404-55745-7*) AMS Pr.

Study of the Primary Group. Edward A. Shils. (Reprint Series in Social Sciences). (C). 1993. reprint ed. pap. text ed. 2.30 (*0-8290-2653-3*, S-262) Irvington.

Study of the Problem of Discrimination Against Indigenous Populations, Vol. V: Conclusions, Proposals & Recommendations. 46p. 1987. 11.00 (*92-1-154060-7*, E.86.XIV.3) UN.

Study of the Professional Criticism of Broadcasting in the U. S., 1920-1955. Ralph L. Smith. Ed. by Christopher H. Sterling. LC 78-21739. (Dissertations in Broadcasting Ser.). 1980. lib. bdg. 40.95 (*0-405-11775-2*) Ayer.

Study of the Pseudorthoceratidae, No. 10 see Palaeontographica Americana: Vol. 2

Study of the Quality of English in Latin Translations. Maxie N. Woodring. LC 78-177626. (Columbia University. Teachers College. Contributions to Education Ser.: No. 187). reprint ed. 37.50 (*0-404-55187-4*) AMS Pr.

Study of the Question of Boundaries Between the Republics of Peru & Ecuador. Vincente Santamaria De Paredes. 1976. lib. bdg. 69.95 (*0-8490-2713-6*) Gordon Pr.

Study of the Relation of the Dutch Lancelot & the Flemish Perchevael Fragments to the Manuscripts of Chretien's Conte del Graal. Mary R. Fuehrer. LC 73-140025. (Catholic University Studies in German: No. 14). reprint ed. 37.50 (*0-404-50234-2*) AMS Pr.

Study of the Relationship Between Race & Ability. L. M. Hunsicker. LC 74-176888. (Columbia University. Teachers College. Contributions to Education Ser.: No. 185). reprint ed. 37.50 (*0-404-55185-8*) AMS Pr.

Study of the Relationship Between the Vocational Home Economics Teacher Training Curricula of a Group of Women's Colleges & Expected Responsibilities of Beginning Teachers. Laura V. Clark. LC 72-176649. (Columbia University. Teachers College. Contributions to Education Ser.: No. 586). reprint ed. 37.50 (*0-404-55586-1*) AMS Pr.

Study of the Results of Planning for Home Economics Education in the Southern States As Organized Under the National Acts for Vocational Education. Druzilla C. Kent. LC 77-176965. (Columbia University. Teachers College. Contributions to Education Ser.: No. 689). reprint ed. 37.50 (*0-404-55689-2*) AMS Pr.

Study of the Securities & Exchange Commission Governance & the Public Interest, 1969-1972. rev. ed. Robert E. Herman. LC 92-34080. (Financial Sector of the American Economy Ser.). 360p. 1992. text ed. 83.00 (*0-8153-1293-8*) Garland.

Study of the Securities Industry, 3 Bks., Set, Pts. 1-9. U. S. Congress Staff. 1982. reprint ed. Set. lib. bdg. 165.00 (*0-89941-228-9*, 201500) W S Hein.

Study of the Short Story. Henry S. Canby. Ed. by Alfred Dashiell. LC 83-45726. reprint ed. 33.00 (*0-404-20050-8*) AMS Pr.

Study of the Small-Mouth Bass, Micropterus Dolomieu (Lacepede) in Rearing Ponds in Ohio. T. H. Langlois. (Bulletin Ser.: No. 33). 1936. 2.00 (*0-86727-032-2*) Ohio Bio Survey.

Study of the Sociability of Elementary School Children. Jui-Ching Hsia. LC 70-176884. (Columbia University. Teachers College. Contributions to Education Ser.: No. 322). reprint ed. 37.50 (*0-404-55322-2*) AMS Pr.

Study of the Social Attitudes & Information on Public Problems of Women Teachers in Secondary Schools. John C. Sullivan. LC 72-177733. (Columbia University. Teachers College. Contributions to Education Ser.: No. 791). reprint ed. 37.50 (*0-404-55791-0*) AMS Pr.

Study of the Socio-Religious Ceremony of Upanayana: Investiture with Sacred Thread in the Sutras & the Dharmasastra. Bharati Barua. (C). 1995. 16.00 (*81-85094-77-2*, Pub. by Punthi Pus II) S Asia.

Study of the Sources of Bunyan's Allegories. James B. Wharey. 1973. 59.95 (*0-8490-1158-2*) Gordon Pr.

Study of the Sources of Bunyan's Allegories(with Special Reference to Deguileville's Pilgrimage of Man. James B. Wharey. LC 68-59038. 136p. (C). 1968. reprint ed. 35.00 (*0-87752-120-4*) Gordian.

Study of the Sources of Han D'Islande & Their Significance in the Literary Development of Victor Hugo. Mary I. O'Connor. LC 76-115357. (Catholic University Romance Languages Ser.: No. 24). reprint ed. 37.50 (*0-404-50324-1*) AMS Pr.

Study of the Sources of the Tales & Romances Written by Nathaniel Hawthorne Before 1853. Elizabeth L. Chandler. (BCL1-PS American Literature Ser.). 64p. 1992. reprint ed. lib. bdg. 59.00 (*0-7812-6723-4*) Rprt Serv.

***Study of the Special Problems & Needs of American Indians with Handicaps Both on & off the Reservation: Appendices.** J. C. O'Connell. 130p. 1987. pap. text ed. write for info. (*1-888557-10-9*, 100104) No Ariz Univ.

***Study of the Special Problems & Needs of American Indians with Handicaps Both on & off the Reservation: Executive Summary.** J. C. O'Connell. 190p. 1987. pap. text ed. write for info. (*1-888557-12-5*, 100103); pap. text ed. write for info. (*1-888557-13-3*, 100102) No Ariz Univ.

Study of the State. Ed. by Henri J. Claessen & Peter Skalnik. (New Babylon Studies in the Social Sciences: No.35). 535p. 1981. 80.00 (*90-279-3348-0*) Mouton.

Study of the Stipitate Hydnums from the Southern Appalachian Mountains - Genera: Bankera, Hydnellum, Phellodon, Sarcodon. Richard E. Baird. (Bibliotheca Mycologica Ser.: Vol. 104). (Illus.). 158p. 1986. pap. 50.00 (*3-443-59005-5*) Lubrecht & Cramer.

Study of the Summer High School. Willis H. Reals. LC 79-177180. (Columbia University. Teachers College. Contributions to Education Ser.: No. 337). reprint ed. 37.50 (*0-404-55337-0*) AMS Pr.

Study of the Teaching of English Composition in Teachers Colleges of the United States, with a Suggested Course of Procedure. Leon R. Meadows. LC 78-177066. (Columbia University. Teachers College. Contributions to Education Ser.: No. 311). reprint ed. 37.50 (*0-404-55311-7*) AMS Pr.

Study of the Test-Performance of American, Mexican & Negro Children see On the Melodic Relativity of Tones

Study of the Theology & the Imagery of Dante's Divina Commedia: Sensory Perception, Reason & Free Will. Sharon Harwood-Gordon. LC 91-31900. (Studies in Italian Literature: Vol. 2). 172p. 1991. lib. bdg. 79.95 (*0-7734-9650-5*) E Mellen.

Study of the Toyota Production System from an Industrial Engineering Viewpoint. rev. ed. Shigeo Shingo. LC 89-60303. (Illus.). 291p. 1989. 50.00 (*0-915299-17-8*) Prod Press.

Study of the Two Experimental Schools of C. N. Starcke & John Dewey. Gra Borup-Nielsen. LC 94-37028. 224p. 1995. text ed. 89.95 (*0-7734-2281-1*) E Mellen.

Study of the Types. Ada R. Habershon. LC 67-24340. 240p. 1975. pap. 10.99 (*0-8254-2850-5*, Kregel Class) Kregel.

Study of the United States Steel Corporation in Its Industrial & Legal Aspects. Horace L. Wilgus. LC 73-2541. (Big Business; Economic Power in a Free Society Ser.). 1979. reprint ed. 21.95 (*0-405-05120-4*) Ayer.

Study of the Upper Limits of the Development of Intelligence. Florence M. Teagarden. LC 75-177723. (Columbia University. Teachers College. Contributions to Education Ser.: No. 156). reprint ed. 37.50 (*0-404-55156-4*) AMS Pr.

Study of the Use of Recycled Paving Material. 52p. (Orig.). (YA). (gr. 12 up). 1994. pap. text ed. 25.00 (*0-7881-0840-9*) DIANE Pub.

Study of the Vernacular Poetry of Ahmad Fu'ad Nigm. Kamal Abdel-Malek. LC 90-15065. (Studies in Arabic Literature: Vol. 12). 177p. 1990. 64.50 (*90-04-08933-0*) E J Brill.

Study of the "Villancico" up to Lope De Vega. M. Paulina St. Amour. LC 78-94170. (Catholic University of America. Studies in Romance Languages & Literatures: No. 21). reprint ed. 37.50 (*0-404-50321-7*) AMS Pr.

Study of the Whole of Man: The Significance of the Seven Principles of Man & the Significance of the Monad. Elsie Benjamin. (Study Ser.: No. 6). 41p. 1981. pap. 6.00 (*0-913004-41-3*) Point Loma Pub.

Study of the Works & Reputation of John Aubrey (1626-1697) with, Emphasis on His 'Brief Lives' Jon Kite. LC 92-23187. (Illus.). 316p. 1992. text ed. 99.95 (*0-7734-9861-3*) E Mellen.

Study of the Works of Manuel Mantero: A Member of the Spanish Generation of 1950. W. Douglas Barnette. LC 95-6073. (Hispanic Literature Ser.: Vol. 25). (Illus.). 164p. 1995. text ed. 79.95 (*0-7734-8983-5*) E Mellen.

Study of Theatrical Vision in Arthur Rimbaud's Illuminations. Gerald Macklin. LC 93-32574. (Studies in French Literature: Vol. 16). 290p. 1993. 89.95 (*0-7734-9349-2*) E Mellen.

Study of Theology. Richard A. Muller. (Foundations of Contemporary Interpretation Ser.: Vol. 7). 240p. 1991. 18.99 (*0-310-41001-0*) Zondervan.

Study of Theology. Gerhard Ebeling. Tr. by Duane A. Priebe. LC 78-5393. 306p. reprint ed. pap. 87.30 (*0-685-16324-5*, 2026983) Bks Demand.

Study of Thinking. Jerome S. Bruner et al. (Social Science Classics Ser.). 352p. 1986. reprint ed. pap. 21.95 (*0-88738-656-3*) Transaction Pubs.

Study of Thomas Hardy. Arthur Symons. LC 77-160427. (Studies in Thomas Hardy: No. 14). (C). 1971. reprint ed. lib. bdg. 75.00 (*0-8383-1297-7*) M S G Haskell Hse.

Study of Thomas Hardy & Other Essays. D. H. Lawrence. Ed. by Bruce Steele. (Cambridge Edition of the Works of D. H. Lawrence). 400p. 1985. text ed. 95.00 (*0-521-25252-0*) Cambridge U Pr.

Study of Thumos in Early Greek Epic. Caroline P. Caswell. (Mnemosyne Ser.: Supplement 114). ix, 85p. 1990. pap. 34.50 (*90-04-09260-9*) E J Brill.

***Study of Time.** Kenneth Koch. 1998. write for info. (*0-375-40136-9*); pap. write for info. (*0-375-70133-8*) Knopf.

Study of Time II: 2nd Conference of the International Society for the Study of Time, Summer, 1973. Ed. by J. T. Fraser et al. (Illus.). ix, 487p. 1975. 100.95 (*0-387-07321-3*) Spr-Verlag.

Study of Time III: 3rd Conference of the International Society for the Study of Time. Ed. by J. T. Fraser et al. 1978. 83.95 (*0-387-90311-9*) Spr-Verlag.

Study of Time IV: Proceedings. Ed. by J. T. Fraser et al. (Illus.). 286p. 1981. 104.95 (*0-387-90594-4*) Spr-Verlag.

Study of Trade among Developing Countries, 1950-1980: An Appraisal of the Emerging Pattern. H. C. Thomas. 242p. 1988. 120.75 (*0-444-70385-3*, North Holland) Elsevier.

Study of Traffic Control & Congestion Control in Broadband ISDN. Yoon D. Chang & David H. Su. (Illus.). 175p. (Orig.). (C). 1994. pap. text ed. 40.00 (*0-7881-0525-6*) DIANE Pub.

Study of Transfer of Training from High School Subjects to Intelligence. Alexander G. Wesman. LC 78-177650. (Columbia University. Teachers College. Contributions to Education Ser.: No. 909). (C). reprint ed. 37.50 (*0-404-55909-3*) AMS Pr.

Study of Turnover. James L. Price. LC 76-56377. (Illus.). 170p. 1977. reprint ed. pap. 48.50 (*0-608-00105-8*, 2060870) Bks Demand.

Study of Twentieth-Century Harmony: Harmony in France to 1914 & Contemporary Harmony, 2 vols. in 1. Rene Lenormand & Mosco Carner. LC 76-40058. (Music Reprint Ser.). 1975. reprint ed. lib. bdg. 32.50 (*0-306-70717-9*) Da Capo.

Study of Two Levels of Bread Enrichment in Children's Diets. Pauline B. Mack et al. (SRCD M Ser.: Vol. 18, No. 2). 1953. pap. 25.00 (*0-527-01558-X*) Periodicals Srv.

Study of Two Methods for Repairing Defects in Line Pipe. John F. Kiefner & A. R. Duffy. 175p. 1974. 12.00 (*0-318-12709-1*, L22275) Am Gas Assn.

***Study of Urban Geography.** 4th ed. write for info. (*0-7131-6589-8*, Pub. by E Arnold UK) Routledge Chapman & Hall.

Study of Urban Geography. 4th ed. Harold Carter. LC 95-40978. 464p. 1995. pap. 34.95 (*0-470-23534-9*, Pub. by E Arnld UK) St Martin.

Study of Urbanization. Philip M > Hauser & Leo F. Schnore. LC 65-24223. 564p. reprint ed. 160.80 (*0-8357-9987-5*, 2013058) Bks Demand.

Study of Value Management & Quantity Surveying Practice. John Kelly & Steven Male. (C). 1988. text ed. 40.00 (*0-85406-398-6*, Pub. by Surveyors Pubns) St Mut.

Study of Values. 3rd ed. Gordon W. Allport et al. teacher ed. 14.64 (*0-395-08460-1*); teacher ed. 2.40 (*0-395-08466-0*) HM.

Study of Variable Stars Using Small Telescopes. Ed. by John R. Percy. (Illus.). 272p. 1987. text ed. 69.95 (*0-521-33300-8*) Cambridge U Pr.

Study of Vasyl' Stefanyk: The Pain at the Heart of Existence. D. S. Struk. LC 72-89110. (Ukrainian Research Foundation Ser.). 200p. 1973. lib. bdg. 13.50 (*0-87287-056-1*) Ukrainian Acad.

Study of Vegetation. Ed. by Marinus J. Werger. (Illus.). 1979. lib. bdg. 146.00 (*90-6193-594-6*) Kluwer Ac.

Study of Verbal Accompaniments to Educational Motion Pictures. Leon H. Westfall. LC 76-177647. (Columbia University. Teachers College. Contributions to Education Ser.: No. 617). (C). reprint ed. 37.50 (*0-404-55617-5*) AMS Pr.

Study of Vermeer. enl. rev. ed. Edward A. Snow. LC 92-21860. (Illus.). 224p. (C). 1993. 45.00 (*0-520-07130-1*); pap. 25.00 (*0-520-07132-8*) U CA Pr.

Study of Vermeer. Edward A. Snow. LC 75-32675. 196p. reprint ed. pap. 55.90 (*0-317-55479-4*, 2029592) Bks Demand.

Study of War. Quincy Wright. LC 83-50443. 466p. 1983. pap. text ed. 25.50 (*0-226-91001-6*, Midway Reprint) U Ch Pr.

Study of War As a Contribution to Peace. Wolf Mendl. LC 82-83955. (Orig.). (C). 1983. pap. 3.00 (*0-87574-247-5*) Pendle Hill.

Study of Welfare State Regimes. Ed. by Jon E. Kolberg. LC 90-32224. (Comparative Public Policy Analysis Ser.). 276p. (gr. 13). 1992. text ed. 63.95 (*0-87332-650-4*) M E Sharpe.

Study of Women Delinquents in New York State. Mabel R. Fernald et al. LC 68-55770. (Criminology, Law Enforcement, & Social Problems Ser.: No. 23). 1968. reprint ed. 26.00 (*0-87585-023-5*) Patterson Smith.

Study of Yoga. J. Ghosh. 276p. 1989. 16.95 (*0-318-36395-X*) Asia Bk Corp.

Study of Young High School Graduates. Margaret Moore. LC 74-177081. (Columbia University. Teachers College. Contributions to Education Ser.: No. 583). reprint ed. 37.50 (*0-404-55583-7*) AMS Pr.

Study of Your Bible. Harold G. Mackay. 1988. pap. 4.00 (*0-937396-68-0*) Walterick Pubs.

Study on Conventional Disarmament. (Disarmament Studies: No. 12). 67p. 9.50 (*92-1-142077-6*, E.85.IX.1) UN.

Study on Defensive Security Concepts & Policies. (Disarmament Studies: No. 26). 64p. Date not set. pap. 20.00 (*92-1-142197-7*, E.93.IX.12) UN.

Study on Depleted Uranium (Tails) & on Uranium Residues from Reprocessing. H. Wingender et al. 105p. 1994. pap. 16.00 (*92-826-6478-3*, CD-NA-15032EN-C, Pub. by Europ Com UK) Bernan Associates.

Study on Deterrence: Its Implications for Disarmament & the Arms Race, Negotiated Arms Reductions & International Security & Other Related Matters. (Study Ser.: No.17). 142p. 1987. 15.00 (*92-1-142127-6*, E.87.IX.2) UN.

Study on Evaluation of Driver Education. William A. Lybrand et al. LC 75-121262. 225p. 1968. 19.00 (*0-403-04515-0*) Scholarly.

***Study on Improving the Single Audit Process.** 1997. lib. bdg. 250.99 (*0-8490-7685-4*) Gordon Pr.

Study on Jerusalem. Hassan bin Talal Crown Prince of Jordan. LC 80-506808. 64p. reprint ed. pap. 25.00 (*0-685-20310-7*, 2030349) Bks Demand.

Study on Papuan Music. Jaap Kunst. LC 75-35130. (Illus.). reprint ed. 30.00 (*0-404-14146-3*) AMS Pr.

Study on Some Smarandache Notions. Charles Ashbacher. Ed. by Marcela Popescu. 75p. (Orig.). (C). 1996. pap. text ed. 7.95 (*1-879585-51-0*) Erhus Univ Pr.

Study on State-of-the-Art of Dioxin from Combustion Sources. Ed. by A. D. Little. 1981. 6.00 (*0-686-34520-7*, H00180) ASME.

Study on the Application of Confidence-Building Measures in Outer Space. (Disarmament Studies: No. 27). 118p. Date not set. pap. 25.00 (*92-1-142205-1*, E.94.IX.6) UN.

Study on the Economic & Social Consequences of the Arms Race & Military Expenditures, No. 19. (Disarmament Studies). 82p. 1989. 9.50 (*92-1-142145-4*, E.89.IX.2) UN.

Study on the Historiography of the British West Indies to the End of the Nineteenth Century. Elsa V. Goveia. LC 75-20036. 192p. 1981. pap. 12.95 (*0-88258-048-5*) Howard U Pr.

Study on the Impact of Liberalization of Inward Cross-Border Mail on Provision. European Commission Staff. 122p. 1995. pap. 25.00 (*92-826-9596-4*, CV-89-95-018ENC, Pub. by Europ Com UK) Bernan Associates.

Study on the Library Resources at the Military Institutions in Japan, the United States, England, France, Belgium, the Netherlands, Germany, & Switzerland. Joseph D. Lowe. LC 90-91743. iii, 28p. 1973. reprint ed. pap. 10.00 (*0-9605506-1-5*) Lowe Pub.

Study on the Presence of Bombesin-Like Peptides & Their Effects on Hormone Release & Cell Multiplication in the Rat Anterior Pituitary. H. Houben. No. 43. 124p. (Orig.). 1991. pap. 37.50 (*90-6186-455-0*, Pub. by Leuven Univ BE) Coronet Bks.

Study on the Pure Theory of Production. Sune Carlson. LC 65-18333. (Reprints of Economic Classics Ser.). vii, 128p. 1965. reprint ed. 27.50 (*0-678-00009-3*) Kelley.

Study on the Rights of Persons Belonging to Ethnic, Religious & Linguistic Minorities. (Study Ser.: No. 5). 114p. 1991. 25.00 (*92-1-154083-6*, 91.XIV.2) UN.

Study on the Synoptic Gospels. Eduardo Martinez Dalmau. 1964. 5.95 (*0-8315-0013-1*) Speller.

S

Study on the Use of Computers by Legislators. Henry C. Trenk & Robert B. Person. 105p. (Orig.). (C). 1994. pap. text ed. 25.00 (*0-7881-0748-8*) DIANE Pub.

Study on Transfer of the Headoffice of a Company from One Member State to Another. European Communities Staff. 62p. 1993. pap. 12.00 (*92-826-5882-1*, C1-79-93-017-EN-C, Pub. by Europ Com UK) Bernan Associates.

Study on Ways & Means of Promoting Transparency in International Transfers of Conventional Arms. (Disarmament Studies: No. 24). 43p. Date not set. pap. 20.00 (*92-1-142189-6*, E.93.IX.6) UN.

Study out the Land. Thomas K. Whipple. LC 76-134158. (Essay Index Reprint Ser.). 1977. 20.95 (*0-8369-2088-0*) Ayer.

Study Outline & Workbook in the Fundamentals of Music. 10th ed. Frank W. Hill et al. 272p. (C). 1991. spiral bd. write for info. (*0-697-10431-1*) Brown & Benchmark.

Study Outline for Chief & Assistant Engineer, Limited & Designated Duty Engineer. V. J. Gianelloni, III. (Illus.). 140p. 1994. pap. text ed. 37.50 (*1-879778-07-6*, BK-104) Marine Educ.

Study Outlines in Physics: Construction & Experimental Evaluation. Jessie Clemensen. LC 71-176654. (Columbia University. Teachers College. Contributions to Education Ser.: No. 553). reprint ed. 37.50 (*0-404-55553-5*) AMS Pr.

Study Paper on Parliamentary Procedure. Ira Grinnell. 1971. 5.00 (*1-55614-008-8*) U of SD Gov Res Bur.

Study Power: Better Study Skills-Greater Success in College. Harley D. Christiansen & Marie L. Vergata. LC 75-5919. 96p. (Orig.). (C). 1975. pap. text ed. 15.95 (*0-915456-00-1*) P Juul Pr.

***Study Power: Study Skills to Improve Your Learning & Your Grades.** William R. Luckie & Wood Smethurst. 128p. 1997. pap. 15.95 (*1-57129-046-X*) Brookline Bks.

Study Power Leader's Guide. American College Testing Program Staff. (Study Power Ser.). 99p. (Orig.). (YA). (gr. 7 up). 1987. teacher ed. 4.00 (*0-937734-63-2*) ACT.

Study Power, Managing Time & Environment. American College Testing Program Staff. (Study Power Ser.). 30p. (Orig.). (YA). (gr. 7 up). 1987. student ed. 1.00 (*0-937734-65-9*) ACT.

Study Power, Preparing for Tests. American College Testing Program Staff. (Study Power Ser.). 14p. (Orig.). (YA). (gr. 7 up). 1987. student ed. 1.00 (*0-937734-69-1*) ACT.

Study Power, Reading Textbooks. American College Testing Program Staff. (Study Power Ser.). 21p. (Orig.). (YA). (gr. 7 up). 1987. student ed. 1.00 (*0-937734-66-7*) ACT.

Study Power Student Workbook Set. American College Testing Program Staff. (Study Power Ser.). (Orig.). (YA). (gr. 7 up). 1987. student ed. 5.00 (*0-937734-64-0*) ACT.

Study Power, Taking Class Notes. American College Testing Program Staff. (Study Power Ser.). 22p. (Orig.). (YA). (gr. 7 up). 1987. student ed., pap. text ed. 1.00 (*0-937734-67-5*) ACT.

Study Power, Taking Tests. American College Testing Program Staff. (Study Power Ser.). 13p. (Orig.). (YA). (gr. 7 up). 1987. student ed. 1.00 (*0-937734-70-5*) ACT.

Study Power, Using Resources. American College Testing Program Staff. (Study Power Ser.). 14p. (Orig.). (YA). (gr. 7 up). 1987. student ed., pap. text ed. 1.00 (*0-937734-68-3*) ACT.

Study Proposal for Assessing Potential for Great Lakes Contamination Via Groundwater. fac. ed. Great Lakes Science Advisory Board, Groundwater Contamination Task Force Staff. 73p. 1985. pap. 25.00 (*0-7837-8618-2*, 2075225) Bks Demand.

Study Reading: A Course in Reading Skills for Academic Purposes. Eric H. Glendinning & Beverly A. Holmstrom. 174p. (C). 1992. pap. text ed. 12.95 (*0-521-39974-2*) Cambridge U Pr.

Study-Reading & Test-Taking Skills. (Fossil Power Plant Startup Training Ser.: Module 1). (Illus.). 69p. spiral bd. 25.00 (*0-87683-358-X*) GP Courseware.

Study-Sarah Churchill. Burton R. Landes. 400p. (Orig.). 1991. reprint ed. pap. write for info. (*0-318-68562-0*) B R Landes.

Study Scores of Historical Styles, Vol. 1. Harry B. Lincoln & Stephen Bonta. 400p. 1986. text ed. write for info. (*0-13-698267-0*) P-H.

Study Scores of Historical Styles, Vol. II. Harry B. Lincoln & Stephen Bonta. (Illus.). 400p. 1987. pap. text ed. write for info. (*0-13-858853-8*) P-H.

Study Scrapbook of Virginia. (Illus.). 5.00 (*0-318-01325-8*) VA Chamber Com.

Study Second Language Acquisition. 1994. 34.95 (*0-19-437189-1*) OUP.

Study Skills. Deem. (C). Date not set. suppl. ed., teacher ed., pap. write for info. (*0-395-66016-5*) HM.

Study Skills. Deem. (C). 1992. teacher ed., pap. 2.76 (*0-395-58812-X*) HM.

Study Skills. Deem. (C). 1992. pap. 28.36 (*0-395-58811-1*) HM.

Study Skills. Goldfarb. (C). 1997. pap. text ed. write for info. (*0-15-503637-8*) HB Coll Pubs.

Study Skills. Goldfarb. (C). 1997. teacher ed., pap. text ed. 26.75 (*0-15-503647-5*) HB Coll Pubs.

Study Skills. Laskey & Roy Gibson. 225p. 1996. pap. 27.00 (*0-205-19152-5*) Allyn.

Study Skills: A Student's Guide for Survival. 2nd ed. Robert A. Carman & Royce W. Adams, Jr. LC 83-5925. (Self-Teaching Guides Ser.: No. 1-581). 272p. (C). 1984. pap. text ed. 16.95 (*0-471-88911-3*) Wiley.

Study Skills: Making the Most of Your Human Computer. Sharon Wooten. 244p. (C). 1996. per., pap. text ed. 27.24 (*0-7872-2340-9*) Kendall-Hunt.

Study Skills: Teaching & Learning Strategies for Mainstream & Specialized Classrooms. Sara Brody. 60p. 1987. teacher ed. 8.00 (*1-886042-00-4*) Larc Pubg.

Study Skills: The Key to Student Success. William Reed. 120p. (C). 1996. per. 20.94 (*0-7872-2596-7*) Kendall-Hunt.

***Study Skills: The Parent Connection.** RCI (Olson) Staff. 64p. 1996. student ed. write for info. incl. vhs (*0-7872-2919-9*) Kendall-Hunt.

***Study Skills: The Parent Connection.** 3rd rev. ed. RCI (Olson) Staff. (Illus.). 49p. 1995. student ed., pap. 7.50 (*0-7872-2917-2*) Kendall-Hunt.

Study Skills: Tools for Active Learning. Abby Marks. 1994. pap. 24.95 (*0-8273-5437-1*) Delmar.

***Study Skills Across the Curriculum: Grades 5-8.** Olson. 786p. 1996. ring bd. 60.00 (*0-7872-2928-8*) Kendall-Hunt.

Study Skills & Notetaking. Gregg Condon. 320p. (C). 1990. teacher ed. 8.00 (*1-56118-335-0*); pap. text ed. 16.95 (*1-56118-334-2*); 8.80 (*1-56118-333-4*) Paradigm MN.

Study Skills & Test-Taking Strategies for Medical Students: Find & Use Your Personal Learning Style. D. D. Shain. (Oklahoma Notes Ser.). 192p. 1994. pap. 17.95 (*0-387-97695-7*) Spr-Verlag.

Study Skills for Academic Success. Cheryl Wecksler. 208p. 1995. pap. 26.95 (*0-8384-3958-6*) Milady Pub.

Study Skills for Academic Writing. John Trzeciak & S. E. Mackay. LC 94-19763. (C). 1994. 9.75 (*0-13-017856-X*) P-H.

Study Skills for Adults Returning to School. 2nd ed. Jerold W. Apps. 240p. 1982. pap. text ed. write for info. (*0-07-002165-1*) McGraw.

Study Skills for Advanced Success. Wecksler. (College ESL Ser.). 1994. teacher ed., pap. 7.95 (*0-8384-4265-X*) Heinle & Heinle.

Study Skills for Advanced Success. Wecksler. (College ESL Ser.). 1994. suppl. ed. 36.95 incl. audio (*0-8384-4288-9*) Heinle & Heinle.

Study Skills for College. Eleanor C. Haburton. LC 82-20388. 224p. 1981. reprint ed. pap. 63.90 (*0-7837-8339-6*, 2049126) Bks Demand.

Study Skills for Life. Concept by L. Ron Hubbard. 128p. (J). (gr. 7-10). 1993. 34.99 (*0-88404-744-X*) Bridge Pubns Inc.

Study Skills for Nurses. Jayne Taylor. LC 92-49336. 1992. write for info. (*0-412-44070-9*) Chapman & Hall.

Study Skills for Nurses. Jayne Taylor. LC 92-49336. 112p. 1992. pap. 28.75 (*1-56593-066-5*, 0380) Singular Publishing.

Study Skills for Nursing: A Practical Guide. Joan W. Parnell & Kevin D. Kendrick. LC 94-26096. 1994. write for info. (*0-443-04686-7*) Churchill.

Study Skills for Science Students. Daniel D. Chiras. Ed. by Westby. 86p. (C). pap. text ed. 8.50 (*0-314-03983-X*) West Pub.

Study Skills for Students in Our Schools. Stephen B. McCarney & Janet Tucci. 206p. (Orig.). 1991. pap. 16.00 (*1-878372-04-1*) Hawthorne Educ Servs.

Study Skills for Students of English as a Second Language. 2nd ed. Richard C. Yorkey. (Illus.). 256p. (gr. 11-12). 1982. text ed. write for info. (*0-07-072316-8*) McGraw.

Study Skills for Today's College Student. Jerold W. Apps. 320p. 1990. teacher ed. 19.95 (*0-07-002465-0*); pap. text ed. write for info. (*0-07-002464-2*) McGraw.

Study Skills for Today's College Students. deluxe ed. Jerold W. Apps. 1994. pap. text ed. write for info. (*0-07-071532-7*) McGraw.

Study Skills GED Student Textbook. Catherine D. Tobias et al. 132p. (Orig.). 1986. pap. text ed. 5.95 (*0-88210-177-3*) Natl Assn Principals.

Study Skills GED Teachers Manual. Elizabeth C. Keroack et al. Ed. by P. Klein. 52p. (Orig.). 1986. pap. 4.95 (*0-88210-178-1*) Natl Assn Principals.

Study Skills Handbook. 1990. 12.95 (*0-19-451226-6*) OUP.

Study Skills Handbook. Jay Amberg. 144p. (Orig.). (J). (gr. 6-10). 1993. pap. 7.95 (*0-673-36098-9*, GoodYrBooks) Addson-Wesley Educ.

Study Skills Handbook: More Than 75 Strategies for Better Learning. Judith Dodge. 1994. pap. 12.95 (*0-590-49510-0*) Scholastic Inc.

Study Skills Instructor's Guide: The Tools for Active Learning. Abby Marks-Beale. 84p. 1994. teacher ed. 16.00 (*0-8273-5439-8*) Delmar.

Study Skills Set. Learning Forum Staff. (Success Products Ser.). (YA). (gr. 8-12). 1989. 130.00 (*0-945525-13-3*) Supercamp.

Study Skills Sorcery. Leslie S. Zakalik. (Study Skills Ser.). 48p. (J). (gr. 4-6). 1978. 6.95 (*0-88160-028-8*, LW 213) Learning Wks.

Study Skills Strategies: Your Guide to Critical Thinking. rev. ed. Uelaine Lengefeld. Ed. by Michael Crisp. LC 93-74051. (Fifty-Minute Ser.). (Illus.). 89p. (Orig.). 1994. pap. 10.95 (*1-56052-260-7*) Crisp Pubns.

***Study Skills Test.** William F. Brown & Bernadette Gadzella. 28p. (Orig.). (YA). 1987. pap. text ed. 3.50 (*1-881936-15-5*) WFB Ent.

Study Skills That Work! Orlando D. Griego. (Illus.). 352p. (Orig.). (C). 1989. pap. text ed. write for info. (*0-318-65855-0*) Griego Educ Servs.

Study Skills Workout, Gr 5-8. Susan C. Bartoletti et al. (Illus.). 90p. (Orig.). 1987. pap. 9.95 (*0-673-18995-3*, GoodYrBooks) Addson-Wesley Educ.

Study Skills Workshop Kit. Incl. Level 1. (J). (gr. 5-9). 1980. (*0-88210-112-9*); Level II. (YA). (gr. 8-10). 1979. (*0-88210-113-7*); 16.50 (*0-317-31958-2*) Natl Assn Principals.

Study Smart. Patty Mayo et al. (Illus.). 59p. (YA). (gr. 5-12). 1990. 42.00 (*0-930599-64-0*) Thinking Pubns.

Study Smart: Ready-to-Use Reading-Skill Skills Activities for Grades 5-12. Antoinette Brescher & Gary W. Abbamont. 280p. 1990. pap. text ed. 29.95 (*0-87628-872-7*) Ctr Appl Res.

Study Smart: The Hands-on, Nuts & Bolts Technique of Earning Higher Grades. Theodore Silver. 1992. pap. 12.00 (*0-679-73864-9*, Villard Bks) Random.

Study Smarter, Not Harder: Your Guide to Successful Learning & Studying in Any Situation. Kevin Paul. 192p. (Orig.). 1996. pap. 14.95 (*1-55180-059-4*) Self-Counsel Pr.

Study Smarter-Save Time-Learn More: A Home Study Course. Michael A. Lisausky. (Home Study Ser.). 40p. student ed. 30.00 (*0-939926-36-9*); audio (*0-939926-35-0*) Fruition Pubns.

Study Smarter, Think Smarter! A Ready-to-Use Study Skills Program for Grades 4-8. Lawrence J. Greene. 256p. 1992. spiral bd 27.95 (*0-87628-873-5*) Ctr Appl Res.

Study Smarts: How to Learn More in Less Time. Judi Kesselman-Turkel & Franklynn Peterson. 64p. (J). 1981. pap. 8.86 (*0-8092-5852-8*) Contemp Bks.

Study Starters: Basic Strategies for Academic Success. Diane P. Kostick. (Illus.). 160p. (J). (gr. 5-9). 1994. 12.99 (*0-86653-797-X*, GA1491) Good Apple.

***Study Strategies for High School Students in the Information Age.** Stephen S. Strichart & Charles T. Mangrum. LC 96-54830. 1997. pap. 24.95 (*0-205-19881-3*) Allyn.

Study Strategies Made Easy: A Practical Plan for School Success. Sandi Sirotowitz & Leslie Davis. LC 96-26195. (Illus.). 156p. (Orig.). (YA). (gr. 6-12). 1996. pap. write for info. (*1-886941-03-3*, 0931) Spec Pr FL.

Study, Study, Study, Study, Study, Study. David L. Riley. (Illus.). 1995. 35.00 (*0-9618976-4-3*) D L Riley.

Study Tactics. William H. Armstrong. 272p. (gr. 10-12). 1983. pap. text ed. 8.95 (*0-8120-2590-3*) Barron.

Study Text II: Pastoral Care of Sick & Dying. 56p. 1984. pap. 3.95 (*1-55586-918-1*) US Catholic.

***Study Time Management.** Lynn Underwood. 1997. pap. text ed. 11.95 (*0-572-02185-2*, Pub. by W Foulsham UK) Trans-Atl Phila.

Study to Evaluate the Stability of Underground Gas Storage Reservoirs. American Gas Association, Pipeline Research Committee, Jr. & H. Reginald Hardy. 404p. 1972. 10.00 (*0-318-12710-5*, L19724) Am Gas Assn.

Study War No More: A Peace Handbook for Youth. Ed. by David S. Young. 107p. reprint ed. pap. 30.50 (*0-7837-5929-0*, 2045728) Bks Demand.

Study Workout for Sixth, Seventh, Eighth Graders, Pt. One: A Workout for the Mind. Patrick R. San Fillipo. 26p. (J). (gr. 6-8). 1991. 34.95 incl. vhs (*0-9630443-1-1*); student ed. 11.95 (*0-9630443-0-3*) Educ Excell Via.

Study Writing. L. Hamp-Lyons & Brendan Heasley. 176p. 1987. pap. text ed. 13.95 (*0-521-31558-1*) Cambridge U Pr.

Study 180 Texas Health Care. John C. Goodman & Merrill Matthews. 1993. 10.00 (*0-685-67209-3*) Natl Ctr Pol.

Studyguide for Topical History of the U. S. Jerry R. Baydo. 225p. 1991. 10.00 (*0-911541-17-9*) Gregory Pub.

Studying a Study & Testing a Test: How to Read the Health Science Literature. 3rd ed. Richard K. Riegelman & Robert P. Hirsch. 352p. 1996. pap. text ed. 29.95 (*0-316-74521-9*) Lppncott-Raven.

Studying a Study & Testing a Test: How to Read the Medical Literature. Richard K. Riegelman. 1981. pap. 19.50 (*0-316-74518-9*) Little.

***Studying Abroad/Learning Abroad: An Abridged Version of the Whole World Guide to Culture Learning.** abr. ed. J. Daniel Hess. LC 97-11428. 149p. (Orig.). 1997. pap. text ed. write for info. (*1-877864-50-1*) Intercult Pr.

Studying Africa in Elementary & Secondary Schools. 3rd ed. Leonard S. Kenworthy. LC 70-105869. (World Affairs Guides). 80p. reprint ed. pap. 25.00 (*0-317-41867-X*, 2026030) Bks Demand.

***Studying Aging & Social Change: Conceptual & Methodological Issues.** Melissa A. Hardy. LC 97-4740. 248p. 1997. text ed. 48.00 (*0-7619-0590-1*); pap. text ed. 22.95 (*0-7619-0591-X*) Sage.

***Studying American Government: A Vade Mecum.** (C). 1996. text ed. 1.56 (*0-669-28255-3*) HM College Div.

Studying American Music. Richard Crawford. (I.S.A.M. Special Publications: No. 3). 24p. (Orig.). 1985. pap. 4.00 (*0-914678-25-6*) Inst Am Music.

Studying & Describing Unwritten Languages. Luc Bouquiaux & Jacqueline M. Thomas. LC 92-80686. xii, 728p. 1992. pap. 50.00 (*0-88312-814-4*); fiche 48.00 (*0-88312-857-8*) Summer Instit Ling.

Studying & Living in Britain. British Council Staff. 1990. pap. 21.00 (*0-7463-0656-3*, Pub. by Northcote UK) St Mut.

***Studying & Living in Britain: The British Council's Guide.** British Council Staff. LC 96-40398. 1997. write for info. (*0-87805-986-5*); pap. write for info. (*0-87805-987-3*) U Pr of Miss.

***Studying & Living in Britain, 1996: A Guide for International Students & Visitors.** (Orig.). 1996. pap. 13.95 (*0-7463-0820-5*, Pub. by Northcote House UK) Trans-Atl Phila.

Studying & Working in France: A Student Guide. Russell Cousins et al. LC 94-12626. 1994. pap. 18.95 (*0-7190-4220-8*, Pub. by Manchester Univ Pr UK) St Martin.

Studying Animal Behavior: Autobiographies of the Founders. Ed. by Donald A. Dewsbury. (Illus.). 512p. 1989. reprint ed. pap. text.ed. 24.00 (*0-226-14410-0*) U Ch Pr.

***Studying Audiences: Shock of the Real.** Virginia Nightingale. 184p. (C). 1996. pap. 17.95 (*0-415-14398-5*) Routledge.

***Studying Audiences: Shock of the Real.** Virginia Nightingale. 184p. (C). (gr. 13). 1996. text ed. 59.95 (*0-415-02447-1*) Routledge.

Studying Behavior in Natural Settings. Richard M. Brandt. LC 81-40189. (Illus.). 416p. 1981. reprint ed. pap. text ed. 30.00 (*0-8191-1830-3*) U Pr of Amer.

***Studying British Cultures: Introduction.** Susan Bassnett. (New Accents Ser.). 200p. (C). 1997. pap. 18.95 (*0-415-11440-3*) Routledge.

***Studying British Cultures: Introduction.** Ed. by Susan Bassnett. (New Accents Ser.). 240p. (C). 1997. text ed. 55.00 (*0-415-16581-4*, Routledge NY) Routledge.

Studying Cell Adhesion. Ed. by P. Bongrand et al. LC 94-36098. 1994. 114.95 (*0-387-57590-1*) Spr-Verlag.

Studying Chemical Equilibria & Applying Le Chatelier's Principle Using Microscale Techniques. Marcia L. Gillette & H. Anthony Neidig. (Modular Laboratory Program in Chemistry Ser.). 16p. (C). 1991. pap. text ed. 1.35 (*0-87540-404-9*, EQUL 404-9) Chem Educ Res.

Studying Chemical Reactions & Writing Chemical Equations. Marcia L. Gillette. (Modular Laboratory Program in Chemistry Ser.). 16p. (C). 1993. pap. text ed. 1.35 (*0-87540-422-7*, REAC 422-7) Chem Educ Res.

Studying Children: Observing & Participating. Draper. 1977. pap. text ed. 15.00 (*0-02-665770-8*) Glencoe.

Studying China in Elementary & Secondary Schools. Leonard S. Kenworthy. LC 74-23808. (World Affairs Guides). 76p. reprint ed. pap. 25.00 (*0-317-41908-0*, 2026033) Bks Demand.

Studying Classical Judaism: A Primer. Jacob Neusner. 192p. (Orig.). 1991. pap. 16.00 (*0-664-25136-6*) Westminster John Knox.

Studying Classrooms. Colin Hook. 303p. (C). 1995. pap. 30.00 (*0-86828-035-6*, Pub. by Deakin Univ AT) St Mut.

Studying Collective Action. Ed. by Mario Diani & Ron Eyerman. (Modern Politics Ser.: Vol. 30). 272p. (C). 1992. 55.00 (*0-8039-8524-X*) Sage.

Studying Creative Writing: "Literatures of the Diaspora" 110p. (Orig.). 1996. pap. write for info. (*0-9652860-0-2*) Diaspora Pr of Am.

Studying Culture: An Introductory Reader. Ed. by Jim McGuigan & Ann Gray. LC 93-7215. 256p. 1993. 60.00 (*0-340-58793-8*, B2562, Pub. by E Arnld UK) St Martin.

***Studying Culture: An Introductory Reader.** 2nd ed. Ann Gray & Jim McGuigan. LC 97-14189. 1997. pap. text ed. 18.95 (*0-340-67688-4*, Pub. by E Arnld UK) St Martin.

Studying Cultures. C. Cherryholmes & G. Manson. (Illus.). (J). (gr. 4). 1979. text ed. 24.64 (*0-07-011984-8*) McGraw.

***Studying Curriculum: Cases & Methods.** Ivor F. Goodson. Ed. by Andy Hargreaves. (Modern Educational Thought Ser.). 160p. 1994. 42.50 (*0-335-19051-0*, Open Univ Pr); pap. 13.99 (*0-335-19050-2*, Open Univ Pr) Taylor & Francis.

Studying Curriculum: Cases & Methods. Ivor F. Goodson. LC 93-46385. 168p. 1994. pap. text ed. 16.95 (*0-8077-3362-8*) Tchrs Coll.

Studying Death to Preserve Life: Genocide & the Politics of Memory. Herbert Hirsch. LC 94-29750. 320p. 1995. pap. 14.95 (*0-8078-4505-1*); text ed. 29.95 (*0-8078-2198-5*) U of NC Pr.

Studying Density Using Salad Oil & Vinegar. Wendy A. Reichenbach. Ed. by H. Anthony Neidig. (Modular Laboratory Program in Chemistry Ser.). 7p. (C). 1993. pap. text ed. 1.35 (*0-87540-393-X*, PROP 393-0) Chem Educ Res.

Studying Diversity in Higher Education. Ed. by Daryl G. Smith et al. LC 85-645339. (New Directions for Institutional Research Ser.: No. 81). 106p. (Orig.). 1994. pap. 19.00 (*0-7879-9963-6*) Jossey-Bass.

***Studying Drama.** write for info. (*0-7131-6450-6*, Pub. by E Arnold UK) Routledge Chapman & Hall.

Studying Effectively. 2nd ed. C. Gilbert Wrenn & Robert P. Larsen. 36p. 1955. reprint ed. pap. 1.65 (*0-8047-1071-6*) Stanford U Pr.

Studying Electrochemical Cells & Reduction Potentials. R. L. Marks. Ed. by H. Anthony Neidig. (Modular Laboratory Program in Chemistry Ser.). 12p. (C). 1992. pap. text ed. 1.35 (*0-87540-418-9*, ELEC 418-9) Chem Educ Res.

Studying Electrochemical Half-Cells & Half-Reactions. Henry Schreiber et al. (Modular Laboratory Program in Chemistry Ser.). 12p. (C). 1995. pap. text ed. 1.35 (*0-87540-450-2*, ELEC 450-2) Chem Educ Res.

Studying Electrochemistry & Establishing the Relative Reactivities of a Series of Metals. James N. Spencer. (Modular Laboratory Program in Chemistry Ser.). 12p. (C). 1993. pap. text ed. 1.35 (*0-87540-419-7*, ELEC 419-7) Chem Educ Res.

Studying Elites Using Qualitative Methods. Ed. by Rosanna Hertz & Jonathan B. Imber. LC 95-2836. (Sage Focus Editions Ser.: Vol. 175). 240p. (C). 1995. 54.00 (*0-8039-7036-6*); pap. 24.95 (*0-8039-7037-4*) Sage.

Studying Engineering: A Road Map to a Successful Career. Raymond B. Landis. (C). 1995. pap. text ed. 22.95 (*0-9646969-0-8*) Discover CA.

Studying Families. Anne P. Copeland & Kathleen M. White. (Applied Social Research Methods Ser.: Vol. 27). (Illus.). 160p. 1991. text ed. 39.95 (*0-8039-3247-2*); pap. text ed. 17.95 (*0-8039-3248-0*) Sage.

Studying for a Driver's License: Reading Level 5. 1993. 13.00 (*0-88336-441-7*) Peoples Pub Grp.

Studying for Biology. 4th ed. Anton E. Lawson. Ed. by Brenda D. Smith. LC 94-20073. (Studying for Ser.). 295p. (C). 1997. pap. text ed. 13.44 (*0-06-500650-X*) Addson-Wesley Educ.

Studying for Biology. Anton E. Lawson. 208p. 1996. reprint ed. pap. 13.95 (*1-886746-78-8*) Talman.

Studying for Chemistry. Smith Little. LC 94-37734. (Studying for Ser.). (Illus.). 200p. (C). 1995. text ed. 14.50 (*0-06-500651-8*) Addson-Wesley Educ.

Studying for Chemistry. Larry Little. 200p. 1996. reprint ed. pap. 13.95 (*1-886746-79-6*) Talman.

An Asterisk (*) at the beginning of an entry indicates that the title is appearing in BIP for the first time.

Studying for History. David Pace & Sharon L. Pugh. Ed. by Brenda D. Smith. LC 95-12331. (Studying for Ser.). (Illus.). 224p. (C). 1996. text ed. 15.50 (0-06-500649-6) Addson-Wesley Educ.

Studying for Mathematics. Lynn Hart & Deborah Najee-Ullah. Ed. by Brenda D. Smith. LC 94-33299. (Studying for Ser.). 192p. (C). 1995. text ed. 13.95 (0-06-500647-X) Addson-Wesley Educ.

Studying for Mathematics. Lynn Hart & Deborah Naje-Ullah. 1996. reprint ed. pap. 12.95 (1-886746-80-X) Talman.

Studying for Psychology. Donna L. Mealey & William D. McIntosh. Ed. by Brenda D. Smith. LC 94-12577. (Studying for Ser.). (Illus.). 208p. (C). 1995. text ed. 15.95 (0-06-500648-8) Addson-Wesley Educ.

Studying for Psychology. Donna L. Mealey. 196p. 1996. reprint ed. pap. 14.95 (1-886746-77-X) Talman.

***Studying for Science: A Guide to Information, Communication & Study Techniques.** White. (Illus.). 216p. (Orig.). 1993. pap. text ed. 10.95 (0-419-14820-5, E & FN Spon) Routledge Chapman & Hall.

Studying for Survival. Frances H. Vigneron. 88p. (Orig.). 1993. pap. 9.95 (1-57087-022-5) Prof Pr NC.

Studying Health & Disease. Ed. by Kevin McConway. LC 93-43194. (Health & Disease Ser.: Bk. 2). 132p. 1994. pap. 26.00 (0-335-19252-1, Open Univ Pr) Taylor & Francis.

Studying Health & Disease. Open University Health & Disease Course Team Staff. (Health & Disease Ser.). 112p. 1985. pap. 32.00 (0-335-15050-0, Open Univ Pr) Taylor & Francis.

Studying History: How & Why. 3rd ed. Robert V. Daniels. LC 80-18406. 128p. 1981. pap. text ed. write for info. (0-13-858738-8) P-H.

Studying Housing Success: A Checklist & Case Study of the Paddox, Oxford. Nicholas D. Smith. (C). 1985. 29.00 (0-685-30263-6, Pub. by Oxford Polytechnic UK) St Mut.

Studying Hygiene Behaviour: Methods, Issues, & Experiences. Ed. by Sandy Cairncross & Vijay Kochar. LC 93-44528. (Illus.). 1994. 36.00 (0-8039-9159-2) Sage.

Studying Implementation: Methodological & Administrative Issues. Walter Williams et al. LC 81-21734. (Chatham House Series on Change in American Politics). 192p. (Orig.). reprint ed. pap. 54.80 (0-8357-3454-4, 2039715) Bks Demand.

Studying in China: A Practical Text for Spoken Chinese. Vivian Ling & James E. Dew. LC 93-74518. 144p. 1993. pap. text ed. 14.95 (0-88727-196-0) Cheng & Tsui.

***Studying in the Content Areas, Social Science.** 2nd ed. Carole Bogue. LC 93-79043. (Illus.). 309p. (C). 1993. pap. text ed. 26.95 (0-943202-43-4) H & H Pub.

***Studying in the Content Areas, the Sciences.** 2nd ed. Carole Bogue. LC 93-79042. (Illus.). 309p. (C). 1993. pap. text ed. 26.95 (0-943202-38-8) H & H Pub.

Studying India in Elementary & Secondary Schools. Leonard S. Kenworthy. LC 74-23809. (World Affairs Guides). 71p. reprint ed. pap. 25.00 (0-317-41905-6, 2026034) Bks Demand.

Studying Interpersonal Communication. Ruth A. Clark. (Interpersonal CommTexts Ser.: Vol. 2). 144p. 1991. 42.00 (0-8039-3305-3); pap. 18.95 (0-8039-3306-1) Sage.

Studying Interpersonal Interaction. Ed. by Barbara M. Montgomery & Steve Duck. LC 90-20933. (Communication Ser.). 346p. 1991. lib. bdg. 39.95 (0-89862-312-X) Guilford Pr.

Studying Interpersonal Interaction. Ed. by Barbara M. Montgomery & Steve Duck. LC 90-20933. (Communication Ser.). 346p. 1993. pap. text ed. 20.95 (0-89862-290-5) Guilford Pr.

Studying, Interpreting, & Applying the Bible. Walter A. Henrichsen & Gayle Jackson. 352p. 1990. pap. 12.99 (0-310-37781-1) Zondervan.

Studying Japan in Elementary & Secondary Schools. Leonard S. Kenworthy. LC 74-23896. (His World Affairs Guides Ser.). (Illus.). 68p. reprint ed. pap. 25.00 (0-685-20334-4, 2056464) Bks Demand.

Studying John: Approaches to the Fourth Gospel. John Ashton. 240p. 1995. text ed. 55.00 (0-19-826355-4) OUP.

Studying Latin America: Essays in Honor of Preston E. James. Ed. by David J. Robinson. LC 80-12413. (Dellplain Latin American Studies: No. 4). 289p. reprint ed. pap. 82.40 (0-317-28159-3, 2022591) Bks Demand.

Studying Law. 2nd ed. Phillip H. Kenny. 1991. U.K. pap. 13.00 (0-406-51270-1, U.K.) MICHIE.

Studying Law. 3rd ed. Phillip H. Kenny. 220p. 1994. pap. text ed. 18.00 (0-406-02435-9, UK) MICHIE.

Studying Law. 5th ed. Christopher Enright. 700p. 1995. pap. 49.00 (1-86287-156-6, Pub. by Federation Pr AU) Gaunt.

Studying Law: An Introduction. Charles D. Kelso & R. Randall Kelso. LC 84-7345. (American Casebook Ser.). 587p. 1984. reprint ed. 38.00 (0-314-81472-8) West Pub.

Studying Law: An Introduction to Legal Research. 2nd ed. J. Clarke Kelso. (C). 1995. text ed. 32.95 (0-256-17300-1) Irwin.

Studying Law: An Introduction to Legal Research. 2nd ed. J. Clarke Kelso. LC 94-45857. (Legal Text Ser.). (C). 1993. pap. 32.95 (0-8205-0446-7) Irwin.

Studying Literary Theory: An Introduction. Roger Webster. 96p. 1990. pap. 9.95 (0-340-50712-8, A4125, Pub. by E Arnold UK) Routledge Chapman & Hall.

Studying Literary Theory: An Introduction. 2nd abr. ed. Roger Webster. 128p. 1995. pap. 12.95 (0-340-58499-8, Pub. by E Arnold UK) Routledge Chapman & Hall.

Studying Literature: A Practical Introduction. Graham Atkin. 224p. 1995. pap. 32.00 (0-13-342742-0) P-H.

***Studying Lives Through Time: Personality & Development.** David C. Funder. 1997. pap. text ed. 19.95 (1-55798-400-X) Am Psychol.

Studying Lives Through Time: Personality & Development. Ed. by Carol Tomlinson-Keasey et al. 452p. 1993. text ed. 39.95 (1-55798-193-0) Am Psychol.

Studying Made Easier. V. Jackson Smith. 65p. (Orig.). (YA). 1995. pap. 6.50 (0-943639-21-2) Anchor Pub Co.

Studying Made Easy: Complete Multi-Media Package. Barbara Keller & Ray Keller. (Illus.). 1993. 49.95 (1-881966-04-6, 26-54-A03) Eagles MT.

Studying Medieval Women: Sex, Gender, Feminism. Ed. by Nancy F. Partner. (Speculum Book). (Illus.). vii, 197p. 1993. pap. 15.00 (0-915651-06-8) Medieval Acad.

Studying Music History: Learning, Reasoning & Writing about Music History & Literature. 2nd ed. David Poultney. LC 95-13540. 288p. (C). 1995. pap. text ed. 41.33 (0-13-190224-5) P-H.

***Studying New Zealand History.** G. A. Wood. 154p. pap. 24.95 (0-908569-63-7) Intl Spec Bk.

***Studying New Zealand History.** Antony Woods. 1996. 29.95 (0-908569-97-1, Pub. by U Otago Pr NZ) Intl Spec Bk.

Studying Organizational Communication: A Case Study of the Farmers Home Administration. Nancy Wyatt & Gerald M. Phillips. Ed. by Lee Thayer. LC 87-33443. (People, Communication, Organization Ser.). 352p. 1988. text ed. 78.50 (0-89391-473-8) Ablex Pub.

Studying Organizational Symbolism: What, How, Why? Michael O. Jones. (Qualitative Research Methods Ser.: Vol. 39). 96p. (C). 1996. 22.95 (0-7619-0219-8); pap. 9.95 (0-7619-0220-1) Sage.

Studying Oxidation-Reduction Reactions. Marcia L. Gillette & H. Anthony Neidig. (Modular Laboratory Program in Chemistry Ser.). 16p. (C). 1995. pap. text ed. 1.35 (0-87540-456-1, REAC 456-1) Chem Educ Res.

Studying People: A Primer in the Ethnics of Social Research. Robert D. Reece & Harvey A. Siegel. LC 86-18059. 272p. (Orig.). 1986. 29.95 (0-86554-220-1, H198); pap. 18.75 (0-86554-221-X, MUP/P028) Mercer Univ Pr.

Studying Personality: Student Booklet. American Psychological Association Staff. (Human Behavior Curriculum Project Ser.). 75p. (Orig.). (gr. 9-12). 1981. pap. text ed. 3.95 (0-8077-2627-3) Tchrs Coll.

Studying Personality: Teachers Manual & Duplication Masters. American Psychological Association Staff. (Human Behavior Curriculum Project Ser.). (Orig.). (gr. 9-12). 1981. pap. 9.95 (0-8077-2628-1) Tchrs Coll.

Studying Persons & Lives. Ed. by Robert A. Zucker et al. (Henry A. Murray Lectures in Personality). 368p. 1989. 42.95 (0-8261-6870-1) Springer Pub.

***Studying Poetry.** write for info. (0-7131-6467-0, Pub. by E Arnold UK) Routledge Chapman & Hall.

Studying Popular Music. R. Middleton. 1990. 95.00 (0-335-15276-7, Open Univ Pr); pap. 39.00 (0-335-15275-9, Open Univ Pr) Taylor & Francis.

Studying Psychology. 4th ed. Brown. 1990. pap. text ed. 4.00 (0-205-13027-5) Allyn.

Studying Public Policy: Policy Cycles & Policy Subsystems. Michael Howlett & M. Ramesh. (Illus.). 248p. 1996. pap. text ed. 29.95 (0-19-540976-0) OUP.

Studying Rhythm. Anne C. Hall. 128p. (C). 1988. pap. text ed. 28.33 (0-13-855651-2) P-H.

***Studying Rhythm.** 2nd ed. Hall. 1997. pap. text ed. 26.67 (0-13-614520-5) P-H.

Studying Russian & Soviet History. Ed. by Abraham S. Ascher. 122p. (Orig.). 1987. pap. 4.50 (0-89994-317-9) Soc Sci Ed.

Studying School Children in Uganda: Four Reports of Exploratory Research. David G. Scanlon et al. LC 74-122748. 85p. reprint ed. 25.00 (0-8357-9607-8, 2017763) Bks Demand.

Studying School Effectiveness. Ed. by David Reynolds. 216p. 1985. text ed. 44.00 (1-85000-023-9, Falmer Pr); pap. text ed. 25.00 (1-85000-024-7, Falmer Pr) Taylor & Francis.

***Studying School Subjects: A Guide.** Colin J. Marsh & Ivor Goodson. 176p. 1996. 69.95 (0-7507-0588-4, Falmer Pr); pap. 24.95 (0-7507-0589-2, Falmer Pr) Taylor & Francis.

Studying Shakespeare: An Introduction. Andrew Gurr. 96p. (C). 1988. pap. text ed. 9.95 (0-7131-6539-1, Pub. by E Arnold UK) Routledge Chapman & Hall.

Studying Smart: Thinking & Study Skills for School & the Workplace. Neild B. Oldham. 260p. 1993. teacher ed. 8.00 (1-56118-529-9); pap. text ed. 16.95 (1-56118-528-0) Paradigm MN.

Studying Smart: Time Management for College Students. rev. ed. Diana S. Hunt & Pam Hait. LC 89-46505. 128p. 1990. pap. 10.00 (0-06-463733-6, PL) HarpC.

Studying Society. J. L. Thompson. (C). 1989. 60.00 (0-09-169961-4, Pub. by S Thornes Pubs UK) St Mut.

Studying Society & Environment: A Handbook for Teachers. Robert Gilbert. 360p. 1996. 69.95 (0-7329-3059-6, Pub. by Macmill Educ AT); pap. 34.95 (0-7329-3060-X, Pub. by Macmill Educ AT) Paul & Co Pubs.

Studying South America in Elementary & Secondary Schools. 2nd ed. Leonard S. Kenworthy. LC 65-19211. (World Affairs Guides). 64p. reprint ed. pap. 25.00 (0-317-41865-3, 2026031) Bks Demand.

Studying Student Attrition. Ed. by Ernest T. Pascarella. LC 81-48576. (New Directions for Institutional Research Ser.: No. IR 36). 1982. pap. 19.00 (0-87589-906-4) Jossey-Bass.

Studying Suzuki Piano: More Than Music. Carole Bigler & Valery Lloyd-Watts. 249p. 1979. pap. text ed. 26.95 (0-87487-586-2) Summy-Birchard.

Studying Teachers' Lives. Ed. by Ivor F. Goodson. 272p. (C). 1992. text ed. 38.00 (0-8077-3155-2); pap. text ed. 18.95 (0-8077-3154-4) Tchrs Coll.

Studying, Teaching & Learning: Trends in Soviet & American Research. Ed. by B. Robert Tabachnick et al. LC 80-27528. (Comparative Education Ser.). 270p. 1981. text ed. 49.95 (0-275-90729-5, C0729, Praeger Pubs) Greenwood.

Studying the Content Areas: Mathematics & Business. Carole Bogue. Ed. by Karen H. Davis. LC 88-81386. (Illus.). 467p. (C). 1988. pap. 28.00 (0-943202-28-0) H & H Pub.

Studying the Effect of Buffering on the Resistance of a Solution to pH Change. George S. Patterson & William E. Good, Jr. Ed. by H. Anthony Neidig. (Modular Laboratory Program in Chemistry Ser.). 11p. (C). 1994. pap. text ed. 1.35 (0-87540-443-X, EQUL 443-x) Chem Educ Res.

Studying the Gospels: An Introduction. Gideon Goosen & Margaret Tomlinson. 1994. pap. 12.95 (0-85574-389-1, Pub. by E J Dwyer AT) Morehouse Pub.

Studying the Historical Jesus: Evaluations of the State of Current Research. Ed. by Craig A. Evans & Bruce D. Chilton. (New Testament Tools & Studies: No. 19). 350p. 1993. 167.50 (90-04-09982-4, NLG250) E J Brill.

Studying the Kinetics of the Solvolysis of 2-Chloro-2-Methylpropane. William H. Brown. Ed. by H. Anthony Neidig. (Modular Laboratory Program in Chemistry Ser.). 12p. (C). 1993. pap. text ed. 1.35 (0-87540-429-4, KINE 429-4) Chem Educ Res.

Studying the Life of Francis of Assisi: A Beginner's Workbook. William B. Hugo. 223p. (Orig.). 1996. pap. 17.95 (0-8199-0970-X, 0970-X) Franciscan Pr.

Studying the Media: An Introduction. Tim O'Sullivan et al. LC 94-14195. 256p. 1995. text ed. 16.95 (0-340-59828-X, Pub. by E Arnld UK) St Martin.

***Studying the Novel.** 3rd ed. Hawthorn. LC 97-6752. 1997. text ed. 14.95 (0-340-69220-0) St Martin.

Studying the Novice Programmer. James C. Spohrer. (Interacting with Computers: IWC Ser.). 504p. 1988. 99.95 (0-8058-0002-6); pap. 45.00 (0-8058-0003-4) L Erlbaum Assocs.

Studying the Old Testament: From Tradition to Canon. Annemarie Ohler. 400p. 47.95 (0-567-09335-2, Pub. by T & T Clark UK) Bks Intl VA.

Studying the Old Testament: From Tradition to Canon. Annemarie Ohler. Tr. by David Cairns from GER. 400p. 1989. pap. 29.95 (0-567-29166-9, Pub. by T & T Clark UK) Bks Intl VA.

***Studying the Parables of Jesus.** Peter R. Jones. LC 97-8700. 1997. write for info. (1-57312-167-3) Smyth & Helwys.

Studying the Presidency. Ed. by George C. Edwards, III & Stephen J. Wayne. LC 82-17472. 320p. (C). 1983. pap. text ed. 18.00 (0-87049-379-5) U of Tenn Pr.

Studying the Sikhs: Issues for North America. Ed. by John S. Hawley & Gurinder S. Mann. LC 92-16469. (SUNY Series in Religious Studies). 217p. (C). 1993. text ed. 64.50 (0-7914-1425-6); pap. text ed. 21.95 (0-7914-1426-4) State U NY Pr.

Studying the Social Worlds of Children. Frances C. Waksler. 282p. 1991. 65.00 (1-85000-910-4, Falmer Pr); pap. 27.00 (1-85000-911-2, Falmer Pr) Taylor & Francis.

Studying the Stoichiometry of the Reaction of Nickel (II) Ion & Hydroxide Ion Using Microscale Techniques. Marcia L. Gillette & H. Anthony Neidig. (Modular Laboratory Program in Chemistry Ser.). 16p. (C). 1991. pap. text ed. 1.35 (0-87540-401-4, STOI 401-4) Chem Educ Res.

Studying the Synoptic Gospels. E. P. Sanders & Margaret Davies. LC 89-35754. 336p. 1989. pap. 22.00 (0-334-02342-4) TPI PA.

Studying the Torah: A Guide to In-Depth Interpretation. Avigdor Bonchek. LC 95-38538. 208p. 1996. 25.00 (1-56821-504-5) Aronson.

***Studying the Torah: A Guide to In-Depth Interpretation.** Avigdor Bonchek. LC 95-38538. 208p. 1997. pap. 19.95 (0-7657-9964-2) Aronson.

Studying the U. S. S. R. in Elementary & Secondary Schools. Leonard S. Kenworthy. LC 77-94510. (World Affairs Guides). 64p. reprint ed. pap. 25.00 (0-317-41914-5, 2026032) Bks Demand.

Studying the Writings of Shoghi Effendi. Ed. by Morten Bergsmo. 216p. (Orig.). 1991. pap. 15.50 (0-85398-336-4) G Ronald Pub.

Studying Training Materials. Larry Mikulecky. 1990. 12.50 (0-13-852328-2) P-H.

Studying War: Anthropological Perspectives, Vol. 2. Ed. by R. E. Downs & Stephen P. Reyna. LC 93-32710. (War & Society Ser.: Vol. 2). 220p. 1993. text ed. 38.00 (2-88124-633-8); pap. text ed. 19.00 (2-88124-634-6) Gordon & Breach.

Studying Weather. Ann Merk & Jim Merk. LC 94-13320. (Weather Report Ser.). (J). (gr. 3 up). 1994. write for info. (0-86593-385-5) Rourke Corp.

***Studying Western Civilization: Reading Maps, Interpreting Documents, Preparing for Exams, a Student's Guide.** Richard Long. (C). 1995. teacher ed., pap. text ed. 2.66 (0-669-12169-X) HM College Div.

***Studying Western Civilization Vol. 1: Reading Maps, Interpreting Documents, Preparing for Exams, a Student's Guide: To 1787, Chpts. 1-19.** Richard Long. (C). text ed. 19.56 (0-669-12168-1) HM College Div.

***Studying Western Civilization Vol. 2: Reading Maps, Interpreting Documents, Preparing for Exams, a Student's Guide: Since 1320, Chpts. 13-20.** Richard Long. (C). text ed. 19.56 (0-669-35366-3) HM College Div.

Studying Women's Writing: An Introduction. Ruth Sherry. 96p. 1989. pap. 9.95 (0-7131-6566-9, Pub. by E Arnold UK) Routledge Chapman & Hall.

***Studying Work in College: A Guide for Work-Study Students.** Curtis Miles. 34p. (Orig.). 1995. pap. text ed. 9.95 (0-943202-53-1) H & H Pub.

Studying Writing: Linguistic Approaches. Ed. by Charles R. Cooper & Sidney Greenbaum. LC 87-33673. (Written Communication Annual Ser.: No. 1). 272p. 1986. reprint ed. pap. 77.60 (0-608-01485-0, 2059529) Bks Demand.

Studying Your Own School: An Educator's Guide to Qualitative Practitioner Research. Gary L. Anderson et al. LC 94-30532. (Illus.). 232p. 1994. 49.95 (0-8039-6113-8); pap. 22.95 (0-8039-6114-6) Corwin Pr.

***Studying Your Workforce: Applied Research Methods & Tools for the Training & Development Practitioner.** Alan B. Clardy. LC 97-4672. 208p. 1997. 45.00 (0-8039-7321-7); pap. 21.95 (0-8039-7322-5) Sage.

Stuettgen, G., Festschrift: Journal: Skin Pharmacology, Vol. 4, No. 3, 1991. Ed. by H. Schaefer. (Illus.). 112p. 1991. pap. 41.75 (3-8055-5465-6) S Karger.

Stufen Level 1: Cassette mit Arbeitsdialogen, Dialogbausteinen und Hoerverstehenstexten. (GER.). (C). 1987. audio 35.25 (3-12-554311-8, Pub. by Klett Edition GW) Intl Bk Import.

Stufen Level 1: Cassetten mit Uebungen zum Phonetikkurs, 2 cass. (GER.). (C). 1987. audio 46.75 (3-12-554312-6, Pub. by Klett Edition GW) Intl Bk Import.

Stufen Level 1: Handbuch fuer den Unterricht. Anne Vorderwuelbecke & Klaus Vorderwuelbecke. 175p. (GER.). (C). 1987. pap. text ed. 22.50 (3-12-554360-6, Pub. by Klett Edition GW) Intl Bk Import.

Stufen Level 2: Cassetten mit Dialogbausteinen und Hoerverstehensuebungen, 2 cass. (GER.). (C). 1987. audio 35.25 (3-12-554321-5, Pub. by Klett Edition GW) Intl Bk Import.

Stufen Level 2: Handbuch fuer den Unterricht. Anne Vorderwuelbecke & Klaus Vorderwuelbecke. 216p. (GER.). (C). 1988. pap. text ed. 22.50 (3-12-554370-3, Pub. by Klett Edition GW) Intl Bk Import.

Stufen Level 2: Kursbuch. Anne Vorderwuelbecke & Klaus Vorderwuelbecke. 193p. (GER.). (C). 1987. pap. text ed. 23.25 (3-12-554320-7, Pub. by Klett Edition GW) Intl Bk Import.

Stufen Level 3: Cassetten mit Hoerverstehenstexten und Phonetikuebungen, 2 cass. (GER.). (C). 1989. audio 46.75 (3-12-554331-2, Pub. by Klett Edition GW) Intl Bk Import.

Stufen Level 3: Handbuch fuer den Unterricht. Anne Vorderwuelbecke & Klaus Vorderwuelbecke. 192p. (GER.). (C). 1990. pap. text ed. 22.50 (3-12-554380-0, Pub. by Klett Edition GW) Intl Bk Import.

Stufen Level 3: Kursbuch. Anne Vorderwuelbecke & Klaus Vorderwuelbecke. 209p. (GER.). (C). 1989. pap. text ed. 23.25 (3-12-554330-4, Pub. by Klett Edition GW) Intl Bk Import.

Stufen Level 4: Cassetten mit Hoerverstehenstexten, Vorlesetexten und Phonetikuebungen. (GER.). (C). 1992. audio 49.00 (3-12-554341-X, Pub. by Klett Edition GW) Intl Bk Import.

Stufen Level 4: Kursbuch. Anne Vorderwuelbecke & Klaus Vorderwuelbecke. 278p. (GER.). (C). 1991. pap. text ed. 28.00 (3-12-554340-1, Pub. by Klett Edition GW) Intl Bk Import.

Stufen des Organischen und der Mensch: Einleitung in die philosophische Anthropologie. 3rd ed. Helmuth Plessner. (Sammlung Goeschen Ser.: No. 2200). 373p. (C). 1975. 22.95 (3-11-005985-1) De Gruyter.

Stufen International Level 1: Lehr- und Arbeitsbuch. Anne Vorderwuelbecke & Klaus Vorderwuelbecke. 183p. (GER.). (C). 1995. pap. text ed. 25.25 (3-12-675280-2, Pub. by Klett Edition GW) Intl Bk Import.

Stufen International Level 1: Lehrerhandbuch, 3 cass. Anne Vorderwuelbecke & Klaus Vorderwuelbecke. (GER.). (C). 1995. audio 54.00 (3-12-675282-9, Pub. by Klett Edition GW) Intl Bk Import.

Stufen International Level 1: Lehrerhandbuch. Anne Vorderwuelbecke & Klaus Vorderwuelbecke. 160p. (GER.). (C). 1996. pap. text ed. 18.00 (3-12-675281-0, Pub. by Klett Edition GW) Intl Bk Import.

Stufen. Kolleg Deutsch als Fremdsprache Level 1: Kursbuch. Anne Vorderwuelbecke & Klaus Vorderwuelbecke. 169p. (GER.). (C). 1986. pap. text ed. 23.25 (3-12-554310-X, Pub. by Klett Edition GW) Intl Bk Import.

Stufenschema: Unterschungen zur Struktur Alttestamentlicher Texte. Theodor Lescow. (Beihefte zur Zeitschrift fuer die Alttestamentliche Wissenschaft Ser.: Bd. 211). x, 282p. (GER.). (C). 1992. lib. bdg. 98.50 (3-11-013768-2) De Gruyter.

Stuff! Good Players Should Know. Dick DeVenzio. (Illus.). 320p. 1983. 19.95 (0-910305-00-5) Fool Court.

***Stuff: Poems from Hollywood.** 29p. (Orig.). 1997. pap. 5.00 (0-89642-386-7) Linden Pubs.

***Stuff: The Secret Lives of Everyday Things.** John C. Ryan & Alan T. Durning. Ed. by Ellen Chu. (Illus.). 88p. (Orig.). (C). 1997. pap. 9.95 (1-886093-04-0) NW Environ Watch.

***Stuff: The Things the World is Made Of.** Ivan Amato. (Illus.). 352p. 1998. pap. 25.00 (0-465-08328-5) Basic.

Stuff see Phonics Is My Way Series

Stuff Americans Are Made of: The Seven Cultural Forces That Define Americans. Joshua Hammond & James Morrison. (Illus.). 288p. 1996. 24.95 (0-02-860829-1) Macmillan.

***Stuff & Anon Sense.** Milton Helder. 80p. Date not set. pap. 5.00 (1-884257-17-8) AGEE Keyboard.

***Stuff & Nonsense.** Laura Cecil. (J). Date not set. lib. bdg. write for info. (0-688-08899-6) Greenwillow.

Stuff & Nonsense. Laura Cecil. LC 89-1647. (Illus.). 96p. (J). (ps up). 1989. 15.95 (0-688-08898-8) Greenwillow.

Stuff Dreams Are Made Of: Housing Provision in Australia 1945-1960. Alastair Greig. 256p. 1995. pap. 29.95 (0-522-84621-1, Pub. by Melbourne Univ Pr AT) Paul & Co Pubs.

An Asterisk (*) at the beginning of an entry indicates that the title is appearing in BIP for the first time.

Stuff I Remember: I Saw It, I Heard It, I Lived It. Elmer Otte. 128p. 1995. write for info. (*0-9648628-5-9*) Folklore Hse.

Stuff I Wish I'd Known: A Practical Guide for High School Speech & Drama Teachers. Toby Heathcotte & Larry Whitesell. LC 94-76738. 166p. (C). 1994. pap. text ed. 15.00 (*0-9640882-0-7*) Mardel Bks.

Stuff It Deluxe: A User's Guide. Fred Terry. Ed. by David Schargel. (Illus.). 130p. 99.95 (*1-878777-02-5*) Aladdin Systs.

Stuff Life's Made Of: A Book about Matter. Jill C. Wheeler. (Kid Physics Ser.). (J). 1997. lib. bdg. 13.99 (*1-56239-630-7*) Abdo & Dghtrs.

*__Stuff Nobody Told Me.__ 2nd ed. Alvin Kou. (Illus.). 138p. 1997. pap. 12.95 (*1-57502-434-9*, PO1322) Morris Pubng.

Stuff of Dreams. Karen E. Young. (Nursery Rhymes Ser.). 15p. (J). (gr. k-2). 1991. pap. text ed. 4.50 (*1-56843-090-6*) BGR Pub.

Stuff of Dreams: Big Book. Karen E. Young. (Nursery Rhymes Ser.). 15p. (J). (gr. k-2). 1991. pap. text ed. 23.00 (*1-56843-043-4*) BGR Pub.

Stuff of Fiction. Gerald W. Brace. LC 71-77391. (C). 1972. pap. text ed. 1.95 (*0-393-00648-4*) Norton.

Stuff of Literature: Physical Aspects of Texts & Their Relation to Literary Meaning. E. A. Levenston. LC 90-28937. 187p. (C). 1992. text ed. 64.50 (*0-7914-0889-2*); pap. text ed. 21.95 (*0-7914-0890-6*) State U NY Pr.

Stuff That Matters for Single Parents. Patricia Lorenz. 260p. 1996. pap. 10.99 (*0-89283-955-4*) Servant.

Stuff That Works Every Single Day. Larry Winget. 1994. pap. 9.95 (*1-881342-03-4*) Win Pubns OK.

Stuff the Lady's Hatbox. Carlton E. Morse. (I Love a Mystery Novel Ser.). 342p. (Orig.). 1988. 16.95 (*0-940249-03-0*); pap. 9.95 (*0-940249-04-9*) Seven Stones Pr.

Stuff We're Made Of: The Positive Approach to Health Through Nutrition. Jorian Jenks. 1959. 5.00 (*0-8159-6829-9*) Devin.

Stuff You Don't Have to Pray About. Susie Shellenberger. LC 95-5616. 176p. (J). 1995. pap. 9.99 (*0-8054-5089-0*, 4250-89) Broadman.

Stuff You Gotta Know: Straight Talk about Real-Life. Guy R. Doud. LC 93-25113. (Illus.). 152p. (Orig.). (YA). (gr. 8-12). 1993. pap. 6.99 (*0-570-04622-X*, 12-3203) Concordia.

Stuffed Aleph: A Family Coloring Book. Pessa K. Twerski. 1983. pap. 2.95 (*0-910818-51-7*) Judaica Pr.

Stuffed Cougar. Ed. by Patrons Association of the Collegiate School Staff. (Illus.). 375p. (Orig.). 1973. pap. 12.95 (*0-681-21703-0*) Collegiate Schls.

Stuffed Cougar, Too. Ed. by Patrons Association of the Collegiate School Staff. (Illus.). 362p. (Orig.). 1992. pap. 12.95 (*0-9634044-0-7*) Collegiate Schls.

*__Stuffed Griffin.__ Utility Club of Griffin Staff. Date not set. pap. text ed. 15.95 (*0-9607584-0-2*) Utility Club.

Stuffed Owl: An Anthology of Bad Verse. Ed. by Dominic B. Lewis & Charles Lee. LC 76-42707. (Illus.). reprint ed. 20.00 (*0-404-15371-2*) AMS Pr.

Stuffed Peacocks. Emily Clark. LC 75-110181. (Short Story Index Reprint Ser.). 1977. 20.95 (*0-8369-3332-X*) Ayer.

Stuffed Shirts. Clare Booth Luce. LC 77-163043. (Short Story Index Reprint Ser.). 1977. reprint ed. 24.95 (*0-8369-3957-3*) Ayer.

Stuffed Spuds. Jeanne Jones. 1995. (*0-7858-0281-9*) Bk Sales Inc.

Stuffed Spuds: One Hundred Light Meals in a Potato. Jeanne Jones. LC 92-6868. 140p. 1992. pap. 8.95 (*0-87131-691-9*) M Evans.

Stuffin' Muffin: Muffin Pan Cooking for Kids. Strom Scherie. (Illus.). 100p. (Orig.). (J). (gr. 4-7). 1982. pap. 18.95 (*0-9606964-9-0*) Yng Peoples Pr.

*__Stuffings: 45 International Recipes to Enhance Fish, Poultry, Meat, Vegetables & Fruit.__ Carole Lalli. 1997. 16.95 (*0-06-757502-1*) HarpC.

Stuffings & An American Sunset: Two Plays. James Prideaux. 1973. pap. 5.25 (*0-8222-0037-6*) Dramatists Play.

StuffIt Deluxe User's Guide 3.0. Michael Miley. Ed. by David Schargel. (Illus.). 290p. 1992. 120.00 (*1-878777-03-3*) Aladdin Systs.

StuffIt SpaceSaver User's Guide 1.0. Michael Miley & David Schargel. (Illus.). 36p. 1992. 59.95 (*1-878777-04-1*) Aladdin Systs.

*__Stufflique.__ 1997. 17.95 (*0-9656084-0-9*) Birch St Clothing.

Stuffy: The Life of Newspaper Pioneer Basil "Stuffy" Walters. Raymond Moscowitz. LC 82-50. (Illus.). 213p. 1982. reprint ed. pap. 60.80 (*0-608-00130-9*, 2060911) Bks Demand.

Stug III: Assault Gun. Hilary Doyle & Tom Jentz. (Illus.). 48p. 1996. pap. 12.95 (*1-85532-537-3*, Pub. by Osprey UK) Stackpole.

Stuka Dive Bombers-Pursuit Bombers-Combat Pilots - A Pictorial Chronicle of German Close-Combat Aircraft to 1945. Gebhard Aders & Werner Held. LC 89-63368. (Illus.). 248p. 1990. 34.95 (*0-88740-216-X*) Schiffer.

Stuka Pilot. Hans-Ulrich Rudel. 240p. 1987. 14.95 (*0-939482-04-5*, Noontide Pr) Legion Survival.

Stuka Pilot: Hans Ulrich Rudel. Gunther Just. Tr. by Edward Force from GER. LC 90-61171. (Illus.). 280p. 1990. 29.95 (*0-88740-252-6*) Schiffer.

Stukey: Genealogy of the Stukey, Ream, Grove, Clem & Denniston Families. E. L. Denniston. (Illus.). 591p. 1991. reprint ed. pap. 89.50 (*0-8328-1879-8*); reprint ed. lib. bdg. 99.50 (*0-8328-1878-X*) Higginson Bk Co.

Stumbling Block: A Sociological Study of the Relationship Between Selected Religious Norms & Drinking Behavior. Jerome H. Skolnick. Ed. by Harriet Zuckerman & Robert K. Merton. LC 79-9028. (Dissertations on Sociology Ser.). 1980. lib. bdg. 44.95 (*0-405-12995-5*) Ayer.

Stumbling Blocks or Stepping Stones: Spiritual Answers to Psychological Questions. Benedict J. Groeschel. 180p. 1987. pap. 9.95 (*0-8091-2896-9*) Paulist Pr.

Stumbling Blocks to Stepping Stones. Shari Rusch. (Illus.). 272p. (Orig.). 1991. pap. 11.95 (*0-9629392-0-X*) Arc WA.

Stumbling on God: Faith & Vision in Mark's Gospel. Christopher Burdon. 120p. reprint ed. pap. 34.20 (*0-7837-5552-X*, 2045327) Bks Demand.

Stumbling to the Priesthood. Vernon J. Schaefer. 200p. 1991. pap. 12.95 (*0-87839-069-3*) North Star.

Stumbling to Zion: Today's Church in Today's World. Maralene Wesner & Miles Wesner. 131p. (Orig.). 1989. pap. 4.95 (*0-936715-24-3*) Diversity Okla.

*__Stumbling Toward Enlightenment.__ Geri Larkin. 1997. pap. text ed. 12.95 (*0-89087-849-8*) Celestial Arts.

*__Stumbling Toward Enlightenment: An Illustrated Crisis Companion.__ Barbara Lewis-Marco. LC 97-2304. 144p. 1997. 14.00 (*0-399-52348-0*, Perigee Bks) Berkley Pub.

Stumbling Toward Maturity. Arnold T. Olson. LC 81-66943. (Heritage Ser.: Vol. 3). 208p. 1981. 8.95 (*0-911802-50-9*) Free Church Pubns.

*__STUMP, a Campaign Journal.__ Scott Jacobs. Ed. by Bruce Bendinger. (Illus.). 252p. (Orig.). 1997. pap. 14.95 (*1-887229-03-5*) Copy Wrkshp.

Stump Ranch Pioneer. Nelle P. Davis. LC 90-42417. (Idaho Yesterdays Ser.). 264p. (YA). 1990. reprint ed. pap. 14.95 (*0-89301-141-X*) U of Idaho Pr.

Stumps. Mark Medoff. 1995. pap. 5.25 (*0-614-03319-5*) Dramatists Play.

Stumpwork Embroidery: A Collection of Fruits, Flowers, Insects. Jane Nicholas. (Illus.). 216p. 1996. 34.95 (*1-86351-183-0*, Pub. by S Milner AT) Sterling.

Stumpy Plunket, the Frog Who Lived in the Elegant Purple Log. Lawrence Stewart. (Illus.). 48p. (J). (gr. k-3). 1995. pap. 7.00 (*0-8059-3782-X*) Dorrance.

Stun Gun Enema. Chris Winkler. 47p. (Orig.). 1989. pap. text ed. 2.95 (*0-944215-03-3*) Ninth St Lab.

Stung by Salt & War: Creative Texts of the Italian Avant-Gardist F.T. Marinetti. Richard Pioli. (Reading Plus Ser.: Vol. 2). 187p. (C). 1987. text ed. 31.50 (*0-8204-0381-4*) P Lang Pubng.

Stunned Myocardium: Properties, Mechanisms, & Clinical Manifestations. Ed. by Robert A. Kloner & Karin Przyklenk. LC 92-49722. (Fundamental & Clinical Cardiology Ser.: Vol. 11). 496p. 1992. 125.00 (*0-8247-8722-6*) Dekker.

Stunning, Hibernation, & Calcium in Myocardial Ischemia & Reperfusion. Ed. by Lionel H. Opie. LC 92-17257. (C). 1992. pap. text ed. 109.50 (*0-7923-1793-9*) Kluwer Ac.

*__Stunning, Hibernation, & Preconditioning: Clinical Pathophysiology of Ischemia.__ Stephen F. Vatner & Guy R. Heyndrickx. 400p. 1997. text ed. write for info. (*0-7817-1207-6*) Lppncott-Raven.

Stunning Way to Die. Joyce Christmas. (Lady Margaret Priam Mystery Ser.: No. 4). 192p. (Orig.). 1991. mass mkt. 4.99 (*0-449-14666-9*, GM) Fawcett.

Stunt Flying with Paper Airplanes. Bob Smith. (Illus.). 32p. (J). (gr. 3 up). 1992. pap. 2.50 (*0-87406-625-5*) Willowisp Pr.

Stunt Guide. John Cann. 1991. pap. 19.95 (*0-9629292-0-4*) Action P A C.

Stunt Guide: Comprehensive Stunt Reference Book for the Entertainment Industry. 3rd ed. John Cann. Ed. by Mark Atteberry. (Illus.). 348p. (C). 1992. spiral bd. 25.00 (*0-9629292-1-2*) Action P A C.

Stunt Island: The Official Strategy Guide. Rick Barba. 256p. 1993. pap. 19.95 (*1-55958-247-2*) Prima Pub.

Stunt Kites! A Complete Flight Manual of Maneuverable Kites. 6th ed. David Gomberg. (Illus.). 90p. 1996. reprint ed. pap. 11.00 (*1-884496-02-4*) Gomberg Kite.

*__Stunt Man: The Autobiography of Yakima Canutt.__ Yakima Canutt & Oliver Drake. LC 96-41114. (Illus.). 288p. 1997. pap. 15.95 (*0-8061-2927-1*) U of Okla Pr.

Stunt Performers. Derek Ware. Ed. by Rebecca Stefoff. LC 91-41209. (Living Dangerously Ser.). (Illus.). 32p. (J). (gr. 5-9). 1992. lib. bdg. 17.26 (*1-56074-045-0*) Garrett Ed Corp.

Stunt Woman. Keith E. Greenberg. Ed. by Bruce Glassman. LC 95-38737. (Risky Business Ser.). (Illus.). 32p. (J). (gr. 2-5). 1996. lib. bdg. 14.95 (*1-56711-159-9*) Blackbirch.

*__Stunted Lives, Stagnant Economies: Poverty, Disease, & Underdevelopment.__ Eileen Stillwaggon. (Illus.). 384p. 1998. 50.00 (*0-8135-2493-8*) Rutgers U Pr.

*__Stunted Lives, Stagnant Economies: Poverty, Disease, & Underdevelopment.__ Eileen Stillwaggon. (Illus.). 384p. 1998. pap. 23.00 (*0-8135-2494-6*) Rutgers U Pr.

Stuntman: A Freelancer's Guide to Learning the Craft & Landing the Jobs. Jack Bucklin. (Illus.). 136p. 1992. pap. 20.00 (*0-87364-673-8*) Paladin Pr.

Stuntman's Daughter. Alice Blanchard. LC 95-26177. 155p. (Orig.). 1996. pap. 14.95 (*1-57441-009-1*) UNTX Pr.

Stunts. Charles L. Grant. 1992. mass mkt. 4.99 (*0-8125-0698-7*) Tor Bks.

Stunts. Carole Simmons Oles. Ed. by Craig Goad et al. (Missouri Chapbook Ser.). 36p. (Orig.). 1992. pap. text ed. 5.00 (*0-9616467-7-2*) GreenTower Pr.

Stupa: Art, Architectonics & Symbolism (Indo-Tibetica I) Giuseppe Tucci. (C). 1988. 50.00 (*81-85179-20-4*, Pub. by Aditya Prakashan II) S Asia.

*__Stupa: Sacred Symbol of Enlightenment.__ Elizabeth Cook & Yeshe De Project Staff. LC 97-12563. (Crystal Mirror Ser.). 1997. pap. write for info. (*0-89800-284-2*) Dharma Pub.

*__Stupa & Its Technology: A Tibeto-Buddhist Perspective.__ Pema Dorjee. (C). 1996. 46.00 (*81-208-1301-4*, Pub. by Motilal Banarsidass II) S Asia.

Stupefaction: Stories & a Novella. Diane Williams. 192p. 1996. 21.00 (*0-679-44186-7*) Knopf.

*__Stupendous Effort: The 87th Indiana in the War of the Rebellion.__ Jack K. Overmyer. LC 96-54581. 1997. write for info. (*0-253-33301-6*) Ind U Pr.

Stupid Bar Tricks. Adam Steinfeld & Bret McCormick. (Illus.). 96p. (Orig.). 1986. pap. 5.95 (*0-939639-00-9*) Now Thats Funny.

Stupid-Beyond-Belief PC Tricks. Bob Levitus. 1992. pap. 19.95 incl. disk (*0-201-63235-7*) Addison-Wesley.

*__Stupid Comics.__ Peter Bagge. 100p. pap. 10.95 (*1-56097-069-3*) Fantagraph Bks.

Stupid Cupid. Ilene Cooper. 128p. (J). (gr. 3-7). 1995. pap. 14.99 (*0-670-85059-4*) Viking Child Bks.

Stupid Cupid. Ilene Cooper. (Holiday 5 Ser.). 144p. (J). (gr. 3-7). 1996. pap. 3.99 (*0-14-036519-2*) Puffin Bks.

Stupid Government Tricks: Outrageous (but True!) Stories of Bureaucratic Bungling & Washington Waste. John J. Kohut. (Illus.). 240p. (Orig.). 1995. pap. 8.95 (*0-452-27314-5*, Plume) NAL-Dutton.

Stupid Jokes for Kids. 224p. (J). (ps-8). 1991. mass mkt. 4.99 (*0-345-37062-7*) Ballantine.

Stupid Mac Tricks. Macintosh Inc. Staff. 1990. pap. 19.95 (*0-201-57046-7*) Addison-Wesley.

Stupid Men Jokes. Nancy Gray. LC 92-37035. 1992. pap. 4.99 (*0-679-74602-1*, Villard Bks) Random.

Stupid Men Jokes. Knott. 1992. mass mkt. 3.99 (*0-312-95119-1*) Tor Bks.

Stupid PC Tricks. Bob Levitus. 1991. pap. 19.95 incl. disk (*0-201-57759-3*) Addison-Wesley.

Stupid Stories: Nonstop Nonsense for Children of All Ages. Robert J. Leonard. (Illus.). 108p. (Orig.). (J). (gr. 5-10). 1989. pap. 5.95 (*0-930753-05-4*) Spect Ln Pr.

Stupid Ways, Smart Ways to Think about God. Michael Shevack & Jack Bemporad. LC 95-12905. (Illus.). 128p. 1995. reprint ed. pap. 8.95 (*0-89243-821-5*, Triumph Books) Liguori Pubns.

Stupid Window Tricks Header Card. Levitus. 1995. pap. text ed. 1.00 (*0-12-799032-1*) Acad Pr.

Stupid Windows Tricks: Making It All Make Nonsense. Bob Levitus. 1992. pap. 19.95 incl. disk (*0-201-60840-5*) Addison-Wesley.

Stupids. Clay Griffith. 112p. (J). 1996. mass mkt. 3.99 (*0-553-48498-2*) Bantam.

Stupids Die. Harry Allard & James Marshall. (Illus.). (J). (gr. k-3). 1981. 14.95 (*0-395-30347-8*) HM.

Stupids Die. Harry Allard & James Marshall. (Illus.). (J). (gr. k-3). 1985. pap. 5.95 (*0-395-38364-1*) HM.

Stupids Have a Ball. Harry Allard. LC 77-27660. (Illus.). (J). (gr. k-3). 1978. 14.95 (*0-395-26497-9*) HM.

Stupids Have a Ball. Harry Allard. LC 77-27660. (Illus.). (J). (gr. k-3). 1984. pap. 5.95 (*0-395-36169-9*) HM.

Stupids Step Out. Harry Allard. LC 73-21698. (Illus.). 32p. (J). (gr. k-3). 1974. 14.95 (*0-395-18513-0*) HM.

Stupids Step Out. Harry Allard. LC 73-21698. (Illus.). 32p. (J). (gr. k-3). 1977. pap. 5.95 (*0-395-25377-2*) HM.

Stupids Step Out. Harry Allard. (Book & Cassette Favorites Ser.). (Illus.). (J). (ps-3). 1989. pap. 8.95 incl. audio (*0-395-52139-4*) HM.

Stupids Take Off. Harry Allard & James Marshall. (Illus.). 32p. (J). (gr. k-3). 1989. 14.95 (*0-395-50068-0*) HM.

Stupids Take Off. Harry Allard. (Illus.). 32p. (J). (gr. k-3). 1993. pap. 5.95 (*0-395-65743-1*) HM.

Sturctural Analysis for Micros see Structural Analysis Software for Micros

Sturcture Argument. 5th ed. Rottenburg. 1996. pap. text ed. 16.50 (*0-312-13412-6*) St Martin.

*__Sturdy Black Bridges on the American Stage: The Portrayal of Black Motherhood in Selected Plays by Contemporary African American Women Playwrights.__ Susanna A. Bosch. Ed. by Richard Martin & Rudiger Schreyer. (Aachen British & American Studies: Vol. 8). (Illus.). 318p. 1996. 63.95 (*3-631-30136-7*) P Lang Pubng.

*__Sturdy Black Bridges on the American Stage: The Portrayal of Black Motherhood in Selected Plays by Contemporary African American Women Playwrights.__ Susanna A. Bosch. Ed. by Richard Martin & Rudiger Schreyer. (Aachen British & American Studies: Vol. 8). (Illus.). 318p. 1996. 63.95 (*0-8204-3179-6*) P Lang Pubng.

Sturdy Econometrics. Edward E. Leamer. LC 94-4208. (Economists of the Twentieth Century Ser.). 392p. 1994. 85.00 (*1-85278-802-X*) E Elgar.

Sturdy Folk: Personal Accounts of Life & Work on the Olympic Peninsula. Ed. & Pref. by Mavis Amundson. 130p. (Orig.). 1995. pap. 9.95 (*0-9610910-2-9*) Western Gull Pub.

Sturgeon: A Genealogical History of the Sturgeons of North America. C. T. McCoy. (Illus.). 239p. 1991. reprint ed. pap. 38.00 (*0-8328-1792-9*); reprint ed. lib. bdg. 48.00 (*0-8328-1791-0*) Higginson Bk Co.

*__Sturgeon Biodiversity & Conservation.__ Vadim J. Birstein et al. LC 97-8149. (Developments in Environmental Biology of Fishes Ser.). 1997. lib. bdg. 248.00 (*0-7923-4517-7*) Kluwer Ac.

Sturgeon Fishes: Developmental Biology & Aquaculture. T. A. Dettlaff et al. Tr. by G. G. Gause & S. G. Vassetzky from RUS. (Illus.). 312p. 1992. 238.95 (*0-387-54744-4*) Spr-Verlag.

Sturgeon Fishing. Larry Leonard. (Illus.). 1987. pap. 8.95 (*0-936608-57-9*) F Amato Pubns.

Sturgis: Guide to the World's Greatest Motorcycle Rally. Gerald Foster. LC 92-45659. (MBI Ser.). (Illus.). 96p. 1993. pap. 14.95 (*0-87938-735-1*) Motorbooks Intl.

Sturgis Illustrated Dictionary of Architecture & Building: An Unabridged Reprint of the 1901-1902, Vol. 1. Russell Sturgis. 1989. pap. 16.95 (*0-486-26025-9*) Dover.

Sturgis Illustrated Dictionary of Architecture & Building: An Unabridged Reprint of the 1901-1902, Vol. 2. Russell Sturgis. 1989. pap. 16.95 (*0-486-26026-7*) Dover.

Sturgis Illustrated Dictionary of Architecture & Building: An Unabridged Reprint of the 1901-1902, Vol. 3. Russell Sturgis. 1989. pap. 16.95 (*0-486-26027-5*) Dover.

Sturgis, Motorcycle Mecca. Martin Garfinkel. 160p. 1990. 29.95 (*1-878627-00-7*); pap. text ed. 19.95 (*1-878627-01-5*) ZG Pub.

Sturgis Thunder in the Hills. Gordon Hanson. 96p. 1994. pap. 14.95 (*0-9627618-6-9*) Billings Gazette.

Sturla the Historian. William P. Ker. 25p. reprint ed. pap. 25.00 (*0-317-08057-1*, 2051176) Bks Demand.

*__Sturlunga Saga: Including the Islendinga Saga of Lawman.__ Gudbrand Vigfusson. (Illus.). reprint ed. pap. 138.50 (*0-317-10728-3*) Bks Demand.

Sturlunga Saga: Including the Islendinga Saga of Lawman Sturla Thordsson & Other Works, 2 vols., 1. Ed. by Gudbrand Vigfusson. (Illus.). reprint ed. pap. 157.30 (*0-317-10727-5*, 2051168) Bks Demand.

Sturlunga Saga, Vol. 1: The Saga of Hvamm-Sturla & the Sage of the Icelanders. Ed. by Julia H. McGrew & George R. Thomas. LC 71-120536. (Library of Scandinavian Literature). (Illus.). 1970. pap. text ed. 9.75 (*0-8290-2036-5*); lib. bdg. 49.00 (*0-8057-3364-7*) Irvington.

Sturlunga Saga, Vol. 2: Shorter Sagas of the Icelanders. Ed. by Julia H. McGrew & George Thomas. LC 71-120536. (Library of Scandinavian Literature). (Illus.). 1974. pap. text ed. 11.75 (*0-8290-2035-7*); lib. bdg. 49.00 (*0-8057-3365-5*) Irvington.

Sturm: A Focus of Expressionism. M. S. Jones. LC 83-72542. (GERM Ser.: Vol. 16). (Illus.). 276p. 1984. 32.50 (*0-938100-26-2*) Camden Hse.

Sturm & Drang: The Robbers, The Soldiers, Storm & Stress, & The Childmurderess. J. Friedrich Von Schiller et al. (German Library: Vol. 14). 324p. 1992. 29.50 (*0-8264-0704-8*); pap. text ed. 16.95 (*0-8264-0705-6*) Continuum.

Sturm-Liouville Operators & Applications. Vladimir A. Marchenko. (Operator Theory Ser.: Vol. 22). 392p. 1986. 150.00 (*0-8176-1794-9*) Birkhauser.

Sturm, Ruger 10-22 Rifle & .44 Magnum Carbine. Duncan Long. (Illus.). 108p. 1988. pap. 12.00 (*0-87364-449-2*) Paladin Pr.

Sturman Collection: Twentieth Century Works on Paper. Tucson Museum of Art Staff et al. LC 86-51143. (Illus.). 43p. 1986. pap. 12.00 (*0-911611-12-6*) Tucson Mus Art.

Sturmgeschutz & its Variants, Vol. II. Walter J. Spielberger. Tr. by James C. Cable from GER. LC 92-60361. (Spielberger German Armor & Military Vehicles Ser.). (Illus.). 256p. 1992. 39.95 (*0-88740-398-0*) Schiffer.

Sturmgeschutz Forty (L-43 & L-48) the Long Gun Versions. Horst Schiebert. LC 91-60860. (Illus.). 48p. 1991. pap. 8.95 (*0-88740-310-7*) Schiffer.

SturmGeschutz III: The Short Gun Versions. Horst Scheibert. Tr. by Edward Force from GER. LC 91-62742. (Illus.). 48p. 1991. pap. 7.95 (*0-88740-350-6*) Schiffer.

Sturmian Theory for Ordinary Differential Equations. William T. Reid. (Applied Mathematical Sciences Ser.: Vol. 31). 559p. 1981. pap. 69.00 (*0-387-90542-1*) Spr-Verlag.

Sturtevant's Edible Plants of the World. Hedrick. 686p. 1972. reprint ed. pap. 13.95 (*0-486-20459-6*) Dover.

Sturz Des Antichrist see Fall of Antichrist

*__Stuti & Stava.__ T. Goudriaan & C. Hooykaas. (Verhandelingen der Koninklijke Nederlandse Akademie van Wetenschappen, Afd. Letterkunde, Nieuwe Reeks Ser.: No. 76). 610p. 1971. pap. text ed. 78.25 (*0-7204-8206-2*) Elsevier.

Stutsbear & the Bionic Busboy: My Secret Diary So Stay Out Unless You Are My Friend This Means You. Walter F. Mercadel. (Orig.). 1994. pap. 8.95 (*0-9634332-1-0*) Lithodendron.

Stutter Control Drill: Mastering Elements of Fluent Speech. Howard Richman. 12p. 1989. student ed., pap. 5.00 (*0-929060-75-X*) Sound Feelings.

Stuttering. Ed. by H. H. Gregory. (Journal: Vol. 46, No. 5, 1994). (Illus.). 56p. 1995. pap. 33.25 (*3-8055-6132-6*) S Karger.

Stuttering. C. Woodruff Starkweather & Janet Givens-Ackerman. Ed. by Harvey Halpern. (Studies in Communicative Disorders). (Orig.). 1996. pap. text ed. 27.00 (*0-89079-699-8*, 7952) PRO-ED.

Stuttering. 2nd ed. Edward G. Conture. 320p. (C). 1989. Casebound. text ed. 66.00 (*0-13-853631-7*) P-H.

*__Stuttering: A Life Bound Up in Words.__ Marty Jezer. LC 96-52955. 256p. 1997. 23.00 (*0-465-08227-4*) Basic.

Stuttering: A Psychoanalytic Study. I. Peter Glauber. Ed. by Helen M. Glauber. LC 82-8125. 208p. 1982. 35.95 (*0-89885-154-8*) Human Sci Pr.

Stuttering: An Integrated Approach to Its Nature & Treatment. Theodore J. Peters & Barry Guitar. (Illus.). 392p. 1990. 42.00 (*0-683-06870-9*) Williams & Wilkins.

Stuttering: An Integration of Contemporary Therapies, No. 16. Theodore Peters & Barry Guitar. LC 80-51679. 1980. pap. 2.00 (*0-933388-15-2*) Stuttering Fnd Am.

Stuttering: Differential Evaluation & Therapy. Hugo H. Gregory. LC 73-4549. (Studies in Communicative Disorders). (C). 1973. pap. text ed. write for info. (*0-672-61291-7*, Bobbs) Macmillan.

Stuttering: Differential Evaluation & Therapy. Hugo H. Gregory. Ed. by Harvey Halpern. LC 86-490. (PRO-ED Studies in Communicative Disorders). (Illus.). 64p. 1986. pap. text ed. 9.00 (*0-89079-093-0*, 1383) PRO-ED.

Stuttering: From Theory to Practice. Margaret Fawcus. 200p. 1995. pap. text ed. 49.95 (*1-56593-497-0*, 1152) Singular Publishing.

Stuttering: Helping the Disfluent Preschool Child. Julie A. Blonigen. (Illus.). 40p. 1996. pap. text ed. 10.95 (*0-937857-64-5*, 1489) Speech Bin.

S

An Asterisk (*) at the beginning of an entry indicates that the title is appearing in BIP for the first time.

Stuttering: Significant Theories & Therapies. 2nd rev. ed. Eugene F. Hahn. Ed. by Elise S. Hahn. xii, 180p. 1956. 32.50 (*0-8047-0376-0*) Stanford U Pr.

Stuttering: The Search for a Cause & Cure. Oliver Bloodstein. LC 92-11153. 199p. 1992. text ed. 55.00 (*0-205-13845-4*, H38458) Allyn.

Stuttering & Other Disorders of Fluency. Ed. by Richard F. Curlee. LC 92-49795. (Current Therapy of Communication Disorders Ser.). 1992. 45.00 (*0-86577-442-0*) Thieme Med Pubs.

Stuttering & Other Fluency Disorders: An Overview for Beginning Clinicians. 2nd ed. Franklin H. Silverman. 1995. text ed. 60.00 (*0-205-17514-7*) Allyn.

Stuttering & Personality Dynamics: Play Therapy, Projective Therapy, & Counseling. Albert T. Murphy & Ruth M. Fitzsimons. LC 60-14180. 527p. reprint ed. pap. 150.20 (*0-317-07907-7*, 2012382) Bks Demand.

Stuttering & Science. William H. Perkins. 156p. 1995. 29.95 (*1-56593-284-6*, 1244) Singular Publishing.

Stuttering & Your Child: Questions & Answers, No. 22. Ed. by Jane Fraser & Edward G. Conture. 64p. 1993. pap. 1.00 (*0-933388-28-4*) Stuttering Fnd Am.

Stuttering Disorders, Vol. 8: Current Therapy of Communication Disorders. William H. Perkins. 255p. 1985. text ed. 24.00 (*0-86577-403-X*) Thieme Med Pubs.

Stuttering Prevented: A Guide for Parents. William H. Perkins. (Illus.). 160p. (Orig.). (C). 1991. pap. text ed. 32.50 (*1-879105-50-0*, 0235) Singular Publishing.

***Stuttering: Science, Therapy, & Practice: The Most Complete Book about Stuttering.** Thomas D. Kehoe. (Illus.). 165p. (Orig.). 1997. pap. 25.00 (*0-9657181-0-7*) Casa Futura.

Stuttering Self-Help for Adults. Morris V. Jones. 144p. (C). 1989. pap. text ed. 34.95 (*0-398-05568-8*) C C Thomas.

Stuttering Therapies: Practical Approaches. Ed. by Celia Levy. 224p. 1987. pap. text ed. 25.95 (*0-7099-4145-5*, Pub. by Croom Helm UK) Routledge Chapman & Hall.

Stuttering Therapy. Cooper. 1996. write for info. (*0-7506-9579-X*) Buttrwrth-Heinemann.

Stuttering Therapy: An Integrated Approach to Theory & Practice. Richard Culatta & Stanley Goldberg. (Illus.). 480p. 1994. text ed. 60.00 (*0-02-326311-3*, Macmillan Coll) P-H.

Stuttering Therapy: Prevention & Intervention with Children, No. 20. Ed. by Gregory H. Hugo & Hugo H. Gregory. LC 85-189819. 152p. pap. 2.00 (*0-933388-22-5*) Stuttering Fnd Am.

Stuttering Therapy, Transfer & Maintenance, No. 19. Jane Fraser. LC 83-240657. 112p. 1985. pap. 2.00 (*0-933388-19-5*) Stuttering Fnd Am.

Stuttering Words. LC 86-82260. (Publications on Stuttering: No. 2). 64p. pap. 1.00 (*0-933388-25-X*) Stuttering Fnd Am.

Stuttgart Nanny Mafia. Susan Fletcher. LC 90-23225. 160p. (J). (gr. 3-7). 1991. lib. bdg. 14.95 (*0-689-31709-3*, Atheneum Bks Young) S&S Childrens.

***Stuttgarter Ballett.** 2nd ed. Hannes Kilian. (Illus.). 271p. (GER.). (C). 1981. 116.00 (*3-921617-45-6*, Pub. by Knstvrlag Weingrtn GW) Intl Bk Import.

***Stuttgarter Ballett: Auf Neuen Wegen.** Gundel Kilian. Tr. by Michael Scuffil. (Illus.). 144p. (ENG & GER.). (C). 1991. 76.00 (*3-8170-4004-0*, Pub. by Knstvrlag Weingrtn GW) Intl Bk Import.

***Stuttgarter und Wiesbadener Emptehlungen: Entstehungsgeschichte und Politischinstitutionelle Innenansichten Gescheiterter Rechtschreibreformversuche von 1950 bis 1965.** Hiltraud Strunk. (GER.). 1992. 94.80 (*3-631-45344-2*) P Lang Pubng.

Stuyvesant. Mark Dunster. 23p. (Orig.). 1991. pap. 5.00 (*0-89642-194-5*) Linden Pubs.

Stuyvesant Square. Margaret Lewerth. 464p. 1989. mass mkt. 4.50 (*0-380-70596-6*) Avon.

Sty of the Blind Pig. Phillip H. Dean. 1972. pap. 5.25 (*0-8222-1091-6*) Dramatists Play.

Stygo. Laura Hendrie. 1995. pap. 11.00 (*0-684-80111-6*, Scribners PB Fict) S&S Trade.

Styka Family Saga. Czeslaw Czaplinski. (Illus.). 202p. 1990. pap. 25.00 (*0-912757-16-7*) Bicenten.

Stylasteridae: Hydrozoa: Hydroida, of the Galapagos Islands. Stephen D. Cairns. LC 85-600176. (Smithsonian Contributions to Zoology Ser.: No. 426). 46p. reprint ed. pap. 25.00 (*0-685-15229-4*, 2027139) Bks Demand.

Style. John Haynes. 128p. (C). 1995. pap. 12.95 (*0-415-10396-7*, C0164) Routledge.

Style. Elsa Klensch & Beryl Meyer. LC 95-11439. 240p. (Orig.). 1995. pap. 14.00 (*0-399-52152-6*, Perigee Bks) Berkley Pub.

***Style.** Richardson. 1997. pap. text ed. 20.00 (*0-205-19957-7*) P-H.

Style: An Anti-Textbook. Richard A. Lanham. LC 73-86906. 144p. 1978. pap. 11.00 (*0-300-02243-3*) Yale U Pr.

Style: Ten Lessons in Clarity & Grace. Williams. (C). 1993. text ed. 20.50 (*0-673-46593-4*) Addson-Wesley Educ.

Style: Ten Lessons in Clarity & Grace. 5th ed. Joseph M. Williams. LC 96-4541. (C). 1997. text ed. 19.95 (*0-673-98243-2*) Addson-Wesley Educ.

Style: The Problem & Its Solution. Bennison Gray. (De Proprietatibus Litterarum, Ser. Major: No. 3). 1969. text ed. 89.25 (*90-279-0441-3*) Mouton.

Style: Toward Clarity & Grace. Joseph M. Williams. 226p. 1995. pap. 9.95 (*0-226-89915-2*) U Ch Pr.

Style & Authenticity in Postmodern Poetry. Jonathan Holden. LC 85-20966. 200p. 1986. text ed. 22.50 (*0-8262-0600-X*) U of Mo Pr.

Style & Class. Sietze Buning. LC 82-14541. 1982. pap. 7.95 (*0-931940-06-0*) Middleburg Pr.

Style & Configuration. Gowen. 1994. 45.00 (*1-85490-298-9*) Academy Ed UK.

Style & Configuration. James Gowen. 1994. pap. 30.00 (*1-85490-297-0*) Academy Ed UK.

Style & Consciousness in Middle English Narrative. John M. Ganim. LC 83-42559. 188p. 1983. reprint ed. pap. 53.60 (*0-7837-9340-5*, 2060081) Bks Demand.

***Style & Evolution of Earliest Motets: Cat. Raisonne B, Vol. 60/2.** Hans Tischler. (Wissenschaftliche Abhandlungen - Musicological Studies). Date not set. write for info. (*0-931902-39-8*) Inst Mediaeval Mus.

Style & Evolution of the Earliest Motets, Pts. 1, 2, 3A & 3B. Incl. Pt. 1. Text. 344p. lib. bdg. 55.00 (*0-685-43105-3*); (Wissenschaftliche Abhandlungen-Musicological Studies: Vol. 40). 1985. write for info. (*0-318-59724-1*) Inst Mediaeval Mus.

Style & Idea: Selected Writings of Arnold Schoenberg. Arnold Schoenberg. Ed. by Leonard Stein. Tr. by Leo Black from GER. LC 84-2604. 560p. 1985. pap. 15.95 (*0-520-05294-3*) U CA Pr.

Style & Idea in the Lyric Suite of Alban Berg. George Perle. LC 95-16154. (Illus.). 68p. 1995. 36.00 (*0-945193-65-3*) Pendragon NY.

Style & Mechanics of Liquefaction-Related Deformation, Lower Absaroka Volcanic Supergroup (Eocene), Wyoming. P. L. Decker. (Special Papers: No. 240). (Illus.). 80p. 1990. pap. 15.00 (*0-8137-2240-3*) Geol Soc.

Style & Music: Theory, History, & Ideology. Leonard B. Meyer. LC 96-17957. xii, 376p. 1997. pap. text ed. 17.95 (*0-226-52152-4*) U Ch Pr.

Style & Orchestration. Gardner Read. LC 77-15884. (Illus.). 320p. 1979. reprint ed. pap. 91.20 (*0-7837-9011-2*, AU00463) Bks Demand.

***Style & Rhetoric in Pindar's Odes.** William H. Race. 229p. 1990. 27.00 (*1-55540-490-1*, 400424); pap. 21.00 (*1-55540-491-X*, 400424) Scholars Pr GA.

Style & Sense: Court Reporting, Transcribing, Legal. Audrey A. Fatooh et al. LC 84-28744. 192p. 1986. spiral bd. 22.95 (*0-88280-109-0*) ETC Pubns.

Style & Sense - for the Legal Profession: A Handbook for Court Reporters, Transcribers, Paralegals & Secretaries. rev. ed. Audrey Fatooh & Barbara R. Mauk. LC 95-16271. 1996. pap. 22.95 (*0-88280-128-7*) ETC Pubns.

Style & Society in Dark Age Greece: The Changing Face of a Pre-Literate Society, 1100-700 BC. James Whitley. (New Studies in Archaeology). (Illus.). 208p. (C). 1991. text ed. 74.95 (*0-521-37383-2*) Cambridge U Pr.

Style & Society in German Literary Expressionism. Egbert Krispyn. LC 64-63741. (University of Florida Humanities Monographs: No. 15). 67p. reprint ed. pap. 25.00 (*0-7837-4923-6*, 2044589) Bks Demand.

Style & Strategy of the Business Letter. Jacqueline Trace. 1986. 12.00 (*0-13-858887-2*) S&S Trade.

Style & Structure in the Praeludia of Dietrich Buxtehude. Lawrence Archbold. LC 85-1064. (Studies in Musicology: No. 82). (Illus.). 357p. reprint ed. pap. 101.80 (*0-8357-1646-5*, 2070345) Bks Demand.

Style & Structure in the Prose of Isaak Babel. Efraim Sicher. 169p. (Orig.). 1986. pap. 19.95 (*0-89357-163-6*) Slavica.

Style & Symbol: Medieval Music: 800-1453. Andrew S. Hughes. (Wissenschaftliche Abhandlungen-Musicological Studies: Vol. 51). 585p. (ENG.). 1989. 90.00 (*0-931902-61-4*) Inst Mediaeval Mus.

Style & Symbolism in Piers Plowman: A Modern Critical Anthology. Ed. by Robert J. Blanch. LC 69-20115. 290p. (Orig.). reprint ed. pap. 82.70 (*0-317-55785-8*, 2029372) Bks Demand.

Style & Temper: Studies in French Fiction, 1925-1960. Wilbur M. Frohock. LC 67-3155. 175p. 1967. reprint ed. pap. 49.40 (*0-7837-4147-2*, 2057995) Bks Demand.

Style & the Man: How & Where to Buy Fine Men's Clothes. Alan Flusser. 400p. 1996. 24.00 (*0-06-270155-X*, HarperStyle) HarpC.

Style & the "Scribbling Women" An Empirical Analysis of Nineteenth-Century American Fiction. Mary P. Hiatt. LC 92-31764. (Contributions in Women's Studies: No. 131). 176p. 1993. text ed. 45.00 (*0-313-28819-4*, GM8819, Greenwood Pr) Greenwood.

Style & Variables in English. Ed. by Timothy Shopen et al. LC 80-23211. 288p. reprint ed. pap. 82.10 (*0-8357-3337-8*, 2039565) Bks Demand.

Style & Vernacular: A Guide to the Architecture of Lane County, Oregon. AIA, Southern Oregon Chapter Staff. (Illus.). 160p. (Orig.). 1983. pap. 9.95 (*0-87595-085-X*) Oregon Hist.

Style & You: Every Woman's Guide to Total Style. Clare Revelli. (Illus.). 96p. 1993. reprint ed. pap. 7.99 (*0-9608092-2-8*) Revelli.

Style-Architecture & Building-Art: Transformations of Architecture in the Nineteenth Century & Its Present Condition. Hermann Muthesius. Tr. & Intro. by Stanford Anderson. LC 94-14964. (Texts & Documents Ser.). (Illus.). 142p. 1994. 29.95 (*0-89236-282-0*, Getty Res Inst); pap. 19.95 (*0-89236-283-9*, Getty Res Inst) J P Getty Trust.

Style As Argument: Contemporary American Nonfiction. Chris Anderson. LC 86-21970. 202p. 1987. pap. 14.95 (*0-8093-1373-1*); text ed. 24.95 (*0-8093-1314-6*) S Ill U Pr.

Style Book: For Journalists & Writers. K. S. Menon. 132p. 1990. text ed. 18.95 (*81-220-0183-1*, Pub. by Konark Pubs Pvt Ltd II) Advent Bks Div.

Style Certain: Les Mots Pour l'Ecrire. 2nd ed. Monique Fol & Paul Barrette. 352p. (C). 1990. text ed. 54.00 (*0-13-945932-4*) P-H.

Style Check: A Concise Guide to Writing & Usage. 416p. 1996. 5.95 (*0-395-75692-8*) HM.

Style, Classification & Ethnicity: Design Categories on Bakuba Raffia Cloth. Dorothy K. Washburn. LC 90-80725. (Transactions Ser.: Vol. 80, Pt. 3). (Illus.). 120p. (C). 1990. pap. 20.00 (*0-87169-803-X*, T803-WAD) Am Philos.

Style contre les Idees: Rabelais, Zola, Sartre et les Autres. Louis-Ferdinand Celine. (FRE.). 1987. pap. 23.95 (*0-7859-3310-7*, 2870272189) Fr & Eur.

Style des Pleiades de Gobineau. Michael Riffaterre. 239p. 1957. 23.95 (*0-8288-7498-0*) Fr & Eur.

***Style Dictionary.** Illus. by Ruben Toledo. 106p. 1997. pap. 29.95 (*0-7892-0348-0*) Abbeville Pr.

Style Follows Function: Architecture of Marcus T. Reynolds. Eugene J. Johnson. (Illus.). 120p. (Orig.). 1993. pap. 24.95 (*1-881324-01-X*) Wash Park.

Style for Actors. Robert Barton. LC 92-16227. 340p. 1993. text ed. 48.95 (*0-87484-958-6*, 958) Mayfield Pub.

Style for Life. Prunella Stack. LC 89-81662. 128p. 9000. 30.00 (*0-7206-0752-3*, Pub. by P Owen Ltd UK) Dufour.

Style for Students. Schall. 1992. pap. text ed. write for info. (*0-07-055096-4*) McGraw.

Style Guide for Desktop Publishing. Charles A. Stanley. Ed. by Elaine Boutwell & Jerry O'Brien. (Illus.). 282p. (Orig.). 1991. pap. 24.95 (*0-9614857-5-2*) Pressure Appli.

Style Guide for the Computer Industry: Read Me First. Sun Technology Publishers Satff. 1996. pap. text ed. 29.95 incl. cd-rom (*0-13-455347-0*) P-H.

***Style Guide to the Use of the Metric System.** 28p. 1996. 5.00 (*0-614-18756-7*) US Metric Assn.

***Style Handbook for African-American Women.** Constance White. 1998. pap. write for info. (*0-399-52379-0*, Perigee Bks) Berkley Pub.

Style Hongrois in the Music of Western Europe. Jonathan Bellman. LC 93-10150. 224p. (C). 1993. text ed. 42.50 (*1-55553-169-5*) NE U Pr.

Style in English. John Nist. LC 72-77824. 1969. pap. 1.75 (*0-672-60904-5*, CR18, Bobbs) Macmillan.

Style in Fiction. Geoffrey N. Leech & M. H. Short. (English Language Ser.). 384p. (C). 1981. pap. text ed. 31.95 (*0-582-29103-8*, 71741) Longman.

Style in History. Peter Gay. 1989. pap. 7.95 (*0-393-30558-9*) Norton.

Style in Modern British Fiction: Studies in Joyce, Lawrence, Forster, Lewis & Green. John Russell. LC 77-22477. (Illus.). 208p. 1978. text ed. 26.50 (*0-8018-2029-4*) Johns Hopkins.

Style in Musical Art. Charles H. Parry. lib. bdg. 25.00 (*0-403-01752-1*) Scholarly.

Style in Musical Art. Charles H. Parry. 438p. 1990. reprint ed. lib. bdg. 89.00 (*0-7812-9128-3*) Rprt Serv.

Style in Old English Poetry: The Test of the Auxiliary. Daniel Donoghue. LC 87-13264. 256p. 1988. text ed. 37.00 (*0-300-03956-5*) Yale U Pr.

Style in Product Design. Graham Vickers. (Issues in Design Ser.). (Illus.). 88p. (C). 1992. pap. 16.95 (*0-85072-277-2*, Pub. by Design Council Bks UK) Ashgate Pub Co.

Style in Prose Fiction. Ed. by Harold C. Martin. LC 59-11178. (Essays of the English Institute Ser.). 1959. text ed. 35.00 (*0-231-02353-7*) Col U Pr.

Style in Prose Fiction see English Institute Essays

Style in Technical Writing. Gary A. Olson et al. (C). 1984. pap. text ed. write for info. (*0-07-554380-X*) McGraw.

Style in Writing: A Prose Reader. Lee Rockas. 431p. (C). 1992. pap. text ed. 31.16 (*0-669-20878-7*); Instr.'s ed. teacher ed. 30.36 (*0-669-28172-7*) HM College Div.

Style Investing: Unique Insight Into Equity Management. Richard Bernstein. LC 94-35163. 238p. 1995. text ed. 60.00 (*0-471-03570-X*) Wiley.

Style Louis XV see Histoire de l'Architecture Classique en France

Style Louis XVI see Histoire de l'Architecture Classique en France

Style Manual for Archival Finding Aids. Corey Seeman. (Illus.). 45p. (Orig.). (C). 1996. pap. 25.00 (*0-7881-2918-X*) DIANE Pub.

***Style Manual for Authors, Editors & Printers.** 480p. 39.95 (*0-644-29770-0*, Pub. by Aust Gov Pub AT) Aubrey Bks.

***Style Manual for Authors, Editors & Printers.** 480p. pap. 24.95 (*0-644-29771-9*, Pub. by Aust Gov Pub AT) Aubrey Bks.

Style Manual for College Students: A Guide to Written Assignments & Papers. rev. ed. Margaret L. Ranald et al. 1982. reprint ed. pap. 10.00 (*0-930146-07-7*) Queens Coll Pr.

Style Manual for Political Science. Michael K. Lane et al. (C). 1993. pap. 4.00 (*1-878147-09-9*) Am Political.

***Style Manual for the Preparation of Standards & Editorial Manuals.** 6th rev. ed. AGMA Technical Committee. (AGMA Information Sheet Ser.: Vol. 900-F96). Date not set. pap. text ed. 30.00 (*1-55589-682-0*) AGMA.

Style Name Directory for Carpets & Rugs. 96p. pap. 30.00 (*0-89275-016-2*) Carpet Rug Inst.

Style of a Law Firm: Eight Gentlemen from Virginia. Anne H. Freeman. (Illus.). 352p. 1989. 24.95 (*0-945575-25-4*) Algonquin Bks.

Style of Bana: An Introduction to Sanskrit Prose Poetry. Robert A. Hueckstedt. 228p. (Orig.). (C). 1986. pap. text ed. 25.50 (*0-8191-4999-3*) U Pr of Amer.

Style of Connectedness: "Gravity's Rainbow" & Thomas Pynchon. Thomas Moore. LC 86-16093. 320p. 1987. text ed. 37.50 (*0-8262-0625-5*, 83-36331) U of Mo Pr.

Style of Hawthorne's Gaze: Regarding Subjectivity. John Dolis. LC 92-33475. 288p. (C). 1993. text ed. 39.95 (*0-8173-0681-1*) U of Ala Pr.

Style of J. S. Bach's Chorale Preludes. 2nd ed. Pref. by Robert L. Tusler. LC 68-13275. (Music Ser.). 1968. reprint ed. lib. bdg. 19.50 (*0-306-70942-2*) Da Capo.

Style of Palestrina & the Dissonance: Music Book Index. Knud Jeppesen. 306p. 1993. reprint ed. lib. bdg. 89.00 (*0-7812-9647-1*) Rprt Serv.

Style of Pope St. Leo the Great, No. 59. William J. Halliwell. (Patristic Studies). 114p. 1984. 26.00 (*0-939738-25-2*) Zubal Inc.

Style of the Century: 1900-1980. Bevis Hillier. (Illus.). 240p. (Orig.). 1990. pap. 20.00 (*0-906969-65-4*) New Amsterdam Bks.

Style of the Kitab-i-Aqdas: Aspects of the Sublime. Suheil B. Bushrui. LC 94-40159. 74p. (C). 1995. 16.00 (*1-883053-08-0*) Univ Pr MD.

***Style Overview Sampler Profile.** 4p. 1994. pap. 5.00 (*1-58034-012-1*, M014S) IML Pubns.

Style Parallax: Why Do Styles of Managing Differ in Effectiveness? Jay Hall. (Illus.). 130p. (Orig.). (C). 1993. pap. text ed. 14.95 (*0-945804-12-1*) Woodstead Pr.

Style, Politics & the Future of Philosophy. Allan Janik. 296p. (C). 1989. lib. bdg. 141.50 (*0-7923-0056-4*, Pub. by Klwr Acad Pubs NE) Kluwer Ac.

Style Profile for Communication at Work. 3rd ed. Susan K. Gilmore & Patrick W. Fraleigh. (Illus.). (NOR.). 1992. pap. 10.00 (*0-938070-07-X*); pap. 10.00 (*0-938070-10-X*); pap. 10.00 (*0-938070-11-8*); pap. 10.00 (*0-938070-24-X*) Friendly Oregon.

Style, Rhetoric, & Rhythm. Morris W. Croll. LC 88-19519. xvi, 450p. 1989. reprint ed. 42.00 (*0-918024-66-8*); reprint ed. pap. 17.50 (*0-918024-67-6*) Ox Bow.

Style, Society, & Person: Archaeological & Ethnological Perspectives. Ed. by Christopher Carr & Jill E. Neitzel. LC 95-2530. (Interdisciplinary Contributions to Archaeology Ser.). 480p. 1995. 69.50 (*0-306-44843-2*, Plenum Pr) Plenum.

Style Sticklers: An Instant Guide for Everybody Who Writes at Work. Jean Rupp. LC 95-80369. 208p. 1998. pap. 12.95 (*1-885221-20-7*) BookPartners.

Style Strategy: Winning the Appearance Game. Jane Segerstrom. LC 88-15877. (Illus.). 160p. 1988. per. 14.95 (*0-936740-12-4*) Triad Pr TX.

Style, Style, Style. Andy Warhol. LC 96-14264. 1997. 10.95 (*0-8212-2320-8*) Bulfinch Pr.

Style Surfing: What to Wear in the Third Millenium. Ted Polhemus. LC 96-60190. (Illus.). 144p. (Orig.). 1996. pap. 22.50 (*0-500-27895-4*) Thames Hudson.

Style Theories as Found in Stylistic Studies of Romance Scholars - 1900-1950. Clare E. Craddock. LC 70-94184. (Catholic University of America. Studies in Romance Languages & Literatures: No. 43). reprint ed. 37.50 (*0-404-50343-8*) AMS Pr.

Style Trends in Pueblo Pottery in the Rio Grande & Little Colorado Cultural Areas from the Sixteenth to the Nineteenth Century. Harry P. Mera. LC 76-43776. (Laboratory of Anthropology, Memoirs: Vol. 3). reprint ed. write for info. (*0-404-15630-4*) AMS Pr.

Style Wheel of Furniture & Decoration. A. Allen Dizik. (Illus.). 12.95 (*0-686-86777-7*) Stratford Hse.

Style Writs for the Sheriff Court. 2nd ed. 450p. 1994. boxed 165.00 (*0-406-02052-3*, UK) MICHIE.

Styled for Living. Ed. by Sherman R. Emery. LC 83-50429. (Illus.). 240p. 1983. 40.00 (*0-943370-00-0*) Inter Design.

StyleMatch America's Designing Duo's New System for Using Your Personal Decorating Style to Create: American's Designing Duo's New System for Using Your Personal Decorating Style to Create a Home You'll Love. Mars Jaffe & Ronn Jaffe. (Illus.). 160p. (Orig.). 1997. pap. 22.50 (*0-8050-3846-9*, Owl) H Holt & Co.

Styles & Structures: Alternative Approaches to College Writing. Charles K. Smith. 340p. (C). 1974. pap. text ed. 22.95 (*0-393-09273-9*) Norton.

Styles & Types of North American Architecture: Social Function & Cultural Expression. Alan Gowans. LC 89-46531. (Illus.). 400p. 1993. pap. 30.00 (*0-06-430175-3*, PL) HarpC.

Styles, Eighteen Fifty to Nineteen Hundred. Kathryn B. Hiesinger. LC 83-6229. (Guides to European Decorative Arts Ser.: No. 2). (Illus.). 48p. (Orig.). 1984. pap. 3.50 (*0-87633-051-0*) Phila Mus Art.

Styles in Painting: A Comparative Study. Paul Zucker. (Illus.). 1950. pap. 7.95 (*0-486-20760-9*) Dover.

***Styles of American Furniture 1860-1960.** Richard Dubrow & Eileen Dubrow. LC 97-16558. 1997. write for info. (*0-7643-0157-8*) Schiffer.

Styles of Creation: Aesthetic Technique & the Creation of Fictional Worlds. Ed. by Eric S. Rabkin & George E. Slusser. LC 91-40086. (Proceedings of the J. Lloyd Eaton Conference of Science Fiction & Fantasy Literature Ser.). 304p. 1993. 45.00 (*0-8203-1455-2*) U of Ga Pr.

Styles of Cultural Activism: From Theory & Pedagogy to Women, Indians, & Communism. Philip Goldstein. LC 92-56922. 1994. 39.50 (*0-87413-489-7*) U Delaware Pr.

Styles of Discourse. Ed. by Nikolaus Coupland. 240p. 1988. lib. bdg. 82.50 (*0-7099-4852-2*, Pub. by Croom Helm UK) Routledge Chapman & Hall.

Styles of Learning & Teaching. Noel Entwistle. 293p. 1990. pap. 32.95 (*0-8464-1487-2*) Beekman Pubs.

Styles of Man-Management in India, Japan & Socialist Countries. Subratesh Ghosh. 1991. 17.00 (*81-204-0547-1*, Pub. by Oxford IBH II) S Asia.

Styles of Ornament. Alexander Speltz. Tr. by David O'Connor. pap. 10.95 (*0-486-20557-6*) Dover.

Styles of Ornament. Alexander Speltz. LC 93-46731. 1994. 14.99 (*0-517-10170-X*, Pub. by Gramercy) Random Hse Value.

Styles of Radical Will. Susan Sontag. 288p. 1991. pap. 12.95 (*0-385-26709-6*, Anchor NY) Doubleday.

Styles of Scientific Thinking in the European Tradition, 3 vols., Set. A. Crombie. 2456p. 1995. 280.00 (*0-7156-2439-3*, Pub. by Duckworth UK) Focus Pub-R Pullins.

S

Styles of Scientific Thought: The German Genetics Community, 1900-1933. Jonathan Harwood. LC 92-15321. (Science & Its Conceptual Foundations Ser.). (Illus.). 456p. (C). 1992. pap. text ed. 27.95 (*0-226-31882-6*); lib. bdg. 75.00 (*0-226-31881-8*) U Ch Pr.

Styles of the Emerging Nation. Ed. by Lisa C. Mullins. (Architectural Treasures of Early America Ser.). (Illus.). 224p. 1988. 19.95 (*0-918678-35-8*) Natl Hist Soc.

Styles of Theater Acting. Sunita Dhir. 1991. text ed. 17.50 (*81-212-0393-7*, Pub. by Gian Publng Hse II) S Asia.

Styles of Urban Policing: Organization, Environment & Police Styles in Selected American Cities. Jeffrey S. Slovak. LC 86-5440. 236p. (C). 1986. text ed. 36.00 (*0-8147-7855-0*) NYU Pr.

Styles of Urban Policing: Organization, Environment & Police Styles in Selected American Cities. Jeffrey S. Slovak. LC 86-5440. 236p. (C). 1988. pap. 17.50 (*0-8147-7875-5*) NYU Pr.

Style's the Man: Reflections on Proust, Fitzgerald, Wharton, Vidal, & Others. Louis Auchincloss. 224p. 1994. text ed. 19.00 (*0-684-19742-1*) S&S Trade.

StyleWrite User Guide. 1992. student ed. 69.00 (*0-933427-54-9*); 99.00 (*0-685-59743-1*) Shipley.

Styling Competition: A Guide to Winning Technique. Emma Ayala. (Illus.). 96p. 1990. pap. 30.95 (*0-87350-359-7*) Milady Pub.

***Styling Street Rods: Practical Hot Rodders Guide.** Larry O'Toole. (Illus.). 144p. 1997. pap. 19.95 (*0-949398-49-7*, Pub. by Graffiti AT) Motorbooks Intl.

Stylistic Arrangements: A Study of William Butler Yeat's "A Vision" Barbara L. Croft. LC 84-45453. (Illus.). 200p. 1987. 36.50 (*0-8387-5087-7*) Bucknell U Pr.

Stylistic Boundaries among Mobile Hunter-Foragers. C. Garth Sampson. LC 87-31431. (Archaeological Inquiry Ser.). (Illus.). 176p. (C). 1988. text ed. 42.00 (*0-87474-838-0*) Smithsonian.

Stylistic Commentary on Phanocles & Related Texts. Katherina Alexander. 168p. (Orig.). 1988. pap. 54.00 (*90-256-0885-X*, Pub. by A M Hakkert NE) Benjamins North Am.

Stylistic Commentary on Theocritus' Idyll, Vol. VII. S. Hatzikosta. xiv, 235p. 1982. pap. 76.00 (*90-256-0844-2*, Pub. by A M Hakkert NE) Benjamins North Am.

Stylistic Criticism of Twentieth-Century Poetry: From Text to Context. Ed. by Pater Verdonk. LC 92-47061. (Interface Ser.). 216p. (C). 1993. pap. 18.95 (*0-415-05863-5*, B2559, Routledge NY) Routledge.

Stylistic Development of Edgar Allen Poe. Richard M. Fletcher. LC 72-94467. (Janua Linguarum, Ser. Practica: No. 55). 192p. 1974. pap. text ed. 40.00 (*90-279-2508-9*) Mouton.

Stylistic Development of Keats. Walter Jackson Bate. LC 83-48836. reprint ed. 23.00 (*0-404-20019-2*) AMS Pr.

Stylistic Developments in Literary & Non-Literary French Prose. Anne Judge & Solange Lamothe. LC 94-39556. (Studies in French Literature: No. 19). 304p. 1995. text ed. 99.95 (*0-7734-9002-7*) E Mellen.

Stylistic Etudes in the Jazz Idiom. 28.00 (*0-7935-5595-7*) H Leonard.

Stylistic Relationship Between Poetry & Prose in the Cantico Espiritual of San Juan De la Cruz. Rosa M. Icaza. LC 76-94191. (Catholic University of America. Studies in Romance Languages & Literatures: No. 54). 1969. reprint ed. 37.50 (*0-404-50354-3*) AMS Pr.

***Stylistic Repetition in the Veda.** J. Gonda. (Verhandelingen der Koninklijke Nederlandse Akademie van Wetenschappen, Afd. Letterkunde, Nieuwe Reeks Ser.: No. 65(3)). 414p. 1959. pap. text ed. 45.00 (*0-7204-8368-9*) Elsevier.

Stylistic Theory & Practice in the Younger Pliny. Federico Gamberini. (Altertumswissenschaftliche Texte und Studien: Vol. 11). xi, 546p. (GER.). 1983. 63.70 (*3-487-07448-6*) G Olms Pubs.

Stylistic Variation in Prehistoric Ceramics. Stephen Plog. (New Studies in Archaeology). (Illus.). 40p. 1980. text ed. 59.95 (*0-521-22581-7*) Cambridge U Pr.

Stylistics. Richard Bradford. LC 96-27990. (The New Critical Idiom Ser.). 224p. (C). 1997. text ed. 49.95 (*0-415-09768-1*, Routledge NY) Routledge.

***Stylistics.** Richard Bradford. 224p. (C). 1997. pap. 10.95 (*0-415-09769-X*) Routledge.

Stylistics: A Practical Coursebook. Laura Wright & Jonathan Hope. LC 94-41574. 224p. (C). 1995. pap. 17.95 (*0-415-11381-4*, C0066) Routledge.

Stylistics: Rethinking the Artforms after Hegel. Richard D. Winfield. LC 95-11121. (SUNY Series in Hegelian Studies). 141p. (C). 1995. text ed. 44.50 (*0-7914-2781-1*) State U NY Pr.

Stylistics: Rethinking the Artforms after Hegel. Richard D. Winfield. LC 95-11121. (SUNY Series in Hegelian Studies). 141p. (C). 1995. pap. text ed. 14.95 (*0-7914-2782-X*) State U NY Pr.

Stylistics & Language Teaching. Suresh Kumar. viii, 188p. 1988. 10.00 (*0-685-62648-2*, Pub. by Kalinga Pubns) Nataraj Bks.

Stylistics of Drama: With Special Focus on Stoppard's Travesties. Peter K. Tan. 248p. (Orig.). 1993. pap. 36.00 (*9971-69-182-5*, Pub. by Singapore Univ Pr SI) Intl Spec Bk.

Stylistics Reader: From Roman Jakobson to the Present. Jean J. Weber. LC 95-38118. 320p. 1996. text ed. 49.95 (*0-340-64621-7*, Pub. by E Arnld UK); text ed. 19.95 (*0-340-64622-5*, Pub. by E Arnld UK) St Martin.

Stylistique. Pierre Guiraud. 126p. 1955. 9.95 (*0-8288-7455-7*) Fr & Eur.

Stylistique Litteraire. Pierre Van Rutten. viii, 207p. 1995. 64.95 (*1-57292-019-X*); pap. 44.95 (*1-57292-018-1*) Austin & Winfield.

Stylites: The Biographies. Tr. by Robert Doran from GRE. (Cistercian Studies: No. 112). 250p. 1992. write for info. (*0-87907-412-4*) Cistercian Pubns.

Stylized Characters' Speech in Thompson Salish Narrative. Steven M. Egesdal. LC 92-64155. xviii, 126p. (Orig.). 1992. pap. 10.00 (*1-879763-09-5*) U MT UMOPL.

***Styll in Love.** LC 97-19364. 1988. write for info. (*0-9657639-0-0*) Van Neste.

Stylometric Authorship Studies in Flavius Josephus & Related Literature. David S. Williams. LC 92-6375. (Jewish Studies: Vol. 12). 236p. 1992. lib. bdg. 89.95 (*0-7734-9518-5*) E Mellen.

Stylometric Study of the New Testament. Anthony Kenny. 160p. 1986. text ed. 60.00 (*0-19-826178-0*) OUP.

Styrbiorn the Strong. Eric R. Eddison. Ed. by R. Reginald & Douglas Melville. LC 77-84222. (Lost Race & Adult Fantasy Ser.). 1978. reprint ed. lib. bdg. 26.95 (*0-405-10975-X*) Ayer.

***Styrene.** (Environmental Health Criteria Ser.: No. 26). 123p. 1983. pap. text ed. 20.00 (*92-4-154086-9*, 1160026) World Health.

Styrene: Ethenylbenzene. Ed. by GDCh-Advisory Committee on Existing Chemicals of Environmental Relevance Staff. LC 93-3182. (BUA Reports: No. 48). 1993. 56.00 (*1-56081-796-8*, VCH) Wiley.

Styrene Polymers to Toys see Encyclopedia of Polymer Science & Engineering

Styrenics & Their Markets. Business Communications Co., Inc. Staff. 202p. 1984. 1,750.00 (*0-89336-385-5*, P-076) BCC.

Styria. (Panorama Bks.). (Illus.). (ENG & FRE.). 3.95 (*0-685-11576-3*) Fr & Eur.

Styrian Estates, 1740-1848: A Century of Transition. Christine L. Mueller. (Modern European History Ser.). 448p. 1987. text ed. 15.00 (*0-8240-8049-1*) Garland.

Styrofoam Ghosts. Julia Vinograd. 50p. (Orig.). 1993. pap. 4.95 (*0-929730-48-8*) Zeitgeist Pr.

***Su Angel de la Guarda Devocionario.** Mark. 1997. pap. 13.95 (*0-684-84457-5*) S&S Trade.

***Su Dinero - Your Money: Frustracion O Libertad? - Frustration or Freedom?** Dayton. 186p. (SPA.). write for info. (*1-56063-946-6*) Editorial Unilit.

Su Embarazo: Semana a Semana. Glade B. Curtis. LC 94-29990. (Illus.). 436p. (SPA.). 1994. pap. 12.95 (*1-55561-061-7*) Fisher Bks.

Su Hijo: Momentos Laves en su Desarrollo desde el Periodo Prenatal Hasta los Seis Anos. T. Berry Brazelton. (Illus.). 560p. 1994. pap. 14.95 (*0-201-40919-4*) Addison-Wesley.

Su Hijo Prodigo. D. James Kennedy. 272p. (SPA.). 1990. pap. 1.50 (*0-8297-0853-7*) Life Pubs Intl.

Su Historia: Los Pentecostales del Siglo Veinte. Fred Foster. Tr. by Jerry Burns & Beth Burns from ENG. (Illus.). 192p. (SPA.). 1989. pap. 7.99 (*0-932581-35-8*) Word Aflame.

Su Nombre Es Jesus-bL-Alumno. Gary Teja. (SPA.). 1989. 1.00 (*1-55955-030-9*) CRC Wrld Lit.

Su Nombre Es Jesus-bL-Maestro. Gary Teja. (SPA.). 1989. 1.50 (*1-55955-031-7*) CRC Wrld Lit.

Su Nombre Es Jesus-C-Alumno. Gary Teja. (SPA.). 1989. 1.00 (*1-55955-038-4*) CRC Wrld Lit.

Su Nombre Es Jesus C-Maestro. Gary Teja. (SPA.). 1989. 1.50 (*1-55955-039-2*) CRC Wrld Lit.

Su Nombre Es Jesus-Db-Alumno. Gary Teja. (SPA.). 1989. 1.00 (*1-55955-028-7*) CRC Wrld Lit.

Su Nombre Es Jesus-Db-Maestro. Gary Teja. (SPA.). 1989. 1.50 (*1-55955-029-5*) CRC Wrld Lit.

Su Obra en Prosa. Domingo Estrada. 346p. 1965. 7.95 (*0-8288-7453-0*) Fr & Eur.

***Su Plan de Negocio.** 4th ed. Dennis J. Sargent et al. Tr. by Maria C. Lewis. (Oregon SBDC network Workbooks Ser.). 87p. (SPA.). 1996. wbk. ed. 20.00 (*1-878475-16-9*) Oregon Small Busn Dev Ctr.

Su Poder Espiritual Y Emocional. Richard D. Dobbins. Tr. by Eliezer Oyola from ENG. Orig. Title: Your Spiritual & Emotional Power. 176p. (SPA.). 1985. pap. 1.50 (*0-8297-0705-0*) Life Pubs Intl.

Su Primer Guia de Meditacion. Goswami Kriuananda. Tr. & Intro. by Naomi Velazquez. 99p. (SPA.). 1993. pap. 7.50 (*0-9613099-9-7*) Temple Kriya Yoga.

***SU Site Excavations at a Mogollon Village, Western New Mexico, Second Season, 1941.** Paul S. Martin. LC 43-6439. (Field Museum of Natural History Anthropological Ser.: Vol. 32, No. 2, February 24, 1943). (Illus.). 197p. 1943. reprint ed. pap. 56.20 (*0-608-02702-2*, 2063367) Bks Demand.

***SU Site Excavations at a Mogollon Village, Western New Mexico, Third Season, 1946.** Paul S. Martin & John B. Rinaldo. LC 47-30981. (Field Museum of Natural History Anthropological Ser.: Vol. 32, No. 3). (Illus.). 133p. 1947. reprint ed. pap. 38.00 (*0-608-02719-7*, 2063384) Bks Demand.

***SU Site Excavations at a Mogollon Village, Western New Mexico, 1939,** Paul S. Martin. LC 41-8504. (Field Museum of Natural History Anthropological Ser.: Vol. 32, No. 1). (Illus.). 122p. 1940. reprint ed. pap. 34.80 (*0-608-02718-9*, 2063383) Bks Demand.

SU Site Excavations at a Mongollon Village, Western New Mexico, 1st, 2nd, & 3rd Seasons. Paul S. Martin. (Field Museum of Natural History Ser.). (Illus.). 1974. reprint ed. 40.00 (*0-527-01892-9*) Periodicals Srv.

***Su Tung Po, Vol. 1.** Demi. 1996. pap. 17.95 (*0-8050-3730-6*) St Martin.

Su Unico Hijo. Leopoldo A. Clarin. Ed. by Carolyn Richmond. (Nueva Austral Ser.: Vol. 104). (SPA.). 1991. pap. text ed. 24.95 (*84-239-1904-8*) Elliots Bks.

SU-15 Flagon: Aircraft Monograph 1. Butowski et al. (Illus.). 48p. 1994. pap. 15.95 (*83-86208-03-1*) Motorbooks Intl.

Su-25 Frogfoot in Action. Hans-Heiri Stapfer. (Aircraft in Action Ser.). (Illus.). 50p. 1992. pap. 7.95 (*0-89747-287-X*, 1129) Squad Sig Pubns.

Su-27 Flanker. Tom Basham. 1996. pap. text ed. 12.95 (*0-7615-0546-6*) Prima Pub.

Sua Majestade, Os Judeus. Goran Larsson. (Illus.). 38p. (POR.). 1996. 3.00 (*1-888235-21-7*) AMI-Jerusalem.

Suarez: Disputation Six, on Formal & Universal Unity. Tr. by James F. Ross. LC 64-7799. (Medieval Philosophical Texts in Translation Ser.: No. 23). 1965. pap. 25.00 (*0-87462-215-8*) Marquette.

Suarez on Individuation. Jorge J. Gracia. Ed. by James Robb. LC 80-84769. (Medieval Philosophical Texts in Translation Ser.: No. 23). 304p. 1981. pap. 25.00 (*0-87462-223-9*) Marquette.

Suasive Art of David Hume. M. A. Box. 304p. 1990. text ed. 39.50 (*0-691-06828-3*) Princeton U Pr.

Sub. Jimmy Jazz. 100p. (Orig.). 1996. pap. 11.00 (*1-884615-15-5*) Incommedo San Diego.

Sub. P. J. Petersen. LC 92-22269. (Illus.). (J). (gr. 2-5). 1993. pap. 13.99 (*0-525-45059-9*) Dutton Child Bks.

Sub. P. J. Petersen. (J). 1995. pap. 4.99 (*0-14-037442-6*) Viking Penguin.

Sub-Acute Spongiform Encephalopathies: Proceedings of a Seminar in the CEC Agricultural Research Programme, Held in Brussels, November 12-14, 1990. Ed. by R. S. Bradley et al. (Current Topics in Veterinary Medicine & Animal Science Ser.). 304p. 1991. lib. bdg. 149.50 (*0-7923-1458-1*) Kluwer Ac.

Sub & Supersonic Experimental Rocket Computer Programs: Fourth Order Range-Kutta, Altitude Prediction, Drag , Center of Pressure. Charles E. Rogers & Jerry Irvine. 50p. 1983. 49.95 (*0-912468-13-0*) CA Rocketry.

Sub-Arcsecond Radio Astronomy. Ed. by R. J. Davis & R. S. Booth. (Illus.). 480p. (C). 1993. 74.95 (*0-521-43472-6*) Cambridge U Pr.

Sub-Contracts DOM 1 & DOM 2: A Guide to Rights & Obligations. Don Riding. LC 96-26491. 247p. 1996. 75.00 (*0-632-04125-0*) Blackwell Sci.

Sub DSL, 3 Vols. 17th ed. Kirby. 1993. 725.00 (*0-8103-8012-9*) Gale.

Sub DSL, 3 Vols. 18th ed. Kirby. 1994. 750.00 (*0-8103-8528-7*) Gale.

Sub DSL, 3 Vols. 20th ed. Gwen Turecki. 1996. 800.00 (*0-8103-5763-1*) Gale.

Sub DSL: Business-Government-Law Libraries, Vol. 1. 20th ed. Gwen Turecki. 1996. 310.00 (*0-8103-5764-X*) Gale.

Sub DSL: Comp Engr Sci Libraries, Vol. 2. 20th ed. Gwen Turecki. 1996. 310.00 (*0-8103-5765-8*) Gale.

Sub DSL: Health Sciences Library, Vol. 3. 20th ed. Zakalik. 1996. 310.00 (*0-8103-5766-6*) Gale.

Sub DSL, Vol. 1: Bus-Govt-Law Libraries. 18th ed. Kirby. 1994. 285.00 (*0-8103-8529-5*) Gale.

Sub DSL, Vol. 2: Comp Engr Sci Libraries, Vol. 2. 17th ed. Kirby. 1993. 275.00 (*0-8103-8014-5*) Gale.

Sub DSL, Vol. 2: Comp Engr Sci Libraries, Vol. 2. 18th ed. Kirby. 1994. 285.00 (*0-8103-8530-9*) Gale.

Sub DSL, Vol. 3: Health Sciences Libr, Vol. 3. 17th ed. Kirby. 1993. 275.00 (*0-8103-8015-3*) Gale.

Sub DSL, Vol. 3: Health Sciences Library, Vol. 3. 18th ed. Kirby. 1994. 285.00 (*0-8103-8531-7*) Gale.

Sub Duty. Grover S. McLeod. 580p. 1986. pap. 19.95 (*1-884150-01-2*) Manchester AL.

Sub Duty. Grover S. McLeod. 581p. 1986. pap. 19.95 (*0-87651-975-3*) Southern U Pr.

***Sub-Epic Stage of the Formulaic Tradition.** A. Hoekstra. (Verhandelingen der Koninklijke Nederlandse Akademie van Wetenschappen, Afd. Letterkunde, Nieuwe Reeks Ser.: No. 75(2)). 76p. 1969. pap. text ed. 15.75 (*0-7204-8414-6*) Elsevier.

Sub Forms. Marc W. Miller. (Harpoon Ser.). (Illus.). 49p. (Orig.). (YA). 1989. pap. 8.00 (*1-55878-019-X*) Game Designers.

Sub-Hardy Hilbert Spaces in the Unit Disk. Donald Sarason. (University of Arkansas Lecture Notes in the Mathematical Sciences Ser.). 112p. 1994. text ed. 57.95 (*0-471-04897-6*) Wiley.

Sub Loco Notes in the Torah of Biblia Hebraica Stuttgartensia. Daniel S. Mynatt. LC 95-6988. (Dissertation Ser.: No. 2). 288p. 1995. pap. 18.95 (*0-941037-33-9*) BIBAL Pr.

***Sub Micron Silicon Devices & Process Technology.** Ter Beek. (Illus.). 608p. 1997. text ed. write for info. (*0-412-72340-9*, Chap & Hall NY) Chapman & Hall.

Sub-Orbital Project Documentation & Computer Runs. Jerry Irvine et al. 50p. 1985. 19.95 (*0-912468-27-0*, SOP) CA Rocketry.

***Sub-Riemannian Geometry.** Andre Bellaiche & J. J. Risler. LC 96-35950. (Progress in Mathematics Ser.). 1996. 84.50 (*0-8176-5476-3*) Birkhauser.

***Sub-Riemannian Geometry.** Ed. by Andre Bellaiche & J. J. Risler. LC 96-35950. (Progress In Mathematics Ser.). 404p. 1996. 84.50 (*3-7643-5476-3*) Birkhauser.

Sub Rosa: Poems. Susan Prospere. 96p. 1993. pap. 8.95 (*0-393-31003-5*) Norton.

Sub Rosa: Strange Tales. Robert Aickman. 1993. reprint ed. lib. bdg. 18.95 (*0-89968-417-3*, Lghtyr Pr) Buccaneer Bks.

Sub-Saharan Africa. Ed. by Chris Allen & Gavin Williams. LC 81-16902. (Sociology of "Developing Societies" Ser.). 240p. 1982. pap. 14.00 (*0-85345-598-8*) Monthly Rev.

Sub-Saharan Africa: A Guide to Information Sources. Ed. by W. A. Skurnik. LC 73-17513. (International Relations Information Guide Ser.: Vol. 3). 144p. 1977. 68.00 (*0-8103-1391-X*) Gale.

Sub-Saharan Africa: A Sub-Continent in Transition. Rukhsana A. Siddiqui. 362p. 1993. 68.95 (*1-85628-427-1*, Pub. by Avebury Pub UK) Ashgate Pub Co.

Sub-Saharan Africa: An Empirical Investigation of Growth, Savings & Investment Performance, 1986-93. Michael T. Hadjimichael et al. (Occasional Paper: No. 118). 86p. 1995. pap. 15.00 (*1-55775-458-6*) Intl Monetary.

Sub-Saharan Africa: An Introduction. Edmund C. Gannon. (JSPES Monograph: No. 6). 1978. pap. 15.00 (*0-930690-09-5*) Coun Soc Econ.

Sub-Saharan Africa: From Crisis to Sustainable Growth. 250p. 1989. English ed., 250p. 20.00 (*0-8213-1349-5*, 11349); French ed.; 250p. 20.00 (*0-8213-1350-9*, 11350) World Bank.

Sub-Saharan African Films & Filmmakers: An Annotated Bibliography, 1987-1992. Nancy J. Schmidt. 418p. 1994. 80.00 (*1-873836-21-X*, Pub. by H Zell Pubs UK) Bowker-Saur.

Sub-Saharan Economic Geology. Ed. by Tom G. Blenkinsop & Paul L. Tromp. (Illus.). 300p. (C). 1995. text ed. 95.00 (*90-5410-610-7*, Pub. by A A Balkema NE) Ashgate Pub Co.

Sub Specie Historiae: Essays in the Manifestations of Historical & Moral Consciousness. John T. Marcus. LC 76-50285. 328p. 1980. 40.00 (*0-8386-2057-4*) Fairleigh Dickinson.

***Sub Survival: A Handbook for the Substitute Elementary Teacher.** 3rd ed. Danna Downing & Fritz Erickson. 150p. 1996. pap. text ed. 18.95 (*1-55691-125-4*, 254) Learning Pubns.

Sub-Tropical Rambles in the Land of the Aphanapteryx: Personal Experiences, Adventures & Wanderings in & Around the Island of Mauritius. Nicholas Pike. LC 72-4081. (Black Heritage Library Collection). 1977. reprint ed. 44.95 (*0-8369-9103-6*) Ayer.

Sub Zero. John Campbell. 352p. (Orig.). 1996. mass mkt. 5.99 (*0-380-78061-5*) Avon.

***Sub-Zero.** Jay Leibold. (Adventures of Batman & Robin Ser.). 1997. pap. text ed. 3.50 (*0-316-17696-6*) Little.

Subacute & Transitional Care Handbook: Defining, Delivering & Improving Care. Steven A. Levenson. Ed. by Kate Aker. 400p. (Orig.). 1996. pap. text ed. 59.95 (*1-886657-08-4*) B Cracom Pub.

***Subacute Care: An Interdisciplinary Curriculum.** AACN Staff. 208p. 1997. 5.00 (*0-7872-3516-4*) Kendall-Hunt.

Subacute Care: Analysis of the Market Opportunities & Competition. Harry Ting. 225p. 1995. ring bd. 895.00 (*1-880874-15-6*) Ctr Hlthcare.

Subacute Care: The Definitive Guide to Hospital Based Nursing Facilities. Mary T. Knapp. LC 94-22126. 204p. 1995. 154.00 (*0-8342-0641-2*, 20641) Aspen Pub.

Subacute Care Operations: A Management Guide for the Free-Standing or Hospital-Based Unit. Laura Z. Hyatt. 250p. (C). 1995. text ed. 75.00 (*1-55738-630-7*) Irwin Prof Pubng.

Subacute Care Services: The Evolving Opportunities & Challenges. Marshall W. Kelly. 200p. (C). 1995. text ed. 55.00 (*1-55738-621-8*) Irwin Prof Pubng.

***Subaltern on the Somme.** Max Plowman. (Great War Ser.: No. 51). 256p. 1996. reprint ed. 34.95 (*0-89839-248-9*) Battery Pr.

Subaltern Studies: Writings on South Asian History & Society, Vol. I. Ed. by Ranajit Guha. (Oxford India Paperbacks Ser.). 251p. 1994. reprint ed. pap. 8.95 (*0-19-563443-8*) OUP.

Subaltern Studies: Writings on South Asian History & Society, Vol. IV. Ed. by Ranajit Guha. (Illus.). 400p. 1988. 28.00 (*0-19-561840-8*) OUP.

***Subaltern Studies: Writings on South Asian History & Society, Vol. IX.** Ed. by Shahid Amin & Dipesh Chakrabarty. (Illus.). 276p. 1997. 29.95 (*0-19-563865-4*) OUP.

Subaltern Studies Vol. 5: Writing on South Asian History & Society, Vol. 5. Ed. by Ranajit Guha. (Oxford India Paperbacks Ser.). (Illus.). 308p. (C). 1996. pap. 10.95 (*0-19-563535-3*) OUP.

Subaltern Studies Vol. VI: Writings on South Asian History & Society. Ed. by Ranajit Guha. (India Paperbacks Ser.). 346p. 1996. reprint ed. pap. 12.95 (*0-19-563536-1*) OUP.

***Subaltern Studies Reader, 1986-1995.** Ranajit Guha. LC 97-18632. 1997. pap. write for info. (*0-8166-2758-4*); pap. write for info. (*0-8166-2759-2*) U of Minn Pr.

Subaltern Studies VII: Writings on South Asian History & Society. Ed. by Partha Chatterjee & Gyanendra Pandey. (Oxford India Paperbacks Ser.). 284p. 1994. reprint ed. pap. 10.95 (*0-19-563362-8*) OUP.

Subaltern Studies, Vol. XIII: Writings on South Asian History & Society. Ed. by David Arnold & David Hardiman. 252p. 1995. 27.00 (*0-19-563411-X*) OUP.

Subaltern Ulysses. Enda Duffy. LC 93-47083. (C). 1994. text ed. 44.95 (*0-8166-2328-7*); pap. text ed. 18.95 (*0-8166-2329-5*) U of Minn Pr.

***Subalterns & Sovereigns: An Anthropological History of Bastar, 1854-1996.** Nandini Sundar. (Illus.). 336p. 1997. 24.95 (*0-19-564116-7*) OUP.

Subaltern's War: Being a Memoir of the Great War from the Point of View of a Romantic Young Man. Charles E. Carrington. LC 72-4273. (World Affairs Ser.: National & International Viewpoints). (Illus.). 236p. 1972. reprint ed. 23.95 (*0-405-04562-X*) Ayer.

Subantarctic Macquarie Island: Environment & Biology. Patricia Selkirk et al. (Illus.). 300p. (C). 1990. text ed. 85.00 (*0-521-26633-5*) Cambridge U Pr.

Subaqueous Slope Failures: Experiments & Modern Occurences. H. Schwarz. (Contributions to Sedimentology Ser.: No. 11). (Illus.). 116p. 1982. pap. text ed. 51.80 (*3-510-57011-1*) Lubrecht & Cramer.

Subarachnoid Haemorrhage. R. P. Sengupta & V. L. McAllister. (Illus.). 390p. 1986. 317.00 (*0-387-15534-1*) Spr-Verlag.

S

An Asterisk (*) at the beginning of an entry indicates that the title is appearing in BIP for the first time.

***Subarachnoid Haemorrhage.** M. Vermeulen et al. (Major Problems in Neurology Ser.: Vol. 25). (Illus.). 140p. 1992. write for info. (*0-7020-1486-9*, Pub. by W B Saunders UK) Saunders.

Subarachnoid Haemorrhage: Aneurysms & Vascular Malformations of the Central Nervous System. R. S. Maurice-Williams. (Illus.). 448p. 1987. 131.50 (*0-685-24836-4*, Yr Bk Med Pubs) Mosby Yr Bk.

Subarachnoid Hemorrhage. Bruce Weir. (Contemporary Neurology Ser.). (Illus.). 325p. (C). 1998. text ed. 120.00 (*0-614-16098-7*) Davis Co.

***Subarachnoid Hemorrhage: Pathophysiology & Management.** Ed. by Joshua B. Bederson. (Neurosurgical Topics Ser.: Vol. 27). (Illus.). 275p. 1996. 95.00 (*1-879284-43-X*) Am Assn Neuro.

Subarctic. Ed. by June Helm. LC 77-17162. (Handbook of North American Indians Ser.: Vol. 6). (Illus.). 838p. 1981. 25.00 (*0-87474-186-6*, HEV6) Smithsonian.

Subarctic Athabascans: A Selected, Annotated Bibliography. Arthur E. Hippler & John R. Wood. LC 74-620010. (ISER Reports: No. 39). 380p. 1974. pap. 15.00 (*0-88353-012-0*) U Alaska Inst Res.

Subarctic Saga: The de Troyes Expedition 1686. W. A. Kenyon. 1994. pap. 4.95 (*0-88854-318-2*, Pub. by Royal Ont Mus CN) U of Toronto Pr.

Subarea Projections Model (SAM) Allocating Enployment & Population, Projecting Household Income, & Land Use Accounting. 45p. 1993. 35.00 (*0-318-22685-5*) Assn Bay Area.

Subaru 1970-84. Chilton Staff. (Total Car Care Ser.). 1996. pap. 22.95 (*0-8019-8790-3*) Chilton.

Subaru 1985-92. 808p. 1992. pap. 21.95 (*0-8019-8259-6*) Chilton.

Subaru 1985-92. Chilton Automotives Editorial Staff. 496p. 1992. pap. 16.95 (*0-8019-8305-3*) Chilton.

Subatomic Physics. 2nd ed. Hans Frauenfelder & Ernest M. Henley. 592p. 1991. text ed. 89.00 (*0-13-859430-9*) P-H.

Subband & Wavelet Transforms: Design & Applications. Ed. by Ali N. Akansu & Mark J. Smith. LC 95-40664. (International Series in Engineering & Computer Science, Natural Language Processing & Machine Translation: No. 340). 472p. (C). 1995. lib. bdg. 95.00 (*0-7923-9645-6*) Kluwer Ac.

Subband Compression of Images: Principals & Examples. T. A. Ramstad et al. LC 95-17786. (Advances in Image Communication Ser.: Vol. 6). 394p. 1995. 178.50 (*0-444-89431-4*) Elsevier.

Subcellular Taxonomy: An Ultrastructural Classification System with Diagnostic Applications. Ed. by A. L. McLay & Peter G. Toner. LC 83-10856. (Ultrastructural Pathology Publication). 86p. 1985. 78.95 (*0-89116-293-3*) Hemisp Pub.

Subcellular Basis of Contractile Failure. Ed. by Borivoj Korecky & Naranjan S. Dhalla. (Developments in Cardiovascular Medicine Ser.). (C). 1990. lib. bdg. 129.50 (*0-7923-0890-5*) Kluwer Ac.

Subcellular Biochemistry Vol. 25: Ascorbic Acid: Biochemistry & Biomedical Cell Biology. Ed. by J. Robin Harris. (Illus.). 425p. (C). 1996. 120.00 (*0-306-45148-4*, Plenum Pr) Plenum.

Subcellular Biochemistry Vol. 26: Myoinositol Phosphates, Phosphoinositides, & Signal Transduction, Vol. 26. Ed. by B. B. Biswas & S. Biswas. (Illus.). 425p. (C). 1996. 125.00 (*0-306-45221-9*, Plenum Pr) Plenum.

Subcellular Biochemistry Vol. 27: Biology of the Lysosome. Ed. by John B. Lloyd et al. (Illus.). 409p. (C). 1997. 129.50 (*0-306-45440-8*, Plenum Pr) Plenum.

***Subcellular Biochemistry Vol. 28: Cholesterol - Its Functions & Metabolism in Biology & Medicine.** Ed. by Robert Bittman. (Illus.). 537p. (C). 139.50 (*0-306-45478-5*, Plenum Pr) Plenum.

Subcellular Factors Immunity. Ed. by Herman Friedman. LC 79-24875. (Annals Ser.: Vol. 332). 625p. 1979. 112.00 (*0-89766-035-8*) NY Acad Sci.

***Subcellular Fractionation: A Practical Approach.** Ed. by John Graham & David Rickwood. (The Practical Approach Ser.: No. 173). (Illus.). 340p. 1997. 110.00 (*0-19-963495-5*, IRL Pr) OUP.

***Subcellular Fractionaton: A Practical Approach.** Ed. by John Graham & David Rickwood. (The Practical Approach Ser.: No. 173). (Illus.). 340p. 1997. pap. 55.00 (*0-19-963494-7*, IRL Pr) OUP.

Subcellular Particles, Structures, & Organelles. Jerold A. Last. Ed. by Allen I. Laskin. LC 73-90306. (Methods in Molecular Biology Ser.: No. 5). (Illus.). 325p. reprint ed. pap. 92.70 (*0-7837-0906-4*, 2041211) Bks Demand.

***Subcellular Structure, Vol. 1.** Abramoff. Date not set. 1.20 (*0-7167-9044-0*) W H Freeman.

Subchapter S Taxation. 3rd ed. Irving M. Grant & William Christian. LC 80-10826. (Tax & Estate Planning Ser.). 1415p. 1990. text ed. 135.00 (*0-07-024072-8*) Shepards.

Subchaser in the South Pacific: A Saga of the U. S. S. SC-761 During World War II. J. Henry Doscher, Jr. LC 94-2271. 1994. 15.95 (*0-89015-947-5*) Sunbelt Media.

Subchronic Toxicities of Industrial & Agricultural Chemicals to Fathead Minnows, Pimephales Promelas. Ed. by D. J. Call & D. L. Geiger. (Subchronic Toxicity Test Ser.). (Illus.). 318p. (Orig.). 1992. pap. 90.00 (*0-9614968-6-X*) Lke Superior Res.

Subcommissural Organ: An Ependymal Brain Gland. Ed. by A. Oksche et al. LC 93-9609. 1993. Alk. paper. 174.00 (*0-387-56336-9*) Spr-Verlag.

***Subcommissural Organ & Reissner's Fiber Complex: An Enigma in the Central Nervous System.** Annie Meiniel et al. (Progress in Histochemistry & Cytochemistry Ser.: Vol. 30, No. 2). (Illus.). vii, 68p. 1996. pap. 50.00 (*3-437-11679-7*, Pub. by G Fischer Verlag GW) Lubrecht & Cramer.

Subconscious & the Superconscious Planes of Mind. W. W. Atkinson. 1991. lib. bdg. 79.95 (*0-8490-4533-9*) Gordon Pr.

Subconscious & the Superconscious Planes of Mind. William W. Atkinson. 200p. 1971. reprint ed. spiral bd. 8.50 (*0-7873-0055-1*) Hlth Research.

Subconscious & the Superconscious Planes of Mind (1909) William W. Atkinson. 200p. 1996. pap. 18.95 (*1-56459-731-8*) Kessinger Pub.

Subconscious Mind & the Chalice. Torkom Saraydarian. LC 91-92891. 400p. 1993. pap. 18.00 (*0-929874-18-8*) TSG Pub Found.

Subconscious Orthodoxy of the Spanish Race. Archimandrite P. DeBallester. Ed. by Orthodox Christian Educational Society Staff. 8p. (Orig.). 1978. reprint ed. pap. 1.50 (*0-938366-46-7*) Orthodox Chr.

Subcontinent in World Politics: India, Its Neighbors & the Great Powers. 2nd rev. ed. Ed. by Lawrence Ziring. LC 82-7634. 268p. 1982. text ed. 55.00 (*0-275-90930-1*, C0930, Praeger Pubs) Greenwood.

Subcontract Management Handbook. George Sammet & Clifton G. Kelley. LC 80-69698. 256p. reprint ed. pap. 73.00 (*0-317-26704-3*, 2023510) Bks Demand.

Subcontracting Electronics: A Management & Technical Guide for Purchasers & Suppliers. David Boswell. LC 92-31693. 1993. text ed. 35.00 (*0-07-707783-0*) McGraw.

Subcontracting under the Federal Acquisition Regulation: A Primer. Vernon J. Edwards. LC 93-2754. 1993. pap. 45.00 (*0-9626190-1-9*) Educ Servs Inst.

Subcontractor's Guide to Residential Construction. Marvin M. Frydenlund. 1997. text ed. 44.00 (*0-07-022654-7*) McGraw.

Subcortical Functions in Language & Memory. Bruce A. Crosson. LC 91-42906. 374p. 1992. lib. bdg. 45.00 (*0-89862-790-7*) Guilford Pr.

Subcortical Visual Systems. Ed. by David J. Ingle & G. E. Schneider. (Journal: Brain, Behavior & Evolution: Vol. 3, No. 1-4). 1970. reprint ed. pap. 73.75 (*3-8055-1149-3*) S Karger.

Subcritical Crack Growth & Fracture of Bridge Steels. (National Cooperative Highway Research Program Report Ser.: No. 181). 82p. 1977. 5.60 (*0-309-02755-1*) Transport Res Bd.

Subcultural Mosaics & Intersubjective Realities: An Ethnographic Research Agenda for Pragmatizing the Social Sciences. Robert Prus. LC 96-32485. 349p. (C). 1997. text ed. 65.50 (*0-7914-3239-4*); pap. text ed. 21.95 (*0-7914-3240-8*) State U NY Pr.

Subcultural Sounds: Micromusics of the West. Mark Slobin. LC 92-34289. (Music - Culture Ser.). 139p. 1993. pap. 15.95 (*0-8195-6261-0*, Wesleyan Univ Pr); text ed. 30.00 (*0-8195-5253-4*, Wesleyan Univ Pr) U Pr of New Eng.

Subculture. Dick Hebdige. 200p. 1981. pap. 14.95 (*0-415-03949-5*) Routledge.

Subculture of Violence: Towards an Integrated Theory in Criminology. Marvin E. Wolfgang & Franco Ferracuti. LC 82-683. 410p. 1982. reprint ed. pap. 116.90 (*0-608-01506-7*, 2059550) Bks Demand.

***Subculture to Clubcultures: An Introduction to Popular Cultural Studies.** Steve Redhead. (Illus.). (C). 1997. text ed. 59.95 (*0-631-19788-5*); pap. text ed. 21.95 (*0-631-19789-3*) Blackwell Pubs.

Subcultures Reader. Ed. by Ken Gelder & Sarah Thornton. LC 96-11488. 456p. 1997. pap. 22.95 (*0-415-12728-9*) Routledge.

Subcultures Reader. Ed. by Ken Gelder & Sarah Thornton. LC 96-11488. 456p. (C). 1997. text ed. 65.00 (*0-415-12727-0*) Routledge.

Subdifferentials: Theory & Applications. Anatoly G. Kusraev & S. S. Kutateladze. (Mathematics & Its Applications Ser.). 408p. (C). 1995. lib. bdg. 189.00 (*0-7923-3389-6*) Kluwer Ac.

Subdivision. Stephen Amidon. 160p. 1992. 18.95 (*0-88001-279-X*) Ecco Pr.

Subdivision Analysis. Douglas D. Lovell & Robert S. Martin. 120p. 1993. 25.00 (*0-922154-11-2*) Appraisal Inst.

Subdivision & Site Plan Handbook. David Listokin & Carole Walker. 461p. 1989. 54.95 (*0-88285-123-3*) Ctr Urban Pol Res.

Subdivision Law & Growth Management. James A. Kushner. LC 91-4140. (Real Property - Zoning Ser.). 1991. ring bd. 145.00 (*0-87632-807-9*) Clark Boardman Callaghan.

***Subdivision Methods for Geometric Design.** Joe Warren. 200p. (C). 1998. pap. text ed. 49.95 (*1-55860-446-4*) Morgan Kaufmann.

Subdivision Regulations in North Carolina: An Introduction. Richard D. Ducker. 16p. 1980. pap. 4.50 (*1-56011-147-X*) Institute Government.

Subdivision, Subsurface Stratigraphy, & Estimated Age Offluvial-Terrace Deposits in Northwestern Tennessee. Donald T. Rodbell. LC 95-9815. (U. S. Geological Survey Bulletin: vol. 2128). write for info. (*0-615-00641-8*) US Geol Survey.

***Subdivisions of the Public Lands.** J. S. Higgins. (Illus.). 234p. (Orig.). 1996. pap. 25.00 (*1-56546-097-9*) Arkansas Res.

Subduction: Insights from Physical Modeling. Alexander I. Shemenda. (Modern Approaches in Geophysics Ser.). 228p. (C). 1994. lib. bdg. 106.00 (*0-7923-3042-0*) Kluwer Ac.

Subduction of Aseismic Oceanic Ridges: Effects on Shape, Seismicity, & Other Characteristics of Consuming Plate Boundaries. Peter R. Yogt et al. LC 75-40900. (Geological Society of America, Special Paper Ser.: No. 172). 63p. reprint ed. pap. 25.00 (*0-685-16450-0*, 2027367) Bks Demand.

***Subduction Top to Bottom.** Gray E. Bebout. LC 96-35932. (Geophysical Monograph Ser.). 1996. write for info. (*0-87590-078-X*) Am Geophysical.

Subduction Zone Magmatism. Yoshiyuki Tatsumi & Steve Eggins. LC 94-44612. (Frontiers in Earth Sciences Ser.). 1995. 45.00 (*0-86542-361-X*) Blackwell Sci.

Subduction Zones, Pt. I. Larry J. Ruff & Hiroo Kanomori. 352p. 1989. 34.50 (*0-8176-1928-3*) Birkhauser.

Subduction Zones, Pt. II. Larry J. Ruff & Hiroo Kanamori. 376p. 1989. 34.50 (*0-8176-2272-1*) Birkhauser.

Subdued Southern Nobility: A Southern Ideal, by One of the Nobility. LC 72-2035. (Black Heritage Library Collection). 1977. reprint ed. 32.95 (*0-8369-9070-6*) Ayer.

Subduing Satan: Religion, Recreation, & Manhood in the Rural South, 1865-1920. Ted Ownby. LC 89-48578. (Fred W. Morrison Series in Southern Studies). (Illus.). xiv, 286p. (C). 1990. 34.95 (*0-8078-1913-1*) U of NC Pr.

Subduing Satan: Religion, Recreation, & Manhood in the Rural South, 1865-1920. Ted Ownby. LC 89-48578. (Fred W. Morrison Series in Southern Studies). (Illus.). xxii, 286p. 1993. reprint ed. pap. 14.95 (*0-8078-4429-2*) U of NC Pr.

Subduing Sovereignty: Sovereignty & the Right to Intervene. Ed. by Marianne Heiberg. 168p. 1994. pap. 19.00 (*1-85567-267-7*, Pub. by Pntr Pubs UK) Bks Intl VA.

***Sube Y Baja.** Scholastic Inc. Staff. (Autobus Magico Ser.). 1997. pap. text ed. 2.99 (*0-590-96429-1*) Scholastic Inc.

Subediting. 2nd ed. Hodgson. 1993. pap. 34.95 (*0-7506-1761-6*) Buttrwrth-Heinemann.

Subfactors: Proceedings of the Taniguchi Symposium on Operator Algebras. H. Araki et al. 304p. 1994. text ed. 74.00 (*981-02-1803-6*) World Scientific Pub.

Subfactors & Knots. V. Jones & Weiss. LC 91-24438. (CBMS Regional Conference Series in Mathematics: No. 80). 113p. 1991. 19.00 (*0-8218-0729-3*, CBMS/80) Am Math.

Subfertile. Tom Mardirosian. 1991. pap. 5.25 (*0-8222-1092-4*) Dramatists Play.

***Subfertility Handbook: A Clinician's Guide.** Ed. by Gab Kovacs. (Illus.). 260p. (C). 1997. text ed. 54.95 (*0-521-56016-0*) Cambridge U Pr.

Subfile Technique for RPG-400 Programmers. 2nd rev. ed. Jonathan Yergin & Wayne Madden. (Technical Publication Ser.). 326p. 1993. pap. 129.00 (*1-884322-11-5*) Duke Commns Intl.

Subfile Technique for RPG/400 Programmers. 2nd ed. Jonathan Yergin & Wayne Madden. 326p. 1993. pap. 89.00 (*1-882419-41-3*) Duke Commns Intl.

Subfiles for RPG Programmers: A Comprehensive User Guide. Michael Catalani. (Illus.). 505p. (Orig.). 1994. pap. 99.00 (*1-883884-18-7*) Midrange Comput.

***Subgenus Hymenanthes, Vol. 39, No. 2.** D. F. Chamberlain. (Revision of Rhododendron Ser.). (Illus.). 1982. 15.00 (*0-11-491994-1*, Pub. by Royal Botanic Edinburgh UK) Balogh.

***Subgenus Rhododendron Sections Rhododendron & Pogonanthum, Vol. 39, No. 1.** J. Cullen. (Revision of Rhododendron Ser.). (Illus.). 1980. 15.00 (*0-11-491649-7*, Pub. by Royal Botanic Edinburgh UK) Balogh.

***Subgenus Tsutsusi, Vol. 47, No. 2.** D. F. Chamberlain & S. J. Rae. (Revision of Rhododendron Ser.). 1990. 40.00 (*0-11-494113-0*, Pub. by Royal Botanic Edinburgh UK) Balogh.

Subgroup Lattices & Symmetric Functions. Lynne M. Butler. LC 94-26457. (Memoirs of the American Mathematical Society Ser.: Vol. 539). 1994. pap. 36.00 (*0-8218-2600-X*, MEMO/112/539) Am Math.

Subgroup Lattices of Groups, Vol. 14. Roland Schmidt. LC 94-20795. (Expositions in Mathematics Ser.: Vol. 14). 576p. (C). 1994. lib. bdg. 157.95 (*3-11-011213-2*) De Gruyter.

Subgroup Structure of the Finite Classical Groups. P. B. Kleidman & Martin W. Liebeck. (London Mathematical Society Lecture Note Ser.: No. 129). 250p. 1990. pap. text ed. 42.95 (*0-521-35949-X*) Cambridge U Pr.

Subgroups of Teichmuller Modular Groups. N. V. Ivanov. LC 92-26912. (Translations of Mathematical Monographs: Vol. 115). 127p. 1992. 39.00 (*0-8218-4594-2*, MMONO/115) Am Math.

Subharmonic Functions, Vol. 2. W. K. Hayman. (London Mathematical Society Monographs: Vol. 20). 875p. 1990. text ed. 155.00 (*0-12-334802-1*) Acad Pr.

Subharmonic Mixing Antenna for Millimeter-Wave Receivers & Oscillationg Slot Antennas for Quasi-Optical Power Combining. fac. ed. Brian K. Kormanyos. (University of Michigan Report: No. RL905). 153p. 1994. pap. 43.70 (*0-7837-7693-4*, 2047450) Bks Demand.

Subhas Chandra Bose: From Kabul to Battle of Imphal. H. N. Pandit. 360p. 1988. text ed. 40.00 (*0-685-19794-8*, Pub. by Sterling Pubs II) Apt Bks.

Subhas Chandra Bose: Man, Mission, Means. Subhash C. Chatopadhyay. (C). 1989. 19.50 (*0-8364-2482-4*, Pub. by Minerva II) S Asia.

Subhas Chandra Bose: The Man & His Mind. Jasobanta Kar. (C). 1988. 17.50 (*81-85195-14-5*, Pub. by Minerva II) S Asia.

Subhas Chandra Bose & Indian Freedom Struggle. Edmund Muller & Arun Bhattacharjee. 1985. 17.50 (*0-8364-1452-7*, Pub. by Ashish II) S Asia.

Subhas Chandra Bose & Middle Class Radicalism: A Study in Indian Nationalism, 1928-1940. Bidyut Chakrabarti. 200p. 1990. text ed. 59.50 (*1-85043-149-3*, Pub. by I B Tauris UK) St Martin.

Subhash Chandra Bose: The Springing Tiger. Hugh Toye. 1970. pap. 2.80 (*0-88253-190-5*) Ind-US Inc.

Subhasitaratnakosa. Vidyakara. Ed. by D. D. Kosambi & V. V. Gokhale. LC 57-9076. (Oriental Ser.: No. 42). 460p. 1957. 27.50 (*0-674-85380-6*) HUP.

Subheadings: A Matter of Opinion. American Society of Indexers Staff. LC 95-8853. 1995. 15.00 (*0-936547-30-8*) Am Soc Index.

***Subhuman Redneck Poems.** Les Murray. 1997. 17.00 (*0-374-27155-0*) FS&G.

Subirrigation & Controlled Drainage. H. W. Belcher & Frank M. D'Itri. 496p. 1994. 69.95 (*1-56670-139-2*, L1139) Lewis Pubs.

Subject. Bernard Lonergan. LC 68-22238. (Aquinas Lectures). (C). 1968. 15.00 (*0-87462-133-X*) Marquette.

Subject Access Systems. Milstead. 1984. text ed. 66.00 (*0-12-498120-8*) Acad Pr.

Subject Access to Visual Resources Collections: A Model for the Computer Construction of Thematic Catalogs. Karen Markey. LC 86-7658. (New Directions in Information Management Ser.: No. 11). 209p. 1986. text ed. 49.95 (*0-313-24031-0*, MSI/) Greenwood.

Subject Analysis: Principles & Procedures. Ed. by Derek Langridge. 146p. 1989. lib. bdg. 32.50 (*0-408-03031-3*) Bowker-Saur.

Subject & Agency in Psychoanalysis: Which Is to Be Master? Frances M. Moran. LC 92-48288. (Psychoanalytic Crosscurrents Ser.). 208p. (C). 1993. 40.00 (*0-8147-5482-1*) NYU Pr.

Subject & Consciousness: A Philosophical Inquiry into Self-Consciousness. Oded Balaban. LC 89-39313. 234p. (C). 1990. lib. bdg. 58.00 (*0-8476-7616-1*) Rowman.

Subject & Object in Renaissance Culture. Ed. by Margreta De Grazia et al. (Studies in Renaissance Literature & Culture). (Illus.). 360p. 1996. pap. text ed. 22.95 (*0-521-45589-8*) Cambridge U Pr.

Subject & Object in Renaissance Culture. Ed. by Margreta De Grazia et al. (Studies in Renaissance Literature & Culture: No. 8). 360p. (C). 1996. text ed. 64.95 (*0-521-45471-9*) Cambridge U Pr.

S

Subject & Psyche. 2nd rev. ed. Robert M. Doran. (Studies in Theology). 1995. pap. 25.00 (*0-87462-627-7*) Marquette.

Subject & Ruler: The Cult of the Ruling Power in Classical Antiquity: Papers Presented at a Conference Held in the University of Alberta on April 13-15, 1994, to Celebrate the 65th Anniversary of Duncan Fishwick. Ed. by Alastair Small. (JRA Supplementary Ser.: No. 17). (Illus.). 264p. (ENG, FRE & GER.). 1996. lib. bdg. 89.50 (*1-887829-17-2*) Jour Roman Arch.

Subject & Strategy. 7th ed. Eschholz. 1996. pap. text ed. 22.00 (*0-312-11528-8*); teacher ed., pap. text ed. 0.26 (*0-312-11529-6*) St Martin.

Subject & Strategy: A Rhetoric Reader. 4th ed. Ed. by Paul A. Eschholz & Alfred F. Rosa. 600p. (C). 1988. Instr's. manual. teacher ed. write for info. (*0-318-62510-5*) St Martin.

Subject & Strategy: A Rhetorical Reader. 6th ed. Ed. by Paul A. Eschholz & Alfred F. Rosa. LC 92-50045. 655p. (C). 1993. pap. text ed. 20.00 (*0-312-06541-8*) St Martin.

Subject & the Self: Lacan & American Psychoanalysis. Ed. by Judith F. Gurewich et al. 1996. pap. 27.00 (*0-7657-0016-6*) Aronson.

Subject As Action: Transformation & Totality in Narrative Aesthetics. Alan Singer. LC 93-34668. (Body in Theory: Histories of Cultural Materialism Ser.). 284p. (C). 1994. text ed. 47.50 (*0-472-10471-3*) U of Mich Pr.

Subject As Action: Transformation & Totality in Narrative Aesthetics. Alan Singer. 1995. pap. 17.95 (*0-472-08383-X*) U of Mich Pr.

Subject Authorities in the Online Environment: Papers from a Conference Program Held in San Francisco June 29, 1987. Ed. by Karen M. Drabenstott. LC 90-20824. (ALCTS Papers on Library Technical Services & Collections: No. 1). (C). 1991. pap. text ed. 10.00 (*0-8389-0558-7*, 0558-7) ALA.

Subject Bibliographies of Government Publications: A Compilation of Books, Reports, & Pamphlets Available from the U. S. Government Printing Office at the Time of Their Publication. Ed. by Pam D. Oliver. 932p. 1989. 85.00 (*1-55888-813-6*) Omnigraphics Inc.

Subject Bibliography of the History of American Higher Education. Compiled by Mark Beach. LC 83-22565. vii, 165p. 1984. text ed. 42.95 (*0-313-23276-8*, BEH/, Greenwood Pr) Greenwood.

Subject Catalog: Of the Library of the State Historical Society of Wisconsin, Madison, Wisconsin, 23 vols., Set. Charles Shetler. LC 78-161601. 1971. text ed. 2,500.00 (*0-8371-3273-8*, WSA/, Greenwood Pr) Greenwood.

Subject Catalog see Catalogs of the Scripps Institution of Oceanography Library

Subject Catalog of the Department Library. 1982. 2,060.00 (*0-8161-1347-5*) Mac Lib Ref.

Subject Catalog of the Institute of Governmental Studies Library, 26 Vols, Set. Ed. by University of California, Berkeley Staff. 1970. 2,830.00 (*0-8161-0907-9*, Hall Library) G K Hall.

Subject Catalog of the Institute of Governmental Studies Library First Supplement. (Reference Ser.). 1978. 825.00 (*0-8161-0963-X*, Hall Library) G K Hall.

Subject Catalog of the Library of the Cornell University School of Hotel Administration, 2 vols., Set. 1981. 255.00 (*0-8161-0421-2*, Hall Library) G K Hall.

Subject Catalog of the Library of the New York Academy of Medicine. New York Academy of Medicine Library Staff. 1970. 3,550.00 (*0-8161-1460-9*, Hall Library) G K Hall.

Subject Catalog of the Library of the New York Academy of Medicine, Supplement 1. New York Academy of Medicine Library Staff. 1980. suppl. ed. 600.00 (*0-8161-1273-8*, Hall Library) G K Hall.

Subject Catalog of the Royal Common Wealth Society, 7 vols. 1994. 880.00 (*0-7838-2246-4*) G K Hall.

Subject Catalog of the World War I Collection. 1970. 310.00 (*0-8161-1424-2*, Hall Library) G K Hall.

Subject Cataloging: A How-to-Do-It Workbook. Terry E. Ferl & Larry Millsap. (How-to-Do-It Ser.). 92p. 1991. 39.95 (*1-55570-099-3*) Neal-Schuman.

Subject Cataloging: Critiques & Innovations. Ed. by Sanford Berman. LC 84-10554. (Technical Services Quarterly Ser.: Vol. 2, Nos. 1-2ca). 224p. 1985. text ed. 49.95 (*0-86656-265-6*) Haworth Pr.

***Subject Cataloging Manual: Classification.** Compiled by Library of Congress, Cataloging Policy & Support Office Staff. 1992. 27.00 (*0-8444-0759-3*) Lib Congress.

Subject Cataloging Manual: Shelflisting. 2nd ed. Compiled by Library of Congress, Cataloging Policy & Support Office Staff. LC 94-41263. 1995. ring bd. 37.00 (*0-615-00423-7*) Lib Congress.

***Subject Cataloging Manual: Subject Headings, 4 vols.** 5th ed. Compiled by Library of Congress, Cataloging Policy & Support Office Staff. 1446p. 1996. 120.00 (*0-8444-0906-5*) Lib Congress.

Subject Catalogue of the House of Commons Parliamentary Papers, 1801-1900, 5 vols. Compiled by Peter Cockton. 4631p. 1988. lib. bdg. 2,089.00 (*0-85964-133-3*) Chadwyck-Healey.

Subject Classification for the Arrangement of Libraries & the Organization of Information with Tables, Indexes, Etc. For the Subdivision of Subjects. James D. Brown. 1976. lib. bdg. 250.00 (*0-8490-2715-2*) Gordon Pr.

Subject Collections, 2 vols. 7th rev. ed. Lee Ash. 2466p. 1993. 275.00 (*0-8352-3141-0*) Bowker.

***Subject Compilations of State Laws: An Annotated Bibliography.** Cheryl R. Nyberg. 1997. 126.50 (*1-889194-00-X*) Boast-Nyberg.

Subject Compilations of State Laws: Cumulative Index 1960-1990. 500p. write for info. (*0-9616293-3-9*) Boast-Nyberg.

Subject Compilations of State Laws: 1960-1979 (1981) Foster & Boast. 1981. 81.50 (*0-313-21255-4*) Boast-Nyberg.

Subject Compilations of State Laws: 1979-83 (1984) Nyberg & Boast. 1984. 75.00 (*0-313-23335-7*) Boast-Nyberg.

Subject Compilations of State Laws 1983-1985: An Annotated Bibliography. Cheryl R. Nyberg. LC 85-73774. 595p. 1986. text ed. 75.00 (*0-9616293-0-4*) Boast-Nyberg.

Subject Compilations of State Laws, 1985-1988: An Annotated Bibliography. Cheryl R. Nyberg. LC 88-93062. 544p. 1989. 80.00 (*0-9616293-1-2*) Boast-Nyberg.

Subject Compilations of State Laws, 1988-1990: An Annotated Bibliography. Cheryl R. Nyberg. 542p. 1991. 95.00 (*0-9616293-2-0*) Boast-Nyberg.

Subject Compilations of State Laws, 1990-1991: An Annotated Bibliography. Cheryl R. Nyberg. 290p. 1992. 100.00 (*0-9616293-4-7*) Boast-Nyberg.

Subject Compilations of State Laws, 1991-1992 (1993) 288p. 1993. 110.00 (*0-9616293-5-5*) Boast-Nyberg.

Subject Compilations of State Laws, 1992-1993 (1994) 265p. 1994. 110.00 (*0-9616293-6-3*) Boast-Nyberg.

Subject Compilations of State Laws, 1993-1994 (1995) 1995. 115.00 (*0-9616293-7-1*) Boast-Nyberg.

Subject Compilations of State Laws, 1994-1995 (1996) 1996. 115.00 (*0-9616293-8-X*) Boast-Nyberg.

Subject Control in Online Catalogs. Ed. by Robert P. Holley. LC 89-19953. (Cataloging & Classification Quarterly Ser.: Vol. 10, Nos. 1-2). (Illus.). 231p. 1989. text ed. 49.95 (*0-86656-793-3*) Haworth Pr.

Subject Cumulative Bibliography of Asian Studies, 1966 to 1970. 1981. 500.00 (*0-8161-1326-2*, Hall Library) G K Hall.

Subject Directory of Special Libraries, 3 vols. 13th ed. Ed. by Brigitte T. Darnay & Janice DeMaggio. 1520p. 1989. Set. 640.00 (*0-8103-5070-X*) Gale.

Subject Directory of Special Libraries, 3 vols. 14th ed. Darnay. 1990. 675.00 (*0-8103-7385-8*) Gale.

Subject Directory of Special Libraries, 3 vols. 15th ed. Kirby. 1991. 695.00 (*0-8103-7390-4*) Gale.

Subject Directory of Special Libraries, 3 vols. 16th ed. Kirby. 1992. 695.00 (*0-8103-5342-3*) Gale.

Subject Directory of Special Libraries, 3 vols., Set. 19th ed. Gwen Turecki. 1995. 785.00 (*0-8103-9110-4*) Gale.

Subject Directory of Special Libraries: Business Government Law Libraries, Vol. 1. 19th ed. Gwen Turecki. 1995. 299.00 (*0-8103-9111-2*) Gale.

Subject Directory of Special Libraries: Computer Engineering Science Libraries, Vol. 2. 19th ed. Gwen Turecki. 1995. 299.00 (*0-8103-9112-0*) Gale.

Subject Directory of Special Libraries: Health Sciences Libraries, Vol. 3. 19th ed. Gwen Turecki. 1995. 299.00 (*0-8103-9113-9*) Gale.

Subject Directory of Special Libraries & Information Centers, Vol. 1: Business, Government & Law Libraries. 17th ed. Kirby. 1993. 275.00 (*0-8103-8013-7*) Gale.

Subject Directory of Special Libraries & Information Centers 1988, 5 vols. 11th ed. Ed. by Brigitte T. Darnay. 1987. Set. 685.00 (*0-8103-4342-8*) Gale.

Subject Directory of Special Libraries & Information Centers 1988: Business & Law Libraries, Vol. 1. 11th ed. Ed. by Brigitee T. Darnay. 381p. 1987. 160.00 (*0-8103-4343-6*) Gale.

Subject Directory of Special Libraries & Information Centers 1988: Education & Information Science Libraries, Vol. 2. 11th ed. Ed. by Brigitte T. Darnay. 279p. 1987. 160.00 (*0-8103-4344-4*) Gale.

Subject Directory of Special Libraries & Information Centers 1988: Health Sciences Libraries, Vol. 3. 11th ed. Ed. by Brigitte T. Darnay. 348p. 1987. 160.00 (*0-8103-4345-2*) Gale.

Subject Directory of Special Libraries & Information Centers 1988: Science & Engineering Libraries, Vol. 5. 11th ed. Ed. by Brigitte T. Darnay. 609p. 1987. 160.00 (*0-8103-4347-9*) Gale.

Subject Directory of Special Libraries & Information Centers 1988: Social Sciences & Humanities Libraries, Vol. 4. 11th ed. Ed. by Brigitte T. Darnay. 794p. 1987. 160.00 (*0-8103-4346-0*) Gale.

Subject Directory of Special Libraries, Vol. 1, Bus.-Govt.-Law Libraries. 14th ed. Darnay. 1990. 250.00 (*0-8103-7386-6*) Gale.

Subject Directory of Special Libraries, Vol. 1: Bus.-Govt.-Law Libraries. 15th ed. Kirby. 1991. 265.00 (*0-8103-5494-2*) Gale.

Subject Directory of Special Libraries, Vol. 1: Bus.-Govt.-Law Libraries. 16th ed. Kirby. 1992. 265.00 (*0-8103-5343-1*) Gale.

Subject Directory of Special Libraries, Vol. 1: Business & Law Libraries. 12th ed. Ed. by Brigitte I. Darnay. 1988. 195.00 (*0-8103-2788-0*) Gale.

Subject Directory of Special Libraries, Vol. 1: Business, Government & Law Libraries. 13th ed. Ed. by Brigitte T. Darnay & Janice DeMaggio. 450p. 1989. 230.00 (*0-8103-5071-8*) Gale.

Subject Directory of Special Libraries, Vol. 2: Comp Engr Sci Libraries. 14th ed. Darnay. 1990. 250.00 (*0-8103-7387-4*) Gale.

Subject Directory of Special Libraries, Vol. 2: Comp. Engr. Sci. Libraries. 15th ed. Kirby. 1991. 265.00 (*0-8103-5495-0*) Gale.

Subject Directory of Special Libraries, Vol. 2: Comp. Engr. Sci Libraries. 16th ed. Kirby. 1992. 265.00 (*0-8103-5344-X*) Gale.

Subject Directory of Special Libraries, Vol. 2: Computers, Science & Engineering Libraries. 13th ed. Ed. by Brigitte T. Darnay & Janice DeMaggio. 700p. 1989. 230.00 (*0-8103-5072-6*) Gale.

Subject Directory of Special Libraries, Vol. 2: Social Science, Humanities, Education Libraries. 12th ed. Ed. by Brigitte I. Darnay. 1988. 195.00 (*0-8103-2789-9*) Gale.

Subject Directory of Special Libraries, Vol. 3: Health Sciences. 13th ed. Ed. by Brigitte T. Darnay & Janice DeMaggio. 370p. 1989. 230.00 (*0-8103-5073-4*) Gale.

Subject Directory of Special Libraries, Vol. 3: Health Sciences Libraries. 12th ed. Ed. by Brigitte I. Darnay. 1988. 195.00 (*0-8103-2790-2*) Gale.

Subject Directory of Special Libraries, Vol. 3: Health Sciences Library. 14th ed. Darnay. 1990. 250.00 (*0-8103-7388-2*) Gale.

Subject Directory of Special Libraries, Vol. 3: Health Sciences Library. 15th ed. Kirby. 1991. 265.00 (*0-8103-5496-9*) Gale.

Subject Directory of Special Libraries, Vol. 3: Health Sciences Library. 16th ed. Kirby. 1992. 265.00 (*0-8103-5345-8*) Gale.

Subject Directory of Special Libraries, Vol. 4: Science & Engineering Libraries. 12th ed. Ed. by Brigitte I. Darnay. 1988. 195.00 (*0-8103-2791-0*) Gale.

Subject Filing: A Guideline. 47p. 1988. pap. 36.00 (*0-933887-29-9*, A4546) ARMA Intl.

Subject Finds a Voice: Foucalt's Turn Towards Subjectivity. Deborah E. Cook. LC 91-39555. (Revisioning Philosophy Ser.: Vol. 11). 180p. (C). 1992. text ed. 39.95 (*0-8204-1821-8*) P Lang Pubng.

Subject for Safety for Junction Boxed for Swimming Pool Lighting Fixtures, UL 1241. 5th ed. (C). 1994. pap. text ed. 330.00 (*1-55989-606-X*) Underwrtrs Labs.

Subject Guide to Australian Books in Print. 3rd ed. 1995. write for info. (*1-875589-83-X*) D W Thorpe.

Subject Guide to Australian Books in Print. 5th ed. Ed. by John Simkin. 1993. 85.00 (*0-909532-95-8*) D W Thorpe.

Subject Guide to Australian Books in Print, 1990. 4th ed. 984p. 1990. lib. bdg. 70.00 (*0-909532-70-2*) D W Thorpe.

Subject Guide to Australian Scientific, Technical & Medical Books in Print. 3rd ed. Ed. by John Simkin. 300p. 1993. pap. 55.00 (*0-909532-94-X*) D W Thorpe.

Subject Guide to Bible Stories. G. Garland. (Illus.). 1996. 27.95 (*0-933062-03-6*) R H Sommer.

Subject Guide to Books in Print 1996-97, 5 vols. rev. ed. Bowker, R. R., Staff. 1996. 359.95 (*0-8352-3800-8*) Bowker.

Subject Guide to Books in Print 1996-97, Vol. 1. Bowker, R. R., Staff. 1996. write for info. (*0-8352-3801-6*) Bowker.

Subject Guide to Books in Print 1996-97, Vol. 2. Bowker, R. R., Staff. 1996. write for info. (*0-8352-3802-4*) Bowker.

Subject Guide to Books in Print 1996-97, Vol. 3. Bowker, R. R., Staff. 1996. write for info. (*0-8352-3803-2*) Bowker.

Subject Guide to Books in Print 1996-97, Vol. 4. Bowker, R. R., Staff. 1996. write for info. (*0-8352-3804-0*) Bowker.

Subject Guide to Books in Print 1996-97, Vol. 5. Bowker, R. R., Staff. 1996. write for info. (*0-8352-3805-9*) Bowker.

***Subject Guide to Books in Print 1997-1998, Vol. 5.** Bowker, R. R., Staff. 1997. write for info. (*0-8352-3962-4*) Bowker.

***Subject Guide to Books in Print, 1997-1998, 5 vols. Bowker, R. R., Staff. 1997. 369.95 (*0-8352-3957-8*) Bowker.**
"...as basic to libraries as shelves." --AMERICAN REFERENCE BOOKS ANNUAL. "There is no excuse for any library lacking this one." --RQ. For the questions that begin, "Are there any books on...," here's the source with more than a million answers! Indexing the more than 1.2 million nonfiction titles from BOOKS IN PRINT 1997-98 under more than 76,000 Library of Congress subject headings, this indispensable tool helps you & your patrons find the latest books on everything from gentrification to immunodiagnosis. & the 1997-98 brings you: * a stand-alone Subject Thesaurus -- listing & cross-referencing all headings from the Subject Guide for easier, more thorough researching * 1,500 new headings -- reflecting the latest trends in more than 130,000 new titles -- & 200,000 entry revisions * the same authoritative bibliographic, ordering, & publisher information found in BOOKS IN PRINT * thousands of publisher-provided annotations that summarize the books themselves. When you need the most trusted & complete research & collection development aid in the book industry, turn to SUBJECT GUIDE TO BOOKS IN PRINT 1997-98. ***Publisher Provided Annotation.***

***Subject Guide to Books in Print 1997-1998, Vol. 1.** Bowker, R. R., Staff. 1997. write for info. (*0-8352-3958-6*) Bowker.

***Subject Guide to Books in Print 1997-1998, Vol. 2.** Bowker, R. R., Staff. 1997. write for info. (*0-8352-3959-4*) Bowker.

***Subject Guide to Books in Print 1997-1998, Vol. 3.** Bowker, R. R., Staff. 1997. write for info. (*0-8352-3960-8*) Bowker.

***Subject Guide to Books in Print 1997-1998, Vol. 4.** Bowker, R. R., Staff. 1997. write for info. (*0-8352-3961-6*) Bowker.

Subject Guide to Children's Books in Print 1996. Ed. by Bowker, R. R., Staff. 1172p. 1996. 155.00 (*0-8352-3686-2*) Bowker.

***Subject Guide to Children's Books in Print, 1997.** 1000p. 1997. 159.00 (*0-8352-3869-5*) Bowker.

***Subject Guide to Children's Books in Print 1997.** Ed. by Bowker, R. R., Staff. 1997. 159.00 (*0-8352-3870-9*) Bowker.

***Subject Guide to Children's Books in Print 1998. Bowker, R. R., Staff. 1100p. 1998. 165.00 (*0-8352-3963-2*) Bowker.**
"...especially useful for...expanding collections to support new curriculum areas."--LIBRARY & INFORMATION SCIENCE ANNUAL. To aid your subject collection activities & help young library patrons research topics of interest, there's no better tool than SUBJECT GUIDE TO CHILDREN'S BOOKS IN PRINT 1998. Here, you'll discover every available fiction & nonfiction children's books in print organized by subject. Turn to the 1998 edition of SUBJECT GUIDE TO CHILDREN'S BOOKS IN PRINT when you need to: * build, update & expand children's & young adult collections * track down children's books on every subject imaginable * assist young readers with research * develop niche areas in your bookstore * choose titles for book talks or lesson plans * cut ordering time & effort with current prices, ISBNs, publishers' telephone numbers & addresses. ***Publisher Provided Annotation.***

Subject Guide to Classical Instrumental Music. Jennifer Goodenberger. LC 89-4129. 171p. 1989. 20.00 (*0-8108-2209-1*) Scarecrow.

Subject Guide to German Books in Print, 7 vols. 19th ed. Ed. by Verlag der Buchhandler-Vereinigung Staff. 12000p. 1996. 435.00 (*3-7657-1939-0*) K G Saur.

Subject Guide to Major United States Government Publications. Ellen P. Jackson. LC 68-25844. 187p. reprint ed. pap. 53.30 (*0-317-41822-X*, 2025613) Bks Demand.

Subject Guide to Microforms in Print 1994. 1450p. 1994. 325.00 (*3-598-11173-8*) K G Saur.

Subject Guide to Microforms in Print 1995. 1450p. 1995. 350.00 (*3-598-11232-7*) K G Saur.

Subject Guide to Microforms in Print 1996. Ed. by Barbara Hopkinson. 1700p. 1996. 430.00 (*3-598-11290-4*) K G Saur.

***Subject Guide to Microforms in Print '97, 2 vols.** Ed. by Barbara Hopkinson. 1997. 435.00 (*3-598-11326-9*) K G Saur.

Subject Guide to Publications of the International Labour Office 1980-85. (International Labour Bibliography Ser.: No. 1). x, 614p. (Orig.). 1987. pap. 27.00 (*92-2-106076-4*) Intl Labour Office.

Subject Guide to Raymond B. Clark's "Maryland & Delaware Genealogist" Ed. by James Dawson. 53p. (Orig.). 1991. pap. 9.75 (*0-685-57107-6*) Unicorn Bkshop.

Subject Guide to Reference Books, 1970-1975. M. Balachandran & S. Balachandran. LC 79-83698. 1980. 60.00 (*0-87650-102-1*) Pierian.

Subject Guide to Statistics in the Presidential Reports of the Brazilian Provinces, 1830-1889. Ann H. Graham. LC 76-620075. (Guides & Bibliographies Ser.: No. 9). 482p. reprint ed. pap. 137.40 (*0-685-15650-8*, 2027331) Bks Demand.

Subject Guide to U. S. Government Reference Sources. 2nd rev. ed. Gayle J. Hardy & Judith S. Robinson. LC 96-17543. 400p. 1996. lib. bdg. 45.00 (*1-56308-189-X*) Libs Unl.

Subject Guide to Women of the World. Katharine J. Phenix. LC 96-14228. 560p. 1996. 75.00 (*0-8108-3190-2*) Scarecrow.

Subject Headings, 5 vols. New York Public Library Staff. 1994. 415.00 (*0-7838-2298-7*, GK Hall) Thorndike Pr.

Subject Headings: A Practical Guide. D. J. Haykin. 1976. lib. bdg. 250.00 (*0-8490-1399-2*) Gordon Pr.

Subject Headings for African-American Materials. Lorene B. Brown. LC 95-10847. xvii, 118p. 1995. pap. text ed. 31.00 (*1-56308-252-7*); cd-rom 45.00 (*1-56308-397-3*) Libs Unl.

***Subject Headings for Children: A List of Subject Headings Used by the Library of Congress with Dewey Numbers Added.** Ed. by Lois Winkel. 500p. 1997. pap. text ed. 80.00 (*0-910608-58-X*) OCLC Forest Pr.

***Subject Headings for Children: List of Headings.** 1997. pap. text ed. 45.00 (*0-910608-62-8*) OCLC Forest Pr.

***Subject Headings for Children Vol. 2: Key Word Index.** 1997. pap. text ed. 45.00 (*0-910608-63-6*) OCLC Forest Pr.

Subject Headings for Church & Synagogue Libraries. 2nd rev. ed. Dorothy B. Kersten. (Guide Ser.: No. 8). (Illus.). 48p. 1990. reprint ed. pap. 8.25 (*0-915324-30-X*) CSLA.

Subject Headings for Real Estate Libraries. 222p. 25.00 (*0-318-15195-2*, NO. 111-855) Natl Assoc Realtors.

***Subject Headings for the Literature of Law & International Law, & Index to LC K Schedules: A Thesaurus of Law Subject Terms.** 5th ed. American Association of Law Libraries Staff. Ed. by Tillie Krieger. LC 96-33358. (AALL Publications: No. 55). xvi, 458p. 1996. 145.00 (*0-8377-0150-3*) Rothman.

Subject in Brazilian Portuguese. Solange de Azambuja Lira. 120p. (C). 1995. 39.95 (*0-8204-2763-2*) P Lang Pubng.

Subject in Question: Departmental Organization & the High School. Leslie S. Siskin & Judith W. Little. (Series on School Reform). 216p. (C). 1995. text ed. 48.00 (*0-8077-3454-3*); pap. text ed. 21.95 (*0-8077-3453-5*) Tchrs Coll.

Subject in Rimbaud: From Self to "Je" Karin J. Dillman. (American University Studies: Romance Languages & Literature: Ser. II, Vol. 23). 155p. (C). 1984. text ed. 20.00 (*0-8204-0200-1*) P Lang Pubng.

Subject Index. (CPL Bibliographies Ser.). 119p. 1979. 10.00 (*0-86602-001-2*, Sage Prdcls Pr) Sage.

***Subject Index, Alphanumerical List, Vol. 00.01.** 1340p. 1997. 66.00 (*0-8031-2467-8*, PCN01-000197-42) ASTM.

Subject Index for Papers Printed in the AWS-WRC Welding Research Supplement of the Welding Journal from 1950 through 1977. 1978. 20.00 (*0-318-18637-3*) Welding Res Coun.

Subject Index of Holy Quran. Afzalur Rahman. 19.95 (*0-933511-68-X*) Kazi Pubns.

Subject Index of Hymns in the English Hymnal & Songs of Praise. Percy Dearmer. 1973. 59.95 (*0-8490-1159-0*) Gordon Pr.

Subject Index of Research Bulletins & Monographs Issued by Federal Emergency Relief Administration & Work Progress Administration, Division of Social Research. U. S. Federal Emergency Relief Administration Staff & U. S. Works Progress Administration Staff. LC 75-45297. (U. S. Government Documents Program Ser.). (Illus.). 110p. 1976. reprint ed. text ed. 55.00 (*0-8371-8716-8*, USSP) Greenwood.

Subject Index to Eighth Circuit Social Security Disability Cases. 79p. 1988. 11.00 (*0-685-30197-4*, 43,590) NCLS Inc.

Subject Index to Feature Articles & Special Reports in Encyclopedia Yearbooks: 1975-1991. Ed. by Sheila Dilbert. 83p. (Orig.). 1992. pap. text ed. 15.00 (*0-9625739-0-6*) Infodatafacts.

Subject Index to International Labor Documentation 1957 to 1964. 1994. 165.00 (*0-7838-2215-4*) G K Hall.

Subject Index to Poetry: A Guide for Adult Readers. Ed. by Herbert Bruncken. 201p. 1998. reprint ed. lib. bdg. 38.50 (*1-55888-986-8*) Omnigraphics Inc.

Subject Index to Sources of Comparative International Statistics. 6th ed. Ed. by F. C. Pieper. 745p. 1979. 200.00 (*0-900246-23-5*) Gale.

Subject Index to the Poems of Edmund Spenser. Charles H. Whitman. (BCL1-PR English Literature Ser.). 261p. 1992. reprint ed. lib. bdg. 79.00 (*0-7812-7230-0*) Rprt Serv.

***Subject Index to the 1990 Census of Population & Housing.** Michael R. Lavin et al. 225p. (Orig.). 1997. pap. 37.95 (*0-9629586-2-X*) Epoch Bks.

Subject Indexes Probability & Statistics Combination, 1940-1984: Sections 60 & 62, 2 vols. (STAPIN Ser.: No. 40-84). pap. 139.00 (*0-8218-0145-7*, STAPIN/40/84) Am Math.

Subject Indexing: An Introductory Guide. Trudi Bellardo. 1991. student ed. 75.00 (*0-87111-388-0*) SLA.

Subject Indexing: Principles & Practices in the 90s-Proceedings Held in Lisbon, Portugal, 17-18 August 1993. Ed. by Robert P. Holey et al. 302p. 1995. 110.00 (*3-598-11251-3*) K G Saur.

Subject India: A Semester Abroad. Jennifer Ladd. LC 89-45010. 176p. 1990. pap. text ed. 7.95 (*0-933662-79-3*) Intercult Pr.

Subject Is Writing: Essays by Teachers & Students. Ed. by Wendy Bishop. LC 92-39430. 278p. 1993. pap. text ed. 24.00 (*0-86709-314-5*, 0314) Boynton Cook Pubs.

Subject Learning in the Primary Curriculum: Issues in English, Science & Mathematics. Ed. by Patricia Murphy et al. 272p. (C). 1995. pap. text ed. 22.95 (*0-415-12537-5*, C0423) Routledge.

An Asterisk (*) at the beginning of an entry indicates that the title is appearing in BIP for the first time.

Subject Matter: Reading Level 10-J. (Single Skills Series). Date not set. pap. 5.65 (*0-89061-381-8*) Jamestown Pubs.
Subject Matter: Reading Level 11-K. (Single Skills Series). Date not set. pap. 5.65 (*0-89061-387-7*) Jamestown Pubs.
Subject Matter: Reading Level 12-L. (Single Skills Series). Date not set. pap. 5.65 (*0-89061-393-1*) Jamestown Pubs.
Subject Matter: Reading Level 3-C. (Single Skills Series). Date not set. pap. 5.64 (*0-89061-364-8*) Jamestown Pubs.
Subject Matter: Reading Level 4-D. (Single Skills Series). Date not set. pap. 5.65 (*0-89061-370-2*) Jamestown Pubs.
Subject Matter: Reading Level 5-E. (Single Skills Ser.). Date not set. pap. 5.65 (*0-89061-326-5*) Jamestown Pubs.
Subject Matter: Reading Level 6-F. (Single Skills Ser.). Date not set. pap. 5.65 (*0-89070-332-9*) Jamestown Pubs.
Subject Matter: Reading Level 7-G. (Single Skills Series). Date not set. pap. 5.65 (*0-89061-338-9*) Jamestown Pubs.
Subject Matter: Reading Level 8-H. (Single Skills Series). Date not set. pap. 5.65 (*0-89061-344-3*) Jamestown Pubs.
Subject Matter: Reading Level 9-I. (Single Skills Series). Date not set. pap. 5.65 (*0-89061-375-3*) Jamestown Pubs.
Subject Matter & Abstraction in Exile. Robert Natkin. (Illus.). 56p. 1993. pap. 9.95 (*1-870626-58-3*, Pub. by Claridge Pr UK) Paul & Co Pubs.
Subject Matter in Health Education: An Analysis & Evaluation of the Contents of Some Courses of Study & Textbooks Dealing with Health & Suggestions for Using Such an Analysis. Ruth M. Strang. LC 70-177814. (Columbia University. Teachers College. Contributions to Education Ser.: No. 222). reprint ed. 37.50 (*0-404-55222-6*) AMS Pr.
Subject-Matter Index of Patents for Inventions Issued by the United States Patent Office from 1790 to 1873, Inclusive, 3 Vols., Set. Ed. by M. D. Leggett. LC 75-24110. (America in Two Centuries Ser.). 1976. reprint ed. 173.95 (*0-405-07737-8*) Ayer.
Subject-Matter Index of Patents for Inventions Issued by the United States Patent Office from 1790 to 1873, Inclusive, 3 Vols., Vol. 1. Ed. by M. D. Leggett. LC 75-24110. (America in Two Centuries Ser.). 1976. reprint ed. 58.95 (*0-405-07738-6*) Ayer.
Subject-Matter Index of Patents for Inventions Issued by the United States Patent Office from 1790 to 1873, Inclusive, 3 Vols., Vol. 2. Ed. by M. D. Leggett. LC 75-24110. (America in Two Centuries Ser.). 1976. reprint ed. 58.95 (*0-405-07739-4*) Ayer.
Subject-Matter Index of Patents for Inventions Issued by the United States Patent Office from 1790 to 1873, Inclusive, 3 Vols., Vol. 3. Ed. by M. D. Leggett. LC 75-24110. (America in Two Centuries Ser.). 1976. reprint ed. 58.95 (*0-405-07740-8*) Ayer.
Subject Matters: Classroom Activity in Math & Social Studies. Susan S. Stodolsky. 33.95p. 1988. 33.95 (*0-226-77511-9*) U Ch Pr.
***Subject Mentoring in the Secondary School.** James Arthur & Joy Davison. 192p. (C). 1997. pap. text ed. 19.95 (*0-415-14892-8*, Routledge NY) Routledge.
Subject, Object, & Other Basic Concepts of Lacanian Psychoanalysis. Bruce Fink. LC 94-49033. 272p. 1995. text ed. 39.50 (*0-691-03760-4*) Princeton U Pr.
Subject-Object Relations in Wordsworth & Lawrence. Donald Gutierrez. LC 86-25049. (Studies in Modern Literature: No. 65). 150p. reprint ed. pap. 42.80 (*0-8357-1781-X*, 2070550) Bks Demand.
Subject of Cinema. Gaston Roberge. (C). 1990. 22.50 (*0-685-49100-5*, Pub. by Seagull Bks II) S Asia.
Subject of Desire: Petrarchan Poetics & the Female Voice in Louise Labe. Deborah L. Baker. LC 96-7181. (Purdue Studies in Romance Literatures: No. 11). 240p. 1996. 34.95 (*1-55753-088-2*) Purdue U Pr.
Subject of Modernism: Narrative Alterations in the Fiction of Eliot, Conrad, Woolf, & Joyce. Tony E. Jackson. LC 94-13175. 224p. 1994. 44.50 (*0-472-10552-3*) U of Mich Pr.
Subject of Modernity. Anthony J. Cascardi. (Literature, Culture, Theory Ser.: No. 3). 296p. (C). 1992. text ed. 59.95 (*0-521-41287-0*); pap. text ed. 19.95 (*0-521-42378-3*) Cambridge U Pr.
Subject of Painting: A Selection by Paul Rogers of 9 Contemporary Painters Working in France. Text by Paul Rogers. (Illus.). 1982. pap. 20.00 (*0-905836-32-4*, Pub. by Museum Modern Art UK) St Mut.
Subject of Philosophy. Philippe Lacoue-Labarthe. Tr. by Thomas Trezise et al. LC 92-29837. (Theory & History of Literature Ser.: Vol. 83). 232p. (ENG & FRE.). (C). 1993. text ed. 19.95 (*0-8166-1697-3*); pap. text ed. 19.95 (*0-8166-1698-1*) U of Minn Pr.
Subject of Rape. Monica Chau et al. (Illus.). 80p. (Orig.). 1993. pap. 12.95 (*0-87427-089-8*) Whitney Mus.
Subject of Semiotics. Kaja Silverman. 316p. 1983. 35.00 (*0-19-503177-6*) OUP.
Subject of Semiotics. Kaja Silverman. 316p. 1984. pap. 19.95 (*0-19-503178-4*) OUP.
Subject of Tragedy. Catherine Belsey. 288p. (Orig.). 1985. 29.95 (*0-416-32700-1*, 9446); pap. text ed. 13.95 (*0-416-32710-9*, 9447) Routledge Chapman & Hall.
Subject of Violence: The Song of Roland & the Birth of the State. Peter Haidu. LC 92-33892. 1993. 39.95 (*0-253-30548-9*) Ind U Pr.
Subject-Oriented Texts: Languages for Special Purposes & Text Theory. Ed. by Hartmut Schroder. (Research in Text Theory Ser.: Vol. 16). viii, 322p. (C). 1991. lib. bdg. 126.15 (*3-11-012568-4*) De Gruyter.
Subject People & Colonial Discourses: Economic Transformation & Social Disorder in Puerto Rico, 1898-1947. Kelvin A. Santiago-Valles. LC 92-30542. (SUNY Series in Society & Culture in Latin America). (Illus.). 304p. (C). 1994. text ed. 59.50 (*0-7914-1589-9*); pap. text ed. 19.95 (*0-7914-1590-2*) State U NY Pr.
***Subject Relations: Unconscious Experience & Relational Psychoanalysis.** Naomi Rucker & Karen Lombardi. LC 97-16984. 224p. (C). 1997. pap. write for info. (*0-415-91423-X*); text ed. write for info. (*0-415-91422-1*) Routledge.
Subject Retrieval in the Seventies New Directions, an International Symposium. LC 70-183149. (Contributions in Librarianship & Information Science Ser.: No. 3). 210p. (C). 1972. text ed. 35.00 (*0-8371-6322-6*, SRS/) Greenwood.
Subject Searching in Library Catalogs: Before & After the Introduction of Online Catalogs. Karen Markey. LC 84-7226. (Library, Information, & Computer Science Ser.: No. 4). (Illus.). 192p. (Orig.). 1984. pap. 21.00 (*0-933418-54-X*) OCLC Online Comp.
***Subject, Theme & Agent in Modern Standard Arabic.** Hussein F. Raof. 288p. 1997. 75.00 (*0-7007-0672-0*, Pub. by Curzon Press UK) Paul & Co Pubs.
Subject to Change. Lois Gould. 224p. 1988. 16.95 (*0-374-27154-2*) FS&G.
***Subject to Change: Guerrilla Television Revisited.** Deirdre Boyle. (Illus.). 304p. 1997. pap. 16.95 (*0-19-511054-4*, 650401Q) OUP.
***Subject to Change: Guerrilla Television Revisited.** Deirdre Boyle. (Illus.). 304p. 1997. 45.00 (*0-19-504334-0*) OUP.
Subject to Change: New Composition Instructors' Theory & Practice. Christine Farris. Ed. by Marcia Tarr. LC 96-52059. (Written Language Ser.). 208p. (Orig.). (C). 1996. text ed. 45.00 (*1-57273-028-5*); pap. text ed. 18.95 (*1-57273-029-3*) Hampton Pr NJ.
Subject to Change: Women's Writing--Feminist Reading. Nancy Miller. (Gender & Culture Ser.). 185p. 1989. pap. text ed. 16.50 (*0-231-06661-9*) Col U Pr.
***Subject to Criticism: Essays.** Lola L. Tostevin. pap. 15.95 (*1-55128-025-6*, Pub. by Mercury Pr CN) LPC InBook.
Subject to Famine: Food Crises & Economic Change in Western India, 1860-1920. Michelle B. McAlpin. LC 82-61376. 304p. 1983. reprint ed. pap. 86.70 (*0-7837-9385-5*, 2060129) Bks Demand.
Subject to Fits. Geoffrey Young. 1980. pap. 10.00 (*0-935724-04-4*) Figures.
Subject to History: Ideology, Class, Gender. Ed. by David Simpson. LC 91-13592. 256p. 1991. 39.95 (*0-8014-2561-1*); pap. 15.95 (*0-8014-9791-4*) Cornell U Pr.
***Subject to Negotiation: Reading Feminist Criticism & American Women's Fictions.** Elaine N. Orr. LC 96-44391. 204p. 1997. text ed. 32.50 (*0-8139-1715-8*) U Pr of Va.
Subject to Others: British Women Writers & Colonial Slavery, 1670-1834. Moira Ferguson. 432p. (C). 1992. pap. 19.95 (*0-415-90476-5*, A6317, Routledge NY) Routledge.
Subject to Ourselves: Social Theory, Psychoanalysis & Postmodernity. Anthony Elliott. 175p. 1996. 52.95 (*0-7456-1422-1*, Pub. by Polity Pr UK); pap. 21.95 (*0-7456-1423-X*, Pub. by Polity Pr UK) Blackwell Pubs.
Subject to Solution: Problems in U. S.-Cuban Relations. Ed. by Wayne S. Smith & E. Morales Dominguez. LC 88-14162. 158p. 1988. lib. bdg. 35.00 (*1-55587-127-5*) Lynne Rienner.
Subject to Whose Authority? Multiple Readings of Romans 13. Jan Botha. LC 93-39944. (Emory Studies in Early Christianity). 274p. 1994. 39.95 (*1-55540-922-9*, 700604) Scholars Pr GA.
***Subject Tonight Is Love: 60 Wild & Sweet Poems of Hafiz.** Daniel Ladinsky. LC 96-92272. 86p. (Orig.). 1996. pap. 10.00 (*0-9657637-0-6*) Pmpkn House.
***Subject with No Object: Strategies for Nominalistic Interpretation of Mathematics.** John P. Burgess & Gideon Rosen. (Illus.). 272p. 1997. 45.00 (*0-19-823615-8*) OUP.
Subjected to Science: Human Experimentation in America Before the Second World War. Susan E. Lederer. (Henry E. Siegrist Series in the History of Medicine). (Illus.). 192p. 1995. text ed. 32.95 (*0-8018-4820-2*) Johns Hopkins.
***Subjected to Science: Human Experimentation in America Before the Second World War.** Susan E. Lederer. 1997. pap. text ed. 15.95 (*0-8018-5709-0*) Johns Hopkins.
Subjecthood & Related Notions: A Contrastive Study of English, German, & Japanese. Itsuki Koya. LC 92-5597. (International Cooper Series in English Language & Literature). 236p. 1992. 48.00 (*3-7643-2740-5*); 42.50 (*0-8176-2740-5*) Birkhauser.
Subjection & Subjectivity: Psychoanalytic Feminism & Moral Philosophy. Diane Tietjens-Meyers. LC 94-20584. (Thinking Gender Ser.). 256p. (C). 1994. pap. 16.95 (*0-415-90508-7*, A6583, Routledge NY); text ed. 62.95 (*0-415-90471-4*, A6579, Routledge NY) Routledge.
Subjection of Women. John Stuart Mill. LC 88-1762. (HPC Classics Ser.). 128p. (C). 1988. pap. text ed. 4.95 (*0-87220-054-X*); lib. bdg. 24.95 (*0-87220-055-8*) Hackett Pub.
Subjection of Women. John Stuart Mill. Ed. by Sue Mansfield. LC 76-3318. (Crofts Classics Ser.). 136p. (C). 1980. pap. text ed. write for info. (*0-88295-116-5*) Harlan Davidson.
Subjection of Women. John Stuart Mill. LC 85-63407. (Great Books in Philosophy). 106p. 1986. pap. 4.95 (*0-87975-335-8*) Prometheus Bks.
Subjection of Women. John Stuart Mill. 1970. pap. 8.95 (*0-262-63038-9*) MIT Pr.
***Subjection of Women.** John S. Mill. LC 96-39387. (Dover Thrift Editions Ser.). 192p. 1997. reprint ed. pap. text ed. 2.00 (*0-486-29601-6*) Dover.
***Subjection of Women: Contemporary Responses to John Stuart Mill.** Ed. & Intro. by Andrew Pyle. (Key Issues Ser.). 340p. 1995. write for info. (*1-85506-409-X*); pap. write for info. (*1-85506-408-1*) Bks Intl VA.
Subjective Agency: A Theory of First Person Expressivity & Its Social Implications. Charles Altieri. 352p. 1994. 60.95 (*1-55786-129-3*) Blackwell Pubs.
Subjective & Objective Evaluation of Sound: International Symposium. E. Ozimek. 320p. 1990. text ed. 104.00 (*981-02-0281-4*) World Scientific Pub.
Subjective Communication. Jose Silva. 3.95 (*0-913343-49-8*) Inst Psych Inc.
Subjective Criticism. David Bleich. LC 77-12968. 320p. 1981. pap. 15.95 (*0-8018-2093-6*) Johns Hopkins.
Subjective Equilibrium Theory of the Farm Household. C. Nakajima. 302p. 1986. 136.25 (*0-444-42646-9*) Elsevier.
Subjective Evolution of Consciousness: The Play of the Sweet Absolute. B. R. Sridhar. 1993. 14.95 (*0-945475-04-7*) Mandala Media.
Subjective Experience of Admission to a Nursing Unit: An Interpretive Study. Ed. by Helen Baker & Alan Pearson. (Research Monographs: No. 6). 1995. pap. 20.00 (*0-7300-1518-1*, Pub. by Deakin Univ AT) St Mut.
Subjective Meaning & Culture: An Assessment Through Word Associations. Lorand B. Szalay & James Deese. LC 78-15561. 176p. reprint ed. pap. 50.20 (*0-8357-4210-5*, 2036987) Bks Demand.
Subjective Probability. Ed. by George Wright & Peter Ayton. 600p. 1994. text ed. 71.95 (*0-471-94443-2*) Wiley.
Subjective Reasoning. John L. Pollock. (Philosophical Studies in Philosophy: No. 8). 266p. 1976. lib. bdg. 104.50 (*90-277-0701-4*, D Reidel) Kluwer Ac.
Subjective Side of Politics. Margo Adair & Sharon Howell. (Illus.). (Orig.). 1988. 3.50 (*1-882098-23-4*) Tools Change.
Subjective Side of Science. Ian I. Mitroff. (Systems Inquiry Ser.). 328p. 1983. reprint ed. pap. 15.95 (*0-914105-21-3*) Intersystems Pubns.
Subjective Side of Strategy Making: Future Orientations & Perceptions of Executives. T. K. Das. LC 86-12344. (Illus.). 292p. 1986. text ed. 49.95 (*0-275-92340-1*, C2340, Praeger Pubs) Greenwood.
Subjective Theory of Organism. James A. Diefenbeck. 1995. 38.50 (*0-7618-0077-8*) U Pr of Amer.
Subjective Truth. Charles Blakemore. 209p. 1993. pap. 7.95 (*1-55523-517-4*) Winston-Derek.
Subjective View: Secondary Qualities & Indexical Thoughts. Colin McGinn. 172p. 1983. pap. 22.00 (*0-19-824695-1*) OUP.
Subjective Vision: Lucinda Bunnen Collections of Photographs. A. D. Coleman. LC 83-81149. (Illus.). 64p. 1983. pap. 6.95 (*0-939802-17-1*) High Mus Art.
Subjective Well-Being. R. Nagpal & H. Sell. (SEARO Regional Health Papers: No. 7). 161p. 1985. pap. text ed. 10.00 (*92-9022-176-3*, 1580007) World Health.
Subjective Well-Being: An Interdisciplinary Perspective. Ed. by F. Strack et al. (International Series in Experimental Social Psychology: Vol. 21). (Illus.). 300p. 1991. text ed. 96.00 (*0-08-037264-3*, CRC Reprint) Franklin.
Subjective Well-Being among Different Age Groups. A. Regula Herzog et al. 115p. (Orig.). 1982. pap. 14.00 (*0-87944-283-2*) Inst Soc Res.
Subjective Well-Being of Young Adults: Trends & Relationships. Willard L. Rodgers & Jerald G. Bachman. LC 88-9455. (ISR Research Report Ser.). 256p. (Orig.). 1988. pap. text ed. 20.00 (*0-87944-323-5*) Inst Soc Res.
Subjectively: Subjectivity & Literature from the Romantics to the Present Day. Ed. by Philip Shaw & Peter Stockwell. 1991. text ed. 49.00 (*0-86187-180-4*) St Martin.
Subjectivism, Intelligibility & Economic Understanding. Ed. by Israel M. Kirzner. LC 85-20831. 336p. (C). 1986. text ed. 40.00 (*0-8147-4589-X*) NYU Pr.
Subjectivities: A History of Self-Representation in Britain, 1832-1920. Regenia Gagnier. (Illus.). 336p. 1991. 48.00 (*0-19-506096-2*) OUP.
***Subjectivity & Intersubjectivity in Modern Philosophy & Psychoanalysis: A Study of Sartre, Binswanger, Lacan & Haberman.** Roger Frie. LC 96-38798. 256p. 1997. 57.50 (*0-8476-8415-6*); pap. 22.95 (*0-8476-8416-4*) Rowman.
Subjectivity & Method in Psychology: Gender, Meaning & Science. Wendy Hollway. (Gender & Psychology Ser.). 160p. (C). 1989. text ed. 69.95 (*0-8039-8207-0*); pap. text ed. 22.95 (*0-8039-8208-9*) Sage.
Subjectivity & Objectivity: Further Aspects of Psychological Growth (An Appendix to Homosexuality: The Psychology of the Creative Process) Paul Rosenfels. LC 86-143018. (Ninth Street Center Monographs). (Orig.). 1974. pap. 3.95 (*0-932961-00-2*) Ninth St Ctr.
Subjectivity & Reduction: An Introduction to the Mind-Body Problem. Barbara Hannan. LC 93-49474. (C). 1994. pap. text ed. 17.95 (*0-8133-1997-8*) Westview.
Subjectivity & Religious Belief. Stephens Evans. LC 82-40062. 238p. (C). 1982. reprint ed. pap. text ed. 23.50 (*0-8191-2665-9*) U Pr of Amer.
Subjectivity & Subjectivisation: Linguistic Perspectives. Ed. by Dieter Stein & Susan Wright. 240p. (C). 1996. text ed. 57.95 (*0-521-47039-0*) Cambridge U Pr.
Subjectivity & Subjugation in Seventeenth-Century Drama & Prose: The Family Romance of French Classicism. Mitchell Greenberg. (Cambridge Studies in French: No. 36). 263p. (C). 1992. text ed. 64.95 (*0-521-41293-5*) Cambridge U Pr.
Subjectivity & the Signs of Love: Discourse, Desire & the Emergence of Modernity in Honore' D'Urfe's "L'Astree" James M. Hembree. LC 95-40412. (American University Studies II: No. 214). 248p. (C). 1997. text ed. 43.95 (*0-8204-2817-5*) P Lang Pubng.
Subjectivity, Identity, & the Body: Women's Autobiographical Practices in the Twentieth Century. Sidonie Smith. LC 92-25022. 240p. 1993. 35.00 (*0-253-35286-X*); pap. 13.95 (*0-253-20789-4*, MB-789) Ind U Pr.
***Subjectivity, Identity, & the Body: Women's Autobiographical Practices in the Twentieth Century.** Sidonie Smith. LC 92-25022. 238p. pap. 67.90 (*0-608-05044-X*, 2059705) Bks Demand.
***Subjectivity in English: Generative Grammar vs. the Cognitive Theory of Epistemic Grounding.** Peter Pelyvas. LC 96-7171. (MetaLinguistica Ser.: Bd. 3). 208p. 1996. pap. 42.95 (*0-8204-2955-4*, PE1369) P Lang Pubng.
***Subjectivity in English: Generative Grammar vs. the Cognitive Theory of Epistemic Grounding.** Peter Pelyvas. Ed. by Andras Kertesz. (Metalinguistica, Debrecen Studies in Linguistics: Vol. 3). (Illus.). 208p. 1996. 42.95 (*3-631-49534-X*) P Lang Pubng.
Subjectivity in Grammar & Discourse: Theoretical Considerations & a Case Study of Japanese Spoken Discourse. Shoichi Iwasaki. LC 92-43831. (Studies in Discourse & Grammar: No. 2). xii, 152p. 1992. 53.00 (*1-55619-368-8*) Benjamins North Am.
Subjectivity in Troubadour Poetry. Sarah Kay. (Cambridge Studies in French: No. 31). 288p. (C). 1990. text ed. 69.95 (*0-521-37238-0*) Cambridge U Pr.
Subjectivity, Information, Systems: Introduction to a Theory of Relativistic Cybernetics, Vol. 12. Guy M. Jumarie. (Studies in Cybernetics: Vol. 12). xviii, 356p. 1986. text ed. 161.00 (*2-88124-011-9*) Gordon & Breach.
Subjectivity, Realism, & Postmodernism: The Recovery of the World in Recent Philosophy. Frank B. Farrell. 336p. (C). 1994. text ed. 59.95 (*0-521-44416-0*) Cambridge U Pr.
Subjectivity, Realism & Postmodernism: The Recovery of the World in Recent Philosophy. Frank B. Farrell. 304p. 1996. pap. text ed. 17.95 (*0-521-56832-3*) Cambridge U Pr.
Subjects & Citizens: Nation, Race, & Gender from Oroonoko to Anita Hill. Ed. by Michael Moon & Cathy N. Davidson. LC 95-10297. 496p. 1995. text ed. 49.95 (*0-8223-1529-7*) Duke.
Subjects & Citizens: Nation, Race, & Gender from Oroonoko to Anita Hill. Ed. by Michael Moon & Cathy N. Davidson. LC 95-10297. 496p. 1995. pap. text ed. 17.95 (*0-8223-1539-4*) Duke.
Subjects & Predicables. John Heintz. LC 73-81805. (Janua Linguarum, Ser. Minor: No. 79). 103p. 1973. pap. text ed. 69.25 (*90-279-2539-9*) Mouton.
Subjects, Citizens, Aliens, & Others: Nationality & Immigration Law. Ann Dummett & Andrew Nichol. (Law in Context Ser.). 336p. (C). 1994. text ed. 50.00 (*0-297-82025-7*); pap. text ed. 25.95 (*0-297-82026-5*) Northwestern U Pr.
***Subjects in Engine Oil Rheology & Tribology.** 1996. 74.00 (*1-56091-866-7*, SP-1209) Soc Auto Engineers.
Subjects in Japanese & English. rev. ed. Yoshihisa Kitagawa. LC 93-38246. (Outstanding Dissertations in Linguistics Ser.). 250p. 1994. text ed. 20.00 (*0-8153-1685-2*) Garland.
Subjects of Analysis. Thomas H. Ogden. LC 93-43113. 240p. 1994. 40.00 (*1-56821-185-6*) Aronson.
Subjects of Analysis. Thomas H. Ogden. 1996. pap. text ed. 25.00 (*1-56821-803-6*) Aronson.
Subjects of Choice: The Process & Management of Pupil & Student Choice. Andrew Stables. LC 94-42938. (Cassell Education Ser.). (Illus.). 208p. 1995. 60.00 (*0-304-32930-4*); pap. 22.50 (*0-304-32928-2*) Cassell.
***Subjects of Deceit: A Phenomenology of Lying.** Alison L. Brown. 224p. (C). 1998. text ed. 59.50 (*0-7914-3673-X*) State U NY Pr.
***Subjects of Deceit: A Phenomenology of Lying.** Alison L. Brown. 224p. (C). 1998. pap. text ed. 19.95 (*0-7914-3674-8*) State U NY Pr.
Subjects of Experience. E. J. Lowe. LC 95-15748. (Studies in Philosophy). 238p. (C). 1996. text ed. 49.95 (*0-521-47503-1*) Cambridge U Pr.
Subjects of Slavery, Agents of Change: Women & Power in Gothic Novels & Slave Narratives... Kari J. Winter. LC 91-32103. (C). 1995. pap. text ed. 16.00 (*0-8203-1788-8*) U of Ga Pr.
Subjects on the World's Stage: Essays on British Literature of the Middle Ages & the Renaissance. Ed. by David G. Allen & Robert A. White. LC 94-42534. (Illus.). 320p. 1995. 43.50 (*0-87413-544-3*) U Delaware Pr.
Subjects or Citizens? The Mennonite Experience in Canada, 1870-1925. Adolf Ens. 280p. 1995. pap. 28.00 (*0-7766-0390-6*, Pub. by Univ Ottawa Pr CN) Paul & Co Pubs.
Subject's Tragedy: Political Poetics, Feminist Theory & Drama. Linda Kintz. 240p. (C). 1992. text ed. 39.50 (*0-472-10385-7*) U of Mich Pr.
Subjects Without Selves: Transitional Texts in Modern Fiction. Gabriele Schwab. LC 93-11692. (Studies in Comparative Literature: No. 43). 298p. 1994. text ed. 36.50 (*0-674-85381-4*) HUP.

S

An Asterisk (*) at the beginning of an entry indicates that the title is appearing in BIP for the first time.

Subjects Worthy of Fame: Essays on Commonwealth Literature in Honour of H. H. Anniah Gowda. A. L. McLeod. 176p. 1989. text ed. 20.00 (81-207-0949-7, Pub. by Sterling Pubs II) Apt Bks.

***Subjekt der Geschichte.** Michael Gans. (Studien und Materialien Zur Geschichte der Philosophie: Band 16). 287p. (GER.). 1993. write for info. (3-487-09767-2) G Olms Pubs.

Subjektive Aesthetik. Joachim Jung. (New Studies in Aesthetics: Vol. 1). 462p. (C). 1987. text ed. 58.00 (0-8204-0519-1) P Lang Pubng.

Subjonctif. 3rd rev. ed. Jacques Cellard. 88p. (FRE.). 1983. pap. 19.95 (0-8288-3354-0) Fr & Eur.

Subjugated Knowledges: Journalism, Gender, & Literature in the Nineteenth Century. Laurel Brake. LC 93-31425. (C). 1994. 45.00 (0-8147-1218-5); pap. 16.00 (0-8147-1219-3) NYU Pr.

Sublanguage: Studies on Language in Restricted Semantic Domains. Ed. by Richard Kittredge & John Lehrberger. (Foundations of Communication & Cognition Ser.). 240p. (C). 1982. text ed. 86.95 (3-11-008244-6) De Gruyter.

Sublethal & Chronic Toxic Effects of Pollutants on Freshwater Fish. R. Muller & R. Lloyd. 371p. 1994. 125.00 (0-85238-207-3) Blackwell Sci.

Sublette Revisited: Stability & Change in a Rural Kansas Community After a Quarter of a Century. William E. Mays. 142p. 1968. pap. 4.95 (0-912598-03-4) Florham.

Sublime. Jonathan Holden. 70p. (Orig.). 1996. pap. 10.95 (1-57441-020-2) UNTX Pr.

Sublime: A Reader in British Eighteenth-Century Aesthetic Theory. Ed. by Andrew Ashfield & Peter De Bolla. 320p. (C). 1996. pap. text ed. 19.95 (0-521-39582-8) Cambridge U Pr.

Sublime: A Reader in British Eighteenth-Century Aesthetic Theory. Ed. by Andrew Ashfield & Peter DeBolla. 320p. (C). 1996. text ed. 59.95 (0-521-39545-3) Cambridge U Pr.

***Sublime Affirmations.** John T. Ferrier. 64p. Date not set. pap. text ed. 6.00 (0-900235-67-5) Order Of The Cross.

Sublime Crime: Fascination, Failure, and Form in Literature of the Enlightenment. Stephanie B. Hammer. LC 92-40551. 240p. (C). 1993. 29.95 (0-8093-1831-8) S Ill U Pr.

Sublime du Quotidien. Herman Parret. (AS-6 Ser.). 286p. (Orig.). (FRE.). 1988. pap. 65.00 (90-272-2266-5) Benjamins North Am.

***Sublime Enjoyment: On the Perverse Motive in American Literature.** Dennis A. Foster. LC 96-40352. (Studies in American Literature & Culture: Vol. 112). 192p. (C). 1997. write for info. (0-521-58437-X) Cambridge U Pr.

***Sublime Figure of History: Aesthetics & Politics in Twentieth-Century China.** Ban Wang. LC 96-48432. 1997. write for info. (0-8047-2846-1) Stanford U Pr.

Sublime Is Now: The Early Work of Barnett Newman. Jeremy Strick. LC 94-65996. (Illus.). 108p. (Orig.). 1994. pap. write for info. (1-878283-42-1) PaceWildenstein.

Sublime Object of Ideology. Slavoj Zizek. 336p. (C). 1989. text ed. 60.00 (0-86091-256-6, A3757, Pub. by Vrso UK); pap. text ed. 19.00 (0-86091-971-4, A3761, Pub. by Vrso UK) Norton.

Sublime Pleasures of Tragedy: A Study of Critical Theory from Dennis to Keats. W. P. Albrecht. LC 75-11896. x, 206p. 1975. 25.00 (0-7006-0135-X) U Pr of KS.

Sublime Puritan: Milton & the Victorians. James G. Nelson. LC 74-8794. (Illus.). 209p. 1974. reprint ed. text ed. 38.50 (0-8371-7586-0, NESP, Greenwood Pr) Greenwood.

***Sublime Revelation: Al-Fath ar-Rabbani.** Shaykh Jilani. 512p. 1996. pap. 29.00 (0-614-21354-1, 1442) Kazi Pubns.

Sublime Savage: James Macpherson & the Poems of Ossian. Fiona J. Stafford. 240p. 1989. 45.00 (0-85224-569-6, Pub. by Edinburgh U Pr UK) Col U Pr.

Sublime Savage: James Macpherson & the Poems of Ossian. Fiona J. Stafford. 208p. 1990. pap. text ed. 20.00 (0-85224-609-9, Pub. by Edinburgh U Pr UK) Col U Pr.

Sublime Smoke: Bold New Flavors Inspired by the Old Art of Barbecue. Bill Jamison & Cheryl A. Jamison. LC 95-48197. (Illus.). 400p. 1996. 29.95 (1-55832-106-3); pap. 16.95 (1-55832-107-1) Harvard Common Pr.

Sublime Thoughts - Situating Emerson & Thoreau in the American Market. Richard F. Teichgraeber, 3rd. LC 94-36088. (New Studies in American Intellectual & Cultural History). 320p. 1995. text ed. 39.95 (0-8018-5000-2) Johns Hopkins.

Sublime Void: On the Memory of the Imagination. Bart Cassiman et al. (Illus.). 280p. 55.00 (90-5544-002-7) Dist Art Pubs.

Sublimeness of Literary Art. J. David Thomas, Jr. LC 94-60447. 59p. 1995. pap. 7.95 (1-55523-696-0) Winston-Derek.

Subliminal: The New Channel to Personal Power. Lee M. Shulman et al. (Illus.). (Orig.). 1990. pap. 9.95 (0-931137-14-4) Infobooks.

Subliminal Ad-Ventures in Erotic Art. Wilson B. Key. (Illus.). 240p. (C). 1992. reprint ed. pap. 14.95 (0-8283-1951-0) Branden Pub Co.

Subliminal Communication: Emperor's Clothes or Panacea? rev. ed. Eldon Taylor. Ed. by Norma Anderson & Suzanne Brady. (Illus.). 144p. 1990. pap. 8.95 (0-940699-01-X) R K Bks.

Subliminal Consciousness. Frederic W. Myers. LC 75-37305. (Occult Ser.). 1976. reprint ed. 58.95 (0-405-07952-4) Ayer.

Subliminal Learning: An Eclectic Approach. Eldon Taylor. Ed. by Norma Anderson et al. (Illus.). 206p. (Orig.). (C). 1988. pap. 12.95 (0-940699-00-1) R K Bks.

Subliminal Power Persuasion. Craig E. Soderholm. 230p. 1995. pap. text ed. write for info. (0-9642241-1-9) Perf Dyn CA.

***Subliminal Power Persuasion, Vol. 1.** Soderholm. 1997. mass mkt. write for info. (0-312-96154-5) St Martin.

Subliminal Technology: Unlocking the Power of Your Own Mind. rev. ed. Eldon Taylor. 30p. 1996. 3.95 (1-55978-037-1) R K Bks.

Subliminal Treatment Procedures: A Clinician's Guide. Paul G. Swingle. LC 90-3857. 192p. 1992. pap. 23.70 (0-943158-77-X, STPBP, Prof Resc Pr) Pro Resource.

Sublimity in the Novels of Ann Radcliffe. Malcolm Ware. (Essays & Studies on English Language & Literature: Vol. 25). (Orig.). 1963. pap. 25.00 (0-8115-0223-6) Periodicals Srv.

Sublimity of Faith. Frank S. Murray. LC 81-81770. (Illus.). 952p. 1982. 25.00 (0-910840-20-2) Kingdom.

Sublunary. Jorge H. Aigla. (Red Ser.). (Illus.). 32p. (Orig.). 6.00 (0-938631-07-1) Pennywhistle Pr.

Submanifolds & Isometric Immersions. Marcos Dajczer et al. LC 90-61664. (Mathematics Lectures: No. 13). viii, 173p. 1990. 30.00 (0-914098-22-5) Publish or Perish.

***Submanifolds of Affine Spaces: An Introduction to Affine Differential Geometry.** 250p. 1998. lib. bdg. 31.00 (981-02-2725-6) World Scientific Pub.

Submarine. Tom Clancy. 352p. 1993. pap. 14.95 (0-425-13873-9) Berkley Pub.

Submarine. large type ed. John Wingate. 416p. 1984. 25.99 (0-7089-1135-8) Ulverscroft.

***Submarine Admiral: From Battlewagons to Ballistic Missiles.** Date not set. 18.95 (0-252-06675-8) U of Ill Pr.

Submarine Admiral: From Battlewagons to Ballistic Missiles. I. J. Galantin. LC 94-42971. (Illus.). 376p. 1995. 26.95 (0-252-02160-6) U of Ill Pr.

Submarine Alliance. John Lambert & David Hill. LC 86-60258. (Anatomy of the Ship Ser.). (Illus.). 96p. 1986. 39.95 (0-87021-688-0) Naval Inst Pr.

***Submarine Badges & Insignia of the World: An Illustrated Reference for Collectors.** Pete Prichard. (Illus.). 136p. 1997. 45.00 (0-7643-0255-8) Schiffer.

Submarine Cave Bivalvia from the Ryukyu Islands. Itaru Hayami & Tomoki Kase. 133p. 1994. 125.00 (0-86008-510-4, Pub. by U of Tokyo JA) Col U Pr.

Submarine Commander. Paul R. Schratz. 400p. 1990. mass mkt. 5.99 (0-671-68466-3) PB.

Submarine Commander: A Story of World War II & Korea. Paul R. Schratz. LC 88-19035. 344p. 1988. 30.00 (0-8131-1661-9) U Pr of Ky.

Submarine Design for the Twenty First Century. Stan Zimmerman. 1993. 274.00 (0-935453-60-1) Pasha Pubns.

Submarine Diary: The Silent Stalking of Japan. Corwin Mendenhall. LC 90-40440. (Bluejacket Paperback Ser.). (Illus.). 308p. 1995. pap. 15.95 (1-55750-582-9) Naval Inst Pr.

***Submarine Fiber Optics Technology & Market Opportunities, 1996.** 279p. 1993. 2,995.00 (0-614-18353-7, IGIC-13) Info Gatekeepers.

***Submarine Insignia of the World.** W. M. Thornton. (Illus.). 192p. 1997. 32.95 (1-55750-843-7) Naval Inst Pr.

Submarine Landslides: Selected Studies in the U. S. Exclusive Economic Zone. D. C. Twichell. (Illus.). 204p. (Orig.). (C). 1994. pap. text ed. 50.00 (0-7881-1246-5) DIANE Pub.

Submarine Pitch. Matt Christopher. (Illus.). 144p. (J). (gr. 3-6). 1992. mass mkt. 3.95 (0-316-14250-6) Little.

Submarine Telecommunication & Power Cables. Cyril C. Barnes. LC 78-304105. (IEE Monograph Ser.: Vol. 20). 222p. reprint ed. pap. 63.30 (0-8357-7041-9, 2033456) Bks Demand.

Submarine Telegraphs: Their History, Construction & Working. Charles D. Bright. LC 74-4669. (Telecommunications Ser.). (Illus.). 744p. 1974. reprint ed. 63.95 (0-405-06035-1) Ayer.

Submarine Versus U Boat. Maritime Books Staff. (C). 1986. text ed. 130.00 (0-685-38782-8, Pub. by Maritime Bks UK) St Mut.

Submarine Wahoo. Gary Davis. 1994. pap. 5.95 (0-382-24753-1, Crstwood Hse) Silver Burdett Pr.

Submarine Wahoo. Gary Davis. LC 94-7102. (Those Daring Machines Ser.). (J). 1994. pap. 5.95 (0-382-24765-5, Crstwood Hse) Silver Burdett Pr.

Submarine Warfare in the Arctic: Option or Illusion? Mark Sakitt. (Occasional Paper of Center for International Security & Arms Control, Stanford University Ser.). 93p. (Orig.). 1988. pap. 12.00 (0-935371-19-2) CFISAC.

Submariner. John O. Coote. 256p. 1991. 22.95 (0-393-03074-1) Norton.

Submariner's World. P. R. Compton-Hall. 144p. 1987. 49.00 (0-85937-303-7, Pub. by K Mason Pubns Ltd UK) St Mut.

Submarines. Tony Gibbons. (Modern Military Techniques Ser.). (Illus.). 48p. (J). (gr. 5 up). 1987. pap. 4.95 (0-8225-9542-7, Lerner Publctns); lib. bdg. 14.95 (0-8225-1383-8, Lerner Publctns) Lerner Group.

***Submarines.** Michael Green. LC 97-5908. (Land & Sea Ser.). (J). 1998. write for info. (1-56065-555-0) Capstone Pr.

Submarines. J. B. Hervey. Ed. by G. Till. (Sea Power Ser.: Vol. 7). (Illus.). 290p. 1994. 50.00 (0-08-040970-9, Pub. by Brasseys UK); pap. 30.00 (0-08-040971-7, Pub. by Brasseys UK) Brasseys Inc.

Submarines. D. White. (Great Bks.). (Illus.). 48p. (J). (gr. 3-8). 1989. lib. bdg. 18.60 (0-86592-452-X) Rourke Corp.

Submarines: Hunters, Killers & Boomers. Consumer Guide Editors. 1990. 9.99 (0-517-03149-3) Random Hse Value.

***Submarines: Leviathans of the Deep.** Timothy L. Francis. LC 97-13129. 1997. write for info. (1-56799-427-X, MetroBooks) M Friedman Pub Grp Inc.

***Submarines & Dirigibles.** Bernie Zubrowski. (J). Date not set. lib. bdg. write for info. (0-688-13918-3, Morrow Junior) Morrow.

Submarines & Other Underwater Craft. Harvey Weiss. LC 89-37614. (Illus.). 64p. (J). (gr. 3-7). 1990. lib. bdg. 13.89 (0-690-04761-4, Crowell Jr Bks) HarpC Child Bks.

***Submarines of September: The Nixon Administration & a Soviet Submarine Base in Cuba.** Patrick J. Haney. (Pew Case Studies in International Affairs). 50p. (C). 1996. text ed. 3.50 (1-56927-372-3) Geo U Inst Dplmcy.

Submarines of the Russian & Soviet Navies, 1718-1990. Norman Polmar & Jurrien Noot. LC 90-6687. (Illus.). 400p. 1991. 65.00 (0-87021-570-1) Naval Inst Pr.

Submarines of the Tsarist Navy: A Pictorial History. Ed. by I. D. Spassky et al. Tr. by Norman Polmar. LC 95-44039. (Illus.). 144p. 1997. 42.50 (1-55750-771-6) Naval Inst Pr.

Submarines, Sacrifice, & Success in the Civil War: A History of the Confederate Submarine Hunley. Mark K. Ragan. LC 95-69553. (Illus.). 240p. 1995. 24.95 (1-886391-04-1); pap. 14.95 (1-886391-05-X) Narwhal Pr.

Submarines with Wings. Terry Treadwell. (Illus.). 192p. (Orig.). 1997. pap. 24.95 (1-880090-29-5) Galde Pr.

Submarinos-Submarines. (Pequena Biblioteca-Little Library). (Illus.). 32p. (SPA.). (J). (gr. 1-4). 1995. 2.95 (1-85697-559-2, Kingfisher LKC) LKC.

Submerged-Arc Welding. Ed. by P. T. Houldcroft. (Illus.). 106p. 1989. pap. 78.00 (1-85573-002-2, Pub. by Woodhead Pubng UK) Am Educ Systs.

Submerged Lands of Texas, Corpus Christi Area: Sediments, Geochemistry, Benthic Macroinvertebrates & Associated Wetlands. W. A. White et al. (Illus.). 154p. 1983. pap. 12.50 (0-318-03338-0) Bur Econ Geology.

Submerged Lands of Texas, Kingsville Area: Sediments, Geochemistry, Benthic Macroinvertebrates, & Associated Wetlands. W. A. White et al. (Illus.). 137p. 1989. pap. 12.50 (0-317-03104-X) Bur Econ Geology.

Submerged Lands of Texas, Port Lavaca Area: Sediments, Geochemistry, Benthic Macroinvertebrates, & Associated Wetlands. W. A. White et al. (Illus.). 165p. 1989. pap. 12.50 (0-317-03105-8) Bur Econ Geology.

Submerged Nations: An Introduction to Theory & Bibliography on One Major Case Study. Vatro Murvar. 93p. 1982. pap. 7.50 (0-931633-01-X) Fnd Soc Stdy.

Submerged Valley & Other Stories. Manoj Das. 159p. (Orig.). 1986. pap. 6.95 (0-941524-26-4) Lotus Light.

Submerging Coasts: The Effects of a Rising Sea Level on Coastal Environments. Eric C. Bird. LC 92-30175. (Coastal Morphology & Research Ser.). 184p. 1993. pap. text ed. 95.00 (0-471-93807-6) Wiley.

Submerging Republican Majority: The 1972 Election in South Dakota. Alan L. Clem. 1973. 1.00 (1-55614-009-6) U of SD Gov Res Bur.

Submerging Villages: Problems & Prospects. Vidyut Joshi. (C). 1987. 11.50 (81-202-0191-4, Pub. by Ajanta II) S Asia.

Submersible Technology & Adapting to Change. Ed. by Society for Underwater Technology Staff. (C). 1988. lib. bdg. 191.00 (0-86010-896-1, Pub. by Graham & Trotman UK) Kluwer Ac.

Submersible Vehicle Systems Design. Ed. by E. Eugene Allmendinger. (Illus.). 425p. 1990. 140.00 (0-614-06721-9) Soc Naval Arch.

***Submersibles & Marine Technologies in Russia's Far East & Siberia.** unabridged ed. Brad Mooney. (WTEC Panel Reports). (Illus.). 139p. (Orig.). 1996. pap. write for info. (1-883712-41-6) Intl Tech Res.

Submicron Multiphase Materials. Ed. by R. Baney et al. (Materials Research Society Symposium Proceedings Ser.: Vol. 274). 185p. 1992. text ed. 66.00 (1-55899-169-7) Materials Res.

Submillimetre Astronomy: Proceedings of the Kona Symposium On Millimetre & Submillimetre Astronomy, Held at Kona, Hawaii, October 3-6, 1988. Ed. by Graeme D. Watt & Adrian S. Webster. (C). 1990. lib. bdg. 137.50 (0-7923-0614-7) Kluwer Ac.

Submillimetre Wave Astronomy. John E. Beckman & John P. Phillips. LC 82-4487. (Illus.). 370p. 1982. text ed. 64.95 (0-521-24733-0) Cambridge U Pr.

Submission & Evaluation of Proposals for Private Power Generation Projects in Developing Countries. Peter A. Cordukes. LC 94-24838. (Discussion Papers: 250). 1994. 8.95 (0-8213-2957-X, 12957) World Bank.

Submission Holds. Key Lincoln. (Orig.). 1994. mass mkt. 4.95 (1-56333-266-3, Badboy) Masquerade.

Submission Reflex. Michael E. Hall & Patricia Dawson. (Illus.). 192p. (Orig.). 1996. pap. 19.95 (1-56072-347-5) Nova Sci Pubs.

Submission to God: Jonah 2. Gary Purdy. (Inter Acta Ser.). (Illus.). 6p. (C). 1994. teacher ed., ring bd. 1.25 (1-885702-47-7, 741-025t, Inter Acta); student ed., ring bd. 3.25 (1-885702-46-9, 741-025s, Inter Acta) WSN Pr.

Submissions to the Royal Commission on Criminal Procedure. NCCL Staff. 1979. 25.00 (0-317-54922-7, Pub. by NCCL UK) St Mut.

Submitting an Idea. 7p. 1974. pap. 1.00 (0-685-42906-7, 537-0012) Amer Bar Assn.

Submitting to a Sinning Husband. Wanda Burkhart. 64p. 1984. pap. 2.95 (0-88144-042-6) Christian Pub.

Submitting to Freedom: The Religious Vision of William James. Bennett Ramsey. (Religion in America Ser.). 208p. 1993. 35.00 (0-19-507426-2) OUP.

Submitting to God's Call: Samuel, David, Isaiah, Ananias, Jesus. Sara Buswell. (Challenge Bible Study Guides Ser.). 112p. (gr. 10). 1993. pap. 5.99 (0-8010-1045-4) Baker Bks.

***Submodular Functions & Electrical Networks.** H. Narayanan. LC 97-4313. (Annals of Discrete Mathematics Ser.). 680p. 1997. write for info. (0-444-82523-1) Elsevier.

Submodular Functions & Optimization. S. Fujishige. (Annals of Discrete Mathematics Ser.: No. 47). 270p. 1991. 131.50 (0-444-88556-0, North Holland) Elsevier.

Submolecular Biology & Cancer. CIBA Foundation Staff. LC 79-14324. (CIBA Foundation Symposium: New Ser.: No. 67). 360p. reprint ed. pap. 102.60 (0-317-29763-5, 2022187) Bks Demand.

Submoveable Subsea Technology. (Advances in Underwater Technology & Offshore Engineering Ser.: Vol. 5). (Illus.). 500p. 1986. lib. bdg. 195.00 (0-86010-771-X) G & T Inc.

Submuloc Show - Columbus Wohs: A Visual Commentary on the Columbus Quincentennial from the Perspective of America's First People. Lucy R. Lippard et al. Ed. by Carla A. Roberts. LC 92-71363. (Illus.). 80p. (Orig.). 1992. pap. 12.50 (1-881388-04-2) Atlatl.

Subnational Movements in South Asia. Ed. by Subrata K. Mitra. LC 94-35982. 224p. (C). 1996. text ed. 59.00 (0-8133-2093-3) Westview.

Subnational Politics in the 1980's: Organization, Reorganization & Economic Development. Ed. by Louis A. Picard & Raphael Zariski. LC 86-20479. 276p. 1986. text ed. 59.95 (0-275-92314-2, C2314, Praeger Pubs) Greenwood.

Subnormal Operators & Representations of Algebras of Bounded Analytic Functions & Other Uniform Algebras. T. Miller et al. LC 86-17381. (Memoirs of the American Mathematical Society Ser.: Vol. 63/354). 125p. 1986. pap. text ed. 26.00 (0-8218-2415-5, MEMO/63/354) Am Math.

Subordinate Sex: A History of Attitudes Towards Women. Vern L. Bullough & Bonnie Bullough. LC 72-91079. 383p. reprint ed. pap. 109.20 (0-317-09711-3, 2014930) Bks Demand.

Subordinated Sex: A History of Attitudes Toward Women. rev. ed. Vern L. Bullough et al. LC 87-23292. 488p. 1988. 50.00 (0-8203-1002-6); pap. 24.95 (0-8203-1003-4) U of Ga Pr.

Subordination: Feminism & Social Theory. Clare Burton. 146p. 1985. text ed. 39.95 (0-86861-718-0, Pub. by Allen Unwin AT); pap. text ed. 18.95 (0-86861-710-5, Pub. by Allen Unwin AT) Paul & Co Pubs.

***Subordination & Equivalence: The Nature & Role of Woman in Augustine & Thomas Aquinas.** Kari E. Borresen. 376p. 1995. reprint ed. pap. 39.00 (90-390-0231-2, Pub. by KOK Pharos NE) Eisenbrauns.

Subordination & Other Topics in Latin. Gualtiero Calboli. LC 89-247. (Studies in Language Companion: Vol. 17). xxix, 691p. (FRE.). 1989. 127.00 (90-272-3018-8) Benjamins North Am.

Subpersonalities: The People Inside Us. John Rowan. 256p. (C). 1990. pap. 17.95 (0-415-04329-8) Routledge.

Subpoemas. Lennart Bruce. 68p. 1974. pap. 6.00 (0-915572-06-0) Panjandrum.

Subpoena George Bush. A. Caleb & D. E. Slaton. 372p. 1993. pap. 18.95 (1-880365-60-X) Prof Pr NC.

Subquantum Kinetics: The Alchemy of Creation. Paul A. LaViolette. (Illus.). 208p. (Orig.). (C). 1994. pap. 15.00 (0-9642025-0-6) Starburst Pubns.

Subramanyan, K. G. Fairy Tales of Oxford & Other Paintings. Contrib. by David Elliott. (Illus.). 1988. pap. 20.00 (0-905836-61-8, Pub. by Museum Modern Art UK) St Mut.

***Subrarachnoid Hemmorage.** Ed. by Yanagihara et al. 755p. 1997. write for info. (0-8247-9519-9) Dekker.

Subrecursion: Functions & Hierarchies. H. E. Rose. (Oxford Logic Guides Ser.). 206p. 1984. 45.00 (0-19-853189-3) OUP.

Subrecursive Programming Systems: Complexity & Succinctness. James S. Royer & John Case. LC 94-26443. (Progress in Theoretical Computer Science Ser.). viii, 252p. 1994. 54.50 (0-8176-3767-2) Birkhauser.

Subregional Security Cooperation in the Third World. William T. Tow. LC 90-36363. 158p. 1990. lib. bdg. 37.00 (1-55587-201-8) Lynne Rienner.

Subregular Germ of Orbital Integrals. Hales. (Memoirs Ser.: No. 476). 142p. 1992. pap. 28.00 (0-8218-2539-9, MEMO/99/476) Am Math.

Subrogation in Insurance Theory & Practice. Horn. (C). 1964. 11.95 (0-256-00651-2) Irwin.

***Subsaharan Africa in the 1990s: Challenges to Democracy & Development.** Ed. by Rukhsana A. Siddiqui. LC 96-44681. 232p. 1997. text ed. 59.95 (0-275-95142-1, Praeger Pubs) Greenwood.

Subsaharan Africa Market Atlas. (Research Reports: No. Q169). 1994. 495.00 (0-85058-780-8) Economist Intell.

Subscribe Now: Building Arts Audiences Through Dynamic Subscription Promotion. 3rd ed. Danny Newman. LC 77-81452. (Illus.). 300p. (C). 1977. pap. 13.95 (0-930452-01-1) Theatre Comm.

Subscriber Guidebook for Employee Leasing Services. T. Joe Willey. LC 88-83864. 130p. 1988. 495.00 (0-944308-00-7) Aegis Consulting.

Subscriber Loop Signaling & Transmission Handbook: Analog. Whitham D. Reeve. LC 91-19685. (Telecommunications Handbook Ser.). (Illus.). 304p. (C). 1992. text ed. 69.95 (0-87942-274-2, PC0268-3) Inst Electrical.

Subscriber Loop Signaling & Transmission Handbook: Digital. Whitham D. Reeve. (Telecommunications Handbook Series). 672p. 1995. 79.95 (0-7803-0440-3, PC3376) Inst Electrical.

Subsea Blowout Preventers & Marine Riser Systems. (Rotary Drilling Ser.: Unit III, Lesson 4). (Illus.). 57p. (Orig.). 1978. pap. text ed. 14.00 (0-88698-052-6, 2-30410) PETEX.

S

An Asterisk (*) at the beginning of an entry indicates that the title is appearing in BIP for the first time.

Subsea Control & Data Acquisition, Vol. 22. Ed. by Society for Underwater Technology Staff. (C). 1990. lib. bdg. 118.50 (*0-7923-0698-8*) Kluwer Ac.

Subsea Control & Data Acquisition for Oil & Gas Production Systems. Ed. by Society for Underwater Technology Staff. LC 94-7723. (Advances in Underwater Technology, Ocean Science, & Offshore Engineering Ser.: Vol. 32). 272p. (C). 1994. lib. bdg. 134.00 (*0-7923-2779-9*) Kluwer Ac.

Subsea International '93: Low Cost Subsea Production Systems. LC 93-18651. (Advances in Underwater Technology, Ocean Science, & Offshore Engineering Ser.: Vol. 30). 180p. 1993. lib. bdg. 92.50 (*0-7923-2243-6*) Kluwer Ac.

Subsea Production Systems - Can Engineering Reduce Pipeline Costs? OCS Publishing Group Staff. 1989. 125.00 (*90-6314-562-4*, Pub. by Lorne & MacLean Marine) St Mut.

Subsea Production Systems - Can Engineering Reduce Pipeline Costs? D. A. Phillips. (C). 1989. 95.00 (*0-89771-731-7*, Pub. by Lorne & MacLean Marine) St Mut.

Subseciva Groningana: Studies in Roman & Byzantine Law, No. V. Bernard H. Stolte. ix, 94p. 1992. pap. 30.00 (*90-6980-058-6*, Pub. by Egbert Forsten NE) Benjamins North Am.

Subseciva Groningana I. Bernard H. Stolte. 142p. (Orig.). (ENG & GER.). 1984. pap. 30.00 (*90-6088-086-2*, Pub. by Boumas Boekhuis NE) Benjamins North Am.

Subseciva Groningana II. Bernard H. Stolte. iv, 146p. (FRE, GER & ITA.). (C). 1985. pap. 32.00 (*90-6980-006-3*, Pub. by Egbert Forsten NE) Benjamins North Am.

Subseciva Groningana III: Studies in Byzantine Law: Proceedings of the Symposium on the Occasion of the Completion of a New Edition of the Basilica, Groningen, June 1-4, 1988. Bernard H. Stolte. x, 154p. (Orig.). (FRE & GER.). 1989. pap. 34.00 (*90-6980-025-X*, Pub. by Egbert Forsten NE) Benjamins North Am.

Subseciva Groningana IV: Studies in Roman & Byzantine Law. Bernard H. Stolte. x, 274p. (Orig.). (ENG, GER & ITA.). 1990. pap. 39.50 (*90-6980-040-3*, Pub. by Egbert Forsten NE) Benjamins North Am.

Subsequent Materials Guide. Martha Miner et al. 7p. 1993. teacher ed. 2.00 (*1-881986-18-7*) Demibach Eds.

Subset FORTRAN-77. Max W. Durgin. (Illus.). 320p. (Orig.). 1983. pap. text ed. 24.95 (*0-935920-11-0*, Ntl Pubs Blck) P-H.

Subset Selection in Regression. Alan J. Miller. (Monographs on Statistics & Applied Probability: No. 40). 224p. (gr. 13). 1990. text ed. 58.95 (*0-412-35380-6*, A3897) Chapman & Hall.

Subsidence: Occurrence, Prediction, & Control. Barry N. Whittaker & D. J. Reddish. (Developments in Geotechnical Engineering Ser.: No. 56). 528p. 1989. 234.00 (*0-444-87274-4*) Elsevier.

Subsidence Due to Fluid Withdrawal. E. C. Donaldson et al. (Developments in Petroleum Science Ser.: Vol. 41). 516p. 1995. 215.00 (*0-444-81820-0*) Elsevier.

Subsidence, Landslip & Ground Heave: With Special Reference to Insurance. G. H. Edwards. (C). 1988. 200.00 (*0-685-32688-8*, Pub. by Witherby & Co UK) St Mut.

Subsidiaries see Northwest's Own Railway - Spokane, Portland & Seattle Railway & Its Subsidiaries

***Subsidiaries of German Firms in the U. S. 1996/97: Tochtergesellschaften Deutscher Unternehmen in den U.S.A.** 22th ed. Ed. by Sven Oehme. 248p. 1996. pap. 100.00 (*0-86640-059-1*) German Am Chamber.

***Subsidies.** Stewart. 1993. pap. text ed. 67.50 (*90-6544-754-7*) Kluwer Ac.

***Subsidies & Competition in the European Union: Generale Bank Lectures 1994-1995.** Ed. by J. Stuyck et al. (Law Ser.: Vol. 6). 92p. (Orig.). 1996. pap. 42.50 (*90-6186-759-2*, Pub. by Leuven Univ BE) Coronet Bks.

Subsidies & Countervailing Measures: Critical Issues for the Uruguay Round. Ed. by Bela Balassa. (Discussion Paper Ser.: No. 55). 170p. 1989. 10.95 (*0-8213-1239-1*, 20055) World Bank.

Subsidies & Environment: Exploring the Linkages. OECD Staff. 218p. (Orig.). 1996. pap. 33.00 (*92-64-14822-1*, Pub. by Org for Econ FR) OECD.

Subsidies & International Trade. Ed. by J. H. Bourgeois. 240p. 1991. pap. 72.00 (*90-6544-529-3*) Kluwer Law Tax Pubs.

Subsidies for the Theatre: A Study of the Central European System of Financing Drama, Opera & Ballet. Wallace Dace. LC 72-84841. 188p. 1973. pap. 7.95 (*0-686-05610-8*) AG Pr.

Subsidies in International Trade. Gary C. Hufbauer & Joanna S. Erb. LC 83-12825. 283p. (Orig.). 1984. 35.00 (*0-88132-004-8*) Inst Intl Eco.

Subsidies to Higher Education: The Issues. Ed. by Howard P. Tuckman & Edward L. Whalen. LC 80-18241. 320p. 1980. text ed. 55.00 (*0-275-90562-4*, C0562, Praeger Pubs) Greenwood.

Subsidized Muse: Public Support for the Arts in the United States. Dick Mietzer. (Modern Revivals in Economics Ser.). 300p. 1993. 59.95 (*0-7512-0142-1*, Pub. by Gregg Pub UK) Ashgate Pub Co.

Subsidized Programs for Low Income People. Ed. by Lloyd Hogan & Vincent R. McDonald. LC 80-53746. 192p. (C). 1981. pap. text ed. 21.95 (*0-87855-864-0*) Transaction Pubs.

Subsidizing Inefficiency: A Study of State Aid & Local Government Productivity. Richard H. Silkman. LC 84-26628. 124p. 1985. text ed. 47.95 (*0-275-90164-5*, C0164, Praeger Pubs) Greenwood.

Subsidizing Shelter: The Relationship Between Welfare Reform & Housing Assistance. Sandra J. Newman & Ann B. Schnare. LC 87-34026. (Urban Institute Report: No. 88-1). (Illus.). 206p. (Orig.). (C). 1988. pap. text ed. 23.00 (*0-87766-414-5*) Urban Inst.

Subsidizing the European Producer. Ed. by Ronald Gerritse. 224p. 1992. text ed. 54.00 (*0-86187-864-7*) St Martin.

Subsidy from Nature. Anthony B. Anderson et al. (Illus.). 256p. 1991. text ed. 37.50 (*0-231-07222-8*) Col U Pr.

***Subsidy Regulation & State Transformation in North America, the GATT & the EU.** Robert O'Brien. LC 97-7120. (International Political Economy Ser.). 1997. write for info. (*0-312-17513-2*) St Martin.

Subsistence Agriculture in Melanesia, 2 vols., 1. Jacques Barrau. (BMB Ser.). 1974. reprint ed. 25.00 (*0-527-02327-2*) Periodicals Srv.

Subsistence Agriculture in Melanesia, 2 vols., 2. Jacques Barrau. (BMB Ser.). 1974. reprint ed. 25.00 (*0-527-02331-0*) Periodicals Srv.

Subsistence & Stone Tool Technology: An Old World Perspective. Bradley Vierra. LC 95-78005. (Anthropological Research Papers: No. 47). (Illus.). xiv, 283p. 1995. pap. 30.00 (*0-936249-12-9*) AZ Univ ARP.

Subsistence & Survival: Rural Ecology in the Pacific. Ed. by Timothy P. Bayliss-Smith & Richard G. Feachem. 1978. text ed. 197.00 (*0-12-083250-X*) Acad Pr.

Subsistence & the North Slope Inupiat: The Effects of Energy Development. John A. Kruse. (ISER Reports: No. 56). 45p. 1982. pap. 6.50 (*0-88353-034-1*) U Alaska Inst Res.

***Subsistence to Supermarket: Food & Agricultural Transformation in South-East Asia.** 396p. 37.95 (*0-644-35093-8*, Pub. by Aust Gov Pub AT) Aubrey Bks.

Subsistence, Trade, & Social Change in Early Bronze Age Palestine. Douglas L. Esse. LC 90-62583. (Studies in Ancient Oriental Civilization: No. 50). (Illus.). xiv, 219p. 1991. pap. 30.00 (*0-918986-66-4*) Orientl Inst Pr IT.

Subsoil Management Techniques. B. A. Stewart. 256p. 1994. 79.95 (*1-56670-020-5*, L1020) Lewis Pubs.

Subsonic Airplane Performance. Amnon Katz. LC 94-32096. 200p. 1994. 29.00 (*1-56091-522-6*, R-142) Soc Auto Engineers.

Subspace Identification for Linear Systems: Theory-Implementation-Applications. Peter Van Overschee. 272p. (C). 1996. lib. bdg. 105.00 (*0-7923-9717-7*) Kluwer Ac.

Substainable Development: Changing Production Patterns, Social Equity & the Environment. 146p. 1991. 17.50 (*92-1-121166-2*, E.91.II.G.5) UN.

Substance: Its Nature & Existence. Joshua Hoffman & Gary S. Rosenkrantz. LC 96-1506. (Problems of Philosophy Ser.). 240p. (C). 1997. pap. 18.95 (*0-415-14032-3*) Routledge.

***Substance: Its Nature & Existence.** Gary S. Rosenkrantz. 240p. (C). 1997. text ed. 65.00 (*0-415-11250-8*) Routledge.

***Substance Abuse.** Joseph W. Sora. LC 97-24825. (Reference Shelf Ser.). 1997. write for info. (*0-8242-0917-6*) Wilson.

Substance Abuse. 3rd ed. Marilynn Bobst. 224p. (C). 1993. pap. 49.95 (*1-878025-51-1*) Western Schls.

Substance Abuse: A Comprehensive Textbook. 2nd ed. Joyce H. Lowinson et al. (Illus.). 1136p. 1992. text ed. 142.00 (*0-683-05211-X*) Williams & Wilkins.

***Substance Abuse: A Comprehensive Textbook.** 3rd ed. Joyce H. Lowinson. LC 96-43039. 1997. write for info. (*0-683-18179-3*) Williams & Wilkins.

Substance Abuse: A Guide to Workplace Issues. American Society for Industrial Security Staff & Norton, O.P. Information Resources Center Staff. 154p. (Orig.). 1990. pap. 35.00 (*1-887056-01-7*) Am Soc Indus Secur.

Substance Abuse: A Multidimensional Assessment & Treatment Approach. Penelope A. Moyers. LC 88-43456. (Illus.). 216p. (C). 1992. pap. text ed. 24.00 (*1-55642-084-6*) SLACK Inc.

Substance Abuse: A Self Teaching Guide for Health Professionals. American Academy of Pediatrics Staff. 193p. 1988. pap. 44.95 (*0-910761-20-5*) Am Acad Pediat.

Substance Abuse: Information for School Counselors, Social Workers, Therapists & Counselors. Gary L. Fisher. LC 95-26504. 384p. 1996. 46.00 (*0-205-16447-1*) Allyn.

Substance Abuse: Pharmacologic, Developmental & Clinical Perspectives. 2nd ed. Gerald A. Bennett. 1991. text ed. 43.50 (*0-8273-4205-5*) Delmar.

Substance Abuse: Prevention & Treatment. Nancy K. Mello. (Encyclopedia of Psychoactive Drugs Ser.: No. 2). (YA). (gr. 7 up). 1988. pap. 8.95 (*0-7910-0807-X*); lib. bdg. 19.95 (*1-55546-219-7*) Chelsea Hse.

Substance Abuse: Special Needs of Racial - Ethnic Minorities. Ed. by Marian M. Pettengill & Pamela A. Schumann. 52p. (Orig.). 1992. pap. 7.00 (*0-685-62294-0*) Midwest Alliance Nursing.

Substance Abuse: The Nation's Number One Health Problem. Brandeis University, Institute for Health Policy Staff. (Key Indicators for Policy Ser.). (Illus.). 68p. (Orig.). 1993. pap. write for info. (*0-942054-08-3*) R W Johnson Found.

Substance Abuse Accounts Auditor. Jack Rudman. (Career Examination Ser.: C-3478). 1994. pap. 29.95 (*0-8373-3478-0*) Nat Learn.

Substance Abuse Among Children & Adolescents: Its Nature, Extent, and Effects from Conception to Adulthood. Ann M. Pagliaro & Louis A. Pagliaro. LC 95-25496. 512p. 1996. text ed. 49.95 (*0-471-58042-2*) Wiley.

Substance Abuse among Ethnic Minorities in America: A Critical, Annotated Bibliography. Howard M. Rebach et al. LC 91-45032. (Library of Sociology: Vol. 20). 480p. 1992. text ed. 76.00 (*0-8153-0066-2*, SS#737) Garland.

Substance Abuse among Women & Parents. James Colliver et al. (Illus.). 62p. (Orig.). (C). 1996. pap. text ed. 25.00 (*0-7881-2746-2*) DIANE Pub.

Substance Abuse & Drugs. 2nd rev. ed. Ed. by Joan Cochran et al. 132p. (Orig.). 1994. pap. text ed. 55.00 (*1-879772-03-5*) Health Studies.

Substance Abuse & Employee Rehabilitation. Robert Thompson. LC 90-2629. 511p. 1990. reprint ed. pap. 145.70 (*0-608-00708-0*, 2061481) Bks Demand.

Substance Abuse & Gang Violence. Ed. by Richard C. Cervantes. (Focus Editions Ser.: Vol. 147). (Illus.). 208p. (C). 1992. 54.00 (*0-8039-4283-4*); pap. 24.95 (*0-8039-4284-2*) Sage.

Substance Abuse & Its Prevention. Mary L. Jones & Patrick Jones. (Family Forum Library Ser.). 16p. 1992. 1.95 (*1-56688-048-3*) Bur For At-Risk.

***Substance Abuse & Mental Health Statistics Sourcebook.** Ed. by Beatrice A. Rouse. (Illus.). 193p. (Orig.). 1996. pap. 35.00 (*0-7881-2985-6*) DIANE Pub.

Substance Abuse & Physical Disability. Ed. by Allen W. Heinemann. LC 92-1443. (Illus.). 270p. 1993. lib. bdg. 49.95 (*1-56024-289-2*) Haworth Pr.

Substance Abuse & Physical Disability. Allen W. Heinemann. 1994. pap. 19.95 (*1-56024-290-6*) Haworth Pr.

Substance Abuse & Psychopathology. Ed. by Arthur I. Alterman. (Applied Clinical Psychology Ser.). 412p. 1985. 80.00 (*0-306-41849-5*, Plenum Pr) Plenum.

Substance Abuse & Psychopathology. Ed. by Steven M. Mirin. LC 84-6291. (Clinical Insights Ser.). 167p. reprint ed. pap. 47.60 (*0-8357-7819-3*, 2036191) Bks Demand.

Substance Abuse & Rehabilitation. Benshoff. (Counseling Ser.). Date not set. text ed. 43.95 (*0-534-34223-X*) Brooks-Cole.

Substance Abuse & the Law. Arbetman. Date not set. pap. text ed. 6.25 (*0-314-78363-6*) West Pub.

Substance Abuse & the New Road to Recovery: A Practioner's Guide. Glenn D. Walters. LC 97-6610. 217p. 1996. 54.95 (*1-56032-427-9*); pap. 24.95 (*1-56032-428-7*) Hemisp Pub.

Substance Abuse As Symptom: A Psychoanalytic Critique of Treatment Approaches & the Cultural Beliefs That Sustain Them. Louis Berger. 372p. 1991. text ed. 39.95 (*0-88163-102-7*) Analytic Pr.

***Substance Abuse Counseling.** Smith & Stevens. 1997. pap. text ed. 38.00 (*0-02-412532-6*) Macmillan.

Substance Abuse Counseling: An Individualized Approach. Judith A. Lewis et al. LC 87-24618. 281p. (C). 1987. text ed. 35.95 (*0-534-08448-6*) Brooks-Cole.

Substance Abuse Counseling: An Individualized Approach. 2nd ed. Judith A. Lewis et al. LC 93-8054. 243p. 1994. text ed. 55.95 (*0-534-20053-2*) Brooks-Cole.

Substance Abuse Counselor. Jack Rudman. (Career Examination Ser.: C-3563). 1994. pap. 29.95 (*0-8373-3563-9*) Nat Learn.

Substance Abuse Curriculum Development in Family Medicine: An Instructor's Manual in Two Parts. 111p. (Orig.). (C). 1994. pap. text ed. 30.00 (*0-7881-0273-7*) DIANE Pub.

Substance Abuse Disorders in Clinical Practice. 2nd ed. Edward C. Senay. 1989. write for info. (*0-8151-7712-7*, Yr Bk Med Pubs) Mosby Yr Bk.

Substance Abuse During Pregnancy & Childhood. Ed. by Ronald R. Watson. LC 94-44482. (Drug & Alcohol Abuse Reviews Ser.: No. 8). 126p. 1995. 59.50 (*0-89603-295-7*) Humana.

Substance Abuse Education: A Manual for Developing Outreach Programs for Parents & Guardians. (Illus.). 99p. (Orig.). (C). 1992. pap. text ed. 20.00 (*1-56806-139-0*) DIANE Pub.

Substance Abuse Education for Nursing: A Model Curriculum, 3 vols. Ed. by Madeline Naegle. 1992. pap. write for info. (*0-685-56350-2*) Natl League Nurse.

Substance Abuse Education for Nursing: A Model Curriculum, 3 vols., Vol. I. Ed. by Madeline Naegle. 624p. 1992. pap. 39.95 (*0-88737-523-5*) Natl League Nurse.

Substance Abuse Education for Nursing: A Model Curriculum, 3 vols., Vol. II. Ed. by Madeline Naegle. 688p. 1992. pap. 49.95 (*0-88737-545-6*) Natl League Nurse.

Substance Abuse Education for Nursing: A Model Curriculum, 3 vols., Vol. III. Ed. by Madeline Naegle. 544p. 1992. pap. 49.95 (*0-88737-546-4*) Natl League Nurse.

Substance Abuse Funding. 1993. 70.00 (*0-937925-88-8*, SUB) Capitol Publns.

Substance Abuse, Homicide & Violent Behavior. Gary Forrest & Robert Gordon. LC 88-5787. 256p. 1991. text ed. 29.95 (*0-89876-154-9*) Gardner Pr.

Substance Abuse I: Drug Abuse. Ed. by Joan Nordquist. (Contemporary Social Issues: A Bibliographic Ser.: No. 16). 64p. (Orig.). (C). 1989. pap. 15.00 (*0-937855-31-6*) Ref Rsch Serv.

Substance Abuse II: Alcohol Abuse: A Bibliography. Ed. by Joan Nordquist. (Contemporary Social Issues: A Bibliographic Ser.: No. 17). 60p. (Orig.). 1990. pap. 15.00 (*0-937855-32-4*) Ref Rsch Serv.

Substance Abuse in Adolescents & Young Adults: A Guide to Treatment. Joseph K. Nowinski. (C). 1990. 29.95 (*0-393-70097-6*) Norton.

Substance Abuse in Children & Adolescents: Intervention & Evaluation. Steven P. Schinke et al. (Developmental Clinical Psychology & Psychiatry Ser.: Vol. 22). (Illus.). 112p. 1991. 39.95 (*0-8039-3748-2*); pap. 17.95 (*0-8039-3749-0*) Sage.

Substance Abuse in Sport: The Realities. 2nd ed. U. S. S. A. (United States Sports Academy) Staff. 176p. (C). 1992. per. 25.95 (*0-8403-7723-1*) Kendall-Hunt.

Substance Abuse in the Family: The Worker & the Corporate Response. (Special Report Series on Work & Family: No. 47). 32p. 1991. 35.00 (*1-55871-269-0*, BSP230) BNA Plus.

Substance Abuse in the Workplace. Reginald L. Campbell & R. Everett Langford. 224p. 1995. 59.95 (*0-87371-131-9*, L131) Lewis Pubs.

Substance Abuse in the Workplace: An Employer Perspective. 69p. 1987. pap. 7.00 (*0-939900-30-0*, PB43) Soc Human Resc Mgmt.

***Substance Abuse Monitoring System, 1996: Minnesota.** (Illus.). 58p. (Orig.). (C). 1996. pap. 20.00 (*0-7881-3725-5*) DIANE Pub.

***Substance Abuse on Campus: A Handbook for College & University Personnel.** Ed. by P. Clayton Rivers & Elsie R. Shore. (Greenwood Educators' Reference Collection Ser.). 1998. text ed. write for info. (*0-313-29310-4*, Greenwood Pr) Greenwood.

Substance Abuse Prevention Activities. Patricia R. Toner. LC 93-14842. (Just for the Health of It Ser.: Unit 6). 1993. pap. 18.95 (*0-87628-879-4*) Ctr Appl Res.

Substance Abuse Prevention Activities for Secondary Students: Ready-to-Use Lessons, Fact Sheets, & Resources for Grades 7-12. Patricia Gerne, Jr. & Timothy Gerne. 256p. 1991. pap. 27.95 (*0-13-876707-6*, 710704) P-H.

Substance Abuse Prevention & Treatment Programs. (YMCA Program Discovery Ser.: Vol. 2, No. 1). 88p. (Orig.). 1991. pap. text ed. 18.00 (*0-87322-324-1*, 5116, YMCA USA) Human Kinetics.

Substance Abuse Prevention Coordinator. Jack Rudman. (Career Examination Ser.: C-3750). 1994. pap. 34.95 (*0-8373-3750-X*) Nat Learn.

Substance Abuse Prevention Handbook. William Callison et al. LC 95-60050. 387p. 1995. pap. text ed. 34.95 (*1-56676-238-3*) Technomic.

Substance Abuse Problems. Sidney Cohen. LC 80-21280. 392p. 1981. text ed. 49.95 (*0-917724-18-6*); pap. text ed. 24.95 (*0-917724-22-4*) Haworth Pr.

Substance Abuse Problems & Programs in Newark: A Needs Assessment for Newark's Fighting Back Initiative. Patricia A. Ebener et al. LC 93-21520. 1994. pap. text ed. 13.00 (*0-8330-1420-X*, MR-282-BGC/DPRC) Rand Corp.

Substance Abuse Problems, Vol. 2: New Issues for the 1980s. Sidney Cohen. LC 80-21280. 323p. 1985. pap. text ed. 24.95 (*0-86656-369-5*) Haworth Pr.

Substance Abuse Problems, Vol. 2: New Issues for the 1980s. Sidney Cohen. LC 80-21280. 323p. 1985. text ed. 49.95 (*0-86656-368-7*) Haworth Pr.

Substance Abuse Program Specialist. Jack Rudman. (Career Examination Ser.: C-3336). 1994. pap. 29.95 (*0-8373-3336-9*) Nat Learn.

Substance Abuse Sourcebook. Ed. by Karen Bellenir. LC 96-9511. (Health Reference Ser.: Vol. 14). 1996. lib. bdg. 75.00 (*0-7808-0038-9*) Omnigraphics Inc.

Substance Abuse Treatment: A Familiy Systems Perspective. Ed. by Edith M. Freeman. (Sourcebooks for the Human Services Ser.: Vol. 25). (Illus.). 330p. (C). 1993. text ed. 52.00 (*0-8039-4889-1*); pap. text ed. 24.95 (*0-8039-4890-5*) Sage.

Substance Abuse Treatment: Considerations for Lesbians & Gay Men see Mart Series

Substance Abuse Treatment Program Assistant. Jack Rudman. (Career Examination Ser.: C-3479). 1994. pap. 27.95 (*0-8373-3479-9*) Nat Learn.

Substance among Other Categories. Joshua Hoffman & Gary S. Rosenkrantz. LC 93-49101. (Studies in Philosophy). (Illus.). 256p. (C). 1994. text ed. 64.95 (*0-521-46101-4*) Cambridge U Pr.

Substance & Essence in Aristotle: An Interpretation of Metaphysics, VII-IX. Charlotte Witt. LC 88-47913. 216p. 1989. 33.50 (*0-8014-2126-8*) Cornell U Pr.

Substance & Essence in Aristotle: An Interpretation of Metaphysics VII-IX. Charlotte Witt. 216p. 1994. pap. 14.95 (*0-8014-8192-9*) Cornell U Pr.

Substance & Function & Einstein's Theory of Relativity. Ernst Cassirer. (C). pap. 8.95 (*0-486-20050-7*) Dover.

Substance & Manner: Studies in Music & the Other Arts. Audrey Davidson. (Illus.). 1977. pap. 4.95 (*0-930276-00-0*) Hiawatha Pr.

Substance & Modern Science. Richard J. Connell. LC 87-73319. 280p. 1988. 19.50 (*0-268-01731-X*); pap. 16.95 (*0-685-31940-7*) Ctr Thomistic.

Substance & Modern Science. Richard J. Connell. LC 87-73319. 1988. pap. text ed. 19.50 (*0-268-01732-8*) U of Notre Dame Pr.

Substance & Practice - Building Technology & the Royal Engineers in Canada. Elizabeth Vincent. 287p. (Orig.). 1993. pap. 20.75 (*0-660-14820-X*, Pub. by Canada Commun Grp CN) Accents Pubns.

Substance & Predication in Aristotle. Frank A. Lewis. 375p. (C). 1992. text ed. 64.95 (*0-521-39159-8*) Cambridge U Pr.

Substance & Separation in Aristotle. Lynne Spellman. 290p. (C). 1995. text ed. 54.95 (*0-521-47147-8*) Cambridge U Pr.

Substance & Shadow. John Marrs. Ed. by Kathleen L. Mendel. LC 94-60397. 64p. (Orig.). (C). 1994. pap. 7.95 (*1-878142-34-8*) Telstar FL.

Substance & Shadow: Or, Morality & Religion in Their Relation to Life, an Essay upon the Physics of Creation. Henry James, Sr. LC 72-915. (Selected Works of Henry James, Sr.: Vol. 8). 1983. reprint ed. 76.50 (*0-404-10088-0*) AMS Pr.

Substance & Shadow: Women & Addiction in the U. S. Stephen R. Kandall. (Illus.). 384p. 1996. 29.95 (*0-674-85360-1*) HUP.

Substance & Style: Instruction & Practice in Copyediting. Mary Stoughton. 351p. (Orig.). 1989. pap. 35.00 (0-935012-11-7) Edit Experts.

Substance & Style: Instruction & Practice in Copyediting. 2nd ed. Mary Stoughton. 352p. (Orig.). (C). 1996. pap. 35.00 (0-935012-18-4) Edit Experts.

Substance, Body & Soul: Aristotelian Investigations. Edwin Hartman. LC 77-71984. 304p. 1977. reprint ed. pap. 86.70 (0-7837-8173-3, 2047878) Bks Demand.

Substance Called Food: How to Understand, Control, & Recover from Addictive Eating. 2nd ed. Gloria Arenson. 256p. 1989. pap. 11.95 (0-8306-3430-4) McGraw-Hill Prof.

Substance Called Food: How to Understand, Control & Recover from Addictive Eating. 2nd ed. Gloria Arenson. 1989. pap. text ed. 12.95 (0-07-156827-1) McGraw.

Substance, Form, & Psyche: An Aristolelean Metaphysics. Montgomery Furth. 304p. 1988. text ed. 65.00 (0-521-34143-4) Cambridge U Pr.

Substance Misuse in Adolescence. Thomas P. Gullotta et al. (Advances in Adolescent Development Ser.: Vol. 7). 240p. 1994. 55.00 (0-8039-5878-1) Sage.

Substance Misuse in Adolescence. Thomas P. Gullotta et al. (Advances in Adolescent Development Ser.: Vol. 7). 1994. pap. 24.95 (0-8039-5879-X) Sage.

Substance of Cervantes. John G. Weiger. 320p. 1985. text ed. 69.95 (0-521-30516-0) Cambridge U Pr.

Substance of Consciousness: An Argument for Interactionism. Matthew Buncombe. (Avebury Series in Philosophy). 240p. 1995. 68.95 (1-85972-271-7, Pub. by Avebury Pub UK) Ashgate Pub Co.

***Substance of Fire: A Screenplay.** Jon R. Baitz. LC 96-48502. 160p. 1996. pap. 9.95 (0-7868-8256-5) Hyperion.

Substance of Fire & Other Plays. Jon R. Baitz. LC 92-16985. 224p. 1991. 24.95 (1-55936-052-6); pap. 12.95 (1-55936-051-8) Theatre Comm.

Substance of Forgetting. Gunnars. 1993. 17.95 (0-88995-085-7, Pub. by Red Deer CN) Orca Bk Pubs.

Substance of Forgetting. Kristjana Gunnars. 128p. 1992. pap. 8.95 (0-88995-092-X, Pub. by Red Deer CN) Orca Bk Pubs.

Substance of Great Achievement. Edwin L. Cole. 1996. pap. 9.99 (0-88419-366-7) Word Pub.

Substance of Spinoza. Errol E. Harris. LC 93-3851. 232p. (C). 1995. text ed. 60.00 (0-391-03827-3) Humanities.

Substance of Style: Perspectives on the American Arts & Crafts Movement. Ed. by Bert Denker. (Illus.). 448p. 1996. 39.95 (0-912724-33-1) Winterthur.

Substance of Things. Charles Capps. 64p. (Orig.). 1989. pap. 4.99 (0-89274-599-1, HH599) Harrison Hse.

Substance of Things Hoped For: A Memoir of African-American Faith. Samuel D. Proctor. LC 95-22665. (Illus.). 288p. (Orig.). 1996. 22.95 (0-399-14089-1, Putnam) Putnam Pub Group.

Substance of Things Hoped for: Fiction & Faith - Outstanding Modern Short Stories. John B. Breslin, Jr. LC 86-16656. 334p. 1987. pap. 8.95 (0-385-24692-7) Georgetown U Pr.

Substance P. Nobel Symposium Staff. Ed. by Ulf S. Von Euler & Bengt Pernow. LC 76-52600. (Illus.). 358p. reprint ed. pap. 102.10 (0-7837-7103-7, 2046932) Bks Demand.

Substance P: Metabolism & Biological Actions. Ed. by C. C. Jordan & P. Oehme. 260p. 1985. 85.00 (0-85066-324-5) Taylor & Francis.

Substance P & Neurokinins. Ed. by J. Henry. (Illus.). 390p. 1987. 175.00 (0-387-96421-5) Spr-Verlag.

Substance P & Related Peptides: Cellular & Molecular Physiology. Ed. by Susan E. Leeman et al. LC 91-27332. (Annals Ser.: Vol. 632). 497p. 1992. pap. 135.00 (0-89766-664-X, QP552) NY Acad Sci.

Substance under Pressure: Artistic Coherence & Evolving Form in the Novels of Doris Lessing. Betsy Draine. LC 82-70556. 240p. 1983. 25.00 (0-299-09230-5) U of Wis Pr.

Substance Use & Delinquency among Inner City Adolescent Males. Paul J. Brounstein et al. LC 90-11970. (Reports: No. 90-3). (Illus.). 156p. (Orig.). (C). 1990. pap. text ed. 18.50 (0-87766-475-7); lib. bdg. 45.00 (0-87766-449-8) Urban Inst.

Substances & Safety. rev. ed. Susan Mercie. 1996. pap. 0.50 (0-89230-201-1) Do It Now.

Substances & Universals in Aristotle's Metaphysics. Theodore Scaltsas. LC 94-8911. 312p. 1994. 39.95 (0-8014-3003-8) Cornell U Pr.

***Substantial Evidence: Life, Death & Justice in Texas.** Bill Hubbard. 304p. 1998. 23.95 (0-88282-160-1) New Horizon NJ.

Substantial Holdings. M. Truman Cooper. (Orig.). 1987. pap. 5.00 (0-317-66653-3) Pudding Hse Pubns.

Substantial Proofs of Being: Osip Mandelstam's Literary Prose. Charles Isenberg. 179p. (Orig.). 1987. pap. 19.95 (0-89357-169-5) Slavica.

Substantial Rehab - New Construction: Housing Production Manual, No. 3. William Duncan. Ed. by Jude Cashman & Peter Werwath. (Housing Production Manuals Ser.). 1990. student ed. 55.00 (0-942901-04-5) Enterprise Foundation.

Substantial Rehabilitation - New Construction. Enterprise Foundation Staff & Rehab Work Group Staff. (Housing Production Manual Ser.). 512p. 1991. text ed. 65.00 (0-442-00814-7) Chapman & Hall.

Substantivableitung Mit -Heit - -Keit, -Ida, -I Im Fruehneuhochdeutschen. Regina Doerfert. (Studia Linguistica Germanica Ser.). xvi, 340p. (GER.). (C). 1994. lib. bdg. 141.55 (3-11-014195-7) De Gruyter.

Substantive Criminal Law. 2nd ed. Wayne R. LaFave & Austin W. Scott, Jr. LC 86-7795. (Criminal Practice Ser.). 1300p. 1986. text ed. write for info. (0-314-98403-8) West Pub.

Substantive Due Process of Law: A Dichotomy of Sense & Nonsense. Frank R. Strong. LC 86-71003. 316p. (C). 1986. lib. bdg. 29.95 (0-89089-313-6) Carolina Acad Pr.

Substantive Evidence in Phonology: The Evidence from Finnish & French. Royal Skousen. LC 74-84242. (Janua Linguarum, Series Minor). (Illus.). 135p. (Orig.). 1975. pap. text ed. 46.15 (90-279-3267-0) Mouton.

Substantive Grammar of Shakespeare's Non-Dramatic Texts. Ashley C. Partridge. LC 75-44106. 232p. 1976. text ed. 20.00 (0-8139-0619-9) U Pr of Va.

Substantivized Adjectives in Old Norse. C. D. Buchanan. (LD Ser.: No. 15). 1974. reprint ed. pap. 25.00 (0-527-00761-7) Periodicals Srv.

Substanz und Qualitaet: Ein Beitrag zur Interpretation der plotinischen Traktate Vi 1, 2, und 3. Klaus Wurm. LC 72-81572. (Quellen und Studien zur Philosophie Ser.: Vol. 5). 276p. (C). 1973. 89.25 (3-11-001899-3) De Gruyter.

Substate Regional Planning in Virginia: A Bibliographical Essay, No. 1086. Walter J. Raymond. 1976. 5.00 (0-686-20402-6, Sage Prdcls Pr) Sage.

Substituent Effects in Radical Chemistry. Ed. by Heinz G. Viehe et al. 1986. lib. bdg. 180.50 (90-277-2340-0) Kluwer Ac.

Substitute. Robert Hawks. 192p. (Orig.). (YA). 1995. mass mkt. 3.99 (0-380-77622-7, Flare) Avon.

Substitute. Nicholas Pine. (Terror Academy Ser.: No. 13). 192p. (Orig.). (YA). 1995. mass mkt. 3.99 (0-425-14534-4) Berkley Pub.

Substitute. Mark Sumner. 224p. 1994. mass mkt. 3.50 (0-06-106188-3, Harp PBks) HarpC.

Substitute. large type ed. Estelle Thompson. (Mystery Ser.). 368p. 1993. 25.99 (0-7089-2977-X) Ulverscroft.

Substitute & Adulterant Plants. S. Garg. (C). 1992. 125.00 (81-7136-021-1, Pub. by Periodical Expert II) St Mut.

***Substitute Bride.** Trisha Alexander. (Special Edition Ser.: No. 1115). 1997. mass mkt. 3.99 (0-373-24115-1, 1-24115-7) Silhouette.

***Substitute Bride.** large type ed. Jasmine Cresswell. (Linford Romance Large Print Ser.). 304p. 1996. pap. 15.99 (0-7089-7958-0, Linford) Ulverscroft.

Substitute Care Providers: Helping Abused & Neglected Children. Kenneth Watson. 76p. (Orig.). (C). 1995. pap. text ed. 25.00 (0-7881-1658-4) DIANE Pub.

Substitute Creature. M. T. Coffin. (Spinetinglers Ser.). 128p. (Orig.). (J). (gr. 3-6). 1995. pap. 3.50 (0-380-77829-7, Camelot) Avon.

Substitute Foods Industry. Business Communications Co., Inc. Staff. 185p. 1986. 1,250.00 (0-89336-481-9, GA-052) BCC.

Substitute for Victory: The Politics of Peacemaking at the Korean Armistice Talks. Rosemary Foot. LC 89-45973. (Cornell Studies in Security Affairs). (Illus.). 248p. 1990. 37.50 (0-8014-2413-5) Cornell U Pr.

Substitute Guest. Grace L. Hill. (Grace Hill Livingston Ser.: Vol. 20). 1991. pap. 4.99 (0-8423-6447-1) Tyndale.

Substitute Ingredients. rev. ed. S. Harold Collins. (Substitute Teaching Ser.). (Illus.). 98p. 1989. 8.95 (0-931993-01-6, GP-001) Garlic Pr OR.

Substitute Mom. Maris Soule. (Romance Ser.). 1996. pap. 3.25 (0-373-19160-X, 1-19160-0) Silhouette.

Substitute Natural Gas from Hydrocarbon Liquids (Oil Gasification) A Bibliography 1960-1973. Library Services Task Force Staff. 62p. 1974. 7.00 (0-318-12711-3, H02074) Am Gas Assn.

Substitute Natural Gas from Hydrocarbon Liquids Symposium - I, March 1973. (Synthetic Fuels Ser.). 455p. 1973. 30.00 (0-910091-43-9) Inst Gas Tech.

Substitute Teacher. Francine Pascal. (Sweet Valley Kids Ser.: No. 3). 80p. (J). (gr. k-3). 1990. pap. 3.50 (0-553-15760-4, Skylark BDD) BDD Bks Young Read.

Substitute Teacher. Jordan Storm. Ed. by Sally Peters. 304p. (Orig.). 1993. mass mkt. 4.99 (0-671-73721-X) PB.

Substitute Teacher. Jean Waricha. (Full House Michelle Ser.: No. 12). (YA). 1997. mass mkt. 3.50 (0-671-00364-X) PB.

***Substitute Teacher Essentials: Idea Booklet & Pocket Folder Organizer.** Karen Sevaly. (Illus.). 16p. (J). (ps-6). 1997. teacher ed., wbk. ed., pap. 3.99 (1-57882-012-X, TF-1263) Teachers Friend Pubns.

Substitute Teacher from Mars. Elaine Moore. LC 93-37527. (Illus.). 96p. (J). (gr. 2-6). 1993. pap. text ed. 2.95 (0-8167-3283-3) Troll Communs.

***Substitute Teacher Handbook, K-8: Expectations, Classroom Management, & Fill-In Activities.** Sara Hacken et al. Ed. by Geoffrey G. Smith. (Illus.). 118p. 1995. teacher ed., pap. text ed. 8.75 (1-890563-00-5) Subs Tchr Train.

***Substitute Teacher Handbook, K-8: Expectations, Classroom Management, & Fill-In Activities.** 2nd ed. Cynthia Murdock et al. Ed. & Illus. by Geoffrey G. Smith. 1997. pap. text ed. 8.95 (1-890563-02-1) Subs Tchr Train.

***Substitute Teacher Handbook, Secondary 9-12: Expectations, Classroom Management, & Fill-In Activities.** Sara Hacken et al. Ed. by Geoffrey G. Smith. (Illus.). 104p. 1995. pap. text ed. 8.75 (1-890563-01-3) Subs Tchr Train.

***Substitute Teacher Handbook, 9-12: Expectations, Classroom Management, & Fill-In Activities.** 2nd ed. Cynthia Murdock et al. Ed. & Illus. by Geoffrey G. Smith. 1997. pap. text ed. 8.95 (1-890563-03-X) Subs Tchr Train.

Substitute Teacher's Handbook: Activities & Projects for Kindergarten Through Grade Six. Mary F. Redwine. 1970. pap. 6.99 (0-8224-6600-7) Fearon Teach Aids.

***Substitute Teacher's Reference Manual.** 2nd ed. Carol A. Jones. LC 97-2646. 1998. write for info. (0-88280-135-X) ETC Pubns.

Substitute Teachers Step by Step Survival Handbook: Elementary Level. Lisa Robinson. (Illus.). 24p. (Orig.). 1994. teacher ed., pap. 6.00 (1-878276-34-4) Educ Systs Assocs Inc.

Substitute Teaching: A Handbook for Hassle-Free Subbing. Barbara Pronin. (Illus.). 241p. 1983. pap. 10.95 (0-312-77484-2) St Martin.

Substitute Teaching: Planning for Success. Ed. by Elizabeth Manera. LC 96-26437. 162p. 1996. spiral bd. 20.00 (0-912099-06-2) Kappa Delta Pi.

Substitute Wife. Anne M. Winston. 1994. mass mkt. 2.99 (0-373-05863-2, 5-05863-1) Harlequin Bks.

Substitutes: Planning for Productivity & Consistency. Randall S. Sprick & Lisa M. Howard. (Library: Management, Motivation & Discipline). 60p. (Orig.). 1996. pap. text ed. 95.00 incl. disk, vhs (1-57035-068-X, 39SUB) Sopris.

Substitutes: Supplementary Materials for School Staff. Randall S. Sprick & Lisa M. Howard. (Library: Management, Motivation & Discipline). 64p. (Orig.). 1996. pap. text ed. 95.00 incl. disk, vhs (1-57035-076-0, 39SUB) Sopris.

Substitutes: The Essentials of Classroom Management. Randall S. Sprick & Lisa M. Howard. (Library: Management, Motivation & Discipline). 33p. (Orig.). 1996. pap. text ed. 95.00 incl. disk, vhs (1-57035-077-9, 39SUB) Sopris.

Substitutes Commodity Exchange Encyclopaedia. Greetings Etc. by Alfreda Staff. 1984. ring bd. 29.95 (0-317-00982-6) Prosperity & Profits.

Substitutes for Asbestos. Business Communications Co., Inc. Staff. 122p. 1988. pap. 1,750.00 (0-89336-524-6, GB-061N) BCC.

Substitutes for Hazardous Chemicals in the Workplace. Goldschmidt & Gitte. 192p. 1996. 39.95 (1-56670-021-3, L1021) Lewis Pubs.

Substitutes for the Saloon: An Investigation Originally Made for the Committee of Fifty. Raymond Calkins. LC 75-137181. (Poverty U. S. A. Historical Record Ser.). 1971. reprint ed. 25.95 (0-405-03119-X) Ayer.

Substitutes for Tripolyphosphate in Detergents. 78p. 1991. 26.00 (92-1-116521-0) UN.

Substitute's Handbook: A Survivor's Guide. John W. Brenot. LC 84-60972. 150p. (Orig.). (C). 1985. pap. text ed. 10.95 (0-88247-729-3) R & E Pubs.

Substituting Agricultural Materials for Petroleum-Based Industrial Products. David Morris & Tom Abeles. LC 86-21350. 33p. 1986. 20.00 (0-917582-46-2) Inst Local Self Re.

Substituting as a Teacher: Being the Best. Debra A. Thomas. 1991. pap. 6.95 (0-88247-866-4) R & E Pubs.

Substituting Ingredients: An A to Z Kitchen Reference. 3rd ed. Becky S. Epstein & Hilary D. Klein. LC 96-3801. (Illus.). 128p. 1996. pap. 9.95 (1-56440-741-1) Globe Pequot.

Substitution: Bilingual Edition. Giulia Niccolai. Tr. by Paul Vangelisti. 1975. per. 2.50 (0-88031-020-0) Invisible-Red Hill.

Substitution Dynamical Systems - Spectral Analysis. M. Queffelec. (Lecture Notes in Mathematics Ser.: Vol. 1294). 240p. 1987. 44.95 (0-387-18692-1) Spr-Verlag.

***Substitution of Materials as a Necessary Aid to the War Effort.** E. J. Wellauer. (Technical Papers). 1942. pap. text ed. 30.00 (1-55589-342-2) AGMA.

Substorms Two: Proceedings of the Second International Conference on Substorms, Fairbanks, Alaska, March 7-11, 1994. Ed. by J. R. Kan et al. (Illus.). (Orig.). (C). 1994. pap. text ed. 35.00 (0-915360-13-6) Geophysical Inst.

Substrata versus Universals in Creole Genesis. Ed. by Pieter Muysken & Norval Smith. LC 86-18856. (Creole Language Library: No. 1). vii, 311p. 1986. 97.00 (0-915027-90-9) Benjamins North Am.

Substrates & Forms for Documentation in Cleanrooms, IES-RP-CC0020.2. 1995. 125.00 (1-877862-48-7) Inst Environ Sci.

Substructural Logics. Kosta Dosen. Ed. by Peter Schroeder-Heister. LC 93-29307. (Studies in Logic & Computation: Vol. 2). (Illus.). 400p. 1994. 65.00 (0-19-853777-8, Clarendon Pr) OUP.

Substructure Analysis & Design. 2nd ed. Paul Andersen. LC 56-6804. 348p. reprint ed. pap. 99.20 (0-317-08677-4, 2012446) Bks Demand.

Substructures of Matter As Revealed with Electroweak Probes: Proceedings of the Thirty-Second Internationale Universit Atswochen fur Kern & Teilchenphysik, Schladming, Austria, 24 February-5 March 1993. Ed. by L. Mathelitsch & W. Plessas. LC 93-44976. (Lecture Notes in Physics Ser.: Vol. 426). 1994. 104.95 (0-387-57575-8) Spr-Verlag.

Subsurface & Outcrop Examination of the Capitan Shelf Margin, Northern Delaware Basin. Ed. by Paul M. Harris & George A. Grover. (Core Workshop Notes Ser.: No. 13). (Illus.). 481p. 1989. pap. 53.00 (0-918985-80-3) SEPM.

***Subsurface Characterization & Monitoring Techniques: A Desk Reference Guide, Vol. 1: Solids & Ground Water.** J. Russell Boulding. (Illus.). 363p. 1996. reprint ed. pap. 50.00 (0-7881-3204-0) DIANE Pub.

***Subsurface Conditions: Geotechnical & Civil Engineering Risk Management.** David J. Hatem. LC 97-12584. 512p. 1997. 69.95 (0-471-15607-8) Wiley.

Subsurface Contamination by Immiscible Fluids: Proceedings of the International Conference Subsurface Contamination by Immiscible Fluids Calgary, Alberta, Canada, 18-20 April 1990. Ed. by K. U. Weyer. (Illus.). 585p. (C). 1991. text ed. 130.00 (90-6191-175-3, Pub. by A A Balkema NE) Ashgate Pub Co.

Subsurface Drainage: Soil-Fluid Interface Phenomena, & Management of Unpaved Surfaces (TRR 1434) Ed. by Naomi Kassabian. (Transportation Research Record Ser.). (Illus.). 104p. 1994. pap. text ed. 25.00 (0-309-05511-3) Transport Res Bd.

Subsurface Exploration for Underground Excavation & Heavy Construction: Proceeding of Specialty Conference Held at New England College, Henniker, NH, August 11-16, 1974 ,(Sponsored by the Engineering Foundation) Engineering Foundation Conference on Subsurface Exploration for Underground Excavation & Heavy Construction. LC 78-320122. 410p. reprint ed. pap. 116.90 (0-685-15540-4, 2026561) Bks Demand.

Subsurface Flow & Contamination: Methods of Analysis & Parameter Uncertainty. Ed. by Miguel A. Marino. (AWRA Monograph Ser.: No. 8). (Illus.). 118p. reprint ed. pap. 33.70 (0-8357-3170-7, 2039433) Bks Demand.

***Subsurface Flow & Transport: A Stochastic Approach.** Ed. by Gedeon Dagan & Shlomo P. Neuman. LC 96-37796. (International Hydrology Ser.). (Illus.). 384p. (C). 1997. text ed. 110.00 (0-521-57257-6) Cambridge U Pr.

***Subsurface Fluid Flow (Ground-Water & Vadose Zone) Modeling, STP 1288.** Ed. by Joseph D. Ritchey & James O. Rumbaugh. LC 96-38424. (Special Technical Publication: Vol. 128). (Illus.). 425p. 1996. text ed. 69.00 (0-8031-2021-4, 04-012880-38) ASTM.

***Subsurface Geologic Investigations of New York Finger Lakes: Implications for Late Quaternary Deglaciation & Environmental Change.** Ed. by H. T. Mullins & N. Eyles. LC 96-35721. (Special Papers: No. 311). 1996. pap. 35.00 (0-8137-2311-6) Geol Soc.

Subsurface Geology: Petroleum, Mining, Construction. 4th ed. Ed. by L. W. LeRoy & D. O. LeRoy. LC 76-51265. 941p. 1977. 21.00 (0-918062-00-4) Colo Sch Mines.

Subsurface Geology: Petroleum, Mining, Construction. 5th ed. Ed. by Jon W. Raese et al. LC 86-18806. (Illus.). 1081p. (C). 1987. 50.00 (0-918062-68-3) Colo Sch Mines.

***Subsurface Hydrological Response to Land Cover & Land Use Changes.** Makoto Taniguchi. LC 97-5204. 1997. text ed. write for info. (0-7923-9931-5) Kluwer Ac.

Subsurface Reservoir Characterization from Outcrop Observations: Proceedings of the 7th IFP Exploration & Production Research Conference, Scarborough, 1992. R. Eschard & B. Doligez. (Colloques & Seminaires Ser.). (Illus.). 212p. 1993. 400.00 (2-7108-0650-9, Pub. by Edits Technip FR) St Mut.

***Subsurface Restoration.** Ed. by C. H. Ward et al. (Applied Groundwater & Hazardous Waste Science Ser.). 504p. (C). 1997. 69.95 (1-57504-060-3, 060-3) Sleeping Bear Software.

Subsurface Transport & Fate Processes. Robert C. Knox et al. 448p. 1992. 69.95 (0-87371-193-9, L193) Lewis Pubs.

***Subsurface Ventilation & Environmental Engineering.** McPherson. (Illus.). 928p. (C). (gr. 13 up). 1993. text ed. 143.95 (0-412-35300-8) Chapman & Hall.

***Subsurface Wealth: The Struggle for Privatization in Argentina.** Guillermo M. Yeatts. LC 97-60187. 232p. 1997. pap. 14.95 (1-57246-075-X) Foun Econ Ed.

Subsymbolic Natural Language Processing: An Integrated Model of Scripts, Lexicon, & Memory. Risto Miikkulainen. LC 92-37285. (Neural Network Modeling & Connectionism Ser.). 422p. (C). 1993. 50.00 (0-262-13290-7, Bradford Bks) MIT Pr.

Subsynchronous Resonance in Power Systems. Ed. by P. M. Anderson et al. LC 89-28366. (Illus.). 282p. 1990. text ed. 49.95 (0-87942-258-0, PC02477) Inst Electrical.

Subtech 1993: Proceedings. Ed. by Society for Underwater Technology Staff. LC 93-32990. (Advances in Underwater Technology, Ocean Science, & Offshore Engineering Ser.: Vol. 31). 1993. lib. bdg. 166.50 (0-7923-2544-3) Kluwer Ac.

Subtech '89, Vol. 23: Fitness for Purpose. Ed. by Society for Underwater Technology Staff. (C). 1990. lib. bdg. 180.50 (0-7923-0742-9) Kluwer Ac.

Subtech '91: Back to the Future. Ed. by Society for Underwater Technology Staff. (C). 1991. lib. bdg. 153.50 (0-7923-1457-3) Kluwer Ac.

Subtenant - To Outwit God. Hanna Krall. Tr. by Jaroslaw Anders et al. from POL. 250p. (Orig.). 1992. 45.95 (0-8101-1050-4); pap. 13.95 (0-8101-1075-X) Northwestern U Pr.

Subterfuge of Art: Language & the Romantic Tradition. Michael Ragussis. LC 78-5845. 256p. reprint ed. pap. 73.00 (0-8357-6623-3, 2035269) Bks Demand.

Subterra: Moving Fortress, Bk. 2. Enrique Barriero & Quique Alcatena. Tr. by Enrique Villagran & Charles Dixon from SPA. (Illus.). 56p. (Orig.). 1989. pap. 8.98 (0-922173-02-8) Four Winds Pub Group.

Subterranean Britain. Ed. by Harriet Crawford. LC 79-16858. 1980. text ed. 29.95 (0-312-77477-X) St Martin.

Subterranean Climbers: Twelve Years in the World's Deepest Chasm. Pierre Chevelier. Tr. by E. M. Hatt. LC 75-34044. (Illus.). 223p. 1975. reprint ed. pap. 6.95 (0-914264-15-X) Cave Bks MO.

Subterranean Hydrology. G. Kovacs et al. LC 80-54120. 1981. 55.00 (0-918334-35-7) WRP.

Subterranean Worlds. Walter Kafton-Minkel. LC 89-84325. 280p. 1989. pap. text ed. 18.95 (1-55950-015-8) Loompanics.

Subterraneans. Jack Kerouac. LC 58-6703. 152p. 1989. pap. 10.95 (0-8021-3186-7, Grove) Grove-Atltic.

Subterraneans. M. D. Willis. (Illus.). 200p. (Orig.). 1996. pap. 16.95 (1-56072-339-4) Nova Sci Pubs.

***Subtext.** Julius Fast. 242p. 3.98 (0-8317-3557-0) Smithmark.

Subtext of Form in the English Renaissance: Proportion Poetical. S. K. Heninger, Jr. LC 92-44786. (Illus.). 232p. (C). 1994. 35.00 (0-271-01070-3); pap. 16.95 (0-271-01071-1) Pa St U Pr.

An Asterisk (*) at the beginning of an entry indicates that the title is appearing in BIP for the first time.

Subtidal Marine Biology of California. Robert Galbraith & Ted Boehler. LC 74-11235. (Illus.). 144p. (Orig.). (C). 1974. pap. 8.95 (*0-87961-026-3*) Naturegraph.

Subtilisin Enzymes: Practical Protein Engineering. Ed. by Richard Bott & Christian Betzel. LC 95-35808. (Advances in Experimental Medicine & Biology Ser.: Vol. 379). 260p. (C). 1995. 79.50 (*0-306-45108-5*) Plenum.

Subtitle C: Nursing Home Reform of the Omnibus Budget Reconciliation Act of 1987. 59p. 1987. pap. 10.00 (*0-685-30154-0*, 40,903B) NCLS Inc.

Subtle Aromatherapy. Patricia Davis. 111p. 1991. pap. 15.95 (*0-85207-227-9*, Pub. by C W Daniel UK) Natl Bk Netwk.

Subtle Aromatherapy. Patricia Davis. (Illus.). 256p. (Orig.). pap. 23.95 (*0-8464-4295-7*) Beekman Pubs.

Subtle Body: Essence & Shadow. David V. Tansley. LC 83-51566. (Art & Imagination Ser.). (Illus.). 96p. 1984. pap. 15.95 (*0-500-81014-1*) Thames Hudson.

Subtle Challenge to God's Authority. Milton G. Crane. LC 88-50302. (Illus.). 144p. (Orig.). 1988. per. 5.50 (*0-945383-03-7*) Teach Servs.

Subtle Deceivers. Wayne H. Miller. Ed. by Denise M. Smith. 203p. (Orig.). 1993. pap. text ed. 9.95 (*0-9634735-0-6*) Hiram Charles.

Subtle Energy. John Davidson. 288p. (Orig.). pap. 23.95 (*0-8464-4296-5*) Beekman Pubs.

Subtle Energy. John Davidson. 190p. 1987. pap. 15.95 (*0-85207-184-1*, Pub. by C W Daniel UK) Natl Bk Netwk.

***Subtle Energy: Awakening to the Unseen Forces in Our Lives.** William Collinge. LC 97-6221. 1998. 24.00 (*0-446-52017-9*) Warner Bks.

Subtle Is the Lord: The Science & Life of Albert Einstein. Abraham Pais. LC 82-2273. (Illus.). 568p. 1982. 35.00 (*0-19-853907-X*) OUP.

Subtle Is the Lord: The Science & Life of Albert Einstein. Abraham Pais. LC 82-2273. (Illus.). 568p. 1983. pap. 16.95 (*0-19-520438-7*) OUP.

Subtle Knot: Creative Scepticism in Seventeenth-Century England. Margaret L. Wiley. LC 68-54994. (Illus.). 303p. 1969. reprint ed. text ed. 55.00 (*0-8371-0753-9*, WISK, Greenwood Pr) Greenwood.

Subtle Magic. large type ed. Meredith Webber. 288p. 1995. 21.50 (*0-263-14629-4*, Pub. by M & B UK) Ulverscroft.

Subtle Power of Spiritual Abuse. Jeff VanVonderen & David Johnson. 240p. (Orig.). 1991. pap. 10.99 (*1-55661-160-9*) Bethany Hse.

Subtle Revolution: Women at Work. Ed. by Ralph E. Smith. 271p. (Orig.). 1979. pap. text ed. 24.00 (*0-87766-260-6*); lib. bdg. 45.00 (*0-87766-259-2*) Urban Inst.

Subtle Seductions see How to Be a "Good Enough" Parent: The Subtle Seductions

Subtle Self: Personal Growth & Spiritual Practice. Judith Blackstone. LC 91-35756. 122p. (Orig.). 1991. pap. 9.95 (*1-55643-066-3*) North Atlantic.

***Subtle Sexism: Current Practices & Prospects for Change.** Nijole V. Benokraitis. LC 96-35662. 400p. 1997. 41.95 (*0-7619-0385-2*); pap. 19.95 (*0-7619-0386-0*) Sage.

Subtle Slant: A Cross-Linguistic Discourse Analysis Model for Evaluating Interethnic Conflict in the Press. Richard G. McGarry. (Illus.). 196p. 1994. 35.00 (*0-9635752-1-X*) Pkway Pubs.

Subtle Sound: The Zen Teachings of Maurine Stuart. Ed. by Roko S. Chayat. 120p. (Orig.). 1996. pap. 10.00 (*0-318-14561-8*) Shambhala Pubns.

Subtle Templates of God. Mike Doney. Ed. by Elizabeth Lake. LC 95-74833. 160p. (Orig.). 1996. pap. 14.95 (*0-89716-603-5*) P B Pubng.

Subtler Language: Critical Readings of Neoclassic & Romantic Poems. Earl R. Wasserman. LC 59-10067. 384p. 1959. reprint ed. pap. 15.95 (*0-8018-0663-1*) Johns Hopkins.

Subtler Magick: The Writings & Philosophy of H. P. Lovecraft. 2nd ed. S. T. Joshi. LC 95-5026. (Milford Series: Vol. 62). 296p. (Orig.). 1996. lib. bdg. 39.00 (*0-916732-58-4*) Borgo Pr.

Subtler Magick: The Writings & Philosophy of H. P. Lovecraft. 2nd expanded rev. ed. S. T. Joshi. LC 95-5026. (Milford Ser.: No. 62). 312p. (Orig.). 1996. pap. 29.00 (*0-916732-59-2*) Borgo Pr.

Subtleties of the Inimitable Mulla Nasrudin. Ed. by Idries Shah. 102p. 1983. reprint ed. 25.00 (*0-86304-021-7*, Pub. by Octagon Pr UK) ISHK.

Subtlety of Sameness: A Theory & Computer Model of Analogy-Making. Robert M. French. LC 95-8723. 320p. 1995. 35.00 (*0-262-06180-5*, Bradford Bks) MIT Pr.

Subtlety of Shaw. Patrick Braybrooke. LC 72-2125. (English Literature Ser.: No. 33). 1972. reprint ed. lib. bdg. 59.95 (*0-8383-1465-1*) M S G Haskell Hse.

***Subtract with Borrowing (Math)** Jo E. Moore. (Mathematics Ser.). (Illus.). 32p. (J). (gr. 3-5). 1996. teacher ed., pap. 2.95 (*1-55799-463-3*, 4065) Evan-Moor Corp.

***Subtract W/O Borrowing (Math)** Jo E. Moore. (Mathematics Ser.). (Illus.). 32p. (J). (gr. 2-3). 1996. teacher ed., pap. 2.95 (*1-55799-452-8*, 4054) Evan-Moor Corp.

Subtracting from Eighteen or Less. Earl Ockenga & Walt Rucker. (Elementary Mathematics Ser.). (Illus.). 16p. (J). (gr. 1). 1990. pap. text ed. 1.25 (*1-56281-135-5*, M135) Extra Eds.

Subtracting from Ten or Less. Earl Ockenga & Walt Rucker. (Elementary Mathematics Ser.). (Illus.). 16p. (J). (gr. 1). 1990. pap. text ed. 1.25 (*1-56281-110-X*, M110) Extra Eds.

***Subtraction.** (Flashboards Ser.). (J). bds. 2.99 (*1-56293-595-X*) McClanahan Bk.

Subtraction. S. Harold Collins. (Straight Forward Math Ser.). 34p. (J). (gr. 1-6). 1986. pap. 3.95 (*0-931993-12-1*, GP-012) Garlic Pr OR.

***Subtraction.** Dorling Kindersley Staff. (My Math Sticker Work Bk.). (Illus.). 16p. (J). 1997. pap. 6.95 (*0-7894-1518-6*) DK Pub Inc.

Subtraction. Karen Evans. (Learn Today for Tomorrow Ser.). (Illus.). 32p. (J). (gr. k-1). 1991. student ed., pap. 2.25 (*1-878624-58-X*) McClanahan Bk.

***Subtraction.** Karen Evans. (J). (gr. k-1). 1997. wbk. ed., pap. text ed. 2.25 (*1-56293-968-8*) McClanahan Bk.

Subtraction. Karen Hilderbrand & Kim M. Thompson. (Rap with the Facts Ser.). (Illus.). 48p. (J). (gr. 1-4). 1991. student ed. 6.99 (*0-9632249-3-X*, TWIN 203) Twin Sisters.

Subtraction. Kim M. Thompson & Karen M. Hilderbrand. (Rap with the Facts Ser.). (Illus.). 24p. (J). (gr. 1-4). 1993. 9.98 incl. audio (*1-882331-21-4*, TWIN 403) Twin Sisters.

Subtraction. Alison Wells. (Discovering Math Ser.). 32p. (J). (gr. 3-5). 1995. lib. bdg. 14.95 (*0-7614-0594-1*, Benchmark NY) Marshall Cavendish.

Subtraction: Basic Math for the Job & Personal Use. Wood. (YA - Adult Education Ser.). 1993. wbk. ed., pap. 5.95 (*0-538-70762-3*) S-W Pub.

Subtraction: No Regrouping. H. S. Lawrence. (Puzzles & Practice Ser.). (Illus.). 30p. (Orig.). (ENG & SPA.). (J). (gr. 1-6). 1992. student ed., pap. 3.95 (*0-931993-50-4*, GP-050) Garlic Pr OR.

Subtraction see Arithmetic Series

Subtraction Facts. Carson & Dellosa. (Home Workbooks Ser.). (Illus.). 64p. (Orig.). (J). (gr. 1-2). 1995. wbk. ed., pap. 2.49 (*0-88724-344-4*, CD6841) Carson-Dellos.

Subtraction Facts in Five Minutes a Day. Susan C. Anthony. (Math Facts in Five Minutes a Day Ser.). 88p. (Orig.). (J). (gr. 2-4). 1995. teacher ed., spiral bd. 11.95 (*1-879478-06-4*, 064) Instr Res Co.

Subtraction Rap. Brad Caudle & Richard Caudle. (Rock 'N Learn Ser.). (Illus.). 24p. (J). (gr. 1 up). 1992. pap. 9.95 (*1-878489-10-0*, RL910) Rock n Learn.

Subtraction Wipe-Off Book. 24p. (J). (gr. 1 up). 1988. pap. 1.95 (*0-590-42042-9*) Scholastic Inc.

Subtraction Wrap-ups: Individual Sets. Marion W. Stuart. (J). (gr. 1-3). text ed. write for info. (*0-943343-02-X*) Lrn Wrap-Ups.

Subtraction 20-10, Level 1. Kitty Wehrli. (Michigan Arithmetic Program Ser.). (J). (gr. 2-3). 1976. 8.50 (*0-89039-178-5*, Ann Arbor Div) Acad Therapy.

Subtraction 20-10, Level 2. Kitty Wehrli. (Michigan Arithmetic Program Ser.). (J). (gr. 2-3). 1976. 8.50 (*0-89039-220-X*, Ann Arbor Div) Acad Therapy.

***Subtropical Convergence Environments: The Coast & Sea in the Southwestern Atlantic.** U. Seeliger et al. LC 96-32225. 332p. 1996. 139.50 (*3-540-61365-X*) Spr-Verlag.

Subtropical Garden. Jacqueline Walker. (Illus.). 176p. 1996. pap. 24.95 (*0-88192-359-1*) Timber.

Subtropical Speculations: An Anthology of Florida Science Fiction. Ed. by Richard Mathews & Rick Wilber. LC 90-37793. 304p. 1991. pap. 8.95 (*0-910923-82-5*) Pineapple Pr.

Subtypes of Learning Disabilities: Theoretical Perspectives & Research. Ed. by Lynne V. Feagans et al. 288p. 1991. text ed. 59.95 (*0-8058-0602-4*) L Erlbaum Assocs.

Subunit Enzymes: Biochemistry & Functions. Ed. by Kurt E. Ebner. LC 74-29697. (Enzymology Ser.: No. 2). (Illus.). 346p. reprint ed. pap. 98.70 (*0-7837-0646-4*, 2040987) Bks Demand.

Subunits in Biological Systems, 3 pts., Pt. C. Ed. by Serge N. Timasheff & Gerald D. Fasman. LC 70-145883. (Biological Macromolecules Ser.: No. 5-7). (Illus.). 355p. reprint ed. pap. 101.20 (*0-7837-0649-9*) Bks Demand.

Subunits in Biological Systems, 3 pts., Pt. A. Ed. by Serge N. Timasheff & Gerald D. Fasman. LC 70-145883. (Biological Macromolecules Ser.: No. 5-7). (Illus.). 422p. reprint ed. pap. 114.00 (*0-7837-0647-2*, 2040988) Bks Demand.

Subunits in Biological Systems, 3 pts., Pt. B. Ed. by Serge N. Timasheff & Gerald D. Fasman. LC 70-145883. (Biological Macromolecules Ser.: No. 5-7). (Illus.). 387p. reprint ed. pap. 110.30 (*0-7837-0648-0*) Bks Demand.

Suburb in the City: Chestnut Hill, Philadelphia, 1850-1990. David R. Contosta. (Illus.). 353p. 1996. pap. text ed. 17.95 (*0-8142-0581-X*) Ohio St U Pr.

Suburban Ambush: Downtown Writing & the Fiction of Insurgency. Robert Siegle. LC 89-33037. (Parallax). (Illus.). 480p. 1989. pap. 16.95 (*0-8018-3854-1*); text ed. 52.00 (*0-8018-3847-9*) Johns Hopkins.

Suburban & Country Homes see Turn-of-the-Century House Designs: With Floor Plans, Elevations & Interior Details of 24 Residences

Suburban & Country Homes Eighteen Ninety-Three. Donald J. Berg. (Yesterday's Home Ser.). (Illus.). 80p. (Orig.). 1985. reprint ed. pap. 8.00 (*0-937214-10-8*) Antiquity Re.

***Suburban Building: Example Basel County.** Dieter Wronsky. 228p. 1996. 59.00 (*3-7643-2629-8*) Birkhauser.

Suburban Burglary: A Time & a Place for Everything. George F. Rengert & John V. Wasilchick. (Illus.). 136p. 1985. pap. text ed. 19.95 (*0-398-06648-5*) C C Thomas.

Suburban Burglary: A Time & a Place for Everything. George F. Rengert & John V. Wasilchick. (Illus.). 136p. (C). 1985. text ed. 29.95 (*0-398-05142-9*) C C Thomas.

Suburban Communities: The Jewishness of American Reform Jews. Gerald L. Showstack. LC 88-10075. (Brown Studies on Jews & Their Societies). 230p. 1988. 39.95 (*1-55540-234-8*, 14-50-05) Scholars Pr GA.

***Suburban Discipline.** Peter J. Lang. LC 97-18862. (Storefront Bks.: Vol. 2). (Illus.). 112p. (Orig.). 1997. pap. 14.95 (*1-56898-106-6*) Princeton Arch.

Suburban Dreaming: An Interdisciplinary Approach to Australian Cities. Ed. by Louise C. Johnson. 210p. 1995. pap. 54.00 (*0-949823-40-6*, Pub. by Deakin Univ AT) St Mut.

Suburban Environment: Sweden & the United States. David Popenoe. LC 76-8091. (Studies of Urban Society). 288p. 1977. lib. bdg. 29.00 (*0-226-67542-4*) U Ch Pr.

Suburban Gangs: The Affluent Rebels. Dan Korem. 283p. 1995. 19.95 (*0-9639103-1-0*) Intl Focus Pr.

Suburban Graffiti. Roy Schneider. 1986. pap. 5.00 (*0-915016-36-2*) Second Coming.

Suburban Growth: Geographical Processes at the Edge of the Western City. Ed. by James Johnson. LC 73-8195. 273p. reprint ed. pap. 77.90 (*0-317-26128-2*, 2024278) Bks Demand.

Suburban Guerrillas: A Novel. Joseph Freda. LC 96-15043. (Hardscrabble Bks.). 224p. 1996. pap. 13.95 (*0-87451-763-X*) U Pr of New Eng.

Suburban Guerrillas: A Novel. Joseph Freda. LC 94-36705. 192p. 1995. 19.95 (*0-393-03768-1*) Norton.

Suburban Land Conversion in the United States: An Economic & Governmental Process. Marion Clawson. LC 70-149239. (Resources for the Future Ser.). (Illus.). 424p. reprint ed. 120.90 (*0-8357-9287-0*, 2017571) Bks Demand.

Suburban Lives. Margaret Marsh. LC 89-36060. (Illus.). 230p. (Orig.). (C). 1990. text ed. 35.00 (*0-8135-1483-5*); pap. text ed. 16.00 (*0-8135-1484-3*) Rutgers U Pr.

Suburban Metaphysics: A Collection of Stories. Ronald J. Rindo. 1990. pap. 7.95 (*0-89823-114-0*) New Rivers Pr.

***Suburban Motel.** George F. Walker. 160p. 1997. pap. 11.95 (*0-88922-379-3*, Pub. by Talonbooks CN) Genl Dist Srvs.

Suburban Nature Guide: How to Discover & Identify the Wildlife in Your Backyard. David Mohrhardt & Richard E. Schinkel. LC 90-10237. (Illus.). 192p. (Orig.). 1991. pap. 16.95 (*0-8117-3080-8*) Stackpole.

Suburban Nightmares. Michael Cherkas et al. 112p. 1990. pap. 10.95 (*0-918348-80-3*, Comics Lit) NBM.

***Suburban Nightmares Vol. 2: Childhood Secrets.** Michael Cherkas & Larry Hancock. (Illus.). 64p. 1996. pap. 9.95 (*1-56163-166-3*) NBM.

Suburban Poems. 2nd ed. Ken Dowen. 1986. pap. 8.00 (*0-933967-05-5*) North Am Edit.

Suburban Racial Dilemma: Housing & Neighborhoods. W. Dennis Keating. LC 93-17865. (Conflicts in Urban & Regional Development Ser.). 288p. 1994. 59.95 (*1-56639-147-4*); pap. 22.95 (*1-56639-148-2*) Temple U Pr.

Suburban Religion: Churches & Synagogues in the American Experience. W. Widick Schroeder et al. LC 74-82113. (Studies in Religion & Society). 266p. 1974. pap. 19.95 (*0-913348-11-2*) Ctr Sci Study.

Suburban Sage. Henry C. Bunner. LC 76-90578. (Short Story Index Reprint Ser.). 1977. 17.95 (*0-8369-3061-4*) Ayer.

Suburban Security. C. C. Goddard. LC 92-70848. (Illus.). 80p. (Orig.). 1992. pap. 8.95 (*0-939427-01-X*) Alpha Pubns OH.

Suburban Sketches. William Dean Howells. LC 78-86146. (Short Story Index Reprint Ser.). (Illus.). 1977. 23.95 (*0-8369-3050-9*) Ayer.

Suburban Sketches. William Dean Howells. (Notable American Authors Ser.). 1992. reprint ed. lib. bdg. 75.00 (*0-7812-3268-6*) Rprt Serv.

Suburban Society. Samuel D. Clark. LC 66-1140. 243p. reprint ed. pap. 69.30 (*0-317-07767-8*, 2019193) Bks Demand.

***Suburban Souls.** 1997. reprint ed. pap. 9.95 (*1-56333-563-8*) Masquerade.

Suburban Souls, Bk. I. 336p. mass mkt. 3.95 (*0-8216-5008-4*) Blue Moon Bks.

Suburban Tokyo: A Comparative Study in Politics & Social Change. Gary D. Allinson. LC 78-62852. (Center for Japanese Studies, UC Berkeley: No. 15). 1979. 52.00 (*0-520-03768-5*) U CA Pr.

Suburban Trend. Harlan P. Douglass. LC 73-124478. (Rise of Urban America Ser.). 1974. reprint ed. 25.95 (*0-405-02450-9*) Ayer.

Suburban Youth in Cultural Crisis. Ralph W. Larkin. LC 78-10742. 272p. 1979. pap. text ed. 16.95 (*0-19-502523-7*) OUP.

***Suburban/Rural Conflicts in Late 19th Century Chicago: Political, Religious & Social Controversies on the North Shore.** Mark A. Zaltman. 1997. 69.95 (*1-57309-125-1*); pap. 49.95 (*1-57309-124-3*) Intl Scholars.

***Suburbia.** Bogosian. LC 96-6555. 1997. pap. 12.95 (*0-312-16615-X*) St Martin.

Suburbia. Eric Bogosian. 1995. pap. 5.25 (*0-8222-1428-8*) Dramatists Play.

Suburbia. Donald N. Rothblatt et al. LC 78-19797. (Praeger Special Studies). 210p. 1979. text ed. 55.00 (*0-275-90414-8*, C0414, Praeger Pubs) Greenwood.

Suburbia: A Guide to Information Sources. Ed. by Joseph Zikmund & Deborah E. Dennis. LC 78-10523. (Urban Studies Information Guide Ser: Vol. 9). 160p. 1979. 68.00 (*0-8103-1435-5*) Gale.

Suburbia: An International Assessment. Donald N. Rothblatt & Daniel J. Garr. LC 85-22111. 336p. 1986. text ed. 39.95 (*0-312-77487-7*) St Martin.

Suburbia: Its People & Their Politics. Robert C. Wood. Ed. by Lewis A. Coser & Walter W. Powell. LC 79-7033. (Perennial Works in Sociology). (Illus.). 1980. reprint ed. lib. bdg. 29.95 (*0-405-12131-8*) Ayer.

Suburbia Re-Examined. Ed. by Barbara M. Kelly. LC 88-29616. (Contributions in Sociology Ser.: No. 78). 256p. 1989. text ed. 55.00 (*0-313-26701-4*, KYS/, Greenwood Pr) Greenwood.

Suburbreal Drive: A Scattering. Mike Miskowski. 36p. (Orig.). 1987. pap. 3.00 (*0-944215-00-9*) Ninth St Lab.

Suburbs. J. John Palen. 1994. pap. text ed. write for info. (*0-07-048128-8*) McGraw.

Suburbs of Cincinnati: Sketches, Historical & Descriptive. Sidney D. Maxwell. LC 73-2907. (Metropolitan America Ser.). 190p. 1977. reprint ed. 15.95 (*0-405-05402-5*) Ayer.

Suburbs of the Arctic Circle. Mary Burns. 158p. 1988. 12.95 (*0-920806-79-1*, Pub. by Penumbra Pr CN) U of Toronto Pr.

Suburbs under Siege: Race, Space, & Audacious Judges. Charles M. Haar. 256p. 1996. text ed. 29.95 (*0-691-04444-9*) Princeton U Pr.

***Subversion & Survival: Informal Economies at the U. S. Mexican Border.** Kathleen A. Staudt. LC 97-12414. 1998. write for info. (*1-56639-567-4*); pap. write for info. (*1-56639-568-2*) Temple U Pr.

Subversion as Foreign Policy: The Secret Eisenhower & Dulles Debacle in Indonesia. Audrey R. Kahin & George M. Kahin. 328p. 1995. 25.00 (*1-56584-244-8*) New Press NY.

***Subversion as Foreign Policy: The Secret Eisenhower & Dulles Debacle in Indonesia.** Audrey R. Kahin & George M. Kahin. (Illus.). 328p. 1997. pap. 18.95 (*0-295-97618-7*) U of Wash Pr.

Subversion de la Semiotica Analisis Estructural de Textos Hispanicos. Emilio Bejel & Ramiro Fernandez. LC 88-72319. 270p. 1988. 20.00 (*0-935318-15-1*) Edins Hispamerica.

***Subversion of Politics: European Autonomous Movements & the Decolonization of Everyday Life.** George Katsiaficas. LC 96-30190. (Revolutionary Studies). (C). Date not set. pap. 19.95 (*0-391-04045-6*) Humanities.

Subversion of Politics: European Autonomous Movements & the Decolonization of Everyday Life. George N. Katsiaficas. LC 96-30190. (Revolutionary Studies). (Illus.). 328p. (C). 1997. text ed. 55.00 (*0-391-04013-8*) Humanities.

***Subversions: Playing with History in Women's Theatre.** Ed. by Gabriele Griffin & Elaine Aston. (Contemporary Theatre Review). 1997. pap. text ed. 21.00 (*90-5702-053-X*, Harwood Acad Pubs) Gordon & Breach.

***Subversions of International Order: Studies in the Political Anthropology of Culture.** John Borneman. LC 97-23444. (SUNY Series in National Identities). 1997. write for info. (*0-7914-3583-0*); pap. write for info. (*0-7914-3584-9*) State U NY Pr.

***Subversive Bible.** Jonathan Magonet. 160p. (Orig.). 1997. pap. 23.00 (*0-334-02671-7*, SCM Pr) TPI PA.

Subversive Crafts. Katy Kline. LC 93-78548. (Illus.). 58p. (Orig.). 1993. pap. 15.00 (*0-938437-44-5*) MIT List Visual Arts.

Subversive Dialogues: Theory in Feminist Therapy. Laura Brown. LC 94-18185. 288p. 1994. 36.00 (*0-465-08322-6*) Basic.

Subversive Discourse: The Cultural Production of Late Victorian Feminist Novels. Rita S. Kranidis. LC 94-29336. 143p. 1995. text ed. 39.95 (*0-312-10739-0*) St Martin.

Subversive Domesticity. Dana Self. (Illus.). 52p. (Orig.). (C). 1996. per. write for info. (*1-887883-01-0*) Ulrich KS.

***Subversive Elements.** Donna E. Smyth. 260p. pap. 8.95 (*0-88961-102-5*, Pub. by Wmns Pr CN) LPC InBook.

Subversive Family: An Alternative History of Love & Marriage. Ferdinand Mount. LC 92-30779. 300p. 1992. 24.95 (*0-02-921992-2*, Free Press) Free Pr.

Subversive Genealogy: The Politics & Art of Herman Melville. Michael P. Rogin. 370p. 1985. pap. 14.95 (*0-520-05178-5*) U CA Pr.

Subversive Heroines: Feminist Resolutions of Social Crisis in the Condition-of-England Novel. Constance D. Harsh. 192p. (C). 1995. text ed. 39.50 (*0-472-10566-3*) U of Mich Pr.

Subversive Imagination: The Artist, Society, & Social Responsibility. Ed. by Carol Becker. LC 93-36230. 256p. (gr. 13). 1994. pap. 16.95 (*0-415-90592-3*, Routledge NY) Routledge.

***Subversive Imaginations: Fantastic Prose & the End of Soviet Literature.** Nadya Peterson. LC 96-52563. (C). 1997. text ed. 49.95 (*0-8133-8920-8*) Westview.

Subversive Intent: Gender Politics & the Avant-Garde. Susan R. Suleiman. (Illus.). 272p. 1990. 34.00 (*0-674-85383-0*) HUP.

Subversive Intent: Gender Politics & the Avant-Garde. Susan R. Suleiman. (Illus.). 296p. (C). 1992. pap. 14.95 (*0-674-85384-9*) HUP.

Subversive Laughter: The Liberating Power of Comedy. Ron Jenkins. 1994. 22.95 (*0-02-916405-2*, Free Press) Free Pr.

Subversive Oratory of Andokides: Politics, Ideology & Decision-Making in Democratic Athens, 410-390 B.C. Anna Missiou. (Classical Studies). (Illus.). 224p. (C). 1992. text ed. 59.95 (*0-521-36009-9*) Cambridge U Pr.

***Subversive Orthodoxy: Traditional Faith & Radical Commitment.** Kenneth Leech. 62p. 6.95 (*0-921846-49-5*) Forward Movement.

Subversive Pleasures: Bakhtin, Cultural Criticism, & Film. Robert Stam. LC 89-2594. (Parallax: Re-Visions of Culture & Society Ser.). 282p. 1992. reprint ed. pap. text ed. 15.95 (*0-8018-4509-2*) Johns Hopkins.

Subversive Psyche: Contemporary Women's Narrative from Argentina & Uruguay. Elia G. Kantaris. (Oxford Hispanic Ser.). 288p. 1996. 65.00 (*0-19-815902-1*) OUP.

Subversive Scribe: Translating Latin American Fiction. Suzanne J. Levine. 224p. 1991. pap. 12.00 (*1-55597-146-6*) Graywolf.

***Subversive Scriptures: Revolutionary Christian Readings of the Bible in Latin America.** LC 96-54056. 1997. pap. 19.00 (*1-56338-200-8*) TPI PA.

S

An Asterisk (*) at the beginning of an entry indicates that the title is appearing in BIP for the first time.

Subversive Sites: Feminist Engagements with Law in India. Ratna Kapur & Brenda Cossman. LC 96-7992. 412p. 1996. 28.00 (*0-8039-9315-3*) Sage.

***Subversive Spirituality.** Eugene H. Peterson. LC 97-21465. 192p. (Orig.). 1997. pap. 16.00 (*0-8028-4297-6*) Eerdmans.

Subversive Spirituality. Eugene Peterson. Ed. by Jim Lyster & John Sharon. 188p. (Orig.). 1994. reprint ed. pap. 16.95 (*1-57383-025-9*) Regent College.

Subversive Stitch: Embroidery & the Making of the Feminine. Rozsika Parker. 247p. (C). 1989. pap. 15.95 (*0-415-90206-1*, A3787, Routledge NY) Routledge.

Subversive Sublimities: Undercurrents in the German Enlightenment. Ed. by Eitel Timm. (GERM Ser.). x, 118p. 1992. 49.50 (*1-879751-15-1*) Camden Hse.

Subversive Vegetarian. Michael Cox & Dresda Crocket. LC 80-635. (Illus.). 129p. (Orig.). 1980. pap. 3.95 (*0-912800-83-6*) Woodbridge Pr.

Subversive Virtue: Asceticism & Authority in the Second-Century Pagan World. James A. Francis. 256p. (C). 1995. 32.50 (*0-271-01304-4*) Pa St U Pr.

Subversive Women: Women's Movements in Africa, Asia, Latin America & the Caribbean. Ed. by Saskia Wieringa. LC 95-40860. 256p. (C). 1996. pap. 22.50 (*1-85649-318-0*, Pub. by Zed Bks Ltd UK); text ed. 59.95 (*1-85649-317-2*, Pub. by Zed Bks Ltd UK) Humanities.

***Subversive Women Series.** Ed. by Marie M. Roberts. 1996. write for info. (*1-85506-261-5*) Bks Intl VA.

Subversive Words: Public Opinion in Eighteenth-Century France. Arlette Farge. Tr. by Rosemary Morris. 240p. 1995. 42.50 (*0-271-01431-8*); pap. 15.95 (*0-271-01432-6*) Pa St U Pr.

Subverting Patriarchy. Alison Lewis. 300p. 1995. 59.95 (*0-85496-322-7*) Berg Pubs.

Subverting Scotland's Past: Scottish Whig Historians & the Creation of an Anglo-British Identity, 1689-1830. Colin Kidd. LC 92-46708. 324p. (C). 1993. text ed. 69.95 (*0-521-43484-X*) Cambridge U Pr.

Subverting the Constitution, India. G. G. Mirchandani. 1977. 12.50 (*0-8364-0030-5*) S Asia.

Subverting the System: D'Aubigne & Calvinism. Catharine R. Coats. (Sixteenth Century Essays & Studies). 160p. 1990. 40.00 (*0-940474-16-6*) Sixteenth Cent.

Subwar 2050 Vol. 1: The Official Strategy Guide. John Possidente. 1994. pap. 19.95 (*1-55958-658-3*) Prima Pub.

Subway Art. Martha Cooper & Henry Chalfant. LC 84-620. (Illus.). 104p. 1988. pap. 17.95 (*0-8050-0678-8*, Owl) H Holt & Co.

***Subway Art, Vol. 1.** M. Cooper. 1984. write for info. (*0-03-071963-1*) H Holt & Co.

Subway Cars of the BMT. James C. Greller. LC 95-9038. (Illus.). 250p. (Orig.). 1995. pap. 35.00 (*0-9645765-1-1*) Xplorer Pr.

Subway Ceramics: A History & Iconography of Mosaic & Bas Relief Signs & Plaques in the New York City Subway System. 2nd ed. Lee Stookey. LC 94-66996. (Illus.). 96p. 1994. pap. 15.00 (*0-9635486-1-1*) L Stookey.

***Subway City: Riding the Trains, Reading New York.** Michael W. Brooks. LC 96-39309. (Illus.). 295p. 1997. 35.00 (*0-8135-2396-6*) Rutgers U Pr.

Subway Etiquette: The Straphanger's Guide to Underground Conduct. Tracey Knight. (Illus.). 96p. (Orig.). 1996. pap. 9.95 (*0-9650594-0-5*) Tek Pr.

Subway Gunman: A Juror's Account of the Bernhard Goetz Trial. Charles Shuttleworth & Mark Lesly. 315p. 1988. 18.95 (*0-945167-08-3*) British Amer Pub.

Subway Hitchhikers: A Novel. Jnana-Devanandashram. LC 90-3358. 176p. (Orig.). 1990. pap. 9.95 (*0-931832-60-8*) Fithian Pr.

Subway Home. Justin Vitiello. 81p. (Orig.). 1994. pap. 9.95 (*0-9617589-9-6*) Lincoln Springs Pr.

Subway Prayer & Other Poems of the Inner City. Thomas Krampf. Ed. by James Cooney. (Illus.). 57p. 1976. pap. 10.00 (*0-9616797-1-9*) Ischua Bks.

Subway Slams. Richard A. Spiegel. (Illus.). 48p. (Orig.). (J). (gr. k-8). 1981. pap. 2.00 (*0-934830-22-3*) Ten Penny.

Subway Sparrow. Leyla Torres. LC 92-55104. (ENG, POL & SPA.). (J). 1993. 15.00 (*0-374-37285-3*) FS&G.

***Subway Sparrow.** Leyla Torres. (Illus.). 32p. (J). (gr. k-3). 1997. pap. 6.95 (*0-374-47129-0*, Sunburst Bks) FS&G.

Subway to the World's Fair. F. A. Kramer. 32p. 1991. pap. 7.95 (*1-882727-03-7*) Bells & Whistles.

***Subzero: The Adventures of Batman & Robin.** James Raven. (Batman Ser.). (J). (gr. 3-7). 1997. pap. 3.50 (*0-614-28846-0*) Little.

Succasunna New Jersey. Sander W. Zulauf. LC 87-71854. 64p. (Orig.). 1987. pap. 7.00 (*0-917020-03-0*) Breaking Point.

Succeed. Rob Narke. LC 83-71420. (Illus.). 336p. (Orig.). 1983. pap. 7.95 (*0-9611336-0-0*) Dreaming.

Succeed: A Handbook on Structuring Managerial Thought. John Allen. (Illus.). 64p. 1986. pap. 8.00 (*0-907791-04-2*) Synerg AZ.

Succeed & Be Happy. Roy Moeller. (Illus.). 100p. (Orig.). 1996. pap. 12.95 (*0-9651952-0-1*) O M A Pub.

Succeed & Grow Rich Through Persuasion. Napoleon Hill. 1989. pap. 4.50 (*0-451-16384-2*, Sig) NAL-Dutton.

Succeed & Grow Rich Through Persuasion. rev. ed. Napoleon Hill. 256p. 1989. pap. 5.99 (*0-451-17412-7*, Sig) NAL-Dutton.

Succeed as Homemaker/Home Health Aide Guide. Lane. (Home Care Aide Ser.). 1994. 12.95 (*0-8273-5530-0*) Delmar.

Succeed at I. Q. Tests. Gilles Azzopardi. 1994. pap. 13.95 (*0-572-01948-3*, Pub. by W Foulsham UK) Trans-Atl Phila.

Succeed at Your Job Interview. George Heaviside. 1996. pap. 9.95 (*0-563-36742-3*, BBC-Parkwest) Parkwest Pubns.

***Succeed for Yourself.** Richard Denny. (Personal Development Ser.). 1997. 24.95 (*0-7494-2132-0*); pap. 15.95 (*0-7494-2133-9*) Kogan Page Ltd.

***Succeed in Business, Germany.** Richard Lord. (Culture Shock Ser.). 1997. pap. 12.95 (*1-55868-354-2*) Gr Arts Ctr Pub.

***Succeed in Business, India.** Douglas Bullis. (Culture Shock Ser.). 1997. pap. 12.95 (*1-55868-319-4*) Gr Arts Ctr Pub.

Succeed with Math: Every Student's Guide to Conquering Math Anxiety. Sheila Tobias. 252p. 1987. pap. 12.95 (*0-87447-259-8*) College Bd.

Succeeding: How to Become an Outstanding Professional, a Career Development Handbook. Lee Harrisberger. LC 93-39066. 245p. (C). 1993. pap. text ed. 17.40 (*0-02-350592-3*, Macmillan Coll) P-H.

Succeeding Against the Odds. John J. Johnson & Lerone Bennett, Jr. LC 88-40571. 1989. 19.95 (*0-446-71010-5*) Warner Bks.

Succeeding Against the Odds: How the Learning Disabled Can Realize Their Promise. Sally L. Smith. 320p. 1993. pap. 12.95 (*0-87477-731-3*, Tarcher Putnam) Putnam Pub Group.

Succeeding Against the Odds: Strategies & Insights from the Learning-Disabled. Sally L. Smith. 320p. 1993. pap. 12.95 (*0-685-74803-0*, Tarcher Putnam) Putnam Pub Group.

Succeeding Against the Odds: The Inspiring Autobiography of One of America's Wealthiest Entrepreneurs. John H. Johnson & Lerone Bennett, Jr. 272p. 1993. reprint ed. pap. 12.95 (*1-56743-002-3*) Amistad Pr.

Succeeding as a Home/Health Aide. Lane. (Home Care Aide Ser.). 1993. teacher ed., pap. 12.00 (*0-8273-3833-3*) Delmar.

Succeeding As a Self-Directed Work Team: 20 Important Questions Answered. rev. ed. Ann Harper & Bob Harper. LC 90-91983. 100p. 1995. pap. 14.95 (*1-880859-00-9*) MW Corp.

Succeeding As a Self-Managed Team: A Practical Guide to Operating As a Self-Managed Work Team. Richard Y. Chang & Mark J. Curtin. (Quality Improvement Ser.). 1994. pap. 12.95 (*1-883553-20-2*) R Chang Assocs.

Succeeding As an Expert Witness: Increasing Your Impact & Income. Harold A. Feder. 252p. 1993. pap. 30.00 (*0-9638385-0-4*) Tageh Pr.

***Succeeding at Jewish Education: How One Synagogue Made It Work.** Joseph Reimer. LC 97-19889. 201p. 1997. pap. 24.95 (*0-8276-0623-0*) JPS Phila.

***Succeeding at the University.** 2nd ed. Joyce Weinsheimer. 134p. (C). 1996. ring bd. 19.63 (*0-7872-2865-6*) Kendall-Hunt.

Succeeding Generations: On the Effects of Investments in Children. Robert H. Haveman & Barbara L. Wolfe. (Illus.). 320p. 1994. 34.95 (*0-87154-377-X*) Russell Sage.

Succeeding Generations: On the Effects of Investments in Children. Robert H. Haveman & Barbara L. Wolfe. 320p. (C). 1995. reprint ed. pap. text ed. 16.95 (*0-87154-380-X*) Russell Sage.

Succeeding in Business As a Christian: The Application of Christian Principles to Business Ventures. Theodore V. Foster. 150p. (Orig.). 1993. pap. 9.95 (*1-883866-01-4*) Clarion Pub.

***Succeeding in China's Telecommunications Market.** 1,995.00 (*0-614-26456-1*) Info Gatekeepers.

Succeeding in College. Reynolds. 1996. pap. text ed. 30.00 (*0-205-16041-7*) P-H.

Succeeding in College with Attention Deficit Disorders: Issues & Strategies for Students, Counselors & Educators. Jennifer Bramer. LC 96-26196. 189p. (Orig.). 1996. pap. 18.00 (*1-886941-06-8*, 0921) Spec Pr FL.

Succeeding in Corporate America: A Case Study of a Black American Against the Odds. William R. Spivey. 1991. 15.95 (*0-533-09488-7*) Vantage.

Succeeding in Corporate America: The Experience of Jewish M.B.A.'s. Samuel Z. Klausner. LC 88-72046. 39p. 1988. pap. 7.50 (*0-87495-100-3*) Am Jewish Comm.

Succeeding in Private Practice: A Business Guide for Psychotherapists. Eileen S. Lenson. (Illus.). 296p. (C). 1993. text ed. 55.00 (*0-8039-4957-X*); pap. text ed. 25.50 (*0-8039-4958-8*) Sage.

Succeeding in Psychology & in College. Schick et al. (Illus.). 40p. (C). 1994. pap. text ed. 7.40 (*0-13-192394-3*) P-H.

Succeeding in Small Business: The One Hundred One Toughest Problems & How to Solve Them. Jane Applegate. 320p. 1993. pap. 13.95 (*0-452-26886-9*, Plume) NAL-Dutton.

Succeeding in the Workplace: Attention Deficit Disorder & Learning Disabilities in the Workplace: a Guide for Success. Kathleen G. Nadeau et al. 154p. (Orig.). 1994. pap. text ed. 25.00 (*1-883560-03-9*) JKL Communs.

Succeeding in the World Without Being of the World. Ken Bridges. LC 93-90236. 71p. (Orig.). (C). 1993. pap. 5.95 (*0-9636330-0-7*) Bridge PA.

Succeeding in World of Work Study. Kimbrell. 1987. 8.88 (*0-02-675570-X*) Macmillan.

***Succeeding in Your Work & Community.** Patricia Duffy. (Hire Learning, Schooling That Works Ser.). 1997. wbk. ed., pap. text ed. 6.95 (*1-56370-190-1*) JIST Works.

Succeeding on Your Own. Rieken. 1986. text ed. 46.50 (*0-15-307000-5*) HR&W Schl Div.

Succeeding with AutoCAD: A Full Course in 2D Drafting & 3D Modelling. Barry Hawkes. LC 95-9897. 1995. write for info. (*0-07-709071-3*) McGraw.

Succeeding with Booch & OMT Methodology. (C). 1997. pap. text ed. 35.95 (*0-8053-2279-5*) Benjamin-Cummings.

Succeeding with Change: Implementing Action-Driven Strategies. Tony Eccles. LC 94-21403. 1995. text ed. 24.95 (*0-07-709004-7*) McGraw.

Succeeding with Change: Implementing Action-Driven Strategies. Tony Eccles. 273p. 1996. pap. text ed. 14.95 (*0-07-709266-X*) McGraw.

Succeeding with Consultants: Self-Assessment for the Changing Nonprofit. Barbara Kibbe & Fred Setterberg. LC 92-9330. 79p. (Orig.). 1992. pap. 19.95 (*0-87954-450-3*) Foundation Ctr.

***Succeeding with Difficult Children, 2 bks., 4 cass.** Christopher J. Nicholls & Raun D. Melmed. (Illus.). 195p. (Orig.). 1994. ring bd. 45.00 incl. audio (*0-9655133-0-0*) Thisisit.

***Succeeding with Difficult Students.** Jeffrey A. Kottler. LC 96-51272. (Practical Skills for Counselors (PSFC) Ser.). (Illus.). 96p. 1997. 31.95 (*0-8039-6470-6*); pap. 12.95 (*0-8039-6471-4*) Corwin Pr.

Succeeding with Difficult Students: Inservice Video Package Leader's Manual. Lee Canter. pap. text ed. write for info. (*0-939007-81-9*) Lee Canter & Assocs.

Succeeding with Difficult Students: New Strategies for Reaching Your Most Challenging Students. Lee Canter & Marlene Canter. 255p. (Orig.). pap. 14.95 (*0-939007-52-5*) Lee Canter & Assocs.

Succeeding with Difficult Students Workbook. Lee Canter. 144p. 1993. student ed. 9.95 (*0-939007-53-3*) Lee Canter & Assocs.

***Succeeding with LD: 20 True Stories about Real People with LD.** Jill Lauren. Ed. by Elizabeth Verdick. LC 96-47404. (Illus.). 152p. (Orig.). 1997. pap. 14.95 (*1-57542-012-0*) Free Spirit Pub.

Succeeding with Objects: Decision Frameworks for Project Management. Adele Goldberg & Kenneth S. Rubin. LC 94-34913. 416p. (C). 1995. text ed. 45.95 (*0-201-62878-3*) Addison-Wesley.

Succeeding with Pointing Dogs, Field Trials & Hunting Tests. Bernard C. Boggs. 500p. 1989. 39.95 (*0-9608838-1-9*) Glenbrier Pub.

***Succeeding with the UML.** Terry Quatrani. (C). 1998. pap. text ed. write for info. (*0-201-31016-3*) Addison-Wesley.

Succeeding/Homemaker/Home Aide. Lane. (Home Care Aide Ser.). 1994. wbk. ed. 13.95 (*0-8273-5365-0*) Delmar.

Succesful Machine Applique. Ed. by S. Gail Reeder. LC 78-72878. (Illus.). 48p. 1978. pap. 6.00 (*0-932946-01-1*) Burdett CA.

Success. Martin Amis. LC 90-50617. 224p. 1991. pap. 11.00 (*0-679-73448-1*, Vin) Random.

Success. Robert B. Graham. LC 71-103512. (Short Story Index Reprint Ser.). 1977. 19.95 (*0-8369-3254-4*) Ayer.

Success. Honor Books Staff. (God's Little Instruction Bks.). 160p. Date not set. pap. 5.99 (*1-56292-084-7*) Honor Bks OK.

***Success.** Roy Lessin. (Priorities Collection). 48p. 1997. 7.99 (*1-881830-42-X*, DS18453) Garborgs.

Success. John O'Brien. 43p. 1984. pap. 3.00 (*0-87129-100-2*, S70) Dramatic Pub.

***Success.** Burt Perlutsky. 1997. pap. 20.95 (*0-7871-1148-1*, Dove Bks) Dove Audio.

Success. Robert H. Schuller. LC 93-18293. (Itty Bitty Bk.). 1993. 4.99 (*0-8407-6307-7*) Nelson.

***Success: A Book of Ideas, Helps, & Examples for All Desiring to Make the Most of Life.** Orison S. Marden. 347p. 1997. pap. 32.00 (*0-89540-360-9*) Sun Pub.

***Success: A Book of Wit & Wisdom.** Ariel Books Staff. 1996. 4.95 (*0-8362-1522-2*, Arie Bks) Andrews & McMeel.

***Success: Becoming a Winner.** Chris Fife. 13p. (Orig.). 1996. pap. 4.00 (*1-890143-07-3*) Kinetic Aesthetics.

Success: Communicating in English. Michael Walker. (Communicating in English). 64p. 1994. pap. text ed. 6.41 (*0-201-58661-4*) Addison-Wesley.

Success: Communicating in English, Level 1. Michael Walker. (Great American English Ser.). (Illus.). 128p. (YA). 1994. teacher ed. 19.00 (*0-201-59516-8*, 59516); text ed. 12.72 (*0-201-59514-1*, 59514); audio 60.00 (*0-201-59517-6*, 59517); vhs 92.11 (*0-201-58891-9*, 58891) Addison-Wesley.

Success: Communicating in English, Level 2. Michael Walker. (Illus.). 1994. teacher ed. 19.00 (*0-201-59520-6*, 59520); audio 60.00 (*0-201-59521-4*, 59521) Longman.

Success: Communicating in English, Level 3. Michael Walker. (Illus.). (YA). 1995. teacher ed. 19.00 (*0-201-59524-9*, 59524); audio 60.00 (*0-201-59525-7*, 59525) Longman.

Success: Communicating in English, Level 4. Michael Walker. (Illus.). (YA). 1994. teacher ed. 19.00 (*0-201-59528-1*, 59528); audio 60.00 (*0-201-59529-X*, 59529) Longman.

Success: Individual, Corporate & National. Hugh Marlow. 416p. (C). 1984. 125.00 (*0-85292-336-8*) St Mut.

Success! Interviews with Performers about Fame, Fortune & Happiness. Brad Zupp. 156p. 1995. pap. text ed. 14.95 (*0-9641002-2-3*) Oasis Pubng.

Success: The Glenn Bland Method. Glenn Bland. 176p. 1983. mass mkt. 4.99 (*0-8423-6689-X*) Tyndale.

Success: What Does It Mean? Sue Riley. LC 77-20992. (What Does It Mean? Ser.). (Illus.). 32p. (J). (ps-2). 1978. lib. bdg. 18.50 (*0-89565-016-9*) Childs World.

Success - the Original Hand Book: Life's Five Greatest Secrets Are Right in Your Hand. Joey Reiman. LC 92-71789. 128p. 1992. 14.95 (*1-56352-044-3*) Longstreet Pr Inc.

Success after 40: Late Bloomers Who Made It Big. Allan Zullo & Bill Hartigan. 192p. (Orig.). 1997. pap. 7.95 (*0-8362-2190-7*) Andrews & McMeel.

***Success Against the Odds.** Hamlyn, Paul Foundation National Commission. 400p. (C). 1996. pap. text ed. 19.95 (*0-415-13526-5*) Routledge.

Success & Crisis in National Health Systems: A Comparative Approach. Ed. by Mark G. Field. (Contemporary Issues in Health, Medicine, & Social Policy Ser.). 320p. 1989. 45.00 (*0-415-01289-9*); pap. 18.95 (*0-415-01290-2*) Routledge.

Success & Enterprise: The Significance of Employee Ownership & Participation. Ed. by Henk Voets & Roger Spear. 205p. 1995. text ed. 55.95 (*1-85628-992-3*, Pub. by Avebury Pub UK) Ashgate Pub Co.

Success & Failure in Housing Provision. Barlow & Duncan. (Policy, Planning & Critical Theory Ser.). 189p. 1994. pap. text ed. 57.95 (*0-08-041029-4*, Prgamon Press) Buttrwrth-Heinemann.

Success & Failure in Israeli Elementary Education: An Evaluation Study with Special Emphasis on Disadvantaged Students. Avram Minkowich. LC 80-19873. 539p. 1981. 49.95 (*0-87855-370-3*) Transaction Pubs.

Success & Failure in Permanent Family Placement. June Thoburn. (Illus.). 112p. 1990. text ed. 55.95 (*0-566-07080-4*, Pub. by Avebury Pub UK) Ashgate Pub Co.

Success & Failure in Small Business. John Lewis et al. LC 83-16447. 304p. 1984. text ed. 58.95 (*0-566-00645-6*, Pub. by Avebury Pub UK) Ashgate Pub Co.

Success & Failure in Small Manufacturing. A. M. Woodruff & T. G. Alexander. LC 73-16632. (Illus.). 124p. 1974. reprint ed. text ed. 35.00 (*0-8371-7203-9*, WOSF, Greenwood Pr) Greenwood.

Success & Failure of Picasso. John Berger. LC 93-13121. 1993. reprint ed. pap. 13.00 (*0-679-73725-1*, Vin) Random.

Success & Failure of the Anglo-American Committee of Inquiry, 1945-1946: Last Chance in Palestine. Allen H. Podet. LC 87-1635. (Jewish Studies: Vol. 3). 384p. 1987. lib. bdg. 99.95 (*0-88946-255-0*) E Mellen.

Success & Failure on Parole in California. 1987. 7.00 (*0-318-32576-4*) Natl Coun Crime.

Success & Happiness, 6. Alexander Verner & Swami Brahma. pap. 2.00 (*0-911662-68-5*) Yoga.

Success & Prosperity Thoughts, Vol. I. Michael Funk & Dellinda Funk. 156p. 1995. pap. 12.95 (*0-9645185-0-3*) Successable Pub.

***Success & Sanity: How to Get Everything You Want Without Losing Everything You Are.** Dan Hegstad. 128p. (Orig.). 1997. wbk. ed., pap. 29.95 incl. audio (*0-9656103-0-6*) Easy St Enterp.

Success & Survival in the Family Owned Business. Pat B. Alcorn. 272p. 1986. pap. 9.95 (*0-446-38326-0*) Warner Bks.

Success & Survival in the Family Owned Business. Pat B. Alcorn. LC 80-28976. 265p. reprint ed. pap. 75.60 (*0-317-58110-4*, AU00346) Bks Demand.

Success & the Christian: The Cost & Criteria of Spiritual Maturity. Aiden W. Tozer. LC 93-74750. 162p. 1994. pap. 8.99 (*0-87509-537-2*) Chr Pubns.

Success & the Fear of Success in Women: A Developmental & Psychodynamic Perspective. David W. Krueger. LC 93-6001. 200p. 1993. pap. 25.00 (*1-56821-114-7*) Aronson.

Success & Time Management. Howard Wight. 1992. pap. 9.95 (*0-9633506-0-9*) Wight Finan Concepts.

Success & Understanding. Jean Piaget. LC 78-16435. (Illus.). 248p. 1978. 25.00 (*0-674-85387-3*) HUP.

***Success As a Customer Service Representative: A Fifty Minute Book.** Lloyd Finch. LC 97-65865. 1997. pap. text ed. 12.95 (*1-56052-421-9*) Crisp Pubns.

Success at Last: Helping Students with AD(H)D Achieve Their Potential. Ed. by Constance Weaver. LC 93-30559. (Illus.). 354p. (C). 1994. pap. text ed. 27.50 (*0-435-08808-4*, 08808) Heinemann.

Success at Statistics: A Worktext with Humor. Fred Pyrczck. (Illus.). 400p. (Orig.). 1995. pap. text ed. 44.95 (*0-9623744-9-0*) Pyrczak Pub.

Success at the Harness Races. Barry Meadow. 1976. reprint ed. pap. 7.00 (*0-87980-320-7*) Wilshire.

Success at Work: A Guide for African-Americans. Anita D. Diggs. LC 92-36603. 128p. 1993. pap. 12.99 (*0-942637-85-2*) Barricade Bks.

Success Begins at Home. Avima D. Lombard. (C). 1994. per. write for info. (*1-56134-306-4*) Dushkin Pub.

Success Breakthrough: Get What You Want from Your Career, Your Relationships, & Your Life. Samuel A. Cypert. 256p. (Orig.). 1993. mass mkt. 4.99 (*0-380-77151-9*) Avon.

***Success Club Manual, Success System, Pt. 6.** (Illus.). 50p. (Orig.). 1995. mass mkt. write for info. (*0-9658371-5-7*) M Goloversic.

Success, Common Sense & the Small Business. Patricia Tway. 176p. (Orig.). 1993. pap. 11.95 (*1-55870-306-3*, Betrwy Bks) F & W Pubns Inc.

Success Curriculum for Remedial Writers. Gerald Camp. (Writing Teachers at Work Ser.). 95p. (C). 1982. pap. text ed. 5.50 (*1-883920-00-0*) Nat Writing Proj.

Success Cybernetics. Uell S. Andersen. 1975. pap. 7.00 (*0-87980-155-7*) Wilshire.

***Success, Dominance & the Superorganism: The Case of the Social Insects.** Edward O. Wilson. LC 97-11141. 1997. pap. write for info. (*0-520-21247-9*) U CA Pr.

Success Easier Than Failure. E. W. Howe. (Collected Works of E. W. Howe). 1988. reprint ed. lib. bdg. 59.00 (*0-7812-1295-2*) Rprt Serv.

Success Easier Than Failure see Collected Works of E. W. Howe

Success! Essential Math with Geometry. 2nd ed. Gustafson. (Mathematics Ser.). 1994. student ed. 24.95 (*0-534-20275-6*) Brooks-Cole.

Success! Essential Math with Geometry. 2nd ed. Gustafson & Frisk. (Mathematics Ser.). 1994. student ed., pap. 21.95 (*0-534-20270-5*) Brooks-Cole.

An Asterisk (*) at the beginning of an entry indicates that the title is appearing in BIP for the first time.

Success Ethic, Education, & the American Dream. Joseph L. DeVitis & John M. Rich. LC 96-3227. (SUNY Series, Education & Culture). 227p. (C). 1996. text ed. 54.50 (*0-7914-2993-8*); pap. text ed. 17.95 (*0-7914-2994-6*) State U NY Pr.

Success Factor. Fred Good. LC 85-50414. 84p. 1985. pap. 3.95 (*0-931117-02-X*) Univ Pub.

Success Factor. Sidney Lecker. LC 85-16135. 111p. reprint ed. pap. 31.70 (*0-8357-4245-8*, 2037033) Bks Demand.

Success Factors for Implementing Change. K. Blache. 393p. 1988. 58.00 (*0-87263-318-7*) SME.

Success Fantasy. Tony Campolo. 184p. 1993. 2.00 (*1-56476-118-5*, 63118, Victor Bks) Chariot Victor.

Success for College Students with Learning Disabilities. S. A. Vogel & P. Adelman. (Illus.). 352p. 1994. 59.95 (*0-387-97763-5*) Spr-Verlag.

***Success for Dummies.** Zig Ziglar. 1998. pap. 19.99 (*0-7645-5061-6*) IDG Bks.

Success Forces. Joseph Sugarman. 210p. (C). 1989. pap. 59.00 (*0-948353-49-X*, Pub. by Oldcastle Bks UK) St Mut.

Success from the Start: Questions & Answers about Gesell Assessments. Pat Eyster. Ed. by Robert Low. 20p. (Orig.). (C). 1990. pap. text ed. 2.00 (*0-318-50108-2*) Programs Educ.

Success from Within: Discovering the Inner State That Creates Personal Fulfillment & Business Success. Jay B. Marcus. LC 90-62354. (Illus.). 200p. 1990. pap. 12.00 (*0-923569-04-9*, G-02) Maharishi U Mgmt Pr.

Success Gems: Your Personal Motivational Success Guide. Jewel D. Taylor. 128p. (Orig.). 1995. pap. 10.00 (*1-884743-02-1*) Quiet Time Pubng.

Success Guide to Managerial Achievement. Robin Stuart-Kotze & Rick Roskin. (C). 1983. pap. 18.95 (*0-8359-7142-2*, Reston) P-H.

***Success Happens with the Positive Alphabet.** Les A. Webster. 1996. spiral bd. write for info. (*1-890197-02-5*); spiral bd. write for info. (*1-890197-03-3*) Les A Webster.

Success, Happiness, Independence: Own Your Own Business. Donald J. Phelan. LC 94-79175. 183p. 1995. 19.95 (*0-944435-31-9*) Glenbridge Pub.

Success How-To's of Money-Making Direct Mail. Galen Stilson & Neal Michaels. (Mail Order Success Ser.: No. 4). 32p. 1985. pap. 12.00 (*0-915665-10-7*) Premier Publishers.

***Success in ACLS: Cases & Critical Thinking.** American Heart Association Staff. 000100p. (C). (gr. 13). 1997. pap. text ed. 9.95 (*0-8151-0916-4*, 28829, Yr Bk Med Pubs) Mosby Yr Bk.

Success in America: The Yeoman Dream & the Industrial Revolution. Rex Burns. LC 75-32482. (Illus.). 224p. 1976. 30.00 (*0-87023-207-X*) U of Mass Pr.

Success in Answering Reference Questions: Two Studies. Frances Benham & Ronald R. Powell. LC 86-14629. (Illus.). 313p. 1987. 32.50 (*0-8108-1940-6*) Scarecrow.

Success in Athletics. Carl Johnson. (Success Sportbooks Ser.). (Illus.). 1977. 12.00 (*0-7195-3375-9*) Transatl Arts.

Success in Bowling: Through Practical Fundamentals. Carol Blassingame & Thomas S. Cross. 80p. 1993. per. 9.39 (*0-8403-8570-6*) Kendall-Hunt.

Success in British History Seventeen Sixty to Nineteen Fourteen. Peter Lane. (Success Sportbooks Ser.). (Illus.). 1978. pap. 12.00 (*0-7195-3483-6*) Transatl Arts.

Success in Circuit Lies: Diderot's Communicational Practice. Rosalina De la Carrera. LC 91-2608. 256p. 1991. 35.00 (*0-8047-1923-3*) Stanford U Pr.

Success in College: The Role of Personal Qualities & Academic Ability. Warren W. Willingham. 240p. (Orig.). 1985. 26.95 (*0-87447-229-6*); pap. 16.95 (*0-87447-228-8*) College Bd.

***Success in College Using the Internet.** Jack Pejsa. 196p. (C). 1997. pap. text ed. 11.56 (*0-395-83016-8*) HM.

Success in Court. Francis L. Wellman. xviii, 404p. 1982. reprint ed. lib. bdg. 35.00 (*0-8377-1326-9*) Rothman.

***Success in Data Response for A-Level Economics.** Gleyns Jones. 154p. (Orig.). 1996. pap. 27.50 (*0-7487-2787-6*, Pub. by Stanley Thornes UK) Trans-Atl Phila.

Success in Football (Soccer) 3rd ed. Mike Smith. (Illus.). 96p. 1984. 12.00 (*0-7195-2822-4*) Transatl Arts.

Success in Managing a Small Business. Henry Kyambalesa. 272p. 1994. 55.95 (*1-85628-924-9*, Pub. by Avebury Pub UK) Ashgate Pub Co.

Success in Marriage-Guaranteed !!! The Secret of Making Friends & Keeping them. John Bryant. (Orig.). 1987. pap. 4.95 (*0-9617444-4-8*) Socratic Pr.

Success in Mathematics. (Success Studybooks Ser.). (Illus.). 609p. 1975. 12.00 (*0-7195-2901-8*) Transatl Arts.

Success in Multi-Level Marketing. Gini G. Scott. 1991. 22.95 (*0-13-877796-9*) P-H.

Success in Multi-Level Marketing. Gini G. Scott. 1991. pap. text ed. 14.95 (*0-13-656315-5*) P-H.

Success in New Home Sales: Developing the Right Mentality & Techniques. Richard Tiller. 160p. 1991. pap. 19.95 (*0-9630722-0-X*) Tiller Mktg.

Success in Newsletter Publishing: A Practical Guide. 314p. 1993. 39.50 (*0-318-03791-2*) Newsletter Pubs Assn.

***Success in Practical Nursing: Personal & Vocational Issues.** 2nd ed. Ed. by Signe S. Hill & Helen A. Howlett. (Illus.). 1993. teacher ed., pap. write for info. (*0-7216-6466-0*) Saunders.

Success in Practical Nursing: Personal & Vocational Issues. 3rd ed. Signe S. Hill & Helen A. Howlett. Ed. by Ilze Rader. LC 96-35766. (Illus.). 448p. 1997. pap. text ed. 21.95 (*0-7216-6877-1*) Saunders.

***Success in Practical Nursing: Personal & Vocational Issues.** 3rd ed. Signe S. Hill & Helen A. Howlett. (Illus.). 1997. teacher ed., pap. write for info. (*0-7216-6878-X*) Saunders.

Success in Reading & Writing. 2nd ed. Jean F. Bernholz & Patricia H. Sumner. (Illus.). 288p. 1991. 27.95 (*0-673-36005-9*, GoodYrBooks) Addson-Wesley Educ.

Success in Reading & Writing. 2nd ed. Barbara J. Blackford & Betty Cramer. (Illus.). 288p. (J). (gr. k). 1991. 27.95 (*0-673-36000-8*, GoodYrBooks) Addson-Wesley Educ.

Success in Reading & Writing: Grade 1. 2nd ed. Henel G. Cappleman. (Illus.). 288p. 1991. 27.95 (*0-673-36001-6*, GoodYrBooks) Addson-Wesley Educ.

Success in Reading & Writing: Grade 2. 2nd ed. Helen G. Cappleman. (Illus.). 288p. 1991. 27.95 (*0-673-36002-4*, GoodYrBooks) Addson-Wesley Educ.

Success in Reading & Writing: Grade 3. 2nd ed. Lisa Lord. (Illus.). 288p. 1991. 27.95 (*0-673-36003-2*, GoodYrBooks) Addson-Wesley Educ.

Success in Reading & Writing: Grade 4. 2nd ed. Patricia H. Sumner & Jean F. Bernholz. (Illus.). 288p. 1991. 27.95 (*0-673-36004-0*, GoodYrBooks) Addson-Wesley Educ.

Success in Reading & Writing: Grade 6. 2nd ed. Lisa Lord. (Illus.). 288p. 1991. 27.95 (*0-673-36006-7*, GoodYrBooks) Addson-Wesley Educ.

Success in Sports. Nick D. Smart. LC 95-8246. (African American Life Ser.). (J). (gr. 2-6). 1995. write for info. (*1-57103-032-8*) Rourke Pr.

Success in the Making: How Smaller U. S. Companies Are Winning New Markets in Japan. (Illus.). 57p. (Orig.). (C). 1994. pap. text ed. 25.00 (*0-7881-1062-4*) DIANE Pub.

Success in the 'Real World' The Graduate's Complete Guide to Making the Most of Your Career (& Your Life)! Kathryn A. Marion. LC 95-90069. 64p. (Orig.). 1995. pap. 5.95 (*0-9645391-5-2*) Educ Reality.

Success Is... Paul H. Dunn. 1983. 6.95 (*0-88494-481-6*) Bookcraft Inc.

Success Is a Choice. Richard C. Nelson. (Orig.). 1979. pap. write for info. (*0-932570-01-1*) Guidelines Pr.

***Success Is a Choice: Ten Steps to Overachieving in Business & Life.** Rick Pitino. 1997. 25.00 (*0-553-47840-0*) Bantam.

***Success Is a Choice: Ten Steps to Overachieving in Business & Life.** Rick Pitino & Bill Reynolds. LC 97-2298. 288p. 1997. 25.00 (*0-553-06668-4*); cd-rom 25.00 (*0-553-45558-3*) Bantam.

Success Is a Fly in the Eye of a Frog. Gene Bedley & Gary Greene. LC 94-68954. 56p. (J). 1995. 20.00 (*1-888353-17-1*) People-Wise.

Success Is a Job in New York . . . The Early Art & Business of Andy Warhol. Donna De Salvo et al. Ed. by Sara Blackburn. LC 89-80466. (Illus.). 92p. (Orig.). 1989. pap. 20.00 (*0-934349-05-3*) Grey Art Gallery Study Ctr.

Success Is a Team Effort. Charles B. Dygert. 95p. 1993. pap. 6.95 (*1-884182-00-3*) Motivat Ent.

Success Is an Inside Job: Heart, Integrity & Intuition, the Secrets to Getting Anything You Want. Lee Milteer. 264p. (Orig.). 1996. pap. 11.95 (*1-57174-031-7*) Hampton Roads Pub Co.

Success Is Never Ending, Failure Is Never Final. Robert H. Schuller. 304p. 1990. mass mkt. 5.99 (*0-553-28182-8*) Bantam.

Success Is No Accident: Learn How to Get What You Want. Lair Ribiero. 112p. 1996. 16.95 (*0-312-14425-3*) St Martin.

***Success Is Not an Accident! Change Your Choices. Change Your Life.** Tommy Newberry. (Illus.). 180p. 1997. 22.00 (*1-886669-07-4*) T Newberry.

Success Is Not an Accident: The Mental Bank Concept. rev. ed. John G. Kappas. (Illus.). 236p. 1982. pap. 14.95 (*0-614-04957-1*) Panorama Van Nuys.

Success Is the Quality of Your Journey. Jennifer James. LC 85-73148. 136p. (Orig.). 1991. pap. 10.00 (*0-937858-66-8*) Newmarket.

Success Is You. Ford & Associates Staff. 144p. 1994. per., pap. text ed. 16.95 (*0-7872-0232-0*) Kendall-Hunt.

***Success: It's Your Birthright: Discover Who You Really Are & Learn How to Co-Control Your Destiny.** 2nd rev. ed. Larry Adebesin & Denise Adebesin. 142p. 1997. reprint ed. pap. write for info. (*0-9651929-8-9*) Enrichment Pub.

***Success: It's Your Birthright: Discover Who You Really Are & Learn: How to Co-Control Your Destiny, Experience Increased Health & Vitality, & Live the Lifestyle of Your Dreams.** Larry Adebesin & Denise Adebesin. 136p. (Orig.). 1997. pap. 12.95 (*0-9651929-0-3*) Enrichment Pub.

***Success Journey: The Process of Living Your Dreams.** John C. Maxwell. LC 96-52135. 240p. 1997. 19.99 (*0-7852-7429-4*) Nelson.

***Success Leaves Clues: Practical Tools for Effective Sales & Marketing.** John Stanton. (Taking Control Ser.). 1997. pap. text ed. 29.95 (*1-56343-161-0*) Merritt Pub.

Success Made Fun. Jim Brancaleone. LC 81-90660. (Orig.). 1981. pap. 14.95 (*0-9601186-2-4*) Brancaleone Educ.

Success Management: How to Get to the Top & Keep Your Sanity Once You Get There. E. Carol Webster. LC 93-84548. 160p. (Orig.). 1993. pap. 19.95 (*0-9636983-0-3*) Privileged Comm.

***Success Memo, Success System.** 190p. (Orig.). 1995. spiral bd. write for info. (*0-9658371-6-5*) M Goloversic.

Success Model: The Five Step System to Completely Revolutionize Your Life. Sam Silverstein. LC 93-87199. 232p. 1994. write for info. (*0-9639468-4-6*) Star Pubng.

Success Modules Chemistry. Timothy Kling. 176p. (C). 1995. pap. text ed., ring bd. 21.00 (*0-7872-1075-7*) Kendall-Hunt.

Success, Motivation & the Scriptures. William H. Cook. LC 74-82582. 224p. 1975. 7.99 (*0-8054-5226-5*, 4252-26) Broadman.

Success Motivation Through the Word. Charles Capps. 272p. 1982. pap. 5.99 (*0-89274-183-X*, HH-183) Harrison Hse.

***Success Nuggets.** Orison S. Marden. 76p. 1997. pap. 6.00 (*0-89540-354-4*) Sun Pub.

Success of Caroline Jones Advertising, Inc. Robert Fleming. (Success Ser.). (Illus.). 96p. (YA). (gr. 5 up). 1996. 15.95 (*0-8027-8353-8*) Walker & Co.

Success of Caroline Jones, Inc. Robert Fleming. (Success Ser.). (Illus.). 112p. (YA). 1996. lib. bdg. 16.85 (*0-8027-8354-6*) Walker & Co.

Success of Failure. Joel Fisher. LC 86-82816. (Illus.). 45p. 1987. 14.00 (*0-916365-20-4*) Ind Curators.

Success of Failures: A True Story of a Learning Disabled Student. Brian Wilson. LC 93-79826. (Illus.). 112p. (Orig.). (YA). (gr. 6-12). 1993. pap. 5.00 (*1-884063-14-4*) Mar Co Prods.

Success of Gordon H. Chong & Associates: An Architect's Success Story. Steven A. Chin. (Success Ser.). (Illus.). 112p. (J). (gr. 4-7). 1996. 15.95 (*0-8027-8307-4*); lib. bdg. 16.85 (*0-8027-8308-2*) Walker & Co.

Success of Hispanic Magazine: A Publishing Success Story. John Garcia. (Success Ser.). (Illus.). 112p. (YA). (gr. 5 up). 1996. 15.95 (*0-8027-8309-0*) Walker & Co.

Success of Navajo Arts & Crafts Enterprise: A Retail Success Story. LeNora B. Trahant. (Success Ser.). (Illus.). 112p. (YA). (gr. 5 up). 1996. 15.95 (*0-8027-8336-8*) Walker & Co.

Success of Political Terrorist Events: An Analysis of Terrorist Tactics & Victim Characteristics, 1968 to 1977. Idris Sharif. 174p. 1995. lib. bdg. 36.50 (*0-7618-0130-8*) U Pr of Amer.

Success of Russian Economic Reform. Brigitte Granville. 153p. (C). 1995. pap. 15.95 (*1-899658-06-8*) Brookings.

Success of the Navajo Arts & Crafts Enterprise: A Retail Success Story. LeNora B. Trahant. (Success Ser.). (Illus.). 112p. (YA). (gr. 5 up). 1996. lib. bdg. 16.85 (*0-8027-8337-6*) Walker & Co.

***Success of the Soul: A Guide to Peace, Purpose & Prosperity.** Subagh S. Khalsa. LC 97-14094. 1997. pap. text ed. 21.95 incl. audio (*0-8048-3103-3*) C E Tuttle.

Success or Failure? Family Planning Programs in the Third World. Donald J. Hernandez. LC 84-6653. (Studies in Population & Urban Demography: No. 4). (Illus.). xviii, 161p. 1985. text ed. 45.00 (*0-313-24401-4*, HSU/, Greenwood Pr) Greenwood.

Success-Oriented P. E. Activities for Secondary Students Success Oriented PE Activities for Secondary Stude: Pre-Game Sports Units & Fitness Motivators Including Cooperative, Interdisciplinary & Critical Thinking Lesson Strands. Bud Turner & Sue Turner. LC 95-25331. 400p. 1996. spiral bd. 29.95 (*0-13-447434-1*) P-H.

Success Oriented Schools: An Educator's Handbook for the 21st Century. Ralph E. Robinson & Barbara A. Beswick. 328p. (Orig.). (C). 1996. pap. text ed. 37.50 (*0-7618-0255-X*) U Pr of Amer.

Success Oriented Supervision. rev. ed. Ed. by Albert St. Denis. 1980. 44.15 (*0-87771-019-8*) Grad School.

Success over Distress: Using Muscle Testing to Help You Master Your Fears, to Expand Your Awareness, & Reach Your Full Potential. Wayne W. Topping. (Illus.). 144p. (Orig.). 1990. student ed., pap. 13.95 (*0-935299-09-2*) Topping Inst.

Success over Stress. Joseph L. Palotta. 184p. 1990. pap. 6.95 (*0-9604852-3-6*) Revelation Hse.

Success over Stress. Paul Terry et al. 52p. 1990. student ed. write for info. (*1-884153-00-3*) Prk Nicollet.

Success Paradigm: Creating Organizational Effectiveness Through Quality & Strategy. Michael E. Friesen & James A. Johnson. LC 95-3265. 232p. 1995. text ed. 55.00 (*0-89930-836-8*, Quorum Bks) Greenwood.

Success Path. James C. Van Houten, Sr. (Illus.). 96p. (Orig.). 1995. pap. 7.95 (*0-9648384-0-0*) Knowledge First.

***Success Principle.** Ronald N. Yeaple. 1996. pap. 15.95 (*0-02-861416-X*) Macmillan.

Success Process. Brown Landone. 233p. 1981. 12.00 (*0-89540-181-9*, SB-181) Sun Pub.

Success Public Communication. 2nd ed. Roy Schwartzman. 144p. (C). 1996. per., pap. text ed. 17.79 (*0-7872-1047-1*) Kendall-Hunt.

Success-Pure & Simple: How to Make It in Business, Sports & the Arts. Dominic N. Certo. LC 83-90470. (Self-Help Bks.). (Illus.). 200p. (Orig.). 1983. reprint ed. pap. 12.95 (*0-915755-00-9*) Hillside Pubns.

***Success Redefined: Notes to a Working Woman.** Lori Giovannoni. LC 97-6417. (Illus.). 128p. (Orig.). 1997. pap. 12.95 (*1-880913-26-7*) Innisfree Pr.

Success Runs in Our Race: The Complete Guide to Effective Networking in the African American Community. George Fraser. 352p. 1996. pap. 12.50 (*0-380-72622-X*) Avon.

Success Runs in Our Race: The Complete Guide to Effective Networking in the African-American Community. George C. Fraser. LC 93-51512. 1994. 25.00 (*0-688-12915-3*) Morrow.

***Success Secrets: A Common Sense Guide to Lifelong Achievement.** Merrill Douglass. 256p. Date not set. pap. 11.99 (*1-56292-189-4*) Honor Bks OK.

Success Secrets of the Motivational Superstars: America's Greatest Speakers Reveal Their Secrets. Michael Jeffreys. LC 96-22802. 511p. 1996. per., pap. 16.00 (*0-7615-0612-8*) Prima Pub.

Success Secrets of the Sales Funnel. Ray Leone. 1992. 24.95 (*1-881196-25-9*) SSS Pub.

Success Signs. Marlene M. Rathgeb. (Illus.). 224p. 1981. pap. 5.95 (*0-312-77486-9*) St Martin.

Success Sparklers: A Treasury of Quips, Quotes & Sparkling Sayings for the Positive Person. 2nd ed. Ivy Conner. 163p. 1990. pap. text ed. 10.95 (*1-878579-02-9*) SUN Pub Co.

***Success Starts Early: How to Prepare Your Children for School & Life Success.** Stan Wonderley. LC 97-3117. (Illus.). 220p. (Orig.). 1997. pap. 14.95 (*0-933025-54-8*) Blue Bird Pub.

Success State of Mind: A Guide for Business People & Students. Don Kracke & Lee Whipple. LC 95-72936. (Illus.). 133p. (Orig.). 1996. pap. 9.95 (*0-9636932-0-4*) Silver Spur.

***Success Stories.** Russell Banks. 192p. 1996. 29.00 (*0-8095-9200-2*) Borgo Pr.

Success Stories. Russell Banks. LC 95-53322. 1996. write for info. (*0-614-95865-2*, PL) HarpC.

Success Stories. Russell Banks. 192p. 1996. pap. text ed. 10.00 (*0-06-092719-4*) HarpC.

Success Stories. Anne C. Ward & Robert L. Sandidge. 1996. pap. 27.50 (*1-57654-002-2*, Creative Core) New Orient Media.

Success Stories: A Multicultural Reader. Joan Weinberg. pap. write for info. (*0-13-150046-5*) P-H.

Success Stories from Drug-Free Schools: A Guide for Educators, Parents & Policymakers. (Illus.). 60p. (Orig.). (C). 1993. pap. text ed. 20.00 (*0-7881-0070-X*) DIANE Pub.

Success Stories in the American Electronics Industry. Ed. by Raymond Martin. 106p. 1991. 15.00 (*1-55822-033-X*) Am Prod & Inventory.

Success Stories on Lowering Health Care Costs by Improving Health Care Quality. M. Daniel Sloan & Jodi B. Torpey. (Illus.). 284p. 1995. pap. 28.00 (*0-87389-262-3*, H0818) ASQC Qual Pr.

Success Strategies. Marge Knoth. (Illus.). 1998. write for info. (*0-927935-12-0*) Valley Pr IN.

Success Strategies. Beatryce Nivens. 1998. pap. 24.95 (*0-525-94062-6*) NAL-Dutton.

Success Strategies: Life's Simple Truths. Joseph Caruso. 179p. 1995. 15.00 (*1-885671-07-5*) Caruso Leader Inst.

Success Strategies for Design Professionals: SuperPositioning for Architecture & Engineering Firms. Weld Coxe et al. LC 92-7581. 152p. (C). 1992. reprint ed. lib. bdg. 36.95 (*0-89464-732-6*) Krieger.

Success Strategies for Investment Real Estate: The Professionals Guide to Better Service & Increased Commissions. 2nd ed. Jerry D. Anderson. Ed. by Helene Berlin. LC 82-61402. (Illus.). 322p. (Orig.). (C). 1985. pap. text ed. 17.95 (*0-913652-33-4*, BK 153) Realtors Natl.

Success Strategies for Women in Business. Ramsey-Wilkes. 224p. 1993. pap. text ed. 19.95 (*0-8403-8166-2*) Kendall-Hunt.

Success Strategies from Heaven. Keith Butler. 112p. 1995. pap. 6.99 (*0-89274-745-5*, HH-745) Harrison Hse.

Success Syndrome: Hitting Bottom When You Reach the Top. Steven Berglas. 300p. 1986. 19.95 (*0-306-42349-9*, Plenum Pr) Plenum.

Success System That Never Fails. W. Clement Stone. 1991. pap. 5.99 (*0-671-73265-X*) S&S Trade.

Success Through a Positive Mental Attitude. Napoleon Hill & W. Clement Stone. 1985. pap. 6.95 (*0-13-859422-8*) P-H.

Success Through a Positive Mental Attitude. Stone. 1991. mass mkt. 6.99 (*0-671-74322-8*, PB Trade Paper) PB.

Success Through a Positive Mental Attitude. Napoleon Hill. 1995. reprint ed. lib. bdg. 29.95 (*1-56849-618-4*) Buccaneer Bks.

Success Through Accepting Responsibility: Principal's Handbook. Jefferson, Thomas, Center Staff. 90p. (J). (gr. k-6). 1987. Grades k-8. teacher ed. 69.95 incl. audio (*0-938308-13-0*) Jefferson Ctr.

Success Through Algebra. Amy Edmondson. (SuperCamp Success Ser.). (YA). (gr. 8-12). 1989. 24.95 (*0-945525-12-5*) Supercamp.

Success Through Color Charisma. Ruth Miller & Sandy Parks. LC 83-73079. 133p. (Orig.). 1983. pap. 12.00 (*0-916359-38-7*) Color Charisma.

Success Through Math Mastery. Learning Forum Staff. (SuperCamp Success Ser.). (YA). (gr. 8-12). 1989. 24.95 (*0-945525-11-7*) Supercamp.

Success Through Mind Power. 2nd ed. Roy Hunter. Ed. by Gil Boyne. 136p. (Orig.). 1986. pap. 7.95 (*0-930298-27-6*) Westwood Pub Co.

Success Through Partnership: An Entrepreneurial Strategy. 2nd ed. Reinhard Mohn. LC 96-7860. 198p. 1996. reprint ed. 19.95 (*0-385-48593-X*) Doubleday.

Success Through Spirituality for Women. Barbara Gray. 1995. 19.95 (*0-9637784-4-7*) B Gray ProActives.

Success Through Teamwork: A Practical Guide to Interpersonal Team Dynamics. Richard Y. Chang. (High Performance Team Ser.). Orig. Title: Managing Team Dynamics. (Illus.). 101p. 1994. pap. 12.95 (*1-883553-25-3*) R Chang Assocs.

Success Through the Stars: An Astrological Guide to Defining & Living a Satisfying Life. Carole Golder. LC 95-4472. 1996. pap. 10.95 (*0-8050-3977-5*, Owl) H Holt & Co.

Success Through Transactional Analysis. Jut Meininger. 224p. 1974. pap. 3.50 (*0-451-12637-8*, Sig) NAL-Dutton.

***Success 2000: Moving into the Millenium with Purpose, Power & Prosperity.** Vicki L. Spina. 256p. 1997. pap. 16.95 (*0-471-17184-0*) Wiley.

Success While Others Fail: Social Movement Unionism & the Public Workplace. Paul Johnston. LC 94-32761. 272p. (Orig.). 1994. 45.00 (*0-87546-334-7*, ILR Press) Cornell U Pr.

Success While Others Fail: Social Movement Unionism & the Public Workplace. Paul Johnston. LC 94-32761. 272p. (Orig.). 1994. pap. 18.95 (*0-87546-335-5*, ILR Press) Cornell U Pr.

***Success with Challenging Students.** Jeffrey A. Kottler. LC 97-21016. (Practical Skills for Counselors Ser.). 1997. write for info. (*0-8039-6651-2*); pap. write for info. (*0-8039-6652-0*) Corwin Pr.

Success with Color Desktop Publishing with CD ROM. Kris Jamsa. 416p. 1997. pap. 49.95 incl. disk (*1-884133-02-9*) Jamsa Pr.

S

S

Success with Educational Software. Frederick Williams & Victoria Williams. LC 85-5679. 192p. 1985. text ed. 49.95 (*0-275-90186-6*, C0186, Praeger Pubs) Greenwood.

Success with Heart Failure: Help & Hope for Those with Congestive Heart Failure. Marc A. Silver. LC 94-28255. (Illus.). 293p. 1994. 23.95 (*0-306-44767-3*, Plenum Insight) Plenum.

Success with House Plants. (Illus.). 1986. write for info. (*1-886614-12-1*) Intl Masters Pub.

Success with House Plants. Reader's Digest Editors. LC 78-59802. (Illus.). 480p. 1981. 26.00 (*0-89577-052-0*) RD Assn.

Success with Internet. Jamsa. (Computer Applications Ser.). 1996. pap. 36.95 (*0-7895-0088-4*) Course Tech.

Success with Internet. Allen Wyatt. 1994. pap. 29.95 incl. disk (*1-884133-01-0*) Jamsa Pr.

Success with Maps, Bk. C. (J). Date not set. pap. 4.25 (*0-590-34356-4*) Scholastic Inc.

Success with Maps, Bk. C. Date not set. teacher ed., pap. 6.25 (*0-590-34357-2*) Scholastic Inc.

Success with Maps, Bk. D. (J). Date not set. pap. 4.25 (*0-590-34358-0*) Scholastic Inc.

Success with Maps, Bk. D. Date not set. teacher ed., pap. 6.25 (*0-590-34359-9*) Scholastic Inc.

Success with Maps, Bk. A. (J). Date not set. pap. 4.25 (*0-590-34352-1*) Scholastic Inc.

Success with Maps, Bk. A. Date not set. teacher ed., pap. 6.25 (*0-590-34353-X*) Scholastic Inc.

Success with Maps, Bk. B. (J). Date not set. pap. 4.25 (*0-590-34354-8*) Scholastic Inc.

Success with Maps, Bk. B. Date not set. teacher ed., pap. 6.25 (*0-590-34355-6*) Scholastic Inc.

Success with Maps, Bk. E. (J). Date not set. pap. 4.25 (*0-590-34360-2*) Scholastic Inc.

Success with Maps, Bk. E. Date not set. teacher ed., pap. 6.25 (*0-590-34361-0*) Scholastic Inc.

Success with Maps, Bk. F. (J). Date not set. pap. 4.25 (*0-590-34362-9*) Scholastic Inc.

Success with Maps, Bk. F. Date not set. teacher ed., pap. 6.25 (*0-590-34363-7*) Scholastic Inc.

Success with Multimedia Programming. Kris Jamsa. pap. 49.95 (*1-884133-11-8*) Jamsa Pr.

Success with Parts. Robert A. Pearson. (Illus.). 42p. (Orig.). 1976. pap. 4.20 (*0-9608378-0-9*) B Pearson.

Success with Rhododendrons & Azaleas. H. Edward Reilly. LC 91-23249. (Illus.). 314p. 1992. 29.95 (*0-88192-211-0*) Timber.

Success with Rhododendrons & Azaleas. H. Edward Reilly. (Illus.). 314p. 1995. pap. 22.95 (*0-88192-331-1*) Timber.

Success with School Gardens: How to Create a Learning Oasis in the Desert. Linda A. Guy et al. LC 96-84767. (Illus.). 144p. (Orig.). 1996. pap. 14.95 (*0-9651987-0-7*) AZ Mstr Grdnrs.

***Success with Soul: New Insights to Achieving Success with Real Meaning.** Doris Pozzi & Stephen Williams. LC 97-60118. (Illus.). 304p. (Orig.). 1997. pap. 14.95 (*0-646-28692-7*) D Welles.

Success with the Gentle Art of Verbal Self Defense. Suzette H. Elgin. 1990. student ed. 99.95 incl. audio (*0-924967-01-3*) Intl Ctr Creat Think.

Success with the Gentle Art of Verbal Self-Defense: Communication Strategies Across the Power Gap. Suzette H. Elgin. 1989. pap. text ed. 14.00 (*0-13-688581-0*) P-H.

***Success with the Scrollsaw.** Zachary Taylor. (Illus.). 160p. 1997. 35.00 (*1-86126-024-5*, Pub. by Crowood Pr UK) Trafalgar.

Success with Windows 95. Kris Jamsa & Naba Barkakati. 480p. 1996. pap. 29.95 (*1-884133-16-9*) Jamsa Pr.

***Success with Windows 95.** Kris Jamsa. 2000p. 1996. cd-rom 49.95 (*1-884133-17-7*) Jamsa Pr.

Success with WordPerfect 7 for Windows 95. Ed Martin. 1997. pap. text ed. 72.00 (*1-57576-028-2*) Que Educ & Trng.

Success with Words: An Easy-to-Use Step-by-Step System That Gives You a More Powerful Vocabulary. 2nd ed. Joan D. Carris & Pat Ordovensky. LC 87-29202. 390p. (Orig.). Date not set. pap. 11.95 (*1-56079-452-6*) Petersons.

Success Without Compromise: There's Only One Way to Succeed & Be Happy. 2nd ed. Richard H. LeTourneau. LC 77-80947. (LeTourneau One-Way Ser.: Vol. 4). 176p. 1985. reprint ed. pap. 5.95 (*0-88207-757-0*) LeTourneau Pr.

Success Without Success. George Burgess. 208p. 1995. mass mkt. 4.99 (*0-88368-369-5*) Whitaker Hse.

Success Yearbook: Three Hundred Sixty-Five Days to Mastery. Dale Ledbetter. (Sales Mastery Ser.). 425p. 1994. pap. 15.95 (*1-884667-00-7*) Gage Res & Develop.

Success, Your Dream & You: A Personal Success Guide to Marketing. Patricia Raskin. LC 90-52808. 224p. 1991. 19.95 (*0-915677-51-2*) Roundtable Pub.

Success, Your Style! Right & Left Brain Techniques for Learning. Nancy L. Matte & Susan H. Henderson. LC 94-41287. 219p. 1995. pap. 27.95 (*0-534-24468-8*) Wadsworth Pub.

***SuccessAbilities.** Paula Ancona. 1997. pap. 14.95 (*1-56370-444-7*, Park Avenue) JIST Works.

SuccessAbilities: 1003 Practical Ways to Keep up, Stand Out & Move Ahead at Work. Paula Ancona. 288p. (Orig.). 1995. pap. 14.95 (*1-886644-00-4*) Chamisa Pr.

Successes & Failures-Flowing Sweet Waters. Bronislav R. Mehl. 1993. 17.95 (*0-533-10058-5*) Vantage.

Successeurs De la Fontaine Au Siecle Des Lumieres (1715-1815) Jean-Noel Pascal. (Eighteenth Century French Intellectual History Ser.: Vol. 3). 288p. (FRE.). (C). 1995. text ed. 57.95 (*0-8204-2534-6*) P Lang Pubng.

Successful Acquisition of Unquoted Companies. 3rd ed. Barrie Pearson. 192p. 1989. text ed. 77.95 (*0-566-02814-X*, Pub. by Gower UK) Ashgate Pub Co.

Successful Activities for Enriching the Language Arts. Betty Coody & David Nelson. (Illus.). 262p. (C). 1986. reprint ed. pap. text ed. 14.95 (*0-88133-195-3*) Waveland Pr.

Successful Administration in Senior Housing: Working with Elderly Residents. Nancy W. Sheehan. (Illus.). 240p. (C). 1992. 46.00 (*0-8039-4524-8*); pap. 21.50 (*0-8039-4525-6*) Sage.

Successful Adoptive Families: A Longitudinal Study of Special Needs Adoption. Victor Groze. LC 95-11264. 184p. 1996. text ed. 49.95 (*0-275-95343-2*, Praeger Pubs) Greenwood.

Successful Advertising Research Methods. Jack B. Haskins & Alice Gagnard-Kendrick. 464p. (C). 1994. text ed. 39.95 (*0-8442-3189-4*, NTC Busn Bks) NTC Pub Grp.

***Successful African American Males: Education Makes a Difference.** Mildred Reese & Thelma Smith. Ed. by Yvette B. McCann. 256p. (YA). (gr. 7-12). 1997. pap. 16.00 (*0-9657163-4-1*) Educ Resources.

Successful Ageing. Gingold. 280p. 1992. pap. 19.95 (*0-19-553206-6*) OUP.

***Successful Aging.** J. W. Rowe & Kahn. 1998. write for info. (*0-375-40045-1*) Pantheon.

Successful Aging: Perspectives from the Behavioral Sciences. Ed. by Paul B. Baltes & Margaret M. Baltes. (European Network on Longitudinal Studies on Individual Development). (Illus.). 400p. (C). 1990. 69.95 (*0-521-37454-5*) Cambridge U Pr.

Successful Aging: Perspectives from the Behavioral Sciences. Ed. by Paul B. Baltes & Margaret M. Baltes. (European Network on Longitudinal Studies on Individual Development). (Illus.). 413p. (C). 1993. pap. text ed. 22.95 (*0-521-43582-X*) Cambridge U Pr.

***Successful Aging: Strategies That Promote Healthy Living.** W. C. Klein & M. Bloom. (Prevention in Practice Library). 190p. (C). 1997. write for info. (*0-306-45664-8*, Plenum Pr); pap. write for info. (*0-306-45663-X*, Plenum Pr) Plenum.

Successful American's Guide to Financial Planning: How to Keep What You've Got & Get More of the Same. Steven R. Kaye. 24.95 (*0-8359-7137-6*) S&S Trade.

Successful Approach to Your Venture Capital Needs: Your Key to a Venture Capital Fortune. Peter C. Forkuo. (Home Entrepreneurs Success Library). 1982. 29.95 (*0-941928-00-4*) P C Forkuo World Ent.

Successful Arbitration: Experience in the Preparation & Presentation of Arbitration Cases. Randy D. Elkin & Thomas L. Hewitt. (Illus.). 128p. 1980. teacher ed. write for info. (*0-8359-7145-7*, Reston) P-H.

Successful Armed Robbery. Harold S. Long. LC 89-63706. 56p. (Orig.). 1990. pap. 8.95 (*1-55950-023-9*, 40065) Loompanics.

Successful Artist Management. enl. rev. ed. Xavier M. Frascogna & H. Lee Hetherington. 288p. 1990. pap. 14.95 (*0-8230-7689-X*, Billboard Bks) Watsn-Guptill.

***Successful Assertiveness.** Dena Michelli. LC 96-32472. 1997. pap. 6.95 (*0-7641-0071-8*) Barron.

Successful Association Leadership: Dimensions of 21st Century Competency for the CEO. Glenn Tecker et al. 164p. 1993. pap. 47.50 (*0-88034-073-8*) Am Soc Assn Execs.

Successful Audit: New Ways to Reduce Risk Exposure & Increase Efficiency. Felix Pomeranz. 512p. 1991. text ed. 65.00 (*1-55623-391-4*) Irwin Prof Pubng.

Successful Bank Asset-Liability Management: A Guide to the Future Beyond GAP. John W. Bitner et al. LC 91-41363. 288p. 1992. text ed. 95.00 (*0-471-52731-9*) Wiley.

Successful Bass Fishing. Ken Schultz. (Illus.). 192p. 1996. pap. text ed. 19.95 (*0-07-057236-4*) McGraw.

Successful Bidding & Tendering. P. D. Marsh. (Gower Business Enterprise Ser.). 179p. 1989. text ed. 25.95 (*0-7045-0619-X*, Pub. by Gower UK) Ashgate Pub Co.

Successful Big Game Hunting. Duncan Gilchrist. (Illus.). 176p. 1987. pap. 12.95 (*0-912299-28-2*) Stoneydale Pr Pub.

Successful Big Game Hunting. Duncan B. Gilchrist. (Illus.). 176p. 1987. 17.95 (*0-685-18747-0*) Stoneydale Pr Pub.

Successful Black & Minority Schools. rev. ed. Ed. by Norma Dabney & Shirley Lewis. 96p. (C). 1990. reprint ed. pap. text ed. write for info. (*0-318-67015-1*) J Richardson.

Successful Black & Minority Schools: Classic Models. rev. ed. Mary R. Hoover et al. 110p. (C). 1990. reprint ed. pap. text ed. 12.00 (*0-685-37973-6*) J Richardson.

Successful Bonsai Growing. Peter D. Adams. (Illus.). 96p. (Orig.). 1996. pap. 10.95 (*0-7063-7439-8*, Pub. by Ward Lock UK) Sterling.

Successful Bonsai Shaping. Peter D. Adams. (Illus.). 128p. pap. 14.95 (*0-943955-70-X*, Trafalgar Sq Pub) Trafalgar.

Successful Bookselling: A Management Training Course. 197p. 1993. pap. 55.00 (*92-3-102838-3*, U8383, Pub. by UNESCO FR) Bernan Associates.

Successful Boss's First 100 Days: The Official Guide for the New Boss. Richard Koch. (Institute of Management Foundation Ser.). 208p. (Orig.). 1994. pap. 22.50 (*0-273-60423-6*, Pub. by Pitman Pub Ltd UK) Trans-Atl Phila.

Successful Bowfishing. Glenn Helgeland. LC 82-74191. (On Target Ser.). (Illus.). 84p. (Orig.). 1984. pap. 4.95 (*0-913305-03-0*) Target Comm.

Successful Branch Management. Stemper. 1990. 42.00 (*1-55520-143-1*) Irwin Prof Pubng.

Successful Breastfeeding. 2nd ed. Royal College of Midwives Staff. (Illus.). 88p. 1991. pap. text ed. 10.00 (*0-443-04460-0*) Churchill.

Successful Business Borrowing: How to Plan & Negotiate a Loan. Kenneth W. Sparks. 240p. 1986. 19.95 (*0-8027-0902-8*) Walker & Co.

Successful Business Communication. John Markham. 201p. 1978. pap. 55.00 (*0-900886-21-8*, Pub. by Witherby & Co UK) St Mut.

Successful Business Forecasting. Joan C. Compton & Stephen B. Compton. 204p. 1989. 21.95 (*0-8306-0207-0*) McGraw-Hill Prof.

Successful Business Operations for Electrical Contractors. Ralph E. Johnson. 1992. text ed. 42.00 (*0-07-032655-X*) McGraw.

Successful Business Plan: Secrets & Strategies. Rhonda M. Abrams. LC 93-21563. (Successful Business Library). (Illus.). 360p. 1993. pap. 27.95 (*1-55571-194-4*) Oasis Pr OR.

Successful Business Plan: Secrets & Strategies. 2nd ed. Rhonda M. Abrams. LC 93-21563. (Successful Business Library). (Illus.). 378p. 1993. ring bd. 49.95 (*1-55571-197-9*); ring bd. 125.95 incl. disk (*1-55571-314-9*) Oasis Pr OR.

Successful Business Plan: Secrets & Strategies. 2nd ed. Rhonda M. Abrams. (Illus.). 334p. 1993. 39.95 incl. disk (*1-55571-199-5*) Oasis Pr OR.

Successful Business Plans for Architects. R. A. McKenzie. 1992. text ed. 42.00 (*0-07-045654-2*) McGraw.

Successful Business Policies. Gerald D. Newbould & George A. Luffman. LC 78-70561. 235p. 1979. text ed. 55.00 (*0-275-90400-8*, C0400, Praeger Pubs) Greenwood.

Successful Business Presentations. Joseph A. Quattrini. (Illus.). 264p. 1989. 19.95 (*0-8306-0335-2*) McGraw-Hill Prof.

Successful Business Presentations. Joseph A. Quattrini. 1990. pap. 15.95 (*0-8306-3055-4*) McGraw-Hill Prof.

Successful Business Presentations with Harvard Graphics 3.0. Management Graphics Limited Staff. (Illus.). 256p. (C). 1992. pap. text ed. 27.95 (*0-201-56890-X*) Addison-Wesley.

Successful Business Speaking. David Thomas & Maridell Fryar. 96p. 1987. pap. 6.60 (*0-8442-5233-6*, NTC Busn Bks) NTC Pub Grp.

***Successful Business Strategies Using Telecommunications Services.** Martin F. Bartholomew. LC 97-19473. 304p. 1997. 59.00 (*0-89006-904-2*) Artech Hse.

Successful Business Uses for Abandoned Service Stations. A. L. Kerth. LC 82-61265. (Illus.). 1982. 35.00 (*0-9601188-2-9*) A L Kerth.

Successful Business Writing. Lassor A. Blumenthal. 112p. (Orig.). 1985. pap. 8.95 (*0-399-51146-6*, Perigee Bks) Berkley Pub.

Successful C for Commercial UNIX Developers. Mohamed M. Osman. LC 96-46060. 1996. pap. text ed. 49.00 incl. disk (*0-89006-642-6*) Artech Hse.

Successful CAD Manager's Handbook. Ralph Grabowski & Richard Huber. LC 93-34297. 290p. 1994. pap. 37.50 (*0-8273-5233-6*) Delmar.

Successful Capital Campaign: From Planning to Victory Celebration. Ed. by H. Gerald Quigg. 188p. 1986. 41.50 (*0-89964-248-9*, 29701) Coun Adv & Supp Ed.

Successful Capital Campaigns: A Guide for Medium to Small. Schwartz & Kihlstedt. LC 96-48720. 200-250p. 1996. 59.00 (*0-8342-0794-X*) Aspen Pub.

Successful Car Buying: How to Come Out a Winner, Whether You Buy New, Buy Used, or Lease. Steve Ross. LC 89-35283. (Illus.). 96p. (Orig.). 1990. pap. 9.95 (*0-8117-2246-5*) Stackpole.

Successful Cardiac Rehabilitation: The Complete Guide for Building Cardiac Rehab Programs. Peggy Pashkow et al. 39.95 (*0-9619796-0-7*) HeartWatchers Pr.

Successful Career Development for Engineers: A Guide For Understanding the Steps to Successful Career Advancement. John Hoschette. 196p. 1994. text ed. 54.95 (*0-471-01718-3*); pap. text ed. 15.95 (*0-471-01727-2*) Wiley.

Successful Career Women: Their Professional & Personal Characteristics. Cecilia A. Northcutt. LC 90-38415. (Contributions in Women's Studies: No. 120). 144p. 1991. text ed. 39.95 (*0-313-27256-5*, NPY, Greenwood Pr) Greenwood.

Successful Carp Fishing. Julian Cundiff. (Illus.). 208p. 1996. 45.00 (*1-85223-902-6*, Pub. by Crowood Pr UK) Trafalgar.

Successful Case Management in Long-Term Care. Joan Quinn. LC 92-49033. (Illus.). 176p. 1993. 26.95 (*0-8261-7750-6*) Springer Pub.

***Successful Catalogs.** Retail Reporting Staff. 1989. 52.50 (*0-688-09001-X*) Morrow.

Successful Catalogs. Steve Warsaw. (Illus.). 256p. 1989. 49.95 (*0-934590-30-3*) Retail Report.

Successful Catering. 3rd ed. Bernard R. Splaver. (Illus.). 312p. 1991. text ed. 52.95 (*0-442-23980-7*) Van Nos Reinhold.

Successful Change Strategies. Taylor. 1995. pap. text ed. 31.50 (*0-13-182890-8*) P-H.

Successful Children Almost Effortlessly: Through Self-Management. Allan E. Harrison. LC 83-81135. 275p. (Orig.). (C). 1983. pap. 14.00 (*0-9611440-0-9*) HEMECO.

***Successful Children, Successful Teaching.** Roger Merry. LC 97-17212. (Enriching the Primary Curriculum - Child, Teacher, Context Ser.). 1997. write for info. (*0-335-19743-4*, Open Univ Pr); pap. write for info. (*0-335-19742-6*, Open Univ Pr) Taylor & Francis.

Successful Children's Choir. Ruth K. Jacobs. 64p. 1984. pap. 5.00 (*0-912222-12-3*) FitzSimons.

Successful Children's Choir. Ruth K. Jacobs. 64p. 1995. reprint ed. pap. 8.95 (*0-9646552-2-5*) F Bock Music.

Successful Children's Parties. rev. ed. Julia Goodwin. (Family Matters Ser.). (Illus.). 96p. 1995. pap. 6.95 (*0-7063-7430-4*, Pub. by Ward Lock UK) Sterling.

Successful Christian Living: As Your Personal Experience. Keith Hershey. (Christian Life Ser.). 30p. (Orig.). 1992. pap. 1.95 (*0-940487-08-X*) Jubilee CA.

Successful Civil Litigation: How to Win Your Case Before You Enter the Courtroom. George Vetter. 1976. 34.50 (*0-13-860205-0*, Busn) P-H.

Successful Classroom: Management Strategies for Regular & Special Education Teachers. Doris Fromberg & Maryanne Driscoll. 200p. (C). 1985. pap. text ed. 18.95 (*0-8077-2771-7*) Tchrs Coll.

***Successful Classroom: Management Strategies for Regular & Special Education Teachers.** Doris P. Fromberg & Maryanne Driscoll. LC 85-2687. 222p. pap. 63.30 (*0-608-05098-9*, 2065654) Bks Demand.

Successful Clay Pigeon Shooting. Ed. by Tony Hoare. (Illus.). 176p. 1992. 39.95 (*1-85223-566-7*, Pub. by Crowood Pr UK) Trafalgar.

Successful Coaching. 2nd ed. Rainer Martens. LC 89-37573. (Illus.). 248p. 1990. pap. text ed. 18.00 (*0-88011-376-6*, PMAR0376) Human Kinetics.

Successful Coaching. 2nd ed. Rainer Martens. LC 96-31259. (Illus.). 280p. 1996. pap. 18.95 (*0-88011-666-8*, PMAR0666) Human Kinetics.

Successful Coaching: National Federation Interscholastic Coaches Education Program. Rainer Martens. LC 90-43427. (Illus.). 248p. 1990. pap. text ed. 18.00 (*0-88011-415-0*, ACEP0064) Human Kinetics.

Successful Coaching: Strategies & Tactics. William F. Stier. (Illus.). 542p. (C). 1995. pap. text ed. 34.95 (*0-89641-238-5*) American Pr.

Successful Cocktail Waitressing. Vickie Karp. 78p. (Orig.). 1983. pap. 3.00 (*0-9612360-0-0*) Karp.

Successful Cold Buffets. Peter Grotz. 1990. text ed. 46.95 (*0-442-30551-6*) Chapman & Hall.

Successful Cold Call Selling. 2nd ed. Lee Boyan. LC 88-48041. 288p. 1989. pap. 16.95 (*0-8144-7718-6*) AMACOM.

Successful Collections: Your Key to Survival. Ed Harrison. Ed. by Susan Taylor. LC 95-72711. (Illus.). x, 185p. (Orig.). 1996. pap. 39.95 (*0-9650526-0-5*) SST Pubns.

***Successful College Athletic Program: The New Standard.** John R. Gerdy. (American Council on Education/Oryx Press Series on Higher Education). 128p. (C). 1997. boxed 29.95 (*1-57356-109-6*) Oryx Pr.

Successful Color Mixtures. Helen Van Wyk. Ed. by Herbert Rogoff. (Illus.). 200p. (Orig.). 1983. pap. text ed. 20.75 (*0-929552-00-8*) Art Instr Assocs.

Successful Commodity Futures Trading: How You Can Make Money in Commodity Markets. Tom Watling & Jonathan Monely. 224p. 1974. 32.95 (*0-8464-0896-1*) Beekman Pubs.

***Successful Communication for Business & Management.** 7th ed. Malra Treece & Betty Kleen. (C). 1997. text ed. 51.00 (*0-13-466682-8*) P-H.

Successful Communication for Business & the Professions. 4th ed. Malra Treece. 525p. 1990. teacher ed. write for info. (*0-318-66385-6*, H23468); teacher ed. 13.33 (*0-685-29838-8*, H23476); trans. 100.00 (*0-685-29839-6*, H23484) P-H.

Successful Communication for Business & the Professions. 6th ed. Malra Treece. LC 93-28778. 598p. (C). 1993. text ed. 78.00 (*0-205-15581-2*) Allyn.

***Successful Communication, Success System, Pt. 4.** (Illus.). 400p. (Orig.). 1995. mass mkt. write for info. (*0-9658371-3-0*) M Goloversic.

Successful Communication Through NLP: A Trainer's Guide. Sally Dimmick. LC 95-2772. 176p. 1995. 54.95 (*0-566-07579-2*, Pub. by Gower UK) Ashgate Pub Co.

***Successful Communication with Alzheimer's Patients: An In-Service Training Manual.** Elizabeth E. Ostuni & Mary J. Santo Pietro. LC 96-54719. 144p. 1997. pap. 30.00 (*0-7506-9564-1*) Buttrwrth-Heinemann.

Successful Communications & Effective Speaking. Millard Bennett & John D. Corrigan. 1976. pap. 4.95 (*0-13-860437-1*, Reward) P-H.

***Successful Computing for Business.** Matt Nicholson. LC 96-35968. (Business Success Ser.). 1997. pap. 6.95 (*0-7641-0058-0*) Barron.

Successful Conference: Programming Methods. Gus Mueller. 90p. (Orig.). 1982. pap. 10.00 (*0-9614097-0-3*) Fern Pubns.

***Successful Cool Storage Projects: From Planning to Operation.** James S. Elleson. (Illus.). 117p. 1997. pap. 63.00 (*1-883413-43-5*) Am Busn Direct.

Successful Corporate Acquisitions: A Complete Guide for Acquiring Companies for Growth & Profit. Jerold Freier. 450p. 1990. text ed. 69.95 (*0-13-860503-3*) P-H.

Successful Corporate Turnarounds: A Guide for Board Members, Financial Managers, Financial Institutions, & Other Creditors. Eugene F. Finkin. LC 86-25280. (Illus.). 229p. 1987. text ed. 59.95 (*0-89930-232-7*, FSC/, Quorum Bks) Greenwood.

Successful Corporate Turnarounds: A Guide for Board Members, Financial Managers, Financial Institutions, & Other Creditors. Eugene F. Finkin. LC 88-15177. 229p. 1988. pap. text ed. 16.95 (*0-275-93108-0*, B3108, Praeger Pubs) Greenwood.

Successful Corporation of the Year 2000, No. 1805. 1994. 295.00 (*0-85058-760-3*) Economist Intell.

Successful Cost Reduction & Control. Burton E. Lipman. 267p. 1978. 29.50 (*0-13-860460-6*) Bell Pub.

***Successful CSR.** Lloyd Finch. LC 97-65865. (Professional Ser.). (Illus.). 140p. (Orig.). 1997. pap. 13.95 (*1-56052-450-2*) Crisp Pubns.

***Successful Customer Care.** John H. Wellemin. LC 96-46466. (Business Success Ser.). 1997. pap. 6.95 (*0-7641-0127-7*) Barron.

Successful Decision-Making. Frank L. Bouquet. (Illus.). 50p. (Orig.). 1994. 29.00 (*1-56216-112-1*); pap. 17.00 (*1-56216-113-X*) Systems Co.

Successful Defence in Criminal Trials. S. K. Shanglo. (C). 1988. 65.00 (*0-685-27929-4*) St Mut.

Successful Delegation: How to Grow Your People, Build Your Team, Free Up Your Time, & Increase Profits & Productivity. Frank F. Huppe. 256p. (Orig.). 1994. pap. 16.95 (*1-56414-142-X*) Career Pr Inc.

Successful Dental Practice in Good Times & Bad. Morton M. Ehudin. 1991. 10.00 (*0-87814-361-0*, D4296) PennWell Bks.

Successful Design of Catalysts: Future Requirements & Development. Ed. by T. Inui. (Studies in Surface Science & Catalysis: No. 44). 356p. 1989. 218.75 (*0-444-87146-2*) Elsevier.

Successful Digital Prepress & Productions. Ihrig. 1996. pap. write for info. (*0-201-41041-9*) Addison-Wesley.

***Successful Direct Mail.** Liz Ferdi. LC 96-34995. (Business Success Ser.). 1997. pap. 6.95 (*0-7641-0074-2*) Barron.

***Successful Direct Mail Design.** Tomoe Nakazawa. (Illus.). 224p. 1997. 75.00 (*4-89444-051-2*, Pub. by PIE Bks JA) Bks Nippan.

Successful Direct Marketing Methods. 5th ed. Robert Stone. LC 93-6716. 640p. 1995. 44.95 (*0-8442-3510-5*, NTC Busn Bks) NTC Pub Grp.

Successful Direct Marketing Methods. 6th ed. Robert Stone. LC 96-9100. 640p. 1996. 49.95 (*0-8442-3003-0*, NTC Busn Bks) NTC Pub Grp.

Successful Direct Marketing Methods. 84th ed. Robert Stone. 1993. 29.95 (*0-8442-3086-3*, NTC Busn Bks) NTC Pub Grp.

Successful Direct Marketing Methods. 89th ed. Robert Stone. 592p. 1994. 34.95 (*0-8442-3180-0*, NTC Busn Bks) NTC Pub Grp.

Successful Dissertations & Theses: A Guide to Graduate Student Research from Proposal to Completion. 2nd ed. David Madsen. LC 91-21687. (Higher & Adult Education - Social & Behavioral Science Ser.). 238p. reprint ed. text ed. 22.00 (*1-55542-389-2*) Jossey-Bass.

Successful Dissertations & Theses: A Guide to Graduate Student Research from Proposal to Completion. David Madsen. LC 82-49039. (Joint Publication in the Jossey-Bass Higher Education Series & the Jossey-Bass Social & Behavioral Science Ser.). 192p. reprint ed. pap. 54.80 (*0-7837-2550-7*, 2042709) Bks Demand.

Successful Diversity Management Initiatives. Patricia Arrendondo. 256p. (C). 1996. 45.00 (*0-8039-7290-3*); pap. 21.95 (*0-8039-7291-1*) Sage.

Successful Dog Breeding: The Complete Handbook of Canine Midwifery. 2nd ed. Chris Walkowicz & Bonnie Wilcox. (Illus.). 240p. 1994. pap. 27.95 (*0-87605-740-7*) Howell Bk.

Successful Dog Training. Michael Kamer. (Illus.). 160p. 1994. 29.95 (*0-7938-0083-8*, TS205) TFH Pubns.

Successful Drug & Alcohol Prevention Programs. Ed. by Eileen V. Coughlin. LC 85-644751. (New Directions for Student Services Ser.: No. 67). 97p. (Orig.). 1994. pap. 19.00 (*0-7879-9996-2*) Jossey-Bass.

Successful Electrical Contracting Methods. Michael Sammaritano. (Illus.). 412p. 1995. ring bd. 149.00 (*1-887720-24-3*) Contracting Pubns.

Successful Engineer: Personal & Professional Skills - A Sourcebook. J. Campbell Martin. LC 92-30123. 1993. text ed. write for info. (*0-07-040725-8*) McGraw.

Successful Enjoyable Selling: How to Get the Best Out of Your Career. Paul W. Richards. LC 95-92731. (Illus.). 152p. (Orig.). 1996. pap. 9.95 (*0-9649313-8-9*) Rainier Pub.

Successful Enrollment Management: A Workbook for Nursing Education Recruitment Professionals. American Association of Colleges of Nursing Staff. Ed. by Barbara K. Redman. 250p. (Orig.). 1989. student ed. 35.00 (*0-922148-01-5*) AACN.

Successful Entrepreneurship. 200p. pap. 69.50 incl. audio (*0-88432-087-1*, S01540) Audio-Forum.

***Successful Environmental Management.** Mark Yoxon. LC 97-24745. (Barron's Educational Ser.). 1998. write for info. (*0-7641-0306-7*) Barron.

Successful Estimating Methods: From Concept to Bid. John D. Bledsoe. (Illus.). 250p. 1992. boxed 64.95 (*0-87629-216-3*, 67287) ACMDG Co.

Successful Exam Technique. C. Coker. 1990. pap. 29.00 (*0-7463-0348-3*, Pub. by Northcote UK) St Mut.

Successful Exhibiting. James W. Dudley. 160p. 1990. 50.95 (*0-8464-1358-2*) Beekman Pubs.

Successful Exhibitor's Handbook: Trade Show Techniques for Beginners & Pros. 3rd ed. Barry Siskind. 264p. 1996. pap. 14.95 (*1-55180-090-X*) Self-Counsel Pr.

Successful Faculty in Academic Medicine: Essential Skills & How to Acquire Them. Ed. by Carole J. Bland et al. LC 89-21921. (Medical Education Ser.: Vol. 12). 336p. 1989. 44.95 (*0-8261-6730-6*) Springer Pub.

Successful Families: Assessment & Intervention. W. Robert Beavers & Robert B. Hampson. (C). 1990. 27.95 (*0-393-70091-7*) Norton.

Successful Family Organizations, Record Keeping, & Genealogy in Family Activities. 3rd ed. Arthur Wallace & Shirley Bousfield. (Illus.). 189p. 1978. pap. 3.95 (*0-937892-02-5*) LL Co.

***Successful Farming, 1850-1870: The Farmer's Best Friend, Vol. 3.** Katie F. Hamilton & A. E. Youman. (Dictionary for Every-Day Wants Ser.). 250p. (Orig.). 1997. pap. 10.00 (*1-889023-07-8*) Metheglin Pr.

Successful Field Service Management. Donald N. McCafferty. LC 79-54842. 191p. reprint ed. pap. 54.50 (*0-317-26903-8*, 2023561) Bks Demand.

Successful Field Trips. Mary D. Lankford. LC 91-38558. 175p. 1992. pap. text ed. 35.00 (*0-87436-638-0*) ABC-CLIO.

Successful Financial Management for the Veterinary Practice. Robert E. Froehlich. 92p. (Orig.). 1987. pap. text ed. 24.95 (*0-941451-01-1*) Am Animal Hosp Assoc.

Successful Fine Art Marketing. Marcia Layton. 256p. 1993. 39.95 (*0-913069-45-0*); pap. 19.95 (*0-913069-39-6*) Consultant Pr.

Successful Fine Art Photography. Harold Davis. (Illus.). 1992. pap. 21.95 (*0-929667-14-X*) Images NY.

Successful Focus Groups: Advancing the State of the Art. Ed. by David L. Morgan. LC 93-6872. (Focus Editions Ser.: Vol. 156). (Illus.). 320p. (C). 1993. text ed. 54.00 (*0-8039-4873-5*); pap. text ed. 24.95 (*0-8039-4874-3*) Sage.

Successful Food Merchandising & Display. Ed. by Martin M. Pegler. (Illus.). 192p. 1989. 49.95 (*0-934590-24-9*) Retail Report.

***Successful Forgiveness, Success System, Pt. 3.** (Illus.). 400p. (Orig.). 1995. mass mkt. write for info. (*0-9658371-2-2*) M Goloversic.

Successful Franchise: A Working Strategy. Ed. by Golden Square Service Ltd., Staff. 144p. 1985. text ed. 40.50 (*0-566-02584-1*, Pub. by Gower UK) Ashgate Pub Co.

Successful Free-Lancing: The Complete Guide to Establishing & Running Any Kind of Free-Lance Business. Marian Faux. 256p. 1983. pap. 9.95 (*0-312-77479-6*) St Martin.

***Successful Freelancing.** rev. ed. Faux. LC 96-43902. 1997. pap. 14.95 (*0-312-15215-9*) St Martin.

***Successful Fund Raising for Higher Education: The Advancement of Learning.** Ed. by Frank H. Rhodes. LC 97-22597. (American Council on Education/Oryx Press Series on Higher Education). 232p. (C). 1997. boxed 34.95 (*1-57356-072-3*) Oryx Pr.

Successful Fund Raising Techniques. 2nd ed. Public Management Institute, Research & Development Staff & Daniel L. Conrad. LC 76-49799. 1985. ring bd. 39.00 (*0-916664-03-1*) Datarex Corp.

Successful Fundraising: A Complete Handbook for Volunteers & Professionals. Joan Flanagan. 320p. 1993. pap. 16.95 (*0-8092-3812-8*) Contemp Bks.

Successful Fundraising for Arts & Cultural Organizations. 2nd ed. Karen B. Hopkins & Carolyn S. Friedman. LC 96-43146. (Illus.). 272p. 1996. pap. 34.95 (*1-57356-029-4*) Oryx Pr.

Successful Gaijin in Japan: How Foreign Companies Are Making It in Japan. Nagami Kishi & David W. Russell. 368p. 1995. 27.95 (*0-8442-3549-0*, NTC Busn Bks) NTC Pub Grp.

***Successful Garden Plans.** LC 96-36423. (Time Life Complete Gardener Ser.). 1996. write for info. (*0-7835-4116-3*) Time-Life.

Successful Gardening. (Illus.). 1989. write for info. (*1-886614-01-6*) Intl Masters Pub.

***Successful Gardening: A-Z of Annuals, Biennials & Bulbs.** Digest Readers Staff. 1997. pap. text ed. 24.95 (*0-89577-923-4*) RD Assn.

***Successful Gardening: A-Z of Deciduous Trees & Shrubs.** Reader's Digest Editors. (Illus.). 176p. 1996. pap. 24.95 (*0-89577-870-X*) RD Assn.

***Successful Gardening: The Garden Problem Solver.** Digest Readers Staff. 1997. pap. text ed. 24.95 (*0-89577-922-6*) RD Assn.

***Successful Gardening: The Practical Gardener, Vol. 1.** Reader's Digest Editors. 176p. 1996. pap. 24.95 (*0-89577-869-6*) RD Assn.

***Successful Gardening Journal: A Seasonal Diary for Your Garden.** Reader's Digest Editors. 144p. 1996. 14.95 (*0-89577-892-0*) RD Assn.

Successful Glamour Photography. John Kelly. (Illus.). 176p. 1983. pap. 22.50 (*0-8174-5924-3*, Amphoto) Watsn-Guptill.

Successful Grant Writing: Strategies for Health & Human Service Professionals. Laura N. Gitlin & Kevin J. Lyons. (Illus.). 235p. 1996. pap. 32.95 (*0-8261-9260-2*) Springer Pub.

***Successful Help, Success System, Pt. 5.** (Illus.). 500p. (Orig.). 1995. mass mkt. write for info. (*0-9658371-4-9*) M Goloversic.

Successful Herbal Remedies. Nelda Gosling. 208p. 1995. mass mkt. 5.50 (*0-06-100895-8*, Harp PBks) HarpC.

Successful Hints on Hunting White Tail Deer. 2nd ed. Bryant W. Conway. 1967. pap. 4.95 (*0-87511-589-6*) Claitors.

***Successful Hiring: A Practical Guide to Interviewing & Selecting Employees.** Mark Cvikota. LC 97-93288. 63p. (Orig.). 1997. pap. 19.95 (*0-9656915-0-0*) Inland Mgmt.

Successful Home Birth & Midwifery: The Dutch Obstetric Model. Ed. by Eva Abraham-Van de Mark. LC 92-42901. 248p. 1993. text ed. 59.95 (*0-89789-295-X*, H295, Bergin & Garvey) Greenwood.

***Successful Home Building: The Inside Track to Building Your Dream Home.** Joseph A. St. Pierre. LC 97-91735. 285p. (Orig.). 1997. pap. 74.95 (*0-9654923-0-3*) Secret Signature.

Successful Home Cell Groups. David Y. Cho & Harold Hostetler. LC 81-80025. 176p. 1981. pap. 7.95 (*0-88270-513-X*) Bridge-Logos.

Successful Homeschool Family Handbook: A Creative & Stress-Free Approach to Homeschooling. 10th large type rev. unabridged ed. Raymond S. Moore & Dorothy N. Moore. LC 93-40688. 300p. 1997. pap. 13.00 (*0-7852-8175-4*) Nelson.

Successful Hunting Strategies. LC 92-60740. (Hunter's Information Ser.). 250p. 1992. write for info. (*0-914697-49-8*) N Amer Outdoor Grp.

Successful Implementation of Concurrent Engineering Products & Processes. Ed. by Sammy G. Shina. LC 93-8487. 1994. text ed. 67.95 (*0-442-01252-7*) Van Nos Reinhold.

Successful Inclusion: Assistance for Teachers of Adolescents with Mild Disabilities. Lynne Chalmers & Barbara Wasson. 64p. (C). 1993. pap. text ed. 12.95 (*1-886979-01-4*) Practicl Pr.

***Successful Induction.** Judy Skeats. (Human Resource Management Ser.). 1996. pap. 16.95 (*0-7494-1956-3*) Kogan Page Ltd.

Successful Industrial Design. Arthur Moss. 76p. 1970. 7.00 (*0-8464-0898-8*) Beekman Pubs.

***Successful Industrial Energy Reduction Programs.** Curl & Fairmont Press Staff. (C). 1997. text ed. 65.00 (*0-13-675059-1*) P-H.

***Successful Industrial Energy Reduction Programs.** Robert S. Curl. LC 97-16391. 1997. write for info. (*0-88173-280-X*) Fairmont Pr.

Successful Industrial Experimentation. Brett Kyle. LC 95-6060. (Illus.). 250p. 1995. 69.95 (*1-56081-050-5*, VCH) Wiley.

Successful Industrial Product Innovation: An Integrative Literature Review. Ed. by C. Anthony Di Benedetto. LC 90-41840. (Bibliographies & Indexes in Economics & Economic History Ser.: No. 7). 184p. 1990. text ed. 55.00 (*0-313-27571-8*, CIK/, Greenwood Pr) Greenwood.

Successful Information Processing. Mary P. Jones. 224p. (Orig.). 1992. pap. 27.50 (*0-7487-1401-4*, Pub. by Stanley Thornes UK) Trans-Atl Phila.

Successful Information Processing. Mary P. Jones. 224p. (Orig.). (C). 1992. pap. 50.00 (*0-7478-1401-5*, Pub. by Stanley Thornes UK) Trans-Atl Phila.

Successful Information System Implementation: The Human Side. Jeffrey K. Pinto. LC 94-24721. (Perspective Ser.). 225p. 1994. pap. 16.95 (*1-880410-37-0*) Proj Mgmt Inst.

Successful Insurance Agency. Fred C. Wootan. Ed. by Scott D. Allen. LC 93-71438. (Illus.). 155p. (C). 1993. text ed. 24.95 (*1-883602-01-7*) Atlantic Digital.

Successful Intelligence. Robert J. Sternberg. 320p. 1996. 23.00 (*0-684-81410-2*) S&S Trade.

***Successful Intelligence: How Pratical & Creative Intelligence Determines Success in Life.** Robert Sternberg. LC 97-17800. 1997. pap. 12.95 (*0-452-27906-2*, Plume) NAL-Dutton.

Successful Interactive Skills for Speech-Language Pathologists & Audiologists. Dorothy Molyneaux & Vera W. Lane. (Excellence in Practice Ser.). 218p. (C). 1989. text ed. 64.00 (*0-8342-0106-2*) Aspen Pub.

Successful Interior Projects Through Effective Contract Documents. Joel Downey et al. 1995. 69.95 (*0-87629-383-6*, 67313) ACMDG Co.

***Successful Interview Skills.** Rebecca Corfield. (Personal Development Ser.). 1992. pap. 12.95 (*0-7494-0614-3*) Kogan Page Ltd.

Successful Interviewing. Marion Sitzmann & Reloy Garcia. 64p. 1986. pap. 6.60 (*0-8442-5229-8*, VGM Career Bks) NTC Pub Grp.

Successful Interviewing for College Seniors. John Shingelton. 1993. pap. 11.95 (*0-8442-4149-0*, VGM Career Bks) NTC Pub Grp.

Successful Interviewing Techniques. Brian Jud. Ed. by Charles Lipka. 20p. (Orig.). (C). 1995. student ed., pap. 1.45 (*1-880218-16-X*) Mktg Dir Inc.

Successful Investing. 5th ed. 1991. 29.95 (*0-671-72835-0*) S&S Trade.

Successful Investing with Fidelity Funds. Ed. by Jack Bowers. LC 94-34101. 1995. 22.95 (*1-55958-647-8*) Prima Pub.

Successful Investing with Fidelity Funds. rev. ed. Jack Bowers. LC 96-47767. 1996. per. 18.00 (*0-7615-0842-2*) Prima Pub.

Successful Investment Strategies. Howard S. Tseng. LC 81-68607. 157p. 1982. pap. 12.88 (*0-686-32448-X*) Am Prudential.

Successful Job Interviewing for the College Graduate. Michael J. Shields. (Illus.). 48p. (Orig.). 1985. 5.00 (*0-9615679-0-2*) Tree of Life.

Successful Job Search: A Step-by-Step Guide for a Successful Job Search in the 1990's. Roxanne S. Rogers. 320p. 1993. 29.95 (*1-884274-00-5*) Rogers Res.

***Successful Job Search: A Workbook.** Jurg Oppliger. 1996. wbk. ed. 27.50 (*0-938609-07-6*) Graduate Group.

Successful Job Search Strategies for the Disabled: Understanding the ADA. Jeffrey G. Allen. 229p. 1994. text ed. 55.00 (*0-471-59234-X*); pap. text ed. 14.95 (*0-471-59235-8*) Wiley.

Successful Keyboarding: An Elementary Approach. Advantage Media Staff. (TE - Keyboarding Ser.). 1986. 53.95 (*0-538-28632-6*) S-W Pub.

Successful Kitchen Operations & Staff Management Handbook. Julia A. Van Duyn. 224p. 1979. 42.95 (*0-686-92162-3*) P-H.

Successful Lab Reports: A Manual for Science Students. Christopher S. Lobban & Marla Schefter. (Illus.). 95p. (C). 1992. text ed. 44.95 (*0-521-40404-5*); pap. text ed. 13.95 (*0-521-40741-9*) Cambridge U Pr.

Successful Land Development: Selected International Project Profiles, World Congress on Land Policy 1986, London, England, July 6-11, 1986. Ed. by Margaret M. Waite & Rachelle L. Levitt. LC 86-50498. (Lincoln Institute Monograph Ser.: No. 86-3). 158p. reprint ed. pap. 45.10 (*0-7837-5771-9*, 2045436) Bks Demand.

Successful Landlocked Salmon Fishing. Bob Newman. 1997. pap. text ed. 17.95 (*0-07-046364-6*) McGraw-Hill Prof.

Successful Large Account Management. Robert B. Miller et al. 240p. 1991. 27.50 (*0-8050-1304-0*) H Holt & Co.

Successful Large Account Management. Robert B. Miller et al. 240p. 1992. reprint ed. pap. 10.99 (*0-446-39356-8*) Warner Bks.

***Successful Leadership.** Carol A. O'Connor. LC 96-17933. (Business Success Ser.). 1997. pap. 6.95 (*0-7641-0072-6*) Barron.

Successful Leasing & Selling of Retail Property. 3rd ed. Grubb & Ellis Company Staff. 304p. 1988. pap. 34.95 (*0-88462-110-3*, 1922-0103) Dearborn Finan.

Successful Life Insurance Selling. Gary Schulte. 256p. 1994. 24.95 (*0-7931-1041-6*, 240118-01) Dearborn Finan.

Successful Litigation Techniques, 8 vols. J. Kelner. 1964. write for info. (*0-8205-1341-5*) Bender.

Successful Living with Chronic Illness. 2nd ed. LFA, Inc. (Lupus Foundation of America, Inc.) Staff. 244p. 1994. per. 14.95 (*0-8403-9101-3*) Kendall-Hunt.

Successful Love & Other Stories. Delmore Schwartz. 256p. 1985. reprint ed. pap. 9.95 (*0-89255-094-5*) Persea Bks.

***Successful Love, Success System, Pt. 2.** (Illus.). 600p. (Orig.). 1997. mass mkt. write for info. (*0-9658371-1-4*) M Goloversic.

Successful Lyric Writing: A Step-by-Step Course & Workbook. Sheila Davis. 292p. 1988. pap. 19.99 (*0-89879-283-5*, Wrtrs Digest Bks) F & W Pubns Inc.

Successful Machine Quilting. Marti Michell. (Illus.). 224p. 1995. pap. 19.95 (*0-696-20432-0*, Meredith Pr) Meredith Bks.

Successful Man-Hunting: How to Find Him, Attract Him, Hold Him. W. Gary Boss. (Illus.). 52p. (Orig.). Date not set. pap. 15.00 (*0-9623763-1-0*) Boss Enterprises.

Successful Management & Problem Solving. 2nd ed. James M. Todd. Orig. Title: Instant Management. 112p. 1993. reprint ed. pap. text ed. 7.99 (*0-936013-19-2*) Herit Pub NC.

Successful Management Consulting. 2nd ed. Wendy M. Greenfield. 192p. 1987. text ed. 95.00 (*0-13-709981-9*) P-H.

S

Successful Management Consulting: Building a Practice with Smaller Company Clients. W. M. Greenfield. 1987. 24.95 (*0-13-863143-3*) P-H.

Successful Management Information Systems. rev. ed. Helen H. Ligon. LC 86-6979. (Research for Business Decisions Ser.: No. 78). 223p. reprint ed. pap. 63.60 (*0-8357-1703-8*, 2070401) Bks Demand.

Successful Management of Ambulatory Surgery Programs, Vol. II. Ed. by Byron Breedlove. LC 85-72162. (Illus.). 469p. 1985. text ed. 127.00 (*0-9603332-4-X*) Am Health Consults.

Successful Management of Redundancy. Paul Lewis. (Human Resource Management in Action Ser.). 272p. 1994. pap. 44.95 (*0-631-18681-6*) Blackwell Pubs.

Successful Management of the Analytical Laboratory. Oscar I. Milner. 176p. 1991. 56.95 (*0-87371-438-5*, L438) Lewis Pubs.

Successful Management Practices: Golf Industry Perspectives. unabridged ed. (NGF Info Pacs Ser.). (Illus.). 200p. (Orig.). 1996. pap. 45.00 (*1-57701-020-5*) Natl Golf.

***Successful Manager.** Geraldine Bown & Catherine Brady. (Women in Management Workbook Ser.). 1991. pap. 15.95 (*0-7494-0518-X*) Kogan Page Ltd.

Successful Manager's Guide to Business: Seven Practical Steps to Producing Your Best Ever Business Plan. David Freemantle. LC 94-17158. 1994. 19.95 (*0-07-707845-4*) McGraw.

Successful Manager's Handbook: Development Suggestions for Today's Managers. rev. ed. Brian L. Davis et al. (Illus.). 808p. 1996. reprint ed. pap. 49.95 (*0-938529-03-X*) Personnel Decisions.

Successful Marketing for Small Business. William A. Cohen & Marshall E. Reddick. LC 80-69699. 288p. reprint ed. pap. 82.10 (*0-317-19830-0*, 2023077) Bks Demand.

***Successful Marketing for the Small Business.** 3rd ed. Dave Patten. (Small Business Ser.). 1995. pap. 15.95 (*0-7494-1527-4*) Kogan Page Ltd.

Successful Marketing Plan. Roman G. Hiebing, Jr. & Scott W. Cooper. 368p. 1995. pap. 34.95 (*0-8442-3199-1*, NTC Busn Bks) NTC Pub Grp.

Successful Marketing Plan: A Disciplined & Comprehensive Approach. 2nd ed. Roman G. Hiebing & Scott W. Cooper. LC 96-28253. 1996. pap. write for info. (*0-8442-3203-3*) NTC Pub Grp.

Successful Marketing Research: The Complete Guide to Getting & Using Essential Information About Your Customers & Competitors. Edward L. Hester. LC 95-45908. 256p. 1995. pap. text ed. 17.95 (*0-471-12380-3*) Wiley.

Successful Marketing Research: The Complete Guide to Getting & Using Essential Information About Your Customers & Competitors. Edward L. Hester. LC 95-45908. 256p. 1995. text ed. 45.00 (*0-471-12381-1*) Wiley.

Successful Marketing Strategies for Nonprofit Organizations. Barry J. McLeish. LC 95-1657. (Nonprofit Law, Finance & Management Ser.). 294p. 1995. text ed. 49.95 (*0-471-10568-6*); pap. text ed. 19.95 (*0-471-10567-8*) Wiley.

Successful Marketing Strategies in American Industry. Jon G. Udell. Ed. by Gay Leslie. (Illus.). 1972. 9.50 (*0-912084-07-3*) Mimir.

Successful Marketing Strategy for High-Tech Firms. Eric Viardot. LC 95-15292. 184p. 1995. 59.00 (*0-89006-770-8*) Artech Hse.

Successful Marketing to the Fifty Plus Consumer. Jeffrey M. Ostroff. 352p. 1989. text ed. 59.95 (*0-13-860271-9*) P-H.

Successful Marketing to the 50 Plus Consumer. Jeffrey M. Ostroff. 1990. pap. 19.95 (*0-13-860297-2*) P-H.

Successful Marriage: A Family Systems Approach to Couples Therapy. W. Robert Beavers. 1985. 24.95 (*0-393-70006-2*) Norton.

Successful Mass Catering & Volume Feeding. rev. ed. Matteo A. Casola. Ed. by Mary Darveau. LC 80-66708. 329p. 1980. reprint ed. text ed. 24.95 (*0-916096-25-4*) Books Bakers.

Successful Math. Bloomfield. Date not set. pap. text ed. write for info. (*0-314-04234-2*) West Pub.

Successful Math Study Skills: Easy-to-Use Step-by-Step Guide to Higher Math Grades. Paul D. Nolting. 208p. 1991. pap. 14.95 (*0-940287-18-8*) Acad Success Pr.

Successful Media Relations: A Practitioner's Guide. Judith Ridgway. LC 84-6128. 214p. 1984. text ed. 54.95 (*0-566-02469-1*, Pub. by Gower UK) Ashgate Pub Co.

Successful Medical Student. John R. Thornborough. 1995. 14.95 (*1-882531-03-5*) ILOC.

Successful Meetings. Public Management Institute Staff. LC 80-80198. 1980. ring bd. 39.00 (*0-916664-23-6*) Datarex Corp.

Successful Men of To-Day: And What They Say of Success. Wilbur F. Crafts. LC 73-2500. (Big Business; Economic Power in a Free Society Ser.). 1973. reprint ed. 20.95 (*0-405-05081-X*) Ayer.

Successful Mentor-Protege Relationships. David M. Lambert. 237p. Date not set. ring bd. 96.00 (*1-56726-026-8*, B566) Holbrook & Kellogg.

Successful Mergers: Planning, Strategy & Execution. Michael Simmons et al. (Waterlow Publications). (Illus.). 250p. 1988. pap. 29.95 (*0-08-036902-2*, Pergamon Pr) Elsevier.

Successful Methods in Cost Engineering. Hira N. Ahuja & Michael A. Walsh. LC 82-17316. 398p. (Orig.). 1986. reprint ed. 51.95 (*0-471-86435-8*, JW) Krieger.

Successful Mini Reef Aquarium. U. Erich Friese. (Illus.). 320p. 1996. 47.95 (*0-7938-2093-6*, TS221) TFH Pubns.

Successful Mission Teams: A Guide for Volunteers. Martha VanCise. Ed. by Susan Hansen. 56p. (Orig.). 1996. pap. 10.95 (*0-614-17621-2*, New Hope) Womans Mission Union.

Successful Models of Community Long Term Care Services for the Elderly. Ed. by Eloise H. Killeffer. LC 89-29378. (Physical & Occupational Therapy in Geriatrics Ser.: Vol. 8, Nos. 1 & 2). (Illus.). 178p. 1990. text ed. 39.95 (*0-86656-987-1*) Haworth Pr.

Successful Movement Challenges: Movement Activities for the Developing Child. Jack Capon. Ed. by Frank Alexander & Diane Alexander. (Illus.). 129p. (Orig.). 1981. pap. 12.00 (*0-915256-07-X*) Front Row.

***Successful Negotiating.** Peter Fleming. LC 97-10350. (Business Success Ser.). 1997. pap. 6.95 (*0-7641-0125-0*) Barron.

Successful Negotiating in Local Government. Ed. by Nancy A. Huelsberg & William F. Lincoln. LC 85-8275. (Practical Management Ser.). (Illus.). 211p. 1985. pap. text ed. 23.95 (*0-87326-045-7*) Intl City-Cnty Mgt.

Successful Negotiating Skills for Women. John Ilich & Barbara S. Jones. 116p. reprint ed. pap. 8.95 (*0-935650-06-7*) Bengal Pr.

***Successful Negotiation.** Robert B. Maddux. (Better Management Skills Ser.). 1988. pap. 12.95 (*1-85091-741-8*) Kogan Page Ltd.

Successful Negotiation: Effective "Win-Win" Strategies & Tactics. 3rd rev. ed. Robert B. Maddux. LC 94-74330. (Fifty-Minute Ser.). (Illus.). 74p. (Orig.). 1995. pap. 10.95 (*1-56052-348-4*) Crisp Pubns.

Successful Negotiation: Trieste 1954: An Appraisal by the Five Participants. Ed. by John C. Campbell. LC 75-2981. 192p. reprint ed. pap. 54.80 (*0-7837-1940-X*, 2042155) Bks Demand.

Successful Negotiation of Commercial Contracts a Businessman's Guide. Patrick Hearn. 142p. 1979. text ed. 63.95 (*0-566-02365-2*, Pub. by Gower UK) Ashgate Pub Co.

Successful Network Marketing for the Twenty-First Century. Rod Nichols. Ed. by Erin Wait. LC 95-18046. (Successful Business Library). (Illus.). 208p. (Orig.). 1995. pap. 15.95 (*1-55571-350-5*) Oasis Pr OR.

***Successful Networking.** Dena Michelli. LC 97-11498. (Business Success Ser.). 1997. pap. 6.95 (*0-7641-0059-9*) Barron.

Successful New Employee Orientation: Assess, Plan, Conduct, & Evaluate Your Program. Jean Barbazette. LC 93-87070. 122p. 1994. ring bd. 79.95 (*0-88390-417-9*, Pfiffr & Co) Jossey-Bass.

Successful New Manager. Joseph T. Straub. LC 94-18779. (WorkSmart Ser.). (Illus.). 112p. 1994. pap. 10.95 (*0-8144-7834-4*) AMACOM.

Successful Nonverbal Communication. 3rd ed. Dale G. Leathers. 432p. 1997. pap. 38.00 (*0-205-26230-9*) Allyn.

Successful Obedience Handling: The New Best Foot Forward. Barbara S. Handler. Ed. by Betty J. McKinney. LC 90-19366. 136p. 1991. pap. 9.95 (*0-931866-51-0*) Alpine Pubns.

Successful Object Sermons. Roderick A. McDonald. (Object Lesson Ser.). 112p. (Orig.). (C). 1990. pap. 6.99 (*0-8010-6270-5*) Baker Bks.

Successful On-Site Manager. Carol S. King et al. LC 83-82536. (Illus.). 353p. 1984. 39.95 (*0-912104-62-7*, 811) Inst Real Estate.

Successful Organized Stockbroker, 2 vols., Set. Paul D. Butt. (Illus.). 83p. (Orig.). pap. 125.00 (*0-9635346-0-2*) Buttonwd Pub.

Successful Parenting for the Military Family. Carol B. Richardson. (Family Forum Library Ser.). 16p. 1993. 1.95 (*1-56688-073-4*) Bur For At-Risk.

***Successful Parenting Guide: Get Ready for School.** Basham. Date not set. pap. text ed. write for info. (*0-582-02621-0*, Pub. by Longman UK) Longman.

Successful Parish Leadership: Nurturing the Animated Parish. Robert G. Duch. LC 89-64499. 224p. (Orig.). (C). 1990. pap. 12.95 (*1-55612-353-1*) Sheed & Ward MO.

Successful Partnering: Fundamentals for Project Owners & Contractors. Hank Schultzel & Paul Unruh. LC 95-21925. (Construction Business & Management Library). 192p. 1996. text ed. 49.95 (*0-471-11465-0*) Wiley.

***Successful Partnerships for the Future: The Administrator-Physician Dynamic.** Mary A. Krill. 98p. (Orig.). 1994. pap. 25.00 (*1-56829-048-9*, 4819) Med Group Mgmt.

Successful Patents & Patenting for Engineers & Scientists. Ed. by Michael A. Lechter et al. LC 94-46193. 432p. 1995. pap. 44.95 (*0-7803-1086-1*, PP4478) Inst Electrical.

Successful Pension Design for Small to Medium-Sized Businesses. 2nd ed. Robert F. Slimmon. (Illus.). 480p. 1987. text ed. 50.00 (*0-13-860255-7*) P-H.

Successful People: What Makes Them That Way? Alice Dunkle. 1987. pap. text ed. 14.00 (*0-910609-14-4*) Gifted Educ Pr.

Successful Perennial Gardening: A Practical Guide. Lewis Hill & Nancy Hill. Ed. by Sarah M. Clarkson. LC 87-45582. (Illus.). 240p. (Orig.). 1988. pap. 18.95 (*0-88266-472-7*, Garden Way Pub) Storey Comm Inc.

***Successful Pharmaceutical Selling: Frank Advice from the Frontlines.** Martin B. Bischoff. LC 97-15126. 1997. 21.95 (*0-7863-1211-4*) Irwin Prof Pubng.

***Successful Pistol Shooting.** Bob Hickey & Art Sievers. (Illus.). 662p. 1996. 49.95 (*0-939414-03-1*) STP.

Successful Pistol Shooting. Frank Leatherdale & Paul Leatherdale. (Illus.). 160p. 1995. 35.00 (*1-85223-883-6*, Pub. by Crowood Pr UK) Trafalgar.

Successful Practice of Law. John E. Tracy. LC 72-6212. (Illus.). 470p. 1973. reprint ed. lib. bdg. 22.50 (*0-8371-6455-9*, TRPL, Greenwood Pr) Greenwood.

***Successful Presentation Skills.** Andrew Bradbury. (Better Management Skills Ser.). 1995. pap. 12.95 (*0-7494-1749-8*) Kogan Page Ltd.

Successful Presentations for Dummies. Malcolm Kushner. 1996. pap. 16.99 (*1-56884-392-5*) IDG Bks.

***Successful Prevention Programs for Children & Adolescents.** J. A. Durlak. (Clinical Child Psychology Library). 202p. (C). 1997. write for info. (*0-306-45645-1*, Plenum Pr) Plenum.

Successful Private Eyes & Private Spies: Private Spies. Barbara L. Thomas & Ralph D. Thomas. (Private Investigation Ser.). 100p. 1986. pap. text ed. 19.95 (*0-317-45231-2*) Thomas Pubns TX.

Successful Private Practice in the 1990s: A New Guide for the Mental Health Professional. Joan K. Beigel & Ralph H. Earle. LC 90-2053. 224p. 1990. pap. text ed. 25.95 (*0-87630-586-9*, 5869) Brunner-Mazel.

Successful Problem Management. Michael Sanderson. LC 78-21050. (Illus.). 237p. reprint ed. pap. 67.60 (*0-8357-8674-9*, 2056830) Bks Demand.

Successful Problem Solving. Dean F. Juniper. 160p. (Orig.). 1995. pap. 11.95 (*0-572-01319-1*, Pub. by Foulsham UK) Assoc Pubs Grp.

Successful Problem Solving. David A. Thomas & Maridell Fryar. 64p. 1991. pap. 6.60 (*0-8442-5239-5*, NTC Busn Bks) NTC Pub Grp.

***Successful Problem Solving & Test Taking: Easy Steps to Passing for Nursing & NCLEX-RN Exams.** 4th rev. ed. Patricia A. Hoefler. (C). 1997. pap. text ed. 29.95 (*1-56533-027-7*) M E D S Inc.

Successful Problem-Solving & Test-Taking for Beginning Nursing Students. Patricia A. Hoefler. Ed. by Amelia R. Hummel. (Illus.). 240p. (C). 1995. 29.95 incl. disk (*1-56533-018-8*, IBK9B) M E D S Inc.

***Successful Problem Solving & Test Taking for Beginning Nursing Students.** 2nd ed. Patricia A. Hoefler. 256p. (Orig.). (C). 1997. pap. text ed. 29.95 (*1-56533-026-9*) M E D S Inc.

Successful Problem-Solving & Test-Taking for Nursing & NCLEX-PN Exams. 2nd ed. Patricia A. Hoefler. Ed. by Amelia R. Hummel & Chellis E. Neal. (Illus.). 166p. (C). 1995. 29.95 incl. disk (*1-56533-014-5*, IBK4) M E D S Inc.

Successful Problem-Solving & Test-Taking for the Advanced Student & the NCLEX-RN: Easy Steps to Passing for the Nursing & The NCLEX-RN Exam. 4th ed. Patricia A. Hoefler. Ed. by Chellis E. Neal & Amelia R. Hummel. (Illus.). 165p. (C). 1995. 29.95 incl. disk (*1-56533-013-7*, IBK1) M E D S Inc.

Successful Product & Business Development. N. Giragosian. 320p. 1978. 75.00 (*0-8247-6770-5*) Dekker.

Successful Product Development: From Research to Results. Nicolette Lemmon. 108p. (Orig.). 1995. pap. 89.00 (*1-889394-20-3*) Credit Union Execs.

***Successful Product Management.** Stephen Morse. (Marketing in Action Ser.). 1994. pap. 22.95 (*0-7494-1129-5*) Kogan Page Ltd.

Successful Professional Practice. Robert P. Levoy. LC 74-97581. (Illus.). 192p. 1970. 39.95 (*0-13-868307-7*, Busn) P-H.

Successful Program Management: Sharpening the Competitive Edge. Arthur E. Mudge. 216p. 1989. text ed. 37.00 (*0-939332-18-3*) J Pohl Assocs.

Successful Program Review: A Practical Guide to Evaluating Programs in Academic Settings. Robert J. Barak & Barbara E. Breier. (Higher Education Ser.). 160p. text ed. 28.95 (*1-55542-241-1*) Jossey-Bass.

Successful Project Management: A Step-by-Step Approach with Practical Examples. 2nd enl. ed. Milton D. Rosenau, Jr. (Project Management Ser.). (Illus.). 320p. 1992. text ed. 59.95 (*0-442-00655-1*) Van Nos Reinhold.

Successful Project Managers: Leading Your Team to Success. O. P. Kharbanda & Jeffrey K. Pinto. (Industrial Engineering Ser.). 421p. 1995. text ed. 36.95 (*0-442-01952-1*) Van Nos Reinhold.

***Successful Promotion by Musicians: The Art of Self-Promotion.** Richard Letts. 224p. 1997. pap. 19.95 (*1-86448-272-9*, Pub. by Allen Unwin AT) Paul & Co Pubs.

***Successful Property Development.** Alan Upson. 1997. pap. text ed. 59.95 (*0-632-02916-1*) Blackwell Sci.

***Successful Proposal Strategies for Small Businesses: Winning Government, Private Sector, & International Contracts.** Robert S. Frey. LC 97-9810. (Technology Management Ser.). 300p. 1997. 59.95 (*0-89006-935-2*) Artech Hse.

Successful Psychiatric Practice: Current Dilemmas, Choices, & Solutions. Edward K. Silberman. (Clinical Practice Ser.: No. 33). 272p. 1995. text ed. 35.00 (*0-88048-486-1*, 8486) Am Psychiatric.

Successful Psychotherapy: A Caring, Loving Relationship. C. H. Patterson & Suzanne C. Hidore. LC 95-52030. 280p. 1997. 40.00 (*1-56821-795-1*) Aronson.

Successful Public Meetings: A Practical Guide for Managers in Government. Elaine Cogan. LC 91-30035. (Public Administration Ser.). 153p. 26.95 (*1-55542-403-1*) Jossey-Bass.

Successful Public Relations Techniques. Public Management Institute Staff. LC 79-93010. 400p. 1979. ring bd. 59.00 (*0-916664-15-5*) Datarex Corp.

Successful Public Speaking. Cheryl Hamilton. (Illus.). 500p. (C). 1996. pap. 37.95 (*0-534-15564-2*) Wadsworth Pub.

Successful Public Speaking: A Practical Guide. William A. Haskins & Joseph M. Staudacher. LC 86-20291. (Illus.). 367p. reprint ed. pap. 104.60 (*0-7837-4511-7*, 2044289) Bks Demand.

Successful Publishing in Scholarly Journals. Bruce A. Thyer. (Survival Skills for Scholars Ser.: Vol. 11). 96p. (C). 1994. text ed. 35.00 (*0-8039-4836-0*); pap. text ed. 15.95 (*0-8039-4837-9*) Sage.

Successful Pubs & Inns. Michael Sargent & Tony Lyle. 200p. 1994. 27.95 (*0-7506-1835-3*) Buttrwrth-Heinemann.

***Successful Purchasing.** Stephen Carter. LC 96-43002. (Business Success Ser.). 1997. pap. 6.95 (*0-7641-0057-2*) Barron.

Successful Quality Management. Frank H. Squires. Ed. by Robert T. Linke. 342p. (Orig.). 1980. pap. 22.50 (*0-933931-03-4*) Hitchcock Pub.

Successful Reading: Key to Our Dynamic Society. Kass-Norman Norman. 264p. 1980. pap. text ed. 20.00 (*0-03-043126-3*) HB Coll Pubs.

Successful Real Estate Brokerage Management. Charles S. Bonnamer. LC 94-66936. 130p. (Orig.). 1994. pap. 19.95 (*0-913825-86-7*, Leg Surv Guides) Sourcebks.

Successful Real Estate Investing in the '90s: A Practical Guide to Profits for the Small Investor. Peter G. Miller. 288p. 1995. pap. 15.00 (*0-06-272062-7*, PL) HarpC.

Successful Real Estate Negotiation. rev. ed. Peter G. Miller & Douglas M. Bregman. LC 93-31859. 320p. 1994. pap. 14.00 (*0-06-273264-1*, Harper Ref) HarpC.

Successful Real Estate Sales Agreements. 4th ed. Erik Jorgensen. 374p. 1988. pap. 17.95 (*0-933800-03-7*) Axiom Pr Pubs.

Successful Recareering: When Changing Jobs Just Isn't Enough. Joyce Schwarz. 192p. (Orig.). 1993. pap. 12.95 (*1-56414-070-9*) Career Pr Inc.

Successful Recruitment Selection: A Practical Guide for Managers. Margaret Dale. 256p. 1995. 45.00 (*0-7494-1422-7*, Pub. by Kogan Pg UK) Cassell.

Successful Reengineering: An In-Depth Guide to Using Information Technology. Daniel Petrozzo & John C. Stepper. (General Engineering Ser.). 250p. 1994. text ed. 29.95 (*0-442-01722-7*) Van Nos Reinhold.

Successful Remodeling. John Reed et al. LC 94-65697. (Illus.). 112p. (Orig.). 1995. pap. 9.95 (*0-89721-269-X*, UPC 05988) Meredith Bks.

Successful Residential Management: The Professional's Guide. Barbara K. Holland. LC 94-29556. (Illus.). 388p. 1994. text ed. 43.95 (*1-57203-005-4*, 700) Inst Real Estate.

Successful Restaurant Design. Regina S. Baraban & Joseph F. Durocher. (Illus.). 256p. 1992. pap. 37.95 (*0-442-01152-0*) Van Nos Reinhold.

Successful Resumes: Resume Development Kit. Steven D. Houseworth. 35p. 1994. pap. 10.00 (*0-9642149-0-3*) Nikwn & Successful.

Successful Resumes & Interviews. Carl Perrin & Peter Dublin. LC 93-4925. 1994. pap. 26.95 (*0-8273-5991-8*) Delmar.

Successful Resumes & Interviews: Instructor's Guide. Carl Perrin. 23p. 1994. 13.00 (*0-8273-5992-6*) Delmar.

***Successful Retailing.** 2nd ed. Paula Wardell. 164p. 1993. pap. 19.95 (*0-936894-40-7*) Upstart Pub.

Successful Retailing: Your Step-by-Step Guide to Avoiding Pitfalls & Finding Profit as an Independent Retailer. Paula Wardell. Ed. by Debra Shouse. 160p. (Orig.). 1990. pap. 24.95 (*0-9625704-8-6*, 610601) Retail Strategies.

***Successful Rifle Shooting.** David Parish. (Illus.). 128p. 1997. 35.00 (*1-86126-019-9*, Pub. by Crowood Pr UK) Trafalgar.

Successful Rose Gardening. Better Homes & Gardens Editors. (Illus.). 224p. 1995. pap. 16.95 (*0-696-20383-9*) Meredith Bks.

Successful Rural Finance Institutions. Jacob Yaron. (Discussion Paper Ser.: No. 150). 135p. 1992. 9.95 (*0-8213-2018-1*, 12018) World Bank.

Successful Sales Assistant's Handbook. New York Institute Of Finance Staff. (Illus.). 288p. student ed. 25.00 (*0-13-860305-7*) NY Inst Finance.

Successful Sales Management: A New Strategy for Modern Sales Managers. Hal Fahner. LC 82-24085. 264p. 1983. 29.95 (*0-13-870402-3*) P-H.

Successful Sales Management: How to Make Your Team the Best. Grant Stewart. (Institute of Management Ser.). 192p. (Orig.). 1993. pap. 39.50 (*0-273-60068-0*, Pub. by Pitman Pub Ltd UK) Trans-Atl Phila.

Successful Sales Meetings: How to Plan, Conduct & Make Sales Meetings Pay Off. James Rapp. 247p. 1990. pap. 29.95 (*0-85013-171-5*) Dartnell Corp.

Successful Sales Promotion. Pran Choudhury et al. (Illus.). 139p. 1992. 27.50 (*0-86311-303-6*, Pub. by Orient Longman Ltd II) Apt Bks.

Successful Sales Promotions. David L. Weiner. 254p. 1993. pap. 55.95 (*0-614-02664-4*) Natl Assn Wholesale Dists.

Successful Salon Management. Milady Publishing Company Staff. (Cosmetology Ser.). 1975. 34.50 (*0-87350-067-9*) Van Nos Reinhold.

Successful Salon Management for Cosmetology Students. Edward J. Tezak. 1985. student ed. 15.95 (*0-87350-411-9*) Milady Pub.

Successful Saltwater Aquariums: A Beginner's Guide. John H. Tullock. Ed. by Omer K. Dersom. (Coralife Ser.). 164p. 1994. 19.95 (*0-9640147-0-X*) Energy Savers.

Successful San Diegans: The Stories Behind San Diego's Most Successful People Both Past & Present. Lee T. Silber. LC 92-94220. (Illus.). 400p. (Orig.). (C). 1993. pap. 15.95 (*0-9628771-1-5*) Tales From Tropics.

Successful School Commmunications: A Manual & Guide for Administrators. William Goldstein & Joseph A. DeVita. (Illus.). 1977. 22.95 (*0-13-872036-3*, Parker Publishing Co) P-H.

Successful School Improvement: The Implementation Perspective & Beyond. Michael G. Fullan. 160p. 1992. 90.00 (*0-335-09576-3*, Open Univ Pr); pap. 27.50 (*0-335-09575-5*, Open Univ Pr) Taylor & Francis.

Successful School Management. Roger Smith. (Introduction to Education Ser.). (Illus.). 208p. 1996. 90.00 (*0-304-32945-2*); pap. 21.00 (*0-304-32947-9*) Cassell.

Successful School Planning & Restructuring: Leadership for the 21st Century. Margaret E. Fitch & Paul J. Malcom. 183p. 1992. pap. text ed. 70.00 (*0-9637959-0-2*) ISD Pub Grp.

Successful Schooling for Economically Disadvantaged At-Risk Youth. Texas Education Agency Dropout Information Agency Staff & Intercultural Development Research Association Staff. 70p. (Orig.). 1989. pap. text ed. 5.00 (*1-878550-43-8*) Inter Dev Res Assn.

Successful Schooling for Everybody. Burton Gorman & William Johnson. Ed. by Stan Elam. 158p. (Orig.). 1990. pap. 19.95 (*1-879639-07-6*) Natl Educ Serv.

Successful Schools for Young Adolescents. Joan Lipsitz. 240p. 1983. 34.95 (*0-87855-487-4*); pap. text ed. 21.95 (*0-87855-947-7*) Transaction Pubs.

Successful Schools Series: Guidebooks to Effective Educational Leadership, 9 bks. Ed. by Fenwick W. English. 1992. boxed 119.00 (*0-8039-6031-X*) Corwin Pr.

Successful Scientific Writing: A Step-by-Step Guide for the Biological & Medical Sciences. Janice R. Matthews et al. (Illus.). 200p. (C). 1996. spiral bd. 19.95 (*0-521-55948-0*) Cambridge U Pr.

Successful Scriptwriting. Jurgen Wolff & Kerry Cox. 364p. 1991. pap. 16.99 (*0-89879-449-8*, Wrtrs Digest Bks) F & W Pubns Inc.

Successful Secondary Schools: Visions of Excellence in American Public Education. Ed. by Bruce L. Wilson & Thomas B. Corcoran. 200p. 1989. 60.00 (*1-85000-200-2*, Falmer Pr); pap. 32.00 (*1-85000-201-0*, Falmer Pr) Taylor & Francis.

Successful Secretary: You, Your Boss, & the Job. Loren B. Belker. LC 81-66239. 224p. reprint ed. pap. 63.90 (*0-317-26943-7*, 2023590) Bks Demand.

Successful Self-Management: A Psychologically Sound Approach to Personal Effectiveness. rev. ed. Paul R. Timm. Ed. by Michael G. Crisp. LC 93-72443. (Fifty-Minute Ser.). (Illus.). 68p. 1994. pap. 10.95 (*1-56052-242-9*) Crisp Pubns.

Successful Self-Publisher: Produce & Market Your Own Best Seller. Dorothy Kavka & Dan Heise. LC 95-71949. (Illus.). 256p. (Orig.). 1996. pap. 19.95 (*1-879260-38-7*) Evanston Pub.

Successful Selling. Brian S. Tracy. 140p. (Orig.). pap. text ed. 5.95 (*1-880461-38-2*) Celebrat Excell.

Successful Selling with NLP: Neuro-Linguistic Programming--The Way Forward in the New Bazaar. Joseph O'Connor & Robin Prior. 1995. pap. 16.00 (*0-7225-2978-3*) Harper SF.

Successful Seminars, Conferences & Workshops. Public Management Institute Staff. LC 80-65013. 400p. 1980. ring bd. 59.00 (*0-916664-19-8*) Datarex Corp.

***Successful Services for Our Children & Families at Risk.** OECD Staff. 340p. (Orig.). 1996. pap. 43.00 (*92-64-15305-5*, 96-96-05-1) OECD.

***Successful Sewing.** Mary G. Westfall. LC 97-395. 432p. 1998. 27.96 (*1-56637-372-7*) Goodheart.

Successful Shark Fishing. A. J. Campell. (Illus.). 176p. 1995. pap. text ed. 17.95 (*0-07-009954-5*) Intl Marine.

Successful Sight Singing, Bk. 1. Nancy Telfer. 180p. 1992. teacher ed. 19.95 (*0-8497-4168-8*, V77T); student ed., pap. text ed. 6.95 (*0-8497-4167-X*, V77S) Kjos.

Successful Sight Singing, Bk. 2. Nancy Telfer. 96p. 1993. student ed., pap. text ed. 6.95 (*0-8497-4171-8*, V82S) Kjos.

Successful Sight Singing, Bk. 2. Nancy Telfer. 220p. 1994. teacher ed. 24.95 (*0-8497-4172-6*, V82T) Kjos.

***Successful Sign Design.** Retail Reporting Staff. 1989. 52.50 (*0-688-09007-9*) Morrow.

***Successful Sign Design.** Retail Reporting Staff. 1992. 52.50 (*0-688-11997-2*) Morrow.

Successful Sign Design. Ed. by Signs of the Times Magazine Editors. (Illus.). 256p. 1989. 34.98 (*0-934590-28-1*) Retail Report.

Successful Sign Design - 2. Signs Of The Times Magazine Editors. (Illus.). 240p. 1992. 49.95 (*0-934590-49-4*) Retail Report.

Successful Simulation: A Practical Approach to Simulation Projects. Stewart Robinson. LC 94-12966. 1994. write for info. (*0-07-707622-2*) McGraw.

Successful Single Parenting. Gary Richmond. 258p. (Orig.). 1989. pap. 8.99 (*0-89081-768-5*) Harvest Hse.

Successful Sitcom Writing. Jurgen Wolff. 208p. 1996. 22.95 (*0-312-14426-1*) St Martin.

An Asterisk (*) at the beginning of an entry indicates that the title is appearing in BIP for the first time.

***Successful Site-Based Management: A Practical Guide.** rev. ed. Larry J. Reynolds. LC 96-51301. (Illus.). 192p. 1996. 69.95 (*0-8039-6559-1*); pap. 29.95 (*0-8039-6560-5*) Sage.

Successful Small Business Management. 6th ed. Leon C. Megginson et al. 880p. (C). 1990. text ed. 56.95 (*0-256-08635-4*) Irwin.

Successful Small Business Management: It's Your Business . . . Mind It! David Seigel & Harold L. Goldman. LC 81-71604. 360p. reprint ed. pap. 102.60 (*0-318-34846-2*, 2030991) Bks Demand.

Successful Small Food Gardens. Louise Riotte. (Illus.). 200p. 1993. 21.95 (*0-88266-816-1*, Garden Way Pub); pap. 11.95 (*0-88266-815-3*, Garden Way Pub) Storey Comm Inc.

Successful Small Gardens. Roy Strong. LC 94-67378. (Illus.). 144p. 1995. 29.95 (*0-8478-1839-X*) Rizzoli Intl.

Successful Small-Scale Farming: An Organic Approach. rev. ed. Karl Schwenke. Ed. by Ben Watson. LC 90-50417. (Illus.). 144p. 1991. reprint ed. pap. 12.95 (*0-88266-642-8*) Storey Comm Inc.

Successful Software Evaluation & Rating: A Quantitative Approach. Michael L. Dean. (Illus.). 250p. (Orig.). 1986. 39.95 (*0-87007-996-4*); pap. 19.95 (*0-87007-997-2*) SourceView.

***Successful Software Process Improvement.** Robert Grady. 350p. (C). 1997. 49.00 (*0-13-626623-1*) P-H.

Successful Soul Winning. Paul Sherrod. (Illus.). 1978. 6.95 (*0-686-14476-7*, 1730394523) P Sherrod.

Successful Southern Gardening: A Practical Guide for Year-round Beauty. Sandra F. Ladendorf. LC 88-20634. (Illus.). x, 294p. (C). 1989. 29.95 (*0-8078-1831-3*); pap. 16.95 (*0-8078-4241-9*) U of NC Pr.

Successful Speaking Vol. 1: The Basics of Public Speaking. Joe Ayres. (Illus.). 200p. (Orig.). (C). 1996. pap. text ed. 22.00 (*0-9651646-0-8*) Commun Vntures.

Successful Speaking Practice: A Nuts & Bolts Approach. C. Stephen Byrum. 75p. (Orig.). 1991. write for info. (*0-924234-22-9*) Milton Pub.

***Successful Special Events: Planning, Hosting & Evaluating.** Barbara R. Levy & Barbara Marion. LC 97-11358. 200p. 1997. pap. write for info. (*0-8342-0935-7*, 09357) Aspen Pub.

***Successful Speech.** William H. Bennett et al. Ed. by Michelle Bailey et al. (Illus.). v, 151p. (Orig.). (YA). (gr. 7-12). 1995. text ed. 39.00 (*1-889510-13-0*); pap. text ed. 29.00 (*1-889510-14-9*) Chmpionship Debate.

***Successful Speech - Teacher's Guide.** William H. Bennett et al. Ed. by Michelle Bailey et al. (Illus.). vi, 261p. (Orig.). 1995. pap. text ed. 45.00 (*1-889510-12-2*) Chmpionship Debate.

Successful Speeches & Toasts: How to Prepare & Deliver Them. Foulsham Editors. 160p. (Orig.). 1995. pap. 7.95 (*0-572-01604-2*, Pub. by Foulsham UK) Assoc Pubs Grp.

Successful Sport Fundraising. William F. Stier, Jr. 280p. (C). 1993. per. write for info. (*0-697-17196-5*) Brown & Benchmark.

Successful Sport Management. Guy Lewis & Herb Appenzeller. 377p. 1985. 60.00 (*0-87215-925-6*) MICHIE.

Successful Staff Development: A How-to-Do-It Manual for Librarians. Marcia Trotta. (How-to-Do-It Manuals Ser.: Vol. 55). 112p. (Orig.). 1995. pap. 39.95 (*1-55570-180-9*) Neal-Schuman.

Successful Stamp Dealing: Tried & Tested Tips & Techniques. Peter Mosiondz. 120p. 1996. pap. text ed. 12.95 (*0-87341-452-7*) Krause Pubns.

Successful Stand-up Comedy: Advice from a Comedy Writer. Gene Perret. 270p. (Orig.). pap. 13.95 (*0-573-69916-X*) S French Trade.

Successful Stock Investing. 2nd ed. 1984. pap. 10.00 (*0-318-19199-7*) Truth Seeker.

Successful Strategic Planning. Stephen G. Haines. Ed. by Robert Racine. LC 93-73141. (Fifty-Minute Ser.). (Illus.). 77p. (Orig.). 1995. pap. 10.95 (*1-56052-251-8*) Crisp Pubns.

Successful Strategic Planning: A Guide for Nonprofit Agencies & Organizations. Patrick J. Burkhart & Suzanne Reuss. (Illus.). 80p. (C). 1993. pap. text ed. 16.95 (*0-8039-4799-2*) Sage.

Successful Strategic Planning: Case Studies. Ed. by Douglas W. Steeples. LC 85-644752. (New Directions for Higher Education Ser.: No. HE 64). 1988. 19.00 (*1-55542-887-8*) Jossey-Bass.

Successful Strategies. Marivaux. Tr. by Timberlake Wertenbaker from FRE. 1992. pap. 5.95 (*0-87129-125-8*, S82) Dramatic Pub.

Successful Strategies & Tools for Computer-Assisted Reporting. Bruce Garrison. LC 96-16112. 265p. 1996. 59.95 (*0-8058-2224-0*); pap. 24.95 (*0-8058-2225-9*) L Erlbaum Assocs.

Successful Strategies for Marketing School Levies. Glenn T. Graham et al. LC 90-62019. (Fastback Ser.: No. 310). (Orig.). (C). 1990. pap. 3.00 (*0-87367-310-7*) Phi Delta Kappa.

Successful Strategies for Positive Relationships in a Changing World: Student Activity Book for "Does Anyone Hear Our Cries for Help?" Bertie R. Synowiec. (Successful Living Ser.). 1996. pap. 34.95 (*1-885335-13-X*) Positive Support.

Successful Strategies for Real Estate Agents: A Step-by-Step System on How to Succeed in Today's Real Estate World. Floyd Wickman. 260p. 1987. 19.95 (*0-939975-01-7*) Exec Pr NC.

Successful Strategies for Sales Managers: A Guide to Get the Best from Salespeople. Floyd Wickman. 249p. 1987. 19.95 (*0-939975-00-9*) Exec Pr NC.

***Successful Strategies for Working (or Living) with Difficult Kids: How to Stay Healthy & Respond Effectively to Disrespectful, Disruptive & Defiant Behavior.** Joyce E. Divinyi. Ed. by Elizabeth Fallon. LC 97-91444. (Illus.). 120p. 1997. pap. write for info. (*0-9656353-4-1*) Wellness Connect.

Successful Strategies for Your Life. Don B. Decker. LC 94-60452. 48p. 1995. 10.95 (*1-55523-694-4*) Winston-Derek.

Successful Student Teaching. F. D. Kreamelmeyer. 179p. (Orig.). (C). 1991. pap. text ed. 14.50 (*1-879215-03-9*) Sheffield WI.

Successful Student Teaching: A Handbook for Elementary & Secondary Student Teachers. Fillmer Hevener, Jr. LC 80-69332. 125p. (C). 1981. per. 9.95 (*0-86548-040-0*) R & E Pubs.

***Successful Study for Degrees.** 2nd ed. Rob Barnes. 208p. 1996. pap. text ed. 14.95 (*0-415-12741-6*) Routledge.

Successful Stuttering Management Program (SSMP) Dorvan H. Breitenfeldt & Delores R. Lorenz. 164p. 1989. student ed. 47.50 (*0-910055-10-6*) East Wash Univ.

Successful Style: A Man's Guide to a Complete Professional Image. Doris Pooser. Ed. by Angie Michael & Phil Trupp. LC 91-18338. (Illus.). 200p. 1990. reprint ed. 16.95 (*0-931961-92-0*) Crisp Pubns.

Successful Subbing: A Survival Guide to Help You Teach Like a Pro. Carol L. Fuery. 58p. 1988. 7.95 (*0-944295-02-9*) Sanibel Sanddollar Pubns.

Successful Supervision. John H. Jackson & Timothy J. Keaveny. (Illus.). 1980. text ed. write for info. (*0-13-872796-1*) P-H.

Successful Surgery: A Doctor's Mind & Body Guide to Help You Through Surgery. Robert Baker. 288p. 1996. pap. 12.00 (*0-671-51900-X*, PB Trade Paper) PB.

Successful System for Pricing & Producing Advertising Services. Edward G. Dorn. LC 95-30851. 1995. write for info. (*0-9631806-7-3*) Cel Pubns.

Successful Tax Reform Lessons from an Analysis of Tax Reform in Six Countries. Cedric T. Sandford. 256p. (C). 1993. 190.00 (*0-9515157-3-X*, Pub. by Fiscal Pubns UK) St Mut.

Successful Teacher: Essays in Secondary School Instruction. Ed. by James L. Kelly. LC 81-23651. 160p. 1982. reprint ed. pap. 45.60 (*0-608-00086-8*, 2060850) Bks Demand.

Successful Team Building. Thomas L. Quick. (AMA Worksmart Ser.). 112p. (Orig.). 1992. pap. 10.95 (*0-8144-7794-1*) AMACOM.

***Successful Team Building.** Graham Willcocks & Steve Morris. LC 96-42929. (Business Success Ser.). 1997. 6.95 (*0-7641-0073-4*) Barron.

Successful Teamwork. CUNA Staff. 128p. 1995. per., pap. text ed. 25.70 (*0-7872-0980-5*, VL01) Kendall-Hunt.

Successful Technical Writing. Bill W. Brown. 349p. 1993. 31.96 (*0-87006-937-3*) Goodheart.

Successful Technique for Criminal Trials. 2nd ed. F. Lee Bailey & Henry B. Rothblatt. LC 84-82304. 1985. 98.00 (*0-685-59849-7*) Clark Boardman Callaghan.

Successful Techniques for Civil Trials. Ronald Carlson. 1992. 105.00 (*0-614-06021-4*, 4007) Natl Prac Inst.

Successful Techniques for Civil Trials. 2nd ed. Ronald L. Carlson. LC 92-72360. 1993. 97.50 (*0-318-00076-8*) Lawyers Cooperative.

Successful Techniques for Higher Profits. Robert Rachlin. LC 80-85150. 260p. 1981. 16.95 (*0-938712-02-0*) Marr Pubns.

Successful Techniques for Improving Productivity in On-Site Construction. Clarkson H. Oglesby et al. (Illus.). 512p. 1988. text ed. write for info. (*0-07-047802-3*) McGraw.

Successful Techniques for Improving Sales: One-Pager Management Tool. Laddie F. Hutar. 54p. 1992. spiral bd. 72.95 (*0-614-06669-7*, 15040) Hutar.

Successful Techniques for Solving Employees Compensation Problems. Don R. Marshall. LC 77-17964. (Illus.). 212p. reprint ed. pap. 60.50 (*0-317-09588-9*, 2020189) Bks Demand.

Successful Telemarketing. Bob Stone & John Wyman. 256p. 1993. 29.95 (*0-8442-3134-7*, NTC Busn Bks) NTC Pub Grp.

Successful Telemarketing. Bob Stone. 1995. pap. 15.95 (*0-8442-3133-9*, NTC Busn Bks) NTC Pub Grp.

Successful Telemarketing: Opportunities & Techniques for Increasing Sales & Profits. Bob Stone & John Wyman. write for info. (*0-318-59698-9*) S&S Trade.

Successful Telemarketing: Opportunities & Techniques for Increasing Sales & Profits. 2nd ed. Bob Stone. 224p. 1995. pap. 19.95 (*0-8442-3296-3*, NTC Busn Bks) NTC Pub Grp.

Successful Telemarketing: The Complete Handbook on Managing a Profitable Telemarketing Operation. Kathy Sisk. 1995. text ed. 59.95 (*0-07-057704-8*) McGraw.

Successful Telemarketing Opportunities & Techniques for Increasing Sales & Profits. 2nd ed. Bob Stone & John Wyman. 224p. 1994. 39.95 (*0-8442-3295-5*, NTC Busn Bks) NTC Pub Grp.

Successful Telephone Selling in the '90's. rev. ed. Martin D. Shafiroff & Robert L. Shook. LC 89-46221. 224p. 1990. pap. 12.00 (*0-06-096491-X*, PL) HarpC.

***Successful Telephone Techniques.** Judith Taylor. (Better Management Skills Ser.). 1994. pap. 12.95 (*0-7494-1178-3*) Kogan Page Ltd.

Successful Temping. Richard Rogers. 1996. 12.95 (*0-02-861060-1*) Macmillan.

Successful Termination. rev. ed. William J. Morin. (Illus.). 44p. (C). 1993. pap. text ed. 10.95 (*1-880030-60-8*) DBM Pub.

***Successful Test Taking: Learning Strategies for Nursing Students.** 3rd ed. Marian B. Sides & Nancy Korchek. 512p. 1998. pap. text ed. write for info. (*0-7817-9202-9*) Lppncott-Raven.

Successful Thoroughbred Investment in a Changing Market. Jack Lohman & Arnold Kirkpatrick. (Illus.). 253p. 1984. 25.00 (*0-929346-10-6*) R Meerdink Co Ltd.

Successful Time Management. 2nd ed. Jack D. Ferner. (Self-Teaching Guides Ser.). 312p. 1995. pap. text ed. 14.95 (*0-471-03392-8*) Wiley.

Successful Time Management for Hospital Administrators. Merrill E. Douglass & Phillip H. Goodwin. LC 79-55063. 150p. reprint ed. pap. 42.80 (*0-317-26716-7*, 2023519) Bks Demand.

***Successful Tourism Marketing.** Susan Briggs. (Marketing & Sales Ser.). 1997. pap. 32.95 (*0-7494-2125-8*) Kogan Page Ltd.

***Successful TQM.** Klaus J. Zink. 200p. 1997. 39.95 (*0-470-23726-0*, EG00) Halsted Pr.

***Successful TQM: Inside Stories from European Quality Award Winners.** Klaus J. Zink. LC 96-28491. 200p. 1997. 65.95 (*0-566-07800-7*, Pub. by Gower UK) Ashgate Pub Co.

Successful Training Practice: A Manager's Guide to Personnel Development. Alan H. Anderson. LC 92-17012. (Human Resource Management in Action Ser.). 1993. pap. 44.95 (*0-631-18766-9*) Blackwell Pubs.

Successful Training Strategies. Jill Casner-Lotto & Work in America Associates Staff. LC 88-42781. (Management Ser.). 450p. 32.95 (*1-55542-101-6*) Work in Amer.

***Successful Transcript.** E. Rushen. Date not set. pap. text ed. write for info. (*0-85896-878-9*) Addison-Wesley.

Successful Transformations? The Creation of Market Economies in Eastern Germany & the Czech Republic. Martin R. Myant. LC 96-23168. (Studies of Communism in Transition). 267p. 1996. 80.00 (*1-85898-495-5*) E Elgar.

Successful Transitions: A Guide Through the Employment Process. 3rd ed. 1987. pap. 7.99 (*1-55549-015-8*) Ed Assocs KY.

Successful Travel Sales. Nancy Chappie. (Illus.). 110p. (C). 1995. pap. text ed. write for info. (*0-9648595-0-5*) Trvl Univ Intl.

Successful Tree Breeding with Index Selection. Paul F. Cotterill & Christine A. Dean. 1989. pap. 35.00 (*0-643-04990-8*, Pub. by CSIRO AT) Aubrey Bks.

Successful Trucking after Deregulation. Thomas J. Hays. Ed. by Barbara Braasch. (Illus.). 300p. (Orig.). (C). 1995. pap. 49.95 (*0-9645222-0-9*) Pac Stand Pub.

Successful Turkey Hunting. J. Wayne Fears. Ed. by Glenn Helgeland. LC 82-74192. (On Target Ser.). (Illus.). 92p. (Orig.). 1984. pap. 5.95 (*0-913305-01-4*) Target Comm.

Successful Use of Teaching Portfolios. Peter Seldin & Associates Staff. 228p. (C). 1993. pap. text ed. 24.95 (*0-9627042-5-3*) Anker Pub.

Successful Vines for the Peninsula: A Selection by the Members of the Western Horticultural Society. Ed. by Elaine S. Levine. LC 96-60292. (Illus.). 104p. (Orig.). 1996. pap. 15.00 (*0-9622226-1-5*) West Hort Soc.

Successful Warmups: Conductor's Edition, Bk. 2. Nancy Telfer. 1996. pap. text ed. 29.95 (*0-8497-4177-7*, V84T) Kjos.

Successful Warmups: Singer's Edition, Bk. 2. Nancy Telfer. 96p. 1996. pap. text ed. 6.95 (*0-8497-4178-5*, V84S) Kjos.

Successful Warmups Bk. 1: Conductor's Edition. Nancy Telfer. 240p. 1995. pap. text ed. 29.95 (*0-8497-4175-0*, V83T) Kjos.

Successful Warmups Bk. 1: Singer's Edition. Nancy Telfer. 96p. 1995. pap. text ed. 6.95 (*0-8497-4174-2*, V83S) Kjos.

Successful Window Dressing & Interior Design: Your Guide to Achieving Excellent Results. Linda M. Ramsay. Ed. by Mary J. Matthews. (Illus.). 336p. 1997. pap. 24.99 (*0-9629918-1-3*) Touch Design.

Successful Women: Their Health & Handwriting. Patricia Wellingham-Jones. LC 89-91640. (Illus.). 206p. (Orig.). 1989. pap. 12.00 (*0-939221-06-3*) Wellingham-Jones.

Successful Women: With Portraits. Sarah K. Bolton. LC 74-936. (Essay Index Reprint Ser.). (Illus.). 1977. reprint ed. 18.95 (*0-518-10143-6*) Ayer.

Successful Women's Events. Madlyn L. Hamblin. 128p. 1995. pap. text ed. 9.99 (*0-8280-0835-3*) Review & Herald.

Successful Wrestling: Coaches' Guide for Teaching Basic to Advanced Skills. Art Keith. LC 89-12098. (Illus.). 160p. (Orig.). 1990. pap. 19.95 (*0-88011-329-4*, PKEI0329) Human Kinetics.

Successful Writing. Nancy Harrison. 168p. 1990. 110.00 (*1-870167-00-7*, Pub. by P Francis UK) St Mut.

***Successful Writing.** 4th ed. Maxine Hairston. (C). Date not set. pap. text ed. write for info. (*0-393-97196-1*) Norton.

Successful Writing: A Guide to Authors of Non-Fiction Books & Articles. George R. Scott. 95p. 1993. pap. 6.95 (*1-874052-02-6*) Paul & Co Pubs.

Successful Writing: A Rhetoric for Advanced Composition. Maxine C. Hairston. (C). 1992. pap. text ed. write for info. (*0-393-96205-9*) Norton.

Successful Writing: A Rhetoric for Advanced Composition. 3rd ed. Maxine C. Hairston. (C). 1992. pap. text ed. 22.95 (*0-393-96204-0*) Norton.

Successful Writing at Work. 3rd ed. Philip C. Kolin. LC 89-80257. 577p. (C). 1990. Instr.'s guide. teacher ed. 2.00 (*0-685-45163-1*) HM College Div.

***Successful Writing at Work.** 4th ed. Philip C. Kolin. (C). 1994. teacher ed., text ed. 2.66 (*0-669-29715-1*) HM College Div.

Successful Writing at Work. 4th ed. Philip C. Kolin. 693p. (C). 1994. pap. text ed. 43.96 (*0-669-29714-3*) HM College Div.

Successfully Different: An Alternative to Divorce. Arnie Wallace & Adryan Russ. LC 89-82471. 192p. (Orig.). 1990. pap. 11.95 (*0-9625341-1-0*) Challenger CA.

Successfully Implementing World-Class Training. Bren D. White. (Illus.). 240p. 1990. 45.00 (*0-9623424-1-6*) Boswell Pub.

Successfully Installing TPM in a Non-Japanese Plant: Total Productive Maintenance. Edward H. Hartmann. LC 92-39939. (Illus.). 221p. (C). 1992. text ed. 39.95 (*1-882258-00-2*, SITPM) TPM Pr.

***Successfully Managing Change.** George Hardy. LC 97-6357. (Business Success Ser.). 1997. pap. 6.95 (*0-7641-0060-2*) Barron.

Successfully Self-Employed: How to Sell What You Do, Do What You Sell, Manage Your Cash in Between. Gregory Brennan. 176p. 1996. pap. 16.95 (*1-57410-000-9*, 5614-4301) Upstart Pub.

Successfully Staffing a Diverse Workplace: A Practical Guide to Building an Effective & Diverse Staff. Maureen Orey. (Workplace Diversity Ser.). (Illus.). 120p. 1995. pap. 12.95 (*1-883553-67-9*) R Chang Assocs.

SuccessGuide, Vol. IV: The Guide to Black Resources in Atlanta, Chicago, Cincinnati, Cleveland, Detroit, Los Angeles, New York City, New Orleans, Philadelphia, Washington D. C., 10 vols., 8 vols. Ed. by George C. Fraser & Margaret Thoren. (Illus.). 2640p. 1993. pap. 239.95 (*1-879355-09-4*) SuccessSource.

SuccessGuide, Vol. IV: The Guide to Black Resources in Atlanta, Chicago, Cincinnati, Cleveland, Detroit, Los Angeles, New York City, New Orleans, Philadelphia, Washington D. C., 10 vols., 8 vols., Set. Ed. by George C. Fraser & Margaret Thoren. (Illus.). 2640p. 1993. write for info. (*1-879355-08-6*); write for info. (*1-879355-11-6*) SuccessSource.

SuccessGuide, Vol. IV: The Guide to Black Resources in Chicago. Ed. by George C. Fraser & Margaret Thoren. (Illus.). 1994. write for info. (*1-879355-13-2*) SuccessSource.

SuccessGuide, Vol. IV: The Guide to Black Resources in Cincinnati-Dayton. Ed. by George C. Fraser & Margaret Thoren. (Illus.). 1993. write for info. (*1-879355-14-0*) SuccessSource.

SuccessGuide, Vol. IV: The Guide to Black Resources in Cleveland. Ed. by George C. Fraser & Margaret Thoren. (Illus.). 1994. write for info. (*1-879355-15-9*) SuccessSource.

SuccessGuide, Vol. IV: The Guide to Black Resources in Detroit. Ed. by George C. Fraser & Margaret Thoren. (Illus.). 1994. write for info. (*1-879355-16-7*) SuccessSource.

SuccessGuide, Vol. IV: The Guide to Black Resources in Los Angeles. Ed. by George C. Fraser & Margaret Thoren. (Illus.). 1993. write for info. (*1-879355-17-5*) SuccessSource.

SuccessGuide, Vol. IV: The Guide to Black Resources in New York City. Ed. by George C. Fraser & Margaret Thoren. (Illus.). 1994. write for info. (*1-879355-18-3*) SuccessSource.

SuccessGuide, Vol. IV: The Guide to Black Resources in Washington, D.C. Ed. by George C. Fraser & Margaret Thoren. (Illus.). 1994. write for info. (*1-879355-19-1*) SuccessSource.

SuccessGuide, Vol. IV: The Networking Guide to Black Resources in Atlanta. Ed. by George C. Fraser & Margaret Thoren. (Illus.). 1994. write for info. (*1-879355-12-4*) SuccessSource.

SuccessGuide 1991: The Guide to Black Resources in Atlanta. Ed. by George C. Fraser & Owen Montague. (Illus.). 352p. (Orig.). 1991. pap. 14.95 (*1-879355-01-9*) SuccessSource.

SuccessGuide 1991: The Guide to Black Resources in Chicago. Ed. by George C. Fraser & Antonio McKinney. 224p. (Orig.). 1991. pap. 14.95 (*1-879355-02-7*) SuccessSource.

SuccessGuide 1991: The Guide to Black Resources in Cincinnati - Dayton. Ed. by George C. Fraser & Jerald L. Tillman. (Illus.). 224p. (Orig.). 1991. pap. 14.95 (*1-879355-03-5*) SuccessSource.

SuccessGuide 1991: The Guide to Black Resources in Cleveland. Ed. by George C. Fraser & Margaret L. Thoren. (Illus.). 224p. (Orig.). 1991. pap. 14.95 (*1-879355-00-0*) SuccessSource.

SuccessGuide 1991: The Guide to Black Resources in Detroit. Ed. by George C. Fraser & Steve Lewis. (Illus.). 224p. (Orig.). 1991. pap. 14.95 (*1-879355-04-3*) SuccessSource.

SuccessGuide 1991: The Guide to Black Resources in New York City. Ed. by George C. Fraser & George K. Walters. (Illus.). 224p. (Orig.). 1991. pap. 14.95 (*1-879355-05-1*) SuccessSource.

SuccessGuide 1991: The Guide to Black Resources in Washington, D. C. Ed. by George C. Fraser & James Carter. (Illus.). 224p. (Orig.). 1991. pap. 14.95 (*1-879355-06-X*) SuccessSource.

Succession. Ian Jones. (Q & A Ser.). 206p. 1995. pap. write for info. (*1-874241-36-8*, Pub. by Cavendish UK) Gaunt.

Succession. Ed. by Linda S. Spedding. 270p. (C). 1991. 72.00 (*1-85352-599-5*, Pub. by HLT Pubns UK) St Mut.

Succession. Ed. by Elizabeth West. 230p. (C). 1990. pap. 75.00 (*1-85352-757-2*, Pub. by HLT Pubns UK) St Mut.

Succession. 2nd ed. Ian Jones. (Q & A Ser.). 280p. 1996. pap. write for info. (*1-85941-273-4*, Pub. by Cavendish UK) Gaunt.

Succession: A Novel of Elizabeth & James. George Garrett. 1991. pap. 12.95 (*0-15-686303-0*, Harvest Bks) HarBrace.

Succession - Cases & Materials. Cherry E. Wright. 1986. U.K. 98.00 (*0-406-56310-1*, U.K.); U.K. pap. 58.00 (*0-406-56311-X*, U.K.) MICHIE.

S

An Asterisk (*) at the beginning of an entry indicates that the title is appearing in BIP for the first time.

Succession & Imperial Leadership among the Mughals 1526-1707. Neeru Misra. (C). 1993. 16.00 (*81-220-0337-0*, Pub. by Konark Pubs II) S Asia.

Succession Between International Organizations. Patrick R. Myers. LC 92-2353. (Publication of the Graduate Institute of International Studies, Geneva). 200p. 1993. 89.95 (*0-7103-0457-9*, B0088) Routledge Chapman & Hall.

Succession in Abandoned Fields: Studies in Central Bohemia, Czechoslovakia. Ed. by J. Osbornova et al. (C). 1990. lib. bdg. 158.50 (*0-7923-0401-2*) Kluwer Ac.

Succession in Fen Woodland Ecosystems in the Dutch Haf District with Special Reference to Betula Pubescens Ehrh. J. Wiegers. (Dissertationes Botanicae Ser.: No. 86). (Illus.). 152p. 1985. pap. text ed. 36.00 (*3-7682-1441-9*) Lubrecht & Cramer.

Succession in the Dehli Sultante. Rekha Pande. 1990. 29.00 (*81-7169-069-6*, Commonwealth) S Asia.

Succession Law in Ireland. James C. Brady. 1989. boxed 106.00 (*1-85475-100-X*, UK) MICHIE.

Succession Laws of Christian Countries with Special Reference to the Law of Primogeniture As It Exists in England. Eyre Lloyd. xi, 108p. 1985. reprint ed. lib. bdg. 20.00 (*0-8377-0816-8*) Rothman.

Succession of Days, 2 vols. in 1. Alex A. Hurst. 356p. 1993. 120.00 (*1-872017-63-0*, Pub. by Book Sales UK) St Mut.

Succession of Fine Lives. Errol Miller. Ed. by Robert Bixby. 36p. 1993. pap. 6.00 (*1-882983-04-1*) March Street Pr.

***Succession of Honorable Victories: The Burnside Expedition in North Carolina.** unabridged ed. Richard A. Sauers. (Illus.). 542p. 1996. text ed. 39.95 (*0-89029-326-0*) Morningside Bkshop.

Succession of Organists: Of the Chapel Royal & the Cathedral of England & Wales from c. 1538. Watkins Shaw. (Oxford Studies in British Church Music). (Illus.). 480p. 1991. 105.00 (*0-19-816175-1*) OUP.

Succession of Shakespere's Works. Ed. by Frederick J. Furnivall. LC 76-137318. reprint ed. 27.50 (*0-404-02663-X*) AMS Pr.

Succession of States in Respect to Treaties, State Property, Archives, & Debts. P. K. Menon. LC 90-22575. (Studies in World Peace: Vol. 6). 265p. 1991. lib. bdg. 89.95 (*0-88946-263-1*) E Mellen.

Succession Ouverte. Driss Charaibi. 192p. (FRE.). 1979. pap. 10.95 (*0-7859-1900-7*, 2070371360) Fr & Eur.

Succession Planning: An Annotated Bibliography & Summary of Commonly Reported Organizational Practices. Lorrina J. Eastman. LC 95-16258. 72p. 1995. pap. text ed. 20.00 (*1-882197-06-2*) Ctr Creat Leader.

Succession Planning: An Ongoing Approach. Rhonda Cooke. (CUES HR Development Ser.). 48p. 1995. pap. 99.00 (*1-889394-21-1*) Credit Union Execs.

Succession Planning for Closely Held Businesses. Galen D. Loven. 123p. 1993. pap. 19.95 (*1-883480-00-0*) Brkthgh Pubns.

Succession Planning Handbook for the Chief Executive. Walter R. Mahler & Stephen J. Drotter. 300p. 1986. 45.00 (*0-914431-01-3*) Mahler Pub Co.

Succession Planning in America's Corporations: How 64 Top Companies Prepare for the Future. Executive KnowledgeWorks Staff. (Illus.). 65p. 1988. spiral bd. 165.00 (*0-943353-05-X*) Exec Knowledge.

Succession-Replacement Planning: Programs & Practices. Joseph Carnazza. 1982. pap. 12.00 (*0-317-11511-1*) CU Ctr Career Res.

Succession Student's Handbook. M. J. De Waal et al. 217p. 1993. pap. write for info. (*0-7021-2915-1*, Pub. by Juta SA) Gaunt.

Succession to Muhammad: A History of Early Islam. Wilferd Madelung. 464p. (C). 1998. text ed. 69.95 (*0-521-56181-7*) Cambridge U Pr.

Succession to Rule under Dehli Sultan. Manoj Kumar Srivastava. 1990. 24.00 (*81-7169-053-X*, Commonwealth) S Asia.

Succession, Wills & Probate. Caroline Sawyer. (Lecture Notes Ser.). 444p. 1995. pap. 36.00 (*1-85941-042-1*, Pub. by Cavendish UK) Gaunt.

Successions of Meniscomyine & Allomyine Rodents (Aplodontidae) in the Oligo-Miocene John Day Formation, Oregon. John M. Rensberger. LC 83-1403. (Publications in Geological Sciences: Vol. 124). 176p. (C). 1983. pap. 30.00 (*0-520-09668-1*) U CA Pr.

Successive Approximation: Survey Recent East European Mathematical Literature. N. Vilenkin & M. Slater. LC 64-14148. (Popular Lectures in Mathematics: Vol. 15). 1964. 43.00 (*0-08-010649-8*, Pub. by Pergamon Repr UK) Franklin.

Successor. Roderic A. Camp. LC 92-34656. 300p. 1993. 11.95 (*0-8263-1420-1*) U of NM Pr.

***Successor.** Dorothy G. Warnke & Thomas E. Warnke. 309p. (Orig.). 1997. mass mkt. 4.99 (*1-55237-295-2*, Pub. by Comnwlth Pub CN) Partners Pubs Grp.

Successor: My Life. Kosho K. Otani. LC 84-23016. (Illus.). 114p. 1985. 18.95 (*0-914910-50-7*) Buddhist Bks.

Successor Generation: Its Challenges & Responsibilities. Robert E. Osgood. 45p. (C). 1983. pap. 21.95 (*0-87855-874-8*) Transaction Pubs.

Successor States & Cooperation Theory. George Macesich. LC 94-6377. 192p. 1994. text ed. 55.00 (*0-275-94936-2*, Praeger Pubs) Greenwood.

Successor States to the U. S. S. R. Ed. by John W. Blaney. LC 94-46162. 333p. 1995. pap. 29.95 (*0-87187-978-6*) Congr Quarterly.

Successor Vision: The United Nations of Tomorrow. Ed. by Peter J. Fromuth. LC 88-23440. (Illus.). 422p. (Orig.). (C). 1988. pap. text ed. 29.00 (*0-8191-6906-4*) U Pr of Amer.

Successors. large type ed. Stuart Seaton. 528p. 1987. 27.99 (*0-7089-8447-9*, Charnwood) Ulverscroft.

Successors of Alexander the Great. C. A. Kinkaid. 192p. 1980. pap. 15.00 (*0-89005-352-9*) Ares.

Succos. Y. Ganz. (ArtScroll Youth Holiday Ser.). (YA). 1991. 8.99 (*0-89906-978-9*) Mesorah Pubns.

Succos: Its Significance, Law, & Prayers. Hersh Goldwurm & Meir Zlotowitz. (ArtScroll Mesorah Ser.). (Illus.). 128p. 1982. 17.99 (*0-89906-166-4*); pap. 14.99 (*0-89906-167-2*) Mesorah Pubns.

Succotash-from My Garden of Memories. Frank W. Whippel. Ed. by Sheila R. Mathison. (Illus.). 300p. (Orig.). 1992. pap. text ed. 12.95 (*0-9633110-0-X*) F W Whipple.

Succoth: A Joyous Holiday. Barbara Soloff-Levy. (J). pap. 1.25 (*0-8167-2203-X*) Troll Communs.

Succubus. Mark Dunster. 11p. 1991. pap. 4.00 (*0-89642-196-1*) Linden Pubs.

Succulent Flora of Southern Africa: A Comprehensive & Authoritative Guide to the Indigenous Succulents of S Africa, Botswana, S-W Africa, Namibia, Angola, Zambia, Zimbabwe, Rhodesia & Mozambique Incorporating the Latest Research & Changes in Nomenclature. Doreen Court. 240p. (C). 1981. text ed. 95.00 (*90-6191-091-9*, Pub. by A A Balkema NE) Ashgate Pub Co.

***Succulent Garden: A Practical Gardening Guide.** Yvonne Cave. LC 96-34044. (Illus.). 100p. (Orig.). 1997. pap. 19.95 (*0-88192-378-8*) Timber.

***Succulent Wild Woman.** Sark. 1997. pap. 15.00 (*0-684-83376-X*, Fireside) S&S Trade.

Succulents: The Illustrated Dictionary. Maurizio Sajeva & Mariangela Constanzo. (Illus.). 240p. 1994. 39.95 (*0-88192-289-7*) Timber.

***Succulents: The Illustrated Dictionary.** Maurizio Sajeva & Mariangela Constanzo. (Illus.). 240p. 1997. reprint ed. pap. 29.95 (*0-88192-398-2*) Timber.

Succumb. Ron Dee. 1994. mass mkt. 5.50 (*0-671-87110-2*) PB.

Such a Candle. Douglas C. Wood. 1980. pap. 8.99 (*0-85234-134-2*, Pub. by Evangelical Pr) Presby & Reformed.

Such a Cloud of Witnesses. rev. ed. Milton G. Crane. LC 91-65119. (Illus.). 80p. 1995. per. 4.95 (*1-57258-045-3*) Teach Servs.

Such a Deal! rev. ed. Jan O'Rear. 96p. 1993. reprint ed. pap. 8.95 (*1-878686-14-3*) Two Lane Pr.

Such a Long Journey. Rohinton Mistry. 1992. pap. 14.00 (*0-679-73871-1*, Vin) Random.

Such a Lovely Couple. Linda Yellin. 352p. (Orig.). 1991. mass mkt. 4.99 (*0-446-36068-6*) Warner Bks.

Such a Noise! Aliana Brodmann. Tr. by David Fillingham from GER. (Illus.). 32p. (J). (gr. k-3). 1989. 11.95 (*0-916291-25-1*) Kane-Miller Bk.

Such a Simple Little Tale: Critical Responses to L. M. Montgomery's Anne of Green Gables. Mavis Reimer. LC 92-7392. (Children's Literature Association Ser.). 210p. 1992. 25.00 (*0-8108-2560-0*) Scarecrow.

Such Agreeable Friends. Gay L. Balliet. 266p. (Orig.). 1987. pap. write for info. (*0-910119-33-3*) SOCO Pubns.

Such Are the Trials: The Civil War Diaries of Jacob Gantz. Ed. by Kathleen Davis. LC 90-48636. (Illus.). 136p. 1991. 22.95 (*0-8138-0947-9*) Iowa St U Pr.

Such As Us: Southern Voices of the Thirties. Ed. by Tom E. Terrill & Jerrold Hirsch. LC 77-14248. xxvi, 302p. (C). 1987. reprint ed. pap. text ed. 13.95 (*0-8078-4191-9*) U of NC Pr.

Such Bright Hopes. Walter R. Scragg. Ed. by Raymond H. Woolsey. 384p. 1987. 9.99 (*0-8280-0389-0*) Review & Herald.

Such Dark Magic. large type ed. Robyn Donald. (Harlequin Ser.). 1993. lib. bdg. 18.95 (*0-263-13419-9*) Thorndike Pr.

Such Dark Magic: Year down Under. Robyn Donald. 1993. mass mkt. 2.99 (*0-373-11611-X*, 1-11611-0) Harlequin Bks.

Such Devoted Sisters. Eileen Goudge. 624p. 1992. pap. 5.99 (*0-451-17337-6*, Sig) NAL-Dutton.

Such Devoted Sisters. Eileen Goudge. 1992. pap. write for info. (*0-451-17216-7*, Sig) NAL-Dutton.

Such Devoted Sisters. large type ed. Eileen Goudge. 905p. 1993. pap. 16.95 (*1-56054-933-5*) Thorndike Pr.

Such Devoted Sisters. Ed. by Shena Mackay. 336p. 1994. reprint ed. 21.95 (*1-55921-110-5*) Moyer Bell.

Such Friends As These. Alexander G. Rose, III & Jeffrey A. Savoye. 1986. pap. 5.00 (*0-910556-24-5*) Enoch Pratt.

Such Good People. Martha W. Hickman. 336p. 1996. 22.95 (*0-446-52040-3*) Warner Bks.

***Such Good People.** Martha W. Hickman. 352p. 1997. mass mkt. 6.50 (*0-446-60467-4*) Warner Bks.

Such Hardworking People: Italian Immigrants in Postwar Toronto. Franca Iacovetta. (Illus.). 328p. 1993. pap. 19.95 (*0-7735-1145-8*, Pub. by McGill CN) U of Toronto Pr.

Such Hardworking People: Italian Immigrants in Postwar Toronto. Franca Lacovetta. (Illus.). 336p. 1992. 55.00 (*0-7735-0874-0*, Pub. by McGill CN) U of Toronto Pr.

Such Is Death. Leo Bruce, pseud. (Carolus Deene Mystery Ser.). 192p. 1985. pap. 5.95 (*0-89733-160-5*) Academy Chi Pubs.

Such Is Death. Leo Bruce, pseud. (Carolus Deene Mystery Ser.). 192p. 1986. 15.00 (*0-89733-159-1*) Academy Chi Pubs.

Such Is Life. Erma L. Milton. 67p. (Orig.). 1996. pap. text ed. 10.95 (*0-9614788-4-5*) Tivoli Pub.

***Such Is My Beloved.** Morley Callaghan. 1996. pap. text ed. 6.95 (*0-7710-9955-X*) McCland & Stewart.

Such Is the Real Nature of Horses. Robert Vavra. LC 79-52901. (Illus.). 1979. 40.45 (*0-688-03504-3*) Morrow.

Such Is the Way of the World: A Journey Through Grief. Barbara S. Brisson. 64p. (Orig.). 1997. pap. 5.95 (*0-8091-3691-0*) Paulist Pr.

Such Men Are Dangerous. Lawrence Block. 192p. 1993. 4.50 (*0-7867-0047-5*) Carroll & Graf.

Such Men As Billy the Kid: The Lincoln County War Reconsidered. Joel Jacobsen. LC 93-42105. (Illus.). xv, 322p. 1994. text ed. 28.00 (*0-8032-2576-8*) U of Nebr Pr.

***Such Men as Billy the Kid: The Lincoln County War Reconsidered.** Joel Jacobsen. LC 93-42105. (Illus.). xv, 322p. 1997. pap. 15.00 (*0-8032-7606-0*, Bison Books) U of Nebr Pr.

Such Nice People. Sandra Scoppettone. 288p. 1981. pap. 2.75 (*0-449-24420-2*, Crest) Fawcett.

Such Pain. Don Bassingthwaite. (World of Darkness: Mage Ser.). 336p. 1995. mass mkt. 4.99 (*0-06-105463-1*, Harp PBks) HarpC.

Such Prompt Eloquence: Language As Agency & Character in Milton's Epics. Leonard Mustazza. LC 86-48007. 176p. 1988. 32.50 (*0-8387-5121-0*) Bucknell U Pr.

Such Silence. Michael Milburn. LC 88-34011. (Alabama Poetry Ser.). 80p. 1989. pap. 9.95 (*0-8173-0430-4*) U of Ala Pr.

***Such Stuff As Dreams.** Norma Johnston. (J). Date not set. write for info. (*0-688-07720-X*, Morrow Junior) Morrow.

Such Sweet Compulsion: The Autobiography of Geraldine Farrar. Geraldine Farrar. LC 72-107802. (Select Bibliographies Reprint Ser.). 1977. 28.95 (*0-8369-5205-7*) Ayer.

Such Sweet Compulsion, the Autobiography of Geraldine Farrar. Geraldine Farrar. LC 70-100656. (Music Ser.). 1970. reprint ed. lib. bdg. 37.50 (*0-306-71863-4*) Da Capo.

Such Sweet Poison. Anne Mather. (Presents Ser.: No. 458). 1992. pap. 2.89 (*0-373-11458-3*, 1-11458-6) Harlequin Bks.

***Such Sweet Sorrow.** Catrin Collier. 352p. 1997. 26.00 (*0-7126-7508-6*, Pub. by Century UK) Trafalgar.

Such Sweet Thunder. 1993. pap. 4.50 (*0-8216-5096-3*, Univ Books) Carol Pub Group.

Such Times. Christopher Coe. 336p. 1994. reprint ed. pap. 10.95 (*0-14-024143-4*, Penguin Bks) Viking Penguin.

Such Waltzing Was Not Easy. Stories. Gordon Weaver. LC 75-2288. (Illinois Short Fiction Ser.). 144p. 1974. 9.95 (*0-252-00533-3*) U of Ill Pr.

Such Was Saratoga. Hugh Bradley. LC 75-1832. (Leisure Class in America Ser.). 1975. reprint ed. 28.95 (*0-405-06901-4*) Ayer.

Such Were the Times: A Personal View of the Lysenko Era in the U. S. S. R. Eleanor D. Manevich. LC 89-64119. 100p. 1990. pap. 9.95 (*0-938875-22-1*) Pittenbruach Pr.

***Suche, Level 2.** Hans M. Enzenberger et al. (Illus.). 200p. (ENG, FRE & GER.). (C). Date not set. pap. text ed. 24.50 (*3-468-47620-5*) Langenscheidt.

***Suche, Level 2.** Hans M. Enzenberger et al. (Illus.). 258p. (ENG, FRE & GER.). (C). Date not set. wbk. ed., pap. text ed. 24.50 (*3-468-47621-3*) Langenscheidt.

***Suche, Level 2.** Hans M. Enzenberger et al. (Illus.). (ENG, FRE & GER.). (C). Date not set. teacher ed., pap. text ed. 24.50 (*3-468-47622-1*) Langenscheidt.

***Suche, Level 2, Glossary.** Hans M. Enzenberger et al. (Illus.). (C). Date not set. pap. text ed. 8.95 (*3-468-47630-2*) Langenscheidt.

***Suche, Level 2, Glossary.** Hans M. Enzenberger et al. (Illus.). (FRE.). (C). Date not set. pap. text ed. 8.95 (*3-468-47631-0*) Langenscheidt.

Suche: Level One Glossary 1 English, Glossary English 1. Enzensberger et al. 62p. 1995. student ed. 8.95 (*3-468-47610-8*) Langenscheidt.

Suche: Level One Textbook 1. Enzensberger et al. 200p. 1993. text ed. 24.50 (*3-468-47600-0*) Langenscheidt.

Suche: Level One Workbook 1. Enzensberger et al. 256p. 1994. student ed. 24.50 (*3-468-47601-9*) Langenscheidt.

Suche Level 1. Enzensberger et al. 256p. 1995. teacher ed. 24.50 (*3-468-47602-7*) Langenscheidt.

Suche Level 1, Glossary French 1. Enzensberger et al. 62p. 1995. student ed. 8.95 (*3-468-47611-6*) Langenscheidt.

Suche Level 1, No. 1. Enzensberger et al. 30p. 1995. trans. 112.65 (*3-468-47606-X*) Langenscheidt.

Suche Level 1, No. 1A. Enzensberger et al. 1994. audio 25.95 (*3-468-47603-5*) Langenscheidt.

Suche Level 1, No. 1B. Enzensberger et al. 1994. audio 12.95 (*3-468-47604-3*) Langenscheidt.

Suche Werkis to Werche: Essays on Piers Plowman in Honor of David C. Fowler. Ed. by Miceal F. Vaughan. (Medieval Texts & Studies: No. 15). (Illus.). 292p. 1993. 36.00 (*0-937191-36-1*) Colleagues Pr Inc.

Sucia Historia de la Liga Antidifamacion de B'nai B'rith. Executive Intelligence Review Editors. (Illus.). 100p. (Orig.). (SPA.). 1994. pap. 7.00 (*0-943235-12-X*) Exec Intel Review.

***Suck: Worst Case Scenarios in Media, Culture, Advertising, & the Internet.** Ed. by Joey Anuff. (Illus.). 224p. 1997. pap. 14.95 (*1-888869-27-5*) HardWired.

Sucker. Carson McCullers. LC 85-29114. (Creative's Classic Short Stories Ser.). 40p. (J). (gr. 4 up). 1986. lib. bdg. 13.95 (*0-88682-053-7*) Creative Ed.

Sucker for Redheads: A Sully Gomez Mystery. Mel Cebulash. LC 93-29070. 1993. 3.95 (*1-56420-006-X*); audio 9.95 (*1-56420-007-8*) New Readers.

Suckers Progress: An Informal History of Gambling in America from the Colonies to Canfield. Herbert Asbury. LC 69-14909. (Criminology, Law Enforcement, & Social Problems Ser.: No. 51). (Illus.). 1969. reprint ed. 25.00 (*0-87585-051-0*) Patterson Smith.

***Suckle: The Status of Basil.** Dave Cooper. 136p. 1996. pap. 14.95 (*1-56097-301-3*) Fantagraph Bks.

Sucralfate: From Basic Science to the Bedside. Ed. by D. Hollander & Guido N. Tytgat. (Illus.). 349p. (C). 1995. 69.50 (*0-306-44740-1*) Plenum.

Sucrose: Properties & Applications. Ed. by Mohammed Mathlouthi & P. Reiser. LC 94-79052. 294p. 1995. 137.95 (*0-7514-0223-0*, Pub. by Akademie Verlag GW) Wiley.

Suctoria und Urceolariidae(Peritricha) Dieter Matthes et al. (Protozoenfauna Ser.: Vol. 7-1). (Illus.). 309p. (GER.). 1988. lib. bdg. 160.00 (*3-437-30497-6*) Lubrecht & Cramer.

Sudafrica: La Revolucion En Camino. Jack Barnes. (Illus.). 75p. (SPA.). 1986. pap. 6.95 (*0-87348-488-6*) Pathfinder NY.

Sudan. Holly A. O'Neill. LC 95-22478. (Country Guide Series Report from the AACRAO-AID Project). 1996. 22.00 (*0-929851-60-9*) Am Assn Coll Registrars.

Sudan. Nick Worrall. 30.00 (*0-7043-2242-0*, Pub. by Quartet UK) Charles River Bks.

Sudan. rev. ed. Daly. (World Bibliographical Ser.). 1992. lib. bdg. 81.00 (*1-85109-187-4*) ABC-CLIO.

Sudan: A Country Study. 4th ed. Library of Congress, Federal Research Division Staff. Ed. by Helen C. Metz. LC 92-21336. (Area Handbook Ser.). 1992. write for info. (*0-8444-0750-X*) Lib Congress.

***Sudan: Ancient Kingdom of the Nile.** Ed. by Dietrich Wilding. (Illus.). 428p. 1997. 85.00 (*2-08-013637-2*, Pub. by Flammarion FR) Abbeville Pr.

Sudan: From Subsistence to Wage Labor. Gaim Kibreab. LC 89-63123. 250p. (C). 1989. 29.95 (*0-932415-49-0*); pap. 9.95 (*0-932415-50-4*) Red Sea Pr.

Sudan: Oxfam Country Profiles. Chris Peters. (Oxfam Country Profiles Ser.). (Illus.). 64p. (C). 1996. pap. 9.95 (*0-85598-316-7*, Pub. by Oxfam UK) Humanities.

Sudan: State & Society in Crisis. Ed. by John O. Voll. LC 91-13026. (Illus.). 184p. 1991. 31.50 (*0-253-36270-9*); pap. 11.95 (*0-253-20683-9*, MB-683) Ind U Pr.

Sudan: State, Capital & Transformation. Ed. by Tony Barnett & Abbas A. Karim. 288p. 1988. lib. bdg. 59.00 (*0-7099-5902-8*, Pub. by Croom Helm UK) Routledge Chapman & Hall.

Sudan: The Gezira Scheme & Agricultural Transition. Tony Barnett & Abbas Abdelkarim. 137p. 1991. text ed. 39.50 (*0-7146-3328-3*, Pub. by F Cass Pubs UK) Intl Spec Bk.

Sudan see Cultures of the World - Group 13

Sudan - Civilian Devastation: Abuses by All Parties in the War in Southern Sudan. Human Rights Watch Africa Staff. 296p. (Orig.). 1994. pap. 15.00 (*1-56432-129-0*) Hum Rts Watch.

Sudan after Nimeiri. Ed. by Peter N. Woodward. (SOAS Series on Contemporary Politics & Culture in the Middle East). 240p. (C). (gr. 13). 1991. text ed. 89.95 (*0-415-00480-2*, A1072) Routledge.

Sudan Campaigns 1881-98. Robert Wilkinson-Latham. (Men-at-Arms Ser.: No. 59). (Illus.). 48p. pap. 11.95 (*0-85045-254-6*, 9011, Pub. by Osprey UK) Stackpole.

Sudan Civil War. Ed. by Martin W. Daly & Ahmad A. Sikainga. 224p. 1993. text ed. 69.50 (*1-85043-515-4*, Pub. by I B Tauris UK) St Martin.

Sudan in Original Photographs. Lesley Forbes & Martin W. Daly. (Illus.). 128p. 1987. text ed. 65.00 (*0-7103-0273-8*) Routledge Chapman & Hall.

Sudan in Pictures. Department of Geography, Lerner Publications. (Visual Geography Ser.). (Illus.). 64p. (YA). (gr. 5 up). 1990. lib. bdg. 19.95 (*0-8225-1839-2*, Lerner Publctns) Lerner Group.

Sudan Memoirs of Carl Christian Giegler Pasha, 1873-1883. Richard Hill. (Fontes Historiae Africanae, Series Varia: Vol. II). (Illus.). 1984. 19.98 (*0-19-726028-4*) David Brown.

Sudan since Nimeiri. Ed. by Peter N. Woodward. 176p. 1988. lib. bdg. 52.50 (*0-7099-5223-6*, Routledge NY) Routledge Chapman & Hall.

Sudan Tales: Reminiscences of Sudan Political Service Wives, 1926-56. Ed. by Rosemary Kenrick. 174p. 1986. 26.95 (*0-906672-31-7*); pap. 18.95 (*0-906672-32-5*) Oleander Pr.

Sudan under Wingate: Administration in the Anglo-Egyptian Sudan, 1899 to 1916. Gabriel R. Warburg. (Illus.). 245p. 1971. 39.50 (*0-7146-2612-0*, Pub. by F Cass Pubs UK) Intl Spec Bk.

Sudan, 1898-1989: The Unstable State. Peter Woodward. LC 89-10953. 273p. 1990. lib. bdg. 42.00 (*1-55587-193-3*) Lynne Rienner.

Sudan 1950-1985: Death of a Dream. Graham F. Thomas. (C). 1990. 90.00 (*1-85077-216-9*, Pub. by Darf Pubs Ltd UK) St Mut.

***Sudan 1990-1992: Food Aid, Famine, & Failure.** (Issue Papers). 1993. pap. 4.00 (*0-614-25347-0*) US Comm Refugees.

***Sudanese Family.** Edika Archibald. (Journey Between Two Worlds Ser.). (Illus.). (J). (gr. 3-6). 1997. pap. 8.95 (*0-614-28838-X*, First Ave Edns) Lerner Group.

Sudbury. Ray Thoms & Kathy Persall. (Illus.). 120p. 32.00 (*1-55046-110-9*, Pub. by Boston Mills Pr CN) Genl Dist Srvs.

Sudbury Region: An Illustrated History. Graeme S. Mount. LC 86-5653. (Illus.). 144p. 1986. 24.95 (*0-89781-177-1*) Am Historical Pr.

***Sudbury River: A Celebration: Photographs by Frank Gohlke.** Rachel R. Lafo et al. LC 93-72473. (Illus.). 40p. (Orig.). Date not set. pap. write for info. (*0-945506-14-7*) DeCordova Mus.

***Sudbury Valley School Experience.** (Illus.). 234p. (Orig.). 1992. pap. 10.00 (*1-888947-01-2*) Sudbury Valley.

***Sudbury Valley School Handbook.** 57p. (Orig.). 1995. pap. 7.00 (*1-888947-14-4*) Sudbury Valley.

***Sudbury Valley School Management Manual.** 282p. (Orig.). 1995. pap. 65.00 (*1-888947-15-2*) Sudbury Valley.

Sudden & Accidental Re-Education of Horse Johnson. Douglas Taylor. 1969. pap. 5.25 (*0-8222-1093-2*) Dramatists Play.

An Asterisk (*) at the beginning of an entry indicates that the title is appearing in BIP for the first time.

Sudden & Gradual: Approaches to Enlightenment in Chinese Thought. Ed. by Peter N. Gregory. LC 87-26688. (Studies in East Asian Buddhism: No. 5). 464p. 1988. text ed. 42.00 (0-8248-1118-6) UH Pr.

Sudden Apprehension: Aspects of Knowledge in Paradise Lost. Lee A. Jacobus. (Studies in English Literature: No. 94). 225p. 1976. text ed. 55.40 (90-279-3253-0) Mouton.

Sudden Cardiac Death. (Technical Report Ser.: No. 726). 25p. 1985. pap. text ed. 4.00 (92-4-120726-4, 1100726) World Health.

Sudden Cardiac Death. Masood Akhtar et al. (Illus.). 700p. 1994. text ed. 99.00 (0-683-00063-2) Williams & Wilkins.

Sudden Cardiac Death. Ed. by A. Bayes De Luna et al. (C). 1990. lib. bdg. 196.50 (0-7923-0716-X) Kluwer Ac.

Sudden Cardiac Death. Sidney Goldstein. LC 94-9562. (Illus.). 346p. 1994. 75.00 (0-87993-589-8) Futura Pub.

Sudden Cardiac Death. Ed. by Mark E. Josephson. LC 93-9180. (Illus.). 448p. 1993. 90.00 (0-86542-199-4) Blackwell Sci.

Sudden Cardiac Death. Ed. by Mark E. Josephson. LC 70-6558. (Cardiovascular Clinics Ser.: Vol. 15 No. 3). (Illus.). 328p. 1985. 50.00 (0-8036-5098-1) Davis Co.

Sudden Cardiac Death. Ed. by Robert J. Myerburg. (Journal: Cardiology: Vol. 74, Suppl. 2, 1987). (Illus.). iv, 72p. 1987. pap. 21.75 (3-8055-4629-7) S Karger.

***Sudden Cardiac Death: Past, Present, & Future.** Ed. by Sandra B. Dunbar et al. LC 96-47804. (American Heart Association Monograph Ser.). (Illus.). 432p. 1997. 78.00 (0-87993-666-5) Futura Pub.

Sudden Cardiac Death: Theory & Practice. Patricia M. Owen. LC 90-14506. 272p. 1991. text ed. 59.00 (0-8342-0200-X) Aspen Pub.

Sudden Cardiac Death & Congestive Heart Failure. Joel Morganroth & E. Neil Moore. 1983. lib. bdg. 99.00 (0-89838-580-6) Kluwer Ac.

Sudden Cardiac Death in the Community. Ed. by Mickey S. Eisenberg et al. LC 83-21156. 163p. 1984. text ed. 45.00 (0-275-91428-3, C1428, Praeger Pubs) Greenwood.

Sudden Cardial Death. Arthar. Date not set. write for info. (1-56372-007-8) Buttrwrth-Heinemann.

Sudden Change of Family. Mary J. Auch. LC 90-55100. 112p. (J). (gr. 3-7). 1990. 13.95 (0-8234-0842-6) Holiday.

Sudden Change of Family. Mary J. Auch. Ed. by Patricia MacDonald. 160p. (J). (gr. 3-6). 1993. reprint ed. mass mkt. 2.99 (0-671-74892-0, Minstrel Bks) PB.

Sudden Coronary Death, Vol. 382. Ed. by Henry M. Greenberg. 484p. 1982. 102.00 (0-89766-153-2); pap. 102.00 (0-89766-154-0) NY Acad Sci.

Sudden Coronary Death: Proceedings of the Paavo Nurmi Symposium, 4th, Helsinki, September 15-17, 1977. Paavo Nurmi Symposium Staff. Ed. by V. Manninen. (Advances in Cardiology Ser.: Vol. 25). (Illus.). 1978. 94.50 (3-8055-2881-7) S Karger.

Sudden Country. large type ed. Loren D. Estleman. (General Ser.). 276p. 1992. pap. 15.95 (0-8161-5429-5, GK Hall); lib. bdg. 19.95 (0-8161-5428-7, GK Hall) Thorndike Pr.

Sudden Dancing. Gene Zeiger. (Amherst Writers & Artists Chapbook Ser.). 40p. (Orig.). 1988. pap. 4.95 (0-941895-03-3) Amherst Wri Art.

Sudden Death. (Mack Bolan Ser.: No. 7). 384p. 1987. mass mkt. 3.95 (0-373-61407-1) Harlequin Bks.

***Sudden Death.** Bird & Falk. (New Trend Fiction B Ser.). (J). 1993. pap. text ed. write for info. (0-582-80043-9, Pub. by Longman UK) Longman.

Sudden Death. Rita Mae Brown. 256p. 1984. mass mkt. 6.50 (0-553-26930-5, Bantam Classics) Bantam.

***Sudden Death.** Kate Chester. (Hear No Evil Ser.). (J). (gr. 6-10). 1997. 3.99 (0-614-29020-1) Scholastic Inc.

Sudden Death. William X. Kienzle. 1986. mass mkt. 5.99 (0-345-32851-5) Ballantine.

Sudden Death. Ed. by Henri E. Kulbertus & Hein J. Wellens. (Developments in Cardiovascular Medicine Ser.: Vol. 4). (Illus.). xiv, 406p. 1980. lib. bdg. 165.00 (90-247-2290-X) Kluwer Ac.

***Sudden Death.** Jackie Manthorne. 1997. pap. text ed. 10.95 (0-921881-43-6, Pub. by Gynergy-Ragweed CN) LPC InBook.

Sudden Death. Steven Mertz. (Orig.). 1995. mass mkt. 5.50 (1-57297-032-4) Blvd Books.

Sudden Death: Cardiac & Other Causes. Donald B. Hackel & Keith A. Reimer. LC 93-70292. (Illus.). 168p. (Orig.). 1993. 75.00 (0-89089-546-5) Carolina Acad Pr.

Sudden Death: Intervention Skills for the Caring Professions. Bob Wright. (Illus.). 180p. 1990. pap. text ed. 26.00 (0-443-04133-4) Churchill.

Sudden Death at the Norfolk Cafe. Winona Sullivan. 1995. mass mkt. 4.99 (0-8041-1213-4) Ivy Books.

Sudden Death Due to Acute Myocardial Infarction. L. Szekeres. LC 85-29941. 296p. 1986. 169.00 (0-8493-6545-7, CRC Reprint) Franklin.

Sudden Death in Infancy, Childhood & Adolescence. Roger W. Byard & Stephen D. Cohle. LC 93-43607. (Illus.). 400p. (C). 1994. text ed. 110.00 (0-521-42031-8) Cambridge U Pr.

Sudden Death in Ischemic Heart Disease. Malcolm D. Silver. LC 95-16590. (Medical Intelligence Unit Ser.). 193p. 1995. 99.00 (1-57059-267-5) R G Landes.

***Sudden Death in Sports.** 100p. (C). 1997. spiral bd. write for info. (0-88011-730-3, COPS0730) Human Kinetics.

Sudden Death, Sudden Change No. 2. Vickie Kaczmarek. 12p. 1993. pap. text ed. 5.00 (1-882472-12-8) Comm Grief Ctr.

Sudden Destruction. Walter E. Adams. Ed. by Candy L. Adams. 190p. 1992. pap. text ed. 7.95 (0-937408-90-5) GMI Pubns Inc.

Sudden Disappearance of Japan: Journeys Through a Hidden Land. J. D. Brown. 225p. (Orig.). 1994. lib. bdg. 39.00 (0-8095-4125-4) Borgo Pr.

Sudden Distances. Lee Upton. 16p. (Orig.). 1988. pap. 5.00 (0-9608802-5-9) Years Pr.

Sudden Dreams. George Evans. LC 91-10107. 106p. (Orig.). 1991. pap. 8.95 (0-918273-86-2) Coffee Hse.

Sudden Endings: Wife Rejection in Happy Marriages. Madeline Bennett. 1991. 22.00 (0-668-09428-1, Arco) Macmillan Gen Ref.

***Sudden Exposure.** Susan Dunlap. 320p. 1997. mass mkt. 5.50 (0-440-21563-3) Dell.

Sudden Exposure: A Jill Smith Mystery. Susan Dunlap. LC 95-30237. (Jill Smith Mystery Ser.). 304p. 1996. 20.95 (0-385-31025-0) Delacorte.

Sudden, Fearful Death. Anne Perry. 1994. mass mkt. 6.99 (0-8041-1283-5) Ivy Books.

Sudden, Fearful Death. large type ed. Anne Perry. LC 93-42207. 1994. lib. bdg. 22.95 (0-7862-0130-4) Thorndike Pr.

Sudden Fiction: American Short-Short Stories. Ed. by Robert Shapard & James Thomas. 280p. 1986. reprint ed. pap. 12.95 (0-87905-265-1) Gibbs Smith Pub.

Sudden Fiction (Continued) 60 New Short-Short Stories. Ed. by Robert Shapard & James Thomas. 320p. 1996. 25.00 (0-393-03830-0); pap. 11.95 (0-393-31342-5, Norton Paperbks) Norton.

Sudden Fiction International. Robert Shapard. 1989. pap. 11.95 (0-393-30613-5) Norton.

Sudden Fictions. Ronald Moran. 59p. pap. 6.00 (1-55780-130-4) Juniper Pr WI.

Sudden Fire. large type ed. Elizabeth Oldfield. (Harlequin Ser.). 1994. lib. bdg. 19.95 (0-263-13778-3) Thorndike Pr.

Sudden Fury. 1994. mass mkt. 3.50 (0-373-61185-4) Harlequin Bks.

Sudden Glory. Vernon F. Anderson. (Caribbean Writers Ser.). 274p. (Orig.). (C). 1987. pap. 9.95 (0-435-98808-5, 98808) Heinemann.

Sudden Glory: Laughter As Subversive History. Barry Sanders. LC 95-5720. 320p. (C). 1995. 27.50 (0-8070-6204-9) Beacon Pr.

Sudden Glory: Laughter As Subversive History. Barry Sanders. 320p. 1996. pap. 15.00 (0-8070-6205-7) Beacon Pr.

Sudden Harbor. Richard Foerster. LC 91-27943. 96p. 1992. pap. 11.95 (0-914061-28-3) Orchises Pr.

Sudden Hearing Loss. Charles P. Kimmelman & Lyon L. Gleich. (Self-Instructional Package Ser.). (Illus.). 43p. (Orig.). (C). 1993. pap. text ed. 25.00 (1-56772-001-3) AAO-HNS.

Sudden Ice. Jim Leeke. LC 87-26771. (Illus.). 188p. (Orig.). 1988. pap. 8.95 (0-89407-073-8) Strawberry Hill.

Sudden Infant Death: Enduring the Loss. 2nd ed. John D. DeFrain et al. 273p. 18.95 (0-669-24544-5, Lexington) Jossey-Bass.

Sudden Infant Death Syndrome: Journal: Pediatrician, Vol. 15, No. 4, 1988. Ed. by David W. Kaplan. (Illus.). 80p. 1988. pap. 37.75 (3-8055-4892-3) S Karger.

Sudden Infant Death Syndrome: Medical Aspects & Psychological Management. Ed. by Jan L. Culbertson et al. LC 88-45399. (Contemporary Medicine & Public Health Ser.). 288p. 1988. text ed. 45.00 (0-8018-3679-4) Johns Hopkins.

Sudden Infant Death Syndrome: Risk Factors & Basic Mechanisms. Ed. by Ronald Harper & Howard Hoffman. LC 87-2365. (Illus.). 1988. 150.00 (0-89335-248-9) PMA Pub Corp.

Sudden Infant Death Syndrome: Who Can Help & How. Ed. by Charles Corr et al. 272p. 1991. 34.95 (0-8261-6720-9) Springer Pub.

Sudden Infant Death Syndrome (SIDS) New Trends in the Nineties. Ed. by Torleiv Rognum. 300p. 1995. 57.00 (82-00-22419-8) Scandnvan Univ Pr.

Sudden Liberating Thought. Kjell Askildsen. Tr. by Sverre Lyngstad from NOR. 237p. 9400. pap. 24.00 (1-870041-24-0, Pub. by Norvik Pr UK) Dufour.

Sudden Loss of Cochlear & Vestibular Function. Ed. by M. Hoke. (Advances in Oto-Rhino-Laryngology Ser.: Vol. 27). (Illus.). x, 198p. 1981. 118.50 (3-8055-2630-X) S Karger.

Sudden Miracles: Eight Women Poets. Ed. by Rhea Tregebov. 1991. pap. 14.95 (0-929005-26-0, Pub. by Second Story Pr CN) LPC InBook.

***Sudden Money.** Susan Bradley. Ed. by Abbey Beagle. Date not set. mass mkt. write for info. (0-9653318-0-6) High Rd Pub.

Sudden Music. Roger White. 200p. 1983. 14.50 (0-85398-162-0); pap. 8.50 (0-85398-163-9) G Ronald Pub.

***Sudden Parade.** Michael Lauchlan. 40p. (Orig.). 1997. pap. text ed. 8.00 (1-56439-057-8) Ridgeway.

***Sudden Prey.** John Sandford. 400p. 1997. mass mkt. 6.99 (0-425-15753-9) Berkley Pub.

Sudden Prey. John Sandford. LC 96-1934. 320p. 1996. 23.95 (0-399-14138-3, Putnam) Putnam Pub Group.

Sudden Prey. large type ed. John Sandford. LC 96-19346. 512p. 1996. 26.95 (0-7838-1832-7, GK Hall) Thorndike Pr.

Sudden Prey. large type ed. John Sandford. LC 96-19346. 1997. pap. 20.00 (0-7838-1829-7, GK Hall) Thorndike Pr.

***Sudden Radiance: Saskatchewan Poetry.** Ed. by Lorna Crozier & Gary Hyland. 14.95 (0-919926-66-5, Pub. by Coteau CN) Genl Dist Srvs.

Sudden Shakespeare: The Shaping of Shakespeare's Creative Thought. Philip Davis. LC 95-48968. 257p. 1996. text ed. 45.00 (0-312-15843-2) St Martin.

Sudden Shelter. Ed. by Jesse D. Jennings et al. LC 81-620691. (University of Utah, Anthropological Papers: No. 103). (Illus.). 339p. (Orig.). reprint ed. pap. 96.70 (0-8357-6853-8, 2035549) Bks Demand.

Sudden Silence. Eve Bunting. 112p. 1990. mass mkt. 4.50 (0-449-70362-2, Juniper) Fawcett.

Sudden Silence. Eve Bunting. 112p. (YA). (gr. 7 up). 1988. 15.00 (0-15-282058-2) HarBrace.

Sudden Sneeze . . . & Others: Senryu. Lesley Einer. 31p. (Orig.). 1991. pap. 4.50 (0-9620822-3-6) Sage Shadow Pr.

Sudden Star. Pamela Sargent. 1979. pap. 1.95 (0-449-14114-4, GM) Fawcett.

Sudden Strangers: The Story of a Gay Son & His Father. Aaron Fricke & Walter Fricke. (Illus.). 128p. 1992. pap. 8.95 (0-312-07855-2) St Martin.

Sudden Switch. Paul McCusker. LC 96-19911. (Time Twists Ser.: No. 1). 144p. (YA). 1996. pap. text ed. 5.99 (0-7459-3611-3) Lion USA.

Sudden Trees & Other Stories. H. E. Francis. LC 91-15541. 160p. 1993. 18.95 (0-913720-76-3) Beil.

Sudden Twists. Burton Goodman. 120p. (J). (gr. 6). 1988. pap. text ed. 12.64 (0-89061-501-2) Jamestown Pubs.

Sudden Twists. Ed. by Jamestown Publishers Staff. 1989. pap. 12.66 (0-8092-0077-5) Jamestown Pubs.

Sudden Victory. Beschloss. 19.95 (0-06-018219-9, HarpT) HarpC.

Sudden Violence: The Art of San Soo. Greg Jones. (Illus.). 256p. 1988. pap. 14.95 (0-87364-465-4) Paladin Pr.

Sudden Wild Magic. Diana W. Jones. 416p. 1994. mass mkt. 4.99 (0-380-71851-0, AvoNova) Avon.

Suddenly. Candace Camp. 1996. mass mkt. 5.99 (1-55166-035-0, 1-66035-6, Mira Bks) Harlequin Bks.

Suddenly. Candace Camp. 408p. 1996. mass mkt. 5.99 (0-614-96285-4) Mira Pubns.

Suddenly. Barbara Delinsky. 480p. 1994. mass mkt. 6.99 (0-06-104200-5, Harp PBks) HarpC.

Suddenly. Sandra Kitt. 1996. pap. text ed. 4.99 (0-7860-0275-1) Kensgtn Pub Corp.

***Suddenly.** McNaughton. (J). 1998. pap. write for info. (0-15-201699-6, HB Juv Bks) HarBrace.

Suddenly! Colin McNaughton. LC 94-12995. (Illus.). 32p. (J). (ps-3). 1995. 14.00 (0-15-200308-8) HarBrace.

Suddenly. large type ed. Barbara Delinsky. LC 94-13166. 567p. 1994. lib. bdg. 23.95 (0-8161-7467-9, GK Hall) Thorndike Pr.

Suddenly: The American Idea Abroad & at Home, 1986-1990. George F. Will. 429p. 1992. pap. 14.95 (0-02-934436-0, Free Press) Free Pr.

Suddenly, a Mortal Splendor. Alexander Blackburn. 309p. 1995. 20.00 (1-880909-23-5) Baskerville.

***Suddenly a Stranger.** large type ed. Paula Lindsay. (Linford Romance Library). 288p. 1996. pap. 15.99 (0-7089-7926-2) Ulverscroft.

Suddenly a Widow. Gretchen Markham. 100p. 1996. pap. 5.00 (1-887146-20-2) Ark Works.

Suddenly Alone: A Progression of Emotions Embraced by a Widow on the Path of Healing. Dolores Dahl. (Illus.). 144p. 1987. pap. 10.95 (0-9608960-5-8) Single Vision.

Suddenly Alone: A Widow's Guide to Financial Security. Ed. by Al King. LC 94-70321. 230p. 1994. pap. 14.95 (0-9622269-9-8) BookPartners.

***Suddenly Alone: How to Prepare for & Survive.** Catherine A. Wannamaker. Ed. by Pages in a Snap, Inc. Staff. (Illus.). v, 300p. 1998. pap. 16.95 (0-9645615-1-4) Equity Enter.

Suddenly Assume see Human Outcry: Chapbook Collection

***Suddenly At His Residence.** large type ed. Christianna Brand. (Linford Mystery Large Print Ser.). 416p. 1997. pap. 16.99 (0-7089-5107-4, Linford) Ulverscroft.

Suddenly Gone, Vol. 1. Dan Mitrione. 1996. mass mkt. 5.99 (0-312-96052-2) St Martin.

Suddenly Gone: The Kansas Murders of Serial Killer Richard Grissom. Dan Mitrione. Ed. by Tom McFarland & Rod Colvin. 300p. 1995. pap. 14.95 (1-886039-23-2) Addicus Bks.

Suddenly in Her Sorbet. Joyce Christmas. 1988. mass mkt. 4.95 (0-449-13311-7, GM) Fawcett.

Suddenly It Was Love. large type ed. Daisy Thomson. (Linford Romance Library). 1995. pap. 15.99 (0-7089-7782-0, Linford) Ulverscroft.

Suddenly It's Christmas. Vernon Thomas. (Writers Workshop Greenbird Ser.). 70p. 1976. 10.00 (0-86578-112-5); 6.00 (0-86578-113-3) Ind-US Inc.

Suddenly It's Evening. Ryah T. Goodman. LC 77-9026. 1977. 5.95 (0-87233-042-7) Bauhan.

***Suddenly Last Summer.** Tennessee Williams. 1969. pap. 5.25 (0-8222-1094-0) Dramatists Play.

Suddenly Last Summer see Four Plays

Suddenly Love. large type ed. Rebecca Flanders. 432p. 1985. 25.99 (0-7089-1386-5) Ulverscroft.

Suddenly No More Time. Emil Gaverluk & Rob Lindsted. 50p. (Orig.). 1994. pap. 2.50 (1-879366-51-7) Hearthstone OK.

Suddenly One Day. Siv Widerberg. Tr. by Tiina Nunnally. LC 93-661. (J). 1993. 13.00 (91-29-62248-4, Pub. by R & S Bks) FS&G.

Suddenly Single! A Lifeline for Anyone Who Has Lost a Love. 2nd ed. Hal Larson & Susan Larson. LC 92-34631. 240p. (Orig.). 1993. pap. 13.95 (1-879904-09-8) Halo Bks.

Suddenly Single Mom: A Practical Guide to Self-Sufficient Survival. T. J. Terry. 183p. 1995. pap. 32.00 (1-887258-00-0) T J Terry.

Suddenly Single Mom: A Practical Guide to Self-Sufficient Survival. rev. ed. T. J. Terry. 190p. 1996. 32.00 (1-887258-23-X) T J Terry.

Suddenly Successful: How Behavioral Optometry Helps You Overcome Learning Health & Behavior Problems. Hazel Dawkins et al. Ed. by Marcia Castaneda & Sally M. Corngold. (Illus.). 306p. 1991. 22.95 (0-943599-14-8) OEPF.

Suddenly Successful Student: A Guide to Overcoming Learning & Behavior Problems. rev. ed. Hazel R. Dawkins et al. Ed. by Sally M. Corngold & Marcia Castaneda. 68p. 1990. reprint ed. lib. bdg. 8.50 (0-943599-15-6) OEPF.

Suddenly Tomorrow Came: A History of the Johnson Space Center. 1994. lib. bdg. 275.00 (0-8490-5793-0) Gordon Pr.

Suddenly We Didn't Want to Die: Memoirs of a World War I Marine. Elton E. Mackin. LC 93-10485. 272p. 1996. pap. 14.95 (0-89141-593-9) Presidio Pr.

Suddenness: On the Moment of Aesthetic Appearance. Karl H. Bohrer. Tr. by Ruth Crowley. LC 93-29695. (European Perspectives Ser.). 253p. (C). 1994. 58.00 (0-231-07524-3) Col U Pr.

Suddha (Nectar) Contemporary Telegu Poetry. Chalam. Tr. by JSRI Narayanana Moorthy. 1990. 22.50 (81-208-0614-X, Pub. by Motilal Banarsidass II) S Asia.

Sudebnik: Quarterly Journal of the Faculty of Law, Moscow School of Social & Economic Sciences & the Vinogradoff Institute of the Faculty of Laws, University College, Longon, Vol. 1. 1996. 225.00 (0-614-14944-4, Pub. by Simmonds & Hill Pubng UK) Gaunt.

S

Sudermann's Frau Sorge: Jugendstill, Archetype, Fairy Tale, Vol. 63. Cordelia Stroinigg. LC 93-23659. (Studies in Modern German Literature: vol. 63). 200p. (C). 1995. text ed. 44.95 (0-8204-2333-5) P Lang Pubng.

Sudeten German Tragedy. Austin J. App. 1984. lib. bdg. 79.95 (0-87700-523-0) Revisionist Pr.

Sudeten Problem, 1933-1938: Volkstumspolitik & the Formulation of Nazi Foreign Policy. Ronald M. Smelser. LC 74-5912. 334p. reprint ed. pap. 95.20 (0-685-23380-4, 2032493) Bks Demand.

Sudhin N. Ghose. S. A. Narayan. (Indian Writers Ser.). 8.50 (0-89253-557-1) Ind-US Inc.

Sudie. Sara Flanigan. 1990. mass mkt. 4.50 (0-312-92501-8) St Martin.

Sudman's Bubble-ology Guide. Louis Pearl. (Illus.). 32p. (Orig.). 1985. pap. 11.95 (0-932165-07-9) Tangent Pr.

Suds in Your Eye. adapted ed. Mary Laswell. 1944. pap. 5.25 (0-8222-1095-9) Dramatists Play.

Sue Coe: Police State. Sue Coe et al. Ed. by Marilyn A. Zeitlin. (Illus.). (Orig.). 1987. pap. text ed. 30.00 (0-935519-07-6) Anderson Gal.

Sue Dolman's Book of Animal Toys. Sue Dolman. (Illus.). 128p. (Orig.). 1996. pap. 14.95 (0-304-34821-X, Pub. by Cassell UK) Sterling.

Sue Likes Blue. Barbara Gregorich. Ed. by Joan Hoffman. (Start to Read! Ser.). (Illus.). 16p. (Orig.). (J). (gr. k-2). 1984. pap. 2.25 (0-88743-011-2, 06011) Sch Zone Pub Co.

Sue Likes Blue. Barbara Gregorich. Ed. by Joan Hoffman. (Start to Read! Ser.). (Illus.). 32p. (Orig.). (J). (gr. k-2). 1992. pap. 3.95 (0-88743-409-6, 06061) Sch Zone Pub Co.

Sue, Settle or Be Silent? A. Anthony Piazza. 1994. pap. 18.95 (0-9635237-0-8) P M C & B.

Suedbayerische Parkrasen-Soziologie und Dynamik bei Unterschiedlicher Pflege. Norbert Mueller. (Dissertationes Botanicae Ser.: Vol. 123). (Illus.). ii, 176p. (GER.). 1988. spiral bd. 45.50 (3-443-64035-4) Lubrecht & Cramer.

***Suede: Interview CD Book.** Date not set. pap. write for info. (1-57899-019-X, MBS Paperbk) Mus Bk Servs.

***Suede: The Illustrated Biography.** York Membery. (Illus.). 48p. 1996. 9.95 (0-7119-3613-7, OP 47484) Omnibus NY.

Suede Holloway. William Baldwin. 1978. pap. 3.95 (0-9602170-0-2) Ars Eterna.

Suedhuegel Kerameikos, Vol. 9. Ursula Knigge. (Kerameikos Ser.). (C). 1976. 276.95 (3-11-004879-5) De Gruyter.

Suedois Sans Peine (One) Swedish for French Speakers (1) Assimil Staff. (FRE & SWE.). 28.95 (0-8288-4392-9, F13090); audio 125.00 (0-685-53045-0) Fr & Eur.

Suedois Sans Peine (Two) Swedish for French Speakers (2) Assimil Staff. (FRE & SWE.). 28.95 (0-8288-4394-5); audio 125.00 (0-685-53046-9) Fr & Eur.

Suena Grande Suenos. Luis Palau. (Serie Cruzada - Crusade Ser.). 36p. (SPA.). 1987. pap. 1.79 (0-8423-6479-X, 498006) Editorial Unilit.

Sueno de America. Esmeralda Santiago. 320p. (SPA.). 1996. 23.00 (0-06-017452-8) HarpC.

***Sueno de America: Novela.** Esmeralda Santiago. 352p. 1997. pap. 13.00 (0-06-092828-X) HarpC.

***Sueno de Felicidad.** Suzannah Davis. (SPA.). 1997. mass mkt. 3.50 (0-373-35185-2, 1-35185-7) Harlequin Bks.

Sueno de la Razon. Antonio B. Vallejo. Ed. by Mariano D. Paco. (Nueva Austral Ser.: No. 248). (SPA.). 1991. pap. text ed. 24.95 (84-239-7248-8) Elliots Bks.

***Sueno de Luna Ilena - Full Moon Dream, Vol. 202.** Noelle B. McCue. (Silhouette Deseo Ser.). (SPA.). 1997. mass mkt. 3.50 (0-373-35202-6, 1-35202-0) Harlequin Bks.

Sueno de Rosita. Mary-Ann S. Bruni. Tr. by Rogelio De Castro from ENG. (Texas Ser.: Vol. 1). (Illus.). 48p. (SPA.). (J). (gr. k-8). 1987. 13.95 (0-935857-02-8); pap. write for info. (0-935857-04-4); write for info. (0-935857-11-7); write for info. (0-935857-12-5) Texart.

Sueno en el Yunque. Graciela Rodriguez et al. (Illus.). 36p. (J). 1993. 12.95 (0-8477-0204-9) U of PR Pr.

Sueno Navideno. I. E. Clark. Tr. by David Barranco from ENG. 17p. (Orig.). (SPA.). 1974. pap. 2.25 (0-88680-027-7) I E Clark.

S

Sueno Que Casi Cambia De Dueno. Luis F. Ulloa. LC 94-31217. 65p. (SPA.). (J). (gr. 7-10). 1995. 15.95 (*0-944957-51-X*) Rivercross Pub.

Sueno (Rimas al Recuerdo) Myriam Y. Aguiar. LC 84-80617. 64p. (Orig.). (SPA.). 1984. pap. 6.00 (*0-89729-348-7*) Ediciones.

Suenos. unabridged ed. Quevedo. (SPA.). pap. 5.95 (*84-410-0047-6*, Pub. by Bookking Intl FR) Distribks Inc.

Suenos: Lo Que Significan Para Usted. Migene Gonzalez-Wippler. LC 96-36418. 1996. pap. text ed. 7.95 (*1-56718-881-8*) Llewellyn Pubns.

Suenos - Dreams. Sabine R. Ulibarri. (Illus.). 116p. (Orig.). (ENG & SPA.). (C). 1994. pap. text ed. 10.95 (*0-938738-12-7*) U TX Pan Am Pr.

Suenos de Cristal. Paulino S. Rodriguez. 144p. (SPA.). 1995. lib. bdg. write for info. (*1-888598-02-6*) P S Rodriguez.

Suenos de On Ilegal. Martin Balarezo. Ed. by MBG Publications Staff. 376p. (Orig.). (SPA.). 1994. pap. text ed. 6.95 (*0-9635531-0-0*) M B G Pubns.

Suenos de un Portugues y Otras Historias. Victor Alperi. LC 95-67274. 101p. 1995. pap. text ed. 20.00 (*0-89295-082-X*) Society Sp & Sp-Am.

Suesswasserfauna Deutchlands. A. Brauer. (Illus.). 1961. reprint ed. 250.00 (*3-7682-0045-0*) Lubrecht & Cramer.

Suesswasserfauna Von Mitteleuropa, Vol. 3-1: Gastrotricha und Nemertini, Plus 2. P. Schwank & Ilse Bartsch. (Illus.). 261p. (GER.). 1990. pap. text ed. 138.60 (*3-437-30606-5*, Pub. by G Fischer Verlag GW) Lubrecht & Cramer.

Suesswasserflora von Mitteleuropa: Chlorophyta I: Phytomonadina, Vol. 9. H. Ettl. Ed. by A. Pascher et al. (Illus.). 807p. (GER.). 1983. lib. bdg. 117.00 (*3-437-30408-9*) Lubrecht & Cramer.

Suesswasserflora von Mitteleuropa: Conjugatophyceae I. Chlorophyta VIII Zygnemales, Vol. 16. J. Z. Kadlubowska. Ed. by A. Pascher & H. Ettl. (Illus.). 532p. (GER.). 1984. lib. bdg. 89.95 (*3-437-30415-1*) Lubrecht & Cramer.

Suesswasserflora von Mitteleuropa: Starmach K. Chrysophyceae und Haptophyceae, Vol. 1. Ed. by A. Pascher. (Illus.). 515p. 1985. lib. bdg. 89.95 (*3-437-30402-X*) Lubrecht & Cramer.

Suesswasserflora von Mitteleuropa: Xanthophyceae, Part 1, Vol. 3. Ed. by J. Gerloff et al. (Illus.). 530p. (GER.). 1978. lib. bdg. 120.00 (*3-437-30250-7*) Lubrecht & Cramer.

Suesswasserflora von Mitteleuropa Vol. 2, Pt. 2: Bacillariophyceae: Bacillariaceae, Epithemiaceae. rev. ed. A. Pascher. Ed. by K. Krammer & H. Lange-Bertalot. (Illus.). 596p. (GER.). 1988. lib. bdg. 109.50 (*3-437-30508-5*) Lubrecht & Cramer.

Suesswasserflora von Mitteleuropa Vol. 23: Pteridophyta und Antophyta, Part 1 - Lycopodiaceae bis Orchidaceae. S. J. Casper & H. D. Krausch. Ed. by A. Pascher et al. (Illus.). 403p. (GER.). 1980. lib. bdg. 85.00 (*3-437-30309-0*) Lubrecht & Cramer.

Suesswasserflora von Mitteleuropa, Vol. 10: Chlorophyta II Tetrasporales, Chlorococcales, Gloeodendrales. rev. ed. A. Pascher. Ed. by H. Ettl & G. Gaertner. (Illus.). 436p. (GER.). 1988. lib. bdg. 103.00 (*3-437-30409-7*) Lubrecht & Cramer.

Suesswasserflora von Mitteleuropa, Vol. 14: Mrozinska, T. Chlorophyta VI. Oedogoniophyceae: Oedogoniales. T. Mrozinska. Ed. by A. Pascher. (Illus.). (GER.). 1985. lib. bdg. 103.00 (*3-437-30413-5*) Lubrecht & Cramer.

Suesswasserflora Von Mitteleuropa, Vol. 2 - Pt. 3: Bacillariophyceae: Centrales, Fragilariaceae, Eunotiaceae. Kurt Krammer. (Illus.). 576p. (GER.). 1991. lib. bdg. 122.20 (*3-437-30541-7*, Pub. by G Fischer Verlag GW) Lubrecht & Cramer.

Suesswasserflora von Mitteleuropa, Vol. 2, Pt. 4: Bacillariophyceae, Achnanthaceae & Index to Pts. 1-4. rev. ed. Kurt Krammer. (Illus.). 437p. (GER.). 1991. lib. bdg. 112.80 (*3-437-30664-2*, Pub. by G Fischer Verlag GW) Lubrecht & Cramer.

Suesswasserflora von Mitteleuropa. Vol. 4: Xanthophyceae, Part 2. A. Rieth. Ed. by A. Pascher et al. (Illus.). 147p. (GER.). 1978. lib. bdg. 44.50 (*3-437-30304-X*) Lubrecht & Cramer.

Suesswasserflora von Mitteleuropa, Vol. 6: Dinophyceae (Dinoflagellida) J. Popovsky et al. (Illus.). 272p. (GER.). 1990. lib. bdg. 75.00 (*3-334-00247-0*, Pub. by G Fischer Verlag GW) Lubrecht & Cramer.

Suesswasserflora von Mitteleuropa, Vol. 20: Schyzomyceten-Bakterien, von J. Haeisler. A. Pascher. Ed. by H. Ettl & J. Gerloff. (Illus.). 588p. (GER.). 1982. lib. bdg. 96.50 (*3-437-30344-9*) Lubrecht & Cramer.

Suesswasserflora von Mitteluropa Vol. 2: Bacillariophyceae Pt. 1: Naviculaceae. Kurt Krammer. (Illus.). 876p. (GER.). 1986. lib. bdg. 143.00 (*3-437-30403-8*) Lubrecht & Cramer.

Suesswasserflora von Suedeuropa, Vol. 24: Pteridophyta und Antophyta, Part 2-Saururaceae bis Asteraceae. A. Pascher. Ed. by H. Ettl et al. (Illus.). 540p. 1981. lib. bdg. 89.95 (*3-437-30341-4*) Lubrecht & Cramer.

Suetonio De Poetis E Biografi Minori. Suetonius. Ed. by W. R. Connor. LC 78-67147. (Latin Texts & Commentaries Ser.). (ENG & LAT.). 1979. reprint ed. lib. bdg. 19.95 (*0-405-11615-2*) Ayer.

Suetonius. A. Wallace-Hadrill. (Classical Paperbacks Ser.). 227p. 1995. pap. 24.95 (*1-85399-451-0*, Pub. by Brstl Class Pr UK) Focus Pub-R Pullins.

Suetonius: Caligula. Ed. by H. Lindsay. (Bristol Latin Texts Ser.). 197p. (LAT.). 1993. pap. 21.95 (*1-85399-375-1*, Pub. by Brstl Class Pr UK) Focus Pub-R Pullins.

Suetonius: Claudius. Ed. by J. Mottershead. 190p. 1986. 19.95 (*0-86292-080-9*, Pub. by Brstl Class Pr UK) Focus Pub-R Pullins.

Suetonius: Divus Augustus. Ed. by J. M. Carter. 236p. 1982. 21.95 (*0-906515-55-6*, Pub. by Brstl Class Pr UK) Focus Pub-R Pullins.

Suetonius: Divus Julius. Ed. by H. Butler & M. Cary. 186p. 1983. reprint ed. 21.95 (*0-86292-026-4*, Pub. by Brstl Class Pr UK) Focus Pub-R Pullins.

Suetonius: Domitian. Ed. by B. Jones. (Latin Texts Ser.). 176p. (LAT.). 1996. pap. 21.95 (*1-85399-454-5*, Pub. by Brstl Class Pr UK) Focus Pub-R Pullins.

Suetonius: Galba, Otho, Vitellus. Ed. by C. Murison. (Bristol Latin Texts Ser.). 208p. (LAT.). 1989. pap. 19.95 (*1-85399-120-1*, Pub. by Brstl Class Pr UK) Focus Pub-R Pullins.

Suetonius: Nero. Ed. by B. Warmington. (Bristol Latin Texts Ser.). 128p. (LAT.). 1977. pap. 19.95 (*0-906515-06-8*, Pub. by Brstl Class Pr UK) Focus Pub-R Pullins.

Suetonius: Tiberius. H. Lindsay. (Latin Texts Ser.). (LAT.). 1995. pap. 20.95 (*1-85399-387-5*, Pub. by Brstl Class Pr UK) Focus Pub-R Pullins.

Sueurs Froides (D'Entre les Morts) Boileau-Narcejac. 192p. (FRE.). 1973. pap. 10.95 (*0-7859-2201-6*, 207036366X) Fr & Eur.

Suez. Keith Kyle. (Illus.). 656p. 1992. pap. 21.95 (*0-312-08311-4*) St Martin.

Suez & Sinai. Harry Browne. LC 72-101536. (Flashpoints Ser.). 136p. reprint ed. pap. 38.80 (*0-317-09516-1*, 2004920) Bks Demand.

Suez Canal. Sean Garrett. Ed. by Malcolm Yapp et al. (World History Program Ser.). (Illus.). 32p. (YA). (gr. 6-11). 1980. reprint ed. pap. text ed. 4.79 (*0-89908-205-X*) Greenhaven.

Suez Canal: Its Past, Present, & Future. Arnold T. Wilson. Ed. by Mira Wilkins. LC 76-29990. (European Business Ser.). (Illus.). 1977. reprint ed. lib. bdg. 21.95 (*0-405-09722-0*) Ayer.

Suez Canal: Letters & Documents Descriptive of Its Rise & Progress in 1854-56. Ferdinand M. De Lesseps. LC 74-83185. (Islam & Mideast Ser.). 1976. reprint ed. 31.00 (*0-8420-1748-8*) Scholarly Res Inc.

Suez Canal Company. Jean B. D'Humieres et al. Ed. by Leonard H. Hartmann. LC 85-90306. (Private Ship Letter Stamps of the World Ser.: Pt. 3). (Illus.). 288p. 1985. 45.00 (*0-917528-07-7*) L H Hartmann.

Suez Crisis. (Flashpoints Ser.). (Illus.). (YA). (gr. 7 up). 1988. lib. bdg. 18.60 (*0-86592-026-5*); lib. bdg. 13.95 (*0-685-58243-4*) Rourke Corp.

Suez Crisis. Anthony Gorst & Lewis Johnman. (Routledge Sources in History Ser.). 192p. (C). 1997. pap. 18.95 (*0-415-11450-0*); text ed. 59.95 (*0-415-11449-7*) Routledge.

Suez Crisis, Nineteen Fifty-Six. Gerald Kurland. Ed. by D. Steve Rahmas. LC 73-78400. (Events of Our Times Ser.: No. 9). 32p. (YA). (gr. 7-12). 1973. lib. bdg. 7.25 (*0-87157-711-9*) SamHar Pr.

Suez Crisis, 1956. Michael G. Fry. (Pew Case Studies in International Affairs). 50p. (C). 1992. pap. text ed. 3.50 (*1-56927-126-7*) Geo U Inst Dplmcy.

Suez-Sinai Crisis: A Retrospective. Ed. by Llan Troen & Moshe Shemesh. 1989. 49.50 (*0-7146-3356-9*, Pub. by F Cass Pubs UK) Intl Spec Bk.

Suffer & Be Still: Women in the Victorian Age. Ed. by Martha Vicinus. LC 71-184524. (Illus.). 256p. 1972. 31.50 (*0-253-35572-9*) Ind U Pr.

Suffer & Be Still: Women in the Victorian Age. Ed. by Martha Vicinus. LC 71-184524. (Illus.). 256p. 1973. pap. 13.95 (*0-253-20168-3*, MB-168) Ind U Pr.

Suffer Little Children. Thomas D. Davis. 208p. 1991. 19.95 (*0-8027-3205-4*) Walker & Co.

***Suffer Little Children: A Sister Fidelma Mystery.** Peter Tremayne. LC 97-8805. 1997. 23.95 (*0-312-15665-0*) St Martin.

Suffer Smoke: Cuentos de Morenci. Elena D. Bjorkquist. LC 96-12336. 1996. pap. 11.95 (*1-55885-168-2*) Arte Publico.

Suffer the Child. Judith Spencer. 1989. pap. 6.99 (*0-671-66852-8*) PB.

Suffer the Children. Janet Pais. 1991. pap. 9.95 (*0-8091-3226-5*) Paulist Pr.

Suffer the Children. John Saul. 384p. 1986. mass mkt. 6.50 (*0-440-18293-X*) Dell.

***Suffer the Children.** David J. Seel. LC 96-71327. (Illus.). 64p. (Orig.). 1996. pap. 12.95 (*1-57736-029-X*) Providence Hse.

Suffer the Children: A Pediatrician's Reflections on Abuse. Rosamond L. Murdock & Mariette Hartley. LC 91-35371. 220p. 1992. 19.95 (*0-929173-09-0*) Health Press.

Suffer the Future: Policy Choices in Southern Africa. Robert I. Rotberg. LC 79-25845. 327p. 1980. 32.00 (*0-674-85401-2*) HUP.

***Suffer the Little Children.** Al Lacy. LC 97-277. (Angel of Mercy Ser.: No. 5). 300p. 1997. pap. 9.99 (*1-57673-039-5*, Multnomah Bks) Multnomah Pubs.

Suffer the Little Children: Two Children's Bureau Bulletins, Original Anthology. Ed. by Leon Stein. LC 77-70552. (Illus.). 1977. lib. bdg. 26.95 (*0-405-10206-2*) Ayer.

Sufferers. Taha Hussein. Tr. by Mona El-Zayyat from ARA. 144p. (C). 1993. 19.95 (*977-424-299-8*, Pub. by Am Univ Cairo Pr UA) Col U Pr.

Sufferers & Healers: The Experience of Illness in Seventeenth-Century England. Lucinda M. Beier. (Social & Economic History Ser.). (Illus.). 288p. 1988. text ed. 69.95 (*0-7102-1053-1*, RKP) Routledge.

Suffering. Dorothee Soelle. Tr. by Everett R. Kalin from GER. LC 75-13036. 192p. 1975. pap. 14.00 (*0-8006-1813-0*, 1-1813, Fortress Pr) Augsburg Fortress.

Suffering: A Care Giver's Guide. John L. Maes. LC 89-27485. 224p. 1990. pap. 12.95 (*0-687-40570-X*) Abingdon.

Suffering: A Test of Theological Method. Arthur C. McGill. LC 82-6934. 130p. 1982. pap. 11.00 (*0-664-24448-3*, Westminster) Westminster John Knox.

Suffering: Human Dimensions Pain-Illness. Betty Ferrell. (Nursing Ser.). 300p. 1995. 49.95 (*0-86720-723-X*) Jones & Bartlett.

Suffering: Indian Perspectives. K. N. Tiwari. 1986. 22.50 (*81-208-0092-3*, Pub. by Motilal Banarsidass II) S Asia.

Suffering: Psychological & Social Aspects in Loss, Grief, & Care. Ed. by Robert DeBellis et al. LC 85-31744. (Loss, Grief & Care Ser.: Vol. 1, Nos. 1 & 2). 196p. 1986. text ed. 49.95 (*0-86656-558-2*) Haworth Pr.

Suffering: Receiving God's Comfort. Jack Kuhatschek. (LifeGuide Bible Studies). 64p. (Orig.). 1992. wbk. ed., pap. 4.99 (*0-8308-1067-6*, 1067) InterVarsity.

***Suffering: Why for God's Sake? Pastoral Research in Theodicy.** Johannes A. Van der Ven & Eric Vossen. (Theologie & Empirie Ser.: Vol. 23). 122p. 1995. pap. 21.50 (*90-390-0122-7*, Pub. by KOK Pharos NE) Eisenbrauns.

Suffering & Evil. John Heagle. (Guidelines for Contemporary Catholics Ser.). (Orig.). 1987. pap. 10.95 (*0-88347-212-0*) Res Christian Liv.

Suffering & Gods Presence. John M. Drescher. 1971. pap. 1.99 (*0-8361-1644-5*) Herald Pr.

Suffering & Hope: The Biblical Vision & the Human Predicament. 2nd ed. J. Christiaan Beker. 144p. (C). 1994. pap. 10.00 (*0-8028-0722-4*) Eerdmans.

Suffering & Ministry in the Spirit: Paul's Defense of His Ministry in Second Corinthians 2:14-3:3. Scott J. Hafemann. LC 90-45907. 275p. 1990. reprint ed. pap. 78.40 (*0-7837-6558-4*, 2046123) Bks Demand.

Suffering & Song. Julia Flora. 1995. pap. 13.95 (*0-7880-0616-9*, 6169) CSS OH.

Suffering & the Beneficent Community: Beyond Libertarianism. Erich H. Loewy. LC 90-46087. (SUNY Series in Ethical Theory). 159p. (C). 1991. pap. text ed. 21.95 (*0-7914-0746-2*) State U NY Pr.

Suffering & the Beneficent Community: Beyond Libertarianism. Erich H. Loewy. LC 90-46087. (SUNY Series in Ethical Theory). 159p. (C). 1991. text ed. 64.50 (*0-7914-0745-4*) State U NY Pr.

Suffering & the Remedy of Art. Harold Schweizer. LC 96-16289. (Illus.). 215p. 1997. text ed. 54.50 (*0-7914-3263-7*); pap. text ed. 17.95 (*0-7914-3264-5*) State U NY Pr.

Suffering Christ on the Cross. Kenneth R. Wichstrom. 1995. 10.95 (*0-533-11262-1*) Vantage.

Suffering from Guilt. Debra Mathers. (Master's Touch Bible Study Ser.). 1994. pap. 3.99 (*0-570-09437-2*, 20-2458) Concordia.

Suffering from Illusion: The Secret Victory of Self-Defeat. Sayers R. Brenner. LC 94-65657. (Illus.). 341p. 1994. reprint ed. pap. 16.95 (*0-9640827-0-5*) Paradox Bks.

Suffering from the Church: Renewal or Restoration? Heinrich Fries. 88p. (Orig.). 1995. pap. 5.95 (*0-8146-2172-4*) Liturgical Pr.

Suffering God: Selected Letters to Galatea & to Papastephanou. Nikos Kazantzakis. Tr. by Philip Ramp. LC 78-75133. 1979. 25.00 (*0-89241-088-4*) Caratzas.

Suffering Grass: Superpowers & Regional Conflict in Southern Africa & the Caribbean. Ed. by Thomas G. Weiss & James G. Blight. LC 91-33977. (Emerging Global Issues Ser.). 182p. 1992. lib. bdg. 37.00 (*1-55587-276-X*) Lynne Rienner.

***Suffering in Silence: Teachers with AIDS & the Moral School Community.** Catherine Zappulla. (Counterpoints: No. 42). 345p. (C). 1997. pap. 29.95 (*0-8204-3668-2*) P Lang Pubng.

Suffering into Joy: What Mother Teresa Teaches about True Joy. Contrib. by Eileen Egan et al. 156p. 1994. pap. 6.99 (*0-89283-876-0*, Charis) Servant.

Suffering Is Optional! The Myth of the Innocent Bystander. Morris L. Haimowitz & Natalie R. Haimowitz. LC 77-72839. (Illus.). (C). 1977. pap. 6.00 (*0-917790-01-4*) Haimowoods.

***Suffering Loss, Seeking Healing: Prayers for Pain-Filled Times.** Evan D. Howard. 1996. pap. text ed. 2.95 (*0-89622-699-9*) Twenty-Third.

Suffering Made Real: American Science & the Survivors at Hiroshima. M. Susan Lindee. LC 94-1832. (Illus.). 300p. 1994. 29.95 (*0-226-48237-5*) U Ch Pr.

***Suffering Mothers in Mid-Victorian Novels.** Natalie McKnight. LC 96-34454. 1996. text ed. 39.95 (*0-312-12295-0*) St Martin.

Suffering of God: An Old Testament Perspective. Terence E. Fretheim. Ed. by Walter Brueggemann. LC 84-47921. (Overtures to Biblical Theology Ser.). 224p. 1984. pap. 16.00 (*0-8006-1538-7*, 1-1538, Fortress Pr) Augsburg Fortress.

Suffering of God According to Martin Luther's Theologia Crucis. Dennis Ngien. LC 94-11414. (American University Studies: Ser. VII, Vol. 181). 304p. (C). 1995. text ed. 46.95 (*0-8204-2582-6*) P Lang Pubng.

***Suffering of Light: Selected Poems of William H. Matheson.** William H. Matheson. LC 96-69808. 122p. (Orig.). 1996. pap. 25.00 (*1-889087-01-7*) P S A Pr.

Suffering of Love: Christ's Descent into the Hell of Human Hopelessness. Regis Martin. LC 95-21586. 173p. 1995. pap. 14.95 (*1-879007-14-2*) St Bedes Pubns.

Suffering of St. Eleutherius. Tr. by Isaac E. Lambertsen from RUS. 16p. (Orig.). 1983. pap. 1.00 (*0-912927-05-4*, X005) St John Kronstadt.

Suffering, of Tests, Trials & Other Troubles. Myrna L. Etheridge. (Illus.). 100p. (Orig.). 1996. pap. 8.00 (*0-937417-03-3*) Etheridge Minist.

Suffering of the Forty Holy Martyrs in Sebaste in Armenia. Orthodox Eastern Church Staff. 1990. pap. 1.00 (*0-89981-122-1*) Eastern Orthodox.

Suffering of the Holy Martyr Dorothy & with Her Christina, Callista, & Thephilus. 2nd rev. ed. Tr. by Holy Nativity Convent Staff from RUS. (Illus.). 28p. 1988. pap. 2.50 (*0-913026-83-2*) St Nectarios.

Suffering of the Holy Venerable-Martyr Stephen the New. Tr. by Isaac E. Lambertsen from RUS. 32p. (Orig.). 1985. pap. 2.50 (*0-912927-14-3*, X014) St John Kronstadt.

Suffering Presence: Theological Reflections on Medicine, the Mentally Handicapped & the Church. Stanley Hauerwas. LC 85-40603. 224p. (Orig.). 1986. pap. text ed. 14.00 (*0-268-01722-0*) U of Notre Dame Pr.

Suffering Self: Pain & Narrative Representation in Early Christianity. Judith Perkins. LC 94-42650. 264p. (C). 1995. pap. 18.95 (*0-415-12706-8*); text ed. 62.95 (*0-415-11363-6*) Routledge.

Suffering, Sex & Other Paradoxes. Richard Holloway. LC 84-62376. 150p. 1985. pap. 10.95 (*0-8192-1358-6*) Morehouse Pub.

Suffering Strong: The Journal of a Westerner in Ethiopia, the Sudan, Eritrea & Chad. Nicholas Mottern. (Current Issues Ser.: No. 3). (Illus.). 110p. 1987. 12.95 (*0-932415-30-X*); pap. 5.95 (*0-932415-31-8*) Red Sea Pr.

Suffering with God: Looking for Hope When Life Falls Apart. Alister E. McGrath. 128p. 1995. pap. 12.99 (*0-310-40691-9*) Zondervan.

***Sufferings of Union Soldiers in Southern Prisons: Transcript of the Andersonville Trial.** Samuel J. Andrews & Helen C. Tregillis. xii, 86p. 1996. reprint ed. pap. 18.50 (*0-7884-0573-X*, A516) Heritage Bk.

Sufferings of Young Werther. Johann Wolfgang Von Goethe. Tr. by Harry Steinhauer. (C). 1969. pap. text ed. 6.95 (*0-393-09880-X*) Norton.

Sufferings of Young Werther & Elective Affinities. Johann Wolfgang Von Goethe. Ed. by Victor Lange. (German Library: Vol. 19). 368p. 1990. 29.50 (*0-8264-0329-8*); pap. text ed. 16.95 (*0-8264-0330-1*) Continuum.

Suffering...Why Me? David Y. Cho. LC 86-70741. 105p. 1986. pap. 4.95 (*0-88270-601-2*) Bridge-Logos.

Sufficent Statistics: Selected Contributions. Vasant S. Huzurbazar. (Statistics: Vol. 19). 280p. 1976. 115.00 (*0-8247-6296-7*) Dekker.

Sufficiency of Hope: Conceptual Foundations of Religion. James L. Muyskens. LC 79-18714. (Philosophical Monographs: Third Annual Ser.: 3rd Annual Ser.). 186p. 1979. 27.95 (*0-87722-162-6*) Temple U Pr.

Sufficiency of Scripture. Noel Weeks. 312p. 1988. 29.99 (*0-85151-523-1*) Banner of Truth.

Sufficient Carbohydrate. Dennis Potter. LC 83-20755. 80p. (Orig.). 1984. pap. 7.95 (*0-571-13261-8*) Faber & Faber.

Sufficient Criterion for a Cone to Be Area-Minimizing. G. Lawlor. LC 91-8060. (Memoirs Ser.: Vol. 91/446). 111p. 1991. pap. 22.00 (*0-8218-2512-7*, MEMO/91/446) Am Math.

Sufficient unto Itself Is the Day: The Ghost Ranch Classes. Rafael Catala. Ed. by Laurie Parker. 80p. (Orig.). 1989. pap. 6.95 (*0-9622517-0-4*) Corrales Infinite.

Sufficiently Radical: Catholicism, Progressivism, & the Bishops' Program of 1919. Joseph M. McShane. LC 86-9735. 319p. 1986. reprint ed. pap. 91.00 (*0-7837-9117-8*, 2049918) Bks Demand.

Suffix Obsession: A Dictionary of All Words Ending in Annual, Ennial, Anthropy, Archy, Cracy, Cide, Culture, Gamy, Gon, Hedron, Lagnia, Latry, Theism, Loquy, Machy, Mancy, Mania, Nym, Phagous, Vorous, Phany, Philia & Phobia. Alan Michaels. LC 92-50941. 196p. 1993. lib. bdg. 32.50 (*0-89950-674-7*) McFarland & Co.

Suffixes: And Other Word-Final Elements of English. Ed. by Laurence Urdang. 376p. 1982. 92.00 (*0-8103-1123-2*) Gale.

Suffocating Mothers: Fantasies of Maternal Origin in Shakespeare's Plays, Hamlet to The Tempest. Janet Adelman. 320p. (C). 1991. pap. 17.95 (*0-415-90039-5*, A1139, Routledge NY) Routledge.

***Suffolk.** Tim Buxbaum. 128p. 1996. pap. 35.00 (*0-7478-0319-6*, Pub. by Shire UK) St Mut.

***Suffolk.** Miles Jebb. (Pimlico County History Guides Ser.). (Illus.). 273p. 1997. pap. 19.95 (*0-7126-5363-5*, Pub. by Pimlico) Trafalgar.

Suffolk Bibliography. A. V. Steward. (Suffolk Records Society Ser.: No. XX). 477p. 1979. 60.00 (*0-85115-115-9*) Boydell & Brewer.

Suffolk Christmas. Ed. by Humphrey Phelps. (Illus.). 160p. 1996. pap. 12.95 (*0-86299-979-0*, Pub. by Sutton Pubng UK) Bks Intl VA.

Suffolk Coast. Russell Edwards. 128p. 1990. pap. 30.00 (*0-86138-054-1*, Pub. by T Dalton UK) St Mut.

Suffolk Committees for Scandalous Ministers, 1644-46. Ed. by Clive Holmes. (Suffolk Records Society Ser.: No. XIII). 128p. 1970. 18.00 (*0-900716-00-2*) Boydell & Brewer.

Suffolk County, Early Long Island Wills of Suffolk County, 1691-1703, with Genealogical & Historical Notes. William S. Pelletreau. (Illus.). 289p. 1995. reprint ed. lib. bdg. 37.50 (*0-8328-4714-3*) Higginson Bk Co.

Suffolk County International Trade Desk Manual: A Guide for Long Island Companies. Ed. by Suffolk County Department of Economic Development Staff. 64p. 1989. write for info. (*0-9619832-1-3*) Island-Metro Pubns.

Suffolk County International Trade Desk Manual: An Export Guide for Long Island Companies. rev. ed. Ed. by Island-Metro Publications, Inc. Staff. 64p. 1990. write for info. (*0-9619832-2-1*) Island-Metro Pubns.

Suffolk County, Long Island in Early Photographs. Ed. by Frederick S. Lightfoot et al. (Americana Ser.). 144p. 1984. pap. 9.95 (*0-486-24672-8*) Dover.

Suffolk Houses. Eric Sandon. (Illus.). 344p. 1977. 79.50 (*0-902028-68-5*) Antique Collect.

An Asterisk (*) at the beginning of an entry indicates that the title is appearing in BIP for the first time.

Suffolk in the Middle Ages: Studies in Places & Place-Names , the Sutton Hoo Ship Burial, Saints, Mummies & Crosses, Domesolay. Norman Scarfe. (Illus.). 212p. 1986. 39.00 (*0-85115-440-9*) Boydell & Brewer.

Suffolk Invasion. Frank Hussey. 200p. (C). 1988. 100.00 (*0-86138-026-6*, Pub. by T Dalton UK) St Mut.

Suffolk Invasion. Frank Hussey. 200p. 1990. pap. 27.00 (*0-86138-027-4*, Pub. by T Dalton UK) St Mut.

Suffolk Observed. M. R. Holmes. (Illus.). 100p. (Orig.). 1994. pap. 24.00 (*0-86025-452-6*, Pub. by I Henry Pubns UK) Players Pr.

Suffolk Parish Vestry Book, 1749-1784, & Newport Parish Vestry Book, 1724-1772. William L. Hopkins. iv, 210p. 1988. pap. 28.00 (*0-8095-8698-3*); lib. bdg. 58.00 (*0-8095-8293-7*) Borgo Pr.

Suffolk Rambles. Jean Pratt & Geoff Pratt. 64p. 1987. 50. 00 (*0-905392-85-X*) St Mut.

***Suffolk Returns from the Census of Religious Worship of 1851.** Ed. by T. C. Timmins. (Suffolk Records Society Ser.: Vol. 39). (Illus.). 304p. 1997. 35.00 (*0-85115-577-4*) Boydell & Brewer.

Suffolk Transnational Law Journal: 1977-1995/96, 19 vols., Set. 655.00 (*0-8377-9154-5*) Rothman.

Suffolk Trilogy: Three Plays for Radio: I Never Killed My German; The Anatolian Head; On the Levitation at St. Michael's. Carey Harrison. (Dramascripts Ser.: Vol. 6). 129p. 1990. pap. 11.95 (*0-906672-62-7*) Oleander Pr.

Suffolk University Law Review: 1967-1995, 29 vols., Set. Bound set. 1,357.50 (*0-8377-9155-3*) Rothman.

Suffolk Village Book. Harold M. West. 176p. 1987. 30.00 (*0-905392-62-0*) St Mut.

Suffolk Words, From "Cullum's History of Hawstead" see English Dialect Society Publications, No. 23: Glossaries XVIII-XXII

Suffrage & Beyond: International Feminist Perspectives. Ed. by Caroline Daley & Melanie Nolan. LC 94-33981. 1994. pap. 19.50 (*0-8147-1871-X*) NYU Pr.

***Suffrage & Power 1918-1928.** Law. Date not set. text ed. write for info. (*1-86064-201-2*, Pub. by I B Tauris UK) St Martin.

Suffrage & Religious Principle: Speeches & Writings of Olympia Brown. Olympia Brown. Ed. by Dana Greene. LC 83-20129. 192p. 1983. 22.50 (*0-8108-1665-2*) Scarecrow.

Suffrage Days: Stories from the Women's Suffrage Movement in Britain, 1865-1918. Sandra S. Holton. 336p. (C). 1996. pap. 24.95 (*0-415-10942-6*); text ed. 65. 00 (*0-415-10941-8*) Routledge.

Suffrage of Elvira. V. S. Naipaul. 208p. 1976. pap. 11.95 (*0-14-002938-9*, Penguin Bks) Viking Penguin.

***Suffragette.** Janet M. Trotter. 320p. 1996. pap. 13.95 (*0-7472-4876-1*, Pub. by Headline UK) Trafalgar.

Suffragettes in Pictures. Diane Atkinston. LC 96-9083. (Illus.). 224p. 1996. pap. 26.95 (*0-7509-1017-8*, Pub. by Sutton Pubng UK) Bks Intl VA.

***Suffragettes to She-Devils.** Liz McQuiston. (Illus.). 240p. 1997. 59.95 (*0-7148-3619-2*, Pub. by Phaidon Press UK) Chronicle Bks.

Sufi: Expressions of the Mystic Quest. Laleh Bakhtiar. LC 87-50252. (Art & Imagination Ser.). (Illus.). 120p. 1997. reprint ed. pap. 16.95 (*0-500-81015-X*) Thames Hudson.

Sufi & Scholar on the Desert Edge: The Heritage of Muhammad b. Ali al-Sanusi. Knut S. Vikor. LC 94-18310. (Islam & Society in Africa Ser.). 1995. 54.95 (*0-8101-1226-4*) Northwestern U Pr.

Sufi Book of Virtue. Abdul K. Al-Qushayri. Tr. by Rabia T. Harris. 1997. pap. text ed. 24.95 (*1-56744-531-4*) Kazi Pubns.

Sufi Brotherhoods in the Sudan. Ali S. Karrar. (Islam & Society in Africa Ser.). 300p. 1992. 49.95 (*0-8101-1045-8*) Northwestern U Pr.

Sufi Doctrine of the Perfect Man. R. A. Nicholson. 1984. reprint ed. pap. 3.95 (*0-916411-48-6*, Near Eastern) Holmes Pub.

Sufi, Eastern Wisdom. LC 92-42264. (Eastern Wisdom Ser.). 64p. 1993. 9.95 (*0-8118-0410-0*) Chronicle Bks.

***Sufi Essays.** Seyyed H. Nasr. 184p. 1996. pap. 16.95 (*0-614-21355-X*, 1184) Kazi Pubns.

Sufi Essays. 2nd ed. Seyyed H. Nasr. LC 91-20958. 184p. 1991. pap. text ed. 16.95 (*0-7914-1052-8*) State U NY Pr.

Sufi Essays. 2nd ed. Seyyed H. Nasr. LC 91-20958. 184p. 1991. text ed. 49.50 (*0-7914-1051-X*) State U NY Pr.

***Sufi Expressions of the Mystic Quest.** Laleh Bakhtiar. 128p. 1996. pap. 14.95 (*0-614-21356-8*, 1185) Kazi Pubns.

***Sufi Heirs of the Prophet: The Indian Naqshbandiyya & the Rise of the Mediating Sufi Shaykh.** Arthur F. Buehler. (Illus.). 240p. 1997. 39.95 (*1-57003-201-7*) U of SC Pr.

Sufi Matriarch: HazratBabajan. Ed. by Kevin Shepherd. 78p. (C). 1989. 60.00 (*0-9508680-1-9*, Pub. by Anthropographia UK) St Mut.

***Sufi Music of India & Pakistan: Sound, Context & Meaning in Qawwali.** Regula B. Qureshi. 266p. 1996. pap. 24.95 (*0-614-21357-6*, 1381); pap. 24.95 (*0-614-21590-0*, 1381) Kazi Pubns.

Sufi Music of India & Pakistan: Sound, Context, & Meaning in Qawwali. Regula B. Qureshi. 284p. 1995. pap. text ed. 24.95 (*0-226-70092-5*) U Ch Pr.

Sufi Mystery. 2nd ed. Ed. by N. P. Archer. 218p. 1988. 25. 00 (*0-900860-79-0*, Pub. by Octagon Pr UK) ISHK.

Sufi Mysticism: An Account, with a Glossary of Their Esoteric Terms. Ed. by H. Wilberforce Clarke. 1994. pap. 6.95 (*1-55818-300-0*, Near Eastern) Holmes Pub.

Sufi Path of Knowledge: Ibn al-Arabi's Metaphysics of Imagination. William C. Chittick. LC 88-7040. 478p. 1989. text ed. 74.50 (*0-88706-884-7*); pap. text ed. 24.95 (*0-88706-885-5*) State U NY Pr.

***Sufi Path of Knowledge: Ibn al-Arabi's Metaphysics of Imagination.** William C. Chittick. 478p. 1996. pap. 24. 95 (*0-614-21358-4*, 1187) Kazi Pubns.

***Sufi Path of Love.** William C. Chittick. 435p. 1996. pap. 19.95 (*0-614-21359-2*, 1188) Kazi Pubns.

Sufi Path of Love: The Spiritual Teachings of Rumi. William C. Chittick. LC 82-19511. (SUNY Series in Islam). 433p. 1984. pap. text ed. 16.95 (*0-87395-724-5*) State U NY Pr.

Sufi Rule for Novices: Kiteab Eadeab Al-Mureidein of Abeu Al-Najeib Al-Suhrawardei. abr. ed. Menahem Milson. LC 74-27750. (Harvard Middle Eastern Studies: No. 17). 99p. reprint ed. pap. 29.70 (*0-7837-4436-6*, 2057965) Bks Demand.

***Sufi Saint of the Twentieth Century.** Martin Lings. 242p. 1996. pap. 15.95 (*0-614-21360-6*, 1189) Kazi Pubns.

Sufi Saint of the Twentieth Century: Shaikh Ahmad al-Alawi. 3rd ed. Martin Lings. (Golden Press Ser.). (Illus.). 132p. 1995. pap. 21.95 (*0-946621-50-0*, Pub. by Islamic Texts UK) Intl Spec Bk.

Sufi Saints & State Power: The Pirs of Sind, 1843-1947. Sarah F. Ansari. (Cambridge Asian Studies Ser.: No. 50). (Illus.). 208p. (C). 1992. text ed. 59.95 (*0-521-40530-0*) Cambridge U Pr.

Sufi Studies: East & West. Ed. by L. F. Williams. 260p. 1973. pap. 15.00 (*0-900860-29-4*, Pub. by Octagon Pr UK) ISHK.

Sufi Studies: East & West. L. F. Williams. 1973. 15.00 (*0-525-21195-0*) NAL-Dutton.

Sufi Symbolism Vol. 1: The Nurbakhsh Encyclopedia of Sufi Symbolism. Javad Nurbakhsh. Tr. by Terry Graham et al. 228p. 1986. 30.00 (*0-933546-12-2*) KNP.

Sufi Symbolism Vol. 2: The Nurbakhsh Encyclopedia of Sufi Terminology. Javad Nurbakhsh. Tr. by Terry Graham. 193p. 1987. 30.00 (*0-933546-31-9*) KNP.

Sufi Symbolism Vol. 3: The Nurbakhsh Encyclopedia of Sufi Terminology: Religions Terminology. Javad Nurbakhsh. Tr. by Terry Graham et al. 263p. 1988. 30. 00 (*0-933546-35-1*) KNP.

Sufi Symbolism Vol. 4: The Nurbakhsh Encyclopedia of Sufi Terminology: the Symbolism of the Natural World. Javad Nurbakhsh. Tr. by Leonard Lewisohn & Terry Graham. 199p. 1990. 30.00 (*0-933546-40-8*) KNP.

Sufi Symbolism Vol. 5: The Nurbakhsh Encyclopedia of Sufi Terminology: Veils, & Clothing, Government, Economics. Javad Nurbakhsh. Tr. by Terry Graham. 194p. 1991. 30.00 (*0-933546-45-9*) KNP.

Sufi Symbolism Vol. 6: The Nurbakhsh Encyclopedia of Sufi Terminology: Titles & Epithets. Javad Nurbakhsh. 141p. 1992. 5.00 (*0-933546-48-3*) KNP.

Sufi Symbolism Vol. 7: The Nurbakhsh Encyclopedia of Sufi Terminology: Comtemplative Disciplines. Javad Nurbakhsh. Tr. by Terry Graham et al. 207p. 1993. 30. 00 (*0-933546-52-1*) KNP.

Sufi Symbolism Vol. 8: The Nurbakhsh Encyclopedia of Sufi Terminology: Inspirations, Revelations, Lights. Javad Nurbakhsh. Tr. by Terry Graham et al. 168p. 1994. 5.00 (*0-933546-53-X*) KNP.

Sufi Symbolism Vol. 9: The Nurbakhsh Encyclopedia of Sufi Terminology: Spiritual Faculties, Spiritual Organs. Javad Nurbakhsh. 181p. 1995. 30.00 (*0-933546-55-6*) KNP.

Sufi Symbolism Vol. 10: The Nurbakhsh Encyclopedia of Sufi Terminology: Spiritual State & Mystical Stations, Vol. XI. Javad Nurbakhsh. Tr. by Terry Graham. 151p. 25.00 (*0-933546-56-4*) KNP.

***Sufi Symbolism Vol. 11: The Nurbakhsh Encyclopedia of Sufi Symbolism.** Javad Nurbakhsh. 161p. 1997. write for info. (*0-933546-59-9*) KNP.

Sufi Thought & Action: An Anthology of Important Papers. Idries Shah et al. 272p. 1990. pap. 17.00 (*0-86304-051-9*, Pub. by Octagon Pr UK) ISHK.

Sufi Tradition in the West. Omar Ali-Shah. 248p. pap. write for info. (*1-883816-00-9*) Alif Pub.

Sufi Vision & Initiation: Meetings with Remarkable Beings. Samuel L. Lewis. Ed. by Neil Douglas-Klotz. LC 86-42579. (Illus.). 398p. (Orig.). 1986. pap. 14.95 (*0-915424-10-X*) PeaceWks Intl Ntwrk.

***Sufi Wisdom.** Marietta T. Stepaniants. 134p. 1996. pap. 14. 95 (*0-614-21361-4*, 1190) Kazi Pubns.

Sufi Wisdom. Marietta T. Stepaniants. LC 93-545. (SUNY Series in Islam). 132p. (C). 1994. text ed. 44.50 (*0-7914-1795-6*); pap. text ed. 14.95 (*0-7914-1796-4*) State U NY Pr.

***Sufi Women.** Javad Nurbakhsh. 202p. 1996. pap. 12.95 (*0-614-21362-2*, 1190) Kazi Pubns.

Sufi Women. rev. ed. Nurbakhsh & Javad Nurrbakhsh. Tr. by Leonard Lewisohn. (Illus.). 263p. 1983. pap. 1.95 (*0-933546-42-4*) KNP.

***Sufi Women: Angels in the Making.** Laleh Bakhtiar. 112p. 1996. pap. 12.95 (*0-614-21559-5*, 1471) Kazi Pubns.

Sufi Women of America: Angels in the Making. Laleh Bakhtiar. 112p. (Orig.). 1996. pap. 12.95 (*1-871031-44-3*) Kazi Pubns.

Suficiente! Lynn Salem & Josie Stewart. Tr. by Mariana Robles. (Illus.). 12p. (J). (gr. 1). pap. 3.50 (*1-880612-28-3*) Seedling Pubns.

Sufis. Idries Shah. LC 64-11299. 480p. 1971. pap. 12.00 (*0-385-07966-4*, Anchor NY) Doubleday.

Sufis. Idries Shah. 404p. 1983. 24.00 (*0-86304-020-9*, Pub. by Octagon Pr UK) ISHK.

***Sufis.** Idris Shah. 460p. 1996. pap. 11.00 (*0-614-21363-0*, 1192) Kazi Pubns.

***Sufis of Andalusia: The Ruh Al-Quds & Al-Durrat Al-Fakhirah.** Muhyiddin I. Arabi. Tr. by R. W. Austin from ARA. 173p. 1988. reprint ed. pap. 12.50 (*0-904975-13-4*, Pub. by Beshara Pubns UK) New Leaf Dist.

Sufis of Bijapur, 1300-1700: Social Roles of Sufis in Medieval India. Richard M. Eaton. LC 77-71978. 391p. reprint ed. pap. 111.50 (*0-7837-1417-3*, 2041771) Bks Demand.

Sufis of Today. Seyyed F. Hossain. (Sufi Research Ser.). 1981. pap. 7.00 (*0-86304-007-1*, Pub. by Octagon Pr UK) ISHK.

***Sufism.** Molana S. Angha. 39p. 1996. pap. 6.00 (*0-910735-98-0*) MTO Printing & Pubn Ctr.

***Sufism.** William Stoddart. 95p. 1996. pap. 5.95 (*0-614-21364-9*, 1193) Kazi Pubns.

Sufism: The Mystical Doctrines & Methods of Islam. William Stoddart. LC 85-16987. (Patterns of World Spirituality Ser.). 91p. 1986. pap. 5.95 (*0-913757-47-0*, New Era Bks) Paragon Hse.

Sufism: The Transformation of the Heart. Llewellyn Vaughan-Lee. LC 95-75550. 224p. (Orig.). 1995. pap. 12.95 (*0-9634574-4-6*) Golden Sufi Ctr.

Sufism: Veil & Quintessence. Frithjof Schuon. LC 81-69573. (Library of Traditional Wisdom). 133p. 1981. pap. 7.00 (*0-941532-00-3*) Wrld Wisdom Bks.

Sufism No. 1: Meaning, Knowledge & Unity. Javad Nurbakhsh. Tr. by Peter Wilson & William Chiltick from PER. 111p. (Orig.). 1991. pap. 0.95 (*0-933546-05-X*) KNP.

Sufism No. 2: Fear & Hope, Contractions & Expansion, Gathering & Dispersion. Javad Nurbakhsh. Tr. by William Chittick from PER. 126p. (Orig.). 1982. pap. 0.95 (*0-933546-07-6*) KNP.

Sufism No. 3: Submission, Contentment, Absence, Presence, Intimacy, Awe, Tranquility, Serenity. Javad Nurbakhsh. Tr. by Leonard Lewisohn & Terry Graham. 133p. 1985. pap. 1.95 (*0-933546-19-X*) KNP.

Sufism No. 4: Repentance, Abstinence, Renunciation, Wariness, Humility, Humbleness, Sincerity. Javad Nurbakhsh. 166p. 1988. pap. 1.95 (*0-933546-33-5*) KNP.

Sufism No. 5: Gratitude, Patience, Trust-in-God, Apsiration, Veracity, Zeal, Valour, Altruism, Shame. Javad Nurbakhsh. Tr. by Terry Graham et al. 158p. 1991. pap. 1.95 (*0-933546-43-2*) KNP.

Sufism & Human Destiny & Sufi Thought in Persian Literature. Mehdi K. Nakosteen. 236p. 1977. 25.00 (*0-936347-17-1*) Iran Bks.

***Sufism & Islam.** Molana S. Angha. 51p. 1996. pap. 6.00 (*0-910735-97-2*) MTO Printing & Pubn Ctr.

Sufism & Islamic Reform in Egypt: The Battle for Islamic Tradition. Julian Johansen. (Oxford Oriental Monographs). 336p. 1996. 80.00 (*0-19-826757-6*) OUP.

***Sufism & Knowledge.** Molana S. Angha. 39p. 1996. pap. 6.00 (*0-910735-94-8*) MTO Printing & Pubn Ctr.

***Sufism & Peace.** Molana S. Angha. 25p. 1996. pap. 6.00 (*0-910735-96-4*) MTO Printing & Pubn Ctr.

Sufism & Psychology. Lynn Wilcox. 256p. (Orig.). 1994. pap. 14.95 (*0-614-01622-3*) Kazi Pubns.

Sufism & Psychology. Lynn Wilcox. 254p. (Orig.). 1994. pap. 15.00 (*1-871031-47-8*) Abjad Bk.

Sufism & Taoism: A Comparative Study of Key Philosophical Concepts. Toshihiko Izutsu. LC 84-78. 493p. 1984. 50.00 (*0-520-05264-1*) U CA Pr.

Sufism & the Islamic Tradition. Sata'at & Lamanat of Shah Waliuilah of Deli. Ed. by D. B. Fry. Tr. by J. N. Jalbani. 127p. 1980. 25.00 (*0-900860-81-2*, Pub. by Octagon Pr UK) ISHK.

***Sufism & Wisdom.** Molana S. Angha. 37p. 1996. pap. 6.00 (*0-910735-95-6*) MTO Printing & Pubn Ctr.

Sufism in India. S. A. Abidi. (C). 1992. 19.00 (*81-224-0418-9*) S Asia.

Sufism, Islam & Jungian Psychology. Ed. by J. Marvin Spiegelman. LC 91-60059. (Religion & Psychology Ser.). 176p. (Orig.). 1991. pap. 12.95 (*1-56184-015-7*) New Falcon Pubns.

***Sufism, Islam & Jungian Psychology.** J. Marvin Spiegelman. 172p. 1996. pap. 12.95 (*0-614-21365-7*, 1197) Kazi Pubns.

Sufism, Mystics, & Saints in Modern Egypt. Valerie J. Hoffman. Ed. by Frederick Denny. LC 95-4373. (Studies in Comparative Religion). (Illus.). 465p. 1995. text ed. 49.95 (*1-57003-055-3*) U of SC Pr.

Sufism of the Rubaiyat or the Secret of the Great Paradox. Norton F. Hazeldine. 56p. 1995. reprint ed. pap. 12.00 (*1-56459-509-9*) Kessinger Pub.

Sufragio Inefectivo: La Falta de Proteccion de los Derechos Politicos en la Legislacion Mexicana. Luis Santos de la Garza. Tr. & Intro. by Andrew A. Reding. (North America Project Special Report Ser.). 34p. (SPA.). 1993. pap. 5.00 (*0-911646-55-8*) World Policy.

Sufrimiento, el Sacrificio, el Triunfo los Ojos del Alma. Thomas W. Petrisko. 384p. 1996. pap. 12.00 (*0-684-81555-9*, Simon Aguilar) S&S Trade.

Sufrimiento Premiado: Comedia Famosa. Lope De Vega Carpio. Ed. by Victor F. Dixon. (Textos B Ser.: No. 5). 177p. (SPA.). (C). 1967. pap. 36.00 (*0-900411-44-9*, Pub. by Tamesis Bks Ltd UK) Boydell & Brewer.

***Sufrir, Por Que Yo?** D. Cho. (SPA.). 5.95 (*0-8297-2034-0*) Life Pubs Intl.

Sug Learns How to Cook. Sylvia W. Dixon. Ed. by Mai T. Angaza. 28p. (Orig.). (J). (gr. 3-10). 1991. pap. 5.00 (*0-9652951-0-9*) S W Dixon.

Sugahtown. Keith Myers. 136p. (Orig.). 1995. pap. 9.95 (*0-9641196-5-X*) Champion Bks.

Sugai. Jean-Clarence Lambert. (Grandes Monografias). (Illus.). 224p. (SPA.). 1993. 175.00 (*84-343-0639-5*) Elliots Bks.

Sugamo Prison, Tokyo: An Account of the Trial & Sentencing of Japanese War Criminals in 1948, by a U. S. Participant. John L. Ginn. LC 92-50424. (Illus.). 311p. 1992. lib. bdg. 42.00 (*0-89950-739-5*) McFarland & Co.

Sugar. Rhoda Nottridge. (Foods We Eat Ser.). (Illus.). 32p. (J). (gr. 1-4). 1990. lib. bdg. 17.50 (*0-87614-418-0*, Carolrhoda) Lerner Group.

Sugar: A User's Guide to Sucrose. N. Pennington. 352p. (gr. 13). 1990. text ed. 78.95 (*0-442-00297-1*) Chapman & Hall.

Sugar: Chemical, Biological & Nutritional Aspects of Sucrose. Ed. by John Yudkin et al. LC 75-30831. 256p. reprint ed. pap. 73.00 (*0-317-41870-X*, 2025741) Bks Demand.

Sugar among the Freaks: Selected Stories by Lewis Nordan. Lewis Nordan. (Front Porch PB Ser.). 312p. (Orig.). 1996. pap. 10.95 (*1-56512-131-7*, 72131) Algonquin Bks.

Sugar & Other Stories. A. S. Byatt. LC 92-50003. 1992. pap. 12.00 (*0-679-74227-1*, Vin) Random.

Sugar & Seasonal Labor Migration - Azucar y Migraciones Estacionales: The Case of Tucuman, Argentina - El Caso de Tucuman, Argentina. John A. Kirchner. LC 80-11605. (University of Chicago, Department of Geography, Research Paper Ser.: No. 192). 189p. 1980. reprint ed. pap. 53.90 (*0-608-02276-4*, 2062917) Bks Demand.

Sugar & Slavery, Family & Race: The Letters & Diary of Pierre Dessalles, Planter in Martinique, 1808-1856. Ed. by Elborg Forster & Robert Forster. LC 95-34519. (Studies in Atlantic History & Culture). 320p. (C). 1996. text ed. 55.00 (*0-8018-5153-X*); pap. text ed. 19.95 (*0-8018-5154-8*) Johns Hopkins.

Sugar & Slavery in Puerto Rico: The Plantation Economy of Ponce, 1800-1850. Francisco A. Scarano. LC 83-40271. 288p. 1984. 22.75 (*0-299-09580-0*) U of Wis Pr.

Sugar & Slaves: The Rise of the Planter Class in the English West Indies, 1624-1713. Richard S. Dunn. LC 75-184229. (Institute of Early American History & Culture Ser.). xx, 359p. 1972. 45.00 (*0-8078-1192-0*) U of NC Pr.

Sugar & Slaves: The Rise of the Planter Class in the English West Indies, 1624-1713. Richard S. Dunn. (Illus.). 384p. 1973. reprint ed. pap. 13.95 (*0-393-00692-1*) Norton.

***Sugar & Spice.** Dewanna Pace. (Our Town Ser.). 288p. 1996. mass mkt. 5.99 (*0-515-11970-9*) Jove Pubns.

Sugar & Spice: Genealogy & Abbreviated Biographies of the Family of Calvert Walke Tazewell & Sophie Goode Tazewell. 2nd ed. Ed. by Calvert W. Tazewell. LC 90-80404. 120p. 1991. pap. 13.00 (*1-878515-10-1*); disk 5.00 (*1-878515-90-X*) W S Dawson.

Sugar & Spice: Sensational Desserts with Vivid Flavors. Carole Bloom. LC 96-13199. 272p. 1996. pap. 14.00 (*1-55788-254-1*, HP Books) Berkley Pub.

Sugar & Spice Advice. Devra N. Speregen. (Full House: Stephanie Ser.: No. 18). (J). 1996. mass mkt. 3.99 (*0-671-56842-6*) PB.

Sugar & Spice & Trial Run. Nigel Williams. (Methuen New Theatrescripts Ser.). 70p. (C). 1988. pap. 7.95 (*0-413-46620-5*, A0277, Pub. by Methuen UK) Heinemann.

Sugar & the Origins of Modern Philippine Society. John A. Larkin. 339p. 1994. 48.00 (*0-520-07956-6*) U CA Pr.

Sugar & the Underdevelopment of Northeastern Brazil, 1500-1970. Kit S. Taylor. LC 78-18423. (University of Florida Monographs: Social Sciences: No. 63). (Illus.). 179p. reprint ed. pap. 51.10 (*0-7837-5078-1*, 2044776) Bks Demand.

Sugar Baby. Karen Young. (Superromance Ser.). 1996. mass mkt. 3.99 (*0-373-70712-6*, 1-70712-4) Harlequin Bks.

Sugar Beach: A Cookbook by the Junior League, Fort Walton Beach, Florida. 1984. 12.95 (*0-9613562-0-0*) Jr Lg Ft Walton.

Sugar Beet Crop. Ed. by D. A. Cooke & R. K. Scott. LC 93-6886. (World Crop Ser.). 704p. (gr. 13). 1993. text ed. 143.95 (*0-412-25130-2*) Chapman & Hall.

Sugar Blues. Dufty. 1993. 5.99 (*0-446-77701-3*) Warner Bks.

Sugar Blues. William Dufty. 256p. 1986. mass mkt. 5.99 (*0-446-34312-9*) Warner Bks.

Sugar Borders. William Fuller. LC 93-86191. 54p. 1993. 8.00 (*1-882022-18-1*) O Bks.

Sugar Bush Connection. Beatrice R. Buszek. 1991. pap. 12. 95 (*0-920852-33-5*, Pub. by Nimbus Publishing Ltd CN) Chelsea Green Pub.

Sugar Busters! Cut Sugar to Trim Fat, Vol. 1. H. Leighton Steward et al. (Illus.). 144p. (Orig.). 1995. 12.95 (*0-9648149-0-0*) Sugar Busters.

Sugar Cage. Connie M. Fowler. Ed. by Maryanne Sacco. 320p. 1993. pap. 10.00 (*0-671-74809-2*, WSP) PB.

Sugar Cakes Cyril. Phillis Gershator. LC 96-1262. (Illus.). (J). 1996. pap. write for info. (*1-57255-224-7*) Mondo Pubng.

***Sugar Camp 1891-1941: The Origin & Early History of a Northern Wisconsin Community.** (Illus.). 99p. (Orig.). 1993. pap. 10.00 (*0-9653745-1-3*) Hodag Pr.

Sugar Cane Industry: An Historical Geography from Its Origins to 1914. J. H. Galloway. (Cambridge Studies in Historical Geography: No. 12). (Illus.). 288p. (C). 1989. 59.95 (*0-521-24853-1*) Cambridge U Pr.

Sugar-Coated Teddy. Edyth Y. Cottrell. LC 75-37441. (Illus.). 80p. (Orig.). 1976. pap. 4.95 (*0-912800-25-9*) Woodbridge Pr.

***Sugar Confectionery & Chocolate Manufacture.** R. Lees & B. Jackson. (Illus.). 380p. 1994. text ed. 95.00 (*0-7514-0114-5*, Pub. by Blackie Acad & Prof UK) Routledge Chapman & Hall.

***Sugar Confectionery Manufacture.** 2nd ed. Ed. by Jackson. (Illus.). 424p. 1995. text ed. 135.00 (*0-7514-0197-8*, Pub. by Blackie Acad & Prof UK) Routledge Chapman & Hall.

Sugar Country. large type ed. Mons Daveson. 1991. pap. 15.99 (*0-7089-6973-9*) Ulverscroft.

Sugar Country Shortline. Wesley Fox. LC 89-80045. (Illus.). 64p. 1989. 29.95 (*0-9604122-3-9*) Fox Pubns.

Sugar Creek: Life on the Illinois Prairie. John M. Faragher. LC 86-5622. 285p. 1986. text ed. 40.00 (*0-300-03545-4*) Yale U Pr.

An Asterisk (*) at the beginning of an entry indicates that the title is appearing in BIP for the first time.

S

Sugar Creek: Life on the Illinois Prairie. John M. Faragher. 1988. pap. 16.00 (0-300-04263-9) Yale U Pr.

Sugar Creek Gang & the Trapline Thief. Paul Hutchens. (Sugar Creek Gang Ser.: Vol. 19). 128p. (J). (gr. 2-7). 1971. mass mkt. 3.99 (0-8024-4821-6) Moody.

Sugar Creek Gang & the Treasure Hunt. Paul Hutchens. (Sugar Creek Gang Ser.: Vol. 12). (J). (gr. 2-7). 1967. mass mkt., pap. 3.99 (0-8024-4814-3) Moody.

Sugar Creek Gang & the Watermelon Mystery. Paul Hutchens. (Sugar Creek Gang Ser.: Vol. 21). (Illus.). 128p. (J). (gr. 2-7). 1971. mass mkt., pap. 3.99 (0-8024-4826-7) Moody.

Sugar Creek Gang & the Western Adventure. Paul Hutchens. (Sugar Creek Gang Ser.: Vol. 24). (J). (gr. 2-7). 1966. mass mkt., pap. 3.99 (0-8024-4824-0) Moody.

Sugar Creek Gang & the White Boat Rescue. Paul Hutchens. (Sugar Creek Gang Ser.: Vol. 31). (J). (gr. 3-7). 1970. mass mkt., pap. 3.99 (0-8024-4833-X) Moody.

Sugar Cup. Annie Sims. (Great Escapes Ser.). 1994. pap. 1.99 (0-373-83275-3, 1-83275-7) Harlequin Bks.

Sugar Dynasty: M. A. Patout & Son, Ltd., 1791-1993. Michael G. Wade. LC 95-69441. (Illus.). 410p. 1995. 29.95 (0-940984-96-2) U of SW LA Ctr LA Studies.

Sugar Economy of Puerto Rico. Arthur D. Gayer et al. 1976. lib. bdg. 59.95 (0-8490-2717-9) Gordon Pr.

Sugar Free: Goodies. Judith S. Majors. LC 87-70318. pap. 6.95 (0-941905-00-4) Apple Pr.

Sugar Free: Hawaiian Cookery. Judith S. Majors. LC 87-70229. pap. 6.95 (0-9602238-9-4) Apple Pr.

Sugar Free: Kids Cookery. Judith S. Majors. LC 79-66220. 1979. pap. 6.95 (0-9602238-1-9) Apple Pr.

Sugar Free . . . . Good & Easy. Judith S. Majors. LC 85-72597. 1985. pap. 5.95 (0-9602238-8-6) Apple Pr.

Sugar Free. . . . Sweets & Treats. Judith S. Majors. LC 82-73049. 1982. pap. 6.95 (0-9602238-6-X) Apple Pr.

Sugar-Free Cakes & Biscuits. 2nd ed. Elbie Lebrecht. 144p. 1989. pap. 8.95 (0-571-15418-2) Faber & Faber.

Sugar-Free Cookbook. Janet Horsley. (Illus.). 36p. (Orig.). 1993. pap. 9.95 (1-85327-084-9, Pub. by Prism Pr UK) Assoc Pubs Grp.

Sugar-Free Desserts. (Favorite All Time Recipes Ser.). (Illus.). 96p. 1993. 7.98 (1-56173-928-6, 2018102) Pubns Intl Ltd.

Sugar Free Desserts, Drinks & Ices. Elbie Lebrecht. 180p. (Orig.). 1993. pap. 10.95 (0-571-16645-8) Faber & Faber.

Sugar Free... Microwavery. Judith S. Majors. LC 80-67167. pap. 6.95 (0-9602238-3-5) Apple Pr.

Sugar Free-That's Me. Judith S. Majors. LC 78-74029. (Illus.). 1978. pap. 6.95 (0-9602238-0-0) Apple Pr.

Sugar-Free Toddlers: Over One Hundred Recipes. Susan Watson. Ed. by Susan Williamson. LC 91-19860. (Illus.). 176p. (Orig.). 1991. pap. 9.95 (0-913589-57-8) Williamson Pub Co.

Sugar Glider. Pauline Reilly. (Picture Roo Bks.). (Illus.). 32p. (J). (gr. 2-6). 1994. pap. 6.95 (0-86417-590-6, Pub. by Kangaroo Pr AT) Seven Hills Bk.

***Sugar Gliders.** C. Macpherson. LC 97-14543. (Complete Pet Owner's Manuals Ser.). 1997. pap. 6.95 (0-7641-0172-2) Barron.

***Sugar Gliders, a Pocket Full of Fun.** Stacy Chancey. (Illus.). 48p. (Orig.). (J). 1996. reprint ed. pap. 16.95 (0-9655629-0-5) Bear Tree.

Sugar Gliders As Your New Pet. Dennis Kelsey-Wood. (Illus.). 93p. 1996. 19.95 (0-7938-0598-8, TS269) TFH Pubns.

Sugar Hacienda of the Marqueses del Valle. Ward J. Barrett. LC 74-110146. (Illus.). 155p. reprint ed. pap. 44.20 (0-8357-7042-7, 2033205) Bks Demand.

Sugar House Hill. Lydia J. Musco. LC 95-78736. (Illus.). 32p. (J). 1995. pap. 8.95 (1-884540-16-3) Haleys.

***Sugar in the Gourd.** Bejamin M. Garrison. 1997. mass mkt. 4.99 (1-55197-280-8, Pub. by Comnwlth Pub CN) Partners Pubs Grp.

Sugar in the Raw: Voices of Young Black Girls in America. Ed. by Rebecca Carroll. LC 96-37527. 1997. pap. 12.00 (0-517-88497-6) Random Hse Value.

Sugar Is Made with Blood: The Conspiracy of la Escalera & the Conflict Between Empires over Slavery in Cuba. Robert L. Paquette. LC 87-34503. (Illus.). 365p. 1990. pap. 19.95 (0-8195-6233-5, Wesleyan Univ Pr) U Pr of New Eng.

Sugar Island Sampler: A Slice of Upper Peninsula Heritage. Bernard Arbic. (Illus.). 160p. (Orig.). 1992. pap. 9.95 (0-9626408-2-4) Priscilla Pr.

Sugar Island Slavery in the Age of Enlightenment: The Political Economy of the Caribbean World. Arthur L. Stinchcombe. 320p. 1996. 45.00 (0-691-02995-4) Princeton U Pr.

Sugar Isn't Everything: A Support Book, in Fiction Form, for the Young Diabetic. Willo D. Roberts. LC 86-17275. 208p. (J). (gr. 4 up). 1987. lib. bdg. 16.00 (0-689-31316-0, Atheneum Bks Young) S&S Childrens.

Sugar Isn't Everything: A Support Book, in Fiction Form, for the Young Diabetic. Willo D. Roberts. LC 88-3358. 192p. (J). (gr. 3-7). 1988. pap. 4.95 (0-689-71225-1, Aladdin Paperbacks) S&S Childrens.

Sugar Land, Texas & the Imperial Sugar Company. R. M. Armstrong. (Illus.). 200p. 1991. 26.95 (0-9629314-0-3) Imperial Holly.

Sugar Loaf Springs: Heber's Elegant Watering Place. Evalena Beary. (Illus.). 120p. 1985. write for info. (0-318-59487-0) River Road Pr.

Sugar Lump, the Orphan Calf. large type ed. Lynn S. Simmons. LC 94-72713. (Illus.). 50p. (C). 1994. boxed 7.95 (0-9642573-0-0) Argyle Bks.

Sugar Maple. Rosamond S. Metcalf. LC 82-595. (Illus.). 40p. (J). (gr. 3-5). 1982. pap. 3.50 (0-914016-87-3) Phoenix Pub.

Sugar Mill Caribbean Cookbook: Casual & Elegant Recipes Inspired by the Islands. Jinx Morgan & Jefferson Morgan. LC 96-9929. (Illus.). 272p. 1996. 29.95 (1-55832-120-9); pap. 14.95 (1-55832-121-7) Harvard Common Pr.

Sugar, My Sweet? Lucy Williams. LC 95-73045. (Red Apple Zoo Series of Nutrition Bks.). (Illus.). 48p. (J). (ps-4). 1996. lib. bdg. 15.95 (0-945080-20-4) Sandridge Pub.

Sugar Pavilion. large type ed. Rosalind Laker. LC 94-1780. 1994. lib. bdg. 24.95 (0-7862-0225-4) Thorndike Pr.

Sugar Petite. Mildred L. McVea. (Illus.). 184p. 1989. pap. 9.95 (0-8071-1622-X) La State U Pr.

Sugar Plantations in the Formation of Brazilian Society, Bahia, Fifteen Fifty to Eighteen Thirty-Five. Stuart B. Schwartz. (Cambridge Latin American Studies: No. 52). 608p. 1986. 95.00 (0-521-30934-4); pap. text ed. 34.95 (0-521-31399-6) Cambridge U Pr.

Sugar Plum. Virginia J. Glist. 186p. (Orig.). 1994. pap. write for info. (1-885591-31-4) Morris Pubng.

Sugar Pond & the Fritter Tree. Jess D. Wilson. LC 81-84550. (Illus.). 215p. 1981. 12.50 (0-935680-09-8) Kentucke Imprints.

Sugar Prince. Fiona Moodie. (Illus.). (J). (ps-3). 1987. 12.95 (1-55774-005-4) Hemed Bks.

Sugar Princess. Sharon Katherine. Ed. by Paul Wood. (Illus.). 31p. (J). 1989. pap. 8.95 (0-685-68779-1) Jungle Pr.

Sugar Problem: Large Costs & Small Benefits. David G. Johnson. LC 74-78952. (Evaluative Studies: No. 14). 96p. reprint ed. pap. 27.40 (0-7837-1088-7, 2041620) Bks Demand.

Sugar Processing: The Development of a Third World Technology. Rachel Kaplinsky. 158p. (Orig.). 1983. pap. 28.50 (0-903031-99-X, Pub. by Intermed Tech UK) Women Ink.

Sugar Rain. Paul Park. 384p. 1990. reprint ed. pap. 3.95 (0-380-71179-6) Avon.

Sugar Ray. Robinson. 31.95 (0-8488-1537-8) Amereon Ltd.

Sugar Ray. Sugar Ray Robinson & Dave Anderson. (Illus.). 400p. 1994. reprint ed. pap. 14.95 (0-306-80574-X) Da Capo.

Sugar Reef Caribbean Cookbook. Devra Dedeaux. 224p. 1991. pap. 13.95 (0-440-50336-1) Dell.

Sugar Scoring System for the Bender Gestalt, Incl. cards. Francee R. Sugar. Ed. by Julie Zinke. 11p. 1995. 3.15 (0-8388-2299-1) Ed Pub Serv.

Sugar Shack. Alma C. Kemp. 1995. 7.95 (0-533-11276-1) Vantage.

***Sugar Snow.** Laura I. Wilder. LC 97-14528. (My First Little House Bks.). (Illus.). (J). 1998. write for info. (0-06-025932-9); lib. bdg. write for info. (0-06-025933-7) HarpC.

Sugar Street. Naguib Mahfouz. Tr. by William M. Hutchins. LC 92-25362. (Cairo Trilogy Ser.: 3). 432p. 1993. pap. 11.95 (0-385-26470-4, Anchor NY) Doubleday.

Sugar Valley Saga. Carroll Gambrell. (Illus.). (Orig.). 1993. pap. 14.95 (0-943487-42-0) Sevgo Pr.

Sugar Water: Hawaii's Plantation Ditches. Carol Wilcox. LC 96-23753. (Illus.). 160p. 1996. text ed. 32.00 (0-8248-1783-4, Kolowalu Bk) UH Pr.

***Sugarbaker's Cookie-Cutter Cookbook: Baking & Decorating Beautiful Cookies for Every Holiday.** Diana C. Butts. 1997. 25.00 (0-684-83318-2, S&S) S&S Trade.

Sugarball: The American Game, the Dominican Dream. Alan M. Klein. (Illus.). 224p. (C). 1991. text ed. 30.00 (0-300-04873-4) Yale U Pr.

Sugarball: The American Game, the Dominican Dream. Alan M. Klein. (Illus.). 224p. 1993. reprint ed. pap. text ed. 17.00 (0-300-05256-1) Yale U Pr.

Sugarbeet Nutrient Deficiency Symptoms: A Color Atlas & Chemical Guide. Albert Ulrich & F. Jackson Hills. 36p. 1969. pap. 3.00 (0-931876-18-4, 4051) ANR Pubns CA.

Sugarbeet Pest Management: Aphid-Borne Viruses. F. J. Hills et al. (Illus.). 12p. (Orig.). 1982. pap. 1.75 (0-931876-60-5, 3277) ANR Pubns CA.

Sugarbeet Pest Management: Leaf Diseases. F. J. Hills et al. (Illus.). 12p. (Orig.). 1982. pap. 1.75 (0-931876-59-1, 3278) ANR Pubns CA.

Sugarbeet Pest Management: Nematodes. Philip S. Roberts & Ivan J. Thomason. (Illus.). 30p. 1981. pap. text ed. 3.00 (0-931876-52-4, 3272) ANR Pubns CA.

Sugarbird Lady. large type ed. Robin Miller. 318p. 1981. 25.99 (0-7089-0615-X) Ulverscroft.

***Sugarbush Spring.** Marsha Chall. Date not set. write for info. (0-688-14907-3); lib. bdg. write for info. (0-688-14908-1) Lothrop.

Sugarcane Crop Logging & Crop Control: Principles & Practices. Harry F. Clements. LC 79-9894. 550p. reprint ed. pap. 156.80 (0-7837-1308-8, 2041456) Bks Demand.

Sugarcane House. Bond. 1997. write for info. (0-15-201446-2) HarBrace.

Sugarcane House. Bond. LC 96-50026. 1997. pap. write for info. (0-15-201447-0) HarBrace.

Sugaring. Jessie Haas. LC 95-38139. (Illus.). (J). Date not set. lib. bdg. write for info. (0-688-14201-X) Greenwillow.

Sugaring. Jessie Haas. LC 95-38139. (Illus.). 24p. (J). (ps up). 1996. 15.00 (0-688-14200-1) Greenwillow.

Sugaring Buckets. Wally Swist. (Mini-Chapbook Ser.: No. 26). 1989. pap. 2.00 (0-913719-93-5) High-Coo Pr.

Sugaring-off Party. Jonathan London. LC 93-21911. (J). 1995. pap. 15.99 (0-525-45187-0) Dutton Child Bks.

Sugaring Season: Making Maple Syrup. Diane Burns. (Photo Bks.). (Illus.). 32p. (J). (ps-5). 1990. lib. bdg. 14.96 (0-87614-420-2, Carolrhoda) Lerner Group.

Sugaring Season: Making Maple Syrup. Diane Burns. (J). (ps-5). 1992. pap. 5.95 (0-87614-554-3, Carolrhoda) Lerner Group.

Sugaring Time. Kathryn Lasky. LC 82-23928. (Illus.). 64p. (J). (gr. 3-7). 1983. lib. bdg. 15.00 (0-02-751680-6, Mac Bks Young Read) S&S Childrens.

Sugaring Time. 95th ed. HB Staff. (J). (gr. 5). 1995. text ed., lib. bdg., pap. text ed. 10.25 (0-15-305226-0) HB Coll Pubs.

Sugaring Time. Kathryn Lasky. LC 86-3468. (Illus.). 64p. (J). (gr. 3-7). 1986. reprint ed. pap. 4.95 (0-689-71081-X, Aladdin Paperbacks) S&S Childrens.

Sugarless: Towards the Year 2000. Ed. by Andrew J. Rugg-Gunn. 208p. 1994. 73.00 (0-85186-495-3, R6495) CRC Pr.

Sugarless Cookery. Florence Murphy. 64p. 1978. pap. 3.95 (0-8323-0306-2) Binford Mort.

Sugarpink Rose. Adela Turin & Nella Bosnia. 32p. 6.95 (0-904613-20-8) Writers & Readers.

Sugarplum Visions: Old Christmases Made New. Susan A. McCreary. LC 83-18300. (Illus.). 160p. 1983. pap. 9.95 (0-9608428-3-7) Straw Patchwork.

Sugars. Rhoda Nottridge. LC 92-21414. (J). (gr. 2-5). 1993. lib. bdg. 14.21 (0-87614-796-1, Carolrhoda) Lerner Group.

Sugars & Sweeteners. Norman Kretchmer. 312p. 1991. 106.95 (0-8493-8835-X, QP702) CRC Pr.

Sugars in Nutrition. Michael Gracey et al. (Nestle Nutrition Workshop Ser.: Vol. 25). 304p. 1991. text ed. 64.50 (0-88167-779-5) Lppncott-Raven.

Sugar's Secrets: Race & the Erotics of Cuban Nationalism. Vera M. Kutzinski. LC 93-7644. (New World Studies). (Illus.). 280p. 1993. text ed. 40.00 (0-8139-1466-3); pap. text ed. 19.50 (0-8139-1467-1) U Pr of Va.

***Sugartime: The Hidden Pleasures of Making Syrup with a Primer for the Novice Sugarer.** Susan C. Hauser. 112p. 1997. 16.95 (1-55821-599-9) Lyons & Burford.

Sugartown. Loren D. Estleman. LC 84-12910. 220p. 1984. 25.00 (0-89366-256-9) Ultramarine Pub.

Sugawara & the Secrets of Calligraphy. Stanleigh H. Jones, Jr. (Translations from the Oriental Classics Ser.). 272p. 1985. text ed. 49.50 (0-231-05974-4); pap. text ed. 18.50 (0-231-05975-2) Col U Pr.

Sugawara No Michizane & the Early Heian Court. Robert Borgen. LC 93-36993. (Illus.). 456p. (C). 1994. reprint ed. pap. text ed. 19.00 (0-8248-1590-4) UH Pr.

Sugerman. Mary McBride. (Historical Ser.). 1994. mass mkt. 3.99 (0-373-28837-9, 1-28837-2) Harlequin Bks.

Suggested Anatomical Landmarks for Entree Ports in Endoscopy. 2nd ed. George Cristino. Ed. by Donna M. Cristino. (Illus.). 223p. (C). 1995. text ed. 220.00 (1-886974-03-9) Inst Knowledge.

Suggested Course Outline for Training NDT Personnel. Vernon L. Stokes. 16p. 1977. pap. 3.75 (0-931403-55-3, 107) Am Soc Nondestructive.

Suggested Fertilizer-Related Policies for Government & International Agencies. T. P. Hignett et al. (Technical Bulletin Ser.: No. T-10). 67p. (Orig.). 1977. pap. 4.00 (0-88090-009-1) Intl Fertilizer.

Suggested Guidelines for Nutrition & Metabolic Management of Adult Patients Receiving Nutrition Support. Ed. by Marion F. Winkler et al. LC 93-851. (Illus.). 1993. spiral bd. write for info. (0-88091-113-1) Am Dietetic Assn.

Suggested Guidelines for Nutrition Care of Renal Patients. 2nd ed. Katy Wilkens & Kathy Schiro. LC 92-10496. 1992. ring bd. 21.00 (0-88091-104-2) Am Dietetic Assn.

Suggested Guidelines for Reducing Adverse Effects of Case Continuances & Delays on Crime Victims & Witnesses. LC 86-71131. 43p. 1986. pap. 6.00 (0-89707-233-2, 509-0024-01) Amer Bar Assn.

Suggested Methods for Analysis of Metals, Ores, & Related Materials. 9th rev. ed. Contrib. by ASTM Committee E-One on Analytical Chemistry for Metals, Ores, & Related Materials Staff. LC 92-13742. Orig. Title: Methods for Analytical Atomic Spectroscopy. 1992. 61.00 (0-8031-1760-4, 03-501092-50) ASTM.

Suggested Pattern Jury Instructions, Vol. I: Civil Cases. 3rd ed. Council of Superior Court Judges of Georgia Committee. 379p. 1994. ring bd. 65.00 (0-89854-152-2) U of GA Inst Govt.

Suggested Pattern Jury Instructions, Vol. II: Criminal Cases. 2nd ed. Council of Superior Court Judges of Georgia Committee. Ed. by Institute of Government Staff. 201p. 1994. ring bd. 65.00 (0-89854-153-0) U of GA Inst Govt.

Suggested Procedures for the Detection & Identification of Certain Finfish & Shellfish Pathogens: Suggested Procedures for the Detection & Identification of Certain Finfish & Shellfish Pathogens. Ed. by John C. Thoesen. LC 90-64152. (Illus.). 1994. student ed., ring bd. 82.50 (0-9625505-2-3) Am Fisheries Soc.

Suggested Program of Teacher Training for Mission Schools Among the Batetela. John G. Barden. LC 75-176517. (Columbia University. Teachers College. Contributions to Education Ser.: No. 853). reprint ed. 37.50 (0-404-55853-4) AMS Pr.

Suggested Safe Practices for Gas Distribution Workers. 53p. 1975. pap. 1.00 (0-318-12712-1, J00400); pap. 0.80 (0-318-59901-5); pap. 0.75 (0-685-73753-5) Am Gas Assn.

Suggested State Legislation, 1941-1995, 54 vols., Set. Ed. by Council of State Governments Staff. LC 72-86156. 1995. reprint ed. lib. bdg. 2,500.00 (0-912004-05-3) Gaunt.

Suggested State Legislation 1986, Vol. 45. Ed. by L. Edward Purcell. 220p. (Orig.). 1986. pap. 15.00 (0-87292-060-7) Coun State Govts.

Suggested State Legislation 1987, Vol. 46. 199p. 1986. pap. 25.00 (0-87292-068-2) Coun State Govts.

Suggested State Legislation 1988, Vol. 47. 321p. 1987. pap. 30.00 (0-87292-075-5) Coun State Govts.

Suggested State Legislation 1989, Vol. 48. 185p. 1988. pap. 30.00 (0-87292-082-8) Coun State Govts.

Suggested State Legislation 1990, Vol. 49. CSG National Committee on Suggested State Legislation Staff. 176p. 1989. pap. 30.00 (0-87292-094-1, SSL 090) Coun State Govts.

Suggested State Legislation, 1991, Vol. 50. CSG National Committee on Suggested State Legislation Staff. 152p. 1990. 30.00 (0-87292-957-4) Coun State Govts.

Suggested State Legislation, 1992, Vol. 51. CSG National Committee on Suggested State Legislation Staff. 192p. 1992. pap. 30.00 (0-87292-965-5, C-010-91) Coun State Govts.

Suggested State Legislation, 1993, Vol. 52. CSG National Committee on Suggested State Legislation Staff. 192p. 1992. pap. 30.00 (0-87292-971-X, C-040-92) Coun State Govts.

***Suggestibility of Children's Recollections: Implications for Eyewitness Testimony.** Ed. by John Doris. 193p. 1991. pap. 19.95 (1-55798-306-2) Am Psychol.

Suggestibility of Children's Recollections: Implications for Eyewitness Testimony. Ed. by John Doris. 193p. 1991. 40.00 (1-55798-118-3) Am Psychol.

Suggestion. Edward G. Warman. 64p. 1997. pap. 5.00 (0-89540-316-1, SB-316) Sun Pub.

Suggestion: Its Law & Applications. C. F. Winbigler. 1991. lib. bdg. 79.95 (0-8490-4269-0) Gordon Pr.

Suggestion & Autosuggestion. Charles Baudouin. 349p. 1993. pap. 27.00 (0-89540-243-2, SB-243) Sun Pub.

Suggestion & Autosuggestion. William W. Atkinson. 217p. 1967. reprint ed. spiral bd. 7.00 (0-7873-0058-6) Hlth Research.

Suggestion & Suggestibility. Ed. by A. V. Gheorghiu et al. (Illus.). xix, 376p. 1989. 93.00 (0-387-19496-7) Spr-Verlag.

Suggestion Box: Ideas for Personal Management. Jennifer G. Friestad & Daniel H. Life. 375p. 1994. 15.00 (1-886299-00-5) Discov From Within.

Suggestion in the Cure of Diseases & the Correction of Vices. George C. Pitzer. 1991. lib. bdg. 79.95 (0-8490-4493-6) Gordon Pr.

Suggestion in the Cure of Diseases & the Correction of Vices. George C. Pitzer. 80p. 1963. reprint ed. spiral bd. 7.00 (0-7873-1093-X) Hlth Research.

Suggestion in the Cure of Diseases & the Correction of Vices (1899) George C. Pitzer. 84p. 1996. pap. 14.95 (1-56459-831-4) Kessinger Pub.

Suggestion, Its Law & Application: The Principles & Practice of Psycho Therapeutics. Charles F. Winbigler. 473p. 1972. reprint ed. spiral bd. 14.00 (0-7873-0977-X) Hlth Research.

Suggestion of His Climate. Tony Nolan. 1977. pap. 5.00 (0-931350-00-X) Moonlight Pubns.

Suggestion Schemes. Alison Jago. 70p. (C). 1979. 51.00 (0-85292-246-9) St Mut.

Suggestion Simplifies. Sidney A. Weltmer. 116p. 1964. reprint ed. spiral bd. 8.50 (0-7873-1092-1) Hlth Research.

Suggestions. Ernest E. Kellett. LC 79-99705. (Essay Index Reprint Ser.). 1977. 20.95 (0-8369-1357-4) Ayer.

Suggestions for Becoming Self Sufficient: An At Your Own Pace Workbook. Center for Self-Sufficiency, Research Division Staff. LC 83-90723. 90p. 1983. ring bd. 25.95 (0-910811-29-6) Ctr Self Suff.

***Suggestions for Ceilings on Desires.** Phyllis Krystal. Date not set. 1.50 (0-614-19430-X) Sathya Sai Bk Ctr.

Suggestions for Improving Juror Utilization in the United States District Court for the Southern District of New York. 99p. 1971. 10.00 (0-318-14446-8) IJA NYU.

Suggestions for Making Money Addressing & Stuffing Envelopes or How to Start a Lettershop Business: A Workbook. rev. ed. Center for Self-Sufficiency Staff. 78p. 1992. ring bd. 25.95 (0-910811-20-2) Prosperity & Profits.

Suggestions for Starting a Business from Businesses That Are Going Out of Business: A Business Workbook. rev. ed. Center for Self-Sufficiency Staff. (Illus.). 67p. 1992. ring bd. 29.95 (0-910811-25-3) Ctr Self Suff.

Suggestions for Successful Living: Positive Ideas for the 7 Areas of Life. David H. Dyson. 72p. 1994. reprint ed. pap. 10.00 (0-9640187-0-5) Leave A Legacy.

Suggestions for the Beginning Teacher of English. 3rd ed. Mercedes A. Saez. 102p. (C). 1972. 1.50 (0-8477-2719-X) U of PR Pr.

Suggestions for the Future Provision of Criminal Lunatics see On the Different Forms of Insanity in Relation to Jurisprudence

Suggestions for the Repression of Crime: With Introduction & Essay Added. Matthew D. Hill. LC 70-172581. (Criminology, Law Enforcement, & Social Problems Ser.: No. 169). 1975. 35.00 (0-87585-169-X) Patterson Smith.

Suggestions for Thought by Florence Nightingale: Selections & Commentaries. Ed. by Michael D. Calabria & Janet A. Macrae. LC 93-37576. (Studies in Health, Illness, & Caregiving). 218p. (Orig.). (C). 1994. text ed. 36.50 (0-8122-3174-0); pap. text ed. 16.95 (0-8122-1501-X) U of Pa Pr.

Suggestions in Design see 1100 Designs & Motifs from Historic Sources

Suggestions in the Planning of a New Hotel. rev. ed. Ad Wittemann. 175p. (Orig.). 1986. pap. 60.00 (0-938481-36-3) Camelot Consult.

Suggestions of Abuse. Michael D. Yapko. 272p. 1994. 22.00 (0-671-87431-4) S&S Trade.

Suggestions on Academical Organisation with Especial Reference to Oxford. Mark Pattison. Ed. by Walter P. Metzger. (Academic Profession Ser.). 1977. lib. bdg. 29.95 (0-405-10027-2) Ayer.

***Suggestions to Authors of the Reports of the United States Geological Survey: Descriptions & Illustrations of Proper Grammatical Usage, Elements of Style, & Methods of Using Scientific Nomenclature.** 1997. lib. bdg. 253.95 (0-8490-7632-3) Gordon Pr.

An Asterisk (*) at the beginning of an entry indicates that the title is appearing in BIP for the first time.

Suggestive-Accelerative Learning & Teaching. Owen L. Caskey. Ed. by Danny G. Langdon. LC 79-26386. (Instructional Design Library). 136p. 1980. 27.95 (*0-87778-156-7*) Educ Tech Pubns.

Suggestive Accelerative Learning Techniques: Theory & Applications. Donald H. Schuster & Charles E. Gritton. 224, xiip. 1986. text ed. 74.00 (*2-88124-055-0*); pap. text ed. 36.00 (*2-88124-054-2*) Gordon & Breach.

Suggestive Inquiry into the Hermetic Mystery. Mary A. Atwood. LC 75-36825. (Occult Ser.). 1976. reprint ed. 56.95 (*0-405-07938-9*) Ayer.

Suggestive Inquiry into the Hermetic Mystery. Mary Anne Atwood. 597p. 1976. reprint ed. 22.00 (*0-911662-64-2*) Yoga.

Suggestopedic Methods & Applications. Ludiger Schiffler. Tr. by Kay U. Herr from GER. LC 92-27764. 196p. 1992. text ed. 70.00 (*2-88124-522-6*); pap. text ed. 29.00 (*2-88124-571-4*) Gordon & Breach.

Suggin Cookbook. Josephine Graham. 164p. 1974. pap. 6.98 (*0-686-09048-9*) J Graham.

Suggin Painting. Josephine Graham. 1976. pap. 3.00 (*0-686-17966-8*) J Graham.

Suharto & His Generals No. 64: Indonesian Military Politics, 1975-83. 4th ed. David Jenkins. 300p. 1997. pap. 12.50 (*0-87763-030-5*) Cornell Mod Indo.

Suhrab & Rustam: A Poem from the Shah Namah of Firdausi. Firdawsi. Tr. by James Atkinson from PER. LC 72-3772. Orig. Title: Soohrab, a Poem. (ENG & PER.). 1972. reprint ed. 50.00 (*0-8201-1103-1*) Schol Facsimiles.

Suhrawardi & the School of Illumination. Mehdi Aminrazavi. (Sufi Ser.). 220p. 1996. 70.00 (*0-7007-0451-5*, Pub. by Curzon Pr UK); pap. 25.00 (*0-7007-0412-4*, Pub. by Curzon Pr UK) Paul & Co Pubs.

Sui Geng: The Hong Kong Marine Police 1841-1950. Iain Ward. 236p. (C). 1991. pap. text ed. 56.00 (*962-209-286-1*, Pub. by Hong Kong U Pr HK) St Mut.

Sui Sin Far - Edith Maude Eaton: A Literary Biography. Annette White-Parks. LC 94-6448. (Illus.). 288p. 1995. text ed. 34.95 (*0-252-02113-4*) U of Ill Pr.

Suicidal Adolescent. Ed. by Moses Laufer. 162p. 1995. pap. text ed. 25.50 (*1-85575-121-6*, Pub. by Karnac Bks UK) Brunner-Mazel.

Suicidal Adolescent. Ed. by Moses Laufer. 162p. 1996. 28.50 (*0-8236-6697-2*, BN 06697) Intl Univs Pr.

Suicidal Adolescents. Patricia A. Davis. 108p. (C). 1983. 29.95 (*0-398-04866-5*) C C Thomas.

Suicidal Behavior in the Asia-Pacific Region. Ed. by Kok L. Peng & Wen-Shing Tseng. 267p. 1992. 59.95 (*9971-69-165-5*, Pub. by Sgapore Univ SI) Coronet Bks.

Suicidal Behaviors: Diagnosis & Management. Ed. by H. L. Resnik. LC 94-32435. 568p. 1995. pap. text ed. 40.00 (*1-56821-263-1*) Aronson.

***Suicidal Behaviour in Adolescents & Adults: Research, Taxonomy & Prevention.** Christopher Bagley & Richard Ramsay. 300p. 1997. text ed. 63.95 (*1-85972-540-6*, Pub. by Ashgate UK) Ashgate Pub Co.

Suicidal Child. Cynthia R. Pfeffer. LC 85-31710. 318p. 1986. lib. bdg. 39.95 (*0-89862-664-1*) Guilford Pr.

Suicidal Corporation: How Big Business Has Failed America. Paul H. Weaver. 1988. 18.95 (*0-317-67757-8*) S&S Trade.

Suicidal Mind. Edwin S. Shneidman. LC 95-42071. 208p. 1996. 25.00 (*0-19-510366-1*) OUP.

Suicidal Narrative in Modern Japan: The Case of Dazai Osamu. Alan Wolfe. 264p. 1990. text ed. 39.50 (*0-691-06774-0*) Princeton U Pr.

Suicidal Patient: Clinical & Legal Standards of Care. Bruce Bongar. 311p. 1991. 39.95 (*1-55798-109-4*) Am Psychol.

Suicidal Patient: Principles of Assessment, Treatment, & Case Management. John A. Chiles & Kirk D. Strosahl. 320p. 1995. text ed. 42.50 (*0-88048-554-X*, 8554) Am Psychiatric.

Suicidal Patient: Recognition, Intervention, Management. Victor M. Victoroff. (Master Works). 1996. pap. 40.00 (*1-56821-810-9*) Aronson.

Suicidal Women: Their Thinking & Feeling Patterns. Charles Neuringer & Dan J. Lettieri. LC 81-6294. 250p. 1982. text ed. 26.95 (*0-89876-023-2*) Gardner Pr.

Suicidal Youth: School-Based Intervention & Prevention. John M. Davis & Jonathan Sandoval. LC 90-25453. (Education & Social & Behavioral Science Ser.). 287p. text ed. 34.95 (*1-55542-329-9*) Jossey-Bass.

***Suicide.** 128p. (Orig.). 1997. mass mkt. 4.99 (*0-8007-8643-2*, Spire) Revell.

Suicide. R. V. Clarke. (Illus.). 145p. 1989. 64.95 (*0-387-97004-5*) Spr-Verlag.

Suicide. Dermot Clifford. 1989. pap. 22.00 (*1-85390-166-0*, Pub. by Veritas IE) St Mut.

Suicide. Laura Dolce. (Encyclopedia of Health Ser.). (Illus.). 112p. (YA). (gr. 7 up). 1992. lib. bdg. 19.95 (*0-7910-0053-2*) Chelsea Hse.

Suicide. Emile Durkheim. 1966. pap. 16.95 (*0-02-908660-4*, Free Press) Free Pr.

***Suicide.** Emile Durkheim. 1997. 17.95 (*0-684-83632-7*, Free Press) Free Pr.

Suicide. Nikolai Erdman. Tr. by Eileen Thalenberg & Alan Richardson. 96p. 1995. lib. bdg. 29.00 (*0-8095-4804-6*) Borgo Pr.

Suicide. Nikolai Erdman. Tr. by Eileen Thalenberg & Alan Richardson. 96p. 1992. pap. 9.95 (*0-88962-137-3*) Mosaic.

Suicide. Stephen A. Flanders. (Library in a Book). 224p. (YA). (gr. 9-12). 1991. 24.95 (*0-8160-1909-6*) Facts on File.

Suicide. Robert E. Long. LC 95-11850. (References Shelf Ser.: Vol. 67, No. 2). 1995. 15.00 (*0-8242-0869-2*) Wilson.

Suicide. Leslie McGuire. (Troubled Society Ser.). (Illus.). 64p. (YA). (gr. 7 up). 1990. lib. bdg. 17.27 (*0-86593-069-4*); lib. bdg. 12.95 (*0-685-46444-X*) Rourke Corp.

Suicide. Anita Russell et al. (Options Ser.). 112p. (gr. 1-8). 1989. teacher ed., pap. 8.00 (*0-920541-65-8*) Peguis Pubs Ltd.

Suicide. Karen O. Savalan. LC 82-61095. 248p. 1982. 14.00 (*0-86690-210-4*, S2363-014) Am Fed Astrologers.

Suicide. Adam Woog. LC 96-9855. (Overview Ser.). (Illus.). (J). (gr. 4-12). 1996. lib. bdg. 17.96 (*1-56006-187-1*) Lucent Bks.

Suicide. 3rd ed. Margaret O. Hyde & Elizabeth H. Forsyth. LC 90-46872. (Illus.). 128p. (YA). (gr. 9-12). 1991. lib. bdg. 22.70 (*0-531-11003-6*) Watts.

Suicide: A Bibliography for Nineteen Fifty to Nineteen Seventy-Four: A Supplement to Death & Dying a Bibliography Nineteen Fifty to Nineteen Seventy-Four. G. Howard Poteet & Joseph C. Santora. LC 76-24093. 1978. 12.50 (*0-87875-108-4*) Whitston Pub.

Suicide: A European Perspective. Nils Retterstol. (Illus.). 220p. (C). 1993. text ed. 59.95 (*0-521-42099-7*) Cambridge U Pr.

Suicide: A Guide to Information Sources. Ed. by David Lester et al. LC 80-71. (Social Issues & Social Problems Information Guide Ser.: Vol. 3). 1980. 68.00 (*0-8103-1415-0*) Gale.

Suicide: A Social & Historical Study. Henry R. Fedden. LC 72-80703. (Illus.). 351p. 1980. reprint ed. 30.95 (*0-405-08498-6*, Pub. by Blom Pubns UK) Ayer.

Suicide: An Essay on Comparative Moral Statistics. Henry Morselli. LC 74-25770. (European Sociology Ser.). 402p. 1975. reprint ed. 29.95 (*0-405-06524-8*) Ayer.

Suicide: Clinical & Epidemiological Studies. Brian Barraclough. 200p. 1987. lib. bdg. 32.50 (*0-7099-5009-8*, Pub. by Croom Helm UK) Routledge Chapman & Hall.

Suicide: How & Where to Find Facts & Get Help. Robert D. Reed & Danek S. Kaus. Ed. by Diane Parker. LC 92-53760. (Abuse Ser.). 48p. 1993. pap. 4.50 (*0-88247-950-4*) R & E Pubs.

Suicide: How God Sustained a Family. Dale A. Byers. LC 91-8836. 128p. (Orig.). 1991. pap. text ed. 7.95 (*0-87227-146-3*, RBP5177) Reg Baptist.

***Suicide: Individual, Cultural, International Perspectives.** 1997. lib. bdg. 25.00 (*1-57230-240-2*, 0240) Guilford Pr.

Suicide: Inside & Out. David K. Reynolds & Norman L. Farberow. LC 75-22661. 1976. pap. 14.95 (*0-520-03506-2*, CAL 370) U CA Pr.

Suicide: Medical Subject Analysis & Research Guide with Bibliography. Sidney J. Hopkins. LC 87-47644. 160p. 1987. 37.50 (*0-88164-588-5*); pap. 34.50 (*0-88164-589-3*) ABBE Pubs Assn.

***Suicide: Opposing Viewpoints.** Ed. by Tamara L. Roleff. LC 97-6697. (Opposing Viewpoints Ser.). (Illus.). (J). (gr. 5-12). 1997. pap. 12.96 (*1-56510-664-4*); lib. bdg. 20.96 (*1-56510-665-2*) Greenhaven.

Suicide: Prevention, Intervention, Postvention. rev. ed. Earl A. Grollman. LC 87-47880. 188p. 1988. pap. 14.00 (*0-8070-2707-3*) Beacon Pr.

Suicide: Problems & Remedies. Shamim Aleem. (Illus.). xii, 124p. (C). 1994. 16.00 (*81-7024-657-1*, Pub. by Ashish Pub Hse II) Nataraj Bks.

Suicide: Questions & Answers - Practical, Medical, Moral & Ethical Aspects. 1991. lib. bdg. 79.95 (*0-8490-5210-6*) Gordon Pr.

Suicide: Reason for Living. Wanda Campbell. 65p. (YA). (gr. 7-12). 1995. pap. 6.95 (*1-57515-049-2*) PPI Pubng.

Suicide: Right or Wrong? Ed. by John Donnelly. (Contemporary Issues Ser.). 212p. (Orig.). (C). 1989. pap. 17.95 (*0-87975-595-4*) Prometheus Bks.

***Suicide: Right or Wrong?** 2nd ed. John Donnelly. (Contemporary Issues in Philosophy Ser.). 1998. pap. text ed. 17.95 (*1-57392-186-6*) Prometheus Bks.

Suicide: Some Things We Know & Some We Don't. M. Russell Ballard. 56p. 1993. 5.95 (*0-87579-766-0*) Deseret Bk.

***Suicide: Teens Talk to Teens.** Marion Crook. 136p. (Orig.). 1997. pap. 12.95 (*1-55180-108-6*) Self-Counsel Pr.

***Suicide: Teens Talk to Teens.** Marion Crook. (YA). 1997. pap. 12.95 (*0-614-27593-8*) Self-Counsel Pr.

Suicide: The Constructive/Destructive Self. Ed. by Coletta A. Klug. LC 96-4678. (Studies in Health & Human Services: Vol. 25). 310p. 1996. text ed. 99.95 (*0-7734-8830-8*) E Mellen.

Suicide: The Forever Decision: For Those Thinking about Suicide, & For Those Who Know, Love, & Counsel Them. Paul G. Quinnett. 144p. 1987. pap. 9.95 (*0-8245-1352-5*) Crossroad NY.

Suicide: The Philosophical Issues. Margaret P. Battlin & J. David. 292p. 1981. 27.00 (*0-7206-0579-2*, Pub. by P Owen Ltd UK) Dufour.

Suicide: The Ultimate Rejection; a Psycho-Social Study. Colin Pritchard. LC 94-43417. 160p. 1995. 79.00 (*0-335-19033-2*); pap. 27.00 (*0-335-19032-4*, Open Univ Pr) Taylor & Francis.

Suicide: The Will to Live vs the Will to Die. Norman Linzer. 240p. 1984. 35.95 (*0-89885-156-4*); pap. 20.95 (*0-89885-190-4*) Human Sci Pr.

Suicide: Theory & Clinical Aspects. Ed. by L. D. Hankoff & Bernice Einsidler. LC 78-55288. 480p. reprint ed. pap. 136.80 (*0-8357-7869-X*, 2036286) Bks Demand.

Suicide: Understanding & Responding. Ed. by Douglas G. Jacobs & Herbert N. Brown. 510p. 1989. 70.00 (*0-8236-6695-6*) Intl Univs Pr.

Suicide: Why?: Eighty-Five Questions & Answers about Suicide. 2nd ed. Adina Wrobleski. LC 93-90614. 92p. 1995. pap. 12.95 (*0-935585-05-2*) Afterwords.

Suicide - Survivors: A Guide for Those Left Behind. 2nd ed. Adina Wrobleski. LC 93-90615. 150p. (Orig.). 1994. pap. 14.95 (*0-935585-06-0*) Afterwords.

***Suicide Academy.** Daniel Stern. LC 97-25066. (Library of Modern Jewish Literature). 206p. 1997. pap. 16.95 (*0-8156-0501-3*) Syracuse U Pr.

Suicide Across the Life Span: Premature Exits. Judith M. Stillion & Eugene E. McDowell. (Series in Death Education, Aging, & Health Care). 325p. 1996. pap. 34.95 (*1-56032-304-3*) Hemisp Pub.

Suicide Across the Life Span: Premature Exits. Judith M. Stillion & Eugene E. McDowell. (Series in Death Education, Aging, & Health Care). 325p. 1996. 79.95 (*1-56032-303-5*) Hemisp Pub.

Suicide after Sixty: The Final Alternative. Marv Miller. LC 79-4246. (Death & Suicide Ser.: Vol. 2). 128p. 1979. pap. 21.95 (*0-8261-2781-9*) Springer Pub.

Suicide among the Elderly in Long-Term Care Facilities. Nancy J. Osgood et al. LC 90-36738. (Contributions to the Study of Aging Ser.: No. 19). 216p. 1990. text ed. 49.95 (*0-313-26522-4*, ODD, Greenwood Pr) Greenwood.

Suicide among Youth: Perspective on Risk & Prevention. Ed. by Cynthia R. Pfeffer. LC 88-36702. 251p. 1989. reprint ed. pap. 71.60 (*0-608-02012-5*, 2062668) Bks Demand.

Suicide & Aging: International Perspectives. Ed. by Jane L. Pearson & Yeates Conwell. LC 96-19793. (Illus.). 256p. 1996. 43.95 (*0-8261-9370-6*) Springer Pub.

Suicide & Attempted Suicide. Ed. by E. M. Brooke. (Public Health Papers: No. 58). 1974. pap. text ed. 8.00 (*92-4-130058-2*, 1110058) World Health.

***Suicide & Attempted Suicide.** Geo Stone & Brian Aldiss. 320p. 1998. 24.00 (*0-7867-0492-6*) Carroll & Graf.

Suicide & Attempted Suicide among Children & Adolescents. Keith E. Hawton. Ed. by Alan E. Kazdin. (Developmental Clinical Psychology & Psychiatry Ser.: Vol. 5). 200p. 1985. text ed. 39.95 (*0-8039-2522-0*); pap. text ed. 17.95 (*0-8039-2523-9*) Sage.

Suicide & Bereavement. Bruce L. Danto et al. 1980. 20.95 (*0-405-12505-4*) Ayer.

Suicide & Clinical Practice. Ed. by Douglas G. Jacobs. LC 91-17193. (Clinical Practice Ser.: No. 21). 189p. 1992. text ed. 28.00 (*0-88048-455-1*, 8455) Am Psychiatric.

Suicide & Depression Among Adolescents & Young Adults. Ed. by Gerald L. Klerman. LC 86-1201. 383p. 1986. text ed. 33.50 (*0-88048-049-1*, 8049) Am Psychiatric.

Suicide & Depression in Late Life: Critical Issues in Treatment. Gary J. Kennedy. LC 95-37313. (Einstein Psychiatry Ser.: Vol. 13). 176p. 1996. text ed. 42.50 (*0-471-12913-5*) Wiley.

Suicide & Homicide: Some Economic, Sociological & Psychological Aspects of Aggression. Andrew F. Henry & James F. Short, Jr. Ed. by Robert J. Kastenbaum. LC 76-19575. (Death & Dying Ser.). (Illus.). 1977. reprint ed. lib. bdg. 23.95 (*0-405-09573-2*) Ayer.

Suicide & Homicide among Adolescents. Paul C. Holinger et al. LC 93-50150. 229p. 1994. lib. bdg. 33.00 (*0-89862-788-5*) Guilford Pubns.

Suicide & Its Prevention: Role of Attitudes in Suicidal Behavior. Ronald W. Maris & Stephen D. Platt. LC 87-29976. (Advances in Suicidology Ser.: Vol. I). (Orig.). 1989. pap. 99.75 (*90-04-08613-7*) E J Brill.

Suicide & Its Psychological Influences: Index of Authors & Subjects with Guide for Rapid Research. rev. ed. Sidney J. Hopkins. LC 94-34384. 171p. 1994. 44.50 (*0-7883-0246-9*); pap. 39.50 (*0-7883-0247-7*) ABBE Pubs Assn.

Suicide & the Elderly. Marilyn Stoner. 70p. (YA). (gr. 7-12). 1993. pap. 6.95 (*1-57515-031-X*) PPI Pubng.

Suicide & the Elderly: An Annotated Bibliography & Review. Compiled by Nancy J. Osgood & John L. McIntosh. LC 86-14935. (Bibliographies & Indexes in Gerontology Ser.: No. 3). 206p. 1986. text ed. 65.00 (*0-313-24786-2*, OSE/, Greenwood Pr) Greenwood.

***Suicide & the Inner Voice: Risk Assessment, Treatment & Case Management.** Robert W. Firestone. LC 96-51212. 352p. 1997. 52.00 (*0-7619-0554-5*); pap. 24.95 (*0-7619-0555-3*) Sage.

Suicide & the Older Adult. Ed. by Antoon A. Leenaars et al. 160p. 1992. lib. bdg. 26.00 (*0-89862-587-4*) Guilford Pr.

Suicide & the School: A Practical Guide to Suicide Prevention. Patrick W. McKee et al. LC 93-12083. (Crisis Intervention Ser.). (Illus.). 160p. (Orig.). 1993. pap. 24.95 (*0-934753-78-4*) LRP Pubns.

Suicide & the Schools: A Handbook for Prevention, Intervention & Rehabilitation. S. W. Johnson & L. J. Miale. (Illus.). 314p. 1987. text ed. 48.95 (*0-398-05302-2*); pap. text ed. 33.95 (*0-398-06638-8*) C C Thomas.

Suicide & the Soul. James Hillman. LC 85-11901. (Dunquin Ser.: No. 8). 191p. 1964. pap. 18.00 (*0-88214-208-9*) Spring Pubns.

***Suicide & the Soul, Vol. 8.** James Hillman. (Dunquin Ser.). 1997. pap. text ed. 19.00 (*0-88214-227-5*) Spr-Verlag.

Suicide & the Unconscious. Ed. by Antoon A. Leenaars & David Lester. LC 95-30948. 312p. 1996. 45.00 (*1-56821-724-2*) Aronson.

Suicide Anyone? John Patrick. 1976. pap. 5.25 (*0-8222-1096-7*) Dramatists Play.

***Suicide As a Cultural Institution in Dostoevsky's Russia.** Irina Paperno. 288p. 1997. 39.95 (*0-8014-3397-5*) Cornell U Pr.

***Suicide As a Cultural Institution in Dostoevsky's Russia.** Irina Paperno. 288p. 1997. pap. 16.95 (*0-8014-8425-1*) Cornell U Pr.

Suicide As a Learned Behavior. David Lester. (Illus.). 144p. 1987. pap. 21.95 (*0-398-06232-3*); text ed. 35.95 (*0-398-05340-5*) C C Thomas.

Suicide As Psychache: A Clinical Approach to Self-Destructive Behavior. Edwin S. Shneidman. LC 92-49478. 272p. 1993. pap. 30.00 (*0-87668-151-8*) Aronson.

Suicide Behind Bars: Prediction & Prevention. David Lester & Bruce L. Danto. LC 92-27480. 176p. 1993. pap. 21.50 (*0-914783-62-9*) Charles.

Suicide Blonde. Darcey Steinke. Ed. by Jane Rosenman. LC 93-28063. 204p. 1994. reprint ed. pap. 10.00 (*0-671-87315-6*, WSP) PB.

Suicide Case: Investigation & Trial of Insurance Claims. LC 87-73032. 82p. 1988. pap. 34.95 (*0-89707-336-3*, 519-0079-01) Amer Bar Assn.

Suicide Charlie. Norman L. Russell. Ed. by Doug Grad. 256p. 1995. mass mkt. 5.99 (*0-671-52279-5*) PB.

Suicide Charlie: A Vietnam War Story. Norman L. Russell. LC 92-29817. 216p. 1993. text ed. 29.95 (*0-275-94521-9*, C4521, Praeger Pubs) Greenwood.

***Suicide Circus: Selected Poems, Vol. 165.** Alexei Kruchenykh. (Sun & Moon Classics Ser.). 1997. pap. text ed. 14.95 (*1-55713-310-7*) Sun & Moon CA.

Suicide et la Morale: Suicide & Morality. Albert Bayet. LC 74-25739. (European Sociology Ser.). 830p. 1975. reprint ed. 66.95 (*0-405-06495-0*) Ayer.

Suicide Excepted. Cyril Hare. (Illus.). (C). 1982. pap. 4.95 (*0-486-24245-5*) Dover.

Suicide Explained: The Australian Experience. Riaz Hassan. 240p. 1996. 59.95 (*0-522-84677-7*, Pub. by Melbourne Univ Pr AT) Paul & Co Pubs.

Suicide for the Terminally Ill. Sallie Stephenson. 50p. (YA). (gr. 7-12). 1992. pap. 6.95 (*1-57515-017-4*) PPI Pubng.

Suicide from a Psychological Perspective. David Lester. 142p. 1988. pap. 24.95 (*0-398-06233-1*) C C Thomas.

Suicide from a Psychological Perspective. David Lester. 142p. (C). 1988. text ed. 37.95 (*0-398-05489-4*) C C Thomas.

Suicide from a Sociological Perspective. David Lester. 138p. 1989. pap. 21.95 (*0-398-06234-X*); text ed. 36.95 (*0-398-05595-5*) C C Thomas.

Suicide in Adolescence. Ed. by Rene F. Diekstra & Keith E. Hawton. 1987. lib. bdg. 92.00 (*0-89838-780-9*) Kluwer Ac.

Suicide in Alcoholism. George E. Murphy. (Monographs in Psychiatry: No. 1). 304p. 1992. 49.95 (*0-19-507153-0*) OUP.

Suicide in America. exp. ed. Herbert Hendin. LC 94-20554. 288p. 1995. 23.00 (*0-393-03688-X*) Norton.

Suicide in America. 2nd expanded ed. Herbert Hendin. 288p. 1996. pap. 14.00 (*0-393-31368-9*, Norton Paperbks) Norton.

***Suicide in American Indians.** David Lester. LC 97-12613. 127p. (C). 1997. lib. bdg. 59.00 (*1-56072-429-3*) Nova Sci Pubs.

Suicide in Children & Adolescents. Syed A. Husain & Trish Vandiver. (Child Behavior & Development Ser.). 302p. 1984. text ed. 32.50 (*0-89335-190-3*) PMA Pub Corp.

Suicide in Children & Adolescents. George MacLean. 144p. 1990. 22.00 (*0-920887-52-X*) Hogrefe & Huber Pubs.

Suicide in Creative Women. David Lester. 189p. (Orig.). (C). 1994. lib. bdg. 69.00 (*1-56072-150-2*) Nova Sci Pubs.

Suicide in Creative Women. David Lester. (Illus.). 161p. (Orig.). 1996. pap. 16.95 (*1-56072-345-9*) Nova Sci Pubs.

Suicide in Henry James's Fiction. Mary J. Joseph. LC 93-2967. (Am. Univ. Studies, XXIV: Vol. 50). 173p. (C). 1994. text ed. 37.95 (*0-8204-2140-5*) P Lang Pubng.

Suicide in Later Life: Recognizing the Warning Signs. Nancy J. Osgood. 168p. 22.95 (*0-669-21214-8*) Free Pr.

Suicide in Rabbinic Literature. Sidney Goldstein. 1988. text ed. 19.95 (*0-88125-147-X*) Ktav.

***Suicide in the Middle Ages: The Violent Against Themselves, Vol. 1.** Alexander Murray. (Illus.). 540p. 1997. 45.00 (*0-19-820539-2*) OUP.

Suicide in Victorian & Edwardian England. Olive Anderson. (Illus.). 488p. 1987. 92.00 (*0-19-820101-X*) OUP.

Suicide Intervention in the Schools. Scott Poland. LC 88-36988. (Guilford School Practitioner Ser.). 214p. 1989. pap. text ed. 20.95 (*0-89862-232-8*); lib. bdg. 49.95 (*0-89862-353-7*) Guilford Pr.

Suicide King. Shelley Singer. 1990. mass mkt. 3.50 (*0-373-26040-7*) Harlequin Bks.

Suicide Legends, Homicide Rumors: The Griffin Mystery. MaryJoy Martin. LC 86-232434. (Illus.). 68p. (Orig.). 1986. pap. write for info. (*0-945319-00-2*) Spes Deo Pubns.

Suicide, No. 12: And a Collection of Other Short Stories. John DiGirolamo. LC 93-93511. 64p. (Orig.). 1994. pap. 8.00 (*1-56002-365-1*, Univ Edtns) Aegina Pr.

Suicide Notes: Predictive Clues & Patterns. Edwin S. Shneidman. 272p. 1988. 42.95 (*0-89885-399-0*) Human Sci Pr.

Suicide of a Child. rev. ed. Adina Wrobleski. Ed. by Joy Johnson. (Illus.). 24p. 1993. reprint ed. pap. 3.25 (*1-56123-021-9*) Centering Corp.

Suicide of a Young Man. Betty Hayes. LC 93-91825. (Illus.). 65p. (Orig.). 1994. pap. 12.95 (*0-9639859-0-6*) Hayes Press.

Suicide of American Churches. Reeves. 1996. 25.00 (*0-02-925967-3*, Free Press) Free Pr.

Suicide of American Churches. Thomas C. Reeves. 288p. 1996. 25.00 (*0-684-82811-1*) Free Pr.

Suicide of an Elite: American Internationalists & Vietnam. Patrick L. Hatcher. LC 89-37829. 448p. 1990. 45.00 (*0-8047-1736-2*) Stanford U Pr.

Suicide of My Son: A Story of Childhood Depression. Trudy Carlson. LC 94-96796. 272p. (Orig.). 1995. per., pap. 16.95 (*0-9642443-1-4*) Benline Pr.

Suicide of the West: An Essay on the Meaning & Destiny of Liberalism. James Burnham. LC 64-14211. 320p. 1985. reprint ed. pap. 9.95 (*0-89526-822-1*) Regnery Pub.

S

***Suicide or Murder: The Strange Death of Governor Meriwether Lewis.** Vardis Fisher. LC 62-12402. 288p. 1962. pap. 16.95 (*0-614-22025-4*) Idaho Ctr Bk.

Suicide or Murder? The Strange Death of Governor Meriwether Lewis. Vardis Fisher. (Illus.). 288p. 1993. reprint ed. pap. 16.95 (*0-8040-0616-4*) Swallow.

Suicide or Survival: The Challenge of the Year 2000. (Insights Ser.: No. 1). 192p. 1978. pap. 9.00 (*92-3-101534-6*, U861, Pub. by UNESCO FR) Bernan Associates.

Suicide over the Life Cycle: Risk Factors, Assessment, & Treatment of Suicidal Patients. Ed. by Susan J. Blumenthal & David J. Kupfer. LC 89-18368. 799p. 1990. text ed. 82.50 (*0-88048-307-5*, 8307) Am Psychiatric.

Suicide Poems. Mike Napoliello. 58p. (Orig.). pap. text ed. 4.50 (*0-9640052-1-2*) US Mrkting.

***Suicide Prevention.** De Leo. LC 97-232. 1997. lib. bdg. write for info. (*0-7923-4468-5*) Kluwer Ac.

Suicide Prevention: A Crisis Intervention Curriculum for Teenagers & Young Adults. Judie Smith. LC 88-8283. 80p. 1989. pap. 14.95 (*1-55691-029-0*, 290) Learning Pubns.

Suicide Prevention: Case Consultations. Ed. by Alan L. Berman. LC 89-26342. (Death & Suicide Ser.: Vol. 10). 176p. 1990. 29.95 (*0-8261-7120-6*) Springer Pub.

Suicide Prevention: The Challenge Confronted- A Manual of Guidance for the Purc. R. Williams & H. G. Morgan. 150p. 1995. pap. text ed. 30.00 (*0-11-321821-4*, HM18214, Pub. by Stationery Ofc UK) Bernan Associates.

Suicide Prevention: Toward the Year 2000. Ed. by Silverman & Maris. 1995. lib. bdg. 25.00 (*0-89862-803-2*, 2803) Guilford Pr.

Suicide Prevention & Control: Index of Modern Authors & Subjects with Guide for Rapid Research. Sidney J. Hopkins. LC 92-43137. 1993. 44.50 (*1-55914-968-X*); pap. 39.50 (*1-55914-969-8*) ABBE Pubs Assn.

Suicide Prevention in Custody Intensive Study Course. Joseph R. Rowan. Ed. by Diane Geiman & Denise Flannery. 192p. 1991. pap. 35.00 (*0-929310-43-8*, 173) Am Correctional.

Suicide Prevention in Custody Intensive Study Course - Final Test. rev. ed. Joseph R. Rowan. Ed. by Diane Geiman & Denise Flannery. 8p. 1992. pap. 19.00 (*1-56991-031-6*) Torah Aura.

Suicide Prevention in Schools. Antoon A. Leenaars & Wenkstern. 1990. 73.95 (*0-89116-954-7*); pap. 39.95 (*1-56032-081-8*) Hemisp Pub.

Suicide Prevention in the Schools: Guidelines for Middle & High School Settings. Dave Capuzzi. LC 93-33197. 128p. 1994. pap. text ed. 23.95 (*1-55620-127-3*, 72581) Am Coun Assn.

Suicide Risk: The Formulation of Clinical Judgement. John T. Maltsberger. LC 86-2415. 176p. (C). 1986. text ed. 13.20 (*0-8147-5398-1*) NYU Pr.

Suicide Risk: The Formulation of Clinical Judgement. John T. Maltsberger. LC 86-2415. 176p. (C). 1988. pap. text ed. 13.20 (*0-8147-5399-X*) NYU Pr.

Suicide Squeeze. David Everson. 1995. mass mkt. 4.99 (*0-8041-1007-7*) Ivy Books.

Suicide Survivor's Handbook: A Guide for the Bereaved & Those Who Wish to Help Them. Trudy Carlson. LC 94-96837. 160p. (Orig.). 1995. per., pap. 14.95 (*0-9642443-0-6*) Benline Pr.

Suicide Syndrome: Origins, Manifestations & Alleviation of Human Self-Destructiveness. Larry Gernsbacher. LC 84-19759. 335p. 1985. pap. 20.95 (*0-89885-376-1*) Human Sci Pr.

Suicide Thoughts & Reflections, 1960-1980. Ed. by Edwin S. Shneidman. LC 81-81844. (Special Issue of Suicide & Life-Threatening Behavior Ser.: Vol. 11). 172p. 1982. 30.95 (*0-89885-090-8*) Human Sci Pr.

Suicide Transport & Immunolesioning. R. G. Wiley. LC 94-40331. (Molecular Biology Intelligence Unit Ser.). 126p. 1994. 89.95 (*1-57059-095-8*) R G Landes.

***Suicide Wall.** Alexander Paul. 320p. (Orig.). 1996. pap. 11.95 (*0-9642761-1-9*) PakDonald Pubng.

Suicide with Assistance: Index of New Information. Shirley S. Taube. LC 95-16340. 1995. 44.50 (*0-7883-0724-X*); pap. 39.50 (*0-7883-0725-8*) ABBE Pubs Assn.

Suicides & Jazzers. Hayden Carruth. (Poets on Poetry Ser.). 176p. (C). 1992. pap. 13.95 (*0-472-06419-3*); text ed. 39.50 (*0-472-09419-X*) U of Mich Pr.

Suicides in Prison. Alison Liebling. LC 92-4230. 256p. (C). (gr. 13). 1992. text ed. 79.95 (*0-415-07559-9*, A9562) Routledge.

Suicidio. 64p. (POR.). 1991. 1.95 (*0-8297-1712-9*) Life Pubs Intl.

***Suicidio.** A. Espinoza. (SPA.). 1.50 (*0-8297-0331-4*) Life Pubs Intl.

***Suicidio - Suicide: Como Saber Cuando Su Adolescente/Riesgo - Knowing When Your Teen Is at Risk.** Anthony. 218p. (SPA.). 1995. write for info. (*1-56063-851-6*) Editorial Unilit.

Suicidology: Essays in Honor of Edwin Shneidman. Ed. by Antoon A. Leenaars. LC 93-12028. 440p. 1993. 45.00 (*0-87668-571-8*) Aronson.

Suid-Afrikaanse Staatsreg. Dion Basson & H. Viljoen. 450p. 1988. pap. write for info. (*0-7021-2011-1*, Pub. by Juta SA) Gaunt.

Suid-Afrikaanse Valutabeheerwetgewing. A. N. Oelofse. 190p. 1991. pap. write for info. (*0-7021-2547-4*, Pub. by Juta SA) Gaunt.

***Suikoden.** PCS Staff. 128p. 1997. per. 14.99 (*0-7615-1068-0*) Prima Pub.

Suing for Medical Malpractice. Frank A. Sloan et al. LC 92-48268. (Illus.). 272p. (C). 1993. 39.95 (*0-226-76279-3*) U Ch Pr.

Suing Government: Citizen Remedies for Official Wrongs. Peter H. Schuck. LC 82-48907. 264p. 1983. text ed. 15.00 (*0-300-02957-8*) Yale U Pr.

Suing Government: Citizen Remedies for Official Wrongs. Peter H. Schuck. LC 82-48907. 264p. 1984. reprint ed. pap. 15.00 (*0-300-03250-1*, Y-508) Yale U Pr.

Suing Judges: A Study of Judicial Immunity. Abimbola Olowofoyeku. 256p. 1994. 55.00 (*0-19-825793-7*) OUP.

Suing the Press. Rodney A. Smolla. 288p. 1987. pap. 10.95 (*0-19-505192-0*) OUP.

Suiseki: The Japanese Art of Miniature Landscape Stones. Felix G. Rivera. LC 96-38067. (Illus.). 192p. (Orig.). 1997. pap. 29.95 (*1-880656-27-2*) Stone Bridge Pr.

Suiseki & Viewing Stones: An American Perspective. Melba L. Tucker. Ed. by Mary H. Bloomer & Peter L. Bloomer. LC 96-4932. (Illus.). 48p. 1996. 17.95 (*0-9634423-2-5*) Stone Lantern.

Suislaw Forest Hikes: A Guide to Oregon's Coast Range. Irene Lilja & Dick Lilja. (Illus.). 64p. (Orig.). 1990. pap. 8.95 (*0-910467-08-0*) Heritage Assocs.

***Suisse Red Guide.** annuals Michelin Travel Publications, Staff. (Red Guide Ser.). (Illus.). 1997. boxed 25.00 (*2-06-006979-3*, 697) Michelin.

***Suisun Marsh History: Hunting & Saving a Wetland.** LC 96-29519. 1997. pap. write for info. (*1-880710-04-8*) Mont Pac Inst.

Suit. Mike Kazaleh. 120p. 1996. pap. 10.95 (*1-883847-19-2*) MU Press.

***Suit up Your Workers for Christian Service.** Eric A. Mayes, Jr. Ed. by Robert Brown. viii, 95p. (Orig.). 1992. pap. write for info. (*1-890025-02-X*) B E A M Oklhma City.

Suit Yourself. (YA). (gr. 10 up). 1991. pap. 6.75 (*1-56191-043-0*, 8230) Meridian Educ.

Suit Yourself: Your Best-Dressed Image Wardrobe Planner. rev. ed. Gail Florin. (Illus.). 60p. 1991. pap. text ed. 6.75 (*0-945247-16-8*) Meridian Educ.

Suit Yourself . . . . Shopping for a Job. Wider Opportunities for Women, Inc. Staff & Roberta Kaplan. LC 80-53209. (Illus.). 52p. (Orig.). 1980. pap. text ed. 7.50 (*0-934966-02-8*) Wider Oppor Women.

***Suit 2.** D. G. Chichester. 1997. 3.99 (*0-671-01173-1*) PB.

Suitable Bodyguard. Kathryn Shay. (Superromance Ser.). 1996. mass mkt. 3.99 (*0-373-70709-6*, 1-70709-0) Harlequin Bks.

Suitable Boy. Vikram Seth. LC 92-54744. 1376p. 1994. reprint ed. pap. 18.00 (*0-06-092500-0*, PL) HarpC.

Suitable Case for Corruption. large type ed. Norman Lewis. 352p. 1985. 25.99 (*0-7089-1390-3*) Ulverscroft.

Suitable Church. Jim Heynen. 80p. 1982. pap. 8.00 (*0-914742-58-2*) Copper Canyon.

Suitable for Framing. Edna Buchanan. 256p. 1995. 21.95 (*0-7868-6047-2*) Hyperion.

Suitable for Framing. Edna Buchanan. 368p. 1996. mass mkt. 4.99 (*0-7868-8901-2*) Hyperion.

Suitable for Framing. large type ed. Edna Buchanan. LC 95-5402. 1995. 25.95 (*1-56895-210-4*) Wheeler Pub.

Suitable for the Wilds: Letters from Northern Alberta, 1929-1931. Mary P. Jackson. Ed. by Janice D. McGinnis. (Illus.). 344p. 1995. 55.00 (*0-8020-0582-9*); pap. 18.95 (*0-8020-7187-2*) U of Toronto Pr.

Suitable Suitor. Alicia Farraday. (Regency Romance Ser.: No. 169). 1992. mass mkt. 2.99 (*0-373-31169-9*, 1-31169-5) Harlequin Bks.

Suitable Vengeance. Elizabeth George. 480p. 1992. mass mkt. 6.50 (*0-553-29560-8*) Bantam.

Suitcase: Refugee Voices from Bosnia & Croatia. Ed. by Julie Mertus et al. LC 96-18199. (Illus.). 256p. (C). 1997. 48.00 (*0-520-20458-1*) U CA Pr.

Suitcase: Refugee Voices from Bosnia & Croatia. Ed. by Julie Mertus et al. LC 96-18199. (Illus.). 256p. (C). 1997. pap. 16.95 (*0-520-20634-7*) U CA Pr.

Suitcase Farming Frontier: A Study in the Historical Geography of the Central Great Plains. Leslie Hewes. LC 72-85031. (Illus.). 305p. reprint ed. pap. 87.00 (*0-7837-1823-3*, 2042023) Bks Demand.

Suitcase Full of Crows: Poems. Carlos Reyes. LC 95-10394. 1995. 10.00 (*1-878325-12-4*) Bluestem Press.

***Suitcase Full of Dreams: The Untold True Story of a Woman Who Dared to Dream!** unabridged ed. Jeanette Thornton & Rita Thornton. (Illus.). 224p. 1996. text ed. 24.95 (*1-889469-00-9*, Med Media Ent) Thornton Sisters.

Suitcase in Berlin. Don Flynn. 192p. 1989. 18.95 (*0-8027-5742-1*) Walker & Co.

***Suitcase Kid.** Jacqueline Wilson. LC 96-29083. (Illus.). (J). 1997. mass mkt. 15.95 (*0-385-32311-5*) Delacorte.

Suitcase of Seaweed & Other Poems. Janet S. Wong. (Illus.). 15.00p. (J). (gr. 4 up). 1996. 15.00 (*0-689-80788-0*, McElderry) S&S Childrens.

Suitcase Scholar Goes to Kenya, Set. Ann Barysh et al. Ed. by Lerner Geography Department Staff. (Suitcase Scholar Ser.). (J). (gr. 4-6). teacher ed., lib. bdg. 66.95 (*0-8225-4001-0*, Lerner Publctns) Lerner Group.

Suitcase Scholar Goes to Mexico, Set. Ann Barysh et al. Ed. by Lerner Geography Department Staff. (Suitcase Scholar Ser.). (Illus.). (J). (gr. 4-6). 1992. teacher ed. 66.95 (*0-8225-4003-7*, Lerner Publctns) Lerner Group.

Suite: Orchid Ska Blues. Norman Weinstein. LC 91-48233. 60p. 1992. pap. 9.95 (*0-7734-9441-3*) E Mellen.

Suite des Erreurs et de la Verite, Vol. IV. 435p. reprint ed. write for info. (*0-318-71411-6*) G Olms Pubs.

***Suite Espanola, Opus 47.** Isaac Albeniz. Ed. by Aaron Stang. 36p. 1985. pap. text ed. 12.95 (*0-7692-1284-0*) Warner Bros.

Suite for Cello & Jazz Piano Trio: Bass & Drums. C. Bolling. 1990. 10.00 (*0-685-32232-7*, SHAT73) Hansen Ed Mus.

Suite for Drury Pond. John Judson. (Haiku Ser.: No. 22). (Orig.). 1989. pap. 5.00 (*1-55780-109-6*) Juniper Pr WI.

Suite for Five Viols. Gillian Platt. (Charney Manor Ser.: No. 7). i, 15p. 1994. pap. text ed. 10.00 (*1-56571-083-5*, CM007) PRB Prods.

Suite for Flute & Jazz Piano. C. Bolling. 1990. pap. text ed. 40.00 (*0-7935-0097-4*, 00490508) H Leonard.

Suite for Flute & Jazz Piano: Solo Flute. C. Bolling. 1990. 6.00 (*0-685-32124-X*, SIL8) Hansen Ed Mus.

Suite for Flute & Piano. C. Bolling. 1990. 6.00 (*0-685-32230-0*, SIL6) Hansen Ed Mus.

Suite for Solo Cello. J. Harbison. 6p. 7.95 (*0-7935-4501-3*, 50482385) H Leonard.

Suite for String Orchestra Score. 64p. pap. 20.00 (*0-7935-5196-X*, 50482511) H Leonard.

Suite for Two Bass Viols. Martha Bishop. (Contemporary Consort Ser.: No. 5). i, 18p. 1990. pap. text ed. 10.00 (*1-56571-003-7*) PRB Prods.

Suite for Two Cellos & Piano. Gian-Carlo Menotti. 44p. 1986. pap. 18.00 (*0-7935-4068-2*, 50291680) H Leonard.

Suite for Viola da Gamba & Harpsichord. Sydney Davidoff. Ed. by Judith Davidoff & Eugenia Earle. (Contemporary Instrumental Ser.: No. 4). i, 14p. 1991. pap. text ed. 10.00 (*1-56571-040-1*) PRB Prods.

Suite for Violin & Jazz Piano. C. Bolling. 1990. 6.00 (*0-685-32239-4*, SIL36) Hansen Ed Mus.

Suite for Violin & Piano. M. Gould. 40p. 1993. pap. 12.95 (*0-7935-2783-X*) H Leonard.

Suite from Bohemia. V. Nelhybel. 1989. pap. text ed. 50.00 (*0-7935-2316-8*, 50481024) H Leonard.

Suite Hebraique: Viola or Violin & Piano. E. Bloch. 16p. 1986. pap. 7.50 (*0-7935-5188-9*, 50286080) H Leonard.

Suite in A Minor Flute & Piano. G. Telemann. 28p. 1986. pap. 8.95 (*0-7935-5432-2*, 50334860) H Leonard.

Suite in C Minor for Two Harpsichords. George F. Handel. Ed. by David Vine. (Early Keyboard Ser.: No. 2). 16p. 1992. pap. text ed. 9.00 (*1-56571-061-4*, EK002) PRB Prods.

Suite Jazz Flute Solos. C. Bolling. 1990. 10.00 (*0-685-32118-5*, SHAT061) Hansen Ed Mus.

Suite of Appearances. limited ed. Mark Strand. (Fine Press Ser.). 12p. Date not set. pap. 45.00 (*0-614-10196-4*) Seluzicki Fine Bks.

Suite of Eight Wood Engravings Based on George Orwell's Novel Animal Farm. limited ed. Eric Holter. (Illus.). 22p. 1991. 125.00 (*0-923980-75-X*) Arundel Pr.

Suite Polonaise. Frederick Davis. LC 93-46261. 64p. 1995. pap. 12.95 (*0-7734-2720-1*, Mellen Poetry Pr) E Mellen.

Suite Pour le Piano. Claude Debussy. 32p. 1987. pap. 4.95 (*0-7935-5110-2*, 50480159) H Leonard.

Suite Statistics & Sediment History. Ed. by William F. Tanner. 230p. 1986. pap. 40.00 (*0-938426-05-2*) FSU Geology.

Suite Thirty-Five. Ed. by Wolfgang Hageney. (Illus.). 208p. (ENG, FRE, GER, ITA & SPA.). 1982. pap. 39.95 (*88-7070-011-9*) Belvedere USA.

Suite Thoughts. Judy Johnson. 68p. 1996. pap. text ed. 19.95 incl. audio (*1-882146-52-2*); pap. text ed. 24.95 incl. disk (*1-882146-53-0*) A D G Prods.

Suite Venitienne - Please Follow Me. Sophie Calle & Jean Baudrillard. Tr. by Dany Barash & Danny Hatfield from FRE. LC 87-73233. (Illus.). 96p. (Orig.). (FRE.). 1988. reprint ed. pap. 11.95 (*0-941920-09-7*) Bay Pr.

Suite 3505: The Story of the Draft Goldwater Movement. F. Clifton White & William J. Gill. 450p. 1993. 19.95 (*1-878802-10-0*); pap. 12.95 (*1-878802-14-3*) J M Ashbrook Ctr Pub Affairs.

Suited to a Tea. Patricia B. Mitchell. 1995. pap. 4.00 (*0-925117-80-3*) Mitchells.

Suites a Five, a Six for Viols & Organ. John Hingeston. Ed. by John Dornenburg. (Viol Consort Ser.: No. 6). i, 162p. 1991. pap. text ed. 50.00 (*1-56571-026-6*) PRB Prods.

Suites A5, A6 for Viols & Organ - Organ Part. rev. ed. John Hingeston. Ed. by John Dornenburg. (Viol Consort Ser.: No. 6). i, 18p. 1994. pap. text ed. 10.00 (*1-56571-100-9*) PRB Prods.

Suites d'un Premier Lit. Eugene Labiche. 9.95 (*0-686-54253-3*) Fr & Eur.

Suites d'une Course: Avec: L'Etoile de Seville. Jules Supervielle. 232p. (FRE.). 1959. pap. 10.95 (*0-7859-1331-9*, 2070261557) Fr & Eur.

Suitor: A Novel of Suspense. Michael Allegretto. 256p. 1993. 19.00 (*0-671-73644-2*) S&S Trade.

Suits to Fit Your Man. Doris Ekern. LC 80-50504. (Illus.). 56p. 1980. pap. 4.50 (*0-933956-05-3*) Sew-Fit.

Sujeto A Cambio: De las Relaciones Del Texto y la Sociedad En la Escritura de Cesar Vallejo (1914-1930) Jose Cerna-Bazan. 416p. (Orig.). (SPA.). 1995. pap. 20.00 (*0-9640795-2-6*) Latinoam Edit.

Sukari: Poetry by Jeanette Adams. 2nd ed. Jeanette Adams. (Illus.). 12p. (Orig.). 1979. pap. 5.00 (*0-9627018-0-7*) J Adams Pubns.

Sukeroku's Double Identity: The Dramatic Structure of Edo Kabuki. Barbara E. Thornbury. (Michigan Papers in Japanese Studies: No. 6). x, 102p. 1982. pap. 5.00 (*0-939512-11-4*) U MI Japan.

Sukey & the Mermaid. Robert D. San Souci. LC 90-24559. (Illus.). 32p. (J). (gr. k-3). 1992. lib. bdg. 15.00 (*0-02-778141-0*, Four Winds Pr) S&S Childrens.

Sukey and The Mermaid. Robert D. San Souci. (Illus.). 32p. (J). (gr. k-4). 1996. 5.99 (*0-689-80718-X*, Aladdin Paperbacks) S&S Childrens.

Sukhamani Sahib: Fountain of Eternal Joy. Swami Rami. LC 88-204663. 247p. (Orig.). (C). 1988. pap. 10.95 (*0-89389-110-X*) Himalayan Inst.

Sukhoi Su-27 'Flanker' Dennis R. Jenkins et al. (World Air Power Journal Special Ser.). (Illus.). 40p. 1994. pap. 9.95 (*1-880588-12-9*) AIRtime Pub.

Sukhothai: Its History, Culture & Art. Betty Gosling. (Asia Collection). (Illus.). 156p. 1991. 55.00 (*0-19-588984-3*) OUP.

Suki. Matthew Lipman. (Philosophy for Children Ser.). 153p. (Orig.). (gr. 9-10). 1978. pap. 10.50 (*0-916834-08-5*, TX86-788) Inst Advncmnt Philos Child.

***Suki & Massry's Therapy of Renal Diseases & Related Disorders.** 3rd ed. Wadi N. Suki & Shaul G. Massry. LC 96-49630. 1997. lib. bdg. write for info. (*0-7923-4368-9*) Kluwer Ac.

Suki & the Invisible Peacock. rev. ed. Joyce K. Blackburn. LC 96-14852. (Illus.). 64p. (J). (gr. 3-5). 1996. 14.95 (*1-881576-69-8*) Providence Hse.

Suki & the Magic Sand Dollar. rev. ed. Joyce K. Blackburn. LC 96-14851. (Illus.). 64p. (J). (gr. 3-5). 1996. 14.95 (*1-881576-70-1*) Providence Hse.

Suki & the Old Umbrella. rev. ed. Joyce K. Blackburn. LC 96-14846. (Illus.). 64p. (J). (gr. 3-5). 1996. 14.95 (*1-881576-71-X*) Providence Hse.

Suki & the Wonder Star. rev. ed. Joyce K. Blackburn. LC 96-14845. (Illus.). 64p. (J). (gr. 3-5). 1996. 14.95 (*1-881576-72-8*) Providence Hse.

Sukkah, 1 vol. (ENG & HEB.). 15.00 (*0-910218-58-7*) Bennet Pub.

Sukkah & the Big Wind. Lily Edelman. (Holiday Series of Picture Storybooks). (Illus.). (J). (gr. k-2). 1976. 5.95 (*0-8381-0716-8*) USCJE.

Sukkot: A Family Seder. Judith Abrams. LC 93-7551. (Illus.). 24p. (J). (ps-6). 1993. pap. 3.95 (*0-929371-75-5*) Kar-Ben.

Sukkot & Simchat Torah Fun for Little Hands. Illus. by Sally Springer. 32p. (J). (ps). 1993. student ed. 3.95 (*0-929371-77-1*) Kar-Ben.

Sukkot-Simhat Torah Anthology. Philip Goodman. LC 72-14058. (Holiday Anthologies Ser.). (Illus.). 476p. 1992. reprint ed. pap. text ed. 15.95 (*0-8276-0302-9*) JPS Phila.

Sukoshi No-Kireina-Kuuki. Alma Burnette. Ed. by Lafe Miller. (Illus.). 28p. (Orig.). (J). (gr. 1-8). 1994. 2.95 (*1-886452-03-2*) Amer Recycling.

Sukraniti. Sukra. Ed. & Tr. by Benoy K. Sarkar. LC 73-3801. (Sacred Books of the Hindus: No. 13). reprint ed. 32.50 (*0-404-57813-6*) AMS Pr.

Sul Ross: Soldier, Statesman, Educator. Judith A. Benner. LC 82-45891. (Centennial Series of the Association of Former Students: No. 13). (Illus.). 276p. 1983. 24.95 (*0-89096-142-5*) Tex A&M Univ Pr.

Sula. Toni Morrison. 1974. 25.00 (*0-394-48044-9*) Knopf.

Sula. Toni Morrison. 1987. pap. 10.95 (*0-452-26349-2*); mass mkt. 6.95 (*0-452-26010-8*, Z5476, Plume) NAL-Dutton.

Sula. Toni Morrison. 1993. pap. 5.99 (*0-451-18240-5*, Sig) NAL-Dutton.

Sulawesi. 2nd ed. Toby A. Volkman. (Regional Guides of Indonesia Ser.). (Illus.). 244p. (Orig.). 1995. pap. 17.95 (*0-8442-9948-0*, Passport Bks) NTC Pub Grp.

Sulawesi: Celebes. Ed. by Ian Caldwell & Toby A. Volkman. Tr. by Sylvia Pessireron & Lisa Scargo from ENG. (Indonesie Reisbibliotheek Ser.). 256p. (DUT.). 1991. pap. 19.95 (*0-945971-38-9*) Periplus.

Sulawesi: Island Crossroads of Indonesia. Toby A. Volkman. (Passport's Regional Guides of Indonesia Ser.). (Illus.). 256p. 1992. pap. 15.95 (*0-8442-9906-5*, Passport Bks) NTC Pub Grp.

Sulawesi: The Celebes. 2nd ed. Ed. by David Pickell & Mike Cooper. 290p. 1995. pap. 19.95 (*962-593-005-1*) Periplus.

Sulawesi Seas: Indonesia's Magnificent Underwater Realm. Mike Severns & Pauline Fiene-Severns. (Illus.). 160p. 1995. text ed. 60.00 (*0-9642269-0-1*) Staples-Ecenbarger.

***Sulayman: The Gifted.** Amina I. Ali. Ed. by J. C. Cinquino. (Prophets' Stories for Children from the Holy Qur'an Ser.: No. 16). (Illus.). 28p. (Orig.). (J). (gr. 4-6). 1996. write for info. (*1-881963-34-9*); pap. 2.50 (*1-881963-35-7*) Al-Saadawi Pubns.

Suleiman: The Magnificent. Andre Clot. 399p. 1993. 30.00 (*1-56131-039-5*) New Amsterdam Bks.

Suleyman & the Ottoman Empire. John Addison et al. Ed. by Malcolm Yapp & Margaret Killingray. (World History Program Ser.). (Illus.). (YA). (gr. 6-11). 1980. reprint ed. pap. text ed. 4.72 (*0-89908-013-8*) Greenhaven.

Suleyman the Magnificent & His Age: The Ottoman Empire in the Early Modern World. Ed. by Metin Kunt & Christine Woodhead. LC 94-49636. 232p. (C). 1995. pap. text ed. 21.50 (*0-582-03827-8*, Pub. by Longman UK) Longman.

***Suleymanname: The Illustrated History of Suleyman the Magnificent.** Esin Atil. 270p. 1996. 75.00 (*0-614-21591-9*, 1199) Kazi Pubns.

Sulfatases of Microbial Origin, Vol. 1. Ed. by K. S. Dodgeson et al. 216p. 1982. 122.00 (*0-8493-6035-8*, QP609, CRC Reprint) Franklin.

Sulfatases of Microbial Origin, Vol. 2. Ed. by K. S. Dodgeson et al. 208p. 1982. 122.00 (*0-8493-6036-6*, CRC Reprint) Franklin.

Sulfate Metabolism & Sulfate Conjugation. Ed. by G. J. Mulder et al. 312p. 1982. 85.00 (*0-8002-3665-3*) Taylor & Francis.

Sulfate-Reducing Bacteria. Ed. by Larry L. Barton. (Biotechnology Handbooks Ser.: Vol. 8). 340p. 1995. 85.00 (*0-306-44857-2*) Plenum.

Sulfate-Reducing Bacteria. 2nd ed. John R. Postgate. LC 83-15307. 250p. 1984. 64.95 (*0-521-25791-3*) Cambridge U Pr.

Sulfate-Reducing Bacteria: Contemporary Perspective. Ed. by J. M. Odom et al. LC 92-2311. (Contemporary Bioscience Ser.). (Illus.). 264p. 1992. 102.95 (*0-387-97865-8*) Spr-Verlag.

An Asterisk (*) at the beginning of an entry indicates that the title is appearing in BIP for the first time.

Sulfated Glycoconjugates in Amelogenesis: Comparative Histochemistry & Evolution of Ectoderm - Derived Hard Tissues. Yasutoku Kogaya. LC 88-20469. (Progress in Histochemistry & Cytochemistry Ser.: No. 29/1). (Illus.). vi, 110p. 1994. pap. 80.00 (*3-437-11585-5*, Pub. by G Fischer Verlag GW) Lubrecht & Cramer.

Sulfation of Drugs & Related Compounds. Gerald J. Mulder. 248p. 1981. 142.00 (*0-8493-5920-1*, RM301, CRC Reprint) Franklin.

Sulfide in Wastewater Collection & Treatment Systems. (ASCE Manual & Report on Engineering Practice: No. 69). 338p. 1989. 48.00 (*0-87262-681-4*) Am Soc Civil Eng.

Sulfide Inclusions in Steel: An International Symposium, 7-8 November, 1974, Port Chester, New York Proceedings. Ed. by John J. DeBarbadillo & Edwin Snape. LC 75-19315. (Materials-Metalworking Technology Ser.: No. 6). (Illus.). 508p. reprint ed. pap. 144.80 (*0-317-09688-5*, 2051903) Bks Demand.

***Sulfilimines & Related Derivates.** Shigeru Oae & Naomichi Furukawa. LC 83-12220. (ACS Monograph Ser.: No. 179). (Illus.). 352p. 1983. reprint ed. pap. 100.40 (*0-608-04360-5*, 2065141) Bks Demand.

Sulfilimines & Related Derivatives. Ed. by Shigeru Oae & Naomichi Furukawa. LC 83-12220. (ACS Monograph: No. 179). 340p. 1983. lib. bdg. 92.95 (*0-8412-0705-4*) Am Chemical.

Sulfinyl, O-Sulfinyl, Sulfonyl, & O-Sulfonyl Radicals, Vol. 4. Alexnader Senning. (Sulfer Reports: Vol. 4, No. 7). 80p. 1985. pap. text ed. 70.00 (*3-7186-0302-0*) Gordon & Breach.

Sulfite Science & Technology, Vol. 4. 3rd ed. Ed. by Michael J. Kocurek et al. (Pulp & Paper Manufacture Ser.). 352p. 1985. 48.00 (*0-919893-22-8*, 0202MS04) TAPPI.

Sulfites, Selenites & Tellurites see Solubility Data Series

Sulfonation & Sulfation - Thorium & Thorium Compounds see Encyclopedia of Chemical Technology

Sulfonyl Isocyanates & Sulfonyl Isothiocyanates, Vol. 1I. J. W. McFarland. (Sulfur Reports). 54p. 1981. pap. text ed. 70.00 (*3-7186-0255-5*) Gordon & Breach.

Sulfur. (Metals & Minerals Ser.). 1993. lib. bdg. 250.95 (*0-8490-8999-9*) Gordon Pr.

Sulfur: New Sources & Uses. Ed. by Michael E. Raymont. LC 82-1645. (ACS Symposium Ser.: No. 183). 1982. 37.95 (*0-8412-0713-5*) Am Chemical.

Sulfur Analogues of Polycyclic Aromatic Hydrocarbons (Thiaarenes) Environmental Occurrence, Chemical & Biological Properties. J. Jacob. (Cambridge Monographs on Cancer Research). 272p. (C). 1990. text ed. 130.00 (*0-521-30120-3*) Cambridge U Pr.

Sulfur Bacteria - STP 650. Ed. by E. Fjerdingstad. 129p. 1985. pap. 15.00 (*0-8031-0582-7*, 04-650000-16) ASTM.

Sulfur-Centered Reactive Intermediates in Chemistry & Biology, Vol. 197. Ed. by C. Chryssostomos & K. D. Asmus. LC 90-14295. (NATO ASI Series A, Life Sciences). (Illus.). 460p. 1990. 135.00 (*0-306-43723-6*, Plenum Pr) Plenum.

Sulfur Compounds in Foods. Ed. by Cynthia J. Mussinan & Mary E. Keelan. LC 94-20826. (ACS Symposium Ser.: Vol. 564). 1994. 79.95 (*0-8412-2943-0*) Am Chemical.

Sulfur Compounds in Fossil Fuels 1, Vol. 3. C. D. Czogalla & F. Boberg. 50p. 1983. pap. text ed. 70.00 (*3-7186-0260-1*) Gordon & Breach.

Sulfur Compounds in Hydrocarbon Pyrolysis, Vol.9. M. Bajus. (Sulfur Reports). 76p. 1989. pap. text ed. 106.00 (*3-7186-4944-6*, Harwood Acad Pubs) Gordon & Breach.

Sulfur-Containing Macroheterocycles, Vol. 6. Alexander Senning. (Sulfur Reports: Vol. 6, No. 3). 119p. 1986. pap. text ed. 101.00 (*3-7186-0371-3*) Gordon & Breach.

Sulfur Dioxide: Applications in Foods, Beverages & Pharmaceuticals. L. C. Schroeter. LC 65-22884. 1966. 155.00 (*0-08-011432-6*, Pub. by Pergamon Repr UK) Franklin.

Sulfur Dioxide & Vegetation: Physiology, Ecology, & Policy Issues. Ed. by William E. Winner et al. LC 83-51323. (Illus.). 624p. 1985. 75.00 (*0-8047-1234-4*) Stanford U Pr.

Sulfur Dioxide, Chlorine, Fluorine & Chlorine Oxides. A. S. Young. 1983. 219.00 (*0-08-026218-X*, Pub. by Pergamon Repr UK) Franklin.

Sulfur Dioxide Control in Pyrometallurgy: Proceedings of a Symposium - Sponsored by the TMS-AIME Pyrometallurgical Committee at the 110th AIME Annual Meeting, Chicago, Illinois, February 22-26, 1981. Metallurgical Society of AIME Staff. Ed. by Terrence D. Chatwin & Nobuo Kikumoto. LC 81-80107. (Conference Proceedings - Metallurgical Society of AIME Ser.). (Illus.). 267p. reprint ed. pap. 76.10 (*0-8357-3556-7*, 2034259) Bks Demand.

Sulfur Extrusion Reactions - Scope & Mechanistic Aspects, Vol. 10. C. R. Williams. (Sulfur Reports). 90p. 1990. text ed. 96.00 (*3-7186-5074-6*, Harwood Acad Pubs) Gordon & Breach.

Sulfur in Agriculture. M. A. Tabatabai. 688p. 1986. 52.00 (*0-89118-089-3*) Am Soc Agron.

Sulfur in Organic & Inorganic Chemistry, 2 vols., Vol. 1. Ed. by Alexander Senning. LC 70-154612. (Illus.). 394p. reprint ed. pap. 112.30 (*0-7837-4850-7*, 2029015) Bks Demand.

Sulfur in Organic & Inorganic Chemistry, Vol. 2. Alexander Senning. LC 70-154612. (Illus.). 376p. reprint ed. pap. 107.20 (*0-8357-3557-5*, 2029015) Bks Demand.

Sulfur in Organic & Inorganic Chemistry, Vol. 3. Ed. by Alexander Senning. LC 70-154612. (Illus.). 478p. reprint ed. pap. 136.30 (*0-8357-3558-3*, 2029015) Bks Demand.

Sulfur in Organic & Inorganic Chemistry, 2 vols., Vol. 4. Ed. by Alexander Senning. LC 70-154612. (Illus.). 454p. reprint ed. pap. 129.40 (*0-7837-4851-5*, 2029015) Bks Demand.

Sulfur in Pesticide Action & Metabolism. Ed. by Joseph D. Rosen et al. LC 81-7916. (ACS Symposium Ser.: No. 158). 1981. 38.95 (*0-8412-0635-X*) Am Chemical.

***Sulfur in Pesticide Action & Metabolism: Based on a Symposium.** Ed. by Joseph D. Rosen et al. LC 81-7916. (ACS Symposium Ser.: Vol. 158). 203p. 1981. reprint ed. pap. 57.90 (*0-608-03039-2*, 2063492) Bks Demand.

Sulfur in Proteins. Yu. M. Torchinsky. (Illus.). 304p. 1981. 140.00 (*0-08-023778-9*, Pub. by Pergamon Repr UK) Franklin.

Sulfur in the Tropics. Graeme Blair. (Technical Bulletin Ser.: No. T-12). (Illus.). 71p. (Orig.). 1979. pap. 4.00 (*0-88090-011-3*) Intl Fertilizer.

***Sulfur, New Sources & Uses.** Ed. by Michael E. Raymont. LC 82-1645. (ACS Symposium Ser.: Vol. 183). 272p. 1982. reprint ed. pap. 77.60 (*0-608-03108-9*, 2063561) Bks Demand.

Sulfur Nutrition & Assimilation in Higher Plants: Regulatory Agricultural & Environmental Aspects. I. Stulen. (Illus.). 1993. 89.00 (*90-5103-084-3*, Pub. by SPB Acad Pub NE) Balogh.

Sulfur Nutrition & Sulfur Assimilation in Higher Plants: Fundamental Environmental & Agricultural Aspects. Ed. by H. Rennenberg et al. (Illus.). 276p. 1990. 89.00 (*90-5103-038-X*, Pub. by SPB Acad Pub NE) Balogh.

***Sulfur Oxides & Suspended Particulate Matter.** (Environmental Health Criteria Ser.: No. 8). 107p. 1979. pap. text ed. 16.00 (*92-4-154068-0*, 1160008) World Health.

Sulfur Poisoning of Nickel Catalysts. C. H. Riesz et al. (Research Bulletin Ser.: No. 10). iv, 23p. 1951. pap. 2.50 (*0-317-56798-5*) Inst Gas Tech.

Sulfur Removal & Recovery from Industrial Processes. Ed. by John B. Pfeiffer. LC 75-11557. (Advances in Chemistry Ser.: No. 139). 1975. 27.95 (*0-8412-0217-6*) Am Chemical.

***Sulfur Removal & Recovery from Industrial Processes.** Ed. by John B. Pfeiffer. LC 75-11557. (Advances in Chemistry Ser.: Vol. 139). 231p. 1975. reprint ed. pap. 65.90 (*0-608-03904-7*, 2064351) Bks Demand.

***Suling (Bamboo Flute of Bali)** 1997. pap. 14.00 (*0-614-29663-3*) Linaria Pr.

***Sulky Sue.** (Little Monsters Ser.). (J). 1997. write for info. (*0-614-21789-X*, Pub. by Splash UK) Assoc Pubs Grp.

Sulla: The Last Republican. Arthur Keaveney. (Classical Lives Ser.). 256p. 1987. reprint ed. pap. 14.95 (*0-7099-3104-2*, Pub. by Croom Helm UK) Routledge Chapman & Hall.

Sulla Lirica Romanza Delle Origini. Guido Errante. 441p. (ITA.). 1943. pap. 15.95 (*0-913298-44-1*) S F Vanni.

Sulla und Seine Zeit im Urteil Ciceros. Hermann Diehl. (Beitrage Zur Altertumswissenschaft Ser.: Band 7). xi, 253p. (GER.). 1988. write for info. (*3-487-09110-0*) G Olms Pubs.

Sullen Weedy Lakes. William Logan. LC 87-46289. 1988. 15.95 (*0-87923-729-5*); pap. 9.95 (*0-87923-730-9*) Godine.

Sullivan-Clinton Campaign in 1779. Alexander C. Flick. 216p. 1993. reprint ed. lib. bdg. 79.00 (*0-7812-5175-3*) Rprt Serv.

Sullivan Co., Tennessee Death Records, 1908-1918. Eddie M. Nikazy. 311p. (Orig.). 1994. pap. text ed. 22.00 (*0-7884-0099-1*) Heritage Bk.

***Sullivan County Gravestone Inscriptions (Taken from Various Cemeteries), 10 vols.** Compiled by G. A. Barber. 1596p. 1997. reprint ed. lib. bdg. 59.50 (*0-8328-6255-X*) Higginson Bk Co.

Sullivan County, Indiana, 1816-1991. Sullivan County Historical Society Staff. LC 90-71730. (Illus.). 352p. 1991. 440.00 (*1-56311-024-5*) Turner Pub KY.

Sullivan County Sketches of Stephen Crane. Stephen Crane. (BCL1-PS American Literature Ser.). 85p. 1993. reprint ed. lib. bdg. 59.00 (*0-7812-6954-7*) Rprt Serv.

Sullivan County Tales & Sketches. Stephen Crane. Ed. by R. W. Stallman. LC 95-11021. (Illus.). 151p. 1995. pap. 15.00 (*0-935796-64-9*) Purple Mnt Pr.

Sullivan County, Tennessee Death Records 1919-1925, Vol. 2. Eddie M. Nikazy. 346p. (Orig.). 1995. pap. 26.00 (*0-7884-0290-0*) Heritage Bk.

Sullivan's Comic Operas: A Critical Appreciation. Thomas F. Dunhill. (Music Ser.). 256p. 1981. reprint ed. lib. bdg. 32.50 (*0-306-76080-0*) Da Capo.

Sullivan's Hollow. Chester Sullivan. LC 78-11434. 112p. 1992. reprint ed. pap. 10.95 (*0-87805-080-9*) U Pr of Miss.

Sullivan's Law. Amanda Clark. 1994. mass mkt. 2.99 (*0-373-03333-8*, 1-03333-1) Harlequin Bks.

Sullivan's Miracle. Lindsay Longford. (Intimate Moments Ser.). 1993. mass mkt. 3.50 (*0-373-07526-X*, 5-07526-2) Silhouette.

Sullivans of Little Horsepen Creek: A Tale of Colonial North Carolina's Regulator Era, Circa: 1760s. Carl Bradfield. (Illus.). 350p. (YA). (gr. 8-12). write for info. (*0-9632319-2-8*) ASDA Pub.

Sullivan's Reef. large type ed. Anne Weale. 1980. 25.99 (*0-7089-0411-4*) Ulverscroft.

Sullivan's Sting. Lawrence Sanders. 368p. 1991. mass mkt. 6.99 (*0-425-12845-8*) Berkley Pub.

Sullivan's Sting. large type ed. Lawrence Sanders. (General Ser.). 428p. 1991. 18.95 (*0-8161-5088-5*) G K Hall.

Sullivan's Sting. large type ed. Lawrence Sanders. (General Ser.). 428p. 1991. lib. bdg. 22.95 (*0-8161-5087-7*, GK Hall) Thorndike Pr.

Sullivan's Woman. Nora Roberts. (NR Flowers Ser.: No. 22). 1992. mass mkt. 3.59 (*0-373-51022-5*, 5-51022-7) Harlequin Bks.

Sully the Seal & Alley the Cat. Lynn Whitehead & Mark Steilen. (Illus.). 48p. (Orig.). (J). (gr. 2-5). 1994. pap. 9.95 (*1-880812-10-X*) S Ink WA.

Sully's Kids. Dawn Stewardson. (Superromance Ser.). 1996. mass mkt. 3.99 (*0-373-70691-X*, 1-70691-0) Harlequin Bks.

Sulphide Minerals. Crystal Chemistry, Parageneses and Systematics. R. I. Kostov & J. M. Stefanova. (Illus.). 212p. 1982. text ed. 44.95 (*3-510-65110-3*) Lubrecht & Cramer.

Sulphides: The Art of Cameo Incrustation. Paul Jokelson & Taylor & Dull, N.Y., N.Y. Staff. LC 68-25513. (Illus.). 159p. 1968. 15.00 (*0-933756-08-9*) Paperwght Pr.

Sulphones in Organic Synthesis. N. S. Simpkins. LC 92-34856. (Tetrahedron Organic Chemistry Ser.: Vol. 10). 381p. 1993. 114.25 (*0-08-040283-6*, Pergamon Pr); pap. 50.00 (*0-08-040284-4*, Pergamon Pr) Elsevier.

Sulphur Cycling on the Continents: Wetlands, Terrestrial Ecosystems & Associated Water Bodies. R. W. Howarth et al. LC 91-26109. (Scientific Committee on Problems of the Environment Ser.). 350p. 1992. text ed. 285.00 (*0-471-93153-5*) Wiley.

Sulphur Dioxide & Nitrogen Oxides in Industrial Waste Gases: Emission, Legislation & Abatement. Ed. by Daniel Van Velzen. 292p. (C). 1991. lib. bdg. 129.50 (*0-7923-1386-0*) Kluwer Ac.

Sulphur in Biology. CIBA Foundation Staff. LC 79-24939. (CIBA Foundation Symposium: New Ser.: No. 72). 324p. reprint ed. pap. 92.40 (*0-317-29756-2*, 2022191) Bks Demand.

Sulphur Nitrides in Organic Chemistry, Vol. 4. S. Mataka et al. 32p. 1984. pap. text ed. 34.00 (*3-7186-0263-6*) Gordon & Breach.

Sulphur Reagents in Organic Synthesis. Ed. by P. Metzner & A. Thuillier. (Best Synthetic Methods Ser.). (Illus.). 224p. 1994. boxed 75.00 (*0-12-690770-6*) Acad Pr.

Sulphur, Selenium, Boron, & Organometallic Compounds see Comprehensive Organic Chemistry

Sulphuric Acid Recovery. 15.00 (*0-318-03195-7*, 7520) Wire Assn Intl.

***Sultan of Spring: A Hunter's Odyssey Through the World of the Wild Turkey.** Bob Saile. (Illus.). 192p. 1998. 22.95 (*1-55821-625-1*) Lyons & Burford.

Sultan Omar Ali Saifuddin III & Britain: The Making of Brunei Darussalam. B. A. Hussainmiya. (Illus.). 482p. (C). 1996. 45.00 (*967-65-3106-5*) OUP.

Sultan Tipu. Fazl Ahmad. (Heroes of Islam Ser.: Bk. 10). 120p. (Orig.). (YA). (gr. 7-12). 1984. pap. 3.50 (*1-56744-237-4*) Kazi Pubns.

Sultan to Sultan: Adventures Among the Masai & Other Tribes of East Africa. Mary Sheldon. LC 72-5615. (Black Heritage Library Collection). 1977. reprint ed. 71.95 (*0-8369-9149-4*) Ayer.

Sultana & Miriam: Two Hundred Fifty Creative Writing Ideas. Diana Doore & Debra Johnson. LC 83-62301. 75p. (Orig.). (C). 1985. pap. text ed. 6.95 (*0-88247-718-8*) R & E Pubs.

Sultana Tragedy: America's Greatest Maritime Disaster. Jerry O. Potter. LC 91-29521. (Illus.). 272p. 1992. 24.95 (*0-88289-861-2*) Pelican.

Sultana's Dream & Selections from the Secluded Ones. Rokeya S. Hossain. Ed. & Tr. by Roushan Jahan. LC 88-11033. 104p. 1988. 19.95 (*0-935312-98-6*); pap. 8.95 (*0-935312-83-8*) Feminist Pr.

Sultanate of Aceh: Relations with the British 1760-1824. Lee Kam Hing. (South-East Asian Historical Monographs). 270p. 1995. 59.00 (*967-65-3055-7*) OUP.

Sultanate of Bornu. P. A. Benton. Tr. by A. Shultze. 401p. 1968. reprint ed. 55.00 (*0-7146-1717-2*, Pub. by F Cass Pubs UK) Intl Spec Bk.

Sultanate of Oman: A Twentieth Century History. Miriam Joyce. LC 95-4268. 152p. 1995. text ed. 47.95 (*0-275-95222-3*, Praeger Pubs) Greenwood.

***Sultan's Daughter.** Chamberlin. LC 96-44192. 1997. 24.95 (*0-312-86203-2*) St Martin.

Sultan's Favourite. large type ed. Helen Brooks. 1995. lib. bdg. 18.95 (*0-263-13963-8*) Thorndike Pr.

Sultan's Gold. Grover S. McLeod. 138p. 1988. 19.95 (*0-87651-976-1*); pap. 16.95 (*0-685-35678-7*) Southern U Pr.

Sultan's Gold: And Other Fleet Type Submarine Stories. Grover S. McLeod. 138p. 1988. 19.95 (*1-884150-04-7*); pap. 16.95 (*1-884150-05-5*) Manchester AL.

***Sultan's Ibrahim Mirza's Haft Awrang: A Princely Manuscript from Sixteenth-Century Iran.** Marianna S. Simpson & Massumeh Farhad. LC 96-49395. 1997. write for info. (*0-300-06802-6*) Yale U Pr.

***Sultan's Kitchen Cookbook.** Ozcan Ozan. 1997. 24.95 (*0-614-19403-2*) C E Tuttle.

***Sultan's Seraglio: An Intimate Portrait of Life at the Ottoman Court.** Ottaviano Bon. 160p. 1996. pap. 19.95 (*0-86356-046-6*, Pub. by Saqi Bks UK) Interlink Pub.

***Sultan's Seraglio: An Intimate Portrait of Life at the Ottoman Court.** Ottaviano Bon. 160p. 1996. 39.95 (*0-86356-215-9*) Intl Spec Bk.

Sultan's Servants: The Transformation of Ottoman Provincial Government, 1550-1650. I. M. Kunt. LC 82-19800. 200p. 1983. text ed. 57.50 (*0-231-05578-1*) Col U Pr.

Sultan's Snakes. Lorna Turpin. (J). (gr. 4 up). 1991. 7.99 (*0-85953-511-8*); pap. 3.99 (*0-85953-512-6*) Childs Play.

***Sultan's Snakes.** Lorna Turpin. (GRE.). (J). 1991. pap. 3.99 (*0-85953-825-7*); pap. 3.99 (*0-85953-559-2*) Childs Play.

***Sultan's Snakes.** Lorna Turpin. (J). 1996. lib. bdg. 11.95 (*0-85953-892-3*) Childs Play.

Sultan's Wives: (That Special Woman!) Tracy Sinclair. (Special Edition Ser.). 1995. pap. 3.75 (*0-373-09943-6*, 1-09943-1) Silhouette.

Sulu Zone, 1768-1898: The Dynamics of External Trade, Slavery, & Ethnicity in the Transformation of a Southeast Asian Maritime State. James F. Warren. 400p. 1981. 64.00 (*9971-69-004-7*, Pub. by Sgapore Univ SI) Coronet Bks.

***Sulzer Centrifugal Pump Handbook.** Sulzer Brothers, Ltd., Staff. ii, 342p. 1989. text ed. 107.50 (*1-85166-442-4*) Elsevier.

Sum Complexities of the Humble Field. Viola Weinberg. (Red Ser.). (Illus.). 32p. (Orig.). 6.00 (*0-938631-06-3*) Pennywhistle Pr.

Sum of All Fears. Tom Clancy. 640p. 1991. 24.95 (*0-399-13615-0*, Putnam) Putnam Pub Group.

Sum of All Fears. Tom Clancy. 928p. (Orig.). 1992. pap. 7.50 (*0-425-13354-0*) Berkley Pub.

Sum of All Fears. large type ed. Tom Clancy. 1507p. 1991. reprint ed. lib. bdg. 26.95 (*1-56054-258-6*) Thorndike Pr.

Sum of All Fears. large type ed. Tom Clancy. 1507p. 1992. pap. 18.95 (*1-56054-947-5*) Thorndike Pr.

Sum of Destructions: Poems. Theodore Weiss. LC 94-11179. 96p. 1994. pap. 9.95 (*0-8071-1933-4*); text ed. 19.95 (*0-8071-1932-6*) La State U Pr.

Sum of Even Powers of Real Linear Forms. B. Reznick. LC 91-44877. (Memoirs Ser.). 155p. 1992. pap. 29.00 (*0-8218-2523-2*, MEMO/96/463) Am Math.

***Sum of Our Choices: Essays in Honour of Eric J. Sharpe.** Ed. by Arvind Sharma. LC 96-43207. (McGill University Studies in Religion). 422p. 1996. pap. 39.95 (*0-7885-0313-8*, 65 00 04) Scholars Pr GA.

Sum of Things. Roland J. Green. (Starcruiser Shenandoah Ser.: No. 3). 384p. 1991. pap. 4.99 (*0-451-45080-9*, ROC) NAL-Dutton.

Sum of Us. David Stevens. 80p. (C). 1995. pap. text ed. 17.95 (*0-86819-441-7*) Aubrey Bks.

SUM Program Beginning Medical Transcription. Linda Campbell et al. 300p. 1994. pap. text ed. 840.00 incl. audio (*0-934385-60-2*) Hlth Prof Inst.

SUM Program Cardiology Transcription Unit. 58p. 1989. pap. text ed. 280.00 (*0-934385-15-7*) Hlth Prof Inst.

SUM Program GI Transcription Unit. 55p. 1989. Incl. 4 one hr. cassettes. pap. text ed. 280.00 (*0-934385-13-0*) Hlth Prof Inst.

SUM Program Orthopedic Transcription Unit. 76p. 1988. Incl. 4 one hr. cassettes. pap. text ed. 280.00 (*0-934385-11-4*) Hlth Prof Inst.

SUM Program Pathology Transcription Unit. 2nd rev. ed. 72p. 1992. pap. text ed. 280.00 incl. audio (*0-934385-65-3*) Hlth Prof Inst.

SUM Program Radiology Transcription Unit. 2nd rev. ed. 72p. 1990. pap. text ed. 210.00 incl. audio (*0-934385-64-5*) Hlth Prof Inst.

Suma Cervantina. Ed. by J. B. Avalle-Arce & E. C. Riley. (Monagrafias A Ser.: No. 14). 452p. (SPA.). (C). 1973. pap. 36.00 (*0-900411-66-X*, Pub. by Tamesis Bks Ltd UK) Boydell & Brewer.

Suma Oriental of Tome Pires & the Book of Francisco Rodrigues. Ed. by Armando Cortesao. 1990. reprint ed. 48.00 (*81-206-0535-7*, Pub. by Asian Educ Servs II) S Asia.

Sumac. Charles Neal. 301p. (Orig.). 1994. pap. write for info. (*0-9638727-0-2*) Flame Grape.

***Sumac Reader.** Ed. by Joseph Bednarik. LC 96-18730. 1997. 17.95 (*0-87013-462-0*) Mich St U Pr.

Sumario de Derecho Procesal Penal Puertorriqueno. 2nd ed. Dora Nevares-Muniz. 296p. (SPA.). 1986. pap. text ed. 20.00 (*0-317-38881-9*); suppl. ed. 10.00 (*0-685-11823-1*) Instituto Desarrollo.

Sumario de Doctrina Cristiana. 5th ed. Louis Berkhof. Tr. by David Vila from ENG. 240p. (SPA.). 1986. pap. 7.25 (*0-939125-05-6*) Evangelical Lit.

Sumario de la Medicina, Francisco Lopez de Villalobos, I-1169: Biblioteca Nacional de Madrid. Maria Nieves-Sanchez. (Medieval Spanish Medical Texts Ser.: No. 13). 8p. (SPA.). 1987. 10.00 incl. fiche (*0-940639-09-2*) Hispanic Seminary.

Sumatra. Ed. by Eric Dey. 288p. 1993. 37.50 (*0-945971-24-9*) Periplus.

Sumatra. 2nd ed. Ed. by Eric Oey. 332p. 1995. pap. 19.95 (*962-593-017-5*) Periplus.

Sumatra: Island of Adventure. Ian Caldwell. (Regional Guides of Indonesia Ser.). 1994. pap. 15.95 (*0-8442-9907-3*, Passport Bks) NTC Pub Grp.

Sumatra: Island of Adventure. 2nd ed. Ian Caldwell. (Regional Guides of Indonesia Ser.). (Illus.). 204p. Date not set. pap. 19.95 (*0-8442-8995-7*, Passport Bks) NTC Pub Grp.

Sumatran Politics & Poetics: Gayo History, 1900-1989. John R. Bowen. (Illus.). 288p. (C). 1991. text ed. 35.00 (*0-300-04708-8*) Yale U Pr.

Sumatran Tiger. Alison Tibbitts & Alan Roocroft. (Animals, Animals, Animals Ser.). (Illus.). 24p. (J). (ps-2). 1992. lib. bdg. 12.95 (*1-56065-105-9*) Capstone Pr.

Sumatripian - From Molecule to Man: An Official Session at the 8th Migraine Trust Symposium - Journal: European Neurology, Vol. 31, No. 5, 1991. Ed. by J. Lance & V. Pfaffenrath. (Illus.). 72p. 1991. pap. 31.50 (*3-8055-5437-0*) S Karger.

***Sumbawanga Safari.** Betty Kilgour. (Illus.). 150p. (Orig.). 1997. pap. 14.95 (*1-55059-142-8*, Pub. by Detselig CN) Temeron Bks.

***Sumemos con el Domino.** Lynette Long. LC 96-53687. (Illus.). 32p. (Orig.). (SPA.). (J). (ps-4). 1997. pap. 6.95 (*0-88106-909-4*) Charlesbridge Pub.

Sumer: Cities of Eden. Ed. by Dale Brown. LC 92-38367. (Lost Civilizations Ser.). (Illus.). 168p. 1993. 19.95 (*0-8094-9887-1*); lib. bdg. 25.93 (*0-8094-9888-X*) Time-Life.

Sumer & the Sumerians. Harriet Crawford. (Illus.). 216p. (C). 1991. text ed. 54.95 (*0-521-38175-4*); pap. text ed. 17.95 (*0-521-38850-3*) Cambridge U Pr.

Sumerian Administrative Documents Dated in the Reigns of the Kings of the Second Dynasty of the Ur from the Temple Archives of Nippur Preserved in Philadelphia. David V. Myhrman. LC 11-1230. (University of Pennsylvania, Babylonian Expedition, Series A: Cuneiform Texts: Vol. 3, Pt. 1). 242p. reprint ed. pap. 69.00 (*0-317-29805-4*, 2052013) Bks Demand.

Sumerian Administrative Documents from the Reigns of ISBI-ERRA. Marc Van de Mieroop. 123p. 1987. text ed. 47.50 (*0-300-03805-4*) Yale U Pr.

Sumerian & Akkadian Administrative Texts: From Pre-Dynastic Times to the End of the Akkad Dynasty. George G. Hackman. LC 78-63527. (Babylonian Inscriptions in the Collection of James B. Nies Ser.: No. 8). reprint ed. 45.00 (*0-404-60138-3*) AMS Pr.

Sumerian & Japanese: A Comparative Language Study. R. Ahlberg. 142, vip. 1991. text ed. 79.00 (*4-915809-50-1*) Gordon & Breach.

Sumerian Archival Texts. William W. Hallo. 67p. 1973. pap. text ed. 38.50 (*0-614-03995-9*, Pub. by Netherlands Inst NE) Eisenbrauns.

***Sumerian Dictionary, Vol. A, Pt. 2.** Ed. by Ake W. Sjoberg. Date not set. 50.00 (*0-924171-35-9*) Peabody Harvard.

Sumerian Dictionary of the University Museum of the University of Pennsylvania, Vol. B. PSD 2. xxvii, 220p. 1984. text ed. 40.00 (*0-934718-64-4*) U PA Mus Pubns.

***Sumerian Dictionary of the University of Pennsylvania Museum Series, 18 vols.** Date not set. write for info. (*0-934718-63-6*) U PA Mus Pubns.

Sumerian Dictionary, Vol. A, Pt. 1. Ed. by Ake W. Sjoberg et al. (PSD Ser.: No. 1-1). xiv, 209p. 1992. text ed. 50.00 (*0-924171-21-9*) U PA Mus Pubns.

Sumerian Economic Texts from the First Dynasty of Isin. Vaughn E. Crawford. LC 78-63528. (Babylonian Inscriptions in the Collection of James B. Nies Ser.: No. 9). reprint ed. 38.00 (*0-404-60139-1*) AMS Pr.

Sumerian Economic Texts from the Umma Archive, Vol. 2. Shin T. Kang. LC 73-84697. (Illus.). 463p. 1973. text ed. 44.95 (*0-252-00425-6*) U of Ill Pr.

Sumerian Gods & Their Representations. I. L. Finkel & M. J. Geller. Date not set. pap. text ed. write for info. (*90-72371-90-9*, Pub. by Styx NE) Eisenbrauns.

Sumerian Grammatical Texts. Stephen H. Langdon. LC 17-16093. (University of Pennsylvania, the University Museum, Publications of the Babylonian Section: Vol. 12, No. 1). 103p. reprint ed. pap. 29.40 (*0-317-28543-2*, 2052028) Bks Demand.

Sumerian Hymnology: The Ersemma. Mark E. Cohen. (Hebrew Union College Annual Supplements Ser.: No. 2). 217p. 1981. 18.75 (*0-87820-601-9*) Hebrew Union Coll Pr.

Sumerian Hymns from Cuneiform Texts in the British Museum. Ed. by Frederick A. Vanderburgh. LC 68-23118. (Columbia University. Contributions to Oriental History & Philology Ser.: No. 1). reprint ed. 29.50 (*0-404-50531-7*) AMS Pr.

Sumerian Literary Fragments from Nippur. J. Heimerdinger. (Occasional Publications of the Babylonian Fund: No. 4). (Illus.). xi, 26p. 1979. text ed. 20.00 (*0-934718-31-8*) U PA Mus Pubns.

Sumerian Liturgical Texts. Stephen H. Langdon. LC 17-16092. (University of Pennsylvania, the University Museum, Publications of the Babylonian Section: Vol. 10, No. 2). 163p. reprint ed. pap. 46.50 (*0-317-28546-7*, 2052026) Bks Demand.

Sumerian Mythology: A Study of Spiritual & Literary Achievement in the Third Millennium B. C. Samuel N. Kramer. LC 88-163. (Illus.). 148p. 1972. reprint ed. text ed. 59.75 (*0-313-26363-9*, KRSM, Greenwood Pr) Greenwood.

Sumerian Records from Drehem. William M. Nesbit. LC 15-2779. (Columbia University. Oriental Studies: No. 8). (Illus.). reprint ed. 32.50 (*0-404-50498-1*) AMS Pr.

Sumerian Roots of the American Preamble. James R. McGuire. pap. 19.95 (*0-685-72080-2*) Lough Erne.

Sumerian Roots of the American Preamble. James T. McGuire. LC 93-81291. (Illus.). 285p. (Orig.). pap. 19.95 (*0-9640880-0-2*) Lough Erne.

Sumerian Vistas: Poems. A. R. Ammons. 1987. pap. 7.95 (*0-393-30425-6*) Norton.

***Sumerians.** Elaine Landau. LC 96-46898. (Cradle of Civilization Ser.). (Illus.). 64p. (J). (gr. 4-6). 1997. lib. bdg. 15.90 (*0-7613-0215-8*) Millbrook Pr.

Sumerians. Pamela Odijk. (Ancient World Ser.). (Illus.). 48p. (J). (gr. 5-8). 1990. 7.95 (*0-382-24268-8*); teacher ed. 4.50 (*0-382-24282-3*); lib. bdg. 14.95 (*0-382-09892-7*) Silver Burdett Pr.

Sumerians. C. Leonard Woolley. LC 79-120570. reprint ed. 37.50 (*0-404-07029-9*) AMS Pr.

Sumerians: Their History, Culture & Character. Samuel N. Kramer. LC 63-11398. (Illus.). 370p. 1971. reprint ed. pap. text ed. 15.95 (*0-226-45238-7*, P422) U Ch Pr.

Sumerki Smertnago Dnya - Twilight of a Mortal Day. Valentin Nikitin. (Orig.). (RUS.). 1990. pap. 8.00 (*2-85065-189-3*) Gnosis Pr.

Sumero-Babylonian Sign List. Samuel A. Mercer. LC 18-16548. (Columbia University. Oriental Studies: No. 14). reprint ed. 34.50 (*0-404-50504-X*) AMS Pr.

Sumerological Studies in Honor of Thorkild Jacobsen: On His Seventieth Birthday, June 7, 1974. Stephen J. Lieberman. LC 75-42584. (Assyriological Studies: No. 20). 332p. 1977. lib. bdg. 24.00 (*0-226-62282-7*) U Ch Pr.

Sumgait Tragedy: Pogroms Against Armenians in Soviet Azerbaijan. Ed. by Samuel Shahmuradian. Tr. by Steven Jones from RUS. LC 90-70361. 344p. 1990. pap. 29.95 (*0-916431-31-2*) Zoryan Ins.

Sumi-E: An Introduction to Ink Painting. Nanae Momiyama. LC 67-15320. (Illus.). 36p. (J). 1967. pap. 6.95 (*0-8048-0554-7*) C E Tuttle.

Sumi-E Book. Yolanda Mayhall. (Illus.). 128p. 1989. pap. 16.95 (*0-8230-5022-X*, Watsn-Guptill) Watsn-Guptill.

Sumi-E Just for You. Hakuho Hirayama. LC 79-84653. (Illus.). 96p. 1980. pap. 25.00 (*0-87011-369-0*) Kodansha.

***Sumi Painting.** T. Mikami. 1996. pap. 12.95 (*4-07-971229-4*) Shufu no Tomo-Sha.

Sumida, Edition I. A. Wallen Burgh. 222p. 1959. write for info. (*0-318-57674-0*) Rural Life.

Sumida-Curious. A. Wollenburg. 256p. 1974. reprint ed. pap. 3.95 (*0-686-02473-7*) Rural Life.

Suminagashi-Zome. Tokutaro Yagi. Tr. by Kyoko Muecke from JPN. (Illus.). 55p. (Orig.). 1991. 650.00 (*0-940592-25-8*) Heyeck Pr.

Summa Artis, 39 vols., Set. Ed. by Jose Pijoan. 19200p. (SPA.). 1989. 1,150.00 (*84-239-5200-2*) Elliots Bks.

Summa Contra Gentiles, 4 bks., Set. Incl. Bk. 1. God. Tr. by Anton C. Pegis. LC 75-19883. 317p. 1975. pap. 13.00 (*0-268-01678-X*); Bk. 2. Creation. Tr. by James F. Anderson. LC 75-19883. 351p. 1975. pap. 13.00 (*0-268-01680-1*); Bk. 3. Providence. , 2 bks. in 1. Tr. by Vernon J. Bourke. LC 75-19883. 560p. 1975. pap. 9.00 (*0-268-01682-8*); Bk. 4. Salvation. Tr. by Charles J. O'Neil. LC 75-19883. 360p. 1975. pap. 13.00 (*0-268-01684-4*); LC 75-19883. 1975. Set pap. 57.50 (*0-268-01676-3*) U of Notre Dame Pr.

Summa Contra Gentiles, Bk. 3: Providence, Vol. 1. St. Thomas Aquinas. LC 75-19883. 1976. pap. 11.50 (*0-268-01686-0*) U of Notre Dame Pr.

Summa Contra Gentiles, Bk. 3: Providence, Vol. 2. St. Thomas Aquinas. LC 75-19883. 1976. pap. 11.50 (*0-268-01688-7*) U of Notre Dame Pr.

Summa Modorum Significandi: Sophismata. Sigerius De Cortraco. (Studies in the History of Linguistics: No. 14). xii, 108p. 1977. 43.00 (*90-272-0955-3*) Benjamins North Am.

Summa Musice: A Thirteenth-Century Manual for Singers. Ed. by Christopher Page. (Musical Texts & Monographs). (Illus.). 250p. (C). 1991. text ed. 75.00 (*0-521-40420-7*) Cambridge U Pr.

Summa of the Christian Life, 3 vols., 1. Louis of Granada. Tr. by Jordan Aumann from SPA. LC 79-65716. 1979. reprint ed. pap. write for info. (*0-89555-118-7*) TAN Bks Pubs.

Summa of the Christian Life, 3 vols., 2. Louis of Granada. Tr. by Jordan Aumann from SPA. LC 79-65716. 1979. reprint ed. pap. write for info. (*0-89555-119-5*) TAN Bks Pubs.

Summa of the Christian Life, 3 vols., 3. Louis of Granada. Tr. by Jordan Aumann from SPA. LC 79-65716. 1979. reprint ed. pap. write for info. (*0-89555-120-9*) TAN Bks Pubs.

Summa of the Christian Life, 3 vols., Set. Louis of Granada. Tr. by Jordan Aumann from SPA. LC 79-65716. 1979. reprint ed. pap. 36.00 (*0-89555-121-7*) TAN Bks Pubs.

Summa of the Summa: The Essential Philosophical Passages of St. Thomas Aquinas' Summa Theologica Edited & Explained for Beginners. Peter Kreeft. LC 90-81772. 539p. (Orig.). 1990. pap. 24.95 (*0-89870-300-X*) Ignatius Pr.

Summa Perfectionis of Pseudo-Geber: A Critical Edition, Translation & Study. William R. Newman. LC 91-25350. (CTAI Ser.: No. 35). iv, 785p. 1991. 267.25 (*90-04-09464-4*) E J Brill.

Summa Philosophiae Naturalis. Paulus Venetus. 262p. 1974. reprint ed. write for info. (*3-487-05006-4*) G Olms Pubs.

Summa Spes. Aleister Crowley. (Orig.). 1993. pap. 5.95 (*1-55818-248-9*) Holmes Pub.

***Summa Theologiae: A Concise Translation.** Thomas Aquinas. 1997. pap. text ed. 29.95 (*0-87061-210-7*) Chr Classics.

***Summa Theologiae: A Concise Translation.** St. Thomas Aquinas. 1997. 45.00 (*0-87061-211-5*) Chr Classics.

Summa Theologica of St. Thomas Aquinas, 5 vols., Set. St. Thomas Aquinas. LC 81-68580. 3104p. 1981. reprint ed. 225.00 (*0-87061-063-5*, 6903); reprint ed. pap. 150.00 (*0-87061-069-4*, 6904) Chr Classics.

Summa Virtutum de Remediis Anime. Ed. by Siegfried Wenzel. LC 82-13430. (Chaucer Library). 352p. 1984. 50.00 (*0-8203-0638-X*) U of Ga Pr.

Summaries: Fragments; General Index see Roman History

Summaries of Judgments, Advisory Opinions & Orders of the International Court of Justice: 1948-1991. 227p. 1992. 30.00 (*92-1-133426-8*) UN.

Summaries of Leading Cases on the Constitution. 13th rev. ed. Paul C. Bartholomew. (Orig.). (C). 1991. pap. text ed. 21.95 (*0-8226-3008-7*) Littlefield.

Summaries of Safety Defect Recall Campaigns for American Motors Corporation Vehicles (1966-1986) Donald J. Schallau. 33p. 1986. 100.00 (*0-685-10656-X*) DJS Ent.

Summaries of Safety Defect Recall Campaigns for Chrysler Corporation Vehicles (1966-1986) Donald J. Schallau. 75p. 1986. 100.00 (*0-933634-04-8*) DJS Ent.

Summaries of Safety Defect Recall Campaigns for Ford Motor Company Vehicles (1966-1986) Donald J. Schallau. 124p. 1986. 100.00 (*0-933634-05-6*) DJS Ent.

Summaries of Safety Defect Recall Campaigns for General Motors Corporation Vehicles (1966-1987) Donald J. Schallau. 134p. 1986. 100.00 (*0-933634-06-4*) DJS Ent.

Summaries of Safety Defect Recall Campaigns for Harley-Davidson Motor Company Vehicles (1966-1986) Donald J. Schallau. 14p. 1986. 100.00 (*0-933634-11-0*) DJS Ent.

Summaries of Safety Defect Recall Campaigns for International Harvester Vehicles (1966-1986) Donald J. Schallau. 37p. 1986. 100.00 (*0-933634-07-2*) DJS Ent.

Summaries of Safety Defect Recall Campaigns for Mack Trucks Inc. Vehicles (1966-1986) Donald J. Schallau. 40p. 1986. 100.00 (*0-933634-08-0*) DJS Ent.

Summaries of Safety Defect Recall Campaigns for Vehicle Tires (All Manufacturers & Distributors), 1966-1986. Donald J. Schallau. 112p. 1986. 100.00 (*0-933634-12-9*) DJS Ent.

Summaries of Safety Defect Recall Campaigns for Volkswagen Vehicles: VW-Porsche-Audi (1966-1986) 36p. 1986. 100.00 (*0-933634-09-9*) DJS Ent.

Summaries of Safety Defect Recall Campaigns for White Motor Corporation Vehicles (1966-1986) Donald J. Schallau. 32p. 1986. 100.00 (*0-933634-10-2*) DJS Ent.

Summaries of State Laws Relating to the Insane. John Koren. Ed. by Gerald N. Grob. LC 78-22570. (Historical Issues in Mental Health Ser.). 1980. reprint ed. lib. bdg. 20.95 (*0-405-11923-2*) Ayer.

Summaries of Three Bilateral Conferences: Held in Beijing & Shanghai; The People's Republic of China. Ed. & Intro. by Robert A. Scalapino. 72p. (C). 1988. pap. text ed. 9.95 (*0-317-91352-2*) Pac Forum.

Summarium Heinrici, Vol. 1: Textkritische Ausgabe der ersten Fassung, Buch I-X. Ed. by Reiner Hildebrandt. LC 73-75487. (Quellen und Forschungen zur Sprach und Kulturgeschichte der Germanischen Voelker Ser.: NF 61). (C). 1974. text ed. 242.30 (*3-11-003750-5*) De Gruyter.

Summarizers: Activity Structures to Support Integration & Retention of New Learning. Jon Saphier & Mary A. Haley. 65p. (Orig.). 1993. student ed. 12.95 (*1-886822-05-0*) Res Better Teach.

Summary: Catechism of the Catholic Church. John R. Klopke. 224p. 1994. pap. text ed. 5.95 (*0-89942-556-9*, 556/04) Catholic Bk Pub.

Summary & Recommendations: Clean Water Act Section 404 Discharge of Dredged & Fill Materials & Section 401 Water Quality Certification Programs in Arizona. Jacqueline Rich & Virginia Coltman. 200p. 1991. pap. text ed. 25.00 (*1-884320-05-8*) ASU Herberger Ctr.

Summary Catalogue of Post-Medieval Western Manuscripts in the Bodleian Library, Oxford: Acquisitions 1916-1975 (SC 37300-55936), 3 vols., Set. Mary Clapinson & T. D. Rogers. 1408p. 1992. 700.00 (*0-19-952109-3*) OUP.

Summary, Conclusions, & Recommendations from Global Change & the Human Prospect: Issues in Population, Science, Technology & Equity. Ed. by Charles F. Blackburn. 36p. (Orig.). 1992. pap. text ed. 2.50 (*0-914446-02-9*) Sigma Xi.

Summary Description of Design Criteria, Codes, Standards, & Regulatory Provisions Typically Used for the Civil & Structural Design of Nuclear Fuel Cycle Facilities, A. 128p. 1988. 17.00 (*0-87262-651-2*) Am Soc Civil Eng.

Summary Dissolution. Harry Polkinhorn. (Illus.). 58p. (Orig.). 1988. pap. 3.00 (*0-926935-06-2*) Runaway Spoon.

Summary Fact Data Sheets (SFDS) Samuel J. Levy. 20p. 1990. ring bd. 24.00 (*1-883467-01-2*) Intl Geometric.

Summary Groundwater Resources of Lebanon County, Pennsylvania. Denise W. Royer. (Water Resource Reports: No. 55). (Illus.). 84p. (Orig.). 1983. pap. 15.30 (*0-8182-0026-X*) Commonweal PA.

Summary Guide to Spanish Florida Missions & Visitas. John H. Hann. 1990. pap. 15.00 (*0-88382-285-7*) AAFH.

Summary, Historical & Political, of the First Planting, Progressive Improvements, & Present State of the British Settlements in North-America. William Douglass. LC 74-141084. (Research Library of Colonial Americana). 1972. reprint ed. 87.95 (*0-405-03279-X*) Ayer.

Summary, Historical & Political, of the First Planting, Progressive Improvements, & Present State of the British Settlements in North America. William Douglass. (Notable American Authors Ser.). 1992. reprint ed. lib. bdg. 75.00 (*0-7812-2681-3*) Rprt Serv.

Summary Information on Master of Social Work Programs: 1994-95. pap. 11.00 (*0-87293-045-9*) Coun Soc Wk Ed.

Summary Injustice: Military Tribunals in Burma. Lawyers Committee for Human Rights Staff. 63p. (Orig.). 1991. pap. 10.00 (*0-934143-41-2*) Lawyers Comm Human.

Summary Judgement Procedure. Andrew Beck. 113p. 1988. boxed 59.00 (*0-409-78853-8*, NZ) MICHIE.

Summary Judgement Procedure Cumulative Supplement. 1992. 20.00 (*0-409-78960-7*, NZ) MICHIE.

Summary Judgment & Other Preclusive Devices. Warren Freedman. LC 88-37481. 210p. 1989. text ed. 69.50 (*0-89930-377-3*, FSJ/, Quorum Bks) Greenwood.

Summary Judgments in Texas: Practice, Procedure & Review. Timothy Patton. 400p. 1994. 115.00 (*0-409-25573-4*); suppl. ed., ring bd. 59.00 (*0-685-74458-2*) MICHIE.

Summary Justice. Lloyd J. Guillory. LC 95-71268. 192p. 1996. 14.95 (*1-887750-05-3*) Rutledge Bks.

Summary of American Law. Martin M. Weinstein. LC 87-82759. 1988. 42.00 (*0-318-37614-8*) Lawyers Cooperative.

Summary of Arizona Community Property Law. Charles M. Smith. 144p. 1981. 12.65 (*0-910039-07-0*) AZ Law Inst.

Summary of Christian Doctrine. Louis Berkhof. 1938. pap. 14.00 (*0-8028-1513-8*) Eerdmans.

Summary of Christian History. rev. ed. Robert A. Baker & John M. Landers. LC 93-11779. 1994. 29.99 (*0-8054-1064-3*, 4210-64) Broadman.

Summary of Christian History see Compendio de la Historia Cristiana

Summary of Conference Agreement on H. R. 3838 (Tax Reform Act of 1986) Joint Committee on Taxation Staff. 73p. 1986. pap. text ed. write for info. (*0-314-34290-7*) West Pub.

Summary of Consumer Research on Health & Diet Attitudes & Knowledge & Use of Food Labels. 60p. (Orig.). (C). 1994. pap. text ed. 25.00 (*0-7881-0707-0*) DIANE Pub.

Summary of Contraindications to Oral Contraceptives. S. C. Knijff et al. (Summary of Oral Contraceptive Data Ser.). (Illus.). 320p. 1997. text ed. 59.00 (*1-85070-691-3*) Prthnon Pub.

Summary of Drug Interactions with Oral Contraceptives. T. B. Geurts et al. Ed. by J. M. Sitsen. (Illus.). 120p. (C). 1993. 39.00 (*1-85070-518-6*) Prthnon Pub.

Summary of Earth Processes & Environments. John Tomikel. LC 80-66211. (Illus.). 166p. (Orig.). (gr. 9-12). 1981. pap. 12.00 (*0-910042-38-1*) Allegheny.

Summary of Employment in Fifty Top-Paying Fields. Work for Hire Staff. 1984. 2.50 (*0-917421-01-9*) Lenox Pub.

***Summary of Evaluations Performed by the Joint FAO/WHO Expert Committee on Food Additives (JECFA)** 376p. 1994. 120.00 (*92-5-103539-3*, Pub. by FAO IT) Bernan Associates.

Summary of Evaluations Performed by the Joint FAO-WHO Expert Committee on Food Additives (JECFA) Ed. by FAO Staff & IPCS Staff. 300p. 1996. ring bd. 175.00 (*0-944398-41-3*) ILSI.

Summary of Evaluations Performed by the Joint FAO-WHO Expert Committee on Food Additives (JECFA) 1956-1993 (First Through Forty-First Meetings) iii, 284p. 1994. pap. text ed. 110.00 (*92-4-156172-6*, 1930059) World Health.

Summary of Financial & Cost Data Survey. 58p. 1988. 1,000.00 (*0-318-35238-9*, FCD) P-PCI.

Summary of Groundwater Resources of Perry County, Pennsylvania. Pref. by Denise W. Royer & Arthur A. Socolow. (Water Resource Reports: No. 59). (Illus.). 70p. 1984. pap. 16.25 (*0-8182-0059-6*) Commonweal PA.

Summary of Highway Product Evaluation Practices & HITEC Needs Survey: Final Report. LC 93-44393. 1994. 25.00 (*0-87262-860-4*) Am Soc Civil Eng.

Summary of Investigations Relating to Reading: July 1, 1982 to June 30, 1983. Samuel Weintraub et al. 352p. reprint ed. pap. 100.40 (*0-317-58125-2*, 2029732) Bks Demand.

Summary of Low-Speed Airfoil Data, No. 2. Michael S. Selig et al. (Illus.). 274p. (Orig.). 1996. pap. 25.00 (*0-9646747-2-6*) Soartech.

Summary of Low-Speed Airfoil Data, Vol. 1. Michael S. Selig et al. (Illus.). 317p. (Orig.). 1995. pap. text ed. 25.00 (*0-9646747-1-8*) Soartech.

Summary of Major Natural Disaster Incidents in the U. S., 1965-85. Claire B. Rubin et al. (Special Publications: No. 17). 47p. 1986. 4.00 (*0-614-01776-9*) Natural Hazards.

Summary of Mississippi Law, 3 vols. & hardbound supplement. Leslie B. Grant. LC 78-76760. 1993. Suppl. 1993. suppl. ed. 360.00 (*0-318-57147-1*) Lawyers Cooperative.

***Summary of Numerical Examples Demonstrating the Procedures for Calculating Geometry Factors for Spur & Helical Gears.** AGMA Technical Committee Staff. (Information Sheet Ser.). 1993. pap. text ed. 60.00 (*1-55589-617-0*) AGMA.

Summary of Oil & Gas Developments in Pennsylvania: 1955 to 1959. William S. Lytle et al. (Mineral Resource Reports: No. 45). (Illus.). 133p. 1984. reprint ed. pap. 15.40 (*0-8182-0036-7*) Commonweal PA.

Summary of One Hundred Second Congress, Second Session, (1992) NCSL State-Federal Relations Staff. (State-Federal Issue Brief Ser.: Vol. 5, No. 5). 13p. 1992. 6.50 (*1-55516-899-X*, 8500-0505) Natl Conf State Legis.

Summary of Precision Bidding. C. C. Wei. 10p. 1978. 1.00 (*0-685-08327-6*) Barclay Bridge.

Summary of Publications & Hearings see Securities Regulation Series

Summary of Reports Presented at April 20, 1985 CMA Production-Management Seminar of Survey of Retail Alterations Problems & Impact of Wider Lining Widths on Clothing Manufacturers Operations. 30p. 1985. 50.00 (*0-318-19703-0*) Clothing Mfrs.

Summary of Reports Presented at April 28, 1984 CMA Production Management Seminar on: New Developments in Trouser Technology, Tailored Clothing Technology Corporation, Manufacturer's Experience with New Technology. 36p. 1984. 50.00 (*0-318-19699-9*) Clothing Mfrs.

Summary of Some of My Research on Organosulphur Compounds: Rotational Isomerism of Vinyl Ethers & Sulfides: The Effect of Organic Sulphur Compounds on Oxidation Processes of Hydrocarbon Fuels, Vol. 7. Alexander Senning et al. (Sulfer Reports: Vol. 7, No. 5). 83p. 1987. pap. text ed. 105.00 (*3-7186-4804-0*) Gordon & Breach.

Summary of Some Properties of Nuclei, Nuclear Radiation, & Reactors. Peter Lindenfeld. 26p. 1981. 6.00 (*0-917853-85-7*, MS3) Am Assn Physics.

Summary of SSA's Procedures for Conducting Continuing Disability Review. Greater Upstate Law Project Staff. 52p. 1986. pap. 5.00 (*0-685-23191-7*, 40,962) NCLS Inc.

Summary of State Ground Water Quality Monitoring Well Regulations. 1989. 75.00 (*0-685-18800-0*) Natl Grnd Water.

Summary of State Mandated Codes: April 1996. Insurance Institute for Property Loss Reduction Staff. (Illus.). 6p. 1996. pap. text ed. write for info. (*1-885312-10-5*) Ins Inst for PLR.

Summary of State Mandated Codes: November 1994. Insurance Institute for Property Loss Reduction Staff. 6p. (Orig.). 1995. pap. text ed. write for info. (*1-885312-03-2*) Ins Inst for PLR.

An Asterisk (*) at the beginning of an entry indicates that the title is appearing in BIP for the first time.

Summary of Symposium on Health Aspects of Exposure to Asbestos in Buildings: How Serious Is the Threat of Asbestos? 40p. 1989. pap. 16.00 (0-685-71676-7, 765) Inst Real Estate.

***Summary of Technical Testimony in the Colorado Water Division 1 Trial.** Nancy Gordon. (Illus.). 140p. (Orig.). (C). 1996. pap. 30.00 (0-7881-3048-X) DIANE Pub.

Summary of the Assessment of the Status of African-Americans, Vol. I. Ed. by Wornie L. Reed. 100p. (Orig.). (C). 1990. pap. 5.95 (1-878358-04-9) U MA W M Trotter Inst.

Summary of the Basics in Solar Energy: Supplement-Tutorials to the 1978 Annual Meeting of the American Section of the International Solar Energy Society. International Solar Energy Society, American Section Staff. Ed. by Karl W. Boer. 1978. pap. text ed. 18.00 (0-89553-013-9) Am Solar Energy.

Summary of the Great Vehicle. Numata Center for Buddhist Translation & Research Staff. Tr. & Intro. by John P. Keenan. LC 92-82069. (BDK English Tripitaka Ser.: Vol. 46-III). 147p. (C). 1992. text ed. 25.00 (0-9625618-6-X) Numata Ctr.

Summary of the Law of Bills of Exchange, Cash Bills, & Promissory Notes: With Notes & References to American Decisions. 4th rev. ed. John Bayley. xii, 426p. 1994. reprint ed. lib. bdg. 52.50 (0-8377-1976-3) Rothman.

Summary of the Law of Contracts. C. C. Langdell. xiv, 278p. 1980. reprint ed. lib. bdg. 26.00 (0-8377-0809-5) Rothman.

Summary of the Law of Patents for Useful Inventions with Forms. William E. Simonds. iv, 360p. 1995. reprint ed. lib. bdg. 45.00 (0-8377-2658-1) Rothman.

Summary of the New Catholic Catechism. James A. Griffin & Albert DiIanni. LC 94-28519. 152p. (Orig.). 1994. pap. 5.95 (0-8189-0714-2) Alba.

Summary of the One Hundred-First Congress: Second Session. (State-Federal Issue Brief Ser.: Vol. 3, No. 5). 12p. 1990. 6.50 (1-55516-887-6, 8500-0305) Natl Conf State Legis.

Summary of the One Hundred First Congress First Session (1989), Vol. 2, No. 11. Office of State-Federal Relations Staff. (State-Federal Issue Brief Ser.: Vol. 2, No. 11). 10p. 1989. pap. text ed. 6.50 (1-55516-881-7, 8500-0211) Natl Conf State Legis.

Summary of the One Hundredth Congress First Session. (State-Federal Issue Brief Ser.: Vol. 2, No. 6). 1989. 6.50 (1-55516-876-0, 8500-0206) Natl Conf State Legis.

Summary of the One Hundredth Congress Second Session. (State-Federal Issue Brief Ser.: Vol. 2, No. 7). 1989. 6.50 (1-55516-877-9, 8500-0207) Natl Conf State Legis.

Summary of the Practice of the Secretary-General as Depository of Multilateral Treaties. 300p. Date not set. 85.00 (92-1-133477-2, E.94.V.15) UN.

Summary of the Principal Legal Decisions Affecting Auditors. Hugh Cocke. Ed. by Richard P. Brief. LC 80-1480. (Dimensions of Accounting Theory & Practice Ser.). 1980. reprint ed. lib. bdg. 17.95 (0-405-13510-6) Ayer.

Summary of the Recommendations of Recent Commission Reports on Improving Undergraduate Education: Five Reports. 48p. 1985. 4.00 (0-318-22554-9, PS-85-3) Ed Comm States.

Summary of the Roman Civil Law, Illustrated by Commentaries on & Parallels from the Mosaic, Canon, Mohammedan, English, & Foreign Law, with an Appendix, Map, & General Index, 4 vols., Set. Patrick M. De Colquhoun. 1988. reprint ed. lib. bdg. 150.00 (0-8377-2036-2) Rothman.

Summary of the Southwest Alluvial Basins, Regional Aquifer-System Analysis, South-Central Arizona & Parts of Adjacent States. T. W. Anderson. 1994. write for info. (0-318-72764-1) US Geol Survey.

Summary of the Study of the New Testament Way of Christian Service. Witness Lee. 50p. 2.00 (0-87083-515-7, 14009001) Living Stream Ministry.

***Summary of U. S. Supreme Court Decisions for the Criminal Justice Community & Database.** Ed. by Angelo DeLeon & Gary Weddle. 240p. 1997. ring bd. 29.95 incl. disk (1-889031-10-0) Looseleaf Law.

Summary of War Damage: Submarines, U. S. Losses & Damage - 7 December 1941 to 15 August 1945. rev. ed. U. S. Navy Staff. LC 89-80589. (Illus.). 60p. (C). 1989. reprint ed. pap. 9.95 (0-944055-03-6) Floating Drydock.

Summary of Yuki Culture. fac. ed. George M. Foster. Ed. by A. L. Kroeber et al. (University of California Publications: No. 5:3). (Illus.). 92p. (C). 1944. reprint ed. pap. 8.45 (1-55567-083-0) Coyote Press.

***Summary Proceedings of the 5th World Congress of Chemical Engineering.** 1996. 25.00 (0-8169-0724-2, P-84) Am Inst Chem Eng.

***Summary Report.** (Next-Generation Manufacturing Project: Vol. I). (Illus.). 54p. (Orig.). 1997. pap. 35.00 (1-885166-13-3) Agility Forum.

Summary Report & Index: Strategies for Europe - Summary Report. Michael Grubb et al. (Renewable Energy Strategies for Europe Ser.: Vol. 5). 80p. (C). 1995. pap. 14.95 (1-85383-282-0, Pub. by Erthscan Pubns UK) Island Pr.

Summary Report of the Atmospheric Deposition Workshop: Held at the Guild Inn in Scarborough, Ontario Between October 29-31, 1986. fac. ed. Workship on Great Lakes Atmospheric Deposition Staff. (Illus.). 47p. 1986. pap. 25.00 (0-7837-8620-4, 2075227) Bks Demand.

Summary Report of Water Sensitivity. (SHRP Interim Reports: No. 003A). 76p. 1989. 5.00 (0-685-41025-0) Transport Res Bd.

Summary Report on Adult College Students. Alan B. Knox. 1959. 2.50 (0-87060-086-9, PUC 8) Syracuse U Cont Ed.

Summary Report on Aging of Asphalt-Aggregate Systems. (SHRP Interim Reports: No. 004A). 100p. 1989. 5.00 (0-685-41022-6) Transport Res Bd.

Summary Report on Elevated Temperature Tests for Asbestos-Free Gasket Materials. LC 90-60976. (MTI Publication: No. 35). (Illus.). 64p. 1990. 53.00 (1-877914-10-X) NACE Intl.

Summary Report on Fatigue Response of Asphalt Mixtures. (SHRP Interim Reports: No. 011A). 147p. 1990. 5.00 (0-685-41023-4) Transport Res Bd.

Summary Report on Low Temperature & Thermal Fatigue Cracking. (SHRP Interim Reports: No. 001A). 83p. 1990. 5.00 (0-685-41024-2) Transport Res Bd.

Summary Report on the Contribution of the Japanese National Committee for IBP, 1964-1974. Japanese Committee for the International Biological Program Staff. Ed. by H. Tamiya. LC 78-670167. (JIBP Synthesis Ser.: No. 20). 244p. 1978. reprint ed. pap. 69.60 (0-608-01559-8, 2061974) Bks Demand.

***Summary Report on the Evaluation of Short-Term Tests for Carcinogens: Collaborative Study on in Vitro Tests.** WHO Staff. (Environmental Health Criteria Ser.: No. 47). 77p. 1985. 15.00 (92-4-154187-3) World Health.

Summary Report on the Evaluation of Short-Term Tests for Carcinogens: Collaborative Study on In Vivo Tests. (Environmental Health Criteria Ser.: No. 109). 96p. 1990. pap. text ed. 18.90 (92-4-157109-8, 1160109) World Health.

Summary Reporting of Financial Information, 2 vols., Set. Deloitte, Haskins & Sells Staff. LC 83-81991. 169p. 1983. 35.00 (0-910586-52-7, 054-83) Finan Exec.

Summary Social, Economic, & Housing Characteristics for the U. S. (Illus.). 110p. (Orig.). (C). 1993. pap. text ed. 30.00 (1-56806-461-6) DIANE Pub.

Summary View of the Courses of Crops in the Husbandry of England & Maryland. John B. Bordley. LC 72-89075. (Rural America Ser.). 1973. reprint ed. 8.00 (0-8420-1477-2) Scholarly Res Inc.

Summary View of the Millennial Church, or United Society of Believers, Commonly Called Shakers. Shakers Staff. LC 72-2993. reprint ed. 57.50 (0-404-10755-9) AMS Pr.

Summary View of the Rights of British America. Thomas Jefferson. 1976. pap. 5.00 (0-940550-07-5) Caxton Club.

Summary View of the Rights of British America. Thomas Jefferson. LC 76-2728. 1977. reprint ed. 50.00 (0-8201-1170-8) Schol Facsimiles.

Summated Rating Scale Construction: An Introduction. Paul E. Spector. (Quantitative Applications in the Social Sciences Ser.: Vol. 82). (Illus.). 96p. (C). 1992. pap. text ed. 9.95 (0-8039-4341-5) Sage.

Summation. Lawrence J. Smith. (Art of Advocacy Ser.). 1978. ring bd. write for info. (0-8205-1030-0); Updates. write for info. (0-318-67988-4) Bender.

Summation Theorems in Structural Stability. Ed. by T. Tarnai. (International Centre for Mechanical Sciences Ser.: No. 354). 222p. 1995. 75.95 (3-211-82704-8) Spr-Verlag.

Summations. Saul Bellow. (Chapbooks in Literature Ser.). 29p. 1987. pap. text ed. 5.00 (0-9614940-9-3) Bennington Coll.

Summe & Substance of the Conference. William Barlow. LC 65-10395. 1965. reprint ed. 50.00 (0-8201-1004-3) Schol Facsimiles.

Summe & Substance of the Conference at Hampton Court, January 14, 1603. William Barlow. LC 74-28829. (English Experience Ser.: No. 711). 1975. reprint ed. 30.00 (90-221-0711-6) Walter J Johnson.

Summer. 1995. 3.98 (0-7858-0301-7) Bk Sales Inc.

Summer. Richard L. Allington & Kathleen Krull. LC 80-25097. (Beginning to Learn about Ser.). (Illus.). 32p. (J). (gr. k-3). 1985. pap. 3.95 (0-8114-8241-3) Raintree Steck-V.

Summer. Nicola Baxter. LC 95-50048. (Toppers Ser.). 24p. (J). 1996. lib. bdg. 15.00 (0-516-09275-8) Childrens.

***Summer.** Nicola Baxter. (Toppers Ser.). 24p. (J). 1997. pap. 4.95 (0-516-26087-1) Childrens.

***Summer.** Karen Bryant-Mole. (Picture This! Ser.). (J). 1997. lib. bdg. write for info. (1-57572-056-6) Rigby Interact Libr.

***Summer.** Gillian Chapman. LC 97-17160. (Seasonal Crafts Ser.). (J). 1997. write for info. (0-8172-4873-0) Raintree Steck-V.

Summer. Chris L. Demarest. 1997. pap. 4.95 (0-15-201391-1) HarBrace.

Summer. Alice Gordon. 1992. pap. 20.00 (0-201-57702-X) Addison-Wesley.

Summer. Ron Hirschi. LC 90-19596. (Illus.). 32p. (J). (ps-3). 1991. pap. 14.99 (0-525-65054-7, Cobblehill Bks) Dutton Child Bks.

Summer. Louis Santrey. LC 82-19384. (Discovering the Seasons Ser.). (Illus.). 32p. (J). (gr. 4-7). 1983. lib. bdg. 11.50 (0-89375-911-2) Troll Communs.

Summer. Lynn M. Stone. LC 93-39058. (As the World Turns Ser.). (J). 1994. write for info. (1-55916-020-9) Rourke Bk Co.

Summer. Ruth Thomson. LC 94-12308. (Get Set...Go! Ser.). (Illus.). 24p. (J). (gr. 1 up). 1994. lib. bdg. 15.40 (0-516-07996-4) Childrens.

Summer. Ruth Thomson. LC 94-12308. (Get Set...Go! Ser.). (Illus.). 24p. (J). (ps-3). 1994. pap. 4.95 (0-516-47996-2) Childrens.

Summer. David Webster. (Exploring Nature Around the Year Ser.). (Illus.). 48p. (J). (gr. 2-4). 1990. pap. 4.95 (0-671-65984-7, Julian Messner) Silver Burdett Pr.

***Summer.** Joanne Weir. (Williams-Sonoma Celebration Ser.). 1997. 21.95 (0-614-27962-3) Time-Life.

Summer. Edith Wharton. 224p. 1993. pap. 3.95 (0-553-21422-5) Bantam.

Summer. Edith Wharton. (Twentieth Century Classics Ser.). 320p. 1987. pap. 4.95 (0-02-055440-0) Macmillan.

Summer. Edith Wharton. 208p. 1993. pap. 4.95 (0-451-52566-3, Sig Classics) NAL-Dutton.

Summer. Edith Wharton. LC 93-18329. 224p. 1993. pap. 9.95 (0-14-018679-4, Penguin Classics) Viking Penguin.

***Summer.** Edith Wharton. lib. bdg. 20.95 (0-8488-1876-8) Amereon Ltd.

Summer. large type ed. Edith Wharton. 1996. lib. bdg. 20.00 (0-7838-1831-9, GK Hall) Thorndike Pr.

Summer. Edith Wharton. 318p. 1991. reprint ed. lib. bdg. 25.00 (0-8095-9073-5) Borgo Pr.

Summer. Edith Wharton. LC 73-115288. 1970. reprint ed. 59.00 (0-403-00259-1) Scholarly.

***Summer: Recipes Inspired by Nature's Bounty.** Joanne Weir. LC 96-35496. (Williams-Sonoma Seasonal Celebration Ser.). 1997. write for info. (0-7835-4607-6) Time-Life.

***Summer: Recipes Inspired by Nature's Bounty.** Joanne Weir. LC 96-35496. (Williams-Sonoma Seasonal Celebration Ser.). 1997. write for info. (1-887451-09-9) Wldon Owen Ref.

Summer Special Edition: Spring Break Special Edition. Katherine Applegate. (YA). (gr. 7 up). 1996. pap. 3.99 (0-671-51041-X, Archway) PB.

Summer see Growing Strong in the Seasons of Life: A Season of Reverance

Summer, a Growing Time. Janet McDonnell. LC 93-1182. (Four Seasons Ser.). (Illus.). 32p. (J). (ps-2). 1993. lib. bdg. 17.40 (0-516-00678-9) Childrens.

Summer Activities. 1988. pap. 14.95 (0-590-70949-6, Scholastic Hardcover) Scholastic Inc.

Summer Activity Book. Clare Beaton. (J). (ps-3). 1994. pap. 4.95 (0-8120-1959-8) Barron.

Summer Adventures. Curtis Casewit. 288p. 1994. pap. 13.00 (0-02-079331-6) Macmillan.

Summer after Summer. Richard Sullivan. 1978. 28.95 (0-405-10860-5, 11858) Ayer.

Summer Ago. George Scarborough. LC 86-6758. 214p. 1986. 13.95 (0-918518-46-6) Iris Pr.

Summer Aide. Jack Rudman. (Career Examination Ser.: C-1498). 1994. pap. 23.95 (0-8373-1498-4) Nat Learn.

Summer Air Conditioning. Seichi Konzo et al. 554p. reprint ed. pap. 157.90 (0-317-10814-X, 2003090) Bks Demand.

Summer & Shiner. Nolan Carlson. LC 92-71256. (Illus.). 158p. (YA). 1992. pap. 6.95 (0-9627947-4-0) Hearth KS.

Summer & Smoke. Tennessee Williams. 1950. pap. 5.25 (0-8222-1097-5) Dramatists Play.

Summer & Smoke see Four Plays

Summer & Smoke see Best American Plays: Third Series, 1945-51

Summer & Winter. Harriet Tidball. LC 76-24010. (Guild Monographs: No. 19). (Illus.). 58p. 1966. pap. 9.95 (0-916658-19-8) Shuttle Craft.

Summer & Winter: A Weave for All Seasons. Donna Sullivan. LC 91-3985. (Illus.). 112p. (Orig.). 1991. pap. 16.95 (0-934026-51-3) Interweave.

Summer Anthology 1993. (S.O.M.O.S. Summer Writers Ser.). 32p. 1993. pap. 6.00 (1-883968-00-3) Blinking Yellow.

Summer at Lonely Beach & Other Stories. Miriam Waddington. 108p. 1995. lib. bdg. 27.00 (0-8095-4587-X) Borgo Pr.

Summer at Lonely Beach & Other Stories. Miriam Waddington. 108p. pap. 8.95 (0-88962-158-6) Mosaic.

Summer at Saint Pierre. large type ed. Pat Lacey. 1991. pap. 15.99 (0-7089-6979-8, Trailtree Bookshop) Ulverscroft.

Summer at the Lake. Andrew M. Greeley. LC 96-6566. 1997. 24.95 (0-312-86082-X) Forge NYC.

***Summer at the Resort: Remembering the Fifties.** rev. ed. Henry G. Starnes. Ed. by Robert Epps. 250p. 1997. pap. 12.00 (0-9657613-0-4) Starnes Pub.

Summer at Willowbank. large type ed. Ivy Preston. (Romance Ser.). 1994. pap. 15.99 (0-7089-7611-5, Linford) Ulverscroft.

Summer Atlas of North American Birds. Ed. by Jeff Price et al. (Illus.). 364p. 1995. text ed. 47.95 (0-12-564660-7) Acad Pr.

Summer Awakening. large type ed. Eric Malpass. 336p. 1983. 25.99 (0-7089-0961-2) Ulverscroft.

Summer Before Dark. Doris Lessing. LC 82-40421. 256p. 1983. pap. 9.00 (0-394-71095-9, Vin) Random.

Summer before the Summer of Love. Marly Swick. LC 95-21750. 224p. 1995. 21.00 (0-06-017254-1, HarpT) HarpC.

Summer before the Summer of Love. Marly Swick. 224p. 1996. pap. 12.00 (0-06-092730-5, PL) HarpC.

Summer Bird Cage. 192p. 1985. pap. 8.95 (0-452-26050-7, Plume) NAL-Dutton.

Summer Bird-Cage. Margaret Drabble. 1985. mass mkt. 6.95 (0-452-25761-1, Plume) NAL-Dutton.

Summer Bird Feeding: Audubon Workshop Guide to Feeding Wild Birds in Summer. John V. Dennis. (Illus.). 130p. 1989. pap. 9.95 (0-9620001-0-8) Audubon Workshop.

Summer Blue: A Novel. Floyd Skloot. LC 94-43106. 218p. 18.95 (0-934257-08-6) Story Line.

Summer Book: From the Heart of the Home. Susan Branch. LC 94-23703. 1995. 23.95 (0-316-10666-6) Little.

***Summer Book Party Package from the Heart of the Home.** Susan Branch. 1997. 23.95 (0-316-10577-5) Little.

Summer Brave. William Inge. Orig. Title: Picnic. 1979. pap. 5.25 (0-8222-1098-3) Dramatists Play.

Summer Bridge Activities: Kindergarten to 1st Grade. Julia A. Hobbs et al. Ed. by J. Wood. (Illus.). 157p. 1995. student ed. 12.95 (1-887923-03-9) Rainbow UT.

Summer Bridge Activities: Preschool to Kindergarten. Julia A. Hobbs et al. Ed. by J. Wood. (Illus.). 139p. 1995. student ed. 12.95 (1-887923-02-0) Rainbow UT.

Summer Bridge Activities: 1st Grade to 2nd Grade. Julia A. Hobbs et al. Ed. by J. Wood. (Illus.). 174p. 1995. student ed. 12.95 (1-887923-04-7) Rainbow UT.

Summer Bridge Activities: 2nd Grade to 3rd Grade. Julia A. Hobbs et al. Ed. by J. Wood. (Illus.). 176p. 1995. student ed. 12.95 (1-887923-05-5) Rainbow UT.

Summer Bridge Activities: 3rd Grade to 4th Grade. Julia A. Hobbs et al. Ed. by J. Wood. (Illus.). 172p. 1995. student ed. 12.95 (1-887923-06-3) Rainbow UT.

Summer Bridge Activities: 4th Grade to 5th Grade. Julia A. Hobbs et al. (Illus.). 180p. (Orig.). 1995. student ed. 12.95 (1-887923-00-4) Rainbow UT.

Summer Bridge Activities Vol. 7: 5th Grade to 6th Grade. Julia A. Hobbs et al. Ed. by Michelle D. Van Leeuwen. (Illus.). 204p. (Orig.). (J). (gr. 5-6). 1996. wbk. ed., pap. 12.95 (1-887923-08-X) Rainbow UT.

Summer Camp. Bobbie Kalman. (Crabapple Ser.). (Illus.). 32p. (J). (ps-3). 1995. lib. bdg. 18.08 (0-86505-620-X) Crabtree Pub Co.

Summer Camp. Bobbie Kalman. (Crabapple Ser.). (Illus.). 32p. (J). (ps-3). 1995. pap. 5.95 (0-86505-720-6) Crabtree Pub Co.

Summer Camp: Great Camps of Algonquin. Liz Lundell. 1995. 42.95 (1-55046-092-7) Genl Dist Srvs.

Summer Camp Creeps. Tim Schoch. 160p. (Orig.). (J). (gr. 3-7). 1987. pap. 2.95 (0-380-75343-X, Camelot) Avon.

***Summer Camp, Ready or Not!** Sandra Belton. (Ernestine & Amanda Ser.). (Illus.). (J). (gr. 3-7). 1997. 16.00 (0-614-29071-6) S&S Childrens.

Summer Camp Scars. David B. Smith. (J). (gr. 7-10). 1994. 5.99 (0-8280-0855-8) Review & Herald.

Summer Campaign. Carla Kelly. 240p. (Orig.). 1989. pap. 3.99 (0-451-15836-9, Sig) NAL-Dutton.

Summer Camps in Canada: A Complete Guide to the Best Summer Camps for Kids & Teenagers. Ann West. 310p. (Orig.). 1995. pap. 15.95 (1-896095-05-4, Pub. by Polestar Bk Pubs CN) Orca Bk Pubs.

Summer Celestial. Stanley Plumly. (American Poetry Ser.: No. 27). 75p. (C). 1985. pap. 7.50 (0-88001-084-3) Ecco Pr.

***Summer Charade.** large type ed. Melinda Hammond. (Linford Romance Large Print Ser.). 304p. 1997. pap. 16.99 (0-7089-5120-1, Linford) Ulverscroft.

Summer Children: Ready or Not for School. 4th ed. James K. Uphoff et al. (Illus.). 114p. 1990. pap. 12.95 (0-9618561-0-6) J&J Pub Co.

Summer City by the Sea. Emil R. Salvini. 1995. 27.95 (0-8135-2261-7) Rutgers U Pr.

Summer Clouds. large type ed. Nina Cariston. 352p. 1996. 25.99 (0-7089-3479-X) Ulverscroft.

Summer Coat, Winter Coat: The Story of a Snowshoe Hare. Doe Boyle. LC 93-13356. (Smithsonian Wild Heritage Collection). (Illus.). 32p. (J). (gr. k-3). 1993. 11.95 (1-56899-015-4); 16.95 incl. audio (1-56899-014-6); audio write for info. (1-56899-016-2) Soundprints.

Summer Coat, Winter Coat: The Story of a Snowshoe Hare. Doe Boyle. (Smithsonian Wild Heritage Collection). (Illus.). 32p. (J). 1995. pap. 4.95 (1-56899-198-3) Soundprints.

Summer Coat, Winter Coat: The Story of a Snowshoe Hare, Incl. toy. Doe Boyle. LC 93-13356. (Smithsonian Wild Heritage Collection). (Illus.). 32p. (J). (gr. k-3). 1993. 25.95 incl. audio (1-56899-018-9); 25.95 incl. audio (1-56899-013-8) Soundprints.

Summer Coat, Winter Coat: The Story of a Snowshoe Hare, Incl. toy. Doe Boyle. (Smithsonian Wild Heritage Collection). (Illus.). 32p. (J). 1995. pap. 14.95 (1-56899-204-1); pap. 14.95 (1-56899-209-2) Soundprints.

Summer Conference. Sarah Winston. LC 90-55171. 224p. 1991. 17.95 (0-8453-4829-9, Cornwall Bks) Assoc Univ Prs.

Summer Cooking with Herbs. Margaret Roberts. LC 94-8636. (Illus.). 104p. 1994. pap. 10.95 (0-8117-3070-0) Stackpole.

Summer Cool: A Jack Paine Mystery. Al Sarrantonio. LC 92-38253. 220p. 1993. 19.95 (0-8027-3235-6) Walker & Co.

Summer Cottages of Edwin Hale Lincoln. Ed. by SnO Publications Staff. (Illus.). 72p. (Orig.). 1981. pap. 15.00 (0-685-04620-6) SnO Pubns.

Summer Cottages of Edwin Hale Lincoln see Pride of Palaces: Lenox Summer Cottages 1883-1933

Summer Cypress. large type ed. Pamela Hill. (Linford Romance Library). 336p. 1995. pap. 15.99 (0-7089-7725-1, Linford) Ulverscroft.

Summer Darkness, Winter Light. Sylvia Halliday. 384p. 1996. mass mkt. 4.99 (0-8217-5260-X, Zebra Kensgtn) Kensgtn Pub Corp.

***Summer Day.** Douglas Florian. (J). Date not set. write for info. (0-688-07584-3); lib. bdg. write for info. (0-688-07585-1) Greenwillow.

Summer Day. Douglas Florian. LC 87-8484. (Illus.). 24p. (J). (ps-1). 1988. 12.95 (0-688-07564-9); lib. bdg. 12.88 (0-688-07565-7) Greenwillow.

Summer Day Is Done. large type ed. Robert T. Stevens. 816p. 1996. 25.99 (0-7089-3510-9) Ulverscroft.

Summer Days. R. Pare. (Illus.). 24p. (J). (ps-8). 1988. 14.95 (1-55037-043-X, Pub. by Annick CN); pap. 4.95 (1-55037-044-8, Pub. by Annick CN) Firefly Bks Ltd.

Summer Days Gone: Thoughts & Reflections. J. P. Ballard. 37p. (Orig.). 1987. pap. text ed. 5.00 (0-9620563-0-8) Common Mans Symposium.

Summer Days with the Treelo Triplets. Mary M. Landis. 192p. 1971. 7.05 (0-686-05591-8) Rod & Staff.

***Summer Daze, Sister Sister.** Quin Harkin. (J). 1997. pap. 3.99 (0-671-00287-2) S&S Trade.

Summer Delights: Cooking with Fresh Herbs. Noel Richardson. (Illus.). 128p. 1986. spiral bd. 9.95 (0-317-60787-1) Aris Bks.

S

S

Summer Delights: Growing & Cooking Fresh Herbs. Noel Richardson. 1994. pap. text ed. 12.95 (*1-895099-47-1*) Gr Arts Ctr Pub.

Summer Desserts. Nora Roberts. (NR Flowers Ser.: No. 23). 1993. mass mkt. 3.59 (*0-373-51023-3*, 5-51023-5) Silhouette.

***Summer Dreams.** 1997. pap. text ed. 4.97 (*1-55748-980-7*) Barbour & Co.

Summer Dresses. Stephanie Hallgren. Ed. by Desert First Works, Inc. 1977. pap. text ed. 2.50 (*0-916556-08-5*) Desert First.

***Summer Driftings among the Lakes.** Frank H. Taylor. (Illus.). 70p. reprint ed. pap. 9.95 (*0-614-26397-2*) Purple Mnt Pr.

Summer Employment Examination. Jack Rudman. (Career Examination Ser.: C-1663). 1994. reprint ed. pap. 23.95 (*0-8373-1663-4*) Nat Learn.

***Summer Engagement.** Emma Stirling. 160p. 1996. 22.00 (*0-7278-4995-6*) Severn Hse.

***Summer Engagement.** large type ed. Emma Stirling. (Ulverscroft Large Print Ser.). 288p. 1997. 27.50 (*0-7089-3765-9*) Ulverscroft.

Summer, Fall, Winter, Spring. (Sesame Street Ser.: No. 18). (J). 1989. pap. 1.49 (*0-553-18401-6*) Bantam.

***Summer Fancy.** Anne Avery. 1997. pap. 5.99 (*0-451-40739-3*, Onyx) NAL-Dutton.

Summer Festivals. Richard Carbotti. (Geronomo Pack Ser.). 8p. (J). (gr. k-2). 1993. pap. write for info. (*1-882563-09-3*) Lamont Bks.

Summer Fill-In Book. Ann M. Martin. (Baby-sitters Little Sister Ser.). 96p. (J). (gr. 2-4). 1995. pap. 2.95 (*0-590-26467-2*) Scholastic Inc.

Summer Folks 'n Year-Round Neighbors: The Bayshore's History Settlement to the 1950s. Ed. by Ann Doud. LC 92-61252. (Illus.). 340p. 1992. lib. bdg. 40.00 (*0-9633751-0-5*) TX Marquee Pub.

Summer Folks 'n Year-Round Neighbors, Vol. 2: The Bayshore's History, Settlement to 1962. Ed. by Linda Bahner-Duncan. LC 92-61252. (Illus.). 350p. 1995. lib. bdg. write for info. (*0-9633751-2-1*) TX Marquee Pub.

Summer Folly. Mary Kingsley. 352p. 1992. mass mkt. 3.99 (*0-8217-3808-9*, Zebra Kensgtn) Kensgtn Pub Corp.

Summer Folly. large type ed. Carol H. Dyke. 1991. pap. 15.99 (*0-7089-6976-3*) Ulverscroft.

Summer for Always. Laura A. Sonnenmark. 160p. (Orig.). (YA). 1995. mass mkt. 3.99 (*0-380-78028-3*, Flare) Avon.

Summer for Secrets. Lou Kassem. 112p. (J). 1989. pap. 2.95 (*0-380-75759-1*, Camelot) Avon.

***Summer for the Gods: The Scopes Trial & America's Continuing Debate over Science & Religion.** Edward J. Larson. LC 97-9648. 336p. 1997. 25.00 (*0-465-07509-6*) Basic.

Summer for Weddings, Vol. 17. Hilda Stahl. (Elizabeth Gail Ser.: Vol. 13). 128p. (YA). (gr. 5 up). 1989. pap. 5.99 (*0-8423-0811-3*) Tyndale.

Summer Frolics. Martin Pyx. (Orig.). 1989. mass mkt. 4.50 (*0-929654-14-5*, 52) Blue Moon Bks.

Summer Fruit. Edon Waycott. 14.95 (*0-00-225106-X*, HarpT) HarpC.

Summer Fruit: Sermons for Pentecost, Middle Third - First Lesson. Richard L. Sheffield. LC 94-1004. (Orig.). 1994. pap. 7.75 (*0-7880-0040-3*) CSS OH.

Summer Fun. Owl Magazine Editors. (Illus.). 128p. (J). (gr. 4 up). 1992. pap. 8.95 (*0-919872-87-5*, Pub. by Greey dePencier CN) Firefly Bks Ltd.

Summer Fun Jumbles: Lazy Day Word Play. (Jumble Ser.). (Illus.). 192p. (Orig.). 1996. pap. 9.95 (*1-57243-114-8*) Triumph Bks.

Summer Furniture: Practical Designs for the Backyard. Thomas Carpenter. (Illus.). 144p. 1994. pap. 18.95 (*0-921820-89-5*, Pub. by Camden Hse CN) Firefly Bks Ltd.

Summer Games: An Olympic Murder Mystery. Sabrina Wylly. LC 96-24569. 288p. 1996. 23.00 (*1-881320-84-7*, Black Belt) Black Belt Comm.

Summer Games for Adults & Children. Hereward Zigo. (Games & Pastimes Ser.: Vol. 6). (Illus.). 64p. 1982. 9.95 (*0-906672-05-8*) Oleander Pr.

Summer Games for Adults & Children. Hereward Zigo. (Games & Pastimes Ser.: Vol. 6). (Illus.). 64p. (J). 1982. pap. 4.95 (*0-906672-06-6*) Oleander Pr.

***Summer Garden: Planning, Preparing, Enjoying.** Jill Billington. 1997. 24.95 (*0-7063-7455-X*) Ward Lock Ltd UK.

Summer Garden Glory: How to Get the Best from Your Garden from Spring Through Autumn. Adrian Bloom. (Illus.). 144p. 1996. 27.00 (*0-00-412744-7*, Pub. by HarpC UK) HarpC.

Summer Gold. John N. Dwyer. LC 70-163364. 72p. 1971. pap. 5.00 (*0-87839-006-5*) North Star.

Summer Hawk. Richard A. Bunch. Ed. by Edward Mycue. (Took Modern Poetry in English Ser.: No. 21). (Illus.). 28p. (Orig.). 1991. pap. 3.00 (*1-879457-23-7*) Norton Coker Pr.

Summer Helmets of the U. S. Army, 1875-1910. 2nd ed. Gordon Chappell. (Illus.). 34p. 1976. reprint ed. pap. 2.00 (*0-943398-05-3*) Wyoming St Mus.

Summer Holds Too Long & Rooting. Leslie C. Tompkins & Lynn H. Burgess. (Juniper Bk. Ser.: No. 52). 50p. 1988. pap. 9.00 (*1-55780-099-5*) Juniper Pr WI.

***Summer Horse.** Bonnie Bryant. (Saddle Club Ser.: No. 67). (YA). 1997. pap. 3.99 (*0-553-48422-2*) Bantam.

Summer House. Alice Thomas Ellis. 352p. 1993. pap. 10.95 (*0-14-023876-X*, Penguin Bks) Viking Penguin.

***Summer House.** Allison McLeay. 1997. 23.95 (*0-312-15666-9*) St Martin.

***Summer House Loon.** large type ed. Anne Fine. (J). 1997. 16.95 (*0-7451-6971-6*, Galaxy Child Lrg Print) Chivers N Amer.

Summer House Sampler: A Collection of Memories & Recipes of Wynnton Elementary School. Ed. by Mimi P. Childs. 264p. 1992. 14.95 (*0-9634091-0-7*) Summer Hse Pr.

Summer Hunting a Prince: The Escape of Charles Edward Stuart. Acair Ltd. Staff. 96p. (C). 1992. text ed. 35.00 (*0-86152-873-5*, Pub. by Acair Ltd UK) St Mut.

Summer I Shrank My Grandmother. Elvira Woodruff. 160p. (J). (gr. 4-7). 1992. pap. 3.99 (*0-440-40640-4*, YB BDD) BDD Bks Young Read.

Summer Ice: Life along the Antarctic Peninsula. Bruce McMillan. LC 93-38831. (Illus.). 48p. (J). (gr. 2-5). 1995. 15.95 (*0-395-66561-2*) HM.

Summer Idea Book: A Creative Idea Book for the Elementary Teacher, Ps-6. Karen Sevaly & Margaret Bolz. (Illus.). 112p. (Orig.). 1990. pap. text ed. 9.95 (*0-943263-17-4*, TF-1604) Teachers Friend Pubns.

Summer in a Jar: Making Pickles, Jams & More. Andrea Chesman. Ed. by Susan Williamson. LC 85-6543. (Illus.). 160p. 1985. pap. 8.95 (*0-913589-14-4*) Williamson Pub Co.

***Summer in America.** Amy W. Cross. (Illus.). 128p. 12.98 (*0-8317-7887-3*) Smithmark.

Summer in Arcady. James L. Allen. (Principle Works of James Lane Allen). 1989. reprint ed. lib. bdg. 79.00 (*0-7812-1731-8*) Rprt Serv.

Summer in Eden. large type ed. Alison A. York. 271p. 1993. 25.99 (*0-7505-0576-1*) Ulverscroft.

Summer in El Salvador. Larry K. Jones. Ed. by Tom McKernan. 310p. 1988. 19.95 (*0-940513-00-5*) World Promos.

Summer in Italy. Sean O'Faolain. 12.95 (*0-8159-6831-0*) Devin.

Summer in the Balkans: Laughter & Tears after Communism. Randall Baker. LC 94-21108. (Books for a World That Works). (Illus.). vi, 202p. 1994. 42.00 (*1-56549-037-1*); pap. 14.95 (*1-56549-036-3*) Kumarian Pr.

Summer in the Spring: Anishinaabe Lyric Poems & Stories. Ed. by Gerald Vizenor. LC 92-32561. (American Indian Literature & Critical Studies: Vol. 6). 1993. pap. 8.95 (*0-8061-2518-7*) U of Okla Pr.

Summer in the Wood. Janet Fitzgerald. (Science Through the Seasons Ser.). (Illus.). 32p. (J). (gr. 1-3). 1991. 15.95 (*0-237-60217-2*, Pub. by Evans Bros Ltd UK) Trafalgar.

Summer in Vermont. large type ed. Rebecca Marsh. LC 93-27184. 1994. lib. bdg. 13.95 (*0-7862-0048-0*) Thorndike Pr.

Summer in Williamsburg. Daniel Fuchs. 380p. 1983. pap., 8.95 (*0-88184-006-8*) Carroll & Graf.

Summer Institute of Linguistics: Its Works & Contributions. Ed. by Ruth M. Brend & Kenneth L. Pike. 1977. pap. 66.15 (*90-279-3355-3*) Mouton.

Summer Intern. Jack Rudman. (Career Examination Ser.: C-1499). 1994. pap. 23.95 (*0-8373-1499-2*) Nat Learn.

Summer Is a Foreign Land: A Play. E. M. Broner. LC 66-21031. 144p. reprint ed. pap. 41.10 (*0-7837-3827-7*, 2043648) Bks Demand.

Summer Is from Winter Until Winter. Sigrid Olesen. (Illus.). 80p. (C). 1980. 4.95 (*0-936748-02-8*); pap. 3.50 (*0-685-01610-2*) Fade In.

Summer Job. Patricia Lakin. LC 94-19720. (My Community Ser.). (Illus.). (J). 1995. lib. bdg. 21.40 (*0-8114-8259-6*) Raintree Steck-V.

Summer Jobs. Aidel Stein. (Baker's Dozen Ser.: No. 14). 155p. (Orig.). (J). 1995. pap. 7.95 (*1-56871-075-5*) Targum Pr.

***Summer Jobs Britain: 1997.** 28th ed. 256p. 1997. pap. 15.95 (*1-85458-156-2*) Petersons.

***Summer Jobs for Students.** 47th ed. Peterson's Staff. (Peterson's Guides Ser.). 1997. pap. text ed. 16.95 (*1-56079-836-X*) Petersons.

Summer Jobs for Students 1996: Where the Jobs Are & How to Get Them. 45th ed. Peterson's Staff. 360p. (C). 1995. pap. 13.95 (*1-56079-495-X*) Petersons.

Summer Jobs for Students 1997. 46th rev. ed. Ed. by Peterson's Staff. 360p. 1996. pap. 16.95 (*1-56079-660-X*) Petersons.

Summer Jobs U. S. A. 1995. 44th ed. 310p. (YA). 1994. pap. 16.95 (*1-56079-397-X*) Petersons.

Summer Journey in the West. Eliza R. Steele. LC 75-123. (Mid-American Frontier Ser.). 1975. reprint ed. 26.95 (*0-405-06888-3*) Ayer.

Summer Key to Trees of Tennessee & the Great Smokies. Royal E. Shanks & Aaron J. Sharp. 24p. 1963. pap. 3.50 (*0-87049-040-0*) U of Tenn Pr.

Summer Kid. Myrna N. Levy. (J). (gr. 1-5). 1991. pap. 5.95 (*0-929005-20-1*, Pub. by Second Story Pr CN) LPC InBook.

Summer King, Winter Fool. Lisa Goldstein. 288p. 1995. mass mkt. 4.99 (*0-8125-3504-9*) Tor Bks.

Summer King, Winter Fool. Lisa Goldstein. 288p. 1995. 4.99 (*0-8125-3503-0*) Tor Bks.

Summer Kitchen. Sandra M. Gilbert & Barbara Hazzard. LC 83-81453. (Illus.). 48p. (Orig.). 1983. pap. 15.00 (*0-940592-14-2*) Heyeck Pr.

Summer Land. Dan Parkinson. 352p. 1989. mass mkt. 3.95 (*0-8217-2683-8*, Zebra Kensgtn) Kensgtn Pub Corp.

Summer Law Study Programs, Nineteen Eighty-Eight: Student Guide to Summer Law Study Programs Offered Throughout the World. 9th rev. ed. Ellen K. Wayne. LC 80-645058. 1988. pap. 17.50 (*0-318-35051-3*) Jt Comm Law Study.

Summer Legs. Anita Hakkinen. (J). 1995. 14.95 (*0-8050-2262-7*) H Holt & Co.

Summer Life. Gary Soto. 160p. (J). 1991. mass mkt. 3.99 (*0-440-21024-0*) Dell.

Summer Light. Roxana Robinson. LC 95-32560. (Hardscrabble Bks.). 211p. (C). 1995. pap. 12.95 (*0-87451-738-9*) U Pr of New Eng.

Summer Lightning. Lydia Browne. 320p. (Orig.). 1995. mass mkt. 4.99 (*0-515-11657-2*) Jove Pubns.

Summer Lightning. Wendy C. Staub. 240p. (J). 1993. mass mkt. 3.50 (*0-06-106778-4*, Harp PBks) HarpC.

Summer Lightning. P. G. Wodehouse. (Fiction Ser.). 256p. 1985. pap. 8.95 (*0-14-000995-7*, Penguin Bks) Viking Penguin.

Summer Like Turnips. LouAnn Gaeddert. LC 88-37380. 80p. (J). (gr. 2-4). 1989. 13.95 (*0-8050-0839-X*, Bks Young Read) H Holt & Co.

Summer Liturgy: A Verse Play. Jeremy Ingalls. LC 85-70744. 136p. (Orig.). 1985. pap. 9.95 (*0-9610662-3-7*) Capstone Edns.

Summer Living: A Cookbook Designed for Easy Summer Living. Ed. by Susan P. Snow. (Illus.). 192p. (Orig.). 1989. pap. text ed. 12.95 (*0-927494-00-0*) Quality Living.

***Summer Love.** Janelle Taylor et al. 352p. 1997. mass mkt. 6.50 (*0-8217-5659-1*, Zebra Kensgtn) Kensgtn Pub Corp.

***Summer Lovers: Strange Bedfellows; First, Best & Only; Granite Man.** Janet Dailey et al. 1997. pap. 9.99 (*0-373-83352-0*, 1-83352-4) Harlequin Bks.

Summer Madness. Susan Lewis. 480p. 1995. mass mkt. 5.99 (*0-06-100562-2*, Harp PBks) HarpC.

Summer Mahogany. large type ed. Janet Dailey. 1995. 20.95 (*0-7862-0349-8*) Thorndike Pr.

Summer Mastitis. Ed. by G. Thomas et al. (Current Topics in Veterinary Medicine & Animal Science Ser.). (C). 1987. lib. bdg. 110.00 (*0-89838-982-8*) Kluwer Ac.

Summer Meditations. Vaclav Havel. 1993. pap. 11.00 (*0-394-28008-3*) Random.

Summer Meditations. Vaclav Havel. Tr. by Paul Wilson from CZE. LC 92-50602. 1993. pap. 12.00 (*0-679-74497-5*, Vin) Random.

Summer Meditations with Native American Elders. Don Coyhis. LC 95-79099. (Meditations with Native American Elders Ser.). 106p. 1995. reprint ed. pap. 9.95 (*1-887874-01-1*) Moh-He-Con-Nuck.

Summer Migrations & Resorts of South Carolina Low-Country Planters. Lawrence F. Brewster. LC 76-115992. (Trinity College Historical Papers: No. 26). reprint ed. 39.50 (*0-404-51776-5*) AMS Pr.

Summer Mockery: The Racial Disturbance in Milwaukee, WI - Summer 1967. Helen Weber. 108p. (Orig.). 1986. pap. 6.95 (*0-9616414-0-1*) Summer Mockery.

Summer Moonshine. P. G. Wodehouse. 240p. 1991. pap. 8.95 (*0-14-002547-2*, Penguin Bks) Viking Penguin.

***Summer Mystagogia.** Bruce Beasley. 96p. (Orig.). 1996. pap. 12.95 (*0-87081-438-9*) Univ Pr Colo.

Summer, Nantucket Drawings. Rose Gonnella. LC 95-94228. (Illus.). 80p. (Orig.). 1995. pap. 24.95 (*0-9646417-0-4*) Waterborn Grp.

Summer Nights. Caroline B. Cooney. (Point Romance Ser.). 176p. (J). (gr. 7-9). 1992. pap. 3.25 (*0-590-45786-1*, Point) Scholastic Inc.

Summer, Nineteen Hundred Nine. Frank Benson. (Fine Art Jigsaw Puzzles Ser.). 1989. 9.95 (*0-934967-46-6*) Battle Rd Pr.

Summer of a Thousand Roses. large type ed. Joyce Bell. (Linford Romance Library). 272p. 1994. pap. 15.99 (*0-7089-7551-8*) Ulverscroft.

***Summer of Betrayal: A Novel.** Hong Ying. Tr. by Martha Avery from CHI. LC 96-51786. 208p. 1997. 22.00 (*0-374-27175-5*) FS&G.

***Summer of Black Widows.** Sherman Alexie. LC 96-9822. 144p. 1996. 22.00 (*1-882413-35-0*); pap. 13.50 (*1-882413-34-2*) Hanging Loose.

Summer of Choices. Lynn Craig. LC 94-4504. (Forever Friends Ser.: Vol. 3). (J). 1994. pap. 5.99 (*0-8407-9241-7*) Nelson.

Summer of Discontent, Seasons of Upheaval: Elite Politics & Rural Insurgency in Yucatan, 1876-1915. Allen Wells & Gilbert M. Joseph. LC 96-10471. 1996. write for info. (*0-8047-2655-8*); pap. write for info. (*0-8047-2656-6*) Stanford U Pr.

Summer of Dreams: The Story of a World's Fair Girl. (Her Story Ser.). 64p. (J). (gr. 4-6). 1993. pap. 3.95 (*0-382-24354-4*); lib. bdg. 9.95 (*0-382-24332-3*) Silver Burdett Pr.

Summer of Enlightment. Cheryl Mildenball. (Black Lace Ser.). 1995. mass mkt. 5.95 (*0-352-32937-8*, Pub. by Virgin Pub UK) London Brdge.

Summer of Fear. Lois Duncan. 224p. (YA). (gr. 7 up). 1977. mass mkt. 4.50 (*0-440-98324-X*, LLL BDD) BDD Bks Young Read.

Summer of Fear. Parker. Date not set. 4.98 (*0-8317-4640-8*) Smithmark.

Summer of Fear. T. Jefferson Parker. 1994. mass mkt. 5.99 (*0-312-95237-6*, Thomas Dunne Bks) St Martin.

***Summer of Fire.** Jill Sheldon. 400p. (Orig.). 1996. mass mkt. 3.99 (*1-85487-709-7*, Pub. by Scarlet Bks UK) London Brdge.

Summer of Fire: Yellowstone 1988. Patricia Lauber. LC 90-23032. (Illus.). 64p. (J). (gr. 4 up). 1991. 19.95 (*0-531-05943-X*) Orchard Bks Watts.

Summer of Forty-Nine. David Halberstam. 1990. mass mkt. 6.99 (*0-380-71075-7*) Avon.

Summer of Forty-Nine. David Halberstam. xvi, 352p. 1994. pap. 10.00 (*0-380-72146-5*) Avon.

Summer of Forty-Two. Herman Raucher. 1991. reprint ed. lib. bdg. 21.95 (*1-56849-079-8*) Buccaneer Bks.

Summer of Horses. Carol Fenner. LC 88-45878. 144p. (Orig.). (J). (gr. 3-6). 1989. pap. 3.99 (*0-394-80480-5*); lib. bdg. 7.99 (*0-394-90480-X*) Knopf Bks Yng Read.

Summer of Innocence. Joanette Richards. (Rainbow Romances Ser.). 160p. 1995. 14.95 (*0-7090-5497-1*, 925, Hale-Parkwest) Parkwest Pubns.

***Summer of Innocence.** large type ed. Jeanette Richards. (Linford Romance Library). 272p. 1996. pap. 15.99 (*0-7089-7905-X*) Ulverscroft.

***Summer of Jack London.** Andrew J. Fenady. 1997. mass mkt. 5.99 (*0-425-16096-3*) Berkley Pub.

Summer of Katya. Trevanian. 256p. 1984. mass mkt. 5.95 (*0-345-31486-7*) Ballantine.

Summer of Lily & Esme. John Quinn. 190p. (Orig.). (J). (gr. 6 up). 1992. pap. 8.95 (*1-85371-208-6*, Pub. by Poolbeg Pr IE) Dufour.

Summer of Love. Gene Anthony. 170p. 1995. 19.95 (*0-86719-421-9*) Last Gasp.

Summer of Love: The Inside Story of LSD, Rock & Roll, Free Love, & High Times in the Wild... Joel Selvin. 1995. pap. 12.95 (*0-452-27407-9*, Plume) NAL-Dutton.

Summer of Love: The Making of Sgt. Pepper. George Martin. (Illus.). 176p. 1994. pap. 17.95 (*0-330-34210-X*, Pub. by Pan Books UK) Trans-Atl Phila.

Summer of Madness. Marion Crook. 192p. (Orig.). (YA). 1995. pap. 6.95 (*1-55143-041-X*) Orca Bk Pubs.

***Summer of Men.** Kate Green. mass mkt. write for info. (*0-06-109101-4*, Harp PBks) HarpC.

Summer of Men. Kate Green. 352p. 1998. 22.00 (*0-06-017986-4*, HarpT) HarpC.

Summer of Missandra. Doris Schick. LC 96-31026. 128p. (Orig.). (J). (gr. 5-9). 1997. pap. 12.95 (*1-880090-35-X*) Galde Pr.

Summer of Mrs. MacGregor. Betty R. Wright. LC 86-45388. 160p. (J). (gr. 3-7). 1986. 15.95 (*0-8234-0628-8*) Holiday.

***Summer of My Amazing Luck.** Miriam Toews. 192p. 1996. pap. 16.95 (*0-88801-205-5*, Pub. by Turnstone CN) LPC InBook.

Summer of My First Pediddle. Steven Moiles. 190p. (Orig.). (YA). (gr. 9-12). 1995. pap. 5.00 (*0-88092-122-6*) Royal Fireworks.

Summer of My German Soldier. Bette Greene. 208p. (J). 1993. mass mkt. 4.99 (*0-440-21892-6*) Dell.

Summer of My German Soldier - Study Guide. Marcia Tretler. Ed. by Joyce Friedland & Rikki Kessler. (Novel-Ties Ser.). (YA). (gr. 6-9). 1993. pap. text ed. 15.95 (*0-88122-131-7*) Lrn Links.

Summer of Pure Ice. limited ed. William M. White. LC 84-70670. (Living Poets' Library: No. 29). (Illus.). 1984. 5.00 (*0-934218-29-3*) Dragons Teeth.

Summer of Rescue: A Novel. Barbara Nelson. LC 95-1262. 1995. pap. 11.00 (*0-684-80114-0*) S&S Trade.

***Summer of Sarah.** Trish Miller. 112p. (Orig.). 1997. mass mkt. 5.99 (*1-55237-392-4*, Pub. by Comnwlth Pub CN) Partners Pubs Grp.

***Summer of Secrets.** Richie T. Cusick. (YA). (gr. 7 up). Date not set. pap. 3.99 (*0-614-19319-2*, Archway) PB.

Summer of Secrets. Grace Thompson. 1994. lib. bdg. 20.00 (*0-7278-4694-9*) Severn Hse.

***Summer of Smoke.** Cameron Dokey. (J). 1997. write for info. (*0-614-29168-2*, Flare) Avon.

Summer of Stanley. Natalie Kinsey-Warnock. LC 94-22685. (Illus.). (J). 1997. pap. 14.99 (*0-525-65177-2*, Cobblehill Bks) Dutton Child Bks.

***Summer of the Black Widow.** Sherman Alexie. 1996. 22.00 (*0-614-20808-4*) Hanging Loose.

Summer of the Bonepile Monster. Aileen K. Henderson. LC 94-33725. (Illus.). 144p. (J). (gr. 3-7). 1995. 14.95 (*1-57131-603-5*); pap. 6.95 (*1-57131-602-7*) Milkweed Ed.

Summer of the Danes. Ellis Peters. 256p. 1992. mass mkt. 5.99 (*0-446-40018-1*, Mysterious Paperbk) Warner Bks.

Summer of the Dragon. Elizabeth Peters. 256p. 1980. pap. 2.25 (*0-449-24291-9*, Crest) Fawcett.

Summer of the Dragon. Elizabeth Peters. 288p. 1989. pap. 4.99 (*0-8125-0754-1*) Tor Bks.

Summer of the Falcon. Jean Craighead George. LC 62-16543. (Trophy Bk.). (Illus.). 153p. (YA). (gr. 5 up). 1979. pap. 3.95 (*0-06-440095-6*, Trophy) HarpC Child Bks.

Summer of the Falcon. Jean Craighead George. 1992. 18.00 (*0-8446-6503-7*) Peter Smith.

Summer of the Great Divide. Linda O. High. LC 95-33532. 176p. (J). (gr. 4-7). 1996. 15.95 (*0-8234-1228-8*) Holiday.

Summer of the Great-Grandmother. Madeleine L'Engle. 245p. 1974. 25.00 (*0-374-27174-7*) FS&G.

Summer of the Great Grandmother. Madeleine L'Engle. (Crosswicks Journal Trilogy Ser.). 245p. 1987. pap. 13.00 (*0-06-254506-X*) Harper SF.

***Summer of the Great-Grandmother: The Crosswicks Journal.** Madeleine L'Engle. 256p. 1996. 35.00 (*0-8095-9224-X*) Borgo Pr.

Summer of the Gun. Will Henry. 224p. 1988. pap. 2.75 (*0-380-70594-X*) Avon.

Summer of the Lost Limb. Janis Good. (Illus.). 110p. (Orig.). (J). (gr. 1-5). 1994. pap. 7.95 (*0-9640365-5-X*) Christ Recollect.

Summer of the Monkeys. Wilson Rawls. 288p. (J). (gr. 4-7). 1992. mass mkt. 4.99 (*0-553-29818-6*) Bantam.

Summer of the Monkeys. Wilson Rawls. LC 75-32295. 240p. (J). 1989. 15.95 (*0-385-11450-8*) Doubleday.

Summer of the Pestilence: A History of the Ravages of the Yellow Fever in Norfolk, Virginia A. D. 1855. 3rd ed. George D. Armstrong. LC 94-67855. 76p. 1995. pap. 10.00 (*1-57000-037-9*) W S Dawson.

Summer of the Red Ferrari. Eva Sanders. 414p. (Orig.). 1996. mass mkt. 5.99 (*0-614-17791-X*, Pub. by Comnwlth Pub CN) Partners Pubs Grp.

Summer of the Redeemers. Carolyn Haines. 1995. pap. 11.95 (*0-452-27402-8*, Plume) NAL-Dutton.

Summer of the Seventeenth Doll. Ray Lawler. LC 58-7670. (Illus.). 142p. 1958. 16.95 (*0-910278-04-0*) Boulevard.

Summer of the Sioux. large type ed. Tim Champlin. LC 93-35695. 1993. lib. bdg. 15.95 (*0-7862-0028-6*) Thorndike Pr.

Summer of the Smoke. large type ed. Luke Short. LC 93-21819. 209p. 1993. lib. bdg. 19.95 (*1-56054-234-9*) Thorndike Pr.

Summer of the Soldiers. Sandra Chastain. 416p. 1993. mass mkt. 4.99 (*1-55817-676-4*, Pinncle Kensgtn) Kensgtn Pub Corp.

Summer of the Storm. Catherine George. (Larger Print Ser.). 1995. pap. 2.99 (*0-373-15591-3*, 1-15591-0); pap. 2.99 (*0-373-03345-1*, 1-03345-5) Harlequin Bks.

Summer of the Storm. large type ed. Catherine George. 1994. 19.95 (*0-263-13930-1*) Thorndike Pr.

Summer of the Swans. (J). pap. 1.95 (*0-590-32525-6*) Scholastic Inc.

***Summer of the Swans.** Betsy Byars. (Scholastic Literature Guide Ser.). (J). 1997. pap. text ed. 3.95 (*0-590-37363-3*) Scholastic Inc.

Summer of the Swans. Betsy C. Byars. (Illus.). 144p. (J). (gr. 5-9). 1981. pap. 3.99 (*0-14-031420-2*, Puffin) Puffin Bks.

Summer of the Swans. Betsy C. Byars. (Illus.). (J). (gr. 7 up). 1970. pap. 15.99 (*0-670-68190-3*) Viking Child Bks.

Summer of the Swans: A Study Guide. Marcia Tretler. (Novel-Ties Ser.). 1985. student ed., teacher ed., pap. text ed. 15.95 (*0-88122-092-2*) Lrn Links.

Summer of '42. Herman Raucher. 23.95 (*0-8488-0310-8*) Amereon Ltd.

Summer of '82. Glen W. Gonder. Ed. by Sharon J. Gonder. 60p. 1996. lib. bdg. 5.00 (*0-614-97212-4*) Osage Bend Pub.

Summer Olympic Games: Exploring International Athletic Competition. Raymond C. Clark & Michael Jerald. (Vocabureader Workbook Ser.: No. 5). (Illus.). 96p. 1987. pap. text ed. 10.50 (*0-86647-021-2*) Pro Lingua.

Summer Olympics. Mark Littleton. (Sports Heroes Ser.). 112p. (J). (gr. 3-7). 1996. pap. 4.99 (*0-310-20266-3*) Zondervan.

Summer Olympics. William McGuire. (Great Moments in Sports Ser.). 32p. (J). (gr. 4). 1990. lib. bdg. 14.95 (*0-88682-318-8*) Creative Ed.

Summer Olympics: A Treasury of Legend & Lore. Bob Fulton. LC 96-10441. 160p. (Orig.). 1996. pap. 12.95 (*0-912083-99-9*) Diamond Communications.

Summer on Campus. 288p. 1995. pap. 15.00 (*0-87447-526-0*) College Bd.

***Summer on Choctaw Mountain.** MaryElizabeth Carpenter. LC 97-23279. (Illus.). 48p. (J). (gr. 3-6). 1997. lib. bdg. 19.95 (*1-55618-162-0*) Brunswick Pub.

***Summer on Kidd's Creek.** Robert Holland. (Illus.). 166p. (Orig.). (J). (gr. 5-10). 1997. pap. 9.95 (*0-9658523-2-6*, C-0002) Frost Hollow.

Summer on the Farm. Janet Fitzgerald. (Science Through the Seasons Ser.). (Illus.). 32p. (J). (gr. 1-3). 1991. 15.95 (*0-237-60221-0*, Pub. by Evans Bros Ltd UK) Trafalgar.

Summer on the Lakes. Margaret Fuller. (Prairie State Bks.). 180p. 1991. 10.95 (*0-252-06164-0*) U of Ill Pr.

Summer on the Lakes. Margaret F. Ossoli. LC 68-24991. (Concordance Ser.: No. 37). 1969. reprint ed. lib. bdg. 75.00 (*0-8383-0225-4*) M S G Haskell Hse.

Summer on the Plains, Eighteen Seventy: From the Diary of Annie Gibson Roberts. Ed. by Brian C. Pohanka. (Illus.). 29.50 (*0-8488-0003-6*, J M C & Co); pap. 21.95 (*0-8488-0028-1*, J M C & Co) Amereon Ltd.

Summer on the Yenesei 1914. Maud D. Haviland. LC 70-115543. (Russia Observed Ser.). (Illus.). 1971. reprint ed. 23.95 (*0-405-03081-9*) Ayer.

Summer on Wheels. Gary Soto. LC 94-18993. 176p. (J). (gr. 4-6). 1995. 13.95 (*0-590-48365-X*) Scholastic Inc.

Summer Opportunities for Kids & Teenagers 1997. 14th rev. ed. Peterson's Staff. 1207p. (Orig.). (YA). 1996. pap. 26.95 (*1-56079-587-5*) Petersons.

Summer Opportunities in Marine & Environmental Science: A Students' Guide to Jobs, Internships & Study, Camp, & Travel Programs. 2nd ed. Joy A. Herriott & Betty G. Herrin. LC 94-96000. (Illus.). 60p. (YA). (gr. 9-12). 1994. pap. 14.95 (*0-9640176-0-1*) White Pond.

Summer Party. Stephen Poliakoff. (Methuen New Theatrescripts Ser.). 59p. (C). 1988. pap. 6.95 (*0-413-47600-6*, A0279, Pub. by Methuen UK) Heinemann.

Summer Patchwork. Rusane Morrison. 1976. 1.50 (*0-685-79010-X*) Oyez.

Summer Patterns, Projects & Plans. Imogene Forte. (Illus.). 80p. (Orig.). 1991. pap. text ed. 8.95 (*0-86530-218-9*, IP 167-9) Incentive Pubns.

Summer People. Maxim Gorky. Tr. by Nicholas Saunders & Frank Dwyer. (Great Translations for Actors Ser.). 112p. 1995. pap. 11.95 (*1-880399-95-4*) Smith & Kraus.

Summer People. Shirley Jackson. 1970. pap. 3.00 (*0-87129-362-5*, S56) Dramatic Pub.

Summer People. Marge Piercy. 416p. 1990. reprint ed. mass mkt. 5.95 (*0-449-21842-2*, Crest) Fawcett.

Summer People, Winter People: A Guide to the Pueblos in the Santa Fe Area. 2nd ed. Sandra A. Edelman. LC 85-22268. (Illus.). 32p. 1986. pap. 4.95 (*0-86534-076-5*) Sunstone Pr.

***Summer Picnic.** Richard Scarry. LC 96-27258. (Busy World of Richard Scarry Ser.). (J). 1997. pap. 3.25 (*0-689-80991-3*, Aladdin Paperbacks) S&S Childrens.

Summer Plague: Polio & Its Survivors. Tony Gould. LC 94-47253. 366p. 1995. 30.00 (*0-300-06292-3*) Yale U Pr.

***Summer Plague: Polio & Its Survivors.** Tony Gould. 1997. pap. text ed. 18.00 (*0-300-07276-7*) Yale U Pr.

***Summer Pleasures.** Elizabeth Marrafino. Date not set. write for info. (*0-345-41992-8*) Ballantine.

Summer Poem. large type ed. Karen Hayes. 512p. 1995. 25.99 (*0-7089-3430-7*) Ulverscroft.

***Summer Programs at New York Colleges for Kids 8-18: 1998-1999.** 2nd ed. Carole Warsawer-Greenblatt. 1997. pap. 18.95 (*0-9651796-7-2*) Summer Prgm Pr.

Summer Programs on College Campuses - Upstate New York '96-'97: For Kids 8-18. Carole Warsawer-Greenblatt. (Illus.). 174p. (Orig.). (J). (gr. 3 up). 1995. pap. 16.95 (*1-55787-139-6*, YP96001) Summer Prgm Pr.

Summer Programs on College Campuses for Kids 8 - 18: Upstate New York 1996 - 1997. Carole Warsawer-Greenblatt. 176p. (J). (gr. 3 up). 1995. pap. 16.95 (*0-9651796-1-3*) Summer Prgm Pr.

Summer Prom Foxtrot. (Ballroom Dance Ser.). 1986. lib. bdg. 79.95 (*0-8490-3428-0*) Gordon Pr.

Summer Prom Foxtrot. (Ballroom Dance Ser.). 1985. lib. bdg. 79.00 (*0-87700-838-8*) Revisionist Pr.

Summer Promise. Robin J. Gunn. (Christy Miller Ser.: Vol. 1). 171p. (Orig.). (YA). 1989. pap. 5.99 (*0-929608-13-5*) Focus Family.

Summer Promises. Diane Schwemm. (Silver Beach Ser.: Vol. 3). 224p. (Orig.). (YA). (gr. 7 up). 1995. mass mkt. 3.99 (*0-553-56722-5*) BDD Bks Young Read.

Summer Queen. Joan D. Vinge. 992p. 1992. mass mkt. 5.99 (*0-446-36251-4*, Aspect) Warner Bks.

Summer Quest. large type ed. Anthea Edgcome. (Linford Romance Library). 272p. 1996. pap. 15.99 (*0-7089-7847-9*, Linford) Ulverscroft.

Summer Rain: A Novel. Marguerite Duras. Tr. by Barbara Bray from FRE. 160p. 1993. reprint ed. pap. 9.00 (*0-02-073040-3*) Macmillan.

Summer Range. Peggy S. Curry. 52p. (Orig.). 1981. 10.00 (*0-937160-05-9*); pap. 5.00 (*0-937160-04-0*) Hi Plains Pr.

Summer Reading Clubs: Complete Plans for 50 Theme-Based Library Programs. Martha S. Simpson. LC 91-51231. 216p. 1992. pap. text ed. 24.95 (*0-89950-721-2*) McFarland & Co.

Summer Resort Life: Tango Teas & All! Edith Gilbert & Pat McKeown. (Illus.). 120p. 1995. pap. 14.95 (*0-9600786-5-7*) Jetiquette.

Summer Rhapsody. large type ed. Nancy John. (General Ser.). 416p. 1993. 25.99 (*0-7089-2925-7*) Ulverscroft.

***Summer Rider.** Bonnie Bryant. (Saddle Club Ser.: No. 68). (YA). 1997. pap. 3.99 (*0-553-48423-0*) BDD Bks Young Read.

Summer Riders. (J). pap. 1.95 (*0-590-31838-1*) Scholastic Inc.

Summer Rock. E. Robert Bayley, Jr. LC 93-93779. 216p. (Orig.). 1994. pap. 10.00 (*1-56002-314-7*, Univ Edtns) Aegina Pr.

***Summer Roses on the Blue Mountains, 1976.** rev. ed. Date not set. pap. 3.40 (*0-614-19022-3*, BA-104) Sathya Sai Bk Ctr.

Summer Rules. Robert Lipsyte. LC 79-2816. (Ursula Nordstrom Bk.). 160p. (YA). (gr. 7 up). 1981. lib. bdg. 14.89 (*0-06-023898-4*) HarpC Child Bks.

***Summer Salads.** Joie Warner. Date not set. write for info. (*0-688-13719-9*) Hearst Bks.

Summer Sands. Sherry Garland. LC 94-6978. (Illus.). 32p. (J). (ps-3). 1995. 15.00 (*0-15-282492-8*, Gulliver Bks) HarBrace.

Summer School Kites. Janet W. Geisz. LC 93-93776. (Illus.). 64p. (J). 1994. pap. 6.00 (*1-56002-311-2*, Univ Edtns) Aegina Pr.

Summer Science Projects. John Williams. LC 96-16450. (Seasonal Science Projects Ser.). (J). 1996. pap. 5.95 (*0-382-39710-X*, Julian Messner); lib. bdg. 11.95 (*0-382-39709-6*, Julian Messner) Silver Burdett Pr.

Summer Scientific Soundings. Ed. by M. Dresden. 300p. (C). 1998. text ed. 32.00 (*981-02-0011-0*) World Scientific Pub.

Summer Secrets. Richie T. Cusick. (YA). (gr. 7 up). 1996. mass mkt. 3.99 (*0-671-54927-8*) PB.

Summer Secrets. Jean Stubbs. 1992. mass mkt. 4.99 (*0-312-92746-0*) St Martin.

Summer Secrets. large type ed. Susan Goodman. 1990. 25.99 (*0-7089-2208-2*) Ulverscroft.

Summer Secrets. large type ed. Jean Stubbs. (General Ser.). 496p. 1993. 25.99 (*0-7089-2869-2*) Ulverscroft.

Summer Seminar in Kathmandu, 1975, 9 papers. ANEF Staff. 119p. 1975. 15.00 (*0-318-17090-6*, 74) Am-Nepal Ed.

Summer Sessions in Public Two-Year Colleges. Raymond J. Young. (AACJC Monographic Ser.). (Illus.). 74p. reprint ed. pap. 25.00 (*0-7837-2478-0*, 2042633) Bks Demand.

Summer Set. David Evans. 312p. (Orig.). 1992. pap. 14.95 (*1-873741-02-2*, Pub. by Millvres Bks UK) LPC InBook.

***Summer Showers in Brindavan, 1972.** Date not set. pap. 3.25 (*0-614-19019-3*, BA-101) Sathya Sai Bk Ctr.

***Summer Showers in Brindavan, 1973.** Date not set. pap. 3.00 (*0-614-19020-7*, BA-102) Sathya Sai Bk Ctr.

***Summer Showers in Brindavan, 1974.** Date not set. pap. 3.00 (*0-614-19021-5*, BA-103) Sathya Sai Bk Ctr.

***Summer Showers in Brindavan, 1977.** Date not set. pap. 1.50 (*0-614-19023-1*, BA-105) Sathya Sai Bk Ctr.

***Summer Showers in Brindavan, 1978.** rev. ed. Date not set. pap. 4.60 (*0-614-19024-X*, BA-106) Sathya Sai Bk Ctr.

***Summer Showers in Brindavan, 1979.** Date not set. pap. 2.00 (*0-614-19025-8*, BA-107) Sathya Sai Bk Ctr.

***Summer Showers in Brindavan, 1990.** Date not set. pap. 3.25 (*0-614-19026-6*, BA-108) Sathya Sai Bk Ctr.

***Summer Showers in Brindavan, 1993.** Date not set. pap. 3.25 (*0-614-19027-4*, BA-109) Sathya Sai Bk Ctr.

Summer Sizzler. 1988. pap. 3.95 (*0-373-48214-0*) Harlequin Bks.

***Summer Sizzlers: Overload; The Leopard's Woman; Lonesome Rider.** Linda Howard et al. 1997. pap. 9.99 (*0-373-48360-0*, 1-48360-1) Harlequin Bks.

Summer Sizzlers & Magic Mondays: School-Age Theme Activities. Edna Wallace. LC 94-69466. (Illus.). 151p. (Orig.). 1994. pap. 16.95 (*0-917505-06-9*) School Age.

Summer Sketches. Dan Simmons. 175p. 1992. text ed. 25.00 (*0-935716-59-9*) Lord John.

Summer Sketches. deluxe ed. Dan Simmons. 175p. 1992. 100.00 (*0-935716-62-9*) Lord John.

Summer Sleep. David Baker. (Poetry Chapbook Ser.). 32p. (Orig.). 1985. pap. 4.00 (*0-937669-19-9*) Owl Creek Pr.

Summer Sleeper. Sandy Berrigan. 43p. 1981. pap. 4.00 (*0-916382-24-9*) Telephone Bks.

Summer Snow & Other Words. Clyde A. Beakley. (Orig.). pap. write for info. (*0-9636782-1-3*) C Beakley.

Summer Sojourn Among the Inns of Court. Cornelius Comegys. x, 131p. Date not set. 34.00 (*0-89941-596-2*, 500280) W S Hein.

Summer Sojourn to the Grand Canyon: The 1898 Diary of Zella Dysart. Ed. by Mona L. McCroskey. LC 96-75066. (Illus.). 108p. (Orig.). 1996. pap. 9.95 (*0-9651067-0-5*) HollyBear Pr.

Summer Soldiers: A Survey & Index of Revolutionary War Courts-Martial. James C. Neagles. LC 85-73273. (Illus.). 290p. 1986. 19.95 (*0-916489-05-1*) Ancestry.

Summer Soldiers: The 1798 Rebellion in Antrim & Down. A. T. Stewart. 296p. 9600. pap. 24.95 (*0-85640-558-2*, Pub. by Blackstaff Pr IE) Dufour.

Summer Song. Susan R. Masters. LC 94-43684. 137p. (J). (gr. 5-7). 1995. 14.95 (*0-395-71127-4*, Clarion Bks) HM.

Summer Souvenirs. Ken Haak. (Illus.). 96p. 1985. pap. 14.95 (*0-312-77554-7*) St Martin.

Summer Special Christmas Edition. Katherine Applegate. (YA). (gr. 7 up). 1996. mass mkt. 3.99 (*0-671-51042-8*) PB.

Summer Sports. Isidro Sanchez & Carme Peris. (World of Sports Ser.). (Illus.). 32p. (J). (ps-1). 1992. pap. 5.95 (*0-8120-4865-2*) Barron.

Summer Spots. Michael J. Rosen. LC 96-23863. 1998. write for info. (*0-15-201534-5*) HarBrace.

Summer Spy. Linda M. Wilson. 96p. (Orig.). (J). (gr. 4-9). 1996. pap. 6.99 (*0-88092-172-2*) Royal Fireworks.

Summer Stargazing: A Practical Guide for Recreational Astronomers. Terence Dickinson. (Illus.). 64p. 1996. 18.95 (*1-55209-014-0*) Firefly Bks Ltd.

Summer Stars. Alan Fisk. 189p. (C). 1992. pap. 27.00 (*0-86383-895-2*, Pub. by Gomer Pr UK) St Mut.

Summer Start: How to Organize Your Best School Year Ever. Pat Fellers & Kathy Gritzmacher. Ed. by Ron Marson. (Master Teacher Ser.). (Illus.). 88p. 1985. teacher ed. 15.00 (*0-941008-61-4*) Tops Learning.

Summer Stock: Behind the Scenes with LBJ in '48. Joe Phipps. LC 92-13118. (Illus.). 338p. 1992. 27.95 (*0-87565-107-0*) Tex Christian.

Summer Storm. Robyn Donald. (Presents Ser.: No. 1408). 1991. pap. 2.79 (*0-373-11408-7*) Harlequin Bks.

Summer Storm. Catherine Hart. 480p. 1996. mass mkt. 5.99 (*0-8439-4073-5*, Leisure Bks) Dorchester Pub Co.

Summer Storm. large type ed. Robyn Donald. 1991. reprint ed. lib. bdg. 18.95 (*0-263-12593-9*) Thorndike Pr.

Summer Storm on the James. Travis DuPriest. (Illus.). 20p. (Orig.). (C). 1991. pap. 5.20 (*1-878142-03-8*) Telstar FL.

Summer Storms. Emma Goldrick. (Presents Plus Ser.). 1993. mass mkt. 2.99 (*0-373-11608-X*, 1-11608-6) Harlequin Bks.

Summer Storms. large type ed. Julia Ashwell. (Linford Romance Library). 256p. 1994. pap. 15.99 (*0-7089-7550-X*) Ulverscroft.

Summer Story. Jill Barklem. (Seasons of Brambly Hedge Ser.). (J). (ps-3). 1989. 8.95 (*0-399-21753-3*, Philomel Bks) Putnam Pub Group.

Summer Stranger. Frances B. Wilson. 1994. 17.95 (*0-8034-9075-5*, 094423) Bouregy.

Summer Strike-Out. Margaret M. Scariano. (Meridian Bks.). (Illus.). 64p. (J). (gr. 3-9). 1989. lib. bdg. 4.95 (*0-87879-617-7*) High Noon Bks.

Summer Sun. Helen Webber. (Illus.). (J). (gr. k-6). 1968. 8.95 (*0-8392-3056-7*) Astor-Honor.

***Summer Sun.** large type unabridged ed. Wilson Call. LC 96-90673. (Illus.). 200p. 1996. 19.95 (*0-9636147-1-1*, 780963) Wilson-Call.

Summer Suns Risin' Lisa W. Nicola. Date not set. 15.95 (*0-8050-4914-2*, Bks Young Read) H Holt & Co.

***Summer Surprise.** Shannon M. Leppard. LC 96-45833. (Adventures of Callie Ann Ser.). 80p. (J). (gr. 2-5). 1997. pap. 3.99 (*1-55661-813-1*) Bethany Hse.

Summer Surrender. Lynda K. Carpenter. 288p. (Orig.). 1995. mass mkt. 4.99 (*0-7865-0082-4*) Diamond.

Summer Switch. Mary Rodgers. LC 79-2690. (Charlotte Zolotow Bk.). 192p. (J). (gr. 5 up). 1982. 14.95 (*0-06-025058-5*); lib. bdg. 12.89 (*0-06-025059-3*) HarpC Child Bks.

Summer Switch. Mary Rodgers. LC 79-2690. (Trophy Bk.). 192p. (YA). (gr. 5 up). 1984. pap. 3.50 (*0-06-440140-5*, Trophy) HarpC Child Bks.

Summer Tales. Johann Beer. Tr. by Gerda Jordan & James Hardin from GER. LC 84-47537. 290p. (Orig.). 1984. pap. 29.45 (*0-8204-0112-9*) P Lang Pubng.

***Summer That Didn't End.** Lynn W. Holt. 1965. write for info. (*0-688-11230-7*) Morrow.

Summer That Didn't End: The Story of the Mississippi Civil Rights Project of 1964. Len Holt. 351p. 1992. reprint ed. pap. 14.95 (*0-306-80469-7*) Da Capo.

Summer the Dolls Toured Europe. Jane S. Bauld. LC 94-69060. (Illus.). 32p. (J). (gr. k-3). 1994. 17.95 (*0-9636274-8-1*) Coming Age Pr.

Summer the Dolls Toured Europe. Illus. by Laura Telford. 32p. (J). (gr. k-3). 1994. pap. 8.95 (*1-885340-02-8*) Coming Age Pr.

Summer the Flowers Had No Scent. D. Miles Nicolai. (Illus.). (J). 1978. pap. 2.75 (*0-933992-00-9*) Coffee Break.

Summer the Flowers Had No Scent. 3rd ed. D. Miles Nicolai. (Color-A-Story Ser.). (Illus.). 28p. (J). (gr. 3-5). 1977. pap. 2.75 (*0-933992-19-X*) Coffee Break.

Summer the Whales Sang. Gloria Montero. (YA). (gr. 5 up). 1995. 16.95 (*0-88862-904-4*); pap. 6.95 (*0-88862-903-6*) Formac Dist Ltd.

***Summer Theatre Directory, 1997.** Ed. by Jill Charles. 150p. 1996. pap. 16.95 (*0-933919-35-2*) Theatre Directories.

Summer Thunder. Brian Shul. (Illus.). 154p. 1993. 40.00 (*0-929823-13-3*) Mach One.

Summer to Die. Lois Lowry. (Illus.). (J). (gr. 3-7). 1977. 14.95 (*0-395-25338-1*) HM.

Summer to Die. Lois Lowry. 128p. (J). 1984. mass mkt. 4.50 (*0-440-21917-5*) Bantam.

Summer Tours in Scotland. Picton Publishing Staff & MacBrayne. (C). 1987. reprint ed. 18.00 (*0-317-90421-3*, Pub. by Picton UK) St Mut.

Summer Tree. Guy G. Kay. (Fionavar Tapestry Ser.: No. 1). 400p. 1992. pap. 5.99 (*0-451-45138-4*, ROC) NAL-Dutton.

Summer Tunes: A Martha's Vineyard Vacation. Patricia McMahon. LC 95-83980. (Illus.). 48p. (J). (gr. 2-5). 1996. 16.95 (*1-56397-572-6*) Boyds Mills Pr.

***Summer Visitor.** Cadman. 1992. pap. text ed. write for info. (*0-17-555979-1*) Addison-Wesley.

***Summer Weekend Cookbook.** Jane Rodmell. (Illus.). 224p. 1997. pap. 24.95 (*0-9696922-2-6*) Firefly Bks Ltd.

Summer Wheels. Eve Bunting. (Illus.). 48p. (J). (gr. 1-5). 1992. 15.00 (*0-15-207000-1*, HB Juv Bks) HarBrace.

Summer Wheels. Eve Bunting. LC 90-49758. (Illus.). 56p. (J). (gr. 2-7). 1996. pap. 6.00 (*0-15-200988-4*, Voyager Bks) HarBrace.

Summer Will End. Dorian Yeager. LC 96-22111. 208p. 1996. 20.95 (*0-312-14743-0*) St Martin.

Summer Wind. Arlene Holliday. 1995. pap. 4.99 (*0-8217-5001-1*) NAL-Dutton.

***Summer Wind.** Gail McFarland. 288p. 1997. mass mkt. 4.99 (*0-7860-0436-3*, Pinncle Kensgtn) Kensgtn Pub Corp.

Summer Wind: The Story of an Immigrant Chinese Politician. Richard Nagasawa. LC 86-50080. 19.95 (*0-87026-063-4*) Westernlore.

***Summer with the Leprechauns: A True Story, Vol. 1.** Tanis Helliwell. LC 96-41441. 208p. (Orig.). 1997. pap. 13.00 (*1-57733-001-3*) B Dolphin Pub.

Summer Without Horses. Bonnie Bryant. (Saddle Club Super Ser.: No. 1). 208p. (J). (gr. 4-7). 1994. 4.50 (*0-553-48149-5*) Bantam.

Summer Woodlands. John R. Quinn. (Illus.). 1980. 9.95 (*0-85699-140-6*) Chatham Pr.

Summer World. Stefan Kanfer. 1989. 22.95 (*0-374-27180-1*) FS&G.

Summer World: The Attempt to Build a Jewish Eden in the Catskills from the Days of the Ghetto to the Rise & Decline of the Borscht Belt. Stefan Kanfer. LC 91-39152. 1992. write for info. (*0-571-12937-4*) Faber & Faber.

Summerdog. Thom Roberts. (Illus.). 128p. (Orig.). (J). (gr. 1 up). 1978. pap. 2.25 (*0-380-01950-7*, Camelot) Avon.

Summerfield Stories. J. M. Ferguson, Jr. LC 84-16443. 98p. 1985. 14.95 (*0-87565-000-7*); pap. 8.95 (*0-87565-010-4*) Tex Christian.

Summerhaven. Linda Masterson. (Illus.). 1979. mass mkt. 1.95 (*0-89083-471-7*, Zebra Kensgtn) Kensgtn Pub Corp.

Summerhill Hounds. J. Robert King. (First Quest Ser.). (Illus.). 055p. (Orig.). (YA). (gr. 5 up). 1995. pap. 3.99 (*0-7869-0196-9*) TSR Inc.

Summerhill School: A New View of Childhood. Alexander S. Neill. Ed. by Albert Lamb. LC 95-33481. 269p. 1995. pap. 12.95 (*0-312-14137-8*, Griffin) St Martin.

Summerhill School: A New View of Childhood. rev. ed. A. S. Neill. Ed. by Albert Lamb. LC 92-34957. 1993. 22.95 (*0-312-08860-4*) St Martin.

***SummerHill Secrets, Vols. 1-5.** Beverly Lewis. 1996. boxed 29.99 (*0-7642-8029-5*) Bethany Hse.

Summerhill Story: The Nineteen Ninety-Two Centennial. Frank P. Alcamo. (Illus.). 1992. pap. 19.95 (*0-935648-37-2*) Halldin Pub.

Summerhills. D. E. Stevenson. 311p. 1976. lib. bdg. 23.95 (*0-89966-162-9*) Buccaneer Bks.

***Summeries of the Ordnance Board of 1863-1868, March 1970 & September 1870.** abr. ed. 128p. (Orig.). 1997. pap. 15.00 (*0-614-28601-8*) Collect Lib.

Summering in Colorado: An 1874 Guide. (Illus.). 1993. reprint ed. pap. 12.50 (*0-910746-36-2*, SUM01) Hope Farm.

Summering in South Africa: Diary of an Indian. Jagdish R. Hiremath. (C). 1993. 14.00 (*81-224-0556-8*) S Asia.

Summering on Nantucket. Ed. by Bruce Courson. (Illus.). 49p. 1986. 9.50 (*0-9607340-6-6*) Nantucket Hist Assn.

Summerland. L. Dean James. 288p. (Orig.). 1994. mass mkt. 4.99 (*0-380-77325-2*, AvoNova) Avon.

Summerland. Ed. by Ryga & Kujundzic. (NFS Canada Ser.). 1993. pap. 17.95 (*0-88922-313-0*) Genl Dist Srvs.

Summerland. Eyvind Skeie. Tr. by Hedwig Durnbaugh from NOR. LC 89-7082. Orig. Title: Summerlandet. (Illus.). 48p. (J). 1989. pap. 6.95 (*0-87178-824-1*, 8241) Brethren.

Summerland: A Western Australian Sesquicentenary Anthology of Poetry & Prose. Ed. by Alec Choate & Barbara Y. Main. 242p. 1995. pap. 8.95 (*0-85564-166-5*, Pub. by Univ of West Aust Pr AT) Intl Spec Bk.

Summerland Affair. large type ed. June Sutton. (Linford Romance Library). 272p. 1994. pap. 15.99 (*0-7089-7510-0*, Linford) Ulverscroft.

Summerlandet see Summerland

Summers & Sabbaticals: Selected Papers on Psychology & Education. Fred S. Keller. 169p. 1986. reprint ed. 19.95 (*0-8290-1968-5*) Irvington.

Summers at the Paul Ranch. George Paul. Ed. by Eldonna Lay. (East County Childhoods Ser.: Vol. 4). (Illus.). 20p. (Orig.). (YA). (gr. 3 up). 1995. pap. 2.50 (*0-9619184-3-8*) E P Lay Assocs.

Summer's Chance. Patricia H. Easton. LC 87-17728. 160p. (YA). (gr. 7 up). 1988. 14.00 (*0-15-200591-9*, Gulliver Bks) HarBrace.

Summer's Chance. Patricia H. Easton. 160p. (YA). (gr. 7 up). 1992. pap. 5.00 (*0-15-282493-6*, Gulliver Bks) HarBrace.

Summer's Day. Joel Meyerowitz. LC 84-40642. (Illus.). 156p. 1987. pap. 17.95 (*0-8129-1195-4*, Times Bks) Random.

Summer's Day. limited ed. Joel Meyerowitz. LC 84-40642. (Illus.). 156p. 1987. 750.00 (*0-8129-1194-6*, Times Bks); 750.00 (*0-8129-1196-2*, Times Bks) Random.

Summer's End. Maribeth Boelts. LC 94-14837. (Illus.). 32p. (J). (gr. k-3). 1995. 14.95 (*0-395-70559-2*) HM.

Summer's End. Robert Hawks. 176p. (Orig.). (YA). (gr. 8 up). 1994. mass mkt. 3.99 (*0-380-77440-2*, Flare) Avon.

Summer's End. Mary Ryan. 352p. 1996. 23.95 (*0-312-14427-X*) St Martin.

Summer's End. Danielle Steel. 384p. 1980. mass mkt. 6.50 (*0-440-18405-3*) Dell.

Summer's End. Todd Strasser. (Lifeguards Ser.). 208p. (YA). (gr. 7-9). 1993. pap. 3.50 (*0-590-46967-3*) Scholastic Inc.

Summer's Exile. Andre Gould. 1995. pap. text ed. 10.95 (*0-85449-202-X*, Pub. by Gay Mens Pr UK) LPC InBook.

***Summers Fly Winters, Vol. 1.** Charles M. Schulz. (J). 1977. write for info. (*0-03-022631-7*) H Holt & Co.

Summers Fly, Winters Walk. Charles M. Schulz. (Illus.). 128p. (J). 1991. pap. 5.95 (*0-8050-1692-9*, Owl) H Holt & Co.

***Summers Fly, Winters Walk.** Charles M. Schulz. (J). 1977. 4.95 (*0-8050-0216-2*) H Holt & Co.

Summer's Gift. Deborah Wood. 320p. (Orig.). 1994. mass mkt. 4.99 (*0-7865-0006-9*) Diamond.

Summers Guide to Coca-Cola. B. J. Summers. (Illus.). 176p. (Orig.). 1996. 19.95 (*0-89145-715-1*, 4708) Collector Bks.

Summer's Illusion. large type ed. Rachael Croft. 256p. 1995. 25.99 (*0-7089-3257-6*) Ulverscroft.

Summers in Star Valley. Matilde Maravillas. 435p. (Orig.). 1991. pap. 14.95 (*0-915214-21-0*) Current.

Summers in Star Valley. 2nd rev. ed. Matilde Maravillas. 454p. (Orig.). 1992. pap. 14.95 (*0-915214-25-3*) Current.

Summers Law. 3rd ed. Date not set. pap. text ed. 46.25 (*0-314-05662-9*) West Pub.

Summer's Lease. G. J. Frahm. (Illus.). 131p. (Orig.). 1989. pap. 8.45 (*0-932914-18-7*) Dordt Coll Pr.

Summer's Lease. John Mortimer. 288p. 1991. pap. 11.95 (*0-14-015827-8*, Penguin Bks) Viking Penguin.

Summers of My Life. Danny P. Clark. (Illus.). 130p. (Orig.). 1989. pap. 11.95 (*0-317-93655-7*) Questar CA.

Summers of Vietnam & Other Poems. Mary Kinzie. LC 89-4116. 145p. 1990. 14.95 (*0-935296-87-5*); pap. 10.95 (*0-935296-83-2*) Sheep Meadow.

Summers on Oil & Gas. write for info. (*0-318-57512-4*) West Pub.

***Summers Pocket Guide to Coca-Cola: Identifications, Current Values, & Circa Dates.** B. J. Summers. (Illus.). 144p. 1997. pap. 9.95 (*1-57432-024-6*, 4952) Collector Bks.

***Summer's Salmon.** A. Rusty Rat. (Illus.). 74p. 1997. 50.00 (*1-886967-05-9*) Meadow Run Pr.

***Summer's Secret.** Sandra Heath. 1997. pap. 4.99 (*0-451-18652-4*, Sig) NAL-Dutton.

Summer's Song. Clara Wimberly. 1999. pap. 4.99 (*0-8217-5106-9*) NAL-Dutton.

Summer's Storm. Denise Domning. 384p. (Orig.). 1994. pap. 4.99 (*0-451-40507-2*, Topaz) NAL-Dutton.

Summerspell. Jean Thesman. LC 94-25737. (J). (gr. 7-10). 1995. 15.00 (*0-671-50130-5*, S&S Bks Young Read) S&S Childrens.

***Summertide.** Charles Sheffield. (Heritage Universe Ser.: Vol. 1). 1991. mass mkt. 4.95 (*0-345-36937-8*, Del Rey) Ballantine.

Summertime. David L. Fleming. LC 85-20827. (Illus.). 410p. (Orig.). 1986. pap. 12.95 (*0-87565-061-9*) Tex Christian.

Summertime. Gershwin. (J). 1998. 16.00 (*0-689-80719-8*) S&S Childrens.

Summertime. Ann Schweninger. (Let's Look at the Seasons Ser.). (Illus.). 32p. (J). (ps-3). 1994. pap. 4.50 (*0-14-054331-7*) Puffin Bks.

Summertime Food. Miriam Ungerer. LC 88-26516. (Illus.). 288p. 1989. 19.95 (*0-394-57535-0*) Random.

Summertime in the Big Woods. Laura Ingalls Wilder. LC 94-48814. (My First Little House Bks.). (Illus.). 40p. (J). (ps-3). 1996. lib. bdg. 11.89 (*0-06-025937-X*) HarpC Child Bks.

***Summertime in the Big Woods.** Laura Ingalls Wilder. LC 94-48814. (My First Little House Bks.). (Illus.). 32p. (J). (ps-3). 1997. 3.25 (*0-694-00949-0*, Festival) HarpC Child Bks.

Summertime in the Big Woods. Laura Ingalls Wilder. LC 94-48814. (My First Little House Bks.). (Illus.). 40p. (J). (ps-3). 1996. 11.95 (*0-06-025934-5*) HarpC Child Bks.

Summertime Puzzle & Fun Book. Elvira Gamiello. (Illus.). (Orig.). (J). (gr. 4-6). 1989. pap. 1.95 (*0-942025-62-8*) Kidsbks.

Summertime Recipes. Joan Peterson & Pete Peterson. 36p. (Orig.). 1981. pap. 3.25 (*0-940844-02-8*) Wellspring.

Summertime Song. Irene Haas. LC 96-17156. (J). 1997. 16.00 (*0-689-50549-3*, McElderry) S&S Childrens.

Summertime Song. Irene Haas. (J). 1997. 16.00 (*0-689-81082-2*, S&S Bks Young Read) S&S Childrens.

SummerTimes: In Celebration of 100 Years of the Muskoka Lakes Association. (Illus.). 192p. 40.00 (*1-55046-081-1*, Pub. by Boston Mills Pr CN) Genl Dist Srvs.

SummerTimes: In Celebration of 100 Years of the Muskoka Lakes Association. deluxe limited ed. (Illus.). 192p. 200.00 (*1-55046-105-2*, Pub. by Boston Mills Pr CN) Genl Dist Srvs.

Summerton. Mark Dunster. 21p. (Orig.). (YA). (gr. 9-12). 1996. pap. 5.00 (*0-89642-295-X*) Linden Pubs.

Summertree. Ron Cowen. 1968. pap. 5.25 (*0-8222-1099-1*) Dramatists Play.

Summerville Days. Carrie Bender. (Whispering Brook Ser.: Bk. 2). 224p. (Orig.). (J). 1996. pap. 7.99 (*0-8361-9040-8*) Herald Pr.

***Summer/Winter Chicken.** Lori Longbotham. LC 97-6247. (Illus.). 144p. (Orig.). 1997. pap. 15.95 (*0-688-15212-0*, Quill) Morrow.

***Summer/Winter Pasta.** Grace Parisi. LC 97-6248. (Illus.). 144p. (Orig.). 1997. pap. 15.95 (*0-688-15213-9*, Quill) Morrow.

Summery of Standard Specifications for Steel Castings see Steel Casting Handbook Supplements

Summing & Nuclear Norms in Banach Space Theory. G. J. Jameson. (London Mathematical Society Student Texts Ser.: No. 8). 192p. 1987. pap. text ed. 23.95 (*0-521-34937-0*) Cambridge U Pr.

Summing Up. W. Somerset Maugham. 208p. 1992. pap. 10.95 (*0-14-018600-X*, Penguin Classics) Viking Penguin.

Summing up. W. Somerset Maugham. LC 75-25377. (Works of W. Somerset Maugham). 1978. reprint ed. 23.95 (*0-405-07830-7*) Ayer.

Summing up: The Science of Reviewing Research. Richard J. Light & David B. Pillemer. LC 84-4506. (Illus.). 224p. 1984. 25.00 (*0-674-85430-6*); pap. 12.95 (*0-674-85431-4*) HUP.

Summing Up the Black Panther Party see Leadership

Summit. Edward Myers. 432p. (Orig.). 1994. pap. 5.99 (*0-451-45419-7*, ROC) NAL-Dutton.

Summit. Charles Taylor. 1996. mass mkt. 6.50 (*0-671-87579-5*) PB.

Summit: A Gold Rush History of Summit County, Colorado. Mary E. Gilliland. LC 80-65781. (Illus.). 336p. (Orig.). (C). 1980. 22.95 (*0-9603624-1-X*); pap. text ed. 13.50 (*0-9603624-0-1*) Alpenrose Pr.

Summit: Climbing the Seven Summits. Robert M. Anderson. 160p. 1995. 65.00 (*0-614-11915-4*, C P Pubs) Crown Pub Group.

Summit: Strengthening Teens' Spiritual Grip. Scharlotte Rich. (Vertical Adventure Ser.: No. 4). 100p. (YA). 1996. pap. text ed. 5.99 (*1-57673-004-2*, Gold & Honey) Multnomah Pubs.

Summit: Treaty of Peace. Edward S. Lax. 90p. (C). 1988. lib. bdg. 30.00 (*0-9620530-0-7*) Hist Bks Ltd.

Summit Beach Park: Akron's Coney Island. Diane D. Francis & David W. Francis. (Illus.). 180p. (Orig.). 1993. pap. 24.95 (*0-9621895-9-6*) Summit Cty Hist Soc.

Summit Centennial: 1892-1992. Summit, South Dakota Centennial Committee Staff. Ed. by Charles D. Floro. 80p. (Orig.). 1992. pap. 5.00 (*1-879765-03-9*) Earth & Sky.

Summit County. Tracy Salcedo. (Twelve Short Hikes Ser.). (Illus.). 32p. (Orig.). 1995. pap. 4.95 (*0-934641-95-1*) Chockstone Pr.

Summit County Cemetery Inscriptions, 2 vols., Vol. 1. 100p. 1980. 7.00 (*0-686-28156-X*) Summit Cnty OH.

Summit County Cemetery Inscriptions, 2 vols., Vol. 2. 100p. 1980. 7.00 (*0-686-28157-8*) Summit Cnty OH.

Summit Guide to the Cascade Volcanoes. Jeff Smoot. (Illus.). 182p. (Orig.). 1992. pap. 14.95 (*0-934641-25-0*) Chockstone Pr.

Summit Hill, the Balloon Route over the Detroit, Toledo & Ironton Railroad. Scott D. Trostel. Ed. by Pat Best. (Ohio Railroad Heritage Ser.). (Illus.). 60p. (Orig.). 1987. pap. 15.95 (*0-925436-01-1*) Cam-Tech Pub.

Summit Ministries Guide to Choosing a College. Ronald H. Nash & J. F. Baldwin. 1995. pap. write for info. (*0-936163-34-8*) Summit Pr CO.

Summit of the Years. John Burroughs. (Works of John Burroughs). 1989. reprint ed. lib. bdg. 79.00 (*0-7812-2197-8*) Rprt Serv.

Summit Springs Battle. Fred H. Werner. (Western Americana Ser.). 200p. (Orig.). 1991. pap. 10.95 (*0-933144-11-3*) Werner Pubn.

Summit Up: Riddles about Mountains. June Swanson. LC 93-19157. (You Must Be Joking! Riddle Bks.). (Illus.). 32p. (J). (gr. 1-4). 1994. lib. bdg. 13.50 (*0-8225-2342-6*, Lerner Publctns) Lerner Group.

Summit Up: Riddles about Mountains. June Swanson. (J). (gr. 1-4). 1994. pap. 3.95 (*0-8225-9658-X*, Lerner Publctns) Lerner Group.

***Summitry in the Americas.** LC 96-40437. 1997. write for info. (*0-88132-242-3*) Inst Intl Eco.

Summits: Climbing the Seven Summits Solo. Robert M. Anderson. LC 95-24209. 1995. 65.00 (*0-517-70200-2*) Crown Pub Group.

Summit's Glory: Sketches of Buchtel College & the University of Akron. George W. Knepper. LC 90-70403. (Illus.). 159p. 1990. 19.95 (*0-9622628-0-3*); pap. 9.95 (*0-9622628-2-X*) U Akron Pr.

Summits Move with the Tide. 2nd ed. Mei-mei Berssenbrugge. 70p. (Orig.). 1982. pap. 4.00 (*0-912678-56-9*, Greenfld Rev Pr) Greenfld Rev Lit.

Summits of God Life: Samadhi & Siddhi. Sri Chinmoy. LC 80-65397. 10p. 1984. reprint ed. pap. 6.95 (*0-88497-145-7*) Aum Pubns.

Summits of Samivel. Samivel. (Illus.). 108p. 1986. 29.95 (*0-9616970-0-8*) Alta House.

Summits of the South: A Visitor's Guide to Twenty-Five Southern Appalachian Peaks. Brian A. Boyd. (Illus.). 112p. (Orig.). 1993. pap. text ed. 8.95 (*0-9625737-5-2*) Ferncreek Pub.

Summon Spirits Cry: A Collection of Poems. Mary Francis. LC 95-79889. 176p. (Orig.). 1996. pap. 11.95 (*0-89870-573-8*) Ignatius Pr.

Summon the Light Within: Daily Exercises & Meditations. Susanne B. Miller. (Illus.). (Orig.). 1995. pap. 3.95 (*1-881217-11-6*) New Atlantean.

Summon up Remembrance. Marzieh Gail. (Illus.). 320p. 1987. 28.50 (*0-85398-258-9*) G Ronald Pub.

***Summon up the Blood.** Celia Wolfe. 1997. 29.95 (*0-85052-537-3*, Pub. by L Cooper Bks UK) Trans-Atl Phila.

Summoned. Megan Marklin. Ed. by Claire Zion. 320p. (Orig.). 1993. mass mkt. 4.99 (*0-671-76098-X*) PB.

Summoned: Poems. Diana O'Hehir. LC 76-16011. (Breakthrough Bks.). 64p. 1976. text ed. 18.95 (*0-8262-0204-7*) U of Mo Pr.

Summoned by Knox: Poems in Scots. Alan N. Bold. 84p. 8500. pap. 12.95 (*0-905075-20-X*, Pub. by Wilfion Bks UK) Dufour.

Summoned by Love. Carlo Carretto. Tr. by Alan Neame from ITA. LC 78-962. Orig. Title: Padre Mio me abbandono a Te. 1978. reprint ed. pap. 10.50 (*0-88344-472-0*) Orbis Bks.

Summoned to Pilgrimage: The Temple As Focus of a Pilgrim People. Velma Ruch. LC 94-10322. 1994. pap. 15.00 (*0-8309-0667-3*) Herald Hse.

Summoners Tale. variorum ed. Geoffrey Chaucer. Ed. by John F. Plummer, 3rd. LC 94-38951. (Chaucer Variorium Ser.: Vol. 2, Pt. 7). (Illus.). 270p. 1995. 49.95 (*0-8061-2744-9*, 2744) U of Okla Pr.

Summoning. Bentley Little. 544p. 1993. mass mkt. 4.50 (*0-8217-4221-3*, Zebra Kensgtn) Kensgtn Pub Corp.

Summoning: Ideas of the Covenant & Interpretive Theory. Ed. by Ellen Spolsky. LC 92-23258. (SUNY Series in Modern Jewish Literature & Culture). 272p. (C). 1993. text ed. 64.50 (*0-7914-1525-2*); pap. text ed. 21.95 (*0-7914-1526-0*) State U NY Pr.

Summoning of Every Man. LC 71-133741. (Tudor Facsimile Texts. Old English Plays Ser.: No. 5). reprint ed. 49.50 (*0-404-53305-1*) AMS Pr.

Summoning Spirits: The Art of Magical Evocation. Konstantinos. LC 95-24724. (Llewellyn's Practical Magic Ser.). (Illus.). 224p. 1995. pap. 14.95 (*1-56718-381-6*) Llewellyn Pubns.

Summoning Tablets of Guilds in Hungary. P. Bagybakay. 1981. 35.00 (*0-317-57365-9*) St Mut.

Summoning Tablets of Guilds in Hungary. Peter Nagybakay. 114p. 1989. 35.00 (*963-13-1066-3*, Pub. by Corvina Bks HU) St Mut.

Summoning the Familiar: Powers & Rites of Common Life. Eileen Gregory. 90p. 1984. pap. 8.00 (*0-911005-04-8*) Dallas Inst Pubns.

***Summoning the Fates.** Z. Budapest. 1998. write for info. (*0-517-70873-6*, Harmony) Crown Pub Group.

Summoning the Gods: Sandpainting of the Native American Southwest. Ronald McCoy. (Plateau Ser.: PL 59: 1). (Illus.). 32p. 1988. pap. 5.95 (*0-89734-059-0*) Mus Northern Ariz.

Summoning Up Remembrance. Henry Stob. LC 94-40625. 1995. pap. text ed. 15.00 (*0-8028-0832-8*) Eerdmans.

Summons. Peter Lovesey. 368p. 1995. 21.95 (*0-89296-551-7*) Mysterious Pr.

Summons. Peter Lovesey. 352p. 1996. mass mkt. 5.99 (*0-446-40369-5*, Mysterious Paperbk) Warner Bks.

Summons. deluxe limited ed. James Dickey. (Poster Poem Ser.). 1988. 50.00 (*0-89723-051-5*) Bruccoli.

Summons. large type ed. Peter Lovesey. (Cloak & Dagger Ser.). 562p. 1995. 24.95 (*0-7862-0560-1*) Thorndike Pr.

Summons & Sign. Dagmar Nick. Tr. by Jim Barnes from GER. LC 80-18367. Orig. Title: Zeugnis & Zeichen. (Illus.). 124p. (Orig.). 1980. pap. 100.00 (*0-933428-02-2*) Chariton Review.

Summons of Death on the Medieval & Renaissance English Stage. Phoebe S. Spinrad. LC 87-5487. 304p. 1987. 52.00 (*0-8142-0443-0*) Ohio St U Pr.

Summons of the Trumpet: U. S.-Vietnam in Perspective. Dave R. Palmer. LC 77-28339. 304p. 1995. pap. 14.95 (*0-89141-550-5*) Presidio Pr.

Summons to Memphis. Peter Taylor. LC 86-45417. 224p. 1986. 15.95 (*0-394-41062-9*) Knopf.

Summons to Memphis. Peter Taylor. 224p. 1987. mass mkt. 4.95 (*0-345-90171-1*) Ballantine.

Summons to Memphis. Peter Taylor. 234p. 1987. mass mkt. 5.99 (*0-345-34660-2*) Ballantine.

Summulae. Dominicus Soto. 286p. 1979. reprint ed. write for info. (*3-487-06833-8*) G Olms Pubs.

SUMMUM: Sealed, Except to the Open Mind. Summum Bonum Amen Ra. LC 87-91265. 126p. (C). 1988. 11.00 (*0-943217-00-8*); student ed. 25.00 (*0-943217-01-6*) Summum.

Summy Piano Solo Package: Advanced, No. 501. (Summy Piano Solo Package Ser.). (Illus.). 32p. (J). (gr. 10-12). 1976. pap. text ed. 5.95 (*0-87487-656-7*) Summy-Birchard.

Summy Piano Solo Package: Elementary, No. 101. (Summy Piano Solo Package Ser.). (Illus.). 32p. (Orig.). (J). (gr. k-2). 1976. pap. text ed. 5.95 (*0-87487-652-4*) Summy-Birchard.

Summy Piano Solo Package: Intermediate, No.301. (Summy Piano Solo Package Ser.). (Illus.). 32p. (Orig.). (J). (gr. 5-8). 1976. pap. text ed. 5.95 (*0-87487-654-0*) Summy-Birchard.

Summy Piano Solo Package: Late Elementary, No.201. (Summy Piano Solo Package Ser.). (Illus.). 32p. (Orig.). (J). (gr. 2-6). 1976. pap. text ed. 5.95 (*0-87487-653-2*) Summy-Birchard.

Summy Piano Solo Package: Late Intermediate, No.401. (Summy Piano Solo Package Ser.). (Illus.). 32p. (Orig.). (J). (gr. 8-10). 1976. pap. text ed. 5.95 (*0-87487-655-9*) Summy-Birchard.

Sumner: John Brown, Second Prolog. Mark Dunster & John Brown. 1980. pap. 4.00 (*0-89642-065-5*) Linden Pubs.

Sumner County, Kansas. Caldwell Messenger Staff. (Illus.). 295p. 1987. 45.00 (*0-88107-096-3*) Curtis Media.

Sumner County, Tennessee: Abstracts of Will Books 1 & 2 (1788-1842) Edythe R. Whitley. 84p. 1995. reprint ed. pap. 12.50 (*0-614-10034-8*, 6340) Clearfield Co.

Sumner County, Tennessee: Index to the Loose Records, 1786 to 1930. Shirley Wilson. 310p. (C). 1988. text ed. 40.00 (*0-317-91242-9*) Richley Enter.

Sumner County Tennessee Court Minutes 1787-1805, 1808-1810. Carol Wells. 353p. (Orig.). 1995. pap. 26.50 (*0-7884-0295-1*) Heritage Bk.

Sumner-Gearing-Class Destroyers: Their Design, Weapons, & Equipment. Robert F. Sumrall. (Illus.). 320p. 1995. 59.95 (*1-55750-786-4*) Naval Inst Pr.

***Sumner Welles.** Welles. LC 97-11579. 1997. 29.95 (*0-312-17440-3*) St Martin.

Sumo: A Pocket Guide. Walter Long. LC 89-50474. (Illus.). 128p. 1989. pap. 9.95 (*0-8048-1594-1*) C E Tuttle.

Sumo: A Pocket Guide. David Shapiro. 1995. pap. 8.95 (*0-8048-2014-7*) C E Tuttle.

Sumo: Le Sport et le Sacre. Laurent R. Martres. (Illus.). 144p. (FRE.). 1985. pap. text ed. 12.95 (*0-916189-01-5*) Graphie Intl.

Sumo & the Woodblock Print Masters. Lawrence Bickford. LC 94-15433. 152p. 1994. 45.00 (*4-7700-1752-9*) Kodansha.

Sumo Bizarro. Dan Piraro. (Illus.). 96p. (Orig.). 1990. pap. 5.95 (*0-87701-774-3*) Chronicle Bks.

Sumo Showdown: The Hawaiian Challenge. Philip Sandoz. 72p. 1993. 29.95 (*0-8048-1895-9*) C E Tuttle.

Sumo, the Wrestling Elephant. Esther Mok. (Illus.). 24p. (J). (gr. 2-5). 1994. pap. 4.95 (*0-943864-68-2*) Davenport.

Sumo Watching. Tsutomu Kakuma & Deborah Iwabuchi. (Illus.). 200p. (Orig.). 1994. pap. 11.95 (*4-89684-236-7*, Pub. by Yohan Pubns JA) Weatherhill.

Sumo Wrestling. Bill Gutman. (Martial Arts Ser.). (Illus.). 48p. (J). (gr. 3-9). 1995. lib. bdg. 17.80 (*1-56065-273-X*) Capstone Pr.

***Sumo Wrestling.** Bill Gutman. (Martial Arts Ser.). (Illus.). 48p. (J). (gr. 3-7). 1995. 18.40 (*0-516-35273-3*) Childrens.

***Sumokella: Hawaii's Cinderella.** Sandi Takayama. (Illus.). 24p. (J). (ps-5). 1997. 9.95 (*1-57306-027-5*) Bess Pr.

Sumptuary Law in Nuernberg: A Study in Paternal Government. Kent R. Greenfield. LC 78-63964. (Johns Hopkins University. Studies in the Social Sciences. Thirtieth Ser. 1912: 2). reprint ed. 36.00 (*0-404-61211-3*) AMS Pr.

Sumptuary Legislation & Personal Regulation in England. Frances E. Baldwin. LC 78-64119. (Johns Hopkins University. Studies in the Social Sciences. Thirtieth Ser. 1912: 1). reprint ed. 41.50 (*0-404-61233-4*) AMS Pr.

Sumptuous Arts at the Royal Abbeys in Reims & Braine: Ornatus Elegantiae, Varietate Stupendes. Madeline H. Caviness. (Illus.). 425p. 1990. text ed. 135.00 (*0-691-04058-3*) Princeton U Pr.

Sumptuous Flaske: European & American Decorted Powder Flasks of the Sixteeth to Nineteenth Centuries. (Illus.). 158p. 1989. pap. 35.00 (*0-917218-38-8*) A Mowbray.

***Sumptuous Patchwork: Patchwork Projects Embellished with Embroidery, Beading, Cording & Stencilling.** Ed. by Christine Donaldson. (Illus.). 128p. 1997. 24.95 (*1-57076-068-3*, Trafalgar Sq Pub) Trafalgar.

***Sumptuous Santa Barbara.** 1996. 17.95 (*0-9649245-0-1*) Devereux Fnd.

Sums & Gaussian Vectors, Vol. X. Vadim Yurinsky. Ed. by A. Dold & F. Takens. (Lecture Notes in Mathematics Ser.: Vol. 1617). 305p. 1995. 64.95 (*3-540-60311-5*) Spr-Verlag.

Sums of Independent Random Variables. V. V. Petrov. Tr. by A. A. Brown. LC 75-5766. (Ergebnisse der Mathematik Ser.: Vol. 82). 360p. 1975. text ed. 69.00 (*0-387-06635-7*) Spr-Verlag.

Sums Through Eighteen. Earl Ockenga & Walt Rucker. (Elementary Mathematics Ser.). (Illus.). 16p. (J). (gr. 1). 1990. pap. text ed. 1.25 (*1-56281-130-4*, M130) Extra Eds.

Sums Through Ten. Earl Ockenga & Walt Rucker. (Elementary Mathematics Ser.). (Illus.). 16p. (J). (gr. 1). 1990. pap. text ed. 1.25 (*1-56281-105-3*, M105) Extra Eds.

Sums, Trimmed Sums & Extremes. Ed. by Marjorie G. Hahn et al. (Progress in Probability Ser.: Vol. 23). ix, 416p. 1990. 57.50 (*0-8176-3542-4*) Birkhauser.

Sumter: The First Day of the Civil War. Robert Hendrickson. 1995. 9.98 (*0-88394-095-7*) Promntory Pr.

Sumter Is Avenged! The Siege & Reduction of Fort Pulaski. Herbert M. Schiller. LC 95-39922. 201p. (C). 1996. 29.95 (*0-942597-86-9*) White Mane Pub.

Sun. (Voyage Through the Universe Ser.). (Illus.). 144p. 1990. 17.27 (*0-8094-6887-5*); lib. bdg. 24.60 (*0-8094-6888-3*) Time-Life.

***Sun.** Isaac Asimov. (J). Date not set. write for info. (*0-688-05459-5*) Lothrop.

***Sun.** Isaac Asimov. (J). Date not set. lib. bdg. write for info. (*0-688-05460-9*) Lothrop.

Sun. George Blattman. 240p. (Orig.). 1985. pap. text ed. 16.95 (*0-88010-148-2*) Anthroposophic.

Sun. Bob Daily. LC 94-2241. (First Bks.). 64p. (J). 1994. lib. bdg. 21.00 (*0-531-20105-8*) Watts.

Sun. Kay Davies & Wendy Oldfield. LC 95-6006. (See for Yourself Ser.). 30p. (J). (gr. k-3). 1995. lib. bdg. 19.97 (*0-8172-4040-3*) Raintree Steck-V.

Sun. Michael George. LC 92-8413. (Vision Bks.). 32p. (J). (gr. 2-6). 1992. lib. bdg. 22.79 (*0-89565-855-0*) Childs World.

Sun. Michael George. (Images Ser.). (J). 1992. lib. bdg. 16.95 (*0-88682-402-8*) Creative Ed.

***Sun.** Michael George. LC 96-47081. (Nature Bks.). 32p. (J). (gr. 1-6). 1997. lib. bdg. 22.79 (*1-56766-385-0*) Childs World.

***Sun.** Caroline Grimshaw. LC 97-22072. (Invisible Journeys Ser.). 1911. write for info. (*0-7166-3002-8*) World Bk.

Sun. Seth D. King. 225p. (Orig.). 1995. pap. 14.00 (*0-9640837-3-6*) Vice Press.

Sun. Patrick Moore. (Illus.). 1968. 4.95 (*0-393-06276-7*) Norton.

An Asterisk (*) at the beginning of an entry indicates that the title is appearing in BIP for the first time.

Sun. Seymour Simon. LC 85-32018. (Illus.). 32p. (J). (ps-3). 1986. 17.00 (0-688-05857-4, Morrow Junior); lib. bdg. 16.93 (0-688-05858-2, Morrow Junior) Morrow.

Sun. Seymour Simon. LC 85-32018. (Illus.). 32p. (J). (ps-3). 1989. pap. 5.95 (0-688-09236-5, Morrow Junior) Morrow.

Sun. Lynda Sorensen. LC 93-14872. (Solar System Ser.). (J). (ps-6). 1993. 12.67 (0-86593-272-7); 9.50 (0-685-66587-9) Rourke Corp.

Sun. M. Stix. (Astronomy & Astrophysics Library). (Illus.). 400p. 1989. 89.00 (0-387-50081-2) Spr-Verlag.

Sun. Gregory L. Vogt. (The Gateway Solar System Ser.). (Illus.). 32p. (J). (gr. 2-4). 1996. lib. bdg. 14.90 (1-56294-600-5) Millbrook Pr.

Sun. Gregory L. Vogt. (Gateway Solar System Ser.). (Illus.). 32p. (J). (gr. 2-4). 1996. 6.95 (0-7613-0160-7) Millbrook Pr.

*Sun. unabridged ed. Paulette Bourgeois. (Starting with Space Ser.). (Illus.). 40p. (J). (gr. 2-6). 1997. 12.95 (1-55074-158-6, Pub. by Kids Can Pr CN) Genl Dist Srvs.

Sun. Robert Daily. (First Bks.). (Illus.). 64p. (J). (gr. 4-6). 1996. reprint ed. pap. 6.95 (0-531-15776-8) Watts.

Sun. Karl O. Kiepenheuer. Tr. by Arnold J. Pomerans. LC 59-7294. (Ann Arbor Science Library). 160p. reprint ed. pap. 45.60 (0-317-09534-X, 2051047) Bks Demand.

Sun: A Laboratory for Astrophysics, Proceedings of the NATO Advanced Study Institute, Held in Crieff, Scotland on 16-29 June 1991. Ed. by Joan T. Schmelz & John C. Brown. LC 92-16845. (NATO Advanced Study Institutes Ser.: Vol. 373). 624p. (C). 1992. lib. bdg. 310.00 (0-7923-1811-0) Kluwer Ac.

Sun: A Play. Gordon Hoban. LC 89-92675. 123p. (Orig.). 1990. pap. 10.95 (0-944204-12-0) Omniun.

Sun: An Introduction. rev. ed. M. Stix. (Astronomy & Astrophysics Library). (Illus.). xiii, 390p. 1991. reprint ed. 79.95 (0-387-53796-1) Spr-Verlag.

Sun: In Praise of the Golden Eye of Heaven. Ed. by Paula Rees. LC 95-43447. 1996. pap. 12.00 (0-06-251261-7) Harper SF.

Sun: Our Daytime Star. Jane B. Moncure. LC 89-24009. (Discovery World Ser.). (Illus.). 32p. (J). (ps-2). 1990. lib. bdg. 21.36 (0-89565-551-9) Childs World.

Sun: Our Future Energy Source. David K. McDaniels. 360p. (C). 1991. reprint ed. lib. bdg. 43.50 (0-89464-594-3) Krieger.

Sun: Our Nearest Star. rev. ed. Franklyn M. Branley. LC 87-47764. (Let's-Read-&-Find-Out Science Bk.). (Illus.). 32p. (J). (ps-3). 1988. lib. bdg. 14.89 (0-690-04678-2, Crowell Jr Bks) HarpC Child Bks.

Sun: Our Very Own Star. Jeanne Bendick. (Early Bird Astronomy Ser.). (Illus.). 32p. (J). (gr. k-2). 1991. pap. 4.95 (1-878841-50-5); lib. bdg. 14.90 (1-878841-02-5) Millbrook Pr.

Sun: Short Stories & Drama. Darrell H. Lum. (Bamboo Ridge Ser.: No. 8). 77p. 1980. pap. 8.00 (0-910043-02-7) Bamboo Ridge Pr.

Sun + Moon Rendezvous. Todd S. Davis. 51p. 1993. pap. 3.00 (0-9635398-0-9); audio 5.00 (0-9635398-1-7) Tertium Non Data.

Sun, Air & Light Baths: How They Cure Disease. (Alternative Medicine Ser.). 1991. lib. bdg. 79.95 (0-8490-4546-0) Gordon Pr.

Sun Also Rises. Ernest Hemingway. (Hudson River Editions Ver.). 248p. 1977. 35.00 (0-684-15327-0) S&S Trade.

Sun Also Rises. Ernest Hemingway. 256p. 1995. pap. 10.00 (0-684-80071-3) S&S Trade.

Sun Also Rises. Ernest Hemingway. 1996. 25.00 (0-684-83051-5) S&S Trade.

Sun Also Rises. large type ed. Ernest Hemingway. LC 94-31301. 1994. lib. bdg. 23.95 (0-8161-5969-6, GK Hall) Thorndike Pr.

Sun Also Rises, 2 vols., Set, Vols. 1 & 2. Ed. by Matthew J. Bruccoli. (Archive of Literary Documents Ser.: Vol. II). 1990. Set; Vol. 1, xvi, 316p.; Vol. 2, pgs. 317-630. lib. bdg. 285.00 (1-55888-267-7) Omnigraphics Inc.

Sun Also Rises: Hemingway. Robert Dunn. (Book Notes Ser.). (C). 1984. pap. 2.50 (0-8120-3443-0) Barron.

Sun Also Rises Notes. Gary Carey. 1968. pap. 3.95 (0-8220-1237-5) Cliffs.

Sun Always Rises. Judy Lyn. 77p. 1990. pap. 9.95 (0-9638550-0-X) Judy Lyn.

Sun Always Shines for the Cool, Midnight Moon at the Greasy Spoon, Eulogy for a Small Time Thief. Miguel Pinero. LC 83-72582. 128p. (Orig.). (C). 1984. pap. 11.00 (0-934770-25-5) Arte Publico.

Sun & a Shield: The Chassidic Dynasty of Dej. Devora Gliksman. LC 96-24707. 1996. 21.95 (0-87306-761-4) Feldheim.

Sun & Cool Stars: Activity, Magnetism, Dynamos: Proceedings of Colloquium No. 130 of the International Astronomical Union, Helsinki, Finland, 17-20 July 1990. Ed. by I. Tuominen et al. (Lecture Notes in Physics Ser.: Vol. 380). x, 530p. 1991. 78.95 (0-387-53955-7) Spr-Verlag.

Sun & Cross: The Development from Megalithic Culture to Early Christianity in Ireland. Jacob Streit. Tr. by Hugh Latham from GER. (Illus.). 224p. 1993. pap. 25.00 (0-86315-157-4, Pub. by Floris Books UK) Anthroposophic.

Sun & Games. Ethel Tiersky & Maxine Chernoff. LC 93-47562. (Attractions Ser.: Bk. 3). 1994. pap. 9.20 (0-8092-3686-9) Contemp Bks.

Sun & Its Secrets. rev. ed. Isaac Asimov et al. (Library of the Universe). (Illus.). (J). (gr. 3 up). 1994. lib. bdg. 18.60 (0-8368-1135-6) Gareth Stevens Inc.

Sun & Moon. Patrick Moore. (Starry Sky Ser.). (Illus.). 24p. (J). (gr. k-3). 1995. lib. bdg. 14.40 (1-56294-622-6) Millbrook Pr.

Sun & Moon. Marcus Pfister. 32p. (J). (gr. 4-7). 1993. pap. 4.95 (0-590-44490-5) Scholastic Inc.

Sun & Moon: Fairy Tales from Korea. Kathleen Seros. LC 82-82510. (Illus.). 61p. (J). (gr. 3-9). 1982. 16.50 (0-930878-25-6) Hollym Intl.

Sun & Moon Guide to Eating Through Literature & Art. Ed. & Intro. by Douglas Messerli. (Illus.). 216p. 1994. 29.95 (1-55713-178-3) Sun & Moon CA.

Sun & Moon Polarity in Your Horoscope. Robert Hughes. LC 77-92771. 12.00 (0-86690-116-7) Am Fed Astrologers.

Sun & Other Things. Peter Carravetta. (Essential Poets Ser.: No. 72). 150p. 1995. 15.00 (1-55071-026-5) Guernica Editions.

Sun & Planetary System. George Teleki. 1982. lib. bdg. 175.00 (90-277-1429-0) Kluwer Ac.

Sun & Shadow. Cathryn Clare. (Shadows Ser.). 1994. mass mkt. 3.50 (0-373-07558-8, 5-07558-5) Silhouette.

*Sun & Shadows Ventures. Bert Murphy. Ed. by Appleyard Communications Staff. (Ventures West Ser.: Vol. 1). (Illus.). 150p. (Orig.). 1996. pap. 9.95 (0-9650298-1-6, SAW298-9077) MBAR Pubng.

Sun & Solar System Debris. William R. Corliss. LC 86-60231. (Catalog of Astronomical Anomalies Ser.). (Illus.). 300p. 1986. 17.95 (0-915554-20-8) Sourcebook.

*Sun & Spoon. Kevin Herkes. LC 96-46259. 144p. (J). (gr. 3 up). 1997. 15.00 (0-688-15232-5) Greenwillow.

Sun & Stars. Lesley Sims. LC 93-28280. (First Starts Ser.). (J). 1994. lib. bdg. 19.97 (0-8114-5505-X) Raintree Steck-V.

Sun & Stars. Lesley Sims. 1995. pap. 4.95 (0-8114-4946-7) Raintree Steck-V.

Sun & Steel. Yukio Mishima. Tr. by John Bester. LC 76-100628. 108p. 1990. pap. 7.00 (0-87011-425-5) Kodansha.

Sun & Storm: The Codex. David B. Pilurs. Ed. by Lenore Caruso & Sara L. Caruso. (Illus.). 96p. (YA). (gr. 7 up). 1993. per. 12.95 (0-9636551-1-6) Storm Pr.

Sun & Storm: The Enchiridion. David B. Pilurs. Ed. by Lenore R. Caruso & Sara L. Caruso. (Illus.). 96p. (YA). (gr. 7 up). 1993. per. 12.95 (0-9636551-0-8) Storm Pr.

Sun & Storm: The Terminus. David B. Pilurs. Ed. by Lenore R. Caruso. (Illus.). 16p. (YA). (gr. 7 up). 1993. 8.95 (0-9636551-2-4, 26635) Storm Pr.

Sun & the Heliosphere in Three Dimensions. Ed. by R. G. Marsden. (Astrophysics & Space Science Library). 1986. lib. bdg. 188.00 (90-277-2198-X) Kluwer Ac.

Sun & the Moon. Gary Mechler et al. LC 94-42421. (National Audubon Society Pocket Guide Ser.). 1995. pap. 7.99 (0-679-76056-3) Knopf.

Sun & the Moon. Niccolo Tucci. LC 94-15577. 676p. 1994. pap. 12.95 (1-55921-126-1) Moyer Bell.

Sun & the Shade: Florida Photography, 1885-1983. Bruce Weber. LC 83-50606. (Illus.). 95p. 1983. pap. 10.00 (0-943411-14-9) Norton Gal Art.

*Sun & the Solar System. Branley. 1996. write for info. (0-8050-5272-0) H Holt & Co.

*Sun & the Stars. Anne Welsbacher. LC 96-26776. (The Universe Ser.). (J). 1997. lib. bdg. 13.95 (1-56239-722-2) Abdo & Dghtrs.

Sun & the Wind. Cornelia Lehn. (Illus.). 32p. (J). (gr. k-5). 1983. 3.95 (0-87303-072-9) Faith & Life.

*Sun & What It Says Endlessly, No. 68. Paul Bennett. 32p. (Orig.). 1995. pap. 7.95 (0-614-24056-5) Pudding Hse Pubns.

Sun Angles for Design. Robert Bennett. LC 78-103157. 1978. pap. 15.00 (0-9601718-1-9) Bennett Arch & Eng.

Sun Artists (Original Series), Nos. 1-8. Ed. by W. Arthur Boord. LC 72-9184. (Literature of Photography Ser.). 1979. reprint ed. 48.95 (0-405-04895-5) Ayer.

Sun As a Star. Roger J. Tayler. (Illus.). 256p. (C). 1996. text ed. 64.95 (0-521-46464-1) Cambridge U Pr.

*Sun As a Star. Roger J. Taylor. (Illus.). 256p. (C). 1996. pap. text ed. 24.95 (0-521-46837-X) Cambridge U Pr.

Sun As a Variable Star. Ed. by H. S. Hudson et al. (Illus.). 380p. (C). 1994. 59.95 (0-521-42006-7) Cambridge U Pr.

Sun As a Variable Star: Solar & Stellar Irradiance Variations, Proceedings of the 143rd IAU Colloquium, Boulder, CO, 1993. Ed. by Judit M. Pap et al. 312p. 1994. 132.00 (0-615-00322-2) Kluwer Ac.

*Sun at Midday: Tales of a Mediterranean Family. Gina Alhadeff. LC 96-26840. 240p. 1997. 23.00 (0-679-41763-X) Pantheon.

*Sun at Midday: Tales of a Mediterranean Family. Gini Alhadeff. LC 97-16762. 240p. (Orig.). 1998. pap. 14.00 (0-88001-578-0) Ecco Pr.

Sun at Midnight. Sandra Field. (Presents Ser.). 1995. pap. 3.25 (0-373-11739-6, 1-11739-9) Harlequin Bks.

Sun at Night. Roger Williamson. LC 88-50313. 125p. (Orig.). 1989. pap. text ed. 6.95 (0-9620218-1-4) Vann Pr.

*Sun at Night. Roger Williamson. 96p. 1997. reprint ed. pap. 2.50 (1-57353-113-8, Eschaton Bks) Eschaton Prods.

Sun at Night: Poems. Brooks Haxton. 76p. 1995. 20.00 (0-679-44179-4) Knopf.

*Sun at Night: Poems. Brooks Haxton. 1997. pap. 14.00 (0-679-76596-4) Knopf.

Sun at the Center: A Primer on Heliocentric Astrology. Philip Sedgwick. LC 90-62430. (Modern Astrology Library). (Illus.). 240p. (Orig.). 1990. pap. 12.95 (0-87542-738-3) Llewellyn Pubns.

Sun Bear: The Path of Power. Sun Bear et al. LC 83-72949. (Illus.). 272p. 1984. pap. 9.95 (0-943404-03-7) Bear Tribe.

Sun Bear: The Path of Power. Sun Bear et al. 272p. 1992. pap. 11.00 (0-671-76529-9) S&S Trade.

Sun Bear the Path of Power: Sun Bear, Wabun & Barry Weinstock. (Illus.). 272p. (Orig.). 1987. pap. 9.95 (0-13-653403-1) S&S Trade.

Sun Bears. Stuart A. Kallen. LC 96-710. (J). 1997. lib. bdg. 13.95 (1-56239-594-7) Abdo & Dghtrs.

Sun Begun. Dragonwagon & Shaffer. Date not set. 16.00 (0-689-81159-4) S&S Childrens.

Sun Begun. Dragonwagon. (J). 1997. 16.95 (0-02-733185-7, Atheneum Bks Young) S&S Childrens.

*Sun Belt Home Plans. LC 96-77234. (Illus.). 256p. (Orig.). 1996. pap. 6.95 (0-938708-71-6) L F Garlinghouse Co.

Sun Betrayed: A Report on the Corporate Seizure of U. S. Solar Energy Development. Ray Reece. LC 79-66992. 234p. 1979. 35.00 (0-89608-072-2); pap. 7.50 (0-89608-071-4) South End Pr.

*Sun Betrayed: A Study of the Corporate Seizure of Solar Energy Development. Ray Reece. 234p. 1979. 49.99 (0-919618-08-1, Pub. by Black Rose Bks CN); pap. 12.99 (0-919618-07-3, Pub. by Black Rose Bks CN) Consort Bk Sales.

Sun Birds & Evergreens: The Nuk-Chuk Stories. Gordon Zima. LC 94-60715. (Illus.). 80p. (J). (gr. 1-5). 1995. pap. 8.95 (1-55523-709-6) Winston-Derek.

Sun-Blazoned. Judy Hogan. 90p. 1983. pap. 5.00 (0-916324-11-7) Carolina Wren.

*Sun Book: Or The Philosopher's Vade Mecum. John Hazelrigg. (Illus.). 189p. 1997. pap. 17.00 (0-89540-330-7, Sun Bks) Sun Pub.

Sun Book: The Philosopher's Vade Mecum. John Hazelrigg. 189p. 1971. reprint ed. spiral bd. 8.50 (0-7873-0387-9) Hlth Research.

Sun Boy: Cou-Yan-Nai: Comanche Indian Story for Children. Weechees. 32p. (J). (gr. 4-9). 1983. pap. 4.95 (0-89992-082-9) Coun India Ed.

Sun Boy & His Hunter's Bow. Weechees. (Sun Boy Ser.). 32p. (J). (gr. 4-8). 1988. pap. 4.95 (0-89992-115-9) Coun India Ed.

Sun Boy & the Angry Panther. Weechees. (Sun Boy Ser.). 32p. (J). (gr. 4-8). 1988. pap. 4.95 (0-89992-114-0) Coun India Ed.

Sun Boy & the Monster of To-Oh-Pah. Weechees. (Sun Boy Ser.). 32p. (J). (gr. 4-8). 1988. pap. 4.95 (0-89992-113-2) Coun India Ed.

*Sun Can Shine Again. Orrie Snyder. LC 97-60122. 352p. (Orig.). 1997. pap. 12.99 (1-57921-006-6) WinePress Pub.

Sun Care Products: The International Market. Euromonitor Staff. 100p. (C). 1988. 2,925.00 (0-685-30320-9, Pub. by Euromonitor Pubns UK) Gale.

Sun Chief: The Autobiography of a Hopi Indian. rev. ed. Leo W. Simmons & Robert V. Hine. (Illus.). 480p. 1963. pap. 16.00 (0-300-00227-0, YW8) Yale U Pr.

Sun Circles & Human Hands. Emma L. Fundaburk. Ed. by Mary D. Foreman. (Illus.). 232p. reprint ed. 24.00 (0-9617083-2-8) Am Bicent Mus.

Sun Clothed Woman. pap. 0.95 (0-937408-08-5) GMI Pubns Inc.

Sun-Clothed Woman & the Manchild. Gordon Lindsay. (Revelation Ser.: Vol. 7). 1962. 1.95 (0-89985-040-5) Christ for the Nations.

Sun Coast Civic Center: A General Office Assistant Simulation. 2nd ed. Norma B. Taylor et al. 1987. pap. 15.95 (0-538-14020-8, N02) S-W Pub.

Sun Country Banker: The Life & the Bank of Samuel Doak Young. Joseph Leach. LC 88-90911. (Illus.). 300p. 1989. 19.95 (0-930208-26-9) Mangan Books TX.

Sun-Damaged Skin. Ronald Marks. 1992. 19.95 (0-614-06225-X); 19.95 (0-614-07393-6, M Dunitz) Scovill Paterson.

Sun Dance. S. W. Brouwer. 312p. 1995. pap. 9.99 (1-56476-427-3, 6-3427, Victor Bks) Chariot Victor.

Sun Dance. Kevin McColley. LC 94-33162. 233p. (YA). (gr. 7 up). 1995. 16.00 (0-689-80008-8) Macmillan.

Sun Dance: A Case History of the Shoshone Bannook Sun Dance. Helene Smith. Ed. by Catherine Snyder. LC 95-2799. (Illus.). 207p. (Orig.). 1995. pap. 17.95 (0-945437-18-8) MacDonald-Sward.

Sun Dance: The Fiftieth Anniversary Crow Indian Sun Dance. Michael Crummett. LC 93-1567. (Illus.). 92p. (Orig.). 1993. pap. 9.95 (1-56044-201-8) Falcon Pr MT.

Sun Dance & Other Ceremonies of the Oglala Division of the Teton Dakota. J. R. Walker. LC 76-43886. (AMNH. Anthropological Papers: Vol. 16, Pt. 2). reprint ed. 45.00 (0-404-15745-9) AMS Pr.

Sun Dance at Turtle Rock. Patricia C. Viglucci. (Illus.). 128p. (Orig.). (J). (gr. 4-7). 1996. pap. 4.95 (0-9645914-9-9, Stone Pine Bks) Patri Pubns.

Sun Dance for Andy Horn. Shelly Frome. 124p. (YA). (gr. 9-12). 1990. 14.95 (0-89992-324-0); pap. 9.95 (0-89992-124-8) Coun India Ed.

Sun Dance of the Crow Indians. Robert H. Lowie. LC 76-43771. (AMNH. Anthropological Papers: Vol. 16, Pt. 1). 1977. reprint ed. 34.50 (0-404-15624-X) AMS Pr.

Sun Dancer. David London. 320p. 1996. 23.00 (0-684-81458-7, S&S) S&S Trade.

Sun Dancer's Passion. Karen A. Bale. (Sweet Medicine's Prophecy Ser.: No. 1). 1981. mass mkt. 3.95 (0-8217-2790-7, Zebra Kensgtn) Kensgtn Pub Corp.

Sun Dances: Prayers & Blessings from the Gaelic. Tr. & Compiled by Alexander Carmichael. 144p. 1990. pap. 9.95 (0-86315-503-0, 448, Pub. by Floris Books UK) Anthroposophic.

*Sun Dancing: A Medieval Vision. Geoffrey Moorhouse. LC 97-8748. 1997. 27.00 (0-15-100277-0) HarBrace.

Sun Day, the Not-Quite Knight. Jane H. Stroschin. (Illus.). 48p. (J). (gr. k-6). 1994. lib. bdg. 15.00 (1-883960-13-4) Henry Quill.

Sun Devils. large type ed. John Armour. (Linford Western Library). 304p. 1992. pap. 15.99 (0-7089-7173-3, Trailtree Bookshop) Ulverscroft.

Sun Dial Time. Don Marquis. LC 79-132119. (Short Story Index Reprint Ser.). 1977. 20.95 (0-8369-3676-0) Ayer.

Sun Dials & Time Dials: A Collection of Working Models to Cut Out & Glue Together. Gerald Jenkins. 1988. pap. 10.95 (0-906212-59-6, Pub. by Tarquin UK) Parkwest Pubns.

Sun Dogs. Robert Olen Butler. 1994. pap. 11.00 (0-8050-3143-X) H Holt & Co.

Sun Dogs & Shooting Stars: A Skywatcher's Guide. Franklyn M. Branley. 128p. (J). 1993. pap. 3.50 (0-380-71848-0, Camelot) Avon.

Sun Downers: VF-11 in World War II. Barrett Tillman. (Gold Wings Ser.). (Illus.). 44p. (C). 1993. pap. 12.95 (0-9625860-8-0) Phalanx Pub.

Sun-Drenched Days, Two-Blanket Nights: A Sportsman Takes Note. Tom Carney. (Illus.). (Orig.). 1995. pap. 10.95 (0-9637085-6-2) Partrdge Pointe.

Sun-Dried Tomatoes. Georgeanne Brennan & Ethel Brennan. (Illus.). 72p. 1995. 9.95 (0-8118-0627-8) Chronicle Bks.

*Sun-Dried Tomatoes! Andrea Chesman. LC 97-24473. (Specialty Cookbooks Ser.). 128p. (Orig.). 1997. pap. 6.95 (0-89594-900-8) Crossing Pr.

Sun, Earth, & Sky. Kenneth R. Lang. LC 95-6109. 1995. 39.95 (3-540-58778-0) Spr-Verlag.

*Sun, Earth & Sky. Kenneth R. Lang. LC 97-8370. 1997. write for info. (3-540-62808-8) Spr-Verlag.

Sun-Earth Buffering & Superinsulation. Don Booth et al. LC 83-72283. (Illus.). 1983. 18.95 (0-9604422-4-3); pap. 14.95 (0-9604422-3-5) Comm Builders.

Sun Earth System. John Streete. LC 95-61059. (Global Change Ser.). (Illus.). 58p. (Orig.). (C). 1996. pap. text ed. 19.00 (0-935702-86-5) Univ Sci Bks.

*Sun-Face Buddha: The Teachings of Ma-Tsu & the Hung-Chou School of Chan. Cheng Chien. LC 92-28980. 170p. pap. 48.50 (0-608-04960-3, 2065539) Bks Demand.

Sun Faced-Moon Faced Haiku, 2 Vols., Vol. 1. Alan Gettis. 32p. 1982. pap. 3.50 (0-913719-20-X) High-Coo Pr.

Sun Faced-Moon Faced Haiku, 2 Vols., Vol. 2. Alan Gettis. 32p. 1982. pap. 3.50 (0-913719-21-8) High-Coo Pr.

Sun Gardens: Victorian Photograms. Anna Atkins & Larry J. Schaaf. (Illus.). 104p. 1985. 40.00 (0-89381-203-X) Aperture.

*Sun Girl & Moon Boy. Yangsook Choi. LC 96-51186. 1997. 17.00 (0-679-88386-X); lib. bdg. 18.99 (0-679-98386-4) Knopf Bks Yng Read.

Sun God's Daughter & King Samvaran: Tapati-Samvaranam & the Kutiyattam Drama Tradition. Tr. by N. P. Unni & Bruce M. Sullivan. (C). 1995. 28.00 (81-7081-311-5, Pub. by Nag Pubs II) S Asia.

Sun God's Island. large type ed. Nina Shaldon. (Linford Romance Library). 1989. pap. 15.99 (0-7089-6794-9) Ulverscroft.

*Sun Has Set. White Wolf Staff. (The Giovanni Chronicles: No. 3). 1998. pap. 15.00 (1-56504-258-1) White Wolf.

Sun Hath Looked upon Me. Calixthe Beyala. (African Writers Ser.). 128p. 1996. pap. 9.95 (0-435-90951-7) Heinemann.

Sun Horse: Native Visions of the New World. Gerald Hausman. LC 92-71218. 144p. 1992. pap. 14.95 (0-914955-08-X) Lotus Light.

Sun in Cancer. Lindy Hough. 118p. (Orig.). 1975. pap. 3.50 (0-913028-34-7) North Atlantic.

Sun in Capricorn. Paul Rosenblatt. 185p. 1989. 18.50 (0-922820-00-7) Watermrk Pr.

*Sun in Glory. large type ed. Harriet Hudson. (Charnwood Large Print Ser.). 672p. 1996. 27.99 (0-7089-8918-7) Ulverscroft.

Sun in the Clouds & Other Essays. Alejo L. Villanueva, Jr. 90p. (Orig.). 1992. pap. 8.75 (971-10-0472-0, Pub. by New Day Pub PH) Cellar.

Sun in the Morning. large type ed. Elizabeth Cadell. 239p. 1996. pap. 21.95 (0-7862-0606-3, Thorndike Lrg Prnt) Thorndike Pr.

Sun in the North. Kathryn G. Black. 215p. 1990. 12.85 (0-9626891-0-6) Dika.

Sun in the Sky. Walter C. O'Kane. LC 50-7404. (Civilization of the American Indian Ser.: No. 30). (Illus.). 274p. reprint ed. 78.10 (0-8357-9742-2, 2016245) Bks Demand.

Sun in the West. Jean Earle. 64p. 1995. pap. text ed. 15.95 (1-85422-138-8, Pub. by Seren Bks UK) Dufour.

Sun in Time. Ed. by Charles P. Sonett et al. LC 91-29614. (Space Science Ser.). (Illus.). 990p. 1992. 70.00 (0-8165-1297-3) Serpents Tail.

*Sun Is a Star & Other Amazing Facts about Space. Kate Petty. (I Didn't Know That Ser.). (Illus.). 32p. (J). (gr. 1-3). 1997. 8.95 (0-7613-0593-9, Copper Beech Bks); lib. bdg. 14.90 (0-7613-0567-X, Copper Beech Bks) Millbrook Pr.

Sun Is Always Shining above the Clouds. Tina B. Polis. 77p. (Orig.). 1993. pap. 12.95 (0-89716-471-7) P B Pubng.

Sun Is Always Shining Somewhere. Allan Fowler. (Rookie Read-about Science Ser.). (Illus.). 32p. (J). (ps-2). 1991. pap. 3.95 (0-516-44906-0); lib. bdg. 17.30 (0-516-04906-2) Childrens.

Sun Is Always Shining Somewhere Big Book. Allan Fowler. (Rookie Read-about Science Big Bks.). (Illus.). 32p. (J). (ps-2). 1991. pap. 32.40 (0-516-49466-X) Childrens.

Sun Is Feminine: A Study on Language & Acquisition in Bilingual Children. T. Taeschner. (Language & Communication Ser.: Vol. 13). (Illus.). 290p. 1983. 92.00 (0-387-12238-9) Spr-Verlag.

Sun Is Not Merciful: Short Stories. Anna L. Walters. LC 85-16177. 136p. (Orig.). 1985. pap. 8.95 (0-932379-10-9); lib. bdg. 18.95 (0-932379-11-7) Firebrand Bks.

Sun Is On. rev. ed. Lindamichelle Baron. (Illus.). 48p. (J). (gr. 1-6). 1982. pap. 5.95 (0-940938-02-2) Harlin Jacque.

S

Sun Is Rising. Sophie Masson. (YA). 1996. pap. 12.95 (0-7022-2789-7, Pub. by Univ Queensland Pr AT) Intl Spec Bk.

Sun Is Shining on the Other Side. Margaret T. Jensen. LC 94-6206. 1994. 24.99 (0-8407-6356-5) Nelson.

Sun Is So Quiet. Nikki Giovanni. LC 95-39357. (Illus.). 32p. (J). (ps up). 1996. 14.95 (0-8050-4119-2, B Martin BYR) H Holt & Co.

Sun Is Up: A Child's Year of Poems. William J. Smith & Carol Ra. LC 94-79620. (Illus.). 32p. (J). (ps-2). 1996. 15.95 (1-56397-029-5) Boyds Mills Pr.

Sun Jack & Rain Jack. Ursel Scheffler. LC 93-39229. (Illus.). 32p. (J). (gr. k up). 1994. lib. bdg. 18.60 (0-8368-1089-9) Gareth Stevens Inc.

***Sun Java Certification Exam Guide.** Cary Jardin. 1997. 69.99 (0-7897-1390-X) Que.

Sun Journey: A Story of Zuni Pueblo. Ann N. Clark. LC 88-70955. (Illus.). 96p. (J). (gr. 3 up). 1988. reprint ed. 19.95 (0-941270-49-1); reprint ed. pap. 9.95 (0-941270-48-3) Ancient City Pr.

Sun King. Nancy Mitford. (Illus.). 312p. 1995. pap. 19.95 (0-14-023967-7, Penguin Bks) Viking Penguin.

***Sun King: Elvis = the Second Coming.** Jeremy Reed. 256p. 1997. 16.95 (1-871592-77-1) Creation Bks.

Sun King: Louis XIV & the New World. Ed. by Steven G. Reinhardt. (Studies in Louisiana Culture: Vol. III). (Illus.). 344p. (Orig.). 1984. write for info. (0-916137-00-7); pap. write for info. (0-916137-01-5) L A Mus Foun.

S

Sun King: The Ascendancy of French Culture During the Reign of Louis XIV. Ed. by David L. Rubin. LC 90-55041. (Illus.). 248p. 1992. 42.50 (0-918016-94-0) Folger Bks.

Sun-Kissed Kitty Learns How to Say "No" Resisting Peer Pressure. Sandra Brown. LC 94-77203. 16p. (J). (gr. 1-4). 1991. 5.95 (1-884063-25-X) Mar Co Prods.

***Sun Light: Poems & Other Words.** Shems Friedlander & Nuri Friedlander. Ed. by Sarah Sullivan. (Illus.). 47p. (Orig.). 1997. pap. 8.95 (1-890506-50-8) Safina Bks.

Sun Lights: A Child's Traditional Values - Communication Skills Educational Program. Norma F. Swanson. 1988. write for info. (0-318-64043-0) Window World NY.

***Sun Lore.** LC 97-17276. 1997. pap. 12.95 (1-56718-343-3) Llewellyn Pubns.

Sun Lore of All Ages. William T. Olcott. 1991. lib. bdg. 79.95 (0-8490-4271-2) Gordon Pr.

Sun-Maid Cookbook. Sun-Maid Growers Staff. LC 79-54948. (Orig.). pap. 5.95 (0-87502-070-4) Benjamin Co.

Sun Maiden & the Crescent Moon: Siberian Folk Tales. James Riordan. LC 90-42586. (International Folk Tale Ser.). 224p. 1991. 24.95 (0-940793-66-0); pap. 11.95 (0-940793-65-2) Interlink Pub.

Sun Men of the Americas. Grace Cooke. 120p. Date not set. pap. 7.95 (0-85487-057-1, Pub. by White Eagle UK) DeVorss.

Sun, Moon & Planets. Lynn Myring. (Explainers Ser.). (J). (gr. 2-5). 1982. pap. 4.50 (0-86020-580-0, Usborne) EDC.

Sun, Moon & Stars, & the Binding of the Years see Florentine Codex, General History of the Things of New Spain

***Sun, Moon & Stars Stamps.** (J). 1996. pap. 12.95 (0-670-87223-7) Viking Child Bks.

Sun, Moon, & Tides: A Collection of Working Models to Cut Out & Glue Together. Gerald Jenkins. 1993. pap. 10.95 (0-906212-76-6, Pub. by Tarquin UK) Parkwest Pubns.

Sun Moon Compendium, 2 Vols. Dorling Kindersley Staff. 1995. write for info. (0-7894-0368-4) HM.

Sun, Moon, Salt. Nancy White. LC 92-62021. (Illus.). 72p. 1993. 10.00 (0-915380-29-3) Word Works.

***Sun Mother Wakes the World.** Diane Wolkenstein. (J). Date not set. write for info. (0-688-13915-9, Morrow Junior); lib. bdg. write for info. (0-688-13916-7, Morrow Junior) Morrow.

Sun My Heart: From Mindfulness to Insight Contemplation. Thich Nhat Hanh. Tr. by Elin Sand et al. from VIE. LC 88-17908. 139p. (Orig.). 1988. pap. 9.50 (0-938077-12-0) Parallax Pr.

Sun Myung Moon & the Unification Church. James Bjornstad. LC 84-70856. 64p. 1984. pap. 4.99 (0-87123-301-0) Bethany Hse.

Sun 'n' Soak: Clothing Optional Naturally. Phil Owensby. (Illus.). 144p. 1994. 19.95 (0-9643762-0-2) Solavescence.

Sun Never Sets: An Historical Essay on Britain & Its Place in the World. Nicholas Tarling. LC 86-81401. 176p. 1986. text ed. 22.50 (0-938719-02-5, Envoy Pr) Apt Bks.

Sun Never Sets: Confronting the Network of Foreign U. S. Military Bases. American Friends Service Committee Staff. Ed. by Joseph Gerson & Bruce Birchard. 400p. (Orig.). 1991. 40.00 (0-89608-400-0); pap. 16.00 (0-89608-399-3) South End Pr.

Sun Never Stops Shining. Gladys J. Booker. 100p. (Orig.). 1991. 10.95 (0-9629641-0-7) E L Booker.

***Sun, Oak, Almond.** W. G. Shepherd. Date not set. 14.95 (0-900977-21-3, Pub. by Anvil Press UK) Dufour.

Sun of Quebec. Joseph A. Altsheler. 25.95 (0-8488-0907-6) Amereon Ltd.

Sun of Quebec. Joseph A. Altsheler. 1993. reprint ed. lib. bdg. 21.95 (0-89968-564-1) Buccaneer Bks.

***Sun of Saratoga.** Joseph Altsheler. Date not set. lib. bdg. 25.95 (0-8488-2121-1) Amereon Ltd.

Sun Oil Co. A Report on the Company's Environmental Policies & Practices. (Illus.). 26p. (C). 1994. reprint ed. pap. text ed. 250.00 (0-7881-0984-7, Coun on Econ) DIANE Pub.

***Sun on a Cloudy Day.** Hanna Mina. Tr. by Bassam Frangieh & Clementina Brown from ARA. 1997. pap. write for info. (1-57889-044-6) Passeggiata.

***Sun on a Cloudy Day.** Hanna Mina. Tr. by Bassam Frangieh & Clementina Brown from ARA. 1997. write for info. (1-57889-045-4) Passeggiata.

Sun, Our Star. Robert W. Noyes. LC 82-11733. (Harvard Books on Astronomy). (Illus.). 271p. reprint ed. pap. 77.30 (0-7837-3861-7, 2043683) Bks Demand.

Sun over Mountain: A Course in Creative Imagination. 3rd ed. Jessica Macbeth. (Illus.). 288p. (Orig.). 1991. pap. 13.95 (0-946551-67-7, Pub. by Gateway Books UK) ACCESS Pubs Network.

Sun Performance & Tuning Sparc & Solaris. Adrian Cockcroft. 288p. 1994. pap. text ed. 38.00 (0-13-149642-5) P-H.

Sun Pictures in Scotland. Graham Smith. (Illus.). 77p. 1989. pap. 7.50 (0-912303-45-X) Michigan Mus.

Sun Pin: The Art of Warfare. Tr. by D. C. Lau & Roger T. Ames. (Illus.). 352p. 1996. 27.50 (0-345-37991-8) Ballantine.

Sun Pin Military Methods. Tr. by Ralph D. Sawyer & Mei-chun L. Sawyer. LC 94-42046. (History & Warfare Ser.). 392p. (C). 1995. pap. text ed. 18.95 (0-8133-8888-0) Westview.

Sun, Planets, Star. John Green. (Little Activity Bks.). (J). 1994. pap. 1.00 (0-486-28097-7) Dover.

Sun Power: A Bibliography of United States Government Documents on Solar Energy. Compiled by Sandra McAninch. LC 80-29037. xx, 944p. 1981. text ed. 135.00 (0-313-20992-8, MSU/, Greenwood Pr) Greenwood.

Sun Power: The Global Solution for the Coming Energy Crisis. Ralph Nansen. 264p. 1996. pap. 14.95 (0-9647021-1-8) Ocean Pr WA.

Sun Rises: A True Account of Events Which Occurred Over 78,000 Years Ago. Robert D. Steele. 1952. pap. 8.95 (0-87505-093-X) Borden.

Sun Rises in the Evening: Monism & Quietism in Western Culture. David Kirby. LC 82-3247. 186p. 1982. 20.00 (0-8108-1536-2) Scarecrow.

Sun Rises, the Star Shines. John Clementson. LC 95-80315. (Illus.). 10p. (J). (ps). 1995. pap. 4.00 (0-15-200316-9, Red Wagon Bks) HarBrace.

Sun Rising on the West: The Saga of Henry Clay & Elizabeth Smith. W. H. Curry. 1979. 20.00 (0-9606940-2-1) Crosby County.

Sun River. Richard Wheeler. 1989. pap. 3.95 (0-8125-1073-9) Tor Bks.

Sun Rock Man. Cid Corman. LC 73-140033. (Orig.). 1970. pap. 1.75 (0-8112-0024-8, NDP318) New Directions.

Sun Rose. Abby Niebauer. 60p. 1985. pap. 14.00 (0-930513-01-0) Blackwells Pr.

Sun, Sand & Cement. T. Taylor. (C). 1989. text ed. 29.95 (0-948032-89-8) St Mut.

Sun, Sand & Sausage Pie: And Beach House Memories. Sally Holbrook. Ed. by Diane MacFarland. LC 91-91372. (Illus.). 112p. 1992. 19.95 (0-9631225-0-9) Sabill Pr.

Sun Sational Bulletin Boards for Holidays & Special Occasions. Becky J. Radtke. (Illus.). 224p. teacher ed. 12.99 (0-86653-685-X, GA1419) Good Apple.

Sun Says When. Alice S. Newton. 80p. 1994. 12.95 (0-8233-0493-0) Golden Quill.

Sun Sense: A Complete Guide to the Prevention, Early Detection, & Treatment of Skin Cancer. Perry Robins. (Illus.). 272p. 1990. pap. 109.95 (0-9627688-0-4) Skin Cancer Fndtn.

Sun Shines at Midnight Too. J. Lamarr Cox. LC 95-76784. (Illus.). 315p. (Orig.). 1995. pap. 13.95 (0-9646440-0-2) Aureole Pub.

Sun Shines for All: Journalism & Ideology in the Life of Charles A. Dana. Janet E. Steele. LC 92-33861. (Illus.). 300p. (C). 1993. text ed. 35.00 (0-8156-2579-0) Syracuse U Pr.

Sun Sign Career Guide. Robert G. Walker & Howard Sasportas. 304p. (Orig.). 1991. mass mkt. 4.50 (0-380-76360-5) Avon.

***Sun Sign Diet.** Gale Black. 1997. pap. 18.95 (0-614-27339-0) Alive & Well.

***Sun Sign Diet: 12 Exclusive Astrological Diets Personally Designed Just for You.** rev. ed. Gayle Black. 430p. 1997. pap. 18.95 (0-9651511-2-3) Alive & Well.

Sun Sign Secrets: The Ultimate Astrological Guide to Yourself. Bernard Fitzwalter. (Illus.). 240p. 1991. reprint ed. pap. 10.00 (1-85538-076-5, Pub. by Aquarian Pr UK) Thorsons SF.

Sun Signs Dieting: Learn to Be Thin with Astrology. Jeanie Innis. 200p. 1993. 8.95 (1-882811-04-6) Skyline Pubns.

Sun Signs from a Polar Star: A Northern Zodiac. Dale DeArmond. (Illus.). 26p. 1993. 120.00 (1-881655-02-4); pap. 8.95 (1-881655-00-8) Old Harbor Pr.

Sun Signs from a Polar Star: A Northern Zodiac. limited ed. Dale DeArmond. (Illus.). 26p. 1993. 55.00 (1-881655-01-6) Old Harbor Pr.

Sun, Snow, Stars, Sky. Catherine Anholt & Laurence Anholt. (Illus.). 32p. (J). 1995. pap. 13.99 (0-670-86196-0) Viking Child Bks.

***Sun Snow Stars Sky.** Catherine Anholt. (J). 1997. pap. 4.99 (0-14-055824-1) Viking Penguin.

***Sun Song.** Jean Marzollo. LC 91-29316. (Picture Bks.). (Illus.). 32p. (J). (gr. k-3). 1997. pap. 5.95 (0-06-443476-1, Trophy) HarpC Child Bks.

Sun Song. Jean Marzollo. LC 91-29316. (Illus.). 32p. (J). 1995. 14.95 (0-06-020787-6, HarpT); lib. bdg. 14.89 (0-06-020788-4, HarpT) HarpC.

Sun Songs: Creation Myths from Around the World. Raymond Van Over. (Orig.). 1980. mass mkt. 4.95 (0-452-00730-5, Mer) NAL-Dutton.

Sun-Spaces. Frances Ottesen. (Illus.). 76p. 1981. 7.95 (0-9605220-0-X) Otafra.

Sun Spaces-Home Additions for Year-Round Natural Living. John H. Mauldin. LC 87-21913. (Illus.). 256p. 1987. 21.95 (0-8306-7816-6, 2816) McGraw-Hill Prof.

Sun Spots. Jacques Devon. Ed. by Rose Johns. (Illus.). 92p. (Orig.). 1988. pap. write for info. (0-318-63128-8) Prairie Rose Pub.

Sun, Stars & Planets. Tom Stacy. LC 90-42979. (Tell Me about Bks.). (Illus.). 40p. (Orig.). (J). (gr. 2-5). 1991. pap. 4.99 (0-679-80862-0) Random Bks Yng Read.

***Sun Still Shone: Professors Talk about Retirement.** Lorraine T. Dorfman. LC 97-16580. 216p. 1997. 21.95 (0-87745-601-1) U of Iowa Pr.

Sun Takes Us Away: New & Selected Poems. Benjamin Saltman. 192p. 1996. pap. 12.95 (0-9639528-7-0, Red Hen Press) Valentine CA.

Sun Technology Papers. M. Hall & J. Barry. (Sun Technical Reference Library). (Illus.). 300p. 1989. 52.95 (0-387-97145-9) Spr-Verlag.

Sun That Never Rose: The Inside Story of Japan's Failed Attempt at Global Financial Dominance. Eugene R. Dattel. 1994. text ed. 27.50 (1-55738-562-9) Irwin Prof Pubng.

Sun That Never Sets. Albert Krassner. 96p. (Orig.). 1991. pap. 7.95 (0-912061-19-7) Veridon Edns.

Sun, the Moon & the Silver Market: Secrets of a Silver Trader. Raymond A. Merriman. 112p. 1992. per. 75.00 (0-930706-19-6) Seek-It Pubns.

Sun, the Moon, & the Stars. Steven Brust. 1996. pap. 11.95 (0-312-86039-0) Orb NYC.

Sun, the Moon, & the Stars. rev. ed. Mae B. Freeman & Ira M. Freeman. LC 78-64604. (Illus.). (J). (gr. 2-4). 1979. 8.95 (0-394-80110-5) Random Bks Yng Read.

Sun, the Rain & the Insulin: Growing up with Diabetes. Joan MacCracken. Ed. by Donna Hoel & Greg Hoel. LC 96-90047. (Illus.). 250p. (Orig.). 1996. pap. 12.95 (0-9646018-5-0) Tiffin Press.

Sun, the Sea, a Touch of the Wind. Rosa Guy. LC 95-7745. 305p. 1995. pap. 22.95 (0-525-24780-7, Dutton) NAL-Dutton.

Sun, the Sea, a Touch of the Wind. Rosa Guy. 320p. 1996. pap. 11.95 (0-452-27551-2, Plume) NAL-Dutton.

Sun, the Wind & Tashira: A Hottentot Tale from Africa. Elizabeth Claire. (Mondo Folktales ser.). (Illus.). 24p. (Orig.). (J). (gr. k-4). 1994. pap. 4.95 (1-879531-20-8); lib. bdg. 9.95 (1-879531-41-0) Mondo Pubng.

Sun, the Wind & Tashira: A Hottentot Tale from Africa, Big Book. Elizabeth Claire. LC 94-8129. (Mondo Folktales ser.). (Illus.). 24p. (Orig.). (J). (gr. k-4). 1994. 23.95 (1-879531-08-9) Mondo Pubng.

Sun, the Wind & the Rain. Lisa W. Peters. LC 87-23808. (Illus.). 32p. (J). (ps-2). 1990. reprint ed. pap. 5.95 (0-8050-1481-0, Owlet BYR) H Holt & Co.

Sun Through the Rain. Lyndon Teeples. 180p. 1972. 14.95 (1-888129-05-0) Story Pubng.

Sun Through the Window. Marci McGill. LC 95-79862. (Illus.). 64p. (J). (gr. 1-4). 1996. pap. 7.95 (1-56397-454-1) Boyds Mills Pr.

Sun-Tzu: Art of War. Tr. by Ralph D. Sawyer. 375p. (C). 1994. pap. text ed. 12.95 (0-8133-1951-X) Westview.

Sun Tzu: Manual for War. Sun Tzu Wu. LC 90-83460. 170p. (Orig.). 1994. pap. 9.95 (0-910169-02-0) ATLI IL.

Sun-Tzu: The Art of War: New Translation Incorporating the Recently Discovered Yin-Ch Ueh-Shan Texts. Tr. & Comment by Roger T. Ames. LC 92-52662. (Illus.). 400p. 1993. 25.00 (0-345-36239-X, Ballantine Trade) Ballantine.

Sun Tzu: The New Translation. Sun-tzu. Ed. by J. H. Huang. LC 92-33951. 1993. pap. 10.00 (0-688-12400-3) Morrow.

Sun Tzu: War & Management. Chou-Hou Wee. 320p. 1996. pap. write for info. (0-201-62858-9) Addison-Wesley.

***Sun Tzu: War & Management.** Chow-Hou Wee. 1996. pap. text ed. 15.00 (0-201-62859-7) Addison-Wesley.

***Sun Tzu & the Art of Business: Six Strategic Principles for Managers.** Mark R. McNeilly. (Illus.). 272p. 1996. 25.00 (0-19-509996-0) OUP.

Sun Tzu on Management: The Art of War in Contemporary Business Strategy. Foo C. Teck. 200p. 1995. pap. 21.95 (981-00-6799-2) Buttrwrth-Heinemann.

Sun Tzu on the Art of War. 292p. 1988. reprint ed. pap. 12.50 (9971-4-9107-9) Heian Intl.

Sun Tzu on the Art of War - A Business Strategy Handbook. Sun Tzu Wu. Tr. by Lionel Giles. 99p. 1991. 12.95 (0-9629505-0-5) Hale Fred Pr.

Sun Tzu's Art of War. Sun Tzu. 1991. lib. bdg. 79.95 (0-8490-4748-X) Gordon Pr.

Sun Tzu's Art of War: The Modern Chinese Interpretation. Tao Hanzhang. Tr. by Yuan Shibing from CHI. LC 87-10168. (Illus.). 128p. 1990. pap. 11.95 (0-8069-6639-4) Sterling.

***Sun Tzu's Art of War for Traders & Investors.** Dean Lundell. LC 96-52325. 200p. 1997. text ed. 19.95 (0-07-039141-6) McGraw.

Sun under Wood: New Poems. Robert Hass. LC 96-19322. 92p. 1996. 22.00 (0-88001-468-7) Ecco Pr.

***Sun under Wood: New Poems.** Robert Hass. 96p. 1998. pap. 15.00 (0-88001-557-8) Ecco Pr.

Sun up, Sun Down. Gail Gibbons. LC 82-23420. (Illus.). 32p. (J). (gr. 1-5). 1983. 15.00 (0-15-282781-1, HB Juv Bks) HarBrace.

Sun up, Sun Down. Gail Gibbons. LC 82-23420. (Voyager Picture Bks.). (Illus.). 32p. (J). (gr. 1-5). 1987. pap. 6.00 (0-15-282782-X, Voyager Bks) HarBrace.

***Sun Valley: The Extraordinary History of the Wood River Valley.** Wendolyn Holland. 304p. 1997. 59.95 (1-56044-587-4, Skyhse) Falcon Pr MT.

Sun Valley Idaho, Vol. I. D. M. Dorward. (Illus.). 33p. 1995. write for info. (0-614-13005-0) Dorward Photo.

Sun Valley Signatures III: A Photographic Portrait of the Sun Valley Area. Photos by David R. Stoecklein. (Illus.). 156p. 1991. 39.95 (0-922029-00-8) Stoecklein Pub.

Sun Valley Story, Vol. I. D. M. Dorward. (Illus.). 32p. (Orig.). 1996. reprint ed. mass mkt., pap. write for info. (0-9615729-2-2) Dorward Photo.

***Sun Virgin.** large type ed. Robert Charles. (Linford Mystery Library). 400p. 1997. pap. 16.99 (0-7089-5024-8, Linford) Ulverscroft.

Sun Walks with Me: A Collection of Poems. Anne-George Telasco. 1996. 8.95 (0-533-11585-X) Vantage.

Sun Wars. R. Borg. 15.00 (1-56076-394-9) Random.

***Sun Weather & Climate.** 1980. 65.00 (0-8103-1018-X, 00006825, Gale Res Intl) Gale.

Sun, Weather, & Climate. John R. Herman & Richard A. Goldberg. (Earth Science Ser.). 360p. 1985. reprint ed. pap. 8.95 (0-486-64796-X) Dover.

Sun Will Shine - Again: An Orphan Boy's Journey Through the Great Depression & the "Big War" Ralph B. Conlee. (Illus.). 328p. 1992. 22.00 (0-9634046-0-1) R B Conlee.

Sun, Wind & Light: Architectural Design Strategies. G. Z. Brown. LC 84-29117. 176p. (C). 1985. pap. text ed. 44.95 (0-471-82063-6) Wiley.

Sun World. Tim Adams. Ed. by Alice Hardy. LC 78-74428. (A-1 Ser.). 4.00 (0-686-24151-7); pap. 8.00 (0-686-24152-5) Central FL Voters.

Sun Worship in India: A Study of Deo Sun-Shrine. A. B. Saran & Gaya Pandey. (C). 1992. text ed. 22.00 (81-7211-030-8, Pub. by Northern Bk Ctr II) S Asia.

Sun Yat-Sen: Frustrated Patriot. C. Martin Wilbur. LC 76-18200. 413p. 1976. text ed. 62.00 (0-231-04036-9) Col U Pr.

Sun Yat-sen see Supplementary Readers for Intermediate Chinese Reader

Sun Yat Sen & the Chinese Republic. Paul M. Linebarger. LC 70-96469. 1969. reprint ed. 34.50 (0-404-03989-8) AMS Pr.

Sun Yat-Sen & the French, 1900-1908. Jeffrey G. Barlow. LC 79-620017. (China Research Monographs: No. 14). 93p. 1979. pap. 2.00 (0-912966-19-X) IEAS.

Sun Yat-sen, His Life & Its Meaning: A Critical Biography. Lyon Sharman. LC 68-17141. xxi, 420p. 1934. 57.50 (0-8047-0609-3) Stanford U Pr.

***Sun Zi: The Art of War.** Comment by Xie Guoliang. 328p. 14.95 (0-8351-3176-9) China Bks.

Sunakorn Drug Prevention Teaching Curriculum. Judy Wood et al. LC 89-50139. 184p. (J). (gr. k-5). 1989. 22.95 (0-938021-42-7) Turner Pub KY.

Sunan Abu Dawud, Vol. I-III. A. Hasan. 69.00 (0-933511-69-8) Kazi Pubns.

Sunan Ibn Majah, Set, Nos. I & II. Muhammad T. Ansari. 952p. (C). 1995. text ed. 39.95 (0-934905-63-0) Kazi Pubns.

Sunan Nasai. Muhammad I. Siddiqi. 526p. (C). 1995. text ed. 19.95 (0-934905-64-9) Kazi Pubns.

Sunbathing with the Professors: Poems of the Eastern Shore. Gilbert Byron. (Illus.). (Orig.). 1982. pap. 5.95 (0-9615275-0-1) Unicorn Bkshop.

Sunbeam Alpine & Tiger: The Complete Story. Graham Robson. 1996. 35.95 (1-85223-941-7) Motorbooks Intl.

Sunbeam S7 & S8. (Super Profile MC Ser.). 11.95 (0-85429-363-9, F363, Pub. by G T Foulis Ltd) Haynes Pubns.

Sunbeams: A Book of Quotations. Sy Safransky. (Illus.). 159p. (Orig.). 1990. pap. 12.95 (1-55643-045-0) North Atlantic.

Sunbeams Level 8: HBJ Reading 1987. Early. (J). 1987. student ed., pap. 32.50 (0-15-330508-8) HB Schl Dept.

***Sunbeam's Spring Picnic.** Alexandra Reid. (Sky Dancer Ser.). (Illus.). 24p. (J). (ps). 1997. 2.50 (0-694-00967-9, Festival) HarpC Child Bks.

Sunbelt Blues: Where Have All the Good Jobs Gone? Ed. by Nancy Peckenham. (Illus.). 64p. (Orig.). 1990. pap. 5.00 (0-943810-46-9) Inst Southern Studies.

Sunbelt Designs: Outdoor Living...Indoors. Ed. by National Plan Service Staff. (Illus.). (Orig.). 1988. pap. 3.95 (0-934039-27-5, A72) Natl Plan Serv.

Sunbelt Stories. V. O. Blum. LC 94-60575. (Illus.). 150p. (Orig.). 1994. pap. 7.95 (0-9620886-1-7) Times Eagle Bks.

Sunbelt Working Mothers: Reconciling Family & Factory. Louise Lamphere et al. LC 92-56789. (Anthropology of Contemporary Issues Ser.). (Illus.). 352p. 1993. 45.00 (0-8014-2788-6); pap. 15.95 (0-8014-8066-3) Cornell U Pr.

Sunbird. Arthur Dobrin. (Illus.). 64p. 15.00 (0-89304-046-0, CCC109); pap. 7.50 (0-89304-012-6) Cross-Cultrl NY.

Sunbird. Wilbur Smith. 1992. mass mkt. 6.99 (0-449-14825-4, GM) Fawcett.

Sunblade. Ginny Odenbach & Linda Osborn. Ed. by Wendy S. Kolsen. (Illus.). 54p. (Orig.). (J). (gr. 3-8). 1995. pap. 3.50 (1-885101-12-0) Writers Pr Srv.

Sunblade: Classroom Set, 31 bks., Set. Osborn Odenbach. Ed. by John Bruyninckx. (Resource Guide, Sunblade Ser.). (Illus.). (Orig.). (J). (gr. 3-7). teacher ed., pap. 112.99 (1-885101-50-3) Writers Pr Srv.

Sunbonnet Family Reunion, Album I: 126 Winning Designs with Complete Instructions. Ed. by Sandra L. Hatch. (Illus.). 168p. (Orig.). 1989. pap. 14.95 (1-882138-01-5) Hse White Birches.

Sunbonnet Family Reunion, Album Two: 126 Winning Designs with Complete Instructions. Ed. by Sandra L. Hatch. (Illus.). 168p. (Orig.). 1990. pap. 14.95 (1-882138-02-3) Hse White Birches.

Sunbonnet Girls, Bk. 1. Kirby. (J). 1998. 15.00 (0-689-80974-3, S&S Bks Young Read) S&S Childrens.

Sunbonnet Girls, Bk. 1. Kirby. (J). 1998. pap. 4.95 (0-689-80969-7, S&S Bks Young Read) S&S Childrens.

Sunbonnet Girls, Bk. 2. Kirby. (J). 1998. 15.00 (0-689-80975-1, S&S Bks Young Read) S&S Childrens.

Sunbonnet Girls, Bk. 2. Kirby. (J). 1998. pap. 4.95 (0-689-80970-0, S&S Bks Young Read) S&S Childrens.

An Asterisk (*) at the beginning of an entry indicates that the title is appearing in BIP for the first time.

Sunbonnet Girls, Bk. 3. Kirby. (J). 1998. 15.00 (*0-689-80976-X*, S&S Bks Young Read) S&S Childrens.

Sunbonnet Girls, Bk. 3. Kirby. (J). 1998. pap. 4.95 (*0-689-80971-9*, S&S Bks Young Read) S&S Childrens.

Sunbonnet Girls, Bk. 4. Kirby. (J). 1998. 15.00 (*0-689-80977-8*, S&S Bks Young Read) S&S Childrens.

Sunbonnet Girls, Bk. 4. Kirby. (J). 1998. pap. 4.95 (*0-689-80972-7*, S&S Bks Young Read) S&S Childrens.

Sunbonnet Sue All Through the Year. Sue Linker. LC 94-6365. 1994. pap. 21.95 (*1-56477-058-3*, B182) That Patchwork.

Sunbonnet Sue Gets It All Together at Home. Jean R. Laury. LC 86-63601. (Adventures of Sunbonnet Sue Ser.). (Illus.). 24p. (Orig.). 1987. pap. 4.95 (*0-8442-2611-4*) Quilt Digest Pr.

Sunbonnet Sue Goes to the Quilt Show. Jean R. Laury. LC 86-63602. (Adventures of Sunbonnet Sue Ser.). (Illus.). 24p. (Orig.). 1987. pap. text ed. 4.95 (*0-8442-2610-6*) Quilt Digest Pr.

Sunbonnet Sue Visits Quilt in a Day. Eleanor Burns. (Illus.). 48p. 1992. 8.95 (*0-922705-38-0*) Quilt Day.

Sunburn. Laurence Shames. LC 94-10865. 288p. 1995. 21.95 (*0-7868-6068-5*) Hyperion.

Sunburn. Laurence Shames. 384p. 1996. mass mkt. 4.99 (*0-7868-8903-9*) Hyperion.

Sunburn. R. L. Stine. Ed. by Patricia MacDonald. (Fear Street Ser.). 176p. (Orig.). (YA). (gr. 7 up). 1993. mass mkt. 3.99 (*0-671-73868-2*, Archway) PB.

Sunburned Prayer. Marc Talbert. LC 94-38682. (J). (gr. 5-9). 1995. pap. text ed. 14.00 (*0-689-80125-4*, S&S Bks Young Read) S&S Childrens.

Sunburned Prayer. Marc Talbert. (J). 1997. 4.50 (*0-689-81326-0*) S&S Childrens.

***Sunburst.** Parke Godwin. Date not set. write for info. (*0-688-14521-3*) Morrow.

Sunburst. Mauricio Magdaleno. Tr. by Anita Brenner from SPA. LC 74-25390. reprint ed. 34.50 (*0-404-58449-7*) AMS Pr.

***Sunburst Alley: A Pictorial Book on the Gibson Les Paul Guitars.** Vic Da Pra. (Illus.). 104p. (Orig.). 1997. pap. 24.95 (*1-57424-034-X*) Centerstream Pub.

***Sunburst Alley: A Pictorial Gallery of the Les Paul Sunburst 1958-1960.** Vic DaPra. (Illus.). 80p. (Orig.). pap. 24.95 (*1-57424-041-2*) Centerstream Pub.

Sunburst Guide to Crochet. Penny Hill. 1994. 4.98 (*0-7858-0007-7*) Bk Sales Inc.

Sunburst Guide to Cross Stitch. Hillary Moore. 1994. 4.98 (*0-7858-0008-5*) Bk Sales Inc.

Sunburst Guide to Knitting. Penny Hill. 1994. 4.98 (*0-7858-0010-7*) Bk Sales Inc.

Sunburst Guide to Needlepoint. Hillary Moore. 1994. 4.98 (*0-7858-0012-3*) Bk Sales Inc.

Sunburst Guide to Patchwork. Hillary Moore. 1994. 4.98 (*0-7858-0009-3*) Bk Sales Inc.

Sunburst Guide to Sewing. Hillary Moore. 1994. 4.98 (*0-7858-0011-5*) Bk Sales Inc.

Sunburst Production Manual. International Export Trading & Supply, Inc. Staff. 86p. 1984. text ed. 20.00 (*0-89904-021-7*); 10.00 (*0-89904-022-5*) Crumb Elbow Pub.

Sunburst Tropical Fruit Company Coo. Nita Groshowski & Mel Meo. (Illus.). 1987. ring bd., vinyl bd. 20.00 (*0-9619064-0-5*) Sunburst Tropical Fruit.

Sunbursts: True Adventures of Toccoa Falls College Missionaries. Lorene Moothart. (Illus.). 232p. (Orig.). 1992. pap. 5.95 (*1-885729-03-0*) Toccoa Falls.

Sunbursts for the Spirit. C. W. Vandenbergh. LC 79-90313. (Sunbursts for the Spirit Ser.: Vol. 1). (Illus.). 56p. (Orig.). 1979. pap. 3.25 (*0-935238-02-6*) Pine Row.

Sunbury, PA. Historical Briefs, Inc. Staff. Ed. by Thomas Antonucci & Michael Antonucci. 176p. 1992. pap. 13.95 (*0-89677-038-9*) Hist Briefs.

***Suncatchers.** Janet R. Parker. (Illus.). (Orig.). 1997. pap. write for info. (*1-886467-17-X*) WJM Press.

Suncatchers. Jamie L. Turner. 400p. 1995. pap. 12.99 (*0-7852-7911-3*) Nelson.

Suncatchers in Minutes. Carolyn Kyle & Teny Nudson. (Illus.). 36p. 1992. pap. 13.95 (*0-935133-40-2*) CKE Pubns.

Suncatchers in My Windows: A Collection of Personal Essays. Odessa Snyder. (Illus.). 196p. (Orig.). 1992. pap. 9.95 (*0-941092-25-9*) Mtn St Pr.

Suncatchers Stained Glass Pattern Book: One Hundred Nineteen Designs. Connie Eaton. (Illus.). 64p. (Orig.). 1987. pap. 4.95 (*0-486-25470-4*) Dover.

Sunchasers. Rebecca Flanders. (American Romance Ser.). 1993. mass mkt. 3.50 (*0-373-16490-4*, 1-16490-4) Harlequin Bks.

SunCoast Civic Center: A General Office. 2nd ed. Taylor & Sanchez. (KM - Office Procedures Ser.). 1987. pap. 14.95 (*0-538-25550-1*) S-W Pub.

Suncoast Guide: Tampa Bay Business Guild Directory. 2nd ed. Ed. by Nancy E. Valmus. 56p. 1992. write for info. (*0-937025-19-4*) Shadowood Pubns.

Suncoast Seasons. Dunedin Youth Guild Staff. (Illus.). 430p. 1984. 13.95 (*0-9613858-0-4*) Dunedin Youth.

SUNCODE Documentation & User's Manual. Larry Palmiter & Terry Wheeling. 235p. 1981. ring bd. 35.00 (*0-934478-29-5*) Ecotope.

Sundance. Peggy Darty. LC 96-30681. 256p. 1996. pap. 8.99 (*0-88070-952-9*, Palisades OR) Multnomah Pubs.

Sundance. Leslie Esdaile. 416p. 1996. mass mkt. 4.99 (*0-7860-0320-0*, Pinncle Kensgtn) Kensgtn Pub Corp.

Sundance. Jonathan London. 1999. pap. 14.99 (*0-525-45404-7*) NAL-Dutton.

Sundance. Richard S. Wheeler. (Skye's West Ser.: No. 6). 352p. (Orig.). 1992. mass mkt. 4.99 (*0-8125-1306-1*) Tor Bks.

Sundance. large type ed. Bill Reno. LC 92-28127. (Nightingale Ser.). 336p. 1993. pap. 14.95 (*0-8161-5630-1*, GK Hall) Thorndike Pr.

Sundance: Dead Man's Canyon - Bring Me His Scalp. large type ed. John Benteen. 1984. 15.95 (*0-7089-1153-6*) Ulverscroft.

Sundance: Death in the Lava. large type ed. John Benteen. (Linford Western Library). 240p. 1985. pap. 15.99 (*0-7089-6082-0*) Ulverscroft.

Sundance: Hangman's Knot. large type ed. Peter McCurtin. (Linford Western Library). 256p. 1989. pap. 15.99 (*0-7089-6718-3*, Linford) Ulverscroft.

Sundance: Iron Men. large type ed. Peter McCurtin. (Linford Western Library). 272p. 1988. pap. 15.99 (*0-7089-6530-X*, Linford) Ulverscroft.

Sundance: Overkill. large type ed. John Benteen. (Linford Western Library). 240p. 1985. pap. 15.99 (*0-7089-6074-X*) Ulverscroft.

Sundance: Silent Enemy. large type ed. John Benteen. (Linford Western Library). 256p. 1985. pap. 15.99 (*0-7089-6078-2*) Ulverscroft.

Sundance: The Cage. large type ed. Peter McCurtin. (Linford Western Library). 368p. 1992. pap. 15.99 (*0-7089-7299-3*, Trailtree Bookshop) Ulverscroft.

Sundance: The Pistoleros. large type ed. John Benteen. (Linford Western Library). 272p. 1993. pap. 15.99 (*0-7089-7309-4*, Linford) Ulverscroft.

Sundance: The Wild Stallions. large type ed. John Benteen. (Linford Western Library). 272p. 1992. pap. 15.99 (*0-7089-7181-4*, Trailtree Bookshop) Ulverscroft.

Sundance, My Uncle. Donna B. Ernst. (Illus.). 170p. (YA). (gr. 9). 1992. 21.95 (*0-932702-96-1*) Creative Texas.

***Sundance Reader.** Connelly. (C). 1996. pap. text ed. write for info. (*0-15-503170-8*) HB Coll Pubs.

Sundance, the Robert Sundance Story. Robert Sundance & Marc Gaede. 240p. (Orig.). (C). 1994. pap. 12.95 (*0-9616019-8-1*) Chaco Pr.

Sundance, the Robert Sundance Story. Robert Sundance & Marc Gaede. 312p. (Orig.). (C). 1995. 19.95 (*0-9616019-9-X*) Chaco Pr.

Sundancer. Edward Hays. LC 82-83135. (Illus.). 64p. (Orig.). 1982. pap. 8.95 (*0-939516-04-7*) Forest Peace.

Sundancer. Briony Shilton. 1996. mass mkt. 7.95 (*1-56201-023-9*, 125) Blue Moon Bks.

Sundancers & River Demons: Essays on Landscape & Ritual. Conger Beasley, Jr. LC 89-5168. 241p. (Orig.). 1990. pap. 16.00 (*1-55728-130-0*) U of Ark Pr.

Sundancer's Woman. Judith E. French. 1996. mass mkt. 5.99 (*0-380-77706-1*) Avon.

Sundancing: The Art & Architecture of James Lambeth. Ed. by Hun B. Im & Courtney Lambeth. LC 92-60943. (Illus.). 208p. 1992. 48.00 (*0-9601678-8-9*); pap. 38.00 (*0-9601678-9-7*) Miami Dog Pr.

***Sundancing at Rosebud & Pineridge.** Thomas E. Mails. (Illus.). 400p. (C). 1997. pap. 29.95 (*1-57178-062-9*) Coun Oak Bks.

Sundara Kandam. Shri Valmiki. 302p. 1984. 8.95 (*0-87481-527-4*, Pub. by Ramakrishna Math II) Vedanta Pr.

Sunday. Thomas Lux. LC 88-63541. (Classic Contemporaries Ser.). 1989. pap. 12.95 (*0-88748-089-6*) Carnegie-Mellon.

Sunday. Phoebe MacAdams. 100p. (Orig.). 1983. pap. 6.00 (*0-939180-20-0*) Tombouctou.

Sunday. Synthia St. James. LC 95-52934. (Illus.). 32p. (J). (gr. k-3). 1996. lib. bdg. 15.95 (*0-8075-7658-1*) A Whitman.

Sunday: A Leaders Weekly Guidebook Year A. Christiane Brusselmans et al. 192p. 1992. text ed. 49.95 (*0-929496-93-0*) Treehaus Comns.

Sunday: Book of Readings Adapted for Children Year A. Christiane Brusselmans et al. 176p. (J). (ps-7). 1989. text ed. 49.95 (*0-929496-38-8*) Treehaus Comns.

Sunday: Book of Readings Adapted for Children, Year B. Christiane Brusselmans et al. 176p. (J). (ps-8). 1990. text ed. 49.95 (*0-929496-57-4*) Treehaus Comns.

Sunday: Book of Readings Adapted for Children Year C. Christiane Brusselmans et al. 176p. (J). text ed. 49.95 (*0-929496-91-4*) Treehaus Comns.

Sunday: Day of Light. H. Boone Porter. 104p. 1988. pap. 6.95 (*0-912405-40-6*) Pastoral Pr.

Sunday: Handbook for Those Who Share the Word with Children. Christiane Brusselmans & Edward Matthews. (Illus.). 36p. (Orig.). 1989. pap. text ed. 7.95 (*0-929496-06-X*) Treehaus Comns.

Sunday: Leaders Weekly Guidebook, Year B. Christiane Brusselmans et al. 160p. (J). (ps-8). 1990. text ed. 49.95 (*0-929496-58-2*) Treehaus Comns.

Sunday: Leaders Weekly Guidebook Year C. Christiane Brusselmans et al. 160p. (J). text ed. 49.95 (*0-929496-92-2*) Treehaus Comns.

Sunday: The Original Feast Day. Joseph A. Fiorenza. 32p. 1989. pap. 2.95 (*0-8146-1815-4*) Liturgical Pr.

Sunday: The Original Feast Day--Study Guide. Joseph A. Fiorenza. 48p. 1989. pap. 2.95 (*0-8146-1814-6*) Liturgical Pr.

***Sunday: Tina Louise.** Tina Louise. LC 97-6791. 1997. write for info. (*0-307-44017-6*) Western Pub.

***Sunday Afternoon, Looking for the Car: The Aberrant Art of Barry Kite.** Alan Bisbort. LC 97-14852. (Illus.). 96p. (Orig.). 1997. pap. 25.00 (*0-7649-0362-4*, A903) Pomegranate Calif.

Sunday Afternoons. Clementa R. Proudfoot. 128p. 1988. write for info. (*0-9621357-0-4*) C R Proudfoot.

***Sunday Afternoons at Garfield Park: Seattle's Black Baseball Teams 1911-1951.** Lyle K. Wilson. LC 96-78997. (Illus.). 148p. (Orig.). 1997. pap. 9.95 (*1-881147-24-X*) Lowell Print.

Sunday Best. John K. Sherman. 1963. 6.95 (*0-87018-057-6*) Ross.

Sunday Bloody Sunday. Drew Mackenzie. 1996. mass mkt. 4.99 (*1-85782-018-5*, Pub. by Blake Publng UK) Seven Hills Bk.

Sunday Came Early This Week. Luleen S. Anderson. 140p. 1982. pap. 11.95 (*0-87073-575-6*) Schenkman Bks Inc.

Sunday Celebrations in the Absence of a Priest. Frwd. by Alan F. Detscher. (Liturgy Documentary Ser.: Vol. 10). 57p. (Orig.). 1996. pap. 5.95 (*1-57455-105-1*) US Catholic.

Sunday Celebrations in the Absence of a Priest: Leader's Edition. 384p. (Orig.). 1997. teacher ed., pap. text ed. 29.95 (*0-8146-2416-2*, Liturg Pr Bks) Liturgical Pr.

***Sunday Celebrations in the Absense of a Priest.** 1994. 26.95 (*0-89942-075-3*, 75/02) Catholic Bk Pub.

Sunday Cook. Grace Howaniec. LC 93-70422. (Illus.). 176p. (Orig.). 1993. pap. 15.95 (*0-942495-27-6*) Amherst Pr.

Sunday Cycles. William C. Gault. 1979. 8.95 (*0-396-07715-3*) WC Stone PMA.

Sunday Dinner. Caleen S. Jennings. 1993. pap. 3.00 (*0-87129-299-8*, SA4) Dramatic Pub.

Sunday Dinner. William H. Willimon. LC 81-52215. 1981. pap. 8.95 (*0-8358-0429-1*) Upper Room Bks.

***Sunday Dinner.** William H. Willimon. 13.35 (*0-687-61114-8*) Abingdon.

Sunday Dismissals for RCIA: Candidates & Catechumens. Mary Milne. 242p. (Orig.). 1993. pap. 19.95 (*0-8146-2145-7*) Liturgical Pr.

Sunday Doll. Mary F. Shura. 112p. 1989. pap. 2.95 (*0-380-70618-0*, Camelot) Avon.

Sunday Doorposts, No. II. Timothy R. Botts. 64p. (Orig.). 1991. pap. 12.95 (*1-55612-462-7*, LL1462) Sheed & Ward MO.

Sunday Doorposts Vol. 2. Timothy R. Botts. (Illus.). 64p. (Orig.). 1987. pap. 12.95 (*1-55612-078-8*) Sheed & Ward MO.

Sunday Drivers: NASCAR Winston Cup Stock Car Racing. Photos by Rick Farnkopf. (Illus.). 176p. 1994. 39.95 (*0-943231-65-5*) Howell Pr VA.

Sunday Facts & Sabbath Fiction: 25 Biblical Reasons Why the Christian Church Worships on Sunday. Russell K. Tardo. 160p. 1992. pap. text ed. 4.95 (*1-881210-06-5*) Faithful Wrd.

Sunday Fun Activities & Ideas, Vol. 2. Karen Finch. 64p. (Orig.). (J). (ps up). 1994. 7.95 (*1-885476-03-5*) Finch Fmly Games.

Sunday Go-to-Meetin' Rebera E. Foston. Ed. by Cynthia E. Garnett. 96p. (Orig.). Date not set. pap. 12.00 (*0-9641709-5-7*) Foston Adolescent.

Sunday Green. 1990. pap. 4.50 (*0-8216-5086-6*, Univ Books) Carol Pub Group.

Sunday Habit. Jim Mele. 1978. pap. 3.00 (*0-916696-07-3*) Cross Country.

Sunday Hell. Butch Holmes. 256p. 1992. mass mkt. 3.95 (*0-87067-391-2*, BH391-2) Holloway.

Sunday Homilies, Cycle C. Herbert F. Smith. LC 91-17927. 236p. (Orig.). 1991. pap. 9.95 (*0-8189-0582-4*) Alba.

Sunday Homilies, Cycle A. Herbert F. Smith. LC 89-32. 223p. (Orig.). 1989. pap. 9.95 (*0-8189-0560-3*) Alba.

Sunday Homilies, 3 vols., Set. Herbert F. Smith. 650p. (Orig.). 1992. pap. 24.95 (*0-8189-0664-2*) Alba.

Sunday Homilies see Sunday Homilies - Cycle B

Sunday Homilies - Cycle B, Cycle B. Herbert F. Smith. LC 90-44789. Orig. Title: Sunday Homilies. 223p. (Orig.). 1992. pap. 9.95 (*0-8189-0597-2*) Alba.

***Sunday Homilies for the Three-Year Cycle.** Liam Swords. 344p. (Orig.). 1995. pap. 19.95 (*1-85607-131-6*, Pub. by Columba Pr IE) Twenty-Third.

***Sunday in America: 75 Photographers Celebrate Faith & Family.** LC 97-22578. 1997. write for info. (*0-310-41060-6*) Zondervan.

Sunday in New York. Norman Krasna. LC 62-13646. (Illus.). 114p. 1962. 16.95 (*0-910278-32-6*) Boulevard.

Sunday in New York. Norman Krasna. 1962. pap. 5.25 (*0-8222-1100-9*) Dramatists Play.

Sunday in New York. 4th ed. Fodor's Staff. 1995. pap. 14.50 (*0-679-02947-8*) Fodors Travel.

Sunday in Sudan. Don Clark. 230p. (Orig.). 1993. pap. 19.95 (*1-884321-00-3*); Computer diskette. disk 9.95 (*1-884321-01-1*) Big Sky Orig.

Sunday in the Park with George. Stephen Sondheim & James Lapine. (Musical Library). (Illus.). 256p. 1991. 19.95 (*1-55783-067-3*); pap. 9.95 (*1-55783-068-1*) Applause Theatre Bk Pubs.

Sunday Is Family Dinners: From Roast Chicken & Mashed Potatoes to Apple Pie & More. Time-Life Books Editors. LC 95-51347. (Everyday Cookbooks Ser.). (Illus.). 128p. 1996. 14.95 (*0-7835-4789-7*) Time-Life.

Sunday Laws of the United States & Leading Judicial Decisions Having Special Reference to the Jews. Albert M. Friedenberg. LC 12-23685. 42p. 1986. reprint ed. pap. 22.50 (*0-89941-475-3*, 304020) W S Hein.

Sunday Lunch. Nora Naish. 1995. pap. 8.99 (*0-7493-2133-4*, Reed Trade) Buttrwrth-Heinemann.

Sunday Lunch. large type ed. Nora Naish. 1995. 25.99 (*0-7089-3277-0*) Ulverscroft.

***Sunday Macaroni Club.** Steve Lopez. LC 96-44062. 1997. 24.00 (*0-15-100264-9*) HarBrace.

Sunday Macaroni Club. Steve Lopez. Date not set. pap. 23.95 (*0-670-86311-4*) Viking Penguin.

Sunday Mealtime Prayers. Michael Kwatera. 72p. (Orig.). 1996. pap. 4.95 (*0-8146-2346-8*, Liturg Pr Bks) Liturgical Pr.

Sunday Morning. Gail Ramshaw. (Illus.). 46p. 1993. 15.95 (*1-56854-005-1*, SUN/AM) Liturgy Tr Pubns.

Sunday Morning. Gail Ramshaw. (Illus.). 48p. (J). (gr. 2-5). 1994. pap. 8.95 (*1-56854-081-7*, PSUNAM) Liturgy Tr Pubns.

Sunday Morning. David Rogers. LC 86-90807. 95p. (Orig.). 1986. pap. 6.95 (*0-9618064-0-0*) D Rogers NY.

***Sunday Morning.** Ed. by David Rogers. 156p. (Orig.). 1997. pap. write for info. (*1-889534-09-9*) Jay St Pubs.

Sunday Morning. 2nd ed. Judith Viorst. LC 92-16928. (Illus.). 40p. (J). (ps-3). 1992. lib. bdg. 13.95 (*0-689-31794-8*, Atheneum Bks Young) S&S Childrens.

Sunday Morning. 2nd ed. Judith Viorst. LC 92-29561. (Illus.). 32p. (J). (gr. k-3). 1993. reprint ed. pap. 3.95 (*0-689-71702-4*, Aladdin Paperbacks) S&S Childrens.

Sunday Morning: Reflections on the Word. Dennis R. Clark. 160p. (Orig.). 1996. pap. 24.95 (*1-55612-861-4*, LL1861) Sheed & Ward MO.

Sunday Morning Atlanta Preaching: Sermons, Afro American, Atlanta. Ed. by Gloria Philpot & Mildred Gunn. 72p. (Orig.). 1994. pap. write for info. (*0-9621362-1-2*) T E Balls Pubns.

Sunday Morning Atlanta, Preaching Vol. II. Ed. & Intro. by Thomas E. Ball. (Illus.). 120p. (Orig.). 1995. pap. 9.95 (*0-9621362-2-0*) T E Balls Pubns.

Sunday Morning Fun Book. Annette H. LaPlaca. (Illus.). 48p. (J). 1995. pap. 5.99 (*0-87788-569-9*) Shaw Pubs.

Sunday Morning in Fascist Spain: A European Memoir, 1948-1953. Willis Barnstone. LC 93-15493. (Illus.). 312p. (C). 1994. 39.95 (*0-8093-1883-0*); pap. 19.95 (*0-8093-1884-9*) S Ill U Pr.

S

***Sunday Morning Live: A Collection of Drama Sketches, Vol. 1.** Willow Creek Staff. Ed. by Steve Pederson. Date not set. vhs 29.95 (*0-310-59339-5*) Zondervan.

Sunday Morning Live: A Collection of Drama Sketches, Vol. 1. Willow Creek Staff. Ed. by Steve Pederson. (Illus.). 96p. 1992. pap. 19.99 (*0-310-59221-6*) Zondervan.

***Sunday Morning Live: A Collection of Drama Sketches, Vol. 2.** Willow Creek Staff. Ed. by Steve Pederson. Date not set. vhs 29.95 (*0-310-59549-5*) Zondervan.

Sunday Morning Live: A Collection of Drama Sketches, Vol. 2. Willow Creek Staff. Ed. by Steve Pederson. (Illus.). 96p. 1993. pap. 19.99 (*0-310-61361-2*) Zondervan.

Sunday Morning Live: A Collection of Drama Sketches, Vol. 3. Willow Creek Staff. Ed. by Steve Pederson. (Illus.). 64p. 1993. vhs 29.99 (*0-310-61479-1*) Zondervan.

Sunday Morning Live: A Collection of Drama Sketches, 6 vols., Vol. 3. Willow Creek Staff. Ed. by Steve Pederson. (Illus.). 64p. 1993. spiral bd. 19.99 (*0-310-61441-4*) Zondervan.

***Sunday Morning Live: A Collection of Drama Sketches, Vol. 4.** Willow Creek Staff. Ed. by Steve Pederson. Date not set. vhs 29.95 (*0-310-61539-9*) Zondervan.

Sunday Morning Live: A Collection of Drama Sketches, Vol. 4. Willow Creek Staff. Ed. by Steve Pederson. 64p. 1993. spiral bd. 19.99 (*0-310-61531-3*) Zondervan.

Sunday Morning Live: A Collection of Drama Sketches, Vol. 5. Willow Creek Staff. Ed. by Steve Pederson. 64p. 1994. spiral bd. 19.99 (*0-310-61541-0*); vhs 29.99 (*0-310-61549-6*) Zondervan.

Sunday Morning Live: A Collection of Drama Sketches, Vol. 6. Willow Creek Staff. Ed. by Steve Pederson. 64p. 1994. spiral bd. 19.99 (*0-310-61551-8*); vhs 29.99 (*0-310-61559-3*) Zondervan.

Sunday Morning Reader's Theater: Nineteen Congregational Worship Resource, Cycle C, Bk. 2, Cycle C. Pamela Urfer. 1994. pap. 11.95 (*0-7880-0214-7*) CSS OH.

Sunday Morning Readers' Theater: Nineteen Congregational Worship Resources. Pamela Urfer. LC 93-43354. 152p. 1994. pap. 11.95 (*1-55673-518-9*, 9405) CSS OH.

Sunday Night Sermons. Edward Fudge. pap. 2.50 (*0-686-12685-8*) E Fudge.

Sunday No Sabbath: A Sermon. John Pocklington. LC 74-28881. (English Experience Ser.: No. 759). 1975. reprint ed. 20.00 (*90-221-0759-0*) Walter J Johnson.

***Sunday Octoechos.** Tr. by Isaac Lambertsen from SLA. 1997. spiral bd. 25.00 (*0-912927-78-X*, X049) St John Kronstadt.

Sunday of Life. Raymond Queneau. Tr. by Barbara Wright from FRE. LC 76-49628. 1977. 5.95 (*0-8112-0645-9*) New Directions.

Sunday of the Living Dead: A Collection of Mormon Humor. Robert Kirby. LC 95-40692. (Illus.). 128p. (Orig.). 1995. pap. 8.95 (*1-885628-49-8*) Buckaroo Bks.

***Sunday on the Farm: Memoirs of a Horseshoer.** Bruce B. Daniels. xi, 164p. 1996. 30.00 (*0-9627965-1-4*) St Eloy.

Sunday Outing. Gloria J. Pickney. LC 93-25383. (Illus.). (J). (gr. k-4). 1994. pap. 14.99 (*0-8037-1198-0*); lib. bdg. 14.89 (*0-8037-1199-9*) Dial Bks Young.

Sunday Outings: A Guide to Scenic Drives & Historical Sights in Marin County. Tacy Dunham. (Marin Trail Guide Ser.). (Illus.). 56p. (Orig.). 1989. pap. 6.95 (*0-685-27209-5*) Cttnwd Pr.

***Sunday Preaching: Brief Homilies for the Sundays of the Three Cycles.** Charles E. Miller. LC 97-7378. 1997. pap. 18.95 (*0-8189-0782-7*) Alba.

Sunday Psalter. Carmelites of Indianapolis Staff. 200p. 1993. pap. 4.95 (*1-886873-06-2*) Carmelites IN.

Sunday Sampler. Kawaski. 229p. 1993. pap. 8.95 (*0-87579-562-5*) Deseret Bk.

Sunday Sampler No. 3: We Believe. Shauna M. Kawasaki. (Illus.). (Orig.). 1994. pap. 8.95 (*0-87579-942-6*) Deseret Bk.

Sunday Sampler, No. Two: Finding Peace. Shauna M. Kawasaki. (Illus.). 231p. 1993. pap. 8.95 (*0-87579-814-4*) Deseret Bk.

***Sunday School.** Gerald Dawe. 48p. 1991. pap. 10.95 (*1-85235-063-6*) Dufour.

Sunday School: The Formation of an American Institution, 1790-1880. Anne M. Boylan. 237p. (C). 1990. reprint ed. pap. 14.00 (*0-300-04814-9*) Yale U Pr.

***Sunday School Craft Encyclopedia.** 16.99 (*0-8307-1770-6*) Regal.

Sunday School Enrollment. Elmer L. Towns. Ed. by Cindy G. Spear. 135p. (Orig.). 1992. ring bd. 59.95 (0-941005-57-7) Chrch Grwth VA.

*Sunday School in the Local Church. Date not set. write for info. (0-8341-1314-7) Nazarene.

Sunday School in the Nineties: Equipping for the Harvest. Ed. by Junus Fulbright. LC 90-62124. 1990. 5.99 (0-87148-815-9) Pathway Pr.

Sunday School Manifesto: In the Image of Her? Elizabeth D. Gray. LC 94-67112. (Illus.). 80p. (Orig.). 1994. pap. 14.95 (0-934512-07-8) Roundtable Pr.

Sunday-School Movement, 1780-1917, & the American Sunday-School Union, 1817-1917. Edwin W. Rice. LC 70-165728. (American Education Ser, No. 2). (Illus.). 1977. reprint ed. 39.95 (0-405-03717-1) Ayer.

*Sunday School Plays for Preschoolers. Hope P. Beck. LC 96-52622. 55p. (Orig.). 1997. pap. write for info. (0-7880-1062-X) CSS OH.

Sunday School Program Builder. Enelle Eder. 1995. pap. 6.99 (0-8341-9288-8) Nazarene.

*Sunday School Songbook, Vol. 1. pap. 12.95 incl. audio (0-87166-138-1, 93966P) Mel Bay.

Sunday School Songs. JTG of Nashville Staff. (J). (ps-3). 1996. 18.95 (1-884832-76-8) JTG Nashville.

Sunday School Standards, No. 960270. LC 81-51621. 1990. 10.99 (0-87148-189-8) Pathway Pr.

Sunday School Teacher's Guide. William S. Deal. pap. 3.99 (0-88019-163-5) Schmul Pub Co.

Sunday School Tooter: Tonette, Soprano Recorder Flutophone & Song Flute. Becker. 1990. 4.95 (0-685-32151-7, H859) Hansen Ed Mus.

*Sunday Search Pamphlet. David R. Mains. (Nineteen Ninety-Seven 50-Day Spiritual Adventure Ser.). 1996. pap. 6.00 (1-57849-020-0) Chapel of Air.

Sunday Sermons: Thoughts of Meditation for Ministers. T. A. Price. LC 95-60633. 192p. (Orig.). 1995. pap. 10.00 (0-936029-38-2) Western Bk Journ.

*Sunday Sermons of the Great Fathers: A Manual of Preaching, Spiritual Reading & Meditation. M. F. Toal & Thomas. LC 96-44004. 1996. write for info. (1-886412-15-4); write for info. (1-886412-16-2); write for info. (1-886412-17-0); write for info. (1-886412-18-9) Preserv Press.

*Sunday Sermons of the Great Fathers: A Manual of Preaching, Spiritual Reading & Meditation, 4 vols. Thomas. Ed. & Tr. by M. F. Toal. LC 96-44004. 1844p. 1996. reprint ed. 129.95 (1-886412-14-6) Preserv Press.

Sunday Service of the Methodists: Twentieth-Century Worship in World-Wide Methodism. Karen B. Tucker. (Kingswood Ser.). 352p. (Orig.). 1996. pap. 17.95 (0-687-01134-5) Abingdon.

Sunday Skaters: Poems. Mary J. Salter. LC 93-33403. 1994. 20.00 (0-679-43109-8) Knopf.

Sunday Skaters: Poems. Mary J. Salter. 112p. 1996. pap. 13.00 (0-679-76567-0) Random.

*Sunday Skaters Signed. Mary J. Salter. 1996. pap. 13.00 (0-676-51728-5) Random.

Sunday Songs Little Play-a-Sound. (J). 1995. write for info. (0-7853-1061-4) Pubns Intl Ltd.

Sunday Spy. William Hood. LC 95-38609. 352p. 1996. 25.00 (0-393-03937-4) Norton.

Sunday Stroll. Paul Borgese. LC 95-82029. (Illus.). 32p. (J). (ps-4). 1996. 15.95 (1-886489-08-4) Laugh & Learn.

Sunday, Sunday. Sandra F. Asher. 1994. 3.00 (0-87129-459-1, S14) Dramatic Pub.

*Sunday Surprise. 24p. (J). 1997. pap. write for info. (0-7814-3024-0, Chariot Bks) Chariot Victor.

Sunday Surprise. Barbara Davoll. (Illus.). 24p. (J). 1988. audio 11.99 (0-89693-616-3, 3-1616, Victor Bks) Chariot Victor.

Sunday Surprise. Barbara Davoll. (Christopher Churchmouse Classics Ser.). (Illus.). 24p. (J). 1988. 8.99 (0-89693-405-5, 6-1405, Victor Bks) Chariot Victor.

Sunday Telegraph Business Finance Directory 1987. G. Bricault. Ed. by J. Carr. (C). 1987. lib. bdg. 215.00 (0-86010-828-7, Pub. by Graham & Trotman UK) Kluwer Ac.

Sunday the Rabbi Stayed Home. Harry Kemelman. (Rabbi Ser.). 224p. 1985. mass mkt. 4.95 (0-449-21000-6) Fawcett.

*Sunday the Rabbi Stayed Home. Harry Kennelman. Date not set. mass mkt. write for info. (0-449-20784-6, Crest) Fawcett.

Sunday Times Self Help Directory. Gillel Price. 300p. 1980. 15.95 (0-8464-1241-1) Beekman Pubs.

Sunday Words for a Monday World. Gaylord L. Lehman. 75p. (Orig.). 1986. pap. 6.95 (0-938828-03-7) Falls Tar.

Sunday Work, 1794-1856. LC 72-2547. (British Labour Struggles Before 1850 Ser.). 1974. 23.95 (0-405-04438-0) Ayer.

Sunday Worship Duet Book: Hymns, Classics, & Songs of Praise. 1993. spiral bd. 15.99 (0-8341-9262-4, MB-656) Lillenas.

Sunday Zebras. Art Holst. 1981. 12.00 (0-9605118-0-6) Forest Pub.

Sunday 3.0 Documentation & User's Manual. Davis Straub. Ed. by Larry Palmiter et al. (Illus.). 57p. 1984. ring bd. 35.00 (0-934478-36-8) Ecotope.

Sundays Are Special: A Storybook to Color. Bessie Dean. 24p. 1979. pap. 4.98 (0-88290-111-7) Horizon Utah.

Sundays at Moosewood Restaurant: Ethnic & Regional Recipes from the Cooks at the Legendary Restaurant. 733p. 1990. pap. 21.50 (0-671-67990-2) S&S Trade.

Sundays at Seven: Choice Words from a Different Light's Gay Writers Series. Ed. by Rondo Mieczkowski. LC 95-83537. 144p. (Orig.). Date not set. pap. 12.00 (1-886360-01-4) Alamo Sq Pr.

Sundays at 2:00 with the Baltimore Colts. Vince Bagli & Norman L. Macht. LC 95-359805. (Illus.). 264p. 1995. pap. 17.95 (0-87033-476-X, Tidewtr Pubs) Cornell Maritime.

Sunday's Child. Edward Phillips. (Stonewall Inn Editions Ser.). 240p. 1988. pap. 7.95 (0-312-02294-8) St Martin.

Sunday's Child: A Planning Guide for Liturgies with Both Children & Adults. Jack Miffleton. 64p. (Orig.). 1989. pap. 7.50 (0-912405-62-7) Pastoral Pr.

Sunday's Children. Ingmar Bergman. Tr. by Joan Tate from SWE. LC 93-40096. 160p. 1995. pap. 9.95 (1-55970-292-3) Arcade Pub Inc.

Sunday's Children: A Novel. Ingmar Bergman. Tr. by Joan Tate from SWE. LC 93-40096. 160p. 1994. 16.95 (1-55970-244-3) Arcade Pub Inc.

Sunday's Children: Prayers in the Language of Children. James L. Bitney & Suzanne Schaffhausen. LC 86-60172. (Illus.). 80p. (Orig.). 1986. 9.95 (0-89390-076-1); pap. 5.95 (0-89390-110-5) Resource Pubns.

Sunday's Ending Too Soon. Charley George. (New American Poetry Ser.: No. 14). 112p. (Orig.). 1993. pap. 10.95 (1-55713-148-1) Sun & Moon CA.

Sunday's Foyer: A Collection of Morman Cartoons. Calvin Grondahl. (Illus.). 96p. 1983. pap. 4.95 (0-9606760-3-1) Sunstone Found.

Sunday's Fun Day, Charlie Brown. Charles M. Schulz. (Illus.). 128p. 1993. pap. 6.95 (0-8050-2891-9) H Holt & Co.

Sunday's Game: A Comprehensive Selection of Game Recipes. Charles R. Shaddox. (Illus.). 203p. 1991. pap. 14.95 (0-9631719-0-9) C R Shaddox.

*Sundays in August. Harry C. Brown. LC 97-25073. 196p. 1997. 26.95 (0-86534-261-X) Sunstone Pr.

Sundays in New York: Pulpit Theology at the Crest of the Protestant Mainstream, 1930-1955. William B. Lawrence. (ATLA Monographs: Vol. 41). 400p. 1996. 49.50 (0-8108-3079-5) Scarecrow.

Sunday's Warriors: The Philadelphia Eagles' Games. Donald P. Campbell. Ed. by Barbara Hope. LC 92-29011. (Illus.). 672p. 1994. pap. 24.95 (0-9627161-5-4) QLP Phila PA.

*Sunday's Warriors: The Philadelphia Eagles' History. 2nd rev. ed. Donald P. Campbell. Ed. by Barbara Hope. LC 95-70751. (Illus.). 669p. 1995. pap. 24.95 (0-9627161-6-2) QLP Phila PA.

Sunday's Women: A Report on Lesbian Life Today. Sasha G. Lewis. LC 78-53655. 229p. reprint ed. pap. 65.30 (0-7837-1385-1, 2041561) Bks Demand.

Sunday's Word: Homilies for Year A. John Heaps. 128p. (Orig.). 1995. pap. 9.95 (0-85574-222-4, Pub. by E J Dwyer AT) Morehouse Pub.

*Sunday's Word: Homilies for Year C. John Heaps. 136p. 1997. pap. 9.95 (0-85574-095-7, Pub. by E J Dwyer AT) Morehouse Pub.

Sundered Soul: A Mythic Tale. Alfred Tella. 226p. (Orig.). 1990. 18.95 (0-89410-694-5, Three Contnts); pap. 8.95 (0-89410-695-3, Three Contnts) Lynne Rienner.

Sundew Stranglers: Plants That Eat Insects. Jerome Wexler. (Illus.). 48p. (J). (gr. 2-6). 1994. pap. 15.99 (0-525-45208-7) Dutton Child Bks.

Sundews: A Sweet & Sticky Death. Victor Gentle. LC 96-5606. (Bloodthirsty Plants! Ser.). (Illus.). (J). 1996. lib. bdg. 15.93 (0-8368-1658-7) Gareth Stevens Inc.

Sundial. Gillian Clarke. (C). 1984. pap. 20.00 (0-85088-540-X, Pub. by Gomer Pr UK) St Mut.

Sundial. Shirley Jackson. 1976. 24.95 (0-8488-0370-1) Amereon Ltd.

Sundial of the Seasons. Hal Borland. 1994. reprint ed. lib. bdg. 32.95 (1-56849-256-1) Buccaneer Bks.

Sundial Years. Alida Harvie. (Illus.). 152p. 1984. 30.00 (0-7212-0663-8, Pub. by Regency Press UK) St Mut.

Sundials. Christopher S. Daniel. 1989. pap. 35.00 (0-85263-808-6, Pub. by Shire UK) St Mut.

Sundials: History, Theory, & Practice. unabridged ed. Rene R. Rohr. Tr. by Gabriel Godin. LC 95-45661. (Illus.). 176p. 1996. reprint ed. pap. text ed. 11.95 (0-486-29139-1) Dover.

Sundials: Their Construction & Use. 3rd ed. R. Newton Mayall & Margaret W. Mayall. LC 73-76242. 256p. 1994. pap. 16.95 (0-933346-71-9) Sky Pub.

Sundials: Theory & Construction. Albert E. Waugh. (Orig.). 1973. pap. 4.95 (0-486-22947-5) Dover.

Sundials, Their Theory & Construction. Albert E. Waugh. (Illus.). 1990. 20.25 (0-8446-4835-3) Peter Smith.

Sundiata: An Epic of Old Mali. D. T. Naine. (C). 1965. pap. text ed. 11.50 (0-582-26475-8, Pub. by Longman UK) Longman.

Sundiata: Lion King of Mali. David Wisniewski. (Illus.). 32p. (J). (gr. k-4). 1992. 16.95 (0-395-61302-7, Clarion Bks) HM.

Sundiver. David Brin. (Uplift Trilogy Ser.). 352p. 1985. mass mkt. 6.50 (0-553-26982-8, Bantam Classics) Bantam.

Sundog. Jim Harrison. pap. 10.00 (0-671-74151-9, WSP) PB.

Sundogs. Lee Maracle. 224p. (Orig.). 1992. pap. 10.95 (0-919441-41-6, Pub. by Theytus Bks Ltd CN) Orca Bk Pubs.

Sundogs & Sunsets. Patricia M. Spross. LC 90-70253. 200p. 1990. pap. 11.95 (0-923568-09-3) Wilderness Adventure Bks.

Sundown. John J. Mathews. LC 88-40214. 328p. 1988. pap. 14.95 (0-8061-2160-2) U of Okla Pr.

Sundown Fiction Collection: Reading Level 3, 22 bks. 1993. audio 275.00 (0-88336-249-X) New Readers.

Sundown Fiction Collection: Reading Level 3, 22 bks., Set. 1993. 55.00 (0-88336-775-0) New Readers.

Sundown Jim. Ernest Haycox. 1989. pap. 2.95 (1-55817-254-8) Kensgtn Pub Corp.

Sundown Jim. large type ed. Ernest Haycox. LC 93-1386. 1993. lib. bdg. 18.95 (1-56054-703-0) Thorndike Pr.

Sundown Murders. Peter James. 157p. (C). 1990. pap. 45.00 (0-86439-094-7, Pub. by Boolarong Pubns AT) St Mut.

Sundown Riders #1. Ralph Compton. 1996. mass mkt. 5.99 (0-312-95862-5) St Martin.

Sundowner. Chris Claremont. 352p. (Orig.). 1994. pap. text ed. 5.50 (0-441-00070-3) Ace Bks.

Sundowner. Phoebe Hesketh. 55p. (Orig.). 9200. pap. 16.95 (1-870612-03-5, Pub. by Enitha Pr UK) Dufour.

Sundry Great Gentlemen: Some Essays in Historical Biography. Marjorie Bowen. LC 68-29192. (Essay Index Reprint Ser.). 1977. reprint ed. 23.95 (0-8369-0230-0) Ayer.

Sundt's Occlusive Cerebrovascular Disease. 2nd rev. ed. Ed. by Fredric B. Meyer. LC 94-18063. 1994. text ed. 165.00 (0-7216-4911-4) Saunders.

Sunfall. Dennis Cooley. 160p. (Orig.). 1996. pap. 13.95 (0-88784-580-0, Pub. by Hse of Anansi Pr CN) Genl Dist Srvs.

*Sunfish Bible. Larry Lewis et al. (Illus.). 368p. (Orig.). 1996. pap. 24.95 (0-9654005-0-6) Omega Cubed.

Sunfishes. rev. ed. Jack Ellis. (Illus.). 160p. 1995. pap. 12.95 (1-55821-356-2) Lyons & Burford.

Sunflash. (Stony Man Ser.: No. 22). 1996. mass mkt. 5.50 (0-373-61906-5, 1-61906-3, Wrldwide Lib) Harlequin Bks.

Sunflower. Margot Dalton. (Superromance Ser.: No. 502). 1992. mass mkt. 3.39 (0-373-70502-6, 1-70502-9) Harlequin Bks.

Sunflower. Marliese Dieckmann. LC 94-65094. (Illus.). 24p. (J). (ps-1). 1994. 12.95 (1-879373-75-0) R Rinehart.

Sunflower. Miela Ford. LC 94-7547. (Illus.). 24p. (J). (ps up). 1995. 16.00 (0-688-13301-0); lib. bdg. 15.93 (0-688-13302-9) Greenwillow.

Sunflower. Charles B. Heiser, Jr. LC 74-15906. (Illus.). 198p. 1981. pap. 15.95 (0-8061-1743-5) U of Okla Pr.

Sunflower. Firouz Hejazi. (Illus.). 96p. (Orig.). (PER.). 1989. pap. 7.00 (0-936347-16-3) Iran Bks.

Sunflower. Jill M. Landis. 1990. mass mkt. 6.50 (0-515-10659-3) Jove Pubns.

Sunflower. Miles MacGregor. Ed. by Nancy R. Thatch. (Books for Students by Students). (Illus.). 29p. (J). (gr. 3-6). 1994. lib. bdg. 14.95 (0-933849-52-4) Landmark Edns.

Sunflower. Mary L. Scott. LC 92-70984. 60p. 1993. 7.95 (1-55523-520-4) Winston-Derek.

Sunflower. P. S. Vasudev. 15.00 (0-89253-776-0); text ed. 6.75 (0-89253-777-9) Ind-US Inc.

*Sunflower: On the Possibilities & Limits of Forgiveness. exp. ed. Simon Wiesenthal. 1997. pap. write for info. (0-8052-1060-1) Schocken.

*Sunflower: On the Possibilities & Limits of Forgiveness. expanded ed. Simon Wiesenthal. 288p. 1997. 24.00 (0-8052-4145-0) Schocken.

*Sunflower Always Faces the Sun. Bette Bottoms. 1997. pap. 5.95 (0-7871-1266-6, Dove Bks) Dove Audio.

*Sunflower Birthday Book. Ed. by Helen Exley. (Artist Notebooks). (Illus.). 80p. 1996. 8.00 (1-85015-783-9) Exley Giftbooks.

Sunflower County. Dave Etter. 441p. (Orig.). 1994. pap. 14.95 (0-944024-24-6) Spoon Riv Poetry.

Sunflower Facing the Sun. Greg Pape. LC 92-5881. (Edwin Ford Piper Poetry Award Ser.). 96p. (Orig.). 1992. pap. 10.95 (0-87745-382-9) U of Iowa Pr.

Sunflower Family. Cherie Winner. LC 95-46110. (Illus.). (J). 1996. lib. bdg. 14.96 (1-57505-007-2, Carolrhoda) Lerner Group.

Sunflower Family. Cherie Winner. 1996. pap. text ed. 7.95 (1-57505-029-3, Carolrhoda) Lerner Group.

*Sunflower Farm, Vol. 2. Lori Ohlson. 62p. 1995. pap. 9.50 (1-56770-326-7) S Scheewe Pubns.

Sunflower Forest. Torey L. Hayden. 416p. 1985. mass mkt. 4.95 (0-380-69922-2) Avon.

Sunflower Girl. Marcia Hoehne. LC 95-32661. (Adventures of Jenna V Ser.: Bk. 4). 160p. (Orig.). (J). (gr. 3-6). 1995. pap. 4.99 (0-89107-858-4) Crossway Bks.

*Sunflower Girl. Hylton. (J). Date not set. 23.95 (0-312-15667-7) St Martin.

Sunflower House. Eve Bunting. LC 95-5422. (Illus.). 32p. (J). (ps-1). 1996. 15.00 (0-15-200483-1) HarBrace.

Sunflower Houses. Sharon Lovejoy. 144p. 1995. pap. 16.95 (1-883010-00-4) Interweave.

Sunflower Houses: Garden Discoveries for Children of All Ages. Sharon Lovejoy. LC 91-29880. (Illus.). 144p. 1991. 24.95 (0-934026-70-X) Interweave.

Sunflower Journal. Cavallini & Company Staff. 1995. 24.00 (1-57489-002-6) Cavallini.

*Sunflower Parable. Liz C. Higgs. (Illus.). 32p. (J). (ps-2). 1997. 7.99 (0-7852-7171-6) Tommy Nelson.

*Sunflower Sal. Janet S. Anderson. LC 96-53906. (Illus.). 32p. (J). (gr. 1-4). 1997. lib. bdg. 15.95 (0-8075-7662-X) A Whitman.

Sunflower Sampler. Ed. by Junior League of Wichita, Inc. Staff. LC 73-88717. 236p. 1993. reprint ed. pap. 9.95 (0-9609676-0-5) Jr League Wichita.

*Sunflower Seeds & Seoul Food: The Best of Frederick C. Klein "On Sports" in the Wall Street Journal. Frederick C. Klein. LC 96-43484. 270p. (Orig.). 1997. pap. 13.95 (1-56625-075-7) Bonus Books.

Sunflower Splendor: Three Thousand Years of Chinese Poetry. Ed. by Wu-Chi Liu & Irving Y. Lo. LC 90-39420. 696p. 1990. reprint ed. 39.95 (0-253-35580-X); reprint ed. pap. 19.95 (0-253-20607-3, MB-607) Ind U Pr.

Sunflower Wild. George J. Brooks. LC 93-93783. 216p. 1994. text ed. 20.95 (1-56002-318-X) Aegina Pr.

Sunflowering. Bob Stanish. 92p. (J). (gr. 4-12). 1977. 9.99 (0-916456-12-9, GA69) Good Apple.

*Sunflowers. Rebecca W. Briccetti. LC 97-13133. 1997. write for info. (1-56799-536-5, Friedman-Fairfax) M Friedman Pub Grp Inc.

Sunflowers. Mary A. McDonald. (Nature Bks.). 32p. (J). (gr. 2-6). 1996. lib. bdg. 22.79 (1-56766-272-2) Childs World.

Sunflowers. Lindsay Porter. (Design Motifs Ser.). (Illus.). 64p. 1996. 9.95 (1-85967-144-6, Lorenz Bks) Anness Pub.

Sunflowers. John F. Prevost. LC 96-1179. (Flowers Ser.). (Illus.). (J). 1996. lib. bdg. 13.99 (1-56239-611-0) Abdo & Dghtrs.

*Sunflowers. Gail Saunders-Smith. LC 97-23580. (J). 1997. write for info. (1-56065-489-9) Capstone Pr.

Sunflowers. Diane M. Sitton. (Illus.). 64p. 1995. pap. 9.95 (0-87905-657-6) Gibbs Smith Pub.

Sunflowers. Compiled by Willard Wattles. LC 78-133077. (Granger Index Reprint Ser.). 1977. 18.95 (0-8369-6207-9) Ayer.

Sunflowers: A Little Treasury of Joy. Running Press Staff. 128p. 1996. 4.95 (1-56138-752-5) Running Pr.

Sunflowers & Shadows. Judith Kott. (Illus.). 38p. spiral bd. 11.95 (1-887965-00-9) Rainbow IL.

Sunflower's Promise: A Zuni Legend. Gloria Dominic. LC 96-9039. (Native American Lore & Legends Ser.). 1996. write for info. (0-86593-430-4) Rourke Corp.

Sung Bibliography. Balazs & Hervonet. 1979. text ed. 65.00 (0-9622011-5-4, CH1586) Col U Pr.

Sung Ceramic Designs. Jan Wirgin. (Illus.). 274p. 1979. 58.50 (0-906610-01-X, Pub. by Bamboo Pub UK) Antique Collect.

Sung Dynasty Uses of the I Ching. Kidder Smith, Jr. et al. 288p. 1990. text ed. 39.50 (0-691-05590-4) Princeton U Pr.

Sung Liturgy: Toward Two Thousand A. D. Ed. by Virgil C. Funk. 194p. (Orig.). 1991. pap. 9.95 (0-912405-79-1) Pastoral Pr.

Sung to Sharyar. E. P. Mathers. 128p. 1987. 70.00 (1-85077-146-4, Pub. by Darf Pubs Ltd UK) St Mut.

Sungates: A Testimony Carved in Wood. Victor Hajdu. Tr. by Rose Stein. (Illus.). (HUN.). 1980. 25.00 (0-933652-16-X) Domjan Studio.

*Sunglasses. (Illus.). 64p. 1996. 15.95 (0-7893-0058-3) Universe.

Sunita Experiment. Mitali Perkins. LC 93-28525. 180p. (J). (gr. 5-9). 1994. pap. 4.50 (1-56282-671-9) Hyprn Child.

Sunita Experiment. Mitali Perkins. LC 92-37267. 144p. (J). (gr. 1-6). 1993. 15.95 (0-316-69943-8, Joy St Bks) Little.

Sunk! Exploring Underwater Archaeology. Geography Department Staff. LC 93-42008. (Buried Worlds Ser.). (YA). (gr. 6 up). 1994. lib. bdg. 22.95 (0-8225-3205-0, Lerner Publctns) Lerner Group.

Sunk Costs & Market Structure: Price Competition, Advertising, & the Evolution of Concentration. John Sutton. (Illus.). 592p. 1991. 55.00 (0-262-19305-1) MIT Pr.

*Sunken Gillnets: Fishing in Bristol Bay, Alaska. William H. Nicholson. 1996. pap. text ed. 14.95 (1-888125-10-1) Publ Consult.

*Sunken Gillnets: Fishing in Bristol Bay, Canada. William Nicholsen. LC 96-70832. (Illus.). 160p. 1996. pap. 14.95 (1-888125-05-5) Publ Consult.

Sunken Nuclear Submarines: A Potential Threat to the Environment. Viking O. Eriksen. (Scandinavian University Press Publication). (Illus.). 177p. 1990. 19.50 (82-00-21019-7) Scandnvan Univ Pr.

Sunken Red. Jeroen Brouwers. Tr. by Adrienne Dixon from DUT. LC 88-19502. 144p. (C). 1988. 15.95 (0-941533-19-0) New Amsterdam Bks.

Sunken Red. Jeroen Brouwers. 144p. 1992. reprint ed. pap. 9.95 (1-56131-025-5) New Amsterdam Bks.

*Sunken Road. Garry Disher. 214p. 1997. pap. 16.95 (1-85702-485-0, Pub. by Fourth Estate UK) Trafalgar.

Sunken Ships & Grid Patterns: 2-D Geometry. Douglas H. Clements et al. Ed. by Priscilla C. Samii et al. (Investigations in Number, Data, & Space Ser.). (Illus.). 179p. (Orig.). 1994. teacher ed., pap. 32.95 (0-86651-817-7, DS21255) Seymour Pubns.

Sunken Ships & Treasures. John C. Fine. LC 86-3652. (Illus.). 128p. (J). (gr. 3 up). 1986. lib. bdg. 16.95 (0-689-31280-6, Atheneum Bks Young) S&S Childrens.

Sunken Teasure: How to Find It. Robert Marx. Ed. by Hal Dawson. LC 90-63186. (Illus.). 402p. 1990. pap. 14.95 (0-915920-74-3) Ram Pub.

Sunken Temple: A Novel by the Author of The Phoenix Tree. Satoko Kizaki. Ed. by Pockell et al. Tr. by Carol A. Flath. 208p. 1994. 22.00 (4-7700-1679-4) Kodansha.

Sunken Treasure. Gail Gibbons. LC 87-30114. (Illus.). 32p. (J). (gr. 1-5). 1988. lib. bdg. 14.89 (0-690-04736-3, Crowell Jr Bks) HarpC Child Bks.

Sunken Treasure. Houghton Mifflin Company Staff. (Literature Experience 1993 Ser.). (J). (gr. 3). 1992. pap. 8.48 (0-395-61793-6) HM.

Sunken Treasure. Marian J. A. Jackson. LC 94-2816. (Miss Danforth Mystery Ser.). 1994. 19.95 (0-8027-3191-0) Walker & Co.

Sunken Treasure. Gail Gibbons. LC 87-30114. (Trophy Nonfiction Bk.). (Illus.). 32p. (J). (gr. 1-5). 1990. reprint ed. pap. 4.95 (0-06-446097-5, Trophy) HarpC Child Bks.

Sunken Treasure on Florida Reefs. 2nd rev. ed. Robert F. Weller. Ed. by Ernie S. Richards. (Illus.). 135p. (YA). 1987. pap. 12.95 (0-9628359-1-9) R Weller.

Sunken Treasures. Houghton Mifflin Company Staff. (Literature Experience 1991 Ser.). (J). (gr. 3). 1990. pap. 8.48 (0-395-55152-8) HM.

Sunken Treaties: Naval Arms Control Between the Wars. Emily O. Goldman. LC 93-31953. 1994. 45.00 (0-271-01033-9); pap. 16.95 (0-271-01034-7) Pa St U Pr.

Sunlight Across the Plains. Catherine Dunbar. 264p. 1995. pap. 10.95 (0-340-59442-X, Pub. by H & S UK) Trafalgar.

Sunlight & Brickwork Vol. 1: Artistic Impressions of Augusta, GA. Illus. by Karen L. Banker. (Rose Cottage Papers). 80p. 1995. pap. 12.00 (1-887106-05-7) McRae Banker.

An Asterisk (*) at the beginning of an entry indicates that the title is appearing in BIP for the first time.

Sunlight & Health: Lowering Cholesterol, Blood Pressure & Blood Sugar Through the Positive Effects of the Sun. 1992. lib. bdg. 88.00 (*0-8490-8815-1*) Gordon Pr.

Sunlight & Man: Normal & Abnormal Photobiologic Responses: Proceedings of the International Conference on Photosensitization & Photoprotection, Held November 6-8, 1972, Tokyo, Japan. International Conference on Photosensitization & Photoprotection Staff. Ed. by Thomas B. Fitzpatrick et al. LC 74-83527. 886p. 1974. reprint ed. pap. 180.00 (*0-608-01200-9*, 2061889) Bks Demand.

Sunlight & Shadow. Ed. by Adams W. Lincoln. LC 76-24669. (Sources of Modern Photography Ser.). (Illus.). 1979. reprint ed. lib. bdg. 19.95 (*0-405-09646-1*) Ayer.

Sunlight & Shadow: The Art of Alfred R. Mitchell, 1888-1972. Thomas R. Anderson & Bruce A. Kamerling. LC 88-11429. (Illus.). 84p. 1988. pap. 24.95 (*0-918740-08-8*) San Diego Hist.

Sunlight & Shadow: or Gleanings from Life Work. John B. Gough. (American Biography Ser.). 542p. 1991. reprint ed. lib. bdg. 99.00 (*0-7812-8151-2*) Rprt Serv.

Sunlight & Shadows. G. Hill. (Illus.). 173p. 1990. 24.50 (*0-940143-93-3*) Safari Pr.

Sunlight & Shadows. Gene Hill. 1996. 24.50 (*0-8227-2965-2*) Petersen Pub.

Sunlight & Shadows: Portraits of Priorities for Living & Dying. L. Richard Batzler. LC 85-82029. (Illus.). 60p. (Orig.). 1986. pap. 4.95 (*0-935710-09-4*) Hid Valley MD.

Sunlight & Song: A Singer's Life. Maria Jeritza. Ed. by Andrew Farkas. Tr. by Frederick H. Martens. LC 76-29942. (Opera Biographies Ser.). (Illus.). 1977. reprint ed. lib. bdg. 30.95 (*0-405-09684-4*) Ayer.

Sunlight Could Save Your Life. Zane R. Kime. LC 80-51038. 312p. 1980. 15.95 (*0-9604268-0-9*); pap. 11.95 (*0-9604268-1-7*) Wrld Hlth Pubns.

Sunlight Dialogues. John C. Gardner. LC 86-40156. 758p. 1987. pap. 16.00 (*0-394-74394-6*, Vin) Random.

Sunlight in the Morning: Songs from the Farm. Rochester Folk Art Guild Staff. (Illus.). 40p. (J). (gr. k-6). 1983. 13.00 (*0-686-40298-7*); audio 6.00 (*0-317-00393-3*) Rochester Folk Art.

***Sunlight, Moonlight.** Amanda Ashley. 400p. (Orig.). 1997. mass mkt. 5.99 (*0-505-52158-X*) Dorchester Pub Co.

Sunlight on a Broken Column. Attia Hosain. 319p. 1981. pap. 5.25 (*0-86578-066-8*) Ind-US Inc.

***Sunlight on a Broken Column.** Rae. LC 97-15510. 1997. 20.95 (*0-312-17039-4*) St Martin.

Sunlight on Water: A Manual for Soul-Full Living. Flo A. Magdalena. Ed. by Jayn A. Zopf & Noel McInnis. (Illus.). 434p. (Orig.). 1996. pap. 19.95 (*1-880914-12-3*) All Worlds Pub.

Sunlight on Your Doorstep. Bradley L. Morison. 1966. 6.95 (*0-87018-044-4*); pap. 2.95 (*0-87018-073-8*) Ross.

***Sunlight, Skycrapers, & Soda Pop: The Wherever-You-Look Science Book.** Andrea T. Bennett & James H. Kessler. LC 97-23687. 1997. pap. text ed. 12.95 (*0-07-001440-X*, Lrning Triangle) McGraw.

***Sunlight Speech That Dispels the Darkness of Doubt.** Thinley Norbu. LC 97-23834. 1998. 25.00 (*1-57062-244-2*) Shambhala Pubns.

***Sunlight Through Rain: A Northwest Haiku Year.** Robert Major & Francine Porad. (Illus.). 58p. (Orig.). 1996. pap. 9.25 (*1-887381-03-1*) Vandina Pr.

Sunlight Works: Solar Science: Educational Activities. Heather Gurley & Bob Larson. (Illus.). 31p. (J). (gr. 1-6). 1993. student ed. 10.00 (*0-9634694-2-8*) Sun Light Wks.

Sunlights & More, 2 vols., Vol. 1. Norma F. Swanson. (Window to the World Educational Materials Ser.). (Illus.). (J). (gr. 4-6). Date not set. 84.95 incl. audio (*0-922049-11-4*) Window World NY.

Sunlit Days. large type ed. Jane Julian. 419p. 1992. 25.99 (*0-7505-0312-2*) Ulverscroft.

Sunlit Path. Mother. 194p. 1987. pap. 7.25 (*81-7058-025-0*, Pub. by SAA II) Aurobindo Assn.

Sunlit Path. Kate Ward. (Rainbow Romances Ser.). 160p. 1993. 14.95 (*0-7090-4910-2*, Hale-Parkwest) Parkwest Pubns.

Sunlit Path. large type ed. Kate Ward. (Linford Romance Library). 272p. 1994. pap. 15.99 (*0-7089-7549-6*) Ulverscroft.

Sunlit Seas. large type ed. Ivy Preston. (Linford Romance Library). 304p. 1994. pap. 15.99 (*0-7089-7535-6*, Linford) Ulverscroft.

Sunlit Slopes. Priscilla Klepser. 68p. 1984. 7.95 (*0-533-05870-8*) Vantage.

Sunlover's Guide: Sun Sense for Outdoor People. David English. (Illus.). 177p. 1991. pap. 14.95 (*0-89716-403-2*) P B Pubng.

***Sunna: Its Obligatory & Exemplary Aspects.** Hamid Algar. 56p. (Orig.). 1997. pap. text ed. 3.50 (*1-889999-01-6*) Islam Pubns Int.

***Sunnah in Islam: The Eternal Relevance of the Teachings & Example of the Prophet, Muhammad.** 2nd rev. ed. Habib-Urrahman Azami. Ed. by Khwaja M. Ul-Hassan & Labiba Hassan. LC 95-77847. (Quranic Studies). 55p. 1995. mass mkt. 6.00 (*1-56316-112-5*) Iqra Intl Ed Fdtn.

Sunne in Splendour. Sharon K. Penman. 944p. 1990. pap. 14.00 (*0-345-36313-2*, Ballantine Trade) Ballantine.

Sunnier Side: Arcadian Tales. Charles Jackson. 320p. 1996. pap. 14.95 (*0-8156-0327-4*) Syracuse U Pr.

Sunnier Side: Twelve Arcadian Tales. Charles R. Jackson. LC 70-157779. (Short Story Index Reprint Ser.). 1977. reprint ed. 21.95 (*0-8369-3891-7*) Ayer.

Sunnier Side of Doubt: What It Is & How to Handle It. Alister E. McGrath. 160p. 1990. pap. 10.99 (*0-310-29661-7*) Zondervan.

***Sunny.** Ann M. Martin. (California Diaries Ser.: No. 2). (J). (gr. 4-8). 1997. mass mkt. 3.99 (*0-590-29836-4*) Scholastic Inc.

Sunny. Mary E. Collura. 160p. (YA). (gr. 7-12). 1991. reprint ed. pap. 4.95 (*0-7736-7289-3*, Pub. by Stoddart Pubng CN) Genl Dist Srvs.

Sunny & Warm. Ann Gasser. 32p. (Orig.). 1994. pap. 3.00 (*1-884257-07-0*) AGEE Keyboard.

Sunny Books - Four-Favorite Tales, 4 bks., Set. Gyo Fujikawa. (Illus.). (J). (ps). reprint ed. Boxed set, four bks., 16 pgs. ea. boxed write for info. (*1-55987-042-7*, Sunny Bks) J B Comns.

Sunny Books - Four-Favorite Tales, 4 bks., Set. Gyo Fujikawa. (Illus.). (J). (ps). 1989. reprint ed. Boxed set, 4 books, 16 pgs. ea. boxed write for info. (*1-55987-040-0*, Sunny Bks) J B Comns.

Sunny Books - Four-Favorite Tales, 4 bks., Set. Gyo Fujikawa. (Illus.). (J). (ps). 1989. reprint ed. Boxed set, four bks., 16 pgs. ea. boxed write for info. (*1-55987-041-9*, Sunny Bks) J B Comns.

Sunny Day. Claire Henley. LC 92-72024. (Illus.). 32p. (J). (ps). 1993. 11.95 (*1-56282-340-X*) Hyprn Child.

Sunny Day Dreams Notebook. 96p. (Orig.). 1990. pap. 5.95 (*0-934672-85-7*) Good Bks PA.

Sunny Days. (Key Words Readers Ser.: A Series, No. 641-8a). (Illus.). 3.50 (*0-7214-0554-1*, Ladybrd) Penguin.

Sunny Days. (Series S05: Set 1). (Illus.). Series S05, Set 1. 4.75 (*0-317-03991-1*, Ladybrd) Penguin.

***Sunny Days.** large type ed. Helga Moray. LC 97-12334. 1997. write for info. (*0-7862-1110-5*, Thorndike Lrg Prnt) Thorndike Pr.

Sunny Days & Starry Nights, a Little Hands Nature Book see Little Hands Nature Book: Earth, Sky, Critters & More

Sunny Days Word Games & Mazes. Elvira Gamiello. (Illus.). (Orig.). (J). (gr. 4-6). 1988. pap. 1.95 (*0-942025-40-7*) Kidsbks.

Sunny Goes to School. Detta Juusola. Ed. by Jacqueline Reina. LC 95-90786. 64p. (J). (gr. 2 up). 1996. pap. 9.95 (*0-9639736-3-0*) Woofspun Pubng.

Sunny Hours. Alice Usher. (Illus.). 40p. (Orig.). (J). (ps-2). 1998. pap. 3.95 (*0-671-75281-2*, Green Tiger S&S) S&S Childrens.

***Sunny Morning.** Serafin A. Quintero & Joaquin A. Quintero. Ed. by William-Alan Landes. Tr. by Lucretia X. Floyd from SPA. 58p. (Orig.). 1996. pap. 6.00 (*0-88734-394-5*) Players Pr.

Sunny Seniors Through Aging Eyes. Betty DeGrace. (Illus.). 78p. 1995. 12.95 (*0-9621266-4-0*) IPPD.

Sunny Side of Castro Street. Dan Vojir. LC 81-14344. (Illus.). 144p. (Orig.). 1982. pap. 6.95 (*0-89407-034-7*) Strawberry Hill.

Sunny Side of Genealogy. Fonda D. Baselt. 102p. 1988. 8.95 (*0-8063-1205-X*, 385) Genealog Pub.

Sunny Side of the Alps: Year-Round Delights in South Tyrol & the Dolomites. Paul Hofmann. (Illus.). 224p. 1996. pap. 12.95 (*0-8050-4710-7*, Owl) H Holt & Co.

***Sunny Side Plucked: New & Selected Poems.** Rita A. Higgins. 160p. 1997. pap. 19.95 (*1-85224-375-9*, Pub. by Bloodaxe Bks UK) Dufour.

Sunny-Side Up. Alma Barkman. (Quiet Time Books for Women). 1984. pap. 4.99 (*0-8024-8431-X*) Moody.

Sunny Side Up. Illus. by Suzy De Poo. 1980. ring bd. 11.95 (*0-9604158-0-7*) Jr League Ft Lauderdale.

Sunny Side Up. Patricia R. Giff. (Kids of the Polk Street School Ser.: No. 11). 80p. (Orig.). (J). (gr. k-3). 1986. pap. 3.50 (*0-440-48406-5*, YB BDD) BDD Bks Young Read.

Sunny Side Up: Break-Through Ideas for Women from One of the Most Loved Speakers in the Church. Lucile Johnson & Arlene Bascom. Ed. by Darla H. Isackson. 125p. (Orig.). 1993. pap. 9.95 (*1-55503-581-7*) Covenant Comms.

Sunny Side up: Diet Cooking the Hospital Way. Indianapolis Community Hospital Staff & Alan McLaren. LC 76-11308. 1977. 22.95 (*0-87949-062-4*) Ashley Bks.

Sunny Side-Up: Effective & Exciting Learning Centers (K-3) Glena Goodwin & Becky McMurray. (Illus.). 280p. (Orig.). 1989. 22.00 (*0-9622803-0-5*) Smith & Brown Pub.

***Sunny-Side Up: Good Morning Recipes to Start Your Day.** Cindy Grubb. LC 96-39084. (Illus.). 64p. (Orig.). 1997. 12.99 (*1-56507-593-5*) Harvest Hse.

Sunny Side Up: Kids Coping with Cancer. (Illus.). 440p. (YA). (gr. 9-12). 1994. 24.95 (*0-939801-03-5*) Bucksnort.

Sunny Slopes of Long Ago. Ed. by Wilson M. Hudson & Allen Maxwell. LC 65-24930. (Texas Folklore Society Publications: No. 33). (Illus.). 204p. 1966. 12.95 (*0-87074-082-2*) UNTX Pr.

Sunny Songs. Lois Youngerman. LC 88-72023. 1989. 12.50 (*0-9618671-1-6*) CKRB Pub.

Sunny South: The Life & Art of William Aiken Walker. Cynthia Seibels. (Illus.). 288p. 1995. 75.00 (*0-9632836-1-8*) R M Hicklin.

Sunny South Maui. Angela K. Kepler. 144p. 1992. pap. 7.95 (*1-56647-012-9*) Mutual Pub HI.

Sunny Stories: The Sheep that Liked to Sing. A. J. Wood. (J). 1989. 1.98 (*0-671-09892-6*) S&S Trade.

Sunny Sunflower. Joan Schwinge. (Illus.). 28p. (J). 1992. pap. 6.95 (*0-9632902-0-7*) Winston Bks.

***Sunnybrook: A True Story with Lies.** Persimmon Blackbridge. 108p. 1996. pap. 15.95 (*0-88974-060-7*, Pub. by Press Gang CN) LPC InBook.

***Sunnybrook: A True Story with Lies.** Persimmon Blackbridge. 1996. 21.95 (*0-88974-068-2*) LPC InBook.

Sunnybrook Garden Tale. Rebecca J. Davis. LC 92-97014. (Illus.). 32p. (J). (gr. 3-5). 1993. lib. bdg. 12.00 (*0-9634032-0-6*) R J Davis.

***Sunny's Legacy: The Poetry of Floyd Alexander Peckel.** Floyd A. Peckel. Ed. & Illus. by Leta Leshe. 44p. (Orig.). 1997. pap. 5.00 (*0-9645451-7-9*) F Swann Pubns.

Sunny's Mittens: Learn-to-Knit - Lovikka Mittens. Robin Hansen. LC 90-61410. (Illus.). 48p. (J). (gr. 3-6). 1990. spiral bd. 12.95 (*0-89272-290-8*) Down East.

Sunnyside Junior High: Piano/Vocal Score. Allison Woyiwada & Rick Woyiwada. 46p. (Orig.). 1992. Piano. pap. 16.00 (*0-88734-025-3*) Players Pr.

Sunnyside Junior High: Vocal/Guitar Score. Allison Woyiwada & Rick Woyiwada. 46p. (Orig.). 1992. Guitar. pap. 10.00 (*0-88734-026-1*) Players Pr.

Sunnyside Junior High (Playscript) Allison Woyiwada. (Orig.). 1991. pap. 10.00 (*0-88734-514-X*) Players Pr.

Sunnyvale: From the City of Destiny to the Heart of the Silicon Valley. Mary J. Ignoffo. LC 94-9363. (Local History Studies: Vol. 35). 1994. pap. 14.95 (*0-935089-17-9*) CA History Ctr.

Sunnyvista City. 1988. pap. 3.50 (*0-19-421908-9*) OUP.

Sunpainters: Eclipse of the Navajo Sun. Baje Whitethorne. LC 94-11146. (Illus.). 32p. (J). (gr. k up). 1994. lib. bdg. 14.95 (*0-87358-587-9*) Northland AZ.

Sunrise. Grace L. Hill. 22.95 (*0-8488-0088-5*) Amereon Ltd.

Sunrise. Grace L. Hill. (Grace Livingston Hill Ser.: Vol. 25). 288p. 1992. pap. text ed. 4.99 (*0-8423-5941-9*) Tyndale.

Sunrise. Julian J. Joyce. LC 91-78176. 73p. (Orig.). 1992. pap. 6.00 (*0-944851-04-5*) Earth Star.

***Sunrise.** Helena C. Pittman. LC 97-2925. (Illus.). (YA). 1998. write for info. (*0-15-201684-8*) HarBrace.

Sunrise. Chassie West. 336p. 1996. mass mkt. 4.99 (*0-06-108110-8*, Harp PBks) HarpC.

Sunrise. White Eagle Staff. 64p. 1958. 6.95 (*0-85487-016-4*, Pub. by White Eagle UK) DeVorss.

Sunrise: A Play in Four Acts. 2nd ed. Isao Yu. Tr. by A. C. Barnes from CHI. 170p. (C). 1978. 11.95 (*0-917056-73-6*, Pub. by Foreign Lang Pr CH) Cheng & Tsui.

Sunrise: A Support Program for Children of Divorced Parents. Virginia McCall. LC 92-26329. 160p. 1992. pap. 12.95 (*0-8091-3330-X*) Paulist Pr.

Sunrise All Day Long: Anthology. (Illus.). 24p. (Orig.). 1986. 5.00 (*0-914473-04-2*) Stone Man Pr.

Sunrise & Shadow. Arthur O. Roberts. LC 84-62861. 112p. (Orig.). 1985. pap. 7.95 (*0-913342-48-3*) Barclay Pr.

Sunrise & Sunset Tables for Key Cities & Weather Stations in the United States. United States Nautical Almanac Office Staff & Gale Research, Inc., Staff. LC 76-24796. 376p. 1977. 92.00 (*0-8103-0464-3*) Gale.

Sunrise at Abadan: The British & Soviet Invasion of Iran, 1941. Richard A. Stewart. LC 88-9720. 303p. 1988. text ed. 59.95 (*0-275-92793-8*, C2793, Praeger Pubs) Greenwood.

Sunrise at Campobello. Dore Schary. 1961. pap. 5.25 (*0-8222-1101-7*) Dramatists Play.

Sunrise at Five. Edward Walsh. LC 89-425. 1991. pap. 14.95 (*0-87949-305-4*) Ashley Bks.

Sunrise at Ten: Johnstown - Another Age. Marie Morgart. LC 90-71995. 203p. (Orig.). 1991. pap. 10.00 (*1-56002-093-8*) Aegina Pr.

Sunrise at the Mayan Temple. Sigmund Brouwer. (Accidental Detective Ser.: Vol. 10). (J). (gr. 3-7). 1992. pap. 4.99 (*0-89693-057-2*, Victor Bks) Chariot Victor.

Sunrise at the Mayan Temple. Sigmund Brouwer. (Accidental Detective Ser.: Vol. 10). 132p. (J). (gr. 3-7). 1995. pap. 5.99 (*1-56476-379-X*, 6-3379, Victor Bks) Chariot Victor.

Sunrise Brighter Still: The Visionary Novels of Frank Waters. Alexander Blackburn. LC 91-18370. 192p. (C). 1991. text ed. 37.95 (*0-8040-0947-3*) Ohio U Pr.

***Sunrise, Day One, Year 2000.** Naseem Javed. LC 96-94408. 1996. pap. 7.00 (*0-9639702-2-4*) Linkbridge Pub.

Sunrise Devotions, No. 2. Compiled by Tim Stearman. 80p. 1991. pap. 2.00 (*0-8341-1395-3*) Beacon Hill.

Sunrise Guns. large type ed. William C. MacDonald. LC 94-33672. (Nightingale Ser.). 264p. 1995. pap. 16.95 (*0-7838-1151-9*, GK Hall) Thorndike Pr.

Sunrise in Fiji. Chaman Nahal. (C). 1988. 21.00 (*0-8364-2367-4*, Pub. by Allied II) S Asia.

***Sunrise in Her Heart.** Dorothy Watts. (Illus.). 128p. (Orig.). 1997. pap. 12.95 (*1-57847-004-8*) Genl Conf Svnth-day.

Sunrise in the West: The Brothers of Gwynedd I. Edith Pargeter. 342p. 1991. pap. 11.95 (*0-7472-3003-X*, Pub. by Headline UK) Trafalgar.

Sunrise Meditations. Anthony Vitale. 64p. 1995. pap. 6.95 (*1-887552-02-2*) Web Pr MI.

Sunrise on the Rappahannock: A River-Lover's Guide to Peace & Happiness. Mary W. Buxton. LC 92-93891. (Illus.). 83p. (Orig.). 1992. pap. 6.50 (*1-880902-05-2*) Rappahannock Pr.

Sunrise on Twenty-First Street. Elizabeth Uhl. LC 91-68088. 56p. 1992. 6.95 (*1-55523-501-8*) Winston-Derek.

Sunrise over the Harbor: A Story about the Meaning of Independence Day. Louise Mandrell & Ace Collins. LC 93-310. (Children's Holiday Adventure Ser.: Vol. 16). (Illus.). 32p. (J). (ps-3). 1993. 12.95 (*1-56530-040-8*) Summit TX.

***Sunrise Shows Late: A Novel.** Eva Mekler. LC 96-43464. 288p. 1997. 21.95 (*1-882593-17-0*) Bridge Wrks.

Sunrise Song. Kathleen Eagle. 384p. (Orig.). 1996. mass mkt. 5.99 (*0-380-77634-0*) Avon.

Sunrise Song. Minnie Gilbert. (Illus.). 96p. 1984. 8.95 (*0-89015-468-6*) Sunbelt Media.

Sunrise, Sunset. Rowland Croucher. 384p. 1996. 12.00 (*1-86371-389-1*) Harper SF.

Sunrise to Eternity: A Study in Jacob Boehme's Life & Thought. John J. Stoudt. LC 79-8626. reprint ed. 34.50 (*0-404-18492-8*) AMS Pr.

***Sunrise Vows.** Carla Cassidy. (Cheyenne Nights Ser.). 1997. mass mkt. 3.75 (*0-373-22419-2*, 1-22419-5) Harlequin Bks.

Sunrise with Seamonsters. Paul Theroux. 1986. pap. 15.00 (*0-395-41501-2*) HM.

Sunrises & Songs: Reading & Writing Poetry in an Elementary Classroom. Amy A. McClure. LC 89-19919. (Illus.). 261p. (Orig.). 1990. pap. text ed. 23.50 (*0-435-08507-7*, 08507) Heinemann.

Sunrising. David Cook. 1990. pap. 9.95 (*0-87951-261-X*) Overlook Pr.

Sunrunner's Fire. Melanie Rawn. (Dragon Prince Ser.: Bk. 3). 480p. 1990. mass mkt. 6.99 (*0-88677-403-9*) DAW Bks.

Suns & Moons. Morag Neil. LC 94-68901. (Illus.). 80p. 1995. 12.95 (*0-8478-1858-6*) Rizzoli Intl.

Suns & Moons. Lindsay Porter. (Design Motifs Ser.). (Illus.). 64p. 1996. 9.95 (*1-85967-139-X*, Lorenz Bks) Anness Pub.

Sun's Asleep Behind the Hill. Mirra Ginsburg. LC 81-6615. (Illus.). 32p. (J). (ps-1). 1982. 16.00 (*0-688-00824-0*); lib. bdg. 15.93 (*0-688-00825-9*) Greenwillow.

***Sun's Breath: Poems of Hafiz.** Daniel Ladinsky. (Illus.). (Orig.). 1997. pap. 15.00 (*0-9657637-5-7*) Pmpkn House.

Sun's Day. Mordicai Gerstein. LC 88-24738. (Illus.). 32p. (J). (ps-1). 1989. 13.00 (*0-06-022404-5*); lib. bdg. 14.89 (*0-06-022405-3*) HarpC Child Bks.

Sun's Family of Planets. Allan Fowler. LC 92-7405. (Rookie Read-about Science Ser.). (Illus.). 32p. (J). (ps-2). 1992. lib. bdg. 17.30 (*0-516-06004-X*) Childrens.

Sun's Family of Planets. Allan Fowler. LC 92-7405. (Rookie Read-about Science Ser.). (Illus.). 32p. (J). (ps-2). 1993. pap. 3.95 (*0-516-46004-8*) Childrens.

Sun's Family of Planets Big Book: Big Book. Allan Fowler. LC 92-7405. (Rookie Read-about Science Ser.). (Illus.). 32p. (J). (ps-2). 1992. pap. 32.40 (*0-516-49631-X*) Childrens.

Sun's Heat from Distant Hills: Tenor & Orchestra Piano Reduction. S. Albert. 32p. 1993. pap. 18.95 (*0-7935-2244-7*) H Leonard.

Suns, Myths & Men. rev. ed. Patrick Moore. LC 68-27145. (Illus.). 1969. 7.95 (*0-393-06364-X*) Norton.

Sun's Not Broken, A Cloud's Just in the Way: On Child-Centered Teaching. Sydney G. Clemens. 137p. (Orig.). 1984. pap. 10.95 (*0-87659-109-8*) Gryphon Hse.

Suns of Independence. Ahmadou Kourouma. Tr. by Adrian Adams from FRE. LC 80-8891. 136p. (C). 1981. pap. 11.50 (*0-8419-0747-1*, Africana) Holmes & Meier.

Suns Without End: Selected Poems by Wilson Reid Ogg. Wilson R. Ogg. (Illus.). 95p. 1988. pap. 5.00 (*0-929707-00-1*) Pinebrook CA.

***Sunscreen Photobiology: Molecular, Cellular & Physiological Aspects.** Francis P. Gasparro. LC 97-21826. (Biotechnology Intelligence Unit (SV) Ser.). 182p. 1997. write for info. (*1-57059-468-6*) R G Landes.

Sunscreens: Development, Evaluation, & Regulatory Aspects. 2nd ed. Ed. by Lowe et al. LC 96-43444. (Cosmetic Science & Technology Ser.: Vol. 15). 816p. 1996. 195.00 (*0-8247-9306-4*) Dekker.

Sunset. 192p. (Orig.). 1995. pap. 5.95 (*1-888736-02-X*) Mangozoo News.

Sunset. 2nd ed. Hanoch Teller. (Illus.). 288p. (YA). (gr. 12). 1988. reprint ed. 15.95 (*0-9614772-2-9*) NYC Pub Co.

Sunset: A History of Parisian Drama in the Last Years of Louis XIV, 1701-1715. Henry C. Lancaster. LC 76-29737. 1977. reprint ed. text ed. 65.00 (*0-8371-9278-1*, LASH, Greenwood Pr) Greenwood.

***Sunset Across India.** Susan E. McCloud. 1997. pap. 9.95 (*1-57008-350-9*) Bookcraft Inc.

***Sunset Across the Waters.** Susan E. McCloud. 1996. 14.95 (*1-57008-285-5*) Bookcraft Inc.

Sunset after Dark. Cherie Bennett. 224p. (Orig.). 1993. pap. 3.99 (*0-425-13772-4*) Berkley Pub.

Sunset after Hours. Cherie Bennett. 224p. (Orig.). 1993. pap. 3.50 (*0-425-13666-3*) Berkley Pub.

Sunset after Midnight. Cherie Bennett. 224p. (Orig.). 1993. pap. 3.99 (*0-425-13799-6*) Berkley Pub.

Sunset & Santiago. Gloria White. 320p. 1997. mass mkt. 5.50 (*0-440-22326-1*) Dell.

Sunset at Blandings. P. G. Wodehouse. 224p. 1991. pap. 8.95 (*0-14-012448-9*, Penguin Bks) Viking Penguin.

Sunset at Rosalie: A Novel. Anne L. McLaughlin. 272p. (Orig.). 1996. pap. 11.95 (*1-880284-15-4*) J Daniel.

Sunset Beach. Jonathan Brannen. (Illus.). 51p. (Orig.). 1991. pap. 5.00 (*0-926935-54-2*) Runaway Spoon.

Sunset Beach. Trip Purcell. 320p. (Orig.). 1996. pap. 12.95 (*1-884570-47-X*) Research Triangle.

Sunset Best Kids Cook Book. (Art-Crafts-Cooking-Drawing Books for Children Ser.). (Illus.). 112p. (J). (gr. k-6). 1995. lib. bdg. 18.95 (*1-56674-104-1*) Forest Hse.

Sunset Best Kids Cookie Book. (Arts-Crafts-Cooking-Drawing Books for Children Ser.). (Illus.). 112p. (J). (gr. k-6). 1995. lib. bdg. 17.95 (*1-56674-084-3*) Forest Hse.

Sunset Best Kids Love-the-Earth Activity Book. Elizabeth L. Hogan. (Environmental - Saving Our Earth Ser.). (Illus.). 96p. (J). (gr. 2-5). 1995. lib. bdg. 16.95 (*1-56674-086-X*) Forest Hse.

Sunset Boulevard. Don Black & Christopher Hampton. 128p. (Orig.). 1993. pap. 8.95 (*0-571-17214-8*) Faber & Faber.

Sunset Boulevard: The Making of the Musical. George Perry. (Illus.). 176p. 1994. 29.95 (*0-8050-2927-3*) H Holt & Co.

Sunset Boulevard Highlights. Andrew Lloyd Webber. 24p. 1993. pap. 9.95 (*0-7935-2779-1*, 00312486) H Leonard.

Sunset by the Chain-Link Fence. Sean T. Dougherty. 30p. 1993. 3.00 (*1-881168-38-7*) Red Danceflr.

Sunset California Freeway: Exit Guide. Bill Cima & Saundra Cima. (Illus.). 352p. (Orig.). 1985. pap. 9.95 (*0-936929-01-4*) Am Travel Pubns.

Sunset Coast. Susan D. Williams. LC 95-15716. 320p. (Orig.). 1995. pap. 11.99 (*0-89107-854-1*) Crossway Bks.

S

Sunset Crater National Monument. Rose Houk. Ed. by Sandra Scott. LC 94-66874. (Illus.). 16p. 1995. pap. 3.95 (*1-877856-46-0*) SW Pks Mnmts.

Sunset Creative Fun Crafts for Kids. (Arts-Crafts-Cooking-Drawing Books for Children Ser.). (Illus.). 80p. (J). (ps-3). 1995. lib. bdg. 16.95 (*1-56674-085-1*) Forest Hse.

Sunset Deceptions. Cherie Bennett. 224p. (Orig.). 1993. pap. 3.99 (*0-425-13905-0*) Berkley Pub.

Sunset Drifters. Majid Amini. Ed. by Christina Koliai. 176p. (Orig.). 1989. pap. 9.95 (*1-877789-01-1*) Afsaneh Pub.

Sunset Embrace. Cherie Bennett. 224p. (Orig.). 1993. pap. 3.99 (*0-425-13840-2*) Berkley Pub.

Sunset Embrace. Sandra Brown. 368p. 1990. mass mkt. 6.50 (*0-446-35685-9*) Warner Bks.

***Sunset Embrace.** Sandra Brown. 1997. mass mkt. 3.99 (*0-446-60564-6*) Warner Bks.

Sunset Embrace. large type ed. Sandra Brown. LC 93-11429. 1993. lib. bdg. 22.95 (*1-56054-786-3*) Thorndike Pr.

Sunset Express. Robert Crais. (Elvis Cole Ser.). 288p. 1996. 21.95 (*0-7868-6096-0*) Hyperion.

***Sunset Express.** Robert Crais. 416p. 1997. mass mkt. 5.99 (*0-7868-8915-2*) Hyperion.

Sunset Fantasy. Cherie Bennett. 224p. (YA). 1994. pap. text ed. 3.99 (*0-425-14458-5*) Berkley Pub.

Sunset Fire. Cherie Bennett. 224p. (YA). (gr. 7-12). 1994. pap. text ed. 3.99 (*0-425-14360-0*) Berkley Pub.

Sunset Fling. Cherie Bennett. 224p. (Orig.). 1995. pap. text ed. 3.99 (*0-425-15026-7*) Berkley Pub.

***Sunset Forever.** Cherie Bennett. 208p. 1997. mass mkt. 3.99 (*0-425-15765-2*) Berkley Pub.

Sunset Gate. Isabel Alden. (Grace Livingston Hill Ser.: Vol. 1). 1995. pap. 4.99 (*0-8423-3175-1*) Tyndale.

Sunset Grill: Poems. Anne Rouse. 64p. 9300. pap. 12.95 (*1-85224-219-1*, Pub. by Bloodaxe Bks UK) Dufour.

Sunset Heart. Cherie Bennett. 224p. (Orig.). (J). (ps-3). 1994. pap. 3.99 (*0-425-14183-7*, Splash) Berkley Pub.

Sunset Heat. Cherie Bennett. (YA). 1992. pap. 3.99 (*0-425-13383-4*) Berkley Pub.

Sunset Holiday. Charlie Bennett. 224p. (Orig.). 1995. pap. text ed. 3.99 (*0-425-15109-3*) Berkley Pub.

Sunset House. large type ed. Winifred Fortescue. 256p. 1996. 21.95 (*1-85695-158-8*, Pub. by ISIS UK) Transaction Pubs.

Sunset Illusions. Cherie Bennett. 224p. (Orig.). (YA). (gr. 7-12). 1994. pap. text ed. 3.99 (*0-425-14336-8*) Berkley Pub.

Sunset Law. large type ed. John B. Hilton. 288p. 1985. 25.99 (*0-7089-1364-4*) Ulverscroft.

***Sunset Limited: A Novel.** James L. Burke. LC 97-23893. 1998. write for info. (*0-385-48842-4*) Doubleday.

Sunset Lines: The Story of the Chicago Aurora & Elgin Railroad, Number 1, Trackage. Larry Plachno. Ed. by Eric Bronsky. (Illus.). 160p. 1987. 32.00 (*0-933449-02-X*) Transport Trails.

Sunset Lines - the Story of the Chicago Aurora & Elgin Railroad, Vol. 2: History. Larry Plachno. LC 86-30751. (Sunset Lines Ser.). (Illus.). 352p. 1990. text ed. 64.00 (*0-933449-10-0*) Transport Trails.

Sunset Magic. Cherie Bennett. 224p. (Orig.). 1994. pap. text ed. 3.99 (*0-425-14290-6*) Berkley Pub.

Sunset Murders. Louise Farr. Ed. by Claire Zion. (Illus.). 392p. 1993. reprint ed. mass mkt. 5.99 (*0-671-70089-8*) PB.

Sunset, No. 01: Sunset Island. Cherie Bennett. (YA). 1991. pap. 3.99 (*0-425-12969-1*, Splash) Berkley Pub.

Sunset, No. 02: Sunset Kiss. Cherie Bennett. 1991. pap. 3.99 (*0-425-12899-7*, Splash) Berkley Pub.

Sunset, No. 03: Sunset Dreams. Cherie Bennett. 1991. pap. 3.99 (*0-425-13070-3*, Splash) Berkley Pub.

Sunset, No. 04: Sunset Farewell. Cherie Bennett. (YA). 1991. pap. 3.99 (*0-425-12772-9*, Splash) Berkley Pub.

Sunset, No. 05: Sunset Reunion. Cherie Bennett. (J). 1991. pap. 3.99 (*0-425-13318-4*, Splash) Berkley Pub.

Sunset of the Confederacy. Morris Schaff. 36.00 (*0-8488-1156-9*) Amereon Ltd.

Sunset of the Confederacy. Morris Schaff. 345p. 1985. reprint ed. 30.00 (*0-942211-82-0*) Olde Soldier Bks.

Sunset of the Romanov Dynasty. Y. Shelayev et al. (Illus.). 343p. (C). 1992. text ed. 60.00 (*5-85255-223-2*) Caratzas.

Sunset of the Sabertooth. Mary P. Osborne. LC 95-34697. (Magic Tree House Ser.: No. 7). (Illus.). (J). (gr. 1-4). 1996. pap. 3.99 (*0-679-86373-7*); lib. bdg. 11.99 (*0-679-96373-1*) Random Bks Yng Read.

Sunset on the Road. Cherie Bennett. (Orig.). 1993. pap. 3.99 (*0-425-13932-8*) Berkley Pub.

Sunset Paradise. Cherie Bennett. 224p. (Orig.). 1992. pap. 3.99 (*0-425-13770-8*) Berkley Pub.

Sunset Park. Photos by Thomas Roma. (Photographers at Work Ser.). (Illus.). 60p. 1997. pap. 15.95 (*1-56098-643-3*) Smithsonian.

***Sunset Pass.** large type ed. Zane Grey. LC 96-42251. (Zane Grey's New Western Ser.). 1996. lib. bdg. 18.95 (*1-57490-047-1*, Sagebrush LP West) T T Beeler.

Sunset Passion. Cherie Bennett. 224p. (Orig.). 1994. pap. 3.99 (*0-425-14397-X*) Berkley Pub.

***Sunset Pond.** Laura A. Smith. (Illus.). 32p. (J). (ps-3). 1997. 14.95 (*0-9658246-3-2*) Flyleaf Publ.

Sunset Possibilities & Other Poems. Gabriel Preil. Tr. by Robert Friend from HEB. (Jewish Poetry Ser.). 150p. 1985. 12.95 (*0-8276-0240-5*); pap. 8.95 (*0-8276-0241-3*) JPS Phila.

Sunset Promises. Cherie Bennett. (Illus.). 224p. 1992. pap. 3.99 (*0-425-13384-2*) Berkley Pub.

***Sunset Promises: Cheyenne Nights.** Carla Cassidy. (Intrigue Ser.). 1997. mass mkt. 3.75 (*0-373-22411-7*, 1-22411-2) Harlequin Bks.

Sunset Railway: To the Midway-Sunset Fields. John F. Bergman. (Illus.). 110p. 1995. 24.95 (*0-943500-14-1*) Kern Historical.

Sunset Recipe Annual: 1993 Edition. Sunset Books Staff. 312p. 1993. 24.99 (*0-376-02694-4*) Sunset Bks Inc.

Sunset Recipe Annual, 1994. Sunset Editors. 288p. 1994. 24.99 (*0-376-02695-2*) Sunset Bks Inc.

Sunset Revenge. Cherie Bennett. 224p. (Orig.). (YA). 1994. pap. 3.99 (*0-425-14228-0*) Berkley Pub.

Sunset Secrets. Cherie Bennett. 1992. pap. 3.99 (*0-425-13319-2*) Berkley Pub.

Sunset Sensation. Cherie Bennett. 224p. (Orig.). (J). 1994. pap. 3.99 (*0-425-14253-1*) Berkley Pub.

Sunset Spirit. Cherie Bennett. 224p. (Orig.). (YA). 1995. pap. text ed. 3.99 (*0-425-15028-3*) Berkley Pub.

Sunset Stranger: It's a Strange World. Cherie Bennett. 224p. (Orig.). (YA). 1994. pap. text ed. 3.99 (*0-425-14129-2*) Berkley Pub.

Sunset Surf. Cherie Bennett. (Orig.). 1993. pap. 3.99 (*0-425-13937-9*) Berkley Pub.

Sunset Tears. Cherie Bennett. 224p. (Orig.). (YA). 1995. pap. text ed. 3.99 (*0-425-15027-5*) Berkley Pub.

Sunset That Was Vanessa. Christopher F. Givan. 24p. (Orig.). 1995. 5.00 (*0-936908-08-4*) Broncho Pr.

Sunset Touch. Cherie Bennett. (YA). 1993. pap. 3.99 (*0-425-13708-2*) Berkley Pub.

Sunset Touch. large type ed. Alex Stuart. 380p. 1989. 25.99 (*0-7089-1968-5*) Ulverscroft.

Sunset Warrior. Eric Van Lustbader. 256p. 1989. mass mkt. 5.99 (*0-449-21646-2*, Crest) Fawcett.

Sunset Warrior. Eric Van Lustbader. 1990. reprint ed. 19.00 (*0-7278-4073-8*) Severn Hse.

Sunset Wedding. Cherie Bennett. 1993. pap. 3.99 (*0-425-13982-4*) Berkley Pub.

Sunset Western Travel Guide 1996 Edition. Ed. by Sunset Books Staff. 352p. 1996. pap. 17.95 (*0-376-06784-5*) Sunset Bks Inc.

Sunset Western Travel Guide 1996 Edition. Ed. by Sunset Books Staff. 352p. 1996. 29.95 (*0-376-06785-3*) Sunset Bks Inc.

Sunset Whispers. Cherie Bennett. 224p. (Orig.). (YA). 1992. pap. 3.99 (*0-425-13386-9*) Berkley Pub.

Sunset Wishes. Cherie Bennett. 224p. (Orig.). 1993. pap. 3.99 (*0-425-13812-7*) Berkley Pub.

Sunset with God. Honor Books Staff. (Quiet Moments with God Ser.). 208p. Date not set. 14.99 (*1-56292-031-6*) Honor Bks OK.

***Sunsets.** Robin J. Gunn. LC 96-47448. 252p. 1997. pap. 8.99 (*1-57673-103-0*, Palisades OR) Multnomah Pubs.

Sunsets. Constance O'Day-Flannery. 416p. (Orig.). 1996. mass mkt. 6.50 (*0-446-60307-4*) Warner Bks.

Sunsets & Glories. Peter Barnes. (Methuen Modern Plays Ser.). 86p. (C). 1990. pap. 9.95 (*0-413-64020-5*, A0491, Pub. by Methuen UK) Heinemann.

Sunsets, Secrets & Surprises. Tracy Stark. LC 96-83467. 64p. 1996. pap. 9.95 (*1-886225-11-7*) Dageforde Pub.

Sunsets, Twilights, & Evening Skies. Aden B. Meinel & Marjorie P. Meinel. (Illus.). 173p. (C). 1991. pap. text ed. 24.95 (*0-521-40647-1*) Cambridge U Pr.

Sunshaker's War. Tom Deitz. 368p. 1990. pap. 3.95 (*0-380-76062-2*) Avon.

Sunshine. Elaine Cannon. 1994. 10.95 (*0-88494-955-9*) Bookcraft Inc.

Sunshine. Illus. by Valerie Coursen. (Notes Ser). 80p. 1996. pap. 3.95 (*1-56138-647-2*) Running Pr.

Sunshine. Norma Klein. 224p. 1976. mass mkt. 3.99 (*0-380-00049-0*, 89506-4, Flare) Avon.

Sunshine. Jan Ormerod. LC 80-84971. (Illus.). (J). (ps up). 1990. pap. 3.95 (*0-688-09353-1*, Mulberry) Morrow.

Sunshine. Joy A. Palmer. LC 92-38437. (What About...? Ser.). (Illus.). 32p. (J). (gr. 2-3). 1992. lib. bdg. 21.40 (*0-8114-3416-8*) Raintree Steck-V.

Sunshine. Joy A. Palmer. (J). (ps-3). 1994. 4.95 (*0-8114-6440-7*) Raintree Steck-V.

Sunshine. Bob Reese. Ed. by Dan Wasserman. (Ten Word Book Ser.). (Illus.). (J). (gr. k-1). 1979. 9.95 (*0-89868-073-5*); pap. 3.95 (*0-89868-084-0*) ARO Pub.

Sunshine. Pat Warren. (Tyler Ser.: No. 506). 1992. mass mkt. 3.99 (*0-373-82506-4*) Harlequin Bks.

Sunshine: Daughter of Sacrifice. Teresa. 216p. 1993. pap. 9.95 (*0-9629875-1-4*) Cornerstn FL.

Sunshine: More Meditations for Children. Maureen Garth. 1995. pap. 11.00 (*1-86371-406-5*) Harper SF.

Sunshine & Forget-Me-Nots: A Grandmother's Legacy of Logic & Laughter. Ellen Yaun. 120p. (Orig.). 1995. pap. text ed. 7.95 (*1-880092-34-4*) Bright Bks TX.

Sunshine & Shadow. Kathleen Harrington. 400p. (Orig.). 1993. mass mkt. 4.50 (*0-380-77058-X*) Avon.

Sunshine & Shadow: The Amish & Their Quilts. (Illus.). 88p. (C). 1991. reprint ed. lib. bdg. 29.00 (*0-8095-7595-7*) Borgo Pr.

Sunshine & Shadow Vol. 1: Recent Painting in Southern California. Contrib. by Joe Goode et al. LC 84-73006. (Illus.). 75p. (Orig.). 1985. pap. 10.00 (*0-911291-10-5*) Fellows Cont Art.

Sunshine & Shadow of Slave Life. Isaac D. Williams. LC 73-168152. reprint ed. 27.50 (*0-404-00262-5*) AMS Pr.

***Sunshine & Shadows.** Elfreda M. Almgren. (Orig.). 1996. pap. write for info. (*1-57553-396-0*) Watermrk Pr.

Sunshine & Shadows. Pamela Browning. (American Romance Ser.: No. 439). 1992. mass mkt. 3.39 (*0-373-16439-4*, 1-16439-1) Harlequin Bks.

Sunshine & Shadows. Roberta Gayle. 352p. 1995. mass mkt. 4.99 (*0-8217-0136-3*, Zebra Kensgtn); mass mkt. 4.99 (*0-7860-0136-4*, Pinncle Kensgtn) Kensgtn Pub Corp.

Sunshine & Shadows Through Time: A Book of Poems. Wayne M. Bushnell. 64p. 1992. boxed 9.95 (*0-87770-561-5*) Ye Galleon.

Sunshine & Smiles. Lighten-Up Staff. (Small Wonders Ser.). 120p. 1994. spiral bd. 4.99 (*1-879127-48-2*) Lighten Up Enter.

Sunshine & Storm in Rhodesia. 2nd ed. Frederick C. Selous. LC 69-18660. (Illus.). 290p. 1969. reprint ed. text ed. 52.50 (*0-8371-4947-9*, SES&, Negro U Pr) Greenwood.

Sunshine & the Moon's Delight: A Centenary Tribute to J. M. Synge. Ed. by Suhbil B. Bushrui. 356p. 7900. 50.00 (*0-900675-55-1*, Pub. by Colin Smythe Ltd UK) Dufour.

Sunshine & the Shadowmaster: The Jones Gang & that Special Woman. Rimmer. 1995. pap. 3.75 (*0-373-09979-7*) Harlequin Bks.

Sunshine at Home & Other Stories. Timothy S. Arthur. LC 77-137722. (American Fiction Reprint Ser.). 1977. reprint ed. 20.95 (*0-8369-7021-7*) Ayer.

***Sunshine at the End of Life.** Margaret Merkel. Ed. by Carolyn S. Zagury. LC 97-60583. 108p. (Orig.). 1997. pap. 12.95 (*1-880254-43-3*) Vista.

Sunshine Basket. Lula Guthrie. (Illus.). 1986. pap. 2.95 (*0-89265-112-1*) Randall Hse.

***Sunshine Box.** Milicent Moss. LC 96-37890. (Illus.). 128p. (J). (gr. 3-9). 1998. 12.99 (*1-57673-132-4*, Gold & Honey) Multnomah Pubs.

***Sunshine Box Journal.** Milicent Moss. (Illus.). (J). (gr. 3-9). 1998. 12.99 (*1-57673-224-X*) Multnomah Pubs.

Sunshine Boys. Neil Simon. 1973. 9.95 (*0-394-48808-3*, 48808) Random.

Sunshine Boys: Lobbyists, Interest Groups & Disclosure Laws. Neil Upmeyer. 1983. 7.50 (*0-943136-18-0*) Ctr Analysis Public Issues.

Sunshine Country. Kristina Roy. 184p. 1984. 5.75 (*0-686-05594-2*) Rod & Staff.

Sunshine Cuisine. Jean-Pierre Brehier & Felicia Gressette. LC 93-24404. 1994. 20.00 (*0-688-13118-2*) Hearst Bks.

***Sunshine for Life's Shadows.** Judy Proffit. (Illus.). 146p. (Orig.). 1997. pap. 9.95 (*1-57090-072-8*) Alexander Bks.

Sunshine, Fruit & Flowers: Santa Clara County, California. Ed. by San Jose Historical Museum Association Staff. (Illus.). 327p. 1986. reprint ed. 24.95 (*0-914139-03-7*) Hist Mus San Jose.

Sunshine Grows the Day. S. Bradford Williams, Jr. LC 83-7314. 80p. (Orig.). 1983. pap. 4.00 (*0-9608522-1-2*) Copper Orchid.

Sunshine Home. Eve Bunting. LC 93-570. (Illus.). (J). (gr. k-3). 1994. 14.95 (*0-395-63309-5*, Clarion Bks) HM.

***Sunshine Jobs: Career Opportunities Working Outdoors.** 2nd ed. Tom Stienstra. Ed. by Janet Connaughton. LC 96-51898. Orig. Title: Careers in the Outdoors. (Illus.). 400p. 1997. 16.95 (*0-911781-15-3*, 5470) Live Oak Pubns.

Sunshine Killers. Giles Tippette. 192p. (Orig.). 1995. mass mkt. 4.50 (*0-515-11535-5*) Jove Pubns.

Sunshine Laws: A Handbook for School Board Members. 140p. 1991. 37.50 (*1-56452-033-1*) NY Boards Assoc.

Sunshine Makes the Seasons. rev. ed. Franklyn M. Branley. LC 85-47540. (Let's-Read-&-Find-Out Science Bk.). (Illus.). 32p. (J). (ps-3). 1985. lib. bdg. 14.89 (*0-690-04482-8*, Crowell Jr Bks) HarpC Child Bks.

Sunshine Mine Disaster. James Brock. 74p. (Orig.). 1995. pap. 12.95 (*0-89301-181-9*) U of Idaho Pr.

Sunshine, Moonshine. Armstrong Jennifer. LC 94-34992. (Early Step into Reading Ser.). 1997. pap. 3.99 (*0-679-86442-3*); lib. bdg. 11.99 (*0-679-96442-8*) Random.

Sunshine of Joy. Helen Steiner Rice. 96p. (gr. 10). 1988. 13.99 (*0-8007-1568-3*) Revell.

Sunshine on Leith: Hibernian's Finest Sons. Simon Pia. (Illus.). 176p. 1996. 29.95 (*1-85158-797-7*, Pub. by Mnstream UK) Trafalgar.

Sunshine on the Prairie: The Story of Cynthia Ann Parker. Jack C. Ramsay, Jr. Ed. by Edwin M. Eakin. (Illus.). 224p. 1990. 16.95 (*0-89015-686-7*) Sunbelt Media.

Sunshine on the Soapsuds. Beneth P. Jones. 86p. (Orig.). 1977. pap. 5.95 (*0-89084-054-7*, 003657) Bob Jones Univ Pr.

Sunshine Preferred: The Philosophy of an Ordinary Woman. Anne Ellis. LC 84-5141. vi, 249p. 1984. reprint ed. pap. 6.95 (*0-8032-6709-6*, Bison Books) U of Nebr Pr.

Sunshine, Rainbows & Friends. Judith Beyl. LC 80-50828. (Illus.). 83p. (Orig.). (J). (ps-k). 1980. pap. 5.95 (*0-933308-01-9*) Harper SF.

Sunshine Riches. Marilyn Forstot. (Lucky in Love Ser.: No. 22). 288p. 1993. mass mkt. 3.50 (*0-8217-4081-4*, Zebra Kensgtn) Kensgtn Pub Corp.

***Sunshine Rider: The First Vegetarian Western.** Ric L. Hardman. LC 97-16244. 1998. write for info. (*0-385-32543-6*) Delacorte.

Sunshine Sensations: The Owl Bay Guide to Florida Gator Tailgating. Lucy Littleton. 128p. 1994. pap. 8.95 (*0-9638568-5-5*) Owl Bay Pubs.

***Sunshine, Shadows, & Sagebrush.** Cactus Smyth. Ed. by Laurie Brown. LC 96-92865. (Illus.). 172p. (Orig.). 1996. pap. 19.95 (*0-9655748-0-6*) Desert Graphics.

***Sunshine Sketches of a Little Town.** Raymond Leacock. 1996. pap. text ed. 6.95 (*0-7710-9984-3*) McCland & Stewart.

Sunshine Sketches of a Little Town. Stephen B. Leacock. LC 71-125228. (Short Story Index Reprint Ser.). 1980. 24.95 (*0-8369-3595-0*) Ayer.

***Sunshine Sketches of Little To.** Stephen Leacock. 1997. 26.95 (*0-7710-5001-1*) McCland & Stewart.

Sunshine Style: A Sunny Caribbee Cookbook for Sunny Climes & Limin Times. Susan Gunter. (Illus.). 240p. (Orig.). 1994. 17.50 (*0-9639423-0-1*); pap. 15.50 (*0-9639423-1-X*) Sunny Caribbee.

Sunshine the Magician's Rabbit. A. Kate Finegan. (Illus.). 64p. (J). (gr. 2-5). 1996. pap. 9.95 (*0-9651689-3-X*) K F Gross.

Sunshine Thoughts Poster Book: Self-esteem Builders for Children. David Thornburg. (Illus.). 48p. 1988. pap. 5.95 (*0-942207-06-8*) Starsong CA.

Sunship Earth: An Acclimatization Program for Outdoor Learning. Steve Van Matre. 138p. 1979. pap. 10.95 (*0-87603-007-X*) Am Camping.

***Sunship III: Perception & Choice for the Journey Ahead.** Steve Van Matre & Bruce Johnson. LC 96-80419. (Illus.). 145p. (Orig.). 1997. pap. 12.95 (*0-917011-03-1*) Inst Earth.

Sunsoft Solaris 2.X for Managers & Administrators. Kent Parkinson et al. (Illus.). 550p. 1995. pap. 34.95 (*0-934605-75-0*, 5084, OnWord Pr) High Mtn.

SunSoft Solaris 2.0 Quick Reference. Onword Press Development Team Staff & Clint Hicks. 256p. 1993. pap. 18.95 (*0-934605-76-9*, 5083, OnWord Pr) High Mtn.

SunSoft Solaris 2.0 User's Guide. Onword Press Development Team Staff & Sam Kimery. 304p. 1994. pap. 29.95 (*0-934605-74-2*, 5082, OnWord Pr) High Mtn.

***Sunsong.** Mordecai & Gordon. Date not set. pap. text ed. write for info. (*0-582-76555-2*, Pub. by Longman UK) Longman.

Sunspacers Trilogy. George Zebrowski. (Illus.). 1996. reprint ed. pap. 14.99 (*1-56504-856-3*, 11013, Borealis) White Wolf.

Sunspcts. Steve Baer. LC 75-20779. 1977. pap. 6.95 (*0-686-21779-9*) Zomeworks Corp.

Sunspots. R. J. Bray & R. E. Loughhead. (Illus.). 1979. reprint ed. pap. 10.95 (*0-486-63731-X*) Dover.

Sunspots: Theory & Observations. Ed. by John H. Thomas & Nigel O. Weiss. LC 92-20041. (NATO ASI Series C, Mathematical & Physical Sciences: Vol. 375). 440p. (C). 1992. lib. bdg. 216.00 (*0-7923-1852-8*) Kluwer Ac.

Sunspots, Dust & Rainfall. George N. Newhall. LC 87-92277. (Illus.). 208p. (Orig.). (C). 1988. text ed. 20.00 (*0-9619881-0-X*); per. 16.00 (*0-9619881-1-8*) S & G Pub.

Sunstar: Sun of Superlove. Superlove Staff. LC 80-53694. (Illus.). 200p. (Orig.). (J). (gr. 7 up). 1980. pap. 7.00 (*0-9602334-1-5*) Superlove.

Sunstone - Piedra De Sol. deluxe ed. Octavio Paz. Tr. by Eliot Weinberger from SPA. LC 91-29993. (Illus.). 64p. 1991. reprint ed. 150.00 (*0-8112-1194-0*) New Directions.

Sunstone - Piedra De Sol. Octavio Paz. Tr. by Eliot Weinberger from SPA. LC 91-29993. (Illus.). 64p. 1991. reprint ed. 18.95 (*0-8112-1197-5*); reprint ed. pap. 8.95 (*0-8112-1195-9*, NDP735) New Directions.

Sunup to Sundown: Watermen of the Chesapeake. 3rd ed. Mick Blackistone. LC 91-73568. (Illus.). 224p. (C). 1988. reprint ed. pap. 13.95 (*0-9627726-4-X*) Blue Crab MD.

Sunward I've Climbed: A Novel...Based on the True Story of Yvette Hamel & the 371st Fighter Group. Annie L. Morgan. LC 94-6583. (Illus.). 320p. 1994. 22.00 (*1-881320-17-0*, Black Belt) Black Belt Comm.

Sunwings Harrowsmith Guide to Solar Addition Architecture. Merilyn S. Mohr. (Illus.). 148p. 1985. pap. 4.99 (*0-920656-37-4*, Pub. by Camden Hse CN) Firefly Bks Ltd.

Sunwise Turn: A Human Comedy of Bookselling. Madge Jenison. 128p. 1993. reprint ed. pap. 12.95 (*1-879923-06-8*) Booksellers Pub.

Sunyata: The Recollections of a Rare-Born Mystic. Ed. by Layena B. Camhi & Elliott Isenberg. 120p. 1990. pap. 12.95 (*1-55643-096-5*) North Atlantic.

Sunzi Speaks: The Art of War. Tr. by Brian Bruya. LC 93-40994. (Illus.). 144p. (CHI & ENG.). pap. 10.95 (*0-385-47258-7*, Anchor NY) Doubleday.

Sunzi Speaks: The Art of War. Tr. by Brian Bruya from ENG. LC 94-33828. (Illus.). 144p. (CHI.). 1996. pap. 10.95 (*0-385-47259-5*, Anchor NY) Doubleday.

Suomalais-Ruotsalainen Tekniikan Ja Kaupan Sawakirja. J. K. Talvitie. 406p. (FIN & SWE.). 1986. 250.00 (*0-8288-2158-5*, F26200) Fr & Eur.

Suomalais-Venalainen Maataloussanasto: Finnish-Russian Agricultural Dictionary. Agopov & Koivu. 282p. (FIN & RUS.). 1986. 195.00 (*0-8288-1182-2*, F22280) Fr & Eur.

***Suomen: 1500 Largest in Finland.** Date not set. 27.95 (*0-8464-4423-2*) Beekman Pubs.

Suomiria: A Fantasy. Douglas A. Menville. LC 75-46307. (Supernatural & Occult Fiction Ser.). 1976. reprint ed. lib. bdg. 26.95 (*0-405-08170-7*) Ayer.

Suor. Jorge Amado. 189p. (FRE.). 1991. pap. 10.95 (*0-7859-2177-X*, 2070384268) Fr & Eur.

Suor Angelica: Vocal Score. Giacomo Puccini. (ENG & ITA.). 1986. pap. 19.95 (*0-7935-5373-3*) H Leonard.

SUP Chapter 9-SSD Plate Bending. Owen F. Hughes. 1991. 32.00 (*0-939773-09-0*) Soc Naval Arch.

SUPCE & SUREA: Publications & Resources for Educators of Adults. Harold Shufflefield. 1983. 5.00 (*0-87060-026-5*, MSS 31) Syracuse U Cont Ed.

Supeconductor Engineering. Ed. by Thomas O. Menash. LC 92-9161. (AIChE Symposium Ser.: No. 287, Vol. 88). 1992. 25.00 (*0-8169-0567-3*) Am Inst Chem Eng.

Super ABC's of the Human Body. Romel Wrenn. (Illus.). 56p. (J). (gr. k-4). 1993. Wkbk. student ed. write for info. (*0-9637869-0-3*) Chldrns Med.

***Super-Absorbent, Biodegradable, Family-Size Baby Blues: A Baby Blues Treasury.** Rick Kirkman & Jerry Scott. (Illus.). 256p. (Orig.). 1997. pap. 12.95 (*0-8362-3657-2*) Andrews & McMeel.

***Super Amos.** Gary Paulsen. (Culpepper Adventures Ser.: No. 30). 80p. (J). 1997. pap. 3.99 (*0-440-41056-8*) Dell.

Super & Parallel Computers & Their Impact on Civil Engineering. Ed. by Manohar P. Kamat. (Sessions Proceedings Ser.). 54p. 1986. 11.00 (*0-87262-551-6*) Am Soc Civil Eng.

An Asterisk (*) at the beginning of an entry indicates that the title is appearing in BIP for the first time.

Super Anti-Coloring Book. Sue Strike. (J). 1997. pap. 8.95 (0-8050-4806-5) H Holt & Co.

Super Art with SuperPaint 3.5. Evelyn Alemanni. LC 93-13554. 1993. pap. text ed. 19.95 (0-8306-4556-X, Windcrest) TAB Bks.

Super Babies: A Handbook of Enriched Accelerated Childhood Development. Robert L. Johnson. LC 81-70940. 144p. reprint ed. pap. 41.10 (0-8357-7681-6, AU00391) Bks Demand.

***Super Baby Food.** Ruth Yaron. LC 96-70596. (Illus.). viii, 450p. 1996. pap. write for info. (0-614-25737-9) F J Roberts.

***Super Baby Food.** Ruth Yaron. LC 96-70596. (Illus.). 460p. (Orig.). 1996. pap. write for info. (0-9652603-0-5) F J Roberts.

Super Banking: Innovative Management Strategies That Work. Richard B. Miller. 250p. 1988. 50.00 (1-55623-114-8) Irwin Prof Pubng.

Super Bible Heroes. Jeffrey Keiser & Deborah Keiser. Ed. by James C. Galvin et al. (LifeGuide Family Bible Studies). (Illus.). 80p. (Orig.). 1995. wbk. ed., pap. 4.99 (0-8308-1111-7, 1111) InterVarsity.

Super Blockbusters Brain Builders. (Creative Child Press Ser.). (Illus.). 278p. (YA). 1991. pap. 2.99 (0-517-02242-7) Random Hse Value.

Super Book of Arts & Crafts. Adrianne Gant et al. (Illus.). 272p. 1990. student ed., pap. 21.50 (1-56472-033-0) Edupress.

Super Book of Home Repairs Remodeling & Building. Larry Eisinger et al. (Illus.). 544p. 1994. 24.95 (0-9637349-0-3) Eisinger Pubns.

Super Bowl. Amy Stevenson. (Great Moments in Sports Ser.). 32p. (J). (gr. 4). 1990. lib. bdg. 14.95 (0-88682-315-3) Creative Ed.

Super Bowl Chronicles: A Sportswriter Reflects on the First 30 Years of America's Game. rev. ed. Jerry Green. (Illus.). 352p. 1995. pap. 14.95 (1-57028-050-9) Masters Pr IN.

Super Bowl Excitement. Angelo G. Resciniti et al. 208p. (YA). (gr. 5 up). 1994. pap. 2.99 (0-87406-716-2) Willowisp Pr.

***Super Bowl Trivia: 75 A to Z Quizzes.** J. M. Colbert. LC 96-90692. 160p. (Orig.). 1996. pap. 14.95 (0-9653182-1-4) Tuff Turtle.

Super Boxers. Ron Wilson et al. 64p. 1983. 5.95 (0-939766-77-9) Marvel Entmnt.

Super Brainy Puzzles. Charles B. Townsend. LC 95-49278. (Illus.). 96p. 1996. 5.95 (0-8069-3898-6) Sterling.

Super Bug Leads Tim Burr to the Gospel in the Woods. Vic Lockman. (Biblical Educational & Recreational Story Book Ser.). (Illus.). 24p. (Orig.). (J). (gr. 8 up). 1991. pap. 3.00 (0-936175-14-1) V Lockman.

***Super Callanetics.** Callan Pinckney. Date not set. write for info. (0-688-05188-X) Morrow.

Super Camper Caper. John Himmelman. (Fix-It Family Ser.). (Illus.). 48p. (J). (ps-3). 1991. pap. 2.95 (0-671-69640-8, Silver Pr NJ) Silver Burdett Pr.

Super Carrier. Peter Albano. 384p. 1994. mass mkt. 4.50 (0-8217-4490-9, Zebra Kensgtn) Kensgtn Pub Corp.

Super Cars Sticker Book. 12p. (J). (ps-6). 1990. pap. 5.99 (0-517-03351-8) Random Hse Value.

Super Challenge. 1990. pap. 1.95 (0-8167-2252-8) Troll Communs.

***Super Challenge.** World Book, Inc. Staff. LC 97-6017. (Mind Benders Ser.). (J). 1997. pap. write for info. (0-7166-4108-9) World Bk.

Super Chief: Earl Warren & His Supreme Court, A Judicial Biography. Bernard Schwartz. (Illus.). 864p. (C). 1984. pap. 25.00 (0-8147-7826-7) NYU Pr.

Super Chief: Train of the Stars. 3rd ed. Stan Repp. LC 80-18725. (Illus.). 258p. 1980. reprint ed. 39.95 (0-87095-081-9) Gldn West Bks.

Super Chops: Jazz Guitar Technique in 20 Weeks. Howard Roberts. LC 79-88145. (Howard Roberts Guitar Manuals Ser.). (Illus.). 87p. 1978. pap. text ed. 12.95 (0-89915-010-1) Playback Mus Pub.

Super Christmas Hits: Easy Guitar. 48p. 1981. pap. 7.95 (0-7935-1960-8, 00699804) H Leonard.

Super Chubby: I Can Make It! Miller. (J). 1997. 4.99 (0-689-80048-7) S&S Childrens.

Super Chubby: Let's Play! Miller. (J). 1997. 4.99 (0-689-80047-9) S&S Childrens.

Super Chubby: Water Play. Miller. (J). 1997. 4.99 (0-689-80046-0) S&S Childrens.

Super Chubby: Wheels Go 'Round. Miller. (J). 1997. 4.99 (0-689-80045-2) S&S Childrens.

Super Cluck. Jane O'Connor & Robert O'Connor. LC 90-32832. (I Can Read Bk.). (Illus.). 64p. (J). (ps-3). 1991. lib. bdg. 14.89 (0-06-024595-6) HarpC Child Bks.

Super Cluck. Jane O'Connor & Robert O'Connor. LC 90-32832. (Trophy I Can Read Bk.). (Illus.). 64p. (J). (gr. k-3). 1993. pap. 3.75 (0-06-444162-8, Trophy) HarpC Child Bks.

Super Colossal Book of Hidden Pictures. Compiled by Highlights for Children Editors. LC 93-72920. 192p. (J). (ps-2). 1994. pap. 7.95 (1-56397-362-6) Boyds Mills Pr.

Super-Colossal Book of Puzzles, Tricks & Games. Sheila A. Barry. (Illus.). 640p. (YA). 1992. reprint ed. 9.99 (0-517-07769-8) Random Hse Value.

***Super Computers.** Charles A. Jortberg. LC 96-28294. (Kids & Computers Ser.). 1997. lib. bdg. 15.95 (1-56239-724-9) Abdo & Dghtrs.

***Super Confidence.** Gael Lindenfield. 240p. 1997. mass mkt. 5.99 (0-06-101108-8, Harp PBks) HarpC.

***Super Cool Science: South Pole Stations, Past, Present, & Future.** Sandra Markle. LC 97-14890. (Illus.). (J). 1997. write for info. (0-8027-8470-4); lib. bdg. write for info. (0-8027-8471-2) Walker & Co.

Super Critter to the Rescue. Mercer Mayer. (Favorite Sound Story Bks.). (Illus.). 24p. (J). 1995. bds. 6.95 (0-307-70900-0, Golden Pr) Western Pub.

***Super Crostics Book, Vol. 4.** Thomas H. Middleton. 1997. pap. 9.00 (0-684-81340-8) S&S Trade.

Super Dave: The Adventures of the World's Most Dangerous Man. Super D. Osborne. LC 94-9309. 1994. 19.95 (1-56530-125-0) Summit TX.

Super-Deep Continental Drilling & Deep Geophysical Sounding. Ed. by K. Fuchs et al. (Exploration of the Deep Continental Crust Ser.). (Illus.). 456p. 1990. 158.95 (0-387-51609-3) Spr-Verlag.

***Super Deluxe with Everything & Other Poems.** Lisa Radon. 36p. (Orig.). 1996. pap. 6.95 (0-9654684-8-8) Big Star.

Super Depth Force: Project Discovery. Irving A. Greenfield. 400p. 1988. mass mkt. 3.95 (0-8217-2352-9, Zebra Kensgtn) Kensgtn Pub Corp.

Super Dooper Jezebel. Tony Ross. 1990. pap. 3.95 (0-374-47342-0) FS&G.

Super Duck: A True Story. Jane S. Williams. Ed. by Robert H. Pruett. (Illus.). 61p. (Orig.). (J). (ps-4). 1990. pap. 9.95 (0-9627635-0-0) Brandylane.

Super-Duper Cookie Caper, No. 22. Laura L. Hope. Ed. by Ann Greenberg. (New Bobbsey Twins Ser.). 96p. (Orig.). 1991. pap. 2.95 (0-671-69294-1, Minstrel Bks) PB.

Super-Duper Jokes. Frederica Young. (J). (gr. 4-7). 1993. 13.00 (0-374-37301-9); pap. 4.95 (0-374-47353-6) FS&G.

Super Duper Pee Wee: Pee Wee Scouts. Judy Delton. 144p. (J). 1995. pap. 3.99 (0-440-40992-6) Dell.

Super-Duper Sleepover Party. Megan Stine. Ed. by Lisa Clancy. (Full House Ser.: No. 2). 96p. (Orig.). (J). (gr. 2-4). mass mkt. 3.50 (0-671-51906-9, Minstrel Bks) PB.

Super Dynamic Kicks. Chong Lee. LC 80-84496. (Korean Arts Ser.). (Illus.). 1980. pap. 9.95 (0-89750-072-5, 409) Ohara Pubns.

Super Easy Hits. (Easy Play Ser.: Vol. 143). 1990. pap. 5.95 (0-7935-0119-9, 00001273) H Leonard.

Super Easy Hits. 1990. pap. 4.95 (0-7935-0174-1, 00001385) H Leonard.

Super Eggs Easter Fun Book. A. P. Folmer. 16p. (J). (ps-3). 1992. pap. 4.99 (0-590-45557-5) Scholastic Inc.

Super Eight Filmaking from Scratch. Bebe F. McClain. (Illus.). 1978. pap. 19.95 (0-13-876110-8) P-H.

Super Empire Strikes Back Official Game Secrets. Rusel DeMaria. 1993. pap. 12.95 (1-55958-452-1) Prima Pub.

Super-Endurance Paper Planes. Edward H. Mathews. (Illus.). 56p. (Orig.). 1992. pap. 13.95 (0-312-08314-9) St Martin.

Super Faculties & Their Culture. Manly P. Hall. pap. 4.95 (0-89314-358-8) Philos Res.

Super Family Vacations: Resort & Adventure Guide. 3rd ed. Martha Shirk & Nancy Klepper. LC 94-36109. 464p. 1995. pap. 16.00 (0-06-273330-3, PL) HarpC.

Super Feds: A Facsimile Selection of Dynamic G-Man Stories from the 1930s. Compiled by Don Hutchison. LC 88-1078. (Starmont Popular Culture Studies: No. 8). viii, 158p. 1988. pap. 21.00 (1-55742-090-4); lib. bdg. 31.00 (1-55742-091-2) Borgo Pr.

Super Field Theories. Ed. by Henry C. Lee et al. LC 87-14159. (NATO ASI Series B, Physics: Vol. 160). (Illus.). 608p. 1987. 135.00 (0-306-42660-9, Plenum Pr) Plenum.

***Super-Fine Valentine.** Bill Cosby. LC 97-16563. (Little Bill Book Ser.). (Illus.). (J). 1997. write for info. (0-590-16401-5); pap. write for info. (0-590-95622-1) Scholastic Inc.

Super Firm: Tough Workouts. Time-Life Books Editors. (Fitness, Health & Nutrition Ser.). (Illus.). 144p. (J). 1989. 17.27 (0-8094-6134-X); lib. bdg. 23.27 (0-8094-6135-8) Time-Life.

Super Fishin' Log. Larry Smith. 190p. (Orig.). 1987. pap. 6.98 (0-685-30430-2) Outdoor Enthusiasts.

Super Fitness Beyond Vitamins. Michael E. Rosenbaum & Dominick Bosco. 1989. pap. 4.95 (0-318-40124-X, Sig) NAL-Dutton.

Super Flyers. Neil Francis. LC 88-19336. (YA). 1988. pap. 6.95 (0-201-14933-8) Addison-Wesley.

Super Foods from Super Soil. Raymond W. Bernard. 1956. spiral bd. 5.50 (0-7873-0993-1) Hlth Research.

Super Formulas, Arts & Crafts: How to Make More Than 360 Useful Products That Contain Honey & Beeswax. Elaine C. White. LC 93-93807. 120p. (Orig.). 1993. pap. 14.95 (0-9637539-7-5) Valley Hills.

Super Fullback. (J). pap. 3.95 (0-590-20608-7) Scholastic Inc.

Super Fun for One: 366 Solo Activities for Kids. Patricia Gordon & Reed C. Snow. LC 96-15943. 208p. (Orig.). 1996. pap. 12.95 (0-8362-2161-3) Andrews & McMeel.

Super Funny School Jokes. Gene Perret. LC 91-22501. (Illus.). 96p. (J). (gr. 2-10). 1991. 14.95 (0-8069-8294-2) Sterling.

Super Funny School Jokes. Gene Perret. LC 91-22501. (Illus.). 96p. (J). (gr. 1-7). 1992. pap. 4.95 (0-8069-8295-0) Sterling.

Super Giant Sports Question & Answer Book. (Creative Child Press Ser.). (Illus.). 278p. (YA). 1991. pap. 2.99 (0-517-02239-7) Random Hse Value.

Super Grandpa see **Supergrandpa**

Super Graphs, Venns & Glyphs: Hundreds of Great Data Collecting Activities to Build Real... Honi Bamberger. 1996. pap. text ed. 16.95 (0-590-67477-3) Scholastic Inc.

Super Groups Bass Lines: Play-It-Like-It-Is-Bass. Ed. by Milton Okun. pap. 9.95 (0-89524-219-2) Cherry Lane.

Super Healing Foods. 192p. (Orig.). 1994. pap. 14.95 (1-57327-012-1, M Pr CA) Busn Concepts.

Super Healing Foods. Frances S. Goulart. 1995. pap. text ed. 13.95 (0-13-108838-6) P-H.

Super Health Through Super Foods: How to Eat High in the Rating Chart. 1992. lib. bdg. 88.75 (0-8490-8792-9) Gordon Pr.

Super-Health Thru Organic Super-Food. Raymond W. Bernard. 163p. 1994. reprint ed. spiral bd. 12.50 (0-7873-1127-8) Hlth Research.

***Super Helping Hero.** (J). 1990. write for info. (1-55513-960-4, Chariot Bks) Chariot Victor.

Super Heroes: A Modern Mythology. Richard Reynolds. (Studies in Popular Culture). (Illus.). 134p. 1994. reprint ed. 35.00 (0-87805-693-9); reprint ed. pap. 13.95 (0-87805-694-7) U Pr of Miss.

***Super Heroes: Sherwoods Star on Target with Robin Hood.** Claire Watts. 1997. 9.95 (0-7166-4503-3) World Bk.

Super Heroes Electronic Game Board from Marvel Comics. Diane Mineau. (Illus.). 12p. (J). (gr. k-2). 1995. 7.99 (0-88705-844-2, Wshng Well Bks) Joshua Morris.

Super-Heroes of the Old Testament: A Course in Moral Education. Donald J. Graff. (J). (gr. 5-6). 1980. teacher ed. 15.25 (1-881678-37-7); student ed. 9.00 (1-881678-38-5) CRIS.

Super-High Definition Images: Beyond HDTV. Naohisa Ohta et al. LC 94-49709. 1995. text ed. 67.00 (0-89006-674-4) Artech Hse.

Super Hits: Trumpet. 48p. 1988. pap. 5.95 (0-7935-3321-X, 00845034) H Leonard.

Super Hormones. William Regelson. 256p. 1996. 23.00 (0-684-83011-6) S&S Trade.

Super Horoscope: Aquarius 1997. 1996. pap. text ed. 6.99 (0-425-15358-4) Berkley Pub.

Super Horoscope: Aries 1997. 1996. pap. text ed. 6.99 (0-425-15348-7) Berkley Pub.

Super Horoscope: Cancer 1997. 1996. pap. text ed. 6.99 (0-425-15351-7) Berkley Pub.

Super Horoscope: Capricorn 1997. 1996. pap. text ed. 6.99 (0-425-15357-6) Berkley Pub.

Super Horoscope: Gemini 1997. 1996. pap. text ed. 6.99 (0-425-15350-9) Berkley Pub.

Super Horoscope: Leo 1997. 1996. pap. text ed. 6.99 (0-425-15352-5) Berkley Pub.

Super Horoscope: Libra 1997. 1996. pap. text ed. 6.99 (0-425-15354-1) Berkley Pub.

Super Horoscope: Pisces 1997. 1996. pap. text ed. 6.99 (0-425-15359-2) Berkley Pub.

Super Horoscope: Sagittarius 1997. 1996. pap. text ed. 6.99 (0-425-15356-8) Berkley Pub.

Super Horoscope: Scorpio 1997. 1996. pap. text ed. 6.99 (0-425-15355-X) Berkley Pub.

Super Horoscope: Taurus 1997. 1996. pap. text ed. 6.99 (0-425-15349-5) Berkley Pub.

Super Horoscope: Virgo 1997. 1996. pap. text ed. 6.99 (0-425-15353-3) Berkley Pub.

Super Hugos. Isaac Asimov. 1992. mass mkt. 5.99 (0-671-72135-6) Baen Bks.

Super-Human Men in History & Religion. Annie Besant. 136p. 1996. pap. 16.95 (1-56459-621-4) Kessinger Pub.

Super Humor Power. Steve Wilson. 184p. 1992. pap. 10.00 (0-9632900-1-0) Steve Wilson.

Super-Hypersonic Aerodynamic & Heat Transfer. Mikohailov. 352p. 1992. 193.95 (0-8493-9309-4, TL571) CRC Pr.

Super Index. Duane Magnani. 1993. pap. 8.95 (1-883858-21-6) Witness CA.

Super-Intense Laser-Atom Physics. Ed. by B. Piraux et al. (NATO ASI Series B, Physics: Vol. 316). (Illus.). 512p. (C). 1994. 129.50 (0-306-44587-5, Plenum Pr) Plenum.

Super-Intense Laster-Atom Physics IV: Proceedings of the NATO Advanced Research Workshop on Super-Intense Laser-Atom Physics, Moscow, Russia, August 5-9, 1995. Ed. by H. G. Muller & M. V. Fedorov. LC 96-14544. (NATO ASI Ser.: Vol. 13). 1996. lib. bdg. 285.00 (0-7923-4048-5) Kluwer Ac.

Super Investment Trends: Cashing in on the Dynamic '90s. James B. Powell. 300p. 1992. text ed. 32.00 (1-55623-500-3) Irwin Prof Pubng.

Super Jazz Duets: Alto Sax. 6.95 (0-7935-4927-2, 00841028) H Leonard.

Super Jazz Duets: Clarinet. 6.95 (0-7935-4926-4, 00841027) H Leonard.

Super Jazz Duets: Flute. 6.95 (0-7935-4925-6, 00841026) H Leonard.

Super Jazz Duets: Trombone. 6.95 (0-7935-4929-9, 00841030) H Leonard.

Super Jazz Duets: Trumpet. 6.95 (0-7935-4928-0, 00841029) H Leonard.

***Super Jesus: A Collection of Doctrinal Essays.** Fred J. Duncan. 128p. (Orig.). 1997. pap. write for info. (0-614-26624-6) Pennington TX.

***Super Jesus: A Collection of Doctrinal Essays.** Fred J. Duncan. 128p. (Orig.). Date not set. pap. write for info. (0-614-30084-3) Pennington TX.

Super Job Search: The Complete Manual for Job-Seekers & Career Changes. 2nd ed. Peter K. Studner. LC 86-50476. (Illus.). 352p. (C). 1995. pap. 22.95 (0-938667-02-5) Jamenair Ltd.

Super Joke Book. Gyles Brandreth. LC 83-397. (Illus.). 128p. (J). (gr. 3 up). 1985. pap. 4.95 (0-8069-6200-3) Sterling.

Super Jumble Puzzle Book. Henri Arnold. (Illus.). 224p. (Orig.). 1991. pap. 8.95 (0-941263-23-1, Tribune) Contemp Bks.

Super Junk Foods That Are Sold As Health Foods. 1992. lib. bdg. 75.00 (0-8490-8801-1) Gordon Pr.

Super Kids & Their Parents. Robert L. Johnson. LC 86-91400. (Exposition-Banner Book Ser.). 191p. reprint ed. pap. 54.50 (0-8357-7680-8, AU00390) Bks Demand.

Super Kids in 30 Minutes a Day. Karen U. Kwiatkowski. LC 94-43565. 1995. 9.95 (1-885003-06-4) R D Reed Pubs.

Super Kids Publishing Company. Debbie Robertson & Patricia Barry. xiii, 354p. 1990. pap. text ed. 25.00 (0-87287-704-3) Teacher Ideas Pr.

Super Kites III. Neil Thorburn. (Super Kites Ser.). 123p. 1991. pap. 8.95 (0-9629354-3-3) N Thorburn.

Super Leadership. Henry P. Simms. 1990. pap. 12.00 (0-425-12356-1, Berkley Trade) Berkley Pub.

Super Luxurious Custom Home Collection, 100 Plans 5000-7900 Square Feet: Collection D. Mike Tecton. (Illus.). (Orig.). 1997. pap. 25.00 (0-922070-23-7, COLLECTION D) M Tecton Pub.

Super Mario Brothers Christmas Favorites: Five Finger Piano. 24p. (J). 1992. pap. 4.95 (0-7935-1496-7, 00290371) H Leonard.

Super Mario Brothers Party Songs for Kids: Five Finger Piano Solos. 24p. (J). 1992. pap. 4.95 (0-7935-1495-9, 00290370) H Leonard.

***Super Mario Kart 64 Unauthorized Game Secrets.** PCS Staff. 96p. 1997. per. 12.99 (0-7615-1078-8) Prima Pub.

Super Mario RPG Unauthorized Secrets. Anthony Lynch. 144p. 1996. per., pap. 12.99 (0-7615-0762-0) Prima Pub.

Super Mario Super Englisch: Woerterbuch fur Kids: English-German, German-English. 2nd ed. Langenscheidt Staff. 576p. (ENG & GER.). 1993. 29.95 (0-7859-8390-2, 3468203705) Fr & Eur.

Super Mario World Secrets: Super Mario Bros. 4 for the Super Nintendo Entertainment System. Rusel DeMaria & Zach Meston. (Secrets of the Games Ser.). (Illus.). 288p. 1991. pap. 12.95 (1-55958-156-5) Prima Pub.

***Super Mario 64: Game Secrets Unauthorized.** PCS Staff. 128p. 1996. per., pap. 12.99 (0-7615-0892-9) Prima Pub.

***Super Mario's Adventures: My Very First Nintendo Game Boy.** Barkan. (J). 1997. 10.95 (0-689-81579-4) S&S Childrens.

Super Marital Sex. Paul P. Pearsall. 448p. 1988. mass mkt. 5.99 (0-8041-0367-4) Ivy Books.

Super Market Crafts. Betty A. Vaughan. (Illus.). 12p. (Orig.). 1983. pap. 1.95 (0-9605172-2-7) BETOM Pubns.

***Super Masks & Fun Face Painting.** Teddy C. Long. LC 96-35803. (J). 1997. 19.95 (1-895569-09-5) Sterling.

***Super Massage.** Inkeles. pap. 16.00 (0-06-251473-3) HarpC.

Super Math Tricks. Zondra Knapp. LC 95-18687. (Illus.). 64p. 1995. pap. 5.95 (1-56565-269-X) Lowell Hse Juvenile.

Super Media: A Cultural Studies Approach. Michael R. Real. (Communication & Human Values Ser.). (Illus.). 282p. (C). 1989. text ed. 52.00 (0-8039-3313-4); pap. text ed. 24.95 (0-8039-3314-2) Sage.

Super Memory. Frankal. 31p. 1993. reprint ed. spiral bd. 5.50 (0-7873-0334-8) Hlth Research.

***Super Memory: A Quick-Action Program for Memory Improvement.** Douglas J. Hermann. 320p. 1997. pap. 12.95 (0-7137-2507-9, Pub. by Blandford Pr UK) Sterling.

Super Memory Super Student, Vol. 1. Harry Lorayne. 1990. pap. 13.95 (0-316-53268-1) Little.

Super Mental Training Book. Robert K. Stevenson. LC 90-91865. (Illus.). 253p. (Orig.). 1990. pap. 19.90 (0-9606252-3-2) Stevenson Intl.

Super Menus for Football Fans. Candy Coleman. (Illus.). 48p. (Orig.). 1981. pap. text ed. 3.00 (0-943768-04-7) C Coleman.

Super Metroid: Unauthorized Game Secrets. Rusel DeMaria. 1994. pap. 14.95 (1-55958-610-9) Prima Pub.

Super Mom's Country Cookin' Cookbook. Ophelia Warner. 400p. 1988. 19.95 (0-89896-089-4) Larksdale.

Super Mom's Country Cookin' Cookbook. Ophelia Warner. LC 86-81520. (Illus.). 386p. 1994. reprint ed. pap. write for info. (0-9643489-0-X) W Roberts.

Super Mom's Organized Scheduler. Gail W. Joyner. 1991. write for info. (0-9628942-0-6) SuperMom.

***Super, Natural Christians: How We Should Love Nature.** Sallie Mcfague. LC 96-50992. 1997. pap. text ed. 15.00 (0-8006-3076-9, Fortress Pr) Augsburg Fortress.

Super NES Games Secrets. Andy Eddy. (Secrets of the Games Ser.). (Illus.). 304p. (Orig.). 1991. pap. 9.99 (1-55958-155-7) Prima Pub.

Super NES Games Secrets, Vol. 2. rev. ed. Rusel DeMaria & Zach Meston. (Illus.). 268p. (Orig.). 1992. pap. 9.95 (1-55958-193-X) Prima Pub.

Super NES Games Secrets, Vol. 3. Rusel DeMaria & Zach Meston. (Secrets of the Games Ser.). (Illus.). 304p. (Orig.). 1992. pap. 11.95 (1-55958-249-9) Prima Pub.

Super NES Games Secrets, Vol. 4. Rusel DeMaria. (Illus.). 412p. (Orig.). 1993. pap. 12.95 (1-55958-378-9) Prima Pub.

Super NES Games Secrets Greatest Tips. Gamepro Magazine Editors. (Illus.). 192p. (Orig.). 1993. pap. 11.95 (1-55958-387-8) Prima Pub.

Super NES Games Unauthorized Power Tips Book. Neil West. (Illus.). 112p. (Orig.). 1993. pap. 14.95 (1-55958-400-9) Prima Pub.

Super NES Games Unauthorized Power Tips Book Vol. 2. Carlton Books Staff. 1994. pap. 14.95 (1-55958-686-9) Prima Pub.

Super Nifty Crafts to Make with Things Around the House. Cambria Cohen. 32p. (J). 1995. pap. 7.95 (1-56565-361-0) Lowell Hse.

Super Nifty Origami Crafts. Andrea Urton. LC 96-17221. (Super Nifty Ser.). (Illus.). 32p. (YA). (gr. 8-12). 1996. pap. 9.95 (1-56565-396-3) Lowell Hse Juvenile.

***Super Number 6: Amazing Facts about the Number Six.** Kitty Higgins. (Birthday Book Ser.). 1998. 6.95 (0-8362-3219-4) Andrews & McMeel.

Super Nutrition for Animals. Nina Anderson et al. (Illus.). 192p. (Orig.). 1997. pap. 12.95 (1-884820-16-6) SAFE GOODS.

Super Nutrition for Men: And the Women Who Love Them. Ann L. Gittleman. 288p. 1996. 19.95 (0-87131-793-1) M Evans.

***Super Nutrition for Men: And the Women Who Love Them.** Ann L. Gittleman. 1997. pap. text ed. 14.95 (0-87131-834-2) M Evans.

Super Nutrition Gardening: How to Grow Your Own Powercharged Foods. William S. Peavy & Warren Peary. LC 92-25950. (Illus.). 248p. pap. 14.95 (0-89529-532-6) Avery Pub.

S

An Asterisk (*) at the beginning of an entry indicates that the title is appearing in BIP for the first time.

***Super-Optimum Solutions & Win-Win Policy: Basic Concepts & Principles.** Stuart S. Nagel. LC 96-54284. 1997. text ed. write for info. (*1-56720-118-0*, Quorum Bks) Greenwood.

Super Origami: Book One. James E. Trodglen, Jr. (Illus.). 44p. (J). 1991. pap. 9.95 (*1-879610-01-9*) Origami Intl.

Super Outer Space Puzzles & Mazes Activity Book. (Super Activity Bks.). (Illus.). 48p. (Orig.). (J). (gr. k-3). 1994. 2.95 (*0-8431-3728-2*) Price Stern Sloan.

Super Paint 3: Everything You Need to Know. Gia Rozells. (Illus.). 320p. (Orig.). 1992. pap. 24.95 (*1-55958-098-4*) Prima Pub.

Super Paper Airplanes. Norman Schmidt. 96p. (J). 1996. pap. 12.95 (*1-895569-07-9*, Pub. by S Milner AT) Sterling.

Super Paper Airplanes: Biplanes to Space Planes. Norman Schmidt. LC 94-35543. (Illus.). 96p. (J). (gr. 4-7). 1995. 19.95 (*1-895569-30-3*, Pub. by Tamos Bks CN) Sterling.

Super Paper Flyers Book & Kit. 1995. 19.95 (*0-8069-3996-6*, Pub. by Tamos Bks CN) Sterling.

Super Parenting in 15 Days: A Back-to-Basics Guide to Parenting Young Children. Tim Stafford. Ed. by Doreen L. Virtue. (Illus.). 42p. (Orig.). 1997. pap. 7.95 (*0-9635826-3-1*) Sharkbait Pr.

Super Parrot. Mirna Benitez. (Real Readers Ser.: Level Red). (Illus.). 32p. (J). (gr. 1-4). 1989. lib. bdg. 21.40 (*0-8172-3503-5*) Raintree Steck-V.

Super Parrot. Mirna Benitez. (Real Reading Ser.: Level Red). (Illus.). 32p. (J). (gr. 1-4). 1989. pap. 3.95 (*0-8114-6704-X*) Raintree Steck-V.

Super-Patriots in America: A Century of Growing Influence. David Kaun & John Ochwat. LC 92-19541. 250p. (C). 1995. text ed. 37.50 (*0-89341-702-5*) Hollowbrook.

Super-Physical Science. A. P. Sinnett. 240p. 1992. pap. 24.95 (*1-56459-263-4*) Kessinger Pub.

Super Potency at Any Age. Edwin Flatto. LC 91-73635. 288p. 1991. 29.98 (*0-941683-09-5*) Instant Improve.

***Super Potency at Any Age.** 5th rev. ed. Edwin Flatto. (Illus.). 286p. 1995. pap. 14.95 (*0-935540-17-2*) Plymouth Pr.

***Super Potency at Any Age.** 5th rev. ed. Edwin Flatto. 1996. lib. bdg. 24.95 (*0-935540-18-0*) Plymouth Pr.

Super Potency at Any Age. 6th rev. ed. Edwin Flatto. (Illus.). 286p. 1996. reprint ed. 24.95 (*0-935540-15-6*) Plymouth Pr.

Super Power. Larry Schreib. (Illus.). 128p. 1979. 18.95 (*0-931472-02-4*) Motorbooks Intl.

Super Power Breathing: For Super Energy, High Health & Longevity. 21th rev. ed. Patricia Bragg & Paul C. Bragg. (Illus.). 128p. Date not set. pap. 6.95 (*0-87790-020-5*) Hlth Sci.

Super Power Rivalry in the Indian Ocean. V. K. Bhasin. 229p. 1981. 24.95 (*0-940500-16-7*, Pub. by S Chand II) Asia Bk Corp.

Super Power Rivalry in the Indian Ocean. V. K. Bhasin. 236p. 1981. text ed. 20.00 (*0-685-43584-9*) Coronet Bks.

Super Power Rivalry in the Indian Ocean. V. K. Bhasin. 238p. 1989. 30.00 (*0-317-52157-8*, Pub. by S Chand II) St Mut.

***Super Powers.** Jones. 1988. pap. text ed. write for info. (*0-582-68482-X*, Pub. by Longman UK) Longman.

Super Powers in the Horn of Africa. Madan M. Sauldie. LC 82-71853. 300p. (C). 1987. text ed. 30.00 (*0-86590-092-2*) Apt Bks.

Super Powers of the Mind: Transform Your Life Through the Twelve Powers. Cody L. Jones. 181p. 1993. pap. 12.00 (*1-878040-07-3*) Personal Growth.

***Super Privacy: The Complete Guide to Personal Privacy & Financial Freedom in Tomorrow's Cashless Society.** Bob Hammond. 144p. 1997. pap. 15.00 (*0-87364-920-6*) Paladin Pr.

Super Procrastinators. Joe Barnes. (Illus.). 224p. 1988. 14.95 (*0-917732-36-7*); pap. text ed. 10.95 (*0-917732-37-5*) Barnes-Bks.

Super Profile: Austin-Healey 'Frogeye' Sprite. Lindsay Porter. (Illus.). 56p. 1983. 12.95 (*0-85429-343-4*, F343, Pub. by G T Foulis Ltd) Haynes Pubns.

Super Profile: Lotus Elan. Graham Armour. 56p. 11.95 (*0-85429-330-2*, F330, Pub. by G T Foulis Ltd) Haynes Pubns.

Super Puppy Training Manual: How to Teach the Best Puppy Training Class You've Ever Had!, Level 1. 2nd ed. Peter J. Vollmer & Nancy Vollmer. (Illus.). 96p. 1989. pap. 25.00 (*1-886056-00-5*) Super Puppy Pr.

Super Puzzles & Fun. Debi Perna. (Illus.). 32p. 1995. pap. 4.95 (*1-895688-25-6*, Pub. by Owl Bks CN) Firefly Bks Ltd.

Super-Radiance: Multiatomic Coherent Emission. M. G. Benedict et al. (Illus.). 376p. 1996. 190.00 (*0-7503-0283-6*) IOP Pub.

Super Reading. Russell G. Stauffer & Jean H. Berg. 295p. (YA). (gr. 10-12). 1981. Includes audiocass. 49.95 incl. audio (*1-55678-036-2*) Learn Inc.

Super Reading Junior. Russell G. Stauffer & Jean H. Berg. 256p. (J). 1981. Includes audiocassettes. 49.95 incl. audio (*1-55678-039-7*) Learn Inc.

Super Reading Secrets. Howard S. Berg. 256p. (Orig.). 1992. mass mkt. 5.99 (*0-446-36299-9*) Warner Bks.

Super-Real Fields: Totally Ordered Fields with Additional Structure. H. Garth & W. H. Woodin. (London Mathematical Society Monographs: Vol. 14). (Illus.). 366p. (C). 1996. 95.00 (*0-19-853991-6*) OUP.

Super Saturday: An Evangelistic Event Full of Exciting Activities for Teens. Marvin S. Osborn & Cindy G. Spear. 105p. 1995. ring bd., vinyl bd. 79.95 incl. audio (*1-57052-016-X*) Chrch Grwth VA.

Super Savvy: How to Get It, How to Use It, How to Make A Fortune with It! Robert E. Levinson. Ed. by Mark T. Lauer. LC 94-14016. 256p. 1994. pap. 14.95 (*1-880539-29-2*) Garrett FL.

Super Scary Stories for Sleep-Overs No. 5. Querida L. Pearce. LC 95-1986. (Scary Stories Ser.). (Illus.). 128p. (J). (gr. 4-7). 1995. pap. 4.95 (*0-8431-3915-3*) Price Stern Sloan.

Super School of the 21st Century. 3rd ed. James J. Asher. (Illus.). 195p. (Orig.). (C). 1996. pap. 19.95 (*1-56018-003-X*) Sky Oaks Prodns.

Super Science! Lisa Blau. (Reader's Theatre Resource Bks.). 118p. 1994. 10.95 (*0-9640333-3-X*) One Heart Educ.

Super Science Concoctions: 50 Mysterious Mixtures for Fabulous Fun. Jill F. Hauser. Ed. by Susan Williamson. LC 95-47894. (Kids Can! Ser.). (Illus.). 160p. (Orig.). (J). (ps up). 1996. pap. 12.95 (*1-885593-02-3*) Williamson Pub Co.

Super Science Fair Projects. Carol Amato. LC 94-5358. (Illus.). 80p. (YA). (gr. 6 up). 1994. pap. 5.95 (*1-56565-141-3*) Lowell Hse Juvenile.

Super Science Fair Sourcebook. Maxine H. Iritz. 1996. pap. text ed. 17.95 (*0-07-032849-8*) McGraw.

***Super Science Secrets.** Sandra Markle. 1997. 14.95 (*1-56352-396-5*) Longstreet Pr Inc.

***Super Science with Simple Stuff! Activities for the Intermediate Grades.** Susan Popelka. 1997. pap. text ed. 21.95 (*0-201-49612-7*) Addison-Wesley.

Super Scripture Activities: Jesus Is My Friend. Mary H. Ross & Jennette Guymon. (J). 1996. pap. 7.95 (*1-55503-861-1*, 01112104) Covenant Comms.

Super Scripture Activities: Tell Me the Stories of Jesus. Mary H. Ross & Jennette Guymon. (J). 1996. pap. 7.95 (*1-55503-860-3*, 01112090) Covenant Comms.

Super Seafood. 96p. 1994. 9.98 (*0-8317-7695-1*) Smithmark.

Super Search-a-Words. (J). (gr. 3-7). 1987. pap. 1.99 (*0-671-63851-3*) S&S Trade.

Super Secret Code Book. Fran Pickering. LC 94-23478. (Illus.). 64p. (J). (gr. 3-7). 1995. pap. 5.95 (*0-8069-0890-4*) Sterling.

Super Secret Codes & Jokes. Elvira Gamiello. (Illus.). (Orig.). (J). (gr. 4-6). 1990. pap. 1.95 (*0-942025-44-X*) Kidsbks.

Super Self-Esteem! 1995. pap. 149.00 incl. audio, vhs (*1-56052-372-7*) Crisp Pubns.

***Super Self-Esteem.** 1995. pap. 24.95 incl. audio (*1-56052-373-5*) Crisp Pubns.

Super Selling Secrets. Rueben Stokes. 1994. pap. 8.95 (*1-55673-936-2*) CSS OH.

Super Seniors, Their Stories & Secrets. Francis R. Line. (Illus.). 175p. (Orig.). 1989. pap. 8.95 (*0-938109-06-5*) Wide Horiz Pr.

Super Senses. Snapshot Staff. (Tab Board Bks.). (Illus.). 10p. 1996. 3.95 (*0-7894-1132-6*) DK Pub Inc.

Super Sentences. Susan Winebrenner. 42p. 1989. pap. 14.95 (*0-936386-53-3*) Creative Learning.

***Super Sexual Orgasm: A Woman's Guide to Ultimate Pleasure.** Barbara Keesling. LC 97-5532. (Illus.). 192p. 1997. 20.00 (*0-06-017479-X*) HarpC.

Super Sharp Pencil & Paper Games. Andrea Angiolino. LC 95-31719. (Illus.). 96p. 1995. pap. 5.95 (*0-8069-3884-6*) Sterling.

Super Shotguns. Duncan Long. (Illus.). 96p. 1992. pap. 18.00 (*0-87364-691-6*) Paladin Pr.

Super Shrink II: Jennifer. Lowman. (C). 1990. teacher ed., pap. text ed. 7.00 (*0-15-584765-1*) HB Coll Pubs.

Super Sight-Reading Secrets: An Innovative, Step-by-Step Program for Musical Keyboard Players of All Levels. 3rd rev. ed. Ed. by Howard Richman. LC 85-90522. 52p. (C). 1986. pap. 9.95 (*0-9615963-0-9*) Sound Feelings.

Super Silly Riddles Dingbats Book. Carole Marsh. (Carole Marsh Dingbats Bks.). (Illus.). (J). (gr. 3-12). 1994. pap. 19.95 (*0-7933-5411-0*); lib. bdg. 29.95 (*0-7933-5410-2*); disk 29.95 (*0-7933-5412-9*) Gallopade Pub Group.

Super Silly Sports Trivia Dingbats Book. Carole Marsh. (Carole Marsh Dingbats Bks.). (Illus.). (J). (gr. 3-12). 1994. pap. 19.95 (*0-7933-5381-5*); lib. bdg. 29.95 (*0-7933-5380-7*); disk 29.95 (*0-7933-5382-3*) Gallopade Pub Group.

Super Simple Birdhouses You Can Make. Charles R. Self. LC 95-20392. (Illus.). 128p. 1995. pap. 10.95 (*0-8069-0858-0*) Sterling.

Super Simple Cooking. B. Layton. (Illus.). 192p. 1994. spiral bd. 5.95 (*1-57166-012-7*) Hearts N Tummies.

Super Simple Quilts. Kathleen Eaton. LC 92-53149. (New Ser.). (Illus.). 112p. 1992. pap. 14.95 (*0-8019-8334-7*) Chilton.

Super 60's Fords: The Inside Story of the Most Powerful Fords Ever Built. John Smith. (Illus.). 128p. 1989. pap. 18.95 (*0-931472-25-3*) Motorbooks Intl.

***Super Skaters.** Random House Value Publishing Staff. 1997. 4.99 (*0-517-18482-6*) Random Hse Value.

Super Sketches for Youth Ministry: Thirty Creative Topical Dramas from Willow Creek Community Church. Debra Poling & Sharon Sherbondy. 192p. (YA). 1991. pap. 12.99 (*0-310-53411-9*) Zondervan.

Super Skin. Nelson L. Novick. (Illus.). 320p. 1991. pap. 13.00 (*0-517-58533-2*, C P Pubs) Crown Pub Group.

Super Skin. Kathryn Marsden. (Illus.). 1993. reprint ed. pap. 12.00 (*0-7225-2798-5*) Thorsons SF.

Super Sleuth Challenge: Crossword Mysteries. Helene Chirinian. 96p. (J). (gr. 4-7). 1994. pap. 3.95 (*1-56565-170-7*) Lowell Hse Juvenile.

Super Slow: The Ultimate Exercise Protocol. 2nd ed. Ken Hutchins. 195p. 1992. pap. 25.00 (*0-9633199-0-6*) Media Support.

***Super Slumber Parties.** Brooks Whitney. LC 97-12894. (Illus.). 64p. (Orig.). (J). (gr. 2-6). 1997. pap. 7.95 (*1-56247-529-0*, Amer Girl Library) Pleasant Co.

Super Smoothies: Taste the Nectar of Life. 2nd rev. ed. Candia L. Cole. LC 96-7197. (Illus.). 1996. 12.95 (*0-88007-214-8*) Woodbridge Pr.

Super Snacks. Jean Warren. (Illus.). 48p. (Orig.). (J). (ps-1). 1992. pap. 6.95 (*0-911019-49-9*, WPH 1601) Warren Pub Hse.

Super Snoop Sam Snout & the Case of the Missing Marble. Anne LeMieux. 64p. (Orig.). (J). (ps-3). 1994. pap. 3.50 (*0-380-77460-7*, Camelot Young) Avon.

Super Snoop Sam Snout & the Case of the Stolen Snowman. Anne LeMieux. 64p. (Orig.). (J). (ps-3). 1994. pap. 3.50 (*0-380-77459-3*, Camelot Young) Avon.

Super Snoop Sam Snout & the Case of the Yogurt-Poker. Anne LeMieux. 64p. (Orig.). (J). (ps-3). 1994. pap. 3.50 (*0-380-77462-3*, Camelot Young) Avon.

Super Sock Sensation. Elaine Weimann & Rita Friedman. (Read to Me Bks.). (Illus.). 30p. (J). (ps-1). 1985. lib. bdg. 12.50 (*0-89796-987-1*) New Dimens Educ.

Super Socks for Courage. Rita Friedman & Elaine Weimann. (Fables from the Letter People Ser.). (Illus.). 30p. (J). (ps-1). 1989. lib. bdg. 12.95 (*0-89796-018-1*) New Dimens Educ.

Super Solar Houses: Saunder's 100 Percent Solar, Low-Cost Designs. William A. Shurcliff. 1983. 12.95 (*0-931790-48-4*) Brick Hse Pub.

***Super Solar System.** Thomas-Cochran. (What a Wonderful World Ser.). 1991. pap. text ed. write for info. (*0-582-90959-7*, Pub. by Longman UK) Longman.

Super Solos. Howard Roberts & Ron Eschete. (Howard Roberts Guitar Manuals Ser.). (Illus.). 48p. 1977. pap. text ed. 9.95 (*0-89915-011-X*) Playback Mus Pub.

Super Songs. pap. 14.95 incl. audio compact disk (*0-7935-4386-X*, 00290026) H Leonard.

Super Songs: Early Elementary Piano Solos. 16p. 1991. pap. 4.95 (*0-7935-0595-X*, 00290257) H Leonard.

Super Songs with Silly Sounds. (Golden Sing Along Bks.). (Illus.). 20p. (J). (ps up). 1992. 16.95 (*0-307-74301-2*, 64301, Golden Pr) Western Pub.

Super Soups. Sally Meddock. Ed. by Jeannine Winquist. 64p. (Orig.). 1986. pap. 3.95 (*0-942320-23-9*) Am Cooking.

Super Source: Color Tiles. (J). (gr. k-2). 1996. pap. text ed. 15.95 (*1-57452-000-8*) Cuisenaire.

Super Source: Color Tiles. (J). (gr. 3-4). 1996. pap. text ed. 15.95 (*1-57452-001-6*) Cuisenaire.

Super Source: Color Tiles. (J). (gr. 5-6). 1996. pap. text ed. 15.95 (*1-57452-002-4*) Cuisenaire.

Super Source: Cuisenaire Rods. Cuisenaire Staff. (J). (gr. k-2). 1996. pap. text ed. 15.95 (*1-57452-003-2*) Cuisenaire.

Super Source: Cuisenaire Rods. Cuisenaire Staff. (J). (gr. 3-4). 1996. pap. text ed. 15.95 (*1-57452-004-0*) Cuisenaire.

Super Source: Cuisenaire Rods. Cuisenaire Staff. (J). (gr. 5-6). 1996. pap. text ed. 15.95 (*1-57452-005-9*) Cuisenaire.

Super Source: Geoboards. Cuisenaire Staff. (J). (gr. k-2). 1996. pap. text ed. 15.95 (*1-57452-006-7*) Cuisenaire.

Super Source: Geoboards. Cuisenaire Staff. (J). (gr. 3-4). 1996. pap. text ed. 15.95 (*1-57452-007-5*) Cuisenaire.

Super Source: Geoboards. Cuisenaire Staff. (J). (gr. 5-6). 1996. pap. text ed. 15.95 (*1-57452-008-3*) Cuisenaire.

***Super Source: Index.** Cuisenaire Staff. 45p. 1996. pap. text ed. write for info. (*0-938587-99-4*) Cuisenaire.

Super Source: Pattern Blocks. Cuisenaire Staff. (J). (gr. k-2). 1996. pap. text ed. 15.95 (*1-57452-009-1*) Cuisenaire.

Super Source: Pattern Blocks. Cuisenaire Staff. (J). (gr. 3-4). 1996. pap. text ed. 15.95 (*1-57452-010-5*) Cuisenaire.

Super Source: Pattern Blocks. Cuisenaire Staff. (J). (gr. 5-6). 1996. pap. text ed. 15.95 (*1-57452-011-3*) Cuisenaire.

Super Source: Snap Cubes. Cuisenaire Staff. (J). (gr. k-2). 1996. pap. text ed. 15.95 (*1-57452-012-1*) Cuisenaire.

Super Source: Snap Cubes. Cuisenaire Staff. (J). (gr. 3-4). 1996. pap. text ed. 15.95 (*1-57452-013-X*) Cuisenaire.

Super Source: Snap Cubes. Cuisenaire Staff. (J). (gr. 5-6). 1996. pap. text ed. 15.95 (*1-57452-014-8*) Cuisenaire.

Super Source: Tangrams. Cuisenaire Staff. (J). (gr. k-2). 1996. pap. text ed. 15.95 (*1-57452-015-6*) Cuisenaire.

Super Source: Tangrams. Cuisenaire Staff. (J). (gr. 3-4). 1996. pap. text ed. 15.95 (*1-57452-016-4*) Cuisenaire.

Super Source: Tangrams. Cuisenaire Staff. (J). (gr. 5-6). 1996. pap. text ed. 15.95 (*1-57452-017-2*) Cuisenaire.

Super Soy! Delicious Protein Without Meat. Barbara Farr. LC 76-2982. (Illus.). 1976. 6.95 (*0-87983-134-0*); pap. 3.95 (*0-87983-102-2*) Keats.

Super Soy: The Miracle Bean. Ruth Winter. 192p. 1996. pap. 11.00 (*0-517-88734-7*, Crown) Crown Pub Group.

Super Speech Adventures. Rita Samuelson. (Lizard Princess Adventure Ser.: Vol. 2). (Illus.). 96p. (J). (gr. k-4). 1991. pap. 10.00 (*0-930599-70-5*) Thinking Pubns.

Super Speech Adventures. Rita Samuelson. (Birthday Party Adventure Ser.: Vol. I). (Illus.). 96p. (J). (gr. k-4). 1991. pap. 10.00 (*0-930599-65-9*) Thinking Pubns.

***Super Spelling Bk. 1.** Cuff. Date not set. pap. text ed. write for info. (*0-582-39104-0*, Pub. by Longman UK) Longman.

***Super Spelling Bk. 2.** Cuff. Date not set. pap. text ed. write for info. (*0-582-39105-9*, Pub. by Longman UK) Longman.

***Super Spelling Bk. 3.** Cuff. Date not set. pap. text ed. write for info. (*0-582-39106-7*, Pub. by Longman UK) Longman.

***Super Spelling Bk. 4.** Cuff. Date not set. pap. text ed. write for info. (*0-582-39107-5*, Pub. by Longman UK) Longman.

***Super Spelling Bk. 5.** Cuff. Date not set. pap. text ed. write for info. (*0-582-39108-3*, Pub. by Longman UK) Longman.

***Super Spelling Bk. 6.** Cuff. Date not set. pap. text ed. write for info. (*0-582-39109-1*, Pub. by Longman UK) Longman.

***Super Spelling Book One.** Mary F. Pecci. (Illus.). 244p. 1997. pap. 19.95 (*0-943220-11-4*) Pecci Educ Pubs.

Super Spelling Fun. Charlie Daniel & Becky Daniel. 64p. (J). (gr. 2-6). 1978. 8.99 (*0-916456-31-5*, GA82) Good Apple.

Super Sport Trucks. Jay H. Smith. (Wheels Ser.). 48p. (J). (gr. 3-4). 1994. lib. bdg. 17.80 (*1-56065-216-0*) Capstone Pr.

***Super Sport Trucks.** Jay H. Smith. (Wheels Ser.). (Illus.). 48p. (J). (gr. 3-6). 1995. 18.40 (*0-516-35216-4*) Childrens.

***Super Sports Cars.** Jackson Jay. (Rollin' Ser.). (Illus.). 48p. (J). (gr. 3-7). 1996. 18.40 (*0-516-20090-9*) Childrens.

Super Springtime Crafts. Holly Hebert. LC 95-26385. (J). (gr. 2-7). 1996. pap. 8.95 (*1-56565-457-9*) Lowell Hse Juvenile.

Super Squats: How to Gain Thirty Pounds of Muscle in Six Weeks. Randall J. Strossen. 120p. (Orig.). 1989. pap. 12.95 (*0-926888-00-5*) IronMind Enterprises.

Super Stain Remover Book. Jack Cassimatis. LC 96-25720. 80p. 1996. pap. 5.95 (*0-8069-9483-5*) Sterling.

Super Standards for Easy Piano. (Easy Piano Ser.). 10.95 (*0-7935-4764-4*, 00310062) H Leonard.

***Super Star.** Judy Katschke. 1996. pap. text ed. 3.95 (*0-8114-9324-5*) Raintree Steck-V.

Super Star Wars Official Game Secrets. Rusel DeMaria. (Illus.). 224p. (Orig.). 1993. pap. 12.95 (*1-55958-405-X*) Prima Pub.

Super Start School. 1991. pap. 3.95 (*0-590-49101-6*) Scholastic Inc.

Super-State: Readings in the Military-Industrial Complex. Ed. by Herbert I. Schiller & Joseph D. Phillips. LC 73-104026. 364p. 1970. pap. text ed. 14.95 (*0-252-00283-0*) U of Ill Pr.

Super States! Puzzles, Games & Fascinating Trivia about the United States. Cindy Barden. Ed. by Judy Mitchell. (Illus.). 192p. (Orig.). (J). (gr. 3-6). 1995. teacher ed., pap. 16.95 (*1-57310-029-3*) Teaching & Lrning Co.

Super Stickers: 52 Full Color Pressure Sensitive Designs. Carolyn Bracken. (Illus.). (J). (gr. k-3). 1993. pap. 3.50 (*0-486-27894-8*) Dover.

Super Stocks. Kenneth L. Fisher. 272p. 1990. per. 22.95 (*1-55623-384-1*) Irwin Prof Pubng.

Super Stocks: The Book That's Changing the Way Investors Think. Kenneth L. Fisher. (Wall Street Wizard Ser.). 248p. 1984. 28.95 (*0-931133-03-3*, Busn Class) Pac Pub Grp.

Super Story Telling. Carol Catron & Barbara Parks. (Preschool-Toddler Ser.). 239p. (J). (ps). 1986. 15.95 (*0-513-01793-3*) Denison.

Super Strassen - Superhighways. Ravenstein Verlag Staff. 1993. pap. text ed. 17.95 (*3-87660-800-7*, Pub. by Ravenstein Vrlg GW) Seven Hills Bk.

Super String Games. Camilla Gryski. LC 88-18365. (Illus.). 80p. (J). (gr. 3 up). 1988. pap. 6.95 (*0-688-07684-X*) Morrow.

Super String Games. Camilla Gryski. 1996. pap. 8.95 (*0-688-15040-3*, Tupelo Bks) Morrow.

***Super Structures.** Dorling Kindersley Staff. (Funfax Eyewitness Library). (J). 1997. pap. 1.95 (*0-7894-1837-1*) DK Pub Inc.

Super Structures. Paul Nash. Ed. by Peter Harris. LC 89-12009. (Illus.). 32p. (J). (gr. 2-4). 1989. lib. bdg. 13.26 (*0-944483-37-2*) Garrett Ed Corp.

Super Structures of the World. Stuart A. Kallen. Ed. by Rosemary Wallner. LC 91-73053. (World Records Library). 202p. (J). 1991. lib. bdg. 12.94 (*1-56239-048-1*) Abdo & Dghtrs.

Super Student/Happy Kid! Sally D. Ketchum. 284p. 1995. pap. 9.95 (*0-9647160-0-3*) Summer Island.

Super Studio: The Guide to a Successful Dance Studio! Debbie Roberts. (Illus.). 160p. (Orig.). 1992. pap. 14.95 (*1-879260-07-7*) Evanston Pub.

***Super Successful Slot Systems.** Donald Currier. 32p. (Orig.). 1996. pap. 10.00 (*1-890030-00-7*) Las Vegas Insider.

Super Sum. Margaret J. Kenney. (Motivated Math Project Activity Booklets). 41p. (Orig.). (YA). (gr. 10-12). 1976. pap. text ed. 2.00 (*0-917916-18-2*) Boston Coll Math.

Super Supplements: Your Guide to Today's Newest Amino Acids & Glandulars. Michael E. Rosenbaum & Dominick Bosco. 288p. 1989. pap. 5.99 (*0-451-15809-1*, Sig) NAL-Dutton.

Super Swindlers: The Incredible Record of America's Greatest Financial Scams. Jonathan Kwitny. 350p. 1993. reprint ed. pap. 5.99 (*1-56171-248-5*, S P I Bks) Sure Seller.

Super Tarot: New Techniques for Improving Your Tarot Reading. Sasha Fenton. (Illus.). 176p. 1991. pap. 11.00 (*1-85538-017-X*, Pub. by Aquarian Pr UK) Thorsons SF.

***Super Teaching.** Eric Jensen. (Illus.). 370p. 1995. 27.00 (*0-9637832-0-3*) Turn Pt Teach.

Super Terrific Pigs. Dick King-Smith. (Illus.). 62p. 1993. pap. 6.95 (*0-575-05457-3*, Pub. by V Gollancz UK) Trafalgar.

Super Toys & Games from Paper. F. Virginia Walter & Teddy C. Long. LC 93-3161. (Illus.). 104p. (YA). (gr. 10-12). 1993. 19.95 (*1-895569-06-0*, Pub. by Tamos Bks CN) Sterling.

Super Toys & Games from Paper. F. Virginia Walter. (Illus.). 104p. 1994. pap. 12.95 (*1-895569-28-1*, Pub. by Tamos Bks CN) Sterling.

Super Treasures of Amazing Knowledge. (Creative Child Press Ser.). (Illus.). 278p. (YA). 1991. pap. 2.99 (*0-685-50837-4*) Random Hse Value.

Super Treasury of Three Hundred Plus Activities, Games, Arts & Crafts. Gayle Vinyard. LC 83-25605. (Illus.). 238p. 1984. pap. 24.95 (*0-89950-106-0*) McFarland & Co.

Super Tuesday: Regional Politics & Presidential Primaries. Barbara Norrander. LC 91-31263. (Illus.). 248p. 1992. text ed. 29.00 (0-8131-1773-9) U Pr of Ky.

Super Tuning Holley Carburetors. Alexander Walordy. (Illus.). 67p. 1987. pap. 14.95 (0-941167-00-3) A Walordy Pr.

Super Tuning Ignition, Carburetors, Cams & Fuel Injection. Alexander Walordy. (Illus.). 67p. (Orig.). (C). 1991. pap. text ed. 14.95 (0-9624323-1-8) A Walordy Pr.

Super Valentine Pop-up Cards. A. P. Folmer. 28p. (J). (ps-3). 1995. pap. 5.95 (0-590-48179-7) Scholastic Inc.

Super Value Classroom Clip Art: Fall, Winter, Spring, & Summer Art for All Occasions! Diane Hook. (Illus.). 480p. 1994. teacher ed. 24.95 (0-88724-321-5) Carson-Dellos.

Super VGA Graphics: Programming Secrets. Steve W. Rimmer. 1993. text ed. 49.95 (0-07-052999-X) McGraw.

Super VGA Graphics: Programming Secrets. Steve W. Rimmer. LC 92-38282. 1993. 44.95 (0-8306-4427-X, Windcrest); pap. 34.45 (0-8306-4428-8, Windcrest) TAB Bks.

Super Vita-Minds: How to Stop Saying I Hate You...to Yourself. 2nd rev. ed. Daya Devi-Doolin. LC 89-92061. 190p. (Orig.). (C). 1997. pap. 19.95 (1-877945-03-X, 150X) Padaran Pubns.

***Super Vixens Dymaxion Lounge.** Hillary Johnson. LC 96-53976. 1997. 20.95 (0-312-15668-5) St Martin.

Super Weird: Strange but True Stories You Won't Believe. Andrea Urton. LC 96-41230. (Illus.). 96p. (J). (gr. 3-7). 1996. pap. 6.95 (1-56565-542-7) Lowell Hse Juvenile.

Super Wings: The Step-by-Step Paper Airplane Book. Peter Clemens & Jose Delgado. 64p. (J). (ps-3). 1992. pap. 4.95 (0-929923-87-1) Lowell Hse.

Super Wings: The Step-by-Step Paper Airplane Book. rev. ed. Peter Clemens & Jose Delgado. (Illus.). 80p. (J). (gr. 3-7). 1996. wbk. ed., pap. 5.95 (1-56565-536-2) Lowell Hse Juvenile.

Super Working Mom's Handbook. Roseann Hirsch. LC 85-8985. 160p. 1986. pap. 8.95 (0-446-38073-3) Warner Bks.

Super Wraps for Kids: Children's Gift Wraps. (J). 1989. 9.99 (0-517-68532-9) Random Hse Value.

Super Years. Charlotte Hale. LC 90-80369. 164p. 1990. pap. 9.95 (0-9625485-0-2) Epiphany GA.

Super 17 Christmas Hits, Vol. 190. 1984. pap. 6.95 (0-7935-2745-7, 00101939) H Leonard.

Super 8 in the Video Age. 4th ed. Bob Brodsky & Toni Treadway. 1997. pap. text ed. 18.00 (0-9610914-4-4) Brodsky & Treadway.

Supera Tus Dificultades de Aprendizaje. Gary Fisher & Rhoda Cummings. (Illus.). 136p. (SPA.). (J). (gr. 8 up). pap. 9.95 (968-860-453-4) Free Spirit Pub.

Superabrasives. General Electric Company Staff. 320p. (C). 1989. pap. text ed. 27.95 (0-07-035587-8) McGraw.

Superabsorbent Polymers: Science & Technology. Ed. by Fredric L. Buchholz & Nicholas A. Peppas. LC 94-34669. (Symposium Ser.: No. 573). (Illus.). 160p. 1994. 49.95 (0-8412-3039-0) Am Chemical.

Superacids & Acidic Melts As Inorganic Chemical Reaction Media. Thomas A. O'Donnell. LC 92-15542. 243p. 1992. 110.00 (1-56081-035-1, VCH) Wiley.

Superalloy 718: Metallurgy & Applications: Proceedings of the International Symposium on the Metallurgy & Applications of Superalloy 718. International Symposium on the Metallurgy & Applications of Superalloy Seven Hundred Eighteen Staff. Ed. by Edward A. Loria. LC 89-60884. 710p. reprint ed. pap. 180.00 (0-7837-6060-4, 2052506) Bks Demand.

Superalloys. Ed. by Peter Allen. 295p. 1984. pap. 295.00 (0-931634-37-7) FIND-SVP.

Superalloys. Chester T. Sims et al. LC 86-32564. 615p. 1987. text ed. 132.00 (0-471-01147-9) Wiley.

Superalloys. American Society for Metals Staff. Ed. by Matthew J. Donachie, Jr. LC 83-71812. (Source Book Ser.). (Illus.). 424p. reprint ed. pap. 120.90 (0-7837-1862-4, 2042063) Bks Demand.

Superalloys: A Technical Guide. Ed. by Elihu F. Bradley. 280p. 1988. 70.00 (0-87170-327-0, 6239) ASM.

***Superalloys: A Technical Guide.** Ed. by Elihu F. Bradley. LC 88-70147. (Illus.). 292p. 1988. reprint ed. pap. 83.30 (0-608-02613-1, 2063271) Bks Demand.

Superalloys Nineteen Eighty: Proceedings of the Fourth International Symposium on Superalloys. Metallurgical Society of AIME, High Temperature Alloys Committee. LC 80-36888. 750p. reprint ed. pap. 180.00 (0-317-10322-9, 2015493) Bks Demand.

Superalloys Nineteen Ninety-Two. Ed. by R. A. Mackay et al. (Illus.). 974p. 1992. 150.00 (0-87339-189-6, 1896) Minerals Metals.

Superalloys 1988: Proceedings of the Sixth International Symposium on Superalloys Sponsored by the High Temperature Alloys Committee of the Metallurgical Society, Held September 18-22, 1988, Seven Springs Mountain Resort, Champion, PA. fac. ed. International Symposium on Superalloys Staff. Ed. by D. N. Duhl et al. LC 88-62071. (Illus.). 899p. 1988. pap. 180.00 (0-7837-8609-3, 2052540) Bks Demand.

***Superalloys 1992: Proceedings of the Seventh International Symposium on Superalloys Sponsored by the TMS Seven Springs International Symposium Committee, in Cooperation with the TMS High Temperature Alloys Committee, ASM International, & the American Society of Mechanical Engineers, Held September 20-24, 1992, Seven Springs Mountain Resort, Champion, PA.** International Symposium on Superalloys Staff. Ed. by S. D. Antolovich et al. LC 92-85044. 924p. 1992. reprint ed. pap. 180.00 (0-608-03825-3, 2062787) Bks Demand.

***Superalloys 1996.** Ed. by R. D. Kissinger et al. (Illus.). 781p. 1996. 170.00 (0-87339-352-X, 352X) Minerals Metals.

Superalloys 718, 625 & Various Derivatives: Proceedings of the International Symposium on the Metallurgy & Applications of Superalloys 718, 625, & Various Derivatives Sponsored by the Minerals, Metals & Materials Society & Cosponsored by ASM International & National Association of Corrosion Engineers, Held June 23-26, 1991, Pittsburgh, PA. fac. ed. International Symposium on the Metallurgy & Applications of Superalloy Seven Hundred Eighteen Staff. Ed. by Edward A. Loria. LC 91-61066. (Illus.). 983p. 1991. pap. 180.00 (0-7837-8610-7, 2052541) Bks Demand.

Superalloys 718, 625, 706 & Various Derivatives: Proceedings of the International Symposium on Superalloys 718, 625, 706 & Various Derivatives Sponsored by the Minerals, Metals & Materials Society & Cosponsored by ASM International & National Association of Corrrosion Engineers, held June 26-29, 1994. Ed. by E. A. Loria & International Symposium on Superalloys Staff. (Illus.). 969p. 1994. 170.00 (0-87339-235-3, 2353) Minerals Metals.

Superando el Dolor: Un Libro Para y Acerca de Adultos Abusados en la Ninez. Eliana Gil. Tr. by Ana I. Ilvento. LC 90-5951. (Illus.). 88p. (SPA.). 1990. pap. 8.95 (1-877872-00-8) Launch Pr.

Superantigens: A Pathogen's View of the Immune System. Ed. by Brigitte T. Huber & Ed Palmer. (Current Communications in Cell & Molecular Biology Ser.: No. 7). (Illus.). 180p. (C). 1993. pap. 39.00 (0-87969-398-3) Cold Spring Harbor.

***Superantigens: Molecular Biology, Immunology & Relevance to Human Disease.** Ed. by Leung et al. LC 96-40407. 624p. 1997. 195.00 (0-8247-9813-9) Dekker.

***Superb Number 7: Amazing Facts about the Number Seven.** Kitty Higgins. (Birthday Book Ser.). 1998. 6.95 (0-8362-3220-8) Andrews & McMeel.

Superb Salads. Anne Willan. LC 93-21802. (Anne Willan's Look & Cook Ser.). (Illus.). 128p. 1993. 16.95 (1-56458-301-5) DK Pub Inc.

Superbaby Syndrome. Jean G. Fitzpatrick. 1990. pap. 8.95 (0-15-686310-3) HarBrace.

Superbase Revealed. Fred Dalgleish. (Illus.). 752p. (Orig.). 1993. pap. 29.95 (1-55958-308-8) Prima Pub.

Superbath: The Blood Washing Method. Benedict Lust. (Illus.). 1982. pap. 2.00 (0-87904-027-0) Lust.

Superbeings. John R. Price. 160p. (Orig.). 1988. reprint ed. mass mkt. 5.99 (0-449-21543-1) Fawcett.

Superbeings: They Are with Us Now...Demonstrating What We All Can Become. 2nd rev. ed. John R. Price. LC 96-44149. 160p. 1997. pap. 12.00 (1-56170-358-3, 399) Hay House.

Superbeuts. Michael J. Phillips. 64p. (Orig.). 1983. pap. 5.00 (0-918342-19-8) Cambric.

Superbike. Edward Packard. (Choose Your Own Adventure Ser.: No. 124). 128p. (J). (gr. 4-7). 1992. pap. 3.50 (0-553-29294-3) Bantam.

Superbike. David A. Russell. 180p. (J). (gr. 4-7). 1993. 3.95 (1-883174-00-7) High Octane.

Superbike. David A. Russell. 168p. pap. 3.95 (1-884559-04-2) Allen Pubng.

Superbike. Jamie Brown. 256p. (YA). (gr. 7-12). 1991. reprint ed. pap. 4.95 (0-7736-7312-1, Pub. by Stoddart Pubng CN) Genl Dist Srvs.

Superbike, Vol. 124. large type ed. Edward Packard. LC 95-21668. (Choose Your Own Adventure Ser.: Vol. 124). (Illus.). 128p. (J). (gr. 4 up). 1995. lib. bdg. 15.93 (0-8368-1407-X) Gareth Stevens Inc.

Superbikes. Roland Brown. 1993. 15.98 (1-55521-860-1) Bk Sales Inc.

Superbikes. Charlie Webster & Mike Morris. LC 95-43800. (Pocket Gems Ser.). (Illus.). (J). 1996. 3.95 (0-8120-6587-5) Barron.

Superbird to the Rescue. Nancy Hayashi. Date not set. pap. write for info. (0-14-037975-4) Viking Penguin.

Superbly Swedish: Recipes & Traditions. Ed. by Martha W. Thompson. LC 83-61944. (Illus.). 88p. 1983. pap. 7.95 (0-941016-10-2) Penfield.

Superboss: The A-Z of Managing People Successfully. David Freemantle. 300p. 1985. text ed. 54.95 (0-566-02588-4, Pub. by Gower UK) Ashgate Pub Co.

***Superboss 2: The New A-Z of Managing People Successfully.** David Freemantle. LC 96-43274. 300p. 1997. text ed. 42.95 (0-566-07811-2, Pub. by Gower UK) Ashgate Pub Co.

Superbounce. Tom Ahern. (Burning Deck Poetry Ser.). 28p. 1983. pap. 3.00 (0-930901-12-6) Burning Deck.

Superbugs: Microorganisms in Extreme Environments. Ed. by Koki Horikoshi & W. D. Grant. (Illus.). x, 299p. 1991. 107.95 (0-387-52825-3) Spr-Verlag.

Supercalc Four: A Ready Reference Manual. Catherine Garrison & Mercedes McGowen. (Illus.). 128p. (C). 1988. pap. text ed. 9.75 (0-201-06389-1) Addison-Wesley.

SuperCalc Illustrated: The Complete Guide to Using the SuperCalc Program. C. Preston Burrow. LC 84-50173. (Illus.). 133p. (Orig.). 1984. pap. 12.95 (0-917065-07-7) Travis Pub Co.

SuperCalc 3: Learning, Using & Mastering. Jerry Willis. 1986. 22.95 (0-8306-0494-4, 2694) McGraw-Hill Prof.

SuperCarnot Heat Engines. Wayne Proell. 439p. 1994. text ed. 200.00 (0-9635505-0-0) Cloud Hill.

Supercarrier: USS George Washington. Christopher Bennett. LC 96-13068. (Enthusiast Color Ser.). (Illus.). 96p. 1996. pap. 12.95 (0-7603-0166-2) Motorbooks Intl.

Supercars. Barrons Educational Staff. LC 95-43796. (Pocket Gems Ser.). (Illus.). (J). 1996. 3.95 (0-8120-6586-7) Barron.

Supercars: The Story of the Dodge Charger Daytona & Plymouth SuperBird. Frank Moriarty. (Illus.). 160p. 1995. 34.95 (1-57427-043-5) Howell Pr VA.

Supercat: Raising the Perfect Feline Companion. Michael W. Fox. (Illus.). 224p. 1991. pap. 19.95 (0-87605-843-8) Howell Bk.

***Supercede.** Thomas A. Lockwood. (New Tutorial Ser.). 1997. pap. 39.99 (0-7645-3143-3) IDG Bks.

***Supercharge Your Health! 150 Easy Ways to Get Strong, Feel Great & Look Your Best.** Gary Null. LC 96-37822. 1997. 6.99 (0-06-273469-5) HarpC.

Supercharge Your Management Role: Making the Transition to Internal Consultant. Mark Thomas & Sam Elbeik. 208p. 1996. pap. 32.95 (0-7506-2546-5) Buttrwrth-Heinemann.

SuperCharge Your Sales Force: Applying the Power of Computers to Get the Best from Your Sales Team. Jon C. Liberman. 225p. 1993. text ed. 22.95 (1-55738-441-X) Irwin Prof Pubng.

Supercharged Bit-Mapped Graphics. Steve W. Rimmer. 664p. 1992. pap. 34.95 (0-8306-3788-5, 4102, Windcrest) TAB Bks.

Supercharged C Graphics: A Programmer's Source Code Toolbox. Lee Adams. (Illus.). 400p. 1989. 34.95 (0-8306-9289-4, Windcrest); pap. 24.95 (0-8306-3289-1, Windcrest) TAB Bks.

Supercharged C Graphics, Quick. Lee Adams. 1991. 24.95 (0-8306-6739-3) McGraw-Hill Prof.

Supercharged C Graphics, Turbo. Lee Adams. 1991. 29.95 (0-8306-6740-7) McGraw-Hill Prof.

Supercharged Gas Coupes: Remembering the "Sixties" Donald R. Montgomery. (Illus.). 192p. 1992. 32.95 (0-9626454-3-5) D Montgomery.

Supercharged Graphics. L. Adams. 1991. 24.95 (0-8306-6658-3) McGraw-Hill Prof.

Supercharged Graphics: A Programmer's Source Code Toolbox. Lee Adams. (Illus.). 400p. 1988. 29.95 (0-8306-0659-9, 2959); pap. 21.95 (0-8306-2959-9) McGraw-Hill Prof.

Supercharged Infield. Matt Christopher. (J). (gr. 4-7). 1994. 3.95 (0-316-14277-8) Little.

Supercharging Corporate Performance: Business Ethics in Action. Francis J. Aguilar. LC 93-5803. 192p. 1994. 25.00 (0-19-508534-5) OUP.

Supercharging MS-DOS. 4th ed. Van Wolverton. (Illus.). 302p. 1994. pap. 25.00 (0-9641851-0-5) Forsyth-Wolf.

Supercharging OS-2 Batch Files & Utilities. David D. Busch. 320p. 1988. pap. 22.95 (0-201-13785-2) Addison-Wesley.

Supercharging the AS/400: A Guide to Performance Management. Ron Fielder & Carolyn Machell. LC 95-5553. 1995. text ed. 40.00 (0-07-707997-3) McGraw.

Superchefs: Signature Recipes from America's New Royalty. Karen G. Zahler. LC 96-1336. 228p. 1996. text ed. 37.50 (0-471-14751-6) Wiley.

Supercheries Litteraires Devoilees, 3 vols. rev. ed. Joseph-Marie Querard. xiv, 66p. 1965. reprint ed. Supplement, xiv, 66p. suppl. ed. write for info. (0-318-71394-2) G Olms Pubs.

Supercheries Litteraires Devoilees, 3 vols., Set. 2nd ed. Joseph-Marie Querard. 1965. reprint ed. write for info. (0-318-71859-6) G Olms Pubs.

Supercheries Litteraires Devoilees, 3 vols., Set. 2nd rev. ed. Joseph-Marie Querard. xii, 1947p. 1965. reprint ed. write for info. (0-318-71393-4) G Olms Pubs.

Supercheries litteraires devoilees, 3 tomes, Set. Joseph-Marie Querard. 150.00 (0-685-35983-2) Fr & Eur.

Superchess: The Official Rules & Game Description. Rolf W. Jacobson. (Illus.). 20p. 1992. pap. 2.95 (0-9634881-0-4); 27.95 (0-9634881-1-2) Green Island.

Supercollider Physics: Proceedings of the Oregon Workshop on High Energy Physics. Ed. by D. Soper. 328p. 1986. text ed. 47.00 (9971-5-0051-5) World Scientific Pub.

Supercollider 1. Ed. by M. McAshan. (Illus.). 840p. 1989. 155.00 (0-306-43365-6, Plenum Pr) Plenum.

Supercollider 2. Ed. by M. McAshan. LC 90-49839. (Illus.). 790p. 1990. 155.00 (0-306-43801-1, Plenum Pr) Plenum.

Supercollider 3. Ed. by John Nonte. (Illus.). 1196p. 1991. 185.00 (0-306-44037-7, Plenum Pr) Plenum.

Supercollider 4: Proceedings of the Fourth International Industrial Symposium on the Super Collider, Held March 4-6, 1992, in Atlanta, Georgia. Ed. by John Nonte. LC 92-30221. 1992. 195.00 (0-306-44254-X, Plenum Pr) Plenum.

Supercollider 5. Ed. by Phyllis Hale. LC 94-3824. (Illus.). 970p. (C). 1994. 195.00 (0-306-44705-3) Plenum.

Supercolliders & Superdetectors: Proceedings of the 19th & 25th Workshops of the Information Eloisatron Project. William A. Barletta & H. Leutz. (Science & Culture Series - Physics). 400p. 1994. text ed. 121.00 (981-02-1595-9) World Scientific Pub.

SuperCommunity Banking: A Super Strategy for Surviving & Thriving in the Year 2000. Anat Bird. 1993. text ed. 42.50 (1-55738-388-X) Irwin Prof Pubng.

Supercommunity Banking Strategies: Taking the Next Steps Toward Market Leadership. Anat Bird. LC 96-38973. 396p. 1996. text ed. 42.50 (0-7863-0966-0) Irwin Prof Pubng.

Supercompilers for Parallel & Vector Computers. Hans Zima. (C). 1991. pap. text ed. 39.75 (0-201-17560-6) Addison-Wesley.

***Supercomputation in Nonlinear & Disordered Systems: Algorithms, Applications & Architectures.** 320p. 1997. 54.00 (981-02-3030-3) World Scientific Pub.

Supercomputational Science. Ed. by R. G. Evans & S. Wilson. LC 90-45241. (Illus.). 340p. 1990. 95.00 (0-306-43663-9, Plenum Pr) Plenum.

Supercomputer. 1995. write for info. (3-598-22412-5) K G Saur.

Supercomputer Algorithms for Reactivity, Dynamics & Kinetics of Small Molecules. Ed. by Antonio Lagana. (C). 1989. lib. bdg. 185.00 (0-7923-0226-5) Kluwer Ac.

Supercomputer & Chemistry: IABG Workshop 1989. Ed. by U. Harms. (Illus.). 152p. 1990. pap. 64.00 (0-387-52915-2) Spr-Verlag.

Supercomputer & Chemistry, No. 2: Debis Workshop 1990. Ed. by U. Harms. (Illus.). vii, 166p. 1991. 106.95 (0-387-54411-9) Spr-Verlag.

Supercomputer Applications. Ed. by Robert W. Numrich. 316p. 1985. 85.00 (0-306-42013-9, Plenum Pr) Plenum.

SuperComputer Applications in Automotive Research & Engineering Development. Ed. by C. Marino. 452p. 1986. 115.00 (0-931215-29-3) Computational Mech MA.

Supercomputer of Today & Tomorrow: The Parallel Processing Revolution. Richard A. Jenkins. (Illus.). 208p. 1986. pap. 14.60 (0-8306-0322-0, 2622P) McGraw-Hill Prof.

Supercomputer Research in Chemistry & Chemical Engineering. Ed. by Lavs F. Jensen & Donald G. Truhlar. LC 87-24127. (Symposium Ser.: No. 353). (Illus.). vii, 429p. 1987. 98.95 (0-8412-1430-1) Am Chemical.

***Supercomputer Research in Chemistry & Chemical Engineering.** Ed. by Klavs F. Jensen & Donald G. Truhlar. LC 87-24127. (ACS Symposium Ser.: Vol. 353). 448p. 1987. reprint ed. pap. 127.70 (0-608-03876-8, 2064323) Bks Demand.

Supercomputer '89. 1989. 33.00 (0-387-51310-8) Spr-Verlag.

Supercomputer '90. 1990. 28.95 (0-387-52792-3) Spr-Verlag.

Supercomputers. Richard K. Miller & Terri C. Walker. LC 88-82059. (Survey on Technology & Markets Ser.: No. 37). 50p. 1989. pap. text ed. 200.00 (1-55865-036-9) Future Tech Surveys.

Supercomputers: A Key to U. S. Scientific, Technological, & Industrial Preeminence. Ed. by J. R. Kirkland & Jesse H. Poore. LC 87-11808. 265p. 1987. text ed. 59.95 (0-275-92622-2, C2622, Praeger Pubs) Greenwood.

Supercomputers: Algorithms, Architectures, & Scientific Computation. Ed. by F. A. Matsen & T. Tajima. 488p. (C). 1986. text ed. 40.00 (0-292-70388-0) U of Tex Pr.

Supercomputers: Directions in Technology & Applications. National Research Council Staff & National Academy of Sciences Staff. 112p. 1989. pap. text ed. 17.00 (0-309-04088-4) Natl Acad Pr.

Supercomputers: Materials, Components, Software. Business Communications Co., Inc. Staff. (Illus.). 236p. 1986. pap. 1,750.00 (0-89336-494-0, G-102) BCC.

Supercomputers: Shaping the Future. Charlene W. Billings. LC 94-44111. (Science Sourcebooks Ser.). 144p. 1995. 17.95 (0-8160-3096-0) Facts on File.

Supercomputers & Parallel Computations. Ed. by D. J. Paddon. (Institute of Mathematics & Its Applications Conference Series, New Ser.). (Illus.). 268p. 1984. 78.00 (0-19-853601-1) OUP.

Supercomputers & Their Performance in Computational Fluid Dynamics. Ed. by Kozo Fujii. (Notes on Numerical Fluid Mechanics Ser.: Vol. 37). xii, 200p. 1993. 48.00 (3-528-07637-2, Pub. by Vieweg & Sohn GW) Informatica.

Supercomputers in Chemistry. Ed. by Peter Lykos & Isaiah Shavitt. LC 81-17630. (ACS Symposium Ser.: No. 173). 1981. 38.95 (0-8412-0666-X) Am Chemical.

***Supercomputers in Chemistry.** Ed. by Peter Lykos & Isaiah Shavitt. LC 81-17630. (ACS Symposium Ser.: No. 173). (Illus.). 288p. 1981. reprint ed. pap. 82.10 (0-608-03239-5, 2063758) Bks Demand.

Supercomputers in Seismic Exploration. Ed. by E. Eisner. LC 88-25410. (Handbook of Geophysical Exploration Ser.). 321p. 1988. text ed. 158.25 (0-08-037018-7, Pergamon Pr) Elsevier.

Supercomputers in Theoretical & Experimental Science. Ed. by Jozef T. Devreese & P. E. Van Camp. 238p. 1985. 89.50 (0-306-42107-0, Plenum Pr) Plenum.

Supercomputers of Today & Tomorrow. 2nd ed. Richard A. Jenkins. (Illus.). 224p. (Orig.). 1989. 24.95 (0-318-41134-2, Windcrest); pap. 16.95 (0-8306-3202-6, Windcrest) TAB Bks.

Supercomputing. Ed. by Elias N. Houstis et al. (Lecture Notes in Computer Science Ser.: Vol. 297). x, 1093p. 1988. pap. 101.00 (0-387-18991-2) Spr-Verlag.

Supercomputing. Ed. by Janusz S. Kowalik. (NATO ASI Series F: Computer & Systems Sciences, Special Programme AET: Vol. 62). (Illus.). x, 425p. 1990. 93.95 (0-387-52691-9) Spr-Verlag.

Supercomputing: Applications, Algorithms, & Architectures for the Future of Supercomputing. Ed. by Jiro Kondo. (Illus.). xvi, 212p. 1991. 93.95 (0-387-70070-6) Spr-Verlag.

Supercomputing & the Transformation of Science. William J. Kaufmann, III & Larry L. Smarr. LC 92-32418. 1995. text ed. write for info. (0-7167-5038-4) W H Freeman.

Supercomputing in Engineering Analysis. Ed. by Hojjat Adeli. (New Generation Computing Ser.: Vol. 1). 376p. 1991. 150.00 (0-8247-8559-2) Dekker.

Supercomputing in Engineering Structures. Ed. by P. Melli & C. A. Brebbia. LC 88-63525. 305p. 1989. 72.00 (0-945824-07-6) Computational Mech MA.

Supercomputing in Fluid Flow: Proceedings of the First International Seminar on Supercomputers in Fluid Flow, Held in Lowell, Massachusetts, October 3-5, 1989. Ed. by T. K. Murthy & C. A. Brebbia. LC 90-84998. (Computational Engineering Ser.). 368p. 1992. 195.00 (0-945824-59-9) Computational Mech MA.

Supercomputing '94. LC 10-639535. 850p. 1994. pap. 170.00 (0-8186-6605-6, PR06605) IEEE Comp Soc.

***Superconducting Accelerator Magnets.** 228p. 1996. lib. bdg. 27.00 (981-02-2790-6) World Scientific Pub.

S

Superconducting Ceramics: Proceedings of the 12th Winter Meeting on Low Temperature Physics. J. L. Heiras et al. (Series on Progress in High Temperature Superconductivity: No. 31). 200p. 1991. text ed. 74.00 (*981-02-0889-8*) World Scientific Pub.

Superconducting D. C. Machines. A. D. Appleton. 1984. write for info. (*0-318-57806-9*) Elsevier.

Superconducting Devices & Their Applications: Proceedings of the 4th International Conference SQUID '91 (Session on Superconducting Devices), Berlin, Fed. Rep. of Germany, June 18-21, 1991. Ed. by H. Koch & H. Lubbig. LC 92-13633. (Physics Ser.: Vol. 64). (Illus.). xv, 603p. 1992. 98.00 (*3-540-55396-7*); 107.95 (*0-387-55396-7*) Spr-Verlag.

Superconducting Electronics. Ed. by M. Nisenoff & Harold Weinstock. (NATO Asi Series F: Vol. 59). (Illus.). 456p. 1989. 107.95 (*0-387-51521-6*) Spr-Verlag.

*__Superconducting Glass-Ceramics in BSCCO: Fabrication via Melting & Its Application.__ 300p. 1997. text ed. 33.00 (*981-02-3204-7*) World Scientific Pub.

Superconducting Levitation: Applications to Bearings & Magnetic Transportation. Francis M. Moon. 295p. 1994. text ed. 72.95 (*0-471-55925-3*) Wiley.

Superconducting Magnets. Martin N. Wilson. (Monographs on Cryogenics: No. 2). (Illus.). 352p. 1987. pap. 55.00 (*0-19-854810-9*) OUP.

Superconducting Quantum Electronics. Ed. by V. Kose. (Illus.). 345p. 1989. 86.95 (*0-387-51176-8*) Spr-Verlag.

Superconducting Super Collider at the Stockbridge, Michigan Site: Community Support & Land Acquisition. Richard W. Stoffle et al. LC 88-8244. (Institute for Social Research, Research Report Ser.). (Illus.). 207p. reprint ed. pap. 59.00 (*0-7837-5247-4*, 2044982) Bks Demand.

Superconducting Technology: Ten Case Studies. Ed. by K. Fossheim. 248p. (C). 1991. pap. 32.00 (*981-02-0694-1*); text ed. 89.00 (*981-02-0628-3*) World Scientific Pub.

Superconductive Particle Detectors. Antonio Barone. (Advances in the Physics of Condensed Matter Ser.: ISI-87). 360p. (C). 1988. text ed. 77.00 (*9971-5-0611-4*) World Scientific Pub.

Superconductiving in Magnetic & Exotic Materials: Proceedings of the Sixth Taniguchi International Symposium, Kashikojima, Japan, Nov. 14-18, 1983. Ed. by T. Matsubara & A. Kotani. (Solid-State Sciences Ser.: Vol. 52). (Illus.). 225p. 1984. 59.95 (*0-387-13324-0*) Spr-Verlag.

Superconductivity. Per F. Dahl. 424p. 1992. 55.00 (*0-88318-848-1*) Spr-Verlag.

Superconductivity. V. L. Ginzburg & E. A. Andrushin. 104p. 1994. text ed. 43.00 (*981-02-1459-6*); pap. text ed. 23.00 (*981-02-1630-0*) World Scientific Pub.

Superconductivity. Ed. by S. K. Joshi et al. 484p. (C). 1990. text ed. 130.00 (*981-02-0150-8*) World Scientific Pub.

*__Superconductivity.__ John B. Ketterson & Shengnian Song. (Illus.). 425p. (C). 1997. text ed. 85.00 (*0-521-56295-3*) Cambridge U Pr.

*__Superconductivity.__ John B. Ketterson & Shengnian Song. (Illus.). 425p. (C). 1997. pap. text ed. 34.95 (*0-521-56562-6*) Cambridge U Pr.

Superconductivity. Charles P. Poole, Jr. et al. (Illus.). 620p. 1996. pap. text ed. 65.00 (*0-12-561456-X*) Acad Pr.

Superconductivity. A. W. Taylor. 110p. 1971. pap. 18.00 (*0-85109-120-2*) Taylor & Francis.

Superconductivity. Michael Tinkham. (Documents on Modern Physics Ser.). 92p. 1965. 271.00 (*0-685-01963-2*) Gordon & Breach.

Superconductivity. 2nd ed. David Shoenberg. (Cambridge Monographs on Physics). 270p. reprint ed. pap. 77.00 (*0-317-09142-5*, 2051478) Bks Demand.

Superconductivity: An Annotated Bibliography with Abstracts. Ed. by A. Bisarsh. 148p. 1995. lib. bdg. 79.00 (*1-56072-106-5*) Nova Sci Pubs.

Superconductivity: Experiments in a New Technology. Dave Prochnow. (Advanced Technology Ser.). (Illus.). 208p. 1988. pap. 14.95 (*0-8306-3132-1*, 3132) McGraw-Hill Prof.

*__Superconductivity: From Basic Physics to the Latest Developments.__ 352p. 1995. 26.00 (*981-02-2583-0*) World Scientific Pub.

Superconductivity: From Basic Physics to the Latest Developments: Lecture Notes of the ICTP Spring College in Condensed Matter on "Superconductivity", Trieste, Italy 27 April - 19 June 1992. Ed. by P. N. Butcher & Yu Lu. 352p. 1995. text ed. 78.00 (*981-02-2456-7*, Pc-P2928) World Scientific Pub.

Superconductivity: Fundamentals & Applications. Werner Buckel. 322p. 1991. 75.00 (*3-527-27893-1*, VCH) Wiley.

Superconductivity: Materials Research Society International Symposium Proceedings - IMAM. Ed. by K. Kitazawa & K. Tachikawa. 1027p. 1989. text ed. 63.00 (*1-55899-035-6*, IMAM-6) Materials Res.

Superconductivity: May 31-June 3, 1988, Sunshine City, Ikebukuro, Tokyo, Japan. MRS International Meeting on Advanced Materials, First, Tokyo, Japan Staff. LC 90-174207. (Proceedings of the MRS International Meeting on Advanced Materials Ser.: No. 6). (Illus.). 1055p. reprint ed. pap. 180.00 (*0-7837-1930-2*, 2042145) Bks Demand.

Superconductivity: McGill Univ. 1968 Summer School Proceedings, 2 vols, Vol. 1. Ed. by P. R. Wallace. 544p. 1969. text ed. 386.00 (*0-677-13810-5*) Gordon & Breach.

Superconductivity: The Next Revolution? Gianfranco Vidali. LC 92-23185. (Illus.). 180p. (C). 1993. text ed. 54.95 (*0-521-37378-6*); pap. text ed. 20.95 (*0-521-37757-9*) Cambridge U Pr.

Superconductivity: Theoretical & Experimental Effects. Ed. by K. N. Shrivastava. (Illus.). 327p. (C). 1996. lib. bdg. 89.00 (*1-56072-360-2*) Nova Sci Pubs.

Superconductivity - Prog in Hts, Vol. 27: Proceedings of the Twenty-Fourth Italian National School on Condensed Matter. Ed. by S. Pace & M. Acquarone. 550p. (C). 1991. text ed. 129.00 (*981-02-0328-4*) World Scientific Pub.

Superconductivity - The Threshold of a New Technology. Jonathan L. Mayo. 1988. pap. 12.95 (*0-8306-9322-X*, 3022P) McGraw-Hill Prof.

Superconductivity & Applications. Ed. by H. C. Ku & P. T. Wu. 476p. (C). 1989. text ed. 151.00 (*9971-5-0953-9*) World Scientific Pub.

Superconductivity & Applications. Ed. by H. S. Kwok et al. (Illus.). 838p. 1990. 155.00 (*0-306-43514-4*, Plenum Pr) Plenum.

Superconductivity & Cryoelectronics. Ed. by W. Krech et al. 216p. (C). 1991. text ed. 61.00 (*981-02-0797-2*) World Scientific Pub.

Superconductivity & Its Applications. Ed. by Y. H. Kao et al. (Conference Proceeding Ser.: No. 251). 792p. 1992. 120.00 (*1-56396-016-8*) Am Inst Physics.

Superconductivity & Its Applications. Ed. by Yi-Han Kao et al. LC 91-55020. (AIP Conference Proceedings Ser.: No. 219). (Illus.). 728p. 1991. 85.00 (*0-88318-835-X*) Am Inst Physics.

Superconductivity & Its Applications: Proceedings of the Sixth Annual Conference, Buffalo, 1992. Ed. by H. S. Kwok et al. (AIP Conference Proceedings Ser.: No. 273). (Illus.). 672p. 1993. text ed. 150.00 (*1-56396-189-X*, AIP) Am Inst Physics.

Superconductivity & Particle Detection: Proceedings of the International Workshop. T. A. Girard et al. 376p. 1995. text ed. 112.00 (*981-02-2006-5*) World Scientific Pub.

Superconductivity & Strongly Correlated Electron Systems. C. Noce et al. 448p. 1994. text ed. 124.00 (*981-02-2038-3*) World Scientific Pub.

Superconductivity in D- & F- Band Metals: Proceedings of the Conference, Univ. of Rochester, 1971, No. 4. American Institute of Physics. Ed. by D. H. Douglass. LC 74-188879. (AIP Conference Proceedings Ser.). 375p. 1972. 14.00 (*0-88318-103-7*) Am Inst Physics.

Superconductivity in Energy Technologies: Assessments, Concepts & New Aspects. 266p. 1990. pap. 195.00 (*0-614-07589-0*, Pub. by Woodhead Pubng UK) Am Educ Systs.

Superconductivity in Science & Technology. Ed. by Morrel H. Cohen. LC 67-25534. 171p. reprint ed. pap. 48.80 (*0-317-08095-4*, 2020047) Bks Demand.

Superconductivity in Ternary Compounds I: Structural, Electronics & Lattices Properties. Ed. by O. Fischer & M. Brian Maple. (Topics in Current Physics Ser.: Vol. 32). (Illus.). 320p. 1982. 80.95 (*0-387-11670-2*) Spr-Verlag.

Superconductivity in Ternary Compounds II: Superconductivity & Magnetism. Ed. by O. Fischer & M. Brian Maple. (Topics in Current Physics Ser.: Vol. 34). (Illus.). 335p. 1982. 69.95 (*0-387-11814-4*) Spr-Verlag.

Superconductivity of Metals & Alloys. Pierre-Gilles de Gennes. (C). 1994. pap. 36.95 (*0-201-40842-2*) Addison-Wesley.

Superconductivity of Metals & Cuprates. J. R. Waldram. LC 96-19055. (Illus.). 220p. 1996. 180.00 (*0-85274-335-1*); pap. 60.00 (*0-85274-337-8*) IOP Pub.

Superconductivity of Transition Metals: Their Alloys & Compounds. S. V. Vonsovsky et al. (Solid-State Sciences Ser.: Vol. 27). (Illus.). 512p. 1982. 86.95 (*0-387-11382-7*) Spr-Verlag.

Superconductivity Sourcebook. V. Daniel Hunt. LC 88-27676. 308p. 1989. text ed. 99.95 (*0-471-61706-7*) Wiley.

Superconductivity Update. Ed. by Richard K. Miller & Matthew Walker. LC 88-45796. 220p. 1990. pap. text ed. 95.00 (*0-88173-071-8*) Fairmont Pr.

Superconductor Component Industry. Business Communications Co., Inc. Staff. 177p. 1988. pap. 1,950.00 (*0-89336-616-1*, GB-106) BCC.

Superconductor Electronics. J. H. Hinken. (Graduate Texts in Contemporary Physics Ser.). (Illus.). 169p. 1989. 59.95 (*0-387-51114-8*) Spr-Verlag.

Superconductor Magnetic Energy Storage. Richard K. Miller & Terri C. Walker. LC 88-80923. (Survey on Technology & Markets Ser.: No. 39). 50p. 1989. pap. text ed. 200.00 (*1-55865-038-5*) Future Tech Surveys.

Superconductors. Miller & Fairmont Press Staff. 1989. pap. text ed. 95.00 (*0-13-876616-9*) P-H.

*__Superconductors.__ A. V. Narlikar. (Illus.). 256p. (Orig.). (C). 1997. pap. text ed. 29.00 (*0-412-63560-7*, Chap & Hall NY) Chapman & Hall.

Superconductors: Conquering Technology's New Frontier. Randy Simon & Andrew Smith. LC 88-17950. (Illus.). 340p. 1988. 23.95 (*0-306-42959-4*, Plenum Pr) Plenum.

Superconductors: Electronics & Computer Applications. Richard K. Miller. LC 89-17028. 270p. 1989. pap. text ed. 95.00 (*0-88173-103-X*) Fairmont Pr.

Superconductors: Proceedings. Ed. by M. Tanenbaum & W. V. Wright. LC 62-18707. 161p. reprint ed. pap. 45.90 (*0-317-08032-6*, 2000686) Bks Demand.

Superconductors: The Irresistible Future. Albert Stwertka. LC 90-19309. (Venture Bks.). (Illus.). 112p. (J). (gr. 7-9). 1991. lib. bdg. 22.00 (*0-531-12526-2*) Watts.

SuperConductors: Transition Temperatures & Characterization of Elements, Alloys & Compounds, Vol. 21. Ed. by R. Flukiger et al. 285p. 1994. 1,408.95 (*0-387-57541-3*) Spr-Verlag.

Superconductors in Power Systems. Jyoti K. Parikh. (C). 1990. text ed. 21.00 (*81-7023-295-3*, Pub. by Allied II) S Asia.

Superconductors. Transition Temperatures & Characterization of Elements, Alloys & Compounds: Subvolume b1: Nb, Nb-Ar ...Nb-Ge. Ed. by R. Flukiger & W. Klose. (Numerical Data & Functional Relationships in Science & Technology Ser.). xxiv, 284p. 1993. 1,100.95 (*0-387-55522-6*) Spr-Verlag.

*__Superconductors Transition Temperatures & Characterization of Elements, Alloys & Compounds Vol. C: O (Without Cuprates)...Sc.__ Ed. by R. Flukiger & W. Klose. (Landolt-Bornstein Ser.: Vol. III, 21). xxviii, 317p. 1997. 1,413.00 (*3-540-56047-5*) Spr-Verlag.

Superconductors with A15 Lattices & Bridge Contacts Based upon Them. Ed. by M. M. Sushchinskiy. (Proceedings of the Lebedev Physics Institute Ser.: Vol. 190, Suppl. 1). 354p. (C). 1991. text ed. 125.00 (*1-56072-011-5*) Nova Sci Pubs.

Superconscious Meditation. Pandit U. Arya. LC 78-102982. 150p. 1978. pap. 12.95 (*0-89389-035-9*) Himalayan Inst.

Superconsciousness: A Guide to Meditation. J. Donald Walters. 256p. (Orig.). 1996. pap. 10.99 (*0-446-67173-8*) Warner Bks.

Superconsciousness Through Meditation. Douglas M. Baker. 1978. pap. 12.50 (*0-906006-75-9*, Pub. by Baker Pubns UK) New Leaf Dist.

Supercontinuum Laser Source. Ed. by R. R. Alfano. (Illus.). 440p. 1989. 130.95 (*0-387-96946-2*) Spr-Verlag.

Superconvergence in Galerkin Finite Element Methods, Vol. XI. Lars B. Wahlbin. Ed. by A. Dold & F. Takens. LC 95-9603. (Lecture Notes in Mathematics Ser.: Vol. 1605). 166p. 1995. 36.95 (*3-540-60011-6*) Spr-Verlag.

Supercounties, U. S. A. G. Etzel Pearcy. LC 75-36700. (Monographs: No.3). (Illus.). 1976. 11.95 (*0-916434-15-X*) Plycon Pr.

Supercourse for the LSAT see LSAT Supercourse

Supercrats. Trevor M. Phillips. 454p. 1989. write for info. (*0-9622708-1-4*) Zubra Pub.

Supercrats. 2nd ed. Trevor M. Phillips. Ed. by Julie A. Phillips. 486p. 1989. write for info. (*0-9622708-2-2*) Zubra Pub.

Supercritical Fluid Engineering Science: Fundamentals & Applications. Ed. by Erdogan Kiran & Joan F. Brennecke. LC 92-33287. (ACS Symposium Ser.: No. 514). (Illus.). 394p. 1992. 98.95 (*0-8412-2513-3*) Am Chemical.

Supercritical Fluid Extraction. Larry T. Taylor. LC 95-42945. (Techniques in Analytical Chemistry Ser.). (Illus.). 200p. 1996. text ed. 49.95 (*0-471-11990-3*, Wiley-Interscience) Wiley.

Supercritical Fluid Extraction. 2nd ed. Mark McHugh & Val J. Krukonis. (Chemical Engineering Technical Ser.). (Illus.). 608p. 1993. 105.00 (*0-7506-9244-8*) Buttrwrth-Heinemann.

Supercritical Fluid Extraction & Chromatography: Techniques & Applications. Ed. by Bonnie A. Carpentier & Michael R. Sevenants. LC 88-3466. (Symposium Ser.: No. 366). (Illus.). ix, 253p. 1988. 65.95 (*0-8412-1469-7*) Am Chemical.

*__Supercritical Fluid Extraction & Chromatography: Techniques & Applications.__ Ed. by Bonnie A. Charpentier & Michael R. Sevenants. LC 88-3466. (ACS Symposium Ser.: Vol. 366). 264p. 1988. reprint ed. pap. 75.30 (*0-608-03888-1*, 2064335) Bks Demand.

Supercritical Fluid Extraction & Its Use in Chromatographic Sample Preparation. Ed. by S. A. Westwood. 1993. 101.00 (*0-8493-7107-4*, QD79) CRC Pr.

*__Supercritical Fluid Processing of Food & Biomaterials.__ Ed. by Rizvi. (Illus.). 280p. 1994. text ed. 141.95 (*0-7514-0184-6*, Pub. by Blackie Acad & Prof UK) Routledge Chapman & Hall.

Supercritical Fluid Science & Technology. Ed. by Keith P. Johnston. LC 89-17521. (ACS Symposium Ser.: No. 406). (Illus.). 536p. 1989. 99.95 (*0-8412-1678-9*) Am Chemical.

Supercritical Fluid Technology. Thomas J. Bruno & James F. Ely. (Illus.). 528p. 1991. 218.95 (*0-8493-6847-2*, TP156) CRC Pr.

Supercritical Fluid Technology: Process Technology Proceedings, No. 3. Ed. by Johan M. Penninger et al. 468p. 1985. 257.50 (*0-444-42552-7*) Elsevier.

Supercritical Fluid Technology: Theoretical & Applied Approaches to Analytical Chemistry. Ed. by Frank V. Bright & Mary E. McNally. LC 92-11434. (ACS Symposium Ser.: No. 488). (Illus.). 384p. 1992. 86.95 (*0-8412-2220-7*) Am Chemical.

Supercritical Fluid Technology in Oil & Lipid Chemistry. Ed. by Jerry W. King & Gary R. List. LC 96-15367. (Illus.). 432p. 1996. 95.00 (*0-935315-71-3*) AOCS Pr.

*__Supercross.__ Joe Bonnello. LC 97-3069. (Enthusiast Color Ser.). (Illus.). 96p. 1997. pap. 12.95 (*0-7603-0320-7*) Motorbooks Intl.

Supercross Motorcycle Racing. Jeff Savage. LC 95-32758. (Action Events Ser.). (J). 1996. pap. 4.95 (*0-382-39292-2*, Crstwood Hse) Silver Burdett Pr.

Supercross Motorcycle Racing. Jeff Savage. LC 95-32758. (Action Events Ser.). (J). 1996. lib. bdg. 14.95 (*0-89686-887-7*, Crstwood Hse) Silver Burdett Pr.

Supercut: Nutrition for the Ultimate Physique. Bill Reynolds & Joyce L. Vedral. (Illus.). 288p. (Orig.). 1985. pap. 13.95 (*0-8092-5387-9*) Contemp Bks.

Superdeep Well of the Kola Peninsula. Ed. by Ye A. Kozlovsky. (Exploration of the Deep Continental Crust Ser.). (Illus.). 590p. 1987. 214.95 (*0-387-16416-2*) Spr-Verlag.

Superdistribution: Objects As Property on the Electronic Frontier. Brad J. Cox. (Illus.). 224p. (C). 1996. pap. text ed. 28.95 (*0-201-50208-9*) Addison-Wesley.

Superdog: Raising the Perfect Canine Companion. Michael W. Fox. 1996. 14.95 (*0-87605-743-1*) Howell Bk.

*__Superdoodle Insects.__ Beverly Armstrong. (Illus.). 32p. (J). (gr. 1-6). 1996. 4.95 (*0-88160-295-7*, LW365) Learning Wks.

*__Superdoodle Pets.__ Beverly Armstrong. (Illus.). 32p. (J). (gr. 1-6). 1996. 4.95 (*0-88160-296-5*, LW366) Learning Wks.

Superduper Collector. Susan C. Poskanzer. LC 85-14051. (Illus.). 48p. (Orig.). (J). (gr. 1-3). 1997. pap. 3.50 (*0-8167-0607-7*) Troll Communs.

Superduper Teddy. Johanna Hurwitz. LC 89-13592. (Illus.). 80p. (J). (gr. k-3). 1990. reprint ed. 12.95 (*0-688-09094-X*, Morrow Junior) Morrow.

Superego: Unconscious Conscience - The Key to the Theory & Therapy of Neurosis. Edmund Bergler. LC 88-13652. 372p. 1989. 47.50 (*0-8236-6252-7*) Intl Univs Pr.

Superfag. Daniel Curzon. 218p. (Orig.). 1996. pap. 9.95 (*0-930650-05-0*) IGNA Books.

Superfairness: Applications & Theory. William J. Baumol. (Illus.). 280p. 1986. pap. 13.95 (*0-262-52131-8*) MIT Pr.

Superfamily of ras-Related Genes. Ed. by D. A. Spandidos. (NATO ASI Series A, Life Sciences: Vol. 220). (Illus.). 338p. 1992. 110.00 (*0-306-44085-7*, Plenum Pr) Plenum.

*__Superfamily with Von Willebrand Factor Va Domains.__ Alfonso Colombatti & Roberto Doliana. LC 96-28891. (Molecular Biology Intelligence Unit Ser.). 200p. 1996. 89.95 (*1-57059-387-6*) R G Landes.

Superficial Estimation. John Wieners. (Illus.). (Orig.). 1987. pap. 5.95 (*0-937815-00-4*) Hanuman Bks.

Superficial Fungal Infections. Ed. by Julian L. Verbov. (New Clinical Applications Dermatology Ser.). 1986. lib. bdg. 82.00 (*0-85200-943-7*) Kluwer Ac.

Superficial Keratitis. Ed. by P. C. Maudgal & L. Missotten. 1981. lib. bdg. 117.50 (*90-6193-801-5*) Kluwer Ac.

Superficial Liposculpture: Manual of Technique. Carson M. Lewis et al. LC 92-49210. 137p. 1996. 180.00 (*0-387-97917-4*) Spr-Verlag.

Superfight No. II: The Story Behind the Fights Between Muhammad Ali & Joe Frazier. Joseph Okpaku. LC 74-74429. 1974. 20.00 (*0-89388-165-1*) Okpaku Communications.

Superfine Particle Technology. Ed. by N. Ichinose et al. (Illus.). 236p. 1992. 159.00 (*0-387-19632-3*) Spr-Verlag.

*__Superfinishes by Chrysler Method.__ M. S. Hutchinson. (Technical Papers). 1939. pap. text ed. 30.00 (*1-55589-449-6*) AGMA.

Superflex: Ms. Olympia's Guide to Building a Strong & Sexy Body. Corinna Everson & Jeff Everson. (Illus.). 224p. (Orig.). 1987. pap. 14.95 (*0-8092-4865-4*) Contemp Bks.

Superfluid Phases of Helium-3. Ed. by P. Wolfe & D. Vollhardt. 300p. 1990. 195.00 (*0-85066-412-8*) Taylor & Francis.

Superfluidity & Superconductivity. 3rd ed. D. R. Tilley & J. Tilley. (Graduate Student Series in Physics). (Illus.). 480p. (C). 1990. pap. 54.00 (*0-7503-0033-7*) IOP Pub.

Superfluous Anarchist: Albert Jay Nock. Michael Wreszin. LC 75-154339. 208p. reprint ed. pap. 59.30 (*0-685-15793-8*, 2027526) Bks Demand.

Superfluous Men & the Post-Stalin Thaw: The Alienated Hero in Soviet Prose During the Decade 1953-1963. Thomas F. Rogers. 1972. text ed. 87.70 (*90-279-2118-0*) Mouton.

Superfluous Things: Material Culture & Social Status in Early Modern China. Craig Clunas. (Illus.). 240p. 1992. text ed. 39.95 (*0-252-01930-X*) U of Ill Pr.

Superflyer: Captain John Champion Flyer. Jonathon J. Thompson, Jr. 40p. (J). (gr. 3-6). 1992. 3.95 (*0-933479-08-5*) Thompson.

Superfoods: Allergy Recipes. Marjorie H. Jones. 36p. 1990. pap. text ed. 3.95 (*0-9634931-0-8*) Mast Ent.

Superfoods: Three Hundred Recipes for Foods That Heal Body & Mind. Dolores Riccio. LC 92-36868. 320p. (Orig.). 1993. 26.95 (*0-446-51753-4*) Warner Bks.

*__Superfoods for Life.__ Dolores Riccio. LC 97-15698. 1998. pap. write for info. (*1-55788-280-0*, HP Books) Berkley Pub.

Superfortress over Japan: Twenty-four Hours with a B-29. Jack Delano et al. (Illus.). 96p. 1996. pap. 15.95 (*0-87938-976-1*) Motorbooks Intl.

Superfudge. Judy Blume. 176p. (J). (gr. 2-6). 1981. mass mkt. 3.99 (*0-440-48433-2*, YB BDD) BDD Bks Young Read.

Superfudge. Judy Blume. LC 80-10439. 176p. (J). (gr. 3-6). 1980. pap. 13.99 (*0-525-40522-4*) Dutton Child Bks.

*__Superfudge.__ Judy Blume. (J). 1996. pap. text ed. 12.95 (*1-56014-665-6*) Santillana.

*__Superfudge.__ Judy Blume. (SPA.). (J). (gr. 6-10). 1996. pap. 12.95 (*0-614-20254-X*) Santillana.

Superfudge: A Study Guide. Marianne Croil. Ed. by Joyce Friedland & Rikki Kessler. (Novel-Ties Ser.). (J). (gr. 2-5). 1991. pap. text ed. 15.95 (*0-88122-574-6*) Lrn Links.

Superfudge see Judy Blume

Superfudge see Judy Blume Collection

Superfund: A Legislative History, 3 Vols., Set. Ed. by Helen C. Needham & Mark Menefee. LC 84-10208. 1982. ring bd. 325.00 (*0-911937-08-0*) Environ Law Inst.

*__Superfund: EPA Has Identified Alternatives to Incineration for Cleaning: UP PCB & Dioxin Contamination.__ (Illus.). 37p. (Orig.). (C). 1996. pap. 20.00 (*0-7881-3022-6*) DIANE Pub.

Superfund: Status, Cost, & Timeliness of Hazardous Waste Site Cleanups. (Illus.). 51p. (C). 1994. pap. text ed. 25.00 (*0-7881-1510-3*) DIANE Pub.

Superfund: The Political Economy of Environmental Risk. John A. Hird. LC 93-44891. (C). 1994. text ed. 48.50 (*0-8018-4806-7*); pap. text ed. 16.95 (*0-8018-4807-5*) Johns Hopkins.

Superfund & Economic Development. Larry Morandi. (State Legislative Reports: Vol. 19, No. 9). 7p. 1994. 5.00 (*1-55516-227-4*, 7302-1909) Natl Conf State Legis.

An Asterisk (*) at the beginning of an entry indicates that the title is appearing in BIP for the first time.

Superfund Claims & Litigation Manual. Cuneo, McKenna & Conner Staff. (Environmental Compliance Handbook Ser.). 236p. 1994. pap. text ed. 50.00 (0-471-11246-1) Wiley.

Superfund Cleanups: Nearing Completion, but Challenges Remain. (Illus.). 59p. (Orig.). (C). 1994. pap. text ed. 30.00 (0-7881-0374-1) DIANE Pub.

Superfund Compliance Handbook. Ed. by W. Lawrence Wallace, Sr. (Environmental Compliance Handbook Ser.: Vol. 5). 1989. pap. 49.95 (1-55840-119-9) Exec Ent Pubns.

Superfund Deskbook. rev. ed. Environmental Law Reporter Staff. 380p. 1992. pap. 85.00 (0-911937-21-8) Environ Law Inst.

Superfund II: A New Mandate. (BNA Special Reports). 165p. 1987. 50.00 (0-87179-923-5) BNA Plus.

Superfund Innovative Technology Evaluation Program: Technology Profiles (1992) (Illus.). 388p. (Orig.). (C). 1993. pap. text ed. 65.00 (1-56806-638-4) DIANE Pub.

Superfund Innovative Technology Evaluation Program: Technology Profiles (1994) 7th ed. (Illus.). 499p. (Orig.). (C). 1995. pap. text ed. 75.00 (0-7881-1676-2) DIANE Pub.

Superfund Innovative Technology Evaluation (SITE) Program: Annual Report to Congress 1993. (Illus.). 51p. (Orig.). (C). 1994. pap. text ed. 25.00 (0-7881-1336-4) DIANE Pub.

Superfund Law & Practice. Bradford F. Whitman. LC 90-86312. 328p. 1991. text ed. 87.50 (0-8318-0572-2, B572) Am Law Inst.

***Superfund Liability & Taxes: Petroleum Industry Shares in Their Historical Context.** Jody M. Perkins & Russell O. Jones. (Illus.). 79p. (Orig.). (C). 1997. pap. text ed. 30.00 (0-7881-3776-X) DIANE Pub.

Superfund Manual: Legal & Management Strategies. 5th ed. 468p. 1993. pap. text ed. 115.00 (0-86587-344-5) Gov Insts.

Superfund Risk Assessment in Soil Contamination Studies. Ed. by Keith B. Hoddinott. LC 92-39698. (Special Technical Publication Ser.: No. STP 1158). (Illus.). 340p. 1993. text ed. 50.00 (0-8031-1445-1, 04-011580-38) ASTM.

Superfund Risk Assessment in Soil Contamination Studies: Second Volume, Vol. 2. Ed. by Keith B. Hoddinott. LC 96-15914. (Special Technical Publication (STP): Vol. 1264). (Illus.). 206p. 1996. text ed. 43.00 (0-8031-2000-1, 04-012640-38) ASTM.

***Superfund Strategy.** Ed. by Chris Elfring & Irene S. Gordon. (Illus.). 282p. 1996. reprint ed. pap. 35.00 (0-7881-3230-X) DIANE Pub.

Supergene & Surficial Ore Deposits: Textures & Fabrics see Handbook of Strata-Bound & Stratiform Ore Deposits

Supergiants! The Biggest Dinosaurs. Don Lessem. LC 96-15418. (J). 1997. 14.95 (0-316-52118-3) Little.

***Supergirl Popup Book.** (J). Date not set. pap. 2.95 (0-448-15300-9) Putnam Pub Group.

***Supergolf: Setup, Swing, & Shotmaking Secrets from the Best of the PGA Hall of Fame.** John Andrisani & Rick Grayson. LC 96-9739. (Illus.). 256p. 1997. 25.00 (0-06-270157-6, Harper Ref) HarpC.

Supergrandpa. David Schwartz. (Illus.). (J). (ps-3). 1991. lib. bdg. 16.93 (0-688-09899-1) Lothrop.

Supergrandpa. David M. Schwartz. Orig. Title: Super Grandpa. (Illus.). (J). (ps-3). 1991. 17.00 (0-688-09898-3) Lothrop.

Supergrass. Linda Holorny. (Illus.). 48p. (Orig.). 1996. pap. 11.95 (0-7119-5497-6, OP 47812) Music Sales.

***Supergrass: The Illustrated Story.** Everett True. (Illus.). 80p. 1996. pap. 14.95 (0-7935-6440-9, 00330228) H Leonard.

Supergrasses: Anti-Terrorist Law Enforcement in Northern Ireland. Steven Greer. 250p. 1995. 59.00 (0-19-825766-X) OUP.

Supergrasses: The Use of Accomplice Evidence in Northern Ireland. Tony Grifford. (C). 1988. 30.00 (0-900137-21-5, Pub. by NCCL UK) St Mut.

Supergravities in Diverse Dimensions: Commentary & Reprints, 2 vols., Set. Ed. by Abdus Salam & E. Sezgin. 1533p. 1989. text ed. 152.00 (9971-5-0119-8); pap. text ed. 76.00 (9971-5-0122-8) World Scientific Pub.

Supergravity & Superstrings: A Geometric Perspective, 3 vols. L. Castellani et al. 2216p. 1991. text ed. 205.00 (9971-5-0037-X); pap. text ed. 113.00 (9971-5-0038-8) World Scientific Pub.

***Supergrowth Companies Entrepreneurs in Action.** John Harrison et al. 219p. 1997. pap. 24.99 (0-7506-2750-6, HD31) Buttrwrth-Heinemann.

Superhard Materials, Convection, & Optical Devices. Ed. by Robert B. Heimann et al. (Crystals - Growth, Properties & Applications Ser.). (Illus.). 200p. 1988. 144.95 (0-387-18602-6) Spr-Verlag.

Superheavy Elements. Krishna Kumar. (Illus.). 168p. 1989. 94.00 (0-85274-097-2) IOP Pub.

Superhero. Ann Hodgman. Ed. by Patricia MacDonald. (Stinky Stanley Ser.: No. 3). (Illus.). 128p. (Orig.). 1994. pap. 3.50 (0-671-78567-2, Minstrel Bks) PB.

Superhero Collectibles: A Pictorial Price Guide. William R. Bruegman, III. Ed. by Joanne M. Bruegman. (Illus.). 200p. (Orig.). 1995. pap. 19.95 (0-9632637-5-7) Toy Scouts.

Superhero Companion Book: A History of Superheroes in Movies Television & Comic Books. William Schoell. (Illus.). 240p. 1995. pap. 14.95 (0-8065-1694-1, Citadel Pr) Carol Pub Group.

Superheroes. John Varley & Ricia Mainhardt. 384p. (Orig.). 1995. pap. 12.00 (0-441-00137-8) Ace Bks.

SuperHeroes. John Varley & Ricia Mainhardt. 1996. mass mkt. 5.99 (0-441-00307-9) Ace Bks.

Superhighway to Wealth: Making Money on the Net. Kristy S. Phillips & Kathleen B. Wilde. 207p. 1995. pap. text ed. 19.95 (0-9649424-0-2) Info Directions.

Superhighway to Wealth: Making Money on the Net. 2nd rev. ed. Kristy S. Phillips & Kathleen B. Wilde. Ed. by Lee R. Phillips. (Illus.). 247p. 1996. pap. 12.95 (0-9649424-1-0) Info Directions.

***Superhormone Promise.** William Regelson. 1997. mass mkt. 6.99 (0-671-01003-4, Pocket Books) PB.

Superhuman Life of Gesar of Ling. Alexandra David-Neel & Lama Yongden. Ed. by Kees W. Bolle. LC 77-79120. (Mythology Ser.). 1978. reprint ed. lib. bdg. 37.95 (0-405-10532-0) Ayer.

Superific Science Series, 12 bks., Set. Jim Conway. teacher ed. 106.99 (1-56417-131-0, GA1110) Good Apple.

Superimmunity: Master Your Emotions & Improve Your Health. Paul P. Pearsall. 304p. 1988. mass mkt. 6.99 (0-449-13396-6, GM) Fawcett.

Superimmunity For Kids: What to Feed Your Children to Keep Them Healthy Now & Prevent Disease in Their Future. Leo Galland. 336p. 1989. pap. 14.95 (0-440-50679-4) Dell.

Superinsulation. P. Russevelt. (C). 1987. 130.00 (0-685-33090-7, Pub. by Interntl Solar Energy Soc UK) St Mut.

Superintendent & the School Board: A Call for Excellence. Max O. Heim et al. LC 89-63743. 223p. 1990. 24.95 (0-914607-28-6) Master Tchr.

Superintendent Building Service (U.S.P.S.) Jack Rudman. (Career Examination Ser.: C-1685). 1994. pap. 34.95 (0-8373-1685-5) Nat Learn.

Superintendent for Administrative Services. Jack Rudman. (Career Examination Ser.: C-2815). 1994. pap. 34.95 (0-8373-2815-2) Nat Learn.

Superintendent of Alarms. Jack Rudman. (Career Examination Ser.: C-2965). 1994. pap. 34.95 (0-8373-2965-5) Nat Learn.

Superintendent of Building Inspection. Jack Rudman. (Career Examination Ser.: C-2282). 1994. reprint ed. pap. 39.95 (0-8373-2282-0) Nat Learn.

Superintendent of Buildings & Grounds. Jack Rudman. (Career Examination Ser.: C-1773). 1994. pap. 29.95 (0-8373-1773-8) Nat Learn.

Superintendent of Construction. Jack Rudman. (Career Examination Ser.: C-1500). 1994. pap. 34.95 (0-8373-1500-X) Nat Learn.

Superintendent of Heating & Ventilation. Jack Rudman. (Career Examination Ser.: C-2380). 1994. pap. 39.95 (0-8373-2380-0) Nat Learn.

Superintendent of Highways. Jack Rudman. (Career Examination Ser.: C-2318). 1994. pap. 39.95 (0-8373-2318-5) Nat Learn.

Superintendent of Laundries. Jack Rudman. (Career Examination Ser.: C-1882). 1994. pap. 34.95 (0-8373-1882-3) Nat Learn.

Superintendent of Plant Operations. Jack Rudman. (Career Examination Ser.: C-2478). 1994. pap. 39.95 (0-8373-2478-5) Nat Learn.

Superintendent of Public Works. Jack Rudman. (Career Examination Ser.: C-2305). 1994. reprint ed. pap. 39.95 (0-8373-2305-3) Nat Learn.

Superintendent of Recreation. Jack Rudman. (Career Examination Ser.: C-652). 1994. pap. 34.95 (0-8373-0652-3) Nat Learn.

Superintendent of Sanitation. Jack Rudman. (Career Examination Ser.: C-2457). 1994. pap. 34.95 (0-8373-2457-2) Nat Learn.

Superintendent of Sewer Service. Jack Rudman. (Career Examination Ser.: C-2141). 1994. reprint ed. pap. 39.95 (0-8373-2141-7) Nat Learn.

Superintendent of Sewers. Jack Rudman. (Career Examination Ser.: C-2276). 1994. reprint ed. pap. 39.95 (0-8373-2276-6) Nat Learn.

Superintendent of Street Lighting. Jack Rudman. (Career Examination Ser.: C-3125). 1994. pap. 39.95 (0-8373-3125-0) Nat Learn.

Superintendent of Wastewater Treatment Plant. Jack Rudman. (Career Examination Ser.: C-2963). 1994. pap. 39.95 (0-8373-2963-9) Nat Learn.

Superintendent of Women's Prisons. Jack Rudman. (Career Examination Ser.: C-1744). 1994. reprint ed. pap. 49.95 (0-8373-1744-4) Nat Learn.

***Superintendent Performance Evaluation: Current Practice & Directions for Improvement.** Carl I. Candoli et al. LC 97-2392. (Evaluation in Education & Human Services Ser.). 1997. lib. bdg. 80.00 (0-7923-9891-2) Kluwer Ac.

Superintendent's Handbook of Financial Management. Raymond S. Schmidgall. 150p. (C). 1996. text ed. 34.95 (1-57504-039-5) Ann Arbor Chelsea.

Superintendents' Leadership in School Reform. Dorothy F. Wissler & Flora I. Ortiz. 180p. 1988. 60.00 (1-85000-261-4, Falmer Pr); pap. 29.00 (1-85000-262-2, Falmer Pr) Taylor & Francis.

Superintending for Contractors: How to Bring Jobs in on Time, on Budget. Paul J. Cook. Orig. Title: Superintending for the General Contractor: Field Project Management. 220p. 1991. pap. 35.95 (0-87629-272-4, 67233) ACMDG Co.

Superintending for the General Contractor: Field Project Management see Superintending for Contractors: How to Bring Jobs in on Time, on Budget

Superintending the Poor: Charitable Ladies & Paternal Landlords in British Fiction. Beth F. Tobin. 183p. 1993. 30.00 (0-300-05559-5) Yale U Pr.

Superior: Journeys on an Inland Sea. Gary McGuffin & Joan McGuffin. LC 95-17071. (Illus.). 160p. 1995. 35.00 (1-55971-483-2) NorthWord.

Superior: The Haunted Shore. Bruce Littejohn & Wayland Drew. (Illus.). 176p. 1983. pap. 19.95 (0-8253-0167-X) Beaufort Bks NY.

Superior: The Haunted Shore. rev. ed. Bruce Littejohn & Wayland Drew. (Illus.). 176p. 1995. pap. 24.95 (1-895565-58-8) Firefly Bks Ltd.

Superior Adventures. Craig Charles. 160p. 1992. pap. 16.95 (1-55971-137-X) NorthWord.

Superior Beings-If They Exist, How Would We Know? Game-Theoretic Implications of Omniscience, Immortality, & Incomprehensibility. Steven J. Brams. (Illus.). 192p. 1983. 54.95 (0-387-91223-1); 37.95 (0-387-90877-3) Spr-Verlag.

***Superior Catholics: Memories of a Parochial Education.** Georgeann Cheney & Theodora Meronek. (Illus.). 150p. (Orig.). 1997. pap. 15.95 (1-886028-23-0) Savage Pr.

Superior Court Practice. H. J. Erasmus. Orig. Title: Nathan, Barnett & Brink. 912p. 1994. pap. 80.00 (0-7021-3213-6, Pub. by Juta SA); ring bd. 90.00 (0-7021-3011-7, Pub. by Juta SA) Gaunt.

Superior Customer Service in Marketing. Stull. (SB - Marketing Education Ser.). 1996. pap. 19.95 (0-538-62868-5) S-W Pub.

Superior Death. Nevada Barr. (Anna Pigeon Ser.: No. 2). 320p. 1995. mass mkt. 6.50 (0-380-72362-X) Avon.

Superior Death. large type ed. Nevada Barr. LC 94-14258. 431p. 1994. lib. bdg. 23.95 (0-8161-7446-6, GK Hall) Thorndike Pr.

Superior Fishing: The Striped Bass, Trout, & Black Bass of the Northern States. Robert B. Roosevelt. LC 84-29451. xxiii, 310p. 1985. reprint ed. pap. 8.95 (0-87351-176-X, Borealis Book) Minn Hist.

Superior Flies. Leonard M. Wright, Jr. (Cortland Library). (Illus.). 96p. 1989. pap. 9.95 (1-55821-042-3) Lyons & Burford.

Superior Force: The Conspiracy Behind the Escape of Goeben & Breslau. Geoffrey Miller. (Illus.). 400p. 1996. pap. 25.00 (0-85958-635-9, Pub. by Univ of Hull Pr UK) Paul & Co Pubs.

Superior Health Through Nutrition. William H. Hay. 179p. 1963. reprint ed. spiral bd. 7.50 (0-7873-0385-2) Hlth Research.

Superior Heartland: A Backwoods History, 2 vols., Set, Vols. I & II. C. Fred Rydholm. 1600p. 1989. write for info. (0-9639948-2-4) Superior Hrtland.

Superior Heartland: A Backwoods History, Vol. I. C. Fred Rydholm. LC 89-90710. 850p. 1989. write for info. (0-9639948-0-8) Superior Hrtland.

Superior Heartland: A Backwoods History, Vol. II. C. Fred Rydholm. 750p. 1989. write for info. (0-9639948-1-6) Superior Hrtland.

Superior Home Designs: A107. Randy Byrne. (Illus.). 32p. 1992. 4.95 (0-934039-39-9) Natl Plan Serv.

Superior Limericks. Irving Superior. Ed. by Sally B. Carr. LC 76-9007. 1976. 22.95 (0-87949-067-5) Ashley Bks.

Superior National Forest: A Complete Recreation Guide for Paddlers, Hikers, Anglers, Campers, Mountain Bikers & Skiers. Robert Beymer. LC 89-3229. (Illus.). 272p. (Orig.). 1989. pap. 12.95 (0-89886-168-3) Mountaineers.

Superior North Shore. Thomas F. Waters. LC 87-13585. (Illus.). 380p. 1987. 24.95 (0-8166-1613-2) U of Minn Pr.

Superior Nutrition. 1994. pap. 8.95 (0-9606948-1-1) Willow Pub.

Superior Peninsula: Seasons in the Upper Peninsula of Michigan. Lon L. Emerick. LC 95-92859. (Illus.). vi, 206p. (Orig.). 1996. pap. 17.95 (0-9650577-5-5, TSP-3) N Country.

Superior Performing Asphalt Pavements (Superpave) The Product of the SHRP Asphalt Research Program. Thomas W. Kennedy et al. (SHRP Ser.: A-410). (Illus.). 156p. (Orig.). (C). 1994. pap. text ed. 15.00 (0-309-05821-X) Natl Res Coun.

Superior Person's Book of Words. Peter Bowler & David Godine. 192p. 1990. reprint ed. mass mkt. 5.99 (0-440-20407-0, LE) Dell.

Superior Person's Guide to Everyday Irritations. Russ Lindway. Ed. by Cliff Carle. (Illus.). 224p. (Orig.). 1990. pap. 4.95 (0-918259-23-1) CCC Pubns.

Superior Person's Second Book of Weird & Wonderous Words. Peter Bowler. (Illus.). 1992. 14.95 (0-87923-928-X) Godine.

Superior Product Development: Managing the Process for Innovative Products. Clement C. Wilson et al. LC 95-7533. 1995. pap. 20.95 (1-55786-509-4) Blackwell Pubs.

Superior Selling: Proven System of Selling Strategies Practiced by Salespeople Everywhere. Brian S. Tracy. 432p. 1995. 25.00 (0-671-86519-6) S&S Trade.

Superior Selling Master Guide. Brooks Group, NASRI Staff. 24p. 1993. spiral bd. 3.00 (0-8403-9108-0) Kendall-Hunt.

Superior Service! 1995. pap. 149.00 incl. audio, vhs (1-56052-368-9) Crisp Pubns.

***Superior Service!** William B. Martin. 1995. pap. 19.95 incl. audio (1-56052-369-7) Crisp Pubns.

Superior Supervision: The Ten Percent Solution. Raymond O. Loen. 171p. 19.95 (0-02-919091-6, Free Press) Free Pr.

Superior Team Development Workshop: Trainer's Package. Dennis C. Kinlaw. 1995. ring bd. 99.95 (0-87425-254-7) HRD Press.

Superior Way: A Cruising Guide to Lake Superior. 2nd ed. Bonnie Dahl. Ed. by Paul L. Hayden. LC 91-76960. (Illus.). 340p. 1992. pap. 29.95 (0-942235-14-2) LSPC Inc.

***Superior Wilderness: Isle Royale National Park.** 2nd rev. ed. Napier Shelton. Orig. Title: The Life of Isle Royale. Date not set. pap. 14.95 (0-614-30220-X) Isle Royale Hist.

Superior Women. Alice Adams. 384p. 1985. mass mkt. 5.99 (0-449-20746-3, Crest) Fawcett.

Superiority & Social Interest: A Collection of Later Writings. Alfred Adler. Ed. by Heinz L. Ansbacher & Rowena R. Ansbacher. 1979. reprint ed. pap. 14.95 (0-393-00910-6) Norton.

Superiority of the Black Athlete. Entine. 1997. pap. 24.00 (0-02-536155-4) Macmillan.

Superiority of the Son. Barry Cunningham. 1990. pap. 3.50 (0-89137-113-3) Quality Pubns.

SuperJournal Project. D. J. Pullinger. 60p. 1994. pap. 52.00 (0-7503-0102-3) IOP Pub.

Superkid! Janice L. Smith. (Trophy Chapter Bk.: No. 3). (Illus.). 96p. (J). (gr. 1-4). 1995. pap. 3.95 (0-06-442005-1, Trophy) HarpC Child Bks.

***Superlative Man.** Herbert Thomas. LC 97-268. 1997. 22.00 (0-374-27209-3) FS&G.

Superlattices & Other Heterostructures: Symmetry & Optical Phenomena. P. E. Pikus & E. L. Ivchenko. LC 94-3452. (Springer Series in Solid-State Sciences: Vol. 110). 1995. 107.95 (0-387-58197-9) Spr-Verlag.

***Superlattices & Other Heterostructures: Symmetry & Optical Phenomena, Vol. 110.** 2nd ed. E. L. Ivchenko & Grigori I. Pikus. LC 96-46761. (Series in Solid-State Sciences). 1997. pap. write for info. (3-540-62030-3) Spr-Verlag.

***SuperLawyers: Profiles of America's Courtroom Celebrities.** Colin Evans. Ed. by Carol Schwartz. 320p. 1997. 17.95 (1-57859-004-3) Visible Ink Pr.

SuperLCCS: Library of Congress Classification Schedules Combined with Additions & Changes Through 1993 for Law & Politcal Science, 11 vols. Ed. by Rita Runchock-Droste & Kathleen Droste. 1994. 1,040.00 (0-8103-9903-2) Gale.

SuperLCCS: Library of Congress Classification Schedules Combined with Additions & Changes Through 1993 for Literature, 14 vols. Ed. by Rita Runchock-Droste & Kathleen Droste. 1994. 1,206.00 (0-8103-9905-9) Gale.

SuperLCCS: Library of Congress Classification Schedules Combined with Additions & Changes Through 1993 for Philosophy & Religion, 5 vols. 93th ed. Ed. by Rita Runchock-Droste & Kathleen Droste. 1994. 410.00 (0-8103-9900-8) Gale.

SuperLCCS: Library of Congress Classification Schedules Combined with Additions & Changes Through 1994 BR-BY. 94th ed. Ed. by Rita Runchock-Droste & Kathleen Droste. 1995. 52.00 (0-8103-6008-X, 033171) Gale.

SuperLEAR Workshop Proceedings. Ed. by C. Amsler. (Institute of Physics Conference Ser.: No. 124). (Illus.). 460p. 1992. 183.00 (0-85498-414-3) IOP Pub.

Superlearning. Sheila Ostrander et al. 360p. 1982. mass mkt. 6.99 (0-440-38424-9, LE) Dell.

Superlearning: Maximize Your Memory. Lynn Schroeder. 1988. 9.95 (0-671-66391-7) S&S Trade.

Superlearning: Optimal Weight. Lynn Schroeder. 1988. 9.95 (0-671-66386-0) S&S Trade.

***Superlearning 2000.** Lynn Schroeder. 1997. mass mkt. 6.99 (0-440-22388-1) Dell.

Superlearning Two Thousand: The New Technologies of Self-Employment. Emily D. Gunter. Ed. by Ruth Hall & Linda Harshberger. (Illus.). 96p. (Orig.). 1993. pap. 9.95 (0-9627145-3-4, Cyrus Pr) Waterside Prodns.

Superlearning und Suggestopadie: Grundlagen-Andwendung-Kritik-Perspektiven. Ruprecht S. Buar et al. 135p. 1990. 30.50 (3-468-49449-1) Langenscheidt.

Superlearning 2000: New, Triple-Fast Ways You Can Learn, Earn, & Succeed in the 21st Century. Lynn Schroeder & Sheila Ostrander. 448p. 1995. reprint ed. pap. 12.95 (0-440-50714-6, Dial Pr) Dell.

Superleverage. Paul Sarnoff. 1991. 24.95 (0-13-877804-3) P-H.

Superlove Says. L. Tom Letchworth. LC 77-71488. 168p. 1977. pap. 4.00 (0-9602334-0-7) Superlove.

Superluminal. Vonda N. McIntyre. LC 83-8568. 298p. 1983. 25.00 (0-89366-189-9) Ultramarine Pub.

Superluminal Radio Sources. Ed. by J. Anton Zensus & Timothy J. Pearson. 300p. 1987. 64.95 (0-521-34560-X) Cambridge U Pr.

Supermagnets, Hard Magnetic Materials. Ed. by Gary J. Long & Fernande Grandjean. (C). 1991. lib. bdg. 275.00 (0-7923-1092-6) Kluwer Ac.

***Supermale.** Alfred Jarry. 1998. pap. text ed. 13.95 (1-878972-25-1) Exact Change.

***Superman.** Golden Books Staff. (J). 1997. pap. text ed. 1.09 (0-307-08705-0) Western Pub.

Superman: At Earth's End. Tom Veitch. Ed. by Carlin. (Illus.). 48p. 1995. pap. 4.95 (1-56389-243-X) DC Comics.

Superman: Attack of the Robot. Joe Edkin. (J). (ps-3). 1996. pap. text ed. 5.95 (0-307-13071-1, Golden Pr) Western Pub.

Superman: Bizarro World. DC Comics Staff. Ed. by Bob Kahan. (Illus.). 128p. 1996. pap. 9.95 (1-56389-260-X) DC Comics.

***Superman: Distant Fires.** Howard Chaykin. 1997. pap. text ed. 5.95 (1-56389-289-8) DC Comics.

Superman: Eradication!: The Origin of the Eradicator. Ed. by Bob Kahan. (Illus.). 160p. 1995. pap. 12.95 (1-56389-193-X) DC Comics.

Superman: Krisis of the Krimson Kryptonite. Ed. by Bob Kahan. (Illus.). 176p. 1996. pap. 12.95 (1-56389-275-8, Paradox) DC Comics.

Superman: Last Son of Krypton. Elliot S. Maggin. 22.95 (0-8488-0118-0) Amereon Ltd.

Superman: Panic in the Sky. Ed. by Mike Carlin. (Illus.). 192p. (J). 1993. pap. 9.95 (1-56389-094-1) DC Comics.

Superman: Shadow Over Metropolis. (Favorite Sound Story Bks.). (Illus.). 20p. (J). (ps). 1995. 9.95 (0-307-70930-2, Golden Pr) Western Pub.

Superman: Speeding Bullets. J. M. DeMatteis. Ed. by Mike Carlin. (Illus.). 48p. (J). 1993. pap. 4.95 (1-56389-117-4) DC Comics.

***Superman: The Death of Clark Kent.** Ed. by Bob Kahan. (Illus.). 320p. 1997. pap. 19.95 (1-56389-323-1) DC Comics.

Superman: The Death of Superman. Ed. by Bob Kahan. (Illus.). 168p. (J). 1992. pap. 4.95 (1-56389-097-6) DC Comics.

Superman: The Earth Stealers. John Byrne. Ed. by Dennis O'Neil. (Illus.). 48p. 1989. pap. 2.95 (*1-56389-067-4*) DC Comics.

***Superman: The Lost Son of Krypton.** Tom Campbell. Ed. by John Sahler. (Magic Touch Talking Bks.). (Illus.). (J). (ps-2). 1997. 19.99 (*1-888208-36-8*) Hasbro.

Superman: The Return of Superman. deluxe ed. Ed. by Bob Kahan. (Illus.). 480p. (J). 1993. pap. 14.95 (*1-56389-149-2*) DC Comics.

Superman: Time & Time Again. DC Comics Staff. Ed. by Bob Kahan. 208p. (J). 1994. pap. 7.50 (*1-56389-129-8*) DC Comics.

Superman: World without a Superman. Ed. by Bob Kahan. (Illus.). 240p. 1993. pap. 7.50 (*1-56389-118-2*) DC Comics.

Superman & Son. Ralph Schoenstein. (Illus.). 156p. 1995. pap. 14.95 (*0-8135-2194-7*) Rutgers U Pr.

Superman & the Flash: Race Around the World. Joe Edkin. (J). (ps-3). 1996. pap. text ed. 3.95 (*0-307-12931-4*, Golden Pr) Western Pub.

Superman Archives, Vol. 1. Jerry Siegel. Ed. by Mark Waid & Richard Bruning. (Illus.). 272p. 1989. 39.95 (*0-930289-47-1*) DC Comics.

Superman Archives, Vol. 2. Jerry Siegel. Ed. by Dale Crane. (Illus.). 272p. 1990. 39.95 (*0-930289-76-5*) DC Comics.

Superman Archives, Vol. 3. Jerry Siegel. Ed. by M. Gold & M. Hill. (Illus.). 272p. 1991. 39.95 (*1-56389-002-X*) DC Comics.

Superman at Fifty: The Persistence. Ed. by Dennis Dooley & Gary Engle. LC 87-15221. (Illus.). 192p. 1987. 16.95 (*0-940601-00-1*) Octavia Ohio.

Superman Collector's Set. (Illus.). (Orig.). 1996. pap. 11.70 (*1-56389-283-9*) DC Comics.

Superman III. William Kotzwinkle. 1983. 2.95 (*0-446-32199-0*); 2.95 (*0-446-32233-4*) Warner Bks.

Superman in Action Comics: Featuring the Complete Covers of the First 25 Years. Mark Waid. (Tiny Folios Ser.). (Illus.). 320p. 1992. pap. 11.95 (*1-55859-595-3*) Abbeville Pr.

Superman Lives. D. C. Comics Staff. 1993. 17.00 (*1-57042-024-6*) Warner Bks.

Superman, No. 2: Featuring the Complete Covers of the Second 25 Years, Vol. 2. Mark Waid. (Tiny Folios Ser.). (Illus.). 320p. 1994. pap. 11.95 (*1-55859-609-7*) Abbeville Pr.

Superman Puzzle & Game Book. DC Comics Staff. 160p. (YA). 1995. 3.99 (*0-8125-7733-7*) Tor Bks.

Superman Sourcebook. Steve Crow. 1989. pap. 10.00 (*0-912771-82-8*) Mayfair Games.

Superman Story, Vol. 1. Marvin Pasko. 160p. 1995. 3.99 (*0-8125-7742-6*) Tor Bks.

Superman Syndrome: Finding God's Stregnth Where You Least Expect it. Jack Kuhatschek. 176p. 1995. 14.99 (*0-310-49771-X*) Zondervan.

Superman vs. Aliens. unabridged ed. Dan Jurgens. (Illus.). 152p. (Orig.). (YA). (gr. 7 up). 1996. pap. 17.95 (*1-56971-167-4*) Dark Horse Comics.

***Superman/Batman: Alternate Destinies.** (Illus.). 232p. 1996. pap. 14.95 (*1-56389-272-3*) DC Comics.

Superman/Batman: Alternate Histories. Ed. by Bob Kahan. (Illus.). 224p. 1996. pap. 14.95 (*1-56389-263-4*) DC Comics.

Superman/Doomsday: Hunter/Prey. Dan Jurgens. Ed. by Bob Kahan. (Illus.). 160p. 1995. pap. 14.95 (*1-56389-201-4*) DC Comics.

Supermanifold: Poems from Ukraine. Stephen Duplij. Ed. by Roger E. Egan, Sr. Tr. by Nina G. Shapiro from RUS. (New Freedoms Poetry Ser.). 96p. (Orig.). pap. write for info. (*0-9632687-2-4*) PenRose Pub.

Supermanifolds. 2nd ed. Bryce DeWitt. (Cambridge Monographs on Mathematical Physics). 400p. (C). 1992. text ed. 135.00 (*0-521-41320-6*); pap. text ed. 47.95 (*0-521-42377-5*) Cambridge U Pr.

Supermanifolds: Theory & Applications. A. Rogers & P. Howe. 300p. 1998. text ed. 53.00 (*981-02-1228-3*) World Scientific Pub.

Supermanifolds Geometrical Methods & Conformal Groups, Lectures on. H. D. Doebner et al. 136p. 1989. text ed. 74.00 (*9971-5-0808-7*) World Scientific Pub.

***Superman's Metropolis.** Jean-Marc et al. Ed. by Mike Carlin. (Illus.). 64p. 1996. pap. 5.95 (*1-56389-242-1*) DC Comics.

Superman's Song: The Story of the Crash Test Dummies. Stephen O'Stick. Date not set. pap. 14.95 (*1-55082-130-X*, Pub. by Quarry Pr CN) LPC InBook.

Superman's World of Krypton. Paul Kupperberg. 160p. 1995. 3.99 (*0-8125-7738-8*) Tor Bks.

Supermarine Aircraft since 1914. rev. ed. C. F. Andrews & E. B. Morgan. (Putnam Aviation Ser.). (Illus.). 399p. 1989. 31.95 (*0-87021-614-7*) Naval Inst Pr.

Supermarine Spitfire. Mike Spick. 1996. 6.99 (*0-517-18463-X*) Random Hse Value.

Supermarket. Gibbons. (J). 14.95 (*0-06-022713-3*, HarpT); lib. bdg. 14.89 (*0-06-022714-1*, HarpT) HarpC.

***Supermarket.** Mickael Taddeo. 1996. pap. text ed. 13.95 (*0-9629316-6-7*) A One Pub.

***Supermarket Branching.** Rebecca J. Hiatt. (Executive Briefing Ser.). 14p. (Orig.). 1996. pap. 39.00 (*1-889394-35-1*) Credit Union Execs.

***Supermarket Design.** Retail Reporting Staff. 1996. 55.00 (*0-688-14593-0*) Morrow.

***Supermarket Design.** Rockport Publishers Editorial Staff. Date not set. Not sold separately (*0-688-08382-X*) Morrow.

Supermarket Design, No. 1. Ed. by Martin M. Pegler. (Illus.). 208p. 1996. 59.95 (*0-934590-79-6*) Retail Report.

***Supermarket Guide: Food Choices for You & Your Family.** Mary A. Hess. (Nutrition Now Ser.). 176p. (Orig.). 1997. pap. 5.95 (*1-56561-110-1*) Chronimed.

Supermarket News Retailers & Wholesalers Directory 1996. 1000p. 1996. pap. 300.00 (*1-56367-092-5*) Fairchild.

Supermarket Nutrition Counter. Annette B. Natow & Jo-Ann Heslin. Ed. by Julie Rubinstein. 608p. (Orig.). 1995. mass mkt. 5.99 (*0-671-78328-9*) PB.

***Supermarket Nutrition Counter.** 2nd ed. Annette B. Natow. 1997. mass mkt. 6.99 (*0-671-89473-0*) PB.

Supermarket Shopper's Guide to Fat Free Foods. Donal O'Reilly. 108p. (Orig.). 1995. pap. 3.95 (*0-9643726-6-5*) Onomy Hse.

Supermarket Sorceress: Spells, Charms, & Enchantments That You Can Make from Supermarket Ingredients. Lexa Roseanne. 1996. pap. 8.99 (*0-312-95768-8*) Tor Bks.

***Supermarket Sorceress Sexy Hex, Vol. 1.** Rosean. 1997. mass mkt. write for info. (*0-312-96328-9*) St Martin.

Supermarket Trap: The Consumer & the Food Industry. rev. ed. Jennifer Cross. LC 75-10806. (Illus.). 318p. reprint ed. pap. 90.70 (*0-317-27929-7*, 2056031) Bks Demand.

***Supermarket Tricks: More Than 125 Ways to Improvise Good Sex.** Jay Wiseman. 128p. (Orig.). 1996. pap. 11.95 (*0-9639763-6-2*) Greenery Pr.

Supermarkets & Department Stores, LB 21-86. BSRIA Staff. (C). 1986. 75.00 (*0-86022-173-3*, Pub. by Build Servs Info Assn UK) St Mut.

Supermarkets Transformed: Understanding Organizational & Technological Innovations. John P. Walsh. LC 92-35961. (Arnold & Caroline Rose Monograph Series of the American Sociological Association). 198p. (C). 1993. text ed. 36.00 (*0-8135-1969-1*) Rutgers U Pr.

Supermassive Black Holes. Ed. by Minas Kafatos. 360p. 1988. text ed. 85.00 (*0-521-34246-5*) Cambridge U Pr.

***Supermax.** Laura Lerman. LC 97-6767. (Illus.). (J). 1998. 11.99 (*0-679-88659-1*); lib. bdg. 13.99 (*0-679-98659-6*) Random.

Supermazes: Thirty Mind Twisters for Puzzle Buffs, Game Nuts, & Other Smart People. Bob Abbott. 80p. 1997. per., pap. 14.00 (*0-7615-0701-9*) Prima Pub.

Supermem: Hebrew Reading & Writing Program. Nily Glaser. 356p. 1991. pap. text ed. 9.95 (*0-9632663-0-6*); pap. text ed. 9.95 (*0-9632663-1-4*) Gan Pub.

Supermembranes & Physics in 2 plus 1 Dimensions. Ed. by Michael J. Duff et al. 468p. (C). 1990. text ed. 118.00 (*981-02-0131-1*) World Scientific Pub.

Supermemory: The Revolution. Sheila Ostrander & Lynn Schroeder. 384p. 1991. 21.95 (*0-88184-691-0*) Carroll & Graf.

Supermen: The Story of Seymour Cray & the Technical Wizards Behind the Supercomputer. Charles J. Murray. LC 96-36448. 1997. text ed. 24.95 (*0-471-04885-2*) Wiley.

Supermom Wonderwife: Tales of Transition. Beverly Kalinin. LC 78-52241. 1978. 3.50 (*0-686-08753-4*) Morningsun Pubns.

SuperMotivation: A Blueprint for Energizing Your Organization from Top to Bottom. Dean R. Spitzer. LC 95-18428. 224p. 1995. 22.95 (*0-8144-0286-0*) AMACOM.

Supernatural. Jillian Powell. (Mysteries of...Ser.). (Illus.). 40p. (J). (gr. 4-6). 1996. lib. bdg. 17.40 (*0-7613-0455-X*, Copper Beech Bks) Millbrook Pr.

Supernatural. Jillian Powell. (Mysteries of...Ser.). (Illus.). 40p. (J). (gr. 4-6). 1996. pap. 6.95 (*0-7613-0470-3*, Copper Beech Bks) Millbrook Pr.

Supernatural: Making Room for the Power of God. A. B. Simpson. 110p. 1994. pap. 7.99 (*0-87509-564-X*) Chr Pubns.

Supernatural & English Fiction. Glen Cavaliero. 320p. 1995. 32.00 (*0-19-212607-5*) OUP.

Supernatural & Mysterious Japan. Catrien Ross. 1995. pap. text ed. 8.95 (*4-900737-37-2*, Pub. by Yen Bks JA) C E Tuttle.

Supernatural & Occult Fiction Series, 63 bks, Set. Douglas A. Menville. 1976. lib. bdg. 1,516.50 (*0-405-08107-3*) Ayer.

Supernatural & Superhuman Unit B: Study Guide, Unit B. Ed. by Deakin University Press Staff. 152p. (C). 1990. pap. 75.00 (*0-7300-0720-0*, HUL305, Pub. by Deakin Univ AT) St Mut.

Supernatural Britain: A Guide to Britain's Most Haunted Locations. Peter Hough. (Illus.). 208p. 1995. pap. 14.95 (*0-7499-1507-2*, Pub. by Piatkus Bks UK) London Brdge.

Supernatural Childbirth. Jackie Mize. 128p. 1993. pap. 7.99 (*0-89274-756-0*, HH-756) Harrison Hse.

Supernatural Evangelism. 2nd rev. ed. James B. Richards. 1997. pap. 12.00 (*0-924748-05-2*) Impact Ministries.

***Supernatural Events in the Life of an Ordinary Man.** Jim Ammerman. 192p. (Orig.). 1996. pap. 10.00 (*1-883893-48-8*) WinePress Pub.

Supernatural Experiences As Recorded in the Four Gospels & the First Chapter of Acts. (Walk with Jesus Ser.). 163p. 1990. pap. 20.00 (*1-57277-526-2*) Script Rsch.

***Supernatural Factfinders.** Smithmark Staff. 1997. 4.98 (*0-7651-9256-X*) Smithmark.

Supernatural Fiction for Teens: More Than 1300 Good Paperbacks to Read for Wonderment, Fear, & Fun. 2nd ed. Cosette Kies. ix, 267p. 1992. lib. bdg. 25.00 (*0-87287-940-2*) Libs Unl.

Supernatural Fiction Writers, Vol. 1. Bleiler. 1985. 110.00 (*0-684-18621-7*, S&S) S&S Trade.

Supernatural Fiction Writers, Vol. 2. Bleiler. 1985. 110.00 (*0-684-18622-5*) Macmillan.

Supernatural Fiction Writers: Fantasy & Horror, 2 vols., Vol. 2. Ed. by E. F. Bleiler. 1169p. 1985. 200.00 (*0-684-17808-7*) S&S Trade.

Supernatural Forces: Belief, Difference, & Power in Contemporary Works by Ethnic Women. Bonnie Winsbro. LC 93-4237. 232p. 1993. pap. 16.95 (*0-87023-880-9*); lib. bdg. 40.00 (*0-87023-879-5*) U of Mass Pr.

Supernatural Fruit of the Holy Spirit. Lester Sumrall. 70p. (C). 1986. pap. text ed. 12.00 (*0-937580-93-7*) LeSEA Pub Co.

Supernatural Horizons: From Glory to Glory. Charles Hunter & Frances Hunter. 1983. pap. 6.95 (*0-917726-52-9*) Hunter Bks.

Supernatural Horror in Literature. H. P. Lovecraft. Ed. by E. F. Bleiler. 1973. reprint ed. pap. 3.95 (*0-486-20105-8*) Dover.

***Supernatural Identity.** 160p. 1996. mass mkt. 5.99 (*0-89274-949-0*, HH949) Harrison Hse.

Supernatural in Gothic Fiction: Horror, Belief, & Literary Change. Robert F. Geary. LC 92-18151. 160p. 1992. text ed. 69.95 (*0-7734-9164-3*) E Mellen.

Supernatural in Relation to the Natural. James McCosh. LC 75-3267. reprint ed. 38.00 (*0-404-59255-4*) AMS Pr.

Supernatural in the Modern German Drama. G. Baerg. 1972. 59.95 (*0-8490-1160-4*) Gordon Pr.

Supernatural in the Tragedies of Euripides. Ernest H. Klotsche. 107p. 1980. 15.00 (*0-89005-343-X*) Ares.

Supernatural in Tragedy (1915) Charles E. Whitmore. 378p. 15.00 (*0-614-09423-2*) Appel.

Supernatural Index: A Listing of Fantasy, Supernatural, Occult, Weird, & Horror Anthologies. Michael Ashley & William G. Contento. LC 95-6290. (Bibliographies & Indexes in Science Fiction, Fantasy & Horror: No. 5). 952p. 1995. text ed. 195.00 (*0-313-24030-2*, Greenwood Pr) Greenwood.

Supernatural Living. A. L. Gill & Joyce Gill. 139p. (SPA.). 1993. spiral bd. 12.95 (*0-941975-18-5*) Power Hse Pub.

Supernatural Living. A. L. Gill & Joyce Gill. 129p. (KOR.). 1993. spiral bd. 12.95 (*0-941975-22-3*) Power Hse Pub.

Supernatural Living: Through the Gifts of the Holy Spirit. 112p. (Orig.). 1995. pap. 9.95 (*0-941975-34-7*) Power Hse Pub.

Supernatural Living: Through the Gifts of the Holy Spirit. A. L. Gill & Joyce Gill. 118p. (RUS.). 1994. spiral bd. 12.95 (*0-941975-30-4*) Power Hse Pub.

Supernatural Overtones. Ron Padgett & Clark Coolidge. 1990. pap. 7.50 (*0-935724-40-0*) Figures.

Supernatural Poetry. Ed. by Gary W. Crawford. (Illus.). 55p. 1995. reprint ed. pap. 4.00 (*0-913045-04-7*) Gothic Pr.

Supernatural Power. James McKeever. 396p. (C). pap. text ed. 9.99 (*0-86694-120-7*) Omega Pubns OR.

Supernatural Power & the Occult. Lynn Walker. 1977. pap. 4.00 (*0-88027-093-4*) Firm Foun Pub.

Supernatural Prayer & Fasting. Richard Booker. 196p. (Orig.). 1993. pap. 8.99 (*1-56043-117-2*) Destiny Image.

Supernatural Provision. Bill Panko & Margaret Panko. 150p. (Orig.). Date not set. pap. 14.95 (*1-885342-27-6*) Creative Ways.

Supernatural Relationships: How to Get Closer to the People You Care For. Ed Gungor. 179p. (Orig.). 1991. pap. 7.99 (*0-9624161-2-6*) Mini Res Fndt.

Supernatural Sleuths. Ed. by Martin H. Greenberg & Charles G. Waugh. 352p. 1996. pap. 5.99 (*0-451-45579-7*) NAL-Dutton.

Supernatural Steam. (Ghost Ser.). (Illus.). 144p. 1993. pap. 7.95 (*0-7117-0593-3*) Seven Hills Bk.

Supernatural Stories. Illus. by Martin Salisbury. LC 96-3381. 224p. (J). (gr. 4-9). 1996. 6.95 (*0-7534-5026-7*, Kingfisher LKC) LKC.

Supernatural Sublime: The Metaphysics of Terror in Anglo-American Romanticism. Jack G. Voller. LC 94-9360. 250p. 1994. lib. bdg. 30.00 (*0-87580-194-3*) N Ill U Pr.

Supernatural Tales. Arthur Conan Doyle. 1995. 27.95 (*0-8488-0752-9*) Amereon Ltd.

Supernatural Tales: Excursions into Fantasy. Vernon Lee. LC 87-60976. 222p. 8700. 27.00 (*0-7206-0680-2*, Pub. by P Owen Ltd UK) Dufour.

Supernatural Tales of Sir Arthur Conan Doyle. Ed. by Peter Haining. (Illus.). 272p. 1995. 21.95 (*0-572-01453-8*, Pub. by Foulsham UK) Assoc Pubs Grp.

Supernatural Tales of Thomas Hardy. Ed. by Peter Haining. 288p. 1995. 21.95 (*0-572-01489-9*, Pub. by Foulsham UK) Assoc Pubs Grp.

Supernatural, the Occult, & the Bible. Gerald A. Larue. 303p. (C). 1990. 26.95 (*0-87975-615-2*) Prometheus Bks.

Supernatural Vanishings: Otherworldly Disappearances. Rodney Davies. LC 95-46883. 192p. 1996. pap. 10.95 (*0-8069-4896-5*) Sterling.

Supernatural Weapon of Love. Bill Panko & Margaret Panko. 112p. 1995. per., pap. 7.95 (*1-885342-01-2*) Creative Ways.

***Supernova.** (Star Wars Adventures Ser.). 15.00 (*0-87431-195-0*, 40066) West End Games.

Supernova. Roger M. Allen & Eric Kotani. 352p. (Orig.). 1991. mass mkt. 4.50 (*0-380-76060-6*) Avon.

Supernova. Russ Ebbets. 150p. 1995. pap. write for info. (*0-9648279-0-5*) Off the Road Pr.

Supernova Search Charts & Handbook. Gregg D. Thompson & James T. Bryan; Jr. (Illus.). 96p. 1990. text ed. 120.00 (*0-521-26721-8*) Cambridge U Pr.

Supernova Story. Laurence A. Marschall. LC 88-17978. (Illus.). 316p. 1988. 22.95 (*0-306-42955-1*, Plenum Pr) Plenum.

Supernova Story. Laurence A. Marschall. LC 93-43454. (Science Library). 344p. (C). 1994. pap. 14.95 (*0-691-03633-0*) Princeton U Pr.

***Supernova Vignettes.** 3rd ed. James A. Green. LC 94-96144. (Physics Ser.: Vol. 1). (Illus.). 250p. 1997. 88.88 (*1-890121-11-8*, 02-01-03) Grnwd Resch.

Supernova 1987A in the Large Magellanic Cloud. Ed. by Minas Kafatos. 420p. 1988. text ed. 100.00 (*0-521-35575-3*) Cambridge U Pr.

Supernovae. Ed. by S. Bludman et al. (Houches Summer School Proceedings Ser.: Vol. 54). 878p. 1994. 305.00 (*0-444-81474-4*, North Holland) Elsevier.

Supernovae. Paul Murdin & Leslie Murdin. 260p. 1985. text ed. 30.95 (*0-521-30038-X*) Cambridge U Pr.

Supernovae. Ed. by A. Petschek et al. (Astronomy & Astrophysics Library). xiii, 293p. 1990. 87.95 (*0-387-97069-X*) Spr-Verlag.

Supernovae. Ed. by David N. Schramm. (Astrophysics & Space Science Library: No. 66). 1977. lib. bdg. 80.00 (*90-277-0806-1*) Kluwer Ac.

Supernovae: A Survey of Current Research. Martin J. Rees & R. Stoneham. 1982. 307.00 (*90-277-1442-8*) Kluwer Ac.

Supernovae: Sixth Jerusalam Winter School for Theoretical Physics. Ed. by T. Piran et al. 344p. (C). 1990. text ed. 74.00 (*9971-5-0963-6*); pap. text ed. 36.00 (*9971-5-0964-4*) World Scientific Pub.

Supernovae: The Tenth Santa Cruz Summer Workshop in Astronomy & Astrophysics, July 9-21, 1989, Lick Observatory. Ed. by S. E. Woosley. (Santa Cruz Summer Workshops Ser.). (Illus.). 792p. 1990. 79.95 (*0-387-97071-1*) Spr-Verlag.

Supernovae & Nucleosynthesis: An Investigation of the History of Matter, from the Big Bang to the Present. David Arnett. (Princeton Series in Astrophysics). 496p. 1996. text ed. 85.00 (*0-691-01148-6*); pap. text ed. 39.50 (*0-691-01147-8*) Princeton U Pr.

Supernovae & Stellar Evolution: Proceedings of the School & Workshop, Goa, Indian, 10-17 March 1989. Ed. by A. Ray & R. Velusamy. 340p. (C). 1991. text ed. 104.00 (*981-02-0657-7*) World Scientific Pub.

Supernovae & Stellar Wind. Tatjana A. Lozinskaya. Tr. by Marc Damashek. (Translation Ser.). (Illus.). 352p. 1990. 120.00 (*0-88318-659-4*) Am Inst Physics.

Supernovae & Supernova Remnants: IAU Colloquium 145. Ed. by Richard McCray & Zhenri Wang. (Illus.). 400p. (C). 1996. text ed. 69.95 (*0-521-46080-8*) Cambridge U Pr.

Supernovae Remnants. Danziger. (International Astronomical Union Symposia Ser.). 1983. pap. text ed. 112.00 (*90-277-1667-6*); lib. bdg. 211.50 (*90-277-1666-8*) Kluwer Ac.

Supernovae Spectra: La Jolla Institute, 1980. Ed. by Roland Meyerhoff & George H. Gillespie. (AIP Conference Proceedings Ser.: No. 63). 173p. 1980. lib. bdg. 18.25 (*0-88318-162-2*) Am Inst Physics.

Supernutrition for Menopause. Ann L. Gittleman. 256p. (Orig.). 1993. mass mkt. 5.99 (*0-671-78100-6*) PB.

Supernutrition for Women. Ann L. Gittleman. 272p. 1991. pap. 13.95 (*0-553-35328-4*) Bantam.

Superorganic. A. L. Kroeber. (Reprint Series in Social Sciences). (C). 1993. reprint ed. pap. text ed. 3.90 (*0-8290-4088-9*, S-154) Irvington.

Superoxide Dismutase, Vol. I. Ed. by Larry W. Oberley. 168p. 1982. 97.00 (*0-8493-6240-7*, QP603, CRC Reprint) Franklin.

Superoxide Dismutase, Vol. II. Ed. by Larry W. Oberley. 192p. 1982. 110.00 (*0-8493-6241-5*, CRC Reprint) Franklin.

Superoxide Dismutase: Pathological States, Vol. III. Ed. by Larry W. Oberley. 280p. 1985. 157.00 (*0-8493-6242-3*, QP603, CRC Reprint) Franklin.

Superoxide Ion: Chemistry & Biological Implications, Vol. I. Igor B. Afanas'Ev. 208p. 1989. 216.00 (*0-8493-5451-X*, QP535) CRC Pr.

Superoxide Ion, Vol. II: Chemistry & Biological Implications. Igor B. Afanas'ev. 208p. 1991. 216.00 (*0-8493-5452-8*, QP535) CRC Pr.

SuperPaint 3.0 for Power Users. Evelyn Alemanni. 256p. 1991. pap. 18.95 (*0-8306-3379-0*, Windcrest) TAB Bks.

Superpave Binder: Performance Graded Asphalt Binder Specification & Testing. (Illus.). 72p. 1994. 12.00 (*0-614-07181-X*, SP-1) Asphalt Inst.

Superpave Level One Mix Design. (Illus.). 128p. 1995. 16.00 (*0-614-07182-8*, SP-2) Asphalt Inst.

Superpave Mix Design Manual for New Construction & Overlays. Ronald J. Cominsky. 172p. (Orig.). (C). 1994. pap. text ed. 15.00 (*0-309-05804-X*, SHRP-A-407) SHRP.

Superpave Mix Design System, Manual of Specifications, Test Methods & Practices. Ed. by J. Youtcheff et al. 253p. (Orig.). (C). 1994. pap. text ed. 20.00 (*0-309-05764-7*, SHRP-A-379) SHRP.

Superplastic Forming: Proceedings of a Symposium. Ed. by Suphal P. Agrawal. LC 84-72936. (Conference Proceedings - American Society for Metals Ser.). (Illus.). 100p. reprint ed. pap. 28.50 (*0-8357-3559-1*, 2034323) Bks Demand.

Superplastic Forming of Structural Alloys: Proceedings of a Symposium. Metallurgical Society of AIME Staff. Ed. by C. H. Hamilton & Neil E. Paton. LC 82-81860. 426p. reprint ed. pap. 121.50 (*0-317-42099-2*, 2026228) Bks Demand.

Superplasticity: Materials Research Society International Symposium Proceedings-IMAM. Ed. by M. Kobayashi & F. Wakai. 317p. 1989. text ed. 52.00 (*1-55899-036-4*, IMAM-7) Materials Res.

Superplasticity: 60 Years after Pearson. Ed. by Norman Ridley. 400p. 1995. 100.00 (*0-901716-77-4*, Pub. by Inst Materials UK) Ashgate Pub Co.

Superplasticity & Superplastic Forming: Proceedings of An International Conference on Superplasticity & Superplastic Forming-Sponsored by the Shaping & Forming & the Titanium Committees of TMS, Held in Blaine, Washington, August 1-4, 1988. fac. ed. International Conference on Superplasticity & Superplastic Forming Staff. Ed. by C. Howard Hamilton & Neil E. Paton. LC 88-62444. 720p. 1988. reprint ed. pap. 180.00 (*0-7837-8305-1*, 2049091) Bks Demand.

An Asterisk (*) at the beginning of an entry indicates that the title is appearing in BIP for the first time.

Superplasticity & Superplastic Forming II. Ed. by A. K. Ghosh & T. K. Bieler. (Illus.). 288p. 1995. 74.00 (*0-87339-300-7*) Minerals Metals.

***Superplasticity in Advanced Materials: ICSAM-97.** Ed. by Atul H. Chokshi. (Materials Science Forum Ser.: Vols. 243-245). (Illus.). 808p. (C). 1997. text ed. 265.00 (*0-87849-759-5*, Pub. by Trans T Pub SZ) Enfield Pubs NH.

Superplasticity in Aerospace. Ed. by Terry R. McNelley & H. C. Heikkenen. LC 88-43025. (Illus.). 400p. 1988. 10.00 (*0-87339-048-2*, 0482) Minerals Metals.

***Superplasticity in Aerospace: Proceedings of a Symposium Sponsored by the Shaping & Forming Committee & Held at the Annual Meeting of the Metallurgicl Society in Phoenix, AZ, January 25-28, 1988.** Ed. by H. Charles Heikkenen et al. LC 88-43025. (Illus.). 381p. pap. 108.60 (*0-608-04884-4*, 2065576) Bks Demand.

Superplasticity in Aerospace No. II: Proceedings of a Symposium Sponsored by the Shaping & Forming Committee & Held at the 119th Annual Meeting of the Metallurgical Society in Anaheim, California, February 19-22, 1990. Minerals, Metals & Materials Society Staff. Ed. by Terry R. McNelley & H. Charles Heikkenen. LC 90-62806. (Illus.). 350p. 1990. reprint ed. pap. 99.80 (*0-608-01699-3*, 2062354) Bks Demand.

Superplasticity in Crystalline Solids. John Pilling & Norman Ridley. 214p. 1989. pap. text ed. 36.00 (*0-901462-56-X*, Pub. by Inst Materials UK) Ashgate Pub Co.

Superplasticity in Metals & Ceramics. T. G. Nieh et al. (Solid State Science Ser.). (Illus.). 300p. (C). 1997. text ed. 74.95 (*0-521-56105-1*) Cambridge U Pr.

Superplasticity in Metals, Ceramics, & Intermetallics Vol. 196: Symposium Proceedings Ser. Ed. by M. J. Mayo et al. 403p. 1990. text ed. 30.00 (*1-55899-085-2*) Materials Res.

Superplasticity of Alloys, Intermetallides & Ceramics. O. A. Kaibyshev. (Illus.). 340p. 1992. 163.95 (*0-387-54907-2*) Spr-Verlag.

Superplasticizers & Other Chemical Admixtures in Concrete. 668p. 1989. pap. 58.95 (*0-685-45551-3*, SP-119BOW6) ACI.

Superplasticizers in Concrete. CANMET-ACI International Symposium on Superplasticizers in Concrete (1st: 1978: Ottawa, Ont) Staff. LC 79-89813. (American Concrete Institute, ACI Publication Ser.: No. SP-62). (Illus.). 433p. reprint ed. pap. 123.50 (*0-685-20779-X*, 2030037) Bks Demand.

Superpollsters: How They Measure & Manipulate Public Opinion in America. David W. Moore. LC 91-30396. 400p. 1992. 21.95 (*0-941423-74-3*) FWEW.

Superpollsters: How They Measure & Manipulate Public Opinion in America. 2nd ed. David W. Moore. (Illus.). 426p. 1995. pap. 15.95 (*1-56858-023-1*) FWEW.

Superpotency. Dudley S. Danoff. 240p. 1993. pap. 10.99 (*0-446-39512-9*) Warner Bks.

Superpower: The Making of a Steam Locomotive. David Weitzman. LC 86-46255. (Illus.). 108p. (J). 1995. 35.00 (*0-87923-671-X*) Godine.

Superpower at Sea: U. S. Ocean Policy. Finn Laursen. LC 83-21222. 224p. 1983. text ed. 55.00 (*0-275-91033-4*, C1033, Praeger Pubs) Greenwood.

Superpower Competition & Crisis Prevention in the Third World. Ed. by Roy Allison & Phil Williams. 293p. (C). 1990. text ed. 64.95 (*0-521-36280-6*) Cambridge U Pr.

Superpower Detente: A Reappraisal. Mike Bowker & Phil Williams. (Royal Institute of International Affairs Ser.: Vol. 2). 288p. (C). 1988. text ed. 39.95 (*0-8039-8041-8*); pap. text ed. 19.95 (*0-8039-8042-6*) Sage.

Superpower Detente & Future of Afghanistan. Jasjit Singh et al. (C). 1990. 27.00 (*81-7050-119-9*, Pub. by Patriot II) S Asia.

Superpower Dilemmas: The U. S. & U. S. S. R. at Century's End. Michael A. Ledeen. 264p. (C). 1991. pap. 24.95 (*0-88738-891-4*) Transaction Pubs.

Superpower Diplomacy in the Horn of Africa. Samuel M. Makinda. LC 86-31379. 272p. 1987. text ed. 49.95 (*0-312-00548-2*) St Martin.

***Superpower Rivalry.** Judges. 1994. pap. text ed. write for info. (*0-582-22667-8*, Pub. by Longman UK) Longman.

Superpower Rivalry & Third World Radicalism: The Idea of National Liberation. S. Neil MacFarlane. LC 84-43081. 236p. (C). 1985. text ed. 36.00 (*0-8018-2671-3*) Johns Hopkins.

Superpower Rivalry in the Indian Ocean: Indian & American Perspectives. Ed. by Selig S. Harrison & K. Subrahmanyam. 320p. 1989. 49.95 (*0-19-505497-0*) OUP.

Superpower Space Race: An Explosive Rivalry Through the Solar System. Robert Reeves. LC 94-28240. (Illus.). 451p. 1994. 28.95 (*0-306-44768-1*, Plenum Pr) Plenum.

Superpower Triumvirs - The United States Faces China & Russia since World War II: Their Geopolitical Intentions & Military Capabilities: Essays on National Security. Joseph D. Lowe. LC 89-91185. (Illus.). xxv, 325p. 1994. 75.00 (*0-930325-12-5*) Lowe Pub.

Superpowers: Being a Forty-Five Year Review of the U. S. A. Soviet Union Political Relationship. Deakin University Press Staff. 95p. (C). 1989. 30.00 (*0-7300-0601-8*, Pub. by Deakin Univ AT) St Mut.

Superpowers & Africa: The Constraints of a Rivalry, 1960-1990. Zaki Laidi. Tr. by Patricia Baudoin. LC 90-10832. (Illus.). 256p. 1990. lib. bdg. 54.00 (*0-226-46781-3*) U Ch Pr.

Superpowers & Client States in the Middle East: The Imbalance of Influence. Ed. by Moshe Efrat & Jacob Bercovitch. 400p. 1991. text ed. 62.95 (*0-415-00490-X*, A5633) Routledge.

Superpowers & Nuclear Arms Control: Rhetoric & Reality. Dennis Menos. LC 89-36700. 192p. 1990. text ed. 49.95 (*0-275-93458-6*, C3458, Praeger Pubs) Greenwood.

Superpowers & Revolution. Ed. by Jonathan R. Adelman. LC 86-21273. 316p. 1986. text ed. 55.00 (*0-275-92166-2*, C2166, Praeger Pubs) Greenwood.

Superpowers & the Middle East. Alan R. Taylor. LC 91-7639. (Contemporary Issues in the Middle East Ser.). 224p. (C). 1991. text ed. 39.95 (*0-8156-2542-1*); pap. text ed. 14.95 (*0-8156-2543-X*) Syracuse U Pr.

Superpowers & the Syrian-Israeli Conflict: Beyond Crisis Management? Helena Cobban. LC 90-25866. (Washington Papers: No. 149). 208p. 1991. pap. text ed. 14.95 (*0-275-93945-6*, B3945, Praeger Pubs) Greenwood.

Superpowers & the Syrian-Israeli Conflict: Beyond Crisis Management? Helena Cobban. LC 90-25866. (Washington Papers: No. 149). 208p. 1991. text ed. 19.95 (*0-275-93944-8*, C3944, Praeger Pubs) Greenwood.

Superpowers & the Third World: Turkish-American Relations & Cyprus. Suha Bolukbasi. LC 88-10343. (Exxon Education Foundation Series on Rhetoric & Political Discourse: Vol. 15). 288p. (Orig.). (C). 1988. pap. text ed. 25.00 (*0-8191-6978-1*, Pub. by White Miller Center); lib. bdg. 49.00 (*0-8191-6977-3*, Pub. by White Miller Center) U Pr of Amer.

Superpowers in Economic Decline. Richard M. Cohen & Peter A. Wilson. (Illus.). 350p. (C). 1990. text ed. 49.50 (*0-685-32668-3*, Crane Russak); pap. text ed. 27.00 (*0-685-32669-1*, Crane Russak) Taylor & Francis.

Superpremium Ice Cream Market. 270p. 1986. 1,250.00 (*0-931634-62-8*) FIND-SVP.

Superpremium Ice Cream Market. Ed. by Peter Allen. 270p. 1989. pap. 1,295.00 (*0-941285-44-8*) FIND-SVP.

SuperPro-crastinators. Joseph E. Barnes. LC 84-71554. 200p. 1985. 14.95 (*0-917732-34-0*, 767); pap. 10.95 (*0-917732-35-9*) Barnes-Bks.

Superprofits & Crises: Modern U. S. Capitalism. Victor Perlo. LC 88-2925. (Illus.). 568p. (C). 1988. 21.00 (*0-7178-0665-0*); pap. 9.95 (*0-7178-0662-6*) Intl Pubs Co.

Superpuppy: How to Choose, Raise & Train the Best Possible Dog for You. Jill Pinkwater & Daniel M. Pinkwater. LC 76-8825. (Illus.). 208p. (J). (gr. 6 up). 1982. pap. 9.95 (*0-89919-084-7*, Clarion Bks) HM.

SuperPuppy: How to Raise the Best Dog You'll Ever Have! 2nd ed. Peter J. Vollmer. (Illus.). 50p. 1988. pap. 8.95 (*1-886056-01-3*) Super Puppy Pr.

SuperPuppy Goes to Puppy Class: How to Train the Best Dog You'll Ever Have! Peter J. Vollmer. (Illus.). 64p. (Orig.). 1992. pap. 8.95 (*1-886056-02-1*) Super Puppy Pr.

Superpuzzles. M. Fowler & R. Parekh. (Superpuzzles Ser.). (Illus.). 144p. (YA). (gr. 6 up). 1995. pap. 14.95 (*0-7460-0735-3*, Usborne) EDC.

Superscaler Microprocessors Design. William M. Johnson. 320p. 1990. text ed. 70.00 (*0-13-875634-1*) P-H.

Superschool & the Superstate: American Education in the Twentieth Century, 1918-1970. Edgar B. Gumbert & Joel H. Spring. LC 73-22226. (Studies in the History of American Education). 222p. reprint ed. pap. 63.30 (*0-317-09296-0*, 2013572) Bks Demand.

Supersearch Software: Two Media Disks - Version 4.0. Peter K. Studner. 45p. 1995. pap. 79.95 (*0-938667-01-7*) Jamenair Ltd.

Supersensible Knowledge. Rudolf Steiner. Tr. by Rita Stebbing from GER. Orig. Title: Die Erkenntnis des Uebersinnlichen in unserer Zeit und deren Bedeutung fuer. 230p. (ENG.). 1988. 20.00 (*0-88010-190-3*); pap. 12.95 (*0-88010-191-1*) Anthroposophic.

Supersensible Physiology & Balance in Teaching. Rudolf Steiner. 15p. 1969. reprint ed. spiral bd. 3.50 (*0-7873-1296-7*) Hlth Research.

Supersensitivity Following Lesions of the Nervous System: An Aspect of the Relativity of Nervous Integration. George W. Stavraky. (Illus.). 220p. reprint ed. pap. 62.70 (*0-317-07847-X*, 2014419) Bks Demand.

Supersheds: The Architecture of Long-Span Large-Volume Buildings. C. J. Wilkinson. 160p. 1991. 64.95 (*0-7506-1221-5*) Buttrwrth-Heinemann.

Supersheds: The Architecture of Long-Span, Large Volume Buildings. 2nd ed. Chris Wilkinson. LC 95-45600. (Architecture New Technology Ser.). (Illus.). 160p. 1996. pap. 37.95 (*0-7506-2490-6*) Buttrwrth-Heinemann.

**Supershrink II: 3.5" ** Joseph Lowman. 119p. (C). 1990. pap. text ed. 35.00 (*0-15-584764-3*) HB Coll Pubs.

**Supershrink II: 5.25" ** Joseph Lowman. 119p. (C). 1990. pap. text ed. 35.00 (*0-15-584763-5*) HarBrace.

SuperSmart Systems: Five Simple, No-Nonsense Steps to Superiority in Reading Speed, Writing, Math & Memory. Edward F. Droge, Jr. 128p. 1994. 19.95 (*0-9637771-1-4*) Crimson Blue.

Supersoaps. Chris Stacey & Darcy Sullivan. 160p. 1988. 45.00 (*1-85283-206-1*, Pub. by Boxtree Ltd UK) St Mut.

***Supersoft X-Ray Sources: Proceedings of the International Workshop Held in Garching, Germany, 28 February-1 March 1996.** Jochen Greiner. LC 96-9905. (Lecture Notes in Physics Ser.: Vol. 472). 356p. 1996. 84.00 (*3-540-61390-0*) Spr-Verlag.

Supersonic Fighter Developments. Roy Braybrook. (Illus.). 225p. 1987. 24.95 (*0-85429-582-8*, F582, Pub. by G T Foulis Ltd) Haynes Pubns.

***Supersonic Flight: Breaking the Sound Barrier & Beyond - The Story of the Bell X-1 & Douglas D-558.** rev. ed. Richard P. Hallion. LC 97-25162. (Illus.). 288p. 1997. 34.95 (*1-85753-253-8*, Pub. by Brasseys UK) Brasseys Inc.

Supersonic Flow & Shock Waves. Richard Courant & K. O. Friedrichs. (Applied Mathematical Sciences Ser.: Vol. 21.). 1992. 83.95 (*0-387-90232-5*) Spr-Verlag.

Supersonic Sounds: A Business Record-Keeping Practice Set. 3rd ed. N. Fritz & Richard H. Wirth. 1981. text ed. 11.96 (*0-07-022562-1*) McGraw.

Superspace & Supergravity: Proceedings of the Nuffield Workshop, Cambridge, June 16-July 12, 1980. Ed. by Stephen W. Hawking & M. Roicek. LC 80-42091. 539p. reprint ed. pap. 153.70 (*0-317-39713-3*, 2055939) Bks Demand.

Superspace or One Thousand & One Lessons in Super Symmetry. S. James Gates, Jr. et al. LC 83-5986. (Frontiers in Physics Ser.). 548p. (C). 1983. 59.25 (*0-8053-3160-3*, Adv Bk Prog) Addison-Wesley.

SuperSpan: The Golden Gate Bridge. Baron Wolman & Tom Horton. LC 82-17746. (Illus.). 96p. (Orig.). 1983. pap. 10.95 (*0-87701-277-6*) Chronicle Bks.

***Superspan: The Golden Gate Bridge.** rev. ed. Tom Horton. (Illus.). 104p. 1997. pap. 12.95 (*0-916290-78-6*) Squarebooks.

Superspeedway Boom, 1959-1964 see Forty Years of Stock Car Racing

Superspies: The Secret Side of Government. Jules Archer. LC 77-72640. (J). (gr. 7-p). 1977. pap. 7.95 (*0-440-08136-X*) Delacorte.

Superstar Sales Manager's Secrets. Barry J. Farber. 128p. (Orig.). 1995. pap. 8.99 (*1-56414-168-3*) Career Pr Inc.

Superstar Sales Secrets. Barry J. Farber. 128p. (Orig.). 1995. pap. text ed. 8.99 (*1-56414-167-5*) Career Pr Inc.

Superstar Series, Vol. 4: Country: Alabama - Highway 101 - The Judds, No. 381. (Easy ABC Music for All Keyboards Ser.). 64p. 1990. pap. 4.95 (*0-7935-0220-9*, HL00001354) H Leonard.

Superstar Workout. Parr & Rudnitsky. pap. write for info. (*0-671-87695-X*) PB.

***Superstar Wrestlers.** Ed. by Michael Benson. 32p. (YA). 1997. pap. 4.95 (*0-934551-18-9*) Starlog Pr.

Superstars: Gay Adult Video Guide. Jamoo. (Illus.). 160p. 1996. pap. 12.95 (*0-9625277-9-3*) Companion Press.

***Superstars: Twelve Lesbians Who Changed the World.** Dell Richards. 12.95 (*0-7867-0955-3*) Carroll & Graf.

Superstars: Twelve Lesbians Who Changed the World. Dell Richards. 256p. 1993. pap. 12.95 (*0-88184-955-3*) Carroll & Graf.

Superstars & Monopoly Wars: Nineteenth-Century Major League Baseball. Tom W. Gilbert. (American Game Ser.). (Illus.). 128p. (YA). (gr. 9-12). 1995. lib. bdg. 22.70 (*0-531-11247-0*) Watts.

Superstars & Super Stats. (Illus.). 48p. (J). (gr. 3 up). 1992. boxed 3.95 (*0-307-22382-5*, 22382, Golden Pr) Western Pub.

***Superstars of Men's Figure Skating.** Pohla Smith. (Male Sports Stars Ser.). (Illus.). 64p. (YA). (gr. 7 up). 1997. lib. bdg. 15.95 (*0-7910-4586-2*) Chelsea Hse.

***Superstars of Men's Pro Wrestling.** (Male Sports Stars Ser.). (Illus.). 64p. (YA). (gr. 7 up). 1997. lib. bdg. 15.95 (*0-7910-4587-0*) Chelsea Hse.

***Superstars of Men's Soccer.** Timothy Urigs. (Male Sports Stars Ser.). (Illus.). 64p. (YA). (gr. 7 up). 1997. lib. bdg. 15.95 (*0-7910-4588-9*) Chelsea Hse.

***Superstars of Men's Swimming & Diving.** Howard Keiser. (Male Sports Stars Ser.). (Illus.). 64p. (YA). (gr. 7 up). 1997. lib. bdg. 15.95 (*0-7910-4589-7*) Chelsea Hse.

***Superstars of Men's Tennis.** Paula Edelson. (Male Sports Stars Ser.). (Illus.). 64p. (YA). (gr. 7 up). 1997. lib. bdg. 15.95 (*0-7910-4590-0*) Chelsea Hse.

***Superstars of NASCAR Activity & Coloring Book.** (Illus.). 44p. (J). (gr. k-4). 1997. pap. 5.95 (*1-890929-08-5*) Comp Motorsport.

***Superstars of Track & Field.** Fred McMane. (Male Sports Stars Ser.). (Illus.). 64p. (YA). (gr. 7 up). 1997. lib. bdg. 15.95 (*0-7910-4591-9*) Chelsea Hse.

***Superstar's of Women's Basketball.** Chelsea House Publishers Staff. 1997. lib. bdg. 15.95 (*0-7910-4389-4*) Chelsea Hse.

***Superstars of Women's Figure Skating.** Pohla Smith. LC 96-45755. (Female Sports Stars Ser.). (Illus.). 64p. (J). (gr. 3 up). 1997. lib. bdg. 15.95 (*0-7910-4392-4*) Chelsea Hse.

***Superstars of Women's Golf.** Barry Wilner. LC 96-45754. (Female Sports Stars Ser.). (Illus.). 64p. (J). (gr. 3 up). 1997. lib. bdg. 15.95 (*0-7910-4390-8*) Chelsea Hse.

***Superstars of Women's Gymnastics.** Joel H. Cohen. LC 96-321555. (Female Sports Stars Ser.). (J). 1997. lib. bdg. 15.95 (*0-7910-4391-6*) Chelsea Hse.

***Superstars of Women's Tennis.** Martin Schwabacher. LC 96-36689. (Female Sports Stars Ser.). (Illus.). 64p. (J). (gr. 3 up). 1997. lib. bdg. 15.95 (*0-7910-4393-2*) Chelsea Hse.

***Superstars of Women's Track & Field.** Rebecca Ferrara. (Female Sports Stars Ser.). (Illus.). 64p. (J). (gr. 3 up). 1997. lib. bdg. 15.95 (*0-7910-4394-0*) Chelsea Hse.

***Superstars on Ice: Figure Skating Champions.** unabridged ed. Patty Cranston. (Illus.). 40p. (Orig.). (YA). (gr. 3 up). 1997. pap. 5.95 (*1-55074-400-3*, Pub. by Kids Can Pr CN) Genl Dist Srvs.

SuperStarters: Activities for Young Children. Bobbye S. Goldstein & Gabriel F. Goldstein. 240p. (J). (ps-3). 17.99 (*0-86653-899-2*, FE0899) Fearon Teach Aids.

Supersticiones y Buenos Consejos. Lydia Cabrera. LC 86-83335. (Coleccion del Chichereku). 62p. (Orig.). (SPA.). 1988. pap. 7.95 (*0-89729-433-5*) Ediciones.

Superstition. F. E. Planer. 377p. 1988. pap. 21.95 (*0-87975-494-X*) Prometheus Bks.

Superstition. Robert G. Ingersoll. (Notable American Authors Ser.). 1992. reprint ed. lib. bdg. 75.00 (*0-7812-3330-5*) Rprt Serv.

Superstition & Force. Henry C. Lea. LC 79-148823. (World History Ser.: No. 48). 1971. reprint ed. lib. bdg. 75.00 (*0-8383-1228-4*) M S G Haskell Hse.

Superstition & the Press. Curtis D. MacDougall. LC 83-61115. (Science & the Paranormal Ser.). 616p. 1983. 41.95 (*0-87975-211-4*); pap. 26.95 (*0-87975-212-2*) Prometheus Bks.

Superstition, Are You Superstitious? Maple. 1979. pap. 2.00 (*0-87980-245-6*) Wilshire.

Superstition in All Ages. Paul H. D'Holbach & Jean Meslier. 1973. 250.00 (*0-87968-108-X*) Gordon Pr.

Superstition in All Ages. Jean Meslier. Tr. by Anna Knoop from FRE. LC 77-161337. (Atheist Viewpoint Ser.). (Illus.). 346p. 1976. reprint ed. 25.95 (*0-405-03795-3*) Ayer.

Superstition in All Ages: Last Will & Testament: Common Sense. Tr. by Jean Meslier & Anna Knoop. 339p. 1974. reprint ed. spiral bd. 12.00 (*0-7873-0609-6*) Hlth Research.

Superstition in All Ages; Last Will & Testament; & Common Sense. Jean Meslier. Tr. by Anna Knoop. 339p. 1996. pap. 24.95 (*1-56459-794-6*) Kessinger Pub.

Superstition Mountain, a Ride Through Time. James Swanson & Tom Kollenborn. LC 81-69495. (Illus.). 240p. 1981. 10.95 (*0-910973-00-8*) Arrowhead AZ.

Superstitions. Peter Lorie. (Illus.). 256p. 1992. 22.50 (*0-671-78183-9*) S&S Trade.

Superstitions from North Carolina, 2 vols., 6. Wayland D. Hand. LC 58-10967. (Frank C. Brown Collection of North Carolina Folklore Ser.). text ed. 45.95 (*0-8223-0258-6*) Duke.

Superstitions from North Carolina, 2 vols., 7. Wayland D. Hand. LC 58-10967. (Frank C. Brown Collection of North Carolina Folklore Ser.). text ed. 45.95 (*0-8223-0259-4*) Duke.

Superstitions from Seven Towns of the United States. Catherine H. Ainsworth. LC 43-7320. (Folklore Bks.). 64p. (J). (ps-12). 1973. 5.00 (*0-933190-00-X*) Clyde Pr.

Superstitions of the Highlands & Islands of Scotland. John G. Campbell. LC 71-173104. (Illus.). 1972. reprint ed. 20.95 (*0-405-08337-8*, Pub. by Blom Pubns UK) Ayer.

Superstitions of the Sea: Digest of Beliefs, Customs, Mystery. James Clary. (Illus.). 360p. 1994. 40.00 (*0-916637-00-X*) Maritime History in Art.

Superstitious. R. L. Stine. 400p. 1996. mass mkt. 6.99 (*0-446-60350-3*) Warner Bks.

Superstitious. R. L. Stine. LC 95-11147. 1995. write for info. (*0-446-51925-1*) Warner Bks.

Superstitious Mind: French Peasants & the Supernatural in the Nineteenth Century. Judith Devlin. LC 86-23341. 336p. 1987. text ed. 40.00 (*0-300-03710-4*) Yale U Pr.

Superstoe. large type ed. William Borden. LC 96-2293. 1996. 23.95 (*1-56895-309-7*) Wheeler Pub.

Superstoe. William Borden. LC 95-70750. 304p. 1996. reprint ed. 22.00 (*0-9642949-5-8*) Orloff Pr.

SuperStor: An Illustrated Tutorial. David J. Strybel. LC 93-3760. (Illus.). 1993. pap. 16.95 (*0-8306-4529-2*, Windcrest) TAB Bks.

Superstring Construction. Ed. by A. N. Schellekens. (Current Physics Sources & Comments Ser.: Vol. 4). 520p. 1989. pap. 68.75 (*0-444-88016-X*) Elsevier.

Superstring Theory, 2 vols., Vol. 1, Introduction. Michael B. Green et al. (Cambridge Monographs on Mathematical Physics). 467p. 1988. pap. text ed. 37.95 (*0-521-35752-7*) Cambridge U Pr.

Superstring Theory, 2 vols., Vol. 2, Phenomenology & Field Theory. Michael B. Green et al. (Cambridge Monographs on Mathematical Physics). 608p. 1988. pap. text ed. 44.95 (*0-521-35753-5*) Cambridge U Pr.

Superstrings. Ed. by P. G. Freund & K. T. Mahanthappa. LC 88-6032. (NATO ASI Series B, Physics: Vol. 175). (Illus.). 360p. 1988. 110.00 (*0-306-42908-X*, Plenum Pr) Plenum.

Superstrings: A Theory of Everything? Ed. by P. C. Davies & J. Brown. (Canto Book Ser.). (Illus.). 242p. (C). 1992. pap. text ed. 10.95 (*0-521-43775-X*) Cambridge U Pr.

Superstrings: Poems. Edward Loomis. (Orig.). 1994. pap. 8.95 (*0-9639443-0-4*) Grafx Bks.

Superstrings: The First Fifteen Years of Superstring Theory, 2 Vols. John J. Schwarz. 1168p. 1985. text ed. 130.00 (*9971-978-66-0*); pap. text ed. 61.00 (*9971-978-67-9*) World Scientific Pub.

Superstrings & Grand Unification: Proceedings of the Winter School on High Energy Physics. Ed. by T. Pradhan. 148p. (C). 1989. pap. 36.00 (*9971-5-0528-2*); text ed. 67.00 (*9971-5-0527-4*) World Scientific Pub.

Superstrings & Particle Theory. Ed. by L. Clavelli & B. Harms. 364p. (C). 1990. text ed. 130.00 (*981-02-0157-5*) World Scientific Pub.

Superstrings & Supergravity. Ed. by A. T. Davies & D. G. Sutherland. (Scottish Universities Summer School in Physics, a NATO Advanced Study Institute Ser.: No. 28). (Illus.). 554p. 1986. 160.00 (*0-905945-11-5*) IOP Pub.

Superstrings & the Search for the Theory of Everything. F. David Peat. 256p. 1989. pap. 14.95 (*0-8092-4257-5*) Contemp Bks.

Superstrings, Anomalies & Unification: Proceedings of the Adriatic Meeting on Particle Physics, 5th, Dubrovnik, Yugoslavia, June 16-28, 1986. Ed. by M. Martinis. 584p. 1987. pap. 47.00 (*9971-5-0233-X*); text ed. 110.00 (*9971-5-0232-1*) World Scientific Pub.

Superstrings, Cosmology, Composite Structures. Ed. by S. James Gates, Jr. & R. N. Mohapatra. 604p. (C). 1987. text ed. 155.00 (*9971-5-0373-5*) World Scientific Pub.

Superstrings, Supergravity, & Unified Theories. Ed. by G. Furlan et al. (ICTP Series in Theoretical Physics: Vol. 2). 560p. 1986. pap. 60.00 (*9971-5-0036-1*); text ed. 150.00 (*9971-5-0035-3*) World Scientific Pub.

Superstrings, Unified Theories & Cosmology: Proceedings of the Summer Workshop on High Energy Physics & Cosmology, Trieste, Italy, June 30-August 15, 1986. Ed. by G. Furlan et al. (ICTP Series in Theoretical Physics: Vol. 3). 464p. 1987. pap. 47.00 (*9971-5-0280-1*); text ed. 144.00 (*9971-5-0271-2*) World Scientific Pub.

Superstrings, Unified Theories & Cosmology 1987. G. Furlan et al. (ICTP Series in Theoretical Physics: Vol. 4). 500p. (C). 1988. pap. 55.00 (*9971-5-0453-7*); text ed. 125.00 (*9971-5-0452-9*) World Scientific Pub.

S

An Asterisk (*) at the beginning of an entry indicates that the title is appearing in BIP for the first time.

Superstrings, Unified Theories & Cosmology, 1988. J. C. Pati et al. (ICTP Series in Theoretical Physics: Vol. 5). 664p. 1989. pap. 53.00 (9971-5-0871-0); text ed. 151.00 (9971-5-0850-8) World Scientific Pub.

Superstrings 1987: Proceedings of the Trieste Spring School on Superstrings, 1987. Ed. by L. Alvarez-Gaume et al. 432p. (Orig.). (C). 1988. pap. 44.00 (9971-5-0518-5, MPH-P549S); text ed. 102.00 (9971-5-0297-6, MPH-P549) World Scientific Pub.

Superstrings '88. Ed. by Michael B. Green et al. 480p. (C). 1989. pap. 46.00 (9971-5-0872-9); text ed. 109.00 (9971-5-0852-4) World Scientific Pub.

Superstrings '89: Spring School & Workshop. Michael B. Green et al. 636p. 1990. text ed. 130.00 (981-02-0138-9) World Scientific Pub.

Superstructuralism. Richard Harland. 224p. (C). 1987. pap. 14.95 (0-415-03952-5) Routledge.

Superstructuralism: The Philosophy of Structuralism & Post-Structuralism. Richard Harland. LC 86-23627. 213p. 1987. 37.50 (0-416-03232-X); pap. 12.95 (0-416-03242-7) Routledge Chapman & Hall.

Supersymmetric Gauge Field Theory & String Theory. D. Bailin & A. Love. (Graduate Student Series in Physics). (Illus.). 322p. 1994. 168.00 (0-7503-0268-2); pap. 51.00 (0-7503-0267-4) IOP Pub.

***Supersymmetric Methods in Quantum & Statistical Physics.** Georg Junker. LC 96-30574. (Texts & Monographs in Physics). (Illus.). 172p. 1996. 44.95 (3-540-61591-1) Spr-Verlag.

Supersymmetric Quantum Cosmology. P. D. D'Eath. (Monographs on Mathematical Physics). (Illus.). 288p. (C). 1996. text ed. 69.95 (0-521-55287-7) Cambridge U Pr.

Supersymmetry: An Introduction with Conceptual & Calculational Details. Ed. by H. Muller-Kirsten & A. Wiedemann. (Lecture Notes in Physics Ser.: Vol. 7). 608p. 1987. text ed. 104.00 (9971-5-0354-9); pap. text ed. 51.00 (9971-5-0355-7) World Scientific Pub.

Supersymmetry: Lectures & Reprints, 2 vols., Set. S. Ferrara. 1376p. 1987. text ed. 123.00 (9971-966-21-2); pap. text ed. 61.00 (9971-966-22-0) World Scientific Pub.

Supersymmetry & Its Applications: Proceedings of the Nuffield Workshop, Cambridge, 24 June to 12 July, 1985. G. Gibbons et al. 500p. 1986. text ed. 90.00 (0-521-30721-X) Cambridge U Pr.

Supersymmetry & Supergravity. rev. ed. Julius Wess & Jonathan Bagger. (Physics Ser.). 190p. 1991. text ed. 65.00 (0-691-08556-0); pap. text ed. 27.50 (0-691-02530-4) Princeton U Pr.

Supersymmetry & Supergravity: A Reprint Volumes in Physics Report. Ed. by M. Jacob. 600p. 1986. text ed. 98.00 (9971-978-74-1); pap. text ed. 60.00 (9971-978-75-X) World Scientific Pub.

Supersymmetry & Supergravity: Proceedings of the Trieste Workshop Sept. 1982 School. Ed. by S. Ferrara et al. 340p. 1983. pap. 33.00 (9971-950-68-5); text ed. 90.00 (9971-950-67-7) World Scientific Pub.

Supersymmetry & Supergravity, 1983: Proceedings of the XIX Winter School & Workshop on Theoretical Physics, Karpacz, Poland, February 14-26, 1983. B. Milewski. 588p. (C). 1983. 98.00 (9971-950-23-5); pap. 52.00 (9971-950-97-9) World Scientific Pub.

Supersymmetry & Supergravity 1984: Proceedings of Trieste Spring School, Italy 1984. Ed. by B. De Wit et al. 500p. 1984. 98.00 (9971-966-75-1); pap. 46.00 (9971-966-76-X) World Scientific Pub.

Supersymmetry & Unification of Fundamental Interaction (Susy 93) Proceedings of the International Workshop. P. Nath. 644p. 1993. text ed. 121.00 (981-02-1593-2) World Scientific Pub.

Supersymmetry in Disorder & Chaos. Konstantin Efetov. (Illus.). 448p. (C). 1996. text ed. 100.00 (0-521-47097-8) Cambridge U Pr.

Supersymmetry, Superfields & Supergravity: An Introduction. P. P. Srivastava. (Graduate Student Series in Physics). (Illus.). 172p. 1986. 42.00 (0-85274-571-0) IOP Pub.

Supersymmetry, Supergravity & Related Topics: Proceedings of the XVth GIFT International Seminar on Theoretical Physics, Sant Feliu de Guixols, Girona, Spain, June 4-9, 1984. Ed. by F. Del Aguila et al. 550p. 1985. 98.00 (9971-966-79-4); pap. 46.00 (9971-966-92-1) World Scientific Pub.

Supersymmetry, Supergravity & Superstrings '86: Proceedings of the Trieste Spring School ICTP, Trieste, Italy 7-15 April 1986. Ed. by B. De Wit et al. 576p. 1987. pap. 49.00 (9971-5-0145-7); text ed. 144.00 (9971-5-0144-9) World Scientific Pub.

Superteam Solution: Successful Teamworking in Organizations. Colin Hasting et al. 208p. 1986. text ed. 51.95 (0-566-02621-X, Pub. by Gower UK) Ashgate Pub Co.

Supertech: How Americans Can Win the Technology Race. Thomas G. Donlan. 360p. 1991. text ed. 32.00 (1-55623-371-X) Irwin Prof Pubng.

Supertough Coatings: Expanding the Performance of Conventional Materials. 117p. 1996. spiral bd. 1,200.00 (1-56217-016-3) Tech Insights.

***Supertoys.** Brian Aldiss. mass mkt. write for info. (0-06-109186-3, Harp PBks) HarpC.

Supertraders: Secrets & Successes of Wall Street's Best & Brightest. Alan Rubenfeld. 1995. per. 19.95 (1-55738-810-5) Irwin Prof Pubng.

SuperTraders: Secrets & Successes of Wall Street's Best & Brightest. rev. ed. Alan Rubenfeld. 225p. 1992. text ed. 24.95 (1-55738-284-0) Irwin Prof Pubng.

Supertrader's - 1994-95 Book of Numbers. Frank A. Taucher. 1994. spiral bd. 59.00 (1-879591-12-X) Mkt Movements.

Supertrader's - 1995-1996 Book of Linear Time Cycles. Frank A. Taucher. 1995. spiral bd. 59.00 (1-879591-16-2) Mkt Movements.

Supertrader's - 1995-96 Book of Ratios. Frank A. Taucher. 1995. spiral bd. 59.00 (1-879591-17-0) Mkt Movements.

Supertrader's Almanac - Book of Spirals. Frank A. Taucher. 1995. pap. 95.00 (1-879591-18-9) Mkt Movements.

Supertrader's Almanac - Reference Manual: Reference Guide & Analytical Techniques for Investors. Frank A. Taucher. 536p. (Orig.). 1991. pap. 55.00 (1-879591-01-4) Mkt Movements.

Supertraining Your Dog. Paul Loeb. 1990. pap. 6.50 (0-671-73209-9) S&S Trade.

Supertrains: Solutions to America's Transportation Gridlock. Joseph Vranich. (Illus.). 432p. 1993. pap. 15.95 (0-312-09468-X) St Martin.

Supertramp: Paris. 1980. 9.95 (0-89898-021-6) Almo Pubns.

Supertrucks. Sloan Walker & Andrew Vasey. LC 85-5379. (Crazy Car Ser.). (Illus.). 48p. (J). (gr. 1-4). 1985. 12.95 (0-8027-6586-6); lib. bdg. 12.85 (0-8027-6606-4) Walker & Co.

Superturbulent Combustion Noise. Battelle Columbus Laboratories Staff et al. 136p. 1976. 5.25 (0-318-12713-X, M40077) Am Gas Assn.

Superunification & Extra Dimensions: Proceedings of the First Torino Meeting on Superunification & Extra Dimensions, Torino, Italy, September 1985. Ed. by P. Fre. 544p. 1986. text ed. 144.00 (9971-5-0101-5) World Scientific Pub.

Supervenience: New Essays. Ed. by Elias E. Savellos & Umit D. Yalcin. (Illus.). 320p. (C). 1995. text ed. 59.95 (0-521-45002-0) Cambridge U Pr.

Supervenience & Materialism. Mark Rowlands. 144p. 1995. 51.95 (1-85972-096-X, Pub. by Avebury Pub UK) Ashgate Pub Co.

Supervenience & Mind: Selected Philosophical Essays. Jaegwon Kim. LC 93-361. (Studies in Philosophy). 448p. (C). 1993. text ed. 65.00 (0-521-43394-0); pap. text ed. 25.95 (0-521-43996-5) Cambridge U Pr.

Supervictim Syndrome: How to Break the Cycle. Thomas R. McCabe. 64p. 1992. pap. 5.95 (1-56246-008-0, P168) Johnsn Inst.

Supervised Boundary Formation. C. M. Orange. 180p. 1994. pap. 57.50 (90-407-1045-7, Pub. by Delft U Pr NE) Coronet Bks.

Supervising. Christina Christenson et al. 336p. 1982. write for info. (0-201-03431-X); teacher ed. write for info. (0-201-03432-8) Addison-Wesley.

Supervising Account Clerk. Jack Rudman. (Career Examination Ser.: C-1884). 1994. pap. 27.95 (0-8373-1884-X) Nat Learn.

Supervising Accountant. Jack Rudman. (Career Examination Ser.: C-1040). 1994. pap. 34.95 (0-8373-1040-7) Nat Learn.

Supervising Addiction Specialist. Jack Rudman. (Career Examination Ser.: C-1501). 1994. pap. 34.95 (0-8373-1501-8) Nat Learn.

Supervising Admitting Clerk. Jack Rudman. (Career Examination Ser.: C-1041). 1994. pap. 27.95 (0-8373-1041-5) Nat Learn.

Supervising Air Pollution Inspector. Jack Rudman. (Career Examination Ser.: C-1502). 1994. pap. 34.95 (0-8373-1502-6) Nat Learn.

Supervising & Law. (Open Learning for Supervisory Management Ser.). 1986. pap. text ed. 19.50 (0-08-070121-3, Pergamon Pr) Elsevier.

Supervising & Managing People. Generation X Staff. (First Books For Business Ser.). (Illus.). 128p. 1996. pap. text ed. 12.00 (0-07-001569-4) McGraw.

Supervising & Marketing. (Open Learning for Supervisory Management Ser.). 1986. pap. text ed. 19.50 (0-08-070064-0, Pergamon Pr) Elsevier.

Supervising Appraiser. Jack Rudman. (Career Examination Ser.: C-1699). 1994. pap. 29.95 (0-8373-1699-5) Nat Learn.

Supervising Appraiser (Real Estate) Jack Rudman. (Career Examination Ser.: C-1680). 1994. pap. 29.95 (0-8373-1680-4) Nat Learn.

Supervising Assessor. Jack Rudman. (Career Examination Ser.: C-1042). 1994. pap. 29.95 (0-8373-1042-3) Nat Learn.

Supervising Audiologist. Jack Rudman. (Career Examination Ser.: C-2237). 1994. pap. 34.95 (0-8373-2237-5) Nat Learn.

Supervising Audit Clerk. Jack Rudman. (Career Examination Ser.: C-887). 1994. pap. 27.95 (0-8373-0887-9) Nat Learn.

Supervising Auditor. Jack Rudman. (Career Examination Ser.: C-2681). 1994. pap. 39.95 (0-8373-2681-8) Nat Learn.

Supervising Automotive Facilities Inspector. Jack Rudman. (Career Examination Ser.: C-2215). 1994. pap. 29.95 (0-8373-2215-4) Nat Learn.

Supervising Automotive Mechanic. Jack Rudman. (Career Examination Ser.: C-2575). 1994. pap. 29.95 (0-8373-2575-7) Nat Learn.

Supervising Beverage Control Investigator. Jack Rudman. (Career Examination Ser.: C-2824). 1994. pap. 29.95 (0-8373-2824-1) Nat Learn.

Supervising Boilermaker. (Career Examination Ser.: C-3623). pap. 34.95 (0-8373-3623-6) Nat Learn.

Supervising Bookkeeper. Jack Rudman. (Career Examination Ser.: C-2682). 1994. pap. 27.95 (0-8373-2682-6) Nat Learn.

Supervising Building Inspector. Jack Rudman. (Career Examination Ser.: C-2840). 1994. pap. 34.95 (0-8373-2840-3) Nat Learn.

Supervising Building Plan Examiner. Jack Rudman. (Career Examination Ser.: C-862). 1994. pap. 34.95 (0-8373-0862-3) Nat Learn.

Supervising Campus Security Officer. Jack Rudman. (Career Examination Ser.: C-1703). 1994. pap. 27.95 (0-8373-1703-7) Nat Learn.

Supervising Cashier. Jack Rudman. (Career Examination Ser.: C-774). 1994. pap. 23.95 (0-8373-0774-0) Nat Learn.

Supervising Child Protective Services Caseworkers. Thomas D. Morton & Marsha K. Salus. 86p. (Orig.). (C). 1995. pap. text ed. 25.00 (0-7881-1920-6) DIANE Pub.

Supervising Children's Counselor. Jack Rudman. (Career Examination Ser.: C-2010). 1994. pap. 34.95 (0-8373-2010-0) Nat Learn.

Supervising Claim Examiner. Jack Rudman. (Career Examination Ser.: C-2322). 1994. pap. 29.95 (0-8373-2322-3) Nat Learn.

Supervising Clerk. Jack Rudman. (Career Examination Ser.: C-775). 1994. pap. 23.95 (0-8373-0775-9) Nat Learn.

Supervising Clerk (Income Maintenance) Jack Rudman. (Career Examination Ser.: C-1706). 1994. pap. 27.95 (0-8373-1706-1) Nat Learn.

Supervising Community Service Worker. Jack Rudman. (Career Examination Ser.: C-2677). 1994. pap. 27.95 (0-8373-2677-X) Nat Learn.

Supervising Computer Operator. Jack Rudman. (Career Examination Ser.: C-776). 1994. pap. 29.95 (0-8373-0776-7) Nat Learn.

Supervising Construction Inspector. Jack Rudman. (Career Examination Ser.: C-1043). 1994. pap. 34.95 (0-8373-1043-1) Nat Learn.

Supervising Consumer Affairs Inspector. Jack Rudman. (Career Examination Ser.: C-1657). 1994. pap. 29.95 (0-8373-1657-X) Nat Learn.

Supervising Counselors & Therapists: A Developmental Approach. Cal D. Stoltenberg & Ursula Delworth. LC 87-45415. (Social & Behavioral Science Ser.). 241p. 31.95 (1-55542-066-4) Jossey-Bass.

Supervising Court Officer. Jack Rudman. (Career Examination Ser.: C-1503). 1994. pap. 27.95 (0-8373-1503-4) Nat Learn.

Supervising Custodial Foreman. Jack Rudman. (Career Examination Ser.: C-1044). 1994. pap. 29.95 (0-8373-1044-X) Nat Learn.

Supervising Demolition Inspector. Jack Rudman. (Career Examination Ser.: C-777). 1994. pap. 34.95 (0-8373-0777-5) Nat Learn.

Supervising Deputy Sheriff. Jack Rudman. (Career Examination Ser.: C-1666). 1994. pap. 29.95 (0-8373-1666-9) Nat Learn.

Supervising Developmental Specialist. Jack Rudman. (Career Examination Ser.: C-924). 1994. pap. 29.95 (0-8373-0924-7) Nat Learn.

Supervising Dietitian. Jack Rudman. (Career Examination Ser.: C-1968). 1994. pap. 29.95 (0-8373-1968-4) Nat Learn.

Supervising Drug & Alcohol Community Coordinator. Jack Rudman. (Career Examination Ser.: C-2777). 1994. pap. 39.95 (0-8373-2777-6) Nat Learn.

Supervising Economist. Jack Rudman. (Career Examination Ser.: C-2202). 1994. pap. 34.95 (0-8373-2202-2) Nat Learn.

Supervising Electrical Inspector. Jack Rudman. (Career Examination Ser.: C-778). 1994. pap. 39.95 (0-8373-0778-3) Nat Learn.

Supervising Electronic Computer Operator. Jack Rudman. (Career Examination Ser.: C-1549). 1994. pap. 29.95 (0-8373-1549-2) Nat Learn.

Supervising Elevator Inspector. Jack Rudman. (Career Examination Ser.: C-1955). 1994. pap. 34.95 (0-8373-1955-2) Nat Learn.

Supervising Emergency Medical Service Specialist. Jack Rudman. (Career Examination Ser.: C-3480). 1994. pap. 34.95 (0-8373-3480-2) Nat Learn.

Supervising Employees with Disabilities: Beyond ADA Compliance. Mary Dickson. Ed. by Brenda Machosky. LC 92-75714. (Fifty-Minute Ser.). 124p. (Orig.). 1993. pap. text ed. 10.95 (1-56052-209-7) Crisp Pubns.

Supervising Employment Consultant (Testing) Jack Rudman. (Career Examination Ser.: C-2464). 1994. pap. 44.95 (0-8373-2464-5) Nat Learn.

Supervising Environmentalist. Jack Rudman. (Career Examination Ser.: C-1586). 1994. pap. 34.95 (0-8373-1586-7) Nat Learn.

Supervising Examiner, Social Services. Jack Rudman. (Career Examination Ser.: C-2140). 1994. reprint ed. pap. 29.95 (0-8373-2140-9) Nat Learn.

Supervising Fire Alarm Dispatcher. Jack Rudman. (Career Examination Ser.: C-1695). 1994. pap. 27.95 (0-8373-1695-2) Nat Learn.

Supervising Fire Marshal (Uniformed) Jack Rudman. (Career Examination Ser.: C-1817). 1994. pap. 39.95 (0-8373-1817-3) Nat Learn.

Supervising Food Inspector. Jack Rudman. (Career Examination Ser.: C-2055). 1994. pap. 34.95 (0-8373-2055-0) Nat Learn.

***Supervising for Success: A Guide for Supervisors.** Tony Moglia. (Fifty Minute Ser.). (Illus.). 120p. (Orig.). 1997. pap. 10.95 (1-56052-460-X) Crisp Pubns.

Supervising Glazier. Jack Rudman. (Career Examination Ser.: C-3751). 1994. pap. 29.95 (0-8373-3751-8) Nat Learn.

Supervising Grants Analyst. Jack Rudman. (Career Examination Ser.: C-2834). 1994. pap. 39.95 (0-8373-2834-9) Nat Learn.

Supervising Hearing Examiner. Jack Rudman. (Career Examination Ser.: C-2327). 1994. pap. 39.95 (0-8373-2327-4) Nat Learn.

Supervising Hearing Officer. Jack Rudman. (Career Examination Ser.: C-2328). 1994. pap. 39.95 (0-8373-2328-2) Nat Learn.

Supervising Highway Engineer. Jack Rudman. (Career Examination Ser.: C-2523). 1994. pap. 39.95 (0-8373-2523-4) Nat Learn.

Supervising Highway Maintenance Supervisor. Jack Rudman. (Career Examination Ser.: C-2632). 1994. pap. 34.95 (0-8373-2632-X) Nat Learn.

Supervising Highway Repairer. (Career Examination Ser.: C-3656). pap. 29.95 (0-8373-3656-2) Nat Learn.

Supervising Hospital Care Investigator. Jack Rudman. (Career Examination Ser.: C-779). 1994. pap. 29.95 (0-8373-0779-1) Nat Learn.

Supervising Housing Groundsman. Jack Rudman. (Career Examination Ser.: C-780). 1994. pap. 29.95 (0-8373-0780-5) Nat Learn.

Supervising Housing Inspector. Jack Rudman. (Career Examination Ser.: C-1045). 1994. pap. 34.95 (0-8373-1045-8) Nat Learn.

Supervising Housing Sergeant. Jack Rudman. (Career Examination Ser.: C-1667). 1994. pap. 39.95 (0-8373-1667-7) Nat Learn.

Supervising Housing Teller. Jack Rudman. (Career Examination Ser.: C-781). 1994. pap. 27.95 (0-8373-0781-3) Nat Learn.

Supervising Human Resources Specialist. Jack Rudman. (Career Examination Ser.: C-1046). 1994. pap. 34.95 (0-8373-1046-6) Nat Learn.

Supervising Human Rights Specialist. Jack Rudman. (Career Examination Ser.: C-1613). 1994. pap. 29.95 (0-8373-1613-8) Nat Learn.

Supervising HVAC Plant Operator. (Career Examination Ser.: C-3752). pap. 39.95 (0-8373-3752-6) Nat Learn.

Supervising Identification Specialist. Jack Rudman. (Career Examination Ser.: C-2513). 1994. pap. 34.95 (0-8373-2513-7) Nat Learn.

Supervising in the Human Services: The Politics of Practice. Stephen M. Holloway & George A. Brager. 320p. 1988. 35.00 (0-02-914810-3, Free Press) Free Pr.

Supervising Incinerator Stationary Engineer. Jack Rudman. (Career Examination Ser.: C-2638). 1994. pap. 34.95 (0-8373-2638-9) Nat Learn.

Supervising Inspector of Markets, Weights & Measures. Jack Rudman. (Career Examination Ser.: C-1047). 1994. pap. 34.95 (0-8373-1047-4) Nat Learn.

Supervising International Banks: Origins & Implications of the Basle Accord. Ethan B. Kapstein. LC 91-43451. (Essays in International Finance Ser.: No. 185). 38p. 1991. pap. text ed. 8.00 (0-88165-092-7) Princeton U Int Finan Econ.

Supervising Investigator. Jack Rudman. (Career Examination Ser.: C-2106). 1994. reprint ed. pap. 29.95 (0-8373-2106-9) Nat Learn.

Supervising Janitor. Jack Rudman. (Career Examination Ser.: C-2065). 1994. reprint ed. pap. 29.95 (0-8373-2065-8) Nat Learn.

Supervising Labor Services Representative. (Career Examination Ser.). Date not set. pap. 39.95 (0-8373-3806-9, C3806) Nat Learn.

Supervising Labor Specialist. Jack Rudman. (Career Examination Ser.: C-2382). 1994. pap. 39.95 (0-8373-2382-7) Nat Learn.

Supervising Laundry Worker. Jack Rudman. (Career Examination Ser.: C-2200). 1994. pap. 29.95 (0-8373-2200-6) Nat Learn.

Supervising Legal Stenographer. Jack Rudman. (Career Examination Ser.: C-2635). 1994. pap. 29.95 (0-8373-2635-4) Nat Learn.

Supervising Manpower Counselor. Jack Rudman. (Career Examination Ser.: C-2437). 1994. pap. 39.95 (0-8373-2437-8) Nat Learn.

Supervising Marketing. (Open Learning for Supervisory Management Ser.). 1986. pap. text ed. 19.50 (0-08-034173-X, Pergamon Pr) Elsevier.

Supervising Meat Inspector. Jack Rudman. (Career Examination Ser.: C-2056). 1994. pap. 34.95 (0-8373-2056-9) Nat Learn.

Supervising Medicaid Claims Examiner. Jack Rudman. (Career Examination Ser.: C-2693). 1994. pap. 34.95 (0-8373-2693-1) Nat Learn.

Supervising Medical Care Representative. Jack Rudman. (Career Examination Ser.: C-3148). 1994. pap. 34.95 (0-8373-3148-X) Nat Learn.

Supervising Medical Services Specialist. Jack Rudman. (Career Examination Ser.: C-3616). 1994. pap. 39.95 (0-8373-3616-3) Nat Learn.

Supervising Medical Social Worker. Jack Rudman. (Career Examination Ser.: C-2630). 1994. pap. 34.95 (0-8373-2630-3) Nat Learn.

Supervising Mortgage Administrator. Jack Rudman. (Career Examination Ser.: C-2312). 1994. reprint ed. pap. 34.95 (0-8373-2312-6) Nat Learn.

Supervising Motor Vehicle License Examiner. Jack Rudman. (Career Examination Ser.: C-2390). 1994. pap. 27.95 (0-8373-2390-8) Nat Learn.

Supervising Motor Vehicle Representative. (Career Examination Ser.: C-3300). 1994. pap. 27.95 (0-8373-3300-8) Nat Learn.

Supervising Museum Instructor. Jack Rudman. (Career Examination Ser.: C-1048). 1994. pap. 29.95 (0-8373-1048-2) Nat Learn.

Supervising Nurse. Jack Rudman. (Career Examination Ser.: C-1883). 1994. pap. 29.95 (0-8373-1883-1) Nat Learn.

Supervising on the Line. Gene Gagnon. (Illus.). 131p. (Orig.). 1988. pap. 12.95 (0-944671-00-4) Margo Pr.

Supervising Painter. Jack Rudman. (Career Examination Ser.: C-3254). 1994. pap. 29.95 (0-8373-3254-0) Nat Learn.

S

***Supervising Paraeducators in School Settings: A Team Approach.** Anna L. Pickett & Kent Gerlach. LC 96-46625. 1997. pap. 29.00 (0-89079-713-7) PRO-ED.

Supervising Parking Enforcement Agent. Jack Rudman. (Career Examination Ser.: C-2143). 1994. reprint ed. pap. 27.95 (0-8373-2143-3) Nat Learn.

Supervising Parking Meter Collector. Jack Rudman. (Career Examination Ser.: C-782). 1994. pap. 27.95 (0-8373-0782-1) Nat Learn.

Supervising Part-Time Employees: A Guide to Better Productivity. Elwood N. Chapman. Ed. by Follin Armfield. LC 93-72501. (Illus.). 85p. (Orig.). 1994. pap. 10.95 (1-56052-243-7) Crisp Pubns.

Supervising Photographer. Jack Rudman. (Career Examination Ser.: C-2504). 1994. pap. 34.95 (0-8373-2504-8) Nat Learn.

Supervising Physical Therapist. Jack Rudman. (Career Examination Ser.: C-2904). 1994. pap. 34.95 (0-8373-2904-3) Nat Learn.

Supervising Physician & Surgeon. Jack Rudman. (Career Examination Ser.: C-2195). 1994. pap. 49.95 (0-8373-2195-6) Nat Learn.

Supervising Plumbing Inspector. Jack Rudman. (Career Examination Ser.: C-1049). 1994. pap. 34.95 (0-8373-1049-0) Nat Learn.

Supervising Police Communications Technician. Jack Rudman. (Career Examination Ser.: C-3618). 1994. pap. 27.95 (0-8373-3618-X) Nat Learn.

Supervising Police Personnel: Back to the Basics. Paul M. Whisenand & George E. Rush. (Illus.). 432p. (C). 1987. text ed. 59.00 (0-13-876178-7) P-H.

Supervising Police Personnel: The 15 Responsibilities. 2nd ed. Paul M. Whisenand & George E. Rush. 304p. 1993. text ed. 77.00 (0-13-878331-4) P-H.

Supervising Probation Officer. Jack Rudman. (Career Examination Ser.: C-2591). 1994. pap. 29.95 (0-8373-2591-9) Nat Learn.

Supervising Professional Conduct Investigator. Jack Rudman. (Career Examination Ser.: C-2299). 1994. reprint ed. pap. 29.95 (0-8373-2299-5) Nat Learn.

Supervising Program Research Specialist. Jack Rudman. (Career Examination Ser.: C-3201). 1994. pap. 39.95 (0-8373-3201-X) Nat Learn.

Supervising Public Health Adviser. Jack Rudman. (Career Examination Ser.: C-3176). 1994. pap. 29.95 (0-8373-3176-5) Nat Learn.

Supervising Public Health Nurse. Jack Rudman. (Career Examination Ser.: C-1748). 1994. reprint ed. pap. 29.95 (0-8373-1748-7) Nat Learn.

Supervising Public Health Sanitarian. Jack Rudman. (Career Examination Ser.: C-2275). 1994. reprint ed. pap. 34.95 (0-8373-2275-8) Nat Learn.

Supervising Real Estate Manager. Jack Rudman. (Career Examination Ser.: C-1860). 1994. pap. 34.95 (0-8373-1860-2) Nat Learn.

Supervising Rent Examiner. Jack Rudman. (Career Examination Ser.: C-1818). 1994. pap. 29.95 (0-8373-1818-1) Nat Learn.

Supervising Sanitary Engineer. Jack Rudman. (Career Examination Ser.: C-2447). 1994. pap. 39.95 (0-8373-2447-5) Nat Learn.

Supervising Sanitation Inspector. Jack Rudman. (Career Examination Ser.: C-2455). 1994. pap. 34.95 (0-8373-2455-6) Nat Learn.

Supervising Security Officer. Jack Rudman. (Career Examination Ser.: C-2205). 1994. pap. 29.95 (0-8373-2205-7) Nat Learn.

Supervising Senior Citizens' Club Leader. Jack Rudman. (Career Examination Ser.: C-2829). 1994. pap. 29.95 (0-8373-2829-2) Nat Learn.

Supervising Social Welfare Examiner. Jack Rudman. (Career Examination Ser.: C-2379). 1994. pap. 29.95 (0-8373-2379-7) Nat Learn.

Supervising Special Officer. Jack Rudman. (Career Examination Ser.: C-1766). 1994. pap. 29.95 (0-8373-1766-5) Nat Learn.

Supervising Stenographer. Jack Rudman. (Career Examination Ser.: C-783). 1994. pap. 23.95 (0-8373-0783-X) Nat Learn.

Supervising Storekeeper. Jack Rudman. (Career Examination Ser.: C-861). 1994. pap. 29.95 (0-8373-0861-5) Nat Learn.

Supervising Street Club Worker. Jack Rudman. (Career Examination Ser.: C-1050). 1994. pap. 29.95 (0-8373-1050-4) Nat Learn.

Supervising Student Employees in Academic Libraries: A Handbook. David A. Baldwin. xvii, 194p. 1991. pap. text ed. 32.00 (0-87287-869-4) Libs Unl.

Supervising Student Internships in Human Services. Ed. by Carlton E. Munson. LC 83-26393. (Clinical Supervisor Ser.: Vol. 2, No. 1). 84p. 1984. text ed. 29.95 (0-86656-301-6) Haworth Pr.

***Supervising Student Teachers the Professional Way.** 5th ed. Henry & Beasley. LC 95-73050. 1996. write for info. (0-916768-09-0) Sycamore Pr.

Supervising Support Investigator. Jack Rudman. (Career Examination Ser.: C-2766). 1994. pap. 29.95 (0-8373-2766-0) Nat Learn.

Supervising System. (Open Learning for Supervisory Management Ser.). 1986. pap. text ed. 19.50 (0-08-070019-5, Pergamon Pr) Elsevier.

Supervising Systems. (Open Learning for Supervisory Management Ser.). 1986. pap. text ed. 19.50 (0-08-034163-2, Pergamon Pr) Elsevier.

Supervising Systems Analyst. Jack Rudman. (Career Examination Ser.: C-2387). 1994. pap. 34.95 (0-8373-2387-8) Nat Learn.

Supervising Tabulator Operator. Jack Rudman. (Career Examination Ser.: C-1681). 1994. pap. 29.95 (0-8373-1681-2) Nat Learn.

Supervising Taxi & Limosine Inspector. Jack Rudman. (Career Examination Ser.: C-2554). 1994. pap. 29.95 (0-8373-2554-4) Nat Learn.

Supervising the Counsellor: A Cyclical Model. Steve Page & Val Wosket. LC 94-8492. (Illus.). 256p. (C). 1994. 62.95 (0-415-10213-8, B4078); pap. text ed. 19.95 (0-415-10212-X, B4074) Routledge.

Supervising the Difficult Employee. Ann M. McGill. LC 94-2845. (Business Skills Express Ser.). 120p. 1994. per. 10.00 (0-7863-0219-4) Irwin Prof Pubng.

Supervising the Law. NEBSM Staff. (Open Learning for Supervisory Management Ser.). 1986. pap. text ed. 19.50 (0-08-034034-2, Pergamon Pr) Elsevier.

***Supervising the PhD: A Guide to Success.** Sara Delamont & Paul Atkinson. 1997. write for info. (0-335-19517-2); pap. write for info. (0-335-19516-4) Taylor & Francis.

Supervising Therapist. Jack Rudman. (Career Examination Ser.: C-2253). 1994. pap. 34.95 (0-8373-2253-7) Nat Learn.

Supervising Thermostat Repairer. (Career Examination Ser.: C-3409). 1994. pap. 27.95 (0-8373-3409-8) Nat Learn.

Supervising Typist. Jack Rudman. (Career Examination Ser.: C-1928). 1994. pap. 23.95 (0-8373-1928-5) Nat Learn.

Supervising Vocational Counselor. Jack Rudman. (Career Examination Ser.: C-2439). 1994. pap. 34.95 (0-8373-2439-4) Nat Learn.

Supervising Water Use Inspector. Jack Rudman. (Career Examination Ser.: C-1051). 1994. pap. 29.95 (0-8373-1051-2) Nat Learn.

Supervising Window Shade Repairer. (Career Examination Ser.). 1997. pap. 29.95 (0-8373-3789-5, C3789) Nat Learn.

Supervising With Authority. (Open Learning for Supervisory Management Ser.). 1986. pap. text ed. 19.50 (0-08-070022-5, Pergamon Pr) Elsevier.

Supervising Youth Division Counselor. Jack Rudman. (Career Examination Ser.: C-2501). 1994. pap. 34.95 (0-8373-2501-3) Nat Learn.

Supervision. Bulin. (C). 1995. student ed., pap. 18.76 (0-395-59139-2) HM.

Supervision. Bulin. (C). 1995. teacher ed., pap. 11.96 (0-395-59140-6) HM.

Supervision. Bulin. (C). 1995. text ed. 52.36 (0-395-59138-4) HM.

Supervision. Samuel C. Certo. (American Bankers Association Edition Ser.). 1995. text ed. 19.00 (0-7863-0503-7) Irwin Prof Pubng.

***Supervision.** Georgia J. Kosmoski. (C). Date not set. text ed. write for info. (1-878016-15-6) Stylex Pub.

Supervision. Moorhead. (C). 1996. suppl. ed., teacher ed., pap. text ed. write for info. (0-03-033083-1); student ed., pap. text ed. write for info. (0-03-033087-4) HB Coll Pubs.

Supervision. Moorhead. (C). 1996. teacher ed., pap. text ed. write for info. (0-03-033089-0) HB Coll Pubs.

Supervision. 2nd ed. 1994. 49.95 (0-387-57400-X) Spr-Verlag.

Supervision. 2nd ed. Bernard Keys & Joy Henshall. 480p. 1990. Net. pap. text ed. 39.50 (0-471-63545-6) Wiley.

Supervision. 2nd ed. Stan Kossen. Date not set. student ed., pap. text ed. 20.50 (0-314-82966-0) West Pub.

Supervision. 2nd ed. Stan Kossen. Ed. by Clyde Perlee & Simon. 532p. (C). 1991. text ed. 52.50 (0-314-76552-2) West Pub.

Supervision. 2nd ed. R. Wayne Mondy et al. 520p. 1990. teacher ed. write for info. (0-318-66378-3, H25067) P-H.

***Supervision.** 2nd ed. Timm. 1992. student ed., pap. 18.95 (0-314-00404-1) S-W Pub.

Supervision. 2nd ed. Paul R. Timm. Ed. by Clyde Perlee & Simon. 443p. (C). 1992. text ed. 56.00 (0-314-93381-6) West Pub.

Supervision. 4th ed. Lloyd L. Byars & Leslie W. Rue. 232p. (C). 1992. student ed., text ed. 19.95 (0-256-12117-6) Irwin.

***Supervision.** 6th ed. Rue. 1998. pap. text ed. 47.60 (0-256-27173-9) McGraw.

Supervision. 8th ed. Plunkett. 1995. text ed. 63.00 (0-13-437955-1) P-H.

Supervision: A Guide to Practice. 4th ed. Jon W. Wiles. LC 95-6543. 1995. text ed. 62.00 (0-02-427641-3, Macmillan Coll) P-H.

Supervision: A Redefinition. 5th ed. Thomas J. Sergiovanni & Robert J. Starratt. LC 92-10031. 1992. text ed. write for info. (0-07-056339-X) McGraw.

***Supervision: A Redefinition.** 6th ed. Thomas J. Sergiovanni & Robert J. Starratt. LC 97-12511. 1997. write for info. (0-07-057891-5) McGraw.

Supervision: A Skill Building Approach. Robert N. Lussier. 528p. (C). 1989. pap. text ed. 45.95 (0-256-06502-0) Irwin.

Supervision: A Skill-Building Approach. 2nd ed. Robert N. Lussier. LC 93-10673. 624p. (C). 1993. Acid-free paper. per. 54.50 (0-256-09050-5) Irwin.

Supervision: ASTD Trainer's Sourcebook. B. H. Williamson. 1996. pap. text ed. 39.95 (0-07-053437-3) McGraw.

Supervision: Building Quality & Diversity Through Leadership. Samuel C. Certo. LC 93-15518. 608p. (C). 1993. per. 54.50 (0-256-11982-1) Irwin.

Supervision: Concepts & Practices Management. 6th ed. Hilgert. (Principles of Management Ser.). 1995. student ed., pap. 22.95 (0-538-83690-3) S-W Pub.

Supervision: Concepts & Practices of Management. 6th ed. Raymond L. Hilgert & Edwin C. Leonard. LC 94-15555. 1995. pap. 60.95 (0-538-83689-X) S-W Pub.

Supervision: Concepts & Practices of Management. 7th ed. Hilgert. LC 97-15180. (GC - Principles of Management Ser.). 1998. pap. 49.95 (0-538-86353-6) S-W Pub.

Supervision: First-Line Management. 5th ed. Lawrence L. Steinmetz & H. Ralph Todd, Jr. 464p. (C). 1991. per. 54.50 (0-256-06669-8) Irwin.

Supervision: Improving Processes for Customer Value. Bounds. (GZ - Supervision Ser.). 1998. text ed. 49.95 (0-538-85942-3) S-W Pub.

Supervision: Key Link to Productivity. 3rd ed. Leslie W. Rue & Lloyd L. Byars. (C). 1990. student ed., pap. text ed. 17.95 (0-256-08192-1) Irwin.

Supervision: Key Link to Productivity. 4th ed. Leslie W. Rue & Lloyd L. Byars. LC 92-14200. (Illus.). 512p. (C). 1992. per. 52.95 (0-256-10525-1) Irwin.

Supervision: Managing for Results. 7th ed. John W. Newstrom & Lester R. Bittel. LC 95-21324. 1995. pap. 25.00 (0-02-802491-5) Glencoe.

Supervision: Quality & Diversity Through Leadership. 2nd ed. Samuel C. Certo. 608p. (C). 1996. 54.50 (0-256-20805-0) Irwin.

Supervision: Skills for Success. J. Alan Hansen. Ed. by Lois Hansen. (Illus.). 161p. (C). 1993. student ed. 14.95 (0-9635737-0-5) Ilum Pr.

Supervision: Techniques & New Dimensions. 2nd ed. Alfred W. Travers. LC 92-24783. 416p. (C). 1992. pap. text ed. 59.00 (0-13-878281-4) P-H.

Supervision: The Art of Management. 4th ed. Frunzi & Savini. 544p. (C). 1996. text ed. 49.00 (0-13-476227-4) P-H.

Supervision: The Direction of People at Work. 5th ed. Warren R. Plunkett. 416p. 1989. teacher ed. write for info. (0-318-64394-4, H17320) P-H.

Supervision: Working with People. 2nd ed. Stephen E. Catt & Donald S. Miller. 515p. (C). 1991. text ed. 11.50 (0-256-10703-3, 050340) Irwin Prof Pubng.

Supervision: Working with People. 2nd ed. Stephen E. Catt & Donald S. Miller. 640p. (C). 1990. text ed. 52.95 (0-256-06904-2) Irwin.

Supervision: Working with People. 2nd ed. Stephen E. Catt & Donald S. Miller. 640p. (C). 1990. student ed. 18.95 (0-256-06905-0) Irwin.

Supervision & Administration: Programs, Positions, Perspectives. Ed. by E. Andrew Mills. (Illus.). 221p. (C). 1991. 22.00 (0-937652-56-3) Natl Art Ed.

Supervision & Facilitator Support Action-Learning Manual: A Guide for Literacy Practitioners. (Literacy Linkage Series Manuals). 27p. (Orig.). 1996. pap. 4.00 (0-932288-96-0) Ctr Intl Ed U of MA.

Supervision & Management: A Guide to Modifying Work Behavior. John N. Marr & Richard T. Roessler. LC 93-36797. (Illus.). 240p. (C). 1994. pap. 20.00 (1-55728-306-0) U of Ark Pr.

Supervision & Management of Quantity Food Preparation. 3rd ed. William J. Morgan, Jr. LC 88-60453. (Illus.). (C). 1988. 36.00 (0-8211-1260-0) McCutchan.

Supervision & Performance: Managing Professional Work in Human Service Organizations. Douglas R. Bunker & Marion H. Wijnberg. LC 88-42779. (Social & Behavioral Science Ser.). 417p. 39.95 (1-55542-099-0) Jossey-Bass.

Supervision & Related Issues: A Handbook for Professionals. Cathy A. Malchiodi & Shirley Riley. 250p. (Orig.). 1996. pap. 24.95 (0-9613309-7-X) Magnolia St Pub.

Supervision & Training: Models, Dilemmas, & Challenges. Ed. by Florence W. Kaslow. LC 85-27037. (Clinical Supervisor Ser.: Vol. 4, Nos. 1 & 2). 259p. 1986. text ed. 49.95 (0-86656-528-0); pap. text ed. 19.95 (0-86656-529-9) Haworth Pr.

Supervision As a Proactive Process: Concepts & Cases. 2nd ed. John C. Daresh & Marsha A. Playko. (Illus.). 397p. (C). 1995. pap. text ed. 25.95 (0-88133-814-1) Waveland Pr.

Supervision Can Be Easy! David K. Lindo. LC 79-17682. 282p. reprint ed. pap. 80.40 (0-317-26952-6, 2023582) Bks Demand.

Supervision Card Course. 1994. 12.95 (0-930137-24-8) Looseleaf Law.

Supervision, Consultation, & Staff Training in the Helping Professions. Florence W. Kaslow et al. LC 77-82919. (Jossey-Bass Social & Behavioral Science Ser.). 368p. reprint ed. pap. 104.90 (0-8357-4896-0, 2037826) Bks Demand.

Supervision for Better Instruction: Practical Techniques for Improving Staff Performance. Marcia K. Knoll. 256p. 1987. 27.50 (0-13-876426-3) P-H.

Supervision for Empowered Workers: View Leadership Styles for Self-Managing Teams. Lloyd Pressel & Robert H. Gardner. 210p. 1992. 24.95 (0-9634821-0-6) Loma Linda Pub.

Supervision for Midwives. Mayes. 227p. 1996. pap. 30.00 (1-898507-14-7) Buttrwrth-Heinemann.

Supervision for Success in Government: A Practical Guide for First Line Managers. Dalton S. Lee & N. Joseph Cayer. (Public Administration Ser.). 225p. 1994. 26.95 (0-685-71219-2) Jossey-Bass.

Supervision for Successful Team Leadership: Your Personal Analysis with the Quesitons & Answers You Need to Know. Lowell F. Masters & Howard D. Richardson. Ed. by S. A. Fish. LC 91-38315. (Illus.). 128p. (Orig.). 1992. pap. 16.95 (0-9630748-0-6) Achieve Pr.

Supervision for Teacher Development. Alan Reiman. LC 97-21568. (C). 1998. pap. text ed. write for info. (0-8013-1539-5) Addison-Wesley.

Supervision for Today's Schools. 4th ed. Peter F. Oliva. 640p. (C). 1993. text ed. 58.95 (0-8013-0778-3, 78807) Longman.

Supervision for Today's Schools. 5th ed. Peter F. Oliva & George E. Pawlas. LC 96-6458. (C). 1997. text ed. 51.95 (0-8013-1650-2) Longman.

Supervision Handbook. Mario J. Ferrari. 175p. 1990. pap. 16.95 (0-87526-378-X) Gould.

Supervision in Action. 4th ed. Claude S. George, Jr. (C). 1985. teacher ed. write for info. (0-8359-7161-9, Reston) P-H.

Supervision in Communication Disorders. Stephen S. Farmer & Judith Farmer. 400p. (C). 1989. write for info. (0-675-20963-3, Merrill Coll) P-H.

Supervision in Early Childhood Education. Joseph J. Caruso & M. Temple Fawcett. (Early Childhood Education Ser.). 256p. 1986. pap. text ed. 18.95 (0-8077-2802-0) Tchrs Coll.

Supervision in Health Education: Principles & Techniques. James H. Humphrey. LC 94-29521. (Illus.). 198p. (C). 1994. pap. 27.95 (0-398-05953-5); text ed. 42.95 (0-398-05932-2) C C Thomas.

Supervision in Social Work. 2nd ed. Alfred Kadushin. LC 84-21397. 608p. 1985. text ed. 39.50 (0-231-06008-4) Col U Pr.

Supervision in Social Work. 3rd ed. Alfred Kadushin. 558p. 1992. text ed. 45.00 (0-231-07108-6) Col U Pr.

Supervision in the Health Care Organizations. Richard I. Lyles & Carl Joiner. LC 85-17799. 245p. 1989. text ed. 33.50 (0-8273-4294-2) Delmar.

Supervision in the Helping Professions. Peter Hawkins & Robin Shohet. 176p. 1989. 85.00 (0-335-09854-1, Open Univ Pr); pap. 29.00 (0-335-09833-9, Open Univ Pr) Taylor & Francis.

Supervision in the Hospitality Industry. 2nd ed. Raphael R. Kavanaugh & Jack D. Ninemeier. LC 90-49672. (Illus.). 312p. 1995. pap. write for info. (0-86612-098-X) Educ Inst Am Hotel.

Supervision in the Hospitality Industry. 2nd ed. Jack Miller et al. LC 91-38368. (Service Management Ser.: No. 1416). 400p. 1992. Net. text ed. 30.50 (0-471-54904-5) Wiley.

***Supervision in the Hospitality Industry.** 2nd ed. Jack E. Miller et al. 1992. pap. text ed. 0.01 (0-471-57820-7) Wiley.

Supervision in Transition. Linda Darling-Hammond & Peter Grimmett. Ed. by Carl Glickman. LC 44-6213. 222p. 1992. pap. 23.95 (0-87120-188-7, 610-92000) Assn Supervision.

Supervision, Key Link to Productivity. 5th ed. Leslie W. Rue & Lloyd L. Byars. LC 95-8206. 480p. (C). 1995. per. 54.50 (0-256-17068-1) Irwin.

Supervision of Applied Training: A Comparative Review. Ed. by DeWayne J. Kurpius et al. LC 76-28640. 279p. 1977. text ed. 75.00 (0-8371-9288-9, KSA/, Greenwood Pr) Greenwood.

Supervision of Bilingual Programs. Juan C. Munguia. Ed. by Francesco Cordasco. LC 77-90555. (Bilingual-Bicultural Education in the U. S. Ser.). 1978. lib. bdg. 26.95 (0-405-11093-6) Ayer.

Supervision of Congregational Ministries: The Reflective Practice of Ministry. C. George Fitzgerald. (JPCP Monograph). 50p. (Orig.). 1993. write for info. (0-929670-08-6) JPCP.

Supervision of District Level Library Media Programs. Blanche M. Woolls. (School Library Media Management Ser.). xviii, 228p. 1990. pap. text ed. 27.00 (0-87287-733-7) Libs Unl.

***Supervision of Health Personnel at District Level.** D. Flahault & M. Piot. 100p. 1988. 18.00 (92-4-154229-2) World Health.

***Supervision of Instruction.** Ed. by Henson. (C). 1998. text ed. write for info. (0-321-01124-4) Addson-Wesley Educ.

***Supervision of Instruction.** 4th ed. Glickman & Gordon. 1997. 56.00 (0-205-27227-4) P-H.

Supervision of Instruction: A Development Approach. 3rd ed. Carl D. Glickman et al. LC 94-22142. 1994. text ed. 63.00 (0-205-16389-0) Allyn.

Supervision of Instruction: Theory into Practice. Wayne K. Hoy & Patrick Forsyth. 320p. 1986. text ed. write for info. (0-07-554370-2) McGraw.

Supervision of Literacy Programs: Teachers As Grass-Roots Change Agents. Lawrence G. Erickson. LC 94-14444. 1994. pap. text ed. 31.00 (0-205-16240-1) Allyn.

Supervision of Ministry Students. Regina Coll. 120p. (Orig.). 1992. pap. 11.95 (0-8146-2040-X) Liturgical Pr.

***Supervision of Police Personnel.** 3rd ed. Whisenand & Rush. 1997. text ed. 61.00 (0-13-616673-3) P-H.

Supervision of Police Personnel. 5th ed. Nathan F. Iannone. LC 93-9096. 382p. (C). 1993. text ed. 73.00 (0-13-064965-1) P-H Gen Ref & Trav.

Supervision of Police Personnel Study Guide. 5th ed. 214p. 1995. 26.95 (1-56325-054-3) Davis Pub Law.

***Supervision of Psychotherapy & Counselling.** Geraldine Shipton. LC 96-33218. 1997. write for info. (0-335-19513-X, Open Univ Pr); pap. write for info. (0-335-19512-1, Open Univ Pr) Taylor & Francis.

Supervision of State Aids. Ross. Date not set. text ed. write for info. (0-7185-1324-X) St Martin.

Supervision of State Aids & Public Undertakings under EEC Law. Ross. 1995. 79.95 (1-85567-298-7) St Martin.

Supervision of Technical Staff. Weston. 1989. 49.00 (0-85186-423-6) CRC Pr.

***Supervision of the Sex Offender.** Georgia Cumming & Maureen Buell. 128p. (Orig.). 1996. pap. 25.00 (1-884444-40-7) Safer Soc.

Supervision of Valves Controlling Water Supplies for Fire Protection. National Fire Protection Association Staff. 1988. 16.75 (0-317-63062-8, 26-88) Natl Fire Prot.

Supervision, Review, & Report Processing. American Institute of Certified Public Accountants Staff. LC 90-1075. (Technical Information for Practitioners Ser.: No. 5). 89p. reprint ed. pap. 25.40 (0-7837-6627-0, 2046214) Bks Demand.

Supervision Strategies for the First Practicum. Susan Neufeldt. 190p. 1995. pap. text ed. 27.95 (1-55620-146-X, 72680) Am Coun Assn.

S

Supervision Test. Jack Rudman. (Teachers License Examination Ser.: S-9). 1994. pap. 49.95 (0-8373-8109-6) Nat Learn.

Supervision Today! Stephen P. Robbins & Sharon L. O'Neil. LC 94-25500. 608p. 1994. pap. text ed. 61.00 (0-13-876848-X) P-H.

***Supervision Today.** 2nd ed. Robbins & Decenzo. 1997. student ed., pap. text ed. 25.33 (0-13-634684-7) P-H.

***Supervision Today.** 2nd ed. Robbins & Decenzo. LC 97-3146. 1997. pap. text ed. 56.00 (0-13-608630-6) P-H.

Supervision Transition! An Employee Guide to Choosing & Moving into a Supervisory Position. Paul O. Radde. Ed. by Larry N. Davis. (Illus.). (Orig.). 1990. pap. 17.95 (0-9625872-0-6) Thriving Pubns.

Supervisor. Jack Rudman. (Career Examination Ser.: C-3510). 1994. pap. 29.95 (0-8373-3510-8) Nat Learn.

Supervisor & on the Job Training. 4th ed. Martin M. Broadwell. 1995. pap. 20.95 (0-201-56363-0) Addison-Wesley.

Supervisor (Buses & Shops) Jack Rudman. (Career Examination Ser.: C-1504). 1994. pap. 29.95 (0-8373-1504-2) Nat Learn.

Supervisor (Cars & Shops) Jack Rudman. (Career Examination Ser.: C-1723). 1994. pap. 29.95 (0-8373-1723-1) Nat Learn.

Supervisor (Child Welfare) Jack Rudman. (Career Examination Ser.: C-784). 1994. pap. 29.95 (0-8373-0784-8) Nat Learn.

Supervisor (Electrical Power) Jack Rudman. (Career Examination Ser.: C-2238). 1994. pap. 29.95 (0-8373-2238-3) Nat Learn.

Supervisor (Electronic Equipment) Jack Rudman. (Career Examination Ser.: C-2193). 1994. pap. 29.95 (0-8373-2193-X) Nat Learn.

Supervisor (Elevators & Escalators) Jack Rudman. (Career Examination Ser.: C-1934). 1994. pap. 29.95 (0-8373-1934-X) Nat Learn.

Supervisor, General Equipment Repair. Jack Rudman. (Career Examination Ser.: C-1458). 1994. pap. 34.95 (0-8373-1458-5) Nat Learn.

Supervisor I (Child Welfare) Jack Rudman. (Career Examination Ser.: C-1806). 1994. pap. 29.95 (0-8373-1806-8) Nat Learn.

Supervisor I (Welfare) Jack Rudman. (Career Examination Ser.: C-1803). 1994. pap. 29.95 (0-8373-1803-3) Nat Learn.

Supervisor II (Child Welfare) Jack Rudman. (Career Examination Ser.: C-1807). 1994. pap. 34.95 (0-8373-1807-6) Nat Learn.

Supervisor II (Welfare) Jack Rudman. (Career Examination Ser.: C-1804). 1994. pap. 34.95 (0-8373-1804-1) Nat Learn.

Supervisor III (Child Welfare) Jack Rudman. (Career Examination Ser.: C-1808). 1994. pap. 34.95 (0-8373-1808-4) Nat Learn.

Supervisor III (Social Service) Jack Rudman. (Career Examination Ser.: C-1951). 1994. pap. 34.95 (0-8373-1951-X) Nat Learn.

Supervisor III (Welfare) Jack Rudman. (Career Examination Ser.: C-1805). 1994. pap. 34.95 (0-8373-1805-X) Nat Learn.

Supervisor (Lighting) Jack Rudman. (Career Examination Ser.: C-1724). 1994. pap. 29.95 (0-8373-1724-X) Nat Learn.

Supervisor (Medical & Psychiatric Social Work) Jack Rudman. (Career Examination Ser.: C-1052). 1994. pap. 34.95 (0-8373-1052-0) Nat Learn.

Supervisor of Building Custodians. Jack Rudman. (Career Examination Ser.: C-1015). 1994. pap. 29.95 (0-8373-1015-6) Nat Learn.

Supervisor of Communications Services. (Career Examination Ser.). pap. 34.95 (0-8373-3778-X, C3778) Nat Learn.

Supervisor of Conservation Areas. Jack Rudman. (Career Examination Ser.: C-3123). 1994. pap. 34.95 (0-8373-3123-4) Nat Learn.

Supervisor of Construction Inspection Services. Jack Rudman. (Career Examination Ser.: C-3139). 1994. pap. 39.95 (0-8373-3139-0) Nat Learn.

Supervisor of Electrical Installations. Jack Rudman. (Career Examination Ser.: C-1507). 1994. pap. 29.95 (0-8373-1507-7) Nat Learn.

Supervisor of Facilities Planning. Jack Rudman. (Career Examination Ser.: C-3021). 1994. pap. 34.95 (0-8373-3021-1) Nat Learn.

Supervisor of Grounds Operations. (Career Examination Ser.: C-2962). 1994. pap. 29.95 (0-8373-2962-0) Nat Learn.

Supervisor of Housing Caretakers. Jack Rudman. (Career Examination Ser.: C-3010). 1994. pap. 29.95 (0-8373-3010-6) Nat Learn.

Supervisor of Licensing. Jack Rudman. (Career Examination Ser.: C-2191). 1994. pap. 29.95 (0-8373-2191-3) Nat Learn.

Supervisor of Marina Maintenance. Jack Rudman. (Career Examination Ser.: C-3130). 1994. pap. 29.95 (0-8373-3130-7) Nat Learn.

Supervisor of Mechanical Installations. Jack Rudman. (Career Examination Ser.: C-1508). 1994. pap. 29.95 (0-8373-1508-5) Nat Learn.

Supervisor of Mechanics (Mechanical Equipment) Jack Rudman. (Career Examination Ser.: C-1484). 1994. pap. 29.95 (0-8373-1484-4) Nat Learn.

Supervisor of Mechanics (Motor Vehicles) Jack Rudman. (Career Examination Ser.: C-3047). 1994. pap. 29.95 (0-8373-3047-5) Nat Learn.

Supervisor of Menagerie. Jack Rudman. (Career Examination Ser.: C-1792). 1994. pap. 29.95 (0-8373-1793-2) Nat Learn.

Supervisor of Motor Repair. Jack Rudman. (Career Examination Ser.: C-1875). 1994. pap. 29.95 (0-8373-1875-0) Nat Learn.

Supervisor of Motor Transport. Jack Rudman. (Career Examination Ser.: C-1509). 1994. pap. 29.95 (0-8373-1509-3) Nat Learn.

Supervisor of Office Services. Jack Rudman. (Career Examination Ser.: C-2533). 1994. pap. 29.95 (0-8373-2533-1) Nat Learn.

Supervisor of Operations. Jack Rudman. (Career Examination Ser.: C-1028). 1994. pap. 34.95 (0-8373-1028-8) Nat Learn.

Supervisor of Park Operations. Jack Rudman. (Career Examination Ser.: C-1752). 1994. pap. 29.95 (0-8373-1752-5) Nat Learn.

Supervisor of Professional Licensing. Jack Rudman. (Career Examination Ser.: C-1029). 1994. pap. 29.95 (0-8373-1029-6) Nat Learn.

Supervisor of Public Parking. Jack Rudman. (Career Examination Ser.: C-1418). 1994. pap. 29.95 (0-8373-1418-6) Nat Learn.

Supervisor of School Maintenance (Construction) Jack Rudman. (Career Examination Ser.: C-1510). 1994. pap. 29.95 (0-8373-1510-7) Nat Learn.

Supervisor of School Maintenance (Mechanical) Jack Rudman. (Career Examination Ser.: C-1511). 1994. pap. 29.95 (0-8373-1511-5) Nat Learn.

Supervisor of Tax Compliance Field Operations. Jack Rudman. (Career Examination Ser.: C-2955). 1994. pap. 34.95 (0-8373-2955-8) Nat Learn.

Supervisor of Traffic Device Maintainers. Jack Rudman. (Career Examination Ser.: C-3052). 1994. pap. 29.95 (0-8373-3052-1) Nat Learn.

Supervisor of Transportation. Jack Rudman. (Career Examination Ser.: C-1813). 1994. pap. 29.95 (0-8373-1813-0) Nat Learn.

Supervisor of Vocational Rehabilitation Unit. Jack Rudman. (Career Examination Ser.: C-1742). 1994. pap. 34.95 (0-8373-1742-8) Nat Learn.

***Supervisor of Volunteer Services.** Jack Rudman. (Career Examination Ser.: Vol. C-3814). 1997. pap. 29.95 (0-8373-3814-X) Nat Learn.

Supervisor of Youth Services. Jack Rudman. (Career Examination Ser.: C-1682). 1994. pap. 29.95 (0-8373-1682-0) Nat Learn.

Supervisor (Power Distribution) Jack Rudman. (Career Examination Ser.: C-423). 1994. pap. 29.95 (0-8373-0423-7) Nat Learn.

Supervisor (Signals) Jack Rudman. (Career Examination Ser.: C-2062). 1994. pap. 29.95 (0-8373-2062-3) Nat Learn.

Supervisor (Social Work) Jack Rudman. (Career Examination Ser.: C-1000). 1994. pap. 29.95 (0-8373-1000-8) Nat Learn.

Supervisor (Stores, Materials & Supplies) Jack Rudman. (Career Examination Ser.: C-1505). 1994. pap. 29.95 (0-8373-1505-0) Nat Learn.

Supervisor (Structures) Jack Rudman. (Career Examination Ser.: C-424). 1994. pap. 29.95 (0-8373-0424-5) Nat Learn.

Supervisor (Structures - Group C) (Iron Work) Jack Rudman. (Career Examination Ser.: C-425). 1994. pap. 29.95 (0-8373-0425-3) Nat Learn.

Supervisor (Telephones) Jack Rudman. (Career Examination Ser.: C-426). 1994. pap. 29.95 (0-8373-0426-1) Nat Learn.

Supervisor (Track) Jack Rudman. (Career Examination Ser.: C-1953). 1994. reprint ed. pap. 29.95 (0-8373-1953-6) Nat Learn.

Supervisor (Turnstiles) Jack Rudman. (Career Examination Ser.: C-427). 1994. pap. 29.95 (0-8373-0427-X) Nat Learn.

Supervisor Universitario de la Practica Docente. Lydia Diaz De Grana. 120p. 1975. pap. 3.00 (0-8477-2707-6) U of PR Pr.

Supervisor (Ventilation & Drainage) Jack Rudman. (Career Examination Ser.: C-1506). 1994. pap. 29.95 (0-8373-1506-9) Nat Learn.

Supervisor (Water & Sewer Systems) Jack Rudman. (Career Examination Ser.: C-2907). 1994. pap. 29.95 (0-8373-2907-8) Nat Learn.

Supervisor (Welfare) Jack Rudman. (Career Examination Ser.: C-0785). 1994. pap. 29.95 (0-8373-0785-6) Nat Learn.

Supervisor y la Prevencion de Accidentes. 96p. 7.50 (0-318-18008-1) Inter-Am Safety.

Supervisors & Teachers: A Private Cold War. 2nd ed. Arthur Blumberg. LC 79-89771. 192p. 1980. 33.00 (0-8211-0133-1) McCutchan.

Supervisor's Big Book of Lists. George Fuller. LC 93-48158. 1994. pap. text ed. 15.95 (0-13-122771-8) P-H.

Supervisor's Big Book of Lists. George Fuller. LC 93-48158. 1994. write for info. (0-13-336850-5) P-H.

Supervisor's Complete Guide to Hazardous Waste & Materials Management. rev. ed. John F. Brady. 1985. ring bd. 99.95 (1-55645-303-5, 303) Busn Legal Reports.

Supervisor's Complete Guide to Leadership Behavior. rev. ed. Richard W. Leatherman. (Illus.). 102p. 1981. 17.50 (0-9603702-1-8) Intl Training.

Supervisor's Factomatic. Jack Horn. LC 86-24391. 490p. 1986. 39.95 (0-317-43315-6, Busn) P-H.

Supervisor's Factomatic. 2nd ed. Jack Horn. LC 93-922. 1993. pap. text ed. 49.95 (0-13-489774-9) P-H Gen Ref & Trav.

Supervisor's Guide. Jerry Brown & Denise Dudley. viii, 68p. (Orig.). 1989. 10.95 (1-878542-01-X, 12-0001) SkillPath Pubns.

Supervisor's Guide to Contract Administration & Grievance Handling. Joseph J. Woodford. 1986. pap. 9.00 (0-913409-05-7) Advisory Pub.

Supervisor's Guide to Documentation & File Building for Employee Discipline. Ronald C. Ruud & Joseph J. Woodford. LC 83-72064. 72p. 1981. pap. 9.00 (0-913409-06-5) Advisory Pub.

Supervisor's Guide to Documenting Employee Discipline. Lee T. Paterson. 60p. 1993. pap. 19.00 (0-250-47232-5) MICHIE.

Supervisor's Guide to Documenting Employee Discipline. 3rd ed. Lee T. Paterson & Michael R. Deblieux. 1991. pap. 19.00 (1-55943-091-5) MICHIE.

Supervisor's Guide to Effective Performance Appraisal. Forest C. Benedict & Cynthia Smith. 38p. 1992. 15.00 (1-878240-07-2) Coll & U Personnel.

Supervisor's Guide to Employee Performance Reviews. 2nd ed. Lee T. Paterson & Michael R. Deblieux. 110p. 1993. pap. 19.00 (1-55943-176-8) MICHIE.

Supervisor's Guide to Federal Labor Relations. 3rd ed. Ed. by Dennis K. Reischl & Ralph R. Smith. 131p. (Orig.). 1993. pap. text ed. 9.95 (0-936295-40-6) FPMI Comns.

Supervisor's Guide to On-The-Job Alcoholism & Drug Problems. Business & Legal Reports Staff. 1986. pap. 9.95 (1-55645-432-5) Busn Legal Reports.

Supervisor's Guide to Preventing Sexual Harassment. Greg Naylor. LC 96-2807. 94p. 1996. spiral bd. 47.00 (0-925773-26-3) M Lee Smith.

Supervisor's Guide to Safety & Health Programs. 80p. 1992. pap. 30.00 (0-943244-87-0) Water Environ.

Supervisors' Guide to Successful Training. William R. Griffin. (Illus.). 1977. pap. text ed. 23.00 (0-9601054-3-3) Cleaning Cons.

Supervisor's Handbook. 2nd ed. Ed. by Career Press Staff. (Business Desk Reference Ser.). 128p. 1993. pap. 8.95 (1-56414-106-3) Career Pr Inc.

Supervisor's Handbook: Techniques for Getting Results Through Others. Mark R. Truitt. 1991. pap. 7.95 (1-55852-056-2) Natl Pr Pubns.

Supervisor's Handbook: Techniques for Getting Results Through Others. 2nd rev. ed. Mark R. Truitt. (Leadership Ser.). (Illus.). 70p. 1988. pap. 9.95 (1-55852-002-3) Natl Pr Pubns.

Supervisors' Handbook for Employee Assistance. Don Reeves. 40p. 1995. pap. 39.99 (1-884937-21-7) Manisses Communs.

Supervisor's Handbook of Mnemonic Devices. Jack Rudman. (Teachers License Examination Ser.: S-10). 1994. pap. 49.95 (0-8373-8110-X) Nat Learn.

Supervisor's Handbook on Maintaining Non-Union Status. rev. ed. Alfred DeMaria. 1986. pap. 9.95 (0-88057-509-3) Exec Ent Pubns.

Supervisor's Handbook on Maintaining Non-Union Status. rev. ed. Alfred T. DeMaria. 80p. 1994. pap. text ed. 19.95 (0-471-11286-0) Wiley.

Supervisor's Log (A Professional's Graffiti) A Handbook for Supervision. June Delano. 176p. (C). 1993. pap. text ed. 18.95 (0-8077-3292-3) Tchrs Coll.

***Supervisor's Portable Answer Book.** George Fuller. 368p. 39.95 (0-13-876632-0) P-H.

Supervisors Portable Answer Book. George G. Fuller. 1989. pap. text ed. 16.95 (0-13-876590-1) P-H.

Supervisor's Right to Know Handbook. rev. ed. Ed. by John F. Brady. 72p. 1988. per. 24.95 (1-55645-305-1, 305) Busn Legal Reports.

Supervisors' Safety Manual. 8th rev. ed. LC 92-85027. (Illus.). 386p. (C). 1992. text ed. 68.95 (0-87912-167-X, 15142-0000) Natl Safety Coun.

***Supervisors' Safety Manual.** 9th ed. National Safety Council Staff. LC 97-8993. 1997. write for info. (0-87912-197-1) Natl Safety Coun.

Supervisor's Safety Meeting Handbook, 2 vols., Set. rev. ed. 1989. ring bd. 199.95 (1-55645-593-3, 110000) Busn Legal Reports.

Supervisor's Script Book. Raymond Dreyfack. 352p. 1996. 39.95 (0-13-460114-9); pap. 15.95 (0-13-476052-2) P-H.

Supervisor's Standard Reference Handbook. 2nd ed. W. H. Weiss. 310p. 1988. 39.95 (0-13-877168-5, Busn) P-H.

Supervisor's Survival Kit: Your First Step into Management. 7th ed. Elwood N. Chapman. LC 92-12433. 1995. pap. text ed. 33.60 (0-13-452525-6) P-H.

Supervisory Acquisition & Enforcement Developments. Thomas P. Vartanian & H. Rodgin Cohen. (Illus.). v, 358p. write for info. (0-318-60752-2) HarBrace.

Supervisory & Middle Managers in Libraries. Martha J. Bailey. LC 80-23049. 218p. 1981. 20.00 (0-8108-1400-5) Scarecrow.

Supervisory Behavior in Education. 3rd ed. Ben M. Harris. (Illus.). 400p. (C). 1985. text ed. write for info. (0-13-877101-4) P-H.

Supervisory Challenge: Principles & Practices. 2nd ed. Jane W. Gibson. 512p. (C). 1994. pap. text ed. 57.00 (0-02-341792-7, Macmillan Coll) P-H.

Supervisory Control of Absenteesim. James V. Findlay & Richard G. Morrison. LC 77-77275. (Illus.). 62p. Incl. transparency masters. ring bd. 69.50 (0-88061-018-2) Intl Loss Cntrl.

Supervisory Couple in Broad-Spectrum Psychotherapy. Wyn Bramley. 180p. (C). 1997. 50.00 (1-85343-353-5); pap. 20.00 (1-85343-354-3) NYU Pr.

Supervisory Electric Engineer. Jack Rudman. (Career Examination Ser.: C-786). 1994. pap. 39.95 (0-8373-0786-4) Nat Learn.

Supervisory Encounter: A Guide for Teachers of Psychodynamic Psychotherapy & Psychoanalysis. Daniel Jacobs et al. LC 94-47180. 1995. 28.50 (0-300-06200-1) Yale U Pr.

***Supervisory Encounter: A Guide for Teachers of Psychodynamic Psychotherapy & Psychoanalysis.** Daniel Jacobs. 1997. pap. text ed. 18.00 (0-300-07277-5) Yale U Pr.

Supervisory General Engineer. Jack Rudman. (Career Examination Ser.: C-787). 1994. pap. 44.95 (0-8373-0787-2) Nat Learn.

Supervisory Handbooks, 3 vols. rev. ed. Dennis J. Murphy. (Speaking from Experience Ser.). Successful Time Management for Supervisors: How to Get More Done, Improve Quality, Meet Deadlines &. pap. 7.50 (1-877948-07-1); Effective Supervision Skills: How to Lead Effectively, Prevent Problems, Praise Genuinely & Get Resu. pap. 7.50 (1-877948-06-3) Prof Train TX.

Supervisory Handbooks, 3 vols. rev. ed. Dennis J. Murphy. (Speaking from Experience Ser.). 47p. 1986. Increasing Employee Motivation: A Guide for Supervisors, 1986, 47p. pap. 7.50 (1-877948-05-5) Prof Train TX.

Supervisory Handbooks, 3 vols., Set. rev. ed. Dennis J. Murphy. (Speaking from Experience Ser.). pap. 15.00 (1-877948-08-X) Prof Train TX.

Supervisory Leadership: Introduction to Instructional Supervision. Allan A. Glatthorn. (C). 1990. text ed. 59.50 (0-673-38134-X) Addson-Wesley Educ.

Supervisory Leadership & the New Factory: Getting Extraordinary Things Done on the Shop Floor. Bud Bilanich. 120p. 1993. pap. 19.95 (0-9638280-0-2) Front Row Pr.

Supervisory Management. 2nd ed. Robert W. Eckles et al. (Management Ser.). 538p. (C). 1989. reprint ed. 56.50 (0-471-05947-1) Krieger.

Supervisory Management. 3rd ed. David Evans. 656p. 1992. text ed. 70.00 (0-304-32551-1); pap. text ed. 26.95 (0-304-32296-2); teacher ed. write for info. (0-304-32546-5) Cassell.

Supervisory Management. 4th ed. David Evans. (Illus.). 640p. 1995. 65.00 (0-304-33129-5) Cassell.

Supervisory Management. 4th ed. David Evans. (Illus.). 640p. 1995. pap. 32.00 (0-304-33131-7) Cassell.

Supervisory Management. 4th ed. Mosley. LC 96-24986. (GC - Principles of Management Ser.). 1997. pap. 55.95 (0-538-85560-6) S-W Pub.

Supervisory Management. 4th ed. Mosley. (GC - Principles of Management Ser.). 1997. student ed., text ed. 15.95 (0-538-85561-4) S-W Pub.

Supervisory Management. 6th ed. P. W. Betts. Orig. Title: Supervisory Studies. 560p. 1993. pap. 48.50 (0-273-60057-5, Pub. by Pitman Pub Ltd UK) Trans-Atl Phila.

Supervisory Management: Art of Empowering. 3rd ed. David Megginson. (GC - Principles of Management Ser.). 1993. student ed., pap. 17.00 (0-538-82247-3) S-W Pub.

Supervisory Management: The Art of Empowering & Developing People. 3rd ed. Donald C. Mosely et al. LC 92-24127. 1993. text ed. 39.00 (0-538-82246-5) S-W Pub.

Supervisory Management: The Art of Working with & Through People. Donald C. Mosley et al. (C). 1985. write for info. (0-538-07660-7, G66) S-W Pub.

Supervisory Management for Health Care Organization. 4th ed. Theo Haimann. 448p. (C). 1990. per. write for info. (0-697-14126-8) Brown & Benchmark.

Supervisory Management for Health Care Organizations. 5th ed. Theo Haimann. 464p. (C). 1993. per. 50.75 (0-697-14127-6) Wm C Brown Pubs.

Supervisory Mechanisms in International Economic Organizations. Ed. by Pieter Van Dijk. 1984. lib. bdg. 231.00 (90-6544-076-3) Kluwer Law Tax Pubs.

Supervisory Personnel Management: Building Work Relationships. Institute of Financial Education Staff. 1988. pap. 29.95 (0-912857-45-5) Inst Finan Educ.

Supervisory Personnel Management: Maximizing Your Effectiveness. Institute of Financial Education Staff. 1988. pap. 29.95 (0-912857-47-1) Inst Finan Educ.

Supervisory Relationships: Exploring the Human Element. Tamara L. Kaiser. 150p. (C). 1997. pap. text ed. 22.95 (0-534-34559-X) Brooks-Cole.

Supervisory Remote Control Systems. R. E. Young. (Control Engineering Ser.: No. 4). (Illus.). 192p. 1977. boxed 42.00 (0-901223-94-8, CE004) Inst Elect Eng.

Supervisory Remote Control Systems. Robert E. Young. LC 77-377600. (IEE Control Engineering Ser.: Vol. 4). (Illus.). 207p. reprint ed. pap. 59.00 (0-685-23326-X, 2032251) Bks Demand.

Supervisory Skills. 2nd ed. Harold M. Emanuel et al. LC 85-81542. 274p. (C). 1990. pap. 25.00 (0-89462-024-X, SM19) IIA.

Supervisory Skills for Nurses. 2nd rev. ed. Gloria York. 248p. (C). 1993. pap. text ed. 49.95 (1-878025-78-3) Western Schls.

***Supervisory Skills for Nurses.** 2nd rev. ed. Gloria York. Ed. by Becky Colgan. 254p. (C). 1996. pap. text ed. 49.95 (1-878025-99-6) Western Schls.

Supervisory Skills in Marketing. Lucy Crawford. Ed. by Eugene L. Dorr. (Occupational Manuals & Projects in Marketing Ser.). (Illus.). (J). (gr. 9-10). 1977. text ed. 12.28 (0-07-013471-5) McGraw.

Supervisory Studies. P. Beats. 49p. (C). 1989. 140.00 (0-685-39844-7, Pub. by Inst Pur & Supply UK) St Mut.

Supervisory Studies: A Managerial Perspective. 5th ed. P. Betts. 512p. (Orig.). 1989. pap. 37.50 (0-273-03071-X, Pub. by Pitman Pub Ltd UK) Trans-Atl Phila.

Supervisory Studies see Supervisory Management

Supervisory Survival: A Practical Guide for the Professional Survival of New, Experienced, & Aspiring Law Enforcement Supervisors. Edward J. Nowicki. LC 93-4274. 1993. pap. 17.95 (1-879411-23-7) Perf Dimensions Pub.

Supervisory Training Approaches & Methods. Compiled by Bradford B. Boyd. 162p. 8.25 (0-318-13287-7, BOSTP) Am Soc Train & Devel.

Supervisory Training Program. 1980. 58.50 (0-318-69883-8, 285500); ring bd. 49.50 (0-685-63186-9, 285600); ring bd. 33.00 (0-685-63187-7, 285600) Am Bankers.

An Asterisk (*) at the beginning of an entry indicates that the title is appearing in BIP for the first time.

Supervisory Training Program: Student Modules. rev. ed. Performance Solutions Staff. Ed. by Gail Watson. 380p. 1993. teacher ed. write for info. (0-318-72221-6); text ed. write for info. (0-89982-323-8) Am Bankers.

Supervixen: Secrets for Building a Lean & Sexy Body. Negrita Jayde. (Illus.). 352p. 1995. pap. 17.95 (0-8092-3440-8) Contemp Bks.

Superwahljahr: The German Elections in 1994. Geoffrey K. Roberts. LC 95-30140. 203p. (C). 1995. text ed. 35.00 (0-7146-4682-2, Pub. by F Cass Pubs UK) Intl Spec Bk.

Superwest. Massimo Mattioli. Ed. by Bernd Metz. Tr. by Tom Leighton from FRE. (Illus.). 48p. 1987. 12.95 (0-87416-035-9) Catalan Communs.

SuperWoman's Rite of Passage: From Midlife to Whole Life. Kathleen F. Lundquist. LC 95-47533. 240p. 1996. pap. 14.95 (1-56718-447-2) Llewellyn Pubns.

Superwomen & the Double Burden: Women's Experience of Change in the Former Soviet Union, Central & Eastern Europe. Ed. by Chris Corrin. (Illus.). 256p. (Orig.). 1992. pap. 16.95 (0-929005-34-1, Pub. by Second Story Pr CN) LPC InBook.

Superwomen Do It Less...A Guide to Having It All: Children, a Career, & a Loving Relationship. Rose M. Ray. Ed. by Nelle Baird. LC 91-65759. (Illus.). (Orig.). 1992. pap. 12.95 (0-9629361-0-3) Yankee Pub.

Superworld 1. Antonio L. Zichichi. LC 89-35914. (Subnuclear Ser.: Vol. 24). (Illus.). 282p. 1990. 89.50 (0-306-43324-9, Plenum Pr) Plenum.

Superworld 2. Antonio L. Zichichi. LC 90-6750. (Subnuclear Ser.: Vol. 25). (Illus.). 572p. 1990. 135.00 (0-306-43493-8, Plenum Pr) Plenum.

Superworld 3. Antonio L. Zichichi. LC 90-7154. (Subnuclear Ser.: Vol. 26). (Illus.). 348p. 1990. 120.00 (0-306-43525-X, Plenum Pr) Plenum.

Superwrite. A. James Lemaster. (KB - Notemaking Ser.). 1990. pap. 18.95 (0-538-60525-1) S-W Pub.

Superwrite: Alphabetic Writing System. A. James Lemaster. (KB - Notemaking Ser.). 1990. pap. 16.95 (0-538-60785-8) S-W Pub.

Superwrite: Alphabetic Writing System. A. James Lemaster. (KB - Notemaking Ser.). 1991. wbk. ed., pap. 15.95 (0-538-60801-3) S-W Pub.

SuperWrite: An Alphabetic Writing System V2, Vol. 2. A. James Lemaster. (KB - Notemaking Ser.). 1992. text ed. 26.95 (0-538-70512-4) S-W Pub.

Superwrite: Notemaking & Study Skills. A. James Lemaster. (KB - Notemaking Ser.). 1991. wbk. ed., pap. 14.95 (0-538-70511-6) S-W Pub.

Superwrite: Notemaking & Study Skills. A. James Lemaster. (KB - Notemaking Ser.). 1992. suppl. ed., pap. 15.95 (0-538-70513-2) S-W Pub.

Superwrite: Notemaking & Study Skills. A. James Lemaster. (KB - Notemaking Ser.). 1992. pap. 15.95 (0-538-61818-3) S-W Pub.

SuperWrite: Notemaking & Study Skills. A. James Lemaster. (KB - Notemaking Ser.). 1992. text ed. 28.95 (0-538-61817-5) S-W Pub.

Superwrite Vol. 1: Alphabetic Writing System, Vol. 1. A. James Lemaster. (KB - Notemaking Ser.). 1991. text ed. 26.95 (0-538-60800-5) S-W Pub.

Superwrite Vol. 2: An Alphabetic Writing System. A. James Lemaster. (KB - Notemaking Ser.). 1992. wbk. ed., pap. 15.95 (0-538-60804-8) S-W Pub.

Superwrite Vol. 2: An Alphabetic Writing System, Vol. 2. A. James Leamaster. (KB - Notemaking Ser.). 1992. text ed. 28.95 (0-538-60803-X) S-W Pub.

Superwrite Alphabetic Writing System: Comprehensive Course, 2 vols., Set. A. James LeMaster. 1991. 43.95 (0-538-61798-5) S-W Pub.

Superwrite, Brief Course: Alphabetic Writing System. 2nd ed. A. James Lemaster. (KB - Notemaking Ser.). 1996. 18.95 (0-538-62845-6); suppl. ed. 314.95 (0-538-62847-2) S-W Pub.

Superwrite Dictionary. A. James Lemaster. (KB - Notemaking Ser.). 1990. pap. 11.95 (0-538-60526-X) S-W Pub.

Superwrite, Post Sec: Alphabetic Writing System. A. James Lemaster. (KB - Notemaking Ser.). 1991. text ed. 22.95 (0-538-70510-8) S-W Pub.

Superzap: IBM-PC Version 1.0. Dale Buscaino & Scott Daniel. Ed. by David Moore & Charles Trapp. (Illus.). 104p. 1985. 49.95 incl. disk (0-932679-00-5) Blue Cat.

Superzorro: Fantastic Mr. Fox. Roald Dahl. 1995. pap. text ed. 8.95 (84-204-3102-8) Santillana.

Superzorro - Fantastic Mr. Fox. Roald Dahl. Tr. by Ramon Buckley. (Illus.). 153p. (SPA.). (J). (gr. 2-4). 1992. pap. write for info. (84-204-0013-0) Santillana.

***Suplemento al Informe de la Consulta Tecnica Sobre Utilizacion y Mercadeo de Pescado en America Latina, Santiago de Chile, 1986.** 227p. (SPA.). 1989. suppl. ed. 30.00 (92-5-302906-4, Pub. by FAO IT) Bernan Associates.

Supper at the Black Pearl. deluxe ed. John Casey. 45p. 1996. 50.00 (0-935716-65-3) Lord John.

Supper Book. Marion Cunningham. (Illus.). 1992. 22.00 (0-679-40144-X) Knopf.

***Supper Book.** Marion Cunningham. 1997. 9.99 (0-517-18384-6) Random Hse Value.

Supper Club: Creative Ideas for Small-Group Fellowship. Michael Kendrick. LC 94-17400. 128p. (Orig.). (gr. 10). 1994. pap. 7.99 (0-8010-5263-7) Baker Bks.

Supper for Crow: A Northwest Coast Indian Tale. Pierr Morgan. LC 93-41665. (J). 1995. 15.00 (0-517-59378-5); lib. bdg. 15.99 (0-517-59379-3) Crown Bks Yng Read.

Supper in the Evening: Pioneer Tales of Michigan. 2nd rev. ed. Al Barnes. LC 67-26278. (Illus.). 254p. 1985. pap. 10.95 (0-915937-01-8) Hor Bks MI.

***Supper of the Lamb.** Louis W. Accola. (Orig.). 1997. pap. 10.95 (0-533-12293-7) Vantage.

***Supper of the Lamb.** Robert Farrar Capon. 1996. 10.98 (0-7651-9829-0) Smithmark.

Supper of the Lord. Deborah J. Baker et al. (Orig.). 1988. pap. 1.95 (1-55673-023-3, 8807) CSS OH.

Suppertime for Frieda Fuzzypaws. (Golden Naptime Tales Series - A Jim Henson Muppet Press Bk.). (Illus.). (J). (ps-3). 1991. write for info. (0-307-12234-4, Golden Books) Western Pub.

Supple Body: The Way to Fitness, Strength & Flexibility. Liliana Djurovic & Sara Black. LC 95-17429. (Illus.). 144p. 1995. 16.00 (0-02-860441-5) Macmillan.

Supple Workout: Abs & Back. Catherine McCrum. (Illus.). 80p. 1996. 14.95 (0-02-861344-9) Macmillan.

Supple Workout: Chest & Shoulders. Mark Bender. (Illus.). 80p. 1996. 14.95 (0-02-861345-7) Macmillan.

Supple Workout: Hips & Thighs. Lorna Malcolm. (Illus.). 80p. 1996. 14.95 (0-02-861346-5) Macmillan.

Supplement: Minimum Standards for Property Management Accounting Service Bureau Syatems. 31p. 1988. pap. 12.00 (0-685-71688-0, 833) Inst Real Estate.

Supplement: Optional Components of a Property Management Software System. 18p. 1986. pap. 12.00 (0-685-71687-2, 935) Inst Real Estate.

Supplement see Census of Medieval & Renaissance Manuscripts in the United States & Canada

Supplement A: The Chemistry of Double-Bonded Functional Groups, Vol. 2. Ed. by Saul E. Patai. LC 88-39812. (Chemistry of Functional Groups Ser.). 797p. 1989. text ed. 780.00 (0-471-91719-2) Wiley.

Supplement A see 1997 PDR Supplements

Supplement a la Revue de la Musique Dramatique en France see Revue de la Musique Dramatique en France

Supplement, Additions et Corrections, Index et Tables see Correspondance

Supplement & General Index see History of the United States Naval Operations in World War Two

Supplement & Index to Holway-Rich Heritage: A History & Genealogy of Two Cape Cod Families, 2 vols., Set. Ed. by Richard T. Holway. LC 92-85465. 246p. 15.00 (0-89725-081-8, 1390a, Penobscot Pr) Picton Pr.

Supplement au Dictionnaire de la Bible, 9 vols., Set. Cazerres et al. (FRE.). 1967. 1,995.00 (0-8288-6691-0, M-6065) Fr & Eur.

Supplement au Voyage de Bougainville: Avec: Pensees Philosophiques, Lettre sur les Aveugles. Denis Diderot & Antoine Adam. 192p. (FRE.). 1972. 10.95 (0-8288-9962-2, F46970) Fr & Eur.

Supplement au Voyage de Cook. Jean Giraudoux. pap. 9.95 (0-685-33929-7) Fr & Eur.

Supplement au Voyage de Cook see Theatre

Supplement Aux Dictionnaire Arabe, 2 vols., set. Reinhart Dozy. 1721p. (ARA & FRE.). 95.00 (0-86685-106-2, LDL1062, Pub. by Librairie du Liban FR) Intl Bk Ctr.

Supplement aux Supercheries Litteraires. J. P. Brunet. 99. 95 (0-685-35982-4) Fr & Eur.

Supplement B see 1997 PDR Supplements

Supplement C: The Chemistry of Triple Bonded Groups, Pt. 1. Saul E. Patai & Zvi Rappoport. (Chemistry of Functional Groups Ser.). 736p. 1983. reprint ed. text ed. 690.00 (0-471-28030-5) Wiley.

Supplement: Concordance of U. S. & German Designations for Metallic Materials see DECHEMA Corrosion Handbook: Corrosive Agents & Their Interaction with Materials

Supplement Constitutional Criminal Procedure. Allen & Kuh. 1990. 14.00 (0-316-03451-7) Little.

Supplement Drawings for Embryology. Graham P. DuShane. LC 55-5121. 49p. reprint ed. pap. 25.00 (0-317-28105-4, 2024091) Bks Demand.

Supplement du Dictionnaire Critique de la Langue Francaise: O-Z. fac. ed. Jean-Francois Feraud. 242p. (FRE.). 1988. pap. 79.95 (0-7859-8115-2, 2859290362) Fr & Eur.

Supplement du Dictionnaire Critique de la Langue Francaise Vol. 1: A-D. fac. ed. Jean-Francois Feraud. 279p. (FRE.). 1988. pap. 79.95 (0-7859-8114-4, 2859290346) Fr & Eur.

Supplement du Dictionnaire Critique de la Langue Francaise Vol. 2: E-N. fac. ed. Jean-Francois Feraud. 299p. (FRE.). 1988. pap. 79.95 (0-7859-8113-6) Fr & Eur.

Supplement D2 Pts. 1 & 2: The Chemistry of Halides, Pseudo-Halides & Azides, Vol. 2. Ed. by Zvi Rappoport & Saul E. Patai. LC 94-18657. (Chemistry of Functional Groups: Vol. 2). 1200p. 1995. text ed. 1,075.00 (0-471-94209-X) Wiley.

Supplement Environmental '88. Anderson. 1988. pap. 10.95 (0-316-03944-6) Little.

Supplement E2: The Chemistry of Hydroxyl, Ether & Peroxide Groups, Vol. 2. Ed. by Saul E. Patai. LC 92-4325. (Chemistry of Functional Groups Ser.). 1250p. 1993. text ed. 1,100.00 (0-471-93045-8) Wiley.

Supplement for Beginning Algebra: Arithmetic Review & Algebra Practice. Gage & Gelbwasser. (J). 1993. pap. text ed. write for info. (0-07-022807-8) McGraw.

Supplement for Introductory Mathematics, Custom Publication. Smith. 1990. pap. text ed. write for info. (0-07-057831-1) McGraw.

Supplement for 1995-1995 with Problems for Business Crime, Cases & Materials. Harry First. (University Casebook Ser.). 165p. 1995. pap. text ed. 9.50 (1-56662-290-5) Foundation Pr.

Supplement Labor '88. Bernard D. Meltzer. 1988. pap. 12. 95 (0-316-56649-7) Little.

Supplement Modern America '89. Douglas Laycock. 1989. 9.95 (0-316-51757-7) Little.

Supplement Modern America '91. Douglas Laycock. 1991. 12.95 (0-316-51761-5) Little.

Supplement of "Helium" Evgenii M. Lifshits & E. L. Andronikashvili. LC 59-8465. 176p. reprint ed. pap. 50. 20 (0-317-08930-7, 2003365) Bks Demand.

Supplement of Reading: Figures of Understanding in Romantic Theory & Practice. Tilottama Rajan. LC 90-55122. 368p. 1990. 47.50 (0-8014-2045-8); pap. 17.95 (0-8014-9749-3) Cornell U Pr.

Supplement Pensions - Profit '87. Russell K. Osgood. 1987. 35.00 (0-316-66616-5) Little.

Supplement Real Estate Tax '81. Morris. 1981. 15.00 (0-316-58393-6) Little.

Supplement Relating to the International Convention for the Prevention of Pollution of the Sea by Oil, 1954. International Maritime Organization Staff. 1981. text ed. 35.00 (0-89771-953-0, Pub. by Intl Maritime Org UK) St Mut.

Supplement Relating to the International Convention on Load Lines, 1966. International Maritime Organization Staff. 1981. text ed. 55.00 (0-89771-977-8, Pub. by Intl Maritime Org UK) St Mut.

Supplement S: The Chemistry of Sulphur-Containing Functional Groups. Ed. by Saul E. Patai & Zvi Rappoport. LC 92-23016. (Chemistry of Functional Groups Ser.). 1120p. 1993. text ed. 890.00 (0-471-93046-6) Wiley.

***Supplement Savvy: A Shopper's Guide to Brand-Name Supplements.** Gail L. Becker. 1997. mass mkt. 6.50 (0-440-22304-0) Dell.

Supplement Ser, 1974. Patons. 1973. 18.00 (0-316-69344-8) Little.

Supplement Series - Materialien und Dokumente, 9 vols., Set. Ed. by Alexander Ritter. 760p. 1993. reprint ed. write for info. (3-487-09316-2) G Olms Pubs.

Supplement Substant '90. Phillip I. Blumberg. 1990. 40.00 (0-316-10077-3) Little.

Supplement to a Bibliography of George Moore. Edwin Gilcher. 200p. 1988. text ed. 42.95 (0-313-27674-9) Greenwood.

Supplement to a "California Flora" Philip A. Munz. 1968. 29.95 (0-520-00904-5) U CA Pr.

Supplement to a Guide to Manuscripts Relating to the American Indian in the Library of the American Philosophical Society. Daythal Kendall. LC 81-65976. (Memoirs Ser.: Vol. 65S). 1983. 15.00 (0-87169-650-9, M65S-KED) Am Philos.

Supplement to a Guide to Source Materials for the Study of Barbados History, 1627-1834. Jerome S. Handler. 114p. 1991. 22.50 (0-916617-35-1) J C Brown.

Supplement to a Programmed Manual for Nursing Home Administrator Examinees. 11th ed. Edmond Boudreaux. 20p. (C). 1995. pap. text ed. 5.00 (1-878199-06-4) Pro Exam Review.

Supplement to Accompany Discrete Mathematics. 2nd ed. Steven Roman. (C). 1989. text ed. 77.50 (0-15-541733-9) SCP.

Supplement to Administrative Law '88. Breyer. 1988. 10.95 (0-316-10786-7) Little.

Supplement to Allibone's Critical Dictionary of English Literature & British & American Authors, 2 vols. J. F. Kirk. 1972. 200.00 (0-8490-1161-2) Gordon Pr.

Supplement to American Law of Property '89. A. James Casner. 1989. 15.95 (0-316-13238-1) Little.

Supplement to Analysis of Workers' Compensation Laws, 1993. 16p. 1993. pap. 10.00 (0-89834-123-X, 0339) Chamber Comm US.

Supplement to Bankruptcy 1994. Baird & Bunchbinder. 1994. suppl. ed. 14.95 (0-316-07685-6) Little.

Supplement to Bankruptcy 1995: 1995 Supplement. Blumberg et al. 1995. suppl. ed. 100.00 (0-316-10189-3) Little.

Supplement to Beck's Theory & Principles of Pleading in Civil Actions. I. Isaacs. 1985. pap. 35.00 (0-409-01237-8, SA) MICHIE.

Supplement to Bell's British Theatre, Farces-1784., 4 vols., Set. Ed. by John Bell. LC 76-44552. (Illus.). 1977. 230. 00 (0-404-00830-5) AMS Pr.

Supplement to Bibliography on Deafness: 1977 to 1979. Ed. by George W. Fellendorf. 1980. pap. text ed. 3.95 (0-88200-139-6, L9435) Alexander Graham.

Supplement to Birds of the World in Philately. Beverly S. Ridgely & Gustavs E. Eglaus. (Illus.). 62p. 1986. pap. text ed. 6.00 (0-935991-00-X) Am Topical Assn.

Supplement to Cargo Work: Guide Lines to the Safe Handling of Roll on-Roll off Vessels. Brown, Son & Ferguson Ltd. Staff. (C). 1987. 60.00 (0-685-45088-0, Pub. by Brwn Son Ferg) St Mut.

Supplement to Cases & Materials on Employment Law, 1994 Statutory. Lance M. Liebman & Mark A. Rothstein. (University Casebook Ser.). 271p. 1994. pap. text ed. 12.95 (1-56662-180-1) Foundation Pr.

Supplement to Charles Evans' American Bibliography. Roger P. Bristol. LC 73-94761. (Bibliographical Society Ser.). 640p. 1970. text ed. 50.00 (0-8139-0287-8) U Pr of Va.

Supplement to Children's Books on Africa & Their Authors. Nancy J. Schmidt. LC 78-24102. (African Bibliography Ser.: Vol. 5). 1979. 37.95 (0-8419-0433-2, Africana) Holmes & Meier.

Supplement to Company Law 1985 Noter-up. 1986. pap. 16.00 (0-409-01876-7, SA) MICHIE.

Supplement to Connecticut Land Use Regulation, 1993. 2nd ed. Terry J. Tondro. 218p. 1994. pap. 55.00 (1-878698-23-0) Atlantic Law.

Supplement to Connecticut Law of Torts, 1993. 3rd ed. Douglass B. Wright et al. 112p. 1993. pap. 50.00 (1-878698-20-6) Atlantic Law.

Supplement to Connecticut Law of Torts, 1994. 3rd ed. Douglass B. Wright et al. 116p. 1994. pap. 55.00 (1-878698-26-5) Atlantic Law.

Supplement to Connecticut Law of Uninsured & Underinsured Motorist Coverage 1994. Jon Belk & Michael C. Jainchill. 84p. 1994. pap. 50.00 (1-878698-27-3) Atlantic Law.

Supplement to Construction Law '90. Geoffrey R. Stone. 1990. 14.00 (0-316-81778-3) Little.

Supplement to Developing Residential Practice: A Source Book. Robin Douglas et al. (C). 1987. 49.00 (0-685-28584-7, Pub. by Natl Inst Soc Work); 45.00 (0-685-40333-5, Pub. by Natl Inst Soc Work) St Mut.

Supplement to "Distribution & Taxonomy of Birds of the World" Charles G. Sibley & Burt L. Monroe, Jr. 112p. 1993. 28.00 (0-300-05549-8) Yale U Pr.

Supplement to Duthie's Flora of the Upper Gangetic Plain & of the Adjacent Siwalik & Sub Himalayan Tracks. M. B. Raizada. 355p. (C). 1976. text ed. 75.00 (0-89771-643-4, Pub. by Intl Bk Distr II) St Mut.

Supplement to Duthie's Flora of the Upper Gangetic Plain & of the Adjacent Siwalik & Sub-Himalayan Tracts. Ed. by M. B. Raizada. 355p. (C). 1976. 75.00 (0-685-21741-8, Pub. by Intl Bk Distr II) St Mut.

Supplement to Employee Discrimination '90. Arno B. Zimmer. 1990. 13.50 (0-316-98820-0) Little.

Supplement to Employment Discrimination in Alabama, 1992. John J. Coleman, III. 39.95 (0-685-61683-5) Southern U Pr.

Supplement to Environmental Law, Cases & Materials, 1993. Roger W. Findley & Daniel A. Darber. (American Casebook Ser.). 83p. 1993. pap. text ed. 8.50 (0-314-02542-1) West Pub.

Supplement to Estate Planning 1994. Casner. 1994. suppl. ed. 295.00 (0-316-12960-7) Little.

***Supplement to Factors Influencing the Durability of Automobile Transmission Gears.** J. O. Almen. (Technical Papers). 1937. pap. text ed. 30.00 (1-55589-244-2) AGMA.

Supplement to Federal Income Taxation, 1985. Boris Brittker et al. (C). 1985. pap. text ed. write for info. (0-318-59076-X) Little.

Supplement to Free Enterprise & Economic Organization: Antitrust, 1993. 6th ed. Louis B. Schwartz et al. (University Casebook Ser.). 334p. 1993. pap. text ed. 15. 50 (1-56662-111-9) Foundation Pr.

Supplement to Genealogical Resources in English Repositories. Joy W. Moulton. (Orig.). (C). 1992. pap. text ed. 4.75 (0-944485-01-4) Hampton OH.

Supplement to Glossary of Indian Medicinal Plants. R. N. Chopra. (C). 1988. 30.00 (0-317-92350-1, Pub. by Scientific UK) St Mut.

Supplement to Gould & Trelease Water Law, 1993. 4th ed. Ed. by George Gould. (American Casebook Ser.). 95p. 1993. pap. text ed. 6.50 (0-314-02638-X) West Pub.

Supplement to Gwinnett County, Georgia, Families, 1818-1968. Alice S. McCabe. 32p. (Orig.). 1988. pap. 5.00 (0-914923-08-0) Gwinnett Hist.

Supplement to Handbook on Injectable Drugs. 8th ed. Lawrence A. Trissel. 96p. (Orig.). 1995. pap. text ed. write for info. (1-879907-54-2) Am Soc Hlth-Syst.

***Supplement to Handbook on Injectable Drugs.** 9th rev. ed. Lawrence A. Trissel. 112p. 1997. pap. text ed. 31.00 (1-879907-72-0, P470S) Am Soc Hlth-Syst.

Supplement to Historical Collections of Coshocton Co., Ohio. William E. Hunt. 208p. 1993. reprint ed. lib. bdg. 25.00 (0-8328-2996-X) Higginson Bk Co.

***Supplement to IEEE Std 802.1D-1990, IEEE Standard 802.6 Distributed Queue Dual Bus (DQDB) Subnetwork of a MAN (ANSI), 802.6k-1992.** 20.00 (1-55937-282-6, SH15891) IEEE Standards.

Supplement to Index of Artists. D. T. Mallett. 1990. 29.00 (0-8446-1298-7) Peter Smith.

Supplement to Interstate Child Custody Disputes, 1990: Practice, Policy & Law. National Center on Women & Family Law Staff. 550p. (Orig.). 1990. pap. text ed. 30. 00 (0-929396-03-0) Natl Ctr Women & Family Law Inc.

Supplement to Investing '89. Barton. 1989. 30.00 (0-316-08284-8) Little.

***Supplement to ISO-IEC 8802-4, 802.4b-1992: 1990, ANSI-IEEE Std 802.4-1990 - Enhancements for Physical Layer Diversity (Redundant Media Control Unit) (ANSI)** 37.00 (1-55937-266-4, SH15735) IEEE Standards.

Supplement to Land Ownership '89. Curtis J. Berger. 1989. 11.50 (0-316-09148-0) Little.

Supplement to Land Use '88. Robert C. Ellickson. 1988. 13. 50 (0-316-23301-3) Little.

Supplement to Land Use '88. Frank Schnidman. 1988. 40. 00 (0-316-77407-3) Little.

Supplement to Land Use '90. Frank Schnidman. 1990. 55. 00 (0-316-77431-6) Little.

***Supplement to Late Roman Pottery.** John W. Hayes. 82p. 1980. pap. 13.50 (0-904152-10-3, Pub. by British Schl Rome UK) David Brown.

Supplement to Making It on Your Own. Nancy Chandler & Jo Wintker. 21p. (Orig.). 1984. pap. text ed. 3.50 (0-89695-013-1) U Tenn CSW.

Supplement to Maritime History. 1985. pap. 5.00 (0-916617-01-7) J C Brown.

Supplement to Mass Tax '87. Jacobs. 1988. 40.00 (0-316-45543-1) Little.

Supplement to Max Farrand's Records of the Federal Convention of 1787. James H. Hutson. LC 86-51340. 512p. 1987. pap. 19.00 (0-300-03904-2, Y-652) Yale U Pr.

Supplement to Mister Warburton's Edition of Shakespeare. Thomas Edwards. LC 76-164762. reprint ed. 24.50 (0-404-02262-6) AMS Pr.

Supplement to Multi-District Litigation '89. Herr. 1989. 40.00 (0-316-35885-1) Little.

Supplement to NBER Report Eight: Recent Economic Changes & the Agenda of Business Cycle Research. Solomon Fabricant. 33p. reprint ed. 20.00 (0-685-61358-5) Natl Bur Econ Res.

Supplement to NBER Report Eleven: Youth, Education, & Work. Jacob A. Mincer. 7p. reprint ed. 20.00 (0-685-61366-6) Natl Bur Econ Res.

S

Supplement to NBER Report Fifteen: The Eurocurrency Market & the Recycling of Petrodollars. Raymond F. Mikesell. 9p. reprint ed. 20.00 (*0-685-61394-1*) Natl Bur Econ Res.

Supplement to NBER Report Five: The Evaluation & Planning of Social Programs. John R. Meyer. 8p. reprint ed. 20.00 (*0-685-61349-6*) Natl Bur Econ Res.

Supplement to NBER Report Four: The New ASA-NBER Survey of Forecasts by Economic Statisticians. Victor Zarnowitz. 10p. reprint ed. 20.00 (*0-685-61347-X*) Natl Bur Econ Res.

Supplement to NBER Report Fourteen: Transportation Solutions to the Energy "Crisis" John R. Meyer. 6p. reprint ed. 20.00 (*0-685-61392-5*) Natl Bur Econ Res.

Supplement to NBER Report Nine: The Quality of Life & Social Indicators. Wilbur J. Cohen. 13p. reprint ed. 20.00 (*0-685-61360-7*) Natl Bur Econ Res.

Supplement to NBER Report One: Composite Indexes of Leading, Coinciding, & Lagging Indicators, 1948-67. Julius Shiskin & Geoffrey H. Moore. 8p. reprint ed. 20.00 (*0-685-61341-0*) Natl Bur Econ Res.

Supplement to NBER Report Seven: Fiftieth Anniversary Colloquia Address. 14p. reprint ed. 20.00 (*0-685-61356-9*) Natl Bur Econ Res.

Supplement to NBER Report Six: National Bureau of Economic Research Fiftieth Anniversary Dinner: Transcript of Proceedings. 30p. reprint ed. 20.00 (*0-685-61353-4*) Natl Bur Econ Res.

Supplement to NBER Report Ten: Productivity in the Tertiary Sector. Solomon Fabricant. 12p. reprint ed. 20.00 (*0-685-61362-3*) Natl Bur Econ Res.

Supplement to NBER Report Thirteen: Common Stock Values & Inflation - The Historical Record of Many Countries. Phillip Cagan. 10p. reprint ed. 20.00 (*0-685-66194-6*) Natl Bur Econ Res.

Supplement to NBER Report Three: The Growing Demand for Medical Care. Victor R. Fuchs. 8p. reprint ed. 20.00 (*0-685-61345-3*) Natl Bur Econ Res.

Supplement to NBER Report Twelve: Setting Environmental Standards: An Economist's View. John R. Meyer. 10p. reprint ed. 20.00 (*0-685-61368-2*) Natl Bur Econ Res.

Supplement to NBER Report Two: Tariff Preferences of Less Developed Countries. Hal B. Lary. 12p. reprint ed. 20.00 (*0-685-61343-7*) Natl Bur Econ Res.

Supplement to Notae Latinae: Abbreviations in Latin MSS. of 850 to 1050 A. D. Doris Bains. xii, 72p. reprint ed. 19.37 (*0-685-66490-2*, 05100366) G Olms Pubs.

Supplement to Postcard of the Falkland Islands, 1988: A Catalogue: 1900-1950. Henry Heyburn & Frances Heyburn. (Illus.). 1990. 45.00 (*0-948251-05-0*, Pub. by Picton UK) St Mut.

Supplement to Railway Stamps. Howard J. Burkhalter & Allen Pollock. 52p. 1988. pap. 5.00 (*0-935991-03-4*) Am Topical Assn.

Supplement to Reference Guide to Minnesota History: A Subject Bibliography 1970-80. Michael Brook & Sarah P. Rubinstein. LC 83-5438. 69p. 1983. pap. 6.95 (*0-87351-160-3*) Minn Hist.

Supplement to Reports on AIDS in the African Press: An Annotated Bibliography. Nancy J. Schmidt. 72p. 1990. pap. 3.00 (*0-941934-61-6*) Indiana Africa.

Supplement to Reversing the Spiral: The Population, Agriculture, & Environment Nexus in Sub-Saharan Africa. Kevin M. Cleaver & G. A. Schreiber. LC 94-22749. (Directions in Development Ser.). 1994. 7.95 (*0-8213-3010-1*, 13010) World Bank.

Supplement to Securities Regulations 1994. Loss. 1994. suppl. ed. 350.00 (*0-316-53283-5*) Little.

Supplement to Security Regulations 1995. Loss. 1995. 385.00 (*0-316-53447-1*) Little.

Supplement to South Carolina Marriages, 1688-1820. Brent H. Holcomb. 57p. 1995. reprint ed. pap. 9.00 (*0-614-10547-1*, 2776) Genealog Pub.

Supplement to Standard Methods. 17th ed. 168p. 1991. pap. 35.00 (*0-685-50830-7*, 10061) Am Pub Health.

Supplement to Standardized Quantity Recipe File - for Quality & Cost Control. Institution Management Department, Iowa State University Staff. 1984. pap. text ed. 29.95 (*0-8138-1566-5*) Iowa St U Pr.

Supplement to Survey of Palestine, Vol. III: Notes Compiled for the Information of the United Nations Special Committee on Palestine, June 1947. LC 90-5245. 160p. (C). 1991. reprint ed. 9.95 (*0-88728-216-4*); reprint ed. pap. 4.95 (*0-88728-217-2*) Inst Palestine.

Supplement to the Bibliography & Abstracts on Thermostat Metals, Vol. STP 288C. 43p. 1974. pap. 4.25 (*0-8031-0765-X*, 04-288030-40) ASTM.

Supplement to the Botany of Bihar & Orissa. Harold A. Mooney. 294p. 1986. reprint ed. 140.00 (*0-685-21849-X*, Pub. by Intl Bk Distr II) St Mut.

Supplement to the Bright Star Catalogue. Dorrit Hoffleit et al. vi, 135p. (Orig.). 1984. pap. 12.00 (*0-914753-01-0*) Yale U Observ.

Supplement to the Catalogue of the Arabic Manuscripts in the British Museum. Charles Rieu. xvi, 935p. reprint ed. write for info. (*0-318-71556-2*) G Olms Pubs.

Supplement to the Check List of Plant & Soil Nematodes, 1961-1965: A Nomenclatorial Compilation. Armen C. Tarjan. LC 60-10226. 129p. reprint ed. pap. 36.80 (*0-685-20540-1*, 2030012) Bks Demand.

Supplement to the Complete Book of Emigrants in Bondage, 1614-1775. Peter W. Coldham. 86p. 1992. 9.00 (*0-8063-1345-5*, 1115) Genealog Pub.

Supplement to the Descendants of Peter Spicer Containing Additions & Corrections. Susan B. Meech. (Illus.). 269p. reprint ed. pap. 42.00 (*0-8328-1653-1*); reprint ed. lib. bdg. 52.00 (*0-8328-1652-3*) Higginson Bk Co.

Supplement to the Dictionary of American Library Biography. Ed. by Wayne A. Wiegand. xix, 184p. 1990. lib. bdg. 45.00 (*0-87287-586-5*) Libs Unl.

Supplement to the Effects of Drugs on Clinical Laboratory Tests. 3rd ed. Ed. by Donald S. Young. 161p. 1991. 60.00 (*0-915274-58-2*) Am Assn Clinical Chem.

Supplement to the Eighteen Fifty-One Davenport Genealogy, Continued to 1876. A. B. Davenport. (Illus.). 437p. 1989. reprint ed. pap. 65.50 (*0-8328-0457-6*); reprint ed. lib. bdg. 72.50 (*0-8328-0456-8*) Higginson Bk Co.

Supplement to the Eleventh Mental Measurements Yearbook. Ed. by Jane E. Conoley & James C. Impara. LC 39-3422. (Mental Measurements Yearbook Ser.). 323p. 1994. pap. 55.00 (*0-910674-34-5*) Buros Inst Mental.

Supplement to the Encyclopedia of the American Constitution. Leonard W. Levy. 704p. 1992. Red binding. 110.00 (*0-02-918678-1*, Free Press) Free Pr.

Supplement to the Fact Book-1986: Statistics & Market Data. rev. ed. (Illus.). 100p. 1986. pap. 39.95 (*0-933641-06-0*) Direct Mkt.

Supplement to the Falkland Islands Catalogue, 1988. Picton Publishing (Chippenham) Ltd. Staff. (C). 1987. 75.00 (*0-685-39332-1*, Pub. by Picton UK) St Mut.

Supplement to the First Amendment & the Fifth Estate, Regulation of Electronic Mass Media. 3rd ed. T. Barton Carter et al. 328p. 1995. suppl. ed., pap. text ed. 8.95 (*1-56662-287-5*) Foundation Pr.

Supplement to the General Catalogue of Photoelectric Magnitudes & Colors of Galaxies in the U, B, V System. Giuseppe Longo & Antoinette De Vaucouleurs. LC 85-51711. (Monographs in Astronomy: No. 3A). 126p. (Orig.). 1985. pap. write for info. (*0-9603796-4-9*) U of Tex Dept Astron.

Supplement to the Guidebook to Making It on Your Own. Nancy Chandler & Jo Wintker. 12p. (Orig.). 1984. pap. text ed. 3.50 (*0-89695-014-X*) U Tenn CSW.

Supplement to the Half-Yearly Army List for the Period Ending 31st December, 1924: War Services of Officers on Retired Pay, Etc. Picton Publishing Staff. 703p. (C). 1987. 245.00 (*0-317-90447-7*, Pub. by Picton UK) St Mut.

Supplement to the Handbook of Middle American Indians, Vol. 1, Archaeology. Ed. by Victoria R. Bricker & Jeremy A. Sabloff. (Illus.). 475p. 1981. text ed. 55.00 (*0-292-77556-3*) U of Tex Pr.

Supplement to the Handbook of Middle American Indians, Vol. 2: Linguistics. Ed. by Victoria R. Bricker & Munro S. Edmonson. LC 83-23562. 156p. 1984. text ed. 35.00 (*0-292-77577-6*) U of Tex Pr.

Supplement to the Handbook of Middle American Indians, Vol. 3: Literatures. Ed. by Victoria R. Bricker & Munro S. Edmonson. LC 85-3361. 207p. 1985. text ed. 35.00 (*0-292-77593-8*) U of Tex Pr.

Supplement to the Handbook of Middle American Indians, Vol. 5: Epigraphy. Ed. by Victoria R. Bricker. LC 91-14769. (Illus.). 203p. 1992. text ed. 40.00 (*0-292-77650-0*) U of Tex Pr.

***Supplement to the Heritage Encyclopedia of Band Music.** William H. Rehrig. Ed. by Paul E. Bierley. LC 96-77526. 1996. 90.00 (*0-918048-12-5*) Integrity.

Supplement to the History of the Later Roman Empire (976-1057 A.D.) Bound with the Patriarchs of Constantinople. J. V. Bury & C. Cobham. 254p. (Orig.). 1986. pap. 20.00 (*0-89005-443-6*) Ares.

Supplement to the Indian Army List, January 1924. Ed. by Government of India, Army Department Staff. 900p. (C). 1987. 336.00 (*0-317-90459-0*, Pub. by Picton UK) St Mut.

Supplement to the Law of Sentencing, Corrections & Prisoner's Rights: Cases & Materials, 1993. 4th ed. Sheldon Krantz & Lynn S. Branham. (American Casebook Ser.). 143p. 1993. pap. text ed. 10.50 (*0-314-02560-X*) West Pub.

Supplement to the Law of Sentencing, Probation, & Parole in North Carolina, 1994: Structured Sentencing Act & Related Legislation, 1993-94. Stevens H. Clarke. 75p. (Orig.). (C). 1994. pap. text ed. 7.50 (*1-56011-227-1*, 91.04B) Institute Government.

Supplement to the List of Indian Fungi. R. N. Tandan. 246p. (C). 1976. text ed. 100.00 (*0-89771-665-5*, Pub. by Intl Bk Distr II) St Mut.

Supplement to the Ninth Mental Measurements Yearbook. Ed. by Jane C. Conoley et al. (Mental Measurements Yearbook Ser.). xiii, 279p. (Orig.). 1988. pap. 55.00 (*0-910674-30-2*) Buros Inst Mental.

***Supplement to the Official Records of the Union & Confederate Armies, 100 vols.** Date not set. 4,000.00 (*1-56837-275-2*) Broadfoot.

***Supplement to the Official Records of the Union & Confederate Armies Pt. I: Reports.** Ed. by Janet B. Hewett et al. (War of the Rebellion the Official Records of the Union & Confederate Armies Ser.: Vol. 8, Serial No. 8). 807p. 1995. Not sold separately (*1-56837-286-8*) Broadfoot.

***Supplement to the Official Records of the Union & Confederate Armies Pt. I: Reports.** Ed. by Janet B. Hewett et al. (War of the Rebellion the Official Records of the Union & Confederate Armies Ser.: Vol. 9, Serial No. 9). 1650p. 1995. Not sold separately (*1-56837-287-6*) Broadfoot.

***Supplement to the Official Records of the Union & Confederate Armies Pt. I: Reports.** Ed. by Janet B. Hewett et al. (War of the Rebellion the Official Records of the Union & Confederate Armies Ser.: Vol. 4, Serial No. 4). 845p. 1995. Not sold separately (*1-56837-293-0*) Broadfoot.

***Supplement to the Official Records of the Union & Confederate Armies Pt. I: Reports.** Ed. by Janet B. Hewett et al. (War of the Rebellion the Official Records of the Union & Confederate Armies Ser.: Vol. 5, Serial No. 5). 715p. 1995. Not sold separately (*1-56837-311-2*) Broadfoot.

***Supplement to the Official Records of the Union & Confederate Armies Pt. I: Reports.** Ed. by Janet B. Hewett et al. (War of the Rebellion the Official Records of the Union & Confederate Armies Ser.: Vol. 10, Serial No. 10). 659p. 1996. Not sold separately (*1-56837-314-7*) Broadfoot.

***Supplement to the Official Records of the Union & Confederate Armies Pt. I: Reports, Vol. 6, Serial No. 6.** Ed. by Janet B. Hewett et al. 916p. 1996. Not sold separately (*1-56837-327-9*) Broadfoot.

***Supplement to the Official Records of the Union & Confederate Armies Pt. II: Record of Events.** Ed. by Janet B. Hewett et al. (War of the Rebellion the Official Records of the Union & Confederate Armies Ser.: Vol. 3, Serial No. 15). 824p. 1995. Not sold separately (*1-56837-283-3*) Broadfoot.

***Supplement to the Official Records of the Union & Confederate Armies Pt. II: Record of Events.** Ed. by Janet B. Hewett et al. (War of the Rebellion the Official Records of the Union & Confederate Armies Ser.: Vol. 4, Serial No. 16). 799p. 1995. Not sold separately (*1-56837-284-1*) Broadfoot.

***Supplement to the Official Records of the Union & Confederate Armies Pt. II: Record of Events.** Ed. by Janet B. Hewett et al. (War of the Rebellion the Official Records of the Union & Confederate Armies Ser.: Vol. 5, No. 17). 812p. 1995. Not sold separately (*1-56837-285-X*) Broadfoot.

***Supplement to the Official Records of the Union & Confederate Armies Pt. II: Record of Events.** Ed. by Janet B. Hewett et al. (War of the Rebellion the Official Records of the Union & Confederate Armies Ser.: Vol. 6, Serial No. 18). 768p. 1995. Not sold separately (*1-56837-292-2*) Broadfoot.

***Supplement to the Official Records of the Union & Confederate Armies Pt. II: Record of Events.** Ed. by Janet B. Hewett et al. (War of the Rebellion the Official Records of the Union & Confederate Armies Ser.: Vol. 7, Serial No. 19). 724p. 1995. Not sold separately (*1-56837-294-9*) Broadfoot.

***Supplement to the Official Records of the Union & Confederate Armies Pt. II: Record of Events.** Ed. by Janet B. Hewett et al. (War of the Rebellion the Official Records of the Union & Confederate Armies Ser.: Vol. 8, Serial No. 20). 763p. 1995. Not sold separately (*1-56837-296-5*) Broadfoot.

***Supplement to the Official Records of the Union & Confederate Armies Pt. II: Record of Events.** Ed. by Janet B. Hewett et al. (War of the Rebellion the Official Records of the Union & Confederate Armies Ser.: Vol. 9, Serial No. 21). 677p. 1995. Not sold separately (*1-56837-297-3*) Broadfoot.

***Supplement to the Official Records of the Union & Confederate Armies Pt. II: Record of Events.** Ed. by Janet B. Hewett et al. (War of the Rebellion the Official Records of the Union & Confederate Armies Ser.: Vol. 10, Serial No. 22). 753p. 1995. Not sold separately (*1-56837-298-1*) Broadfoot.

***Supplement to the Official Records of the Union & Confederate Armies Pt. II: Record of Events.** Ed. by Janet B. Hewett et al. (War of the Rebellion the Official Records of the Union & Confederate Armies Ser.: Vol. 11, Serial No. 23). 737p. 1995. Not sold separately (*1-56837-299-X*) Broadfoot.

***Supplement to the Official Records of the Union & Confederate Armies Pt. II: Record of Events.** Ed. by Janet B. Hewett et al. (War of the Rebellion the Official Records of the Union & Confederate Armies Ser.: Vol. 12, Serial No. 24). 835p. 1995. Not sold separately (*1-56837-302-3*) Broadfoot.

***Supplement to the Official Records of the Union & Confederate Armies Pt. II: Record of Events.** Ed. by Janet B. Hewett et al. (War of the Rebellion the Official Records of the Union & Confederate Armies Ser.: Vol. 13, Serial No. 25). 814p. 1995. Not sold separately (*1-56837-303-1*) Broadfoot.

***Supplement to the Official Records of the Union & Confederate Armies Pt. II: Record of Events.** Ed. by Janet B. Hewett et al. (War of the Rebellion the Official Records of the Union & Confederate Armies Ser.: Vol. 14, Serial No. 26). 816p. 1995. Not sold separately (*1-56837-304-X*) Broadfoot.

***Supplement to the Official Records of the Union & Confederate Armies Pt. II: Record of Events.** Ed. by Janet B. Hewett et al. (War of the Rebellion the Official Records of the Union & Confederate Armies Ser.: Vol. 15, Serial No. 27). 839p. 1995. Not sold separately (*1-56837-307-4*) Broadfoot.

***Supplement to the Official Records of the Union & Confederate Armies Pt. II: Record of Events.** Ed. by Janet B. Hewett et al. (War of the Rebellion the Official Records of the Union & Confederate Armies Ser.: Vol. 16, Serial No. 28). 860p. 1995. Not sold separately (*1-56837-309-0*) Broadfoot.

***Supplement to the Official Records of the Union & Confederate Armies Pt. II: Record of Events.** Ed. by Janet B. Hewett et al. (War of the Rebellion the Official Records of the Union & Confederate Armies Ser.: Vol. 17, Serial No. 29). 826p. 1995. Not sold separately (*1-56837-312-0*) Broadfoot.

***Supplement to the Official Records of the Union & Confederate Armies Pt. II: Record of Events.** Ed. by Janet B. Hewett et al. (War of the Rebellion the Official Records of the Union & Confederate Armies Ser.: Vol. 18, Serial No. 30). 833p. 1995. Not sold separately (*1-56837-313-9*) Broadfoot.

***Supplement to the Official Records of the Union & Confederate Armies Pt. II: Record of Events.** Ed. by Janet B. Hewett et al. (War of the Rebellion the Official Records of the Union & Confederate Armies Ser.: Vol. 19, Serial No. 31). 819p. 1995. Not sold separately (*1-56837-315-5*) Broadfoot.

***Supplement to the Official Records of the Union & Confederate Armies Pt. II: Record of Events.** Ed. by Janet B. Hewett et al. (War of the Rebellion the Official Records of the Union & Confederate Armies Ser.: Vol. 20, Serial No. 32). 810p. 1996. Not sold separately (*1-56837-317-1*) Broadfoot.

***Supplement to the Official Records of the Union & Confederate Armies Pt. II: Record of Events.** Ed. by Janet B. Hewett et al. (War of the Rebellion the Official Records of the Union & Confederate Armies Ser.: Vol. 21, Serial No. 33). 815p. 1996. Not sold separately (*1-56837-318-X*) Broadfoot.

***Supplement to the Official Records of the Union & Confederate Armies Pt. II: Record of Events.** Ed. by Janet B. Hewett et al. (War of the Rebellion the Official Records of the Union & Confederate Armies Ser.: Vol. 22, Serial No. 34). 798p. 1996. Not sold separately (*1-56837-319-8*) Broadfoot.

***Supplement to the Official Records of the Union & Confederate Armies Pt. II: Record of Events.** Ed. by Janet B. Hewett et al. (War of the Rebellion the Official Records of the Union & Confederate Armies Ser.: Vol. 23, Serial No. 35). 817p. 1996. Not sold separately (*1-56837-322-8*) Broadfoot.

***Supplement to the Official Records of the Union & Confederate Armies Pt. II: Record of Events.** Ed. by Janet B. Hewett et al. (War of the Rebellion the Official Records of the Union & Confederate Armies Ser.: Vol. 24, Serial No. 36). 753p. 1996. Not sold separately (*1-56837-323-6*) Broadfoot.

***Supplement to the Official Records of the Union & Confederate Armies Pt. II: Record of Events.** Ed. by Janet B. Hewett et al. (War of the Rebellion the Official Records of the Union & Confederate Armies Ser.: Vol. 25, Serial No. 37). 789p. 1996. Not sold separately (*1-56837-324-4*) Broadfoot.

***Supplement to the Official Records of the Union & Confederate Armies Pt. II: Record of Events.** Ed. by Janet B. Hewett et al. (War of the Rebellion the Official Records of the Union & Confederate Armies Ser.: Vol. 26, Serial No. 38). 841p. 1996. Not sold separately (*1-56837-325-2*) Broadfoot.

***Supplement to the Official Records of the Union & Confederate Armies Pt. II: Record of Events, Vol. 28, Serial No. 40.** Ed. by Janet B. Hewett et al. 841p. 1996. Not sold separately (*1-56837-295-7*) Broadfoot.

***Supplement to the Official Records of the Union & Confederate Armies Pt. II: Record of Events, Vol. 29, Serial No. 41.** Ed. by Janet B. Hewett et al. 846p. 1996. Not sold separately (*1-56837-328-7*) Broadfoot.

***Supplement to the Official Records of the Union & Confederate Armies Pt. II: Record of Events, Vol. 30, Serial No. 42.** Ed. by Janet B. Hewett et al. 828p. 1996. Not sold separately (*1-56837-329-5*) Broadfoot.

***Supplement to the Official Records of the Union & Confederate Armies Pt. II: Records of Events, Vol. 27, Serial No. 39.** Ed. by Janet B. Hewett et al. 778p. 1996. write for info. (*1-56837-326-0*) Broadfoot.

Supplement to the Official Records of the Union & Confederate Armies Vol. 1: Part I - Reports. Ed. by Janet B. Hewett et al. 754p. 1994. Not sold separately (*1-56837-276-0*) Broadfoot.

Supplement to the Official Records of the Union & Confederate Armies Vol. 1: Serial 13, Part II - Record of Events. Alabama. Ed. by Janet B. Hewett. 962p. 1994. Not sold separately (*1-56837-279-5*) Broadfoot.

Supplement to the Official Records of the Union & Confederate Armies Vol. 2: Part I - Reports. Ed. by Janet B. Hewett et al. 788p. 1994. Not sold separately (*1-56837-277-9*) Broadfoot.

Supplement to the Official Records of the Union & Confederate Armies Vol. 2: Serial 14, Part II - Record of Events. Arizona, Arkansas. Ed. by Janet B. Hewett. 853p. 1994. Not sold separately (*1-56837-281-7*) Broadfoot.

Supplement to the Official Records of the Union & Confederate Armies Vol. 3: Part I - Reports. Ed. by Janet B. Hewett et al. 809p. 1994. Not sold separately (*1-56837-280-9*) Broadfoot.

Supplement to the Philocalia: The Second Century of Saint John of Karpathos. David Balfour & Mary Cunningham. Ed. by Nomikos M. Vaporis. LC 89-7449. (Archbishop Iakovos Library of Ecclesiastical & Historical Sources: No. 16). 150p. (Orig.). (C). 1994. pap. text ed. 14.95 (*0-917653-34-3*) Hellenic Coll Pr.

Supplement to the Pre-Islamic Coinage of Eastern Arabia. D. T. Potts. (Carsten Niebuhr Institute Publications (CNI): No. 16). (Illus.). 100p. 1994. 65.00 (*87-7289-272-2*, Pub. by Mus Tusculanum DK) Paul & Co Pubs.

Supplement to the Second Edition of Rodd's Chemistry of Carbon Compounds, Vol. 1, Pts F & G. Ed. by M. F. Ansell. 404p. 1983. 286.00 (*0-444-42183-1*) Elsevier.

Supplement to the Second Edition of Rodd's Chemistry of Carbon Compounds, Vol. IV: Heterocyclic Compounds. 476p. 1994. 311.25 (*0-444-89932-4*) Elsevier.

Supplement to the Sheffield Glossary. S. O. Addy. (English Dialect Society Publications: No. 62). 1974. reprint ed. pap. 25.00 (*0-8115-0482-4*) Periodicals Srv.

Supplement to the Sociology of Invention. S. C. Gilfillan. (Illus.). 1971. 10.00 (*0-911302-16-6*) San Francisco Pr.

Supplement to the Supreme Court & Magistrate's Courts Legislation Handbook. Taitz & Kelbrick. 146p. 1992. pap. 12.00 (*0-409-05829-7*, SA) MICHIE.

An Asterisk (*) at the beginning of an entry indicates that the title is appearing in BIP for the first time.

Supplement to the Swiss Federal Code of Obligations, 1988. Tr. by Simon L. Goren. ii, 10p. 1988. pap. 5.00 (*0-8377-0621-1*) Rothman.

Supplement to the Tenth Mental Measurements Yearbook. Ed. by Jack J. Kramer & Jane C. Conoley. LC 39-3422. (Mental Measurements Yearbook Ser.). xii, 321p. (Orig.). 1990. pap. 65.00 (*0-910674-32-9*, Bison Books) U of Nebr Pr.

Supplement to the Tuckerman Tables. Michael H. Houlden & F. Richard Stephenson. LC 86-71019. (Memoirs Ser.: Vol. 170). 564p. 1986. pap. 35.00 (*0-87169-170-1*, M170-STF) Am Philos.

Supplement to the Twelfth Mental Measurements Yearbook. James C. Impara. 1996. pap. text ed. 60.00 (*0-910674-43-4*) Buros Inst Mental.

Supplement to the 1810 Census of Virginia. Netti Schreiner-Yantis. LC 70-165302. 320p. 1971. 25.00 (*0-89157-009-8*) GBIP.

Supplement to Torrey's New England Marriages Prior to Seventeen Hundred. Melinde L. Sanborn. 80p. 1992. 12.50 (*0-685-48611-7*, 5142) Genealog Pub.

Supplement to Trial Ethics 1994. Underwood. 1994. suppl. ed. 95.00 (*0-316-88817-6*) Little.

Supplement to Trusts 1995. Fratcher. 1995. suppl. ed. 245. 00 (*0-316-29430-6*) Little.

Supplement to Using Maps & Aerial Photography in Your Genealogical Research. Marilyn Lind. LC 85-80941. (Illus.). 43p. (Orig.). 1985. pap. text ed. 5.50 (*0-937463-07-8*) Linden Tree.

Supplement to Who's Who in America 1991-1992. 46th ed. 1293p. 1991. 167.00 (*0-8379-7102-0*) Marquis.

Supplement to 1894 "History of Dudley Family" Dudley. 96p. 1993. reprint ed. pap. 18.00 (*0-8328-3798-9*); reprint ed. lib. bdg. 28.00 (*0-8328-3797-0*) Higginson Bk Co.

Supplement Zu Hain und Panzer: Beitrage Zur Inkunabelbibliographie. Konrad Burger. vii, 440p. 1966. reprint ed. 160.00 (*0-318-71749-2*) G Olms Pubs.

Supplement 1950-1954 see Short Story Index: Basic Volume, 1900-1949

Supplement 1953 see Short Story Index: Basic Volume, 1900-1949

Supplement 1955-1958 see Short Story Index: Basic Volume, 1900-1949

Supplement 1959-1963 see Short Story Index: Basic Volume, 1900-1949

Supplement 1964-1968 see Short Story Index: Basic Volume, 1900-1949

Supplement 1969-1973 see Short Story Index: Basic Volume, 1900-1949

Supplement (1971-1986) to Robert G Albion's Naval & Maritime History: An Annotated Bibliography. Benjamin W. Labaree. 232p. 1988. pap. 13.95 (*0-913372-46-3*) Mystic Seaport.

Supplement, 1974-1978 see Short Story Index: Basic Volume, 1900-1949

Supplementa: Zu den Neutestamentlichen und den Kirchengeschichtlichen Entwurfen. Kurt Aland. viii, 516p. (C). 1990. lib. bdg. 152.35 (*3-11-012142-5*) De Gruyter.

Supplemental Apology for the Believers in the Shakespeare Papers. George Chalmers. 656p. 1971. reprint ed. 45.00 (*0-7146-2536-1*, Pub. by F Cass Pubs UK) Intl Spec Bk.

Supplemental Apology for the Believers in the Shakespeare-Papers: Being a Reply to Mr. Malone's Answer. George Chalmers. LC 70-96374. (Eighteenth Century Shakespeare Ser.: No. 26). viii, 656p. 1971. reprint ed. lib. bdg. 57.50 (*0-678-05141-0*) Kelley.

Supplemental Applications & Topics. Baum. (Barnett Math Ser.). 192p. (C). 1991. pap. text ed. 21.00 (*0-02-306770-5*, Macmillan Coll) P-H.

Supplemental Chapters to Accompany Calculus. 6th ed. Michael Penna. (C). 1996. ring bd. 6.50 (*0-201-43155-6*) Addison-Wesley.

Supplemental Check List of Kentucky Imprints, 1788-1820, Including the Original Printing of the Original Kentucky Copyright Ledger, 1800-1854. Ed. by J. W. Townsend. (Historical Records Survey Monographs). 1942. 25.00 (*0-527-01925-9*) Periodicals Srv.

Supplemental Checklist of Fantastic Literature. Ed. by Bradford M. Day. LC 74-15962. (Science Fiction Ser.). 160p. 1976. reprint ed. 13.95 (*0-405-06327-X*) Ayer.

Supplemental Class III Archaeological Survey of the Phase A, Reach 3 Corridor, Tucson Aqueduct, Central Arizona Project: Late Sedentary & Early Classic Period Tucson Basin Hohokam Occupation in the Lower Santa Cruz River Basin, Marana to Rillito, Arizona see Class III Survey of the Tucson Aqueduct Phase A Corridor, Central Arizona Project

*__Supplemental Index to Robert's Rules of Order Newly Revised, 1990 Edition.__ 100p. (Orig.). 1997. pap. 8.00 (*1-884048-16-1*) Natl Assn Parliamentarians.

Supplemental Instruction: Improving First-Year Student Success in High-Risk Courses. Deanna C. Martin & David R. Arendale. (Freshman Year Experience Monograph: No. 7). 57p. (Orig.). 1993. pap. 25.00 (*1-889271-05-5*) Nat Res Ctr.

Supplemental Instruction: Increasing Achievement & Retention. Ed. by Deanna C. Martin & David R. Arendale. LC 85-644763. (New Directions for Teaching & Learning Ser.: No. 60). 110p. (Orig.). 1994. pap. 19.00 (*0-7879-9999-7*) Jossey-Bass.

Supplemental Instructional Resources, Basics: Bridging Vocational & Academic Skill - Instructional Program Development. National Center for Research in Vocational Education Staff. 1987. 7.95 (*0-317-03915-6*, SP300DB) Ctr Educ Trng Employ.

Supplemental Irrigation in the Near East & North Africa. Ed. by Eugene R. Perrier & Abdul B. Salkini. 628p. 1991. lib. bdg. 242.00 (*0-7923-1006-3*) Kluwer Ac.

Supplemental Materials for First Year Polish. Leonard A. Polakiewicz. (Illus.). lxii, 212p. (Orig.). (POL.). (C). 1991. pap. text ed. 16.95 (*0-89357-215-2*) Slavica.

Supplemental New Testament Archaeology. Dan P. Cole. Ed. by Hershel Shanks. 48p. (Orig.). (C). 1995. pap. text ed. 99.50 incl. sl. (*1-880317-42-7*) Biblical Arch Soc.

Supplemental Papers to Bentham & Hooker's Genera Plantarum. G. Bentham & J. D. Hooker. 1971. reprint ed. 175.00 (*3-7682-0706-4*) Lubrecht & Cramer.

Supplemental Problems to Organic Chemistry. Marye A. Fox & James K. Whitesell. (Chemistry Ser.). 32p. (C). 1995. pap. text ed. 10.00 (*0-86720-912-7*) Jones & Bartlett.

Supplemental Process Guide for Congregations: Defining the Role of the Non-Jew in the Synagogue. Ed. by Dru Greenwood. 96p. 1993. pap. 10.00 (*0-685-72158-2*, 280061) UAHC.

Supplemental Report on the Elevated-Temperature Properties of Chromium-Molybdenum Steels - DS6-S2. 140p. 1986. pap. 30.00 (*0-8031-0816-8*, 05-006002-40) ASTM.

Supplemental Report on the Elevated Temperature Properties of Chromium-Molybdenum Steels, DS6-S1. 70p. 1966. pap. 2.25 (*0-8031-0815-X*, 05-006001-40) ASTM.

Supplemental Studies in Math, Vol. 1. Eliseo R. Martinez & Irma C. Martinez. (Math Ser.). (Illus.). 73p. (J). (ps-1). 1985. student ed. 8.75 (*1-878300-00-8*) Childrens Work.

Supplemental Tables of Molecular Orbital Calculations, 2 vols, Set. Andrew Streitwieser. 1965. 707.00 (*0-08-010219-0*, Pub. by Pergamon Repr UK) Franklin.

Supplemental Warp Patterning. Harriet Tidball. LC 76-24008. (Guild Monographs: No. 17). (Illus.). 46p. 1966. pap. 9.95 (*0-916658-17-1*) Shuttle Craft.

Supplementary Cases in Everyday Law. Babbie Mason. (LA - Business Law Ser.). 1991. wbk. ed., pap. 17.95 (*0-538-60968-0*) S-W Pub.

Supplementary Cementing Materials for Use in Blended Cements. 130p. 1996. pap. 40.00 (*0-89312-142-8*, RD112T) Portland Cement.

Supplementary Enrichment Vocabulary: Preliminary Edition, Lessons 1-40. Raji M. Rammuny. 82p. (C). 1994. pap. text ed. 9.00 (*1-57074-145-X*) Greyden Pr.

Supplementary Grammar Notes to "An Introduction to Modern Japanese", Pt. 1: Lessons 1-15. Mutsuko E. Simon. LC 86-71897. xv, 138p. (C). 1986. 17.95 (*0-939512-29-7*) U MI Japan.

Supplementary Grammar Notes to "An Introduction to Modern Japanese", Pt. 2: Lessons 16-30. Mutsuko E. Simon. LC 86-71897. x, 172p. (C). 1987. 17.95 (*0-939512-32-7*) U MI Japan.

*__Supplementary Grammar 1.__ Elsworth. 1988. pap. text ed. write for info. (*0-582-01407-7*, Pub. by Longman UK) Longman.

*__Supplementary Grammar 2.__ Dawson. 1988. pap. text ed. write for info. (*0-582-01406-9*, Pub. by Longman UK) Longman.

Supplementary Materials for Puntos de Partida. 4th ed. Sharon Foerster & Jean Miller. 1993. pap. text ed. write for info. (*0-07-021454-9*) McGraw.

Supplementary Mutagenicity Tests: UKEMS Recommended Procedures. Ed. by David J. Kirkland & Margaret Fox. (Illus.). 175p. (C). 1994. text ed. 59.95 (*0-521-45073-X*) Cambridge U Pr.

Supplementary Note to "A Bibliography of the Works of Samuel Daniel" see Charles Viner's General Abridgement of Law & Equity

Supplementary Notes on American Menispermaceae: Parts VI & VII. B. A. Krukoff & Rupert C. Barneby. (Memoirs Ser.: Vol. 22(2)). 89p. 1971. pap. 11.00 (*0-89327-075-X*) NY Botanical.

Supplementary Notes on the American Species of Erythrina: Field Studies of Central American Species see Memoirs of the New York Botanical Garden: No. 20(2)

Supplementary Notes on the American Species of Strychnos Pt. VII. B. A. Krukoff. (Memoirs Ser.: Vol. 12 (2)). (Illus.). 94p. 1965. 10.00 (*0-89327-046-6*) NY Botanical.

Supplementary Notes on the American Species of Strychnos Pts. VIII & IX. B. A. Krukoff & Rupert C. Barneby. (Memoirs Ser.: Vol. 20 (1)). (Illus.). 97p. 1969. 10.00 (*0-89327-067-9*) NY Botanical.

Supplementary Readers for Intermediate Chinese Reader, 5 vols. Incl. Vol. 1. White Haired Girl. Chi-Yu Ho. 1976. 5.95 (*0-685-73244-4*); Vol. 1. White Haired Girl. Chi-Yu Ho. 1976. pap. 5.95 (*0-88710-116-X*); Vol. 2. Red Detachment of Women. Chi-Yu Ho. 1976. 5.95 (*0-685-73245-2*); Vol. 2. Red Detachment of Women. Chi-Yu Ho. 1976. (*0-88710-117-8*); Vol. 3. Episodes from Dream of the Red Chamber. Louise H. Li. 1976. pap. (*0-318-51880-5*); Vol. 3. Episodes from Dream of the Red Chamber. Louise H. Li. 1976. 4.95 (*0-88710-118-6*); Vol. 4. Sun Yat-sen. Yung Teng Chia-Yee. 1976. 5.95 (*0-685-73246-0*); Vol. 5. Wu Sung Kills a Tiger. Yung Teng Chia-Yee. 1976. 5.95 (*0-685-73247-9*); 1976. write for info. (*0-88710-120-8*) Yale Far Eastern Pubns.

Supplementary Report see Report of the Federal Trade Commission on Agricultural Income Inquiry

Supplementary Report of the Land Planning Committee to the National Resources Board, Washington, DC, 1935-1942: Proceedings of the U. S. National Resources Committee & Land Planning, Public Works & Land Use Committee, 1971. United States National Resources Committee & Land Planning, Public Works & Rural Land Use Committee. (Land Planning Report Ser.). 1972. reprint ed. 87.95 (*0-405-04535-2*) Ayer.

Supplementary Report on the Cladoniae of Connecticut. Alexander W. Evans. (Connecticut Academy of Arts & Sciences Ser., Trans.: Vol. 35). 1944. pap. 49.50 (*0-685-22908-4*) Elliots Bks.

Supplementary Russian-English Dictionary. Stephen Marder. xv, 522p. (Orig.). (ENG & RUS.). 1995. reprint ed. pap. 27.95 (*0-89357-253-5*) Slavica.

Supplementary Sensorimotor Area. Hans Lders. 544p. 1995. text ed. 125.00 (*0-7817-0268-2*) Lppncott-Raven.

Supplementary Solos: Level 1. David Kraehenbuehl et al. Ed. by Frances Clark & Louise Goss. (Frances Clark Library for Piano Students). 32p. (J). (gr. k-12). 1979. pap. text ed. 5.95 (*0-87487-105-0*) Summy-Birchard.

Supplementary Solos: Level 2. David Kraehenbuehl et al. Ed. by Frances Clark & Louise Goss. (Frances Clark Library for Piano Students). 32p. (J). (gr. k-12). 1980. pap. text ed. 5.95 (*0-87487-106-9*) Summy-Birchard.

Supplementary Solos: Levels 3 & 4. Roger Grove et al. Ed. by Louise Goss & Francis Clark. (Frances Clark Library for Piano Students). 48p. (J). (gr. k-12). 1974. pap. 7.95 (*0-87487-140-9*) Summy-Birchard.

Supplementary Studies on the Systematics of the Genus Perdita (Hymenoptera, Andrenidae), Pt. 2. Philip H. Timberlake. LC 77-635326. (University of California Publications in Social Welfare: No. 85). (Illus.). 73p. reprint ed. pap. 25.00 (*0-8357-6857-0*, 2035555) Bks Demand.

Supplementary Study of Hazardous Materials Transportation in Texas. Contrib. by Leigh Boske & Susan Hadden. (Policy Research Project Report: No. 88). 134p. 1988. pap. 12.00 (*0-89940-695-5*) LBJ Sch Pub Aff.

Supplementary Texts in Mongolian Script for First Year Reading. (Mongolia Society Special Papers: No. 4). 1965. spiral bd. 7.50 (*0-910980-24-1*) Mongolia.

Supplementary Ways for Increasing International Stability. Ed. by Peter Kopacek. LC 96-37961. (IFAC Postprint Ser.). 170p. 1996. pap. 67.00 (*0-08-042378-7*, Pergamon Pr) Elsevier.

Supplementay Principles & Recommendations for Population & Housing Censuses. 143p. 1990. 17.00 (*92-1-161317-5*, 90.XVII.9) UN.

Supplementing Literature Programs: Selected Titles. Mary M. Eble & Jeanne L. Renton. LC 93-2156. 276p. 1993. 42.50 (*0-8108-2658-5*) Scarecrow.

Supplements: fasc. 1-2: al-Abbas b. Ahmad b.Tulun-Basbas. 1980 see Encyclopaedia of Islam: New Edition

Supplements: fasc. 3-4: Basbas-Djawhar. 1981 see Encyclopaedia of Islam: New Edition

Supplements: fasc. 5-6: Djawhar-al-Iraki. 1982 see Encyclopaedia of Islam: New Edition

Supplements to a Course in Miracles: Psychotherapy & The Song of Prayer. 112p. 1996. pap. 9.95 (*0-670-86994-5*) Studio Bks.

Supplements to a Course in Miracles: Psychotherapy: Purpose, Process, & Practice & the Song of Prayer: Prayer, Forgiveness, Healing. Inner Peace Foundation Staff. 112p. 1996. pap. 9.95 (*0-14-025848-5*, Viking) Viking Penguin.

Supplements to the Monthly Vital Statistics Report: Advance Reports, 1986 PHS 90-1953. (Vital & Health Statistics Ser. 24: Compilations of Data on Natality, Mortality, Marriage, Divorce, & Induced Terminations of Pregnancy: No. 3). 145p. 1989. 8.00 (*0-685-61590-1*, 017-022-01107-7) Natl Ctr Health Stats.

Supplements to the Monthly Vital Statistics Report: Advance Reports, 1987 PHS 90-1954. (Vital & Health Statistics Ser. 24: Compilations of Data on Natality, Mortality, Marriage, Divorce, & Induced Terminations of Pregnancy: No. 4). 144p. 1990. 7.50 (*0-685-61589-8*, 017-022-01118-2) Natl Ctr Health Stats.

Supplements to the Second Edition of Rodd's Chemistry of Carbon Compounds: Supplement to Vol. IV: Heterocyclic Compounds, Part B: Five-Membered Heterocyclic Compounds with a Single Hetero-Atom in the Ring; Alkaloids, Dyes & Pigments. Ed. by M. F. Ansell. 318p. 1985. 259.25 (*0-444-42485-7*) Elsevier.

Supplements to the Second Edition of Rodd's Chemistry of Carbon Compounds, Vol. III: Aromatic Compounds; Part H: Polycarbocyclic Compounds with More Than Thirteen Atoms in the Fused-Riding System. Ed. by M. F. Ansell. 140p. 1988. 128.00 (*0-444-42989-1*) Elsevier.

Supplements to the Second Edition of Rodd's Chemsitry of Carbon Compounds - Volume IV: Heterocyclic Compounds; Part K. Ed. by M. F. Ansell. 626p. 1989. 476.75 (*0-444-87399-6*) Elsevier.

Supplements to the 2nd Edition of Rodd's Chemistry of Carbon Compounds: Heterocyclic Compounds, Vol. 4. Ed. by M. F. Ansell. 272p. 1987. 233.50 (*0-444-42792-9*) Elsevier.

Supplements to the 2nd Edition of Rodd's Chemistry of Carbon Compounds: Supplement to Vol. 1: Aliphatic Compounds; Part E: Unsaturated Acyclic Hydrocarbons, Trihydric Alcohols, Their Oxidation Products & Derivatives. Ed. by M. F. Ansell. 510p. 1983. 383.50 (*0-444-42236-6*) Elsevier.

*__Supplements to the 2nd Edition of Rodd's Chemistry of Carbon Compounds Vol. IV, Pt. F: Six-Membered Heterocyclic Compounds with a Single Nitrogen Atom in the Ring; Pyridine, Polymethylenepyridines, Quinoline, Isoquinoline & Their Derivatives.__ M. F. Ansell. 252p. 1987. 208.75 (*0-444-42821-6*) Elsevier.

*__Supplements to the 2nd Edition of Rodd's Chemistry of Carbon Compounds Vol. IV, Pt. G: Six-Membered Ring Compounds Where the Hetero-Atom is Phosphorus, Arsenic, Antimony or Bismuth.__ M. F. Ansell. 460p. 1987. 370.50 (*0-444-42897-6*) Elsevier.

*__Supplements to the 2nd Edition of Rodd's Chemistry of Carbon Compounds Vol. IV, Pt. L: Fused-Ring Heterocyclic Compounds Containing Three or More Nitrogen Atoms; Purines & Related Ring Systems; Nucleosides; Nucleotides & Nucleic Acids; Pteridines, Alloxazines, Flavins & Related Compounds.__ M. F. Ansell. 276p. 1988. 233.50 (*0-444-42978-6*) Elsevier.

Supplementum Adnotationum Super Lucanum III: Libri viii-x. Ed. by Giuseppe A. Cavajoni. (Classical & Byzantine Monographs: No. 16). viii, 165p. (Orig.). (LAT.). 1990. pap. 56.00 (*90-256-0982-1*, Pub. by A M Hakkert NE) Benjamins North Am.

Supplementum Comicum. Ioannes Demianczuk. 158p. 1967. reprint ed. write for info. (*0-318-70908-2*) G Olms Pubs.

Supplementum Epigraphicum Graecum, Vol. XXVI. Ed. by H. W. Pleket & R. S. Stroud. 550p. 1979. 75.00 (*0-89005-429-0*) Ares.

Supplementum Epigraphicum Graecum, Vol. XXIX. Ed. by H. W. Pleket & R. S. Stroud. (SEG Ser.). 544p. 1982. 110.00 (*0-89005-432-0*) Ares.

Supplementum Epigraphicum Graecum, Vol. XXX. Ed. by H. W. Pleket & R. S. Stroud. (SEG Ser.). 634p. 1983. 110.00 (*0-89005-433-9*) Ares.

Supplementum Epigraphicum Graecum, Vol. XXXI. Ed. by H. W. Pleket & R. S. Stroud. (SEG Ser.). 500p. 1984. 110.00 (*0-89005-434-7*) Ares.

Supplementum Epigraphicum Graecum, Vol. XXXII. 2nd ed. Ed. by H. W. Pleket & R. S. Stroud. (SEG Ser.). xxi, 550p. (GRE.). 1985. 110.00 (*0-89005-439-8*) Ares.

Supplementum Epigraphicum Graecum, Vol. XXXIII. 550p. 110.00 (*0-89005-557-2*) Ares.

Supplementum Epigraphicum Graecum, Vol. XXXIV. 575p. 110.00 (*0-89005-440-1*) Ares.

Supplementum Epigraphicum Graecum, Vol. XXXV. 617p. 110.00 (*0-89005-441-X*) Ares.

Supplementum Epigraphicum Graecum, Vol. XXXVI. 588p. 120.00 (*0-685-59656-7*) Ares.

Supplementum Epigraphicum Graecum, Vol. XXXVII. 680p. 110.00 (*0-685-59657-5*) Ares.

Supplementum Epigraphicum Graecum, Vol. XXXVIII. 699p. 110.00 (*0-685-70915-9*) Ares.

Supplementum Epigraphicum Graecum: Index to Vols. XXVI-XXXV. 599p. 115.00 (*0-685-59658-3*) Ares.

Supplementum Epigraphicum Graecum: Vols. 1-25 & Index Vols. 11-20, 8 Vols., Set. Ed. by J. J. Hondius & A. G. Woodhead. 1984. reprint ed. 900.00 (*0-89005-428-2*) Ares.

Supplementum Epigraphicum Graecum an Index to Volumes XXVI-XXXV (1976-1985) 900p. 1990. 125.00 (*90-5063-037-5*, Pub. by Gieben NE) Benjamins North Am.

Supplementum Epigraphicum Graecum XXXV, 1986. xxiv, 564p. 1989. 91.00 (*90-5063-043-X*, Pub. by Gieben NE) Benjamins North Am.

Supplementum Festivum: Studies in Honor of Paul Oskar Kristeller. Ed. by John Monfasani et al. LC 87-18422. (Medieval & Renaissance Texts & Studies: Vol. 49). (Illus.). 672p. 1987. 60.00 (*0-86698-033-4*, MR49) MRTS.

Supplementum Hellenisticum. Ed. by Heinz-Gunther Nesselrath et al. 863p. (GRE.). 1983. 476.95 (*3-11-008171-7*) De Gruyter.

Supplementum Inscriptionum Atticarum I. Ed. by Al N. Oikonomides. 1976. 45.00 (*0-89005-126-7*) Ares.

Supplementum Inscriptionum Atticarum II. Ed. by Al N. Oikonomides. 1978. 45.00 (*0-89005-249-2*) Ares.

Supplementum Inscriptionum Atticarum III. Ed. by Al. N. Oikonomides. 1979. 45.00 (*0-89005-275-1*) Ares.

Supplementum Inscriptionum Atticarum IV. Ed. by Al N. Oikonomides. 1980. 45.00 (*0-89005-377-4*) Ares.

Supplementum Inscriptionum Atticarum V. Ed. by Al N. Oikonomides. 1984. 45.00 (*0-89005-531-9*) Ares.

Supplementum Inscriptionum Atticarum VI: The Latin Inscriptions of Athens & Attica. Ed. by M. C. Miller. (Inscriptiones Atticae Ser.). (Illus.). viii, 189p. (LAT.). (C). 1992. text ed. 45.00 (*0-89005-532-7*) Ares.

Supplementum Inscriptionum Atticarum, VII. M. C. Miller. 1996. 45.00 (*0-89005-533-5*, SIA07) Ares.

Suppliant Maidens, Persians, Prometheus, Seven Against Thebes see Tragedies

Suppliant Women. Euripides. Tr. by Rosanna Warren & Stephen Scully. LC 94-14161. (Greek Tragedy in New Translations Ser.). 112p. 1995. pap. 7.95 (*0-19-504553-X*) OUP.

Suppliant Women see Euripides: Four Tragedies

Suppliants see Ten Greek Plays in Contemporary Translations

Suppliants see Prometheus Bound & Other Plays

Suppliants see Works

Suppliants & Other Dramas: Persians, Seven Against Thebes, Fragments, Prometheus Bound. rev. ed. Aeschylus. Ed. & Tr. by Michael Ewans. (Everyman Paperback Classics Ser.). 312p. (C). 1996. pap. 7.50 (*0-460-87755-0*, Everyman's Classic Lib) C E Tuttle.

Supplicacyon for the Beggers. Simon Fish. Ed. by F. J. Furnivall. (EETS, ES Ser.: No. 13). 1974. reprint ed. 35. 00 (*0-527-00229-1*) Periodicals Srv.

Supplication Made to the Privy Counsel. Walter Travers. LC 76-57419. (English Experience Ser.: No. 833). 1977. reprint ed. lib. bdg. 15.00 (*90-221-0833-3*) Walter J Johnson.

Supplicatory Canon to St. Anastasia the Deliverer from Potions. (Illus.). 32p. (Orig.). 1990. pap. 3.00 (*0-913026-37-9*) St Nectarios.

Supplices, Hercules, Ion, Troiades, Electra, Iphigenia Taurica see Fabulae

Supplied Life: Selected Portions for Daily Reading. Bill Freeman. 410p. (Orig.). 1995. pap. 10.00 (*0-914271-70-9*) Mnstry Wrd.

S

Supplier Certification: A Continuous Improvement Strategy. Richard A. Maass et al. (Supplier Quality Ser.). 141p. (Orig.). 1990. pap. 27.00 (*0-87389-083-3*, H0592) ASQC Qual Pr.

Supplier Certification II: A Handbook for Achieving Excellence Through Continuous Improvement 5th Edition. 5th ed. Peter L. Grieco, Jr. LC 92-5830. 550p. 1995. 49.95 (*0-945456-08-5*) PT Pubns.

Supplier Management Handbook. Ed. by James L. Bossert. LC 93-41960. 364p. 1994. 47.00 (*0-87389-284-4*, H0840) ASQC Qual Pr.

Supplier Mold Compound Preform Manufacturing Process Characterization. Charles E. Bobbitt, Jr. LC 92-23857. (Six Sigma Research Institute Ser.). 1992. pap. write for info. (*0-201-63433-3*) Addison-Wesley.

Supplier Opportunites into the 21st Century: A Look to the Future for Suppliers. Automotive Consulting Group, Inc. Staff. Date not set. 495.00 (*0-614-95832-6*) Wards Comm.

Supplier Price Analysis: A Guide for Purchasing, Accounting, & Financial Analysts. Richard G. Newman. LC 91-33084. 200p. 1992. text ed. 55.00 (*0-89930-545-8*, NSR/, Quorum Bks) Greenwood.

Supplier Profiles Directory of SCADA Products - Systems - Services: The Sourcebook of Products, Systems, & Services for Supervisory Control & Data Acquisition (SCADA) Professionals, 1988-89. Michael A. Marullo. 211p. 1988. pap. 40.00 (*0-9622280-0-1*) cfari pr.

Supplier Profiles Directory of SCADA Products - Systems - Services, 1992-93. Pref. by Michael A. Marullo. 265p. 1993. pap. 50.00 (*0-9622280-2-8*) cfari pr.

Supplier Profiles Directory of SCADA Products, Systems & Services: 1990-91 Edition. Michael A. Marullo. 259p. (Orig.). 1991. pap. 45.00 (*0-685-48472-6*) cfari pr.

Supplier Profiles Directory of SCADA Products, Systems, Services. Ed. by Elizabeth A. Clark. 364p. 1994. pap. 75.00 (*0-9644786-0-9*) AM-FM Intl.

***Supplier Profiles Directory of SCADA Products, Systems, Services 1996/1997 Edition.** 3rd ed. Ed. by John Kayser & Mary B. Murray. 364p. 1996. pap. 75.00 (*0-9644786-1-7*) AM-FM Intl.

Supplier Quality Management: Foundations. Bob Checkaneck et al. Ed. by Mari-Lynn Hankinson. (AT&T Quality Library). (Illus.). 111p. (Orig.). 1994. pap. 19.95 (*0-932764-43-6*) AT&T Customer Info.

Supplier Quality Management: Monitoring & Improvement. Upendra Chivukula et al. Ed. by Mari-Lynn Hankinson. (AT&T Quality Library). (Illus.). 139p. (Orig.). 1994. pap. 19.95 (*0-932764-48-7*) AT&T Customer Info.

Supplier Quality Management: Selection & Qualification. Andrew Griffin & David Klinger. Ed. by Mari-Lynn Hankinson. (AT&T Quality Library). (Illus.). 124p. (Orig.). 1994. pap. 19.95 (*0-932764-45-2*) AT&T Customer Info.

Supplier Selection & Improvement. Thomas J. Gehrke. LC 92-23868. (Six Sigma Research Institute Ser.). 1992. write for info. (*0-201-63434-1*) Addison-Wesley.

Suppliers Directory, 1990. CBA Service Corp. Staff. 1990. 67.95 (*0-317-03835-4*) Chr Bksellers.

***Suppliers to Multinationals: Linkage Programs to Strengthen Local Companies in Developing Countries.** Joseph Battat et al. (FIAS Occasional Paper Ser.: No. 6). 46p. 1996. 7.95 (*0-8213-3746-7*, 13746) World Bank.

Supplies & Materials Management. H. K. Compton. 518p. (C). 1985. 195.00 (*0-685-39932-X*, Pub. by Inst Pur & Supply UK) St Mut.

Supplies & Materials Management. H. K. Compton. 518p. (C). 1989. 175.00 (*0-685-36126-8*, Pub. by Inst Pur & Supply UK) St Mut.

Supply & Costs in the U. S. Petroleum Industry: Two Econometric Studies. Franklin M. Fisher. LC 77-86394. (Resources for the Future, Inc. Publications). 192p. reprint ed. 42.50 (*0-404-60332-7*) AMS Pr.

Supply & Demand for College Graduates in the South, 1985. Marilu H. McCarty & Eva C. Galambos. 1978. pap. text ed. 2.50 (*0-686-23907-5*) S Regional Ed.

Supply & Demand for Finance of Small Enterprises in Ghana. Ernest Aryeetey et al. (Discussion Papers: No. 251). 126p. 1994. 8.95 (*0-8213-2964-2*, 12964) World Bank.

Supply & Demand for Foster Family Care in the Southeast. George Thomas et al. 115p. 1977. 3.50 (*0-318-16358-6*, B26) Regional Inst Social Welfare.

Supply & Installation of Plant & Equipment: Standard Bidding Documents. 216p. 1996. 14.95 (*0-8213-3535-9*, 13535) World Bank.

Supply & Marketing Constraint on Latin American Manufacturing Exports. Intro. by Hugh H. Schwartz. (Illus.). 259p. (Orig.). 1991. pap. text ed. write for info. (*0-940602-35-0*) IADB.

Supply & Price Outlook for Crops. S. L. Bapna & K. R. Rao. 262p. 1987. 18.50 (*81-204-0218-9*, Pub. by Oxford IBH II) S Asia.

Supply Belcher: The Collected Works. Linda Davenport. LC 56-5. 144p. 1996. text ed. 65.00 (*0-8153-2427-8*) Garland.

Supply Catalog: U. S. General Services Administration. (Illus.). 1022p. (Orig.). (C). 1995. pap. text ed. 95.00 (*0-7881-1958-3*) DIANE Pub.

Supply Chain Management. William C. Copacino. 200p. 1997. 45.00 (*1-57444-074-8*) St Lucie Pr.

Supply Chain Optimization: Building the Strongest Total Business Network. Charles C. Poirier & Stephen E. Reiter. LC 96-7814. 312p. 1996. 32.95 (*1-881052-93-1*) Berrett-Koehler.

Supply Clerk. Jack Rudman. (Career Examination Ser.: C-3340). 1994. pap. 23.95 (*0-8373-3340-7*) Nat Learn.

Supply-Demand Model of Health Care Financing with an Application to Zaire. Ricardo A. Bitran. LC 93-20079. (EDI Technical Materials Ser.). 92p. 1994. 23.95 (*0-8213-2342-3*, 12342) World Bank.

***Supply Estimates - Revised & Supplementary Estimates: 1996-97 Spring Supplementary EStimates.** Stationery Office. 1997. pap. 40.00 (*0-10-268597-5*, HM85975, Pub. by Stationery Ofc UK) Bernan Associates.

Supply Management: Material for Management Training in Agricultural Cooperatives MATCOM, Viena. xii, 92p. 1986. 31.50 (*92-2-102365-6*) Intl Labour Office.

Supply Management Toolbox: How to Manage Your Suppliers. Peter L. Grieco, Jr. Ed. by Steven Marks. LC 94-1144. 154p. 1995. pap. 26.95 (*0-945456-11-5*) PT Pubns.

Supply of Concepts. Irving Silverman. LC 88-27103. 197p. 1989. text ed. 55.00 (*0-275-93275-3*, C3275, Praeger Pubs) Greenwood.

Supply of Natural Resources: The Case of Oil & Natural Gas. Robert M. Spann. Ed. by Stuart Bruchey. LC 78-22748. (Energy in the American Economy Ser.). (Illus.). 1979. lib. bdg. 15.95 (*0-405-12013-3*) Ayer.

Supply of Residential Mortgage Valuations: A Report on the Supply in the UK Monopolies & Mergers Commission Report. HMSO Staff. (Command Papers: No. 2542). 238p. 1994. pap. 40.00 (*0-10-125422-9*, HM54229, Pub. by Stationery Ofc UK) Bernan Associates.

Supply Ship Operations. Vic Gibson. (Illus.). 208p. 1993. pap. 42.95 (*0-7506-0780-7*) Buttrwrth-Heinemann.

Supply-Side Economics: A Critical Appraisal. Intro. by Richard H. Fink. LC 82-51294. (Illus.). 488p. 1982. text ed. 65.00 (*0-313-27067-8*, U7067, Greenwood Pr); pap. text ed. 21.95 (*0-313-27068-6*, P7068, Greenwood Pr) Greenwood.

Supply-Side Economics in the Nineteen Eighties: Conference Proceedings. Federal Reserve Bank of Atlanta Staff & Emory University Law & Economics Center Staff. LC 82-15025. (Illus.). 572p. 1982. text ed. 49.95 (*0-89930-045-6*, FSU/, Quorum Bks) Greenwood.

Supply-Side Portfolio Strategies. Ed. by Victor A. Canto & Arthur B. Laffer. LC 87-13091. 200p. 1988. text ed. 49.95 (*0-89930-286-6*, LFP/, Quorum Bks) Greenwood.

Supply-Side Revolution: An Insider's Account of Policymaking in Washington. Paul C. Roberts. (Illus.). 328p. 1984. 37.00 (*0-674-85620-1*) HUP.

Supply-Side Revolution: An Insider's Account of Policymaking in Washington. Paul C. Roberts. 328p. 1986. pap. text ed. 10.95 (*0-674-85621-X*) HUP.

Supply Side Revolution in Britain. Patrick Minford. 272p. 1991. 80.00 (*1-85278-426-1*) E Elgar.

***Supply Side Revolution in Britain.** Patrick Minford. 272p. 1991. pap. 25.00 (*1-85278-428-8*) E Elgar.

Supply Side Solution. Ed. by Bruce Bartlett & Timothy P. Roth. LC 83-7619. (Illus.). 304p. reprint ed. pap. 86.70 (*0-8357-4829-4*, 2037766) Bks Demand.

Supply-Side Tax Policy: Its Relevance to Developing Countries. Ved P. Gandhi et al. LC 87-29890. xi, 388p. 1987. pap. 20.00 (*0-939934-91-4*) Intl Monetary.

Supply-Side Tax Policy: Its Relevance to Developing Countries. Ved P. Gandhi. LC 87-29890. 400p. reprint ed. pap. 114.00 (*0-685-23685-4*, 2032119) Bks Demand.

Supply Story: Professional Substitutes in Education. Ed. by Shiela Galloway & Marlene Morrison. LC 94-2460. 192p. 1994. 75.00 (*0-7507-0282-6*, Falmer Pr); pap. 27.00 (*0-7507-0283-4*, Falmer Pr) Taylor & Francis.

Supplycacyon of Soulys: Agaynst the Supplycacyon of Beggars. Thomas More. LC 72-220. (English Experience Ser.: No. 353). 88p. 1971. reprint ed. 25.00 (*90-221-0353-6*) Walter J Johnson.

***Supplying & Servicing Retailers.** (Survive & Prosper Ser.). 80p. 19.95 (*0-644-32431-7*, Pub. by Aust Gov Pub AT) Aubrey Bks.

Supplying Household Heating Services by High Temperature Circulating Liquids & Vapors. E. F. Davis et al. (Research Bulletin Ser.: No. 3). iv, 23p. 1948. pap. 2.50 (*0-685-18028-X*) Inst Gas Tech.

Supplying Quality Multinutrient Fertilizers in the Latin American & Caribbean Region: Emphasizing Bulk Blending & the Complementary Role of Granulation. Ed. by J. J. Schultz & E. D. Frederick. LC 90-4560. (Special Publications: No. SP-14). (Illus.). 236p. (Orig.). 1990. pap. text ed. 40.00 (*0-88090-089-X*) Intl Fertilizer.

Supplying Repression: U. S. Support for Authoritarian Regimes Abroad. rev. ed. Michael T. Klare et al. 165p. (C). 1981. 9.95 (*0-89758-033-8*); pap. 4.95 (*0-89758-024-9*) Inst Policy Stud.

Supplying the Mining World: The Mining Equipment Manufacturers of San Francisco, 1850-1900. Lynn R. Bailey. (Illus.). 1996. 36.95 (*0-87026-096-0*) Westernlore.

Supplying the Nuclear Arsenal: American Production Reactors, 1942-1992. Rodney P. Carlisle & Joan M. Zenzen. LC 95-44410. (Illus.). 296p. (C). 1996. text ed. 48.00 (*0-8018-5207-2*) Johns Hopkins.

Supplying the Troops: General Somervell & American Logistics in WW II. John K. Ohl. LC 93-39869. (Illus.). 325p. 1994. lib. bdg. 32.00 (*0-87580-185-4*) N Ill U Pr.

***Supplying Vaccines: An Economic Analysis of Critical Issues.** Ed. by Mark V. Pauly et al. LC 95-7993. 225p. (YA). (gr. 12 up). 1996. 99.00 (*90-5199-231-9*, 231-9) IOS Press.

Supplying War. Martin L. Van Creveld. LC 77-5550. 295p. 1979. pap. text ed. 19.95 (*0-521-29793-1*) Cambridge U Pr.

Supplying Water & Saving the Environment for Six Billion People. Ed. by Udai P. Singh & Otto J. Helweg. 200p. 1990. pap. text ed. 25.00 (*0-87262-786-1*) Am Soc Civil Eng.

***Supplyisms: A Navy Supply-Type's Handbook for Comic Relief Afloat & Ashore.** Carla M. Albritton. (Illus.). ix, 132p. (Orig.). 1996. pap. 6.95 (*0-9653458-0-7*) C M Albritton.

Support & Replacement of the Failing Heart. Ed. by O. H. Frazier et al. 400p. 1995. text ed. 149.95 (*0-397-51508-1*) Lppncott-Raven.

***Support & Seduction: A History of Corsets & Bras.** Beatrice Fontanel. LC 97-14551. 1997. text ed. write for info. (*0-8109-4086-8*) Abrams.

Support Collection Supervisor. (Career Examination Ser.: C-3753). pap. 29.95 (*0-8373-3753-4*) Nat Learn.

Support Collector. Jack Rudman. (Career Examination Ser.: C-2800). 1994. pap. 23.95 (*0-8373-2800-4*) Nat Learn.

Support Costs in the Defense Budget: The Submerged One-Third: A Staff Paper. Martin Binkin. LC 72-646. (Studies in Defense Policy). 59p. reprint ed. pap. 25.00 (*0-685-16381-4*, 2027739) Bks Demand.

Support Every Outbreak of Protest & Rebellion see Strategic Outlook & Alliances

Support for Families. Peter Burke & Katy Cigno. 176p. (C). 1996. 55.95 (*1-85628-983-4*, Pub. by Avebury Pub UK) Ashgate Pub Co.

Support for Microenterprises: Lessons for Sub-Saharan Africa. Maryke Dessing. (Technical Paper Ser.: No. 122). 84p. 1990. 7.95 (*0-8213-1553-6*, 11553) World Bank.

Support for Parents & Infants: A Manual for Parent Organization & Professionals. Ed. by C. F. Boukydis. 256p. 1986. 29.95 (*0-7102-0038-2*, 0038W, RKP) Routledge.

Support for the American Welfare State: The View of Congress & the Public. Fay L. Cook & Edith J. Barrett. (Illus.). 320p. 1992. text ed. 54.50 (*0-231-07618-5*); pap. text ed. 18.00 (*0-231-07619-3*) Col U Pr.

Support for the Poor in the Mishnaic Law of Agriculture: Tractate Peah. Roger Brooks. LC 83-8719. (Brown Judaic Studies: No. 43). 220p. (C). 1983. pap. 22.00 (*0-89130-632-3*, 14 00 43) Scholars Pr GA.

Support Group Leaders Guide. Jennie Newbrough & Carol Greenwood. 150p. 1993. pap. 12.95 (*1-56616-005-7*, 572047) Aglow Communs.

Support Group Manual: A Training Manual for Conducting Support Programs for Parents Who Have Interrupted Pregnancies Secondary to Fetal Anomalies. Kathleen J. Delp & Molly A. Minnick. (Illus.). 56p. (Orig.). 1995. pap. 14.95 (*1-878526-41-3*) Pineapple MI.

Support Groups: Current Perspectives on Theory & Practice. Ed. by Maeda J. Galinsky & Janice H. Schopler. LC 95-44465. (Social Work with Groups Ser.: Vol. 18, No. 1). 123p. 1996. text ed. 29.95 (*1-56024-763-0*) Haworth Pr.

Support Groups - The Human Face of the HIV-AIDS Epidemic: A Handbook for Health Care Professionals, People with AIDS, Their Loved Ones, & the Community-at-Large. Gail Barouh. LC 92-81221. x, 94p. 1992. pap. 10.00 (*1-881305-00-7*) LIAAC.

Support Groups for Caregivers of the Aged: A Training Manual for Facilitators. Harriet Rzetelny & Joanna Mellor. LC 84-167188. 72p. (Orig.). 1981. pap. 7.50 (*0-88156-008-1*) Comm Serv Soc NY.

Support Groups for Children. Kathleen O'Rourke & John C. Worzbyt. 425p. 1996. pap. 36.95 (*1-56032-395-7*) Hemisp Pub.

Support Groups for Practicing Special Education Professionals. Lynne Cook & National Clearinghouse for Professions in Special Education Staff. (Professional Action Ser.). 56p. 1992. pap. text ed. 10.00 (*0-86586-228-1*, R640) Coun Exc Child.

Support Investigator. Jack Rudman. (Career Examination Ser.: C-2765). 1994. pap. 27.95 (*0-8373-2765-2*) Nat Learn.

Support Networks for Inclusive Schooling: Interdependent Integrated Education. Susan B. Stainback. LC 89-48390. 288p. 1990. pap. text ed. 25.00 (*1-55766-041-7*, 0417) P H Brookes.

Support of Schools in Colonial New York by the Society for the Propagation of the Gospel in Foreign Parts. William W. Kemp. LC 78-176933. (Columbia University. Teachers College. Contributions to Education Ser.: No. 56). reprint ed. 37.50 (*0-404-55056-8*) AMS Pr.

Support of Schools in Colonial New York by the Society for the Propagation of the Gospel in Foreign Parts. William W. Kemp. LC 72-89192. (American Education: Its Men, Institutions, & Ideas. Series 1). 1970. reprint ed. 15.95 (*0-405-01430-9*) Ayer.

Support of State Educational Programs by Dedication of Specific Revenues & by General Revenue Appropriations: A Study of Certain Factors Which Relate to the Adoption & Use of These General Policies by State Governments. William I. Pearman. LC 75-177147. (Columbia University. Teachers College. Contributions to Education Ser.: No. 591). reprint ed. 37.50 (*0-404-55591-8*) AMS Pr.

Support of the Acutely Failing Liver. A. A. Demetriou. (Medical Intelligence Unit Ser.). 100p. 1994. 89.95 (*1-879702-37-1*) R G Landes.

Support of the Shaken Sangat: Meetings with Three Masters. A. S. Oberoi. Ed. by Russell Perkins. LC 84-50911. (Illus.). 256p. (Orig.). 1984. pap. 15.00 (*0-89142-043-6*) Sant Bani Ash.

Support of Underground Excavations in Hard Rock. Ed. by E. Hoek et al. (Illus.). 300p. (C). 1995. pap. 19.50 (*90-5410-187-3*, Pub. by A A Balkema NE); text ed. 45.00 (*90-5410-186-5*, Pub. by A A Balkema NE) Ashgate Pub Co.

Support Organizations for the Engineering Community. National Research Council Staff. (Engineering Education & Practice in the United States Ser.). 80p. 1986. pap. text ed. 10.50 (*0-309-03629-1*) Natl Acad Pr.

Support Patterns at the United Nations. Jack E. Vincent. 322p. (C). 1992. pap. text ed. 34.50 (*0-8191-8234-6*); lib. bdg. 54.00 (*0-8191-8233-8*) U Pr of Amer.

Support Practice Handbook: Preparation, Negotiation, Trial. Neil Hurowitz. 628p. 1985. suppl. ed. 80.00 (*0-930273-14-1*); suppl. ed. 40.00 (*0-930273-77-X*) MICHIE.

Support Services: Issues for Education, Health & Social Service Professionals. Jonathan Solity & Graham Bickler. (Introduction to Education Ser.). (Illus.). 176p. 1993. 75.00 (*0-304-32706-9*); pap. 25.00 (*0-304-32704-2*) Weidner & Sons.

Support Services & the Curriculum: A Practical Guide to Collaboration. Penny Lacey & Jeanette Lomas. 224p. 1993. pap. 29.00 (*1-85346-222-5*, Pub. by D Fulton UK) Taylor & Francis.

Support Services Renewal in Education Vol. 1: Educational Leadership for the 21st Century. Leroy G. Baruth & M. Lee Manning. Ed. by William J. Bailey. (Educational Leadership for the 21st Century Ser.: Vol. 1). 274p. 1995. 39.95 (*1-56676-203-0*, 762030) Technomic.

Support Staff Desk Manual. 199p. 1988. 23.00 (*0-685-30186-9*, 44,365) NCLS Inc.

***Support Structure for the European Superhighway.** 4,995.00 (*0-614-26457-X*) Info Gatekeepers.

Support Worker Training. Chandler. 1991. pap. text ed. 23.00 (*0-7020-1562-8*) HarBrace.

Support Your Local Pastor: Practical Ways to Encourage Your Minister. Wes Roberts. LC 95-38505. pap. 9.00 (*0-89109-923-9*) NavPress.

Support Your Local Wizard, 3 vols. in 1. Diane Duane. 480p. 1990. 12.98 (*1-56865-010-8*, GuildAmerica) Dblday Direct.

Supported Beams & Slabs. (Craftsman Ser.). 103p. 1989. pap. 14.50 (*0-685-45546-7*, CCS-3BOW6) ACI.

Supported Complex & High Risk Coronary Angioplasty. Ed. by Fayez A. Shawl. (Interventional Cardiology Ser.). (C). 1991. lib. bdg. 132.00 (*0-7923-1121-3*) Kluwer Ac.

Supported Employment. Ed. by Paul Wehman et al. 344p. 1992. 39.50 (*0-9626521-7-2*) PRO-ED.

Supported Employment: Models, Methods & Issues. Frank R. Rusch. (Illus.). 400p. (C). 1990. text ed. 39.95 (*0-685-30431-0*) Sycamore Pub.

Supported Employment: Models, Methods, & Issues. Frank R. Rusch. 450p. 1990. text ed. 67.95 (*0-534-21660-9*) Brooks-Cole.

Supported Employment: Strategies for Integration of Workers with Disabilities. Ed. by Paul Wehman et al. 1995. reprint ed. write for info. (*0-89079-655-6*) PRO-ED.

Supported Employment & TBI. 2nd ed. Ed. by William H. Burke. (Professional Series on Traumatic Brain Injury: Vol. 18). 64p. (Orig.). 1995. pap. 9.50 (*1-882855-38-8*) HDI Pubs.

Supported Employment for Persons with Developmental Disabilities. Mit Arnold. 126p. 1992. pap. 21.95 (*0-398-06009-6*); text ed. 31.95 (*0-398-05780-X*) C C Thomas.

Supported Employment for Persons with Disabilities: Focus on Excellence. Ed. by P. Wehman & J. Kregel. (Illus.). 268p. 1989. 38.95 (*0-89885-446-6*) Human Sci Pr.

Supported Metal Complexes: A New Generation of Catalysts. F. R. Hartley. LC 85-19362. 1985. lib. bdg. 168.50 (*90-277-1855-5*) Kluwer Ac.

***Supported Reagents: Preparation, Analysis & Applications.** J. H. Clark et al. 1992. text ed. 55.00 (*0-471-18779-8*) Wiley.

***Supporting American Industry: Rhetoric & Reality.** Richard D. Bingham. LC 97-20514. 304p. (C). (gr. 13). 1997. 55.95 (*1-56324-596-5*) M E Sharpe.

Supporting an Adoption. Pat Holmes. 23p. 1986. reprint ed. pap. 3.50 (*0-9611872-1-2*) Our Child Pr.

Supporting & Strengthening Families: Methods, Strategies & Practices. Ed. by Carl J. Dunst et al. LC 93-50893. 1994. pap. 30.00 (*0-914797-94-8*) Brookline Bks.

Supporting & Unique Military Electromagnetic Compatibility Standards of the United States. John D. Osburn. LC 88-80526. (Electromagnetic Interference & Compatibility Ser.: Vol. 12). (Illus.). 276p. 1988. 65.00 (*0-944916-12-0*) emf-emi Control.

Supporting Art & Culture. DeGrazia. 12.95 (*0-317-07058-4*) Lieber-Atherton.

Supporting Art & Culture: One-Thousand One Questions on Policy. Alfred De Grazia. 1992. 12.00 (*0-940268-30-2*) Metron Pubns.

Supporting Cast: A Study of Flat & Minor Characters. David Galef. LC 92-14766. 240p. (C). 1993. 35.00 (*0-271-00885-7*) Pa St U Pr.

***Supporting Change & Develop, in the Primary School.** Sullivan. 1991. text ed. write for info. (*0-582-08945-X*, Pub. by Longman UK) Longman.

***Supporting Chidren & Parents Through Family Changes.** Ed. by Anne B. Smith & Nicola J. Taylor. 134p. 1996. pap. 39.95 (*1-877133-07-8*, Pub. by U Otago Pr NZ) Intl Spec Bk.

Supporting Children with Communication Difficulties in Inclusive Settings. Richard L. Schiefelbusch et al. Orig. Title: Early Language Intervention: Supporting Children with Communication Difficulties in Inclusive Settings. (Illus.). 512p. (C). 1996. pap. 49.33 (*0-02-379272-8*, Macmillan Coll) P-H.

Supporting Children with Disabilities in Community Programs: The Teaching Research Integrated Preschool. Joyce Peters & Teaching Research Early Childhood Training Department Staff. (Illus.). 165p. (Orig.). (C). 1993. pap. text ed. 20.00 (*0-685-64739-0*) Teaching Res.

Supporting Civil Society: The Political Role of Non-Governmental Organizations in Central America. Laura MacDonald. LC 94-43333. (International Political Economy Ser.). 1997. text ed. 59.95 (*0-312-12535-6*) St Martin.

Supporting Classroom Instruction Through the School Media Center: A Collection of Case Studies. Ed. by George K. Sheppard. 53p. (Orig.). 1984. pap. 5.95 (*0-914677-02-0*) Contemp Issues.

***Supporting Community Care: The Contribution of Housing Benefit.** Steve Griffiths. 1995. 48.00 (*1-899942-01-7*, Pub. by Natl Inst Soc Work) St Mut.

Supporting Community Employment Schemes: Roles & Skills of Workers. Paul Henderson. (C). 1987. 30.00 (*0-685-40337-8*, Pub. by Natl Inst Soc Work) St Mut.

Supporting Details: Reading Level 10-J. (Single Skills Series). Date not set. pap. 5.65 (*0-89061-383-4*) Jamestown Pubs.

Supporting Details: Reading Level 11-K. (Single Skills Series). Date not set. pap. 5.65 (*0-89061-389-3*) Jamestown Pubs.

Supporting Details: Reading Level 12-L. (Single Skills Series). Date not set. pap. 5.65 (*0-89061-395-8*) Jamestown Pubs.

Supporting Details: Reading Level 4-D. (Single Skills Series). Date not set. pap. 5.65 (*0-89061-372-9*) Jamestown Pubs.

Supporting Details: Reading Level 5-E. (Single Skills Series). Date not set. pap. 5.65 (*0-89061-328-1*) Jamestown Pubs.

Supporting Details: Reading Level 6-F. (Single Skills Series). Date not set. pap. 5.65 (*0-89061-334-6*) Jamestown Pubs.

Supporting Details: Reading Level 7-G. (Single Skills Series). Date not set. pap. 5.65 (*0-89061-340-0*) Jamestown Pubs.

Supporting Details: Reading Level 8-H. (Single Skills Series). Date not set. pap. 5.65 (*0-89070-346-9*) Jamestown Pubs.

Supporting Details: Reading Level 9-I. (Single Skills Series). Date not set. pap. 5.65 (*0-89070-377-9*) Jamestown Pubs.

Supporting Emotional Needs of Family Members: A Module for Training Early Intervention Special Education Personnel. Infant Hearing Resource Staff. (Early Intervention Series II). 34p. (Orig.). (C). 1994. pap. text ed. 89.00 incl. vhs (*1-883204-02-X*) Infant Hearing Resc.

Supporting Emotional Needs of Family Members: A Module for Training Personnel Serving Families of Deaf & Hard of Hearing Infants & Young Children. Ed. by Valerie Schuyler. (Early Intervention Ser.). 39p. (C). 1993. 89.00 incl. vhs (*0-9618297-4-5*) Infant Hearing Resc.

Supporting Families. (State Legislative Reports: Vol. 19, No. 13). 7p. 1994. 5.00 (*1-55516-378-5*, 7302-1913) Natl Conf State Legis.

Supporting Families. 184p. 1995. pap. 45.00 (*0-11-495716-9*, HM57169, Pub. by Stationery Ofc UK) Bernan Associates.

Supporting Grassroots Organizations. Ed. by Thomas F. Carroll & John D. Montgomery. (Lincoln Institute of Land Policy Monograph Ser.: No. 87-1). 145p. reprint ed. pap. 41.40 (*0-7837-5770-0*, 2045435) Bks Demand.

***Supporting Language & Literacy: A Handbook for Those Who Assist in Early Years Settings.** Suzi Clipson-Boyles. 80p. 1996. pap. 22.95 (*1-85346-438-4*, Pub. by D Fulton UK) Taylor & Francis.

Supporting Language Learning in Everyday Life. Judith F. Duchan. LC 94-29227. (School-Age Children Ser.). 224p. (Orig.). (C). 1994. pap. text ed. 39.95 (*1-56593-221-8*, 0581) Singular Publishing.

Supporting Low Income Neighborhood Organizations: A Guide for Community Foundations. Steven E. Mayer & David Scheie. Ed. by Mary Lilya. (Illus.). 1989. write for info. (*0-9624428-2-8*) Rainbow Research.

***Supporting Numeracy: A Handbook for Those Who Assist in Early Years Settings.** Rita Headington. 80p. 1997. pap. 24.95 (*1-85346-454-6*, Pub. by D Fulton UK) Taylor & Francis.

Supporting Peace: America's Role in an Israel-Syria Peace Agreement: Report of a Washington Institute Study Group. A. J. Bacevich et al. LC 94-24119. 1994. pap. 16.95 (*0-944029-59-0*) Wash Inst NEP.

***Supporting Players of Television 1959-1983.** Jack Ward. LC 96-94626. (Illus.). xii, 388p. 1996. 34.95 (*0-9653481-0-5*) Lakeshre West.

***Supporting Players of Television 1959-1983.** Jack Ward. LC 96-94626. (Illus.). xii, 387p. 1996. pap. 24.95 (*0-9653481-1-3*) Lakeshre West.

Supporting Saints: Life Stories of Nineteenth-Century Mormons. Ed. by Cannon & Whittaker. (Specialized Monograph Ser.: Vol. 1). 12.95 (*0-88494-565-0*) Bookcraft Inc.

Supporting Special Educational Needs in Secondary School Classrooms. Jane Lovey. (Roehampton Teaching Studies). 160p. 1995. pap. 24.95 (*1-85346-339-6*, Pub. by D Fulton UK) Taylor & Francis.

Supporting Struggling Readers. Barbara J. Walker. (Pippin Teacher's Library). 96p. 1992. pap. text ed. 14.50 (*0-88751-048-5*, 00717) Heinemann.

Supporting the Changing Family: A Guide to the Parent-to-Parent Model. B. Reschly. 31p. 1979. pap. 10.95 (*0-929816-61-7*) High-Scope.

Supporting the Eighteen Percent: The Experience of the Six LEA's. Harriet Gross & Caroline Gipps. 200p. 1987. 47.00 (*1-85000-141-3*, Falmer Pr) Taylor & Francis.

Supporting the Move to Whole Language: A Handbook for School Leaders. Kathy Barclay & Elizabeth Boone. LC 92-40245. 1995. 24.95 (*0-590-49222-5*, 1576b296 1993) Scholastic Inc.

Supporting the Pediatric Transfusion Recipient. Ed. by Linda A. Chambers & Linda A. Issitt. LC 94-32346. (Illus.). 161p. (C). 1994. 50.00 (*1-56395-032-4*) Am Assn Blood.

Supporting the Sky. Patricia B Griffith. 289p. 1996. 23.95 (*0-399-14128-6*, Putnam) Putnam Pub Group.

Supporting the Spirit of Learning: What Teaching Would Be Like If Process Were Content. Arthur L. Costa & Rosemarie M. Liebmann. LC 96-10144. 320p. 1996. 69.95 (*0-8039-6311-4*); pap. 29.95 (*0-8039-6312-2*) Corwin Pr.

Supporting Whole Language: Stories of Teacher & Institutional Change. Ed. by Constance Weaver & Linda Henke. LC 91-28226. 245p. 1992. pap. text ed. 23.50 (*0-435-08704-5*, 08704) Heinemann.

Supporting Young Adolescents: A Guide to Leading Parent Meetings. rev. ed. Linda Barr. Ed. by Hank Resnik. (Skills for Adolescence Ser.). (Illus.). 128p. 1988. 15.00 (*0-933419-27-9*) Quest Intl.

Supporting Young Adults Who Are Deaf-Blind in Their Communities: A Transition Planning Guide for Service Providers, Families, & Friends. Jane M. Everson. 384p. 1995. pap. 39.95 (*1-55766-161-8*) P H Brookes.

Supporting Young Learners 1: Ideas for Preschool & Day Care Providers. Ed. by Nancy A. Brickman & Lynn S. Taylor. LC 91-21317. 324p. 1991. pap. 25.95 (*0-929816-34-X*) High-Scope.

Supporting Young Learners 2: Ideas for Child Care Providers & Teachers. Nancy A. Brickman. LC 96-18555. 328p. 1996. 25.95 (*1-57379-006-0*) High-Scope.

Supporting Yourself As an Artist: A Practical Guide. 2nd ed. Deborah A. Hoover. (Illus.). 272p. 1989. pap. 12.95 (*0-19-505972-7*) OUP.

Supportive & Active Psychotherapies: A Dynamic Approach. Paul A. Dewald. LC 93-74969. 354p. 1995. pap. 35.00 (*1-56821-221-6*) Aronson.

Supportive Care in Cancer Patients. Ed. by H. J. Senn & L. Schmid. (Recent Results in Cancer Research Ser.: Vol. 108). (Illus.). 350p. 1988. 137.00 (*0-387-17150-9*) Spr-Verlag.

Supportive Care in Cancer Therapy. Ed. by Donald J. Higby. (Cancer Treatment & Research Ser.). 1983. lib. bdg. 176.50 (*0-89838-569-5*) Kluwer Ac.

***Supportive Care of Children with Cancer.** 2nd ed. Arthur R. Ablin. 1998. pap. text ed. 29.95 (*0-8018-5727-9*) Johns Hopkins.

Supportive Care of Children with Cancer: Current Therapy & Guidelines from the Children's Cancer Group. Ed. by Arthur R. Ablin. LC 92-48869. (Johns Hopkins Series in Hematology - Oncology). 120p. 1993. text ed. 65.00 (*0-8018-4629-3*); pap. text ed. 28.95 (*0-8018-4630-7*) Johns Hopkins.

***Supportive Care of the Cancer Patient.** Ed. by Chris Williams & John W. Swetenham. (Illus.). 288p. 1997. 55.00 (*0-340-56171-8*, Pub. by Ed Arnold UK) OUP.

Supportive Fellow Speakers & Cooperative Conversations: Discourse Topics & Topical Actions, Participant Roles & 'Recipient Action' in a Particular Type of Everyday Conversation. Wolfram Bublitz. LC 88-10119. xii, 308p. (C). 1988. 83.00 (*1-55619-047-6*) Benjamins North Am.

Supportive Interviewing in Human Service Organizations: Fundamental Skills for Gathering Information & Encouraging Productive Change. Kenneth France & Michelle Kish. LC 94-34468. (Illus.). 320p. (C). 1994. pap. 43.95 (*0-398-05955-1*); text ed. 65.95 (*0-398-05937-3*) C C Thomas.

Supportive Ministries. Michael Landsman. 32p. (Orig.). 1992. pap. 3.95 (*0-88270-702-7*) Bridge-Logos.

Supportive Network. Claire G. Wenger. 1984. 38.75 (*0-317-40641-8*, Pub. by Natl Inst Soc Work) St Mut.

***Supportive School Supervision: A Guide for Teachers & Administrators.** Stanley W. Rothstein & Raymond C. Garubo. LC 97-21993. (Greenwood Educators' Reference Collection Ser.). 1998. text ed. write for info. (*0-313-29652-9*, Greenwood Pr) Greenwood.

Supportive Therapy: A Psychodynamic Approach. Lawrence H. Rockland. LC 89-42801. 320p. (C). 1989. 37.00 (*0-465-08337-4*) Basic.

Supportive Therapy for Borderline Patients: A Psychodynamic Approach. Lawrence H. Rockland et al. LC 92-1538. (Diagnosis & Treatment of Mental Disorders Ser.). 308p. 1992. lib. bdg. 36.95 (*0-89862-182-8*) Guilford Pr.

Supportive Therapy in Haematology. Ed. by P. C. Das et al. LC 85-4977. 1985. lib. bdg. 176.00 (*0-89838-700-0*) Kluwer Ac.

Suppose a Man. John Levy. 1977. 4.00 (*0-685-88979-3*) Elizabeth Pr.

Suppose the Wolf Were an Octopus: Grades K-2. Bagley & Foley. (J). 1992. pap. 9.99 (*0-89824-087-5*) Trillium Pr.

Suppose the Wolf Were an Octopus: Grades 3-4. Bagley. (J). 1992. pap. 9.99 (*0-89824-096-4*) Trillium Pr.

Suppose the Wolf Were an Octopus: Grades 5-6. Bagley. (J). 1992. pap. 9.99 (*0-89824-097-2*) Trillium Pr.

Suppose You Were a Kitten. Phyllis J. Neuberger. LC 82-91105. (Illus.). (J). (gr. 1-3). 1982. pap. 2.95 (*0-9610050-0-9*) P J Neuberger.

Supposed to Fly: A Sequence from Pilsen, Czechoslovakia. Miroslav Holub. Tr. by Ewald Osers from CZE. (Illus.). 160p. 9600. pap. 16.95 (*1-85224-274-4*, Pub. by Bloodaxe Bks UK) Dufour.

***Supposedly Fun.** Wallace. 1998. pap. 13.95 (*0-316-92528-4*) Little.

***Supposedly Fun Thing I'll Never Do Again: Essays & Ruminations.** David F. Wallace. 353p. 1997. 23.95 (*0-316-91989-6*) Little.

Supposes. Dick Gackenbach. (Illus.). 32p. (J). (ps-3). 1989. 13.00 (*0-15-200594-3*, Gulliver Bks) HarBrace.

Supposing the Subject. 288p. (C). (gr. 13). 1994. pap. text ed. 19.00 (*1-85984-075-2*, B4682, Pub. by Vrso UK) Norton.

Supposing the Subject. Ed. by Joan Copjec. 288p. (C). (gr. 13). 1994. text ed. 60.00 (*1-85984-980-6*, B4678, Pub. by Vrso UK) Norton.

***Supposition Error: A Novel.** A. D. Manning. (Illus.). 313p. (Orig.). 1996. pap. 12.95 (*0-9644636-3-6*) Parlay Enter.

Suppressed & Incredible Inventions. John Freeman. 1987. reprint ed. spiral bd. 14.00 (*0-7873-1091-3*) Hlth Research.

Suppressed Book About Slavery. Ed. by George W. Carleton. LC 68-28987. (American Negro: His History & Literature. Series 1). (Illus.). 1978. reprint ed. 21.95 (*0-405-01806-1*) Ayer.

Suppressed Commentaries on the Wiseian Forgeries: Addendum to an Enquiry. William B. Todd. LC 77-89555. (Bibliographical Monograph: No. 1). (Illus.). 49p. 1974. reprint ed. 15.00 (*0-87959-052-1*) U of Tex H Ransom Ctr.

Suppressed Inventions. 1991. lib. bdg. 79.95 (*0-8490-4608-4*) Gordon Pr.

Suppressed Inventions & How They Work. 1986. lib. bdg. 79.95 (*0-8490-3605-4*) Gordon Pr.

***Suppressed Inventions & Other Discoveries: Revealing the World's Greatest Secrets of Science.** Jonathan Eisen. 1997. pap. text ed. 14.95 (*0-89529-809-0*) Avery Group Inc.

Suppressed Madness of Sane Men: Forty-Four Years of Exploring Psycho-Analysis. Marion Milner. (Illus.). 250p. (C). 1987. pap. 19.95 (*0-422-61690-7*, Pub. by Tavistock UK); lib. bdg. 49.50 (*0-422-61020-8*, Pub. by Tavistock UK) Routledge Chapman & Hall.

***Suppressed Madness of Sane Men: Forty-Four Years of Exploring Psychoanalysis.** Marion Milner. (The New Library of Psychoanalysis Ser.: Vol. 3). 318p. (C). 1987. pap. text ed. 22.95 (*0-415-03673-9*) Routledge.

***Suppressed Murder of Wyatt Earp.** rev. ed. Glenn G. Boyer. (Illus.). 168p. 1997. lib. bdg. 39.95 (*1-890670-07-3*) Hist Research.

Suppressed Sister: A Relationship in Novels by Nineteenth- & Twentieth-Century British Women. Amy K. Levin. LC 91-55127. 160p. 1992. 29.50 (*0-8387-5211-X*) Bucknell U Pr.

Suppressed Truth About the Assassination of Abraham Lincoln. Burke McCarty. 255p. 1960. reprint ed. 20.00 (*0-686-29301-0*, Chedney) A-albionic Res.

Suppressed Truth about the Assassination of Abraham Lincoln. Burke McCarty. 272p. 1993. reprint ed. spiral bd. 10.50 (*0-7873-0595-2*) Hlth Research.

Suppressed Truth About the Assassination of Lincoln. Burke McCarty. 1972. 250.00 (*0-87968-169-1*) Gordon Pr.

Suppression of a People: Torture & Imprisonment in Tibet. Physicians for Human Rights Staff. (Illus.). 62p. 1989. pap. 6.00 (*0-614-14416-7*) Phy Human Rights.

Suppression of John F. Deitz: An Episode of the Progressive Era in Wisconsin. Paul H. Hass. (Wisconsin Stories Ser.). 55p. 1979. pap. 1.75 (*0-87020-184-0*) State Hist Soc Wis.

Suppression of the African Slave-Trade. W. E. B. Du Bois. 27.95 (*0-8488-1289-1*) Amereon Ltd.

Suppression of the African Slave-Trade to the U. S. 1638-1870. W. E. B. Du Bois. (History - United States Ser.). 335p. 1992. reprint ed. lib. bdg. 89.00 (*0-7812-6153-8*) Rprt Serv.

Suppression of the African Slave-Trade to the United States of America. W. E. B. Du Bois. 344p. 1987. reprint ed. lib. bdg. 26.95 (*0-89966-588-8*) Buccaneer Bks.

Suppression of the African Slave Trade to the United States of America, 1638-1870. W. E. B. Du Bois. 325p. 1970. reprint ed. 26.95 (*0-87928-011-5*) Corner Hse.

Suppression of the African Slave Trade, 1638-1870. W. E. B. Du Bois. LC 65-18803. xx, 336p. 1970. pap. text ed. 17.95 (*0-8071-0149-4*) La State U Pr.

Suppression of the Automobile: Skullduggery at the Crossroads. David Beasley. LC 87-31788. (Contributions in Economics & Economic History Ser.: No. 81). 192p. 1988. text ed. 49.95 (*0-313-26144-X*, BSY/, Greenwood Pr) Greenwood.

Suppression of the Monasteries in the West Country. J. H. Bettey. (Illus.). 224p. 1990. 28.00 (*0-86299-594-9*, Pub. by Sutton Pubng UK) Bks Intl VA.

Suppressor B Lymphocytes. R. V. Petrov et al. Tr. by V. E. Tatarchenko from RUS. (Soviet Medical Reviews, Immunology Series Supplement: Vol. 1). 208p. 1988. text ed. 287.00 (*3-7186-4800-8*) Gordon & Breach.

Suppressor Cells & Their Factors. Ed. by Randall S. Krakauer & John D. Clough. 184p. 1981. 109.00 (*0-8493-6185-0*, QR185, CRC Reprint) Franklin.

Suppressor Cells in Human Disease. Ed. by James S. Goodwin. LC 81-5565. (Immunology Ser.: No. 14). 375p. reprint ed. pap. 106.90 (*0-7837-3348-8*, 2043306) Bks Demand.

Suppressors, 6 Vols. 1986. lib. bdg. 1,200.00 (*0-8490-3590-2*) Gordon Pr.

Suprachiasmatic Nucleus: The Mind's Clock. R. Moore & S. Reppert. Ed. by Donald F. Klein et al. (Illus.). 488p. 1991. 88.00 (*0-19-506250-7*) OUP.

Suprafamilial Authority & Economic Process in Micronesian Atolls see Commerce des Hommes

Supramental Manifestation on Earth. Sri Aurobindo. 108p. 1988. pap. 3.50 (*81-7058-311-X*, Pub. by SAA II) Aurobindo Assn.

Supramolar Structure & Function: Dubrovnik, Yugoslavia, Sept. 16-28, 1988. Ed. by Greta Pifat-Mrzljak. 288p. 1988. text ed. 77.00 (*9971-5-0656-4*) World Scientific Pub.

Supramolecular Architecture: Synthetic Control in Thin Films & Solids. Ed. by Thomas Bein. LC 92-14921. (ACS Symposium Ser.: Vol. 499). (Illus.). 469p. 1992. 97.95 (*0-8412-2460-9*) Am Chemical.

Supramolecular Chemistry: An Introduction. Fritz Vogtle. LC 90-48199. 337p. 1991. text ed. 265.00 (*0-471-92802-X*) Wiley.

Supramolecular Chemistry: An Introduction. Fritz Vogtle. 337p. 1993. pap. text ed. 59.95 (*0-471-94061-5*) Wiley.

Supramolecular Chemistry: Proceedings of the Second NATO Science Forum, Taormina (Sicily), Italy, December 15-18, 1991. Vincenzo Balzani & Lee De Cola. LC 92-5813. (NATO Advanced Study Institutes Series C, Mathematical & Physical Sciences: No. 371). 476p. (C). 1992. lib. bdg. 204.50 (*0-7923-1759-9*) Kluwer Ac.

Supramolecular Chemistry I: Directed Synthesis & Molecular Recognition. Ed. by Eicke R. Weber. (Topics in Current Chemistry Ser.: Vol. 165). (Illus.). 336p. 1993. 174.95 (*0-387-56280-X*) Spr-Verlag.

Supramolecular Chemistry II. Ed. by International Editorial Board Staff. (Topics in Current Chemistry Ser.: Vol. 175). 158p. 1995. 141.95 (*3-540-58800-0*) Spr-Verlag.

Supramolecular Chemistry II. E. Weber. (Topics in Current Chemistry Ser.: Vol. 175). 158p. 1995. 129.00 (*0-354-05880-0*) Spr-Verlag.

Supramolecular Chemistry of Anions. Ed. by Antonio Bianchi et al. 250p. 1996. 69.95 (*1-56081-906-5*, VCH) Wiley.

***Supramolecular Chemistry of Anions.** Antonio Bianchi et al. LC 97-7640. 1997. text ed. 69.95 (*0-471-18622-8*) Wiley.

Supramolecular Control of Structure & Reactivity. Ed. by Andrew D. Hamilton. LC 96-944. (Perspectives in Supramolecular Chemistry Ser.: Vol. 3). 1996. write for info. (*0-471-95920-0*) Wiley.

Supramolecular Photochemistry. Ed. by Vincenzo Balzani. (C). 1987. lib. bdg. 204.50 (*90-277-2593-4*) Kluwer Ac.

Supramolecular Stereochemistry, Vol. 473. Ed. by Jay S. Siegel. LC 95-31284. (NATO ASI Ser.). 1995. lib. bdg. 143.00 (*0-7923-3702-6*) Kluwer Ac.

Supranational & Constitutional Courts in Europe: Functions & Sources. Ed. by Igor I. Kavass. LC 92-6043. 404p. 1992. text ed. 85.00 (*0-89941-789-2*, 307460) W S Hein.

Supremacy of Christ. Ajith Fernando. LC 95-15316. 288p. (Orig.). 1995. pap. 14.99 (*0-89107-855-X*) Crossway Bks.

Supremacy of God. Ilon. LC 80-66408. 1980. pap. 4.50 (*0-9600958-6-1*) Birth Day.

Supremacy of God in Preaching. John Piper. LC 90-34898. 128p. (Orig.). 1990. pap. text ed. 7.99 (*0-8010-7112-7*) Baker Bks.

Supreme. Phillip Mahoney. 80p. 1989. pap. 7.95 (*1-55643-053-1*) North Atlantic.

Supreme Ambition see Climbing the Blue Mountain: A Guide for the Spiritual Journey

Supreme Command. Cohen. Date not set. 24.00 (*0-02-906070-2*, Free Press) Free Pr.

Supreme Court. Barbara Aria. LC 94-9797. (First Bks.). 64p. (J). (gr. 4-6). 1994. lib. bdg. 21.00 (*0-531-20180-5*) Watts.

Supreme Court. Rae Bains. LC 84-2736. (Illus.). 32p. (J). (gr. 3-6). 1985. pap. text ed. 3.50 (*0-8167-0273-X*) Troll Communs.

Supreme Court. Richard Bernstein & Jerome Agel. LC 88-21027. (Into the Third Century Ser.). (YA). (gr. 7 up). 1989. 12.95 (*0-8027-6834-2*); lib. bdg. 13.85 (*0-8027-6835-0*) Walker & Co.

***Supreme Court.** Catherine Reef. (Places in American History Ser.). (Illus.). 72p. (J). (gr. 4). 1997. pap. 7.95 (*0-382-24722-1*, Dillon Silver Burdett) Silver Burdett Pr.

Supreme Court. William H. Rehnquist. LC 88-29737. 1989. pap. 13.00 (*0-688-08668-3*, Quill) Morrow.

Supreme Court. Dana R. Ulloth. Ed. by Christopher H. Sterling. LC 78-21744. (Dissertations in Broadcasting Ser.). 1980. lib. bdg. 21.95 (*0-405-11780-9*) Ayer.

Supreme Court. 3rd ed. Arnold Petersen. 1971. pap. text ed. 0.75 (*0-935534-30-X*) NY Labor News.

Supreme Court. 4th ed. Lawrence Baum. 280p. 1991. 30.95 (*0-87187-619-1*) Congr Quarterly.

Supreme Court: A Citizen's Guide. Robert J. Wagman. (Illus.). 288p. 1993. 22.95 (*0-88687-692-3*, Pharos) Wrld Almnc.

Supreme Court: A Paper Doll Book. Andy Mayer & Jim Becker. (Illus.). 40p. (Orig.). 1993. pap. 9.99 (*0-312-09397-7*) St Martin.

Supreme Court: Judicial Process & Judicial Politics. Arthur A. North. LC 66-17855. (Orig.). 1966. pap. text ed. 8.95 (*0-89197-435-0*) Irvington.

Supreme Court: Myth & Reality. Arthur S. Miller. LC 77-91106. (Contributions in American Studies: No. 38). xvii, 288p. 1978. text ed. 55.00 (*0-313-20046-7*, MSC/, Greenwood Pr) Greenwood.

Supreme Court: Palladium of Freedom. Alpheus T. Mason. LC 62-18443. 217p. reprint ed. pap. 61.90 (*0-317-29150-5*, 2055629) Bks Demand.

Supreme Court: Trends & Developments, Set, Vols. 1-5. Jesse H. Choper et al. Set. 150.00 (*1-55917-683-0*, 811B) Natl Prac Inst.

Supreme Court: Trends & Developments, Vol. 4: 1981-82. Jesse H. Choper et al. 40.00 (*1-55917-681-4*, 800B) Natl Prac Inst.

Supreme Court: Trends & Developments, Vol. 5: 1982-83. Jesse H. Choper et al. 40.00 (*1-55917-682-2*, 810B) Natl Prac Inst.

Supreme Court: Views from the Inside. Alan F. Westin. LC 83-6722. 192p. 1983. reprint ed. text ed. 49.75 (*0-313-24062-0*, WSUP, Greenwood Pr) Greenwood.

Supreme Court A to Z: A Ready Reference Encyclopedia. Ed. by Elder Witt. 528p. 1994. 129.00 (*1-56802-053-8*) Congr Quarterly.

Supreme Court Act Fifty-Nine of 1959 & the Magistrates' Courts Act 32 of 1944. 7th ed. H. J. Erasmus & Owen J. Barrow. 520p. 1992. pap. 37.00 (*0-7021-2929-1*, Pub. by Juta SA) Gaunt.

Supreme Court Act Fifty-Nine of 1959 & the Magistrates' Courts Act 32 of 1944. 8th ed. H. J. Erasmus & Owen J. Barrow. 534p. 1994. pap. 40.00 (*0-7021-3110-5*, Pub. by Juta SA) Gaunt.

Supreme Court Act 59 of 1959 & The Magistrates' Courts Act 32 of 1944. 9th ed. H. J. Erasmus & Owen J. Barrow. 271p. 1995. pap. 39.00 (*0-7021-3344-2*, Pub. by Juta SA) Gaunt.

***Supreme Court Act 59 of 1959 & the Magistrates' Courts Act 32 of 1944.** 10th ed. J. H. Erasmus & O. J. Barrow. 259p. 1996. pap. 52.00 (*0-7021-3576-3*, Pub. by Juta SA) Gaunt.

***Supreme Court & American Constitutionalism.** Ed. by Bradford P. Wilson & Ken Masugi. (Ashbrook Series on Constitutional Politics). 275p. 1997. 68.00 (*0-8476-8658-2*) Rowman.

***Supreme Court & American Constitutionalism.** Ed. by Bradford P. Wilson & Ken Masugi. (Ashbrook Series on Constitutional Politics). 275p. (Orig.). 1997. pap. 23.95 (*0-8476-8659-0*) Rowman.

Supreme Court & Confessions of Guilt. Otis H. Stephens. LC 73-8777. 250p. reprint ed. pap. 71.30 (*0-7837-3024-1*, 2042916) Bks Demand.

Supreme Court & Constitutional Democracy. John Agresto. LC 83-45928. 192p. 1984. pap. 13.95 (*0-8014-9277-7*) Cornell U Pr.

Supreme Court & Constitutional Theory, 1953-1993. Ronald Kahn. LC 93-39805. 326p. 1994. pap. 17.95 (*0-7006-0711-0*) U Pr of KS.

Supreme Court & Constitutional Theory, 1953-1993. Ronald Kahn. LC 93-39805. 326p. 1995. 35.00 (*0-7006-0666-1*) U Pr of KS.

Supreme Court & Full Bench Election Cases (1950-1989), 2 vols., Set. P.L.A. Staff. (C). 1989. 455.00 (*0-685-46479-2*) St Mut.

Supreme Court & Full Bench on Transfer of Property: Dealing with Digest of Cases 1950-1988, 1989. M. S. Ansari. (C). 1988. 165.00 (*0-685-36471-2*) St Mut.

Supreme Court & Individual Rights. 2nd ed. Congressional Quarterly, Inc. Staff & Elder Witt. 351p. (Orig.). 1988. pap. 32.95 (*0-87187-465-2*) Congr Quarterly.

Supreme Court & Individual Rights. 3rd ed. Joan Biskupic & Elder Witt. LC 96-8220. 370p. 1996. pap. 34.95 (*1-56802-239-5*) Congr Quarterly.

Supreme Court & Judicial Choice: The Role of Provisional Review in a Democracy. Paul R. Dimond. LC 88-26709. 250p. 1989. text ed. 37.50 (*0-472-10103-X*) U of Mich Pr.

Supreme Court & Judicial Function. Ed. by Philip B. Kurland. 292p. 1976. pap. text ed. 7.50 (*0-226-46401-6*) U Ch Pr.

Supreme Court & Judicial Review. Robert K. Carr. LC 74-98215. xiv, 304p. 1970. reprint ed. text ed. 59.75 (*0-8371-3261-4*, CAJR, Greenwood Pr) Greenwood.

Supreme Court & Judicial Review in American History. Kermit L. Hall. LC 85-47508. (Bicentennial Essays on the Constitution Ser.). 60p. 1985. pap. 7.00 (*0-87229-030-1*) Am Hist Assn.

***Supreme Court & Juvenile Justice.** Christopher P. Manfredi. LC 97-18993. 288p. 1997. 35.00 (*0-7006-0851-6*) U Pr of KS.

Supreme Court & Legal Change: Abortion & the Death Penalty. Lee Epstein & Joseph F. Kobyalka. LC 92-53618. (Thornton H. Brooks Series in American Law & Society). xviii, 418p. (C). 1992. 49.95 (*0-8078-2051-2*); pap. 19.95 (*0-8078-4384-9*) U of NC Pr.

Supreme Court & Libel. Clifton O. Lawhorne & Howard R. Long. LC 80-21161. (New Horizons in Journalism Ser.). 176p. 1981. 19.95 (*0-8093-0998-X*) S Ill U Pr.

Supreme Court & Magistrates' Courts Legislation Handbook. Taitz & Kelbrick. 512p. 1990. pap. 52.00 (*0-409-05827-0*, SA) MICHIE.

Supreme Court & Patents & Monopolies. Ed. by Philip B. Kurland. 208p. 1975. pap. text ed. 7.50 (*0-226-46404-0*) U Ch Pr.

Supreme Court & Political Questions. Charles G. Post. LC 78-64164. (Johns Hopkins University. Studies in the Social Sciences. Thirtieth Ser. 1912: 4). reprint ed. 29.50 (*0-404-61274-1*) AMS Pr.

Supreme Court & Public Prayer: The Need for Restraint. Charles E. Rice. LC 64-18392. 216p. reprint ed. pap. 61.60 (*0-7837-0466-6*, 2040789) Bks Demand.

Supreme Court & Puerto Rico: The Doctrine of Separate & Unequal. Juan R. Torruella. LC 84-7572. 320p. 1985. 10.50 (*0-8477-3031-X*) U of PR Pr.

Supreme Court & Sovereign States. Charles Warren. LC 75-87626. (American Scene Ser.). 160p. 1972. reprint ed. lib. bdg. 25.00 (*0-306-71807-3*) Da Capo.

Supreme Court & Supreme Law. Ed. by Edmond N. Cahn. LC 68-55629. (Illus.). ix, 250p. 1968. reprint ed. text ed. 65.00 (*0-8371-0335-5*, CASC, Greenwood Pr) Greenwood.

Supreme Court & the American Family: Ideology & Issues. Eva R. Rubin. LC 85-21865. (Contributions in American Studies: No. 85). 251p. 1986. text ed. 55.00 (*0-313-25157-6*, RSU/, Greenwood Pr) Greenwood.

Supreme Court & the Attitudinal Model. Harold J. Spaeth & Jeffrey A. Segal. (Illus.). 435p. (C). 1993. text ed. 59.95 (*0-521-41130-0*); pap. text ed. 19.95 (*0-521-42293-0*) Cambridge U Pr.

Supreme Court & the Bicentennial. William O. Douglas. LC 77-77835. (Leverton Lectures: No. 4). 99p. 1978. 19.50 (*0-8386-2064-7*) Fairleigh Dickinson.

Supreme Court & the Commander in Chief. Clinton Rossiter. Ed. by Richard P. Longaker. LC 76-12815. 280p. 1976. pap. 15.95 (*0-8014-9161-4*) Cornell U Pr.

Supreme Court & the Constitution: Readings in American Constitutional History. 3rd ed. Ed. by Stanley I. Kutler. (C). 1984. pap. text ed. 19.95 (*0-393-95437-4*) Norton.

Supreme Court & the Decline of Constitutional Aspiration. Gary J. Jacobsohn. LC 86-6489. (Philosophy & Society Ser.). 192p. (C). 1986. pap. 23.00 (*0-8476-7607-2*) Rowman.

Supreme Court & the Electoral Process. Richard Claude. LC 70-94885. 314p. reprint ed. pap. 89.50 (*0-317-07954-9*, 2015687) Bks Demand.

Supreme Court & the Mass Media: Selected Cases, Summaries, & Analyses. Douglas S. Campbell. LC 89-26567. 256p. 1990. text ed. 55.00 (*0-275-93421-7*, C3421); pap. text ed. 16.95 (*0-275-93549-3*, B3549) Greenwood.

Supreme Court & the News Media. David L. Grey. LC 68-17732. 206p. reprint ed. 58.80 (*0-8357-9473-3*, 2015423) Bks Demand.

***Supreme Court & the Powers of the American Government.** Joan Biskupic & Elder Witt. LC 96-9856. 434p. 1996. pap. 34.95 (*1-56802-324-3*) Congr Quarterly.

Supreme Court & the Second Bill of Rights: The Fourteenth Amendment & the Nationalization of Civil Liberties. Richard C. Cortner. 374p. 1981. 35.00 (*0-299-08390-X*) U of Wis Pr.

Supreme Court & Unconstitutional Legislation. Blaine F. Moore. LC 68-56672. (Columbia University. Studies in the Social Sciences: No. 133). reprint ed. 31.50 (*0-404-51133-3*) AMS Pr.

Supreme Court As Final Arbiter in Federal-State Relations, 1789-1957. John R. Schmidhauser. LC 73-7676. 241p. 1973. reprint ed. text ed. 59.75 (*0-8371-6945-3*, SCFA, Greenwood Pr) Greenwood.

Supreme Court at Work. CQ Inc. Staff. 351p. 1990. 24.95 (*0-87187-540-3*) Congr Quarterly.

***Supreme Court at Work.** 2nd ed. Joan Biskupic & Elder Witt. LC 96-29102. 402p. 1996. pap. 34.95 (*1-56802-323-5*) Congr Quarterly.

Supreme Court Bar: Legal Elites in the Washington Community. Kevin T. McGuire. LC 93-3074. (Constitutionalism & Democracy Ser.). 320p. (C). 1993. text ed. 40.00 (*0-8139-1449-3*) U Pr of Va.

Supreme Court Bibliography. Fenton S. Martin & Robert U. Goehlert. 564p. 1990. 220.00 (*0-87187-554-3*) Congr Quarterly.

Supreme Court Book. Paul Deegan. Ed. by Bob Italia. LC 92-13715. (Supreme Court Justices Ser.). (J). 1992. lib. bdg. 14.98 (*1-56239-097-X*) Abdo & Dghtrs.

Supreme Court Cases. (C). 1989. 704.00 (*0-89771-694-9*) St Mut.

Supreme Court Cases. Zenov. Date not set. teacher ed., pap. text ed. write for info. (*0-314-02320-8*) West Pub.

Supreme Court Cases - 1969 to 1988 Vol. IV & Supplement Vol., 84 vols. Eastern Book Co., Staff. (C). 1989. write for info. (*0-318-65543-8*) St Mut.

Supreme Court Cases (Cri.) E. B. C. Staff. (C). 1991. ring bd. 200.00 (*0-89771-466-0*) St Mut.

Supreme Court Cases (Criminal), 1980 to 1988, 19 vols. Eastern Book Co. Staff. (C). 1989. 2,660.00 (*0-685-27890-5*) St Mut.

Supreme Court Cases, L & S. (C). 1989. 252.00 (*0-89771-696-5*) St Mut.

Supreme Court Cases (L & S) E. B. C. Staff. (C). 1991. ring bd. 180.00 (*0-89771-467-9*) St Mut.

Supreme Court Cases (Labour & Service), 1973 to 1988, 16 vols. Ed. by Eastern Book Co. Staff. (C). 1989. 2,240.00 (*0-685-27891-3*) St Mut.

Supreme Court Cases (Labour & Services) Eastern Book Co. Staff. (C). 1990. 130.00 (*0-685-38605-8*) St Mut.

Supreme Court Cases Labour & Services, 16 vols., Set. deluxe ed. Eastern Book Co. Staff. (C). 1988. ring bd. 600.00 (*0-685-25170-5*) St Mut.

Supreme Court Cases (Tax) E. B. C. Staff. (C). 1991. ring bd. 50.00 (*0-89771-468-7*) St Mut.

Supreme Court Cases (Taxation), 1973 to 1988, 16 vols. Eastern Book Co. Staff. (C). 1989. 1,600.00 (*0-685-27892-1*) St Mut.

Supreme Court Cases 1969-1988, 84 vols., Set. deluxe ed. Eastern Book Co. Staff. (C). 1988. ring bd. 2,050.00 (*0-685-25166-7*) St Mut.

Supreme Court Cases, 1990 Supplement. E. B. C. Staff. (C). 1991. ring bd. 180.00 (*0-89771-469-5*) St Mut.

Supreme Court Cases, 1991, Vol. 1. E. B. C. Staff. (C). 1991. ring bd. 180.00 (*0-89771-470-9*) St Mut.

Supreme Court Civil Procedure: New South Wales. 2nd ed. P. W. Young. 1987. Australia. 83.00 (*0-409-49385-6*, A.T.); Australia. pap. 61.00 (*0-409-49386-4*, A.T.) MICHIE.

Supreme Court Compendium: Data, Decision, & Developments. Jeffrey S. Segal et al. LC 93-23845. 741p. 1993. pap. 38.95 (*0-87187-770-8*) Congr Quarterly.

Supreme Court Compendium: Data, Decision, & Developments. Jeffrey S. Segal et al. LC 93-23845. 741p. 1994. 58.95 (*0-87187-771-6*) Congr Quarterly.

Supreme Court Compendium: Data, Decisions, & Developments. 2nd ed. Jeffrey S. Segal et al. LC 96-33603. 744p. 1996. 62.95 (*1-56802-168-2*); pap. 41.95 (*1-56802-167-4*) Congr Quarterly.

Supreme Court Confronts Abortion: The Briefs, Argument, & Decision in Planned Parenthood v. Casey. Ed. by Leon Friedman. LC 93-10947. 502p. 1993. 37.50 (*0-374-27203-4*, Noonday); pap. 17.00 (*0-374-52377-0*, Noonday) FS&G.

Supreme Court Crisis. Merlo J. Pusey. LC 74-171699. (FDR & the Era of the New Deal Ser.). 108p. 1972. reprint ed. lib. bdg. 19.50 (*0-306-70389-0*) Da Capo.

Supreme Court Decennial Digest 1981-1990, Vol. I. Surendra Malik. (C). 1993. 180.00 (*81-7012-505-7*, Pub. by Eastern Book II) St Mut.

Supreme Court Decennial Digest 1981-1990, Vol. II. Surendra Malik. (C). 1993. 180.00 (*81-7012-515-4*, Pub. by Eastern Book II) St Mut.

Supreme Court Decennial Digest 1981-1990, Vol. III. Surendra Malik. (C). 1993. 180.00 (*81-7012-519-7*, Pub. by Eastern Book II) St Mut.

Supreme Court Decisions Series, 9 vols., Set. (Illus.). 96p. (YA). (gr. 6 up). 1994. lib. bdg. 143.82 (*0-8050-3714-4*) TFC Bks NY.

Supreme Court Digest. write for info. (*0-318-57484-5*) West Pub.

Supreme Court Economic Review. Ed. by Harold Demsetz & Ernest Gellhorn. 288p. 1995. lib. bdg. 60.00 (*0-913969-68-0*) U Pr of Amer.

Supreme Court Economic Review, Vol. 1. Ed. by Peter H. Aranson. 250p. 1994. reprint ed. lib. bdg. 60.00 (*0-913969-66-4*, G Mason Univ Pr) Univ Pub Assocs.

Supreme Court Economic Review, Vol. 2. Ed. by Peter H. Aranson. 300p. 1994. reprint ed. lib. bdg. 60.00 (*0-913969-67-2*, G Mason Univ Pr) Univ Pub Assocs.

Supreme Court Economic Review, Vol. 5. Ed. by Harold Demsetz et al. 1996. lib. bdg. 45.00 (*0-226-28687-8*) U Ch Pr.

Supreme Court Economic Review Vol. 4. Ed. by Harold Demsetz & Ernest Gellhorn. 216p. 1995. lib. bdg. 45.00 (*0-226-28685-1*) U Ch Pr.

***Supreme Court Explained.** Ellen Greenberg. LC 96-39582. 1997. pap. 12.95 (*0-393-31638-6*) Norton.

***Supreme Court Explained.** Ellen Greenberg. LC 96-39582. 192p. (C). 1997. 19.95 (*0-393-04097-6*) Norton.

Supreme Court from Taft to Burger. enl. rev. ed. Alpheus T. Mason. LC 78-19084. 352p. 1979. pap. text ed. 16.95 (*0-8071-0469-8*) La State U Pr.

Supreme Court Guide to Words & Phrases. G. Goyle. (C). 1990. 90.00 (*0-89771-135-1*) St Mut.

***Supreme Court Holding a Criminal Term, No. 14056: The United States vs. Charles J. Guiteau.** Date not set. 155.95 (*0-405-05231-6*) Ayer.

Supreme Court Holding a Criminal Term No. 14056: The United States vs. Charles J. Guiteau, 2 vols, Set. LC 73-2422. (Mental Illness & Social Policy; the American Experience Ser.). reprint ed. 141.00 (*0-685-00517-8*) Ayer.

Supreme Court in American Democracy. David G. Barnum. LC 92-50012. (Illus.). 352p. (C). 1993. pap. text ed. 20.00 (*0-312-06106-4*) St Martin.

Supreme Court in American Democracy. David G. Barnum. LC 92-50012. (Illus.). 352p. (C). 1993. text ed. 39.95 (*0-312-08686-5*) St Martin.

Supreme Court in Modern Role. rev. ed. Carl B. Swisher. LC 79-26664. (New York University, James Stokes Lectureship on Politics Ser.). ix, 221p. 1980. reprint ed. text ed. 55.00 (*0-313-22279-7*, SWSU, Greenwood Pr) Greenwood.

Supreme Court in Quest of Identity. Gobind Das. (C). 1989. 125.00 (*0-89771-760-0*, Pub. by Eastern Book II) St Mut.

Supreme Court in the American System of Government. Robert H. Jackson. LC 55-9696. (Godkin Lectures, Harvard University: 1955). 101p. reprint ed. pap. 28.80 (*0-317-09854-3*, 2005678) Bks Demand.

Supreme Court in the Early Republic: The Chief Justiceships of John Jay & Oliver Ellsworth. William R. Casto. LC 94-18750. (Chief Justiceships of the United States Supreme Court Ser.). 292p. 1995. text ed. 49.95 (*1-57003-033-2*) U of SC Pr.

Supreme Court in the Federal Judicial System. 4th ed. Stephen L. Wasby. LC 92-27512. 1993. 28.95 (*0-8304-1312-X*) Nelson-Hall.

Supreme Court in the Mirror of Justices. Felix Frankfurter. (Reprint Series in Social Sciences). (C). 1993. reprint ed. pap. text ed. 1.00 (*0-8290-3433-1*, PS-87) Irvington.

Supreme Court in United States History, Vols. 1 & 2. rev. ed. Charles Warren. (Illus.). 1987. reprint ed. Vol. - 1 xvi, 814 vol.2 - x, 812. pap. 125.00 (*0-8377-2741-3*) Rothman.

Supreme Court Journal, Nineteen Seventy-One to Nineteen Eighty-Five, 30 vols., Set. Eastern Book Co. Staff. (C). 1987. 3,000.00 (*0-685-25178-0*) St Mut.

Supreme Court Judgement on Prime Minister's Election Case. Surendra Malik. 283p. 1975. 75.00 (*0-317-54841-7*) St Mut.

Supreme Court Justice Is Appointed. David J. Danelski. LC 80-21229. (Studies in Political Science). x, 242p. 1980. reprint ed. text ed. 59.75 (*0-313-22652-0*, DASJ, Greenwood Pr) Greenwood.

Supreme Court Justice Joseph Story: Statesman of the Old Republic. R. Kent Newmyer. LC 84-11886. (Studies in Legal History). (Illus.). 508p. reprint ed. pap. 144.80 (*0-7837-6854-0*, 2046683) Bks Demand.

Supreme Court Justices: A Biographical Dictionary. Ed. by Melvin Urofsky. LC 94-10028. (Illus.). 586p. 1994. text ed. 75.00 (*0-8153-1176-1*, H1851) Garland.

Supreme Court Justices: Illustrated Biographies 1789-1995. 2nd ed. Ed. by Clare Cushman. LC 93-1446. (Illus.). 588p. 1997. 48.95 (*1-56802-127-5*); pap. 33.95 (*1-56802-126-7*) Congr Quarterly.

***Supreme Court Justices & Their Court in the Stream of History.** Kermit L. Hall. LC 96-31268. (Equal Justice under Law Ser.). 1996. write for info. (*0-926019-93-7*) Carlson Pub.

Supreme Court Labour & Service Digest (1950-1986), 4 vols. Ed. by S. Malik. (C). 1989. 415.00 (*0-685-27880-8*) St Mut.

Supreme Court Labour & Services Digest, Vol. V. Surendra Malik. (C). 1991. 95.00 (*0-685-39657-6*) St Mut.

Supreme Court Labour & Services Digest: 1987-1990. Surendra Malik. (C). 1991. 200.00 (*0-89771-700-7*) St Mut.

Supreme Court Labour & Services Digest, 1950 to 1986, 4 vols., Set. Eastern Book Co. Staff. (C). 1988. 300.00 (*0-685-25676-6*) St Mut.

Supreme Court Labour & Services Digest, 1950-1982, 3 vols. Surendra Malik. 1532p. 1983. 750.00 (*0-317-54846-8*) St Mut.

Supreme Court Labour & Services Digest, 1950-1989, 5 vols., Set. Ed. by Surendra Malik. (C). 1989. 200.00 (*0-685-38609-0*) St Mut.

Supreme Court Labour & Services Digest, 1950-1989, 5 vols., Set, Vols. I-IV. Surendra Malik. (C). 1991. Set. 400.00 (*0-685-39644-4*) St Mut.

Supreme Court Labour & Services Digest, 1950-1989, 5 vols., V. Ed. by Surendra Malik. (C). 1989. write for info. (*0-318-68183-8*) St Mut.

Supreme Court Labour & Services Digest, 1950-1989, 5 vols., Vol. III, 1979-1982. Ed. by Surendra Malik. (C). 1989. 40.00 (*0-685-38607-4*) St Mut.

Supreme Court Labour & Services Digest, 1950-1989, 5 vols., Vol. IV, 1983-1986. Ed. by Surendra Malik. (C). 1989. 40.00 (*0-685-38608-2*) St Mut.

Supreme Court Labour & Services Digest, 1950-1989, 5 vols., Vols. I & II, 1950-1978. Ed. by Surendra Malik. (C). 1989. 130.00 (*0-685-38606-6*) St Mut.

Supreme Court Labour & Services Digest (1987-1990), Vol. V. Ed. by Surendra Malik. (C). 1991. text ed. 160.00 (*0-89771-490-3*) St Mut.

Supreme Court Labour Judgements, 1950-83, 13 vols. Ed. by Joshi Prasad & Kharbanda Prasad. (C). 1990. 100.00 (*0-89771-303-6*) St Mut.

Supreme Court Labour Judgments 1984-1987. I. C. Joshi. (C). 1988. 320.00 (*0-685-36497-6*) St Mut.

Supreme Court Law Review, Vol. 7. Ed. by Edward Belobaba & Eric Gertner. 1985. 143.00 (*0-409-86947-3*) MICHIE.

Supreme Court Law Review, 1990, Vol. 1. Gertner Belobara. 632p. 1991. text ed. 165.00 (*0-409-89766-3*) MICHIE.

Supreme Court Law Review, 1990-1991, Vol. 3. Gertner Belobaba. 552p. 1993. text ed. 165.00 (*0-409-90842-8*) MICHIE.

Supreme Court Law Review, 1991, Vol. 2. Gertner Belobaba. 616p. 1992. text ed. 165.00 (*0-409-90663-8*) MICHIE.

Supreme Court Mandal Commission Case 1992. Surendra Malik. (C). 1993. 62.50 (*81-7012-498-0*, Pub. by Eastern Book II) St Mut.

Supreme Court of Canada Reports Service, 7 vols., Set. ring bd. 315.00 (*0-409-82050-4*, CN) MICHIE.

Supreme Court of Iowa. 97p. 1971. 3.00 (*0-318-14447-6*) IJA NYU.

Supreme Court of North Carolina & Slavery. Bryce R. Holt. LC 73-109913. (Duke University. Trinity College Historical Society. Historical Papers: No. 17). reprint ed. 30.00 (*0-404-53167-9*) AMS Pr.

Supreme Court of Queensland: History, Jurisdiction, Procedure. B. H. McPherson. 464p. 1989. boxed 120.00 (*0-409-49444-5*, Austral) MICHIE.

Supreme Court of the United States. Charles E. Hughes. LC 38-34022. 1966. pap. text ed. 21.00 (*0-231-08567-2*) Col U Pr.

Supreme Court of the United States. Michael Kronenwetter. LC 95-13477. (American Government in Action Ser.). (Illus.). 112p. (YA). (gr. 6 up). 1996. lib. bdg. 18.95 (*0-89490-536-8*) Enslow Pubs.

Supreme Court of the United States. Photos by Fred J. Maroon. (Illus.). 176p. 1996. pap. 24.95 (*1-56566-097-8*) Thomasson-Grant.

Supreme Court of the United States. Fred J. Maroon & Suzy Maroon. LC 95-31708. (Illus.). 192p. 45.00 (*0-9650308-0-6*) Lickle Pubng.

***Supreme Court of the United States.** Fred J. Maroon & Suzy Maroon. LC 95-31708. (Illus.). 192p. pap. 24.95 (*0-9650308-1-4*) Lickle Pubng.

Supreme Court of the United States: An Introduction. Thomas G. Walker & Lee Epstein. LC 92-50015. 207p. (C). 1992. pap. text ed. 10.00 (*0-312-06269-9*) St Martin.

Supreme Court of the United States: Its History & Influence in Our Constitutional System. Westel W. Willoughby. LC 78-64251. (Johns Hopkins University. Studies in the Social Sciences. Thirtieth Ser. 1912: 7). reprint ed. 37.50 (*0-404-61355-1*) AMS Pr.

Supreme Court of the United States Hearings & Reports On Successful & Unsuccessful Nominations of Supreme Court Justices By the Senate Judiciary Committee: 1916-1990 & 1983 Supplement, 11 vols. Ed. by Roy M. Mersky & J. Myron Jacobstein. LC 75-13630. (Illus.). 1977. fiche 205.00 (*1-57588-269-8*, 301031) W S Hein.

Supreme Court of the United States Hearings & Reports on Successful & Unsuccessful Nominations of Supreme Court Justices by the Senate Judiciary Committee: 1916-1994 & 1983 Supplement, 10 vols. in 38. Ed. by Roy M. Mersky & J. Myron Jacobstein. LC 75-13630. (Illus.). 1977. Set (incl. 1983 supplement). lib. bdg. 3,495.00 (*0-930342-48-8*, 301030) W S Hein.

Supreme Court of the United States, Summary of the October, 1980 Term. G. Kenneth Reiblich. 1983. write for info. (*0-318-58311-9*) West Pub.

Supreme Court of Trinidad & Tobago, 5 vols., Set. 1985. 295.00 (*1-57588-366-X*, 302640) W S Hein.

Supreme Court on Church & State. Robert S. Alley. (Illus.). 464p. 1988. pap. 24.00 (*0-19-505029-0*) OUP.

Supreme Court on Constitutional Aspect of Labour Law. H. L. Kumar. (C). 1989. 350.00 (*0-685-27919-7*) St Mut.

Supreme Court on Criminal Law, 1950-1990, 3 vols., Vol. 1. J. K. Soonava. (C). 1990. 200.00 (*0-89771-165-3*) St Mut.

Supreme Court on Equal Pay for Equal Work. Vidya B. Mishra. (C). 1989. 125.00 (*0-685-36495-X*) St Mut.

Supreme Court on Essential Commodities Act, 1955. Surendra Malik. 161p. 1984. 120.00 (*0-317-54843-3*) St Mut.

Supreme Court on Essential Commodities Act, 1984: With Supplement. Ed. by Surendra Malik. (C). 1987. reprint ed. 45.00 (*0-685-39714-9*) St Mut.

S

An Asterisk (*) at the beginning of an entry indicates that the title is appearing in BIP for the first time.

Supreme Court on Full Bench Motor Vehicle & Compensation Cases, 1950-1990. A. Arora & K. Kalra. (C). 1990. 120.00 (*0-89771-192-0*) St Mut.
Supreme Court on Hindu Law. Surendra Malik. 247p. 1977. 115.00 (*0-317-54845-X*) St Mut.
Supreme Court on Interpretation of Statutes. Surendra Malik. (C). 1977. 35.00 (*0-685-39669-X*) St Mut.
Supreme Court on Law of Limitation, 1950-1979. Surendra Malik. 226p. 1981. 75.00 (*0-317-54844-1*) St Mut.
Supreme Court on Law of Limitation, 1950-1979. Surendra Malik. (C). 1981. 40.00 (*0-685-39630-4*) St Mut.
Supreme Court on Preventive Detention from 1950 to Present. S. Surendra Malik. 478p. 1985. 270.00 (*0-317-54842-5*) St Mut.
Supreme Court on Preventive Detention, 1950- Surendra Malik. (C). 1991. 95.00 (*0-685-39581-2*) St Mut.
Supreme Court on Preventive Detention (1950 up to Date) Surendra Malik. (C). 1991. 95.00 (*0-685-39730-0*) St Mut.
Supreme Court on Public Servants & Disciplinary Action, 1980-1987: 1988 Edition. P. N. Sharma. (C). 1988. 175.00 (*0-685-36461-5*) St Mut.
Supreme Court on Rent Control & Eviction. Surendra Malik. (C). 1992. 200.00 (*0-89771-792-9*, Pub. by Eastern Book II); 100.00 (*81-7012-471-9*, Pub. by Eastern Book II) St Mut.
Supreme Court on Sales Tax Nineteen Fifty to Nineteen Eighty-Eight. Ed. by B. L. Mittal. (C). 1988. 150.00 (*0-685-36452-6*) St Mut.
Supreme Court on Sales Tax (1950-1988) M. M. Mittal. (C). 1988. 150.00 (*0-685-27885-9*) St Mut.
Supreme Court on Tenancy & Land Laws: 1950-1990. Ed. by Surendra Malik. (C). 1991. 135.00 (*0-89771-682-5*) St Mut.
Supreme Court on Trial. Charles S. Hyneman. LC 73-20501. 308p. 1974. reprint ed. text ed. 65.00 (*0-8371-7326-4*, HYSC, Greenwood Pr) Greenwood.
Supreme Court on Words & Phrases. Surendra Malik. (C). 1993. 140.00 (*81-7012-510-3*, Pub. by Eastern Book II) St Mut.
Supreme Court Politics: The Institution & Its Procedure. Susan L. Bloch. Ed. by Thomas G. Krattenmaker. LC 94-9272. 698p. 1994. pap. text ed. 39.00 (*0-314-03492-7*) West Pub.
Supreme Court Politics: The Institution & Its Procedure, Teacher's Manual to Accompany. Susan L. Bloch. Ed. by Tom Krattenmaker. (American Casebook Ser.). 17p. 1994. pap. text ed. write for info. (*0-314-04153-2*) West Pub.
Supreme Court Practice: For Practice in the Supreme Court of the United States. 7th ed. Stephen M. Shapiro et al. LC 93-21082. 1030p. 1993. text ed. 175.00 (*0-87179-786-0*, 0786) BNA Books.
***Supreme Court Practice: 1997 Supplement.** Robert L. Stern et al. (Orig.). 1997. pap. 65.00 (*1-57018-095-4*, 1095) BNA Books.
Supreme Court Practice & Procedure. B. R. Agarwala. (C). 1992. 250.00 (*0-89771-796-1*, Pub. by Eastern Book II) St Mut.
Supreme Court Practice & Procedure. John Fage. 1980. 60.00 (*0-686-97116-7*, Pub. by Fourmat Pub UK) St Mut.
Supreme Court Practice & Procedure. John Fage. 150p. 1987. 104.00 (*1-85190-036-5*, Pub. by Fourmat Pub UK) St Mut.
Supreme Court Practice & Procedure. 5th ed. B. R. Agarwala. (C). 1989. 200.00 (*0-685-39545-6*) St Mut.
Supreme Court Practice & Procedure. 5th ed. John Fage & Gary Whitehead. 183p. 1992. 65.00 (*1-85190-150-7*, Pub. by Tolley Pubng UK) St Mut.
Supreme Court, Race, & Civil Rights. Abraham L. Davis & Barbara L. Graham. LC 95-12923. 512p. (C). 1995. 68.00 (*0-8039-7219-9*); pap. 31.50 (*0-8039-7220-2*) Sage.
Supreme Court Reborn: Constitutional Revolution in the Age of Roosevelt. William E. Leuchtenburg. 352p. 1995. text ed. 30.00 (*0-19-508613-9*) OUP.
Supreme Court Reborn: The Constitutional Revolution in the Age of Roosevelt. William E. Leuchtenburg. 368p. 1996. reprint ed. pap. 15.95 (*0-19-511131-1*) OUP.
Supreme Court Review, 1960. Ed. by Philip B. Kurland. LC 60-14353. 335p. 1960. lib. bdg. 30.00 (*0-226-46410-5*) U Ch Pr.
Supreme Court Review, 1961. Ed. by Philip B. Kurland. LC 60-14353. 339p. 1961. lib. bdg. 30.00 (*0-226-46411-3*) U Ch Pr.
Supreme Court Review, 1962. Ed. by Philip B. Kurland. LC 60-14353. 334p. 1962. lib. bdg. 30.00 (*0-226-46412-1*) U Ch Pr.
Supreme Court Review, 1963. Ed. by Philip B. Kurland. LC 60-14353. 364p. 1963. lib. bdg. 30.00 (*0-226-46414-8*) U Ch Pr.
Supreme Court Review, 1964. Ed. by Philip B. Kurland. LC 60-14353. 323p. 1964. lib. bdg. 30.00 (*0-226-46415-6*) U Ch Pr.
Supreme Court Review, 1965. Ed. by Philip B. Kurland. LC 60-14353. 295p. 1965. lib. bdg. 30.00 (*0-226-46416-4*) U Ch Pr.
Supreme Court Review, 1966. Ed. by Philip B. Kurland. LC 60-14353. 408p. 1966. lib. bdg. 30.00 (*0-226-46417-2*) U Ch Pr.
Supreme Court Review, 1967. Ed. by Philip B. Kurland. LC 60-14353. 317p. 1967. lib. bdg. 30.00 (*0-226-46418-0*) U Ch Pr.
Supreme Court Review, 1968. 1,968th ed. Ed. by Philip B. Kurland. LC 60-14357. 254p. 1968. lib. bdg. 30.00 (*0-226-46419-9*) U Ch Pr.
Supreme Court Review, 1969. Ed. by Philip B. Kurland. LC 60-14353. 454p. 1969. lib. bdg. 30.00 (*0-226-46420-2*) U Ch Pr.
Supreme Court Review, 1970. Ed. by Philip B. Kurland. LC 60-14353. 274p. 1970. lib. bdg. 30.00 (*0-226-46421-0*) U Ch Pr.
Supreme Court Review, 1971. Ed. by Philip B. Kurland. LC 60-14353. 330p. (C). 1971. lib. bdg. 30.00 (*0-226-46422-9*) U Ch Pr.
Supreme Court Review, 1973. Ed. by Philip B. Kurland. LC 60-14353. viii, 260p. 1974. lib. bdg. 30.00 (*0-226-46424-5*) U Ch Pr.
Supreme Court Review, 1974. Ed. by Philip B. Kurland. LC 60-14353. 416p. 1975. lib. bdg. 30.00 (*0-226-46425-3*) U Ch Pr.
Supreme Court Review, 1975. Ed. by Philip B. Kurland. LC 60-14353. 188p. 1976. lib. bdg. 30.00 (*0-226-46426-1*) U Ch Pr.
Supreme Court Review, 1976. Ed. by Philip B. Kurland. LC 76-14353. 352p. 1977. lib. bdg. 30.00 (*0-226-46428-8*) U Ch Pr.
Supreme Court Review, 1977. Ed. by Philip B. Kurland. LC 60-14353. (Supreme Court Review Ser.). 353p. 1978. lib. bdg. 36.00 (*0-226-46429-6*) U Ch Pr.
Supreme Court Review, 1978. Ed. by Philip B. Kurland & Gerhard Casper. LC 60-14353. 418p. 1979. lib. bdg. 40.00 (*0-226-46431-8*) U Ch Pr.
Supreme Court Review, 1979. Ed. by Philip B. Kurland & Gerhard Casper. LC 60-14353. 404p. 1980. lib. bdg. 42.00 (*0-226-46432-6*) U Ch Pr.
Supreme Court Review, 1980. Ed. by Philip B. Kurland & Gerhard Casper. LC 60-14353. 376p. 1981. lib. bdg. 40.00 (*0-226-46433-4*) U Ch Pr.
Supreme Court Review, 1981. Philip B. Kurland et al. LC 60-14353. 448p. 1982. lib. bdg. 40.00 (*0-226-46434-2*) U Ch Pr.
Supreme Court Review, 1982. 2nd ed. Ed. by Philip B. Kurland et al. LC 60-14353. (Supreme Court Review Ser.). 388p. (C). 1983. lib. bdg. 40.00 (*0-226-46435-0*) U Ch Pr.
Supreme Court Review, 1983. Ed. by Philip B. Kurland et al. LC 60-14353. 634p. 1984. lib. bdg. 47.00 (*0-226-46436-9*) U Ch Pr.
Supreme Court Review, 1984. Ed. by Philip B. Kurland et al. LC 60-14353. vii, 418p. 1985. lib. bdg. 42.00 (*0-226-46437-7*) U Ch Pr.
Supreme Court Review, 1985. Philip Kurland. 432p. 1986. lib. bdg. 45.00 (*0-226-46438-5*) U Ch Pr.
Supreme Court Review, 1986. Ed. by Philip B. Kurland et al. LC 60-14353. 402p. 1987. lib. bdg. 45.00 (*0-226-46439-3*) U Ch Pr.
Supreme Court Review, 1987. Philip B. Kurland et al. 428p. 1988. lib. bdg. 45.00 (*0-226-46440-7*) U Ch Pr.
Supreme Court Review, 1988. Ed. by Philip B. Kurland et al. LC 60-14353. xii, 281p. 1989. lib. bdg. 47.50 (*0-226-46441-5*) U Ch Pr.
Supreme Court Review, 1989. Ed. by Gerhard Casper & Dennis J. Hutchinson. LC 60-14353. 360p. 1990. lib. bdg. 51.00 (*0-226-09571-1*) U Ch Pr.
Supreme Court Review 1990. Ed. by Gerhard Casper & Dennis J. Hutchinson. 328p. 1991. lib. bdg. 42.50 (*0-226-09573-8*) U Ch Pr.
Supreme Court Review, 1991. Ed. by Dennis J. Hutchinson et al. 400p. 1992. lib. bdg. 49.50 (*0-226-09574-6*) U Ch Pr.
Supreme Court Review, 1992. Ed. by Dennis J. Hutchinson et al. (Supreme Court Review Ser.). 400p. 1993. pap. text ed. 45.00 (*0-226-36247-7*) U Ch Pr.
Supreme Court Review 1993. Ed. by Hutchinson Dennis J. et al. 456p. 1994. lib. bdg. 45.00 (*0-226-36248-5*) U Ch Pr.
Supreme Court Review, 1994. Ed. by Dennis J. Hutchinson et al. 552p. 1995. lib. bdg. 54.00 (*0-226-36311-2*) U Ch Pr.
Supreme Court Review, 1995. Dennis J. Hutchinson et al. (Supreme Court Review Ser.). 380p. 1996. lib. bdg. 54.00 (*0-226-36312-0*) U Ch Pr.
***Supreme Court Review, 1996.** Dennis J. Hutchinson. 1997. lib. bdg. 54.00 (*0-226-36313-9*) U Ch Pr.
Supreme Court Rules. Robert L. Stern et al. 1995. pap. 45.00 (*1-57018-023-7*) BNA Books.
Supreme Court Rules Nineteen Sixty-Six. K. K. Malik. 119p. 1984. 90.00 (*0-317-54869-7*) St Mut.
Supreme Court Secret: Justice Scalia's Secret Involvement with an Appellee. John M. Fritz. 1994. pap. write for info. (*0-930179-24-2*) Johns Enter.
Supreme Court Services Law Judgements, 1950-1988. J. S. Kalra. (C). 1990. 100.00 (*0-685-54411-7*) St Mut.
Supreme Court Speaks. United States Supreme Court Staff & Jerre S. Williams. LC 71-121509. (Essay Index Reprint Ser.). 1977. reprint ed. 31.95 (*0-8369-1855-X*) Ayer.
Supreme Court Statecraft: The Rule of Law & Men. Wallace Mendelson. LC 85-2489. 362p. 1985. reprint ed. pap. 103.20 (*0-608-00181-3*, 2060963) Bks Demand.
Supreme Court Under Marshall & Taney. R. Kent Newmyer. Ed. by John H. Franklin & A. S. Eisenstadt. LC 68-29540. (American History Ser.). 192p. (C). 1969. pap. text ed. write for info. (*0-88295-746-5*) Harlan Davidson.
Supreme Court Under Warren. Gerald Kurland. Ed. by D. Steve Rahmas. LC 72-89222. (Topics of Our Times Ser.: No. 5). 32p. 1973. lib. bdg. 7.25 (*0-87157-805-0*) SamHar Pr.
Supreme Court Watch 1995. David M. O'Brien. Date not set. write for info. (*0-393-03869-6*) Norton.
Supreme Court Watch 1995: An Annual Supplement. David M. O'Brien. (C). 1995. pap. text ed. 11.95 (*0-393-96892-8*) Norton.
Supreme Court Watch 1996. David M. O'Brien. (C). Date not set. pap. text ed. 12.95 (*0-393-97047-7*) Norton.
Supreme Court Yearbook. Kenneth Jost. 270p. 1994. 33.95 (*0-87187-815-1*); pap. text ed. 23.95 (*0-87187-813-5*) Congr Quarterly.
Supreme Court Yearbook, 1989-1990. Joan Biskupic. 1991. 33.95 (*0-87187-590-X*); pap. 23.95 (*0-87187-591-8*) Congr Quarterly.
Supreme Court Yearbook 1990-1991. Joan Biskupic. 250p. 1991. 33.95 (*0-87187-637-X*); pap. 23.95 (*0-87187-638-8*) Congr Quarterly.
Supreme Court Yearbook, 1991-1992. Joan Biskupic. 250p. 1992. 33.95 (*0-87187-716-3*); pap. 23.95 (*0-87187-715-5*) Congr Quarterly.
Supreme Court Yearbook, 1992-1993. Ed. by Kenneth Jost. 298p. 1994. 33.95 (*0-87187-796-1*) Congr Quarterly.
Supreme Court Yearbook, 1992-1993. Ed. by Kenneth Jost. 298p. 1994. pap. 23.95 (*0-87187-795-3*) Congr Quarterly.
Supreme Court Yearly Digest for 1982. Surendra Malik. (C). 1983. 55.00 (*0-685-39735-1*) St Mut.
Supreme Court Yearly Digest for 1985. Surendra Malik. (C). 1986. 100.00 (*0-685-39734-3*) St Mut.
Supreme Court Yearly Digest for 1986. Surendra Malik. (C). 1987. 100.00 (*0-685-39732-7*) St Mut.
Supreme Court Yearly Digest for 1988. Ed. by Surendra Malik. (C). 1989. 140.00 (*0-685-39733-5*) St Mut.
Supreme Court Yearly Digest for 1991. Surendra Malik. (C). 1992. 320.00 (*0-89771-780-5*, Pub. by Eastern Book II) St Mut.
Supreme Court Yearly Digest for 1992. Surendra Malik. (C). 1993. 180.00 (*81-7012-500-6*, Pub. by Eastern Book II) St Mut.
Supreme Court Yearly Digest, 1989. Surendra Malik. (C). 1990. 195.00 (*0-685-36438-0*) St Mut.
Supreme Court Yearly Digest, 1990. Surendra Malik. (C). 1990. 110.00 (*0-89771-329-X*) St Mut.
Supreme Court Yearly Digest, 1990. Surendra Malik. (C). 1991. text ed. 220.00 (*0-89771-491-1*) St Mut.
Supreme Court's Constitution. Bernard Siegan. LC 86-16190. 305p. 1987. pap. 21.95 (*0-88738-671-7*) Transaction Pubs.
Supreme Doctrine: Psychological Studies in Zen Thought. 2nd ed. Hubert Benoit. 234p. 1995. pap. 19.95 (*1-898723-14-1*, Pub. by Sussex Acad Pr UK) Intl Spec Bk.
Supreme Folly. Rodney R. Jones & Gerald F. Uleman. 208p. 1993. pap. 6.95 (*0-393-30941-X*) Norton.
***Supreme Gallantry: Malta's Role in the Allied Victory 1939-1945.** Tony Spooner. (Illus.). 345p. 1996. 55.00 (*0-7195-5706-2*, Pub. by John Murray UK) Trafalgar.
Supreme Identity. Alan W. Watts. 1972. pap. 9.00 (*0-394-71835-6*, Vin) Random.
Supreme Instants: The Photography of Edward Weston. Beaumont Newhall. 191p. 1986. 50.00 (*0-317-53697-4*) Little.
Supreme Life: The History of a Negro Life Insurance Company. Robert C. Puth. LC 75-41780. (Companies & Men: Business Enterprises in America Ser.). 1976. 27.95 (*0-405-08095-6*) Ayer.
Supreme Philosophy of Man. 7th ed. Alfred A. Montapert. LC 70-119515. 1977. 10.00 (*0-9603174-2-2*) Bks of Value.
Supreme Philosophy of Man: The Laws of Life. Alfred A. Montapert. 1977. pap. 4.95 (*0-87505-368-8*) Borden.
***Supreme Self.** 2nd ed. Abhayananda. LC 97-21590. 1998. write for info. (*0-914557-10-6*) Atma Bks.
Supreme Self: A Modern Upanishad. Swami Abhayananda. (Illus.). 180p. (Orig.). 1984. pap. 9.95 (*0-914557-01-7*) Atma Bks.
***Supreme Souvenir Company.** James Stevenson. (J). Date not set. write for info. (*0-688-05137-5*); lib. bdg. 99.98 (*0-688-05139-1*) Greenwillow.
***Supreme Souvenir Factory.** James Stevenson. (J). Date not set. lib. bdg. 99.98 (*0-688-07783-8*) Greenwillow.
***Supreme Way: Inner Teachings of the Southern Mountain Tao.** Loy Ching-Yuen. Tr. by Trevor Carolan & Du Liang from CHI. LC 96-39808. 120p. (Orig.). 1997. pap. 11.95 (*1-55643-239-9*) North Atlantic.
***Supreme Wisdom.** Elijah Muhammad. 64p. Date not set. reprint ed. pap. 5.95 (*1-884855-13-X*) Secretarius.
Supreme Wisdom, Vol. 2. Elijah Muhammad. 96p. 1957. pap. 6.95 (*1-56411-080-X*) Untd Bros & Sis.
***Supreme Wisdom, Vol. 2.** Elijah Muhammad. 96p. Date not set. reprint ed. pap. 6.95 (*1-884855-19-9*) Secretarius.
Supreme Wisdom Bk. 1: Solution to the So-Called Negroes' Problem. Elijah Muhammad. 56p. 1957. pap. 4.95 (*1-56411-079-6*) Untd Bros & Sis.
Supremely Abominable Crimes: The Trial of Knights Templar. Edward Burman. 304p. 1995. 21.95 (*0-85031-928-5*, Pub. by A & B UK) London Brdge.
***Supremely Abominable Crimes: The Trial of the Knights of Templar.** Edward Burman. 304p. (Orig.). 1997. write for info. (*0-7490-0268-9*, Pub. by A & B UK) London Brdge.
Supremely Political: The Role of Ideology & Presidential Management in Unsuccessful Supreme Court Nominations. John Massaro. LC 89-21622. (SUNY Series on the Presidency). 272p. 1990. text ed. 21.50 (*0-7914-0301-7*) State U NY Pr.
Supremes: Triumph & Tragedy. rev. ed. Marianne Ruuth. (Illus.). 256p. 1995. mass mkt. 4.95 (*0-87067-749-7*, BH749-7) Holloway.
Supressed Persian: An Anthology of Forbidden Literature. Paul Sprachman. (Bibliotheca Iranica Ser.: No. 2). 170p. 1995. lib. bdg. 29.95 (*1-56859-034-2*) Mazda Pubs.
Supression of Immoral Traffic in Women & Girls Act, 1956. Mazhar Husain. 236p. 1979. 80.00 (*0-317-54675-9*) St Mut.
Suprise Twist. Melissa Lowell. (Silver Blades Ser.: Vol. 11). 144p. (J). (gr. 4-7). 1995. pap. 3.50 (*0-553-48317-X*, Skylark BDD) BDD Bks Young Read.
Suprised by Laughter. Terry Lindvall. 432p. 1996. 22.99 (*0-7852-7689-0*) Nelson.
Suprofen. Ed. by M. E. Rosenthale. (Journal: Pharmacology: Vol. 27, Suppl. 1). (Illus.). viii, 96p. 1983. pap. 30.50 (*3-8055-3789-1*) S Karger.
Sur Baudelaire, Flaubert et Morand. Marcel Proust. (FRE.). 1987. pap. 24.95 (*0-7859-3309-3*, 2870271980) Fr & Eur.
Sur Das: Poet, Singer, Saint. John S. Hawley. LC 84-40327. (Publications on Asia of the School of International Studies: No. 40). (Illus.). 256p. (C). 1984. text ed. 30.00 (*0-295-96102-3*) U of Wash Pr.
Sur de Mexico, Cruce de Caminos para las Pajaros Migratorios: Southern Mexico: Crossroads for Migratory Birds. Russell Greenbert. (Illus.). 32p. (ENG & SPA.). (YA). 1994. pap. 5.00 (*1-881230-01-5*) Smiths Migratory.
Sur Gratien et les Decretales. Adam Vetulani & Waclaw Uruszczak. (Collected Studies: No. CS308). 336p. 1990. text ed. 109.95 (*0-86078-256-5*, Pub. by Variorum UK) Ashgate Pub Co.
Sur la Linio: Rakontoj Kaj Noveloj. Georgo Kamaco. 40p. (ESP.). 1991. pap. 4.50 (*1-882251-01-6*) Eldonejo Bero.
Sur la Poesie. Rene Char. 35p. 1974. 8.95 (*0-7859-0687-8*, F93360) Fr & Eur.
Sur la Politique Rationnelle. Alphonse D. Lamartine. 164p. 1978. reprint ed. 49.95 (*0-7859-5361-2*) Fr & Eur.
Sur la Route. Jack Kerouac. 436p. (FRE.). 1976. pap. 11.95 (*0-7859-2367-5*, 2070367665) Fr & Eur.
Sur la Voie Glorieuse. Anatole France. 102p. 1916. 25.00 (*0-686-55878-2*) Fr & Eur.
Sur L'amour. Pierre Teilhard De Chardin. pap. 6.25 (*0-685-36602-2*) Fr & Eur.
Sur l'Art et les Artistes. Denis Diderot. 220p. (FRE.). 1967. 27.95 (*0-8288-9954-1*, F46790) Fr & Eur.
Sur le Bonheur. Pierre Teilhard De Chardin. pap. 6.25 (*0-685-36603-0*) Fr & Eur.
Sur le Materialisme: De l'Atomisme a la Dialectique Revolutionnaire. Phillipe Sollers. 192p. (FRE.). 1974. pap. 17.95 (*0-7859-1240-1*, 2020019671) Fr & Eur.
Sur le Reve. Sigmund Freud. (FRE.). 1990. pap. 10.95 (*0-7859-2821-9*) Fr & Eur.
Sur le Vif. Jarausch & Tufts. 1993. pap. 25.50 (*0-8384-4008-8*) Heinle & Heinle.
Sur le Vif. Jarausch & Tufts. 1993. student ed., pap. 25.50 (*0-8384-4009-6*) Heinle & Heinle.
Sur Le Vif. Jarausch. (College French Ser.). 1993. teacher ed., pap. 28.75 (*0-8384-4014-2*) Heinle & Heinle.
Sur Le Vif. Jarausch. (College French Ser.). 1993. suppl. ed., pap. 27.75 (*0-8384-4013-4*) Heinle & Heinle.
Sur Le Vif. Jarausch. (College French Ser.). 1993. teacher ed., pap. 15.00 (*0-8384-4010-X*); suppl. ed., teacher ed. 11.95 incl. audio (*0-8384-4012-6*); suppl. ed. 26.95 incl. audio (*0-8384-4011-8*) Heinle & Heinle.
Sur l'Eau. Guy De Maupassant. (FRE.). 1972. 10.95 (*0-8288-9623-2*, M2458) Fr & Eur.
Sur les Cimes du Desespoir. E. M. Cioran. (FRE.). 1991. pap. 12.95 (*0-7859-3166-X*, 22530577819) Fr & Eur.
Sur les Femmes. Henry De Montherlant. 14.95 (*0-685-36988-9*) Fr & Eur.
Sur les sections analytiques de la courbe universelle de Teichmuller. John H. Hubbard. LC 75-41604. (Memoirs Ser.: No. 4/166). 137p. 1976. pap. 22.00 (*0-8218-1866-X*, MEMO/4/166) Am Math.
Sur l'Histoire Economique de la France Medievale: La Route, le Fleuve, la Foire. Robert-Henri Bautier. Ed. by O. Guyotjeannin. (Collected Studies: No. CS 340). 360p. 1991. text ed. 103.95 (*0-86078-293-X*, Pub. by Variorum UK) Ashgate Pub Co.
Sur Plusieurs Beaux Sujects: Wallace Stevens' Commonplace Book, a Facsimile & Transcription. Wallace Stevens. Ed. by Milton J. Bates. LC 88-61760. (Illus.). 128p. 1989. 27.50 (*0-8047-1549-1*) Stanford U Pr.
Sur Quelques Myrionemacees. C. Sauvageau. 1897. reprint ed. 40.00 (*3-7682-0705-6*) Lubrecht & Cramer.
Sur Quelques Themes Erotique et Mystiques De Gita-Govinda: L'Andalouise Ou les Hesperides. Marguerite Yourcenar. 50p. (FRE.). 1985. 18.95 (*0-7859-0507-3*, 2903059608) Fr & Eur.
Sur Racine. Roland Barthes. (FRE.). 1979. pap. 11.95 (*0-7859-0661-8*, F13010) Fr & Eur.
Sur un Air De Navaja. Raymond Chandler. 256p. (FRE.). 1987. pap. 10.95 (*0-7859-2067-6*, 2070378497) Fr & Eur.
***Sura-Sura: A Text for Intermediate Japanese.** Chie Imaizumi & Masahiko Seto. 181p. (Orig.). (C). 1997. pap. text ed. 24.95 (*0-88710-186-0*) Yale Far Eastern Pubns.
***Surah Al-Fatihah: Foundation of the Qur'an.** Hamid Algar. 52p. (Orig.). 1997. pap. text ed. 5.00 (*1-889999-00-8*) Islam Pubns Int.
Sure As Strawberries. Sue A. Alderson. (Illus.). 32p. (J). (gr. 4-7). 1992. 12.95 (*0-88995-087-3*, Pub. by Red Deer CN) Orca Bk Pubs.
Sure As the Dawn. Donald E. Mansell & Vesta W. Mansell. LC 93-3782. 1993. 10.99 (*0-8280-0723-3*) Review & Herald.
Sure Can Use a Little Good News: 12 Gospel Plays in Rhyme. Jeffrey E. Burkart. LC 96-5315. 112p. 1996. 13.99 (*0-570-04866-4*, 12-3357) Concordia.
Sure Death of a Mouse. Dan Crawford. 256p. (Orig.). 1994. mass mkt. 4.99 (*0-441-00024-X*) Ace Bks.
Sure Foundation: Aleut Churches in World War II. Barbara S. Smith et al. (Illus.). 80p. 1994. pap. text ed. 11.95 (*0-9609308-2-5*) Aleutian.
Sure Guide to Heaven. Joseph Alleine. (Puritan Paperbacks Ser.). Orig. Title: Alarm to the Unconverted. 148p. 1995. pap. 4.99 (*0-85151-081-7*) Banner of Truth.
Sure-Hire Cover Letters. Robbie M. Kaplan. 150p. 1994. pap. 10.95 (*0-8144-7854-9*) AMACOM.
Sure-Hire Resumes. Robbie M. Kaplan. LC 94-6026. 188p. 1994. pap. 10.95 (*0-8144-7871-9*) AMACOM.
Sure I Believe! So What? J. M. Boice. 10.99 (*1-85792-095-3*, Pub. by Christian Focus UK) Spring Arbor Dist.

S

An Asterisk (*) at the beginning of an entry indicates that the title is appearing in BIP for the first time.

Sure I Can Rollerskate on Jell-O! Judith H. Pettigrew. (Illus.). 108p. (Orig.). 1989. pap. 8.95 (0-9622899-2-2) Creative Consort Inc.

Sure of You. Armistead Maupin. 272p. 1994. pap. 12.00 (0-06-092484-5, PL) HarpC.

Sure on This Shining Night Opus 13 No. 3. S. Barber. 8p. 1986. pap. 1.25 (0-7935-5481-0, 50308930) H Leonard.

Sure Reward. B. J. Smagula. 120p. 1995. pap. 8.95 (1-55622-047-2, Seaside Pr) Wordware Pub.

Sure Shot & Other Poems. Erica Funkhouser. 1993. pap. 9.95 (0-395-67282-1) HM.

Sure Signs: New & Selected Poems. Ted Kooser. LC 79-21725. (Poetry Ser.). 112p. 1980. pap. 12.95 (0-8229-5313-7) U of Pittsburgh Pr.

Sure Songs & Other Selected Poems. 110p. 1993. 12.95 (0-930061-57-8) Interspace Bks.

Sure Steps to Reading & Spelling: The Weiss Method of Teaching English. rev. ed. M. Herbert Weiss. 1976. text ed. write for info. (0-916720-07-1); pap. text ed. 6.75 (0-916720-02-0) Weiss Pub.

Sure Thing. Brian Chilcote. (Inter Acta Ser.). (Illus.). 4p. (C). 1994. student ed., ring bd. 3.25 (0-9629245-1-2, 741-002s, Inter Acta) WSN Pr.

Sure Thing. Brian Chilcote. (Inter Acta Ser.). (Illus.). 6p. (C). 1994. teacher ed., ring bd. 1.25 (0-9629245-2-0, 741-002t, Inter Acta) WSN Pr.

Sure Thing. Melissa Hartman. 208p. 1994. pap. 9.95 (1-56280-078-7) Naiad Pr.

Sure Thing. Warren Murphy. 448p. 1988. mass mkt. 4.50 (1-55817-129-0, Pinncle Kensgtn) Kensgtn Pub Corp.

Sure Thing: Sports & Gambling. Jeff Savage. LC 96-25629. (J). 1996. write for info. (0-8225-3303-0) Lerner Group.

Sure Thing: What We Believe & Why. Cornelius Plantinga, Jr. LC 86-8280. (Illus.). 300p. (YA). (gr. 8-10). 1986. teacher ed. 13.75 (0-930265-28-9); text ed. 16.95 (0-930265-27-0) CRC Pubns.

Sure Thing Commodity Trading. Larry Williams & Michelle Noseworthy. 1977. 50.00 (0-930233-04-2) Windsor.

Sure-Thing Options Trading: A Money-Making Guide to the New Listed Stock & Commodity Options Markets. George Angell. LC 84-6812. 288p. 1984. pap. 13.95 (0-452-26110-4, Plume) NAL-Dutton.

Sure to Endure. Danny Lynchard. 43p. 1983. pap. 1.95 (0-88144-043-4) Christian Pub.

Sure You Can! Extra-Musical Guidance for the Young Choral Conductor. Theron Kirk. LC 77-76867. 1978. pap. text ed. 15.95 (0-916656-02-0, MFBK 02) Mark Foster Mus.

***Sure You Fit In.** O. Virginia Phillips. (Illus.). 200p. 1997. 15.00 (0-614-29853-9) Fmily Connect.

***Surefire Strategies for Growing Your Home-Based Business.** David Schaefer. 208p. (Orig.). 1997. pap. 16.95 (1-57410-090-4, 5615-8601, Upstart) Dearborn Finan.

Surefire Way to Better Spelling: A Revolutionary Strategy to Turn Poor Spellers into Pros. Robert C. Dixon. 288p. (Orig.). 1993. pap. 10.95 (0-312-09463-9, Thomas Dunne Bks) St Martin.

Surefoot Mule. Bob Reese. (Grand Canyon Ser.). (Illus.). (J). (gr. k-6). 1987. 9.95 (0-89868-197-9); pap. 3.95 (0-89868-198-7) ARO Pub.

***Surely You're Joking, Mr. Feynman! Adventures of a Curious Character.** Richard P. Feynman. (Illus.). 352p. 1997. pap. 13.95 (0-393-31604-1) Norton.

Surena, General Des Parthes. Pierre Corneille. 248p. 1970. 12.95 (0-7859-0693-2, F35970) Fr & Eur.

Surest Path: The Political Treatise of a Nineteenth-Century Muslim Statesman. khayr al Funisi. Tr. by Leon C. Brown. LC 67-25399. (Middle Eastern Monographs: No. 16). 190p. 1990. 5.00 (0-674-85695-3) HUP.

Surest Ways to Get a Job, Se, Pts. I & II. Arthur A. Hawkins, II. 137p. 1992. Set. pap. 19.95 (1-881297-39-X) Info Res Lab.

Surest Ways to Get a Job, Set, Pts I & II. Arthur A. Hawkins, II. 137p. 1992. Set. pap. text ed. 19.95 (1-881297-38-1) Info Res Lab.

Surest Ways to Get a Job, Pt. I: Ways to Get the Job Done. Arthur A. Hawkins, II. 67p. 1992. pap. 12.95 (1-881297-43-8); pap. text ed. 12.95 (1-881297-44-6) Info Res Lab.

Surest Ways to Get a Job, Pt. II: Ways to Get What You Deserve. Arthur A. Hawkins, II. 54p. 1992. pap. 12.95 (1-881297-48-9); pap. text ed. 12.95 (1-881297-49-7) Info Res Lab.

Suresvara's Vartika on Asva & Asvamedha Brahaman. Shoul Hino. (C). 1990. 12.75 (81-208-0643-3, Pub. by Motilal Banarsidass II) S Asia.

Suresvara's Vartika on Madhu Brahmana. Ed. by K. P. Jog & Shoun Hino. (C). 1988. 11.00 (81-208-0438-4, Pub. by Motilal Banarsidass II) S Asia.

Suresvara's Vartika on Purusavidha Brahmana. K. P. Jog. (Advaita Tradition Ser.: Vol. 5). (C). 1993. text ed. 36.00 (81-208-1112-7, Pub. by Motilal Banarsidass II) S Asia.

Suresvara's Vartika on Saptanna Brahmana. Ed. by Shoun Hino & K. P. Jog. Tr. by K. P. Jog. (C). 1995. 22.00 (81-208-1283-2, Pub. by Motilal Banarsidass II) S Asia.

***Suresvara's Vartika on Sisu & Murtamurta Brahmana.** Ed. by K. P. Jog & S. Hino. Tr. by S. Hino. (C). 1996. 14.00 (81-208-1382-0, Pub. by Motilal Banarsidass II) S Asia.

Suresvara's Vartika on Udgitha Brahmana. Ed. & Tr. by K. P. Jog. (C). 1991. 18.00 (0-685-50016-0, Pub. by Motilal Banarsidass II) S Asia.

Surety Law Topical Index. American Bar Association, Tort & Insurance Practice Staff. LC 87-62071. 608p. 1993. pap. 64.95 (0-89707-320-7, 519-0225) Amer Bar Assn.

Surf - El Oleaje. Juan Fortez y Bravo. Tr. & Illus. by Curtis Williams. 248p. (C). 1989. 15.99 (1-878382-04-7); 19.99 (1-878382-05-5); pap. 11.99 (1-878382-03-9); pap. text ed. 23.99 (1-878382-06-3); lib. bdg. 27.99 (1-878382-07-1); 7.99 (1-878382-02-0) Book Gallery.

Surf City: The California Sound. Friedman-Fairfax & Sony Music Staff. (Life, Times & Music Book/CD Ser.). 1995. pap. 16.98 incl. audio compact disk (1-56799-182-3, Friedman-Fairfax) M Friedman Pub Grp Inc.

Surf Club. Ed Harsen. 32p. (Orig.). 1982. pap. 3.00 (0-935252-35-5) Street Pr.

Surf Fishing. Joe Malat. 40p. (Orig.). 1993. pap. 3.80 (0-940844-75-3) Wellspring.

Surf Fishing for Stripers & Blues. William A. Muller. (Illus.). 100p. 1991. 10.95 (0-9625187-4-3) Wavecrest Comns.

Surf Fishing the Atlantic Coast. Eric Burnley. LC 88-39541. (Illus.). 192p. (Orig.). 1989. pap. 14.95 (0-8117-2301-1) Stackpole.

Surf Fishing with the Experts. Richard Reina & William A. Muller. (With the Experts Ser.). (Illus.). 242p. 1984. text ed. 14.95 (0-9625187-0-0) Wavecrest Comns.

Surf Fishing with the Experts. 2nd ed. Muller & Richard Reina. (With the Experts Ser.). (Illus.). 242p. pap. 11.95 (0-9625187-5-1) Wavecrest Comns.

Surf Gecko to the Rescue! Bruce Hale. (Illus.). 32p. (J). (ps-4). 1991. write for info. (0-9621280-1-5) Wrds & Picts Pubng.

Surf Goddesses: Beauty Meets the Beach. Photos by Sam Kash. LC 95-32174. (Illus.). 157p. 1995. pap. 25.95 (0-942154-95-9) Radius Pr.

Surf Guitar. Ed. by Roy Zimmerman. (Illus.). 144p. (Orig.). 1996. pap. 19.95 (1-56922-074-3, 07-4026) Creat Cncpts.

Surf Lifesavers of Australia. Jill B. Bruce. (Illus.). 64p. 1993. 12.95 (0-86417-480-2, Pub. by Kangaroo Pr AT) Seven Hills Bk.

Surf Monkeys. Jay Leibold. (Choose Your Own Adventure Ser.: No. 131). 128p. (J). (gr. 4-7). 1993. pap. 3.25 (0-553-29301-X) Bantam.

***Surf of Sparrows' Songs.** Sasenarine Persaud. 1997. pap. 11.95 (0-920661-60-2, Pub. by TSAR CN) LPC InBook.

Surf on the Internet. J. C. Herz. 1996. pap. 11.95 (0-316-36009-0) Little.

Surf Otters: Trick or Treat. Amye Rosenberg. (J). 1995. pap. 2.95 (0-689-80379-6, Litl Simon S&S) S&S Childrens.

Surf Otters: Very Merry Christmas. Amye Rosenberg. (J). 1995. pap. 2.95 (0-689-80380-X, Litl Simon S&S) S&S Childrens.

Surf, Sand & Streetcars: A Mobile History of Santa Cruz, California. Charles S. McCaleb. LC 95-11081. 1995. reprint ed. write for info. (0-940283-06-9) Santa Cruz Hist.

Surface! Alexander Fullerton. 176p. 1984. pap. 6.00 (0-583-12295-7, Pub. by Granada UK) Academy Chi Pubs.

Surface. Laura Mullen. 88p. (Orig.). 1991. 10.95 (0-252-06187-X) U of Ill Pr.

***Surface: Contemporary Photography in Art & Media.** (Illus.). 220p. 1997. pap. 49.95 (3-927258-45-8) Gingko Press.

Surface Acoustic Wave in Inhomogenous Media. S. V. Biryukov. (Series on Wave Phenomena: Vol. 20). 1995. write for info. (0-387-58460-9) Spr-Verlag.

Surface Acoustic Wave in Inhomogenous Media. S. V. Biryukov. (Series on Wave Phenomena: Vol. 20). 1995. 99.95 (3-540-58460-9) Spr-Verlag.

Surface Acoustic Waves & Signal Processing. Michel Feldmann & Jeannine Henaff. (Acoustics Library). 405p. 1989. text ed. 59.00 (0-89006-308-7) Artech Hse.

Surface Active Ethylene Oxide Adducts. N. Schonfeldt. LC 69-19089. 1969. 418.00 (0-08-012819-X, Pub. by Pergamon Repr UK) Franklin.

Surface Activities of Proteins: Chemical & Physical Modifications. Shlomo Magdassi. LC 96-25981. 336p. 1996. 150.00 (0-8247-9532-6) Dekker.

***Surface Alloying by Ion, Electron & Laser Beams: Papers Presented at the 1985 ASM Materials Science Seminar Held October 12-13, 1985, Toronto, Ontario, Canada.** Ed. by S. T. Picraux et al. LC 86-71028. (Illus.). 429p. 1987. reprint ed. pap. 122.30 (0-608-02649-2, 2063308) Bks Demand.

Surface Analysis by Electron Spectroscopy: Measurement & Interpretation. G. C. Smith. (Updates in Applied Physics & Electrical Technology Ser.). (Illus.). 160p. (C). 1994. 49.50 (0-306-44806-8, Plenum Pr) Plenum.

Surface Analysis Methods in Materials Science. Ed. by D. J. O'Connor et al. (Surface Sciences Ser.: Vol. 23). (Illus.). 480p. 1992. 79.00 (0-387-53611-6) Spr-Verlag.

Surface Analysis of Paper. Ed. by Terrance E. Conners & Sujit Banerjee. 375p. 1995. 136.95 (0-8493-8992-5, 8992) CRC Pr.

Surface Analysis Techniques & Applications, No. 84. Roscoe Randell & Neagel. 1990. 109.00 (0-85186-597-6) CRC Pr.

Surface Analysis Techniques for Metallurgical Applications: A Symposium. Symposium on Surface Analysis Techniques for Metallurgical Applications Staff. Ed. by R. S. Carbonara & J. R. Cuthill. LC 75-39442. (ASTM Special Technical Publication Ser.: No. 596). (Illus.). 156p. reprint ed. pap. 44.50 (0-7837-4701-2, 2044847) Bks Demand.

Surface Analysis with STM & AFM: Experimental & Theoretical Aspects of Image Analysis. Sergei N. Magonov & Myung-Hwan Whangbo. (Illus.). 300p. 1996. 125.00 (3-527-29313-2, VCH) Wiley.

Surface Analytical Techniques for Probing Biomaterial Processes. Ed. by John Davies et al. LC 96-6084. 192p. 1996. 99.95 (0-8493-8352-8) CRC Pr.

Surface Anatomy. Backhouse. 1991. write for info. (0-8151-0372-7, Yr Bk Med Pubs) Mosby Yr Bk.

***Surface Anatomy.** Jewell. 1998. pap. text ed. write for info. (0-7216-7421-6) Saunders.

Surface Anatomy: The Anatomical Basis of Clinical Examination. John S. Lumley. (Illus.). 104p. 1990. pap. text ed. 21.95 (0-443-04084-2) Churchill.

Surface Anatomy: The Anatomical Basis of Clinical Examination. 2nd ed. John S. Lumley. LC 96-10352. (Illus.). 1996. write for info. (0-443-05302-2) Churchill.

Surface & Colloid Chemistry in Advanced Ceramics Processing. Ed. by Pugh & Bergstrom. (Surfactant Science Ser.: Vol. 51). 376p. 1993. 165.00 (0-8247-9098-7) Dekker.

Surface & Colloid Chemistry in Natural Waters & Water Treatment. Ed. by R. Beckett. LC 90-21580. (Illus.). 150p. 1990. 65.00 (0-306-43802-X, Plenum Pr) Plenum.

Surface & Colloid Science, Vol. 12. Ed. by Egon Matijevic. LC 67-29459. 484p. 1982. 115.00 (0-306-40616-0, Plenum Pr) Plenum.

Surface & Colloid Science, Vol. 13. Ed. by Egon Matijevic & Robert J. Good. 288p. 1984. 95.00 (0-306-41322-1, Plenum Pr) Plenum.

Surface & Colloid Science, Vol. 14. Ed. by Egon Matijevic. LC 67-29459. (Illus.). 404p. 1987. 105.00 (0-306-42421-5, Plenum Pr) Plenum.

Surface & Colloid Science, Vol. 15. Ed. by Egon Matijevic. (Illus.). 325p. 1992. 95.00 (0-306-44150-0, Plenum Pr) Plenum.

Surface & Colloid Science in Computer Technology. K. L. Mittal. LC 87-12273. (Illus.). 456p. 1987. 110.00 (0-306-42602-1, Plenum Pr) Plenum.

Surface & Defect Properties of Solids, Vols. 1-7. Incl. Vol. 1. 1970-71 Literature. LC 72-78528. 1972. 30.00 (0-85186-250-0); Vol. 2. 1971-72 Literature. LC 72-78528. 1973. 34.00 (0-85186-260-8); Vol. 3. 1972-73 Literature. LC 72-78528. 1974. 30.00 (0-85186-270-5); Vol. 4. 1973-74 Literature. LC 72-78528. 1975. 38.00 (0-85186-280-2); Vol. 5. 1974-75 Literature. LC 72-78528. 1976. 43.00 (0-85186-290-X); Vol. 6. 1975-76 Literature. LC 72-78528. 1977. 68.00 (0-85186-300-0); Vol. 7. . Ed. by M. W. Roberts & J. M. Thomas. LC 72-78528. 1978. 57.00 (0-85186-310-8); LC 72-78528. write for info. (0-318-50487-1) Am Chemical.

Surface & Dermal Sampling for Toxic Exposures. Shirley A. Ness. Date not set. text ed. 75.95 (0-442-01465-1) Van Nos Reinhold.

Surface & Ground Water Quality: Pollution Prevention, Remediation, & the Great Lakes. American Water Resources Association Staff. Ed. by Aaron A. Jennings & N. Earl Spangenberg. LC 90-85959. (American Water Resources Association Technical Publication Ser.: Vol. TPS-91-1). (Illus.). 284p. (Orig.). 1991. reprint ed. pap. 81.00 (0-7837-9221-2, 2049972) Bks Demand.

Surface & Interface Analysis, ECASIA '85: Proceedings of the European Conference on Applications of Surface & Interface Analysis. David Briggs. 128p. 1996. text ed. 440.00 (0-471-91160-7) Wiley.

Surface & Interface Characterization by Electron Optical Methods. Ugo Valdre. LC 88-28989. (NATO ASI Series B, Physics: Vol. 191). (Illus.). 328p. 1988. 95.00 (0-306-43086-X, Plenum Pr) Plenum.

Surface & Interface Characterization in Corrosion. S. Shah. (Illus.). 266p. 1994. 154.00 (1-877914-61-4) NACE Intl.

Surface & Interfacial Aspects of Biomedical Polymers Vol. 1: Surface Chemistry & Physics. Ed. by Joseph D. Andrade. 486p. 1985. 120.00 (0-306-41741-3, Plenum Pr) Plenum.

Surface & Interfacial Aspects of Biomedical Polymers, Vol. 2: Protein Adsorption. Ed. by Joseph D. Andrade. 338p. 1985. 110.00 (0-306-41742-1, Plenum Pr) Plenum.

Surface & Near-Surface Chemistry of Oxide Materials. Ed. by J. Nowotny. (Materials Science Monographs: Vol. 47). 714p. 1988. 300.75 (0-444-42954-9, North Holland) Elsevier.

Surface & Subsurface Hydrology. Ed. by Hubert J. Morel-Seytoux et al. LC 78-68496. 1979. 35.00 (0-918334-28-4) WRP.

Surface & Subsurface Mapping in Hydrogeology. M. Erdelyi. Ed. by Janos Galfi. 383p. (C). 1988. 150.00 (963-05-4658-2, Pub. by Akad Kiado HU) St Mut.

Surface & Symbol: Giuseppe Terragni & the Architecture of Italian Rationalism. Thomas Schumacher. LC 90-42728. (Illus.). 296p. 1991. pap. 29.95 (0-910413-76-2) Princeton Arch.

***Surface Application of Paper Chemicals.** Brander. (Illus.). 304p. 1997. text ed. write for info. (0-7514-0370-9, Pub. by Blackie Acad & Prof UK) Routledge Chapman & Hall.

Surface Area. L. Cesari. (Annals of Mathematics Studies: No. 35). 1956. 45.00 (0-527-02752-9) Periodicals Srv.

Surface at the Pole: The Extraordinary Voyages of the USS Skate. James F. Calvert. LC 95-46460. (Bluejacket Bks.). (Illus.). 236p. 1996. pap. 14.95 (1-55750-119-X) Naval Inst Pr.

Surface Bait Subtleties: Topwater Tactics for Muskies. John Dettloff. LC 95-182635. 1995. 12.95 (1-57223-028-2) Idyll Arbor.

Surface-Based Air Defense System Analysis Software & User's Manual. Robert H. Macfadzean & James M. Johnson. (Radar Software Library). 300p. 1992. student ed. write for info. incl. disk (0-89006-457-1) Artech Hse.

Surface-Based Air Defense Systems Analysis. Robert H. Macfadzean. (Radar Library). 460p. 1992. text ed. write for info. (0-89006-451-2) Artech Hse.

Surface Characteristics of Fibers & Textiles. Ed. by Martin J. Schick. LC 75-10346. (Fiber Science Ser.: No. 7, Pt. 1). 432p. reprint ed. pap. 123.20 (0-318-35002-5, 2030862) Bks Demand.

Surface Characteristics of Fibers & Textiles, Pt. 2. Martin J. Schick. (Fiber Science Ser.: Vol. 7). 272p. 1977. 140.00 (0-8247-6531-1) Dekker.

Surface Characteristics of Roadways: International Research & Technologies, STP 1031. Ed. by W. E. Meyer & J. Reichert. LC 90-35195. (Special Technical Publication (STP) Ser.). (Illus.). 600p. 1990. text ed. 99.00 (0-8031-1391-9, 04-010310-08) ASTM.

***Surface Characterization of Advanced Polymers.** Luigia Sabbatini & Pier G. Zamboni. (Illus.). xvi, 304p. 1993. 140.00 (3-527-28512-1, VCH) Wiley.

Surface Characterization of Advanced Polymers. Ed. by Luigia Sabbatini & Pier G. Zambonin. LC 92-33556. 312p. 1993. write for info. (1-56081-270-2, VCH) Wiley.

Surface Characterization of Biomaterials. Ed. by Buddy D. Ratner. (Progress in Biomedical Engineering Ser.: No. 6). 346p. 1988. 184.50 (0-444-43016-4) Elsevier.

Surface Chemistry & Beam-Solid Interactions Vol. 201: Materials Research Society Symposium Proceedings. Ed. by H. Atwater et al. 637p. 1991. text ed. 55.00 (1-55899-093-3) Materials Res.

Surface Chemistry of Froth Flotation. Jan Leja. 744p. 1981. 145.00 (0-306-40588-1, Plenum Pr) Plenum.

Surface Chemistry of Oxides. Royal Society of Chemistry Staff. 1992. 28.00 (0-85990-386-9) CRC Pr.

***Surface Cleaning, Finishing & Coating.** 9th ed. ASM Surface Treating & Coating Div. Council Staff. LC 82-13844. (Metals Handbook Ser.: Vol. 5). (Illus.). 736p. 1982. reprint ed. pap. 180.00 (0-608-03984-5, 2064715) Bks Demand.

Surface Coal Mining Effects on Ground Water Recharge. fac. ed. National Research Council U. S. Staff. LC 90-60773. (Illus.). 169p. 1990. pap. 48.20 (0-7837-7567-9, 2047320) Bks Demand.

Surface Coal Mining Reclamation Pt. 1: 15 Years of Progress, 1977-1992. (Illus.). 53p. (Orig.). (C). 1995. pap. text ed. 20.00 (0-7881-1893-5) DIANE Pub.

***Surface Coatings: Raw Materials & Their Usage.** 3rd ed. Oil & Colour Chemists' Association Staff. (Illus.). 640p. 1993. text ed. 147.95 (0-412-55210-8, Chap & Hall NY) Chapman & Hall.

Surface Coatings: Science & Technology. 2nd ed. Ed. by Swaraj Paul. 931p. 1996. text ed. 165.00 (0-471-95818-2) Wiley.

***Surface Coatings: Science & Technology.** Paul Swaraj. LC 83-23252. (Illus.). 751p. 1985. reprint ed. pap. 180.00 (0-608-02606-9, 2063264) Bks Demand.

***Surface Coatings for Advanced Materials.** Ed. by R. P. Agarwala. (Materials Science Forum Ser.: Vol. 246). (Illus.). 292p. (C). 1997. text ed. 88.00 (0-87849-749-8, Pub. by Trans T Pub SZ) Enfield Pubs NH.

Surface Coatings, Vol. 1: Raw Materials & Their Usage. 2nd ed. Oil & Colour Chemists' Association of Australia Staff. LC 83-7262. 388p. (gr. 13). 1983. text ed. 101.95 (0-412-25660-6, NO. 6860) Chapman & Hall.

Surface Complexation Modelling: Hydrous Ferric Oxide. David A. Dzombak. LC 89-35596. 393p. 1990. text ed. 134.00 (0-471-63731-9) Wiley.

Surface Conditioning of Vacuum Systems: AVS Series 8. Ed. by Robert Langley et al. LC 89-82542. (AIP Conference Proceedings Ser.: No. 199). (Illus.). 184p. 1990. lib. bdg. 70.00 (0-88318-756-6) Am Inst Physics.

Surface Contamination: Proceedings Symposium, Gatlinburg, June 1964. B. Fish. LC 66-17932. 1967. 185.00 (0-08-011918-2, Pub. by Pergamon Repr UK) Franklin.

Surface Crack: Physical Problems & Computational Solutions. Presented at the Winter Annual Meeting of ASME, New York, N. Y., November 26-30, 1972. Ed. by J. L. Swedlow. LC 72-88547. 208p. reprint ed. pap. 59.30 (0-317-08113-6, 2016841) Bks Demand.

Surface Crack Growth: Models, Experiments, & Structures. Walter G. Reuter. Ed. by John H. Underwood & James C. Newman, Jr. LC 89-49360. (Special Technical Publication (STP) Ser.: No. 1060). (Illus.). 425p. 1990. text ed. 88.00 (0-8031-1284-X, 04-010600-30) ASTM.

Surface Crystallographic Information Service: A Handbook of Surface Structures. J. M. MacLaren et al. (C). 1987. pap. text ed. 101.50 (90-277-2554-3) Kluwer Ac.

Surface Crystallography. Maclaren. 1987. lib. bdg. 152.00 (90-277-2503-9) Kluwer Ac.

Surface Crystallography: An Introduction to Low Energy Election Diffraction. L. J. Clarke. LC 84-11804. (Wiley-Interscience Publications). (Illus.). 343p. reprint ed. pap. 97.80 (0-7837-1885-3, 2042086) Bks Demand.

Surface Crystallography by LEED: Theory, Computation & Structural Results. M. A. Van Hove & S. Y. Tong. (Chemical Physics Ser.: Vol. 2). (Illus.). 1979. 56.95 (0-387-09194-7) Spr-Verlag.

Surface Defects in Cold Rolled Strip & Sheet. H. G. Grunhofer et al. (Illus.). 48p. (FRE & GER.). 1967. pap. 75.00 (3-514-00040-9, Pub. by Woodhead Pubng UK) Am Educ Systs.

Surface Defects in Concrete. 32p. 1974. pap. 11.95 (0-924659-03-3, 3910) Aberdeen Group.

Surface Defects in Hot Rolled Flat Steel Products. H. G. Grunhofer et al. (Illus.). 41p. (FRE & GER.). 1978. pap. 59.95 (3-514-00210-X, Pub. by Woodhead Pubng UK) Am Educ Systs.

Surface Defects on Cold Rolled, Uncoated Sheet: Quadralingual: German, English, French, Spanish. 2nd ed. H. G. Grunhofer et al. 50p. (FRE & GER.). 1995. 85.00 (0-614-17073-7, Pub. by Woodhead Pubng UK) Am Educ Systs.

Surface Delineation of Functional Areas at a Mississippian Ceremonial Center. Dan M. Healan. Ed. by Carl H. Chapman. LC 72-93556. (Memoir Ser.: No. 10). 49p. (Orig.). 1972. pap. 2.00 (0-943414-26-1) MO Arch Soc.

Surface Design for Fabric. Richard M. Proctor & Jennifer F. Lew. LC 81-7420. (Illus.). 192p. 1984. pap. 24.95 (0-295-96087-6) U of Wash Pr.

Surface Design for Fabric. rev. ed. Richard M. Proctor & Jennifer F. Lew. (Illus.). 192p. 1995. pap. 27.95 (0-295-97446-X) U of Wash Pr.

An Asterisk (*) at the beginning of an entry indicates that the title is appearing in BIP for the first time.

Surface Designer's Art: Contemporary Fabric Printers Painters & Dyers. Intro. by Katherine Westphal. LC 92-42334. (Illus.). 176p. 1993. 45.00 (*0-937274-67-4*) Lark Books.

***Surface Deterioration of Gear Teeth.** J. O. Almen. (Technical Papers). 1948. pap. text ed. 30.00 (*1-55589-247-7*) AGMA.

Surface Diagnostics in Tribology - Fundamental Principles & Applications. K. Miyoshi & Y. W. Chung. LC 93-36748. (Series on Modern Tribology: Vol. 1). 352p. 1993. text ed. 121.00 (*981-02-1516-9*) World Scientific Pub.

Surface Disinfectants, No. C-178. 192p. 1993. 2,250.00 (*1-56965-000-4*) BCC.

Surface Disordering: Growth, Roughening & Phase Transitions. Ed. by R. Jullien et al. 310p. 1993. lib. bdg. 125.00 (*1-56072-098-0*) Nova Sci Pubs.

Surface Disposal of Sewage Sludge. (Illus.). 41p. (Orig.). (C). 1995. pap. text ed. 20.00 (*0-7881-2356-4*) DIANE Pub.

***Surface Durability Rating Standards for Spur, Helical, & Herringbone Gearing: A Recapitulation of Their Derivation.** W. P. Schmitter. (Technical Papers). 1955. pap. text ed. 30.00 (*1-55589-250-7*) AGMA.

Surface Electrochemistry: A Molecular Level Approach. John O. Bockris & S. U. Khan. (Illus.). 976p. (C). 1993. 79.50 (*0-306-44298-1*, Plenum Pr); pap. 42.50 (*0-306-44339-2*, Plenum Pr) Plenum.

***Surface Electron Transfer Processes.** George Mclendon et al. 1995. text ed. 85.00 (*0-471-18553-1*) Wiley.

Surface Electron Transfer Processes. R. J. Miller et al. LC 94-22662. (Illus.). viii, 376p. 1995. 79.95 (*1-56081-036-X*, VCH) Wiley.

Surface Electronic Transport Phenomena in Semiconductors. V. N. Dobrovolsky & V. G. Litovchenko. Tr. by E. M. Pestryakov. (Semiconductor Science & Technology Ser.: No. 2). (Illus.). 240p. 1991. 85.00 (*0-19-852034-4*) OUP.

Surface Emitting Semiconductor Lasers & Arrays. Ed. by Gary A. Evans & Jacob M. Hammer. (Quantum Electronics - Principles & Applications Ser.). (Illus.). 505p. 1993. text ed. 122.00 (*0-12-244070-6*) Acad Pr.

Surface Engineering. Ed. by Ram Kossowsky & Subhash C. Singhal. 1984. lib. bdg. 276.50 (*90-247-3093-7*) Kluwer Ac.

Surface Engineering, 3 vols., Vol. I: Fundamentals of Coatings. Ed. by P. K. Datta & J. S. Gray. 370p. 1993. 105.00 (*0-85186-665-4*, Q) CRC Pr.

Surface Engineering, 3 vols., Vol. II: Engineering Applications. Ed. by P. K. Datta & J. S. Gray. 342p. 1993. 105.00 (*0-85186-675-1*, R8667) CRC Pr.

Surface Engineering, 3 vols., Vol. III: Process Technology & Surface Analysis. Ed. by P. K. Datta & J. S. Gray. 312p. 1993. 105.00 (*0-85186-685-9*, R8668) CRC Pr.

Surface Engineering: Papers Presented at the 1993 International Conference. Ed. by P. Mayr. (Illus.). 590p. 1993. 105.00 (*3-88355-189-9*, Pub. by DGM Metallurgy Info GW) IR Pubns.

Surface Engineering: Processes & Applications. Ken N. Strafford. LC 94-61268. 380p. 1994. pap. text ed., pap. 79.95 (*1-56676-154-9*) Technomic.

Surface Engineering: Second International Conference. Welding Institute Staff et al. Ed. by I. A. Bucklow. (Welding Institute Conference Proceedings Ser.). (Illus.). 532p. 1988. pap. 285.00 (*0-85300-224-X*, Pub. by Woodhead Pubng UK) Am Educ Systs.

Surface Engineering: Solutions to Corrosion & Wear-Related Failures. Ed. by P. K. Datta & J. S. Burnell-Gray. 352p. 1996. 285.00 (*1-85573-260-2*, Pub. by Woodhead Pubng UK) Am Educ Systs.

***Surface Engineering by Lasers.** Hosson. (Illus.). 288p. (C). 1997. text ed. write for info. (*0-412-63470-8*, Chap & Hall NY) Chapman & Hall.

Surface Enhanced Raman Scattering. Ed. by Richard K. Chang & Thomas E. Furtak. LC 81-22739. 450p. (C). 1982. 95.00 (*0-306-40907-0*, Plenum Pr) Plenum.

Surface Enhanced Raman Vibrational Studies at Solid-Gas Interfaces. I. Pockrand. (Tracts in Modern Physics Ser.: Vol. 104). (Illus.). 160p. 1984. 56.00 (*0-387-13416-6*) Spr-Verlag.

***Surface Fatigue Life of Contour Induction Hardened AISI 1552 Gears.** Dennis Townsend & Mike Chaplin. (1995 Fall Technical Meeting). 1995. pap. text ed. 30.00 (*1-55589-654-5*) AGMA.

Surface Finish & Its Measurements. Jean M. Bennett. 1000p. (Orig.). 1992. text ed. 150.00 (*1-55752-264-2*) Optical Soc.

Surface Fissures in the Hueco Bolson & Adjacent Basins, West Texas. R. W. Baumgardner, Jr. & B. R. Scanlon. (Illus.). 44p. 1992. pap. 3.50 (*0-317-05171-7*, GC92-2) Bur Econ Geology.

Surface Flow. Ed. by W. G. Gray. (Progress in Engineering Ser.). 120p. 1984. pap. 46.00 (*0-931215-01-3*) Computational Mech MA.

Surface Forces. B. V. Derjaguin et al. Tr. by J. A. Kitchener from RUS. LC 87-13599. (Illus.). 460p. 1987. 120.00 (*0-306-11011-3*, Consultants) Plenum.

Surface Forces & Surfactant System: Progress in Colloid & Polymer Science, Vol. 74. Ed. by J. C. Ericksson et al. 1987. 90.00 (*0-387-91309-2*) Spr-Verlag.

Surface Forces & Surfactant Systems. J. C. Eriksson et al. (Progress in Colloid & Polymer Science Ser.: Vol. 74). 128p. 1987. 54.00 (*0-318-32637-X*) Spr-Verlag.

Surface Geochemistry in Petroleum Exploration. Steven A. Tedesco. LC 94-28118. 208p. (gr. 13). 1994. text ed. 89.95 (*0-412-99301-5*) Chapman & Hall.

***Surface Hardening of Gear Teeth.** D. VandeVate. (Technical Papers). 1939. pap. text ed. 30.00 (*1-55589-336-8*) AGMA.

Surface Impoundments: Design, Construction & Operation. Robert P. Hartley. LC 91-43029. (Pollution Technology Review Ser.: No. 209). (Illus.). 183p. 1992. 45.00 (*0-8155-1302-X*) Noyes.

Surface Infrared & Raman Spectroscopy. W. Suetaka & John T. Yates. (Methods of Surface Characterization Ser.: Vol. 3). 260p. 1995. 59.50 (*0-306-44963-3*) Plenum.

Surface Inhomogeneities on Late-Type Stars. Ed. by P. B. Byrne & D. J. Mullan. (Lecture Notes in Physics Ser.: Vol. 397). 355p. 1992. 74.95 (*0-387-55310-X*) Spr-Verlag.

Surface Interest: Textiles of Today. Harriet Tidball. LC 61-2332. (Guild Monographs: No. 2). (Illus.). 22p. 1961. pap. 9.95 (*0-916658-02-3*) Shuttle Craft.

***Surface-Launched Acoustic Wave Sensors: Chemical Sensing & Thin-Film Characterization.** Michael Thompson & David Stone. LC 96-44729. (Chemical Analysis Ser.). 1997. text ed. 69.95 (*0-471-12794-9*) Wiley.

Surface-Level Ozone Exposures & Their Effects on Vegetation. A. S. Lefohn. 384p. 1991. 102.00 (*0-87371-169-6*, L169) Lewis Pubs.

Surface Line Dispatcher. Jack Rudman. (Career Examination Ser.: C-788). 1994. pap. 23.95 (*0-8373-0788-0*) Nat Learn.

Surface Line Operator. Jack Rudman. (Career Examination Ser.: C-789). 1994. pap. 19.95 (*0-8373-0789-9*) Nat Learn.

Surface Mechanics. Frederick F. Ling. LC 72-10012. 336p. reprint ed. pap. 95.80 (*0-317-11062-4*, 2006492) Bks Demand.

Surface Mechanics: Papers Presented at a Symposium Held November 16-21, 1969, at the ASME Winter Annual Meeting in Los Angeles. American Society of Mechanical Engineers. Ed. by Frederick F. Ling. LC 72-101588. 188p. reprint ed. pap. 53.60 (*0-317-42028-3*, 2025966) Bks Demand.

Surface Micromachined Capacitive Tactile Image Sensor. M. R. Wolffenbuttel. 136p. (Orig.). 1994. pap. 48.50 (*90-6275-967-X*, Pub. by Delft U Pr NE) Coronet Bks.

Surface Mine Reclamation Manual. E. S. Lyle, Jr. 299p. 1986. 66.50 (*0-444-01014-9*) P-H.

Surface Mining. 2nd ed. Ed. by B. A. Kennedy. LC 90-62378. (Illus.). 1206p. (C). 1990. 82.00 (*0-87335-102-9*, 102-9) SMM&E Inc.

Surface Mining. Ed. by Eugene P. Pfleider et al. LC 68-24169. (Seeley W. Mudd Ser.). (Illus.). 1083p. reprint ed. pap. 180.00 (*0-8357-8338-3*, 2033974) Bks Demand.

Surface Mining & Quarrying: Mechanization, Technology & Capacity. T. Shaw & Vladimir Pavlovic. 400p. 1992. write for info. (*0-13-878901-0*) P-H.

Surface Mining Environmental Monitoring & Reclamation Handbook. Ed. by Lyle V. Sendlein et al. 750p. 1983. 131.00 (*0-444-00791-1*) P-H.

Surface Mining Equipment. James W. Martin et al. LC 82-81951. (Illus.). 450p. 1982. 37.95 (*0-9609060-0-2*) Martin Consult.

Surface Modeling for CAD - CAM. B. K. Choi. (Advances in Industrial Engineering Ser.: No. 11). 390p. 1991. 184.00 (*0-444-88482-3*) Elsevier.

Surface Modeling Using Autosurf. Cheng. LC 96-25870. (General Engineering Ser.). 1996. pap. 24.95 (*0-534-95694-7*) PWS Pubs.

Surface Modelling by Computer: Conference Proceedings. 114p. 1977. 21.00 (*0-7277-0029-4*, Pub. by T Telford UK) Am Soc Civil Eng.

Surface Modification Engineering, 2 Vols., Vol. I. Ed. by Ram Kossowsky. 352p. 1989. 134.00 (*0-8493-4769-6*, TA418) CRC Pr.

Surface Modification Engineering, 2 Vols., Vol. II. Ed. by Ram Kossowsky. 256p. 1989. 123.00 (*0-8493-4770-X*, TA418) CRC Pr.

Surface Modification Industry Reviews. Moran & Horn. 1995. 1,500.00 (*0-614-10928-0*, DSM94) BCC.

***Surface Modification of Polymeric Biomaterials: Proceedings of the American Chemical Society Division of Polymer Chemistry International Symposium Held in Anaheim, California, April 2-6, 1995.** Ed. by Buddy D. Ratner & David G. Castner. LC 96-40102. (Illus.). 202p. (C). 85.00 (*0-306-45512-9*, Plenum Pr) Plenum.

Surface Modification of Polymers, No. P-214. 204p. 1994. 2,650.00 (*1-56965-305-4*) BCC.

Surface Modification Technologies: Proceedings of the First International Conference on Surface Modification Technology. International Conference on Surface Modifications & Coatings (1985: Toronto: Ontario) Staff. Ed. by T. S. Sudarshan & D. G. Bhat. LC 88-61506. (Illus.). 335p. reprint ed. pap. 95.50 (*0-7837-6059-0*, 2052505) Bks Demand.

***Surface Modification Technologies: Proceedings of the First International Conference on Surface Modification Technology Sponsored by the TMS Mechanical Metallurgy Committee, 117th TMS Annual Meeting, Phoenix, AZ, January 25-28, 1988.** International Conference on Surface Modifications & Coatings (1985: Toronto: Ontario) Staff. Ed. by T. S. Sudarshan & D. G. Bhat. LC 88-61506. (Illus.). 335p. 1988. reprint ed. pap. 95.50 (*0-608-02488-0*, 2063132) Bks Demand.

Surface Modification Technologies: Proceedings of the Ninth International Conference on Surface Modification Technologies Held on October 29 - November 3, 1995 at Cleveland, Ohio, Vol. IX. Ed. by T. S. Sudarshan et al. 608p. 1996. 220.00 (*1-86125-000-2*, Pub. by Inst Materials UK) Ashgate Pub Co.

***Surface Modification Technologies No. 6: Proceedings of the Sixth International Conference on Surface Modification Technologies Held in Chicago, U. S. A., November 2-5, 1992.** International Conference on Surface Modifications & Coatings (1985: Toronto: Ontario) Staff. Ed. by T. S. Sudarshan & J. Braza. LC 93-78980. (Illus.). 926p. pap. 180.00 (*0-608-04976-X*, 2065593) Bks Demand.

Surface Modification Technologies II: Proceedings of the Second International Conference on Surface Modification Technologies. International Conference on Surface Modification Technology Staff. Ed. by T. S. Sudarshan & D. G. Bhat. LC 88-61506. (Illus.). 353p. reprint ed. pap. 100.70 (*0-7837-6067-1*, 2052513) Bks Demand.

Surface Modification Technologies III: Proceedings of the Third International Conference Held in Neuchatel, Switzerland, August 28-September 1, 1989. International Conference on Surface Modification Technology Staff. Ed. by T. S. Sudarshan et al. LC 89-63290. 909p. reprint ed. pap. 180.00 (*0-7837-6068-X*, 2052514) Bks Demand.

Surface Modification Technologies IV: Proceedings of the Fourth International Conference Held in Paris, France, November 6-9, 1990. fac. ed. Minerals, Metals & Materials Society Staff. Ed. by T. S. Sudarshan et al. LC 91-60269. (Illus.). 1032p. 1991. pap. 180.00 (*0-7837-8611-5*, 2052542) Bks Demand.

Surface Modification Technologies IX. Ed. by T. S. Sudarshan et al. (Illus.). 608p. 1996. 220.00 (*0-87339-295-7*) Minerals Metals.

Surface Modification Technologies V. Ed. by T. S. Sudarshan. 800p. 1992. 198.00 (*0-901716-13-8*, Pub. by Inst Materials UK) Ashgate Pub Co.

Surface Modification Technologies VIII. Ed. by T. S. Sudarshan & M. Jeandin. 976p. 1995. text ed. 200.00 (*0-901716-69-3*, Pub. by Inst Materials UK) Ashgate Pub Co.

Surface Modifications & Coatings: Proceedings of an International Conference. International Conference on Surface Modifications & Coatings (1985: Toronto: Ontario) Staff. Ed. by Richard B. Sisson, Jr. LC 86-70859. (Illus.). 473p. reprint ed. pap. 134.90 (*0-318-39725-0*, 2033084) Bks Demand.

Surface Mount & Related Technologies. Ginsberg. (Electrical Engineering & Electronics Ser.: Vol. 57). 368p. 1989. 140.00 (*0-8247-8073-6*) Dekker.

Surface Mount Capacitors U. S. Markets, Technologies & Opportunities: A 1993-1998 Technical-Economic Analysis. Dennis M. Zogbi. 338p. (Orig.). 1994. pap. 1,800.00 (*0-929717-21-X*) Paumanok Pubns.

Surface Mount Guidelines for Process Control, Quality, & Reliability. David Boswell. 1992. text ed. 30.00 (*0-07-707571-4*) McGraw.

Surface Mount Technology. Richard K. Miller & Terri C. Walker. LC 88-81649. (Survey on Technology & Markets Ser.: No. 58). 50p. 1989. pap. text ed. 200.00 (*1-55865-057-1*) Future Tech Surveys.

Surface Mount Technology. Rudolf Strauss. LC 93-44368. (Illus.). 384p. 1994. 69.95 (*0-7506-1862-0*) Buttrwrth-Heinemann.

***Surface Mount Technology.** 2nd ed. Ray P. Prasad. LC 96-40513. 1997. write for info. (*0-412-12921-3*) Chapman & Hall.

Surface Mount Technology: Principles & Practice. 2nd ed. Ray P. Prasad. (Electrical Engineering Ser.). 1995. 69.95 (*0-442-01862-2*) Van Nos Reinhold.

Surface Mount Technology: Recent Japanese Developments. Ed. by TechSearch International Staff. LC 92-53186. (Illus.). 336p. (C). 1992. text ed. 79.95 (*0-7803-0407-1*, PC0302-0) Inst Electrical.

Surface Mount Technology: The Future for Electronics Assembly. Stephen McClelland. (Illus.). 200p. 1987. pap. 173.00 (*0-387-17430-3*) Spr-Verlag.

Surface Mount Technology: The Handbook of Materials & Methods. Bernard S. Matisoff et al. (Illus.). 448p. 1989. 48.50 (*0-8306-3130-5*, 3130) McGraw-Hill Prof.

Surface-Mount Technology for PC Boards. rev. ed. James K. Hollomon, Jr. (Illus.). 309p. (C). 1995. reprint ed. pap. 26.95 (*0-7906-1060-4*) Prompt Publns.

Surface Mount Technology Glossary Terms & Definitions. Phil Farrow & Debra Kopp. 77p. (Orig.). 1994. pap. 40.00 (*1-885045-01-8*) ITM.

Surface Mount Technology Handbook. Vern Solberg. (Illus.). 528p. 1990. 49.95 (*0-8306-9478-1*, 3478) McGraw-Hill Prof.

Surface Mount Technology in Electronics. 185p. 1989. 2,450.00 (*0-89336-689-7*, G-118) BCC.

***Surface Mount Technology Terms & Concepts.** Debra Kopp. LC 97-14824. 1997. pap. text ed. 24.95 (*0-7506-9875-6*) Buttrwrth-Heinemann.

Surface Mount Technology with Fine Pitch Components: The Manufacturing Issues. Hans Danielsson. LC 94-72638. 242p. (gr. 13). 1994. text ed. 83.95 (*0-412-55340-6*) Chapman & Hall.

Surface of Earth. Reynolds Price. 1995. pap. 14.00 (*0-684-81339-4*) S&S Trade.

Surface of His Earth: Philosophical Musings from the West. Daniel D. Tranel. 200p. 1995. pap. 14.95 (*0-89745-188-0*) Sunflower U Pr.

Surface of the Earth: An Introduction to Geotechnical Science. Peter J. Williams. LC 81-3683. (Illus.). 228p. (Orig.). (C). 1982. pap. text ed. 14.95 (*0-582-30043-6*) Longman.

Surface Operations in Petroleum Production, Vol. I. G. V. Chilingarian et al. (Developments in Petroleum Science Ser.: No. 19A). 822p. 1987. 369.25 (*0-444-42473-3*) Elsevier.

Surface Operations in Petroleum Production, Vol. II. Ed. by G. V. Chilingarian et al. (Developments in Petroleum Science Ser.: No. 19B). 562p. 1989. 277.25 (*0-444-42677-9*) Elsevier.

Surface Organometallic Chemistry: Molecular Approaches to Surface Catalysis. Ed. by Jean-Marie Basset et al. (C). 1988. lib. bdg. 157.50 (*90-277-2724-4*) Kluwer Ac.

***Surface Oxide Films.** Ed. by J. A. Bardwell. (Illus.). 322p. 1996. 52.00 (*1-56677-168-4*, PV96-18) Electrochem Soc.

Surface Phases on Silicon: Preparation, Structures, & Properties. V. G. Lifshits et al. 275p. 1994. text ed. 129.00 (*0-471-94846-2*) Wiley.

Surface Phenomena. C. Suits & H. Way. LC 60-7068. (Collected Works of Irving Langmuir: Vol. 9). 1961. 238.00 (*0-08-009361-2*, Pub. by Pergamon Repr UK) Franklin.

Surface Phenomena & Additives in Water-Based Coatings & Printing Technology. Ed. by M. K. Sharma. (Illus.). 312p. 1992. 95.00 (*0-306-44103-9*, Plenum Pr) Plenum.

Surface Phenomena & Fine Particles in Water-Based Coatings & Printing Technology. Ed. by M. K. Sharma & F. J. Micale. LC 91-11802. (Illus.). 320p. 1990. 95.00 (*0-306-43724-4*, Plenum Pr) Plenum.

Surface Phenomena & Latexes in Waterborne Coatings & Printing Technologies: Proceedings of an International Symposium Held in Conjunction with the Twenty-Third Annual Meeting of the Fine Particle Society, July 13-17, 1992, Las Vegas, Nevada. Ed. by Mahendra K. Sharma. 225p. (C). 1995. 85.00 (*0-306-45106-9*) Plenum.

Surface Phenomena in Hemorheology: Their Theoretical, Experimental & Clinical Aspects, Vol. 416. Ed. by Alfred L. Copley & Geoffrey V. Seaman. 155.00 (*0-89766-226-1*); pap. 155.00 (*0-89766-227-X*) NY Acad Sci.

Surface Phonons. Ed. by W. Kress et al. (Surface Sciences Ser.: Vol. 21). (Illus.). 304p. 1991. 69.95 (*0-387-52721-4*) Spr-Verlag.

Surface Photochemistry. Ed. by Mazakazu Anpo. (Photoscience & Photoengineering Ser.: Vol. 1). 200p. 1996. text ed. 125.00 (*0-471-95031-9*) Wiley.

Surface Physics. Ed. by Xianoyuan Li. (China Center of Advanced Science & Technology (World Laboratory) Symposium - Workshop Proceedings Ser.). 1992. pap. text ed. 72.00 (*2-88124-860-8*) Gordon & Breach.

Surface Physics & Related Topics: Festschrift for Xie Xide. Ed. by F. J. Yang et al. 392p. (C). 1991. text ed. 118.00 (*981-02-0555-4*) World Scientific Pub.

Surface Physics of Liquid Crystals. A. A. Sonin. 192p. 1995. text ed. 60.00 (*2-88124-995-7*) Gordon & Breach.

***Surface Plane.** Martha Boles & Rochelle Newman. 1996. reprint ed. pap. text ed. 33.95 (*0-697-35578-0*) Pythagorean Pr.

Surface Plasmons. H. Raether. (Tracts in Modern Physics Ser.: Vol. 111). (Illus.). 150p. 1988. 71.95 (*0-387-17363-3*) Spr-Verlag.

Surface Plotter. Myers. (Mathematics Ser.). 1991. pap. 14.95 (*0-534-13725-3*) Brooks-Cole.

Surface Plotter. Myers. (Mathematics Ser.). 1991. 53.95 (*0-534-13716-4*); 53.95 (*0-534-13719-9*) Brooks-Cole.

Surface Preparation: The State of the Art. Bernard R. Appleman & Harold E. Hower. 234p. 1985. pap. text ed. 40.00 (*0-938477-06-4*) SSPC.

Surface Preparation & Microscopy of Materials. Brian Bousfield. 342p. 1992. text ed. 265.00 (*0-471-93181-0*) Wiley.

Surface Preparation Techniques for Adhesive Bonding. Raymond F. Wegman. LC 88-34528. 150p. 1989. 42.00 (*0-8155-1198-1*) Noyes.

Surface Processes & Landforms. Don J. Easterbrook. LC 92-20847. (Illus.). 544p. (C). 1992. text ed. 80.00 (*0-02-331250-5*, Macmillan Coll) P-H.

Surface Processing & Laser Assisted Chemistry: Proceedings of Symposium E, European-Materials Research Society Spring Conference, Strasbourg, France, 29 May-1 June, 1990. Ed. by I. W. Boyd et al. (European Materials Research Society Symposia Proceedings Ser.: No. 18). 260p. 1991. 179.50 (*0-444-88947-7*) Elsevier.

***Surface Production Operations, Vol. 1.** 2nd ed. Ken Arnold & Maurice Stewart, Jr. 1998. 115.00 (*0-88415-821-7*, 5821) Gulf Pub.

***Surface Production Operations, Vol. 2.** 2nd ed. Ken Arnold & Maurice Stewart, Jr. 1998. 115.00 (*0-88415-822-5*, 5822) Gulf Pub.

Surface Production Operations Vol. 1: Design of Oil-Handling Systems & Facilities. Ken Arnold & Maurice Stewart, Jr. LC 86-345. (Illus.). 414p. 1986. 89.00 (*0-87201-173-9*) Gulf Pub.

Surface Production Operations Vol. 2: Design of Gas-Handling Systems & Facilities. 522p. 1988. 89.00 (*0-87201-175-5*) Gulf Pub.

Surface Profile of Anti-Corrosion Paints. John D. Keane et al. (Illus.). 165p. 1976. pap. text ed. 45.00 (*0-938477-13-7*) SSPC.

Surface Properties & Catalysis by Non-Metals. Ed. by J. P. Bonnelle et al. 1983. lib. bdg. 187.00 (*90-277-1607-2*) Kluwer Ac.

Surface Properties of Layered Structures. Ed. by G. Benedek. LC 92-26745. (Physics & Chemistry of Materials with Low-Dimensional Structures Ser.: Vol. 16). 352p. (C). 1992. lib. bdg. 188.00 (*0-7923-1961-3*) Kluwer Ac.

Surface Reactions. Ed. by Robert J. Madix. LC 93-49867. (Surface Sciences Ser.: Vol. 34). 1994. 75.95 (*0-387-57605-3*) Spr-Verlag.

Surface Resonant Photoionisation of Atoms. G. G. Telegin. 200p. 1995. pap. 93.00 (*1-898326-29-0*, Pub. by Cambdge Intl UK) Am Educ Systs.

Surface Roughness & Scattering. LC 92-80626. (Technical Digest Series, 1992: Vol. 14). 200p. (Orig.). 1992. pap. 75.00 (*1-55752-242-1*) Optical Soc.

Surface Roughness Effects in Hydrodynamic & Mixed Lubrication: Presented at the Winter Annual Meeting of the American Society of Mechanical Engineers, Chicago, Illinois, November 16-21, 1980. American Society of Mechanical Engineers Staff. Ed. by S. M. Rohde & H. S. Cheng. LC 80-69179. (Illus.). 217p. reprint ed. pap. 61.90 (0-8357-2830-7, 2039066) Bks Demand.

***Surface Rupture of the 1957 Gobi-Altay, Mongolia, Earthquake.** Ed. by R. A. Kurushin et al. LC 97-19774. (Special Paper Ser.: No. 320). (Illus.). 1997. pap. write for info. (0-8137-2320-5) Geol Soc.

Surface Scattering Experiments with Conduction Electrons. Dieter Schumacher. LC 92-33496. (Tracts in Modern Physics Ser.: Vol. 128). 1992. 97.95 (0-387-56106-4) Spr-Verlag.

Surface Science: An Introduction. John B. Hudson. 336p. 1991. 68.95 (0-7506-9159-X) Buttrwrth-Heinemann.

Surface Science: Lectures on Basic Concepts & Applications - Proceedings of the Sixth Latin American Symposium on Surface Physics (SLAFS-6), Cusco, Peru, September 3-7, 1990. Ed. by F. A. Ponce & M. Cardona. (Proceedings in Physics Ser.: Vol. 62). (Illus.). xiii, 525p. 1992. 144.95 (0-387-53604-3) Spr-Verlag.

Surface Science: Principles & Applications: Proceeding of the Australian-German Workshop, Australia, December 2-5, 1991. Ed. by Russel F. Howe et al. LC 93-16744. (Proceedings in Physics Ser.: Vol. 73). 1993. 108.95 (0-387-56539-6) Spr-Verlag.

***Surface Science: Principles & Current Applications.** R. J. MacDonald et al. LC 96-31370. 374p. 1996. 109.50 (3-540-61405-2) Spr-Verlag.

Surface Science: Proceedings of the International Course, Trieste, Jan. 16-April 10, 1974, 2 Vols., 1. International Course Staff. (Illus.). 302p. 1976. pap. 95.00 (92-0-130375-0, ISP396-1, Pub. by IAEA AU) Bernan Associates.

Surface Science: The First Thirty Years. Ed. by C. B. Duke. 1064p. 1994. 126.75 (0-444-81813-8, North Holland) Elsevier.

***Surface Science: The First Thirty Years.** C. B. Duke. 1064p. 1994. pap. 57.75 (0-444-81827-8, North Holland) Elsevier.

Surface Science Investigations in Tribology: Experimental Approaches. Ed. by Yip-Wah Chung et al. LC 92-1263. (ACS Symposium Ser.: No. 485). (Illus.). 256p. 1992. 59.95 (0-8412-2205-3) Am Chemical.

Surface Science of Catalysis: In Situ Probes & Reaction Kinetics. Ed. by Daniel J. Dwyer & Friedrich M. Hoffmann. LC 91-41322. (Symposium Ser.: No. 482). (Illus.). 275p. 1992. 59.95 (0-8412-2189-8) Am Chemical.

Surface Science of Metal Oxides. Victor E. Henrich & P. A. Cox. LC 93-18566. (Illus.). 425p. (C). 1994. text ed. 95.00 (0-521-44389-X) Cambridge U Pr.

Surface Science of Metal Oxides. Victor H. Henrich & P. A. Cox. (Illus.). 478p. 1996. pap. text ed. 39.95 (0-521-56687-8) Cambridge U Pr.

Surface Science Techniques. Walls. 196p. 1994. text ed. 65.00 (0-08-042148-2, Pergamon Pr) Elsevier.

Surface Scientists's Guide to Organometallic Chemistry. Mark R. Albert & John T. Yates, Jr. LC 86-25937. (Illus.). xiii, 200p. 1987. 54.95 (0-8412-1003-9) Am Chemical.

Surface Segregation Phenomena. Dowben & Miller. 440p. 1990. 287.00 (0-8493-6893-6, TN690) CRC Pr.

Surface Stability. Rhythm & News Staff. Ed. by T. N. Rhys-Jones. (Characterisation of High-Temperature Materials Ser.: No. 6). (Illus.). 296p. 1989. pap. text ed. 52.50 (0-901462-61-6, Pub. by Inst Materials UK) Ashgate Pub Co.

Surface Streets. David James. (Illus.). 50p. (Orig.). 1982. pap. 4.95 (0-930090-15-2) Applezaba.

Surface Strength Terminology. rev. ed. Technical Association of the Pulp & Paper Industry Staff. LC 83-50017. (Illus.). 47p. reprint ed. pap. 25.00 (0-7837-6056-6, 2045869) Bks Demand.

Surface Strength Terminology. 2nd rev. ed. Ed. by J. Lind et al. (Illus.). 42p. 1993. pap. 40.00 (0-89852-411-3, 0101R111) TAPPI.

Surface Strength Terminology: A Project of the Printing Committee of the Coating & Graphic Arts Division. Technical Association of the Pulp & Paper Industry Staff. LC 83-50017. 75p. reprint ed. pap. 25.00 (0-317-30461-5, 2024915) Bks Demand.

Surface Structure: The Interface of Autonomous Components. Robert Fiengo. LC 80-14680. (Language & Thought Ser.). 213p. 1981. 33.95 (0-674-85725-9) HUP.

***Surface, Structure, & Interpretation.** Mark Steedman. LC 96-31618. (Linguistic Inquiry Monograph Ser.: No. 30). (Illus.). 144p. 1996. pap. 12.50 (0-262-69193-0) MIT Pr.

***Surface, Structure, & Interpretation.** Mark Steedman. LC 96-31618. (Linguistic Inquiry Ser.: No. 30). (Illus.). 144p. 1997. 25.00 (0-262-19379-5) MIT Pr.

Surface Structures of Microorganisms & Their Interactions with the Mammalian Host, Vol. 18. Ed. by E. Schrinner et al. 267p. 1988. 95.00 (3-527-26899-5, VCH) Wiley.

Surface Studies with Lasers. Ed. by F. R. Aussenegg et al. (Chemical Physics Ser.: Vol. 33). (Illus.). 270p. 1983. 55.95 (0-387-12598-1) Spr-Verlag.

Surface Subsidence Engineering. Syd S. Peng. LC 92-80558. 161p. (C). 1992. 73.50 (0-87335-114-2, 114-2) SMM&E Inc.

Surface Syntax of English: A Formal Model within the Meaning-Text Framework. Igor K. Mel'cuk & Nikolai V. Pertsov. LC 86-6884. (Linguistic & Literary Studies in Eastern Europe: No. 13). xv, 526p. 1986. 190.00 (90-272-1515-4) Benjamins North Am.

***Surface Temper Etch Inspection after Grinding.** 2nd rev. ed. AGMA Technical Committee Staff. (ANSI/AGMA Standard Ser.). 1992. pap. text ed. 35.00 (1-55589-577-8) AGMA.

***Surface Tempering Caused by Grinding.** G. Murphy. (Technical Papers). 1953. pap. text ed. 30.00 (1-55589-223-X) AGMA.

Surface Tension. Marisa De Franceschi. 324p. 1994. pap. 13.00 (0-920717-94-2) Guernica Editions.

Surface Tension. Elaine Equi. LC 89-38597. 69p. (Orig.). 1989. pap. 8.95 (0-918273-54-4) Coffee Hse.

Surface Tension. Bruce Zimmerman. 320p. 1996. 24.00 (0-06-017610-5) HarpC.

Surface Tension: Lesbian & Straight Women Write about Their Relationships. Meg Daly. 256p. 1996. pap. 12.00 (0-684-80221-X, Touchstone Bks) S&S Trade.

Surface Tension: Poems. Steve Phillips. LC 95-53754. (Illus.). 64p. 1996. 12.95 (0-7734-2680-9, Mellen Poetry Pr) E Mellen.

Surface Tension & Adsorption with the Collaboration of A. Bellemans. Raymond Defay & I. Prigogine. LC 61-71787. 464p. reprint ed. pap. 132.30 (0-317-08947-1, 2003639) Bks Demand.

Surface Tension & Bubbles. Alan Ward. (Experimenting With Ser.). (Illus.). 48p. (J). (gr. 3-8). 1991. lib. bdg. 14.95 (0-7910-1513-0) Chelsea Hse.

Surface-Tension-Driven Flows. Ed. by G. P. Nietzel & M. K. Smith. LC 93-73260. 88p. pap. 35.00 (0-7918-1024-0) ASME.

Surface Texture: Profile Measurement. Benjamin S. Fultz. (Illus.). 96p. 1984. pap. text ed. 30.00 (0-938477-22-6) SSPC.

***Surface Textures.** Anita Shackelford. LC 97-1123. 1997. write for info. (0-89145-890-5, Am Quilters Soc) Collector Bks.

Surface Textures versus Skidding: Measurements, Frictional Aspects & Safety Features of Tire-Pavement Interactions. Symposium on Surface Texture & Standard Surfaces (1974: Washington, D.C.). LC 75-3829. (ASTM Special Technical Publication Ser.: No. 583). 158p. pap. 45.10 (0-317-58263-1, 2056397) Bks Demand.

Surface Thoughts. Aaron Simmons. (Illus.). 48p. (Orig.). (YA). (gr. 5-12). 1993. pap. 5.00 (1-882913-01-9) Thornton LA.

Surface Topography & Body Deformity: Proceedings of 5th International Symposium on Surface Topography & Body Deformity, September 19-October 1, 1989, Vienna, Austria. Ed. by Hermann Neugebauer & Gerhard Windischbaur. 240p. (Orig.). 1990. pap. 65.00 (1-56081-303-2, Pub. by G Fischer Verlag GW) Lubrecht & Cramer.

Surface Topography & Spinal Deformity. Ed. by J. Harris & A. Turner-Smith. 252p. 1986. pap. 80.00 (3-437-10962-6, Pub. by G Fischer Verlag GW) Lubrecht & Cramer.

Surface Topography & Spinal Deformity: Proceedings of the 6th International Symposium, Sept. 19-20, 1990 Estril. A. Alberti et al. (Illus.). 218p. (Orig.). 1992. pap. 100.00 (1-56081-335-0, Pub. by G Fischer Verlag GW) Lubrecht & Cramer.

***Surface Transportation: Research Funding, Federal Role, & Emerging Issues.** (Illus.). 42p. (Orig.). (C). 1996. pap. 25.00 (0-7881-3584-8) DIANE Pub.

Surface Treatment & Finishing of Aluminium. R. G. King & D. W. Hopkins. LC 87-16070. (Pergamon Materials Engineering Practice Ser.). 150p. 1988. 76.00 (0-08-031137-7, Pub. by Pergamon Repr UK) Franklin.

Surface Treatment & Finishing of Aluminum & Its Alloys. FMJ Intl. Publ. Ltd. Staff. (C). 1989. 610.00 (0-685-46630-2, Pub. by Fuel Metallurgical Jrnl UK) St Mut.

***Surface Warfare.** 1997. lib. bdg. 250.99 (0-8490-6167-9) Gordon Pr.

Surface Warships: An Introduction to Design Principles. P. J. Gates. Ed. by Geoffrey Till. (Sea Power Ser.: Vol. 3). 193p. 1987. 40.00 (0-08-034753-3, Pub. by Brasseys UK); 25.00 (0-08-034754-1, Pub. by Brasseys UK) Brasseys Inc.

Surface Water & Ecology Symposium, Vol. 7: WEF Annual Conference, 1993. 427p. 1993. pap. 150.00 (1-881369-47-1) Water Environ.

Surface Water Drainage for Low-Income Communities. v, 88p. (ENG, FRE & SPA.). 1991. pap. text ed. 16.00 (92-4-154416-3, 1150352) World Health.

Surface Water Impoundments, 2 vols., Set. Ed. by H. G. Stefan. LC 81-67445. 1724p. 1981. pap. 125.00 (0-87262-271-1) Am Soc Civil Eng.

Surface Water Quality: Have the Laws Been Successful? Ruth Patrick. (Illus.). 247p. 1992. text ed. 42.50 (0-691-08769-5) Princeton U Pr.

Surface Water Quality & Ecology Symposia, Vol. 7: WEF 1992 Annual Conference. 1992. pap. 150.00 (1-881369-10-2) Water Environ.

Surface Water-Quality Modeling. Steve Chapra. LC 96-15461. (Illus.). 784p. 1996. text ed. 53.00 (0-07-011364-5) McGraw.

Surface Water-Quality Modeling. Steven C. Chapra. LC 96-15461. 1996. disk write for info. (0-07-843306-1) McGraw.

Surface Water Treatment: The New Rules. Harry Von Huben. 92p. 1991. pap. 33.00 (0-89867-536-7, NO. 20249) Am Water Wks Assn.

Surface Waters Acidification Programme. Ed. by B. J. Mason. 400p. (C). 1991. text ed. 120.00 (0-521-39533-X) Cambridge U Pr.

Surface-Wave Devices for Signal Processing. D. P. Morgan. (Studies in Electrical & Electronic Engineering: No. 19). 432p. 1991. reprint ed. pap. 67.50 (0-444-88845-4) Elsevier.

Surface Wave Filters: Design, Construction & Use. Ed. by Herbert Matthews. LC 77-3913. 535p. reprint ed. pap. 152.50 (0-317-09163-8, 2019522) Bks Demand.

Surface Waves & Discontinuities. P. Malischewsky. (Developments in Solid Earth Geophysics Ser.: Vol. 16). 1988. 144.50 (0-444-98959-5) Elsevier.

Surface Waves in Plasmas & Solids: Proceedings of the Second International Conference on Surface Waves in Plasmas & Solids, Ohrid, Yugoslavia 5-11 September 1985. Ed. by S. Vukovic. 712p. 1986. text ed. 131.00 (9971-5-0139-2) World Scientific Pub.

Surface Waves in Solids & Layered Structures, Acoustoelectronics '89: 2nd-4th International Symposium-Conference. M. Borissov et al. 480p. 1990. text ed. 151.00 (981-02-0091-9) World Scientific Pub.

Surface X-Ray & Neutron Scattering: Proceedings of the 2nd International Conference Physik Zentrum, Bad Honnef, FRG, June 25-28, 1991. Ed. by H. Zabel & I. K. Robinson. (Proceedings in Physics Ser.: Vol. 61). (Illus.). xi, 256p. 1992. 75.95 (0-387-54896-3) Spr-Verlag.

Surface/Interface & Stress Effects in Electronic Materials Nanostructures: Materials Research Society Symposium Proceedings, Vol. 405. Ed. by S. M. Prokes et al. (MRS Symposium Proceedings Ser.: Vol. 405). 546p. 1996. 73.00 (1-55899-308-8, 405) Materials Res.

Surfaces. Avrum Stroll. LC 87-35541. (Illus.). 240p. 1988. pap. text ed. 15.95 (0-8166-1694-9) U of Minn Pr.

Surfaces: Visual Research for Artists, Architects & Designers. Judy A. Juracek. (Illus.). 335p. 1996. 85.00 incl. cd-rom (0-393-73007-7) Norton.

Surfaces Aleatoires. M. Wschebor. (Lecture Notes in Mathematics Ser.: Vol. 1147). vii, 111p. 1985. 29.95 (0-387-15688-7) Spr-Verlag.

Surfaces & Coatings Related to Paper & Wood. Ed. by R. H. Marchessault & Christen Skaar. LC 66-27617. (C). 1967. 39.95 (0-8156-5017-5) Syracuse U Pr.

Surfaces & Interfaces in Ceramic & Ceramic-Metal Systems. Ed. by Joseph A. Pask & Anthony Evans. LC 81-5878. (Materials Science Research Ser.: Vol. 14). 768p. 1981. 125.00 (0-306-40726-4, Plenum Pr) Plenum.

Surfaces & Interfaces of Ceramic Materials. Ed. by Louis C. Dufour et al. (C). 1989. lib. bdg. 348.50 (0-7923-0447-0) Kluwer Ac.

Surfaces & Interfaces of Solids. Hans Luth. LC 92-28267. (Surface Sciences Ser.: Vol. 15). 1993. 89.00 (0-387-52681-1) Spr-Verlag.

Surfaces & Interfaces of Solids. 2nd ed. Hans Luth. LC 93-32523. (Illus.). 500p. 1993. 64.50 (0-387-56840-9) Spr-Verlag.

Surfaces & Interfaces of Solids. 3rd ed. Hans Luth. LC 96-38355. (Illus.). 487p. 1997. 49.00 (3-540-58576-1) Spr-Verlag.

Surfaces & Masks. Clarence Major. LC 88-23673. 91p. (Orig.). 1988. pap. 8.95 (0-918273-43-9) Coffee Hse.

Surfaces de Riemann. Eric Reyssat. (Progress in Mathematics Ser.: No. 77). 256p. 1989. 60.50 (0-8176-3441-X) Birkhauser.

Surfaces Fibrees en Courbes de Genre Deux. G. Z. Xiao. (Lecture Notes in Mathematics Ser.: Vol. 1137). ix, 103p. 1985. 29.95 (0-387-15662-3) Spr-Verlag.

Surfaces, Interfaces, & Colloids: Principles & Applications. Drew Myers. 433p. 1991. 49.50 (1-56081-033-5, VCH) Wiley.

Surfaces of Nonpositive Curvature. Patrick Eberlein. LC 79-15112. (Memoirs Ser.: No. 20/218). 90p. 1979. pap. 17.00 (0-8218-2218-7, MEMO/20/218) Am Math.

Surfaces of Normal & Malignant Cells. Richard O. Hynes. LC 78-16184. (Illus.). 479p. reprint ed. pap. 136.60 (0-685-20633-5, 2030418) Bks Demand.

***Surfaces, Vacuum, & Their Applications.** Ed. by Isaac Hernandez-Calderon. (Conference Proceeding Ser.: No. 378). 704p. 1996. 165.00 (1-56396-418-X, AIP) Am Inst Physics.

Surfacing. Margaret Atwood. LC 95-36575. 272p. 1996. pap. 10.95 (0-553-37780-9) Bantam.

Surfacing. Margaret Atwood. 240p. 1987. mass mkt. 5.99 (0-449-21375-7, Crest) Fawcett.

Surfact Modification Technologies, No. 6. Ed. by T. S. Sudarshan & J. F. Braza. (Illus.). 830p. 1993. 10.00 (0-87339-217-5, 2175) Minerals Metals.

Surfactant Adsorption & Surface Solubilization. Ed. by Ravi Sharma. LC 95-44680. (ACS Symposium Ser.: Vol. 615). 416p. 1996. 97.95 (0-8412-3333-0) Am Chemical.

***Surfactant Aggregation.** Clint. (Illus.). 296p. (C). 1991. text ed. 166.95 (0-216-92905-9, Pub. by Blackie Acad & Prof UK) Routledge Chapman & Hall.

Surfactant Aggregation. J. H. Clint. 320p. 1991. 117.50 (0-412-02481-0, A4214, Blackie & Son-Chapman NY) Routledge Chapman & Hall.

Surfactant-Based Mobility Control: Progress in Miscible-Flood Enhanced Oil Recovery. Ed. by Duane H. Smith. LC 88-16675. (Symposium Ser.: No. 373). (Illus.). x, 449p. 1988. 94.95 (0-8412-1491-3) Am Chemical.

***Surfactant-Based Mobility Control: Progress in Miscible-Flood Enhanced Oil Recovery.** Duane H. Smith. LC 88-16675. (ACS Symposium Ser.: No. 373). (Illus.). 461p. 1988. reprint ed. pap. 131.40 (0-608-03281-6, 2063799) Bks Demand.

Surfactant-Based Separation Processes. John F. Scamehorn. (Surfactant Science Ser.: Vol. 33). 360p. 1989. 180.00 (0-8247-7929-0) Dekker.

Surfactant Biodegradation. 2nd expanded rev. ed. Swisher. (Surfactant Science Ser.: Vol. 18). 1116p. 1986. 295.00 (0-8247-6938-4) Dekker.

Surfactant-Enhanced Subsurface Remediation: Emerging Technologies. Robert C. Knox et al. LC 95-15245. (Symposium Ser.: Vol. 594). 312p. 1995. 84.95 (0-8412-3225-3) Am Chemical.

Surfactant in Clinical Practice: Proceedings of an International Symposium, Parma, June 4-5, 1990. Bengt D. Robertson. Ed. by Stefano Parmigiani et al. LC 93-5629. 240p. 1993. text ed. 53.00 (3-7186-5279-X) Gordon & Breach.

***Surfactant in Lung Injury & Lung Transplantation.** James F. Lewis & Richard J. Novick. (Medical Intelligence Unit Ser.). 218p. 1997. 89.95 (1-57059-432-5) R G Landes.

Surfactant-Polymer Chemical Flooding, No. 1. (SPE Reprint Ser.). 288p. 1988. reprint ed. 20.00 (1-55563-012-X, 30524) Soc Petrol Engineers.

Surfactant-Polymer Chemical Flooding, No. 2. (SPE Reprint Ser.). 224p. 1988. reprint ed. 17.50 (1-55563-014-6, 30555) Soc Petrol Engineers.

Surfactant Science & Technology. 2nd ed. Drew Myers. 360p. 1992. 49.50 (1-56081-586-8, VCH) Wiley.

Surfactant Solutions: New Methods of Investigations. Zana. (Surfactant Science Ser.: Vol. 22). 496p. 1986. 215.00 (0-8247-7623-2) Dekker.

Surfactant System of the Lungs. Konrad Morgenroth & M. Newhouse. viii, 112p. (C). 1988. lib. bdg. 79.25 (3-11-011387-2) De Gruyter.

Surfactant Systems: Their Chemistry, Pharmacy & Biology. D. Attwood & Alexander T. Florence. 736p. (C). (gr. 13). 1983. text ed. 132.50 (0-412-14840-4, 6714) Chapman & Hall.

Surfactant Therapy for Lung Disease. Robertson & Taeusch. (Lung Biology in Health & Disease Ser.: Vol. 84). 702p. 1995. 195.00 (0-8247-9502-4) Dekker.

Surfactants. Tharwat F. Tadros. 1984. text ed. 94.00 (0-12-682180-1) Acad Pr.

Surfactants & Colloids in the Environment. Ed. by M. J. Schwuger & F. H. Haegel. (Progress in Colloid & Polymer Science Ser.: Vol. 95). 180p. 1994. 81.95 (0-387-91484-6) Spr-Verlag.

Surfactants & Interfacial Phenomena. 2nd ed. Milton Rosen. LC 88-5404. 431p. 1989. text ed. 92.95 (0-471-83651-6) Wiley.

Surfactants & Macromolecules: Self-Assembly at Interfaces & in Bulk. Ed. by B. Lindman et al. (Progress in Colloid & Polymer Science Ser.: Vol. 82). 200p. 1991. 148.00 (0-387-91367-X) Spr-Verlag.

Surfactants & the Lining of the Lung. Emile M. Scarpelli. LC 87-29861. (Contemporary Medicine & Public Health Ser.). (Illus.). 160p. 1988. text ed. 60.00 (0-8018-3633-6) Johns Hopkins.

Surfactants Europa. Ed. by Gordon L. Hollis. 459p. 1995. 149.95 (0-85404-804-9) CRC Pr.

Surfactants in Agrochemicals. Tharwat F. Tadros. LC 94-37159. (Surfactant Science Ser.: Vol. 54). 280p. 1994. text ed. 125.00 (0-8247-9100-2) Dekker.

Surfactants in Analytical Chemistry: Applications of Organized Amphiphilic Media. E. Pramauro & E. Pellizzetti. (Comprehensive Analytical Chemistry Ser.: Vol. 31). 540p. 1996. text ed. 262.50 (0-444-89033-5) Elsevier.

Surfactants in Chemical-Process Engineering. Darsh T. Wasan. Ed. by Shah Ginn. (Surfactant Science Ser.: Vol. 28). 560p. 1988. 195.00 (0-8247-7830-8) Dekker.

***Surfactants in Cosmetics.** 2nd ed. Ed. by Rhein & Martin M. Rieger. LC 97-57. (Surfactant Science Ser.). 656p. 1997. 195.00 (0-8247-9805-8) Dekker.

Surfactants in Cosmetics. Ed. by Martin M. Rieger. LC 84-28718. (Surfactant Science Ser.: No. 16). (Illus.). 498p. reprint ed. pap. 142.00 (0-7837-4775-6, 2044530) Bks Demand.

Surfactants in Emerging Technology. Rosen. (Surfactant Science Ser.: Vol. 26). 232p. 1987. 145.00 (0-8247-7801-4) Dekker.

Surfactants in Solution. Arun K. Chattopadhyay & K. L. Mittal. LC 96-23963. (Surfactant Science Ser.: Vol. 64). 440p. 1996. 175.00 (0-8247-9792-2) Dekker.

Surfactants in Solution, 3 Vols., Set. Ed. by K. L. Mittal. LC 83-19170. 712p. 1984. 325.00 (0-685-07795-0, Plenum Pr) Plenum.

Surfactants in Solution, Set, Vols. 7-10. Ed. by K. L. Mittal. (Illus.). 2107p. 1990. Set. 395.00 (0-685-51856-6, Plenum Pr) Plenum.

Surfactants in Solution, 3 Vols., Vol. 1. Ed. by K. L. Mittal. LC 83-19170. 712p. 1984. 125.00 (0-306-41483-X, Plenum Pr) Plenum.

Surfactants in Solution, 3 Vols., Vol. 2. Ed. by K. L. Mittal. LC 83-19170. 718p. 1984. 125.00 (0-306-41484-8, Plenum Pr) Plenum.

Surfactants in Solution, 3 Vols., Vol. 3. Ed. by K. L. Mittal. LC 83-19170. 740p. 1984. 125.00 (0-306-41485-6, Plenum Pr) Plenum.

Surfactants in Solution, Vol. 7. Ed. by K. L. Mittal. (Illus.). 535p. 1989. 135.00 (0-306-43332-X, Plenum Pr) Plenum.

Surfactants in Solution, Vol. 8. Ed. by K. L. Mittal. LC 83-19170. (Illus.). 476p. 1990. 135.00 (0-306-43333-8, Plenum Pr) Plenum.

Surfactants in Solution, Vol. 9. Ed. by K. L. Mittal. (Illus.). 548p. 1989. 135.00 (0-306-43334-6, Plenum Pr) Plenum.

Surfactants in Solution, Vol. 10. Ed. by K. L. Mittal. (Illus.). 548p. 1989. 135.00 (0-306-43335-4, Plenum Pr) Plenum.

Surfactants in Solution, Vol. 11. Ed. by K. L. Mittal & D. O. Shah. (Illus.). 658p. (C). 1992. 155.00 (0-306-44186-1, Plenum Pr) Plenum.

Surfactants in Solution, Vol. 4. Ed. by K. L. Mittal. 550p. 1987. 135.00 (0-306-42468-1, Plenum Pr) Plenum.

Surfactants in Solution, Vol. 4, Set, Vols. 5 & 6. Ed. by K. L. Mittal. 550p. 1987. Set with Vol. 5 & 6. 325.00 (0-685-18004-2, Plenum Pr) Plenum.

Surfactants in Solution, Vol. 5. Ed. by K. L. Mittal. 575p. 1987. 135.00 (0-306-42469-X, Plenum Pr) Plenum.

An Asterisk (*) at the beginning of an entry indicates that the title is appearing in BIP for the first time.

Surfactants in Solution, Vol. 5, Set, Vols. 4 & 6. Ed. by K. L. Mittal. 575p. 1987. Set with Vol. 4 & 6. 325.00 (*0-685-18005-0*, Plenum Pr) Plenum.

Surfactants in Solution, Vol. 6. Ed. by K. L. Mittal. 600p. 1987. 135.00 (*0-306-42470-3*, Plenum Pr) Plenum.

Surfactants in Solution, Vol. 6, Set, Vols. 4 & 5. Ed. by K. L. Mittal. 600p. 1987. Set with Vol.4 & 5. 325.00 (*0-685-18006-9*, Plenum Pr) Plenum.

Surfactants in Textile Processing. Datyner. (Surfactant Science Ser.: Vol. 14). (Illus.). 224p. 1983. 145.00 (*0-8247-1812-7*) Dekker.

Surfactantsystem der Lunge. Konrad Morgenroth & M. Newhouse. viii, 110p. (C). 1986. lib. bdg. 79.25 (*3-11-011015-6*) De Gruyter.

Surfboard. rev. ed. Stephen M. Shaw et al. (Illus.). 72p. (JPN.). (YA). (gr. 8 up). 1993. 14.95 (*0-912750-04-9*) Transmedia.

***Surfeit of Guns: A Sir Robert Carey Mystery.** P. F. Chisholm. LC 97-7080. 233p. 1997. 20.95 (*0-8027-3304-2*) Walker & Co.

Surfeit of Lampreys. large type ed. Ngaio Marsh. 1983. 15. 95 (*0-7089-0990-6*) Ulverscroft.

Surfer. Linda Cargill. 176p. (J). (gr. 7-9). 1995. mass mkt. 3.99 (*0-590-22215-5*) Scholastic Inc.

Surfer Sex: True Gay Encounters from Australia. Rusty Winter. 96p. (Orig.). 1985. pap. 10.00 (*0-917342-10-0*) Gay Sunshine.

Surfer Tools. Christopher Monro. LC 92-36130. 1993. pap. 45.00 (*0-442-01506-2*) Van Nos Reinhold.

Surfergrrrls: Look, Ethel! An Internet Guide for Us! Laurel Gilbert & Crystal Kile. LC 96-13645. 252p. (Orig.). 1996. pap. 15.00 (*1-878067-79-6*) Seal Pr WA.

Surfers. Photos by Patrick Cariou. (Illus.). 192p. 1997. 60. 00 (*1-57687-010-3*, pwerHse Bks) pwerHse Cultrl.

Surfers. limited ed. Text by Dan Duane & Matt Warshaw. (Illus.). 192p. 1997. boxed 175.00 (*1-57687-011-1*, pwerHse Bks) pwerHse Cultrl.

Surfer's Guide to Florida. Amy Vansant. LC 94-42566. (Illus.). 144p. (Orig.). 1995. pap. 14.95 (*1-56164-073-5*) Pineapple Pr.

Surfer's Guide to Hawaii. Greg Ambrose. LC 91-70850. (Illus.). 160p. 1991. pap. 11.95 (*0-935848-90-8*) Bess Pr.

Surfers of the Zuvuya: Tales of Intergalactic Travel. 2nd ed. Jose Arguelles. LC 88-18091. 180p. (Orig.). 1988. pap. 15.00 (*0-939680-55-6*) Bear & Co.

Surfers, Soulies, Skinheads & Skaters: Street Style from the Forties to the Nineties. Amy De La Haye & Cathie Dingwall. 160p. 1996. 40.00 (*0-87951-689-5*) Overlook Pr.

Surfer's Start-Up: A Beginner's Guide to Surfing. Doug Werner. LC 94-41284. (Start-Up Sports Ser.: Vol. 1). (Illus.). 112p. (Orig.). 1993. pap. 9.95 (*0-934793-47-6*) Tracks Pubng.

Surfer's Start-Up: A Beginner's Guide to Surfing. Doug Werner. 112p. 1993. lib. bdg. 29.00 (*0-8095-5915-3*) Borgo Pr.

Surfers Travel Guide: A Handbook to Surf Paradise. Chris Ahrens. (Illus.). 225p. (Orig.). (YA). pap. 14.95 (*1-9640858-1-X*) Chubasco Pubng.

Surffrage & Beyond: International Feminist Perspectives. Ed. by Caroline Daley & Melanie Nolan. LC 94-33981. 1994. 55.00 (*0-8147-1870-1*) NYU Pr.

Surficial Geology: Building with the Earth. John E. Costa & Victor R. Baker. (Illus.). 510p. (C). 1990. reprint ed. text ed. 80.00 (*1-878907-17-4*) TechBooks.

Surfiction: Fiction Now & Tomorrow. 2nd ed. Ed. by Raymond Federman. LC 80-54657. viii, 316p. 1981. 18. 00 (*0-8040-0651-2*) Swallow.

Surfin' Guitars: Instrumental Surf Bands of the Sixties. 2nd ed. Robert J. Dalley. (Rock & Roll Remembrances Ser.: No. 13). (Illus.). 382p. 1996. lib. bdg. 55.00 (*1-56075-042-1*) Popular Culture.

***Surfin' the Internet: Practical Ideas from A to Z.** Annette Lamb et al. (Illus.). 332p. (Orig.). (C). 1996. pap. text ed. 26.95 (*0-9641581-2-4*) Vision to Action.

Surfin' the Net: The Little Black Book for Your Computer. Anita Stumbo. (Little Black Bks.: No. 2). 128p. (Orig.). 1997. pap. 5.95 (*1-886110-08-5*) Addax Pubng.

Surfin'ary: A Dictionary of Surfing Terms & Surfspeak. Trevor Cralle. (Illus.). 240p. (Orig.). 1991. pap. 19.95 (*0-89815-422-7*) Ten Speed Pr.

***Surfing.** Larry D. Brimner. LC 97-9428. (First Book Ser.). (J). 1997. write for info. (*0-531-20315-8*) Watts.

Surfing. John Conway. (Illus.). 128p. 1989. pap. 18.95 (*0-8117-2278-3*) Stackpole.

Surfing. Jeremy Evans. LC 92-43227. (Adventurers Ser.). (Illus.). 48p. (J). (gr. 5-6). 1994. lib. bdg. 13.95 (*0-89686-824-9*, Crstwood Hse) Silver Burdett Pr.

Surfing. Sam George. 128p. 1994. pap. 10.95 (*1-56799-028-2*) M Friedman Pub Grp Inc.

Surfing. Bill Gutman. (Action Sports Ser.). 48p. (J). (gr. 3-4). 1994. lib. bdg. 17.80 (*1-56065-235-7*) Capstone Pr.

***Surfing.** Bill Gutman. (Action Sports Ser.). (Illus.). 48p. (J). (gr. 3-4). 1995. 18.40 (*0-516-35235-0*) Childrens.

Surfing. Scott Hays. LC 93-32164. (Pro-Am Sports Ser.). (J). 1993. write for info. (*0-86593-349-9*) Rourke Corp.

Surfing: A History of the Ancient Hawaiian Sport. Ben R. Finney & James D. Houston. LC 95-52233. 120p. 1996. pap. 25.00 (*0-87654-594-0*) Pomegranate Calif.

Surfing, a Royal Sport. Jack London. Ed. by A. S. Ash. 19p. (C). 1994. pap. 2.00 (*0-942208-12-9*) Bandanna Bks.

Surfing California. Allan B. Wright. LC 73-78956. 176p. (Orig.). 1973. pap. 9.95 (*0-911449-02-7*) Mountain Sea.

Surfing for Success. Stull. 1996. pap. text ed. write for info. (*0-13-495417-3*) P-H.

Surfing Guide to Southern California. David Stern & Bill Cleary. LC 63-17835. 256p. 1977. 19.95 (*0-911449-06-X*) Mountain Sea.

Surfing Hawaii. Bank Wright. LC 72-81871. (Illus.). 96p. (Orig.). 1971. pap. 7.95 (*0-911449-07-8*) Mountain Sea.

Surfing Himalayas. Frederick Lenz. 1995. pap. 16.95 (*1-55927-370-4*) St Martin.

Surfing Huge Waves with Ease. Fred Van Dyke. 64p. 1992. pap. 8.95 (*1-56647-008-0*) Mutual Pub HI.

***Surfing Made Easy.** Craig Furnas. 60p. (Orig.). 1997. pap. 10.00 (*0-614-30079-7*) CJF.

***Surfing on Finnegans Wake.** Marshall McLuhan. 18.95 (*1-56176-911-8*) Mystic Fire.

Surfing on the Internet: A Nethead's Adventures On-Line, Vol. 1. J. C. Herz. LC 94-24795. 1995. 19.95 (*0-316-35958-0*) Little.

***Surfing on the Ocean of Numbers: A Few Smarandache Notions & Similar Topics.** unabridged ed. Henry Ibstedt. (Illus.). 73p. (Orig.). 1997. pap. 11.95 (*1-879585-57-X*) Erhus Univ Pr.

Surfing South West. Ed. by Dave Hunter. (C). 1989. pap. text ed. 24.95 (*0-85025-302-0*, Pub. by Tor Mark Pr UK) St Mut.

***Surfing Success in Management.** Stull & Simkins. 1997. pap. text ed. write for info. (*0-13-648478-6*) P-H.

Surfing the Consciousness Net: The Adventures of Dani Mellon Du Pont. Timothy Leary. 1995. pap. 12.95 (*0-86719-410-3*) Last Gasp.

Surfing the Himalayas: Conversations & Travels with Master Fwap. Frederick Lenz. 256p. 1995. 14.95 (*0-312-14147-5*) St Martin.

Surfing the Himalayas: Conversations & Travels with Master Fwap, Vol. 1. Frederick Lenz. 1995. 14.95 (*0-446-52034-9*) Warner Bks.

***Surfing the Himilayas.** Lenz. LC 96-44195. 1996. pap. 9.95 (*0-312-15217-5*) St Martin.

Surfing the Internet with NetScape. Daniel A. Tauber et al. LC 95-67726. 332p. 1995. 19.99 (*0-7821-1740-6*) Sybex.

Surfing the Internet with Netscape Navigator 3. Daniel A. Tauber. 402p. 1996. pap. text ed. 22.99 incl. disk (*0-7821-1929-8*) Sybex.

***Surfing the Internet with Netscape X.** Daniel A. Tauber. 1996. pap. text ed. 22.99 incl. cd-rom (*0-7821-2055-5*) Sybex.

Surfing the Microsoft Network. Wallace Wang. 352p. 1995. pap. write for info. (*0-13-341942-8*) P-H.

Surfing the Waves of Musical Acoustics. Russell F. Pinizzotto. (Orig.). (C). 1995. pap. 21.16 (*1-56870-178-0*) RonJon Pub.

Surfing Tomorrow: Essays on the Future of American Fiction. Ed. by Lance Olsen. 105p. 1995. per. 9.95 (*1-884754-22-8*) Potpourri Pubns.

Surfing with the Great White Shark. Kenny Doudt. LC 92-90967. 88p. (Orig.). (YA). pap. 8.95 (*0-9633342-7-1*) Shark-Bite.

***Surfman!** Donna Hill. LC 97-16739. 1998. write for info. (*0-395-86614-6*, Clarion Bks) HM.

***Surfriders: In Search of the Perfect Wave.** Matt Warshaw. (Illus.). 128p. 1997. 40.00 (*1-887656-10-3*) Tehabi Bks.

Surf's Up. Mercer Mayer. (LC & the Critter Kids Mini-Novels Ser.). (Illus.). 72p. (J). (ps-3). 1994. 3.50 (*0-307-15982-5*, Golden Books) Western Pub.

***Surf's Up! A Website Workbook for Basic French.** Linda Moehle-Vieregge et al. (Illus.). 268p. (FRE.). 1997. 14. 95 (*0-88432-934-8*, B29348) Audio-Forum.

***Surf's Up! A Website Workbook for Basic German.** Linda Moehle-Vieregge et al. (Illus.). (Orig.). (GER.). 1996. wbk. ed., pap. 14.95 (*0-88432-922-4*, B29224) Audio-Forum.

Surf's Up: The Beach Boys on Record, 1961-81. Brad Elliott. Ed. by Thomas Schultheiss. (Rock & Roll Reference Ser.: No. 6). (Illus.). 512p. 1991. reprint ed. lib. bdg. 39.50 (*1-56075-022-7*) Popular Culture.

Surf's Up for Laney. Claire Caldwell. 187p. (YA). (gr. 7 up). 1995. pap. 49.95 (*0-671-53390-8*) PB.

Surfside Resort: A Business Pub Simulation. Sullivan. (DF - Computer Applications Ser.). 1993. pap. 23.95 (*0-538-70732-1*) S-W Pub.

Surge & Decline: A Study of Electoral Change. Angus Campbell. (Reprint Series in Social Sciences). (C). 1993. reprint ed. pap. text ed. 1.00 (*0-8290-3655-5*, PS-38) Irvington.

Surge & Thunder: Trends of Civilization & Culture. Charles G. Shaw. LC 75-3377. reprint ed. 47.50 (*0-404-59371-2*) AMS Pr.

***Surge Protection (C62) 1995 Edition.** 210.00 (*1-55937-505-1*, SH94275) IEEE Standards.

Surge Protection for Electronics Seminar Papers. 1990. 80. 00 (*0-86022-306-X*, Pub. by Build Servs Info Assn UK) St Mut.

***Surge Tectonics: A New Hypothesis of Global Geodynamics.** Arthur A. Meyerhoff. (Solid Earth Science Library). 340p. (C). 1996. lib. bdg. 156.00 (*0-7923-4156-2*) Kluwer Ac.

Surge to Freedom: The End of Communist Rule in Eastern Europe. J. F. Brown. LC 90-44883. 350p. 1991. text ed. 49.95 (*0-8223-1126-7*); pap. text ed. 21.95 (*0-8223-1145-3*) Duke.

Surgeon. Francis Roe. 416p. (Orig.). 1994. pap. 5.99 (*0-451-18024-0*, Sig) NAL-Dutton.

Surgeon. Jack Rudman. (Career Examination Ser.: C-790). 1994. pap. 44.95 (*0-8373-0790-2*) Nat Learn.

Surgeon! A Year in the Life of an Innercity Surgeon. Richard T. Caleel & John Littell. 1988. pap. 3.95 (*0-317-62245-5*) St Martin.

Surgeon & the Hospital in the Civil War. Albert G. Hart. 1987. pap. 10.00 (*0-942211-54-5*) Olde Soldier Bks.

***Surgeon Ashore.** large type ed. Ann Jennings. (Linford Romance Library). 304p. 1997. pap. 16.99 (*0-7089-5032-9*) Ulverscroft.

Surgeon for Lucinda. James Scotland. Ed. by William-Alan Landes. 55p. (Orig.). 1996. pap. 5.00 (*0-88734-379-1*) Players Pr.

Surgeon General's National Workshop: Implementation Strategies for Improving Hispanic-Latino Health. Ed. by Antonia C. Novello & Lydia E. Soto-Torres. (Illus.). 51p. (Orig.). (C). 1994. pap. text ed. 25.00 (*0-7881-1518-9*) DIANE Pub.

Surgeon General's Report. Pruitt. (C). 1994. pap. text ed. 17.00 (*0-03-010248-0*) HB Coll Pubs.

Surgeon General's Report on Nutrition & Health. U. S. Department of Health & Human Resources Staff. 1989. pap. 18.95 (*0-914629-96-4*) Prima Pub.

Surgeon General's Report on Nutrition & Health. U. S. Department of Health & Human Services Staff. 128p. 1989. mass mkt. 6.95 (*0-446-39061-5*) Warner Bks.

Surgeon General's Report on Nutrition & Health: Summary & Recommendations. C. Everett Koop. 78p. (Orig.). (C). 1994. pap. text ed. 25.00 (*0-7881-0744-5*) DIANE Pub.

Surgeon General's Workshop on Drunk Driving: Proceedings. 106p. (Orig.). (C). 1993. pap. text ed. 30. 00 (*1-56806-378-4*) DIANE Pub.

Surgeon in the Snow. large type ed. Lydia Balmain. (Magna Romance Ser.). 250p. 1992. 25.99 (*0-7505-0400-5*) Ulverscroft.

Surgeon of His Honour. Pedro Calderon de la Barca. Tr. by Roy Campbell & Everett W. Hesse from SPA. LC 77-13711. 1978. reprint ed. text ed. 52.50 (*0-8371-9871-2*, CASU, Greenwood Pr) Greenwood.

***Surgeon Parke's African Journey 1887-1889.** J. B. Lyons. 282p. 9400. 39.95 (*1-874675-20-1*) Dufour.

Surgeon Royal. large type ed. Margaret Barker. 274p. 1993. 25.99 (*0-7505-0552-4*) Ulverscroft.

Surgeon with a Secret. large type ed. Quenna Tilbury. 307p. 1989. 25.99 (*0-7089-1951-0*) Ulverscroft.

Surgeons at the Bailey: English Forensic Medicine to 1878. Thomas R. Forbes. LC 85-8191. (Illus.). 271p. reprint ed. pap. 77.30 (*0-7837-3318-6*, 2057722) Bks Demand.

***Surgeon's Care.** large type ed. Lucy Clark. (Mills & Boon Large Print Ser.). 288p. 1997. 22.50 (*0-263-15004-6*) Ulverscroft.

Surgeon's Choice. large type ed. Hazel Fisher. (Magna Romance Ser.). 245p. 1992. 25.99 (*0-7505-0437-4*) Ulverscroft.

Surgeon's Civil War: The Letters & Diaries of Daniel M. Holt, M.D. Ed. by James M. Greiner et al. (Illus.). 304p. 1994. pap. 18.00 (*0-87338-538-1*) Kent St U Pr.

Surgeon's Daughter. large type ed. Drusilla Douglas. 1994. 25.99 (*0-7505-0749-7*, Pub. by Magna Print Bks UK) Ulverscroft.

Surgeon's Daughter. large type ed. Kathleen Treves. (Linford Romance Library). 336p. 1985. pap. 15.99 (*0-7089-6053-7*) Ulverscroft.

Surgeon's Dilemma. large type ed. Mary Howard. 384p. 1983. 25.99 (*0-7089-0974-4*) Ulverscroft.

Surgeon's Fight to Rebuild Men. Fred Albee. (American Autobiography Ser.). 270p. 1995. reprint ed. lib. bdg. 79. 00 (*0-7812-8441-4*) Rprt Serv.

***Surgeon's Guide to Endoscopic & Laparoscopic Ultrasonography of the Colon, Rectum, & Anus.** Ed. by Wong et al. LC 96-52546. (Illus.). 1997. text ed. write for info. (*0-89640-338-6*) Igaku-Shoin.

Surgeon's Knot. large type ed. Arthur Young. 448p. 1983. 25.99 (*0-7089-1037-8*) Ulverscroft.

Surgeon's Mate. Patrick O'Brian. 1994. 22.50 (*0-393-03707-X*) Norton.

Surgeon's Mate. Patrick O'Brian. 384p. 1992. pap. 12.95 (*0-393-30820-0*) Norton.

Surgeon's Nurse. large type ed. Ann Gilmer. (Romance Ser.). 256p. 1993. 25.99 (*0-7089-2986-9*) Ulverscroft.

Surgeon's Sister. large type ed. Quenna Tilbury. 288p. 1989. 25.99 (*0-7089-2034-9*) Ulverscroft.

Surgeons, Smallpox, & the Poor: A History of Medicine & Social Conditions in Nova Scotia, 1749-1799. Allan E. Marble. (Illus.). 352p. 1993. 39.95 (*0-7735-0988-7*, Pub. by McGill CN) U of Toronto Pr.

***Surgeons, Smallpox, & the Poor: A History of Medicine & Social Conditions in Nova Scotia, 1749-1799.** Allan E. Marble. (Illus.). 376p. 1997. pap. 55.00 (*0-7735-1639-5*, Pub. by McGill CN) U of Toronto Pr.

Surgeon's Surgeon: Theodor Billroth, 1829-1894, Vol. 1. Karel B. Absolon. (Illus.). 1979. 25.00 (*0-87291-129-2*) Coronado Pr.

Surgeon's Surgeon: Theodor Billroth (1829-1894), Vol. II. Karel B. Absolon. (Illus.). 232p. 1981. 28.50 (*0-87291-146-2*) Coronado Pr.

Surgeon's Surgeon see Belle Epoque of Surgery: The Life & Times of Theodor Billroth

Surgeon's Surgeon (Theodor Billroth 1829-1894) see Grossmeister der Chirurgie (Theodor Billroth 1829-1894)

Surgeon's Surgeon, Vol. 3: Theodor Billroth (1829-1894) Karel B. Absolon. (Illus.). 280p. 1987. 30.00 (*0-87291-163-2*) Coronado Pr.

Surgery. Ed. by Bruce E. Jarrell & R. Anthony Carabasi, III. LC 95-2245. (National Medical Series for Independent Study). 1995. pap. 28.00 (*0-683-06271-9*) Williams & Wilkins.

***Surgery.** Taylor. 1998. pap. text ed. write for info. (*0-7216-7642-1*) Saunders.

Surgery. 2nd ed. (National Medical Ser.). 1990. 27.00 (*0-685-75191-0*) Williams & Wilkins.

Surgery. 2nd ed. John H. Davis & George F. Sheldon. 2000p. (C). (gr. 13). 1994. text ed. 140.00 (*0-8016-7169-8*) Mosby Yr Bk.

Surgery. 2nd ed. Bruce E. Jarrell & R. Anthony Carabasi, III. (National Medical Ser.). (Illus.). 570p. 1990. 27.00 (*0-683-06270-0*) Williams & Wilkins.

Surgery. L. Skrbic. (Illus.). 127p. (Orig.). (C). 1991. reprint ed. write for info. (*0-9626486-1-2*) Postgraduate Med Rev Ed.

***Surgery: A Clinical Approach.** Michael J. Stamos & Edward Passaro. LC 96-41027. 1996. write for info. (*0-443-08995-7*) Churchill.

Surgery: An Illustrated History. Ira M. Rutkow. LC 93-9820. (Illus.). 512p. (C). (gr. 13). 1993. text ed. 129.00 (*0-8016-6078-5*) Mosby Yr Bk.

Surgery: Clinical Manual. Richard M. Stillman. (Illus.). 663p. 1989. pap. text ed. 29.95 (*0-8385-1283-6*, A1283-9) Appleton & Lange.

Surgery: One Hundred & Fifty Years Ago. C. B. Tilanus. Ed. by H. T. Deelman. 1977. reprint ed. 12.50 (*0-85409-953-0*) Charles River Bks.

Surgery: Pretest Self-Assessment & Review. 7th ed. Ed. by Thomas K. King et al. LC 93-42940. (Clinical Sciences PreTest Ser.). 324p. 1994. pap. text ed. 17.95 (*0-07-052065-8*) McGraw-Hill HPD.

***Surgery: PreTest Self-Assessment & Review.** 8th ed. Ed. by Peter L. Geller & Richard S. Nitzberg. LC 97-20617. (Pretest Clinical Science Ser.). (Illus.). 336p. 1997. pap. 17.95 (*0-07-052533-1*) McGraw-Hill HPD.

Surgery: Review for New National Boards. Glenn W. Geelhoed. LC 94-79792. (Illus.). 246p. 1994. pap. 25.00 (*0-9632873-5-4*) J & S Pub VA.

Surgery: Scientific Principles & Practice. 2nd ed. Lazar Greenfield. LC 96-21918. 1784p. 1996. text ed. 110.00 (*0-397-51481-6*) Lppncott-Raven.

***Surgery: Scientific Principles & Practice.** 2nd ed. Lazar J. Greenfield et al. 1996. text ed. 134.95 (*0-397-51817-X*); text ed. 134.95 (*0-397-51832-3*) Lppncott-Raven.

***Surgery: 1997 Edition.** rev. ed. Samuel E. Wilson. 98p. 1997. pap. 12.75 (*1-881528-28-6*) Current Clin Strat.

Surgery & Arthroscopy of the Knee. Ed. by W. E. Muller & W. Hackenbruch. (Illus.). 800p. 1988. 199.00 (*0-387-17982-8*) Spr-Verlag.

Surgery & Pathology of the Middle Ear. Ed. by Jean F. Marquet. 1985. lib. bdg. 233.50 (*0-89838-707-8*) Kluwer Ac.

***Surgery & Recovery: How to Reduce Anxiety & Promote Healthy Healing.** Kaye Olson. 224p. 1997. pap. 12.95 (*1-890394-03-3*) Rhodes & Easton.

Surgery & Support of the Premature Infant. Ed. by P. Puri. (Modern Problems in Pediatrics Ser.: Vol. 23). (Illus.). x, 210p. 1985. 130.50 (*3-8055-4073-6*) S Karger.

Surgery, Anesthetics, & Radiology Scoring Guidelines. 60p. 1989. write for info. (*0-86688-201-4*) Joint Comm Hlthcare.

Surgery Annual, 1982, Vol. 14. Lloyd M. Nyhus. (Illus.). 1982. text ed. 90.00 (*0-8385-8719-4*, A8719-5) Appleton & Lange.

Surgery Annual, 1983, Vol. 15. Lloyd M. Nyhus. (Illus.). 416p. 1983. text ed. 90.00 (*0-8385-8721-6*, A8721-1) Appleton & Lange.

Surgery Annual, 1984, Vol. 16. Lloyd M. Nyhus. LC 69-18093. (Illus.). 432p. (C). 1984. text ed. 90.00 (*0-8385-8722-4*, A87229) Appleton & Lange.

Surgery Annual, 1987, Vol. 19. Ed. by Lloyd M. Nyhus. (Illus.). 384p. 1986. text ed. 90.00 (*0-8385-8794-1*, A8794-8) Appleton & Lange.

Surgery Annual, 1988, Vol. 20. Ed. by Lloyd M. Nyhus. (Illus.). 384p. 1988. text ed. 90.00 (*0-8385-8728-3*, A8728-6) Appleton & Lange.

Surgery Annual 1990. Lloyd M. Nyhus. 1990. text ed. 90. 00 (*0-8385-8735-6*) Appleton & Lange.

Surgery Annual, 1991, Vol. 23, Pt. 1. Ed. by Lloyd M. Nyhus. (Illus.). 242p. (C). 1990. text ed. 90.00 (*0-8385-8743-7*, A8743-5) Appleton & Lange.

Surgery Annual, 1991, Vol. 23, Pt. 2. Ed. by Lloyd M. Nyhus. (Illus.). 194p. (C). 1991. text ed. 90.00 (*0-8385-8744-5*, A8744-3) Appleton & Lange.

Surgery Annual, 1992, Vol. 24, Pt. 1. Ed. by Lloyd M. Nythus. 258p. (C). 1991. text ed. 90.00 (*0-8385-8745-3*, A8745-0) Appleton & Lange.

Surgery Annual, 1992, Vol. 24, Pt. 2. Lloyd M. Nyhus. (Illus.). 272p. 1992. text ed. 90.00 (*0-8385-8748-8*, A8748-4) Appleton & Lange.

Surgery Annual, 1993, Pt. 2. Lloyd M. Nyhus. (Illus.). 272p. 1993. text ed. 90.00 (*0-8385-8749-6*, A8749-2) Appleton & Lange.

Surgery Annual 1993, Vol. 25, Pt. 1. Lloyd M. Nyhus. (Illus.). 272p. (C). 1993. text ed. 90.00 (*0-8385-8798-4*, A8798-9) Appleton & Lange.

Surgery Annual 1994. Lloyd M. Nyhus. (Illus.). 288p. 1994. text ed. 90.00 (*0-8385-8531-0*, A8531-4) Appleton & Lange.

Surgery Annual 1995. Lloyd M. Nyhus. (C). 1995. text ed. 90.00 (*0-8385-7992-2*, A8799-7) Appleton & Lange.

Surgery at the District Hospital: Obstetrics, Gynaecology, Orthopaedics, & Traumatology. Ed. by J. Cook et al. 207p. (ENG, FRE, RUS & SPA.). 1991. pap. text ed. 22.50 (*92-4-154413-9*, 1150351) World Health.

***Surgery Book.** Youngson. 1997. pap. 17.95 (*0-312-15218-3*) St Martin.

Surgery Book: Seventy-Five of the Most Common Operations Illustrated & Explained. Robert M. Youngson. (Illus.). 448p. 1993. 27.95 (*0-312-09398-5*) St Martin.

Surgery Electives: What to Know Before the Doctor Operates, 2nd Edition, with Internet Addresses. 2nd ed. John McCabe. Ed. by Miriam Ingersol. LC 95-71658. 400p. 1996. pap. 19.95 (*1-884702-22-8*) Carmania Bks.

Surgery for Anaesthetists. Richard Zorab. 1989. 193.00 (*0-632-01371-0*) CRC Pr.

***Surgery for Bone & Soft-Tissue Tumors.** Ed. by Michael Simon & Dempsey Springfield. (Illus.). 1000p. 1997. text ed. 265.00 (*0-397-51396-8*) Lppncott-Raven.

Surgery for Cancer of the Larynx & Related Structures. 2nd ed. Carl E. Silver. Ed. by Larry McGrew. LC 95-17699. (Illus.). 288p. 1996. text ed. 135.00 (*0-7216-5266-2*) Saunders.

S

Surgery for Cancer of the Larynx & Related Structures. Carl E. Silver. LC 81-12242. (Illus.). 264p. reprint ed. pap. 75.30 (*0-7837-2580-9*, 2042739) Bks Demand.

Surgery for Cerebrovascular Disease. 2nd ed. Ed. by Wesley S. Moore. (Illus.). 736p. 1996. text ed. 220.00 (*0-7216-3624-1*) Saunders.

Surgery for Congenital Heart Defects. 2nd ed. Ed. by J. Stark & M. De Leval. LC 92-49450. (Illus.). 608p. 1993. text ed. 279.00 (*0-7216-3648-9*) Saunders.

***Surgery for Dental Students.** 4th ed. M. Woodruff & H. E. Berry. (Illus.). 370p. 1984. pap. write for info. (*0-632-01171-8*) Blackwell Sci.

Surgery for Endocrinological Diseases & Malformations in Childhood. Ed. by M. W. Gauderer & T. A. Angerpointner. (Progress in Pediatric Surgery Ser.: Vol. 26). (Illus.). 176p. 1991. 137.00 (*0-387-52524-6*) Spr-Verlag.

Surgery for Gastrointestinal Cancer: A Multidisciplinary Approach. Ed. by Harold J. Wanebo et al. LC 96-14257. 864p. 1996. text ed. 179.00 (*0-397-51518-9*) Lppncott-Raven.

***Surgery for Hyperopia & Presbyopia.** Ed. by Neal A. Sher. LC 96-24160. (Illus.). 1997. text ed. write for info. (*0-89640-340-8*) Igaku-Shoin.

***Surgery for Hyperopia & Presbyopia.** Neal A. Sher. LC 96-24160. 1997. write for info. (*4-260-14340-9*) Igaku-Shoin.

***Surgery for Hyperopia & Presbyopia.** Neal A. Sher. LC 96-24160. 1997. write for info. (*0-683-30333-3*) Williams & Wilkins.

Surgery for Mechanical Complications of Myocardial Infarction. Ed. by Tirone E. David. LC 93-23998. (Illus.). 252p. 1993. 156.00 (*1-879702-67-3*, R) CRC Pr.

Surgery for Morbid Obesity. John H. Linner. (Illus.). 275p. 1984. 138.00 (*0-387-90888-9*) Spr-Verlag.

Surgery for Newton. Paul D. Chan. (Current Clinical Strategies Ser.). 343p. (C). 1995. 34.95 incl. disk (*1-57443-004-1*) Educ Res Lab.

Surgery for Phonatory Disorders. Harvey M. Tucker. LC 81-38539. (Monographs in Clinical Otolaryngology: No. 3). (Illus.). 140p. reprint ed. pap. 39.90 (*0-7837-2587-6*, 2042749) Bks Demand.

Surgery for Rheumatoid Arthritis: A Comprehensive Team Approach. Mack L. Clayton & Charley J. Smyth. (Illus.). 414p. 1992. text ed. 99.00 (*0-443-08217-0*) Churchill.

Surgery for Spinal Cord Injuries. Ed. by Steven R. Garfin & Bruce E. Northrup. LC 93-258. (Principles & Techniques in Spine Surgery Ser.). 336p. 1993. text ed. 126.00 (*0-7817-0075-2*) Lppncott-Raven.

Surgery for Stroke. Greenhalgh. 1993. pap. text ed. 165.00 (*0-7020-1759-0*) HarBrace.

Surgery in AIDS. Forse. text ed. write for info. (*0-7216-5139-9*) Saunders.

Surgery in America: From the Colonial Era to the Twentieth Century. 2nd ed. A. S. Earle. LC 83-17808. (Illus.). 350p. 1983. text ed. 105.00 (*0-275-91389-9*, C1389, Praeger Pubs) Greenwood.

Surgery in & Around the Brain Stem & Third Ventricle. Ed. by Madjid Samii. (Illus.). 625p. 1986. 333.00 (*0-387-16581-9*) Spr-Verlag.

Surgery in Gynecological Oncology. A. P. Heintz. Ed. by C. Thomas Griffiths. (Developments in Oncology Ser.). 1983. lib. bdg. 158.50 (*0-89838-604-7*) Kluwer Ac.

Surgery in Rheumatoid Arthritis. Ed. by Ian F. Goldie. (Reconstruction Surgery & Traumatology Ser.: Vol. 18). (Illus.). vi, 214p. 1981. 88.00 (*3-8055-1445-X*) S Karger.

Surgery in the Elderly. Goldman. Date not set. write for info. (*0-7506-1374-2*) Buttrwrth-Heinemann.

Surgery in the Retroperitoneal Space. Rosenshein & Rock. 1989. 125.00 (*0-397-50949-9*) Lppncott-Raven.

Surgery in World War II 2 vols., Set. 1995. lib. bdg. 599.99 (*0-8490-6582-8*) Gordon Pr.

Surgery Nutrition Handbook. Mary Marian et al. LC 95-16240. (Nutrition Handbooks Ser.: Vol. 4). 96p. (gr. 13). 1995. pap. text ed. 15.95 (*0-412-07521-0*, Chap & Hall NY) Chapman & Hall.

Surgery of Anus, Rectum & Colon. Keighley. 1993. text ed. 439.00 (*0-7020-1278-5*) HarBrace.

Surgery of Basal Cell Carcinoma. Daniel Marchac. (Illus.). 130p. 1987. 150.00 (*0-387-18034-6*) Spr-Verlag.

***Surgery of Congenital Heart Disease: The Pediatric Cardiac Care Consortium 1984-1995.** Ed. by James H. Moller. (Perspectives in Pediatric Cardiology Ser.: Vol. 6). 1997. write for info. (*0-87993-678-9*) Futura Pub.

Surgery of Cranial Base Tumors. Laligam N. Sekhar & Ivo P. Janecka. 896p. 1992. text ed. 257.50 (*0-88167-877-5*, 2378) Lppncott-Raven.

Surgery of Cranial Base Tumors. Laligam N. Sekhar & Ivo P. Janecka. 896p. 1993. sl. 341.50 (*0-7817-0052-3*) Lppncott-Raven.

Surgery of Facial Bone Fractures. Ed. by Craig A. Foster & John E. Sherman. (Illus.). 273p. 1987. text ed. 95.00 (*0-443-08436-X*) Churchill.

Surgery of Female Incontinence. 2nd rev. ed. Ed. by S. L. Stanton & Emil A. Tanagho. (Illus.). 304p. 1986. 218.00 (*0-387-15821-9*) Spr-Verlag.

Surgery of Genitourinary Pelvic Tumors: An Anatomic Atlas. Edison J. Pontes. 136p. 1993. text ed. 124.95 (*0-471-58831-8*) Wiley.

***Surgery of Hand-Unit in Adults & Children, 2 vols.** Hosein A. Motamed. Incl. Vol. I. . LC 77-78228. (Illus.). 1997. reprint ed. (*0-910161-03-8*); Vol. II. . LC 77-78228. (Illus.). 1997. reprint ed. (*0-910161-04-6*); LC 77-78228. reprint ed. 450.00 (*0-910161-02-X*) Motamed Med Pub.

Surgery of Infants & Children: Scientific Principles & Practice. Keith T. Oldham. LC 96-43070. 1,888p. 1996. text ed. 250.00 (*0-397-51417-4*) Lppncott-Raven.

Surgery of Inflammatory Bowel Disorders: Vol. 14, CSI. Lee & Nolan. (Illus.). 1987. pap. 15.00 (*0-443-03439-7*) Churchill.

Surgery of Liver Disease in Children. Edward R. Howard. (Illus.). 288p. 1991. text ed. 185.00 (*0-7506-1360-2*) Buttrwrth-Heinemann.

Surgery of Male Infertility. Ed. by Marc Goldstein. LC 94-7749. (Illus.). 336p. 1994. text ed. 85.00 (*0-7216-6693-0*) Saunders.

Surgery of Peripheral Nerves. G. Morello & F. Pluchino. (Surgical Technique Ser.: Vol. XIV). 392p. 1988. text ed. 250.00 (*1-57235-043-1*) Piccin NY.

Surgery of Skull Base Meningiomas: With a Chapter on Pathology by G. F. Walter. Madjid Samii & M. Ammirati. (Illus.). 150p. 1993. 175.00 (*0-387-54016-4*) Spr-Verlag.

Surgery of Skull Base Tumors. Ed. by C. Gary Jackson. (Illus.). 291p. 1991. text ed. 135.00 (*0-443-08596-X*) Churchill.

Surgery of Spine Trauma. Ed. by Paul R. Meyer, Jr. (Illus.). 867p. 1989. text ed. 175.00 (*0-443-08122-0*) Churchill.

Surgery of Spine Trauma. Ed. by Paul R. Meyer, Jr. LC 88-23790. (Illus.). 879p. 1989. reprint ed. pap. 180.00 (*0-7837-9590-4*, 2060339) Bks Demand.

Surgery of Stomach, Duodenum & Small Intestine. 2nd ed. J. L. Sawyers & H. William Scottq. (Illus.). 968p. 1991. 175.00 (*0-86542-141-2*) Blackwell Sci.

Surgery of the Abdominal Wall. Ed. by J. P. Chevrel. Tr. by E. Goldstein from FRE. (Illus.). 290p. 1986. 238.00 (*0-387-12640-6*) Spr-Verlag.

Surgery of the Alimentary Tract: Mesentary Vasculature, Hernias, Small Intestine, Peritoneum, Omentum, Mesentary & Retroperitoneum, Surgical Nutrition, 5 vols., Set. 2nd ed. Richard T. Shackelford & George D. Zuidema. (Illus.). 600p. 1986. 490.00 (*0-7216-8087-9*) Saunders.

Surgery of the Arteria Profunda Femuralis. Ed. by Marco P. Merlini. LC 94-12558. 1994. 132.00 (*0-387-58067-0*) Spr-Verlag.

***Surgery of the Arteries to the Head.** Ramon Berguer & Edouard Kieffer. (Illus.). 236p. 1992. 189.00 (*0-387-97748-1*) Spr-Verlag.

Surgery of the Biliary Tract. Ed. by James Toouli. LC 92-49459. (Illus.). 408p. 1993. text ed. 125.00 (*0-443-04361-2*) Churchill.

Surgery of the Carotoid & Vertebral Arteries: For the Prevention of Stroke. Allan Callow. LC 95-15498. 434p. 1996. 150.00 (*0-683-01369-6*) Williams & Wilkins.

Surgery of the Cervical Spine. Howard S. An. (Illus.). 350p. 1994. 150.00 (*0-683-00128-0*) Williams & Wilkins.

Surgery of the Cervical Spine. Emery. Date not set. text ed. write for info. (*0-7216-5780-X*) Saunders.

Surgery of the Chest. 6th rev. ed. John A. Waldhausen et al. LC 95-21444. (Illus.). 000672p. (C). (gr. 13). 1995. text ed. 134.00 (*0-8151-9249-5*) Mosby Yr Bk.

Surgery of the Chest, 2 vols., Set. 6th ed. David C. Sabiston, Jr. & Frank C. Spencer. LC 94-22780. (Illus.). 2272p. 1995. text ed. 299.00 (*0-7216-5271-9*) Saunders.

Surgery of the Colon, Rectum, & Anus. Patrick W. Mazier et al. LC 93-40034. (Illus.). 992p. 1994. text ed. 239.00 (*0-7216-4689-1*) Saunders.

***Surgery of the Colon, Rectum & Anus.** 5th ed. Ed. by Fielding & Goldberg. (Rob & Smith's Operative Surgery Ser.). (Illus.). 940p. (C). 1993. text ed. 165.95 (*0-7506-1255-X*, Chap & Hall NY) Chapman & Hall.

Surgery of the Cranial Nerves of the Posterior Fossa. Ed. by Daniel L. Barrow. (Neurosurgical Topics Ser.: Bk. 13). (Illus.). 322p. 1993. 95.00 (*1-879284-02-2*) Am Assn Neuro.

***Surgery of the Craniovertebral Junction.** Curtis A. Dickman et al. LC 97-25003. 1997. write for info. (*3-13-107181-8*, Pub. by G Thieme GW) Thieme Med Pubs.

***Surgery of the Craniovertebral Junction.** Robert F. Spetzler et al. LC 97-25003. (Illus.). 784p. 1997. 249.00 (*0-86577-681-4*) Thieme Med Pubs.

Surgery of the Diencephalon. Ed. by Robert N. Holtzman & B. M. Stein. (Contemporary Perspectives in Neurosurgery Ser.: Vol. 1). (Illus.). 320p. 1989. 70.00 (*0-306-43054-1*, Plenum Med Bk) Plenum.

Surgery of the Ear & Temporal Bone. Ed. by Joseph B. Nadol, Jr. & Harold F. Schuknecht. (Illus.). 494p. 1992. text ed. 194.50 (*0-88167-803-1*, 2287) Lppncott-Raven.

Surgery of the Ear & Temporal Bone. Ed. by Joseph B. Nadol, Jr. & Harold F. Schuknecht. (Illus.). 494p. 1993. sl. 315.00 (*0-88167-935-6*) Lppncott-Raven.

Surgery of the Esophagus, Stomach, & Small Intestine. 5th ed. Ed. by Christopher Wastell et al. LC 94-21059. 1040p. 1995. text ed. 199.95 (*0-316-92442-3*) Lppncott-Raven.

Surgery of the Eye, 2 vols. Hoyt & Keates. Ed. by Stephen R. Waltman et al. (Illus.). 1204p. 1988. 280.00 (*0-443-08354-1*) Churchill.

Surgery of the Eyelid, Orbit, & Lacrimal System. Ed. by William B. Stewart. LC 93-19768. (Ophthalmology Monographs). 1993. write for info. (*1-56055-069-4*) Am Acad Ophthal.

Surgery of the Eyelids & Orbit: An Anatomical Approach. Bradley N. Lemke & Robert C. Della Rocca. (Illus.). 1989. text ed. 175.00 (*0-8385-7500-5*, A7500-0) Appleton & Lange.

***Surgery of the Foot.** Sigvard T. Hansen. 1996. text ed. write for info. (*0-397-51811-0*) Lppncott-Raven.

Surgery of the Foot. Kent K. Wu. LC 85-19849. 551p. reprint ed. pap. 157.10 (*0-7837-2755-0*, 2043135) Bks Demand.

Surgery of the Foot & Ankle. Helal. 893p. 1995. text ed. 175.00 (*0-397-51423-9*) Lppncott-Raven.

Surgery of the Foot & Ankle. Kenneth A. Johnson. (Illus.). 320p. 1989. text ed. 155.00 (*0-88167-398-6*) Lppncott-Raven.

Surgery of the Foot & Ankle. 6th rev. ed. Ed. by Roger A. Mann & Michael J. Coughlin. LC 92-19174. Orig. Title: Surgery of the Foot & Ankle. 1703p. (C). (gr. 13). 1992. text ed. 280.00 (*0-8016-6683-X*) Mosby Yr Bk.

Surgery of the Foot & Ankle see Surgery of the Foot & Ankle

Surgery of the Gallbladder & Bile Ducts. Lawrence M. Way & Carlos A. Pellegrini. (Illus.). 726p. 1987. text ed. 147.00 (*0-7216-9139-0*) Saunders.

Surgery of the Hand & Upper Extremity, 1. Clayton A. Peimer. write for info. (*0-07-049388-X*) McGraw.

Surgery of the Hand & Upper Extremity, 2. Clayton A. Peimer. write for info. (*0-07-049389-8*) McGraw.

Surgery of the Hand & Upper Extremity, 2 vols., Set. Ed. by Clayton A. Peimer. LC 95-32395. 2336p. 1996. text ed. 295.00 (*0-07-049293-X*) McGraw-Hill HPD.

Surgery of the Head & Neck. 3rd ed. Robert A. Wise & Harvey W. Baker. LC 73-93801. (AHandbook of Operatiave Surgery Ser.). 379p. reprint ed. pap. 108.10 (*0-317-29898-4*, 2021839) Bks Demand.

Surgery of the Heart & Aorta. Cooley. pap. text ed. write for info. (*0-7216-4371-X*) Saunders.

Surgery of the Hip Joint. Ed. by Raymond G. Tronzo. LC 72-79357. 856p. reprint ed. pap. 180.00 (*0-317-27958-0*, 2056019) Bks Demand.

Surgery of the Hip Joint, Vol. 1. 2nd ed. Ed. by Raymond G. Tronzo. (Illus.). 490p. 1984. 186.00 (*0-387-90922-2*) Spr-Verlag.

Surgery of the Hip Joint, Vol. 2. 2nd ed. Ed. by Raymond G. Tronzo. (Illus.). 465p. 1987. 296.00 (*0-387-96275-1*) Spr-Verlag.

Surgery of the Intracranial Venous System: Embryology, Anatomy, Pathophysiology, Neuroradiology, Diagnosis, & Treatments. Ed. by A. Hakuba. (Illus.). 616p. 1996. 250.00 (*4-431-70167-2*) Spr-Verlag.

Surgery of the Iris & the Ciliary Body: Proceedings of the Ophthalmic Microsurgery Study Group, 4th, Lund, Sweden, July 4-7, 1972. Ophthalmic Microsurgery Study Group Staff. Ed. by E. Palm & G. Mackensen. (Advances in Ophthalmology Ser.: Vol. 30). 300p. 1975. 158.50 (*3-8055-1844-7*) S Karger.

Surgery of the Knee. 2nd ed. Ed. by John N. Insall. (Illus.). 1344p. 1993. text ed. 250.00 (*0-443-08734-2*) Churchill.

Surgery of the Larynx. Byron J. Bailey & Hugh F. Biller. (Illus.). 471p. 1985. text ed. 135.00 (*0-7216-1472-8*) Saunders.

Surgery of the Larynx & Trachea. Dedo. (Illus.). 352p. (C). 1990. 125.00 (*1-55664-063-3*) Mosby Yr Bk.

Surgery of the Leg & Foot. August Rutt. (Hackenbroch Ser.). 1980. text ed. 135.00 (*0-7216-4446-5*) Saunders.

Surgery of the Lip. Ed. by K. Calhoun & C. Stiernberg. (American Academy of Facial Plastic & Reconstructive Surgery Monograph). (Illus.). 112p. 1991. pap. text ed. 79.00 (*0-86577-409-9*) Thieme Med Pubs.

Surgery of the Liver & Biliary Tract. Ed. by L. H. Blumgart. (Illus.). 1568p. 1988. text ed. 425.00 (*0-443-03149-5*) Churchill.

Surgery of the Liver & Biliary Tract. 2nd ed. Ed. by Leslie H. Blumgart. LC 94-5894. (Illus.). 350.00 (*0-443-04500-3*) Churchill.

Surgery of the Liver & Intrahepatic Bile Ducts. I. Fagarasanu. Ed. by Henry J. Heimlich. LC 77-86984. (Illus.). 490p. 1972. 27.60 (*0-87527-007-7*) Green.

Surgery of the Male Reproductive Tract. Ed. by Larry I. Lipshultz et al. (Clinics in Andrology Ser.: No. 2). (Illus.). 275p. 1980. lib. bdg. 175.00 (*90-247-2315-9*) Kluwer Ac.

Surgery of the Mandible. Byron J. Bailey. Ed. by Richard Holt. (American Academy of Facial Plastic & Reconstructive Surgery Monograph). 1987. text ed. 87.00 (*0-86577-239-8*) Thieme Med Pubs.

***Surgery of the Mouth & Jaws.** Ed. by J. R. Moore. (Illus.). 880p. 1986. write for info. (*0-632-00736-2*) Blackwell Sci.

Surgery of the Musculoskeletal System, 5 vols. 2nd ed. Ed. by C. McCollister Evarts. (Illus.). 5214p. 1990. text ed. 550.00 (*0-443-08516-1*) Churchill.

Surgery of the Musculoskeletal System, 1. Ed. by C. McCollister Evarts. LC 83-7865. (Illus.). 1138p. reprint ed. pap. 180.00 (*0-8357-7919-X*) Bks Demand.

Surgery of the Musculoskeletal System, 2. Ed. by C. McCollister Evarts. LC 83-7865. (Illus.). 1168p. reprint ed. pap. 180.00 (*0-8357-7920-3*) Bks Demand.

Surgery of the Musculoskeletal System, 3. Ed. by C. McCollister Evarts. LC 83-7865. (Illus.). 1142p. reprint ed. pap. 180.00 (*0-8357-7921-1*) Bks Demand.

Surgery of the Musculoskeletal System, 4. Ed. by C. McCollister Evarts. LC 83-7865. (Illus.). reprint ed. write for info. (*0-8357-7922-X*) Bks Demand.

Surgery of the Musculoskeletal System, Vols. 1-4. Ed. by C. McCollister Evarts. LC 83-7865. (Illus.). reprint ed. pap. 160.00 (*0-685-74197-4*, 2036348) Bks Demand.

Surgery of the Neck. P. G. Cevese et al. (Surgical Technique Ser.: Vol. XII). 422p. 1988. text ed. 250.00 (*1-57235-037-7*) Piccin NY.

Surgery of the Neurogenic Bladder. P. Magasi. 148p. (C). 1982. 54.00 (*963-05-2892-4*, Pub. by Akad Kiado HU) St Mut.

Surgery of the Newborn. Neill V. Freeman et al. 1994. 165.00 (*0-443-04346-9*) Churchill.

Surgery of the Oesophagus. Ed. by Glyn G. Jamieson. (Illus.). 960p. 1988. text ed. 225.00 (*0-443-03409-5*) Churchill.

Surgery of the Oesophagus. 2nd ed. Thomas P. J. Hennessy & A. Cuschieri. (Illus.). 368p. 1992. 185.00 (*0-7506-1498-6*) Buttrwrth-Heinemann.

Surgery of the Pancreas. John R. Brooks. (Illus.). 528p. 1983. text ed. 135.00 (*0-7216-2082-5*) Saunders.

Surgery of the Pancreas. Ed. by Michael Trede & David C. Carter. LC 93-12700. 700p. 1993. text ed. 225.00 (*0-443-04427-9*) Churchill.

***Surgery of the Pancreas.** 2nd ed. M. Trede & David C. Carter. LC 97-7856. 1997. write for info. (*0-443-05522-X*) Churchill.

Surgery of the Paranasal Sinuses. 2nd ed. Blitzer et al. (Illus.). 480p. 1991. text ed. 165.00 (*0-7216-3583-0*) Saunders.

***Surgery of the Peripheral Nerve.** S. E. Mackinnon. (Illus.). 662p. 1988. 189.00 (*0-86577-283-5*) Thieme Med Pubs.

Surgery of the Posterior Fossa. Ed. by William A. Buchheit & Raymond C. Truex, Jr. LC 78-73554. (Seminars in Neurological Surgery Ser.). 197p. 1979. reprint ed. pap. 56.20 (*0-608-00315-8*, 2061032) Bks Demand.

Surgery of the Sellar Region & Paranasal Sinuses. Ed. by Madjid Samii. (Illus.). xxii, 583p. 1991. 325.00 (*0-387-53697-3*) Spr-Verlag.

Surgery of the Shoulder: Proceedings of the Sixth International Congress on Surgery of the Shoulder, Held in Helsinki, 27 June-1 July 1995 & Stockholm, 2-4 July 1995. Ed. by Martti Vastamaki & Pekka Jalovaara. LC 95-11221. (International Congress Ser.: Vol. 1085). 536p. 1995. 275.50 (*0-444-81913-4*, Excerpta Medica) Elsevier.

Surgery of the Skull Base. Madjid Samii. (Illus.). 512p. 1989. 373.00 (*0-387-18448-1*) Spr-Verlag.

***Surgery of the Skull Base: An Interdisciplinary Approach.** Madjid Samii & Wolfgang Draf. 525p. 1989. 342.00 (*3-540-18448-1*) Spr-Verlag.

Surgery of the Small & Large Intestine. Herbert B. Greenlee. LC 72-85707. (Handbook of Operative Surgery Ser.). 426p. reprint ed. pap. 121.50 (*0-318-34995-7*, 2030843) Bks Demand.

Surgery of the Spinal Cord. August Livshitz. Tr. by V. E. Tatarchenko from RUS. LC 90-4997. 440p. 1991. 65.00 (*0-8236-6257-8*) Intl Univs Pr.

Surgery of the Spinal Cord: Potential for Regeneration & Recovery. Ed. by Robert N. Holtzman & B. M. Stein. (Contemporary Perspectives in Neurosurgery Ser.). (Illus.). 344p. 1991. 133.00 (*0-387-97625-6*) Spr-Verlag.

Surgery of the Spine: A Combined Orthopaedic & Neurosurgical Approach. G. F. Findlay & R. Owen. (Illus.). 1264p. 1992. 395.00 (*0-632-03021-6*) Blackwell Sci.

Surgery of the Spine: Surgical Anatomy & Operative Approaches. R. Louis. (Illus.). 328p. 1983. 288.00 (*0-387-11412-2*) Spr-Verlag.

Surgery of the Stomach. Ed. by H. D. Becker et al. (Illus.). 390p. 1988. 284.00 (*0-387-17116-9*) Spr-Verlag.

Surgery of the Temporomandibular Joint. 2nd ed. D. A. Keith. (Illus.). 336p. 1992. 125.00 (*0-86542-211-7*) Blackwell Sci.

***Surgery of the Third Ventricle.** 2nd ed. Michael L. Apuzzo. LC 96-29699. 1997. write for info. (*0-683-00249-X*) Williams & Wilkins.

Surgery of the Thymus. Ed. by J. C. Givel. (Illus.). 360p. 1990. 238.00 (*0-387-16315-8*) Spr-Verlag.

Surgery of the Thyroid & Parathyroid Gland. 3rd ed. Cady & Rossi. (Illus.). 368p. 1990. text ed. 99.00 (*0-7216-3462-1*) Saunders.

Surgery of the Upper Respiratory System, Vol. 1. 3rd ed. William W. Montgomery. LC 96-5668. 1996. write for info. (*0-683-06121-6*) Williams & Wilkins.

Surgery of the Upper Respiratory System, Vol. 2. 2nd ed. William W. Montgomery. LC 78-9004. (Illus.). 760p. 1988. text ed. 110.00 (*0-8121-1142-7*) Williams & Wilkins.

Surgery of Vertebrobasilar Aneurysms: London, Ontario, Experience on 1,767 Patients. C. G. Drake et al. 400p. 1996. 185.00 (*3-211-82696-3*) Spr-Verlag.

***Surgery Office Manual.** (Office Manual Ser.). 200p. 1995. ring bd. 145.00 (*1-890018-08-2*) Anadem Pubng.

Surgery on Call. 2nd ed. Leonard G. Gomella. 1995. pap. text ed. 23.95 (*0-8385-8746-1*) Appleton & Lange.

Surgery on Codimension 2 Submanifolds. M. H. Freedman. LC 77-23944. (Memoirs Ser.: No. 12/191). 93p. 1977. pap. 21.00 (*0-8218-2191-1*, MEMO/12/191) Am Math.

Surgery on File, 4 Vols., Set. Diagram Group Staff. Date not set. ring bd. 275.00 (*0-8160-1084-6*) Facts on File.

Surgery on File: Eye, Ear, Nose & Throat Surgery. Diagram Group Staff. (Illus.). 128p. 1989. ring bd. 85.00 (*0-8160-1770-0*) Facts on File.

Surgery on File: Obstetrics & Gynecology. Diagram Group Staff. (Illus.). 128p. 1988. ring bd. 85.00 (*0-8160-1768-9*) Facts on File.

Surgery on File: Orthopedics & Trauma Surgery. Diagram Group Staff. (Illus.). 128p. 1988. ring bd. 85.00 (*0-8160-1771-9*) Facts on File.

Surgery on File: Pediatrics. Diagram Group Staff. (Illus.). 128p. 1988. ring bd. 85.00 (*0-8160-1769-7*) Facts on File.

Surgery on Simply-Connected Manifolds. W. Browder. LC 70-175907. (Ergebnisse der Mathematik und Ihrer Grenzgebiete Ser.: Vol. 65). 140p. 1972. 42.95 (*0-387-05629-7*) Spr-Verlag.

Surgery Review: A Self-Assessment Study Manual. Ed. by M. D. Ram. LC 87-14466. 225p. 1987. pap. 32.50 (*0-941022-09-9*) Davies Pubng.

Surgery Study Cards. Gott. 1989. pap. text ed. 72.00 (*0-7216-2804-4*) Saunders.

Surgery Survival Guide: A Manual for Interns & Medical Students. 3rd ed. Michael S. Godin. (Illus.). 128p. 1993. pap. 16.95 (*0-9621594-2-5*) Bluebelle Med Co.

Surgery Theory & Geometry of Representations. T. Tom Dieck & I. Hambleton. (DMV Seminar Ser.: No. 11). 124p. 1988. 44.50 (*0-8176-2204-7*) Birkhauser.

Surgery, Transplantation, Oral Medicine, Neurophysiology & Psychology see Medical Primatology 1972: Selected Papers, Proceedings

Surgery Upper GI Tract. 5th ed. Jamison. (Operative Surgery Ser.). Date not set. write for info. (*0-7506-0317-8*) Chapman & Hall.

Surgery with Coefficients. G. A. Anderson. (Lecture Notes in Mathematics Ser.: Vol. 591). 1977. 13.00 (*3-540-08250-6*) Spr-Verlag.

Surges-McKay: History of the Surges-McKay Families; Also Allied Families, Pflueger, Reibel, Bouville, Beaune. J. R. Crossman. (Illus.). 60p. 1994. reprint ed. pap. 13.50 (*0-8328-4092-0*) Higginson Bk Co.

Surges, Sags & Spikes: Protecting Your Personal Computer from Electrical Power Problems. rev. ed. Mark Waller. (Illus.). 240p. (C). 1992. reprint ed. pap. 19.95 (*0-7906-1019-1*) Prompt Publns.

Surgical Adhesives & Sealants: Current Technology & Applications. Ed. by David Sierra & Renato Saltz. LC 95-61620. 260p. 1995. pap. 69.95 (*1-56676-327-4*) Technomic.

Surgical Anatomy. 2nd ed. Healey, Jr. (Illus.). 352p. (gr. 13). 1990. 79.00 (*1-55664-127-3*) Mosby Yr Bk.

Surgical Anatomy: The Embryologic & Anatomic Basis of Modern Surgery. John E. Skandalakis & William C. Wood. (Illus.). 450p. 1996. text ed. 125.00 (*1-57626-004-6*) Quality Med Pub.

Surgical Anatomy & Techniques: A Resident's Pocket Manual. John E. Skandalakis et al. LC 94-17332. (Illus.). 674p. 1996. 34.00 (*0-387-94081-2*) Spr-Verlag.

Surgical Anatomy of Head & Neck. J. Krmpotic-Nenanic et al. (Illus.). 345p. 1988. 454.00 (*0-387-17414-1*) Spr-Verlag.

Surgical Anatomy of the Ear & Temporal Bone. Bruce Proctor. (Illus.). 240p. 1989. text ed. 79.00 (*0-86577-295-9*) Thieme Med Pubs.

Surgical Anatomy of the Face. Wayne F. Larrabee, Jr. & Kathleen H. Makielski. LC 92-21808. 240p. 1992. text ed. 152.50 (*0-88167-945-3*) Lppncott-Raven.

Surgical Anatomy of the Face, Set. Wayne F. Larrabee, Jr. & Kathleen H. Makielski. LC 92-21808. 240p. 1993. sl. 184.00 (*0-7817-0053-1*) Lppncott-Raven.

Surgical Anatomy of the Nose. M. Eugene Tardy, Jr. (Illus.). 128p. 1990. text ed. 115.50 (*0-88167-636-5*, 2098) Lppncott-Raven.

Surgical Anatomy of the Orbit. Barry M. Zide & Glenn W. Jelks. (Illus.). 88p. 1985. text ed. 115.50 (*0-88167-054-5*) Lppncott-Raven.

Surgical Anatomy of the Orbit, Set. Barry M. Zide & Glenn W. Jelks. (Illus.). 88p. 1985. sl. 205.00 (*0-88167-203-3*) Lppncott-Raven.

Surgical & Dental Instruments: Snowden & Brother (1860) & John Weiss & Son (1863) James M. Edmonson & Snowden & Brother Staff. LC 97-13781. (Illus.). 340p. 1997. reprint ed. 125.00 (*0-930405-72-2*, NP33942) Norman SF.

Surgical & Interventional Cardiovascular Pathology: Basic Principles & Clinical Correlations. Schoen. 320p. 1989. text ed. 115.00 (*0-7216-2457-X*) Saunders.

Surgical & Medical Instruments & Equipment Industry. 390p. 1990. 850.00 (*0-686-32755-1*) Busn Trend.

Surgical & Medical Management of Venous Disease. Seshadri Raju. LC 96-31993. 1995. 110.00 (*0-683-07111-4*) Williams & Wilkins.

Surgical & Prosthetic Voice Restoration after Total & Subtotal Laryngectomy: Proceedings of the 6th International Congress, San Sebastian, 29 September-1 October 1995. Ed. by J. Algaba. (International Congress Ser.: No. 1112). 432p. 1996. text ed. 200.75 (*0-444-82345-X*, Excerpta Medica) Elsevier.

Surgical Approach to Head & Neck Anatomy. Dolwick. 1993. write for info. (*0-397-50970-7*) Lppncott-Raven.

Surgical Approaches for Internal Fixation. T. Ruedi et al. (Illus.). 180p. 1983. 154.00 (*0-387-12809-3*) Spr-Verlag.

Surgical Approaches to Cutaneous Melanoma. Ed. by C. M. Balch. (Pigment Cell Ser.: Vol. 7). (Illus.). viii, 212p. 1985. 136.00 (*3-8055-4055-8*) S Karger.

Surgical Approaches to the Facial Skeleton. Ed. by Edward Ellis, III & Michael F. Zide. LC 94-27364. (Illus.). 223p. 1995. 189.00 (*0-683-02794-8*) Williams & Wilkins.

Surgical Approaches to the Foot & Ankle. George B. Holmes, Jr. 224p. 1994. text ed. 95.00 (*0-07-030029-1*) McGraw-Hill HPD.

Surgical Approaches to the Spine. Todd A. Albert et al. (Illus.). 272p. 1997. text ed. 125.00 (*0-7216-4554-2*) Saunders.

Surgical Approaches to the Spine: An Atlas of Surgical Anatomy. Robert G. Watkins. (Illus.). 190p. 1983. 234.00 (*0-387-90758-0*) Spr-Verlag.

***Surgical Approaches to the Vessels.** Ed. by Alain Branchereau & Ramon Berguer. 1997. write for info. (*0-87993-664-9*) Futura Pub.

Surgical Arena. Peter Grant. LC 93-84589. 308p. 1993. 21.95 (*0-938539-11-6*) Newmark Pub.

Surgical Art of Harvey Cushing. Ed. by Peter M. Black. (Illus.). 192p. 1992. 45.00 (*1-879284-10-3*) Am Assn Neuro.

Surgical Atlas of External Rhinoplasty: Decortication Approach. Slobodan B. Jugo. LC 95-8380. (Illus.). 1995. write for info. (*0-443-04690-5*) Churchill.

Surgical Atlas of Gynecologic Oncology. Ed. by Donald D. Gallup & O. Eduardo Talledo. LC 93-32871. 1994. text ed. 87.00 (*0-7216-3980-1*) Saunders.

***Surgical Atlas of Sports Medicine.** Miller. Date not set. text ed. write for info. (*0-7216-7307-4*) Saunders.

Surgical Attending Rounds. F. Lee & C. Dyke. 450p. 1992. pap. 29.50 (*0-8121-1470-1*) Williams & Wilkins.

Surgical Audit. 2nd ed. Alan B. Pollock & Mary Evans. 296p. 1993. 85.00 (*0-7506-0774-2*) Buttrwrth-Heinemann.

Surgical Beauty Racket. Kendall Moore & Sally Thompson. LC 78-51044. 1979. 22.95 (*0-87949-126-4*) Ashley Bks.

Surgical Care: Physiologic Approach to Clinical Management. Ed. by Robert E. Condon & Jerome J. DeCosse. LC 79-21864. 487p. reprint ed. pap. 138.80 (*0-7837-1474-2*, 2057169) Bks Demand.

***Surgical Care for the Elderly.** 2nd ed. R. Benton Adkins, Jr. & H. William Scott, Jr. LC 97-23283. 656p. 1997. text ed. write for info. (*0-7817-1450-8*) Lppncott-Raven.

Surgical Care in the United States: A Policy Perspective. Ed. by Madelon L. Finkel. LC 88-606. (Contemporary Medicine & Public Health Ser.). 336p. 1988. text ed. 40.00 (*0-8018-3638-7*) Johns Hopkins.

Surgical Care, No. 2. Ed. by Robert E. Condon & Jerome DeCosse. LC 82-26127. 442p. reprint ed. pap. 126.00 (*0-7837-1483-1*, 2057178) Bks Demand.

Surgical Care of Voice Disorders. W. J. Gould & V. L. Lawrence. (Disorders of Human Communication Ser.: Vol. 7). (Illus.). 130p. 1984. 54.95 (*0-387-81777-8*) Spr-Verlag.

Surgical Complications: A Self-Instructional Guide, Bk. 4. 3rd rev. ed. Dale S. Bloomquist et al. Ed. by James R. Hooley & James R. Whitacre. (Illus.). 64p. 1983. pap. 7.95 (*0-89939-041-2*) Stoma Pr.

Surgical Complications & Wound Healing in the Small Animal Practice. Joseph Harari. LC 92-20695. (Illus.). 432p. 1993. pap. text ed. 61.00 (*0-7216-3984-4*) Saunders.

Surgical Consultations: Update 1. Beahrs et al. 512p. 1993. 75.00 (*0-8151-0552-5*, Yr Bk Med Pubs) Mosby Yr Bk.

Surgical Consultations: Update 2. Beahrs et al. 512p. 1994. 75.00 (*0-8151-0553-3*, Yr Bk Med Pubs) Mosby Yr Bk.

Surgical Consultations: Update 3. Beahrs et al. 512p. 1995. 75.00 (*0-8151-0554-1*, Yr Bk Med Pubs) Mosby Yr Bk.

Surgical Consultations: Update 4. Beahrs et al. 1996. 75.00 (*0-8151-0555-X*, Yr Bk Med Pubs) Mosby Yr Bk.

Surgical Correction of Dentofacial Deformities, 3 vols., 1. William H. Bell et al. LC 76-27050. 1980. text ed. 220.00 (*0-7216-1675-5*) Saunders.

Surgical Correction of Dentofacial Deformities, 3 vols., 2. William H. Bell et al. LC 76-27050. 1980. text ed. 220.00 (*0-7216-1707-7*) Saunders.

Surgical Correction of Dentofacial Deformities, 3 vols., 3. Ed. by William H. Bell et al. LC 76-27050. (Illus.). 2565p. 1985. 135.00 (*0-7216-1740-9*) Saunders.

Surgical Critical Care. Howard Corwin. Date not set. write for info. (*0-393-71031-9*) Norton.

Surgical Critical Care. Moylan. 600p. (gr. 13). 1994. text ed. 135.00 (*1-55664-163-X*, Yr Bk Med Pubs) Mosby Yr Bk.

Surgical Critical Care. John A. Weigelt. LC 94-44206. (Illus.). 416p. 1995. text ed. 99.00 (*0-7216-3368-4*) Saunders.

***Surgical Cross Coder: Cross-Reference CPT to ICD-9 HCPCS & Other Major Code Groups.** (Illus.). (Orig.). 1997. pap. 79.95 (*1-56337-194-4*) Medicode Inc.

Surgical Decision Making. F. T. De Dombal. LC 92-49547. (Illus.). 164p. 1993. pap. text ed. 42.50 (*0-7506-0704-1*) Buttrwrth-Heinemann.

Surgical Decision Making. 3rd ed. Lawrence Norton et al. (Illus.). 368p. 1992. text ed. 89.50 (*0-7216-6598-5*) Saunders.

Surgical Dermatology. David J. Eedy et al. LC 95-52144. (Illus.). 288p. 1996. pap. 99.95 (*0-632-03425-4*) Blackwell Sci.

Surgical Dermatology: Advances in Current. Henry H. Roenigk. 567p. (C). (gr. 13). 1993. 135.00 (*0-8151-7414-4*, Yr Bk Med Pubs) Mosby Yr Bk.

Surgical Dermatopathology. Ed. by M. E. Maloney et al. (Illus.). 608p. 1995. write for info. (*0-86542-299-0*) Blackwell Sci.

Surgical Diagnosis & Management, No. 2. Dunn. 640p. 1991. pap. 49.95 (*0-632-02782-7*) Blackwell Sci.

Surgical Diagnosis & Methods of Examination. B. P. Chatterjee. (C). 1989. 150.00 (*0-89771-366-4*, Pub. by Current Dist II) St Mut.

***Surgical Diagnostic & Therapeutic Instruments.** J. J. Stanek. (Illus.). 174p. 1986. write for info. (*0-632-01177-7*) Blackwell Sci.

Surgical Disease of the Billary Tract & Pancreas. Braasch & Tompkins. 800p. (C). (gr. 13). 1994. text ed. 140.00 (*0-8016-6684-8*) Mosby Yr Bk.

Surgical Diseases in Pregnancy. Ed. by L. A. Cibils. (Clinical Perspectives in Obstetrics & Gynecology Ser.). (Illus.). xi, 208p. 1990. 80.00 (*0-387-97203-X*) Spr-Verlag.

***Surgical Diseases of the Pancreas.** 2nd ed. John M. Howard. LC 97-22075. 1997. write for info. (*0-683-18019-3*) Williams & Wilkins.

Surgical Diseases of the Pancreas. John M. Howard et al. LC 85-15847. 978p. reprint ed. pap. 180.00 (*0-7837-2716-X*, 2043096) Bks Demand.

Surgical Diseases of the Pleura & Chest Wall. R. Maurice Hood. (Illus.). 269p. 1986. text ed. 80.00 (*0-7216-1401-9*) Saunders.

***Surgical Diseases of the Spleen.** J. R. Hiatt et al. LC 96-41244. (Illus.). 345p. 1996. 149.00 (*3-540-61781-7*) Spr-Verlag.

***Surgical Diseases of the Tropics: Handbook.** Ricardo V. Cohen & Frederico Aun. LC 96-27741. (On Call In... Ser.). 362p. write for info. (*1-57059-356-6*) R G Landes.

Surgical Disorders of the Fourth Ventricle. Alan R. Cohen. 512p. 1995. 195.00 (*0-86542-360-1*) Blackwell Sci.

Surgical Disorders of the Peripheral Nerves. 2nd ed. Herbert Seddon. LC 75-9991. 350p. reprint ed. pap. 99.80 (*0-8357-3376-9*, 2039622) Bks Demand.

Surgical Disorders of the Sacrum. Ed. by James R. Doty & Setti S. Rengachary. LC 93-2421. 320p. 1993. 99.00 (*0-86577-494-3*) Thieme Med Pubs.

Surgical Disorders of the Shoulder. Ed. by Michael S. Watson. (Illus.). 662p. 1991. text ed. 200.00 (*0-443-03889-9*) Churchill.

***Surgical Efficiency & Economy: Proceedings of the 3rd World-Conference.** P. Dohrmann et al. 1997. pap. 99.00 (*0-86577-733-0*) Thieme Med Pubs.

Surgical Emergencies in Children: A Practical Guide. Ed. by Peter A. Raine et al. LC 94-27819. (Illus.). 416p. 1994. 130.00 (*0-7506-1389-0*) Buttrwrth-Heinemann.

Surgical Emergencies in the Newborn. J. Alexander Haller & James L. Talbert. LC 79-135685. 163p. reprint ed. pap. 46.50 (*0-317-07970-0*, 2014548) Bks Demand.

Surgical Endocrinology. John Lynn & Stephen Bloom. (Illus.). 592p. 1993. 250.00 (*0-7506-1390-4*) Buttrwrth-Heinemann.

Surgical Endocrinology: Clinical Syndromes. 2nd ed. Stanley R. Friesen & Norman W. Thompson. LC 65-10267. (Illus.). 400p. 1990. text ed. 120.00 (*0-397-50861-1*, Lippnctt) Lppncott-Raven.

Surgical Endodontics. J. Gutmann. (Illus.). 468p. 1991. 65.00 (*1-56386-030-9*) Ishiyaku Euro.

Surgical Endodontics: A Colour Manual. 2nd ed. Ian E. Barnes et al. (Illus.). 128p. 1991. text ed. 85.00 (*0-7236-1571-3*) Buttrwrth-Heinemann.

Surgical Endoscopy. Ed. by Thomas L. Dent. LC 85-5298. (Illus.). 551p. reprint ed. pap. 159.60 (*0-8357-7611-5*, 2056934) Bks Demand.

Surgical Exposure of the Spine: An Extensile Approach. Ed. by AANS Publications Committee & Edward C. Benzel. (Neurosurgical Special Topics Ser.). (Illus.). 200p. 1995. 95.00 (*1-879284-25-1*) Am Assn Neuro.

Surgical Exposures in Orthopaedic Surgery: The Anatomic Approach. Stanley Hoppenfeld & Piet DeBoer. (Illus.). 640p. 1984. text ed. 165.00 (*0-397-50597-3*, 65-07628, Lippnctt) Lppncott-Raven.

Surgical Exposures in Orthopaedics. 2nd ed. Stanley Hoppenfeld. 624p. (C). 1994. text ed. 165.00 (*0-397-51044-6*) Lppncott-Raven.

Surgical Geriatric Gynecology. V. Jaluvka. (Contributions to Gynecology & Obstetrics Ser.: Vol. 7). (Illus.). x, 174p. 1980. pap. 65.75 (*3-8055-3070-6*) S Karger.

Surgical Gynecologic Oncology. Ed. by E. Burghardt et al. LC 92-49606. 1993. 249.00 (*0-86577-473-0*) Thieme Med Pubs.

Surgical Gynecologic Techniques. F. Novak. 422p. 1978. text ed. 112.00 (*1-57235-025-3*) Piccin NY.

Surgical Hemotherapy. Ed. by P. Lundsgaard-Hansen. (Bibliotheca Haematologica Ser.: No. 46). (Illus.). viii, 252p. 1980. pap. 72.00 (*3-8055-0361-X*) S Karger.

Surgical Infections. Ed. by Donald E. Fry. (Illus.). 787p. 1995. text ed. 99.95 (*0-316-29426-8*) Lppncott-Raven.

Surgical Infections: Diagnosis & Treatment. Ed. by Jonathan L. Meakins. LC 93-29195. (Illus.). 500p. (C). 1993. text ed. 89.00 (*0-89454-016-5*) Sci Am Medicine.

Surgical Infectious Diseases. 3rd ed. Howard Simmons. LC 94-20995. (C). 1994. text ed. 195.00 (*0-8385-8754-2*, A8754-2) Appleton & Lange.

Surgical Instruments: A Pocket Guide. Maryann P. Wells & Mary Bradley. (Illus.). 392p. 1992. pap. text ed. 28.00 (*0-7216-4311-6*) Saunders.

Surgical Instruments in Greek & Roman Times. J. G. Milne. (Illus.). 201p. 1991. 25.00 (*0-89005-127-5*) Ares.

Surgical Instruments of the Hindus, 2 vols. Girindranath Mukhopadhyaya. LC 75-23714. reprint ed. 65.00 (*0-404-13340-1*) AMS Pr.

Surgical Intensive Care. George T. Shires. LC 92-48912. (Illus.). 1475p. 1993. text ed. 99.95 (*0-316-78083-7*) Lppncott-Raven.

Surgical Intern Pocket Survival Guide. Ronald Chamberlain. 78p. 1993. pap. text ed. 7.50 (*0-9634063-5-3*) Intl Med Pub.

Surgical Intuition: What It Is & How to Get It. Ed. by Robert M. Hamm & Charles M. Abernathy. LC 93-77760. (Illus.). 436p. 1995. text ed. 39.95 (*1-56053-059-6*) Hanley & Belfus.

Surgical Judgement Using Decision Sciences. John R. Clarke. LC 83-24594. (Surgical Science Ser.: Vol. III). 124p. 1984. text ed. 45.00 (*0-275-91425-9*, C1425, Praeger Pubs) Greenwood.

Surgical Management. 2nd rev. ed. Geoffrey D. Chisholm et al. Ed. by R. C. Williamson. 848p. 1991. 135.00 (*0-7506-0025-X*) Buttrwrth-Heinemann.

Surgical Management of Cerebrovascular Disease. Ed. by R. Eugene Zierler. LC 94-20311. 416p. 1994. text ed. 80.00 (*0-07-072792-9*) McGraw-Hill HPD.

Surgical Management of Crohn's Disease & Ulcerative Colitis. Devinder Kumar & John Alexander-Williams. LC 93-4186. 1993. 192.00 (*0-387-19730-3*) Spr-Verlag.

Surgical Management of Crohn's Disease & Ulcerative Joints. Devinder Kumar & John Alexander-Williams. (Illus.). 260p. 1993. write for info. (*3-540-19730-3*) Spr-Verlag.

Surgical Management of Deformities in Leprosy & Other Peripheral Neuropathies. Noshir H. Antia et al. (Illus.). 172p. 1993. 39.95 (*0-19-563058-0*) OUP.

Surgical Management of Degenerative Arthritis of the Lower Limb. Ed. by Richard L. Cruess & Nelson S. Mitchell. LC 75-20440. (Illus.). 248p. reprint ed. 70.70 (*0-8357-9421-0*, 2014539) Bks Demand.

Surgical Management of Epilepsy. Ed. by Allen R. Wyler & Bruce P. Hermann. (Illus.). 420p. 1993. text ed. 85.00 (*0-7506-9416-5*) Buttrwrth-Heinemann.

Surgical Management of External Diseases of the Eye. Susan M. Stenson. LC 94-32668. (Illus.). 344p. 1995. 145.00 (*0-89640-274-6*) Igaku-Shoin.

Surgical Management of Morbid Obesity. Ed. by Ward O. Griffen, Jr. & Kenneth J. Printen. LC 87-5368. (Science & Practice of Surgery Ser.: No. 12). 320p. 1987. reprint ed. pap. 91.20 (*0-608-01295-5*, 2062041) Bks Demand.

Surgical Management of Neurovascular Disease. 3rd ed. Robert G. Ojemann et al. LC 94-40513. (Illus.). 1995. 175.00 (*0-683-06629-3*) Williams & Wilkins.

Surgical Management of Rheumatoid Arthritis. Beddow. 194p. 1989. 175.00 (*0-7236-1007-X*) Buttrwrth-Heinemann.

Surgical Management of Soft Tissue Sarcomas. Myron Arlen & Ralph C. Marcove. (Illus.). 344p. 1987. text ed. 135.00 (*0-7216-1399-3*) Saunders.

Surgical Management of Sterility. E. Cittadini et al. 150p. 1976. text ed. 24.00 (*1-57235-057-1*) Piccin NY.

Surgical Management of the Burn Wound. David M. Heimbach & Loren H. Engrav. (Illus.). 176p. 1984. text ed. 159.00 (*0-89004-914-9*) Lppncott-Raven.

***Surgical Management of the Diabetic Patient.** Ed. by Michael Bergman & Gregorio A. Sicard. LC 90-9064. 425p. 1991. reprint ed. pap. 121.20 (*0-608-03387-1*, 2064084) Bks Demand.

***Surgical Management of Tumors of the Oropharynx.** Steven M. Zeitels & Arnold Komisar. LC 97-16822. (Continuing Education Program Ser.). 1997. pap. write for info. (*1-56772-056-0*) AAO-HNS.

***Surgical Management of Vascular Disease.** Ed. by Peter R. Bell et al. (Illus.). 1436p. 1992. write for info. (*0-7020-1514-8*, Pub. by W B Saunders UK) Saunders.

***Surgical Methods in Rigidity.** F. T. Farrell. (Tata Institute Lectures on Mathematics & Physics Ser.). 100p. 1997. pap. 29.95 (*3-540-58977-5*) Spr-Verlag.

Surgical Neuroangiography, Vol. 1. P. Lasjaunias & A. Berenstein. (Functional Anatomy of Craniofacial Arteries Ser.). (Illus.). 450p. 1994. 215.00 (*0-387-16534-7*) Spr-Verlag.

Surgical Neuroangiography, Vol. 2. P. Lasjaunias & A. Berenstein. (Endovascular Treatment of Craniofacial Lesions Ser.). (Illus.). 450p. 1996. 199.00 (*0-387-16535-5*) Spr-Verlag.

Surgical Neuroangiography, Vol. 3. A. Berenstein & P. Lasjaunias. (Illus.). 420p. 1994. 215.00 (*0-387-17501-6*) Spr-Verlag.

Surgical Neuroangiography, Vol. 4: Endocascular Treatment of Cerebral Problems. A. Berenstein & P. Lasjaunias. (Illus.). 425p. 1993. 215.00 (*0-387-17500-8*) Spr-Verlag.

Surgical Neuroangiography, Vol. 5: Endocascular Treatment of Spine & Spinal Cord. A. Berenstein & P. Lasjaunias. (Illus.). 320p. 1994. 215.00 (*0-387-55043-7*) Spr-Verlag.

Surgical Nurse. large type ed. Ruth Ives. (Linford Romance Library). 336p. 1988. pap. 10.95 (*0-7089-6575-X*, Linford) Ulverscroft.

Surgical Nursing. Bonnie Allbaugh. Ed. by Kathy V. Gettrust. LC 93-26626. (Plans of Care for Specialty Practice Ser.). 436p. 1994. pap. 30.50 (*0-8273-6297-8*) Delmar.

Surgical Nursing. 2nd ed. Mary J. Evans & Mary Ann Black. (Clinical Rotation Guide Ser.). (Illus.). 160p. 1994. pap. 16.95 (*0-87434-736-X*) Springhouse Pub.

Surgical Nutrition. 1996. 117.00 (*3-540-59291-1*) Spr-Verlag.

Surgical Nutrition: Strategies in Critically Ill Patients. Rifat Latifi. Ed. by Stanley Dudrick. LC 95-4265. (Medical Intelligence Unit Ser.). 212p. 1995. 89.00 (*1-57059-154-7*) R G Landes.

Surgical Obstetrics. Plauche. 1991. text ed. 110.00 (*0-7216-3049-9*) Saunders.

Surgical Oncology. Allen-Mersh. 480p. (gr. 13). 1995. text ed. 119.95 (*0-412-48940-6*) Chapman & Hall.

Surgical Oncology. McCardle. 332p. 1990. 175.00 (*0-407-01700-3*) Buttrwrth-Heinemann.

***Surgical Oncology.** Raphael E. Pollock. LC 97-5016. (Cancer Treatment & Research Ser.). 1997. lib. bdg. write for info. (*0-7923-9900-5*) Kluwer Ac.

Surgical Oncology. Ed. by U. Veronesi et al. (Illus.). 1000p. 1989. 304.00 (*0-387-17770-1*) Spr-Verlag.

Surgical Ophthalmology One. F. C. Blodi et al. (Illus.). 592p. 1991. 327.00 (*0-387-52105-4*) Spr-Verlag.

Surgical Ophthalmology Two. Ed. by F. C. Blodi et al. (Illus.). 728p. 1992. 298.00 (*0-387-52107-0*) Spr-Verlag.

Surgical-Orthodontic Treatment: A Contemporary Synthesis. William R. Proffit & White. (Illus.). 752p. (C). (gr. 13). 1990. text ed. 199.00 (*0-8016-5291-X*) Mosby Yr Bk.

Surgical Orthodontics: Diagnosis & Treatment. W. Van Der Kwast et al. (Illus.). 120p. 1993. text ed. 45.00 (*90-5383-179-7*, Pub. by VU Univ Pr NE) Paul & Co Pubs.

Surgical Orthodontics, No. 2: Techniques & Instrumentation. W. Van Der Kwast et al. (Illus.). 140p. 1994. 40.00 (*90-5383-231-9*, Pub. by VU Univ Pr NE) Paul & Co Pubs.

***Surgical Path of Kidney, Bladder & Prostate.** Tomaszewsk. 1997. text ed. write for info. (*0-7216-3738-8*) Saunders.

Surgical Pathology. Alberto M. Marchevsky. (Lung Biology in Health & Disease Ser.: Vol. 44). 736p. 1990. 215.00 (*0-8247-8106-6*) Dekker.

Surgical Pathology. W. E. Thomas & J. H. Smith. LC 92-15537. (Colour Guide Ser.). 160p. 1992. pap. 19.95 (*0-443-03252-1*) Churchill.

Surgical Pathology, 2 vols. 2nd ed. Walter F. Coulson. LC 65-7743. (Illus.). 1824p. 1988. text ed. 245.00 (*0-397-50609-0*, Lippnctt) Lppncott-Raven.

Surgical Pathology Dissection. William H. Westra. 50p. 1996. 98.00 (*0-387-94715-9*) Spr-Verlag.

Surgical Pathology Dissection: An Illustrated Guide. William H. Westra et al. LC 95-24467. (Illus.). 208p. 1996. 49.00 (*0-387-94567-9*) Spr-Verlag.

***Surgical Pathology of Laryngeal Neoplasms.** Ed. by Ferlito. (Illus.). 504p. 1995. text ed. 155.00 (*0-412-58010-1*, Chap & Hall NY) Chapman & Hall.

Surgical Pathology of Prostate & Seminal Vesicles. Joseph Kovi. 336p. 1988. 191.00 (*0-8493-4804-8*, RC899) CRC Pr.

Surgical Pathology of the Breast. K. Rogers & A. J. Coup. 348p. 1990. 95.00 (*0-7236-0965-9*) Buttrwrth-Heinemann.

Surgical Pathology of the Breast. Weidner. 1998. text ed. write for info. (*0-7216-1755-7*) HarBrace.

S

Surgical Pathology of the Female Reproductive System & Peritoneum. Ed. by Stephen S. Sternberg & Stacey E. Mills. 318p. 1990. text ed. 99.50 (*0-88167-726-4*) Lppncott-Raven.

Surgical Pathology of the Head & Neck, Pt. B. Barnes. 1000p. 1985. Vol. 2. 235.00 (*0-8247-7269-5*) Dekker.

Surgical Pathology of the Head & Neck, Set, Pt. A. Barnes. 896p. 1985. Vol. 1. 235.00 (*0-8247-7216-4*) Dekker.

Surgical Pathology of the Lymph Nodes & Related Organs. 2nd ed. Ed. by Elaine S. Jaffe. LC 94-13094. (Major Problems in Pathology Ser.: Vol. 16). 1994. text ed. 79.00 (*0-7216-5136-4*) Saunders.

***Surgical Pathology of the Mediastinum.** 2nd ed. Alberto M. Marchevsky & Mamoru Kaneko. LC 91-23675. reprint ed. pap. 100.40 (*0-608-04705-8*, 2065426) Bks Demand.

Surgical Pathology of the Mouth & Jaws. Roderick A. Cawson et al. (Illus.). 376p. 1996. text ed. 275.00 (*0-7236-0840-7*) Buttrwrth-Heinemann.

Surgical Pathology of the Nervous System & Its Coverings. 2nd ed. Peter C. Burger & F. Stephen Vogel. LC 81-16250. (Illus.). 755p. reprint ed. pap. 180.00 (*0-8357-6557-1*, 2035922) Bks Demand.

Surgical Pathology of the Nervous System & Its Coverings. 3rd ed. Peter C. Burger et al. (Illus.). 737p. 1991. text ed. 159.95 (*0-443-08687-7*) Churchill.

Surgical Pathology of the Ovaries. Peter Russell & Patricia Bannatyne. (Illus.). 539p. 1989. text ed. 199.00 (*0-443-03535-0*) Churchill.

***Surgical Pathology of the Ovaries.** 2nd ed. Peter Russell & Annabelle Farnsworth. LC 97-9201. 1997. write for info. (*0-443-05384-7*) Churchill.

Surgical Pathology of the Pituitary Gland. Ricardo V. Lloyd. (Illus.). 271p. 1992. text ed. 67.00 (*0-7216-6459-8*) Saunders.

Surgical Pathology of the Salivary Glands. Albert Ellis & Auclair. (Illus.). 608p. 1991. text ed. 87.00 (*0-7216-3224-6*) Saunders.

Surgical Pathophysiology. Ed. by A. Aasen. 452, xiiip. 1990. text ed. 145.00 (*3-7186-5038-X*, Harwood Acad Pubs) Gordon & Breach.

Surgical Pediatric Otolaryngology: Head Neck Surgery. Steven D. Handler et al. (Illus.). 400p. 1996. text ed. 125.00 (*0-86577-153-7*) Thieme Med Pubs.

Surgical Pharmacology of the Eye. Ed. by Marvin L. Sears & Ahti Tarkkanan. LC 84-24974. (Illus.). 608p. 1985. reprint ed. pap. 173.30 (*0-7837-9572-6*, 2060321) Bks Demand.

Surgical Practice. 6th ed. M. Hobsley. 1993. 55.00 (*0-340-55153-4*, Pub. by E Arnold UK) Routledge Chapman & Hall.

Surgical Principles. Ed. by Irving Taylor & Stephen Karran. LC 96-4700. (Arnold Publication Ser.). 224p. 1996. pap. 59.50 (*0-340-61379-3*, Pub. by E Arnold UK) Routledge Chapman & Hall.

Surgical Problems Affecting the Patient with Cancer: Interdisciplinary Management. Ed. by Alan T. Lefor. 424p. 1995. text ed. 79.50 (*0-397-51402-6*) Lppncott-Raven.

Surgical Problems in the AIDS Patient. Samuel E. Wilson & Russell A. Williams. LC 94-7074. (Illus.). 312p. 1994. 75.00 (*0-89640-247-9*) Igaku-Shoin.

Surgical Radiology: A Complement in Radiology & Imaging to the Sabiston-Davis-Christopher Textbook of Surgery, 3 vols., 1. J. George Teplick & Marvin E. Haskin. (Illus.). 1152p. 1981. text ed. 163.00 (*0-7216-8781-4*) Saunders.

Surgical Radiology: A Complement in Radiology & Imaging to the Sabiston-Davis-Christopher Textbook of Surgery, 3 vols., 2. J. George Teplick & Marvin E. Haskin. (Illus.). 1152p. 1981. text ed. 173.00 (*0-7216-8782-2*) Saunders.

Surgical Radiology: A Complement in Radiology & Imaging to the Sabiston-Davis-Christopher Textbook of Surgery, 3 vols., 3. J. George Teplick & Marvin E. Haskin. (Illus.). 1152p. 1981. text ed. 173.00 (*0-7216-8791-1*) Saunders.

Surgical Radiology: A Complement in Radiology & Imaging to the Sabiston-Davis-Christopher Textbook of Surgery, 3 vols., Set. J. George Teplick & Marvin E. Haskin. (Illus.). 1152p. 1981. text ed. 459.00 (*0-7216-8783-0*) Saunders.

Surgical Recall. Lorne Blackbourne. (Illus.). 352p. 1994. pap. 26.00 (*0-683-00835-8*) Williams & Wilkins.

***Surgical Recall.** 2nd ed. Lorne H. Blackbourne. LC 97-25166. (Recall Ser.). 1997. write for info. (*0-683-30102-0*) Williams & Wilkins.

Surgical Reflections: Images in Paint & Prose. Seymour I. Schwartz. LC 92-49796. (Illus.). 183p. 1993. 79.00 (*0-942219-48-1*) Quality Med Pub.

Surgical Rejuvenation of the Face. 2nd ed. Baker & Gordon. (Illus.). 640p. (C). (gr. 13 up). 1995. text ed. 264.00 (*0-8016-0153-3*) Mosby Yr Bk.

Surgical Repair & Reconstruction in Rheumatoid Disease. 2nd rev. ed. A. Benjamin et al. (Illus.). xviii, 254p. 1993. reprint ed. 247.00 (*0-387-19727-3*) Spr-Verlag.

Surgical Scripts: Master Surgeons Think Aloud about 43 Common Surgical Problems. Charles M. Abernathy & Robert M. Hamm. LC 93-39297. 200p. 1994. 21.95 (*1-56053-119-3*) Hanley & Belfus.

Surgical Secrets. Abernathy. 1986. 22.95 (*0-8016-0070-7*) Mosby Yr Bk.

Surgical Signs. Bruce Campbell & Martin Cooper. LC 93-3750. (Colour Guide Ser.). 1994. pap. text ed. 19.95 (*0-443-04005-2*) Churchill.

Surgical Solution: A History of Involuntary Sterilization in the United States. Philip R. Reilly. LC 90-5090. 208p. 1991. 28.00 (*0-8018-4096-1*) Johns Hopkins.

***Surgical Standards in Obstetrics.** Margaret Burns. 190p. 1995. spiral bd. 95.00 (*1-879575-66-3*) Acad Med Sys.

Surgical Systems & Accessories. (Market Research Reports: No. 310). (Illus.). 156p. 1992. 795.00 (*0-317-05117-2*) Theta Corp.

Surgical Teaching: Practice Makes Perfect. Neal A. Whitman & Peter Lawrence. 136p. 1991. text ed. 30.00 (*0-940193-08-6*) Univ UT Sch Med.

Surgical Technique in Gynecological Oncology. Shepherd & John M. Monaghan. Date not set. write for info. (*0-7506-1312-2*) Buttrwrth-Heinemann.

Surgical Technique of Total Hip Arthroplasty. Richard H. Rothman & William Hozack. 350p. 1995. text ed. write for info. (*0-7817-0156-2*) Lppncott-Raven.

Surgical Techniques. Ronald A. Malt. 1985. text ed. 162.00 (*0-7216-1219-9*) HarBrace.

***Surgical Techniques: Tools of the Trade & Rules of the Road.** Edwin A. Deitch. LC 97-5053. (Illus.). 432p. 1997. pap. text ed. 39.95 (*0-397-51393-3*) Lppncott-Raven.

Surgical Techniques in Experimental Farm Animals. F. A. Harrison. (Illus.). 150p. 1995. 83.00 (*0-19-854258-5*) OUP.

Surgical Techniques of the Temporal Bone & Skull Base. Herbert Silverstein & Seth Rosenberg. (Illus.). 225p. 1992. text ed. 98.50 (*0-8121-1530-9*) Williams & Wilkins.

Surgical Technologist. Ronald R. Smith. Ed. by Diane Parker. LC 92-50920. (Smith's Career Notes Ser.). 24p. 1993. pap. 2.50 (*1-56875-006-4*) R & E Pubs.

Surgical Technologist Certifying Exam Study Guide. Ed. by Association of Surgical Technologists Staff. 158p. (Orig.). 1995. pap. text ed. 29.95 (*0-926805-07-X*) Assn Surgical.

Surgical Technology: Principles & Practice. 3rd ed. Joanna R. Fuller. LC 92-49085. (Illus.). 752p. 1993. text ed. 56.95 (*0-7216-4064-8*) Saunders.

Surgical Technology International Vol. V: International Developments in Surgery & Research. Ed. by Zoltan Szabo et al. (Illus.). 500p. 1996. text ed. 95.00 (*0-9643425-4-5*); pap. text ed. 115.00 (*0-9643425-5-3*) Univ Med Pr.

Surgical Technology International III: International Developments in Surgery & Surgical Research. Ed. by Morris D. Kerstein et al. (Illus.). 604p. 1994. pap. text ed. 95.00 (*0-9643425-0-2*) Univ Med Pr.

Surgical Technology International III: International Developments in Surgery & Surgical Research. Ed. by Morris D. Kerstein et al. (Illus.). 604p. 1994. text ed. 115.00 (*0-9643425-1-0*) Univ Med Pr.

Surgical Technology International IV: International Developments in Surgery & Surgical Research. Ed. by Zoltan Szabo et al. (Illus.). 465p. 1995. pap. text ed. 95.00 (*0-9643425-2-9*) Univ Med Pr.

Surgical Technology International IV: International Developments in Surgery & Surgical Research. Ed. by Zoltan Szabo et al. (Illus.). 465p. 1995. text ed. 115.00 (*0-9643425-3-7*) Univ Med Pr.

Surgical Technology International VI: International Development in Surgery & Surgical Research. Ed. by Zoltan Szabo et al. (Illus.). 500p. 1996. text ed. 95.00 (*0-9643425-6-1*) Univ Med Pr.

Surgical Technology International VI: International Development in Surgery & Surgical Research. Ed. by Zoltan Szabo et al. (Illus.). 500p. 1996. text ed. 115.00 (*0-9643425-7-X*) Univ Med Pr.

Surgical Thoracoscopy. D. Gossot et al. (Illus.). 124p. 1993. 95.00 (*0-387-59577-5*) Spr-Verlag.

Surgical Thoracoscopy. Rolf Inderbitzi. LC 93-28475. 1994. 118.00 (*0-387-56894-8*) Spr-Verlag.

Surgical Transcription in Obstetrics & Gynecology. John E. Turrentine. (Illus.). (C). 1993. 34.95 (*1-85070-512-7*) Prthnon Pub.

Surgical Treatment of Anal Incontinence. C. V. Mann & R. E. Glass. (Illus.). xiii, 160p. 1991. 232.00 (*0-387-19640-4*) Spr-Verlag.

***Surgical Treatment of Anal Incontinence.** 2nd ed. Charles V. Mann & Richard Glass. LC 96-36555. 1996. 149.00 (*3-540-76061-X*) Spr-Verlag.

Surgical Treatment of Aortic Aneurysms. Denton A. Cooley. (Illus.). 215p. 1986. text ed. 110.00 (*0-7216-1398-5*) Saunders.

Surgical Treatment of Aortic Dissection. Hans G. Borst et al. LC 95-37913. 357p. 1995. 119.95 (*0-443-07531-X*) Churchill.

Surgical Treatment of Astigmatism. Ed. by James P. Gills et al. LC 94-856. 186p. 1994. 89.00 (*1-55642-220-2*) SLACK Inc.

Surgical Treatment of Bronchial Carcinoma. J. Hasse. (Illus.). 160p. 1986. 103.00 (*0-387-16230-5*) Spr-Verlag.

Surgical Treatment of Chronic Pancreatitis: New Standards. Ed. by John P. Neoptolemos et al. (Journal: Digestive Surgery Ser.: Vol. 13, No. 2, 1996). (Illus.). 96p. 1996. pap. 54.00 (*3-8055-6323-X*) S Karger.

Surgical Treatment of Congenital Heart Disease. 3rd ed. Grady L. Hallman et al. LC 86-21062. 245p. reprint ed. pap. 69.90 (*0-7837-2713-5*, 2043093) Bks Demand.

***Surgical Treatment of Epilepsy.** William H. Theodore. (Epilepsy Research Ser.: Vol. 5). xxii, 250p. 1992. 220.75 (*0-444-89474-8*) Elsevier.

Surgical Treatment of Hepatic Metastases of Colorectal Diseases: Report of the 94th French Congress of Surgery. Ed. by B. Nordlinger & D. Jaeck. (Monographs of the French Surgical Association). 140p. 1993. 100.00 (*0-387-55142-5*) Spr-Verlag.

Surgical Treatment of Metastatic Cancer. Michael T. Lotze. LC 97-5524. 650p. 1997. text ed. 139.00 (*0-397-51474-3*) Lppncott-Raven.

Surgical Treatment of Middle Ear Cholesteatoma. M. Wayoff et al. (Advances in Oto-Rhino-Laryngology Ser.: Vol.36). (Illus.). x, 238p. 1987. 156.00 (*3-8055-4441-3*) S Karger.

Surgical Treatment of the Epilepsies. fac. ed. Ed. by Jerome Engel, Jr. LC 85-43520. (Illus.). 747p. pap. 180.00 (*0-7837-7278-5*, 2047028) Bks Demand.

Surgical Treatment of the Epilepsies. 2nd ed. Ed. by Jerome Engel, Jr. LC 92-49518. 816p. 1993. text ed. 142.00 (*0-88167-988-7*) Lppncott-Raven.

Surgical Word Book. 2nd ed. Claudia J. Tessier. 1991. pap. text ed. 39.00 (*0-7216-2128-7*) Saunders.

Surgical Wound. Ed. by Peter Dineen. LC 81-8163. (Illus.). 238p. reprint ed. pap. 67.90 (*0-8357-7646-8*, 2056971) Bks Demand.

Surgvision: The First Video Atlas of General Surgery. Ed. by Nelson Gurll. 300p. (C). 1990. 595.00 (*0-944903-06-1*) Adams Pub Group.

Suri & Co. Tales of a Persian Teenage Girl. Mahshid Amirshahi. Tr. by J. E. Knorzer from IRA. (Modern Middle Eastern Literature in Translation Ser.). 100p. (Orig.). 1995. pap. 9.95 (*0-292-70463-1*) U of Tex Pr.

Surimi Technology. Ed. by Lanier & Lee. (Food Science & Technology Ser.: Vol. 50). 536p. 1992. 205.00 (*0-8247-8470-7*) Dekker.

Surinaamse Slangeninkleur: Surinam Snakes in Color. Joep Moonen et al. (Illus.). 119p. 1979. pap. 29.95 (*0-88359-016-6*) R Curtis Pubng.

Surinam: Politics, Economics & Society. H. E. Chin. (Marxist Regimes Ser.). 220p. 1987. text ed. 49.00 (*0-86187-516-8*); text ed. 17.50 (*0-86187-517-6*) St Martin.

***Suriname.** LC 97-17786. (Major World Nations Ser.). (Illus.). 120p. (YA). (gr. 5 up). 1997. lib. bdg. 19.95 (*0-7910-4748-2*) Chelsea Hse.

Suriname. Noelle B. Beatty. (Let's Visit Places & Peoples of the World Ser.). (Illus.). 96p. (J). (gr. 5 up). 1988. lib. bdg. 19.95 (*1-55546-196-4*) Chelsea Hse.

Suriname. Rosemarijn Hoefte. (World Bibliographical Ser.). 1991. lib. bdg. 65.00 (*1-85109-103-3*) ABC-CLIO.

Suriname. Carolyn S. Lieberg. LC 95-2692. (Enchantment of the World Ser.). (Illus.). 172p. (J). (gr. 5-9). 1995. lib. bdg. 30.00 (*0-516-02638-0*) Childrens.

Suriname: Recent Developments Relating to Human Rights: Report of a Mission to Suriname in February, 1981. John Griffiths. 38p. reprint ed. pap. 25.00 (*0-685-16097-1*, 2027736) Bks Demand.

***Suriname: Statistical Annex.** Jose S. Lizondo. (IMF Staff Country Report Ser.: Vol. 96/34). 42p. pap. 25.00 (*0-608-04858-5*, 2065517) Bks Demand.

Suriname see Statements of the Laws of the OAS Member States in Matters Affecting Business

Suriname & the Netherlands Antilles: An Annotated English-Language Bibliography. Enid Brown. LC 92-10786. 293p. 1992. 32.50 (*0-8108-2576-7*) Scarecrow.

Suriname Folk-Lore. Melville J. Herskovits & Frances S. Herskovits. LC 71-82365. (Columbia Univ. Contributions to Anthropology Ser.: No. 27). (Illus.). reprint ed. 67.50 (*0-404-50577-5*) AMS Pr.

Suriname Planatlas. 65.00 (*0-8270-2837-7*) OAS.

Surly Bonds of Earth. Edward D. McKenzie. (Illus.). 160p. 1987. 20.00 (*0-9617909-0-3*) E D McKenzie.

Surly Tim & Other Stories. Frances Hodgson Burnett. LC 77-103500. (Short Story Index Reprint Ser.). 1977. 21.95 (*0-8369-3242-0*) Ayer.

Surname Detective: Investigating Surname Distribution in England, 1086-Present Day. Colin D. Rogers. LC 94-24441. 1995. text ed. 59.95 (*0-7190-4047-7*, Pub. by Manchester Univ Pr UK) St Martin.

Surname Directory, 1983. Ed. by Joan Pate. 123p. (Orig.). 1991. pap. 10.00 (*1-879766-06-X*) OCG Society.

Surname Directory, 1986. Ed. by Joan Pate. 194p. (Orig.). 1986. pap. 8.00 (*1-879766-07-8*) OCG Society.

Surname Directory, 1989. Ed. by Joan Pate. 190p. (Orig.). 1989. pap. 10.00 (*1-879766-08-6*) OCG Society.

Surname Directory, 1992, No. 4. Intro. by Joan Pate. 182p. (Orig.). 1992. pap. 10.00 (*1-879766-18-3*) OCG Society.

Surname Index to Forty-Three Westmoreland County, PA. Cemeteries, Vol. 2. Bob Closson & Mary Closson. 127p. 1986. lib. bdg. 9.50 (*0-933227-52-3*) Closson Pr.

Surname Index to History of the Upper Ohio Valley, Set, Vols. 1 & 2. Leila S. Francy. 46p. 1993. pap. text ed. 6.00 (*1-55856-133-1*) Closson Pr.

Surname Index to Sixty-Five Volumes of Colonial & Revolutionary Pedigrees. Rodney G. Crowther. 143p. lib. bdg. 17.25 (*0-915156-27-X*) Natl Genealogical.

Surname Register. 2nd ed. 446p. 1989. per. 25.00 (*0-685-28280-5*) Conejo Val Geneal.

Surname Register: Births, Marriages & Deaths of 15,000 Ancestors Researched by the Members of the Conejo Valley Genealogical Society. 2nd rev. ed. Conejo Valley Genealogical Society, Inc. Staff. Ed. by William P. Marlatt. 1989. pap. text ed. write for info. (*0-9622138-0-2*) Conejo Val Geneal.

Surnames: Determining Origins with Biographical & Ethnic References. Diane S. Ptak. LC 95-92174. 30p. 1995. pap. 14.00 (*1-886905-06-1*) D S Ptak.

Surnames: Their Meanings & Origins. Diane S. Ptak. LC 95-92176. 30p. 1993. pap. 14.00 (*1-886905-04-5*) D S Ptak.

***Surnames & Genealogy: A New Approach.** George Redmonds. LC 96-54888. 1997. write for info. (*0-88082-052-7*) New Eng Hist.

Surnames & Genetic Structure. Gabriel W. Lasker. (Cambridge Studies in Biological Anthropology). 150p. 1985. text ed. 42.95 (*0-521-30285-4*) Cambridge U Pr.

Surnames for Women: A Decision-Making Guide. Susan J. Kupper. LC 89-43654. 157p. 1990. pap. 24.95 (*0-89950-496-5*) McFarland & Co.

Surnames in the United States Census of 1790: An Analysis of National Origins of the Population. 334p. 1995. reprint ed. pap. 28.50 (*0-685-60325-3*, 100) Clearfield Co.

***Surnames of Devon.** David Postles. (Illus.). 332p. 1995. 34.00 (*0-904920-25-9*, Pub. by Leopards Head Pr UK) David Brown.

Surnames of Ireland. Edward MacLysaght. 314p. 1991. reprint ed. pap. 9.50 (*0-7165-2366-3*, Pub. by Irish Acad Pr IE) Intl Spec Bk.

***Surnames of Lancashire.** Richard McKinley. 501p. 1981. 24.00 (*0-904920-05-4*, Pub. by Leopards Head Pr UK) David Brown.

***Surnames of Oxfordshire.** Richard McKinley. 312p. 1977. 16.00 (*0-904920-01-1*, Pub. by Leopards Head Pr UK) David Brown.

Surnames of Scotland: Genealogy & Surnames with Some Heraldic & Biographical Notes. William Anderson. 1991. reprint ed. pap. 15.00 (*0-89979-054-2*) British Am Bks.

Surnames of Scotland: Their Origin, Meaning & History. George F. Black. LC 47-1716. 838p. 1946. reprint ed. 50.00 (*0-87104-172-3*) NY Pub Lib.

***Surnames of Sussex.** Richard McKinley. 483p. 1988. 34.00 (*0-904920-14-3*, Pub. by Leopards Head Pr UK) David Brown.

***Surnames of the United Kingdom: A Concise Etymological Dictionary, 2 vols. in 1.** Henry Harrison. 622p. 1996. reprint ed. 45.00 (*0-614-23493-X*, 2580) Clearfield Co.

Surnames of the United Kingdom: A Concise Etymological Dictionary, 2 vols., Set. Henry Harrison. reprint ed. write for info. (*0-318-71914-2*) G Olms Pubs.

Surnames of Wales: For Family Historians & Others. John Rowlands & Sheila Rowlands. (Illus.). 229p. 1996. pap. 19.95 (*0-8063-1516-4*, 5032) Genealog Pub.

***Surpassing Greatness of His Power.** Rick Joyner. LC 97-20962. 224p. (Orig.). 1997. pap. 10.99 (*0-88368-481-0*) Whitaker Hse.

***Surpassing Greatness of His Power: Ministry in the Power of the Spirit.** Rick Joyner. 226p. 1996. pap. 8.00 (*1-878327-50-X*, RJI-015) Morning NC.

Surpassing Ourselves: An Enquiry into the Nature & Implications of Expertise. Carl Bereiter & Marlene Scardamalia. LC 93-28840. 304p. 1993. 52.95 (*0-8126-9204-7*); pap. 19.95 (*0-8126-9205-5*) Open Court.

Surpassing Righteousness: Evangelism & Ethics in the Sermon on the Mount. W. Clyde Tilley. LC 92-25421. 180p. 1992. pap. 10.95 (*1-880837-03-X*) Smyth & Helwys.

Surpassing the Love of Men: Romantic Friendship & Love Between Women from the Renaissance To... Lillian Faderman. 1994. pap. 15.00 (*0-688-13330-4*, Quill) Morrow.

Surpassing Threats & Rewards: Newer Plateaus for Couples & Coupling. Ed. & Intro. by Barbara J. Brothers. LC 94-44765. (Journal of Couples Therapy). (Illus.). 144p. 1995. lib. bdg. 29.95 (*1-56024-723-1*) Haworth Pr.

Surpassing Wit: Oliver St. John Gogarty, His Poetry & His Prose. James F. Carens. LC 78-12644. 304p. 1979. text ed. 51.50 (*0-231-04642-1*) Col U Pr.

Surplus Compendium. Michael Sullivan. (Illus.). 96p. (Orig.). 1979. pap. 15.00 (*0-317-93999-8*) Arete Systs.

***Surplus Federal Computers for Schools: An Assessment of the Early Implementation of E. O. 12999.** Thomas K. Glennan & Critical Technologies Institute Rand Corp. Staff. LC 97-17421. 1997. write for info. (*0-8330-2510-4*) Rand Corp.

Surplus Koan Totem, Bk. 2. Lewis Koch. 1993. 15.00 (*0-932526-44-6*) Nexus Pr.

***Surplus Lines Insurance Practices.** Ed. by William R. Feldhaus. LC 96-79435. 219p. (C). 1996. pap. text ed. 24.00 (*0-89462-110-6*, 16202) Am Inst FCPCU.

***Surplus Lines Insurance Principles & Issues.** Ed. by William R. Feldhaus. LC 96-76202. 291p. (Orig.). (C). 1996. pap. text ed. 26.00 (*0-89462-099-1*, ASLI161) IIA.

Surplus of Memory: Chronicle Warsaw Ghetto Uprising. Yitzchak Zuckerman. Ed. & Tr. by Barbara Harshav. LC 92-31230. 708p. 1993. 35.00 (*0-520-07841-1*) U CA Pr.

Surplus People: Forced Removals in South Africa. Laurine Platzky & Cherryl Walker. LC 82-95958. 250p. 1985. pap. text ed. 16.95 (*0-86975-255-3*, Pub. by Ravan Pr ZA) Ohio U Pr.

Surplus Population. abr. rev. ed. William Corbett. 48p. 1994. pap. 5.95 (*0-948688-07-6*, Pub. by Pelagian Pr UK) AK Pr Dist.

Surplus Powerlessness. Michael Lerner. LC 85-62314. 320p. 1986. 14.95 (*0-935933-01-8*); pap. 9.95 (*0-935933-02-6*) Inst Labor & Mental.

Surplus Powerlessness: The Psychodynamics of Everyday Life & the Psychology of Individual & Social Transformation. Michael Lerner. LC 91-7279. 424p. (C). 1991. pap. 18.50 (*0-391-03706-4*) Humanities.

Surplus Revenue of Eighteen Thirty-Seven. Edward G. Bourne. (Works of Edward Gaylord Bourne). 1989. reprint ed. lib. bdg. 79.00 (*0-7812-2007-6*) Rprt Serv.

Surplus Utilisation in Agriculture. Ratan Khasnabis & Jyoti P. Chakrabarti. 1989. 22.00 (*81-7022-255-9*, Pub. by Concept II) S Asia.

Surplus Values Revisited. Benjamin A. Medeiros. 1993. 14.95 (*0-533-10394-0*) Vantage.

***Surprise.** Date not set. 20.00 (*0-8464-4424-0*) Beekman Pubs.

***Surprise!** Sally Noll. LC 96-36979. (Illus.). 24p. (J). (ps up). 1997. 15.00 (*0-688-15170-1*); lib. bdg. 14.93 (*0-688-15171-X*) Greenwillow.

Surprise! Mary Packard. (My First Reader Ser.). (Illus.). 28p. (J). (ps-2). 1990. pap. 3.95 (*0-516-45360-2*); lib. bdg. 15.50 (*0-516-05360-4*) Childrens.

***Surprise!** Laura E. Williams. (Let's Have a Party Ser.: No. 4). (Illus.). (J). 1997. pap. 3.99 (*0-380-78921-3*) Avon.

Surprise!, Level 3. Elizabeth Butler. (Let Me Read Ser.). (J). 1996. 2.95 (*0-673-36342-2*, GoodYrBooks) Addson-Wesley Educ.

Surprise! Level 1, Blue. Jane Fine. (Easy-to-Read Ser.). (Illus.). 32p. (J). (ps-2). 1996. pap. 3.50 (0-14-038029-9) Puffin Bks.

Surprise at Logan School. Connie Griffith. (Tootie McCarthy Ser.: Bk. 2). 128p. (Orig.). (J). (gr. 5-8). 1993. pap. 6.99 (0-8010-3856-1) Baker Bks.

Surprise Attack. John Kerrigan, pseud. 224p. 1996. 22.00 (0-7278-4946-8) Severn Hse.

Surprise Attack: Lessons for Defense Planning. Richard K. Betts. LC 82-70887. 318p. 1982. 36.95 (0-8157-0930-7); pap. 16.95 (0-8157-0929-3) Brookings.

Surprise Attack: The Victim's Perspective. Ephraim Kam. LC 88-15395. (Illus.). 304p. 1988. 36.50 (0-674-85745-3) HUP.

Surprise Attack in Mathematical Problems. Lloyd A. Graham. (Illus.). (Orig.). 1968. pap. 5.95 (0-486-21846-5) Dover.

Surprise Box. Libby Hathorn. LC 93-28957. (Voyages Ser.). (Illus.). (J). 1994. 4.25 (0-383-03778-6) SRA McGraw.

Surprise! Christ Comes! Barney Schroeder. 1989. pap. 2.75 (1-55673-143-4, 9868) CSS OH.

***Surprise Christmas Bride.** Child. 1997. mass mkt. 3.50 (0-373-76112-0) Harlequin Bks.

Surprise de l'Amour: La Second Surprise de l'Amour. Pierre de Marivaux. (FRE.). 1991. pap. 12.95 (0-7859-3165-1, 2253057290) Fr & Eur.

Surprise Endings. Robin J. Gunn. (Christy Miller Ser.: Vol. 4). 160p. (Orig.). (YA). 1991. pap. 5.99 (1-56179-024-9) Focus Family.

Surprise Endings: Ten Good Things about Bad Things. Ron Mehl. 180p. 1993. pap. 9.99 (0-88070-828-X, Multnomah Bks) Multnomah Pubs.

***Surprise Family.** Lynn Reiser. (J). Date not set. pap. 4.95 (0-688-15476-X, Mulberry) Morrow.

Surprise Family. Lynn W. Reiser. LC 93-16249. (Illus.). 32p. (J). (ps up). 1994. 16.00 (0-688-11671-X); lib. bdg. 15.93 (0-688-11672-8) Greenwillow.

Surprise for Easter: A Revolving Picture Book. Pete Bowman. (Illus.). 12p. (Orig.). (J). (ps-2). 1992. pap. 11.95 (0-689-71552-8, Aladdin Paperbacks) S&S Childrens.

Surprise for Mom see Set 2

***Surprise for Santa.** Emma J. James. (Illus.). 32p. (Orig.). (J). (ps-3). pap. text ed. write for info. (1-885935-02-1) Appalchn Log.

***Surprise Garden.** Zoe Hall. LC 97-9735. (Illus.). (J). 1998. write for info. (0-590-10075-0, Blue Sky Press); pap. write for info. (0-590-10076-9) Scholastic Inc.

Surprise Gospel Objectalks for Childrens' Church, 6 vols., 1. Arnold C. Westphal. (Orig.). 1979. 4.95 (0-915398-12-5) Visual Evangels.

Surprise Gospel Objectalks for Childrens' Church, 6 vols., 2. Arnold C. Westphal. (Orig.). 1979. 4.95 (0-915398-13-3) Visual Evangels.

Surprise Gospel Objectalks for Childrens' Church, 6 vols., 3. Arnold C. Westphal. (Orig.). 1979. 4.95 (0-915398-14-1) Visual Evangels.

Surprise Gospel Objectalks for Childrens' Church, 6 vols., 4. Arnold C. Westphal. (Orig.). 1979. 4.95 (0-915398-15-X) Visual Evangels.

Surprise Gospel Objectalks for Childrens' Church, 6 vols., 5. Arnold C. Westphal. (Orig.). 1979. 4.95 (0-915398-16-8) Visual Evangels.

Surprise Gospel Objectalks for Childrens' Church, 6 vols., 6. Arnold C. Westphal. (Orig.). 1979. 4.95 (0-915398-17-6) Visual Evangels.

Surprise Gospel Objectalks for Childrens' Church, 6 vols., Nos. 1-6. Arnold C. Westphal. (Orig.). 1979. write for info. (0-318-56348-7) Visual Evangels.

Surprise Images in Nature Aha!, Vol. 3. Richard Burrill. (Somewhere Behind the Eyes Ser.: Vol. 3). (Illus.). 96p. (J). (gr. 4-12). 1996. pap. text ed. 10.95 (1-878464-19-1) Anthro Co.

***Surprise in Mommy's Tummy.** (J). (ps-3). Date not set. 5.50 (0-89259-115-3) Am Trust Pubns.

Surprise in the Wardrobe. Val Willis. (J). (gr. 4-8). 1990. 15.00 (0-374-37309-4) FS&G.

Surprise Island. Gertrude C. Warner. LC 49-49618. (Boxcar Children Mysteries Ser.: No. 2). (Illus.). (J). (gr. 2-7). 1949. reprint ed. pap. 3.95 (0-8075-7674-3); reprint ed. lib. bdg. 13.95 (0-8075-7673-5) A Whitman.

Surprise, Larousse Dictionnaire des Sens Perdus. Alain Duchesne. 288p. (FRE.). 1991. pap. 45.00 (0-7859-7642-6, 2033300315) Fr & Eur.

Surprise of Being. Fernando Pessoa. Tr. by James Greene & Clara de Azevedo Mafra from POR. LC 86-82063. 64p. 8700. 25.00 (0-946162-23-9, Pub. by Angel Bks UK); pap. 13.95 (0-946162-24-7, Pub. by Angel Bks UK) Dufour.

Surprise of Germantown: Or, the Battle of Cliveden, October 4th, 1777. Thomas J. McGuire. (Illus.). 121p. (C). 1995. pap. text ed. 11.95 (0-939631-77-6) Thomas Publications.

Surprise Package: (Under the Mistletoe) Lynn Bulock. (Romance Ser.). 1994. pap. 2.75 (0-373-19053-0, 1-19053-7) Silhouette.

Surprise Paper Tearing Talks, No. 9. Arnold C. Westphal. 1976. pap. 4.95 (0-915398-08-7) Visual Evangels.

Surprise Party. Nicole Davidson. 192p. (Orig.). (J). (gr. 5). 1993. pap. 3.50 (0-380-76996-4, Flare) Avon.

Surprise Party. Gerald Dorset. (Illus.). 16p. 1980. 10.00 (0-934714-16-9); boxed 3.00 (0-934714-15-0) Swamp Pr.

Surprise Party. Sharon Gordon. LC 81-4869. (Illus.). 32p. (J). (gr. k-2). 1981. lib. bdg. 12.95 (0-89375-521-4) Troll Communs.

Surprise Party. Sharon Gordon. LC 81-4869. (Illus.). 32p. (J). (gr. k-2). 1996. pap. 3.95 (0-89375-522-2) Troll Communs.

Surprise Party. Pat Hutchins. LC 86-7255. (Illus.). 32p. (J). (ps-3). 1986. lib. bdg. 14.95 (0-02-745930-6, Mac Bks Young Read) S&S Childrens.

Surprise Party. Annabelle Prager. LC 87-20649. (Step into Reading Bks.). (Illus.). 48p. (J). (gr. 1-3). 1988. pap. 3.99 (0-394-89596-7); lib. bdg. 7.99 (0-394-99596-1) Random Bks Yng Read.

Surprise Party. R. L. Stine. (Fear Street Ser.). (Orig.). (YA). (gr. 7 up). mass mkt. 3.99 (0-671-73561-6, Archway) PB.

Surprise Party. Pat Hutchins. LC 91-10599. (Illus.). 32p. (J). (gr. k-3). 1991. reprint ed. pap. 3.95 (0-689-71543-9, Aladdin Paperbacks) S&S Childrens.

Surprise Party: Big Book. Pat Hutchins. LC 91-10599. (Illus.). 32p. (J). (gr. k-3). 1991. reprint ed. pap. 16.95 (0-689-71542-0, Aladdin Paperbacks) S&S Childrens.

Surprise Present. Nick Ward. (Illus.). 16p. (J). 1987. pap. 3.95 (0-19-272142-9) OUP.

***Surprise Spell.** Gill Davies. (Little Spooky Window Book Ser.). (Illus.). 13p. (J). (ps-1). 1997. bds. 3.99 (1-57584-166-5) Rdrs Dgst Yng Fam.

Surprise Stories. unabridged ed. Lynne Backer. Ed. by Mary L. Muffoletto. (Illus.). 64p. 1996. pap. 6.95 (1-889369-13-6, TI0050) Teaching Ink.

***Surprise Studded Springtime.** Becky Daniel. (Illus.). 192p. (Orig.). 1996. pap. text ed. 12.95 (1-56490-026-6) G Grimm Assocs.

Surprise, Surprise! Annette Broadrick. 1993. mass mkt. 4.99 (0-373-48262-0, 5-48262-5) Silhouette.

Surprise! Surprise! Michael Foreman. LC 95-919. (Illus.). 32p. (J). (ps-3). 1995. 14.00 (0-15-200038-0) HarBrace.

Surprise! Surprise! Francine Pascal. (Sweet Valley Kids Ser.: No. 1). 80p. (J). (ps-3). 1989. pap. 3.50 (0-553-15758-2, Skylark BDD) BDD Bks Young Read.

Surprise! Surprise! Virginia Vail. LC 89-31346. (Horse Crazy Ser.). (Illus.). 128p. (J). (gr. 4-6). 1997. pap. 2.95 (0-8167-1658-7) Troll Communs.

Surprise! Surprise! Gyo Fujikawa. (Illus.). 16p. (J). (ps). 1989. reprint ed. bds. 6.95 (1-55987-007-9, Sunny Bks) J B Comns.

Surprise! Surprise! It's Grandfather's Birthday! Barbara A. Porte. LC 96-6342. (Illus.). 32p. (J). (gr. k up). 1997. 15.00 (0-688-14157-9); lib. bdg. 14.93 (0-688-14158-7) Greenwillow.

Surprise, Thomas! A Thomas the Tank Engine Book. W. Awdry. (Chunky Flap Bks.). (Illus.). 22p. (J). (ps). 1994. 3.99 (0-679-85446-0) Random Bks Yng Read.

Surprise Visit. Thomas Fink. 57p. (Orig.). 1993. pap. text ed. 8.00 (0-934450-54-4) Unmuzzled Ox.

Surprised by Faith. rev. ed. Donald A. Bierle. 120p. 1993. pap. write for info. (0-9647488-0-0) HIS Minist.

Surprised by Faith: A Scientist Shares His Personal, Life-Changing Discoveries about God, the Bible & Personal Fulfillment. Don Bierle. 120p. (Orig.). 1996. pap. 8.99 (1-883002-33-8) Emerald WA.

***Surprised by God.** Stephen Arterburn & Rob Wilkins. LC 96-43831. 1997. 16.99 (1-56179-465-1) Focus Family.

***Surprised by God.** Stephen Arterburn. 1997. audio 22.99 (1-56179-489-9) Focus Family.

***Surprised by Grace: A Journey Beyond Personal Enlightenment.** Amber Terrell. LC 97-90029. (Illus.). viii, 241p. (Orig.). 1997. pap. 14.50 (0-9656670-0-6) True Lght Pub.

Surprised by Joy. C. S. Lewis. 22.95 (0-8488-1078-3) Amereon Ltd.

Surprised by Joy: The Shape of My Early Life. C. S. Lewis. LC 56-5329. 248p. 1956. 14.95 (0-15-187011-X) HarBrace.

Surprised by Joy: The Shape of My Early Life. C. S. Lewis. LC 56-5329. 1966. pap. 10.00 (0-15-687011-8, Harvest Bks) HarBrace.

Surprised by Joy: The Shape of My Early Life. C. S. Lewis. 1995. 16.00 (0-15-100185-5) HarBrace.

Surprised by Suffering. R. C. Sproul. 214p. 1994. pap. 10.99 (0-8423-6624-5) Tyndale.

Surprised by Suffering. large type ed. R. C. Sproul. (Large Print Christian Classics Ser.). 1991. reprint ed. pap. 12.95 (0-8027-2653-4) Walker & Co.

Surprised by the Power of the Spirit: A Former Dallas Seminary Professor Discovers that God Speaks & Heals Today. Jack Deere. LC 93-22158. 256p. 1993. 17.99 (0-310-58790-5) Zondervan.

Surprised by the Power of the Spirit: A Former Dallas Seminary Professor Discovers That God Speaks & Heals Today. Jack Deere. 304p. 1996. pap. 10.99 (0-310-21127-1) Zondervan.

Surprised by the Spirit. Edward Farrell. 1971. pap. 8.95 (0-87193-030-7) Dimension Bks.

Surprised by the Voice of God: How God Speaks Today Through Prophecies, Dreams, & Visions. Jack Deere. 256p. 1996. 18.99 (0-310-46200-2) Zondervan.

Surprised by the Voice of God: How God Speaks Today Through Prophets, Dreams, & Visions. Jack Deere. 1995. audio 14.99 (0-310-41418-0) Zondervan.

Surprised by Truth: 11 Converts Give the Biblical & Historical Reasons for Becoming Catholic. Ed. & Intro. by Patrick Madrid. 280p. (Orig.). 1994. pap. 11.99 (0-9642610-8-1) Basilica Pr.

***Surprise/Picture.** John Spiers. (J). Date not set. pap. 3.95 (0-448-41483-X) Putnam Pub Group.

Surpriser: The Life of Rowland, Lord Hill. Gordon L. Teffeteller. LC 81-72058. (Illus.). 272p. 1983. 38.50 (0-87413-212-6) U Delaware Pr.

Surprises. Etienne Delessert. LC 93-27453. (Yok-Yok Ser.). (Illus.). 32p. (J). (gr. 1-8). 1994. 10.95 (0-88682-643-8, 97931-098) Creative Ed.

Surprises. Burton Goodman. 144p. (J). (gr. 4). 1990. pap. 11.97 (0-89061-675-2) Jamestown Pubs.

Surprises! Dick Hilliard & Beverly Valenti-Hilliard. LC 81-52714. (Center Celebration Ser.). (Illus.). 64p. (Orig.). (J). (gr. 1 up). 1981. pap. text ed. 4.95 (0-89390-031-1) Resource Pubns.

Surprises. Ed. by Lee B. Hopkins. LC 83-47712. (Harper I Can Read Bk.). (Illus.). 64p. (J). (gr. k-3). 1984. lib. bdg. 14.89 (0-06-022585-8) HarpC Child Bks.

Surprises. Lee B. Hopkins. LC 83-47712. (Charlotte Zolotow Bk.). (Illus.). 64p. (J). (gr. k-3). 1986. pap. 3.50 (0-06-444105-9, Trophy) HarpC Child Bks.

Surprises. Kenneth G. Mills. (Illus.). 135p. 1980. 17.95 (0-919842-06-2, KGOB4) Sun-Scape Ent.

Surprises by the River: The Prophecy of Ezekiel. Jon L. Berquist. 168p. (Orig.). 1993. pap. 11.99 (0-8272-3432-5) Chalice Pr.

Surprises in Theoretical Physics. Rudolf Peierls. LC 79-84009. (Physics Ser.). 176p. 1979. pap. text ed. 16.95 (0-691-08242-1) Princeton U Pr.

Surprises of Life. Georges E. Clemenceau. Tr. by Grace Hall. LC 77-132113. (Short Story Index Reprint Ser.). 1977. 20.95 (0-8369-3670-1) Ayer.

Surprising Adventures of the Magical Monarch of Mo & His People. L. Frank Baum. (Illus.). (J). (ps-4). 1968. pap. 6.95 (0-486-21892-9) Dover.

Surprising Effects of Sympathy: Marivaux, Diderot, Rousseau, & Mary Shelley. David Marshall. (Illus.). x, 296p. 1988. 33.00 (0-226-50710-6) U Ch Pr.

Surprising Gift: The Story of Holden Village, Church Renewal Center. Charles P. Lutz. (Illus.). 144p. (Orig.). 1987. pap. 6.00 (0-9618617-0-3) Holden Village.

Surprising Lands Down Under. Ed. by Donald J. Crump. LC 89-14499. (Special Publications Series 24: No. 3). (Illus.). (YA). 1989. 12.95 (0-87044-714-9); lib. bdg. 12.95 (0-87044-719-X) Natl Geog.

***Surprising Mary.** Mitch Finley. (Illus.). 112p. (Orig.). 1997. pap. 7.95 (1-878718-37-1) Resurrection.

Surprising Myself. Christopher Bram. LC 86-82182. 400p. 1987. pap. 17.95 (1-55611-007-3) D I Fine.

Surprising Myself. Christopher Bram. 1988. pap. 12.95 (0-8050-0669-X, Owl) H Holt & Co.

Surprising Myself. Jean Fritz. LC 93-12001. (Meet the Author Ser.). (Illus.). 32p. (J). (gr. 2-5). 1992. 13.95 (1-878450-37-9) R Owen Pubs.

Surprising Science: 180 Fun & Challenging Science Brain Teasers for Kids: Level 1, Budding Genius. Jack De Waard & Nancy De Waard. 192p. (J). (gr. 3-5). 1996. pap. 9.95 (0-673-36311-2, GoodYrBooks) Addson-Wesley Educ.

Surprising Science: 180 Fun & Challenging Science Brain Teasers for Kids: Level 2, Genius. Jack De Waard & Nancy De Waard. 192p. (J). (gr. 4-6). 1996. pap. 9.95 (0-673-36312-0, GoodYrBooks) Addson-Wesley Educ.

Surprising Science Puzzles. Erwin Brecher. LC 94-16838. (Illus.). 96p. 1994. 14.95 (0-8069-0698-7) Sterling.

Surprising Science Puzzles. Erwin Brecher. (Illus.). 96p. 1996. pap. 5.95 (0-8069-0699-5) Sterling.

Surprising Side of Grace: Appreciating God's Loving Anger. Steven Bly. LC 94-11149. 192p. 1994. pap. 8.99 (0-929239-89-X) Discovery Hse Pubs.

Surprising Stories. Saki, pseud. (J). 1996. pap. 3.99 (0-590-74568-9) Scholastic Inc.

***Surprising Stories from People Jesus Met.** Mikal Keefer & John Cutshall. 112p. (Orig.). 1998. pap. 15.99 (1-55945-716-3) Group Pub.

Surprising Swimmers. Anthony D. Fredericks. LC 95-35667. (World of Discovery Ser.). (Illus.). 48p. (J). (gr. 3-9). 1996. 9.95 (1-55971-543-X) NorthWord.

Surprising Truth about Depression: Medical Breakthroughs that Can Work for You. Herbert Wagemaker & Peter D. Bellis. 192p. 1994. pap. 10.99 (0-310-40101-1) Zondervan.

Surprising Years: Understanding Your Changing Adolescent. rev. ed. Cliff Schimmels & Hank Resnik. Ed. by Linda Barr & Marba Wojcicki. (Skills for Adolescence Ser.). (Illus.). 144p. (Orig.). 1988. pap. text ed. 6.85 (0-933419-25-2) Quest Intl.

Surprizing Adventures of John Roach, Mariner of Whitehaven. 2nd ed. John Roach. 864p. 1986. reprint ed. pap. 8.00 (0-913129-14-3) La Tienda.

Surprizing Narrative: Olaudah Equiano & the Beginnings of Black Autobiography. Angelo Costanzo. LC 86-25748. (Contributions in Afro-American & African Studies: No. 104). 156p. 1987. text ed. 45.00 (0-313-25633-0, CZO/, Greenwood Pr) Greenwood.

Surpula Lacrymans: Fundamental Biology & Control Strategies. Ed. by D. H. Jennings & A. F. Bravery. LC 91-4222. 217p. 1991. text ed. 179.00 (0-471-93058-X, Wiley-L) Wiley.

Surrational Images. Photos by Scott Mutter. (Illus.). 96p. (C). 1992. 28.95 (0-252-01935-0) U of Ill Pr.

Surreal Gourmet: Real Food for Pretend Chefs. Bob Blumer. Ed. by Nion McEvoy. (Illus.). 96p. 1992. pap. 14.95 (0-8118-0121-7) Chronicle Bks.

Surreal Gourmet Entertains: High-Fun, Low-Stress Dinner Parties for 6 to 12 People. Bob Blumer. LC 94-42916. (Illus.). 120p. 1995. pap. 16.95 (0-8118-0804-1) Chronicle Bks.

Surreal Numbers. Donald E. Knuth. LC 74-5998. (C). 1974. pap. text ed. 16.25 (0-201-03812-9) Addison-Wesley.

Surrealism. Jacqueline Chenieux-Gendron. Tr. by Vivian Folkenflik from FRE. (European Perspectives Ser.). 224p. 1990. text ed. 49.50 (0-231-06810-7) Col U Pr.

Surrealism. Jacqueline Chenieux-Gendron. 1994. pap. 16.50 (0-231-06811-5) Col U Pr.

***Surrealism.** Smithmark Staff. (Art Movements Ser.). 1997. 16.98 (0-7651-9489-9) Smithmark.

Surrealism. Yves Duplessis. Tr. by Paul Capon. LC 77-17880. 158p. 1978. reprint ed. text ed. 49.75 (0-313-20110-2, DUSU, Greenwood Pr) Greenwood.

Surrealism. Julien Levy. LC 68-9469. 1968. reprint ed. 18.95 (0-405-00299-8, Ind Pubns) Ayer.

Surrealism. Julien Levy. (Illus.). 202p. 1995. reprint ed. pap. 17.95 (0-306-80663-0) Da Capo.

Surrealism. Patrick Waldberg. LC 96-61460. (World of Art Ser.). (Illus.). 128p. 1997. reprint ed. pap. 14.95 (0-500-20040-8) Thames Hudson.

***Surrealism: Surrealist Visuality.** Silvano Levy. LC 96-36461. 1997. 50.00 (0-8147-5128-8); pap. 20.00 (0-8147-5127-X) NYU Pr.

Surrealism: The Road to the Absolute. Anna A. Balakian. LC 76-87200. (Illus.). 33p. (C). 1987. pap. text ed. 17.00 (0-226-03560-3) U Ch Pr.

Surrealism & Communism: The Early Years. Alan Rose. LC 91-2231. (American University Studies: History: Ser. IX, Vols. 96). 343p. (C). 1991. text ed. 49.95 (0-8204-1384-4) P Lang Pubng.

Surrealism & Film. J. H. Matthews. LC 75-163624. 226p. reprint ed. pap. 64.50 (0-685-16170-6, 2056146) Bks Demand.

Surrealism & Quebec Literature: History of a Cultural Revolution. Andre G. Bourassa. Tr. by Mark Czarnecki. LC 84-238283. (University of Toronto Romance Ser.: No. 50). 409p. reprint ed. pap. 116.60 (0-7837-1229-4, 2041366) Bks Demand.

Surrealism & the Book. Renee R. Hubert. LC 86-16099. 408p. 1987. 85.00 (0-520-05719-8) U CA Pr.

Surrealism & the Book. Renee R. Hubert. 1992. pap. 27.50 (0-520-08089-0) U CA Pr.

Surrealism & the Occult: Shamanism, Magic, Alchemy, & the Birth of an Artistic Movement. Nadia Choucha. (Illus.). 144p. 1992. pap. 12.95 (0-89281-373-3) Inner Tradit.

Surrealism & Women. Ed. by Mary A. Caws et al. (Illus.). 246p. 1991. pap. 15.95 (0-262-53098-8) MIT Pr.

Surrealism in Exile & the Beginning of the New York School. Martica Sawin. LC 95-10961. (Illus.). 456p. 1995. 45.00 (0-262-19360-4) MIT Pr.

***Surrealism in Exile & the Beginning of the New York School.** Martica Sawin. (Illus.). 496p. 1997. reprint ed. pap. 25.00 (0-262-69201-5) MIT Pr.

Surrealism, Insanity, & Poetry. J. H. Matthews. LC 82-3165. (Illus.). 168p. 1982. 39.95 (0-8156-2273-2) Syracuse U Pr.

Surrealism of the Movies. William Earle. 1986. pap. 19.95 (0-913750-02-6) Transaction Pubs.

Surrealismo Poetico en el Mundo Europeo y el Extremo Oriente: La Propagacion del Surrealismo Europeo al Japon y a Corea, y un Comparativo de la Poesia Vanguardista. Whangbai Bahk. LC 91-23030. (American University Studies: Romance Languages & Literature: Ser. II, Vol. 167). 240p. (SPA.). (C). 1992. text ed. 41.95 (0-8204-1531-6) P Lang Pubng.

Surrealism Pro & Con. Kenneth Burke et al. 1973. pap. 4.50 (0-910664-27-7) Gotham.

Surrealism, Quantum Philosophy, & World War I. Virginia P. Williams. (Modern European History Ser.). 336p. 1987. text ed. 15.00 (0-8240-8068-8) Garland.

Surrealisme au Service de la Revolution. Andre Breton. 59.95 (0-686-51938-8, S9634) Fr & Eur.

Surrealisme au Service de la Revolution, Nos. 1-6. Ed. by Andre Breton. LC 68-28661. (Contemporary Art Ser.). (Illus.). (FRE.). 1968. reprint ed. 52.95 (0-405-00707-8) Ayer.

Surrealisme Desocculte: Manifeste du Surrealisme, 1924. Bernard-Paul Robert. LC 76-469238. 195p. (FRE.). 1975. reprint ed. pap. 55.60 (0-608-02192-X, 2062862) Bks Demand.

Surrealisme et le Mythe. Annette Tamuly. LC 93-24887. (American University Studies II: Vol. 208). 304p. (FRE.). (C). 1995. text ed. 49.95 (0-8204-2272-X) P Lang Pubng.

Surrealismo en Cataluna. R. Maria Malet et al. (Illus.). 208p. (SPA.). 1993. 150.00 (84-343-0546-1) Elliots Bks.

Surrealist Art. Sarane Alexandrian. (World of Art Ser.). (Illus.). (Orig.). 1985. pap. 14.95 (0-500-20097-1) Thames Hudson.

***Surrealist Art: The Bergman Collection at the Art Institute of Chicago.** Dawn Ades. LC 96-61200. (World of Art Ser.). (Illus.). 208p. (Orig.). 1997. pap. 34.95 (0-500-23711-5) Thames Hudson.

***Surrealist Look: An Erotic of Encounter.** Mary A. Caws. LC 96-44541. 228p. 1997. 37.50 (0-262-03244-9) MIT Pr.

Surrealist Mind. J. H. Matthews. LC 88-43398. 240p. 1991. 40.00 (0-945636-06-7) Susquehanna U Pr.

Surrealist Movement in England. Paul C. Ray. LC 70-145626. 331p. 1971. 20.00 (0-685-10518-0) Lib Soc Sci.

Surrealist Painting. Simon Wilson. (Color Library Ser.). (Illus.). 128p. (C). 1994. reprint ed. pap. 14.95 (0-7148-2722-3, Pub. by Phaidon Press UK) Chronicle Bks.

Surrealist Parade. Wayne Andrews. LC 89-14037. (Illus.). 192p. 1990. 22.95 (0-8112-1126-6); pap. 11.95 (0-8112-1127-4, NDP689) New Directions.

Surrealist Philosophy. 2nd ed. Tom Hibbard & Joseph A. Uphoff. LC 87-17519. 46p. 1987. pap. text ed. 3.00 (0-943123-00-3) Arjuna Lib Pr.

Surrealist Poetry in English. Xenophon. Ed. & Intro. by Edward B. Germain. 352p. 1993. pap. 13.95 (0-14-018486-4, Penguin Classics) Viking Penguin.

Surrealist Poetry in France. J. H. Matthews. LC 71-96815. 254p. reprint ed. pap. 72.40 (0-8357-3125-1, 2039386) Bks Demand.

***Surrealist Prints.** Ed. by Gilbert E. Kaplan. LC 96-52626. (Illus.). 160p. 1997. 45.00 (0-8109-6339-6) Abrams.

Surrealist Vision & Technique: Drawings & Collages from the Pompidou Center & the Picasso Museum, Paris. Clark V. Poling. (EMILOP Ser.: Vol. 8). (Illus.). 115p. (Orig.). 1996. pap. 29.95 (0-9638169-7-7) M C Carlos Mus.

Surrealist Voice of Robert Desnos. Mary Ann Caws. LC 76-25145. (Illus.). 208p. 1977. 27.50 (0-87023-223-1) U of Mass Pr.

S

An Asterisk (*) at the beginning of an entry indicates that the title is appearing in BIP for the first time.

Surrealists Look at Art. Ed. by Louis Aragon et al. Tr. by Michael Palmer from FRE. LC 85-81092. (Illus.). 256p. (Orig.). (C). 1990. 50.00 (*0-932499-08-2*) Lapis Pr.

***Surreality.** Ed. by Die Gestalten Staff. (Localizer 1.2 Ser.). 160p. (Orig.). 1996. 44.00 (*3-931126-03-X*, Pub. by Die Gestalten GW) Consort Bk Sales.

***Surrena's Choice.** Susan Paul. 1997. mass mkt. 4.99 (*1-55237-139-5*, Pub. by Comnwlth Pubns Inc CN) Anthem America.

Surrender. (Pocket Power Ser.). 16p. (Orig.). 1986. pap. 1.25 (*0-89486-325-8*, 5449B) Hazelden.

***Surrender.** Lyn Bulock. 286p. (Orig.). 1997. pap. 8.99 (*1-57673-187-1*) Multnomah Pubs.

***Surrender.** Lynn Bulock. LC 97-17221. 1997. pap. text ed. 8.99 (*1-57673-104-9*, Multnomah Bks) Multnomah Pubs.

Surrender. Kathleen Eagle. 1995. mass mkt. 5.50 (*0-373-20116-8*) Harlequin Bks.

***Surrender.** Heather Graham. 1998. mass mkt. 6.99 (*0-451-40690-7*, Onyx) NAL-Dutton.

Surrender. Metsy Hingle. (Desire Ser.). 1996. mass mkt. 3.25 (*0-373-05978-7*, 1-05978-1) Silhouette.

Surrender. Charlotte Lamb. (Presents Ser.). 1993. pap. 2.89 (*0-373-11540-7*, 1-11540-1) Harlequin Bks.

Surrender. Amanda Quick. 352p. 1990. mass mkt. 6.50 (*0-553-28594-7*) Bantam.

Surrender. Rochelle Wayne. 416p. 1995. mass mkt. 4.99 (*0-8217-5067-4*, Zebra Kensgtn) Kensgtn Pub Corp.

Surrender. large type ed. Amanda Quick. LC 94-17375. 1994. 25.95 (*1-56895-103-5*) Wheeler Pub.

Surrender: A Guide for Prayer. Jacqueline Bergan & S. Marie Schwan. (Take & Receive Ser.). 153p. (Orig.). 1986. pap. 6.95 (*0-88489-171-2*) St Marys.

Surrender: The Secret to Perfect Peace & Happiness. Gregory L. Jackson, Sr. LC 94-27759. 1994. 7.99 (*0-8280-0733-0*) Review & Herald.

Surrender a Dream. Jill Barnett. Ed. by Linda Marrow. 384p. (Orig.). 1991. mass mkt. 5.50 (*0-671-72341-3*) PB.

Surrender & Catch: Experience & Inquiry Today. Kurt H. Wolff. (Synthese Library: No. 105). 422p. 1976. lib. bdg. 117.50 (*90-277-0758-8*, D Reidel) Kluwer Ac.

Surrender & Catch: Experience & Inquiry Today. Kurt H. Wolff. (Synthese Library: No. 105). 422p. 1977. pap. text ed. 46.00 (*90-277-0765-0*, D Reidel) Kluwer Ac.

Surrender & Other Stories. Mabel Seguin. (C). 1996. pap. text ed. 11.95 (*0-582-25833-2*, Pub. by Longman UK) Longman.

Surrender in Scarlet. Patricia Camden. 400p. (Orig.). 1991. mass mkt. 4.50 (*0-380-76262-5*) Avon.

***Surrender in Silk.** Susan Mallery. (Intimate Moments Ser.). 1997. mass mkt. 3.99 (*0-373-07770-X*, 1-07770-0) Silhouette.

Surrender My Heart. Lois Greiman. 384p. (Orig.). 1993. mass mkt. 4.50 (*0-380-77181-0*) Avon.

Surrender My Love. Johanna Lindsey. 432p. (Orig.). 1994. mass mkt. 6.50 (*0-380-76256-0*) Avon.

Surrender My Love. large type ed. Johanna Lindsey. LC 94-34502. 403p. 1994. 23.95 (*0-7838-1124-1*, GK Hall) Thorndike Pr.

Surrender None: The Legacy of Gird. Elizabeth Moon. 544p. 1990. mass mkt. 5.99 (*0-671-69878-8*) Baen Bks.

Surrender, Occupation, & Private Property in International Law: An Evaluation of U. S. Practice in Japan. Nisuke Ando. (Oxford Monographs in International Law). (Illus.). 224p. 1991. 72.00 (*0-19-825411-3*) OUP.

Surrender of an Empire. Nesta H. Webster. 1973. 250.00 (*0-8490-1162-0*) Gordon Pr.

Surrender of An Empire. Nesta H. Webster. 392p. 1931. reprint ed. pap. 6.00 (*0-913022-07-1*) CPA Bk Pub.

Surrender of an Empire. Nesta H. Webster. 392p. 1931. reprint ed. pap. 11.95 (*0-945001-06-1*) GSG & Assocs.

Surrender of Nora. Maura Seger. (Intimate Moments Ser.). 1995. pap. 3.50 (*0-373-07617-7*, 1-07617-3) Silhouette.

Surrender Proceedings, April Ninth, 1865, Appomattox Court House. Frank P. Cauble. (Illus.). 141p. 1987. 12.95 (*0-930919-40-8*) H E Howard.

Surrender Sweet Stranger. Dewanna Pace. 1988. 3.95 (*0-517-00652-9*) Random Hse Value.

Surrender the Dream. Debra Dier. 448p. (Orig.). 1993. mass mkt., pap. text ed. 4.99 (*0-8439-3405-0*) Dorchester Pub Co.

***Surrender the Heart.** Nina Beaumont. 1997. mass mkt. 4.99 (*0-373-28962-6*, 1-28962-8) Harlequin Bks.

Surrender the Night. Christine Monson. 400p. 1987. pap. 3.95 (*0-380-89969-8*) Avon.

Surrender the Night. Susan P. Teklits. 432p. 1994. mass mkt. 4.50 (*0-06-108279-1*, Harp PBks) HarpC.

Surrender the Pink. Carrie Fisher. Ed. by Bill Grose. 1991. reprint ed. mass mkt. 5.99 (*0-671-66641-X*, Pocket Star Bks) PB.

***Surrender to God Within: Pathwork at the Soul Level.** Eva Pierrakos. Ed. & Intro. by Donovan Thesenga. x, 204p. (Orig.). 1997. pap. 14.95 (*0-9614777-5-X*) Pathwork Pr.

Surrender to Love. Rosemary Rogers. 624p. 1982. mass mkt. 5.99 (*0-380-80630-4*) Avon.

Surrender to the Dawn. Annee Cartier. 384p. Date not set. pap. 4.99 (*0-7860-0228-X*, Pinncle Kensgtn) Kensgtn Pub Corp.

Surrender to the Fury. Cara Miles. 384p. (Orig.). 1992. mass mkt. 4.50 (*0-380-76452-0*) Avon.

***Surrendering to Motherhood: Losing Your Mind, Finding Your Soul.** Iris Krasnow. LC 96-3076. 224p. 1997. 22.95 (*0-7868-6217-3*) Hyperion.

Surrendering to the Real Things: The Archetypal Experience of C. Wordsworth Crockett. Jeff Gundy. (Poetry Chapbooks Ser.: No. 2). 16p. (Orig.). 1986. pap. 2.50 (*0-936044-04-7*) Pikestaff Pr.

Surrender...or Fight? One Woman's Victory over Cancer. Beatrice H. Hoek & Melanie Jongsma. LC 94-31021. 96p. (Orig.). (gr. 10). 1995. pap. 6.99 (*0-8010-4401-4*) Baker Bks.

Surreptitious Printing in England, 1550 to 1640. Denis B. Woodfield. 203p. 1973. 25.00 (*0-914930-04-4*) Biblio Soc Am.

Surreptitious Printing in England 1550-1640. Denis B. Woodfield. 212p. 1973. 25.00 (*0-614-16154-1*) Oak Knoll.

Surreptitious Speech: "Presence Africaine" & the Politics of Otherness, 1947-1987. Ed. by V. Y. Mudimbe. (Illus.). 490p. 1992. pap. text ed. 24.95 (*0-226-54507-5*); lib. bdg. 71.50 (*0-226-54506-7*) U Ch Pr.

***Surrey.** John Drewett. 120p. 1996. pap. 35.00 (*0-614-19444-X*, Pub. by Shire UK) St Mut.

Surrey: A Photographic Record 1850-1920. John Janaway. 96p. 1987. 65.00 (*0-905392-38-8*) St Mut.

Surrey: Henry the Eighth, Pt. 6. Mark Dunster. 1980. pap. 4.00 (*0-89642-061-2*) Linden Pubs.

Surrey of One Hundred Years Ago. Aylwin Guilmant. (Illus.). 1994. 38.00 (*0-7509-0371-6*, Pub. by Sutton Pubng UK) Bks Intl VA.

Surrey Rambles. Derek Palmer. 64p. 1987. 35.00 (*0-905392-77-9*) St Mut.

Surrey Village Book. Graham Collyer. 168p. 1987. 30.00 (*0-905392-32-9*) St Mut.

Surrey Walks. (Ordnance Survey Pathfinder Guides Ser.). (Illus.). 80p. 1993. pap. 14.95 (*0-7117-0610-7*) Seven Hills Bk.

Surrey with the Fringe on Top. Illus. by James Warhola. LC 92-2462. (J). 1993. pap. 14.00 (*0-671-79456-6*, S&S Bks Young Read) S&S Childrens.

Surrogate Dad. Marion S. Collins. (Intimate Moments Ser.). 1994. mass mkt. 3.50 (*0-373-07610-X*, 1-07610-8) Silhouette.

Surrogate Gun. Jack Cummings. 224p. 1992. mass mkt. 3.50 (*1-55817-607-1*, Pinncle Kensgtn) Kensgtn Pub Corp.

Surrogate Gun. Jack Cummings. 192p. 1990. 17.95 (*0-8027-4102-9*) Walker & Co.

Surrogate Gun. large type ed. Jack Cummings. 339p. 1990. lib. bdg. 14.95 (*1-56054-007-9*) Thorndike Pr.

Surrogate Juries. Walter F. Abbott. LC 90-80485. 265p. 1990. 80.00 (*0-8318-0607-9*, B607) Am Law Inst.

Surrogate Markers to Assess Efficacy of Treatment in Chronic Liver Diseases: Proceedings of the International Falk Workshop Held in Basel, Switzerland, October 23-24, 1995. Ed. by J. Reichen & R. E. Poupon. LC 96-17380. 1996. lib. bdg. 98.00 (*0-7923-8705-8*) Kluwer Ac.

Surrogate Motherhood. Martha A. Field. LC 88-17459. 224p. 1988. 32.00 (*0-674-85748-8*) HUP.

Surrogate Motherhood. Martha A. Field. 232p. 1990. pap. 14.95 (*0-674-85749-6*) HUP.

Surrogate Motherhood: A Worldwide View of the Issues. Diederika Pretorius. (American Series in Behavioral Sciences & Law: No. 1085). 262p. 1994. pap. 38.95 (*0-398-06331-1*) C C Thomas.

Surrogate Motherhood: A Worldwide View of the Issues. Diederika Pretorius. (American Series in Behavioral Sciences & Law: No. 1085). 262p. (C). 1994. text ed. 56.95 (*0-398-05787-7*) C C Thomas.

Surrogate Motherhood: Conception in the Heart. Helena Ragone. (C). 1994. pap. text ed. 21.50 (*0-8133-1979-X*) Westview.

Surrogate Motherhood: Politics & Privacy. Ed. by Larry Gostin. LC 89-45474. (Medical Ethics Ser.). 384p. 1990. 12.95 (*0-253-32604-4*) Ind U Pr.

Surrogate Motherhood, Women's Rights, & the Working Class. Cindy Jaquith. 23p. 1988. pap. 2.50 (*0-87348-495-9*) Pathfinder NY.

Surrogate Parenting: An Annotated Review of the Literature. Sara Robbins. LC 84-1824. (CompuBibs Ser.: No. 3). 40p. 1984. pap. 10.00 (*0-914791-04-4*) Vantage Info.

Surrogate Parenting Contract Legislation Enacted: 1987, 1988, & 1989. (State Legislative Reports: Vol. 15, No. 2). 10p. 1990. 5.00 (*1-55516-258-4*, 7302-1502) Natl Conf State Legis.

Surrogate Proletariat: Moslem Women & Revolutionary Strategies in Soviet Central Asia, 1919-1929. Gregory J. Massell. LC 73-16047. 491p. 1974. reprint ed. pap. 140.00 (*0-7837-9384-7*, 2060128) Bks Demand.

Surrogates & Other Mothers: The Debates over Assisted Reproduction. Ruth Macklin. LC 93-5988. 240p. 1994. pap. 19.95 (*1-56639-180-6*) Temple U Pr.

Surrogate's Court Clerk. Jack Rudman. (Career Examination Ser.: C-2135). 1994. reprint ed. pap. 27.95 (*0-8373-2135-2*) Nat Learn.

Surrogate's Court Procedure Act, N.Y.S. 200p. 1997. ring bd. 10.95 (*0-930137-13-2*) Looseleaf Law.

Surrounded. D'Arcy McNickle. LC 77-91886. (Zia Bks.). 311p. 1978. pap. 12.95 (*0-8263-0469-9*) U of NM Pr.

Surrounded by Dangerous Things. Carol Poster. 48p. 1995. pap. 7.00 (*1-880286-17-3*) Singular Speech Pr.

***Surrounded by Dangers of All Kinds: The Mexican War Letters of Lieutenant Theodore Laidley.** Ed. by James M. McCaffrey. LC 97-22086. (War & the Southwest Ser.: Vol. 6). (Illus.). 240p. 1997. 25.00 (*1-57441-034-2*) UNTX Pr.

Surrounded by Headhunters. Sandra Klaus. (Illus.). 32p. (J). (gr. k-6). 1986. 8.99 (*1-55976-076-1*) CEF Press.

Surrounded by Love.... Kimberly R. Rinehart. Ed. by Georgia M. Rettmer. (Illus.). 1990. pap. 3.95 (*0-942865-11-1*) It Takes Two.

Surrounded by the Cross Fire. Peter R. Doyle. LC 94-10277. (Daring Adventures Ser.: No. 4). 1994. pap. 5.99 (*1-56179-258-6*) Focus Family.

Surry County: Virginia Publick Claims. Janice L. Abercrombie & Richard Slatten. (Virginia Publick Claims Ser.). ix, 19p. 1991. pap. 5.00 (*0-8095-8701-7*) Borgo Pr.

Surry County: Virginia Publick Claims. Janice L. Abercrombie & Richard Slatten. (Virginia Publick Claims Ser.). ix, 19p. (C). 1991. reprint ed. lib. bdg. 25.00 (*0-8095-8364-X*) Borgo Pr.

Surry County Marriages, 1768-1825. Catherine L. Knorr. 124p. 1982. reprint ed. 16.00 (*0-89308-256-2*, VA 14) Southern Hist Pr.

Surry County, N. C., Court Minutes, 1768-1789, Vols. 1 & 2. W. O. Absher. 168p. 1985. pap. 18.50 (*0-89308-554-5*) Southern Hist Pr.

Surry County, N. C., Deeds, 1779-1797, Bks. D, E, & F. 128p. 1985. pap. 15.00 (*0-89308-555-3*) Southern Hist Pr.

Surry County, North Carolina Marriage Bonds & Certificates, 1783-1868, 2 vols., Set. Francis T. Ingmire. 220p. 1994. pap. 30.00 (*0-8095-8699-1*); lib. bdg. 60.00 (*0-8095-8130-2*) Borgo Pr.

Surry County, North Carolina, Wills, 1771-1827: Annotated Genealogical Abstracts. Jo W. Linn. 215p. 1992. 25.00 (*0-8063-1346-3*, 3380) Genealog Pub.

Surry County, Virgina Deed Book 4 (1742-1747) T.L.C. Genealogy Staff. LC 91-66028. 95p. (Orig.). 1991. spiral bd. 15.00 (*1-57445-007-7*) TLC Genealogy.

Surry County, Virginia, Court Orders, 1741-1751: An Every-Name Index. T.L.C. Genealogy Staff. 106p. (Orig.). 1992. spiral bd. 12.00 (*1-57445-008-5*) TLC Genealogy.

Surry County, Virginia Deeds & Estate Accounts, 1733-1755. William L. Hopkins. iv, 163p. 1994. pap. 30.00 (*0-8095-8700-9*); lib. bdg. 60.00 (*0-8095-8299-6*) Borgo Pr.

Surry County Virginia Register of Free Negroes. Ed. by Dennis Hodgins. 339p. (Orig.). 1995. pap. 30.00 (*1-888192-20-8*) VA Geneal Soc.

Surry County Wills, Estate Accounts & Inventories, 1730-1800. Lyndon H. Hart, III. 182p. 1983. pap. 25.00 (*0-89308-325-9*) Southern Hist Pr.

Surry Light Artillery of Virginia: Under the Stars & Bars. Jones, Jr. Ed. by Lee A. Wallace. (Illus.). 425p. 1975. reprint ed. 30.00 (*0-89029-020-2*) Morningside Bkshop.

Surry of Eagle's Nest: Or, the Memoirs of a Staff Officer Serving in Virginia. John E. Cooke. LC 68-23718. (Americans in Fiction Ser.). 484p. reprint ed. lib. bdg. 34.00 (*0-8398-0273-0*) Irvington.

Surry of Eagle's Nest: Or, the Memoirs of a Staff Officer Serving in Virginia. John E. Cooke. (Americans in Fiction Ser.). 484p. (C). 1986. reprint ed. pap. text ed. 8.95 (*0-8290-2037-3*) Irvington.

Sursis. Jean-Paul Sartre. (Chemins des Liberte Ser.: Bk. 2). (FRE.). 1976. pap. 13.95 (*0-8288-3780-5*, F125282) Fr & Eur.

Sursis. Jean-Paul Sartre. (Folio Ser.: No. 866). 1976. pap. 10.95 (*2-07-036866-1*) Schoenhof.

Sursum Corda: Teaching Urban Youths to Read. John C. Hirsh. LC 90-22544. 116p. (Orig.). (C). 1991. pap. text ed. 7.95 (*0-87840-520-8*) Georgetown U Pr.

Sursum Corda! The Collected Letters of Malcolm Lowry, 1926-1946, Vol. I. Malcolm Lowry. Ed. by Sherrill E. Grace. (Illus.). 736p. (C). 1995. 49.95 (*0-8020-0748-1*) U of Toronto Pr.

***Sursum Corda! Vol. 2: The Collected Letters of Malcolm Lowry: 1947-1957.** Ed. by Sherrill E. Grace. 800p. 1996. 60.00 (*0-8020-4118-3*) U of Toronto Pr.

Surti Touch: Adventures in Indian Cooking. Malvi Doshi. LC 80-21487. (Illus.). 224p. (Orig.). 1980. pap. 9.95 (*0-89407-042-8*) Strawberry Hill.

Surtsey: The Newest Place on Earth. Kathryn Lasky. LC 92-52990. (Illus.). 64p. (J). (gr. 3-7). 1992. 15.95 (*1-56282-300-0*); lib. bdg. 15.89 (*1-56282-301-9*) Hyprn Child.

Surtsey: The Newest Place on Earth. Kathryn Lasky. LC 92-52990. (Illus.). 64p. (J). (gr. 3-7). 1994. pap. 6.95 (*0-7868-1004-1*) Hyprn Child.

Suruma. 186p. (Orig.). (SPA.). 1990. pap. 15.00 (*0-9615403-4-6*) Dos Pasos Ed.

Surveill Militarism & Drama. Breight. LC 96-27991. 1996. text ed. 59.95 (*0-312-16406-8*) St Martin.

Surveillance. Ed. by Deborah Irmas & Branda Miller. (Illus.). 55p. (Orig.). (C). 1987. pap. 10.00 (*0-937335-02-9*) LA Contemp Exhib.

Surveillance & Target Acquisition. (Brassey's Battlefield Weapons Systems & Technology Ser.: Vol. 7). 160p. 1983. text ed. 43.00 (*0-08-028334-9*, Pergamon Pr); pap. text ed. 23.00 (*0-08-028335-7*, Pergamon Pr) Elsevier.

Surveillance & Target Aquisition Systems. 2nd ed. M. A. Richardson et al. (Land Warfare - New Battlefield Weapons Systems & Technology Series into the 21st Century). (Illus.). 240p. 1997. 32.95 (*1-85753-137-X*, Pub. by Brasseys UK) Brasseys Inc.

Surveillance Audio Amplifiers: The Cult of Electronic Super-Hearing. Mick Tyner. (Illus.). 277p. (Orig.). 1990. pap. 29.95 (*0-940401-54-1*) Trentland Pr.

Surveillance Countermeasures: A Serious Guide to Detecting, Evading, & Eluding Threats to Personal Privacy. ACM IV Security Services Staff. (Illus.). 144p. 1994. pap. 20.00 (*0-87364-763-7*) Paladin Pr.

Surveillance for Agricultural Prices & Trade: A Handbook for Colombia. Alberto Valdes & Barry Schaeffer. LC 95-2099. (Technical Papers: Vol. 268). 102p. 1995. 8.95 (*0-8213-3117-5*, 13117) World Bank.

Surveillance for Agricultural Prices & Trade: A Handbook for the Dominican Republic. Alberto Valdes & Barry Schaeffer. LC 95-814. (Technical Papers: Vol. 267). 80p. 1995. 7.95 (*0-8213-3116-7*, 13116) World Bank.

***Surveillance for the Prevention & Control of Health Hazards Due to Antibiotic-Resistant Enterobacteria: Report of a WHO Meeting, 1978.** (Technical Report Ser.: No. 624). 54p. 1978. pap. text ed. 6.00 (*92-4-120624-1*, 1100624) World Health.

Surveillance in the Stacks: The FBI's Library Awareness Program. Herbert N. Foerstel. LC 90-38419. (Contributions in Political Science Ser.: No. 266). 184p. 1991. text ed. 49.95 (*0-313-26715-4*, FFG, Greenwood Pr) Greenwood.

***Surveillance of Acute Viral Respiratory Infections in Europe: Report on a WHO Symposium.** (Euro Reports & Studies Ser.: No. 47). 65p. 1981. pap. text ed. 5.00 (*92-890-1213-7*) World Health.

Surveillance of Agricultural Price & Trade Policies: A Handbook for Argentina. Alberto Valdes & Barry Schaeffer. 80p. 1995. 7.95 (*0-8213-3333-X*) World Bank.

Surveillance of Agricultural Price & Trade Policies: A Handbook for Chile. Alberto Valdes & Barry Schaeffer. 88p. 1995. 7.95 (*0-8213-3323-2*, 13323) World Bank.

Surveillance of Agricultural Price & Trade Policies: A Handbook for Ecuador. Alberto Valdes et al. LC 95-50508. (Technical Paper Ser.: No. 314). 84p. 1996. 7.95 (*0-8213-3527-8*, 13527) World Bank.

Surveillance of Agricultural Price & Trade Policies: A Handbook for Paraguay. Alberto Valdes & Barry Schaeffer. LC 96-27955. (World Bank Technical Papers: No. 327). 72p. 1996. 7.95 (*0-8213-3694-0*, 13694) World Bank.

***Surveillance of Agricultural Price & Trade Policy in Latin America During Major Policy Reforms.** Alberto Valdes. LC 96-37184. (Discussion Papers: No. 349). 80p. 1996. 7.95 (*0-8213-3836-6*) World Bank.

Surveillance of Agricultural Prices & Trade: A Handbook for Uruguay. Alberto Valdes & Barry Schaeffer. 76p. 1995. 7.95 (*0-8213-3306-2*, 13306) World Bank.

***Surveillance of Drinking-Water Quality.** WHO Staff. (WHO Monograph Ser.: No. 63). 135p. 1976. 29.00 (*92-4-140063-3*) World Health.

Surveillance of Morbidity & Mortality Module 4: Facilitator's Guide. Martine Hilton. (Primary Health Care Management Advancement Programme (PHC MAP) Modules Ser.). 58p. 1993. pap. text ed. write for info. (*1-882839-18-8*) Aga Khan Fnd.

Surveillance of Morbidity & Mortality Module 4: User's Guide. Pierre Claquin et al. (Primary Health Care Management Advancement Programme (PHC MAP) Modules Ser.). 126p. 1993. pap. text ed. write for info. (*1-882839-15-3*) Aga Khan Fnd.

Surveillance of Reproductive Health in the U. S. Survey of Activity Within & Outside Industry. Maureen Hatch et al. LC 85-71881. (Orig.). 1985. pap. text ed. 20.00 (*0-89364-053-0*, 847-8800) Am Petroleum.

Surveillance, Power & Modernity: Bureaucracy & Discipline from 1700 to the Present Day. Christopher Dandeker. 250p. 1990. text ed. 49.95 (*0-312-04222-1*) St Martin.

Surveillance, Privacy, & the Law: Employee Drug Testing & the Politics of Social Control. John Gilliom. LC 94-176. (Law, Meaning, & Violence Ser.). 200p. 1994. 34.50 (*0-472-10493-4*) U of Mich Pr.

Surveillance, Privacy, & the Law: Employee Drug Testing & the Politics of Social Control. John Gilliom. (C). 1996. pap. 19.95 (*0-472-08416-X*) U of Mich Pr.

Surveiller et Punir: Naissance de la Prison. Michel Foucault. (Tel Ser.). 315p. (FRE.). 1975. pap. 23.95 (*2-07-072968-0*) Schoenhof.

Surveiors Dialogue... for All Men to Peruse, That Have to Do with the Revenues of Land, or the Manurance, Use or Occupation. Third Time Imprinted & Enlarged. John Norden. LC 79-84126. (English Experience Ser.: No. 945). 280p. 1979. reprint ed. lib. bdg. 26.00 (*90-221-0945-3*) Walter J Johnson.

Survey Accounting. Joseph G. Louderback. Date not set. teacher ed., pap. text ed. write for info. (*0-314-01400-4*); student ed., pap. text ed. 21.75 (*0-314-01401-2*) West Pub.

Survey & Evaluation of Factors Affecting Heat Transfer Performance & Cost of Steam Condensers. North Carolina State University Staff. 93p. 1967. 13.95 (*0-317-34551-6*, 104) Intl Copper.

***Survey & Excavations in Southern Ecuador.** Donald Collier & John V. Murra. LC 43-11409. (Field Museum of Natural History Anthropological Ser.: Vol. 35, May 15, 1943). (Illus.). 227p. 1943. reprint ed. pap. 64.70 (*0-608-02701-4*, 2063366) Bks Demand.

Survey & Excavations North & East of Navajo Mountain, Utah, 1959-1962. Alexander J. Lindsay, Jr. et al. (Glen Canyon Ser.: No. 8). 400p. 1968. pap. 12.50 (*0-685-14708-8*, BS-45) Mus Northern Ariz.

***Survey & Planning Grant 1980.** Ed. by N. H. Hannan. (Illus.). 552p. 1992. reprint ed. pap. 50.00 (*0-614-28422-8*) Albert Hse Pub.

Survey & Public Opinion Research: Grades Five to Twelve. 2nd ed. Lois F. Roets. 120p. (J). (gr. 3 up). 1988. 16.00 (*0-911943-14-5*) Leadership Pub.

Survey & Statistical Computing: Proceedings of an International Conference Organized by the Study Group on Computers in Survey Analysis, Bristol, U. K. September 24-26, 1992. Ed. by Andrew Westlake et al. LC 92-26712. 502p. 1992. 165.00 (*0-444-89779-8*, North Holland) Elsevier.

Survey Coordinator's Handbook: Winning Strategies for Your JCAHO Survey. (Illus.). 250p. (Orig.). 1996. pap. text ed. 97.00 (*1-885829-33-7*) Opus Communs.

Survey Design & Analysis Using TURBOSTATS. Mike Hart. LC 93-3296. 160p. 1993. pap. 26.95 (*0-412-54830-5*) Chapman & Hall.

Survey Drafting: Drafting Practices in Surveying & Engineering Offices. 3rd ed. Gurdon H. Wattles. LC 81-52885. 382p. 1981. teacher ed. 28.00 (*0-9606962-0-2*) Wattles Pubns.

Survey Economics. Tucker. Date not set. 18.25 (*0-314-04673-9*) West Pub.

An Asterisk (*) at the beginning of an entry indicates that the title is appearing in BIP for the first time.

Survey Errors & Survey Cost. Robert M. Groves. LC 89-5674. 590p. 1989. text ed. 129.00 (*0-471-61171-9*) Wiley.

Survey Graphic. Ed. by Alain L. Locke. (Illus.). 92p. 1980. reprint ed. pap. 10.00 (*0-933121-05-9*) Black Classic.

Survey Handbook. Arlene Fink. (Survey Kit Ser.: Vol. 1). 144p. 1995. pap. 16.95 (*0-8039-5934-6*) Sage.

Survey in Basic Christianity. Jean Gibson. (Believer's Bible Lessons Ser.). 1979. pap. 9.50 (*0-937396-41-9*) Walterick Pubs.

Survey in Comfort: A Tool for Archaeoastronomical Studies. David S. Dearborn. (Astronomy & Astrophysics Ser.). (Illus.). 60p. 1985. pap. 15.00 (*0-934525-01-3*); disk 50.00 (*0-934525-03-X*) West Research.

Survey in Comfort: A Tool of Archaeoastronomical Studies. David S. Dearborn. (Astronomy & Astrophysics Ser.). (Illus.). 60p. 1985. 50.00 incl. disk (*0-934525-02-1*) West Research.

Survey in Zeelandia of Formosa. Lin Yung. (Asian Folklore & Social Life Monographs: No. 96). (CHI.). 1977. 14.00 (*0-89986-328-0*) Oriental Bk Store.

Survey Interviewing: Theory & Techniques. Ed. by Terence W. Beed & Robert J. Stimson. 224p. (C). 1985. text ed. 34.95 (*0-86861-436-X*) Routledge Chapman & Hall.

Survey Kit, 9 vols., Set. Arlene Fink. 1995. pap. 132.55 (*0-8039-7388-8*) Sage.

***Survey Measurement & Process Quality.** Ed. by Lars Lyberg et al. 808p. 1997. 94.95 (*0-471-16559-X*) Wiley.

Survey Method: The Contribution of Surveys to Sociological Explanation. Catherine Marsh. (Contemporary Social Research Ser.: No. 6). 272p. (C). 1982. pap. text ed. 19.95 (*0-04-310015-5*) Routledge Chapman & Hall.

Survey Methodology & Uses. Albert Parker. Ed. by Laurie Bryant. 15p. (Orig.). 1979. pap. 9.00 (*0-317-04922-4*) Natl Coun Econ Dev.

***Survey Methodology for Temperate Marine Habitats.** Michael Kingsford & Chris Battershill. (Illus.). 160p. (Orig.). (C). 1996. pap. 39.95 (*0-908812-54-X*, Pub. by Canterbury Univ NZ) Aubrey Bks.

Survey Methods & Statistical Summary of Nonfuel Minerals. (Metals & Minerals Ser.). 1993. lib. bdg. 250.95 (*0-8490-8965-4*) Gordon Pr.

Survey Methods in Community Medicine: Epidemiological Studies, Programme Evaluation, Clinical Trials. 4th ed. J. H. Abramson. (Illus.). 339p. 1990. pap. text ed. 32.00 (*0-443-04196-2*) Churchill.

Survey of a Public School System. Henry L. Smith. LC 75-177774. (Columbia University. Teachers College. Contributions to Education Ser.: No. 82). reprint ed. 37.50 (*0-404-55082-7*) AMS Pr.

Survey of Accounting. Ronald J. Huefner & Robert P. Derstine. 1988. text ed. write for info. (*0-07-030822-5*) McGraw.

Survey of Accounting. Joseph G. Louderback, III et al. Ed. by Fenton. LC 92-24023. 700p. (C). 1993. text ed. 63.00 (*0-314-01041-6*) West Pub.

Survey of Accounting. Richard G. Schroeder & Charles P. Zlatkovich. 783p. (C). 1990. text ed. 59.95 (*0-256-07007-5*, 01-2816-01) Irwin.

Survey of Accounting. James D. Stice. (AB - Accounting Principles Ser.). Date not set. pap. 55.95 (*0-538-84617-8*) S-W Pub.

***Survey of Accounting.** James D. Stice. (AB - Accounting Principles Ser.). Date not set. student ed., pap. 23.95 (*0-538-87324-8*) S-W Pub.

***Survey of Accounting.** Carl S. Warren. (Miscellaneous/Catalogs Ser.). Date not set. text ed. 68.95 (*0-538-87085-0*) S-W Pub.

Survey of Accounting: Selected Chapters. 2nd ed. David H. Marshall. (C). 1994. text ed. 34.00 (*0-256-18085-7*) Irwin.

Survey of Accounting: What the Numbers Mean. 2nd ed. David H. Marshall. LC 92-16798. 640p. (C). 1992. text ed. 71.75 (*0-256-11301-7*) Irwin.

Survey of Accounting: What the Numbers Mean. 2nd ed. David H. Marshall. 320p. (C). 1992. student ed., text ed. 24.50 (*0-256-11328-9*) Irwin.

***Survey of Accounting Practices in the European Oil & Gas Industry.** Institute of Petroleum Accounting Staff. 79p. 1997. pap. 25.00 (*0-926969-03-X*) UNTIPA.

Survey of Adult Aphasia & Related Language Disorders. 2nd ed. G. Albyn Davis. LC 92-49840. 400p. (C). 1992. text ed. 70.00 (*0-13-878018-8*) P-H.

Survey of Advanced Microprocessor Architectures. Andrew M. Veronis. (Illus.). 416p. 1991. text ed. 59.95 (*0-442-00120-7*) Van Nos Reinhold.

Survey of Advanced Sales. 6th ed. Dearborn-R & R Newkirk Staff. LC 96-20652. 1996. write for info. (*0-7931-2141-8*) Dearborn Trade.

Survey of African Marriage & Family Life. Arthur Phillips. LC 74-15079. reprint ed. 67.50 (*0-404-12128-4*) AMS Pr.

Survey of Agriculture Economics Literature, Vol. 4. Ed. by Lee R. Martin. (Illus.). 1064p. (C). 1991. text ed. 59.95 (*0-8166-1942-5*) U of Minn Pr.

Survey of American Economic Fiction. Lisle A. Rose. (BCL1-PS American Literature Ser.). 22p. 1993. reprint ed. lib. bdg. 59.00 (*0-7812-6593-2*) Rprt Serv.

Survey of American Foreign Relations: 1928, 1929, 2 vols. Charles P. Howland. Ea. 89.50 (*0-686-50174-8*) Elliots Bks.

Survey of American Gambling Attitudes & Behavior. Maureen Kallick et al. 560p. (Orig.). 1979. pap. 25.00 (*0-87944-245-X*) Inst Soc Res.

Survey of American Gambling Attitudes & Behavior. Maureen Kallick et al. LC 79-89198. (Institute for Social Research, Research Report Ser.). 580p. reprint ed. pap. 165.30 (*0-7837-5253-9*, 2044990) Bks Demand.

Survey of American Genealogical Periodicals & Periodical Indexes. Ed. by Kip Sperry. LC 78-55033. (Genealogy & Local History Ser.: Vol. 3). 216p. 1978. 68.00 (*0-8103-1401-0*) Gale.

Survey of American Law. Schneemana. (Paralegal Ser.). 1994. teacher ed., pap. 15.00 (*0-8273-6079-7*) Delmar.

Survey of American Poetry: Civil War & Aftermath (1861-1889)., Vol. V+ Granger Book Company, Editorial Board Staff. LC 81-83526. 400p. 1985. lib. bdg. 39.95 (*0-89609-217-8*) Roth Pub Inc.

Survey of American Poetry: Early Nineteenth Century, 1800-1829. Ed. by Granger Book Company, Editorial Board Staff. LC 81-83526. (Series II: Vol. III). 286p. 1984. 39.95 (*0-89609-215-1*) Roth Pub Inc.

Survey of American Poetry: First Great Period, 1830-1860. Granger Book Company, Editorial Board Staff. LC 81-83526. (Series II: Vol. IV). 1984. 39.95 (*0-89609-216-X*) Roth Pub Inc.

Survey of American Poetry: Revolutionary Era. 1766-1799, Vol. II. Granger Book Company, Editorial Board Staff. LC 81-83526. 200p. 1983. 39.95 (*0-89609-214-3*) Roth Pub Inc.

Survey of American Poetry: Twilight Interval, 1890-1912, Vol. VI. Granger Book Company, Editorial Board Staff. LC 81-83526. 400p. 1986. 39.95 (*0-89609-218-6*) Roth Pub Inc.

Survey of American Poetry, Vol. I: Colonial Period (1607-1765) Granger Book Company, Editorial Board Staff. LC 81-83526. 220p. 1982. 39.95 (*0-89609-213-5*) Roth Pub Inc.

Survey of American Poetry, Vol. IX: World War II & Aftermath (1940-1950) Roth Publishing, Inc. Staff. LC 81-83526. 1986. 39.95 (*0-89609-221-6*) Roth Pub Inc.

Survey of American Poetry, Vol. VII: Poetic Renaissance (1913-1919) Roth Publishing, Inc. Staff. LC 81-83526. 380p. 1986. 39.95 (*0-89609-219-4*) Roth Pub Inc.

Survey of American Poetry, Vol. VIII: Interval Between World Wars (1920-1939) Roth Publishing, Inc. Staff. LC 81-83526. 380p. 1986. 39.95 (*0-89609-220-8*) Roth Pub Inc.

Survey of American Poetry, Vol. X: Midcentury to 1984. Roth Publishing, Inc. Staff. LC 81-83526. 370p. 1986. 39.95 (*0-89609-222-4*) Roth Pub Inc.

Survey of Ancient Peruvian Art. Philip A. Means. (Connecticut Academy of Arts & Sciences Ser., Trans.: Vol. 21). 1917. pap. 75.00 (*0-685-44363-9*) Elliots Bks.

Survey of Applicable, Vol. II. Maia & Karel Rektorys. 1994. write for info. (*0-7923-0681-3*) Kluwer Ac.

Survey of Applicable Mathematics, 2 vols. 2nd rev. ed. Karel Rektorys. (Mathematics & Its Applications Ser.). 1769p. 1994. lib. bdg. 595.00 (*0-7923-0679-1*) Kluwer Ac.

Survey of Arab History. rev. ed. Bernard G. Weiss & Arnold H. Green. 320p. 1988. pap. 22.50 (*977-424-180-0*, Pub. by Am Univ Cairo Pr UA) Col U Pr.

Survey of Archeological Resources & an Evaluation of Buried Site Potential in Northwestern Oklahoma County, Oklahoma. Jack L. Hofman et al. (Archeological Resource Survey Report). (Illus.). 101p. (C). 1990. pap. text ed. 9.00 (*1-881346-24-2*) Univ OK Archeol.

Survey of Arts Administration Training: 1991-1992. rev. ed. Ed. by E. Arthur Prieve. LC 91-12452. 96p. (Orig.). 1991. pap. 11.95 (*0-915400-90-1*, ACA Bks) Am Council Arts.

Survey of Asia's Energy Prices. Anil K. Malhotra. LC 94-16612. (Technical Papers: Vol. 248). 1994. 11.95 (*0-8213-2860-3*, 12860) World Bank.

Survey of Basic Accounting. 2nd ed. Roland F. Salmonson et al. (C). 1976. 17.95 (*0-256-01890-1*) Irwin.

Survey of Basic Skills: Grade Six, Rationale & Content. California Department of Education Staff. 72p. 1982. pap. 6.00 (*0-8011-0267-7*) Calif Education.

Survey of Bible Doctrine. Charles C. Ryrie. LC 72-77958. 192p. (C). 1972. pap. 10.99 (*0-8024-8438-7*) Moody.

***Survey of Biology Lecture Outlines.** John M. DeBow. 231p. (C). 1995. wbk. ed. 18.84 (*1-890756-00-8*, 36121-1) VisionKeeper.

Survey of Biomedical & Clinical Engineering Department in U. S. Hospitals, 1985. Allan F. Pacela. 27p. (Orig.). 1985. pap. text ed. 40.00 (*0-930844-18-1*) Quest Pub.

Survey of Black Newspapers in America. Intro. by Henry G. La Brie, III. LC 80-80551. (Mass Communication & Journalism Ser.). 72p. (Orig.). 1980. 6.00 (*0-89080-034-0*) Mercer Hse.

Survey of British Commonwealth Affairs, 2 vols., Set. William K. Hancock. LC 74-15049. reprint ed. 62.50 (*0-404-12084-9*) AMS Pr.

Survey of British Commonwealth Affairs: Problems of Wartime Cooperation & Post-War Change, 1939-1952. Nicholas Mansergh. 470p. 1968. reprint ed. 47.50 (*0-7146-1496-3*, Pub. by F Cass Pubs UK) Intl Spec Bk.

Survey of British Poetry, Vol. Four: Nineteenth Century. Ed. by Roth Publishing, Inc. Staff. 400p. 1992. 59.95 (*0-89609-277-1*) Roth Pub Inc.

Survey of British Poetry, Vol. I: Old English to Renaissance. Ed. by Roth Publishing, Inc. Staff. 442p. 1988. 59.95 (*0-89609-274-7*) Roth Pub Inc.

Survey of British Poetry, Vol. II: Cavalier to Restoration, Vol. 2. Ed. by Roth Publishing, Inc. Staff. 365p. 1989. 59.95 (*0-89609-275-5*) Roth Pub Inc.

Survey of British Poetry, Vol. III: Eighteenth Century. Ed. by Roth Publishing, Inc. Staff. LC 88-60329. 438p. 1991. 59.95 (*0-89609-276-3*) Roth Pub Inc.

Survey of Bromide in Drinking Water & Impacts on DBP Formation. (Illus.). 108p. 1995. pap. 56.00 (*0-89867-783-1*, 90662) Am Water Wks Assn.

Survey of Buddhism: Its Doctrines & Methods Through the Ages. 7th ed. Sangharakshita. 544p. 1996. reprint ed. pap. 24.95 (*0-904766-65-9*) Windhorse Pubns.

Survey of Cable Subscribers: Viewing Preferences for Channels 4, 13, & 19. CAUR Staff. 25p. (Orig.). 1985. pap. 2.50 (*1-55719-037-2*) U NE CPAR.

Survey of Calculus. Wiggins. (Mathematics Ser.). 1996. text ed. 77.95 (*0-534-92874-9*) PWS Pubs.

Survey of Carpentry Masterpieces. Ed. by G. Lister Sutcliffe. (Modern Carpenter Joiner & Cabinet-Maker Ser.: Vol. 5). (Illus.). 128p. 1990. reprint ed. 19.95 (*0-918678-59-5*) Natl Hist Soc.

Survey of Cenozoic Volcanism on Mainland Asia. J. L. Whitford-Stark. (Special Papers: No. 213). (Illus.). 82p. 1987. pap. 1.00 (*0-8137-2213-6*) Geol Soc.

Survey of Chemical & Biological Warfare. John Cookson & Judith Nottingham. LC 79-128595. 428p. reprint ed. pap. 122.00 (*0-8357-3560-5*, 2034338) Bks Demand.

***Survey of Chemicals Being Tested for Carcinogenicity.** (IARC Information Bulletin Ser.: No. 9). 294p. 1981. text ed. 41.00 (*92-832-1309-2*) World Health.

***Survey of Chemicals Being Tested for Carcinogenicity.** (IARC Information Bulletin Ser.). 326p. 1982. text ed. 42.00 (*92-832-1310-6*) World Health.

***Survey of Chemicals Being Tested for Carcinogenicity.** (IARC Information Bulletin Ser.: No. 11). 368p. 1984. text ed. 50.00 (*92-832-1311-4*) World Health.

***Survey of Chemicals Being Tested for Carcinogenicity.** M. Ghess & J. Wilbourn. (IARC Information Bulletin Ser.: No. 13). 413p. 1988. text ed. 43.00 (*92-832-1313-0*) World Health.

Survey of Chester County Pennsylvania Architecture. Margaret B. Schiffer. LC 76-4683. 396p. 1976. 35.00 (*0-916838-02-1*) Schiffer.

Survey of Chinese Aviation Industry 1995-1996. annuals (CHI & ENG.). 1995. 255.00 (*7-80046-907-7*, V189, Pub. by HUWEI Cnslts CH) Am Overseas Bk Co.

Survey of Choral Music. Homer Ulrich. (Harbrace History of Musical Forms Ser.). 245p. (C). 1973. pap. text ed. 17.50 (*0-15-584863-1*) HB Coll Pubs.

Survey of Christian Ethics. Edward L. Long, Jr. 352p. 1982. pap. 18.95 (*0-19-503242-X*) OUP.

Survey of Christian Hymnody. rev. ed. William J. Reynolds & Milburn Price. LC 87-81996. (Illus.). 300p. 1987. pap. text ed. 24.95 (*0-916642-32-1*, 904) Hope Pub.

Survey of Church History. J. D. O'Donnell. 1973. pap. 6.95 (*0-89265-009-5*) Randall Hse.

Survey of Citizen Attitudes & Opinions Regarding the Austin, Texas, Police Department & Its Relations with the Community. James W. Stevens et al. 68p. (Orig.). 1986. pap. text ed. 8.00 (*0-936440-72-4*) U TX SUPA.

Survey of Commercial Turnkey CAD-CAM Systems. 2nd ed. 96.00 (*0-686-31441-7*) C I M Systems.

Survey of Communication Disorders. John M. Palmer. (Illus.). 288p. 1990. 39.00 (*0-683-06743-5*) Williams & Wilkins.

Survey of Communication Disorders: A Social & Behavioral Perspective. Marylou P. Gelfer. LC 95-11270. 1995. text ed. write for info. (*0-07-023453-1*) McGraw.

Survey of Community Workers in the United Kingdom. David Francis et al. (C). 1984. 50.00 (*0-685-40336-X*, Pub. by Natl Inst Soc Work) St Mut.

Survey of Company Car Schemes 1993-94. Peter Burgess. 160p. 1993. 135.00 (*0-85459-768-9*, Pub. by Tolley Pubng UK) St Mut.

Survey of Compounds Which Have Been Tested for Carcinogenic Activity. 1995. lib. bdg. 2,995.99 (*0-8490-6706-5*) Gordon Pr.

***Survey of Compounds Which Have Been Tested for Carcinogenic Activity, 2 vols.** 1997. lib. bdg. 600.99 (*0-8490-8143-2*) Gordon Pr.

Survey of Constantin Brancusi's Work. Sandra Miller. (Clarendon Studies in the History of Art). (Illus.). 256p. 1995. 68.00 (*0-19-817514-0*) OUP.

Survey of Constitutional Development in China. Hawkling L. Yen. LC 72-76693. (Columbia University. Studies in the Social Sciences: No. 104). reprint ed. 32.50 (*0-404-51104-X*) AMS Pr.

Survey of Contemporary Literature, 12 vols., Set. Ed. by Frank N. Magill. LC 77-79874. 8531p. 1977. lib. bdg. 350.00 (*0-89356-050-2*) Salem Pr.

Survey of Contemporary Music. Cecil Gray. LC 75-93341. (Essay Index Reprint Ser.). 1977. 21.95 (*0-8369-1294-2*) Ayer.

Survey of Contemporary Music. 2nd ed. Cecil Gray. LC 78-163551. 266p. 1973. reprint ed. text ed. 59.75 (*0-8371-6211-4*, GRCM, Greenwood Pr) Greenwood.

Survey of Contemporary Music. Cecil Gray. 266p. 1990. reprint ed. lib. bdg. 69.00 (*0-685-45702-8*) Rprt Serv.

Survey of Contemporary Toxicology, Vol. 1. Ed. by Anthony T. Tu. LC 79-25224. 367p. reprint ed. pap. 104.60 (*0-8357-3561-3*, 2032003) Bks Demand.

Survey of Contemporary Toxicology, Vol. 2. Ed. by Anthony T. Tu. LC 79-25224. (Illus.). 248p. reprint ed. pap. 70.70 (*0-8357-3562-1*, 2056809) Bks Demand.

Survey of Corporate Government Affairs Departments. Rebecca S. Fahrlander. 48p. (Orig.). 1984. pap. 3.50 (*1-55719-004-6*) U NE CPAR.

Survey of Corrosion Inhibitors & Related Additives to Improve the Corrosion Resistance & Heat Transfer of Copper & Its Alloys. Battelle Memorial Institute Staff. 59p. 1969. 8.85 (*0-317-34552-4*, 148) Intl Copper.

Survey of Covenant History. Walter R. Roehrs. 208p. 1989. 15.95 (*0-570-04244-5*, 15-2197) Concordia.

Survey of Criminal History Information Systems (1992) 60p. (Orig.). (C). 1994. pap. text ed. 30.00 (*0-7881-0401-2*) DIANE Pub.

Survey of Criminal History Information Systems (1993) With Supplementary Information on Presale Firearm Check (1994) (Illus.). 74p. (Orig.). (C). 1995. pap. text ed. 30.00 (*0-7881-1904-4*) DIANE Pub.

Survey of Criminal Law. 2nd ed. Hall. (Paralegal Ser.). 1997. teacher ed. 10.50 (*0-8273-7571-9*) Delmar.

Survey of Criminal Law. 2nd ed. Daniel Hall. (Paralegal Ser.). (Illus.). 352p. 1996. pap. 35.95 (*0-8273-7570-0*) Delmar.

Survey of Cripples in New York City: Under the Auspices of a Special Committee on Survey of Cripples. Henry C. Wright. Ed. by William R. Phillips & Janet Rosenberg. LC 79-6014. (Physically Handicapped in Society Ser.). 1980. reprint ed. lib. bdg. 15.95 (*0-405-13137-2*) Ayer.

Survey of Cuban Revistas, 1902-1958. Anno. & Compiled by Roberto Esquenazi-Mayo. LC 92-20930. 1993. write for info. (*0-8444-0758-5*) Lib Congress.

Survey of Current Structural Research. (Manual & Report on Engineering Practice Ser.: No. 51). 335p. 1970. pap. 30.00 (*0-87262-225-8*) Am Soc Civil Eng.

Survey of Damage to Historic Adobe Buildings after the January 1994 Northridge Earthquake. E. Leroy Tolles et al. LC 96-19185. (GCI Scientific Program Reports Ser.). (Illus.). 176p. (Orig.). 1996. pap. 20.00 (*0-89236-391-6*, Getty Conservation Inst) J P Getty Trust.

Survey of Development Control Issues. Keith Thomas. (C). 1988. 59.00 (*0-685-30248-2*, Pub. by Oxford Polytechnic UK) St Mut.

Survey of Direct U. S. Private Capital Investment in Research & Development Facilities in Japan. (Illus.). 124p. (Orig.). (C). 1993. pap. text ed. 60.00 (*1-56806-534-5*) DIANE Pub.

***Survey of Distance Learning Programs in Higher Education.** Primary Research Group Staff. 100p. 1997. pap. 85.00 (*1-57440-009-6*) Primary Research.

Survey of Distributed Multimedia: Research, Standards & Products. Ed. by Chris Adie. 150p. (Orig.). (C). 1993. pap. text ed. 50.00 (*0-7881-0039-4*) DIANE Pub.

Survey of Early American Design. Ed. by Lisa C. Mullins. (Architectural Treasures of Early America Ser.). (Illus.). 248p. 1987. 19.95 (*0-918678-20-X*) Natl Hist Soc.

***Survey of Early American Design.** Ed. by Russell F. Whitehead et al. (Architectural Treasures of Early America Ser.). (Illus.). 224p. 1977. 16.95 (*0-405-10071-X*) Arno Press.

Survey of Early Childhood Abilities. Karen G. Codding. 1987. teacher ed., pap. 15.00 (*0-931421-10-1*); student ed. 14.00 (*0-931421-23-3*); 8.00 (*0-931421-21-7*); 26.00 (*0-931421-24-1*); lp 22.00 (*0-931421-22-5*) Psychol Educ Pubns.

Survey of Ecological Economics. Ed. by Rajaram Krishnan et al. (Frontier Issues in Economic Thought Ser.: No. 1). 350p. 1995. text ed. 49.95 (*1-55963-410-3*) Island Pr.

Survey of Ecological Economics. Ed. by Rajaram Krishnan et al. (Frontier Issues in Economic Thought Ser.: No. 1). 350p. (C). 1995. pap. text ed. 24.95 (*1-55963-411-1*) Island Pr.

Survey of Economic & Social Conditions in Africa. 202p. 1995. pap. 28.00 (*92-1-125067-6*, E.95.II.K.1) UN.

Survey of Economic & Social Conditions in Africa, 1985-1986. 1988. 19.00 (*92-1-125052-8*, E.88.II.K.1) UN.

Survey of Economic & Social Conditions in Africa, 1986-1987. 161p. 19.00 (*92-1-125053-6*, E. 88. II.K.12) UN.

Survey of Economic & Social Conditions in Africa, 1987-1988. 161p. 1988. 19.00 (*92-1-125055-2*, 90-II.K.1) UN.

Survey of Economic & Social Developments in the ESCWA Region. 250p. 1990. 49.00 (*92-1-128120-2*, 90.II.L.10) UN.

Survey of Economic & Social Developments in the ESCWA Region. 264p. 1994. pap. 42.00 (*92-1-128147-4*, E.94.II.L.11) UN.

Survey of Economic & Social Developments in the ESCWA Region in the 1980s. 254p. 1990. 35.00 (*0-685-39213-9*, 90.II.L.2) UN.

Survey of Economic Theory on Technological Change & Employment. Alexander Gourvitch. LC 66-23421. (Reprints of Economic Classics Ser.). xiii, 252p. 1966. reprint ed. 37.50 (*0-678-00113-8*) Kelley.

Survey of Economics. Clark. (AB - Accounting Principles Ser.). 1997. pap. 54.95 (*0-538-84677-1*) S-W Pub.

Survey of Economics. Clark. (Miscellaneous/Catalogs Ser.). (C). 1997. pap. 22.95 (*0-538-86853-8*) S-W Pub.

Survey of Economics. Irvin B. Tucker, III. LC 94-3692. 492p. (C). 1995. pap. text ed. 50.25 (*0-314-04019-6*) West Pub.

Survey of Economics. 2nd ed. Ali Hekmat et al. 358p. (C). 1996. pap. text ed. 41.50 (*1-56226-284-X*) CT Pub.

Survey of Economics. 2nd ed. James Lassiter & James Gilbertie. 527p. (C). 1992. pap. text ed. 50.56 (*1-56226-118-5*) CT Pub.

***Survey of Economics.** 2nd ed. Tucker. (HB - Economics Ser.). 1998. student ed., pap. 17.95 (*0-538-87775-8*); text ed. 48.95 (*0-538-87772-3*) S-W Pub.

Survey of Electronics. Oppenheimer. (C). 1990. teacher ed., pap. text ed. 38.25 (*0-03-020843-2*) HB Coll Pubs.

Survey of Electronics. Samuel L. Oppenheimer. 500p. (C). 1990. text ed. 40.00 (*0-03-020842-4*) SCP.

Survey of Employee Benefits. John Wilkinson. 140p. 1991. 135.00 (*0-85459-587-2*, Pub. by Tolley Pubng UK) St Mut.

Survey of Energy Demand Elasticity Estimates in Developing Countries. Corazon M. Siddavao. (Technical Memorandum Ser.: No. 80-7). 79p. reprint ed. pap. 25.00 (*0-317-42012-7*, 2025970) Bks Demand.

Survey of English Dialects: The Dictionary & Grammar. Clive Upton et al. LC 93-20391. 512p. (C). (gr. 13). 1994. text ed. 185.00 (*0-415-02029-8*, B0245) Routledge.

Survey of English Literature, 1830-1880, 2 vols., Set. Oliver Elton. LC 75-41016. (BCL Ser. II). reprint ed. 75.00 (*0-404-14900-6*) AMS Pr.

Survey of English Spelling. Edward M. Carney. LC 93-3378. 544p. (C). (gr. 13). 1993. text ed. 79.95 (*0-415-09270-1*, B0010) Routledge.

S

Survey of Equipment for Small-Scale Motive Power & Electricity Generation from Wood & Agricultural Residues. Ed. by E. A. Williams & A. P. Robinson. 1993. pap. 25.00 (*0-85954-324-2*, Pub. by Nat Res Inst UK) St Mut.

Survey of European Nuclear Policy, 1985-87. Ed. by Harald Muller. 240p. 1989. text ed. 55.00 (*0-312-02796-6*) St Martin.

Survey of Extensible Programming Language see Annual Review in Automatic Programming

Survey of Factors Affecting the Use of Copper in Steel. Southern Research Institute Staff. 58p. 1966. 8.70 (*0-317-34553-2*, 84) Intl Copper.

Survey of Family Literacy in the United States. Ed. by Lesley M. Morrow. 140p. 1995. pap. 14.95 (*0-87207-131-6*) Intl Reading.

Survey of Federal Writers' Project Manuscript Holdings in State Depositories. Anne Banks & Robert Carter. 32p. 1985. pap. 6.00 (*0-87229-028-X*) Am Hist Assn.

Survey of Financial & Managerial Accounting. 5th ed. Roger H. Hermanson et al. 607p. (C). 1988. 21.95 (*0-256-06977-8*) Irwin.

Survey of Finite Mathematics. Marvin Marcus. LC 92-43550. (Illus.). 496p. 1993. reprint ed. pap. 12.95 (*0-486-67553-X*) Dover.

Survey of FLES Practices see Current Issues in Language Teaching

Survey of Foliar Flavonoids in the Aceraceae. Thomas J. Delendick. LC 89-29446. (Memoirs Ser.: No. 54). (Illus.). 136p. 1990. pap. 33.50 (*0-89327-343-0*) NY Botanical.

Survey of Folklife along the Big South Fork of the Cumberland River. Benita J. Howell. (University of Tennessee, Department of Anthropology, Report of Investigations Ser.: No. 30). (Illus.). 454p. reprint ed. pap. 129.40 (*0-685-20455-3*, 2029848) Bks Demand.

Survey of Foreign Laws & Regulations Affecting International Franchising. 2nd ed. LC 89-81634. 912p. 1989. 140.00 (*0-89707-509-9*, 503-0081) Amer Bar Assn.

Survey of French Literature, 2 vols. rev. ed. Morris Bishop. Incl. Vol. 1. Middle Ages to 1800. rev. ed. 462p. (C). 1965. text ed. 40.00 (*0-15-584963-8*); Vol. 2. Nineteenth & Twentieth Centuries. rev. ed. 462p. (C). 1965. text ed. 52.25 (*0-15-584964-6*); 462p. (C). 1965. Set text ed. write for info. (*0-685-02107-6*) HB Coll Pubs.

Survey of Functional Neuroanatomy. Bill Garoutte. LC 80-84809. (Illus.). 217p. (C). 1982. pap. text ed. 9.75 (*0-930010-04-3*) Jones Med.

Survey of Functional Neuroanatomy. 3rd ed. Bill Garoutte. (Illus.). 224p. (C). 1994. pap. text ed. 15.00 (*0-9643644-0-9*) Mill Valley Med.

Survey of Gas Utility & Pipeline Research & Development. Institute of Gas Technology Staff & J. Glenn Seay. 246p. 1972. pap. 10.00 (*0-318-12715-6*, M21173) Am Gas Assn.

Survey of Graduate Students & Postdoctorates in Science & Engineering: Technical Notes & Data Summaries. Ed. by J. G. Huckenpohler. (Illus.). 73p. (Orig.). (C). 1994. pap. text ed. 25.00 (*0-7881-1431-X*) DIANE Pub.

Survey of Graves in the Cemeteries of Northwest Pasco County, Florida. West Pasco County Genealogical Society Staff. Ed. by Berangere Boisselle. (Illus.). 151p. (C). 1984. 22.00 (*0-9614369-0-5*) West Pasco County Genealogical.

Survey of Greek Alchemy. Frank S. Taylor. LC 79-8627. reprint ed. 31.50 (*0-404-18493-6*) AMS Pr.

Survey of Health Care Reform: Fifty States & Washington, D.C. Dolores A. Sands. 200p. (Orig.). (C). 1994. pap. text ed. 4.00 (*0-7881-0750-X*) DIANE Pub.

***Survey of Health Reform in Central Asia.** Jeni G. Klugman & George Schieber. (Technical Paper Ser.: No. 344). 68p. 1997. pap. 7.95 (*0-8213-3804-8*, 13804) World Bank.

Survey of Hidden Variables Theories. F. J. Belinfante. 376p. (C). 1973. text ed. 166.00 (*0-08-017032-3*, Pub. by Pergamon Repr UK) Franklin.

Survey of High-Level Synthesis Systems. Ed. by Robert A. Walker & Raul Camposano. (C). 1991. lib. bdg. 81.00 (*0-7923-9158-6*) Kluwer Ac.

Survey of Hinduism. 2nd ed. Klaus K. Klostermaier. LC 93-46778. 715p. (C). 1994. text ed. 59.50 (*0-7914-2109-0*) State U NY Pr.

Survey of Hinduism. 2nd ed. Klaus K. Klostermaier. LC 93-46778. 715p. (C). 1994. pap. text ed. 21.95 (*0-7914-2110-4*) State U NY Pr.

Survey of Hinduism. Klaus K. Klostermaier. (Illus.). 656p. 1990. reprint ed. 42.50 (*0-317-99943-5*, Pub. by M Manoharial II) Coronet Bks.

Survey of Historic Costume. 2nd ed. Phyllis G. Tortora & Keith Eubank. LC 93-72152. 522p. 1994. text ed. 55.00 (*1-56367-003-8*) Fairchild.

Survey of Independent Presses, 1989-1990: Sorted & Analyzed by Number of Titles in Print. Laing Research Services Staff. 70p. 1990. 95.00 (*0-938106-08-2*) Laing Res Servs.

Survey of Independent Presses, 1989-1990: Sorted & Analyzed by Publisher's Annual Gross Revenue. Laing Research Services Staff. 70p. 1990. 95.00 (*0-938106-11-2*) Laing Res Servs.

Survey of Indian Metal Sculpture. B. Bandopadhyay. 217p. 1987. 99.95 (*0-318-36259-3*) Asia Bk Corp.

Survey of Indian Metal Sculpture. B. Bandyopahyay. 217p. 1987. 65.00 (*0-8364-2035-7*, Pub. by Usha II) S Asia.

Survey of Indian River Archeology, Florida. Irving Rouse. LC 76-43813. (Yale Univ. Publications in Anthropology: No. 45). 376p. reprint ed. 52.50 (*0-404-15668-1*) AMS Pr.

Survey of Indian Sculpture. S. K. Saraswati. (Illus.). 1975. 28.50 (*0-685-13820-8*) Coronet Bks.

Survey of Industrial Chemistry. 2nd rev. ed. Philip J. Chenier. LC 92-19693. (Illus.). xv, 528p. 1992. 55.00 (*1-56081-082-3*, VCH) Wiley.

***Survey of Industrial Chemistry.** 2nd rev. ed. Philip J. Chenier. 1992. text ed. 69.95 (*0-471-18798-4*) Wiley.

Survey of Industrial Chemistry. Philip J. Chenier. 440p. (C). 1990. reprint ed. lib. bdg. 55.25 (*0-89464-504-8*) Krieger.

Survey of Industrial Robots. 2nd ed. 143.00 (*0-686-31442-5*) C I M Systems.

Survey of Inmates of State Correctional Facilities, 1979. 2nd ed. U. S. Department of Justice, Bureau of Justice Statistics Staff. LC 81-85743. 1981. write for info. (*0-89138-941-5*) ICPSR.

Survey of Instructional Development Models. Kent L. Gustafson. 68p. 1991. 7.50 (*0-937597-32-5*, IR-91) ERIC Clear.

Survey of Intermediate Sanctions. 59p. (Orig.). (C). 1993. pap. text ed. 25.00 (*1-56806-815-8*) DIANE Pub.

Survey of International Arbitration Sites. 3rd ed. American Arbitration Association Staff. LC 84-81526. 175p. 1993. reprint ed. pap. 15.00 (*0-943001-09-9*) Am Arbitration.

Survey of International Arbitrations. Alexander M. Stuyt. (C). 1990. lib. bdg. 196.00 (*0-7923-0522-1*) Kluwer Ac.

Survey of Israel's History. rev. ed. Leon J. Wood & David O'Brien. 416p. 1986. 26.99 (*0-310-34770-X*, 06506) Zondervan.

Survey of Japanese Collections in the United States. Naomi Fukuda. LC 81-4481. (Michigan Papers in Japanese Studies: No. 4). x, 182p. 1981. pap. 5.00 (*0-939512-09-2*) U MI Japan.

Survey of Japanese Studies in the United States: The 1990s. Rhoads Murphey. LC 96-22246. (Occasional Papers). 125p. (Orig.). 1996. pap. 15.00 (*0-924304-27-8*) Assn Asian Studies.

Survey of Jewish Affairs 1982. Ed. by William Frankel. LC 83-48732. 289p. 1984. 35.00 (*0-8386-3206-8*) Fairleigh Dickinson.

Survey of Jewish Affairs 1983. Ed. by William Frankel. 320p. 1985. 35.00 (*0-8386-3244-0*) Fairleigh Dickinson.

Survey of Jewish Affairs, 1985. Ed. by William Frankel. 280p. 1986. 35.00 (*0-8386-3269-6*) Fairleigh Dickinson.

Survey of Jewish Affairs 1987. William Frankel. LC 84-645587. (Illus.). 304p. 1988. 30.00 (*0-8386-3322-6*) Fairleigh Dickinson.

Survey of Jewish Affairs, 1988. Ed. by William Frankel. LC 84-645587. 280p. 1989. 35.00 (*0-8386-3343-9*) Fairleigh Dickinson.

***Survey of Knot Theory.** Akio Kawauchi. 440p. 1996. 89.50 (*3-7643-5124-1*) Birkhauser.

Survey of Labor Relations. 2nd ed. Lee Balliet. LC 87-864. 224p. 1987. reprint ed. pap. 63.90 (*0-608-00709-9*, 2061482) Bks Demand.

Survey of Legal Literature on Woman Offenders. S. Livesay. i, 16p. 1975. pap. 2.00 (*0-938876-01-5*) Entropy Ltd.

Survey of Lie Groups & Lie Algebras with Applications & Computational Methods. J. G. Belinfante & Bernard Kolman. (Classics in Applied Mathematics Ser.: No. 02). xi, 164p. 1989. pap. 31.00 (*0-89871-243-2*, CL02) Soc Indus-Appl Math.

Survey of Linguistic Theories. Ed. by Jerold A. Edmondson & Donald A. Burquest. xi, 243p. 1992. pap. 25.00 (*0-88312-642-7*); fiche 20.00 (*0-88312-583-8*) Summer Instit Ling.

Survey of Lubbock's Growth As a Medical Center, 1909-1954. William R. Dunnagan. 65p. 1980. 5.00 (*0-911618-05-8*) West Tex Mus.

Survey of Macro Processors: A Machine-Independent Assembly Language for Systems Programs see Annual Review in Automatic Programming

Survey of Maintenance & Management Needs in Omaha Housing Authority's Apartments for Senior Citizens. Rebecca S. Fahrlander & Joan V. Holley. 46p. (Orig.). 1982. pap. 3.50 (*1-55719-017-8*) U NE CPAR.

Survey of Major Issues & Trends Relevant to the Management of Elementary & Secondary Education. vi, 42p. (Orig.). 1993. pap. 7.00 (*0-86552-121-2*) U of Oreg ERIC.

Survey of Marketing Research, 1983: Organization, Functions, Budget, Compensation. Ed. by Dik W. Twedt. LC 84-259. (Illus.). 77p. reprint ed. pap. 25.00 (*0-8357-6872-4*, 2035570) Bks Demand.

Survey of Mass Communication. Ronald G. Hicks. LC 77-8438. 372p. (C). 1977. pap. text ed. 12.95 (*0-88289-164-2*) Pelican.

***Survey of Mathematics.** 4th ed. Allen Angel. (C). 1993. pap. text ed. 48.50 (*0-201-30065-6*) Addison-Wesley.

Survey of Mathematics: With Applications. 3rd ed. Allen R. Angel & Stuart R. Porter. (Illus.). 761p. (C). 1989. teacher ed. 12.95 (*0-201-13698-8*); text ed. 49.50 (*0-201-13696-1*); student ed., pap. text ed. 18.25 (*0-201-13697-X*); 12.95 (*0-201-15468-4*) Addison-Wesley.

Survey of Mathematics with Applications. 4th ed. Allen Angel. (C). 1993. student ed., pap. text ed. 16.95 (*0-201-54996-4*) Addison-Wesley.

Survey of Mathematics with Applications. 5th ed. Allen Angel. Ed. by Karen Guardino. LC 96-43388. 736p. (C). 1997. text ed. 58.50 (*0-201-84600-4*) Addison-Wesley.

Survey of Mathematics with Applications. 5th ed. Allen Angel. (C). 1997. student ed., pap. text ed. 21.50 (*0-201-80957-5*) Addison-Wesley.

***Survey of Mathematics with Applications: With Right Triangle Trigonometry Appendix.** 5th ed. Allen Angel. Ed. by Karen Guardino. LC 96-43388. 768p. (C). 1997. text ed. 58.50 (*0-201-85761-8*) Addison-Wesley.

Survey of Matrix Theory & Matrix Inequalities. Marvin Marcus & Henryk Minc. 192p. 1992. reprint ed. pap. 6.95 (*0-486-67102-X*) Dover.

Survey of Medical Neuroscience. Robert M. Beckstead. 408p. 1996. pap. 34.95 (*0-387-94488-5*) Spr-Verlag.

***Survey of Medieval Castles of Anatolia II Vol. II: Nicomedia.** Clive Foss. (Monographs: Vol. 21). (Illus.). 112p. 1996. 35.00 (*1-898249-07-5*, Pub. by Brit Inst Arch UK) David Brown.

Survey of Medieval Iberian Coinages. 2nd rev. ed. John F. Lhotka & P. K. Anderson. LC 88-72079. 128p. 1989. reprint ed. pap. 15.00 (*0-942666-54-2*) S J Durst.

Survey of Mental Health Nursing Practices see Critical Behaviors in Psychiatric-Mental Health Nursing: Monograph

***Survey of Metaphysics & Esoterism.** Frithjof Schuon. 224p. (Orig.). 1996. pap. 12.95 (*0-614-21241-3*, 1203) Kazi Pubns.

Survey of Metaphysics & Esoterism. Frithjof Schuon. LC 86-13261. (Library of Traditional Wisdom). 110p. (Orig.). 1986. pap. 12.00 (*0-941532-06-2*) Wrld Wisdom Bks.

Survey of Metropolitan Courts Final Report. Maxine B. Virtue. LC 50-62646. (Michigan Legal Publications). xxx, 315p. Date not set. 40.00 (*1-57588-367-8*, 301840) W S Hein.

Survey of Minimal Surfaces. Robert Osserman. 192p. 1986. reprint ed. pap. 8.95 (*0-486-64998-9*) Dover.

***Survey of Minority-Owned Business Enterprises: Asians & Pacific Islanders, American Indians, & Alaska Natives.** Ewen Wilson & Ruth A. Runyan. (Illus.). 120p. (Orig.). (C). 1996. pap. 35.00 (*0-7881-3654-2*) DIANE Pub.

***Survey of Minority-Owned Business Enterprises: Black.** Ewen Wilson & Ruth A. Runyan. (Illus.). 121p. (Orig.). (C). 1996. pap. 35.00 (*0-7881-3652-6*) DIANE Pub.

***Survey of Minority-Owned Business Enterprises: Hispanic.** Ewen Wilson & Ruth A. Runyan. (Illus.). 151p. (Orig.). (C). 1996. pap. 35.00 (*0-7881-3653-4*) DIANE Pub.

***Survey of Models for Tumor-Immune System Dynamics.** Ed. by J. A. Adam & N. Bellomo. LC 96-38754. 332p. 1996. 75.00 (*0-8176-3901-2*) Birkhauser.

***Survey of Modern Algebra.** 5th rev. ed. Garrett Birkhoff & Saunders Mac Lane. LC 97-372. (Illus.). 512p. (C). 1996. text ed. 59.00 (*1-56881-068-7*) AK Peters.

Survey of Modern English. Stephan Gramley & Michael Patzold. LC 92-5427. 400p. (C). 1992. pap. 25.00 (*0-415-04957-1*, A7364) Routledge.

Survey of Modern English. Stephan Gramley & Michael Patzold. LC 92-5427. 400p. (C). (gr. 13). 1992. text ed. 79.95 (*0-415-04956-3*, A7360) Routledge.

Survey of Modern Grammars. 2nd ed. Herndon. 374p. (C). 1976. pap. text ed. 28.00 (*0-03-089675-4*) HB Coll Pubs.

Survey of Modernist Poetry. Laura R. Jackson & R. Graves. LC 76-95444. (Studies in Poetry: No. 38). 1969. reprint ed. lib. bdg. 75.00 (*0-8383-1200-4*) M S G Haskell Hse.

Survey of Modernist Poetry. Laura R. Jackson & Robert Graves. LC 76-145263. 1971. reprint ed. 39.00 (*0-403-01178-7*) Scholarly.

Survey of Modernist Poetry. Laura J. Riding. (BCL1-PR English Literature Ser.). 295p. 1992. reprint ed. lib. bdg. 79.00 (*0-7812-7073-1*) Rprt Serv.

Survey of Musical Instrument Collections in the United States & Canada. Ed. by Music Library Association Committee. 135p. 1974. 8.50 (*0-318-14925-7*); pap. 6.50 (*0-318-14927-3*) Music Library Assn.

Survey of Mutualistic Communities in America. Ralph Albertson. LC 72-2934. (Communal Societies in America Ser.). reprint ed. 31.50 (*0-404-10700-1*) AMS Pr.

Survey of National & International Standards Applicable to Building Energy & Management Systems. A. Howlett. (C). 1988. 105.00 (*0-86022-210-1*, Pub. by Build Servs Info Assn UK) St Mut.

Survey of Nebraska Women's Employment Participation, Attitudes, & Needs. Murray Frost. 105p. (Orig.). 1979. pap. 6.50 (*1-55719-063-1*) U NE CPAR.

Survey of New Testament. Paul Benware. 144p. (C). 1994. student ed., pap. text ed., spiral bd. 19.89 (*0-7872-0313-0*) Kendall-Hunt.

Survey of Nonlinear Dynamics ("Chaos Theory") R. L. Ingraham. 100p. (C). 1991. text ed. 36.00 (*981-02-0777-8*) World Scientific Pub.

Survey of Nonmetal Mineral Industry in China. 248p. 1993. 205.00 (*0-614-11849-2*, Pub. by HUWEI Cnslts CH) Am Overseas Bk Co.

Survey of Nucleonic Heat Transfer Research & Development. American Society of Mechanical Engineers Staff. LC 72-185848. (American Society of Mechanical Engineers Handbook: Vol. 1). 44p. reprint ed. pap. 25.00 (*0-317-09936-1*, 2016900) Bks Demand.

Survey of Numerical Mathematics, 2 vols., I. David M. Young & Robert T. Gregory. 1248p. 1988. reprint ed. pap. text ed. 14.95 (*0-486-65691-8*) Dover.

Survey of Numerical Mathematics, 2 vols., II. David M. Young & Robert T. Gregory. 1248p. 1988. reprint ed. pap. text ed. 14.95 (*0-486-65692-6*) Dover.

Survey of Numismatic Research, 1966-71, 3 vols. Ed. by P. Naster et al. 1133p. 1973. 20.00 (*0-89722-069-2*) Am Numismatic.

Survey of Objective Studies of Psychoanalytic Concepts. Robert R. Sears. LC 79-4476. 156p. 1979. reprint ed. text ed. 59.75 (*0-313-21249-X*, SESO, Greenwood Pr) Greenwood.

Survey of Old Testament Introduction. 2nd expanded rev. ed. Gleason L. Archer. 1996. 32.99 (*0-8024-8200-7*) Moody.

Survey of Organism Form & Function Laboratory Manual. Kevin Murray. 128p. (C). 1994. per., pap. text ed. 20.95 (*0-8403-9873-5*) Kendall-Hunt.

Survey of Organizational & Instructional Practices in Michigan Middle Schools, 1988. Katherine Gilliland. Ed. by Louis G. Romano. 1988. pap. 3.50 (*0-918449-12-X*) MI Middle Educ.

Survey of Organizations. James C. Taylor & David G. Bowers. LC 72-619571. 172p. 1972. 16.00 (*0-87944-124-0*) Inst Soc Res.

Survey of Painting in the Deccan. Stella Kramrisch. 1983. 55.50 (*0-8364-2616-9*, Pub. by Munshiram Manoharial II) S Asia.

Survey of Palestine, Vol. I: Prepared in December 1945 & January 1946 for the Information of the Anglo-American Committee of Inquiry. Intro. by J. V. Shaw. LC 90-5245. 544p. (C). 1991. reprint ed. 19.95 (*0-88728-211-3*); reprint ed. pap. 12.50 (*0-88728-213-X*) Inst Palestine.

Survey of Palestine, Vol. II: Prepared in December 1945 & January 1946 for the Information of the Anglo-American Committee of Inquiry. LC 90-5245. 616p. (C). 1991. reprint ed. 19.95 (*0-88728-214-8*); reprint ed. pap. 12.50 (*0-88728-215-6*) Inst Palestine.

Survey of Paralegalism. Buckley. (Paralegal Ser.). 1995. text ed. 41.95 (*0-8273-6206-4*) Delmar.

Survey of Paralegalism. Buckley. (Paralegal Ser.). 1995. teacher ed. 14.00 (*0-8273-6207-2*) Delmar.

Survey of Persian Art, Vol. XV: Pre-Islamic Bibliography. Arthur U. Pope. Ed. by Phyllis Ackerman. lib. bdg. 85.00 (*4-89360-020-6*, Pub. by Prsnlly Oriented JA) Mazda Pubs.

Survey of Persian Art, Vol. XVI: Islamic Bibliography. Arthur U. Pope. Ed. by Phyllis Ackerman. lib. bdg. 85.00 (*4-89360-021-4*, Pub. by Prsnlly Oriented JA) Mazda Pubs.

Survey of Persian Art, Vols. I-XVI: From Prehistoric Times to the Present, Set. Arthur U. Pope. Ed. by Phyllis Ackerman. (Illus.). 3816p. lib. bdg. 1,495.00 (*4-89360-011-7*, Pub. by Prsnlly Oriented JA) Mazda Pubs.

Survey of Persian Art, Vols. IV & IX: Potery & Faience, Set. Arthur U. Pope. Ed. by Phyllis Ackerman. 353p. lib. bdg. 145.00 (*4-89360-014-1*, Pub. by Prsnlly Oriented JA) Mazda Pubs.

Survey of Persian Art, Vols. V-a & X: Art of the Book, Set. Arthur U. Pope. Ed. by Phyllis Ackerman. (Illus.). 186p. lib. bdg. 145.00 (*4-89360-015-X*, Pub. by Prsnlly Oriented JA) Mazda Pubs.

Survey of Persian Art, Vols. V-b & XI: Textiles, Set. Arthur U. Pope. Ed. by Phyllis Ackerman. (Illus.). 262p. lib. bdg. 145.00 (*4-89360-016-8*, Pub. by Prsnlly Oriented JA) Mazda Pubs.

Survey of Persian Art, Vols. VI-a & XII: Carpets, Set. Arthur U. Pope. Ed. by Phyllis Ackerman. (Illus.). 209p. lib. bdg. 170.00 (*4-89360-017-6*, Pub. by Prsnlly Oriented JA) Mazda Pubs.

Survey of Persian Handicraft. Jay Gluck & Sumi H. Gluck. Ed. by Carl J. Penton. (Illus.). 416p. 1992. 95.00 (*4-89360-024-9*, Pub. by Prsnlly Oriented JA) Mazda Pubs.

***Survey of Persian Handicraft.** deluxe ed. J. Gluck & S. Gluck. 1996. 320.00 (*4-89360-025-7*, Pub. by Prsnlly Oriented JA) Mazda Pubs.

Survey of Physical Science: Lecture Notes. Paul Tayler. 200p. (C). 1995. pap. text ed., spiral bd. 18.63 (*0-7872-1909-6*) Kendall-Hunt.

Survey of Physical Theory. Max Planck. LC 93-6110. 128p. 1994. reprint ed. pap. text ed. 6.95 (*0-486-67867-9*) Dover.

***Survey of Practical Mathematics with Applications.** Dauhrice Gibson & Janice McFatter. 492p. (C). 1996. per., pap. text ed. 39.84 (*0-7872-2469-3*) Kendall-Hunt.

Survey of Precast Prestressed Concrete Parking Structures. 73p. 1988. 24.00 (*0-318-35235-4*, R&D7) P-PCI.

Survey of Preconditioned Iterative Methods. A. M. Bruaset. LC 95-6872. (Pitman Research Notes in Mathematics Ser.). 1995. write for info. (*0-615-00667-1*) Longman.

Survey of Prehistoric Sites in the Region of Flagstaff, Arizona. Harold S. Colton. (Bureau of American Ethnology Bulletins Ser.). 69p. 1995. lib. bdg. 79.00 (*0-7812-4104-9*) Rprt Serv.

Survey of Prehistoric Sites in the Region of Flagstaff, Arizona. Harold S. Colton. reprint ed. 59.00 (*0-403-03702-6*) Scholarly.

Survey of Press Freedom in Latin America 1985-1986. Ed. by Cecilio J. Morales, Jr. et al. 64p. (Orig.). 1986. pap. 8.95 (*0-937551-00-7*) Coun Hemispheric Aff.

Survey of Priests Ordained Five to Nine Years. Eugene F. Hemrick & Dean R. Hoge. (Illus.). 72p. (Orig.). 1991. pap. 6.00 (*1-55833-071-2*) Natl Cath Educ.

Survey of Primitive Money: The Beginnings of Currency. Alison H. Quiggin. LC 76-44779. reprint ed. 47.50 (*0-404-15964-8*) AMS Pr.

Survey of Public Attitudes Toward Refugees & Immigrants: Report of Findings. 1984. write for info. (*0-318-60435-3*) US Comm Refugees.

***Survey of Public Education in the Nation's Urban School Districts - 1995: Triennial Report.** 136p. (Orig.). 1996. pap. 35.00 (*0-88364-204-2*) Natl Sch Boards.

Survey of Rapid Prototyping End-Users: First Generation a Smashing Success, End-Users Waiting for Next Generation Systems. Market Intelligence Staff. 425p. (Orig.). 1992. 1,695.00 (*1-56753-398-1*) Frost & Sullivan.

Survey of Recent Christian Ethics. Edward L. Long, Jr. 230p. 1982. pap. 16.95 (*0-19-503160-1*) OUP.

Survey of Recent Developments in China (Mainland & Taiwan), 1985-1986, No. 2. Ed. by Hungdah Chiu & Jaw-ling J. Chang. 222p. 1987. 8.00 (*0-942182-82-0*, 79) Occasional Papers.

Survey of Research in Economic & Social History of India. R. S. Sharma. 1986. 30.00 (*81-202-0142-6*, Pub. by Ajanta II) S Asia.

An Asterisk (*) at the beginning of an entry indicates that the title is appearing in BIP for the first time.

Survey of Resistivities of Water from Subsurface Formations in West Texas & Southeastern New Mexico. Society of Professional Well Log Analysts Staff & Society of Professional Well Log Analysts. 248p. 1982. 17.00 (*0-89520-316-2*, 31632) Soc Petrol Engineers.

Survey of Retail Furniture Distribution in France. 1981. 110.00 (*0-317-43722-4*) St Mut.

Survey of Russian Music: Music Book Index. Michel D. Calvocoressi. 142p. 1993. reprint ed. lib. bdg. 69.00 (*0-7812-9567-X*) Rprt Serv.

Survey of Salaries & Responsibilities for Hospital Biomedical - Clinical Engineering & Technology Personnel, 1992. Allan F. Pacela. (Illus.). 24p. (Orig.). 1992. pap. 80.00 (*0-930844-36-X*) Quest Pub.

Survey of Salary, Benefits & Staffing Patterns of Community Mental Health Providers, 1991. 106p. 1991. pap. 34.50 (*1-883066-05-0*) Natl Comm Mental.

Survey of Sardis & the Major Monuments Outside the City Walls. George M. Hanfmann & Jane C. Waldbaum. LC 75-1746. (Archaeological Exploration of Sardis Monograph: No. 1). (Illus.). 396p. 1976. 45.00 (*0-674-85751-8*) HUP.

Survey of Selected Local Government Energy Emergency Planning Programs. 84p. 1982. 15.00 (*0-318-17337-9*, DG/82-321) Pub Tech Inc.

Survey of Selected States Regarding Collective Bargaining Laws for State Employees & Experiences under Those Laws. Dan Fernbach & Jane R. Henkel. 78p. (Orig.). (C). 1994. pap. text ed. 25.00 (*0-7881-1315-1*) DIANE Pub.

Survey of Semiconductor Physics, Vol. II: Barriers, Junctions, Surfaces & Devices. Karl W. Boer. (Illus.). 1488p. 1992. text ed. 89.95 (*0-442-00672-1*) Van Nos Reinhold.

Survey of Significant Federal Court Decisions on Rights of Federal Employees. 123p. 1981. pap. text ed. 15.00 (*1-56986-135-8*) Federal Bar.

Survey of SLA Software Users. Special Libraries Association Staff. LC 88-138051. (SLA Research Ser.: No. 1). 178p. reprint ed. pap. 50.80 (*0-7837-4047-6*, 2043876) Bks Demand.

Survey of Slum & Squatter Settlements. (Human Settlements, Planning & Development Ser.: No. 225). (Illus.). 197p. 1982. 60.00 (*0-907567-24-X*, Tycooly Pub); pap. 40.00 (*0-907567-25-8*, Tycooly Pub) Weidner & Sons.

Survey of Social Psychology. 3rd ed. Leonard Berkowitz. 544p. (C). 1986. text ed. 43.25 (*0-03-070438-3*) HB Coll Pubs.

Survey of Social Science, 5 vols., Set. Ed. by Frank N. Magill. LC 91-29798. (Economics Ser.). 2494p. (YA). (gr. 9-12). 1991. lib. bdg. 375.00 (*0-89356-725-6*) Salem Pr.

Survey of Social Science, 6 vols., Set. Ed. by Frank N. Magill. LC 93-34708. (Psychology Ser.). 2698p. 1993. lib. bdg. 425.00 (*0-89356-732-9*) Salem Pr.

Survey of Social Science, 5 vols., Set. Frank N. Magill. LC 95-30408. (Government & Politics Ser.). 2222p. 1995. lib. bdg. 375.00 (*0-89356-745-0*) Salem Pr.

Survey of Social Science: Sociology Series, 5 vols., Set. Ed. by Frank N. Magill. LC 94-31770. 2244p. 1994. lib. bdg. 375.00 (*0-89356-739-6*) Salem Pr.

Survey of Some Japanese Tax Laws. Eric V. De Becker. LC 78-78358. (Studies in Japanese Law & Government). 182p. 1979. reprint ed. text ed. 69.50 (*0-313-26984-X*, U6984, Greenwood Pr) Greenwood.

Survey of Sources at the Rockefeller Archive Center for the Study of African-American History & Race Relations. Kenneth W. Rose et al. Ed. by Lois Sherman. 120p. (Orig.). (C). pap. write for info. (*1-884354-01-7*) IN Univ Ctr.

Survey of State Housing Trust Fund Programs: Existing & Proposed. Anne Hoskins & Claudia Jadrijevic. 50p. 1990. 10.00 (*0-685-56598-X*) CPA Washington.

Survey of State IRM Organizational Structures: NASIRE Biannual Report, 1991-92. 150p. 1992. pap. 50.00 (*0-87292-969-8*, C-033-92) Coun State Govts.

Survey of State-Level Involvement in Distance Education at the Elementary & Secondary Levels. Richard England. 34p. (C). 1991. pap. 12.50 (*1-877780-04-9*) ACSDE.

Survey of State Welfare Reforms: Final Report, July 1994. Julie Strawn et al. Ed. by Karen Glass. 78p. (Orig.). 1994. pap. 15.00 (*1-55877-193-X*) Natl Governor.

Survey of Taiwanese Family-Life. Toshio Ikeda. (Asian Folklore & Social Life Monographs: No. 11). (JPN.). 1972. 18.00 (*0-89986-014-1*) Oriental Bk Store.

***Survey of Test Methods in Fluid Filtration.** Peter R. Johnston. LC 94-37795. (Illus.). 181p. pap. 51.60 (*0-608-05080-6*, 2065634) Bks Demand.

Survey of the Administration of Criminal Justice in Oregon: Final Report on 1771 Felony Cases in Multnomah County Report Number One. Wayne L. Morse & Ronald H. Beattie. LC 74-3838. (Criminal Justice in America Ser.). 1974. reprint ed. 24.95 (*0-405-06155-2*) Ayer.

Survey of the Almagest. Olaf Pedersen. (Acta Historica Scientarium Ser.: No. 30). (Illus.). 454p. 1974. pap. 57. 50 (*87-7492-087-1*, D-751, Pub. by Odense Universitets Forlag DK) Coronet Bks.

Survey of the Benthis Algal Vegetation of the Dyrafjordur, Northwest Iceland. I. M. Munda. (Offprint from Nova Hedwigia Ser.: No. 29). (Illus.). 1978. pap. text ed. 30.00 (*3-7682-1201-7*) Lubrecht & Cramer.

Survey of the Bible. G. Campbell Morgan. (World Classic Library). 639p. 1994. reprint ed. 19.99 (*0-529-10061-4*, WCL1) World Publng.

Survey of the Bible: A Treasury of Bible Information. 4th ed. William Hendriksen. (Illus.). 512p. (gr. 10). 1995. pap. 14.99 (*0-8010-5415-X*) Baker Bks.

Survey of the Bible - Chinese Edition. David Dawson. Tr. by John Leung. 58p. (CHI.). 1989. pap. 9.50 (*1-56582-030-4*) Christ Renew Min.

Survey of the Birdlife of Northwestern Florida. Francis M. Weston. (Tall Timbers Resaerch Station Bulletin Ser.: No. 5). 151p. reprint ed. pap. 43.10 (*0-685-15975-2*, 2026818) Bks Demand.

Survey of the Books of History. J. D. O'Donnell & Ralph Hampton, Jr. 1976. pap. 3.95 (*0-89265-032-X*) Randall Hse.

Survey of the Books of Poetry. J. D. O'Donnell & Ralph Hampton, Jr. 1976. pap. 2.95 (*0-89265-033-8*) Randall Hse.

Survey of the Commercial Agency. Campbell et al. 1984. lib. bdg. 95.00 (*90-6544-181-6*) Kluwer Law Tax Pubs.

Survey of the Environmental Knowledge, Comprehension, of the Secondary Level Students & Teachers in the Philippines. Leticia Cortes. (Environment Problems & Solutions Ser.). 191p. 1991. text ed. 20.00 (*0-8240-9298-8*) Garland.

Survey of the General Epistles & Revelation. Stanley Outlaw et al. 1976. pap. 3.95 (*0-89265-036-2*) Randall Hse.

Survey of the Great Dukes State of Tuscany, in 1596. Robert Dallington. LC 74-80171. (English Experience Ser.: No. 650). 74p. 1974. reprint ed. 20.00 (*90-221-0650-0*) Walter J Johnson.

Survey of the Hebrew Bible. Vahan H. Tootikian. 208p. 1990. 20.00 (*0-8187-0120-X*) Harlo Press.

Survey of the History of African Art. Cole & Visona. 1996. pap. text ed. 39.95 (*0-13-442187-6*) P-H.

Survey of the Honour of Denbigh 1334. Ed. by P. Vinogradoff & F. Morgan. (British Academy, London, Records of the Social & Economic History of Wngland & Wales. Series: Vol. 1). 1974. reprint ed. pap. 60.00 (*0-8115-1241-X*) Periodicals Srv.

Survey of the Impact of Manufactured Exports from Industrializing Countries in Asia & Latin America: Must Export-Oriented Growth Be Disruptive? Lawrence G. Franko. LC 79-91759. (Committee on Changing International Realities Ser.). 56p. 1979. 4.50 (*0-89068-051-5*) Natl Planning.

Survey of the International Sale of Goods. Ed. by Louis Lafili et al. 375p. 1986. lib. bdg. 97.50 (*90-6544-241-3*) Kluwer Ac.

Survey of the Irish in England (1872) Ed. by Alan O'Day. 174p. 1990. boxed 45.00 (*1-85285-010-8*) Hambledon Press.

Survey of the Major Prophets. Ralph Hampton, Jr. & Robert E. Picirilli. 1976. pap. 1.95 (*0-89265-034-6*) Randall Hse.

Survey of the Management & Utilization of Electronics Data Processing Systems in Admission, Records, & Registration, 1969-70. American Association of Collegiate Registrars & Admissions Officers Staff. 139p. reprint ed. pap. 39.70 (*0-317-26616-0*, 2024076) Bks Demand.

Survey of the Negro Convention Movement. Howard H. Bell. LC 74-94129. (American Negro: His History & Literature. Series 3). 1970. reprint ed. 21.95 (*0-405-01915-7*) Ayer.

Survey of the New Testament. Paul N. Beware. (Everyman's Bible Commentary Ser.). 1990. pap. 12.99 (*0-8024-2092-3*) Moody.

Survey of the New Testament. David L. Fletcher. (C). 1993. student ed. 9.54 (*1-56870-100-4*) RonJon Pub.

Survey of the New Testament. Robert E. Picirilli et al. (Orig.). 1984. pap. 9.95 (*0-89265-090-7*) Randall Hse.

Survey of the New Testament. 3rd ed. Robert H. Gundry. 400p. 1994. 26.99 (*0-310-59550-9*) Zondervan.

Survey of the New Testament (Everyman's Bible Commentary) see Panorama del Nuevo Testamento

Survey of the Non-Pronominal Non-Formative Affixes of the Blackfoot Verb. Christianus C. Uhlenbeck. reprint ed. write for info. (*3-253-02068-1*) Adlers Foreign Bks.

Survey of the Old Testament. David L. Fletcher. (C). 1993. student ed. 11.71 (*1-56870-099-7*) RonJon Pub.

Survey of the Old Testament. Andrew E. Hill & John H. Walton. 448p. 1991. 26.99 (*0-310-51600-5*) Zondervan.

Survey of the Old Testament. Robert E. Picirilli et al. (Orig.). 1984. pap. 9.95 (*0-89265-089-3*) Randall Hse.

Survey of the Old Testament. rev. ed. Paul N. Benware. (Everyman's Bible Commentary Ser.). 1993. pap. 12.99 (*0-8024-2093-1*) Moody.

Survey of the Old Testament: Student Notes. William H. Marty. 228p. (C). 1996. pap. text ed., spiral bd. 19.42 (*0-8403-7603-0*) Kendall-Hunt.

Survey of the Old Testament (Everyman's Bible Commentary) see Panorama del Antiguo Testamento

***Survey of the Old Testament Introduction.** Gleason Archer. (Orig.). 1996. pap. 29.99 (*0-8024-8201-5*) Moody.

Survey of the Pentateuch. Stanley Outlaw & J. D. O'Donnell. 93p. 1975. pap. 3.95 (*0-89265-027-3*) Randall Hse.

Survey of the Pretended Holy Dicipline. Richard Bancroft. LC 78-38148. (English Experience Ser.: No. 428). 472p. 1972. reprint ed. 75.00 (*90-221-0428-1*) Walter J Johnson.

Survey of the Roman, or Civil Law: An Extract from Gibbon's History of the Decline & Fall of the Roman Empire. Edward Gibbon. Tr. by W. Gardiner. viii, 232p. 1996. reprint ed. lib. bdg. 37.50 (*0-8377-2216-0*) Rothman.

Survey of the Scientific Manuscripts in the Egyptian National Library. David A. King. LC 85-29369. (American Research Center in Egypt, Catalogs Ser.: Vol. 5). (Illus.). xiv, 332p. 1986. pap. text ed. 52.50 (*0-936770-12-0*, Pub. by Amer Res Ctr Egypt UA) Eisenbrauns.

Survey of the Scientific Manuscripts in the Egyptian National Library. David A. King. LC 85-29369. (American Research Center in Egypt, Catalogs Ser.: Vol. 5). (Illus.). xiv, 332p. 1986. text ed. 65.00 (*0-936770-14-7*, Pub. by Amer Res Ctr Egypt UA) Eisenbrauns.

Survey of the Scofill(s) s in England & America, Seven Hundred Years of History & Genealogy. H. Brainerd. (Illus.). 586p. 1993. reprint ed. pap. 89.00 (*0-8328-3060-7*); reprint ed. lib. bdg. 99.00 (*0-8328-3059-3*) Higginson Bk Co.

Survey of the Shores & Islands of the Persian Gulf 1820-1829, 5 vols. Intro. by A. S. Cook. (Illus.). 378p. (C). 1989. reprint ed. lib. bdg. 1,095.00 (*1-85207-190-7*, Pub. by Archive Editions UK) N Ross.

Survey of the Social & Business Usage of Arithmetic. Guy M. Wilson. LC 74-177633. (Columbia University. Teachers College. Contributions to Education Ser.: No. 100). reprint ed. 37.50 (*0-404-55100-9*) AMS Pr.

Survey of the Spherical Space Form Problem, Vol. 2. James F. Davis. (Mathematical Reports: vol.2, pt. 2). xii, 60p. 1986. text ed. 52.00 (*3-7186-0250-4*) Gordon & Breach.

Survey of the State of Maine in Reference to Its Geographical Features, Statistics & Political Economy. Moses Greenleaf. LC 71-128108. 1970. 2.50 (*0-913764-00-0*) Maine St Mus.

***Survey of the State of the Art in Human Language Technology.** Ed. by Giovanni Varile & Antonio Zampolli. (Studies in Natural Language Processing). 530p. (C). 1997. 49.95 (*0-521-59277-1*) Cambridge U Pr.

Survey of the Summe of Church-Discipline, Bk. II. John Cotton. (Works of John Cotton Ser.). 1990. reprint ed. lib. bdg. 79.00 (*0-7812-2320-2*) Rprt Serv.

Survey of the Summe of Church-Discipline Wherein the Way of the Congregational Churches of Christ in New England Is Warranted & Cleared, by Scripture & Argument. Thomas Hooker. LC 78-141113. (Research Library of Colonial Americana). 1972. reprint ed. 44.95 (*0-405-03326-5*) Ayer.

Survey of the Teaching of English to Non-English Speakers in the United States. Harold B. Allen. Ed. by Francesco Cordasco. LC 77-90403. (Bilingual-Bicultural Education in the U. S. Ser.). 1978. reprint ed. lib. bdg. 23.95 (*0-405-11072-3*) Ayer.

Survey of the Turkish Empire. William Eton. LC 73-6278. (Middle East Ser.). 1973. reprint ed. 41.95 (*0-405-05334-7*) Ayer.

Survey of the Universe. Paul Tayler. 176p. (C). 1995. pap. 16.41 (*0-7872-1826-X*) Kendall-Hunt.

Survey of Thermodynamics. Martin Bailyn. LC 93-28712. 480p. 1994. text ed. 65.00 (*0-88318-797-3*, AIP) Am Inst Physics.

Survey of Tidal River Systems in the Northern Territory & Their Crocodile Populations: Monographs, Nos. 2-8. Harry Messel. Incl. No. 2. Victoria & Fitzmaurice River Systems. 52p. 1979. pap. 28.00 (*0-08-023098-9*); No. 3. Adelaide, Daly & Moyle Rivers. 58p. 1979. pap. 28.00 (*0-08-023099-7*); No. 4. Alligator Region River System: Murgenella & Cooper's Creeks; East, South & West Alligator Rivers & Wildman River. 70p. 1979. pap. 28. 00 (*0-08-024789-X*); No. 5. Goodmadeer & King River Systems: Majarie, Wurugoij & All Night Creeks. 62p. 1979. pap. 28.00 (*0-08-024790-3*); No. 6. Some River & Creek Systems on Melville & Grant Islands: North & South Creeks on Grant Island. 64p. 1979. pap. 28.00 (*0-08-024784-9*); No. 7. Liverpool-Tomkinson River Systems & Nungbulgarri Creek. 84p. 1979. pap. 28.00 (*0-08-024785-7*); No. 8. Some Rivers & Creeks on the Western Shore of the Gulf of Carpentaria: Rose River, Muntak Creek; Hart, Walker & Koolatong Rivers. 40p. 1979. pap. 28.00 (*0-08-024786-5*); (Illus.). 1979. Set pap. write for info. (*0-318-55231-0*) Elsevier.

Survey of Trace Forms of Algebraic Number Fields. P. E. Connor & R. Perlis. (Series in Pure Mathematics: Vol. 2). 328p. 1984. text ed. 55.00 (*9971-966-04-2*); pap. text ed. 30.00 (*9971-966-05-0*) World Scientific Pub.

Survey of Traditional Chinese Medicine. Claude Larre et al. Tr. by Sarah E. Stang. (Illus.). 231p. (Orig.). (FRE.). 1986. pap. 20.00 (*0-912381-00-0*) Trad Acupuncture.

Survey of Twentieth Century Revival Movements in North America. Richard M. Riss. 208p. 1988. pap. 9.95 (*0-913573-72-8*) Hendrickson MA.

Survey of U. S. Naval Affairs, 1865-1917. Paolo E. Coletta. LC 87-10394. (Illus.). 272p. (Orig.). (C). 1987. lib. bdg. 50.50 (*0-8191-6397-X*) U Pr of Amer.

Survey of U. S. Naval Affairs, 1865-1917. Paolo E. Coletta. LC 87-10394. (Illus.). 272p. (Orig.). (C). 1987. pap. text ed. 26.00 (*0-8191-6398-8*) U Pr of Amer.

Survey of Ufologists & Their Use of the Library. George M. Eberhart. 24p. (C). 1978. pap. 2.00 (*0-929343-52-2*) J A Hynek Ctr UFO.

Survey of Underground Gas Storage Facilities in the United States & Canada 1978. 64p. 1978. pap. 4.00 (*0-318-12716-4*, XU0678) Am Gas Assn.

Survey of United States & Total World Production, Proved Reserves, & Remaining Recoverable Resources of Fossil Fuels & Uranium, as of December 31, 1982. Joseph D. Parent. xviii, 250p. 1984. pap. 30.00 (*0-910091-52-8*) Inst Gas Tech.

Survey of United States History. Ralph Hymes. 112p. (C). 1994. per. 19.89 (*0-8403-9566-3*) Kendall-Hunt.

Survey of University Presses, 1989-1990. Laing Research Services Staff. 70p. 1990. 95.00 (*0-938106-09-0*) Laing Res Servs.

Survey of Urban Arterial Design Standards. (Illus.). 91p. 1969. 10.00 (*0-917084-21-7*) Am Public Works.

Survey of Vegetation in Glen Canyon Reservoir Basin. Angus M. Woodbury et al. (Glen Canyon Ser.: No. 5). reprint ed. 20.00 (*0-404-60636-9*) AMS Pr.

Survey of Vegetation in the Curecanti Reservoir Basins. Angus M. Woodbury et al. (Upper Colorado Ser.: No. 6). reprint ed. 17.50 (*0-404-60656-3*) AMS Pr.

Survey of Vegetation in the Flaming Gorge Basin. Angus M. Woodbury et al. (Upper Colorado Ser.: No. 2). reprint ed. 30.00 (*0-404-60645-8*) AMS Pr.

Survey of Vegetation in the Navajo Reservoir Basin. Angus M. Woodbury et al. (Upper Colorado Ser.: No. 4). reprint ed. 25.00 (*0-404-60651-2*) AMS Pr.

Survey of Vertebrate Pretectal Areas & the Accessory Optic System. Ed. by J. Wallman & K. V. Fite. (Journal: Brain, Behavior Evolution: Vol. 26, No. 2, 1985). (Illus.). 76p. 1985. pap. 44.00 (*3-8055-4247-X*) S Karger.

Survey of Western Civilization. Richard D. Goff et al. LC 86-24606. (Illus.). 854p. (C). 1987. Instr's. manual. teacher ed., pap. text ed. write for info. (*0-314-34775-5*) West Pub.

Survey of Western Civilization, I. Richard D. Goff et al. LC 86-24606. (Illus.). 854p. (C). 1987. pap. text ed. 44. 25 (*0-314-26135-4*) West Pub.

Survey of Western Civilization, II. Richard D. Goff et al. LC 86-24606. (Illus.). 854p. (C). 1987. pap. text ed. 44. 25 (*0-314-26137-0*) West Pub.

Survey of Western Civilization, No. I. Richard D. Goff et al. LC 86-24606. (Illus.). 854p. (C). 1987. Study Guide I. student ed., pap. text ed. 20.00 (*0-314-34776-3*) West Pub.

Survey of Western Civilization, No. II. Richard D. Goff et al. LC 86-24606. (Illus.). 854p. (C). 1987. Study Guide II. student ed., pap. text ed. 20.00 (*0-314-35865-X*) West Pub.

Survey of Western Civilization, Set. Richard D. Goff et al. LC 86-24606. (Illus.). 854p. (C). 1987. text ed. 62.50 (*0-314-26133-8*) West Pub.

Survey of Western Civilization, Vol. I. 2nd ed. Cassar et al. Date not set. pap. text ed. write for info. (*0-07-022616-4*) McGraw.

Survey of Western Civilization, Vol. 2. Cassar et al. 1994. pap. text ed. write for info. (*0-07-011231-2*) McGraw.

Survey of Western Civilization: Volume B. Richard D. Goff et al. 513p. (C). 1987. pap. text ed. 41.00 (*0-314-58348-3*) West Pub.

Survey of Western Civilization: Volume C. Richard D. Goff et al. 854p. (C). 1987. pap. text ed. 41.00 (*0-314-58492-7*) West Pub.

Survey of Western Music to 1750. S. B. Potter. (Illus.). 445p. (C). 1993. pap. text ed. 17.95 (*0-910648-05-0*) Gamut Music.

Survey of Western Palestine. Charles Warren & Claude R. Conder. LC 78-63371. (Crusades & Military Orders Ser.: Second Series). reprint ed. 41.50 (*0-404-17047-1*) AMS Pr.

Survey of Western Palestine, 3 vols., Set. Claude R. Conder. Ed. by E. H. Palmer & Walter Besant. LC 78-63331. (Crusades & Military Orders Ser.: Second Series). (Illus.). reprint ed. 155.00 (*0-404-17010-2*) AMS Pr.

***Survey of Western Palestine 1882-1888.** Ed. by H. H. Kitchener & C. R. Conder. Date not set. reprint ed. lib. bdg. write for info. (*0-614-25974-6*, Pub. by Archive Editions UK) N Ross.

Survey of Work Done in the Military History of India. S. N. Prasad. 1976. 6.50 (*0-88386-939-X*) S Asia.

Survey of Workers Compensation Laws. Alliance of American Insurers Staff. 73p. 1995. pap. text ed. 20.00 (*1-887271-00-7*) Alliance Am Insurers.

***Survey of Workers Compensation Laws.** rev. ed. 78p. 1996. pap. write for info. (*1-887271-27-9*) Alliance Am Insurers.

***Survey of Workers Compensation Laws.** rev. ed. 84p. 1997. pap. 20.00 (*1-887271-28-7*) Alliance Am Insurers.

Survey on a Shoestring: A Manual for Small-Scale Language Survey. Frank Blair. LC 90-71834. xii, 141p. 1991. pap. 11.00 (*0-88312-644-3*); fiche 12.00 (*0-88312-266-9*) Summer Instit Ling.

Survey on Drug Prevalence & Attitudes in the Dominican Republic. Development Associates, Inc. Staff. 115p. 1993. pap. text ed. 15.00 (*1-879839-03-2*) Develop Assocs.

Survey on Drug Prevalence & Attitudes in Urban Panama. Joel M. Jutkowitz et al. LC 92-34132. 1992. pap. write for info. (*1-879839-02-4*) Develop Assocs.

***Survey on Job Descriptions.** Patricia A. Cervenka. LC 97-1733. (Briefs in Law Librarianship Ser.). 1997. write for info. (*0-8377-9315-7*) Rothman.

***Survey on Knot Theory.** 1996. text ed. 89.50 (*0-8176-5124-1*) Spr-Verlag.

Survey on Lawyer Discipline Systems. 60p. 1989. pap. 12. 95 (*0-685-43620-9*, 561-0094) Amer Bar Assn.

Survey on Sanskrit Grammar in Tibetan Language. Narendra K. Dash. (C). 1993. 32.00 (*81-7320-011-4*, Pub. by Agam II) S Asia.

Survey on the Teaching of Professional Responsibility. ABA, Center for Professional Responsibility Staff. 27p. 1987. pap. 8.95 (*0-318-36473-5*, 561-0074) Amer Bar Assn.

Survey on the Ways in Which States Interpret Their International Obligations. Paul Guggenheim. Bd. with Mission on the Teaching of the Social Sciences in Pakistan.; Research Councils in the Social Sciences.; Social Sciences in Secondary Schools.; Research Councils in the Social Sciences Addenda. (UNESCO Social Science Clearing House Report Ser.: Nos. 1 & 6). 1974. reprint ed. Set pap. (*0-8115-3323-9*) Periodicals Srv.

Survey, or Topographical Description of France. with a New Mappe. John Eliot. LC 79-84104. (English Experience Ser.: No. 923). (Illus.). 116p. 1979. reprint ed. lib. bdg. 20.00 (*90-221-0923-2*) Walter J Johnson.

S

Survey Principles Manual. Training Technologies Staff. (Sc - Marketing Research). 1997. text ed. 37.95 (*0-538-86537-7*) S-W Pub.

Survey Questions. Jean M. Converse & Stanley Presser. (Quantitative Applications in the Social Sciences Ser.: Vol. 63). 96p. (Orig.). 1986. pap. text ed. 9.95 (*0-8039-2743-6*) Sage.

***Survey Questions & Secret Rules: Introduction.** Tracey Wright & Jan Makros. Ed. by Catherine Anderson & Beverly Cory. (Investigations in Number, Data, & Space Ser.). (Illus.). 136p. (Orig.). 1997. teacher ed., pap. 22.95 (*1-57232-468-6*, 43704) Seymour Pubns.

Survey Report Form. rev. ed. 1992. pap. write for info. (*0-932915-08-6*) Accredit Assn Ambulatory.

Survey Research. 2nd ed. Charles H. Backstrom & Gerald D. Hursh-Cesar. LC 81-1738. 436p. (C). 1986. text ed. 88.00 (*0-02-305080-2*, Macmillan Coll) P-H.

Survey Research: A Computer-Assisted Introduction. William S. Bainbridge. 370p. (C). 1989. pap. 40.95 (*0-534-09774-X*) Wadsworth Pub.

Survey Research by Telephone. rev. ed. James H. Frey. (Library of Social Research: Vol. 150). 240p. 1989. pap. 24.95 (*0-8039-2985-4*) Sage.

Survey Research by Telephone. 2nd rev. ed. James H. Frey. (Library of Social Research: Vol. 150). 240p. 1989. 54.00 (*0-8039-2984-6*) Sage.

Survey Research Designs: Towards a Better Understanding of Their Costs & Benefits. Ed. by R. W. Pearson & R. F. Boruch. (Lecture Notes in Statistics Ser.: Vol. 38). v, 129p. 1986. 39.95 (*0-387-96428-2*) Spr-Verlag.

Survey Research for Geographers. Ira M. Sheskin. LC 84-73382. (Resource Publications in Geography). 112p. (Orig.). 1985. pap. 15.00 (*0-89291-187-5*) Assn Am Geographers.

Survey Research for Geographers. Ira M. Sheskin. (Orig.). (C). 1985. 75.00 (*0-317-62318-4*, Pub. by Scientific UK) St Mut.

Survey Research for Geographers. Ira M. Sheskin. (Orig.). (C). 1986. text ed. 35.00 (*81-85046-50-6*, Pub. by Scientific Pubs II) St Mut.

Survey Research for Public Administration. David H. Folz. LC 95-50178. 1996. pap. 15.95 (*0-7619-0153-1*) Sage.

Survey Research for Public Administration. David H. Folz. LC 95-50178. 204p. (C). 1996. 35.00 (*0-7619-0152-3*) Sage.

Survey Research Handbook. Pamela L. Alreck & Robert B. Settle. LC 84-71129. 350p. 1984. text ed. 52.50 (*0-87094-529-7*) Irwin Prof Pubng.

Survey Research Handbook. Robert G. Settle et al. (C). 1994. pap. 75.95 (*0-256-18375-9*) Irwin.

Survey Research Handbook. 2nd ed. Pamela L. Alreck & Robert B. Settle. LC 94-7619. (Marketing Ser.). 470p. (C). 1994. per. 39.00 (*0-256-10321-6*) Irwin.

Survey Research Handbook: Guidelines & Strategies for Conducting a Survey. 2nd ed. Robert G. Settle. 496p. 1994. text ed. 50.00 (*0-7863-0358-1*) Irwin Prof Pubng.

Survey Research in the Social Sciences. Ed. by Charles Y. Glock. LC 67-25911. 544p. 1967. 50.00 (*0-87154-331-1*) Russell Sage.

Survey Research Methods. 2nd ed. Earl Babbie. 395p. (C). 1990. pap. 41.95 (*0-534-12672-3*) Wadsworth Pub.

Survey Research Methods. 2nd ed. Floyd J. Fowler, Jr. (Applied Social Research Methods Ser.: Vol. 1). (Illus.). 152p. (C). 1993. text ed. 39.95 (*0-8039-5048-9*); pap. text ed. 17.95 (*0-8039-5049-7*) Sage.

Survey Research Project Manual. Monica A. Longmore et al. 192p. (C). 1996. pap. text ed. 20.50 (*0-314-06110-X*) West Pub.

Survey Responses: An Evaluation of Their Validity. Ellen J. Wentland & Kent W. Smith. (Illus.). 207p. 1993. text ed. 53.00 (*0-12-744030-5*) Acad Pr.

Survey, Review & Buyers' Guide see Tutorial Guide to CAD-CAM, CAE Systems

Survey Sampling. J. Leslie Kish. 643p. 1965. text ed. 99.95 (*0-471-48900-X*) Wiley.

Survey Sampling. Leslie Kish. 643p. 1995. pap. text ed. 42.95 (*0-471-10949-5*) Wiley.

***Survey Sampling.** Lohr. 1998. pap. 55.95 (*0-534-35361-4*) Brooks-Cole.

Survey Sampling Principles. E. K. Foreman. (Statistics: Textbooks & Monographs: Vol. 120). 496p. 1991. 160.00 (*0-8247-8407-3*) Dekker.

Survey Search & Seizure. B. Malik. (C). 1988. 375.00 (*0-685-25678-2*) St Mut.

Survey Sources: For U. S. & International Employee Pay & Benefit Surveys. 3rd rev. ed. Ed. by Mae L. Ding. 1997. pap. 265.00 (*0-9633931-2-X*) Prsnl Systs Assocs.

Survey, Testing, & Documentation Assembly & Offense Areas Live Fire Maneuver Range, Fort Irwin, San Bernardino County, California. fac. ed. Contrib. by W. T. Eckhardt & M. Jay Hatley. (Fort Irwin, Miscellaneous Reports). (Illus.). 260p. (C). 1982. reprint ed. pap. text ed. 23.05 (*1-55567-520-4*) Coyote Press.

Survey to Determine the Attitudes of Industry for an Expanded WRC Welding Research Program. 1978. 25.00 (*0-318-18636-5*) Welding Res Coun.

Survey Vessels of the World. Oilfield Publications Limited Staff. 350p. (C). 1993. 515.00 (*1-870945-37-9*, Pub. by Oilfield Pubns UK) St Mut.

Survey Vessels of the World. Oilfield Publications Limited Staff. (Vessels of the World Ser.). (Illus.). 138p. 1995. pap. 285.00 (*1-870945-72-7*, Pub. by Oilfld Pubns Ltd UK) Am Educ Systs.

Surveying. (Illus.). 64p. (J). (gr. 6-12). 1984. pap. 2.40 (*0-8395-3327-6*, 33327) BSA.

Surveying. Heribert Kahmen & Wolfgang Faig. 474p. (C). 1988. lib. bdg. 129.95 (*3-11-008303-5*) De Gruyter.

Surveying. 3rd ed. Charles B. Breed. 495p. 1971. Net. text ed. write for info. (*0-471-10070-6*) Wiley.

Surveying. 3rd ed. Jack C. McCormac. LC 94-6281. 400p. 1994. pap. text ed. 54.00 (*0-13-031162-6*) P-H.

***Surveying.** 6th ed. A. Bannister. (C). 1992. pap. text ed. 54.95 (*0-582-07688-9*, Pub. by Longman UK) Longman.

Surveying. 9th ed. Francis H. Moffitt & Harry Bouchard. (C). 1992. text ed. 79.37 (*0-06-500059-5*) Addson-Wesley Educ.

Surveying: Principles & Applications. 2nd ed. Barry F. Kavanagh & Glenn Bird. 800p. 1988. boxed 40.00 (*0-318-37861-2*) P-H.

Surveying: Principles & Applications. 4th ed. Barry F. Kavanagh & S. J. Bird. LC 95-3157. 700p. 1995. text ed. 81.00 (*0-13-438300-1*) P-H.

***Surveying: Solutions Manual.** 10th ed. Mofitt. (C). 1998. teacher ed., pap. text ed. write for info. (*0-673-97132-5*) Addison-Wesley.

Surveying: With Construction Applications. 3rd ed. Barry F. Kavanagh. LC 96-5561. 1996. text ed. 71.00 (*0-13-449679-5*) P-H.

***Surveying a Dynamical System: A Study of the Gray Scott Reaction in a Twophase Reactor.** Khalid Alhumaizi. 1995. pap. 78.95 (*0-582-24688-1*, Pub. by Longman UK) Longman.

Surveying & Charting of the Seas. W. Langeraar. (Elsevier Oceanography Ser.: No. 37). 612p. 1984. 162.50 (*0-444-42278-1*, I-540-83) Elsevier.

Surveying & Mapping for Field Scientists. W. Ritchie et al. (Illus.). 192p. (C). 1988. pap. text ed. 51.95 (*0-582-30086-X*) Longman.

Surveying & Navigation for Geophysical Exploration. L. Harold Spradley. LC 84-19769. (Illus.). 289p. 1985. text ed. 54.00 (*0-934634-87-4*) Intl Human Res.

Surveying & Restoring Classic Boats. J. C. Winters. LC 92-28984. (Illus.). 200p. 1993. 35.00 (*0-924486-42-2*) Sheridan.

Surveying Buildings. Malcolm Hollis & Charles Gibson. 234p. (C). 1986. 150.00 (*0-85406-464-8*, Pub. by Surveyors Pubns) St Mut.

Surveying Derelict Land. Edwin M. Bridges. (Monographs on Soil & Resources Survey: No. 13). (Illus.). 146p. 1987. 65.00 (*0-19-854566-5*) OUP.

Surveying Employees: A Practical Guidebook. John E. Jones. 1996. pap. text ed. 24.95 (*0-87425-305-5*) HRD Press.

Surveying Fiberglass Sailboats: A Step-by-Step Guide for Buyers & Owners. Henry C. Mustin. 1993. pap. text ed. 17.95 (*0-87742-347-4*) Intl Marine.

Surveying Fiberglass Sailboats: A Step by Step Guide for Buyers & Owners. Henry C. Mustin. 1994. pap. text ed. 17.95 (*0-07-044248-7*) McGraw.

Surveying Flip Chart. Jack D. Keen. 50p. (C). 1995. 22.00 (*1-56569-047-8*) Land Survey.

Surveying for Civil Engineers. 2nd ed. Philip C. Kissam. (C). 1981. text ed. write for info. (*0-07-034882-0*) McGraw.

Surveying for Construction. 4th ed. William Irvine. LC 94-48598. 1995. 16.95 (*0-07-707998-1*) McGraw.

Surveying Fundamentals. 2nd ed. Jack C. McCormac. 608p. 1990. text ed. 81.00 (*0-13-878026-9*) P-H.

Surveying Fundamentals: A Tutorial Approach. D. M. Edwards et al. (Illus.). 1977. pap. text ed. 9.90 (*0-89534-006-2*) Am Print Co.

Surveying Handbook. Russell C. Brinker. LC 87-8217. (Illus.). 1100p. 1987. text ed. 105.00 (*0-442-21423-5*) Chapman & Hall.

Surveying Handbook. 2nd ed. Ed. by Russell Brinker & Roy Minnick. LC 94-5241. 912p. (gr. 13). 1995. text ed. 99.95 (*0-412-98511-X*) Chapman & Hall.

Surveying Handbook. 2nd ed. Russell C. Brinker. 1993. text ed. 129.95 (*0-442-01062-1*) Chapman & Hall.

Surveying Historic Buildings. Jennifer E. Attebery. (Local History Technical Leaflets Ser.). (Illus.). 16p. (Orig.). 1985. pap. 1.50 (*0-931406-11-0*) Idaho State Soc.

Surveying Immigrant Communities: Policy Imperatives & Technical Challenges. Julie DaVanzo & Jennifer Hawes-Dawson. LC 94-38284. 178p. 1994. pap. 15.00 (*0-8330-1594-X*) Rand Corp.

Surveying Instructions for the Survey of Public Lands: Answers a Study Supplement. John E. Keen. 61p. (C). 1995. pap. text ed. 20.00 (*1-56569-005-2*) Land Survey.

Surveying Instructions for the Survey of Public Lands: Questions a Study Supplement. John E. Keen. 180p. (C). 1995. pap. text ed. 30.00 (*1-56569-004-4*) Land Survey.

Surveying Instrumentation & Coordinate Computation Workshop Lecture Notes. 3rd ed. Joseph F. Dracup et al. 208p. 1979. 20.90 (*0-317-32471-3*, S260) Am Congrs Survey.

Surveying Instrumentation-Coordinate Computation Workshop Lecture Note. Joseph F. Dracup et al. 208p. 1979. pap. 25.00 (*0-614-06115-6*, S260) Am Congrs Survey.

Surveying Instruments. Fritz Deumlich. 336p. (C). 1981. text ed. 85.40 (*3-11-007765-5*) De Gruyter.

Surveying Instruments: Their History. Edmond R. Kiely. 1979. reprint ed. 34.00 (*0-686-25583-6*) CARBEN Survey.

Surveying Instruments & Their Operational Principles. Ed. by L. Fialovsky. (Developments in Geotechnical Engineering Ser.: No. 62). 760p. 1991. 198.75 (*0-444-98829-7*) Elsevier.

Surveying Instruments & Their Operational Principles. Lajos Fialovszky & Holeczy Gyula. 273p. 1991. 120.00 (*0-614-04416-2*, Pub. by Akad Kiado HU) St Mut.

Surveying Marine Damage: A Thorough & Substantial Handbook. C. B. Thompson. 542p. 1995. 135.00 (*1-85609-067-1*, Pub. by Witherby & Co UK) St Mut.

Surveying Measurements & Their Analysis. R. B. Buckner. (Illus.). 288p. (C). 1983. text ed. 48.00 (*0-910845-11-5*, 480) Landmark Ent.

Surveying Natural Populations. Ed. by Lee-Ann C. Hayek & Martin A. Buzas. (Illus.). 448p. 1996. 60.00 (*0-231-10240-2*); pap. 24.00 (*0-231-10241-0*) Col U Pr.

Surveying Practice. 3rd ed. Philip C. Kissam. (Illus.). 1977. text ed. 39.95 (*0-07-034901-0*) McGraw.

Surveying Practice. 4th ed. Jerry A. Nathanson & Philip C. Kissam. 608p. 1988. text ed. 37.95 (*0-07-034903-7*) Glencoe.

***Surveying Principles for Civil Engineers: Review for the Engineering Surveying Section of the California Special Civil Engineer Examination.** Paul A. Cuomo. LC 97-12592. 150p. (Orig.). 1997. pap. 24.95 (*1-888577-08-8*) Prof Pubns CA.

Surveying Public Opinion. Sondra M. Rubenstein. LC 94-16428. 425p. 1995. pap. 37.95 (*0-534-17856-1*) Wadsworth Pub.

***Surveying Review for the Civil Engineer Exam.** 3rd ed. Shu-Hsien Liu. 12p. (Orig.). 1996. pap. 24.50 (*1-57645-017-1*) Engineering.

Surveying Reviewer: For the Civil Engineering License Examination. Frank Talania. (Illus.). 250p. 1995. pap. 32.00 (*0-929176-16-2*) Burdick & Landreth Co.

Surveying Small Craft. 3rd ed. Ian Nicolson. (Illus.). 224p. 1994. 29.95 (*0-924486-58-9*) Sheridan.

Surveying Subjective Phenomena, 2 vols., I. Ed. by Charles F. Turner & Elizabeth Martin. LC 83-61131. 1088p. 1985. 49.95 (*0-87154-882-8*) Russell Sage.

Surveying Subjective Phenomena, 2 vols., II. Ed. by Charles F. Turner & Elizabeth Martin. LC 83-61131. 1088p. 1985. 55.00 (*0-87154-883-6*) Russell Sage.

Surveying Subjective Phenomena, 2 vols., Set. Ed. by Charles F. Turner & Elizabeth Martin. LC 83-61131. 1088p. 1985. 90.00 (*0-87154-881-X*) Russell Sage.

***Surveying the Canadian Pacific: Memoir of a Railroad Pioneer.** R. M. Rylatt. 1991. pap. 24.95 (*0-7748-0568-4*, Pub. by U BC Pr) U of Wash Pr.

Surveying the Courtroom: A Land Expert's Guide to Evidence & Civil Procedure. John Briscoe. 199p. 1985. 60.00 (*0-910845-21-2*, 958) Landmark Ent.

Surveying the Forty-Ninth Parallel: 1858-61. Ed. by Herman J. Deutsch. (Illus.). 17p. 1962. pap. 1.00 (*0-917048-24-5*) Wash St Hist Soc.

***Surveying the Land.** Lynn Turnage. LC 97-10160. (Roots of Youth Ministry Ser.). 1997. write for info. (*1-57895-008-2*) Bridge Resources.

Surveying the Land: Skills & Exercises in U. S. Historical Geography, 2 vols., Vol. I: To 1877. Robert B. Grant. 106p. (C). 1996. 15.96 (*0-669-27111-X*) HM College Div.

Surveying the Land: Skills & Exercises in U. S. Historical Geography, 2 vols., Vol. II: From 1865. Robert B. Grant. 92p. (C). 15.96 (*0-669-27112-8*) HM College Div.

***Surveying the Library Landscape: The Inspection Visits of the University of Illinois Library School.** Thomas D. Walker. (Occasional Papers: No. 206). 49p. (Orig.). 1996. pap. 10.00 (*0-614-24096-4*) U of Ill Grad Sch.

Surveying the Mahele: Mapping the Hawaiian Land Revolution. Gary L. Fitzpatrick & Riley M. Moffat. LC 95-37752. (Palapala'aina Ser.: Vol. 2). (Illus.). 132p. 1995. 65.00 (*0-915013-17-7*) Editions Ltd.

Surveying the New Testament. William H. Marty. 196p. 1996. spiral bd. 20.01 (*0-8403-7025-3*) Kendall-Hunt.

Surveying the Scriptures. Robert Hoggard. 1981. pap. 3.95 (*0-86544-013-1*) Salv Army Suppl South.

Surveying the South: Studies in Regional Sociology. John S. Reed. LC 93-8561. 168p. (Orig.). (C). 1993. pap. 15.95 (*0-8262-0915-7*) U of Mo Pr.

Surveying the South: Studies in Regional Sociology. John S. Reed. LC 93-8561. 168p. (Orig.). (C). 1993. text ed. 30.00 (*0-8262-0914-9*) U of Mo Pr.

Surveying the Texas & Pacific Land Grant West of the Pecos River. J. J. Bowden. (Southwestern Studies: No. 46). 1975. pap. 5.00 (*0-87404-104-X*) Tex Western.

Surveying Theory & Practice. 6th ed. Raymond E. Davis et al. (Illus.). 1120p. 1981. text ed. write for info. (*0-07-015790-1*) McGraw.

Surveying Victims: A Study of the Measurement of Criminal Victimization, Perceptions of Crime & Attitudes to Criminal Justice. Richard F. Sparks et al. LC 76-52393. 286p. reprint ed. pap. 81.60 (*0-685-20653-X*, 2030439) Bks Demand.

Surveyor. Jack Rudman. (Career Examination Ser.: C-3032). 1994. pap. 29.95 (*0-8373-3032-7*) Nat Learn.

Surveyor in Court. ACSM Staff. 40p. 1975. pap. 12.00 (*0-614-06114-8*, S270) Am Congrs Survey.

Surveyors & Statesmen. Sarah S. Hughes. LC 79-56069. 196p. 1980. 25.00 (*0-686-77533-3*) VA Surveyors.

Surveyor's Guide. B. F. Dorr. 1978. reprint ed. pap. 12.00 (*0-686-25542-9*, 514) CARBEN Survey.

Surveyor's Guide to Electromagnetic Distance Measurement. Ed. by J. J. Saastamoinen. LC 68-79061. 203p. reprint ed. pap. 57.90 (*0-317-08362-7*, 2019159) Bks Demand.

Surveyor's Hand. Anne Cherner. LC 81-70100. 80p. (Orig.). 1981. pap. 10.00 (*0-9607302-0-6*) Compton Pr.

***Surveyors of the Ancient Mississippi Valley.** P. Clay Sherrod & Martha A. Rolingson. (Illus.). 155p. 1987. pap. 10.00 (*1-56349-055-2*, RS28) AR Archaeol.

Surveys: Historic & Economic. William J. Ashley. LC 66-21366. (Reprints of Economic Classics Ser.). xxviii, 476p. 1966. reprint ed. 49.50 (*0-678-00170-7*) Kelley.

Surveys & Experiments in Education Research. James F. McNamara. LC 94-60492. 220p. 1994. pap. text ed. 29.95 (*1-56676-167-0*) Technomic.

Surveys & Soundings in European Literature. Hermann J. Weigand. Ed. by A. Leslie Willson. LC 66-10931. 370p. 1966. reprint ed. pap. 105.50 (*0-7837-9473-8*, 2060215) Bks Demand.

Surveys for Travellers, Emigrants & Others. John H. Melish. LC 75-22829. (America in Two Centuries Ser.). 1976. 33.95 (*0-405-07701-7*) Ayer.

Surveys from Exile Vol. 2: Political Writings. Karl Marx. Ed. & Intro. by David Fernbach. 384p. 1993. pap. 10.95 (*0-14-044572-2*, Penguin Classics) Viking Penguin.

Surveys in Applied Mathematics, Vol. 1. Ed. by Joseph B. Keller et al. 280p. 1995. 75.00 (*0-306-44993-5*, Plenum Pr) Plenum.

Surveys in Applied Mathematics, Vol. 2. Mark Freidlin et al. (Illus.). 280p. (C). 1995. 75.00 (*0-306-45060-7*, Plenum Pr) Plenum.

Surveys in Combinatorics, 1989. Ed. by J. Siemons. (London Mathematical Society Lecture Note Ser.: No. 141). 228p. (C). 1989. pap. text ed. 47.95 (*0-521-37823-0*) Cambridge U Pr.

Surveys in Combinatorics, 1991. Ed. by A. D. Keedwell. (London Mathematical Society Lecture Note Ser.: No. 166). (Illus.). 312p. (C). 1992. pap. text ed. 44.95 (*0-521-40766-4*) Cambridge U Pr.

Surveys in Combinatorics, 1993. Ed. by K. Walker. (London Mathematical Society Lecture Note Ser.: No. 187). (Illus.). 250p. (C). 1993. pap. text ed. 39.95 (*0-521-44857-3*) Cambridge U Pr.

Surveys in Combinatorics, 1995. Ed. by Peter Rowlinson. (London Mathematical Society Lecture Note Ser.: No. 218). (Illus.). 300p. (C). 1995. pap. text ed. 42.95 (*0-521-49797-3*) Cambridge U Pr.

***Surveys in Combinatorics, 1997.** Ed. by R. A. Bailey. (London Mathematical Society Lecture Note Ser.: Vol. 241). (Illus.). 250p. (C). 1997. pap. write for info. (*0-521-59840-0*) Cambridge U Pr.

Surveys in Differential Geometry. S. Yau & C. C. Hsiung. LC 91-7410. 320p. 1991. pap. 31.00 (*0-8218-0168-6*, DIFGEO/1) Am Math.

Surveys in Econometrics. Ed. by L. Oxley et al. (Illus.). 400p. (C). 1995. pap. 36.95 (*0-631-19065-1*) Blackwell Pubs.

Surveys in Economics, Vol. 1. Ed. by Andrew J. Oswald. 256p. (C). 1991. pap. 27.95 (*0-631-17973-9*) Blackwell Pubs.

Surveys in Economics, Vol. 2. Ed. by Andrew T. Oswald. 312p. (C). 1991. pap. 27.95 (*0-631-17975-5*) Blackwell Pubs.

Surveys in International Trade. David Greenaway & L. Alan Winters. (Illus.). 320p. 1994. pap. 33.95 (*0-631-18589-5*) Blackwell Pubs.

Surveys in Parapsychology. Rhea A. White. LC 76-119. 496p. 1976. 29.50 (*0-8108-0906-0*) Scarecrow.

Surveys in Set Theory. A. R. Mathias. LC 83-10106. (London Mathematical Society Lecture Note Ser.: No. 87). 256p. 1983. pap. 44.95 (*0-521-27733-7*) Cambridge U Pr.

Surveys in Social Research. David A. De Vaus. LC 85-9146. (Contemporary Social Research Ser.: No. 11). 240p. 1986. text ed. 55.00 (*0-04-312023-7*); pap. text ed. 18.95 (*0-04-312024-5*) Routledge Chapman & Hall.

Surveys in Social Research. 2nd ed. David A. De Vaus. 346p. (C). 1990. pap. text ed. 21.95 (*0-04-445722-7*) Routledge Chapman & Hall.

Surveys in Social Research. 3rd ed. David A. De Vaus. 400p. (C). 1992. pap. text ed. 24.95 (*1-86373-099-0*, Pub. by Allen Unwin AT) Paul & Co Pubs.

Surveys in Social Work. 4th ed. David De Vaus. 424p. 1996. pap. 29.95 (*1-86373-939-4*, Pub. by Allen Unwin AT) Paul & Co Pubs.

Surveys in Transaction Costs, Markets & Hierarchies. Ed. by Christos N. Pitelis. LC 92-30554. 1993. pap. 27.95 (*0-631-18898-3*) Blackwell Pubs.

Surveys of Applied Economics, Vol. 1. LC 73-82638. 288p. (C). 1973. text ed. 32.50 (*0-312-77735-3*) St Martin.

Surveys of Applied Economics, Vol. 2. Ed. by Royal Economic Society Staff & Social Studies Research Council Staff. LC 73-82638. 1977. text ed. 35.00 (*0-312-77770-1*) St Martin.

Surveys of Australian Psychology. Ed. by N. T. Feather. 280p. 1985. text ed. 25.95 (*0-86861-607-9*); pap. text ed. 13.95 (*0-86861-599-4*) Routledge Chapman & Hall.

Surveys of Consumers, 1974-75: Contributions to Behavioral Economics. Ed. by Richard T. Curtin. LC 72-619718. 336p. 1976. 16.00 (*0-87944-209-3*) Inst Soc Res.

Surveys of Drinking & Abstaining: Urban, Suburban & National Studies. (Journal of Studies on Alcohol: Suppl. No. 6). 1972. 9.00 (*0-911290-01-X*) Rutgers Ctr Alcohol.

Surveys of Fisheries Resources. Donald R. Gunderson. LC 92-21522. 256p. 1993. text ed. 69.95 (*0-471-54735-2*) Wiley.

Surveys of Research in Transportation Technology: Presented at the Winter Annual Meeting of the ASME, November 11-15, 1973. Ed. by E. Diamant et al. LC 73-90322. (American Society of Mechanical Engineers, Applied Mechanics Division Ser.: Vol. 5). (Illus.). 182p. reprint ed. pap. 51.90 (*0-317-10236-2*, 2016808) Bks Demand.

Surveys of the Confederate Postmasters' Provisionals. Francis J. Crown, Jr. LC 81-52857. 1984. lib. bdg. 50.00 (*0-88000-124-0*) Quarterman.

Surveys of the Member States' Powers to Investigate & Sanction Violations of. European Commision Staff. 92p. 1995. pap. text ed. 18.00 (*92-826-9069-5*, Pub. by Europ Com UK) Bernan Associates.

Surveys of Tidal River Systems in the Northern Territory & Their Crocodile Population. Harry Messel et al. (Monographs: No. 1). (Illus.). 464p. 1982. 155.00 (*0-08-024819-5*, G135, Pergamon Pr) Elsevier.

Surveys of Tidal River Systems in the Northern Territory & Their Crocodile Population: Monograph, No. 18. Ed. by Harry Messel et al. (Illus.). 308p. 1985. 135.00 (*0-08-029858-3*, Pergamon Pr) Elsevier.

Surveys of Tidal River Systems in the Northern Territory & Their Crocodile Populations. Harry Messel et al. (Monographs: No. 17). (Illus.). 92p. 1981. pap. 28.00 (*0-08-024818-7*, Pergamon Pr) Elsevier.

An Asterisk (*) at the beginning of an entry indicates that the title is appearing in BIP for the first time.

Surveys of Tidal River Systems in the Northern Territory & Their Crocodile Populations. Harry Messel. (Monographs: No. 15). (Illus.). 368p. 1982. 135.00 (*0-08-024831-4*, Pergamon Pr) Elsevier.

Surveys of Tidal River Systems in the Northern Territory & Their Crocodile Populations. Incl. Tidal Waterways of Castlereagh Bay & Hutchinson & Cadell Straits: Bennett, Darbitla, Djigaglia Djabura, Ngandadauda Creeks & the Glyde & Woolen Rivers. 1980. pap. 35.00 (*0-08-024801-2*); Tidal Waterways of Arnhem Bay: Darwarunga, Habgood, Baralminer, Gobalpa, Coromuro, Cato, Peter John & Burungbirinung Rivers. 1980. pap. 33.00 (*0-08-024803-9*); Tidal Waterways on the South-Western Coast of the Gulf of Carpentaria: Limmen Bight Towns, Roper, Phelp & Wilson Rivers; Nayarnpi, Wungguliyanga, Painnyilatya, Mangkurdurrungku & Yiwapa Creeks. 1980. pap. 26.00 (*0-08-024804-7*); Tidal Waterways on the Southern Coast of the Gulf of Carpentaria: Calvert, Robinson, Wearyan & McArthur Rivers & Some Intervening Creeks. 1980. pap. 28.00 (*0-08-024805-5*); Tidal Waterways of the Van Diemen Gulf: Ilamary; River, Iwalg, Saltwater & Minimini: Creeks & Coastal Arms on Cobourg Peninsula. Resurveys of the Alligator Region Rivers. 1980. pap. 31.00 (*0-08-024806-3*); Some River & Creek Systems on the West Coast of Cape York Peninsula in the Gulf of Carpentaria: Nassau, Staaten & Gilbert Rivers & Duck Creek. 1981. pap. 33.00 (*0-08-024807-1*); (Monographs: Nos. 9-14 & 16). (Illus.). 1980. Set pap. write for info. (*0-318-55232-9*) Elsevier.

Surveys of Tidal River Systems in the Northern Territory of Australia: Resurveys of the Tidal Waterways of Van Diemen Gulf & the Southern Gulf of Carpentaria 1984 & 1985. Harry Messel et al. (Surveys of Tidal Rivers Ser.: No. 19). (Illus.). 118p. 1986. 86.00 (*0-08-029882-6*, PPA) Elsevier.

Surveys of Tidal Waterways in the Kimberley Region, Western Australia & Their Crocodile Populations: Monograph 20 - Tidal Waterways of the Kimberley Surveyed During 1977, 1978 & 1986. Harry Messel et al. (Surveys of Tidal Rivers Ser.: No. 20). 256p. 1988. 83.00 (*0-08-034429-1*, Pergamon Pr) Elsevier.

Surveys, Polls, Censuses, & Forecasts Directory. 284p. 1983. 245.00 (*0-8103-1692-7*) Gale.

Surveys 2: Eight State-of-the Art Articles on Key Areas in Language Teaching. Ed. by Valerie Kinsella. LC 82-45961. (Cambridge Language Teaching Library). 156p. 1983. pap. 15.95 (*0-521-27047-2*) Cambridge U Pr.

Survivable Networks. Grover. 1996. text ed. 70.00 (*0-13-494576-X*) P-H.

Survival. Peter David. (Star Trek: The Next Generation, Starfleet Academy Ser.: No. 3). (Illus.). 128p. (Orig.). (J). (gr. 3-6). mass mkt. 3.99 (*0-671-87086-6*, Minstrel Bks) PB.

Survival, 29 bks. Betty L. Hall. (YA). (gr. 11-12). Date not set. write for info. (*0-614-08425-3*) Westwood Pr.

Survival. Nancy Lord. LC 90-27025. 161p. (Orig.). 1991. pap. 10.95 (*0-918273-84-6*) Coffee Hse.

***Survival.** Anthony Masters. LC 97-24773. (True Stories Ser.). 1997. pap. text ed. 7.95 (*0-8069-9657-9*) Sterling.

Survival. Susan Onion et al. (Interdisciplinary Units Ser.). 1995. pap. text ed. 14.95 (*1-55734-604-6*) Tchr Create Mat.

Survival. Nancy Polette. (Illus.). 48p. (Orig.). 1991. pap. 5.95 (*0-913839-93-0*) Pieces of Lrning.

Survival. R. W. Richards. Ed. by Jeff Bogart. (Story of the New Southland Ser.: Bk. I). (Illus.). 252p. (YA). 1995. pap. text ed. 13.95 (*0-9625502-4-8*) RoKarn Pubns.

***Survival.** Thomas-Cochran. (What a Wonderful World 1 Ser.). 1991. pap. text ed. write for info. (*0-582-90951-1*, Pub. by Longman UK) Longman.

Survival. R. Wosch. 1992. 17.99 (*0-89906-872-3*); pap. 14.99 (*0-89906-873-1*) Mesorah Pubns.

Survival: A Guide to Living on Your Own. Joan B. Kelly & Valerie M. Chamberlain. (Illus.). 1979. text ed. 27.40 (*0-07-033870-1*) McGraw.

Survival: A Manual That Could Save Your Life. Chris Janowsky & Gretchen Janowsky. (Illus.). 208p. 1986. pap. 18.00 (*0-87364-506-5*) Paladin Pr.

Survival: A Novel of the Donner Party. K. C. McKenna. 320p. (Orig.). 1994. mass mkt. 4.99 (*0-515-11405-7*) Jove Pubns.

Survival: A Sequential Program for College Writing. 5th rev. ed. 390p. 1995. pap. text ed. 24.95 (*0-917962-32-X*) T H Peek.

Survival: How to Prevail in Hostile Environments. Xavier Maniguet. Tr. by Ivanka Roberts from ENG. LC 93-16118. 464p. (ENG & FRE). 1994. 35.00 (*0-8160-2518-5*) Facts on File.

Survival! In the Desert. Susan Landsman. 112p. (Orig.). (J). 1993. pap. 3.50 (*0-380-76601-9*, Camelot) Avon.

Survival! In the Jungle. Susan Landsman. 112p. (Orig.). (YA). 1993. pap. 3.50 (*0-380-76605-1*, Camelot) Avon.

Survival: Live off the Land in the City & Country. Pagnar Benson & Devon Christensen. 262p. (C). 1983. pap. 9.95 (*0-8065-0867-1*, Citadel Pr) Carol Pub Group.

Survival: The Ten Rules for Success in Petroleum Marketing. Bruce F. McCall. 145p. 15.00 (*0-685-65573-3*) Mkters Assn of Am.

Survival: Your First 72 Hours. Ellen Wilfley. (Illus.). 90p. 1995. pap. text ed. 7.95 (*0-9644552-6-9*) SunRise Pbl.

Survival Against All Odds: The First 100 Years of Anatolia College. Everett Stephens & Mary Stephens. (Illus.). 224p. 1986. lib. bdg. 37.50 (*0-89241-421-9*) Caratzas.

Survival among the Kurds: A Study of the Yezidis. John S. Guest. LC 92-17867. 1993. 89.95 (*0-7103-0456-0*, B0089) Routledge Chapman & Hall.

Survival Analysis. Ed. by John Crowley et al. LC 82-84316. (IMS Lecture Notes - Monograph Ser.: Vol. 2). x, 302p. 1982. pap. 25.00 (*0-940600-02-1*) Inst Math.

Survival Analysis. John P. Klein & Melvin L. Moeschberger. LC 96-9006. (Statistics for Biology & Health Ser.). 352p. 1997. 59.95 (*0-387-94829-5*) Spr-Verlag.

Survival Analysis. Rupert G. Miller, Jr. LC 81-4437. (Probability & Mathematical Statistics: Applied Probability & Statistics Section Ser.). 238p. 1981. pap. text ed. 84.95 (*0-471-09434-X*, Wiley-Interscience) Wiley.

Survival Analysis: A Practical Approach. Mahesh K. Parmar & David Machin. LC 95-32240. 150p. 1995. text ed. 45.00 (*0-471-93640-5*) Wiley.

Survival Analysis: A Self-Learning Text. David G. Kleinbaum. LC 95-18632. (Springer Series in Statistics). 264p. 1997. 44.95 (*0-387-94543-1*) Spr-Verlag.

Survival Analysis - State of the Art: Proceedings of the NATO Advanced Research Workshop on Survival Analysis & Related Topics, Columbus, Ohio, U. S. A., 23-28 June 1991. Ed. by John P. Klein & Prem K. Goel. 464p. (C). 1992. lib. bdg. 177.00 (*0-7923-1634-7*) Kluwer Ac.

Survival Analysis Using the SAS System: A Practical Guide. Paul D. Allison. 296p. (C). 1997. pap. 37.95 (*1-55544-279-X*, BR55233) SAS Inst.

Survival & Change in the Third World. B. Crow et al. 376p. (C). 1988. pap. 19.95 (*0-19-520717-3*) OUP.

Survival & Consolidation: The Foreign Policy of Soviet Russia, 1918-1921. Richard K. Debo. 532p. 1992. 60.00 (*0-7735-0828-7*, Pub. by McGill CN) U of Toronto Pr.

Survival & Emergency Uses of Parachute. 1995. lib. bdg. 250.96 (*0-8490-6659-X*) Gordon Pr.

Survival & Growth: Management Strategies for the Small Firm. Theodore Cohn & Roy A. Lindberg. LC 73-92163. 240p. reprint ed. pap. 68.40 (*0-317-29948-4*, 2051700) Bks Demand.

Survival & Profit in Rural Java: The Case of an East Javanese Village. Sven Cederroth. (SIAS Monographs: No. 63). 330p. (C). 1995. text ed. 49.00 (*0-7007-0294-6*, Pub. by Curzon Press UK) UH Pr.

Survival & Progress: The Afro-American Experience. L. Alex Swan. LC 80-1197. (Contributions in Afro-American & African Studies: No. 58). (Illus.). xxiii, 251p. 1981. text ed. 38.50 (*0-313-22480-3*, SSU/, Greenwood Pr) Greenwood.

Survival & Regeneration: Detroit's American Indian Community. Edmund J. Danziger, Jr. LC 90-29857. (Great Lakes Bks.). (Illus.). 262p. 1991. text ed. 29.95 (*0-8143-2348-0*, Great Lks Bks) Wayne St U Pr.

Survival & Religion: Biological Evolution & Cultural Change. Ed. by Eric L. Jones & Vernon Reynolds. LC 95-9880. 1996. text ed. 75.00 (*0-471-95507-8*) Wiley.

Survival & Sociology: Vindicating the Human Subject. Kurt H. Wolff. 124p. (C). 1990. 34.95 (*0-88738-357-2*) Transaction Pubs.

Survival & the Bomb: Methods of Civil Defense. Ed. by Eugene Paul Wigner. LC 69-16003. 317p. reprint ed. pap. 90.40 (*0-317-12974-0*, 2015520) Bks Demand.

Survival Arts of the Primitive Paiutes. Margaret M. Wheat. LC 67-30392. (Illus.). xiii, 140p. 1967. pap. 16.95 (*0-87417-048-6*) U of Nev Pr.

Survival at Sea. Ron Brandt. (Illus.). 88p. 1994. pap. 15.95 (*0-87364-770-X*) Paladin Pr.

Survival! at Sea. Susan Landsman. 112p. (Orig.). 1993. pap. 3.50 (*0-380-76603-5*, Camelot) Avon.

***Survival at Sea: A Training & Instruction Manual.** 100p. 14.95 (*0-644-24262-0*, Pub. by Aust Gov Pub AT) Aubrey Bks.

Survival at Sea: The Lifeboat & Liferaft. C. H. Wright. (C). 1988. 110.00 (*0-85174-555-5*, Pub. by Brwn Son Ferg) St Mut.

Survival at Sea: The Lifeboat & Liferaft. 4th ed. C. H. Wright. (Illus.). 353p. 1988. pap. text ed. 45.00 (*0-85174-540-7*) Sheridan.

Survival Bartering. Duncan Long. LC 86-80537. 56p. 1986. pap. text ed. 8.00 (*0-915179-37-7*) Loompanics.

Survival Behind the Wheel: Safety, Knowledge, Strategy, Performance for All Who Drive. 3rd rev. ed. Gilbert N. Drake. (Illus.). 136p. 1995. pap. 12.95 (*0-9644384-0-2*) SafeWheels Pr.

***Survival Bible for Women in Medicine.** Kathryn K. Ko. LC 97-15485. 1997. write for info. (*1-85070-752-9*) Prthnon Pub.

Survival Books, Nineteen Eighty-One. Bruce Clayton. LC 81-80117. (Illus.). 180p. (Orig.). 1981. pap. 14.95 (*0-939216-00-0*) Media West.

***Survival by Association: Supply Management Landscapes of the Eastern Caribbean.** Barbara M. Welch. 384p. 1996. 55.00 (*0-7735-1370-1*, Pub. by McGill CN) U of Toronto Pr.

Survival Camp. Eve Bunting. LC 92-11689. (Author's Signature Collection). (Illus.). (J). (gr. 3-8). 1992. lib. bdg. 12.79 (*0-89565-970-0*) Childs World.

Survival Dancing. Anselm Hollo. 28p. (Orig.). 1995. pap. 5.00 (*1-887289-00-3*) Rodent Pr.

Survival English. Lee Mosteller & Bobbi Paul. (Illus.). 200p. (C). 1985. pap. text ed. 8.50 (*0-13-879172-4*) P-H.

Survival English: English Through Conversations, BK. 1B. Lee Mosteller & Bobbi Paul. (Illus.). 144p. 1988. pap. text ed. 5.25 (*0-13-879222-4*) P-H.

Survival English: English Through Conversations, Bk. 2B. Lee Mosteller & Michele A. Haight. (Illus.). 128p. 1988. pap. text ed. 5.25 (*0-13-879263-1*) P-H.

Survival English Three. Lee Mosteller. 192p. 1994. pap. text ed. 11.25 (*0-13-878166-4*) P-H.

Survival English 1A. 2nd ed. Lee Mosteller & Bobbi Paul. 144p. 1993. pap. 7.50 (*0-13-016593-X*) P-H.

Survival English 1B. 2nd ed. Lee Mosteller & Bobbi Paul. 144p. 1993. pap. 7.50 (*0-13-016601-4*) P-H.

Survival English 2. 2nd ed. Lee Mosteller & Bobbi Paul. 240p. 1994. pap. text ed. 11.25 (*0-13-016650-2*) P-H.

Survival English 2A. 2nd ed. Lee Mosteller & Bobbi Paul. pap. write for info. (*0-13-016619-7*) P-H.

Survival English 2B. 2nd ed. Lee Mosteller & Bobbi Paul. pap. write for info. (*0-13-016627-8*) P-H.

Survival English 3A. Lee Mosteller. write for info. (*0-13-017005-4*) P-H.

Survival English 3B. Lee Mosteller. pap. write for info. (*0-13-017013-5*) P-H.

Survival Factor. Mike Birkhead & Tim Birkhead. 208p. (C). 1990. 60.00 (*1-85283-245-2*, Pub. by Boxtree Ltd UK) St Mut.

Survival Factor: An Action Guide to Improving Your Business Today. V. Daniel Hunt. 256p. (C). 1994. 75.00 (*0-939246-65-1*) Wiley.

Survival Factor: An Action Guide to Improving Your Business Today. V. Daniel Hunt. 256p. 1995. text ed. 27.95 (*0-471-13181-4*) Wiley.

Survival-Fighting Knives. Leroy Thompson. (Illus.). 104p. 1986. pap. 18.00 (*0-87364-347-X*) Paladin Pr.

Survival for Busy Women. exp. ed. Emilie Barnes. (Orig.). 1993. pap. 8.99 (*1-56507-065-8*) Harvest Hse.

Survival for Yachtsmen. C. H. Wright. (C). 1987. suppl. ed. 100.00 (*0-85174-489-3*) St Mut.

Survival Game. Philip Kerrigan. 256p. 1989. mass mkt. 3.95 (*0-380-70682-2*) Avon.

***Survival Games.** Charles Gaines. LC 97-12379. 240p. 1997. 22.00 (*0-87113-684-8*, Atlntc Mnthly) Grove-Atltic.

Survival Games Personalities Play. Eve Delunas. LC 92-64111. 304p. (Orig.) (C). 1992. pap. 15.00 (*0-931104-35-1*) Sunflower Ink.

Survival Gardening: Enough Nutrition to Live on... Just in Case. 2nd ed. John A. Freeman. (Illus.). 104p. 1983. pap. 8.95 (*0-9607730-5-3*) Johns Pr.

Survival Gardening Cookbook: Low Cost Nutritious. John A. Freeman. Ed. by Grace B. Freeman. (Illus.). 104p. (Orig.). 1985. pap. 10.95 (*0-9607730-8-8*) Johns Pr.

Survival Gear. Rita Moir. 176p. (Orig.). 1994. pap. 12.95 (*0-919591-81-7*, Pub. by Polestar Bk Pubs CN) Orca Bk Pubs.

***Survival Guide: Tips for Coping for Patients of Spiritual Healing.** Michelle E. Cappel. (Illus.). 50p. (Orig.). 1997. pap. 10.95 (*0-9653666-1-8*) M E Cappel.

***Survival Guide for Activity Professionals.** 2nd rev. ed. Richelle N. Cunninghis. Ed. by Nancy DeBolt. LC 97-16966. 92p. 1997. pap. 12.00 (*1-882883-16-0*, 313) Idyll Arbor.

Survival Guide for Anatomy & Physiology: A Topical Review for Board Examination Review for RN, RT, PA, LPN, PA, PT, OT, DH & MLT Health Occupations. W. Charles Plenielk. Ed. by William C. Kleinelp. 140p. (Orig.). (C). 1994. 15.95 (*0-929941-17-9*) Wood River Pubns.

***Survival Guide for Black Men in America: You Don't Have to Be Extinct.** Xavier C. Dicks. 300p. 1997. 24.95 (*0-9647003-2-8*) Farry Bell.

Survival Guide for College Students with ADD or LD. Kathleen G. Nadeau. LC 94-15724. (Illus.). 64p. 1994. pap. 9.95 (*0-945354-63-0*) Magination Pr.

Survival Guide for Crafters: Dreams Don't Just Happen. Barbara Massie. 47p. 1994. pap. text ed. 6.95 (*1-884053-06-8*) Magnolia AR.

Survival Guide for Kids with LD: Learning Differences. Gary Fisher & Rhoda Cummings. Ed. by Nancy Nielsen. LC 89-37084. (Self-Help for Kids Ser.). (Illus.). 104p. (Orig.). (J). (gr. 2 up). 1990. pap. 9.95 (*0-915793-18-0*); audio 10.00 (*0-915793-20-2*) Free Spirit Pub.

Survival Guide for Nursing Students. Philip Burnard & Paul Morrison. (Illus.). 128p. 1993. pap. text ed. 25.00 (*0-7506-1589-3*) Buttrwrth-Heinemann.

Survival Guide for Older Americans. Martin R. Cramer & Sanford I. Ruden. 188p. pap. text ed. 17.95 (*0-9640843-0-9*) Camco Enter.

Survival Guide for Parents: How to Avoid Screwing up Your Kids or Losing Your Own Sanity. Mickey Michaels. LC 94-74608. 125p. 1995. pap. 9.95 (*0-9644761-1-8*) Possibility Pr.

Survival Guide for Parents of Gifted Kids: How to Understand, Live with, & Stick Up for Your Gifted Child. Sally Y. Walker. LC 91-9449. (Illus.). 152p. (Orig.). 1991. pap. 10.95 (*0-915793-28-8*) Free Spirit Pub.

Survival Guide for Road Warriors: Essentials for the Mobile Lawyer. Daniel S. Coolidge. 176p. 1996. pap. text ed. 29.95 (*1-57073-298-1*) Amer Bar Assn.

Survival Guide for Teenagers with LD: (Learning Differences) Rhoda Cummings & Gary Fisher. Ed. by Pamela Espeland. LC 93-6798. (Illus.). 200p. (Orig.). (YA). (gr. 7 up). 1993. pap. 11.95 (*0-915793-51-2*); audio 19.95 (*0-915793-56-3*) Free Spirit Pub.

Survival Guide for the Elementary - Middle School Counselor. John J. Schmidt. 288p. 1991. spiral bd. 32.95 (*0-87628-801-8*) Ctr Appl Res.

Survival Guide for the Evolving Insurance Crisis. Edward D. Curry. Ed. by Letha S. Curry. (Illus.). 174p. (Orig.). 1995. pap. 39.95 (*0-9633590-2-9*) Target Mktg-Mgmt.

Survival Guide for The First-Year Special Education Teacher. rev. ed. Mary Kemper Cohen et al. LC 94-31388. 1994. pap. text ed. 12.00 (*0-86586-256-7*, P335R) Coun Exc Child.

Survival Guide for the Florida Teacher. Barbara A. Murray & Kenneth T. Murray. 100p. (Orig.). 1995. pap. text ed. 16.95 (*0-9644512-1-2*) IntraCoast Pub.

***Survival Guide for the Groom to Be or How Not to Let Sex Become a Fond Memory. Maureen Moss. Ed. by Beth Meyer. (Illus.). 128p. (Orig.). 1996. pap. 9.95 (*0-9651310-1-7*) Constant Concepts.**

Survival Guide for the Jr. High - Middle School Math Teacher. G. Baur & D. Pigford. 1983. 22.95 (*0-13-879156-2*, Busn) P-H.

Survival Guide for the Mariner. Robert J. Meurn. LC 93-7990. (Illus.). 240p. 1993. text ed. 25.00 (*0-87033-444-1*) Cornell Maritime.

Survival Guide for the New Millennium: How to Survive the Coming Earth Changes. Byron R. Kirkwood. LC 92-41591. 112p. (Orig.). 1993. pap. 9.95 (*0-931892-54-6*) B Dolphin Pub.

Survival Guide for the Preschool Teacher. Jean R. Feldman. 336p. 1990. pap. 27.95 (*0-685-39262-7*) P-H.

Survival Guide for the Secondary School Counselor. Kenneth Hitchner. 256p. 1987. spiral bd. 32.95 (*0-87628-781-X*) Ctr Appl Res.

Survival Guide for the Unemployed: A Philadelphia Unemployment Project Handbook. rev. ed. (Illus.). 96p. (YA). (gr. 12 up). 1994. pap. text ed. 10.00 (*0-7881-0842-5*) DIANE Pub.

Survival Guide for Today's Career Woman. Victoria L. Rayner. 208p. (Orig.). 1994. pap. 19.95 (*0-924272-06-6*) Info Net Pub.

***Survival Guide of the Entrepreneurial Woman.** (Illus.). 350p. 1997. pap. 24.95 (*1-56559-931-4*) HGI Mrktng.

Survival Guide to Buying Art. Doug Thompson. 32p. (Orig.). 1991. pap. 4.95 (*0-9630775-0-3*) Make It Simple.

Survival Guide to Computer Contracts: How to Select & Negotiate for Business Computer Systems. Jeff Monassebian. Ed. by Marcy J. Gordon. LC 96-83000. (Illus.). 304p. 1996. pap. 24.95 (*0-9650971-7-X*) Applicat Pubng.

Survival Guide to Confirmation: The Candidate's Guide. Stephen Gomez. 64p. 1993. 20.00 (*0-85439-437-0*, Pub. by St Paul Pubns UK) St Mut.

Survival Guide to Confirmation: The Catechist's Guide. Stephen Gomez. 80p. 1993. 24.00 (*0-85439-436-2*, Pub. by St Paul Pubns UK) St Mut.

Survival Guide to End-User Computing. Ed. by Naomi Karlen. 384p. 1994. 49.95 (*0-7913-2015-4*) Warren Gorham & Lamont.

Survival Guide to Rats & Stats. Jerry Kroth. (Illus.). 192p. (C). 1988. pap. text ed. 15.95 (*0-936618-02-7*) Genotype.

Survival Guide to School-Age Child Care. Betsy Arns. (Illus.). 254p. (Orig.). (C). 1988. pap. text ed. 19.95 (*0-317-93309-4*) Schl-Age Wkshops Pr.

Survival Guide to the Last Times. James A. Aderman. Ed. by William E. Fischer. (Bible Class Course for Young Adults Ser.). (Illus.). 36p. (Orig.). 1987. teacher ed. 5.50 (*0-938272-31-4*, 22-2195); pap. text ed. 3.50 (*0-938272-30-6*, 22-2194) WELS Board.

Survival Guide to the Stress of Organizational Change. Price Pritchett & Ron Pound. 30p. (Orig.). 1995. pap. 5.95 (*0-944002-16-1*) Pritchett Assocs.

***Survival Guide to the Stress of Organizational Change.** Price Pritchett & Ron Pound. 30p. (Orig.). (FRE.). 1996. pap. 5.95 (*0-944002-24-2*) Pritchett Assocs.

Survival Handbook for Preschool Parents. Helen W. Smith. 159p. 1990. pap. 10.98 (*0-88290-400-0*) Horizon Utah.

Survival Handbook for Small Business. rev. ed. Frieda Carrol. LC 80-70496. 73p. 1992. ring bd. 35.95 (*0-9605246-4-9*) Prosperity & Profits.

Survival Improvised Weapons. (Weaponry Ser.). 1986. lib. bdg. 79.95 (*0-8490-3846-4*) Gordon Pr.

Survival in Ashes. William W. Johnstone. (Ashes Ser.: No. 12). 1990. mass mkt. 3.95 (*0-8217-3098-3*, Zebra Kensgtn) Kensgtn Pub Corp.

Survival in Auschwitz. Primo Levi. (U Ser.). 1995. pap. 11.00 (*0-684-82680-1*) S&S Trade.

Survival in Groups: The Basics of Group Membership. Tom Douglas. LC 95-15367. 167p. 1995. 79.00 (*0-335-19413-3*, Open Univ Pr); pap. write for info. (*0-335-19412-5*, Open Univ Pr) Taylor & Francis.

Survival in Sarajevo: How a Jewish Community Came to the Aid of Its City. 1995. pap. 29.95 (*3-85447-572-1*) Dist Art Pubs.

***Survival in Simplicissimus & Mutter Courage.** Cara M. Horwich. (Studies in Modern German Literature: Vol. 81). 168p. (C). 1997. text ed. 38.95 (*0-8204-3058-7*) P Lang Pubng.

Survival in Space. Richard Harding. 256p. 1989. 22.00 (*0-415-00253-2*) Routledge.

Survival in the Academy: A Guide for Beginning Academics. Gerald M. Phillips et al. LC 93-44472. (Hampton Press - SCA Applied Communication Ser.). 288p. 1994. pap. text ed. 24.95 (*1-881303-69-1*) Hampton Pr NJ.

Survival in the Air Age. U. S. President's Air Policy Commission. Ed. by Richard H. Kohn. LC 78-22406. (American Military Experience Ser.). 1980. reprint ed. lib. bdg. 17.95 (*0-405-11880-5*) Ayer.

Survival in the Doldrums: The American Women's Rights Movement, 1945 to the 1960s. Leila J. Rupp & Verta Taylor. 256p. 1987. 30.00 (*0-19-504938-1*) OUP.

Survival in the Doldrums: The American Women's Rights Movement, 1945 to the 1960s. Leila J. Rupp & Verta Taylor. (Illus.). 256p. (C). 1990. reprint ed. pap. 21.50 (*0-8142-0516-X*) Ohio St U Pr.

S

Survival! in the Mountains. Susan Landsman. 112p. (Orig.). (J). 1993. pap. 3.50 (*0-380-76602-7*, Camelot) Avon.

Survival in the Organization: Gunnar Hjelholt Looks Back at the Concentration Camp from an Organizational Perspective. Benedicte Madsen & Soren Willert. Tr. by Edith Matteson. (Illus.). 96p. (C). 1996. pap. 9.95 (*87-7288-539-4*, Pub. by Aarhus Univ Pr DK) David Brown.

Survival in the Software Jungle. Mark Norris. LC 95-33001. 256p. 1995. 55.00 (*0-89006-831-3*) Artech Hse.

Survival in the Square. Dwight Hawkins & Morrie Greenberg. LC 89-9762. (Illus.). 160p. (Orig.). 1989. pap. 5.95 (*0-9622652-0-9*) Brooke-Richards.

Survival in the '90's: A Guide for Outdoor Enthusiasts. Bob Newman. (Illus.). 224p. (Orig.). 1995. pap. 15.95 (*0-89732-191-X*) Menasha Ridge.

Survival in Youth Ministry. Robert P. Stamschror. 120p. (Orig.). 1994. pap. 6.95 (*0-88489-317-0*) St Marys.

Survival Instincts. Marissa Piesman. LC 96-16050. 224p. 1997. 20.95 (*0-385-31358-6*) Delacorte.

***Survival Instincts.** Marissa Piesman. (A Nina Fischman Mystery Ser.). 1997. mass mkt. 5.99 (*0-440-22453-5*, Dell Trade Pbks) Dell.

Survival into the Twenty-First Century. Viktoras Kulvinskas. Ed. by Hermine Hurlbut & Joan Newman. (Illus.). 1975. pap. 21.95 (*0-933278-04-7*) Twen Fir Cent.

Survival Japanese: How to Communicate Without Fuss or Fear - Instantly. Boye L. De Mente. 126p. (Orig.). 1992. pap. 5.95 (*0-8048-1681-6*) C E Tuttle.

Survival Jobs: 118 Ways to Make Money While Pursuing Your Dreams. Deborah Jacobson. LC 95-61685. 218p. (Orig.). 1996. pap. 15.95 (*0-9648526-8-3*) Windtree Pubng.

Survival Kit. rev. ed. J. Grubbs. Ed. & Illus. by Joan Abell. (J). (gr. 7-8). pap. 28.00 (*1-56611-039-4*); lib. bdg. 32.00 (*1-56611-011-4*) Jones.

***Survival Kit Family Haggadah: Everything a Family Needs to Create An Enjoyable, Educational Experience.** Shimon Apisdorf. 1997. pap. text ed. 8.95 (*1-881927-11-3*) Leviathan OH.

Survival Kit for Growing Christians. Marlene LeFever. (Bible Discovery Guide Ser.). 32p. (J). (gr. 4-6). 1988. 1.50 (*0-87788-796-9*); pap. text ed. 3.50 (*0-87788-797-7*) Shaw Pubs.

***Survival Kit for Multicultural Living.** Ellen Summerfield. LC 97-2357. 1997. pap. 17.95 (*1-877864-49-8*) Intercult Pr.

Survival Kit for Overseas Living: For Americans Planning to Live & Work Abroad. 3rd ed. L. Robert Kohls. 181p. (C). 1996. pap. text ed. 11.95 (*1-877864-38-2*, 306R) Intercult Pr.

Survival Kit for Teachers & Parents. 2nd ed. Myrtle T. Collins & Susan J. Benjamin. LC 92-43037. 1993. 12.95 (*0-673-36035-0*, GoodYrBooks) Addson-Wesley Educ.

Survival Kit for the Secondary School Art Teacher. Helen D. Hume. 288p. 1990. pap. text ed. 34.95 (*0-87628-798-4*) Ctr Appl Res.

Survival Kit for the Special Education Teacher. Roger Pierangelo. LC 93-44763. 1994. pap. 29.95 (*0-87628-870-0*) Ctr Appl Res.

Survival Kit for Those Who Sit: Simple Office Exercises to Boost Your Energy & Productivity. Ruth Lindsey & Douglas D. Gorrie. LC 89-10211. (Illus.). 128p. (Orig.). 1989. pap. 8.95 (*0-913581-10-0*) Publitec.

Survival Kit for Today's Family. Bill R. Swetmon. LC 93-37611. 115p. 1994. pap. 8.95 (*1-55622-034-0*, Seaside Pr) Wordware Pub.

Survival Kit for Wives. Donald Martin & Renee Martin. 1986. pap. 12.95 (*0-394-74361-X*, Villard Bks) Random.

Survival Licks & Bar Room Tricks. Mark & Junior. (Illus.). 76p. 1991. pap. text ed. 8.95 (*0-931759-51-X*) Centerstream Pub.

Survival Manual for Consumers: Get Mad then Get Even. James McTigue. (Self Confidence - Self Competence Ser.). 200p. (Orig.). 1987. pap. 11.95 (*0-932123-03-1*) Stone Trail Pr.

Survival Manual for Men in Divorce. Carol Wilson et al. 96p. 1995. per., pap. text ed. 10.95 (*0-8403-9788-7*) Kendall-Hunt.

Survival Manual for the Independent Woman Traveler. limited ed. Roberta Mendel. LC 82-80695. 128p. (Orig.). 1982. pap. 14.00 (*0-936424-06-0*) Pin Prick.

Survival Manual for Women in Divorce. Carol Wilson et al. 96p. 1995. per., pap. text ed. 10.95 (*0-8403-9787-9*) Kendall-Hunt.

Survival Medical Guide, Vol. 2. George Settar. 200p. (SPA.). 1979. 49.95 (*0-8288-6896-4*) Fr & Eur.

Survival Medical Guide, Vol. 3. George Settar. 200p. (GER.). 1979. 49.95 (*0-8288-6897-2*) Fr & Eur.

Survival Medical Guide, Vol. 4. George Settar. 200p. (RUM.). 1979. 49.95 (*0-8288-6898-0*) Fr & Eur.

Survival Medical Guide, Vol. 7. George Settar. 200p. (JPN.). 1979. 49.95 (*0-8288-6900-6*) Fr & Eur.

Survival Medical Guide, Vol. 8. George Settar. 200p. (CHI.). 1979. 49.95 (*0-8288-6901-4*) Fr & Eur.

Survival Medical Guide, Vol. 10. George Settar. 200p. (RUS.). 1979. 49.95 (*0-8288-6903-0*) Fr & Eur.

Survival Medical Guide, Vol. 11. George Settar. 200p. (DUT.). 1979. 49.95 (*0-8288-6904-9*) Fr & Eur.

Survival Medical Guide, Vol. 12. George Settar. 200p. (GRE.). 1979. 49.95 (*0-8288-6905-7*) Fr & Eur.

Survival Medical Guide, Vol. 13. George Settar. 200p. (SWE.). 1979. 49.95 (*0-8288-6906-5*) Fr & Eur.

Survival Medical Guide - Medicine, Vol. 9. George Settar. 200p. (POR.). 1979. 49.95 (*0-8288-6902-2*) Fr & Eur.

Survival Medical Guide-Medicine, Vol. 6. George Settar. 200p. (ITA.). 1979. 49.95 (*0-8288-6899-9*) Fr & Eur.

Survival Models & Data Analysis. Regina C. Elandt-Johnson & Norman L. Johnson. LC 79-22836. (Probability & Mathematical Statistics: Applied Probability & Statistics Section Ser.). 457p. 1980. text ed. 137.00 (*0-471-03174-7*) Wiley.

***Survival Models & Their Estimation.** 2nd rev. ed. Dick London. (C). 1997. pap. text ed. 47.50 (*1-56698-268-5*) Actex Pubns.

Survival Munitions: How to Reuse Spent Primers, How to Make Your Own Small Arms Rifle Powder, Flash Powder for Hand Grenades, Land Mines & Napalm from Everyday Supermarket Items. (Weaponry Ser.). 1986. lib. bdg. 79.95 (*0-8490-3844-8*) Gordon Pr.

Survival of American Democracy: Virtual Reality vs. Actual Reality, a Metaphor, & Irony of Christianity. Bruce P. Burns. LC 96-68693. 233p. (Orig.). 1996. pap. 12.95 (*1-882792-25-4*) Proctor Pubns.

***Survival of American Democracy: Virtual Reality vs. Actual Reality, a Metaphor, & Irony of Christianity.** Bruce P. Burns. LC 96-68693. 233p. (Orig.). 1996. 21.95 (*1-882792-30-0*) Proctor Pubns.

Survival of Cancer Patients in Europe: The EUROCARE Study. M. Sant et al. (IARC Scientific Publications: No. 132). 463p. 1995. pap. 98.00 (*92-832-2132-X*) OUP.

Survival of Charles Darwin: A Biograph of a Man & An Idea. Ronald W. Clark. 1986. mass mkt. 5.95 (*0-380-69991-5*) Avon.

Survival of Civilization. John D. Hamaker & Donald A. Weaver. (Illus.). 218p. (Orig.). 1982. pap. 12.00 (*0-941550-00-1*) Hamaker-Weaver.

Survival of Corporatism During the New Deal Era, 1933-1945. Intro. by Robert F. Himmelberg. LC 93-48672. (Business & Government in America since 1870 Ser.: Vol. 6). 432p. 1994. text ed. 70.00 (*0-8153-1408-6*) Garland.

Survival of Empire: Portuguese Trade & Society in China & the South China Sea, 1630-1754. G. B. Souza. (Illus.). 300p. 1986. text ed. 65.00 (*0-521-24855-8*) Cambridge U Pr.

Survival of Ethiopian Independence. Sven Rubenson. LC 78-1367. (Illus.). 437p. 1978. pap. 35.00 (*0-8419-0375-1*, Africana) Holmes & Meier.

Survival of Food Crops & Livestock in the Event of Nuclear War: Proceedings. Ed. by David W. Bensen & Arnold H. Sparrow. LC 77-170334. (AEC Symposium Ser.). 762p. 1971. 26.75 (*0-87079-219-9*, CONF-700909); fiche 9.00 (*0-87079-220-2*, CONF-700909) DOE.

Survival of Freedom. Ed. by Jerry Pournelle & John F. Carr. 384p. 1981. pap. 2.95 (*0-449-24435-0*) Fawcett.

Survival of Mechanical Systems in Transient Environments: Presented at the Winter Annual Meeting of the American Society of Mechanical Engineers, New York, December 2-7, 1979. American Society of Mechanical Engineers Staff. Ed. by Thomas L. Geers & Pin Tong. LC 79-54424. (AMD Ser.: Vol. 36). (Illus.). 195p. reprint ed. pap. 55.60 (*0-8357-2854-4*, 2039089) Bks Demand.

Survival of Pagan Gods: The Mythological Tradition & Its Place in Renaissance Humanism & Art. J. Seznec. Tr. by B. F. Sessions. 392p. 1995. pap. text ed. 17.95 (*0-691-02988-1*) Princeton U Pr.

Survival of Small Business. Ed. by Vincent P. Carosso & Stuart Bruchey. LC 78-18155. (Small Business Enterprise in America Ser.). 1979. lib. bdg. 28.95 (*0-405-11512-1*) Ayer.

Survival of the Adversary Culture. Paul Hollander. 299p. (C). 1991. 21.95 (*1-56000-554-8*) Transaction Pubs.

Survival of the Bark Canoe. John McPhee. (Illus.). 146p. 1975. 18.95 (*0-374-27207-7*) FS&G.

Survival of the Bark Canoe. John McPhee. (Illus.). 132p. 1982. pap. 9.00 (*0-374-51693-6*) FS&G.

Survival of the Black Family: The Institutional Impact of American Social Policy. K. Sue Jewell. LC 88-2338. 207p. 1988. text ed. 55.00 (*0-275-92985-X*, C2985, Praeger Pubs) Greenwood.

Survival of the Black Family: The Institutional Impact of American Social Policy. K. Sue Jewell. LC 88-2338. 207p. 1989. pap. text ed. 15.95 (*0-275-93504-3*, B3504, Praeger Pubs) Greenwood.

Survival of the Fitter: Lives of Some African Engineers. John Powell. 127p. (Orig.). 1995. pap. 20.95 (*0-614-16423-0*, Pub. by Intermed Tech UK) Women Ink.

***Survival of the Fittest.** Jonathan Kellerman. 384p. 1997. 24.95 (*0-553-08923-4*) Bantam.

***Survival of the Fittest, Vol. 120.** Franklin W. Dixon. (Hardy Boys Casefiles Ser.). (J). 1997. mass mkt. 3.99 (*0-671-56120-0*, Archway) PB.

Survival of the Fittest: Keeping Healthy in Travel & Service. Christine Aroney-Sine. 1994. 9.95 (*0-912552-88-3*) MARC.

Survival of the Fittest: New Product Development During the 90's. Philip A. Himmelfarb. 1992. 19.95 (*0-13-879313-1*, Busn) P-H.

Survival of the Gods: Classical Mythology in Medieval Art. Brown University, Department of Art Staff. LC 86-72762. (Illus.). 226p. (Orig.). 1986. pap. text ed. 20.00 (*0-933519-10-9*) D W Bell Gallery.

***Survival of the Hessian Nobility, 1770-1870.** Gregory W. Pedlow. LC 87-25720. 318p. 1988. reprint ed. pap. 90.70 (*0-608-02915-7*, 2063979) Bks Demand.

Survival of the Individual. Apa Pant. 176p. 1983. text ed. 20.00 (*0-86131-400-X*, Pub. by Orient Longman Ltd II) Apt Bks.

Survival of the Pagan Gods: The Mythological Tradition & Its Place in Renaissance Humanism & Art. Jean Seznec. Tr. by Barbara Sessions. (Bollingen Ser.: Vol. 38). (Illus.). 108p. 1972. pap. 15.95 (*0-691-01783-2*, Bollingen) Princeton U Pr.

Survival of the Sanest: Order & Disorder in a Pretrial Psychiatric Clinic. Robert J. Menzies. 310p. 1989. text ed. 40.00 (*0-8020-5827-2*); pap. text ed. 18.95 (*0-8020-6737-9*) U of Toronto Pr.

Survival of the Soul & Its Evolution after Death. Pierre Cornillier. 1972. lib. bdg. 250.00 (*0-87968-498-4*) Krishna Pr.

Survival of the Spirit: Chiricahua Apaches in Captivity. H. Henrietta Stockel. LC 92-39772. (Illus.). 360p. 1993. 24.95 (*0-87417-208-X*) U of Nev Pr.

Survival of the Unfittest. Charles W. Armstrong. 1973. 59.95 (*0-8490-1163-9*) Gordon Pr.

Survival of the Unlike. Liberty H. Bailey. 1991. 60.00 (*0-936128-25-9*) De Young Pr.

Survival on a Westward Trek, 1858-1859: The John Jones Overlanders. Ed. by Dwight L. Smith. LC 89-31053. (Illus.). 176p. (C). 1989. 26.95 (*0-8214-0921-2*) Ohio U Pr.

Survival on Montague Island. Ralph Soberg. (Illus.). 64p. (Orig.). 1990. pap. 6.50 (*0-9625429-0-3*) Hardscratch Pr.

Survival on the Battle Field. Robert K. Spear. LC 87-50245. 200p. (Orig.). 1987. pap. 14.95 (*0-86568-093-0*, 335) Unique Pubns.

***Survival or Extinction.** Ed. by H. Synge & H. Townsend. ix, 250p. 1979. pap. 15.00 (*0-9504876-2-7*, Pub. by Royal Botnic Grdns UK) Balogh.

Survival or Hegemony? The Foundations of Israeli Foreign Policy. Samuel J. Roberts. LC 73-8134. (Studies in International Affairs: No. 20). 175p. reprint ed. pap. 49.90 (*0-317-41684-7*, 2025852) Bks Demand.

Survival or Suicide. Ed. by Harry H. Moore. LC 77-134118. (Essay Index Reprint Ser.). 1977. 20.95 (*0-8369-2001-5*) Ayer.

Survival Packet, 2 Vols. 1986. lib. bdg. 79.95 (*0-8490-3845-6*) Gordon Pr.

Survival Papers. Daryl Sharp. 1995. pap. 15.00 (*0-919123-34-1*, Pub. by Inner City CN) BookWorld Dist.

Survival Papers: Applied Jungian Psychology. Daryl Sharp. LC 91-30857. 256p. (Orig.). 1991. pap. 9.95 (*0-87542-724-3*) Llewellyn Pubns.

Survival Pattern of the Rural Poor. M. Sadeque. (C). 1990. text ed. 29.00 (*81-85119-82-1*, Pub. by Northern Bk Ctr II) S Asia.

Survival Poaching. Ragnar Benson. (Illus.). 250p. 1980. text ed. 24.95 (*0-87364-183-3*) Paladin Pr.

Survival Probabilities: The Goal of Risk Theory. Hilary L. Seal. LC 78-8599. (Wiley Series in Probability & Mathematical Statistics). 113p. reprint ed. pap. 32.30 (*0-317-41972-2*, 2025979) Bks Demand.

Survival Pronunciation: Vowel Contrasts. Ellen Hecht & Gerry Ryan. (Illus.). (C). 1982. 7.78 (*0-13-879321-2*) Alemany Pr.

Survival Psychology. John Leach. 232p. (C). 1994. 45.00 (*0-8147-5090-7*) NYU Pr.

Survival Reading. 1980. pap. 2.95 (*0-590-49042-7*, Scholastic Hardcover) Scholastic Inc.

***Survival Reading Skills.** Tekla White. (Real-Life Reading Activities Ser.). (Illus.). 64p. (J). (gr. 4-6). 1996. teacher ed., pap. 7.95 (*1-55799-596-6*, 573) Evan-Moor Corp.

Survival Retreat: A Total Plan for Retreat Defense. Ragnar Benson. (Illus.). 136p. 1983. pap. 10.00 (*0-87364-275-9*) Paladin Pr.

Survival Routines for Professionals: Moving Toward Corporate Success. Thomas C. Cannon. (Illus.). 176p. (C). 1988. text ed. 29.20 (*0-13-879271-2*) P-H.

Survival Sense for Pilots & Passengers. Robert C. Stoffel. LC 80-70906. (Illus.). 224p. 1987. pap. 9.95 (*0-913724-24-6*) Emerg Response Inst.

Survival Series, Bk. 1. Duey & Bale. LC 97-3578. 1998. 3.99 (*0-689-81308-2*) S&S Childrens.

Survival Series, Bk. 2. Duey & Bale. LC 97-3172. 1998. 3.99 (*0-689-81309-0*) S&S Childrens.

Survival Series, Bk. 3. Duey & Bale. 1998. 3.99 (*0-689-81310-4*) S&S Childrens.

Survival Series, Bk. 4. Suranna. 1998. 3.99 (*0-689-81311-2*) S&S Childrens.

Survival Shooting: Handguns & Shotguns. T. Given. 1986. lib. bdg. 79.95 (*0-8490-3700-X*) Gordon Pr.

Survival Skills. Libby Roberts. (All Action Ser.). (Illus.). 48p. (J). (gr. 3-4). 1993. 9.50 (*0-8225-2481-3*, Lerner Publctns) Lerner Group.

Survival Skills. L. Smith. (Superskills Ser.). (Illus.). 48p. (YA). (gr. 6-10). 1987. pap. 5.95 (*0-7460-0169-X*) EDC.

Survival Skills: Living Strong As a Christian When Times Get Tough. Randy Petersen. (1993 50-Day Spiritual Adventure Ser.). (Illus.). 64p. (Orig.). (YA). (gr. 7-12). 1992. student ed., pap. text ed. 4.99 (*1-879050-08-0*) Chapel of Air.

Survival Skills for Center Directors. Ed. by Roger Neugebauer. (Best of Exchange Ser.). 48p. (Orig.). (C). 1994. pap. 10.00 (*0-942702-11-5*) Child Care.

Survival Skills for Changing Times: Purposeful Christian Living in the '90s. Chapel of the Air Ministries Staff. (1993 50-Day Spiritual Adventure Ser.). (Illus.). 48p. (Orig.). 1992. student ed., pap. text ed. 4.99 (*1-879050-07-2*) Chapel of Air.

Survival Skills for Changing Times: Purposeful Christian Living in the '90s Leader's Manual. Chapel of the Air Ministries Staff. (1993 50-Day Spiritual Adventure Ser.). (Illus.). 90p. 1992. ring bd. 39.99 (*1-879050-12-9*) Chapel of Air.

Survival Skills for Managers. Marlene Wilson. LC 80-54241. (Illus.). 264p. (Orig.). (C). 1981. pap. text ed. 14.95 (*0-9603362-1-4*) Volunteer Mgmt.

Survival Skills for Single Parents. Paul J. Ciborowski. 182p. 1988. 14.95 (*0-935465-04-9*) Stratmar Ed Sys.

Survival Skills for Teachers Series, 4 bks. 1993. pap. 9.95 (*0-318-72968-7*) Corwin Pr.

Survival Skills...A Job Finding Guide. Neva N. Harden. LC 88-82651. (Illus.). 58p. (Orig.). 1989. pap. text ed. 12.95 (*0-913945-54-4*) Horizon Comms.

Survival Song, Pt. 2. John Bennett. 120p. 1985. pap. 4.00 (*0-912824-35-2*) Vagabond Pr.

Survival Song, Pt. 3. John Bennett. 120p. 1985. pap. 4.00 (*0-912824-36-0*) Vagabond Pr.

Survival Source: When Parents Divorce. Nancy A. Burcham. 73p. (YA). (gr. 7-12). 1993. pap. 6.95 (*1-57515-036-0*) PPI Pubng.

Survival Spanish: A Pocket Guide for the Medical Professional. Theodore P. Skaarup. 150p. (Orig.). 1991. spiral bd. 14.95 (*1-879671-01-8*) Key-Logic.

***Survival Spanish for Correctional Staff.** Sam L. Slick & Jeanne Mullaney. 61p. 1997. teacher ed., ring bd. 37.50 incl. audio (*1-888467-06-1*) Command Spanish.

Survival Spanish for Emergency Responders. James Serrato. Ed. by Sandra Serrato. (Illus.). 234p. (Orig.). (SPA.). 1992. pap. text ed. 16.95 (*0-9635324-0-5*) Streetwise Tech.

***Survival Spanish for Highway Drug Interdiction.** Sam L. Slick. 66p. 1997. teacher ed., ring bd. 37.50 incl. audio (*1-888467-02-9*) Command Spanish.

***Survival Spanish for Jail Facilities.** Sam L. Slick. 68p. 1997. teacher ed., ring bd. 37.50 incl. audio (*1-888467-05-3*) Command Spanish.

Survival Spanish for Law Enforcement Officers. Sam L. Slick. 40p. 1992. text ed. 32.00 (*1-888467-00-2*) Command Spanish.

***Survival Spanish for Narcotics Officers.** Sam L. Slick. 65p. 1997. teacher ed., ring bd. 37.50 incl. audio (*1-888467-03-7*) Command Spanish.

***Survival Spanish for Probation Officers.** Sam L. Slick. 90p. 1997. teacher ed., ring bd. 37.50 incl. audio (*1-888467-04-5*) Command Spanish.

***Survival Stories: Memoirs of Crisis.** Kathryn Rhett. LC 96-52427. 1997. 23.95 (*0-385-48449-6*) Doubleday.

Survival Strategies: Paris & New York. Ed. by George G. Wynne. 165p. 1979. pap. text ed. 21.95 (*0-87855-749-0*) Transaction Pubs.

***Survival Strategies for Africans in America: 13 Steps to Freedom.** Anthony T. Browder. LC 89-80061. (From the Browder File Ser.: Vol. II). (Illus.). 163p. (Orig.). 1996. pap. 15.00 (*0-924944-10-2*) Inst Karmic.

Survival Strategies for Agricultural Cooperatives. Charles E. French et al. LC 79-20528. (Illus.). 288p. 1980. reprint ed. pap. 82.10 (*0-608-00096-5*, 2060861) Bks Demand.

***Survival Strategies for Christian Colleges & Universities: A Leader's Guide to Managing in Turbulent Times.** Melissa Morris-Olson. 122p. 1996. pap. 14.50 (*0-9652730-0-8*) Coal Christian Coll.

Survival Strategies for Couples: A Self-Help Book. John Wright. LC 85-43505. 231p. 1986. 27.95 (*0-87975-319-6*) Prometheus Bks.

Survival Strategies for New Scientists. Carl J. Sindermann. LC 87-14193. (Illus.). 264p. 1987. 17.95 (*0-306-42703-6*, Plenum Pr) Plenum.

Survival Strategies for Parenting Your ADD Child: Dealing with Obsessions, Compulsions, Depression, Explosive Behavior & Rage. George T. Lynn. (Illus.). 290p. (Orig.). 1996. pap. 12.95 (*1-887424-19-9*) Underwood Bks.

Survival Strategies for the Holidays. Barbara Dan. 100p. (Orig.). 1995. 7.95 (*1-884898-08-4*) Eden Pubng NV.

Survival Strategies for the New Workplace. Campbell. 1995. pap. 11.00 (*0-671-87584-1*, Fireside) S&S Trade.

Survival Strategies in Early Life Stages of Marine Resources: Proceedings of an International Workshop, Yokohama, Japan, October 1994. Ed. by Y. Watanabe et al. (Illus.). 378p. (C). 1996. text ed. 99.00 (*90-5410-637-9*, Pub. by A A Balkema NE) Ashgate Pub Co.

Survival Strategies of the Algae. Ed. by Greta A. Fryxell. LC 82-12865. (Illus.). 176p. 1983. text ed. 52.95 (*0-521-25067-6*) Cambridge U Pr.

Survival Suggestions for Libraries: A Self Paced Workbook. rev. ed. Bibliotheca Press Staff. 1995. reprint ed. ring bd. 25.95 (*0-939476-48-7*, Biblio Pr) Prosperity & Profits.

***Survival Tactics: Cooperation & Conflict in Animal Societies.** Raghavendra Gadagkar. LC 97-9447. 1997. write for info. (*0-674-17055-5*) HUP.

Survival Tales of John Hersey. Nancy L. Huse. LC 82-50825. 217p. (C). 1983. 18.50 (*0-87875-238-2*) Whitston Pub.

Survival Techniques. (C). 1989. 105.00 (*0-89771-702-3*, Pub. by Lorne & MacLean Marine) St Mut.

Survival Techniques. Lorne & MacLean Marine & Offshore Publications Staff. (C). 1985. 75.00 (*0-685-33872-X*, Pub. by Lorne & MacLean Marine) St Mut.

An Asterisk (*) at the beginning of an entry indicates that the title is appearing in BIP for the first time.

Survival Techniques. OCS Marine Staff. (C). 1989. text ed. 110.00 (*0-906314-01-1*, Pub. by Lorne & MacLean Marine) St Mut.

Survival Themes in Fiction for Children & Young People. 2nd ed. Binnie T. Wilkin. LC 93-26421. 211p. 1993. 27.50 (*0-8108-2676-3*) Scarecrow.

Survival Thinking: For Police & Corrections Officers. James L. Lockard. 260p. 1991. pap. 33.95 (*0-398-06243-9*) C C Thomas.

Survival Thinking: For Police & Corrections Officers. James L. Lockard. 260p. (C). 1991. text ed. 49.95 (*0-398-05728-1*) C C Thomas.

Survival This Way: Interviews with American Indian Poets. Joseph Bruchac. LC 87-16224. (Sun Tracks Ser.: Vol. 15). 363p. 1990. reprint ed. pap. 19.95 (*0-8165-1178-0*) U of Ariz Pr.

Survival Till Seventeen. Leonard Feeney. (American Autobiography Ser.). 88p. 1995. reprint ed. lib. bdg. 69.00 (*0-7812-8515-1*) Rprt Serv.

Survival Tips for a Single Parent. Jeanette Johnson. Ed. by Penny E. Wheeler. 32p. 1988. pap. 0.89 (*0-8280-0450-1*) Review & Herald.

Survival Tips for Working Moms: Two Hundred Ninety-Seven Real Tips from Real Moms. Linda G. Pillsbury. LC 93-87732. (Illus.). 192p. (Orig.). 1994. pap. 10.95 (*0-9622036-5-3*) Prspctive Pub.

Survival Training: Search & Rescue. Ed. by M. M. Rastellini. (Illus.). 579p. (Orig.). (C). 1994. pap. text ed. 75.00 (*0-7881-0314-8*) DIANE Pub.

Survival Trip. Lee Mountain. (Attention Span Stories Ser). (Illus.). 48p. (Orig.). 1978. pap. text ed. 8.65 (*0-89061-146-7*, 582) Jamestown Pubs.

Survival Workbook. David A. Wilson. (Illus.). 50p. 1989. student ed., pap. 15.00 (*0-934852-33-2*) Lorien Hse.

Survival Writing: Staying Alive on Paper. Stephen Gladis. 80p. 1996. per., pap. text ed. 7.95 (*0-8403-3822-8*) Kendall-Hunt.

Survival 101: Strategies for Building Wealth & Financial Freedom in the Nineties. E. L. Anderson, III. 1992. 10.95 (*0-533-10263-4*) Vantage.

Survival 21: Futurology for the 21st Century. Robert Roman. 17.50 (*0-912314-00-1*) Academy Santa Clara.

***Survivalist's Little Book of Wisdom.** David Scott. LC 96-38155. (Little Books of Wisdom). 160p. (Orig.). 1997. pap. 5.95 (*1-57034-064-1*) ICS Bks.

Survivalist's Medicine Chest. Ragnar Benson. (Illus.). 80p. 1982. pap. 10.00 (*0-87364-256-2*) Paladin Pr.

Survivals: Poems. Edwin Honig. 1964. pap. 3.95 (*0-8079-0120-2*) October.

Survivals & New Arrivals: The Old & New Enemies of the Catholic Church. Hilaire Belloc. LC 91-67652. 167p. 1993. pap. 9.00 (*0-89555-454-2*) TAN Bks Pubs.

Survivals of Greek Zoological Illuminations in Byzantine Manuscripts. Z. Kadar. 138p. (C). 1978. 165.00 (*963-05-1187-8*, Pub. by Akad Kiado HU) St Mut.

Survivant. Andree Chedid. (FRE.). 1992. pap. 10.95 (*0-7859-3285-2*, 2277231711) Fr & Eur.

Survivant. Jules Supervielle. (Folio Ser.: No. 1280). 222p. (FRE.). 1928. 6.95 (*2-07-037280-4*) Schoenhof.

Survive! S. S. Gorman. Ed. by Lisa Clancy. (High-Fives Ser.). 128p. (J). 1992. pap. 2.99 (*0-671-74503-4*, Minstrel Bks) PB.

***Survive Alive.** John Bartleson. (Illus.). 16p. (J). (gr. k-3). 1996. pap. 2.50 (*1-883697-47-6*) Hara Pub.

***Survive Alive Life Safety Kit.** John Bartleson. (J). (gr. k-3). 1996. pap. 27.00 (*1-883697-48-4*) Hara Pub.

Survive & Profit. David Moreau. 1996. pap. 17.95 (*0-7871-0640-2*, Dove Bks) Dove Audio.

***Survive & Prosper.** 2nd ed. Tony Boffey. (Small Business Ser.). 1994. pap. 14.95 (*0-7494-1276-3*) Kogan Page Ltd.

Survive & Thrive after Fifty-Five. Vada L. Barkley. 160p. (Orig.). 1987. pap. 8.95 (*0-89265-130-X*) Randall Hse.

Survive in Five Languages. C. Farnes. (Essential Guides Ser.). (Illus.). 64p. (YA). (gr. 8 up). 1993. pap. 6.95 (*0-7460-1034-6*); lib. bdg. 14.95 (*0-88110-623-2*) EDC.

Survive Information Overload: The 7 Best Ways to Manage Your Workload by Seeing the Big Picture. Kathryn Alesandrini. 225p. 1992. 27.50 (*1-55623-721-9*) Irwin Prof Pubng.

***Survive Little Buddy.** Irene Kucholick. 284p. (Orig.). 1997. mass mkt. 4.99 (*1-55197-704-4*, Pub. by Comnwlth Pub CN) Partners Pubs Grp.

Survive the Night (Heartbreakers) Marilyn Pappano. (Intimate Moments Ser.). 1996. mass mkt. 3.99 (*0-373-07703-3*, 1-07703-1) Silhouette.

Survive the Savage Sea. Dougal Robertson. (Illus.). 224p. 1994. pap. 14.95 (*0-924486-73-2*) Sheridan.

Survive the Savage Sea. large type ed. Dougal Robertson. (Non-Fiction Ser.). 448p. 1986. 15.95 (*0-7089-1409-8*) Ulverscroft.

Survive This Day. Bernard Jensen. 1976. pap. 9.95 (*0-932615-18-X*) B Jensen.

***Survive to Win: The Inspiring Story of One Man Who Overcame Incredible Odds & Came Out a Champion.** Bob Watson. LC 97-10200. 1997. 19.99 (*0-7852-7193-7*) Nelson.

Survived to Tell: The Autobiography of Edward Keonjian. Edward Keonjian. LC 96-24330. (Illus.). 288p. 1996. 28.95 (*0-86534-252-0*) Sunstone Pr.

Surviving. Henry Green. Date not set. pap. 11.95 (*0-14-018773-1*, Viking) Viking Penguin.

Surviving: A Guide for Victims, Families, Friends & Professionals. Allison Brittsan & Clarene Shelley. 175p. (Orig.). 1994. pap. 14.95 (*0-9626437-4-2*) Biblio Unlimited.

Surviving a Competitive Healthcare Market: Strategies for the 21st Century. Jana B. Knol. 175p. (Orig.). 1995. pap. text ed. 39.95 (*0-07-600781-2*, ME116) Practice Mgmt Info.

Surviving a Japanese P.O.W. Camp: Father & Son Endure Internment in Manila During World War II. Peter R. Wygle. Ed. by Eugene D. Wheeler. LC 91-11652. (Illus.). 224p. (Orig.). 1991. pap. 9.95 (*0-934793-30-1*) Pathfinder CA.

Surviving a Japanese P.O.W. Camp: Father & Son Endure Internment in Manila During World War II. Peter R. Wygle. 224p. (Orig.). 1991. reprint ed. lib. bdg. 33.00 (*0-8095-5900-5*) Borgo Pr.

Surviving a Layoff. Harry S. Dahlstrom. (Illus.). 50p. (Orig.). 1994. pap. text ed. 3.99 (*0-940712-76-8*) Dahlstrom & Co.

Surviving a Nuclear Powered Family. Candi McLean. (Illus.). 119p. (Orig.). 1992. pap. 14.95 (*1-55059-045-6*) Temeron Bks.

Surviving a Writer's Life. Suzanne Lipsett. LC 93-22857. 240p. 1995. pap. 10.00 (*0-06-250658-7*) Harper SF.

Surviving Addiction Workbook: Practical Tips on Developing a Recovery Plan. rev. ed. Dennis C. Daley & Judy Miller. 32p. 1997. pap. 11.50 (*1-55691-065-7*, 657) Learning Pubns.

Surviving Adverse Seasons. Stories. Barry Targan. LC 79-20191. (Illinois Short Fiction Ser.). 176p. 1979. 9.95 (*0-252-00787-5*); text ed. 14.95 (*0-252-00786-7*) U of Ill Pr.

Surviving after High School: Overcoming Life's Hurdles. Arthur J. Heine. LC 90-91976. (Illus.). 248p. (Orig.). (YA). 1995. 22.95 (*0-9628376-0-1*); pap. 14.95 (*0-9628376-1-X*) J-Mart Pr.

***Surviving after High School: Overcoming Life's Hurdles.** Arthur J. Heine. (Orig.). 1996. 14.95 (*0-9628376-5-2*) J-Mart Pr.

Surviving Alzheimer's: A Guide for Families. Florian Raymond. 1994. 10.95 (*0-943873-00-2*) Elder Bks.

Surviving an Auto Accident: A Guide to Your Physical, Economic, & Emotional Recovery. Robert Saperstein & Dana Saperstein. 208p. 1994. lib. bdg. 35.00 (*0-8095-5919-6*) Borgo Pr.

Surviving an Auto Accident: A Guide to Your Physical, Economic, & Emotional Recovery. Robert Saperstein & Dana Saperstein. LC 94-2303. 208p. 1994. pap. 8.95 (*0-934793-55-7*) Pathfinder CA.

***Surviving An Eating Disorder: Strategies for Family & Friends.** rev. ed. Michele Siegel et al. 256p. 1997. pap. 13.00 (*0-06-095233-4*, PL) HarpC.

Surviving an Eating Disorder: Strategies for Family & Friends. Michele Siegel et al. LC 87-45668. 256p. 1989. reprint ed. pap. 12.50 (*0-06-091553-6*, PL 1553, PL) HarpC.

Surviving & Enjoying Your Adolescent. I. J. Barrish & Harriet H. Barrish. LC 89-38432. (Coping Parent Ser.). 96p. (Orig.). 1989. pap. 7.95 (*0-933701-42-X*) Westport Pubs.

Surviving & Other Essays. Bruno Bettelheim. LC 79-22029. 1980. pap. 16.00 (*0-394-74264-8*, Vin) Random.

Surviving & Prospering in a Business Partnership. 2nd ed. Jay Jacobsen. Ed. by Julie Lefevre. (Successful Business Library). (Illus.). 180p. 1988. pap. 19.95 (*1-55571-072-7*); ring bd. 39.95 (*1-55571-041-7*) Oasis Pr OR.

Surviving & Prospering in the Managed Mental Health Care Marketplace. Tracy Todd. Ed. by Bruce D. Forman. LC 94-17985. (Practice Management Ser.). 106p. (Orig.). 1994. pap. 18.20 (*1-56887-004-3*, SPMBP, Prof Resc Pr) Pro Resource.

Surviving & Thriving in Today's Economy. Louis L. Kristan. 170p. (Orig.). 1990. pap. text ed. 7.95 (*0-9627439-0-9*) L L Kristan.

Surviving As a Teacher: The Legal Dimension. rev. ed. Fred Hartmeister. LC 94-23092. (Illus.). 306p. (Orig.). 1994. pap. 18.95 (*0-944496-43-1*) Bonus Books.

Surviving as Indians: The Challenge of Self-Government. Menno Boldt. LC 93-215302. 384p. 1994. pap. 19.95 (*0-8020-7767-6*) U of Toronto Pr.

Surviving Betrayal: Counseling An Adulterous Marriage. Donald R. Harvey. LC 94-29017. 224p. (Orig.). (C). 1994. pap. 13.99 (*0-8010-4396-4*) Baker Bks.

***Surviving Breast Cancer.** Charlotte Higgins-Lee. 64p. 1997. pap. 7.00 (*0-8059-4116-9*) Dorrance.

Surviving Cancer. Kay D. Quain. LC 88-62065. 126p. 1988. pap. 7.95 (*1-55612-156-3*) Sheed & Ward MO.

Surviving Catastrophic Earth Changes. G. Cope Schellhorn. LC 94-75685. (Illus.). 196p. (Orig.). 1994. pap. 12.95 (*1-881852-08-3*) Horus Hse Pr.

***Surviving Child Sexual Abuse: A Handbook for Helping Women Challenge Their Past.** 2nd ed. Liz Hall & Siobhan Lloyd. 400p. 1993. 95.00 (*0-7507-0152-8*, Falmer Pr) Taylor & Francis.

Surviving Child Sexual Abuse: A Handbook for Helping Women Challenge Their Past. 2nd ed. Liz Hall & Siobhan Lloyd. 272p. 1993. pap. 35.00 (*0-7507-0153-6*, Falmer Pr) Taylor & Francis.

Surviving Childhood Cancer: A Guide for Families. Margot J. Fromer. 240p. 1995. text ed. 21.95 (*0-88048-668-6*, 8668) Am Psychiatric.

***Surviving Church Conflict.** Dave Peters. LC 96-40869. 160p. (Orig.). 1997. pap. 10.99 (*0-8361-9051-3*) Herald Pr.

***Surviving Crisis: Twenty Prominent Authors Write about Events that Shaped Their Lives.** Ed. by Lee Gutkind. LC 97-12387. (Creative Nonfiction Reader Ser.). 240p. 1997. 15.95 (*0-87477-889-1*, Tarcher Putnam) Putnam Pub Group.

***Surviving Day 1 with Windows NT 4.0.** Phoenix Publishing Systems Staff. 96p. 1996. 12.99 (*0-7897-0995-3*) Que.

Surviving Day 1 with Windows 95. Phoenix Publishing Systems Staff. (Illus.). 96p. (Orig.). 1995. pap. 99.90 (*0-7897-0579-6*) Que.

Surviving Death: A Practical Guide to Caring for the Dying & the Bereaved. rev. ed. Charles Meyer. LC 91-65169. 200p. 1991. pap. 9.95 (*0-89622-486-4*) Twenty-Third.

***Surviving Death: Eternal Consciousness & the Self-Perpetuating Universe.** J. Robert Adams. 1997. pap. 14.95 (*1-56315-082-4*) Sterling Hse.

Surviving Death: Evidence of the Afterlife. Geoff Viney. 320p. (Orig.). 1994. pap. 14.95 (*0-312-10436-7*) St Martin.

***Surviving Debt: A Guide for Consumers.** 2nd rev. ed. Jonathan Sheldon et al. LC 96-92323. 352p. 1996. pap. 15.00 (*1-881793-40-0*) Nat Consumer Law.

Surviving Debt: Counseling Families in Financial Trouble. National Consumer Law Center, Inc. Staff. LC 92-81748. 272p. (Orig.). 1992. pap. 15.00 (*1-881793-07-9*) Nat Consumer Law.

Surviving Denali: A Study of Accidents on Mount McKinley, 1903-90. 2nd ed. Jonathan Waterman. (Illus.). 264p. 1991. pap. 20.00 (*0-930410-48-3*) Amer Alpine Club.

Surviving Dependence: Voices of African American Elders. Mary M. Ball & Frank Whittington. 287p. 1995. 43.95 (*0-89503-125-6*) Baywood Pub.

Surviving Desire. Ally Acker. 72p. (Orig.). 1994. pap. 7.95 (*0-9633481-7-5*, Garden St) Valentine CA.

Surviving Disaster Stress: What to Do Before, During & after Any Crisis to Prevent Pos-Traumatic Stress Disorders. Donald E. Dossey. (Illus.). 256p. 1997. pap. 14.95 (*0-925640-08-5*) Outcomes Unltd.

Surviving Divorce: Men Beyond Marriage. Peter Ambrose et al. LC 82-22717. 206p. 1983. text ed. 40.50 (*0-86598-122-1*) Rowman.

Surviving Divorce: Women's Resources after Separation. Mavis Maclean. 166p. (C). 1991. pap. text ed. 32.00 (*0-8147-5462-7*) NYU Pr.

***Surviving Divorce in Kansas City.** Michael J. Albano et al. LC 96-93102. 100p. (Orig.). 1997. pap. 15.95 (*0-9656174-0-8*) L Sanchez.

Surviving Doomsday. C. Bruce Sibley. (C). 1977. pap. 65.00 (*0-7219-0780-6*, Pub. by Scientific UK) St Mut.

Surviving Environmental Challenges of the 1990s: Lessons for Ports, Terminals & Waterways - Major Presentations. 188p. 1989. 25.00 (*0-934292-08-6*) Natl Waterways.

Surviving Exercise. Judy Alter. 1990. pap. 10.95 (*0-395-50073-7*) HM.

***Surviving Family Life: The Seven Crises of Living Together.** Sonya Rhodes & Josleen Wilson. 299p. (Orig.). 1986. pap. 11.95 (*1-57171-029-9*) Lincoln-Rembrandt.

Surviving Family Life: The Seven Crises of Living Together. Sonya Rhodes & Josleen Wilson. 299p. 1986. reprint ed. pap. 11.95 (*0-935005-06-4*) Lincoln-Rembrandt.

Surviving Fieldwork. Nancy Howell. (Special Publication: No. 26). 1990. 15.00 (*0-913167-38-X*) Am Anthro Assn.

***Surviving Financial Crisis.** (Master's Touch Bible Study Ser.). 1996. pap. 3.99 (*0-570-09554-9*, 20-2595) Concordia.

Surviving Financial Disaster. Richard L. Strohm. 88p. 1991. pap. 9.95 (*0-9630356-0-6*) Makai.

Surviving Freshman Composition: Straight Talk about How to Get the Best Possible Start in Your College Career. Scott Edelstein. 192p. (Orig.). 1988. pap. 7.95 (*0-8184-0463-0*) Carol Pub Group.

Surviving Global Slavery: Living under the New World Order. Robert K. Spear. (Illus.). 164p. (Orig.). 1992. pap. 9.95 (*0-9622627-8-1*) U Force Dynamics.

***Surviving Globalism.** Schrecker. LC 97-891. 1997. text ed. 79.95 (*0-312-17474-8*) St Martin.

***Surviving Graduate School Part Time.** Von V. Pittman. LC 97-4584. (Graduate Survival Skills Ser.: Vol. 1). 169p. 1997. 42.00 (*0-7619-0439-5*); pap. 19.95 (*0-7619-0440-9*) Sage.

Surviving Grief...& Learning to Live Again. Catherine M. Sanders. LC 91-43605. 240p. 1992. pap. text ed. 15.95 (*0-471-53471-4*) Wiley.

Surviving Hard Times. Ian Gale. 160p. (Orig.). 1993. pap. 10.95 (*0-86417-487-X*, Pub. by Kangaroo Pr AT) Seven Hills Bk.

Surviving Hard Times: The Working People of Lowell. Ed. by Mary H. Blewett. LC 81-86362. (Illus.). xii, 178p. (Orig.). 1982. pap. 6.95 (*0-942472-05-5*) Lowell Museum.

Surviving, Healing & Growing: The How to Survive the Loss of a Love Workbook. Melba Colgrove et al. 198p. 1991. pap. 11.95 (*0-931580-46-3*) Prelude Press.

***Surviving High School.** Michael Riera. LC 96-45273. 160p. (Orig.). 1997. pap. 14.95 (*0-89087-825-0*) Celestial Arts.

Surviving Homework: Tips from Teens. Amy Nathan. (Illus.). 80p. (J). (gr. 5-8). 1996. lib. bdg. 17.90 (*1-56294-185-2*) Millbrook Pr.

Surviving Hostage Situations. Robert K. Spear & D. Michael Moak. Ed. by James Robinson. (Illus.). 144p. (Orig.). (C). 1989. pap. 10.95 (*0-9622627-0-6*) U Force Dynamics.

Surviving Hostage Situations. 2nd ed. Robert K. Spear & D. Michael Moak. (Illus.). 144p. (Orig.). 1991. reprint ed. pap. 14.95 (*0-9622627-5-7*) U Force Dynamics.

Surviving Hypoxia: Mechanisms of Control & Adaptation. Lutz. 592p. 1993. 121.95 (*0-8493-4226-0*, RB150) CRC Pr.

Surviving in College. David J. Yarington. 1977. pap. text ed. write for info. (*0-672-61372-7*) Macmillan.

Surviving in Corrections: A Guide for Corrections Professionals. David B. Kalinich & Terry Pitcher. (Illus.). 206p. 1984. 38.95 (*0-398-04999-8*); pap. 24.95 (*0-398-06196-3*) C C Thomas.

Surviving in General Music I. Michael D. Bennett. 97p. (Orig.). 1979. pap. 9.95 (*0-934019-00-2*) Memphis Musicraft.

***Surviving in Healthcare.** Enzmann. LC 97-11563. (Illus.). 400p. (C). (gr. 13). 1997. pap. text ed. 42.00 (*0-8151-2447-3*, 30821, Yr Bk Med Pubs) Mosby Yr Bk.

***Surviving in Losses.** Raffaele Manzi. Ed. by Sharon Manzi. 454p. (Orig.). (C). 1996. pap. text ed. 30.00 (*0-9644029-2-0*) Means NJ.

Surviving in Ministry: Navigating the Pitfalls, Experiencing the Renewals. Robert R. Lutz & Bruce T. Taylor. 1990. pap. 11.95 (*0-8091-3156-0*) Paulist Pr.

Surviving in Prison. Harold S. Long. LC 90-62804. (Illus.). 136p. (Orig.). 1990. pap. 14.95 (*1-55950-044-1*, 40070) Loompanics.

Surviving in Schools in the 1990s: Strategic Management of School Environments. James R. Tompkins & Patricia L. Tompkins-McGill. LC 92-33169. (C). 1993. pap. text ed. 28.50 (*0-8191-8920-0*); lib. bdg. 54.50 (*0-8191-8919-7*) U Pr of Amer.

Surviving in the City: The Urban Informal Sector in Latin America. J. J. Thomas. Date not set. pap. 14.95 (*0-7453-0828-7*, Pub. by Pluto Pr UK) LPC InBook.

Surviving in the City: The Urban Informal Sector in Latin America. J. J. Thomas. LC 95-3549. (Critical Studies on Latin America). 1995. 55.00 (*0-7453-0827-9*, Pub. by Pluto Pr UK) LPC InBook.

Surviving in the Jungle: What You Really Need to Know to Market Your Business Without Losing Your Shirt. Linda J. Nash & Martha G. Kampen. (Illus.). 153p. (Orig.). 1993. pap. 12.95 (*0-9636702-0-4*) PRISM MO.

Surviving in the Newspaper Business: Newspaper Management in Turbulent Times. Jim Willis. LC 87-37685. 223p. 1988. text ed. 49.95 (*0-275-92862-4*, C2862, Praeger Pubs) Greenwood.

Surviving in the Newspaper Business: Newspaper Management in Turbulent Times. Jim Willis. LC 87-37685. 223p. 1988. pap. text ed. 15.95 (*0-275-92863-2*, B2863, Praeger Pubs) Greenwood.

Surviving in the Sunshine: An Entertainment Industry Guide & Date Book for Florida. Marion J. Caffey. 350p. 1989. write for info. (*0-318-65038-X*) Sunshine Pubns.

Surviving in the Workplace. Earl Harrell & Cassandra Harrell. LC 93-72063. 70p. (Orig.). 1993. pap. 6.95 (*0-9625203-1-4*) E T Pub Co.

***Surviving in Two Worlds: Contemporary Native American Voices.** Lois Crozier-Hogle et al. Ed. by Jay Leibold. LC 96-25378. (Illus.). 287p. 1997. 35.00 (*0-292-74694-6*); pap. 14.95 (*0-292-74695-4*) U of Tex Pr.

Surviving Indonesia's Gulag. Carmel Budiardjo. 1996. pap. 17.95 (*0-304-33562-2*, Pub. by Cassell Pubng UK) LPC InBook.

Surviving Infertility: A Compassionate Guide Through the Emotional Crisis of Infertility. rev. ed. Linda P. Salzer. LC 90-56098. 336p. 1991. reprint ed. pap. 14.00 (*0-06-097382-X*, PL) HarpC.

Surviving Infidelity: Making Decisions, Recovering from the Pain. Gloria G. Harris & Rona Subotnik. 192p. (Orig.). 1993. pap. 7.95 (*1-55850-299-8*) Adams Media.

Surviving Last Period on Fridays & Other Desperate Situations: Cottonwood Game Book. Cheryl M. Thurston. 58p. (Orig.). (YA). (gr. 5-12). 1986. pap. text ed. 14.95 (*1-877673-01-3*, G) Cottonwood Pr.

Surviving Life in the Fast Lane. Tim Kimmel. 96p. 1990. pap. 6.00 (*0-89109-293-5*) NavPress.

Surviving Mental Illness: Stress, Coping & Adaptation. Agnes B. Hatfield & Harriet P. Lefley. LC 93-20492. 206p. 1993. pap. text ed. 19.95 (*0-89862-022-8*); lib. bdg. 42.00 (*0-89862-124-0*) Guilford Pr.

Surviving Ministry. Ronald W. Sisk. LC 96-34104. 192p. (Orig.). 1997. pap. text ed. 14.95 (*1-880837-48-X*) Smyth & Helwys.

Surviving Motherhood. Donna L. Montgomery. (Illus.). 200p. (Orig.). 1986. pap. 6.95 (*0-938577-00-X*) St Johns Pub.

Surviving Myths Unit D: Study Guide, Unit D. Deakin University Press Staff. 164p. (C). 1991. pap. 105.00 (*0-7300-0724-3*, HUL306, Pub. by Deakin Univ AT) St Mut.

Surviving Nursing. 2nd ed. Emily E. Smythe. LC 94-60006. (Illus.). 304p. (C). 1993. pap. 49.95 (*1-878025-57-0*) Western Schls.

Surviving Nursing: A Coping Manual. Emily E. Smythe. 300p. 1984. pap. write for info. (*0-201-16418-3*, Health Sci) Addison-Wesley.

Surviving on the Edge: The On the Edge Player's Survival Guide. Peter Hentges et al. (On the Edge Ser.). 224p. 1995. pap. 9.95 (*1-887801-22-7*, Atlas Games) Trident MN.

Surviving on the Job. Jay Como. 1983. 10.48 (*0-02-670180-4*); teacher ed. 10.48 (*0-02-670190-1*) Glencoe.

Surviving on the Texas Frontier: The Journal of a Frontier Orphaned Girl in Early Texas. Sarah H. Hall. Ed. by Paula M. Marks. LC 94-12612. 160p. 1996. 19.95 (*0-89015-986-6*, Eakin Pr) Sunbelt Media.

Surviving Poor. Xandra Kayden. 1990. text ed. 24.95 (*0-02-917231-4*, Free Press) Free Pr.

Surviving Popular Psychology: Debriefing the Me Degeneration. Clint Weyand. 148p. (Orig.). 1980. pap. 8.95 (*0-938292-13-7*) Being Bks.

***Surviving Post-Socialism: Local Strategies & Regional Responses.** Frances Pine & Susan Bridger. LC 97-8843. 240p. (C). 1998. text ed. write for info. (*0-415-15850-8*) Routledge.

Surviving Pregnancy Loss. Rochelle Friedman & Bonnie Gradstein. 1982. 16.95 (*0-316-29349-0*); pap. 10.95 (*0-316-29348-2*) Little.

Surviving Pregnancy Loss: A Complete Sourcebook for Women & Their Families. Rochelle Friedman & Bonnie Gradstein. 320p. 1995. pap. 15.95 (*0-8065-1758-1*, Citadel Pr) Carol Pub Group.

S

Surviving Procedures after a Sexual Assault. 3rd ed. Megan Ellis. 1988. pap. 9.50 (*0-88974-011-9*, Pub. by Press Gang CN) LPC InBook.

***Surviving Production: The Art of Production Management for Film & Television.** Deborah S. Patz. 400p. 1997. pap. 26.95 (*0-941188-60-4*) M Wiese Prodns.

Surviving Salvation: The Ethiopian Jewish Family in Transition. Ruth Westheimer & Steven Kaplan. (Illus.). 170p. (C). 1993. 25.00 (*0-8147-9253-7*) NYU Pr.

Surviving Schizophrenia: A Manual for Families, Consumers & Providers. 3rd ed. E. Fuller Torrey. LC 94-10533. (Illus.). 409p. 1995. pap. 14.00 (*0-06-095076-5*, HarpT) HarpC.

Surviving School Micropolitics: Strategies for Administrators. Jane C. Lindle. LC 94-60924. 168p. 1994. text ed. 29.95 (*1-56676-175-1*) Technomic.

Surviving School Reform: A Year in the Life of One School. Laraine K. Hong. LC 96-3791. (Series on School Reform). 216p. 1996. 46.00 (*0-8077-3521-3*); pap. 21.95 (*0-8077-3520-5*) Tchrs Coll.

Surviving Secrets: The Experience of Abuse for the Child, the Adult, & the Helper. Moira Walker. LC 92-9376. 1992. 85.00 (*0-335-09764-2*, Open Univ Pr); pap. 25.00 (*0-335-09763-4*, Open Univ Pr) Taylor & Francis.

Surviving Sexual Abuse. Marya McCrae. (Master's Touch Bible Study Ser.). 1994. pap. 3.99 (*0-570-09521-2*, 20-2462) Concordia.

Surviving Sexual Contradiction. Dimen. 1986. 19.95 (*0-02-531620-6*) Macmillan.

Surviving Sexual Violence. Liz Kelly. LC 88-22033. xi, 273p. (Orig.). 1989. pap. text ed. 16.95 (*0-8166-1753-8*) U of Minn Pr.

Surviving Sibling Rivalry. Lee Canter. (Illus.). 48p. (Orig.). 1993. pap. 5.95 (*0-939007-77-0*) Lee Canter & Assocs.

Surviving Sisters. Gail Pass. 252p. 1989. reprint ed. pap. 8.95 (*0-941483-16-9*) Naiad Pr.

Surviving Sixteen, No. 3: Did You Hear about Amber? Cherie Bennett. (High Flyer Ser.). 224p. (J). (gr. 7 up). 1993. pap. 3.50 (*0-14-036318-1*, Puffin) Puffin Bks.

Surviving Sixth Grade. Lana S. Newlin. Ed. by Cathy Morey. (Illus.). 90p. (J). (gr. 5-7). 1990. 16.95 (*0-9625413-0-3*); pap. 9.95 (*0-9625413-1-1*) Christmans.

Surviving Spins. Fred DeLacerda. LC 89-15527. (Illus.). 134p. 1989. 19.95 (*0-8138-0142-7*) Iowa St U Pr.

Surviving Stress at Work: How Four Thousand GE Managers Learned to Cope. David R. Frew & Carl A. Jackson. (Illus.). 150p. (Orig.). 1991. pap. 9.95 (*0-685-38853-0*) Gannon U Pr.

Surviving Success: A Common Sense Guide for the Celebrity. S. Gary Spicer. Ed. by Deborah E. DiRezze. (Orig.). 1990. pap. 12.95 (*0-9626062-0-0*) Clark & Maybelle.

Surviving Summers with Kids: Funfilled Activities for All. Rita B. Herron. Ed. by Diane Parker. LC 93-2275. 125p. 1993. pap. 9.95 (*1-56875-052-8*) R & E Pubs.

***Surviving Technological Innovation in the Pacemaker Industry, 1959-1990.** rev. ed. Catherine M. Banbury. LC 96-46669. (Studies on Industrial Productivity). (Illus.). 201p. 1997. text ed. 49.00 (*0-8153-2796-X*) Garland.

Surviving Teen Pregnancy: Your Choices, Dreams, & Decisions. rev. ed. Shirley M. Arthur. Ed. by Jeanne W. Lindsay. LC 95-33735. (Illus.). 192p. (YA). (gr. 6-12). 1996. 17.95 (*1-885356-05-6*); pap. 11.95 (*1-885356-06-4*) Morning Glory.

Surviving the AIDS Plague. Taki N. Anagnoston. Ed. by Carla Hewitt. (Illus.). 340p. (Orig.). (C). 1991. pap. text ed. 14.95 (*0-922356-44-0*) Amer West Pubs.

Surviving the Americans: The Continued Struggle of the Jews after Liberation. Robert L. Hilliard. LC 96-30277. 240p. 1997. 22.00 (*1-888363-32-0*) Seven Stories.

Surviving the Asic Experience. John Schroeter. 240p. 1991. text ed. 72.00 (*0-13-877838-8*) P-H.

Surviving the Breakup: How Children & Parents Cope with Divorce. Judith S. Wallerstein & Joan B. Kelly. 352p. 1996. pap. 14.50 (*0-465-08345-5*) HarpC.

Surviving the Cold. David Barton. (QRL Poetry Bks.: XXII). 1981. 20.00 (*0-614-06388-4*) Quarterly Rev.

Surviving the Comfort Zone. Roy Masters. Ed. by Dorothy Baker. LC 91-73149. 193p. (Orig.). 1991. pap. text ed. 15.95 (*0-933900-15-5*) Foun Human Under.

Surviving the Coming Mutual Fund Crisis. Donald Christensen. LC 94-1677. 1994. 22.95 (*0-316-14145-3*) Little.

Surviving the Coming Mutual Fund Crisis: How You Can Take Defensive Measures to Protect Your... Donald Christensen. 1995. pap. 13.95 (*0-316-13782-0*) Little.

Surviving the Contained Depression of the 1990's. S. Jay Levy & David Levy. LC 92-56827. 96p. 16.00 (*0-679-42401-6*) Random.

Surviving the Cut: Natural Forest Management in the Humid Tropics. Nels Johnson & Bruce Cabarle. 100p. 1993. Large format. pap. 14.95 (*0-915825-90-2*, JOLAP) World Resources Inst.

Surviving the Dalkon Shield IUD: Women vs. the Pharmaceutical Industry. Karen M. Hicks. (Athene Ser.). 208p. (C). 1993. text ed. 37.00 (*0-8077-6271-7*); pap. text ed. 16.95 (*0-8077-6270-9*) Tchrs Coll.

Surviving the Darkness. Grace H. Ketterman. LC 93-5899. Orig. Title: Depression Hits Every Family. 1993. pap. 12.99 (*0-8407-9275-1*) Nelson.

***Surviving the Day: An American POW in Japan.** Frank J. Grady & Rebecca Dickson. LC 96-51072. (Illus.). 288p. 1997. 32.95 (*1-55750-340-0*) Naval Inst Pr.

Surviving the Death of a Child. John Munday & Frances Wohlenhaus-Munday. 96p. (Orig.). 1995. pap. 10.00 (*0-664-25566-3*) Westminster John Knox.

Surviving the Demise of Solo Practice: Mental Health Practitioners Prospering in the Era of Managed Care. Ed. by Nicholas A. Cummings et al. LC 96-14756. 1996. 47.50 (*1-887841-03-2*, Psychosocial) Intl Univs Pr.

Surviving the Design of a 200 RISC Microprocessor: Lessons Learned. Veljko Milutinovic. LC 95-52094. 200p. 1996. pap. 35.00 (*0-8186-7343-5*, BPO7343) IEEE Comp Soc.

Surviving the Dole Years: The 1930s - a Personal Story. Mick Masson. 200p. 1994. pap. 27.95 (*0-86840-285-0*, Pub. by New South Wales Univ Pr AT) Intl Spec Bk.

Surviving the Eighties. Lewis B. Mayhew. LC 79-88773. (Jossey-Bass Series in Higher Education). 366p. reprint ed. pap. 104.40 (*0-7837-0183-7*, 2040479) Bks Demand.

Surviving the Epidemic of Suicide. Bill Steele. 113p. (YA). (gr. 7-12). 1994. pap. 6.95 (*1-57515-055-7*) PPI Pubng.

***Surviving the Fall: A Physician's Coming of Age in the AIDS Epidemic.** Peter A. Selwyn. LC 97-15292. 1998. write for info. (*0-300-07126-4*) Yale U Pr.

Surviving the Feminization of America: How to Keep Women from Ruining Your Life. Rich Zubaty. LC 93-85156. (Illus.). 448p. (Orig.). 1994. pap. 19.95 (*1-882342-04-6*) Panther IL.

Surviving the Fire: Mother Courage & WWII. Ed. by Lilo Klug. LC 89-22926. (Illus.). 146p. 1989. pap. 9.95 (*0-940880-24-5*) Open Hand.

Surviving the Fire: Mother Courage & WWII. Ed. by Lilo Klug. LC 89-22926. (Illus.). 146p. (YA). (gr. 10-12). 1989. 19.95 (*0-940880-23-7*) Open Hand.

Surviving the Flood. Stephen Minot. LC 85-63551. (Illus.). 306p. 1986. reprint ed. 22.00 (*0-933256-62-0*) Second Chance.

Surviving the Future. Tekonsha. Ed. & Intro. by Chief Little Summer. 224p. (Orig.). 1994. pap. 16.95 (*1-880440-09-1*) Piqua Pr.

Surviving the Global Financial Crisis: The Economics of Hope for Generation X. Paul Hellyer. 1996. pap. text ed. 18.95 (*0-9694394-3-1*, Pub. by Chimo Media CN) Login Pubs Consort.

Surviving the Hazardous Materials Incident, Pt. I. 3rd ed. OnGuard Inc. Staff & Randy R. Bruegman. Ed. by Joe R. Varela & Susan Peterson. 304p. 1996. student ed., pap. text ed. 12.95 (*1-56916-200-X*, 20HAZ P1) OnGuard.

Surviving the Hazardous Materials Incident, Pt. 2. 2nd ed. OnGuard Inc. Staff. 288p. 1995. pap. text ed. 12.95 (*1-56916-213-1*); teacher ed., ring bd. 34.95 (*1-56916-214-X*) OnGuard.

***Surviving the Heartbreak of Choosing Death for Your Pet: Your Personal Guide for Dealing with Pet Euthanasia.** Linda M. Peterson. LC 96-94369. 160p. (Orig.). 1997. pap. 12.95 (*0-9652572-2-3*) Greentree Pub PA.

Surviving the Holocaust: The Kovno Ghetto Diary. Avraham Tory. Tr. by Jerzy Michalowicz. (Illus.). 604p. 1990. 45.00 (*0-674-85810-7*) HUP.

Surviving the Holocaust: The Kovno Ghetto Diary. Avraham Tory. 604p. (C). 1991. pap. text ed. 16.95 (*0-674-85811-5*) HUP.

Surviving the Law. CWL. LC 86-61881. (Breaking the Law Ser.: Vol. 2). (Illus.). 55p. (Orig.). 1986. pap. 18.00 (*0-939856-62-X*) Tech Group.

Surviving the Loss of a Loved One. Anthony M. Coniaris. 1992. pap. 9.95 (*0-937032-89-1*) Light&Life Pub Co MN.

Surviving the Media Jungle. David Chagall. 208p. 1996. pap. 10.99 (*0-8054-6263-5*, 4262-63) Broadman.

Surviving the Millennium: American Global Strategy, the Collapse of the Soviet Empire, & the Question of Peace. Hall Gardner. LC 93-23477. 280p. 1994. text ed. 59.95 (*0-275-94754-8*, Praeger Pubs) Greenwood.

Surviving the Nineties & Winning. Baxter D. Wellmon. 184p. (C). 1990. 24.95 (*0-9622176-3-8*) Air Acad Pr.

Surviving the Not So Golden Years: Vital Medical & Financial Strategies for Anyone Planning to Grow Old. M. Therese Young. 292p. 1990. 17.95 (*1-56171-005-9*) Sure Seller.

Surviving the One Computer Classroom: A Handbook for Classroom Teachers. Stanley C. Coy. 39p. (Orig.). (C). 1992. pap. 6.50 (*1-881459-01-2*) Eagle Pr SC.

***Surviving the PC University: The Best of Heterodoxy.** Peter Collier & David Horowitz. 368p. 1996. pap. 9.95 (*1-886442-06-1*) Ctr Study Popular.

Surviving the Prodigal Years: How to Love Your Wayward Child Without Ruining Your Own Life. Marcia Mitchell. 175p. (Orig.). 1995. pap. 8.99 (*1-883002-12-5*) Emerald WA.

Surviving the Research Process. Lisbeth Hockey. 1995. pap. 30.00 (*0-7300-1372-3*, Pub. by Deakin Univ AT) St Mut.

***Surviving the Search: Sexuality, Spirituality & Love.** Christopher Pramuk. Ed. by Kathy Coffey. 40p. (Orig.). (YA). 1997. pap. 4.95 (*1-889108-26-X*) Liv Good News.

Surviving the Second Civil War: The Land Rights Battle... & How to Win It. Timothy R. Walters. 192p. (Orig.). 1994. pap. 12.95 (*0-9641935-0-7*) Rawhide Wstrn.

Surviving the Secret. Kathryn Rodriguez & Pamela W. Vredevelt. LC 92-6327. 224p. 1993. reprint ed. pap. 8.99 (*0-8007-5442-5*) Revell.

Surviving the Sermon: A Guide to Preaching for Those Who Have to Listen. David J. Schlafer. LC 92-19363. 132p. 1992. pap. 10.95 (*1-56101-064-2*) Cowley Pubns.

Surviving the Squeeze. Stephen M. Pollan. 320p. 1994. pap. 10.00 (*0-02-081168-3*) Macmillan.

Surviving the Start-Up Years in Your Own Business. Joyce S. Marder. (Illus.). 172p. (Orig.). 1991. pap. 7.95 (*1-55870-200-8*, Betrwy Bks) F & W Pubns Inc.

Surviving the Storm: A Family's Struggle & Ultimate Victory over Cancer. Janet Selbst & Leslie Selbst. (Illus.). 168p. (Orig.). 1996. pap. 16.95 (*1-56072-315-7*) Nova Sci Pubs.

Surviving the Storm: A Memoir. Chen Xuezhao. Ed. by Jeffrey C. Kinkley. Tr. by Ti Hua & Caroline Greene from CHI. LC 90-21300. (Foremoters Legacies Ser.). 176p. (gr. 13). 1990. 57.95 (*0-87332-601-6*, East Gate Bk) M E Sharpe.

Surviving the Storm: A Memoir. Chen Xuezhao. Ed. by Jeffrey C. Kinkley. Tr. by Ti Hua & Caroline Greene. LC 92-1300. (Foremothers Legacies Ser.). 176p. (gr. 13). 1995. pap. text ed. 17.95 (*1-56324-553-1*, East Gate Bk) M E Sharpe.

Surviving the Storms: Memory of Stalin's Tyranny. Helen Dmitriew. LC 92-62075. (Illus.). 218p. 1992. text ed. 21.95 (*0-912201-31-2*) CSU Pr Fresno.

***Surviving the Streets: Girls Living on Their Own.** rev. ed. Rachel Pfeffer. LC 96-46547. (Children of Poverty Ser.). (Illus.). 174p. 1997. text ed. 37.00 (*0-8153-2617-3*) Garland.

Surviving the Swastika: Scientific Research in Nazi Germany. Kristie Macrakis. LC 93-19919. (Illus.). 256p. 1993. 42.00 (*0-19-507010-0*) OUP.

Surviving the Tweenage Years see Too Young to Drive, Too Old to Ride: Surviving Your Child's Middle School Years

Surviving the Unexpected: A Curriculum Guide for Wilderness Survival & Survival from Natural & Man Made Disasters. 3rd rev. ed. Ed. by Daniel E. Fear. (Illus.). 91p. 1974. spiral bd. 10.00 (*0-913724-00-9*) Emerg Response Inst.

Surviving the Unexpected Wilderness Emergency: A Text for Body Management Under Stress. 6th rev. ed. Eugene H. Fear. LC 73-78035. (Illus.). (C). 1979. pap. 10.00 (*0-913724-02-5*) Emerg Response Inst.

***Surviving the Western State of Mind.** Ed. by Gennie Nord. (Illus.). 178p. (Orig.). 1997. pap. 15.00 (*1-889367-06-0*) Up the Creek.

Surviving the 20th Century Diet: Scientific Solutions to a Diet Gone Wrong. abr. ed. Mary R. Swope. (Illus.). 79p. (Orig.). 1996. pap. text ed. 6.95 (*0-9606936-6-1*) Swope Enter.

Surviving Together: The Olaf Palme Lectures on Common Security, 1988. Ed. by Radmila Nakarada & Jan Oberg. 214p. 1989. text ed. 49.95 (*1-85521-067-3*, Pub. by Dartmth Pub UK) Ashgate Pub Co.

Surviving Trauma: Loss & Literature. David Aberbach. 202p. 1989. 32.50 (*0-300-04557-3*) Yale U Pr.

Surviving Trench Warfare: Technology & the Canadian Corps, 1914-1918. Bill Rawling. 320p. 1992. 50.00 (*0-8020-5017-4*); pap. 19.95 (*0-8020-6002-1*) U of Toronto Pr.

Surviving When Someone You Love Was Murdered: A Professional's Guide to Group Grief Therapy for Families & Friends of Murder Victims. Lula M. Redmond. 170p. (Orig.). (C). 1989. pap. 24.95 (*0-9624592-0-8*) Psychological Consult.

Surviving with Kids: A Lifeline for Overwhelmed Parents. Wayne Bartz & Richard Rasor. LC 78-13328. (Illus.). 192p. 1978. pap. 8.95 (*0-915166-55-0*) Impact Pubs CA.

Surviving with the Biosphere: Proceedings of the Fourth International Conference on Environmental Future. Ed. by Nicholas Polunin & John H. Burnett. (Illus.). 561p. 1994. 79.00 (*0-7486-0314-X*, Pub. by Edinburgh U Pr UK) Col U Pr.

Surviving Without a Secretary: A Guide to Productivity. Jean Q. Manzo. Ed. by Janis Paris. LC 96-83619. (Fifty Minute Ser.). 99p. (Orig.). 1996. pap. 10.95 (*1-56052-393-X*) Crisp Pubns.

Surviving Without Romance: African Women Tell Their Stories. Mary L. Cummings. LC 90-48573. 224p. (Orig.). 1991. pap. 9.99 (*0-8361-3538-5*) Herald Pr.

Surviving Your Adolescents: How to Manage & Let Go of Your 13 to 18 Year Olds. rev. ed. Thomas W. Phelan. (Illus.). 168p. 1993. pap. 12.95 (*0-9633861-0-7*) Child Mgmt.

Surviving Your Boss: How to Cope with Office Politics & Get on with Your Job. Ann D. Clark & Patt Perkins. 224p. 1996. 19.95 (*1-55972-336-X*, Birch Ln Pr) Carol Pub Group.

Surviving Your Boss: How To Cope with Office Politics & Get on with Your Job. Ann D. Clark & Patt Perkins. 224p. 1996. pap. 12.95 (*0-8065-1803-0*, Citadel Pr) Carol Pub Group.

Surviving Your Child's Dating Years: 7 Vital Skills to Help Your Child Build Healthy Relationships. Bobbie Reed. LC 95-7305. (How to Family Ser.). 160p. 1995. pap. 8.99 (*0-570-04826-5*, 12-3268) Concordia.

Surviving Your Crises, Reviving Your Dreams. Donald E. Watson. 256p. (Orig.). 1994. pap. 12.95 (*0-938179-37-3*) Mills Sanderson.

Surviving Your Dissertation: A Comprehensive Guide to Content & Process. Kjell E. Rudestam & Rae R. Newton. 208p. (C). 1992. text ed. 46.00 (*0-8039-4562-0*); pap. text ed. 19.50 (*0-8039-4563-9*) Sage.

Surviving Your Dog's Adolescence: A Positive Training Program. Carol L. Benjamin. LC 93-17879. (Illus.). 224p. 1993. pap. 20.00 (*0-87605-742-3*) Howell Bk.

Surviving Your Friend's Divorce: 10 Rules to Help You Both. Mary K. Leatherman. 112p. (Orig.). 1996. pap. 8.95 (*0-87946-135-7*) ACTA Pubns.

Surviving Your Future: A Journey Through Time from Our Glorious Beginnings to Our Not-So-Glorious Future... Can You Survive It? Phyllis Zylstra. LC 94-69223. 96p. (Orig.). 1995. pap. 7.95 (*0-9644140-0-7*) Olia Bks.

Surviving Your Health Care. Michael M. Warren. LC 93-91539. 300p. (Orig.). 1995. pap. 16.95 (*0-9627775-3-6*) Ledero Pr.

***Surviving Your Next Object-Oriented Project.** Ed. by Alistar Cockburn. (C). 1998. pap. text ed. write for info. (*0-201-49834-0*) Addison-Wesley.

Surviving Your Partner's Job Loss: The Complete Guide to Rescuing Your Marriage & Family from Today's Economy. Jill Jukes & Ruthan Rosenberg. LC 92-46162. 216p. 1993. pap. 12.95 (*1-882605-00-4*) Natl Pr Bks.

Surviving Your Role As a Lawyer. 2nd rev. ed. David H. Barber. (Illus.). 166p. 1987. pap. text ed. 17.95 (*0-915667-07-X*) Spectra Pub Co.

Surviving Your Seasons of Change. Adelle Penn-Brown. Ed. by Phyllis Mackell. (Orig.). 1991. pap. 1.95 (*0-9629630-0-3*) V I Christian Min.

Surviving Your Two-Year-Old. Janet Poland. 1995. pap. 59.88 (*0-312-95654-1*); mass mkt. 4.99 (*0-312-95582-0*) Tor Bks.

Surviving "60 Minutes" & the Other News Magazine Shows. James E. Lukaszewski. 16p. 1995. pap. 40.00 (*1-883291-16-X*) Lukaszewski.

Survivor. Moshe Garbarz & Elie Garbarz. Tr. by Jean-Jacques Garbarz. LC 91-31212. (Illus.). 274p. 1992. 29.95 (*0-8143-2372-3*) Wayne St U Pr.

Survivor. Paul Gillon. Ed. by Bernd Metz. Tr. by Dwight Decker from FRE. (Illus.). 49p. (Orig.). 1990. pap. 10.95 (*0-87416-116-9*) Catalan Communs.

Survivor. Michael Greenwald. Ed. by Dougal Robertson. 584p. 1989. 34.95 (*0-931297-02-8*); pap. 26.95 (*0-931297-03-6*) Blue San Diego.

Survivor. Arun Joshi. 136p. 1975. pap. 2.50 (*0-88253-777-6*) Ind-US Inc.

Survivor. Tabitha King. LC 96-26347. 1997. pap. 24.95 (*0-525-94241-6*) NAL-Dutton.

Survivor. Knute Lee. LC 84-81767. 224p. 1984. pap. 9.95 (*0-8187-0057-2*) Harlo Press.

Survivor. Fritz Raddatz. Tr. by Ralph Manheim. 1989. 15.95 (*0-316-73213-3*) Little.

Survivor. Rae Wilder. 300p. write for info. (*0-318-69935-4*) Longitude & Lat.

Survivor. large type ed. Champlin. Date not set. 20.00 (*0-7838-1672-3*, GK Hall) Thorndike Pr.

Survivor. large type ed. James Herbert. 336p. (Orig.). 1984. 27.99 (*0-7089-8165-8*) Ulverscroft.

Survivor, Vol. 1. rev. ed. Kurt Saxon. (Illus.). 480p. 1988. pap. text ed. 25.00 (*1-881801-06-3*) Atlan Formularies.

Survivor, Vol. 2. Kurt Saxon. 464p. 1988. pap. text ed. 25.00 (*1-881801-07-1*) Atlan Formularies.

Survivor, Vol. 3. Kurt Saxon. 464p. 1992. pap. text ed. 25.00 (*1-881801-08-X*) Atlan Formularies.

Survivor, Vol. 4. Kurt Saxon. 464p. 1992. pap. text ed. 25.00 (*1-881801-09-8*) Atlan Formularies.

Survivor: A Western Story. Tim Champlin. LC 96-6304. 1996. 16.95 (*0-7862-0661-6*, Five Star) Mac Lib Ref.

Survivor: An Anatomy of Life in the Death Camps. Terrence Des Pres. (Illus.). 230p. 1980. pap. 11.95 (*0-19-502703-5*) OUP.

Survivor: The True Story of the Sinking of the Doggerbank. Hans Herlin. Tr. by John Brownjohn. 224p. 1995. 39.50 (*0-85052-409-1*, Pub. by L Cooper Bks UK) Trans-Atl Phila.

Survivor & Other Poems. Tadeusz Rozewicz. Tr. by Magnus J. Krynski & Robert A. Maguire. LC 76-3034. (Lockert Library of Poetry in Translation). 180p. reprint ed. pap. 51.30 (*0-8357-4202-4*, 2036981) Bks Demand.

Survivor from a Dead Age: The Memoirs of Louis Lozowick. Ed. by Virginia H. Marquardt. (Illus.). 320p. 1997. 34.95 (*1-56098-696-4*) Smithsonian.

Survivor in Limbo. Sigmund Weiss. LC 90-92241. (Illus.). 88p. 1991. pap. 7.95 (*1-878116-06-1*) JVC Bks.

Survivor in Us All: Four Young Sisters in the Holocaust. Erna F. Rubinstein. LC 86-10844. 185p. (YA). (gr. 8 up). 1986. pap. text ed. 15.00 (*0-208-02129-9*, Archon Bks) Shoe String.

Survivor of a Tarnished Ministry. Betty E. De Blase. 176p. (Orig.). 1983. pap. text ed. 6.95 (*0-913621-00-5*) Truth CA.

Survivor of the Edmund Fitzgerald. Joan Skelton. 100p. 1985. 7.95 (*0-920806-80-5*, Pub. by Penumbra Pr CN) U of Toronto Pr.

Survivor of the Holocaust. Jack Eisner. 302p. 1996. pap. 11.00 (*1-57566-104-7*, Knsington) Kensgtn Pub Corp.

Survivor Personality. Al Siebert. LC 96-11324. 288p. (Orig.). 1996. reprint ed. pap. 12.00 (*0-399-52230-1*, Perigee Bks) Berkley Pub.

Survivor Prayers: Talking with God about Childhood Sexual Abuse. Catherine J. Foote. LC 93-44220. 96p. (Orig.). 1994. pap. 9.00 (*0-664-25435-7*) Westminster John Knox.

Survivor Psychology: The Darkside of a Mental Health Mission. Susan Smith. 233p. (Orig.). (C). 1995. pap. 14.95 (*0-89777-138-9*, Upton Bks) Sirs Inc.

***Survivor Syndrome: Medical & Psychological Consequences of the Holocaust.** Leon Deutsch. 270p. 1996. pap. 19.95 (*1-55022-249-X*, Pub. by E C W Pr CN) Aubrey Bks.

***Survivors.** Eleanor H. Ayer. (Holocaust Library). (Illus.). (J). (gr. 4-12). 1997. lib. bdg. 17.96 (*1-56006-096-4*) Lucent Bks.

Survivors. Clint Berrywell. 196p. 1983. pap. 5.00 (*0-942698-13-4*) Trends & Events.

Survivors. Jean Lorrah. Ed. by Dave Stern. (Star Trek: The Next Generation Ser.: No. 4). (Orig.). 1991. mass mkt. 5.50 (*0-671-74290-6*) PB.

Survivors: A New Vision of Endangered Wildlife. Photos & Text by James Balog. (Illus.). 160p. 1990. 49.50 (*0-8109-3908-8*) Abrams.

Survivors: A Personal Story of the Holocaust. Jacob Biber. LC 85-22415. (Studies in Judaica & the Holocaust: No. 2). 204p. 1986. pap. 23.00 (*0-89370-470-9*); lib. bdg. 33.00 (*0-89370-370-2*) Borgo Pr.

Survivors: An Oral History of the Armenian Genocide. Donald E. Miller & Lorna T. Miller. LC 92-18439. 1993. 27.50 (*0-520-07984-1*) U CA Pr.

Survivors: And Other New York Poems. Ilsa Gilbert. 24p. (Orig.). 1985. pap. 3.50 (*0-934776-05-9*) Bard Pr.

Survivors: Children of the Holocaust. Judith Hemmendinger. 200p. (Orig.). 1986. reprint ed. 15.95 (*0-915765-24-1*) Natl Pr Bks.

An Asterisk (*) at the beginning of an entry indicates that the title is appearing in BIP for the first time.

***Survivors: Faces of Those in Need.** Robert Cotner & Kenneth Baillie. (Illus.). 52p. (Orig.). 1997. pap. 25.00 (*0-9657275-0-5*) Slvation Army.

Survivors: How to Keep Your Best People on Board after Downsizing. Gayle Caplan & Mary K. Teese. LC 96-20606. 264p. 1996. 25.95 (*0-89106-091-X*, 7893) Davies-Black.

Survivors: Jewish Refugees in Birmingham, 1933-1945. Birmingham Jewish History Research Group Staff & Zoe Josephs. (Illus.). 217p. 1988. pap. 25.00 (*1-869922-02-6*) Denali Press.

Survivors: Poems. Frederick Feirstein. LC 74-12385. 1976. 12.50 (*0-89366-125-2*); pap. 7.50 (*0-89366-126-0*) Ultramarine Pub.

Survivors: Vietnam POWs Tell Their Story. Zalin Grant. (Illus.). 355p. reprint ed. pap. 14.95 (*0-306-80561-8*) Da Capo.

Survivors: Women of the Southwest. Rita K. Chegin. LC 91-66179. (Illus.). 176p. (Orig.). 1991. pap. 9.95 (*0-9622940-4-7*) Yucca Tree Pr.

***Survivors - A World War II Novel.** J. L. McCabe & Jim Collins. 1997. pap. text ed. write for info. (*0-942465-20-2*) Summertree Bks.

Survivors & Others. Robert Drake. LC 87-5644. 208p. 1987. 24.95 (*0-86554-253-8*, MUP H-218); pap. 14.95 (*0-86554-254-6*, MUP/P041) Mercer Univ Pr.

Survivors & Partners: Healing the Relationships of Survivors of Sexual Abuse. (Orig.). 1991. pap. 9.95 (*0-9629960-4-1*) Heron Hill.

Survivor's Guide: A Guide for Teenage Girls Who Are Survivors of Sexual Abuse. Sharice A. Lee. LC 94-45028. 1995. 25.00 (*0-8039-5780-7*); pap. text ed. 12.95 (*0-8039-5781-5*) Sage.

Survivors Guide for Government Executives: How to Succeed in Washington. John H. Trattner. LC 89-5519. 106p. (Orig.). (C). 1989. pap. text ed. 15.75 (*0-8191-7431-9*, Excellence in Plastics); lib. bdg. 33.00 (*0-8191-7430-0*, Excellence in Plastics) U Pr of Amer.

Survivor's Guide to Family Preparedness. John R. Sauer. Ed. by Anderson & Shirley Jurjovec. (Common Sense Survival Guide Ser.: Vol. 7). (Illus.). 32p. (Orig.). 1996. mass mkt. 5.95 (*1-889399-09-4*) SAI Pubng.

Survivor's Guide to Home Schooling. Luanne Shackelford & Susan White. LC 88-70691. 177p. 1988. pap. 9.99 (*0-89107-503-8*) Crossway Bks.

Survivor's Guide to Library Research: A Simple Systematic Approach to Using the Library & Writing. William B. Badke. 128p. 1990. pap. 9.99 (*0-310-53111-X*) Zondervan.

***Survivor's Guide to Secure IT Centre Design.** M. Faithful & S. Watt. vi, 114p. 1991. 200.00 (*1-85617-037-3*, Pub. by Elsvr Adv Tech UK) Elsevier.

Survivor's Guide to Step-Parenting. Jim Stokes. (Illus.). (Orig.). 1992. pap. 11.95 (*0-933025-24-6*) Blue Bird Pub.

Survivor's Guide to Writing. Freed. 1992. pap. text ed. write for info. (*0-07-021913-3*) McGraw.

Survivors in the Shadows: An Endangered Mammal Postcard Collection. Lawrence Ormsby. (Illus.). 20p. (Orig.). 1994. pap. 7.95 (*0-87358-581-X*) Northland AZ.

Survivor's Manual: A Book of Poems. Janice H. Mikesell. LC 90-80133. 52p. (Orig.). 1990. reprint ed. pap. 8.00 (*0-9621112-1-X*) Hens Teeth.

Survivors of Childhood Cancer: A Physician & Nurse. Schwartz et al. 280p. (C). (gr. 13). 1994. pap. text ed. 50.00 (*0-8016-6521-3*) Mosby Yr Bk.

Survivors of Suicide. Rita Robinson. (Orig.). 1992. pap. 9.95 (*0-87877-174-3*) Newcastle Pub.

Survivors of the Holocaust in Poland: A Portrait Based on Jewish Community Records, 1944-1947. Lucjan Dobroszycki. LC 94-17363. 164p. (gr. 13). 1994. text ed. 48.95 (*1-56324-463-2*) M E Sharpe.

Survivor's Primer & Up-Dated Retreater's Bibliography. Don Stephens & Barbie Stephens. (Illus.). 1976. pap. 12.00 (*0-686-21855-8*) Stephens Pr.

Survivor's Sourcebook. John R. Sauer. Ed. by Anderson & Shirley Jurjovec. (Illus.). 150p. (Orig.). 1996. pap. 39.95 (*1-889399-00-0*) SAI Pubng.

Survivors, Victims & Perpetrators: Essays on the Nazi Holocaust. Ed. by Joel E. Dimsdale. LC 79-24834. (Illus.). 474p. 1980. pap. text ed. 45.95 (*0-89116-351-4*) Hemisp Pub.

Survivorship Analysis for Clinical Studies. Harris & Albert. (Statistics: Textbooks & Monographs: Vol. 114). 224p. 1990. 115.00 (*0-8247-8400-6*) Dekker.

Surya & Sun Cult in Indian Art, Culture, Literature, Thought. Shanti Lal Nagar. (C). 1995. 120.00 (*81-7305-056-2*, Pub. by Aryan Bks Intl II) S Asia.

***Surya-Sevana: The Way to God of a Balinese Siva Priest.** C. Hooykaas. (Verhandelingen der Koninklijke Nederlandse Akademie van Wetenschappen, Afd. Letterkunde, Nieuwe Reeks Ser.: No. 72(3)). 226p. pap. 32.50 (*0-7204-8421-9*) Elsevier.

Surya Siddhanta: A Textbook of Hindu Astronomy. Ed. by Phanindralal Gangooly. (C). 1989. reprint ed. 27.00 (*81-208-0612-3*, Pub. by Motilal Banarsidass II) S Asia.

Sus. Barrie Keeffe. 28p. (C). 1988. pap. 7.95 (*0-413-46870-4*, A0280) Heinemann.

Sus Derechos de Credito en Estados Unidos. Lucio Ortiz. (Orig.). (SPA.). (YA). (gr. 9-12). 1989. pap. 6.00 (*0-685-28998-2*) Publicaciones Nuevos.

Sus Hijos, Barro En Sus Manos. Gloria Ricardo. 26p. 1992. pap. 1.15 (*1-885630-12-3*) HLM Producciones.

Sus Hijos y el Rock. Bob Larson. 45p. (SPA.). 1990. pap. 2.49 (*0-945792-75-1*, 498047) Editorial Unilit.

Sus Signos de Fertilidad: Aprenda a Conocerlos y Utilizarlos Para Lograr o Evitar el Embrazo en Forma Natural. Merryl Winstein. (Illus.). 192p. 1996. pap. 12.95 (*0-9619401-5-8*) Smooth Stone Pr.

Susan & God. Rachel Crothers. 1947. pap. 5.25 (*0-8222-1102-5*) Dramatists Play.

Susan & Gordon Adopt a Baby. Judy Freudberg & Tony Geiss. LC 86-2951. (Sesame Street Bks.). (Illus.). 24p. (J). (ps-2). 1986. 10.99 (*0-394-88341-1*) Random Bks Yng Read.

Susan B. Anthony. Cynthia F. Klingel & Dan Zadra. (We the People Ser.). (Illus.). 32p. (J). 1987. lib. bdg. 14.95 (*0-88682-164-9*) Creative Ed.

***Susan B. Anthony.** Darlene Resling & Albert Lindel. (Our Changing Lives Ser.). (Illus.). 64p. (YA). (gr. 4-12). 1997. pap. text ed. 7.95 (*1-55596-167-3*, LW2000) Learning Well.

***Susan B. Anthony.** Peter Roop & Connie Roop. LC 97-13731. (Lives & Times Ser.). (J). 1997. lib. bdg. write for info. (*1-57572-563-0*) Rigby Interact Libr.

Susan B. Anthony: A Crusader for Womanhood. AESOP Enterprises, Inc. Staff & Gwendolyn J. Crenshaw. (Heroes & Sheroes Ser.). 14p. (J). (gr. 3-12). 1991. pap. write for info. incl. audio (*1-880771-09-8*) AESOP Enter.

Susan B. Anthony: And Justice for All. Jeanne Gehret. (Illus.). 120p. (J). (gr. 4 up). 1994. 14.95 (*0-9625136-9-5*); pap. 6.95 (*0-9625136-8-7*) Verbal Images Pr.

Susan B. Anthony: Champion of Women's Rights. Helen A. Monsell. LC 86-10716. (Childhood of Famous Americans Ser.). (Illus.). 192p. (J). (gr. 2-6). 1986. reprint ed. pap. 4.95 (*0-02-041800-0*) Macmillan.

Susan B. Anthony: Mini-Play. (Women's Studies). (J). (gr. 5 up). 1974. 6.50 (*0-89550-365-4*) Stevens & Shea.

Susan B. Anthony: Rebel, Crusader, Humanitarian. Alma Lutz. LC 75-37764. 1976. reprint ed. 27.95 (*0-89201-017-7*) Zenger Pub.

***Susan B. Anthony: Voice for Women's Voting Rights.** Martha E. Kendall. LC 96-30386. (Historical American Biographies Ser.). 128p. (YA). (gr. 6 up). 1997. lib. bdg. 18.95 (*0-89490-780-8*) Enslow Pubs.

Susan B. Anthony - A Biography: A Singular Feminist. Kathleen L. Barry. LC 88-1228. (Illus.). 416p. (C). 1988. text ed. 32.00 (*0-8147-1105-7*) NYU Pr.

Susan B. Anthony: Fighter for Women's Rights see Junior World Biographies

Susan B. Anthony Slept Here. Jurate Kazikas. 1994. write for info. (*0-8129-2360-X*) Random.

Susan B. Anthony, The Woman Who Changed the Mind of a Nation. Rheta C. Dorr. LC 74-100519. reprint ed. 47.50 (*0-404-00626-4*) AMS Pr.

Susan B. Anthony: Woman Suffragist see American Women of Achievement

Susan Butcher & the Iditarod Trail. Ellen M. Dolan. LC 92-36837. (J). 1993. 14.95 (*0-8027-8211-6*); lib. bdg. 15.85 (*0-8027-8212-4*) Walker & Co.

Susan Butcher & the Iditarod Trail. Ellen M. Dolan. (Illus.). 112p. (YA). (gr. 5 up). 1996. pap. 6.95 (*0-8027-7496-2*) Walker & Co.

Susan Butcher, Sled Dog Racer. Ginger Wadsworth. LC 93-36093. (Achievers Ser.). (Illus.). 64p. (J). (gr. 4-9). 1994. lib. bdg. 17.50 (*0-8225-2878-9*, Lerner Publctns) Lerner Group.

Susan Clegg & Her Friend Mrs. Lathrop. Anne French. LC 71-94723. (Short Story Index Reprint Ser.). 1977. 19.95 (*0-8369-3102-5*) Ayer.

Susan Clegg & Her Neighbors' Affairs. Anne French. LC 70-150474. (Short Story Index Reprint Ser.). 1977. reprint ed. 19.95 (*0-8369-3814-3*) Ayer.

Susan Cooper. Mikkelsen. Date not set. 22.95 (*0-8057-7813-6*, Twayne) Scribnrs Ref.

Susan Glaspell. Arthur E. Waterman. LC 66-17062. (Twayne's United States Authors Ser.). 1966. pap. text ed. 7.75 (*0-8290-0016-X*); lib. bdg. 17.95 (*0-89197-958-1*) Irvington.

Susan Glaspell. Arthur E. Waterman. (Twayne's United States Authors Ser.). 1966. pap. 13.95 (*0-8084-0288-9*, T101) NCUP.

Susan Glaspell: A Research & Production Sourcebook. Mary E. Papke. LC 92-42696. (Modern Dramatists Research & Production Sourcebooks Ser.: No. 4). 320p. 1993. text ed. 75.00 (*0-313-27383-9*, PSA, Greenwood Pr) Greenwood.

Susan Glaspell's Century of American Women: A Critical Interpretation of Her Work. Veronica Makosky. LC 92-23329. 184p. 1993. 38.00 (*0-19-507866-7*) OUP.

***Susan Irvine's Rose Gardens.** Susan Irvine. 1997. pap. text ed. 24.95 (*1-875657-83-5*, Pub. by Hyland Hse AT) Seven Hills Bk.

Susan Jeffers Connection. Will C. Howell. 1991. pap. 9.99 (*0-86653-980-8*) Fearon Teach Aids.

Susan Kahn. Lincoln Rothschild. LC 79-5388. (Illus.). 164p. 1980. 45.00 (*0-87982-031-4*) Art Alliance.

Susan L. Mitchell. Richard M. Kain. LC 78-126275. (Irish Writers Ser.). 1975. 8.50 (*0-8387-7768-6*); pap. 1.95 (*0-8387-7627-2*) Bucknell U Pr.

Susan Lenox: Her Fall & Rise, 2 vols., Set. David C. Phillips. (Collected Works of David G. Phillips). 1988. reprint ed. lib. bdg. 99.00 (*0-7812-1346-0*) Rprt Serv.

Susan Lenox: Her Fall & Rise, 2 vols., Set. David G. Phillips. LC 68-57548. (Muckrakers Ser.). 1076p. reprint ed. lib. bdg. 16.00 (*0-8398-1568-9*) Irvington.

Susan Lenox: Her Fall & Rise, 2 vols., Set. David G. Phillips. (Muckrakers Ser.). 1076p. 1986. reprint ed. pap. text ed. 12.50 (*0-8290-2038-1*) Irvington.

Susan Lenox, Her Fall & Rise, 2 vols. in 1. David G. Phillips. LC 70-121842. (Illus.). reprint ed. 35.00 (*0-404-05029-8*) AMS Pr.

Susan Lenox: Her Fall & Rise see Collected Works of David G. Phillips

Susan Perl's Park Peepl. Monica Bayley & Susan Perl. LC 81-67306. (Illus.). 7.95 (*0-915696-25-8*) Determined Prods.

Susan Rothenberg. Joan Simon. (Illus.). 198p. 1991. 75.00 (*0-8109-3753-0*) Abrams.

Susan Rothenberg: Exhibition Catalogue. Michael Auping. LC 92-4189. 159p. 1992. pap. 19.95 (*0-914782-82-7*) Buffalo Fine-Albrght-Knox.

Susan Rothenberg - The Prints: A Catalogue Raisonne. Rachel R. Maxwell et al. (Illus.). 104p. (Orig.). (C). 1987. pap. 20.00 (*0-944751-00-8*) Maxwells Busn.

Susan Seddon Boulet: The Goddess Paintings. Illus. by Susan S. Boulet. LC 93-87362. 128p. 1994. 40.00 (*1-56640-975-6*); pap. 29.95 (*1-56640-957-8*) Pomegranate Calif.

Susan Shatter: Light in Darkness. Ed. by Neil Winkel. (Illus.). 12p. (Orig.). 1993. 10.00 (*0-9626097-1-4*) Fischbach Gal.

Susan Smith: Victim or Murderer. George A. Rekers. LC 95-79296. 230p. 1995. 21.95 (*0-944435-38-6*) Glenbridge Pub.

Susan Sontag: Mind As a Passion. Liam Kennedy. LC 95-911. 208p. 1995. text ed. 35.00 (*0-7190-3785-9*, Pub. by Manchester Univ Pr UK) St Martin.

Susan Sontag: Mind As a Passion. Liam Kennedy. LC 95-911. 1997. text ed. 19.95 (*0-7190-3786-7*, Pub. by Manchester Univ Pr UK) St Martin.

***Susan Sontag an Annotated Bibliography.** (Bibliographies of Modern Critics & Critical Schools Ser.). Date not set. text ed. 29.00 (*0-8240-5731-7*) Garland.

Susan Sontag Reader. limited ed. Susan Sontag. 446p. 1982. 60.00 (*0-374-27216-6*) FS&G.

Susann Folk Cross-Stitch Charts see Charted Folk Designs for Cross-Stitch Embroidery

Susanna Foo Chinese Cuisine: The Fabulous Flavors & Innovative Recipes of North America's Finest Chinese Cook. Susanna Foo. Ed. by Rux Martin. LC 95-9052. (Illus.). 352p. 1995. 35.00 (*1-881527-94-8*) Chapters Pub.

Susanna, "Jeanie," & "The Old Folks at Home" The Songs of Stephen C. Foster from His Time to Ours. 2nd ed. William W. Austin. LC 87-13931. (Music in American Life Ser.). 456p. 1989. text ed. 34.95 (*0-252-01476-6*); pap. text ed. 14.95 (*0-252-06069-5*) U of Ill Pr.

Susanna McGavock Carter: The Trusted Housekeeper Slave of General William Giles Harding of Nashville's Belle Meade Plantation. Emma W. Bragg. LC 93-71143. (Illus.). 30p. (Orig.). 1993. 25.00 (*0-9611930-3-4*) E W Bragg.

Susanna Moodie: Letters of a Lifetime. Carl Ballstadt et al. 400p. 1985. 35.00 (*0-8020-2580-3*) U of Toronto Pr.

Susanna Moodie: Letters of a Lifetime. Ed. by Carl Ballstadt et al. (Illus.). 400p. 1993. pap. 19.95 (*0-8020-7385-9*) U of Toronto Pr.

Susanna, Mother of the Wesleys. Rebecca L. Harmon. (Abingdon Classics Ser.). 175p. 1991. reprint ed. pap. 5.95 (*0-687-40767-2*) Abingdon.

Susanna of the Alamo: A True Story. John Jakes. LC 85-27143. (Illus.). 32p. (J). (gr. 1-5). 1986. 14.00 (*0-15-200592-7*, Gulliver Bks) HarBrace.

Susanna of the Alamo: A True Story. John Jakes. (Illus.). 32p. (J). (gr. 1-5). 1990. pap. 7.00 (*0-15-200595-1*, Gulliver Bks) HarBrace.

Susanna Siegelbaum Gives up Guys. June Foley. 160p. (YA). (gr. 7-9). 1992. pap. 3.25 (*0-590-43700-3*) Scholastic Inc.

Susanna Wesley. Arnold Dallimore. LC 92-41948. 176p. (gr. 10). 1993. pap. 9.99 (*0-8010-3018-8*) Baker Bks.

Susanna Wesley. Charles Ludwig. LC 84-60314. (Sower Ser.). 195p. (J). (gr. 3-6). 1984. pap. 7.99 (*0-88062-110-9*) Mott Media.

Susanna Wesley. 4th ed. Frederick E. Maser. 31p. 1987. reprint ed. pap. 1.00 (*1-880927-01-2*) Gen Comm Arch.

Susanna Wesley: A Remarkable Woman & Mother. George W. Rice. 56p. 1990. pap. 2.49 (*0-8341-1349-X*) Beacon Hill.

Susanna Wesley: Servant of God. Sandy Dengler. (YA). (gr. 5 up). 1987. mass mkt. 5.99 (*0-8024-8414-X*) Moody.

Susanna Wesley: The Complete Writings. Ed. by Charles Wallace, Jr. LC 95-8821. 560p. 1997. 65.00 (*0-19-507437-8*) OUP.

Susannah & the Elders. Patrick Smith. (Illus.). 101p. (Orig.). 1992. pap. 11.00 (*0-942908-11-2*) Pancake Pr.

Susannah & the Sandman. Monika Laimgruber. (Illus.). (J). Date not set. 15.95 (*1-55858-601-6*); lib. bdg. 15.88 (*1-55858-602-4*) North-South Bks NYC.

Susannah's Secret. large type ed. Katrina Wright. (Linford Romance Library). 208p. 1992. pap. 15.99 (*0-7089-7278-0*, Trailtree Bookshop) Ulverscroft.

Susanneke. C. J. Van Doornik. Tr. by Miriam Slaa from DUT. LC 94-38672. (Illus.). 34p. (J). 1994. pap. 4.50 (*0-921100-61-2*) Inhtce Pubns.

***Susan's Special Christmas.** Mason Ellis. LC 96-53953. (Illus.). 32p. (Orig.). (J). 1997. 9.99 (*1-56507-608-7*) Harvest Hse.

Susato Motet Anthologies, Vol. 2. Ed. by Richard Sherr. LC 56-5. (Sixteenth-Century Motet Ser.: Vol. 16). 344p. 1995. text ed. 110.00 (*0-8240-7916-7*) Garland.

Susato Motet Anthologies: Liber Nonus Ecclesiasticarum Cantionum Quinque Vocum...(Antwerp: Susato, 1554)/ Liber Decimus Ecclesiasticarum Cantionum Quinque Vocum...(Antwerp: Susato, 1555) Richard Sherr. (Sixteenth-Century Motet Ser.: Vol. 17). 352p. 1996. text ed. 100.00 (*0-8240-7917-5*) Garland.

Susato Motet Anthologies: Liber Quintus Ecclesiasticarum Cantionum Quinque Vocum Vulgo Moteta Vocant, Tam Ex Veteri Quam Ex Novo Testamento, Ab Optimis Quibusque Huius Aetatis Musicis Compositarum Omnes Primi Toni Antae Nunquam Excusus. Ed. by Richard Sherr. LC 95-700111. (Sixteenth-Century Motet Ser.: No. 15). 344p. 1995. text ed. 100.00 (*0-8240-7915-9*) Garland.

Susato Motet Anthologies: Liber Undecimus Ecclesiasticarum, Vol. 4. Ed. by Richard Sherr. LC 56-5. (Sixteenth-Century Motet Ser.: Vol. 18). 506p. 1996. text ed. 150.00 (*0-8240-7918-3*) Garland.

***Susceptibility Tensors for Nonlinear Optics.** S. V. Popov et al. LC 95-12396. (Optics & Optoelectronics Ser.). (Illus.). 194p. 1995. disk 500.00 (*0-7503-0344-1*) IOP Pub.

Susceptibility Tensors for Nonlinear Optics. S. V. Popov et al. LC 95-12396. (Optics & Optoelectronics Ser.). (Illus.). 194p. 1995. 200.00 (*0-7503-0253-4*) IOP Pub.

Susceptibility to Inhaled Pollutants. Ed. by Mark J. Utell & Robert Frank. LC 89-32217. (Special Technical Publication Ser.: No. STP 1024). (Illus.). 245p. 1989. text ed. 55.00 (*0-8031-1262-9*, 04-010240-17) ASTM.

Susceptible to the Sacred: The Psychological Experience of Ritual. Bani Shorter. LC 95-38888. 160p. 1996. pap. 15.95 (*0-415-12620-7*) Routledge.

Susceptible to the Sacred: The Psychological Experience of Ritual. Bani Shorter. LC 95-38888. 160p. (C). 1996. text ed. 49.95 (*0-415-12619-3*) Routledge.

Susceptible Visual Apparatus. Cronly-Dillon. 1991. 137.00 (*0-8493-7516-9*, QP474) CRC Pr.

Sushi. Mia Detrick. LC 81-12224. (Illus.). 96p. (Orig.). 1981. pap. 10.95 (*0-87701-238-5*) Chronicle Bks.

***Sushi.** K. Yamamoto. 1996. 6.98 (*0-7858-0675-X*) Bk Sales Inc.

Sushi & Sourdough: A Novel. Tooru J. Kanazawa. LC 89-35376. 256p. 1991. reprint ed. pap. 12.95 (*0-295-97083-9*) U of Wash Pr.

Sushi at Home. Kay Shimizu. (Illus.). 142p. 1994. bds. 22.00 (*0-87040-930-1*) Japan Pubns USA.

Sushi for Parties. Ken Kowasumi. 80p. 17.00 (*1-56836-956-5*) FS&G.

Sushi for Parties: Maki-Zushi & Nigiri-Zushi. Ken Kawasumi. (Illus.). 80p. (Orig.). 1995. pap. 17.00 (*0-87040-956-5*) Japan Pubns USA.

Sushi Made Easy. Nobuko Tsuda. LC 82-7097. (Illus.). 152p. (JPN.). 1982. pap. 10.95 (*0-8348-0173-6*) Weatherhill.

Susie Bright's Sexual Reality: A Virtual Sex World Reader. Susie Bright. 154p. (Orig.). 1992. 24.95 (*0-939416-58-1*); pap. 9.95 (*0-939416-59-X*) Cleis Pr.

***Susie Bright's Sexual State of the Union.** Susie Bright. LC 96-44603. 251p. 1997. 24.00 (*0-684-80023-3*) S&S Trade.

Susie Bright's Sexwise: America's Favorite X-Rated Intellectual Does Dan Quayle, Catharine MacKinnon, Stephen King, Camille Paglia, Nicholson Baker, Madonna, the Black Panthers & the GOP. Susie Bright. LC 94-47330. 180p. 1995. pap. 10.95 (*1-57344-002-7*) Cleis Pr.

Susie Cooper: An Elegant Affair. Bryn Youds. LC 96-60054. (Illus.). 80p. 1996. pap. 24.95 (*0-500-27888-1*) Thames Hudson.

***Susie Cooper Productions.** Anne Eatwell. (Illus.). 107p. pap. 24.95 (*0-948107-88-X*, Pub. by V&A Ent UK) Antique Collect.

Susie Goes Shopping. Rose Greydanus. (Illus.). 32p. (J). (gr. k-2). 1997. pap. 2.50 (*0-89375-289-4*) Troll Communs.

Susie King Taylor: Destined to Be Free. Denise Jordan. (Illus.). 48p. (J). (gr. 3 up). 1994. 13.00 (*0-940975-49-1*); pap. 5.00 (*0-940975-50-5*) Just Us Bks.

***Susie Mae's New School.** Margaree K. Mitchell. (J). Date not set. write for info. (*0-688-15221-X*); lib. bdg. write for info. (*0-688-15222-8*) Lothrop.

Susie Plants a Seed. Judy Mullican. (Little Bks.). (Illus.). 8p. (Orig.). (J). (ps-k). 1995. pap. text ed. 10.95 (*1-57332-065-X*); pap. text ed. 10.95 (*1-57332-066-8*) HighReach Lrning.

Susie Sexpert's Lesbian Sex World. Susie Bright. 160p. (Orig.). 1991. pap. 9.95 (*0-939416-35-2*) Cleis Pr.

***Susipyne Pasauliai.** Nijole Grazulis. LC 97-71770. (Illus.). 96p. (Orig.). (LIT.). 1997. pap. 15.00 (*1-886060-07-X*) Galerija.

Suspect. Judy Baer. (Cedar River Daydreams Ser.: Bk. 24). (YA). (gr. 7-10). 1996. mass mkt. 4.99 (*1-55661-834-4*) Bethany Hse.

Suspect. Reginald Denham. 1944. pap. 5.25 (*0-8222-1103-3*) Dramatists Play.

Suspect. Jo Leigh. 1994. 3.50 (*0-373-07569-3*) Silhouette.

Suspect. Georges Simenon. 1991. 17.95 (*0-15-137057-5*) HarBrace.

Suspect. L. R. Wright. 224p. 1986. mass mkt. 7.99 (*0-7704-2122-9*) Bantam.

Suspect. Laurali R. Wright. 224p. 1987. pap. 5.95 (*0-14-010477-1*, Penguin Bks) Viking Penguin.

***Suspect.** large type ed. Nicholas Rhea. (Dales Large Print Ser.). 340p. 1997. pap. 18.99 (*1-85389-722-1*) Ulverscroft.

Suspect Community. Paddy Hillyard. (Law & Social Theory Ser.). (C). 1993. text ed. 28.00 (*0-7453-0728-0*) Westview.

Suspect Community: People's Experiences of the Prevention of Terrorism Acts in Britain. Paddy Hillyard. 300p. pap. 22.95 (*0-7453-0726-4*, Pub. by Pluto Pr UK) LPC InBook.

Suspect Community: People's Experiences of the Prevention of Terrorism Acts in Britain. Paddy Hillyard. LC 92-42289. 300p. (C). 73.50 (*0-7453-0727-2*, Pub. by Pluto Pr UK) LPC InBook.

Suspect Documents: Their Scientific Examination. Wilson R. Harrison. LC 80-22803. (Illus.). 594p. 1981. text ed. 59.95 (*0-88229-759-7*) Nelson-Hall.

Suspect Groom. Cassie Miles. (Intrigue Ser.). 1995. mass mkt. 3.50 (*0-373-22332-3*, 1-22332-0) Harlequin Bks.

Suspect in Smoke. Carolyn Keene. (Nancy Drew Mystery Stories Ser.: No. 114). 160p. (J). (gr. 3-6). 1993. pap. 3.99 (*0-671-79301-2*, Minstrel Bks) PB.

Suspect to Change. Will Humble. (Illus.). 32p. (Orig.). 1996. pap. 3.25 (*0-88680-420-5*) I E Clark.

Suspects. Thomas Berger. LC 95-42513. 294p. 1996. 23.00 (*0-688-11925-5*) Morrow.

Suspects. William J. Caunitz. 384p. 1987. mass mkt. 6.50 (*0-553-26705-1*) Bantam.

Suspended. Stephen Kapetanovich. (Illus.). 40p. (Orig.). 1994. pap. text ed. 6.95 (1-56315-034-4) Sterling Hse.

Suspended Adolescence: Help for Parents of Chemical Abusers. rev. ed. Richard De Santis & Gerald Manney. (Illus.). 70p. 1989. pap. 7.95 (0-9627723-0-5) Beech Hill Pubns.

Suspended Animation. W. E. Davis. LC 94-9509. (Gil Beckman Mystery Ser.: Bk. 1). 192p. (Orig.). 1994. pap. 8.99 (0-89107-802-9) Crossway Bks.

*__Suspended Animation.__ large type ed. Wally Davis. LC 96-51738. (Gil Beckman Mystery Ser.). 1997. 22.95 (0-7862-1013-3) Thorndike Pr.

Suspended Animation: Six Essays on the Preservation of Bodily Parts. Frank Gonzalez-Crussi. LC 95-12650. (Illus.). 1995. pap. 16.00 (0-15-600231-0, Harvest Bks) HarBrace.

Suspended Fictions: Reading Novels by Manuel Puig. Lucille Kerr. 280p. 1987. text ed. 29.95 (0-252-01329-8) U of Ill Pr.

*__Suspended License: Censorship & the Visual Arts.__ Ed. by Elizabeth C. Childs. LC 97-16469. (Samuel & Althea Stroum Book Ser.). (Illus.). 400p. 1997. pap. 25.00 (0-295-97627-6) U of Wash Pr.

Suspended Matter in the Aquatic Environment. Doeke Eisma. LC 92-27025. 1993. 163.95 (0-387-55825-X) Spr-Verlag.

Suspended Music: Chime-Bells in the Culture of Bronze Age China. Lothar Von Falkenhausen. (Illus.). 567p. 1994. 70.00 (0-520-07378-9) U CA Pr.

Suspended Sentence: A Guide for Writers. Roscoe C. Born. LC 93-24797. 224p. (C). 1993. 15.95 (0-8138-2401-X) Iowa St U Pr.

*__Suspense.__ Parnell Hall. 1998. 23.00 (0-89296-624-6) Mysterious Pr.

Suspense: Conceptualizations, Theoretical Analyses, & Empirical Explorations. Ed. by Peter Vorderer et al. (LEA's Communication Ser.). 376p. 1996. pap. 36.00 (0-8058-1966-5); text ed. 79.95 (0-8058-1965-7) L Erlbaum Assocs.

Suspense: Four Great Novels of Intrigue: A Collection Consisting of Orient Express, This Gun. Graham Greene. 1995. 12.98 (0-88365-907-7) Galahad Bks.

Suspense in the Formula Story. George N. Dove. LC 89-61585. 144p. (C). 1989. 25.95 (0-87972-455-2); pap. 12.95 (0-87972-456-0) Bowling Green Univ Popular Press.

Suspension & Steering. James G. Hughes. 256p. (C). 1987. pap. text ed. write for info. (0-15-584985-9, SUSPEN) HB Coll Pubs.

Suspension & Steering. Knowles. 128p. 1994. 19.50 (0-8273-6889-5) Delmar.

Suspension & Steering. Knowles. (Today's Technician Ser.). 544p. 1996. 150.00 (0-8273-6912-3) Delmar.

Suspension & Steering. Knowles. (Automotive Technology Ser.). 1997. student ed. 14.95 (0-8273-7659-6) Delmar.

Suspension & Steering. Don Knowles. LC 94-12957. (Today's Technician Ser.). 848p. 1994. pap. 53.50 (0-8273-6185-8) Delmar.

Suspension of Henry Adams: A Study of Manner & Matter. Vern Wagner. LC 68-26875. 269p. reprint ed. pap. 76.70 (0-7837-3780-7, 2043599) Bks Demand.

Suspension of the Power of Alienation, & Postponement of Vesting, Under the Laws of New York, Michigan, Minnesota & Wisconsin. Stewart Chaplin. xxxix, 370p. 1981. reprint ed. lib. bdg. 30.00 (0-8377-0428-6) Rothman.

Suspension or Termination of Treaties on Grounds of Breach. Mohammed M. Gomaa. LC 96-12170. 1996. lib. bdg. 97.00 (90-411-0226-4, Pub. by M Nijhoff NE) Kluwer Ac.

Suspensions. Terry Ehret et al. 62p. 1990. pap. write for info. (0-9625104-4-0) White Mtn Pr.

Suspensions. 2nd ed. Terry Ehret et al. (Illus.). 62p. 1990. pap. write for info. (0-318-66579-4) White Mtn Pr.

Suspensions: Fundamentals & Applications in the Petroleum Industry. Ed. by Laurier L. Schramm. (Advances in Chemistry Ser.: Vol. 251). 1995. 134.95 (0-8142-3136-5) Am Chemical.

*__Suspensions: Fundamentals & Applications in the Petroleum Industry.__ Ed. by Laurier L. Schramm. (ACS Advances in Chemistry Ser.: No. 251). (Illus.). 700p. 1996. 134.95 (0-8412-3136-2) Am Chemical.

Suspensions & Steering Technology: 1996 International Congress & Exposition. (Special Publications). 187p. 1996. pap. 74.00 (1-56091-766-0, SP-1136) Soc Auto Engineers.

Suspensions & Their Relationship to Vehicle Roll Stability: Eleven Papers. 104p. 1992. 19.00 (1-56091-306-1, SP-940) Soc Auto Engineers.

Suspensory Behavior, Locomotion, & Other Behaviors of Captive Gibbons: Cognition see Gibbon & Siamang: A Series of Volumes on the Lesser Apes

Suspicion. Julia Grice. 288p. 1994. mass mkt. 4.99 (0-8125-1091-7) Tor Bks.

*__Suspicion.__ Heggan. 1998. mass mkt. 5.99 (1-55166-305-8) Harlequin Bks.

Suspicion. Judith McWilliams. (Historical Ser.). 1994. mass mkt. 3.99 (0-373-28815-8, 1-28815-8) Harlequin Bks.

Suspicion. Marilyn Pappano. 416p. 1997. mass mkt. 6.50 (0-446-60355-4) Warner Bks.

Suspicion: A Novel. McCrum. LC 96-39013. 256p. 1997. 23.00 (0-393-04046-1) Norton.

Suspicion & Silence: The Right to Silence in Criminal Investigations. Ed. by David Morgan & Geoffrey Stephenson. 168p. 1994. text ed. 38.00 (1-85431-380-0, Pub. by Blackstone Pr UK) Gaunt.

Suspicion of Guilt. Barbara J. Parker. 432p. 1996. mass mkt., pap. 5.99 (0-451-17703-7, Sig) NAL-Dutton.

Suspicion of Guilt. large type ed. Barbara J. Parker. LC 95-16352. 1995. 25.95 (1-56895-232-5) Wheeler Pub.

Suspicion of Innocence. Barbara J. Parker. 1994. 20.95 (0-525-93747-1, Dutton) NAL-Dutton.

Suspicion of Innocence. Barbara J. Parker. 432p. 1994. pap. 5.99 (0-451-17340-6, Sig) NAL-Dutton.

*__Suspicion of Innocence.__ Barbara J. Parker. 344p. 4.98 (0-8317-4569-X) Smithmark.

Suspicion of Innocence. large type ed. Barbara J. Parker. LC 94-6064. 602p. 1994. reprint ed. lib. bdg. 22.95 (0-7862-0212-2) Thorndike Pr.

Suspicions. Connie Bennett. (Intrigue Ser.). 1995. pap. 3.50 (0-373-22311-0, 1-22311-4) Harlequin Bks.

Suspicion's Gate. Justine Davis. (Intimate Moments Ser.: No. 423). 1992. mass mkt. 3.39 (0-373-07423-9, 5-07423-2) Harlequin Bks.

Suspicious Affair. large type ed. Barbara Metzger. LC 95-9788. 299p. 1995. reprint ed. pap. 19.95 (0-7838-1297-3, GK Hall) Thorndike Pr.

Suspicious Characters. Julia Vinograd. (Illus.). 60p. (Orig.). 1990. pap. 4.95 (0-929730-19-4) Zeitgeist Pr.

Suspicious Death Scene Investigation. Ed. by Peter Vanezis. (Arnold Publication). (Illus.). 208p. 1996. 65.00 (0-340-55863-6) OUP.

Suspicious Minds: A Radio Play Developing Listening Strategies & Lifeskills. S. Begin et al. (YA). 1990. audio 37.95 (0-8013-0288-9, 75938) Longman.

*__Suspicious River.__ Kasischke. 1997. pap. 12.00 (0-395-86002-4) HM.

Suspicious River. Laura Kasischke. LC 95-46801. 224p. 1996. 22.95 (0-395-77397-0) HM.

Suspicious Wounds. Bernard Holland. LC 95-76895. 103p. 1995. 15.00 (0-9646700-0-3) LIA Pub.

Suspiciously Simple History of Science & Invention: Without the Boring Bits. 2nd ed. John Farman. (Illus.). 246p. (Orig.). (YA). (gr. 7-12). 1994. pap. 14.95 (0-330-32807-7, Pub. by Macmlln UK) Trans-Atl Phila.

Susquehanna: NYS & WR. John Krause & Ed Crist. (Illus.). 100p. 1991. reprint ed. pap. 16.95 (0-911868-80-1, C80) Carstens Pubns.

Susquehanna: River of Dreams. Susan Q. Stranahan. LC 92-45039. (Illus.). 336p. (C). 1993. 35.00 (0-8018-4602-1) Johns Hopkins.

Susquehanna Heartland. Ruth H. Seitz. LC 91-67908. (Pennsylvania's Cultural & Natural Heritage Ser.). 120p. 1992. 24.95 (1-879441-78-0) RB Bks.

Susquehanna River Guide. Christopher Beatty. LC 95-61569. (Illus.). 112p. (Orig.). 1995. pap. 9.95 (0-9639705-7-7) Ecopress.

Susquehanna, River of Dreams. Susan Q. Stranahan. (Illus.). 336p. 1995. pap. 15.95 (0-8018-5147-5) Johns Hopkins.

Susquehanna's Indians. Barry C. Kent. (Pennsylvania Historical & Museum Commission Anthropological Ser.: No. 6). (Illus.). 438p. 1984. pap. 16.95 (0-89271-024-1) Pa Hist & Mus.

Susquehannock: An Anthology of Bioregional Literature. Ed. by Walt Franklin & Michael Czarnecki. 52p. 1986. pap. 5.95 (0-9613465-4-X) Great Elm.

Susquehannock Vocabulary. Thomas C. Holm. Ed. by Claudio R. Sallvucci. 1996. reprint ed. 22.95 (0-9644234-4-8) Evol Pubng & Manuf.

*__Sussex.__ Desmond Seward. (Pimlico County History Guides Ser.). (Illus.). 304p. 1997. pap. 19.95 (0-7126-5133-0, Pub. by Pimlico) Trafalgar.

Sussex Christmas. Shaun Payne. (Illus.). 160p. 1991. pap. 15.00 (0-86299-747-X, Pub. by Sutton Pubng UK) Bks Intl VA.

Sussex County: Virginia Publick Claims. Janice L. Abercrombie & Richard Slatten. (Virginia Publick Claims Ser.). ix, 28p. 1992. pap. 5.00 (0-8095-8703-3) Borgo Pr.

Sussex County: Virginia Publick Claims. Janice L. Abercrombie & Richard Slatten. (Virginia Publick Claims Ser.). ix, 28p. (C). 1992. reprint ed. lib. bdg. 25.00 (0-8095-8365-8) Borgo Pr.

Sussex County, a Tale of Three Centuries. Writers Program, Virginia Staff. LC 73-3659. (American Guide Ser.). 1942. reprint ed. 16.00 (0-404-57959-0) AMS Pr.

Sussex County Marriages, 1754-1810. Catherine L. Knorr. 118p. 1980. reprint ed. 16.00 (0-89308-257-0, VA 20) Southern Hist Pr.

Sussex County, New Jersey, Marriages. Howard E. Case. vi, 358p. (Orig.). 1993. pap. 24.00 (1-55613-702-8) Heritage Bk.

Sussex County, Virginia Deeds & Estate Accounts, 1684-1733. William L. Hopkins. 213p. 1994. pap. 30.00 (0-8095-8702-5); lib. bdg. 60.00 (0-8095-8371-2) Borgo Pr.

Sussex County, Virginia Wills, 1754-1764. T.L.C. Genealogy Staff. LC 91-75355. 131p. (Orig.). 1991. spiral bd. 15.00 (1-57445-009-3) TLC Genealogy.

Sussex Customs, Curiosities & Country Lore. Tony Wales. (C). 1989. 39.00 (1-85455-036-5, Pub. by Ensign Pubns & Print UK) St Mut.

Sussex Garland. Tony Wales. 128p. 1987. 30.00 (0-905392-64-7) St Mut.

Sussex Ghosts. Judy Middleton. 96p. 1987. 30.00 (0-905392-90-6) St Mut.

Sussex Murders, County Murders & Mysteries. David Briffett. (C). 1989. 45.00 (1-85455-045-4, Pub. by Ensign Pubns & Print UK) St Mut.

Sussex of One Hundred Years Ago. Aylwin Weller. (Illus.). 128p. 1991. 35.00 (0-86299-968-5, Pub. by Sutton Pubng UK) Bks Intl VA.

Sussex Scandals. Rupert Taylor. 96p. 1987. 30.00 (0-905392-81-7) St Mut.

Sussex Seams: A Collection of Travel Writing. Ed. by Paul Foster. (Illus.). 160p. Date not set. pap. 15.95 (0-7509-1191-3, Pub. by Sutton Pubng UK) Bks Intl VA.

*__Sussex Spaniel: AKC Rank #139.__ John R. Lewis, Jr. (Rare Breed Ser.). (Illus.). 96p. 1997. 19.95 (0-7938-0776-X, RX-126) TFH Pubns.

Sustainability: A Systems Approach. Tony Clayton & Nicholas J. Radcliffe. (Illus.). 256p. 1996. write for info. (1-85383-314-2, Pub. by Erthscan Pubns UK); pap. write for info. (1-85383-319-3, Pub. by Erthscan Pubns UK) Island Pr.

Sustainability: Economics, Ecology, & Justice. John B. Cobb, Jr. LC 92-20552. (Ecology & Justice Ser.). 200p. 1992. pap. 17.50 (0-88344-823-8) Orbis Bks.

Sustainability: Systems Approach. Anthony M. Clayton & Nicholas J. Radcliffe. (C). 1996. pap. text ed. 29.95 (0-8133-3185-4) Westview.

Sustainability Analysis Module 9: Facilitator's Guide. Mary Millar. (Primary Health Care Management Advancement Programme (PHC MAP) Modules Ser.). 55p. 1993. pap. text ed. write for info. (1-882839-16-1) Aga Khan Fnd.

Sustainability Analysis Module 9: User's Guide. Jack Reynolds & Wayne Stinson. (Primary Health Care Management Advancement Programme (PHC MAP) Modules Ser.). 105p. 1993. pap. text ed. write for info. (1-882839-07-2) Aga Khan Fnd.

*__Sustainability & Global Environmental Policy: New Perspectives.__ Ed. by Andrew K. Dragun & Kristin M. Jakobsson. LC 97-14363. 336p. 1997. 80.00 (1-85898-630-3) E Elgar.

Sustainability & Optimality of Public Debt. M. Carlberg. (Illus.). X, 217p. 1995. 61.00 (3-7908-0834-2) Spr-Verlag.

Sustainability & Policy: Limits to Economics. Michael Common. (Illus.). 360p. (C). 1995. text ed. 59.95 (0-521-43001-1); pap. text ed. 19.95 (0-521-43605-2) Cambridge U Pr.

Sustainability & the Wealth of Nations: First Steps in an Ongoing Journey. Ismail Serageldin. LC 95-51679. (Environmentally Sustainable Development Occasional Papers: No. 5). 28p. 1996. 7.95 (0-8213-3551-0, 13551) World Bank.

*__Sustainability, Growth, & Poverty Alleviation: A Policy & Agroecological Perspective.__ Stephen A. Vosti et al. LC 97-1816. 1997. write for info. (0-8018-5607-8) Johns Hopkins.

Sustainability of a Government Targeted Credit Program: Evidence from Bangladesh. Shahidur R. Khandker et al. LC 95-46678. (Discussion Papers: No. 316). 110p. 1996. 8.95 (0-8213-3516-2, 13516) World Bank.

Sustainability of Irrigated Agriculture: Proceedings of the NATO Advanced Research Workshop, Vimeiro, Portugal, March 21-26, 1994. Ed. by L. S. Pereira et al. LC 96-205. (NATO ASI Series E: Applied Sciences: Vol. 213). (C). 1996. lib. bdg. 315.00 (0-7923-3936-3) Kluwer Ac.

*__Sustainability of Rice Farming.__ Ed. by D. J. Greenland. 320p. 1997. 90.00 (0-85199-163-7, Pub. by CAB Intntl UK) OUP.

*__Sustainability of Rice-Wheat Production Systems in Asia.__ FAO Staff. (Illus.). 216p. (C). 1995. 55.00 (1-886106-50-9) Science Pubs.

Sustainability of Urban Systems: A Cross-National Evolutionary Analysis of Urban Innovation. Peter Nijkamp. 323p. 1990. text ed. 68.95 (1-85628-094-2, Pub. by Avebury Pub UK) Ashgate Pub Co.

Sustainability of Water & Sanitation Systems. Ed. by John Pickford et al. 168p. (Orig.). 1996. pap. 32.50 (1-85339-339-8, Pub. by Intermed Tech UK) Women Ink.

Sustainable Agricultural Development: The Role of International Cooperation: Proceedings of the Twenty-First International Conference of Agricultural Economists. G. H. Peters et al. (International Association of Agricultural Economists Ser.). 736p. 1992. 59.95 (1-85521-272-2, Pub. by Dartmth Pub UK) Ashgate Pub Co.

Sustainable Agricultural Systems. Ed. by Rattan Lal et al. (Illus.). 696p. 1990. 60.00 (0-935734-21-X) Soil & Water Conserv.

Sustainable Agriculture: Concepts, Issues & Policies in OECD Countries. 50p. (Orig.). 1995. pap. 17.00 (92-64-14646-6, Pub. by Org for Econ FR) OECD.

Sustainable Agriculture & the Environment: Perspectives on Growth & Constraints. Ed. by Vernon W. Ruttan. 189p. (C). 1991. pap. text ed. 52.00 (0-8133-8507-5) Westview.

Sustainable Agriculture & the Environment in the Humid Tropics. National Research Council, Board on Agriculture Staff. LC 92-36869. 720p. (C). 1993. text ed. 49.95 (0-309-04749-8) Natl Acad Pr.

Sustainable Agriculture & the 1995 Farm Bill. Task Force of Scientists Staff. LC 95-10780. (Illus.). 32p. (Orig.). 1995. pap. 50.00 (1-887383-00-X) CAST.

*__Sustainable Agriculture Directory of Expertise.__ 3rd ed. Cynthia Arnold et al. 400p. (Orig.). 1997. pap. text ed. 50.00 (0-7881-3830-8) DIANE Pub.

Sustainable Agriculture Directory of Expertise: Seven Hundred Seventeen People & Groups Who Can Help You Farm Longer, More Safely & More Profitably. 300p. (Orig.). (C). 1994. pap. text ed. 40.00 (0-7881-0512-4) DIANE Pub.

Sustainable Agriculture in Africa. Ed. by E. Ann McDougall. LC 89-81235. (Comparative Studies in African-Caribbean Literature Ser.). 345p. (C). 1990. 45.00 (0-86543-147-7); pap. 14.95 (0-86543-148-5) Africa World.

Sustainable Agriculture in California: A Guide to Information. Steven Mitchell & David Bainbridge. 198p. (Orig.). 1991. pap. 15.00 (1-879906-01-5, 3348) ANR Pubns CA.

Sustainable Agriculture in California: Proceedings of a Research Symposium, Sacramento, California, March 15-16, 1990. Ed. by David Chaney. 256p. (Orig.). 1991. pap. text ed. 15.00 (1-879906-02-3, 3348) ANR Pubns CA.

*__Sustainable Agriculture in Central America.__ J. P. Groot et al. LC 97-9144. 1997. write for info. (0-312-17555-8) St Martin.

Sustainable Agriculture in Egypt. Ed. by Mohamed A. Faris & Mahmood H. Khan. LC 93-19486. 280p. 1993. lib. bdg. 40.00 (1-55587-370-7) Lynne Rienner.

Sustainable Agriculture in Print: Current Books. Jane P. Gates. 24p. (Orig.). (C). 1995. pap. text ed. 20.00 (0-7881-2042-5) DIANE Pub.

Sustainable Agriculture in Print: Current Books & Definitions & Terms - Bibliography. Mary V. Gold. 52p. (Orig.). (C). 1994. pap. text ed. 25.00 (0-7881-1450-6) DIANE Pub.

*__Sustainable Agriculture in Print: Current Periodicals.__ Suzanne DeMuth. 130p. (C). 1996. reprint ed. pap. 35.00 (0-7881-3382-9) DIANE Pub.

Sustainable Agriculture in Temperate Zones. Ed. by Charles Francis et al. LC 89-39543. 487p. 1990. text ed. 95.00 (0-471-62227-3) Wiley.

Sustainable Agriculture in the American Midwest: Lessons from Natural & Human History, Prospects for the Future. Ed. by Gregory McIsaac & William R. Edwards. LC 93-45671. (Environment & the Human Condition Ser.). 312p. 1994. text ed. 32.95 (0-252-02100-2) U of Ill Pr.

Sustainable Agriculture Systems. Ed. by J. L. Hatfield & D. L. Karlen. LC 93-26659. 336p. 1993. 89.95 (1-56670-049-3, L1049) Lewis Pubs.

*__Sustainable America: A New Concensus for Prosperity, Opportunity, & a Healthy Environment for the Future.__ Ed. by Nita Congress. (Illus.). 186p. (Orig.). 1996. pap. 35.00 (0-7881-3351-9) DIANE Pub.

*__Sustainable America: National Environmental Policy for the 21st Century-the U. S. Agenda 21.__ Ed. by Daniel Sitarz. 250p. 1998. pap. 15.95 (0-935755-54-3, EarthPress) Nova Pub IL.

Sustainable Animal Production from Small Farm Systems in South-East Asia. C. Devendra. (Animal Production & Health Papers: No. 106). 152p. 1993. pap. 17.00 (92-5-103168-1, F31681, Pub. by FAO IT) Bernan Associates.

*__Sustainable Aquaculture.__ John E. Bardach. LC 96-44727. 280p. 1997. 69.95 (0-471-14829-6) Wiley.

Sustainable Architecture: Principles, Paradigms, & Case Studies. 8th ed. James Steele. LC 96-45681. 320p. 1997. text ed. 49.95 (0-07-060949-7) McGraw.

Sustainable Cities. Graham Haughton & Colin Hunter. (Regional Policy & Development Ser.: No. 7). 250p. 1994. pap. 29.50 (1-85302-234-9) Taylor & Francis.

Sustainable Cities: Concepts & Strategies for Eco-City Development. Ed. by Bob Walter et al. LC 92-90568. (Illus.). 354p. (Orig.). 1992. pap. 20.00 (0-9633511-0-9) Eco-Home Media.

Sustainable Clean Water. R. P. Lim et al. (Advances in Limnology Ser.: Heft 28). (Illus.). 571p. 1987. pap. text ed. 180.00 (3-510-47026-5) Lubrecht & Cramer.

Sustainable Communities: A Community Action Guide. Dorothy Craig. Ed. by Susan Boyd & Burks Lapham. (Community Action Guides Ser.). (Illus.). (Orig.). (YA). (gr. 6-12). 1997. pap. 4.00 (0-937345-09-1) CONCERN.

Sustainable Communities: A New Design Synthesis for Cities, Suburbs, & Towns. Sim Van der Ryn & Peter Calthorpe. LC 83-4676. (Illus.). 238p. 1991. reprint ed. pap. 20.00 (0-87156-629-X) Sierra.

Sustainable Community Development: Principles & Concepts. Chris Maser. 300p. (Orig.). 1996. pap. 39.95 (1-57444-070-5) St Lucie Pr.

Sustainable Construction: Proceedings of the First International Conference. Ed. & Intro. by Charles J. Kibert. (Illus.). 900p. (C). 1994. pap. text ed. 100.00 (0-9643886-1-8) U of FL Construction.

Sustainable Corporate Growth: A Model & Management Planning Tool. John J. Clark et al. LC 88-6755. 322p. 1989. text ed. 65.00 (0-89930-238-6, CKS/, Quorum Bks) Greenwood.

Sustainable Democracy. Adam Przeworski. 160p. (C). 1995. text ed. 44.95 (0-521-48261-5); pap. text ed. 14.95 (0-521-48375-1) Cambridge U Pr.

Sustainable Democracy: Individuality & the Politics of Growth. John Buell & Thomas S. DeLuca, Jr. LC 96-9976. 192p. 1996. 39.95 (0-7619-0221-X); pap. 17.95 (0-7619-0222-8) Sage.

*__Sustainable Development.__ Neil Harrison. 250p. 1997. write for info. (1-55587-564-5) Lynne Rienner.

*__Sustainable Development.__ Neil Harrison. 250p. 1997. pap. write for info. (1-55587-582-3) Lynne Rienner.

Sustainable Development. Ed. by Bholeshwar Nath et al. 365p. 1996. 29.00 (90-5487-115-6, Pub. by VUB Univ Pr BE) Paul & Co Pubs.

Sustainable Development. Olav S. Stokke. 132p. 1992. text ed. 30.00 (0-7146-3449-2, Pub. by F Cass Pubs UK) Intl Spec Bk.

Sustainable Development, 2 vols., Set. Ed. by N. L. Gupta. (C). 1993. 84.00 (81-7033-181-1, Pub. by Rawat II) S Asia.

Sustainable Development: Challenges & Opportunities in the Developing World. Jennifer A. Elliott. LC 93-17692. (Introductions to Development Ser.). 128p. (C). 1993. pap. 13.95 (0-415-06954-8) Routledge.

Sustainable Development: Changing Production Patterns, Social Equity & the Environment. 146p. 1992. 17.50 (0-685-52977-0) UN.

Sustainable Development: Citizens, Unions & the Corporations. Laurie E. Adkin. (Illus.). 250p. 1996. 48.99 (1-55164-081-3, Pub. by Black Rose Bks CN); pap. 19.99 (1-55164-080-5, Pub. by Black Rose Bks CN) Consort Bk Sales.

*__Sustainable Development: Creating Agents of Change.__ Ed. by J. DuBose & J. Vanegas. 176p. 1996. write for info. (0-939204-55-X) Eng Found.

An Asterisk (*) at the beginning of an entry indicates that the title is appearing in BIP for the first time.

Sustainable Development: Economics & Environment in the Third World. David Pearce et al. (Illus.). 232p. 1990. text ed. 80.00 (1-85278-167-X) E Elgar.

Sustainable Development: Exploring the Contradictions. Michael Redclift. 200p. (C). 1987. pap. 14.95 (0-415-05085-5); text ed. 47.50 (0-416-90240-5) Routledge Chapman & Hall.

***Sustainable Development: Implications for World Peace.** Ed. by Antonio R. Magalhaes & Sean McKaughan. (Tom Slick World Peace Ser.). 200p. 1997. pap. 20.00 (0-89940-007-8) LBJ Sch Pub Aff.

Sustainable Development: Linkages & Partnerships for the Developing World. (Illus.). 50p. (Orig.). (C). 1993. pap. text ed. 20.00 (0-7881-0027-0) DIANE Pub.

Sustainable Development: Population & the Environment: Proceedings of a Workshop on Sustainable Development in Sub-Saharan Africa. Ed. by Cynthia Green. 214p. (Orig.). 1994. pap. write for info. (0-89492-104-5) Acad Educ Dev.

Sustainable Development: Principles, Analysis & Policies. Ian Moffatt. LC 96-13441. 224p. 1996. 65.00 (1-85070-731-6) Prthnon Pub.

Sustainable Development: Science, Ethics, & Public Policy. Ed. by John Lemons & Donald A. Brown. LC 95-10769. (Environmental Science & Technology Library). 304p. (C). 1995. lib. bdg. 149.00 (0-7923-3500-7) Kluwer Ac.

Sustainable Development - the U. K. Strategy. HMSO Staff. (Command Papers: No. 2426). 267p. 1994. pap. 45.00 (0-10-124262-X, HM4262X, Pub. by Stationery Ofc UK) Bernan Associates.

Sustainable Development & Environmental Assessment: Perspectives on Planning for a Common Future. Peter Jacobs & Barry Sadler. (Illus.). 184p. (Orig.). (C). 1993. pap. text ed. 30.00 (1-56806-450-0) DIANE Pub.

Sustainable Development & Environmental Management of Small Islands. Ed. by W. Beller et al. (Man & the Biosphere Ser.: Vol. 5). (Illus.). 420p. 1990. 65.00 (1-85070-267-5) Prthnon Pub.

Sustainable Development & Good Governance. Ed. by Konrad Ginther et al. LC 94-46498. 508p. (C). 1995. lib. bdg. 175.00 (0-7923-3341-1, Pub. by M Nijhoff NE) Kluwer Ac.

Sustainable Development & International Law. Ed. by Winfried Lang. LC 95-7301. 1995. lib. bdg. 120.00 (1-85966-179-3, Pub. by Graham & Trotman UK) Kluwer Ac.

Sustainable Development & Persons with Disabilities: The Process of Self-Empowerment. Yash Tandon. Ed. by Christine Fowles. (Illus.). 128p. (Orig.). 1995. pap. write for info. (0-9650657-0-7) African Dev Fnd.

Sustainable Development & Poverty Alleviation in Sub-Saharan Africa: The Case of Botswana. Charles Perrings. (Series of ILO Studies). 1996. text ed. 65.00 (0-312-12833-9) St Martin.

***Sustainable Development & Preservation of the Oceans: The Challenges of UNCLOS & Agenda 21.** Law of the Sea Institute Staff et al. LC 97-4222. 1997. write for info. (0-911189-32-7) Law Sea Inst.

Sustainable Development & the Biosphere: Concepts & Principles. William E. Rees. (Teilhard Studies: No. 23). 1990. 3.50 (0-89012-061-7) Am Teilhard.

Sustainable Development & the Energy Industries. Ed. by Nicola Steen. 240p. (C). 1994. pap. 24.95 (1-85383-210-3) Brookings.

Sustainable Development Concepts: An Economic Analysis. John Pezzey. LC 92-35724. (Environment Paper Ser.: No. 2). 90p. 1992. 7.95 (0-8213-2278-8, 12278) World Bank.

Sustainable Development Conference Proceedings Set, 2 vols. 400p. 1994. pap. 19.00 (1-56091-559-5, P277) Soc Auto Engineers.

Sustainable Development Curriculum Framework for World History & Cultures. Ed. by Jeffrey L. Brown & Paula Gotsch. 1991. pap. 20.00 (0-614-02992-9) Amer Forum.

Sustainable Development Curriculum Framework for World History & Cultures: Lessons on the Environment Development & Equity. Jeffrey L. Brown et al. (Illus.). 300p. (Orig.). 1991. pap. 20.00 (0-928630-00-5) Global Learning.

Sustainable Development for A Democratic South Africa. Ed. by Ken Cole. LC 94-7199. 1994. text ed. 49.95 (0-312-12205-5) St Martin.

***Sustainable Development in a Developing World: Integrating Socio-Economic & Environmental Appraisal.** C. H. Kirkpatrick & Norman Lee. LC 97-22295. 1998. write for info. (1-85898-581-1) E Elgar.

***Sustainable Development in Africa: Prospects for the Twenty-First Century.** Ed. by Valentine U. James. 270p. 1997. pap. 54.95 (1-57309-187-1, Cath Scholar Pr) Intl Scholars.

***Sustainable Development in Africa: Prospects for the Twenty-First Century.** Ed. by Valentine U. James. 270p. 1997. 74.95 (1-57309-188-X, Cath Scholar Pr) Intl Scholars.

Sustainable Development in Central Asia. Ed. by Shirin Akiner et al. 240p. 1996. 75.00 (0-7007-0419-1, Pub. by Curzon Pr UK) Paul & Co Pubs.

Sustainable Development in the Lake Baikal Region: A Model Territory for the World. Ed. by Valentin A. Koptyug & Martin Uppenbrink. LC 95-44201. (NATO ASI Ser.: Partnership Sub-Series 2: Environment: Vol. 6). 372p. 1995. 196.95 (3-540-60560-6) Spr-Verlag.

Sustainable Development in the Sahel: Proceedings of the 4th Sahel Workshop, January 6 - 8, 1992. Knud Tybirk. (AAU Reports: No. 29). 132p. (C). 1992. pap. text ed. 12.95 (0-614-12694-0, Pub. by Aarhus Univ Pr DK) David Brown.

***Sustainable Development in the Southeastern Coastal Zone.** Ed. by F. John Vernberg et al. LC 97-9203. (Belle W. Baruch Library in Marine Science: No. 20). (Illus.). 535p. 1997. 65.00 (1-57003-198-3) U of SC Pr.

Sustainable Development in Third World Countries: Applied & Theoretical Perspectives. Ed. by Valentine U. James. LC 95-30661. 280p. 1996. text ed. 69.50 (0-275-95307-6, Praeger Pubs) Greenwood.

***Sustainable Development in Western Europe: Coming to Terms with Agenda 21.** Timothy O'Riordan & Heather Voisey. LC 97-17430. 1997. write for info. (0-7146-4830-2); pap. write for info. (0-7146-4376-9, Pub. by F Cass Pubs UK) Intl Spec Bk.

Sustainable Development Introduction Guide. David Reid. 1995. 20.00 (1-85383-241-3, Pub. by Erthscan Pubns UK) Island Pr.

Sustainable Development of Agriculture. Ed. by Jyoti K. Parikh. (C). 1988. lib. bdg. 180.50 (90-247-3642-0) Kluwer Ac.

Sustainable Development of Dry-Land Agriculture in India. Ed. by R. P. Singh. 536p. 1995. pap. 400.00 (0-614-09716-9, Pub. by Scientific Pubs II) St Mut.

Sustainable Development of Dryland Agriculture in India. R. P. Singh. 536p. 1994. pap. 150.00 (81-7233-092-8, Pub. by Scientific Pubs II) St Mut.

Sustainable Development of the Rural Poor. B. Pomod & N. Murari Ballal. 1992. 27.50 (81-7040-278-6, Pub. by Himalaya II) Apt Bks.

***Sustainable Development on the North Atlantic Margin: Selected Contributions to the 13th International Seminar on Marginal Regions.** Ed. by Byron et al. 300p. 1997. text ed. 63.95 (1-85972-649-6, Pub. by Ashgate UK) Ashgate Pub Co.

Sustainable Dryland Farming: Combining Farmer Innovation & Medic Pasture in a Mediterranean Climate. Lynne Chatterton & Brian Chatterton. (Illus.). 352p. (C). 1996. text ed. 90.00 (0-521-33141-2) Cambridge U Pr.

Sustainable Economy for the 21st Century. Juliet B. Schor. (Open Magazinie Pamphlet Ser.: No. 31). 28p. (Orig.). (C). 1995. pap. text ed. 4.00 (1-884519-11-3) Open Media.

Sustainable Energy: Options for New Zealand. Keith Dawber & Dai Redshaw. (Illus.). 208p. (C). 1996. pap. 24.95 (0-908569-95-5, Pub. by U Otago Pr NZ) Intl Spec Bk.

Sustainable Energy Developments in Europe & North America. (ECE Energy Ser.: No. 6). 217p. 60.00 (92-1-116499-0, E.91.II.E.2) UN.

***Sustainable Energy Strategy.** 1996. lib. bdg. 255.99 (0-8490-6354-X) Gordon Pr.

Sustainable Energy Systems: Pathways for Australian Energy Reform. Ed. by Stephen Dovers. (Illus.). 248p. (C). 1995. text ed. 59.95 (0-521-43099-2) Cambridge U Pr.

Sustainable Environmental Economics & Management: Principles & Practice. R. Kerry Turner. LC 93-10000. 320p. 1993. text ed. 49.95 (0-470-22163-1); pap. text ed. 29.95 (0-470-22164-X) Halsted Pr.

Sustainable Environmental Economics & Management: Principles & Practices. Ed. by R. Kerry Turner. LC 93-10000. 389p. 1993. pap. text ed. 55.00 (0-471-94781-4) Wiley.

Sustainable Environmental Law, 1996 Pocket Part. 1996. text ed. write for info. (0-314-20333-8) West Pub.

***Sustainable Farm Enterprises.** Jim Richardson. (RRP Ser.). (Illus.). 144p. 1996. pap. write for info. (0-7506-8939-0, 31044) Buttrwrth-Heinemann.

***Sustainable Farming.** Walsingham. (Illus.). 304p. 1997. text ed. 43.00 (0-412-72120-1, Chap & Hall NY) Chapman & Hall.

Sustainable Farming Guide Book. Douglas Gunnink. (Illus.). 85p. (Orig.). (C). 1994. pap. text ed. 30.00 (0-7881-0195-1) DIANE Pub.

***Sustainable Financing Mechanisms for Coral Reef Conservation: Proceedings of a Workshop.** Ed. by Anthony J. Hooten & Marea E. Hatziolos. (Environmentally Sustainable Development Occasional Papers: No. 9). 126p. 1995. 8.95 (0-8213-3490-5, 13490) World Bank.

Sustainable Fish Farming: Proceedings of the First International Symposium of Sustainable Fish Farming, Oslo, Norway, August 1984. Ed. by Helge Reinertsen & Herborg Haaland. (Illus.). 350p. (Orig.). (C). 1996. text ed. 99.00 (90-5410-567-4, Pub. by A A Balkema NE) Ashgate Pub Co.

Sustainable Food Production: A Manual of Sustainable Methods of Plant Production Helpful in Meeting Food Needs Everywhere. Don Sobkoviak & Lois Sobkoviak. (Food Mission Ser.). 88p. 1995. pap. 15.00 (0-9645839-0-9) SAND Inst Intl.

***Sustainable Food Security in West Africa.** Date not set. text ed. 250.00 (0-7923-9919-6) Kluwer Ac.

Sustainable Forest Management. Ian Ferguson. (Illus.). 176p. 1996. 75.00 (0-19-553604-5) OUP.

Sustainable Forestry: Philosophy, Science & Economics. Chris Maser. LC 94-5192. (Illus.). 400p. (Orig.). 1994. pap. 39.95 (1-884015-16-6) St Lucie Pr.

***Sustainable Forestry Challenges for Developing Countries.** Gerardo Mery. Ed. by Matti Palo. LC 96-27711. (Environmental Science & Technology Library). 400p. (C). 1996. lib. bdg. 144.00 (0-7923-3738-7) Kluwer Ac.

***Sustainable Forests: Global Challenges & Local Solutions.** Ed. by O. Thomas Bouman & David G. Brand. LC 95-52446. (Journal of Sustainable Forestry Ser.: Vols. 4 & 5). 392p. (C). 1996. 69.95 (1-56022-055-4, Food Products); pap. text ed. 29.95 (1-56022-058-9, Food Products) Haworth Jrnl Co-Edits.

***Sustainable Global Communities in the Information Age: Visions from Futures Studies.** Ed. by Kaoru Yamaguchi. LC 97-11602. (Praeger Studies on the 21st Century). 248p. 1997. text ed. 59.95 (0-275-96063-3, Praeger Pubs); pap. text ed. 24.95 (0-275-96062-5, Praeger Pubs) Greenwood.

***Sustainable Grand Canyon Workshop.** Nancy Clanton et al. (Illus.). 116p. (C). 1996. reprint ed. pap. 35.00 (0-7881-3476-0) DIANE Pub.

Sustainable Growth of Agriculture in India. S. K. Mishra. 135p. 1994. 50.00 (81-85880-30-1, Pub. by Print Hse II) St Mut.

Sustainable Harvest & Marketing of Rain Forest Products. Ed. by Mark J. Plotkin & Lisa Famolare. LC 91-43278. 325p. (Orig.). 1992. 40.00 (1-55963-169-4); pap. 20.00 (1-55963-168-6) Island Pr.

Sustainable Human Development & Agriculture. (Guidebook Ser.). (Illus.). (Orig.). 1994. pap. text ed. write for info. (0-9637044-5-1) PACT Pubns.

Sustainable Industrialization. David Wallace. 94p. (Orig.). 1996. pap. 15.95 (1-85383-352-5) Coun Foreign.

Sustainable International Development. Compiled by Poonam Smith-Sreen. LC 92-620873. 40p. (Orig.). 1992. pap. text ed. 4.50 (0-941872-61-0) MSU Dept Res Dev.

***Sustainable Investment & Resource Use.** J. Jeffers. (Man & the Biosphere Ser.). Orig. Title: Pastoralism in Transition. 350p. 1992. 89.00 (92-3-102748-4, U6747, Pub. by UNESCO-Bangkok TH) Bernan Associates.

Sustainable Investment & Resource Use. Ed. by M. D. Young. (Illus.). 176p. (C). 1992. text ed. 60.00 (0-85070-381-6, Pub. by CSIRO AT) Aubrey Bks.

Sustainable Investment & Resource Use: Equity, Environmental Integrity & Economic Efficiency. M. D. Young. (Man & the Biosphere Ser.: Vol. 9). (Illus.). 200p. (C). 1992. 65.00 (1-85070-381-7) Prthnon Pub.

Sustainable Land Use Planning. Ed. by Hubert N. Van Lier. LC 94-1633. 376p. 1994. 197.75 (0-444-81835-9) Elsevier.

***Sustainable Landscapes & Gardens.** Wesley A. Groesbeck & Jan Striefel. (Illus.). 1997. write for info. (0-614-28413-9) Environ Resources.

Sustainable Management of Natural Resources. T. N. Khushoo & Manju Sharma. (Indian National Science Academy Ser.). 1993. text ed. 35.00 (0-7069-5609-5, Pub. by Vikas II) S Asia.

Sustainable Management of Soils. Ed. by Rattan Lal & B. A. Stewart. (Advances in Soil Science Ser.). 576p. 1995. 79.95 (1-56670-076-0, L1076) Lewis Pubs.

***Sustainable Management of Tropical Catchments.** Ed. by David Harper & Tony Brown. text ed. 96.00 (0-471-96914-1) Wiley.

Sustainable Mobility & Least-Cost Access, Pt. 4: Low Carbon Transportation Futures in Western Europe. Florentin Krause et al. (Energy Policy in the Greenhouse: Vol. 2). 200p. (Orig.). 1993. pap. 80.00 (1-883774-07-1) IPSEP.

***Sustainable Peace: The Role of the U. N. & Regional Organizations.** Connie Peck. LC 97-26019. (Carnegie Commission on Preventing Deadly Conflict Ser.). 224p. 1997. 59.00 (0-8476-8560-8) Rowman.

***Sustainable Peace: The Role of the U. N. & Regional Organizations.** Connie Peck. LC 97-26019. (Carnegie Commission on Preventing Deadly Conflict Ser.). 224p. 1997. pap. 19.95 (0-8476-8561-6) Rowman.

Sustainable Practices for Vegetable Production in the South. Mary Peet. (Illus.). 184p. 1996. pap. text ed. 28.95 (0-941051-55-2) Focus Pub-R Pullins.

Sustainable Reconstruction of Highland & Headwater Regions: Proceedings of the 3rd International Symposium on Headwater Control, New Delhi, October 6-8, 1995. R. B. Singh & Martin J. Haigh. (Illus.). 694p. (Orig.). (C). 1996. text ed. 115.00 (90-5410-719-7, Pub. by A A Balkema NE) Ashgate Pub Co.

Sustainable Resource Development in the Third World. D. D. Southgate. 192p. 1988. pap. 140.00 (81-7089-100-0, Pub. by Intl Bk Distr II) St Mut.

***Sustainable Rural Developement.** Sheperd. Date not set. text ed. 65.00 (0-312-17763-1) St Martin.

***Sustainable Rural Development.** Ed. by Henk De Haan & Michael Redclift. (Illus.). 190p. 1997. text ed. 59.95 (1-85972-595-3, Pub. by Avebury Pub UK) Ashgate Pub Co.

Sustainable School Reform: The District Context. Lawrence W. Lezotte. Ed. by Barbara C. Jacoby. 283p. 1992. pap. 32.50 (1-883247-01-2) Effect Schls.

Sustainable Settlement & Development of the Onchocerciasis Control Programme Area: Proceedings of a Ministerial Meeting. Ed. by John Elder & Laura Cooley. LC 95-45681. (Technical Paper Ser.: No. 310). 192p. 1995. 10.95 (0-8213-3515-4) World Bank.

***Sustainable Settlement & Development of the Onchocerciasis Control Programme Area: Proceedings of a Ministerial Meeting.** John Elder & Laura Cooley. (Technical Paper Ser.: No. 310). 192p. (FRE.). 1996. 10.95 (0-8213-3538-3, 13538) World Bank.

Sustainable Settlement in the Brazilian Amazon. Anna De Almeida & Joao S. Campari. (World Bank Publication). 190p. (C). 1996. 32.95 (0-19-521104-9) OUP.

Sustainable Sewerage: Guidelines for Community Schemes. R. A. Reed. 112p. (Orig.). 1995. pap. 15.50 (1-85339-305-3, Pub. by Intermed Tech UK) Women Ink.

***Sustainable Small Schools: A Handbook for Rural Communities.** Craig B. Howley & John M. Eckman. 157p. (Orig.). 1997. pap. text ed. 15.00 (1-880785-16-1) ERIC-CRESS.

Sustainable Tourism? European Experiences. Ed. by G. K. Priestley et al. 224p. 1996. 63.00 (0-85199-100-9, Pub. by CAB Intntl UK) OUP.

Sustainable Tourism: Principles & Practice. Bernard Lane & Bill Bramwell. 256p. 1996. pap. text ed. 42.00 (0-471-95761-5) Wiley.

Sustainable Tourism in Australia. Rob Harris & Leiper. 1995. pap. 41.95 (0-7506-8919-6) Buttrwrth-Heinemann.

Sustainable Tourism in Islands & Small States: Case Studies, Vol. 2. Ed. by Lino Briguglio et al. (Island Studies). (Illus.). 352p. 1996. pap. 90.00 (1-85567-371-1, Pub. by Pntr Pubs UK) Bks Intl VA.

Sustainable Tourism in Islands & Small States: Issues & Policies, Vol. 1. Ed. by Lino Briguglio et al. (Island Studies). (Illus.). 256p. 1996. boxed, pap. 90.00 (1-85567-370-3, Pub. by Pntr Pubs UK) Bks Intl VA.

Sustainable Tourist Development. Ed. by P. Nijkamp & H. Coccossis. 224p. 1995. 55.95 (1-85972-177-X, Pub. by Avebury Pub UK) Ashgate Pub Co.

Sustainable Transport: Priorities for Policy Reform. LC 96-16621. (Development in Practice Ser.). 114p. 1996. 12.95 (0-8213-3598-7) World Bank.

Sustainable Transport in Central & Eastern European Cities. OECD ECMT Staff. 430p. (Orig.). 1996. pap. 65.00 (92-821-1211-X, Pub. by Org for Econ FR) OECD.

Sustainable Water Resources Management in Arid Countries. Ed. by Eric Schiller. (Canadian Journal of Development Studies, 1992). 226p. 1992. 40.00 (0-614-06678-6) Intl Water Resc.

Sustainable World: Defining & Measuring Sustainability. Ed. by Thaddeus C. Trzyna. LC 94-25490. 1995. 28.00 (1-880028-02-6) Cal Inst Public.

Sustained Attention in Human Performance. Ed. by Joel S. Warm. LC 83-19846. (Studies in Human Performance Ser.: No. 1-507). 368p. 1984. text ed. 150.00 (0-471-10322-5) Wiley.

Sustained Release Medications. Ed. by J. C. Johnson. LC 80-23455. (Chemical Technology Review Ser.: No. 177). (Illus.). 412p. 1981. 54.00 (0-8155-0826-3) Noyes.

Sustained Timed Writings. 4th ed. Robert L. Grubbs & James L. White. 96p. 1982. text ed. 10.96 (0-07-025063-4) McGraw.

Sustainers & Sustainability: Attitudes, Attributes, & Actions for Global Survival. Leonard W. Doob. LC 95-7982. 192p. 1995. text ed. 52.95 (0-275-95314-9, Praeger Pubs) Greenwood.

***Sustaining a World-Class Organizational Culture.** Frank Ashby. (Improving Human Performance Ser.). 1998. 39.00 (0-88415-279-0, 5279) Gulf Pub.

***Sustaining Agricultural Profitability Through Research: Challenges & Progress: Proceedings, 34th Annual Meeting of the Agricultural Research Institute, October 8-10, 1985.** 231p. pap. 25.00 (0-614-24238-X) Agri Research Inst.

***Sustaining Amazonia.** Hall. Date not set. text ed. 59.95 (0-7190-4698-X) St Martin.

Sustaining & Strengthening Stewardship. James Kelley. 48p. (Orig.). 1995. pap. 3.95 (0-8146-2326-3, Liturg Pr Bks) Liturgical Pr.

Sustaining Cities in Europe. Peter Nijkamp & Adriaan Perrels. 1994. 49.95 (1-85383-229-4, Pub. by Erthscan Pubns UK); pap. 24.95 (1-85383-203-0, Pub. by Erthscan Pubns UK) Island Pr.

Sustaining Coastal Resources: Economics & the Natural Sciences. Ed. by Charles S. Colgan. (Orig.). 1995. pap. 11.95 (0-939561-23-9) Univ South ME.

Sustaining Development in Mineral Economies: The Resource Curse Thesis. Richard M. Auty. LC 92-2484. 256p. (C). (gr. 13). 1993. text ed. 69.95 (0-415-09482-8, B0148) Routledge.

Sustaining Domestic Budget Deficits in Open Economies. Farrokh K. Langdana. 208p. (C). (gr. 13). 1990. text ed. 74.95 (0-415-03735-2, A3700) Routledge.

Sustaining Earth: Response to the Environmental Threat. Ed. by D. J. Angell et al. LC 90-9120. 200p. 1991. text ed. 55.00 (0-312-05702-4) St Martin.

Sustaining Earth: Response to the Environmental Threat. Ed. by D. J. Angell et al. 200p. 1994. text ed. 22.95 (0-312-12083-4) St Martin.

***Sustaining Economic Growth: The Positive Impact of the Michigan Incubator Industry 1985-1996.** Lawrence A. Molnar et al. 1996. pap. 29.95 (1-887183-37-X) NBIA.

Sustaining Export-Oriented Development: Ideas from East Asia. Ed. by Ross Garnaut et al. (Trade & Development Ser.). (Illus.). 272p. (C). 1995. text ed. 59.95 (0-521-48304-2) Cambridge U Pr.

Sustaining Hand: Community Leadership & Corporate Power. rev. ed. Bryan D. Jones & Lynn W. Bachelor. LC 93-12434. (Studies in Government & Public Policy). 296p. 1993. pap. 14.95 (0-7006-0599-1) U Pr of KS.

Sustaining Hand: Community Leadership & Corporate Power. 2nd rev. ed. Bryan D. Jones & Lynn W. Bachelor. LC 93-12434. (Studies in Government & Public Policy). 296p. 1993. 29.95 (0-7006-0598-3) U Pr of KS.

Sustaining High Performance: The Strategic Transformation to a Customer-Focused Learning Organization. Stephen Haines & Katie McCoy. LC 94-46633. 280p. 1995. 44.95 (1-884015-55-7) St Lucie Pr.

Sustaining Innovation As an American Competitive Advantage. Andre L. Delbecq. (Urban Studies: No. 7). 46p. (Orig.). 1989. pap. 6.00 (0-913749-09-5) U MD Urban Stud.

***Sustaining Innovation in South Gate: A Framework for Restructuring City Government.** Brent Keltner. LC 96-34471. 1996. pap. 15.00 (0-8330-2442-6, MR-804-CSG) Rand Corp.

***Sustaining Joy.** Shirley Knapp & Nanette McLane. ix, 56p. 1996. spiral bd. 14.95 (0-9656110-0-0) Northwinds Prods.

Sustaining Knock Your Socks off Service. Ron Zemke & Thomas K. Connellan. 150p. 1993. pap. 17.95 (0-8144-7824-7) AMACOM.

Sustaining Law Practice Excellence. J. Edwin Dietel. LC 92-71400. 276p. 1992. text ed. 90.00 (0-8318-0688-5, B688) Am Law Inst.

S

Sustaining Local Literacies. Ed. by David Barton. LC 93-50655. 108p. 1994. 39.95 (*1-85359-227-7*, Pub. by Multilingual Matters UK) Taylor & Francis.

Sustaining Marine Fisheries. National Research Council Staff. 100p. (C). 1997. 24.95 (*0-309-05526-1*) Natl Acad Pr.

Sustaining Our Water Resources. National Research Council, Water Science & Technology Board Staff. 128p. (Orig.). (C). 1993. pap. text ed. 25.00 (*0-309-04948-2*) Natl Acad Pr.

Sustaining Primary Health Care. Anne LaFond. LC 95-16318. 1995. text ed. 49.95 (*0-312-12732-4*) St Martin.

Sustaining Quality Advantages in Financial Services. James J. Lynch. (C). 1994. 175.00 (*0-7478-1828-2*, Pub. by Stanley Thornes UK) Trans-Atl Phila.

Sustaining Rapid Development in East Asia & the Pacific. LC 93-3075. (Development in Practice Ser.). (Illus.). 139p. 1993. 8.95 (*0-8213-2386-5*, 12386) World Bank.

Sustaining Relief with Development: Strategic Issues for the Red Cross & Red Crescent. Ian McAllister. LC 93-75. 280p. (C). 1993. Alk. paper. lib. bdg. 112.00 (*0-7923-2163-4*) Kluwer Ac.

Sustaining Safe Sex: Gay Communities Respond to AIDS. Susan Kippax et al. 228p. 1993. 75.00 (*0-7507-0133-1*, Falmer Pr); pap. 27.50 (*0-7507-0134-X*, Falmer Pr) Taylor & Francis.

Sustaining the Common Good: A Christian Perspective on the Global Economy. John B. Cobb, Jr. 128p. (Orig.). 1994. pap. 12.95 (*0-8298-1010-2*) Pilgrim OH.

Sustaining the Earth. John Young. LC 90-4856. 225p. 1990. text ed. 25.00 (*0-674-85820-4*) HUP.

Sustaining the Earth. John Young. 240p. 1992. pap. text ed. 10.95 (*0-674-85821-2*) HUP.

Sustaining the Earth: An Integrated Approach. G. Tyler Miller, Jr. 360p. 1994. pap. 28.75 (*0-534-21432-0*) Wadsworth Pub.

Sustaining the Earth: An Integrated Approach. 2nd ed. G. Tyler Miller, Jr. LC 95-18546. (Biology Ser.). 325p. (C). 1996. pap. 38.95 (*0-534-23922-6*) Wadsworth Pub.

***Sustaining the Earth: An Integrated Approach.** 3rd ed. G. Tyler Miller, Jr. LC 97-384. (Wadsworth Biology Ser.). (C). 1997. pap. text ed. 38.95 (*0-534-52884-8*) Wadsworth Pub.

Sustaining the Earth: Choosing Consumer Products That Are Safe for You, Your Family, & the Earth. Debra Dadd-Redalia. LC 93-49649. 352p. 1994. pap. 15.00 (*0-688-12335-X*) Hearst Bks.

Sustaining the Earth: Role of Multilateral Development Institutions. Patti L. Petesch & Maurice J. Williams. LC 93-5875. (Policy Essay Ser.: No. 9). 112p. (C). 1993. pap. text ed. 9.95 (*1-56517-011-3*) Overseas Dev Council.

Sustaining the Earth: The Past, Present, & Future of the Green Revolution. John Young. 225p. pap. 24.95 (*0-86840-260-5*, Pub. by New South Wales Univ Pr AT) Intl Spec Bk.

Sustaining the Future: Activities for Environmental Education in U. S. History. Ed. by Jeffrey L. Brown. 270p. (Orig.). 1995. pap. 25.00 (*0-928630-03-X*) Global Learning.

***Sustaining the Vision: A Collection of Articles & Papers on Research in School Librarianship.** Ed. by Laurel A. Clyde. 331p. 1996. 35.00 (*0-614-31081-4*) IASL.

***Sustaining the Vision: Selected Papers from the 24th Annual Conference of the International Association of School Librarianship, Worcester College of Education, Worcester, England, U. K., July 17-21, 1995.** Ed. by Donald Adcock. 180p. 25.00 (*1-890861-18-9*) IASL.

***Sustaining the Vision - School Library Imperatives for the 21st Century: Selected Papers from the 25th Annual Conference of the International Association of School Librarianship, Ocho Rios, Jamaica, July 16-August 3, 1996.** Ed. by Donald Adcock. 180p. 1997. 25.00 (*1-890861-20-0*) IASL.

Sustaining the Wings: A Fifty-Year History of Sheppard Air Force Base: 1941-1991. Gary W. Boyd et al. (Illus.). 160p. 1991. 20.00 (*0-915323-04-4*) Midwestern St U Pr.

Sustaining Total Quality. Ed. by Theresa Brothers & Elizabeth Miranda. (Report: No. 1025). 54p. (Orig.). 1993. pap. text ed. 100.00 (*0-8237-0473-4*) Conference Bd.

Sustaining Utterance: Discourses on Chasidic Thought. Adin Steinsaltz. LC 89-6939. 144p. 1996. pap. 18.00 (*1-56821-997-0*) Aronson.

Sustaining Utterance: Discourses on Chasidic Thought. Adin Steinsaltz. LC 89-6939. 144p. 1992. reprint ed. 25.00 (*0-87668-845-8*) Aronson.

***Sustenance.** Aaron Anstett. (Minnesota Voices Project Ser.: Vol. 78). (Illus.). 88p. (Orig.). 1997. pap. 12.95 (*0-89823-173-6*) New Rivers Pr.

Sustineo Alas: Keep Them Flying. Eric P. Dundatscheck. LC 93-90390. (Illus.). 275p. (Orig.). 1993. pap. 14.95 (*0-9636497-0-1*) Erisys.

Susto: A Folk Illness. Ed. by Arthur J. Rubel et al. LC 84-214. (Comparative Studies of Health Systems & Medical Care: Vol. 12). (Illus.). 170p. 1985. 45.00 (*0-520-05196-3*) U CA Pr.

Susto: A Folk Illness. Ed. by Arthur J. Rubel et al. (Comparative Studies of Health Systems & Medical Care: Vol. 12). (Illus.). 195p. 1991. reprint ed. pap. 15.00 (*0-520-07634-6*) U CA Pr.

***Susuism & Susueconomics - What Susu Is: An Economic System that Stresses Collective Savings & Independence.** unabridged ed. Paul Barton. (Orig.). 1996. pap. 12.00 (*1-56411-138-5*, 4BBG0142) Untd Bros & Sis.

Susurrus. Jane B. Gillespie. LC 87-16829. (Orig.). 1987. pap. 8.95 (*0-87233-091-5*) Bauhan.

Susy & Grand Unification from Strings to Collider Phenomenology: Proceedings of the 3rd CSIC Workshop; Madrid, Spain Jan-Feb 1985. Ed. by J. Mustrede Leon et al. 530p. 1986. text ed. 117.00 (*9971-978-62-8*) World Scientific Pub.

Susy & Mark Twain. Ed. by Edith C. Salsbury. Date not set. reprint ed. lib. bdg. 30.95 (*0-8488-1769-9*) Amereon Ltd.

Sut Lovingood Yarns. George W. Harris. (Notable American Authors Ser.). 1992. reprint ed. lib. bdg. 75.00 (*0-7812-3014-4*) Rprt Serv.

Sut Lovingood's Nat'ral Born Yarnspinner: Essays on George Washington Harris. Ed. by James E. Caron & M. Thomas Inge. (Illus.). 344p. 1996. text ed. 44.95 (*0-8173-0821-0*) U of Ala Pr.

Sut Lovingood's Yarns. George W. Harris. Ed. by M. Thomas Inge. (Masterworks of Literature Ser.). 1966. pap. 14.95 (*0-8084-0290-0*) NCUP.

Suteindo Garasu: Stained Glass. Kenneth Fenter. (American Family in Japan Ser.). (Illus.). 256p. (Orig.). 1991. pap. 10.45 (*0-930693-08-6*) Cross Cult Pr.

Sutherland Statutory Construction, 7 vols., Set. C. Sands. LC 84-22974. 1990. 575.00 (*0-685-09242-9*) Clark Boardman Callaghan.

Sutherland's Handbook for Bicycle Mechanics. 6th ed. Howard Sutherland. Ed. by Leigh Moorhouse & Mark Huie. (Illus.). 680p. 1995. 140.00 (*0-914578-09-X*) Sutherland Pubns.

Sutherland's Handbook of Coaster Brakes & Internally Geared Hubs. 3rd ed. Howard Sutherland et al. (Illus.). 122p. (Orig.). 1992. reprint ed. pap. 39.50 (*0-914578-08-1*) Sutherland Pubns.

Sutler Paper Money. Kenneth Keller. (Illus.). 256p. 1994. pap. 50.00 (*0-912317-20-5*) World Exo.

Sutliff: A History of the American & Puritanical Family of Sutliff or Sutliffe, Spelled Sutcliffe in England, & a Genealogy of All the Descendants Through Nathaniel Sutliff, Jr. S. M. Sutliff, Jr. (Illus.). 199p. 1992. reprint ed. pap. 31.00 (*0-8328-2425-9*); reprint ed. lib. bdg. 41.00 (*0-8328-2424-0*) Higginson Bk Co.

Sutpen's Design: Interpreting Faulkner's "Absalom, Absalom!" Dirk Kuyk, Jr. 192p. 1990. text ed. 30.00 (*0-8139-1260-1*) U Pr of Va.

Sutra & Other Stories. Simin Daneshvar. Tr. by Hassan Javadi & Amin Neshati from PER. LC 94-17049. 1994. 24.95 (*0-934211-42-6*) Mage Pubs Inc.

Sutra in Forty-Two Sections. Tr. by Buddhist Text Translation Society from CHI. (Illus.). 114p. (Orig.). 1977. pap. 5.00 (*0-917512-15-4*) Buddhist Text.

Sutra in Forty-Two Sections Spoken by the Buddha, Bilingual Edition: A Simple Explanation by the Venerable Master Hsuan Hua. Ed. by Buddhist Text Translation Society Staff & Buddhist Text Translation Society. 347p. 1995. 12.00 (*0-88139-184-0*) Buddhist Text.

Sutra of Golden Light. Tr. by R. E. Emmerick from SAN. (C). 1970. 22.00 (*0-86013-051-7*, Pub. by Pali Text) Wisdom MA.

***Sutra of Maitreya's Attaining Buddahood.** Tr. by Buddhist Church of Diamond Springs Staff from CHI. 110p. (Orig.). 1996. pap. text ed. write for info. (*0-614-22004-1*, Buddhist Bliss) Buddhist Ch.

***Sutra of the Merit & Virtue of the Past Vows of Medicine Master Vaidurya Light Tathagata: A Simple Explanation.** Uan H. Hs. LC 97-409. 1997. write for info. (*0-88139-306-1*) Buddhist Text.

Sutra of the Past Vows of Earth Store Bodhisattva. Tr. by Buddhist Text Translation Society Staff from CHI. LC 74-18135. (Illus.). 235p. (Orig.). 1982. 16.00 (*0-917512-09-X*) Buddhist Text.

Sutra of the Past Vows of Earth Store Bodhisattva. Tr. by Buddhist Text Translation Society Staff from CHI. LC 74-18135. (Illus.). 120p. (Orig.). 1982. pap. text ed. 7.00 (*0-88139-502-1*) Buddhist Text.

Sutra of the Past Vows of Earthstore Bodhisattva: The Collected Lectures of Tripitaka Master Hsuan Hua. Husan Hua. Tr. by Heng Ching from CHI. (IASWR Ser.). 235p. 1974. 12.75 (*0-686-47598-4*, S-10); pap. 6.75 (*0-915078-00-7*, S-11) Inst Adv Stud Wld.

Sutra on the Eight Realizations of the Great Beings. Thich Nhat Hanh. Tr. by Diem T. Truong & Carole Melkonian from VIE. 22p. 1987. pap. 3.50 (*0-938077-07-4*) Parallax Pr.

Sutra on Upasaka Precepts. Numata Center for Buddhist Translation & Research Staff. Tr. & Intro. by Bhiksuni Shih Heng-ching. LC 91-60120. (BDK English Tripitaka Ser.: Vol. 45-II). 224p. (C). 1994. text ed. 30.00 (*0-9625618-5-1*) Numata Ctr.

Sutra Spoken by Vimilakirti. Ed. by Kevin R. O'Neil. pap. 6.00 (*0-86627-009-4*) Crises Res Pr.

***Sutra Vahini (The Realization of Fatherhood of God & Brotherhood of Man)** Sai B. Sathya. Date not set. pap. 1.75 (*0-614-19045-2*, BA-314) Sathya Sai Bk Ctr.

Sutta-Nipata. Ed. by Dines Andersen & Helmer Smith. LC 78-70124. reprint ed. 34.00 (*0-404-17383-7*) AMS Pr.

Sutta-Nipata: A New Translation from the Pali Canon. Ed. & Tr. by H. Saddhatissa. 160p. (C). 1987. pap. text ed. 16.00 (*0-7007-0181-8*, Pub. by Curzon Press UK) UH Pr.

Sutta Nipata: Or Dialogues & Discourses of Gotama Buddha. Intro. by Swamy M. Coomara. LC 78-70125. 1980. reprint ed. 34.00 (*0-404-17384-5*) AMS Pr.

Sutter. Julian Dana. 1992. reprint ed. lib. bdg. 75.00 (*0-7812-5022-6*) Rprt Serv.

Sutter Buttes: A Naturalist's View. Walt Anderson. LC 82-90753. (Illus.). 326p. (Orig.). (C). 1983. pap. 16.00 (*0-9610722-1-0*) Nat Select.

Sutter Buttes of California: A Study of Plio-Pleistocene Volcanism. Howell Williams & G. H. Curtis. (UC Publications in Social Sciences: Vol. 116). 1979. reprint ed. 35.00 (*0-520-03808-8*) U CA Pr.

Sutter of California. James Dana. lib. bdg. 69.00 (*0-403-08971-9*) Scholarly.

Sutter of California: A Biography. Julian Dana. LC 74-11308. (Illus.). 423p. 1974. reprint ed. text ed. 35.00 (*0-8371-7644-1*, DASC, Greenwood Pr) Greenwood.

Sutter's Own Story. Erwin G. Gudde. 1992. reprint ed. lib. bdg. 75.00 (*0-7812-5042-0*) Rprt Serv.

Sutter's Secret, No. 172. Jon Sharpe. 176p. 1996. mass mkt. 4.99 (*0-451-18540-4*, Sig) NAL-Dutton.

Sutton Hoo: Fifty Years After. R. T. Farrell & C. Neuman de Veguar. (American Early Medieval Studies: No. II). 201p. pap. 27.00 (*0-685-66175-X*) Am Erly Medieval.

Sutton Hoo Research Committee: Bulletins 1983-1993. Ed. by Martin Carver. (Illus.). 336p. (C). 1993. 71.00 (*0-85115-341-0*, Boydell Pr) Boydell & Brewer.

Sutton Hoo Viking Ship Burial. R. Bruce-Mitford. (C). 1988. 40.00 (*0-900657-46-4*, Pub. by W Sessions UK) St Mut.

Sutton Place: Uncommon Community by the River. Christopher Gray. (Illus.). 80p. (Orig.). 1997. pap. 14.95 (*0-614-17754-5*) Sutton Area Commun.

Sutton's American Sign Language Dictionary. 2nd ed. Valerie J. Sutton. 300p. 1994. ring bd. 45.00 (*0-914336-56-8*) Ctr Sutton Movement.

***Sutton's Law. unabridged ed. Jane M. Orient & Linda J. Wright. LC 97-72143. 299p. 1997. 21.95 (*0-9641077-1-6*) Hacienda Pub.**

There's a brand new health care system at Texas University Regional Preventive Healthcare - EquaCare, an ideal marriage of medicine & economics. However, in internist Maggie Altman's opinion, it doesn't do a very good job of making sick people well. And Maggie becomes even more critical of EquaCare when the wrong patients die - people who don't have life-threatening illnesses, people like her patient Frank Post. Her quest for the truth of what happened to Post leads her into the inner workings of the new EquaCare system & ultimately to a horrifying conclusion: that someone is meddling with EquaCare at TURPH, someone whom patients are just assets or liabilities to be managed for maximum profit. She has a short list of suspects: Steven Blaine, chief resident & king of the computer printouts who roams the halls of TURPH at night; & Milton Silber, former professor of medicine who claims to have no interest in EquaCare or medicine any longer but who, nonetheless, makes clandestine visits to TURPH. Finally, when an attempt is made on her life, Maggie realizes that she's attracted the attention of someone very powerful, someone whose identity she'd better uncover before there's another death at TURPH - hers.

Publisher Provided Annotation.

Suttons Synagogue: Or the English Centurion (A Sermon) Percival Burrell. LC 74-28822. (English Experience Ser.: No. 647). 1974. reprint ed. 15.00 (*90-221-0647-0*) Walter J Johnson.

Suttree. Cormac McCarthy. 1994. 22.75 (*0-8446-6792-7*) Peter Smith.

Suttree. Cormac McCarthy. 1992. pap. 13.00 (*0-679-73632-8*, Vin) Random.

Sutureless Cataract Surgery: An Evolution Toward Minimally Invasive Technique. Ed. by Donald Sanders et al. LC 91-66239. 210p. 1991. 95.00 (*1-55642-198-2*) SLACK Inc.

Sutures. Christopher Sanford. LC 92-22249. 165p. 1993. 18.95 (*0-939149-73-7*) Soho Press.

Suum Cuique. Oscar G. Sonneck. LC 70-76916. (Essay Index Reprint Ser.). 1977. 20.95 (*0-8369-0031-6*) Ayer.

Suvarnadvipa Ancient Indian Colonies in the Far East, 2 vols., Set. R. C. Majumdar. (C). 1986. 110.00 (*81-212-0040-7*) S Asia.

Suwanee River Tales. Sherwood Bonner. LC 73-38641. (Black Heritage Library Collection). (Illus.). 1977. reprint ed. 30.95 (*0-8369-8999-6*) Ayer.

***Suwannee River: Strange Green Land.** Cecile H. Matschat. lib. bdg. 23.95 (*0-8488-2004-5*) Amereon Ltd.

Suye Mura: A Japanese Village. John F. Embree. LC 94-24004. (Michigan Classics in Japanese Studies: No. 14). xxvii, 354p. 1995. reprint ed. pap. 18.95 (*0-939512-68-8*) U MI Japan.

Suzann Says, Vol. I. Ollie. (Illus.). 48p. (Orig.). 1992. pap. 5.95 (*0-9624100-6-3*) Bell Buckle.

Suzanne. D. Belloc. 160p. (FRE.). 1990. pap. 10.95 (*0-7859-2134-6*, 2070382168) Fr & Eur.

Suzanne Ciani: Dream Songs. Suzanne Ciani. 88p. 1995. otabind 14.95 (*0-7935-4393-2*, 00306027) H Leonard.

Suzanne Ciani: New Age Piano. 112p. 1991. pap. 14.95 (*0-7935-0293-4*, 00490470) H Leonard.

Suzanne De Passe: Motown's Boss Lady. Mark Mussari. Ed. by Richard G. Young. LC 91-28541. (Wizards of Business Ser.). (Illus.). 64p. (J). (gr. 4-8). 1992. lib. bdg. 17.26 (*1-56074-026-4*) Garrett Ed Corp.

Suzanne et le Pacifique. Jean Giraudoux. pap. 9.95 (*0-685-33930-0*) Fr & Eur.

Suzanne et les Jeunes Hommes. Georges Duhamel. (Chronique Des Pasquier Ser.: Vol. IX). 374p. (FRE.). 1977. pap. 11.95 (*0-7859-1849-3*, 2070369234) Fr & Eur.

Suzanne et les Jeunes Hommes see Chronique des Pasquier

Suzanne et les Juenes Hommes see Chronique des Pasquier

Suzanne Helmuth & Jock Reynolds: Photographas & Documents, 1975-1985. Philip Brookman. (Illus.). 44p. 1986. 10.00 (*0-939982-06-4*) Sesnon Art Gall.

***Suzanne Somers' Eat Great, Lose Weight.** Suzanne Somers. 1997. 23.00 (*0-517-70861-2*) Crown Pub Group.

Suzanne Valadon. Therese D. Rosinsky. (Women Artists Ser.). 1994. pap. 14.95 (*0-87663-777-2*) Universe.

Suzanne Valadon. Jeanine Warnod. (CAL Art Ser.). (Illus.). 1985. 14.95 (*0-517-54499-7*, Crown) Crown Pub Group.

Suzanne Valadon: The Complete Work. Paul Petrides. (Illus.). 370p. (FRE.). 1971. 475.00 (*1-55660-068-2*) A Wofsy Fine Arts.

Suzanne Vega - Days of Open Hand. Ed. by Milton Okun. pap. 14.95 (*0-89524-545-0*) Cherry Lane.

Suzanne Vega - Solitude Standing. Ed. by Milton Okun. pap. 12.95 (*0-89524-345-8*) Cherry Lane.

***Suzanne Vega - 99.9.** Ed. by Carol Cuellar. 72p. (Orig.). (C). 1992. pap. text ed. 18.95 (*0-7692-0861-4*, VF1867) Warner Brothers.

Suzanne White's Guide to Love. Suzanne White. 1996. pap. 14.00 (*0-614-97669-3*) Harper SF.

Suzanne White's Guide to Love: A Unique Blend of Zodiac-Based & Chinese Astrology That Shows You How to Find Your Perfect Mate. Suzanne White. LC 95-50729. 384p. 1996. pap. 14.00 (*0-06-251297-8*) Harper SF.

Suzanne White's Original Chinese Astrology Book. Suzanne White. LC 89-51949. (Illus.). 359p. 1990. pap. 8.95 (*0-8048-1645-X*) C E Tuttle.

Suzanne's African Adventure: A Visit to Cucu's Land. Barbara S. Muchene & Munene Muchene. Ed. by Shirley L. Wagner. LC 92-75821. (Illus.). 90p. (Orig.). (J). (gr. 3-6). 1993. pap. 9.95 (*1-878398-18-0*) Blue Note Pubns.

***Suzanne's Natural Food.** Suzanne Marquardt. Date not set. pap. 7.95 (*0-88999-328-9*, Pub. by Lancelot Pr CN) BookWorld Dist.

Suzanne's 10th Birthday. Suzy Cox. 64p. (Orig.). (J). (gr. 1-6). 1995. per. 9.95 (*0-9645042-0-0*) Suzy Cox.

Suzi Castle's Deliciously Healthy Favorite Foods Cookbook: Over 250 Mouth-Watering Recipes Low-Fat, Sugar-Free & Quick & Easy. Suzi Castle. LC 95-94689. (Illus.). 132p. (Orig.). 1996. pap. 14.95 (*0-9647423-2-2*) Hlth Cookbks.

Suzi, Sam, George & Alice. Beverley Birch & Sally Gardner. (Illus.). 32p. (J). (ps-1). 1994. 17.95 (*0-370-31771-8*, Pub. by Bodley Head UK) Trafalgar.

Suzi Sinzinnati. Joe D. Bellamy. 1989. 18.95 (*0-916366-56-1*) Pushcart Pr.

Suzie. Stan T. Stanley. 424p. (Orig.). 1995. mass mkt. 6.99 (*1-896329-53-5*, Pub. by Comnwlth Pub CN) Partners Pubs Grp.

Suzie A. Alan Haig-Brown. (Illus.). 112p. (Orig.). (J). 1991. pap. 8.95 (*0-88865-068-X*, Pub. by Pacific Educ Pr CN) Orca Bk Pubs.

Suzuki. Mick Walker. (Illus.). 128p. 1993. pap. 15.95 (*1-85532-298-6*, Pub. by Osprey Pubng Ltd UK) Motorbooks Intl.

Suzuki: GS550 Fours, 1977-1986 - Service, Repair, Performance. (Illus.). pap. 25.95 (*0-89287-273-X*, M373) Clymer Pub.

Suzuki ALT/LT125 & 185: 1983-87. 3rd ed. (Illus.). 207p. (Orig.). Date not set. reprint ed. pap. 25.95 (*0-89287-523-2*, M381) Clymer Pub.

Suzuki Bass School Vol. 1: Bass Part, Vol. 1. Shinichi Suzuki. (Suzuki Method Ser.). 24p. 1991. pap. text ed. 6.95 (*0-87487-370-3*) Summy-Birchard.

Suzuki Bass School Vol. 3: Bass Part. Contrib. by Shinichi Suzuki. 32p. 1996. pap. text ed. 6.95 (*0-87487-376-2*) Summy-Birchard.

Suzuki Bass School Vol. 3: Piano Accompaniment. Contrib. by Shinichi Suzuki. 28p. 1996. pap. text ed. 6.95 (*0-87487-377-0*) Summy-Birchard.

Suzuki Bass School, Vol. 1: Piano Accompaniment. Shinichi Suzuki. (Suzuki Method Ser.). 24p. 1993. 6.95 (*0-87487-372-X*) Summy-Birchard.

Suzuki Bass School, Vol. 2: Bass Part. Shinichi Suzuki. (Suzuki Bass School Ser.). 15p. (JPN.). 1993. pap. text ed. 6.95 (*0-87487-371-1*, Suzuki Method) Summy-Birchard.

Suzuki Bass School, Vol. 2: Piano Accompaniment. Shinichi Suzuki. (Suzuki Bass School Ser.). 18p. (JPN.). 1993. pap. text ed. 6.95 (*0-87487-374-6*, Suzuki Method) Summy-Birchard.

Suzuki Cello School: Cello Part, Vol. 2. rev. ed. Shinichi Suzuki. (Suzuki Method Ser.). 20p. 1992. pap. text ed. 6.95 (*0-87487-481-5*) Summy-Birchard.

Suzuki Cello School: Cello Part, Vol. 3. rev. ed. Shinichi Suzuki. (Suzuki Method Ser.). 28p. 1992. pap. text ed. 6.95 (*0-87487-483-1*) Summy-Birchard.

Suzuki Cello School: Piano Accompaniment, Vol. 2. rev. ed. Shinichi Suzuki. (Suzuki Method Ser.). 24p. 1992. pap. text ed. 6.95 (*0-87487-482-3*) Summy-Birchard.

Suzuki Cello School: Piano Accompaniment, Vol. 3. rev. ed. Shinichi Suzuki. (Suzuki Method Ser.). 24p. 1992. pap. text ed. 6.95 (*0-87487-484-X*) Summy-Birchard.

Suzuki Cello School: Piano Accompaniment, Vol. 5. Shinichi Suzuki. (Suzuki Cello School (Suzuki Method) Ser.). 24p. (J). (gr. k-12). 1983. pap. text ed. 6.95 (*0-87487-270-7*, Suzuki Method) Summy-Birchard.

***Suzuki Cello School Vol. 9: Cello Part & Piano Accompaniment.** Shinichi Suzuki. 56p. 1996. pap. text ed. 11.95 (*0-87487-365-7*) Summy-Birchard.

***Suzuki Cello School Vol. 10: Cello Part & Piano Accompaniment.** Shinichi Suzuki. 64p. 1996. pap. text ed. 11.95 (*0-87487-366-5*) Summy-Birchard.

Suzuki Cello School, Cello Part, Vol. 1. rev. ed. Shinichi Suzuki. (Suzuki Method Ser.). 24p. 1991. pap. text ed. 6.95 (*0-87487-479-3*) Summy-Birchard.

Suzuki Cello School, Cello Part, Vol. 8. Shinichi Suzuki. 16p. 1991. pap. text ed. 6.95 (*0-87487-361-4*) Summy-Birchard.

Suzuki Cello School, Cello Part, Vol. 7. Shinichi Suzuki. (Suzuki Cello School Ser.). 24p. (J). (gr. k-12). 1987. pap. text ed. 6.95 (*0-87487-360-6*, Suzuki Method) Summy-Birchard.

Suzuki Cello School, Piano Accompaniment, Vol. 1. rev. ed. Shinichi Suzuki. (Suzuki Method Ser.). 24p. 1982. pap. text ed. 6.95 (*0-87487-480-7*) Summy-Birchard.

Suzuki Cello School, Piano Accompaniment, Vol. 8. Shinichi Suzuki. 25p. 1991. pap. text ed. 7.50 (*0-87487-363-0*) Summy-Birchard.

Suzuki Cello School, Vol. 4: Cello Part. Shinichi Suzuki. (Suzuki Cello School (Suzuki Method) Ser.). 16p. (J). (gr. k-12). 1983. pap. text ed. 6.50 (*0-87487-266-9*, Suzuki Method) Summy-Birchard.

Suzuki Cello School, Vol. 4: Piano Accompaniment. Shinichi Suzuki. (Suzuki Cello School (Suzuki Method) Ser.). 24p. (J). (gr. k-12). 1983. pap. text ed. 6.95 (*0-87487-269-3*, Suzuki Method) Summy-Birchard.

Suzuki Cello School, Vol. 5: Cello Part. Shinichi Suzuki. (Suzuki Cello School (Suzuki Method) Ser.). 24p. (J). (gr. k-12). 1983. pap. text ed. 6.50 (*0-87487-267-7*, Suzuki Method) Summy-Birchard.

Suzuki Cello School, Vol 6: Cello Part. Shinichi Suzuki. 16p. (J). (gr. k-12). 1984. pap. text ed. 6.50 (*0-87487-268-5*, Suzuki Method) Summy-Birchard.

Suzuki Cello School, Vol. 6: Piano Accompaniments. Shinichi Suzuki. (Suzuki Cello School (Suzuki Method) Ser.). 24p. (Orig.). (J). (gr. 6-12). 1984. pap. text ed. 6.95 (*0-87487-271-5*, Suzuki Method) Summy-Birchard.

Suzuki Cello School, Vol. 7: Piano Accompaniments. Shinichi Suzuki. (Suzuki Cello School Ser.). 32p. (J). (gr. k-12). 1987. pap. text ed. 6.95 (*0-87487-362-2*, Suzuki Method) Summy-Birchard.

Suzuki Changed My Life. Maasaki Honda. (Illus.). 320p. 1976. pap. text ed. 16.95 (*0-87487-084-4*, Suzuki Method) Summy-Birchard.

Suzuki Concept: An Introduction to a Successful Method for Early Music Education. Ed. by Elizabeth Mills & Therese Murphy. (Illus.). 220p. 1973. 9.95 (*0-87297-002-7*) Diablo.

Suzuki Concept: An Introduction to a Successful Method for Early Music Education. Ed. by Elizabeth Mills & Therese Murphy. (Illus.). 220p. 1973. pap. 7.95 (*0-87297-003-5*) Diablo.

***Suzuki DR250-350, 1990-1994.** (Illus.). Date not set. reprint ed. pap. 25.95 (*0-89287-602-6*, M476) Intertec Pub.

Suzuki Flute School: Piano Accompaniments, Vol. 2. Shinichi Suzuki. 16p. (Orig.). (gr. k-6). 1971. pap. text ed. 6.95 (*0-87487-168-9*, Suzuki Method) Summy-Birchard.

Suzuki Flute School, Flute Part, Vol. 2. Shinichi Suzuki. 15p. 1971. 6.50 (*0-87487-167-0*) Summy-Birchard.

Suzuki Flute School, Flute Part, Vol. 6. Shinichi Suzuki. 16p. 1988. 6.50 (*0-87487-381-9*) Summy-Birchard.

Suzuki Flute School, Flute Part, Vol. 7. Shinichi Suzuki. 16p. 1988. 6.50 (*0-87487-383-5*) Summy-Birchard.

Suzuki Flute School, Piano Accomp, Vol. 6. Shinichi Suzuki. 31p. 1988. 6.95 (*0-87487-382-7*) Summy-Birchard.

Suzuki Flute School, Piano Accomp, Vol. 7. Shinichi Suzuki. 26p. 1988. 6.95 (*0-87487-384-3*) Summy-Birchard.

Suzuki Flute School, Vol. 1: Flute Part. Shinichi Suzuki. 24p. (gr. k-6). 1971. pap. text ed. 6.95 (*0-87487-165-4*) Summy-Birchard.

Suzuki Flute School, Vol. 1: Piano Accompaniments. Shinichi Suzuki. 24p. (Orig.). 1971. pap. text ed. 6.95 (*0-87487-166-2*, Suzuki Method) Summy-Birchard.

Suzuki Flute School, Vol. 10: Flute Part. Shinichi Suzuki. (Suzuki Flute School Ser.). 20p. (JPN.). 1993. pap. text ed. 6.95 (*0-87487-695-8*) Summy-Birchard.

Suzuki Flute School, Vol. 10: Piano Accompaniment. Shinichi Suzuki. (Suzuki Flute School Ser.). 32p. (JPN.). 1993. pap. text ed. 8.95 (*0-87487-696-6*) Summy-Birchard.

Suzuki Flute School, Vol. 11: Flute Part. Shinichi Suzuki. (Suzuki Flute School Ser.). 24p. (JPN.). 1993. pap. text ed. 6.95 (*0-87487-697-4*) Summy-Birchard.

Suzuki Flute School, Vol. 11: Piano Accompaniment. Shinichi Suzuki. (Suzuki Flute School Ser.). 48p. (JPN.). 1993. pap. text ed. 8.95 (*0-87487-698-2*) Summy-Birchard.

Suzuki Flute School, Vol. 3: Flute Part. Shinichi Suzuki. 16p. (Orig.). (gr. k-8). 1971. pap. text ed. 6.95 (*0-87487-169-7*, Suzuki Method) Summy-Birchard.

Suzuki Flute School, Vol. 3: Piano Accompaniments. Shinichi Suzuki. 32p. (Orig.). 1971. pap. text ed. 6.95 (*0-87487-170-0*, Suzuki Method) Summy-Birchard.

Suzuki Flute School, Vol. 4: Flute Part. Shinichi Suzuki. 16p. (Orig.). (gr. k-8). 1971. pap. text ed. 6.50 (*0-87487-171-9*, Suzuki Method) Summy-Birchard.

Suzuki Flute School, Vol. 4: Piano Accompaniments. Shinichi Suzuki. 24p. (Orig.). 1971. pap. text ed. 6.95 (*0-87487-172-7*, Suzuki Method) Summy-Birchard.

Suzuki Flute School, Vol. 5: Flute Part. Shinichi Suzuki. 24p. (gr. 6-12). 1971. pap. text ed. 6.95 (*0-87487-173-5*, Suzuki Method) Summy-Birchard.

Suzuki Flute School, Vol. 5: Piano Accompaniments. Shinichi Suzuki. 32p. (Orig.). 1971. pap. text ed. 6.95 (*0-87487-174-3*, Suzuki Method) Summy-Birchard.

Suzuki Flute School, Vol. 8: Flute Part. Shinichi Suzuki. (Suzuki Flute School Ser.). 20p. (JPN.). 1993. pap. text ed. 6.95 (*0-87487-691-5*) Summy-Birchard.

Suzuki Flute School, Vol. 8: Piano Accompaniment. Shinichi Suzuki. (Suzuki Flute School Ser.). 48p. (JPN.). 1993. pap. text ed. 8.95 (*0-87487-692-3*) Summy-Birchard.

Suzuki Flute School, Vol. 9: Flute Part. Shinichi Suzuki. (Suzuki Flute School Ser.). 16p. (JPN.). 1993. pap. text ed. 6.95 (*0-87487-693-1*) Summy-Birchard.

Suzuki Flute School, Vol. 9: Piano Accompaniment. Shinichi Suzuki. (Suzuki Flute School Ser.). 40p. (JPN.). 1993. pap. text ed. 8.95 (*0-87487-694-X*) Summy-Birchard.

***Suzuki GSR750, 1988-1992 GSX750F Katana, 1989-1994.** abr. ed. (Illus.). Date not set. pap. 25.95 (*0-89287-627-1*, M478) Intertec Pub.

***Suzuki GSX R750.** Gary Pinchin. (Illus.). 200p. 1997. 35.95 (*1-86126-082-2*, Pub. by Crowood UK) Motorbooks Intl.

Suzuki GS1100 Chain Drive, 1980-1981: 1980-1981 (Service, Repair, Performance) David Sales. (Illus.). (Orig.). Date not set. reprint ed. pap. 25.95 (*0-89287-353-1*, M378) Intertec Pub.

Suzuki GS400-450 Twins, 1977-1987 Chain Drive: GS400-450 Twins 1977-1987 Service, Repair, Performance. (Illus.). Date not set. reprint ed. pap. 25.95 (*0-89287-237-3*, M372) Intertec Pub.

***Suzuki GS500 Twins, 1989-1996.** LC 96-79022. (Illus.). (Orig.). 1996. pap. 25.95 (*0-89287-671-9*, M484) Intertec Pub.

***Suzuki GS550, 1977-1986.** 7th ed. (Illus.). Date not set. reprint ed. pap. 25.95 (*0-89287-664-6*, M373) Intertec Pub.

Suzuki GS650, 1981-1983: Service Repair Performance. 2nd ed. (Illus.). 326p. Date not set. reprint ed. pap. 25.95 (*0-89287-367-1*, M364) Intertec Pub.

Suzuki GS750 Fours, 1977-82: Service, Repair, Performance. (Illus.). pap. 25.95 (*0-89287-189-X*, M370) Clymer Pub.

***Suzuki GS750, 1977-1982.** 5th ed. (Illus.). Date not set. reprint ed. pap. 25.95 (*0-89287-667-0*, M370) Intertec Pub.

Suzuki GS850-1100 Shaft Drive, 1979-1984: Service, Repair, Maintenance. 3rd ed. (Illus.). (Orig.). Date not set. reprint ed. pap. 25.95 (*0-89287-305-1*, M376) Intertec Pub.

Suzuki Guitar School: Piano Accompaniment, Vol. 1. Shinichi Suzuki. (Suzuki Method Ser.). 31p. 1991. pap. text ed. 6.95 (*0-87487-389-4*) Summy-Birchard.

Suzuki Guitar School, Guitar Part, Vol. 1. Shinichi Suzuki. 24p. 1991. pap. text ed. 6.95 (*0-87487-388-6*) Summy-Birchard.

Suzuki Harp Ensemble Music. Barbara Meixner. 29p. 1994. pap. text ed. 6.95 (*0-87487-753-9*) Summy-Birchard.

Suzuki Harp School, Vol. 2. Mary K. Waddington. 24p. 1995. pap. text ed. 6.95 (*0-87487-291-X*) Summy-Birchard.

Suzuki Harp School, Vol. 1. Mary K. Waddington. Ed. by Shinichi Suzuki. (Suzuki Harp Method Ser.). 32p. (Orig.). 1985. pap. text ed. 6.95 (*0-87487-290-1*, Suzuki Method) Summy-Birchard.

Suzuki Images. Arthur Montzka & Craig Timmerman. LC 88-62934. 64p. (Orig.). 1988. pap. text ed. 19.95 (*0-9621416-0-7*) Shar Prods.

Suzuki in the String Class: An Adaptation of the Teachings of Shinichi Suzuki. Paul Zahtilla. LC 70-178376. 193p. reprint ed. teacher ed., pap. 55.10 (*0-317-26425-7*, 2024981) Bks Demand.

Suzuki Katana 600, 1988-1993 GSX-R750-1100, 1986-1987. 2nd ed. (Illus.). Date not set. reprint ed. pap. 25.95 (*0-89287-590-9*, M383) Intertec Pub.

***Suzuki King Quad/Quad Runner 250, 1987-1995.** LC 94-79864. (Illus.). (Orig.). 1995. pap. 25.95 (*0-89287-643-3*, M483) Intertec Pub.

Suzuki LS650 Savage Single, 1986-1988: LS650 Savage Single, 1986-1988. (Illus.). Date not set. reprint ed. pap. 25.95 (*0-89287-517-8*, M384) Intertec Pub.

Suzuki LT230 & LT250, 1985-1990: Service, Repair, Maintenance. 2nd ed. (Illus.). (Orig.). Date not set. reprint ed. pap. 25.95 (*0-89287-608-5*, M475) Clymer Pub.

Suzuki Parent's Diary. Carroll Morris. 88p. 1984. pap. text ed. 10.95 (*0-87487-590-0*) Summy-Birchard.

Suzuki Pianist's List of Supplementary Materials. Beverly T. Fest. 32p. 1991. pap. text ed. 6.95 (*0-87487-591-9*) Summy-Birchard.

Suzuki Piano Ensemble Music Vol. 1: 1 Piano, 4 Hands. Barbara Meixner. 22p. 1995. pap. text ed. 6.95 (*0-87487-749-0*) Summy-Birchard.

Suzuki Piano Ensemble Music Vol. 1: 2 Pianos, 4 Hands. Barbara Meixner. 25p. 1995. pap. text ed. 6.95 (*0-87487-750-4*) Summy-Birchard.

Suzuki Piano Ensemble Music Vol. 2: 2 Pianos, 4 Hands. Barbara Meixner. 32p. 1995. pap. text ed. 6.95 (*0-87487-751-2*) Summy-Birchard.

Suzuki Piano Ensemble Music Vols. 3-4: 2 Pianos, 4 Hands. Barbara Meixner. 30p. 1995. pap. text ed. 6.95 (*0-87487-752-0*) Summy-Birchard.

Suzuki Piano School. rev. ed. Shinichi Suzuki. (Suzuki Piano School Ser.). 32p. (J). (ps-3). 1996. pap. text ed. 6.95 (*0-87487-473-4*, Suzuki Method) Summy-Birchard.

Suzuki Piano School, Vol. 2. rev. ed. Shinichi Suzuki. 24p. 1995. pap. text ed. 6.95 (*0-87487-474-2*) Summy-Birchard.

Suzuki Piano School, Vol. 3. Shinichi Suzuki. (Suzuki Piano School Ser.). 32p. (FRE, GER, JPN & SPA.). (gr. k-12). 1970. pap. text ed. 6.95 (*0-87487-162-X*, Suzuki Method) Summy-Birchard.

Suzuki Piano School, Vol. 4. Shinichi Suzuki. (Suzuki Piano School Ser.). 32p. (FRE, GER, JPN & SPA.). (gr. 3-12). 1978. pap. text ed. 6.95 (*0-87487-163-8*, Suzuki Method) Summy-Birchard.

Suzuki Piano School, Vol. 5. Shinichi Suzuki. (Suzuki Piano School Ser.). 48p. (JPN.). (gr. 4-12). 1973. pap. text ed. 6.95 (*0-87487-442-4*, Suzuki Method) Summy-Birchard.

Suzuki Piano School, Vol. 6. Shinichi Suzuki. (Suzuki Piano School Ser.). 48p. (JPN.). (gr. 4-12). 1973. pap. text ed. 6.95 (*0-87487-443-2*, Suzuki Method) Summy-Birchard.

Suzuki Piano School, Vol. 7. rev. ed. Shinichi Suzuki. (Suzuki Method Ser.). 31p. 1992. reprint ed. 6.95 (*0-87487-444-0*) Summy-Birchard.

Suzuki Quad Racer, 1985-1988. (Illus.). Date not set. reprint ed. pap. 25.95 (*0-89287-446-5*, M380) Clymer Pub.

Suzuki Repertory Group Lessons for Violin & Viola. Carolyn M. Meyer. 84p. 1993. pap. text ed. 12.95 (*0-87487-435-1*) Summy-Birchard.

Suzuki RM 125-500 Single Shock: 1981-1988 Service, Repair, Performance. (Illus.). 242p. 1985. pap. 25.95 (*0-89287-385-X*, M379) Clymer Pub.

***Suzuki RM125-500 Single Shock, 1981-1988.** 2nd ed. (Illus.). Date not set. reprint ed. pap. 25.95 (*0-89287-666-2*, M379) Intertec Pub.

Suzuki RM50-400 Twin Shock, 1975-1981: Service, Repair, Performance. 3rd ed. (Illus.). Date not set. reprint ed. pap. 25.95 (*0-89287-196-2*, M371) Intertec Pub.

***Suzuki RM80-250, 1989-1995.** (Illus.). (Orig.). 1996. pap. 25.95 (*0-89287-658-1*, M386) Intertec Pub.

Suzuki Viola School, Vol. A. Ed. by Doris Preucil & Shinichi Suzuki. (Piano Accompaniment Ser.). 64p. (J). (gr. k-12). 1982. pap. text ed. 10.95 (*0-87487-245-6*, Suzuki Method) Summy-Birchard.

Suzuki Viola School: Piano Accompaniments, Vol. 3. Doris Preucil. Ed. by Shinichi Suzuki. 32p. (J). (gr. k-12). 1983. pap. text ed. 6.95 (*0-87487-246-4*, Suzuki Method) Summy-Birchard.

Suzuki Viola School: Piano Accompaniments, Vol. 4. Shinichi Suzuki. Ed. by Doris Preucil. 64p. (J). (gr. k-12). 1983. pap. text ed. 10.95 (*0-87487-275-8*, Suzuki Method) Summy-Birchard.

Suzuki Viola School: Viola Part, Vol. 3. Shinichi Suzuki. Ed. by Doris Preucil. (Suzuki Viola School Ser.). 24p. (J). (gr. k-12). 1983. pap. text ed. 6.95 (*0-87487-243-X*, Suzuki Method) Summy-Birchard.

Suzuki Viola School: Viola Part, Vol. 4. Shinichi Suzuki. Ed. by Doris Preucil. (Suzuki Viola School Ser.). 32p. (J). (gr. k-12). 1983. pap. text ed. 6.95 (*0-87487-244-8*, Suzuki Method) Summy-Birchard.

Suzuki Viola School, Piano Accompaniments, Vol. 5. Shinichi Suzuki. (Suzuki Viola School Ser.). 52p. (J). (gr. k-12). 1986. pap. text ed. 8.95 (*0-87487-250-2*, Suzuki Method) Summy-Birchard.

Suzuki Viola School, Viola Part, Vol. 1. Doris Preucil. Ed. by Shinichi Suzuki. (Suzuki Viola School Ser.). 32p. (J). (gr. k-12). 1981. pap. text ed. 6.95 (*0-87487-241-3*) Summy-Birchard.

Suzuki Viola School, Viola Part, Vol. 2. Doris Preucil. Ed. by Shinichi Suzuki. (Suzuki Viola School Ser.). 32p. (J). (gr. k-12). 1982. pap. text ed. 6.95 (*0-87487-242-1*) Summy-Birchard.

Suzuki Viola School, Viola Part, Vol. 5. Shinichi Suzuki. Ed. by Doris Preucil. (Suzuki Cello School Ser.). 32p. 1986. pap. text ed. 6.95 (*0-87487-249-9*) Summy-Birchard.

Suzuki Viola School, Vol. 6: Piano Accompaniment. Shinichi Suzuki. (Suzuki Viola School Ser.). 40p. (JPN.). 1993. pap. text ed. 10.95 (*0-87487-492-0*) Summy-Birchard.

Suzuki Viola School, Vol. 6: Viola Part. Shinichi Suzuki. (Suzuki Viola School Ser.). 32p. (JPN.). 1993. pap. text ed. 8.50 (*0-87487-491-2*) Summy-Birchard.

Suzuki Violin Method in American Music Education. rev. ed. John Kendall. 40p. 1985. pap. text ed. 5.95 (*0-87487-280-4*, Suzuki Method) Summy-Birchard.

***Suzuki Violin Method in American Music Education.** John D. Kendall. LC 72-96899. 32p. 1978. reprint ed. pap. 25.00 (*0-608-04209-9*, 2064946) Bks Demand.

Suzuki Violin School: Piano Accompaniments, Vol. 5. 39p. (FRE, GER, JPN & SPA.). 1971. pap. text ed. 7.50 (*0-87487-153-0*) Summy-Birchard.

Suzuki Violin School, Piano Accompaniments, Vol. 1. Shinichi Suzuki. 24p. 1978. pap. text ed. 6.95 (*0-87487-145-X*, Suzuki Method) Summy-Birchard.

Suzuki Violin School, Piano Accompaniments, Vol. 2. Shinichi Suzuki. 32p. (FRE, GER, JPN & SPA.). 1970. pap. text ed. 6.95 (*0-87487-147-6*, Suzuki Method) Summy-Birchard.

Suzuki Violin School, Piano Accompaniments, Vol. 3. Shinichi Suzuki. 32p. (FRE, GER, JPN & SPA.). 1970. pap. text ed. 6.95 (*0-87487-149-2*, Suzuki Method) Summy-Birchard.

Suzuki Violin School, Piano Accompaniments, Vol. 4. Shinichi Suzuki. 32p. (FRE, GER, JPN & SPA.). 1970. pap. text ed. 6.95 (*0-87487-151-4*, Suzuki Method) Summy-Birchard.

Suzuki Violin School, Piano Accompaniments, Vol. B. Shinichi Suzuki. (Suzuki Violin School Ser.). 192p. (JPN.). 1980. pap. text ed. 24.95 (*0-87487-228-6*) Summy-Birchard.

Suzuki Violin School, Violin Part, Vol. 1. Shinichi Suzuki. 32p. 1978. pap. text ed. 6.95 (*0-87487-144-1*) Summy-Birchard.

Suzuki Violin School, Violin Part, Vol. 2. Shinichi Suzuki. 24p. 1978. pap. text ed. 6.95 (*0-87487-146-8*) Summy-Birchard.

Suzuki Violin School, Violin Part, Vol. 3. Shinichi Suzuki. 24p. 1978. pap. text ed. 6.95 (*0-87487-148-4*) Summy-Birchard.

Suzuki Violin School, Violin Part, Vol. 4. Shinichi Suzuki. 24p. 1978. 6.95 (*0-87487-150-6*) Summy-Birchard.

Suzuki Violin School, Violin Part, Vol. 5. Shinichi Suzuki. 24p. 1978. 6.95 (*0-87487-152-2*) Summy-Birchard.

Suzuki Violin School, Violin Part, Vol. 6. Shinichi Suzuki. (Suzuki Violin School Ser.). 24p. (FRE, GER, JPN & SPA.). (gr. 5-12). 1978. pap. text ed. 6.95 (*0-87487-154-9*) Summy-Birchard.

Suzuki Violin School, Violin Part, Vol. 7. Shinichi Suzuki. (Suzuki Violin School Ser.). 24p. (FRE, GER, JPN & SPA.). (gr. 6-12). 1978. pap. text ed. 6.95 (*0-87487-156-5*) Summy-Birchard.

Suzuki Violin School, Violin Part, Vol. 8. Shinichi Suzuki. (Suzuki Violin School Ser.). 24p. (FRE, GER, JPN & SPA.). (gr. 6-12). 1978. pap. text ed. 6.95 (*0-87487-158-1*) Summy-Birchard.

Suzuki Violin School, Violin Part, Vol. 9. Shinichi Suzuki. (Suzuki Violin School Ser.). 48p. (JPN.). (gr. 6-12). 1975. pap. text ed. 8.50 (*0-87487-225-1*) Summy-Birchard.

Suzuki Violin School, Violin Part, Vol. 10. Shinichi Suzuki. (Suzuki Violin School Ser.). 48p. (JPN.). (gr. 6-12). 1976. pap. text ed. 8.50 (*0-87487-226-X*) Summy-Birchard.

Suzuki Violinist. William Starr. 142p. 1976. pap. text ed. 16.95 (*0-87487-605-2*) Summy-Birchard.

Suzuki Vitara - The Enthusiast's Companion. Nigel Fryatt. (Illus.). 112p. 1995. 24.95 (*0-947981-93-4*, Pub. by Motor Racing UK) Motorbooks Intl.

***Suzuki VS700-800 Intruder, 1985-1994.** (Illus.). (Orig.). 1995. pap. 25.95 (*0-89287-629-8*, M481) Intertec Pub.

Suzuki 125-400cc, 1964-1981: 125-400cc Singles, 1964-1981 Service, Repair, Performance. 5th ed. (Illus.). Date not set. reprint ed. pap. 25.95 (*0-89287-280-2*, M369) Intertec Pub.

Suzuki 2-140 hp Outboards, 1977-1984: 2-140 HP 1977-1984. (Illus.). 368p. (Orig.). Date not set. reprint ed. pap. 34.95 (*0-89287-406-6*, B780) Intertec Pub.

Suzuki 2-225 hp Outboards, 85-91. 1991. 32.95 (*0-89287-556-9*, B-781) Intertec Pub.

Suzuki 380-750cc, 1972-1977: 380-750cc Triples, 1972-1977 Service, Repair, Maintenance. 4th ed. Clymer Publications Staff. (Illus.). Date not set. reprint ed. pap. 25.95 (*0-89287-285-3*, M368) Intertec Pub.

Suzy & the Mouse King. Jan Wahl. (Illus.). 78p. (J). 1992. lib. bdg. 12.95 (*0-940696-34-7*) Monroe County Lib.

***Suzy, Fair Suzy.** large type ed. Lawrence Lazuli. (Illus.). 32p. (Orig.). (J). (gr. k-4). 1997. pap. 7.95 (*1-882521-05-6*) Stones Pt Pr.

Suzy Frelinghuysen & George L. K. Morris: American Abstract Artists Aspects of Their Work & Collection. Debra B. Balken & Deborah M. Rothschild. LC 92-50485. (Illus.). 64p. (Orig.). 1993. pap. 18.95 (*0-913697-14-1*) U of Pa Pr.

Suzy Lake: Points of Reference. Martha Hanna. 48p. 1993. pap. text ed. 10.95 (*0-88884-564-2*, Pub. by CN Mus Contemporary Photo CN) U Ch Pr.

Suzy McKee Charnas, Octavia Butler, Joan Vinge. Marleen S. Barr et al. Ed. by Roger C. Schlobin. LC 85-2715. (Starmont Reader's Guide Ser.: Vol. 23). (Orig.). 1986. pap. 21.00 (*0-916732-91-6*); lib. bdg. 31.00 (*0-916732-92-4*) Borgo Pr.

***Suzy Mule.** Barbara DeRubertis. LC 96-53889. (Illus.). 32p. (Orig.). (J). (ps-2). 1997. pap. 4.95 (*1-57565-026-6*); pap. 7.95 incl. audio (*1-57565-036-3*) Kane Pr.

Suzy Prudden's Exercise Program for Young Children. Suzy Prudden. LC 82-40506. (Illus.). 192p. 1983. pap. 6.95 (*0-89480-371-9*, 371) Workman Pub.

Suzy Q: Restoring A '63 Corvette Sting Ray. Ed. by Cars & Parts Magazine Staff. (Illus.). 258p. 1996. pap. text ed. 12.95 (*1-880524-19-8*) Cars & Parts.

Suzy's Secret Snoop Society. Mary Anderson. (J). (gr. 3-7). 1991. pap. 2.95 (*0-380-75917-9*, Camelot) Avon.

SU(3) X SU(2) X U(1) & Beyond: Proceedings of the XIIIth GIFT International Seminar on Theoretical Physics & Xth Winter Meeting on Fundamentals Physics Masella, Girona, Spain, Jan. 28-Feb. 6, 1982. Ed. by A. Ferrando et al. 516p. 1983. 98.00 (*9971-950-79-0*) World Scientific Pub.

Svaha. Charles DeLint. 320p. 1994. reprint ed. pap. 4.50 (*0-8125-3409-3*) Tor Bks.

Svahilsko-Cesky-Svahilsky Kapesni Slovnik: Swahili-Czech-Swahili. Kropacek. 578p. (CZE & SWA.). 1980. 19.95 (*0-8288-1700-6*, M14012) Fr & Eur.

Svalbard: Land Beyond the North Cape. Olle Carlsson & Stefan Lundgren. 64p. 1994. 15.95 (*0-9641652-0-1*) Spec Expedit.

Svalbard Treaty: From Terra Nullius to Norwegian Sovereignty. Geir Ulfstein. 440p. 1995. 99.00 (*82-00-22713-8*) Scandnvan Univ Pr.

***Svalikhita Jivani: The Autobiography of Srila Bhaktivinda Thakur.** Kedarnatha Dutta & Shukavak Das. 180p. 1994. pap. 25.00 (*1-889756-29-6*) Sanskrit Relgns Inst.

Svan-English Dictionary. Chato Gudjedjiani & Letas Palmaitis. LC 85-4089. (Anatolian & Caucasian Studies). 1985. 55.00 (*0-88206-062-7*) Caravan Bks.

Svarfdale Saga: And Other Tales. Tr. by W. Bryant Bachman, Jr. & Guomundur Erlingsson from ICE. LC 94-4900. 142p. (Orig.). 1994. lib. bdg. 29.00 (*0-8191-9513-8*) U Pr of Amer.

Svayamvara & Other Poems. Jayanta Mahapatra. (Redbird Ser.). 1976. 6.75 (*0-89253-558-X*); 4.00 (*0-89253-091-X*) Ind-US Inc.

SVD & Signal Processing, Two: Algorithms, Analysis & Applications. R. Vaccaro. 512p. 1991. 96.50 (*0-444-88896-9*) Elsevier.

SVD & Signaling Processing III: Algorithms, Architectures, & Applications. Ed. by Marc Moonen & Bart De Moor. LC 95-3193. 498p. 1995. 210.50 (*0-444-82107-4*) Elsevier.

Svedectvo a Evanjelizacia. Vladimir Uhri. 36p. (Orig.). (SLO.). 1996. pap. 1.75 (*1-56983-035-5*) New Creat WI.

Svend Borberg's Sinner & Saint - Synder OG Helgen 1939. Tr. by Rosco N. Tolman from DAN. LC 91-29117. 140p. 1991. 69.95 (*0-7734-9918-0*) E Mellen.

Svendsen Essent Oils Aromatic. 1985. lib. bdg. 90.00 (*90-247-3195-X*, Pub. by M Nijhoff NE) Kluwer Ac.

Svengali's Secrets & Memoirs of the Golden Age. J. H. Duval. 5.95 (*0-8315-0014-X*) Speller.

S

An Asterisk (*) at the beginning of an entry indicates that the title is appearing in BIP for the first time.

S

Svensk-Dansk Ordbog: Swedish-Danish Dictionary. V. Palmgen & E. Hartmann. 251p. (DAN & SWE.). 1978. 39.95 (0-8288-5273-1, M1287) Fr & Eur.
Svensk Ordbok (Swedish Dictionary) S. Allen. 1513p. (SWE.). 1986. 195.00 (0-8288-2071-6, F60690) Fr & Eur.
Svensk-Turkish Ordbok. 4th ed. M. Guner. 173p. (TUR.). 1981. 95.00 (0-8288-1647-6, F 14821) Fr & Eur.
***Sverdlovsk Oblast: Economy, Industry, Government, Business.** 2nd rev. ed. Russian Information & Business Center, Inc. Staff. (Russian Regional Business Directories Ser.). (Illus.). 200p. 1997. pap. 99.00 (1-57751-427-0) Russ Info & Busn Ctr.
***Sverre Fehn: Works & Projects, 1949-1996.** Gennaro Postiglione. (Illus.). 320p. 1997. 75.00 (1-885254-64-4) Monacelli Pr.
Sveshnikov Sicilian. Mikhail Krasenkov. 1996. pap. 21.95 (1-85744-123-0, Pub. by Cadogan Books UK) Macmillan.
Svet V Labirintakh (Light in Labyrinths) Literary Scetches. Alexander Viazmensky. LC 90-45052. (Illus.). 97p. (Orig.). (RUS.). 1990. pap. 4.00 (0-916201-08-2) M I P Co.
Svetasvatara Upanisad. Tr. by Swami Tyagisananda. (ENG & SAN.). pap. 2.95 (0-87481-418-9) Vedanta Pr.
Svetasvatara Upanisad, 2 pts. in 1. Varma S. Siddhesvar. LC 73-3810. (Sacred Books of the Hindus: Vol. 18, Pt. 2). reprint ed. 18.00 (0-404-57840-3) AMS Pr.
Svetlana Beriosova: A Biography. A. H. Franks. (Series in Dance). 1978. reprint ed. 25.00 (0-306-79537-X) Da Capo.
Svetliaki: Ironicheskaia Metafizika. Igor Efimov, pseud. LC 91-11620. 120p. (Orig.). (RUS.). 1991. pap. 8.00 (1-55779-041-8) Hermitage.
Svidetelstvo Obvineniya, Vol. I, 1987. Vladimir Stepanov. (Illus.). 350p. 20.00 (0-9616413-2-0) Multilingual.
Svidetelstvo Obvineniya, Vol. II, 1987. Vladimir Stepanov. 279p. 15.00 (0-9616413-3-9) Multilingual.
Svidetelstvo Obvineniya, Vol. III, 1988. Vladimir Stepanov. 275p. 15.00 (0-9616413-4-7) Multilingual.
Svjatejshij Tikhon, Patrijarkh Moskovskij i Vseja Rossij. 80p. 1965. pap. 3.00 (0-317-29216-1) Holy Trinity.
Svjatoj Ioann (Pommer) Arkiepiskop Rihskij i Latvijskij. Lugmilla Koehler. (Illus.). 72p. 1985. pap. 3.00 (0-317-29224-2) Holy Trinity.
Svjelij Otrok: Sbornik Statej o Tsarevichje Mutchenikje Alekseje i drugikh Tsarstvennikh Mutchenikakh. (Illus.). 105p. reprint ed. pap. 5.00 (0-317-29229-3) Holy Trinity.
Svoboda: A Select Index, 4 vols., Set. Compiled by Walter A. Anastazievsky et al. LC 89-82654. (Orig.). 1994. pap. 85.00 (0-685-67718-4) Immig His Res.
Svoboda: A Select Index, 4 vols., Vol. 1: 1893-1899. Compiled by Walter A. Anastazievsky et al. LC 89-82654. xix, 406p. (Orig.). 1990. pap. 25.00 (0-932833-10-1) Immig His Res.
Svoboda: A Select Index, 4 vols., Vol. 2: 1900-1907. Compiled by Walter A. Anastazievsky et al. LC 89-82654. xlvi, 410p. (Orig.). 1991. pap. 25.00 (0-932833-11-X) Immig His Res.
Svoboda: A Select Index, 4 vols., Vol. 3: January 1908-July 1914. Compiled by Walter A. Anastazievsky et al. LC 89-82654. xlv, 407p. (Orig.). 1993. pap. 25.00 (0-932833-17-9) Immig His Res.
Svoboda - A Select Index, Vol. 4: August 1914 to December 1918. Ed. by Walter A. Anastazievsky. LC 89-82654. xlv, 394p. (Orig.). (C). 1994. pap. text ed. 25.00 (0-932833-14-4) Immig His Res.
***Svoe Vremia - One's Own Time.** Valery Chershnia. LC 96-8479. 106p. (Orig.). (RUS.). 1996. pap. 9.00 (1-55779-079-5) Hermitage.
SVR4 Multiprocessor for Intel Installation Guide. AT&T Staff & Unix System Laboratories Staff. 1992. pap. text ed. 17.00 (0-13-879487-1) P-H.
SVR4 Multiprocessor for Intel Program Supplement. AT&T Staff & Unix System Laboratories Staff. 1992. pap. text ed. 18.00 (0-13-879453-7) P-H.
SVR4 Multiprocessor for Intel System Administrative Supplement. AT&T Staff & Unix System Laboratories Staff. 1992. pap. text ed. 67.00 (0-13-879438-3) P-H.
SV40 Chromosome Model for Studies of Anticancer Drugs That Disrupt Mammalian DNA Replication. Robert M. Snapka. (Molecular Biology Intelligence Unit Ser.). 192p. 1996. 89.00 (0-412-10521-7) R G Landes.
***SV40 Replicon Model for Analysis of Anticancer Drugs.** Robert M. Snapka. (Biotechnology Intelligence Unit Ser.). 1996. 69.95 (0-12-653630-9) Acad Pr.
Swadeshi: The Quest for Self-Reliance. Marilyn Turkovich & Julian C. Hollick. (Passages to India Ser.). (C). 1989. spiral bd. 20.00 (1-56709-020-6) Indep Broadcast.
Swadeshi Bank from South India: A History of the Indian Bank 1907-1982. R. K. Seshadri. (Illus.). 249p. 1982. text ed. 27.50 (0-86131-341-0, Pub. by Orient Longman Ltd II) Apt Bks.
Swag. Elmore Leonard. 240p. 1984. mass mkt. 5.99 (0-440-18424-X) Dell.
Swagger Religionists: The Great Unrest. Marie Corelli. 10p. 1971. reprint ed. spiral bd. 5.00 (0-7873-0220-1) Hlth Research.
Swaggering Soldier see Pot of Gold & Other Plays
Swags Etc. Cy DeCosse Incorporated Staff. LC 96-26996. (Creative Touches Ser.). 64p. 1996. pap. 9.95 (0-86573-876-9) Cowles Creative.
Swagtown. L. S. Riker. 1992. mass mkt. 3.99 (0-312-92694-4) St Martin.
Swahili: A Foundation for Speaking, Reading & Writing. Thomas J. Hinnebusch & Sarah M. Mirza. LC 78-65430. (Illus.). 296p. 1978. Bilingual ed. pap. 22.50 (0-8191-0659-3) U Pr of Amer.
Swahili: Conversation & Grammar. 2nd ed. John Indakwa. LC 72-84022. 520p. reprint ed. pap. 148.20 (0-317-26821-X, 2024309) Bks Demand.
Swahili: Idiom & Identity of an African People. Alamin M. Mazrui & Ibrahim N. Shariff. LC 93-9903. 1994. 45.95 (0-86543-310-0); pap. 14.95 (0-86543-311-9) Africa World.
Swahili: Reconstructing the History & Language of An African Society, 800-1500. Thomas G. Spear. LC 84-3659. (Ethnohistory Ser.). (Illus.). 160p. 1985. pap. text ed. 18.95 (0-8122-1207-X) U of Pa Pr.
***Swahili - English Mini-Books Set with Audio, 11 bks.** Claudia Schwalm. (Illus.). (ENG & SWA.). (J). (gr. k-6). 1997. pap. 21.95 incl. audio (0-614-24743-8) Cultural Cnnect.
Swahili & Sabaki: A Linguistic History. Derek Nurse & Thomas J. Hinnebusch. LC 93-4560. (Problems in Linguistics Ser.: Vol. 121). 1993. 85.00 (0-520-09775-0) U CA Pr.
Swahili Basic Course. Foreign Service Institute Staff. 560p. (SWA.). 1980. pap. text ed. 225.00 incl. audio (0-88432-041-3, AFW426) Audio-Forum.
Swahili Cassette Pack. Berlitz Editors. (Cassette Pack Ser.). (Illus.). 192p. 1995. 16.95 incl. audio (2-8315-1391-X) Berlitz.
Swahili Chronicle of Ngazija. Said B. Ahmed. Ed. by Lyndon Harries. (African Humanities Ser.). (Illus.). 136p. (Orig.). 1977. pap. text ed. 10.00 (0-941934-20-9) Indiana Africa.
Swahili Coast, 2nd to 19th Centuries: Islam, Christianity & Commerce in Eastern Africa. G. S. Freeman-Grenville. (Collected Studies: No. CS275). (Illus.). 284p. (C). 1988. reprint ed. lib. bdg. 89.95 (0-86078-223-9, Pub. by Variorum UK) Ashgate Pub Co.
***Swahili Complete Course, 2 cass.** 2nd ed. D. V. Perrott. (Teach Yourself Ser.). 320p. pap. 24.95 incl. audio (0-8442-3835-X) NTC Pub Grp.
Swahili Dictionary. D. V. Perrott. 184p. (ENG & SWA.). 1995. pap. 14.95 (0-8442-3838-4, Teach Yourslf) NTC Pub Grp.
Swahili-English Dictionary. F. Johnson. 42.50 (0-87557-079-8) Saphrograph.
Swahili English Dictionary. G. Madan. 442p. (ENG & SWA.). 1992. 59.95 (0-8288-8458-7) Fr & Eur.
Swahili-English Dictionary. Charles W. Rechenbach & Angelica W. Gesuga. LC 67-31438. 653p. reprint ed. pap. 180.00 (0-318-39759-5, 2033133) Bks Demand.
Swahili-English, English-Swahili Practical Dictionary. Nicholas Awde. 465p. (Orig.). (ENG & SWA.). 1998. pap. 16.95 (0-7818-0480-9) Hippocrene Bks.
Swahili-French Dictionary: Dictionnaire Swahili-Francais. A. Lenselaer. 646p. (FRE & SWA.). 1983. 175.00 (0-8288-1100-8, F60950) Fr & Eur.
Swahili Language: A Descriptive Language. E. N. Myachina. (Languages of Asia & Africa Ser.). 96p. (Orig.). (C). 1981. pap. 19.95 (0-7100-0849-X, RKP) Routledge.
Swahili Origins: Swahili Culture & the Shungwaya Phenomenon. James De Vere Allen. Ed. by John Middleton. LC 92-14316. (Eastern African Studies). 416p. (C). 1993. text ed. 39.95 (0-8214-1030-X); pap. text ed. 19.95 (0-8214-1044-X) Ohio U Pr.
Swahili Phrase Book. Berlitz Editors. LC 73-20999. (Phrase Bk.). 192p. 1995. pap. 6.95 (2-8315-0938-6) Berlitz.
Swahili Phrasebook. Robert Leonard. 104p. (Orig.). 1988. pap. 2.95 (0-86442-025-0) Lonely Planet.
Swahili-Russian-Swahili Dictionary. A. Kutuzov. 696p. (RUS & SWA.). 1987. 24.95 (0-8288-0799-X, M9119) Fr & Eur.
Swahili-Speaking Peoples of Zanzibar & the East African Coast: Arabs, Shirazi & Swahili. Adriann H. Prins. LC 68-5550. (Ethnographic Survey of Africa: East Central Africa Ser.: Pt. 12). 157p. reprint ed. pap. 44.80 (0-8357-6965-8, 2039025) Bks Demand.
Swahili Syntax. Anthony J. Vitale. 260p. 1981. 83.10 (90-70176-38-6); pap. 57.70 (90-70176-25-4) Mouton.
Swahili Tales. Edward Steere. LC 78-63225. (Folktale Ser.). reprint ed. 38.00 (0-404-16164-2) AMS Pr.
***Swahili/English Mini-Books Set with Audio, 11 bks.** Claudia Schwalm. (Illus.). (Orig.). (ENG & SWA.). (J). (ps-7). 1997. pap. write for info. incl. audio (0-614-24473-0) Cultural Cnnect.
SWALCAP: A Guide for Librarians & Systems Managers. Jane Gosling. 129p. 1987. 49.95 (0-566-03539-1, Pub. by Gower UK) Ashgate Pub Co.
Swale: A History of the Holy River of St. Paulinus. David Morris. 1995. pap. 45.00 (1-85072-152-1, Pub. by W Sessions UK) St Mut.
Swallow. Sabrina Crewe. LC 96-4832. (Life Cycles Bks.). (J). 1996. lib. bdg. 21.40 (0-8172-4373-9) Raintree Steck-V.
Swallow: Genealogy of the Swallow Family, 1666-1910. Baker, North & Ellis Staff. (Illus.). 217p. 1992. reprint ed. pap. 34.50 (0-8328-2202-7); reprint ed. lib. bdg. 44.50 (0-8328-2201-9) Higginson Bk Co.
Swallow: Life Cycles: A Circular Pop-up Book. David Hawcock. LC 94-73276. (Life Cycles Ser.). (Illus.). 12p. (J). (ps-3). 1995. 6.95 (0-7868-0101-8) Hyprn Child.
Swallow Barn: or A Sojourn in the Old Dominion. John P. Kennedy. (BCL1-PS American Literature Ser.). 422p. 1992. reprint ed. lib. bdg. 99.00 (0-7812-6776-5) Rprt Serv.
Swallow Barn: or A Sojourn in the Old Dominion. Novel. John P. Kennedy. LC 85-23215. (Library of Southern Civilization). xxix, 506p. 1986. pap. text ed. 19.95 (0-8071-1322-0) La State U Pr.
Swallow-Book. Ernst Toller. LC 74-7005. (Studies in German Literature: No. 13). 1974. lib. bdg. 75.00 (0-8383-1902-5) M S G Haskell Hse.
Swallow Island. Julia Ferrari. (Illus.). 28p. 1981. 85.00 (0-939622-14-9) Four Zoas Night Ltd.
Swallow Right-or Else! Daniel Garliner. LC 78-75294. 108p. 1979. 7.65 (0-87527-195-2) Green.
Swallow Shelter & Associated Sites. Gardiner F. Dalley. (Anthropological Papers: No. 96). (Illus.). 1978. pap. 17.50 (0-87480-143-5) U of Utah Pr.
Swallowdale. Arthur Ransome. LC 84-48802. (Illus.). 448p. 1985. pap. 11.95 (0-87923-572-1) Godine.
Swallowdale. Arthur Ransome. 1995. reprint ed. lib. bdg. 24.95 (1-56849-673-7) Buccaneer Bks.
***Swallowed by a Snake: The Gift of the Masculine Side of Healing.** Thomas R. Golden. 136p. 1997. pap. 13.95 (0-9654649-0-3) Golden Healing.
Swallowing Disorders Treatment Manual. Edward Hardy & Natalie M. Robinson. Ed. by Cindy Drolet & C. Gilles-Brown. (Illus.). 154p. (Orig.). 1993. pap. text ed. 41.00 (1-883315-05-0) Imaginart Pr.
Swallowing Dust. Robert J. Stout. 1976. pap. 1.50 (0-88031-033-2) Invisible-Red Hill.
Swallowing Paradise. Teresa Ferenc. Ed. by Richard Seehuus & Richard Jackson. Tr. by Lusia Slomkowska from POL. 16p. (Orig.). 1992. pap. 4.00 (1-881489-02-7) Poetry Miscellany.
***Swallowing Stones.** Joyce McDonald. LC 97-1402. (J). 1997. write for info. (0-385-32309-3) Delacorte.
Swallowing the Anchor. William McFee. LC 70-128275. (Essay Index Reprint Ser.). 1977. 21.95 (0-8369-1986-6) Ayer.
Swallowing the Scroll: Late in a Prophetic Tradition with Poetry of Susan Howe & John Taggart. Lew Daly. 1994. pap. 5.00 (1-879645-08-4) Garlic MA.
Swallows & Amazons. Arthur Ransome. LC 84-48803. 352p. 1985. pap. 11.95 (0-87923-573-X) Godine.
Swallows & Amazons. Arthur Ransome. 1995. reprint ed. lib. bdg. 24.95 (1-56849-672-9) Buccaneer Bks.
Swallows in the Birdhouse. Stephen Swinburne. (Illus.). 32p. (J). (gr. k-3). 1996. lib. bdg. 16.40 (1-56294-182-8) Millbrook Pr.
Swallow's Nest: A Feminine Reading of the Psalms. Marchiene V. Reinstra. 1992. pap. 18.95 (0-377-00248-8) Friendship Pr.
Swallowtail Butterflies: An Action Plan for Their Conservation. Tim R. New & N. M. Collins. (Illus.). 40p. 1991. pap. 16.00 (2-8317-0061-2, Pub. by IUCN SZ) Island Pr.
Swallowtail Butterflies of East Africa. R. H. Carcasson. 1984. 30.00 (0-317-07177-7) St Mut.
Swallowtail Butterflies of the Americas: A Study in Biological Dynamics, Ecological Diversity, Biosystematics, & Conservation. Hamilton A. Tyler et al. (Illus.). 376p. (Orig.). 1994. 49.50 (0-945417-90-X); student ed., pap. 24.50 (0-945417-91-8) Sci Pubs.
Swallowtail Butterflies of the Americas: A Study in Biological Dynamics, Ecological Diversity, Biosystematics, & Conservation. deluxe ed. Hamilton A. Tyler et al. (Illus.). 376p. (Orig.). 1994. 150.00 (0-945417-92-6) Sci Pubs.
Swami: Encounters with Modern Mystics. Doug Boyd. 330p. 1995. pap. 15.95 (0-89389-142-8) Himalayan Inst.
Swami Adbhutananda: Teachings & Reminiscences. Swami Chetanananda. LC 80-50962. (Illus.). 175p. 1980. pap. 6.95 (0-916356-59-0) Vedanta Soc St Louis.
Swami Akhandananda. Swami Annadananda. Tr. by N. C. Bhattachavya from BEN. 304p. 1994. pap. 6.95 (81-85301-04-2, Pub. by Advaita Ashrama II) Vedanta Pr.
Swami & Friends. R. K. Narayan. LC 80-16119. 192p. 1980. pap. 10.95 (0-226-56831-8) U Ch Pr.
Swami Chinmayananda: Journey of a Master: The Man, the Path, the Teaching. Nancy Patchen. 335p. 1989. pap. 15.00 (1-880687-17-8) Chinmaya Pubns.
Swami Dayanand Sarswati. Krishna S. Arya. 355p. 1987. 23.00 (81-85054-22-3, Pub. by Manohar II) S Asia.
Swami Dayananda Saraswati: His Biography & Teachings. Lala L. Rai. Ed. by S. K. Bhatia. iv, 104p. 1991. text ed. 22.50 (81-85047-76-6, Pub. by Reliance Pub Hse II) Apt Bks.
Swami on Rye: Max in India. Maira Kalman. LC 95-9749. (Illus.). 40p. (J). (gr. 3 up). 1995. pap. 16.00 (0-670-85646-0, Viking) Viking Penguin.
Swami Ramakrishnananda: The Apostle the South. Tapasyananda. 276p. 1973. pap. 4.95 (0-87481-453-7, Pub. by Ramakrishna Math II) Vedanta Pr.
Swami Sahajanand & the Peasants of Jharkhand: A View from 1941. Ed. by Walter Hauser. (C). 1995. text ed. 40.00 (81-7304-108-3, Pub. by Manohar II) S Asia.
***Swami Trigunatita: His Life & Work.** Sister Gargi, pseud. (Illus.). 434p. (Orig.). 1997. pap. write for info. (0-9612388-3-6) Vedanta Soc N Cal.
Swami Vijnanananda: A Short Life & Spiritual Discourses. Compiled by Apurvananda. 173p. 1987. pap. 3.50 (0-87481-547-9, Pub. by Ramakrishna Math II) Vedanta Pr.
Swami Vijnanananda: His Life & Sayings. Swami Vishwashrayananda. Tr. by Devavrata Basu Ray from BEN. 72p. 1981. pap. 1.95 (0-87481-502-9, Pub. by Advaita Ashrama II) Vedanta Pr.
Swami Vivekananda. K. R. Iyengar. 81p. 1988. pap. 4.50 (0-910261-14-8, Pub. by Samata Bks II) Lotus Light.
***Swami Vivekananda: A Reassessment.** P. Sil Narasingha. LC 96-29425. (Illus.). 256p. 1997. 41.50 (0-945636-97-0) Susquehanna U Pr.
Swami Vivekananda: Selected Speeches & Writings. Ed. by Bimal Prasad. (Orig.). (C). 1994. 12.00 (0-7069-7552-9, Pub. by Vikas II) S Asia.
Swami Vivekananda: The Educator. V. Sukumaran Nair. 1987. text ed. 11.95 (81-207-0610-2, Pub. by Sterling Pubs II) Apt Bks.
Swami Vivekananda & the Indian Quest for Socialism. Arun K. Biswas. 300p. 35.00 (0-8364-1949-9, KL Mukhopadhyay) S Asia.
***Swami Vivekananda in San Francisco.** 2nd ed. Ashokananda. 72p. (Orig.). 1990. pap. 3.95 (0-9612388-2-8) Vedanta Soc N Cal.
Swami Vivekananda in the West: New Discoveries, Vol. II. Marie L. Burke. (Illus.). 457p. 1985. 8.95 (0-87481-219-4, Pub. by Advaita Ashrama II) Vedanta Pr.
Swami Vivekananda in the West: New Discoveries: His Prophetic Mission, Vol. 1. Marie L. Burke. (Illus.). 515p. text ed. 9.95 (0-87481-218-6, Pub. by Advaita Ashrama II) Vedanta Pr.
Swami Vivekananda in the West: New Discoveries the World Teacher, Pt. III. Marie L. Burke. (Illus.). 639p. 1987. 8.95 (0-87481-220-8, Pub. by Advaita Ashrama II) Vedanta Pr.
Swami Vivekananda in the West Vol. IV, Pt. 2: New Discoveries: The World Teacher. Marie L. Burke. (Illus.). 640p. 1988. 8.95 (0-87481-221-6, Pub. by Advaita Ashrama II) Vedanta Pr.
Swami Vivekananda in the West Vol. 5: New Discoveries: A New Gospel. (Illus.). 455p. 1988. 8.95 (0-87481-222-4, Pub. by Advaita Ashrama II) Vedanta Pr.
Swami Vivekananda in the West Vol. 6, Pt. 2: New Discoveries: A New Gospel. Marie L. Burke. (Illus.). 461p. 1988. 8.95 (0-87481-223-2, Pub. by Advaita Ashrama II) Vedanta Pr.
Swami Vivekananda's Contribution to the Present Age. Swami Satprakashananda. LC 77-91628. (Illus.). 249p. 1978. 9.50 (0-916356-58-2) Vedanta Soc St Louis.
Swamiji & His Message. 2.50 (0-614-17336-1) Vedanta Pr.
***Swamp.** Donald Silver. (Illus.). 48p. (J). (gr. 1-4). 1997. pap. text ed. 10.95 (0-07-057926-1) McGraw.
Swamp Angel. Anne Isaacs. LC 93-43956. (Illus.). 40p. (J). (ps-4). 1994. pap. 15.99 (0-525-45271-0) Dutton Child Bks.
Swamp Angel. Anne Isaacs. 1998. pap. 5.99 (0-14-055908-6) Viking Penguin.
***Swamp Angel.** Ethel Wilson. 1996. pap. text ed. 6.95 (0-7710-8958-9) McCland & Stewart.
***Swamp Angel.** large type ed. Ethel Wilson. 1997. pap. 21.95 (1-55041-314-7, Pub. by Fitzhenry & Whiteside CN) Iowa St U Pr.
Swamp Candles. Ralph Burns. LC 95-50367. (Iowa Poetry Prize, 1995 Ser.). 78p. (Orig.). 1996. pap. 10.95 (0-87745-539-2) U of Iowa Pr.
***Swamp Cats.** Jeffrey Love. 176p. (Orig.). 1996. pap. 11.95 (0-9653524-0-4) Russn Hill Pr.
Swamp Fire. Patricia Potter. 1995. mass mkt. 4.99 (1-55166-078-4, 1-66078-6, Mira Bks) Harlequin Bks.
Swamp Fox. Robert D. Bass. LC 59-5368. (Illus.). 1982. pap. 11.95 (0-87844-051-8) Sandlapper Pub Co.
Swamp Furies. Anne Schraff. Ed. by Liz Parker. (Take Ten Bks.). (Illus.). 45p. (Orig.). (J). (gr. 6-12). 1992. pap. text ed. 3.95 (1-56254-056-4) Saddleback Pubns.
Swamp Gravy: Folk Tales of South Georgia. Debra C. Jones et al. 336p. 1994. 16.95 (0-9643054-0-2); pap. 12.95 (0-9643054-1-0) Colquitt-Miller Arts Coun.
Swamp Life. Theresa Greenaway. LC 92-53489. (Look Closer Ser.). (Illus.). 32p. (J). (gr. 1-4). 1993. 9.95 (1-56458-211-6) DK Pub Inc.
Swamp Man. rev. ed. Donald Goines. 224p. (Orig.). 1995. mass mkt. 4.95 (0-87067-962-7, BH962-7) Holloway.
Swamp Monster. Rick Detorie. (Magic Answer Bks.). (J). 1989. pap. 1.95 (0-8125-7315-3) Tor Bks.
Swamp Monsters. Mary B. Christian. LC 82-1574. (Easy-to-Read Bks.). (Illus.). 56p. (J). (ps-3). 1983. pap. 4.95 (0-8037-7614-4) Dial Bks Young.
Swamp Monsters. Houghton Mifflin Company Staff. (Literature Experience 1993 Ser.). (J). (gr. 2). 1992. pap. 8.48 (0-395-61772-3) HM.
Swamp Monsters Level 3, Yellow. Mary B. Christian. LC 82-1574. (Easy-to-Read Ser.). (Illus.). (J). (gr. 1-4). 1994. pap. 3.50 (0-14-036841-8, Puffin) Puffin Bks.
Swamp of the Hideous Zombies. Geoffrey Hayes. LC 96-883. (J). 1996. pap. 3.99 (0-679-87696-0) Random.
Swamp of the Hideous Zombies. Geoffrey Hayes. (Graveyard Creeper Ser.: No. 1). (J). 1996. lib. bdg. 11.99 (0-679-97696-5) Random.
Swamp Pop: Cajun & Creole Rhythm & Blues. Shane K. Bernard. (American Made Music Ser.). (Illus.). 232p. (C). 1996. 50.00 (0-87805-875-3); cd-rom 16.00 (0-87805-896-6) U Pr of Miss.
Swamp Robber. Paul Hutchens. (Sugar Creek Gang Ser.: Vol. 1). (J). (gr. 2-7). 1966. mass mkt., pap. 3.99 (0-8024-4801-1) Moody.
***Swamp Robber.** Paul Hutchens. (Sugar Creek Gang Ser.: No. 1). 128p. (J). 1997. mass mkt. 4.99 (0-8024-7005-X) Moody.
Swamp Sailors: Riverine Warfare in the Everglades, 1835-1842. George E. Buker. LC 74-186326. (Illus.). 152p. 1975. 16.95 (0-8130-0352-0) U Press Fla.
***Swamp Sailors in the Second Seminole War.** George E. Buker. LC 96-36994. (Florida Sand Dollar Bks.). (Illus.). 148p. 1997. reprint ed. pap. 16.95 (0-8130-1514-6) U Press Fla.
***Swamp Screamer: At Large with the Florida Panther.** Charles Fergus. 1997. pap. text ed. 12.00 (0-86547-514-8, North Pt Pr) FS&G.
Swamp Screamers: At Large with the Florida Panther. Charles Fergus. LC 95-6752. 224p. 1996. 25.00 (0-86547-491-5, North Pt Pr) FS&G.
Swamp Secrets. Carla Cassidy. 1993. mass mkt. 3.50 (0-373-27004-6, 5-27004-6) Silhouette.
Swamp Song: A Natural History of Florida's Swamps. Ron Larson. LC 95-9806. (Illus.). 231p. 1995. pap. 19.95 (0-8130-1355-0) U Press Fla.
Swamp Stomp. Stickland Henrie. 1996. pap. 19.95 (0-385-25619-1) Doubleday.
Swamp Thing. Mayer. (Illus.). 32p. (J). (ps-3). 1995. pap. text ed. 3.50 (0-307-16660-0, Golden Books) Western Pub.

An Asterisk (*) at the beginning of an entry indicates that the title is appearing in BIP for the first time.

Swamp Thing Love & Death. Ed. by KC Carlson. 208p. 1990. pap. 19.95 (*0-930289-54-4*, Vertigo) DC Comics.
Swamp Thing Love & Death. Alan Moore. 1990. pap. 17.95 (*0-446-39192-1*) Warner Bks.
Swamp to Sugar Bowl: Pioneer Days in Belle Glade. Lawrence E. Will. (Illus.). 240p. 1984. pap. 5.00 (*0-614-12725-4*) Great Outdoors.
Swamp Water. Vereen Bell. LC 80-24570. (Brown Thrasher Bks.). 282p. 1981. reprint ed. pap. 14.95 (*0-8203-0546-4*) U of Ga Pr.
Swamp Water & Wiregrass: Historical Sketches of Coastal Georgia. George A. Rogers & R. Frank Saunders. LC 84-701. x, 254p. 1984. 19.95 (*0-86554-099-3*, MUP/H091) Mercer Univ Pr.
Swamp Yankee. E. Otis Dyer. LC 94-92172. (Illus.). 240p. (Orig.). 1994. pap. 18.00 (*0-88492-052-6*) W S Sullwold.
Swamped! Nathan Aaseng. LC 95-10388. (Grubstake Adventures Ser.). 80p. (J). 1995. pap. 5.99 (*0-8066-2788-3*, Augsburg) Augsburg Fortress.
***Swampland.** Brian E. Ableman. (Habitats Ser.). 1997. 23.00 (*0-516-20743-1*) Childrens.
***Swamplands of the Soul: New Life in Dismal Places.** James Hollis. (Studies in Jungian Psychology by Jungian Analysts: No. 73). 35p. 1996. pap. 16.00 (*0-919123-74-0*, Pub. by Inner City CN) BookWorld Dist.
Swamps. Sheila Gore. LC 91-45081. (Our Planet Ser.). (Illus.). 32p. (J). (gr. 4-6). 1993. lib. bdg. 12.95 (*0-8167-2755-4*) Troll Communs.
Swamps. Sheila Gore. LC 91-45081. (Our Planet Ser.). (Illus.). 32p. (J). (gr. 4-6). 1997. pap. 4.95 (*0-8167-2756-2*) Troll Communs.
Swamps & Marshes. Chris Arvetis & Carole Palmer. LC 93-33675. (Where Are We? Ser.). (Illus.). (J). (gr. 4 up). 1994. 3.95 (*0-528-83676-5*) Rand McNally.
Swamps & Marshes. Francene Sabin. LC 84-2717. (Illus.). 32p. (J). (gr. 3-6). 1985. pap. text ed. 3.50 (*0-8167-0281-0*) Troll Communs.
***Swamps of Sleethe.** Jack Prelutsky. (J). Date not set. write for info. (*0-688-07778-1*); lib. bdg. write for info. (*0-688-07779-X*) Greenwillow.
***Swampscott, MA.** Ken Turino. (Images of America Ser.). pap. 16.99 (*0-7524-0521-7*, Arcdia) Chalford.
Swan. Naomi Campbell. 357p. 1994. pap. 20.00 (*0-434-00097-3*, Reed Trade) Buttrwrth-Heinemann.
Swan. Naomi Campbell. 1996. mass mkt. 5.99 (*0-7493-2208-X*, Reed Trade) Buttrwrth-Heinemann.
Swan. Elizabeth Egloff. 1994. pap. 5.25 (*0-8222-1383-4*) Dramatists Play.
Swan. Virginia Mayo. (Illus.). 32p. (J). (ps-3). 1994. 12.95 (*0-8120-6408-9*); pap. 5.95 (*0-8120-1938-5*) Barron.
Swan. Vivian A. Phillips. (Illus.). 20p. (Orig.). (J). Date not set. pap. text ed. write for info. (*1-888413-02-6*) Seasoning Quilting.
Swan: A Storybook for Adults & Other Children. Jerri Curry. (Illus.). 21p. (YA). (gr. 7 up). 1988. 13.95 incl. audio (*0-944586-00-7*) WIN Pub.
Swan - The Second Voyage. Jim Moore. (Illus.). 250p. 1994. 22.95 (*0-924486-45-7*) Sheridan.
Swan Among the Indians: Life of James Swan, 1818-1900. Lucile McDonald. LC 72-85230. (Illus.). 280p. 1972. 14.95 (*0-8323-0066-7*) Binford Mort.
Swan & Shadow: Yeats' Dialogue with History. Thomas R. Whitaker. LC 89-9861. (Critical Studies in Irish Literature: Vol. 1). 340p. 1989. pap. 14.95 (*0-8132-0680-4*) Cath U Pr.
Swan at the Well: Shakespeare Reading Chaucer. E. Talbot Donaldson. LC 84-21913. 192p. 1985. text ed. 32.00 (*0-300-03349-4*) Yale U Pr.
Swan Boats at Four. large type ed. George V. Higgins. 432p. 1996. pap. 21.95 (*0-7862-0632-2*, Thorndike Lrg Prnt) Thorndike Pr.
Swan Bride. Betina Lindsey. Ed. by Caroline Tolley. 288p. (Orig.). 1990. mass mkt. 5.50 (*0-671-68914-2*) PB.
Swan Dive. Jeremiah Healy. 1991. mass mkt. 4.50 (*0-671-74329-5*) PB.
Swan Flyway: The Tundra Swan. Dana Limpert. LC 92-42381. (Smithsonian Wild Heritage Collection). (Illus.). 32p. (J). (gr. k-3). 1993. 11.95 (*0-924483-95-4*); 16.95 incl. audio (*0-924483-96-2*); audio write for info. (*0-924483-99-7*) Soundprints.
Swan Flyway: The Tundra Swan. Dana Limpert. (Smithsonian Wild Heritage Collection). (Illus.). 32p. (J). (gr. k-3). 1995. pap. 4.95 (*1-56899-138-X*) Soundprints.
Swan Flyway: The Tundra Swan, Incl. toy. Dana Limpert. LC 92-42381. (Smithsonian Wild Heritage Collection). (Illus.). 32p. (J). (gr. k-3). 1993. 25.95 incl. audio (*0-924483-97-0*) Soundprints.
Swan Flyway: The Tundra Swan Including 8" Stuffed Toy, Incl. toy. Dana Limpert. (Smithsonian Wild Heritage Collection). (Illus.). 32p. (J). (gr. k-3). 1995. pap. 14.95 (*1-56899-144-4*) Soundprints.
Swan Lake. Anthea Bell. LC 86-9509. (Illus.). 28p. (J). (gr. 1 up). 1991. pap. 15.95 (*0-88708-028-6*, Picture Book Studio) S&S Childrens.
Swan Lake. Margot Fonteyn. (Illus.). 32p. (J). 1989. 16.00 (*0-15-200600-1*, Gulliver Bks) HarBrace.
Swan Lake. Mark Helprin. (Illus.). 112p. (J). (gr. 4-7). 1992. pap. 12.95 (*0-395-64647-2*) HM.
Swan Lake. Rachel Isadora. (Illus.). 32p. (J). (ps-3). 1996. pap. 5.95 (*0-698-11370-5*, Paperstar) Putnam Pub Group.
Swan Maiden. Robert G. Sauber. LC 93-34605. (Illus.). 32p. (J). (ps-3). 1994. lib. bdg. 15.95 (*0-8234-1088-9*) Holiday.
Swan Princess. Francine Hughes. 32p. (J). (ps-3). 1994. pap. 2.95 (*0-590-22203-1*) Scholastic Inc.
Swan Princess. A. L. Singer. 104p. (J). (gr. 4-7). 1994. pap. 3.50 (*0-590-22204-X*) Scholastic Inc.
Swan Road. Rebecca Brandewyne. 384p. (Orig.). 1994. mass mkt. 5.99 (*0-446-32701-8*) Warner Bks.
Swan Road. large type ed. Rebecca Brandewyne. LC 93-47341. 578p. (Orig.). 1994. lib. bdg. 22.95 (*0-7862-0132-0*) Thorndike Pr.
Swan Road. Rebecca Brandewyne. 384p. (Orig.). 1995. reprint ed. 22.00 (*0-7278-4758-9*) Severn Hse.
Swan Song. Edmund Crispin. LC 80-80453. 192p. 1980. 14.95 (*0-8027-5420-1*) Boulevard.
Swan Song. Robert R. McCammon. Ed. by Sally Peters. 1987. pap. 7.50 (*0-671-74103-9*) PB.
Swan Song. large type ed. Edmund Crispin. (Linford Mystery Library). 311p. 1987. pap. 15.99 (*0-7089-6361-7*, Linford) Ulverscroft.
Swan Song. Edmund Crispin. 192p. reprint ed. lib. bdg. 20.95 (*0-89190-692-4*, Rivercity Pr) Amereon Ltd.
Swan Song. Edmund Crispin. 1993. reprint ed. lib. bdg. 16.95 (*1-56849-195-6*) Buccaneer Bks.
***Swan Song: Reflections on Perth & Western Australia 1956-1995.** George Seddon. pap. 24.95 (*0-86422-428-1*, Pub. by Univ of West Aust Pr AT) Intl Spec Bk.
Swan Star. Betina Lindsey. 1994. mass mkt. 5.50 (*0-671-79939-8*) PB.
Swan Valley Journal. Edward L. Foss. LC 94-71889. 223p. (Orig.). 1994. pap. 14.00 (*1-56044-306-5*) Falcon Pr MT.
Swan Villa. Martin Walser. Tr. by Leila Vennewitz. 1982. 14.95 (*0-03-059372-7*) H Holt & Co.
Swan Witch. Betina Lindsey. Ed. by Carolyn Tolley. 256p. (Orig.). 1993. mass mkt. 4.99 (*0-671-75171-9*) PB.
Swander: History of the Swander Family. J. I. Swander. (Illus.). 143p. 1992. reprint ed. pap. 23.00 (*0-8328-2332-5*); reprint ed. lib. bdg. 33.00 (*0-8328-2331-7*) Higginson Bk Co.
Swander: History of the Swander Family. J. I. Swander. 143p. 1992. reprint ed. pap. 21.50 (*0-8328-2605-7*); reprint ed. lib. bdg. 31.50 (*0-8328-2604-9*) Higginson Bk Co.
Swanfall: Journey of the Tundra Swans. Tom Horton. (Illus.). 48p. (J). (gr. 1-3). 1991. 15.95 (*0-8027-8106-3*); lib. bdg. 16.85 (*0-8027-8107-1*) Walker & Co.
Swank Prank. Bertrand Gauthier. (First Novels Ser.). (Illus.). 64p. (J). (gr. 1-4). 1995. pap. 4.95 (*0-88780-092-0*); bds. 14.95 (*0-88780-093-9*) Formac Dist Ltd.
Swank Talk. Bertrand Gauthier. Tr. by Sarah Cummins from FRE. (First Novels Ser.). (Illus.). 64p. (Orig.). (J). (gr. 1-4). 1992. 14.95 (*0-88780-209-5*, Pub. by Formac Pubng CN) Formac Dist Ltd.
Swank Talk. Bertrand Gauthier. (First Novels Ser.). (Illus.). 64p. (Orig.). (J). (gr. 1-4). 1995. pap. 4.95 (*0-88780-208-7*); bds. 14.95 (*0-614-04044-2*) Formac Dist Ltd.
Swann. Dan Sherman. 1979. pap. 1.95 (*0-449-24132-7*, Crest) Fawcett.
Swann. Carol Shields. 320p. 1990. pap. 11.95 (*0-14-013429-8*, Penguin Bks) Viking Penguin.
Swann Song. Gibbs Davis. 176p. (YA). (gr. 7 up). 1989. mass mkt. 2.50 (*0-380-75609-9*, Flare) Avon.
Swann's Way. Arthur James Ltd. Staff. 280p. (C). 1993. 59.00 (*0-85305-329-4*, Pub. by J Arthur Ltd UK) St Mut.
Swann's Way. Marcel Proust. Tr. by C. K. Scott-Moncrieff. 1965. pap. text ed. write for info. (*0-07-553647-1*, T67) McGraw.
***Swann's Way.** Marcel Proust. 1982. pap. 20.00 (*0-394-71182-3*) Random.
Swann's Way. Marcel Proust. 1986. reprint ed. lib. bdg. 21.95 (*0-89966-581-0*) Buccaneer Bks.
Swann's Way: In Search of Lost Time, Vol. 1. Marcel Proust. Tr. by C. K. Moncrieff & Terence Kilmartin from FRE. LC 92-25657. (In Search of Lost Time Ser.). 644p. 1992. 19.50 (*0-679-60005-1*, Modern Lib) Random.
Swann's Way: Remembrance of Things Past. Marcel Proust. Tr. by C. K. Scott-Moncrieff & Terence Kilmartin. (International Ser.). 480p. 1989. pap. 13.00 (*0-679-72009-X*, Vin) Random.
Swanny's Ways. Steve Katz. (New American Fiction Ser.: No. 33). 554p. 1995. 22.95 (*1-55713-209-7*) Sun & Moon CA.
Swans. Dafila Scott. LC 95-32902. (WorldLife Library). (Illus.). 72p. 1995. pap. 14.95 (*0-89658-320-1*) Voyageur Pr.
***Swans.** Lynn M. Stone. LC 96-27707. (Early Bird Nature Bks.). (J). 1996. write for info. (*0-8225-3019-8*, Lerner Publctns) Lerner Group.
Swans & Amber. Dorothy B. Thompson. LC 88-7716. (Illus.). 216p. 1988. reprint ed. pap. 8.50 (*0-87661-945-6*) Am Sch Athens.
Swans & Amber: Some Early Greek Lyrics. Dorothy B. Thompson. LC 49-6415. 201p. reprint ed. pap. 57.30 (*0-317-28162-3*, 2014434) Bks Demand.
Swans & Storks, Sparrows & Doves: Sketches for an Imaginative Zoology. Karl Konig. 60p. 1990. pap. 12.95 (*0-86315-046-2*, 1191, Pub. by Floris Books UK) Anthroposophic.
Swan's Gift. Brenda Seabrooke. LC 94-41788. (Illus.). (J). (ps up). 1995. 15.95 (*1-56402-360-5*) Candlewick Pr.
Swan's Gift. Brenda Seabrooke. LC 94-41788. (Illus.). 32p. (J). (gr. k-3). 1996. reprint ed. pap. 5.99 (*1-56402-970-0*) Candlewick Pr.
Swan's How to Pick the Right People Program. William S. Swan. LC 88-27888. 284p. 1989. pap. text ed. 19.95 (*0-471-62188-9*) Wiley.
***Swan's Island.** Elizabeth Spires. 64p. 1997. reprint ed. pap. 12.95 (*0-88748-249-X*) Carnegie-Mellon.
Swans of Brhyadr. Vivienne Couldrey. 224p. 1981. pap. 1.75 (*0-449-50166-3*, Coventry) Fawcett.
Swans of the World: In Nature, History, Myth & Art. A. Lindsay Price. (Illus.). 196p. 1995. 26.95 (*0-933031-81-5*) Coun Oak Bks.
Swan's Reach. large type ed. Margaret Way. (Linford Romance Library). 304p. 1985. pap. 15.99 (*0-7089-6059-6*) Ulverscroft.
***Swan's Stories.** H. C. Andersen & Brian Alderson. LC 96-47197. (Illus.). (J). 1997. 19.99 (*1-56402-894-1*) Candlewick Pr.
***Swans Way.** Becky L. Weyrich. 1997. pap. 5.50 (*0-8217-5783-0*) Kensgtn Pub Corp.
Swanscombe Skull. A. T. Marston. Bd. with Report on the Swanscombe Skull. LC 78-72701. LC 78-72701. reprint ed. 27.50 (*0-404-18271-2*) AMS Pr.
Swansea: An Illustrated History. Ed. by Glanmor Williams. (Illus.). 386p. (C). 1992. 75.00 (*0-7154-0714-7*, Pub. by C Davies Pubs) St Mut.
Swansea - City Guide. Peter Stead. 112p. (C). 1992. 39.00 (*0-7154-0717-1*, Pub. by C Davies Pubs) St Mut.
Swansea Bay's Green Mantle. Mary E. Gillham. 427p. (C). 1989. 95.00 (*0-685-61443-3*, Pub. by D Brown & Sons Ltd UK) St Mut.
Swansea Girl: A Memoir. Barbara Hardy. 216p. 9400. 32.00 (*0-7206-0904-6*, Pub. by P Owen Ltd UK) Dufour.
Swansea Porcelain. W. D. John et al. 97p. (C). 1989. 295.00 (*0-685-66200-4*, Pub. by D Brown & Sons Ltd UK) St Mut.
Swansea Porcelain: Shapes & Decoration. A. E. Jones & Leslie Joseph. 288p. (C). 1989. 450.00 (*0-905928-84-9*, Pub. by D Brown & Sons Ltd UK) St Mut.
Swanson: Easy Low-Fat Broth Recipes. Swanson Staff. 1996. 12.95 (*0-696-20556-4*) Meredith Bks.
***Swanson: Easy Low-Fat Broth Recipes.** Swanson Staff. 1996. pap. 9.95 (*0-696-20639-0*) Meredith Bks.
Swansongs: Poems. Susan J. Lenier. (Modern Poets Ser.: Vol. 12). (Illus.). (Orig.). 1982. 15.00 (*0-906672-04-X*); pap. 8.95 (*0-906672-03-1*) Oleander Pr.
Swap. Norma Klein. 320p. 1984. mass mkt. 3.75 (*0-380-68528-0*) Avon.
***Swap.** George Layton. LC 96-40447. 192p. (YA). (gr. 4 up). 1997. 16.95 (*0-399-23148-X*, Putnam) Putnam Pub Group.
Swap & Derivative Financing: The Global Reference to Products Pricing Applications & Markets. 2nd ed. Satyajit Das. 1993. text ed. 95.00 (*1-55738-542-4*) Irwin Prof Pubng.
Swap Financing. Satyajit Das. (Illus.). xxxv, 661p. 1989. pap. 148.50 (*0-455-20831-X*, Pub. by Law Bk Co AT) Gaunt.
Swap Literacy: A Comprehensible Guide. Elizabeth Ungar. LC 96-83204. (Bloomberg Professional Library). (Illus.). 176p. 1996. 40.00 (*1-57660-001-7*) Bloomberg NJ.
Swapping. Shirley Lowe & Angela Ince. 240p. 1988. 17.95 (*0-316-53381-5*) Little.
Swapping Stories: Folktales from Louisiana. Ed. by Carl Lindahl et al. 352p. 1997. 45.00 (*0-87805-930-X*); pap. 20.00 (*0-87805-931-8*) U Pr of Miss.
Swaps. Stephen F. Meyers. 480p. 1996. 99.00 (*0-412-61160-0*) Chapman & Hall.
Swaps: The Legal Aspects of Economic Substance. Paul Goris. Ed. by Max Foster. LC 93-33346. 544p. (C). 1994. lib. bdg. 175.00 (*1-85333-910-5*, Pub. by Graham & Trotman UK) Kluwer Ac.
Swaps & Financial Derivatives. Satyajit Das. 1500p. 1996. 277.00 (*0-946559-62-7*, Pub. by IFR Pub UK) Am Educ Systs.
Swaps & Financial Engineering: A Self-Study Guide to Mastering & Applying Swaps. Coopers & Lybrand Staff. 1994. per. 55.00 (*1-55738-592-0*) Irwin Prof Pubng.
Swaps & Other Derivatives in Nineteen Ninety-Two. (Corporate Law & Practice Course Handbook, 1985-86 Ser.). 395p. 1992. pap. 70.00 (*0-685-69496-8*); vhs 950.00 (*0-685-69497-6*) PLI.
SWAPs & Other Derivatives in 1995. (Corporate Law & Practice Course Handbook, 1985-86 Ser.). 520p. 1995. pap. 99.00 (*0-685-69717-7*, B4-7095) PLI.
SWAPs & Other Derivatives in 1996. (Corporate Law & Practice Course Handbook, 1985-86 Ser.). Date not set. pap. 99.00 (*0-614-17203-9*, B4-7122) PLI.
Swaps Compendium. Ed. by John Watson & Gavin Gray. 240p. 1995. 245.00 (*1-85564-258-1*, Pub. by Euromoney UK) Am Educ Systs.
Swaps Handbook: Swaps & Related Risk Management Instruments. Kenneth R. Kapner & John F. Marshall. 1990. 110.00 (*0-13-879297-6*) NY Inst Finance.
Swaps Market. 2nd ed. John F. Marshall & Kenneth R. Kapner. LC 92-73929. 258p. (C). pap. text ed. 31.00 (*1-878975-16-1*) Blackwell Pubs.
Swaps Training Manual Complete. Richard Flavell. 225p. 1995. 325.00 (*1-85564-122-4*, Pub. by Euromoney UK) Am Educ Systs.
Swaraj: Cultural & Political. Pramatha N. Bose. 1986. reprint ed. 32.50 (*0-8364-1950-2*, Pub. by Usha II) S Asia.
Swaraj in One Year. 2nd ed. Mohandas K. Gandhi. 1921. 20.00 (*0-404-02676-1*) AMS Pr.
Sward & Johnston, Biographical Sketches of Augustana Leaders. Oscar N. Olson. LC 56-5870. (Augustana Historical Society Publications: No. 15). 80p. 1955. pap. 3.00 (*0-910184-15-1*) Augustana.
Swarm Studies & Inelastic Electron-Molecule Collisions. Ed. by L. C. Pitchford et al. (Illus.). xi, 403p. 1986. 119.95 (*0-387-96402-9*) Spr-Verlag.
***Swarm Warning.** I. K. Swobud. (Masked Rider Ser.). (J). 1997. pap. 3.99 (*0-614-28638-7*) Blvd Books.
***Swarming Independence.** Colin Standish & Russell Standish. (Orig.). 1996. pap. 8.95 (*0-614-30874-7*) Hartland Pubns.
Swarms of Ions & Electrons in Gases. Ed. by W. Lindinger et al. (Illus.). 320p. 1984. 60.95 (*0-387-81823-5*) Spr-Verlag.
Swarovski: The Magic of Crystal. Vivienne Becker & John B. Taylor. LC 94-31129. 1995. 39.95 (*0-8109-4454-5*) Abrams.
Swartkrans Ape-Man: Paranthropus Crassidens. Robert Broom & J. T. Robinson. LC 76-44697. reprint ed. 47.50 (*0-404-15911-7*) AMS Pr.
Swartz Proof Product Defect. Edward M. Swartz. LC 85-50535. 1985. 98.00 (*0-685-59884-5*) Clark Boardman Callaghan.
Swartzia (Leguminosae, Caesalpinioideae, Swartzieae) Richard S. Cowan. LC 67-14268. (Flora Neotropica Monographs: No. 1). (Illus.). 228p. 1987. reprint ed. pap. text ed. 15.00 (*0-89327-320-1*) NY Botanical.
***Swash Letter Alphabets.** Dan X. Solo. LC 96-41110. (Illus.). 1996. pap. 8.95 (*0-486-29332-7*) Dover.
Swashbuckler. Lee Lynch. 288p. (Orig.). 1985. pap. 8.95 (*0-930044-66-5*) Naiad Pr.
Swashbuckler. James Moloney. (Storybridge Ser.). 96p. (J). (gr. 4-7). 1995. pap. 9.95 (*0-7022-2825-7*, Pub. by Univ Queensland Pr AT) Intl Spec Bk.
Swastika: Constructing the Symbol. Malcolm Quinn. LC 94-4683. (Material Cultures Ser.). (Illus.). 192p. (C). (gr. 13). 1994. 45.00 (*0-415-10095-X*, B4879) Routledge.
Swastika Night. Katharine Burdekin. LC 85-12980. 208p. (Orig.). 1985. reprint ed. pap. 9.95 (*0-935312-56-0*) Feminist Pr.
Swastika on the Synagogue Door. 2nd ed. Leonard Romm. LC 94-46454. (Lazarus Family Mystery Ser.). (Illus.). 168p. (Orig.). (J). (gr. 6-9). 1994. reprint ed. pap. 5.95 (*1-881283-05-4*) Alef Design.
Swastika Outside Germany. Donald M. McKale. LC 77-22304. 304p. reprint ed. pap. 86.70 (*0-8357-7043-5*, 2033316) Bks Demand.
Swastika Smashers: Eighty-Second Airborne Heroes. S. S. Edward. 180p. 1994. pap. 14.95 (*1-883500-07-9*) RAMSI Bks.
SWAT: Strategic Weapons & Tactics for Executives: Handbook for Implementing Strategic Advantage Through Technology. John J. Donovan. (Illus.). 180p. 1988. 15.95 (*0-685-24279-X*) Cambridge Tech Grp Inc.
***SWAT Battle Tactics: How to Organize, Train, & Equip a SWAT Team for Law Enforcement or Self-Defense.** Pat Cascio & John McSweeney. (Illus.). 128p. 1996. pap. 17.00 (*0-87364-900-1*) Paladin Pr.
Swat It! see Set 4
***SWAT Leadership & Tactical Planning: The SWAT Operator's Guide to Combat Law Enforcement.** Tony L. Jones. (Illus.). 128p. 1996. pap. 18.00 (*0-87364-897-8*) Paladin Pr.
SWAT Ninety: Second Scandinavian Workshop on Algorithm Theory Bergen, Sweden, July 11-14, 1990 Proceedings. Ed. by J. R. Gilbert et al. (Lecture Notes in Computer Science Ser.: Vol. 447). vi, 417p. 1990. 47.00 (*0-387-52846-6*) Spr-Verlag.
***Swat Patrol: Pledge Paddling on Fraternity Row.** B. D. Ross. 84p. 1994. pap. 11.95 (*0-9645291-8-1*) A D Thompson.
SWAT (Special Weapons & Tactics) Phillip L. Davidson. (Illus.). 148p. 1979. 27.95 (*0-398-03890-2*) C C Thomas.
Swat Team. Hans Halberstadt. (Power Ser.). (Illus.). 128p. 1994. pap. 16.95 (*0-87938-877-3*) Motorbooks Intl.
S.W.A.T. Team Operations. Burt Rapp. LC 90-60904. (Illus.). 160p. (Orig.). 1990. pap. 18.95 (*1-55950-035-2*, 58065) Loompanics.
SWAT Teams: Explosive Face-Offs with America's Deadliest Criminals. Robert L. Snow. (Illus.). 300p. (C). 1996. 24.95 (*0-306-45266-9*, Plenum Pr) Plenum.
***Swat 2.** Prima Publishing Staff. 1997. pap. 19.99 (*0-7615-1116-4*) Prima Pub.
Swatch: Almost Everything You Need to Know about Dealing & Collecting Swatches. 232p. 1995. spiral bd. 35.00 (*0-913902-66-7*) Heart Am Pr.
Swatch: Almost Everything You Need to Know about Dealing & Collecting Swatches. Ehrhardt. (Illus.). 232p. 1995. spiral bd. 200.00 (*0-913902-65-9*) Heart Am Pr.
Swath. John Perlman. 1978. 20.00 (*0-686-59675-7*); pap. 8.00 (*0-686-59676-5*) Elizabeth Pr.
Swatting the Mosquitoes of Marriage. Marian V. Liautaud. 240p. 1994. pap. 9.99 (*0-310-40511-4*) Zondervan.
Swayam's Authentic Cook Book. Swayam P. Singh. LC 87-91273. 70p. 1988. pap. 12.95 (*0-318-41283-7*) S Singh.
Swayam's Authentic Cook Book of India. Swayam P. Singh. 70p. 1988. pap. 12.95 (*0-318-42479-7*) S Singh.
Swayam's Authentic Cookbook of India: Healthy No Preservatives Recipes. rev. ed. Swayam P. Singh. Ed. by Mike Danovich. 100p. 1987. reprint ed. pap. 12.95 (*0-935380-01-9*) S Singh.
Swayam's India Cook Book. Swayam P. Singh. Ed. by Mike Donavich. write for info. (*0-318-62773-6*) S Singh.
Swaying: Essays on Intercultural Love. Ed. by Jessie C. Grearson & Lauren B. Smith. LC 95-33941. 238p. 1995. pap. 14.95 (*0-87745-527-9*); text ed. 27.95 (*0-87745-526-0*) U of Iowa Pr.
Swazi. B. O. Oluikpe. LC 96-32821. (Heritage Library of African Peoples: Set 4). (Illus.). 64p. (YA). (gr. 7-12). 1997. lib. bdg. 15.95 (*0-8239-2012-7*, D2012-7) Rosen Group.
Swazi: A South African Kingdom. 2nd ed. Hilda Kuper. 208p. (C). 1986. pap. text ed. 13.50 (*0-03-070239-9*) HB Coll Pubs.
Swaziland. Ettagale Blauer & Jason Laure. LC 96-2024. (Enchantment of the World Ser.). 128p. (J). 1996. lib. bdg. 30.00 (*0-516-20020-8*) Childrens.
Swaziland. Balem Nyeko. (World Bibliographical Ser.: No. 24). 135p. 1983. lib. bdg. 45.00 (*0-903450-35-6*) ABC-CLIO.
Swaziland. rev. ed. Compiled by Balam Nyeko. (World Bibliographical Ser.: Vol. 24). 241p. 1995. lib. bdg. 64.50 (*1-85109-226-9*) ABC-CLIO.
Swear Like a Trooper: A Dictionary of Military Terms & Phrases. Compiled by William Priest. (Illus.). 200p. 1997. write for info. (*1-883522-13-7*) Rockbridge Pub.

Swearing: A Social History of Foul Language, Oaths & Profanity in English. Geoffrey Hughes. (Language Library). 296p. 1991. 36.95 (*0-631-16593-2*) Blackwell Pubs.

Sweat. Zora Neale Hurston. Ed. by Cheryl A. Wall. 200p. (C). 1996. 35.00 (*0-8135-2315-X*); pap. text ed. 14.00 (*0-8135-2316-8*) Rutgers U Pr.

Sweat: Stories & a Novella. Lucy J. Bledsoe. LC 95-16106. 164p. (Orig.). 1995. pap. 10.95 (*1-878067-64-8*) Seal Pr WA.

Sweat & the Gold. Harriet M. Savitz. (Illus.). 154p. (Orig.). 1984. pap. 7.95 (*0-685-10575-X*) Veep.

Sweat of the Sun & Tears of the Moon: Gold & Silver in Pre-Columbian Art. Andre Emmerich. LC 77-72685. (Illus.). 1977. reprint ed. 75.00 (*0-87817-208-4*) Hacker.

Sweat of the Sun, Tears of the Moon: A Chronicle of an Incan Treasure. Peter Lourie. 320p. 1991. text ed. 19.95 (*0-689-12111-3*, Atheneum S&S) S&S Trade.

***Sweat of Their Brow: A History of Work in Latin America.** David McCreery. (Latin American Realities Ser.). 220p. Date not set. text ed. 61.95 (*0-7656-0207-5*); pap. text ed. 22.95 (*0-7656-0208-3*) M E Sharpe.

***Sweat Testing: Sample Collection & Quantitative Analysis; Approved Guideline (1994)** Contrib. by Vicky LeGrys. 1994. 75.00 (*1-56238-188-1*, C34-A) Natl Comm Clin Lab Stds.

"Sweat" Triumph of Selfworth. Dylotta Dye. 48p. (Orig.). (J). 1994. pap. 3.90 (*1-885148-00-3*) Lavots Press.

***Sweat Your Prayers: Unveiling the Mysteries of the Soul.** Gabrielle Roth. (Inner Work Bk.). 320p. 1998. 23.95 (*0-87477-878-6*, Tarcher Putnam) Putnam Pub Group.

Sweater Design in Plain English. Maggie Righetti. (Illus.). 352p. (Orig.). 1990. pap. 14.95 (*0-312-05164-6*) St Martin.

Sweater Design Workbook. Gail Selfridge. LC 90-56185. (Illus.). 126p. (Orig.). 1991. pap. 14.95 (*0-934026-65-3*) Interweave.

Sweater for Candyce. Shawn Strannigan. (I Can Understand Ser.). (Illus.). 24p. (J). (ps-2). 1995. pap. 2.99 (*0-7847-0293-4*, 03460) Standard Pub.

***Sweater Weather.** Maggie Hardy. (Illus.). 70p. (Orig.). 1996. pap. 9.95 (*0-9646284-0-6*) Carmel Commun.

Sweater Workshop. Jacqueline Fee. (Interweave Press Bks.). 1986. spiral bd. 16.95 (*0-685-53955-5*) Contemp Bks.

Sweater Workshop. Jacqueline Fee. LC 83-80246. (Illus.). 192p. 1986. spiral bd. 19.95 (*0-934026-12-2*) Interweave.

Sweaters: Twenty-Eight Contemporary Designs in the Norwegian Tradition. Tone Takle & Lise Kolstad. Tr. by Robin O. Hansen from NOR. (Illus.). 128p. (Orig.). 1992. pap. 19.95 (*0-934026-76-9*) Interweave.

Sweaters by Hand: Designs for Spinners & Knitters. Helene Rush & Rachael Emmons. LC 88-32898. (Illus.). 160p. 1988. pap. 17.95 (*0-934026-37-8*) Interweave.

Sweaters from a New England Village: Twenty Original Patterns Featuring Harrisville Designs Yarn. Candace Strick. LC 95-72159. (Illus.). 128p. 1996. pap. 21.95 (*0-89272-358-0*) Down East.

Sweaters from Penobscot Bay. Janey Todd & Ben G. Henneke. (North Island Designs Ser.: Vol. V). (Illus.). 96p. pap. 17.95 (*0-9620763-2-5*) N Island Designs.

Sweaterscapes of the American West: A Collection of Designs for Machine or Hand Knitters. Lynne Barr & Douglas Barr. (Illus.). 80p. 1993. spiral bd. 17.95 (*0-89272-323-8*) Down East.

Sweaterscapes of the North Country: Unique Intarsia Patterns for Machine or Hand Knitters. Lynne Barr & Douglas Barr. LC 91-74034. (Illus.). 72p. 1991. spiral bd. 16.95 (*0-89272-310-6*) Down East.

Sweatlodge Participation among Nez Perce Women. Carol J. Carman. 121p. (C). 1989. pap. text ed. 11.65 (*1-55567-069-5*) Coyote Press.

Sweatshirts with Style. Mary Mulari. LC 93-8197. (Illus.). 124p. 1993. pap. 15.95 (*0-8019-8392-4*) Chilton.

Sweatshop Strife: Class, Ethnicity, & Gender in the Jewish Labour Movement of Toronto, 1900-1939. Ruth A. Frager. LC 92-94700. (Social History of Canada Ser.: No. 47). 300p. 1992. 60.00 (*0-8020-5968-6*); pap. 20.95 (*0-8020-6895-2*) U of Toronto Pr.

Sweaty Palms: The Neglected Art of Being Interviewed. rev. ed. H. Anthony Medley. (Illus.). 194p. 1992. reprint ed. pap. 8.95 (*0-89815-403-0*) Ten Speed Pr.

***Swede: The Will to Win: A Profile of Andrew J. Oberlander, M. D.** 2nd ed. David H. Oberlander. LC 96-92267. (Illus.). 125p. 1996. reprint ed. pap. 8.95 (*0-9654493-1-9*) D H Oberlander.

Swede, the Horse Who Didn't Forget. large type ed. William O. Beazley. (White Horse Ser.). (Illus.). 46p. (Orig.). (J). (gr. k-5). 1989. spiral bd., pap. 7.95 (*1-884758-07-X*) W O Beazley.

Sweden. (Insight Guides Ser.). 1993. pap. 22.95 (*0-395-66235-4*) HM.

***Sweden.** (Major World Nations Ser.). (Illus.). 120p. (YA). (gr. 5 up). 1997. lib. bdg. 19.95 (*0-7910-4749-0*) Chelsea Hse.

Sweden. Mary Alderton. (Blue Guides Ser.). (Illus.). 448p. 1995. pap. 24.00 (*0-393-31271-2*, Norton Paperbks) Norton.

Sweden. Donna Bailey. LC 91-22052. (Where We Live Ser.). (Illus.). 32p. (J). (gr. 1-4). 1992. lib. bdg. 21.40 (*0-8114-2567-3*) Raintree Steck-V.

Sweden. Walter Imber & Wolf Tieze. LC 78-66110. (Illus.). 1979. 50.00 (*0-89674-004-8*) J J Binns.

Sweden. Intro. by C. Johnson. (Panorama Bks.). (Illus.). (FRE.). 3.95 (*0-685-11577-1*) Fr & Eur.

Sweden. Lars Nordstrom. LC 89-81616. 160p. 1990. 39.95 (*1-55868-023-3*) Gr Arts Ctr Pub.

***Sweden.** OECD Staff. (Development Cooperation Review Series, 1996: No. 19). 66p. (Orig.). 1996. pap. 18.00 (*92-64-15285-7*, 43-96-13-1) OECD.

Sweden. Ralph Zickgraf. (Let's Visit Places & Peoples of the World Ser.). (Illus.). 96p. (J). (gr. 5 up). 1988. lib. bdg. 19.95 (*1-55546-797-0*) Chelsea Hse.

Sweden: A Royal Treasury, 1550-1700. Ed. by Michael Conforti & Guy Walton. LC 88-5225. (Illus.). 194p. (Orig.). 1988. pap. 14.95 (*0-89468-111-7*) Natl Gallery Art.

Sweden: A Short Survey of the Kingdom of Sweden. LC 79-84139. (English Experience Ser.: No. 956). 116p. 1979. reprint ed. lib. bdg. 15.00 (*90-221-0956-9*) Walter J Johnson.

Sweden: A Study of the Educational System of Sweden and A Guide to the Academic Placement of Students in Educational Institutions in the United States: Country Report 1994. Kathleen Zanotti & Karlene N. Dickey. LC 94-32898. (PIER World Education Ser.). 1995. 50.00 (*0-929851-23-4*) Am Assn Coll Registrars.

Sweden: Coat of Arms Ore Values 1858-1872. Per Sjoman et al. Ed. by Lauson Stone et al. Tr. by Sven Ahman from SWE. (Illus.). 113p. (Orig.). 1984. pap. text ed. 17.50 (*0-936493-04-6*) Scand Philatelic.

Sweden: Its People & Industry, 2 vols. Ed. by Raoul Gordon. 1976. lib. bdg. 250.00 (*0-8490-2719-5*) Gordon Pr.

Sweden: Lion Type Stamps 1862-1872 & Ring Type Stamps 1872-1892. George Menzinsky. (Illus.). 123p. (Orig.). 1985. pap. text ed. 17.50 (*0-936493-05-4*) Scand Philatelic.

Sweden: Penal Code of Sweden. (American Series of Foreign Penal Codes: Vol. 17). x, 114p. 1972. 15.00 (*0-8377-0037-X*) Rothman.

Sweden: The Middle Way on Trial. Marquis W. Childs. LC 79-24714. (Illus.). 197p. reprint ed. pap. 56.20 (*0-8357-3743-8*, 2036469) Bks Demand.

Sweden: The Nation's History. enl. ed. Franklin D. Scott. LC 88-6931. 704p. (C). 1988. reprint ed. pap. text ed. 29.95 (*0-8093-1489-4*) S Ill U Pr.

Sweden see Cultures of the World - Group 4

***Sweden & European Integration.** Lee Miles. LC 97-13479. (Illus.). 330p. 1997. text ed. 59.95 (*1-85521-629-9*, Pub. by Ashgate UK) Ashgate Pub Co.

Sweden & the American Revolution. Adolph B. Benson. 1926. 20.00 (*0-686-17387-2*) R S Barnes.

Sweden & the American Revolution. Adolph B. Benson. 228p. 1992. reprint ed. pap. 21.00 (*0-685-66227-6*, 9049) Clearfield Co.

Sweden at the Edge: Lessons for American & Swedish Managers. Ed. by Michael Maccoby. LC 90-44875. (Innovations in Organizations Ser.). 260p. (C). 1991. text ed. 32.95 (*0-8122-8153-5*) U of Pa Pr.

Sweden in Pictures. Ed. by Lerner Publications, Department of Geography Staff. (Visual Geography Ser.). (Illus.). 64p. (YA). (gr. 5 up). 1993. lib. bdg. 19.95 (*0-8225-1872-4*, Lerner Publctns) Lerner Group.

Sweden Pocket Guide. Berlitz Editors. (Pocket Guides Ser.). 160p. 1994. pap. 7.95 (*2-8315-2679-5*) Berlitz.

***Sweden Skilling Banco Stamps, 1855-1858 & Black Local Stamp & 1862 Provisional of Local Stamp Type.** George Menzinsky et al. Ed. by Lauson Stone et al. Tr. by Sven Ahman. (Illus.). 91p. 1985. pap. text ed. 17.50 (*0-936493-06-2*) Scand Philatelic.

Sweden, the Welfare State. Wilfrid Fleisher. LC 72-10696. (Illus.). 255p. 1973. reprint ed. text ed. 35.00 (*0-8371-6611-X*, FLSW, Greenwood Pr) Greenwood.

***Sweden Visions & Verse of a Land & Its People Collector's Postcard Book.** Illus. by Bobbie Peterson. (Collector's Postcard Bks.). 22p. (Orig.). (ENG & SWE.). 1996. pap. 9.95 (*1-881988-22-8*) Paulstad Inc.

Swedenborg: A Hermetic Philosopher. Ethan A. Hitchcock. 1972. 59.95 (*0-8490-1164-7*) Gordon Pr.

Swedenborg: Buddha of the North. D. T. Suzuki. LC 95-46033. (Swedenborg Studies Monograph Ser.: Vol. 5). (Illus.). 160p. (Orig.). (C). 1996. pap. 11.95 (*0-87785-184-0*) Swedenborg.

Swedenborg: Buddha of the North. Daissetz T. Suzuki. LC 95-46033. (Swedenborg Studies Monograph Ser.: Vol. 5). (Illus.). 160p. (Orig.). (C). 1996. 16.95 (*0-87785-185-9*) Swedenborg.

Swedenborg: Life & Teaching. rev. ed. George Trobridge. Ed. by R. H. Tafel, Jr. LC 92-60086. 176p. 1992. reprint ed. 16.95 (*0-87785-139-5*); reprint ed. pap. 10.95 (*0-87785-142-5*) Swedenborg.

***Swedenborg & Esoteric Islam.** Henry Corbin. 150p. 1996. pap. 11.00 (*0-614-21242-1*, 1424); pap. 11.00 (*0-614-21685-0*, 1424) Kazi Pubns.

Swedenborg & Esoteric Islam: Two Studies. Henry Corbin. Tr. by Leonard Fox from FRE. LC 94-30687. (Swedenborg Studies: No. 4). 168p. 1995. pap. text ed. 9.95 (*0-87785-183-2*) Swedenborg.

Swedenborg & Kant: E. Swedenborg's Mystical View of Humankind & the Dual Nature of Humankind in I. Kant. Gottlieb Florschutz. (Swedenborg Studies: No. 2). 26, vp. 1993. pap. text ed. 4.95 (*0-87785-181-6*) Swedenborg.

Swedenborg & the New Age. Edmund A. Beaman. LC 77-134422. (Communal Societies in America Ser.). reprint ed. 37.50 (*0-404-08458-3*) AMS Pr.

Swedenborg Epic. Cyriel O. Sigstedt. LC 78-137269. (Illus.). reprint ed. 57.50 (*0-404-05999-6*) AMS Pr.

Swedenborg Researcher's Manual: A Research Reference Manual for Writers of Academic Dissertations, & for Other Scholars. William R. Woofenden. 366p. 1988. 19.95 (*0-915221-65-9*) Swedenborg Sci Assn.

Swedenborg Rite & the Great Masonic Leaders of the Eighteenth Century. Samuel Beswick. 210p. 1994. reprint ed. pap. 16.95 (*1-56459-424-6*) Kessinger Pub.

Swedenborg's Journal of Dreams. Emanuel Swedenborg. LC 86-70341. 194p. 1986. pap. 8.95 (*0-87785-133-6*) Swedenborg.

Swedenborg's Journal of Dreams, 1743-1744. rev. ed. Emanuel Swedenborg. Ed. by G. E. Klemming. Tr. by J. J. Wilkinson from SWE. 120p. 1989. pap. 9.00 (*0-915221-67-5*) Swedenborg Sci Assn.

Swedenborg's 1714 Airplane. Henry Soderberg. 87p. 1988. 9.95 (*0-87785-138-7*) Swedenborg.

Sweden's Best Stories: An Introduction to Swedish Fiction. Ed. by Hanna A. Larsen. Tr. by Charles W. Stork from SWE. LC 70-37276. (Short Story Index Reprint Ser.). 1977. reprint ed. 23.95 (*0-8369-4087-3*) Ayer.

Sweden's Capital Imports & Exports. Jucker Fleetwood & Erin Elver. Ed. by Mira Wilkins. LC 76-29743. (European Business Ser.). (Illus.). 1977. reprint ed. lib. bdg. 18.95 (*0-405-09760-3*) Ayer.

Swedes: From Whence They Came. Jack R. Evans. LC 92-85013. (Little History Ser.). (Illus.). 166p. (Orig.). 1993. pap. 9.95 (*1-877882-05-4*) SCW Pubns.

Swedes: In Their Homeland, in America, in Connecticut. David E. O'Connor & Arthur E. Soderlind. (Peoples of Connecticut Ser.). 238p. 1983. 8.00 (*0-685-09449-9*) I N Thut World Educ Ctr.

Swedes & Dutch at New Castle. C. A. Weslager. (Orig.). 17.95 (*0-912608-71-4*); pap. 9.95 (*0-912608-50-1*) Mid Atlantic.

Swedes & Finns in New Jersey. Federal Writers' Project, New Jersey. LC 73-3640. (American Guide Ser.). (Illus.). reprint ed. 49.50 (*0-404-57940-X*) AMS Pr.

Swedes & the Swedish Settlements in North America, 2 Vols. Helge Nelson. Ed. by Franklyn D. Scott. LC 78-15197. (Scandinavians in America Ser.). (Illus.). 1979. reprint ed. lib. bdg. 50.95 (*0-405-11654-3*) Ayer.

Swedes in America, 1638-1938. A. Benson & Allan Hedin. LC 73-98681. (American History & Americana Ser.: No. 47). 1969. reprint ed. lib. bdg. 75.00 (*0-8383-0326-9*) M S G Haskell Hse.

Swedes in America, 1638-1938. Adolph B. Benson. (History - United States Ser.). 614p. 1993. reprint ed. lib. bdg. 109.00 (*0-7812-4869-8*) Rprt Serv.

Swedes in Wisconsin. Frederick Hale. LC 82-23272. (Illus.). 32p. 1983. pap. 3.00 (*0-87020-217-0*) State Hist Soc Wis.

Swedish. (Cassette Pack Ser.). 192p. 1994. 16.95 incl. audio (*2-8315-1482-7*) Berlitz.

Swedish. 2nd ed. Gladys Hird. LC 78-74534. 288p. 1980. pap. text ed. 29.95 (*0-521-22644-9*) Cambridge U Pr.

Swedish: A Comprehensive Reference Grammar. Philip Holmes & Ian Hinchliffe. LC 92-44014. 496p. (C). (gr. 13). 1993. pap. 35.00 (*0-415-08208-0*, B0744, Routledge NY) Routledge.

***Swedish: An Essential Grammar.** Philip Holmes & Ian Hinchliffe. LC 96-41334. (Routledge Grammars Ser.). 192p. (ENG & SWE.). (C). 1997. pap. write for info. (*0-415-16048-0*); text ed. write for info. (*0-415-16160-6*) Routledge.

Swedish - English Business Dictionary. 943p. (ENG & SWE.). 215.00 (*0-946760-04-7*) IBD Ltd.

Swedish, A Practical Grammar. rev. ed. Allan L. Rice. LC 58-13379. 110p. reprint ed. pap. 31.40 (*0-685-16044-0*, 2026950) Bks Demand.

Swedish-American Landmarks: Where to Go & What to See. Alan H. Winquist. Ed. by Beth Allen. LC 94-43200. (Illus.). 322p. (Orig.). 1995. pap. 24.95 (*0-9609620-3-4*) Swedish Council.

Swedish-American Life in Chicago: Cultural & Urban Aspects of an Immigrant People, 1850-1930. Ed. by Philip J. Anderson & Dag Blanck. (Ethnic History of Chicago Ser.). 408p. 1992. text ed. 42.50 (*0-252-01829-X*) U of Ill Pr.

Swedish-American Newspapers: A Guide to the Microfilms Held by Swenson Swedish Immigration Research Center. Compiled by Lilly Setterdahl. LC 81-68299. (Augustana College Library Publications: No. 35). 36p. 1981. pap. 3.00 (*0-910182-41-8*) Augustana Coll.

Swedish-American Periodicals. E. Walfred Erickson. Ed. by Franklyn D. Scott. LC 78-15206. (Scandinavians in America Ser.). 1979. lib. bdg. 18.95 (*0-405-11635-7*) Ayer.

***Swedish Americans.** Allyson McGill. LC 96-36783. (The Immigrant Experience Ser.). (J). 1997. 19.95 (*0-7910-4551-X*); pap. 9.95 (*0-7910-4552-8*) Chelsea Hse.

Swedish & Finnish Glossary of Gastronomy: Gastronomisk Ordlista. L. Perkio. 90p. (FIN & SWE.). 1985. 35.00 (*0-8288-0846-5*, F34200) Fr & Eur.

Swedish & German Economics & Law Dictionary: Fachwoerterbuch Fuer Recht und Wirtschaft. 2nd ed. Gunter Parsenow. 520p. (GER & SWE.). 1985. 195.00 (*0-8288-0825-2*, M7399) Fr & Eur.

Swedish & Soviet Energy Problems. Ed. by Kurt Wickman. 373p. (Orig.). 1987. pap. 42.50 (*91-540-9274-4*) Coronet Bks.

***Swedish Art of Building.** Ed. by Joran Lindvall. (Illus.). 255p. 1992. 99.50 (*91-520-0287-X*, Pub. by Almqvist & Wiksell SW) Coronet Bks.

Swedish Basic Course. Foreign Service Institute Staff. 384p. 1982. pap. text ed. 185.00 incl. audio (*0-88432-045-6*, AFK501) Audio-Forum.

Swedish Beauty Secrets. Paavo Airola. 48p. 1984. pap. 3.95 (*0-932090-07-9*) Health Plus.

Swedish Bullionist Controversy: P. N. Christiernin's Lectures on the High Price of Foreign Exchange in Sweden, 1761. P. N. Christiernin. Ed. by Robert V. Eagly. LC 74-161990. (American Philosophical Society, Memoirs Ser.: Vol. 87). 129p. reprint ed. pap. 36.80 (*0-317-27884-3*, 2025137) Bks Demand.

Swedish Church. Herbert M. Waddams. LC 81-7021. (Illus.). viii, 70p. 1981. reprint ed. text ed. 45.00 (*0-313-22184-7*, WASW, Greenwood Pr) Greenwood.

Swedish Code of Judicial Procedure. rev. ed. Ed. by Anders Bruzelius & Krister Thelin. (American Series of Foreign Penal Codes: No. 24). xvii, 253p. 1979. 28.50 (*0-8377-0044-2*) Rothman.

Swedish Commentators on America: Sixteen Thirty-Eight to Eighteen Sixty-Five. Esther E. Larson. Ed. by Franklyn D. Scott. LC 78-15194. (Scandinavians in America Ser.). 1979. reprint ed. lib. bdg. 17.95 (*0-405-11647-0*) Ayer.

Swedish Diplomats at Cromwell's Court. M. Roberts. (Camden Fourth Ser.: No. 36). 336p. 27.00 (*0-86193-117-3*) David Brown.

Swedish Economic Thought: Explorations & Advances. Ed. by Lars Jonung. LC 92-19680. (Illus.). 272p. (C). (gr. 13). 1993. text ed. 74.95 (*0-415-05413-3*, A9898) Routledge.

Swedish Economy. Ed. by Barry P. Bosworth & Alice M. Rivlin. LC 86-29920. 338p. 1987. 18.95 (*0-8157-1042-9*) Brookings.

Swedish-English - English-Swedish Dictionary. M. Bergstrom et al. 744p. 1993. 40.50 (*91-27-71515-9*, Pub. by Natur och Kulturs) IBD Ltd.

Swedish-English - English-Swedish Medical & Pharmaceutical Dictionary. 3rd rev. ed. Clive K. Cressy. 682p. (SWE.). 1992. 255.00 (*91-970984-4-2*) IBD Ltd.

Swedish-English - English-Swedish Standard Dictionary. rev. ed. Vincent Petty. 804p. 1995. pap. 19.95 (*0-7818-0379-9*) Hippocrene Bks.

Swedish-English--English-Swedish Medical & Pharmaceutical Dictionary. 3rd ed. Clive K. Cressy. 682p. (ENG & SWE.). 1992. 248.00 (*0-7859-8923-4*) Fr & Eur.

Swedish-English Comprehensive Dictionary. 888p. (ENG & SWE.). 1996. 60.00 (*0-7818-0462-0*) Hippocrene Bks.

Swedish-English Comprehensive Dictionary. 888p. (ENG & SWE.). 1996. pap. 39.50 (*0-7818-0474-4*) Hippocrene Bks.

Swedish-English Dictionary. Berlitz Editors. (Bilingual Pocket Dictionaries Ser.). 300p. (ENG & SWE.). 1989. pap. 6.95 (*2-8315-0943-2*) Berlitz.

Swedish-English Dictionary. Ruben Nojd & M. Angstrom. (ENG & SWE.). 39.50 (*0-87557-082-8*) Saphrograph.

Swedish-English, English-Swedish Dictionary: Svensk-Engelsk-Svensk Ordbok. Astrid Tornberg. 468p. (ENG & SWE.). 1986. 29.95 (*0-8288-0525-3*, M5885) Fr & Eur.

Swedish-English, English-Swedish Medical Dictionary. 2nd ed. Clive Cressy. 547p. (ENG & SWE.). 1988. lib. bdg. 195.00 (*0-8288-3312-5*, F136120) Fr & Eur.

Swedish-English, English-Swedish Technical Dictionary. 10th ed. E. Engstroem. 975p. (ENG & SWE.). 1989. Swedish-English, 10th ed., 1989, 975p. 121.00 (*0-88431-266-6*) IBD Ltd.

Swedish-English, English-Swedish Technical Dictionary. 13th ed. E. Engstroem. 955p. (ENG & SWE.). 1989. English-Swedish, 13th ed., 1989, 955p. 121.00 (*0-88431-267-4*) IBD Ltd.

Swedish-English Technical Dictionary. E. Engstrom. 375p. (ENG & SWE.). 1989. reprint ed. 250.00 (*0-8288-0676-4*, M10054) Fr & Eur.

Swedish Exodus. Lars Ljungmark. Tr. by Kermit B. Westerberg. 192p. (C). 1996. pap. 14.95 (*0-8093-2047-9*) Swedish-Am.

Swedish Experiment in Family Politics: The Myrdals & the Interwar Population Crisis. Allan Carlson. 314p. 1989. 44.95 (*0-88738-299-1*) Transaction Pubs.

Swedish Family Odyssey. Charles H. Hendricks. 400p. 1995. 25.00 (*0-9645422-0-X*) Hendricks Fam.

Swedish Farmers' Movement & Government Agricultural Policy. Michele Micheletti. LC 89-16206. 227p. 1990. text ed. 55.00 (*0-275-93398-9*, C3398, Praeger Pubs) Greenwood.

Swedish Film Classics: A Pictorial Study or Twenty-Five Films from 1913-1957. Alexsander Kwiatkowski. (Illus.). 144p. (C). 1983. pap. 9.95 (*0-486-24304-4*) Dover.

Swedish-Finnish Technical Dictionary: Ruotsalais-Suomalainen Tekniikan Ja Kaupan Sanakirja. J. K. Talvitie. 368p. (FIN & SWE.). 1986. 250.00 (*0-8288-2157-7*, F26210) Fr & Eur.

Swedish Folk Art: All Tradition Is Change. Ed. by Mats Widbom & Barbro S. Klein. LC 94-4165. 1995. 60.00 (*0-8109-3849-9*) Abrams.

Swedish Folktales & Legends. Ed. by Lone T. Blecher & George Blecher. (Illus.). 416p. 1995. pap. 17.00 (*0-679-75841-0*) Pantheon.

Swedish-French Dictionary: Svensk-Fransk Fackordbok. R. Lofmarker & G. Pioud. 320p. (FRE & SWE.). 1984. 125.00 (*0-8288-0831-7*, F63000) Fr & Eur.

Swedish-French, French-Swedish Dictionary: Svensk-Fransk-Svensk Ordbok. Ruben Nojd. 450p. (FRE & SWE.). 1986. 49.95 (*0-8288-1681-6*, F57114) Fr & Eur.

Swedish-French Technical Dictionary: Svensk - Fransk Teknisk Ordbok: Dictionnaire Technique Suedois-Francais. E. Engstrom. 412p. (FRE & SWE.). 1982. 150.00 (*0-8288-2150-X*, M14457) Fr & Eur.

Swedish-German Technical Dictionary: Svensk - Tysk Tecknis Ordbok. 6th ed. E. Engstrom. 412p. (GER & SWE.). 1985. 150.00 (*0-8288-2151-8*, F26510) Fr & Eur.

Swedish Glass Factories: Production Catalogues 1915-1960. Ed. by Helmut Ricke et al. (Illus.). 442p. (ENG, GER & SWE.). 1995. 185.00 (*3-7913-0804-1*, Pub. by Prestel GW) te Neues.

Swedish-Hungarian Concise Dictionary. Janos Feher & Gyorgy Lako. 1024p. 1992. 45.00 (*963-05-6400-9*, Pub. by Akad Kiado HU) St Mut.

Swedish-Hungarian Dictionary: Sved-Magyar Szotar. 4th ed. Gyorgy Lako. 1024p. (HUN & SWE.). 1985. 49.95 (*0-8288-1674-3*, M8583) Fr & Eur.

Swedish-Icelandic Dictionary: Svensk-Islandsk Ordbok. G. Holm & A. Davidsson. 849p. (ICE & SWE.). 1982. 150.00 (*0-8288-1104-0*, M2831) Fr & Eur.

Swedish Immigrants in Lincoln's Time. Nels Hokanson. Ed. by Franklyn D. Scott. LC 78-15187. (Scandinavians in America Ser.). 1979. reprint ed. lib. bdg. 28.95 (*0-405-11640-3*) Ayer.

Swedish Imperial Experience, 1560-1718. Michael Roberts. LC 78-58799. 166p. 1984. pap. 19.95 (*0-521-27889-9*) Cambridge U Pr.

Swedish in Three Months. (Hugo's Language Bks.). 192p. 1993. pap. 9.95 (*0-85285-188-X*) Hunter NJ.

Swedish in Three Months. (Hugo's Language Bks.). 1993. 49.95 incl. audio (*0-85285-189-8*) Hunter NJ.

Swedish Literature in America. A. H. Edgren. 1972. 59.95 (*0-8490-1165-5*) Gordon Pr.

Swedish Lotto Systems: Guaranteed & Tested Strategies. Thomas Ollson. (LOMAP Ser.: Vol. 4). (Illus.). 80p. 1986. pap. 9.95 (*0-936918-08-X*) Intergalactic NJ.

Swedish Mecca of the Plains: A Novel about Lindsborg, Kansas, & the Smoky Valley During the Middle Years. Robert E. Segerhammer. LC 93-25917. (Saga of Smoky Hill Ser.: Vol. 2). (Illus.). 1993. 15.00 (*0-918331-04-8*) Smoky Valley Hist.

Swedish Mentality. Ake Daun. Tr. by Jan Teeland from ENG. LC 95-15481. 240p. 1996. pap. 16.95 (*0-271-01502-0*) Pa St U Pr.

Swedish Mentality. Ake Daun. Tr. by Jan Teeland from ENG. LC 95-14585. 240p. 1996. 35.00 (*0-271-01501-2*) Pa St U Pr.

Swedish-Norwegian Dictionary: Svensk-Norsk Ordbok. 223p. (NOR & SWE.). 1981. 95.00 (*0-8288-1034-6*, M3342) Fr & Eur.

***Swedish Nuclear Dilemma: Energy & the Environment.** William D. Nordhaus. LC 97-19258. (Illus.). 184p. 1997. 39.00 (*0-915707-84-5*) Resources Future.

Swedish Passenger Arrivals in New York 1820-1850. Nils W. Olsson. LC 67-21056. 392p. 1967. 5.00 (*0-318-03677-0*) Swedish-Am.

Swedish Philosopher Axel Haegerstroem & His Relationship to Finland's Struggle to Preserve Her Legal Order, 1899-1917. Jacob W. Sundberg. ix, 77p. (Orig.). 1983. pap. text ed. 10.00 (*0-8377-1129-0*) Rothman.

Swedish Phrase Book. (Hugo's Phrasebks.). 128p. (Orig.). 1989. pap. 4.95 (*0-85285-138-3*) Hunter NJ.

Swedish Phrase Book. Berlitz Editors. (Phrase Bk.). 192p. 1994. pap. 6.95 (*2-8315-0886-X*) Berlitz.

Swedish Place-Names in North America. Otto R. Landelius. Ed. by Raymond Jarvi. Tr. by Karin Franzen. LC 84-14192. 376p. 1985. text ed. 34.95 (*0-8093-1204-2*) S Ill U Pr.

Swedish-Polish, Polish-Swedish Dictionary. L. Sikorski. (POL & SWE.). 1992. write for info. (*0-8288-7277-5*, F33180) Fr & Eur.

Swedish Proverbs. Compiled by Joanne Asala. 63p. 1994. pap. 10.95 (*0-941016-98-6*) Penfield.

Swedish Recipes. Ed. by G & R Publishing Staff. (Uni-Bks.). 160p. (Orig.). 1994. pap. text ed. 3.00 (*1-56383-036-1*, 7200) G & R Pub.

Swedish Room. Lars Sjoberg & Ursula Sjoberg. (Illus.). 192p. 1994. 45.00 (*0-679-42981-6*) Pantheon.

Swedish Room. Lars Sjoberg & Ursula Sjoberg. (Illus.). 192p. 1996. pap. 25.00 (*0-679-75839-9*) Pantheon.

Swedish-Russian Dictionary. D. Milanova. 760p. (RUS & SWE.). 1973. 59.95 (*0-8288-6331-8*, M-9077) Fr & Eur.

Swedish Settlement on the Delaware, 2 vols., Set. Amandus Johnson. 1993. reprint ed. lib. bdg. 150.00 (*0-7812-5474-4*) Rprt Serv.

Swedish Settlements on the Delaware, 1638-1664, 2 vols., Set. Amandus Johnson. (Illus.). 1080p. 1996. reprint ed. pap. 80.00 (*0-614-16613-6*, 3030) Clearfield Co.

Swedish-Spanish Dictionary: Svensk-Spansk Ordbok (Esselte) A. Akerlund. 389p. (SPA & SWE.). 1984. 49.95 (*0-8288-1069-9*, M2815) Fr & Eur.

Swedish Swatches: Yellow, Blue, Red & Green Series in Color Photos. Malin Selander. (Illus.). 64p. 1990. 19.95 (*0-9625586-0-5*) Unicorn Bks & Crafts.

Swedish Sweaters. Britt-Marie Christoffersson. Ed. by John Kelsey. LC 90-11129. (Illus.). 144p. 1990. 17.95 (*0-942391-80-2*, 070126) Taunton.

Swedish Texans. Larry Scott. 1992. 15.95 (*0-86701-044-4*) U of Tex Inst Tex Culture.

Swedish Theatre of Chicago, 1868-1950. Henriette C. Naeseth. LC 51-14886. (Augustana College Library Publications: No. 22). 390p. 1951. 4.95 (*0-910182-17-5*) Augustana Coll.

Swedish Theatre of Chicago, 1869-1950. Henriette C. Naeseth. LC 51-14886. (Augustana Historical Society Publications: Vol. 12). 390p. 1951. 4.95 (*0-910184-12-7*) Augustana.

Swedish Travel Pack. (Hugo's Travel Packs Ser.). 128p. (Orig.). 1990. Includes audio cassette. pap. 14.95 (*0-85285-142-1*) Hunter NJ.

Swedish Wage Negotiation System. Anders Olsson. 220p. 1990. text ed. 52.95 (*1-85521-203-X*, Pub. by Dartmth Pub UK) Ashgate Pub Co.

Swedish Women's Writing 1850-1995: Women in Context Series. Helena Forsas-Scott. LC 96-47339. (Women in Context Ser.). (C). 1997. pap. 29.95 (*0-485-92003-4*, Pub. by Athlone Pr UK) Humanities.

Swedish Women's Writing 1850-1995: Women in Context Series: Women Writing 1850-1990. Helena Forsas-Scott. LC 96-47339. (Women in Context Ser.). (C). 1997. 85.00 (*0-485-91003-9*, Pub. by Athlone Pr UK) Humanities.

Swedish Writers. Stanley H. Barkan & Siv Cedering. 1991. boxed 75.00 (*0-89304-949-2*); boxed 50.00 (*0-685-49069-6*) Cross-Cultrl NY.

***Swedish/English Dictionary.** Berlitz Editors. 368p. 1998. pap. 7.95 (*2-8315-6385-2*) Berlitz.

Sweeney Astray. Seamus Heaney. LC 84-1512. 96p. 1984. 25.00 (*0-374-27221-2*) FS&G.

Sweeney Astray. Seamus Heaney. LC 84-1512. 96p. 1985. pap. 9.00 (*0-374-51894-7*) FS&G.

Sweeney Astray. limited ed. Seamus Heaney. LC 84-1512. 96p. 1984. 60.00 (*0-374-27222-0*) FS&G.

Sweeney Todd: Demon Barber of the Barbary Coast. Tim Kelly. 52p. 1978. pap. 4.00 (*0-88680-189-3*) I E Clark.

Sweeney Todd: The Demon Barber of Fleet Street. Stephen Sondheim & Hugh Wheeler. Ed. by Jonathan Dodd. (Musical Library). (Illus.). 256p. 1991. 19.95 (*1-55783-065-7*); pap. 9.95 (*1-55783-066-5*) Applause Theatre Bk Pubs.

***Sweeney Todd - Vocal Selections.** Stephen Sondheim. Ed. by Sy Feldman. 40p. (Orig.). 1997. pap. text ed. 100.00 (*1-57623-970-5*, VAL2021A) Warner Brothers.

***Sweeney Todd, the Demon Barber of Fleet Street: Vocal Selections.** Ed. by Sy Feldman. 44p. (Orig.). (C). 1996. pap. text ed. 12.95 (*1-57623-562-9*, VAL2020A) Warner Brothers.

Sweeney's Flight. Seamus Heaney. (Illus.). 1992. 35.00 (*0-374-27219-0*) FS&G.

Sweeney's Honor. Brian Garfield. 192p. 1980. pap. 1.95 (*0-449-24330-3*, Crest) Fawcett.

Sweeney's Run. Jack D. Hunter. 336p. 1994. mass mkt. 4.99 (*0-8125-1339-8*) Tor Bks.

Sweep. Cy K. Jones. Ed. by T. H. Cornell. 76p. (Orig.). 1996. pap. 12.00 (*0-9652018-1-3*) Bloody Someday.

Sweep of Probability. George N. Schlesinger. LC 90-70848. 224p. (C). 1991. text ed. 33.50 (*0-268-01738-7*) U of Notre Dame Pr.

Swee'pea & Other Playground Legends: Tales of Drugs, Violence & Basketball. John Valenti & Ron Naclerio. LC 90-45321. (Illus.). 256p. pap. 16.95 (*0-935576-39-8*) Kesend Pub Ltd.

Swee'pea & Other Playground Legends: Tales of Drugs, Violence & Basketball. John Valenti & Ron Naclerio. LC 90-45321. (Illus.). 268p. 1990. 26.95 (*0-935576-38-X*) Kesend Pub Ltd.

***Sweeper in the Sky: The Life of Maria Mitchell.** Helen Wright. LC 97-11262. (Illus.). 288p. 1997. 24.95 (*1-883551-70-6*, College Ave Pr); pap. 16.95 (*1-883551-43-9*, College Ave Pr) Attic Studio Pub.

Sweeper to Saint: Stories of Holy India. Baba Hari Dass. Ed. by Ma Renu. LC 80-52021. (Illus.). 208p. (Orig.). 1980. pap. 8.95 (*0-918100-03-8*) Sri Rama.

***Sweepers.** P.T. Deutermann. Date not set. 23.95 (*0-312-15669-3*) St Martin.

Sweeping It Under the Drug: A Complete Book about Recreational Drugs & How to Create a Great Life Without Them. Dennis Marcellino. LC 88-2083. 192p. 1988. pap. 9.95 (*0-945272-04-9*) Lighthouse.

Sweeping the Cobwebs. Lillien J. Martin & Clare De Grucy. Ed. by Robert J. Kastenbaum. LC 78-22209. (Aging & Old Age Ser.). 1979. reprint ed. lib. bdg. 17.95 (*0-405-11823-6*) Ayer.

***Sweeping up Dreams: Lyrics As Poetry.** Tim Henderson. 1996. pap. 10.95 (*0-9649407-2-8*) Sun Cntry Pubns.

Sweeping up the Heart. Betty R. Bryant. 60p. (Orig.). 1993. pap. 12.50 (*0-914125-04-4*) Serif Pr.

Sweeping up the Heart: A Father's Lament for His Daughter. Paul W. Nisly. LC 92-4565. 108p. 1992. pap. 8.95 (*1-56148-069-X*) Good Bks PA.

Sweepstakes Secrets. 1991. lib. bdg. 79.95 (*0-8490-4110-4*) Gordon Pr.

Sweet Addiction. Charlotte Lamb. (Presents Ser.). 1993. pap. 2.89 (*0-373-11530-X*, 1-11530-2) Harlequin Bks.

Sweet Afton. Christopher Howell. LC 91-19109. 72p. (C). 1991. 16.50 (*0-918323-05-3*, True Directs); pap. 8.50 (*0-918323-04-5*, True Directs) Black Riv Pr.

Sweet Amity's Fire. Lee Scofield. 352p. 1993. mass mkt. 4.50 (*0-06-108149-3*, Harp PBks) HarpC.

Sweet & Gentle Struggle: Francis de Dales on the Necessity of Spiritual Friendship. Terence A. McGoldrick. LC 96-8817. 558p. 1996. lib. bdg. 59.50 (*0-7618-0416-1*) U Pr of Amer.

***Sweet & Low.** Becker. 1988. pap. 7.95 (*0-671-64991-4*) PB.

Sweet & Lowdown: America's Popular Song Writers. Warren Craig. LC 77-20223. 1978. 45.00 (*0-8108-1089-1*) Scarecrow.

Sweet & Maxwell's EC Intellectual Property Materials. Ed. by Anna Booy & Audrey Horton. 1994. pap. 52.00 (*0-421-51200-8*) Sweet & Maxwell.

Sweet & Natural: Fruit Sweetened. Sue E. Willett. (Health Ser.). 160p. (Orig.). 1991. pap. text ed. 3.00 (*1-56383-007-8*, 9070) G & R Pub.

Sweet & Natural Baking: Sugar-Free, Flavorful Recipes from Mani's Bakery. Mani Niall. LC 96-100. (Illus.). 132p. 1996. pap. 17.95 (*0-8118-1049-6*) Chronicle Bks.

Sweet & Natural Desserts: East West's Best & Most Wholesome, Sugar- & Dairy-Free Treats. Ed. by East West Journal Editors. (Illus.). 120p. (Orig.). 1986. pap. 7.95 (*0-936184-05-1*) Boston Common Pr.

Sweet & Sassy: Counted Cross Stitch Designs for Children & Beginners. Kathy Anderson. 32p. (Orig.). (J). 1983. pap. 5.98 (*0-88290-216-4*) Horizon Utah.

Sweet & Savory Sauces: More than 60 Recipes that Make Any Meal a Special Occasion. Lorraine Bodger. LC 95-23391. (Illus.). 1995. 15.00 (*0-684-81157-X*, S&S) S&S Trade.

Sweet & Scrumptious Chocolate. Ed. by Linda Piepenbrink. LC 92-63183. 52p. 1993. 4.95 (*0-89821-102-6*, 11655) Reiman Pubns.

Sweet & Silly Muppet Poems. Jack Prelutsky. (First Little Golden Bks.). (Illus.). 24p. (J). (ps-3). 1992. 1.09 (*0-307-10249-1*, Golden Books) Western Pub.

***Sweet & Simple Country Cross-Stitch.** Lori Gardner. LC 96-37979. (Illus.). 128p. 1997. 24.95 (*0-8069-9341-3*, Pub. by D & C Pub UK) Sterling.

Sweet & Simple Country Quilts. Jenni Dobson. LC 96-5185. (Illus.). 144p. 1996. 27.95 (*0-8069-9497-5*) Sterling.

Sweet & Sour. large type ed. Andrew A. Rooney. LC 92-40343. (Basic Ser.). 350p. 1993. reprint ed. lib. bdg. 22.95 (*1-56054-628-X*) Thorndike Pr.

Sweet & Sour: One Woman's Chinese Adventure, One Man's Chinese Torture. Brooks Robards & Jim Kaplan. LC 95-67939. 200p. (Orig.). 1995. pap. 14.95 (*0-9645250-0-3*) Smmrst Pr.

Sweet & Sour: Stories from the Working World of Police, Social Workers, Lawyers, Judges, Gaolers & Occasional Villains. Rod Settle. 181p. 1995. pap. 19.95 (*1-86287-182-5*, Pub. by Federation Pr AU) Gaunt.

Sweet & Sour: Tales from China. Carol Kendall. (J). (gr. 4-7). 1990. pap. 7.95 (*0-395-54798-9*, Clarion Bks) HM.

Sweet & Sour: Uncle Rolf's Guide to Eating in New York's Chinatown. Rolf Myller. 48p. 1991. pap. 5.95 (*0-9631810-3-3*) Cato Pub.

Sweet & Sour Animal Book. Langston Hughes. (Illus.). 48p. (J). 1994. 16.95 (*0-19-509185-X*) OUP.

***Sweet & Sour Animal Book.** Langston Hughes & Ben Vereen. (Iona & Peter Opie Library of Children's Literature). (Illus.). (J). 1997. pap. 9.95 (*0-19-512030-2*) OUP.

Sweet & Sour Milk. Nuruddin Farah. 242p. (Orig.). 1992. pap. 12.00 (*1-55597-159-8*) Graywolf.

***Sweet & Sour Secrets.** Patricia T. Kienzle. (Illus.). 32p. (J). (gr. 2-3). 1991. teacher ed. pap. 3.95 (*1-890798-03-7*) P T Kienzle.

Sweet & Sugar Free: Nutritional Sweets Cookbook. Karen E. Barkie. 5.95 (*0-317-05971-8*) Hypoglycemia Foun.

Sweet & Sugarfree: An All Natural Fruit-Sweetened Dessert Cookbook. Karen E. Barkie. LC 82-5606. 192p. 1982. pap. 7.95 (*0-312-78066-4*) St Martin.

Sweet Angel Band: And Other Stories. R. M. Kinder. (Orig.). 1991. pap. 11.95 (*0-9627460-2-9*) Helicon Nine Eds.

Sweet Annie's Pass. Marilyn Pappano. (Intimate Moments Ser.). 1993. mass mkt. 3.50 (*0-373-07512-X*, 5-07512-2) Silhouette.

Sweet Anointing. Tom Franks. 144p. (Orig.). 1989. pap. 6.95 (*0-88144-141-4*) Mercedes Ministries.

Sweet Apple Gardening Book. Celestine Sibley. 224p. 1989. 12.95 (*0-934601-68-2*) Peachtree Pubs.

Sweet Aroma, Falling in Love: Inspirational Thoughts from a Country Girl's Diary. Myrtle W. McGrew. LC 91-77500. (Illus.). 192p. (Orig.). 1992. pap. 8.95 (*0-9624398-8-6*) Abel II Pub.

Sweet Awakening. Marjorie Farrell. 384p. (Orig.). 1995. mass mkt. 4.99 (*0-451-40492-0*, Topaz) NAL-Dutton.

***Sweet Baby.** Sala. 1998. mass mkt. 5.99 (*1-55166-416-X*) Harlequin Bks.

Sweet Baby Coming. Eloise Greenfield. (Illus.). 14p. (J). (ps). 1994. 5.95 (*0-694-00578-9*, Festival) HarpC Child Bks.

Sweet Bamboo: A Saga of a Chinese American Family. Louise L. Larson. LC 89-62055. (Illus.). viii, 227p. (Orig.). 1990. pap. 12.95 (*0-930377-02-8*) Chinese Hist CA.

Sweet Bargain. Kate Moore. 224p. (Orig.). 1993. mass mkt. 3.99 (*0-380-77056-3*) Avon.

Sweet Betrayal. large type ed. Helen Brooks. 1994. lib. bdg. 19.95 (*0-263-13647-7*) Thorndike Pr.

Sweet Betsy from Pike. (Vocal Score Ser.). 056p. 1983. pap. 15.00 (*0-88188-474-X*, 00448614) H Leonard.

***Sweet Beulah Land.** Date not set. pap. 1.20 (*0-8341-9226-8*) Lillenas.

Sweet Bird of Youth. Tennessee Williams. 1962. pap. 5.25 (*0-8222-1104-1*) Dramatists Play.

Sweet Bird of Youth. Tennessee Williams. (Three by Tennessee Williams). 1976. pap. write for info. (*0-318-54501-2*) NAL-Dutton.

Sweet Bird of Youth. Tennessee Williams. LC 59-9492. 144p. 1959. pap. 8.95 (*0-8112-0596-7*, NDP409) New Directions.

Sweet Bird of Youth see Three by Tennessee Williams

***Sweet Bitter Love.** unabridged ed. Rita Schiano. LC 96-69426. 256p. (Orig.). 1996. pap. 10.99 (*1-883061-15-6*) Rising NY.

Sweet Blood. Pat Graversen. 256p. 1992. mass mkt. 4.50 (*0-8217-3907-7*, Zebra Kensgtn) Kensgtn Pub Corp.

Sweet Bondage. Lilian Barnes. (Rainbow Romances Ser.). 160p. 1993. 14.95 (*0-7090-4911-0*, Hale-Parkwest) Parkwest Pubns.

***Sweet Bread Machine Cookbook.** Melissa Clark. 192p. 1997. mass mkt. 5.99 (*0-425-15695-8*) Berkley Pub.

Sweet Breath of Life: A Salute to Your Magnificent Being. Luzanne Lucas. LC 95-92000. 160p. 1995. 16.95 (*0-9645269-6-4*) Desirata Pr.

Sweet Bunch of Daisies: Folk Songs from Alabama: A Collection of over 265 - Words & Music. LC 89-61565. (Illus.). 300p. 1991. 24.95 (*1-938991-41-9*) Colonial Pr AL.

Sweet By 'N' By. Frank Higgins. 1996. pap. 5.25 (*0-8222-1551-9*) Dramatists Play.

Sweet Chance. Carole Howey. mp. (Orig.). 1995. mass mkt., pap. text ed. 4.99 (*0-8439-3733-5*) Dorchester Pub Co.

Sweet Chariot: Slave Family & Household Structure in Nineteenth-Century Louisiana. Ann P. Malone. LC 91-50787. (Fred W. Morrison Series in Southern Studies). (Illus.). xvi, 369p. (C). 1992. 45.00 (*0-8078-2026-1*) U of NC Pr.

Sweet Chariot: Slave Family & Household Structure in Nineteenth-Century Louisiana. Ann P. Malone. LC 91-50787. (Fred W. Morrison Series in Southern Studies). (Illus.). 383p. (C). 1996. pap. text ed. 17.95 (*0-8078-4590-6*) U of NC Pr.

Sweet Charity. 1994. pap. 10.95 (*1-57007-037-7*, XW1652) Astor Bks.

***Sweet Charity.** Rachel Wilson. (Homespun Ser.). 304p. 1997. mass mkt. 5.99 (*0-515-12134-7*) Jove Pubns.

Sweet Charity: The Role & Workings of Voluntary Organisations. Ed. by Chris Hanvey & Terry Philpot. 240p. (C). 1996. pap. 18.95 (*0-415-13801-9*); text ed. 65.00 (*0-415-13800-0*) Routledge.

Sweet Charity - Broadway Vocal Selections. 1986. pap. 10.95 (*0-89898-471-8*) Warner Brothers.

Sweet Cheat. large type ed. Meg Alexander. 350p. 1996. 21.50 (*0-263-14688-X*, Pub. by M & B UK) Ulverscroft.

Sweet Cheat Gone. Alannah Knight. 192p. 1992. 19.00 (*0-7278-4379-6*) Severn Hse.

Sweet Cherry Wine. Carol Schmidt. 272p. 1994. pap. 9.95 (*1-56280-063-9*) Naiad Pr.

Sweet Clara & the Freedom Quilt. Deborah Hopkinson. LC 91-11601. (Illus.). 40p. (J). (gr. k-5). 1993. 16.00 (*0-679-82311-5*); lib. bdg. 16.99 (*0-679-92311-X*) Knopf Bks Yng Read.

Sweet Clara & the Freedom Quilt. Deborah Hopkinson. (Illus.). 32p. (J). 1995. pap. 6.99 (*0-679-87472-0*) Random.

Sweet Clover: A Romance of the White City. Clara L. Burnham. LC 92-70330. (Great Lakes Romances Ser.). 256p. (Orig.). 1992. reprint ed. pap. 8.95 (*0-923048-80-4*) Bigwater Pub.

Sweet Comfort for Feeble Saints. Charles H. Spurgeon. 1978. mass mkt. 0.75 (*1-56186-336-X*) Pilgrim Pubns.

Sweet Confessions. 224p. 1991. pap. 4.50 (*0-88184-777-1*) Carroll & Graf.

***Sweet Confessions.** 4.50 (*0-7867-0777-1*) Carroll & Graf.

Sweet Corn: Poems. James Stevenson. 64p. (J). (gr. 3-8). 1995. 15.00 (*0-614-14519-8*) Greenwillow.

***Sweet Corn: Poems.** James Stevenson. (Illus.). 64p. (J). (gr. 3 up). 1995. 15.00 (*0-688-12647-2*) Greenwillow.

Sweet Creek Holler. Ruth White. 168p. (YA). (gr. 7 up). 1988. 16.00 (*0-374-37360-4*) FS&G.

Sweet Creek Holler. Ruth White. (YA). (gr. 5 up). 1992. pap. 4.50 (*0-374-47375-7*) FS&G.

Sweet Dalliance. Lisa Bingham. Ed. by Caroline Tolley. 256p. (Orig.). 1994. mass mkt. 5.50 (*0-671-88711-4*) PB.

Sweet Danger. Margery Allingham. 256p. 1988. mass mkt. 5.95 (*0-14-008779-6*, Penguin Bks) Viking Penguin.

Sweet Dark Places: Poetry by Leslea Newman. Leslea Newman. 110p. (Orig.). 1991. pap. 8.95 (*0-939821-01-X*) Pride OH.

Sweet Days Die. William Morris. (Poetry Ser.). (Illus.). 96p. 1996. 19.95 (*1-85793-644-2*, Pub. by Pavilion UK) Trafalgar.

Sweet Days of Discipline. Fleur Jaeggy. Tr. by Tim Parks from ITA. LC 93-9196. 112p. (Orig.). 1993. pap. 9.95 (*0-8112-1235-1*, NDP758) New Directions.

Sweet Deal. John Westermann. LC 91-42130. 224p. 1992. 18.95 (*0-939149-56-7*) Soho Press.

Sweet Deal. John Wastermann. Ed. by Paul McCarthy. 320p. 1993. reprint ed. mass mkt. 5.50 (*0-671-79170-2*) PB.

Sweet Death. Bill Waggoner. 192p. 1992. 19.95 (*0-8027-3208-9*) Walker & Co.

Sweet Death, Kind Death. Amanda Cross. 244p. 1987. mass mkt. 5.99 (*0-345-35254-8*) Ballantine.

Sweet Decadence. Lisa Bingham. 1996. mass mkt., pap. 5.99 (*0-671-88713-0*, PB Trade Paper) PB.

Sweet Deceiver. April Ashmore. 384p. 1994. mass mkt. 4.50 (*0-8217-4701-0*, Zebra Kensgtn) Kensgtn Pub Corp.

Sweet Deceiver. Angie Ray. 336p. 1995. mass mkt. 4.99 (*0-06-108379-8*, Harp PBks) HarpC.

Sweet Deception. Mary M. Douglas. 122p. (Orig.). 1996. spiral bd., pap. 18.50 (*0-9643764-2-3*) Wildot Pr.

Sweet Deception. Vanessa Hale. 1995. 17.95 (*0-8034-9102-6*, 095121) Bouregy.

***Sweet Deception.** Susan Kearney. (Intrigue Ser.: No. 428). 1997. mass mkt. 3.75 (*0-373-22428-1*, 1-22428-6) Harlequin Bks.

Sweet Deceptions: Create Decadent Desserts Without All That Fat (or Guilt)! Patty A. Neeley. LC 95-42385. 1996. spiral bd. 14.95 (*0-7615-0287-4*) Prima Pub.

Sweet Defiance. Lisa Bingham. 1995. mass mkt. 5.99 (*0-671-88712-2*) PB.

Sweet Diamond Dust: And Other Stories. Rosario Ferre. 208p. 1996. pap. 10.95 (*0-452-27748-5*, Plume) NAL-Dutton.

Sweet Disorder & the Carefully Careless. Robert Maxwell. LC 93-32943. (Princeton Papers on Architecture: No. 2). (Illus.). 336p. (Orig.). 1994. pap. 19.95 (*1-56898-005-1*) Princeton Arch.

Sweet Dream Luke Lion. Kidsbooks Inc. Staff. mass mkt. 2.98 (*1-56156-340-4*) Kidsbks.

***Sweet Dream Pie.** Audrey Wood. LC 96-54644. (Illus.). (J). 1998. write for info. (*0-590-96204-3*, Blue Sky Press) Scholastic Inc.

Sweet Dreams. Kate Daniel. 224p. (YA). 1992. mass mkt. 3.50 (*0-06-106720-2*, Harp PBks) HarpC.

Sweet Dreams. Shelley Duvall. 8p. (J). 1992. pap. 11.98 incl. cd-rom (*1-56668-144-8*, 70505-2); pap. 7.98 incl. audio (*1-56668-142-1*, 70405-4) BMG Kidz.

Sweet Dreams. Robin J. Gunn. LC 94-6239. (Christy Miller Ser.: Vol. 11). (J). 1994. pap. 5.99 (*1-56179-255-1*) Focus Family.

***Sweet Dreams.** Jane Johnson. Ed. by Patrick Caton. 365p. 1997. spiral bd., pap. 6.50 (*1-56245-309-2*) Great Quotations.

Sweet Dreams. Barbara J. Neasi. LC 87-15083. (Rookie Reader Ser.). (Illus.). 32p. (J). (ps-2). 1987. pap. 3.50 (*0-516-42084-4*); lib. bdg. 15.00 (*0-516-02084-6*) Childrens.

Sweet Dreams. rev. ed. John Preston. (Mission of Alex Kane Ser.). 1992. reprint ed. mass mkt. 4.95 (*1-56333-062-8*, Badboy) Masquerade.

Sweet Dreams: A Garden Lullaby. Bobbi McPeak-Bailey. (Illus.). 48p. (Orig.). (J). (gr. k-3). 1995. pap. 9.95 (*0-9625005-4-2*) Wee Pr.

S

S

Sweet Dreams: A Lift-the-Flap Bedtime Story. Sue Porter. (Illus.). 24p. (J). 1996. 14.95 (*0-7894-1104-0*) DK Pub Inc.

Sweet Dreams: Bedtime Poems & Lullabyes. Bruce Lansky. (J). (ps-k). 1996. 15.00 (*0-671-57046-3*, S&S) S&S Trade.

Sweet Dreams: Bedtime Poems, Songs, & Lullabies. Bruce Lansky. (Illus.). 1996. 15.00 (*0-671-53479-3*); write for info. (*0-88166-246-1*) Meadowbrook.

Sweet Dreams: Heirloom Quilts for Babies. Deborah Gordon & Helen Frost. (Illus.). 72p. (Orig.). 1995. pap. 17.95 (*0-9633917-3-9*) First Star AZ.

Sweet Dreams: Sexuality, Gender & Popular Fiction. Ed. by Susannah Radstone. (C). 1988. pap. 19.95 (*0-85315-672-7*, Pub. by Lawrence & Wishart UK) NYU Pr.

Sweet Dreams: The Art of Bessie Pease Gutman. Pamela Prince & Bessie Pease. 1985. 14.95 (*0-517-55672-3*, Harmony) Crown Pub Group.

***Sweet Dreams: 3 Sleepytime Books of Poems, Prayers & Lullabies.** Joan W. Anglund. (J). 11.95 (*0-614-19250-1*, Litl Simon S&S) S&S Childrens.

Sweet Dreams & Monsters: A Beginner's Guide to Dreams & Nightmares & Things That Go Bump under the Bed. Peter Mayle. (Illus.). (J). (gr. k-up). 1986. 9.95 (*0-517-55972-2*, Harmony) Crown Pub Group.

Sweet Dreams Big Book. (Rookie Readers Big Bks.). (Illus.). 32p. (J). (ps-2). 1990. pap. 32.40 (*0-516-49456-2*) Childrens.

Sweet Dreams, Clown-Arounds. Joanna Cole. LC 93-13038. (Parents Magazine Read Aloud Original Ser.). (Illus.). (J). 1994. lib. bdg. 17.27 (*0-8368-0976-9*) Gareth Stevens Inc.

Sweet Dreams, Clown-Arounds. Joanna Cole. LC 85-6348. (Illus.). 48p. (J). (ps-3). 1985. 5.95 (*0-8193-1138-3*) Parents.

Sweet Dreams, Irene. Jan Burke. 256p. 1995. mass mkt. 4.99 (*0-380-72350-6*) Avon.

Sweet Dreams, Irene. Jan Burke. LC 93-31179. 1994. 18.00 (*0-671-78210-X*) S&S Trade.

Sweet Dreams, My Darling. Anne Joseph. 1990. mass mkt. 3.95 (*1-55817-414-1*, Pinncle Kensgtn) Kensgtn Pub Corp.

Sweet Dreams My King. Terry Page. (Illus.). 24p. (J). (gr. 2-6). 1996. pap. text ed. 4.00 (*1-887864-61-X*); lib. bdg. 7.00 (*1-887864-22-9*) Boo Bks.

Sweet Dreams My King Coloring Book. Terry Page. (Illus.). 32p. (J). (ps-5). 1996. pap. 3.00 (*1-887864-23-7*) Boo Bks.

Sweet Dreams Nantucket. Tom Simms. LC 84-62252. (Illus.). 128p. (Orig.). 1985. pap. 12.95 (*0-932493-00-9*) Rejected Works.

Sweet Dreams of the Wild Vol. 1: Poems for Bedtime. Rebecca K. Dottlich. LC 94-60259. (Illus.). 32p. (J). (ps-k). 1996. 15.95 (*1-56397-180-1*, Wordsong) Boyds Mills Pr.

Sweet Dreams Robyn: A Father Writes about His Daughter's Struggle with Leukemia. Dan Rothermel. Ed. by Joy Johnson. (Illus.). 74p. 1991. pap. 5.50 (*1-56123-026-X*) Centering Corp.

Sweet Dreams, Serena. large type ed. Marjorie Everett. LC 93-10507. 1993. pap. 13.95 (*1-56054-747-2*) Thorndike Pr.

Sweet Dreams, Spot! Eric Hill. (Soft Spots Ser.). (Illus.). 8p. (J). (gr. k-1). 1984. 4.95 (*0-399-21069-5*, Putnam) Putnam Pub Group.

Sweet Dreams, Tweety. Jean Lewis. (Golden Little Super Shape Bks.). (Illus.). 24p. (J). (ps). 1993. pap. 1.49 (*0-307-10552-0*, Golden Books) Western Pub.

Sweet Dried Apples: A Vietnamese Wartime Childhood. Rosemary Breckler. LC 95-518. (Illus.). 32p. (J). (ps-3). 1996. 15.95 (*0-395-73570-X*) HM.

***Sweet Ember.** Barbara Delinsky. 256p. 1997. mass mkt. 5.99 (*0-06-101098-7*, Harp PBks) HarpC.

Sweet Enchantment. Elizabeth Graham. 384p. 1995. mass mkt. 4.99 (*0-8217-5043-7*, Zebra Kensgtn) Kensgtn Pub Corp.

Sweet Enchantress. Parris A. Bonds. 448p. (Orig.). 1991. mass mkt., pap. text ed. 4.99 (*0-8439-3177-9*) Dorchester Pub Co.

Sweet Enemy & Love on Trial. Diana Palmer. (Diana Palmer Duets Ser.: No. 1). 1990. mass mkt. 3.25 (*0-373-48222-1*) Harlequin Bks.

Sweet Enemy Mine. Ana Leigh. 448p. (Orig.). 1991. mass mkt., pap. text ed. 4.50 (*0-8439-3114-0*) Dorchester Pub Co.

Sweet Eros & Witness: Two One-Act Plays. Terrence McNally. 1969. pap. 5.25 (*0-8222-1105-X*) Dramatists Play.

Sweet Escape. Susan Macias. 304p. (Orig.). 1994. mass mkt. 4.99 (*0-7865-0025-5*) Diamond.

Sweet Everlasting. Patricia Gaffney. 384p. (Orig.). 1993. pap. 4.99 (*0-451-40375-4*, Topaz) NAL-Dutton.

Sweet Everlasting: A Novel. Judson Mitcham. LC 95-24474. 200p. 1996. 22.95 (*0-8203-1807-8*) U of Ga Pr.

***Sweet Everlasting: A Novel.** Judson Mitcham. 1997. mass mkt. 6.99 (*0-380-73027-8*) Avon.

Sweet Evil. Stephen Singular. 288p. (Orig.). 1994. mass mkt. 4.99 (*0-380-76795-3*) Avon.

Sweet Fancy. Sally Martin. 224p. (Orig.). 1994. mass mkt. 3.99 (*0-380-77398-8*) Avon.

Sweet Fifteen. Diane G. Bertrand. LC 94-32656. 224p. (YA). (gr. 6-12). 1995. 12.95 (*1-55885-122-4*); pap. 7.95 (*1-55885-133-X*) Arte Publico.

***Sweet Fifteen.** Diane G. Bertrand. (YA). (gr. 6-12). 1996. pap. text ed. 7.95 (*1-55885-184-4*) Arte Publico.

Sweet Flypaper of Life. rev. ed. Langston Hughes. 112p. 1985. reprint ed. 28.95 (*0-88258-152-X*) Howard U Pr.

Sweet Foolishness. Nicole Cynthia. 36p. (Orig.). 1985. pap. 2.95 (*0-9609794-2-5*) A Foster.

Sweet Fortune. Jayne Ann Krentz. 352p. 1991. mass mkt. 5.99 (*0-671-72854-7*) PB.

***Sweet Fortune.** large type ed. Jayne Ann Krentz. (General Ser.). 458p. 1992. lib. bdg. 21.95 (*0-8161-5412-0*, GK Hall) Thorndike Pr.

***Sweet Friction.** Marcus Van Heller. 560p. 1997. mass mkt. 7.95 (*0-7867-0451-9*) Carroll & Graf.

Sweet Friday Island. Theodore Taylor. LC 93-32435. 176p. (YA). (gr. 7 up). 1994. 11.00 (*0-15-200009-7*); pap. 5.00 (*0-15-200012-7*) HarBrace.

Sweet Gogarty. Matthew Hochberg. LC 75-19570. (Illus.). 111p. (C). 1975. pap. 12.50 (*0-913204-04-8*) December Pr.

Sweet Grapes: How to Stop Being Infertile & Start Living Again. Jean W. Carter & Michael P. Carter. LC 89-34135. 144p. 1989. pap. 12.00 (*0-944934-01-3*) Perspect Indiana.

Sweet Grass. Andy Juniper. 176p. 1995. lib. bdg. 39.00 (*0-8095-4859-3*) Borgo Pr.

Sweet Grass. Andy Juniper. 176p. pap. 12.95 (*0-88962-573-5*) Mosaic.

Sweet Grass. Andy Juniper. 169p. 1994. pap. 14.95 (*0-88962-575-1*) Mosaic.

Sweet Harvests On. Sam Silva. (Dog River Review Poetry Ser.). (Illus.). 24p. (Orig.). 1992. pap. 3.00 (*0-916155-20-X*) Trout Creek.

Sweet Health. Aaron Maree. (Illus.). 128p. 1996. 19.00 (*0-207-18428-3*) HarperColl Wrld.

Sweet Hearts. Jill M. Landis et al. 320p. (Orig.). 1993. mass mkt. 4.99 (*1-55773-855-6*) Diamond.

Sweet Heat. Dave DeWitt & Melissa Stock. 192p. (Orig.). 1996. pap. 16.95 (*0-89815-817-6*) Ten Speed Pr.

Sweet Hereafter: A Novel. Russell Banks. LC 90-56404. 272p. 1992. pap. 12.00 (*0-06-092324-5*, PL) HarpC.

Sweet Hollow. Stories. Lou V. Crabtree. LC 83-14934. 106p. 1984. pap. 9.95 (*0-8071-1133-3*) La State U Pr.

Sweet Home: Invisible Cities in the Afro-American Novel. Charles Scruggs. LC 92-30830. 272p. (C). 1993. text ed. 45.00 (*0-8018-4502-5*) Johns Hopkins.

Sweet Home: Invisible Cities in the Afro-American Novel. Charles Scruggs. LC 92-30830. 272p. 1995. pap. text ed. 15.95 (*0-8018-5127-0*) Johns Hopkins.

Sweet Home Alabama: Food for Family & Friends from the Heart of the South. Junior League of Huntsville Staff. 192p. 1995. 21.95 (*0-9618113-2-3*) J L Huntsville.

Sweet Home Chicago. Joel Lipmann. 1980. pap. 2.00 (*0-686-70612-9*) Quixote.

Sweet Home Chicago: Przewodnik Po Chicago. Jan Kaluza. Ed. by Polish Book Fair, Inc. Staff. (Illus.). 150p. 1995. pap. 12.00 (*1-885889-65-8*) Home Tutor.

Sweet Home Chicago: The Real City Guide. 4th rev. ed. Ed. by Amy Teschner. LC 93-234194. (Illus.). 496p. 1992. pap. 13.95 (*1-55652-161-8*) Chicago Review.

Sweet Home in the Oregon Cascades. Margaret S. Carey & Patricia H. Hainline. (Illus.). 140p. 1979. pap. 7.95 (*0-934784-04-3*) Calapooia Pubns.

Sweet Home, Saturday Night. David Baker. 96p. 1991. pap. 12.00 (*1-55728-203-X*) U of Ark Pr.

Sweet, Hot & Blue: St. Louis' Musical Heritage. Lyn D. Cunningham & Jimmy Jones. LC 88-27353. (Illus.). 255p. 1989. lib. bdg. 45.00 (*0-89950-302-0*) McFarland & Co.

Sweet Hour of Prayer. 3rd ed. Don DeWelt. 56p. 1986. 2.99 (*0-89900-144-0*) College Pr Pub.

Sweet Illusion. large type ed. Angela Carson. 358p. 1994. 25.99 (*0-7505-0634-2*, Pub. by Magna Print Bks UK) Ulverscroft.

Sweet Illusions. Walter D. Myers. 146p. (Orig.). (YA). 1987. 14.95 (*0-915924-14-5*); pap. 7.95 (*0-915924-15-3*) Tchrs & Writers Coll.

Sweet Indulgences: Desserts for Every Occasion. Norman Kolpas. 1993. pap. write for info. (*1-56799-022-3*, Friedman-Fairfax) M Friedman Pub Grp Inc.

Sweet Inspirations: A Sugar Free Dessert Cookbook. 4th ed. Patti Lynch. (Illus.). 150p. 1992. reprint ed. pap. 12. 95 (*0-9620469-0-6*) Sweet Inspirations.

***Sweet Inspirations: Life's Golden Rulebook.** Nubia Levon. (Orig.). 1997. pap. 12.99 (*1-890254-49-5*) Innov Pub Concepts.

***Sweet Intimacy Spa.** Restrepo. 208p. 1997. pap. 10.00 (*0-06-092822-0*) HarpC.

Sweet Iris. Aileen Humphrey. 336p. (Orig.). 1994. pap. text ed. 4.99 (*0-515-11381-6*) Jove Pubns.

Sweet Is the Word: Reflections on the Prophets, Principles, & Promises of the Book of Mormon. Marilyn Arnold. LC 96-12275. 1996. write for info. (*1-55503-925-1*) Covenant Comms.

Sweet Justice. Mary L. Baxter. 384p. (Orig.). 1994. mass mkt. 5.50 (*0-446-36494-0*) Warner Bks.

Sweet Kate. large type ed. Lucy Gillen. (Romance Ser.). 304p. 1992. 25.99 (*0-7089-2639-8*) Ulverscroft.

Sweet Kids: How to Balance Diabetes Control & Good Nutrition with Family Peace. Betty P. Brackenridge & Richard Rubin. LC 96-20277. 256p. 1996. pap. 14.95 (*0-945448-67-8*) Am Diabetes.

Sweet Killough: Let Go Your Anchor. Maurice Hayes. (Illus.). 219p. 9500. pap. 15.95 (*0-85640-528-0*, Pub. by Blackstaff Pr IE) Dufour.

Sweet Kiss of Summer. Francine Pascal. (Sweet Valley University Ser.: No. 23). 240p. (YA). (gr. 9 up). 1996. mass mkt. 3.99 (*0-553-56707-1*, Sweet Valley) BDD Bks Young Read.

Sweet Knight Times. Andrea Edwards. (Special Edition Ser.: No. 740). 1992. mass mkt. 3.39 (*0-373-09740-9*, 5-09740-7) Harlequin Bks.

Sweet La-La Land. Robert Campbell. Ed. by Jane Chelius. 320p. 1991. reprint ed. mass mkt. 4.99 (*0-671-73236-6*) PB.

***Sweet Land of Liberty.** Charles C. Coffin. 12.95 (*0-938558-48-X*) Noble Pub Assocs.

***Sweet Land of Liberty? The Black Struggle for Civil Rights in Twentieth-Century America.** Robert Cook. LC 97-8579. (Studies in Modern History). 1997. write for info. (*0-582-21531-5*); pap. write for info. (*0-582-21532-3*) Longman.

Sweet Land of Liberty? The Supreme Court & Individual Rights. Henry M. Holzer. 198p. 1983. 14.95 (*0-917572-03-3*) Common Sense.

Sweet Lavender. Margaret E. Porter. 224p. 1993. pap. 3.99 (*0-451-17728-2*, Sig) NAL-Dutton.

Sweet Lavender. Margaret E. Porter. (Regency Romance Ser.). 224p. 1992. 19.95 (*0-8027-1205-3*) Walker & Co.

Sweet Liar. Jude Deveraux. Ed. by Linda Marrow. 384p. (Orig.). 1992. pap. 17.00 (*0-671-79190-7*) PB.

Sweet Liar. Jude Deveraux. Ed. by Linda Marrow. (Orig.). 1993. pap. 6.99 (*0-671-68974-6*) PB.

Sweet Liar. large type ed. Jude Deveraux. LC 92-38592. (General Ser.). 586p. (Orig.). 1993. pap. 18.95 (*0-8161-5623-9*) G K Hall.

***Sweet Liberty.** Joseph O'Connor. 384p. 1997. pap. 14.95 (*1-57098-151-5*) R Rinehart.

Sweet Liberty: Travels in Irish America. Joseph O'Conner. 367p. 1996. 24.95 (*1-57098-105-1*) R Rinehart.

***Sweet Liberty: Travels in Irish America.** Joseph O'Conner. 384p. (Orig.). 1997. pap. 17.95 (*0-330-33323-2*, Pub. by Picador UK) Trans-Atl Phila.

***Sweet Lies.** Viveca Carlyle. 352p. 1997. mass mkt. 4.99 (*0-7860-0425-8*, Pinncle Kensgtn) Kensgtn Pub Corp.

Sweet Lies & Rainbow Skies. Jane M. Choate. 1993. 17.95 (*0-8034-9015-1*) Bouregy.

Sweet Lies & Rainbow Skies. large type ed. Jane M. Choate. LC 95-9787. (Nightingale Ser.). 192p. 1995. reprint ed. pap. 17.95 (*0-7838-1290-6*, GK Hall) Thorndike Pr.

Sweet Little Jesus Boy: A Soliloquy. Robert H. McGimsey. 32p. 1973. pap. 2.95 (*0-911336-53-2*) Sci of Mind.

Sweet Lorain. Bruce Weigl. 1996. 29.95 (*0-8101-5053-0*); pap. 11.95 (*0-8101-5054-9*) TriQuarterly.

Sweet Love Survive. Susan Johnson. 320p. 1996. mass mkt. 5.99 (*0-553-56329-7*, Fanfare) Bantam.

Sweet Lucy Wine. Stories. Dabney Stuart. LC 91-21245. 128p. 1992. 18.95 (*0-8071-1707-2*) La State U Pr.

Sweet Lullaby. Lorraine Heath. 304p. (Orig.). 1994. mass mkt. 4.99 (*1-55773-987-0*) Diamond.

Sweet Madness: A Study of Humor. William F. Fry, Jr. LC 63-17821. (Paperbounds Ser.: No. PB-3). 1968. pap. 8.95 (*0-87015-163-0*) Pacific Bks.

Sweet Magnolia. Virginia L. Kroll. LC 93-11966. (Illus.). 32p. (J). (ps-4). 1995. 14.95 (*0-88106-415-7*); pap. 6.95 (*0-88106-414-9*); lib. bdg. 15.88 (*0-88106-416-5*) Charlesbridge Pub.

Sweet Maple: Life, Lore & Recipes from the Sugarbush. James Lawrence & Rux Martin. LC 93-24090. 224p. 1993. 29.95 (*1-881527-00-X*); pap. 19.95 (*1-881527-01-8*) Chapters Pub.

***Sweet-Maria' Italian Cookie Tray: A Cookbook.** Maria B. Sanchez. 1997. pap. 13.95 (*0-312-15670-7*, Griffin) St Martin.

Sweet Marmalade, Sour Oranges: Contemporary Portuguese Women's Fiction. Ed. & Intro. by Alice Clemente. LC 92-73209. 217p. (Orig.). 1994. pap. text ed. 12.50 (*0-943722-20-9*) Gavea-Brown.

Sweet Medicine. David Seals. 1994. pap. 10.00 (*0-517-88188-8*) Crown Pub Group.

Sweet Medicine: Sites of Indian Massacres, Battlefields, & Treaties. Drex Brooks. LC 94-6689. (Illus.). 175p. (C). 1995. 26.95 (*0-8263-1538-0*) U of NM Pr.

Sweet Memories. LaVyrle Spencer. 384p. 1988. pap. 4.50 (*0-373-97078-1*) Harlequin Bks.

Sweet Memories. LaVyrle Spencer. (Mira Bks.). 1995. mass mkt. 5.99 (*1-55166-057-1*, 1-66057-0, Mira Bks) Harlequin Bks.

Sweet Memories: Victorian Photograph Album. Nancy Akmon & Roni Akmon. (Illus.). 12p. 1996. 11.95 (*1-884807-16-X*) Blushing Rose.

Sweet Memories Still. Natalie Kinsey-Warnock. (J). 1997. pap. 14.99 (*0-525-65230-2*) NAL-Dutton.

Sweet Miss Seeton. Hamilton Crane. (Heron Carvic's Miss Seeton Ser.). 272p. 1996. 21.95 (*0-425-15471-8*, Prime Crime) Berkley Pub.

***Sweet Miss Seeton.** Hamilton Crane. 256p. 1997. reprint ed. mass mkt. 5.99 (*0-425-15962-0*, Prime Crime) Berkley Pub.

Sweet Mother: Modern African Music. Wolfgang Bender. Tr. by Wolfgang Freis. (Chicago Studies in Ethnomusicology). (Illus.). 256p. 1991. pap. 17.95 (*0-226-04254-5*) U Ch Pr.

Sweet Mystery: A Book of Remembering. Judith H. Paterson. LC 95-13113. 288p. 1996. 23.00 (*0-374-27226-3*) FS&G.

***Sweet Mystery: A Southern Memoir of Family Alcoholism, Mental Illness, & Recovery.** Judith H. Paterson. 1997. pap. text ed. 12.00 (*0-374-52499-8*, Noonday) FS&G.

Sweet Myth-tery of Life. Robert L. Asprin. 240p. 1995. mass mkt. 5.50 (*0-441-00194-7*) Ace Bks.

Sweet Myth-tery of Life. Robert L. Asprin. LC 93-47256. (Illus.). 1994. write for info. (*0-89865-891-8*) Donning Co.

Sweet Myth-tery of Life. limited ed. Robert L. Asprin. LC 93-47256. (Illus.). 1994. write for info. (*0-89865-892-6*) Donning Co.

Sweet 'n' Slow. 3rd ed. Patricia B. Mitchell. 1992. pap. 4.00 (*0-925117-62-5*) Mitchells.

***Sweet Nightingale.** large type ed. Sheila Bishop. (Large Print Ser.). 384p. 1996. 25.99 (*0-7089-3642-3*) Ulverscroft.

Sweet Nothings. Claire Bocardo. 544p. 1993. mass mkt. 4.50 (*0-8217-4366-X*, Zebra Kensgtn) Kensgtn Pub Corp.

Sweet Nothings: An Anthology of Rock & Roll in American Poetry. Ed. by Jim Elledge. LC 93-11795. 312p. 1994. 29.95 (*0-253-31936-6*); pap. 15.95 (*0-253-20864-5*) Ind U Pr.

Sweet Nothings: The Art of Light & Luscious Desserts. Jill O'Connor. LC 92-25616. (Illus.). 112p. 1993. pap. 12.95 (*0-8118-0289-2*) Chronicle Bks.

Sweet on Construction Industry Contracts: Major AIA Documents. 2nd ed. J. Sweet. 142p. 1994. pap. 52.00 (*0-471-02360-4*) Wiley.

Sweet on Construction Industry Contracts: Major AIA Documents. 2nd ed. J. Sweet. 208p. 1995. suppl. ed., pap. 50.00 (*0-471-11211-9*) Wiley.

Sweet on Construction Industry Contracts: Major AIA Documents, Vol. 1. 3rd ed. Jonathan J. Sweet & Justin Sweet. LC 95-44565. 1996. text ed. 115.00 (*0-471-12551-2*, Wiley-Liss) Wiley.

Sweet on Construction Industry Contracts: Major AIA Documents, Vol. 2. 3rd ed. Jonathan J. Sweet & Justin Sweet. LC 95-44565. 1996. text ed. 115.00 (*0-471-12552-0*, Wiley-Liss) Wiley.

Sweet on Construction Industry Contracts: Major AIA Documents, Vol. 2. 3rd ed. Justin Sweet & Jonathan J. Sweet. LC 95-44565. 1996. text ed. 240.00 (*0-471-12550-4*) Wiley.

***Sweet on Construction Law.** Justin Sweet. LC 97-18487. 1997. pap. write for info. (*1-57073-443-7*) ABA Prof Educ Pubns.

Sweet on My Lips: The Love Poems of Mirabai. Louise L. Levi. LC 96-83816. 112p. (Orig.). 1997. pap. 12.95 (*1-887276-04-1*, Coolgrve Pr) Cool Grove Pub.

A cycle of 24 poems ornamented by historical & cultural facets of the work as well as the translator's personal experience. "Mirabai's spiritual vision & poetic genius shine through these pages. Verses of wounded pathos & soaring ecstasy are rendered here as vividly as if they had been spoken yesterday, yet with the incantatory power of sacred text. Levi's translations, brilliant in their lucidity, usher the reader directly into the heart of Mira's rare, impassioned devotion."--Miranda Shaw. "The beautiful poems of Mirabai have been BEAUTIFULLY translated from the Middle Hindi by Louise Landes Levi, & they should serve as a fine key to this tantric poet's consciousness."--Lawrence Ferlinghetti. "The West has St. Teresa d'Avila - the East has Mirabai. Whosoever understands them both understands all there is to understand."-- Claudio Rugafiori. Louise Landes Levi was born in 1944 in New York City & now lives in Italy. She studied Indian music living in North India for nearly three years, principally in Bombay. Her travels led her to the principal sites of Mira's hagiography & to a native speaker of Mira's 16th century Braj Bhasha. Ms. Levi is the author of 20 books, chap books & pamphlets & performs her own poetry in Europe & the United States. Translator from the French of Rene Dumal & Henri Michaux. ***Publisher Provided Annotation.***

***Sweet on My Lips: The Love Poems of Mirabai.** Louise L. Levi. LC 96-83816. 112p. (Orig.). 1997. 18.00 (*1-887276-07-6*, Coolgrve Pr) Cool Grove Pub.

Sweet Ones: Poems. Len Roberts. LC 87-63529. (Lakes & Prairies Ser.). 72p. (Orig.). 1988. pap. 6.95 (*0-915943-24-7*) Milkweed Ed.

Sweet Onions & Sour Cherries: A Cookbook for Market Day. Jeannette Ferrary & Louise Fiszer. (Illus.). 320p. 1992. 25.00 (*0-671-70084-7*) S&S Trade.

Sweet Panic/Blinded by the Sun. Poliakoff. 1996. pap. 15. 95 (*0-413-70700-8*, Pub. by Methuen UK) Heinemann.

Sweet Pea: The Autobiography of a Diabetic. Gloria P. Hightower. LC 94-71843. 1994. pap. 10.95 (*0-8158-0503-9*) Chris Mass.

Sweet Persuasion: The Illustrated Guide to Closing the Sale. Paul Karasik. (Illus.). (Orig.). 1993. pap. 7.95 (*0-13-177312-7*) P-H.

Sweet Persuasion: The Illustrated Guide to Unparalleled Management Success. Paul Karasik. 1993. pap. 7.95 (*0-13-756255-1*) P-H.

Sweet Peter Deeder. rev. ed. Odie Hawkins. 224p. (Orig.). 1983. mass mkt. 5.99 (*0-87067-365-3*, BH365) Holloway.

***Sweet Peter Deeter.** Odie Hawkins. 1997. pap. 5.99 (*0-87067-882-5*) Holloway.

Sweet Piracy. Jennifer Blake. 256p. 1993. lib. bdg. 20.00 (*0-7278-4490-3*) Severn Hse.

Sweet Poison. Margaret Gibson. 192p. 1995. pap. 10.00 (*0-00-647962-6*) HarpC.

***Sweet Porridge.** Pierr Morgan. Date not set. 14.95 (*0-399-21984-6*) Putnam Pub Group.

***Sweet Potato.** Kay Farmer & Cindy Yarberry. (Illus.). 96p. (Orig.). (J). (ps-3). 1990. pap. 26.95 (*1-57543-013-4*) Mar Co Prods.

Sweet Potato: An Untapped Food Resource. Jennifer A. Woolfe. 659p. (C). 1992. text ed. 135.00 (*0-521-40295-6*) Cambridge U Pr.

***Sweet Potato Biscuits & Other Stories.** 162p. (Orig.). 1996. pap. 12.00 (*0-9654018-0-4*) C T Goolsby.

Sweet Potato Pie. Anne Rockwell. LC 94-34990. (Early Step into Reading Ser.). (Illus.). (J). 1996. pap. 3.99 (*0-679-86440-7*) Random.

An Asterisk (*) at the beginning of an entry indicates that the title is appearing in BIP for the first time.

Sweet Potato Pie. Anne Rockwell. LC 94-34990. (Step into Reading Ser.: No. 2). (Illus.). (J). 1996. lib. bdg. 11.99 (0-679-96440-1) Random.

Sweet Potato Products: A Natural Resource for the Tropics. Ed. by John C. Bouwkamp. 280p. 1985. 160.00 (0-8493-5428-5, TP444, CRC Reprint) Franklin.

Sweet Potato Technology for the 21st Century. Ed. by Walter A. Hill et al. LC 92-61944. (Illus.). 596p. 1992. 60.00 (0-9625021-3-8) Tuskegee U Schl Agr Home Econ.

Sweet Prairie Passion. F. Rosanne Bittner. (Savage Destiny Ser.: No. 1). 1996. mass mkt. 5.99 (0-8217-5342-8, Zebra Kensgtn) Kensgtn Pub Corp.

Sweet Promise. Janet Dailey. 1991. mass mkt. 3.50 (0-373-83232-X) Harlequin Bks.

Sweet Promise. Janet Dailey. 1996. pap. 5.99 (0-373-83329-6, 1-83329-2) Harlequin Bks.

Sweet Promise. Layle Giusto. 240p. 1994. mass mkt. 4.99 (0-7860-0085-6, Pinncle Kensgtn) Kensgtn Pub Corp.

Sweet Promised Land. Robert Laxalt. (Basque Ser.). (Illus.). 200p. 1988. reprint ed. pap. 18.00 (0-87417-137-7) U of Nev Pr.

Sweet Promises. Edith Bach-Hall. 157p. (Orig.). 1996. mass mkt. 4.99 (1-55197-080-5, Pub. by Comnwlth Pub CN) Partners Pubs Grp.

Sweet Promises: A Reader in Indian-White Relations in Canada. Ed. by J. R. Miller. 448p. 1991. pap. text ed. 24.95 (0-8020-6818-9) U of Toronto Pr.

Sweet Reason. Henle. (C). 1995. pap. text ed. write for info. (0-7167-2430-8) W H Freeman.

Sweet Reason: Rhetoric & the Discourses of Modernity. Susan Wells. LC 95-46870. 264p. (C). 1996. pap. text ed. 18.95 (0-226-89337-5) U Ch Pr.

Sweet Reason: Rhetoric & the Discourses of Modernity. Susan Wells. LC 95-46870. (C). 1996. lib. bdg. 52.00 (0-226-89336-7) U Ch Pr.

Sweet Rebel. large type ed. Juliet Gray. (Linford Romance Library). 304p. 1993. pap. 15.99 (0-7089-7333-7, Linford) Ulverscroft.

Sweet Recovery: A Young Woman's Emotional Ride with Diabetes, Vision Loss, & an Eating Disorder...to Health & Freedom. Denise J. Bradley. LC 91-66399. (Illus.). 175p. (Orig.). 1992. pap. 9.95 (0-9630526-1-6); lib. bdg. 24.95 (0-9630526-2-4) Upbeat Prods.

Sweet Refrain. Margie Walker. 304p. 1994. mass mkt. 4.99 (0-7860-0041-4, Pinncle Kensgtn) Kensgtn Pub Corp.

Sweet Remedy. Linda P. Ashour. 336p. 1996. 23.00 (0-684-81833-7, S&S) S&S Trade.

Sweet Revenge. Regina Barreca. 1995. 23.00 (0-517-59757-8, Harmony) Crown Pub Group.

Sweet Revenge. Richard F. Beaird. 416p. (Orig.). 1986. mass mkt. 3.50 (0-8217-1904-1, Zebra Kensgtn) Kensgtn Pub Corp.

***Sweet Revenge.** Rueben Cross. 40p. 1996. pap. 7.00 (0-8059-3922-9) Dorrance.

Sweet Revenge. Debra Franklin. 1996. pap. 3.99 (0-8217-5177-8) NAL-Dutton.

Sweet Revenge. Carolyn Keene. Ed. by Ann Greenberg. (Nancy Drew Files Ser.: No. 61). 160p. (Orig.). (YA). (gr. 6 up). 1991. pap. 3.50 (0-671-73065-7, Archway) PB.

Sweet Revenge. Patricia Pellicane. pap. 3.50 (0-317-61761-3) PB.

Sweet Revenge. Nora Roberts. 384p. 1989. mass mkt. 6.50 (0-553-27859-2) Bantam.

Sweet Revenge. Nora Roberts. 384p. 1996. 16.95 (0-553-10514-0) Bantam.

Sweet Revenge. Jenna Ryan. 1996. mass mkt. 3.75 (0-373-22393-5, 1-22393-2) Harlequin Bks.

***Sweet Revenge.** Rumiko Takahashi. (Return of Lum Urusei Yatsura Ser.). 1997. pap. text ed. 15.95 (1-56931-193-5, Viz Comics) Viz Commns Inc.

Sweet Revenge: Ten Plays of Bloody Murder. Marvin Kaye & Marilyn Stasio. 832p. 1992. 12.99 (1-56865-007-8, GuildAmerica) Dblday Direct.

***Sweet Revenge: The Wicked Delights of Getting Even.** Regina Barreca. 304p. 1997. reprint ed. mass mkt. 6.99 (0-425-15766-0) Berkley Pub.

Sweet Revenge of Melissa Chavez: A Novel. Neil Davidson. LC 95-25953. 178p. (YA). (gr. 9 up). 1995. lib. bdg. 18.95 (0-936389-39-7) Tudor Pubs.

Sweet Rewards. Melinda Mcrae. 1996. mass mkt. 5.99 (0-451-40647-8, Onyx) NAL-Dutton.

Sweet Rose of Friendship. (Cherished Moments Ser.). (Illus.). 1995. 9.99 (1-57051-043-1) Brownlow Pub Co.

***Sweet Rosie O'Grady.** Joan Jonker. 314p. 1997. pap. 11.95 (0-7472-5374-9, Pub. by Headline UK) Trafalgar.

Sweet Ruin. Tony Hoagland. LC 92-50252. (Brittingham Prize in Poetry Ser.). 92p. (Orig.). (C). 1992. pap. 10.95 (0-299-13584-5) U of Wis Pr.

Sweet Sacrifice. Elizabeth Bailey. (Regency Romance Ser.). 1993. mass mkt. 2.99 (0-373-31194-X, 1-31194-3) Harlequin Bks.

Sweet Salt. Ray Locke. LC 89-60774. 224p. (Orig.). 1990. pap. 12.95 (0-915677-43-1) Roundtable Pub.

Sweet Salt, A Novel. Robert Mayer. 132p. (Orig.). 1984. 14.95 (0-933553-02-1); pap. 9.95 (0-933553-03-X) Mariposa Print Pub.

***Sweet Sarah Ross.** Julie Tetel. (North Point Ser.). 1997. mass mkt. 4.99 (0-373-28965-0, 1-28965-1) Harlequin Bks.

Sweet, Saucy & a Little Bit Naughty. Beatrice Watson. 100p. 1993. 14.95 (0-9637737-0-4) Black Beas.

Sweet Savage Eden. Heather X. Graham. (American Woman Ser.). 400p. (Orig.). (YA). 1989. mass mkt. 6.50 (0-440-20235-3) Dell.

Sweet Savage Heart. Janelle Taylor. 576p. 1993. mass mkt. 4.99 (0-8217-3829-1, Zebra Kensgtn) Kensgtn Pub Corp.

Sweet Savage Heart. Janelle Taylor. 1995. pap. 5.99 (0-8217-5276-6) NAL-Dutton.

Sweet Savage Love. Rosemary Rogers. (Steve & Ginny Ser.: Bk. 1). 640p. 1976. mass mkt. 5.99 (0-380-00815-7) Avon.

Sweet, Savage Splendor. Lauren Wilde. 448p. 1993. mass mkt. 4.50 (0-8217-4061-X, Zebra Kensgtn) Kensgtn Pub Corp.

Sweet Savannah. Thelma W. Smothers. Ed. by Jo J. Pitt & Debbie B. Lumpkins. 224p. (YA). (gr. 8 up). 1994. lib. bdg. 20.00 (1-882188-06-3) Magnolia Mktg.

Sweet-Scented Name, & Other Fairy Tales, Fables, & Stories. Fedor K. Teternikov. Ed. by Stephen Graham. LC 73-37565. (Short Story Index Reprint Ser.). 1977. reprint ed. 20.95 (0-8369-4124-1) Ayer.

Sweet Scented Rose. Sheila Pickles. 1995. 7.99 (0-517-15662-8) Random.

Sweet Scented Rose: A Treasure of Verse & Prose. Ed. by Sheila Pickles. LC 93-25562. 1996. 25.00 (0-517-59681-4, Harmony) Crown Pub Group.

Sweet Science. A. J. Liebling. (Autographed Sports Classics Ser.). 1981. reprint ed. 24.95 (0-941372-06-5) Holtzman Pr.

Sweet Scoop: Fat-Free & Low-Fat Frozen Desserts. Ed. by Cole Group Staff. LC 95-45658. (Cooking Companion Ser.). 1996. pap. 7.95 (1-56426-818-7) Cole Group.

Sweet Seasons: Santa Barbara in Time & Color. Patti Jacquemain. (Illus.). 112p. 1991. 55.00 (0-929702-01-8); pap. 28.00 (0-929702-02-6) Mission Creek.

Sweet Seasons: Santa Barbara in Time & Color. limited ed. Patti Jacquemain. (Illus.). 112p. 1991. 190.00 (0-929702-03-4) Mission Creek.

***Sweet Second Summer of Kitty Malone.** Matt Cohen. 232p. 1993. pap. 14.95 (1-55082-071-0, Pub. by Quarry Pr CN) LPC InBook.

Sweet Seduction. Wanda Owen. 448p. 1996. mass mkt. 4.99 (0-8217-5402-5, Zebra Kensgtn) Kensgtn Pub Corp.

Sweet Seduction. Julie Tetel. 1993. mass mkt. 3.99 (0-373-28767-4, 1-28767-1) Harlequin Bks.

***Sweet Seduction.** Stella Whitelaw. (Scarlet Ser.). (Orig.). 1997. mass mkt. 3.99 (1-85487-958-8, Pub. by Scarlet Bks UK) London Brdge.

Sweet Sensations. Julie Tetel. (Historical Ser.). 1993. mass mkt. 3.99 (0-373-28782-8, 1-28782-0) Harlequin Bks.

Sweet-Shop Owner. Graham Swift. LC 92-56342. 1993. pap. 10.00 (0-679-73980-7, Vin) Random.

Sweet Silver Blues. Glen Cook. 256p. 1990. reprint ed. pap. 5.50 (0-451-45070-1, ROC) NAL-Dutton.

Sweet Singer. Marla Martin. (J). (gr. 2-4). 1976. 2.55 (0-686-15487-8) Rod & Staff.

Sweet Singer of Israel: Unfinished Poems & Devotional Thoughts. Max I. Reich. LC 70-38312. (Biography Index Reprint Ser.). 1977. reprint ed. 17.95 (0-8369-8127-8) Ayer.

Sweet Sinner. Diana Hamilton. (Presents Ser.). 1996. mass mkt. 3.50 (0-373-11841-4, 1-11841-3) Harlequin Bks.

Sweet Sinner. large type ed. Diana Hamilton. (Harlequin Romance Ser.). 1995. 20.95 (0-263-14236-1) Thorndike Pr.

Sweet Sister Lyric. Jeremy Reed. 80p. 9600. pap. 16.95 (1-870612-62-0, Pub. by Enitha Pr UK) Dufour.

***Sweet Sixteen.** Ellen Harris. Date not set. write for info. (0-688-12144-6) Morrow.

Sweet Sixteen. Gail Herman. (YA). (gr. 6 up). 1996. pap. text ed. 3.99 (0-590-67449-8) Scholastic Inc.

Sweet Sixteen & Never Been Killed. Richard Posner. Ed. by Patricia MacDonald. 256p. (Orig.). (J). (gr. 7 up). 1993. pap. 3.50 (0-671-86506-4, Archway) PB.

Sweet Skin. Don Wilsun. (Illus.). 144p. (Orig.). 1993. pap. 10.00 (1-878888-12-9) Nine Muses.

Sweet Smart Xylitol, Vol. 1. John Peldyak. 110p. (Orig.). 1996. pap. 7.95 (1-57502-161-7, PO759) Morris Pubng.

Sweet Smelling Myrrh: The Autobiography of Madame Guyon. abr. ed. Ed. by Abbie C. Morrow. 192p. 1996. reprint ed. pap. 9.99 (0-88019-348-4) Schmul Pub Co.

Sweet Smells of Christmas. Patricia M. Scarry. (Golden Scratch & Sniff Bks.). (Illus.). 32p. (J). (ps-2). 1970. 6.95 (0-307-13527-6, Golden Pr) Western Pub.

Sweet, Soft, & Country. Pat McClure. (Illus.). 32p. 1984. pap. 6.50 (0-941284-25-5) J Shaw Studio.

Sweet Song of Love. Merline Lovelace. (Historical Ser.). 1994. mass mkt. 3.99 (0-373-28830-1, 1-28830-7) Harlequin Bks.

Sweet Songs for Gentle Americans: The Parlor Song in America, 1790-1860. Nicholas E. Tawa. LC 78-71394. 1980. 22.95 (0-87972-130-8) Bowling Green Univ Popular Press.

***Sweet Sorcery.** Ashland Price. 384p. 1997. mass mkt. 4.99 (0-8217-5604-4, Zebra Kensgtn) Kensgtn Pub Corp.

Sweet Sorghum. R. Ferraris. 1988. pap. 18.00 (0-643-04860-X, Pub. by CSIRO AT) Aubrey Bks.

Sweet Soul Music: Rhythm & Blues & the Southern Dream of Freedom. Peter Guralnick. (Illus.). 480p. 1994. pap. 18.00 (0-06-096049-3, PL6049, PL) HarpC.

Sweet Spanish Bride. Donna Whitfield. 384p. (Orig.). 1994. mass mkt. 4.50 (0-380-77626-X) Avon.

***Sweet Starfire.** Jayne A. Krentz. 1997. write for info. (0-7862-0911-9) Thorndike Pr.

Sweet Starfire. Jayne Ann Krentz. 1986. mass mkt. 4.95 (0-445-20034-0) Warner Bks.

Sweet Street Blues. rev. ed. Lawrence Blaine. 224p. (Orig.). 1985. mass mkt. 2.50 (0-87067-260-6, BH260-6) Holloway.

Sweet Strings of Love. Kay D. Rozzo. LC 94-18538. (Chloe Celeste Chronicles Ser.: Vol. 3). 1994. pap. 11.99 (0-8163-1221-4) Pacific Pr Pub Assn.

Sweet Success. Jana Ellis. LC 89-36348. (Merivale Mall Ser.). 160p. (J). (gr. 7 up). 1989. pap. text ed. 2.50 (0-8167-1673-0) Troll Communs.

Sweet Success: How NutraSweet Created a Billion Dollar Business. Joseph E. McCann. 300p. 1990. text ed. 30.00 (1-55623-268-3) Irwin Prof Pubng.

Sweet Sue. A. R. Gurney. 1987. pap. 5.25 (0-8222-1106-8) Dramatists Play.

Sweet Sue's Adventure. S. Campbell. 1980. pap. 3.00 (0-933062-11-7) R H Sommer.

Sweet Suffering: Woman As Victim. Natalie Shainess. LC 83-18762. 256p. 1984. write for info. (0-672-52766-9) Macmillan.

Sweet Summer: Growing up with & Without My Dad. Bebe Moore Campbell. 272p. 1990. pap. 12.00 (0-345-36694-8) Ballantine.

Sweet Summer: Growing Up With & Without My Dad. Bebe Moore Campbell. 1996. mass mkt. 6.50 (0-449-14984-6) Fawcett.

Sweet Summer Storm. Amy E. Saunders. 400p. (Orig.). 1994. mass mkt., pap. text ed. 4.99 (0-8439-3650-9) Dorchester Pub Co.

Sweet Surprise. Pamela Folse. (Illus.). 32p. (J). (ps-7). 1995. lib. bdg. 14.95 (1-884725-11-2) Blue Heron LA.

Sweet Surprises: Notes from the Heart. ICB Staff. (Love Notes Ser.). (Illus.). 112p. (Orig.). 1995. per., pap. 5.95 (1-57102-051-9, Ideals Child) Hambleton-Hill.

Sweet Surrender. 8.00 (0-9615622-0-X) McElyea Pubns.

Sweet Surrender. Catherine Coulter. LC 99-943913. 1985. pap. 5.99 (0-451-15694-3, Onyx) NAL-Dutton.

Sweet Surrender. Julie Tetel. (Historical Ser.). 1995. pap. 4.50 (0-373-28855-7, 1-28855-4) Harlequin Bks.

Sweet Suspicions. Julie Tetel. (Historical Ser.: No. 728). 1992. mass mkt. 3.99 (0-373-28728-3, 1-28728-3) Harlequin Bks.

Sweet, Sweet Basket. Margie W. Clary. Ed. by Barbara Stone. LC 94-39551. (Illus.). 40p. (J). (gr. k-7). 1995. 15.95 (0-87844-127-1) Sandlapper Pub Co.

Sweet, Sweet Fig Banana. Phillis Gershator. LC 95-32087. (Illus.). 32p. (J). (ps-2). 1996. lib. bdg. 14.95 (0-8075-7693-X) A Whitman.

Sweet Sweetback's Baadasssss Song. 2nd ed. Melvin Van Peebles. Ed. by Lois Douglass & Marva Allen. (Voices of Conscience Ser.). (Illus.). 216p. (JPN.). (C). 1994. reprint ed. 17.95 (1-883545-01-3) Shields Pub.

Sweet Swing Blues on the Road. Wynton Marsalis & Frank Stewart. LC 93-4740. 1994. 29.95 (0-393-03514-X) Norton.

Sweet Swing'n Golf. 2nd ed. Thomas S. Cross. (Illus.). 179p. (Orig.). (C). 1995. pap. text ed. 12.95 (0-87563-553-9) Stipes.

Sweet Tales. 220p. 1990. pap. 4.50 (0-88184-606-6) Carroll & Graf.

***Sweet Tales.** 4.50 (0-7867-0606-6) Carroll & Graf.

Sweet Talk. Stephanie Vaughn. 1990. 16.95 (0-394-57605-5) Random.

Sweet Talk: The Language of Love. Susan Ferraro. 224p. 1995. 17.00 (0-671-79234-2) S&S Trade.

Sweet Talkers. Kathleen K. (Orig.). 1994. pap. 12.95 (1-56333-192-6, R Kasak Bks) Masquerade.

***Sweet Talkers.** 2nd rev. ed. Kathleen K. 1997. reprint ed. mass mkt. 6.95 (1-56333-516-6, Rhinoceros) Masquerade.

Sweet Talking the System. Ed. by Andrew Douglas. (Instrument Pilots Library). 192p. 1993. 23.95 (1-879620-14-6) Belvoir Pubns.

Sweet Temptations Natural Dessert Book: Delicious Desserts that Need No Cooking. Frances Kendall. LC 87-22675. (Illus.). 274p. pap. 10.95 (0-89529-355-2) Avery Pub.

Sweet Terror. Mark Crose. 1995. pap. 3.50 (0-8217-4641-3) NAL-Dutton.

Sweet Texas Dreams. Dana Ransom. 352p. 1996. mass mkt. 4.99 (0-8217-5517-X, Zebra Kensgtn) Kensgtn Pub Corp.

Sweet Things. A. Wilkes. (First Cookbooks Ser.). (Illus.). 24p. (J). (gr. 1-4). 1993. pap. 4.50 (0-7460-0227-0, Usborne) EDC.

Sweet Thursday. John Steinbeck. 1979. mass mkt. 7.00 (0-14-004889-8, Penguin Bks) Viking Penguin.

Sweet Thursday. John Steinbeck. 288p. 1996. pap. 9.95 (0-14-018750-2, Penguin Classics) Viking Penguin.

***Sweet Tibby Mack.** Roz D. Fox. (Matchmaker, Matchmaker Ser.). 1997. mass mkt. 3.99 (0-373-70746-0, 1-70746-2) Harlequin Bks.

Sweet to Shore. Jan Robinson. 288p. 1990. pap. 14.95 (0-9612686-4-6) Ship-Shore.

Sweet Tooth. Laura N. Montenegro. LC 93-49643. 32p. (J). (gr. k-3). 1995. 14.95 (0-395-68078-6) HM.

Sweet Tooth. Yves Navarre. Tr. by Donald Watson from FRE. 1980. 14.95 (0-7145-3522-2) Riverrun NY.

Sweet Touch. Lorna Balian. (Illus.). 52p. (Orig.). (J). (ps-6). 1994. reprint ed. lib. bdg. 14.95 (1-881772-26-8) Humbug Bks.

Sweet Tranquility. Donna Bell. 224p. 1997. mass mkt. 4.99 (0-8217-5544-7, Zebra Kensgtn) Kensgtn Pub Corp.

Sweet Treason. Patricia Gaffney. 448p. (Orig.). 1992. mass mkt., pap. text ed. 4.99 (0-8439-3247-3) Dorchester Pub Co.

Sweet Treasures of Aloha & Other Poems. June A. Elliott. 60p. (Orig.). 1995. pap. write for info. (1-57553-012-0) Watermrk Pr.

Sweet Treats. Aaron Maree. (Illus.). 64p. 1993. 10.00 (0-207-18037-7, Pub. by Angus & Robertson AT) HarpC.

Sweet Uprisings. Carol Morris. (Illus.). 18p. (Orig.). 1990. pap. 5.00 (0-9608802-7-5) Years Pr.

***Sweet Valentine.** Val Daniels. (Romance Ser.). 1997. 3.25 (0-373-03446-6, 1-03446-1) Harlequin Bks.

***Sweet Valley Blizzard!** Created by Francine Pascal. (Sweet Valley Kids Ser.: No. 74). (Orig.). (J). 1998. pap. 3.50 (0-553-48343-9) BDD Bks Young Read.

Sweet Valley Clean-Up. Francine Pascal. (Sweet Valley Kids Ser.: No. 27). 80p. (J). 1992. pap. 2.99 (0-553-15923-2) Bantam.

Sweet Valley High. Francine Pascal. 1995. 8.98 (1-57042-243-5) Warner Bks.

Sweet Valley High. Francine Pascal. 1995. 8.98 (1-57042-244-3) Warner Bks.

Sweet Valley High, No. 56: Lost at Sea. Francine Pascal. 160p. (YA). 1989. pap. 3.50 (0-553-27970-X) Bantam.

Sweet Valley High, No. 57: Teacher Crush. Francine Pascal. 144p. (YA). 1989. pap. 2.95 (0-553-28079-1) Bantam.

Sweet Valley High Super Edition: Spring Break. Francine Pascal. (Sweet Valley High Ser.: No. 3). 240p. (Orig.). (YA). 1986. mass mkt. 4.50 (0-553-25537-1) Bantam.

Sweet Valley High Super Thriller, No. 3. Created by Francine Pascal. 240p. (Orig.). (YA). 1988. mass mkt. 3.99 (0-553-27554-2) Bantam.

Sweet Valley High Supers, 4 vols., Set. Francine Pascal. 1991. boxed, mass mkt. 14.00 (0-553-61820-2) Bantam.

Sweet Valley Kids, No. 28: Elizabeth Meets Her Hero. Francine Pascal. 80p. (J). (ps-3). 1992. pap. 2.99 (0-553-15924-0) Bantam.

Sweet Valley Kids, No. 29: Andy & the Alien. Francine Pascal. 80p. (J). (ps-3). 1992. pap. 2.99 (0-553-15925-9) Bantam.

Sweet Valley Slumber Party. Francine Pascal. (Sweet Valley Kids Ser.: No. 22). 80p. (J). (gr. 4-7). 1991. pap. 3.50 (0-553-15934-8) Bantam.

Sweet Valley Trick or Treat. Francine Pascal. (Sweet Valley Kids Ser.: No. 12). 80p. (J). (gr. 4-7). 1990. pap. 3.50 (0-553-15825-2) Bantam.

Sweet Valley Twins, 4 vols., No. 02, Set. Francine Pascal. (Orig.). 1991. boxed, pap. 11.85 (0-553-61815-6) Bantam.

Sweet Valley Twins, 10 bks., Set. large type ed. Jamie Suzanne. (YA). (gr. 7-12). 1990. reprint ed. 99.50 (1-55905-074-8) Grey Castle.

***Sweet Valley University, 4 Vols.** Francine Pascal. (Sweet Valley University Ser.). 1994. mass mkt. 15.96 (0-553-63493-3) Bantam.

Sweet Vengeance. Kat Martin. 1993. mass mkt. 6.50 (0-312-95095-0) St Martin.

Sweet Vengeance. June L. Shiplett. (Historical Ser.: No. 710). 1992. mass mkt. 3.99 (0-373-28710-0) Harlequin Bks.

Sweet Vengeance. large type ed. Rowan Edwards. 304p. 1992. pap. 15.99 (0-7089-7141-5, Trailtree Bookshop) Ulverscroft.

Sweet Vidalia Onions/Blue Ribbon Recipes. Evelyn Rogers. 122p. 1995. pap. 8.95 (0-9614318-3-0) Rogers Cookbooks.

Sweet Vietnam. Richard Parque. 288p. 1984. mass mkt. 3.50 (0-8217-1423-6, Zebra Kensgtn) Kensgtn Pub Corp.

Sweet Voices of Lahaina: Life Story of Maui's Fabulous Gardens. Mary C. Richards. (Illus.). 91p. 1990. 9.95 (0-89610-170-3) Island Heritage.

Sweet Water & Polar: Poems from the Length of a Marriage. Aminta Marks. LC 92-81196. 177p. (Orig.). 1992. pap. 12.00 (0-9626898-1-5) Grindstone Pr.

Sweet Water River. Eugenia Moore. LC 90-92340. (Illus.). 72p. 1991. pap. 7.95 (1-878116-05-3) JVC Bks.

Sweet Water-Stolen Land. Philip McLaren. 1993. pap. 14.95 (0-7022-2551-7, Pub. by Univ Queensland Pr AT) Intl Spec Bk.

Sweet Waters, a Chilean Farm. Charles J. Lambert. LC 75-14091. (Illus.). 212p. 1975. reprint ed. text ed. 55.00 (0-8371-8201-8, LASWA, Greenwood Pr) Greenwood.

Sweet Whispers, Brother Rush. Virginia Hamilton. 224p. 1983. mass mkt. 4.50 (0-380-65193-9, Flare) Avon.

Sweet Whispers, Brother Rush. Virginia Hamilton. 224p. (J). (gr. 7 up). 1982. 17.95 (0-399-20894-1, Philomel Bks) Putnam Pub Group.

Sweet Wild World: Selections from Thoreau's Journals. Illus. by Georgia Dearborn. 142p. (Orig.). (C). 1982. 12.95 (0-89182-059-0); pap. 6.95 (0-89182-060-4) Charles River Bks.

Sweet Will. Levine. 1985. pap. 5.95 (0-689-11586-5, Atheneum S&S) S&S Trade.

Sweet William. Jessica Palmer. 1995. mass mkt. 5.50 (0-671-88017-9) PB.

Sweet William: A Memoir of Old Horse. John Hawkes. 272p. 1994. reprint ed. pap. 10.95 (0-14-023616-3, Penguin Bks) Viking Penguin.

***Sweet Wind, Wild Wind.** Elizabeth Lowell. 1997. pap. 5.50 (1-55166-288-4, 1-66288-1, Mira Bks) Harlequin Bks.

Sweet Wine or Sour Grapes? Brad Harford. Ed. by Reba Harford. (Illus.). viii, 104p. (Orig.). 1995. pap. 10.00 (0-9650947-0-7) WinePress AZ.

Sweet Women Lie. large type ed. Loren D. Estleman. LC 90-47663. 296p. 1990. reprint ed. lib. bdg. 7.95 (1-56054-070-2) Thorndike Pr.

Sweet Words So Brave: The Story of African American Literature. Barbara K. Curry & James M. Brodie. LC 96-18995. (Illus.). 64p. (J). (gr. 3 up). 1996. 24.95 (1-55933-179-8) Zino Pr.

***Sweetapple Farm.** Wendy Smith. (Illus.). 32p. (J). (gr. 1-3). 1997. 17.95 (0-09-176744-X, Pub. by Hutchnson UK) Trafalgar.

Sweetbitter. Reginald Gibbons. 440p. 1994. 21.95 (0-913089-51-6) Broken Moon.

Sweetbitter. Reginald Gibbons. 432p. 1996. pap. 11.95 (0-14-025242-8, Viking) Viking Penguin.

Sweetbriar. Jude Deveraux. 1991. pap. 6.99 (0-671-74382-1) PB.

***Sweetbriar Summer.** Brenda Wilbee. LC 96-43379. 1997. 11.99 (0-8007-5619-3) Revell.

Sweetbriar Summit. Christine Rimmer. 1994. mass mkt. 3.50 (0-373-09896-0, 1-09896-1) Harlequin Bks.

Sweetco: Business Model & Activity File. 2nd ed. Lester R. Bittel et al. 320p. 1984. pap. text ed. 13.95 (0-07-005516-5) McGraw.

***Sweetcorn.** Pam Robson. LC 97-6910. (What's for Lunch? Ser.). (J). 1998. write for info. (0-516-20823-3) Childrens.

S

Sweetener Market. 270p. 1994. 1,095.00 (*0-318-03904-4*) Busn Trend.

Sweeteners: Discovery, Molecular Design, & Chemoreception. Ed. by D. Eric Walters et al. LC 90-21814. (ACS Symposium Ser.: No. 450). (Illus.). 352p. 1991. 84.95 (*0-8412-1903-6*) Am Chemical.

Sweeteners: Health Effects. Ed. by Gary M. Williams. LC 87-629727. (Illus.). 250p. 1988. 50.00 (*0-911131-96-5*) Princeton Sci Pubs.

Sweeter Music. Charlotte V. Allen. (Orig.). 1994. reprint ed. lib. bdg. 19.00 (*0-7278-4595-0*) Severn Hse.

***Sweeter Savage Love.** Sandra Hill. 400p. (Orig.). 1997. mass mkt. 5.99 (*0-505-52212-8*, Love Spell) Dorchester Pub Co.

Sweeter Than Candy. Rhodesia Jackson. LC 96-9311. 388p. 1997. pap. 14.00 (*0-9637282-1-0*) Orgena Ent.

Sweeter Than Chocolate. Helen Wingo. LC 96-96391. 192p. 1996. 17.95 (*0-8034-9210-3*, Avalon Bks) Bouregy.

Sweeter Than Dreams. 1996. pap. 5.96 (*1-57566-070-9*) Kensgtn Pub Corp.

Sweeter Than Dreams. Olga Bicos. 512p. 1995. mass mkt. 4.99 (*0-8217-0142-8*, Zebra Kensgtn) Kensgtn Pub Corp.

Sweeter Than Honey. Jesse B. Deloe. pap. 5.99 (*0-88469-105-5*) BMH Bks.

Sweeter Than Honey. Paul N. Tassell. 142p. 1978. pap. 3.50 (*0-87227-068-8*, RBP5073) Reg Baptist.

Sweeter Than Honey: Ethiopian Women & Revolution: Testimonies of Tigrayan Women. Ed. by Nell Druce & Jenny Hammond. LC 90-60727. (Illus.). 184p. (C). 1990. 35.00 (*0-932415-55-5*); pap. 11.95 (*0-932415-56-3*) Red Sea Pr.

Sweeter Than Sin. Sara Orwig. 368p. (Orig.). 1992. mass mkt. 4.99 (*0-446-36084-8*) Warner Bks.

***Sweeter Than Wine.** Stephani Mittman. 384p. 1997. mass mkt. 5.50 (*0-440-22180-3*) Dell.

Sweeter That the Rose. LC 93-85969. 1994. 24.95 (*0-942237-34-X*) Leisure AR.

Sweeter the Juice: A Family Memoir in Black & White. Shirlee T. Haizlip. 1994. 22.00 (*0-671-79235-0*) S&S Trade.

Sweeter the Juice: A Family Memoir in Black & White. Shirlee T. Hazlip. 1995. pap. 11.00 (*0-671-89933-3*, Touchstone Bks) S&S Trade.

Sweetest Berry on the Bush. Nubia Kai. LC 92-63010. (Illus.). 121p. (Orig.). (J). 1993. pap. 8.00 (*0-88378-059-3*) Third World.

Sweetest Fig. Chris Van Allsburg. LC 93-12692. (Illus.). (J). (gr. 4 up). 1993. 17.95 (*0-395-67346-1*) HM.

***Sweetest Hour: Tikkun Chatzot.** Ed. by Avrohom Greenbaum. 150p. 1993. pap. 10.00 (*0-930213-50-5*) Breslov Res Inst.

Sweetest Impression of Life: The James Family & Italy. Ed. by James Tuttleton & Agostino Lombardo. (C). 1990. 50.00 (*0-8147-8183-7*) NYU Pr.

Sweetest Song. Gary P. Walton. (Illus.). 45p. (Orig.). 1988. pap. 5.00 (*0-9621606-0-1*) Pea Pod Pr.

Sweetest Song: The Song of Solomon Expressed Through the Lives of Saints & Martyrs. Richard Wurmbrand. LC 93-18513. 1993. pap. 5.00 (*0-551-01652-3*) Living Sacrifice Bks.

Sweetest Thing. large type ed. Emma Blair. (Charnwood Large Print Ser.). 1995. 27.99 (*0-7089-8832-6*, Charnwood) Ulverscroft.

Sweetest You Can Find: Life in Eastern Guadalupe County, Texas, 1851-1951, As Seen in the History of Selected Schools & Communities. Josephine B. Etlinger. LC 87-50533. (Illus.). xvi, 384p. 1987. 15.00 (*0-934955-10-7*) Watercress Pr.

Sweetfeed: A Mike Flint Murder Mystery. R. Austin Healy. LC 96-75857. 256p. 1996. 24.95 (*0-8338-0230-5*) Marshall Jones.

Sweetgrass. Cass Dalglish. Ed. by Ray Howe. 134p. (Orig.). (C). 1992. pap. 10.95 (*0-9627860-3-9*) Lone Oak MN.

Sweetgrass. Jan Hudson. 160p. (YA). (gr. 7-9). 1991. pap. 3.99 (*0-590-43486-1*) Scholastic Inc.

Sweetheart. Kate Daniel. 240p. (YA). 1993. mass mkt. 3.50 (*0-06-106735-0*, Harp PBks) HarpC.

Sweetheart. Peter McGehee. (Stonewall Inn Editions Ser.). 224p. 1993. pap. 8.95 (*0-312-09399-3*) St Martin.

Sweetheart for Valentine. Lorna Balian. (Illus.). 32p. (J). (ps-3). 1988. reprint ed. 12.95 (*0-687-37109-0*) Humbug Bks.

Sweetheart Jewelry & Collectibles. Nick Snider. LC 95-68862. (Illus.). 160p. (Orig.). 1995. pap. 29.95 (*0-88740-834-6*) Schiffer.

Sweetheart Schottische. (Ballroom Dance Ser.). 1986. lib. bdg. 79.95 (*0-8490-3415-9*) Gordon Pr.

Sweetheart Schottische. (Ballroom Dance Ser.). 1985. lib. bdg. 60.00 (*0-87700-799-3*) Revisionist Pr.

***Sweetheart Season.** Karen K. Fowler. 1998. pap. write for info. (*0-345-41642-2*) Ballantine.

***Sweetheart Season.** large type ed. Karen J. Fowler. (Niagara Large Print Ser.). 1996. 27.99 (*0-7089-5849-4*) Ulverscroft.

Sweetheart Season: A Novel. Karen J. Fowler. 320p. 1996. 23.00 (*0-8050-4737-9*) H Holt & Co.

Sweetheart Treasures, Sharing the Value of Sexual Purity: A Guide for Parents, Concerned Adults & Young People. Catherine E. Wood. Ed. by Scott Inboden et al. (Sweetheart Treasures Ser.). 87p. (J). (gr. 5-12). 1994. pap. 6.95 (*0-9642092-0-9*) Treas Values.

Sweethearts of Sixties TV. Ron Smith. 224p. (Orig.). 1993. pap. 5.50 (*1-56171-206-X*, S P I Bks) Sure Seller.

Sweethearts of Sleeping Bear Bay. Donna Winters. Ed. by Anne Severance. LC 91-70068. (Great Lakes Romances Ser.). (Illus.). 208p. 1995. reprint ed. pap. 8.95 (*0-923048-77-4*) Bigwater Pub.

Sweethearts of the Sage: Biographies & Filmographies of 258 Actresses Appearing in Western Movies. Buck Rainey. LC 91-52639. (Illus.). 652p. 1992. lib. bdg. 95.00 (*0-89950-565-1*) McFarland & Co.

Sweetie: A Sugar-Coated Nightmare. (Wellinworld Tapes & Books for Children: 2-9). 36p. (J). (ps-4). 1985. 8.95 (*0-88684-175-5*); audio write for info. (*0-318-59507-9*) Listen USA.

Sweetie: The Screenplay. Gerard Lee & Jane Campion. 1991. pap. 12.95 (*0-7022-2371-9*, Pub. by Univ Queensland Pr AT) Intl Spec Bk.

Sweetie Pie: More Than a Love Story. Barry Casebolt & Sara Casebolt. LC 95-67297. 236p. 1995. 17.95 (*0-9643937-3-5*) Rutledge Bks.

***Sweetie Pie: The Richard Simmons Private Collection of Dazzling Desserts.** Richard Simmons. (J). 1997. 22.00 (*1-57719-276-1*) GT Pubng Corp.

Sweetie Pie Cafe Cookbook. Judith A. Cleaver. Date not set. spiral bd., pap. 10.95 (*0-9650481-0-1*) Two Girls Flying.

Sweetly Be! A Muscadine Book. Rose B. Stevens. LC 90-43224. 200p. 1990. 17.95 (*0-87805-465-0*) U Pr of Miss.

Sweet'ner Dearest: Bittersweet Vignettes about Aspartame (NutraSweet) H. J. Roberts. LC 92-64347. (Illus.). 300p. 1992. pap. 19.95 (*0-9633260-1-5*); audio 19.95 (*0-9633260-0-7*) Sunshine Sentinel.

***Sweetness.** Ed. by J. Dobbing. (Illus.). 282p. 1987. 55.00 (*3-540-17045-6*, 170456) Spr-Verlag.

***Sweetness: The Biological, Behavioral & Social Aspects.** (Illus.). 1995. pap. text ed. 12.50 (*0-944398-51-0*) ILSI.

***Sweetness: The Biological, Behavioural & Social Aspects.** (Concise Monographs). (Illus.). 22p. 1995. write for info. (*0-9943985-1-4*, 398510) ILSI.

Sweetness & Light. Kip Wilcox & Lisa Cowden. (Illus.). 272p. 1996. pap. 17.00 (*0-679-75608-6*) Random.

Sweetness & Light: The "Queen Anne" Movement, 1860-1900. Mark Girouard. LC 77-30113. (Illus.). 272p. 1984. reprint ed. pap. 27.50 (*0-300-03068-1*, Y-491) Yale U Pr.

Sweetness & Power: The Place of Sugar in Modern History. Sidney W. Mintz. 1986. pap. 13.95 (*0-14-009233-1*, Penguin Bks) Viking Penguin.

***Sweetness from Starch - Manual for Making Maltose from Starch.** Nguyen Guyhn & John Cecil. 40p. 1996. pap. 10.00 (*92-5-103780-9*, F37809, Pub. by FAO IT) Bernan Associates.

***Sweetness of Honey & the Sting of Bees: A Book of Love.** Michelle Lovric & Nikiforos D. Mardas. 96p. 1997. 14.95 (*1-55670-680-4*) Stewart Tabori & Chang.

Sweetness of the Fig: Aboriginal Women in Transition. Virginia Huffer et al. LC 80-21658. (Illus.). 244p. 1981. 30.00 (*0-295-95790-5*) U of Wash Pr.

Sweetness to the Soul. Jane Kirkpatrick. 424p. 1995. pap. text ed. 11.99 (*0-88070-765-8*, Multnomah Bks) Multnomah Pubs.

Sweet'ning Relationships. Thomas A. Gregg. LC 95-68515. 120p. 1995. pap. 12.95 (*1-57197-002-9*) Pentland Pr.

Sweets for My Sweet. Jane Bolitho. 224p. 1996. 22.00 (*0-7278-4883-6*) Severn Hse.

Sweets 'n Eats: The Goodie Guide to Greater Pasadena. Jan W. Castro. 1992. pap. 6.95 (*0-9624023-2-X*) J C West Prodns.

Sweetser: Set Sweetser & His Descendants. P. S. Sweetser. 427p. 1991. reprint ed. pap. 65.00 (*0-8328-2176-4*); reprint ed. lib. bdg. 75.00 (*0-8328-2175-6*) Higginson Bk Co.

***SweetSips: Making Your Own Liqueurs & Cordials at Home.** Charles Thomas. (Illus.). 40p. (Orig.). 1995. spiral bd., pap. 6.95 (*0-9652643-0-0*) C Thomas.

***SweetSips 2: Wining & Dining with Homemade Liqueurs.** Charles Thomas. (Illus.). 90p. (Orig.). 1996. spiral bd., pap. 9.95 (*0-9652643-1-9*) C Thomas.

***SweetSmart Xylitol: Sweeten Your Smile.** John Peldyak. (Illus.). 52p. (Orig.). 1996. pap. write for info. (*1-57502-341-5*) Morris Pubng.

Sweetwater. Knut Faldbakken et al. 184p. 9400. 30.00 (*0-7206-0911-9*, Pub. by P Owen Ltd UK) Dufour.

***Sweetwater.** Dorothy Garlock. 512p. 1997. mass mkt. 6.50 (*0-446-60255-8*) Warner Bks.

Sweetwater. Laurence Yep. LC 72-9867. (Trophy Bk.). (Illus.). 224p. (J). (gr. 5 up). 1983. pap. 3.50 (*0-06-440135-9*, Trophy) HarpC Child Bks.

Sweetwater: Gunslinger 201. William H. LaBarge & Robert L. Holt. Ed. by Ernest J. Gentle. LC 83-73237. (Illus.). 192p. 1983. 14.60 (*0-8168-8515-X*, 28515, TAB-Aero) TAB Bks.

Sweetwater: Gunslinger 201. 6th ed. Robert L. Holt & William H. LaBarge. (Illus.). 190p. 1983. reprint ed. 19.95 (*0-930926-22-6*) Calif Fin Pubns.

Sweetwater Gunslinger Two Hundred One. William H. LaBarge & Robert L. Holt. (Illus.). 192p. 14.95 (*0-685-47251-5*, 28515, TAB-Aero) TAB Bks.

Sweetwater Gunslinger 201. William H. Labarge. 1991. 14.95 (*0-8306-8515-4*) McGraw-Hill Prof.

***Sweetwater Ranch.** Geoffrey Norman. 464p. 31.50 (*0-7089-3671-7*) Ulverscroft.

Sweetwater Run: The Story of Buffalo Bill Cody & the Pony Express. Andrew Glass. LC 95-52228. (Illus.). 48p. (J). (gr. 1-5). 1996. 15.95 (*0-385-32220-8*) Delacorte.

Sweetwater Sea Saga. Virginia M. Soetebier. (Illus.). xii, 120p. (Orig.). 1991. pap. 9.95 (*0-939923-18-1*) M & W Pub Co.

Sweetwater Seduction. Joan Johnston. 384p. (Orig.). 1991. mass mkt. 4.50 (*0-440-20561-1*) Dell.

Sweetwater, Storms, & Spirits: Stories of the Great Lakes. Ed. by Victoria Brehm. LC 89-20682. 352p. (Orig.). 1991. 37.50 (*0-472-10144-7*); pap. 16.95 (*0-472-08151-9*) U of Mich Pr.

Sweetwater Wisdom: A Native American Spiritual Way. Wendy Crockett. LC 97-4155. 108p. (Orig.). 1997. pap. 11.95 (*0-8245-1485-8*) Crossroad NY.

Swell-Looking Babe. Jim Thompson. LC 91-50071. (Vintage Crime - Black Lizard Ser.). 160p. 1991. pap. 9.00 (*0-679-73311-6*, Vin) Random.

Swell Season. Josef Skvorecky. Tr. by Paul Wilson from CZE. LC 85-16257. 226p. 1986. reprint ed. pap. 8.50 (*0-88001-090-8*) Ecco Pr.

Swelling. John M. Bennett. (Illus.). 38p. (Orig.). 1988. pap. 3.00 (*0-926935-05-4*) Runaway Spoon.

Swelling My Song in Vagabond Shoes: Re-entering the Corporate Life. Richard E. Petitti. (Self Realization Bks.: Bk. IX). (Illus.). 100p. 1986. pap. 10.00 (*0-938582-12-7*) Sensitive Man.

Swenson's Pediatric Surgery. 5th ed. John Raffensperger. (Illus.). 994p. 1989. text ed. 175.00 (*0-8385-8757-7*, A8757-5) Appleton & Lange.

Swept Away. Katherine Applegate. (Ocean City Ser.: No. 8). 240p. (J). 1995. mass mkt. 3.99 (*0-06-106285-5*, Harp PBks) HarpC.

Swept Away. Dafydd A. Hugh. 256p. (YA). (gr. 7 up). 1996. mass mkt. 4.50 (*0-06-106289-8*) HarpC.

Swept Away. Julie Tetel. 352p. (Orig.). 1989. mass mkt. 3.95 (*0-445-20922-4*, Mysterious Paperbk) Warner Bks.

***Swept Away.** Julie T. Andresen. 355p. 1997. reprint ed. pap. 12.50 (*0-9654499-0-4*) Windows on Hist.

Swept Away: The Mountain. Hugh D. Ab. 256p. 1996. mass mkt. 4.50 (*0-06-106290-1*) HarpC.

Swept Away: The Pit. Dafydd A. Hugh. 240p. 1996. mass mkt. 4.50 (*0-06-106291-X*, Harp PBks) HarpC.

***Swept Away No. 1.** Dafydd Hugh. mass mkt. write for info. (*0-06-106436-X*, Harp PBks) HarpC.

Swept Back to a Texas Future. Peggy P. Freeman. (Illus.). 40p. (J). (gr. 4-7). 1991. pap. 7.95 (*0-937460-72-9*) Hendrick-Long.

Swerve. Sheri D. Wilson. 1994. per. 12.95 (*0-88978-274-1*, Pub. by Arsenal Pulp CN) LPC InBook.

Swerving Straight: Poems, Selected & New. Thomas Johnson. LC 81-3457. 112p. 1981. 10.00 (*0-934184-07-0*); pap. 5.00 (*0-934184-08-9*) Alembic Pr.

Swetnam Arraigned by Women. LC 75-133742. (Tudor Facsimile Texts. Old English Plays Ser.: No. 136). reprint ed. 49.50 (*0-404-53436-8*) AMS Pr.

***Swettenham.** H. S. Barlow. (Illus.). 783p. 1995. 50.00 (*983-99915-1-5*, Pub. by Southdene Sendirian MY) SE Asia.

Sweynheym & Pannartz & the Origins of Printing in Italy: German Technology & Italian Humanism in Renaissance Rome. deluxe ed. Edwin Hall. 132p. 1991. bds., boxed 450.00 (*0-9628568-0-0*) P J Pirages.

S'Wheat Relief. Brenda Sillasen. 119p. 1995. pap. 10.95 (*0-9638163-3-0*) Hisel Bk Ends.

SWI Schlagwortindex Teil II: Zu SfB Systematik fur Bibliotheken ASB Allgemeine Systematik fur Offentliche Bibliotheken SSD Systematik Stadtbibliothek Duisburg. Compiled by Verein der Bibliothekare an Offentlichen Bibliotheken Staff. 245p. 1992. pap. text ed. 43.00 (*3-598-10830-3*) K G Saur.

Swidden Agriculture in Indonesia: The Subsistence Strategies of the Kalimantan Kantu' Michael R. Dove. (New Babylon Studies in the Social Sciences: No. 43). (Illus.). xx, 515p. 1985. 129.25 (*3-11-009592-0*) Mouton.

Swidden Fallow Agroforestry in the Peruvian Amazon. Ed. by W. M. Denevan & Christine Padoch. LC 87-30785. (Advances in Economic Botany Ser.: Vol. 5). (Illus.). 108p. (C). 1988. pap. 22.25 (*0-89327-325-2*) NY Botanical.

Swift. Leslie Stephen. Ed. by John Morley. (English Men of Letters Ser). reprint ed. lib. bdg. 27.50 (*0-404-51731-5*) AMS Pr.

Swift. Carl C. Van Doren, pseud. LC 76-12127. reprint ed. 26.50 (*0-404-15239-2*) AMS Pr.

Swift. Carl C. Van Doren. (BCL One-PR English Literature Ser.). 279p. 1992. reprint ed. lib. bdg. 79.00 (*0-7812-7413-3*) Rprt Serv.

Swift: An Introduction. Ricardo Quintana. LC 79-17607. 204p. 1980. reprint ed. text ed. 55.00 (*0-313-22052-2*, QUST, Greenwood Pr) Greenwood.

Swift: Madness & Art. Ed. by Brynmill Pr. Ltd. Staff. (C). 1989. 35.00 (*0-907839-12-6*, Pub. by Brynmill Pr Ltd UK) St Mut.

Swift: The Man, His Works, & the Age: Dr. Swift, Vol. II. Irvin Ehrenpreis. 800p. 1983. text ed. 40.00 (*0-317-54487-X*) HUP.

Swift: The Man, His Works, & the Age: Mr. Swift & His Contemporaries, Vol. I. Irvin Ehrenpreis. 360p. 1962. 42.50 (*0-674-85830-1*) HUP.

Swift & His Circle. Robert W. Jackson. LC 79-76905. (Essay Index Reprint Ser.). 1977. 15.95 (*0-8369-0019-7*) Ayer.

Swift & His Contexts. Ed. by John I. Fischer et al. LC 89-107. (Studies in the Eighteenth Century: No. 14). 1989. 39.50 (*0-404-63514-8*) AMS Pr.

Swift & Scatological Satire. Jae Num Lee. LC 76-129807. 158p. 1976. text ed. 29.95 (*0-8263-0196-7*) Irvington.

***Swift & Sure: Bringing Certainty & Finality to Criminal Punishment.** William J. Cornelius. LC 96-34997. 1997. 22.95 (*1-57105-037-X*) Bridge St Bks.

***Swift Arrow.** Josephine C. Edwards. LC 97-60096. 128p. (J). 1997. reprint ed. per. 8.95 (*1-57258-080-1*) Teach Servs.

Swift As the Wind: The Cheetah. Barbara J. Esbensen. LC 95-666. (Illus.). 32p. (J). (gr. 1-4). 1996. 15.95 (*0-531-09497-9*); lib. bdg. 16.99 (*0-531-08797-2*) Orchard Bks Watts.

Swift Family. Compiled by K. W. Swift. 170p. 1991. reprint ed. pap. 28.00 (*0-8328-2178-0*); reprint ed. lib. bdg. 38.00 (*0-8328-2177-2*) Higginson Bk Co.

Swift Flows the River. Nard Jones. LC 48-10158. 449p. 1964. 14.95 (*0-8323-0114-0*) Binford Mort.

Swift Flows the River: Log Driving in Oregon. Dow Beckham. (Illus.). 207p. (Orig.). (C). 1992. pap. text ed. 15.95 (*0-930998-04-9*) Arago Bks.

Swift in Ireland. Richard A. King. LC 79-171231. (English Literature Ser.: No. 33). 1972. reprint ed. lib. bdg. 75.00 (*0-8383-1338-8*) M S G Haskell Hse.

Swift Justice: Murder & Vengeance in a California Town. Harry Farrell. LC 92-34395. 1992. pap. 10.95 (*0-312-08901-5*) St Martin.

Swift Potomac's Lovely Daughter: Two Centuries at Georgetown Through Students' Eyes. Ed. by Joseph Durkin. LC 89-48744. (Illus.). 446p. (Orig.). 1990. pap. 14.95 (*0-87840-501-1*) Georgetown U Pr.

Swift Progress of Population: A Demographic History of the Philadelphia Region, 1642-1859. Susan E. Klepp. LC 90-55893. (Memoirs Ser.: Vol. 187). (Illus.). 344p. (C). 1990. 35.00 (*0-87169-187-6*, M187-KLS) Am Philos.

Swift Rivers. Cornelia Meigs. (Newbery Honor Roll Ser.). (Illus.). 288p. (Orig.). (J). (gr. 4-7). 1994. reprint ed. pap. 6.95 (*0-8027-7419-9*) Walker & Co.

Swift Runner. Colin A. Thomson. (Illus.). 114p. 1984. 17.95 (*0-920490-40-9*) Temeron Bks.

Swift Shoe Company. Craig G. Harms & Stanley W. Huff. (C). 1987. pap. text ed. 25.95 (*0-256-05710-9*) Irwin.

Swift, Temple, & the Du Cros Affair Pt. 1: An Answer to a Scurrilous Pamphlet, Lately Printed, Intituled, a Letter from Monsieur de Cros, to the Lord: And Lettre de Mondieur Du Cros, a Mylord. Intro. by David L. Woolley. LC 92-24238. (Augustan Reprints Ser.: Nos. 239-240). 1986. reprint ed. 21.50 (*0-404-70239-2*, PR3728) AMS Pr.

Swift, Temple, & the Du Cros Affair, Letter from Monsieur de Cros...Being an Answer to Sir Wm. Temple's Memoirs, Concerning What Passed from the Year 1672 until the Year 1679 Pt. 2: And Reflections upon Two Pamphlets...Lately Published; One Called, a Letter from Monsieur de Cros, Concerning the Memoirs of Christendom, & the Other, an Answer. Intro. by J. A. Downie. (Augustan Reprints Ser.: Nos. 241-242). 1987. reprint ed. 21.50 (*0-404-70241-4*) AMS Pr.

***Swift Thunder.** Champlin. 1998. 20.00 (*0-7862-1160-1*) Thorndike Pr.

Swift to Hear, Slow to Speak. Jerry Butler. 1975. pap. 4.95 (*0-89137-511-2*) Quality Pubns.

***Swift Victory: Essays on the Gifts of the Holy Spirit.** 211p. 1997. reprint ed. 19.95 (*0-912141-49-2*) Roman Cath Bks.

Swift, Vol. 2: Dr. Swift, Vol. 2. Irvin Ehrenpreis. 800p. (C). 1967. 48.00 (*0-674-85832-8*) HUP.

Swiftest. Kenneth Rudeen. (Illus.). 1966. 5.50 (*0-393-07443-9*) Norton.

***Swiftest Eagle.** large type ed. Alice Dwyer-Joyce. (Large Print Ser.). 352p. 1997. 27.50 (*0-7089-3700-4*) Ulverscroft.

Swiftly Tilting Planet. Madeleine L'Engle. 256p. (YA). (gr. 7 up). 1979. mass mkt. 4.50 (*0-440-90158-8*, LLL BDD) BDD Bks Young Read.

Swiftly Tilting Planet. Madeleine L'Engle. LC 78-9648. 288p. (J). (gr. 5 up). 1978. 17.00 (*0-374-37362-0*) FS&G.

Swiftly Tilting Planet. Madeleine L'Engle. 288p. (J). (gr. 4-7). 1981. pap. 4.50 (*0-440-40158-5*) Dell.

Swiftly Tilting Planet. large type ed. Madeleine L'Engle. LC 93-21812. (J). 1993. Alk. paper. 15.95 (*1-56054-710-3*) Thorndike Pr.

Swift's Anatomy of Misunderstanding: A Study of Swift's Epistemological Imagination in "A Tale of a Tub" & "Gulliver's Travels" Frances Louis. 220p. 1981. 52.50 (*0-389-20074-3*, 06804) B&N Imports.

***Swifts & Spiny Lizards.** Ray Hunziker. (Illus.). 64p. 1998. pap. 9.95 (*0-7938-0280-6*, RE-132) TFH Pubns.

Swift's Landscape. Carole Fabricant. LC 94-45617. (C). 1995. reprint ed. pap. text ed. 16.95 (*0-268-01754-9*) U of Notre Dame Pr.

Swift's Most Valuable Friend. Sybil Le Brocquy. LC 68-26028. 128p. 6800. 18.95 (*0-8023-1165-2*) Dufour.

Swift's Narrative Satires: Author & Authority. Everett Zimmerman. LC 83-45176. 210p. 1983. 30.00 (*0-8014-1595-0*) Cornell U Pr.

Swift's Parody. Robert Phiddian. (Cambridge Studies in Eighteenth-Century English Literature & Thought Ser.: No. 26). 236p. (C). 1995. text ed. 59.95 (*0-521-47437-X*) Cambridge U Pr.

Swift's Poetic Worlds. Louise K. Barnett. LC 80-54538. 224p. 1982. 32.50 (*0-87413-187-1*) U Delaware Pr.

Swift's Politics: A Study in Disaffection. Ian Higgins. (Cambridge Studies in Eighteenth-Century English Literature & Thought: No. 20). 225p. (C). 1994. text ed. 59.95 (*0-521-41814-3*) Cambridge U Pr.

Swift's Silver Mines & Related Appalachian Treasures. Michael S. Steely. (Illus.). 272p. (Orig.). 1995. pap. 17.95 (*1-57072-036-3*) Overmountain Pr.

Swift's Tory Politics. F. P. Lock. LC 83-8155. 100p. 1984. 32.50 (*0-87413-252-5*) U Delaware Pr.

Swiftwater People. Bert Russell. (Oral History Ser.: No. 2). 1979. 11.95 (*0-930344-05-7*); pap. 8.95 (*0-930344-02-2*) Lacon Pubs.

Swiftwater Rescue: A Manual for the Rescue Professional. Slim Ray. (Illus.). 360p. (Orig.). 1997. pap. text ed. 24.95 (*0-9649585-0-3*) CFS Pr.

Swifty: My Life & Good Times. Irving Lazar & Annette Tapert. LC 94-47215. 1995. 24.00 (*0-684-80418-2*) S&S Trade.

Swifty: The Autobiography of Irving Lazar. Swifty Lazar. 1995. 24.00 (*0-671-52505-0*) S&S Trade.

Swim! Eve Rice. LC 95-25081. (Illus.). 24p. (J). (ps up). 1996. 15.00 (*0-688-14274-5*); lib. bdg. 14.93 (*0-688-14275-3*) Greenwillow.

Swim at Your Own Risk: Adventure Mystery for Kids Ages 8-12. Allen Robbins. (Spider Tales Ser.). (Orig.). (J). (gr. 3-7). 1995. 14.00 (*0-922242-76-3*) Bepuzzled.

An Asterisk (*) at the beginning of an entry indicates that the title is appearing in BIP for the first time.

Swim Bay Area: A Guide to Swimming Pools in the San Francisco Bay Area. Nancy Mackay & Vivian M. Pisano. (Illus.). 192p. (Orig.). 1988. pap. 8.95 (*0-943937-00-0*) Swimming Across West.

Swim, Bike, Run. Glenn Town & Todd Kearney. LC 93-24695. (Illus.). 240p. 1993. pap. 16.95 (*0-87322-513-9*, PTOW0513) Human Kinetics.

Swim Community Educator. Canadian Red Cross Society Staff. (gr. 13). 1996. write for info. (*0-8151-1531-8*) Mosby Yr Bk.

Swim for the Health of It. Ernest W. Maglischo & Cathy Ferguson Brennan. LC 84-60886. 144p. (Orig.). (C). 1985. pap. text ed. 14.95 (*0-87484-588-2*, 588) Mayfield Pub.

Swim Free. Laura Sanborn & Lorraine Eberhardt. (Illus.). 32p. (J). (gr. 6-12). 1982. pap. 6.95 (*0-910715-00-9*) Search Public.

Swim in the Void. Gary Horn. LC 88-70450. (Illus.). 64p. (Orig.). 1988. pap. 7.95 (*0-916383-58-X*) Aegina Pr.

***Swim Like a Fish.** Ellen Schecter. (J). 1997. pap. 4.50 (*0-553-37583-0*, Bank St); pap. 4.50 (*0-553-53133-6*, Bank St) BDD Bks Young Read.

Swim, Number Nine Duckling. Susan Akass. LC 94-71349. (Illus.). 32p. (J). (ps-2). 1995. 13.95 (*1-56397-421-5*) Boyds Mills Pr.

Swim Polar Bear, Swim! Joan Stimson. (J). 1996. 13.95 (*0-8120-6634-0*); pap. text ed. 5.50 (*0-8120-9888-9*) Barron.

***Swim Suit Confidence.** Sharon Abrahamson. Ed. & Illus. by Victoria Rivas. 36p. Date not set. pap. 4.50 (*1-889289-13-2*) Ye Olde Font Shoppe.

***Swim the Silver Sea, Joshie Otter.** Nancy W. Carlstrom. (Illus.). 32p. (Orig.). (J). (ps-1). 1997. pap. 5.95 (*0-698-11447-7*, Paperstar) Putnam Pub Group.

Swim Through the Sea. Kristin J. Pratt. (Illus.). 44p. (Orig.). (J). (ps-7). 1994. 16.95 (*1-883220-03-3*); pap. 7.95 (*1-883220-04-1*) Dawn CA.

Swim with the Dolphins: How Women Can Succeed in Corporate America on Their Own Terms. Connie Glaser & Barbara S. Smalley. 336p. 1996. pap. 12.99 (*0-446-67184-3*) Warner Bks.

***Swim with the Sharks.** Harvey Mackay. 1996. pap. 12.95 (*0-449-91148-9*) Fawcett.

***Swim with the Sharks.** Gordy Slack. (I Wish I Could Ser.). (Illus.). 48p. (J). (gr. 4-7). 1997. pap. 6.95 (*1-57098-116-7*) R Rinehart.

Swim with the Sharks Without Being Eaten Alive. Harvey Mackay. 352p. 1989. mass mkt. 6.99 (*0-8041-0426-3*) Ivy Books.

Swim with the Sharks Without Being Eaten Alive: Outsell, Outmanage, Outmotivate & Outnegotiate Your Competition. Harvey Mackay. LC 87-24757. 224p. 1988. 20.00 (*0-688-07473-1*) Morrow.

***SwimLog.** Tim Hauts. (Illus.). 176p. (Orig.). 1997. pap. 12.95 (*1-57028-147-5*) Masters Pr IN.

Swimmer. Eleanor Perry. LC 67-17163. 127p. 1967. 16.95 (*0-910278-70-9*) Boulevard.

***Swimmer.** Peter M. Sacks. LC 97-5870. (Phoenix Poets Ser.). 1996. pap. 10.95 (*0-226-73343-2*); lib. bdg. 21.00 (*0-226-73342-4*) U Ch Pr.

Swimmer: An Integrated Computational Model of a Perceptual-Motor System. William Uttal. (Scientific Psychology Ser.). 248p. 1992. text ed. 59.95 (*0-8058-1070-6*) L Erlbaum Assocs.

Swimmer: The Journey of the Alaskan Salmon. Shelley R. Gill. (Illus.). (J). 1995. 15.95 (*0-934007-23-3*); pap. 8.95 (*0-934007-24-1*) Paws Four Pub.

Swimmer & Team. Don Gambril & Alfred Bay. LC 84-9036. (Illus.). 117p. (Orig.). 1985. pap. 9.95 (*0-9615634-0-0*) Alfred Bay.

***Swimmer in the Deep Blue Dream.** Sara Berkeley. 156p. 8900. pap. 9.95 (*1-85186-092-4*) Dufour.

Swimmer in the Rain. Robert Wallace. LC 78-74988. (Poetry Ser.). 1979. pap. 11.95 (*0-915604-57-4*) Carnegie-Mellon.

Swimmer Manuscript: Cherokee Sacred Formulas & Medicinal Prescriptions. James Mooney. (Bureau of American Ethnology Bulletins Ser.). 319p. 1995. lib. bdg. 99.00 (*0-7812-4099-9*) Rprt Serv.

Swimmer. Poems. Susan Ludvigson. LC 83-25593. 53p. 1984. 13.95 (*0-8071-1155-4*) La State U Pr.

Swimmers. Jillian Powell. (J). (ps-2). 1992. lib. bdg. 6.95 (*0-87614-703-1*, Carolrhoda) Lerner Group.

Swimmers Guide: Directory of Pools for Fitness Swimmers. 2nd rev. ed. Bill Haverland & Tom Saunders. (Illus.). 349p. 1995. pap. 16.95 (*0-9635960-1-2*) ALSA Pubng.

***Swimmers, Take Your Marks!** Janet E. Gill. (Swim Team Ser.: No. 1). (J). (gr. 3-7). 1997. pap. 3.99 (*0-380-78672-9*, Camelot) Avon.

***Swimming.** LC 96-52602. (Successful Sports Ser.). (J). 1997. lib. bdg. write for info. (*1-57572-199-6*) Rigby Interact Libr.

Swimming. (Take up Sports! Ser.). (Illus.). 64p. pap. 4.95 (*1-56757-055-0*) Appleton Comms.

***Swimming.** Amateur Swimming Association Staff. (Know the Sport Ser.). (Illus.). 48p. 1997. pap. 5.95 (*0-8117-2835-8*) Stackpole.

Swimming. Donna Bailey. LC 90-36527. (Sports World Ser.). (Illus.). 32p. (J). (gr. 1-4). 1990. pap. 3.95 (*0-8114-4716-2*); lib. bdg. 21.40 (*0-8114-2852-4*) Raintree Steck-V.

Swimming. Peter Brooke-Ball. (Butterfly Bks.). (J). 1990. 8.95 (*0-86685-478-9*) Intl Bk Ctr.

***Swimming.** Brown & Benchmark Staff. (Elements of Learning Ser.). 120p. (C). 1997. per. write for info. (*0-697-29465-X*) Brown & Benchmark.

Swimming. David L. Costill et al. (Handbook of Sports Medicine & Science Ser.). (Illus.). 224p. 1982. pap. text ed. 30.00 (*0-632-03027-5*, BCOS3027, Pub. by Blackwell UK) Human Kinetics.

Swimming. Walter Cryer. 128p. (Orig.). (C). 1991. pap. text ed. 14.95 (*0-89787-616-4*) Gorsuch Scarisbrick.

Swimming. Sean McSweeney & Rebecca Sampson. (Sportscene Ser.). (Illus.). 64p. (YA). (gr. 7-10). 1993. 24.95 (*0-7134-7128-X*, Pub. by Batsford UK) Trafalgar.

Swimming. John Verrier. (Successful Sports Ser.). (J). 1996. lib. bdg. write for info. (*1-57572-071-X*) Rigby Interact Libr.

Swimming. Barry Wilner. (How to Play the All-Star Way Ser.). 1996. lib. bdg. 21.34 (*0-8114-6596-9*) Raintree Steck-V.

Swimming. 5th ed. Betty J. Vickers & William Vincent. 112p. (C). 1988. per. write for info. (*0-697-07283-5*) Brown & Benchmark.

Swimming. 6th ed. Betty J. Vickers & William J. Vincent. 112p. (C). 1993. per. write for info. (*0-697-12664-1*) Brown & Benchmark.

***Swimming.** 7th ed. Vincent Vickers. 1999. pap. text ed. 8.00 (*0-697-34536-X*) McGraw.

Swimming: A Step-By-Step Guide. Gene Dabney. LC 89-27346. (Be the Best! Ser.). (Illus.). 64p. (J). (gr. 4-8). 1990. lib. bdg. 11.89 (*0-8167-1945-4*) Troll Communs.

Swimming: A Step-By-Step Guide. Gene Dabney. LC 89-27346. (Be the Best! Ser.). (Illus.). 64p. (J). (gr. 4-8). 1997. pap. 3.95 (*0-8167-1946-2*) Troll Communs.

Swimming: Easy Sports Reader. Burt & Hog. (Illus.). 16p. (J). (ps-1). 1996. pap. 2.49 (*1-55734-897-9*) Tchr Create Mat.

Swimming: Gift for Life, Vol. I. Elise T. Lawton. (Illus.). 64p. 1986. pap. text ed. 3.00 (*0-9617193-0-3*) Lawton E T.

Swimming: Index of Modern Information with Bibliography. Irwin E. Herold. LC 88-47799. 150p. (Orig.). 1988. 44.50 (*0-88164-878-7*); pap. 39.50 (*0-88164-879-5*) ABBE Pubs Assn.

Swimming: Skills of the Game. John Verrier. (Illus.). 128p. 1996. pap. 19.95 (*1-85223-898-4*, Pub. by Crowood Pr UK) Trafalgar.

Swimming: Steps to Success. 2nd ed. David G. Thomas. LC 95-42642. (Steps to Success Activity Ser.). (Illus.). 168p. 1996. pap. 14.95 (*0-87322-846-4*, PTHO0846) Human Kinetics.

***Swimming Across the Hudson.** Joshua Henkin. 230p. 1997. 24.95 (*0-399-14116-2*, Putnam) Putnam Pub Group.

Swimming Against the Current in Contemporary Philosophy: Occasional Essays & Papers. Henry B. Veatch. LC 88-18940. (Studies in Philosophy & the History of Philosophy). 337p. 1990. 44.95 (*0-8132-0681-2*) Cath U Pr.

Swimming Against the Tide: Feminist Dissent on the Issue of Abortion. Ed. by Angela Kennedy. 144p. 1996. pap. 17.50 (*1-85182-267-4*, Pub. by Four Cts Pr IE) Intl Spec Bk.

Swimming Against the Tide: Turkish Trade Reform in the 80's. Anne O. Krueger & Okan Akton. 250p. 1992. pap. 14.95 (*1-55815-178-8*) ICS Pr.

Swimming & Aquatics Today. Ron Ballatore & William Miller. Ed. by Clyde Perlee. 227p. (C). 1990. pap. text ed. 21.25 (*0-314-50329-3*) West Pub.

Swimming & Diving. Robert Sandelson. LC 91-16117. (Olympic Sports Ser.). (Illus.). 48p. (J). (gr. 6). 1991. lib. bdg. 13.95 (*0-89686-670-X*, Crstwood Hse) Silver Burdett Pr.

Swimming & Diving. David Smale. (The Summer Olympics Ser.). 32p. (J). (gr. 4-8). 1995. 14.79 (*1-887068-04-X*) Smart Apple.

Swimming & Diving. David Smale. 32p. 1995. 14.79 (*1-887068-08-2*) Smart Apple.

Swimming & Diving. John Verrier. LC 95-39283. (Olympic Library). (J). 1996. write for info. (*1-57572-039-6*) Rigby Interact Libr.

Swimming & Diving. rev. ed. American Red Cross Staff. 368p. (gr. 13). 1995. pap. text ed. 21.00 (*0-8151-0595-9*) Mosby Yr Bk.

Swimming & Diving Bag Kit. American Red Cross Staff. 1992. 60.00 (*0-8016-6904-9*) Mosby Yr Bk.

Swimming & Health Instruction, Sr. H.S. Jack Rudman. (Teachers License Examination Ser.: T-62). 1994. pap. 27.95 (*0-8373-8062-6*) Nat Learn.

Swimming & Lifesaving Manual. Royal Life Saving Society-Australia Staff. 228p. (gr. 13). 1994. pap. text ed. write for info. (*0-8151-7324-5*) Mosby Yr Bk.

Swimming & Water Safety. Canadian Red Cross Society Staff. 320p. (gr. 13). 1995. pap. text ed. 9.19 (*0-8151-1498-2*) Mosby Yr Bk.

Swimming & Water Safety. Canadian Red Cross Society Staff. 320p. (gr. 13). 1995. pap. text ed. 9.19 (*0-8151-1953-4*) Mosby Yr Bk.

Swimming at Midnight: Selected Shorter Poems. John Matthias. LC 95-1278. 156p. 1995. text ed. 26.95 (*0-8040-0984-8*) Ohio U Pr.

Swimming at Midnight: Selected Shorter Poems. John Matthias. 132p. 1995. pap. text ed. 11.95 (*0-8040-0985-6*) Swallow.

Swimming at Twelve Mile. J. D. Carpenter. 70p. 1979. 3.95 (*0-920806-01-5*) U of Toronto Pr.

Swimming Book. Ginny L. Winter. (Illus.). (J). (gr. k-3). 1964. 8.95 (*0-8392-3037-0*) Astor-Honor.

***Swimming Cat Cove: An Allison O'Neil Mystery.** Lauren W. Douglas. LC 96-45477. 224p. (Orig.). 1997. pap. 11.95 (*1-56280-168-6*) Naiad Pr.

Swimming Coaching. Joseph Dixon. (Illus.). 192p. 1996. pap. 35.00 (*1-85223-998-0*, Pub. by Crowood Pr UK) Trafalgar.

Swimming Dragon: A Chinese Way to Fitness, Energy & a Very Long Life. T. K. Shih. (Illus.). 120p. (Orig.). 1988. pap. 9.95 (*0-88268-063-3*) Station Hill Pr.

Swimming Even Faster: A Comprehensive Guide to the Science of Swimming. 2nd ed. Ernest W. Maglischo. LC 92-41324. 704p. (C). 1993. pap. 41.95 (*1-55934-036-3*, 1036) Mayfield Pub.

Swimming Everyone. 2nd ed. Messner. 186p. 1992. pap. text ed. 14.95 (*0-88725-180-3*) Hunter Textbks.

Swimming for Fitness. George Austin & Jon Noble. pap. 10.95 (*0-7136-5687-5*, Pub. by A&C Black UK) Talman.

Swimming for Fitness. George Austin & Noble. pap. 15.95 (*0-7136-4040-5*, 93299, Pub. by A&C Black UK) Talman.

Swimming for Seniors. Edward J. Shea. LC 85-23787. 144p. (Orig.). 1986. pap. 13.95 (*0-88011-271-9*, PSHE0271) Human Kinetics.

Swimming for Total Fitness: A Progressive Aerobic Program. Jane Katz & Nancy P. Bruning. LC 92-31877. 384p. 1993. pap. 17.50 (*0-385-46821-0*) Doubleday.

Swimming in Clear Water. William O. Boggs. 1989. 3.50 (*0-941127-08-7*) Dacotah Terr Pr.

Swimming in Silk. Darren Williams. 204p. (Orig.). 1996. pap. 14.95 (*1-86373-849-5*, Pub. by Allen & Unwin Aust Pty AT) IPG Chicago.

Swimming in the Congo. Margaret Meyers. LC 95-17162. 300p. (Orig.). 1995. pap. 13.95 (*1-57131-006-1*) Milkweed Ed.

***Swimming in the Sea of the Talmud.** Michael Katz & Gershon Schwartz. LC 97-6195. 1997. pap. 24.95 (*0-8276-0607-9*) JPS Phila.

Swimming in the Starry River. Reid. 1995. mass mkt. 5.99 (*0-312-95683-5*) Tor Bks.

Swimming in the Starry River. P. Carey Reid. 384p. 1994. 19.95 (*0-7868-6005-7*) Hyperion.

Swimming in the Starry River. Paul C. Reid. LC 95-41213. 384p. (J). 1995. pap. 11.95 (*0-312-14136-X*) St Martin.

Swimming in the Sun: Discovering the Lord's Prayer with Francis of Assisi & Thomas Merton. Albert Haase. 216p. 1993. pap. 9.95 (*0-86716-193-0*) St Anthony Mess Pr.

***Swimming in the Volcano.** Bob Shacochis. 520p. 3.98 (*0-7651-0135-1*) Smithmark.

Swimming in the Volcano. Bob Shacochis. (Contemporary American Fiction Ser.). 528p. 1994. pap. 11.95 (*0-14-023658-9*, Penguin Bks) Viking Penguin.

Swimming in the Volcano: A Novel. Bob Shacochis. Ed. by B. Grossman. 608p. 1993. text ed. 22.00 (*0-684-19260-8*) S&S Trade.

Swimming into the Twenty-First Century. Cecil M. Colwin. LC 90-28869. (Orig.). 1993. pap. 19.95 (*0-87322-456-6*, PCOL0456) Human Kinetics.

***Swimming Lesson.** Antonio Jocson & J. E. Chon. (Muddy Tom's Wacky Adventures: Vol. 3). (Illus.). 31p. (J). (gr. k-3). 1997. 11.95 (*1-890963-02-X*) Lib Bell.

Swimming Lessons: And Other Stories from Firozsha Baag. Rohinton Mistry. 1997. pap. 12.00 (*0-679-77632-X*) Random.

Swimming Lessons: New & Selected Poems. Nancy Willard. 240p. 1996. 25.00 (*0-679-44639-7*) Knopf.

Swimming Made Easy & Fun: Step by Step Advice for Beginning & Advanced Swimmers. Linda Delzeit. 224p. (C). 1991. pap. text ed. 15.69 (*0-8403-6991-3*) Kendall-Hunt.

Swimming Man Burning: A Rip-Roaring Novel of the American West. Terrence Kilpatrick. LC 93-7852. (Western Literature Ser.). 248p. 1993. reprint ed. pap. 13.00 (*0-87417-219-5*) U of Nev Pr.

Swimming Out of the Collective Unconscious. Maxine Combs. pap. 4.95 (*0-9612158-3-6*) Signal Bks.

Swimming Past Iceland. Jackson Wheeler. LC 93-80195. (Illus.). 56p. (Orig.). 1993. pap. 8.95 (*0-9638843-1-X*) Mille Grazie.

Swimming Pool. 1991. mass mkt. 3.95 (*0-8217-3679-5*, Zebra Kensgtn) Kensgtn Pub Corp.

***Swimming Pool.** Claudette C. Mitchell et al. (Visions: African-American Experiences: Vol. 26). (Illus.). 8p. (Orig.). (J). (gr. k-1). 1996. pap. text ed. 3.00 (*1-57518-068-5*) Arborlake.

Swimming Pool. Mary R. Rinehart. 1985. mass mkt. 3.50 (*0-8217-1686-7*, Zebra Kensgtn) Kensgtn Pub Corp.

***Swimming Pool.** Mary R. Rinehart. 1997. mass mkt. 5.50 (*0-8217-5634-6*) Kensgtn Pub Corp.

***Swimming Pool.** Mary R. Rinehart. 336p. 1997. mass mkt. 5.50 (*1-57566-157-8*, Knsington) Kensgtn Pub Corp.

Swimming Pool Book: Everything You Need to Know to Design, Build, & Landscape the Perfect Pool. Tom Griffiths. LC 94-13683. 144p. 1995. 27.50 (*0-671-88292-9*) S&S Trade.

Swimming Pool Library. Alan Hollinghurst. (International Ser.). 1989. pap. 13.00 (*0-679-72256-4*, Vin) Random.

***Swimming Pool Operator.** Jack Rudman. (Career Examination Ser.: Vol. C-3819). 1997. pap. 27.95 (*0-8373-3819-0*) Nat Learn.

***Swimming Pool Sunday.** Wickham. Date not set. write for info. (*0-312-18188-4*) St Martin.

Swimming Pools. Kent Keegan & Pamela J. Keegan. Ed. by Shirley M. Horowitz & Gail Kummings. LC 81-69642. (Illus.). 160p. 1982. pap. 9.95 (*0-932944-50-7*) Creative Homeowner.

Swimming Pools. Stewart. Ed. by John Patrick. (Lothian Australian Garden Ser.). (Illus.). 64p. (Orig.). 1995. pap. 10.95 (*0-85091-500-7*, Pub. by Lothian Pub AT) Seven Hills Bk.

***Swimming Pools: A Guide to Their Planning, Design, & Operation.** 4th ed. Ed. by M. Alexander Gabrielsen. LC 86-15255. (Illus.). 327p. 1987. reprint ed. pap. 93.20 (*0-608-04282-X*, 2065061) Bks Demand.

Swimming Pools - Before, During, & After. Manny Garcia. (Illus.). 110p. (Orig.). 1993. pap. 34.50 (*0-9636812-0-6*) M Garcia.

Swimming Pools at War. Yves Navarre. Tr. by Donald Watson from FRE. (Publications: No. 1). 168p. (Orig.). 1982. pap. 8.95 (*0-913745-00-6*) Ubu Repertory.

Swimming Public Brochure. American Red Cross Staff. (gr. 13). 1996. write for info. (*0-8151-0969-5*) Mosby Yr Bk.

Swimming, Snow. Paulette B. Alden. (Winter Book Ser.: No. 6). 42p. 1993. 175.00 (*1-879832-05-4*); lib. bdg. 75.00 (*1-879832-06-2*) MN Ctr Book Arts.

***Swimming the Channel.** Friedman. LC 97-15601. 1997. 14.95 (*0-8050-5444-8*) H Holt & Co.

Swimming the Channel. Jim Neville. 192p. 1994. 18.95 (*0-312-11337-4*, Thomas Dunne Bks) St Martin.

Swimming the Channel: A Widow's Journey to Life. Sally Friedman. 256p. 1996. 22.00 (*0-374-27230-1*) FS&G.

Swimming the English Channel. Susan Bright. (Fastbook 1985 Ser.). 20p. 1985. 6.00 (*0-685-10808-2*) Plain View.

Swimming the Mystic Mile & Other Stories. Jean R. Smith. 120p. 1993. pap. 12.95 (*1-882063-28-7*, Heritage Hse) Cottage Pr MA.

***Swimming Through the Grand Hotel.** Judith Kazantzis. 80p. 1997. pap. 17.95 (*1-900564-20-3*, Pub. by Enitha Pr UK) Dufour.

Swimming Through Troubled Water, Proceedings of the Special Session on Shrimp Culture, Aquaculture '95. Ed. by Craig L. Browdy & J. Stephen Hopkins. (Illus.). 253p. (C). 1995. pap. text ed. 35.00 (*0-9624529-8-X*) World Aquaculture.

***Swimming to Atlantis.** unabridged ed. Charles J. Hebert. Ed. by Winter C. Neil. 296p. 1997. 17.95 (*0-9653145-0-2*, 97-01) Pontalba Pr.

Swimming to Cambodia. Spalding Gray. LC 85-20875. 127p. 1985. pap. 8.95 (*0-930452-50-X*) Theatre Comm.

***Swimming to the Moon.** E. G. Curtsinger. 236p. 1996. per., pap. 15.00 (*0-941179-42-7*) Latitudes Pr.

Swimming Upstream: A Complete Guide to the College Application Process for the Learning Disabled Student. Diane W. Howard. (Illus.). 140p. (Orig.). (YA). (gr. 8-12). 1989. student ed., pap. write for info. (*0-9623524-0-3*) Hunt Hse Pub.

Swimming Upstream: A Complete Guide to the College Application Process for the Learning Disabled Student. Diane W. Howard. 79p. (Orig.). 1994. pap. text ed. 22.99 (*0-9623524-4-6*) Hunt Hse Pub.

Swimming Upstream: Teaching & Learning Psychotherapy in a Biological Era. Jerry M. Lewis. LC 90-2671. 208p. 1991. text ed. 31.95 (*0-87630-612-1*) Brunner-Mazel.

Swimming with Dolphins. Erin Pizzey. 368p. 1995. mass mkt. 5.50 (*0-06-100558-4*, Harp PBks) HarpC.

Swimming with the Whales. Ella T. Ellis. 1996. mass mkt. 4.50 (*0-449-70456-4*, Juniper) Fawcett.

Swimming with the Whales. Ella T. Ellis. (J). 1995. 14.95 (*0-8050-3306-8*) H Holt & Co.

Swimmy. Leo Lionni. LC 63-8504. (Illus.). 40p. (J). (ps-2). 1963. 16.00 (*0-394-81713-3*) Knopf Bks Yng Read.

Swimmy. Leo Lionni. LC 63-8504. (Illus.). 40p. (J). (ps-2). 1963. lib. bdg. 18.99 (*0-394-91713-8*) Knopf Bks Yng Read.

Swimmy. Leo Lionni. LC 63-8504. (Children's Paperbacks Ser.). (Illus.). 32p. (J). (ps-6). 1973. pap. 5.99 (*0-394-82620-5*) Knopf Bks Yng Read.

***Swimsuit Issue & Sport: Hegemonic Masculinity & Sports Illustrated.** Laurel R. Davis. LC 96-38825. (Suny Series on Sport, Culture & Social Relations Ser.). 168p. 1997. 54.50 (*0-7914-3391-9*); pap. write for info. (*0-7914-3392-7*) State Univ of New York.

***Swimsuit Model Photography.** Cliff Hollenbeck. 1997. pap. text ed. 29.95 (*0-936262-57-5*) Amherst Media.

Swimsuits: Drafting & Design. Lee J. McFarland. 80p. 1989. pap. 12.00 (*1-883763-00-2*) Kideko Hse.

Swinburne. Samuel C. Chew. (BCL1-PR English Literature Ser.). 335p. 1992. reprint ed. lib. bdg. 89.00 (*0-7812-7677-2*) Rprt Serv.

Swinburne. Harold G. Nicolson. (BCL1-PR English Literature Ser.). 207p. 1992. reprint ed. lib. bdg. 79.00 (*0-7812-7706-X*) Rprt Serv.

Swinburne. Harold G. Nicolson. LC 70-145208. 1971. reprint ed. 39.00 (*0-403-00807-7*) Scholarly.

Swinburne: An Estimate. John Drinkwater. (BCL1-PR English Literature Ser.). 215p. 1992. reprint ed. lib. bdg. 79.00 (*0-7812-7678-0*) Rprt Serv.

Swinburne: The Critical Heritage. Ed. by Clyde K. Hyder. 1970. 69.50 (*0-7100-6656-2*, RKP) Routledge.

Swinburne & His Gods: The Roots & Growth of an Agnostic Poetry. Margot K. Louis. 256p. (C). 1990. text ed. 49.95 (*0-7735-0715-9*, Pub. by McGill CN) U of Toronto Pr.

Swinburne Letters, Vol. 3: 1875-1877. Algernon C. Swinburne. Ed. by Cecil Y. Lang. LC 59-12698. reprint ed. pap. 85.80 (*0-317-29712-0*, 2022043) Bks Demand.

Swinburne Letters, Vol. 5: 1883-1890. Algernon C. Swinburne. Ed. by Cecil Y. Lang. LC 59-12698. reprint ed. pap. 74.50 (*0-317-29713-9*) Bks Demand.

Swinburne Letters, 6 vols., Vols. 1-5. Algernon C. Swinburne. Ed. by Cecil Y. Lang. Incl. Vol. 1. 1854-1869. (Illus.). i, 316p. 1959. 50.00 (*0-300-00665-9*); Vol. 2. 1869-1875. vi, 378p. 1959. 50.00 (*0-300-00666-7*); write for info. (*0-318-56529-3*) Yale U Pr.

Swinburne's Literary Career & Fame. Clyde K. Hyder. LC 75-30031. (Romantic & Victorian Criticism Ser.). (Illus.). 400p. (C). 1989. reprint ed. 45.00 (*0-404-14034-3*) AMS Pr.

Swinburne's Poems & Ballads: A Criticism. William M. Rossetti. LC 73-130623. reprint ed. 21.50 (*0-404-05416-1*) AMS Pr.

Swinburne's Theory of Poetry. Thomas E. Connolly. LC 64-17576. 144p. 1965. text ed. 19.50 (*0-87395-013-5*) State U NY Pr.

Swindle: How a Man Named John Grambling Cheated Banks out of Thirty-Six Million. Brian Rosner. 350p. 1990. 30.00 (*1-55623-291-8*) Irwin Prof Pubng.

Swindle of Ethnic Minorities. 1991. lib. bdg. 69.95 (*0-8490-4440-5*) Gordon Pr.

Swindler see Two Spanish Picaresque Novels

S

S

Swindler & Other Stories. Ethel M. Dell. LC 72-140329. (Short Story Index Reprint Ser.). 1977. 23.95 (0-8369-3721-X) Ayer.

Swindler, Spy, Rebel: The Confidence Woman in Nineteenth-Century America. Kathleen DeGrave. 286p. 1995. 37.50 (0-8262-1005-8) U of Mo Pr.

***Swindler's Treasure, Vol. 4.** Lois W. Johnson. LC 97-4670. (Riverboat Adventures Ser.). (J). (gr. 3-8). 1997. pap. 5.99 (1-55661-354-7) Bethany Hse.

Swindon: History & Guide. John Chandler. (History & Guide Ser.). (Illus.). 128p. 1992. pap. 16.00 (0-7509-0190-X, Pub. by Sutton Pubng UK) Bks Intl VA.

Swindon to Gloucester Line. Colin G. Maggs. (Illus.). 128p. 1991. 29.00 (0-7509-0000-8, Pub. by Sutton Pubng UK) Bks Intl VA.

Swine AI Book: A Field & Laboratory Technicians' Guide to Artificial Insemination in Swine. Glen Almond et al. Ed. by Ruth Cronje. (Illus.). 108p. (Orig.). (C). 1994. 19. 95 (0-9640737-0-6) Swine AI Pubns.

***Swine AI Book: A Field & Laboratory Technicians Guide to Artificial Insemination in Swine.** 2nd rev. ed. Glen Almond et al. (Illus.). 120p. (SPA.). (C). 1997. pap. text ed. 25.00 (0-9640737-1-4) Swine AI Pubns.

Swine As Models in Biomedical Research. Ed. by Michael Swindle et al. LC 91-35337. (Illus.). 328p. 1992. text ed. 59.95 (0-8138-1472-3) Iowa St U Pr.

Swine Farrowing Handbook: Housing & Equipment. William H. Friday et al. Ed. by Midwest Plan Service Personnel Staff. LC 91-3581. (Illus.). 80p. (Orig.). 1992. pap. 7.00 (0-89373-084-X, MWPS-40) MidWest Plan Serv.

Swine Flu Conspiracy. John Deaux. 1997. 18.95 (0-89896-262-5) Larksdale.

Swine Housing & Equipment Handbook. 4th ed. Midwest Plan Service Engineers Staff. LC 82-2292. (Illus.). 112p. 1983. pap. 8.00 (0-89373-054-8, MWPS-8) MidWest Plan Serv.

Swine in Biomedical Research, Vol. 1. Ed. by M. E. Tumbleson. 684p. 1986. 135.00 (0-306-42414-2, Plenum Pr) Plenum.

Swine in Biomedical Research, Vol. 2. Ed. by M. E. Tumbleson. 690p. 1986. 135.00 (0-306-42415-0, Plenum Pr) Plenum.

Swine in Biomedical Research, Vol. 3. Ed. by M. E. Tumbleson. 750p. 1986. 135.00 (0-306-42416-9, Plenum Pr) Plenum.

Swine in Cardiovascular Research. H. Stanton & H. Mersmann. LC 85-30734. 200p. 1986. 116.00 (0-8493-6565-1, CRC Reprint) Franklin.

Swine in Cardiovascular Research, Vol. 1. H. Stanton & H. Mersmann. LC 85-30734. 1986. reprint ed. 111.00 (0-8493-6564-3, CRC Reprint) Franklin.

***Swine Inseminators' Handbook.** Glen Almond et al. (Illus.). 80p. (Orig.). (C). 1997. pap. text ed. 15.00 (0-9640737-2-2) Swine AI Pubns.

Swine Medicine. Wolf. 1998. text ed. write for info. (0-7216-5841-5) Saunders.

Swine Practice. Boden. 1991. pap. text ed. 42.00 (0-7020-1557-1) HarBrace.

Swine Production. Clarence E. Bundy et al. (gr. 10-12). 1976. text ed. 31.52 (0-13-879783-8) P-H.

Swine Production & Nutrition. Wilson G. Pond & Jerome H. Maner. (Illus.). 733p. 1984. text ed. 76.95 (0-87055-450-6) AVI.

***Swine Science.** M. E. Ensminger & Richard Parker. (Illus.). (YA). (gr. 9-12). 1984. 73.25 (0-8134-3117-4) Interstate.

Swine Science. 5th ed. M. E. Ensminger & Richard Parker. LC 82-84359. (Illus.). (gr. 9-12). 1984. 66.60 (0-8134-2289-2) Interstate.

Swine Science. 5th ed. M. E. Ensminger & Richard Parker. LC 82-84359. (Illus.). (YA). (gr. 9-12). 1984. text ed. 54. 95 (0-8134-3108-5) Interstate.

Swine Snafu. J. Bianchi. (Illus.). 24p. (J). (ps-8). 1988. 12. 95 (0-921285-14-0, Pub. by Bungalo Bks CN); pap. 4.95 (0-921285-12-4, Pub. by Bungalo Bks CN) Firefly Bks Ltd.

Swineherd. Hans Christian Andersen. 1995. 3.98 (0-8317-1077-2) Smithmark.

Swineherd. Illus. by Lisbeth Zwerger. LC 94-32153. (J). Date not set. 14.95 (1-55858-428-5) North-South Bks NYC.

Swine's Wedding. Daniel E. Weiss. LC 96-68815. 216p. (C). 1997. text ed. 17.99 (1-85242-419-2, High Risk Bks) Serpents Tail.

Swing. Earl Atkinson. (Ballroom Dance Ser.). 1983. lib. bdg. 250.00 (0-87700-470-6) Revisionist Pr.

***Swing.** Gary Gildner. (Illus.). 28p. (Orig.). 1996. pap. 20. 00 (0-931659-29-9) Limberlost Pr.

***Swing.** deluxe limited ed. Gary Gildner. (Illus.). 28p. (Orig.). 1996. 50.00 (0-931659-30-2) Limberlost Pr.

***Swing: Mastering the Principles of the Game.** Nick Price & Lorne Rubinstein. LC 96-52267. 240p. 1997. 30.00 (0-679-44670-2) Knopf.

Swing & Early Progressive Piano Styles see Jazz Improvisation

Swing Changes: Big-Band Jazz in New Deal America. David W. Stowe. LC 93-47000. (Illus.). 337p. 1994. 29. 95 (0-674-85825-5, STOSWJ) HUP.

Swing Changes: Big-Band Jazz in New Deal America. David W. Stowe. (Illus.). 344p. 1996. pap. 16.95 (0-674-85826-3) HUP.

Swing Dancer, Version 1.0: A Swing Dancer's Manual. Craig R. Hutchinson. LC 88-90818. (Illus.). 212p. (Orig.). (C). 1988. pap. 20.00 (0-317-89759-4) Potomac Swing Dance Club.

Swing, Dawn of a New Era: The Alternative Lifestyle. Cathy Marks & Steve Marks. LC 94-75819. 320p. 1994. 24.95 (0-9640903-0-9) M S W Pubng.

Swing Directory of Social Welfare Information Networks. National Inst. for Social Work Staff. (C). 1988. 35.00 (0-685-31908-3, Pub. by Natl Inst Soc Work) St Mut.

Swing Easy, Hit Hard. Julius Boros. LC 95-11835. (Illus.). 160p. 1995. pap. 14.95 (1-55821-416-X) Lyons & Burford.

Swing Era: The Development of Jazz, 1930-1945. Gunther A. Schuller. (History of Jazz Ser.: Vol. 11). (Illus.). 944p. 1991. reprint ed. pap. 17.95 (0-19-507140-9) OUP.

Swing Era New York: The Jazz Photographs of Charles Peterson. W. Royal Stokes. (Illus.). 256p. 1994. 49.95 (1-56639-227-6) Temple U Pr.

Swing Era New York: The Jazz Photographs of Charles Peterson. W. Royal Stokes. (Illus.). 232p. (C). 1996. pap. 24.95 (1-56639-464-3) Temple U Pr.

Swing Fiddle, an Introduction. Ryan J. Thomson. (Illus.). 75p. (Orig.). (C). 1990. pap. 10.95 (0-931877-19-9) Captain Fiddle Pubns.

Swing for a Lifetime. Bob Taski & Jim Flick. Ed. by Sally Peters. (Golf Digest Ser.: Vol. 1). 96p. (Orig.). 1992. pap. 10.00 (0-671-75869-1) PB.

Swing Hammer Swing! Jeff Torrington. LC 93-47299. 1994. 23.95 (0-15-187427-1) HarBrace.

Swing Hammer Swing! Jeff Torrington. 416p. 1995. pap. 13.00 (0-15-600197-7) HarBrace.

Swing II, after the Dawn. Cathy Marks & Steve Marks. 320p. 1995. 24.95 (0-9640903-2-5) M S W Pubng.

Swing Kings. Friedman-Fairfax & Sony Music Staff. (Life, Times & Music Book/CD Ser.). 1995. pap. 16.98 incl. audio compact disk (1-56799-076-2, Friedman-Fairfax) M Friedman Pub Grp Inc.

***Swing Kings.** Julie Koerner. (Musicbooks Ser.). 1997. 13. 50 incl. audio compact disk (1-56799-358-3, Friedman-Fairfax) M Friedman Pub Grp Inc.

Swing Legacy. Chip Deffaa. (Studies in Jazz: No. 9). (Illus.). 393p. 1989. 42.50 (0-8108-2282-2) Scarecrow.

Swing Low: Black Men Writing. Ed. & Compiled by Rebecca Carroll. LC 94-33373. 1995. 22.50 (0-517-59981-3, Crown); pap. 12.00 (0-517-88324-4, Crown) Crown Pub Group.

Swing Low, Sweet chariot: The Mortality Cost of Colonizing Liberia in the Nineteenth Century. Antonio McDaniel. (Illus.). 213p. 1995. 34.00 (0-226-55724-3) U Ch Pr.

Swing Made Easy. (Ballroom Dance Ser.). 1985. lib. bdg. 79.95 (0-87700-675-X) Revisionist Pr.

Swing Out: Great Negro Dance Bands. Gene Fernett. (Illus.). 176p. 1993. pap. 14.95 (0-306-80501-4) Da Capo.

Swing Shift: Building the Liberty Ships. Joseph Fabry. LC 81-14449. (Illus.). 224p. (Orig.). 1982. pap. 7.95 (0-89407-049-5) Strawberry Hill.

Swing Sisters. Jeane Westin. 560p. 1994. mass mkt. 4.99 (1-55817-782-5, Pinncle Kensgtn) Kensgtn Pub Corp.

Swing Sisters. Jeane Westin. 576p. 1991. text ed. 22.95 (0-684-19222-5) S&S Trade.

Swing, Swing, Swing: The Life & Times of Benny Goodman. Ross Firestone. (Illus.). 512p. 1993. 29.95 (0-393-03371-6) Norton.

Swing, Swing, Swing: The Life & Times of Benny Goodman. Ross Firestone. 1994. pap. 14.95 (0-393-31168-6) Norton.

Swing That Music. Louis Armstrong. (Illus.). 200p. 1993. reprint ed. pap. 12.95 (0-306-80544-8) Da Capo.

Swing That Pail. Louisa M. Burger. (Orig.). 1991. pap. 7.50 (0-912449-37-3) Floating Island.

Swing the Clubhead. Ernest Jones. LC 85-30241. (Illus.). 126p. 1983. reprint ed. 13.95 (0-914178-91-1) Golf Digest.

Swing the Next: A Second Collection of Squares, Contras, Triplets, & Circles. Ted Sannella. (Illus.). 206p. 1996. spiral bd. 28.00 (0-917024-08-7) Country Dance & Song.

Swing Thoughts: The Keys to Improving Your Game from Golf's Greatest Pros. Ed. by Don Wade. LC 92-42263. 240p. 1993. 16.95 (0-8092-3912-4) Contemp Bks.

Swing Thoughts: The World's Greatest Golfers Share Their Keyes to Mastering the Game. Don Wade. 240p. 1994. pap. 12.95 (0-8092-3638-9) Contemp Bks.

Swing to Bop: An Oral History of the Transition in Jazz in the 1940's. Ira Gitler. 352p. 1987. pap. 13.95 (0-19-505070-3) OUP.

Swing Your Partner: Old Time Dances of New Brunswick & Nova Scotia. Lois S. Fahs. 1939. pap. 21.95 (0-931814-01-4) Comn Studies.

Swingbeds: Assessing Flexible Health Care in Rural Communities. Ed. by Joshua M. Wiener. LC 86-73150. (Dialogues on Public Policy Ser.). 140p. 1987. pap. 11. 95 (0-8157-9283-2) Brookings.

Swinger of Birches: Poems of Robert Frost for Young People. Robert Frost. LC 82-5517. (Illus.). 80p. (J). (gr. 4 up). 1982. 21.95 (0-916144-92-5); pap. 14.95 (0-916144-93-3); pap. 23.90 incl. audio (0-88045-102-5, 102-5); audio 8.95 (0-88045-099-1) Stemmer Hse.

***Swingers.** Favreau. LC 96-37966. 1997. pap. 9.95 (0-7868-8261-1) Little.

Swingers. Maria Yourglich & Anita Yourglich. LC 91-38819. 1992. pap. 13.95 (0-87949-361-5) Ashley Bks.

***Swingers & Crooners: The Art of Jazz Singing.** Leslie Gourse. LC 96-31529. (Art of Jazz Ser.). (J). 1997. lib. bdg. 22.00 (0-531-11321-3) Watts.

***Swingers & Crooners: The Art of Jazz Singing.** Leslie Gourse. (The Art of Jazz Ser.). 1997. pap. text ed. 6.95 (0-531-15837-3) Watts.

Swinger's Showcase over 40 Great Songs. 160p. (Orig.). 1994. pap. 16.95 (0-89724-244-0) Warner Brothers.

Swingers Three. Cherri Grant. 224p. (Orig.). 1990. mass mkt. 3.95 (0-87067-338-6) Holloway.

***Swingin' & Singin' & Getting Merry like Christmas.** Maya Angelou. 1997. mass mkt. 12.00 (0-553-38005-2) Bantam.

Swingin' at the Savoy: The Memoir of a Jazz Dancer. Norma Miller. LC 96-20104. (Illus.). 310p. 1996. 29.95 (1-56639-494-5) Temple U Pr.

Swingin' Round the Cirkle. David R. Locke. LC 72-91085. (American Humorists Ser.). (Illus.). 307p. reprint ed. lib. bdg. 26.50 (0-8398-1167-5) Irvington.

Swinging Approach to Racquetball. Charles Smith & Don Jones. 64p. (C). 1994. pap. text ed., spiral bd. 8.35 (0-8403-9616-3) Kendall-Hunt.

Swinging below a Star. (Strategies Program Ser.). 1991. pap. 23.24 (0-8123-6908-4); text ed. 20.12 (0-8123-6907-6) McDougal-Littell.

Swinging Big Bands: Into the Nineties. Al Raymond. 245p. 1992. pap. 20.00 (0-9634600-0-5) Harmony Pr PA.

Swinging Caravan. Achmed Abdullah. LC 75-103485. (Short Story Index Reprint Ser.). 1977. 20.95 (0-8369-3077-0) Ayer.

Swinging High: Dr. Wise Reader. Francis H. Wise. Ed. by Joyce M. Wise. (Learn to Read Ser.: No. 8). (Illus.). 21p. (C). 1983. pap. 1.50 (0-915766-61-2) Wise Pub.

Swinging in the Wind: Kids: Survivors of a Crisis. Kathleen L. Peabody & Margaret L. Mooney. Ed. by Bettye Ellison & Peter Libby. LC 92-50632. (Illus.). 144p. (Orig.). (C). 1992. pap. text ed. 12.95 (0-9629350-9-3) Sharp Pub.

Swinging on a Rainbow. Charles D. Perkins. LC 91-78393. (Illus.). 32p. (J). (gr. 1-4). 1992. 14.95 (0-86543-286-4); pap. 6.95 (0-86543-287-2) Africa World.

Swinging on a Star. Michael Leeds & Johnny Burke. 1996. pap. 6.00 (0-8222-1523-3) Dramatists Play.

***Swinging on a Tune: Songs for the Very Small & the Very Tall.** 2nd rev. ed. Alice Eberhart-Wright. Ed. by Carol F. Marshall. (Illus.). 110p. (J). (ps-1). 1996. reprint ed. pap. 15.00 (0-9657482-0-0) A Eberhart-Wright.

Swinging the Dream. Erenberg. 1995. 29.95 (0-226-21516-4) U Ch Pr.

Swinging the Maelstrom: New Perspectives on Malcolm Lowry. Ed. by Sherrill Grace. 1992. 55.00 (0-7735-0862-7, Pub. by McGill CN) U of Toronto Pr.

Swinging Tree. Janet R. Showalter. (Orig.). (J). (gr. k-5). 1995. pap. text ed. 5.95 (0-9646464-5-5) Heritage Inspirations.

Swinging Tree: I Am Special Childrens Story Books. Carol T. Plum. 32p. (J). (gr. 3-8). 1989. pap. text ed. 3.95 (0-87973-013-7, 13); lib. bdg. 6.95 (0-87973-016-1, 16) Our Sunday Visitor.

Swinging with Gar. Gar Witherspoon. (Illus.). 114p. (Orig.). 1987. pap. 9.95 (0-9618178-0-1) G Witherspoon.

Swingle: History of the Swingle Family. C. F. Martzolff. (Illus.). 212p. 1995. reprint ed. pap. 33.00 (0-8328-4846-8); reprint ed. lib. bdg. 43.00 (0-8328-4845-X) Higginson Bk Co.

Swinglische Bekenntnis see Accompt Rekenynge & Confession of the Faith of Huldrik Zwinglius

***Swings & Misses: Moribund Labor Relations in Professional Baseball.** Kenneth M. Jennings. LC 97-11085. 1997. text ed. write for info. (0-275-95797-7, Praeger Pubs) Greenwood.

Swing's the Thing. Ben Hines & Bob McBee. LC 85-6349. 112p. (Orig.). (J). 1986. pap. 9.95 (0-9609500-1-X) McBee Sports.

Swingtime Favorites: Playin' Jazz. (Easy Piano Ser.). 48p. 1987. pap. 6.95 (0-7935-2014-2, 00366235) H Leonard.

Swinson: Group Accounting. Christopher Swinson. 200p. 1993. pap. 80.00 (0-406-50019-3) MICHIE.

Swirling. Dale Pendell. 44p. 1986. boxed 5.00 (1-882623-04-5) Exiled-Am Pr.

Swirling Flow Problems at Intakes: Hydraulic Structures Design Manual, No. 1. Ed. by J. Knauss. 168p. (C). 1987. text ed. 85.00 (90-6191-643-7, Pub. by A A Balkema NE) Ashgate Pub Co.

***Swirly Whirly.** Joseph Greenbaum, Jr. 232p. (Orig.). 1997. mass mkt. 4.99 (1-55237-189-1, Pub. by Comnwlth Pub CN) Partners Pubs Grp.

***Swish!** Bill Martin & Michael Sampson. LC 96-44216. (Illus.). (J). 1997. 14.95 (0-8050-4498-1) H Holt & Co.

Swiss - Bernese Oberland: A Summer Guide with Specific Trips to the Mountains, Lakes & Villages. Philip H. Alspach & Loretta H. Alspach. LC 92-71079. 104p. 1992. pap. 16.95 (0-9632235-3-4) Intercon CA.

Swiss Account. Paul Erdman. 384p. 1993. mass mkt. 5.99 (0-8125-2016-5) Tor Bks.

Swiss Alps. Passport Books Editors. 120p. 1994. pap. 17.95 (0-8442-9969-3, Passport Bks) NTC Pub Grp.

Swiss Army Knife Companion: The Improbable History of the World's Handiest Knife. Rick Wall. LC 86-62852. (Illus.). 64p. (Orig.). 1986. pap. text ed. 7.95 (0-9618035-0-9) Swiss Army Knife Soc.

Swiss at War 1300-1500. Douglas Miller. (Men-at-Arms Ser.: No. 94). (Illus.). 48p. pap. 11.95 (0-85045-334-8, 9030, Pub. by Osprey UK) Stackpole.

Swiss Ball Applications for Orthopedic & Sports Medicine: A Guide for Home Exercise Programs Utilizing the Swiss Ball. Joanne Posner-Mayer. Ed. by Jauna Hyer et al. (Illus.). 250p. (C). 1995. pap. text ed. 29.95 (0-9645341-4-2) Ball Dynam.

Swiss Bank Accounts. 1992. lib. bdg. 275.95 (0-8490-5290-4) Gordon Pr.

Swiss Bank Accounts. Michael A. Jones. 1990. text ed. 24. 95 (0-07-155923-X) McGraw.

Swiss Bank Accounts: A Personal Guide to Ownership, Benefits & Use. Michael A. Jones. 204p. 1989. 22.95 (0-8306-4046-0, Liberty Hse) TAB Bks.

Swiss Bank Accounts: Investments Through Swiss Banks. William Von Graz. LC 88-92323. 96p. (Orig.). 1989. pap. 15.95 (0-922958-01-7) H W Parker.

Swiss Banks. 1992. lib. bdg. 250.00 (0-8490-5272-6) Gordon Pr.

Swiss Colonists in 19th Century America. Adelrich Steinach. 512p. 1995. reprint ed. 49.50 (0-89725-223-3, 1607) Picton Pr.

***Swiss Company Law.** Bruno Becchio. LC 96-3332. 1996. lib. bdg. 130.00 (90-411-0967-6) Kluwer Ac.

***Swiss Democracy.** 2nd ed. Linder. Date not set. text ed. 69.95 (0-312-17756-9) St Martin.

Swiss Emigration Book. Cornelia Schrader-Muggenthaler. 216p. 1993. text ed. 22.95 (1-55856-144-7) Closson Pr.

Swiss Equity Market. Henri B. Meier. LC 85-12195. (Illus.). xiv, 210p. 1986. text ed. 49.95 (0-89930-147-9, MEQ/, Quorum Bks) Greenwood.

Swiss Family Robinson. Robert Louis Stevenson. (YA). (gr. 7 up). 1996. pap. 2.99 (0-614-15792-7) Tor Bks.

Swiss Family Robinson. Johann Wyss. Ed. by John Seelye. (World's Classics Ser.). (Illus.). 560p. 1992. pap. 9.95 (0-19-282724-3, 12461) OUP.

Swiss Family Robinson. Johann Wyss. Ed. by Naunerle Farr. (Now Age Illustrated IV Ser.). (Illus.). (J). (gr. 4-12). 1978. pap. text ed. 2.95 (0-88301-323-1) Pendulum Pr.

Swiss Family Robinson. Johann Wyss. Ed. by Naunerle Farr. (Now Age Illustrated IV Ser.). (Illus.). (J). (gr. 4-12). 1978. student ed. 1.25 (0-88301-347-9) Pendulum Pr.

Swiss Family Robinson. Johann Wyss. Ed. by Raymond James. LC 89-33888. (Illustrated Classics Ser.). (Illus.). 48p. (J). (gr. 3-6). 1990. lib. bdg. 12.89 (0-8167-1875-X) Troll Communs.

Swiss Family Robinson. Johann Wyss. Ed. by Raymond James. LC 89-33888. (Illustrated Classics Ser.). (Illus.). 48p. (J). (gr. 3-6). 1996. pap. 4.95 (0-8167-1876-8) Troll Communs.

***Swiss Family Robinson.** Johann Wyss. Ed. by Malvina Vogel. (Great Illustrated Classics Ser.: Vol. 11). (Illus.). 240p. (J). (gr. 3-6). 1990. 9.95 (0-86611-962-0) Playmore Inc.

Swiss Family Robinson. Johann D. Wyss. LC 94-5858. (Everyman's Library Children's Classics). (J). 1994. 13. 95 (0-679-43640-5, Evrymans Lib Childs) Knopf.

Swiss Family Robinson. Johann D. Wyss. Date not set. lib. bdg. 26.95 (0-8488-0108-3) Amereon Ltd.

Swiss Family Robinson. Johann D. Wyss. (J). 1990. pap. 4.95 (0-451-52481-0, Sig Classics) NAL-Dutton.

Swiss Family Robinson. Johann D. Wyss & Robert Louis Stevenson. 1996. mass mkt., pap. 2.99 (0-8125-4306-8) Tor Bks.

Swiss Family Robinson. Johann D. Wyss. (Young Reader's Christian Library). 224p. (J). 1994. pap. text ed. 1.39 (1-55748-552-6) Barbour & Co.

Swiss Family Robinson. Johann D. Wyss. (Airmont Classics Ser.). (YA). (gr. 5 up). 1964. mass mkt. 1.95 (0-8049-0013-2, CL-13) Airmont.

Swiss Family Robinson. Johann D. Wyss. 320p. 1992. pap. 3.50 (0-553-21403-9, Bantam Classics) Bantam.

***Swiss Family Robinson.** Johann D. Wyss. (Young Collector's Illustrated Classics Ser.). (Illus.). 192p. (J). (gr. 3-7). write for info. (1-56156-459-1) Kidsbks.

Swiss Family Robinson. Johann D. Wyss. (Illus.). (J). (gr. 4-6). 1949. 16.95 (0-448-06022-1, G&D) Putnam Pub Group.

Swiss Family Robinson. Johann D. Wyss. 1997. pap. 2.95 (0-89375-416-1) Troll Communs.

Swiss Family Robinson. Johann D. Wyss. (J). 1996. pap. 3.99 (0-14-036718-7) Viking Penguin.

Swiss Family Robinson. Johann D. Wyss. (First Illustrated Classics Ser.). (Illus.). 240p. (J). (ps-6). Date not set. pap. 2.95 (0-614-97963-3) Landoll.

Swiss Family Robinson. Johann D. Wyss. (Illustrated Classics Ser.). (Illus.). 240p. (J). (ps-6). Date not set. 9.95 (1-56987-117-5) Landoll.

Swiss Family Robinson. Johann D. Wyss. (Illustrated Landoll Classics Ser.). (Illus.). 224p. (J). (ps-6). Date not set. pap. text ed. 3.95 (1-56987-400-X) Landoll.

Swiss Family Robinson. Johann D. Wyss. 1981. reprint ed. lib. bdg. 25.95 (0-89966-421-0) Buccaneer Bks.

Swiss Family Robinson: Junior Novelization. Disney Press Staff. (J). 1996. pap. 4.95 (0-7868-4084-6) Disney Pr.

***Swiss Family Robinson Readalong.** Johann Wyss. (Illustrated Classics Collection 4). 64p. 1994. pap. 14.95 incl. audio (0-7854-0773-1, 40526) Am Guidance.

***Swiss Family Robinson/Robinson Crusoe.** Smithmark Staff. (Classic Library Collection). 1996. 12.98 (0-7651-9984-X) Smithmark.

Swiss Federal Code of Obligations (As of January 1, 1984) Simon L. Goren. LC 86-26076. xiii, 305p. 1987. 65.00 (0-8377-2207-1) Rothman.

Swiss Foreign Direct Investment in the United States 1974-1994. Francis M. Jeffries. 300p. (Orig.). 1995. pap. 125. 00 (1-878974-19-X) Jeffries & Assocs.

Swiss German Dialect & Romance Patois. William G. Moulton. (LD Ser.: No. 34). 1941. pap. 25.00 (0-527-00780-3) Periodicals Srv.

Swiss Higher Schools of Engineering & Swiss Higher Schools of Economics & Business Administration. Karlene N. Dickey & Karen Lukas. 1991. pap. 20.00 (0-910054-95-9) Am Assn Coll Registrars.

***Swiss Holiday.** Elizabeth Yates & Gloria Repp. LC 96-29206. (J). 1996. pap. 6.49 (0-89084-889-0, 100537) Bob Jones Univ Pr.

Swiss Lake & Mire Environments During the last 15,000 Years. Ed. by G. Lang. (Dissertationes Botanicae Ser.: No. 87). (Illus.). 428p. 1985. pap. 104.00 (3-7682-1447-8) Lubrecht & Cramer.

Swiss Life in Town & Country. Alfred T. Story. LC 77-87714. 312p. 1983. reprint ed. 62.50 (0-404-16508-7) AMS Pr.

Swiss Migration to America: The Swiss Mennonites. Leo Schelbert. Ed. by Francesco Cordasco. LC 80-891. (American Ethnic Groups Ser.). 1981. lib. bdg. 42.95 (0-405-13452-5) Ayer.

Swiss Money Secrets: How You Can Legally Hide Your Money. Adam Starchild. 128p. 1996. pap. 15.00 (0-87364-855-2) Paladin Pr.

An Asterisk (*) at the beginning of an entry indicates that the title is appearing in BIP for the first time.

Swiss Musical Boxes: Musical Novelties & Clocks. LC 84-24607. (Illus.). 36p. (Orig.). 1985. reprint ed. pap. 4.95 (*0-930163-25-7*) Arlington Bk.

Swiss Nature Doctor's Book of 12 Health- Restoring Treatments. A. Vogel. 16p. (Orig.). 1990. pap. 2.95 (*0-87983-522-2*) Keats.

Swiss Nature Doctor's Guide to a Healthier Heart & Circulatory System. A. Vogel. 16p. (Orig.). 1990. pap. 2.95 (*0-87983-519-2*) Keats.

Swiss Nature Doctor's Healthful Advice on Natural Diet. A. Vogel. 16p. (Orig.). 1990. pap. 2.95 (*0-87983-521-4*) Keats.

Swiss Nature Doctor's Home Treatment of Common Ailments. A. Vogel. 16p. (Orig.). 1990. pap. 2.95 (*0-87983-517-6*) Keats.

Swiss Nature Doctor's Recommended Natural Foods for Health & Vitality. A. Vogel. 16p. (Orig.). 1990. pap. 2.95 (*0-87983-520-6*) Keats.

Swiss Nature Doctor's Secrets of Therapeutic Herbs. A. Vogel. 16p. (Orig.). 1990. pap. 15.00 (*0-87983-518-4*) Keats.

Swiss Neutrality & Security: Armed Forces, National Defence & Foreign Policy. Marko Milivojevic & Pierre Maurer. LC 89-28949. 272p. 1991. 55.00 (*0-85496-608-0*) Berg Pubs.

Swiss Press & Foreign Affairs in World War II. Frederick H. Hartmann. LC 60-62782. (University of Florida Monographs, Social Sciences: No. 5). 96p. reprint ed. pap. 27.40 (*0-8357-6716-7*, 2035350) Bks Demand.

Swiss Secrets. Carolyn Keene. Ed. by Anne Greenberg. (Nancy Drew Files Series, Passport to Romance Trilogy: No. 72, No. 1). 160p. (YA). (gr. 6 up). mass mkt. 3.99 (*0-671-73076-2*, Archway) PB.

Swiss Shooting Talers & Medals. Delbert R. Kraus. (Illus.). 1984. reprint ed. 12.00 (*0-915262-71-1*) S J Durst.

Swiss Surnames: A Complete Register, 3 vols. Frwd. by Lewis B. Rohrbach. LC 41-18702. 1995. 149.50 (*0-89725-206-3*, 1630) Picton Pr.

***Swiss Timepiece Makers 1775-1975, 2 vols.** Kathleen W. Pritchard. LC 97-4050. 1800p. 1997. 125.00 (*0-914659-79-0*) Phoenix Pub.

Swiss Way of Welfare: Lessons for the Western World. Ralph Segalman. LC 85-19153. 224p. 1985. text ed. 55.00 (*0-275-92044-5*, Greenwood Pr) Greenwood.

Swiss Without Halos. J. Christopher Herold. LC 79-9792. 271p. 1979. reprint ed. text ed. 59.75 (*0-313-21268-6*, HESH, Greenwood Pr) Greenwood.

Swiss Wristwatches: Chronology of Worldwide Success. Gisbert Brunner & Christian Pfeiffer-Belli. LC 90-63793. (Illus.). 248p. 1991. 69.95 (*0-88740-301-8*) Schiffer.

Switch. Torsten Barring. (Orig.). 1992. mass mkt. 4.95 (*1-56333-061-X*, Badboy) Masquerade.

Switch. William Bayer. 352p. 1985. pap. 4.99 (*0-451-15356-1*, Sig) NAL-Dutton.

Switch. Elmore Leonard. 224p. 1990. mass mkt. 4.99 (*0-440-20831-9*) Dell.

Switch. McColley. LC 96-30917. (J). 1997. 16.00 (*0-689-81122-5*) S&S Childrens.

***Switch.** Kevin McColley. (J). 1997. pap. text ed. 4.50 (*0-689-81527-1*, Atheneum Bks Young) S&S Childrens.

Switch. large type ed. Elmore Leonard. LC 93-24852. 258p. 1993. pap. 17.95 (*0-8161-5653-0*, GK Hall) Thorndike Pr.

Switch Bitch. Roald Dahl. 144p. 1989. pap. 10.95 (*0-14-004179-6*, Penguin Bks) Viking Penguin.

Switch Cat. large type ed. Garry Disher. LC 94-21002. (Illus.). 32p. (J). (ps-2). 1995. 14.95 (*0-395-71643-8*) Ticknor & Fields.

Switch Engineering Handbook. John R. Mason. 1992. text ed. 64.50 (*0-07-040769-X*) McGraw.

Switch Hitters: Lesbians Write Gay Male Erotica & Gay Men Write Lesbian Erotica. Ed. by Carol Queen & Lawrence Schimel. 200p. (Orig.). 1996. pap. 12.95 (*1-57344-021-3*); lib. bdg. 24.95 (*1-57344-022-1*) Cleis Pr.

Switch-Level Timing Simulation of MOS VLSI Circuits. Vasant Rao et al. (C). 1988. lib. bdg. 91.00 (*0-89838-302-1*) Kluwer Ac.

Switch Level VLSI. Randall E. Bryant. (C). 1996. text ed. write for info. (*0-201-07404-4*) Addison-Wesley.

Switch Mode Power Conversion: Basic Theory & Design. Sum. (Electrical Engineering & Electronics Ser.: Vol. 22). 336p. 1984. 99.75 (*0-8247-7234-2*) Dekker.

Switch On, Switch Off. Melvin Berger. LC 88-17638. (Let's-Read-&-Find-Out Science Bk.). (Illus.). 32p. (J). (gr. k-3). 1989. lib. bdg. 14.89 (*0-690-04786-X*, Crowell Jr Bks) HarpC Child Bks.

Switch on, Switch Off. Melvin Berger. LC 88-17638. (Trophy Let's-Read-&-Find-Out Bk.). (Illus.). 32p. (J). (gr. k-3). 1990. pap. 4.95 (*0-06-445097-X*, Trophy) HarpC Child Bks.

Switch on to Love. large type ed. Irene Lawrence. (Linford Romance Library). 224p. 1993. pap. 15.99 (*0-7089-7470-8*, Trailtree Bookshop) Ulverscroft.

Switch-Reference & Discourse Representation. Lesley Stirling. (Cambridge Studies in Linguistics: No. 63). 381p. (C). 1993. text ed. 80.00 (*0-521-40229-8*) Cambridge U Pr.

Switch Reference & Universal Grammar: Proceedings of a Symposium on Switch Reference & Universal Grammar, Winnipeg, May 1981. Ed. by John Haiman & Pamela Munro. (Typological Studies in Language: No. 2). xv, 337p. 1983. 71.00 (*90-272-2866-3*); pap. 37.95 (*90-272-2862-0*) Benjamins North Am.

Switch Reference in Koasati Discourse. David P. Rising. LC 92-80355. xii, 90p. 1992. pap. 8.00 (*0-88312-813-6*); fiche 8.00 (*0-88312-859-4*) Summer Instit Ling.

***Switch Virtual Networking.** Brian Dorling et al. 1996. 40.00 (*0-614-20318-X*) P-H.

Switcharound. Lois Lowry. 128p. (J). (gr. k-6). 1991. pap. 3.50 (*0-440-48415-4*, YB BDD) BDD Bks Young Read.

Switcharound. Lois Lowry. 1985. 16.00 (*0-395-39536-4*) HM.

Switchback. Robin Stevenson & Tom Bade. 1988. pap. write for info. (*0-318-63240-3*, Zebra Kensgtn) Kensgtn Pub Corp.

Switchback. Collin Wilcox. 1995. pap. text ed. 5.95 (*0-8050-4233-4*) H Holt & Co.

Switchback: (Or) Lost Child in the Terror Zone. Murray Mednick. (Classics Ser.: No. 159). 60p. (Orig.). 1997. pap. 9.95 (*1-55713-309-3*) Sun & Moon CA.

Switchblade: The Ace of Blades. Ragnar Benson. (Illus.). 104p. 1989. pap. 12.00 (*0-87364-500-6*) Paladin Pr.

Switchboard Operator. Jack Rudman. (Career Examination Ser.: C-883). 1994. pap. 19.95 (*0-8373-0883-6*) Nat Learn.

Switchboard Supervisor. Jack Rudman. (Career Examination Ser.: C-884). 1994. pap. 27.95 (*0-8373-0884-4*) Nat Learn.

Switched. R. L. Stine. (Fear Street Ser.). (YA). (gr. 7 up). 1995. mass mkt. 3.99 (*0-671-86839-X*, Archway) PB.

Switched Capacitor Circuits. A. Dabrowski. (Illus.). 272p. 1996. 74.95 (*0-412-75270-0*) Chapman & Hall.

Switched Capicitor Filters: Theory, Analysis & Design. Anandmohan et al. 500p. 1995. text ed. 74.00 (*0-13-879818-4*, 330201) P-H.

***Switched-Current Design & Implementation of Oversampling AD Converters, Vol. 412.** Nanxiong Tan. LC 97-17309. (Analog Circuits & Signal Processing & Computer Science Ser.). 1997. write for info. (*0-7923-9963-3*) Kluwer Ac.

***Switched Local Area Networks.** Roese. (ITCP-US Computer Science Ser.). 1997. pap. 44.99 incl. cd-rom (*1-85032-896-X*) ITCP.

Switched Mode Power Supplies: Design & Construction. H. W. Whittington et al. 216p. 1992. text ed. 98.00 (*0-471-93346-5*) Wiley.

***Switched Mode Power Supplies: Design & Construction.** 2nd ed. H. W. Whittington et al. LC 96-51437. (Electronic & Electrical Engineering Research Ser.). 1997. write for info. (*0-471-96772-6*) Wiley.

***Switched Mode Power Supplies: Design & Construction.** 2nd ed. H. W. Whittington et al. LC 96-51437. (Electronic & Electrical Engineering Research Studies Ser.). 1997. write for info. (*0-86380-203-6*) Research Service.

Switched-Mode Power Supplies in Practice. Otmar Kilgenstein. 329p. 1989. text ed. 215.00 (*0-471-92004-5*) Wiley.

***Switched-Mode Servo Systems: For Tracking & Instrumentation.** James A. Green. LC 94-77826. (Engineering Ser.: Vol. 3). (Illus.). 120p. 1997. 62.88 (*1-890121-19-3*, 03-04-01) Grnwd Resch.

Switched-on Living: Simple Ways to Use the Mind-Body Connection to Energize Your Life. Jerry V. Teplitz & Norma Eckroate. (Illus.). 120p. (Orig.). 1994. pap. 10.95 (*1-878901-93-1*) Hampton Roads Pub Co.

Switched Reluctance Motors & Their Control. T. J. Miller. LC 92-82559. (Monographs in Electrical & Electronic Engineering: No. 31). 216p. 1993. 85.00 (*0-19-859387-2*, Clarendon Pr) OUP.

Switched Reluctance Motors & Their Controls. Tim Miller & James R. Hendershot, Jr. 300p. 1992. 150.00 (*1-881855-02-3*) Magna Physics.

Switched Reluctance Motors, Inverters & Controls: A Reference Book of Collected Papers since 1988. 500p. 1992. 150.00 (*1-881855-01-5*) Magna Physics.

***Switchers.** Thompson. (J). 1998. 14.89 (*0-7868-2328-3*) Hyprn Child.

***Switchers 2.** Thompson. (J). 1999. 17.89 (*0-7868-2329-1*) Hyprn Child.

Switches. Sinclair. 1988. pap. 42.95 (*0-632-02068-7*) Buttrwrth-Heinemann.

***Switchgear & Control Handbook.** 3rd ed. Ed. by Robert W. Smeaton & William H. Ubert. (Illus.). 1024p. 1997. text ed. 99.95 (*0-07-058451-6*) McGraw.

Switchgear & Switchboard Apparatus Industry: A Product-by-Product Marketing Analysis & Competitor Profile. 250p. 1994. 1,095.00 (*0-317-55204-X*) Busn Trend.

Switching & Finite Automata Theory. 2nd ed. Zvi Kohavi. Ed. by Edward A. Feigenbaum & Richard W. Hamming. (McGraw-Hill Computer Science Ser.). (Illus.). (C). 1978. text ed. write for info. (*0-07-035310-7*) McGraw.

Switching Hour. Barkan. LC 96-2966. (Real Monsters: 2). (J). 1996. 3.99 (*0-689-80870-4*) S&S Trade.

Switching Machines. Perrin. 1972. lib. bdg. 129.50 (*90-277-0196-2*) Kluwer Ac.

Switching Machines. 2nd ed. Perrin. 1972. lib. bdg. 135.00 (*90-277-0197-0*) Kluwer Ac.

***Switching Market & Opportunities, 1996.** (China Telecom-2000 Ser.: Vol. 3). 1995. 2,995.00 (*0-614-18325-1*, IGIC-03) Info Gatekeepers.

Switching On. Paul Dennison. 1981. 12.95 (*0-942143-06-X*, 1) Edu-Kinesthetics.

Switching Phenomena in High-Voltage Circuit Breakers. Ed. by Kunio Nakanishi. (Electrical Engineering & Electronics Ser.: Vol. 75). 296p. 1991. 140.00 (*0-8247-8543-6*) Dekker.

Switching, Protection & Distribution in Low-Voltage Networks: Handbook with Selection Criteria & Planning Guidelines for Switchgear, Switchboards & Distribution Systems. Petra Belzner et al. 659p. 1994. 55.00 (*3-89578-000-6*, VCH) Wiley.

Switching Systems & Applications. Fraidoon Mazda. (Telecommunication Ser.). (Illus.). 288p. 1996. pap. 28.95 (*0-240-51456-4*, Focal) Buttrwrth-Heinemann.

Switching the Odds. Phyllis Knight. (Stonewall Inn Mysteries Ser.). 240p. 1993. 8.95 (*0-312-09400-0*) St Martin.

Switching the Odds: A Lil Ritchie Mystery. Phyllis Knight. 224p. 1992. 17.95 (*0-685-52429-9*) St Martin.

Switching Theory in Space Technology: Proceedings of the (Application of Switching Theory in Space Technology Symposium) Symposium, Sunnyvale, CA, 1962. Ed. by Howard Aiken et al. LC 63-10730. (Illus.). 367p. reprint ed. pap. 104.60 (*0-317-09300-2*, 2002905) Bks Demand.

Switching Well. Peni R. Griffin. LC 92-38442. 224p. (J). (gr. 5-9). 1993. lib. bdg. 16.00 (*0-689-50581-7*, McElderry) S&S Childrens.

Switching Well. Peni R. Griffin. 224p. (J). (gr. 5 up). 1994. pap. 4.99 (*0-14-036910-4*) Puffin Bks.

Switchmode Power Supply Handbook. Keith Billings. 1989. text ed. 75.00 (*0-07-005330-8*) McGraw.

Switchstance. Phoebe Matthews. 176p. (Orig.). (YA). (gr. 7 up). 1989. pap. 2.95 (*0-380-75729-X*, Flare) Avon.

Switzerland. (Panorama Bks.). (Illus.). (FRE.). 3.95 (*0-685-11578-X*) Fr & Eur.

Switzerland. (Insight Guides Ser.). 1993. pap. 21.95 (*0-395-66442-X*) HM.

Switzerland. (Essential Guides Ser.). 1994. pap. 7.95 (*0-8442-8934-5*, Passport Bks) NTC Pub Grp.

Switzerland. (Driving Tours Ser.). 1995. pap. 18.00 (*0-671-51751-1*, P-H Travel) P-H Gen Ref & Trav.

Switzerland. Berlitz Editors. (Pocket Guides Ser.). 192p. 1992. 10.95 (*2-8315-2359-1*) Berlitz.

Switzerland. Charles A. Heatwole. LC 94-9860. (American Geographical Society Around the World Program Ser.). 1995. 18.95 (*0-939923-47-5*); pap. 13.95 (*0-939923-46-7*) M & W Pub Co.

Switzerland. Walter Imber & Fritz Auf Der Maur. LC 78-53351. (Illus.). 1979. 50.00 (*0-89674-003-X*) J J Binns.

Switzerland. Insight Guides Staff. (Illus.). 384p. 1985. pap. 15.95 (*0-317-19990-0*) P-H.

Switzerland. Hiro Kishikawa. (Classic Hotels of the World Ser.: No. 4). (Illus.). 192p. 1995. 85.00 (*4-309-71594-X*, Pub. by Kawadeshobo Shinsha JA) Bks Nippan.

Switzerland. Heinz K. Meier. (World Bibliographical Ser.). 1990. lib. bdg. 98.00 (*1-85109-107-6*) ABC-CLIO.

***Switzerland.** Smithmark Staff. (World Traveler Ser.). 1996. 14.98 (*0-8317-3602-X*) Smithmark.

Switzerland. rev. ed. Martin Hintz. LC 86-9581. (Enchantment of the World Ser.). (Illus.). 128p. (J). (gr. 5-9). 1994. lib. bdg. 30.00 (*0-516-02790-5*) Childrens.

***Switzerland.** 2nd ed. Mark Honan. (Illus.). 368p. 1997. pap. 16.95 (*0-86442-404-3*) Lonely Planet.

Switzerland: A Guide to the Monty & Capital Markets. 1996. ring bd. 170.00 (*1-85564-409-6*, Pub. by Euromoney UK) Am Educ Systs.

Switzerland: A Study of the Educational System of Switzerland & a Guide to the Academic Placement of Students from Switzerland in Educational Institutions of the United States. Karlene N. Dickey. LC 81-1240. (World Education Ser.). 142p. reprint ed. pap. 40.50 (*0-685-24141-6*, 2033013) Bks Demand.

Switzerland: A View from Boston. Ed. by Philip J. McNiff. 1984. pap. 10.00 (*0-89073-077-6*) Boston Public Lib.

Switzerland: Off the Beaten Track. Kenneth Loveland et al. LC 93-4065. (Illus.). 285p. (Orig.). 1993. pap. 14.95 (*1-56440-300-9*, Pub. by Moorland Pubng UK) Globe Pequot.

Switzerland: Phaidon Cultural Guides. 1985. 15.95 (*0-13-879875-3*) S&S Trade.

Switzerland: Picturesque & Descriptive. Joel Cook. 1977. lib. bdg. 59.95 (*0-8490-2721-7*) Gordon Pr.

***Switzerland: Recent Economic Developments.** Harilaos Vittas. (IMF Staff Country Report Ser.: Vol. 96/31). (Illus.). 44p. pap. 25.00 (*0-608-04855-0*, 2065514) Bks Demand.

***Switzerland: Selected Background Issues.** International Monetary Fund Staff. (IMF Staff Country Report Ser.: Vol. 96/32). (Illus.). 56p. pap. 25.00 (*0-608-04856-9*, 2065515) Bks Demand.

Switzerland: The Summit of Europe. Margaret Schrepfer. LC 88-35913. (Discovering Our Heritage Ser.). (Illus.). 144p. (J). (gr. 5 up). 1989. lib. bdg. 14.95 (*0-87518-405-7*, Dillon Silver Burdett) Silver Burdett Pr.

Switzerland: You Have to See It to Believe It. Geraldine S. Fulenwider. 1996. pap. 7.95 (*0-533-11644-9*) Vantage.

Switzerland see Cultures of the World - Group 8

Switzerland--in Pictures. Lerner Publications, Department of Geography Staff. LC 95-2807. (Visual Geography Ser.: Vol. 27, No. 16). (Illus.). (J). 1996. lib. bdg. 19.95 (*0-8225-1895-3*, Lerner Publctns) Lerner Group.

Switzerland & Liechtenstein 1992-93. rev. ed. (Frommer's Comprehensive Travel Guide Ser.). (Illus.). 564p. 1991. pap. 19.00 (*0-13-327313-X*, P-H Travel) P-H Gen Ref & Trav.

Switzerland & the European Common Market. Rene Schwok. LC 90-25837. 144p. 1991. text ed. 47.95 (*0-275-93645-7*, C3645, Praeger Pubs) Greenwood.

Switzerland As a Financial Center. Philippe Braillard. (C). 1988. lib. bdg. 265.50 (*90-247-3639-0*) Kluwer Ac.

Switzerland at Its Best. Robert S. Kane. (World at Its Best Travel Ser.). (Illus.). 268p. 1995. pap. 12.95 (*0-8442-9565-5*, Passport Bks) NTC Pub Grp.

Switzerland at the Beginning of the Sixteenth Century. John M. Vincent. LC 72-149671. reprint ed. 29.50 (*0-404-06768-9*) AMS Pr.

Switzerland by Rail. Anthony J. Lambert. LC 95-11392. (Bradt Rail Guides Ser.). (Illus.). 416p. (Orig.). 1996. pap. 17.95 (*1-56440-701-2*, Pub. by Bradt Pubns UK) Globe Pequot.

Switzerland Green Guide. Michelin Staff. 1991. pap. 19.95 (*0-7859-9169-7*) Fr & Eur.

Switzerland Green Guide. Ed. by Michelin Travel Publications, Staff. (JPN.). 1991. per. 36.00 (*4-408-01306-4*, 9564) Michelin.

Switzerland Green Guide. 2nd ed. Ed. by Michelin Travel Publications, Staff. 1995. per. 20.00 (*2-06-701563-X*, 563) Michelin.

***Switzerland Green Guide.** 3rd ed. Michelin Staff. (Green Guides Ser.). (Illus.). 1997. per. 20.00 (*2-06-156303-1*, 1563) Michelin.

Switzerland Green Guide English Edition. Michelin Staff. pap. 17.95 (*0-7859-7194-7*, 206701563X) Fr & Eur.

Switzerland Green Guide Japanese Edition. Michelin Staff. (FRE.). pap. 36.00 (*0-614-00389-X*, 4408013064) Fr & Eur.

Switzerland (Hotel & Restaurant Guide) 1996. Michelin Staff. 1996. 24.95 (*0-7859-9902-7*) Fr & Eur.

Switzerland in English Prose & Poetry. Arnold H. Lunn. 1976. lib. bdg. 59.95 (*0-8490-2720-9*) Gordon Pr.

Switzerland in Perspective. Ed. by Janet E. Hilowitz. LC 90-32459. (Contributions in Sociology Ser.: No. 92). 240p. 1991. text ed. 59.95 (*0-313-26089-3*, HSW, Greenwood Pr) Greenwood.

Switzerland in Perspective. George Soloveytchik. LC 82-11781. 306p. 1982. reprint ed. text ed. 59.75 (*0-313-23363-2*, Greenwood Pr) Greenwood.

***Switzerland Map.** 1996. 8.95 (*2-06-700427-1*, 427) Michelin.

Switzerland Red Guide. Michelin Staff. 1994. 24.95 (*0-7859-7171-8*, 2060069491) Fr & Eur.

***Switzerland Unwrapped.** Date not set. text ed. 29.95 (*1-86064-300-0*, Pub. by I B Tauris UK) St Martin.

***Switzerland '98.** Fodors Travel Staff. 1997. pap. 19.50 (*0-679-03540-0*) Fodors Travel.

Switzerland's Private International Law. 2nd ed. Tr. by Pierre A. Karrer et al. LC 93-35596. 1993. write for info. (*90-6544-778-4*) Kluwer Law Tax Pubs.

Switzerland's Private International Law Statute 1987: The Swiss Code on Conflict of Laws & Related Legislation. Pierre A. Karrer & Karl W. Arnold. 302p. 1989. 100.00 (*90-6544-290-1*) Kluwer Law Tax Pubs.

Switzerland's Role As an International Financial Center. Benedicte V. Christensen. (Occasional Paper Ser.: No. 45). 40p. 1986. pap. 7.50 (*0-939934-74-4*) Intl Monetary.

Switzler's Illustrated History of Missouri, from 1541-1877. William F. Switzler. LC 75-125. (Mid-American Frontier Ser.). (Illus.). 1975. reprint ed. 53.95 (*0-405-06890-5*) Ayer.

Swivel-Chair Logger. Bert Webber. 1977. 9.95 (*0-87770-163-6*); pap. 6.95 (*0-87770-174-1*) Ye Galleon.

Swoon Rocket. Bill Luoma. 1996. pap. 6.00 (*0-935724-74-5*) Figures.

Swoop. P. G. Wodehouse. (Illus.). 126p. 1993. pap. write for info. (*0-87008-144-6*) JAS Heineman.

Swoose. Dick King-Smith. (Illus.). 56p. (J). (gr. 2-5). 1994. 12.95 (*1-56282-658-1*); lib. bdg. 12.89 (*1-56282-659-X*) Hyprn Child.

Swoose: Odyssey of a B-17. Herbert S. Brownstein. (Illus.). 240p. 1993. 29.95 (*1-56098-196-2*) Smithsonian.

Swoosh: The Unauthorized Story of Nike & the Men Who Played There. J. B. Strasser & Laurie Becklund. LC 92-54426. (Illus.). 560p. 1993. reprint ed. pap. 14.00 (*0-88730-622-5*) Harper Busn.

Swope of G. E. The Story of Gerard Swope & General Electric in American Business. David Loth. LC 75-41769. (Companies & Men: Business Enterprises in America Ser.). 1976. reprint ed. 33.95 (*0-405-08084-0*) Ayer.

Sword. Michael K. Baker. LC 84-90678. 303p. (J). (gr. 5-p). 1985. pap. 8.00 (*0-932543-00-6*); text ed. 8.00 (*0-932543-01-4*) M B Pub.

Sword. A. J. Gates. LC 87-40424. 212p. 1987. pap. 9.95 (*1-55523-085-7*) Winston-Derek.

Sword. Agnar Thordarson. Tr. by Paul Schach from ICE. LC 77-125259. (Library of Scandinavian Literature). 1970. lib. bdg. 6.25 (*0-8057-3369-8*) Irvington.

Sword: The General Book V. David Drake & S. M. Stirling. (General Ser.: Bk. V). 352p. 1995. mass mkt. 5.99 (*0-671-87647-3*) Baen Bks.

Sword & Brush: The Spirit of the Martial Arts. Dave Lowry. LC 95-5653. (Illus.). 144p. (Orig.). 1995. pap. 14.00 (*1-57062-112-8*) Shambhala Pubns.

Sword & Citadel: The Sword of the Lictor/The Citadel of the Autarch. Gene Wolfe. 416p. 1994. pap. 14.95 (*0-312-89018-4*) Orb NYC.

***Sword & Dollar, Vol. 1.** 2nd ed. Date not set. pap. text ed. write for info. (*0-312-11610-1*) St Martin.

Sword & Firearm Collection of the Society of the Cincinnati in the Anderson House Museum. John Brewer Brown. LC 65-25758. (Illus.). 120p. 1965. 10.00 (*0-318-16567-8*) Anderson Hse Mus.

Sword & Mitre: Government & Episcopate in France & England in the Age of Aristocracy. Norman Ravitch. 1966. text ed. 35.40 (*3-11-200273-3*) Mouton.

Sword & Pen: Poems of Nineteen Fifteen from Dundee & Tayside. Ed. by Hilda D. Spear & Bruce Pandrich. 136p. 1989. pap. text ed. 14.00 (*0-08-037960-5*, Pub. by Aberdeen U Pr) Macmillan.

Sword & Scalpel. large type ed. Frank G. Slaughter. 1979. 12.00 (*0-7089-0386-X*) Ulverscroft.

Sword & Scalpel: A Surgeon's Story of Faith & Courage. Robert L. Foster & Lorry Lutz. Ed. by M. B. Steele. 240p. (Orig.). pap. 10.95 (*0-939497-21-2*) Promise Pub.

Sword & Sorceress, No. 13. Marion Z. Bradley. 1996. mass mkt. 5.99 (*0-88677-703-8*) DAW Bks.

***Sword & Sorceress, Vol. XIV.** Ed. by Marion Z. Bradley. 1997. mass mkt. 5.99 (*0-614-27731-0*) DAW Bks.

Sword & the Chain. Joel Rosenberg. (Guardians of the Flame Ser.: Bk. 2). 256p. 1987. pap. 3.95 (*0-451-15982-9*, ROC) NAL-Dutton.

Sword & The Chain. Joel Rosenberg. (Guardians of the Flame Ser.). 256p. 1984. pap. 4.99 (*0-451-45351-4*, ROC) NAL-Dutton.

Sword & the Circle: King Arthur & the Knights of the Round Table. Rosemary Sutcliff. 264p. (J). (gr. 7 up). 1994. pap. 3.99 (*0-14-037149-4*) Puffin Bks.

S

Sword & the Cross: A History of the Church in Lithuania. Saulius Suziedelis. LC 88-61211. (Illus.). 200p. (Orig.). 1988. pap. 9.95 (*0-87973-416-7*, 416) Our Sunday Visitor.

Sword & the Cross: Reflections on Command & Conscience. James H. Toner. LC 91-32209. 200p. 1992. text ed. 49.95 (*0-275-94212-0*, C4212, Praeger Pubs) Greenwood.

Sword & the Dollar. Michael J. Parenti. 240p. 1988. 16.95 (*0-312-02295-6*) St Martin.

Sword & the Flame. Stephen R. Lawhead. (Dragon King Trilogy Ser.: Bk. 3). 384p. 1992. mass mkt. 5.99 (*0-380-71631-3*, AvoNova) Avon.

Sword & the Flame, Bk. 3. Stephen R. Lawhead. (Dragon King Trilogy Ser.: Vol. 3). 320p. 1996. pap. 13.00 (*0-310-20504-2*) Zondervan.

Sword & the Flute-Kali & Krsna: Dark Visions of the Terrible & the Sublime in Hindu Mythology. David R. Kinsley. LC 73-91669. (Hermeneutics: Studies in the History of Religions: No. 4). 175p. 1975. pap. 14.95 (*0-520-03510-0*) U CA Pr.

***Sword & the Jungle.** Alan Savage. 288p. 1996. 22.00 (*0-7278-4964-6*) Severn Hse.

Sword & the Lotus. Osho Rajneesh. Ed. by Ma Dhyan Sagar. (Talks in the Himalayas Ser.). 338p. 1989. 21.95 (*3-89338-075-2*, Pub. by Rebel Hse GW) Osho America.

Sword & the Mind. Yagyu Munenori. Tr. by Hiroaki Sato from JPN. LC 85-8899. (Illus.). 144p. 1986. 19.95 (*0-87951-209-1*) Overlook Pr.

Sword & the Mind. Yagyu Munenori. Tr. by Hiroaki Sato. 144p. 1988. pap. 11.95 (*0-87951-256-3*) Overlook Pr.

Sword & the Ploughshare: Autonomous Peace Initiatives in East Germany. John Sandford. (C). 1983. pap. 7.50 (*0-85036-303-9*, Pub. by Merlin Pr UK) Humanities.

Sword & the Same: Sword Book of the Honcho-Gunkiko & Book of the Same. Henry Joly. (Illus.). 200p. 1970. pap. 35.00 (*0-87556-619-7*) Saifer.

Sword & the Scalpel. Alan Savage. 288p. 1996. 22.00 (*0-7278-4906-9*) Severn Hse.

Sword & the Scepter: The Problem of Militarism in Germany. Gerhard A. Ritter. Tr. by Heinz Norden. Incl. Vol. 1. Prussian Tradition 1740-1890. LC 68-31041. 338p. 1988. lib. bdg. 25.00 (*0-945726-18-X*); Vol. 1. Prussian Tradition 1740-1890. LC 68-31041. 338p. 1988. pap. 12.95 (*0-945726-13-9*); Vol. 2. European Powers & the Wilhelminian Empire, 1890-1914. LC 68-31041. 328p. 1970. lib. bdg. 25.00 (*0-945726-19-8*); Vol. 2. European Powers & the Wilhelminian Empire, 1890-1914. LC 68-31041. 328p. 1970. pap. 12.95 (*0-945726-14-7*); Vol. 3. Tragedy of Statesmanship: Bethmann Hollweg As War Chancellor (1914-1917). LC 68-31041. 612p. 1988. lib. bdg. 35.00 (*0-945726-20-1*); Vol. 3. Tragedy of Statesmanship: Bethmann Hollweg As War Chancellor (1914-1917). LC 68-31041. 612p. 1988. pap. 16.95 (*0-945726-15-5*); Vol. 4. Reign of German Militarism & the Disaster of 1918. LC 68-31041. 496p. 1988. lib. bdg. 35.00 (*0-945726-21-X*); Vol. 4. Reign of German Militarism & the Disaster of 1918. LC 68-31041. 496p. 1988. pap. 14.95 (*0-945726-16-3*); LC 68-31041. 1174p. 1988. reprint ed. Set pap. 49.95 (*0-945726-17-1*) Scholars Bookshelf.

Sword & the Scepter: The Problem of Militarism in Germany, Set. Gerhard A. Ritter. Tr. by Heinz Norden. Incl. Vol. 1. Prussian Tradition 1740-1890. LC 68-31041. 338p. 1988. lib. bdg. 25.00 (*0-945726-18-X*); Vol. 1. Prussian Tradition 1740-1890. LC 68-31041. 338p. 1988. pap. 12.95 (*0-945726-13-9*); Vol. 2. European Powers & the Wilhelminian Empire, 1890-1914. LC 68-31041. 328p. 1970. lib. bdg. 25.00 (*0-945726-19-8*); Vol. 2. European Powers & the Wilhelminian Empire, 1890-1914. LC 68-31041. 328p. 1970. pap. 12.95 (*0-945726-14-7*); Vol. 3. Tragedy of Statesmanship: Bethmann Hollweg As War Chancellor (1914-1917). LC 68-31041. 612p. 1988. lib. bdg. 35.00 (*0-945726-20-1*); Vol. 3. Tragedy of Statesmanship: Bethmann Hollweg As War Chancellor (1914-1917). LC 68-31041. 612p. 1988. pap. 16.95 (*0-945726-15-5*); Vol. 4. Reign of German Militarism & the Disaster of 1918. LC 68-31041. 496p. 1988. lib. bdg. 35.00 (*0-945726-21-X*); Vol. 4. Reign of German Militarism & the Disaster of 1918. LC 68-31041. 496p. 1988. pap. 14.95 (*0-945726-16-3*); LC 68-31041. 1174p. 1988. reprint ed. Set lib. bdg. 99.50 (*0-945726-22-8*) Scholars Bookshelf.

Sword & the Shadow. Sylvia Thorpe. 240p. 1976. pap. 1.50 (*0-449-22945-9*, Crest) Fawcett.

Sword & the Sickle. Mulk R. Anand. (C). 1984. 11.00 (*0-8364-2793-9*, Pub. by Arnold Pubs II) S Asia.

Sword & the Sickle. Mulk-Raj Anand. 386p. 1984. 12.00 (*0-86578-242-3*) Ind-US Inc.

***Sword & the Sorceress, Vol. 14.** (J). 1997. pap. 5.99 (*0-88677-741-0*) DAW Bks.

Sword & the Stone. Catherine Storr. (Legends & Folktales Ser.). (J). (ps-3). 1993. pap. 4.95 (*0-8114-7147-0*) Raintree Steck-V.

Sword & the Trowel: Works of C. H. Spurgeon in His Magazine, 7 vols., Set, Vols. 1-7, 1865-1884. Charles H. Spurgeon. reprint ed. pap. 97.00 (*1-56186-221-5*) Pilgrim Pubns.

Sword & the Trowel: Works of C. H. Spurgeon in His Magazine, 7 vols., Vol. 1, 1865-66-67. Charles H. Spurgeon. 1975. reprint ed. pap. 13.00 (*1-56186-207-X*) Pilgrim Pubns.

Sword & the Trowel: Works of C. H. Spurgeon in His Magazine, 7 vols., Vol. 2, 1868-69-70. Charles H. Spurgeon. 1975. reprint ed. pap. 13.00 (*1-56186-208-8*) Pilgrim Pubns.

Sword & the Trowel: Works of C. H. Spurgeon in His Magazine, 7 vols., Vol. 3, 1871-72-73. Charles H. Spurgeon. 1977. reprint ed. pap. 13.00 (*1-56186-209-6*) Pilgrim Pubns.

Sword & the Trowel: Works of C. H. Spurgeon in His Magazine, 7 vols., Vol. 4, 1874-75-76. Charles H. Spurgeon. 1978. reprint ed. pap. 13.00 (*1-56186-212-6*) Pilgrim Pubns.

Sword & the Trowel: Works of C. H. Spurgeon in His Magazine, 7 vols., Vol. 5, 1877-78-79. Charles H. Spurgeon. 1983. reprint ed. pap. 15.00 (*1-56186-215-0*) Pilgrim Pubns.

Sword & the Trowel: Works of C. H. Spurgeon in His Magazine, 7 vols., Vol. 6, 1880-81-82. Charles H. Spurgeon. 1989. reprint ed. pap. 15.00 (*1-56186-219-3*) Pilgrim Pubns.

Sword & the Trowel: Works of C. H. Spurgeon in His Magazine, 7 vols., Vol. 7, 1883-84. Charles H. Spurgeon. 1997. reprint ed. pap. 15.00 (*1-56186-222-3*) Pilgrim Pubns.

Sword & Womankind: The Influence of the Sword Upon Moral & Social Status of Women. E De Beaumont & A. Allinson. 1977. lib. bdg. 59.95 (*0-8490-2722-5*) Gordon Pr.

Sword at Sunrise. Alan Evans. 272p. 1994. 26.95 (*0-340-60320-8*, Pub. by H & S UK) Trafalgar.

Sword at Sunset. Rosemary Sutcliff. 512p. 1987. mass mkt. 4.50 (*0-8125-8852-5*) Tor Bks.

Sword Bearer. John White. LC 86-2860. (Archives of Anthropos Ser.: Bk. 1). (Illus.). 295p. (Orig.). (J). (gr. 4 up). 1986. pap. 11.99 (*0-87784-590-5*, 590) InterVarsity.

Sword Blades & Poppy Seed. Amy Lowell. LC 78-64046. (Des Imagistes: Literature of the Imagist Movement Ser.). 256p. reprint ed. 39.50 (*0-404-17129-X*) AMS Pr.

Sword-Breaker. Jennifer Roberson. (Novels of Tiger & Del: No. 4). 464p. 1991. mass mkt. 5.99 (*0-88677-476-4*) DAW Bks.

Sword Dance of the Generalissimos. Pat'rick N. Pugh. 1995. pap. 7.95 (*1-883184-14-2*) PNP.

Sword Dancer, Bk. 1. Jennifer Roberson. 288p. 1986. mass mkt. 5.50 (*0-88677-376-8*) DAW Bks.

***Sword Dancing: A History.** Stephen D. Corrsin. (Illus.). 256p. 1996. 45.00 (*1-874312-25-7*, Pub. by Drake Intl Serv UK) Intl Spec Bk.

Sword Fighting: A Scripture Memory Curriculum for Home & School. Karyn Henley. (Illus.). 117p. (C). 1993. pap. 8.95 (*1-879541-21-1*, SF1) Allen Thomas Pub.

Sword for a Dragon. Christopher B. Rowley. 480p. (Orig.). 1993. pap. 6.99 (*0-451-45235-6*, ROC) NAL-Dutton.

Sword for the Convicted: Representing Indigent Defendants on Appeal. David T. Wasserman. LC 89-25909. (Contributions in Criminology & Penology Ser.: No. 30). 304p. 1990. text ed. 59.95 (*0-313-26881-9*, WQC/, Greenwood Pr) Greenwood.

Sword from the Rock: Investigation into the Origins of Epic Literature & Development of the Hero. Gertrude R. Levy. 1976. lib. bdg. 59.95 (*0-8490-2723-3*) Gordon Pr.

Sword in Anglo-Saxon England: Its Archaeology & Literature. Hilda Ellis Davidson. (Illus.). 288p. (C). 1994. reprint ed. 53.00 (*0-85115-355-0*) Boydell & Brewer.

Sword in the Age of Chivalry. R. Ewart Oakeshott. (Illus.). 203p. (C). 1995. reprint ed. 63.00 (*0-85115-362-3*) Boydell & Brewer.

Sword in the Sand: A Treatise on the Muslim Tradition & Its Challenge to the Christian World. Nasser Lotfi. Ed. by Marsha Kearns. 104p. (Orig.). 1991. pap. write for info. (*1-878353-14-4*) Silent Partners.

Sword in the Stone. (Classics Ser.). 96p. (J). (ps-3). 1994. 7.98 (*1-57082-052-X*) Mouse Works.

Sword in the Stone. Grace Maccarone. (Hello Reader! Ser.). (Illus.). 32p. (J). 1992. pap. 3.50 (*0-590-45527-3*, 043, Cartwheel) Scholastic Inc.

Sword in the Stone. T. H. White. LC 92-24808. (Illus.). 256p. (J). 1993. 21.95 (*0-399-22502-1*, Philomel Bks) Putnam Pub Group.

Sword in the Stone. T. H. White. 288p. (YA). (gr. 7 up). 1978. mass mkt. 4.99 (*0-440-98445-9*, LE) Dell.

***Sword in the Sun: Dialogue with an Angel.** Anthony Duncan. (Illus.). 212p. (Orig.). 1997. pap. 14.95 (*0-9650839-4-2*) Sun Chalice.

Sword in the Tree. Clyde R. Bulla. LC 56-5699. (Illus.). 128p. (J). (gr. 2-5). 1962. lib. bdg. 14.89 (*0-690-79909-8*, Crowell Jr Bks) HarpC Child Bks.

Sword Is Forged. Evangeline Walton. LC 82-19653. 347p. 1983. 25.00 (*0-89366-161-9*) Ultramarine Pub.

Sword-Maker. Jennifer Roberson. 464p. 1989. mass mkt. 5.99 (*0-88677-379-2*) DAW Bks.

Sword Master: Highlander 1st Edition Box of 12 Decks. Mike Sager. 107.40 (*1-887032-33-9*) Thund Castle.

Sword Master: Highlander 1st Edition Box of 36 Packs. Mike Sager. 88.20 (*1-887032-34-7*) Thund Castle.

Sword Master: Highlander 1st Edition 16 Card Pack. Mike Sager. 2.45 (*1-887032-22-3*) Thund Castle.

Sword Master: Highlander 1st Edition 56 Card Deck. Mike Sager. 8.95 (*1-887032-32-0*) Thund Castle.

Sword Master: Highlander 3rd Edition Box 36 Packs. Mike Sager. 88.20 (*1-887032-40-1*) Thund Castle.

Sword, Miter, & Cloister: Nobility & the Church in Burgundy, 980-1198. Constance B. Bouchard. LC 86-29158. (Illus.). 416p. 1987. 55.00 (*0-8014-1974-3*) Cornell U Pr.

Sword of Antietam. Joseph A. Altsheler. 1993. reprint ed. lib. bdg. 21.95 (*0-89968-566-8*) Buccaneer Bks.

Sword of Antietam: The Story of the Nation's Crisis. Joseph A. Altsheler. (Joseph A. Altsheler Civil War Ser.). 1985. 27.95 (*0-89190-986-9*) Amereon Ltd.

Sword of Bedwyr. R. A. Salvatore. (Crimson Shadow Ser.: Bk. 1). 320p. 1996. mass mkt. 5.99 (*0-446-60272-8*, Aspect) Warner Bks.

***Sword of Bone.** (Echoes of War Military History Ser.). 1996. pap. 10.95 (*0-907675-60-3*, Pub. by Ashland Buchan & Enright UK) Cimino Pub Grp.

Sword of Camelot. Gilbert Morris. (Seven Sleepers Ser.: Vol. 3). (YA). 1995. pap. 5.99 (*0-8024-3683-8*) Moody.

Sword of Chaos. Marion Zimmer Bradley. (Darkover Ser.). 1982. pap. 3.50 (*0-88677-172-2*) DAW Bks.

Sword of Christendom: The Work of Catholic Action for the Reign of Christ the King. Stephen P. DeLallo. 312p. (Orig.). 1994. pap. 9.95 (*0-935952-51-9*) Angelus Pr.

Sword of Denis Anwyck. Maylan Schurch. LC 92-22127. (J). 1992. pap. 7.99 (*0-8280-0658-X*) Review & Herald.

Sword of Fire & Shadow. Diana L. Paxson & Adrienne Martin-Barnes. LC 94-49015. 1995. 22.00 (*0-688-14156-0*, AvoNova) Avon.

Sword of Fire & Shadow. Diana L. Paxson. 1996. mass mkt. 5.99 (*0-380-75803-2*) Avon.

Sword of Flame. Maggie Furey. 416p. 1996. mass mkt. 6.50 (*0-553-56527-3*, Spectra) Bantam.

Sword of General Englund: A Novel of Murder in the Dakota Territory, 1876. Donald Honig. 288p. 1996. 20.00 (*0-684-80321-6*) S&S Trade.

***Sword of Gnosis.** Jacob Needleman. 1996. pap. 21.95 (*0-614-21366-5*, 1205) Kazi Pubns.

Sword of His Mouth: Forceful & Imaginative Language in Synoptic Sayings. Robert C. Tannehill. LC 75-18948. (Society of Biblical Literature. Semeia Supplements Ser.: No. 1). 234p. 1975. reprint ed. pap. 66.70 (*0-7837-5452-3*, 2045217) Bks Demand.

Sword of Honour Trilogy. Evelyn Waugh. 1994. 20.00 (*0-679-43136-5*) Knopf.

Sword of Imagination: Memoirs of a Half-Century of Literary Conflict. Russell Kirk. LC 95-11108. (Illus.). 509p. 1995. 35.00 (*0-8028-3765-4*) Eerdmans.

Sword of Islam. Raphael Sabatini. 1976. reprint ed. lib. bdg. 27.95 (*0-89190-745-9*, Rivercity Pr) Amereon Ltd.

Sword of Knowledge. C. J. Cherryh et al. LC 94-24611. 816p. 1995. 15.00 (*0-671-87645-7*) Baen Bks.

***Sword of Macleod.** Karen Fox. 320p. (Orig.). 1997. mass mkt. 4.99 (*0-505-52160-1*) Dorchester Pub Co.

Sword of Maiden's Tears. Rosemary Edghill. 288p. 1994. mass mkt. 4.99 (*0-88677-622-8*) DAW Bks.

Sword of Mary, Vol. 2. Esther Friesner. (Orig.). 1996. pap. 5.99 (*1-56504-936-5*, 13200, Borealis) White Wolf.

Sword of Moses: An Ancient Book of Magic. Tr. by Moses Gaster from HEB. 1992. reprint ed. pap. 8.95 (*1-55818-163-6*, Near Eastern) Holmes Pub.

Sword of Nemesis. Robert E. Tracy. LC 73-18609. reprint ed. 45.00 (*0-404-11419-9*) AMS Pr.

Sword of No Blade. Joan Baxter. LC 92-1773. (Illus.). 195p. (Orig.). 1992. pap. 11.95 (*0-87728-748-1*) Weiser.

***Sword of Nuada.** Garry H. Leuziere. (Druid Trilogy Ser.: Bk. I). 364p. 1998. pap. 13.95 (*1-58006-028-5*, Dreamscape Pr) Sovereign.

Sword of Orion. Robin White. 1996. mass mkt. 6.99 (*0-449-14953-6*) Fawcett.

Sword of Orion. Robin A. White. 1995. mass mkt. 5.99 (*0-449-28709-2*) Fawcett.

Sword of Roele. Wolfgang Baur. 1996. 12.95 (*0-7869-0374-0*) TSR Inc.

Sword of Samurai Cat. Mark E. Rogers. 1991. pap. 7.95 (*0-312-85156-1*) St Martin.

Sword of Scandinavia. Ronald L. Tarnstrom. LC 94-90244. (Armed Forces Handbooks Ser.). (Illus.). 444p. (Orig.). 1996. pap. 24.95 (*0-922037-13-2*) Trogen Bks.

Sword of Shannara. Terry Brooks. (Shannara Ser.: Bk. 1). 736p. 1983. mass mkt. 6.99 (*0-345-31425-5*, Del Rey) Ballantine.

Sword of Shannara. Terry Brooks. (Shannara Ser.: Bk. 1). 1996. mass mkt. 6.99 (*0-345-90957-7*, Del Rey) Ballantine.

***Sword of Shannara.** Terry Brooks. (Shannara Ser.). 1997. mass mkt. 6.99 (*0-345-91127-X*, Del Rey) Ballantine.

Sword of Testimony. Blaine M. Yorgason & Brenton Yorgasen. (Gospel Power Ser.). 40p. (Orig.). 1989. pap. text ed. 3.50 (*0-929985-24-9*) Jackman Pubng.

Sword of the Archangel: Fascist Ideology in Romania. Radu Ioanid. (East European Monographs: No. 292). 320p. 1990. text ed. 54.50 (*0-88033-189-5*) Col U Pr.

Sword of the Devil. Carolyn Gray. 1994. lib. bdg. 22.00 (*0-7278-4622-1*) Severn Hse.

Sword of the Lord. Everitt M. Fjordbak. 101p. 1975. pap. text ed. 2.95 (*1-882449-05-3*) Messenger Pub.

Sword of the Lord & Gideon. James C. Kelly & William C. Baker. LC 80-15899. 1980. pap. 2.95 (*0-913239-02-X*) Appalach Consortium.

Sword of the North. Richard W. White. LC 83-147510. 400p. 1983. 18.95 (*0-89803-122-2*) Jameson Bks.

***Sword of the Prophets.** Mark A. Garland. 336p. 1997. mass mkt. 5.99 (*0-671-87776-3*) Baen Bks.

Sword of the Samurai: The Classical Art of Japanese Swordsmanship. George R. Parulski, Jr. (Illus.). 144p. 1985. 34.95 (*0-87364-332-1*) Paladin Pr.

***Sword of the Samurai: With Michael Reaves.** Steve Perry. 1990. pap. write for info. (*0-553-24052-8*) Bantam.

Sword of the Spirit. John Christopher. (J). (gr. 6-12). 1984. 17.75 (*0-8446-6158-9*) Peter Smith.

***Sword of the Spirit.** Audrey Mrofchak. 250p. (Orig.). Date not set. pap. text ed. write for info. (*1-882972-95-3*) Queenship Pub.

Sword of Tipu Sultan. B. S. Gidwani. 372p. 1989. 8.50 (*0-318-37005-0*) Asia Bk Corp.

***Sword of Tortuga.** LC 94-90573. 303p. (Orig.). 1994. pap. 12.00 (*0-9658878-0-4*) Pirate-Privateer.

Sword of Truth. Ed. by Gilbert Morris. LC 94-7013. (Wakefield Dynasty Ser.). 422p. 1994. pap. 11.99 (*0-8423-6228-2*) Tyndale.

Sword of Truth: The Life & Times of Shehu Usuman Dan Fodio. Mervyn Hiskett. (Islam & Society in Africa Ser.). 232p. (C). 1994. reprint ed. pap. 19.95 (*0-8101-1115-2*) Northwestern U Pr.

Sword of Winter. Marta Randall. LC 83-4830. 271p. 1983. 25.00 (*0-89366-160-0*) Ultramarine Pub.

Sword of Wisdom. Sheng-Yen Chang. LC 90-84026. 237p. 1991. pap. 12.00 (*0-9609854-5-X*) Dharma Drum Pubs.

Sword of Youth. James L. Allen. (Principle Works of James Lane Allen). 1989. reprint ed. lib. bdg. 79.00 (*0-7812-1740-7*) Rprt Serv.

***Sword or the Scroll? Dilemmas of Religion & Military Service in Israel.** Stuart A. Cohen. (Sherman Lectures: Vol. 3). 112p. 1997. text ed. 22.00 (*90-5702-083-1*, Harwood Acad Pubs) Gordon & Breach.

Sword Over America. Richard Ruhling. (Illus.). 55p. (Orig.). pap. 2.00 (*0-317-55134-5*) Total Health.

Sword Play. Victor Milan. (Forgotten Realms Arcane Age Netheril Trilogy Ser.: Bk. 1). 1996. pap. 5.99 (*0-7869-0492-5*) TSR Inc.

Sword Point. Harold Coyle. 1990. pap. 6.50 (*0-671-73712-0*, Pocket Star Bks) PB.

Sword-Singer, Bk. 2. Jennifer Roberson. 384p. 1988. mass mkt. 5.99 (*0-88677-447-0*) DAW Bks.

***Sword Sorceress.** Marion Z. Bradley. 1998. mass mkt. 5.99 (*0-88677-768-2*) DAW Bks.

Swordbearer. Glen Cook. 1992. mass mkt. 4.99 (*0-8125-3330-5*) Tor Bks.

Swordbearers: Supreme Command in the First World War. Correlli Barnett. LC 74-19057. (Illus.). 416p. 1975. reprint ed. pap. 15.95 (*0-253-20175-6*, MB 175) Ind U Pr.

***Swordfish.** Hugo Claus. Tr. by Ruth Levitt from FLE. (Unesco Collection of Representative Works, Series of Translations from the Literature of the Union of Soviet Socialist Republics). 168p. 9700. 27.95 (*0-7206-0985-2*, Pub. by P Owen Ltd UK) Dufour.

Swordfish Tooth. Cynthia Zarin. 1989. write for info. (*0-394-56797-8*) Knopf.

Swordpoint. large type ed. John Harris. 464p. 1982. 25.99 (*0-7089-0878-0*) Ulverscroft.

Swords Against Carthage. Friedrich Donauer. Tr. by F. T. Cooper. LC 61-12878. (Illus.). (J). (gr. 7-11). 1932. 21.00 (*0-8196-0112-8*) Biblo.

Swords Against Darkness, No. 1. Andrew J. Offutt. 1990. mass mkt. 3.95 (*0-8217-2972-1*, Zebra Kensgtn) Kensgtn Pub Corp.

Swords Against Darkness, No. 5. Ed. by Andrew J. Offutt. 1981. mass mkt. 2.50 (*0-89083-839-9*, Zebra Kensgtn) Kensgtn Pub Corp.

Swords & Blades of the American Revolution. George C. Neumann & Frank J. Kravic. LC 91-66957. (Illus.). 288p. 1991. reprint ed. 35.95 (*0-9605666-9-4*); reprint ed. pap. 23.95 (*1-880655-00-4*) Scurlock Pub.

Swords & Ploughshares: Or, the Supplanting of the System of War by the System of Law. Lucia A. Mead. LC 71-143431. (Peace Movement in America Ser.). xiv, 249p. 1972. reprint ed. lib. bdg. 28.95 (*0-89198-079-2*) Ozer.

Swords & Plowshares. Maxwell D. Taylor. (Quality Paperbacks Ser.). (Illus.). 472p. 1990. reprint ed. pap. 14.95 (*0-306-80407-7*) Da Capo.

Swords & Plowshares: The United States & Disarmament 1898-1979. Patrick J. Gallo. 101p. (Orig.). 1980. pap. 31.95 (*0-89126-090-0*) MA-AH Pub.

Swords & Roses. Joseph Hergesheimer. LC 70-167355. (Essay Index Reprint Ser.). 1977. reprint ed. 21.95 (*0-8369-2650-1*) Ayer.

Swords & Roses. Joseph Hergesheimer. (History - United States Ser.). 327p. 1992. reprint ed. lib. bdg. 89.00 (*0-7812-6179-1*) Rprt Serv.

Swords & Scimitars. Linda L. Chaikin. LC 96-45768. (Royal Pavilions Ser.: No. 1). 288p. 1996. pap. 9.99 (*1-55661-881-6*) Bethany Hse.

***Swords & Sword Makers of the War of 1812.** Richard H. Bezdek. (Illus.). 104p. 1997. text ed. 40.00 (*0-87364-927-3*) Paladin Pr.

Swords Around a Throne: Napoleon's Grande Armee. John R. Elting. (Illus.). 550p. 1988. 50.00 (*0-02-909501-8*, Free Press) Free Pr.

***Swords Around a Throne: Napoleon's Grande Armee.** John R. Elting. LC 96-45720. (Illus.). 784p. 1997. reprint ed. pap. 19.95 (*0-306-80757-2*) Da Capo.

Swords Beneath Camelot: The Quest for Excalibur. Lane Riosley. (Illus.). 23p. (Orig.). (J). (gr. 3 up). 1992. pap. 3.00 (*1-57514-264-3*, 1047) Encore Perform Pub.

Swords from Public Collections in the Commonwealth of Pennsylvania. Ed. by Bruce S. Bazelon. (Illus.). 127p. 1987. pap. 12.00 (*0-917218-26-4*) A Mowbray.

***Swords in Myrtle Dress'd: Towards a Rhetoric of Sodom: Gay Readings of Homosexual Politics & Poetics in the Eighteenth Century.** Jon T. Rowland. LC 97-21641. 1997. write for info. (*0-8386-3760-4*) Fairleigh Dickinson.

Swords in the North. Paul L. Anderson. LC 57-9448. 270p. (J). (gr. 7-11). 1935. 21.00 (*0-8196-0103-9*) Biblo.

Swords into Ploughshares. Mary H. Jones. LC 70-109757. (Illus.). 374p. 1971. reprint ed. text ed. 35.00 (*0-8371-4247-4*, JOSP, Greenwood Pr) Greenwood.

Swords into Ploughshares: A "Home Front" Anthology. Ed. by Sandra Gurvis. (Vietnam Generation Ser.). 178p. (Orig.). (C). 1991. pap. text ed. 15.00 (*0-9628524-1-4*) Burning Cities Pr.

Swords into Plowshares. Ed. by Arthur J. Laffin & Anne Montgomery. 350p. 1996. pap. 18.00 (*1-879175-18-5*) Fortkamp.

Swords into Plowshares: A Collection of Plays about Peace & Social Justice. Ingrid Rogers. LC 82-24492. 281p. 1983. reprint ed. pap. 80.10 (*0-608-02168-7*, 2062837) Bks Demand.

Swords Into Plowshares: Converting to a Peace Economy. Michael Renner. 70p. (Orig.). 1990. pap. 5.00 (*0-916468-97-6*) Worldwatch Inst.

Swords into Plowshares: The Problems & Progress of International Organization. 4th ed. Inis L. Claude, Jr. 1984. pap. text ed. write for info. (*0-07-554636-1*) McGraw.

An Asterisk (*) at the beginning of an entry indicates that the title is appearing in BIP for the first time.

Swords into Plowshares: Theological Reflections on Peace. Roger Burrgraeve & Marc Vervenne. (Louvain Theological & Pastoral Monographs). 208p. (Orig.). 1992. pap. 25.00 (0-8028-0568-X) Eerdmans.
Swords of Anjou. Mario Pei. 310p. 1953. 8.95 (0-913298-66-2) S F Vanni.
Swords of Lightning: Special Forces & the Changing Face of Warfare. Terry White. (Illus.). 192p. 1992. 24.95 (0-08-040976-8, Pub. by Brasseys UK) Brasseys Inc.
Swords of Shakespeare: An Illustrated Guide to Stage Combat Choreography in the Plays of Shakespeare. J. D. Martinez. (Illus.). 272p. 1996. lib. bdg. 45.00 (0-89950-959-2) McFarland & Co.
***Swords of Tallera.** Charles Gramlich. 246p. (Orig.). 1997. mass mkt. 4.99 (1-55197-815-6, Pub. by Comnwlth Pub CN) Partners Pubs Grp.
Swords of the Britons. A. J. Young. 200p. 1984. 40.00 (0-7212-0624-7, Pub. by Regency Press UK) St Mut.
Swords of the Horseclans. Robert Adams. (Horseclans Ser.: No. 2). 1983. pap. 2.95 (0-451-14025-7, E9988, Sig) NAL-Dutton.
Swords of the Legion. Harry Turtledove. (Videssos Cycle Ser.: Bk. 4). 408p. 1987. mass mkt. 5.99 (0-345-33070-6, Del Rey) Ballantine.
Swords of the Rainbow. Eric Garber. Ed. by Jewelle Gomez. 352p. (Orig.). 1996. pap. text ed. 11.95 (1-55583-266-0) Alyson Pubns.
Swords of the Samurai. (Illus.). 1981. pap. 14.95 (0-87422-049-1) Wash St U Pr.
Swords of the Swashbucklers. Bill Mantlo & Jackson Guice. 64p. 1984. 5.95 (0-87135-002-5) Marvel Entmnt.
Swords, Samurai & Suzuribako. Marcy A. Wasilewski. (Illus.). 28p. (J). (gr. 3-8). 1979. 2.50 (0-916746-52-6) Springfield Lib & Mus.
Swords, Ships & Sugar: A History of Nevis to 1900. 4th ed. Vincent K. Hubbard. LC 95-70424. 192p. 1996. pap. 14.95 (0-9633818-5-7) Premiere Edits.
Swordsman. Terry L. Craig. 304p. (Orig.). 1987. pap. 7.95 (0-9618852-0-3) Berachah Pub.
Swordsmen & Saurians. Krenkel. (Illus.). 1990. 39.95 (0-913035-72-6); pap. 19.95 (0-913035-55-6) Eclipse Bks.
***Swordsmen in Power: War & Politics under the English Republic 1649-1660.** Roger Hainsworth. (Illus.). 320p. 1997. 35.95 (0-7509-0571-9, Pub. by Sutton Pubng UK) Bks Intl VA.
Swordsmen of the Screen: From Douglas Fairbanks to Michael York. Jeffrey Richards. (Cinema & Society Ser.). (Illus.). 312p. 1980. pap. 10.95 (0-7100-0681-0, RKP) Routledge.
Swordsmith Family of Tsuda Sukehiro. Kizu. 1991. pap. 4.95 (0-910704-18-X) Hawley.
Swordsmith Minamoto no Kiyomaro. Kizu. 1993. pap. 4.95 (0-910704-35-X) Hawley.
Swordsmith Nagasone Kotetsu Okisato. Kizu. 1990. pap. 4.95 (0-910704-07-4) Hawley.
Swordsmith Suishinshi Masahide. Kizu. 1991. pap. 5.95 (0-910704-19-8) Hawley.
Swordsmith Taikei Naotane. Hawley & Kizu. 1990. pap. 5.95 (0-910704-09-0) Hawley.
Swordsmiths of Kaga Province in the Shinto Era. Kizu. 1991. pap. 4.95 (0-910704-11-2) Hawley.
Swordsmiths of Satsuma Province. Kizu. 1991. pap. 4.95 (0-910704-12-0) Hawley.
Swordsmiths Sa of Chikuzen Province. Kizu. 1992. pap. 4.95 (0-910704-32-5) Hawley.
Swordsmiths Tadayoshi. Kizu. 1991. pap. 4.95 (0-910704-17-1) Hawley.
Swordspoint. Ellen Kushner. 288p. 1994. mass mkt. 4.99 (0-8125-3644-4) Tor Bks.
***Swordtails: Keeping & Breeding Them in Captivity.** Herbert R. Axelrod & Myron Gordon. (Illus.). 64p. 1997. pap. 6.95 (0-7938-0365-9, RE-616) TFH Pubns.
Swordtails & Platies. Herbert R. Axelrod & Lothar Wischnath. (Illus.). 191p. 1991. text ed. 79.95 (0-86622-090-9, TS-131) TFH Pubns.
Sworn Book of Honourius the Magician. Tr. by Daniel J. Driscoll. LC 76-57011. 1983. 20.00 (0-935214-00-3) Heptangle.
Sworn Enemies. Carol Matas. 144p. (YA). 1994. mass mkt. 3.99 (0-440-21900-0) Dell.
Sworn of the Altar of God: A Religious Biography of Thomas Jefferson. Edwin S. Gaustad. (Library of Religious Biography). 260p. (Orig.). 1996. pap. 15.00 (0-8028-0156-0) Eerdmans.
Sworn to Silence. Jennifer Baker. (Class Secrets Ser.: No. 3). (YA). (gr. 7 up). 1995. mass mkt. 3.99 (0-671-51035-5) PB.
***Sworn to Silence.** Vickie York. (Intrigue Ser.: No. 421). 1997. mass mkt. 3.75 (0-373-22421-4, 1-22421-1) Harlequin Bks.
SWOT: Jurisprudence. 4th ed. Raymond I. Wacks. 268p. 1995. pap. 18.00 (1-85431-475-0, Pub. by Blackstone Pr UK) Gaunt.
SWOT - A Level Law. Nick Johnson & Alan Pannett. 240p. (C). 1990. 90.00 (1-85431-007-0, Pub. by Blackstone Pr UK) St Mut.
SWOT a Level Law. N. Johnson & A. Plannett. (C). 1991. text ed. 65.00 (1-85431-187-5, Pub. by Blackstone Pr UK) Gaunt.
SWOT a Level Law. 2nd ed. Nick Johnson & Simon Cooper. 1995. 8.95 (1-85431-469-6, Pub. by Blackstone Pr UK) Gaunt.
SWOT Commercial & Consumer Law. Graham Stephenson & Peter Clark. 228p. (C). 1990. 90.00 (0-685-40605-9, Pub. by Blackstone Pr UK) St Mut.
Swot Commercial & Consumer Law. Ed. by Graham Stephenson & Peter Clark. 228p. (C). 1993. text ed. 20.00 (1-85185-232-8, Pub. by Blackstone Pr UK) Gaunt.
Swot Commercial & Consumer Law. 3rd ed. Graham Stephenson & Peter Clark. 229p. 1995. pap. 20.00 (1-85431-474-2, Pub. by Blackstone Pr UK) Gaunt.
SWOT Company Law. Allan Blake & Helen Bond. 240p. (C). 1990. 80.00 (1-85431-055-0, Pub. by Blackstone Pr UK) St Mut.
SWOT Company Law. 5th ed. Allan Blake & Helen J. Bond. 275p. 1996. pap. 22.00 (1-85431-478-5, Pub. by Blackstone Pr UK) Gaunt.
SWOT Constitutional & Administrative Law. Robert Lee. 204p. (C). 1990. 80.00 (1-85431-030-5, Pub. by Blackstone Pr UK) St Mut.
SWOT Constitutional & Administrative Law. 4th ed. Mark Stallworthy. 252p. 1995. pap. 22.00 (1-85431-337-1, Pub. by Blackstone Pr UK) Gaunt.
SWOT Conveyancing. Ed. by B. Walker. (C). 1991. pap. 25.50 (1-85431-180-8, Pub. by Blackstone Pr UK) Gaunt.
SWOT Conveyancing. 2nd ed. Bridget Walker. 247p. 1995. pap. 22.00 (1-85431-413-0, Pub. by Blackstone Pr UK) Gaunt.
SWOT Criminal Law. Christopher Ryan & Gary Scanlan. 238p. (C). 1990. 80.00 (1-85431-034-8, Pub. by Blackstone Pr UK) St Mut.
SWOT Criminal Law. 4th ed. Christopher Ryan. 286p. 1995. pap. 22.00 (1-85431-339-8, Pub. by Blackstone Pr UK) Gaunt.
SWOT EC Law. Nigel Foster. 264p. 1993. pap. 22.00 (1-85431-064-X, Pub. by Blackstone Pr UK) Gaunt.
SWOT EC Law. 2nd ed. Nigel Foster. 286p. 1995. pap. 18.00 (1-85431-480-7, Pub. by Blackstone Pr UK) Gaunt.
SWOT Employment Law. Ann Holmes. 240p. (C). 1990. 90.00 (1-85431-008-9, Pub. by Blackstone Pr UK) St Mut.
Swot Employment Law. H. Homes & P. Painter. 239p. (C). 1988. 110.00 (0-685-39837-4, Pub. by Inst Pur & Supply UK) St Mut.
SWOT Employment Law. 3rd ed. A. E. Holmes. 281p. 1995. pap. 22.00 (1-85431-340-1, Pub. by Blackstone Pr UK) Gaunt.
SWOT English Legal System. Ed. by D. Howarth. (C). 1992. 20.00 (1-85431-203-0, Pub. by Blackstone Pr UK) Gaunt.
SWOT English Legal System. David Howarth. 256p. (C). 1990. 85.00 (1-85431-006-2, Pub. by Blackstone Pr UK) St Mut.
SWOT English Legal System. 3rd ed. Stephen R. Wilson. 260p. 1996. pap. 22.00 (1-85431-479-3, Pub. by Blackstone Pr UK) Gaunt.
SWOT Equity & Trusts. Ed. by P. Todd. (C). 1991. 100.00 (1-85431-151-4, Pub. by Blackstone Pr UK) Gaunt.
SWOT Equity & Trusts. Paul Todd. 200p. (C). 1990. 90.00 (1-85431-033-X, Pub. by Blackstone Pr UK) St Mut.
SWOT Equity & Trusts. 5th ed. Paul Todd. 193p. 1996. pap. 22.00 (1-85431-500-5, Pub. by Blackstone Pr UK) Gaunt.
SWOT Family Law. Duncan Bloy. 240p. (C). 1990. 85.00 (1-85431-031-3) St Mut.
SWOT Family Law. 4th ed. Duncan Bloy. 250p. 1995. pap. 22.00 (1-85431-341-X, Pub. by Blackstone Pr UK) Gaunt.
SWOT International Law. Steven Wheatley. 181p. 1996. pap. 22.00 (1-85431-501-3, Pub. by Blackstone Pr UK) Gaunt.
SWOT Jurisprudence. Raymond I. Wacks. 222p. (C). 1990. 80.00 (1-85431-080-1, Pub. by Blackstone Pr UK) Gaunt.
SWOT Land Law. Denise Artis & John Houghton. 190p. (C). 1990. 80.00 (1-85431-053-4, Pub. by Blackstone Pr UK) St Mut.
SWOT Land Law. 4th ed. D. Artis & John T. Houghton. 202p. 1995. pap. 22.00 (1-85431-383-5, Pub. by Blackstone Pr UK) Gaunt.
SWOT Law of Contract. Richard Taylor. 238p. (C). 1990. 80.00 (1-85431-054-2, Pub. by Blackstone Pr UK) St Mut.
SWOT Law of Contract. 5th rev. ed. Richard D. Taylor. 238p. 1995. pap. 22.00 (1-85431-338-X, Pub. by Blackstone Pr UK) Gaunt.
Swot Law of Evidence. Christopher Carr & John Beaumont. 214p. (C). 1990. 90.00 (1-85431-035-6) St Mut.
Swot Law of Evidence. 4th ed. Chris Carr & John Beaumont. 210p. 1996. pap. 22.00 (1-85431-486-6, Pub. by Blackstone Pr UK) Gaunt.
SWOT Law of Succession. Ian Jones. 1993. 8.95 (1-85431-199-9, Pub. by Blackstone Pr UK) Gaunt.
SWOT Law of Torts. Peter Clark & Graham Stephenson. 178p. (C). 1990. 92.00 (1-85431-029-1, Pub. by Blackstone Pr UK) St Mut.
SWOT Law of Torts. 4th ed. P. Clark & G. Stephenson. 168p. 1995. pap. 22.00 (1-85431-343-6, Pub. by Blackstone Pr UK) Gaunt.
SWOT Revenue Law. Derek Martin. 278p. (C). 1990. 90.00 (0-906322-91-X, Pub. by Blackstone Pr UK) St Mut.
SWOT (Success Without Tears) Equity & Trusts. 4th ed. 196p. 1994. pap. 22.00 (1-85431-342-8) Gaunt.
SX-Seventy Art. LC 79-2426. (Illus.). 140p. 1979. 20.00 (0-912810-23-8) Lustrum Pr.
Syama Prasad Mookerjee: Founder of Jana Sangh. S. R. Bakshi. (C). 1992. 32.00 (0-685-59773-3, Pub. by Anmol II) S Asia.
Sybaris & Other Homes. Edward E. Hale. LC 70-155158. (Utopian Literature Ser.). 1979. reprint ed. 20.95 (0-405-03551-9) Ayer.
Sybase & Client-Server Computing. Alex Berson & George Anderson. LC 94-44228. (Computer Communications Ser.). 1995. write for info. (0-00-700503-2) McGraw.
Sybase & Client/Server Computing: Featuring System II. 2nd ed. Alex Berson & Geroge Anderson. (Illus.). 650p. 1996. pap. text ed. 54.95 (0-07-006080-0) McGraw.
Sybase Architecture & Administration. John Kirkwood. 1993. text ed. 62.00 (0-13-100330-5) P-H.
***Sybase Client-Server Explorer.** James Bean. 1996. pap. text ed. 44.99 incl. cd-rom (1-57610-045-6) Coriolis Grp.
Sybase Database Administrator's Handbook. Brian Hitchcock. LC 95-38350. 1995. pap. text ed. 53.00 (0-13-357477-6) P-H.
***Sybase Database Administrator's Reference Library, 3 vols.** Rob Gillette. 1996. 119.95 (0-13-651424-3) P-H.
***SyBase DBA Companion: An Introduction to Database Administration.** Brian Hitchcock. LC 97-6036. 1997. pap. 49.95 (0-13-652389-7) P-H.
***Sybase Developer's Handbook.** Daniel Worden. (Illus.). 743p. 1997. pap. text ed., pap. 49.95 incl. cd-rom (0-12-763950-0, AP Prof) Acad Pr.
***SyBase Developer's Reference.** Casciato Ventures, Inc. Staff. 1997. pap. 44.95 (0-13-616921-X) P-H.
Sybase Performance Tuning Strategies. Ronald Phillips & Bonnie O'Neil. 176p. (C). 1996. text ed. 31.95 (0-13-494865-3) P-H.
SYBASE Replication Server. Clifford. 1991. 50.00 (0-07-011513-3) McGraw.
SYBASE Replication Server. Charles B. Clifford. LC 95-18169. 1995. text ed. 45.00 (0-07-011515-X) McGraw.
Sybase SQL Anywhere: Secrets of the Watcom SQL Masters: PowerBuilder Developer's Journal. Joe Celko & Michael MacDonald. (SQL Training Ser.: No. I). (Illus.). 480p. (Orig.). 1996. pap. 37.75 (1-886141-05-3) SYS-Con Pubns.
SyBase SQL Anywhere Developer's Guide. Ian Richmond & Derek Ball. (Illus.). 400p. 1998. pap. 39.99 (1-85032-860-9) ITCP.
Sybase SQL Server on the World Wide Web. Edward Ashley & Beth Epperson. LC 96-19186. 400p. 1996. pap. 36.95 (1-85032-815-3) ITCP.
***Sybase SQL Server Performance & Tuning.** Paulsell. (ITCP-US Computer Science Ser.). 1997. pap. 49.95 (1-85032-883-8) ITCP.
Sybase SQL Server Performance Tuning. Shaibal Roy. 656p. (C). 1996. text ed. 54.00 (0-13-442997-4) P-H.
Sybase SQL Server Survival Guide. Jim Panttaja. LC 96-10798. 384p. 1996. pap. text ed. 36.95 (0-471-12745-0) Wiley.
Sybase SQL Server 11: An Administrator's Guide. John E. Kirkwood. (Illus.). 52p. 1996. pap. 42.95 (1-85032-287-2) ITCP.
Sybase SQL Server 11 DBA Survival Guide. 2nd ed. Northern Lights Consulting Staff. 656p. 1996. 49.99 incl. cd-rom (0-672-30888-6) Sams.
Sybase SQL Server 11 Unleashed. Northern Lights Consulting Staff. 1152p. 1996. 59.99 incl. cd-rom (0-672-30909-2) Sams.
Sybase Stored Procedures. Gonzales. (C). 1997. text ed. 33.75 (0-13-488884-7) P-H.
Sybase System II: Secrets of the Sybase Masters: Sybase Developer's Journal. Jeff Garbus & Michael MacDonald. (Illus.). 576p. (Orig.). 1996. pap. 43.95 (1-886141-08-8) SYS-Con Pubns.
Sybase Systems Management. Karen Hogoboom. LC 96-18153. 700p. 1996. 44.95 (0-13-455353-5) P-H.
Sybil. Flora R. Schreiber. (Illus.). 464p. 1989. mass mkt. 6.99 (0-446-35940-8) Warner Bks.
Sybil. Louis Auchincloss. LC 75-108840. 284p. 1972. reprint ed. text ed. 35.00 (0-8371-3728-4, AUSY, Greenwood Pr) Greenwood.
Sybil. Benjamin Disraeli. Ed. by Sheila Smith. (World's Classics Ser.). 480p. 1981. reprint ed. pap. 7.95 (0-19-281551-2) OUP.
Sybil: The Glide of Her Tongue. Gillian Hanscombe. 128p. 1993. pap. 11.95 (1-875559-05-1, Pub. by SpiniFex Pr AT) LPC InBook.
Sybil, or the Two Nations. Benjamin Disraeli. Ed. by Tom Braun. 304p. 1980. pap. 10.95 (0-14-043134-9, Penguin Classics) Viking Penguin.
Sybil Rides for Independence. Drollene Brown. Ed. by Abby Levine. LC 84-17219. (Illus.). 48p. (J). (gr. 2-5). 1985. 12.95 (0-8075-7684-0) A Whitman.
Sybil: Tancred see Works of Benjamin Disraeli
Sycamore - Oriole. Ken McCullough. Ed. by Dale K. Boyer. LC 91-71532. (Ahsahta Press Modern & Contemporary Poets of the West Ser.). 60p. (Orig.). 1991. pap. 6.95 (0-916272-50-8) Ahsahta Pr.
Sycamore Canyon Jewelers: A Computerized Payroll Accounting Practice Set Release 3.0 & Release 3.5. Carol Yacht. 200p. (C). 1996. 22.85 (0-256-21759-9) Irwin.
Sycamore Shores. Clark B. Fireston. 1993. reprint ed. lib. bdg. 89.00 (0-7812-5360-8) Rprt Serv.
Sycamore Street. C. B. Christiansen. LC 92-33685. (Illus.). 48p. (J). (gr. 1-3). 1993. lib. bdg. 13.95 (0-689-31784-0, Atheneum Bks Young) S&S Childrens.
Sycamores & More. Josephine F. Collitt. (Illus.). 70p. 1995. pap. 7.50 (0-9648441-2-3) J F Collitt.
Sycophancy in Athens & Capital Punishment in Ancient Athens. John O. Lofbarg & Irving Barkan. Ed. by Gregory Vlastos. LC 78-14609. (Morals & Law in Ancient Greece Ser.). 1979. reprint ed. lib. bdg. 17.95 (0-405-11585-7) Ayer.
SYD. Deana L. Jensen. (Illus.). 304p. (Orig.). 1991. pap. 13.95 (0-9615793-2-3) D L Jensen.
***Syd - Sydney.** Ramonia G. O'Bannon. 40p. (Orig.). 1997. pap. 8.99 (1-55237-324-X, Pub. by Comnwlth Pub CN) Partners Pubs Grp.
Syd Solomon: A Dialogue with Nature. Meg Perlman & Kevin Dean. Ed. by Kathleen G. Chilson. LC 90-63244. (Illus.). 1990. pap. 9.95 (0-916758-31-1) Ringling Mus Art.
Sydney. (Insight Guides Ser.). 1993. pap. 21.95 (0-395-66293-1) HM.
Sydney. (Eyewitness Travel Guides Ser.). 264p. 1996. pap. 22.95 (0-7894-1069-9) DK Pub Inc.
Sydney. Berlitz Editors. (Pocket Guides Ser.). (Illus.). 144p. 1993. pap. 7.95 (2-8315-0714-6) Berlitz.
***Sydney.** John Melick. 1997. pap. 18.50 (0-06-277213-9, Access NY) HarpC.
***Sydney.** 3rd ed. Tom Smallman. (Illus.). 304p. 1997. pap. 12.95 (0-86442-510-4) Lonely Planet.
Sydney. 4th ed. Frommer Staff. (Frommer's Travel Guides Ser.). 1995. 12.95 (0-02-860060-6) Macmillan.
Sydney: City Guide. 2nd ed. Jon Murray. (Illus.). 280p. 1994. pap. 9.95 (0-86442-227-X) Lonely Planet.
Sydney: Sydney-Smith & Clagett-Price Genealogy, with the Lewis, Montgomery, Harrison, Hawley, Moorhead, Rixey, et al. Lucy M. Price. (Illus.). 324p. 1992. reprint ed. pap. 49.50 (0-8328-2741-X); reprint ed. lib. bdg. 59.50 (0-8328-2740-1) Higginson Bk Co.
Sydney: Travel Guide. Globe Pequot Press Staff. 1996. pap. text ed. 9.95 (1-85368-548-8) Globe Pequot.
Sydney & Frances Lewis Contemporary Art Fund Collection. Rebecca Massie. LC 80-14914. (Illus.). 112p. (Orig.). 1980. pap. 5.00 (0-917046-09-9) Va Mus Arts.
Sydney & New South Wales. Anne Matthews. (Illustrated Travel Guides from Thomas Cook Ser.). (Illus.). 192p. 1994. pap. 12.95 (0-8442-9050-5, Passport Bks) NTC Pub Grp.
Sydney by Ferry & Foot. 4th ed. John Gunter. (Illus.). 176p. 1995. pap. 11.95 (0-86417-621-X, Pub. by Kangaroo Pr AT) Seven Hills Bk.
Sydney Camm & the Hurricane: Perspectives on the Master Fighter Designer & His Finest Achievement. Ed. by John W. Fozard. LC 90-62901. (Illus.). 224p. (C). 1991. text ed. 49.00 (1-56098-034-6) Smithsonian.
Sydney Downtown. Jo Dirks. (Illus.). 192p. (Orig.). 1993. pap. 14.95 (0-86417-445-4, Pub. by Kangaroo Pr AT) Seven Hills Bk.
***Sydney Duck.** Morris L. West. Date not set. write for info. (0-688-05103-0) Morrow.
Sydney, Herself. Colby Rodowsky. 176p. (YA). (gr. 7 up). 1989. 12.95 (0-374-30649-4) FS&G.
Sydney, Herself. Colby Rodowsky. (YA). (gr. 7 up). 1993. pap. 4.95 (0-374-47390-0, Sunburst Bks) FS&G.
Sydney, Invincible. Colby Rodowsky. LC 94-22440. 160p. (YA). (gr. 7 up). 1995. 14.00 (0-374-37365-5) FS&G.
Sydney Laurence, Painter of the North. Kesler E. Woodward. LC 89-70471. (Illus.). 152p. 1990. reprint ed. pap. 27.95 (0-295-96953-9) U of Wash Pr.
Sydney Mouse Coloring Book. Trudy K. Austin. (Illus.). 12p. (Orig.). 1995. pap. 2.00 (0-9640210-5-6) Jackson Harbor.
Sydney Omarr - Horoscope 1993: Aquarius. Sydney Omarr. 1992. pap. 3.99 (0-451-17296-5, Sig) NAL-Dutton.
Sydney Omarr - Horoscope 1993: Aries. Sydney Omarr. 1992. pap. 3.99 (0-451-17286-8, Sig) NAL-Dutton.
Sydney Omarr - Horoscope 1993: Cancer. Sydney Omarr. 1992. pap. 3.99 (0-451-17289-2, Sig) NAL-Dutton.
Sydney Omarr - Horoscope 1993: Capricorn. Sydney Omarr. 1992. pap. 3.99 (0-451-17295-7, Sig) NAL-Dutton.
Sydney Omarr - Horoscope 1993: Gemini. Sydney Omarr. 1992. pap. 3.99 (0-451-17288-4, Sig) NAL-Dutton.
Sydney Omarr - Horoscope 1993: Leo. Sydney Omarr. 1992. pap. 3.99 (0-451-17290-6, Sig) NAL-Dutton.
Sydney Omarr - Horoscope 1993: Libra. Sydney Omarr. 1992. pap. 3.99 (0-451-17292-2, Sig) NAL-Dutton.
Sydney Omarr - Horoscope 1993: Pisces. Sydney Omarr. 1992. pap. 3.99 (0-451-17297-3, Sig) NAL-Dutton.
Sydney Omarr - Horoscope 1993: Sagittarius. Sydney Omarr. 1992. pap. 3.99 (0-451-17294-9, Sig) NAL-Dutton.
Sydney Omarr - Horoscope 1993: Scorpio. Sydney Omarr. 1992. pap. 3.99 (0-451-17293-0, Sig) NAL-Dutton.
Sydney Omarr - Horoscope 1993: Taurus. Sydney Omarr. 1992. pap. 3.99 (0-451-17287-6, Sig) NAL-Dutton.
Sydney Omarr - Horoscope 1993: Virgo. Sydney Omarr. 1992. pap. 3.99 (0-451-17291-4, Sig) NAL-Dutton.
Sydney Omarr Aquarius, 1994. Sydney Omarr. 1993. pap. 3.99 (0-451-17655-3, Sig) NAL-Dutton.
Sydney Omarr Aquarius, 1995. Sydney Omarr. 1994. pap. 3.99 (0-451-18117-4) NAL-Dutton.
Sydney Omarr Aquarius 1996. Sydney Omarr. 1995. mass mkt. 4.50 (0-451-18451-3, Sig) NAL-Dutton.
Sydney Omarr Aries, 1994. Sydney Omarr. 1993. pap. 3.99 (0-451-17661-8, Sig) NAL-Dutton.
Sydney Omarr Aries, 1995. Sydney Omarr. 1994. pap. 3.99 (0-451-18120-4) NAL-Dutton.
Sydney Omarr Aries 1996. Sydney Omarr. 1995. mass mkt. 4.50 (0-451-18450-5, Sig) NAL-Dutton.
Sydney Omarr Cancer, 1994. Sydney Omarr. 1993. pap. 3.99 (0-451-17659-6, Sig) NAL-Dutton.
Sydney Omarr Cancer, 1995. Sydney Omarr. 1994. pap. 3.99 (0-451-18119-0) NAL-Dutton.
Sydney Omarr Cancer 1996. Sydney Omarr. 1995. mass mkt. 4.50 (0-451-18454-8, Sig) NAL-Dutton.
Sydney Omarr Capricorn, 1994. Sydney Omarr. 1993. pap. 3.99 (0-451-17654-5, Sig) NAL-Dutton.
Sydney Omarr Capricorn, 1995. Sydney Omarr. 1994. pap. 3.99 (0-451-18116-6) NAL-Dutton.
Sydney Omarr Capricorn 1996. Sydney Omarr. 1995. mass mkt. 4.50 (0-451-18452-1, Sig) NAL-Dutton.
Sydney Omarr Gemini, 1994. Sydney Omarr. 1993. pap. 3.99 (0-451-17658-8, Sig) NAL-Dutton.
Sydney Omarr Gemini, 1995. Sydney Omarr. 1994. pap. 3.99 (0-451-18115-8) NAL-Dutton.
Sydney Omarr Gemini 1996. Sydney Omarr. 1995. mass mkt. 4.50 (0-451-18455-6, Sig) NAL-Dutton.
Sydney Omarr Leo, 1994. Sydney Omarr. 1993. pap. 3.99 (0-451-17662-6, Sig) NAL-Dutton.
Sydney Omarr Leo, 1995. Sydney Omarr. 1994. pap. 3.99 (0-451-18121-2) NAL-Dutton.
Sydney Omarr Libra, 1994. Sydney Omarr. 1993. pap. 3.99 (0-451-17665-0, Sig) NAL-Dutton.

S

Sydney Omarr Libra, 1995. Sydney Omarr. 1994. pap. 3.99 (*0-451-18124-7*) NAL-Dutton.

Sydney Omarr Pisces, 1994. Sydney Omarr. 1993. pap. 3.99 (*0-451-17656-1*, Sig) NAL-Dutton.

Sydney Omarr Pisces 1995. Sydney Omarr. 1994. pap. 3.99 (*0-451-18118-2*, Sig) NAL-Dutton.

Sydney Omarr Pisces 1996. Sydney Omarr. 1995. mass mkt. 4.50 (*0-451-18459-9*, Sig) NAL-Dutton.

Sydney Omarr Sagittarius, 1994. Sydney Omarr. 1993. pap. 3.99 (*0-451-17664-2*, Sig) NAL-Dutton.

Sydney Omarr Sagittarius, 1995. Sydney Omarr. 1994. pap. 3.99 (*0-451-18123-9*) NAL-Dutton.

Sydney Omarr Sagittarius 1996. Sydney Omarr. 1995. mass mkt. 4.50 (*0-451-18458-0*, Sig) NAL-Dutton.

Sydney Omarr Scorpio, 1995. Sydney Omarr. 1994. pap. 3.99 (*0-451-18122-0*) NAL-Dutton.

Sydney Omarr Scorpio 1996. Sydney Omarr. 1995. mass mkt. 4.50 (*0-451-18460-2*, Sig) NAL-Dutton.

Sydney Omarr Taurus, 1994. Sydney Omarr. 1993. pap. 3.99 (*0-451-17653-7*, Sig) NAL-Dutton.

Sydney Omarr Taurus, 1995. Sydney Omarr. 1994. pap. 3.99 (*0-451-18113-1*) NAL-Dutton.

Sydney Omarr Taurus 1996. Sydney Omarr. 1995. mass mkt. 4.50 (*0-451-18461-0*, Sig) NAL-Dutton.

Sydney Omarr Virgo, 1994. Sydney Omarr. 1993. pap. 3.99 (*0-451-17652-9*, Sig) NAL-Dutton.

Sydney Omarr Virgo, 1995. Sydney Omarr. 1994. pap. 3.99 (*0-451-18112-3*) NAL-Dutton.

Sydney Omarr Virgo 1996. Sydney Omarr. 1995. mass mkt. 4.50 (*0-451-18462-9*, Sig) NAL-Dutton.

Sydney Omarr Virgo 1997. Signet Staff. 1996. mass mkt. 4.99 (*0-451-18840-3*, Sig) NAL-Dutton.

Sydney Omarr's Astrological Guide for You in 1995. Sydney Omarr. 288p. (Orig.). 1994. pap. 4.50 (*0-451-18163-8*, Sig) NAL-Dutton.

Sydney Omarr's Astrological Guide for You in 1996. Sydney Omarr. 288p. (Orig.). 1995. mass mkt. 4.99 (*0-451-18495-5*, Sig) NAL-Dutton.

Sydney Opera House: Sydney 1957-73: Jorn Utzon. Philip Drew. (Architecture in Detail Ser.). (Illus.). 60p. (Orig.). (C). 1995. pap. 29.95 (*0-7148-3297-9*, Pub. by Phaidon Press UK) Chronicle Bks.

Sydney Pocket Guidebook. Little Hills Press Editorial Board Staff. (Illus.). 128p. 1996. pap. 9.95 (*1-86315-082-X*) Pelican.

Sydney Smith: A Biography & a Selection. Gerald W. Bullett. LC 77-138578. (Illus.). 1971. reprint ed. text ed. 65.00 (*0-8371-5777-3*, BUSS, Greenwood Pr) Greenwood.

***Sydney Swans.** Steve Christo. 80p. 1996. pap. 19.95 (*0-86840-424-1*, Pub. by New South Wales Univ Pr AT) Intl Spec Bk.

***Sydney the Kangaroo Shares with You a Story of a Tender Nature.** Beverly Mitchell. (Illus.). 9p. (J). (gr. k-3). 1997. pap. 6.00 (*0-8059-4079-0*) Dorrance.

Sydney the Wandering Sardine. Helen Howard. Ed. by Doris Berdahl. (Illus.). 114p. (J). (gr. 3-4). 1995. 14.95 (*0-9646546-0-1*) Glenwood Pr.

Sydney Tunnels. Brian Kennedy & Barbara Kennedy. (Illus.). 96p. (Orig.). 1993. pap. 14.95 (*0-86417-525-6*, Pub. by Kangaroo Pr AT) Seven Hills Bk.

Sydney Wildflower Bushwalks. Jane Mundy. (Illus.). 96p. pap. 13.95 (*0-86417-335-0*, Pub. by Kangaroo Pr AT) Seven Hills Bk.

Syed Amanuddin: His Mind & Art. A. N. Dwivedi. vii, 143p. 1988. text ed. 25.00 (*81-207-0824-5*, Pub. by Sterling Pubs II) Apt Bks.

Sykes' Regular Infantry Division, 1861-1864: A History of Regular United States Infantry Operations in the Civil War's Eastern Theater. Timothy J. Reese. LC 90-42746. (Illus.). 488p. 1990. lib. bdg. 57.50 (*0-89950-447-7*) McFarland & Co.

Syllabaire Elamite: Histore & Paliographie. M. J. Steve. (Civilisations Du Proche-Orient Ser.: Series 2, Vol. 1). 176p. 1992. pap. 45.00 (*0-614-11311-3*, Pub. by Recherches et Pubns SZ) Eisenbrauns.

Syllabi for Music Methods Courses. Rosemary Watkins. 278p. (C). 1992. teacher ed. 20.00 (*1-56545-012-4*, 1044) Music Ed Natl.

Syllabic Inscriptions from Byblos. George E. Mendenhall. 194p. 1986. text ed. 40.00 (*0-8156-6077-4*, Am U Beirut) Syracuse U Pr.

Syllabification & Accent in the Paradise Lost. George D. Brown. LC 73-39543. reprint ed. 29.50 (*0-404-01129-2*) AMS Pr.

Syllabification & Consonant Cooccurrence Conditions. Greg Lamontagne. LC 96-53690. (Outstanding Dissertations in Linguistics Ser.). 270p. 1997. 59.00 (*0-8153-2559-2*) Garland.

Syllable in Dutch. Mieke Trommelen. (Publications in Language Sciences). xii, 187p. 1983. pap. 42.35 (*90-6765-016-1*) Mouton.

Syllable Structure & Stress In Dutch. Harry V. Hulst. (Linguistic Models Ser.: No. 8). 276p. 1985. pap. 44.65 (*90-6765-038-2*) Mouton.

Syllable, Word, Nexus, Cursus. Ernst Pulgram. (Janua Linguarum, Ser.: No. 81). 1970. pap. text ed. 40.80 (*90-279-0706-4*) Mouton.

Syllables of Sky: Studies in South Indian Civilzation in Honour of Velcheru Narayana Rao. David Shulman. (Illus.). 492p. (C). 1996. 29.95 (*0-19-563549-3*) OUP.

Syllables, Tone, & Verb Paradigms. Ed. by William R. Merrifield & Calvin R. Rensch. (Publications in Linguistics: No. 95). 130p. (Orig.). 1990. fiche 12.00 (*0-88312-630-3*) Summer Instit Ling.

Syllabus: Legal Issues Affecting Poor Children. 191p. 1986. 20.00 (*0-685-30183-4*, 42,610) NCLS Inc.

Syllabus - European Seminars on Diagnostic & Interventional Radiology (ESDIR), Rome, Italy: Functional MRI. P. Pavone & Plinio Rossi. LC 96-26790. 160p. 1996. pap. 79.50 (*3-540-75025-8*) Spr-Verlag.

Syllabus der Pflanzenfalien: Kapitael V, 2 - Bryophytina, Laubmoose. 13th ed. A. Engler. Ed. by J. Gerloff et al. (Illus.). 109p. (GER.). 1983. pap. 35.00 (*3-443-02001-1*) Lubrecht & Cramer.

Syllabus der Pflanzenfamilien, 2 vols. 12th ed. A. Engler. Incl. Vol. 1. Allgemeiner Teil: Bakterien Bis Gymnospermen. 1964. 60.00 (*3-443-39015-3*); Vol. 2. Angiospermen Vebersicht Ueber Die Florengebiete der Erde. 1964. 95.00 (*3-443-39016-1*); (Illus.). write for info. (*0-318-54145-9*) Lubrecht & Cramer.

Syllabus Design. 1988. 14.50 (*0-19-437139-5*) OUP.

Syllabus for Advanced Ceramics. F. Carlton Ball. LC 77-187486. (C). pap. 3.95 (*0-935066-03-9*) Keramos Bks.

Syllabus for Land Surveyor Examinations. 2nd ed. Charles Safford. (Illus.). 160p. 1989. pap. 40.00 (*0-910845-12-3*, 722) Landmark Ent.

Syllabus for Mandarin Primer. Rulan C. Pian. (Illus.). 118p. reprint ed. pap. 33.70 (*0-7837-4178-2*, 2059027) Bks Demand.

Syllabus for the Surgeon's Secretary. 4th rev. ed. Jeannette A. Szulec & Z. Szulec. (Illus.). 1144p. 1991. 95.00 (*0-913092-03-7*) Medical Arts.

Syllabus in English of the Documents Relating to England & Other Kingdoms, 3 Vols, Set. Great Britain, Public Record Office Staff. LC 78-168243. reprint ed. 275.00 (*0-404-03130-7*) AMS Pr.

Syllabus of Chinese Civilization. Mason J. Gentzler. LC 72-197083. (Companions to Asian Studies). 119p. reprint ed. pap. 34.00 (*0-317-11187-6*, 2015209) Bks Demand.

Syllabus of Examinations. Imperial Society of Teachers of Dancing Staff. (Ballroom Dance Ser.). 1986. lib. bdg. 79.95 (*0-8490-3333-0*) Gordon Pr.

Syllabus of Examinations. Imperial Society of Teachers of Dancing Staff. (Ballroom Dance Ser.). 1985. lib. bdg. 74.95 (*0-87700-863-9*) Revisionist Pr.

Syllabus of Indian Civilization. Leonard A. Gordon & Barbara S. Miller. LC 70-168868. (Companions to Asian Studies). 182p. (C). 1971. pap. text ed. 19.50 (*0-231-03560-8*) Col U Pr.

Syllabus of Japanese Civilization. 2nd ed. H. Paul Varley. LC 72-195883. (Companions to Asian Studies). 110p. reprint ed. pap. 31.40 (*0-7837-0432-1*, 2040755) Bks Demand.

Syllabus of Medieval History, Three Hundred Ninety-Five to Thirteen Hundred. Dana C. Munro. 1980. lib. bdg. 49.95 (*0-8490-3193-1*) Gordon Pr.

Syllabus Sourcebook on Media & Women. Ed. by Dana Densmore. 48p. 1980. 5.50 (*0-930470-06-0*) Womens Inst Free Press.

***Syllabus. 5th Radiological Refresher Course: Chest, Musculoskeleton, G.I. & Abdomen, Urinary Tract.** L. Dalla Palma. 200p. 1996. pap. 79.50 (*3-540-75019-3*) Spr-Verlag.

Sylloge Inscriptionum Graecarum, 4 vols., Set. Wilhelm Dittenberger. 2512p. (GER.). 1960. reprint ed. write for info. (*0-318-70443-9*) G Olms Pubs.

Sylloge Inscriptionum Graecarum et Latinarum Macedoniae, 2 vols. Margarites Demitsas. 1046p. 1980. 140.00 (*0-89005-324-3*) Ares.

Sylloge Nummorum Graecorum: The Collection of the American, Lucania, Pt. 2. American Numismatic Society Staff. LC 61-19327. (Illus.). reprint ed. pap. 25.00 (*0-7837-6971-7*, 2037460) Bks Demand.

Sylloge Nummorum Graecorum Pt. 3: The Collection of the American Numismatic Society: Brattium Sicily 1: Abacaenum-Eryx. Hyla A. Troxell. (Sylloge Nummorum Graecorum Ser.). (Illus.). 38p. 1975. pap. 75.00 (*0-89722-063-3*) Am Numismatic.

Sylloge Nummorum Graecorum Pt. 4: The Collection of the American Numismatic Society: Sicily 2: Galaria-Styella. Eva Jaunzems. (Illus.). 25p. 1978. pap. 75.00 (*0-89722-175-3*) Am Numismatic.

Sylloge Nummorum Graecorum Pt. 5: The Collection of the American Numismatic Society: Sicily 3: Syracuse - Siceliotes. Denyse Berend. (Illus.). 108p. 1988. pap. 75.00 (*0-89722-224-5*) Am Numismatic.

Sylloge Nummorum Graecorum Pt. 6: The Collection of the American Numismatic Society: Palestine-South Arabia. Ya'akov Meshorer. (Illus.). 54p. 1981. text ed. 100.00 (*0-89722-187-7*) Am Numismatic.

Sylloge Nummorum Graecorum Pt. 7: The Collection of the American Numismatic Society: Macedonia I: Cities, Traco-Macedonian Tribes, Paeonian Kings. Nancy M. Waggoner. (Illus.). 43p. 1987. text ed. 60.00 (*0-89722-216-4*) Am Numismatic.

Sylloge Nummorum Graecorum Pt. 8: The Collection of the American Numismatic Society: Macedonia 2: Alexander I - Philip II. Hyla A. Troxell. (Illus.). 44p. 1994. text ed. 75.00 (*0-89722-245-8*) Am Numismatic.

***Sylloge of Coins of the British Isles: Ashmolean III, Henry VII.** D. M. Metcalf. 1976. 19.98 (*0-19-725960-X*) David Brown.

***Sylloge of Coins of the British Isles Vol. 21: Coins in Yorkshire Collections.** E. J. Pirie. 1975. 19.98 (*0-19-725939-1*) David Brown.

***Sylloge of Coins of the British Isles Vol. 22, Pt. V: Royal Coll. Copenhagen.** G. Galster. 1975. 36.00 (*0-19-725949-9*) David Brown.

Sylloge of Coins of the British Isles Vol. 25: Helsinki. Tuukka Talvio. (Illus.). 1978. 60.00 (*0-19-725979-0*) David Brown.

Sylloge of Coins of the British Isles Vol. 26: East Anglia. T. H. Clough. 1980. 75.00 (*0-19-725991-X*) David Brown.

Sylloge of Coins of the British Isles Vol. 27: Lincolnshire Collection. Anthony J. Gunstone. (Illus.). 1981. 80.00 (*0-19-725993-6*) David Brown.

Sylloge of Coins of the British Isles Vol. 28: Index Vols. 1-20. Veronica Smart. 1981. 45.00 (*0-19-726002-0*) David Brown.

Sylloge of Coins of the British Isles Vol. 29: Merseyside. M. Warhurst. (Illus.). 1982. 65.00 (*0-19-726007-1*) David Brown.

Sylloge of Coins of the British Isles Vol. 30: American Collections. Jeremiah D. Brady. (British Academy Ser.). (Illus.). 1982. 19.98 (*0-19-726011-X*) David Brown.

Sylloge of Coins of the British Isles Vol. 32: Ulster, Pt. II. Wilfred A. Seaby. (Sylloge of Coins of the British Isles British Academy Ser.: Vol. 21). 88p. 1984. 27.00 (*0-19-726030-6*) David Brown.

Sylloge of Coins of the British Isles Vol. 36: Berlin. N. Bernd Kluge. (Illus.). 192p. 1987. 80.00 (*0-19-726048-9*) David Brown.

Sylloge of Coins of the British Isles Vol. 37: Polish Museums. N. Andrzej Mikolajczyk. (Sylloge of Coins of the British Isles British Academy Ser.: Vol. 37). (Illus.). 88p. 1987. 45.00 (*0-19-726063-2*) David Brown.

Sylloge of the United States Holdings in the National Numismatic Collection of the Smithsonian Institution, Vol. 1: Gold Coins, 1785-1834. Cory Gillilland. LC 92-6897. (Illus.). 152p. (C). 1993. text ed. 62.00 (*1-56098-160-1*) Smithsonian.

Syllogism. Paul Thom. (Analytica Ser.). 312p. 1981. lib. bdg. 99.00 (*3-88405-002-8*) Philosophia Pr.

Syllogismes de l'Amertume. E. M. Cioran. (FRE.). 1987. pap. 10.95 (*0-7859-2809-X*, 2070324494) Fr & Eur.

Syllogismes de l'Amertume. E. M. Cioran. (Folio Essais Ser.: No. 79). (FRE.). pap. 8.95 (*2-07-032449-4*) Schoenhof.

Syllogisms. Clifton A. Wiles. LC 88-80476. (Illus.). 51p. (Orig.). 1988. pap. 5.95 (*0-9614593-4-4*) hell box.

Syllogistic Philosophy or Prolegomena to Science, 2 vols. Francis E. Abbot. LC 75-3013. (Philosophy in America Ser.). reprint ed. 115.00 (*0-404-59005-5*) AMS Pr.

Syllogistik Des Aristoteles, 2 vols. in 3, Set. Heinrich Maier. xxiv, 1195p. 1969. reprint ed. write for info. (*0-318-70973-2*) G Olms Pubs.

Sylow Theory Formations & Fitting Classes in Locally Finite Groups. Martyn R. Dixon. (Series in Algebra). 320p. 1994. text ed. 48.00 (*981-02-1795-1*) World Scientific Pub.

Sylva. Jean Vercors. 285p. (FRE.). 1992. pap. 18.95 (*0-7859-1454-4*, 0-7859-1454-4); pap. 3.95 (*0-686-55142-7*) Fr & Eur.

Sylva Sylvarum: Or a Natural History in Ten Centuries & Miscellaneous Philosophical Tracts. Francis Bacon. 190p. 1996. pap. 17.95 (*1-56459-639-7*) Kessinger Pub.

Sylvan. Mark Dunster. 23p. (Orig.). 1995. pap. 4.00 (*0-89642-256-9*) Linden Pubs.

Sylvan. Judy V. Witt. (Illus.). 88p. 1996. 24.95 (*1-883911-07-9*) Brandylane.

Sylvan Delta. Catherine Harris. (Illus.). 48p. (Orig.). 1993. pap. 9.00 (*1-880516-08-X*) Left Hand Bks.

***Sylvan Path: A Journey Through America's Forests.** Gary Ferguson. LC 96-46058. 1997. 20.95 (*0-312-15219-1*) Thomas Dunne Bks.

Sylvania: Majestic Forests & Deep, Clear Waters. Bonnie Peacock. LC 87-401098. 60p. 1986. 9.95 (*0-9620008-0-9*) Peacock MI.

Sylvanus Thayer: A Biography. James W. Kershner. 1981. 49.95 (*0-405-14092-4*) Ayer.

Sylvester Ahola: The Gloucester Gabriel. Dick Hill. LC 93-11425. (Studies in Jazz: No. 14). (Illus.). 222p. 1993. 39.50 (*0-8108-2625-9*) Scarecrow.

Sylvester & the Magic Pebble. William Steig. LC 80-12314. (Illus.). 32p. (J). (gr. k-4). 1987. pap. 5.95 (*0-671-66269-4*, S&S Bks Young Read) S&S Childrens.

Sylvester & the Magic Pebble. William Steig. LC 80-12314. (Illus.). 32p. (J). (gr. k-4). 1988. pap. 15.00 (*0-671-66154-X*, S&S Bks Young Read) S&S Childrens.

Sylvester & the Magic Pebble: A Study Guide. Garrett Christopher. Ed. by Joyce Friedland & Rikki Kessler. (Little Novel-Ties Ser.). (J). (gr. k-3). 1991. pap. text ed. 14.95 (*0-88122-595-9*) Lrn Links.

Sylvester & the Magic Pebble: With Puzzle. William Steig. (J). (gr. k up). 1995. pap. 9.95 (*0-689-80417-2*, Atheneum Bks Young) S&S Childrens.

Sylvester Bear Overslept. Jan Wahl. LC 79-4095. (Illus.). 48p. (J). (ps-3). 1979. 5.95 (*0-8193-1003-4*); lib. bdg. 5.95 (*0-8193-1004-2*) Parents.

Sylvester Judd's New England. Richard D. Hathaway. LC 81-17854. (Illus.). 362p. 1982. 40.00 (*0-271-00307-3*) Pa St U Pr.

Sylvester: or The Wicked Uncle. Georgette Heyer. 1976. 24.95 (*0-8488-0695-6*) Amereon Ltd.

Sylvester the Jester. Michael P. Waite. LC 91-38875. 32p. (J). (ps-3). 1992. pap. 9.99 (*0-7814-0033-3*, Chariot Bks) Chariot Victor.

Sylvia. Emmanuel Berl. (FRE.). 1972. pap. 10.95 (*0-7859-1718-7*, 2070362655) Fr & Eur.

Sylvia. Howard Fast. 240p. 1992. 17.95 (*1-55972-128-6*, Birch Ln Pr) Carol Pub Group.

Sylvia. A. R. Gurney. 1996. pap. 5.25 (*0-8222-1496-2*) Dramatists Play.

Sylvia. Leonard Michaels. LC 92-16541. 144p. 1992. 10.00 (*1-56279-029-3*) Mercury Hse Inc.

Sylvia. large type ed. Howard Fast. 480p. 1992. reprint ed. lib. bdg. 20.95 (*1-56054-567-4*) Thorndike Pr.

Sylvia: A Novel. Upton Sinclair. LC 79-115276. 1971. reprint ed. 49.00 (*0-403-00291-5*) Scholarly.

Sylvia Bashline's Savory Game Cookbook. Sylvia G. Bashline. 176p. 1989. pap. write for info. (*0-9622756-0-3*) Iron Blue.

Sylvia Beach & the Lost Generation: A History of Literary Paris in the Twenties & Thirties. Noel R. Fitch. (Illus.). 1985. pap. 16.95 (*0-393-30231-8*) Norton.

***Sylvia Game.** Vivien Alcock. LC 96-53109. (J). 1997. pap. 4.95 (*0-395-81650-5*) HM.

Sylvia Pankhurst. Barbara. LC 96-19740. 1996. text ed. 55.00 (*0-312-16268-5*) St Martin.

***Sylvia Pankhurst.** Winslow. 1996. text ed. 19.95 (*0-312-16329-0*) St Martin.

Sylvia Pankhurst Reader. Ed. by Kathryn Dodd. LC 92-31627. 1993. text ed. 59.95 (*0-7190-2888-4*, Pub. by Manchester Univ Pr UK); text ed. 19.95 (*0-7190-2889-2*, Pub. by Manchester Univ Pr UK) St Martin.

Sylvia Plath. Susan Bassnet. LC 86-22293. (Women Writers Ser.). 176p. 41.00 (*0-389-20687-3*, N8245); pap. 14.00 (*0-389-20688-1*, N8246) B&N Imports.

Sylvia Plath. Lynn F. Chapman. LC 93-3354. (Voices in Poetry Ser.). (J). 1994. lib. bdg. 17.95 (*0-88682-614-4*) Creative Ed.

Sylvia Plath. Hall. 1998. 22.95 (*0-8057-7838-1*) Macmillan.

Sylvia Plath. Pashupati Jha. 1993. text ed. 22.50 (*81-85231-09-5*, Pub. by Creative Pubs II) Advent Bks Div.

Sylvia Plath. Robyn Marsack. (Open Guides to Literature Ser.). 112p. 1992. 75.00 (*0-335-09353-1*, Open Univ Pr); pap. 22.00 (*0-335-09352-3*, Open Univ Pr) Taylor & Francis.

Sylvia Plath. Ed. by Linda Wagner-Martin. (Critical Heritage Ser.). 320p. 1988. text ed. 49.95 (*0-415-00910-3*) Routledge.

***Sylvia Plath.** Ed. by Linda Wagner-Martin. (Critical Heritage Ser.). 346p. (C). 1997. text ed. 15.00 (*0-415-15942-3*) Routledge.

Sylvia Plath: A Biography. Linda Wagner-Martin. (Vermilion Bks.). (Illus.). 304p. 1988. pap. 12.95 (*0-312-02325-1*) St Martin.

Sylvia Plath: A Reference Guide, 1973-1988. Sheryl L. Meyering. (Reference Guides to Literature Ser.). 288p. 1989. 45.00 (*0-8161-8929-3*, Hall Reference) Macmillan.

Sylvia Plath: An Annotated Bibliography. Stephen Tabor. (Twentieth Century Literary Bibliographies Ser.). 268p. 1987. text ed. 47.50 (*0-313-27706-0*) Greenwood.

Sylvia Plath: Collected Poems. Sylvia Plath. Ed. by Ted Hughes. 350p. 1991. reprint ed. lib. bdg. 43.00 (*0-8095-9057-3*) Borgo Pr.

Sylvia Plath: Confessing the Fictive Self. Toni Saldivar. LC 91-45858. (Writing about Women: Feminist Literary Studies: Vol. 3). 213p. (C). 1992. text ed. 32.95 (*0-8204-1665-7*) P Lang Pubng.

Sylvia Plath: New Views on the Poetry. Gary Lane. LC 78-20515. 280p. reprint ed. pap. 79.80 (*0-685-15476-9*, 2026323) Bks Demand.

Sylvia Plath: Poetry & Existence. David Holbrook. 320p. (C). 1988. reprint ed. pap. 19.95 (*0-485-12062-3*, Pub. by Athlone Pr UK) Humanities.

Sylvia Plath: The Woman & the Work. Ed. by Edward Butscher. 242p. 7900. 30.00 (*0-7206-0545-8*, Pub. by P Owen Ltd UK) Dufour.

Sylvia Plath: The Wound & the Cure of Words. Stephen G. Axelrod. 272p. 1992. reprint ed. pap. text ed. 14.95 (*0-8018-4374-X*) Johns Hopkins.

Sylvia Plath see Modern Critical Views Series

Sylvia Porter's a Home of Your Own. Sylvia Porter. 176p. 1989. pap. 7.95 (*0-380-89755-5*) Avon.

Sylvia Porter's Four Hundred & Forty-Two Tax Saving Tips, 1989. Sylvia Porter. 256p. (Orig.). 1988. mass mkt. 6.95 (*0-380-89996-5*) Avon.

Sylvia Porter's Four Hundred Ninety-Five Tax-Savings Tips: 1990 Edition. Sylvia Porter. 288p. (Orig.). 1989. pap. 7.95 (*0-380-89997-3*) Avon.

Sylvia Porter's Guide to Your Health Care: How You Can Have the Best Health Care for Less. Sylvia Porter. 304p. 1990. pap. 9.95 (*0-380-89758-X*) Avon.

Sylvia Porter's Love & Money. Sylvia Porter. 256p. 1986. mass mkt. 3.95 (*0-380-89753-9*) Avon.

Sylvia Porter's New Money Book for the 80's. Sylvia Porter. 1328p. 1980. pap. 10.95 (*0-380-51060-X*) Avon.

Sylvia Porter's Your Financial Security: Making Your Money Work at Every Stage of Your Life. Sylvia Porter. 240p. 1989. reprint ed. pap. 8.95 (*0-380-89754-7*) Avon.

Sylvia Rimm on Raising Kids. Sylvia B. Rimm. (Illus.). 244p. (Orig.). 1992. pap. 15.00 (*0-937891-09-6*) Apple Pub Wisc.

Sylvia Sleigh: Invitation to a Voyage & Other Works. Ed. by Dennis Adrian. LC 89-61866. (Illus.). 38p. (Orig.). 1990. pap. 9.95 (*0-944110-42-8*) Milwauk Art Mus.

Sylvia Stark: A Pioneer. Victoria Scott & Ernest Jones. (Illus.). 64p. (Orig.). (J). (gr. 4-12). 1992. pap. 6.95 (*0-940880-38-5*); lib. bdg. 12.95 (*0-940880-37-7*) Open Hand.

Sylviad: Or, Minstrelsy of Nature in the Wilds of North America. Anthony P. Heinrich. (Earlier American Music Ser.: No. 28). 338p. 1990. reprint ed. lib. bdg. 59.50 (*0-306-77324-4*) Da Capo.

Sylvia's Lovers. Elizabeth C. Gaskell. Ed. by Andrew Sanders. (World's Classics Ser.). 533p. 1982. pap. 9.95 (*0-19-281571-7*) OUP.

***Sylvia's Lovers.** Elizabeth C. Gaskell. 1997. pap. 11.95 (*0-14-043422-4*) Viking Penguin.

Sylvia's Soul Food: Recipes from Harlem's World-Famous Restaurant. Sylvia Woods & Christopher Styler. LC 92-16524. 160p. 1992. 18.00 (*0-688-10012-0*) Hearst Bks.

Sylvie: Recollections of Valois. Gerard De Nerval. LC 77-10266. (Illus.). 168p. reprint ed. 55.00 (*0-404-16318-1*) AMS Pr.

Sylvie & Bruno. Lewis Carroll. (Illus.). 448p. 1988. reprint ed. pap. 8.95 (*0-486-25588-3*) Dover.

***Sylvie Believes.** Danielle Ponsolle. (Life with Sylvie Ser.: Vol. 11). (Illus.). 24p. (J). (ps). 1997. 12.95 (*1-890309-51-6*) Tern Bk Co.

An Asterisk (*) at the beginning of an entry indicates that the title is appearing in BIP for the first time.

***Sylvie Feels.** Danielle Ponsolle. (Life with Sylvie Ser.: Vol. 12). (Illus.). 24p. (J). (ps). 1997. 12.95 (*1-890309-50-8*) Tern Bk Co.

***Sylvie Goes to the Park Bk. 2.** Danielle Ponsolle. (Life with Sylvie Ser.: Bk. 2). (Illus.). 24p. (J). (ps-k). 1997. 12.95 (*0-9655782-1-6*, Tern Bks) Tern Bk Co.

***Sylvie Goes to the Zoo Bk. 3.** Danielle Ponsolle. (Life with Sylvie Ser.: Bk. 3). (Illus.). 24p. (J). (ps-k). 1997. 12.95 (*0-9655782-2-4*, Tern Bks) Tern Bk Co.

***Sylvie Hears Bk. 9.** Danielle Ponsolle. (Life with Sylvie Ser.: Bk. 9). (Illus.). 24p. (J). (ps-k). 1997. 12.95 (*0-9655782-8-3*, Tern Bks) Tern Bk Co.

***Sylvie Imagines Bk. 10.** Danielle Ponsolle. (Life with Sylvie Ser.: Bk. 10). (Illus.). 24p. (J). (ps-k). 1997. 12.95 (*0-9655782-9-1*, Tern Bks) Tern Bk Co.

***Sylvie Sees Bk. 8.** Danielle Ponsolle. (Life with Sylvie Ser.: Bk. 8). (Illus.). 24p. (J). (ps-k). 1997. 12.95 (*0-9655782-7-5*, Tern Bks) Tern Bk Co.

***Sylvie's Back Yard Bk. 1.** Danielle Ponsolle. (Life with Sylvie Ser.: Bk. 1). (Illus.). 24p. (J). (ps-k). 1997. 12.95 (*0-9655782-0-8*, Tern Bks) Tern Bk Co.

Symantec C++ Vol. 1: Object Oriented Programming Fundamentals for the MacIntosh. Dan P. Sydow. 1994. pap. 39.95 (*1-55958-633-8*) Prima Pub.

***Symantec Visual Cafe Sourcebook.** Cary Jardin & Pam Dixon. LC 97-3078. 1996. pap. text ed. 39.99 (*0-471-17804-7*) Wiley.

Symbiogenesis: A Macro-Mechanism of Evolution - Progress Towards a Unified Theory of Evolution Based on Studies in Cell Biology. Werner Schwemmler. x, 225p. (C). 1989. lib. bdg. 56.95 (*0-89925-589-2*); lib. bdg. 56.95 (*3-11-012132-8*) De Gruyter.

Symbiosis. Daniela Gioseffi. 26p. 1997. pap. 5.00 (*0-614-07914-4*, Hummingbird Folios) Ladybug Publ.

Symbiosis: Contemplation & Action. Luigi Faccenda. Ed. & Tr. by Immaculata Press Staff. LC 91-71757. (Illus.). 88p. (Orig.). (ITA.). 1992. pap. text ed. 3.65 (*0-9625953-1-4*) Immaculata Pr.

Symbiosis: Popular Culture & Other Fields. Ed. by Ray B. Browne & Marshall W. Fishwick. LC 88-71361. 224p. (C). 1988. 31.95 (*0-87972-439-0*); pap. 15.95 (*0-87972-440-4*) Bowling Green Univ Popular Press.

Symbiosis: Writing & an Academic Culture. Kim Kipling et al. LC 92-28900. 140p. (C). 1993. pap. text ed. 24.00 (*0-86709-313-7*, 0313) Boynton Cook Pubs.

Symbiosis & Separation: Towards a Psychology of Culture. Richard A. Koenigsberg. LC 88-93056. 89p. (Orig.). 1989. pap. 20.00 (*0-915042-20-7*) Lib Soc Sci.

Symbiosis As a Source of Evolutionary Innovation: Speciation & Morphogenesis. Ed. by Lynn Margulis & Rene Fester. 408p. 1991. 45.00 (*0-262-13269-9*) MIT Pr.

Symbiosis in Cell Evolution: Microbial Evolution in the Archean & Proterozoic Eons. 2nd ed. Lynn Margulis. LC 92-14565. (C). 1995. text ed. write for info. (*0-7167-7028-8*); pap. text ed. write for info. (*0-7167-7029-6*) W H Freeman.

Symbiosis In Parent-Offspring Interactions. Howard Moltz. Ed. by Leonard A. Rosenblum. 300p. 1983. 65.00 (*0-306-41410-4*, Plenum Pr) Plenum.

Symbiosis of Human & Artifact, 2vols. Ed. by Y. Anzai et al. (Advances in Human Factors/Ergonomics Ser.: Vol. 20 A-B). 2296p. 1995. 450.75 (*0-444-81795-6*, North Holland) Elsevier.

Symbiosis of Plants & Microbes. D. Werner. (Illus.). 392p. (gr. 13). 1992. text ed. 158.95 (*0-412-36230-9*, A7624) Chapman & Hall.

Symbiosis of Work & Technology. Ed. by Jos Benders et al. LC 94-44626. 1995. pap. write for info. (*0-7484-0317-5*) Taylor & Francis.

Symbiotic Character. Stephen M. Johnson. 1991. 27.95 (*0-393-70115-8*) Norton.

Symbiotic Community: E. W. Mueller's Approach to the Rural Social Crisis. Gilson A. Waldkoenig. LC 96-24603. 182p. 1996. pap. text ed. 24.50 (*0-7618-0440-4*); lib. bdg. 44.50 (*0-7618-0439-0*) U Pr of Amer.

Symbiotic Interactions. A. E. Douglas. (Illus.). 160p. 1994. pap. 35.00 (*0-19-854294-1*) OUP.

Symbiotic Nitrogen Fixation: Proceedings of the 14th North American Conference on Symbiotic Nitrogen Fixation, University of Minnesota, St. Paul Minnesota, U. S. A. July 25-29, 1993. Ed. by Peter H. Graham. 208p. (C). 1994. lib. bdg. 106.00 (*0-7923-2781-0*) Kluwer Ac.

Symbiotic Nitrogen Fixation in Plants. Ed. by P. S. Nutman. LC 75-2732. (International Biological Programme Ser.: No. 7). (Illus.). 652p. 1976. text ed. 155.00 (*0-521-20645-6*) Cambridge U Pr.

Symbiotic Nitrogen Fixation Technology. Elkan. (Books in Soils, Plants & the Environment: Vol. 13). 456p. 1987. 235.00 (*0-8247-7751-4*) Dekker.

***Symbiotic N2 Fixation of Crop Legumes: Achievements & Perspectives.** A. P. Hansen. (Hohenheim Tropical Agricultural Ser.: No. 2). (Illus.). 248p. 1994. pap. 49.00 (*3-8236-1235-2*, Pub. by Backhuys Pubs NE) Balogh.

Symbiotic Phenomenon. Ed. by Joanna Mikolajewska et al. (C). 1988. lib. bdg. 175.00 (*90-277-2723-6*) Kluwer Ac.

Symbol - Letter Tracking. 10.00 (*0-87879-732-7*, Ann Arbor Div); 10.00 (*0-87879-733-5*, Ann Arbor Div); 10. 00 (*0-87879-734-3*, Ann Arbor Div) Acad Therapy.

Symbol & Archetype: A Study in the Meaning of Existance. Martin Lings. viii, 141p. 1991. 26.95 (*1-870196-04-X*, Pub. by Islamic Texts UK) Intl Spec Bk.

Symbol & Archetype: A Study in the Meaning of Existance, Vol. 1. Martin Lings. 138p. 1991. pap. 14.95 (*1-870196-05-8*, Pub. by Islamic Texts UK) Intl Spec Bk.

***Symbol & Archetype: A Study of the Meaning of Existence.** Martin Lings. 142p. 1996. pap. 14.95 (*0-614-21243-X*, 1206) Kazi Pubns.

Symbol & Empowerment: Paul Tillich's Post-Theistic System. Richard Grigg. LC 85-7214. xvi, 148p. 1985. text ed. 14.50 (*0-86554-163-9*, MUP H153) Mercer Univ Pr.

Symbol & Idea in Henry Adams. Melvin E. Lyon. LC 67-20597. 338p. reprint ed. pap. 96.40 (*0-7837-6019-1*, 2045831) Bks Demand.

Symbol & Image in Celtic Religious Art. Miranda Green. 336p. 1989. 45.00 (*0-415-03419-1*, A3719) Routledge.

Symbol & Image in Celtic Religious Art. Miranda Green. (Illus.). 296p. (C). 1992. pap. 17.95 (*0-415-08076-2*, A9589) Routledge.

Symbol & Magic in Egyptian Art. Richard H. Wilkinson. LC 93-60424. (Illus.). 224p. 1994. 24.95 (*0-500-23663-1*) Thames Hudson.

Symbol & Meaning Beyond the Closed Community: Essays in Mesoamerican Ideas. Gary H. Gossen. LC 86-82620. (Studies on Culture & Society: Vol. 1). (Illus.). 278p. (Orig.). (C). 1987. pap. text ed. 25.00 (*0-942041-10-0*) Univ Albany IFMS.

Symbol & Myth: Humbert De Superville's Essay on Absolute Signs in Art. Barbara Stafford. LC 76-19842. 206p. 1979. 65.00 (*0-87413-120-0*) U Delaware Pr.

Symbol & Myth in Ancient Poetry. Herbert A. Musurillo. LC 77-2395. 220p. 1977. reprint ed. text ed. 55.00 (*0-8371-9554-3*, MUSM, Greenwood Pr) Greenwood.

Symbol & Neurosis: Selected Papers of Lawrence S. Kubie. Ed. by Herbert J. Schlesinger & Eugene B. Brody. LC 77-92177. (Psychological Issues Monograph: No. 44, Vol. 11, No. 4). 280p. 1978. 42.50 (*0-8236-6291-8*); pap. 37.50 (*0-8236-6290-X*) Intl Univs Pr.

Symbol & Privilege: The Ritual Context of British Royalty. Ilse Hayden. LC 86-25093. 214p. 1987. 17.95 (*0-8165-0906-9*) U of Ariz Pr.

Symbol & Sacrament: A Contemporary Sacramental Theology. rev. ed. Michael G. Lawler. 500p. (C). 1994. reprint ed. pap. 19.95 (*1-881871-10-X*) Creighton U Pr.

Symbol & Sacrament: A Contemporary Sacramental Theology. 2nd rev. ed. Michael G. Lawler. 500p. (C). 1994. reprint ed. 29.95 (*1-881871-11-8*) Creighton U Pr.

Symbol & Sacrament: A Sacramental Reinterpretation of Christian Existence. Louis-Marie Chauvet. 592p. (Orig.). 1994. 39.95 (*0-8146-6124-6*, Pueblo Bks) Liturgical Pr.

Symbol & Satire in the French Revolution: With 171 Illustrations. Ernest F. Henderson. 1977. lib. bdg. 69.95 (*0-8490-2724-1*) Gordon Pr.

Symbol & Show: Pan-American Exposition of 1901. Austin Fox. (Illus.). 128p. 1986. pap. 13.95 (*0-681-64104-5*) Meyer Enter.

Symbol & Substance in Japanese Lacquer: Lacquer Boxes from the Collection of Elaine Ehrenkranz. Barbara T. Okada. (Illus.). 192p. 1995. 60.00 (*0-8348-0316-X*) Weatherhill.

Symbol & the Symbolic: Ancient Egypt, Science, & the Evolution of Consciousness. R. A. Schwaller De Lubicz. Tr. by Robert Lawlor & Deborah Lawlor from FRE. LC 81-13375. (Illus.). 100p. 1981. reprint ed. pap. 8.95 (*0-89281-022-X*) Inner Tradit.

Symbol Art: Thirteen Squares, Circles & Triangles from Around the World. Leonard E. Fisher. LC 85-42805. (Illus.). 64p. (J). (gr. 4-6). 1986. 16.95 (*0-02-735270-6*, Four Winds Pr) S&S Childrens.

***Symbol Articulation.** Lorraine Arcuri. (Illus.). 406p. 1996. spiral bd. 34.00 (*1-884135-28-5*) Mayer-Johnson.

Symbol Communication Technique (SCT) A Self-Motivating Method of Learning to Write. rev. ed. Alfred W. Munzert. Ed. by Karen K. Elskamp. LC 70-134719. 88p. 1987. pap. 8.95 (*0-917292-04-9*) H-U Public.

Symbol Discrimination & Sequencing. W. Edwards & S. Edwards. (Ann Arbor Tracking Program Ser.). (J). (gr. 2). 1976. student ed. 12.00 (*0-87879-730-0*, Ann Arbor Div); student ed. 12.00 (*0-87879-731-9*, Ann Arbor Div) Acad Therapy.

Symbol Discrimination Series: Books 1, 2. Ann Arbor Publishers Editorial Staff. (Illus.). 16p. (gr. k-1). 1974. write for info. (*0-318-56865-9*, Ann Arbor Div) Acad Therapy.

Symbol Discrimination Series: Books 1, 2, Bk. 1, Levels 1-3. Ann Arbor Publishers Editorial Staff. (Symbol Discrimination Ser.). (Illus.). 16p. (gr. k-1). 1974. Book 1, Levels 1, 2, 3. 7.00 (*0-87879-724-6*, Ann Arbor Div) Acad Therapy.

Symbol Discrimination Series: Books 1, 2, Bk. 2, Levels 4-6. Ann Arbor Publishers Editorial Staff. (Symbol Discrimination Ser.). (Illus.). 16p. (gr. k-1). 1974. Book 2, Levels 4, 5, 6. 7.00 (*0-87879-725-4*, Ann Arbor Div) Acad Therapy.

Symbol Formation. Ed. by Heinz Werner & Bernard Kaplan. 530p. (C). 1984. pap. text ed. 39.95 (*0-89859-370-0*) L Erlbaum Assocs.

Symbol, Myth, & Culture: Essays & Lectures of Ernst Cassirer, 1935-1945. Ernst Cassirer. Ed. by Donald P. Verene. LC 78-9887. 316p. reprint ed. pap. 90.10 (*0-8357-3742-X*, 2036468) Bks Demand.

Symbol, Myth, & Rhetoric: The Politics of Culture in an Armenian-American Population. Jenny Phillips. LC 87-45788. (Immigrant Communities & Ethnic Minorities in the U. S. & Canada Ser.: No. 23). 1989. 47.50 (*0-404-19433-8*) AMS Pr.

Symbol of Man. G. Wilson Knight. 192p. 1984. 40.00 (*0-317-43712-7*, Pub. by Regency Press UK) St Mut.

Symbol of the Soul from Holderlin to Yeats: A Study in Metonymy. Suzanne Nalbantian. LC 76-25550. 159p. reprint ed. pap. 45.40 (*0-8357-4574-0*, 2037483) Bks Demand.

Symbol of Wilderness: Echo Park & the American Conservation Movement. Mark W. Harvey. LC 93-46955. 329p. 1994. 18.95 (*0-8263-1542-9*) U of NM Pr.

Symbol Signs. 2nd ed. American Institute of Graphic Arts Staff. (Illus.). 248p. 1994. pap. 29.95 (*0-8230-6325-9*, Watson-Guptill Bks) Watsn-Guptill.

Symbol, Status, & Personality. Samuel I. Hayakawa. LC 63-1772. 188p. 1966. pap. 5.95 (*0-15-687611-6*, Harvest Bks) HarBrace.

Symbol Stones of Scotland. Anthony Jackson. 269p. (C). 1987. 60.00 (*0-907618-10-3*, Pub. by Orkney Pr UK); pap. 45.00 (*0-907618-16-2*, Pub. by Orkney Pr UK) St Mut.

Symbol, Story, & Ceremony: Using Metaphor in Individual & Family Therapy. Gene Combs & Jill Freedman. (C). 1990. 29.95 (*0-393-70092-5*) Norton.

Symbol, Substance, Science - The Societal Issues of Food Biotechnology: Conference Proceedings, June 28 & 29, 1993. Pref. by W. Steven Burke & Alvin L. Young. xi, 146p. (Orig.). 1993. pap. text ed. 20.00 (*0-945597-24-X*) NC Biotech Ctr.

Symbol, Sword, & Shield: Defending Washington During the Civil War. Benjamin F. Cooling, III. LC 91-26949. (Illus.). 319p. (C). 1991. reprint ed. 27.95 (*0-942597-24-9*) White Mane Pub.

Symbol Theory. Norbert Elias. (Theory, Culture & Society Ser.: Vol. 9). 160p. 1991. 55.00 (*0-8039-8418-9*); pap. 21.95 (*0-8039-8419-7*) Sage.

Symbola, Bd. II: Kleine Schriften Zur Literatur- und Kulturgeschichte der Antike. Hildebrecht Hommel. 492p. 1988. write for info. (*0-318-70762-4*) G Olms Pubs.

Symbolae Ad Mycologiam Fennicam. Peter A. Karsten. 1966. reprint ed. 128.00 (*3-7682-0352-2*) Lubrecht & Cramer.

Symbolae Berolinenses fur Dieter Harlfinger. Ed. by Friederike Berger et al. vi, 457p. (GER.). 1993. pap. 108.00 (*90-256-1047-1*, Pub. by A M Hakkert NE) Benjamins North Am.

Symbolae Biblicae et Mesopotamicae: Francisco Mario Theodoro De Liagre Bohl Dedicatae. Ed. by M. A. Beek et al. (Illus.). viii, 416p. 1973. pap. text ed. 175.00 (*0-614-03987-8*, Pub. by Netherlands Inst NE) Eisenbrauns.

Symbolae Mycologicae & Supplements. L. Fuckel. (Illus.). 1966. reprint ed. 160.00 (*3-7682-0358-1*) Lubrecht & Cramer.

Symbolae Osloenses, Vol. LXV. Ed. by Egil Kraggerud et al. (Scandinavian University Press Publication). 177p. 1990. 52.00 (*82-00-02994-8*) Scandnvan Univ Pr.

Symbolae Osloenses, Vol. LXVI. Ed. by Egil Kraggerud. (Scandinavian University Press Publication). 150p. 1991. 52.00 (*82-00-21244-0*, 12305) Scandnvan Univ Pr.

Symbolae Osloenses, Vol. LXVII. Ed. by Egil Kraggerud. (Scandinavian University Press Publication). 150p. 1992. 52.00 (*82-00-21511-3*) Scandnvan Univ Pr.

Symbolae Osloenses, Vol. LXVIII. Ed. by Egil Kraggerud. (Scandinavian University Press Publication). 151p. 1993. 52.00 (*82-00-21734-5*) Scandnvan Univ Pr.

Symbolae Osloenses, Vol. LXIX. Ed. by Egil Kraggerud. 150p. 1995. 52.00 (*82-00-21967-4*) Scandnvan Univ Pr.

Symbolaeographia Which Termed the Art, Description of Instruments, Covenants, Contracts, Etc. William West. LC 74-28892. (English Experience Ser.: No. 768). 1975. reprint ed. 60.00 (*90-221-0768-X*) Walter J Johnson.

Symbolic Analysis Cross Culturally: The Rorschach Test. George A. De Vos & L. Bryce Boyer. (C). 1989. 58.00 (*0-520-06086-5*) U CA Pr.

Symbolic Analysis for Automated Design of Analog Integrated Circuits. Georges G. Gielen & Willy M. Sansen. (C). 1991. lib. bdg. 92.00 (*0-7923-9161-6*) Kluwer Ac.

Symbolic Analysis for Parallelizing Compilers. Mohammad R. Haghighat. 168p. (C). 1995. lib. bdg. 90.00 (*0-7923-9623-5*) Kluwer Ac.

***Symbolic Analysis in Analog Integrated Circuit Design.** Heinrich Floberg. LC 97-22121. (Analog Circuits, Signal Processing & Computer Science Ser.: Vol. 413). 1997. write for info. (*0-7923-9969-2*) Kluwer Ac.

Symbolic Analysis of Analog Circuits: Techniques & Applications. Ed. by Lawrence P. Huelsman & Georges G. Gielen. LC 92-40211. (International Series in Engineering & Computer Science, VLSI, Computer Architecture, & Digital Screen Processing). 88p. (C). 1993. lib. bdg. 105.00 (*0-7923-9324-4*) Kluwer Ac.

***Symbolic Analysis Techniques: Applications to Analog Design Automation.** Ed. by Francisco V. Fernandez et al. LC 97-18498. 480p. 1997. 110.00 (*0-7803-1075-6*, PC4283) Inst Electrical.

Symbolic & Algebraic Computation. 1990. pap. 40.95 (*0-201-54892-5*) Addison-Wesley.

Symbolic & Algebraic Computation. Ed. by P. Gianni. (Lecture Notes in Computer Science Ser.: Vol. 358). xi, 545p. 1989. pap. 58.00 (*0-387-51084-2*) Spr-Verlag.

Symbolic & Algebraic Computation by Computers: Proceedings of the International Symposium, 2nd, Institute of Physical & Chemical Research (RIKEN), Saitama, Japan, August 21-22, 1984. Ed. by N. Inada & T. Soma. (Series in Computer Science: Vol. 2). 256p. 1985. text ed. 61.00 (*9971-5-0021-3*) World Scientific Pub.

Symbolic & Connectionist Approach to Legal Information Retrieval. Daniel E. Rose. 328p. 1994. text ed. 59.95 (*0-8058-1388-8*) L Erlbaum Assocs.

Symbolic & Decorative Art of the Osage People. Louis F. Burns. Tr. by Dhegiha Sioux. (Illus.). 124p. (Orig.). 1995. pap. 34.50 (*0-942574-10-9*) Ciga Pr.

Symbolic & Mythological Animals. J. C. Cooper. 1992. pap. 17.00 (*1-85538-118-4*) Thorsons SF.

Symbolic & Numerical Computation for Artificial Intelligence. Ed. by Bruce Donald et al. (Computational Mathematics & Applications Ser.). (Illus.). 369p. 1992. text ed. 89.00 (*0-12-220535-9*) Acad Pr.

Symbolic & Quantitative Approaches to Reasoning & Uncertainty: European Conference ECSQARU '93, Granada, Spain, November 8-10, 1990: Proceedings. Ed. by Michael Clarke et al. LC 93-34942. (Lecture Notes in Computer Science Ser.: Vol. 747). 1993. 55.95 (*0-387-57395-X*) Spr-Verlag.

Symbolic & Quantitative Approaches to Uncertainty: European Conference ECSQAU Marseille, France, October 15-17, 1991 Proceedings. Ed. by Robert Kruse et al. (Lecture Notes in Computer Science Ser.: Vol. 548). xi, 362p. 1991. 47.00 (*0-387-54659-6*) Spr-Verlag.

Symbolic Art of Gogol: Essays on His Short Fiction. James B. Woodward. 131p. 1982. 18.95 (*0-89357-093-1*) Slavica.

Symbolic Communication: Signifying Calls & Police Response. Peter K. Manning. (Organization Studies: No. 9). 290p. 1989. 40.00 (*0-262-13234-6*) MIT Pr.

Symbolic Communities: The Persistence & Change of Chicago's Local Communities. Albert Hunter. LC 74-75612. (Studies of Urban Society). xviii, 254p. (C). 1982. reprint ed. pap. text ed. 9.95 (*0-226-36081-4*) U Ch Pr.

Symbolic Computation: Applications to Scientific Computing. Robert Grossman. LC 89-19701. (Frontiers in Applied Mathematics Ser.: No. 5). 186p. 1989. pap. 28.50 (*0-89871-239-4*) Soc Indus-Appl Math.

Symbolic Computation: Computers in Pure & Applied Mathematics. Ilan Vardi. 1994. 47.95 incl. disk (*0-387-94147-9*) Spr-Verlag.

Symbolic Computation in Undergraduate Mathematics. Ed. by Zaven A. Karian. LC 92-64063. (MAA Notes Ser.). 200p. 1992. pap. 34.95 (*0-88385-082-6*, NTE-24) Math Assn.

Symbolic Computing with LISP & Prolog. Robert A. Mueller & Rex L. Page. LC 88-23414. 469p. 1988. Net. pap. text ed. 36.00 (*0-471-60771-1*) Wiley.

Symbolic Consciousness: A Commentary on Love's Body. William C. Shepherd. LC 76-26582. (American Academy of Religion. Aids for the Study of Religion Ser.: No. 4). 88p. reprint ed. pap. 25.10 (*0-7837-5406-X*, 2045170) Bks Demand.

***Symbolic Construction of Community.** Anthony P. Cohen. (Key Ideas Ser.). 150p. (C). 1985. pap. text ed. 12.95 (*0-415-04616-5*) Routledge.

Symbolic Construction of Community. Anthony P. Cohen. (Key Ideas Ser.). 150p. 1985. pap. 8.95 (*0-85312-855-3*, 9583, Pub. by Tavistock-E Horwood UK) Routledge Chapman & Hall.

Symbolic Crusade: Status Politics & the American Temperance Movement. 2nd ed. Joseph R. Gusfield. LC 85-28858. 240p. 1986. pap. text ed. 11.95 (*0-252-01312-3*) U of Ill Pr.

Symbolic Crusade: Status Politics & the American Temperance Movement. Joseph R. Gusfield. LC 80-13342. viii, 198p. 1980. reprint ed. text ed. 52.50 (*0-313-22423-4*, GUSC, Greenwood Pr) Greenwood.

Symbolic Defense: The Cultural Significance of the Strategic Defense Initiative. Edward T. Linenthal. LC 88-32111. (Illus.). 176p. 1989. text ed. 21.95 (*0-252-01619-X*) U of Ill Pr.

Symbolic Defense: The Cultural Significance of the Strategic Defense Initiative. fac. ed. Edward T. Linenthal. LC 88-32111. (Illus.). 160p. 1989. reprint ed. pap. 45.60 (*0-7837-8076-1*, 2047829) Bks Demand.

Symbolic Directions in Modern Astrology. Carter. 1984. pap. 9.95 (*0-7229-5145-0*) Theos Pub Hse.

Symbolic Directions in Modern Astrology. Charles E. Carter. 88p. 1974. reprint ed. spiral bd. 7.00 (*0-7873-0159-0*) Hlth Research.

Symbolic Dramatic Play-Literacy Connection. Joyce Wilkinson. 18.00 (*0-536-58235-1*) Ginn Pr.

Symbolic Dynamics & Hyperbolic Groups. Michel Coornaert & Athanase Papadopoulos. LC 93-9394. (Lecture Notes in Mathematics Ser.: Vol. 1539). 1993. Acid-free paper. 30.95 (*0-387-56499-3*) Spr-Verlag.

Symbolic Dynamics & Its Applications: (Proceedings of a Conference in Honor of Roy L. Adler Held July 28 to August 2, 1991) Ed. by Peter Walters. LC 92-20203. (Contemporary Mathematics Ser.: Vol. 135). 452p. 1992. 55.00 (*0-8218-5146-2*, CONM/135) Am Math.

Symbolic Dynamics of Trapezoidal Maps. J. D. Louck & N. Metropolis. (Mathematics & Its Applications Main Ser.). 1986. lib. bdg. 141.00 (*90-277-2197-1*) Kluwer Ac.

Symbolic Earth: Discourse & Our Creation of the Environment. Ed. by James G. Cantrill & Christine L. Oravec. LC 96-5956. 486p. 1996. pap. 19.95 (*0-8131-0883-7*); text ed. 45.00 (*0-8131-1973-1*) U Pr of Ky.

Symbolic Economies: After Marx & Freud. Jean-Joseph Goux. Tr. by Jennifer C. Gage from FRE. LC 89-17469. (Illus.). 280p. 1990. 47.50 (*0-8014-2042-3*); pap. 16.95 (*0-8014-9612-8*) Cornell U Pr.

Symbolic Essays. Manly P. Hall. pap. 5.95 (*0-89314-822-9*) Philos Res.

Symbolic Exchange & Death. Jean Baudrillard. Tr. by Ian Grant. (Theory, Culture & Society Ser.: Vol. 25). 288p. (C). 1993. text ed. 59.95 (*0-8039-8398-0*); pap. text ed. 22.95 (*0-8039-8399-9*) Sage.

Symbolic Execution. D. Ince & D. Coward. (ITCP-UK Computer Science Ser.). 192p. 1994. pap. 49.95 (*0-412-58340-2*) Chapman & Hall.

Symbolic Experience: A Study of Poems by Pedro Salinas. Rupert C. Allen. LC 81-10307. 190p. 1982. reprint ed. pap. 54.20 (*0-608-01659-4*, 2062314) Bks Demand.

Symbolic Function: Psychoanalysis & the Philosophy of Language. Gemma Corradi-Fiumara. 1992. text ed. 55. 95 (*0-631-17317-X*) Blackwell Pubs.

Symbolic Function: Psychoanalysis & the Philosophy of Language. Gemma Corradi-Fiumara. 1992. pap. text ed. 24.95 (*0-631-18372-8*) Blackwell Pubs.

Symbolic Functioning in Childhood. Ed. by Nancy R. Smith & Margery B. Franklin. 256p. 1979. 49.95 (*0-89859-491-X*) L Erlbaum Assocs.

Symbolic Images in Art As Therapy. R. M. Simon. LC 95-39590. 224p. (C). 1997. text ed. 69.95 (*0-415-12227-9*) Routledge.

***Symbolic Images in Art as Therapy.** Rita Simon. 224p. (C). 1997. pap. 18.95 (*0-415-12228-7*) Routledge.

Symbolic Imagination: Coleridge & the Romantic Tradition. J. Robert Barth. LC 76-44333. (Princeton Essays in Literature Ser.). 173p. reprint ed. pap. 49.40 (*0-8357-3310-6*, 2039533) Bks Demand.

Symbolic Immortality: The Tlingit Potlatch of the Nineteenth Century. Sergei Kan. LC 88-38200. (Series in Ethnographic Inquiry). 384p. 1989. text ed. 35.00 (*0-87474-686-8*) Smithsonian.

Symbolic Immortality: The Tlingit Potlatch of the Nineteenth Century. Sergei Kan. LC 88-38200. (Series in Ethnographic Inquiry). (Illus.). 384p. (C). 1993. reprint ed. pap. text ed. 15.95 (*1-56098-309-4*) Smithsonian.

Symbolic Integration: Transcendental Functions, Vol. 1. Manuel Bronstein. LC 96-41956. 256p. 1997. 49.00 (*3-540-60521-5*) Spr-Verlag.

Symbolic Interaction: An Introduction to Social Psychology. Ed. by Nancy J. Herman & Larry T. Reynolds. LC 93-79473. 501p. (Orig.). 1994. text ed. 42.95 (*1-882289-22-6*); pap. text ed. 28.95 (*1-882289-21-8*) Gen Hall.

Symbolic Interaction & Cultural Studies. Ed. by Howard S. Becker & Michal M. McCall. LC 89-48060. 294p. 1990. pap. text ed. 17.95 (*0-226-04118-2*) U Ch Pr.

Symbolic Interaction & Ethnographic Research: Intersubjectivity & the Study of Human Lived Experience. Robert Prus. LC 94-49571. 301p. 1995. text ed. 59.50 (*0-7914-2701-3*); pap. text ed. 19.95 (*0-7914-2702-1*) State U NY Pr.

***Symbolic Interactionism.** 6th ed. Charon. 1997. pap. 24.00 (*0-13-671694-6*) P-H.

Symbolic Interactionism: An Introduction, An Interpretation, An Intergration. 5th ed. Joel M. Charon. LC 94-31698. 240p. 1994. pap. text ed. 28.00 (*0-13-122953-2*) P-H.

Symbolic Interactionism: Genesis, Varieties & Critcisms. Bernard N. Meltzer et al. (Monographs in Social Theory). 1977. reprint ed. pap. 13.95 (*0-7100-8056-5*, RKP) Routledge.

Symbolic Interactionism: Perspective & Method. Herbert Blumer. 1986. pap. 14.95 (*0-520-05676-0*) U CA Pr.

Symbolic Interactionism & Cultural Studies: The Politics of Interpretation. Norman K. Denzin. Ed. by Charles Lemert. (Twentieth-Century Social Theory Ser.). 224p. 1992. text ed. 56.95 (*1-55786-059-9*); pap. text ed. 23.95 (*1-55786-291-5*) Blackwell Pubs.

Symbolic Interactionism As Affect Control. Neil J. MacKinnon. LC 93-38563. (SUNY Series in the Sociology of Emotions). 245p. 1994. pap. text ed. 21.95 (*0-7914-2042-6*) State U NY Pr.

Symbolic Interactionism As Affect Control. Neil J. MacKinnon. LC 93-38563. (SUNY Series in the Sociology of Emotions). 245p. 1994. text ed. 64.50 (*0-7914-2041-8*) State U NY Pr.

Symbolic Language of Ancient Art & Mythology. Richard P. Knight. (Illus.). 460p. 1993. reprint ed. pap. 49.95 (*1-56459-410-6*) Kessinger Pub.

Symbolic Language of Geometrical Figures. Omraam M. Aivanhov. (Izvor Collection: Vol. 218). 152p. (Orig.). 1985. pap. 6.95 (*2-85566-366-0*, Pub. by Prosveta FR) Prosveta USA.

Symbolic Leaders: Public Dramas & Public Men. Orrin E. Klapp. LC 64-23369. 1964. 37.50 (*0-202-30024-2*); pap. 4.95 (*0-8290-0688-5*) Irvington.

Symbolic Logic. Smith. (Brooks-Cole One-Unit Series in Precalculus Mathematics). (C). 1991. pap. 17.95 (*0-534-14931-6*) Brooks-Cole.

Symbolic Logic. 2nd ed. John Venn. LC 79-119161. 1971. lib. bdg. 29.50 (*0-8284-0251-5*) Chelsea Pub.

Symbolic Logic. 5th ed. Irving M. Copi. 416p. (C). 1979. text ed. 42.00 (*0-02-324980-3*, Macmillan Coll) P-H.

Symbolic Logic: A Conceptual Approach. 2nd ed. Douglass D. McFerran. 68p. 1993. per. 21.99 (*0-8403-8354-1*) Kendall-Hunt.

Symbolic Logic: A First Course. 2nd ed. Hardegree. 1994. pap. text ed. write for info. (*0-07-026268-3*) McGraw.

Symbolic Logic & Mechanical Theorem Proving. Chin-Liang Chang & Richard C. Lee. (Computer Science & Applied Mathematics Ser.). 1973. text ed. 45.00 (*0-12-170350-9*) Acad Pr.

Symbolic Logic & the Game of Logic. Lewis Carroll. pap. 6.95 (*0-486-20492-8*) Dover.

Symbolic Message of Illness. Calin Pop. Ed. by Rodney Charles & Izabelle Hubert. (Illus.). 230p. 1997. 21.95 (*1-887472-16-9*) Sunstar Pubng.

Symbolic Method of Coleridge, Baudelaire & Yeats. Anca Vlasopolos. LC 82-20079. 219p. reprint ed. pap. 62.50 (*0-318-39788-9*, 2033190) Bks Demand.

Symbolic Model Checking. Kenneth L. McMillan. LC 93-24859. 216p. (C). 1993. lib. bdg. 94.00 (*0-7923-9380-5*) Kluwer Ac.

Symbolic Mythology & Translation of a Lost & Forgotten Language (1917) John M. Woolsey. 224p. 1993. reprint ed. pap. 17.95 (*1-56459-416-5*) Kessinger Pub.

Symbolic Network Analysis. P. M. Lin. (Studies in Electrical & Electronic Engineering: No. 41). 310p. 1991. 170.00 (*0-444-87389-9*) Elsevier.

Symbolic-Numeric Analysis of Dynamic Systems in Engineering. Kreuzer. 1995. write for info. (*0-8493-7372-7*) CRC Pr.

Symbolic-Numeric Data Analysis & Learning. Ed. by E. Diday & Y. Lechevallier. 612p. (C). 1991. text ed. 195.00 (*1-56072-042-5*) Nova Sci Pubs.

Symbolic Order: A Contemporary Reader on the Arts in Education. Ed. by Peter Abbs. 370p. 1989. 75.00 (*1-85000-593-1*, Falmer Pr); pap. 35.00 (*1-85000-594-X*, Falmer Pr) Taylor & Francis.

Symbolic Persons in the Masques of Ben Jonson. Allan H. Gilbert. LC 79-85910. (BCL Ser.: I). reprint ed. 34.50 (*0-404-02759-8*) AMS Pr.

Symbolic Projection for Image Information Retrieval & Spatial Reasoning. Ed. by S. K. Chang et al. (Signal Processing & Its Applications Ser.). (Illus.). 336p. 1996. boxed 59.95 (*0-12-168030-4*) Acad Pr.

Symbolic Prophecy of the Great Pyramid. Lewis H. Spencer. LC 37-3808. (Illus.). 192p. 1936. pap. 12.95 (*0-912057-55-6*, 502070) RO AMORC.

Symbolic Quantitative Approaches to Reasoning & Uncertainty: European Conference ECSQARU '95, Fribourg, Switzerland, July 1995: Proceedings. Ed. by Christine Froidevaux & Jurg Kohlas. 430p. 1995. 68.00 (*3-540-60112-0*) Spr-Verlag.

Symbolic Quest: Basic Concepts of Analytical Psychology. Edward C. Whitmont. 352p. 1991. pap. 16.95 (*0-691-02454-5*) Princeton U Pr.

Symbolic Recipes: Scientific Computing with Maple. R. M. Corless. 1994. 35.00 (*0-387-94210-6*) Spr-Verlag.

Symbolic Regression Psychology. Paul D. Fairweather & Donovan Johnson. 231p. (C). 1982. text ed. 19.50 (*0-8290-0420-3*) Irvington.

Symbolic Self Completion. R. A. Wicklund & P. M. Gollwitzer. 256p. (C). 1982. text ed. 49.95 (*0-89859-213-5*) L Erlbaum Assocs.

Symbolic Software for Interactive Descriptions of Dynamic Systems. G. Paul Wilhelmij. 1991. pap. 29.95 (*1-55860-194-5*) Morgan Kaufmann.

Symbolic Space: French Enlightenment Architecture & Its Legacy. Richard A. Etlin. LC 93-50194. 262p. 1994. 40.00 (*0-226-22084-2*) U Ch Pr.

Symbolic Space: French Enlightenment Architecture & Its Legacy. Richard A. Etlin. xxvi, 236p. 1996. pap. text ed. 19.95 (*0-226-22085-0*) U Ch Pr.

Symbolic Species: Coevolution of Language & the Brain. Terrance Deacon. LC 96-31115. (Illus.). 352p. 1997. 29.95 (*0-393-03838-6*) Norton.

Symbolic State Politics: Education Funding in Ohio, 1970-1980. Linda L. Bennett. LC 83-48760. (American University Studies: Political Science: Ser. X, Vol. 1). 164p. (C). 1983. pap. text ed. 17.35 (*0-8204-0052-1*) P Lang Pubng.

Symbolic Structures: The Role of Composition in Signaling Meaning in Italian Medieval Art. Michael Grillo. LC 93-34841. (American University Studies XX: Vol. 20). 432p. (C). 1997. text ed. 59.95 (*0-8204-2268-1*) P Lang Pubng.

Symbolic Teachings: or Masonry & Its Message. Thomas M. Stewart. 249p. 1992. reprint ed. pap. 35.00 (*0-922802-76-9*) Kessinger Pub.

Symbolic Theories in Applied Communication Research: Bormann, Burke & Fisher. John F. Cragan & Donald C. Shields. Ed. by Gary L. Kreps. LC 94-49142. (Speech Communication Association Applied Communication Ser.). 368p. 1995. text ed. 72.50 (*1-881303-77-2*) Hampton Pr NJ.

Symbolic Theories in Applied Communication Research: Bormann, Burke & Fisher. Donald C. Shields. LC 94-49142. (Speech Communication Association Applied Communication Ser.). 368p. 1995. pap. text ed. 28.50 (*1-881303-78-0*) Hampton Pr NJ.

Symbolic Uses of Politics. With a New Afterword. Murray Edelman. LC 84-16195. 232p. 1985. pap. text ed. 10.95 (*0-252-01202-X*) U of Ill Pr.

Symbolic Values of Foreign Language Use: From the Japanese Case to a General Sociolinguistic Perspective. Herald Haarmann. (Contributions to the Sociology of Language Ser.: No. 51). xiv, 291p. (C). 1989. lib. bdg. 103.10 (*0-89925-485-3*) Mouton.

Symbolic Vision in Biblical Tradition. Susan Niditch. LC 83-8643. (Harvard Semitic Monographs). 270p. (C). 1983. 17.00 (*0-89130-627-7*, 04 00 30) Scholars Pr GA.

***Symbolic Visual Learning.** Ed. by Katsuchi Ikeuchi & Manuela Velosa. (Illus.). 384p. 1997. 75.00 (*0-19-509870-6*) OUP.

Symbolic World of Federico Garcia Lorca. Rupert C. Allen. LC 72-80890. 1972. 20.00 (*0-8263-0245-9*) Lib Soc Sci.

***Symbolic Worlds: Art, Science, Language, Ritual.** Israel Scheffler. 224p. (C). 1996. text ed. 49.95 (*0-521-56425-5*) Cambridge U Pr.

Symbolical Language of Ancient Art & Mythology. Richard P. Knight. 1976. lib. bdg. 59.95 (*0-8490-2725-X*) Gordon Pr.

Symbolical Masonry: An Interpretation of the Three Degrees. H. L. Haywood. 380p. 1996. pap. 24.95 (*1-56459-592-7*) Kessinger Pub.

Symbolically Speaking. D. Douglas Schneider. Ed. by Michael Von Bruck. (Illus.). 85p. (J). (ps up). 1987. pap. 5.95 (*0-939169-01-0*) Inst Glbl Educ.

Symbolik und Mythologie der Alten Volker, 4 vols. in 2. Georg F. Creuzer. (Volkskundliche Quellen, Reihe V Ser.). xvi, 3022p. (GER.). 1990. reprint ed. 800.00 (*3-487-04371-8*) G Olms Pubs.

Symbolik und Mythologie der Alten Volker Besonders der Griechen, 6 Vols. Georg F. Creuzer. Ed. by Kees W. Bolle. LC 77-79119. (Mythology Ser.). (Illus.). (GER.). 1978. reprint ed. lib. bdg. 357.95 (*0-405-10531-2*) Ayer.

Symbolism. Charles Chadwick. (Critical Idiom Ser.). 1971. pap. 8.95 (*0-416-60910-4*, 2129) Routledge Chapman & Hall.

Symbolism. Michael Gibson. 1995. 39.99 (*3-8228-9324-2*) Taschen Amer.

***Symbolism.** Michael Gibson. (Big Art Ser.). 1997. pap. text ed. 19.99 (*3-8228-8570-3*) Taschen Amer.

Symbolism. Robert Goldwater. LC 77-82780. (Illus.). 1979. pap. text ed. 25.00 (*0-06-430095-1*, IN-95, Icon Edns) HarpC.

***Symbolism.** Milton A. Pottenger. LC 94-78131. (Astro-Cards Reprints Ser.). (Illus.). 312p. 1996. reprint ed. pap. text ed. 25.00 (*1-885500-15-7*, AR1) Astro-Cards.

Symbolism: A Bibliography of Symbolism As an International & Multi-Disciplinary Movement. Compiled by David L. Anderson. LC 74-17460. 160p. (C). 1975. text ed. 44.00 (*0-8147-0555-3*) NYU Pr.

Symbolism: A Comprehensive Dictionary. Compiled by Steven Olderr. LC 85-42833. 159p. 1986. lib. bdg. 28.50 (*0-89950-187-7*) McFarland & Co.

Symbolism: A Treatise on the Soul of Things; How the Natural World Is but a Symbol of the Real World; the Modern Church, with Its Spire & Cross, & the Bible Account of Noah's Ark Symbols of the Phallic Religion. Milton A. Pottenger. (Illus.). 312p. pap. 24.95 (*1-56459-464-5*) Kessinger Pub.

***Symbolism: Exposition of the Doctorinal Differences Between Catholics & Protestants As Evidenced by Their Symbolical Writings.** Johann A. Mohler. LC 96-51962. 552p. 1997. pap. 29.95 (*0-8245-1665-6*) Crossroad NY.

Symbolism: Its Meaning & Effect. Alfred N. Whitehead. LC 58-10916. viii, 88p. 1985. 20.00 (*0-8232-1137-1*); pap. 12.50 (*0-8232-1138-X*) Fordham.

Symbolism: The Manichean Vision: A Study in the Art of James, Conrad, Woolf & Stevens. Daniel J. Schneider. LC 74-12841. 247p. reprint ed. pap. 70.40 (*0-8357-2946-X*, 2039202) Bks Demand.

Symbolism & After: Essays on Russian Poetry in Honour of Georgette Donchin. A. McMillin. 245p. 1992. 65.95 (*1-85399-297-6*, Pub. by Brstl Class Pr UK) Focus Pub-R Pullins.

Symbolism & Art Nouveau. A. Mackintosh. LC 77-76764. (Modern Movements in Art Ser.). 1978. reprint ed. pap. 3.50 (*0-8120-0882-0*) Barron.

Symbolism & Classicism in Modern Literature. David Rubio. 1972. 59.95 (*0-8490-1167-1*) Gordon Pr.

Symbolism & Growth: The Religious Thought of Horace Bushnell. David L. Smith. Ed. by Wendell S. Dietrich. LC 80-14600. (American Academy of Religion Academy Ser.). 190p. (C). 1981. pap. 15.95 (*0-89130-410-X*, 01 01 36) Scholars Pr GA.

Symbolism & Interpretation. Tzvetan Todorov. Tr. by Catherine Porter from FRE. LC 82-5078. (Illus.). 176p. 1982. 35.00 (*0-8014-1269-2*) Cornell U Pr.

Symbolism & Reality: A Study in the Nature of Mind. Charles W. Morris. LC 86-17602. (Foundations of Semiotics Ser.: No. 15). v, 105p. (C). 1993. 53.00 (*90-272-3287-3*) Benjamins North Am.

Symbolism & Surrealism. (Shorewood Art Programs for Education Ser.). 20p. 1975. teacher ed. 107.00 (*0-88185-061-6*); 143.00 (*0-685-07237-1*) Shorewood Fine Art.

Symbolism from Poe to Mallarme: The Growth of a Myth. Joseph Chiari. LC 76-114096. 208p. (C). 1970. reprint ed. 50.00 (*0-87752-020-8*) Gordian.

Symbolism in Ancient Chinese Art. Hugo Munsterberg. LC 84-82430. (Illus.). 250p. 1986. lib. bdg. 50.00 (*0-87817-303-X*) Hacker.

Symbolism in the Fourth Gospel: Meaning, Mystery, Community. Craig R. Koester. LC 94-31476. 1995. 22.00 (*0-8006-2893-4*, Fortress Pr) Augsburg Fortress.

Symbolism in the Poetry of Sri Aurobindo. Syamala Kallury. (C). 1989. 20.00 (*81-7017-257-8*, Pub. by Abhinav II) S Asia.

Symbolism of Churches & Church Ornaments. Gulielmus Durantis. 1980. lib. bdg. 64.95 (*0-8490-3166-4*) Gordon Pr.

Symbolism of Churches & Church Ornaments: A Translation of the First Book of the Rationale Divinorum Officiorum. Gulielmus Durantis. Ed. by John M. Neale & Benjamin Webb. reprint ed. 28.00 (*0-404-04653-3*) AMS Pr.

Symbolism of Color. Ellen Conroy. (Illus.). 80p. 1996. reprint ed. pap. 9.95 (*0-87877-236-7*) Newcastle Pub.

Symbolism of Color: The Beauty & Magic of Color Has Been a Vital Part of Living, Religion & Mysticism. Faber Birren. (Illus.). 196p. (gr. 9-12). 1988. 15.95 (*0-8065-1099-4*, Citadel Pr); pap. 7.95 (*0-8065-1109-5*, Citadel Pr) Carol Pub Group.

Symbolism of Evil. Paul Ricoeur. LC 67-11506. 1969. reprint ed. pap. 18.00 (*0-8070-1567-9*, BPA18) Beacon Pr.

Symbolism of Freemasonry. Jirah D. Buck. 17.00 (*0-685-19503-1*) Powner.

Symbolism of Freemasonry. Albert G. Mackey. 17.00 (*0-685-19504-X*) Powner.

Symbolism of Freemasonry: Its Science, Philosophy, Legends, Myths & Symbols. Albert G. Mackey. 375p. 1994. pap. 24.95 (*1-56459-469-6*) Kessinger Pub.

Symbolism of Habitat: An Interpretation of Landscape in the Arts. Jay Appleton. LC 89-24811. (Jessie & John Danz Lectures). (Illus.). 104p. 1990. 17.50 (*0-295-96940-7*) U of Wash Pr.

Symbolism of Hinduism: A Hermeneutic Approach. Tribhuwan Kapur. (C). 1988. 16.00 (*81-212-0245-0*, Pub. by Gian Publng Hse II) S Asia.

Symbolism of Light & Color. Manly P. Hall. 32p. 1976. reprint ed. pap. 4.95 (*0-89314-376-6*) Philos Res.

Symbolism of Style: Art As Therapy. Rita Simon. LC 91-32552. (Illus.). 240p. (Orig.). (C). 1991. pap. text ed. 19.95 (*0-415-04131-7*, A7114, Tavistock) Routledge.

Symbolism of Subordination: Indian Identity in a Guatemalan Town. Kay B. Warren. (Illus.). 237p. 1989. reprint ed. pap. 12.95 (*0-292-77621-7*) U of Tex Pr.

Symbolism of the Biblical World: Ancient Near Eastern Iconography & the Book of Psalms. Othmar Keel. Tr. by Timothy J. Hallett from GER. (Illus.). 422p. 1996. reprint ed. text ed. 36.50 (*1-57506-014-0*) Eisenbrauns.

Symbolism of the Celtic Cross. Derek Bryce. LC 95-19403. (Illus.). 128p. (Orig.). 1995. pap. 9.95 (*0-87728-850-X*) Weiser.

***Symbolism of the Cross.** Rene Guenon. Tr. by Angus Macnab from FRE. (Perennial Wisdom Ser.). 148p. 1996. reprint ed. pap. 17.95 (*0-900588-21-7*) S Perennis.

Symbolism of the Divine Comedy. Jefferson B. Fletcher. LC 71-168043. reprint ed. 22.50 (*0-404-02438-6*) AMS Pr.

Symbolism of the Stupa. Adrian Snodgrass. (Studies on Southeast Asia: No. 1). (Illus.). 469p. (Orig.). (C). 1988. pap. text ed. 20.00 (*0-87727-700-1*) Cornell SE Asia.

Symbolism of the Stupa. Adrian Snodgrass. (C). 1992. reprint ed. text ed. 32.00 (*81-208-0781-2*, Pub. by Motilal Banarsidass II) S Asia.

Symbolism of the Tarot. P. D. Ouspensky. Tr. by A. L. Pogossky from RUS. (Illus.). 64p. 1976. reprint ed. pap. 2.50 (*0-486-23291-3*) Dover.

Symbolism of the Tarot: A Long-Lost Classic Resurrected. P. D. Ouspensky. 75p. 1995. pap. 18.95 (*0-87877-229-4*) Newcastle Pub.

Symbolism of Vanitas in the Arts, Literature & Music: Comparative & Historical Studies. Ed. by Liana DeGirolalmi-Cheney. LC 89-13788. (Illus.). 288p. 1993. lib. bdg. 89.95 (*0-88946-399-9*) E Mellen.

Symbolism on Greek Coins. Agnes Baldwin. LC 76-62839. (Illus.). 1977. reprint ed. lib. bdg. 20.00 (*0-915262-10-X*) S J Durst.

Symbolism, the Sacred, & the Arts. Mircea Eliade. 208p. 1992. pap. text ed. 14.95 (*0-8264-0618-1*) Continuum.

Symbolism Through the Ages. Kathryn D. Henry. 1988. pap. 14.95 (*0-89314-423-1*) Philos Res.

Symbolisme de la Salette. Paul Claudel. 64p. (FRE.). 1952. 10.95 (*0-7859-1125-1*, 2070215237) Fr & Eur.

Symbolist Aesthetics & Early Abstract Art: Sites of Imaginary Space. Dee Reynolds. (Cambridge Studies in French: No. 51). (Illus.). 320p. (C). 1995. text ed. 59.95 (*0-521-42102-0*) Cambridge U Pr.

Symbolist Art. Edward Lucie-Smith. (World of Art Ser.). (Illus.). 216p. 1985. pap. 14.95 (*0-500-20125-0*) Thames Hudson.

Symbolist Art Theories: A Critical Anthology. Henri Dorra. LC 93-32264. 1994. 40.00 (*0-520-07742-3*) U CA Pr.

Symbolist Art Theories: A Critical Anthology. Henri Dorra. LC 93-32264. (Illus.). 396p. (C). 1996. pap. 15.95 (*0-520-07768-7*) U CA Pr.

Symbolist Dead City. Friedman. LC 90-44652. (Studies in Comparative Literature). 224p. 1990. reprint ed. 20.00 (*0-8240-5972-7*) Garland.

Symbolist Generation. Pierre L. Mathieu. LC 89-43610. (Illus.). 250p. 1991. 50.00 (*0-8478-1218-9*) Rizzoli Intl.

Symbolist Home & the Tragic Home: Mallarme & Oedipus. Richard E. Goodkin. LC 84-9280. (Purdue University Monographs in Romance Languages: Vol. 13). xv, 203p. (Orig.). 1984. pap. 47.00 (*90-272-1723-8*) Benjamins North Am.

Symbolist Movement: A Critical Appraisal. Anna A. Balakian. LC 77-76044. 320p. (C). 1977. pap. text ed. 14.00 (*0-8147-0994-X*) NYU Pr.

Symbolist Movement in Literature. Arthur Symons. LC 79-166209. (Studies in Comparative Literature: No. 35). 1971. lib. bdg. 75.00 (*0-8383-1316-7*) M S G Haskell Hse.

Symbolist Movement in Literature. Arthur Symons. LC 77-11488. (Symbolists Ser.). 208p. 1980. reprint ed. 27.50 (*0-404-16348-3*) AMS Pr.

***Symbolist Movement in the Literature of European Languages.** A. Balakian. 1984. pap. 245.00 (*963-05-3895-4*, Pub. by Akad Kiado HU) St Mut.

Symbolist Prints of Edvard Munch: The Vivian & David Campbell Collection. Elizabeth Prelinger & Michael Park-Taylor. (Illus.). 224p. 1996. 50.00 (*0-300-06952-9*) Yale U Pr.

Symbolist Theater: The Formation of an Avant-Garde. Frantisek Deak. LC 92-35799. (PAJ Bks.). 320p. 1993. text ed. 45.00 (*0-8018-4382-0*); pap. text ed. 14.95 (*0-8018-4598-X*) Johns Hopkins.

Symbolistes et Decadents. Adam. Ed. by Pakenham. (Exeter French Texts Ser.: Vol. 70). 104p. (FRE.). Date not set. pap. text ed. 19.95 (*0-85989-300-6*, Pub. by Univ Exeter Pr UK) Northwestern U Pr.

Symbolistes et decadents. Gustave Kahn. LC 77-10272. reprint ed. 52.50 (*0-404-16324-6*) AMS Pr.

Symbolization: Proposing a Developmental Paradigm for a New Psychoanalytic Theory of Mind. Anna Aragno. LC 97-15905. 432p. 1997. 65.00 (*0-8236-6294-2*) Intl Univs Pr.

Symbolization & Creativity. Susan K. Deri. LC 83-26482. xii, 364p. 1984. 52.50 (*0-8236-6292-6*) Intl Univs Pr.

Symbolizing America. Ed. by Herve Varenne. LC 85-24694. xvi, 290p. 1986. pap. text ed. 13.00 (*0-8032-9603-7*, Bison Books) U of Nebr Pr.

Symbolizing Society: Stories, Rites & Structure in a Catholic High School. Nancy Lesko. (Education Policy Perspectives Ser.). 170p. 1988. 60.00 (*1-85000-302-5*, Falmer Pr); pap. 28.00 (*1-85000-307-6*, Falmer Pr) Taylor & Francis.

Symbology: The Use of Symbols in Visual Communications, 4th Communications Conference, Art Directors Club, New York Staff. Ed. by Elwood Whitney. LC 70-167307. (Essay Index Reprint Ser.). 1977. reprint ed. 39.95 (*0-8369-2579-3*) Ayer.

Symbols: A Silent Language. Jan Adkins. LC 78-2977. (Illus.). 64p. 1984. pap. 4.95 (*0-8027-7216-1*) Walker & Co.

Symbols: Myth, Magic, Fact, & Fancy. Fred Rosebury. LC 74-22888. (Illus.). 411p. reprint ed. pap. 117.20 (*0-685-23681-1*, AU00358) Bks Demand.

An Asterisk (*) at the beginning of an entry indicates that the title is appearing in BIP for the first time.

Symbols: Our Universal Language. LC 62-20744. 1962. pap. 7.50 (*0-912504-44-7*) Sym & Sign.

Symbols: Public & Private. Raymond Firth. LC 72-11806. (Symbol, Myth & Ritual Ser.). 469p. 1975. pap. 16.95 (*0-8014-9150-9*) Cornell U Pr.

Symbols & Artifacts: Views of the Corporate Landscape. Ed. by Pasquale Gagliardi. (Studies in Organization: No. 24). (Illus.). xiv, 428p. (C). 1990. lib. bdg. 106.15 (*3-11-012012-7*) De Gruyter.

Symbols & Artifacts: Views of the Corporate Landscape. Ed. by Pasquale Gagliardi. (Communication & Social Order Ser.). (Illus.). 445p. 1990. reprint ed. pap. text ed. 34.95 (*0-202-30428-0*) Aldine de Gruyter.

Symbols & Emblems of Early & Medieval Christian Art. Louisa Twining. 1980. lib. bdg. 85.00 (*0-8490-3197-4*) Gordon Pr.

Symbols & Language in Sacred Christian Architecture. Radu Dragan & Augustin Ioan. LC 95-38447. (Illus.). 136p. 1996. 69.95 (*0-7734-8870-7*) E Mellen.

Symbols & Meanings in School Mathematics. David Pimm. LC 94-39323. 240p. (C). 1995. pap. 17.95 (*0-415-11385-7*, C0464); text ed. 59.95 (*0-415-11384-9*, C0463) Routledge.

Symbols & Political Quiescence. Murray Edelman. (Reprint Series in Political Science). (C). 1993. reprint ed. pap. text ed. 1.00 (*0-8290-3495-1*, PS-460) Irvington.

Symbols & Salvation: Paul Tillich's Doctrine of Religious Symbols & His Interpretation of the Symbols of the Christian Tradition. Donald F. Dreisbach. 250p. (Orig.). (C). 1992. lib. bdg. 54.50 (*0-8191-8788-7*) U Pr of Amer.

Symbols & Symptoms: In Which Medical Education & Its Relationship to the Humanities Is Considered. Frank C. Wilson. LC 95-81760. 125p. 1996. write for info. (*1-878208-70-5*) Guild Pr IN.

Symbols & Terms of the Church. Mark P. Bangert. 24p. 1990. pap. 1.50 (*0-8066-2522-8*, 23-1957) Augsburg Fortress.

Symbols & Their Meaning. Rudolph F. Norden. 64p. 1985. pap. 4.99 (*0-570-03949-5*, 12-2883) Concordia.

Symbols As Power: The Papacy Following the Investiture Contest. Mary Stroll. LC 90-27757. (BSIH Ser.: No. 24). (Illus.). xxiii, 238p. 1991. 99.50 (*90-04-09374-5*) E J Brill.

Symbols Come Alive in the Sand. Evalyn T. Dundas. (Illus.). 151p. 1989. pap. 16.95 (*0-904575-41-1*, Coventure Ltd) Sigo Pr.

Symbols Come Alive in the Sand. Evalyn T. Dundas. (Illus.). 151p. (C). 1991. 27.50 (*0-904575-42-X*, Coventure Ltd) Sigo Pr.

Symbols, Computation, & Intentionality: A Critique of the Computational Theory of Mind. Steven W. Horst. LC 95-37156. (Illus.). 340p. 1996. 45.00 (*0-520-20052-7*) U CA Pr.

Symbols, Conflict, & Identity: Essays in Political Anthropology. Zdzislaw Mach. LC 92-22553. (SUNY Series in Anthropological Studies of Contemporary Issues). 297p. (C). 1993. text ed. 64.50 (*0-7914-1465-5*); pap. text ed. 21.95 (*0-7914-1466-3*) State U NY Pr.

Symbols, Diagrams & Circuits. Bergwall. (Electronics Technology Ser.). 1991. 85.00 (*0-8273-4808-8*) Van Nos Reinhold.

Symbols, Dreams, & Visions. Morton T. Kelsey. (Wellspring Bks.). 128p. 1988. pap. 8.95 (*0-916349-60-8*) Amity Hse Inc.

Symbols for All Seasons: Environmental Planning for Cycles A, B, & C. Catherine H. Krier. LC 88-15050. 184p. (Orig.). (C). 1988. pap. 9.95 (*0-89390-125-3*) Resource Pubns.

Symbols for Designers. Arnold Whittick. (Illus.). 1972. reprint ed. 51.00 (*1-55888-231-6*) Omnigraphics Inc.

***Symbols for Gear Terms.** A. H. Candee. (Technical Papers: Vol. 96). 1930. pap. text ed. 30.00 (*1-55589-148-9*) AGMA.

Symbols for the Various Functions of Document Handling Equipment. Association for Information & Image Management Staff. 12p. 1993. pap. 39.00 (*0-89258-273-1*, MS54) Assn Inform & Image Mgmt.

***Symbols, Impossible Numbers, & Geometric Entanglements: British Algebra Through the Commentaries on Newton's "Universal Arithmetick"** Helena M. Pycior. (Illus.). 320p. (C). 1997. text ed. 74.95 (*0-521-48124-4*) Cambridge U Pr.

Symbols in Art & Religion: Indian & Comparative Perspectives. Ed. by Karel Werner. (School of Oriental Studies, University of Durham (U. K.) Indological Ser.: No. 2). (Illus.). 260p. (C). 1990. text ed. 45.00 (*0-913215-69-4*, Pub. by Curzon Press UK) UH Pr.

Symbols in Life & Art. James A. Leith. 224p. 1987. 55.00 (*0-7735-0616-0*, Pub. by McGill CN) U of Toronto Pr.

Symbols of American Libraries. 1975. lib. bdg. 250.00 (*0-8490-1168-X*) Gordon Pr.

Symbols of Ancient Egypt in the Late Period (21st Dynasty) Beatrice L. Goff. (Religion & Society Ser.). 1979. text ed. 165.40 (*90-279-7622-8*) Mouton.

***Symbols of Ancient Gods.** Rhiannon Ryall. (Orig.). 1997. pap. 21.95 (*1-86163-008-5*, Pub. by Capall Bann Pubng UK) Holmes Pub.

***Symbols of Catholicism.** Le Gail. 1997. 40.00 (*2-908228-94-7*, Pub. by Assouline FR) Rizzoli Intl.

Symbols of Change: Urban Transition in a Zambian Community. Bennetta Jules-Rosette. LC 81-2122. (Modern Sociology Ser.). (Illus.). 224p. 1981. pap. 39.50 (*0-89391-085-6*); text ed. 73.25 (*0-89391-064-3*) Ablex Pub.

Symbols of Church Seasons & Days. John Bradner. LC 77-70805. (Illus.). (Orig.). 1977. pap. 6.95 (*0-8192-1228-8*) Morehouse Pub.

Symbols of Community: The Cultural System of a Swedish Church. Peter G. Stromberg. LC 85-30229. (Anthropology of Form & Meaning Ser.). 127p. 1986. 23.50 (*0-8165-0967-0*) U of Ariz Pr.

Symbols of Democracy. Ithiel De Sola Pool. LC 81-6229. (Hoover Institute Studies, Series C: Symbols: No. 4). xi, 80p. 1981. reprint ed. text ed. 59.75 (*0-313-22517-6*, POSD, Greenwood Pr) Greenwood.

Symbols of Dreams. Jerry L. Rothermel. 95p. (Orig.). (C). 1987. reprint ed. pap. 4.95 (*0-944386-03-2*) SOM Pub.

Symbols of Eternity: The Art of Landscape Painting in China. Michael Sullivan. LC 78-65393. (Illus.). 111p. reprint ed. pap. 30.00 (*0-7837-3949-4*, 2043778) Bks Demand.

Symbols of Excellence: Precious Materials As Expressions of Status. Grahame Clark. (Illus.). 150p. 1986. text ed. 42.95 (*0-521-30264-1*) Cambridge U Pr.

Symbols of Faith: A Visual Journey to Historic Churches of New Mexico. Joan B. Baker & Judith Tobin. (Illus.). 56p. (Orig.). 1993. pap. 22.00 (*0-9637342-0-2*); 15.00 (*0-9637342-1-0*) Bunbury Pr.

Symbols of God's Love: Codes & Passwords. Jeanne S. Fogle. Ed. by Mary Jean Ducket & W. Ben Lane. LC 86-12014. (Illus.). 32p. (Orig.). (J). (gr. k-3). 1986. pap. 10.00 (*0-664-24050-X*, Westminster) Westminster John Knox.

Symbols of Heraldry Explained. (Illus.). 112p. 1980. pap. 9.95 (*0-9502455-5-0*, Pub. by Heraldic Art IE) Irish Bks Media.

Symbols of Ideal Life: Social Documentary Photography in America, 1890-1950. Maren Stange. (Illus.). 208p. (C). 1989. text ed. 49.95 (*0-521-32441-6*) Cambridge U Pr.

Symbols of Ideal Life: Social Documentary Photography in America, 1890-1950. Maren Stange. (Illus.). 208p. (C). 1992. pap. text ed. 21.95 (*0-521-42429-1*) Cambridge U Pr.

***Symbols of Islam.** Chebel. Date not set. 40.00 (*2-84323-007-1*) St Martin.

***Symbols of Judaism.** Marc-Alain Ouaknin. (Illus.). 128p. 1996. 40.00 (*2-908228-35-1*) St Martin.

Symbols of Judaism: The Challenge to Learn & Create. pap. 4.00 (*0-686-96080-7*) USCJE.

***Symbols of Kwanzaa.** Fred Crump, Jr. LC 96-61182. (Illus.). 44p. (J). (gr. k-4). 1997. pap. 3.95 (*1-55523-812-2*) Winston-Derek.

Symbols of Light. Michael S. Djanti. LC 91-67744. (Illus.). 88p. 1993. pap. 9.00 (*1-56002-131-4*, Univ Edtns) Aegina Pr.

Symbols of Montana. Rex C. Myers & Norma B. Ashby. 32p. (Orig.). 1989. reprint ed. pap. 3.50 (*0-917298-26-8*, 4537) MT Hist Soc.

Symbols of New York. 1985. pap. write for info. (*0-89359-076-2*) Afton Pub.

Symbols of Power. Ed. by Vina Mazumdar. 373p. 1979. 19.95 (*0-318-37080-8*) Asia Bk Corp.

Symbols of Recovery: The Twelve Steps at Work in the Unconscious. Richard D. Grant, Jr. 72p. 1991. pap. text ed. 9.95 (*1-878287-27-3*) Type & Temperament.

Symbols of Sacrifice. Richard J. Hull, II. 1991. pap. 3.25 (*1-55673-281-3*, 9114) CSS OH.

Symbols of Sacrifice: Lenten Congregational Resources, Year 3. Richard J. Hull, II. 1992. pap. 3.25 (*1-55673-513-8*) CSS OH.

Symbols of Sacrifice: Year 2. Richard J. Hull, II. 1991. pap. 3.25 (*1-55673-384-4*, 9202) CSS OH.

Symbols of Substance: Court & State in Nayaka Period Tamilnadu. Velcheru N. Rao et al. (Illus.). 388p. 1993. 55.00 (*0-19-563021-1*) OUP.

Symbols of Survival: The Art of Will MacLean. Duncan MacMillan. (Illus.). 120p. 1993. 34.95 (*1-85158-419-6*, Pub. by Mnstream UK) Trafalgar.

Symbols of the Church. 6th ed. (Ichthus Ser.). 1987. pap. 3.95 (*0-687-18301-4*) Abingdon.

Symbols of the Holy Spirit. Tom Adcox. 51p. 1993. pap. write for info. (*0-9636261-0-8*) Abund Life Bks.

Symbols of the Season: Exciting Epiphany Experiences. Jude D. Fournier & Phyllis Vos Wezeman. 83p. 1991. pap. 9.95 (*1-877871-26-5*, 2615) Ed Ministries.

Symbols of the Soul: Therapy & Guidance Through Fairy Tales. Birgitte Brun et al. 128p. 1993. 39.95 (*1-85302-107-5*) Taylor & Francis.

***Symbols of Tibetan Buddhism.** Levenson. 1997. 40.00 (*2-908228-86-6*, Pub. by Assouline FR) Rizzoli Intl.

Symbols of Trade. Stanley Sacharow. (Illus.). 163p. 1983. 14.50 (*0-88108-003-9*); pap. 9.95 (*0-910158-98-3*) Art Dir.

Symbols, Pictures, & Quantum Reality: On the Theoretical Foundations of the Physical Universe. W. Schommers. (Foundations of Natural Science & Technology Ser.). 264p. 1995. text ed. 55.00 (*981-02-2056-1*) World Scientific Pub.

***Symbols, Sex & the Stars: An Outline of the Origins of Moon & Sun Worship, Astrology, Sex Symbolism, Mystic Meaning of Numbers, the Cabala, & Many Popular Customs, Myths, Superstitions & Religious Beliefs.** 2nd ed. Ernest Busenbark. (Illus.). 396p. 1997. reprint ed. pap. 22.95 (*1-885395-19-1*) Book Tree.

Symbols, Signs & Letters. Martin Andersch. (Illus.). 256p. 1989. 75.00 (*0-8306-5506-9*) TAB Bks.

Symbols, Signs & Signets. Ernst Lehner. (Illus.). 1950. pap. 7.95 (*0-486-22241-1*) Dover.

Symbols, Signs & Signets. Ernst Lehner. (Illus.). 1990. 21.50 (*0-8446-0771-1*) Peter Smith.

Symbols That Stand for Themselves. Roy Wagner. LC 85-16448. (Illus.). 162p. 1986. pap. text ed. 12.00 (*0-226-86929-6*) U Ch Pr.

Symbols, the News Magazines & Martin Luther King. Richard Lentz. LC 89-12852. 384p. 1990. text ed. 47.50 (*0-8071-1523-1*) La State U Pr.

Symbols vs. Neurons? Ed. by Joachim Stender & Tom Addis. (Frontiers in Artificial Intelligence & Applications Ser.: Vol. 9). 252p. (gr. 12). 1990. pap. 65.00 (*90-5199-039-1*, Pub. by IOS Pr NE) IOS Press.

Symeon Neos Theologos, Hymnen Einleitung und kritischer Text. Ed. by Athanasios Kambylis. (Supplementa Byzantina Ser.: Vol. 3). (C). 1976. 619.25 (*3-11-004888-4*) De Gruyter.

Symeon the Holy Fool: Leontius's "Life" & the Late Antique City. Derek Krueger. LC 94-41651. (Transformation of the Classical Heritage Ser.: Vol. 25). 1996. 35.00 (*0-520-08911-1*) U CA Pr.

Symeon, the New Theologian: The Discourses. C. J. De Catanzaro. LC 80-82414. (Classics of Western Spirituality Ser.). 416p. 1980. pap. 19.95 (*0-8091-2230-8*) Paulist Pr.

Symeonis Monachi Opera Omnia, 2 vols., Set. Ed. by Thomas Arnold. Incl. Vol. 1. Historia Ecclesiae Dunelmensis. 1974. (*0-8115-1143-X*); Vol. 2. Historia Regum. 1974. (*0-8115-1144-8*); (Rolls Ser.: No. 75). 1974. reprint ed. 140.00 (*0-685-10007-3*) Periodicals Srv.

Symetric Bends: How to Join Two Lengths of Cord. Roger E. Miles. (Series on Knots & Everything). 150p. 1995. text ed. 32.00 (*981-02-2194-0*) World Scientific Pub.

Symetry in Chaos: A Search for Pattern in Mathematics, Art, & Nature. Michael Field & Martin Golubitsky. (Illus.). 232p. (C). 1996. pap. 22.50 (*0-19-853688-7*) OUP.

Symlog: A Manual for the Case Study of Groups. Robert F. Bales et al. LC 79-7480. (Illus.). 1979. 50.00 (*0-02-901300-3*, Free Press) Free Pr.

Symlog Case Study Kit: With Instructions for a Group Self-Study. Robert F. Bales. LC 79-7480. 1980. pap. 19.95 (*0-02-901310-0*, Free Press) Free Pr.

SYMLOG Field Theory: Organizational Consultation, Value Differences, Personality & Social Perception. Ed. by Sharon E. Hare & A. Paul Hare. LC 96-21250. 280p. 1996. text ed. 69.50 (*0-275-95635-0*, Praeger Pubs) Greenwood.

Symlog Practitioner: Applications of Small Group Research. Ed. by Richard B. Polley et al. LC 87-37684. (Illus.). 427p. 1988. text ed. 69.50 (*0-275-92364-9*, C2364, Praeger Pubs) Greenwood.

Symmachie Und Spondai: Untersuchungen Zum Griechischen Voelkerrecht der Archaischen Und Klassischen Zeit (8. - 5. Jahrhundert V. Chr.) Ernst Baltrusch. (Untersuchungen Zur Antiken Literatur Und Geschichte Ser.: No. 43). xi, 274p. (GER.). (C). 1994. lib. bdg. 144.65 (*3-11-013745-3*) De Gruyter.

Symmachus, Quintas Aurelius: Concordantiae in Q. Aurelii Symmachi Opera - A Concordance to Symmachus, 2 vols., Set. Quintus A. Symmachus. Ed. by Valeria Lomanto. (Alpha-Omega, Reihe A Ser.: Vol. LIV). 1148p. 1983. 193.70 (*3-487-07439-7*) G Olms Pubs.

Symmetric & G-Algebras: With Applications to Group Representations. Gregory Karpilovsky. (C). 1990. lib. bdg. 167.00 (*0-7923-0761-5*) Kluwer Ac.

Symmetric Approach to the Labor Market: An Application of the SEM Method. Evelien Eggink. (Tinbergen Institute Research Ser.: No. 83). 232p. 1994. pap. 26.50 (*90-5170-307-4*, Pub. by Thesis Pubs NE) IBD Ltd.

Symmetric Automorphisms of Free Products. Darryl McCullough & Andy Miller. (Memoirs of the American Mathematical Society Ser.: No. 582). 1996. pap. 35.00 (*0-8218-0459-6*, MEMO/122/582) Am Math.

Symmetric Function & Allied Tables. F. N. David et al. 278p. 1966. lib. bdg. 32.50 (*0-85264-702-6*) Lubrecht & Cramer.

Symmetric Functions & Hall Polynomials. 2nd ed. I. G. Macdonald. (Mathematical Monographs). 400p. 1995. 95.00 (*0-19-853489-2*) OUP.

Symmetric Group: Representations, Combinatorial Algorithms, & Symmetric Functions. Carl Sagan. 216p. (C). (gr. 13). 1991. text ed. 67.95 (*0-534-15540-5*) Chapman & Hall.

Symmetric Group in Quantum Chemistry. Ruben Pauncz. 352p. 1995. 115.95 (*0-8493-8291-2*, 8291) CRC Pr.

***Symmetric Inverse Semigroups.** Stephen Lipscomb. LC 96-26968. (Mathematics Surveys & Monographs: Vol. 46). 1996. 49.00 (*0-8218-0627-0*, SURV/46) Am Math.

Symmetric Properties of Real Functions, TBC. Thomson. (Pure & Applied Mathematics Ser.: Vol. 183). 472p. 1994. 165.00 (*0-8247-9230-0*) Dekker.

Symmetric Spaces: Short Courses Presented at Washington University. Ed. by William M. Boothby et al. LC 74-182213. (Pure & Applied Mathematics Ser.: No. 8). (Illus.). 502p. reprint ed. pap. 143.10 (*0-317-08008-3*, 2021506) Bks Demand.

Symmetric Structures in Banach Spaces. W. B. Johnson et al. LC 79-10225. (Memoirs Ser.: No. 19/217). 298p. 1980. reprint ed. pap. 22.00 (*0-8218-2217-9*, MEMO/19/217) Am Math.

Symmetrical Components. C. F. Wagner & R. D. Evans. LC 82-14051. 454p. 1982. reprint ed. lib. bdg. 49.50 (*0-89874-556-X*) Krieger.

Symmetrical Components for Power Systems Engineering. Blackburn. (Electrical Engineering & Electronics Ser.: Vol. 85). 448p. 1993. 110.00 (*0-8247-8767-6*) Dekker.

Symmetrical English. John B. Watson. 1989. pap. 14.95 (*0-02-026241-8*) Macmillan.

Symmetrie. 2nd ed. Hermann Weyl. (Science & Society Ser.: No. 11). 158p. (GER.). (C). 1980. 54.50 (*0-8176-1280-7*) Birkhauser.

Symmetrie, Gruppe, Dualitat. Erhard Scholz. (Science Networks Ser.: No. 1). 404p. (GER.). 1989. 105.00 (*0-8176-1974-7*) Birkhauser.

Symmetries. Tom Johnson. 1981. 6.00 (*0-938690-02-7*) Two Eighteen.

Symmetries. Richard Kostelanetz. 1983. pap. 12.00 (*0-918406-24-2*) Future Pr.

Symmetries. deluxe ed. Richard Kostelanetz. 1983. 100.00 (*0-918406-25-0*) Future Pr.

Symmetries & Curvature Structure in General Relativity. G. S. Hall. (Lecture Notes in Physics Ser.). 300p. 1998. text ed. 61.00 (*981-02-1051-5*) World Scientific Pub.

Symmetries & Differential Equations. G. W. Bluman & S. Kumei. (Applied Mathematical Sciences Ser.: Vol. 81). (Illus.). xiii, 412p. 1996. 59.00 (*0-387-96996-9*) Spr-Verlag.

Symmetries & Fundamental Interactions in Nuclei. E. Henley & W. Haxton. 500p. 1995. text ed. 109.00 (*981-02-2057-X*) World Scientific Pub.

Symmetries & Integrability of Difference Equations. D. Levi et al. LC 96-26796. (CRM Proceedings & Lecture Notes Ser.: Vol. 9). 1996. 98.00 (*0-8218-0601-7*, CRMP/9) Am Math.

Symmetries & Laplacians. David Gurarie. LC 92-15115. (Mathematics Studies: Vol. 174). 454p. 1992. 169.25 (*0-444-88612-5*, North Holland) Elsevier.

Symmetries & Nonlinear Phenomena: Paipa, Columbia, Feb. 22-26, 1988. Ed. by D. Levi & Pavel Winternitz. 472p. 1988. text ed. 102.00 (*9971-5-0663-7*) World Scientific Pub.

Symmetries & Nonlinear Phenomena: Paipa, Columbia, Feb. 22-26, 1988. Ed. by Pavel Winternitz. 472p. 1988. pap. 52.00 (*9971-5-0701-3*) World Scientific Pub.

Symmetries & Nuclear Structure. Richard A. Meyer & Vladimir Paar. (Nuclear Science Research Conference Ser.: Vol. 13). 640p. 1987. text ed. 198.00 (*3-7186-0400-0*) Gordon & Breach.

Symmetries & Reflections. Eugene P. Wigner. LC 79-89843. 1979. reprint ed. pap. 18.00 (*0-918024-16-1*) Ox Bow.

Symmetries & Semiclassical Features of Nuclear Dynamics. Ed. by A. Raduta. (Lecture Notes in Physics Ser.: Vol. 279). 1987. 50.95 (*0-387-17926-7*) Spr-Verlag.

Symmetries & Singularity Structures: Integrability & Chaos in Nonlinear Dynamical Systems. Ed. by M. Lakshmanan & M. Daniel. (Research Reports in Physics). (Illus.). 256p. 1991. 71.95 (*0-387-53092-4*) Spr-Verlag.

Symmetries, Asymmetries & the World of Particles. T. D. Lee. (Illus.). 80p. 1987. 15.00 (*0-295-96519-3*) U of Wash Pr.

Symmetries Gauge Fields Strings & Fundamental Interact: Mathematical Techniques in Gauge & String Theories. T. Dass. 1993. write for info. (*81-224-0470-7*, Pub. by Wiley Estrn II) Franklin.

Symmetries in Modern Physics. U. Fano & A. Ravi Rau. (Illus.). 333p. 1996. boxed 59.95 (*0-12-248455-X*) Acad Pr.

Symmetries in Physics. Ed. by A. Frank et al. (Illus.). 391p. 1992. 64.95 (*0-387-55148-4*) Spr-Verlag.

Symmetries in Physics. W. D. Ludwig & C. Falter. (Solid-State Sciences Ser.: Vol. 64). (Illus.). 470p. 1988. 66.00 (*0-387-18021-4*) Spr-Verlag.

Symmetries in Physics: Group Theory Applied to Physical Problems. 2nd ed. W. D. Ludwig & C. Falter. LC 95-39620. (Springer Series in Solid-State Sciences: Vol. 64). 473p. 1996. student ed., teacher ed., pap. 69.00 (*3-540-60284-4*) Spr-Verlag.

Symmetries in Physics (1600-1980) Proceedings. M. G. Doncel et al. 696p. 1988. text ed. 75.00 (*84-7488-148-X*) World Scientific Pub.

Symmetries in Science, Vol. 2. Ed. by Bruno Gruber & Romuald Lenczewski. 590p. 1986. 135.00 (*0-306-42461-4*, Plenum Pr) Plenum.

Symmetries in Science, Vol. 3. Ed. by Bruno Gruber & F. Iachello. (Illus.). 624p. 1989. 145.00 (*0-306-43148-3*, Plenum Pr) Plenum.

Symmetries in Science IV: Biological & Biophysical Systems. Ed. by Bruno Gruber & J. H. Yopp. LC 90-6766. (Illus.). 250p. 1990. 85.00 (*0-306-43502-0*, Plenum Pr) Plenum.

Symmetries in Science V: Algebraic Systems, Their Representations, Realizations, & Physical Applications. Ed. by Bruno Gruber et al. (Illus.). 612p. 1991. 145.00 (*0-306-43895-X*, Plenum Pr) Plenum.

Symmetries in Science VI: From the Rotation Group to Quantum Algebras. Ed. by B. Gruber. (Illus.). 766p. 1994. 149.50 (*0-306-44584-0*, Plenum Pr) Plenum.

Symmetries in Science VII: Spectrum-Generating Algebras & Dynamic Symmetries in Physics. Ed. by B. Gruber & T. Otsuka. (Illus.). 646p. 1994. 145.00 (*0-306-44586-7*, Plenum Pr) Plenum.

Symmetries in Science VIII No. VIII: Proceedings of a Symposium Held in Bregenz, Austria, August 8-12, 1994. Ed. by Bruno Gruber. LC 95-36857. (Illus.). 465p. (C). 1995. 125.00 (*0-306-45119-0*, Q172, Plenum Pr) Plenum.

***Symmetries, Lie Algebras & Representations: A Graduate Course for Physicists.** Jurgen Fuchs & Chrisotph Schweigert. (Cambridge Monographs on Mathematical Physics). (Illus.). 464p. (C). 1997. text ed. 100.00 (*0-521-56001-2*) Cambridge U Pr.

Symmetries of Culture: Theory & Practice of Plane Pattern Analysis. Dorothy K. Washburn & Donald W. Crowe. LC 87-27924. 304p. 1991. reprint ed. pap. 35.00 (*0-295-97084-7*) U of Wash Pr.

Symmetries of Equations of Quantum Mechanics. W. I. Fushchich & A. G. Nikitin. LC 94-11784. 1994. 75.00 (*0-89864-069-5*) Allerton Pr.

Symmetries of Islamic Geometrical Patterns. Jan A. Syed & Amer S. Salman. 350p. 1994. text ed. 44.00 (*981-02-1704-8*) World Scientific Pub.

Symmetries of Maxwell's Equations. W. I. Fushchich & A. G. Nikitin. (C). 1987. lib. bdg. 146.00 (*90-277-2320-6*) Kluwer Ac.

S

Symmetries of Nature: A Handbook for Philosophy of Nature & Science. Klaus Mainzer. LC 95-50834. (Illus.). 681p. (C). Date not set. 188.00 (3-11-012990-6, Q172) De Gruyter.

Symmetries, Topology, & Resonances in Hamiltonian Mechanics. Valery V. Kozlov. LC 95-1802. 1995. write for info. (3-540-57039-X) Spr-Verlag.

Symmetries, Topology, & Resonances in Hamiltonian Mechanics. Valery V. Kozlov. LC 95-1802. (Ergebnisse der Mathematik und ihrer Grenzgebiete: Vol. 31). (Illus.). 402p. 1995. 154.95 (0-387-57039-X) Spr-Verlag.

Symmetry. Ed. by Istvan Hargittai. (International Series in Modern Applied Mathematics & Computer Science). 1000p. 1986. 140.00 (0-685-14183-7, Pergamon Pr) Elsevier.

Symmetry. Laura Moriarty. Ed. by Cydney Chadwick. 120p. (Orig.). 1995. pap. text ed. 9.95 (1-880713-04-7) AVEC Bks.

Symmetry. Hermann Weyl. 176p. 1946. pap. 10.95 (0-691-02374-3) Princeton U Pr.

Symmetry: A Basis for Synthesis Design. Tse-Lok Ho. LC 95-5007. 1995. text ed. 94.95 (0-471-57376-0) Wiley.

Symmetry: A Design System for Quiltmakers. Ruth B. McDowell. Ed. by Barbara K. Kuhn & Harold Nadel. LC 93-40036. (Illus.). 144p. (Orig.). 1995. pap. 21.95 (0-914881-78-7, 10098) C & T Pub.

Symmetry: A Unifying Concept. Istvan Hargittai & Magdolna Hargittai. LC 93-42632. (Illus.). 240p. 1995. pap. 18.00 (0-679-76945-5) Shelter Pubns.

Symmetry: Unifying Human Understanding. Ed. by Istvan Hargittai. (International Series in Modern Applied Mathematics & Computer Science: Vol. 10). 1058p. 1986. 462.00 (0-08-033986-7, C110, D110, H100, E110, K105, Pergamon Pr) Elsevier.

Symmetry Analysis & Exact Solutions of Equations of Nonlinear Mathematical Physics. W. I. Fushchich et al. LC 92-44788. (Mathematics & Its Applications Ser.: Vol. 246). 460p. (C). 1993. lib. bdg. 236.50 (0-7923-2146-4) Kluwer Ac.

Symmetry & Combinatorial Enumeration in Chemistry. S. Fujita. (Illus.). ix, 368p. 1991. 53.95 (0-387-54126-8) Spr-Verlag.

Symmetry & Separation of Variables. Willard Miller, Jr. (Encyclopedia of Mathematics & Its Applications Ser.: No. 4). 1984. 69.95 (0-521-30224-2) Cambridge U Pr.

Symmetry & Simplicity in Physics: A Symposium on the Occasion of Sergio Fubini's 65 Birthday. W. M. Alberico & S. Sciuto. 232p. 1995. text ed. 81.00 (981-02-2048-0) World Scientific Pub.

Symmetry & Spectroscopy. Daniel C. Harris. 1989. pap. 14.95 (0-486-66144-X) Dover.

***Symmetry & Structural Properties of Condensed Matter.** 500p. 1997. 64.00 (981-02-3026-5) World Scientific Pub.

Symmetry & Structural Properties of Condensed Matter. Ed. by T. Lulek et al. 440p. (C). 1991. text ed. 137.00 (981-02-0422-1) World Scientific Pub.

Symmetry & Structural Properties of Condensed Matter: Proceedings of the 2nd International School of Theoretical Physics. W. Florek et al. 504p. 1993. text ed. 109.00 (981-02-1166-X) World Scientific Pub.

Symmetry & Structural Properties of Condensed Matter: Proceedings of the 3rd International School on Theoretical Physics. T. Lulek et al. 524p. 1995. text ed. 109.00 (981-02-2059-6) World Scientific Pub.

Symmetry & Structure: Readable Group Theory for Chemists. 2nd ed. Sidney F. Kettle. LC 94-39498. 416p. 1995. text ed. 74.95 (0-471-95547-7); pap. text ed. 39.95 (0-471-95476-4) Wiley.

Symmetry & Structures of Crystals. M. O'Keefe & B. G. Hyde. 600p. 1997. text ed. 97.00 (981-02-1701-3) World Scientific Pub.

Symmetry & Topology in Chemical Reactivity. Pieter E. Schipper. 284p. 1994. text ed. 74.00 (981-02-1542-8) World Scientific Pub.

Symmetry As a Developmental Principle in Nature & Art. W. Hahn. 400p. 1998. text ed. 74.00 (981-02-2363-3) World Scientific Pub.

Symmetry Breaking for Compact Lie Groups. Michael Field. (Memoirs of the American Mathematical Society Ser.: Vol. 574). 1996. pap. 43.00 (0-8218-0435-9, MEMO/120/574) Am Math.

Symmetry, Causality, Mind. Michael Leyton. (Illus.). 640p. 1992. 55.00 (0-262-12163-8, Bradford Bks) MIT Pr.

***Symmetry Discovered: Concepts & Applications in Nature & Science.** enl. ed. Joe Rosen. (Illus.). 160p. 1997. reprint ed. pap. text ed. 6.95 (0-486-29433-1) Dover.

Symmetry Groups: Theory & Chemical Applications. Robert L. Flurry, Jr. (Illus.). 1980. text ed. write for info. (0-13-880013-8) P-H.

Symmetry in Chaos: A Search for Pattern in Mathematics, Art & Nature. Michael Field & Martin Golubitsky. LC 92-14023. (Illus.). 200p. 1992. 39.95 (0-19-853689-5) OUP.

Symmetry in Physics. Ed. by Joe Rosen. 160p. 1982. 26.00 (0-917853-86-5, RB34) Am Assn Physics.

***Symmetry in Plants.** 600p. 1998. 59.00 (981-02-2621-7) World Scientific Pub.

***Symmetry in Science: An Introduction to the General Theory.** J. Rosen. 234p. 1996. pap. 29.95 (0-387-94836-8) Spr-Verlag.

Symmetry in Science: An Introduction to the General Theory. Joseph Rosen. LC 94-30622. 1995. 49.95 (0-387-94375-7) Spr-Verlag.

Symmetry Methods in Physics, in Memory of Professor YA. A. Smorodinsky Vols. 1 & 2: Proceedings of the International Workshop on Symmetry Methods in Physics, Dubna, Russia, 1993, 2 vols., Vol. 2. Ed. by A. N. Sissakian et al. 602p. (Orig.). (C). 1995. 95.00 (1-57485-006-7) Hadronic Pr Inc.

Symmetry, No. 2: Unifying Human Understanding. Istvan Hargittai. (International Series in Modern Applied Mathematics & Computer Science: Vol. 18). 1085p. 1989. 150.75 (0-08-037237-6, Pergamon Pr) Elsevier.

Symmetry of Biorhythms & Reactivity. A. P. Dubrov. Tr. by H. Szamuely from RUS. 268p. 1989. text ed. 375.00 (2-88124-692-3) Gordon & Breach.

Symmetry of Crystals. E. S. Fedorov. LC 75-146982. (American Crystallographic Association Monograph Ser.: Vol. 7). 315p. 1971. 25.00 (0-686-60371-0) Polycrystal Bk Serv.

Symmetry of Sailing: The Physics of Sailing for Yachtsmen. Ross Garrett. (Illus.). 278p. 1996. pap. 29.95 (1-57409-000-3) Sheridan.

Symmetry Operator Program. Drew. 32p. 1992. 250.00 (0-19-268034-X) OUP.

Symmetry Orbits. Hugo F. Verheyen. LC 93-31298. (Design Science Collections Ser.). 236p. 1995. 75.00 (0-8176-3661-7) Birkhauser.

Symmetry Patterns. Alan Wiltshirl. 32p. (Orig.). 1991. pap. 7.50 (0-906212-73-1, Pub. by Tarquin UK) Parkwest Pubns.

Symmetry Principles & Magnetic Symmetry in Solid State Physics. S. J. Joshua. (Graduate Student Series in Physics). (Illus.). 288p. 1991. 140.00 (0-7503-0070-1); pap. 45.00 (0-7503-0071-X) IOP Pub.

Symmetry, Rigid Motion & Patterns. Donald Crowe. (Hi Map Ser.: No. 4). (Illus.). pap. text ed. 9.99 (0-614-05325-0, HM 5604) COMAP Inc.

Symmetry Rules for Chemical Reactions: Orbital Topology & Elementary Processes. Ralph G. Pearson. LC 76-10314. 557p. reprint ed. pap. 158.80 (0-317-28061-9, 2055771) Bks Demand.

Symmetry Through the Eyes of a Chemist. Istvan Hargittai & Magdolna Hargittai. LC 86-24617. (Illus.). 458p. 1986. 160.00 (3-527-26409-4, VCH) Wiley.

Symmetry Through the Eyes of a Chemist. 2nd ed. Istvan Hargittai & Magdolna Hargittai. (Illus.). 461p. 1995. pap. 39.50 (0-306-44852-1, Plenum Pr) Plenum.

Symmetry Through the Eyes of a Chemist. 2nd ed. Istvan Hargittai et al. (Illus.). 461p. 1995. 85.00 (0-306-44851-3, Plenum Pr) Plenum.

Symmetry Violations in Subatomic Physics: Proceedings of the 6th Summer Institute in Theoretical Physics. Ed. by B. Castel & P. J. O'Donnell. 240p. (C). 1989. text ed. 93.00 (9971-5-0908-3) World Scientific Pub.

Symmetry Wave Trading Method. Michael Gur. 1993. 65.00 (0-930233-54-9) Windsor.

Symmetry with Pattern Blocks. Arthur Wiebe. 24p. (J). (gr. 3-9). 1985. student ed. 5.95 (1-878669-30-3, CTA-4766) Crea Tea Assocs.

Symmetry 2. Hargittai. (International Series in Modern Applied Mathematics). 1989. 110.00 (0-08-037238-4) Elsevier.

Symozia: Voyage of Discovery. J. C. Symmes. LC 74-16520. (Science Fiction Ser.). (Illus.). 248p. 1975. reprint ed. 25.95 (0-405-06312-1) Ayer.

Sympathetic Attractions: Magnetic Practices, Beliefs, & Symbolism in Eighteenth-Century England. Patricia Fara. LC 96-10785. 328p. 1996. text ed. 45.00 (0-691-01099-4) Princeton U Pr.

Sympathetic Introspection for Three Recorders. Suan Guess-Hanson. (Contemporary Consort Ser.: No. 22). 3p. 1992. pap. text ed. 0.60 (1-56571-067-3, CC022) PRB Prods.

Sympathetic Magic. Michael Blumenthal. LC 80-50812. (Illus.). 96p. (Orig.). (C). 1980. 60.00 (0-931956-04-8); pap. 12.00 (0-931956-03-X); 60.00 (0-686-70197-6) Water Mark.

Sympathetic Manifesto: Poems. Doren Robbins. LC 87-42791. 91p. (Orig.). 1987. pap. 7.95 (0-912288-26-4) Perivale Pr.

Sympathetic Response: George Eliot's Fictional Rhetoric. Mary E. Doyle. LC 80-65908. (Illus.). 192p. 1981. 29.50 (0-8386-3065-0) Fairleigh Dickinson.

Sympathetic Strikes & Sympathetic Lockouts. Frederick S. Hall. LC 78-76665. (Columbia University. Studies in the Social Sciences: No. 26). reprint ed. 29.50 (0-404-51026-4) AMS Pr.

Sympathetic Understanding of the Child: Birth to Sixteen. 3rd ed. David Elkind. LC 93-43166. 1994. pap. text ed. 27.00 (0-205-15018-7) Allyn.

Sympathetic Undertaker. Biyi Bandele. (African Writers Ser.). 208p. 1993. pap. 9.95 (0-435-90592-9, 90592) Heinemann.

***Sympathomimetic Enantiomers in the Treatment of Asthma: The Proceedings of a Meeting Held by the Section of Respiratory Medicine, the Royal Society of Medicine, London, October 1995.** Ed. by J. F. Costello. LC 96-44595. (Illus.). 136p. 1997. text ed. 48.00 (1-85070-776-6) Prthnon Pub.

Sympathy & Science: Women Physicians in American Medicine. Regina M. Morantz-Sanchez. 480p. 1987. pap. 12.95 (0-19-504985-3) OUP.

Sympathy for the Devil. Kent Anderson. 1989. mass mkt. 4.95 (0-446-35222-5) Warner Bks.

Sympathy for the Devil. Holly Lisle. 256p. 1996. mass mkt. 5.99 (0-671-87703-8) Baen Bks.

Sympathy of Souls. Albert Goldbarth. LC 90-31254. 177p. (Orig.). 1990. pap. 9.95 (0-918273-77-3) Coffee Hse.

Symphonia: A Critical Edition of the "Symphonia Armonie Celestium Revelationum" (Symphony of the Harmony of Celestial Revelations) St. Hildegard of Bingen. Ed. & Tr. by Barbara Newman. LC 88-47739. 344p. 1988. 45.00 (0-8014-2009-1); pap. 13.95 (0-8014-9514-8) Cornell U Pr.

Symphonic & Chamber Music Score & Parts Bank Thematic Catalogue of the Facsimile Archive of 18th & Early 19th Century Autographs, Manuscripts, & Printed Copies at the Ph.D Program in Music of the Graduate School of the City University of New York. Ruth H. Rowen. LC 95-39268. (Thematic Catalogues Ser.: Vol. 24). 1996. 62.00 (0-945193-84-X) Pendragon NY.

Symphonic Classics: Masterpieces from Orchestral & Chamber Repertory, Transcribed for Solo Piano. (Piano Solos Ser.). 126p. (Orig.). 1990. pap. 10.95 (0-7935-0060-5, HL00490204) H Leonard.

Symphonic Concert, Band Manuscript. 8.95 (1-56222-095-0, 94516) Mel Bay.

Symphonic Duets in Bass Clef: Thirty-Eight Pedagocical & Performance Duets in Bass Clef. Vladislav Blazhevich. Ed. by Reginald H. Fink. 94p. 1992. student ed. 19.95 (0-918194-25-3) Accura.

Symphonic Masterpieces. Olin Downes. LC 72-5560. (Essay Index Reprint Ser.). 1977. reprint ed. 24.95 (0-8369-2987-X) Ayer.

Symphonic Masterpieces. Olin Downes. (Music Book Index Ser.). 294p. 1992. reprint ed. lib. bdg. 79.00 (0-7812-9479-7) Rprt Serv.

Symphonic Music: Its Evolution since the Renaissance. Homer Ulrich. LC 52-12033. 352p. 1952. text ed. 60.00 (0-231-01908-4) Col U Pr.

Symphonic Poems of Franz Liszt. Keith Johns. LC 96-46052. (FLSS Ser.: No. 3). 1997. 54.00 (0-945193-40-8) Pendragon NY.

Symphonic Silences. Opal V. Oehler. 1996. 10.00 (0-533-11300-8) Vantage.

Symphonic Suite for Orchestra: Full Score. K. Husa. 80p. 1993. pap. 20.00 (0-7935-2629-9) H Leonard.

Symphonie Fantastique. Hector Berlioz. Ed. by Edward T. Cone. (Critical Scores Ser.). (C). 1971. pap. text ed. 10.95 (0-393-09926-1) Norton.

Symphonie Pastorale. Andre Gide. (FRE.). 1972. pap. 10.95 (0-8288-3688-4, F116670); pap. 10.95 (0-7859-2259-8, 2070360180) Fr & Eur.

Symphonie Pastorale. Andre Gide. Ed. by Justin O'Brien & M. Shackleton. 126p. (FRE.). (C). 1954. pap. text ed. 11.96 (0-669-27383-X) HM College Div.

Symphonie Pastorale. Andre Gide. (Folio Ser.: No. 18). (FRE.). 1972. pap. 6.95 (2-07-036018-0) Schoenhof.

Symphonie Pastorale. Andre Gide. 1972. write for info. (0-318-63601-8) Fr & Eur.

Symphonie Pastorale. large type ed. Andre Gide. 181p. 1990. 22.95 (1-85290-023-7, Pub. by ISIS UK) Transaction Pubs.

Symphonie Pastorale et la Porte Etroite De Gide. Marc Dambre. 214p. (FRE.). 1991. pap. 12.95 (0-7859-2181-8, 2070384403) Fr & Eur.

Symphonies Bk. 1: Piano. Ludwig van Beethoven. 152p. 1986. per. 15.95 (0-7935-1538-6, 50260120) H Leonard.

Symphonies Bk. 2: Piano. Ludwig van Beethoven. 164p. 1986. per. 15.95 (0-7935-4084-4, 50260130) H Leonard.

Symphonies Concertantes I. Ed. by Ernest Warburton. (Johann Christian Bach, 1735-1782 The Collected Works). 465p. 1985. text ed. 115.00 (0-8240-6079-2) Garland.

Symphonies Concertantes II. Ed. by Ernest Warburton. (Johann Christian Bach, 1735-1782 The Collected Works). 1988. text ed. 115.00 (0-8240-6080-6) Garland.

Symphonies De Beethoven. 13th ed. J. G. Prod'homme. LC 76-52485. (Music Reprint Ser.). (Illus.). (FRE.). 1977. reprint ed. lib. bdg. 55.00 (0-306-70859-0) Da Capo.

Symphonies for the Piano: Centennial Edition. J. Brahms. 160p. 1994. otabind 12.95 (0-7935-3232-9, 50482125) H Leonard.

Symphonies I. Ed. by Ernest Warburton. LC 83-48727. (Johann Christian Bach: The Collected Works). 350p. 1985. text ed. 95.00 (0-8240-6075-X) Garland.

Symphonies II. Ed. by Ernest Warburton. (Johann Christian Bach: The Collected Works). 450p. 1985. text ed. 105.00 (0-8240-6076-8) Garland.

Symphonies III. Johann C. Bach. Ed. by Ernest Warburton. (Johann Christian Bach Ser.). 480p. 1990. text ed. 125.00 (0-8240-6077-6) Garland.

Symphonies in Color: The Paintings of Malcah Zeldis. Ori Z. Soltes. 16p. (Orig.). 1992. pap. 4.00 (1-881456-02-1) B B K Natl Jew Mus.

Symphonies IV. Johann C. Bach. Ed. by Ernest Warburton. (Johann Christian Bach Ser.). 400p. 1989. text ed. 85.00 (0-8240-6078-4) Garland.

Symphonies Nos. 1 & 2 in Full Score. Gustav Mahler. 1987. pap. 14.95 (0-486-25473-9) Dover.

Symphonies of Gustav Mahler: A Critical Discography. Compiled by Lewis M. Smoley. LC 86-14222. (Discographies Ser.: No. 23). 206p. 1986. text ed. 65.00 (0-313-25189-4, SSY/, Greenwood Pr) Greenwood.

Symphonies of Mozart. Georges P. Saint-Foix. 1980. lib. bdg. 55.00 (0-8490-3191-5) Gordon Pr.

Symphonies of Mozart: Music Book Index. Georges P. Saint-Foix. 188p. 1993. reprint ed. lib. bdg. 69.00 (0-7812-9611-0) Rprt Serv.

Symphonies of Ralph Vaughan Williams. Elliott S. Schwartz. LC 81-12513. (Music Reprint Ser.). (Illus.). 242p. 1982. reprint ed. lib. bdg. 32.50 (0-306-76137-8) Da Capo.

Symphonies, Shamrocks & Songs: Poems. Marian G. McNeely. Ed. by M. A. Myers. LC 91-77716. 75p. (Orig.). 1991. pap. text ed. 7.95 (1-879183-15-3) Bristol Banner.

Symphonies, Vol. 6: Symphony No. 1 in E-flat, op. 20; Symphony No. 2 in D Minor, op. 49; Symphony No. 5 in C Minor, op. 102. Ed. by Clive Brown. (Selected Works of Louis Spohr, 1784-1859). 440p. 1988. text ed. 45.00 (0-8240-1505-3) Garland.

***Symphony.** Charles Grant. LC 96-42992. (Millennium Quartet Ser.: Bk. 1). 1997. 23.95 (0-312-86274-1) St Martin.

Symphony. Yvalth Noel. LC 92-70526. 50p. (Orig.). 1992. pap. 6.95 (0-9631147-1-9) A S Abrathyn-Arnold.

Symphony. 2nd ed. Louise E. Cuyler. LC 95-13538. (Detroit Monographs in Musicology-Studies in Music: No. 16). 248p. 1995. 45.00 (0-89990-072-0) Info Coord.

Symphony. 2nd ed. Preston Stedman. 512p. 1992. text ed. 59.00 (0-13-880055-3) P-H.

Symphony. Ed. by Ralph Hill. 1988. reprint ed. lib. bdg. 79.00 (0-7812-0369-4) Rprt Serv.

Symphony. Ed. by Ralph Hill. LC 72-181174. 416p. 1961. reprint ed. 59.00 (0-403-01578-2) Scholarly.

Symphony: A Concert Guide. Michael Steinberg. (Illus.). 678p. 1995. 39.95 (0-19-506177-2) OUP.

Symphony: A Listener's Manual. 2nd ed. Orville Shetney. 258p. 1990. 22.95 (0-945483-04-X) E Bowers Pub.

Symphony & Drama, 1850-1900 see Oxford History of Music

Symphony & the Symphonic Poem. 6th rev. ed. Earl V. Moore & Theodore E. Heger. LC 57-63375. (C). 1974. text ed. 15.95 (0-914004-01-8) Ulrich.

Symphony, Eighteen Hundred to Nineteen Hundred. Ed. by Paul H. Lang. LC 75-77392. (Music Anthology Ser.). (C). 1969. pap. text ed. 34.95 (0-393-09865-6) Norton.

Symphony Fantastique & Harold in Italy in Full Score. Hector Berlioz. (Music Scores & Music to Play Ser.). 320p. 1984. reprint ed. pap. 11.95 (0-486-24657-4) Dover.

Symphony for the Sheep. C. M. Millen. LC 95-43097. (Illus.). 32p. (J). 1996. 14.95 (0-395-76503-X) HM.

Symphony Hall, Boston. H. Earle Johnson. LC 78-31124. (Music Reprint Ser.). 1979. reprint ed. lib. bdg. 42.50 (0-306-79518-3) Da Capo.

Symphony in B Minor: The Passion of Peter Ilitch Tchaikovsky. Larry Holdridge. LC 78-2284. (Illus.). 64p. 1978. 10.95 (0-916144-26-7); pap. 3.95 (0-916144-27-5) Stemmer Hse.

Symphony in Counterpoint: An Overture to Hope. Margaret F. Moylan. 7p. 1994. pap. 5.95 (0-9642109-0-8) Parkinsonian.

Symphony in Norway, Vol. I. Ed. by Barry S. Brook. LC 81-13252. (Symphony 1720-1840 Ser.: Vol. 11, Series F). 320p. 1981. 25.00 (0-8240-3810-X) Garland.

Symphony in Poland. Ed. by Barry S. Brook. (Symphony 1720-1840 Series F: Vol. 21). 398p. 1982. text ed. 25.00 (0-8240-3820-7) Garland.

Symphony Mastery. Daniel H. Harris. 432p. 1985. text ed. 38.95 (0-13-880022-7) P-H.

Symphony No. Four for Orchestra. Elie Siegmeister. 159p. 1981. pap. 50.00 (0-8258-0188-5, 05049) Fischer Inc NY.

Symphony No. One: Opus 23. John K. Paine. LC 73-171077. (Earlier American Music Ser.: No. 1). 180p. 1972. reprint ed. lib. bdg. 32.50 (0-306-77301-5) Da Capo.

Symphony No. Thirty-Five in D, K. 385: The Haffner Symphony. Wolfgang Amadeus Mozart. 1968. pap. 8.00 (0-19-385289-6) OUP.

Symphony No. Two: In B Flat, Opus 21. George W. Chadwick. LC 71-170930. (Earlier American Music Ser.: No. 3). 216p. 1972. reprint ed. 35.00 (0-306-77304-X) Da Capo.

Symphony No. 2: Score. J. Harbison. 104p. 1993. per. 20.00 (0-7935-2487-3) H Leonard.

Symphony No. 3 Score Critical Edition: The Camp Meeting "Smyth" 1990. write for info. (0-7935-0037-0) H Leonard.

Symphony No. 4: Brahms. Kenneth Hull. Date not set. write for info. (0-393-03800-9) Norton.

Symphony of Animals. Illus. by Walter Anderson. LC 96-14276. 144p. 1996. 50.00 (0-87805-909-1) U Pr of Miss.

Symphony of Color: Stained Glass at First Church. Patricia H. Rodgers. (Illus.). 63p. (Orig.). 1990. pap. write for info. (0-9626196-0-4) United Ch Cambridge.

Symphony of Color: The World of Kelly Fitzpatrick. Montgomery Museum of Fine Arts Staff. Ed. by Margaret L. Ausfeld. LC 90-25173. (Illus.). 72p. (ps-12). 1991. pap. 18.00 (0-89280-028-3) Montgomery Mus.

Symphony of Creation: The Heavens. Linda Draper. (Illus.). 200p. (Orig.). 1989. pap. 14.95 (0-317-93518-6) Camenae Twins.

Symphony of Flavors: A Classic Collection of Recipes. Christine Askew et al. LC 90-64430. 288p. 1991. 14.95 (0-9629059-0-9) Sir Deb.

Symphony of Hearts. Manjiri Prabhu. (C). 1994. text ed. 7.00 (81-7167-183-7, Pub. by Rupa II) S Asia.

Symphony of Life: Letters by Ludwig van Beethoven. Ludwig van Beethoven. Tr. by Ulrich L. Steindorff. LC 74-24037. reprint ed. 17.50 (0-404-12860-2) AMS Pr.

Symphony of Light. Jack McKinney. (Robotech Ser.: No. 12). 224p. 1987. mass mkt. 5.99 (0-345-34145-7, Del Rey) Ballantine.

Symphony of Love. Elmer A. Spiezio. 168p. 1994. 16.95 (1-57087-059-4) Prof Pr NC.

Symphony of Manufacturing. F. G. Hopkins. LC 93-87427. 200p. (C). 1994. 25.00 (0-9639870-0-3) Oakland Cnslt.

Symphony of New Testament Hymns. Robert J. Karris. LC 96-25645. 184p. (Orig.). 1996. pap. 14.95 (0-8146-2425-1, Liturg Pr Bks) Liturgical Pr.

Symphony of the Heart. Renee F. Schwarz. (Illus.). 107p. 1993. 17.95 (0-88400-169-5) Shengold.

Symphony of the Zodiac. 2nd ed. Torkom Saraydarian. LC 79-53516. 1988. 20.00 (0-911794-04-2); pap. 18.00 (0-911794-05-0) Aqua Educ.

***Symphony of Whales.** Schuch. (J). 1998. write for info. (0-15-100289-4); write for info. (0-15-201670-8, HB Juv Bks) HarBrace.

An Asterisk (*) at the beginning of an entry indicates that the title is appearing in BIP for the first time.

Symphony on Ice: The Protopopovs. A. Shelukhin. Tr. by Beatrice Yusem. 64p. 1992. pap. 15.00 (*0-9631758-9-0*) Platoro Pr.

Symphony Orchestras of the United States: Selected Profiles. Ed. by Robert R. Craven. LC 85-7637. 544p. 1986. text ed. 65.00 (*0-313-24072-8*, CRU/, Greenwood Pr) Greenwood.

Symphony Orchestras of the World. Robert R. Craven. LC 86-29452. 491p. 1987. text ed. 105.00 (*0-313-24073-6*, CRW/, Greenwood Pr) Greenwood.

Symphony Revealed. Dan Shaffer. write for info. (*0-318-58232-5*) P-H.

Symphony since Beethoven. Felix Weingartner. 1972. 59.95 (*0-8490-1169-8*) Gordon Pr.

Symphony since Beethoven. Felix Weingartner. 1980. lib. bdg. 49.95 (*0-8490-3143-5*) Gordon Pr.

Symphony Themes. Raymond M. Burrows. 295p. reprint ed. lib. bdg. 59.00 (*0-685-14863-7*) Rprt Serv.

Symphony Writers since Beethoven. Felix Weingartner. Tr. by Arthur Bles from GER. LC 77-109878. (Illus.). vii, 168p. 1969. reprint ed. text ed. 49.75 (*0-8371-4369-1*, WESW) Greenwood.

Symphony Writers since Beethoven. Felix Weingartner. 168p. 1990. reprint ed. lib. bdg. 59.00 (*0-7812-9117-8*) Rprt Serv.

Symphony Writers since Beethoven. Felix Weingartner. 168p. 1991. reprint ed. lib. bdg. 69.00 (*0-7812-9330-8*) Rprt Serv.

Symphony, 1825-1914. D. Kern Holoman. (Studies in Musical Genres & Repertories). (Illus.). 1996. 45.00 (*0-02-871105-X*) Schirmer Bks.

Symphony #4. Kenneth Hull. (Critical Editions Ser.). (C). Date not set. pap. text ed. write for info. (*0-393-96677-1*, Norton Paperbks) Norton.

Symphorien Champier & the Reception of the Occultist Tradition in Renaissance France. Brian Copenhaver. 1978. text ed. 102.35 (*90-279-7647-3*) Mouton.

Symplectic Cobordism & the Computation of Stable Stems. Stanley O. Kochman. LC 93-17167. (Memoirs of the American Mathematical Society Ser.: No. 496). 88p. 1993. pap. 29.95 (*0-8218-2558-5*, MEMO/104/496) Am Math.

Symplectic Cobordism Ring, No. I. Stanley O. Kochman. LC 79-27872. (Memoirs Ser.: No. 228). 206p. 1980. pap. 21.00 (*0-8218-2228-4*, MEMO/24/228) Am Math.

Symplectic Cobordism Ring, No. II. Stanley O. Kochman. LC 79-27872. (Memoirs Ser.: No. 271). 170p. 1982. pap. 19.00 (*0-8218-2271-3*, MEMO/40/271) Am Math.

Symplectic Fibrations & Multiplicity Diagrams. Victor Guillemin et al. (Illus.). 224p. (C). 1996. text ed. 49.95 (*0-521-44323-7*) Cambridge U Pr.

Symplectic Geometry. Ed. by D. A. Salamon. (London Mathematical Society Lecture Note Ser.: No. 192). 300p. (C). 1994. pap. text ed. 44.95 (*0-521-44699-6*) Cambridge U Pr.

Symplectic Geometry. 2nd ed. A. T. Fomenko. (Advanced Studies in Contemporary Mathematics). 512p. 1995. text ed. 110.00 (*2-88124-901-9*) Gordon & Breach.

Symplectic Geometry, Vol. 5. A. T. Fomenko. (Advanced Studies in Contemporary Mathematics). xiv, 388p. 1988. text ed. 385.00 (*2-88124-657-5*) Gordon & Breach.

Symplectic Geometry: An Introduction Based on the Seminar in Bern in 1992. B. Aebischer. (Progress in Mathematics Ser.: No. 124). 256p. 1994. 49.50 (*3-7643-5064-4*); 49.50 (*0-8176-5064-4*) Birkhauser.

Symplectic Geometry & Mathematical Physics: Actes du Colloque en l'Honneur de Jean-Marie Souriau. Ed. by P. Donato et al. (Progress in Mathematics Ser.: Vol. 99). xiii, 478p. 1991. 96.50 (*0-8176-3581-5*) Birkhauser.

Symplectic Geometry & Quantization: A Symposium on Symplectic Geometry & Quantization Problems, July 1993, Japan. Ed. by Yoshiaki Maeda et al. LC 94-25115. (Contemporary Mathematics Ser.: Vol. 179). 1994. pap. 51.00 (*0-8218-0302-6*, CONM/179) Am Math.

Symplectic Geometry & Secondary Characteristic Classes. Izu Vaisman. (Progress in Mathematics Ser.: No. 72). 232p. 1987. 57.50 (*0-8176-3356-1*) Birkhauser.

Symplectic Geometry, Groupoids & Integrable Systems. P. Dazord & Alan Weinstein. (Mathematical Sciences Research Institute Publications: Vol. 20). (Illus.). 328p. 1991. 69.95 (*0-387-97526-8*) Spr-Verlag.

Symplectic Groups. O. Timothy O'Meara. LC 78-19101. (Mathematical Surveys & Monographs). 122p. 1978. reprint ed. pap. 49.00 (*0-8218-1516-4*, SURV/16) Am Math.

Symplectic Invariants & Hamiltonian Dynamics. Helmut Hofer & Eduard Zehnder. LC 94-28461. (Advanced Texts Ser.). 360p. 1994. 59.50 (*0-8176-5066-0*) Birkhauser.

***Symplectic Manifolds with No Kahler Structure, Vol. 166.** John Oprea & Aleksy Tralle. LC 97-20491. (Lecture Notes in Mathematics Ser.). 1997. pap. write for info. (*3-540-63105-4*) Spr-Verlag.

Symplectic Matrices, First Order Systems & Special Relativity. M. Kauderer. 250p. 1994. text ed. 64.00 (*981-02-0829-4*); pap. text ed. 30.00 (*981-02-1984-9*) World Scientific Pub.

Symplectic Techniques in Physics. Victor Guillemin & Shlomo Sternberg. 468p. (C). 1990. pap. text ed. 35.95 (*0-521-38990-9*) Cambridge U Pr.

Symplectic Twist Maps. C. Gole. (Advanced Series in Nonlinear Dynamics). 150p. (C). 1998. text ed. 36.00 (*981-02-0589-9*) World Scientific Pub.

Symposia & Symposium Publications: A Guide for Organisers, Lecturers, & Editors of Scientific Meetings. A. A. Manten. LC 76-837. (Illus.). 176p. reprint ed. pap. 50.20 (*0-317-09783-0*, 2051677) Bks Demand.

Symposia Gausina Conference B: Statistical Sciences: Proceedings of the 2nd Gauss Symposium, Munich, Germany, August 2-7, 1993. Ed. by Volker Mammitzsch & Hans Schneeweiss. (Symposia Gaussiana Ser.). x, 342p. (C). 1995. lib. bdg. 148.95 (*3-11-014412-3*) De Gruyter.

Symposia Gaussina Conference A: Mathematics & Theoretical Physics: Proceedings of the 2nd Gauss Symposium, Munich, Germany, August 2-7, 1993. Ed. by Minaketan Behara et al. LC 95-14935. (Symposia Gaussiana Ser.). xx, 745p. (C). 1995. lib. bdg. 198.95 (*3-11-014476-X*) De Gruyter.

Symposia Mathematica, vol. 14. Symposiama. 1975. text ed. 204.00 (*0-12-612214-8*) Acad Pr.

Symposia Mathematica, vol. 15. Symposiama. 1976. text ed. 204.00 (*0-12-612215-6*) Acad Pr.

Symposia Mathematica, vol. 21. Symposiama. 1978. text ed. 204.00 (*0-12-612221-0*) Acad Pr.

Symposia Mathematica, vol. 22. Symposiama. 1978. text ed. 204.00 (*0-12-612222-9*) Acad Pr.

Symposia Mathematica, vol. 23. Symposiama. 1980. text ed. 157.00 (*0-12-612223-7*) Acad Pr.

***Symposia Mathematica, Vol. 25A.** Symposiama. 1981. text ed. 157.00 (*0-12-612225-3*) Acad Pr.

Symposia Mathematica, Vol. 26. (Serial Publication Ser.). 243p. 1982. text ed. 157.00 (*0-12-612226-1*) Acad Pr.

Symposia Mathematica, Vol. 29. Ed. by M. W. Baldoni-Silva & A. W. Knapp. 309p. 1990. text ed. 117.00 (*0-12-612229-6*) Acad Pr.

Symposia Mathematica, Vol. 31. Ed. by M. W. Baldoni-Silva & A. W. Knapp. (Illus.). 261p. 1990. text ed. 135.00 (*0-12-612231-8*) Acad Pr.

Symposia Mathematica Vol. 32: Problems in the Theory of Surfaces & Their Classification. Ed. by F. Catanese et al. 410p. 1992. text ed. 117.00 (*0-12-612232-6*) Acad Pr.

Symposia of the Royal Entomological Society of London: Insect Polymorphism. Ed. by J. S. Kennedy. 115p. 1984. 50.00 (*0-317-07178-5*) St Mut.

Symposia of the Royal Entomological Society of London: Insect Reproduction. K. C. Highnam. 120p. 1984. 50.00 (*0-317-07179-3*) St Mut.

Symposia of the Royal Entomological Society of London: Insect Ultrastructure. A. C. Neville. 190p. 1984. 45.00 (*0-317-07180-7*) St Mut.

Symposia of the Zoological Society of London, Vol. 51. (Serial Publications). 1984. text ed. 126.00 (*0-12-613351-4*) Acad Pr.

Symposia on Theoretical Physics & Mathematics: Lectures Presented at the Anniversary Symposium of the Institute of Mathematical Sciences, Madras, India, 8 Vols., Vol. 1. Institute of Mathematical Sciences (India). Ed. by Alladi Ramakrishnan. LC 65-31184. 1963. pap. 45.30 (*0-317-11136-1*, 2019402) Bks Demand.

Symposia on Theoretical Physics & Mathematics: Lectures Presented at the Anniversary Symposium of the Institute of Mathematical Sciences, Madras, India, 8 Vols., Vol. 2. Institute of Mathematical Sciences (India). Ed. by Alladi Ramakrishnan. LC 65-31184. 1964. pap. 62.00 (*0-317-11137-X*) Bks Demand.

Symposia on Theoretical Physics & Mathematics: Lectures Presented at the Anniversary Symposium of the Institute of Mathematical Sciences, Madras, India, 8 Vols., Vol. 3. Institute of Mathematical Sciences (India). Ed. by Alladi Ramakrishnan. LC 65-31184. 1964. pap. 48.50 (*0-317-11138-8*) Bks Demand.

Symposia on Theoretical Physics & Mathematics: Lectures Presented at the Anniversary Symposium of the Institute of Mathematical Sciences, Madras, India, 8 Vols., Vol. 5. Institute of Mathematical Sciences (India). Ed. by Alladi Ramakrishnan. LC 65-31184. 1965. pap. 57.50 (*0-317-11139-6*) Bks Demand.

Symposia on Theoretical Physics & Mathematics: Lectures Presented at the Anniversary Symposium of the Institute of Mathematical Sciences, Madras, India, 8 Vols., Vol. 7. Institute of Mathematical Sciences (India). Ed. by Alladi Ramakrishnan. LC 65-31184. 1966. pap. 51.30 (*0-317-11140-X*) Bks Demand.

Symposia on Theoretical Physics & Mathematics: Lectures Presented at the Anniversary Symposium of the Institute of Mathematical Sciences, Madras, India, 8 Vols., Vol. 8. Institute of Mathematical Sciences (India). Ed. by Alladi Ramakrishnan. LC 65-31184. 1967. pap. 53.00 (*0-317-11141-8*) Bks Demand.

Symposia on Theoretical Physics & Mathematics: Lectures Presented at the Anniversary Symposium of the Institute of Mathematical Sciences, Madras, India, 8 Vols., Vol. 9. Institute of Mathematical Sciences (India). Ed. by Alladi Ramakrishnan. LC 65-31184. 1968. pap. 72.30 (*0-317-11142-6*) Bks Demand.

Symposia on Theoretical Physics & Mathematics: Lectures Presented at the Anniversary Symposium of the Institute of Mathematical Sciences, Madras, India, 8 Vols., Vol. 10. Institute of Mathematical Sciences (India). Ed. by Alladi Ramakrishnan. LC 65-31184. 1969. pap. 42.80 (*0-317-11143-4*) Bks Demand.

Symposia on Water Resources Education, a Lifetime of Learning: Changing Roles in Water Resources Management & Policy. American Water Resources Association Staff. LC 93-71755. (American Water Resources Association Technical Publication Ser.: Vol. TPS-93-2). (Illus.). 732p. 1993. reprint ed. pap. 180.00 (*0-7837-9225-5*, 2049976) Bks Demand.

***Symposium.** Ed. by Theodor Damian et al. 99p. 1996. pap. text ed. write for info. (*1-888067-03-9*) Romanian Inst.

Symposium. Plato. Ed. by Kenneth J. Dover. LC 78-67430. (Cambridge Greek & Latin Classics Ser.). 196p. 1980. pap. text ed. 21.95 (*0-521-29523-8*) Cambridge U Pr.

Symposium. Plato. Tr. by Paul Woodruff from GRE. LC 89-30960. (HPC Classics Ser.). 110p. (C). 1989. pap. 6.95 (*0-87220-076-0*); lib. bdg. 27.95 (*0-87220-077-9*) Hackett Pub.

Symposium. Plato. Tr. by Robin A. Waterfield. LC 93-566. (World's Classics Ser.). 160p. (ENG & GER.). 1994. pap. 6.95 (*0-19-282908-4*) OUP.

Symposium. Plato. 1996. 13.50 (*0-679-60197-X*, Modern Lib) Random.

Symposium. Plato. Tr. & Intro. by Walter Hamilton. (Classics Ser.). 128p. 1952. pap. 8.95 (*0-14-044024-0*, Penguin Classics) Viking Penguin.

Symposium. Muriel Spark. 192p. 1992. pap. 9.00 (*0-380-71553-8*) Avon.

***Symposium, Vol. I, No. 1, 1994.** Theodor Damian et al. 37p. 1994. pap. 8.00 (*1-888067-00-4*) Romanian Inst.

***Symposium, Vol. II, No. 1, 1995.** Theodor Damian et al. 60p. 1995. pap. 6.00 (*1-888067-01-2*) Romanian Inst.

Symposium: A New Look at Some Old Sites, No. 6. Ed. by Gary S. Breschini & Trudy Haversat. (Archives of California Prehistory Ser.: No. 6). 86p. (Orig.). pap. 7.75 (*1-55567-037-7*) Coyote Press.

Symposium: Factors that Regulate the Wax & Wane of Algal Populations. Ed. by R. G. Wetzel. (International Association of Theoretical & Applied Limnology Communications Ser.: No. 19). (Illus.). 318p. 1971. pap. text ed. 104.00 (*3-510-52019-X*) Lubrecht & Cramer.

Symposium: Looking at the Principles Behind Affirmative Action. Richard A. Wasserstrom & William B. Reynolds. (Working Papers on Civil Rights). 1988. 2.50 (*0-318-33315-5*, CR1) IPPP.

Symposium: Patterns of Land Utilization & Other Papers: American Ethnological Society Proceedings, 1961. Ed. by Viola E. Garfield. LC 84-45548. 1988. reprint ed. pap. 45.00 (*0-404-62655-6*) AMS Pr.

Symposium & Phaedrus. Plato. 96p. 1993. reprint ed. pap. text ed. 1.00 (*0-486-27798-4*) Dover.

Symposium & the Phaedo. Plato. Ed. & Tr. by Raymond Larson. LC 79-55931. (Crofts Classics Ser.). 144p. (Orig.). (C). 1980. pap. text ed. write for info. (*0-88295-122-X*) Harlan Davidson.

Symposium & The Phaedrus: Plato's Erotic Dialogues. Plato. LC 92-35391. (SUNY Series in Ancient Greek Philosophy). 214p. (C). 1993. pap. text ed. 11.95 (*0-7914-1618-6*) State U NY Pr.

Symposium by God & the Devil. John R. Stahl. (Illus.). 32p. (C). 1971. 30.00 (*0-945303-00-9*) Evanescent Pr.

Symposium for the Marketing of Higher Education, 1992, November 15-17, 1992, Atlanta, Georgia. LC 92-42186. 1992. 75.00 (*0-87757-227-5*) Am Mktg.

Symposium Graeco-Arabicum II: Bochum 3-5 Marz, 1987. Ed. by Gerhard Endress. (Archivum Graeco-Arabicum Ser.: No. 1). xvi, 204p. (GER.). 1989. 53.00 (*90-6032-315-7*, Pub. by Gruner NE) Benjamins North Am.

Symposium in Immunology, 2 vols. Ed. by M. M. Eibl et al. LC 93-7837. 1993. Alk. paper. 79.95 (*0-387-56478-0*) Spr-Verlag.

Symposium in Immunology. Ed. by M. M. Eibl & C. Huber. (Humoral Immunodeficiencies Ser.: 3). 285p. 1994. pap. 85.00 (*0-387-57126-4*) Spr-Verlag.

Symposium in Immunology V Vol. 5: Antiviral Immunity. Ed. by M. M. Eibl et al. (Illus.). 132p. 1996. pap. 109.00 (*3-540-60061-2*) Spr-Verlag.

Symposium in Memory of Kei Mori: Studies in Economic Dynamics. L. R. Klein. 100p. 1995. text ed. 48.00 (*981-02-2054-5*) World Scientific Pub.

Symposium in Music Education: A Festschrift for Charles Leonhard. Ed. by Richard Colwell. LC 81-71592. 329p. 1982. 15.00 (*0-686-38473-3*) U IL Sch Music.

Symposium of Law Publishers. Ed. by Thomas Woxland & Robert Berring. LC 91-32424. (Legal Reference Services Quarterly Ser.: Vol. 11, Nos. 3-4). 166p. 1992. 39.95 (*1-56024-229-9*) Haworth Pr.

Symposium of Law Publishers. Ed. by Thomas Woxland. LC 91-32424. (Legal Reference Services Quarterly Ser.: Vol. 11, Nos. 3-4). 166p. 1996. pap. 19.95 (*0-7890-6049-3*) Haworth Pr.

***Symposium of North Eastern Accelerator Personnel.** 350p. 1998. 54.00 (*981-02-3035-4*) World Scientific Pub.

Symposium of Plato. Plato. Tr. by Benjamin Jowett. 1996. pap. 4.95 (*0-8283-1456-X*, 17, Intl Pocket Lib) Branden Pub Co.

Symposium of Plato. Plato. Tr. by Tom Griffith. (Illus.). 144p. 1993. pap. 15.95 (*0-520-06695-2*) U CA Pr.

Symposium of Plato. Plato. Ed. by John A. Brentlinger. Tr. by Suzy Q. Groden. LC 79-103478. (Illus.). 144p. (C). 1970. pap. 13.95 (*0-87023-076-X*) U of Mass Pr.

***Symposium of Plato.** Ed. by Rowe. (Classical Texts Ser.). Date not set. write for info. (*0-85668-614-X*, Pub. by Aris & Phillips UK) David Brown.

***Symposium of Plato.** Ed. by Rowe. (Classical Texts Ser.). Date not set. pap. write for info. (*0-85668-615-8*, Pub. by Aris & Phillips UK) David Brown.

Symposium of the International Society for Research in Stereoencephalotomy, 7th, Sao Paulo, June 24, 1977. Ed. by Philip L. Gildenberg. (Advances in Stereoencephalotomy Ser.: Vol. 8). (Illus.). 1978. pap. 78.50 (*3-8055-2946-5*) S Karger.

Symposium of the Whole: A Range of Discourse Toward an Enthnopoetics. Jerome Rothenberg & Diane Rothenberg. 526p. (C). 1983. pap. 16.00 (*0-520-04531-9*) U CA Pr.

Symposium on Advanced Manufacturing, 1988: Proceedings. Ed. by R. William De Vore. LC 86-63797. (Illus.). 150p. 1988. pap. 10.00 (*0-89779-072-3*, UKY BU147) OES Pubns.

Symposium on Air-Pollution Measurement Methods. LC 63-21664. (American Society for Testing & Materials: No. 352). 84p. reprint ed. pap. 25.00 (*0-317-10904-9*, 2000117) Bks Demand.

Symposium on Algebraic Topology, in Honor of Jose Adem: Proceedings. Ed. by Samuel Gitler. LC 82-13812. (Contemporary Mathematics Ser.: Vol. 12). 357p. 1982. pap. 35.00 (*0-8218-5010-5*, CONM/12) Am Math.

Symposium on Applications of Micro-Electronics, 27th March, 1968, University of Birmingham. LC 73-435862. (Institution of Electrical Engineers Conference Report Ser.: No. 49). 88p. reprint ed. pap. 25.10 (*0-317-10137-4*, 2007387) Bks Demand.

Symposium on Atomic Energy & Its Implications. LC 74-84341. (Essay Index Reprint Ser.). 1977. 22.95 (*0-8369-1110-5*) Ayer.

Symposium on Automatic Control in Electricity Supply, 29-31 March, 1966 in Manchester, England. Automatic Control in Electricity Supply Staff. (IEE Conference Publication Ser.: No. 16, Pt. 1). (Illus.). 392p. reprint ed. pap. 111.80 (*0-317-09932-9*, 2051588) Bks Demand.

***Symposium on Building Partnerships for Women's Health: Implications for Managed Care.** Leslie R. Wolfe & Karen Schneider. 24p. (Orig.). 1997. pap. 10.00 (*1-877966-41-X*) Ctr Women Policy.

Symposium on Byzantine Medicine. Ed. by John Scarborough. LC 85-25967. (Dumbarton Oaks Papers: No. 38). (Illus.). 298p. 1985. 40.00 (*0-88402-139-4*) Dumbarton Oaks.

Symposium on Central California Archaeology: Problems, Programs, & Interdisciplinary Approaches. fac. ed. Ed. by Freddie Curtis. (Sacramento Anthropological Society, Sacramento State College Ser.: No. 3). (Illus.). 128p. 1965. reprint ed. pap. text ed. 11.50 (*1-55567-558-1*) Coyote Press.

Symposium on Cherokee & Iroquois Culture. William N. Fenton & John Gulick. (Bureau of American Ethnology Bulletins Ser.). 292p. 1995. lib. bdg. write for info. (*0-7812-4180-4*) Rprt Serv.

Symposium on Cinema in Developing Countries. 171p. 1979. 12.95 (*0-318-36278-3*) Asia Bk Corp.

Symposium on Cleaning & Materials Processing for Electronics & Space Apparatus. American Society for Testing & Materials Staff. LC 63-15794. (American Society for Testing & Materials: No. 342). 273p. reprint ed. pap. 77.90 (*0-317-08016-4*, 2000138) Bks Demand.

Symposium on Community Studies in Anthropology: American Ethnological Society Proceedings, 1963. American Ethnological Society Staff. LC 84-45550. 1988. reprint ed. pap. 35.00 (*0-404-62657-2*) AMS Pr.

Symposium on Conodont Biostratigraphy, Ohio State University, 1969. Geological Society of America Conodont Biostratigraphy Symposium Staff. Ed. by Walter C. Sweet & Stig M. Bergstrom. (Geological Society of America, Memoir Ser.: No. 127). 515p. reprint ed. pap. 146.80 (*0-317-28379-0*, 2025461) Bks Demand.

Symposium on Corrosion Fundamentals: A Series of Lectures Presented at the University of Tennessee Corrosion Conference at Knoxville on March 1-3, 1955. Ed. by Anton De Brasunas & E. E. Stansbury. LC 56-13073. 261p. reprint ed. pap. 74.40 (*0-317-10658-9*, 2022212) Bks Demand.

Symposium on Creation VI. Donald W. Patten. 1977. pap. 3.95 (*0-685-52492-2*) Pacific Mer.

Symposium on Daniel, 7 vols., Set. Ed. by Frank B. Holbrook. (Daniel & Revelation Committee Ser.: Vol. 2). 557p. (Orig.). 1986. Vol. 2. pap. 12.95 (*0-925675-01-6*) BRI DC.

Symposium on Design for Elevated Temperature Environment. Ed. by S. Y. Zamrik. LC 79-173043. 67p. reprint ed. pap. 25.00 (*0-317-10994-4*, 2013307) Bks Demand.

Symposium on Diseases of Fishes & Shellfishes. Stanislas F. Snieszko. LC 72-114052. (Special Publication Ser.: No. 5). 528p. 1970. text ed. 13.00 (*0-913235-04-0*) Am Fisheries Soc.

Symposium on Drought in Botswana. Ed. by Madalon T. Hinchey. 15.00 (*0-87451-171-2*) Clark U Pr.

Symposium on Dynamic Behavior of Materials. American Society for Testing & Materials Staff. LC 63-20729. (American Society for Testing & Materials Special Technical Publication Ser.: No. 336). 323p. reprint ed. pap. 92.10 (*0-317-10854-9*, 2000144) Bks Demand.

Symposium on Environmental Issues in Photofinishing: Advanced Printing of Paper Summaries. Symposium on Environmental Issues in Photofinishing, Los Angeles, CA Staff. (Illus.). 90p. reprint ed. pap. 25.70 (*0-7837-1642-7*, 2041936) Bks Demand.

Symposium on Fatigue & Symposium on Human Factors in Equipment Design, 2 Vols. Ed. by W. F. Floyd et al. LC 77-70494. (Illus.). 1977. reprint ed. lib. bdg. 35.95 (*0-405-10165-1*) Ayer.

Symposium on Fatigue Tests of Aircraft Structures: Low-Cycle, Full-Scale, & Helicopters. American Society for Testing & Materials Staff. LC 63-15793. (American Society for Testing & Materials: No. 338). 279p. reprint ed. pap. 79.60 (*0-317-09223-5*, 2000142) Bks Demand.

Symposium on Flameproofing, Intrinsic Safety & Other Safeguards in Electrical Instrument Practice, 27th April, 1962. (Institution of Electrical Engineers Conference Report Ser.: No. 3). 96p. reprint ed. pap. 27.40 (*0-317-10109-9*, 2007382) Bks Demand.

***Symposium on Gear Tooth Finishing.** AGMA Technical Committee. (Technical Papers: Vol. 129.01). 1948. pap. text ed. 30.00 (*1-55589-134-9*) AGMA.

Symposium on God's Deliverance: A 15 Part Examination of God's Work of Deliverance. Michael D. Juzwick. 1996. spiral bd. 19.95 (*1-887412-07-7*) Light Eternal Pubns.

Symposium on Graphite Fiber Composites: An Integrated Approach to Their Development & Use Presented at ASME Winter Meeting, Pittsburgh, PA., Nov. 1967. American Society of Mechanical Engineers, Rubber & Plastic Division Staff. LC 67-31228. 77p. reprint ed. pap. 25.00 (*0-317-08656-1*, 2012303) Bks Demand.

Symposium on Ground Water. Ed. by Gerard P. Lennon. LC 91-21956. 320p. 1991. pap. text ed. 35.00 (*0-87262-817-5*) Am Soc Civil Eng.

S

An Asterisk (*) at the beginning of an entry indicates that the title is appearing in BIP for the first time.

Symposium on High Temperature Composites: Special Conference of the American Society for Composites. LC 89-50847. 305p. 1989. 49.95 (*0-87762-700-2*) Technomic.

Symposium on Hong Kong: 1997. Ed. by Hungdah Chiu. (Occasional Papers-Reprints Series in Contemporary Asian Studies: No. 3-1985 (68)). 100p. (Orig.). (C). 1986. reprint ed. pap. 4.00 (*0-942182-70-7*) Occasional Papers.

***Symposium on Incremental Motion Control Systems & Devices: 24th Annual Proceedings.** Ed. by Benjamin C. Kuo. (Illus.). 325p. 1995. 95.00 (*0-931538-18-1*) Incremental Motion.

Symposium on Incremental Motion Control Systems & Devices: 25th Annual Proceedings. Ed. by Benjamin C. Kuo. (Illus.). 330p. 1996. 99.00 (*0-931538-19-X*) Incremental Motion.

Symposium on Incremental Motion Control Systems & Devices, 10th Annual: Proceedings. Ed. by Benjamin C. Kuo. (Illus.). 362p. 1981. 50.00 (*0-931538-03-3*) Incremental Motion.

Symposium on Incremental Motion Control Systems & Devices, 11th Annual: Proceedings. Ed. by Benjamin C. Kuo. (Illus.). 332p. 1982. 50.00 (*0-931538-04-1*) Incremental Motion.

Symposium on Incremental Motion Control Systems & Devices, 12th Annual: Proceedings. Ed. by Benjamin C. Kuo. (Illus.). 320p. 1983. 50.00 (*0-931538-05-X*) Incremental Motion.

Symposium on Incremental Motion Control Systems & Devices, 13th Annual: Proceedings. Ed. by Benjamin C. Kuo. (Illus.). 350p. 1984. 50.00 (*0-931538-06-8*) Incremental Motion.

Symposium on Incremental Motion Control Systems & Devices, 14th Annual: Proceedings. Ed. by Benjamin C. Kuo. (Illus.). 432p. 1985. 60.00 (*0-931538-07-6*) Incremental Motion.

Symposium on Incremental Motion Control Systems & Devices, 15th Annual: Proceedings. Ed. by Benjamin C. Kuo. (Illus.). 398p. 1986. 60.00 (*0-931538-08-4*) Incremental Motion.

Symposium on Incremental Motion Control Systems & Devices, 16th Annual: Proceedings. Ed. by Benjamin C. Kuo. (Illus.). 370p. 1987. 70.00 (*0-931538-09-2*) Incremental Motion.

Symposium on Incremental Motion Control Systems & Devices, 17th Annual: Proceedings. Ed. by Benjamin C. Kuo. (Illus.). 360p. 1988. 70.00 (*0-931538-10-6*) Incremental Motion.

Symposium on Incremental Motion Control Systems & Devices, 18th Annual: Proceedings. Ed. by Benjamin C. Kuo. (Illus.). 357p. 1989. 75.00 (*0-931538-11-4*) Incremental Motion.

Symposium on Incremental Motion Control Systems & Devices, 19th: Proceedings. Ed. by Benjamin C. Kuo. (Illus.). 450p. 1990. 85.00 (*0-931538-12-2*) Incremental Motion.

Symposium on Incremental Motion Control Systems & Devices, 20th Annual Proceedings. Ed. by Benjamin C. Kuo. (Illus.). 1991. 85.00 (*0-931538-13-0*) Incremental Motion.

Symposium on Incremental Motion Control Systems & Devices, 21st Annual Proceedings. Ed. by Benjamin C. Kuo. (Illus.). 1992. 90.00 (*0-931538-14-9*) Incremental Motion.

Symposium on Incremental Motion Control Systems & Devices, 22nd Annual Proceedings. Ed. by Benjamin C. Kuo. (Illus.). 1993. 90.00 (*0-931538-16-5*) Incremental Motion.

Symposium on Incremental Motion Control Systems & Devices. 23rd Annual Proceedings. Ed. by Benjamin C. Kuo. (Illus.). 1994. 90.00 (*0-931538-17-3*) Incremental Motion.

Symposium on Incremental Motion Control Systems & Devices, 8th. Incremental Motion & Control Systems & Devices Symposium Staff. LC 73-647018. (Illus.). 1979. 45.00 (*0-931538-01-7*) Incremental Motion.

Symposium on Information & Communication in Chemistry see International Congress of Pure & Applied Chemistry, 24th, Hamburg, 1973: Proceedings

Symposium on Language & Culture: American Ethnological Society Proceedings, 1962. Ed. by Viola E. Garfield & Wallace L. Chafe. LC 84-45549. 1988. reprint ed. pap. 35.00 (*0-404-62656-4*) AMS Pr.

Symposium on Law & Outer Space, 3rd Annual (1991) 90p. 1991. pap. text ed. 15.00 (*1-56986-173-0*) Federal Bar.

Symposium on Law & Outer Space, 4th Annual. 65p. 1992. 15.00 (*1-56986-228-1*, SPC-92-65) Federal Bar.

Symposium on Local Diversity in Iroquois Culture. William N. Fenton. (Bureau of American Ethnology Bulletins Ser.). 187p. 1995. lib. bdg. 79.00 (*0-7812-4149-9*) Rprt Serv.

Symposium on Local Diversity in Iroquois Culture. Intro. by William N. Fenton. (Illus.). 187p. 1990. reprint ed. pap. 25.00 (*1-878592-08-4*); reprint ed. lib. bdg. 49.00 (*1-878592-09-2*) Native Amer Bk Pubs.

Symposium on Local Diversity in Iroquois Culture. Ed. by William N. Fenton. reprint ed. 49.00 (*0-403-03704-2*) Scholarly.

Symposium on Lubricants for Automotive Equipment. American Society for Testing & Materials Staff. LC 63-15729. (American Society for Testing & Materials: No. 334). 259p. reprint ed. pap. 73.90 (*0-317-09152-2*, 2000122) Bks Demand.

Symposium on Lucunar Infarcts: Clinical Aspects & Diagnostic Examinations: Ravenna, April 1989. Ed. by G. G. Rebucci et al. (Journal: European Neurology: Vol. 29, Suppl. 2, 1989). 50p. (C). 1989. pap. 22.50 (*3-8055-5124-X*) S Karger.

Symposium on Materials for Aircraft, Missiles, & Space Vehicles. American Society for Testing & Materials Staff. LC 63-20730. (American Society for Testing & Materials: 345). 149p. reprint ed. pap. 42.50 (*0-317-09214-6*, 2000136) Bks Demand.

Symposium on Measurement in Unsteady Flow: Presented at the ASME Hydraulic Division Conference, Worcester, Mass., May 21-23, 1962. American Society of Mechanical Engineers Staff. LC 63-2546. 118p. reprint ed. pap. 33.70 (*0-317-11163-9*, 2050440) Bks Demand.

Symposium on Mechatronics 1993. Ed. by Tsu-Chin Tsao et al. 309p. pap. 70.00 (*0-7918-1020-8*) ASME.

Symposium on Medical Therapy in Glaucoma. Ed. by Erik L. Greve. (Documenta Ophthalmologica Proceedings Ser.: Vol. 12). 1977. lib. bdg. 70.50 (*90-6193-152-5*) Kluwer Ac.

Symposium on Mineral Resources of the Southeastern United States: 1949 Proceedings. Frances G. Snyder. 272p. reprint ed. pap. 77.60 (*0-317-29304-4*, 2022223) Bks Demand.

Symposium on Mining, Hydrology, Sedimentology & Reclamation: Proceedings, 1986. R. William DeVore & Donald H. Graves. LC 83-60966. (Illus.). 283p. (Orig.). 1986. pap. 10.00 (*0-89779-067-7*, UKY BU142) OES Pubns.

Symposium on Mining, Hydrology, Sedimentology & Reclamation, 1988: Proceedings. Ed. by Donald H. Graves & R. William De Vore. LC 83-60966. (Illus.). 248p. 1988. pap. 10.00 (*0-89779-073-1*, UKY BU148) OES Pubns.

Symposium on New Approaches to the Study of Religion: American Ethnological Society Proceedings, 1964. Ed. by June Helm. LC 84-45551. 1988. reprint ed. pap. 45.00 (*0-404-62658-0*) AMS Pr.

Symposium on Newer Structural Materials for Aerospace Vehicles. LC 65-16809. (American Society for Testing & Materials Special Technical Publication Ser.: No. 379). 125p. reprint ed. pap. 35.70 (*0-317-09248-0*, 2000735) Bks Demand.

Symposium on Nuclear Energy & Latin American Development: Proceedings. AEC Technical Information Center Staff. 164p. 1968. pap. 18.95 (*0-87079-358-6*, PRNC-112); fiche 9.00 (*0-685-73232-0*) DOE.

Symposium on Nucleic Acid Metabolism of Placenta & Fetus. Ed. by T. Hayashi. (Journal: Gynecologic Investigation: Vol. 8, No. 3). (Illus.). 1977. 24.00 (*3-8055-2771-3*) S Karger.

Symposium on Oneness Pentecostalism 1986. Ed. & Intro. by J. L. Hall. LC 86-19024. (Orig.). (C). 1986. pap. 7.95 (*0-932581-03-X*) Word Aflame.

Symposium on Oneness Pentecostalism 1988 & 1990: Eleven Studies Exploring Historical, Biblical, & Theological Perceptions As Related to the Oneness Movement. LC 90-36543. 389p. (Orig.). 1990. pap. 8.99 (*0-932581-72-2*) Word Aflame.

Symposium on Organic Reaction Mechanisms, No. 19. Royal Society of Chemistry Staff. 1990. 14.00 (*0-85186-139-3*) CRC Pr.

Symposium on Paleolimnology. Ed. by David Frey. (Communications of the International Association of Theoretical & Applied Limnology: No. 17). (Illus.). 448p. (Orig.). 1969. pap. text ed. 115.00 (*3-510-52017-3*, Pub. by E Schweizerbartsche GW) Lubrecht & Cramer.

Symposium on Parenthood & Husbandry: A Three Phase Examination of Biblical & Cooperative Parental Oversight. Michael D. Juzwick. 1997. spiral bd. 17.95 (*1-887412-01-8*) Light Eternal Pubns.

***Symposium on Pharmacology of Learning & Retention, Vol. 4.** B. Knoll. 1974. pap. 50.00 (*963-05-0192-9*, Pub. by Akad Kiado HU) St Mut.

Symposium on Photofinishing Technology: 2nd International: Programs & Paper Summaries. Society of Photographic Scientists & Engineers Staff. Ed. by Kenneth T. Lassiter. 56p. reprint ed. pap. 25.00 (*0-317-28479-7*, 2019236) Bks Demand.

Symposium on Photomorphogenesis. Ed. by Song Pill-Soon. 1978. pap. 21.00 (*0-08-022677-9*, Pergamon Pr) Elsevier.

Symposium on Polyamines, 1-3 June 1990, Albere, Trento, Italy, Vol. 9. J. V. Bannister. (Life Chemistry Reports). 273p. 1991. pap. text ed. 289.00 (*3-7186-5225-0*, Harwood Acad Pubs) Gordon & Breach.

Symposium on Polyamines, 2-4 May 1991, Alghero, Sardinia, Vol. 10. J. V. Bannister & D. Cocco. (Life Chemistry Reports). 170p. 1993. pap. text ed. 397.00 (*3-7186-5339-7*) Gordon & Breach.

Symposium on Radiation Effects on Metals & Neutron Dosimetry. American Society for Testing & Materials Staff. LC 63-12698. (American Society for Testing & Materials Special Technical Publication Ser.: Special Technical Publication, No. 341). 415p. reprint ed. pap. 118.30 (*0-317-10870-0*, 2000139) Bks Demand.

Symposium on Recent Advances in the Chemistry of Colouring Matters, No. 4. Royal Society of Chemistry Staff. 1989. 7.00 (*0-85186-029-X*) CRC Pr.

Symposium on Recent Developments in Nondestructive Testing of Missiles & Rockets. American Society for Testing & Materials Staff. (American Society for Testing & Materials: No. 350). 121p. reprint ed. pap. 34.50 (*0-317-09141-7*, 2000116) Bks Demand.

Symposium on Research Amateur Astronomy. Ed. by S. Edberg. (ASP Conference Series Proceedings: Vol. 33). 280p. 1992. 28.00 (*0-937707-52-X*) Astron Soc Pacific.

Symposium on Resource Use & Conservation of the African Great Lakes, Bujumbara, 1989. R. H. Lowe-McConnell et al. (International Association of Theoretical & Applied Limnology Communications Ser.: No. 23). (Illus.). 128p. 1992. pap. text ed. 44.30 (*3-510-52023-8*, Pub. by E Schweizerbartsche GW) Lubrecht & Cramer.

Symposium on Revelation, Bk. 1: Introductory & Exegetical Studies, 7 vols. Intro. by Frank B. Holbrook. LC 92-3102. (Daniel & Revelation Committee Ser.: Vol. 6). (Illus.). 399p. (Orig.). 1992. pap. 12.95 (*0-925675-14-8*) BRI DC.

Symposium on Revelation, Bk. 2: Exegetical & General Studies, 7 vols. Ed. by Frank B. Holbrook. LC 92-3102. (Daniel & Revelation Committee Ser.: Vol. 7). (Illus.). 465p. 1992. pap. 12.95 (*0-925675-15-6*) BRI DC.

Symposium on Saprobiology. Ed. by Vladimir Sladecek. (Limnology Report: No. 9). (Illus.). 249p. (Orig.). 1978. pap. text ed. 73.50 (*3-510-47007-9*, Pub. by E Schweizerbartsche GW) Lubrecht & Cramer.

Symposium on Semiconductor Modeling & Simulation 1993. IEEE, Electron Devices Society Staff. Ed. by Institute of Electrical & Electronics Engineers, Inc. Staff. LC 93-77325. 90p. 1993. pap. write for info. (*0-7803-1225-2*, 93TH0538-9); fiche write for info. (*0-7803-1226-0*, 93TH0538-9) Inst Electrical.

Symposium on Small Hydropower & Fisheries. Ed. by F. W. Olson et al. LC 85-72260. 497p. 1985. text ed. 28.00 (*0-913235-37-7*, 85-72260) Am Fisheries Soc.

Symposium on Spectrochemical Analysis for Trace Elements. American Society for Testing & Materials Staff. LC 58-3176. (American Society for Testing & Materials Special Technical Publication Ser.: No. 221). 85p. reprint ed. pap. 25.00 (*0-317-09810-1*, 2000112) Bks Demand.

Symposium on Spectroscopy. American Society for Testing & Materials Staff. LC 60-9523. (American Society for Testing & Materials: No. 269). 251p. reprint ed. pap. 71.60 (*0-317-09560-9*, 2000106) Bks Demand.

Symposium on Standards for Filament-Wound Reinforced Plastics. American Society for Testing & Materials Staff. LC 62-22246. (American Society for Testing & Materials Special Technical Publication Ser.: Special Technical Publication, No. 327). 336p. reprint ed. pap. 95.80 (*0-317-10780-1*, 2000120) Bks Demand.

Symposium on Stress-Strain-Time-Temperature Relationships in Materials. American Society for Testing & Materials Staff. LC 62-22248. (American Society for Testing & Materials Special Technical Publication Ser.: Special Publication, No. 325). 135p. reprint ed. pap. 38.50 (*0-317-10835-2*, 2000133) Bks Demand.

Symposium on Support & Testing of Large Astronomical Mirrors: Proceedings Held in Tuscon, Arizona, December 4-6, 1966. Ed. by David L. Crawford et al. (Arizona University, Optical Sciences Center, Technical Report Ser.: Vol. 30). 260p. reprint ed. pap. 74.10 (*0-317-28566-1*, 2055253) Bks Demand.

Symposium on Surface Mining, Hydrology, Sedimentology & Reclamation, 1984: Proceedings. Ed. by R. William DeVore & Donald H. Graves. LC 83-60966. (Illus.). 492p. (Orig.). 1984. pap. 10.00 (*0-89779-062-6*, UKY BU136) OES Pubns.

Symposium on Surface Mining, Hydrology, Sedimentology & Reclamation, 1985: Proceedings. R. William DeVore & Donald H. Graves. LC 83-60966. (Illus.). 439p. (Orig.). 1985. pap. 10.00 (*0-89779-064-2*, UKY BU139) OES Pubns.

Symposium on Teaching Intelligence, a Report. 97p. (Orig.). (C). 1995. pap. text ed. 35.00 (*0-7881-1641-X*) DIANE Pub.

Symposium on Technology & Social Change in Foreign Cultures. (Reports on Technology & Social Change Ser.). 334p. 1973. 15.00 (*0-945271-23-9*) ISU-CIKARD.

Symposium on the Alkali Metals, No. 22. Royal Society of Chemistry Staff. 1989. 20.00 (*0-85186-169-5*) CRC Pr.

Symposium on the Biological Significance of Estuaries. Ed. by Philip A. Douglas & Richard H. Stroud. 1971. 4.00 (*0-686-21854-X*) Sport Fishing.

Symposium on the Chemical & Physical Effects of High-Energy Radiation on Inorganic Substances. American Society for Testing & Materials Staff. LC 64-14646. (American Society for Testing & Materials Special Technical Publication Ser.: No. 359). 119p. reprint ed. pap. 34.00 (*0-317-09795-4*, 2000748) Bks Demand.

Symposium on the Chemical Basis of Heredity. Symposium on the Chemical Basis of Heredity Staff. Ed. by William D. McElroy & Bentley Glass. LC 57-7151. (Contribution of the McCollum-Pratt Institute Ser.: No. 153). (Illus.). 862p. reprint ed. pap. 180.00 (*0-8357-8339-1*, 2034157) Bks Demand.

***Symposium on the Development & Management of Fisheries in Small Water Bodies.** (Summary of Proceedings & Selected Papers, Accra 1987). 195p. (ENG & FRE.). 1989. 25.00 (*92-5-002871-7*, Pub. by FAO IT) Bernan Associates.

Symposium on the House Sparrow (Passer domesticus) & European Tree Sparrow (P. montanus) in North America. Ed. by S. Charles Kendeigh. 121p. 1973. 6.00 (*0-943610-14-1*) Am Ornithologists.

Symposium on the Orion Nebula to Honor Henry Draper, December 4-5, 1981. Ed. by A. E. Glassgold & P. J. Huggins. 338p. 1982. 65.00 (*0-89766-180-X*, VOL. 395C); pap. write for info. (*0-89766-181-8*) NY Acad Sci.

Symposium on the Phycology of Large Lakes of the World. Ed. by M. Munawar. (Limnology Report: No. 22). (Illus.). (Orig.). 1985. pap. text ed. 87.50 (*0-317-63452-6*, Pub. by E Schweizerbartsche GW) Lubrecht & Cramer.

Symposium on the Pressuremeter & Its Marine Applications: Paris, April 19-20, 1982. Editions Technip Staff. (Illus.). 440p. (C). 1982. pap. 485.00 (*2-7108-0434-4*, Pub. by Edits Technip FR) St Mut.

Symposium on the Siting of Nuclear Facilities: Proceedings. (Illus.). 1975. pap. 100.00 (*92-0-020175-X*, ISP384, Pub. by IAEA AU) Bernan Associates.

Symposium on the Solution Properties/Natural Polymers, No. 23. Royal Society of Chemistry Staff. 1989. 17.00 (*0-85186-179-2*) CRC Pr.

Symposium on the Tom C. Clark Papers. 50p. 1987. 15.00 (*0-935630-24-4*) U of Tex Tarlton Law Lib.

Symposium on the Use of Isotopes in Biology & Medicine, University of Wisconsin, 1947. Use of Isotopes In Biology & Medicine Staff et al. LC 48-2939. 468p. reprint ed. pap. 133.40 (*0-317-41734-7*, 2021131) Bks Demand.

Symposium on Trazodone. Ed. by C. L. Cazzullo et al. (Journal: Neuropsychobiology: Vol. 15, Suppl. 1, 1986). (Illus.). iv, 52p. 1986. pap. 22.50 (*3-8055-4338-7*) S Karger.

Symposium on Two & One Fourth Chrome One Molybdenum Steel in Pressure Vessels & Piping: Held as Part of the 25th Annual Petroleum- Engineering Conference, & The Second Annual Pressure Vessels & Piping Conference, September 16-17, 1970, Denver, CO. Adolph O. Schaefer. LC 75-28161. 216p. reprint ed. pap. 61.60 (*0-685-23445-2*, 2032699) Bks Demand.

Symposium on VLSI Circuits, 1993. IEEE, Solid State Circuits Council Staff. Ed. by Institute of Electrical & Electronics Engineers, Inc. Staff. LC 93-77782. 130p. 1993. pap. text ed. write for info. (*0-7803-1260-0*, 93CH3304-3); lib. bdg. write for info. (*0-7803-1261-9*, 93CH3304-3); fiche write for info. (*0-7803-1262-7*, 93CH3304-3) Inst Electrical.

Symposium on VLSI Circuits, 1994. IEEE, Solid State Circuits Council Staff. Ed. by Institute of Electrical & Electronics Engineers, Inc. Staff. LC 94-75833. 144p. 1994. pap. text ed. write for info. (*0-7803-1918-4*); lib. bdg. write for info. (*0-7803-1919-2*, 94CH3434-8); fiche write for info. (*0-7803-1920-6*) Inst Electrical.

Symposium on VLSI Technology, 1994. IEEE, Electronic Devices Society Staff. Ed. by Institute of Electrical & Electronics Engineers, Inc. Staff. LC 90-655131. 144p. 1994. pap. text ed. write for info. (*0-7803-1921-4*); lib. bdg. write for info. (*0-7803-1922-2*, 94CH3433-0); fiche write for info. (*0-7803-1923-0*) Inst Electrical.

Symposium on Water-Use Data for Water Resources Management: Proceedings. Symposium on Water-Use Data for Water Resources Management Staff. Ed. by Marvin Waterstone & R. John Burt. LC 88-71321. (American Water Resources Association Technical Publication Ser.: No. TPS-88-2). (Illus.). 872p. reprint ed. pap. 180.00 (*0-7837-1090-9*, 2041622) Bks Demand.

Symposium Papers & Related Information on Nondestructive Testing for Pipe Systems: Sponsored by Institute of Gas Technology, June 7-10, 1976, Chicago, Illinois. Institute of Gas Technology Staff. LC 76-382339. 335p. reprint ed. pap. 95.50 (*0-317-30071-7*, 2019243) Bks Demand.

Symposium Plato. Benjamin E. Jowett. 64p. (C). 1956. pap. text ed. 6.00 (*0-02-360760-2*, Macmillan Coll) P-H.

Symposium sur les tumeurs cutanees des enfants. Gent. November 1978. Ed. by J. De Bersaques. (Journal: Dermatologica: Vol. 161, Suppl. 1, 1980). (Illus.). iv, 160p. 1981. pap. 14.50 (*3-8055-2238-X*) S Karger.

Symposium to Honor C C Lin. D. Benney et al. 452p. 1988. text ed. 102.00 (*9971-5-0245-3*) World Scientific Pub.

Symposium Toward the Development of a Geoscience Information System: Proceedings of the Sixth Annual Meeting of the Geoscience Information Society, November 1, 1971, Washington D. C. Geoscience Information Society Staff. (Geoscience Information Society Proceedings Ser.: Vol. 2). 106p. reprint ed. pap. 30.30 (*0-7837-5623-2*, 2045532) Bks Demand.

Symposium Transsonicum, No. III. Ed. by J. Zierep & H. Oertel. (International Union of Theoretical & Applied Mechanics Symposia Ser.). (Illus.). 506p. 1989. 126.95 (*0-387-50202-5*) Spr-Verlag.

Symposium Transsonicum 2. Ed. by K. Oswatitsch & D. Rues. (International Union of Theoretical & Applied Mechanics Symposia Ser.). 1976. 86.95 (*0-387-07526-7*) Spr-Verlag.

Symposium Zoological Society London, No. 50. Ed. by Marcia Edwards & Unity McDonnell. (Serial Publication Ser.). 336p. 1982. text ed. 164.00 (*0-12-613350-6*) Acad Pr.

Symposiums see Republic & Other Works

Sympotica: A Symposium on the Symposion. Oswyn Murray. (Illus.). 368p. 1995. pap. 42.00 (*0-19-815004-0*) OUP.

Symptom Analysis: A Method of Brief Therapy. M. Gerald Edelstein. (C). 1990. 21.95 (*0-393-70094-1*) Norton.

Symptom Analysis & Physical Diagnosis. 2nd ed. Ed. by A. Davis et al. 328p. 1985. text ed. 42.00 (*0-08-029870-2*); pap. text ed. 25.95 (*0-08-029869-9*) Elsevier.

Symptom-Context Method: Symptoms As Opportunities in Psychotherapy. Lester Luborsky. 422p. 1996. text ed. 39.95 (*1-55798-354-2*, 431-6730) Am Psychol.

***Symptom-Focused Psychiatric Drug Therapy for Managed Care: With 100 Clinical Cases.** Sonny Joseph. LC 96-26946. 510p. 1997. pap. 24.95 (*0-7890-0194-2*) Haworth Pr.

***Symptom-Focused Psychiatric Drug Therapy for Managed Care: With 100 Clinical Cases.** Sonny Joseph. LC 96-26946. (Illus.). 510p. (C). 1997. 89.95 (*0-7890-0133-0*, Hawrth Medical) Haworth Pr.

Symptom Management Algorithms for Palliative Care. Linda D. Seaman. 104p. 1996. pap. 11.50 (*1-888411-00-7*) Intellicard.

Symptom Management in Advanced Cancer. Robert G. Twycross. LC 95-34888. 1995. write for info. (*1-85775-058-6*, Radcliffe Med Pr) Scovill Paterson.

Symptom Management in Multiple Sclerosis. 2nd ed. Randall T. Schapiro. LC 86-72100. (Illus.). 151p. 1994. pap. 19.95 (*0-939957-60-4*) Demos Vermande.

An Asterisk (*) at the beginning of an entry indicates that the title is appearing in BIP for the first time.

Symptom Management Proceedings. Ed. by Patricia J. Larson. (C). 1995. pap. 25.00 (*0-943671-13-2*) UCSF Schl Nursing.

Symptom of Beauty. Francette Pacteau. LC 93-38507. (Essays in Art & Culture Ser.). 232p. 1994. 35.00 (*0-674-85987-1*) HUP.

Symptom of Beauty: Essays in Art & Culture. Francette Pacteau. (Essays in Art & Culture Ser.). (Illus.). 232p. (Orig.). (C). 1995. pap. text ed. 19.95 (*0-674-85988-X*) HUP.

Symptom-Oriented Guide to Adverse Drug Reactions. Mark L. Braunstein & John D. James. 560p. pap. write for info. (*0-07-032252-X*) McGraw.

Symptom Path to Enlightenment: The New Dynamics of Self-Organization in Hypnotherapy: an Advanced Manual for Beginners. Ernest L. Rossi. Ed. by Kathryn L. Rossi. (Illus.). 367p. (Orig.). 1996. pap. 29.95 (*0-9651985-0-2*) Palisades Gateway.

Symptom Reduction Through Clinical Biofeedback. Ivan Wentworth-Rohr. 273p. (C). 1984. 45.95 (*0-89885-135-1*); pap. 20.95 (*0-89885-366-4*) Human Sci Pr.

Symptom Solver: Understanding-&-Treating-the Most Common Male Health Concerns. Alisa Bauman & Brian Kaufman. Ed. by Men's Health Books Staff. LC 96-22076. 1996. pap. 14.95 (*0-87596-357-9*) Rodale Pr Inc.

Symptomatology & Differential Diagnosis: A Conspectus of Clinical Semeiographies. R. C. Schafer. LC 85-71673. (Illus.). 1088p. 1986. text ed. 90.00 (*0-9606618-1-6*, K-18) Am Chiro Assn.

Symptoms. Isadore Rosenfeld. 512p. 1994. mass mkt. 6.99 (*0-553-56813-2*) Bantam.

Symptoms: Their Causes & Cures. Prevention Magazine Health Book Editors. 736p. 1996. reprint ed. mass mkt. 6.99 (*0-553-56989-9*) Bantam.

Symptoms: Their Causes & Cures - How to Understand & Treat 265 Health Concerns. Ed. by Prevention Magazine Staff et al. LC 93-23014. 660p. 1994. 29.95 (*0-87596-179-7*) Rodale Pr Inc.

Symptoms & Signs of Substance Misuse. Margaret M. Stark & J. J. Payne-James. (Greenwich Medical Media Ser.). 80p. 1996. pap. 19.95 (*1-900151-10-3*) OUP.

***Symptoms & Solution.** Jay Goldstein. 1993. pap. 4.99 (*0-425-13919-0*) Berkley Pub.

Symptoms & Treatment of a Child's Learning Disorders & Academic Disorders: Handbook for Parents. Morrison F. Gardner. 1990. pap. 1.95 (*0-931421-62-4*) Psychol Educ Pubns.

Symptoms in the Mind. 2nd ed. Sims. 1995. pap. text ed. 50.00 (*0-7020-1788-4*) Saunders.

Symptoms in the Pharmacy: A Guide to the Management of Common Symptoms. 2nd ed. Alison Blenkinsopp & Paul Paxton. LC 94-11238. 256p. 1994. pap. 32.95 (*0-632-03609-5*, Pub. by Blckwell Sci Pubns UK) Blackwell Sci.

Symptoms of a Finer Age. Joe Amato. (White Noise Poetry Ser.). 96p. (Orig.). 1995. pap. 12.00 (*1-885215-12-6*, Viet Nam Gnrtn) Burning Cities Pr.

Symptoms of Depression. Charles G. Costello. LC 92-18109. (Series on Personality Processes). 336p. 1993. text ed. 80.00 (*0-471-54304-7*) Wiley.

Symptoms of Disease in Childhood. T. J. David. LC 95-7187. 1995. 49.95 (*0-632-03635-4*) Blackwell Sci.

Symptoms of Love: An Exciting Approach to a Range of Love Poems. (C). 1989. 45.00 (*1-871014-01-8*, Pub. by Desk Top Bks UK) St Mut.

Symptoms of Psychopathology: A Handbook. C. G. Costello. LC 78-88309. 693p. (C). reprint ed. 180.00 (*0-8357-9988-3*, 2055186) Bks Demand.

Symptoms of Schizophrenia. Charles G. Castello. LC 93-16759. (Series on Personality Processes). 336p. 1993. text ed. 72.50 (*0-471-54875-8*) Wiley.

Symptoms, Signs & Syndromes. Champney. 1979. pap. text ed. 20.00 (*0-7020-0712-9*) HarBrace.

Symptons & Early Warning Signs: A Comprehensive New Guide to More Than 600 Medical Symptoms & What They Mean. Michael Apple et al. Ed. by Peter Curtis & Carolyn Curtis. 1995. pap. 15.95 (*0-452-27113-4*, Plume) NAL-Dutton.

***Symptotic Behaviour of Linearly Transformed Sums of Random Variables.** LC 97-17692. 1997. text ed. 395.00 (*0-7923-4632-7*) Kluwer Ac.

Synaesthesia: Classic & Contemporary Readings. Baron-Cohen. (Illus.). 256p. 1996. 54.95 (*0-631-19763-X*) Blackwell Pubs.

Synaesthesia: Classic & Contemporary Readings. Baron-Cohen. (Illus.). 256p. 1996. pap. 22.95 (*0-631-19764-8*) Blackwell Pubs.

Synagogue. Sarah Feldman. (Let's Explore Being Jewish Ser.). (Illus.). 16p. (J). (gr. 1-2). 1996. pap. 1.75 (*0-87441-599-3*) Behrman.

Synagogue. rev. ed. C. H. Kraeling. 1979. 150.00 (*0-87068-331-4*) Ktav.

Synagogue: The Complete History of the Art & Architecture of the Synagogue. Harold A. Meek. (Illus.). 240p. (C). 1995. 59.95 (*0-7148-2932-3*, Pub. by Phaidon Press UK) Chronicle Bks.

Synagogue in Jewish Life. J. Kohn. 1988. 6.95 (*0-87068-381-0*) Ktav.

Synagogue in Late Antiquity. Lee I. Levine. (JTS & the American Schools of Oriental Research Ser.). 1987. pap. 19.95 (*0-685-19157-5*); bds. 26.95 (*0-317-64344-4*) Jewish Sem.

Synagogue in the Central City: Temple Israel of Greater Miami, 1922-1972. Charlton W. Tebeau. LC 71-85107. (Illus.). 144p. 1972. 7.95 (*0-87024-239-3*) U of Miami Pr.

***Synagogue Life in Northern Nevada.** LC 96-61053. (Orig.). 1996. pap. 12.95 (*0-936029-46-3*) Western Bk Journ.

Synagogue Survival Kit. Jordan L. Wagner. LC 96-39695. 368p. 1997. 30.00 (*1-56821-967-9*) Aronson.

Synagogues & Churches of Ancient Palestine. Leslie J. Hoppe. 152p. (Orig.). 1994. pap. text ed. 11.95 (*0-8146-5754-0*, M Glazier) Liturgical Pr.

***Synagogues of Europe: Architecture, History, Meaning.** Carol H. Krinsky. Date not set. 33.00 (*0-8446-6906-7*) Peter Smith.

Synagogues of Europe: Architecture, History, Meaning. unabridged ed. Carol H. Krinsky. (Illus.). 461p. reprint ed. pap. 27.95 (*0-486-29078-6*) Dover.

Synagogues of Kentucky: Architecture & History. Lee S. Weissbach. (Perspectives on Kentucky's Past Ser.). (Illus.). 200p. 1995. 24.95 (*0-8131-1912-X*) U Pr of Ky.

Synagogues of London. Paul Lindsay. LC 92-21435. (Illus.). 144p. 1992. pap. 19.50 (*0-85303-258-0*, Pub. by Vallentine Mitchell UK); text ed. 35.00 (*0-85303-241-6*, Pub. by Vallentine Mitchell UK) Intl Spec Bk.

Synagogues of New York City: A History of Jewish New York. (Illus.). 199p. (Orig.). Date not set. pap. 24.95 (*1-878741-25-X*) Israelowitz Pub.

Synagogues of New York's Lower East Side. Jo R. Fine & Gerard R. Wolfe. LC 75-15126. (Illus.). (C). 1978. text ed. 23.60 (*0-8147-2559-7*) NYU Pr.

Synagogues of the United States. Oscar Israelowitz. (Illus.). 200p. 1992. 29.95 (*1-878741-11-X*); pap. 24.95 (*1-878741-09-8*) Israelowitz Pub.

Synagogues, Temples & Congregations of Maryland, 1830-1990. Earl Pruce. 255p. 1993. pap. 15.00 (*1-883312-00-0*) Jew Hist Soc MD.

Synapse: Function, Plasticity, & Neurotrophism. M. Kuno. (Illus.). 350p. 1995. 49.95 (*0-19-854687-4*) OUP.

***Synapse: In Development, Health, & Disease.** Ed. by E. Edward Bittar et al. (Advances in Organ Biology Ser.: Vol. 2). 416p. 1997. 128.50 (*0-7623-0222-4*) Jai Pr.

Synapses, Circuits, & the Beginnings of Memory. Gary Lynch. (Cognitive Neuroscience Ser.). (Illus.). 152p. (C). 1986. 25.00 (*0-262-12114-X*, Bradford Bks) MIT Pr.

Synaptic Connections: Neuroscience Memory Cards. S. Parker Haberly & Kenneth E. Kratz. 1000p. 1996. 45.00 (*1-56593-639-6*, 1324) Singular Publishing.

Synaptic Modification, Neuron Selectivity & Nervous System Organization. Ed. by William Levy et al. 280p. (C). 1985. text ed. 59.95 (*0-89859-344-1*) L Erlbaum Assocs.

Synaptic Modifications & Memory: An Electrophysiological Analysis. Leon L. Voronin. LC 93-6851. (Studies of Brain Function: Vol. 19). 1993. Alk. paper. 219.95 (*0-387-56325-3*) Spr-Verlag.

Synaptic Organization of the Brain. 3rd ed. Ed. by Gordon M. Shepherd. (Illus.). 576p. 1990. pap. 35.00 (*0-19-506256-6*) OUP.

***Synaptic Organization of the Brain.** 4th ed. Ed. by Gordon Shepherd. (Illus.). 656p. 1997. pap. 39.95 (*0-19-511824-3*) OUP.

***Synaptic Organization of the Brain.** 4th ed. Ed. by Gordon Shepherd. (Illus.). 656p. 1997. 60.00 (*0-19-511823-5*) OUP.

Synaptic Plasticity. Ed. by Carl W. Cotman. LC 85-9784. 579p. 1985. lib. bdg. 89.95 (*0-89862-654-4*) Guilford Pr.

Synaptic Plasticity: Molecular, Cellular, & Functional Aspects. Ed. by Michel Baudry et al. LC 93-19699. (Illus.). 1993. 50.00 (*0-262-02359-8*, Bradford Bks) MIT Pr.

Synaptic Plasticity in the Hippocampus. Ed. by H. L. Haas & G. Buzsaki. (Illus.). 120p. 1988. 81.50 (*0-387-18599-2*) Spr-Verlag.

Synaptic Receptors: Isolation & Molecular Biology. Eduardo D. De Robertis. LC 74-80624. (Modern Pharmacology-Toxicology Ser.: No. 4). (Illus.). 405p. reprint ed. pap. 115.50 (*0-7837-0897-1*, 2041202) Bks Demand.

Synaptic Transmission: Cellular & Molecular Basis. Herbert Zimmerman. (Science Briefings Ser.). (Illus.). 168p. (C). 1994. text ed. 58.00 (*0-19-521065-4*); pap. text ed. 32.00 (*0-19-521073-5*) OUP.

Synaptic Transmission & Neuronal Interaction. fac. ed. Ed. by Michael V. Bennett. LC 73-83886. (Society of General Physiologists Ser.: No. 28). (Illus.). 400p. pap. 114.00 (*0-7837-7532-6*, 2046972) Bks Demand.

Synastry: Understanding Human Relationships Through Astrology. Ronald Davison. 335p. 1983. 14.95 (*0-943358-05-1*) Aurora Press.

Synaxaires Byzantins, Menologes, Typica. Hippolyte Delehaye. (Collected Studies: No. CS66). 322p. (C). 1977. reprint ed. lib. bdg. 102.95 (*0-86078-010-4*, Pub. by Variorum UK) Ashgate Pub Co.

Synchronic & Diachronic Approaches to Linguistic Variation & Change. fac. ed. Georgetown University Round Table on Languages & Linguistics Staff. Ed. by Thomas J. Walsh. LC 58-31607. 367p. 1989. reprint ed. pap. 104.60 (*0-7837-7797-3*, 2047553) Bks Demand.

Synchronic Chinese-Western Daily Calendar 1341-1661 A.D. Keith Hazelton. (Ming Studies Research Ser.). 321p. 1984. pap. 32.00 (*1-886108-00-5*) UMN Ming Studies.

Synchronic or Diachronic? A Debate on Method in Old Testament Exegesis. Ed. by Johannes C. De Moor. (Oudtestamentische Studi En: No. 34). 1995. 88.50 (*90-04-10342-2*) E J Brill.

Synchronic Phonology of Mandarin Chinese. Chin-Chuan Cheng. LC 72-88180. (Monographs on Linguistic Analysis: No. 4). 81p. (Orig.). 1973. pap. text ed. 32.35 (*90-279-2407-4*) Mouton.

Synchronicities. Miyoko Tanahashi. 1976. pap. 2.00 (*0-936072-02-4*) Soc New Lang Study.

Synchronicity. F. David Peat. 256p. 1987. pap. 13.95 (*0-553-34676-8*, New Age Bks) Bantam.

Synchronicity: Science, Myth & the Trickster. 2nd ed. Allan Combs & Mark Holland. 200p. (Orig.). (C). 1995. pap. 10.95 (*1-56924-845-1*) Marlowe & Co.

Synchronicity: Synchronicity & a Causal Connecting Principle. Carl G. Jung. Ed. by G. Adler. Tr. by R. F. Hull. (Bollingen Ser.: Vol. 20). 142p. 1973. pap. 9.95 (*0-691-01794-8*) Princeton U Pr.

Synchronicity: The Anatomy of Coincidence. Text by Carolyn North. LC 94-11735. (Fringe Ser.: Vol. 3). 1994. 3.95 (*0-916147-44-4*) Regent Pr.

Synchronicity: The Inner Path of Leadership. Peter M. Senge. LC 96-948. 256p. 1996. 24.95 (*1-881052-94-X*) Berrett-Koehler.

Synchronicity & Reunion: The Genetic Connection of Adoptees & Birthparents. LaVonne H. Stiffler. 189p. 1992. pap. 9.95 (*0-9634410-0-0*) L H Stiffler.

***Synchronicity As Spiritual Guidance.** Mark Thurston. LC 97-631. (Illus.). 251p. (Orig.). 1997. pap. 14.95 (*0-87604-377-5*, 474) ARE Pr.

Synchronicity Guidebook...High-Tech Meditation. Cynthia Larsen & Paul Shannon. LC 93-74177. (Illus.). 120p. (Orig.). 1994. pap. write for info. (*1-884068-20-0*) Amethyst Pub.

Synchronicity, Science, & Soulmaking. Victor Mansfield. 270p. 1995. pap. 18.95 (*0-8126-9304-3*) Open Court.

Synchronization: From Reel to Reel - A Complete Guide for the Synchronization of Audio, Film & Video. Jeff Rona. (Illus.). 128p. (Orig.). 1990. pap. 16.95 (*0-88188-905-9*, 00239235) H Leonard.

***Synchronization & Control of Distributed Systems & Programs.** Michel Raynal & Jean-Michel Helary. LC 90-12210. (Wiley Series in Parallel Computing). (Illus.). 134p. reprint ed. pap. 38.20 (*0-608-05306-6*, 2065844) Bks Demand.

Synchronization & Linearity: An Algebra for Discreet Event Systems. Francois L. Baccelli et al. (Probability & Mathematical Statistics Ser.). 489p. 1993. text ed. 156.00 (*0-471-93609-X*) Wiley.

Synchronization Design for Digital Systems. Teresa H. Meng. (C). 1990. lib. bdg. 85.50 (*0-7923-9128-4*) Kluwer Ac.

Synchronization in Digital Communications, Vol. 1: Phase-, Frequency-Locked Loops, & Amplitude Control. Heinrich Meyr & Gerd Ascheid. LC 89-22445. (Series in Telecommunications). 510p. 1990. text ed. 99.00 (*0-471-50193-X*) Wiley.

Synchronization in Real-Time Systems: A Priority Inheritance Approach. Ed. by Ragunathan Rajkumar. 208p. (C). 1991. lib. bdg. 81.00 (*0-7923-9211-6*) Kluwer Ac.

Synchronization in Science & Technology. Ed. by I. I. Blekhman. 350p. 1988. 68.00 (*0-7918-0003-2*, 800032) ASME Pr.

Synchronized Swimming. Stephen Corey. 66p. (Orig.). 1984. pap. 9.95 (*0-942979-14-1*) Livingston U Pr.

Synchronized Swimming. Stephen Corey. LC 85-50561. 88p. (Orig.). 1985. 13.95 (*0-930501-03-9*); pap. 7.50 (*0-930501-01-2*) Swallows Tale Pr.

Synchronous Machines Theory & Performance. Charles Concordia. (General Electric Ser.). (Illus.). 234p. reprint ed. pap. 66.70 (*0-317-08837-8*, 2011865) Bks Demand.

***Synchronous Management Vol. 1: Profit-Based Manufacturing for the 21st Century.** Mokshagundam L. Srikanth & Michael Umble. LC 96-34929. 1997. pap. write for info. (*0-943953-06-5*) Spectrum CT.

***Synchronous Management: Profit-Based Manufacturing for the 21st Century Vol. 2: Implementation Issues & Case Studies.** M. Michael Umble & Mokshagundam L. Srikanth. (Illus.). 250p. (Orig.). 1997. pap. write for info. (*0-943953-07-3*) Spectrum CT.

Synchronous Manufacturing: Principles for World-Class Excellence. Michael Umble & Mokshagundam L. Srikanth. LC 95-23324. (Illus.). 270p. (Orig.). 1995. pap. 29.95 (*0-943953-05-7*) Spectrum CT.

Synchronous Manufacturing Workbook: Principles for World-Class Excellence. Mokshagundam L. Srikanth & Albert E. Podzunas. (Illus.). 55p. (Orig.). 1990. pap. 24.95 (*0-943953-02-2*) Spectrum CT.

Synchronous Packet Radio Using the Software Approach: AX.25 Protocal, Vol. 2. Robert M. Richardson. Ed. by T. F. Belvins. 280p. 1984. 22.00 (*0-940972-08-5*) Richcraft Eng.

Synchronous Packet Radio Using the Software Approach: Vancouver Protocol, Vol. 1. Robert M. Richardson. Ed. by T. F. Blevins. 223p. 1983. 22.00 (*0-940972-07-7*) Richcraft Eng.

Synchronous Programming of Reactive Systems. Nicolas Halbwachs. LC 92-38480. (Kluwer International Series in Engineering & Computer Science: No. 215). 184p. (C). 1992. lib. bdg. 99.00 (*0-7923-9311-2*) Kluwer Ac.

***Synchronous Reluctance Motors.** R. G. March. (Technical Papers). 1970. pap. text ed. 30.00 (*1-55589-428-3*) AGMA.

Synchronous Transfer: Asychronous Transfer Mode - A Technical Overview. Harry J. R. Dutton & Lenhard. 336p. (C). 1995. pap. text ed. 52.00 (*0-13-520446-1*) P-H.

Synchrontron Radiation in Materials Research Vol. 143: Materials Research Society Symposium Proceedings. Ed. by R. Clarke et al. 304p. 1989. text ed. 30.00 (*1-55899-016-X*) Materials Res.

Synchrony & Diachrony of the Balkan Infinitive: A Study in Areal, General, & Historical Linguistics. Brian Joseph. LC 83-5351. (Cambridge Studies in Linguistics: Supplementary Volumes). 250p. 1983. text ed. 65.00 (*0-521-27318-8*) Cambridge U Pr.

Synchroservice! The Innovative Way to Build a Dynasty of Customers. Richard J. Schonberger & Edward M. Knod, Jr. LC 94-2259. 300p. 1994. text ed. 32.50 (*0-7863-0245-3*) Irwin Prof Pubng.

Synchrotron Light: Applications & Related Instrumentation II. Aldo F. Craievich. 312p. (C). 1990. text ed. 92.00 (*981-02-0088-9*) World Scientific Pub.

Synchrotron Light, Applications & Related Instrumentation: Proceedings of the 1st Workshop. Aldo F. Craievich. 320p. 1989. text ed. 108.00 (*9971-5-0843-5*) World Scientific Pub.

Synchrotron Radiation. Ed. by Giorgio Margaritondo & J. H. Weaver. (Reprint Bks.). 128p. 1986. pap. text ed. 26.00 (*0-917853-19-9*, RB46) Am Assn Physics.

Synchrotron Radiation: Selected Experiments in Condensed Matter Physics. Ed. by W. Czaja. (Monte Verita Ser.). viii, 179p. 1991. 53.00 (*0-8176-2594-1*) Spr-Verlag.

Synchrotron Radiation: Techniques & Applications. Ed. by C. Kunz. LC 78-24275. (Topics in Current Physics Ser.: Vol. 10). (Illus.). 1979. 78.95 (*0-387-09149-1*) Spr-Verlag.

Synchrotron Radiation & Dynamic Phenomena. A. Beswick. (Conference Proceeding Ser.: No. 258). 500p. 1992. 120.00 (*1-56396-008-7*) Am Inst Physics.

Synchrotron Radiation & Its Applications. I. M. Ternov et al. LC 85-8717. 388p. 1985. text ed. 612.00 (*3-7186-0236-9*) Gordon & Breach.

Synchrotron Radiation in Chemistry & Biology, Vol. I. Ed. by M. J. Dewar et al. (Topics in Current Chemistry Ser.: Vol. 145). (Illus.). 240p. 1988. 141.95 (*0-387-18385-X*) Spr-Verlag.

Synchrotron Radiation in Diffraction Studies. Workshop: Using Synchrotron Radiation for Diffraction. American Crystallographic Association Annual Meeting August 18-23, 1985 Progrm & Abstracts, Vol. 13. 75p. 1985. pap. 10.00 (*0-317-43249-4*) Polycrystal Bk Serv.

Synchrotron Radiation in Structural Biology. Ed. by R. M. Sweet & Avril D. Woodhead. (Basic Life Sciences Ser.: Vol. 51). (Illus.). 372p. 1989. 89.50 (*0-306-43256-0*, Plenum Pr) Plenum.

Synchrotron Radiation in the Biosciences. Ed. by B. Chance et al. LC 93-33962. (Illus.). 816p. (C). 1994. 155.00 (*0-19-853986-X*, Old Oregon Bk Store) OUP.

Synchrotron Radiation Research. Ed. by Herman Winick & Seb Doniach. LC 80-14378. (Illus.). 776p. 1980. 145.00 (*0-306-40363-3*, Plenum Pr) Plenum.

Synchrotron Radiation Research Vol. 1: Advances in Surface & Interface Science: Techniques. Ed. by R. Z. Bachrach. (Illus.). 486p. 1992. 120.00 (*0-306-43872-0*, Plenum Pr) Plenum.

Synchrotron Radiation Research Vol. 2: Advances in Surface & Interface Science: Issues & Technology. Ed. by R. Z. Bachrach. (Illus.). 396p. 1992. 105.00 (*0-306-43873-9*, Plenum Pr) Plenum.

***Synchrotron Radiation Sources: A Primer.** 528p. 1995. text ed. 33.00 (*981-02-2424-9*) World Scientific Pub.

Synchrotron Radiation Sources: A Primer. Herman Winick. 544p. 1995. text ed. 83.00 (*981-02-1856-7*) World Scientific Pub.

Synchrotron Radiation Sources & Their Applications: Proceedings of the 30th Scottish Universities' Summer School in Physics, Aberdeen, 1985. Ed. by I. C. Munro & N. Greaves. (Scottish Universities Summer School in Physics, a NATO Advanced Study Institute Ser.: No. 30). (Illus.). 520p. 1989. 208.00 (*0-905945-13-1*) IOP Pub.

***Synchrotron Radiation Techniques in Industrial, Chemical, & Materials Science: Proceedings of the Combined Symposia on Applications of Synchrotron Research to Materials Science Held in Washington, D. C., August 1995, & Applications of Synchrotron Radiation in Chemistry & Related Fields Held in Chicago, Illinois, August 1995.** Ed. by Kevin L. D'Amico et al. LC 96-41921. 290p. (C). 1996. 89.50 (*0-306-45389-4*) Plenum.

***Synchrotron Radiation Theory & Its Development: In Memory of I. M. Ternov (1921-1996)** 450p. 1997. text ed. 60.00 (*981-02-3156-3*) World Scientific Pub.

Synchrotron Techniques in Interfacial Electrochemistry: Proceedings of the NATO Advanced Research Workshop, Funchal, Madeira, Portugal, December 14-18, 1992. Ed. by C. A. Melendres. (NATO Advanced Science Institutes C: Mathematical & Physical Sciences Ser.). 500p. (C). 1994. lib. bdg. 247.00 (*0-7923-2844-2*) Kluwer Ac.

Syncopated Gospel & Bible-Related Songs for Minnesotans Who Don't Go to Church Much. Allen M. Blair. 13p. 1987. pap. 6.25 (*0-930366-38-7*) Northcountry Pub.

Syncopated Minnesota Novelties for Young People in Schools & Other Bad Places. Al Blair. 22p. 1988. pap. 12.75 (*0-930366-54-9*) Northcountry Pub.

Syncopated Rhythms - for the Contemporary Drummer. C. Kerrigan. 104p. 1990. pap. 11.95 (*0-931759-44-7*) Centerstream Pub.

Syncopated Songs That Are Banned in Forade, Starbuck & Thief River Falls. Al Blair. 14p. 1988. pap. 7.25 (*0-930366-35-2*) Northcountry Pub.

***Syncope.** R. T. Ross. (Major Problems in Neurology Ser.: Vol. 18). (Illus.). 176p. 1989. write for info. (*0-7020-1326-9*, Pub. by W B Saunders UK) Saunders.

***Syncope: Mechanisms & Management.** Ed. by Blair P. Grubb et al. LC 97-24424. 1997. write for info. (*0-87993-683-5*) Futura Pub.

Syncope: The Philosophy of Rapture. Catherine Clement. Tr. by Sally O'Driscoll. LC 94-7610. 1994. text ed. 44.95 (*0-8166-1977-8*); pap. text ed. 19.95 (*0-8166-1978-6*) U of Minn Pr.

Syncope & Falls in the Older Patient. R. A. Kenny. 360p. (gr. 13). 1995. text ed. 110.00 (*0-412-56810-1*) Chapman & Hall.

Syncope of the Old English Present Endings: A Dialect Criterion. J. Hedberg. (Lund Studies in English: Vol. 12). 1974. reprint ed. pap. 45.00 (*0-8115-0555-3*) Periodicals Srv.

Syncreny: An Introduction. Evan Porter. LC 86-62684. 220p. 1987. pap. 7.95 (*0-940683-00-8*) Society Pubng.

Syncretic Religion of Lin Chao-En. Judith A. Berling. LC 79-25606. (Institute for Advanced Studies of World Religions; Neo-Confucian Studies). 1980. text ed. 60.00 (*0-231-04870-X*) Col U Pr.

Syncretic Society. Felipe G. Casals. Tr. by Guy Daniels from FRE. LC 80-6455. 103p. reprint ed. pap. 29.40 (*0-685-23732-X*, 2032773) Bks Demand.

Syncretism: The Art of the 21st Century. Alternative Museum Staff. LC 90-86368. (Orig.). 1991. pap. text ed. 8.00 (*0-932075-35-5*) Alternative Mus.

Syncretism - Anti-Syncretism: The Politics of Religious Synthesis. Ed. by Charles Stewart & Rosalind Shaw. LC 93-46102. (European Association of Cultural Anthropologists Ser.). 240p. (C). 1994. text ed. 59.95 (*0-415-11116-1*, B4679, Routledge NY) Routledge.

Syncretism - Anti-Syncretism: The Politics of Religious Synthesis. Ed. by Charles Stewart & Rosalind Shaw. LC 93-46102. (European Association of Cultural Anthropologists Ser.). 240p. (C). 1994. pap. 17.95 (*0-415-11117-X*, B4683, Routledge NY) Routledge.

Syncretism of Ch'an & Pure Land Buddhism. Heng-Ching Shin. LC 91-36700. (Asian Thought & Culture Ser.: Vol. 9). 279p. (C). 1992. text ed. 48.95 (*0-8204-1681-9*) P Lang Pubng.

S

***Syncretistic Religious Communities in the Near East: Collected Papers of the International Symposium "Alevism in Turkey & Comparable Syncretistic Religious Communities in the Near East in the Past & Present", Berlin, 14-17 April 1995.** Ed. by Krisztin Kehl-Bodrogi et al. (Numen Book Ser.: Vol. 76). 273p. 1997. 93.75 (*90-04-10861-0*) E J Brill.

Syndic. Cyril Kornbluth. 1993. reprint ed. lib. bdg. 18.95 (*0-89968-347-9*, Lghtyr Pr) Buccaneer Bks.

Syndical & Corporative Institutions of Italian Fascism. G. Lowell Field. (Columbia University. Studies in the Social Sciences: No. 443). reprint ed. 32.50 (*0-404-51433-2*) AMS Pr.

Syndicalism. Intro. by James R. Barrett. 64p. 1990. reprint ed. pap. 9.00 (*0-88286-187-5*); reprint ed. lib. bdg. 24.95 (*0-88286-188-3*) C H Kerr.

Syndicalism & Revolution in Spain. Antonio Bar. (History of Anarchism Ser.). 1981. lib. bdg. 250.00 (*0-8490-3208-3*) Gordon Pr.

Syndicalism & the General Strike. Arthur Lewis. 1976. lib. bdg. 59.95 (*0-8490-2696-2*) Gordon Pr.

Syndicalism in France: A Study of Ideas. Jeremy Jennings. LC 89-24114. 387p. 1990. text ed. 45.00 (*0-312-04027-X*) St Martin.

Syndicalism in France, by Louis Levine. Lewis L. Lorwin & Jean A. Flexner. LC 76-127443. (Columbia University. Studies in the Social Sciences: No. 116). reprint ed. 39.50 (*0-404-51116-3*) AMS Pr.

Syndicalist: Reproduced in Facsimile 1912-1914. Intro. by Geoff Brown. 104p. 1975. 57.50 (*0-685-71536-1*, Pub. by Spokesman Bks UK) Coronet Bks.

Syndicalist Legacy: Trade Unions & Politics in Two French Cities in the Era of World War I. Kathryn E. Amdur. LC 86-1633. (Working Class in American History Ser.). 496p. 1986. text ed. 44.95 (*0-252-01238-0*) U of Ill Pr.

***Syndicate in the Sun.** Hank Messick. Date not set. lib. bdg. 23.95 (*0-8488-1810-5*) Amereon Ltd.

Syndicate Wars Unauthorized Secrets. Prima Development Staff. 240p. 1996. per. 19.99 (*0-7615-0089-8*) Prima Pub.

***Syndicate Wife.** Hank Messick. Date not set. lib. bdg. 29.95 (*0-8488-1811-3*) Amereon Ltd.

Syndicate Wife. 2nd ed. Hank Messick. 214p. 1995. reprint ed. 29.95 (*0-9650243-0-X*) For The Love Bks.

Syndicated Credits Market. I. D Bond. (Bank of England Economics Division Discussion Papers: 22). 97p. reprint ed. pap. 27.70 (*0-317-42232-4*, 2025768) Bks Demand.

Syndicated Lending. Ed. by Tony Rhodes. 370p. Date not set. pap. 170.00 (*1-85564-078-3*, Pub. by Euromoney UK) Am Educ Systs.

Syndicated Lending. 2nd ed. Ed. by Tony Rhodes. 400p. 1995. pap. 170.00 (*1-85564-518-1*, Pub. by Euromoney UK) Am Educ Systs.

Syndicated Television: The First Forty Years, 1947-1987. Hal Erickson. LC 89-42583. 432p. 1989. lib. bdg. 55.00 (*0-89950-410-8*) McFarland & Co.

Syndication Success Stories. Greg James. 176p. (Orig.). pap. 16.95 (*0-910019-26-6*) Lghthse Pub Gp.

***Syndrome of D-Glyceric Acidemia with Hyperglycinemia.** Steen Kolvraa. 71p. 1988. 24.00 (*87-7288-186-0*, Pub. by Aarhus Univ Pr DK) David Brown.

Syndrome of Nonverbal Learning Disabilities: Neurodevelopmental Manifestations. Byron P. Rourke. LC 95-3981. 1995. lib. bdg. 46.95 (*0-89862-155-0*) Guilford Pr.

Syndromes for the Layperson: Now I Know What's Wrong With Me. Eustace A. Dixon. 108p. 1988. 8.95 (*0-942848-04-7*) Eureka Pubns.

Syndromes of Atherosclerosis: Correlations of Clinical Imaging & Pathology. Ed. by Valentin Fuster. (American Heart Association Monographs). (Illus.). 576p. 1996. 85.00 (*0-87993-638-X*) Futura Pub.

Syndromes of the Head & Neck. 3rd ed. Robert J. Gorlin et al. (Oxford Monographs on Medical Genetics: No. 19). (Illus.). 1056p. 1990. 195.00 (*0-19-504518-1*) OUP.

Syndromic Living. Robert E. McDaniel. 153p. (Orig.). 1989. pap. 9.95 (*0-9623475-0-7*) Zanni Pubs.

Syner Abs II. Jerry Robinson. (Illus.). 46p. 1990. pap. 14.95 (*0-944831-27-3*) Health Life.

Synergetic Computers & Cognition: A Top-down Approach to Neural Nets. H. Haken. (Synergetics Ser.: Vol. 50). (Illus.). 240p. 1991. 76.95 (*0-387-53030-4*) Spr-Verlag.

Synergetic Economics: Time & Change in Nonlinear Economics. W. B. Zhang. (Synergetics Ser.: Vol. 53). (Illus.). xv, 246p. 1991. 98.00 (*0-387-52904-7*) Spr-Verlag.

Synergetic Stew: Explorations in Dymaxion Dining. Buckminster Staff. (Illus.). 120p. (Orig.). 1982. 6.95 (*0-911573-00-3*) Buckminster Fuller.

Synergetics. Taylor Hay & Joanna Hay. 224p. 1990. pap. 13.00 (*0-671-67397-1*) S&S Trade.

***Synergetics: An Introduction.** 1983. 86.95 (*0-387-12356-3*) Spr-Verlag.

Synergetics: Chaos, Order, Self-Organization. Michael Bushev. 252p. 1994. text ed. 53.00 (*981-02-1286-0*) World Scientific Pub.

Synergetics: From Microscopic to Macroscopic Order. Ed. by E. Frehland. (Synergetics Ser.: Vol. 22). (Illus.). 280p. 1984. 78.95 (*0-387-13131-0*) Spr-Verlag.

Synergetics: Strength & Fracture of Metallic Materials. V. S. Ivanova. 140p. 1995. boxed 55.00 (*1-898326-18-5*, Pub. by Cambdge Intl UK) Am Educ Systs.

Synergetics Dictionary: The Mind of R. Buckminster Fuller, 4 vols., Set. Fuller & Edgar J. Applewhite. 2800p. 1986. text ed. 150.00 (*0-8240-8729-1*) Garland.

Synergetics of Cognition. Ed. by H. Haken & M. Stadler. (Synergetics Ser.: Vol. 45). (Illus.). 415p. 1990. 77.00 (*0-387-51929-7*) Spr-Verlag.

***Synergetics of Measurement, Prediction & Control, Vol. XX.** I. Grabec & W. Sachse. (Synergetics Ser.: Vol. 68). (Illus.). 458p. 1997. 98.00 (*0-387-57048-9*) Spr-Verlag.

Synergetics of the Brain. Ed. by H. Haken et al. (Synergetics Ser.: Vol. 23). (Illus.). 390p. 1983. 86.95 (*0-387-12960-X*) Spr-Verlag.

Synergetics, Order & Chaos. Ed. by M. G. Velarde. 752p. (C). 1988. text ed. 138.00 (*9971-5-0717-X*) World Scientific Pub.

Synergic Power: Beyond Domination, Beyond Permissiveness. 2nd ed. James H. Craig & Marguerite Craig. LC 79-67184. (Illus.). 164p. 1979. pap. 6.95 (*0-914158-28-7*) ProActive Pr.

***Synergiemanagement im Handel: Grundzuge Einer Handelsbetrieblichen Synergiekonzeption unter Berucksichtigung Empirischer Untersuchungen im Deutschen Konsumguterhandel.** Bodo Reinke. (Illus.). xxiv, 262p. (GER.). 1996. 54.95 (*3-631-30464-1*) P Lang Pubng.

Synergistic Approach Stuttering Therapy. Bloom. 1996. write for info. (*0-7506-9527-7*) Buttrwrth-Heinemann.

Synergize Your Spine. Paul Holmquist. Ed. by Colleen Holmquist. (Illus.). 29p. (Orig.). (C). 1996. 17.00 (*0-9643397-0-6*) Synergy Phys.

Synergogy: A New Strategy for Education, Training, & Development. Jane S. Mouton & Robert R. Blake. LC 83-23898. (Joint Publication in the Jossey-Bass Management Series & the Jossey-Bass Social & Behavioral Science Ser.). 206p. reprint ed. pap. 58.80 (*0-7837-2549-3*, 2042708) Bks Demand.

Synergy: Increasing Productivity with People, Ideas, & Things. Richard O. Wolfe. 112p. 1995. per. 19.89 (*0-8403-8462-9*) Kendall-Hunt.

Synergy: Transforming America's High Schools Through Integrated Thematic Instruction. Karen D. Olsen. (Illus.). 278p. (Orig.). 1995. pap. 24.95 (*1-878631-25-X*) Bks Educators.

Synergy Between Dynamics & Reactivity at Clusters & Surfaces: Proceedings of the NATO ARW, Drymen, Scotland, July 3-8, 1994. Ed. by Louis J. Farrugia. LC 95-17086. (NATO ASI Ser.: Series C, Mathematical & Physical Sciences: Vol. 465). 376p. (C). 1995. lib. bdg. 184.00 (*0-7923-3522-8*) Kluwer Ac.

Synergy Church: A Strategy for Integrating Small Groups & Sunday School. Michael C. Mack. LC 95-47637. 208p. (Orig.). (C). 1996. pap. 13.99 (*0-8010-9009-1*) Baker Bks.

***Synergy Myth: And Other Ailments of Business Today.** Harold Geneen. 1997. 24.95 (*0-312-14724-4*) St Martin.

Synergy, No. 3: New Science Fiction. Ed. by George Zebrowski. (Harvest-HBJ Original Ser). 256p. 1988. pap. 8.95 (*0-15-687702-3*) HarBrace.

***Synergy Project: Facilitator's Guide.** 138p. 1995. pap. 49.95 incl. vhs (*0-614-30578-0*, SM-95-1B) Ed Comm States.

Synergy Session. Lynn M. Buess. LC 80-67932. (Illus.). 113p. (Orig.). 1980. pap. 4.95 (*0-87516-427-7*) DeVorss.

Synergy Trap. Mark L. Sirower. LC 96-44862. 192p. 1997. 25.00 (*0-684-83255-0*) S&S Trade.

Synergy '86: Conference Proceedings, June 16-18, 1986, Universal City, CA. Synergy '86 (1986: Universal City, CA) Staff. LC 86-61093. (Illus.). 392p. reprint ed. pap. 111.80 (*0-8357-6498-2*, 2035869) Bks Demand.

Synermergency: A Clarion Call to Anything But Arms. rev. ed. James J. Pacifico. LC 91-92488. 184p. 1992. 8.95 (*0-9632022-4-3*); lib. bdg. 24.95 (*0-9632022-1-9*); 13.00 (*0-9632022-3-5*) Holy Grail.

Synermergency: A Clarion Call to Anything But Arms. 2nd rev. ed. James J. Pacifico. LC 91-92488. (Illus.). 212p. (C). Date not set. pap. 24.95 (*0-9632022-2-7*) Holy Grail.

Synermergency: A Clarion Call to Anything But Arms. 2nd rev. ed. James J. Pacifico. LC 91-92488. 184p. 1992. 24.95 (*0-9632022-0-0*) Holy Grail.

SynerShape: A Scientific Weight-Loss Guide. Health for Life Staff. (Illus.). 24p. 1984. pap. 11.95 (*0-944831-04-4*) Health Life.

Synerstretch: For Total Body Flexibility. Health for Life Staff. (Illus.). 32p. 1984. 11.95 (*0-944831-05-2*) Health Life.

Synesius of Cyrene: Philosopher & Bishop. A. Gardner. 1977. lib. bdg. 59.95 (*0-8490-2697-0*) Gordon Pr.

Synesius of Cyrene: Philosopher-Bishop. Jay Bregman. LC 81-10293. (Transformation of the Classical Heritage Ser.: Vol. II). 1982. 50.00 (*0-520-04192-5*) U CA Pr.

Synesthesia. R. E. Cytowic. (Neuropsychology Ser.). (Illus.). 315p. 1989. 111.95 (*0-387-96807-5*) Spr-Verlag.

Synesthesia: Sound & Vision in Contemporary Art. Don Bacigalupi. LC 94-67647. (Illus.). 41p. (Orig.). 1994. pap. 5.00 (*1-883502-02-0*) San Ant Mus Art.

***Synethetic & Natural Phenols.** J. H. Tyman. LC 96-28442. (Studies in Organic Chemistry: Vol. 52). 720p. 1996. 364.25 (*0-444-88164-6*) Elsevier.

Synethetic Coordination Chemistry: Theory of Practice. Julian A. Davies et al. 500p. 1996. text ed. 104.00 (*981-02-2084-7*) World Scientific Pub.

Synextensional Magmatism in the Basin & Range Province: A Case Study from the Eastern Great Basin. P. B. Gans et al. Ed. by G. A. Mahood & E. Schermer. (Special Papers: No. 233). (Illus.). 60p. 1989. pap. 5.00 (*0-8137-2233-0*) Geol Soc.

Synfuels: The Problems & the Promise. E. J. Hoffman. LC 81-68123. 347p. 1982. 29.50 (*0-9601552-4-4*) Energon Co.

Synge: The Medieval & the Grotesque. Toni O'Brien - Johnson. (Irish Literary Studies: Vol. # 11). 210p. 8200. 35.00 (*0-86140-104-2*, Pub. by Colin Smythe Ltd UK) Dufour.

***Synge: Three Plays.** John Millington Synge. 1997. pap. 5.95 (*0-451-52651-1*, Sig Classics) NAL-Dutton.

Synge & the Ireland of His Time. William Butler Yeats. (BCL1-PR English Literature Ser.). 42p. 1992. reprint ed. lib. bdg. 59.00 (*0-7812-7688-8*) Rprt Serv.

Synge, J. M. A Biography. Robin Skelton. 1983. pap. 3.95 (*0-8159-6847-7*) Devin.

***Synge Letters: Bishop Edward Synge to His Daughter Alicia.** Mary L. Legg. 576p. 9600. 70.00 (*1-874675-49-X*) Dufour.

Syngenesis & Epigenesis in the Formation of Mineral Deposits. Ed. by A. Wauschkuhn et al. (Illus.). 660p. 1985. 158.95 (*0-387-13845-5*) Spr-Verlag.

Synge's First Symphony: The Aran Islands. William E. Hart. 136p. (Orig.). (C). 1993. pap. text ed. 19.95 (*0-910919-08-9*) Mariel Pubns.

Synge's Guide to Aran Islands. Ruth W. Shaw. 1983. pap. 7.95 (*0-8159-6835-3*) Devin.

Synge's The Aran Islands. Arnold Goldman. 42p. 9100. pap. 8.95 (*0-86140-330-4*) Dufour.

Syngman Rhee. Robert T. Oliver. LC 72-13864. (Illus.). 380p. 1973. reprint ed. text ed. 65.00 (*0-8371-6759-0*, OLSR, Greenwood Pr) Greenwood.

Synnove Solbakken. Bjornstjerne Bjornson. Tr. by Julie Sutter. LC 79-38341. (Select Bibliographies Reprint Ser.). 1977. 18.95 (*0-8369-6758-5*) Ayer.

Synod of Sixteen Seventy-Two: Acts & Decrees of the Jerusalem Synod Held Under Dositheus, Containing the Confession Published Name of Cyril Lukaris. Orthodox Eastern Church Staff. Tr. by J. N. Robertson. LC 78-81769. 1969. reprint ed. 41.50 (*0-404-03567-1*) AMS Pr.

Synod of Sleuths: Essays on Judeo-Christian Detective Fiction. Ed. by Jon L. Breen & Martin H. Greenberg. 169p. 1990. 22.50 (*0-8108-2382-9*) Scarecrow.

Synodicon Vetus. Ed. by John Duffy & John Parker. LC 79-52935. (Dumbarton Oaks Texts: Vol. 5). 209p. 1979. 35.00 (*0-88402-088-6*) Dumbarton Oaks.

Synods of the Polish National Catholic Church, 1904-1958. Ed. by Casimir J. Grotnik. 608p. 1993. 89.50 (*0-88033-269-7*, 372) East Eur Monographs.

Synon AD-Interface Reference Manual. 55p. 1991. write for info. (*1-56380-026-8*) Synon Ltd.

Synon Developer's Guide for the AS 400. John Porter. 1995. text ed. 45.00 (*0-07-050667-1*) McGraw.

Synon Entry: An Application Generator for the AS-400, 2 vols., Set. 1991. write for info. incl. disk (*1-56380-013-6*) Synon Ltd.

Synon Entry: An Application Generator for the AS-400, Concepts Release 3.0, 2 vols. 600p. 1991. Vol. 1: Concepts Release 3.0, 600p. write for info. (*1-56380-014-4*) Synon Ltd.

Synon Entry: An Application Generator for the AS-400, Reference, 2 vols., Vol. 2. 300p. 1991. write for info. (*1-56380-015-2*) Synon Ltd.

Synon Entry: An Application Generator for the AS-400, Release 2.1.2, 2 vols., Set. 1991. write for info. incl. disk (*1-56380-007-1*) Synon Ltd.

Synon Entry: An Application Generator for the AS-400, Release 2.1.2, Concepts, 2 vols., Vol. 1. 580p. 1991. write for info. (*1-56380-008-X*) Synon Ltd.

Synon Entry: An Application Generator for the AS-400, Release 2.1.2, Reference, 2 vols., Vol. 2. 270p. 1991. write for info. (*1-56380-009-8*) Synon Ltd.

Synon Entry Training Example (2.1.2) 310p. 1991. write for info. (*1-56380-018-7*) Synon Ltd.

Synon-1E: Utilities for the AS-400, Release 3.0, 2 vols., Set. 1991. write for info. incl. disk (*1-56380-010-1*) Synon Ltd.

Synon-1E: Utilities for the AS-400, Release 3.0, Command Handbook Reference, 2 vols. 435p. 1991. Command Handbook Reference, 435p. write for info. (*1-56380-012-8*) Synon Ltd.

Synon-1E: Utilities for the AS-400, Release 3.0, Concepts Guide, 2 vols. 365p. 1991. Concepts Guide, 365p. write for info. (*1-56380-011-X*) Synon Ltd.

Synon-2E: An Application Generator for the AS-400, Release 3.0, 2 vols., Set. 1991. student ed. write for info. incl. disk (*1-56380-003-9*) Synon Ltd.

Synon-2E: An Application Generator for the AS-400, Release 3.0, Concepts, 2 vols., Vol. 1. 740p. 1991. student ed. write for info. (*1-56380-004-7*) Synon Ltd.

Synon-2E: An Application Generator for the AS-400, Release 3.0, Reference, 2 vols., Vol. 2. 440p. 1991. student ed. write for info. (*1-56380-005-5*) Synon Ltd.

Synon-2E Worked Example (3.0) 200p. 1991. student ed. write for info. (*1-56380-023-3*); Implementation Techniques, 20p. disk write for info. (*1-56380-028-4*) Synon Ltd.

Synon-2G: An Application Generator for the AS-400 - Release 2.1, 2 vols., Set. 1991. 60.00 (*1-56380-000-4*) Synon Ltd.

Synon-2G: An Application Generator for the AS-400 - Release 2.1, Vol. 1: Concepts. 710p. 1991. write for info. (*1-56380-001-2*) Synon Ltd.

Synon-2G: An Application Generator for the AS-400 - Release 2.1, Vol. 2: Reference. 408p. 1991. write for info. (*1-56380-002-0*) Synon Ltd.

Synon-2G: An Application Generator for the AS-400 (3.0), 2 vols., Set. 1991. write for info. incl. disk (*1-56380-020-9*) Synon Ltd.

Synon-2G: An Application Generator for the AS-400 (3.0), Concepts, 2 vols., Vol. 1. 750p. 1991. write for info. (*1-56380-021-7*) Synon Ltd.

Synon-2G: An Application Generator for the AS-400 (3.0), Reference, 2 vols., Vol. 2. 425p. 1991. write for info. (*1-56380-022-5*) Synon Ltd.

Synon-2G Concepts & Facilities 2.1, 2 bks., No. I. 230p. 1991. write for info. (*1-56380-016-0*) Synon Ltd.

Synon-2G Concepts & Facilities 2.1, 2 bks., No. II. 175p. 1991. write for info. (*1-56380-017-9*) Synon Ltd.

Synon-2G Worked Example. 643p. 1991. 60.00 (*1-56380-006-3*); disk write for info. (*0-318-68462-4*) Synon Ltd.

Synon-2G Worked Example (3.0) 400p. 1991. write for info. incl. disk (*1-56380-024-1*) Synon Ltd.

Synonym Dictionary: Synonymwoerterbuch: Sinnverwandte Ausdruecke der Deutschen Sprache. 3rd ed. Herbert Gorner & Guenter Kempcke. 643p. (GER.). 1986. 29.95 (*0-8288-1974-2*, M15175) Fr & Eur.

Synonym Finder. rev. ed. J. I. Rodale. LC 78-11440. 1368p. 1978. 29.95 (*0-87857-236-8*, 10-342-2) Rodale Pr Inc.

Synonym Finder. rev. ed. Rev. by J. I. Rodale et al. 376p. 1986. pap. 14.99 (*0-446-37029-0*) Warner Bks.

Synonym for Love. Alison Moore. LC 94-40442. 256p. 1995. text ed. 19.95 (*1-56279-074-9*) Mercury Hse Inc.

Synonym for Love. Alison Moore. 1996. pap. 10.95 (*0-452-27622-5*, Plume) NAL-Dutton.

Synonymized Checklist of the Vascular Flora of the United States, Canada, & Greenland. John T. Kartesz & Rosemarie Kartesz. xlviii, 494p. 1980. 55.00 (*0-8078-1422-9*) U of NC Pr.

Synonyms: Individual Sets. Marion W. Stuart. text ed. write for info. (*0-943343-08-9*) Lrn Wrap-Ups.

Synonyms, Antonyms, & Homonyms. Carson & Dellosa. (Home Workbooks Ser.). (Illus.). 64p. (Orig.). (J). (gr. 1-3). 1995. wbk. ed., pap. 2.49 (*0-88724-331-2*, CD6828) Carson-Dellos.

Synonyms, Antonyms, Homonyms. Sheldon L. Tilkin. (Horizons II Ser.). (Illus.). 24p. (J). (gr. 3-4). 1980. student ed., pap. 3.95 (*0-89403-603-3*) EDC.

Synonyms for "Child", "Boys", "Girl" in Old English: An Etymological-Semiasiological Investigation. H. Back. (Lund Studies in English: Vol. 2). 1974. reprint ed. pap. 45.00 (*0-8115-0545-6*) Periodicals Srv.

Synonymy & Linguistic Analysis. Roy Harris. LC 73-160625. (Language & Style Ser.: No. 12). 172p. reprint ed. pap. 49.10 (*0-685-15366-5*, 2026524) Bks Demand.

Synonymy & Semantic Classification. Karen S. Jones. 256p. 45.00 (*0-85224-517-3*, Pub. by Edinburgh U Pr UK) Col U Pr.

Synopse des Lois du Pentateuque. Guy Lasserre. 242p. 1994. text ed. 102.00 (*90-04-10202-7*) E J Brill.

Synopses of Results of the First Programme on Optimization of the Production & Utilisation of Hydrocarbons. Commission of the European Communities, Directorate-General Telecommunications, Information Industries & Innovation Staff. 1000p. (C). 1993. lib. bdg. 328.50 (*1-85333-879-6*, Pub. by Graham & Trotman UK) Kluwer Ac.

Synopsis. Guy R. Mermier. (Medieval & Renaissance Monograph). (Orig.). 1988. pap. 5.00 (*0-941107-02-7*) MARC Pub Co.

***Synopsis: An Annual Index of Greek Studies - 1992.** Ed. by Andrew Dimarogonas. 320p. 1997. text ed. 125.00 incl. 3.5 hd (*90-5702-541-8*, ECU104, Harwood Acad Pubs) Gordon & Breach.

Synopsis: Painting, Architecture, Sculpture. 2nd ed. Alvar Aalto. (Geschichte und Theorie der Architektur Ser.: No. 12). (Illus.). 240p. (ENG, FRE & GER.). 1980. 57.00 (*0-8176-1109-6*) Birkhauser.

Synopsis Fungorum Carolinea Superioris. L. D. Von Schweinitz. 1976. reprint ed. 12.00 (*3-7682-1065-0*) Lubrecht & Cramer.

Synopsis Fungorum in America Boreali Media Degentium. L. D. Schweinitz. 1962. reprint ed. 80.00 (*3-7682-0117-1*) Lubrecht & Cramer.

Synopsis Hepaticarum. K. M. Gottsche et al. 1967. reprint ed. 130.00 (*3-7682-0516-9*) Lubrecht & Cramer.

***Synopsis Human Anatomy And Physiology.** Vande Graaff. 1997. student ed., pap. text ed. 18.00 (*0-697-03397-X*) McGraw.

Synopsis Juris Gentium, Vol. 1. Ed. by Edwig Von Bar. LC 95-77194. (Classics in International Law Reprint Ser.: No. 6). (LAT.). 1995. reprint ed. 85.00 (*0-89941-949-6*, 310130) W S Hein.

Synopsis Methodica Animalium Quadrupedum et Serpentini Generis. John Ray. Ed. by Keir B. Sterling. LC 77-81111. (Biologists & Their World Ser.). (LAT.). 1978. reprint ed. lib. bdg. 31.95 (*0-405-10694-7*) Ayer.

Synopsis Methodica Avium & Piscium. John Ray. Ed. by William Derham & Keir B. Sterling. LC 77-81111. (Biologists & Their World Ser.). (Illus.). (LAT.). 1978. reprint ed. lib. bdg. 39.95 (*0-405-10695-5*) Ayer.

Synopsis, Nineteen Ninety-One to Ninety-Two, Vol. 3. Guy R. Mermier. 124p. 1993. text ed. 49.95 (*0-7734-9237-2*) E Mellen.

Synopsis of American History. 6th ed. Charles C. Sellers et al. (C). 1984. teacher ed. write for info. (*0-318-62577-6*) HM.

An Asterisk (*) at the beginning of an entry indicates that the title is appearing in BIP for the first time.

Synopsis of American History. 7th rev. ed. Charles C. Sellers et al. (Illus.). 544p. (C). 1992. pap. text ed. 28.25 (*0-929587-74-X*) I R Dee.

***Synopsis of American History: Complete Edition.** 8th ed. Neil R. McMillen & Charles C. Bolton. LC 97-1450. 1997. pap. text ed. 28.25 (*1-56663-160-2*) I R Dee.

***Synopsis of American History Vol. 1: Through Reconstruction.** 8th ed. Date not set. pap. text ed. 22.25 (*1-56663-161-0*) I R Dee.

***Synopsis of American History Vol. 2: Since the Civil War.** 8th ed. Date not set. pap. text ed. 22.25 (*1-56663-162-9*) I R Dee.

Synopsis of American History, Vol. I: Through Reconstruction. 7th rev. ed. Charles C. Sellers et al. (Illus.). 256p. (C). 1992. pap. text ed. 22.25 (*0-929587-75-8*) I R Dee.

Synopsis of American History, Vol. II: Since the Civil War. 7th rev. ed. Charles C. Sellers et al. (Illus.). 352p. (C). 1992. pap. text ed. 22.25 (*0-929587-76-6*) I R Dee.

Synopsis of Ayurveda: Based on Susruta Sanhita. G. D. Singhal & T. J. Patterson. 250p. 1993. 27.95 (*0-19-562540-4*) OUP.

***Synopsis of Biological Data on the Grass Carp, Ctenopharyngodon Idella (Cuvier & Valenciennes, 1844)** 90p. 1984. 12.00 (*92-5-101359-4*, Pub. by FAO IT) Bernan Associates.

Synopsis of Common Surgical Procedures. Ed. by Balazs I. Bodai. LC 92-49577. (Illus.). 277p. 1993. pap. text ed. 29.95 (*0-8121-1220-2*) Williams & Wilkins.

Synopsis of Complete Dentures. Charles W. Ellinger. LC 74-23703. 365p. reprint ed. pap. 104.10 (*0-317-28606-4*, 2055422) Bks Demand.

Synopsis of Critical Care. 3rd ed. William J. Sibbald. 352p. 1988. pap. 42.00 (*0-683-07709-0*) Williams & Wilkins.

Synopsis of Diseases of the Chest. 2nd rev. ed. J. A. Pare & Robert G. Fraser. LC 93-25873. (Illus.). 732p. 1993. reprint ed. text ed. 99.00 (*0-7216-3669-1*) Saunders.

Synopsis of English Syntax. Eugene A. Nida. (Janua Linguarum, Series Practica: No. 19). (Orig.). 1966. pap. text ed. 40.00 (*90-279-2430-9*) Mouton.

Synopsis of Eugen Bleuler's Dementia Praecox or the Group of Schizophrenias. Ed. by Nathan S. Kline. (Monograph Series on Schizophrenia). 57p. 1966. 27.50 (*0-8236-6320-5*) Intl Univs Pr.

Synopsis of Fevers & Their Treatment. 12th ed. J. H. Lawson. 1977. pap. 15.95 (*0-8151-5335-X*, Yr Bk Med Pubs) Mosby Yr Bk.

***Synopsis of Four Gospels.** Orchard. (Studies of the New Testament & Its World). 49.95 (*0-567-09331-X*, Pub. by T & T Clark UK) Bks Intl VA.

***Synopsis of General Pathology for Surgeons.** Dennis W. Cotton. LC 97-938. 1997. write for info. (*0-7506-3592-4*) Buttrwrth-Heinemann.

Synopsis of Gynecologic Oncology. 3rd ed. C. Paul Morrow & Duane E. Townsend. LC 87-2112. (Illus.). 602p. reprint ed. pap. 171.60 (*0-7837-6248-8*, 2045960) Bks Demand.

Synopsis of Gynecologic Oncology. 4th ed. C. Paul Morrow et al. LC 93-50. 576p. 1993. text ed. 92.00 (*0-443-08861-6*) Churchill.

Synopsis of Gynecology. Johnson & Ann S. Symonds. Date not set. write for info. (*0-7506-1354-8*) Buttrwrth-Heinemann.

***Synopsis of Human Anatomy & Physiology.** Kent M. Van De Graaff et al. 672p. (C). 1996. text ed. write for info. (*0-697-04296-0*) Wm C Brown Pubs.

Synopsis of Infectious & Tropical Diseases. 3rd ed. Woodruff & Wright. 354p. 1987. pap. 42.50 (*0-7236-0826-1*) Buttrwrth-Heinemann.

Synopsis of Integrated Pest Management in Developing Countries in the Tropics. Integrated Pest Management Working Group Staff. 1991. pap. 25.00 (*0-85954-296-3*, Pub. by Nat Res Inst UK) St Mut.

Synopsis of Intensive Care Medicine. L. I. Worthley. LC 93-17403. 1994. 89.95 (*0-443-04638-7*) Churchill.

Synopsis of Lectures on Medical Science. Alva Curtis. 27p. 1958. reprint ed. spiral bd. 5.00 (*0-7873-0232-5*) Hlth Research.

Synopsis of Minor Oral Surgery. George Dimitroulis. LC 96-23371. 1997. write for info. (*0-7236-1094-0*) Wright UK.

Synopsis of Neuroanatomy. 4th ed. Howard A. Matzke & Floyd M. Foltz. (Illus.). 185p. 1983. pap. 15.95 (*0-19-503244-6*) OUP.

Synopsis of Neuropsychiatry. Ed. by Stuart C. Yudofsky & Robert E. Hales. LC 93-44844. 660p. 1994. pap. text ed. 45.00 (*0-88048-691-0*, 8691) Am Psychiatric.

Synopsis of North American Desmids Pt. 2: Desmidiaceae: Placodermae, 5 Sections, Sect. 1. Gerald W. Prescott et al. LC 70-183418. (Illus.). 285p. reprint ed. Section 1, 285p. pap. 81.30 (*0-8357-3791-8*, 2036522) Bks Demand.

Synopsis of North American Desmids Pt. 2: Desmidiaceae: Placodermae, 5 Sections, Sect. 2. Gerald W. Prescott et al. LC 70-183418. (Illus.). 423p. reprint ed. Section 2, 423. pap. 120.60 (*0-8357-3792-6*, 2036522) Bks Demand.

Synopsis of North American Desmids Pt. 2: Desmidiaceae: Placodermae, 5 Sections, Sect. 3. Gerald W. Prescott et al. LC 70-183418. (Illus.). 730p. reprint ed. Section 3, 730p. pap. 180.00 (*0-8357-3793-4*, 2036522) Bks Demand.

Synopsis of North American Desmids Pt. 2: Desmidiaceae: Placodermae, 5 Sections, Sect. 4. Gerald W. Prescott et al. LC 70-183418. (Illus.). 710p. reprint ed. Section 4, 710p. pap. 180.00 (*0-8357-3794-2*, 2036522) Bks Demand.

Synopsis of North American Desmids Pt. 2: Desmidiaceae: Placodermae, 5 Sections, Sect. 5. Gerald W. Prescott et al. LC 70-183418. (Illus.). 127p. reprint ed. Section 5, 127p. pap. 36.20 (*0-8357-3795-0*, 2036522) Bks Demand.

Synopsis of Obstetrics. Johnson & Ann S. Symonds. Date not set. write for info. (*0-7506-1348-3*) Buttrwrth-Heinemann.

Synopsis of Old Icelandic Grammar. Alan Bower. 80p. (C). 1994. pap. 24.00 (*0-9643394-1-2*) Stonehill MI.

Synopsis of Operative ENT. Maurice R. Hawthorne & Brian J. Bingham. (Illus.). 360p. 1992. pap. 95.00 (*0-7506-1359-9*) Buttrwrth-Heinemann.

Synopsis of Oral Pathology. 7th ed. Bhaskar. 832p. (C). (gr. 13). 1986. text ed. 61.95 (*0-8016-1243-8*) Mosby Yr Bk.

Synopsis of Orthopedics. Howard An. (Illus.). 480p. 1991. text ed. 65.00 (*0-86577-383-1*) Thieme Med Pubs.

Synopsis of Otolaryngology. 5th ed. Roger F. Gray & Maurice R. Hawthorne. (Illus.). 624p. 1992. 95.00 (*0-7506-1358-0*) Buttrwrth-Heinemann.

Synopsis of Paediatrics. Alex Habel. (Illus.). 664p. 1993. 115.00 (*0-7506-1352-1*) Buttrwrth-Heinemann.

Synopsis of Pediatric Emergency Care. Ed. by Jagannath S. Surpure. LC 92-49571. 544p. 1993. text ed. 75.00 (*1-56372-011-6*, Andover Med Pubs) Buttrwrth-Heinemann.

Synopsis of Pediatric Emergency Medicine. Ed. by Gary R. Fleisher & Stephen Ludwig. LC 94-39410. 1995. 65.00 (*0-683-03261-5*) Williams & Wilkins.

Synopsis of Pharmacology for Students in Dentistry. Thomas J. Pallasch & Richard M. Oksas. LC 74-8951. 152p. reprint ed. 43.40 (*0-8357-9422-9*, 2014571) Bks Demand.

***Synopsis of Spine Surgery.** Howard S. An. LC 97-747. 1997. write for info. (*0-683-18097-5*) Williams & Wilkins.

Synopsis of the Birds of India & Pakistan: Together with Those of Nepal, Bhutan, Bangladesh, & Sri Lanka. 2nd ed. S. Dillon Ripley. (Illus.). 680p. 1988. 35.00 (*0-19-562164-6*) OUP.

***Synopsis of the Books of Adam & Eve.** Ed. by Gary Anderson & Michael E. Stone. 88p. 1994. pap. 14.95 (*1-55540-964-4*, 063505) Scholars Pr GA.

Synopsis of the Books of Adam & Eve. Ed. by Gary A. Anderson & Michael E. Stone. LC 94-2747. (SBL Early Judaism & Its Literature Ser.). 88p. 1994. 24.95 (*1-55540-963-6*, 063505) Scholars Pr GA.

Synopsis of the Chrysididae in America North of Mexico. R. M. Bohart & Lynn S. Kimsey. (Memoir Ser.: No.33). (Illus.). 266p. 1982. 35.00 (*1-56665-031-3*) Assoc Pubs FL.

Synopsis of the First Three Gospels With the Addition of the Johannine Parallels. Albert Huck & Heinrich Greeven. 1981. 40.00 (*0-8028-3568-6*) Eerdmans.

Synopsis of the Hebrew Bible. W. R. Brookman. Date not set. write for info. (*1-56563-135-8*) Hendrickson MA.

***Synopsis of the Herpetofauna of Mexico, 6 vols.** Hobart M. Smith & Rozella B. Smith. Incl. Vol. 1 Analysis of the Literature on the Mexican Axolotl. 1971. 10.00 (*0-910914-06-0*); Vol. 2 Analysis of the Literature Exclusive of the Mexican Axolotl. 1973. 12.50 (*0-910914-07-9*); Vol. 3 Source Analysis & Index for Mexican Reptiles. 1976. 25.00 (*0-910914-08-7*); Vol. 4 Source Analysis & Index for Mexican Amphibians. 1976. 12.50 (*0-910914-09-5*); Vol. 5 Guide to Mexican Amphisbaenians & Crocodilians. 1977. 12.50 (*0-910914-10-9*); Vol. 6 Guide to Mexican Turtles. 1980. 40.00 (*0-910914-11-7*); 112.00 (*0-614-28549-6*) J Johnson.

Synopsis of the Herpetofauna of Mexico, Vol. VII. Hobart M. Smith & Rozella B. Smith. LC 92-36642. 1096p. (C). 1993. 75.00 (*0-87081-284-X*) Univ Pr Colo.

Synopsis of the Heteroptera or True Bugs of the Galapagos Islands. Richard C. Froeschner. LC 84-600217. (Smithsonian Contributions to Zoology Ser.: No. 407). 88p. reprint ed. pap. 25.10 (*0-317-30173-X*, 2025355) Bks Demand.

Synopsis of the Indian Tribes Within the U. S. East of the Rocky Mountains & in British & Russian Possessions in North America. Albert Gallatin. LC 78-168093. reprint ed. 52.50 (*0-404-07127-9*) AMS Pr.

Synopsis of the Law of Libel & the Right of Privacy. Bruce W. Sanford. 1986. pap. 2.95 (*0-915106-19-1*) Newspaper Ent.

Synopsis of the Law of Nations, Vol. 2. Tr. by John P. Bate. LC 95-77196. (Classics in International Law Reprint Ser.: No. 6). 1995. reprint ed. 100.00 (*1-57588-267-1*, 310140) W S Hein.

Synopsis of the Lichen Genus Xanthoparmelia (Vaino) Hale (Ascomycotina, Parmeliaceae) Mason E. Hale. LC 89-600293. (Smithsonian Contributions to Botany Ser.: No. 74). 254p. reprint ed. pap. 72.40 (*0-8357-2748-3*, 2039862) Bks Demand.

Synopsis of the Marine Prosobranch Gastropod & Bivalve Mollusks in Alaskan Waters. Nora R. Foster. (IMS Reports: No. R81-3). 499p. 37.50 (*0-914500-14-7*) U of AK Inst Marine.

Synopsis of the Military Career of General Joseph Wheeler: Commander of the Cavalry Corps, Army of the West. Ed. & Intro. by George R. Stewart. LC 88-12272. (Eyewitness Accounts of the Civil War Ser.). (Illus.). 38p. (C). 1988. reprint ed. pap. 10.00 (*0-942301-05-6*) Birm Pub Lib.

Synopsis of the North American Microtine Rodents. E. Raymond Hall & E. Lendell Cockrum. (Museum Ser.: Vol. 5, No. 27). 126p. 1953. pap. 4.00 (*0-686-80288-8*) U KS Nat Hist Mus.

Synopsis of the Stratigraphy in the Western Grand Canyon, Arizona. George H. Billingsley. (Research Ser.). 36p. 1978. pap. 3.50 (*0-685-14700-2*, RS-16) Mus Northern Ariz.

Synopsis of Treatments of Psychiatric Disorders. 2nd ed. Ed. by Glen O. Gabbard & Sarah D. Atkinson. LC 96-43619. 1143p. 1996. pap. text ed. 60.00 (*0-88048-859-X*, 8859) Am Psychiatric.

Synopsis '96: Specialist Cardiological Investigations. J. Roquebrune. Date not set. write for info. (*0-397-58732-5*) Lppncott-Raven.

Synoptic Approach to the Riddle of Existence: Toward an Adequate World View for a World Civilization. Arthur W. Munk. LC 77-818. 264p. 1977. 12.75 (*0-87527-165-0*) Green.

Synoptic Climatology in Environmental Analysis: A Primer. Brent M. Yarnal. (Belhaven Studies in Climatology). 195p. 1994. text ed. 89.00 (*0-471-94796-2*) Wiley.

Synoptic Climatology in Environmental Analysis. Brent M. Yarnal. 256p. 1993. 69.95 (*1-85293-117-5*, Belhaven) Halsted Pr.

Synoptic Climatology of the Westerlies: Process & Patterns. Jay R. Harman. LC 91-58672. (Resource Publications for College Geography). (Illus.). 80p. (C). 1992. pap. 15.00 (*0-89291-208-1*) Assn Am Geographers.

Synoptic Concordance of Aramaic Inscriptions. Walter E. Aufrecht & John Hurd. (International Concordance Library: Vol. I). 1975. pap. 20.00 (*0-935106-24-3*) Biblical Res Assocs.

Synoptic-Dynamic Meteorology in Midlatitudes: Observations & Theory of Weather Systems, Vol. II. Howard B. Bluestein. (Illus.). 557p. (C). 1993. 69.00 (*0-19-506268-X*) OUP.

Synoptic-Dynamic Meteorology in Midlatitudes, Vol. One: Principles of Kinematics & Dynamics. Howard B. Bluestein. (Illus.). 416p. (C). 1992. text ed. 65.00 (*0-19-506267-1*) OUP.

Synoptic Eddies in the Ocean. A. S. Monin et al. 1986. lib. bdg. 194.00 (*90-277-1925-X*) Kluwer Ac.

Synoptic Flora of Mysore District. R. R. Rao & B. A. Razi. (International Bioscience Monographs: No. 7). 694p. 1981. 65.00 (*0-88065-180-6*, Messers Today & Tomorrow) Scholarly Pubns.

Synoptic Food Composition Tables. P. Cok et al. 444p. 1987. pap. text ed. 40.00 (*1-57235-046-6*) Piccin NY.

Synoptic Gospels: An Introduction. Keith F. Nickle. LC 79-92069. (Orig.). 1980. pap. 13.00 (*0-8042-0422-5*, John Knox) Westminster John Knox.

Synoptic Gospels Today. Joseph Kudasiewicz. Tr. by Sergius Wroblewski from POL. LC 96-17362. 352p. (Orig.). 1996. pap. 18.95 (*0-8189-0726-6*) Alba.

Synoptic History of Classical Rhetoric. 2nd ed. James J. Murphy et al. 316p. (Orig.). (C). 1995. pap. 19.95 (*1-880393-19-0*, Hermagoras) L Erlbaum Assocs.

Synoptic Meteorology Exercises & Readings, Vol. 1. Constantine N. Zois. (Meteorology/Oceanography Workbooks). 1995. lab manual ed. 25.00 (*1-888950-04-8*) Xenon Hse.

Synoptic Meteorology Exercises & Readings, Vol. 2. Constantine N. Zois. (Meteorology/Oceanography Workbooks). 1995. lab manual ed. 25.00 (*1-888950-05-6*) Xenon Hse.

Synoptic Meteorology Exercises & Readings, Vol. 3. Constantine N. Zois. (Meteorology/Oceanography Workbooks). 1995. lab manual ed. 25.00 (*1-888950-06-4*) Xenon Hse.

Synoptic Meteorology in China. C. Bao. (Illus.). vi, 269p. 1988. 103.95 (*0-387-16715-3*) Spr-Verlag.

Synoptic Problem: A Critical Analysis. William R. Farmer. LC 76-13764. xi, 308p. 1981. 18.95 (*0-915948-02-8*, MUP-H005) Mercer Univ Pr.

Synoptic Problem: An Introduction. Robert H. Stein. 292p. (C). 1995. reprint ed. pap. 14.99 (*0-8010-2019-0*) Baker Bks.

Synoptic Vision: Essays on the Philosophy of Wilfrid Sellars. C. F. Delaney et al. LC 76-22406. 1977. text ed. 23.00 (*0-268-01596-1*) U of Notre Dame Pr.

Synorgon Diet: How to Achieve Healthy Weight in a World of Excess. Randy L. Wysong. (Illus.). 271p. 1993. pap. 12.95 (*0-918112-06-0*) Inquiry Pr.

Synphore Dans "la Jeune Parque" De Paul Valery. Grace Campbell. LC 74-28038. (Romance Monographs: No. 12). 1975. 13.00 (*84-399-3510-2*) Romance.

***Synposis of the Parasites of Fishes of Canada: (1978-1993)** T. E. McDonald & L. Margolis. (Canadian Special Publication of Fisheries & Aquatic Sciences). 265p. (Orig.). 1995. pap. 45.00 (*0-660-15902-3*, Pub. by NRC Res Pr CN) Aubrey Bks.

Synsedimentary Faulting & Sediment-Hosted Submarine-Hydrothermal Mineralizations in the Late Palaeozoic Rhenish Basin (Germany) 1989. W. Werner. (Geotektonische Forschungen Ser.: No. 71). (Illus.). 305p. 1989. pap. text ed. 125.00 (*3-510-50037-7*) Lubrecht & Cramer.

Synseeds: Applications of Synthetic Seeds to Crop Improvement. Vicki J. Redenbaugh. 496p. 1992. 232.00 (*0-8493-4906-0*) CRC Pr.

Syntactic Analysis of Sea Island Creole. Irma A. Cunningham. LC 90-26133. (Publications of the American Dialect Society: No. 75). 160p. 1991. pap. text ed. 17.00 (*0-8173-0537-8*) U of Ala Pr.

Syntactic & Structural Pattern Recognition: Theory & Applications. Ed. by H. Bunke & A. Sanfeliu. 564p. (C). 1990. text ed. 99.00 (*9971-5-0552-5*); pap. text ed. 61.00 (*9971-5-0566-5*) World Scientific Pub.

Syntactic Argumentation & the Structure of English. Scott Soames & David M. Perlmutter. LC 78-65471. 1979. pap. 18.95 (*0-520-03833-9*) U CA Pr.

Syntactic Argumentation, Vol. 1: Text. Donna J. Napoli & Emily N. Rando. LC 79-17605. 430p. reprint ed. pap. 122.60 (*0-7837-6334-4*, 2046047) Bks Demand.

Syntactic Argumentation, Vol. 2: Teacher's Guide. Donna J. Napoli & Emily N. Rando. LC 79-17605. 45p. reprint ed. pap. 25.00 (*0-7837-6335-2*, 2046047) Bks Demand.

Syntactic Case & Morphological Case in the History of English. Ans Van Kemenade. xi, 249p. 1987. pap. 57.70 (*90-6765-342-X*) Mouton.

Syntactic Categories & Grammatical Relations: The Cognitive Organization of Information. William Croft. 344p. 1991. pap. text ed. 37.50 (*0-226-12090-2*) U Ch Pr.

Syntactic Change: Toward a Theory of Historical Syntax. Jan T. Faarlund. (Trends in Linguistics, Studies & Monographs: No. 50). x, 222p. (C). 1990. lib. bdg. 72.35 (*3-11-012651-6*) Mouton.

Syntactic Change & Syntactic Reconstruction: A Tagmemic Approach. John R. Costello. LC 83-60279. (Publications in Linguistics: No. 68). 78p. (Orig.). 1983. fiche 8.00 (*0-88312-404-1*) Summer Instit Ling.

Syntactic Change in Germanic: Aspects of Language Change in Germanic with Particular Reference to Middle Dutch. Kate Burridge. LC 92-23195. (Current Issues in Linguistic Theory Ser.: No. 89). xii, 287p. 1992. 76.00 (*1-55619-146-4*) Benjamins North Am.

***Syntactic Change in Medieval French Verb-Second & Null Subjects.** Barbara S. Vance. LC 97-23495. (Studies in Natural Language & Linguistic Theory). 1997. write for info. (*0-7923-4669-6*) Kluwer Ac.

Syntactic Derivation of Tagalog Verbs. Videa P. De Guzman. LC 78-11029. (Oceanic Linguistics Special Publication Ser.: No. 16). 432p. reprint ed. pap. 123.20 (*0-8357-8535-1*, 2034838) Bks Demand.

S

***Syntactic Development.** LC 96-46257. 1997. lib. bdg. 75.00 (*0-226-62075-1*) U Ch Pr.

***Syntactic Development.** LC 96-46257. 1997. pap. text ed. 27.95 (*0-226-62077-8*) U Ch Pr.

Syntactic Development of the Infinitive in Indo-European. Dorothy Disterheft. 220p. (Orig.). 1980. pap. 22.95 (*0-89357-058-3*) Slavica.

Syntactic Factors in Memory? Samuel Fillenbaum. (Janua Linguarum, Series Minor: No. 168). 1973. pap. text ed. 20.80 (*90-279-2421-X*) Mouton.

Syntactic Iconicity & Linguistic Freezes: The Human Dimension. Ed. by Marge E. Landsberg. (Studies in Anthropological Linguistics: No. 9). ix, 444p. (C). 1995. lib. bdg. 183.10 (*3-11-014227-9*) Mouton.

Syntactic Parsing Strategies in Italian: The Minimal Chain Principle. Marica De Vincenzi. 256p. (C). 1991. lib. bdg. 120.00 (*0-7923-1274-0*) Kluwer Ac.

***Syntactic Phenomena English.** 2nd ed. McCawley. LC 97-11825. 1996. lib. bdg. 110.00 (*0-226-55627-1*); lib. bdg. 49.95 (*0-226-55629-8*) U Ch Pr.

Syntactic Phenomena of English, Vol. 1. James D. McCawley. (Illus.). 416p. 1988. pap. text ed. 22.50 (*0-226-55624-7*) U Ch Pr.

Syntactic Phenomena of English, Vol. 2. James D. McCawley. (Illus.). 466p. 1988. pap. text ed. 22.50 (*0-226-55626-3*) U Ch Pr.

Syntactic Phrase Structure Phenomena in Noun Phrases & Sentences. Ed. by Christa Bhatt et al. LC 89-18430. (Linguistik Aktuell Ser.: Vol. 6). ix, 187p. 1989. 44.00 (*90-272-2726-8*) Benjamins North Am.

Syntactic Recoverability of Null Arguments. Yves Roberge. 224p. (C). 1990. text ed. 55.00 (*0-7735-0732-9*, Pub. by McGill CN) U of Toronto Pr.

Syntactic Revolution. Abraham L. Gillespie. Ed. by Richard Milazzo. LC 75-22994. (Illus.). 190p. (C). 1981. pap. 12.95 (*0-915570-05-X*) Oolp Pr.

Syntactic Structure in Rimbaud's "Illuminations" Susan W. Fusco. LC 89-70094. (Romance Monographs: No. 49). 1990. pap. 28.00 (*84-599-2850-0*) Romance.

Syntactic Structures. Noam Chomsky. (Janua Linguarum, Series Minor: No. 4). 1978. 13.95 (*0-89925-090-4*) Mouton.

Syntactic Study of Egyptian Colloquial Arabic. Saad M. Gamal-Eldin. (Janua Linguarum, Ser. Practica: No. 34). 1967. pap. text ed. 95.40 (*90-279-0648-3*) Mouton.

Syntactic Theory: A Unified Approach. Robert D. Borsley. (Illus.). 256p. 1995. text ed. 22.50 (*0-7131-6543-X*, A6314, Pub. by E Arnld UK) St Martin.

Syntactic Theory & First Language Acquisition: Cross-Linguistic Perspectives, 2 vols., Set. Ed. by Barbara Lust et al. 1994. text ed. 125.00 (*0-8058-1575-9*) L Erlbaum Assocs.

Syntactic Theory & First Language Acquisition Cross-Linguistic Perspectives Vol. 1: Heads, Projections & Learnability. Ed. by Barbara Lust et al. 376p. 1994. text ed. 79.95 (*0-8058-1351-9*) L Erlbaum Assocs.

Syntactic Theory & First Language Acquisition Cross-Linguistic Perspectives Vol. 2: Binding, Dependences & Learnability. Ed. by Barbara Lust et al. 568p. 1994. text ed. 99.95 (*0-8058-1350-0*) L Erlbaum Assocs.

***Syntactic Theory & the Structure of English: A Minimalist Approach.** Andrew Radford. (Cambridge Textbooks in Linguistics Ser.). 528p. (C). 1997. text ed. 69.95 (*0-521-47125-7*); pap. text ed. 24.95 (*0-521-47707-7*) Cambridge U Pr.

Syntactic Typology: Studies in the Phenomenology of Language. Ed. by Winfred P. Lehmann. LC 78-56377. 477p. 1978. 22.50 (*0-292-77545-8*) U of Tex Pr.

Syntactic Variables: Resumptive Pronouns & A' Binding in Palauan. Carol Georgopoulos. 252p. (C). 1991. lib. bdg. 149.50 (*0-7923-1293-7*) Kluwer Ac.

Syntactica: NeXStep Edition. Richard K. Larson et al. (Illus.). 140p. 1996. pap. 25.00 (*0-262-62106-1*) MIT Pr.

Syntactical & Critical Concordance to the Greek Text of Baruch & the Epistle of Jeremiah. R. A. Martin. (Computer Bible Ser.: Vol. XII). (GRE.). 1977. pap. 49.95 (*0-935106-09-X*) Biblical Res Assocs.

Syntactical Causes of Case Reduction in Old French. G. G. Laubscher. (Elliott Monographs: Vol. 7). 1921. 30.00 (*0-527-02611-5*) Periodicals Srv.

Syntactical Concordance to the Correlated Greek & Hebrew Text of Ruth. R. A. Martin & Sylvio Scorza. (Computer Bible Ser.: Vol. 30). 279p. (Orig.). 1988. pap. 89.95 (*0-935106-26-X*) Biblical Res Assocs.

Syntagma Musicum of Michael Praetorius, Vol. 2: De Organographica. Michael Praetorius. Tr. by Harold Blumenfeld. LC 79-20847. (Music Reprint Ser.). (Illus.). 1980. reprint ed. 29.50 (*0-306-70563-X*) Da Capo.

Syntagma Musicum, Tomus Secundus se Organographie. Michael Praetorius. Ed. by Robert Eitner. (Publikation alterer praktischer und theoretischer Musikwerke, XV. & XVI. Jhs. Ser.: Vol. 13). (Illus.). (GER.). 1966. reprint ed. lib. bdg. 75.00 (*0-8450-1713-6*) Broude.

Syntagma Musicum Two: (Translated from the Edition of 1619) - De Organographia, Pts. I & II. Michael Praetorius. Ed. & Tr. by David Z. Crookes. (Early Music Ser.: No. 7). (Illus.). 174p. 1991. reprint ed. pap. 37.50 (*0-19-816260-X*) OUP.

Syntagma of the Evidences of the Christian Religion. Robert Taylor. 191p. 1992. pap. 19.95 (*1-56459-172-7*) Kessinger Pub.

Syntagma of the Evidences of the Christian Religion. Robert Taylor. 191p. 1985. reprint ed. spiral bd. 16.50 (*0-7873-0856-0*) Hlth Research.

Syntaktische Forscshungen auf dem Gebiet des Spatlateins. Dag Norberg. (Universitets Arsskrift Ser.: No. 9). 283p. 1990. reprint ed. write for info. (*3-487-09347-2*) G Olms Pubs.

S

Syntax. Blaser. (NFS Canada Ser.). 1993. pap. 8.95 (*0-88922-209-6*) Genl Dist Srvs.

Syntax. Ralph Gibson. LC 82-83708. (Illus.). 80p. 1983. 24.95 (*0-912810-39-4*) Lustrum Pr.

Syntax: A Functional-Typological Introduction, Vol. II. T. Givon. LC 84-6195. xxvi, 554p. 1991. 74.00 (*1-55619-096-4*); pap. 24.95 (*1-55619-097-2*) Benjamins North Am.

Syntax: A Functional-Typological Introduction, Vol. 1. T. Givon. LC 84-6195. xx, 464p. (C). 1984. 62.00 (*0-915027-07-0*); pap. text ed. 24.95 (*0-915027-08-9*) Benjamins North Am.

Syntax: A Linguistics Introduction to Sentence Structure. 2nd ed. Keith Brown & Jim Miller. (Illus.). 384p. 1991. pap. 22.50 (*0-04-445561-5*, A8202) Routledge Chapman & Hall.

***Syntax: A Minimalist Introduction.** Andrew Radford. 200p. (C). 1997. text ed. 54.95 (*0-521-58122-2*); pap. text ed. 16.95 (*0-521-58914-2*) Cambridge U Pr.

Syntax: Linguistic Introduction to Sentence Structure. 2nd ed. Keith Brown & Jim Miller. (Illus.). 384p. (Orig.). (C). 1992. pap. 22.95 (*0-415-08421-0*, Routledge NY) Routledge.

***Syntax: Structure, Meaning, & Function.** Robert D. Van Valin, Jr. & Randy J. LaPolla. (Textbooks in Linguistics Ser.). 850p. (C). 1997. text ed. 74.95 (*0-521-49565-2*) Cambridge U Pr.

***Syntax: Structure, Meaning, & Function.** Robert D. Van Valin, Jr. & Randy J. LaPolla. (Textbooks in Linguistics Ser.). 850p. (C). 1997. pap. text ed. 29.95 (*0-521-49915-1*) Cambridge U Pr.

Syntax: Theory & Problems. Donna J. Napoli. (Illus.). 416p. (C). 1993. pap. text ed. 39.00 (*0-19-507946-9*) OUP.

Syntax Vol. 9.2: Ein Internationales Handbuch Zeitgenoessischer Forchung - An International Handbook of Contemporary Research. Ed. by Joachim Jacobs et al. (Handbooks of Linguistics & Communication Science). xii, 611p. (GER.). (C). 1995. lib. bdg. 383.10 (*3-11-014263-5*) De Gruyter.

Syntax see Universals of Human Language

Syntax & Human Experience. Nicolas Ruwet. Ed. & Tr. by John Goldsmith. LC 90-23535. (Studies in Contemporary Linguistics). 362p. 1991. pap. text ed. 29.00 (*0-226-73222-3*) U Ch Pr.

Syntax & Interpretation of the Relative Clause Constructure in Swahili, 4 vols., Set. Ed. by Camillia N. Barrett-Keach. (Outstanding Dissertations in Linguistics Ser.). 1985. text ed. 15.00 (*0-8240-5432-6*) Garland.

Syntax & Parsing. Paul Gorrell. (Cambridge Studies in Linguistics: No. 76). 196p. (C). 1995. text ed. 47.95 (*0-521-45282-1*) Cambridge U Pr.

Syntax & Piagetian Operational Thought: A Developmental Study of Bilingual Children. Ruth V. Tremaine. LC 75-5749. 145p. 1975. reprint ed. pap. 41.40 (*0-7837-6346-8*, 2046058) Bks Demand.

Syntax & Pragmatics in Functional Grammar. Ed. by M. Bolkestein et al. (Functional Grammar Ser.). xiv, 223p. 1985. pap. 50.00 (*90-6765-097-8*) Mouton.

Syntax & Pragmatics of Anaphora: A Study with Special Reference to Chinese. Yan Huang. (Cambridge Studies in Linguistics: No. 70). 352p. (C). 1994. text ed. 65.00 (*0-521-41887-9*) Cambridge U Pr.

Syntax & Semantics, Vol. 20. Ed. by Geoffrey J. Huck & Almerindo E. Ojeda. 306p. 1987. text ed. 118.00 (*0-12-613520-7*) Acad Pr.

Syntax & Semantics Vol. 19: The Syntax of Pronominal Cities, Vol 19. Hagit Borer. 365p. 1986. text ed. 118.00 (*0-12-613519-3*) Acad Pr.

Syntax & Semantics Vol. 28: Small Clauses. Ed. by Anna Cardinaletti & Maria T. Guasti. (Illus.). 333p. 1995. text ed. 79.95 (*0-12-613528-2*) Acad Pr.

Syntax & Semantics of Middle Constructions: A Study with Special Reference to German. Sarah M. Fagan. (Cambridge Studies in Linguistics: No. 60). 240p. (C). 1992. text ed. 69.95 (*0-521-41060-6*) Cambridge U Pr.

Syntax & Semantics of Spanish Presentational Sentence-Types. Margarita Suner. LC 82-12122. (Romance Languages & Linguistics Ser.). 382p. reprint ed. pap. 108.90 (*0-7837-6345-X*, 2046057) Bks Demand.

Syntax & Semantics of the English Verb Phrase. Michael Grady. LC 75-118277. (Janua Linguarum, Ser. Practica: No. 112). (Illus.). (Orig.). 1970. pap. text ed. 40.00 (*90-279-0745-5*) Mouton.

Syntax & Semantics of the Verb in Classical Greek: An Introduction. 2nd ed. Albert Rijksbaron. 199p. (C). 1994. 30.00 (*90-70265-36-2*, Pub. by Gieben NE) Benjamins North Am.

Syntax & Semantics of Verb Morphology in Modern Aramaic. Robert D. Hoberman. (American Oriental Ser.: Vol. 69). xii, 226p. 1989. 32.00 (*0-940490-69-2*) Am Orient Soc.

Syntax & Semantics, Vol. 14: Tense & Aspect. Ed. by John P. Kimball & Philip Tedesch. 1981. text ed. 118.00 (*0-12-613514-2*) Acad Pr.

Syntax & Semantics, Vol. 16: The Syntax of Native American Languages. Eung-Do Cook & Donna B. Gerdts. LC 83-17265. (Serial Publication Ser.). 1984. text ed. 118.00 (*0-12-613516-9*) Acad Pr.

Syntax & Semantics, Vol. 22: Structure & Case Marking in Japanese. Ed. by Shigeru Miyagawa & Stephen Anderson. 259p. 1989. pap. text ed. 61.00 (*0-12-606103-3*) Acad Pr.

Syntax & Semantics, Vol. 23: The Syntax of the Modern Celtic Languages. Ed. by Stephen R. Anderson & Randall Hendrick. 262p. 1990. text ed. 102.00 (*0-12-613523-1*); pap. text ed. 55.00 (*0-12-606104-1*) Acad Pr.

Syntax & Semantics, Vol. 24: Modern Icelandic Syntax. Ed. by Stephen R. Anderson et al. 443p. 1990. pap. text ed. 69.00 (*0-12-606105-X*) Acad Pr.

Syntax & Semantics, Vol. 25: Perspectives on Phrase Structure: Heads & Licensing. Ed. by Stephen R. Anderson & Susan Rothstein. 264p. 1991. pap. text ed. 50.00 (*0-12-606106-8*) Acad Pr.

Syntax & Semantics, Vol. 26: Syntax & the Lexicon. Tim Stowell & Eric Wehrli. (Illus.). 298p. 1992. text ed. 95.00 (*0-12-613526-6*); pap. text ed. 51.00 (*0-12-606107-6*) Acad Pr.

Syntax & Semantics, Vol. 27: The Syntactic Structure of Hungarian. Ed. by Ferenc Kiefer & Katalin F. Kiss. (Illus.). 475p. 1994. text ed. 84.00 (*0-12-613527-4*) Acad Pr.

Syntax & Speech. William E. Cooper & Jeanne Paccia-Cooper. LC 80-16614. (Cognitive Science Ser.: No. 3). 284p. 1980. 36.00 (*0-674-86075-6*) HUP.

Syntax & Style. Clarence E. Schneider. LC 72-97330. 342p. 1974. pap. 14.95 (*0-88316-019-6*) Chandler & Sharp.

Syntax & Style in Old English: A Comparison of the Two Versions of Waerferth's Translation of Gregory's Dialogues. David Yerkes. LC 81-14200. (Medieval & Renaissance Texts & Studies: Vol. 5). 112p. 1982. 24.00 (*0-86698-011-3*, MR5) MRTS.

Syntax Criticism of Johannine Literature, the Catholic Epistles & the Gospel Passion Accounts. Raymond A. Martin. LC 89-13567. (Studies in the Bible & Early Christianity: Vol. 18). 200p. 1989. lib. bdg. 89.95 (*0-88946-618-1*) E Mellen.

Syntax Criticism of the Synoptic Gospels. Raymond A. Martin. LC 87-5646. (Studies in Bible & Early Christianity: Vol. 10). 232p. 1987. lib. bdg. 99.95 (*0-88946-610-6*) E Mellen.

Syntax of Anaphoric Binding. Mary Dalrymple. LC 93-20413. (CSLI Lecture Notes Ser.: No. 36). 196p. 1993. text ed. 54.95 (*1-881526-07-0*); pap. text ed. 19.95 (*1-881526-06-2*) CSLI.

Syntax of Apollonius Dyscolus. Fred W. Householder. (Studies in the History of Linguistics: Vol. 23). vi, 281p. (C). 1981. 65.00 (*90-272-4504-5*) Benjamins North Am.

Syntax of Classical Greek from Homer to Demosthenes: First Part-The Syntax of the Simple Sentence Embracing the Doctrine of the Moods & TENSES, Second Part-The Syntax of Simple Sentence Continued Embracing the Doctrine of the Article. Basil L. Gildersleeve. 1980. reprint ed. 64.50 (*90-6088-071-4*, Pub. by Boumas Boekhuis NE) Benjamins North Am.

Syntax of Contemporary French: A Pedagogical Handbook & Reference Grammar. Wolf Hollerbach. LC 93-42113. 526p. (Orig.). (C). 1994. pap. text ed. 37.50 (*0-8191-9380-1*) U Pr of Amer.

Syntax of Coordination. Robert R. Van Oirsouw. 250p. 1987. lib. bdg. 75.00 (*0-7099-2639-1*, Pub. by Croom Helm UK) Routledge Chapman & Hall.

Syntax of Early Latin, 2 vols. in 1. Charles E. Bennett. xxi, 409p. 1982. reprint ed. 185.00 (*3-487-01345-2*) G Olms Pubs.

Syntax of English Phrasal Verbs. Kazimierz A. Sroka. LC 74-151657. (Janua Linguarum, Series Practica: No. 129). 216p. (Orig.). 1972. pap. text ed. 50.00 (*90-279-2218-7*) Mouton.

***Syntax of Hungarian Noun Phrases: A Lexical-Functional Approach.** Tibor Laczk'o. LC 95-48818. (MetaLinguistica Ser.: Bd. 2). 97p. 1996. pap. 42.95 (*0-8204-2960-0*, 68728) P Lang Pubng.

Syntax of Il Fiore & of Dante's Inferno As Evidence in the Question of the Authorship of Il Fiore. Mary D. Ramacciotti. LC 72-115356. (Catholic University of America: No. 12). reprint ed. 37.50 (*0-404-50312-8*) AMS Pr.

Syntax of Japanese Honorifics. Gary D. Prideaux. (Janua Linguarum, Series Practica: No. 102). 1970. pap. text ed. 50.00 (*90-279-0741-2*) Mouton.

Syntax of Mandarin Interrogatives. Earl Rand. LC 78-626766. (University of California Publications in Social Welfare: Vol. 55). (Illus.). 123p. reprint ed. pap. 35.10 (*0-317-10083-1*, 2011788) Bks Demand.

Syntax of Masoretic Accents in the Hebrew Bible. James D. Price. LC 90-20265. (Studies in the Bible & Early Christianity: Vol. 27). 344p. 1990. lib. bdg. 99.95 (*0-88946-510-X*) E Mellen.

Syntax of Modern Arabic Prose, Vol. 1: The Simple Sentence. Vicente Cantarino. LC 69-16996. 184p. reprint ed. pap. 52.50 (*0-685-20425-1*, 2056415) Bks Demand.

Syntax of Modern Literary Ukrainian. George Y. Shevelov. 1963. text ed. 172.35 (*90-279-0186-4*) Mouton.

Syntax of Moods & Tenses of New Testament Greek. Ernest D. Burton. 240p. 1898. 35.95 (*0-567-01002-3*, Pub. by T & T Clark UK) Bks Intl VA.

Syntax of Negation. Liliane Haegeman. (Cambridge Studies in Linguistics: No. 75). 388p. (C). 1995. text ed. 69.95 (*0-521-46492-7*) Cambridge U Pr.

Syntax of New Testament Greek. James A. Brooks & Carlton L. Winbery. LC 78-51150. 186p. 1978. pap. text ed. 15.50 (*0-8191-0473-6*) U Pr of Amer.

***Syntax of Nonfinite Complementation: An Economy Approach.** Zeljko B. Skovic. LC 97-14912. (Linguistic Inquiry Monograph Ser.). 1997. write for info. (*0-262-02429-2*); pap. write for info. (*0-262-52236-5*) MIT Pr.

Syntax of Norwegian Passive Constructions. Tor A. Afarli. LC 92-17859. (Linguistik Aktuell - Linguistics Today Ser.: No. 7). xii, 178p. 1992. 50.00 (*1-55619-225-8*) Benjamins North Am.

Syntax of Noun Phrases: Configuration, Parameters & Empty Categories. Alessandra Giorgi & Giuseppe Longobardi. (Cambridge Studies in Linguistics: No. 57). (Illus.). 312p. (C). 1991. text ed. 70.00 (*0-521-37004-3*); pap. text ed. 24.95 (*0-521-37902-4*) Cambridge U Pr.

Syntax of Number, Person, & Gender: A Theory of Phi-Features. Johan Kerstens. LC 93-26398. (Linguistic Models Ser.: No. 18). x, 276p. (C). 1993. lib. bdg. 113.85 (*3-11-013603-1*) Mouton.

Syntax of Reflexivization. Martin Everaert. (Publications in Language Sciences). xi, 330p. (Orig.). (C). 1986. pap. 75.40 (*90-6765-153-2*) Mouton.

Syntax of Romanian: Comparative Studies in Romance. Carmen Dobrovie-Sorin. Vol. 40. 1993. 109.00 (*0-685-67322-7*) Mouton.

Syntax of Romanian: Comparative Studies in Romance. Carmen Dobrovie-Sorin. (Studies in Generative Grammar: No. 40). xx, 296p. (C). 1993. lib. bdg. 121.55 (*3-11-013541-8*) Mouton.

Syntax of Scope. Joseph Aoun & Yen-Hui A. Li. LC 92-30929. (Linguistic Inquiry Monographs: Vol. 21). (Illus.). 190p. 1993. 37.50 (*0-262-01133-6*); pap. 18.95 (*0-262-51068-5*) MIT Pr.

Syntax of Sentence & Text: A Festschrift for Frantisek Danes. Ed. by Svetla Cmejrkova & Frantisek Sticha. LC 94-12314. (Linguistic & Literary Studies in Eastern Europe: No. 42). 1994. lib. bdg. 75.00 (*1-55619-267-3*) Benjamins North Am.

Syntax of Serial Verbs: An Investigation into Serialization in Sranan & Other Languages. Mark Sebba. LC 86-31017. (Creole Language Library: Vol. 2). xv, 218p. 1987. 52.00 (*0-915027-95-X*) Benjamins North Am.

Syntax of Social Life: The Theory & Method of Comparative Narratives. Peter Abell. 192p. 1987. 49.95 (*0-19-827271-5*) OUP.

Syntax of Spanish Reflexive Verbs: The Parameters of the Middle Verb. Sandra S. Babcock. LC 74-106468. (Janua Linguarum, Ser. Practica: No. 105). (Orig.). 1970. pap. text ed. 33.85 (*90-279-0742-0*) Mouton.

Syntax of Spoken Brazilian Portuguese. Earl W. Thomas. LC 69-11280. 383p. 1969. reprint ed. pap. 109.20 (*0-608-00492-8*, 2061311) Bks Demand.

Syntax of Subjects. Koichi Tateishi. LC 94-15069. 280p. 1994. 49.95 (*1-881526-46-1*); pap. 24.95 (*1-881526-45-3*) CSLI.

Syntax of Subjects. Koichi Tateishi. 1995. pap. 24.95 (*0-521-52645-0*) Cambridge U Pr.

Syntax of the Celtic Languages: A Comparative Perspective. Ed. by Ian G. Roberts & Robert D. Borsley. 380p. (C). 1996. text ed. 59.95 (*0-521-48160-0*) Cambridge U Pr.

Syntax of the Declinable Words in the Roman de la Rose. M. Calixta Garvey. LC 74-94208. (Catholic University in Romance Languages & Literatures Ser.: No. 13). reprint ed. 37.50 (*0-404-50313-6*) AMS Pr.

Syntax of the Gesta Francorum. John J. Gavigan. (L. D. Mono. Ser.: No.37). 1943. pap. 25.00 (*0-527-00783-8*) Periodicals Srv.

Syntax of the Moods & Tenses of New Testament Greek. Ernest D. Burton. LC 76-25360. 238p. 1976. 16.99 (*0-8254-2256-6*, Kregel Class) Kregel.

Syntax of the Moods & Tenses of the Greek Verb. William W. Goodwin. 472p. 1992. reprint ed. 25.00 (*0-9637069-1-8*) W H Allen Bksell.

Syntax of the Old French Subjunctive. Frede Jensen. LC 73-79890. (Janua Linguarum, Ser. Practica: No. 220). 134p. (Orig.). 1974. pap. text ed. 49.25 (*90-279-2691-3*) Mouton.

Syntax of the Old Spanish Subjunctive. Frede Jensen & Thomas A. Lathrop. (Janua Linguarum, Series Practica: No. 182). 1973. pap. text ed. 40.00 (*90-279-2450-3*) Mouton.

Syntax of the Simple Sentence in Proto - Germanic. Paul J. Hopper. LC 72-94524. (Janua Linguarum, Series Practica: No. 143). 104p. (Orig.). 1975. pap. text ed. 36.95 (*90-279-3282-4*) Mouton.

Syntax Today. Keith Brown. (Approaches to Linguistics Ser.). 256p. (C). 1992. pap. write for info. (*0-521-42452-6*) Cambridge U Pr.

Syntax Today. Keith Brown. (Approaches to Linguistics Ser.). 256p. (C). 1994. write for info. (*0-521-41401-6*) Cambridge U Pr.

Syntaxe Comparative Francais-Anglais. Jeanne Ambrose. 123p. (FRE.). 29.50 (*0-916379-42-6*) Scripta.

Syntaxe des Verbes de mouvement en Coreen Contemporain. Chai-Song Hong. LC 84-28391. (Lingvisticae Investigationes Supplementa Ser.: No. 12). xv, 309p. (FRE.). 1985. 65.00 (*90-272-3122-2*) Benjamins North Am.

Syntaxe du Francais. Pierre Guiraud. 126p. 1970. 9.95 (*0-8288-7454-9*) Fr & Eur.

Syntaxe du Francais Moderne, 2 tomes, Set. Le Bidois. 35.90 (*0-685-36655-3*); 60.95 (*0-8288-7865-X*, F135480) Fr & Eur.

Synthese Eurosibereinne, Phytosociologique & Phytogeographique de la Classe des Festuco-Brometea. J. M. Royer. (Dissertationes Botanicae Ser.: Vol. 178). (Illus.). 296p. (FRE.). 1991. pap. text ed. 91.00 (*3-443-64090-7*) Lubrecht & Cramer.

Syntheses & Separations Using Functional Polymers. Sherrington. 454p. 1988. text ed. 340.00 (*0-471-91848-2*) Wiley.

Synthesis. Theodore Enslin. 400p. 1975. pap. 6.00 (*0-913028-36-3*) North Atlantic.

Synthesis. Torkom Saraydarian. 1983. pap. 2.50 (*0-911794-18-2*) Aqua Educ.

***Synthesis.** 2nd ed. Fowler & Pidcock. 1988. teacher ed., pap. text ed. write for info. (*0-17-555698-9*) Addison-Wesley.

Synthesis: An Introduction to the History, Theory & Practice of Electronic Music. rev. ed. Herbert A. Deutsch. LC 85-30824. (Illus.). 132p. (Orig.). 1976. pap. 15.95 (*0-88284-348-6*, 1439) Alfred Pub.

Synthesis: The Hermetic Tarot. T. Byron G. (Illus.). 76p. (Orig.). (C). 1988. pap. text ed. 8.95 (*1-879352-01-X*) Mini-Novel Pub.

Synthesis - Mechanism - Polymer Drugs. Ed. by International Board of Experts Staff. (Advances in Polymer Science Ser.: Vol. 97). (Illus.). 168p. 1990. 118.95 (*0-387-52834-2*) Spr-Verlag.

Synthesis & Analysis in Materials Processing: Characterization & Diagnostics of Ceramics & Metal Particulate Processing. Ed. by E. J. Lavernia et al. LC 89-61036. (Illus.). 100p. 1989. 10.00 (*0-87339-106-3*, 1063) Minerals Metals.

***Synthesis & Analysis in Materials Processing: Characterization & Diagnostics of Ceramics & Metal Particulate Processing: Proceedings of a Symposium/Sponsored by the TMS Synthesis & Analysis in Materials Processing Committee, Held During the 1989 TMS Annual Meeting, Las Vegas, Nevada, February 28-March 3, 1989.** Ed. by Enrique J. Lavernia et al. LC 89-61036. (Illus.). 104p. pap. 29.70 (*0-608-04979-4*, 2065596) Bks Demand.

Synthesis & Application of Lanthanide-Doped Materials. Ed. by B. G. Potter, Jr. & A. J. Bruce. (Ceramic Transactions Ser.: No. 67). (Illus.). 150p. 1996. 90.00 (*1-57498-012-2*, CT067) Am Ceramic.

Synthesis & Applications of Isotopically Labelled Compounds, 1991: Proceedings of the Fourth International Symposium, Toronto, Canada, 3-7 September 1991. Ed. by E. Buncel & George W. Kabalka. LC 92-20005. 784p. 1992. 412.50 (*0-444-89280-X*) Elsevier.

Synthesis & Applications of Isotopically Labelled Compounds 1994: 1994 Proceedings of the Fifth International Symposium, Strasburg, France, 20-24 June 1994. Ed. by J. Allen & R. Voges. 935p. 1995. text ed. 215.00 (*0-471-95143-9*) Wiley.

Synthesis & Backward Reference in Husserl's Logical Investigations. Jay Lampert. LC 94-23102. (Phaenomenologica Ser.: Vol. 131). 232p. 1995. lib. bdg. 96.00 (*0-7923-3105-2*, Pub. by Klwr Acad Pubs NE) Kluwer Ac.

Synthesis & Characterization of Inorganic Compounds. William L. Jolly. (Illus.). 590p. (C). 1991. reprint ed. pap. text ed. 39.95 (*0-88133-578-9*) Waveland Pr.

Synthesis & Characterization of Oligomers. Constantin V. Uglea & Ioan A. Negulescu. (Illus.). 384p. 1991. 232.95 (*0-8493-4954-0*, QD352) CRC Pr.

Synthesis & Chemistry of Agrochemicals. Ed. by Don R. Baker et al. LC 87-22304. (Symposium Ser.: No. 355). (Illus.). ix, 571p. 1987. 89.95 (*0-8412-1434-4*) Am Chemical.

***Synthesis & Chemistry of Agrochemicals.** Ed. by Don R. Baker et al. LC 87-22304. (ACS Symposium Ser.: Vol. 355). 488p. 1987. reprint ed. pap. 139.10 (*0-608-03878-4*, 2064325) Bks Demand.

Synthesis & Chemistry of Agrochemicals III. Ed. by Don R. Baker et al. LC 92-27345. (ACS Symposium Ser.: Vol. 504). (Illus.). 456p. 1992. 109.95 (*0-8412-2473-0*) Am Chemical.

Synthesis & Chemistry of Agrochemicals IV. Ed. by Don R. Baker et al. (ACS Symposium Ser.: No. 584). (Illus.). 506p. 1995. 129.95 (*0-8412-3091-9*) Am Chemical.

***Synthesis & Coordination Behaviour of N-alkylamino Sugars & Derivatives.** Hendrik Lammers. (Illus.). 199p. (Orig.). 1995. pap. 59.50 (*90-407-1187-9*, Pub. by Delft U Pr NE) Coronet Bks.

Synthesis & Counseling in Astrology: The Professional Manual. Noel Tyl. LC 94-5937. (Illus.). 893p. 1994. pap. 29.95 (*1-56718-734-X*) Llewellyn Pubns.

Synthesis & Degradation-Rheology & Extrusion. Ed. by H. J. Cantow et al. (Advances in Polymer Science Ser.: Vol. 47). (Illus.). 170p. 1982. 62.00 (*0-387-11774-1*) Spr-Verlag.

Synthesis & Fuction Control of Biofunctionality Materials. Ed. by T. Tsuruta et al. LC 93-167294. (New Functionality Materials Ser.: Vol. B). 400p. 1993. 153.25 (*0-444-81613-5*, North Holland) Elsevier.

Synthesis & Modeling of Intermittent Estuaries. Ed. by W. R. Cuff & M. Tomczak, Jr. (Lecture Notes on Coastal & Estuarine Studies: Vol. 3). 302p. 1983. pap. 42.00 (*0-387-12681-3*) Spr-Verlag.

An Asterisk (*) at the beginning of an entry indicates that the title is appearing in BIP for the first time.

Synthesis & Optimization of Digital Circuits. Giovanni De Micheli. LC 93-43595. 1994. text ed. write for info. (*0-07-016333-2*) McGraw.

Synthesis & Other Virtual Realities. Mary Rosenblum. LC 95-43950. (Illus.). 288p. 1996. 21.95 (*0-87054-170-6*, Arkham Hse) Arkham.

Synthesis & Photosynthesis. (Advances in Polymer Science Ser.: Vol. 123). (Illus.). 263p. 1995. 188.95 (*3-540-58908-2*) Spr-Verlag.

Synthesis & Polymerization of Metal-Containing Monomers. Anatoly D. Pomogailo & Vladimir S. Savostyanov. LC 93-49461. 192p. 1994. 95.95 (*0-8493-2863-2*, 2863) CRC Pr.

Synthesis & Processing of Ceramics: Scientific Issues. Ed. by W. E. Rhine et al. (Symposium Proceedings Ser.: Vol. 249). 581p. 1992. text ed. 17.50 (*1-55899-143-3*) Materials Res.

Synthesis & Processing of Nanocrystalline Powder: A Collection of Papers from the 1996 TMS Annual Meeting & Exhibition in Anaheim, California, February 4-8, 1996. Ed. by D. L. Bourell. (Illus.). 315p. 1996. 84.00 (*0-87339-315-5*, 3155) Minerals Metals.

Synthesis & Properties of Advanced Catalytic Materials: 1994 MRS Fall Meeting, Boston, MA. Ed. by Dick A. Nagaki et al. (MRS Symposium Proceedings Ser.: Vol. 368). 394p. 1995. 72.00 (*1-55899-270-7*) Materials Res.

***Synthesis & Properties of Advanced Materials.** Ed. by Carl McHargue. LC 96-41137. 304p. (C). 1996. lib. bdg. 158.00 (*0-7923-9816-5*) Kluwer Ac.

Synthesis & Properties of Low-Dimensional Materials, Vol. 313. Ed. by Joel S. Miller & Arthur J. Epstein. (Annals Ser.). 828p. 1978. pap. 82.00 (*0-89072-069-X*) NY Acad Sci.

Synthesis & Properties of Metastable Phases: Proceedings of a Symposium - Sponsored by the TMS-AIME Alloy Phases Committee at the Fall Meeting of the Metallurgical Society of AIME, Pittsburgh, PA, October 5-9, 1980. Metallurgical Society of AIME Staff. Ed. by E. S. Machlin & T. J. Rowland. LC 80-85205. (Conference Proceedings Ser.). 203p. reprint ed. pap. 57.90 (*0-8357-2519-7*, 2052399) Bks Demand.

Synthesis & Properties of Polymers. Ed. by G. E. Zaikov. 1995. 77.00 (*1-56072-257-6*) Nova Sci Pubs.

Synthesis & Structure of Macromolecules. Cold Spring Harbor Symposia on Quantitative Biology Staff. LC 34-8174. (Cold Spring Harbor Symposia on Quantitative Biology Ser.: Vol. 28). (Illus.). 630p. 1963. pap. 179.60 (*0-7837-8979-3*, 2049760) Bks Demand.

Synthesis & Technique in Inorganic Chemistry. 2nd ed. Robert J. Angelici. (Illus.). 235p. (C). 1987. pap. text ed. 34.50 (*0-935702-53-9*) Univ Sci Bks.

Synthesis Approach to Digital System Design. Ed. by Petra Michel. (International Series in Engineering & Computer Science, VLSI, Computer Architecture, & Digital Screen Processing). 432p. (C). 1992. lib. bdg. 126.00 (*0-7923-9199-3*) Kluwer Ac.

Synthesis bei Kant: Das Problem der Verbindung von Vorstellungen. Hansgeorg Hoppe. 252p. 1983. 99.25 (*3-11-008981-5*) De Gruyter.

Synthesis, Characterization, & Theory of Polymeric Networks & Gels. Ed. by Shaul M. Aharoni. LC 92-26765. 1992. 105.00 (*0-306-44306-6*, Plenum Pr) Plenum.

Synthesis for Control Dominated Circuits: Selected Papers from the IFIP WG10.2 - WG10.5 Workshops, Grenoble, France, April & September 1992. Ed. by Gabriele Saucier & Jacques Trilhe. LC 93-14919. (Computer Science & Technology Ser.). 464p. 1993. pap. 153.25 (*0-444-81479-5*, North Holland) Elsevier.

Synthesis, High Pressure Effects & Some Miscellaneous Aspects. Ed. by Anant Narlikar. (Studies of High Temperature Superconductors: Vol. 16). 307p. 1995. 97.00 (*1-56072-251-7*) Nova Sci Pubs.

Synthesis Imaging in Radio Astronomy: A Collection of Lectures from the Third NRAO Synthesis Imaging Summer School. Ed. by R. A. Perley et al. (ASP Conference Series Proceedings: Vol. 6). 509p. 1989. 28.00 (*0-937707-23-6*) Astron Soc Pacific.

Synthesis, Instruments & Prospects: Energy Sources for Europe. Michael Grubb et al. (Renewable Energy Strategies for Europe Ser.: Vol. 4). 120p. (C). 1995. pap. 14.95 (*1-85383-287-1*, Pub. by Erthscan Pubns UK) Island Pr.

Synthesis Novel in Latin America: A Study on Joao Guimaraes Rosa's Grande Sertao: Veredas. Eduardo D. Coutinho. LC 91-10289. (Studies in the Romance Languages & Literatures: No. 237). 170p. (C). 1991. pap. 29.95 (*0-8078-9241-6*) U of NC Pr.

Synthesis of Acetylenes, Allenes & Cumulenes: A Laboratory Manual. L. Bradsma & H. D. Verkruijsse. (Studies in Organic Chemistry: Vol. 8). 276p. 1981. 162.00 (*0-444-42009-6*) Elsevier.

Synthesis of Biocomposite Materials: Chemical & Biological Modified Natural Polymers. 320p. 1992. 172.00 (*0-8493-6771-9*, TA418) CRC Pr.

Synthesis of Carbon Phosphorus Bonds. Ed. by Robert Engel. LC 87-22932. 160p. 1988. 138.00 (*0-8493-4930-3*, QD412, CRC Reprint) Franklin.

Synthesis of Carboxylic Acids, Esters & Their Derivatives - Updates. James F. Wolfe & Michael A. Ogliaruso. LC 90-43886. (Chemistry of Functional Groups Ser.). 684p. 1991. text ed. 525.00 (*0-471-91717-6*) Wiley.

Synthesis of Current & Projected Concrete Highway Technology. David Whiting et al. 285p. (Orig.). (C). 1993. pap. text ed. 15.00 (*0-309-05272-6*, SHRP-C-345) SHRP.

Synthesis of Digital Design from Recursive Equations. Steven D. Johnson. (ACM Distinguished Dissertation Ser.). (Illus.). 200p. 1984. 32.50 (*0-262-10029-0*) MIT Pr.

Synthesis of Electrical Networks. H. Baher. LC 83-21905. (Illus.). 299p. reprint ed. pap. 85.30 (*0-8357-4609-7*, 2037542) Bks Demand.

Synthesis of Existing Knowledge & Practice in the Field of Educational Partnerships. 1994. lib. bdg. 250.00 (*0-8490-8588-8*) Gordon Pr.

***Synthesis of Finite State Machines: Functional Optimization.** Timothy Kam. LC 96-47092. 296p. (C). 1996. lib. bdg. 110.00 (*0-7923-9842-4*) Kluwer Ac.

***Synthesis of Finite State Machines: Logic Optimization.** LC 97-7693. 1997. lib. bdg. 115.00 (*0-7923-9892-0*) Kluwer Ac.

Synthesis of Fused Heterocycles, Vol. 47. G. P. Ellis. LC 86-28944. (Chemistry of Heterocyclic Compounds, a Series of Monographs: Vol. 47, Pt. 2). 1430p. 1992. text ed. 565.00 (*0-471-93070-9*) Wiley.

Synthesis of Fused Heterocycles, Vol. 47. Gwyn P. Ellis. LC 86-28944. (Chemistry of Heterocyclic Compounds, a Series of Monographs: Vol. 47, Pt. 1). 660p. 1987. reprint ed. text ed. 945.00 (*0-471-91431-2*) Wiley.

Synthesis of High-Silica Aluminosilicate Zeolites. P. A. Jacobs & J. A. Martens. 390p. 1987. 238.25 (*0-444-42814-3*) Elsevier.

Synthesis of Holarctic Miridae: Distribution, Biology, & Origin, with Emphasis on North America. A. Wheeler. (Thomas Say Monographs: Vol. 15). 306p. 1992. 50.00 (*0-938522-39-6*, TS15) Entomol Soc.

Synthesis of Lactones & Lactams. Michael A. Ogliaruso & James F. Wolfe. Ed. by Saul E. Patai & Zvi Rappoport. LC 92-28932. (Updates from the Chemistry of Functional Groups Ser.). 1085p. 1993. text ed. 625.00 (*0-471-93734-7*) Wiley.

Synthesis of Lanthanide & Actinide Compounds. Ed. by G. Meyer & L. R. Morss. (C). 1991. lib. bdg. 188.00 (*0-7923-1018-7*) Kluwer Ac.

Synthesis of Marine Natural Products, No. 1: Terpenoids. K. F. Albizati et al. Ed. by Paul J. Scheuer. (Bioorganic Marine Chemistry Ser.: Vol. 5). (Illus.). xi, 280p. 1992. 172.95 (*0-387-54375-9*) Spr-Verlag.

Synthesis of Marine Natural Products, No. 2: Nonterpenoids. K. F. Albizati et al. Ed. by Paul J. Scheuer. (Bioorganic Marine Chemistry Ser.: Vol. 6). (Illus.). xi, 322p. 1992. 172.95 (*0-387-54376-7*) Spr-Verlag.

Synthesis of Microporous Materials, 2 vols., Set, Vols. 1-2. Ed. by Mario Occelli & Harry E. Robson. (Illus.). 932p. (gr. 13). 1992. Set. text ed. 245.95 (*0-442-01116-4*) Chapman & Hall.

Synthesis of Microporous Materials, 2 vols., Vol. 1: Molecular Sieves. Ed. by Mario Occelli & Harry E. Robson. (Illus.). 932p. (gr. 13). 1992. text ed. 151.95 (*0-442-00661-6*) Chapman & Hall.

Synthesis of Microporous Materials, 2 vols., Vol. 2: Expanded Clays & Other Microporous Solids. Ed. by Mario Occelli & Harry E. Robson. (Illus.). 932p. (gr. 13). 1992. text ed. 151.95 (*0-442-00662-4*) Chapman & Hall.

Synthesis of Natural Products: Problems of Stereoselectivity, Vol. 1. Frantisek Turecek. LC 85-29943. 248p. 1986. 140.00 (*0-8493-6406-X*, CRC Reprint) Franklin.

Synthesis of Natural Products: Problems of Stereoselectivity, Vol. 2. Frantisek Turecek. LC 85-29943. 296p. 1986. 167.00 (*0-8493-6407-8*, CRC Reprint) Franklin.

Synthesis of Natural Products see Eleventh IUPAC International Symposium on Chemistry: Bulgarian Academy of Sciences

Synthesis of Natural Products Problems of Stereoselectivity, Set, Vols. I & II. Pavel Kocovsky et al. 1986. Set. 289.00 (*0-8493-6418-3*, QD415) CRC Pr.

Synthesis of Natural Products Problems of Stereoselectivity, Vol. I. Pavel Kocovsky et al. 248p. 1986. write for info. (*0-318-61545-2*) CRC Pr.

Synthesis of Natural Products Problems of Stereoselectivity, Vol. II. Pavel Kocovsky et al. 304p. 1986. write for info. (*0-318-61546-0*) CRC Pr.

Synthesis of Optically Active Alpha Amino Acids. Williams. (Tetrahedron Organic Chemistry Ser.). Date not set. text ed. write for info. (*0-08-042076-1*, Pergamon Pr); pap. text ed. write for info. (*0-08-042077-X*, Pergamon Pr) Elsevier.

Synthesis of Optically Active Alpha-Amino Acids. R. M. Williams. (Organic Chemistry Ser.: No. 7). (Illus.). 410p. 1989. pap. text ed. 48.00 (*0-08-035939-6*) Elsevier.

Synthesis of Optically Active Alpha-Amino Acids. R. M. Williams. (Organic Chemistry Ser.: No. 7). (Illus.). 410p. 1989. text ed. 125.00 (*0-08-035940-X*, Pergamon Pr) Elsevier.

Synthesis of Parallel Algorithms. John H. Reif. 1993. 59.95 (*1-55860-135-X*) Morgan Kaufmann.

Synthesis of Penicillin, Cephalosporin C, & Analogs. Maghar S. Manhas & Ajay K. Bose. LC 69-13151. (New Directions in Organic Chemistry Ser.). 132p. reprint ed. pap. 37.70 (*0-685-16176-5*, 2027101) Bks Demand.

***Synthesis of Polymers for Plastic Optical Fibers, 3 vols., Vols. 1-3.** Alexander Baran. 1995. 495.00 (*0-614-18422-3*) Info Gatekeepers.

Synthesis of Porous Materials: Zeolites, Clays & Nanostuctures. Ed. by Mario L. Occelli & Henri Kessler. LC 96-32685. (Chemical Industries Ser.: Vol. 69). 744p. 1996. 195.00 (*0-8247-9759-0*) Dekker.

Synthesis of Power Distribution to Manage Signal Integrity in Mixed-Signal IC. Balsha R. Stanisic et al. LC 96-14899. 208p. (C). 1996. lib. bdg. 95.00 (*0-7923-9734-7*) Kluwer Ac.

Synthesis of Results from Scientific Drilling in the Indian Ocean. Ed. by Robert Duncan & David Rea. LC 92-34422. (Geophysical Monograph Ser.: Vol. 70). 1993. 48.00 (*0-87590-822-5*) Am Geophysical.

Synthesis of Science & Religion: Critical Essays & Dialogues. Ed. by T. D. Singh & Ravi V. Gomatam. LC 87-34129. (Illus.). 451p. 1988. text ed. 29.95 (*0-941525-01-5*) Bhaktvdnta Institute.

Synthesis of Self, 4 vols., Vol. 1. Roy M. Mendelsohn. LC 87-25798. (Illus.). 370p. 1987. 60.00 (*0-306-42711-7*, Plenum Med Bk) Plenum.

Synthesis of Self, 4 vols., Vol. 2. Roy M. Mendelsohn. LC 87-25798. (Illus.). 272p. 1987. 60.00 (*0-306-42712-5*, Plenum Med Bk) Plenum.

Synthesis of Self, 4 vols., Vol. 3. Roy M. Mendelsohn. LC 87-25798. (Illus.). 392p. 1987. 60.00 (*0-306-42713-3*, Plenum Med Bk) Plenum.

Synthesis of Self, 4 vols., Vol. 4. Roy M. Mendelsohn. LC 87-25798. (Illus.). 266p. 1987. 60.00 (*0-306-42714-1*, Plenum Med Bk) Plenum.

Synthesis of Strontium Iodate Monohydrate. M. Royer et al. Ed. by H. Anthony Neidig. (Modular Laboratory Program in Chemistry Ser.). 12p. (C). 1987. pap. text ed. 1.35 (*0-87540-341-7*, SYNT 341-7) Chem Educ Res.

Synthesis of Subsonic Airplane Design. E. Torenbeek. 1982. reprint ed. lib. bdg. 98.00 (*90-247-2724-3*) Kluwer Ac.

Synthesis of Sulphones, Suphoxides & Cyclic Sulphides. K. Schank et al. Ed. by Saul E. Patai & Zvi Rappoport. (Chemistry of Functional Groups Ser.). 720p. 1994. text ed. 395.00 (*0-471-93970-6*) Wiley.

Synthesis of the Caledonian Rocks of Britain. Ed. by D. J. Fettes & A. L. Harris. 1986. lib. bdg. 143.00 (*90-277-2235-8*) Kluwer Ac.

Synthesis of the Horoscope. Ernest Grant & Catherine Grant. LC 88-70466. (Grant Textbook Ser.: Vol. 3). 144p. 1988. 18.50 (*0-86690-343-7*, G2811-014) Am Fed Astrologers.

Synthesis of Traditional & Modern in the Evolution of Third World Societies. Nodari A. Simonia. LC 91-823. (Contributions in Political Science Ser.: No. 289). 192p. 1992. text ed. 49.95 (*0-313-28144-0*, SNZ, Greenwood Pr) Greenwood.

Synthesis of Yoga. Sri Aurobindo. LC 91-76706. 889p. 1992. 34.95 (*0-941524-66-3*); pap. 29.95 (*0-941524-65-5*) Lotus Light.

Synthesis of Yoga. Sri Aurobindo. 899p. 1988. 19.00 (*81-7058-011-0*, Pub. by SAA II); pap. 16.00 (*81-7058-257-1*, Pub. by SAA II) Aurobindo Assn.

Synthesis of Yoga. Sri Aurobindo. (Life Companion Library). 1984p. 15.95 (*0-89744-017-X*) Auromere.

Synthesis of Yoga. 6th ed. Sri Aurobindo. 1979p. 18.50 (*0-89744-931-2*) Auromere.

***Synthesis Plus.** Fowler. 1993. student ed., pap. text ed. write for info. (*0-17-556638-0*) Addison-Wesley.

***Synthesis, Processing & Modeling of Advanced Materials: 2nd ASM Paris Conference.** F. H. Froes & T. Khan. 372p. 1993. 70.00 (*0-614-24010-7*, 9205) ASM.

Synthesis, Reactions & Selected Physico-Chemical Properties of 1,3- & 1,2- Tetrachalcogenafulvalenes, Vol. 7. G. Schukat et al. 86p. 1987. pap. text ed. 88.00 (*3-7186-0398-5*) Gordon & Breach.

Synthesis, Storage & Secretion of Adrenal Catecholamines: Proceedings of a Satellite Symposium to the 8th International Congress of Pharmacology, 19-24 July 1981, Tokyo, Japan. Ed. by F. Izumi et al. (Illus.). 302p. 1982. 81.00 (*0-08-028012-9*, Pergamon Pr) Elsevier.

Synthesis Structure & Properties of the First Examples of Germacyclopropenes (Germirenes) & 1,2-Digermacyclobutenes. O. M. Nefedov et al. (SSR Chemistry Reviews Ser.). 64p. 1988. 39.00 (*0-318-39941-5*) Gordon & Breach.

Synthesis Using Vilsmeier Reagents. Ed. by Charles M. Marson & Paul R. Giles. 256p. 1994. 96.95 (*0-8493-7869-9*, 7869) CRC Pr.

Synthesis with Style. Steve DeFuria & Joe Scacciaferro. (Ferro Technologies Ser.). (Illus.). 120p. (Orig.). 1989. pap. 19.95 (*0-88188-868-0*, HL 00239057) H Leonard.

Synthesis/Characterization & Novel Applications of Molecular Sieve Materials Vol. 233: Materials Research Society Symposium Proceedings. Ed. by V. A. Maroni et al. 303p. 1991. text ed. 68.00 (*1-55899-127-1*) Materials Res.

Synthesis/Processing of Lightweight Metallic Materials. Ed. by F. H. Froes et al. (Illus.). 382p. 1996. 76.00 (*0-87339-316-3*, 3163) Minerals Metals.

Synthesizer. John Bates. (Topics in Music Ser.). (Illus.). 48p. 1988. pap. 11.95 (*0-19-321337-0*) OUP.

Synthesizer Basics. rev. ed. Ed. by Keyboard Magazine Editors. (Keyboard Synthesizer Library). (Illus.). 136p. 1988. pap. 14.95 (*0-88188-714-5*, HL00183705) H Leonard.

Synthesizer Generator. T. W. Reps & T. Teitelbaum. (Texts & Monographs in Computer Science). (Illus.). xiii, 310p. 1988. 70.95 (*0-387-96857-1*) Spr-Verlag.

Synthesizer Generator: The Synthesizer Reference Manual, 2 vols., Set. T. W. Reps & T. Teitelbaum. (Texts & Monographs in Computer Science). (Illus.). 1989. 55.00 (*0-387-97100-9*) Spr-Verlag.

Synthesizer Generator Reference Manual. 3rd ed. T. W. Reps & T. Teitelbaum. (Texts & Monographs in Computer Science). (Illus.). viii, 165p. 1990. 36.95 (*0-387-96910-1*) Spr-Verlag.

Synthesizer Performance & Real-Time Techniques. Jeff Pressing. LC 91-39700. (Computer Music & Digital Audio Ser.: Vol. 8). (Illus.). 462p. (C). 1992. 49.95 (*0-89579-257-5*) A-R Eds.

Synthesizer Programming. Ed. by Dominic Milano. (Keyboard Magazine Synthesizer Library). (Illus.). 120p. (Orig.). 1987. pap. 14.95 (*0-88188-550-9*, HL00183703) H Leonard.

Synthesizers & Computers. rev. ed. Ed. by Keyboard Magazine Editors. 136p. 1987. pap. 14.95 (*0-88188-716-1*, HL 00183707) H Leonard.

Synthesizers in the Elementary Music Classroom: An Integrated Approach. Jackie Wiggins. (Illus.). 64p. (Orig.). (C). 1991. teacher ed. 11.00 (*1-56545-005-1*, 1047) Music Ed Natl.

Synthesizing Alum. Marcia L. Gillette & H. Anthony Neidig. (Modular Laboratory Program in Chemistry Ser.). 12p. (C). 1995. pap. text ed. 1.35 (*0-87540-451-0*, SYNT 451-0) Chem Educ Res.

Synthesizing Alum & Observing Some Chemistry of Aluminum. Marcia L. Gillette & H. Anthony Neidig. (Modular Laboratory Program in Chemistry Ser.). 12p. (C). 1995. pap. text ed. 1.35 (*0-87540-452-9*, SYNT 452-9) Chem Educ Res.

Synthesizing & Analyzing a Coordination Compound of Nickel (II) Ion, Ammonia, & Chloride Ion. George S. Patterson. Ed. by H. Anthony Neidig. (Modular Laboratory Program in Chemistry Ser.). 16p. (C). 1994. pap. text ed. 1.35 (*0-87540-433-2*, SYNT 433-2) Chem Educ Res.

Synthesizing Aspirin. Robert L. Glogovsky. Ed. by H. Anthony Neidig. (Modular Laboratory Program in Chemistry Ser.). 8p. (C). 1994. pap. text ed. 1.35 (*0-87540-439-1*, SYNT 439-1) Chem Educ Res.

Synthesizing Construction & Marketing in Economic Development. Low S. Pheng. 272p. 1995. text ed. 63.95 (*1-85972-219-9*, Pub. by Avebury Pub UK) Ashgate Pub Co.

***Synthesizing Nature-Nurture: Prenatal Roots of Instinctive Behavior.** Gilbert Gottlieb. LC 96-50907. (John M. MacEachran Memorial Lectures). 200p. 1997. write for info. (*0-8058-2548-7*); pap. write for info. (*0-8058-2870-2*) L Erlbaum Assocs.

Synthesizing Synchronous Systems by Static Scheduling in Space-Time. B. Lisper. (Lecture Notes in Computer Science Ser.: Vol. 362). vi, 263p. 1989. 37.00 (*0-387-51156-3*) Spr-Verlag.

Synthesthesia. limited ed. Terence McKenna. (Illus.). 40p. 1992. 1,500.00 (*1-887123-04-0*) Granary Bks.

Synthetic Actors in Computer-Generated 3D Films. N. Magnenat-Thalmann & Daniel Thalmann. Ed. by Toshiyasu L. Kunii. (Computer Science Workbench Ser.). (Illus.). 144p. 1990. 82.74 (*0-387-52214-X*) Spr-Verlag.

Synthetic Adhesives & Sealants. Ed. by W. C. Wake. LC 86-19037. (Critical Reports on Applied Chemistry). 139p. 1987. text ed. 249.00 (*0-471-91287-5*) Wiley.

Synthetic Adjuvants. Arlette Adam. LC 85-6331. (Modern Concepts in Immunology Ser.). 256p. 1985. text ed. 75.00 (*0-471-86450-1*) Krieger.

Synthetic Analgesics, Pt. 2A: Morphinans. J. Hellerbach & O. Schnider. LC 59-13814. (International Series Mono in Organic Chemistry: Vol. 8). 1966. 95.00 (*0-08-010895-4*, Pub. by Pergamon Repr UK) Franklin.

Synthetic & Organic Food Additives Markets. 189p. 1992. 1,950.00 (*0-945235-64-X*) Lead Edge Reports.

Synthetic & Other Non-Metallic Fiber Reinforcement of Concrete. 84p. 1994. pap. 39.25 (*0-614-02508-7*, C28BOW6) ACI.

Synthetic Antidiarrheal Drugs: Synthesis - Preclinical & Clinical Pharmacology. Ed. by William Van Bever & Harbans Lal. LC 76-8605. (Modern Pharmacology-Toxicology Ser.: No. 7). (Illus.). 302p. reprint ed. pap. 86.10 (*0-7837-0982-X*, 2041289) Bks Demand.

Synthetic Aperture Radar. J. P. Fitch. (Illus.). 170p. 1987. 54.00 (*0-387-96665-X*) Spr-Verlag.

Synthetic Aperture Radar. John J. Kovaly. LC 76-42314. (Artech Radar Library). (Illus.). 357p. reprint ed. pap. 101.80 (*0-685-20802-8*, 2030128) Bks Demand.

Synthetic Aperture Radar: Systems & Signal Processing. John C. Curlander & Robert N. McDonough. LC 90-29175. (Remote Sensing & Image Processing Ser.). 672p. 1991. text ed. 135.00 (*0-471-85770-X*) Wiley.

Synthetic-Aperture Radar & Electronic Warfare. Walter W. Goj. LC 92-21739. (Radar Library). 135p. (C). 1992. text ed. 49.00 (*0-89006-566-7*) Artech Hse.

Synthetic Application of 1,3-Dithiolium & 1,3-Oxathiolium Cations. K. Hirai et al. 38p. 1983. pap. text ed. 101.00 (*3-7186-0157-5*) Gordon & Breach.

Synthetic Binders in Paper Coatings: A Project of the Coating Binders Committee. Technical Association of the Pulp & Paper Industry Staff. Ed. by Alvin R. Sinclair. LC 75-7557. (TAPPI Monographs: No. 37). 151p. reprint ed. pap. 43.10 (*0-317-28872-5*, 2020305) Bks Demand.

***Synthetic Biodegradable Polymer Scaffolds.** Ed. by A. Atala et al. LC 96-45700. (Tissue Engineering Ser.). 348p. 1997. 99.00 (*0-8176-3919-5*) Birkhauser.

Synthetic Chemistry: Nitroxides. Volodarsky. 240p. 1993. 172.95 (*0-8493-4590-1*, QP305) CRC Pr.

Synthetic Diamond: Emerging CVD Science & Technology. Ed. by Karl E. Spear & John P. Dismukes. LC 93-7128. (Electrochemical Society Ser.). 663p. 1994. text ed. 99.95 (*0-471-53589-3*) Wiley.

Synthetic Dyes for Natural Fibers. rev. ed. Linda Knutson. LC 86-80912. (Illus.). 168p. 1986. reprint ed. pap. 12.00 (*0-934026-23-8*) Interweave.

Synthetic Economics. Henry L. Moore. LC 67-18571. (Reprints of Economic Classics Ser.). vii, 186p. 1967. reprint ed. 35.00 (*0-678-00233-9*) Kelley.

Synthetic Fabric Coverings. Don Stits. LC 92-46751. (Illus.). 198p. 1990. pap. text ed. 7.95 (*0-89100-307-X*, EA-307) IAP.

Synthetic Fibers for the Wet System & Thermal Bonding Applications Seminar, 1986: Boston Park Plaza, Boston, MA, October 9-10. Technical Association of the Pulp & Paper Industry Staff. (TAPPI Notes Ser.). (Illus.). 77p. pap. 25.00 (*0-317-58155-4*, 2029693) Bks Demand.

Synthetic Fibre Materials. Ed. by H. Brody. (Polymer Science & Technology Ser.). 384p. 1994. pap. 162.75 (*0-582-06267-5*) Longman.

S

An Asterisk (*) at the beginning of an entry indicates that the title is appearing in BIP for the first time.

Synthetic Filament Yarn: Texturing Technology. Ali Demir & Hassan M. Behery. LC 95-23400. 1996. text ed. 74.00 (*0-13-440025-9*) P-H.

Synthetic Fluorine Chemistry. George A. Olah et al. LC 91-25155. 416p. 1992. text ed. 127.00 (*0-471-54370-5*) Wiley.

Synthetic Fuel Technology Development in the United States: A Retrospective Assessment. Michael Crow et al. LC 88-12596. 187p. 1988. text ed. 55.00 (*0-275-93083-1*, C3083, Praeger Pubs) Greenwood.

Synthetic Fuels. Giogio Beghi. 1985. lib. bdg. 172.50 (*90-277-2016-9*) Kluwer Ac.

Synthetic Fuels: A Resource Guide. 1991. lib. bdg. 75.00 (*0-8490-4805-2*) Gordon Pr.

Synthetic Fuels from Coal: Overview & Assessment. Larry L. Anderson & David A. Tillman. LC 79-17786. (Wiley-Interscience Publications). 172p. reprint ed. pap. 49.10 (*0-317-26175-4*, 2025184) Bks Demand.

Synthetic Fuels from Coal: Status of the Technology. Ed. by P. F. Paul et al. (C). 1988. pap. text ed. 178.50 (*1-85333-103-1*, Pub. by Graham & Trotman UK) Kluwer Ac.

Synthetic Fuels from Oil Shale & Tar Sands (Symposium III) 707p. 1983. 75.00 (*0-910091-48-X*) Inst Gas Tech.

Synthetic Fuels from Oil Shale Symposium I, December 1979. (Synthetic Fuels Ser.). 684p. 1980. 60.00 (*0-910091-44-7*) Inst Gas Tech.

Synthetic Fuels from Oil Shale Symposium II. 624p. 1981. 60.00 (*0-910091-45-5*) Inst Gas Tech.

Synthetic Fuels Processing: Comparative Economics. Ed. by Arnold H. Pelofsky. LC 76-41472. (Illus.). 487p. reprint ed. pap. 138.80 (*0-7837-3351-8*, 2043309) Bks Demand.

Synthetic Fuels Research: A Bibliography. 4th ed. Ruby L. Mathison. 218p. 1980. pap. 15.00 (*0-318-12717-2*, H01980) Am Gas Assn.

Synthetic Functional Fluids & Lubricants, No. YC-179. John Bruce. (Illus.). 152p. 1994. 2,650.00 (*1-56965-006-3*) BCC.

***Synthetic, Imitation & Treated Gemstones.** M. O'Donoghue. LC 97-14620. 1997. pap. 39.00 (*0-7506-3173-2*) Buttrwrth-Heinemann.

Synthetic Lubricants & High Performance Functional Fluids. Ed. by Ronald L. Shubkin. LC 92-25564. (Chemical Industries Ser.: Vol. 48). 616p. 1992. 199.00 (*0-8247-8715-3*) Dekker.

Synthetic Materials for Non-Linear Optics & Electronics: Proceedings of Symposium E, 1992 E-MRS Spring Conference, Strasbourg, France, June 1992. Ed. by Yosh Maruyama et al. (European Materials Research Society Symposia Proceedings Ser.: Vol. 35). 480p. 1993. 250.00 (*0-444-89909-X*, North Holland) Elsevier.

Synthetic Membranes, 2 vols., Set. Albin F. Turbak. Incl. Desalination. LC 81-1259. 1981. 54.95 (*0-8412-0622-8*); Hyper & Ultrafiltration Uses. LC 81-1259. 1981. 54.95 (*0-8412-0623-6*); LC 81-1259. (ACS Symposium Ser.: Nos. 153 & 154). 1981. 94.95 (*0-8412-0625-2*) Am Chemical.

Synthetic Membranes, Vol. 5. Ed. by Maynard B. Chenoweth. (MMI Press Symposium Ser.: Vol. 5). 288p. 1986. text ed. 220.00 (*3-7186-0327-6*) Gordon & Breach.

***Synthetic Membranes: Based on the 20th Anniversary Symposium Honoring Drs. Loeb & Sourirajan, Vol. 1.** Ed. by Albin F. Turbak. LC 81-1259. (ACS Symposium Ser.: Vols. 153-154). 479p. 1981. reprint ed. pap. 136.60 (*0-608-03043-0*, 2063496) Bks Demand.

***Synthetic Membranes: Based on the 20th Anniversary Symposium Honoring Drs. Loeb & Sourirajan, Vol. 2.** Ed. by Albin F. Turbak. LC 81-1259. (ACS Symposium Ser.: Vols. 153-154). 485p. 1981. reprint ed. pap. 138.30 (*0-608-03044-9*, 2063496) Bks Demand.

Synthetic Membranes & Membrane Separation Processes. Matsurra. 480p. 1993. 103.95 (*0-8493-4202-3*) CRC Pr.

Synthetic Methods for Carbohydrates. Ed. by Hassan S. El Khadem. LC 76-58888. (ACS Symposium Ser.: No. 39). 1977. 29.95 (*0-8412-0365-2*) Am Chemical.

***Synthetic Methods for Carbohydrates.** Hassan S. El Khadem. LC 76-58888. (ACS Symposium Ser.: Vol. 39). 295p. 1976. reprint ed. pap. 84.10 (*0-608-03559-9*, 2064278) Bks Demand.

Synthetic Methods of Organometallic & Inorganic Chemistry Vol. 1: Literature, Laboratory Techniques, & COmmon Starting Materials. Ed. by Wolfgang A. Herrmann. LC 95-49908. 182p. 1995. 87.00 (*0-86577-627-X*) Thieme Med Pubs.

***Synthetic Methods of Organometallic & Inorganic Chemistry Vol. 2: Groups 1, 2, 13, & 14.** Ed. by W. A. Herrmann. 310p. 1996. 135.00 (*0-86577-653-9*) Thieme Med Pubs.

***Synthetic Methods of Organometallic & Inorganic Chemistry Vol. 3: Phosphorus, Arsenic, Antimony, & Bismuth.** Ed. by W. A. Herrmann. 228p. 1996. 135.00 (*0-86577-654-7*) Thieme Med Pubs.

***Synthetic Methods of Organometallic & Inorganic Chemistry Vol. 4: Sulfur, Selenium, & Tellurium.** Ed. by W. A. Herrmann. 200p. 1997. 87.00 (*0-86577-661-X*) Thieme Med Pubs.

***Synthetic Methods of Organometallic & Inorganic Chemistry Vol. 5: Copper, Silver, Gold, Zinc, Cadmium, & Mercury.** Ed. by W. A. Herrmann. 200p. 1997. 87.00 (*0-86577-662-8*) Thieme Med Pubs.

***Synthetic Methods of Organometallic & Inorganic Chemistry Vol. 6: Lanthanides & Actinides.** Ed. by W. A. Herrmann. 200p. 1997. 87.00 (*0-86577-663-6*) Thieme Med Pubs.

***Synthetic Methods of Organometallic & Inorganic Chemistry Vol. 7: Transition Metals, Pt. 1.** W. A. Herrmann. 300p. 1997. 129.00 (*0-86577-664-4*) Thieme Med Pubs.

***Synthetic Methods of Organometallic & Inorganic Chemistry Vol. 7: Transition Metals, Pt. 2.** W. A. Herrmann. 300p. 1997. 129.00 (*0-86577-665-2*) Thieme Med Pubs.

Synthetic Microstructures in Biological Research. Ed. by Joel M. Schnur et al. LC 92-48767. (Illus.). 246p. (C). 1993. 75.00 (*0-306-44347-3*, Plenum Pr) Plenum.

Synthetic Nuvism. Contrib. by Barry Blinderman. (Illus.). 16p. 1995. 5.00 (*0-945558-14-7*) ISU Univ Galls.

Synthetic Oligosaccharides: Indispensable Probes for the Life Sciences. Ed. by Pavol Kovac. LC 94-16835. (ASC Symposium Ser.: Vol. 560). 1994. 79.95 (*0-8412-2930-9*) Am Chemical.

Synthetic Organic Chemicals, U. S. Production & Sales (1993) (Illus.). 220p. (Orig.). (C). 1995. pap. text ed. 5.00 (*0-7881-1644-4*) DIANE Pub.

Synthetic Organic Chemistry. (Topics in Current Chemistry Ser.: Vol. 130). (Illus.). 250p. 1985. 111.95 (*0-387-15810-3*) Spr-Verlag.

Synthetic Organic Electrochemistry. 2nd ed. Albert S. Fry. LC 88-38317. 339p. 1989. text ed. 99.95 (*0-471-63396-8*) Wiley.

Synthetic Organic Photochemistry. Ed. by William M. Horspool. LC 84-10480. 552p. 1984. 130.00 (*0-306-41449-X*, Plenum Pr) Plenum.

Synthetic Peptides in the Search for T & B Cell Epitopes. Rajnavolgyi. (Molecular Biology Intelligence Unit Ser.). 200p. 1994. 89.95 (*1-57059-160-1*) R G Landes.

Synthetic Polymeric Membranes: A Structural Perspective. 2nd ed. Robert E. Kesting. LC 85-6162. 348p. 1985. text ed. 140.00 (*0-471-80717-6*) Wiley.

Synthetic Polymeric Membranes: Proceedings of the 29th Microsymposium on Macromolecules, Prague, Czechoslovakia, July 7-10, 1986. Ed. by J. Kahovec & Blahoslav Sedlacek. xiv, 717p. (Orig.). 1987. lib. bdg. 276.95 (*3-11-010823-2*) De Gruyter.

Synthetic Polymers. D. Feldman & Barbalata. (Illus.). 320p. 1996. 89.95 (*0-412-71040-4*) Chapman & Hall.

Synthetic Polymers-Building the Giant Molecule. Fred W. Billmeyer. LC 77-171279. (Science Study Ser.). 204p. reprint ed. pap. 58.20 (*0-685-15256-1*, 2026508) Bks Demand.

Synthetic Polypeptides As Antigens. Ed. by M. H. Van Regenmortel et al. (Laboratory Techniques in Biochemistry & Molecular Biology Ser.: No. 19). 228p. 1988. pap. 40.00 (*0-444-80974-0*) Elsevier.

Synthetic Polypeptides As Antigens. Ed. by Mare H. Van Regenmortel et al. (Laboratory Techniques in Biochemistry & Molecular Biology Ser.: No. 19). 350p. 1989. 148.25 (*0-444-80975-9*) Elsevier.

Synthetic Process & Control of Functionality Materials. Ed. by T. Tsuruta et al. LC 93-167312. (New Functionality Materials Ser.: Vol. C). 792p. 1993. 238.50 (*0-444-81616-X*, North Holland) Elsevier.

Synthetic Programming Made Easy. Keith Jarett. (Illus.). 192p. (Orig.). (C). 1982. pap. text ed. 9.95 (*0-9612174-0-5*, 146) EduCALC Pubns.

Synthetic Programming on the HP-41C. William C. Wickes. (Illus.). 96p. (Orig.). (C). 1980. pap. 10.95 (*0-9625258-0-4*) Larken Pubns.

***Synthetic Pyrethroids.** Ed. by Michael Elliott. LC 77-1810. (ACS Symposium Ser.: Vol. 42). 241p. 1977. reprint ed. pap. 68.70 (*0-608-03833-4*, 2064280) Bks Demand.

Synthetic Repertory, 3 vols., Set. 4th ed. (ENG, FRE & GER.). 1992. pap. text ed. 190.00 (*3-7760-1342-7*, Pub. by K F Haug Pubs) Medicina Bio.

Synthetic Rubber: A Project That Had to Succeed. Vernon Herbert & Attilio Bisio. LC 85-948. (Contributions in Economics & Economic History Ser.: No. 63). (Illus.). xi, 243p. 1985. text ed. 59.95 (*0-313-24634-3*, BSR/, Greenwood Pr) Greenwood.

Synthetic Rubber: The Story of an Industry. Attilio Bisio. (Illus.). 58p. 40.00 (*0-9638167-1-3*) IIOSRP.

Synthetic Rubber in the Soviet Union. Vayentin Sazykin & Adrian Troitski. 68p. 1992. 90.00 (*0-9638167-0-5*) IIOSRP.

Synthetic Rubbers: Processes & Economic Data. Ed. by Jean-Pierre Arlie. 128p. (C). 1992. pap. 200.00 (*2-7108-0619-3*, Pub. by Edits Technip FR) St Mut.

Synthetic Securities. S. Partridge-Hicks & Piers Hartland-Swann. 200p. 1994. pap. 135.00 (*1-870031-86-5*, Pub. by Euromoney UK) Am Educ Systs.

Synthetic Spaces: Holography at MIT. Dana Friis-Hansen & Betsy Connors. (Illus.). 10p. 1990. pap. 2.00 (*0-938437-33-X*) MIT List Visual Arts.

Synthetic Substrates & Synthetic Inhibitors: The Use of Chromogenic Substrates in Studies of the Haemostatic Mechanism. Ed. by M. Blomback & P. Brakman. (Haemostasis Journal: Vol. 7, Nos. 2-3). (Illus.). 1978. pap. 30.50 (*3-8055-2907-4*) S Karger.

Synthetic Substrates in Clinical Blood Coagulation Assays. Ed. by H. R. Lijnen et al. (Developments in Hematology & Immunology Ser.: No. 1). 142p. 1980. lib. bdg. 61.00 (*90-247-2409-0*) Kluwer Ac.

Synthetic Uses of Anodic Substitution Reactions. Lennart Eberson & Klas Nyberg. 1977. pap. 14.00 (*0-08-021583-1*, Pergamon Pr) Elsevier.

Synthetic Utility of Sulfur-Containing Dianions, Vol. 1. K. Tanaka & A. Kaji. (Sulfur Reports: Vol. 2). 34p. 1980. pap. text ed. 56.00 (*3-7186-0039-0*) Gordon & Breach.

Synthetic Vaccines, 2 vols., Set. R. Arnon. 1987. reprint ed. 203.00 (*0-8493-4658-4*, CRC Reprint) Franklin.

Synthetic Vaccines, Vol. I. Arnon. 168p. 1987. 101.00 (*0-8493-4659-2*) CRC Pr.

Synthetic Vaccines, Vol. II. Arnon. 176p. 1987. 103.00 (*0-8493-4660-6*) CRC Pr.

Synthetic Worlds. T. L. Kunit et al. 250p. 1994. text ed. 55.00 (*0-471-95321-0*) Wiley.

Synthetic Zeolites, 2 vols., Vol. 2. S. P. Zhdanov et al. Tr. by N. F. Standen. 768p. 1990. Set. text ed. 581.00 (*2-88124-675-3*) Gordon & Breach.

Synthetic Zeolites Vol. 1: Crystallization, Structural & Chemical Modification of Crystals, Vol. 1. S. P. Zhdanov et al. Tr. by N. F. Standen. xiv, 296p. 1990. text ed. 310.00 (*2-88124-720-2*) Gordon & Breach.

Synthetic Zeolites Vol. 2: Absorption & Molecular Properties of Zeolites, Vol. 2. S. P. Zhdanov et al. Tr. by N. F. Standen. xiv, 428p. 1990. text ed. 414.00 (*2-88124-721-0*) Gordon & Breach.

Synthon Model of Organic Chemistry & Synthesis Design. J. Kcoa et al. (Lecture Notes in Chemistry Ser.: Vol. 51). vii, 207p. 1989. 38.95 (*0-387-50932-1*) Spr-Verlag.

Syntonics: A Dynamic New Program for Total Health & Happiness. Robert Kronemeyer. LC 93-40328. 1994. text ed. 27.95 (*0-13-879552-5*) P-H Gen Ref & Trav.

Syphilis: Werewolf of Medicine. Herbert M. Shelton. 150p. reprint ed. spiral bd. 13.50 (*0-7873-1004-2*) Hlth Research.

Syphilis & Other Venereal Diseases. William J. Brown et al. LC 77-88803. 263p. reprint ed. pap. 75.00 (*0-317-55361-5*, 2029170) Bks Demand.

Syphilis in Shakespeare's England. Johannes Fabricius. 380p. 1994. pap. 24.95 (*1-85302-270-5*) Taylor & Francis.

Syphilis: or A Poetical History of the French Disease. Fracastorius. 1972. 69.95 (*0-8490-1170-1*) Gordon Pr.

Syphilis, Puritanism & Witchcraft: A Historical Explanation in Light of Medicine & Psychoanalysis. Stanislav Andreski. 224p. 1989. text ed. 45.00 (*0-312-02702-8*) St Martin.

Syphilis Serology: Principles & Practice. G. D. Wasley & Helen H. Wong. (Illus.). 168p. 1989. 39.95 (*0-19-261530-0*) OUP.

Syphilis Today & among the Ancients, 3 vols. in 2, Set. Frederic Buret. LC 72-9627. reprint ed. 81.50 (*0-404-57422-X*) AMS Pr.

Syr Gawayne. Frederic Madden. 1972. 59.95 (*0-8490-1171-X*) Gordon Pr.

Syr Gawayne: A Collection of Ancient Romance Poems by Scottish & English Authors. Ed. by Frederic Madden. LC 71-144420. (Bannatyne Club. Edinburgh. Publications: No. 61). reprint ed. 49.50 (*0-404-52772-8*) AMS Pr.

Syracuse: The Heart of New York. Alexis O'Neill. 1988. 34.95 (*0-89781-275-1*, 5219) Am Historical Pr.

***Syracuse & Its Environs: A History, 3 vols. in 2.** Franklin H. Chase. (Illus.). 3385p. 1997. reprint ed. lib. bdg. 140.00 (*0-8328-6256-8*) Higginson Bk Co.

Syracuse & the Underground Railroad. Evamarie Hardin. 8p. 1989. pap. 2.95 (*1-883582-06-7*) Erie Canal Mus.

Syracuse Black Community, 1970: A Comparative Study. Seymour Sacks & Ralph Andrew. LC 73-21186. (Occasional Papers: No. 41). 77p. 1974. pap. 3.00 (*0-87060-065-6*, OCP 41) Syracuse U Cont Ed.

***Syracuse China.** Cleota Reed & Stan Skoczen. LC 97-14548. 272p. 1997. 60.00 (*0-8156-0474-2*) Syracuse U Pr.

***Syracuse China & the Railroads.** Richard W. Luckin. (Illus.). 1998. 50.00 (*0-614-29636-6*) RK Pub.

Syracuse Community-Referenced Curriculum Guide for Students with Moderate & Severe Disabilities. Luanna H. Meyer. LC 89-9876. 416p. (Orig.). (C). 1989. reprint ed. spiral bd. 53.95 (*1-55766-027-1*, 0271) P H Brookes.

Syracuse Dine-a-Mate. 280p. 1994. pap. 20.00 (*1-57393-009-1*) Dine-A-Mate.

***Syracuse Dine-a-Mate Book.** 256p. 1996. pap. text ed. 30.00 (*1-57393-051-2*) Dine-A-Mate.

Syracuse Journal of International Law & Commerce: 1972-1996, 22 vols., Set. Bound set. 777.50 (*0-8377-9156-1*) Rothman.

Syracuse Landmarks: An AIA Guide to Downtown & Historic Neighborhoods. Evamaria Hardin. LC 92-35000. (Illus.). 400p. (C). 1993. pap. text ed. 16.95 (*0-8156-0273-1*) Syracuse U Pr.

Syracuse Landmarks: The AIA Guide to Downtown & Historic Neighborhoods. Evamaria Hardin. LC 92-35000. 1993. 49.95 (*0-8156-2599-5*) Syracuse U Pr.

***Syracuse, NY.** Onodaga Historical Association Staff. (Images of America Ser.). 1997. pap. 16.99 (*0-7524-0551-9*, Arcdia) Chalford.

Syracuse, NY 1940's. Historical Briefs, Inc. Staff. Ed. by Thomas Antonucci & Michael Antonucci. 176p. 1991. pap. 13.95 (*0-89677-022-2*) Hist Briefs.

Syracuse, the Fairest Greek City: Ancient Art from the Museo Archeologico Regionale Paolo Orsi. Bonna D. Wescoat. (Illus.). 123p. 1994. pap. text ed. 24.95 (*88-7813-252-7*) U of Pa Pr.

Syracuse Then & Now: The Urban Landscape. Erie Canal Museum Staff. 52p. 1990. pap. 4.95 (*1-883582-04-0*) Erie Canal Mus.

Syracuse University: The Tolley Years, 1942-1969. John R. Greene & Karrie A. Baron. (Illus.). 400p. (C). 1996. text ed. 29.95 (*0-8156-2701-7*, GRSU) Syracuse U Pr.

Syracuse University History. William F. Galpin. Incl. Vol. 1. Pioneer Days. LC 52-2118. (Illus.). 270p. 1952. 29.95 (*0-318-55908-0*); LC 52-2118. 1952. 29.95 (*0-8156-2010-1*) Syracuse U Pr.

Syracuse University History: The Critical Years, Vol.3. Richard Wilson et al. LC 52-2118. (Illus.). 464p. 1984. text ed. 29.95 (*0-8156-8108-9*) Syracuse U Pr.

Syreta. Dwight A. Osborne. pap. 5.95 (*0-9632817-5-5*) Osborne Bks.

Syria. Margaret Beaton. LC 88-18697. (Enchantment of the World Ser.). (Illus.). 128p. (J). (gr. 5-9). 1988. lib. bdg. 30.00 (*0-516-02708-5*) Childrens.

Syria. Garland G. Parker. (Pelham Guides Ser.). 45p. (C). 1996. write for info. (*0-929851-99-4*) Am Assn Coll Registrars.

Syria. Ian J. Seccombe. (World Bibliographical Ser.: No. 73). 341p. 1987. lib. bdg. 65.00 (*1-85109-018-5*) ABC-CLIO.

***Syria: A Historical & Architectural Guide.** Warwick Ball. (Illus.). 224p. 1996. pap. 24.95 (*0-905906-96-9*, Pub. by Scorpion Pub UK) Interlink Pub.

Syria: Development & Monetary Policy. Edmund Y. Asfour. LC 59-13357. (Middle Eastern Monographs: No. 1). (Illus.). 164p. 1959. pap. 5.95 (*0-674-86190-6*) HUP.

Syria: Fragile Mosaic of Power. Martha N. Kessler. (Illus.). 143p. (Orig.). (C). 1995. reprint ed. pap. text ed. 35.00 (*0-7881-2346-7*) DIANE Pub.

Syria: Society, Culture, & Polity. Ed. by Richard T. Antoun & Donald Quataert. LC 90-10251. (SUNY Series in Middle Eastern Studies). 144p. (C). 1991. text ed. 65.50 (*0-7914-0713-6*); pap. text ed. 21.95 (*0-7914-0714-4*) State U NY Pr.

Syria: The Desert & the Sown. Gertrude L. Bell. LC 73-6270. (Middle East Ser.). 1979. reprint ed. 35.95 (*0-405-05325-8*) Ayer.

Syria see Cultures of the World - Group 10

Syria & Egypt under the Last Five Sultans of Turkey, 2 Vols. Ed. by Edward B. Barker. LC 73-6269. (Middle East Ser.). 1979. reprint ed. 56.95 (*0-405-05324-X*) Ayer.

***Syria & Iran: Middle Powers in a Penetrated Regional System.** Anoushiravan Ehteshami & Raymond A. Hinnebusch. 248p. (C). 1997. text ed. 59.95 (*0-415-15675-0*) Routledge.

Syria & Iran: Rivalry & Co-operation. Hussein Agha & Ahmad S. Khalidi. (Chatham House Papers). 128p. 1995. 50.00 (*1-85567-234-0*, Pub. by Pntr Pubs UK) Bks Intl VA.

Syria & Iran: Rivalry & Co-Operation. Hussein Agha & Ahmad S. Khalidi. (Chatham House Papers). 128p. 1995. pap. 15.95 (*1-85567-235-9*, Pub. by Pntr Pubs UK) Bks Intl VA.

Syria & Iran: Rivalry & Cooperation. Hussein J. Agha & Ahmad S. Khalidi. LC 95-22262. 1995. reprint ed. pap. write for info. (*0-87609-181-8*) Coun Foreign.

Syria & Israel. David W. Felder. (Illus.). 44p. 1996. pap. text ed. 8.95 (*0-910959-50-1*, B&G 10A) Wellington Pr.

Syria & Israel: From War to Peacemaking. Moshe Ma'oz. 320p. 1995. 55.00 (*0-19-828018-1*) OUP.

Syria & Lebanon. Michael Haag. (Cadogan Guides Ser.). (Illus.). 400p. (Orig.). 1995. pap. 18.95 (*1-86011-025-8*, Pub. by Cadogan Bks UK) Globe Pequot.

Syria & Lebanon. Albert H. Hourani. 1967. 20.00 (*0-86685-015-5*) Intl Bk Ctr.

Syria & Lebanon. Nicola A. Ziadeh. (Arab Background Ser.). 312p. 1968. 18.00 (*0-86685-034-1*, LDL0341, Pub. by Librairie du Liban FR) Intl Bk Ctr.

Syria & Lebanon: A Political Essay. Albert H. Hourani. 1977. lib. bdg. 59.95 (*0-8490-2714-4*) Gordon Pr.

Syria & Lebanon under French Mandate, 1968. Stephen H. Longrigg. (Arab Background Ser.). 1967. 18.00 (*0-86685-021-X*) Intl Bk Ctr.

Syria & the French Mandate: The Politics of Arab Nationalism, 1920-1945. Philip S. Khoury. (Middle Eastern History Ser.). 720p. 1986. text ed. 90.00 (*0-691-05486-X*); pap. text ed. 29.95 (*0-691-00843-4*) Princeton U Pr.

Syria & the Lebanese Crisis. Adeed I. Dawisha. LC 80-85. 200p. 1980. text ed. 39.95 (*0-312-78203-9*) St Martin.

Syria & the Middle East Peace Process. Alasdair Drysdale & Raymond A. Hinnebusch. LC 91-23949. 256p. 1991. reprint ed. pap. 73.00 (*0-608-02007-9*, 2062663) Bks Demand.

Syria Beyond the Peace Process. Daniel Pipes. (Policy Papers: Vol. 40). 1996. 16.95 (*0-944029-64-7*) Wash Inst NEP.

Syria in Pictures. Lerner Publications, Department of Geography Staff. (Visual Geography Ser.). (Illus.). 64p. (YA). (gr. 5 up). 1992. lib. bdg. 19.95 (*0-8225-1867-8*, Lerner Publctns) Lerner Group.

Syria the Desert & the Sown. G. L. Bell. 352p. 1984. 250.00 (*1-85077-062-X*, Pub. by Darf Pubs Ltd UK) St Mut.

Syria under Islam: Empire on Trial, 634-1097. Kamal S. Salibi. LC 77-24197. 1977. 35.00 (*0-88206-013-9*) Caravan Bks.

Syria under the Ba'th, 1963-1966: Army-Party Symbiosis. Itamar Rabinovitch. 276p. 1972. boxed 44.95 (*0-87855-163-8*) Transaction Pubs.

Syria Unmasked: The Suppression of Human Rights by the Asad Regime. Human Rights Watch - Middle East Staff. (Human Rights Watch Bks.). 224p. (C). 1991. text ed. 30.00 (*0-300-05115-8*) Yale U Pr.

Syria Unmasked: The Suppression of Human Rights by the Asad Regime. Human Rights Watch - Middle East Staff. (Human Rights Watch Bks.). 224p. (C). 1993. pap. 20.00 (*0-300-05786-5*) Yale U Pr.

Syria, 1945-1986: Politics & Society. Derek Hopwood. 176p. 1988. 55.00 (*0-04-445039-7*) Routledge Chapman & Hall.

Syria, 1945-1986: Politics & Society. Derek Hopwood. LC 87-32433. 176p. (C). 1988. pap. text ed. 27.95 (*0-04-445046-X*) Routledge Chapman & Hall.

Syria 3000 to 300 B. C. A Handbook of Political History. Horst Klengel. 263p. 1993. 150.00 (*0-685-67330-8*, Pub. by Akademie Verlag GW) Wiley.

Syriac Chronicle Known As That of Zachariah of Mitylene. Zacharias. LC 76-24991. (Byzantine Texts: No. 5). reprint ed. 57.50 (*0-404-60005-0*) AMS Pr.

Syriac Chronicle of Pseudo-Dionysius of Tel-Mahre: A Study in the History of Historiography. Witold Witakowski. (Studia Semitica Upsaliensia: Vol. 9). 182p. (Orig.). 1987. pap. text ed. 41.00 (*91-554-1967-4*, Pub. by Uppsala Univ Acta Univ Upsaliensis SW) Coronet Bks.

Syriac Language of Peshitta & Old Syriac Versions of Matthew: Syntactic Structure, Inner-Syriac Developments & Translation Technique, Vol. 22. Jan Joosten. LC 95-16571. (Studies in Semitic Languages & Linguistics). 223p. 1996. 127.00 (*90-04-10036-9*) E J Brill.

Syriac Perspectives on Late Antiquity. Sebastian Brock. (Collected Studies: No. CS199). 336p. (C). 1984. reprint ed. lib. bdg. 94.95 (*0-86078-147-X*, Pub. by Variorum UK) Ashgate Pub Co.

Syriac Text see Nestorian Collection of Christological Texts

Syriac Version of the Psalms of Solomon. Joseph L. Trafton. (Society of Biblical Literature Septuagint & Cognate Studies Ser.). 276p. (C). 1985. 34.95 (*0-89130-910-1*, 06-04-11); pap. 22.95 (*0-89130-911-X*, 06 04 11) Scholars Pr GA.

Syriac Version of the Wisdom of Ben Sira Compared to the Greek & Hebrew Materials. Milward D. Nelson. LC 87-28674. (Society of Biblical Literature Dissertation Ser.). 216p. 1989. 18.95 (*1-55540-193-7*, 06 21 07); pap. 12.95 (*1-55540-194-5*, 06 21 07) Scholars Pr GA.

Syrian Christians in Muslim Society: An Interpretation. Robert M Haddad. LC 81-6202. (Princeton Studies on the Near East). viii, 118p. 1981. reprint ed. text ed. 38. 50 (*0-313-23054-4*, HASYC, Greenwood Pr) Greenwood.

Syrian Desert. Christina P. Grant. LC 78-63341. (Crusades & Military Orders Ser.: Second Series). (Illus.). reprint ed. 41.00 (*0-404-17017-X*) AMS Pr.

Syrian Goddess (De Dea Syria) Attributed to Lucian. Harold W. Attridge & Robert A. Oden. LC 76-135. (Texts & Translations Ser.: No. 9). 69p. reprint ed. pap. 25.00 (*0-7837-5459-0*, 2045224) Bks Demand.

Syrian Hamster in Toxicology & Carcinogenesis: Proceedings - Symposium on the Syrian Hamster in Toxicology & Carcinogenesis Research, Boston, November 30-December 2, 1977. Ed. by F. Homburger. (Progress in Experimental Tumor Research Ser.: Vol. 24). (Illus.). 1979. 130.50 (*3-8055-2890-6*) S Karger.

Syrian Intervention in Lebanon. Naomi Weinberger. (Illus.). 352p. 1986. text ed. 55.00 (*0-19-504010-4*) OUP.

Syrian Ismailism: The Ever Living Line of Imamate A.D. 1100-1260. Nasseh A. Mirza. 220p. 1996. 70.00 (*0-7007-0506-6*, Pub. by Curzon Pr UK); pap. 25.00 (*0-7007-0507-4*, Pub. by Curzon Pr UK) Paul & Co Pubs.

Syrian Pageant: The History of Syria & Palestine, 1000 B.C. to A.D. 1945. Wilfrid T. Castle. 1977. lib. bdg. 59. 95 (*0-8490-2716-0*) Gordon Pr.

Syrian Social Nationalist Party: An Ideological Analysis. Labib Zuwiyya-Yamak. LC 66-24812. (Middle Eastern Monographs: No. 14). (Illus.). 183p. 1966. pap. 4.50 (*0-674-86236-8*) HUP.

Syrian Tetradrachmas of Caracalla & Macrinus. 1980. reprint ed. lib. bdg. 30.00 (*0-915262-57-6*) S J Durst.

***Syrians: A Travelogue 1992-1994.** Laurence Deonna. Tr. by Christopher Snow from FRE. Orig. Title: Syriens, Syriennes. (Illus.). 160p. 1997. 24.00 (*1-57889-041-1*); pap. 14.00 (*1-57889-040-3*) Passeggiata.

Syriens, Syriennes see Syrians: A Travelogue 1992-1994

Syringobulbia: A Contribution to the Pathophysiology of the Brainstem. N. Jonesco-Sisesti. Ed. & Tr. by R. T. Ross. LC 86-9489. 328p. 1986. text ed. 75.00 (*0-275-92123-9*, C2123, Praeger Pubs) Greenwood.

***Syringomyelia & the Chiari Malformations.** Ed. by John A. Anson et al. (Neurosurgical Topic Ser.: Vol. 26). (Illus.). 250p. 1997. 95.00 (*1-879284-42-1*) Am Assn Neuro.

Syringomyelia, Vol. 4: Current Concepts in Diagnosis & Treatment. Ulrich Batzdorf. (Illus.). 228p. 1991. 78.00 (*0-683-00475-1*) Williams & Wilkins.

Syrinx Or a Sevenfold History. W. Warner. Ed. by Wallace A. Bacon. LC 72-128939. (Northwestern University. Humanities Ser.: No. 26). reprint ed. 31.50 (*0-404-50726-3*) AMS Pr.

***Syrische Chronik des Josua Stylites.** Andreas Luther. (Untersuchungen Zur Antiken Literatur Und Geschichte Ser.: Vol. 49). (Illus.). viii, 307p. (GER.). (C). 1997. lib. bdg. 146.70 (*3-11-015470-6*) De Gruyter.

Syrische Grammatik. Arthur Ungnad. xi, 223p. (GER.). 1992. reprint ed. write for info. (*3-487-09635-8*) G Olms Pubs.

Syrische Kirchenbau. Hermann W. Beyer. (Studien zur Spaetantiken Kunstgeschichte: Vol. 1). (Illus.). viii, 183p. (C). 1978. reprint ed. 138.50 (*3-11-005705-0*) De Gruyter.

Syrohexaplaric Psalter. Robert J. Hiebert. (Society of Biblical Literature Septuagint & Cognate Studies Ser.). 370p. 1990. 29.95 (*1-55540-431-6*, 06 04 27); pap. 19.95 (*1-55540-432-4*, 06 04 27) Scholars Pr GA.

Systat for Desktop Analysis. Leland Wilkinson. 1993. pap. 39.95 (*0-442-01633-6*) Chapman & Hall.

***Systat for Students 6.0.** (Illus.). 116p. (C). 1996. pap. text ed. 61.00 (*0-13-659970-2*) P-H.

Systat Getting Started with Windows. Systat Inc. Staff. 1994. pap. text ed. 21.80 (*0-13-437237-9*) P-H.

Systat Graphics for Windows. Systat Inc. Staff. 1994. pap. text ed. 30.60 (*0-13-437062-7*) P-H.

***SyStat 6.0 for Windows: Command Reference.** SPSS Inc. Staff. (C). 1996. pap. text ed. 21.80 (*0-13-654310-3*) P-H.

***SyStat 6.0 for Windows: Data.** SPSS Inc. Staff. (C). 1996. pap. text ed. 24.00 (*0-13-654485-1*) P-H.

***SyStat 6.0 for Windows: Graphics.** SPSS Inc. Staff. (C). 1996. pap. text ed. 30.60 (*0-13-654393-6*) P-H.

***Systat 7.0: Command Reference.** (C). 1997. pap. text ed. 20.60 (*0-13-644618-3*) P-H.

***Systat 7.0 Graphics.** SPSS Inc., Staff. 1997. pap. text ed. 29.00 (*0-13-676909-8*) P-H.

***Systat 7.0 New Statistics.** 1997. pap. text ed. 30.60 (*0-13-644627-2*) P-H.

***Systat 7.0 Statistics.** 1997. pap. text ed. 29.00 (*0-13-679739-3*) P-H.

***System.** Peter Kuper. Ed. by Bob Kahan. (Illus.). 104p. 1997. pap. 12.95 (*1-56389-322-3*) DC Comics.

System: As Uncovered by the San Francisco Graft Prosecution. Franklin Hichborn. LC 69-14933. (Criminology, Law Enforcement, & Social Problems Ser.: No. 38). 1969. reprint ed. 24.00 (*0-87585-038-3*) Patterson Smith.

System: The American Way of Politics at the Breaking Point. Haynes Johnson & David S. Broder. 560p. 1996. 25.95 (*0-316-46969-6*) Little.

***System: The American Way of Politics at the Breaking Point.** Haynes Johnson & David S. Broder. 1997. pap. 15.95 (*0-316-11145-7*) Little.

System Administration Vol. 1: For Intel Processors (SVR4.2 MP) UNIX Staff. (Illus.). 464p. (C). 1994. pap. text ed. 65.00 (*0-13-158023-X*) P-H.

System Administration Vol. 2: For Intel Processors (SVR4.2 MP) Unix System Laboratories Staff. (Illus.). 736p. (C). 1994. pap. text ed. 65.00 (*0-13-158031-0*) P-H.

System Administration NetWare 3.12: For Novell Test No. 50-130; NetWare 3.1x Administration. 4th rev. ed. Muhammad Zafar. (CNE Training Manual Ser.). (Illus.). 278p. 1996. text ed. 75.00 (*1-57739-001-6*) PC Age.

System Administration NetWare 4.1: For Novell Test No. 50-152; NetWare v4.1 Administration. rev. ed. Muhammad Zafar. (CNE Training Manual Ser.). (Illus.). 326p. 1996. text ed. 100.00 (*1-57739-008-3*) PC Age.

***System Administrator's Guide to Directory Services.** 1997. 59.99 (*0-7897-1262-8*) Macmillan.

System Administrator's Guide to Sun Workstations. G. Becker & Kathy Slattery. (Sun Technical Reference Library). (Illus.). 296p. 1994. 48.95 (*0-387-97250-1*) Spr-Verlag.

***System Administrator's Guide to Windows NT Server.** Date not set. 49.99 (*0-7897-1307-1*) Macmillan.

System Aids in Constructing Consultation Programs. William J. Van Melle. LC 81-13132. (Computer Science: Artificial Intelligence Ser.: No. 11). (Illus.). 185p. reprint ed. pap. 52.80 (*0-8357-1232-X*, 2070354) Bks Demand.

System Analysis. McLeod. (C). 1994. student ed., pap. text ed. 28.00 (*0-03-076686-9*) HB Coll Pubs.

System Analysis & Design: A Project Approach. David Harris. 576p. (C). 1994. pap. text ed. 32.00 (*0-03-097377-5*) Dryden Pr.

System Analysis & Design Projects. Jack D. Harpool et al. (C). 1986. text ed. 39.95 (*0-8016-2068-6*) Irwin.

System Analysis & Mathematical Modeling in the U. S. S. R. Avgustin Tuzhilin. Ed. by Cynthia Corell. (Illus.). 133p. (Orig.). 1983. pap. text ed. 75.00 (*0-317-89524-9*) Delphic Associates.

System Analysis for Creep in Materials & Structures. P. Samarin. (Advanced Series in Mathematical Science & Engineering). 1996. pap. write for info. (*1-885978-22-7*) Wrld Fed Pubs.

System & Dialectics of Art: Annotated from Unpublished Writings. John Graham. LC 74-160670. (Illus.). 237p. reprint ed. pap. 67.60 (*0-8357-4034-X*, 2036726) Bks Demand.

System & History in Philosophy: On the Unity of Thought & Time, Text & Explanation, Solitude & Dialogue, Rhetoric & Truth in the Practice of Philosophy & Its History. Adriaan T. Peperzak. LC 85-27679. (SUNY Series in Contemporary Continental Philosophy). 172p. (Orig.). 1986. text ed. 64.50 (*0-88706-273-3*); pap. text ed. 21.95 (*0-88706-275-X*) State U NY Pr.

System & Profits: Early Management Accounting at Dupont & General Motors. Thomas H. Johnson. Ed. by Richard P. Brief. LC 80-1458. (Dimensions of Accounting Theory & Practice Ser.). 1980. lib. bdg. 31. 95 (*0-405-13481-9*) Ayer.

System & Revelation: The Philosophy of Franz Rosenzweig. Stephane Moses. Tr. by Catherine Tihanyi. LC 91-29532. 318p. 1992. 39.95 (*0-8143-2128-3*) Wayne St U Pr.

System & Signal Analysis. Chi-Tsong Chen. 576p. (C). 1989. text ed. 62.75 (*0-03-005694-2*); Solutions manual. teacher ed. write for info. (*0-03-027918-6*) SCP.

***System & Signal Analysis.** 2nd ed. Chi-Tsong Chen. (The/ Oxford Series in Electrical & Computer Engineering). 736p. 1994. 69.00 (*0-19-510722-5*); pap. 26.50 (*0-19-511456-6*) OUP.

System & Signal Analysis. 2nd ed. Chi-Tsong Chen. (Illus.). 88p. (C). 1994. student ed., pap. text ed. write for info. (*0-03-000089-4*) OUP.

System & Structure: Essays in Communication & Exchange. 2nd ed. Anthony Wilden. (Illus.). 1980. 45.00 (*0-422-76700-X*, 2585, Pub. by Tavistock UK); pap. 22. 00 (*0-422-76710-7*, 2879, Pub. by Tavistock UK) Routledge Chapman & Hall.

System & Theory of Geosciences, 2 pts., 1. Ed. by Herbert H. Uhlig. 103p. (C). 1975. pap. 23.00 (*0-08-019664-0*, Pergamon Pr) Elsevier.

System & Theory of Geosciences, 2 pts., Pt. 2. Ed. by Herbert H. Uhlig. 103p. (C). 1975. pap. 23.00 (*0-08-019670-5*, Pergamon Pr) Elsevier.

System & Unsystem: How American Society Works. Joseph A. Raffaele. 388p. 1974. 18.95 (*0-470-70274-5*); pap. 11.95 (*0-470-70483-7*) Schenkman Bks Inc.

***System & Writing in the Philosophy of Jacques Derrida.** 253p. 1993. pap. text ed. 19.95 (*0-521-44852-2*) Cambridge U Pr.

System & Writing in the Philosophy of Jacques Derrida. Christopher Johnson. LC 92-16567. (Cambridge Studies in French: No. 40). 1993. 59.95 (*0-521-41492-X*) Cambridge U Pr.

System Anylsis. 4th ed. James C. Wetherbe. Date not set. teacher ed., pap. text ed. write for info. (*0-314-03412-9*) West Pub.

System Applications Guide. Ed. by Walt Kester & James Bryant. (Analog Devices Technical Reference Bks.). (Illus.). 800p. (Orig.). 1993. pap. 30.00 (*0-916550-13-3*) Analog Devices.

System Approach to the Relationship Between Consumption & Wealth. S. G. Hall & K. D. Patterson. (Bank of England. Discussion Papers. Technical Ser.: No. 38). 16p. reprint ed. pap. 25.00 (*0-7837-2666-X*, 2043030) Bks Demand.

System Aranearum. Alexander Petrunkevitch. (Connecticut Academy of Arts & Sciences Ser., Trans.: Vol. 29). 1928. pap. 75.00 (*0-685-22807-X*) Elliots Bks.

System Architecture, 80486. Tom Shanley. (Architecture Ser.). 90p. 1992. pap. 14.95 (*1-881609-01-4*) Mindshare Pr.

System Behavior & System Modeling - Mac. Arthur A. Few. LC 95-61062. (Illus.). 100p. (Orig.). (C). 1996. pap. text ed. 31.00 incl. disk (*0-935702-88-1*) Univ Sci Bks.

System Behavior & System Modeling - Windows. Arthur A. Few. LC 95-61062. (Illus.). 112p. (Orig.). (C). 1996. pap. text ed. 31.00 (*0-935702-83-0*) Univ Sci Bks.

System BIOS for IBM PCs, Compatibles & EISA Computers: The Complete Guide to ROM-Based System Software. 2nd ed. Phoenix Technologies Staff. (Illus.). 604p. 1991. pap. 34.95 (*0-201-57760-7*) Addison-Wesley.

***System Book for Family Law: A Forms & Procedures Handbook, 2 vols.** Leonard L. Loeb et al. 900p. 1993. ring bd. 165.00 incl. disk (*0-945574-00-2*) State Bar WI CLE Bk Div.

System de l'Incanto des Galees du Marche a Venise: (Fin XIIIe-Milieu XVe Siecle) Doris Stockly. (Fin XIIIe-Milieu XVe Siecle Ser.). 365p. (FRE.). 1994. 159.50 (*90-04-10002-4*) E J Brill.

System der Leibnizschen Logik. Wolfgang Lenzen. (Foundations of Communication & Cognition Ser.). xvi, 235p. (C). 1990. lib. bdg. 83.10 (*3-11-012353-3*) De Gruyter.

System der Pragmatischen Suffixmorpheme Des Wogulischen Dialekts an der Tawda: Aus Dem Ungarischen Ubersetzt von Regina Hessky. Laszlo Honti. (Janua Linguarum, Ser.: No. 246). 1976. pap. 35. 40 (*90-279-3406-1*) Mouton.

System der Wissenschaften nach Gegenstanden und Methoden see System of the Sciences According to Objects & Methods

System Description of the Marijuana Trade. Michael T. Childress. LC 93-26051. 1994. pap. 13.00 (*0-8330-1430-7*, MR-235-A/DPRC) Rand Corp.

System Design Approaches to Public Services. John H. Burgess. LC 76-737. (Illus.). 300p. 1978. 38.50 (*0-8386-1892-8*) Fairleigh Dickinson.

System Design for Computer Applications. Hyman N. Laden & Thomas R. Gildersleeve. LC 63-17363. 336p. reprint ed. pap. 95.80 (*0-317-09782-2*, 2007075) Bks Demand.

System Design Guidelines for Reliability. Ed. by Howard K. Dicken. (Illus.). 1990. 135.00 (*1-878266-04-7*) DM Data.

System Design Modeling & Metamodeling. J. P. Van Gigch. (Illus.). 440p. 1990. 85.00 (*0-306-43740-6*, Plenum Pr) Plenum.

System Design with the MC68020, MC68030, & MC68040 32-Bit Microprocessors. Asghar Noor. LC 92-12923. 587p. 1994. text ed. 59.95 (*0-442-31886-3*) Van Nos Reinhold.

System Designs into Silicon. J. C. Forskitt & J. Johansson. (Illus.). 264p. 1993. pap. 80.00 (*0-7503-0114-7*) IOP Pub.

System Development & Ada. Ed. by A. Nico Habermann & Ugo MOntanari. (Lecture Notes in Computer Science Ser.: Vol. 275). v, 305p. 1987. 39.00 (*0-387-18341-8*) Spr-Verlag.

System Development Auditing: Traditional & New Development Methodologies & Packaged Software. D. B. Dunmore. (Illus.). 354p. 1988. text ed. 60.00 (*0-940706-22-9*) Management Advisory Pubns.

***System Development Auditor.** Z. G. Ruthberg et al. 130p. 1991. 313.00 (*1-85617-116-7*, Pub. by Elsvr Adv Tech UK) Elsevier.

System Development Charges for Water, Wastewater, & Stormwater Facilities. Arthur C. Nelson. 192p. 1995. 59.95 (*1-56670-037-X*, L1037) Lewis Pubs.

***System Disorders & Atrophies, Pt. I.** Pierre J. Vinken et al. (Handbook of Clinical Neurology Ser.: Vol. 21). 636p. 1975. 423.00 (*0-7204-7221-0*) Elsevier.

***System Disorders & Atrophies, Pt. II.** Pierre J. Vinken et al. (Handbook of Clinical Neurology Ser.: Vol. 22). 586p. 1975. 393.25 (*0-7204-7222-9*) Elsevier.

System Disorders & Atrophies see Handbook of Clinical Neurology

System Dynamics. 2nd ed. Katsuhiko Ogata. 656p. 1992. text ed. 85.00 (*0-13-855941-4*) P-H.

***System Dynamics.** 3rd ed. Ogata. 1997. text ed. 85.00 (*0-13-675745-6*) P-H.

System Dynamics: A Unified Approach. 2nd ed. Dean C. Karnopp et al. LC 90-12110. 514p. 1990. text ed. 89.95 (*0-471-62171-4*) Wiley.

System Dynamics & Modeling. Rolf Clark. (Topics in Operations Research Ser.). iii, 163p. 1988. pap. 15.00 (*1-877640-08-5*) INFORMS.

***System Dynamics in Economic & Financial Models.** C. Heij. LC 97-17075. (Series in Financial Economics & Quantitative Analysis). 1997. write for info. (*0-471-96934-6*) Wiley.

***System Effects: Complexity in Political & Social Life.** Robert Jervis. LC 97-1108. 1997. write for info. (*0-691-02624-6*) Princeton U Pr.

***System Engineering Approach to Imaging.** Norman S. Kopeika. LC 96-37101. 1997. write for info. (*0-8194-2377-7*) SPIE.

System Engineering Management. Benjamin S. Blanchard. LC 90-44134. (New Dimensions in Engineering Ser.). 392p. 1991. text ed. 89.95 (*0-471-50676-1*) Wiley.

***System Engineering Management.** 2nd ed. Benjamin S. Blanchard. LC 97-3546. 1997. 69.95 (*0-471-19086-1*) Wiley.

System Engineering Planning & Enterprise Identity. Jeffrey O. Grady. LC 94-31150. (Systems Engineering Ser.). 400p. 1995. 79.95 (*0-8493-7832-X*) CRC Pr.

System Enquiry: A System Dynamics Approach. Eric F. Wolstenholme. 238p. 1990. text ed. 47.95 (*0-471-92783-X*) Wiley.

System Fault Diagnostics, Reliability & Related Knowledge-Based Approaches, Set. Ed. by Spyros G. Tzafestas. (C). 1987. lib. bdg. 180.50 (*90-277-2550-0*) Kluwer Ac.

System Fault Diagnostics, Reliability & Related Knowledge-Based Approaches, Vol. I: Fault Diagnostics & Reliability. Ed. by Spyros G. Tzafestas. (C). 1987. lib. bdg. 180.50 (*90-277-2551-9*) Kluwer Ac.

System Files & Devices for Intel Processors (SVR4.2 MP) Unix System Laboratories Staff. (Illus.). 704p. (C). 1994. pap. text ed. 80.00 (*0-13-158130-9*) P-H.

System Files & Devices Reference. Unix System Laboratories Staff. 1993. pap. text ed. 32.00 (*0-13-177189-2*) P-H.

System for Advancement in the Fire Service. Arthur R. Couvillon. LC 88-83385. 130p. 1990. pap. 9.95 (*0-938329-56-1*) Info Guides.

System for Ophthalmic Dispensing. 2nd ed. Clifford W. Brooks & Irving Borish. (Illus.). 581p. 1996. text ed. 80. 00 (*0-7506-9481-5*) Buttrwrth-Heinemann.

System for Ophthalmic Dispensing. Clifford W. Brooks & Irving M. Borish. LC 76-5734. (Illus.). 472p. 1979. reprint ed. 75.00 (*0-7506-9000-3*) Buttrwrth-Heinemann.

System for Settlement of Disputes under the United Nations Convention on the Law of the Sea. A. O. Adede. LC 86-5373. (Publications on Ocean Development: Vol. 10). 1987. lib. bdg. 132.00 (*90-247-3324-3*) Kluwer Ac.

System for Teaching Business Education. Adele F. Schrag & Robert P. Poland. 576p. 1987. pap. text ed. 50.37 (*0-07-055602-4*) Glencoe.

System for the Romanization of Arabic. (National Information Standards Ser.). 1989. reprint ed. 20.00 (*0-88738-989-9*, Z39.12) Transaction Pubs.

System FORE, 5 Vols. Ed. by Eric Bagai & Judith Bagai. (Illus.). 1328p. (C). 1979. student ed. 90.00 (*0-943292-00-X*, Flaming Sparrow) Foreworks.

System FORE Handbook. Eric Bagai & Judith Bagai. (System FORE Ser.: Vol. 1). 96p. (Orig.). (C). 1979. pap. text ed. 7.00 (*0-943292-01-8*, Flaming Sparrow) Foreworks.

System Identification. T. S. Soderstrom. 640p. 1989. boxed 56.40 (*0-13-881236-5*) P-H.

System Identification. 2nd ed. Ellen J. Ljung. 1996. text ed. 75.00 (*0-13-656695-2*) P-H.

System Identification: Parameter & State Estimation. Pieter Eykhoff. LC 73-2781. (Illus.). 575p. 1974. reprint ed. pap. 163.90 (*0-7837-9505-X*, 2060255) Bks Demand.

System Identification: Theory for the User. Lennart Ljung. (Illus.). 384p. 1987. text ed. 86.00 (*0-13-881640-9*) P-H.

System Identification & Control Design Using P.I.M. Plus Software. Ioan D. Landau. 272p. 1990. text ed. 69.00 (*0-13-880782-5*) P-H.

***System Identification & Robust Control: A Case Study Approach.** Steen Tffner-Clausen. LC 96-42695. (Advances in Industrial Control Ser.). 1996. 69.00 (*3-540-76087-3*) Spr-Verlag.

System Identification Based on Riemannian Geometry: Theory & Algorithms. Ralf Peeters. (Tinbergen Institute Ser.). 368p. 1994. pap. 28.50 (*90-5170-246-9*, Pub. by Thesis Pubs NE) IBD Ltd.

System Identification for Self-Adaptive Control. W. D. Davies. LC 70-128756. 394p. reprint ed. pap. 112.30 (*0-317-08013-X*, 2022540) Bks Demand.

System Identification 1997 (SYSID '97) Ed. by Y. Sunahara. (IFAC Postprint Ser.). 1997. pap. text ed. write for info. (*0-08-042592-5*, Pergamon Pr) Elsevier.

System Identification of Vibrating Structures: Mathematical Models from Test Data Presented at 1972 Winter Annual Meeting of the American Society of Mechanical Engineers. Ed. by W. D. Pilkey & R. Cohen. LC 72-92594. (Illus.). 206p. reprint ed. pap. 58. 80 (*0-317-08340-6*, 2019473) Bks Demand.

System Identification (SYSID '94) M. Blanke & T. S. Soderstrom. LC 95-17156. (IPPV IFAC Ser.). 1700p. 1995. pap. 286.50 (*0-08-042225-X*, Pergamon Pr) Elsevier.

System Identification Tutorials. Ed. by R. Isermann. (Automatica Ser.: Vol. 16, No. 5). (Illus.). 88p. 1981. pap. text ed. 7.00 (*0-08-027302-5*, Pergamon Pr) Elsevier.

System in Black Language. David Sutcliffe & John Figueroa. (Multilingual Matters Ser.: No. 77). 192p. 1992. 99.00 (*1-85359-130-0*, Pub. by Multilingual Matters UK); pap. 34.90 (*1-85359-129-7*, Pub. by Multilingual Matters UK) Taylor & Francis.

***System in Denial: Nelson vs. the United States.** Marcus Nelson-Giavanni. Ed. by John Pritchard. (Illus.). 416p. 1997. 23.95 (*0-914207-11-3*) Cornucopia Pubns.

System Integration. Jeffrey O. Grady. LC 94-5639. (Systems Engineering Ser.). 272p. 1994. 71.95 (*0-8493-7831-1*) CRC Pr.

System Integration, Vol. 8. Ed. by James E. Rush. LC 83-9584. (Library Systems Evaluation Guides Ser.). (Illus.). 240p. 1987. 59.50 (*0-912803-08-8*) Rush Assoc.

An Asterisk (*) at the beginning of an entry indicates that the title is appearing in BIP for the first time.

S

***System Made Me Do It! A Life Changing Approach to Office Politics.** Susan M. Osborn. LC 96-94879. (Illus.). 176p. (Orig.). 1997. pap. 19.95 (*0-9655368-0-7*) LifeThread Pubns.

System Manager's Bible. Brillhart. 1996. pap. text ed. 39.00 (*0-13-443680-6*) P-H.

System Modeling & Optimization, Vol. 197. Ed. by J. Henry et al. (Lecture Notes in Control & Information Sciences Ser.). 976p. 1994. 139.95 (*0-387-19893-8*) Spr-Verlag.

System Modeling & Optimization: Proceedings. Eleventh IFIP Conference Staff. Ed. by P. Thoft-Christensen. (Lecture Notes in Control & Information Sciences Ser.: Vol. 59). x, 892p. 1984. 105.95 (*0-387-13185-X*) Spr-Verlag.

***System Modeling & Visual Simulaiton in Industry.** Peter Darnell. 1997. text ed. 59.99 (*1-85032-802-9*) ITCP.

***System Modelling & Control.** 3rd ed. write for info. (*0-340-54379-5*, Pub. by E Arnold UK) Routledge Chapman & Hall.

***System Modelling & Optimization.** Dolezal & J. Fidler. (Illus.). 672p. 1995. text ed. 156.50 (*0-412-71880-4*, Chap & Hall NY) Chapman & Hall.

System Modelling & Optimization. Masao Iri & K. Yajma. (Lecture Notes in Control & Information Sciences Ser.: Vol. 113). (Illus.). 787p. 1988. 158.95 (*0-387-19238-7*) Spr-Verlag.

System Modelling & Optimization. Ed. by A. Prekopa et al. (Lecture Notes in Control & Information Sciences Ser.: Vol. 84). (Illus.). 1060p. 1986. pap. 153.00 (*0-387-16854-0*) Spr-Verlag.

System Modelling & Optimization: Proceedings of the 14th IFIP-Conference, Leipzig, GDR, July 3-7, 1989. Ed. by H. J. Sebastian et al. (Lecture Notes in Control & Information Sciences Ser.: Vol. 143). (Illus.). x, 960p. 1990. pap. 148.00 (*0-387-52659-5*) Spr-Verlag.

System Modelling & Optimization: Proceedings of the 15th IFIP Conference, Zurich, Switzerland, 2-6 September 1991. Ed. by P. Kall et al. LC 92-18536. (Lecture Notes in Control & Information Sciences Ser.: Vol. 180). (Illus.). 967p. 1992. 240.95 (*0-387-55577-3*) Spr-Verlag.

System of Accentuation for Sumero-Akkadian Signs. Clarence E. Keiser. LC 78-63553. (Yale Oriental Series: Researches: No. 9). reprint ed. 20.00 (*0-404-60279-7*) AMS Pr.

System of Adult Education in Yugoslavia. Dusan Savicevic. LC 69-17692. (Notes & Essays Ser.: No. 59). (C). 1968. pap. text ed. 2.50 (*0-87060-023-0*, NES 59) Syracuse U Cont Ed.

System of Aeronautics. John Wise. (Illus.). 319p. 1980. 24.95 (*0-87770-227-6*) Ye Galleon.

***System of Ambition?** Black. 1991. pap. text ed. write for info. (*0-582-00475-6*, Pub. by Longman UK) Longman.

System of Ambition? British Foreign Policy, 1660-1793. Jeremy Black. (Studies in Modern History). (Illus.). 336p. (C). 1991. text ed. 56.50 (*0-582-08014-2*, 78817) Longman.

System of Architectural Ornament. Louis Sullivan. 1968. 50.00 (*0-87130-018-4*); pap. 40.00 (*0-87130-019-2*) Eakins.

System of Ayurveda. Shiv Sharma. (C). 1993. text ed. 9.00 (*81-85557-02-0*, Pub. by Low Price II) S Asia.

System of Botany-Descriptive & Analytical. J. D. Hooker. 1066p. 1986. reprint ed. pap. 175.00 (*0-7855-0394-3*, Pub. by Intl Bks & Periodicals II) St Mut.

System of Case Taking in Medicine. S. Sarkar. (C). 1989. 30.00 (*0-89771-360-5*, Pub. by Current Dist II) St Mut.

System of Complete Medical Police: Selections from Johann Peter Frank. Johann P. Frank. Ed. by Erna Lesky. LC 75-39820. 493p. reprint ed. pap. 140.60 (*0-317-07932-8*, 2020757) Bks Demand.

System of Courtly Love. Lewis F. Mott. LC 65-26458. (Studies in Comparative Literature: No. 35). (C). 1969. reprint ed. lib. bdg. 75.00 (*0-8383-0599-7*) M S G Haskell Hse.

System of Criminal Law: Cases & Materials - New South Wales. Dirk J. Meure et al. 1040p. 1979. Australia. pap. 98.00 (*0-409-30441-7*, A.T.) MICHIE.

System of Economic Contradictions: or The Philosophy of Misery. Pierre J. Proudhon. Tr. by Benjamin R. Tucker. LC 75-38261. (Evolution of Capitalism Ser.). 482p. 1978. reprint ed. 30.95 (*0-405-04134-9*) Ayer.

System of English Grammar. Ralph B. Long & Dorothy R. Long. LC 75-159449. 531p. (C). 1980. reprint ed. text ed. 12.00 (*0-8477-3325-4*); reprint ed. pap. text ed. 9.60 (*0-8477-3326-2*) U of PR Pr.

System of Experimental Design: Engineering Methods to Optimize Quality & Minimize Costs, 2 vols., Set. Genichi Taguchi. 1176p. 1987. 150.00 (*0-527-91621-8*, 916218) Qual Resc.

System of Figure Skating: 1880. T. Vandervell & H. Witham. (Illus.). 200p. 1983. pap. 25.00 (*0-87556-710-X*) Saifer.

System of Five Cakras in Kubjikamatatantra 14-16. Dory Heilijgers-Seelen. (Groningen Oriental Studies: No. 9). x, 330p. 1994. 57.00 (*0-614-07064-3*, Pub. by Egbert Forsten NE) Benjamins North Am.

System of Government in the Living Body Series, 10 vols. Betty Y. Ho. Ed. by Betty Elkan. LC 92-26675. (Illus.). 1015p. (Orig.). 1994. Set. pap. 120.00 (*0-9600148-8-8*) Juvenescent.

System of Government under the Holy Prophet. S. Abul Ala Maududi. 32p. (Orig.). 1985. pap. 4.95 (*1-56744-395-8*) Kazi Pubns.

System of International Comparisons of Gross Product & Purchasing Power. Irving B. Kravis et al. LC 73-19352. (United Nations International Comparison Project: Phase One Ser.). (Illus.). 310p. reprint ed. pap. 88.40 (*0-7837-5381-0*, 2045145) Bks Demand.

System of Law & Courts Governing New South Wales. 2nd ed. W. L. Morrison. 1985. pap. 71.00 (*0-409-49263-9*, AT) MICHIE.

System of Logic. 8th ed. John Stuart Mill. (C). 1986. reprint ed. pap. text ed. 27.25 (*0-935005-34-X*); reprint ed. lib. bdg. 32.95 (*0-935005-29-3*) Lincoln-Rembrandt.

***System of Logic & History of Logical Doctrines: 1871 Edition.** Friedrich Ueberweg. 624p. 1996. reprint ed. write for info. (*1-85506-201-1*) Bks Intl VA.

System of Marker Variables for the Field of Learning Disabilities. Barbara K. Keogh et al. LC 81-18202. (Alexander R. Luria Research Monograph Ser. in Learning Disabilities: No. 1). 104p. reprint ed. pap. 29.70 (*0-8357-3987-2*, 2036685) Bks Demand.

System of Metaphysics. George S. Fullerton. LC 68-23290. 1968. reprint ed. text ed. 95.00 (*0-8371-0079-8*, FUSM, Greenwood Pr) Greenwood.

System of Metaphysics. George S. Fullerton. 1968. reprint ed. 39.00 (*0-403-00125-0*) Scholarly.

System of Moral Philosophy, in Three Books, 2 vols., Vol. 5. Francis Hutcheson. Ed. by Bernhard Fabian. (System of Moral Philosophy Ser.: Vol. 1, 3 bks.). 358p. 1990. reprint ed. lib. bdg. 110.00 (*3-487-02256-7*) G Olms Pubs.

System of Moral Philosophy, in Three Books, 2 vols., Vol. 6. Francis Hutcheson. Ed. by Bernhard Fabian. (System of Moral Philosophy Ser.: Vol. 2, 3 bks.). 380p. 1990. reprint ed. lib. bdg. 110.00 (*3-487-02257-5*) G Olms Pubs.

System of National Accounts. 246p. 1970. 17.00 (*92-1-161132-6*) UN.

System of National Accounts 1993. OECD Staff. 711p. (Orig.). 1994. 85.00 (*92-1-161352-3*) OECD.

System of Nomenclature for Terpene Hydrocarbons: Acyclics, Monocyclics, Bicyclics. American Chemical Society, Division of Organic Chemistry Staff & Industrial & Engineering Chemistry. LC 55-4170. (American Chemical Society Advances in Chemistry Ser.: No. 14). 110p. reprint ed. pap. 31.40 (*0-317-08703-7*, 2050183) Bks Demand.

System of Objects. Jean Baudrillard. 200p. (C). 1996. pap. text ed. 18.00 (*1-85984-068-X*, Pub. by Vrso UK) Norton.

System of Objects. Jean Baudrillard. 208p. (C). (gr. 13 up). 1996. text ed. 65.00 (*1-85984-943-1*, Pub. by Vrso UK) Norton.

System of Oratory, 2 vols., Set. John Ward. (Anglistica & Americana Ser.: No. 24). 1969. reprint ed. 128.70 (*0-685-66527-5*, 05102065) G Olms Pubs.

System of Orthopaedic Medicine. Ombregt. 1995. text ed. 160.00 (*0-7020-1595-4*) Saunders.

System of Physical Examination. D. P. Kingsford & D. T. Liley. 36p. 1991. pap. text ed. 15.00 (*0-07-452808-4*) McGraw-Hill HPD.

System of Plotinus. Hermetic Truth Society Staff. 1985. reprint ed. pap. 8.95 (*0-916411-75-3*) Holmes Pub.

System of Pragmatic Idealism, Vol. One: Human Knowledge in Idealistic Perspective. Nicholas Rescher. (Illus.). 367p. 1991. text ed. 55.00 (*0-691-07391-0*) Princeton U Pr.

System of Pragmatic Idealism, Vol. 2: The Validity of Values - A Normative Theory of Evaluative Rationality. Nicholas Rescher. 296p. 1993. text ed. 55.00 (*0-691-07393-7*) Princeton U Pr.

System of Primary Particle: First Step in the Search for the Ultimate Particle. Yecheskiel Zamir. LC 90-91407. (Avkoan Theory Ser.: Vol. 1-d). 89p. (Orig.). 1990. pap. text ed. 18.95 (*0-9614730-5-3*) Y Z Pubns.

System of Professions: An Essay on the Division of Expert Labor. Andrew Abbott. xvi, 452p. 1988. pap. text ed. 22.50 (*0-226-00069-9*) U Ch Pr.

System of Protection & Industrial Development in Zimbabwe. Lindani B. Ndlovu. 246p. 1994. 59.95 (*1-85628-870-6*, Pub. by Avebury Pub UK) Ashgate Pub Co.

System of Public Sacrifice in Fourth-Century Athens. Vincent J. Rosivach. LC 93-47180. (American Philological Association, American Classical Studies: No. 34). 171p. 1994. 29.95 (*1-55540-942-3*, 400434); pap. 19.95 (*1-55540-943-1*, 40 04 34) Scholars Pr GA.

***System of Regulating Documents in Construction Principal Provisions: Snip 10-01-94.** Russia's Minstroy Staff. (Snip Building Codes of Russia Ser.). (Illus.). iv, 40p. (Orig.). 1996. ring bd. 6.95 (*1-57937-001-2*) Snip Register.

System of Rights. Rex Martin. 528p. 1993. 59.00 (*0-19-827374-6*) OUP.

***System of Rights.** Rex Martin. 448p. 1997. reprint ed. pap. 19.95 (*0-19-829293-7*) OUP.

System of Scientific Medicine. Howard Berliner. 180p. 1985. 29.95 (*0-422-79520-8*, 9822, Pub. by Tavistock UK); pap. 13.95 (*0-422-79530-5*, 9829, Pub. by Tavistock UK) Routledge Chapman & Hall.

System of Social Science: Papers Relating to Adam Smith. 2nd ed. Andrew S. Skinner. 304p. (C). 1996. 65.00 (*0-19-823334-5*, Clarendon Pr) OUP.

System of Stages for Correlation of Magallanes Basin Sediments. Manley L. Natland et al. LC 74-75964. (Geological Society of America, Memoir Ser.: No. 139). 202p. reprint ed. pap. 57.60 (*0-317-28976-4*, 2023735) Bks Demand.

System of Target Selection Applied by the German Air Force in WW II. (USAF Historical Studies: No. 186). 481p. 1956. reprint ed. pap. 56.95 (*0-89126-161-3*) MA-AH Pub.

System of Taxation in China in the Tsing Dynasty, 1644-1911. Shao-Kwan Chen. LC 79-120215. (Columbia University. Studies in the Social Sciences: No. 143). 1970. reprint ed. 39.50 (*0-404-51143-0*) AMS Pr.

System of Taxation in the Russian Oil & Gas Industry & Attraction of Foreign Investments. Yu N. Shvemberger. 97p. 1995. 150.00 (*0-614-04181-3*) Gaunt.

System of the Hungarian Sentence Patterns. Janos Zsilka. LC 66-63663. (Uralic & Altaic Ser.: Vol. 67). 1967. pap. text ed. 15.00 (*0-87750-023-1*) Res Inst Inner Asian Studies.

System of the Laws of the State of Connecticut, 2 Vols., Set. Zephaniah Swift. LC 73-37991. (American Law Series: The Formative Law). 962p. 1972. reprint ed. 60.95 (*0-405-04036-9*) Ayer.

System of the Laws of the State of Connecticut, 2 Vols., Vol. 1. Zephaniah Swift. LC 73-37991. (American Law Series: The Formative Law). 962p. 1972. reprint ed. 30.95 (*0-405-04037-7*) Ayer.

System of the Laws of the State of Connecticut, 2 Vols., Vol. 2. Zephaniah Swift. LC 73-37991. (American Law Series: The Formative Law). 962p. 1972. reprint ed. 30.95 (*0-405-04038-5*) Ayer.

System of the Science of Music & Practical Composition: Incidentally Comprising What Is Usually Understood by the Term Through Bass. Johann B. Logier. LC 76-20715. (Music Reprint Ser.). 1976. reprint ed. lib. bdg. 42.50 (*0-306-70793-4*) Da Capo.

System of the Sciences According to Objects & Methods. Paul Tillich. LC 80-67078. Orig. Title: Das System der Wissenschaften nach Gegenstanden und Methoden. 288p. 1981. 22.50 (*0-686-76167-7*) Bucknell U Pr.

System of the Sciences According to Objects & Methods. Paul Tillich. Tr. & Intro. by Paul Wiebe. Orig. Title: Das System der Wissenschaften nach Gegenstanden und Methoden. 240p. 1981. 34.50 (*0-8387-5013-3*) Bucknell U Pr.

System of the Vedanta. Paul Deussen. (C). 1990. reprint ed. 15.00 (*81-85395-88-8*, Pub. by Low Price II) S Asia.

System of Transcendental Idealism. F. W. Schelling. Tr. & Intro. by Peter Heath. 248p. (Orig.). 1993. pap. text ed. 16.50 (*0-8139-1458-2*) U Pr of Va.

System of Transcendental Idealism (1800) F. W. Schelling. LC 78-6638. 248p. 1978. text ed. 28.50 (*0-8139-0780-2*) U Pr of Va.

System of Vectorcardiographic Interpretation. Abner C. Witham. LC 74-83118. 484p. reprint ed. pap. 138.00 (*0-317-58157-0*, 2029742) Bks Demand.

System of Water Quality from the Biological Point of View. Ed. by Vladimir Sladecek. (Limnology Report: No. 7). (Illus.). 222p. (Orig.). 1973. pap. text ed. 68.50 (*3-510-47005-2*, Pub. by E Schweizerbartsche GW) Lubrecht & Cramer.

System One Thousand & Thirty-Two: Reference Booklet. rev. ed. Karen Molloy. 91p. 1987. spiral bd. 12.00 (*0-317-63455-0*) CompuServe Data Tech.

System One Thousand & Thirty-Two Primer. rev. ed. Nina Zolotow & Ken Jackson. (Illus.). 125p. 1987. spiral bd. 25.00 (*0-912055-14-6*) CompuServe Data Tech.

System Operation see CEGB: Modern Power Station-System Practice - MPSP

System Operation see Modern Power Station Practice

***System Reliability.** Klaassen. (Mechanical Engineering Ser.). 1990. pap. 51.95 (*0-340-50142-1*) Van Nos Reinhold.

System Reliability Theory: Models & Statistical Methods. Arnljot Hyland & Marvin Rausand. (Series in Probability & Mathematical Statistics). 640p. 1994. text ed. 84.95 (*0-471-59397-4*) Wiley.

System Safety: Including Department of Defense Standards. Donald Layton. 200p. 1989. text ed. 39.95 (*0-938862-64-2*) Weber Systems.

System Safety Engineering & Management. Harold E. Roland & Brian Moriarty. (Wiley Interscience Ser.). 368p. 1983. 34.95 (*0-317-01156-1*, 1-09695-4) DeLeuw-Cather Co.

***System Safety Engineering & Risk Assessment: A Practical Approach.** Nicholas J. Bahr. LC 97-10526. 1997. boxed write for info. (*1-56032-416-3*) Hemisp Pub.

System Safety Engineering Management. 2nd ed. Harold E. Roland & Brian Moriarty. LC 90-12109. 367p. 1990. text ed. 89.95 (*0-471-61816-0*) Wiley.

System Safety Two Thousand: A Practical Guide for Planning, Managing, & Conducting System Safety Programs. Joe Stephenson. LC 90-42038. 368p. 1991. text ed. 67.95 (*0-442-23840-1*) Van Nos Reinhold.

***System Security: A Management Perspective.** David Oppenheimer et al. Ed. & Frwd. by Dan Geer. (Orig.). 1997. pap. text ed. 7.50 (*1-880446-85-5*) USENIX Assn.

System 7.5 Book for Macintosh Users. Don Crabb. (Illus.). 400p. (Orig.). 1994. 25.00 (*1-56830-109-X*) Hayden.

System Shock. Justin Richards. (Dr. Who Missing Adventures Ser.). 1995. mass mkt. 5.95 (*0-426-20445-X*, Pub. by Virgin Pub UK) London Brdge.

System Shock Clue Book: I.C.E. Breaker. Tuesday Frase. (Illus.). 96p. (Orig.). 1994. pap. 14.95 (*0-929373-19-7*) Origin Syst.

System Shock Strategies & Secrets. Bernie Yee. LC 95-69357. 204p. 1995. 14.99 (*0-7821-1722-8*, Strategies & Secrets) Sybex.

System Simulation & Scientific Computing: Proceedings of Beijing International Conference on System Simulation & Scientific Computing, Beijing, China, 23-26 October 1989, 2 vols., Set. Ed. by Wen C. Yuan et al. LC 89-23059. (International Academic Publishers Ser.). 2000p. 1990. 315.00 (*0-08-037881-1*, 1303; 1101; 1102; 1808, Pub. by IAP UK) Elsevier.

System Simulation Programming Styles & Languages. Wolfgang Kreutzer. 352p. (C). 1986. text ed. 32.25 (*0-201-12914-0*) Addison-Wesley.

System Simulation with Digital Computer. Narsingh Deo. (Illus.). 224p. (C). 1983. 38.00 (*0-13-881789-8*) P-H.

System Software: An Introduction to Systems Programming. Leland L. Beck. 496p. 1985. text ed. write for info. (*0-201-10950-6*) Addison-Wesley.

System Software: An Introduction to Systems Programming. 2nd ed. Leland L. Beck. (Illus.). 480p. (C). 1990. text ed. 50.50 (*0-201-50945-8*) Addison-Wesley.

System Software: An Introduction to Systems Programming. 3rd ed. Leland L. Beck. 500p. (C). 1997. text ed. 45.95 (*0-201-42300-6*) Addison-Wesley.

System Software & Software Systems: Programming Support Environment. T. Rus & D. Rus. 250p. 1998. text ed. 46.00 (*981-02-1256-9*) World Scientific Pub.

System Software & Software Systems: Systems Methodology for System Software. R. Rus & D. Rus. 388p. 1993. text ed. 48.00 (*981-02-1254-2*) World Scientific Pub.

System Software & Tools for High Performance Computing Environments. Paul C. Messina & Thomas A. Sterling. xix, 160p. 1993. pap. 5.00 (*0-89871-326-9*) Soc Indus-Appl Math.

System Structure & Control: Preprints of the IFAC Workshop, Prague, Czechoslovakia, 3-5 September 1992. Vladimir Strejc. LC 92-40441. 508p. 1992. pap. 121.75 (*0-08-042057-5*, Pergamon Pr) Elsevier.

System Structure & Control 1995. Ed. by M. Guglielmi. LC 96-39667. (IFAC Proceedings Ser.). 616p. 1996. pap. 96.00 (*0-08-042356-6*, Pergamon Pr) Elsevier.

System, Structure & Experience: Toward a Scientific Theory of Mind. Ervin Laszlo. (Current Topics of Contemporary Thought Ser.: Vol. 1). xii, 112p. 1969. text ed. 109.00 (*0-677-02360-X*) Gordon & Breach.

System Structure Theory. unabridged ed. Ronald W. Cutburth. 105p. 1996. spiral bd. 12.00 (*1-878291-30-0*) Love From Sea.

***System Synthesis, 10th International Symposium.** LC 10-801820. 175p. 1997. pap. 80.00 (*0-8186-7949-2*) IEEE Comp Soc.

System Synthesis, 8th International Symposium on (ISSS '95) LC 10-801820. 192p. 1995. pap. 50.00 (*0-8186-7076-2*, PR07076) IEEE Comp Soc.

System Synthesis, 9th International Symposium On: ISSS 96. LC 10-801820. 160p. 1996. pap. 50.00 (*0-8186-7563-2*) IEEE Comp Soc.

System Test & Diagnosis. William R. Simpson & John W. Sheppard. LC 94-19248. 400p. (C). 1994. lib. bdg. 108.50 (*0-7923-9475-5*) Kluwer Ac.

System-Theoretic Methods in Economic Modelling, No. II. Ed. by S. Mittnik. (International Series in Modern Applied Mathematics & Computer Science: No. 22). 209p. 1989. 39.50 (*0-08-037932-X*, Pergamon Pr) Elsevier.

System-Theoretic Methods in Economic Modelling I. Ed. by S. Mittnik. (International Series in Modern Applied Mathematics & Computer Science). 184p. 1989. 39.50 (*0-08-037228-7*, Pergamon Pr) Elsevier.

System-Theoretical Modelling in Surface Water Hydrology. Ian Douglas. Ed. by Dietrich Barsch et al. (Physical Environment Ser.: Vol. 6). (Illus.). 200p. 1991. 118.95 (*0-387-51272-1*) Spr-Verlag.

System Theory. R. Rohrer. write for info. (*0-318-51860-0*) Entropy Ltd.

System Thirty-four Teacher's Guide. Douglas D. Minkema. 48p. (gr. 9-12). text ed. 110.00 (*0-9610582-7-7*) Apollo Com.

System Training: Emission & Performance - ATTP. New York State Staff. (Automotive Technology Ser.). 1993. pap. 36.95 (*0-8273-6759-7*) Delmar.

System und Phylogenie der Lebewesen. Physikalische, chemische und biologische Evolution., Vol. 1. Edwin Moehn. (Illus.). 884p. 1984. lib. bdg. 198.00 (*3-510-65117-0*) Lubrecht & Cramer.

System V ABI MIPS Processor Supplement. AT&T Staff. 224p. 1991. pap. text ed. 28.00 (*0-13-880170-3*) P-H.

System V Abi Mips Processor Supplement. 3rd ed. Unix System Laboratories Staff. 1994. pap. text ed. 21.00 (*0-13-104688-8*) P-H.

System V Guide to Unix & Xenix. Douglas W. Topham. xxii, 733p. 1990. 60.95 (*0-387-97021-5*) Spr-Verlag.

System V Interface Definition. AT&T Staff. 1991. pap. 43.50 (*0-201-56653-2*) Addison-Wesley.

System V Interface Definition. AT&T Staff. (C). 1991. pap. text ed. 45.95 (*0-201-56654-0*) Addison-Wesley.

System V Interface Definition, Vol. 1. 3rd ed. Unix Staff. (C). 1991. pap. text ed. 45.95 (*0-201-56652-4*) Addison-Wesley.

System V, Interface Definition, Vol. 4. 3rd ed. AT&T Staff. 1991. pap. 43.50 (*0-201-56655-9*) Addison-Wesley.

System V Interface Definition, Vol. V. 3rd ed. UNIX System Laboratories Staff. (UNIX Ser.). (Illus.). 784p. (C). 1991. pap. text ed. 49.50 (*0-201-56656-7*) Addison-Wesley.

System V Interface Definition, Vol. 6. 3rd ed. Unix System Laboratories Staff. (C). 1993. pap. text ed. 35.50 (*0-201-52480-5*) Addison-Wesley.

***System Validation & Verification.** Jeffrey O. Grady. LC 97-22214. (Systems Engineering Ser.). 1997. write for info. (*0-8493-7838-9*) CRC Pr.

System-Wide Analysis of International Consumption Patterns. Saroja Selvanathan. LC 93-10998. (Advanced Studies in Theoretical & Applied Econometrics: Vol. 29). 364p. (C). 1993. Acid-free paper. lib. bdg. 133.00 (*0-7923-2344-0*) Kluwer Ac.

System Works! Hank Virgona. LC 76-42218. (Graphic Arts, Painting & Sculpture Ser.). (Illus.). 1977. lib. bdg. 25.00 (*0-306-70856-6*) Da Capo.

System 1022 Host Language Interface User's Reference Manual. rev. ed. Andrew Garland et al. 201p. 1987. ring bd. 45.00 (*0-912055-21-9*) CompuServe Data Tech.

System 1022 Primer. Ken Jackson. (Illus.). 149p. (Orig.). 1982. spiral bd. 25.00 (*0-912055-00-6*) CompuServe Data Tech.

An Asterisk (*) at the beginning of an entry indicates that the title is appearing in BIP for the first time.

System 1022 User's Reference Manual. rev. ed. Andrew Garland et al. 661p. 1987. ring bd. 65.00 (*0-912055-22-7*) CompuServe Data Tech.

System 1022-1032 Conversion Guide. Alex Humez et al. Ed. by Shirley Stone. 150p. 1988. ring bd. 45.00 (*0-912055-25-1*) CompuServe Data Tech.

System 1032 Forms Guide. rev. ed. Lynda Urgotis. (Illus.). 139p. 1986. ring bd. 27.00 (*0-912055-18-9*) CompuServe Data Tech.

System 1032 Host Language Interface User's Guide. rev. ed. Joshua Goldman & Nina Zolotow. (Illus.). 134p. 1986. ring bd. 32.00 (*0-912055-20-0*) CompuServe Data Tech.

System 1032 PCI Guide. Mena Paton. Ed. by Shirley Stone. 50p. (Orig.). pap. text ed. 20.00 (*0-912055-24-3*) CompuServe Data Tech.

System 1032 Reference Booklet. rev. ed. Karen Molloy. Ed. by Shirley Stone. 91p. 1987. spiral bd. 12.00 (*0-912055-23-5*) CompuServe Data Tech.

System 1032 User's Guide. Nina Zolotow et al. (Illus.). 910p. 1986. ring bd. 65.00 (*0-912055-19-7*) CompuServe Data Tech.

System-36 Migration Alternatives: Issues & Answers. Teresa Elms et al. 160p. 1991. pap. 65.00 (*1-880738-01-5*) Elms Info Servs.

System 360-370 Job Control Language & the Access Methods. Reino Hannula. LC 76-23986. (Illus.). (C). 1977. pap. text ed. 21.56 (*0-201-02755-0*) Addison-Wesley.

System 370-390 Job Control Language. 3rd ed. Gary D. Brown. 480p. 1991. pap. text ed. 46.95 (*0-471-53465-X*) Wiley.

System 370-390 Job Control Language. 3rd ed. Gary D. Brown. 464p. 1991. text ed. 55.00 (*0-471-53594-X*) Wiley.

System 7 Revealed. Anthony Meadow. 1991. pap. 22.95 (*0-201-55040-7*) Addison-Wesley.

System 7.1: The Complete Sourcebook. 2nd ed. Gordon M. Campbell. LC 93-16179. (Illus.). 400p. 1993. pap. 32.95 (*0-8306-4361-3*, Windcrest) TAB Bks.

System 7.1 for Macintosh Introduction. 150p. 1993. 29.95 (*1-57533-027-X*) Comput Confidence.

System 7.5 Book: Getting the Most from Your New Macintosh Operating System. 3rd ed. Craig Danuloff. (Illus.). 736p. 1994. pap. 24.95 (*1-56604-129-5*) Ventana Communs.

System 7.5 for Macintosh Introduction. 150p. 1995. 29.95 (*1-57533-028-8*) Comput Confidence.

Systema Antialorum, Secundum Ordines, Genera, Species. J. C. Fabricius. 1970. reprint ed. 52.00 (*90-6123-060-8*) Lubrecht & Cramer.

***Systema Elementare Universae Jurisprudentiae Naturalis in Usum Praelectionum Academicarum Adornatum, Band 39.** Daniel Nettelbladt. 806p. (GER.). 1996. reprint ed. 158.00 (*3-487-10284-6*) G Olms Pubs.

System...a Glimpse of Eternity. Bob Gidel & Kathy Bostwick. (Illus.). 254p. 1983. pap. 10.95 (*0-9623887-1-8*) Andaraeon.

Systema Helminthum: Acanthocephala, Vol. 5. Satyu Yamaguti. 423p. 1985. pap. 175.00 (*0-7855-0399-4*, Pub. by Intl Bks & Periodicals II) St Mut.

Systema Helminthum: Manogenea & Aspidoeotylea, Vol. 4. Satyu Yamaguti. 699p. 1985. pap. 175.00 (*0-7855-0398-6*, Pub. by Intl Bks & Periodicals II) St Mut.

Systema Helminthum: The Cestodes of Vertebrates, Vol. 2. Satyu Yamaguti. 860p. 1985. pap. 175.00 (*0-7855-0396-X*, Pub. by Intl Bks & Periodicals II) St Mut.

Systema Helminthum: The Digenetic Trematodes of Vertebrates & the Digenetic Trematodes of Vertebrates, Vol. 1, Pts. 1-2. Satyu Yamaguti. 1575p. 1985. pap. 315.00 (*0-7855-0395-1*, Pub. by Intl Bks & Periodicals II) St Mut.

Systema Helminthum: The Nematodes of Vertebrates, Vol. 3, Pts. 1-2. Satyu Yamaguti. 1261p. 1985. pap. 300.00 (*0-7855-0397-8*, Pub. by Intl Bks & Periodicals II) St Mut.

Systema Naturae: Tomus II, Vegetabilia. 10th ed. Carl Linnaeus. 1964. reprint ed. 112.50 (*3-7682-0219-4*) Lubrecht & Cramer.

Systema Naturae 1735. Carl Linnaeus. 30p. 1964. reprint ed. text ed. 55.00 (*90-6004-104-6*, Pub. by B De Graaf NE) Coronet Bks.

Systemantics: How Systems Work and Especially How They Fail. John Gall. LC 76-50820. 1977. write for info. (*0-8129-0674-8*, Times Bks) Random.

Systemantics: The Underground Text of Systems Lore. rev. ed. John Gall. LC 86-82290. (Illus.). xxi, 319p. 1986. pap. 17.95 (*0-9618251-0-3*) General Syst Pr.

Systematic Aesthetics. Richard D. Winfield. LC 95-8153. 272p. 1995. 49.95 (*0-8130-1368-2*) U Press Fla.

Systematic Analysis in Dispute Resolution. Ed. by Stuart S. Nagel & Miriam K. Mills. LC 90-22125. 304p. 1991. text ed. 69.50 (*0-89930-623-3*, NSA, Quorum Bks) Greenwood.

Systematic Analysis of Bipolar & MOS Transistors. Ugur Cilingiroglu. LC 92-43084. (Materials Ser.). 220p. 1993. text ed. 55.00 (*0-89006-625-6*) Artech Hse.

Systematic Analysis of Surface-Active Agents. 2nd ed. Milton J. Rosen & Henry A. Goldsmith. LC 78-173678. (Chemical Analysis Ser.: Vol. 12). 617p. reprint ed. pap. 175.90 (*0-317-28059-7*, 2055772) Bks Demand.

Systematic & Applied Entomology: An Introduction. Ed. by Ian Naumann. 496p. 1994. pap. 49.95 (*0-522-84518-5*, Pub. by Melbourne Univ Pr AT) Paul & Co Pubs.

Systematic & Ecological Relationships of the Water Snakes Natrix Sipedon & N. Fasciata in Alabama & the Florida Panhandle. Terry D. Schwaner & Robert H. Mount. (Occasional Papers: No. 45). 44p. 1976. 1.00 (*0-317-04885-6*) U KS Nat Hist Mus.

***Systematic & Ethical Public Relations Campaigns.** 2nd ed. Mark McElreath. 464p. (C). 1997. per. write for info. (*0-07-114584-2*) McGraw.

Systematic & Historical Exposition of Roman Law: In the Order of a Code. 4th ed. W. A. Hunter. Tr. by Ashton Cross from LAT. 1134p. 1992. reprint ed. 105.00 (*1-56169-001-5*) Gaunt.

Systematic & Historical Exposition of Roman Law: In the Order of a Code. William A. Hunter. Tr. by J. Ashton Cross. LC 93-79715. lvi, 927p. 1994. reprint ed. 195.00 (*1-56169-073-2*) Gaunt.

Systematic Approach to Advertising Creativity. Stephen Baker. LC 78-23814. (Illus.). 288p. reprint ed. pap. 82.10 (*0-8357-3612-1*, AU00397) Bks Demand.

Systematic Approach to Digital Logic Design. Frederic J. Mowle. LC 75-18156. (Electrical Engineering Ser.). 500p. (C). 1976. text ed. write for info. (*0-201-04920-1*); teacher ed. write for info. (*0-201-04921-X*) Addison-Wesley.

Systematic Approach to Instructional Design. 2nd ed. Clifford H. Edwards. 307p. (C). 1995. pap. text ed. 18.80 (*0-87563-602-0*) Stipes.

Systematic Approach to Maintenance. (Transportation Research Record Ser.: No. 1183). 82p. 1988. 12.00 (*0-309-04723-4*) Transport Res Bd.

Systematic Approach to Mineral Identification. Betty M. James. (Illus.). 250p. (Orig.). 1996. pap. 21.95 (*0-9651286-1-X*) Petrograph.

Systematic Approach to Tsetse & TrypanOsomiasis Control. FAO Staff. (Animal Production & Health Papers: No. 121). 200p. 1995. pap. 30.00 (*92-5-003554-3*, F35543, Pub. by FAO IT) Bernan Associates.

Systematic Arrangement of Lord Coke's First Institute of the Laws of England, Set, Vols. I-III. 2nd ed. J. H. Thomas. Ed. by Bernard D. Reams, Jr. LC 86-62936. (Historical Writings in Law & Jurisprudence Ser.: No. 5A). 1986. reprint ed. 162.00 (*0-89941-519-9*, 304550) W S Hein.

Systematic Aspects of Biocompatibility, Vol. 2. Ed. by D. F. Williams. 240p. 1981. 135.00 (*0-8493-6622-4*, RA1231) CRC Pr.

Systematic Bibliography: A Practical Guide to the Work of Compilation. 4th rev. ed. Antony M. Robinson & A. L. Robinson. LC 79-40542. 135p. reprint ed. pap. 38.50 (*0-7837-5325-X*, 2045064) Bks Demand.

Systematic Botany. 4th ed. Subhash C. Datta. (C). 1988. pap. 15.00 (*81-224-0013-2*) S Asia.

Systematic Catalogue of the Soft Scale Insects (Homoptera: Coccoidea, Coccidae) of the World: With Data on Geographical Distribution, Host Plants, Biology, & Economics Importance. Yair Ben-Dov. LC 93-9502. (Flora & Fauna Handbook Ser.: No. 9). (Illus.). x, 350p. (Orig.). 1993. pap. 89.95 (*1-877743-13-5*) Sandhill Crane.

Systematic Cause Analysis Technique - SCAT. Date not set. write for info. (*0-88061-124-3*) Intl Loss Cntrl.

Systematic Cause Analysis Technique (SCAT) - Part. Date not set. write for info. (*0-88061-123-5*) Intl Loss Cntrl.

Systematic Classic of Acupuncture, MoxiBustion. 800p. 1994. 79.95 (*0-936185-29-5*) Blue Poppy Pr.

Systematic Classification of Types of Intermetallic Structures. P. I. Kripyakevich. LC 64-24936. (Illus.). 37p. reprint ed. pap. 25.00 (*0-317-09528-5*, 2020666) Bks Demand.

Systematic Classroom Observation. Paul Croll. (Social Research & Educational Studies). 220p. 1986. pap. 33.00 (*1-85000-107-3*, Falmer Pr) Taylor & Francis.

Systematic Corporate Planning. Argent. 1976. pap. 55.95 (*0-442-30741-1*) Chapman & Hall.

Systematic Data Collection. Susan C. Weller & A. Kimball Romney. (Qualitative Research Methods Ser.: Vol. 10). 96p. (C). 1988. text ed. 22.95 (*0-8039-3073-9*); pap. text ed. 9.95 (*0-8039-3074-7*) Sage.

Systematic Desensitization: Student Guide. Justin Lucian. 1976. pap. text ed. 6.95 (*0-89420-000-3*, 480011); audio 37.80 (*0-89420-186-7*, 480000) Natl Book.

Systematic Design for Instruction. 3rd ed. Walter Dick & Lou Carey. (C). 1990. pap. text ed. 42.00 (*0-673-38772-0*) Addson-Wesley Educ.

Systematic Design of Instruction. 4th ed. Walter Dick & Lou Carey. LC 95-34392. (Illus.). 416p. (C). 1996. text ed. 46.95 (*0-673-99084-2*) Addson-Wesley Educ.

Systematic Destruction of American Education. 1992. lib. bdg. 179.95 (*0-8490-5563-6*) Gordon Pr.

Systematic Destruction of American Education. 1996. lib. bdg. 250.75 (*0-8490-5939-9*) Gordon Pr.

Systematic Dictionary of English Adverbs, Vol. 3. Ed. by Collet's Holdings, Ltd. Staff. 296p. 1983. 50.00 (*0-317-42838-1*) St Mut.

Systematic Electronic Troubleshooting. James Perozzo. (Electronics Technology Ser.). 1989. pap. 36.95 (*0-8273-3288-2*) Delmar.

***Systematic Entworking for Corporate & Personal Sustainable Success.** Roger Hayes. 160p. 1997. pap. 17.95 (*0-304-33814-1*); text ed. 60.00 (*0-304-33813-3*) Cassell.

Systematic Enumeration of the Species of Calmus & Daemonorops with Diagnoses of the New Ones. O. Beccari. 230p. 1979. reprint ed. 40.00 (*0-685-54015-4*, Pub. by Intl Bk Distr II) St Mut.

Systematic Fault Diagnosis: Principles & Documentation. EEMUA Staff. (Handbook Ser.: No. 37). 1987. 100.00 (*0-317-58048-5*, Pub. by EEMUA UK) St Mut.

***Systematic Fieldwork, Vol. 1.** Oswald Werner et al. LC 85-26152. 416p. 1987. reprint ed. pap. 118.60 (*0-608-03370-7*, 2059635) Bks Demand.

***Systematic Fieldwork, Vol. 2.** Oswald Werner et al. LC 85-26152. 360p. 1987. reprint ed. pap. 102.60 (*0-608-03371-5*, 2059635) Bks Demand.

Systematic Geomorphology. Adrian E. Scheidegger. (Illus.). 300p. 1987. 73.95 (*0-387-82001-9*) Spr-Verlag.

Systematic Glossary of Selected Economics & Social Terms. Isaac Paenson. 450p. (ENG, FRE, RUS & SPA.). 1982. 175.00 (*0-8288-0153-3*, M 8172) Fr & Eur.

Systematic Glossary of Terminology of Statistical Methods: English, French, Spanish & Russian. Isaac Paenson. LC 63-10029. (ENG, FRE, RUS & SPA.). 1970. 235.00 (*0-08-012285-X*) Franklin.

Systematic Glossary of the Terminology of Statistical Methods. Isaac Paenson. 544p. (ENG, FRE, RUS & SPA.). 1982. 295.00 (*0-8288-2354-5*, M8173) Fr & Eur.

Systematic Golf: A Complete Golf Instruction Course. Mike Palmer. LC 92-38184. (Illus.). 160p. 1993. pap. 16.95 (*0-8069-0329-5*) Sterling.

Systematic Guide to the Case Law of the European Court of Human Rights, 1960-1994. Ed. by Peter Kempees. LC 94-42241. 1996. text ed. 485.00 (*0-7923-3281-4*) Kluwer Ac.

Systematic Hebrew, Pt. C. Shahar Yonay & Rina Yonay. (J). (gr. 7). 1986. 13.45 (*0-9616783-0-5*) S Yonay.

Systematic Hebrew, Pt. D. Shahar Yonay & Rina Yonay. (J). (gr. 8-9). 1987. 14.95 (*0-9616783-1-3*) S Yonay.

Systematic Hebrew, Pt. A. Shahar Yonay & Rina Yonay. (J). (gr. 5). 1988. 11.95 (*0-9616783-2-1*) S Yonay.

Systematic Hebrew, Pt. B. Shahar Yonay & Rina Yonay. (J). (gr. 6). 1988. 11.95 (*0-9616783-3-X*) S Yonay.

***Systematic Identification of Organic Compounds.** 7th ed. Ralph L. Shriner & R. C. Fuson. LC 97-5545. 1997. write for info. (*0-471-59748-1*) Wiley.

Systematic Identification of Organic Compounds: A Laboratory Manual. 6th ed. Ralph L. Shriner et al. LC 79-13365. 604p. 1980. Net. text ed. 51.00 (*0-471-78874-0*) Wiley.

***Systematic Innovation: An Introduction to the Theory of Inventive Problem Solving (TR12)** John Terninko & Alla Zusman. (Illus.). 200p. 1997. 18.95 (*1-57444-111-6*) St Lucie Pr.

***Systematic Innovation (TRIZ) Teopnr Pewehnr N30dpetatbernx 3a8ay - Theory of Inventive Problem Solving (Tips)** John Terninko. Ed. by Mary A. Kahl & Maggie Rogers. (TRIZ Ser.). (Illus.). 150p. 1996. pap. text ed. 40.00 (*1-882382-11-0*) Respons Mgmt.

Systematic Instruction in Mathematics for the Middle & High School Years see Secondary Mathematics Instruction: An Integrated Approach

Systematic Instruction in Science for the Middle & High School Years see Secondary Science Instruction: An Integrated Approach

Systematic Instruction of People with Severe Handicaps. 3rd ed. Martha E. Snell. 544p. (C). 1990. text ed. 66.00 (*0-675-20468-2*, Merrill Coll) P-H.

Systematic Intervention with Disturbed Children. Ed. by Marvin I. Fine. LC 83-21519. 275p. 1984. text ed. 37.00 (*0-88331-204-2*) Luce.

Systematic Interviewing Communication Skills for Professional Effectiveness: Communication Skills for Professional Effectiveness. John M. Dillard & Robert R. Reilley. 384p. (C). 1990. pap. text ed. 38.20 (*0-675-20824-6*, Merrill Coll) P-H.

Systematic Introduction to Expert Systems: Knowledge Representations & Problem Solving Methods. Frank Puppe. LC 93-14650. 1993. 59.00 (*0-387-56255-9*) Spr-Verlag.

Systematic Introduction to Improvisation on the Pianoforte: Opus 200. Alice Mitchell et al. Ed. by Gordon T. Anderson. LC 82-17225. (Longman Music Ser.). 128p. (C). 1983. text ed. write for info. (*0-582-28329-9*) Macmillan.

Systematic Japanese. Gene Nishi. 268p. (Orig.). 1997. pap. 16.00 (*0-87040-980-8*) Kodansha.

Systematic Litigation Planning. Stephen E. Gottlieb. LC 78-8522. 63p. reprint ed. pap. 25.00 (*0-685-16022-X*, 2056177) Bks Demand.

Systematic Maintenance Organisation. P. Priel. 1990. 40.00 (*0-7121-1926-4*, Pub. by Northcote UK) St Mut.

Systematic Management of Human Resources. Richard B. Peterson & Lane Tracy. LC 78-55826. 1979. text ed. write for info. (*0-201-05814-6*); write for info. (*0-201-05815-4*) Addison-Wesley.

Systematic Medication Profile Review. 3rd ed. Quentin M. Srnka & Timothy H. Self. 151p. (Orig.). (C). 1991. pap. 15.00 (*0-910769-26-5*) Am Coll Apothecaries.

***Systematic Methods for Chemical Process Design.** Lorenz T. Biegler et al. LC 96-52100. (C). 1997. text ed. 85.00 (*0-13-492422-3*) P-H.

***Systematic Methods of Scientific Discovery: Papers from the 1995 Spring Symposium.** Ed. by Raul Valdez-Perez. (Technical Reports). (Illus.). 130p. (Orig.). 1995. spiral bd. 25.00 (*0-929280-86-5*) AAAI Pr.

Systematic Monograph of the Tongue Soles of the Genus Cynoglossus Hamilton-Buchanan (Pisces, Cynoglossidae) A. G. Menon. LC 76-608109. (Smithsonian Contributions to Zoology Ser.: No. 238). 133p. reprint ed. pap. 38.00 (*0-317-28685-4*, 2055286) Bks Demand.

Systematic Musculoskeletal Examination: Including Manual Diagnostic Techniques. Herbert Frisch. Tr. by Terry C. Telger. LC 93-30002. 1994. 150.00 (*0-387-51782-0*) Spr-Verlag.

Systematic Musculoskeletal Examination: Including Manual Medicine Diagnostic Techniques. Herbert Frisch. Tr. by Terry C. Telger from GER. (Illus.). 505p. 1993. write for info. (*3-540-51782-0*) Spr-Verlag.

Systematic Nature of Jewish Theology: Two Examples. Heinz M. Graupe. LC 95-31547. 130p. 1995. 24.95 (*0-89733-423-X*) Academy Chi Pubs.

Systematic Nature of Jewish Theology: Two Examples. Heinz M. Graupe. LC 95-31547. 130p. 1995. pap. 14.95 (*0-89733-422-1*) Academy Chi Pubs.

Systematic New Product Development. 2nd ed. G. Douglas et al. 196p. 1983. text ed. 63.00 (*0-566-02412-8*, Pub. by Gower UK) Ashgate Pub Co.

Systematic Planning for Educational Change. William G. Cunningham. LC 81-84692. 323p. 1982. text ed. 41.95 (*0-87484-551-3*, 551) Mayfield Pub.

Systematic Positions see Handbook of Social Psychology

***Systematic Problem Solving & Decision Making.** Sandy Pokras. (Better Management Skills Ser.). 1990. pap. 12.95 (*0-7494-0159-1*) Kogan Page Ltd.

Systematic Quality Management. Gary B. Clark. 1996. 65.00 (*0-89189-312-1*) Am Soc Clinical.

Systematic Relationships of Neotropical Horned Frogs, Genus Hemiphractus: Anura: Hylidae. Linda Trueb. (Occasional Papers: No. 29). 60p. 1974. pap. 1.00 (*0-686-80386-8*) U KS Nat Hist Mus.

Systematic Relationships of the Tribe Phyllotini: Muridae: Sigmodontinae of South America. Janet K. Braun. (Illus.). 50p. (Orig.). 1993. pap. 10.00 (*1-883090-04-0*) OK Museum.

Systematic Reuse: Issues in Initiating & Improving a Reuse Program: Proceedings of the International Workshop on Systematic Reuse, Liverpool, 8-9 January 1996. Ed. by Marjan Sarshar. (BCS Software Reuse Specialist Group Ser.). 117p. 1995. pap. 59.00 (*3-540-76012-1*) Spr-Verlag.

Systematic Review of the Marsupial Frogs: Hylidae: Gastrotheca, of the Andes of Ecuador. William E. Duellman. (Occasional Papers: No. 22). 27p. 1974. pap. 1.00 (*0-686-80347-7*) U KS Nat Hist Mus.

Systematic Reviews. Ed. by Iain Chalmers & Douglas Altman. (Illus.). 128p. (Orig.). 1995. pap. text ed. 31.00 (*0-7279-0904-5*, Pub. by BMJ Pubng Grp UK) Amer Coll Phys.

Systematic Revision of Diplocentrid Scorpions (Diplocentridae) from Circum - Caribbean Lands. Oscar F. Francke. (Special Publications: No. 14). (Illus.). 92p. (Orig.). 1978. pap. 7.00 (*0-89672-062-4*) Tex Tech Univ Pr.

Systematic Revision of the Deep-Sea Subfamily Lipomerine of the Isopod Crustacean Family Munnopsidae. George D. Wilson. (Bulletin of the Scripts Institution of Oceanography Ser.). 1989. 27.50 (*0-520-09745-9*) U CA Pr.

Systematic Revision of the Genus Cybianthus Subgenus Grammadenia (Myrsinaceae) J. J. Pipoly. LC 87-11221. (Memoirs Ser.: Vol. 43). (Illus.). 76p. 1987. pap. 17.50 (*0-89327-314-7*) NY Botanical.

Systematic Safety Management in the Air Traffic Services. Richard Profit. 150p. 135.00 (*1-85564-470-3*, Pub. by Euromoney UK) Am Educ Systs.

Systematic Safety Training. Hendrick. (Occupational Safety & Health Ser.: Vol. 19). 360p. 1990. 145.00 (*0-8247-8238-0*) Dekker.

Systematic Screening for Behavior Disorders (SSBD) Observation Training Manual, 3 vols. 136p. 1992. teacher ed., pap. text ed. write for info. (*0-944584-43-8*) Sopris.

Systematic Screening for Behavior Disorders (SSBD) Program Kit, 3 vols., Kit. 2nd ed. Hill M. Walker & Herbert H. Severson. 368p. 1992. Set, kit incl. SSBD manuals, videotape, forms for screening in 25 classrooms, user's guide & adminis. teacher ed., pap. text ed. 195.00 incl. vhs (*0-944584-73-X*, 19KIT) Sopris.

Systematic Screening for Behavior Disorders (SSBD) Technical Manual. 80p. 1992. teacher ed., pap. text ed. write for info. (*0-944584-42-X*) Sopris.

Systematic Screening for Behavior Disorders (SSBD) User's Guide & Administration Manual. 152p. 1992. teacher ed., pap. text ed. write for info. (*0-944584-44-6*) Sopris.

Systematic Selling: How to Influence the Buying Decision Process. Terry A. Mort. LC 77-5937. 198p. reprint ed. pap. 56.50 (*0-317-26910-0*, 2023552) Bks Demand.

Systematic Settlements: A Practical Guide for the PI Specialist. 2nd ed. Sanford W. Hornwood & I. Lucretia Hollingsworth. LC 85-82120. 1986. 135.00 (*0-685-59910-8*) Clark Boardman Callaghan.

Systematic Significance of Leaf Structure in the Tribe Sclerieae (Cyperacae see Memoirs of the New York Botanical Garden: No. 16

Systematic Sociology: An Introduction to the Study of Society. Karl Mannheim. Ed. by J. S. Eros & W. A. Stewart. LC 83-22743. (International Library of Sociology & Social Reconstruction). xxx, 169p. 1984. reprint ed. text ed. 49.75 (*0-313-24378-6*, MASY) Greenwood.

Systematic Sociology: On the Basis of the Beziehungslehre & Gebildelehre. Leopold Von Wiese. LC 73-14186. 798p. 1974. reprint ed. 44.95 (*0-405-05532-3*) Ayer.

***Systematic Sociology (1957)** Intro. by Bryan Turner. (Karl Mannheim Ser.: Vol. 8). 1997. 105.00 (*0-415-15084-1*) Routledge.

Systematic Software Development Using VDM. 2nd ed. Bobbie Jones. 350p. 1990. pap. text ed. 47.20 (*0-13-880733-7*) P-H.

Systematic Status & Relationships of the Hylid Frog Nyctimantis Rugiceps Boulenger. William E. Duellman & Linda Trueb. (Occasional Papers: No. 58). 14p. 1976. pap. 1.00 (*0-686-80350-7*) U KS Nat Hist Mus.

Systematic Studies in Polygonaceae of Kashmir Himalaya. A. H. Munshi & G. N. Javeid. 215p. (C). 1986. 275.00 (*81-85046-32-8*, Pub. by Scientific UK) St Mut.

Systematic Studies in the Melastomataceae: Bellucia, Loreya & Macairea. Susanne S. Renner. LC 88-39155. (Memoirs Ser.: No. 50). (Illus.). 111p. 1989. pap. 24.00 (*0-89327-335-X*) NY Botanical.

S

S

Systematic Studies of Darters of the Subgenus Catonotus (Percidae), with the Description of a New Species from Caney Fork, Tennessee. Marvin E. Braasch & Lawrence M. Page. (Occasional Papers: No. 78). 10p. 1979. 1.00 (*0-317-04822-8*) U KS Nat Hist Mus.

Systematic Studies of Darters of the Subgenus Catonotus (Percidae), with the Description of a New Species from the Lower Cumberland & Tennessee River Systems. Lawrence M. Page & Marvin E. Braasch. (Occasional Papers: No. 60). 18p. 1976. pap. 1.00 (*0-686-79828-7*) U KS Nat Hist Mus.

Systematic Studies of Darters of the Subgenus Catonotus with the Description of a New Species from the Duck River System. Lawrence M. Page & Marvin E. Braasch. (Occasional Papers: No. 63). 18p. 1977. pap. 1.00 (*0-686-79827-9*) U KS Nat Hist Mus.

Systematic Studies of the Genus Pyrrhopappus (Compositae, Cichorieae) David K. Northington. (Special Publications: No. 6). 38p. 1974. pap. 2.00 (*0-89672-031-4*) Tex Tech Univ Pr.

Systematic Succession Planning: Building Leadership from Within. Rebecca L. Wolfe. LC 95-83113. (Fifty-Minute Ser.). (Illus.). 126p. (Orig.). 1996. wbk. ed., pap. 10.95 (*1-56052-380-8*) Crisp Pubns.

Systematic Supervision for Physical Education. Lynda E. Randall. LC 92-2930. (Illus.). 264p. 1992. text ed. 42.00 (*0-87322-363-2*, BRAN0363) Human Kinetics.

Systematic Survey of the Mesozoic Bivalvia from Japan. Ed. by Itaru Hayami. 249p. 1976. 52.50 (*0-86008-152-4*, Pub. by U of Tokyo JA) Col U Pr.

Systematic Survey of the Paleozoic & Mesozoic Gastropoda & Paleozoic Bivalvia from Japan. Ed. by Itaru Hayami & Tomoki Kase. 153p. 1978. 44.50 (*0-86008-198-2*, Pub. by U of Tokyo JA) Col U Pr.

Systematic Systems Approach: An Integrated Method for Solving Systems Problems. Thomas H. Athey. (Illus.). 416p. (C). 1982. text ed. 47.00 (*0-13-880914-3*) P-H.

Systematic Tabulation of Indo-European Animal Names. E. Gottlieb. (LD Ser.: No. 8). 1931. pap. 25.00 (*0-527-00754-4*) Periodicals Srv.

Systematic Teaching Strategies. James S. Cangelosi. (Orig.). (C). 1992. teacher ed. write for info. (*0-8013-0930-1*); pap. text ed. 40.95 (*0-8013-0633-7*, 79195) Longman.

***Systematic Theology.** Louis Berkhof. LC 96-32290. 989p. 1996. 45.00 (*0-8028-3820-0*) Eerdmans.

Systematic Theology, 8 vols. in 4. Lewis S. Chafer. LC 92-34956. 2864p. 1993. 150.00 (*0-8254-2340-6*) Kregel.

Systematic Theology, 3 Vols in 1. Augustus H. Strong. 1200p. 1977. 48.00 (*0-8170-0177-8*) Judson.

Systematic Theology, 3 vols. in 1. Paul Tillich. LC 51-2235. 950p. 1967. 75.00 (*0-226-80336-8*) U Ch Pr.

***Systematic Theology.** abr. ed. Charles Hodge. Ed. by Edward N. Gross. LC 97-18567. 585p. 1997. reprint ed. pap. 22.99 (*0-87552-224-6*) Presby & Reformed.

Systematic Theology. R. L. Dabney. 903p. 1996. reprint ed. 37.99 (*0-85151-453-7*) Banner of Truth.

***Systematic Theology, Vols. 1-2, Set.** James L. Garrett, Jr. 75.00 (*0-8028-2427-7*) Eerdmans.

Systematic Theology, 3 Vols, Set. Charles Hodge. 1949. 100.00 (*0-8028-8135-1*) Eerdmans.

Systematic Theology, 2 vols., Set. John Miley. 1108p. 1989. reprint ed. 39.95 (*0-943575-09-5*) Hendrickson MA.

Systematic Theology, Vol. I. James L. Garrett, Jr. 726p. (C). 1990. text ed. 35.00 (*0-8028-2425-0*) Eerdmans.

Systematic Theology, Vol. 1. Wolfhart Pannenberg. Tr. by Geoffrey W. Bromiley from GER. xiv, 460p. (C). 1991. 45.00 (*0-8028-3656-9*) Eerdmans.

Systematic Theology, Vol. 1. Paul Tillich. LC 51-2235. 312p. 1973. pap. text ed. 11.95 (*0-226-80337-6*, P556) U Ch Pr.

Systematic Theology, Vol. 2. Wolfhart Pannenberg. Tr. by Geoffrey W. Bromiley. 515p. (C). 1994. text ed. 45.00 (*0-8028-3707-7*) Eerdmans.

Systematic Theology, Vol. 2. Paul Tillich. LC 51-2235. xii, 200p. (C). 1975. pap. text ed. 10.95 (*0-226-80338-4*, P633) U Ch Pr.

Systematic Theology: A Modern Protestant Approach. Kenneth Cauthen. LC 86-23807. (Toronto Studies in Theology: Vol. 25). 520p. 1986. lib. bdg. 119.95 (*0-88946-769-2*) E Mellen.

Systematic Theology: A Pentecostal Perspective. Gary McGee. Ed. by Stanley M. Horton et al. LC 93-23568. (Logion Press Ser.). 704p. 1994. text ed. 32.95 (*0-88243-319-9*, 02-0319) Gospel Pub.

Systematic Theology: Biblical, Historical & Evangelical, Vol. 02. James L. Garrett. 1995. 45.00 (*0-8028-2426-9*) Eerdmans.

Systematic Theology: Life & the Spirit History & the Kingdom of God, Vol. 3. Paul Tillich. LC 51-2235. 446p. 1976. reprint ed. pap. text ed. 19.95 (*0-226-80339-2*, P706) U Ch Pr.

Systematic Theology: Perspectives from Liberation Theology. Ed. by Jon Sobrino & Ignacio Ellacuria. LC 95-50123. 350p. 1996. pap. 24.00 (*1-57075-068-8*) Orbis Bks.

Systematic Theology: Roman Catholic Perspectives. Ed. by Francis S. Fiorenza & John P. Galvin. Incl. Systematic Theology Vol. 1: Roman Catholic Perspectives. LC 91-678. 352p. 1991. 29.00 (*0-8006-2460-2*, 1-2460, Fortress Pr); Systematic Theology Vol. 2: Roman Catholic Perspectives. LC 91-678. 384p. 1991. 29.00 (*0-8006-2461-0*, 1-2461, Fortress Pr); 52.00 (*0-8006-2459-9*, Fortress Pr) Augsburg Fortress.

***Systematic Theology: The Triune God, Vol. 1.** Robert W. Jensen. 304p. 1997. 49.95 (*0-19-508648-1*) OUP.

***Systematic Theology of the Christian Faith.** Robert L. Reymond. LC 97-12939. 1997. 39.99 (*0-8499-1317-9*) Word Pub.

Systematic Theology, Vol. 1, Roman Catholic Perspectives see **Systematic Theology: Roman Catholic Perspectives**

Systematic Theology, Vol. 2, Roman Catholic Perspectives see **Systematic Theology: Roman Catholic Perspectives**

Systematic Thinking for Social Action. Alice M. Rivlin. LC 74-161600. 150p. 1971. 28.95 (*0-8157-7478-8*); pap. 10.95 (*0-8157-7477-X*) Brookings.

***Systematic Trading: A Reasonable Approach for Successful Trading.** Joseph B. Stowell. (Illus.). 145p. 150.00 (*1-886977-04-6*) Money Mgmt Inst.

Systematic Training for Effective Parenting Leader's Manual. rev. ed. Don Dinkmeyer, Sr. & Gary D. McKay. 1989. 38.95 (*0-88671-299-8*, 6203) Am Guidance.

Systematic Training for Effective Parenting of Teens - Step-Teen: Leader's Guide. rev. ed. Don Dinkmeyer, Sr. et al. (Systematic Training for Effective Parenting of Teens Ser.). 135p. 1990. pap. text ed. 38.95 (*0-88671-403-6*, 5752) Am Guidance.

Systematic Training for Effective Parenting Parent's Handbook. rev. ed. Gary D. McKay & Don Dinkmeyer, Sr. 1989. pap. text ed. 14.95 (*0-88671-298-X*, 6202) Am Guidance.

Systematic Training for Effective Teaching: Teacher's Handbook. Don Dinkmeyer et al. (Illus.). 291p. (Orig.). (C). 1980. pap. text ed. 26.95 (*0-913476-75-7*, 5005) Am Guidance.

Systematic Training for Effective Teaching (STET) Leader's Manual. Don Dinkmeyer, Jr. et al. 149p. 1980. vinyl bd. 42.95 (*0-913476-74-9*, 5002) Am Guidance.

Systematic Training for Effective Teaching (STET) Teacher's Resource Book: Activities for Teachers & Students. Gary D. McKay et al. (Illus.). 161p. (Orig.). (C). 1980. pap. 16.95 (*0-913476-76-5*, 5007) Am Guidance.

***Systematic Training in Skills of V. Satir.** Loeschen. LC 97-10297. (Counseling Ser.). 1998. pap. 38.95 (*0-534-23172-1*) Wadsworth Pub.

Systematic Training Program Design: Maximizing Effectiveness & Minimizing Liability. Sallie Gordon. LC 93-31031. 432p. 1994. text ed. 64.00 (*0-13-100389-5*) P-H.

Systematic Translation of Hindi-Urdu into English. Anoop Chandola. LC 79-127886. 365p. 1970. pap. 25.95 (*0-8165-0289-7*) U of Ariz Pr.

Systematic Treatment of Fruit Types. Richard W. Spjut. LC 93-6139. (Memoirs Ser.: Vol. 70). (Illus.). 181p. 1994. pap. text ed. 24.95 (*0-89327-383-X*) NY Botanical.

Systematic View of the Science of Jurisprudence. Sheldon Amos. xxii, 545p. 1982. reprint ed. lib. bdg. 39.50 (*0-8377-0210-0*) Rothman.

Systematic Vocabulary of Terminology. Rachel Boutin-Quesnel et al. 38p. (FRE.). 1985. pap. 29.95 (*0-8288-9391-8*) Fr & Eur.

Systematics. C. J. Humphries et al. 1997. pap. 39.95 (*0-632-03636-2*) Blackwell Sci.

Systematics: A New Approach to Systems Analysis. Kit Grindley. (Illus.). 1977. text ed. 13.95 (*0-89433-020-9*) Petrocelli.

Systematics: Search for Miraculous Management. Saul Kuchinsky. (Illus.). 271p. (Orig.). pap. 14.95 (*0-934254-12-5*) Claymont Comm.

Systematics & Biology of the Genus Macrocneme Hubner (Lepidoptera-Ctencuhidae) Robert E. Dietz, 4th. LC 93-49869. (Publications in Entomology: Vol. 113). 1994. pap. 22.00 (*0-520-09780-7*) U CA Pr.

Systematics & Bionomics of Anthophora: The Bomboides Group & Species Groups of the New World (Hymenoptera: Apoidea, Anthophoridae) fac. ed. Robert W. Brooks. LC 82-40445. (University of California Publications in Entomology: No. 98). (Illus.). 96p. 1983. reprint ed. pap. 27.40 (*0-7837-8128-8*, 2047935) Bks Demand.

***Systematics & Cell Structure, No. 7.** Ed. by P. A. Lemke. (Mycota: Vol. VII). Date not set. write for info. (*3-540-58008-5*) Spr-Verlag.

Systematics & Conservation Evaluation. Ed. by C. J. Humphries et al. (Systematics Association Special Ser.: Vol. 50). (Illus.). 464p. 1994. 115.00 (*0-19-857771-0*) OUP.

Systematics & Ecology of the Sea-Urchin Genus Centrostephanus: Echinodermata: Echinodea, from the Atlantic & Eastern Pacific Oceans. David L. Pawson & John E. Miller. LC 83-600054. (Smithsonian Contributions to the Marine Sciences Ser.: No. 20). 20p. reprint ed. pap. 25.00 (*0-317-29916-6*, 2021766) Bks Demand.

Systematics & Economic Botany of the Oenocarpus - Jessenia (Palmae) Complex. Michael J. Balick. LC 86-23455. (Advances in Economic Botany Ser.: Vol. 3). (Illus.). 148p. 1986. pap. 24.65 (*0-89327-311-2*) NY Botanical.

Systematics & Evolution of Cordylanthus (Scrophulariaceae-Pedicularieae) Tsan I. Chuang & Lawrence R. Heckard. Ed. by Christiane Anderson. LC 86-3546. (Systematic Botany Monographs: Vol. 10). (Illus.). 105p. 1986. pap. 13.00 (*0-912861-10-X*) Am Soc Plant.

Systematics & Evolution of Dicerandra (Labiatae) R. B. Huck. (Phanerogamarum Monographiae: Vol. 19). (Illus.). 344p. 1987. text ed. 115.00 (*3-443-78001-6*) Lubrecht & Cramer.

Systematics & Evolution of the Greater Antillean Hylid Frogs. Linda Trueb & Michael J. Tyler. (Occasional Papers: No. 24). 60p. 1974. pap. 1.00 (*0-686-80385-X*) U KS Nat Hist Mus.

Systematics & Evolution of the Ranunculiflorae. Ed. by Uwe Jensen & Joachim W. Kadereit. LC 95-464. (Plant Systematics & Evolution Ser.: Suppl. 9). 260p. 1996. 222.00 (*3-211-82721-8*) Spr-Verlag.

Systematics & Evolutionary Relationships of Spiny Pocket Mice, Genus Liomys. Hugh H. Genoways. (Special Publications: No. 5). (Illus.). 368p. (Orig.). 1973. pap. 10.00 (*0-89672-030-6*) Tex Tech Univ Pr.

Systematics & Nesting Behavior of Australian Bembix Sand Wasps - (Hymenoptera, Sphecidae) Evans & Matthews. (Memoir Ser.: No. 20). (Illus.). 1973. 45.00 (*1-56665-018-6*) Assoc Pubs FL.

Systematics & the Origin of Species. Ernst W. Mayr. Ed. by Stephen J. Gould & Niles Eldridge. LC 82-4215. (Classics in Evolution Ser.). 384p. 1982. reprint ed. pap. text ed. 24.50 (*0-231-05449-1*) Col U Pr.

Systematics & the Properties of the Lanthanides. Ed. by Shyama Sinha. 1983. lib. bdg. 230.00 (*90-277-1613-7*) Kluwer Ac.

Systematics & Zoogeography of Middle American Shrews of the Genus Cryptotis. Jerry R. Choate. (Museum Ser.: Vol. 19, No. 3). 123p. 1970. 6.25 (*0-317-04961-5*) U KS Nat Hist Mus.

Systematics, Breeding & Seed Production of Potatoes. Tr. by A. K. Dhote from RUS. 219p. (C). 1986. text ed. 55.00 (*90-6191-452-3*, Pub. by A A Balkema NE) Ashgate Pub Co.

Systematics, Ecology, & Biodiversity Crisis. Ed. by Niles Eldridge. (Illus.). 329p. 1992. text ed. 44.50 (*0-231-07528-6*) Col U Pr.

Systematics Fluid Inclusions in Diagenetic Minerals. Robert H. Goldstein & T. James Reynolds. (Short Course Notes Ser.: No. 31). (Illus.). 212p. 1994. pap. 48.00 (*1-56576-008-5*) SEPM.

Systematics, Historical Ecology, & North American Freshwater Fishes. Ed. by Richard L. Mayden. LC 92-19781. xvi, 969p. 1992. 99.50 (*0-8047-2162-9*) Stanford U Pr.

Systematics of a Species Complex in the Deep-Sea Genus Eurycope, with a Revision of Six Previously Described Species (Crustacea, Isopoda, Eurycopidae) George D. Wilson. LC 83-5917. (Bulletin of the Scripps Institution of Oceanography, University of California, San Diego Ser.: No. 25). 72p. 1982. pap. 25.00 (*0-7837-8435-X*, 2049237) Bks Demand.

Systematics of Acmella (Asteraceae-Heliantheae) Robert K. Jansen. Ed. by Christiane Anderson. LC 85-15844. (Systematic Botany Monographs: Vol. 8). (Illus.). 115p. (Orig.). 1985. pap. 13.00 (*0-912861-08-8*) Am Soc Plant.

Systematics of Antirrhinum (Scrophulariaceae) in the New World. David M. Thompson. Ed. by Christiane Anderson. (Systematic Botany Monographs: Vol. 22). (Illus.). 142p. (Orig.). 1988. pap. 17.00 (*0-912861-22-3*) Am Soc Plant.

Systematics of Bees of the Genus Eufriesea (Hymenoptera, Apidae) Lynn S. Kimsey. LC 81-7400. (University of California Publications in Entomology: No. 95). 137p. 1982. pap. 39.10 (*0-7837-7488-5*, 2049210) Bks Demand.

Systematics of Chusquea Section Swallenochloa, Section Verticillatae, Section Serpentes, & Section Longifoliae (Poaceae-Bambusoideae) Lynn G. Clark. Ed. by Christiane Anderson. (Systematic Botany Monographs: Vol. 27). (Illus.). 127p. (Orig.). 1989. pap. 15.00 (*0-912861-27-4*) Am Soc Plant.

Systematics of Clermontia (Campanulaceae- Lobelioideae) Thomas G. Lammers. Ed. by Christiane Anderson. (Systematic Botany Monographs: Vol. 32). (Illus.). 97p. 1991. Smyth-sewn, acid-free paper. pap. 13.00 (*0-912861-32-0*) Am Soc Plant.

Systematics of Columnea Section Pentadenia & Section Stygnanthe (Gesneriaceae) Vol. 44. James F. Smith. Ed. by Christiane Anderson. (Systematic Botany Monographs). (Illus.). 89p. 1994. pap. 11.00 (*0-912861-44-4*) Am Soc Plant.

Systematics of Coursetia (Leguminosae-Papilionoideae) Matt Lavin. Ed. by Christiane Anderson. (Systematic Botany Monographs: Vol. 21). (Illus.). 167p. 1988. pap. 20.00 (*0-912861-21-5*) Am Soc Plant.

Systematics of Cryosophila (Palmae) Randall J. Evans. Ed. by Christiane Anderson. (Systematic Botany Monographs: Vol. 46). (Illus.). 70p. 1995. pap. 9.00 (*0-912861-46-0*) Am Soc Plant.

Systematics of Epilobium (Onagraceae) in China. Chia-jui Chen et al. Ed. by Christiane Anderson. (Systematic Botany Monographs: Vol. 34). (Illus.). 209p. 1992. pap. 25.00 (*0-912861-34-7*) Am Soc Plant.

***Systematics of Erisma (Vochysiaceae)** Maria L. Kawasaki. LC 97-24319. (Memoirs of the New York Botanical Garden Ser.). 1997. write for info. (*0-89327-417-8*) NY Botanical.

Systematics of Frankenia (Frankeniaceae) in North & South America. M. A. Whalen. Ed. by Christiane Anderson. (Systematic Botany Monographs: Vol. 17). (Illus.). (Orig.). 1987. pap. 11.00 (*0-912861-17-7*) Am Soc Plant.

Systematics of Middle American Mastiff Bats of the Genus Molossus. Patricia G. Dolan. (Special Publications: No. 29). (C). 1989. pap. 12.00 (*0-89672-203-1*) Tex Tech Univ Pr.

Systematics of Montanoa (Asteraceae-Heliantheae) Vicki Ann Funk. LC 82-7878. (Memoirs Ser.: Vol. 36). (Illus.). 133p. 1982. pap. 10.00 (*0-89327-243-4*) NY Botanical.

Systematics of Nearctic Telenomus: Classification & Revisions of the Podisi & Phymatae Species Groups (Hymenopetra Scelionidae) Norman F. Johnson. Ed. by Veda M. Cafazzo & Karen J. Reese. (Bulletin New Ser.: Vol. 6, No. 3). 113p. 1984. 10.00 (*0-86727-094-2*) Ohio Bio Survey.

Systematics of North American Daphnia. John L. Brooks. (Connecticut Academy of Arts & Sciences Ser., Trans.: Vol. 13). 1957. pap. 100.00 (*0-685-22858-4*) Elliots Bks.

***Systematics of Oenothera Section Oenothera Subsection Oenothera (Onagraceae)** Werner Dietrich et al. Ed. by Christiane Anderson. (Illus.). 234p. 1997. 30.00 (*0-912861-50-9*) Am Soc Plant.

Systematics of Oenothera Section Oenothera Subsection Raimannia & Subsection Nutantigemma (Onagraceae) Werner Dietrich & Warren L. Wagner. Ed. by Christiane Anderson. (Systematic Botany Monographs: Vol. 24). (Illus.). 91p. (Orig.). 1988. pap. 10.50 (*0-912861-24-X*) Am Soc Plant.

Systematics of Oropogon (Alectoriaceae) in the New World. Theodore L. Esslinger. Ed. by Christiane Anderson. (Systematic Botany Monographs: Vol. 28). (Illus.). 111p. (Orig.). 1989. pap. 13.50 (*0-912861-28-2*) Am Soc Plant.

Systematics of Pappobolus (Asteraceae- Heliantheae) Jose L. Panero. Ed. by Christiane Anderson. (Systematic Botany Monographs: Vol. 36). (Illus.). 195p. 1993. pap. 25.00 (*0-912861-36-3*) Am Soc Plant.

Systematics of Polystichum in Western North America North of Mexico. David H. Wagner. LC 79-14584. (Pteridologia Ser.: No. 1). (Illus.). 64p. 1979. pap. 10.00 (*0-933500-00-9*) Am Fern Soc.

Systematics of Rhynchospora Section Dichromena. W. W. Thomas. LC 84-4872. (Memoirs Ser.: Vol. 37). (Illus.). 116p. 1984. pap. 21.00 (*0-89327-251-5*) NY Botanical.

Systematics of Serjania (Sapindaceae), Pt. I. Pedro Acevedo-Rodriquez. LC 92-18033. (Memoirs Ser.: Vol. 67). 96p. 1993. pap. 15.50 (*0-89327-377-5*) NY Botanical.

Systematics of Simple Sulfide Structures. rev. ed. Tibor Zoltai. 93p. 1974. pap. 4.50 (*0-686-47229-2*) Polycrystal Bk Serv.

Systematics of Simsia (Compositae-Heliantheae) David M. Spooner. Ed. by Christiane Anderson. (Systematic Botany Monographs: Vol. 30). (Illus.). 90p. 1990. pap. 11.00 (*0-912861-30-4*) Am Soc Plant.

Systematics of Smaller Asian Night Birds Based on Voice. Joe T. Marshall. 58p. 1978. 7.00 (*0-943610-25-7*) Am Ornithologists.

Systematics of Tetramerium (Acanthaceae) Thomas F. Daniel. Ed. by Christiane Anderson. LC 86-10852. (Systematic Botany Monographs: Vol. 12). (Illus.). 134p. 1986. pap. 16.50 (*0-912861-12-6*) Am Soc Plant.

Systematics of the Acutae Group of Carex (Cyperaceae) in the Pacific Northwest. Lisa A. Standley. Ed. by Christiane Anderson. LC 85-9024. (Systematic Botany Monographs: Vol. 7). (Illus.). 106p. (Orig.). 1985. pap. 13.00 (*0-912861-07-X*) Am Soc Plant.

Systematics of the Annual Species of Muhlenbergia (Poaceae-Eragrostideae) Paul M. Peterson & Carol R. Annable. Ed. by Christiane Anderson. (Systematic Botany Monographs: Vol. 31). (Illus.). 109p. 1991. pap. 13.50 (*0-912861-31-2*) Am Soc Plant.

Systematics of the Chrysoxena Group of Genera: Lepidoptera, Tortricidae, Euliini. John W. Brown & Jerry A. Powell. (Publications in Entomology: Vol. 111). (C). 1992. pap. 17.00 (*0-520-09765-3*) U CA Pr.

Systematics of the Colletidae Based on Mature Larvae with Phenetic Analysis of Apoid Larvae (Hymenoptera, Apoidea) Ronald J. McGinley. LC 80-15362. (University of California Publications in Social Welfare: No. 91). (Illus.). 333p. reprint ed. pap. 95.00 (*0-685-24002-9*, 2031587) Bks Demand.

***Systematics of the Fig Wasp Parasites of the Genus Apocrypta Coquerel.** S. A. Ulenberg. (Verhandelingen der Koninklijke Nederlandse Akademie van Wetenschappen, Afd. Natuurkunde Ser.: No. 83). 176p. 1985. pap. text ed. 50.00 (*0-444-85630-7*) Elsevier.

Systematics of the Genus Didelphis: Marsupialia: Didelphidae in North & Middle America. Alfred L. Gardner. (Special Publications: No. 4). (Illus.). 81p. (Orig.). 1973. pap. 4.00 (*0-89672-029-2*) Tex Tech Univ Pr.

Systematics of the Legume Genus Harpalyce: Leguminosae. Lotoideae. Thomas S. Elias. Incl. Monographs of the Genus Hamelia: Rubiaceae. LC 66-6394. 1976. (*0-318-54703-1*); LC 66-6394. (Memoirs Ser.: Vol. 26, No. 4). (Illus.). 144p. 1976. pap. 16.00 (*0-89327-001-6*) NY Botanical.

Systematics of the Neotropical Characiform Genus Potamorhina. Richard P. Vari. LC 84-1398. (Smithsonian Contributions to Zoology Ser.: No. 400). 40p. reprint ed. pap. 25.00 (*0-317-26576-8*, 2023958) Bks Demand.

Systematics of the Neotropical Characiform Genus Steindachnerina Fowler: Pisces: Ostariophysi. Richard P. Vari. LC 90-26412. (Smithsonian Contributions to Zoology Ser.: No. 507). (Illus.). 122p. reprint ed. pap. 34.80 (*0-7837-0544-1*, 2040872) Bks Demand.

Systematics of the Neotropical Characiform Genus Curimata Bosc: Pisces: Characiformes. Richard P. Vari. LC 89-600023. (Smithsonian Contributions to Zoology Ser.: No. 474). (Illus.). 67p. reprint ed. pap. 25.00 (*0-8357-6440-0*, 2035811) Bks Demand.

Systematics of the Neotropical Characiform Genus Cyphocharax Fowler: Pisces: Ostariophysi. Richard P. Vari. LC 91-45327. (Smithsonian Contributions to Zoology Ser.: No. 529). (Illus.). 141p. reprint ed. pap. 40.20 (*0-7837-3404-2*, 2043364) Bks Demand.

Systematics of the Neotropical Species of Thelyoteris Section Cyclosorus. Alan R. Smith. LC 70-635327. (University of California Publications in Social Welfare: Vol. 59). (Illus.). 151p. reprint ed. pap. 43.10 (*0-685-23660-9*, 2014702) Bks Demand.

Systematics of the New World Species of Marsilea (Marsileaceae) David M. Johnson. Ed. by Christiane Anderson. LC 86-7949. (Systematic Botany Monographs: Vol. 11). (Illus.). 87p. 1986. pap. 10.00 (*0-912861-11-8*) Am Soc Plant.

An Asterisk (*) at the beginning of an entry indicates that the title is appearing in BIP for the first time.

Systematics of the Onocleoid Ferns. Robert M. Lloyd. LC 72-170330. (University of California Publications in Social Welfare: Vol. 61). (Illus.). 99p. reprint ed. pap. 28.30 (0-685-23659-5, 2014704) Bks Demand.

Systematics of the Trans-Andean Species of Creagrutus: Ostariophysi: Characiformes: Characidae. Antony S. Harold & Richard P. Vari. LC 93-48088. (Smithsonian Contributions to Zoology Ser.: No. 551). (Illus.). 35p. reprint ed. pap. 25.00 (0-7837-7049-9, 2046860) Bks Demand.

Systematics of Three Species of Woodrats (Genus Neotom) in Central North America. Elmer C. Birney. (Miscellaneous Publications: No. 58). 173p. 1973. 9.00 (0-317-04956-9) U KS Nat Hist Mus.

Systematics of Timonius subgenus Abbottia Vol. 42: (Rubiaceae-Guettardeae) Steven P. Darwin. Ed. by Christiane Anderson. (Systematic Botany Monographs). (Illus.). 86p. 1994. pap. 11.00 (0-912861-42-8) Am Soc Plant.

Systematics of Tuberous Lomatiums (Umbelliferae) Mark A. Schlessman. Ed. by Christiane Anderson. LC 84-6399. (Systematic Botany Monographs: Vol. 4). (Illus.). 55p. (Orig.). 1984. pap. 8.50 (0-912861-04-5) Am Soc Plant.

Systematische Grammatikvermittlung und Spracharbeit: Im Deutschunterrichtfur Auslandische Jugendliche. Herrad Von Meese. 223p. 1984. 24.50 (3-468-49431-9) Langenscheidt.

Systematische Schachtraining. Sergiu Samarian. (Illus.). 152p. (GER.). 1992. write for info. (3-283-00313-0) G Olms Pubs.

Systematischer Katalog der Deutschen Staatsbibliothek Berlin, Bis 1955. 1991. write for info. incl. fiche (0-318-71810-3) G Olms Pubs.

Systematischer Katalog der Kartenabteilung in der Deutschen Staatsbibliothek Berlin Bis 1945. 1991. write for info. incl. fiche (0-318-71811-1) G Olms Pubs.

Systematiscshes Verzeichnis der Abhandlungen in den Schulschriften, 5 vols. in 3, Set. Rudolf Klussmann. xxxix, 1873p. 1976. reprint ed. write for info. (3-487-05848-0) G Olms Pubs.

Systematisierung von Infusionsloesungen und Grundlagen der Infusionstherapie. I. W. Hahnefeld. (Beitraege zur Infusionstherapie und Klinische Ernaehrung Ser.: Band 5). (Illus.). 112p. 1980. pap. 17.00 (3-8055-1395-X) S Karger.

Systematization of Radiotherapy & the Techniques of Irradiating Cancer Patients, Vol. 3. M. Sh. Weinberg. (Soviet Medical Reviews Ser.: Vol. 3, No. 1). 68, ivp. 1989. pap. text ed. 56.00 (3-7186-4915-2) Gordon & Breach.

Systematization of Russian Government: Social Evolution in the Domestic Administration of Imperial Russia, 1711-1905. fac. ed. George L. Yaney. LC 72-85613. 446p. 1973. reprint ed. pap. 127.20 (0-7837-8066-4, 2047819) Bks Demand.

Systematized Abbreviation-Related Dermatopathology Software (SARDS) Reference Manual. Spencer D. Albright, III. 1989. Basic Version. write for info. incl. disk (0-318-65958-1); Advanced Version. write for info. incl. disk (0-318-65959-X) S Albright.

Systematized Prevention of Oral Disease: Theory & Practice. Lars Granath & William D. McHugh. 288p. 1986. 142.00 (0-8493-5163-4, RK60, CRC Reprint) Franklin.

Systeme D 2.0. James S. Noblitt. (College Spanish Ser.). 1991. teacher ed., pap. 19.95 (0-8384-2630-1) Heinle & Heinle.

Systeme de la Nature ou des Lois du Monde Physique et Du Monde Moral, 2 vols., Set. Paul H. D'Holbach. xl, 1009p. 1974. reprint ed. 225.00 (3-487-05377-2) G Olms Pubs.

Systeme de l'Agression. Marquis de Sade. 256p. (FRE.). 1972. pap. 20.95 (0-7859-5479-1) Fr & Eur.

Systeme der kumulativen Logik. J. Wolfgang Degen. (Analytica Ser.). 265p. (GER.). 1984. 92.00 (3-88405-038-9) Philosophia Pr.

Systeme des Residences D'Hiver et D'Ete Chez les Nomades et les Chefs Hongrois au Xe Siecle. Gy Gyorffy. v, 111p. (Orig.). (FRE.). (C). 1976. pap. text ed. 26.95 (3-11-013298-2) Mouton.

***Systeme Micro-Informatique pour la Formation & l'Aide a la Planification Agricole: Description Technique.** 181p. (FRE.). 1987. 30.00 (92-5-202609-6, Pub. by FAO IT) Bernan Associates.

Systeme Palatial en Orient, en Grece et a Rome: Acts du Colloqie de Strasbourg, 19-22 Juin 1985. Ed. by E. Levy. (Travaux du Centre de Recherche sur le Proche Orient et la Grece Antiques Ser.: Vol. 9). (Illus.). 502p. 1987. pap. 114.00 (90-04-08520-3) E J Brill.

Systeme Social, 3 vols. in 1. Paul H. D'Holbach. viii, 558p. 1969. reprint ed. 130.00 (0-318-71353-5) G Olms Pubs.

Systeme Social Oder Naturliche Principien der Moral und der Politik. Paul-Henri T. D'Holbach. xi, 552p. 1969. reprint ed. 130.00 (0-318-71461-2) G Olms Pubs.

***Systementwurf einer Management-Erfolgsrechnung als Instrument des Controlling: Am Beispiel einer Gemeinnutzigen Non-Profit-Organisation fur Praventiv- und Sozialmedizin.** Kurt Zischg. (Europaische Hochschulschriften: Reihe 5: Bd. 1822). 235p. (GER.). 1996. pap. 44.95 (3-631-49529-3) P Lang Pubng.

Systemes de la Mode. Roland Barthes. (FRE.). 1983. pap. 18.95 (0-7859-0669-X, F13020) Fr & Eur.

***Systemes de Suivi pour le Developpement Agricole Annexe 1: Le Systeme de Suivi des Effets de l'Office de Mise en Valeur Agricole du Loukos (Maroc)** 91p. (FRE.). 1987. 12.00 (92-5-201229-X, Pub. by FAO IT) Bernan Associates.

Systemes des Equations Differentielles, 3 Vols. in 1. J. A. Lappo-Danilevskii. LC 53-7110. 35.00 (0-8284-0094-6) Chelsea Pub.

Systemes Echantillonnes Nonlineaires-Exercises et Problemes. P. Vidal. (Theorie des Systemes Ser.). 114p. (FRE.). 1969. text ed. 161.00 (0-677-50500-0) Gordon & Breach.

Systemic Analysis of Judaism. Jacob Neusner. LC 87-32401. (Brown Judaic Studies). 144p. 1988. 30.95 (1-55540-204-6, 14-01-37) Scholars Pr GA.

Systemic Approach to Consultation. David Campbell. 102p. 1992. pap. text ed. 21.95 (1-85575-073-2, Pub. by Karnac Bks UK) Brunner-Mazel.

Systemic Approaches to Training in Child Protection. Gerrilyn Smith. (Systemic Thinking & Practice Ser.). 120p. 1993. pap. text ed. 24.95 (1-85575-019-8, Pub. by Karnac Bks UK) Brunner-Mazel.

Systemic Autoimmunity. Ed. by Bigazzi & Seymour Reichlin. (Immunology Ser.: Vol. 54). 320p. 1991. 180.00 (0-8247-8550-9) Dekker.

Systemic Behavioral Approach: A Behavioral-Systemic Approach. Ed. by Joan Atwood. (Social Welfare Ser.). 400p. (C). 1992. pap. text ed. 29.95 (0-8304-1300-6) Nelson-Hall.

Systemic Cardiac Embolism. Ed. by Michael D. Ezekowitz. LC 93-37225. (Fundamental & Clinical Cardiology Ser.: Vol. 18). 424p. 1993. 150.00 (0-8247-9151-7) Dekker.

Systemic Change: Touchstones for the Future School. Ed. by Patrick M. Jenlink. LC 95-79278. (Illus.). 304p. (Orig.). 1995. pap. 39.95 (0-932935-63-X, 1344) IRI-SkyLght.

Systemic Change & Stabilization in Eastern Europe. Laszlo Csaba. 152p. 1991. 55.95 (1-85521-204-8, Pub. by Dartmth Pub UK) Ashgate Pub Co.

Systemic Change in Education. Ed. by Charles M. Reigeluth & Robert J. Garfinkle. LC 93-36654. 184p. 1994. 34.95 (0-87778-271-7) Educ Tech Pubns.

Systemic Competitiveness: New Governance Patterns for Industrial Development. Klaus Esser et al. LC 96-440. (GDI Book Ser.: No. 7). 172p. (Orig.). 1996. pap. 22.50 (0-7146-4251-7, Pub. by F Cass Pubs UK) Intl Spec Bk.

Systemic Crisis: Problems in Society, Politics, & World Order. William D. Perdue. (Illus.). 550p. (C). 1993. pap. text ed. 26.75 (0-03-055347-4) HB Coll Pubs.

Systemic Disease & the Nasal Airway. Ed. by Thomas V. McCaffrey. LC 92-49198. (Rhinology & Sinusology Ser.). 1993. 55.00 (0-86577-466-8) Thieme Med Pubs.

Systemic Diseases, Part I see Handbook of Clinical Neurology

Systemic Drugs for Skin Diseases. Wolverton & Wilkin. 400p. 1991. pap. text ed. 67.00 (0-7216-2987-3) Saunders.

Systemic Functional Approaches to Discourse: Selected Papers from the 12th International Systemic Workshop. Ed. by James D. Benson et al. LC 87-31461. (Advances in Discourse Processes Ser.: Vol. 26). 384p. 1988. text ed. 78.50 (0-89391-403-7) Ablex Pub.

***Systemic Functional Grammar in Natural Language Generation: Linguistic Description & Computational Representation.** Elke Teich. LC 97-2549. (Communication in Artificial Intelligence Ser.). 1997. write for info. (0-304-70168-8) Cassell.

Systemic Group Therapy: A Triadic Model. Jeremiah Donigian & Richard Malnati. LC 96-17211. (Counseling Ser.). 115p. (C). 1997. pap. text ed. 15.95 (0-534-34518-2) Brooks-Cole.

Systemic Harpoon into Family Games: Preventive Interventions in Therapy. Giuliana Prata. LC 90-2157. 192p. 1990. text ed. 32.95 (0-87630-591-5) Brunner-Mazel.

Systemic Hormones, Neurotransmitters & Brain Development. Ed. by G. Doerner & S. M. McCann. (Monographs in Neural Sciences: Vol. 12). (Illus.). x, 222p. 1986. 158.50 (3-8055-4287-9) S Karger.

Systemic Ichthyology: A Collection of Readings. Ed. by David Greenfield. 1972. 39.50 (0-8422-5024-7); pap. text ed. 24.95 (0-8290-0674-5) Irvington.

Systemic Lupus Erythematosus. Ed. by Peter A. Miescher. LC 95-1128. 240p. 1995. 92.00 (0-387-59039-0) Spr-Verlag.

Systemic Lupus Erythematosus. 2nd ed. Robert G. Lahita. (Illus.). 1002p. 1992. text ed. 179.00 (0-443-08785-7) Churchill.

Systemic Lupus Erythematosus. Ed. by Robert G. Lahita. LC 86-11007. (Illus.). 1024p. reprint ed. pap. 180.00 (0-7837-2586-8, 2042748) Bks Demand.

Systemic Lupus Erythematosus. Marian W. Ropes. LC 75-31988. 179p. reprint ed. pap. 51.10 (0-7837-6089-2, 2059135) Bks Demand.

Systemic Lupus Erythematosus: Clinical & Theoretical Aspects. Julian L. Verbov et al. (Illus.). 220p. (C). 1973. text ed. 26.00 (0-8422-7104-X) Irvington.

Systemic Lupus Erythematosus: Renal Vasculitis. Adalberto Sessa. LC 92-23672. (Contributions to Nephrology Ser.: Vol. 99). (Illus.). viii, 152p. 1992. 128.75 (3-8055-5603-9) S Karger.

Systemic Ocular Assessment. Anastas F. Pass. (Illus.). 256p. 1997. text ed. 50.00 (0-7506-9566-8) Buttrwrth-Heinemann.

Systemic Pathology of Fish: A Text & Atlas of Comparative Tissue Responses in Diseases of Teleosts. Hugh W. Ferguson. LC 88-13739. (Illus.). 274p. (C). 1989. text ed. 69.95 (0-8138-0147-8) Iowa St U Pr.

Systemic Pathology, Vol. 1: Nose, Throat & Ears. 3rd ed. Ed. by I. Friedmann. (Illus.). 416p. 1986. text ed. write for info. (0-443-03097-9) Churchill.

Systemic Pathology, Vol. 2: Blood & Bone Marrow. 3rd ed. Ed. by S. N. Wickramasinghe. (Illus.). 490p. 1986. text ed. 159.00 (0-443-03099-5) Churchill.

Systemic Perspectives on Discourse, Vol. 1. Ed. by James Benson et al. LC 84-28466. (Advances in Discourse Processes Ser.: Vol. 15). 400p. 1985. text ed. 78.50 (0-89391-193-3) Ablex Pub.

Systemic Perspectives on Discourse, Vol. 2. James Benson & William Greaves. Ed. by Roy O. Freedle. LC 84-28466. (Advances in Discourse Processes Ser.: Vol. 16). 308p. 1985. text ed. 78.50 (0-89391-202-6) Ablex Pub.

Systemic Psychotherapy with Families, Couples, & Individuals. Guido L. Burbatti et al. LC 92-9280. 224p. 1993. 35.00 (0-87668-390-1) Aronson.

Systemic Radiotherapy with Monoclonal Antibodies: Options & Problems. Ed. by H. Bihl & M. Wannenmacher. (Recent Results in Cancer Research Ser.: Vol. 141). 192p. 1996. 135.00 (3-540-60209-7) Spr-Verlag.

Systemic Reform: Perspectives on Personalizing Education. 1996. lib. bdg. 250.95 (0-8490-6916-5) Gordon Pr.

Systemic Religious Education. Timothy A. Lines. LC 86-20383. 264p. (Orig.). 1987. pap. 18.95 (0-89135-057-8) Religious Educ.

Systemic Sclerosis. Ed. by Philip J. Clements & Daniel E. Furst. LC 95-15204. 657p. 1995. 125.00 (0-683-01740-3) Williams & Wilkins.

Systemic Sclerosis: Scleroderma. Ed. by Malcolm I. Jayson & Carol M. Black. LC 87-37122. 362p. 1988. reprint ed. pap. 103.20 (0-608-01631-4, 2062216) Bks Demand.

Systemic Sclerosis, Scleroderma. Ed. by Malcolm I. Jayson & Carol M. Black. 362p. 1988. text ed. 275.00 (0-471-90846-0) Wiley.

Systemic Shock. Dean Ing. 320p. 1992. mass mkt. 4.99 (0-8125-0038-5) Tor Bks.

Systemic Sociology. Ramkrishna Mukherjee. (Illus.). 256p. (C). 1993. text ed. 26.00 (0-8039-9126-6) Sage.

Systemic Text Generation As Problem Solving. Terry Patten. (Studies in Natural Language Processing). (Illus.). 275p. 1988. text ed. 49.95 (0-521-35076-X) Cambridge U Pr.

Systemic Therapist, Vol. I. Ed. by Bradford P. Keeney et al. 137p. (Orig.). 1990. pap. text ed. 18.00 (0-9626461-1-3) Systemic Therapy.

Systemic Therapist, Vol. II. Ed. by Bradford P. Keeney. (Orig.). 1991. pap. text ed. 18.00 (0-9626461-2-1) Systemic Therapy.

Systemic Treatment of Families Who Abuse. Eliana Gil. LC 95-18734. (Psychology Ser.). 263p. 27.95 (0-7879-0153-9) Jossey-Bass.

Systemic Treatment of Incest: A Therapeutic Handbook. Terry S. Trepper & Mary J. Barrett. LC 89-9739. (Psychosocial Stress Ser.: No. 15). 304p. 1989. text ed. 32.95 (0-87630-560-5) Brunner-Mazel.

Systemic Treatment Selection: Toward Targeted Therapeutic Interventions. Larry E. Beutler & John F. Clarkin. LC 89-71203. (Integrative Psychotherapy Ser.: No. 3). 384p. 1990. text ed. 49.95 (0-87630-576-1) Brunner-Mazel.

Systemic Vasculitides. Jacob Churg. Ed. by Andrew Churg. LC 90-15649. (Illus.). 408p. 1991. 192.50 (0-89640-195-2) Igaku-Shoin.

Systemic Vasculitis: The Biological Basis. Leroy. (Inflammatory Disease & Therapy Ser.: Vol. 11). 600p. 1992. 210.00 (0-8247-8650-5) Dekker.

***Systemic Violence: How Schools Hurt Children.** Ed. by Juanita R. Epp. 192p. 1996. 69.95 (0-7507-0581-7, Falmer Pr); pap. 24.95 (0-7507-0582-5, Falmer Pr) Taylor & Francis.

Systemic Violence in Education: Promise Broken. Ed. by Juanita R. Epp & Ailsa M. Watkinson. LC 96-36301. (SUNY Series, Education & Culture). 220p. (C). 1997. text ed. 54.50 (0-7914-3295-5); pap. text ed. 17.95 (0-7914-3296-3) State U NY Pr.

Systemic Work with Organizations: A New Model for Managers & Change Agents. Ed. by David Campbell et al. (Karnac Bks.). 206p. 1995. pap. text ed. 32.95 (1-85575-100-3, Pub. by Karnac Bks UK) Brunner-Mazel.

***Systemische Organisationsentwicklung: Eine Evolutionare Strategie fur Kleine und Mittlere Organisationen 3, Korrigierte Auflage.** Walter Hafele. (Europaische Hochschulschriften: Reihe 5: Bd. 1087). 229p. (GER.). 1996. 43.95 (3-631-30320-3) P Lang Pubng.

Systemology & Linguistic Aspects of Cybernetics, Vol. 16. G. P. Melnikov. (Studies in Cybernetics: Vol. 16). 440p. 1988. text ed. 435.00 (2-88124-665-6) Gordon & Breach.

***Systems: A Look at Criminal Justice.** 7th ed. George F. Cole. 1998. pap. text ed. 25.95 (0-534-52708-6) Wadsworth Pub.

Systems: Approaches, Theories, Applications. Ed. by William E. Hartnett. (Epistome Ser.: No. 3). 215p. 1977. lib. bdg. 112.00 (90-277-0822-3, D Reidel) Kluwer Ac.

Systems: Concepts, Methodologies, & Applications. 2nd ed. Brian Wilson. LC 90-12021. 391p. 1990. text ed. 75.00 (0-471-92716-3) Wiley.

Systems: Decomposition, Optimisation & Control. Madan G. Singh & Andre Titli. 1978. text ed. 291.00 (0-08-022150-5, Pub. by Pergamon Repr UK) Franklin.

Systems: How They Work & How They Fail. 1991. lib. bdg. 79.95 (0-8490-4638-6) Gordon Pr.

Systems - Agriculture, Pollution, & Politics: How They Interact Within the Chesapeake Bay. CGS Staff. 192p. (C). 1996. pap. text ed. 26.25 (0-7872-2518-5) Kendall-Hunt.

Systems Analysis. 1996. lib. bdg. 250.75 (0-8490-5946-1) Gordon Pr.

Systems Analysis: How to Establish Quality of a New Product from Inception to Design Planning. Ronald W. Cutburth. Ed. by Rebecca Rodolff. (Illus.). 100p. 1994. ring bd. 12.00 (1-878291-25-4) Love From Sea.

Systems Analysis & Design. H. L. Capron. (Illus.). 525p. (C). 1986. text ed. 44.25 (0-8053-2241-8); pap. text ed. 11.95 (0-8053-2243-4); student ed. 11.95 (0-8053-2242-6) Benjamin-Cummings.

Systems Analysis & Design. Perry Edwards. 1993. pap. text ed. write for info. (0-07-019573-0) McGraw.

Systems Analysis & Design. Michael L. Gibson. (DC - Introduction to Computing Ser.). 1995. student ed., pap. 18.95 (0-87709-545-0) S-W Pub.

Systems Analysis & Design. Harris. (C). 1995. teacher ed., pap. text ed. 52.00 (0-03-011614-7) HB Coll Pubs.

Systems Analysis & Design. David Harris. (C). 1994. teacher ed., pap. text ed. 38.00 (0-03-011617-1) HB Coll Pubs.

***Systems Analysis & Design.** David Harris. 252p. (C). 1994. pap. text ed. 21.00 (0-03-011618-X) HB Coll Pubs.

Systems Analysis & Design. Margaret S. Wu & Shih-Yen Wu. Ed. by Szilagyi. LC 93-38908. 600p. (C). 1994. text ed. 63.75 (0-314-02702-5) West Pub.

Systems Analysis & Design. Don Yeates et al. 464p. (Orig.). 1994. pap. 57.50 (0-273-60066-4, Pub. by Pitman Pub Ltd UK) Trans-Atl Phila.

Systems Analysis & Design. 2nd ed. Elias M. Awad. 544p. (C). 1985. text ed. 60.95 (0-256-02824-9) Irwin.

Systems Analysis & Design. 2nd ed. Gary B. Shelly. 1995. pap. 42.00 (0-87709-631-7) Course Tech.

Systems Analysis & Design. 3rd ed. Kendall. 928p. 1994. text ed. 86.00 (0-13-436692-1) P-H.

Systems Analysis & Design. 3rd ed. Kenneth E. Kendall & Julie E. Kendall. LC 94-30969. 1996. text ed. 82.21 (0-13-148883-X) P-H.

S

***Systems Analysis & Design, Incl. VAW for DOS & instr. manual, transparency.** Gary B. Shelly et al. 640p. 1995. text ed. write for info. (0-7895-0144-9) Course Tech.

***Systems Analysis & Design, Incl. VAW for Windows, instr. manual, transparency.** 2nd ed. Gary B. Shelly et al. 640p. 1995. text ed. write for info. (0-7895-0143-0) Course Tech.

Systems Analysis & Design: A Case Study Approach. 2nd ed. Robert J. Thierauf. 512p. (C). 1986. write for info. (0-675-20229-9, Merrill Coll) P-H.

Systems Analysis & Design: A Comprehensive Methodology with CASE. Michael L. Gibson & Cary T. Hughes. LC 93-39103. 808p. 1994. text ed. 58.95 (0-87709-247-8) Course Tech.

Systems Analysis & Design: A Structured Approach. William S. Davis. 432p. (C). 1983. teacher ed. write for info. (0-201-10272-2); text ed. 33.50 (0-201-10271-4) Addison-Wesley.

Systems Analysis & Design: A Systematic View. 2nd ed. William S. Davis. (Illus.). 480p. (C). 1992. pap. text ed. write for info. (0-201-55711-8) Addison-Wesley.

Systems Analysis & Design: Alternative Structured Approaches. write for info. (0-318-60707-7) P-H.

Systems Analysis & Design: An Organizational Approach. Raymond McLeod, Jr. 804p. (C). 1993. text ed. 69.25 (0-03-055154-4) Dryden Pr.

Systems Analysis & Design: An Organizational Approach. Raymond McLeod, Jr. 804p. (C). 1994. disk 29.75 (0-03-003028-5) Dryden Pr.

Systems Analysis & Design: An Organizational Approach. Raymond McLeod, Jr. 498p. (C). 1994. teacher ed., pap. text ed. 88.25 (0-03-076682-6) Dryden Pr.

Systems Analysis & Design: Best Practices. 4th ed. James C. Wetherbe & Nicholas P. Vitalari. Ed. by Clyde Perlee. LC 93-11455. 400p. (C). 1994. text ed. 57.50 (0-314-02679-7) West Pub.

***Systems Analysis & Design & the Transition to Objects Project Workbook.** Sandra D. Dewitz. 1996. pap. text ed. write for info. (0-07-016768-0) McGraw.

Systems Analysis & Design Methods. 2nd ed. Jeffrey L. Whitten et al. 797p. (C). 1989. text ed. 67.95 (0-256-07493-3) Irwin.

Systems Analysis & Design Methods. 2nd ed. Jeffrey L. Whitten et al. 152p. (C). 1989. 19.95 (0-256-07494-1) Irwin.

Systems Analysis & Design Methods. 3rd ed. Jeffrey L. Whitten et al. LC 93-34091. 896p. (C). 1993. text ed. 72.75 (0-256-09360-1) Irwin.

Systems Analysis & Design Methods. 3rd ed. Jeffrey L. Whitten et al. LC 93-34091. 1993. teacher ed. write for info. (0-256-10132-9) Irwin.

Systems Analysis & Design Methods. 3rd ed. Jeffrey L. Whitten et al. 188p. (C). 1993. student ed., text ed. 21.50 (0-256-09361-X) Irwin.

Systems Analysis & Design Methods. 4th ed. Jeffrey L. Whitten & Lonnie Bentley. LC 97-8260. 896p. (C). 1997. 72.75 (0-256-19906-X) Irwin.

***Systems Analysis & Design Methods.** 4th ed. Jeffrey L. Whitten et al. LC 97-8260. 1997. write for info. (0-256-23826-X) Irwin.

Systems Analysis & Design Methods: International Version. 2nd ed. Jeffrey L. Whitten et al. 797p. (C). 1989. per. 30.95 (0-256-07787-8) Irwin.

Systems Analysis & Design Methods, Management Information Systems. 3rd ed. Jeffrey L. Whitten et al. (C). 1994. pap. text ed. 33.95 (0-256-18467-4) Irwin.

Systems Analysis & Design with Modern Methods. Leonard Fertuck. 672p. (C). 1993. pap. text ed. 56.91 (0-697-22324-8) Irwin.

Systems Analysis & Design with Modern Methods. 2nd ed. Leonard Fertuck. 688p. (C). 1994. per. 59.95 (0-697-16218-4) Bus & Educ Tech.

Systems Analysis & Design with Modern Methods: A Case Study. Leonard Fertuck. 32p. (C). 1991. 7.97 (0-697-13492-X) Irwin.

Systems Analysis & Policy Planning: Applications in Defense. Ed. by Edward S. Quade & W. I. Boucher. LC 68-22241. 480p. reprint ed. pap. 136.80 (0-685-15495-5, 2026274) Bks Demand.

Systems Analysis & Project Management. 3rd ed. David I. Cleland & William R. King. (Illus.). 512p. (C). 1983. text ed. write for info. (0-07-011311-4) McGraw.

Systems Analysis & Simulation. 1989. 71.95 (0-387-97093-2) Spr-Verlag.

Systems Analysis & Simulation. Ed. by Achim Sydow et al. (Advances in Simulation Ser.: Vol. 1). (Illus.). 428p. 1989. 71.95 (*0-387-97091-6*) Spr-Verlag.

Systems Analysis & Simulation, 1985: Proceedings of the 2nd International Symposium on Systems Analysis & Simulation, Berlin, GDR, 26-31 August, 1985. Ed. by Achim Sydow et al. 1986. 84.00 (*0-08-034024-5*, Pub. by PPL UK) Elsevier.

Systems Analysis & Social Planning: Human Problems of Post-Industrial Society. Robert Boguslaw. 1982. text ed. 29.50 (*0-8290-0111-5*) Irvington.

Systems Analysis & Social Planning: Human Problems of Post Industrial Society. Robert Boguslaw. (C). 1986. reprint ed. pap. text ed. 14.95 (*0-8290-2011-X*) Irvington.

Systems Analysis Applied to Livestock Production. Thomas Cartwright & Harvey Blackburn. 1995. text ed. write for info. (*0-8493-8751-5*) CRC Pr.

Systems Analysis Applied to Management of Water Resources: Proceedings of Fourth IFAC Symposium, Rabat, Morocco, October 11-13 1988. Ed. by M. Jellali. (IFAC Proceedings Ser.: IFPS 8911). (Illus.). 200p. 1989. 94.00 (*0-08-035733-4*, Pergamon Pr) Elsevier.

Systems Analysis Approach to Selecting, Designing & Implementing Automated Systems, No. 9102. Edward J. Kazlauskas & Lawrence O. Picus. 110p. 1991. 30.00 (*0-910170-58-4*) Assn Sch Busn.

Systems Analysis Design - Study Guide & Cases. Burch. (DC - Introduction to Computing Ser.). 1992. student ed., pap. 18.95 (*0-87835-871-4*) Course Tech.

Systems Analysis, Design & Development. Perry Edwards. LC 84-28979. 508p. (C). 1985. text ed. 45.25 (*0-03-000142-0*) HB Coll Pubs.

Systems Analysis, Design, & Implementation. John Burch. 900p. 1992. text ed. 59.95 (*0-87835-818-8*) Course Tech.

Systems Analysis, Design, & the Transition to Objects. Sandra Dewitz. 1996. text ed. write for info. (*0-07-016763-X*) McGraw.

Systems Analysis for Applications: Software Design. David B. Brown & Jeffrey A. Herbanek. (Illus.). 466p. (C). 1984. text ed. 39.95 (*0-8162-1160-4*) Holden-Day.

Systems Analysis for Civil Engineers. Paul J. Ossenbruggen. LC 83-14595. 571p. 1984. Net. text ed. 55.50 (*0-471-09889-2*) Wiley.

Systems Analysis for Production Operations, Vol. 3. C. Carl Pegels. (Studies in Operations Research). 472p. 1976. text ed. 228.00 (*0-677-04710-X*) Gordon & Breach.

Systems Analysis for Social Scientists. F. Cortes et al. LC 73-23061. 352p. reprint ed. 100.40 (*0-8357-9990-5*, 2016464) Bks Demand.

Systems Analysis in Forage Crops Production & Utilization. Ed. by R. W. Van Keuren. (Illus.). 64p. 1975. pap. 4.00 (*0-89118-508-9*) Crop Sci Soc Am.

Systems Analysis in Health Care. Ed. by Vijay Mahajan & C. Carl Pegels. LC 78-19461. 504p. 1979. text ed. 75.00 (*0-275-90384-2*, C0384, Praeger Pubs) Greenwood.

Systems Analysis in Political Science: A Marxist Critique of David Easton. A. K. Baruah. 208p. (C). 1987. 37.95 (*81-85024-25-1*, Pub. by Uppal Pub Hse II) Asia Bk Corp.

Systems Analysis in Public Policy: A Critique. rev. ed. Ida R. Hoos. LC 82-48766. 320p. (C). 1983. pap. 13.95 (*0-520-04952-7*) U CA Pr.

Systems Analysis in Water Quality Management: Proceedings of a Symposium Held in London, U. K., 30 June-2 July 1987. Ed. by M. B. Beck. (Advances in Water Pollution Control Ser.: No. 3). (Illus.). 445p. 1987. 105.75 (*0-08-035585-4*, Pergamon Pr) Elsevier.

Systems Analysis of Ecosystems. Ed. by G. S. Innis & R. V. O'Neill. (Statistical Ecology Ser.: Vol. 9). 1979. 45.00 (*0-89974-006-5*) Intl Co-Op.

Systems Analysis of Imagery. Gardner Lord. (C). 1992. text ed. 21.00 (*0-913412-64-3*) Brandon Hse.

Systems Analysis of the Global Boreal Forest. Ed. by Herman H. Shugart et al. (Illus.). 545p. (C). 1992. text ed. 125.00 (*0-521-40546-7*) Cambridge U Pr.

Systems Analysis Project: Case Book. Margaret S. Wu. Ed. by Szilagyi. 160p. (C). 1994. pap. text ed. 21.75 (*0-314-02894-3*) West Pub.

Systems Analysis Techniques. Barbara Robinson & Mary Prior. (Illus.). 288p. 1995. pap. 23.95 (*1-85032-183-3*) ITCP.

Systems Analyst. Jack Rudman. (Career Examination Ser.: C-2168). 1994. reprint ed. pap. 29.95 (*0-8373-2168-9*) Nat Learn.

Systems & Computer Science. Conference on Systems & Computer Science, 1965: University of Western Ontario. Ed. by John F. Hart & Satoru Takasu. LC 68-114245. 261p. reprint ed. pap. 74.40 (*0-317-10999-5*, 2014240) Bks Demand.

Systems & Control: An Introduction to Linear Sampled & Nonlinear Systems. T. Dougherty. 672p. 1995. text ed. 68.00 (*981-02-2346-3*) World Scientific Pub.

Systems & Control Encyclopedia: Theory, Technology, Applications, 8 Vols. Ed. by Madan G. Singh. LC 86-15085. (Illus.). 5686p. 1987. 3,795.25 (*0-08-028709-3*, Pergamon Pr) Elsevier.

Systems & Control Encyclopedia Supplementary, Vol. 1. Madan G. Singh. 658p. 1990. 354.50 (*0-08-035933-7*, Pergamon Pr) Elsevier.

Systems & Control Encyclopedia Supplementary, Vol. 2. Ed. by Madan G. Singh. 454p. 1992. 354.50 (*0-08-040601-7*, Pergamon Pr) Elsevier.

***Systems & Control in the Twenty-First Century.** LC 96-45612. (Progress in Systems & Control Theory Ser.). 1996. 95.00 (*0-8176-3881-4*) Birkhauser.

Systems & Decision Making: A Management Science Approach. Hans G. Daellenbach. 545p. 1994. pap. text ed. 65.00 (*0-471-95094-7*) Wiley.

Systems & Development: The Minnesota Symposia on Child Psychology, Vol. 22. Esther Thelen. (Minnesota Symposium on Child Psychology Ser.). 264p. 1989. 55.00 (*0-8058-0409-9*) L Erlbaum Assocs.

Systems & Images. Ed. by John Sunderland. 102p. 1995. pap. text ed. 33.00 (*3-7186-5723-6*, Harwood Acad Pubs) Gordon & Breach.

Systems & Issues in ITS. 122p. 1995. 44.00 (*1-56091-677-X*, SP-1106) Soc Auto Engineers.

Systems & Management Science by Extremal Methods: Research Honoring Abraham Charnes at Age 70. Ed. by Fred Y. Phillips. 608p. (C). 1992. lib. bdg. 219.00 (*0-7923-9139-X*) Kluwer Ac.

Systems & Models for Developing Programs for the Gifted & Talented. Ed. by Joseph S. Renzulli. 1986. pap. text ed. 38.95 (*0-936386-44-4*) Creative Learning.

***Systems & Networks: Mathematical Theory & Applications, 2 vols.** Reinhard Mennicken. text ed. write for info. (*3-05-501676-9*) Wiley.

Systems & Networks Vol. 1: Mathematical Theory & Applications: Proceedings: Key Invited Lectures: International Symposium MTNS '93 (1993: Regensburg, Germany) Ed. by Uwe Helmke et al. (Mathematical Research Ser.: Vol. 77). 930p. 1995. 120.00 (*3-05-501573-8*, Pub. by Akademie Verlag GW) Wiley.

Systems & Procedures for the Modern Office: A Simulation Approach. 2nd rev. ed. Judith C. Simon & Lillian H. Chaney. LC 92-10224. Orig. Title: Procedures for the Modern Office. 1992. pap. text ed. 25.65 (*0-13-880477-X*) P-H.

Systems & Procedures Including Office Management Information Sources. Ed. by Chester Morrill, Jr. LC 67-31261. (Management Information Guide Ser.: No. 12). 380p. 1967. 68.00 (*0-8103-0812-6*) Gale.

Systems & Processes: Collected Works in Sociology. Ed. by Mario Reda et al. (C). 1968. pap. 19.95 (*0-8084-0292-7*) NCUP.

Systems & Regions in Global Politics: An Empirical Study of Diplomacy, International Organization & Trade. Tom Nierop. text ed. 59.95 (*0-470-22040-6*) Wiley.

Systems & Regions in Global Politics: An Empirical Study of Diplomacy, International Organization & Trade 1950-1991. Tom Nierop. LC 93-46291. (Belhaven Studies in Political Geography). 244p. 1995. text ed. 65.00 (*0-471-94942-6*) Wiley.

Systems & Signals. N. Levan. (University Series in Modern Engineering). 173p. 1983. pap. 33.00 (*0-387-90900-1*) Spr-Verlag.

Systems & Signals. 2nd rev. ed. N. Levan. LC 86-31158. (University Series in Modern Engineering). 176p. (C). 1987. text ed. 29.50 (*0-911575-40-5*) Optimization Soft.

Systems & Signals. 3rd enl. rev. ed. N. Levan. LC 92-28882. (University Series in Modern Engineering). 240p. 1992. pap. text ed. 39.00 (*0-911575-63-4*) Optimization Soft.

Systems & Technologies Instructor Guide Kit. American Production & Inventory Control Society Staff. 1995. 600.00 (*1-55822-074-7*) Am Prod & Inventory.

Systems & Technologies Reprints. American Production & Inventory Control Society Staff. 239p. 1995. 21.00 (*1-55822-041-0*) Am Prod & Inventory.

Systems & Technologies Student Guide. American Production & Inventory Control Society Staff. 1995. 37.00 (*1-55822-075-5*) Am Prod & Inventory.

Systems & Technology for Advanced Manufacturing. Ed. by Keith M. Gardiner. LC 82-61726. (Manufacturing Update Ser.). 270p. reprint ed. pap. 77.00 (*0-317-41896-3*, 2026161) Bks Demand.

Systems & Theories in Psychology. 4th ed. Melvin H. Marx & W. A. Cronan-Hillix. (Psychology Ser.). 576p. 1987. text ed. write for info. (*0-07-040680-4*); Instr's. man. teacher ed., pap. text ed. write for info. (*0-07-040681-2*) McGraw.

Systems & Transforms with Applications in Optics. Athanasios Papoulis. LC 81-5995. 484p. (C). 1981. reprint ed. lib. bdg. 51.50 (*0-89874-358-3*) Krieger.

Systems Application Architecture: Common Programming Interface. James Martin et al. LC 93-18129. 320p. 1993. text ed. 66.00 (*0-13-785916-3*) P-H.

Systems Application Architecture: The IBM SAA Strategy. L. Robert Libutti. 1990. pap. 24.95 (*0-8306-3516-5*) McGraw-Hill Prof.

Systems Application Architecture for the 1990s: A Guide for MIS Managers & End Users. Jud Breslin & John McGann. 1997. text ed. write for info. (*0-89930-484-2*, BFH, Quorum Bks) Greenwood.

Systems Approach in Vision: Proceedings of a Workshop Held in Amsterdam, the Netherlands, 27-29 August 1984. Ed. by D. Regan et al. (Illus.). 226p. 1986. 55.00 (*0-08-032033-3*, Pub. by PPL UK) Elsevier.

Systems Approach to Air Pollution Control. Robert J. Bibbero & Irving G. Young. LC 74-8905. 542p. reprint ed. pap. 154.50 (*0-317-11255-4*, 2055157) Bks Demand.

Systems Approach to AMT Deployment. Denis R. Towill. Ed. by John E. Cherrington. (Advanced Manufacturing Ser.). (Illus.). 260p. 1993. write for info. (*3-540-19790-7*) Spr-Verlag.

Systems Approach to AMT Deployment. Ed. by Denis R. Towill & John E. Cherrington. LC 92-44415. 1993. 202.95 (*0-387-19790-7*) Spr-Verlag.

Systems Approach to Architecture. A. Benjamin Handler. LC 79-100397. (Elsevier Architectural Science Ser.). 192p. reprint ed. pap. 54.80 (*0-317-10850-6*, 2007768) Bks Demand.

Systems Approach to Computer-Integrated Design & Manufacturing. Nanua Singh. LC 94-40012. 643p. 1995. text ed. write for info. (*0-471-58517-3*) Wiley.

***Systems Approach to Golfing: Systems Approach.** unabridged ed. Richard E. Heyl. Ed. by Tade Sullivan & Michelle Wright. (Illus.). 176p. 1996. text ed. 22.95 (*0-9653532-1-4*) Leaning Pine Pub.

***Systems Approach to Golfing College Edition: Systems Approach.** 2nd rev. ed. Richard E. Heyl. Ed. by Tade Sullivan. (Illus.). 136p. (C). 1996. pap. text ed. 16.00 (*0-9653532-0-6*) Leaning Pine Pub.

Systems Approach to Hydrology: Proceedings of the Bilateral U. S.-Japan Seminar in Hydrology, 1st, Honolulu, Jan. 11-17, 1971. Ed. by Vujica Yevjevich. LC 71-168496. 1971. 35.00 (*0-918334-02-0*) WRP.

Systems Approach to Instructional Design. Ed. by Thomas T. Liao & David C. Miller. LC 77-86497. (Technology of Learning Systems Ser.: Vol. 1). (Illus.). 1978. pap. 10.00 (*0-89503-004-7*) Baywood Pub.

Systems Approach to Literature: Mythopoetics of Chekhov's Four Major Plays. Vera Zubarev. LC 96-25009. (Contributions to the Study of World Literature Ser.). 192p. 1997. text ed. 55.00 (*0-313-30193-X*) Greenwood.

Systems Approach to Problem Solving from Corporate Markets to National Missions. George K. Chacko. LC 89-3925. 227p. 1989. text ed. 55.00 (*0-275-93203-6*, C3203, Praeger Pubs) Greenwood.

Systems Approach to Programmable Controllers. Fred Swainston. 400p. 1991. teacher ed., pap. 13.50 (*0-8273-4669-7*) Delmar.

Systems Approach to Programmable Controllers. Fred Swainston. 400p. 1991. pap. 33.95 (*0-8273-4670-0*) Delmar.

Systems Approach to Quality Improvement. William F. Roth, Jr. LC 91-4204. 208p. 1991. text ed. 47.95 (*0-275-94107-8*, C4107, Praeger Pubs) Greenwood.

Systems Approach to Recreation Programming. Frederick C. Patterson. LC 87-12682. (Illus.). 181p. (C). 1991. reprint ed. pap. text ed. 14.95 (*0-88133-593-2*) Waveland Pr.

Systems Approach to Small Group Interaction. 5th ed. Stewart L. Tubbs. LC 94-20888. 1994. text ed. 29.95 (*0-07-065512-X*) McGraw.

***Systems Approach to Small Group Interaction.** 6th ed. Stewart L. Tubbs. LC 97-11605. 1997. write for info. (*0-07-065526-X*) McGraw.

Systems Approach to Training & Development. A. K. Sah. 240p. 1991. text ed. 37.50 (*81-207-1259-5*, Pub. by Sterling Pubs II) Apt Bks.

Systems Approach to Wood Structures. 101p. 1994. 40.00 (*0-935018-69-7*, 7312) Forest Prod.

Systems Approaches for Agricultural Development: Proceedings of the International Symposium on Systems Approaches for Agricultural Development, 2-6 December 1991, Bangkok, Thailand. Ed. by F. W. De Vries et al. LC 92-20496. (System Approaches for Sustainable Agricultural Development Ser.: Vol. 2). 560p. (C). 1992. lib. bdg. 294.50 (*0-7923-1880-3*) Kluwer Ac.

Systems Approaches to Developmental Neurobiology. Ed. by P. A. Raymond et al. (NATO ASI Series A, Life Sciences: Vol. 192). (Illus.). 204p. 1990. 75.00 (*0-306-43594-2*, Plenum Pr) Plenum.

Systems Architecting: Creating & Building Complex Systems. Eberhardt Rechtin. 352p. 1990. text ed. 81.00 (*0-13-880345-5*) P-H.

Systems Architecture: Hardware & Software in Information Systems. 2nd ed. Stephen D. Burd. LC 93-3688. (C). 1994. text ed. 55.95 (*0-87835-876-5*, BF8765) S-W Pub.

Systems Atlas of Male Human Anatomy. Engineering Animation Inc. Staff. Ed. by Ron Worthington. 120p. (C). (gr. 13). 1996. spiral bd. 19.95 (*0-8151-8654-1*) Mosby Yr Bk.

Systems-Based Approach to Policymaking. Ed. by Kenyon B. De Greene. LC 93-538. 384p. (C). 1993. lib. bdg. 124.00 (*0-7923-9336-8*) Kluwer Ac.

***Systems Big Books.** (Early Science Ser.). (Illus.). (Orig.). (J). (ps-2). 1996. pap. 74.00 (*1-56784-356-5*) Newbridge Comms.

***Systems-Centered Therapy for Groups.** Yvonne M. Agazarian. LC 97-3418. 1997. lib. bdg. 40.00 (*1-57230-195-3*, 0195) Guilford Pubns.

***Systems Challenge: Getting the Clinical Information Support You Need to Improve Patient Care.** Ed. by Nancy A. Kreider & Becky J. Haselton. LC 97-9523. 200p. 1997. pap. text ed. 40.00 (*1-55648-199-3*, 040100) AHPI.

***Systems Change Approach to Substance Abuse Prevention.** Ed. by Jacob U. Gordon. LC 96-39801. (Studies in Health & Human Services: Vol. 26). 212p. 1997. text ed. 89.95 (*0-7734-8781-6*) E Mellen.

Systems Change Strategies in Educational Settings. Richard I. Arends & Jane H. Arends. LC 77-22315. (New Vistas in Counseling Ser.: Vol. III). 120p. 1977. 32.95 (*0-87705-310-3*) Human Sci Pr.

Systems Construction & Analysis: A Mathematical & Logical Framework. Norman Fenton & Gillian Hill. LC 92-1487. (International Series in Software Engineering). 1992. 18.95 (*0-07-707431-9*) McGraw.

Systems Consultation: A New Perspective for Family Therapy. Ed. by Lyman C. Wynne et al. LC 86-4778. (Guilford Family Therapy Ser.). 487p. 1986. pap. text ed. 26.95 (*0-89862-908-X*); lib. bdg. 52.50 (*0-89862-068-6*) Guilford Pr.

Systems Control Clerk. Jack Rudman. (Career Examination Ser.: C-3571). 1994. pap. 23.95 (*0-8373-3571-X*) Nat Learn.

Systems Control Theory for Power Systems. Ed. by Joe H. Chow & Petar V. Koktovic. LC 94-44183. (IMA Volumes in Mathematics & Its Applications: Vol. 6). 1995. 75.95 (*0-387-94438-9*) Spr-Verlag.

Systems Design: VLSI for Digital Signal Processing, Vol. II. B. A. Bowen & William R. Brown. (Illus.). 432p. 1985. text ed. 40.00 (*0-317-20146-8*) P-H.

Systems Design in the Fourth Generation Object-Based Development Using dBASE 3.0 & dBASE 4.0. John A. Lehman. LC 90-48154. 381p. 1991. Net. text ed. 36.00 (*0-471-52752-1*) Wiley.

Systems Design of Education: A Journey to Create the Future. Bela H. Banathy. LC 90-19155. (Illus.). 240p. 1991. 37.95 (*0-87778-229-6*) Educ Tech Pubns.

Systems Design under CICS Command & VSAM. Alex Varsegi. (Illus.). 272p. 1987. 28.95 (*0-8306-2843-6*, 2843, TAB/TPR) TAB Bks.

Systems Design Under CICS Command & VSAM. Alex Varsegi. 1987. text ed. 28.95 (*0-07-157575-8*) McGraw.

Systems Design with Advanced Microprocessors. Ed. by John Freer. 282p. (C). 1987. text ed. 200.00 (*0-273-02679-8*, Pub. by Pitman Pubng UK) St Mut.

Systems Developer. (Career Examination Ser.: C-3754). pap. 34.95 (*0-8373-3754-2*) Nat Learn.

Systems Development: A Practical Approach. William Amadio. 1989. text ed. write for info. (*0-07-558072-1*) McGraw.

Systems Development: A Practical Approach. William Amadio. 500p. (C). 1988. text ed. 24.00 (*0-394-39232-9*) Mitchell Pub.

Systems Development: Analysis, Design & Implementation. 2nd ed. Alan L. Eliason. (C). 1990. text ed. 72.95 (*0-673-39867-6*) Addson-Wesley Educ.

Systems Development & Project Management Study Guide. 3rd ed. Richard Marr et al. 179p. 1994. pap. text ed. 25.00 (*1-877796-12-3*) IDMA.

Systems Development Management. Ed. by Ian A. Gilhooley & Maryellen MacIsaac. 1992. ring bd. 395.00 (*0-87769-266-1*) Warren Gorham & Lamont.

Systems Development Management. Ed. by Paul C. Tinnirello. ring bd. 464.00 (*0-685-69689-8*, ASDM) Warren Gorham & Lamont.

Systems Development Through the AD - Cycle: Using the Techniques & Tools of the 90's. Glenn R. Lowry. 592p. (C). 1995. write for info. (*0-697-20225-9*) Bus & Educ Tech.

Systems Development Through the AD - Cycle: Using the Techniques & Tools of the 90's. Glenn R. Lowry. 224p. (C). 1995. student ed., pap. write for info. (*0-697-20240-2*); student ed., pap. write for info. (*0-697-20241-0*) Bus & Educ Tech.

Systems Development Using Structured Techniques. M. Bull. 368p. 1989. pap. 42.95 (*0-412-31020-1*); text ed. 89.95 (*0-412-31010-4*, A3691) Chapman & Hall.

***Systems Developmet: Analysis, Design & Implementation.** 3rd ed. Ed. by Eliason. (C). 1996. text ed. write for info. (*0-321-01400-6*) Addson-Wesley Educ.

Systems Documentation: Techniques of Persuasion in Large Organizations. Frank Whitehouse. 1973. 32.00 (*0-8464-0906-2*) Beekman Pubs.

***Systems Dynamics.** Palm. 1998. text ed. 47.96 (*0-256-11449-8*) Irwin.

Systems Ecology: An Introduction. Howard T. Odum. LC 82-8650. reprint ed. pap. 178.80 (*0-7837-2809-3*, 2057663) Bks Demand.

Systems Economics: Concepts, Models, & Multidisciplinary Perspectives. Ed. by Karl A. Fox & Don G. Miles. LC 86-27586. (Illus.). 270p. 1987. reprint ed. pap. 77.00 (*0-608-00032-9*, 2060798) Bks Demand.

Systems Education: Perspectives, Programs, & Methods. Ed. by Bela H. Banathy. (Systems Inquiry Ser.). 177p. 1983. pap. 16.95 (*0-914105-02-7*) Intersystems Pubns.

Systems Engineering. Aslaksen & Belcher. 440p. 1992. pap. text ed. 57.00 (*0-13-880402-8*) P-H.

Systems Engineering. Andrew P. Sage. LC 92-19523. (Series in Systems Engineering). 624p. 1992. text ed. 79.95 (*0-471-53639-3*) Wiley.

Systems Engineering: An Approach to Information-Based Design. George A. Hazelrigg. 544p. (C). 1996. text ed. 80.00 (*0-13-461344-9*) P-H.

Systems Engineering: Principles & Practice of Computer-Based Systems Engineering. Bernard Thome. (Software-Based Systems Ser.). 394p. 1992. text ed. 85.00 (*0-471-93552-2*) Wiley.

Systems Engineering & Analysis. 2nd ed. Benjamin S. Blanchard & Walter J. Fabrycky. 720p. 1990. text ed. 86.67 (*0-13-880758-2*) P-H.

Systems Engineering & Management **see IFAC '96: 13th World Congress Proceedings**

***Systems Engineering Design.** 4th ed. Ed. by Bloom. (C). 1996. text ed. 13.50 (*0-673-67649-8*) Addison-Wesley.

***Systems Engineering for Commercial Aircraft.** Scott Jackson. LC 97-845. (Illus.). 250p. 1997. text ed. 59.95 (*0-291-39846-4*, Pub. by Ashgate UK) Ashgate Pub Co.

***Systems Engineering Guidebook: A Process for Developing Systems & Products.** James N. Martin. LC 96-36435. (Systems Engineering Ser.). 275p. 1996. 49.95 (*0-8493-7837-0*) CRC Pr.

Systems Engineering in Public Administration: Proceedings of the IFIP TC8-WG8.5 Working Conference on Systems Engineering in Public Administration, Ludenberg, Germany, 3-5 March 1993. Conference on Systems Engineering Staff. Ed. by Hinrich E. G. Bonin. (IFIP Transactions A: Computer Science & Technology Ser.: Vol. A-36). 174p. 1993. pap. 89.00 (*0-444-81560-0*, North Holland) Elsevier.

Systems Engineering Management: Achieving Total Quality. James A. Lacy. 336p. 1991. 36.95 (*0-8306-2304-3*) McGraw-Hill Prof.

Systems Engineering Management: Achieving Total Quality. James A. Lacy. LC 91-21576. (Illus.). 336p. 1995. reprint ed. text ed. 70.00 (*0-9644627-0-2*) J Lacy Consult.

Systems Engineering Management Guide. (Orig.). 1992. lib. bdg. 300.00 (*0-8490-5504-0*) Gordon Pr.

An Asterisk (*) at the beginning of an entry indicates that the title is appearing in BIP for the first time.

Systems Engineering Methods. Harold Chestnut. LC 67-17336. (Wiley Series on Systems Engineering & Analysis). 404p. reprint ed. pap. 115.20 (*0-317-08335-X*, 2051601) Bks Demand.
Systems Engineering Models of Human Machine Interactions. William B. Rouse. (Systems Science & Engineering Ser.: Vol. 6). 152p. 1980. 60.25 (*0-444-00366-5*) P-H.
Systems Engineering of Education: Anasynthesis of the Education & Training Supersystem, No. 9. Leonard C. Silvern. (C). 1970. pap. 2.00 (*0-87657-126-7*) Ed & Training.
Systems Engineering of Education: Application of Systems Thinking to the Administration of Instruction, 2 vols., No. 2. Leonard C. Silvern. LC 75-27690. (Illus.). 178p. (C). 1976. 25.00 (*0-87657-114-3*) Ed & Training.
Systems Engineering of Education: General Systems Model for Effective Curriculums, No. 7. Leonard C. Silvern. (Illus.). (C). 1971. 25.00 incl. audio (*0-87657-120-8*) Ed & Training.
Systems Engineering of Education: Logos Language for Flowchart Modeling, No. 10. Leonard C. Silvern. (C). 1970. student ed. 60.00 incl. audio, sl. (*0-87657-108-9*) Ed & Training.
Systems Engineering of Education: Model for Producing a System, Set. Leonard C. Silvern. (C). 1970. 20.00 (*0-87657-109-7*) Ed & Training.
Systems Engineering of Education: Model for Producing Models, No. 13. Leonard C. Silvern. (C). 1971. audio, sl. 25.00 (*0-87657-111-9*) Ed & Training.
Systems Engineering of Education: Preparing Occupational Instruction, No. 19. Leonard C. Silvern. LC 77-74289. (C). 1977. text ed. 18.00 (*0-87657-115-1*, ETC 3.1.3. 219) Ed & Training.
Systems Engineering of Education: Principles of Computer-Assisted Instruction Systems, No. 6. Leonard C. Silvern. LC 70-76367. (Illus.). (C). 1970. 15.00 (*0-87657-104-6*) Ed & Training.
Systems Engineering of Education: Quantitative Concepts for Education Systems, No. 5. Leonard C. Silvern. LC 69-19555. (Illus.). iv, 144p. (C). 1972. 16.00 (*0-87657-105-4*) Ed & Training.
Systems Engineering of Education: Quantitative Models for Occupational Teacher Utilization of Government Published Information, No. 8. Leonard C. Silvern & Carl N. Brooks. LC 79-91932. (Illus.). (C). 1969. 10.00 (*0-87657-101-1*) Ed & Training.
Systems Engineering of Education: Roles of Feedback & Feedforward During Simulation, No. 18. Leonard C. Silvern. LC 74-79181. (C). 1974. text ed. 6.00 (*0-87657-113-5*) Ed & Training.
Systems Engineering of Education: Simulating a Real-Life Problem on the General System Model for Effective Curriculums, No. 15. Leonard C. Silvern. (Illus.). (C). 1972. student ed. 30.00 incl. audio (*0-87657-121-6*) Ed & Training.
Systems Engineering of Education: Synthesis As a Process, No. 16. Leonard C. Silvern. LC 73-76218. (C). 1973. audio, sl. 40.00 (*0-87657-122-4*) Ed & Training.
Systems Engineering of Education: System Conceptualizations, No. 17. Leonard C. Silvern. (C). 1973. audio, sl. 80.00 (*0-87657-125-9*) Ed & Training.
Systems Engineering of Education: Systems Analysis & Synthesis Applied Quantitatively to Create an Instructional System, No. 4. Leonard C. Silvern. LC 65-27696. (Illus.). 120p. (C). 1969. text ed. 18.00 (*0-87657-124-0*) Ed & Training.
Systems Engineering of Education: Systems Analysis & Synthesis Applied to Occupational Instruction in Secondary Schools, No. 3. Leonard C. Silvern. LC 67-31679. (Illus.). 99p. (C). 1967. text ed. 10.00 (*0-87657-123-2*) Ed & Training.
Systems Engineering of Education: Systems Techniques for Pretesting Mediated Instructional Materials, No. 14. Jay M. Sedlik. LC 79-162916. (Illus.). (C). 1971. text ed. 18.00 (*0-87657-112-7*) Ed & Training.
Systems Engineering of Education: Systems Using Feedback, No. 12. Leonard C. Silvern. (C). 1971. student ed. 45.00 incl. audio, sl. (*0-87657-110-0*) Ed & Training.
Systems Engineering of Education: The Evolution of Systems Thinking in Education, No. 1. 3rd ed. Leonard C. Silvern. LC 73-150823. (Illus.). vi, 128p. (C). 1975. 20.00 (*0-87657-107-0*) Ed & Training.
Systems Engineering Tools. Harold Chestnut. LC 65-19484. (Wiley Series on Systems Engineering & Analysis). (Illus.). 664p. reprint ed. pap. 180.00 (*0-317-08334-1*, 2055158) Bks Demand.
Systems Engineering Using SDL-92. Anders Olsen et al. LC 94-31557. 480p. 1994. 167.50 (*0-444-89872-7*, North Holland) Elsevier.
***Systems Engineering with Models & Objects.** David W. Oliver et al. LC 97-4055. (Illus.). 350p. 1997. text ed. 60.00 (*0-07-048188-1*) McGraw.
Systems Engineer's Handbook: A Guide to Building VME & VXI Systems. Ed. by John Black. (Illus.). 1112p. 1992. text ed. 89.00 (*0-12-102820-8*) Acad Pr.
Systems Far from Equilibrium: Sitges Conference. Ed. by Luis Garrido. (Lecture Notes in Physics Ser.: Vol. 132). 403p. 1980. 39.95 (*0-387-10251-5*) Spr-Verlag.
Systems for Administrative Office Support. 4th ed. Walter A. Brower, Jr. et al. LC 93-4814. 1993. write for info. (*0-02-801025-6*) Glencoe.
Systems for Cytogenetic Analysis in Vicia Faba L. Ed. by G. P. Chapman & S. A. Tarawali. (Advances in Agricultural Biotechnology Ser.). 1984. lib. bdg. 107.50 (*90-247-3089-9*) Kluwer Ac.
***Systems for Financing Newly Emerging Private Enterprises in Transition Economies.** OECD Staff. 148p. (Orig.). 1997. pap. 28.00 (*92-64-15405-1*, 14-97-01-1, Pub. by Org for Econ FR) OECD.
Systems-For Managing Change. William M. Mayon-White. 1996. pap. text ed. 38.00 (*0-13-878125-7*) P-H.
Systems for Success: A "How to" Manual for Today's Interior Designer. Kate Halverson. LC 89-51681. (Illus.). 370p. 1990. student ed. 39.95 (*0-9623401-1-1*) Weston Comns.
***Systems for Success: Strategies for Maximum Efficiency in Landscape Installation & Nursery Production.** Dwight Hughes, Jr. Ed. by Julie Higginbotham. (Illus.). 100p. 1996. pap. write for info. (*0-9655037-0-4*) D Hughes Systs.
***Systems for Sustainability: People, Organizations, & Environments.** Ed. by F. A. Stowell et al. LC 97-25876. (Illus.). (C). 1997. write for info. (*0-306-45615-X*, Plenum Pr) Plenum.
Systems in Action. R. J. Allen & Bennett P. Lientz. (C). 1978. pap. text ed. 30.00 (*0-673-16150-1*) Addson-Wesley Educ.
Systems in Crisis: New Imperatives of High Politics at Century's End. Charles F. Doran. (Cambridge Studies in International Relations: No. 16). (Illus.). 304p. (C). 1991. text ed. 59.95 (*0-521-40185-2*); pap. text ed. 19.95 (*0-521-31237-X*) Cambridge U Pr.
Systems in English Grammar: An Introduction for Language Teachers. Peter A. Master. LC 95-15946. 1995. pap. 29.95 (*0-13-156837-X*) P-H.
Systems in Transition. Cheney. (DC - Introduction to Computing Ser.). 1997. pap. 57.95 (*0-7895-0193-7*) Course Tech.
Systems Inquiring - Applications, Theory, Philosophy & Methodology: Proceedings of the Society for General Systems Research, 1985, Set. Ed. by Bela H. Banathy. 1200p. 1985. pap. text ed. 86.00 (*0-914105-36-1*) Intersystems Pubns.
Systems Integration & Ancillary Facilities see Design Handbook of Wastewater Systems
Systems Management. John S. Baumgartner. LC 79-11634. 521p. reprint ed. pap. 148.50 (*0-685-15907-8*, 2026799) Bks Demand.
Systems Management: Management Protocols API (XMP) X/Open Staff. (Illus.). 218p. (C). 1994. pap. text ed. 50.00 (*0-13-353491-X*) P-H.
Systems Management: Version 2. 2nd ed. 236p. (C). 1996. pap. text ed. 49.00 (*0-13-496373-3*) P-H.
Systems Management Backup. 1997. pap. text ed. 54.00 (*0-13-496399-7*) P-H.
Systems Management, First IEEE International Workshop. LC 93-77036. 168p. 1994. pap. text ed. 40.00 (*0-8186-3820-6*, 3820) IEEE Comp Soc.
Systems Management for Information Technology & Software Engineering. Andrew P. Sage. LC 94-23585. (Wiley Series in Systems Engineering). 624p. 1995. text ed. 74.95 (*0-471-01583-0*) Wiley.
***Systems Management in a Distributed Environment.** 300p. (C). 1996. pap. text ed. 49.00 incl. cd-rom (*0-13-496100-5*) P-H.
Systems Management under UNIX. Nigel Backhurst & Paul Davies. 232p. 1987. text ed. 25.95 (*1-85058-049-9*, Pub. by Sigma Pr UK) Bk Clearing Hse.
Systems Management, 2nd IEEE International Workshop On. LC 96-83311. 200p. 1996. pap. 50.00 (*0-8186-7442-3*, PRO7442) IEEE Comp Soc.
Systems Methodologies, Isomorphies & Applications: Proceedings of the Society for General Systems Research, 1984, Set, Vols. 1 & 2. Ed. by August W. Smith. 660p. 1984. Set. pap. text ed. 66.00 (*0-914105-29-9*) Intersystems Pubns.
Systems Methodology for the Management Sciences. Michael C. Jackson. (Contemporary Systems Thinking Ser.). (Illus.). 306p. 1991. 59.50 (*0-306-43877-1*, Plenum Pr) Plenum.
Systems Migration: A Complete Reference. Alan R. Simon. 1993. text ed. 64.95 (*0-442-30853-1*) Van Nos Reinhold.
Systems Modeling & Computer Simulation. Kheir. (Electrical Engineering & Electronics Ser.: Vol. 94). 760p. 1995. 125.00 (*0-8247-9421-4*) Dekker.
Systems Modelling for Energy Policy. Ed. by Derek Bunn & Erik Larsen. LC 96-47600. 1997. text ed. 80.00 (*0-471-95794-1*) Wiley.
Systems, Models, & Feedback: Theory & Applications. Ed. by Aldo Isidori & T. J. Tarn. (Progress in Systems & Control Theory Ser.: Vol. 12). (Illus.). 393p. 1992. 109.50 (*0-8176-3633-1*) Birkhauser.
Systems, Models & Measures: Formal Approaches to Computing & Information Technology (FACIT) S. A. Schuman. xvii, 335p. 1994. 55.95 (*0-387-19753-2*) Spr-Verlag.
Systems Network Architecture: A Tutorial. Ed. by Anton Meijer. 224p. (C). 1987. text ed. 225.00 (*0-273-02842-1*, Pub. by Pitman Pubng UK) St Mut.
Systems Nurse: Designing Health Care Systems for Quality Care Delivery to All People. T. J. Terry. 96p. 1994. pap. 46.00 (*1-887258-01-9*) T J Terry.
Systems Nurse: Designing Health Care Systems for Quality Care Delivery to All People. 2nd rev. ed. T. J. Terry. 102p. 1996. 46.00 (*1-887258-22-1*) T J Terry.
Systems of Cities & Facility Location. Pierre Hansen et al. (Fundamentals of Pure & Applied Economics Ser.: Vol. 22). 122, xp. 1987. pap. text ed. 48.00 (*3-7186-0403-5*) Gordon & Breach.
***Systems of Consanguinity & Affinity of the Human Family.** Lewis H. Morgan. LC 96-53016. (Illus.). xxv, 604p. 1997. pap. text ed. 38.00 (*0-8032-8230-3*, Bison Books) U of Nebr Pr.
Systems of Continuing Education: Priority to District Health Personnel. (Technical Report Ser.: No. 803). 50p. (ENG, FRE & SPA.). 1990. pap. text ed. 8.00 (*92-4-120803-1*, 1100803) World Health.
Systems of Control in International Adjudication & Arbitration: Breakdown & Repair. W. Michael Reisman. LC 91-33033. 188p. 1992. text ed. 34.95 (*0-8223-1202-6*) Duke.
Systems of Discourse: Structures & Semiotics in the Social Sciences. George V. Zito. LC 83-26668. (Contributions in Sociology Ser.: No. 51). (Illus.). xiv, 158p. 1984. text ed. 42.95 (*0-313-24446-4*, ZSD/, Greenwood Pr) Greenwood.
Systems of Electrical Supply & Distribution. C. Duncan & E. G. Stocks. 60p. (C). 1984. pap. 35.00 (*0-85973-010-7*, Pub. by S Thornes Pubs UK) St Mut.
Systems of Equations, Bk. 9 see Key to Algebra Series
Systems of Evolution Equations. Yu A. Mitripolsky et al. 1992. lib. bdg. 153.00 (*0-7923-2054-9*) Kluwer Ac.
Systems of Family Therapy: An Adlerian Integration. Robert Sherman & Don Dinkmeyer. LC 86-29897. 322p. 1987. text ed. 39.95 (*0-87630-457-9*) Brunner-Mazel.
Systems of Formal Logic. I. H. Hackstaff. 365p. 1966. lib. bdg. 112.00 (*90-277-0077-X*, D Reidel) Kluwer Ac.
Systems of Frequency Curves. William Elderton & Norman L. Johnson. LC 69-10571. 224p. reprint ed. pap. 63.90 (*0-317-26324-2*, 2024451) Bks Demand.
Systems of Higher Education in Twelve Countries: A Comparative View. Nell P. Eurich. LC 81-1245. 172p. 1981. text ed. 85.00 (*0-275-90611-6*, C0611, Praeger Pubs) Greenwood.
***Systems of Innovation: Technologies, Institutions & Organizations.** Charles Edquist. LC 96-27375. (Science, Technology & the International Political Economy Ser.). 1997. write for info. (*1-85567-452-1*, Pub. by Pntr Pubs UK); pap. write for info. (*1-85567-453-X*, Pub. by Pntr Pubs UK) Bks Intl VA.
Systems of Land Tenure in Various Countries. Ed. by John W. Probyn. LC 75-153000. (Select Bibliographies Reprint Ser.). 1977. reprint ed. 30.95 (*0-8369-5752-0*) Ayer.
Systems of Linear Equations. Steven Roman. (Illus.). 84p. (Orig.). (C). 1992. pap. text ed. write for info. (*1-878015-11-7*) Innov Textbooks.
Systems of Linear Inequalities. A. S. Solodovnikov. Tr. by Lawrence M. Glasser & Thomas P. Branson from RUS. LC 79-16106. (Popular Lectures in Mathematics). 92p. 1980. pap. text ed. 10.00 (*0-226-76786-8*) U Ch Pr.
Systems of Logic. Norman M. Martin. 336p. (C). 1989. pap. text ed. 24.95 (*0-521-36770-0*) Cambridge U Pr.
Systems of Microdifferential Equations. Masaki Kashiwara. Tr. by Teresa M. Fernandes. (Progress in Mathematics Ser.: No. 34). 200p. (C). 1983. 45.00 (*0-8176-3138-0*) Birkhauser.
Systems of Partial Differential Equations & Lie Pseudogroups, Vol. 14. J. F. Pommaret. (Mathematics & Its Applications Ser.). xiv, 412p. 1978. text ed. 274.00 (*0-677-00270-X*) Gordon & Breach.
Systems of Political Control & Bureaucracy in Human Societies: American Ethnological Society Proceedings, 1958. Ed. by Verne F. Ray. LC 84-45545. 1988. reprint ed. pap. 35.00 (*0-404-62652-1*) AMS Pr.
Systems of Prosodic & Paralinguistic Features in English. David Crystal & Randolph Quirk. (Janua Linguarum, Ser. Minor: No. 39). (Orig.). 1964. pap. text ed. 26.15 (*90-279-0574-6*) Mouton.
Systems of Psychotherapy: A Transtheoretical Analysis. 2nd ed. James O. Prochaska. 442p. (C). 1984. boxed 48.95 (*0-534-10708-7*) Brooks-Cole.
Systems of Psychotherapy: A Transtheoretical Analysis. 3rd ed. James O. Prochaska & John C. Norcross. LC 93-41023. 540p. 1994. text ed. 60.95 (*0-534-22290-0*) Brooks-Cole.
Systems of Quasilinear Equations & Their Applications to Gas Dynamics. B. L. Rozdestvenskii & N. N. Janenko. LC 82-24488. (Translations of Mathematical Monographs: Vol. 55). 676p. 1983. 198.00 (*0-8218-4509-8*, MMONO/55) Am Math.
Systems of Reductions. 1987. student ed. 94.00 (*0-387-18598-4*) Spr-Verlag.
Systems of Rehearsal: Stanislavsky, Brecht, Grotowski & Peter Brook. Shomit Mitter. LC 92-43. 224p. (C). (gr. 13). 1992. pap. 15.95 (*0-415-06784-7*, A7101); text ed. 52.95 (*0-415-06783-9*, A7097) Routledge.
Systems of Representation in Children: Development & Use. Ed. by Chris Pratt & Alison F. Garton. LC 92-25523. (Developmental Psychology & Its Applications Ser.). 283p. 1993. text ed. 105.00 (*0-471-92501-2*) Wiley.
Systems of Society: An Introduction to Social Science. 6th ed. Manuel G. Mendoza. 780p. (C). 1995. pap. text ed. 49.56 (*0-669-39319-3*) HM College Div.
***Systems of Society: An Introduction to Social Science.** 6th ed. Manuel G. Mendoza. (C). 1995. teacher ed., text ed. 2.66 (*0-669-39320-7*) HM College Div.
***Systems of Society with "Newsweek"** 6th ed. (C). 1995. text ed. 56.36 (*0-669-39374-6*) HM College Div.
Systems of Survival: A Dialogue on the Moral Foundations of Commerce & Politics. Jane Jacobs. 1994. pap. 13.00 (*0-679-74816-4*) Random.
***Systems of the World.** Date not set. 22.00 (*0-8464-4425-9*) Beekman Pubs.
Systems of Units, National & International Aspects: A Symposium Organized by Section M on Engineering. American Association for the Advancement of Science Staff. Ed. by Carl F. Kayan. LC 59-15335. (American Association for the Advancement of Science Publication Ser.: No. 57). 307p. reprint ed. pap. 87.50 (*0-317-27548-8*, 2015170) Bks Demand.
Systems of War & Peace. Theodore Caplow & Louis Hicks. LC 94-44517. 288p. (C). 1995. pap. text ed. 28.50 (*0-8191-9858-7*); lib. bdg. 59.50 (*0-8191-9857-9*) U Pr of Amer.
Systems of Water Statistics in the ECE Region. 123p. 1986. 15.00 (*92-1-116373-0*) UN.
Systems One Thousand & Thirty-Two Reference Booklet. rev. ed. Karen Molloy. 91p. 1987. spiral bd. 12.00 (*0-317-61662-5*) CompuServe Data Tech.
Systems One Thousand & Twenty-Two Primer. Ken Jackson. 142p. 1982. spiral bd. 25.00 (*0-317-61663-3*) CompuServe Data Tech.
Systems Optimization Methodology. V. V. Kolbin. 500p. 1997. text ed. 99.00 (*981-02-1589-4*) World Scientific Pub.
Systems Panel Reports. Commission on Engineering & Technical Systems Staff. (Star 21: Strategic Technologies for the Army in the Twenty-First Century Ser.: Vol. 3). 800p. 1992. pap. 66.00 (*0-309-04636-X*) World Scientific Pub.
Systems Perspective of Parenting: The Individual, the Family, & the Social Network. Thomas W. Roberts. LC 93-41870. 414p. 1994. pap. 43.95 (*0-534-15546-4*) Brooks-Cole.
Systems Programmer. Jack Rudman. (Career Examination Ser.: C-2187). 1994. pap. 27.95 (*0-8373-2187-5*) Nat Learn.
Systems Programming. Donald E. Merusi. 1996. pap. text ed. 56.00 (*0-13-490558-X*) P-H.
Systems Programming for Small Computers. Daniel H. Marcellus. (C). 1984. pap. 23.95 (*0-13-881656-5*) P-H.
Systems Programming for Windows 95: C/C++ Programmer's Guide to VxDs, I/O Devices, & Operating System Extensions. Walter Oney. (Programming Ser.). 736p. 1996. pap. 39.95 incl. cd-rom (*1-55615-949-8*) Microsoft.
Systems Project Management. Ed. by Don Yeates. 296p. (C). 1986. pap. text ed. 140.00 (*0-273-02388-8*, Pub. by Pitman Pubng UK) St Mut.
Systems Prospects: The Next Ten Years of Systems Research. Ed. by Robert L. Flood et al. LC 89-48013. (Illus.). 390p. 1989. 95.00 (*0-306-43398-2*, Plenum Pr) Plenum.
Systems Quality - Reliability. Intel Corporation Staff. 160p. (Orig.). 1990. pap. 20.00 (*1-55512-091-1*) Intel Corp.
Systems Quality & Reliability. 1991. pap. text ed. 21.95 (*0-07-031222-2*) McGraw.
Systems Reliability & Risk Analysis. 2nd rev. ed. Ernst G. Frankel. (C). 1988. lib. bdg. 157.50 (*90-247-3665-X*, Pub. by Graham & Trotman UK) Kluwer Ac.
Systems Reliability, Maintainability & Management. Balhir Dhillon. (Illus.). 376p. 1983. text ed. 32.50 (*0-89433-195-7*) Petrocelli.
Systems Representation of Global Climate Change Models: Foundation for a Systems Science Approach. N. Sreenath. LC 92-45818. (Lecture Notes in Control & Information Sciences Ser.). 1993. 79.00 (*0-387-19824-5*) Spr-Verlag.
Systems Requirements Analysis (SRA) Jeffrey O. Grady. LC 92-34871. 496p. 1993. text ed. 55.00i (*0-07-023994-0*) McGraw.
Systems Requirements & Process Reengineering: A Modeling & Prototyping Guide. Stephen J. Andriole. LC 96-19092. 1996. text ed. 45.00 (*0-07-001974-6*) McGraw.
Systems Research II: Methodological Problems. Ed. by J. M. Gvishiani. (Advances in Systems Research Ser.). (Illus.). 280p. 1985. 138.00 (*0-08-030556-3*, Pub. by PPL UK) Franklin.
Systems Research, Operation Research Vol. 44. Gy. Szepesi & B. Szekely. 154p. 1980. 30.00 (*963-05-1761-2*, Pub. by Akad Kiado HU) St Mut.
Systems Science: Addressing Global Issues. Ed. by Frank A. Stowell et al. LC 93-19328. 1993. 135.00 (*0-306-44522-0*, Plenum Pr) Plenum.
Systems Science & Engineering. Ching Weimin. (International Academic Publishers Ser.). 1000p. 1989. 265.00 (*0-08-036387-3*, Pergamon Pr) Elsevier.
Systems Science in Health Care: Proceedings of the International Conference on Systems in Health Care, July 1980, Montreal, Quebec, Canada. C. Tilquin. LC 81-94784. 1888p. 1981. 829.00 (*0-08-025370-9*, Pergamon Pr) Elsevier.
Systems Selling Strategies. Mack Hanan & James Cribbin. LC 77-25034. 205p. reprint ed. pap. 58.50 (*0-317-10206-0*, 2022620) Bks Demand.
Systems-Sensitive Leadership: Empowering Diversity Without Polarizing the Church. Michael C. Armour & Don Browning. LC 95-2490. 1995. pap. 12.99 (*0-89900-736-8*) College Pr Pub.
***Systems Set.** (Early Science Ser.). (Illus.). (Orig.). (J). (ps-2). 1996. pap. 229.00 (*1-56784-355-7*) Newbridge Comms.
Systems Software. Frank Maddix. 1990. pap. text ed. 22.95 (*0-13-877713-6*) P-H.
Systems, Software, & Quality Engineering: Theory & Fundamentals. Arthur E. Ferdinand. LC 93-15896. 1993. 59.95 (*0-442-01730-8*) Van Nos Reinhold.
Systems Software Tools. Ted J. Biggerstaff. (Illus.). 320p. 1986. text ed. 32.00 (*0-13-821869-2*) P-H.
Systems Software Tools, Software Builder's Kit Version 1.0. rev. ed. Ted J. Biggerstaff. 48p. 1987. write for info. (*0-318-61641-6*) P-H.
***Systems Support Aide.** Jack Rudman. (Career Examination Ser.: Vol. C-3811). 1997. pap. 29.95 (*0-8373-3811-5*) Nat Learn.
Systems That Learn: An Introduction to Learning Theory for Cognitive & Computer Scientist. Daniel N. Osherson et al. (Learning, Development & Conceptual Change Ser.). 232p. 1990. pap. 12.95 (*0-262-65024-X*, Bradford Bks) MIT Pr.
Systems That Work: Government Financial Manuals, Analyses & Operating Procedures. Municipal Finance Officers Association Staff & Girard Miller. (Illus.). ix, 273p. write for info. (*0-318-60754-9*) Municipal.

S

Systems Theory & Family Therapy: A Primer. Raphael J. Becvar & Dorothy S. Becvar. LC 81-43721. 104p. (Orig.). (C). 1982. pap. text ed. 14.75 (*0-8191-2444-3*); lib. bdg. 49.00 (*0-8191-2443-5*) U Pr of Amer.

Systems Theory & Scientific Philosophy: An Application of the Cybernetics of W. Ross Ashby to Personal & Social Philosophy, the Philosophy of Mind, & the Problems of Artificial Intelligence. John Bryant. 288p. (Orig.). (C). 1991. pap. text ed. 28.50 (*0-8191-8304-0*); lib. bdg. 56.50 (*0-8191-8303-2*) U Pr of Amer.

***Systems Theory Applied to Television Station Management in the Competitive Marketplace.** William G. Covington. LC 97-25128. 1997. pap. write for info. (*0-7618-0824-8*) U Pr of Amer.

Systems Theory for Organization Development. Ed. by Thomas G. Cummings. LC 79-42906. (Wiley Series on Individuals, Groups & Organizations). 380p. reprint ed. pap. 108.30 (*0-685-15464-5*, 2026691) Bks Demand.

Systems Theory in Immunology. Ed. by C. Bruni. (Lecture Notes in Biomathematics Ser.: Vol. 32). 273p. 1980. 36.95 (*0-387-09728-7*) Spr-Verlag.

Systems Theory Research, 18. Systems Theory Research Staff. reprint ed. pap. 81.50 (*0-317-28435-5*, 2020694) Bks Demand.

Systems Theory Research, 19. Systems Theory Research Staff. reprint ed. pap. 81.80 (*0-317-28436-3*) Bks Demand.

Systems Theory Research, 20. Systems Theory Research Staff. reprint ed. pap. 69.50 (*0-317-28437-1*) Bks Demand.

Systems Theory Research, 21. Systems Theory Research Staff. reprint ed. pap. 66.30 (*0-317-28438-X*) Bks Demand.

Systems Theory Research, 22. Systems Theory Research Staff. reprint ed. pap. 75.30 (*0-317-28439-8*) Bks Demand.

Systems Theory Research, 23. Systems Theory Research Staff. reprint ed. pap. 80.30 (*0-317-28440-1*) Bks Demand.

Systems Thinking. Nicolas Kramer & Jacob De Smit. 1977. pap. text ed. 50.00 (*90-207-0587-3*) Kluwer Ac.

Systems Thinking for Harassed Managers. Nano McCaughan & Barry Palmer. 160p. 1994. pap. text ed. 27.95 (*1-85575-055-4*, Pub. by Karnac Bks UK) Brunner-Mazel.

Systems Thinking in Action. Ed. by Michael C. Jackson & P. Keys. 1985. pap. 25.00 (*0-08-033413-X*, Pub. by PPL UK) Elsevier.

Systems Thinking in Europe. Ed. by Michael C. Jackson et al. (Illus.). 602p. 1991. 125.00 (*0-306-44013-X*, Plenum Pr) Plenum.

Systems Thinking in Library & Information Management. David A. Smith. LC 81-152172. (Illus.). 142p. reprint ed. pap. 40.50 (*0-7837-5326-8*, 2045065) Bks Demand.

***Systems Thinking Manager.** text ed. 50.00 (*0-471-97071-9*) Wiley.

Systems Thinking, Systems Practice. Peter B. Checkland. LC 80-41381. 330p. 1981. text ed. 100.00 (*0-471-27911-0*) Wiley.

Systems Thinking Tools: A User's Reference Guide. Daniel H. Kim. Ed. by Kellie T. Wardman. (Toolbox Reprint Ser.). (Illus.). 55p. (Orig.). 1994. pap. 15.00 (*1-883823-02-1*) Pegasus Comm.

Systems to Support Health Policy Analysis: Theory, Models, & Uses. David H. Gustafson et al. LC 91-20880. (Illus.). 431p. (C). 1992. text ed. 42.00 (*0-910701-73-3*, 0907) Health Admin Pr.

Systems Tools for Project Planning. Peter Delp. LC 77-7588. 1976. pap. text ed. 15.00 (*0-89249-021-7*) Intl Development.

Systems Training in Emissions & Performance. NYS Department of Motor Vehicles Staff & Nicholas J. Positano. LC 92-14877. 1993. pap. 23.95 (*0-8273-5588-2*) Delmar.

Systems Transfer Characteristics of Firms in Spain: A Comparative Management Study of American & Spanish Business Organizations. Bernard D. Estafen. (International Business Research Institute Ser.: No. 5). 160p. 1973. 5.00 (*0-87925-005-4*) Ind U Busn Res.

Systems Understanding Aid. 4th ed. Alvin A. Arens & D. Dewey Ward. Orig. Title: Systems Understanding Aid for Auditing. (Illus.). 148p. (Orig.). (C). 1995. pap. text ed. 22.95 (*0-912503-10-6*) Armond-Dalton.

Systems Understanding Aid - Microcomputer Version. 3rd ed. Alvin A. Arens et al. 160p. (Orig.). (C). 1989. pap. text ed. 18.95 incl. disk (*0-912503-08-4*) Armond-Dalton.

Systems Understanding Aid for Auditing. 3rd ed. Alvin A. Arens & D. Dewey Ward. 128p. (Orig.). (C). 1989. pap. text ed. 18.95 (*0-912503-06-8*) Armond-Dalton.

Systems Understanding Aid for Auditing see Systems Understanding Aid

Systems Understanding Aid for Financial Accounting. 3rd ed. Donald E. Kieso et al. 128p. (Orig.). (C). 1989. pap. text ed. 15.95 (*0-912503-07-6*) Armond-Dalton.

Systems Understanding Aid for Financial Accounting. 4th ed. Donald E. Kieso et al. (Illus.). 148p. (Orig.). (C). 1995. pap. text ed. 22.95 (*0-912503-11-4*) Armond-Dalton.

Systems View of Education: Concepts & Principles for Effective Practice. Bela H. Banathy. LC 92-7928. (Illus.). 224p. (Orig.). 1992. 34.95 (*0-87778-245-8*) Educ Tech Pubns.

Systems View of the World. Ervin Laszlo. LC 71-188357. 131p. 1972. pap. 7.95 (*0-8076-0636-7*) Braziller.

Systems View of the World: A Holistic Vision for Our Time. Ervin Laszlo. LC 96-711. (Advances in Systems Theory, Complexity & the Human Sciences Ser.). 112p. 1996. pap. 14.95 (*1-57273-053-6*) Hampton Pr NJ.

Systems with Hysteresis. M. A. Krasnosel'Skii & A. V. Pokrovskii. (Illus.). xviii, 410p. 1989. 149.95 (*0-387-15543-0*) Spr-Verlag.

Systems with Small Dissipation. V. B. Braginsky et al. Tr. by Erast Gliner. LC 85-20876. (Illus.). xii, 160p. 1986. pap. text ed. 18.00 (*0-226-07073-5*) U Ch Pr.

Systmatic Index of Recent & Pleistocene Planktonic Foraminifera. Tsunemasa Saito et al. LC 81-188860. reprint ed. pap. 54.20 (*0-608-01545-8*, 2061954) Bks Demand.

Systolic Algorithms. D. J. Evans. (International Journal of Computer Mathematics: Vol. 25, Nos. 3-4). iv, 108p. 1988. pap. text ed. 440.00 (*2-88124-690-7*) Gordon & Breach.

Systolic Algorithms, Vol. 3. Ed. by D. J. Evans. (Topics in Computer Mathematics Ser.). 449p. 1991. text ed. 176.00 (*2-88124-804-7*) Gordon & Breach.

Systolic Array Optimizing Compiler. Monica S. Lam. (C). 1988. lib. bdg. 75.50 (*0-89838-300-5*) Kluwer Ac.

Systolic Array Parallelizing Compiler. Ping S. Tseng. (C). 1990. lib. bdg. 69.00 (*0-7923-9122-5*) Kluwer Ac.

Systolic Arrays. J. McCanny et al. 720p. 1989. boxed 61.60 (*0-13-473422-X*) P-H.

Systolic Computations. M. A. Frumkin. (Mathematics & Its Applications MASS Ser.). 336p. (C). 1992. lib. bdg. 172.50 (*0-7923-1708-4*) Kluwer Ac.

Systolic Parallel Processing. Nikolay Petkov. LC 92-39979. (Advances in Parallel Computing Ser.: Vol. 5). 712p. 1992. 229.25 (*0-444-88769-5*, North Holland) Elsevier.

Systolic Signal Processing Systems. Earl E. Swartzlander. (Electrical Engineering & Electronics Ser.: Vol. 42). 416p. 1987. 175.00 (*0-8247-7717-4*) Dekker.

Syzygy. Sarah Brock. 32p. 1995. pap. 5.00 (*0-930502-42-6*) Pine Pr.

***Syzygy: The Union of Opposites: An Artist at the Boundary of the Void & the Manifest.** Margot Weiss. (Illus.). 75p. (Orig.). 1998. pap. 24.95 (*0-9653370-1-4*) Sephiran Pr.

***Szabo Dezso Es a Magyar Miniszterelnokok.** 2nd ed. Ed. by Gyula Gombos. 148p. 1995. pap. 6.00 (*963-7871-04-7*) Occidental.

Szamuzott a Szabadsag Igazaban. Istvan Eszterhas. 1978. per. 10.00 (*0-912404-10-8*) Alpha Pubns.

Szechuan Cooking: 56 Easy-to-Follow Recipes. Ed. by Brian Klingborg. (Illus.). 78p. 1993. pap. 10.95 (*0-914929-75-5*, Pub. by Hilt Pubng HK) ACCESS Pubs Network.

Szechwan & the Chinese Republic: Provincial Militarism & Central Power, 1911-1938. Robert A. Kapp. LC 73-77155. (Yale Historical Publications: Miscellany: No. 96). (Illus.). 208p. reprint ed. pap. 59.30 (*0-317-11081-0*, 2022008) Bks Demand.

Szechwan Style Chinese Cuisine. Weichuan. Ed. by Lee H. Lin. (Illus.). 96p. (CHI & ENG.). 1993. pap. 19.95 (*0-941676-31-5*) Wei-Chuan Pub.

Szekely & Bartok: The Story of a Friendship. Claude Kenneson. LC 93-33524. 572p. 1994. 39.95 (*0-931340-70-5*, Amadeus Pr) Timber.

Szeletian: And the Transition from Middle to Upper Paleolithic in Central Europe. P. Allsworth-Jones. 448p. 1986. 135.00 (*0-19-813401-0*) OUP.

Szellemi Honvedelem, Vol. 1. Zoltan Szabo. LC 88-92811. 344p. (HUN.). 1988. pap. 20.00 (*0-911050-64-7*) Occidental.

Szentendre. Peter Korniss. (Illus.). 68p. 1989. 47.00 (*963-13-3883-5*, Pub. by Corvina Bks HU) St Mut.

Szentendre. Tahin et al. (Illus.). 96p. 1989. 27.00 (*963-13-2820-1*, Pub. by Corvina Bks HU) St Mut.

Szerelmes Foldrajz. 2nd ed. Zoltan Szabo. LC 63-14466. 198p. 1964. 6.00 (*0-911050-20-5*) Occidental.

Szigeti on the Violin. Joseph Szigeti & Spike Hughes. LC 78-6800. 1979. reprint ed. pap. 5.95 (*0-486-23763-X*) Dover.

Szivarvany, No. 22. 160p. 1987. pap. 10.00 (*0-936398-44-2*) Framo Pub.

Szivarvany, No. 23. 160p. 1987. pap. 10.00 (*0-936398-45-0*) Framo Pub.

Szlachta Kalwinska W Polsce. Szymon Konarski. 362p. (POL.). 1994. 45.00 (*0-614-02648-2*) Szwede Slavic.

Szombathelyi Ferenc Visszaemlekezesei. Ed. by Peter Gosztonyi. 64p. 1980. 6.00 (*0-911050-50-7*) Occidental.

Szomoru Vasarnap. Gustavo Agrait. LC 88-29642. 118p. (Orig.). 1989. pap. 6.95 (*0-8477-3632-6*) U of PR Pr.

Szuletesnap korul: Vazlat egy letunt korszakrol (1950-1953)-Krudy Gyula Szellemenek. Rozsa Ignacz. x, 111p. 1983. 29.00 (*0-933104-15-4*) Jupiter Pr.

Szycher's Dictionary of Biomaterials & Medical Devices. Michael Szycher. LC 91-67901. 270p. 1992. text ed. 79.95 (*0-87762-882-3*) Technomic.

Szycher's Dictionary of Medical Devices. Michael Szycher. LC 95-60052. 220p. 1995. text ed. 79.95 (*1-56676-275-8*) Technomic.

Szymanowski. Teresa Chylinska. Tr. by A. T. Jordan. (Library of Polish Studies: Vol. 1). (Illus.). 1973. text ed. 10.00 (*0-917004-04-3*) Kosciuszko.

***Szymanowski.** Christopher Palmer. (BBC Music Guides Ser.). 104p. 1996. 7.95 (*0-563-20136-3*, BB 11133, Pub. by BBC UK) Parkwest Pubns.

Szymanowski as Post-Wagnerian: The Love Songs of Hafiz, Op. 24. Stephen C. Downes. LC 93-41942. (Outstanding Dissertations in Music from British Universities Ser.). 376p. 1994. text ed. 86.00 (*0-8153-1634-8*) Garland.

2 Corinthians see IVP New Testament Commentary Series

1787-May, 1788 see Papers of Alexander Hamilton

1782-1786 see Papers of Alexander Hamilton

1759-1761 see Correspondance Complete de Diderot

1789-Present: Chapters 22-35 see Societies & Cultures in World History

1779-1781 see Papers of Alexander Hamilton

1768-1778 see Papers of Alexander Hamilton

1770-1771 see Correspondance Complete de Diderot

1771 see Correspondance Complete de Diderot

1771-1772 see Correspondance Complete de Diderot

1776-1784 see Correspondance Complete de Diderot

1773-1774 see Correspondance Complete de Diderot

1768 see Correspondance Complete de Diderot

1765-1766 see Correspondance Complete de Diderot

1769 see Correspondance Complete de Diderot

1767 see Correspondance Complete de Diderot

1766 see Correspondance Complete de Diderot

1713-1757 see Correspondance Complete de Diderot

17th Through 19th Centuries see Western European Costume & Its Relation to the Theatre

6G Ash-Tip & Its Contents: Cultic & Administrative Discard from the Temple? see Abu Salabikh Excavations

1668-1669 see Correspondence of Henry Oldenburg

Standard 1973 see Prix Nobel en

Standard 1973 see Evaluation of Some Pesticide Residues in Food 1971: Monographs

Standard 1973 see Standard

"Sultangalievisme" au Tatarstan see Mouvements Nationaux Chez les Musulmans de Russie

S110 Member Services. 3rd ed. Ewing & CUNA Staff. 128p. 1995. per., pap. text ed. 21.14 (*0-7872-0210-X*) Kendall-Hunt.

S200 Lending Process. 3rd ed. Ewing & CUNA Staff. 128p. 1995. per., pap. text ed. 21.14 (*0-7872-0386-6*) Kendall-Hunt.

S220 Collections. 3rd ed. Ewing & CUNA Staff. 144p. 1995. per., pap. text ed. 21.14 (*0-7872-0392-0*) Kendall-Hunt.

S300 Basic Accounting. 2nd ed. Ewing & CUNA Staff. 96p. 1995. per., pap. text ed. 21.14 (*0-7872-0207-X*) Kendall-Hunt.

S36 Power Tools: Tips & Techniques from "NEWS 3X/400" Ed. by Chuck Lundgren. 747p. (Orig.). 1991. pap. 89.00 (*0-9628743-0-2*) Duke Commns Intl.

S410 Mortgage Lending. CUNA (Ewing) Staff. 160p. 1994. per. 21.14 (*0-8403-9419-5*) Kendall-Hunt.

S420 Loan Marketing. 2nd ed. CUNA (Ewing) Staff. 176p. 1995. per., pap. text ed. 21.14 (*0-7872-0970-8*) Kendall-Hunt.

***S510 Successful Sales Techniques.** CUNA Staff. 112p. 1996. per., pap. text ed. 21.14 (*0-7872-2924-5*) Kendall-Hunt.

T

***T.** Sarah Kirsch. 32p. 1995. 7.00 (*1-874400-05-9*, Pub. by Reality St Edits UK) SPD-Small Pr Dist.

t. Ed. by Jeanette R. Paxson. (Oil & Gas Production Ser.). (Illus.). 107p. (Orig.). 1982. pap. text ed. 15.00 (*0-88698-119-0*, 3.30210) PETEX.

***T. A. C. S. S. The Real Big Brother Story!** LC 95-90991. 104p. (Orig.). 1997. pap. 8.00 (*1-56002-639-1*, Univ Edtns) Aegina Pr.

T. A. for Tots (& Other Prinzes) anniversary ed. Alvyn M. Freed. (Transactional Analysis for Everybody Ser.). (Illus.). 144p. 1997. pap. 14.95 (*0-915190-73-7*, JP9073-7) Jalmar Pr.

T. A. P. P. Sources: A National Directory of Teenage Pregnancy Prevention Programs. Dominique Treboux. 565p. 1989. 42.50 (*0-8108-2277-6*) Scarecrow.

T A Today: A New Introduction to Transactional Analysis. Ian Stewart & Vann Joines. 342p. (C). 1987. pap. text ed. 19.95 (*1-870244-00-1*, Pub. by Lifespace UK) V Joines.

T. A. Z. The Temporary Autonomous Zone, Ontological Anarchy, Poetic Terrorism. Hakim Bey. 150p. 1991. pap. 6.00 (*0-936756-76-4*) Autonomedia.

T. B. Manuscript. Jennifer Shennan. 1997. write for info. (*0-945193-32-7*) Pendragon NY.

T. B. of Advanced Practical Physics. C. Chattopadhyay et al. (C). 1989. 45.00 (*0-89771-405-9*, Pub. by Current Dist II) St Mut.

T. B. of Gynaecology & Contraception. 9th ed. D. Dawn. (C). 1988. 100.00 (*0-685-36190-X*, Pub. by Current Dist II) St Mut.

T. B. of Obstetrics & Neonatology. 12th ed. D. Dawn. (C). 1990. 130.00 (*0-685-36191-8*, Pub. by Current Dist II) St Mut.

T-Backs, T-Shirts, Coat, & Suit. E. L. Konigsburg. LC 93-18427. 176p. (J). (gr. 4-8). 1993. lib. bdg. 14.00 (*0-689-31855-3*, Atheneum Bks Young) S&S Childrens.

T-Backs, T-Shirts, Coat & Suit. E. L. Konigsburg. LC 94-27288. 176p. (J). (gr. 5-9). 1995. pap. text ed. 3.95 (*0-7868-1027-0*) Hyprn Child.

***T-Ball.** Claudette C. Mitchell et al. (Visions: African-American Experiences: Vol. 27). (Illus.). 8p. (Orig.). (J). (gr. k-1). 1996. pap. text ed. 3.00 (*1-57518-069-3*) Arborlake.

T-Ball U. S. A. Parents Guide to Teeball. H. W. Broido. (Illus.). 128p. (Orig.). 1996. pap. 12.95 (*1-57028-082-7*) Masters Pr IN.

T-Bird: Forty Years of Thunder. John Gunnell. LC 95-76856. (Illus.). 304p. 1995. pap. text ed. 24.95 (*0-87341-365-2*, ATH01) Krause Pubns.

T-Boat Handbook: A Guide to the Operation of Small Inspected Passenger Vessels. Ed. by Richard A. Block. 206p. 1991. pap. 20.00 (*0-934114-76-5*, BK-115) Marine Educ.

T Bone N Weasel. Jon Klein. 1987. pap. 5.25 (*0-8222-1112-2*) Dramatists Play.

T-Bone Trouble. Nancy Levene. LC 90-32906. 128p. (J). (gr. 3-6). 1990. pap. 4.99 (*1-55513-765-2*, Chariot Bks) Chariot Victor.

T-Bone Walker Blues Vital Guitar. Richard DeVinck. (Illus.). 128p. (Orig.). 1994. pap. 19.95 (*0-614-14365-9*, 07-4033) Creat Cncpts.

T-Bone's Tent. Kate Green. (Fossil Family Tales Ser.). (Illus.). 32p. (J). (gr. k-4). 1992. lib. bdg. 22.79 (*0-89565-782-1*) Childs World.

***"T" Book: Testing: Critical Components in the Identification of Dyslexia.** Jane F. Greene & Louisa C. Moats. (Orton Emeritus Ser.). 5.00 (*0-614-29500-9*) Orton Dyslexia.

T-Boy & the Trial for Life. Timothy J. Edler. (Tim Edler's Tales from the Atchafalaya Ser.). (Illus.). 36p. (J). (gr. k-8). 1978. pap. 6.00 (*0-931108-02-0*) Little Cajun Bks.

T-Boy in Mossland. Timothy J. Edler. (Tim Edler's Tales from the Atchafalaya Ser.). (Illus.). 48p. (J). (gr. k-8). 1978. pap. 6.00 (*0-931108-03-9*) Little Cajun Bks.

T-Boy the Little Cajun. Timothy J. Edler. (Tim Edler's Tales from the Atchafalaya Ser.). (Illus.). 36p. (J). (gr. k-8). 1978. pap. 6.00 (*0-931108-01-2*) Little Cajun Bks.

***T. C. (Testosterone Curse), The Journal of E. Z. Gottcha.** Mary Wells-Noyes. 1996. 16.95 (*1-887361-03-0*) Wolf Wise Pub.

T. C. Cannon: He Stood in the Sun. Joan Frederick. LC 95-12152. (Illus.). 224p. 1995. 40.00 (*0-87358-603-4*) Northland AZ.

T. C. Hammond. Warren Nelson. 178p. 1994. pap. 9.99 (*0-85151-672-6*) Banner of Truth.

T Cell Activation in Health & Disease Disorders of Immune Regulation-Infection & Autoimmunity. Ed. by Marc Feldmann et al. 264p. 1989. text ed. 69.00 (*0-12-252682-1*) Acad Pr.

***T-Cell Autoimmunity & Multiple Sclerosis.** Marco Londei. 200p. 1997. 89.95 (*0-412-14011-X*) R G Landes.

T-Cell Dependent & Independent B-Cell Activation. Snow. 288p. 1990. 142.00 (*0-8493-6819-7*, SB611) CRC Pr.

T-Cell-Directed Immunointervention. Ed. by Jean-Francois Bach. LC 92-49921. (Frontiers in Pharmacology & Therapeutics Ser.). (Illus.). 336p. 1993. 145.00 (*0-632-03105-0*) Blackwell Sci.

T Cell Hybridomas. M. J. Taussig. 296p. 1985. 167.00 (*0-8493-5202-9*, QR185, CRC Reprint) Franklin.

T-Cell Paradigms in Parasitic & Bacterial Infections. Ed. by S. H. Kaufmann. (Current Topics in Microbiology & Immunology Ser.: Vol. 155). (Illus.). 145p. 1990. 89.00 (*0-387-51515-1*) Spr-Verlag.

T Cell Receptor Genes. Ed. by John I. Bell et al. (Illus.). 504p. 1995. 115.00 (*0-19-262418-0*); pap. 53.00 (*0-19-262419-9*) OUP.

T-Cell Receptor Use in Human Autoimmune Diseases. Ed. by Mark M. Davis & Joel Buxbaum. (Annals of the New York Academy of Sciences Ser.: Vol. 756). 1995. write for info. (*0-89766-915-0*); pap. write for info. (*0-614-08004-5*) NY Acad Sci.

T-Cell Receptor Use in Human Autoimmune Diseases: Proceedings. Ed. by Mark M. Davis & Joel Buxbaum. LC 95-19479. (Annals of the New York Academy of Sciences Ser.: Vol. 756). 464p. 1995. pap. 175.00 (*0-89766-916-9*) NY Acad Sci.

T-Cell Receptors. Ed. by Tak W. Mak. LC 87-38495. (Illus.). 254p. 1988. 69.50 (*0-306-42708-7*, Plenum Pr) Plenum.

T-cell Signaling of Macrophage Activation: Cell Contact-Dependent & Cytokine Signals. Robert D. Stout & Jill Suttles. LC 95-18865. (Molecular Biology Intelligence Unit Ser.). 178p. 1995. 79.00 (*1-57059-271-3*) R G Landes.

T-Cell Subsets & Cytokines Interplay in Infectious Diseases. Ed. by A. S. Mustafa et al. (Illus.). 222p. 1996. 248.00 (*3-8055-6122-9*) S Karger.

T Cell Subsets in Infectious & Autoimmune Diseases. Nicholas A. Mitchison. (Ciba Foundation Symposium Ser.: Vol. 195). 300p. 1996. text ed. 79.95 (*0-471-95720-8*) Wiley.

T-Cell Vaccination & Autoimmune Disease. Jingwu Zhang & Jef Raus. LC 95-1239. (Medical Intelligence Unit Ser.). 174p. 1995. 79.00 (*1-57059-254-3*) R G Landes.

T-Cells & Sympathy: Monologues in the Age of AIDS. Michael Kearns. LC 95-17109. 142p. 1995. pap. 10.95 (*0-435-08676-6*, 08676) Heinemann.

T-Class Submarine. Paul J. Kemp. LC 90-61162. (Illus.). 192p. 1990. 37.95 (*1-55750-826-7*) Naval Inst Pr.

***T. D. Jakes Habla a los Hombres.** Jakes. 144p. (SPA.). pap. write for info. (*0-7899-0332-6*) Editorial Unilit.

***T. D. Jakes Portable for Women.** T. D. Jakes. 1996. pap. write for info. (*0-614-20842-4*) Albury Pub.

T. D. Jakes Speaks to Men. T. D. Jakes. 1996. pap. text ed. 5.99 (*1-880089-86-6*) Albury Pub.

T. D. Jakes Speaks to Women. T. D. Jakes. 1996. pap. text ed. 5.99 (*1-880089-87-4*) Albury Pub.

T. E. Hulme. Michael Roberts. LC 72-169106. (English Biography Ser.: No. 31). 1971. reprint ed. lib. bdg. 59.95 (*0-8383-1342-6*) M S G Haskell Hse.

T. E. Lawrence. Charles Edmonds. LC 76-52954. (English Biography Ser.: No. 31). 1977. lib. bdg. 75.00 (*0-8383-2177-1*) M S G Haskell Hse.

T. E. Lawrence. Jeremy Wilson. (Illus.). 248p. 1988. 50.00 (*0-904017-85-0*, Pub. by Natl Port Gall UK) Antique Collect.

T. E. Lawrence: A Bibliography. Philip O'Brien. (G. K. Hall Reference Bks.). 416p. 1988. lib. bdg. 60.00 (*0-318-32523-3*, Hall Reference) Macmillan.

T. E. Lawrence: A Bibliography. Elizabeth W. Duval. LC 74-185877. (Reference Ser.: No. 44). 1972. reprint ed. lib. bdg. 75.00 (*0-8383-1385-X*) M S G Haskell Hse.

T. E. Lawrence: A Portrait in Paradox Controversy & Caricature in the Biographies of T. E. Lawrence. Jill M. Phillips. 600p. 1975. 250.00 (*0-8490-1172-8*) Gordon Pr.

T. E. Lawrence: Letters to E. T. Leeds. Ed. & Intro. by J. M. Wilson. (Illus.). 140p. 1988. 150.00 (*0-904845-80-X*, Pub. by Whittington Pr UK) Granary Bks.

T. E. Lawrence: Poems. Ed. by Gwendolyn MacEwen. 80p. 1995. lib. bdg. 29.00 (*0-8095-4588-8*) Borgo Pr.

T. E. Lawrence: Soldier, Writer, Legend: New Essays. Ed. by Jeffrey Meyers. LC 88-29720. 192p. 1989. text ed. 45.00 (*0-312-02770-2*) St Martin.

T. E. Lawrence: The Selected Letters. Malcolm Brown. (Illus.). 564p. 1994. pap. 16.95 (*1-56924-995-4*) Marlowe & Co.

T. E. Lawrence see Notable Biographies

T. E. Lawrence by His Friends. Ed. by A. W. Lawrence. 576p. 1980. reprint ed. 75.00 (*0-87752-196-4*) Gordian.

T. E. Lawrence Poems. Gwendolyn MacEwen. 80p. reprint ed. pap. 9.95 (*0-88962-172-1*) Mosaic.

T. E. Lawrence Revisited. Tabachnick. LC 97-21412. 1997. 22.95 (*0-8057-7800-4*, Twayne) Scribnrs Ref.

T. E. Lawrence's Translation of Homer's Odyssey. Homer. Ed. by Bernard M. Knox. Tr. by T. E. Lawrence. 384p. 1991. 27.50 (*0-19-506818-1*) OUP.

T. E. T. (Teacher Effectiveness Training) Thomas Gordon. 14.95 (*0-317-63114-4*) McKay.

***T. Evetts Haley: A True Texas Legend.** Bill Modisett. 232p. 1996. write for info. (*0-9650623-0-9*) Stked Plains TX.

***T. Evetts Haley: A True Texas Legend.** Bill Modisett. 232p. 1996. pap. write for info. (*0-9650623-1-7*) Stked Plains TX.

T-Factor Diet. Martin Katahn. 384p. 1994. mass mkt. 6.99 (*0-553-56560-5*) Bantam.

T-Factor Fat Gram Counter. Ed. by Jamie Pope-Cordle & Martin Katahn. 1989. pap. 3.49 (*0-393-30655-0*) Norton.

T-Factor Fat Gram Counter. exp. rev. ed. Jamie Pope & Martin Katahn. 80p. 1995. pap. 5.95 (*0-393-31331-X*, Norton Paperbks) Norton.

T Factor Fat Gram Counter with Three Week Recording Diary. rev. ed. Martin Katahn. 1992. pap. 69.80 (*0-393-30902-9*) Norton.

T for Texas: A State Full of Folklore. Ed. by Francis E. Abernethy. LC 82-70089. (Publications of the Texas Folklore Society: No. 44). (Illus.). 250p. (Orig.). 1982. 15.95 (*0-935014-03-9*) E-Heart Pr.

T-Form Organization: Using Technology to Design Organizations for the 21st Century. Henry C. Lucas, Jr. (Management Ser.). 272p. 29.95 (*0-7879-0167-9*) Jossey-Bass.

T. G. Masaryk: Against the Current, 1882-1914. H. Gordon Skilling. LC 93-29636. 1994. 39.50 (*0-271-01042-8*) Pa St U Pr.

T. G. Masaryk Revisited. Hanus J. Hajek. (East European Monographs: No. 139). 194p. 1983. text ed. 60.00 (*0-88033-030-9*) East Eur Monographs.

T. G. Masaryk (1850-1937), Vol. 1: Thinker & Politician. Ed. by Stanley B. Winters. 400p. 1990. text ed. 55.00 (*0-312-02681-1*) St Martin.

T. G. Masaryk (1850-1937), Vol. 2: Thinker & Critic. Ed. by Robert B. Pynsent. 400p. 1989. text ed. 55.00 (*0-312-02680-3*) St Martin.

T. G. Masaryk (1850-1937), Vol. 3: Statesman & Cultural Force. Ed. by Harry Hanak. LC 89-4215. 272p. 1990. text ed. 49.95 (*0-312-03096-7*) St Martin.

T-Groups & Therapy Groups in a Changing Society. Dee G. Appley & Alvin E. Winder. LC 73-10934. (Jossey-Bass Behavioral Science Ser.). 232p. reprint ed. 66.20 (*0-8357-9350-8*, 2013913) Bks Demand.

T. H. Huxley: Man's Place in Nature. James G. Paradis. LC 78-5492. 240p. 1978. reprint ed. pap. 68.40 (*0-7837-8911-4*, 2049622) Bks Demand.

T. H. Huxley on Education: A Selection of His Writings. Thomas H. Huxley. LC 72-154507. (Cambridge Texts & Studies in the History of Education). 240p. reprint ed. pap. 68.40 (*0-317-26091-X*, 2024417) Bks Demand.

T. H. White & the Matter of Britain: A Literary Overview. Martin Kellman. LC 87-24677. (Studies in the Historical Novel: Vol. 2). 256p. 1988. lib. bdg. 89.95 (*0-88946-231-3*) E Mellen.

T. H. White's The Once & Future King. Elisabeth Brewer. (Arthurian Studies: Vol. 30). 246p. (C). 1993. 53.00 (*0-85991-393-7*, DS Brewer) Boydell & Brewer.

T-Hangar Tales. Joe Juptner. 120p. 1995. pap. 17.95 (*0-911139-18-4*) Flying Bks.

T-Hold Kubotan. Takayuki Kubota. 28p. (Orig.). 1983. pap. 3.95 (*0-86568-111-2*, 1181) Unique Pubns.

***T. I. P. - Thoughts in Passing.** John G. Coulson. LC 96-90882. (Orig.). 1997. pap. 10.95 (*0-533-12203-1*) Vantage.

T in CETA: Local & National Perspectives. Ed. by Sar A. Levitan & Garth L. Mangum. LC 81-19791. 433p. 1981. text ed. 14.00 (*0-911558-94-2*); pap. text ed. 10.00 (*0-911558-93-4*) W E Upjohn.

T Is for "Terrific", Mahji's ABC's. Mahji Hall. LC 88-62371. 32p. (Orig.). (J). (ps-3). 1989. pap. text ed. 4.95 (*0-940880-22-9*); lib. bdg. 9.95 (*0-940880-21-0*) Open Hand.

T Is for Texas. Anne Bustard. LC 89-35633. (Illus.). 32p. (J). (ps-2). 1990. 12.95 (*0-89658-113-6*) Voyageur Pr.

T Is for Think: Thinking Fun with the Alphabet. Greta Rasmussen & Ted Rasmussen. LC 94-61645. (Illus.). 64p. 1995. pap. 8.95 (*0-936110-17-1*) Tin Man Pr.

T Is for Tortilla: A Southwestern Alphabet Book. Jody Alpers. (Illus.). 30p. (J). (gr. k-6). 1993. pap. 6.95 (*0-9640533-0-6*) Libros de Ninos.

T Is for Touching. Carol Grimm & Becky Montgomery. (J). (gr. k up). 1985. teacher ed. 79.95 incl. vhs (*0-914633-09-0*); teacher ed. 95.00 incl. vhs (*0-914633-08-2*); teacher ed. write for info. (*0-914633-05-8*) Rape Abuse Crisis.

T. J. & the Big Trout River Vandals. Weddle L. Massey. LC 91-14678. 94p. (Orig.). (J). (gr. 4-7). 1991. pap. 3.95 (*0-87227-148-X*, RBP5180) Reg Baptist.

T. J. & the Nobody House. Weddle L. Massey. LC 90-8702. 95p. (Orig.). (J). (gr. 3-7). 1990. pap. text ed. 3.95 (*0-87227-145-5*, RBP5174) Reg Baptist.

T. J. & the Somebody Club. Weddle L. Massey. LC 92-5342. 108p. (J). 1992. 3.95 (*0-87227-176-5*, RBP5210) Reg Baptist.

T. J. Flopp. Stephen E. Cosgrove. LC 89-9329. (Stephen Cosgrove's Value Tales Ser.). (Illus.). 32p. (J). (gr. k-4). 1990. lib. bdg. 21.36 (*0-89565-660-4*) Childs World.

***T. J. James Habla a las Mujeres.** Jakes. 160p. (SPA.). pap. write for info. (*0-7899-0333-4*) Editorial Unilit.

T. J. Jemison, Sr. Story. Theodore J. Jemison, Sr. LC 94-34944. 1994. write for info. (*0-910683-27-1*) Townsnd-Pr.

T. J. Ryan: A Political Biography. D. J. Murphy. 1990. pap. 29.95 (*0-7022-2289-5*, Pub. by Univ Queensland Pr AT) Intl Spec Bk.

***T. J.'s Story: A Book about a Boy Who Is Blind.** Arlene Schulman. LC 97-25129. (J). 1997. write for info. (*0-8225-2586-0*) Lerner Group.

T. L. C. Barbara Delinsky. 1994. mass mkt. 4.99 (*1-55166-010-5*, 1-66010-9, Mira Bks) Harlequin Bks.

T. L. C. Barbara Delinsky. 1995. mass mkt. 4.99 (*0-373-83310-5*, 1-83310-2) Harlequin Bks.

T-Lymphocyte & Inflammatory Cell Research in Asthma. Ed. by Georges Jolles et al. (Illus.). 392p. 1993. text ed. 89.00 (*0-12-388170-6*) Acad Pr.

T Lymphocyte Differentiation in the Human Thymus, 4, Vol. 2. Ed. by Marion D. Kendall & M. A. Ritter. 324p. 1989. text ed. 191.00 (*3-7186-4932-2*) Gordon & Breach.

T Lymphocytes: Structure, Functions, Choices. Ed. by Franco Celada & Benvenuto Pernis. LC 92-49284. (NATO ASI Series A, Life Sciences: Vol. 233). 1992. 85.00 (*0-306-44258-2*, Plenum Pr) Plenum.

T-Lymphocytes & Their Receptors in Immunologic Recognition. B. D. Brondz. 496p. 1988. text ed. 752.00 (*3-7186-4801-6*) Gordon & Breach.

***T. M. Allen (Pioneer Preacher of KY & MO)** Alvin Jennings. 224p. (Orig.). 1976. pap. 6.95 (*0-933672-00-4*, C-1740) Star Bible.

***T. M. Healy: The Rise & Fall of Parnell & the Establishment of the Irish Free State.** Frank Callanan. 320p. 1996. 32.95 (*1-85918-009-4*, Pub. by Cork Univ IE) Intl Spec Bk.

T. Macci Plauti Aulularia: With Critical & Exegetical Notes & an Introduction. Plautus. Ed. by W. R. Connor. LC 78-67156. (Latin Texts & Commentaries Ser.). (ENG & LAT.). 1979. reprint ed. lib. bdg. 19.95 (*0-405-11623-3*) Ayer.

T. Macci Plauti Epidicus. Plautus. Ed. by W. R. Connor. (Latin Texts & Commentaries Ser.). (ENG & LAT.). 1979. reprint ed. lib. bdg. 37.95 (*0-405-11600-4*) Ayer.

T. Macci Plauti Pseudolus. Plautus. Ed. by W. R. Connor. LC 78-11622. (Latin Texts & Commentaries Ser.). (ENG & LAT.). 1979. reprint ed. lib. bdg. 15.95 (*0-405-11622-5*) Ayer.

T. Macci Plauti Rudens. Plautus. Ed. by W. R. Connor & Edward A. Sonnenschein. LC 78-67153. (Latin Texts & Commentaries Ser.). (ENG & LAT.). 1979. reprint ed. lib. bdg. 25.95 (*0-405-11620-9*) Ayer.

T. Max Lawton: Memories Through Eyes of the Heart. William A. Farrar, Jr. 100p. 1991. 14.95 (*0-9630165-0-4*) W A Farrar.

T-Money & Wolf. Kevin Willmott & Ric Averill. 1994. 5.25 (*0-87129-347-1*, T95) Dramatic Pub.

T. N. Hasselquist. O. Fritiof Ander. Ed. by Franklyn D. Scott. LC 78-15208. (Scandinavians in America Ser.). 1979. reprint ed. lib. bdg. 23.95 (*0-405-11630-6*) Ayer.

T-Neck. Bobbi. 63p. (J). 1992. pap. 5.95 (*0-9626608-4-1*) Magik NY.

T-Neck. 2nd rev. ed. 180p. (J). (gr. 5 up). 1993. pap. 7.95 (*0-9626608-5-X*) Magik NY.

T-Nonc: The Cajun Environmentalist. Elvis J. Cavalier. (Illus.). 32p. (J). (gr. k-7). 1995. lib. bdg. 14.95 (*1-884725-04-X*) Blue Heron LA.

T-Nonc: The Cajun Environmentalist & T-Nonc's School Lessons on the Environment, 2 vols., Set. Elvis J. Cavalier. Ed. by Carolyn P. Gorman. (Illus.). (J). (gr. k-7). 1995. teacher ed., pap. 25.00 (*1-884725-07-4*) Blue Heron LA.

T-O-R-A-H see Kadima Kesher Series

T. P. Flanagan. S. B. Kennedy. 96p. 1996. 45.00 (*1-85182-215-1*, Pub. by Four Cts Pr IE); pap. 25.00 (*1-85182-216-X*, Pub. by Four Cts Pr IE) Intl Spec Bk.

T. P. Flanagan. limited ed. S. B. Kennedy. 1996. boxed 125.00 (*1-85182-217-8*, Pub. by Four Cts Pr IE) Intl Spec Bk.

T. P. O'Connor & the Liverpool Irish. L. W. Brady. (Royal Historical Society: Studies in History: No. 39). (Illus.). 320p. 1983. 63.00 (*0-901050-92-X*) Boydell & Brewer.

T-Pierre Frog & T-Felix Frog Go to School. Betty Mire. LC 93-74275. (Illus.). 32p. (Orig.). (J). (gr. 1-3). 1994. lib. bdg. 6.95 (*0-9639378-0-4*) Cajun Bay Pr.

T. Q. M. Toolkit: A Handbook of Practical Techniques for Quality Management. Jenny Waller et al. 1996. 79.95 (*0-89397-447-1*, Pub. by Kogan Page UK) Nichols Pub.

***T. R.** Noel F. Busch. Date not set. write for info. (*0-688-05675-X*) Morrow.

T-R-A-I-N up the Children. Linda J. Burba & Keith V. Burba. 112p. 1985. pap. 6.99 (*0-8341-1062-8*) Beacon Hill.

***T. Rex & the Crater of Doom.** Walter Alvarez. 236p. 1997. 24.95 (*0-691-01630-5*) Princeton U Pr.

T. S. Bayer, 1694-1738: A Study of a Pioneer Sinologist. Knud Lundbaek. (SIAS Monographs: No. 54). (Illus.). 256p. (C). 1986. pap. text ed. 21.00 (*0-7007-0189-3*, Pub. by Curzon Press UK) UH Pr.

***T. S. Eliot, 2 vols.** (Collected Critical Heritage Ser.). 832p. (C). 1997. text ed. 50.00 (*0-415-15949-0*) Routledge.

***T. S. Eliot.** Ed. by Grant. (Critical Heritage Ser.). 408p. (C). 1997. text ed. 35.00 (*0-415-15947-4*) Routledge.

***T. S. Eliot.** Ed. by Michael Grant. (Critical Heritage Ser.). 424p. (C). 1997. text ed. 35.00 (*0-415-15948-2*) Routledge.

T. S. Eliot. Philip R. Headings. (Twayne's United States Authors Ser.). 1964. pap. 13.95 (*0-8084-0293-5*, T57) NCUP.

T. S. Eliot. Compiled by Richard March & M. J. Tambimuttu. LC 68-55850. (Essay Index Reprint Ser.). 1977. 21.95 (*0-8369-0676-4*) Ayer.

T. S. Eliot: A Collection of Critical Essays. Ed. by Hugh Kenner. 1962. pap. 4.95 (*0-13-274324-8*, Spectrum IN) Macmillan Gen Ref.

T. S. Eliot: A Literary Life. Tony Sharpe. LC 91-9079. (Literary Lives Ser.). 176p. 1991. text ed. 35.00 (*0-312-06203-6*) St Martin.

T. S. Eliot: A Study of His Writings by Several Hands. B. Rajan. LC 65-15865. (Studies in T. S. Eliot: No. 11). 1969. reprint ed. lib. bdg. 75.00 (*0-8383-0545-8*) M S G Haskell Hse.

T. S. Eliot: A Symposium for His Seventieth Birthday. Ed. by Neville Braybrooke. LC 68-58773. (Essay Index Reprint Ser.). 1977. reprint ed. 23.95 (*0-8369-0100-2*) Ayer.

T. S. Eliot: A Virgilian Poet. Gareth Reeves. LC 88-23373. 192p. 1989. text ed. 39.95 (*0-312-02474-6*) St Martin.

T. S. Eliot: An Anthology of Recent Criticism. Ed. by Tapan K. Basu. 1993. 27.95 (*81-85753-01-6*, Pub. by Pencraft International II) Advent Bks Div.

T. S. Eliot: Essays from the Southern Review. Ed. by James Olney. (Illus.). 368p. 1988. 90.00 (*0-19-818575-8*) OUP.

T. S. Eliot: Homage from India. P. Lal. 12.00 (*0-88253-300-2*) Ind-US Inc.

T. S. Eliot: Man & Poet, 2 vols. Ed. by Laura Cowan. (Man & Poet Ser.). 1990. Vol. 1. 45.00 (*0-943373-09-3*); Vol. 1. pap. 25.00 (*0-943373-10-7*) Natl Poet Foun.

T. S. Eliot: Man & Poet, Vol. II. Ed. by Sebastian Knowles & Scott Leonard. (Man & Poet Ser.). 425p. 1992. pap. 25.00 (*0-943373-12-3*) Natl Poet Foun.

T. S. Eliot: Man & Poet, Vol. II. Ed. by Sebastian Knowles & Scott Leonard. (Man & Poet Ser.). 425p. 1992. 45.00 (*0-943373-11-5*) Natl Poet Foun.

T. S. Eliot: Mystic, Son, & Lover. Donald J. Childs. LC 96-24155. 1997. text ed. 45.00 (*0-312-16417-3*) St Martin.

T. S. Eliot: Poet & Dramatist. Joseph Chiari. LC 79-158. 167p. 1979. reprint ed. 50.00 (*0-87752-218-9*) Gordian.

T. S. Eliot: The Critical Heritage, 2 vols., Vol. 1. Michael Grant. (Critical Heritage Ser.). 388p. 1982. Vol.1, 388p. 55.00 (*0-7100-9224-5*, RKP) Routledge.

T. S. Eliot: The Dialectical Structure of His Theory of Poetry. Fei-Pai Lu. LC 66-13877. 182p. reprint ed. pap. 51.90 (*0-317-28152-6*, 2024098) Bks Demand.

T. S. Eliot: The Modernist in History. Ed. by Ronald Bush. (Cambridge Studies in American Literature & Culture: No. 51). 144p. (C). 1991. text ed. 49.95 (*0-521-39074-5*) Cambridge U Pr.

T. S. Eliot: The Philosopher Poet. Alzina S. Dale. LC 88-4457. (Wheaton Literary Ser.). 209p. 1988. 17.99 (*0-87788-832-9*) Shaw Pubs.

T. S. Eliot: The Poems. Martin Scofield. (British & Irish Authors Ser.). 276p. 1988. pap. text ed. 17.95 (*0-521-31761-4*) Cambridge U Pr.

T. S. Eliot: The Poet & His Critics. Robert H. Canary. LC 81-20516. (Poet & His Critics Ser.). 407p. 1982. reprint ed. pap. 116.00 (*0-7837-9677-3*, 2060405) Bks Demand.

T. S. Eliot see Modern Critical Views Series

T. S. Eliot - The Critic: A Study in Critical Ideology & Method. Sourindra Mitra. xx, 279p. 1985. 16.00 (*0-685-67631-5*, Pub. by Mittal Pubs Dist II) Nataraj Bks.

T. S. Eliot & American Philosophy: The Harvard Years. Manju Jain. 352p. (C). 1993. text ed. 69.95 (*0-521-41766-X*) Cambridge U Pr.

T. S. Eliot & Dante. Dominic Manganiello. LC 88-15871. 192p. 1989. text ed. 39.95 (*0-312-02104-6*) St Martin.

T. S. Eliot & Eugene O'Neill: The Dream & the Nightmare. Ed. by V. R. Prasad. (C). 1991. 20.00 (*81-202-0313-5*, Pub. by Ajanta II) S Asia.

T. S. Eliot & Hermeneutics: Absence & Interpretation in "The Waste Land" Harriet Davidson. LC 84-21757. 143p. 1985. text ed. 25.00 (*0-8071-1208-9*) La State U Pr.

***T. S. Eliot & Ideology.** 211p. 1997. pap. text ed. 17.95 (*0-521-62760-5*) Cambridge U Pr.

T. S. Eliot & Ideology. Kenneth Asher. (Cambridge Studies in American Literature & Culture: No. 86). 240p. (C). 1995. text ed. 54.95 (*0-521-45284-8*) Cambridge U Pr.

T. S. Eliot & Indian Philosophy. Amar K. Singh. 176p. 1990. text ed. 25.00 (*81-207-1100-9*, Pub. by Sterling Pubs II) Apt Bks.

T. S. Eliot & Indic Traditions: A Study in Poetry & Belief. Cleo M. Kearns. LC 86-13687. 256p. 1987. text ed. 65.00 (*0-521-32439-4*) Cambridge U Pr.

T. S. Eliot & Mysticism: The Secret History of Four Quartets. Paul Murray. LC 89-34363. 300p. 1991. text ed. 39.95 (*0-312-03531-4*) St Martin.

T. S. Eliot & the Ideology of Four Quartets. John X. Cooper. 256p. (C). 1996. text ed. 54.95 (*0-521-49629-2*) Cambridge U Pr.

T. S. Eliot & the Language of Poetry. F. Tekacs. (Studies in Modern Philology: Vol. 6). 150p. (C). 1989. pap. 45.00 (*963-05-5324-4*, Pub. by Akad Kiado HU) St Mut.

T. S. Eliot & the Lay Reader. Ethel M. Stephenson. 1972. 250.00 (*0-87968-085-7*) Gordon Pr.

T. S. Eliot & the Lay Reader. Ethel M. Stephenson. (Studies in T. S. Eliot: No. 11). 1970. reprint ed. pap. 39.95 (*0-8383-0101-0*) M S G Haskell Hse.

T. S. Eliot & the Myth of Adequation. Alan Weinblatt. LC 83-17863. (Studies in Modern Literature: No. 29). 204p. reprint ed. pap. 58.20 (*0-8357-1465-9*, 2070585) Bks Demand.

T. S. Eliot & the Philosophy of Criticism. Richard M. Shusterman. 236p. 1988. text ed. 65.00 (*0-231-06742-9*) Col U Pr.

T. S. Eliot & the Poetics of Literary History. Gregory S. Jay. LC 83-748. xii, 256p. 1983. text ed. 35.00 (*0-8071-1099-X*) La State U Pr.

T. S. Eliot & the Politics of Voice: The Argument of the Waste Land. John X. Cooper. LC 87-10896. (Studies in Modern Literature: No. 79). 133p. reprint ed. pap. 38.00 (*0-8357-1824-7*, 2070640) Bks Demand.

T. S. Eliot & the Use of Memory. Grover C. Smith. LC 96-7254. 1996. write for info. (*0-614-13390-4*) Bucknell U Pr.

T. S. Eliot & the Use of Memory. Grover C. Smith. LC 96-7254. 1996. 33.50 (*0-8387-5328-0*) Bucknell U Pr.

T. S. Eliot & Walt Whitman. S. Musgrove. 1972. 200.00 (*0-87968-012-1*) Gordon Pr.

T. S. Eliot & Walt Whitman. S. Musgrove. LC 72-100773. (Studies in Comparative Literature: No. 35). (C). 1970. reprint ed. lib. bdg. 49.95 (*0-8383-0332-3*) M S G Haskell Hse.

T. S. Eliot, Anti-Semitism & Literary Form. Anthony Julius. 336p. (C). 1995. text ed. 54.95 (*0-521-47063-3*) Cambridge U Pr.

T. S. Eliot Collection of the University of Texas at Austin. Illus. by William R. Holman. LC 70-169270. (Tower Bibliographical Ser.: No. 9). 1975. 25.00 (*0-87959-042-4*) U of Tex H Ransom Ctr.

T. S. Eliot Companion: Life & Works. F. B. Pinion. 304p. 1989. pap. 24.00 (*0-333-49817-8*, Pub. by Papermac UK) Trans-Atl Phila.

T. S. Eliot, Wallace Stevens, & the Discourses of Difference. Michael Beehler. LC 86-11393. 182p. 1987. text ed. 30.00 (*0-8071-1269-0*) La State U Pr.

T. S. Eliot's Ariel Poems: The Poetics of Recovery. John H. Timmerman. LC 94-17435. 1994. 35.00 (*0-8387-5286-1*) Bucknell U Pr.

T. S. Eliot's Concept of Language: A Study of Its Development. Harry T. Antrim. LC 76-634405. (University of Florida Humanities Monographs: No. 35). 84p. reprint ed. pap. 25.00 (*0-7837-4967-8*, 2044633) Bks Demand.

T. S. Eliot's Drama: A Research & Production Sourcebook. Randy Malamud. LC 91-46960. (Modern Dramatists Research & Production Sourcebooks Ser.: No. 2). 328p. 1992. text ed. 55.00 (*0-313-27813-X*, MTK, Greenwood Pr) Greenwood.

T. S. Eliot's Dramatic Pilgrimage: A Progress in Craft As an Expression of Christian Perspective. Daven M. Kari. LC 90-24913. (Studies in Art & Religious Interpretation: Vol. 13). 220p. 1991. lib. bdg. 89.95 (*0-88946-688-2*) E Mellen.

T. S. Eliot's Dramatic Theory & Practice: From Sweeney Agonistes to the Elder Statesman. Carol H. Smith. LC 77-5156. 258p. 1977. reprint ed. 50.00 (*0-87752-201-4*) Gordian.

T. S. Eliot's Impersonal Theory of Poetry. Mowbray Allan. LC 73-489. 189p. 1974. 29.50 (*0-8387-1311-4*) Bucknell U Pr.

T. S. Eliot's Major Poems & Plays Notes. Robert B. Kaplan. 1965. pap. 3.95 (*0-8220-1246-4*) Cliffs.

T. S. Eliot's Murder in the Cathedral see Modern Critical Interpretations

T. S. Eliot's Negative Way. Eloise K. Hay. LC 81-23747. 224p. 1982. reprint ed. pap. 63.90 (*0-7837-6071-X*, 2059117) Bks Demand.

T. S. Eliot's Personal Waste Land: Exorcism of the Demons. James E. Miller. LC 76-40424. 1977. 28.50 (*0-271-01237-4*) Pa St U Pr.

T. S. Eliot's Silent Voices. John T. Mayer. 368p. 1990. 49.95 (*0-19-505668-X*) OUP.

T. S. Eliot's "The Waste Land" A Critical Study. V. Rai. 1974. lib. bdg. 69.95 (*0-8490-1173-6*) Gordon Pr.

T. S. Eliot's The Waste Land see Modern Critical Interpretations

***T. S. Eliot's Use of Popular Science.** Manju Jaidka. LC 96-40159. (Studies in British Literature: Vol. 27). 184p. 1997. text ed. 79.95 (*0-7734-8658-5*) E Mellen.

T. S. Elliot's Shakespeare Criticism. Sudhakar Marathe. 1989. 20.00 (*81-7018-534-3*, Pub. by BR Pub II) S Asia.

T. S. Elliot's the Waste Land. Gareth Reeves. 1995. pap. text ed. 19.95 (*0-13-320722-6*) P-H.

T. S. Kuhn & Social Science. Barry Barnes. LC 81-58454. 192p. 1982. text ed. 43.00 (*0-231-05436-X*); pap. text ed. 17.00 (*0-231-05437-8*) Col U Pr.

T. S. Stribling: Pioneer Realist in Modern Southern Literature. Edward J. Piacentino. 194p. (Orig.). (C). 1988. pap. text ed. 20.00 (*0-8191-6720-7*) U Pr of Amer.

T Series MG: A Collector's Guide. Graham Robson. (Collector's Guide Ser.). (Illus.). 128p. 1981. 27.95 (*0-900549-51-3*, Pub. by Motor Racing UK) Motorbooks Intl.

T Series Tribute. Ed. by Richard L. Knudson. (Illus.). 192p. 1986. boxed 100.00 (*0-938253-00-X*) NEMGTRL.

T-Shirt. (Design Library: Vol. 6). (Illus.). 80p. (Orig.). 1996. pap. 14.95 (*3-927258-31-8*) Gingko Press.

T-Shirt. 1996. 5.00 (*3-540-14568-0*) Spr-Verlag.

***T-Shirt.** Compiled by Rockport Publishers Editorial Staff. (Design Library). (Illus.). 80p. pap. write for info. (*1-56496-245-8*) Rockport Pubs.

T-Shirt Airbrushing: The Step-by-Step Guide & Showcase. Cliff Stieglitz. (Illus.). 144p. 1995. 27.99 (*1-56496-146-X*) Rockport Pubs.

T-Shirt Book. Scott Fresener. LC 95-13401. (Illus.). 96p. 1995. pap. 14.95 (*0-87905-686-X*) Gibbs Smith Pub.

T-Shirt Designs. Kathy Sandmann. (Illus.). 48p. (Orig.). 1987. pap. 9.95 (*0-937679-01-1*) Sewing Sampler.

***T-Shirt Fun: Fabulous T-Shirt Designs & Creations.** (Creative Fun Ser.). (Illus.). 64p. (J). (gr. 3-7). 1997. 7.95 (*1-85967-508-5*, Lorenz Bks) Anness Pub.

T

T-Shirt Japanese Versus Necktie Japanese: Two Levels of Politeness. Hiroko Fukuda. Tr. by Charles M. De Wolf. (Power Japanese Ser.). 128p. 1995. pap. 10.00 (*4-7700-1834-7*) Kodansha.

T-Shirt Paints. June Ford. (You Can Do It! Ser.). (Illus.). 72p. (Orig.). (J). (ps up). 1994. pap. 12.95 (*1-56530-158-7*) Summit TX.

***T-Shirt Printer's Survival Manual.** Michael P. Shanley & Nita G. Coldiron. (Illus.). 229p. (Orig.). 1992. pap. 27.95 (*1-889920-00-2*, TSPSM) S&C Enterprises.

***T-Shirt Printer's Survival Manual.** 2nd ed. Michael P. Shanley & Nita G. Coldiron. LC 96-92698. (Illus.). 213p. (Orig.). 1996. pap. 29.95 (*1-889920-01-0*, TSPSM2) S&C Enterprises.

***T-Shirts.** Arlene Erlbach. LC 97-14335. (How It's Made). (Illus.). 1998. write for info. (*0-8225-2392-2*) Lerner Group.

***T-Shirts for Fun or Profit.** Eric M. Meyers. (Illus.). 88p. (Orig.). (YA). (gr. 6 up). 1996. pap. 12.95 (*0-9653537-6-1*) True North.

T. Subba Row Collected Writings. Henk J. Spierenburg. LC 96-48587. (Secret Doctrine Reference Ser.). (Illus.). 500p. 1997. 30.00 (*0-913510-69-6*) Wizards.

T. Tembarom. Frances Hodgson Burnett. 22.95 (*0-8488-0254-3*) Amereon Ltd.

***T. U. L. I. P. The Five Disputed Points of Calvinism.** 2nd ed. Ben L. Rose. LC 96-32985. 64p. 1996. pap. 9.95 (*1-57736-021-4*) Providence Hse.

T. V. A. Lessons for International Application. Herman Finer. LC 77-172008. (FDR & the Era of the New Deal Ser.). (Illus.). 1972. reprint ed. lib. bdg. 39.50 (*0-306-70378-5*) Da Capo.

T. V. A. & the Grass Roots: A Study in the Sociology of Formal Organization. Philip Selznick. LC 65-25023. 1979. pap. 13.00 (*0-520-05227-7*) U CA Pr.

***T. V. Dinners: Culinary Highlights from Classic T. V.** Pat Katzman & Barry Katzman. 208p. 1997. pap. 12.00 (*1-57297-254-8*) Blvd Books.

T. W. Bate & Dunheved Ironworks. William H. Jones. (C). 1989. 30.00 (*1-85022-020-4*, Pub. by Dyllansow Truran UK) St Mut.

T. W. Robertson & the Prince of Wales's Theatre. Daniel Barrett. LC 93-21442. (AUS XXVI: Vol. 23). 304p. (C). 1995. text ed. 49.95 (*0-8204-2369-6*) P Lang Pubng.

T. X. Margarita's: Guide to Modern Cocktails. Bryan Diehl. 60p. 1992. pap. 8.95 (*0-9643225-0-1*) T X Margarita.

T. X. Margarita's: New American Guide to Modern Cocktails. Bryan Diehl. 102p. 1994. 18.50 (*0-9643225-1-X*) T X Margarita.

T-Zero. Italo Calvino. Tr. by William Weaver. LC 76-14789. (Helen & Kurt Wolff Bk.). 152p. 1976. pap. 9.00 (*0-15-692400-5*, Harvest Bks) HarBrace.

T-34 in Action. Steven J. Zaloga. (Armor in Action Ser.). (Illus.). 50p. (Orig.). 1983. reprint ed. pap. 7.95 (*0-89747-112-1*, 2020) Squad Sig Pubns.

T-34 Mentor in Action. Lou Drendel. (Aircraft in Action Ser.). (Illus.). 50p. 1990. pap. 7.95 (*0-89747-249-7*, 1107) Squad Sig Pubns.

T-34-76 Medium Tank 1941-45. Steven J. Zaloga. (New Vanguard Ser.). (Illus.). 48p. 1994. pap. 12.95 (*1-85532-382-6*, 9344, Pub. by Osprey UK) Stackpole.

***T-34-85 Medium Tank: 1944-94.** Jim Kinnear & Steven J. Zaloga. (New Vanguard Ser.: No. 20). 48p. 1996. pap. 12.95 (*1-85532-535-7*, Pub. by Osprey UK) Stackpole.

T-6: A Pictorial Record of the Harvard, Texan & Wirraway. Peter Smith. (Illus.). 160p. 1995. 34.95 (*0-7603-0191-3*) Motorbooks Intl.

T-72. Steven J. Zaloga. (New Vanguard Ser.). (Illus.). 48p. 1993. pap. 12.95 (*1-85532-338-9*, 9341, Pub. by Osprey UK) Stackpole.

***TA Experience: Preparing for Multiple Roles: Selected Readings from the 3rd National Conference on the Training & Employment of Graduate Teaching Assistants.** Ed. by Karron G. Lewis. 448p. (Orig.). 1993. pap. 42.95 (*0-913507-55-5*) New Forums.

TA for Kids (& Grownups Too) 3rd rev. ed. Alvyn M. Freed & Margaret Freed. LC 77-81761. (Transactional Analysis for Everybody Ser.). (Illus.). (J). (gr. 4-7). 1977. pap. 9.95 (*0-915190-09-5*, JP9009-5) Jalmar Pr.

TA for Teens (& Other Important People) Alvyn M. Freed. LC 76-19651. (Transactional Analysis for Everybody Ser.). (Illus.). 258p. (YA). (gr. 8-12). 1976. pap. 21.95 (*0-915190-03-6*, JP9003-6) Jalmar Pr.

TA for Tots Coloring Book. Alvyn M. Freed. (Transactional Analysis for Everybody Ser.). (J). (ps-3). 1976. pap. 1.95 (*0-915190-33-8*, JP9033-8) Jalmar Pr.

Ta-Poo-Ach Means Apple. Barbara Genet. LC 85-60009. (Illus.). 46p. (J). (ps-3). 1985. 8.00 (*0-86705-015-2*) A R E Pub.

Ta'ammulat. Malik Bin-Nabi. (Mushkilat al-Hadarah Ser.). 220p. 1979. pap. 6.95 (*1-57547-025-X*) Dar Al-Fikr.

Ta'anith, 1 vol. (ENG & HEB.). 15.00 (*0-910218-62-5*) Bennet Pub.

TAAS Master Math: Teacher's Handbook for Texas Assessment of Academic Skills, Gr. Eight-Gr. Nine. Janine Graft & Daniel McNamee. Ed. by Lori Mammen. (Illus.). 144p. (Orig.). 1990. pap. text ed. 17.95 (*0-944459-17-X*) ECS Lrn Systs.

TAAS Master Math, Exit Level: Teacher's Handbook for Texas Assessment of Academic Skills. Daniel McNamee & Janine Graft. Ed. by Lori Mammen. (Illus.). 144p. (Orig.). 1990. pap. text ed. 17.95 (*0-944459-18-8*) ECS Lrn Systs.

TAAS Master Math, Grades Four & Five: Teacher's Handbook for Texas Assessment of Academic Skills. Beverly Cunningham et al. (Illus.). 144p. (Orig.). 1990. pap. text ed. 17.95 (*0-944459-15-3*) ECS Lrn Systs.

TAAS Master Math, Grades Two & Three: Teacher's Handbook for Texas Assessment of Academic Skills. Beverly Cunningham et al. (Illus.). 144p. (Orig.). 1990. pap. text ed. 17.95 (*0-944459-14-5*) ECS Lrn Systs.

TAAS Master Reading, Exit Level: Teacher's Handbook for Texas Assessment of Academic Skills. Lori Mammen et al. (Illus.). 112p. (Orig.). 1990. pap. text ed. 14.95 (*0-944459-23-4*) ECS Lrn Systs.

TAAS Master Reading, Gr. Four-Five: Teacher's Handbook for Texas Assessment of Academic Skills. Beverly Cunningham et al. (Illus.). 112p. (Orig.). 1990. pap. text ed. 14.95 (*0-944459-20-X*) ECS Lrn Systs.

TAAS Master Reading, Gr. Two-Gr. Three: Teacher's Handbook for Texas Assessment of Academic Skills. Beverly Cunningham et al. (Illus.). 112p. (Orig.). 1990. pap. text ed. 14.95 (*0-944459-19-6*) ECS Lrn Systs.

TAAS Master Reading, Grades 6-7: Teacher's Handbook for Texas Assessment of Academic Skills. Lori Mammen et al. (Illus.). 112p. (Orig.). 1990. pap. text ed. 14.95 (*0-944459-21-8*) ECS Lrn Systs.

TAAS Master Science. Elizabeth Klar & Lori Mammen. (Illus.). 1994. teacher ed., pap. text ed. 19.95 (*0-944459-94-3*) ECS Lrn Systs.

TAAS Master Science. Linda Pruski et al. (Illus.). 1994. teacher ed., pap. text ed. 19.95 (*0-944459-93-5*) ECS Lrn Systs.

TAAS Master Social Studies Grade Eight. Lori Mammen. (TAAS Master Ser.). (Illus.). 144p. (Orig.). 1993. pap. 19.95 (*0-944459-91-9*) ECS Lrn Systs.

TAAS Master Social Studies Grade Four. Lori Mammem. (TAAS Master Ser.). (Illus.). 144p. 1993. pap. text ed. 19.95 (*0-944459-92-7*) ECS Lrn Systs.

TAAS Master Student Practice Book: Math. Ed. by Lori Mammen. (Illus.). 144p. (J). (gr. 3). 1996. pap. text ed. 18.95 (*1-57022-079-4*, ECS0794) ECS Lrn Systs.

TAAS Master Student Practice Book: Math. Ed. by Lori Mammen. (Illus.). 128p. (J). (gr. 4). 1996. pap. text ed. 16.95 (*1-57022-081-6*, ECS0816) ECS Lrn Systs.

TAAS Master Student Practice Book: Math. Ed. by Lori Mammen. (Illus.). 160p. (J). (gr. 5). 1996. pap. text ed. 19.95 (*1-57022-084-0*, ECS0840) ECS Lrn Systs.

TAAS Master Student Practice Book: Math. Ed. by Lori Mammen. (Illus.). 144p. (YA). (gr. 10). 1996. pap. text ed. 20.95 (*1-57022-093-X*) ECS Lrn Systs.

TAAS Master Student Practice Book: Math. Ed. by Lori Mammen. (Illus.). 144p. (J). (gr. 6). 1996. pap. text ed. 20.95 (*1-57022-086-7*, ECS0867) ECS Lrn Systs.

TAAS Master Student Practice Book: Math. Ed. by Lori Mammen. (Illus.). 144p. (J). (gr. 7). 1996. pap. text ed. 20.95 (*1-57022-088-3*, ECS0883) ECS Lrn Systs.

TAAS Master Student Practice Book: Math. Ed. by Lori Mammen. (Illus.). 144p. (J). (gr. 8). 1996. pap. text ed. 20.95 (*1-57022-090-5*, ECS0905) ECS Lrn Systs.

TAAS Master Student Practice Book: Reading. Ed. by Lori Mammen. (Illus.). 96p. (J). (gr. 3). 1996. pap. text ed. 13.95 (*1-57022-080-8*, ECS0808) ECS Lrn Systs.

TAAS Master Student Practice Book: Reading. Ed. by Lori Mammen. (Illus.). 96p. (J). (gr. 4). 1996. pap. text ed. 13.95 (*1-57022-082-4*, ECS0824) ECS Lrn Systs.

TAAS Master Student Practice Book: Reading. Ed. by Lori Mammen. (Illus.). 96p. (J). (gr. 5). 1996. pap. text ed. 13.95 (*1-57022-085-9*, ECS0859) ECS Lrn Systs.

TAAS Master Student Practice Book: Reading. Ed. by Lori Mammen. (Illus.). 96p. (J). (gr. 6). 1996. pap. text ed. 13.95 (*1-57022-087-5*, ECS0875) ECS Lrn Systs.

TAAS Master Student Practice Book: Reading. Ed. by Lori Mammen. (Illus.). 96p. (J). (gr. 8). 1996. pap. text ed. 17.95 (*1-57022-091-3*, ECS0913) ECS Lrn Systs.

TAAS Master Student Practice Book: Reading. Ed. by Lori Mammen. (Illus.). 96p. (J). (gr. 7). 1996. pap. text ed. 17.95 (*1-57022-089-1*, ECS0891) ECS Lrn Systs.

TAAS Master Student Practice Book: Reading. Ed. by Lori Mammen. (Illus.). 96p. (YA). (gr. 10). 1996. pap. text ed. 17.95 (*1-57022-094-8*, ECS0948) ECS Lrn Systs.

TAAS Master Student Practice Book: Writing. Ed. by Lori Mammen. (Illus.). 112p. (J). (gr. 4). 1996. pap. text ed. 15.95 (*1-57022-083-2*, ECS0832) ECS Lrn Systs.

TAAS Master Student Practice Book: Writing. Ed. by Lori Mammen. (Illus.). 112p. (J). (gr. 8). 1996. pap. text ed. 18.95 (*1-57022-092-1*, ECS0921) ECS Lrn Systs.

TAAS Master Student Practice Book: Writing. Ed. by Lori Mammen. (Illus.). 112p. (YA). (gr. 10). 1996. pap. text ed. 18.95 (*1-57022-095-6*, ECS0956) ECS Lrn Systs.

TAAS Master Writing, Exit Level: Teacher's Handbook for Texas Assessment of Academic Skills. Lori Mammen. 112p. (Orig.). 1990. pap. text ed. 14.95 (*0-944459-13-7*) ECS Lrn Systs.

TAAS Master Writing, Gr. Eight-Gr. Nine: Teacher's Handbook for Texas Assessment of Academic Skills. Lori Mammen. (Illus.). 128p. 1990. pap. text ed. 15.95 (*0-944459-12-9*) ECS Lrn Systs.

TAAS Master Writing, Grade 2 - Grade 3: Teacher's Handbook for Texas Assessment of Academic Skills. Lori Mammen. (Illus.). 128p. (Orig.). 1990. pap. text ed. 15.95 (*0-944459-09-9*) ECS Lrn Systs.

TAAS Master Writing, Grades Four & Five: Teacher's Handbook for Texas Assessment of Academic Skills. Lori Mammen. (Illus.). 128p. (Orig.). 1990. pap. text ed. 15.95 (*0-944459-10-2*) ECS Lrn Systs.

TAAS Master Writing, Grades Six & Seven: Teacher's Handbook for Texas Assessment of Academic Skills. Lori Mammen. (Illus.). 128p. 1990. pap. text ed. 15.95 (*0-944459-11-0*) ECS Lrn Systs.

TAAS Practice Test: Exit Level Math. (Illus.). 16p. (J). 1995. pap. write for info. (*1-57022-075-1*, ECS0751) ECS Lrn Systs.

TAAS Practice Test: Exit Level Reading. (Illus.). 16p. (YA). (gr. 11). 1995. pap. write for info. (*1-57022-076-X*) ECS Lrn Systs.

TAAS Practice Test: Exit Level Writing. (Illus.). 16p. (YA). 1995. pap. write for info. (*1-57022-077-8*, ECS0778) ECS Lrn Systs.

TAAS Practice Test: Math. (Illus.). 16p. (J). (gr. 3). 1995. pap. write for info. (*1-57022-061-1*, ECS0611) ECS Lrn Systs.

TAAS Practice Test: Math. (Illus.). 16p. (J). (gr. 4). 1995. pap. write for info. (*1-57022-062-X*, ECS062X) ECS Lrn Systs.

TAAS Practice Test: Math. (Illus.). 16p. (J). (gr. 5). 1995. pap. write for info. (*1-57022-063-8*, ECS0638) ECS Lrn Systs.

TAAS Practice Test: Math. (Illus.). 16p. (J). (gr. 6). 1995. pap. write for info. (*1-57022-064-6*, ECS0646) ECS Lrn Systs.

TAAS Practice Test: Math. (Illus.). 16p. (J). (gr. 7). 1995. pap. write for info. (*1-57022-065-4*, ECS0654) ECS Lrn Systs.

TAAS Practice Test: Math. (Illus.). 16p. (J). (gr. 8). 1995. pap. write for info. (*1-57022-066-2*, ECS0662) ECS Lrn Systs.

TAAS Practice Test: Reading. (Illus.). 16p. (J). (gr. 3). 1995. pap. write for info. (*1-57022-067-0*, ECS0670) ECS Lrn Systs.

TAAS Practice Test: Reading. (Illus.). 16p. (J). (gr. 4). 1995. pap. write for info. (*1-57022-068-9*, ECS0689) ECS Lrn Systs.

TAAS Practice Test: Reading. (Illus.). 16p. (J). (gr. 5). 1995. pap. write for info. (*1-57022-069-7*, ECS0697) ECS Lrn Systs.

TAAS Practice Test: Reading. (Illus.). 16p. (J). (gr. 6). 1995. pap. write for info. (*1-57022-070-0*, ECS0700) ECS Lrn Systs.

TAAS Practice Test: Reading. (Illus.). 16p. (J). (gr. 7). 1995. pap. write for info. (*1-57022-071-9*, ECS0719) ECS Lrn Systs.

TAAS Practice Test: Reading. (Illus.). 16p. (J). (gr. 8). 1995. pap. write for info. (*1-57022-072-7*, ECS0727) ECS Lrn Systs.

TAAS Practice Test: Writing. (Illus.). 16p. (J). (gr. 4). 1995. pap. write for info. (*1-57022-073-5*, ECS0735) ECS Lrn Systs.

TAAS Practice Test: Writing. (Illus.). 16p. (J). (gr. 8). 1995. pap. write for info. (*1-57022-074-3*, ECS0743) ECS Lrn Systs.

TAAS Quick Review Mathematics: Exit Level. Janine Graft. (Illus.). 112p. 1992. pap. text ed. 14.95 (*0-944459-35-8*) ECS Lrn Systs.

TAAS Quick Review Mathematics: Grade 5. Elizabeth Klar & Beverly Cunningham. (Illus.). 112p. 1992. pap. text ed. 14.95 (*0-944459-32-3*) ECS Lrn Systs.

TAAS Quick Review Mathematics: Grade 7. Beverly Cunningham & Elizabeth Klar. (Illus.). 112p. 1992. pap. text ed. 14.95 (*0-944459-33-1*) ECS Lrn Systs.

TAAS Quick Review Mathematics: Grade 9. Ed. by Daniel McNamee. (Illus.). 112p. 1992. pap. text ed. 14.95 (*0-944459-34-X*) ECS Lrn Systs.

TAAS Quick Review Reading: Exit Level. Lori Mammen. (Illus.). 96p. 1992. pap. text ed. 12.95 (*0-944459-39-0*) ECS Lrn Systs.

TAAS Quick Review Reading: Grade 4. Violette Parker & Lori Mammen. (Illus.). 96p. 1992. pap. text ed. 12.95 (*0-944459-36-6*) ECS Lrn Systs.

TAAS Quick Review Reading, Grade 8. Lori Mammen. (Illus.). 96p. 1992. pap. 12.95 (*0-944459-38-2*) ECS Lrn Systs.

TAAS Quick Review Writing: Exit Level. Lori Mammen. 64p. 1991. pap. text ed. 9.95 (*0-944459-30-7*) ECS Lrn Systs.

TAAS Quick Review Writing: Grade 3. Lori Mammen. (Illus.). 64p. 1991. pap. text ed. 9.95 (*0-944459-26-9*) ECS Lrn Systs.

TAAS Quick Review Writing: Grade 5. Lori Mammen. (Illus.). 64p. 1991. pap. text ed. 9.95 (*0-944459-27-7*) ECS Lrn Systs.

TAAS Quick Review Writing: Grade 7. Lori Mammen. 64p. 1991. pap. text ed. 9.95 (*0-944459-28-5*) ECS Lrn Systs.

TAAS Quick Review Writing: Grade 9. Lori Mammen. 64p. 1991. pap. text ed. 9.95 (*0-944459-29-3*) ECS Lrn Systs.

***TAB Electronics & Computer Yellow Pages: Equipment, Components, & Supplies.** Andrew Yoder. (Illus.). 800p. 1996. pap. text ed. 29.95 (*0-07-076510-3*) McGraw.

TAB Electronics Guide to Understanding Electricity & Electronics. G. Randy Slone. 1996. pap. text ed. 19.95 (*0-07-058216-5*) McGraw.

TAB Electronics Guide to Understanding Electricity & Electronics. G. Randy Slone. 1996. text ed. 26.95 (*0-07-058215-7*) McGraw-Hill Prof.

TAB Electronics Technician's Online Resource Reference. Stephen J. Bigelow. LC 96-42140. (Illus.). 384p. 1997. text ed. 44.95 (*0-07-036219-X*); pap. text ed. 24.95 (*0-07-036220-3*) McGraw.

***Tab Electronics Yellow Pages: Equipment, Components, & Supplies.** Andrew Yoder. 1996. text ed. 49.95 (*0-07-076512-X*) McGraw.

TAB-McGraw-Hill Encyclopedia of Popular Electronics. Stan Gibilisco. LC 96-39022. (Illus.). 1008p. 1996. text ed. 69.50 (*0-07-024190-2*) McGraw.

TAB Service Manual for CCTV & MATV. Robert L. Goodman. 1991. pap. text ed. 18.95 (*0-07-155752-0*) McGraw.

TAB Service Manual for CCTV & MATV. Robert L. Goodman. (Illus.). 294p. 1991. 25.95 (*0-8306-7343-1*, 3343) TAB Bks.

Tab Service Manual for CCTV & MATV. Robert L. Goodman. 1991. pap. 18.95 (*0-8306-3343-X*) McGraw-Hill Prof.

"Tab-Slide-Guide" for All Major Keys of the Lee Oskar Melody Maker Ten-Hole Diatonic Harmonica, No. 3. R. Charles Potter. 6.95 (*0-9646765-3-2*) Charles Publns.

"Tab-Slide-Guide" for All Major Keys of the Ten-Hole Diatonic Harmonica, No. 1. R. Charles Potter. 6.95 (*0-9646765-1-6*) Charles Publns.

"Tab-Slide-Guide" for All Natural Minor Keys of the Ten-Hole Diatonic Harmonica, No. 2. R. Charles Potter. 6.95 (*0-9646765-2-4*) Charles Publns.

Tab Writing Book. (Illus.). 64p. 1977. pap. 7.95 (*0-8256-0187-8*, OK63305, Oak) Music Sales.

Tabacundo, No. 10. James Hoxeng et al. Tr. by Carla Clason & Yvonne Villanueva from SPA. (Technical Notes Ser.). 28p. (Orig.). 1976. Span. pap. 2.00 (*0-932288-23-5*) Ctr Intl Ed U of MA.

Tabanini of Thailand above the Isthumus of Kra. John J. Burton. LC 76-56190. (Illus.). 165p. (Orig.). 1978. 15.00 (*0-911836-10-1*) Entomological Repr.

Tabaqat-I-Akbari. Tr. by B. De. 1990. reprint ed. 25.00 (*81-85418-03-9*, Pub. by Low Price II) S Asia.

Tabaqat-i-Akbari of Khwajah Nizamuddin Ahmad: (A History of India from the Early Musabhman Invasions to the Thirty-Eighth Year of the Reign of Akbar), 3 vols., Set. Ed. by Baini Prashad. Tr. by Brajendranath. (C). 1992. reprint ed. 28.00 (*81-85418-90-X*, Pub. by Low Price II) S Asia.

***Tabard.** Michael A. Buggs. (Illus.). 64p. (Orig.). (J). (gr. 2-6). pap. 15.00 (*0-9657723-0-6*) Buggs Bks.

Tabasco Cookbook: 125 Years of America's Favorite Pepper Sauce. Paul McIlhenny & Barbara Hunter. LC 92-5520. 144p. 1993. 15.00 (*0-517-58965-6*, C P Pubs) Crown Pub Group.

Tabatha's Tickle. Robin Wilde. (Orig.). 1997. mass mkt. 6.50 (*1-56333-468-2*) Masquerade.

Tabbakh al Lebanie: Lebanese Cooking. Ibrahim Mouzannar. (Illus.). 200p. (ARA.). 16.95 (*0-86685-278-6*, LDL2786, Pub. by Librairie du Liban FR) Intl Bk Ctr.

Tabbles of Bower. Jennifer Bloomer. (Swanson Lectures). 50p. 1991. pap. write for info. (*1-880337-01-0*) Cranbrook Acad.

Tabbner's Nursing Care: Theory & Practice. 2nd ed. Ed. by Jackie Chandler. (Illus.). 782p. (Orig.). 1991. pap. text ed. 38.50 (*0-443-04030-3*) Churchill.

Tabby: A Story in Pictures. Aliki. LC 94-18523. 32p. (J). 1995. 13.95 (*0-06-024915-3*); lib. bdg. 13.89 (*0-06-024916-1*) HarpC.

Tabby Cat. Stuart A. Kallen. LC 95-10525. (J). (gr. k-3). 1995. lib. bdg. 13.99 (*1-56239-447-9*) Abdo & Dghtrs.

Tabby Cat Wants That. Outlet Book Co. Staff. (J). 1991. 3.99 (*0-517-05682-8*) Random Hse Value.

Tabel o Rangakh - Rangtabelle - Table des Rangs - Table of Ranks: 1722-1917. Timothy F. Boettger. (Illus.). 50p. (Orig.). (ENG, FRE, GER & RUS.). Date not set. pap. 15.95 (*0-9651330-8-7*) T F Boettger.

Tabellae Defisionis de la Sicilia Griega. Maria Del Amor Lopez Jimeno. (C & BM Ser.: No. 22). 269p. (SPA.). 1992. pap. 52.00 (*90-256-1002-1*, Pub. by A M Hakkert NE) Benjamins North Am.

Taber: Descendants of Jos. & Philip, Sons of Philip Taber from Rhode Island, Conn. & Long Island. A. A. Wright & A. H. Wright. 86p. 1995. reprint ed. pap. 17.00 (*0-8328-4848-4*); reprint ed. lib. bdg. 27.00 (*0-8328-4847-6*) Higginson Bk Co.

Taberna Pauperum: The Development of a New Background to the Nativity of Christ in the Fourteenth & Fifteenth Centuries in the North. Israel Oren. LC 93-31501. (Hermeneutics of Art Ser.: Vol. 3). 1994. write for info. (*0-8204-2073-5*) P Lang Pubng.

Tabernacle. N. Levine. (Illus.). 144p. 1990. boxed 125.00 (*1-871055-15-6*) Soncino Pr.

Tabernacle. Martin R. DeHaan. 185p. 1979. reprint ed. pap. 11.99 (*0-310-23491-3*, 9502P) Zondervan.

Tabernacle: A Study Guide to Discover the True Meaning of the Tabernacle. Dean Guest. (Illus.). 60p. (C). 1991. reprint ed. pap. 3.95 (*1-879667-01-0*) Dove Pr TX.

Tabernacle: Camping with God. Stephen F. Olford. LC 78-173686. 187p. 1971. 14.99 (*0-87213-675-2*) Loizeaux.

***Tabernacle: God's Perfect Plan of Salvation to All Mankind.** 2nd rev. ed. Hugh B. McGowan. (Illus.). 152p. 1997. reprint ed. pap. text ed. 7.95 (*0-9657661-0-1*) Impact Minist.

Tabernacle: Its Priests & Its Services. rev. ed. William Brown. 232p. 1996. 19.95 (*1-56563-195-1*); pap. 12.95 (*1-56563-229-X*) Hendrickson MA.

Tabernacle: Patterns & Directions for a Scale Model. Winifred E. Griffith. (Illus.). (Orig.). 1986. pap. 6.95 (*0-914598-58-9*) Padre Prods.

Tabernacle in the Wilderness. David Little. LC 89-36832. 1989. Pkg. of 5. pap. 14.95 (*0-87213-561-6*) Loizeaux.

Tabernacle in the Wilderness. David Little. LC 89-36832. 59p. 1989. pap. 2.99 (*0-87213-520-9*) Loizeaux.

Tabernacle in the Wilderness. John Ritchie. LC 82-178. 120p. (C). 1982. reprint ed. pap. 5.99 (*0-8254-3616-8*) Kregel.

Tabernacle in the Wilderness see Tabernaculo en el Desierto

Tabernacle of David. rev. ed. Kevin J. Conner. (Illus.). 286p. 1986. 11.95 (*0-914936-94-8*) BT Pub.

Tabernacle of Israel: Its Structure & Symbolism. James Strong. LC 85-8100. (Illus.). 118p. 1987. pap. 9.99 (*0-8254-3745-8*, Kregel Class) Kregel.

Tabernacle of Moses. Kevin J. Conner. (Illus.). 128p. 1988. 10.95 (*0-914936-93-X*) BT Pub.

Tabernacle: Plans for the Sanctuary see Torah Anthology: Meam Lo'ez

Tabernacle, Priesthood & the Offerings. Henry W. Soltau. LC 72-88590. 488p. pap. 14.99 (*0-8254-3750-4*) Kregel.

Tabernacle Talks Today. R. P. Daniel. pap. 5.95 (*0-88172-020-8*) Believers Bkshelf.

Tabernacle Types & Teaching. Edward Laity. 1980. pap. 3.95 (*0-86544-011-5*) Salv Army Suppl South.

***Tabernaculo.** E. Blattner. (SPA.). pap. 1.95 (*0-8297-0601-1*) Life Pubs Intl.

Tabernaculo en el Desierto. John Ritchie. Orig. Title: The Tabernacle in the Wilderness. (Illus.). 144p. (SPA.). 1987. pap. 4.99 (*0-8254-1616-7*, Edit Portavoz) Kregel.

***Tabernaculo y la Igelsia.** G. Edwards. (SPA.). 6.95 (*0-8297-0998-3*) Life Pubs Intl.

An Asterisk (*) at the beginning of an entry indicates that the title is appearing in BIP for the first time.

Taber's Cyclopedic Medical Dictionary. 18th deluxe ed. Ed. by Clayton L. Thomas. (Illus.). 2439p. (C). 1997. text ed. 69.00 (0-8036-0195-6) Davis Co.

Taber's Cyclopedic Medical Dictionary: (Not Thumb-Indexed) 18th ed. Ed. by Clayton L. Thomas. (Illus.). 2439p. (C). 1997. text ed. 29.95 (0-8036-0194-8) Davis Co.

Taber's Cyclopedic Medical Dictionary: (Thumb-Indexed) 18th ed. Ed. by Clayton L. Thomas. (Illus.). 2439p. (C). 1997. text ed. 32.95 (0-8036-0193-X) Davis Co.

***Taber's Indexed Medical Dictionary, 1997.** 18th ed. pap. 36.00 (0-614-26996-2, 4726) Medicode Inc.

Taber's Medical Word Book with Pronunciations. Ed. by Clayton L. Thomas. LC 90-2948. 876p. (C). 1990. pap. text ed. 19.95 (0-8036-8265-4) Davis Co.

***Taber's Plain Medical Dictionary, 1997.** 18th ed. pap. 33. 00 (0-614-26997-0, 4727) Medicode Inc.

Tabibito (the Traveler) Hideki Yukawa. Tr. by L. M. Brown & R. Yoshida. 224p. 1982. text ed. 47.00 (9971-950-09-X); pap. text ed. 21.00 (9971-950-10-3) World Scientific Pub.

***Tabitha, No. 4.** 112p. (J). Date not set. write for info. (0-7814-0241-7, Chariot Bks) Chariot Victor.

Tabitha: The Fabulous Flying Feline. Carol A. Timmel. LC 96-13693. (Illus.). (J). 1996. 15.95 (0-8027-8448-8); pap. 16.85 (0-8027-8449-6) Walker & Co.

Tabitha Bible Class, Vol. I. Sharon Bryan. 1987. teacher ed., pap. 5.75 (0-89137-819-7); student ed., pap. 4.95 (0-89137-818-9) Quality Pubns.

Tabitha Bible Class, Vol. III. Sharon Fleck. 75p. 1996. pap. 5.75 (0-89137-827-8) Quality Pubns.

Tabitha Bible Class, Vol. III. Sharon Fleck. (Illus.). 34p. (J). (gr. 4-10). 1996. pap. 4.95 (0-89137-826-X) Quality Pubns.

Tabitha Jones. 2nd ed. Jane Weinberger. (Illus.). 40p. (Orig.). (J). (ps-4). 1985. pap. 3.95 (0-932433-07-3) Windswept Hse.

Tabitha Stories. A. N. Wilson. LC 96-43463. (Illus.). 48p. (Orig.). (J). (gr. 1-4). 1997. pap. 6.99 (0-7636-0161-6) Candlewick Pr.

Tabitha's Tease. Robin Wilde. (Orig.). 1996. mass mkt. 5.95 (1-56333-387-2) Masquerade.

***Tabla Cronologica de los Cinco Mundos - Chronological Chart of the Five Worlds.** Whitcomb. (Tablas Cronologicas - Chronological Chart Ser.). (SPA.). write for info. (1-56063-929-6) Editorial Unilit.

***Tabla Cronologica del Nuevo Testamento - Chronological Chart of the New Testament.** Boyer. (Tablas Cronologicas - Chronological Chart Ser.). (SPA.). write for info. (1-56063-935-0) Editorial Unilit.

***Tabla Cronologica del Periodo Intertestamentario - Chronological Chart of the Period Between the Testaments.** Boyer. (Tablas Cronologicas Ser.). (SPA.). write for info. (1-56063-934-2) Editorial Unilit.

***Tabla Cronologica/Cautividad Babilonica I-II - Chart of Babylonia Captivity I-II.** Whitcomb. (Tablas Cronologicas - Chronological Chart Ser.). (SPA.). write for info. (1-56063-933-4) Editorial Unilit.

Tabla de Composicion de Alimentos de Uso Corriente en Puerto Rico. Escuela de Economia Domestica Staff. 31p. 1986. pap. 2.00 (0-8477-2305-4) U of PR Pr.

***Tabla de los Patriarcas y Jueces de A. T. - Chart of the O. T. Patriarchs & Judges.** Whitcomb. (Tablas Cronologicas - Chronological Chart Ser.). (SPA.). write for info. (1-56063-931-8) Editorial Unilit.

***Tabla de los Reyes/Profetas del A. T. - Chart of the O. T. Kings & Prophets.** Witcomb. (Tablas Cronologicas Ser.). (SPA.). write for info. (1-56063-932-6) Editorial Unilit.

***Tabla Legacy of Taranath Rao: Pranava Tala Prajna: Technique & Repertoire for the Drums of the Classical Music of North India.** Jeffrey M. Feldman. LC 95-68090. 205p. 1995. pap. 22.95 (0-9643694-6-X) Digitala.

Tabla, Lessons & Practice. 2nd ed. Aloke Dutta. (Illus.). 190p. (Orig.). 1995. pap. 20.00 (0-9646771-0-5) A Dutta.

Tabla of Lucknow: A Cultural Analysis of a Musical Tradition. James Kippen. (Cambridge Studies in Ethnomusicology). (Illus.). 264p. 1988. text ed. 80.00 (0-521-33528-0) Cambridge U Pr.

Tabla of Lucknow: A Cultural Analysis of a Musical Tradition. James Kippen. (Cambridge Studies in Ethnomusicology). (Illus.). 264p. 1988. digital audio 19. 95 (0-521-33529-9) Cambridge U Pr.

Tablado de Marionetas para Educacion de Principes. Ramon Del Valle-Inclan. Ed. by Cesar Oliva. (Nueva Austral Ser.: Vol. 129). (SPA.). 1991. pap. text ed. 17.95 (84-239-1929-3) Elliots Bks.

***Tablao Flamenco.** Mercedes A. Sanchez. (SPA.). pap. write for info. (0-89729-538-2) Ediciones.

Table. Monique Hooker. 1996. pap. 14.95 (0-8050-4867-7) H Holt & Co.

Table. Monique Hooker. LC 97-403. 1997. 27.50 (0-8050-4866-9) H Holt & Co.

Table. Diane Von Furstenberg. 160p. 1996. 40.00 (0-679-44757-1) Random.

Table Alphabetical of Hard Usual English Words. Robert Cawdry. LC 66-12119. 1977. reprint ed. 50.00 (0-8201-1007-8) Schol Facsimiles.

Table & Floor Games: Easy to Make - Fun to Play. Liz Wilmes & Dick Wilmes. Orig. Title: Make Take Games. (Illus.). 262p. (Orig.). 1994. pap. 19.95 (0-943452-16-3) Building Blocks.

Table Attendant Training. Donald McHugh. LC 83-720057. (Series 925). (Orig.). 1983. student ed. 8.00 (0-8064-0401-9); audio, vhs 169.00 (0-8064-0402-7) Bergwall.

Table aux Creves. Marcel Ayme. 1929. pap. 29.95 (0-8288-9054-4) Fr & Eur.

Table aux Creves. Marcel Ayme. (FRE.). 1990. reprint ed. pap. 12.95 (0-7859-1699-7, 2070361160) Fr & Eur.

Table Beckons: Thoughts & Recipes from the Kitchen of Alain Senderens. Alain Senderens. Tr. by Michael Krondl from FRE. LC 93-15912. (Illus.). 1993. 22.00 (0-374-12909-6) FS&G.

Table Before Me. Pauline E. Cramer. 127p. 1992. pap. 0.97 (0-8163-1079-3) Pacific Pr Pub Assn.

Table Blessings: Mealtime Prayers Throughout the Year. Victor-Antoine D'Avila-Latourrette. LC 94-71884. (Illus.). 176p. (Orig.). 1994. pap. 12.95 (0-87793-538-6) Ave Maria.

Table Book. William Hone. 1972. 59.95 (0-8490-1174-4) Gordon Pr.

***Table, Chair, Bear.** Jane Feder. 1997. pap. 5.95 (0-395-85075-4) HM.

Table, Chair, Bear: A Room in Many Languages. Jane Feder. LC 92-40529. (Illus.). 32p. (J). (ps-2). 1995. 13.95 (0-395-65938-8) Ticknor & Flds Bks Yng Read.

***Table Chic: Ideas & Themes for Creative Tables.** Kelly Hoppen. 1997. 25.00 (1-57145-651-1) Advan Mktg Servs.

***Table de Concordances Rythmique et Syntaxique d'Emaux et Camees.** Theophile Gautier. 525p. 1995. write for info. (3-487-09843-1) G Olms Pubs.

Table de Flandes: The Chess Master. Arturo P. Reverte. 1995. pap. 16.95 (0-679-76090-3, Vin) Random.

Table de la Bibliographie de Voltaire par Bengesco: Geneva, 1953, Vol. 1. Jean Malcolm. 1974. 30.00 (0-8115-0898-6) Periodicals Srv.

Table Decorating. New Holland Publ. Ltd. Staff. (C). 1989. 50.00 (0-685-32436-2, Pub. by New Holland Pubs UK) St Mut.

Table Decorating Book. George A. Saint. (Illus.). 112p. 1995. pap. 19.95 (1-57076-032-2, Trafalgar Sq Pub) Trafalgar.

Table Decoration. Pamela Westland. 1994. 14.98 (0-7858-0156-1) Bk Sales Inc.

Table Decorations. Jan Bridge. (Illus.). 64p. 1995. 9.99 (0-517-14171-X) Random Hse Value.

Table d'Hote. Daniel Boulanger. 273p. (FRE.). 1985. pap. 11.95 (0-7859-2023-4, 2070376974) Fr & Eur.

Table d'Hote. large type ed. Douglas Clark. 315p. 1981. 25. 99 (0-7089-0603-6) Ulverscroft.

Table-Driven Strategies for Rapid SAS Applications Development. Tanya Kolosova & Samuel Berestizhevsky. 230p. (C). 1995. pap. 34.95 (1-55544-245-5, BR55198) SAS Inst.

Table Flowers. Shane Connolly. (Illus.). 128p. 1996. 24.95 (1-57076-041-1, Trafalgar Sq Pub) Trafalgar.

Table Food Composition 1.1. Date not set. pap. text ed. write for info. (0-314-04882-0) West Pub.

***Table for Two.** (Collector's Ser.: Vol. 40). (Illus.). 64p. (Orig.). 1995. pap. write for info. (0-942320-52-2) Am Cooking.

Table for Two. Alisa Bair. 200p. (Orig.). 1997. pap. 8.95 (1-56148-218-8) Good Bks PA.

Table for Two: Making a Good Marriage Better. Cary A. Friedman. 1992. pap. 8.95 (0-944070-98-1) Feldheim.

Table for Two: Meat - & - Dairy - Free Recipes for Two. Joanne Stepaniak. LC 95-26091. 192p. (Orig.). 1996. pap. 12.95 (1-57067-019-6) Book Pub Co.

Table Formatting, Microcomputer/Keyboarding/ Formatting Applications. Crawford et al. (TA - Typing/ Keyboarding Ser.). 1986. pap. 13.95 (0-538-26130-7) S-W Pub.

***Table Graces.** Compiled by Lois L. Kaufman. (Charming Petites Ser.). (Illus.). 80p. 1997. 4.95 (0-88088-821-0) Peter Pauper.

Table in the Sky. Lee Minor. LC 88-51386. 53p. (J). (gr. k-3). 1989. 5.95 (1-55523-197-7) Winston-Derek.

Table in the Wilderness. Angus Kinnear. 200p. 1978. pap. 5.99 (0-8423-6900-7) Tyndale.

Table in the Wilderness. Watchman Nee. 1979. pap. 5.95 (0-87508-422-2) Chr Lit.

Table in Tuscany: Classic Recipes from the Heart of Italy. Leslie Forbes. (Illus.). 160p. 1991. pap. 16.95 (0-87701-832-4) Chronicle Bks.

Table Knives & Forks. Simon Moore. 1995. pap. 25.00 (0-7478-0295-5, Pub. by Shire UK) St Mut.

Table Layout & Decoration. Audrey Ellis. (Illus.). 1978. 14. 95 (0-8464-0907-0) Beekman Pubs.

Table Legs. Paul Lyons. LC 89-25840. 160p. (C). 1989. 15. 95 (0-941533-42-5) New Amsterdam Bks.

***Table, les Oiseaux! - Bird Feeding Banquet.** Michael Martchenko. (Droles D'Histories Ser.). (Illus.). 24p. (FRE.). (J). (ps up). 1996. pap. 4.95 (2-89021-184-3, Pub. by Les Editions CN) Firefly Bks Ltd.

Table Mountain Complex as Derived from a Synthesis of 124 Archaeological Sites Clustered in Stratified Biological, Geographical & Geological Zones. Ronald V. May. (Illus.). 119p. (C). 1987. reprint ed. pap. text ed. 10.65 (1-55567-431-3) Coyote Press.

Table Mountain Quartzite & Moose Formation (New Names) & Associated Rocks of the Middle Proterozoic Belt Supergroup, Highland Mountains, Southwestern Montana. Ed. by J. Michael O'Neill. LC 95-3665. (Belt Supergroup in the Highland Mountains & Probable Equivalent Rocks in the Pioneer & Anaconda Ranges Bulletin Ser.: Vol. 2121). 1995. write for info. (0-615-00519-5) US Geol Survey.

Table Number Seven. large type ed. Victor Canning. 321p. 1989. 25.99 (0-7089-1970-7) Ulverscroft.

Table of Contents. John McPhee. 293p. 1985. 19.95 (0-374-27241-7) FS&G.

Table of Contents. John McPhee. 294p. 1986. pap. 12.00 (0-374-52008-9) FS&G.

Table of Food Composition 93. Date not set. pap. text ed. write for info. (0-314-02442-5) West Pub.

Table of Green Fields. Guy Davenport. LC 93-18677. 160p. 1993. 21.95 (0-8112-1251-3) New Directions.

Table of Integrals, Series, & Products. 5th ed. J. S. Gradshteyn & J. M. Ryzhjk. Ed. by Alan Jeffrey. 1204p. 1993. text ed. 65.00 (0-12-294755-X) Acad Pr.

Table of Inwardness. Calvin Miller. LC 84-9134. 120p. (Orig.). 1984. pap. 10.99 (0-87784-832-7, 832) InterVarsity.

Table of Isotopes, Vol. 1. 8th ed. Richard B. Firestone. Ed. by Virginia S. Shirley. 3000p. 1996. write for info. (0-471-07730-5) Wiley.

Table of Isotopes, Vol. 2. 8th ed. Richard B. Firestone. Ed. by Virginia S. Shirley. LC 95-46439. 1996. text ed. 0.01 (0-471-14917-9) Wiley.

Table of Isotopes, 2 vols., Vol. 2. 8th ed. Richard B. Firestone. Ed. by Virginia S. Shirley. LC 95-46439. 1996. text ed. 295.00 (0-471-14918-7) Wiley.

Table Of Isotopes, Vol. 2. 8th ed. Richard B. Firestone. Ed. by Virginia S. Shirley. 1996. 145.00 (0-471-16405-4) Wiley.

Table of Judgments: Critique of Pure Reason A67-76; B92-101. Reinhard Brandt. Tr. by Eric Watkins. (North American Kant Society Studies in Philosophy: Vol. 4). ix, 151p. (Orig.). (C). 1996. pap. text ed. 20.00 (0-924922-24-9); lib. bdg. 39.00 (0-924922-74-5) Ridgeview.

Table of Laser Lines in Gases & Vapors. 3rd enl. rev. ed. (Optical Sciences Ser.: Vol. 2). 1980. 50.95 (0-387-10347-3) Spr-Verlag.

Table of Offerings: Seventeen Years of Acquisitions of Egyptian & Ancient Near Easter Art by William Kelly Simpson for the Museum of Fine Arts, Boston. Museum of Fine Arts, Egyptian Department Staff & William K. Simpson. Ed. by Cynthia M. Purvis. LC 87-50312. (Illus.). 112p. 1987. pap. 13.00 (0-87846-280-5) Mus Fine Arts Boston.

Table of Proceedings in Juvenile Courts. Shaw & Sons Ltd. Staff. (C). 1984. 22.00 (0-7219-0189-1, Pub. by Scientific UK) St Mut.

Table of Public Statutes: Table of Acts & Responsible Ministers, No. 1, Issue 94-1. 338p. (Orig.). 1994. pap. 64.95 (0-660-59107-3, Pub. by Canada Commun Grp CN) Accents Pubns.

Table of Radioactive Isotopes. Edgardo Browne & Richard B. Firestone. LC 86-9069. 1056p. 1986. text ed. 225.00 (0-471-84909-X) Wiley.

Table of Remembrance: Communion Meditations. Bill Norris & Judy Norris. 104p. (Orig.). 1991. pap. text ed. 6.99 (0-89900-372-9) College Pr Pub.

Table of the Lord. Dominic Scotto. 73p. (Orig.). 1991. pap. text ed. 5.95 (0-932506-78-X, 678X) St Bedes Pubns.

Table of the Sin Function & Sin Squared Function for Values from 2 Degrees to 87 Degrees. H. Anne Plettinger. 46p. 1965. pap. 63.00 (0-677-01100-8) Gordon & Breach.

***Table Olives.** Garrido Fernandez et al. (Illus.). 256p. 1997. text ed. 99.00 (0-412-71810-3, Chap & Hall NY) Chapman & Hall.

Table Prayers: New Prayers, Old Favorites, Songs, & Responses. Compiled by Mildred Tengbom. LC 77-72451. 128p. 1977. pap. 5.99 (0-8066-1594-X, 10-6185, Augsburg) Augsburg Fortress.

Table Rapping & Automatic Writing, 4. Alexander Verner & Swami Brahma. pap. 2.00 (0-911662-28-6) Yoga.

Table Rock. large type ed. Les Savage, Jr. LC 93-29691. 1993. lib. bdg. 19.95 (0-8161-5863-0, GK Hall) Thorndike Pr.

Table Rock. Les Savage, Jr. LC 92-43526. 184p. 1993. reprint ed. 19.95 (0-8027-1267-3) Walker & Co.

Table Rock Basin in Barry County, Missouri. Lee M. Adams. Ed. by Carl H. Chapman. (Memoir Ser.: No. 1). (Illus.). 63p. (Orig.). 1950. pap. 1.50 (0-943414-17-2) MO Arch Soc.

Table Rocks of Jackson County: Islands in the Sky. Chris Reyes et al. LC 93-91595. (Illus.). 142p. (Orig.). (C). 1994. pap. 14.00 (0-9637486-0-2) Last Minute.

Table Saw Basics. Roger W. Cliffe. LC 84-8676. (Basics Ser.). (Illus.). 128p. 1991. pap. 10.95 (0-8069-7216-5) Sterling.

Table Saw Book. R. Cristoforo. 1991. 23.95 (0-8306-5304-X) McGraw-Hill Prof.

Table Saw Book. R. J. De Cristoforo. 1987. text ed. 23.95 (0-07-157033-0); pap. text ed. 22.95 (0-07-157042-X) McGraw.

Table Saw Book. R. J. De Cristoforo. (Illus.). 352p. 1987. 23.95 (0-8306-7789-5, 2789); pap. 16.95 (0-8306-2789-8) McGraw-Hill Prof.

Table Saw Book. Kelly Mehler. 192p. 1993. pap. 25.95 (1-56158-011-2) Taunton.

***Table Saw Shop Reference Book.** Roger Cliffe. 1998. write for info. (0-8069-9779-6) Sterling.

Table Saw Techniques. Roger W. Cliffe. LC 84-8676. (Illus.). 352p. 1984. pap. 17.95 (0-8069-7912-7) Sterling.

***Table Saw Techniques.** rev. ed. Roger Cliffes. LC 97-19321. 1997. 18.95 (0-8069-4268-1) Sterling.

Table Setting: East Meets West. Kuwako Takahashi. (Illus.). 144p. 1992. 39.95 (4-07-975138-9, Pub. by Shufunomoto Co Ltd JA) C E Tuttle.

Table Setting Guide. rev. ed. Sharon E. Dlugosch. LC 90-2353. (Illus.). 80p. (Orig.). 1990. pap. 8.95 (0-918420-11-3) Brighton Pubns.

Table Settings. Robin Emmerson. 1989. pap. 25.00 (0-7478-0139-8, Pub. by Shire UK) St Mut.

***Table Settings: 100 Inspirational Stylings, Themes & Layouts, with over 60 Sensational Step-by-Step Projects.** Tessa Evelegh. (Illus.). 160p. 1997. 27.50 (1-85967-380-5, Lorenz Bks) Anness Pub.

Table Swift Construction Manual. Richard Schneider & Myrna Schneider. (Spinster-Helper Ser.). (Illus.). (Orig.). 1984. pap. 1.95 (0-936984-04-X) Schneider Pubs.

Table Talk. A. Bronson Alcott. 208p. 1969. 15.00 (0-87556-010-5) Saifer.

***Table Talk.** Luther. (Great Devotional Classics Ser.). pap. 1.85 (0-687-61133-4) Abingdon.

***Table Talk.** Luther. pap. 2.00 (0-8358-0052-0) Upper Room Bks.

Table Talk. Mimi Wilson & Mary B. Lagerborg. LC 94-14105. 1994. spiral bd. 10.99 (1-56179-254-3) Focus Family.

Table Talk. Amos B. Alcott. (Works of Amos Bronson Alcott). 1989. reprint ed. lib. bdg. 79.00 (0-685-27408-X) Rprt Serv.

Table-Talk. Amos B. Alcott. (BCL1-PS American Literature Ser.). 178p. 1992. reprint ed. lib. bdg. 69.00 (0-7812-6667-X) Rprt Serv.

Table Talk: A Maundy Thursday Resource. Marion Fairman. 16p. (Orig.). 1995. pap. 3.50 (0-7880-0290-2) CSS OH.

Table Talk: An Inside Look at Teacher Negotiations from Both Sides of the Table. James Q. Harty. 210p. (Orig.). 1992. pap. write for info. (0-9631255-0-8) EduPRESS PA.

Table Talk: Appalachian Meals & Memories. Sidney S. Farr. 174p. (C). 1994. 29.95 (0-8229-3785-9); pap. 15.95 (0-8229-5533-4) U of Pittsburgh Pr.

Table Talk: From Bridge to Brunches. Becky Bowdre et al. (Illus.). 202p. (Orig.). 1986. spiral bd. 8.00 (0-9616705-0-9) Table Talk Bridge.

Table Talk: Martin Luther. Robert Van De Weyer. 320p. 1995. pap. 12.00 (0-00-627937-6) Harper SF.

Table Talk: Resources for the Communion Meal. Ed. by Jane E. McAvoy. 112p. (Orig.). 1993. pap. 8.99 (0-8272-3632-8) Chalice Pr.

Table Talk! Three Hundred Sixty-Five Ways to Reclaim the Family Dinner Hour. Steve Bennett & Ruth Bennett. (Illus.). 236p. (Orig.). 1993. pap. 6.95 (1-55850-300-5) Adams Media.

Table-Talk: 1689. John Selden. Ed. by Edward Arber. 1972. reprint ed. 15.00 (0-87556-314-7) Saifer.

Table-Talk of G. B. S. Archibald Henderson. LC 74-16315. (George Bernard Shaw Ser.: No. 92). 1974. lib. bdg. 75. 00 (0-8383-1890-8) M S G Haskell Hse.

Table-Talk of John Selden: With a Biographical Preface & Notes by S.W. Singer; to Which Is Added Spare Minutes; Or, Resolved Meditations & Premeditated Resolutions by Arthur Warwick. rev. ed. John Selden. LC 74-39207. (Select Bibliographies Reprint Ser.). 1977. reprint ed. 23.95 (0-8369-6809-3) Ayer.

Table Talk of W. H. Auden. Alan Ansen. Ed. by Nicholas Jenkins. LC 90-7414. 134p. 1990. 15.95 (0-86538-072-4) Ontario Rev NJ.

Table Tennis. (Take up Sports! Ser.). (Illus.). 64p. pap. 4.95 (1-56757-056-9) Appleton Comms.

***Table Tennis.** Date not set. 35.95 (0-8464-4426-7) Beekman Pubs.

Table Tennis. Martin Sklorz. (EP Sports Ser.). (Illus.). 1971. 6.95 (0-7158-0582-7) Charles River Bks.

Table Tennis. Gordon Steggal. (Skills of the Game Ser.). (Illus.). 122p. 1990. pap. 19.95 (1-85223-159-9, Pub. by Crowood Pr UK) Trafalgar.

Table Tennis: Steps to Success. Larry Hodges. LC 92-37606. (Steps to Success Activity Ser.). (Illus.). 160p. 1993. pap. 14.95 (0-87322-403-5, PHOD0403) Human Kinetics.

Table Tennis: The Sport. Scott Preiss. 80p. (C). 1991. per. write for info. (0-697-13635-3) Brown & Benchmark.

Table Tennis Education Program. Escalade Sports Staff. 160p. 1994. per., pap. text ed. 14.99 (0-7872-0225-8) Kendall-Hunt.

Table, the Donkey & the Stick. Jacob W. Grimm & Wilhelm K. Grimm. (Illus.). (J). (ps-3). 1976. lib. bdg. 7.95 (0-07-022701-2) McGraw.

Table Top Football. Klutz Press Staff. 30p. 1993. pap. 8.95 (1-878257-50-1) Klutz Pr.

Table Top Lightning. Lloyd F. Richie. 33p. 1992. 15.00 (0-914119-26-5) Tesla Bk Co.

***Table-Top Science: Intermediate.** Linda Allison. (Illus.). 96p. (Orig.). (J). (gr. 3-6). 1997. pap. 11.95 (1-57612-019-8, MM2051) Monday Morning Bks.

***Table-Top Science: Primary.** Linda Allison. (Illus.). 96p. (Orig.). (J). (gr. 1-3). 1997. pap. 11.95 (1-57612-018-X, MM2050) Monday Morning Bks.

Table Where Rich People Sit. Byrd Baylor. LC 93-1251. (Illus.). 32p. (J). 1994. text ed. 15.00 (0-684-19653-0, Atheneum Bks Young) S&S Childrens.

Table Without Flies, Please. Bill Griffith. (Illus.). 120p. 1990. 14.95 (1-56097-032-4) Fantagraph Bks.

Tableau Politique de la France de L'ouest Sous la Troisieme Republique: The Political Map of Western France Under the Third Republic. Andre Siegfried. LC 74-25784. (European Sociology Ser.). 566p. 1975. reprint ed. 46.95 (0-405-06537-X) Ayer.

Tableaux, Charades, & Pantomimes: Adapted Alike to Parlor Entertainments, School & Church Exhibitions, & for Use on the Amateur Stage. LC 70-167485. (Granger Index Reprint Ser.). 1977. reprint ed. 17.95 (0-8369-6290-7) Ayer.

Tableaux Culturels de la France. J. S. Ravise. (C). 1984. 75. 00 (0-85950-206-6, Pub. by S Thornes Pubs UK) St Mut.

Tableaux Etudes, Opus 33 & 39. Sergei Rachmaninoff. 104p. 1985. pap. 12.95 (0-7935-3164-0, 00123087) H Leonard.

Tableaux Vivants. (Orig.). 1993. mass mkt. 4.95 (1-56333-121-7) Masquerade.

Tables. Amos B. Alcott. (Works of Amos Bronson Alcott). 1989. reprint ed. lib. bdg. 79.00 (0-685-27410-1) Rprt Serv.

Tables, Vol. 10. 4th ed. John H. Wigmore. 1988. 145.00 (0-316-93984-6) Little.

Tables Alphabetiques des Noms Cites, 4 vols., Set. Stendhal. 195.00 (0-686-55082-X) Fr & Eur.

Tables & Chairs. LC 95-1912. (Best of Fine Woodworking Ser.). 1995. pap. 14.95 (1-56158-100-3) Taunton.

T

Tables & Desks. LC 93-49732. (Art of Woodworking Ser.). 144p. 1994. 19.95 (*0-8094-9512-0*) Time-Life.

Tables & Figures for Use with Thermodynamics. 5th ed. Kenneth Wark. 128p. 1988. pap. text ed. write for info. (*0-07-068288-7*) McGraw.

Tables & Nomograms of Hydrochemical Analysis. Igor' I Sokolov. LC 60-13952. 89p. reprint ed. pap. 25.40 (*0-317-09355-X*, 2020662) Bks Demand.

Tables & Other Facts & Figures. (Basic Math Ser.: No. 678-5). (Illus.). (gr. 1-3). 3.50 (*0-7214-0663-7*, Ladybrd) Penguin.

Tables, Data & Formulae for Engineers. A. Greer & D. J. Hancox. 96p. (C). 1988. boxed 39.00 (*0-85950-023-3*, Pub. by S Thornes Pubs UK) St Mut.

Tables, Data & Formulae for Engineers & Mathematicians. 2nd rev. ed. A. Greer & D. J. Hancox. 104p. (C). 1989. pap. 21.00 (*0-7487-0077-3*, Pub. by S Thornes Pubs UK) St Mut.

Tables for Active Filter Design: Based on Cauer MCPER Functions. Mario Biey & Amedeo Premoli. LC 84-73279. (Illus.). 576p. 1985. reprint ed. pap. 164.20 (*0-7837-9770-2*, 2060498) Bks Demand.

Tables for Aspect Research. Gauquelin F. Schneider. 128p. 1986. pap. 9.95 (*0-917086-90-2*) ACS Pubns.

Tables for Estimating Median Fatigue Limits. Robert E. Little. LC 80-69062. (ASTM Special Technical Publication Ser.: No. 731). 184p. reprint ed. pap. 52.50 (*0-8357-5555-X*, 2035185) Bks Demand.

Tables for Microscopic Identification of Ore Minerals. E. W. Uytenbogaardt & E. A. Burke. (Earth Science Ser.). 430p. 1985. reprint ed. pap. 13.95 (*0-486-64839-7*) Dover.

Tables for Normal Sampling with Unknown Variances: The Student Distribution & Economically Optimal Sampling Plans. Jerome Bracken & Arthur Schliefer. LC 64-13716. 208p. reprint ed. pap. 59.30 (*0-317-08675-8*, 2002196) Bks Demand.

Tables for Normal Tolerance Limits, Sampling Plans & Screening. Robert E. Odeh & D. B. Owen. LC 79-27905. (Statistics, Textbooks & Monographs: No. 32). 332p. reprint ed. pap. 94.70 (*0-7837-7135-5*, 2052529) Bks Demand.

Tables for Statisticians. J. White et al. 80p. (C). 1979. pap. 21.00 (*0-85950-462-X*, Pub. by S Thornes Pubs UK) St Mut.

Tables for the Automotive Trade: Special Edition Within the Scope of Tech. Coop. in Vocational Training. 14th ed. G. Hamm & G. Burk. 1986. reprint ed. write for info. (*0-85226-350-3*, Pub. by Wiley Estrn II) Franklin.

Tables for the Calculation of Friction in Internal Flows. H. R. Wallingford & D. I. Barr. 331p. 1995. 86.40 (*0-7277-2046-5*) Am Soc Civil Eng.

Tables for the Design & Analysis of Stiffened Steel Plates. Noel W. Murray & Georg Thierauf. 197p. 1981. 54.00 (*3-528-08673-4*, Pub. by Vieweg & Sohn GW) Informatica.

Tables for Traffic Management & Design. 2nd ed. Theodor Frankel. LC 76-29193. (Traffic Ser.). (Illus.). 84p. (C). 1983. pap. text ed. 15.95 (*1-56016-015-2*) ABC TeleTraining.

Tables for Use in High Resolution Mass Spectrometry. D. Henneberg & K. Casper. Incl. Chemical Formulae from Mass Determinations. LC 75-130645. (*0-318-59376-9*); LC 75-130645. 208p. reprint ed. pap. 59.30 (*0-317-29340-0*, 2024031) Bks Demand.

Tables from NESC-1990. rev. ed. (Illus.). 64p. 1989. pap. 28.00 (*1-55937-016-5*, SH12658) IEEE Standards.

Tables of Angular Scattering Functions for Heterodisperse Systems of Spheres. Mukul Yajnik et al. LC 68-57471. 1304p. reprint ed. pap. 180.00 (*0-7837-3578-2*, 2043437) Bks Demand.

Tables of Ascendants & Midheavens. Ernest R. Grant. 136p. 1954. 10.00 (*0-86690-108-6*, G1151-014) Am Fed Astrologers.

Tables of Bessel Transforms. F. Oberhettinger. LC 72-88727. 289p. 1972. 42.95 (*0-387-05997-0*) Spr-Verlag.

Tables of Bullet Performance. Philip Mannes. Ed. by Dave Wolfe. 407p. (Orig.). 1980. text ed. 17.50 (*0-935632-06-9*); pap. text ed. 17.50 (*0-935632-05-0*) Wolfe Pub Co.

Tables of Clebsch-Gordan, Racah, & Subduction Coefficients of SU(n) Groups. Jin-Quan Chen & Pei-Ning Wang. 240p. 1987. text ed. 114.00 (*9971-5-0072-8*); pap. text ed. 64.00 (*9971-5-0073-6*) World Scientific Pub.

Tables of Diurnal Planetary Motion. 176p. 11.00 (*0-86690-055-1*, A1005-014) Am Fed Astrologers.

Tables of Dominant Weight Multiplicities for Representations of Simple Lie Algebras. Bremner et al. (Pure & Applied Mathematics Ser.: Vol. 90). 352p. 1985. 145.00 (*0-8247-7270-9*) Dekker.

Tables of Experimental Data Used for the Correlation of the Thermophysical Properties of Ethane. (Illus.). 165p. (Orig.). (C). 1994. pap. text ed. 65.00 (*0-7881-1126-4*) DIANE Pub.

Tables of Functions with Formulae & Curves. 4th ed. Eugene Jahnke & Fritz Emde. 1945. pap. text ed. 8.95 (*0-486-60133-1*) Dover.

Tables of Houses Campanus. Astro Numeric Service Staff. LC 77-77345. 208p. 1977. 12.00 (*0-86690-054-3*, A2005-054) Am Fed Astrologers.

Tables of Houses for U. S. Latitudes. abr. ed. Magnus Jensen. 14p. 1970. reprint ed. spiral bd. 4.50 (*0-7873-0474-3*) Hlth Research.

Tables of Houses Koch. Astro Numeric Service Staff. LC 77-77346. 208p. 1977. 15.00 (*0-86690-251-1*, A2006-054) Am Fed Astrologers.

Tables of Houses Placidus. Astro Numeric Service Staff. LC 77-77344. 208p. 1977. 14.00 (*0-86690-252-X*, A2007-054) Am Fed Astrologers.

Tables of Indefinite Integrals. G. Petit Bois. 1906. pap. text ed. 7.95 (*0-486-60225-7*) Dover.

Tables of Indefinite Integrals. A. P. Prudnikov et al. 192p. 1989. text ed. 91.00 (*2-88124-710-5*) Gordon & Breach.

Tables of Integrals & Other Mathematical Data. 4th ed. Herbert B. Dwight. (C). 1961. write for info. (*0-02-331170-3*, Macmillan Coll) P-H.

Tables of Intensities for the Calibration of Infrared Spectroscope Measurements in the Liquid Phase: International Union of Pure & Applied Chemistry, Physical Chemistry Division, Commission on Molecular Structure & Spectroscopy. John E. Bertie et al. 272p. 1995. 69.50 (*0-86542-926-X*) Blackwell Sci.

Tables of Ion Implantation Spatial Distribution. A. F. Burenkov et al. 462p. 1986. text ed. 347.00 (*2-88124-071-2*) Gordon & Breach.

Tables of Lame Polynomials. F. Arscott & I. M. Khabaza. (Mathematical Tables Ser.). 172.00 (*0-08-009739-1*, Pub. by Pergamon Repr UK) Franklin.

Tables of Light-Scattering Functions: Relative Indices of Less Than Unity & Infinity. Richard Henry Boll. LC 57-7175. reprint ed. pap. 93.00 (*0-317-08493-3*, 2011234) Bks Demand.

Tables of Light Scattering Functions for Spherical Particles. William J. Pangonis. LC 56-12604. 123p. reprint ed. pap. 35.10 (*0-7837-3790-4*, 2043610) Bks Demand.

Tables of Magic. George Baxter. 160p. 1996. pap. 9.95 (*1-55622-486-9*) Wordware Pub.

Tables of Mellin Transforms. F. Oberhettinger. vii, 275p. 1975. 43.95 (*0-387-06942-9*) Spr-Verlag.

Tables of Normalized Associations Legendre Polynomials. S. Belousov & D. Brown. LC 62-17650. (Mathematical Tables Ser.: Vol. 18). 1962. 176.00 (*0-08-009723-5*, Pub. by Pergamon Repr UK) Franklin.

Tables of Planetary Phenomena. 2nd rev. ed. Neil F. Michelsen. 249p. 1996. pap. 29.95 (*0-935127-31-3*) ACS Pubns.

Tables of Principal Unitary Representations Fedorov Groups. D. Faddeyev & Prabir Basu. LC 63-18934. (Mathematical Tables Ser.: Vol. 34). 1964. 74.00 (*0-08-010056-2*, Pub. by Pergamon Repr UK) Franklin.

Tables of Random Permutations. Lincoln E. Moses & Robert V. Oakford. LC 63-12041. 233p. 1963. 37.50 (*0-8047-0148-2*) Stanford U Pr.

Tables of Scattering Functions for Heterodisperse Systems. Arthur F. Stevenson & Wilfried Heller. LC 61-8315. 221p. reprint ed. pap. 63.00 (*0-7837-3579-0*, 2043438) Bks Demand.

Tables of Screening Design. Donald J. Wheeler. 305p. (C). 1989. pap. 40.00 (*0-945320-05-1*) SPC Pr.

Tables of Spectral Data for Structure Determination of Organic Compounds. 2nd ed. E. Pretsch et al. (Chemical Laboratory Practice Ser.). xiii, 415p. 1996. 59.95 (*0-387-51202-0*) Spr-Verlag.

Tables of Standard Electrode Potentials. Guilio Milazzo & Sergio Caroli. LC 77-8111. 437p. reprint ed. pap. 124.60 (*0-685-20767-6*, 2030411) Bks Demand.

Tables of the Hypergeometric Probability Distribution. Gerald J. Lieberman & Donald B. Owen. vi, 726p. 1961. 79.50 (*0-8047-0057-5*) Stanford U Pr.

Tables of the Incomplete Beta Function. Karl Pearson. 205p. 1968. lib. bdg. 100.00 (*0-521-05922-4*) Lubrecht & Cramer.

Tables of the Incomplete Beta-Function. Karl Pearson. 505p. 1968. 160.00 (*0-85264-704-2*) St Mut.

Tables of the Motion of the Moon, 3 vols., Set. Ernest Brown & Henry B. Hedrick. 1920. pap. 750.00 (*0-685-89789-3*) Elliots Bks.

Tables of the Non-Central t-Distribution: Density Function, Cumulative Distribution Function & Percentage Points. George J. Resnikoff & Gerald J. Lieberman. LC 57-7832. x, 389p. 1957. 57.50 (*0-8047-0492-9*) Stanford U Pr.

Tables of the SU(mn) SU(m) x SU(n) Coefficients of Fractional Parentage. J. Q. Chen et al. 456p. 1991. text ed. 74.00 (*981-02-0113-3*) World Scientific Pub.

Tables of Thomson Functions: Their First Derivatives. L. Nosova & Prabir Basu. LC 61-12445. (Mathematical Tables Ser.). 1961. 191.00 (*0-08-009518-6*, Pub. by Pergamon Repr UK) Franklin.

***Tables on the Prairie.** Joyce V. Smith. 1997. pap. text ed. 8.99 (*1-57673-188-X*, Multnomah Bks) Multnomah Pubs.

Tables Thermodynamic & Transport Properties: Air Argon Carbon Dioxide, Carbon Monoxide, Hydrogen, Nitrogen, Oxygen & Steam. 5th ed. J. Hilsenrath & H. Hoge. LC 60-14940. 1960. 211.00 (*0-08-009315-9*, Pub. by Pergamon Repr UK) Franklin.

Tables Turned. James Bonar. LC 70-107918. (Reprints of Economic Classics Ser.). vii, 135p. 1970. reprint ed. 29.50 (*0-678-00633-4*) Kelley.

Tables You Can Customize. Ernie Conover. (Betterway Woodworking Plans Ser.). (Illus.). 128p. (Orig.). 1995. pap. 19.99 (*1-55870-397-7*, Betrwy Bks) F & W Pubns Inc.

Tableservice Techniques. Bruce H. Axler. 1974. pap. 3.95 (*0-672-96116-4*, Bobbs) Macmillan.

Tablet. Bill Myers. LC 92-34301. (Journeys to Fahrah Ser.: Vol. 4). (Illus.). 144p. (Orig.). (J). (gr. 3 up). 1992. pap. 5.99 (*1-55661-299-0*) Bethany Hse.

Tablet & the Scroll: Near Eastern Studies in Honor of William W. Hallo. Ed. by Mark E. Cohen et al. LC 92-42780. 1993. 58.00 (*0-9620013-9-2*) CDL Pr.

Tablet of Carmel. Baha'u'llah. 55p. 1992. 21.95 (*1-870989-13-9*); pap. 13.25 (*1-870989-14-7*) Bahai.

Tablet of My Heart: Journal Writing for Spiritual Growth. Ramona Czer. LC 91-61109. 144p. (Orig.). 1991. pap. 7.99 (*0-8100-0382-1*, 12N1754) Northwest Pub.

Tablet of the Heart: God & Me. Abdu'l-Baha. Ed. by Betty J. Fisher. (Illus.). (J). (ps-2). 1987. lib. bdg. 10.00 (*0-87743-207-4*) Bahai.

Tablet of Visitation. deluxe limited ed. Baha'u'lla'h. Tr. by Shoghi Effendi from ARA. LC 94-96884. (Illus.). 32p. 1995. 1,000.00 (*0-9645136-0-9*) Taraz Pubng.

***Tabletalk: Story Sharing for Families.** Carol Eipers. (Illus.). 64p. 1997. pap. 24.95 (*1-55612-969-6*, LI1969) Sheed & Ward MO.

***Tableting Specification Manual.** 4th ed. American Pharmaceutical Association Staff. Ed. by Linda Young. (Illus.). 128p. 1995. spiral bd. 125.00 (*0-917330-67-6*) Am Pharm Assn.

Tabletop Learning Series, Games: Some Old, Some New, All Fun to Do. Imogene Forte. Ed. by Susan Oglander. LC 83-82331. (Tabletop Learning Ser.). (Illus.). 80p. (Orig.). (J). (gr. k-6). 1983. pap. text ed. 4.95 (*0-86530-093-3*, IP-933) Incentive Pubns.

Tabletop Vignettes. Sharon Dlugosch. LC 91-39054. 144p. 1991. pap. 9.95 (*0-918420-16-4*) Brighton Pubns.

Tabletops: Easy, Practical, Beautiful Ways to Decorate. Ohrbach. 1997. 25.00 (*0-517-70332-7*) Random Hse Value.

Tablets. A. Bronson Alcott. 208p. 1969. reprint ed. 15.00 (*0-87556-011-3*) Saifer.

Tablets from Fort Shalmaneser see Cuneiform Texts from Nimrud

Tablets I-XXVI. Armand Schwerner. 1989. pap. 16.00 (*0-947757-17-1*, Pub. by Atlas Pr UK) Serpents Tail.

Tablets of Baha'u'llah Revealed after the Kitab-i-Aqdas. Baha'u'llah. Tr. by Habib Taherzadeh from PER. 299p. 1994. 11.00 (*0-87743-174-4*) Bahai.

Tablets of Baha'u'llah Revealed after the Kitab-i-Agdas. Baha'u'llah. Tr. by Habib Taherzadeh from PER. LC 88-6250. 299p. 1988. 3.95 (*0-87743-216-3*) Bahai.

Tablets of Ebla: Concordance & Bibliography. Scott G. Beld et al. LC 84-5939. x, 70p. (Orig.). (C). 1984. pap. 10.00 (*0-931464-21-8*) Eisenbrauns.

***Tablets of Inspiration: A Personal Journal.** Burliss E. Parker, Jr. 224p. 1997. pap. 13.95 (*0-9647028-5-1*) Sowers Press.

Tablets of Stone. John G. Reisinger. 120p. (Orig.). 1989. pap. write for info. (*0-925703-05-2*) Crown MA.

Tablets of Stone, Hearts of Flesh: A Positive Approach to the Ten Commandments. Thomas G. Caserta. 70p. 1996. pap. 3.50 (*0-8198-7387-X*) Pauline Bks.

Tablets of the Divine Plan: Revealed by 'Abdu'l-Baha to the North American Baha'is. Abdu'l-Baha. 144p. 1993. pap. 3.00 (*0-87743-233-3*) Bahai.

Tablets XVI-XVIII. Armand Schwerner. 1976. pap. 20.00 (*0-686-67895-8*) Heron Pr.

Tablettes Cuneiformes De Tello Au Musee d'Istambul: Datant De l'Epoque De la IIIe Dynastie d'Ur. B. Lafont & F. Yildiz. 296p. 1989. pap. text ed. 56.00 (*90-6258-065-3*, Pub. by Netherlands Inst NE) Eisenbrauns.

Tablettes de Buis d'Apronenia Avtia. Pascal Quignard. (FRE.). 1989. pap. 15.95 (*0-7859-2940-1*) Fr & Eur.

Tablettes de la Vie et la Mort. Matthieu. Ed. by Smith. (Exeter French Texts Ser.: Vol. 40). 82p. (FRE.). Date not set. pap. text ed. 19.95 (*0-85989-196-8*, Pub. by Univ Exeter Pr UK) Northwestern U Pr.

Tablettes d'epoch d'Ur III de Princeton Theological Seminary. Marcel Sigrist. (Occasional Publications of the Samuel Noah Kramer Fund: No. 10). (Illus.). 93p. 1990. text ed. 45.00 (*0-934718-97-0*) U PA Mus Pubns.

Tabloid Design for the Organizational Press: A Compendium of Design. Raymond Dorn. (Illus.). 63p. (Orig.). 1983. pap. 15.00 (*0-931368-14-6*) Ragan Comm.

***Tabloid Dreams: Stories.** Robert O. Butler. 1997. pap. text ed. 12.00 (*0-8050-5589-4*) H Holt & Co.

Tabloid Dreams: Stories. Robert Olen Butler. 203p. 1996. 22.50 (*0-8050-3131-6*) H Holt & Co.

***Tabloid History of the World.** Kevin McDonough. (Illus.). 224p. 1997. pap. 9.95 (*0-7868-8223-9*) Hyperion.

***Tabloid History of the World.** Kevin McDonough. 1997. pap. text ed. 59.70 (*0-7868-9944-1*) Hyperion.

Tabloid Journalism: An Annotated Bibliography of English-Language Sources. LC 96-8942. (Bibliographies & Indexes in Mass Media & Communications: No. 10). 200p. 1996. text ed. 65.00 (*0-313-29544-1*, Greenwood Pr) Greenwood.

***Tabloid Television: Popular Journalism & the "Other News"** John Langer. LC 97-12734. (Communication & Society Ser.). 1997. write for info. (*0-415-06636-0*) Routledge.

Tabo Monastery & Buddhism in the Trans-Himalaya: Thousand Years of Existence of the Tabo Chos-khor. O. C. Handa. (C). 1994. text ed. 110.00 (*81-85182-96-5*, Pub. by Indus Pub II) S Asia.

Taboo. Angela E. Dreyer. LC 83-62045. 87p. 1983. pap. 3.95 (*0-914241-00-1*) Macanna-Rose.

Taboo. David S. Ryan. 191p. 1984. pap. 8.95 (*0-905116-14-3*) Seven Hills Bk.

***Taboo.** large type ed. Ellen Archer. (Black Satin Romance Ser.). 336p. 1996. 25.99 (*1-86110-013-2*) Ulverscroft.

Taboo. Elizabeth Gage. Ed. by Claire Zion. LC 92-25327. 576p. 1993. reprint ed. mass mkt. 5.99 (*0-671-78644-X*, Pocket Star Bks) PB.

Taboo, No. 1. Ed. by Stephen R. Bissette & John Totleben. (Illus.). 112p. (Orig.). 1988. pap. 9.95 (*0-922003-00-9*) Spiderbaby Grafix Pubns.

Taboo, No. 2. Ed. by Stephen R. Bissette & John Totleben. (Illus.). 112p. (Orig.). 1989. pap. 9.95 (*0-922003-01-7*) Spiderbaby Grafix Pubns.

Taboo, Vol. 2. Ed. by Joe L. Kincheloe et al. 224p. (C). 1995. pap. text ed. 15.00 (*0-614-09449-6*) P Lang Pubng.

Taboo, Vol. 3. Ed. by Stephen R. Bissette & Nancy J. O'Connor. (Illus.). 144p. (Orig.). 1989. pap. 9.95 (*0-922003-02-5*) Spiderbaby Grafix Pubns.

Taboo, Vol. 4. Ed. by Stephen R. Bissette & Nancy J. O'Connor. Tr. by Randy Lofficier & Jean-Marc Lofficier. (Illus.). 144p. (Orig.). (FRE.). 1990. pap. write for info. (*0-922003-03-3*) Spiderbaby Grafix Pubns.

Taboo: Sex, Identity & Erotic Subjectivity in Anthropological Fieldwork. Ed. by Don Kulick & Margaret Willson. 224p. (C). (gr. 13). 1995. text ed. 59.95 (*0-415-08818-6*, C0173) Routledge.

Taboo: Sex, Identity & Erotic Subjectivity in Anthropological Fieldwork. Ed. by Don Kulick & Margaret Willson. 224p. (C). 1995. pap. 17.95 (*0-415-08819-4*, C0174) Routledge.

Taboo - "The Ecstasy of Evil" The Psychopathology of Sex & Religion. 2nd ed. Christopher S. Hyatt et al. LC 91-66752. 240p. 1991. pap. 14.95 (*1-56184-039-4*) New Falcon Pubns.

Taboo & the Perils of the Soul see Golden Bough

Taboo (Export Edition) Elizabeth Gage. 1993. mass mkt. 5.99 (*0-671-86985-X*) PB.

Taboo in Culture. 1991. lib. bdg. 79.95 (*0-8490-4625-4*) Gordon Pr.

Taboo, Magic, Spirits: A Study of Primitive Elements in Roman Religion. Eli E. Burriss. LC 72-114489. x, 250p. 1972. reprint ed. text ed. 35.00 (*0-8371-4724-7*, BUTA, Greenwood Pr) Greenwood.

Taboo No More: The Phallus in Fact, Fantasy & Fiction. Mark Thorn. (Illus.). 202p. 1990. 29.95 (*0-944007-63-5*) Sure Seller.

***Taboo Scarf & Other Tales.** Weinberg. Date not set. pap. write for info. (*0-312-18189-2*) St Martin.

Tabooed Jung: Marginalization & Influence. Christine Gallant. 192p. (C). 1996. 35.00 (*0-8147-3087-6*) NYU Pr.

Taboos in German Literature. Ed. by David A. Jackson. LC 95-52174. 224p. 1996. 49.95 (*1-57181-881-2*) Berghahn Bks.

Tabor Family Album. Edward H. Blair. 1978. 2.95 (*0-913488-06-2*) Timberline Bks.

Tabor Sacramental Preparation, Parent Man. Kate Dooley & Maureen Gallagher. 64p. (Orig.). 1987. pap. 6.50 (*0-89505-513-9*, T1860) Tabor Pub.

Tabor Sacramental Preparation, Parish Man. James Bitney & Yvette Nelson. 64p. (Orig.). 1987. pap. text ed. 6.95 (*0-89505-512-0*, T1850) Tabor Pub.

Tabu & Dancing Elephants. Rene Deetlefs. Date not set. pap. write for info. (*0-14-037976-2*) Viking Penguin.

Tabu & the Dancing Elephants. Ed. & Retold by Rene Deetlefs. LC 94-25905. (Illus.). (J). 1995. pap. 14.99 (*0-525-45226-5*) Dutton Child Bks.

Tabu Linguistico en Mexico: El Lenguaje erotico de los mexicanos. Larry M. Grimes. LC 78-52419. 1978. pap. 15.00 (*0-916950-09-3*); lib. bdg. 24.00 (*0-916950-10-7*) Biling Rev-Pr.

***TABU Search.** Fred Glover & Fred Laguna. LC 97-24688. 1997. write for info. (*0-7923-9965-X*) Kluwer Ac.

***Tabula Imperii Romani: Map of the Roman Empire, Coptos.** Compiled by D. Meredith. (Illus.). 1958. pap. 5.00 (*0-85431-253-6*, Pub. by Soc Antiquaries UK) David Brown.

***Tabula Imperii Romani: Map of the Roman Empire, Cyrene.** Compiled by R. G. Goodchild. (Illus.). 16p. 1954. pap. 5.00 (*0-85431-252-8*, Pub. by Soc Antiquaries UK) David Brown.

***Tabula Imperii Romani: Map of the Roman Empire, Lepcis Magna.** Compiled by R. G. Goodchild. (Illus.). 14p. 1954. pap. 5.00 (*0-85431-251-X*, Pub. by Soc Antiquaries UK) David Brown.

Tabula Imperii Romani, Iudaea, Palaestina, Eretz Israel in the Hellenistic, Roman & Byzantine Periods: Maps & Gazetteer. Yoram Tsafrir et al. (Illus.). 274p. 1994. 59.50 (*965-208-107-8*) Jour Roman Arch.

Tabula of Cebes. John Fitzgerald & L. Michael White. LC 82-19118. (Society of Biblical Literature Texts & Translations Ser.). 236p. (C). 1983. pap. 20.95 (*0-89130-601-3*, 06 02 24) Scholars Pr GA.

Tabula Rasa: A Constructivist Novel. Richard Kostelanetz. LC 78-61089. 1978. pap. 200.00 (*0-932360-27-0*) Archae Edns.

Tabula Rasa: On the Manifest Need for Fundamental Philosophical Redirection. Somos, pseud. 104p. (Orig.). 1989. pap. 8.50 (*0-9623445-0-8*) Logos Found.

Tabula Rasula. Jed Rasula. LC 85-30378. (Illus.). 96p. 1986. pap. 5.50 (*0-930794-62-1*) Station Hill Pr.

Tabula Rosa. Rachel B. DuPlessis. 110p. 1987. pap. 8.50 (*0-937013-19-6*) Potes Poets.

Tabulae Phycologicae, 20 vols. in four. F. T. Kuetzing. (Bibliotheca Phycologica Ser.: No. 32). 1977. reprint ed. lib. bdg. 975.00 (*3-7682-1143-6*) Lubrecht & Cramer.

Tabulate Corals & Echinoderms from the Pennsylvanian Winterset Limestone, Hogshooter Formation, Northeastern Oklahoma, No. 279 see Bulletins of American Paleontology: Vol. 64

Tabulator Operator. Jack Rudman. (Career Examination Ser.: C-800). 1994. pap. 23.95 (*0-8373-0800-3*) Nat Learn.

Tabulatur Buch see Monuments of Music & Music Literature in Facsimile: Series One

***Tac & Tuk.** Carolee W. Henney. LC 92-75411. (Illus.). 16p. (J). (gr. 2-4). 1993. lib. bdg. 12.95 (*0-9626580-4-9*) Aton Pr.

Tac-Tickle: Pure Strategy. Harry D. Ruderman. 1966. 3.00 (*0-911624-06-6*) Wffn Proof.

TAC-U. S. A. Directory: 1991. 1991. 8.00 (*0-685-41036-6*) Athletics Cong.

Tacachale: Essays on the Indians of Florida & Southeastern Georgia During the Historic Period. Ed. by Jerald T. Milanich & Samuel Proctor. LC 94-6039. (Ripley P. Bullen Monographs). 232p. 1994. pap. text ed. 18.95 (*0-8130-1297-X*) U Press Fla.

***Tacachale: Essays on the Indians of Florida & Southwestern Georgia During the Historic Period.** Ed. by Jerald Milanich & Samuel Proctor. LC 77-20051. (Ripley P. Bullen Monographs in Anthropology & History Ser.: Vol. 1). 229p. reprint ed. pap. 65.30 (*0-608-04496-2*, 2065241) Bks Demand.

An Asterisk (*) at the beginning of an entry indicates that the title is appearing in BIP for the first time.

Tachechena. Jack Metzler. 238p. 1992. text ed. 8.99 (*1-56043-655-7*) Destiny Image.

***Taches d'Encre.** H. Jay Siskin et al. 192p. (FRE.). (C). 1996. pap. text ed. 36.76 (*0-669-32707-7*) HM College Div.

***Taches d'Encre.** H. Jay Siskin et al. (FRE.). (C). 1996. teacher ed., text ed. 2.66 (*0-669-41834-X*) HM College Div.

Tachi-Yokuts, Indians of the San Joaquin Valley: Indians of the San Joaquin Valley, Their Lives, Songs & Stories. Marjorie W. Cummins. Ed. by Kathleen Vander Meer & California State University, Fresno Staff. (Illus.). 174p. 1978. 16.03 (*0-914330-23-3*) M W Cummins.

Tachycardias. Ed. by Borys Surawicz et al. (Developments in Cardiovascular Medicine Ser.). 1984. lib. bdg. 254.00 (*0-89838-588-1*) Kluwer Ac.

Tachycardias: Mechanisms & Management. 2nd ed. Ed. by Mark E. Josephson & Hein J. Wellens. LC 92-48867. (Bakken Research Center Ser.). (Illus.). 512p. 1993. 97.00 (*0-87993-549-9*) Futura Pub.

Tachydromiinae (Diptera Empididae) of Fennoscandia & Denmark. M. Chvala. (Fauna Entomologica Scandinavica Ser.: No. 3). (Illus.). 336p. 1975. pap. 50.00 (*87-87491-04-4*) Lubrecht & Cramer.

Tachygraphischen Abkurzungen der Griechischen Handschriften. Oskar Lehmann. vi, 111p. 1965. reprint ed. write for info. (*0-318-70957-0*) G Olms Pubs.

Tachykinin Receptors. Ed. by Stephen H. Buck. LC 94-13436. (Receptors Ser.). 640p. 1994. 125.00 (*0-89603-266-3*) Humana.

Tachyon Web. Christopher Pike. (YA). (gr. 9 up). 1997. mass mkt. 3.99 (*0-671-69060-4*) PB.

Tacit Bargaining & Stable Proliferation in South Asia. Neil Joeck. (CISA Working Papers: No. 66). 21p. (Orig.). 1989. pap. 15.00 (*0-86682-084-1*) Ctr Intl Relations.

Tacit Bargaining, Arms Races, & Arms Control. George W. Downs & David M. Rocke. LC 90-33589. (Illus.). 248p. (C). 1990. text ed. 47.50 (*0-472-09450-5*); pap. text ed. 19.95 (*0-472-06450-9*) U of Mich Pr.

Tacit Dimension. Michael Polanyi. 1983. 17.25 (*0-8446-5999-1*) Peter Smith.

Tacit Organization, Vol. 8. Virginia H. Ingersoll & Guy B. Adams. Ed. by Judith A. Levy. LC 92-17685. (Contemporary Studies in Applied Behavioral Science: Vol. 8). 280p. 1992. 73.25 (*1-55938-297-X*) Jai Pr.

Taciturn Text: The Fiction of Robert Penn Warren. Randolph P. Runyon. 288p. 1991. 45.00 (*0-8142-0530-5*) Ohio St U Pr.

Taciturne. Roger Martin du Gard. 238p. (FRE.). 1932. pap. 12.95 (*0-7859-1285-1*, 2070242439) Fr & Eur.

Tacitus. R. Martin. (Classical Paperbacks Ser.). 256p. 1994. pap. 24.95 (*1-85399-431-6*, Pub. by Brstl Class Pr UK) Focus Pub-R Pullins.

Tacitus. Ronald Mellor. 200p. (C). (gr. 13). 1994. pap. 17.95 (*0-415-91002-1*, B4411) Routledge.

Tacitus: Annals I. Ed. by N. Miller. (Bristol Latin Texts Ser.). (LAT.). pap. 19.95 (*1-85399-358-1*, Pub. by Brstl Class Pr UK) Focus Pub-R Pullins.

Tacitus: Annals XIV. Ed. by E. C. Woodcock. (Bristol Latin Texts Ser.). 196p. (LAT.). 1992. pap. 17.95 (*1-85399-315-8*, Pub. by Brstl Class Pr UK) Focus Pub-R Pullins.

Tacitus: Annals XV, Annals XV. N. Miller. (Latin Texts Ser.). (LAT.). 1994. pap. 18.95 (*1-85399-434-0*, Pub. by Brstl Class Pr UK) Focus Pub-R Pullins.

***Tacitus: Germania.** Ed. by J. Anderson. 296p. (Orig.). 1996. pap. text ed. 31.95 (*1-85399-503-7*, Pub. by Brstl Class Pr UK) Focus Pub-R Pullins.

Tacitus: Histories III. Ed. by K. Wellesley. (Bristol Latin Texts Ser.). 258p. (LAT.). 1972. 49.95 (*0-424-06190-2*) Focus Pub-R Pullins.

Tacitus: The Classical Heritage. Ed. by Ronald Mellor. LC 95-6076. (Classical Heritage Ser.: Vol. 6). 304p. 1995. text ed. 58.00 (*0-8153-0933-3*) Garland.

Tacitus - Concordantia Tacitea, 2 vols., Set. Ed. by D. R. Blackman & G. G. Betts. (Alpha-Omega, Reihe A Ser.: Bd. LXXIV). 1932p. (GER.). 1986. 480.00 (*3-487-07748-5*) G Olms Pubs.

Tacitus' Agricola, Germany, & Dialogue on Orators. rev. ed. Tr. & Intro. by Herbert W. Benario. LC 90-48807. (Oklahoma Series in Classical Culture: Vol. 8). (Illus.). 160p. 1991. 28.95 (*0-8061-2321-4*) U of Okla Pr.

Tacitus & the Tacitean Tradition. Ed. by T. J. Luce & A. J. Woodman. LC 92-25050. (Magie Classical Publications). 240p. (C). 1993. text ed. 39.50 (*0-691-06988-3*) Princeton U Pr.

Tacitus, Annalen, 2 vols., Bd. I: Ab Excessu Divi Augusti I-IV. Ed. by Karl Nipperdey & Georg Andresen. 466p. (GER.). 1978. write for info. (*3-296-15751-4*) G Olms Pubs.

Tacitus, Annalen, 2 vols., Bd. II: Ab Excessu Divi Augusti XI-XVI. Ed. by Karl Nipperdey & Georg Andresen. 347p. (GER.). 1978. write for info. (*3-296-15752-2*) G Olms Pubs.

Tacitus' Histories: Handbook. Tacitus. Ed. by P. V. Jones. (Cambridge Latin Texts Ser.). 80p. 1975. pap. text ed. 13.95 (*0-521-20489-5*) Cambridge U Pr.

Tacitus the Sententious Historian: A Sociology of Rhetoric in Annales 1-6. Patrick Sinclair. LC 93-47590. (C). 1995. 32.50 (*0-271-01333-8*) Pa St U Pr.

Tacitus the Sententious Historian: A Sociology of Rhetoric in Annales 1-6. Patrick Sinclair. 200p. 1995. 32.50 (*0-02-710133-9*) Pa St U Pr.

Tack: Care & Cleaning. Cherry Hill. 1991. pap. 2.95 (*0-88266-653-3*, Garden Way Pub) Storey Comm Inc.

Tack & Clothing. Susan McBane. (WLRS Ser.). (Illus.). 112p. 1996. pap. 10.95 (*0-7063-7427-4*, Pub. by Ward Lock UK) Sterling.

Tack Buyer's Guide. Charlene Strickland. (Illus.). 315p. (Orig.). 1988. pap. 19.95 (*0-914327-22-4*) Breakthrgh NY.

Tack Now, Skipper. Owen Parker. 1979. 29.95 (*0-8464-0065-0*) Beekman Pubs.

Tackett. Lyn Nofziger. LC 93-8244. 192p. 1993. 16.95 (*0-89526-495-1*) Regnery Pub.

Tackett & the Saloon Keeper. Lyn Nofziger. 1994. 16.95 (*0-89526-480-3*) Regnery Pub.

Tackett & the Teacher. Lyn Nofziger. LC 93-45949. 192p. 1994. 16.95 (*0-89526-488-9*) Regnery Pub.

Tackle & Technique for Taking Trout. Dave Hughes. LC 89-11371. (Illus.). 192p. (Orig.). 1990. pap. 14.95 (*0-8117-2309-7*) Stackpole.

Tackle Care: The Tackle Maintenance Handbook. C. Boyd Pfeiffer. (Illus.). 160p. (Orig.). 1987. pap. 12.95 (*0-941130-56-8*) Lyons & Burford.

Tackle Without a Team. Matt Christopher. LC 88-22644. (Illus.). 128p. (J). (gr. 3-7). 1989. 15.95 (*0-316-14067-8*) Little.

Tackle Without a Team. Matt Christopher. (J). (gr. 4-7). 1993. mass mkt. 3.95 (*0-316-14268-9*) Little.

Tackling Accountants' Liability: A Glimpse into the Future. James C. Emerson. 100p. (Orig.). 1991. pap. 195.00 (*0-943945-07-0*) Emerson WA.

Tackling Bullying in Your School: A Practical Handbook for Teachers. Ed. by Sonia Sharp & Peter K. Smith. LC 93-47626. 208p. (Orig.). (C). 1994. pap. 25.00 (*0-415-10374-6*, B4412, Routledge NY) Routledge.

Tackling Discrimination at the Workplace: An Analysis of Sex Discrimination in Britain. Brian Chiplin & Peter J. Sloane. LC 82-4384. (Cambridge Management & Industrial Relations Ser.: No. 2). (Illus.). 190p. 1983. 47.95 (*0-521-24565-6*) Cambridge U Pr.

Tackling Drug Problems in Public Housing: A Guide for Police. Deborah L. Weisel. 117p. 1990. pap. 16.50 (*1-878734-19-9*) Police Exec Res.

Tackling Dyslexia: The Bangor Way. Ann Cooke. 148p. 1993. 29.99 (*1-56593-370-2*, 0429) Singular Publishing.

Tackling Environmental Problems Across the Media of Land, Water, & Air. Feng Liu. LC 93-379. (CPL Bibliographies Ser.: No. 289). 20p. 1993. pap. 10.00 (*0-86602-289-9*, Sage Prdcls Pr) Sage.

Tackling Fear of Crime: A Starter Kit. H. M. S. O. Staff. 106p. 1995. pap. text ed. 40.00 (*0-11-341135-9*, HM11359, Pub. by Stationery Ofc UK) Bernan Associates.

Tackling Gridlock. Connie Hartline et al. (Special Reports: No. 56). (Illus.). 46p. (Orig.). 1991. pap. text ed. 35.00 (*0-917084-35-7*) Am Public Works.

***Tackling Life Head On: Lessons for Kids' Lives with Ronnie Lott As "Coach"** Manuel J. Costa. LC 97-19984. 1997. write for info. (*0-917479-17-3*) Guild Psy.

Tackling Notre Dame. Virginia M. Black. LC 83-82713. (Illus.). 250p. 1984. pap. 6.95 (*0-87319-030-0*) Hallberg Pub Corp.

Tackling Poverty in Rural Mexico, Set. (Toward a Better World Ser.). (YA). (gr. 9-12). 1981. student ed., teacher ed., text ed. 60.00 incl. flmstrp (*0-8213-0074-1*, 10074) World Bank.

Tackling Racism in Europe: An Examination of Anti-Discrimination Law in Practice. Martin MacEwen. 224p. 1995. 38.95 (*0-85496-857-1*); pap. 16.95 (*1-85973-047-7*) Berg Pubs.

***Tackling Single Parenting: From a Man's Point of View.** Steve Horner. LC 96-96904. 304p. 1996. pap. 17.95 (*0-9654086-0-4*) S Horner.

Tackling Strategic Problems: The Role of Group Decision Support. Ed. by Colin Eden & Jim Radford. 224p. (C). 1990. 45.00 (*0-8039-8259-3*); pap. 18.95 (*0-8039-8260-7*) Sage.

Tackling the Inner Cities: The Nineteen Eighties Reviewed, Prospects for the 1990s. Ed. by Susanne MacGregor & Ben Pimlott. (Illus.). 304p. 1990. 79.00 (*0-19-827737-7*) OUP.

Tackling the Team. Marco Vassi. 188p. 1993. pap. 16.95 (*0-933256-85-X*) Second Chance.

Tackling Toxics in Everyday Products: A Directory of Organizations. Nancy Lilienthal et al. LC 91-29961. 192p. 1992. pap. 19.95 (*0-918780-56-X*) INFORM NY.

***Tacky in Trouble.** Lester. 1998. 14.95 (*0-395-86113-6*) HM.

Tacky the Penguin. Helen Lester. LC 87-30684. (Illus.). 32p. (J). (ps-3). 1988. 14.95 (*0-395-45536-7*) HM.

Tacky the Penguin. Helen Lester. (Illus.). 32p. (J). (gr. k-3). 1990. pap. 5.95 (*0-395-56233-3*) HM.

Tacoma. Ed. by Richard C. Anderson. 120p. 1988. 39.95 (*0-685-22942-4*) Baker Anderson.

Tacoma: Tomorrow's City - Today. Denny MacGougan. LC 96-4821. (Urban Tapestry Ser.). (Illus.). 192p. 1996. 39.50 (*1-881096-28-9*) Towery Pub.

Tacoma Public Utilities Story: The First 100 Years. John S. Ott & Dick Malloy. LC 93-60904. (Illus.). 300p. 1993. 30.00 (*0-9637684-0-9*); pap. 20.00 (*0-9637684-1-7*) Tacoma Pub Util.

Tacoma, WA. (Streetfinder Ser.). (Illus.). 1995. pap. 15.95 (*0-528-91373-5*) Rand McNally.

***Tacoma/Olympia Metro Business Directory 1996-1997.** American Business Directories Staff. 1632p. 1996. boxed 225.00 (*1-56105-900-5*) Am Busn Direct.

***Tacoma/Olympia Metro Business Directory 1997-1998.** rev. ed. American Business Directories Staff. 1632p. 1997. boxed 295.00 (*1-56105-987-0*) Am Busn Direct.

***Tacos on the Tundra: The Story of Pepe's North of the Border.** Lyn Kidder. (Illus.). 225p. 1996. pap. 15.00 (*0-9654826-2-6*) Bonaparte Bks.

Tacos, Tempura & Teem Gok. Nancy Lee & Linda Oldham. LC 78-75120. 80p. (J). (ps-8). 1979. 3.95 (*0-931178-02-9*) Hands on Pubns.

Tac's Island. Ruth Y. Radin. 80p. (J). (gr. 2-9). 1997. reprint ed. pap. 2.95 (*0-8167-1320-0*) Troll Communs.

Tact in Court Containing Sketches of Cases Won by Skill, Wit, Art, Tact, Courage & Eloquence with Practical Illustrations in Letters of Lawyers Giving Their Best Rules for Winning Cases. 3rd rev. ed. J. W. Donovan. 135p. 1983. reprint ed. lib. bdg. 20.00 (*0-8377-0517-7*) Rothman.

Tact in Court or How Lawyers Win: Containing Sketches of Cases Won by Skill, Wit, Art, Tact, Courage & Eloquence with Trial Rules & Illustrations. J. W. Donovan. LC 88-80856. 124p. 1988. reprint ed. 39.00 (*0-912004-66-5*) Gaunt.

Tact of Teaching: The Meaning of Pedagogical Thoughtfulness. Max Van Manen. LC 91-11349. (SUNY Series, the Philosophy of Education). 240p. 1991. text ed. 64.50 (*0-7914-0667-9*); pap. text ed. 21.95 (*0-7914-0668-7*) State U NY Pr.

Tactful God: Dom Gregory Dix, Priest, Monk, & Scholar. Simon Bailey. 304p. (Orig.). 1995. pap. 19.95 (*0-85244-340-4*, Pub. by Gracewing UK) Morehouse Pub.

Tactful Toughness Workbook. Pennie Myers & Don W. Nance. (Orig.). 1994. pap. text ed. 25.00 (*0-9620723-5-4*) MAS.

Tactical Communications Conference Proceedings, 1994. IEEE, Fort Wayne Section Staff. Ed. by IEEE, Institute of Electrical & Electronics Engineers, Inc. Staff. LC 94-76918. 300p. 1994. pap. write for info. (*0-7803-2004-2*, 94TH0678-3); fiche write for info. (*0-7803-2005-0*) Inst Electrical.

Tactical Counterintelligence. 1989. lib. bdg. 79.95 (*0-8490-3981-9*) Gordon Pr.

Tactical Counterintelligence. 1991. lib. bdg. 79.95 (*0-8490-4090-6*) Gordon Pr.

Tactical Deception. 1990. lib. bdg. 79.95 (*0-8490-3985-1*) Gordon Pr.

Tactical Decisions in a Personal Injury Case. Paul L. Stritmatter. (ATLA Monograph Ser.). 36p. (Orig.). 1988. pap. write for info. (*0-941916-48-0*) ATLA Pr.

Tactical Deductions from the War of 1870-1871. Albrecht Von Boguslawski. 160p. 1996. pap. 15.95 (*0-9649188-2-X*) Absinthe Pr.

***Tactical Display for Soldiers: Human Factors Considerations.** National Research Council Staff. LC 96-39712. 246p. (Orig.). 1997. pap. text ed. 45.00 (*0-309-05638-1*, Joseph Henry Pr) Natl Acad Pr.

Tactical Edge: Surviving High-Risk Patrol. Charles Remsberg. LC 85-73162. (Illus.). 544p. (C). 1986. text ed. 39.95 (*0-935878-05-X*) Calibre Pr.

Tactical Electronic Warfare. (Military Science Ser.). 1991. lib. bdg. 76.00 (*0-8490-4202-X*) Gordon Pr.

Tactical Employment of Antiarmor Platoons, Companies & Battalions. 1995. lib. bdg. 259.95 (*0-8490-6653-0*) Gordon Pr.

Tactical Employment of Mortars. 1991. lib. bdg. 79.95 (*0-8490-4091-4*) Gordon Pr.

Tactical Employment of Mortars. 1995. lib. bdg. 255.95 (*0-8490-6656-5*) Gordon Pr.

Tactical Employment of Riot Control Agent CS. 1995. lib. bdg. 250.75 (*0-8490-6557-7*) Gordon Pr.

Tactical Employment of Riot Control Agent CS. 1995. lib. bdg. 256.95 (*0-8490-6617-4*) Gordon Pr.

Tactical Exercise. Evelyn Waugh. LC 78-167471. (Short Story Index Reprint Ser.). 1980. reprint ed. 20.95 (*0-8369-3997-2*) Ayer.

***Tactical Experiments HRM.** Kroeck. (C). 1993. 48.95 incl. 3.5 ld (*0-03-098292-8*) HB Coll Pubs.

Tactical Fly Fishing: For Trout & Sea Trout on River & Stream. Pat O'Reilly. (Illus.). 272p. 1991. 45.00 (*1-85223-294-3*, Pub. by Crowood Pr UK) Trafalgar.

Tactical Handcuffing for Chain- & Hinged-Style Handcuffs. John G. Peters, Jr. (Illus.). 304p. (Orig.). (C). 1989. pap. 15.00 (*0-923401-00-8*) Reliapon Police Prods.

Tactical Ingenuity Pyramid & Thinker's Manual. James E. Lukaszewski. 12p. 1990. pap. 10.00 (*1-883291-00-3*) Lukaszewski.

Tactical Intelligence: Army Needs to Reconsider & Test All-Source Analysis System Alternative. (Illus.). 53p. (Orig.). (YA). (gr. 12 up). 1994. pap. text ed. 30.00 (*0-7881-0788-7*) DIANE Pub.

***Tactical Intelligence: Army Needs to Reconsider & Test All-Source Analysis System Alternative.** (Illus.). 40p. 1994. pap. text ed. 40.00 (*1-57979-128-X*) BPI Info Servs.

Tactical Job Searching: Concentrates on Sure-Fire Career Strategies. 128p. 1991. pap. 12.96 (*0-685-49168-4*) Artek Pr Inc.

Tactical Land Clearing. 1995. lib. bdg. 259.95 (*0-8490-6608-5*) Gordon Pr.

Tactical Marksman: A Complete Training Manual for Police & Practical Shooters. Dave M. Lauck. (Illus.). 176p. 1996. pap. 35.00 (*0-87364-881-1*) Paladin Pr.

Tactical Neutralization Techniques. Gregory J. Connor & Matthew Summers. (Illus.). 300p. 1988. pap. text ed. 19.80 (*0-87563-326-9*) Stipes.

Tactical Nuclear Operations. (Military Science Ser.). 1991. lib. bdg. 75.00 (*0-8490-4201-1*) Gordon Pr.

Tactical Nuclear Weapons: European Perspectives. 360p. 1978. 45.00 (*0-85066-129-3*) Taylor & Francis.

Tactical Pistol: Advanced Gunfighting Concepts & Techniques. Gabriel Suarez. (Illus.). 216p. pap. 25.00 (*0-87364-864-1*) Paladin Pr.

***Tactical Shotgun: The Best Techniques & Tactics for Employing the Shotgun in Personal Combat.** Gabriel Suarez. (Illus.). 232p. 1996. pap. 25.00 (*0-87364-898-6*) Paladin Pr.

Tactical Textiles: A Genealogy of the Boise Peace Quilt Project. Angeline Kearns Blain. 112p. (C). 1996. per., pap. text ed. 16.74 (*0-8403-9683-X*) Kendall-Hunt.

Tactics. 2nd ed. Ed. by Rodney Pattisson. 96p. (C). 1993. text ed. 65.00 (*0-906754-75-5*, Pub. by Fernhurst Bks UK) St Mut.

Tactics: A Guide to Tactical Marketing & Management. John Hathaway-Bates. 1987. 29.50 (*0-910333-03-3*) Nerthus Pubns.

Tactics: Cara a Cara. Joseph R. Scott, Jr. & Catherine S. Meisel-Valdez. (Illus.). 112p. (Orig.). (SPA.). (YA). (gr. 9-11). 1993. pap. text ed. 11.00 (*1-877653-22-5*, 11) Wayside Pub.

Tactics: Conversaciones Entres Dos. Joseph R. Scott, Jr. (Illus.). 96p. (Orig.). (SPA.). (YA). (gr. 9-12). 1996. pap. text ed. 10.00 (*1-877653-37-3*, 35) Wayside Pub.

Tactics: Conversations à Deux. Joseph Scott. 90p. (Orig.). (FRE.). (YA). (gr. 7-12). 1990. pap. text ed. 10.00 (*1-877653-09-8*) Wayside Pub.

Tactics: The Art & Science of Success. Edward De Bono. 192p. 1984. 17.95 (*0-316-17790-3*) Little.

***Tactics & Mindsets: A Source Book on Asian Crime & Culture.** Douglas D. Daye. 400p. 1996. text ed. 64.95 (*0-8493-8116-9*, 8116) CRC Pr.

Tactics & Techniques in Psychoanalytic Therapy, Vol. 1. Ed. by Peter L. Giovacchini. LC 72-144143. 768p. 1993. pap. 35.00 (*1-56821-110-4*) Aronson.

Tactics & Techniques in Psychoanalytic Therapy Vol. II: Countertransference. Ed. by Peter L. Giovacchini. LC 72-144143. 480p. Date not set. pap. 50.00 (*0-7657-0015-8*) Aronson.

Tactics & Techniques in Psychoanalytic Therapy, Vol. III: Implications of Winnicott's Contributions. Ed. by Peter L. Giovacchini. LC 72-144143. 296p. 1990. 40.00 (*0-87668-789-3*) Aronson.

Tactics & Techniques of Community Intervention. 3rd ed. Ed. by John E. Tropman et al. LC 94-66870. 482p. (C). 1995. pap. text ed. 40.00 incl. 5.25 hd (*0-87581-391-7*) Peacock Pubs.

Tactics at Gettysburg. A. T. Cowell. 81p. 1987. reprint ed. 9.00 (*0-942211-05-7*) Olde Soldier Bks.

Tactics Face a Face. Joseph R. Scott, Jr. (Illus.). 96p. (FRE.). (YA). (gr. 7-12). 1988. reprint ed. pap. text ed. 10.00 (*1-877653-08-X*) Wayside Pub.

Tactics for Criminal Patrol: Vehicle Stops, Drug Discovery & Officer Survival. Charles Remsberg. LC 95-67002. (Illus.). 520p. 1995. text ed. 39.95 (*0-935878-12-2*) Calibre Pr.

Tactics for Improving Parenting Skills (TIPS) Bob Algozzine & James E. Ysseldyke. 210p. 1995. teacher ed., pap. 19.50 (*1-57035-035-3*, 77TIPS) Sopris.

Tactics for Preserving Open Space: A Survey & Analysis of Local Governments' Park Land Acquisition Techniques. Elise M. Bright. 51p. (Orig.). 1990. pap. text ed. 10.00 (*0-936440-80-5*) U TX SUPA.

Tactics for Teaching. 2nd ed. Thomas C. Lovitt. (Illus.). 368p. (C). 1994. pap. text ed. 43.00 (*0-02-371813-7*, Macmillan Coll) P-H.

Tactics for Trout. Dave Hughes. LC 90-9488. (Illus.). 224p. (Orig.). 1990. pap. 14.95 (*0-8117-2403-4*) Stackpole.

Tactics of Change: Doing Therapy Briefly. Richard Fisch et al. LC 81-48665. (Social & Behavioral Science Ser.). 322p. 28.95 (*0-87589-521-2*) Jossey-Bass.

Tactics of Duty. William H. Keith, Jr. (Battletech Ser.: No. 19). 1995. mass mkt. 4.99 (*0-451-45382-4*) NAL-Dutton.

***Tactics of End-Games.** Jeno Ban. LC 97-22514. (Illus.). 214p. 1997. reprint ed. pap. text ed. 7.95 (*0-486-29705-5*) Dover.

Tactics of Legal Reasoning. Pierre Schlag & David Skover. LC 86-70367. 118p. (C). 1986. pap. text ed. 10.00 (*0-89089-309-8*); lib. bdg. 19.95 (*0-89089-308-X*) Carolina Acad Pr.

Tactics of Organic Synthesis. Tse-Lok Ho. 450p. 1994. text ed. 69.95 (*0-471-59896-8*) Wiley.

Tactics of Psychotherapy: An Application of Psychoanalytic Theory to Psychotherapy. William F. Murphy. LC 65-19462. 1965. 67.50 (*0-8236-6360-4*) Intl Univs Pr.

Tactics of Scientific Research: Evaluating Experimental Data in Psychology. Murray Sidman. LC 60-13278. (Illus.). x, 428p. (C). 1988. reprint ed. pap. text ed. 18.00 (*0-9623311-0-4*) Authors Coop.

Tactics of Small Boat Racing. Stuart H. Walker. (Illus.). 352p. 1991. pap. 17.00 (*0-393-30801-4*) Norton.

Tactics, Techniques & Concepts of Anti-Armor Warfare. (Military Science Ser.). 1991. lib. bdg. 79.95 (*0-8490-4200-3*) Gordon Pr.

Tactics to Tackle Thinking: Creative Activities for the English Classroom. Pat Watson & Johanna Wrinkle. (Illus.). 80p. 1992. pap. text ed. 10.95 (*0-944459-43-9*) ECS Lrn Systs.

Tactics to Take You to the Top. Mary A. Hogue & Mary D. Litchford. 125p. (C). 1992. pap. write for info. (*1-881457-01-X*) Cont Mgmt Cnslts.

Tactile Aids for the Hearing Impaired. Summers. 270p. 1992. pap. 87.75 (*1-56593-582-9*, 0233) Singular Publishing.

Tactile Graphics. Polly Edman. LC 92-12198. 544p. 1992. text ed. 87.00 (*0-89128-194-0*) Am Foun Blind.

Tactile Sensors: A Survey on Technology & Markets, No. 6. Richard K. Miller & Terri C. Walker. LC 88-80484. 54p. 1988. pap. text ed. 200.00 (*1-55865-005-9*) Future Tech Surveys.

Tactile Sensors for Robotics & Medicine. Ed. by John G. Webster. LC 88-10794. 365p. 1988. text ed. 136.00 (*0-471-60607-3*) Wiley.

Tactile Vessel: New Basket Form. Jack L. Larsen. (Illus.). 100p. (Orig.). 1989. pap. 19.95 (*0-9616623-3-6*) Erie Art Mus.

Tactique au XIII siecle, 2 vols., Set. Henri M. Delpech. LC 78-63493. reprint ed. 110.00 (*0-404-17140-0*) AMS Pr.

Tacto. Chelsea House Publishers Staff. 1996. lib. bdg. 14.95 (*0-7910-4009-7*) Chelsea Hse.

Tactrust Handbook. 1986. 7.50 (*0-317-65149-8*) Athletics Cong.

Tactual Perception: A Sourcebook. Ed. by William Schiff & Emerson Foulke. LC 81-10172. (Illus.). 500p. 1982. text ed. 85.00 (*0-521-24095-6*) Cambridge U Pr.

Tad & Dad. Stephen Mooser & Lin Oliver. LC 87-40340. (Catch the Reading Bug Ser.). (Illus.). (J). (ps-2). 1990. 4.95 (*1-55782-023-6*, Warner Juvenile Bks) Little.

***Tad & Mr. Boom.** Conrad Gaiser. (Illus.). (J). (gr. k-3). 1997. pap. 7.00 (*0-8059-4016-2*) Dorrance.

Tad Gonopolis & His Adventures in the Slumberyard, No. 3. Uncle Hyggly. (Gonopolis Family Ser.). (Illus.). 48p. (J). (gr. 3-6). 1987. pap. 8.95 (*0-935583-03-3*) Wounded Coot.

Tad Lincoln: White House Wildcat. David R. Collins. (Illus.). 48p. (J). (gr. 1-4). 1995. pap. 7.95 (*1-878668-40-4*); lib. bdg. 14.95 (*1-878668-33-1*) Disc Enter Ltd.

Tad Savinar: Talk Radio. Roger Hull. (Illus.). 1983. pap. 2.00 (*0-914435-08-6*) Marylhurst Art.

TAD-Schrift: Twenty Years of Mystery Fandom in The Armchair Detective. J. Randolph Cox. LC 87-36810. viii, 111p. (C). 1987. reprint ed. pap. 17.00 (*0-941028-05-4*, Brownstone Bks); reprint ed. lib. bdg. 27.00 (*0-8095-6401-7*, Brownstone Bks) Borgo Pr.

Tadao Ando. Ed. & Intro. by Francesco Dal Co. (Illus.). 524p. 1995. 75.00 (*0-7148-3471-8*, Pub. by Phaidon Press UK) Chronicle Bks.

Tadao Ando. Kenneth Frampton. (Illus.). 80p. 1991. pap. 19.95 (*0-87070-198-3*) Mus of Modern Art.

Tadao Ando. Mirko Zandini. (Architectural Monographs: No. 14). (Illus.). 128p. 1990. pap. 30.00 (*1-85490-007-2*) Academy Ed UK.

Tadao Ando. Mirko Zandini. (Architectural Monographs: No. 14). (Illus.). 128p. 1990. 45.00 (*1-85490-010-2*) Academy Ed UK.

Tadao Ando. 2nd ed. Masao Furuyama. LC 95-22062. (Studiopaperback Ser.). 216p. 1995. pap. 24.95 (*0-8176-5583-2*) Birkhauser.

***Tadao Ando.** 2nd ed. Masao Furuyama. (Studio Paperback Ser.). 1995. pap. write for info. (*3-7643-5583-2*) Birkhauser.

***Tadao Ando.** 2nd expanded ed. Masao Furuyama. (Illus.). 248p. 1996. pap. text ed. 34.50 (*3-7643-5437-2*) Birkhauser.

Tadao Ando: An Architectural Monograph. (Illus.). 150p. 1990. 45.00 (*0-312-04033-4*); pap. 30.00 (*0-312-03985-9*) St Martin.

Tadao Ando: Buildings & Sketches. Werner Blaser. 170p. 1989. 108.50 (*0-8176-2327-2*) Birkhauser.

Tadao Ando: Dormant Lines. Kazuki Negishi et al. (Illus.). 48p. 1991. 30.00 (*0-614-14666-6*) Harvard Univ Graduate Schl of.

***Tadao Ando: The Colors of Light.** limited ed. Richard Pare. (Illus.). 272p. 1996. 450.00 (*0-7148-3541-2*, Pub. by Phaidon Press UK) Chronicle Bks.

***Tadao Ando: The Colours of Light.** Richard Pare. (Illus.). 272p. 1996. 95.00 (*0-7148-3374-6*, Pub. by Phaidon Press UK) Chronicle Bks.

Taddeo Alderotti & His Pupils: Two Generations of Italian Medical Learning. Nancy G. Siraisi. LC 80-7554. 486p. 1981. reprint ed. pap. 138.60 (*0-7837-9445-2*, 2060187) Bks Demand.

Taddeo Gaddi: Critical Reappraisal & Catalogue Raisonne. Andrew Ladis. (Illus.). 288p. 1983. text ed. 70.00 (*0-8262-0382-5*) U of Mo Pr.

Taddy McFinley & the Great Grey Grimly. Heidi Salter. Ed. by Nancy R. Thatch. LC 89-31820. (Books for Students by Students). (Illus.). 26p. (J). (gr. 3-8). 1989. lib. bdg. 14.95 (*0-933849-21-4*) Landmark Edns.

Tadeo Ortiz, Mexican Colonizer & Reformer. W. H. Timmons. (Southwestern Studies: No. 43). 1974. 5.00 (*0-87404-101-5*) Tex Western.

Tadeusz Myslowski Towards Organic Geometry 1972-1994: 163 Selected Photographic Images on Japanese Paper. Tadeusz Myslowski. (Illus.). 176p. 1994. text ed. 75.00 (*0-9640648-0-4*) I Hockman Fine.

***Tadhkaratul Auliya.** Farid U. Attar. Tr. by Bankey Behari. 213p. 1996. 12.95 (*0-614-21367-3*, 1209) Kazi Pubns.

Tadhkirat Al-Muluk. Richards. (Gibb Memorial Trust Ser.: Vol. 16). 1943. 39.95 (*0-906094-12-7*, Pub. by Aris & Phillips UK) David Brown.

Tadpole. Jules Tasca. 1974. pap. 5.25 (*0-8222-1107-6*) Dramatists Play.

Tadpole & Frog. Christine Back & Barrie Watts. LC 86-10049. (Stopwatch Ser.). (Illus.). 25p. (J). (gr. k-4). 1986. pap. 3.95 (*0-382-24021-9*, Silver Pr NJ); lib. bdg. 9.95 (*0-382-09285-6*, Silver Pr NJ) Silver Burdett Pr.

***Tadpole Tales: Readers Theatre for Young Children.** Anthony D. Fredericks. (Illus.). 115p. (J). (gr. 1-3). 1997. pap. 18.50 (*1-56308-547-X*) Libs Unl.

Tadpole to Frog. Oliver S. Owen. LC 94-11370. (Lifewatch Ser.). (J). 1994. lib. bdg. 14.98 (*1-56239-291-3*) Abdo & Dghtrs.

Tadpole to Frog Pop-Up. Elizabeth Rodger. (Illus.). 8p. (J). 1996. pap. 4.95 (*0-590-54346-6*, Cartwheel) Scholastic Inc.

Tadpoles. Elaine Pascoe. Ed. by Nicole Bowman. LC 95-40848. (Nature Close-up Ser.). (Illus.). 48p. (YA). (gr. 3-7). 1996. lib. bdg. 16.95 (*1-56711-179-3*) Blackbirch.

***Tadpoles of the Forested Regions of Borneo.** Robert F. Inger. LC 85-71159. (Field Museum of Natural History, Publication 184, Anthropological Ser.: No. 26). 96p. 1985. reprint ed. pap. 27.40 (*0-608-03791-5*, 2064651) Bks Demand.

***TAE Algebra I.** Nichols. 1986. pap. text ed. 78.25 (*0-03-002163-4*) HR&W Schl Div.

***TAE Algebra II.** Nichols. 1986. pap. text ed. 84.00 (*0-03-002174-X*) HR&W Schl Div.

Tae Allez, Viens: Holt French. annuals 1996. text ed. 69.25 (*0-03-094020-6*) HR&W Schl Div.

***TAE Geometry.** Nichols. 1986. pap. text ed. 77.00 (*0-03-002187-1*) HR&W Schl Div.

Tae Kwon Do. Bill Gutman. (Action Sports Ser.). 48p. (J). (gr. 3-9). 1995. lib. bdg. 17.80 (*1-56065-266-7*) Capstone Pr.

***Tae Kwon Do.** Bill Gutman. (Martial Arts Ser.). (Illus.). 48p. (J). (gr. 3-7). 1995. 18.40 (*0-516-35266-0*) Childrens.

Tae Kwon Do. Michael Teitelbaum. (Illus.). 24p. (Orig.). (J). 1990. pap. 2.50 (*0-942025-88-1*) Kidsbks.

Tae Kwon Do: Secrets of Korean Karate. Sihak H. Cho. 256p. 1992. pap. 21.95 (*0-8048-1704-9*) C E Tuttle.

Tae Kwon Do: Techniques & Training. Kyong M. Lee. LC 95-52503. (Illus.). 160p. 1996. pap. 12.95 (*0-8069-5955-X*) Sterling.

Tae Kwon Do: The Korean Martial Art & National Sport. Richard Chun. LC 74-1799. (Illus.). 544p. 1976. 55.00i (*0-06-010779-0*, HarpT) HarpC.

Tae Kwon Do: The Ultimate Reference Guide to the World's Most Popular Martial Art. Yeon Hee Park et al. (Illus.). 224p. 1991. reprint ed. pap. 12.95 (*0-8160-2542-8*) Facts on File.

Tae Kwon Do: The Ultimate Reference to the World's Most Popular Martial Art. Hee P. Yeon et al. (Illus.). 224p. 1989. 24.95 (*0-8160-1521-X*) Facts on File.

Tae Kwon Do: Traditional Art & Modern Sport. Eddie Ferrie. (Illus.). 160p. 1993. pap. 29.95 (*1-85223-757-0*, Pub. by Crowood Pr UK) Trafalgar.

Tae Kwon Do Basics. Keith D. Yates & H. Bryan Robbins. LC 96-52503. (Illus.). 128p. 1992. pap. 5.95 (*0-8069-8756-1*) Sterling.

Tae Ven Conmigo! Holt Spanish. annuals 1996. text ed. 69.25 (*0-03-093991-7*) HR&W Schl Div.

Taegeuk Forms of Taekwon Do. Pu G. Gwon. Ed. by Mike Lee. LC 83-63602. (Korean Arts Ser.). 224p. (Orig.). 1984. pap. 14.95 (*0-89750-097-0*, 435) Ohara Pubns.

Taekwon-Do. Richard Chun. 55.00 (*0-685-70709-1*) Wehman.

Taekwon-Do Hyungs for Blue & Red Belt Levels. James S. Benko. LC 81-82100. (Illus.). 121p. (Orig.). 1981. pap. 15.00 (*0-937314-04-8*, 048S) ITA Inst.

***Taekwon-Do Patterns: White Belt to 1st Degree Black Belt.** James S. Benko. (Illus.). 160p. (Orig.). 1997. pap. 38.00 (*0-937314-28-5*) ITA Inst.

Taekwon-Do, Self-Defense Against Weapons. James S. Benko. LC 80-82015. (Illus.). 111p. 1981. pap. 15.00 (*0-937314-00-5*, 005S) ITA Inst.

Taekwondo. Jerry Craven. LC 94-4086. (Illustrated History of Martial Arts Ser.). (J). 1994. write for info. (*0-86593-367-7*) Rourke Corp.

Taekwondo: White Belt to Yellow Belt. Taekwondo Association Staff. pap. 34.95 (*0-7136-4104-5*, 93359, Pub. by A&C Black UK) Talman.

Taekwondo Dinosaurs: How Dinosaurs Train to Get Their Black Belts. Y. H. Park. (Illus.). 32p. (J). 1994. pap. 5.95 (*0-9637151-4-3*) YH Pk Taekwondo.

Taekwondo for Children. Y. H. Park. 1994. pap. text ed. 9.95 (*0-9637151-5-1*) YH Pk Taekwondo.

Taekwondo for Children: The Ultimate Reference Guide for Children Interested in the World's Most Popular Martial Art. Y. H. Park & Jeff Leibowitz. (Illus.). 128p. (Orig.). (J). (gr. 4-8). 1994. pap. 9.95 (*0-9637151-0-0*) YH Pk Taekwondo.

Taekwondo Kyorugi: Olympic Style Sparring. Kuk H. Chung & Kyung M. Lee. LC 94-26035. 144p. 1994. pap. 12.95 (*1-880336-05-7*) Turtle CT.

***Taekwondo Techniques & Tactics.** Y. H. Park & Thomas D. Seabourne. LC 96-37724. (Martial Arts Ser.). (Illus.). 192p. (Orig.). 1997. pap. 15.95 (*0-88011-644-7*, PPAR0644) Human Kinetics.

***Tae's Sonata.** Haemi Balgassi. LC 96-29081. (J). 1997. 14.00 (*0-395-84314-6*, Clarion Bks) HM.

Taezhnyi Brodiaga. Mikhail Dyomin. LC 84-62843. 336p. (Orig.). 1986. pap. 19.00 (*0-89830-094-0*) Russica Pubs.

Tafelband see Opicinus de Canistris: Weltbild & Bekenntnisse Eines Avignonesischen Klerikers des 14 Jahrhunderts

Taff Trail: Official Guide. 2nd ed. Jeff Vinter. LC 93-5316. (Illus.). 128p. Date not set. pap. 12.95 (*0-7509-0341-4*, Pub. by Sutton Pubng UK) Bks Intl VA.

Taff Vale Railway. Donald S. Barrie. (C). 1985. 39.00 (*0-85361-027-4*) St Mut.

Taffy of Torpedo Junction. Nell W. Wechter. LC 96-8050. 160p. (C). 1996. pap. 9.95 (*0-8078-4619-8*) U of NC Pr.

***Taffy's Family.** Cooper Edens & Alexandra Day. (Michael di Capua Bks.). (Illus.). 32p. (J). (ps up). 1997. 12.95 (*0-06-205149-0*); lib. bdg. 12.89 (*0-06-205150-4*) HarpC Child Bks.

Tafhimul - Quran: Urdu Translation & Commentary, 6 vols., Set. A. A. Maudadi. 150.00 (*0-933511-70-1*) Kazi Pubns.

Taflak Lysandra. L. Neil Smith. (Thomas Paine Maru Ser.). 240p. (Orig.). 1988. mass mkt. 3.50 (*0-380-75323-5*) Avon.

Tafsir ul-Quran, 4 vol. set. Abdul M. Maulana. 2800p. (C). 1985. text ed. 69.00 (*1-56744-216-1*) Kazi Pubns.

Taft. Ann Patchett. 1995. mass mkt. 5.99 (*0-8041-1388-2*) Ivy Books.

***Taft Annual Review 1991.** 1991. 55.00 (*0-914756-82-6*, 00004692) Taft Group.

Taft Corporate Giving Directory. 90th ed. 1017p. 1989. 395.00 (*0-914756-80-X*, 100861-99584) Taft Group.

Taft Corporate Giving Directory. 91th ed. 1017p. 1990. 395.00 (*0-914756-81-8*, 101398-M99348) Taft Group.

Taft Corporate Giving Directory, 1992: Comprehensive Profiles & Analyses of Major American Corporate Philanthropic Programs. 92th rev. ed. Ed. by Susan Elnicki & Taft Corporation Staff. 1084p. 1991. 395.00 (*1-879784-14-9*, 600226) Taft Group.

Taft Foundation Reporter. 90th ed. 850p. 1989. 327.00 (*0-914756-63-X*, 100862-99584) Taft Group.

Taft Museum: A Cincinnati Legacy. Ed. by Dottie L. Lewis. (Illus.). 63p. (Orig.). 1988. pap. text ed. 7.50 (*0-911497-09-9*) Cinc Hist Soc.

Taft Museum: Its History & Collections, 2 vols., Set. Ed. by Edward J. Sullivan. LC 94-16313. (Illus.). 728p. 1995. boxed 195.00 (*1-55595-056-6*) Hudson Hills.

Taft Strategic Atlas: U. S. Health Care Reform. Frederick I. Taft. 686p. (Orig.). 1993. pap. 39.00 (*0-9635808-0-9*) Pub Strategy.

Taft Strategic Atlas: U. S. Health Care Reform. Frederick I. Taft. Ed. by Michael A. Salatka. (Illus.). (Orig.). 1993. pap. 39.00 (*0-9635808-1-7*) Pub Strategy.

Taft. Taft Family Gathering: Proceedings at the Meeting of the Taft Family at Uxbridge, Mass, 1874. 103p. 1991. reprint ed. pap. 19.00 (*0-8328-1982-4*); reprint ed. lib. bdg. 29.00 (*0-8328-1981-6*) Higginson Bk Co.

Taft, Wilson, Harding, & Coolidge. Michael Weber. LC 96-770. (Complete History of Our Presidents Ser.: No. 8). (J). 1996. write for info. (*0-86593-416-9*) Rourke Corp.

Tag: You're Dead! John Peel. LC 92-19939. (High Flyer Ser.). 128p. (J). (gr. 3-7). 1992. pap. 2.99 (*0-14-036053-0*) Puffin Bks.

TAG - Technical Assistance Guide: A Directory of Resources for New York Nonprofit Organizations. 75p. 1997. pap. text ed. 12.00 (*0-88156-161-4*) Comm Serv Soc NY.

Tag Against Time. Helen H. Vick. LC 95-45371. 188p. (YA). (gr. 6-12). 1996. 15.95 (*1-57140-006-0*, Harbinger CO); pap. 9.95 (*1-57140-007-9*, Harbinger CO) R Rinehart.

***Tag Against Time.** Helen H. Vick. 48p. (YA). (gr. 6-12). 1996. teacher ed., pap. 9.95 (*1-57140-014-1*, Harbinger CO) R Rinehart.

Tag-along Timothy Tours Alaska. Jean Richardson. Ed. by Edwin M. Eakin. (Illus.). 48p. (J). (gr. 2-3). 1989. pap. 6.95 (*0-89015-706-5*) Sunbelt Media.

Tag-along Timothy Tours Texas. Jean Richardson. (Illus.). (J). 1992. 10.95 (*0-89015-817-7*) Sunbelt Media.

Tag Team Studs. Clay Caldwell. (Orig.). 1996. mass mkt. 6.50 (*1-56333-465-8*, Badboy) Masquerade.

Tagalog - English Picture Dictionary. Claudia Schwalm. (Illus.). 89p. (J). (gr. k-6). 1995. 22.95 incl. audio (*1-57371-010-5*) Cultural Cnnect.

Tagalog Beginning Course. Neonetta C. Cabrera et al. Tr. by J. Donald Bowen. (Illus.). 526p. 1968. Incl. 24 audio cassettes. pap. text ed. 295.00 incl. audio (*0-88432-103-7*, AFTG10) Audio-Forum.

Tagalog Dictionary. Teresita V. Ramos. LC 71-152471. (PALI Language Texts, Philippines Ser.). 374p. (Orig.). (TAG.). (C). 1971. pap. text ed. 15.00 (*0-87022-676-2*) UH Pr.

Tagalog for Beginners. Teresita V. Ramos & Videa P. De Guzman. LC 77-148651. (Pacific & Asian Linguistics Institute. PALI Language Texts: Philippines Ser.). 875p. reprint ed. pap. 180.00 (*0-317-55727-0*, 2029584) Bks Demand.

Tagalog Newspaper Reader. (ENG & TAG.). 1990. audio 20.00 (*0-931745-68-3*) Dunwoody Pr.

Tagalog Newspaper Reader. Annabelle M. Sarra & R. David Zorc. LC 89-85771. 271p. (ENG & TAG.). 1990. 43.00 (*0-931745-66-7*) Dunwoody Pr.

***Tagalog (Pilipino) Language Survival Kit.** 2nd ed. (Illus.). 200p. 1998. pap. 5.95 (*0-86442-432-9*) Lonely Planet.

Tagalog Reference Grammar. Paul Schachter & Fe T. Otanes. 600p. 1972. 60.00 (*0-520-04943-8*) U CA Pr.

Tagalog-Russian Dictionary. deluxe ed. M. Cruz & S. P. Ignashev. 388p. (RUS & TAG.). 1959. 14.95 (*0-8288-6846-8*, M-9052) Fr & Eur.

Tagalog Slang Dictionary. R. David Zorc et al. LC 90-86224. 128p. 1991. 25.00 (*0-931745-56-X*) Dunwoody Pr.

Tagalog Structures. Teresita V. Ramos. LC 75-152472. (PALI Language Texts, Philippines Ser.). 186p. (Orig.). (C). 1971. pap. text ed. 14.00 (*0-87022-677-0*) UH Pr.

Tage Erlander: Serving the Welfare State, 1946-1969. Olof Ruin. Tr. by Michael F. Metcalf from SWE. LC 89-37755. (Policy & Institutional Studies). (Illus.). 378p. 1990. 49.95 (*0-8229-3631-3*) U of Pittsburgh Pr.

Tage Frid Teaches Woodworking: Furnituremaking, Bk. 3. Tage Frid. LC 78-65178. (Illus.). 240p. 1985. text ed. 21.95 (*0-918804-40-X*) Taunton.

Tage Frid Teaches Woodworking: Joinery, Bk. 1. Tage Frid. LC 78-65178. (Illus.). 224p. 1979. 21.95 (*0-918804-03-5*) Taunton.

Tagebuch der Anne Frank. Anne Frank. 320p. (GER.). 1992. pap. 11.75 (*3-596-11377-6*, Pub. by Fischer Taschbch Verlag GW) Intl Bk Import.

Tagebuch Einer Reise in Inner-Arabien, 2 vols., Vol. I. Julius Euting. (Illus.). 258p. reprint ed. write for info. (*0-318-71504-X*) G Olms Pubs.

Tagebuch Einer Reise in Inner-Arabien, 2 vols., Vol. II. Julius Euting. (Illus.). 304p. reprint ed. write for info. (*0-318-71505-8*) G Olms Pubs.

Tagebuch Einer Reise in Inner-Arabien, Vol. II: XIII. Julius Euting. (Illus.). 304p. reprint ed. Vol. II: xiii, 304p. write for info. (*0-318-71506-6*) G Olms Pubs.

***Tagebuch of Ernst Silge U. S. N.** Frank H. Pierce, 3rd. (Illus.). (Orig.). 1996. pap. 25.00 (*0-7884-0489-X*, P316) Heritage Bk.

Tagebucher von Joseph Goebbels: Samtliche Fragmente. Teil I: Die Handschriftlichen Tagebucher. Juli 1924 bis Juli 1941, 4 vols. & index. Ed. by Elke Frohlich. 3380p. (GER.). 1987. lib. bdg. 235.00 (*3-598-21915-6*) U Pubns Amer.

Tagebucher von Joseph Goebbels, Teil II: Diktate 1941 bis 1945, 15 vols. Ed. by Elke Frohlich. (GER.). 1995. lib. bdg. 1,305.00 (*3-598-21920-2*) U Pubns Amer.

Tagebuecher 1953 - 1952. Thomas Mann. Ed. by Inge Jens. 978p. (GER.). 1995. 115.25 (*3-10-048214-X*, Pub. by S Fischer GW) Intl Bk Import.

Taggard Point: Shapes, Bk. 2. Mark Rivers. 208p. (Orig.). (YA). 1995. mass mkt. 3.99 (*0-425-14726-6*) Berkley Pub.

Taggard Point: The Clown, Bk. 4. Mark Rivers. 176p. (Orig.). 1995. mass mkt. 3.99 (*0-425-15016-X*) Berkley Pub.

Taggard Point Bk. 1: The Forever House. Mark Rivers. 176p. (Orig.). 1995. pap. text ed. 3.99 (*0-425-14567-0*) Berkley Pub.

Taggard Point Bk. 3: When the Dead Scream. Mark Rivers. 176p. (Orig.). (YA). 1995. mass mkt. 3.99 (*0-425-14880-7*) Berkley Pub.

Taggart. Louis L'Amour. 160p. 1982. mass mkt. 3.99 (*0-553-25477-4*) Bantam.

Taggart. Louis L'Amour. 1996. reprint ed. mass mkt. 3.99 (*0-553-24577-5*) Bantam.

Tagging Procedures. Center for Occupational Research & Development Staff. (EUTEC Power Plant Operator Curriculum Ser.). (Illus.). 18p. (C). 1985. pap. text ed. write for info. (*1-55502-223-5*) CORD Commns.

Tagmemic Analysis of Mexican Spanish Clauses. Ruth M. Brend. (Janua Linguarum, Ser. Practica: No. 52). 1968. text ed. 73.85 (*90-279-0662-9*) Mouton.

Tagmemic Comparison of the Structure of English & Vietnamese Sentences. Duong T. Binh. LC 74-123126. (Janua Linguarum, Ser. Practica: No. 110). (Orig.). 1971. pap. text ed. 110.80 (*90-279-1598-9*) Mouton.

Tagmemics, Discourse & Verbal Art. Kenneth L. Pike. LC 81-9541. (Michigan Studies in the Humanities: No. 3). (C). 1981. pap. 6.00 (*0-936534-02-8*) Mich Studies Human.

Tagore & Radhakrishnan: A Study in Religious Perspective. Jaya Mukherjee. 120p. 1992. 12.00 (*81-85078-79-3*, Pub. by Janaki Prakashan II) Nataraj Bks.

Tagore-Gandhi Controversy. M. K. Gandhi & Rabindranath Tagore. Ed. by R. K. Prabhu. 155p. (Orig.). 1983. pap. 3.50 (*0-934676-52-6*) Greenlf Bks.

Tagore, India & Soviet Union. A. P. Gnatyuk Danil'chuk. 400p. 1986. 48.50 (*0-8364-1831-X*, Pub. by Firma KLM II) S Asia.

Tagore, Rabindranath, a Collection of His Life & Work. Rabindranath Tagore Festival Committee. (Illus.). 80p. 1986. pap. 40.00 (*0-905836-56-1*, Pub. by Museum Modern Art UK) St Mut.

Tagore Reader. Rabindranath Tagore. Ed. by Amiya Chakravarty. 1966. pap. 18.00 (*0-8070-5971-4*, BP234) Beacon Pr.

Tagore Testament. Rabindranath Tagore. Tr. by Indu Dutt from BEN. 115p. 1979. pap. 3.95 (*0-88253-188-3*) Ind-US Inc.

Tagore's Last Poems. rev. ed. Shyamasree Devi & P. Lal. 29p. (BEN.). 1980. 8.00 (*0-86578-120-6*); pap. 4.00 (*0-86578-121-4*) Ind-US Inc.

Tagores of Jorasanko. Hironmoy Banerjee. Tr. by Biplab K. Majumdar. (C). 1995. 35.00 (*81-212-0488-7*, Pub. by Gian Publng Hse II) S Asia.

Tagraume - Bilder im Lichte der Aufklarung. G. Lammel. 296p. (GER.). 1992. text ed. 59.00 (*3-364-00263-0*) Gordon & Breach.

Tags. Carole Eastman & Blair Eastman. 44p. 1991. pap. 3.95 (*0-9634052-0-9*) Eastman & Co.

Tags - Travel, Activities, Games & Stuff: Complete Travel Guide & License Plate Game. (Illus.). 216p. (Orig.). 1994. pap. 14.95 (*1-884187-24-2*) AMICA Pub Hse.

Taguchi Methods: A Hands on Approach. Glen S. Peace. (Illus.). 384p. 1993. 55.95 (*0-201-56311-8*) Addison-Wesley.

Taguchi Methods: Applications in World Industry. Ed. by A. Bendell. (Illus.). 250p. 1989. 89.00 (*0-387-50657-8*) Spr-Verlag.

Taguchi Methods: Design of Experiments. Genichi Taguchi. (Quality Engineering Ser.). 370p. 1993. 45.00 (*0-941243-18-4*) ASI Pr.

Taguchi Methods: On Line Production. Genichi Taguchi. (Quality Engineering Ser.). 370p. 1993. 55.00 (*0-941243-17-6*) ASI Pr.

Taguchi Methods: Research & Development. Genichi Taguchi. Ed. by Seiso Konishi & Yuin Wu. LC 92-13700. (Quality Engineering Ser.: Vol. 1). 376p. 1993. 45.00 (*0-941243-16-8*) ASI Pr.

Taguchi Methods: Special Issue of Quality Reliability Engineering. Ed. by Norman C. Harris et al. 205p. 1988. pap. text ed. 105.00 (*0-471-92046-0*) Wiley.

Taguchi Methods & QFD: Hows & Whys for Management. Ed. by Nancy E. Ryan. LC 88-22182. (Illus.). 110p. 1988. 16.50 (*0-941243-04-4*) ASI Pr.

Taguchi Methods Orthogonal Arrays & Linear Graphs: Tools for Quality Engineering. G. Taguchi & Seiso Konishi. Tr. by J. Kennedy et al. from JPN. 72p. 1987. student ed., pap. 9.50 (*0-941243-01-X*) ASI Pr.

Taguchi on Robust Technology Development: Bringing Quality Engineering Upstream. Genichi Taguchi. LC 92-30947. 136p. 1993. 24.95 (*0-7918-0028-8*) ASME.

Taguchi Techniques for Quality Engineering: Loss Function, Orthogonal Experiments, Parameter & Tolerance Design. 2nd ed. P. J. Ross. LC 95-15415. 329p. 1996. text ed. 49.00 (*0-07-053958-8*) McGraw.

Tah-Koo Wah-Kan: Or, The Gospel among the Dakotas. Stephen R. Riggs. LC 78-38460. (Religion in America, Ser. 2). 534p. 1972. reprint ed. 36.95 (*0-405-04081-4*) Ayer.

Tah Tye: The Last 'Possum in the Pouch. Mary A. Fontenot. LC 96-23872. (Illus.). 32p. (J). (ps-7). 1996. lib. bdg. 14.95 (*1-884725-10-4*) Blue Heron LA.

***Taheebo.** Rita Elkins. (The Woodland Health Ser.). 1997. pap. text ed. 3.95 (*1-885670-40-0*) Woodland UT.

Tahirih: The Poetry of Qurratu'l-'Ayn. Ed. by Amin Banani. 1996. 19.95 (*0-933770-55-3*) Kalimat.

Tahirih the Pure. rev. ed. Martha L. Root. LC 80-39945. (Illus.). 1981. reprint ed. boxed 12.95 (*0-933770-14-6*) Kalimat.

*Tahiti. Roseline Ngcheong-Lum. LC 96-40213. (Cultures of the World Ser.: Group 14). (Illus.). 128p. (YA). (gr. 5 up). 1997. lib. bdg. 23.95 (0-7614-0682-4) Marshall Cavendish.

Tahiti. P. I. Nordmann. 1972. 250.00 (0-8490-1175-2) Gordon Pr.

Tahiti. Henry Adams. Ed. by Robert E. Spiller. LC 47-3845. (Illus.). 216p. 1976. reprint ed. 50.00 (0-8201-1213-5) Schol Facsimiles.

Tahiti: The Marriage of Loti. Pierre P. Loti-Viaud. Tr. by Clara Bell. 217p. 1987. pap. 19.95 (0-7103-0231-2, 02312) Routledge Chapman & Hall.

Tahiti & French Polynesia: A Travel Survival Kit. 4th ed. Tony Wheeler & Rob Kay. (Illus.). 400p. 1997. pap. 16.95 (0-86442-287-3) Lonely Planet.

Tahiti Nui. Eric Debischop. Tr. by Edward Young. (Illus.). 1959. 15.95 (0-8392-1109-0) Astor-Honor.

Tahiti-Polynesia Handbook. 3rd ed. David Stanley. (Moon Travel Handbook Ser.). (Illus.). 243p. (Orig.). 1996. pap. 13.95 (1-56691-037-4) Moon Trvl Hdbks.

Tahitian & English Dictionary. John Davies. LC 75-35188. reprint ed. 42.50 (0-404-14217-6) AMS Pr.

Tahitian-English, English-Tahitian Dictionary. Leonard Clairmont. 32.50 (0-87559-053-5) Shalom.

Tahitian Transformation: Gender & Capitalist Development in a Rural Society. Victoria S. Lockwood. LC 92-24045. (Women & Change in the Developing World Ser.). 180p. (C). 1993. pap. text ed. 16.95 (1-55587-391-X); lib. bdg. 40.00 (1-55587-317-0) Lynne Rienner.

Tahitians: Mind & Experience in the Society Islands. Robert I. Levy. LC 73-77136. (Illus.). xxviii, 576p. 1975. reprint ed. pap. text ed. 21.95 (0-226-47607-3, P649) U Ch Pr.

Tahlequah. Virginia Brunner. LC 94-60011. (Illus.). 1994. 35.00 (0-936029-34-X) Western Bk Journ.

Tahoe: An Environmental History. Douglas H. Strong. LC 83-6523. (Illus.). 210p. reprint ed. pap. 59.90 (0-7837-6185-6, 2045907) Bks Demand.

Tahoe: The Complete Guide: Including Reno & Surrounding Area. Ken Castle. (Illus.). 704p. (Orig.). 1995. pap. 18.95 (0-935701-02-8) Foghorn Pr.

*Tahoe: The Complete Guide to Outdoor Recreation, Sightseeing, & Nightlife in the Lake Tahoe Basin, Including Reno. 2nd ed. Ken Castle. (Complete Guide Ser.). (Illus.). 700p. 1997. pap. 20.95 (1-57354-024-2) Foghorn Pr.

Tahoe City Yesterdays. Carol Van Etten. (Illus.). 134p. 1987. pap. 24.95 (0-913814-28-8) Nevada Pubns.

*Tahoe Heritage: The Bliss Family of Glenbrook, Nevada. Sessions S. Wheeler. (Illus.). 176p. (Orig.). 1997. pap. 15.95 (0-87417-299-3) U of Nev Pr.

Tahoe Place Names. Barbara Lekisch. Ed. by Peter Browning. LC 88-80574. (Illus.). 192p. (Orig.). (C). 1988. pap. 14.95 (0-944220-01-0) Great West Bks.

Tahoe Sierra. 3rd ed. Jeffrey P. Schaffer. LC 87-6198. (Illus.). 320p. 1987. pap. 14.95 (0-89997-082-6) Wilderness Pr.

Tahoe Times - the Receptionist Office Job. 2nd ed. Butler. (KM - Office Procedures Ser.). 1985. 24.95 (0-538-25820-9) S-W Pub.

Tahoe-Yosemite Trail. 5th ed. Thomas Winnett. LC 87-6216. 136p. 1987. pap. 11.95 (0-89997-084-2) Wilderness Pr.

Tahquamenan Country: A Look at Its Past. Charles S. Taylor. (Illus.). 150p. 1991. 15.00 (0-9614344-9-X) Historical Soc MI.

Tahquamenon in Michigan's Upper Peninsula. John S. Penrod. (YA). (gr. 7 up). 1988. pap. 5.00 (0-942618-12-2) Penrod-Hiawatha.

Tahquitz & Suicide Rocks. Intro. by Chuck Wilts. LC 79-87634. (Illus.). 208p. 1973. pap. 9.50 (0-930410-07-6) Amer Alpine Club.

Tahquitz Exchange. Bernnie Reese et al. (Orig.). (YA). (gr. 12). 1993. pap. write for info. (0-9628802-3-X) DeChamp CA.

*Tahuri. Ngahuia Te Awekotuku. (International Connections Ser.). 104p. pap. 9.95 (0-88961-183-1, Pub. by Wmns Pr CN) LPC InBook.

Tai Ahoms & the Stars: Three Ritual Texts to Ward off Danger. Ed. by B. J. Terwiel & Ranoo Wichasin. Tr. by Ranoo Wichasin. (Studies on Southeast Asia: No. 10). 170p. 1992. pap. text ed. 16.00 (0-87727-709-5) Cornell SE Asia.

Tai Chen on Mencius: Explorations in Words & Meaning. Ann-ping Chin & Mansfield Freeman. 232p. (C). 1990. text ed. 35.00 (0-300-04654-5) Yale U Pr.

Tai Chen's Inquiry into Goodness: A Translation of the Yuan Shan, with an Introductory Essay. Chung-ying Cheng. LC 70-113573. 184p. reprint ed. pap. 52.50 (0-7837-3984-2, 2043814) Bks Demand.

Tai Chi. Ed. by Peter Albright. LC 95-37899. (Naturally Better Boo Ser.). 64p. 1996. 12.95 (0-02-860831-3) Macmillan.

Tai Chi. Cheng & Smith. 29.95 (0-685-22124-5) Wehman.

*Tai Chi: Flowing Movements for Harmony & Balance. Paul Tucker. (New Life Library). (Illus.). 64p. 1997. 9.95 (1-85967-503-4, Lorenz Bks) Anness Pub.

Tai Chi: For Stress Control & Relaxation. Gary Khor. (Illus.). 165p. 1994. reprint ed. pap. 11.95 (0-89346-795-2) Heian Intl.

T'ai Chi: Ten Minutes to Health. Chia S. Pang & Goh E. Hock. LC 85-22388. (Illus.). 132p. (Orig.). 1986. pap. 17.95 (0-916360-30-X) CRCS Pubns CA.

Tai Chi: The Supreme Ultimate. Lawrence Galante. LC 84-50665. (Illus.). 177p. 1982. pap. 10.95 (0-87728-497-0) Weiser.

T'ai-Chi: The Supreme Ultimate Exercise for Health, Sport, & Self-Defense. Man-Ch'ing Cheng & Robert W. Smith. LC 67-23009. (Illus.). 112p. 1967. 29.95 (0-8048-0560-1) C E Tuttle.

*Tai Chi Beginner (Taijiquan) Yang Style of Shaolin Chi Mantis. 2nd ed. Zhen Shen-Lang. Ed. by Michelle McCarty. LC 96-68710. (Tai Chi (Taijiquan) Ser.). (Illus.). 208p. (Orig.). (YA). (gr. 7-12). 1997. 24.88 (1-885910-04-5); teacher ed. 31.88 (1-885910-06-1); wbk. ed., pap. 12.88 (1-885910-01-0) Shaolin Commns.

Tai Chi Beginner (Taijiquan) Yang Style of Shaolin Chi Mantis. 2nd ed. Zhen Shen-Lang & Sifu R. O'Connor. Ed. by Michelle McCarty. LC 96-68710. (Tai Chi (Taijiquan) Ser.). (Illus.). 208p. (Orig.). (YA). (gr. 7-12). 1997. pap. 18.88 (1-885910-00-2) Shaolin Commns.

T'ai Chi Boxing Chronicle. Kuo Lien-Ying. Tr. by Guttman from CHI. LC 93-40412. (Illus.). 141p. (Orig.). (C). 1994. pap. 14.95 (1-55643-177-5) North Atlantic.

*T'ai Chi Changes: T'ai Chi According to the Book of Changes. Stuart A. Olson. 180p. Date not set. otabind 1.95 (1-889633-02-X) Jade Forest.

*Tai Chi Chi Kung I. M. Chia. 1996. 14.95 (0-935621-12-1) Heal Tao Bks.

T'ai Chi Chih: Joy Thru Movement. Justin F. Stone. LC 96-5633. (Illus.). 98p. (Orig.). 1996. pap. text ed. 14.95 (1-882290-02-X) Good Karma.

T'ai-Chi Ch'uan. Yang Ming-shih. (Quick & Easy Ser.). (Illus.). 60p. (Orig.). 1974. pap. 6.95 (4-07-973783-1, Pub. by Shufunomoto Co Ltd JA) C E Tuttle.

T'ai Chi Ch'uan: A Simplified Method of Calisthenics for Health & Self Defense. Cheng Man-ch'ing. Tr. by Beauson T'seng from CHI. (Illus.). 160p. (Orig.). 1981. pap. 11.95 (0-913028-85-1) North Atlantic.

T'ai Chi Ch'uan: Body & Mind in Harmony (Integration of Meaning & Method) Sophia Delza. LC 84-23916. 244p. 1985. pap. 18.95 (0-88706-030-7) State U NY Pr.

T'ai-Chi Ch'uan: Embracing the Pearl. Robert Chuckrow. (Illus.). 151p. (Orig.). 1995. pap. 22.95 (0-9645919-0-1) Rising Mist.

Tai-Chi Ch'uan: Its Effects & Practical Application. 3rd ed. Yearniing K. Chen. (Illus.). 192p. 1996. reprint ed. pap. 9.95 (0-87877-043-7) Newcastle Pub.

Tai-Chi Ch'uan: Its Effects & Practical Application. Yen-Lin Chen. LC 80-19810. vi, 184p. 1993. reprint ed. pap. 23.00 (0-89370-995-6); reprint ed. lib. bdg. 33.00 (0-89370-643-4) Borgo Pr.

Tai Chi Chuan: Roots & Branches. Nigel Sutton. 136p. 1996. pap. 8.95 (0-8048-2072-4) C E Tuttle.

Tai-Chi Ch'uan: The Chinese Way. Foen Tjoeng Lie. LC 87-35928. (Illus.). 128p. (Orig.). 1988. pap. 10.95 (0-8069-6826-5) Sterling.

Tai Chi Ch'uan: The Gentle Workout for Mind & Body. Yue S. Wei. LC 95-17865. (Illus.). 128p. 1995. pap. 10.95 (0-8069-1366-5) Sterling.

T'ai Chi Ch'uan: The Internal Tradition. Ron Sieh. (Illus.). 90p. (Orig.). 1992. pap. 9.95 (1-55643-128-7) North Atlantic.

T'ai Chi Ch'uan: The Martial Side. Michael Babin. (Illus.). 152p. 1992. pap. 16.00 (0-87364-679-7) Paladin Pr.

Tai Chi Chuan: The Twenty-Seven Forms. Marshall Ho'o. Ed. by Mike Lee. LC 86-51059. (Chinese Arts Ser.). 112p. 1986. pap. 10.95 (0-89750-109-8, 449) Ohara Pubns.

T'ai Chi Ch'uan: Yang Style. Yang Jwing-Ming. LC 81-50513. (Illus.). 250p. (Orig.). 1981. pap. 12.50 (0-86568-023-X, 210) Unique Pubns.

T'ai Chi Ch'uan & I Ching: A Choreography of Body & Mind. Liu Da. LC 79-183640. 1987. pap. 11.00 (0-06-091309-6, PL-1309, PL) HarpC.

T'ai Chi Ch'uan & Meditation. Da Liu. LC 85-25071. (Illus.). 192p. 1991. pap. 14.00 (0-8052-0993-X) Schocken.

Tai Chi Ch'uan & Qigong: Techniques & Training. Manfred Grosser. LC 96-12879. (Illus.). 144p. 1996. pap. 12.95 (0-8069-5957-6) Sterling.

T'ai-chi Ch'uan Experience: Reflections & Perceptions on Body-Mind Harmony. Sophia Delza. Ed. & Intro. by Robert C. Neville. 330p. 1996. pap. 19.95 (0-7914-2898-2); text ed. 59.50 (0-7914-2897-4) State U NY Pr.

T'ai Chi Ch'uan for Health & Self-Defense: Philosophy & Practice. T. T. Liang. 1977. pap. 10.00 (0-394-72461-5, Vin) Random.

Tai Chi Chuan Martial Applications: Advanced Yang Style Tai Chi Chuan. 2nd rev. ed. Jwing-Ming Yang. Ed. by Alan Dougall. LC 96-60388. (Martial Arts-Internal Ser.). Orig. Title: Advanced Yang Style Tai Chi Chuan. (Illus.). 384p. (Orig.). 1996. pap. 22.95 (1-886969-44-2, B008R) YMAA Pubn.

T'ai Chi Ch'uan Ta Wen: Questions & Answers on T'a Chi Ch'uan. Chen Wei-Ming. Tr. by Benjamin Pang Jeng Lo & Robert Smith from CHI. 64p. (Orig.). 1985. pap. 7.95 (0-938190-67-9) North Atlantic.

T'ai Chi Ch'uan the Philosophy of Yin & Yang & Its Applications. Douglas Lee. Ed. by Charles Lucas. LC 76-6249. (Chinese Arts Ser.). (Illus.). 1976. pap. text ed. 11.95 (0-89750-044-X, 317, Wehman) Ohara Pubns.

Tai Chi Chuan's Internal Secrets. Doc Fai Wong & Jane Hallander. (Illus.). 160p. (Orig.). 1991. pap. 12.95 (0-86568-138-4, 250) Unique Pubns.

T'ai Chi Classics. Waysun Liao. LC 89-43316. (Illus.). 296p. (Orig.). 1990. pap. 15.00 (0-87773-531-X) Shambhala Pubns.

Tai Chi Combat. Paul Crompton. pap. 17.95 (1-874250-25-1, 93162) Talman.

Tai Chi for Beginners: 10 Minutes to Health & Fitness. Claire Hooton. 160p. (Orig.). 1996. pap. 14.00 (0-399-52207-7, Perigee Bks) Berkley Pub.

*Tai Chi for Longevity with Polynesian & Alsharqi Techniques. Angelie Bliss. (Illus.). 136p. (Orig.). 1998. pap. 15.95 (0-9651438-5-6) Air & Water King.

Tai Chi for Two: The Practice of Push Hands. Paul Crompton. pap. 17.95 (1-874250-40-5, 93306, Pub. by P H Crompton UK) Talman.

T'ai Chi Handbook: Exercise, Meditation, Self-Defense. Herman Kauz. LC 73-10552. (Illus.). 192p. 1974. pap. 14.95 (0-385-09370-5, Dolp) Doubleday.

Tai Chi Journey. John Lash. 1993. pap. 13.95 (1-85230-120-1) Element MA.

*Tai Chi Made Easy: Step-By-Step Guide to Health & Relaxation. LC 96-37162. 1997. write for info. (1-882606-25-6) Peoples Med Soc.

T'ai Chi Ruler: Chinese Yoga for Health & Longevity. Terry Dunn. 128p. 1996. pap. text ed. 15.95 (0-938045-14-8) Dragon Door.

T'ai Chi Swordplay. Xing Yanling. (Illus.). 145p. (Orig.). 1992. pap. 29.00 (0-87040-850-X) Japan Pubns USA.

Tai Chi Theory & Martial Power: Advanced Yang Style Tai Chi Chuan. 2nd rev. ed. Jwing-Ming Yang. Ed. by Alan Dougall. LC 96-60387. (Chinese Martial Arts-Internal Ser.). Orig. Title: Advanced Yang Style Tai Chi Chuan. (Illus.). 288p. (Orig.). 1996. pap. 19.95 (1-886969-43-4, B007R) YMAA Pubn.

T'ai Chi Touchstones: Yang Family Secret Transmissions. 3rd ed. Ed. by Douglas Wile. (Illus.). 159p. (Orig.). 1983. pap. 11.95 (0-912059-01-X) Sweet Ch I Pr.

*Tai Chi Training in China: Masters, Teachers & Coaches. Howard Thomas. (Illus.). 224p. 1997. pap. 25.00 (1-874250-70-7, Pub. by P H Crompton UK) Talman.

T'ai Chi Workbook. Paul Crompton. LC 87-9736. (Illus.). 157p. 1987. pap. 19.00 (0-87773-424-0) Shambhala Pubns.

Tai-chung, Taiwan: Structure & Function. Clifton W. Pannell. LC 72-91223. (University of Chicago, Department of Geography, Research Paper Ser.: No. 144). 214p. 1973. reprint ed. pap. 61.00 (0-608-02269-1, 2062910) Bks Demand.

Tai in Tai Context. Ed. by Richard A. O'Connor. (Crossroads Ser.: Ser. 5.1). 122p. (Orig.). 1990. pap. 5.00 (1-877979-90-2) SE Asia.

Tai-Ji Fitness: Its Principles & Basic Training. Xiaonan Zhang. 1990. write for info. (0-9625392-0-1) Zhang Import & Export.

TAI Mathematics Classroom Set. (J). (gr. 3). 1995. 550.00 (0-88106-175-1, M300) Charlesbridge Pub.

TAI Mathematics Classroom Set. (J). (gr. 4). 1995. 550.00 (0-88106-176-X, M400) Charlesbridge Pub.

TAI Mathematics Classroom Set. (J). (gr. 5). 1995. 550.00 (0-88106-177-8, M500) Charlesbridge Pub.

TAI Mathematics Classsroom Set. (J). (gr. 6 up). 1995. 550.00 (0-88106-178-6, M600) Charlesbridge Pub.

TAI Mathematics Implementation Guide. 1995. 5.00 (0-88106-170-0, M055) Charlesbridge Pub.

TAI Mathematics Monitor Book. 1995. 6.50 (0-88106-168-9, M053) Charlesbridge Pub.

TAI Mathematics Resource Room Set. 1995. 275.00 (0-88106-179-4, M950) Charlesbridge Pub.

TAI Mathematics Review Units Book. 1995. 6.00 (0-88106-167-0, M054) Charlesbridge Pub.

TAI Mathematics Teacher Resource Book. 1995. 75.00 (0-88106-169-7, M051) Charlesbridge Pub.

TAI Mathematics Test Book. 1995. 6.50 (0-88106-166-2, M052) Charlesbridge Pub.

Tai-Pan. James Clavell. 736p. 1976. mass mkt. 7.99 (0-440-18462-2) Dell.

Tai-Pan. James Clavell. 1983. 24.95 (0-385-31448-5) Delacorte.

Tai-Pan see James Clavell Library

Tai Race, Elder Brother of the Chinese. William C. Dodd. 1976. lib. bdg. 59.95 (0-8490-2726-8) Gordon Pr.

T'ai Shan: An Account of the Sacred Eastern Peak of China. Dwight C. Baker. 1973. lib. bdg. 250.00 (0-87968-474-7) Krishna Pr.

Tai Yu Shan: Traditional Ecological Adaptation in a South Chinese Island. Armando Da Silva. (Asian Folklore & Social Life Monographs: No. 32). 1972. 14.00 (0-89986-032-X) Oriental Bk Store.

*TAICHI: A Personal Learning Experience, 2 vols. 2nd ed. Arthur T. Orawski. LC 95-61881. (Illus.). 1818p. 1996. lib. bdg. 276.00 incl. vhs (0-9633995-2-7) TIPRAC.

*TAICHI: A Personal Learning Experience, Supplement to 1st Edition. Arthur T. Orawski. (Illus.). 1996. lib. bdg. 84.00 (0-9633995-1-9) TIPRAC.

Taif: The Summer Capital of Saudi Arabia. Angelo Pesce. 120p. (C). 1995. 100.00 (0-907151-27-2, Pub. by IMMEL Pubng UK) St Mut.

Taiga. Elizabeth Kaplan. LC 95-38923. (Biomes Ser.). 64p. (J). (gr. 3-5). 1996. lib. bdg. 17.95 (0-7614-0135-0, Benchmark NY) Marshall Cavendish.

Taiga. April P. Sayre. (Exploring Earth's Biomes Ser.). (Illus.). 64p. (J). (gr. 5-8). 1994. lib. bdg. 15.98 (0-8050-2830-7) TFC Bks NY.

Taiga's True Views: The Language of Landscape Painting in Eighteenth-Century Japan. Melinda Takeuchi. (Illus.). 232p. (C). 1992. 65.00 (0-8047-1915-2) Stanford U Pr.

Taiga's True Views: The Language of Landscape Painting in Eighteenth-Century Japan. Melinda Takeuchi. 1994. pap. 22.50 (0-8047-2343-5); pap. 24.95 (0-8047-2088-6) Stanford U Pr.

Taigman's Advanced Cardiology: In Plain English. Syd Canan et al. LC 94-48021. 1995. pap. 28.75 (0-89303-999-3) P-H.

Taiji Chin Na. Jwing-Ming Yang. Ed. by James O'Leary, Jr. (Illus.). 288p. (Orig.). 1995. per., pap. 24.95 (0-940871-37-8, B022) YMAA Pubn.

Taijutsu: Ninja Art of Unarmed Combat. Charles Daniel. LC 86-51212. 200p. (Orig.). 1986. pap. 12.95 (0-86568-085-X, 125) Unique Pubns.

Taijutsu Tactics: Ninja Close-Quarter Grappling. Omoto Saiji. (Illus.). 112p. 1987. pap. 14.50 (0-87364-401-8) Paladin Pr.

Taiko: A Novel. Eiji Yoshikawa. Ed. by Moriyasu & Chaline. Tr. by William S. Wilson from JPN. 940p. 1992. 35.00 (4-7700-1570-4) Kodansha.

Tail Arse Charlie. John Millet. 24p. 1984. pap. 2.00 (0-317-07609-4) Samisdat.

Tail Code: The Complete History of USAF Tactical Aircraft Tail Code Markings. Patrick Martin. LC 93-84496. (Illus.). 176p. 1994. 45.00 (0-88740-513-4) Schiffer.

Tail End Charlies! Navy Combat Fighter Pilots at War's End. Roy D. Erickson. Ed. by Henry Sakaida. (Illus.). 272p. 1995. 30.00 (0-9646821-0-9) R D Erickson.

Tail Feathers from Mother Goose: The Opie Rhyme Book. Iona A. Opie & P. Opie. (Illus.). 124p. (J). 1991. 7.99 (0-517-05555-4) Random Hse Value.

*Tail Gunner: Squadron Leader. R. C. Rivaz. (Illus.). 128p. 1996. 14.99 (0-7509-1327-4, Pub. by Sutton Pubng UK) Bks Intl VA.

Tail Gunner's Tale. Gerald E. McDowell. 1991. 17.95 (0-533-09100-4) Vantage.

*Tail of Adventure. Tam Uyen Vo. (Illus.). (J). (gr. 2 up). 1995. pap. text ed. 4.95 (0-9654498-1-5) Voco Pub.

Tail of the Dragon: New Dance, 1976-1982. Marcia B. Siegel. LC 91-522. (Illus.). 251p. 1991. text ed. 44.95 (0-8223-1156-9); pap. text ed. 15.95 (0-8223-1166-6) Duke.

Tail of the Storm. Alan Cockrell. LC 94-26404. (Illus.). 248p. 1995. pap. 24.95 (0-8173-0772-9) U of Ala Pr.

Tail of Two Murders. Melissa Cleary. 192p. (Orig.). 1993. pap. 4.99 (0-425-15809-8, Prime Crime) Berkley Pub.

*Tail Stories: An Aspect of Love of Pets. Elmer A. Spiezio. (Illus.). 70p. (Orig.). (J). 1996. pap. 10.95 (1-57502-328-8) Morris Pubng.

Tail Tales. Sally Markham-David. LC 93-6631. (J). 1994. pap. write for info. (0-383-03718-2) SRA McGraw.

Tail Toes Eyes Ears Nose. Marilee R. Burton. LC 87-33276. (Illus.). 32p. (J). (ps-1). 1988. lib. bdg. 14.89 (0-06-020874-0) HarpC Child Bks.

Tail Waggings of Maggie. Margaret W. Baender. (Illus.). 64p. (J). (gr. 8-10). 1982. pap. 6.00 (0-88100-012-4) Philmar Pub.

Tailchaser's Song. Tad Williams. 400p. 1986. mass mkt. 6.99 (0-88677-374-1, 040) DAW Bks.

Taildraggers High. Larry Sutton. LC 85-47592. 161p. (J). (gr. 5 up). 1985. 11.95 (0-374-37372-8) FS&G.

Tailed Head-Hunters of Nigeria: An Account of an Official's Seven Years of Experience in the Northern Nigerian Pagan Belt, & a Description of the Manners, Habits & Customs of Some of Its Native Tribes. Arthur J. Tremearne. (B. E. Ser.: No. 133). 1989. 32.00 (0-8115-3058-2) Periodicals Srv.

*Tailey Whaley: A Tale of a Whale with a Whale of a Tail. (Illus.). 38p. (J). (ps-6). 1997. 14.95 (0-9657214-4-2) Trident Pub.

Tailgate Fever Cookbook: Arizona. Susan M. Shaffer et al. LC 92-32292. (Illus.). 1992. pap. 9.95 (0-914846-66-3) Golden West Pub.

*Tailgate Meetings That Work! A Guide to Effective Construction Safety Training, National Edition. 324p. 1997. ring bd. 90.00 (1-882417-17-8, 9655) Am Conf Govt Indus Hygienist.

Tailgate Parties. Susan Wyler. (Particular Palate Cookbook Ser.). 1984. pap. 6.95 (0-517-55441-0, Harmony) Crown Pub Group.

Tailgate Picnics for the Southwest Conference. Candy Coleman. (Illus.). 48p. (Orig.). 1981. pap. text ed. 4.00 (0-943768-05-5) C Coleman.

Tailgater's Handbook. Joe Drozda. (Illus.). 256p. (Orig.). 1996. pap. 14.95 (1-57028-093-2) Masters Pr IN.

Tailgating at Texas: A Recipe Guide to Texas Longhorn Tailgating. Lucy Littleton. (Illus.). 1995. pap. 8.95 (1-885623-07-0) Owl Bay Pubs.

Tailgating in T-Town: The Owl Bay Guide to Crimson Tide Tailgating. Lucy Littleton. 128p. 1994. pap. 8.95 (0-9638568-4-7) Owl Bay Pubs.

*Tailgating Without a Hitch: Tailgate Cooking Made Fun. Kathy C. Merrill. LC 96-70134. 100p. (Orig.). 1996. pap. 12.95 (1-882792-32-7) Proctor Pubns.

Tailhook, 1991, Pt. 2: Events at the Thirty-Fifth Annual Tailhook Symposium. (Illus.). 212p. (Orig.). (C). 1993. pap. text ed. 40.00 (0-7881-0117-X) DIANE Pub.

*Tailings & Mine Waste 1997: Proceedings of the Fourth International Conference, Fort Collins, Colorado, 13-17 January 1997. (Illus.). 802p. (C). 1996. text ed. 115.00 (90-5410-857-6, Pub. by A A Balkema NE) Ashgate Pub Co.

Tailings & Mine Waste 94: Proceedings of the First International Conference, Fort Collins, January 1994. (Illus.). 272p. (C). 1994. text ed. 80.00 (90-5410-364-7, Pub. by A A Balkema NE) Ashgate Pub Co.

Tailings & Mine Waste '95: Proceedings of the 2nd International Conference, Fort Collins, CO, USA, 17-20 January 1995. Second International Conference Staff. (Illus.). 140p. 1995. 55.00 (90-5410-526-7) Balkema RSA.

Tailings & Mine Waste 96: Proceedings of the Third International Conference, Fort Collins, Colorado, 16-19 January, 1996. (Illus.). 676p. (C). 1996. text ed. 115.00 (90-5410-594-1, Pub. by A A Balkema NE) Ashgate Pub Co.

Tailings Management: Problems & Solutions in the Mining Industry. G. M. Ritcey. (Process Metallurgy Ser.: No. 6). 970p. 1989. 348.25 (0-444-87374-0) Elsevier.

*Tailless Aircraft. (Mechanical Engineering Ser.). 1997. text ed. 59.95 (0-340-61402-1, Pub. by E Arnold UK) Routledge Chapman & Hall.

Tailless Batrachians of Europe, 2 parts in one. George A. Boulenger. Ed. by Keir B. Sterling. LC 77-81096. (Biologists & Their World Ser.). (Illus.). 1978. reprint ed. lib. bdg. 42.95 (0-405-10679-3) Ayer.

Tailleur de Gloucester. Beatrix Potter. (Illus.). 58p. (FRE.). (J). 1991. 9.95 (0-7859-3630-0, 2070560767) Fr & Eur.

Tailleur de Gloucester. Beatrix Potter. (Gallimard Ser.). 58p. (FRE.). (J). 1991. 10.95 (2-07-056076-7) Schoenhof.

An Asterisk (*) at the beginning of an entry indicates that the title is appearing in BIP for the first time.

Tailor. Jack Rudman. (Career Examination Ser.: C-1512). 1994. pap. 34.95 (*0-8373-1512-3*) Nat Learn.

Tailor Boy. Jane G. Austin. (Works of Jane (Goodin) Austin). 1989. reprint ed. lib. bdg. 79.00 (*0-685-44732-4*) Rprt Serv.

Tailor of Gloucester. Beatrix Potter. (Original Peter Rabbit Bks.: No. 3). (J). 1987. pap. 5.95 (*0-7232-3462-0*) Warne.

Tailor of Gloucester. Beatrix Potter. (World of Peter Rabbit & Friends Ser.). (Illus.). 60p. (J). 1993. pap. 16.00 (*0-7232-4094-9*) Warne.

Tailor of Gloucester. Beatrix Potter. LC 88-11510. (Illus.). 44p. (J). (ps up). 1991. pap. 14.95 (*0-88708-080-4*, Rabbit) S&S Childrens.

Tailor of Gloucester. Beatrix Potter. (J). (gr. 2 up). 1995. pap. 10.95 incl. audio (*0-689-80362-1*, Rabbit) S&S Childrens.

Tailor of Gloucester. Beatrix Potter. (World of Peter Rabbit & Friends Ser.). (Illus.). 36p. (J). (ps-3). 1993. pap. 4.99 (*0-7232-4137-6*) Warne.

Tailor of Gloucester. Beatrix Potter. (Illus.). 57p. (J). (gr. k-3). 1973. reprint ed. pap. 1.75 (*0-486-20176-7*) Dover.

Tailor of Gloucester: Lift-the-Flap Book. Beatrix Potter. (Illus.). 24p. (J). (ps-1). 1994. pap. 11.99 (*0-7232-4147-3*) Warne.

***Tailor of Panama.** John Le Carre. 320p. 1996. 25.00 (*0-679-45480-2*); 25.00 (*0-679-45446-2*) Knopf.

***Tailor of Panama.** John Le Carre. 1997. mass mkt. 6.99 (*0-345-42043-8*) Ballantine.

***Tailor of Panama.** John Le Carre. 1996. pap. 25.00 (*0-679-77413-0*) Random.

***Tailor of Panama.** large type ed. John Le Carre. 512p. 1996. pap. 25.95 (*0-7838-1933-1*) Random Hse Lrg Prnt.

Tailored Metal Catalysts. Yasuhiro Iwasawa. 1985. lib. bdg. 157.50 (*90-277-1866-0*) Kluwer Ac.

Tailored Urologic Imaging. Anthony F. Laili. LC 80-16566. (Illus.). 335p. reprint ed. pap. 95.50 (*0-685-23362-6*, 2032298) Bks Demand.

Tailoring: Traditional & Contemporary Techniques. Linda Thiel & Marie Ledbetter. (Illus.). 384p. 1980. text ed. 60.00 (*0-8359-7534-7*, Reston) P-H.

Tailoring: Traditional & Contemporary Techniques. Linda Thiel & Marie Ledbetter. (Illus.). 384p. 1981. teacher ed. write for info. (*0-8359-7535-5*, Reston) P-H.

Tailoring & Repair. rev. ed. (Illus.). 170p. 1985. 10.00 (*0-318-18629-2*) Master Design.

Tailoring Environmental Standards to Control Contract Requirements: Proceedings of the 1st National Conference & Workshop, June 1984. LC 62-38584. 200p. (Orig.). 1984. pap. text ed. 75.00 (*0-915414-79-1*) Inst Environ Sci.

Tailoring Genes for Crop Improvements: An Agricultural Perspective. Ed. by George Bruening et al. (Basic Life Sciences Ser.: Vol. 41). (Illus.). 223p. 1987. 65.00 (*0-306-42579-3*, Plenum Pr) Plenum.

***Tailoring Ladies Jackets: Step-by-Step Instructions.** Mary E. Flury. (Illus.). 88p. Date not set. 8.95 (*1-883375-03-7*) Sew-Pro Wrkshop.

Tailoring Multiphase & Composite Ceramics. Ed. by Richard E. Tressler et al. (Materials Science Research Ser.: Vol. 20). 796p. 1986. 125.00 (*0-306-42381-2*, Plenum Pr) Plenum.

Tailoring of Mechanical Properties of Si3N4: Proceedings of the NATO Advanced Research Workshop on Tailoring of High Temperature Properties of Si3N4 Ceramics, 276. Ed. by Michael J. Hoffmann & G. Petzow. LC 94-33304. (NATO Advanced Science Institutes Series C: Vol. 276). 476p. (C). 1994. lib. bdg. 243.00 (*0-7923-3119-2*) Kluwer Ac.

Tailoring of the Belle Epoque: Vincent's Systems of Cutting All Kinds of Tailor-Made Garments (1903) rev. ed. W. D. Vincent. Ed. by R. L. Shep. LC 90-92047. Orig. Title: Vincent's Systems of Cutting All Kinds of Tailor-Made Garments. (Illus.). 304p. 1991. pap. 24.95 (*0-914046-11-X*) R L Shep.

Tailoring Process. Bystrom. (OX - Home Economics Ser.). 1985. wbk. ed., pap. 33.95 (*0-538-32310-8*) S-W Pub.

Tailoring Software for Multiple Processor Systems. Karsten Schwan. LC 84-28081. (Computer Science: Distributed Database Systems Ser.: No. 16). 201p. reprint ed. pap. 57.30 (*0-8357-1645-7*, 2070417) Bks Demand.

Tailoring Technics: Tailoring with Fusibles, Manageable Custom Tailoring. 2nd ed. Margaret Komives. LC 90-90224. (Illus.). 100p. 1991. pap. 14.95 (*1-878017-01-2*) Maggi K Ent.

Tailoring Your Tastes. Linda Omichinski & Heather W. Hildebrand. (Illus.). 176p. 1995. pap. 14.95 (*1-895569-34-6*, Pub. by Tamos Bks CN) Sterling.

Tailpipe Trucker. Clay Caldwell. 1995. mass mkt. 5.95 (*1-56333-296-5*, Badboy) Masquerade.

Tails & Tales: Small Farming in New England. Suze Craig. LC 93-79739. (Illus.). 224p. (Orig.). 1993. pap. 15.00 (*1-883977-05-3*) Lind Hill Pr.

***Tails from the Barkside.** Brian Kilcommons & Sarah Wilson. LC 97-13196. (Illus.). 1997. 18.00 (*0-446-52150-7*) Warner Bks.

Tails' of a Dog Psychoanalyst. C. W. Meisterfeld. LC 78-58492. (Illus.). 1978. 19.95 (*0-9601292-2-7*) M R K.

Tails of Flame. Gerald Holt. 208p. (J). (gr. 3-6). 1996. pap. 4.95 (*0-7736-7431-4*, Pub. by Stoddart Pubng CN) Genl Dist Srvs.

Tails of Quince & Flute in Semer Wood. Jeannie Ferber. (Illus.). 120p. (J). (gr. 4 up). 1995. 21.00 (*1-885934-02-5*) Andover Green.

Tails of the Blue Lady. Rose C. Gregory. 66p. 1995. 10.95 (*0-9648631-0-3*) Latchkey Hse.

Tails Up! Ray R. Kepley. LC 80-81060. (Illus.). 466p. 1980. 15.95 (*0-9604248-0-6*) Kepley.

Tailwater Trout in the South: An Angler's Guide. Jimmy Jacobs. LC 96-12520. 256p. 1996. pap. 18.00 (*0-88150-335-5*, Backcountry) Countryman.

Tailypo. Joanna Galdone. LC 77-23289. (J). (ps-4). 1984. pap. 6.95 (*0-395-30084-3*, Clarion Bks) HM.

Tailypo. Paul Galdone. 1994. pap. 8.95 incl. audio (*0-395-69174-5*) Ticknor & Flds Bks Yng Read.

Tailypo! Jan Wahl. LC 90-39491. (Illus.). 32p. (J). (ps-2). 1991. 14.95 (*0-8050-0687-7*, Bks Young Read) H Holt & Co.

Tailypo! Jan Wahl. LC 90-39491. (Illus.). 32p. (J). (ps-2). 1996. pap. 5.95 (*0-8050-4907-X*, B Martin BYR) H Holt & Co.

Tailypo: A New Fangled Tall Tale. Illus. by Sterling Brown. 32p. (J). (ps-3). 1996. lib. bdg. 15.95 (*0-8234-1249-0*) Holiday.

Taima-Taima. Ed. by Claudio Ochsenius & Ruth Gruhn. 138p. 1992. pap. 11.00 (*1-55889-874-3*) Ctr Study First Am.

Taimanov & Knights Tour Benoni. John L. Watson. 86p. (Orig.). 1985. pap. 6.00 (*0-931462-39-8*) Chess Ent.

Taimanov's Selected Games. Mark Taimanov. 1996. pap. 19.95 (*1-85744-150-8*) Macmillan.

Tain. Tr. by Thomas Kinsella. (Illus.). 320p. 1970. pap. 15.95 (*0-19-281090-1*) OUP.

Tain of the Mirror. Rodolphe Gasche. LC 86-4673. 384p. 1986. 38.00 (*0-674-86700-9*) HUP.

Tain of the Mirror: Derrida & the Philosophy of Reflection. Rodolphe Gasche. 360p. 1988. reprint ed. pap. 16.95 (*0-674-86701-7*) HUP.

Taine & Brunetiere on Criticism. Giovanni Gullace. 158p. 1982. 10.00 (*0-87291-160-8*) Coronado Pr.

Taine's Notes on England. Hippolyte A. Taine. LC 74-142704. (Essay Index Reprint Ser.). 1977. 23.95 (*0-8369-2139-9*) Ayer.

Taino: The Activity Book. Edwin Fontanez. (Illus.). 48p. (Orig.). (ENG & SPA.). (J). (gr. 4 up). 1996. pap. write for info. (*0-9640868-3-2*) Exit Studio.

***Taino Indian: A Native American Experience.** Saul Torres. 50p. 1996. pap. 10.00 (*1-888867-02-7*) Biblos Pr.

***Tainos.** Michael Dorris. (SPA.). (J). 1996. pap. text ed. 10.95 (*84-204-4757-9*) Santillana.

Tainos: Rise & Decline of the People Who Greeted Columbus. Irving Rouse. (Illus.). 232p. (C). 1993. pap. 13.00 (*0-300-05696-6*) Yale U Pr.

***Tainos de Borinquen: Puerto Rico Before Columbus.** Ciro Sepulveda. (Illus.). 50p. (Orig.). (ENG & SPA.). (J). (gr. 3-5). 1996. pap. 10.00 (*1-888867-03-5*) Biblos Pr.

Taint of Madness: Insanity & Dread Within Asylum Walls. Eric Rowe et al. (Call of Cthulhu Roleplaying Game Ser.). (Illus.). 124p. (Orig.). 1995. pap. 18.95 (*1-56882-042-9*, 2354) Chaosium.

Tainted: The Virus That Will End Life on Earth. Kevin Hogan. (Illus.). (Orig.). 1996. pap. 14.00 (*0-9635085-4-7*) Network Three Thous.

***Tainted Blood.** Andrew Billings. 544p. 1997. mass mkt. 6.99 (*0-515-12046-4*) Jove Pubns.

Tainted Blood: A Frightening Possibility. Thomas C. McCollum, 3rd. 368p. 1996. 25.00 (*1-880404-11-7*, Shoji Bks) Bkwrights.

Tainted Breeze: The Great Hanging at Gainesville, Texas 1862. Richard B. McCaslin. LC 93-15835. (Illus.). 264p. (C). 1993. text ed. 32.50 (*0-8071-1825-7*) La State U Pr.

***Tainted Breeze: The Great Hanging at Gainesville, Texas, 1862.** Richard B. McCaslin. (Illus.). 256p. 1997. pap. 13.95 (*0-8071-2219-X*) La State U Pr.

Tainted Evidence. Robert Daley. 448p. 1994. mass mkt. 5.99 (*0-446-60083-0*, Warner Vision) Warner Bks.

Tainted Evidence. Robert Daley. 1995. pap. 5.99 (*0-446-36083-X*) Warner Bks.

Tainted Goddesses: Female Film Stars of the Third Reich. Cinzia Romani. Ed. by D. Teal. Tr. by Bob Connolly from ITA. (Illus.). 182p. 1992. pap. 19.95 (*0-9627613-1-1*) Sarpedon.

Tainted Greatness: Antisemitism & Cultural Heroes. Ed. by Nancy A. Harrowitz. LC 93-5724. (Themes in the History of Philosophy Ser.). 288p. 1994. 59.95 (*1-56639-153-9*); pap. 24.95 (*1-56639-161-X*) Temple U Pr.

Tainted Love. Alison Fraser. (Presents Ser.). 1995. mass mkt. 3.25 (*0-373-11753-1*, 1-11753-0) Harlequin Bks.

Tainted Love. large type ed. Alison Fraser. (Harlequin Romance Ser.). 1995. 20.95 (*0-263-14211-6*, Pub. by Mills & Boon UK) Thorndike Pr.

***Tainted Million.** Susan Trott. 200p. (Orig.). 1996. pap. 11.95 (*0-9653524-1-2*) Russn Hill Pr.

Tainted Souls & Painted Faces: The Rhetoric of Fallenness in Victorian Culture. Amanda Anderson. LC 93-17254. (Reading Women Writing Ser.). 256p. 1993. 39.95 (*0-8014-2781-9*); pap. 15.95 (*0-8014-8148-1*) Cornell U Pr.

Tainted Treats: A Collection of Horror Tales, Poems, & Drawings. R. Payne Cabeen. LC 94-69984. (Streamline Pictures Bks.). (Illus.). 208p. (Orig.). 1994. pap. 12.95 (*1-57300-052-3*, Streamline Pic Bks) Streamline Ent.

Tainted Treats: A Collection of Horror Tales, Poems, & Drawings. deluxe ed. R. Payne Cabeen. LC 94-69984. (Streamline Pictures Bks.). (Illus.). 208p. (Orig.). 1994. pap. 22.95 (*1-57300-051-5*, Streamline Pic Bks) Streamline Ent.

Tainted Truth: The Manipulation of Fact in America. Cynthia Crossen. 272p. 1994. 23.00 (*0-671-79285-7*) S&S Trade.

Tainted Truth: The Manipulation of Fact in America. Cynthia Crosson. 272p. 1996. pap. 12.00 (*0-684-81556-7*) S&S Trade.

Tainted War: Culture & Identity in Vietnam War Narratives. Lloyd B. Lewis. LC 84-27929. (Contributions in Military History Ser.: No. 44). xvi, 193p. 1985. text ed. 49.95 (*0-313-23723-9*, LVW/, Greenwood Pr) Greenwood.

Tainyi Sovetnik. Loseff Lev. LC 87-35388. 128p. (Orig.). (RUS.). 1988. pap. 8.00 (*0-938920-97-9*) Hermitage.

Taipan: The World's Most Dangerous Snake. Philip Kendall & Paul Masci. (Illus.). 96p. (Orig.). 1996. pap. 16.95 (*0-86417-596-5*, Pub. by Kangaroo Pr AT) Seven Hills Bk.

Taipan Traders. Anthony Lawrence. (Illus.). 96p. 1994. 40.00 (*962-7283-07-X*, Pub. by FormAsia HK) Weatherhill.

Taipans: Hong Kong's Merchant Princes. Colin N. Crisswell. (Illus.). 292p. 1991. pap. 18.95 (*0-19-585373-3*, 12303) OUP.

Taipei. Roger M. Selya. (World Cities Ser.). 224p. 1994. text ed. 49.95 (*0-470-22024-4*) Halsted Pr.

Taipei. Roger M. Selya. (Belhaven World Cities Ser.). 224p. 1995. text ed. 70.00 (*0-471-94981-7*) Wiley.

Taipei Conference on Prostaglandin & Leukotriene Research. Taipei Conference on Prostaglandin & Leukotriene Research Staff. Ed. by Bengt Samuelsson et al. (Advances in Prostaglandin, Thromboxane & Leukotriene Research Ser.: No. 19). (Illus.). 763p. 1989. reprint ed. pap. 180.00 (*0-608-00612-2*, 2061199) Bks Demand.

Taipi. Herman Melville. (FRE.). 1984. pap. 17.95 (*0-7859-4199-1*) Fr & Eur.

Taiping Ideology: Its Sources, Interpretations & Influences. Vincent Y. Shih. LC 66-19571. (Publications on Asia of the School of International Studies: No. 15). 576p. 1967. pap. 10.00 (*0-295-95243-1*) U of Wash Pr.

Taiping Rebel: The Deposition of Li Hsiu-Ch'eng. Charles A. Curwen. LC 76-8292. (Cambridge Studies in Chinese History, Literature & Institutions). 365p. reprint ed. pap. 104.10 (*0-685-20544-4*, 2030588) Bks Demand.

***Taiping Rebellion.** Shunshin Chin. Tr. by Joshua Fogel from CHI. 672p. (C). (gr. 13). 1998. text ed. 85.00 (*0-7656-0099-4*, East Gate Bk); pap. text ed. 35.00 (*0-7656-0100-1*, East Gate Bk) M E Sharpe.

Taiping Rebellion: Documents & Comments. Franz Michael. Ed. by Chung-Li Chang. Incl. Vol. 2. . LC 66-13538. 756p. 1971. 35.00 (*0-295-73959-2*); Vol. 3. . LC 66-13538. 1107p. 1971. 35.00 (*0-295-73960-6*); LC 66-13538. (Publications on Asia of the Institute for Comparative & Foreign Area Studies: No. 14, Pt. 2). 1971. write for info. (*0-318-56165-4*) U of Wash Pr.

Taiping Revolutionary Movement. Yu-wen Chien. Ed. by Adrienne Suddard. LC 72-91299. 633p. reprint ed. pap. 180.00 (*0-8357-8340-5*, 2033770) Bks Demand.

Tairora Culture: Contingency & Pragmatism. James B. Watson. LC 82-23776. (Anthropological Studies in the Eastern Highlands of New Guinea: Vol. 5). (Illus.). 346p. 1983. 40.00 (*0-295-95799-9*) U of Wash Pr.

Taisce Duan: A Treasury of Irish Poems with Translations in English. Ed. by Jo O'Donoghue. 270p. (Orig.). 1993. pap. 19.95 (*1-85371-118-7*, Pub. by Poolbeg Pr IE) Dufour.

Taiseido's Pocket Romanized Japanese-English Dictionary. M. Takahashi. 1596p. (ENG & JPN.). 1984. pap. 75.00 (*0-8288-0467-2*, F48850) Fr & Eur.

Tait & LaPlante's Handbook of Connecticut Evidence. 2nd ed. Colin C. Tait. 608p. 1987. 125.00 (*0-316-83178-6*) Little.

Tait Family. Judson F. Sandlin. (Illus.). 250p. 1987. reprint ed. write for info. (*0-9621399-0-4*); reprint ed. pap. 15.00 (*0-685-24961-1*); reprint ed. lib. bdg. 30.00 (*0-685-44553-4*) J F Sandlin.

Taitiriya Samhita of the Black Yajurveda, 10 vols. Ed. by A. Mahadeva & K. Rangacharya. (C). 1986. reprint ed. 185.00 (*81-208-0228-4*, Pub. by Motilal Banarsidass II) S Asia.

Taitiriya Upanisat. Tr. by Srisa C. Vidyarnava & Mohan L. Sandal. LC 73-3824. (Sacred Books of the Hindus: No. 30, Pt 3). reprint ed. 17.00 (*0-404-57833-0*) AMS Pr.

Taittiriya Upanisad. Swami M. Prasad. (C). 1994. 14.00 (*81-246-0014-7*, Pub. by DK Pubs Dist II) S Asia.

Taittiriya Upanishad. 3.00 (*0-87481-045-0*) Vedanta Pr.

Taittiriya Upanishad: With the Commentaries of Sri Sankaracharya, Sri Sureshvaracharya & Sayana (Sri Vidyaranya) Tr. by Alladi M. Sastri from MAR. 1996p. 1989. 27.95 (*0-910261-08-3*, Pub. by Samata Bks II) Lotus Light.

Taiwan. 1989. pap. 19.95 (*0-685-28255-4*) P-H.

Taiwan. Berlitz Editors. (Pocket Guides Ser.). (Illus.). 128p. 1991. 6.95 (*2-8315-0574-7*) Berlitz.

Taiwan. Alice Cromie. LC 94-6120. (Enchantment of the World Ser.). (Illus.). 128p. (J). (gr. 5-9). 1994. lib. bdg. 30.00 (*0-516-02627-5*) Childrens.

Taiwan. Patrick J. Kennedy. (Pelham Guides Ser.). 30p. (C). 1996. 22.00 (*0-929851-87-0*) Am Assn Coll Registrars.

Taiwan. Paul Mooney. (China Guides Ser.). (Illus.). 256p. 1995. pap. 15.95 (*0-8442-9824-7*, 9824-7, Passport Bks) NTC Pub Grp.

Taiwan. William Russell. LC 93-48341. (Islands in the Sea Ser.). (J). 1994. write for info. (*1-55916-033-0*) Rourke Bk Co.

Taiwan. annot. ed. Ed. by Wei-Chin Lee. (World Bibliographical Ser.: No. 113). 250p. 1990. lib. bdg. 69.00 (*1-85109-091-6*) ABC-CLIO.

Taiwan. large type ed. Christopher Wood. 528p. 1986. 25.99 (*0-7089-1480-2*) Ulverscroft.

***Taiwan.** 7th ed. Insight Guides Staff. (Insight Guides Ser.). 1997. pap. 22.95 (*0-395-85060-6*) HM.

Taiwan: A History. Murray A. Rubinstein. 450p. (C). (gr. 13). 1997. text ed. 62.95 (*1-56324-815-8*, East Gate Bk) M E Sharpe.

Taiwan: A History. Murray A. Rubinstein. 450p. (C). (gr. 13). 1997. pap. text ed. 24.95 (*1-56324-816-6*, East Gate Bk) M E Sharpe.

Taiwan: A Travel Survival Kit. 3rd ed. Robert Storey. (Illus.). 360p. (Orig.). 1994. pap. 14.95 (*0-86442-228-8*) Lonely Planet.

Taiwan: Beyond the Economic Miracle. Ed. by Denis F. Simon & Michael Y. Kau. LC 91-28561. (Taiwan in the Modern World Ser.). 428p. (C). (gr. 13). 1992. text ed. 69.95 (*0-87332-879-5*, East Gate Bk); pap. text ed. 29.95 (*1-56324-215-X*, East Gate Bk) M E Sharpe.

***Taiwan: Lisa Lin's Painting "Making Mooncakes"** Jacquiline Touba et al. LC 96-37695. (Young Artists of the World Ser.). 1997. lib. bdg. write for info. (*0-8239-5104-9*) Rosen Group.

Taiwan: Nation-State or Province? 2nd ed. John F. Copper. (Nations of the Modern World: Asia Ser.). 250p. (C). 1996. pap. text ed. 22.00 (*0-8133-2091-7*) Westview.

Taiwan: National Identity & Democratization. Alan M. Wachman. LC 94-12659. (Taiwan in the Modern World Ser.). 312p. (C). (gr. 13). 1994. text ed. 69.95 (*1-56324-398-9*, East Gate Bk); pap. text ed. 26.95 (*1-56324-399-7*, East Gate Bk) M E Sharpe.

Taiwan: Studies in Chinese Local History. Ed. by Leonard H. Gordon. LC 78-108096. (East Asian Institute Ser.). 124p. 1970. text ed. 29.50 (*0-231-03376-1*) Col U Pr.

Taiwan see Cultures of the World - Group 11

***Taiwan & Chinese Nationalism: National Identity & Status in International Society.** Christopher Hughes. (Politics in Asia Ser.). 256p. (C). 1997. text ed. 65.00 (*0-415-15768-4*) Routledge.

Taiwan & the Asia-Pacific in the 1990s. 3rd ed. Ed. by Gary Klintworth. 224p. pap. 24.95 (*1-86373-594-1*, Pub. by Allen Unwin AT) Paul & Co Pubs.

Taiwan & the Geopolitics of the Asian-American Dilemma. Jen-kun Fu. LC 91-29225. 160p. 1992. text ed. 49.95 (*0-275-94130-2*, C4130, Praeger Pubs) Greenwood.

Taiwan & the United Nations: Conflict Between Domestic Politics & International Objectives. Harvey J. Feldman. (Essays in Public Policy Ser.: Vol. 64). 16p. 1995. pap. 5.00 (*0-8179-5692-1*) Hoover Inst Pr.

Taiwan at the Crossroads: Human Rights, Political Development, & Social Change on the Beautiful Island. Marc J. Cohen. LC 89-113005. (Illus.). 431p. 1988. pap. 10.95 (*0-9604518-0-3*) Asia Resource.

Taiwan Business: The Portable Encyclopedia for Doing Business with Taiwan. Christine Genzberger et al. LC 93-45978. (Country Business Guide Ser.). 310p. 1994. pap. 24.95 (*0-9631864-5-0*) Wrld Trade Pr.

Taiwan-China Economic Connection: Democracy & Development Across the Taiwan Straits. Tse-Kang Leng. LC 96-8991. (Transitions: Asia & Asian America Ser.). 1996. text ed. 59.00 (*0-8133-2982-5*) Westview.

Taiwan-China Economic Connection: Democracy & Development across the Taiwan Straits. Tse-Kang Leng. LC 96-8991. (Transitions: Asia & Asian America Ser.). (C). 1996. pap. text ed. 19.95 (*0-8133-9006-0*) Westview.

Taiwan Enterprises in Global Perspective. Ed. by N. T. Wang. LC 91-36418. (Taiwan in the Modern World Ser.). 384p. (C). (gr. 13). 1992. text ed. 69.95 (*1-56324-071-8*, East Gate Bk) M E Sharpe.

Taiwan in a Transformed Global Setting. Ed. by David T. Lee & Robert L. Pfaltzgraff, Jr. (Institute for Foreign Policy Analysis Ser.). 147p. 1995. pap. 11.95 (*0-02-881138-0*) Brasseys Inc.

Taiwan in China's Foreign Relations, 1836-1874. Sophia S. Yen. LC 65-7577. 416p. reprint ed. pap. 118.60 (*0-317-11218-X*, 2010227) Bks Demand.

Taiwan in Pictures. Ed. by Lerner Publications, Department of Geography Staff. (Visual Geography Ser.). (Illus.). 64p. (YA). (gr. 5 up). 1991. lib. bdg. 19.95 (*0-8225-1865-1*, Lerner Publctns) Lerner Group.

Taiwan Journal: Ten Historic Days. John Tomikel. LC 79-53164. (Illus.). 1979. 11.95 (*0-910042-37-3*); pap. 9.95 (*0-910042-36-5*) Allegheny.

Taiwan Political Miracle: Essays on Political Development, Elections & Foreign Relations. John F. Copper. 1995. pap. text ed. write for info. (*0-7618-0113-8*); lib. bdg. write for info. (*0-7618-0112-X*) U Pr of Amer.

***Taiwan Product Guide.** Ed. by C. DePaula. 350p. 1997. pap. 100.00 (*0-915344-72-6*) Todd Pubns.

Taiwan Relations Act: A Decade of Implementation. Ed. by William B. Bader & Jeffrey T. Bergner. 210p. (C). 1989. 14.95 (*1-55813-028-4*) Hudson Instit IN.

Taiwan Relations Act & Sino-American Relations, No. 5. Hungdah Chiu. 34p. 1990. 4.00 (*0-925153-11-7*, 100) Occasional Papers.

Taiwan Relations Act & the Defense of the Republic of China. Edwin K. Snyder et al. LC 80-81294. (Policy Papers in International Affairs: No. 12). 132p. 1980. pap. text ed. 7.50 (*0-87725-512-1*) U of Cal IAS.

Taiwan Trade Directory. 1987. lib. bdg. 250.00 (*0-8490-3909-6*) Gordon Pr.

Taiwanese Ballads: A Catalogue. Wolfram Eberhard. (Asian Folklore & Social Life Monographs: No. 22). 1972. 14.00 (*0-89986-024-9*) Oriental Bk Store.

Taiwanese Culture, Taiwanese Society: A Critical Review of Social Science Research Done on Taiwan. Stephen O. Murray & Keelung Hong. LC 93-48342. 250p. (Orig.). (C). 1994. pap. text ed. 28.50 (*0-8191-9434-4*); lib. bdg. 49.50 (*0-8191-9433-6*) U Pr of Amer.

Taiwanese Folk Literature, 2 vols. Teito Hirasawa. (Asian Folklore & Social Life Monographs: Nos. 78 & 79). (JPN.). 1917. 22.00 (*0-89986-290-X*) Oriental Bk Store.

Taiwan's Capital Market Reform: The Financial & Legal Issues. Brian W. Semkow. 350p. 1995. 68.00 (*0-19-828891-3*) OUP.

Taiwan's Changing Rural Society, 2 vols. Wu Tsong-Shien. (Asian Folklore & Social Life Monographs: Nos. 44-45). (CHI & ENG.). 1972. 25.00 (*0-89986-043-5*) Oriental Bk Store.

Taiwan's Democratization: Forces Behind the New Momentum. Jaushieh J. Wu. (Studies on Contemporary Taiwan). (Illus.). 224p. 1995. text ed. 70.00 (*0-19-586499-9*) OUP.

T

An Asterisk (*) at the beginning of an entry indicates that the title is appearing in BIP for the first time.

Taiwan's Development: Implications for Contending Political Economy Paradigms. Cal Clark. LC 89-7494. (Contributions in Economics & Economic History Ser.: No. 100). 283p. 1989. text ed. 59.95 (0-313-25448-6, CTE, Greenwood Pr) Greenwood.

Taiwan's Economic Role in East Asia. Chi Schive. LC 95-2644. (Significant Issues Ser.: Vol. 17, No. 2). 117p. (C). 1995. pap. 14.95 (0-89206-319-X) CSI Studies.

Taiwan's Electoral Politics & Democratic Transition: Riding the Third Wave. Ed. by Hung-mao Tien. LC 95-627. (Taiwan in the Modern World Ser.). (Illus.). 272p. (C). (gr. 13). 1995. text ed. 52.95 (1-56324-670-8, East Gate Bk) M E Sharpe.

Taiwan's Electoral Politics & Democratic Transition: Riding the Third Wave. Ed. by Hung-mao Tien. LC 95-627. (Taiwan in the Modern World Ser.). (Illus.). 272p. (C). 1995. pap. text ed. 22.95 (1-56324-671-6, East Gate Bk) M E Sharpe.

*Taiwan's Expanding Role in the International Arena. Ed. by Maysing H. Yang. LC 96-40275. (Taiwan In The Modern World Ser.). 244p. (C). (gr. 13). 1997. text ed. 52.95 (1-56324-968-5, East Gate Bk); pap. text ed. 24.95 (1-56324-992-8, East Gate Bk) M E Sharpe.

Taiwan's Financial Markets & Institutions: The Legal & Financial Issues of Deregulation & Internationalization. Brian W. Semkow. LC 92-7507. 264p. 1992. text ed. 55.00 (0-89930-742-6, SQG, Quorum Bks) Greenwood.

*Taiwan's Leading Corporations. Dun & Bradstreet Staff. 755p. 1995. 380.00 (957-99683-0-6) Dun & Bradstreet.

Taiwan's Political & Economic Growth in the Late Twentieth Century. Daniel A. Metraux. LC 91-37670. 172p. 1991. lib. bdg. 79.95 (0-7734-9636-X) E Mellen.

Taiwan's Recent Elections: Fulfilling the Democratic Process, No. 6. John F. Copper. 174p. 1990. 8.00 (0-925153-12-5, 101) Occasional Papers.

*Taiwan's Role in the East Asian Economy: Implications for the U. S.-Asia Relations. Robert W. Radtke. 56p. (Orig.). 1997. 5.00 (0-87848-519-8, X88465) Asia Soc.

Taiwan's Security & United States Policy: Executive & Congressional Strategies. Michael S. Frost. (Occasional Papers-Reprints Series in Contemporary Asian Studies: No. 4). 39p. (Orig.). 1982. pap. text ed. 4.00 (0-942182-48-0) Occasional Papers.

*Taiwan's Security in the Changing International System. Dennis V. Hickey. LC 96-34628. 240p. 1996. lib. bdg. 49.95 (1-55587-627-7, 876277) Lynne Rienner.

Taiwan's Social Construction, Nineteen Forty-Five to Nineteen Seventy-Five. Yang Chai-Ling. (Asian Folklore & Social Life Monograph: No . 77). (CHI.). 1976. 14.00 (0-89986-255-1) Oriental Bk Store.

Taiwan's 1991 & 1992 Non-Supplemental Elections: Reaching a Higher State of Democracy. John F. Copper. LC 94-6040. 180p. 1994. pap. text ed. 21.50 (0-8191-9480-8); lib. bdg. 46.50 (0-8191-9479-4) U Pr of Amer.

*Taize, a Meaning to Life. Oliver Clement. LC 97-23089. 1997. trans. write for info. (1-57999-007-X) GIA Pubns.

*Taj Mahal. Christine Moorcroft. LC 97-15619. (Great Buildings Ser.). 1998. write for info. (0-8172-4920-6) Raintree Steck-V.

Taj Mahal. Amina Okada & M. C. Joshi. (Illus.). 240p. 1993. 75.00 (1-55859-617-8) Abbeville Pr.

Taj Mahal. Usha Rai. LC 87-14739. (Illus.). 160p. 1987. 75.00 (0-86565-078-0) Vendome.

Taj Mahal: The Illumined Tomb: An Anthology of Seventeenth-Century Mughal & European Documentary Sources. Ed. by W. E. Begley & Z. A. Desai. (Illus.). 392p. 1990. text ed. 45.00 (0-295-96944-X) U of Wash Pr.

Tajaliat. Mir-Ghotbeddin M. Angha. 104p. (PER.). 1982. 16.00 (0-910735-15-8); pap. 11.00 (0-910735-16-6) MTO Printing & Pubn Ctr.

Tajar Tales. 36p. 1967. pap. 4.95 (0-87603-040-1) Am Camping.

Tajar Tales. Jane S. Ward. LC 93-71385. (Illus.). 48p. (J). (ps-4). 1993. reprint ed. Colorized pictures, music & song added. lib. bdg. 14.95 (1-883338-01-8); reprint ed. Book & cassette set. lib. bdg. 19.95 incl. audio (1-883338-00-X) Classic Wrks.

Tajikistan. Djalili. LC 97-17189. 1997. text ed. write for info. (0-312-16143-3) St Martin.

Tajikistan. Ed. by Lerner Geography Department Staff. (Then & Now Ser.). (Illus.). 64p. (YA). (gr. 5 up). 1993. lib. bdg. 22.95 (0-8225-2816-9, Lerner Publctns) Lerner Group.

Tajikistan: Economic Review. International Monetary Fund Staff. 46p. 1992. pap. 10.00 (1-55775-257-5) Intl Monetary.

Tajikistan: The Transition to a Market Economy. Reza Ghasimi & International Bank for Reconstruction & Development Staff. (Country Study). 1994. 15.95 (0-8213-3105-1) World Bank.

Tajin Totonac. Isabel T. Kelly & Angel Palerm. LC 76-44746. reprint ed. 38.75 (0-404-15865-X) AMS Pr.

Tajmahal: The True Story. P. N. Oak. Orig. Title: The Tajmahal is a Temple Palace. (Illus.). 336p. (Orig.). 1989. pap. 10.95 (0-9611614-4-2) A Ghosh.

Tajmahal & Its Incarnation. R. Nath. 232p. 1985. 49.95 (0-318-36975-3) Asia Bk Corp.

Tajmahal is a Temple Palace see Tajmahal: The True Story

*Tak... Just So... Victor Pavlenkov. LC 95-96060. (Illus.). 70p. (Orig.). 1995. pap. 4.95 (0-9637035-3-6) FC-Izdat.

Tak Eto Bylo - It Was Like This: One Family Story, Russia - U. S. A., 1950-1990. Paulina Rayevsky. LC 92-72486. (Illus.). 370p. (Orig.). (RUS.). 1992. 16.00 (0-911971-73-4) Effect Pub.

Taka, Taka Strauss Polka Set. William Starr & Constance Starr. (Sounds of Symphony Ser.). 1988. pap. text ed. 22.00 (0-87487-614-1) Summy-Birchard.

Takahiro Kondo, Painter & Potter. Ed. by Jane Wilkinson & Ruta Noreika. (Illus.). 72p. 1995. pap. 19.95 (0-948636-73-4, 6734, Pub. by Natl Mus Scotland UK) A Schwartz & Co.

Takao & Grandfather. Houghton Mifflin Company Staff. (Literature Experience 1993 Ser.). (J). (gr. 5). 1992. pap. 9.16 (0-395-61815-0) HM.

*Takasaki Masaharu: An Architecture of Cosmology. Takasaki Masaharu. (Illus.). 160p. (Orig.). 1998. pap. 35.00 (1-56898-121-X) Princeton Arch.

Takashi's Voyage: The Wreck of the Sindia. Lucinda Hathaway. (Illus.). 112p. (YA). (gr. 8-11). 1995. 12.00 (0-945582-24-2) Down the Shore Pub.

Take. Eugene Izzi. 1988. pap. 3.50 (0-318-33000-8) St Martin.

Take. Eugene Izzi. 1988. pap. 3.50 (0-312-91120-3) St Martin.

Take. Bill James. (Detective Colin Harpur Novel Ser.). 240p. 1994. reprint ed. 20.00 (0-88150-294-4) Countryman.

Take a Bible Break. W. E. McCumber. 116p. 1986. pap. 6.99 (0-8341-1080-6) Beacon Hill.

*Take a Bite of Music, It's Yummy. Mary A. Hall. (Illus.). 50p. 1982. reprint ed. pap. 8.00 (0-9609466-0-8); reprint ed. audio 10.00 (0-614-26651-3) NEAEYC.

*Take a Bite Out of Job Hunting. John Kingman. Ed. by Annette Fancher. (Illus.). 184p. 1997. pap. 12.95 (0-9645104-0-5) Pantera Pub.

Take a Bite...It's Light! Low Fat Recipes Collected by Chris Brito-Millard, Certified Personal Trainer. rev. ed. Chris Brito-Millard. (Illus.). 168p. 1995. 14.95 (0-9649659-0-9) B A Brito.

Take a Bow Jody. Audrey Eaton & Jane Kennedy. (Illus.). 8p. (Orig.). (J). (gr. k-1). 1995. pap. 3.50 (1-880612-47-X) Seedling Pubns.

Take a Break. (English As a Second Language Course Ser.). 272p. 1988. pap. text ed. 49.50 incl. audio (0-88432-197-5, S32516) Audio-Forum.

Take a Break, Vol. 1. 2nd ed. Albert DiNicola. (Orig.). 1986. pap. write for info. (0-318-59205-3) Lumen Series.

Take a Break: Two-Minute Devotions for the Workplace. Robert J. Strand. LC 91-77476. 208p. 1992. pap. 5.95 (0-88243-679-1, 02-0679) Gospel Pub.

*Take a Break - Everybody Needs One: Call to Worship. Ernst Nusmann. LC 96-38670. 130p. (Orig.). 1997. pap. 15.25 (0-7880-0846-3) CSS OH.

Take a Camel to Lunch: And Other Adventures for Mature Travelers. Nancy O'Connell. (Mature Reader Ser.). (Illus.). 228p. (Orig.). 1991. pap. 8.95 (1-55867-024-6) Bristol Pub Ent CA.

Take a Chance. Gary J. Cooper. (J). (gr. 2-8). 1993. 18.95 (0-937857-46-7, 1544) Speech Bin.

Take a Chance, Gramps! Jean D. Okimoto. (J). (gr. 3-7). 1996. mass mkt. 3.99 (0-8125-4323-8) Tor Bks.

Take a Chance, Gramps!, Vol. 1. Jean D. Okimoto. (J). (gr. 4-7). 1990. 15.95 (0-316-63812-9, Joy St Bks) Little.

Take a Chance on Me. Clint Berryhill. 268p. 1983. pap. 5.00 (0-685-07464-1) Trends & Events.

Take a Chance to Be First. Avis. 1986. 16.95 (0-02-504410-9) Macmillan.

Take a Deep Breath: The Kids' Play-Away Stress Book. Lawrence E. Shapiro. (Play & Read Ser.). (Illus.). 83p. (Orig.). (J). (ps-6). 1992. pap. 19.95 (1-882732-02-2) Ctr Applied Psy.

Take a Giant Step, Unit 5. (Networks Ser.). 1991. 7.45 (0-88106-739-3) Charlesbridge Pub.

Take a Giant Step Activity Book, Unit 5. (Networks Ser.). 1991. 3.90 (0-88106-741-5, N214) Charlesbridge Pub.

Take a Girl Like You. large type ed. Kingsley Amis. (Romance Ser.). 688p. 1993. 25.99 (0-7089-2927-3) Ulverscroft.

Take a Hike. Cathy E. Dubowski. (Secret World of Alex Mack Ser.: No. 7). (J). (gr. 3-6). 1996. pap. 3.99 (0-671-56309-2) S&S Trade.

*Take a Hike! Family Walks in the Rochester Area. Susan J. Freeman & Richard E. Freeman. (Illus.). 160p. (Orig.). 1997. pap. 16.95 (0-9656974-6-0) Footprint Pr NY.

Take a Hike: Riddles about Football. Rick Walton & Ann Walton. LC 92-27011. (You Must Be Joking! Ser.). (Illus.). (J). (gr. 1-4). 1993. lib. bdg. 13.50 (0-8225-2340-X, Lerner Publctns) Lerner Group.

Take a Hike: Riddles about Football. Rick Walton & Ann Walton. (J). (gr. 1-4). 1993. pap. 3.95 (0-8225-9640-7, Lerner Publctns) Lerner Group.

Take a Hike! The Sierra Club Beginner's Guide to Hiking & Backpacking. Lynne Foster. (Illus.). 176p. (J). (gr. 4-7). 1991. pap. 10.95 (0-316-28948-5, Joy St Bks) Little.

Take a Look: An Introduction to the Experience of Art. Rosemary Davidson. (Illus.). 128p. (J). (gr. 4-7). 1994. pap. 18.99 (0-670-84478-0) Viking Child Bks.

Take a Look at a Good Book: The Third Collection of Additive Alphametics for the Connoisseur. Steven Kahan. LC 96-16547. 1996. pap. 15.95 (0-89503-142-6) Baywood Pub.

Take a Look at Snakes. Betsy C. Maestro. (Illus.). 40p. (J). 1992. 14.95 (0-590-44935-4, Scholastic Hardcover) Scholastic Inc.

*Take a Look at Snakes. Betty Maestro. (J). 1997. pap. text ed. 5.99 (0-590-44936-2) Scholastic Inc.

Take a Look at Yourself: Self-in-System Sensitizers. Barry Oshry. (Notes on Power Ser.). (Orig.). 1978. pap. text ed. 10.50 (0-910411-05-0) Power & Sys.

Take a Look, It's in a Book: How Television Is Made at Reading Rainbow. Ronnie Krauss. LC 96-25984. (Illus.). 32p. (J). (gr. k-3). 1997. 15.95 (0-8027-8488-7); lib. bdg. 16.85 (0-8027-8489-5) Walker & Co.

*Take a Moment & Create Your Life! A Guide to the Life-Creating Process. Joanne C. Rodasta. LC 96-92601. (Illus.). 144p. (Orig.). 1997. pap. 9.95 (0-9652628-0-4) Spiritsmith.

Take a New Bearing: Skills & Sensitive Strategies for Sharing Spiders, Stars, Shelters, Safety, & Solitude. Phyllis M. Ford. LC 91-2007. (Illus.). 264p. (Orig.). 1991. pap. 17.95 (0-87603-119-X) Am Camping.

Take a Number. Janet Dawson. (Northern California Mysteries Ser.). 1994. mass mkt. 4.99 (0-449-22183-0) Fawcett.

*Take a Number: Poetry in E-Motion. Jennifer Maybury. LC 97-65874. (Illus.). 144p. (Orig.). 1997. pap. 10.95 (1-889120-08-1) StarsEnd Creations.

Take a Quick Bow! 26 Short Plays for Classroom Fun. Pamela Marx. 192p. (J). (gr. 1-4). 1996. pap. 12.95 (0-673-36316-3, GoodYrBooks) Addson-Wesley Educ.

Take a Ride. Pootler & Pillion. LC 93-86728. (Illus.). 32p. (J). (ps-1). 1994. pap. 8.95 (0-9638479-3-7) Magnolia MA.

Take a Stand! Daniel Weizmann. LC 96-1117. 64p. (J). (gr. 2 up). 1996. 6.95 (0-8431-7997-X) Price Stern Sloan.

*Take a thousand Eggs or More: A Translation of Medieval Recipes from Harleian MS.279, Harleian MS.4016, & Extracts of Ashmole MS.1439, Laud MS.553, & Douce MS.55, with over 100 Recipes Adapted to Modern Cookery, 2 vols. 2nd ed. Cindy Renfrow. (Illus.). 670p. (Orig.). 1997. spiral bd., pap. 27.00 (0-9628598-4-2) C Renfrow.

*Take a Walk: 100 Walks Through Natural Places in the Puget Sound Region. Sue M. Hacking. LC 96-51000. (Illus.). 224p. (Orig.). 1997. pap. 15.95 (1-57061-085-1) Sasquatch Bks.

Take a Walk in Their Shoes. Glennette T. Turner. LC 89-9700. 176p. (J). (gr. 4-8). 1989. pap. 15.99 (0-525-65006-7, Cobblehill Bks) Dutton Child Bks.

Take a Walk in Their Shoes: Biographies of Fourteen Outstanding African Americans - with Skits about Each to Act Out. Glennette T. Turner. LC 92-19524. (Illus.). 176p. (J). (gr. 3-7). 1992. pap. 6.99 (0-14-036250-9) Puffin Bks.

Take a Walk, Johnny. Margaret Hillert. (Illus.). (J). (ps-2). 1981. pap. 5.10 (0-8136-5611-7); lib. bdg. 7.95 (0-8136-5111-5) Modern Curr.

Take a Walk with Me. Kaitlin M. Smith. (Illus.). 12p. (J). (gr. k-3). 1993. pap. 10.95 (1-56606-019-2) Bradley Mann.

Take a Whistler's Walk. Joyce G. Reed. (Illus.). 77p. (J). (gr. 4-9). 1988. 12.95 (0-943487-08-0); pap. 4.95 (0-943487-07-2) Sevgo Pr.

*Take a Woman's Word for It: The Dictionary According to Women. Cy DeBoer. Ed. by Cliff Carle. 1997. pap. 5.95 (1-57644-047-8) CCC Pubns.

Take Action. Love. 1994. pap. 5.99 (0-517-13492-6) Random Hse Value.

Take Action: 18 Proven Strategies for Advancing in Today's Business World. Susan Bixler & Lisa Scherrer. 1997. pap. 12.95 (0-449-91061-X) Fawcett.

Take Action Against Drug Abuse: How to Start a Volunteer Anti-Drug Program in Your Community. (Illus.). 53p. (Orig.). (C). 1994. pap. text ed. 25.00 (0-7881-0383-0) DIANE Pub.

Take Advantage of the Ever Increasing Value of Your Money. Malcolm Haley. LC 76-58116. 1977. 4.95 (0-918582-01-6) Tenameca.

*Take All to Nebraska. Sophus Winther. LC 75-11672. 314p. pap. 89.50 (0-608-05111-X, 2065670) Bks Demand.

Take-Along Crafts. Susan P. Curtis. (Illus.). 72p. (Orig.). 1982. pap. 2.50 (0-918178-28-2) Simplicity.

Take Along Stories, 16 vols. Incl. Vol. 1. Bake a Cake. Jean Pennington. (Illus.). 8p. (Orig.). (J). (gr. 2-3). 1996. pap. Not sold separately (0-89084-801-7); Vol. 2. Scamper Sam. Gloria Repp. (Illus.). 8p. (Orig.). (J). (gr. 2-3). 1996. pap. Not sold separately (0-89084-800-9); Vol. 3. What Can King Do?. Lelani Mortland. (Illus.). 8p. (Orig.). (J). (gr. 2-3). 1996. pap. Not sold separately (0-89084-802-5); Vol. 4. Fish! Fish! Fish!. Elaine Bradley. (Illus.). 8p. (Orig.). (J). (gr. 2-3). 1996. pap. Not sold separately (0-89084-803-3); Vol. 5. Tracker Tom. Milly Howard. (Illus.). 8p. (Orig.). (J). (gr. 2-3). 1996. pap. Not sold separately (0-89084-804-1); Vol. 6. Gift from God. Milly Howard. (Illus.). 8p. (Orig.). (J). (gr. 2-3). 1996. pap. Not sold separately (0-89084-805-X); Vol. 7. My Butterfly Net. Tammie Jacobs. (Illus.). 8p. (Orig.). (J). (gr. 2-3). 1996. pap. Not sold separately (0-89084-806-8); Vol. 8. Off to School. Jamie Turner. (Illus.). 8p. (Orig.). (J). (gr. 2-3). 1996. pap. Not sold separately (0-89084-807-6); Vol. 9. Lots of Pots. Elaine Bradley. (Illus.). 8p. (Orig.). (J). (gr. 2-3). 1996. pap. Not sold separately (0-89084-808-4); Vol. 10. Fixed Up. Joyce E. Voelker. (Illus.). 8p. (Orig.). (J). (gr. 2-3). 1996. pap. Not sold separately (0-89084-811-4); Vol. 11. Zoo. Milly Howard. (Illus.). 8p. (Orig.). (J). (gr. 2-3). 1996. pap. Not sold separately (0-89084-812-2); Vol. 12. At the Mountain. Elaine Bradley. (Illus.). 8p. (Orig.). (J). (gr. 2-3). 1996. pap. Not sold separately (0-89084-813-0); Vol. 13. Gifts from the Sky. Dawn L. Watkins & Ann Bailes. (Illus.). 8p. (Orig.). (J). (gr. 2-3). 1996. pap. Not sold separately (0-89084-814-9); Vol. 14. Quackless. Debra White. (Illus.). 8p. (Orig.). (J). (gr. 2-3). 1996. pap. Not sold separately (0-89084-815-7); Vol. 15. What's in the Thicket?. Elizabeth Koon. (Illus.). 8p. (Orig.). (J). (gr. 2-3). 1996. pap. Not sold separately (0-89084-816-5); Vol. 16. Can Joan Smile?. Jamie Turner. (Illus.). 8p. (Orig.). (J). (gr. 2-3). 1996. pap. Not sold separately (0-89084-817-3); 1996. pap. 19.95 (0-89084-818-1, 087221) Bob Jones Univ Pr.

*Take America Back. John C. Hagee. Ed. by Connie Reece. 48p. (Orig.). 1996. pap. 5.00 (1-56908-027-5) Global Evang.

Take Ami Pro 3.0 to the Edge. Gerry M. Litton. (Customizing Ser.). (Illus.). 560p. (Orig.). 1993. pap. 29.95 incl. disk (1-56276-089-0, Ziff-Davis Pr) Que.

Take & Make Holy. Mari W. Zimmerman. 198p. (Orig.). 1995. pap. 12.00 (1-56854-094-9, TAKMAK) Liturgy Tr Pubns.

Take & Read: Spiritual Reading: An Annotated List. Eugene H. Peterson. 135p. (Orig.). 1996. pap. text ed. 10.00 (0-8028-4096-5) Eerdmans.

Take Another Little Piece of My Heart. Pamela Des Barres. 1993. mass mkt. 5.50 (0-425-13945-X) Berkley Pub.

Take Another Look. E. Carini. (J). (ps-3). 1969. pap. 1.50 (0-685-03910-2) P-H.

Take Another Look at Guidance: Proven Methods to Help You Sail Through Life's Tough Choices. Bob Mumford. 192p. 1993. pap. 7.95 (1-884004-01-6) Lifechangers.

Take Another Look at Linear Bass Patterns. William L. Fowler. LC 82-90965. (Illus.). 82p. 1983. pap. text ed. 10.00 (0-943894-01-8) Fowler Music.

Take Another Look at the Keyboard. rev. ed. William L. Fowler. LC 82-90364. (Illus.). 76p. 1986. pap. text ed. 10.00 (0-943894-11-5) Fowler Music.

Take Anywhere Puppets. Elaine Cole & David Cole. (Illus.). 16p. (Orig.). 1994. pap. 8.95 (1-883426-13-8) Chldrns Outrch.

Take Back Plenty. Colin Greenland. 496p. (Orig.). 1992. mass mkt. 4.99 (0-380-76395-8, AvoNova) Avon.

Take Back the Apples. Frank D. Vari & Rosemary V. Pennell. 96p. (Orig.). 1993. pap. 8.95 (0-9638053-0-4) Bettina Pub.

Take Back the Light: A Feminist Reclamation of Spirituality & Religion. Sheila Ruth. LC 93-6061. (New Feminist Perspectives Ser.). 240p. (Orig.). (C). 1994. text ed. 52.50 (0-8476-7879-2); pap. text ed. 14.95 (0-8226-3031-1) Rowman.

Take Back the Night. Dennis Foley. 1996. mass mkt. 5.99 (0-8041-0725-4) Ivy Books.

Take Back the Night. Dee Holmes. (Intimate Moments Ser.). 1993. mass mkt. 3.39 (0-373-07495-6, 5-07495-0) Silhouette.

Take Back the Night. Francine Pascal. (Sweet Valley University Ser.: No. 11). 240p. (YA). (gr. 9-12). 1995. pap. 3.99 (0-553-56656-3) Bantam.

Take Back the Night: Women on Pornography. Ed. by Laura Lederer. LC 80-23701. 352p. 1980. pap. 10.50 (0-688-08728-0, Quill) Morrow.

Take Back Your Government: A Practical Handbook for the Private Citizen. Robert A. Heinlein. 304p. 1992. mass mkt. 5.99 (0-671-72157-7) Baen Bks.

*Take Back Your Krown. K. Hummit Hatshepsitu. (Illus.). 110p. 1996. lib. bdg. 25.00 (0-9655432-0-X) Khummit Nubian.

Take Back Your Life: How to Regain Your Personal Freedom. Arthur W. Lamb. 168p. 1992. pap. 12.95 (0-9631757-6-9) Pin Oak Pr.

Take Back Your Power: A Working Woman's Response to Sexual Harassment. Jennifer Coburn. LC 95-9548. 92p. 1995. pap. 10.00 (0-910383-13-8) Ism Pr.

Take Care. Claudia Jolles et al. (Illus.). 72p. 1995. write for info. (1-884692-02-8) Swiss Inst.

Take Care! A Transdisciplinary Approach to the Development of Health & Safety Programs. Wendy J. Ashcroft & Suzanne C. Smith. 372p. (Orig.). 1993. teacher ed., pap. 35.00 (0-9634229-2-8) Scalars Pub.

Take Care! Preventing Child Sexual Abuse. Clodagh Corcoran. 132p. 1987. pap. 7.95 (1-85371-000-8, Pub. by Poolbeg Pr IE) Dufour.

*Take Care in Middle & Beyond. Verrilli. Date not set. pap. write for info. (0-312-18191-4) St Martin.

*Take Care in the Childbearing. Verrilli. Date not set. pap. write for info. (0-312-18190-6) St Martin.

Take Care of Brown Bear. Harriet Ziefert. (Illus.). 12p. (J). (ps). 1995. pap. 6.99 (0-670-85458-1) Viking Child Bks.

Take Care of Me. Chana R. Jacobs. Ed. by Dina Rosenfeld. (Illus.). 32p. (J). (ps-1). 1989. 8.95 (0-922613-06-0); pap. 6.95 (0-922613-07-9) Hachai Pubns.

Take Care of Millie: Reading Level 3. Jessie R. Hull. (Sundown Fiction Collection). 64p. 1993. 3.95 (0-88336-216-3); audio 9.95 (0-88336-262-7) New Readers.

Take Care of the Heart You Have. Nancy Gibson et al. Ed. by Susan D. Allen & Colleen A. Holloran. (Illus.). 56p. pap. text ed. 3.75 (0-916999-14-9) HERC Inc.

Take Care of Your Child. Robert H. Pantell. (C). 1988. pap. 51.95 (0-201-48834-5) Addison-Wesley.

*Take Care of Your Child: U. S. Benefits. Robert H. Pantell. 1996. pap. write for info. (0-201-15451-X) Addison-Wesley.

Take Care of Your Heart: The Complete Book of Heart Facts. Ezra A. Amsterdam & Ann M. Holmes. LC 82-12068. 355p. reprint ed. pap. 101.20 (0-7837-1364-9, 2041512) Bks Demand.

Take Care of Yourself. Bill Gutman. (J). 1996. lib. bdg. 16.98 (0-8050-4144-3) H Holt & Co.

Take Care of Yourself. 3rd ed. Donald M. Vickery. (SPA.). 1988. pap. write for info. (0-201-69458-1) Addison-Wesley.

Take Care of Yourself. 5th ed. Donald M. Vickery. 1993. pap. write for info. (0-201-62710-8) Addison-Wesley.

Take Care of Yourself. 5th ed. Donald M. Vickery. 1995. pap. write for info. (0-201-40710-8) Addison-Wesley.

Take Care of Yourself. 6th ed. Donald M. Vickery. 448p. 1996. pap. 18.00 (0-201-48989-9) Addison-Wesley.

*Take Care of Yourself. 6th ed. Donald M. Vickery. 1996. pap. 2.45 (0-201-15450-1) Addison-Wesley.

Take Care of Yourself: A Health Care Workbook for Beginning ESL Students. Marianne Brems et al. LC 93-7377. 256p. 1993. pap. 11.25 (0-13-882317-0) Prentice ESL.

T

Take Care of Yourself: Blue Cross & Blue Shield of North Carolina. Donald M. Vickery. 1995. pap. write for info. (0-201-48976-7) Addison-Wesley.

Take Care of Yourself: Coastal Health Plan. 4th ed. Donald M. Vickery. 1992. pap. write for info. (0-201-63258-6) Addison-Wesley.

Take Care of Yourself: Deseret Mutual Health Version. Donald M. Vickery. 1992. pap. write for info. (0-201-62282-3) Addison-Wesley.

Take Care of Yourself: Energy for Life. 4th ed. Donald M. Vickery. 1992. pap. write for info. (0-201-63205-5) Addison-Wesley.

Take Care of Yourself: Franciscan Skemp Healthcare. 6th ed. Donald M. Vickery. 1996. pap. write for info. (0-201-69459-X) Addison-Wesley.

Take Care of Yourself: Health Track. 5th ed. Donald M. Vickery. 1995. pap. write for info. (0-201-48990-2) Addison-Wesley.

Take Care of Yourself: Healthplus Version. Donald M. Vickery. 1990. pap. write for info. (0-201-62284-X) Addison-Wesley.

***Take Care of Yourself: Newport Naval Hospital.** 6th ed. Donald M. Vickery. 1996. pap. write for info. (0-201-15452-8) Addison-Wesley.

Take Care of Yourself: Sanus Special Edition. 4th ed. Donald M. Vickery. 1992. pap. write for info. (0-201-62260-2) Addison-Wesley.

Take Care of Yourself: Special Edition for Mesa Insurance. 5th ed. Donald M. Vickery. 1995. pap. write for info. (0-201-47991-5) Addison-Wesley.

Take Care of Yourself: The Consumer's Guide to Medical Care. Donald M. Vickery. 1986. pap. 14.95 (0-201-08091-5) Addison-Wesley.

Take Care of Yourself: U. S. Benefits. 5th ed. Donald M. Vickery. 1993. pap. write for info. (0-201-62721-3) Addison-Wesley.

Take Care of Yourself: Wisconsin Educational Association Insurance. 5th ed. Donald M. Vickery. 1995. pap. write for info. (0-201-48977-5) Addison-Wesley.

Take Care of Yourself: Your Personal Guide to Self-Care & Preventing Illness. 5th ed. Donald M. Vickery & James F. Fries. LC 92-48678. 1993. pap. 17.95 (0-201-63292-6) Addison-Wesley.

Take Care with Yourself: A Young Person's Guide to Understanding, Preventing & Healing from the Hurts of Child Abuse. Laurie A. White & Steven L. Spencer. (Illus.). 36p. (Orig.). (J). (gr. k-7). 1983. English edition. pap. 5.95 (0-9612024-0-8); pap. (0-318-57557-4) White & Spencer.

***Take Charge.** Sarah E. Hutchinson & Stacey Sawyer. 1992. text ed. 27.95 (0-07-413222-9); text ed. 27.95 (0-07-413223-7) Irwin.

Take Charge! A Guide to Feeling Good. W. W. Johnston & Ed D. Kern. (Illus.). 159p. (Orig.). 1986. pap. 7.95 (0-9619220-1-X) Acorn Endeavors.

Take Charge! A "How-to" Approach for Solving Every Day Problems. Joseph J. Bannon. LC 91-61668. (Illus.). 157p. (Orig.). 1992. pap. 9.95 (0-915611-46-5) Sagamore Pub.

Take Charge! A Step-by-Step Guide to Managing Your Money. Henrietta Humphreys. 92p. (Orig.). 1989. pap. 8.95 (0-685-30001-3) Gatehouse Bks.

Take Charge: A Strategic Guide for Blind Job Seekers. Rami Rabby & Diane Croft. 336p. (Orig.). 1990. pap. text ed. 13.95 (0-939173-16-6); audio 9.95 (0-939173-18-2); disk 9.95 (0-939173-19-0) Natl Braille Pr.

Take Charge: A Strategic Guide for Blind Job Seekers. braille ed. Rami Rabby & Diane Croft. 336p. (Orig.). 1990. 9.95 (0-939173-17-4) Natl Braille Pr.

***Take Charge: A Student-Centered Approach to English, Bk. 1.** Edna T. Diolata. 1997. pap. text ed. write for info. (0-07-044427-7) McGraw.

Take Charge: Economic Development in Small Communities. Economic Development in Small Communities Work Group. 280p. 1990. student ed., ring bd. 18.00 (0-685-60770-4, RRD 153) NCRCRD.

Take Charge! How to Manage Your Customer Relationships. Grace Major. LC 92-60371. (Executive Edition Ser.). 266p. (Orig.). 1992. teacher ed. 149.00 (0-9632406-2-5); text ed. 27.95 (0-9632406-1-7); pap. text ed. 27.95 (0-9632406-0-9) Sigma Bks.

Take Charge: The Leader Who Makes a Difference. Eric Swanson. (Inter Acta Ser.). (Illus.). 6p. (C). 1994. teacher ed., ring bd. 1.25 (1-57334-003-0, 741-067t, Inter Acta); student ed., ring bd. 3.25 (1-57334-002-2, 741-067s, Inter Acta) WSN Pr.

Take-Charge Guide to Type I Diabetes. American Diabetes Association Staff. LC 94-17538. (Illus.). 288p. 1996. pap. 16.95 (0-945448-35-X) Am Diabetes.

Take Charge Now: Surviving the Classroom - Tips for Motivating & Inspiring All Teachers. Rita Herron. Ed. by Diane Parker. LC 94-28199. 150p. (Orig.). 1996. pap. 9.95 (1-56875-069-2) R & E Pubs.

Take Charge of Your Baby's Development: From Day One Through Toilet-Training, Boy Version. Joanne Burnett. (Illus.). 340p. (Orig.). 1995. ring bd., pap. 54.95 (0-9647389-1-0) Tous Bks.

Take Charge of Your Baby's Development: From Day One Through Toilet-Training, Girl Version. Joanne Burnett. (Illus.). 340p. (Orig.). 1995. ring bd., pap. 54.95 (0-9647389-2-9) Tous Bks.

***Take Charge! of Your Baby's Development: From Day One Through Toilet-Training, Unisex Version.** Joanne Burnett. (Illus.). 250p. 1997. spiral bd. 21.95 (0-9647389-3-7) Tous Bks.

Take Charge of Your Career: Survive & Profit from a Mid-Career Change. 2nd ed. Daniel Moreau. 258p. 1996. pap. 15.00 (0-8129-2829-6, Times Business) Kiplinger Bks.

Take Charge of Your Child's Health: A Guide to Recognizing Symptoms & Treating Minor Illnesses at Home. George Wootan & Sarah Verney. (Illus.). 320p. 1992. pap. 18.00 (0-517-57365-2, Crown) Crown Pub Group.

Take Charge of Your Diabetes: A Guide for Patients. (Illus.). 72p. (Orig.). (C). 1993. pap. 20.00 (0-7881-0113-7) DIANE Pub.

Take Charge of Your Financial Future: Straight Talk on Managing Your Money from the Financial Analyst Who Defied Donald Trump. Marvin B. Roffman & Michael J. Schwager. 272p. 1996. pap. 12.95 (0-8065-1718-2, Citadel Pr) Carol Pub Group.

Take Charge of Your Health. Terry Paul. 1995. pap. text ed. 12.95 (1-56066-439-8) Great Performance.

Take Charge of Your Health. Paul Terry. 1995. pap. text ed. 12.95 (1-56066-603-X) Great Performance.

Take Charge of Your Health: Healing with Yogatherapy & Nutrition. Christopher S. Kilham. (Illus.). 176p. (Orig.). 1985. pap. 22.00 (0-87040-632-9) Japan Pubns USA.

Take Charge of Your Health: Professional Secrets You Need to Know to Obtain the Best Medical Care. Stephen Astor. LC 91-90283. 216p. (Orig.). 1991. pap. 12.95 (0-915001-07-1) Two As.

Take Charge of Your Hospital Stay: A "Start Smart" Guide for Patients & Care Partners. Karen K. McCann. LC 94-26399. 341p. 1994. 24.95 (0-306-44765-7, Plenum Insight) Plenum.

***Take Charge of Your Job Search! A Handbook to Empower Unemployed People to Find Their Own Jobs.** Frances Curiel. LC 96-30051. 101p. (Orig.). 1997. pap. 20.00 (1-883302-11-0) Trning Res.

Take Charge of Your Life! Patricia Ross & Jodi Owens-Kristenson. LC 95-43173. 383p. 1996. 38.64 (1-56637-279-8) Goodheart.

Take Charge of Your Life. 4th ed. Patricia D. Cota-Robles. Ed. by Elvira Dunlap & Kay Meyer. 179p. reprint ed. pap. 8.95 (0-9615287-0-2) New Age Study Human.

Take Charge of Your Life: What to Do When Someone in Your Family Has a Drinking or Other Drug Problem. Martin Fleming. 32p. 1993. pap. 5.95 (1-56246-070-6, P263) Johnsn Inst.

Take Charge of Your Life Therapy. R. W. Alley. Ed. by Lisa Engelhardt. LC 94-70290. 88p. 1995. pap. 4.95 (0-87029-271-4) Abbey.

Take Charge of Your Medical Practice...Before Someone Else Does It for You: Practical Practice Managment for the Managed Care Market. Neil Baum & Elaine Zablocki. LC 96-6738. 224p. 1996. 60.00 (0-8342-0799-0, 20799) Aspen Pub.

Take Charge of Your PC: By Learning DOS & Computer Fundamentals. Woody Greene. (Illus.). 121p. (YA). 1995. student ed., pap. text ed. 13.95 (1-887281-02-9) Labyrinth CA.

***Take Charge of Your Student Loan & Win: The Guerrilla Guide to Researching, Repaying, & Ridding Yourself of Student Loan Debt.** Anne Stockwell. LC 97-2060. 1997. write for info. (0-06-273435-0, PL) HarpC.

***Take Comfort: Creative Group Guide.** Wesley Haystead. 160p. 1997. pap. 15.99 (0-7847-0575-5, 40325) Standard Pub.

Take Command Mr. Farragut. Peter Roop & Connie Roop. LC 95-31666. (Illus.). 160p. (J). (gr. 2 up). Date not set. 15.00 (0-688-12043-1) Lothrop.

Take Control: Weight Reduction. Judd Biasiotto. (Illus.). 134p. (Orig.). 1986. pap. 8.00 (0-933079-05-2) World Class Enterprises.

Take Control: You Don't Have to be a Victim of Crime. Bob Portenier. Ed. by Shannon Littlejohn. (Illus.). 128p. (Orig.). 1994. pap. 9.95 (1-880652-38-2) Wichita Eagle.

***Take Control Curriculum: A. D. H. D.** Robert C. Smith, Jr. et al. LC 96-77635. 50p. (Orig.). (YA). (gr. 6-12). 1996. wbk. ed., pap. 13.95 (1-884063-94-2) Mar Co Prods.

Take Control of Your Career: A Development Guide. Boyle-Delp. 144p. 1992. spiral bd. 15.95 (0-8403-7368-6) Kendall-Hunt.

Take Control of Your Health: A Woman's Guide to Staying Well at Any Age. Prevention Magazine Editors. 1996. pap. 12.95 (0-87596-336-6) Rodale Pr Inc.

Take Control of Your Money: With the Moneywise Money Management System. Richard D. Ivie. 229p. (Orig.). 1993. pap. 19.95 (0-9633644-0-5) Moneywise Pub.

Take Control of Your Own Health Care Decisions: A State by State Guide to Preparing Your Living Will & Appointing Your Health Care Agent, with Forms: Regional Edition: Midwest & Great Lakes Edition. Phillip Williams. 310p. (Orig.). 1995. Midwest & Great Lakes Regional ed., incl. Illinois, Indiana, Iowa, Michigan, Minnesota, Missouri, Ne. pap. 24.95 (0-936284-24-2) P Gaines Co.

Take Control of Your Student Loans. Robin Leonard. LC 97-14062. 336p. 1997. pap. text ed. 19.95 (0-87337-358-8) Nolo Pr.

Take Courage: Psalms of Support & Encouragement. William J. Byron. 192p. (Orig.). 1995. pap. 10.95 (1-55612-751-0) Sheed & Ward MO.

Take Credit for Improving Our World. Feitelberg. 1993. pap. text ed. write for info. (0-07-020506-X) McGraw.

Take Each Day One Step at a Time: Poems to Inspire & Encourage the Journey to Recovery: a Collection from Blue Mountain Arts. LC 94-34185. 1994. pap. 7.95 (0-88396-395-7) Blue Mtn Pr CO.

Take 'Em Along: Sharing the Wilderness with Your Children. Barbara J. Euser. LC 86-31908. (Illus.). 128p. (Orig.). 1987. pap. 7.95 (0-917895-12-6) Johnson Bks.

Take Excel for Windows to the Edge. Rupley. 1995. 39.95 (1-56276-109-9, Ziff-Davis Pr) Que.

Take Fantastic Home Videos: How Anyone Can Shoot Great Videos! John Fuller. (Illus.). 128p. 1996. pap. 12.95 (0-936262-37-0) Amherst Media.

Take Five. Westley M. Pederson. 1983. pap. 3.00 (0-87129-268-8, T64) Dramatic Pub.

***Take Five.** Scott. 1991. pap. text ed. write for info. (0-582-87483-1, Pub. by Longman UK) Longman.

***Take Five: A Christmas Cookbook.** 1996. pap. 12.00 (0-9645899-2-3) Wimmer Bk Dist.

Take Five: Collected Poems. Kenneth A. McClane. LC 87-23699. (Contributions in Afro-American & African Studies: No. 109). 296p. 1988. text ed. 49.95 (0-313-25761-2, MTA/, Greenwood Pr) Greenwood.

Take Five! Devotions for Men, 3 vols., Set. Robert W. Busha. 1994. boxed, pap. text ed. 21.99 (0-8054-5371-7, 4253-71) Broadman.

Take Five! Devotions to Strengthen a Man at His Work. Ed. by Robert Busha. LC 93-45614. 1994. 7.99 (0-8054-5366-0, 4253-66) Broadman.

Take Five! Devotions to Strengthen a Man's Life in Christ. Ed. by Robert Busha. LC 93-45607. 1994. 7.99 (0-8054-5368-7, 4253-68) Broadman.

Take Five! Devotions to Strengthen a Man's Relationship. Ed. by Robert Busha. LC 93-45613. 1994. 7.99 (0-8054-5367-9, 4253-67) Broadman.

Take Five: Prayers for the Workplace. Simeon Thole. 64p. 1989. pap. 1.95 (0-8146-1839-1) Liturgical Pr.

Take Five! 5 Minutes with Bill Quick. William K. Quick. Ed. by Mary I. Levack. LC 96-92122. 90p. (Orig.). 1996. pap. write for info. (1-57502-159-5, PO755) Morris Pubng.

Take Five, a Cookbook. Debbye Dabbs. 236p. 1995. pap. text ed. 12.00 (0-9645899-0-7) D Dabbs.

Take Four Hearts. large type ed. Joan Terry. (Ulverscroft). 384p. 1994. 25.99 (0-7089-3067-0) Ulverscroft.

***Take God at His Word Vol. 1: Experience the Power of Giving.** Kregg Hood. 48p. (Orig.). 1996. pap. 4.95 (0-8344-0271-8, SPASB1) Sweet Pub.

Take God's Hand. Betty Mire. 64p. 1990. per. write for info. (0-8187-0128-5) Harlo Press.

Take Good Care. Mary Engelbreit. (Illus.). 48p. 1993. 4.95 (0-8362-4617-9) Andrews & McMeel.

Take Heart. Lisa Higdon. 272p. 1996. mass mkt. 5.99 (0-515-11898-2) Jove Pubns.

Take Heart. Oglesby Paul. LC 86-3170. (Francis A. Countway Library of Medicine). (Illus.). 336p. 1986. 19.95 (0-674-86745-9) HUP.

Take Heart. Molly Peacock. 1989. pap. 12.00 (0-679-72196-7) McKay.

Take Heart! A Proven Step-by-Step Program to Improve Your Heart's Health. Terence Kavanagh. 352p. (Orig.). 1992. pap. 16.95 (1-55013-377-2, Pub. by Key Porter Bks CN) Firefly Bks Ltd.

Take Heart: The Life & Prescription for Living of Paul Dudley White. Oglesby Paul. (Illus.). 366p. 1986. 18.95 (0-317-04059-6) F A Countway.

Take Heart: Your Life After Coronary Artery Bypass Surgery. Rita Dervin et al. (Illus.). 64p. 1990. pap. text ed. 3.50 (0-916999-08-4) HERC Inc.

Take Heart, Catechist: Twenty Stories for Guidance & Growth. John Van Bemmel. LC 90-71135. 112p. (Orig.). 1991. pap. 5.95 (0-89622-459-7, C50) Twenty-Third.

Take Heart, O Ye of Little Faith. Annette G. Cooper. 1995. pap. 7.95 (0-533-11434-9) Vantage.

Take Heed. Watchman Nee. Ed. by Stephen Kaung & Herbert L. Fader. 204p. (Orig.). 1991. pap. 5.00 (0-935008-74-8) Christian Fellow Pubs.

Take Her Deep! I. J. Galantin. Ed. by Paul McCarthy. 1991. mass mkt. 4.95 (0-671-73651-5) PB.

***Take Hold.** Merrill Leffler. 1997. 7.50 (0-931848-95-4) Dryad Pr.

***Take Hold of Life!** Mike Leatherwood. 176p. (Orig.). (YA). (gr. 7-12). 1997. pap. 10.99 (1-57782-020-7) Discipleshp.

Take Hold of Your Future: A Career Planning Guide. JoAnn Harris-Bowlsbey et al. (Illus.). 218p. 1991. 11.95 (1-56009-006-5); teacher ed. write for info. (1-56009-005-7) ACT.

Take Hold upon the Future: Letters on Writers & Writing, 1938-1946. William Everson & Lawrence C. Powell. Ed. by William R. Eshelman. LC 94-6471. 634p. 1994. 69.50 (0-8108-2878-2) Scarecrow.

Take-Home Learning Totes. Cheryl S. Taylor. 96p. teacher ed. 10.99 (0-86653-755-4, GA1470); teacher ed. 10.99 (0-86653-768-6, GA1471) Good Apple.

Take Home Poems. Matt Meyers. LC 95-90080. 72p. (Orig.). 1995. pap. 4.95 (0-9646336-0-4) M Meyers.

Take-Home Science: Independent Activities for Science & Technology. Jenny Feely. LC 94-33824. 80p. 1994. pap. text ed. 16.50 (0-435-08365-1, 08365) Heinemann.

Take-Home Stories. Richelle R. Selleck. 96p. (J). (ps-2). 1990. 11.99 (0-86653-567-5, GA1169) Good Apple.

Take Home the Pizza Pals, 6 bks., Set. Tish Rabe & Lisa A. Marsoli. (Illus.). 48p. (J). (gr. 2-6). 1996. bds., boxed 9.99 (0-88705-967-8) Rdrs Dgst Yng Fam.

***Take It & Like It.** Thomas Cipullo. 106p. (Orig.). 1997. pap. 10.95 (0-9655112-7-8) A T Cipullo.

Take It Away. (Sesame Street Ser.: No. 16). (J). 1989. pap. 1.49 (0-553-18399-0) Bantam.

Take It Back: The Fine Art of Returning Almost Anything. Arlene Singer et al. (Illus.). 160p. (Orig.). 1991. pap. 9.95 (0-915765-74-8) Natl Pr Bks.

***Take It Easy.** David Hill. LC 96-37550. 1997. pap. 14.99 (0-525-45763-1) NAL-Dutton.

Take It Easy: American Idioms & Two Word Verbs for Students of English As a Foreign Language. Pamela McPartland. (English As a Second Language Ser.). 176p. 1981. pap. text ed. 15.95 (0-13-882902-0) P-H.

Take It Easy: American Idioms & Two Word Verbs for Students of English As a Foreign Language. Pamela McPartland. (English As a Second Language Ser.). 176p. 1981. 17.50 (0-13-882910-1) P-H.

Take-It-Easy Good-Times Cookbook. Patricia B. Mitchell. 1991. pap. 4.00 (0-925117-51-X) Mitchells.

Take It from Here: GCSE & Standard Grade Project Work Through the Short Story. Ed. by Rosemary Moor. 128p. (C). 1989. 39.00 (0-7487-0064-1, Pub. by S Thornes Pubs UK) St Mut.

Take It from Me: Practical & Inspiring Career Advice from the Celebrated & the Successful. Michael Levine. 208p. (Orig.). 1996. pap. 12.00 (0-399-52217-4, Perigee Bks) Berkley Pub.

Take It from the Top! How to Earn Your Living in Radio & T.V. Voice-Overs. Alice Whitfield. LC 91-66985. (Illus.). 175p. (Orig.). (C). 1992. pap. 19.95 (0-9631048-0-2) Ring-U-Turkey Pr.

Take It Like a Man: The Autobiography of Boy George. Boy George. 544p. 1996. pap. 13.00 (0-06-092761-5) HarpC.

Take It Like a Man: The Autobiography of Boy George. Boy George & Spencer Bright. LC 95-22573. (Illus.). 500p. 1995. 25.00 (0-06-017368-8, HarpT) HarpC.

Take It Off & Keep It Off: Based on the Successful Methods of Overeaters Anonymous. Helen Lerner. 176p. (Orig.). 1989. pap. 8.95 (0-8092-4493-4) Contemp Bks.

Take It or Leave It. Raymond Federman. LC 75-21556. 426p. 1976. pap. 8.95 (0-914590-23-5) Fiction Coll.

***Take It or Leave It.** 2nd rev. ed. 426p. 1997. pap. 12.95 (1-57366-030-2) Fiction Coll.

Take It to the Hoop. Ed. by Daniel Rudman. (Illus.). 300p. (Orig.). 1980. 25.00 (0-913028-80-0) North Atlantic.

Take It to the Mat. Bobby Douglas. 140p. 1993. pap. 15.95 (0-9635812-0-1) Sigler Print.

Take It While It's There. James Gala. 86p. (C). 1989. text ed. 55.00 (1-872795-66-8, Pub. by Pentland Pr UK) St Mut.

Take Jesus for Example. Thomas Babaja. (Illus.). 66p. (Orig.). 1985. pap. text ed. 3.50 (0-942345-20-7) Dovehaven Pr Ltd.

Take Judaism, for Example: Studies Toward the Comparison of Religions. Jacob Neusner. LC 92-17940. 244p. 1992. 69.95 (1-55540-743-9, 24 00 51) Scholars Pr GA.

Take Me Along. Lynn Videon et al. (J). 1987. pap. 9.99 (0-8224-6719-4) Fearon Teach Aids.

Take Me for a Ride: Coming of Age in a Destructive Cult. Mark E. Laxer. 200p. 1993. pap. 14.00 (0-9638108-3-9) Outer Rim Pr.

***Take Me Home.** John Denver. Date not set. 5.99 (0-517-17632-7) Random Hse Value.

Take Me Home: An Autobiography. John Denver. 1994. 22.00 (0-517-59537-0, Harmony) Crown Pub Group.

Take-Me-Home: Notes on the Church Year for Children. Ed. by Peter Mazar. (Illus.). 128p. (Orig.). (J). (gr. 1-8). 1991. pap. 15.00 (0-929650-52-2, TAKHOM) Liturgy Tr Pubns.

Take Me Home, Country Roads. 30.00 (0-7935-5216-8, 00868001) H Leonard.

Take Me Home, Too. Peter Mazar. (Illus.). 128p. (Orig.). (J). (gr. 1-6). 1997. pap. 15.00 (1-56854-180-5, TKHOM2) Liturgy Tr Pubns.

Take Me Like a Photograph. 2nd ed. Chocolate Waters. 1980. pap. 7.00 (0-935060-02-2) Eggplant Pr.

Take Me Out! Houghton Mifflin Company Staff. (Literature Experience 1991 Ser.). (J). (gr. 4). 1990. pap. 9.16 (0-395-55163-3) HM.

Take Me Out of the Ball Game, Vol. 8. (McGee & Me! Ser.: Vol. 8). 92p. (J). 1990. pap. 5.99 (0-8423-4113-7) Tyndale.

Take Me Out to the Ball Game. (Little Golden Sound Story Bks.). (Illus.). 24p. (J). 1995. bds. 6.95 (0-307-74831-6, Golden Pr) Western Pub.

Take Me Out to the Ball Game: A Book of History, Hits, & Heroes. Ariel Books Staff. (Illus.). 40p. 1995. 6.95 (0-8362-4732-9, Arie Bks) Andrews & McMeel.

Take Me Out to the Ballgame. Maryann Kovalski. LC 92-10155. (Illus.). 32p. (J). (gr. k-3). 1993. 14.95 (0-590-45638-5) Scholastic Inc.

Take Me Out to the Ballgame. Jack Norworth. LC 91-18555. (Illus.). 40p. (J). (ps up). 1992. lib. bdg. 16.00 (0-02-735991-3, Four Winds Pr) S&S Childrens.

Take Me to Coney Island. Miriam Packer. (Prose Ser.: No. 25). 185p. 1993. pap. 13.00 (0-920717-92-6) Guernica Editions.

***Take Me to the Dance.** Poole & Denise. 1993. pap. text ed. write for info. (0-17-556286-5) Addison-Wesley.

Take Me to Your Leader: A Game about Presidential Elections. Edward Dye. (Illus.). 12p. (gr. 4-12). 1982. 9.95 (0-910141-02-9, KP116) Kino Pubns.

Take Me to Your Liter: Science & Math Jokes. Illus. by Gregory Filling. 40p. (J). (gr. 2-5). 1991. lib. bdg. 13.95 (0-945912-13-7) Pippin Pr.

Take Me Under the Sea: The Dream Merchants of the Deep. Thomas N. Burgess. LC 93-87618. (Illus.). 272p. (Orig.). 1994. pap. 13.95 (0-9639840-0-4) Ocean Archives.

Take Me Where the Good Times Are. Robert Cormier. 224p. (YA). 1991. mass mkt. 3.99 (0-440-21096-8, YB BDD) BDD Bks Young Read.

Take Me with You! Songbook. Peter Alsop. (J). 1988. 11.00 (0-8256-1116-4) Moose Schl Records.

Take My Advice. rev. ed. Ed. by John E. Rotelle. 64p. 1987. pap. 1.00 (0-941491-02-1) Augustinian Pr.

***Take My Breath Away.** Meg O'Brien. 1997. mass mkt. 5.99 (0-312-96158-8) St Martin.

Take My Hand. Dawn Colclasure. 48p. (Orig.). 1993. pap. write for info. (1-56167-129-0) Am Literary Pr.

Take My Hand: An Angel's Journey. Louise Shelby. (Illus.). 32p. (J). 1995. 15.95 (0-9642776-1-1) In the Weeds.

Take My Hand: Physical Guided Action. Tony LoBue. Ed. by Barbara Burke. (Illus.). (Orig.). 1989. pap. text ed. 5.95 (0-9625492-0-7) T LoBue.

An Asterisk (*) at the beginning of an entry indicates that the title is appearing in BIP for the first time.

Take My Headache. David Wellen & Matthew Wellen. (Illus.). 64p. (Orig.). 1990. pap. 4.50 (*0-9620605-2-6*) Vacuum Bks.

Take My Life. Audrey J. Williamson. 64p. 1982. pap. 4.99 (*0-8341-0812-7*) Beacon Hill.

Take My Rooks. Yasser Seirawan & Nikolay Minev. Ed. by Jonathan Berry et al. (Illus.). xvi, 95p. (Orig.). 1991. pap. 12.95 (*1-879479-01-X*) ICE WA.

Take My Word: Autobiographical Innovations of Ethnic American Working Women. Anne E. Goldman. LC 95-6078. 274p. 1996. pap. 16.00 (*0-520-20097-7*) U CA Pr.

Take My Word: Autobiographical Innovations of Ethnic American Working Women. Anne E. Goldman. LC 95-6018. 274p. (C). 1996. 40.00 (*0-520-20096-9*) U CA Pr.

***Take My Yoke upon You.** John Polis. 98p. 1997. pap. 7.99 (*1-884369-53-7*, EBED Pubns) McDougal Pubng.

Take 'n' Talk. Lorna D. Smith. 175p. 1995. pap. 9.50 (*0-9632467-9-8*) ApronStrings.

Take New York Home: The First 3-Dimensional Pop-up Map of New York. Cari J. Pearlman. (Illus.). (YA). (gr. 1-12). 1994. 11.50 (*0-929644-01-8*) MultiMap.

Take No As a Starter: The Life of Richard L. Graves, Set. Intro. by J. Francis Brown, IV. 661p. 1980. lib. bdg. 84.50 (*1-56475-080-9*); fiche write for info. (*1-56475-354-9*) U NV Oral Hist.

Take No Farewells. Robert Goddard. 576p. 1992. mass mkt. 7.99 (*0-552-13562-3*) Bantam.

Take No Prisoners. Mack Nasty. LC 90-62143. 128p. (Orig.). 1990. pap. 12.95 (*1-55950-043-3*, 19169) Loompanics.

***Take No Prisoners.** Prima Publishing Staff. 1997. pap. 19.99 (*0-7615-1201-2*) Prima Pub.

Take Notes. June Biesch. (Paper Moon Bks.). 30p. (Orig.). pap. text ed. 5.00 (*1-884438-02-4*) Epiphany AR.

Take Notes. 2nd ed. Ron Fry. (How to Study Ser.). 128p. (C). 1994. pap. 6.95 (*1-56414-076-8*) Career Pr Inc.

***Take Now, Pay Later.** large type ed. Joanna Dessau. (Ulverscroft Large Print Ser.). 272p. 1997. 27.50 (*0-7089-3715-2*) Ulverscroft.

Take-Off Companies. Ed. by Raymond W. Smilor & Robert L. Kuhn. LC 85-16745. 204p. 1985. text ed. 55.00 (*0-275-90226-9*, C0226, Praeger Pubs) Greenwood.

Take-Off for Taiwan. Ed. by Peter Ferdinand. LC 96-3019. 128p. 1996. 39.95 (*1-85567-115-8*, Pub. by Pntr Pubs UK); pap. 15.95 (*1-85567-116-6*, Pub. by Pntr Pubs UK) Bks Intl VA.

Take Off from Within. Ervin Seale. 120p. 1993. reprint ed. pap. 8.95 (*0-87516-658-X*) DeVorss.

Take-Off Tappers. Bonnie Nemeth. Ed. by Wolf Nemeth & Debby Bouldin. (Timeless Tap Ser.: Level 3, Bk. 3, Vol. 3). (Illus.). 72p. (Orig.). (J). (gr. 1-3). 1996. pap. 12.00 (*1-888199-53-9*) Dance Innovators.

***Take off with Measuring.** Sally Hewitt. (J). (gr. k up). 1997. pap. text ed. 4.95 (*0-8172-4268-6*) Raintree Steck-V.

***Take off with Numbers.** Sally Hewitt. (J). (gr. k up). 1997. pap. text ed. 4.95 (*0-8172-4265-1*) Raintree Steck-V.

***Take off with Puzzles.** Sally Hewitt. (J). 1996. pap. text ed. 4.95 (*0-8172-4270-8*) Raintree Steck-V.

***Take off with Shapes.** Sally Hewitt. (J). 1996. pap. text ed. 4.95 (*0-8172-4269-4*) Raintree Steck-V.

***Take off with Sorting & Sets.** Sally Hewitt. (Take off with... Ser.). (Illus.). (J). (gr. 2-5). 1997. pap. 4.95 (*0-614-28913-0*) Raintree Steck-V.

***Take off with Time.** Sally Hewitt. (J). 1996. pap. text ed. 4.95 (*0-8172-4266-X*) Raintree Steck-V.

Take Off Your Glasses & See: A Mind - Body Approach to Expanding Your Eyesight & Insight. Jacob Liberman. 288p. 1995. pap. 14.00 (*0-517-88604-9*) Crown Pub Group.

Take off Your Glasses & See: How to Heal Your Eyesight & Expand Your Insight. Jacob Liberman. LC 94-32101. 1995. 21.00 (*0-517-59859-0*) Crown Pub Group.

Take off Your Mask. Ludwig Eidelberg. LC 48-4537. 231p. reprint ed. pap. 65.90 (*0-317-10378-4*, 2010699) Bks Demand.

Take off Your Shoes: A Guide to the Nature of Reality. Stefan C. Nadzo. LC 81-66185. 140p. (Orig.). 1981. pap. 5.95 (*0-937226-01-7*) Laugh Cat.

***Take off 10 Years in 10 Weeks.** Judith Wills. 1996. pap. 16.95 (*0-614-20761-4*) RD Assn.

Take One. Sean Croyston. 112p. 1995. pap. 19.95 (*0-86819-438-7*) Aubrey Bks.

Take One: Television Directors on Directing. Jack Kuney. LC 89-72126. 191p. 1990. pap. text ed. 16.95 (*0-275-93546-9*, Praeger Pubs) Greenwood.

Take One: The Control Room Insights of Ten TV Directors. Jack Kuney. LC 89-17225. (Contributions to the Study of Popular Culture Ser.: No. 25). 191p. 1990. text ed. 49.95 (*0-313-26384-1*, KUI/, Greenwood Pr) Greenwood.

Take One As Needed. Oscar London. 224p. (Orig.). 1989. pap. 8.95 (*0-89815-297-6*) Ten Speed Pr.

Take One Hand. Cynthia Todd & Debbie Ziemann. (Sing Me a Song Ser.). (Illus.). 25p. (J). (gr. k-6). 1990. lib. bdg. 9.95 (*1-879056-05-4*) Alpenhorn Pr.

Take-Out City. Cynthia Lawrence. 208p. 1993. 18.95 (*0-88184-942-1*) Carroll & Graf.

***Take Out Your Crayons.** Julie Howard. 25p. (J). reprint ed. 5.95 (*0-937690-34-1*) Wrld Lib Pubns.

Take Over. Jeffrey C. Wright. (Orig.). 1983. pap. 6.00 (*0-915124-85-8*, Toothpaste) Coffee Hse.

Take-Over. large type ed. Mary Raymond. 304p. 1986. 25.99 (*0-7089-1546-9*) Ulverscroft.

Take-overs & Mergers. Chandrasegar. xiii, 553p. 1995. write for info. (*0-409-99714-5*, ASIA) MICHIE.

Take Paradise. Orval Lund. 1989. 2.50 (*0-941127-05-2*) Dacotah Terr Pr.

Take Part - Take One: Pupils' Book. J. Burgen. (C). 1986. 30.00 (*0-85950-557-X*, Pub. by S Thornes Pubs UK) St Mut.

Take Part - Take One: Teacher's Book. Stanley Thornes. (C). 1986. 25.00 (*0-85950-558-8*, Pub. by S Thornes Pubs UK) St Mut.

Take Part Art. Bob Gregson. (J). (gr. 3-6). 1990. pap. 15.99 (*0-8224-6781-X*) Fearon Teach Aids.

Take, Read: Scripture, Textuality, & Cultural Practice. Wesley A. Kort. LC 95-48947. (C). 1996. 38.50 (*0-271-01591-8*); pap. 19.95 (*0-271-01592-6*) Pa St U Pr.

Take Six: Behind the Scenes with the Parables. Mark Vander Vennen. (Prime-Time Bible Studies). 64p. (Orig.). (YA). (gr. 9-12). 1992. teacher ed. 8.45 (*1-56212-011-5*, 1210-3054) CRC Pubns.

Take Stage! How to Direct & Produce a Lesbian Play. Carolyn Gage. LC 96-44777. 1997. 38.50 (*0-8108-3263-9*) Scarecrow.

***Take Ten, Vol. 1.** Carver. Date not set. pap. text ed. write for info. (*0-312-15712-6*); wbk. ed., pap. text ed. write for info. (*0-312-15732-0*); pap. text ed. write for info. (*0-312-15730-4*) St Martin.

***Take Ten, Vol. 2.** Carver. Date not set. pap. text ed. write for info. (*0-312-15713-4*); wbk. ed., pap. text ed. write for info. (*0-312-15731-2*); pap. text ed. write for info. (*0-312-15729-0*) St Martin.

Take Ten: New 10-Minute Plays. E. Lave & N. Sheilgold. LC 96-53571. 1997. pap. 14.00 (*0-679-77282-0*) McKay.

Take Ten Steps to Successful Research: Grades 5-8. Liz C. Rothlein & Anita M. Meinbach. (Illus.). 82p. (Orig.). 1988. pap. 9.95 (*0-673-38087-4*, GoodYrBooks) Addson-Wesley Educ.

***Take That: Talk Back.** Luke Taylor. (Illus.). 32p. 1996. 9.95 (*0-7119-4300-1*, OP 47734) Omnibus NY.

Take That, Mr. Smugglesdorf! Mary M. Douglas. LC 96-90100. 123p. (Orig.). 1996. spiral bd., pap. 22.50 (*0-9643764-3-1*) Wildot Pr.

Take the Ball & Run: A Rugby Anthology Selected by Godfrey Smith. Godfrey Smith. (Illus.). 256p. 1996. pap. 15.95 (*1-85793-764-3*, Pub. by Pavilion UK) Trafalgar.

***Take the Big Picture.** James Reaney. 176p. 1986. pap. 8.95 (*0-88984-087-3*, Pub. by Porcupines Quill CN) Genl Dist Srvs.

Take the Fear Out of Asking for Major Gifts. James A. Donovan. 103p. (Orig.). 1994. pap. write for info. (*0-9639875-1-8*) Donovan Mgmt.

Take the High Ground: An Executive's Guide to Total Quality Management. Dave McLaughlin. LC 90-6469. (Illus.). viii, 187p. 1990. 19.95 (*0-931541-17-4*) Mancorp Pub.

Take the I.Q. Test. Philip J. Carter & Ken A. Russell. (Illus.). 128p. (Orig.). 1989. pap. 5.95 (*0-7137-2054-9*, Pub. by Blandford Pr UK) Sterling.

***Take the Journey: 34 Daily Devotions to Help You Go Against the Flow.** Les Christie. 130p. (Orig.). 1997. pap. 5.99 (*0-89900-714-7*) College Pr Pub.

Take the Lead. Stan Seckler. (Illus.). 40p. 1991. pap. 8.95 (*1-56516-006-1*) H Leonard.

Take the Lead for Trombone. 1995. pap. 9.95 (*0-7935-5167-6*, 00030058) H Leonard.

Take the Lead for Trombone: Basic Manual for the Lead Trombonist in a Jazz Ensemble. Steve Wiest. (Illus.). 40p. (Orig.). (C). 1993. pap. 8.95 (*1-56516-061-4*) H Leonard.

Take the Lead for Trumpet: Basic Manual for the Lead Trumpet in a Jazz Ensemble. Dominic Spera. (Illus.). 32p. (Orig.). (C). 1992. pap. 8.95 (*1-56516-060-6*) H Leonard.

Take the Money & Strut! A Private Investigator's Guide To Collecting a Bad Debt. Fay Faron. 128p. (Orig.). 1988. pap. 9.95 (*0-9620096-0-1*) Creighton-Morgan.

Take the Money & Strut see Nasty Bit of Business: A Private Eye's Guide to Collecting a Bad Debt

***Take the Mummy & Run.** Ellen Weiss & Mel Friedman. (Carmen Sandiego Mystery Ser.). (Illus.). 144p. (J). (gr. 3-7). 1997. pap. 4.50 (*0-06-440664-4*, Trophy) HarpC Child Bks.

Take the Mystery Out of Boat Maintenance. Lawrence A. Diamond. (Illus.). 1989. 22.50 (*0-393-03335-X*) Norton.

Take the Mystery Out of Media: Make Your Publicity Newsworthy. Lorraine B. Kingdon. 144p. (Orig.). 1994. pap. 12.95 (*0-9640861-0-7*) Commun Skills.

Take the Pain Out of Painting - Interiors. Glenn Haege. Ed. by Kathleen Stief. (Illus.). 264p. (Orig.). 1993. per. 14.97 (*1-880615-19-3*) Master Handyman.

Take the Pain Out of Painting! Exteriors. Glenn Haege. Ed. by Kathleen Stief. (Illus.). 224p. 1993. reprint ed. Perfect bdg. per. 12.95 (*1-880615-15-0*) Master Handyman.

Take the Pizza & Run: And Other Stories for Children about Stewardship. Barbara DeGrote-Sorensen. (Illus.). 32p. (J). 1992. pap. 5.99 (*0-8066-2599-6*, 10-25996) Augsburg Fortress.

Take the Plane. Muriel Vallet. (Illus.). 10p. (J). (gr. k-3). 1993. pap. 10.95 (*1-895583-59-4*) MAYA Pubs.

***Take the Reins.** rev. ed. John L. Moore. LC 96-50947. 224p. 1997. 12.99 (*0-7852-7226-7*) Nelson.

Take the Rich off Welfare. Mark Zapezauer & Arthur Naiman. LC 96-34351. (Real Story Ser.). 192p. (Orig.). 1996. pap. 9.00 (*1-878825-31-3*) Odonian Pr.

Take the Road to Creativity & Get off Your Dead End. David P. Campbell. 136p. 1985. pap. 8.95 (*0-912879-91-2*) Ctr Creat Leader.

Take the Stand. Charles B. Graham. LC 96-19677. 192p. 1996. pap. 11.99 (*0-8054-6267-8*, 4262-67) Broadman.

Take the Time. Frank J. Valentino. 100p. 1992. lib. bdg. write for info. (*1-880764-00-8*) Northwind NJ.

Take the Tour: For a Taste of Colonial Edenton. St. Paul's Episcopal Church Women. (Illus.). 300p. 1995. spiral bd. 17.00 (*0-9643218-0-7*) Saint Pauls Epis Chur.

***Take the Tyme.** S. T. Wakon. iv, 155p. 1997. pap. 7.95 (*0-9658146-0-2*) Power Pub.

Take the Witness! Alfred Cohn & Joe Chisholm. xii, 315p. 1996. reprint ed. 82.00 (*1-56169-211-5*) Gaunt.

Take Them up Tenderly: A Collection of Profiles. Margaret C. Harriman. LC 72-5763. (Essay Index Reprint Ser.). 1977. reprint ed. 25.95 (*0-8369-2991-8*) Ayer.

Take These Chains from My Heart. Phyllis George. Ed. & Selected by Teresa George. LC 94-47248. 144p. (Orig.). 1995. pap. 8.00 (*0-380-77874-2*) Avon.

***Take These Men.** Cyril Joly. (Echoes of War Military History Ser.). 1996. pap. 10.95 (*0-907675-40-9*, Pub. by Ashland Buchan & Enright UK) Cimino Pub Grp.

Take Things As They Happen. Matthew V. Smith. (Illus.). 19p. (J). (gr. k-3). 1994. pap. 11.95 (*1-56606-029-X*) Bradley Mann.

Take Thirty Dictionary. Ernest Beaucamp & Dorothea Hansen. (gr. 12). 1971. pap. 9.75 (*0-89420-099-2*, 219905) Natl Book.

Take Thirty Shorthand: Student Syllabus, 2 vols., 1. Ernest Beaucamp & Dorothea Hansen. (YA). (gr. 11-12). 1976. pap. text ed. 9.95 (*0-89420-097-6*, 218999) Natl Book.

Take Thirty Shorthand: Student Syllabus, 2 vols., 2. Ernest Beaucamp & Dorothea Hansen. (YA). (gr. 11-12). 1976. 8.95 (*0-89420-098-4*, 219105); audio 192.75 (*0-89420-211-1*, 177700) Natl Book.

Take This Book & Call Me in the Morning! Mary McBride & Veronica McBride. Ed. by Helen Duffy. (Illus.). 104p. (Orig.). 1993. pap. 5.95 (*0-9627601-5-3*) Bros Grinn.

***Take This Book to the Dentist with You.** Charles B. Inlander. 1998. pap. text ed. 14.95 (*1-882606-27-2*) Peoples Med Soc.

Take This Book to the Gynecologist with You. Gale Malesky. 1991. pap. 9.95 (*0-201-52379-5*) Addison-Wesley.

Take This Book to the Gynecologist with You. Karen Morales. 1991. pap. 9.95 (*0-201-52380-9*) Addison-Wesley.

***Take This Book to the Hospital with You: A Consumer Guide to Surviving Your Hospital Stay.** Charles B. Inlander & Ed Weiner. LC 96-44013. 1997. write for info. (*1-882606-70-1*) Peoples Med Soc.

Take This Book to the Hospital with You: A Consumer Guide to Surviving Your Hospital Stay. rev. ed. Charles B. Inlander. LC 92-38767. 1993. 7.99 (*0-517-08921-1*) Random Hse Value.

Take This Book to the Hospital with You: A Consumer Guide to Surviving Your Hospital Stay. 3rd ed. Charles B. Inlander. 1993. pap. 14.95 (*1-882606-03-5*) Peoples Med Soc.

Take This Book to the Pediatrician with You: The Guide to Your Child's Health. Charles B. Inlander. 1992. pap. 14.95 (*0-9627334-6-6*) Peoples Med Soc.

Take This Book to the Pediatrician with You: The Guide to Your Child's Health. Charles B. Inlander & J. Lynne Dodson. LC 93-40935. 1994. 5.99 (*0-517-10015-0*) Random Hse Value.

Take This Exit: Rediscovering the Iowa Landscape. Ed. by Robert F. Sayre. (Illus.). 340p. 1989. pap. 18.95 (*0-8138-0199-0*) Iowa St U Pr.

Take This House, Please! The Complete Guide to Buying Real Estate Owned by Lenders, 2 vols., 1. John Beck & Ronald Starr. Ed. by Jonathan Albert. 535p. (Orig.). 1985. pap. 65.00 (*0-934521-00-X*) Unlimited Golden Pr.

Take This House, Please! The Complete Guide to Buying Real Estate Owned by Lenders, 2 vols., 2. John Beck & Ronald Starr. Ed. by Jonathan Albert. 535p. (Orig.). 1985. pap. 65.00 (*0-934521-01-8*) Unlimited Golden Pr.

Take This House, Please! The Complete Guide to Buying Real Estate Owned by Lenders, 2 vols., Set. John Beck & Ronald Starr. Ed. by Jonathan Albert. 535p. (Orig.). 1985. spiral bd. 95.00 (*0-934521-02-6*) Unlimited Golden Pr.

Take This Job & Leave It: How to Get Out of a Job You Hate & into a Job You Love. Bill Radin. 192p. 1993. pap. 12.95 (*1-56414-057-1*) Career Pr Inc.

Take This Job & Love It: A Personal Guide to Career Empowerment. Diane Tracy. 1996. pap. text ed. 10.95 (*0-07-065304-6*) McGraw.

Take This Job & Sell It! The Recruiter's Handbook. Richard Mackie. LC 93-33890. (Illus.). 176p. (Orig.). 1994. pap. 24.95 (*0-936609-30-3*) QED Ft Bragg.

***Take This Work & Love It.** Dennis Jaffe & Cynthia D. Scott. Ed. by Janis Paris. LC 96-86722. 270p. (Orig.). 1997. pap. 14.95 (*1-56052-420-0*) Crisp Pubns.

***Take Three.** Susan Aizenberg et al. Ed. by Askold Melnyczuk. (AGNI New Poets Ser.: Vol. 2). 96p. (Orig.). 1997. pap. 12.95 (*1-55597-254-3*) Graywolf.

Take Three. Thomas S. Ellis et al. Ed. by Askold Melnyczuk. LC 95-81003. (AGNI New Poets Ser.: No. 1). 130p. (Orig.). 1996. pap. 12.95 (*1-55597-239-X*) Graywolf.

Take Time for Fitness. Paul Terry et al. 52p. 1990. student ed. write for info. (*1-884153-03-8*) Prk Nicollet.

Take Time to Laugh: It's the Music of the Soul. Eve B. Hatchett. Ed. by Frances Cowden. LC 93-79789. (Illus.). 58p. 1993. pap. 6.00 (*1-884289-00-2*) Grandmother Erth.

Take Time to Talk: A Resource for Apraxia Therapy, Esophageal Speech Training, Aphasia Therapy, & Articulation Therapy. 2nd ed. Patricia F. White. LC 96-14174. 200p. 1996. spiral bd. 25.00 (*0-7506-9783-0*) Buttrwrth-Heinemann.

Take to the Sky. Laurie Lawlor. (Heartland Ser.: No. 2). (J). (gr. 3-6). 1996. mass mkt. 3.99 (*0-671-53717-2*) PB.

Take Two: A Life in Movies & Politics. enl. ed. Philip Dunne. LC 91-43377. (Illus.). 408p. 1992. reprint ed. pap. 17.95 (*0-87910-157-1*) Limelight Edns.

Take Two: Adating the Contemporary American Novel to Film. Ed. by Barbara T. Upack. LC 93-72985. (Illus.). 198p. (C). 1994. 45.95 (*0-87972-641-5*); pap. 18.95 (*0-87972-642-3*) Bowling Green Univ Popular Press.

Take Two & Hit to Right. Art Molen. 1976. 21.95 (*0-8488-1575-0*) Amereon Ltd.

***Take Two Aspirin & See Yourself in the Morning.** Robert A. Norman. LC 97-12867. 260p. (Orig.). 1997. pap. 16.95 (*0-931541-62-X*) Mancorp Pub.

***Take Two at Bedtime.** Margery Allingham. Date not set. lib. bdg. 20.95 (*0-8488-1951-9*) Amereon Ltd.

Take Two Crackers & Call Me in the Morning! A Real Life Guide for Surviving Morning Sickness. Miriam Erick. Ed. by Tim Champion. LC 95-80416. (Illus.). 72p. (Orig.). 1995. pap. 8.50 (*0-9613063-5-1*) Grinnen-Barrett Pub Co.

Take Two Roots & Call Me in the Morning. Wilsdon. LC 94-16076. 80p. (J). 1994. write for info. (*0-7167-6570-5*); pap. write for info. (*0-7167-6572-1*) W H Freeman.

Take Up My Cross. (Illus.). 80p. 1996. 9.95 (*1-57036-235-1*) Turner Pub GA.

Take up the Bodies: Theater at the Vanishing Point. Herbert Blau. LC 81-19774. (Illus.). 328p. 1985. pap. text ed. 12.95 (*0-252-01245-3*) U of Ill Pr.

Take up Thy Bed & Walk. David Hinshaw. Ed. by William R. Phillips & Janet Rosenberg. LC 79-6905. (Physically Handicapped in Society Ser.). (Illus.). 1980. reprint ed. lib. bdg. 28.95 (*0-405-13114-3*) Ayer.

Take up Your Life: Spiritual Guidance for the Real World. Janet C. Spring. 216p. 1996. 19.95 (*0-8048-3091-6*) C E Tuttle.

Take Us to Your Mall: A FoxTrot Collection. Bill Amend. (Illus.). 128p. 1995. pap. 8.95 (*0-8362-1780-2*) Andrews & McMeel.

Take What You Want. large type ed. Gordon Nimse. (Dales Mystery Ser.). 422p. 1993. pap. 17.99 (*1-85389-372-2*) Ulverscroft.

Take WordPerfect to the Edge. Shadel. 1993. 29.95 (*1-56276-083-1*, Ziff-Davis Pr) Que.

Take Your Agenda, I'm Going to Tahiti! Dick Starr & Bill Genicevitch. (Illus.). 300p. (Orig.). 1995. pap. 29.00 (*1-888221-00-3*) Results Now.

Take Your Brother by the Hand. Joachim Oppenheimer. LC 91-71463. (Illus.). 186p. (Orig.). 1991. pap. 17.95 (*0-9629401-0-0*) J Oppenheimer.

Take Your Case to Peoples' (Small Claims) Court. 16p. 1990. pap. 3.95 (*0-918734-25-8*) Reymont.

Take Your Hands off My Attitude: Your Right to a Bad Attitude; Alyce P. Cornyn-Selby. 48p. (Orig.). 1987. pap. 8.95 (*0-941383-02-4*) Beynch Pr.

Take Your Hat Off When the Flag Goes By. Janeen Brady. (Illus.). 22p. (Orig.). (J). (gr. k-6). 1987. student ed. 2.95 (*0-944803-31-8*); 1.50 (*0-944803-33-4*); audio 10.95 (*0-944803-32-6*) Brite Music.

Take Your Hat Off When the Flag Goes By, 20 vols., Set. Janeen Brady. (Illus.). 22p. (Orig.). (J). (gr. k-6). 1987. student ed. 15.00 (*0-944803-34-2*) Brite Music.

Take Your Hat Off When the Flag Goes By: Songbook. Janeen Brady. (Illus.). 22p. (Orig.). (J). (gr. k-6). 1987. 8.95 (*0-944803-29-6*) Brite Music.

Take Your Kids to Europe. Cynthia W. Harriman. (Illus.). 304p. (Orig.). 1994. pap. 13.95 (*0-9630601-1-2*) Mason-Grant.

***Take Your Kids to Europe: The Overseas Travel Guide for Thinking Families.** 3rd ed. Cynthia W. Harriman. LC 97-17730. (Illus.). 320p. 1997. pap. 16.95 (*0-7627-0127-7*) Globe Pequot.

Take Your Life off Hold. Ted Dreier. LC 87-12065. 210p. 1987. 6.99 (*1-55591-020-3*); pap. 4.99 (*1-55591-038-6*) Fulcrum Pub.

Take Your Mark on Vacation. Linda Gidre et al. (Summer Work Bks.). (Illus.). 50p. (J). (gr. 1-2). Date not set. wbk. ed. 6.95 (*0-9641274-2-3*) TYM Pubng.

Take Your Mark on Vacation. Linda Gidre et al. (Summer Work Bks.). (Illus.). 50p. (YA). (gr. 1-2). Date not set. wbk. ed. 6.95 (*0-9641274-3-1*) TYM Pubng.

Take Your Mark on Vacation, Level 4. Tracy Clark et al. Ed. by Christine Currie et al. (Summer Workbooks Ser.). (Illus.). (J). (gr. 3-4). 1994. student ed. 6.95 (*0-9641274-0-7*) TYM Pubng.

Take Your Mark on Vacation, Level 5. Tracy Clark et al. Ed. by Christine Currie et al. (Summer Workbooks Ser.). (Illus.). 52p. (J). (gr. 4-5). 1994. student ed. 6.95 (*0-9641274-1-5*) TYM Pubng.

Take Your Pet: A Guide of Accommodations for Pets & Their Owners. Ed. by Arthur Frank. 440p. (Orig.). 1990. pap. 9.95 (*0-9626885-0-9*) Artco Offset.

***Take Your Pet Along.** Heather Walters. 1997. pap. text ed. 14.95 (*0-9648913-2-8*) MCE.

Take Your Pet Along: 1001 Places to Stay with Your Pet. Heather M. Walters. 287p. 1995. pap. text ed. 14.95 (*0-9648913-0-1*) MCE.

***Take Your Pet Too! Fun Things to Do - Great U. S. Vacations.** Heather M. Walters. (Pet Travel Ser.). 300p. Date not set. 16.95 (*0-9648913-1-X*) MCE.

***Take Your Pick: Text.** Woolcott. 1992. pap. text ed. write for info. (*0-17-555999-6*) Addison-Wesley.

Take Your Place in History: A Personal Chronology. Kurt Florman. 176p. (Orig.). 1993. pap. text ed. 17.00 (*1-55613-818-0*) Heritage Bk.

***Take Your Time: Finding Balance in a Hurried World.** Eknath Easwaran. LC 97-3832. 240p. 1997. 16.95 (*0-7868-6221-1*) Hyperion.

Take Your Tricks: Over Six Hundred Declare Play Tips You Can Take to the Bank. Edwin B. Kantar. 1993. pap. 10.95 (*1-882180-04-6*) Griffin CA.

Take Your Victory! Corbin Nash. 42p. (Orig.). 1996. pap. 5.00 (*0-9649747-0-3*) Chrstian Outreach.

Take 22. J. Crist. Date not set. pap. write for info. (*0-14-009462-8*, Penguin Bks) Viking Penguin.

***Take 3.** Forrester & Savage. 1991. student ed., pap. text ed. write for info. (*0-17-556455-8*) Addison-Wesley.

***Takecharge Computing for Teachers.** Pam Dixon. 1997. pap. 24.99 (*0-7645-0256-5*) IDG Bks.

*TakeCharge Computing for Teens & Parents. Dixon. 1996. pap. 24.99 (0-7645-0101-1) IDG Bks.

*Takecharge Computing for Teens & Parents. Pam Dixon. 1997. pap. 24.99 (0-7645-0257-3) IDG Bks.

Takedown. (Super Bolan Ser.). 1994. mass mkt. 4.99 (0-373-61434-9, 1-61434-6) Harlequin Bks.

Takedown. Matt Christopher. (Illus.). (J). (gr. 3-7). 1990. 15.95 (0-316-13930-0) Little.

Takedown: The Pursuit & Capture of Kevin Mitnick, America's Most Wanted Computer Outlaw - By the Man Who Did It. Tsutomu Shimomura & John Markoff. 336p. 1996. 24.95 (0-7868-6210-6) Hyperion.

*Takedown: The Pursuit & Capture of Kevin Mitnick, America's Most Wanted Computer Outlaws - by the Man Who Did It. Tsutomu Shimomura & John Markoff. 528p. 1996. mass mkt. 5.99 (0-7868-8913-6) Hyperion.

Takelma Texts & Grammar, Vol. VIII. Ed. by Victor Golla. (Collected Works of Edward Sapir). 606p. (C). 1990. lib. bdg. 139.00 (3-11-012329-0) Mouton.

Taken: Inside the Alien-Human Abduction Agenda. Karla Turner. 288p. 1994. pap. 16.95 (0-9640899-0-4) Kelt Works.

*Taken at Gunpoint. Tina Knight & Roscoe Knight. 708p. (Orig.). 1996. pap. 10.00 (1-883893-45-3) WinePress Pub.

Taken at the Flood. Agatha Christie. 240p. 1984. pap. text ed. 5.50 (0-425-06803-X) Berkley Pub.

Taken at the Flood. John Gunther. (Illus.). 380p. 1990. reprint ed. lib. bdg. 29.95 (0-89966-729-5) Buccaneer Bks.

Taken by a Stranger. Lin Summerfield. LC 94-26335. 252p. 1995. 21.95 (0-8027-3194-5) Walker & Co.

Taken by Storm. Sandra Field. (Presents Ser.). 1993. pap. 2.89 (0-373-11557-1, 1-11557-5) Harlequin Bks.

Taken by Storm. Danelle Harmon. 400p. (Orig.). 1995. mass mkt. 4.99 (0-380-78003-8) Avon.

Taken by Storm. large type ed. Sandra Field. 1992. reprint ed. lib. bdg. 18.95 (0-263-13130-0, Pub. by Mills & Boon UK) Thorndike Pr.

Taken by Storm: The Media, Public Opinion, & U. S. Foreign Policy in the Gulf War. Ed. by W. Lance Bennett & David L. Paletz. LC 93-45527. 341p. 1994. pap. 15.95 (0-226-04259-6) U Ch Pr.

Taken by Surprise: Travel After Fifty. Ester G. Mock. Ed. by Diane Parker. LC 90-50899. 130p. 1991. pap. 5.95 (0-88247-860-5) R & E Pubs.

Taken by Surprise: Travel after Sixty. Esther G. Mock. LC 91-61315. 128p. 1991. pap. 6.95 (0-88247-880-X) R & E Pubs.

Taken by You. Connie Mason. 1996. mass mkt. 5.50 (0-380-77998-6) Avon.

Taken Captive: A Japanese POW's Story. Ooka Shohei. Ed. & Tr. by Wayne P. Lammers from JPN. LC 95-35865. 352p. 1996. text ed. 27.95 (0-471-14285-9) Wiley.

Taken for Granted. large type ed. Caroline Anderson. 288p. 1995. 21.50 (0-263-14513-1, Pub. by M & B UK) Ulverscroft.

Taken for Granted: How Grant Thornton's Business Climate Index Leads States Astray. Corporation for Enterprise Development Staff et al. 101p. (Orig.). 1986. pap. 10.00 (0-9605804-3-3) Corp Ent Dev.

Taken for Pearls: New Poems. Tony Curtis. 64p. 1994. pap. 14.95 (1-85411-087-X, Pub. by Seren Bks UK) Dufour.

Taken In: American Gullibility & the Reagan Mythos. Stephen Ducat. (Illus.). 161p. 1988. pap. 12.95 (0-943685-00-1) Life Sci Pr.

Taken in Marriage. Thomas Babe. 1979. pap. 5.25 (0-8222-1108-4) Dramatists Play.

Taken on Trust. Terry Waite. 1993. 24.95 (0-15-187849-8) HarBrace.

Taken on Trust. Terry Waite. 400p. 1994. mass mkt. 7.99 (0-7704-2615-8) Bantam.

Taken on Trust: An Autobiography. Terry Waite. LC 95-36417. 1995. pap. 15.00 (0-688-14384-9) Morrow.

Taken to Extremes: Education in the Far North. Frank Darnell & Anton Hoem. 320p. 1996. 39.90 (82-00-22588-7) Scandnvan Univ Pr.

*Taken to the Cleaners. Dolores Johnson. 1997. mass mkt. 5.50 (0-440-22370-9) Dell.

Taken to the Stage: The Education of an Actress. Mimi Kennedy. LC 96-22833. (Career Development Ser.). 272p. 1996. 24.95 (1-57525-024-1) Smith & Kraus.

*Takeoff. Delguidice. 1997. 20.00 (0-15-100331-9) HarBrace.

*Takeoff: Eight Experiences of Flying. Daniele Del Giudice & Joseph Farrell. LC 96-45987. 1997. 20.00 (0-15-100269-X) HarBrace.

Takeoffs & Landings. Leighton Collins. 1982. text ed. 19.95 (0-02-527240-3) Macmillan.

*Takeout Stakeout. Gallagher. (Mystery Files of Shelby Woo Ser.). (J). 1997. mass mkt. 3.99 (0-671-01152-9) PB.

Takeover. Stephen W. Frey. LC 95-9851. 389p. 1995. pap. 19.95 (0-525-93985-7, Dutton) NAL-Dutton.

Takeover. Stephen W. Frey. 1996. mass mkt. 6.99 (0-451-18478-5, Sig) NAL-Dutton.

Takeover. Stephen W. Frey. 1996. pap. 6.99 (0-451-18928-0, Sig) NAL-Dutton.

Takeover. Saburo Shiroyama. 1991. 12.95 (0-533-09463-1) Vantage.

*Takeover. Sam Volard. LC 96-32171. 225p. 1997. 37.95 (0-566-07728-0, Pub. by Gower UK) Ashgate Pub Co.

Takeover. large type ed. Stephen W. Frey. 484p. 1995. 24.95 (0-7838-1486-0) Thorndike Pr.

Takeover: How Euroman Changed the World, 2 vols. large type ed. Arthur Niehoff. LC 96-75697. Orig. Title: The Other Side of History. 231p. (Orig.). (C). 1996. pap. 13.95 (0-9643072-2-7) Hominid Pr.

Takeover Bids. Michael Pescod. 1989. write for info. (0-406-10369-0) MICHIE.

Takeovers, 3 vols., Set. Ed. by A. Cosh & A. Hughes. (International Library of Management). (Illus.). 1500p. 1996. text ed. 149.95 (1-85521-556-X, Pub. by Dartmth Pub UK) Ashgate Pub Co.

Takeovers: A Strategist's Manual for Business Combinations in the 1990s. 2nd ed. Ralph C. Ferrara et al. LC 93-17362. 550p. 1993. boxed 95.00 (1-56257-216-4) MICHIE.

Takeovers & Freezeouts, 5 vols., Set. Martin Lipton & Erica H. Steinberger. 2000p. 1978. 290.00 (0-317-01347-5, 00551) NY Law Pub.

Takeovers & the Public Interest: The Hume Report on Corporate Takeovers. Alan Peacock & Graham Bannock. (Aberdeen University Press Bks.). 156p. 1991. pap. text ed. 25.90 (0-08-041206-8, Pub. by Aberdeen U Pr) Macmillan.

*Takeovers Law & Strategy. Rodd Levy. 265p. 1996. pap. 85.00 (0-455-21398-4, Pub. by Cavendish UK) Gaunt.

Takeovers, Mergers, & the Regional Economy. Brian Ashcroft & James H. Love. (Scottish Industrial Policy Ser.). 256p. 1993. text ed. 65.00 (0-7486-0400-6, Pub. by Edinburgh U Pr UK) Col U Pr.

Takers River of Gold. Jerry Ahern & S. A. Ahern. 1985. mass mkt. 3.50 (0-373-62402-6) Harlequin Bks.

Takes One to Know One: An Alison Kaine Mystery. Kate Allen. LC 96-8841. 200p. (Orig.). 1996. pap. 10.95 (0-934678-74-X) New Victoria Pubs.

Takin' It to the Streets: A Sixties Reader. Ed. by Alexander Bloom & Winifred Breines. 656p. 1995. 47.00 (0-19-506623-5); pap. text ed. 20.95 (0-19-506624-3) OUP.

*Taking. Donald Beman. 368p. (Orig.). 1997. mass mkt. 4.99 (0-8439-4202-9) Dorchester Pub Co.

Taking: The Collected Social & Political Writings of Irving Layton, 1935-1977. Ed. & Intro. by Howard Aster. 244p. pap. 8.95 (0-88962-057-1) Mosaic.

Taking a Bath? Find Out Why Cutting of Genitals is Hygienic! Hard Facts & Myths on Female Circumcision. Lynda B. Ukemenam. (Illus.). 250p. (Orig.). (C). 1994. pap. text ed. 12.99 (1-885974-00-0) St Candid Hse.

Taking a Bite Out of Crime: The Impact of a National Prevention Campaign. Garrett J. O'Keefe et al. LC 96-25179. 176p. 1996. pap. 19.95 (0-8039-5989-3) Sage.

*Taking a Bite Out of Crime: The Impact of the National Citizens' Crime Prevention Media Campaign. Dennis P. Rosenbaum et al. 176p. 1996. 45.00 (0-8039-5988-5) Sage.

Taking a Chance on God: Liberating Theology for Gays, Lesbians, & Their Lovers, Families & Friends - With a New Preface. John J. McNeill. 288p. 1996. pap. 14.00 (0-8070-7945-6) Beacon Pr.

Taking a Chance on Love. Gina F. Wilkins. (Temptation Ser.: No. 392). 1992. mass mkt. 2.99 (0-373-25492-X, 1-25492-9) Harlequin Bks.

Taking a Look at Your Leadership Styles see How to be a More Effective Church Leader: A Special Edition for Pastors & Other Church Leaders

*Taking a New Tack on Nonpoint Water Pollution. 66p. 1995. pap. 14.00 (0-614-30377-X, S4) Terrene Inst.

Taking a Risk: An Historical & Hysterical Look at the Purveyors of Death, Doom, & Destruction. Robin Willis. 120p. (C). 1988. pap. 135.00 (0-948691-59-X, Pub. by Witherby & Co UK) St Mut.

Taking a Stand: A Guide to the Research Paper with Readings. Clark. (C). 1992. text ed. 28.95 (0-673-46027-4) Addson-Wesley Educ.

Taking a Stand: A Guide to the Researched Paper with Readings. 2nd ed. Irene L. Clark. (Illus.). 704p. (C). 1996. text ed. 30.50 (0-673-99509-7) Addson-Wesley Educ.

Taking a Stand: A Guide to the Researched Papers with Readings. 2nd ed. Clark. 752p. Date not set. teacher ed., pap. write for info. (0-673-99510-0) Addson-Wesley Educ.

Taking a Stand: Child Psychiatrists in Custody, Access & Disputed Adoption Cases. British Agencies for Adoption & Fostering Editors. (C). 1989. 39.00 (0-903534-55-X, Pub. by Brit Ag for Adopt & Fost UK) St Mut.

Taking a Stand: Essays in Honour of John Beckwith. Ed. by Timothy McGee. 320p. 1995. 65.00 (0-8020-0583-7) U of Toronto Pr.

Taking a Stand: The Clash of Leaders, Ideas & Strategies. Aaron Klieman. LC 90-44345. (American Zionism Ser.: Vol. 4). 300p. 1991. reprint ed. text ed. 35.00 (0-8240-7352-5) Garland.

Taking a Stand: The Story of the Ottumwa Brethren. Victor Knowles & William E. Paul. LC 96-21467. 1996. write for info. (0-89900-761-9) College Pr Pub.

Taking a Stand for God. Gregory R. Owyang. 226p. (Orig.). 1987. pap. 3.50 (0-945304-00-5) FCBC.

Taking a Stand on Banking. Helen P. Rogers. 64p. (Orig.). 1991. pap. 6.95 (0-915915-18-9) Wellington Pubns.

Taking a Stand on Civil Rights. Helen P. Rogers. LC 91-66842. 80p. (Orig.). 1991. pap. 6.95 (0-915915-19-7) Wellington Pubns.

Taking a Stand on Education. Helen P. Rogers. LC 91-67469. 80p. (Orig.). 1991. pap. text ed. 6.95 (0-915915-11-1) Wellington Pubns.

Taking a Stand on Health Care. Helen P. Rogers. LC 91-75100. 64p. (Orig.). 1991. pap. 6.95 (0-915915-08-1) Wellington Pubns.

Taking a Stand on Housing. Helen P. Rogers. LC 91-75106. 64p. (Orig.). 1991. pap. 6.95 (0-915915-15-4) Wellington Pubns.

Taking a Stand on Our National Debt. Helen P. Rogers. LC 91-66841. 128p. (Orig.). 1991. pap. 6.95 (0-915915-10-3) Wellington Pubns.

Taking a Stand on Poverty. Helen P. Rogers. LC 91-67468. 96p. (Orig.). 1991. pap. 6.95 (0-915915-17-0) Wellington Pubns.

Taking a Stand on Regulation. Helen P. Rogers. LC 91-75101. 96p. (Orig.). 1991. pap. 6.95 (0-915915-13-8) Wellington Pubns.

Taking a Stand on Taxes. Helen P. Rogers. 90p. (Orig.). 1991. pap. 6.95 (0-915915-16-2) Wellington Pubns.

Taking a Stand on the Environment. Helen P. Rogers. LC 91-67467. 90p. (Orig.). 1991. pap. 6.95 (0-915915-12-X) Wellington Pubns.

Taking a Stand on U. S. Competitiveness. Helen P. Rogers. LC 91-67462. 128p. (Orig.). 1991. pap. 6.95 (0-915915-14-6) Wellington Pubns.

Taking a Walk Caminando. Rebecca Emberley. (Illus.). (SPA.). (J). (ps-3). 1994. 5.95 (0-316-23471-0) Little.

*Taking Action: An Environmental Guide for You & Your Community. Ed. by Adam Rogers. 224p. 1995. pap. text ed. 14.95 (92-807-1568-2) UN.

Taking Action: Working Together for Positive Change in Your Community. Constance Mungall & Elizabeth Amer. (Reference Ser.). (Illus.). 200p. (Orig.). 1992. Canadian Edition. pap. 10.95 (0-88908-532-3) Self-Counsel Pr.

Taking Action: Writing, Reading, Speaking & Listening Through Simulation Games. Lynn Q. Troyka & Jerrold Nudelman. (Illus.). 176p. (C). 1975. pap. text ed. 27.20 (0-13-882571-8) P-H.

*Taking Action to Reduce Poverty in Sub-Saharan Africa. LC 96-32180. (Development in Practice Ser.). 168p. 1997. 20.00 (0-8213-3698-3, 13698) World Bank.

Taking Active Charge of Your Life: Facilitator's Manual. Ed Harmon & Marge Jarmin. (Illus.). 149p. (J). (gr. 5-12). 1987. reprint ed. pap. 175.00 incl. flmstrp, vhs (0-918588-09-X, 401) Barksdale Foun.

Taking Active Charge of Your Life Kit. Ed Harmon & Marge Jarmin. (Illus.). 149p. 1987. reprint ed. Incl. facilitator's manual & video or filmstrip. pap., vinyl bd. 175.00 incl. vhs (0-918588-25-1, 401) Barksdale Foun.

Taking Advantage of Media: A Manual for Parents & Teachers. Laurene K. Brown. 208p. 1986. 19.95 (0-7102-0402-7, RKP) Routledge.

Taking Advantage of Postscript. John F. Sherman. 336p. (C). 1992. spiral bd. write for info. (0-697-14032-6) Bus & Educ Tech.

Taking Ancient Mythology Economically. Morris Silver. LC 92-31192. 354p. 1992. 106.50 (90-04-09706-6) E J Brill.

Taking & Defending Depositions in Commercial Cases 1993. (Litigation & Administrative Practice Course Handbook, 1983-84 Ser.: Vol. 469). 375p. 1993. 70.00 (0-685-69736-3, H4-5161) PLI.

Taking & Enforcing Security in China, Vol. 1. 158p. 1993. 270.00 (962-7708-04-6, Pub. by Euromoney UK) Am Educ Systs.

Taking & Enforcing Security in China, Vol. 2. 205p. 1995. 270.00 (962-7708-29-1, Pub. by Euromoney UK) Am Educ Systs.

Taking Animals Seriously: Mental Life & Moral Status. David DeGrazia. 380p. (C). 1996. text ed. 59.95 (0-521-56140-X); pap. text ed. 18.95 (0-521-56760-2) Cambridge U Pr.

Taking Apart the Poco Poco: A Novel. Richard Francis. 1995. 21.00 (0-684-80337-2) S&S Trade.

Taking Asthma to Camp: A Fictional Story about Asthma Camp. Kim Gosselin. LC 95-79633. (Children's Asthma Ser.). (Illus.). 32p. (Orig.). (J). (gr. k-6). 1995. pap. 9.95 (0-9639449-2-4) JayJo Bks.

Taking Asthma to School. Kim Gosselin. (Special Kids in School Ser.: Vol. 2). (Illus.). 24p. (J). (gr. k-6). 1995. pap. 9.95 (0-9639449-1-6) JayJo Bks.

Taking Back America: The Revolution Begins. Michael W. Haga. LC 94-74475. 390p. (C). 1995. pap. 19.95 (1-881872-17-3) Acclaim Pub.

Taking Back Control of Your Life: Overcoming Poor Self Esteem, Put Downs & Victimization. Claire Stevens. LC 92-85233. (Illus.). 102p. (Orig.). 1993. pap. 12.95 (0-9635094-9-7) Sterling MA.

*Taking Back Dignity: How to Get Employment Stay Off Wellfare & Improve Your Life. Lawrence Edwards. (Illus.). 150p. (Orig.). 1998. pap. 19.95 (0-9658283-0-1, Bridge-C Suc) Bridge-C.

Taking Back My Life. Nancy Ziegenmeyer & Larkin Warren. 224p. 1993. mass mkt. 4.99 (0-380-72038-8) Avon.

Taking Back My Name. Maria M. Gillan. 20p. (Orig.). 1992. pap. 3.75 (0-614-14182-6) Lincoln Springs Pr.

*Taking Back My Yesterdays: Lessons in Forgiving & Moving Forward with Your Life. Linda H. Hollies. LC 97-25343. 176p. (Orig.). 1997. pap. 10.95 (0-8298-1208-3) Pilgrim OH.

Taking Back Our Neighborhoods: Building Communities That Work. Mary I. Wachter & Cynthia Tinsley. 244p. 1996. 19.95 (1-57749-015-0) Fairview Press.

Taking Back Our Streets: My Life Fighting Crime in America. Willie L. Williams & Bruce Henderson. 320p. 1996. 23.00 (0-684-80277-5) S&S Trade.

Taking Back Tomorrow: A School Leader's Guide to Violence, Security & Safeguarding Our School Children. Thomas S. Shannon. 174p. (Orig.). 1995. pap. 14.95 (0-88364-190-9) Natl Sch Boards.

Taking Big Bucks: Solving the Whitetail Riddle. Ed Wolff. (Illus.). 176p. 1987. 17.95 (0-912299-25-8); pap. 12.95 (0-685-18746-2) Stoneydale Pr Pub.

Taking Books to Heart: How to Develop a Love of Reading in Your Child - For Parents of Children 2 to 9. Paul Copperman. LC 86-7923. 288p. 1986. pap. 10.95 (0-201-05717-4) Addison-Wesley.

Taking Breaks. Barbara L. McCombs & Linda Brannan. (Skills for Job Success Ser.). (Illus.). 32p. (Orig.). 1990. student ed., pap. 4.95 (1-56119-041-1) Educ Pr MD.

Taking Breaks. Barbara L. McCombs & Linda Brannan. (Skills for Job Success Ser.). (Illus.). 32p. (Orig.). (YA). (gr. 7-12). 1990. teacher ed. 1.95 (1-56119-042-X); disk 39.95 (1-56119-121-3) Educ Pr MD.

Taking Breaks, Set. Barbara L. McCombs & Linda Brannan. (Skills for Job Success Ser.). (Illus.). 32p. (Orig.). (YA). (gr. 7-12). 1990. student ed., teacher ed. 44.95 (1-56119-079-9) Educ Pr MD.

Taking Care: Medication Management for Older People. rev. ed. Justin L. Faherty. 1994. pap. 0.50 (0-89230-128-7) Do It Now.

Taking Care: Monitoring Power Dynamics & Relational Boundaries in Pastoral Care & Counseling. Carrie Doehring. 192p. (Orig.). 1995. pap. 16.95 (0-687-35934-1) Abingdon.

Taking Care: Premium Edition. Random House Staff. 1997. pap. write for info. (0-679-77795-4) Random.

Taking Care: Self-Care for 100 Common Symptons & 25 Long-Term Ailments. Random House Staff. LC 96-41153. 1997. pap. 12.00 (0-679-77794-6) Random.

Taking Care: Short Stories. Joy Williams. 1985. pap. 11.00 (0-394-72912-9, Vin) Random.

Taking Care: The Legacy of Soma Weiss, Eugene Stead, and Paul Beeson. William Hollingsworth. (Illus.). 331p. 1994. pap. 16.00 (1-57087-038-1) Prof Pr NC.

Taking Care: Understanding & Encouraging Self-Protective Behavior. Ed. by Neil Weinstein. (Illus.). 320p. 1987. text ed. 64.95 (0-521-32435-1) Cambridge U Pr.

Taking Care of Aging Family Members: A Practical Guide. enl. rev. ed. Wendy Lustbader & Nancy R. Hooyman. LC 93-24322. 322p. 1993. pap. 17.95 (0-02-919518-7, Free Press) Free Pr.

Taking Care of Aging Family Members: A Practical Guide. 2nd enl. rev. ed. Wendy Lustbader & Nancy R. Hooyman. LC 93-24322. 322p. 1993. 24.95 (0-02-919517-9, Free Press) Free Pr.

*Taking Care of Baby. Joanna Cole. (J). Date not set. lib. bdg. write for info. (0-688-13898-5, Morrow Junior) Morrow.

*Taking Care of Baby. Joanna Cole. (J). 0009. write for info. (0-688-13897-7, Morrow Junior) Morrow.

Taking Care of Business: How to Become More Efficient & Effective Using ISO 9000. Greg Hutchins. 256p. 1995. text ed. 27.50 (0-471-13204-7) Wiley.

Taking Care of Business: One Hundred One Ways to Keep Your Customers Coming Back (Without Whining, Groveling or Giving Away the Store) 2nd ed. Ron Zemke & Dick Schaaf. 127p. 1991. 14.97 (0-943210-07-0) Lakewood Pubns.

Taking Care of Business: Quality Lessons from the Corner Office to the Factory Floor. Greg Hutchins. LC 93-61780. 224p. 1994. 24.00 (0-939246-58-9, TM 7712) Wiley.

Taking Care of Business: The Dictionary of Contemporary Business Terms. Ed. by Donald L. Caruth & Steven A. Stovall. 330p. 1996. pap. 14.95 (0-8442-0902-3) NTC Pub Grp.

Taking Care of Caregivers: For Families & Others Who Care for People with Alzheimer's Disease & Other Forms of Dementia. D. Jeanne Roberts. (Illus.). 200p. (Orig.). 1991. pap. 14.95 (0-923521-09-7) Bull Pub.

*Taking Care of Dad (After All This, I End up with Alzheimer's) A True Life Story. Ann M. Longobardi. 108p. (Orig.). 1997. mass mkt. 4.99 (1-55237-288-X, Pub. by Comnwlth Pub CN) Partners Pubs Grp.

Taking Care of Me: (So I Can Take Care of Others) Barbara Carlson et al. LC 94-23012. (Tools for Everyday Parenting Ser.). (Illus.). 104p. (Orig.). 1997. lib. bdg. 18.95 (1-884734-03-0) Parenting Pr.

Taking Care of Me: (So I Can Take Care of Others) Glo Wellman et al. LC 94-23012. (Tools for Everyday Parenting Ser.). (Illus.). 104p. (Orig.). 1997. pap. 9.95 (1-884734-02-2) Parenting Pr.

*Taking Care of Me: The Habits of Happiness. Mary K. Mueller. 186p. (Orig.). 1997. pap. 12.95 (0-9654372-0-5) Insight Inc.

Taking Care of Mommy. Paula Linden & Susan Gross. (Family Bk. Ser.). 239p. 1983. pap. 7.95 (0-318-19491-0) M E Pinkham.

Taking Care of Mrs. Carroll. Paul Monette. (Stonewall Inn Editions Ser.). 288p. 1988. pap. 9.95 (0-312-01515-1) St Martin.

Taking Care of Our Own: A Year in the Life of a Small Hospital. Susan Garrett. 192p. 1995. pap. 10.95 (0-452-27271-8, Plume) NAL-Dutton.

*Taking Care of Residents: A Customer Service Approach. Pennie Myers & Don W. Nance. 61p. 1997. wbk. ed., pap. text ed. 25.00 (0-9620723-6-2) MAS.

Taking Care of Rosie. Lynn Salem & Josie Stewart. (Illus.). 8p. (J). (gr. k-1). 1992. pap. 3.50 (1-880612-05-4) Seedling Pubns.

Taking Care of Safety. Roger Saunders. 256p. 1991. pap. 83.00 (0-273-03507-X, Pub. by Pitman Pubng UK) St Mut.

Taking Care of Terrific. Lois Lowry. 176p. (J). (gr. 4-7). 1984. pap. 3.99 (0-440-48494-4, YB BDD) BDD Bks Young Read.

Taking Care of Terrific. Lois Lowry. LC 82-23331. 160p. (J). (gr. 5 up). 1983. 15.95 (0-395-34070-5) HM.

Taking Care of the Earth. Billy Goodman. (Golden Little Look-Look Bks.). (Illus.). 24p. (J). (ps-3). 1992. 1.49 (0-307-11532-1, 11532, Golden Books) Western Pub.

*Taking Care of the Earth: Kids in Action. Larry Pringle. LC 95-76352. (Illus.). (J). (gr. 2-5). 1997. pap. 7.95 (1-56397-634-X) Boyds Mills Pr.

Taking Care of the Earth: Kids in Action, Vol. 1. Laurence Pringle. LC 95-76352. 64p. (J). (gr. 4-8). 1996. 14.95 (1-56397-326-X) Boyds Mills Pr.

T

An Asterisk (*) at the beginning of an entry indicates that the title is appearing in BIP for the first time.

Taking Care of Today & Tomorrow: A Resource Guide for Health, Aging & Long-Term Care. George J. Pfeiffer & Louise Williams. LC 87-71285. (Illus.). 288p. 1989. pap. 14.95 (*0-9616506-1-3*) Ctr Corporate Hlth.

Taking Care of Yoki. Barbara Campbell. LC 85-46040. (Trophy Bk.). 160p. (J). (gr. 3-7). 1986. reprint ed. pap. 3.95 (*0-06-440173-1*, Trophy) HarpC Child Bks.

***Taking Care of Your Body & Its Fine Parts A to Z.** 2nd rev. ed. Anna M. Saccheri & S & H Publishing Staff. (Illus.). 27p. (Orig.). (J). (gr. 2-4). 1988. pap. 5.95 (*0-9656854-1-1*) S & H Pub.

Taking Care of Your Cat. Sheldon L. Gerstenfeld. LC 79-2338. (Illus.). 1979. pap. 9.95 (*0-201-03059-4*) Addison-Wesley.

Taking Care of Your Cat. Helen Piers. (Young Pet Owner's Guides Ser.). (Illus.). 32p. (YA). 1992. pap. 4.95 (*0-8120-4873-3*) Barron.

Taking Care of Your Child. rev. ed. Robert H. Pantell et al. 1990. pap. 15.95 (*0-201-08278-0*) Addison-Wesley.

***Taking Care of Your Child.** 5th ed. Pantell. 1998. pap. write for info. (*0-201-32815-1*) Addison-Wesley.

Taking Care of Your Child: A Parent's Guide to Complete Medical Care. 4th ed. Robert H. Pantell et al. (Illus.). 608p. 1993. pap. 17.95 (*0-201-63293-4*) Addison-Wesley.

Taking Care of Your Corporation Vol. 1: Director & Shareholder Meetings Made Easy. Tony Mancuso. 300p. 1994. pap. 26.95 (*0-87337-223-9*) Nolo Pr.

Taking Care of Your Corporation Vol. 2: Key Corporate Decisions Made Easy. Anthony Mancuso. 1995. pap. 39.95 incl. disk (*0-87337-276-X*) Nolo Pr.

Taking Care of Your Dog. Helen Piers. (Young Pet Owner's Guides Ser.). (Illus.). 32p. (YA). 1992. pap. 4.95 (*0-8120-4874-1*) Barron.

Taking Care of Your Gerbils: Young Pet Owner's Guides Ser. Helen Piers. Ed. by Matthew M. Vriends. LC 92-26959. 32p. (J). 1993. pap. 4.95 (*0-8120-1369-7*) Barron.

Taking Care of Your Goldfish. Helen Piers. Ed. by Matthew M. Vriends. LC 92-32170. (Young Pet Owner's Guides Ser.). 32p. (J). 1993. pap. 4.95 (*0-8120-1368-9*) Barron.

Taking Care of Your Guinea Pig. Helen Piers. (Young Pet Owner's Guides Ser.). 32p. (J). (gr. 3 up). 1993. pap. 4.95 (*0-8120-1367-0*) Barron.

Taking Care of Your Hamster. Helen Piers. (Young Pet Owner's Guides Ser.). 32p. (J). 1992. pap. 5.95 (*0-8120-4695-1*) Barron.

Taking Care of Your New Baby: A Guide to Infant Care. Jeanne W. Driscoll & Marsha Walker. (Illus.). 208p. Date not set. mass mkt. 5.95 (*0-89529-693-4*) Avery Pub.

Taking Care of Your Parakeet. Helen Piers. (Young Pet Owner's Guides Ser.). 32p. (J). (gr. 3 up). 1993. pap. 4.95 (*0-8120-1370-0*) Barron.

Taking Care of Your Rabbit. Helen Piers. (Young Pet Owner's Guides Ser.). 32p. (J). 1992. pap. 5.95 (*0-8120-4697-8*) Barron.

Taking Cash Out of the Closely Held Corporation. 4th ed. Lawrence C. Silton. 460p. 69.95 (*0-13-882713-3*, Busn) P-H.

Taking Cash Out of the Closely-Held Corporation: Taking Opportunities, Strategies & Techniques. 3rd ed. Lawrence C. Silton. LC 84-25249. 380p. 1984. text ed. 59.95 (*0-87624-536-X*, Inst Busn Plan) P-H.

***Taking Center Stage: Drama in America.** Amy K. Rathburn. 1997. pap. 16.95 (*0-472-08393-7*) U of Mich Pr.

***Taking Center Stage: Drama in America.** Amy K. Rathburn. (Orig.). 1997. teacher ed., pap. 14.95 (*0-472-08431-3*) U of Mich Pr.

Taking Center Stage: Feminism in Contemporary U. S. Drama. Janet Brown. LC 91-23952. 177p. 1991. 22.50 (*0-8108-2448-5*) Scarecrow.

Taking Chances. Kristin Hungenberg. 1993. 17.95 (*0-8034-9024-0*) Bouregy.

Taking Chances. Rebecca H. Lee. (Town Called Harmony Ser.). 288p. (Orig.). 1994. mass mkt. 4.99 (*0-7865-0022-0*) Diamond.

Taking Chances. Janelle Taylor. 544p. 1993. mass mkt. 4.50 (*0-8217-4259-0*, Zebra Kensgtn) Kensgtn Pub Corp.

***Taking Chances.** Laurie A. Ward. 195p. (Orig.). 1997. mass mkt. 4.99 (*1-55237-156-5*, Pub. by Comnwlth Pub CN) Partners Pubs Grp.

Taking Chances. Fredrick Burnham. 140p. 1994. reprint ed. 35.00 (*1-879356-32-5*) Wolfe Pub Co.

Taking Chances. Janelle Taylor. 560p. 1996. reprint ed. 24.00 (*0-7278-4737-6*) Severn Hse.

Taking Chances: Abortion & the Decision Not to Contracept. Kristin Luker. LC 74-22965. 200p. 1975. pap. 11.95 (*0-520-03594-1*) U CA Pr.

Taking Chances: Derrida, Psychoanalysis, & Literature. Ed. by Joseph H. Smith & William Kerrigan. LC 83-49198. 216p. 1984. 34.50 (*0-8018-3232-2*) Johns Hopkins.

Taking Chances: Derrida, Psychoanalysis, & Literature. Ed. by Joseph H. Smith & William Kerrigan. LC 83-49198. (Psychiatry & the Humanities Ser.: No. 7). 216p. 1988. reprint ed. pap. 13.95 (*0-8018-3749-9*) Johns Hopkins.

Taking Chances: Essays on Rational Choice. Jordan H. Sobel. (Cambridge Studies in Probability, Induction & Decision Theory). 368p. (C). 1994. text ed. 69.95 (*0-521-41635-3*) Cambridge U Pr.

Taking Chances, Making Choices. Helen Lawrence. 148p. (C). 1993. pap. text ed. write for info. (*1-884155-04-9*) Day & Nite Pub.

Taking Chances with Sex. Christine DeVault. 1990. pap. 3.95 (*0-941816-77-X*) ETR Assocs.

Taking Charge. C. G. Baker. LC 93-15038. (Karate Club Ser.: No. 7). 144p. (J). (gr. 3-7). 1993. pap. 3.50 (*0-14-036568-0*, Puffin) Puffin Bks.

***Taking Charge.** Beschloss. 1997. 30.00 (*0-684-80407-7*) S&S Trade.

Taking Charge. Created by Francine Pascal. (Sweet Valley Twins Ser.: No. 26). 112p. (Orig.). (J). 1989. pap. 3.25 (*0-553-15669-1*) Bantam.

Taking Charge: A Guide to People Management in Today's Public Sector. Alan Fowler. 98p. (C). 1993. pap. 35.00 (*0-614-03377-2*, Pub. by IPM Hse UK) St Mut.

***Taking Charge: A Parent & Teacher Guide to Loving Discipline.** 2nd ed. JoAnne Nordling. LC 91-50982. 300p. 1997. pap. 14.95 (*1-56875-189-3*, 189-3) R & E Pubs.

Taking Charge: A Personal Guide to Managing Projects & Priorities. Michael E. Feder. viii, 78p. (Orig.). 1989. 10.95 (*1-878542-04-4*, 12-0005) SkillPath Pubns.

Taking Charge: A Practical Guide for Leaders. 1995. lib. bdg. 251.99 (*0-8490-6740-5*) Gordon Pr.

Taking Charge: A Practical Guide for Leaders. Perry M. Smith. 234p. (Orig.). (C). 1995. pap. text ed. 40.00 (*0-7881-2068-9*) DIANE Pub.

***Taking Charge: A Woman's Guide to Fitness & Long Life.** Marcia Sheridan. Ed. by Jeanne Ewing. (Illus.). 320p. 1997. pap. 29.95 (*1-884690-00-9*) Owl Press.

Taking Charge: An Introduction to Electricity. Larry Schafer. (Illus.). 160p. 1992. pap. text ed. 18.95 (*0-87355-110-9*) Natl Sci Tchrs.

Taking Charge: Crisis Intervention in Criminal Justice. Anne T. Romano. LC 89-37995. (Contributions in Criminology & Penology Ser.: No. 25). 208p. 1990. text ed. 55.00 (*0-313-26890-8*, RTA/, Greenwood Pr) Greenwood.

Taking Charge: Every Woman's Action Guide to Personal, Political & Professional Success. Joan S. Lester. 250p. (Orig.). 1996. pap. 14.95 (*1-57324-052-4*) Conari Press.

Taking Charge: How Communities Are Planning Their Futures. Ronald L. Thomas et al. (Special Report Ser.). 86p. (Orig.). 1988. pap. text ed. 29.95 (*0-87326-935-7*) Intl City-Cnty Mgt.

Taking Charge: How to Coach Yourself to Quality Living. Charlene Bell. (Illus.). 242p. (Orig.). 1992. pap. 14.95 (*0-9624320-0-8*) Sunburst IA.

Taking Charge: How to Master the Eight Most Common Fears of Long-Term Illness. Irene Pollin & Susan K. Golant. 288p. 1996. pap. 14.00 (*0-8129-2700-1*, Times Bks) Random.

Taking Charge: Making the Right Choices. 2nd ed. Perry M. Smith. LC 88-16960. (Illus.). 280p. (Orig.). pap. 12.95 (*0-89529-522-9*) Avery Pub.

Taking Charge: Management & Marketing for the Media Arts. Ed. by Evelyn Goldstein et al. 165p. 1986. pap. 27.50 (*0-915339-01-3*) Media All.

***Taking Charge: Managing Life's Struggles.** Marilyn Kielbasa & Michael Theisen. Ed. by Thomas Zanzig. (Horizons Ser.: Level II, Minicourse 4). (Illus.). 80p. (Orig.). (YA). (gr. 10-11). 1996. student ed., pap. text ed. 9.95 (*0-88489-382-0*) St Marys.

Taking Charge: Mastering the Eight Fears of Chronic Illness. Irene Pollin & Susan K. Golant. LC 93-29434. 1994. 23.00 (*0-8129-2258-1*, Times Bks) Random.

Taking Charge: Nursing, Suffrage, & Feminism in America, 1873-1920. Sandra B. Lewenson. LC 93-11137. (Development of American Feminism Ser.: Vol. 1). 368p. 1993. text ed. 60.00 (*0-8240-6897-1*) Garland.

Taking Charge: State Action on School Reform in the 1980s. Denis P. Doyle et al. 150p. (Orig.). (C). 1991. pap. text ed. 18.50 (*1-55813-038-1*) Hudson Instit IN.

Taking Charge: Strategic Leadership in the Middle Game. Stephen A. Stumpf & Thomas P. Mullen. 240p. 1991. text ed. write for info. (*0-13-851999-4*) P-H.

Taking Charge: Survival Skills for the Take Charge Nurse. Biggers & Vivian. 32p. (gr. 13). 1996. pap. text ed. 129.95 (*0-8151-1297-1*) Mosby Yr Bk.

Taking Charge: Teenagers Talk about Life & Physical Disabilities. Kay H. Kriegsman et al. (Illus.). 186p. (YA). (gr. 7-12). 1992. pap. 14.95 (*0-933149-46-8*) Woodbine House.

Taking Charge: The Electric Automobile in America. Michael B. Schiffer. LC 93-49483. (Illus.). 240p. 1994. 24.95 (*1-56098-355-8*) Smithsonian.

Taking Charge: Time Management for Personal & Professional Productivity. Eric W. Skopec & Laree Kiely. (Illus.). 208p. 1991. pap. 22.95 (*0-201-55039-3*) Addison-Wesley.

Taking Charge: 236 Proven Principles of Effective Leadership. Byrd Buggett. LC 95-39699. 128p. 1995. 12.95 (*1-55853-358-3*) Rutledge Hill Pr.

Taking Charge & Letting Go: A Breakthrough Strategy for Creating & Managing the Horizontal Company. Bert A. Spector. LC 95-3609. 1995. 24.50 (*0-02-930385-0*, Free Press) Free Pr.

Taking Charge of ADHD: The Complete, Authoritative Guide for Parents. Russell A. Barkley. LC 95-37424. 302p. 1995. pap. text ed. 16.95 (*0-89862-099-6*) Guilford Pr.

Taking Charge of Change. Shirley M. Hord et al. LC 87-70644. 98p. 1987. pap. text ed. 10.00 (*0-87120-144-5*, 611-87022) Assn Supervision.

***Taking Charge of Change.** Smith. 1997. pap. 13.00 (*0-201-91604-5*) Addison-Wesley.

Taking Charge of Change: Ten Principles for Managing People & Performance. Douglas K. Smith. LC 95-32314. 304p. 1996. 25.00 (*0-201-48408-0*) Addison-Wesley.

Taking Charge of Infertility. Patricia I. Johnston. LC 93-44146. 272p. 1994. 21.95 (*0-944934-07-2*) Perspect Indiana.

Taking Charge of Infertility. Patricia I. Johnston. LC 93-44146. 272p. 1995. pap. 14.00 (*0-944934-08-0*) Perspect Indiana.

Taking Charge of Manufacturing: How Companies Are Combining Technological & Organizational Innovations to Compete Successfully. John E. Ettlie. LC 87-46333. (Management Ser.). 213p. 32.95 (*1-55542-086-9*) Jossey-Bass.

***Taking Charge of Menopause Workbook.** Robert M. Dosh et al. 195p. (Orig.). 1997. pap. 17.95 (*1-57224-060-1*) New Harbinger.

Taking Charge of My Life: An Anthology of Writing by New Writers. Ed. by Literacy Volunteers of New York City Staff. (New Writers' Voices Ser.). 64p. (Orig.). 1991. pap. text ed. 3.50 (*0-929631-37-4*, Signal Hill) New Readers.

Taking Charge of My Life: Choices, Changes & Me. Ed Harmon & Marge Jarmin. LC 88-988. (Illus.). 184p. (Orig.). (YA). (gr. 5-12). 1988. pap. 9.95 (*0-918588-10-3*, 410) Barksdale Foun.

Taking Charge of My Life: Personal Essays by Today's College Students. 1993. pap. text ed. 2.00 (*0-944210-62-7*) Townsend NJ.

***Taking Charge of My Mind & Body: A Girls' Guide to Outsmarting Alcohol, Drug, Smoking, & Eating Problems.** Gladys Folkers & Jeanne Engelmann. Ed. by Elizabeth Verdick. LC 96-46732. (Illus.). 208p. (Orig.). (J). 1997. pap. 13.95 (*1-57542-015-5*) Free Spirit Pub.

Taking Charge of Organizational Conflict: A Guide to Handling the Demands of Human Interactions. David Cowan. Ed. by Dianne Schilling. 165p. (Orig.). 1995. teacher ed., pap. 14.95 (*1-56499-019-2*) Innerchoice Pub.

Taking Charge of Your Career Direction, Vols. I-III. 3rd ed. Robert D. Lock. 1996. teacher ed. write for info. (*0-534-34045-8*) Brooks-Cole.

Taking Charge of Your Career Direction: Career Planning Guide, Bk. 1. 2nd ed. Robert D. Lock. LC 91-17083. 400p. (C). 1992. pap. 18.75 (*0-534-13656-7*) Brooks-Cole.

Taking Charge of Your Career Direction: Career Planning Guide, Bk. I. 3rd ed. Robert D. Lock. LC 95-43468. (Counseling Ser.: Bk. 1). 350p. 1996. pap. 27.95 (*0-534-34000-8*) Brooks-Cole.

Taking Charge of Your Child's Education: Nine Steps to Becoming a Learning Ally. Terry Mallen. LC 94-72481. (Illus.). 200p. (Orig.). 1995. pap. 14.95 (*0-9642369-9-0*) Acumen Pr.

Taking Charge of Your Fertility: The Definitive Guide to Natural Birth Control & Pregnancy Achievement. Toni Weschler. LC 95-13496. (Illus.). 400p. 1995. pap. 22.00 (*0-06-095053-6*) HarpC.

Taking Charge of Your Life in a World Out of Control. Van Crouch. 160p. 1996. 9.99 (*1-56292-128-2*) Honor Bks OK.

Taking Charge of Your Medical Fate. Lawrence C. Horowitz. LC 88-2001. (Illus.). 288p. 1988. 18.95 (*0-394-56336-0*) Random.

Taking Charge of Your Smoking. Joyce D. Nash. 124p. (Orig.). 1981. student ed. 14.95 (*0-915950-50-2*) Bull Pub.

Taking Charge of Your Social Life. rev. ed. Eileen Gambrill & Cheryl Richey. (Illus.). 346p. 1988. reprint ed. 17.95 (*0-9619781-0-4*) Behavioral Options.

Taking Charge on the Job: Techniques for Assertive Management. Lyn Taetzsch. Ed. by Eileen Benson. 1978. 15.95 (*0-917386-22-1*) Exec Ent Pubns.

Taking Charge Through Home Schooling: Personal & Political Empowerment. M. Larry Kaseman & Susan D. Kaseman. LC 91-126496. 287p. (Orig.). 1991. pap. 12.95 (*0-9628365-0-8*) Koshkonong Pr.

Taking Charge/Managing Conflict. Joseph B. Stulberg. 175p. 27.95 (*0-669-14014-7*, Lexington) Jossey-Bass.

Taking Child Abuse Seriously. Violence Against Children Study Group Staff. 250p. (Orig.). (C). 1989. pap. 19.95 (*0-04-445322-1*) Routledge Chapman & Hall.

Taking Children Seriously. Richard Hubbard. 12.99 (*0-551-02291-4*) Zondervan.

Taking Christianity to China: Alabama Missionaries in the Middle Kingdom, 1850-1950. Wayne Flynt & Gerald W. Berkley. LC 96-12145. (Illus.). 384p. (C). 1997. text ed. 34.95 (*0-8173-0833-4*) U of Ala Pr.

***Taking Command.** John O. Moench. (Illus.). 495p. 1996. 34.95 (*1-877597-05-8*) Malia Enterprises.

Taking Command of Enable. 3rd rev. ed. Yvonne Johnson. (Command Ser.). 360p. 1985. reprint ed. pap. text ed. 21.95 (*0-937141-00-3*) Key Pubns KY.

Taking Command of Ventura on the IBM-PC. Gary Hart. Ed. by Yvonne Johnson. (Command Ser.). 1988. pap. 21.95 (*0-937141-02-X*) Key Pubns KY.

Taking Control. Dennis Daley & Judy Miller. 1993. pap. 12.95 (*1-55691-095-9*, 959) Learning Pubns.

***Taking Control.** Una-Mary Parker. 314p. 1997. pap. 11.95 (*0-7472-5139-8*, Pub. by Headline UK) Trafalgar.

Taking Control. Mary H. Ponce. LC 87-70272. 128p. (Orig.). 1987. pap. 9.50 (*0-934770-70-0*) Arte Publico.

***Taking Control: Autonomy in Language Learning.** V. Pemberton. 352p. (Orig.). 1996. pap. 52.50 (*962-209-407-4*, Pub. by Hong Kong Univ Pr HK) Coronet Bks.

Taking Control: Historical Adventure. rev. ed. Ann Love. 1996. reprint ed. pap. 5.00 (*0-88092-998-7*) Royal Fireworks.

Taking Control: Living with the Mitral Valve Prolapse Syndrome. Kristine A. Scordo. 198p. (Orig.). 1993. pap. 19.95 (*0-938100-99-8*) Camden Hse.

***Taking Control: Living with the Mitral Valve Prolapse Syndrome.** 2nd rev. ed. Kristine A. Scordo. (Illus.). 190p. (Orig.). pap. 20.00 (*0-9650689-0-0*) Kardinal Pubng.

Taking Control: Politics in the Information Age. Morley Winograd & Dudley Buffa. 288p. 1996. 25.00 (*0-8050-4489-2*) H Holt & Co.

Taking Control: Power & Education in First Nations Education. Celia Haig-Brown. 256p. 1994. pap. 24.95 (*0-7748-0493-9*, Pub. by U BC Pr) U of Wash Pr.

Taking Control: Vitalizing Education. Myles I. Friedman. LC 93-19090. 216p. 1993. text ed. 59.95 (*0-275-94199-X*, C4199, Praeger Pubs) Greenwood.

Taking Control of Arthritis. large type ed. Fred G. Kantrowitz. 578p. 1991. reprint ed. 21.95 (*1-56054-235-7*) Thorndike Pr.

Taking Control of Arthritis. large type ed. Fred G. Kantrowitz. 578p. 1992. reprint ed. pap. 15.95 (*1-56054-957-2*) Thorndike Pr.

Taking Control of Your Career & Quality Lifestyle: Taking Control of Your Ship on the Career Sea of Life. Robert E. Ripley & Marie J. Ripley. LC 93-70694. (Illus.). 191p. 1993. pap. 19.95 (*0-9621133-3-6*, B009) Carefree Pr.

Taking Control of Your Financial Future: Making Smart Investment Decisions With Stocks & Mutual Funds. Thomas E. O'Hara. LC 94-25001. 272p. 1994. text ed. 25.00 (*0-7863-0139-2*) Irwin Prof Pubng.

Taking Control of Your Headaches: How to Get the Treatment You Need. Paul N. Buckro et al. LC 95-9413. 180p. (Orig.). 1995. pap. 14.95 (*0-89862-787-7*) Guilford Pr.

***Taking Control of Your Life: A Gynecologist's Personal Guide.** James A. Schaller. LC 96-40108. 360p. 1997. 24.95 (*1-57733-018-8*); pap. 16.95 (*1-57733-004-8*) B Dolphin Pub.

Taking Control of Your Life: The Secrets of Successful Enterprising Women. Gail Blanke & Kathleen Walas. 1990. 17.95 (*0-942361-18-0*) MasterMedia Pub.

Taking Control of Your Office Records: A Managers Guide. Katherine Ascher. LC 83-6133. (Professional Librarian Ser.). 264p. 1986. 25.00 (*0-8161-1883-3*, Hall Reference) Macmillan.

***Taking Control of Your Thoughts.** Billy J. Daugherty. 32p. (Orig.). (YA). 1996. pap. 0.50 (*1-56267-059-X*) Victory Ctr OK.

Taking Control Process: Beyond Light Duty. Richard K. Pimentel et al. Ed. by Barbara Wexler & Anita L. Wright. 135p. (C). 1995. 89.00 (*0-942071-31-X*) M Wright & Assocs.

Taking Decisions. (Open Learning for Supervisory Management Ser.). 1986. pap. text ed. 19.50 (*0-08-070025-X*, Pergamon Pr) Elsevier.

Taking Depositions. James F. Cirrincione. 480p. 1994. pap. 38.50 (*0-934753-38-5*) LRP Pubns.

Taking Diabetes to School. Kim Gosselin. LC 93-80544. (Special Kids in School Ser.: Vol. 1). (Illus.). 24p. (J). (gr. k-6). 1994. pap. 9.95 (*0-9639449-0-8*) JayJo Bks.

Taking Discipleship Seriously: A Radical Biblical Approach. Tom Sine. 80p. 1985. pap. 9.00 (*0-8170-1085-8*) Judson.

Taking Dutch Further. (Hugo's Language Courses Ser.). 192p. 1994. pap. 7.95 (*0-85285-213-4*); audio 39.95 (*0-85285-214-2*) Hunter NJ.

***Taking Eden: Poems.** Robert Clinton. LC 97-5657. 80p. 1998. 20.95 (*1-889330-09-4*); pap. 12.95 (*1-889330-10-8*) Sarabande Bks.

Taking Education Seriously. John Wilson & Barbara Cowell. 180p. 1989. pap. 28.00 (*1-85000-539-7*, Falmer Pr) Taylor & Francis.

Taking Europe Seriously: The Rise of the EC. Simon Serfaty. 180p. 1992. text ed. 35.00 (*0-312-06231-1*) St Martin.

Taking Every Thought Captive. Alaine Pakkala. 112p. 1994. write for info. (*1-886461-32-5*) Lydia Press.

Taking Flight. Early. 1983. text ed. 48.00 (*0-15-331269-6*) HB Schl Dept.

***Taking Flight.** Shipman. 1998. 26.00 (*0-684-81131-6*) S&S Trade.

***Taking Flight.** Vicki Van Meter. 1999. pap. 4.99 (*0-14-037663-1*) Penguin.

Taking Flight. Lawrence Watt-Evans. (Orig.). 1993. mass mkt. 4.99 (*0-345-37715-X*, Del Rey) Ballantine.

***Taking Flight: A Book about Flight.** Scholastic Inc., Staff. (Magic School Bus Ser.). (J). 1997. pap. text ed. 2.99 (*0-590-73871-2*) Scholastic Inc.

Taking Flight: A Book of Story-Meditations. Anthony De Mello. 192p. 1990. pap. 10.95 (*0-385-41371-8*) Doubleday.

***Taking Flight: Education & Training for Aviation Careers.** Ed. by Janet S. Hansen & Clinton V. Oster. 192p. 1997. pap. text ed. 37.00 (*0-309-05676-4*) Natl Acad Pr.

Taking Flight: My Story. Vicki Van Meter & Dan Gutman. LC 94-44067. (Illus.). 96p. (J). 1995. pap. 14.99 (*0-670-86260-6*, Viking) Viking Penguin.

Taking Flight: Story of the Wright Brothers & Other Pioneers. Krensky. 1998. pap. 3.99 (*0-689-81224-8*) S&S Childrens.

Taking Flight: The Story of the Wright Brothers & Other Pioneers. Krensky. (J). 1998. 15.00 (*0-689-81225-6*) S&S Childrens.

Taking Freedom Too Seriously? An Essay on Analytic & Post-Analytic Political Philosophy. W. J. Norman. LC 91-9677. (Political Theory & Political Philosophy Ser.). 200p. 1991. text ed. 15.00 (*0-8153-0137-5*) Garland.

Taking French Further. (Hugo's Language Courses Ser.). 192p. 1994. pap. 7.95 (*0-85285-211-8*); audio 39.95 (*0-85285-212-6*) Hunter NJ.

Taking Fund Raising Seriously: Advancing the Practice & Profession of Raising Money. Ed. by Dwight F. Burlingame & Lamont J. Hulse. LC 91-18232. (Nonprofit Sector-Public Administration Ser.). 332p. text ed. 34.95 (*1-55542-388-4*) Jossey-Bass.

Taking Giving Seriously. Paul G. Schervish. Ed. by Patricia Dean & Lois Sherman. 104p. (Orig.). 1993. pap. 9.95 (*1-884354-00-9*) IN Univ Ctr.

Taking Glasnost Seriously: Toward an Open Soviet Union. Micheal Novak. LC 87-34895. 224p. 1988. pap. 9.75 (*0-8447-3642-2*) Am Enterprise.

T

Taking Good Care: A Handbook for Care Assistants. Jenyth Worsley. 144p. (C). 1989. 59.00 (0-86242-072-5, Pub. by Age Concern Eng UK) St Mut.

*Taking Heaven by Storm: Methodism & the Rise of Popular American Religion. John Wigger. (Religion in America). (Illus.). 320p. 1997. 55.00 (0-19-510452-8) OUP.

Taking Hold: My Journey into Blindness. Sally H. Alexander. LC 94-12302. (J). 1994. text ed. 14.95 (0-02-700402-3, Mac Bks Young Read) S&S Childrens.

*Taking Hold of Torah: Jewish Commitment & Community in America. Arnold M. Eisen. LC 97-1150. (Helen & Martin Schwartz Lectures in Jewish Civilization). 1997. write for info. (0-253-33314-8) Ind U Pr.

Taking Hole of the Future: The ABC's of Strategic Planning. Jean Wincek & Colleen O'Malley. (Illus.). 66p. (Orig.). 1995. pap. 11.00 (1-55833-148-4) Natl Cath Educ.

*Taking Humor Seriously in Children's Literature: Literature-Based Mini-Units & Humorous Books for Children, Ages 5-12. Patricia L. Roberts. LC 97-15547. (School Library Media Ser.: No. 11). 256p. 1996. 36.00 (0-8108-3209-7) Scarecrow.

Taking Humour Seriously. Jerry Palmer. LC 93-15323. 224p. (C). 1994. pap. 16.95 (0-415-10267-7) Routledge.

Taking Humour Seriously. Jerry Palmer. LC 93-15323. 224p. (C). (gr. 13). 1994. text ed. 62.95 (0-415-10266-9) Routledge.

Taking Initiative: The Nineteen Ninety Citizens' Movement to Raise California Alcohol Excise Taxes to Save Lives. Advocacy Institute Staff. 115p. 1992. pap. text ed. 15.00 (1-882215-03-6) Advocacy Inst.

Taking Issue. Ed. by Dan Garrett. (Drama Anthologies Ser.). (Illus.). 108p. (Orig.). (YA). 1990. pap. 15.00 (0-333-46709-4, Pub. by Macmillan Ed UK) Players Pr.

*Taking It. Michael Cadnum. 1997. pap. 3.99 (0-14-037570-8) Penguin.

Taking It. Michael Cadnum. 135p. (YA). (gr. 7 up). 1995. pap. 14.99 (0-670-86130-8) Viking Child Bks.

*Taking It All. large type ed. Sharon Kendrick. (Mills & Boon Large Print Ser.). 288p. 1997. 22.50 (0-263-15000-3) Ulverscroft.

Taking It Home: Stories from the Neighborhood. Tony Ardizzone. LC 95-11027. (Sunsinger Bks. - Illinois Short Fiction). 152p. 1996. 12.95 (0-252-06483-6) U of Ill Pr.

Taking It Like a Man: Suffering, Sexuality, & the War Poets: Brooke, Sassoon, Owen, Graves. Adrian Caesar. LC 92-30538. 1993. text ed. 69.95 (0-7190-3834-0, Pub. by Manchester Univ Pr UK) St Martin.

Taking It Lying Down: Sexuality & the Uncherished Mother. Frances Hudson & Bernard Ineichen. 228p. (C). 1992. text ed. 32.00 (0-8147-3484-7) NYU Pr.

*Taking It to the Streets: The Social Protest Theater of Luis Valdez & Amiri Baraka. Harry J. Elam, Jr. LC 96-45790. (Theater--Theory/Text/Performance Ser.). (C). 1997. 37.50 (0-472-10793-3) U of Mich Pr.

Taking Japan Seriously: A Confucian Perspective on Leading Economic Issues. Ronald Dore. LC 86-61030. x, 264p. 1987. 42.50 (0-8047-1350-2); pap. 14.95 (0-8047-1401-0) Stanford U Pr.

Taking Jesus Seriously. David Jackman. 9.99 (1-85792-066-X, Pub. by Christian Focus UK) Spring Arbor Dist.

Taking Judaism Personally. Judy Petsonik. 1996. 23.00 (0-02-925098-6, Free Press) Free Pr.

Taking Judiasm Personally. Judy Petsonik. 320p. 1996. 25.00 (0-684-82809-X) Free Pr.

Taking Laughter Seriously. John Morreall. LC 82-5858. 144p. (C). 1983. pap. 21.95 (0-87395-643-5); text ed. 64.50 (0-87395-642-7) State U NY Pr.

Taking Liberties. Enright & Morton. (Law in Context Ser.). 220p. (C). 1994. text ed. 60.00 (0-297-82029-X) Northwestern U Pr.

Taking Liberties. Duncan Forbes. 66p. 9400. pap. 12.95 (1-870612-27-2, Pub. by Enitha Pr UK) Dufour.

Taking Liberties: AIDS & Cultural Politics. Ed. by Erica Carter & Simon Watney. 240p. 1991. pap. 14.95 (1-85242-147-9) Serpents Tail.

Taking Liberties: Gay Men's Essays on Politics, Culture & Sex. Ed. by Michael Bronski. (Orig.). 1996. pap. 12.95 (1-56333-456-9, R Kasak Bks) Masquerade.

Taking Liberties: National Barriers to the Free Flow of Ideas. Elizabeth Hull. LC 89-22888. 173p. 1990. text ed. 45.00 (0-275-93043-2, C3043, Greenwood Pr) Greenwood.

*Taking Liberties & Into. Dave Carley. LC 93-228796. 1997. pap. text ed. 10.95 (0-88754-512-2, Pub. by Playwrights CN Pr CN) Theatre Comm.

Taking Life Seriously: A Study of the Argument of the Nicomachean Ethics. Francis Sparshott. (Toronto Studies in Philosophy). 479p. 1996. pap. 24.95 (0-8020-7179-1) U of Toronto Pr.

Taking Life Seriously: A Study of the Argument of the Nicomachean Ethics. Francis Sparshott. LC 93-94629. (Toronto Studies in Philosophy). 479p. (C). 1996. 60.00 (0-8020-2953-1) U of Toronto Pr.

Taking Light from Each Other. Jean Burden. (University of Central Florida Contemporary Poetry Ser.). 96p. (C). 1992. pap. 10.95 (0-8130-1114-0); lib. bdg. 19.95 (0-8130-1113-2) U Press Fla.

Taking Lives: Genocide & State Power. 3rd enl. ed. Irving L. Horowitz. LC 79-66341. 230p. (C). 1981. pap. 21.95 (0-87855-882-9) Transaction Pubs.

*Taking Lives: Genocide & State Power. 4th ed. Irving L. Horowitz. LC 96-32315. 1996. 44.95 (1-56000-308-1) Transaction Pubs.

Taking Lives: Genocide & State Power. 4th expanded rev. ed. Irving L. Horowitz. LC 96-32315. 256p. 1996. pap. text ed. 24.95 (1-56000-877-6) Transaction Pubs.

Taking Measures Across the American Landscape. James Corner. LC 96-1557. (Illus.). 208p. 1996. 45.00 (0-300-06566-3) Yale U Pr.

Taking Men Alive: Catching Men for Christ. Charles G. Trumbull. LC 90-41520. 1990. pap. 7.99 (0-8007-5375-5) Revell.

Taking Money Out of Your Corporation: Perfectly Legal Methods to Maximize Your Income. M. John Storey. LC 92-28508. 198p. 1993. text ed. 75.00 (0-471-58044-9); pap. text ed. 17.95 (0-471-58043-0) Wiley.

Taking Money Seriously. David E. Laidler. 200p. 1990. pap. 29.95 (0-262-12148-4) MIT Pr.

Taking More Birds. Don Carlisle & Dolph Adams. (Illus.). 160p. 1993. 19.95 (1-55821-231-0) Lyons & Burford.

Taking More Birds: A Practical Handbook for Success at Sporting Clays & Wing Shooting. Dan Carlisle & Dolph Adams. (Illus.). 160p. 1995. pap. 15.95 (1-55821-473-9, 24739) Lyons & Burford.

Taking My Cat to the Vet. Susan Kuklin. LC 88-5052. (Illus.). 32p. (J). (ps-k). 1988. lib. bdg. 13.95 (0-02-751233-9, Bradbury S&S) S&S Childrens.

Taking Names & Pointing Fingers. Staajabu & V. S. Chochezi. (Illus.). 128p. 1996. pap. 10.00 (0-9642340-3-3) Straight Out.

Taking Nature into Action: A Report to the Club of Rome. Van. 1995. 17.00 (0-387-94533-4) Spr-Verlag.

Taking Note: Improving Your Observational Notetaking. Brenda M. Power. (Orig.). (C). 1996. pap. text ed. 12.50 (1-57110-035-0) Stenhse Pubs.

Taking Notes in the Classroom: A Guide to Higher Grades, Preparation for Exams, Reduced Study Time, Less Stress. Elizabeth C. Kells. (Orig.). (YA). (gr. 10-12). 1993. pap. text ed. 7.95 (0-9634458-7-1) Pubs Northeast.

Taking Notice. Hacker. 1990. pap. 2.00 (0-918314-15-1) Out & Out.

Taking Notice. Marilyn Hacker. LC 79-28166. 128p. 1980. pap. 5.95 (0-394-73917-5) Knopf.

Taking of Evidence Abroad: Practical Handbook on the Operation of the Hauge Convention of 18 March 1970 on the Taking of Evidence Abroad in Civil or Commercial Matters. 126p. 1984. 38.00 (90-6215-112-4, Pub. by Maklu Uitgevers BE) Gaunt.

Taking of Evidence in International Arbitral Proceedings. Institute of International Business Law & Practice Staff. 175p. (Orig.). 1990. pap. text ed. 75.00 (92-842-0086-5, Pub. by ICC Pub SA FR) ICC Pub.

Taking of Hill 610: And Other Essays on Friendship. Paul N. McCloskey, Jr. 220p. 1992. 12.95 (0-9635186-0-7) Eaglet Bks.

Taking of Mariasburg. Julian F. Thompson. 288p. (YA). (gr. 7 up). 1988. pap. 12.95 (0-590-41247-7, Scholastic Hardcover) Scholastic Inc.

Taking of Room 114. Mel Glenn. LC 96-45545. 1997. pap. 16.99 (0-525-67548-5) NAL-Dutton.

Taking of the Waters. John Shannon. LC 93-72442. 404p. (Orig.). 1994. pap. 13.00 (0-9639050-1-5); disk 10.00 (0-9639050-2-3) J Brown Bks.

Taking Off. Bruce Bennett. LC 91-27165. 96p. (Orig.). 1992. pap. 10.00 (0-914061-26-7) Orchises Pr.

Taking Off: And Other Coming of Age Stories by American Teen Writers. Ed. by R. James Stahl & Kathryn Kulpa. LC 94-48919. (American Teen Writer Ser.). 144p. (Orig.). (YA). (gr. 7-12). 1996. pap. 9.75 (1-886427-02-X) Merlyns Pen.

Taking Off: Beginning Listening. T. Forest & J. Huizenga. (Illus.). 1989. pap. text ed. 14.79 (0-8013-0119-X, 75783); audio 47.51 (0-8013-0534-9, 78410) Longman.

Taking off: Planes Then & Now. Steven Otfinoski. LC 96-18677. (Here We Go! Ser.). 32p. (J). (gr. 1). 1997. lib. bdg. 14.95 (0-7614-0407-4, Benchmark NY) Marshall Cavendish.

*Taking off Quantities: Civil Engineering. Spain. (Illus.). 224p. (Orig.). 1995. pap. text ed. 29.00 (0-419-20400-8, E & FN Spon) Routledge Chapman & Hall.

Taking off the Blindfold. Gyeorgos C. Hatonn. (Phoenix Journals). 202p. 1994. pap. 6.00 (1-56935-038-8) Phoenix Source.

Taking on Death: A Daily Spiritual Program Through the Great & Holy Lenten Fast of the Orthodox Christian Church. Tasos Dimiris. (Illus.). 109p. (Orig.). 1995. student ed., pap. text ed. 37.95 (1-884090-08-7) Ecumenics Intl.

Taking on General Motors: A Case Study of the UAW Campaign to Keep GM Van Nuys Open. Eric Mann. (Illus.). 408p. (Orig.). (C). 1987. pap. 20.00 (0-89215-141-2) U Cal LA Indus Rel.

Taking on Goliath: Party Formation, Party System Change, & Democratization in Mexico. Kathleen Bruhn. LC 95-47061. (C). 1996. pap. 22.50 (0-271-01587-X); text ed. 55.00 (0-271-01586-1) Pa St U Pr.

Taking on the Heart of Christ: Meditations & Devotions. John H. Newman. 1990. pap. 5.95 (0-87193-276-8) Dimension Bks.

Taking on the World. Robert W. Merry. 1997. pap. 17.95 (0-14-014984-8) Viking Penguin.

Taking on the World: Joseph & Stewart Alsop, Guardians of the American Century. Robert W. Merry. LC 95-9445. 672p. 1996. pap. 34.95 (0-670-83868-3, Viking) Viking Penguin.

Taking Our Cities for God. John Dawson. LC 89-80822. 220p. 1989. pap. 8.99 (0-88419-241-5) Creation House.

Taking Our Photo. Pauline Cartwright. LC 92-31950. (Voyages Ser.). (Illus.). (J). 1993. 3.75 (0-383-03595-3) SRA McGraw.

*Taking Our Pulse: The Health of America's Women. Iris F. Litt. LC 97-9512. 1997. write for info. (0-8047-2828-3); pap. write for info. (0-8047-3137-3) Stanford U Pr.

Taking Our Time: Feminist Perspectives on Temporality. Frieda J. Forman & Caoran Sowton. (Athene Ser.). (Illus.). 256p. 1989. text ed. 40.00 (0-08-036478-0); pap. text ed. 15.95 (0-08-036477-2) Elsevier.

Taking Our Time: Feminist Perspectives on Temporality. Ed. by Frieda J. Forman & Caoran Sowton. (Athene Ser.). 210p. (C). 1989. pap. text ed. 16.95 (0-8077-6219-9) Tchrs Coll.

Taking Our Time: Remaking the Temporal Order. Mike Donaldson. 216p. (C). 1996. pap. 24.95 (1-875560-64-5, Pub. by Univ of West Aust Pr AT) Intl Spec Bk.

Taking Out Moscow: Talking about Trident. Church of Scotland Society, Religion & Technology Project Staff. 106p. (C). 1992. pap. 32.00 (0-86153-148-5, Pub. by St Andrew UK) St Mut.

Taking Out the Trash: A No-Nonsense Guide to Recycling. Jennifer Carless. LC 91-43855. 249p. (Orig.). 1992. 35.00 (1-55963-171-6); pap. 16.00 (1-55963-170-8) Island Pr.

Taking Over. large type ed. S. Lowe & A. Ince. 1990. 25.99 (0-7089-2307-0) Ulverscroft.

Taking Part: A Twentieth-Century Life. Robert Josephy. LC 92-44857. (Singular Lives: The Iowa Series in North American Autobiography). (Illus.). 239p. 1993. 22.95 (0-87745-412-4) U of Iowa Pr.

Taking Part in Community Care Planning: The Involvement of User Groups, Career Groups & Voluntary Groups. Averil Osborn. (C). 1991. 60.00 (0-946505-84-5, Pub. by Age Concern Eng UK) St Mut.

Taking Parts: Ingredients for Leadership, Participation, & Empowerment. Mary J. Bona et al. Ed. by Eloise A. Buker et al. LC 93-45519. 284p. (Orig.). (C). 1994. pap. text ed. 34.00 (0-8191-9397-6) U Pr of Amer.

Taking Pictures. William R. Zwikl. LC 89-25161. (Illus.). 160p. 1989. text ed. 9.95 (0-930973-10-0) Canal Hist Tech.

Taking Pictures for Profit: The Complete Guide to Selling Your Work. Lee Frost. (Illus.). 128p. 1996. 24.95 (0-7153-0312-0, Pub. by D & C Pub UK) Sterling.

Taking Pictures of God: Meditations. Bruce T. Marshall. LC 96-612. 1996. pap. 7.00 (1-55896-341-3, Skinner Hse Bks) Unitarian Univ.

Taking Population Out of the Equation: Reformulating I Equals PAT. H. Patricia Hynes. LC 93-80310. (Illus.). 55p. (Orig.). 1993. pap. text ed. write for info. (0-9630083-1-5) Inst Women Tech.

Taking Population Seriously. Frances M. Lappe & Rachel Schurman. (Illus.). 90p. 1990. pap. 7.95 (0-935028-53-6) Inst Food & Develop.

Taking Property & Just Compensation: Lew & Economics Perspectives of the Takings Issue. Ed. by Nicholas Mercuro. (Recent Economic Thought Ser.). 240p. (C). 1992. lib. bdg. 96.50 (0-7923-9233-7) Kluwer Ac.

Taking Reform Seriously: Perspectives on Public Interest Liberalism. Michael W. McCann. LC 86-47647. 348p. 1986. pap. 18.95 (0-8014-9415-X) Cornell U Pr.

Taking Refuge: Lao Buddhists in North America. Penny Van Esterik. vii, 148p. (Orig.). 1993. pap. 15.95 (1-881044-04-1) ASU Prog SE Asian.

*Taking Responsibility. Branden. 1997. pap. 12.00 (0-684-83248-8, Fireside) S&S Trade.

Taking Responsibility. Brown & Keller. 1990. 4.95 (1-56456-102-X, 402X) W Gladden Found.

Taking Responsibility, 25 bks., Set. Brown & Keller. 1990. 57.75 (1-56456-103-8, 402) W Gladden Found.

Taking Responsibility: Adult & Continuing Education. Field. Date not set. pap. 12.95 (0-7453-0932-1, Pub. by Pluto Pr UK) LPC InBook.

Taking Responsibility: Art, Design & Performing Arts. Goulding. Date not set. pap. 12.95 (0-7453-0933-X, Pub. by Pluto Pr UK) LPC InBook.

Taking Responsibility: Art, Design & Performing Arts. Ken Goulding. LC 94-33849. (Environmental Agenda Ser.). write for info. (0-7453-0093-6) Westview.

Taking Responsibility: Humanities & Social Sciences. Wylie. Date not set. pap. 12.95 (0-7453-0926-7, Pub. by Pluto Pr UK) LPC InBook.

Taking Responsibility: Overview. Khan. pap. 12.95 (0-614-08712-0, Pub. by Pluto Pr UK); pap. 5.95 (0-7453-1027-3, Pub. by Pluto Pr UK) LPC InBook.

Taking Responsibility: Rural Environment. Peters. Date not set. pap. 12.95 (0-7453-0935-6, Pub. by Pluto Pr UK) LPC InBook.

Taking Responsibility: Science & Technology. Blackmore. Date not set. pap. 12.95 (0-7453-0927-5, Pub. by Pluto Pr UK) LPC InBook.

Taking Responsibility: Self-Reliance & the Accountable Life. Nathaniel Branden. LC 95-36640. 256p. 1996. 22.00 (0-684-81083-2) S&S Trade.

Taking Responsibility: Sport, Leisure, Hospitality & Tourism. Roberts. Date not set. pap. 12.95 (0-7453-0931-3, Pub. by Pluto Pr UK) LPC InBook.

Taking Responsiblity: Built Environment. Samantha Woods. LC 94-35060. (Environmental Agenda Ser.). (C). pap. 12.95 (0-7453-0930-5, Pub. by Pluto Pr UK) LPC InBook.

Taking Responsibility: Engineering. Duffell. (C). pap. 12.95 (0-7453-0928-3, Pub. by Pluto Pr UK) LPC InBook.

Taking Responsibility: Health & Wellbeing. Barwise. LC 94-33850. (Environmental Agenda Ser.). (C). pap. 12.95 (0-7453-0929-1, Pub. by Pluto Pr UK) LPC InBook.

Taking Responsibility: Information Technology. Richard Ennals. (Environmental Agenda Ser.). (C). pap. 12.95 (0-7453-0934-8, Pub. by Pluto Pr UK) LPC InBook.

Taking Responsibility: Management & Business. Roome. LC 94-33847. (Environmental Agenda Ser.). (C). pap. 12.95 (0-7453-0925-9, Pub. by Pluto Pr UK) LPC InBook.

Taking Rights Seriously. Ronald D. Dworkin. 386p. 1977. 34.50 (0-674-86710-6) HUP.

Taking Rights Seriously. Ronald D. Dworkin. 386p. 1978. pap. 15.95 (0-674-86711-4) HUP.

*Taking Risks. Sharon Kendrick. (Mills & Boon Large Print Ser.). 288p. 1997. 22.50 (0-263-14936-6) Ulverscroft.

Taking Risks: The Management of Uncertainty. Kenneth R. MacCrimmon & Donald A. Wehrung. (Illus.). 384p. 1988. pap. 16.95 (0-02-919563-2, Free Press) Free Pr.

*Taking Root: The Origins of the Canadian Jewish Community. Gerald Tulchinksy. (Illus.). 368p. 1997. pap. 19.95 (0-7737-5862-3, Pub. by Stoddart Pubng CN) Genl Dist Srvs.

Taking Root: The Origins of the Canadian Jewish Community. Gerald J. Tulchinsky. LC 92-28210. (Brandeis Series in American Jewish History, Culture, & Life). (Illus.). 367p. 1993. 40.00 (0-87451-609-9) U Pr of New Eng.

Taking Root: The Workshop Center at City College. Beth Alberty et al. 45p. (Orig.). (C). 1983. pap. 3.00 (0-317-45084-0) City Coll Wk.

Taking Root to Fly: Articles on Functional Anatomy. 3rd rev. ed. Irene Dowd. (Illus.). 96p. (C). 1995. pap. text ed. 16.00 (0-9645805-0-0) I Dowd.

Taking Scarlet As a Real Colour. Evelyn Conlon. 176p. 9300. pap. 13.95 (0-85640-501-9, Pub. by Blackstaff Pr IE) Dufour.

Taking Security Interests in Personal Property. Edwin E. Smith. LC 92-60337. 131p. 1992. pap. text ed. 45.00 (0-944490-46-8) Mass CLE.

Taking Security Interests in Personal Property: Spring 1993 Action Guide. Morris W. Hirsch. Ed. by Kay E. Tindel. 85p. 1993. pap. text ed. 47.00 (0-88124-629-8, BU-11163) Cont Ed Bar-CA.

Taking Seizure Disorders to School: A Story about Epilepsy. Kim Gosselin. LC 95-81787. (Special Kids in School Ser.: Vol. 3). (Illus.). 32p. (Orig.). (J). (gr. k-6). 1996. pap. 9.95 (0-9639449-3-2) JayJo Bks.

Taking Sides. Stephen Green. 370p. 1987. pap. 9.95 (0-915597-54-3) Amana Bks.

*Taking Sides. Ronald Harwood. 1997. pap. 5.25 (0-8222-1566-7) Dramatists Play.

*Taking Sides. Ronald Harwood. 1996. pap. 9.95 (0-571-17772-7) Faber & Faber.

Taking Sides. Gary Soto. 144p. (J). (gr. 3-7). 1991. 16.00 (0-15-284076-1, HB Juv Bks) HarBrace.

Taking Sides. Gary Soto. LC 91-11082. 144p. (J). (gr. 3-7). 1992. pap. 8.00 (0-15-284077-X) HarBrace.

*Taking Sides: A Speaking Text for Advanced & Intermediate Students. Kevin B. King. LC 96-61011. (Orig.). 1997. pap. 15.95 (0-472-08418-6) U of Mich Pr.

*Taking Sides: A Speaking Text for Advanced & Intermediate Students. Kevin B. King. LC 96-61011. (Orig.). 1997. teacher ed. 16.95 (0-472-08422-4) U of Mich Pr.

*Taking Sides: Clashing Views on Controversial Bioethical Issues. 7th ed. Carol Levine. (C). 1997. per. write for info. (0-697-37535-8) Brown & Benchmark.

*Taking Sides: Clashing Views on Controversial Economic. 7th ed. Thomas R. Swartz & Frank J. Bonello. (C). 1997. text ed. write for info. (0-697-39265-1) Wm C Brown Pubs.

Taking Sides: Clashing Views on Controversial Economic Issues. 7th ed. Frank Bonello & Thomas R. Swartz. (C). 1996. 17.50 (0-256-23049-8) Irwin.

Taking Sides: Clashing Views on Controversial Economic Issues. 7th ed. Ed. by Thomas R. Swartz & Frank J. Bonello. LC 94-47618. (Illus.). 432p. (C). 1995. per. 13.95 (1-56134-329-3) Dushkin Pub.

*Taking Sides: Clashing Views on Controversial Educational Issues. 9th ed. James Noll. (C). 1997. per. write for info. (0-697-37534-X) Brown & Benchmark.

*Taking Sides: Clashing Views on Controversial Issues. 4th ed. Richard C. Monk. (C). 1997. text ed. write for info. (0-697-39263-5) Wm C Brown Pubs.

Taking Sides: Clashing Views on Controversial Issues. 5th ed. Robert T. Francoeur. 384p. (C). 1996. per. write for info. (0-697-31292-5) Wm C Brown Pubs.

Taking Sides: Clashing Views on Controversial Issues. 7th ed. John T. Rourke. 384p. (C). 1996. per. write for info. (0-697-31296-8) Wm C Brown Pubs.

*Taking Sides: Clashing Views on Controversial Issues. 7th ed. John T. Rourke. 384p. (C). 1997. text ed. write for info. (0-697-39277-5) Wm C Brown Pubs.

Taking Sides: Clashing Views on Controversial Issues in Business Ethics. 4th ed. Lisa H. Newton & Maureen M. Ford. 384p. (C). 1996. per. write for info. (0-697-31291-7) Wm C Brown Pubs.

Taking Sides: Clashing Views on Controversial Issues in Childhood & Society. Ed. by Robert L. DelCampo & Diana S. DelCampo. LC 95-121. 416p. (C). 1995. per. 13.95 (1-56134-333-1) Dushkin Pub.

*Taking Sides: Clashing Views on Controversial Issues in Drugs Society. 2nd ed. Raymond Goldberg. (C). 1997. text ed. write for info. (0-697-39264-3) Wm C Brown Pubs.

*Taking Sides: Clashing Views on Controversial Issues in Family & Personal Relationships. 3rd ed. Gloria W. Bird & Michael J. Sporakowski. (C). 1996. per. write for info. (0-697-35715-5) Wm C Brown Pubs.

*Taking Sides: Clashing Views on Controversial Issues in Family Personal Relationships. 3rd ed. Gloria W. Bird & Michael J. Sporakowski. (C). 1997. text ed. write for info. (0-697-39268-6) Wm C Brown Pubs.

*Taking Sides: Clashing Views on Controversial Issues in Health & Society. 2nd ed. Eileen L. Daniel. (C). 1997. text ed. write for info. (0-697-39269-4) Wm C Brown Pubs.

*Taking Sides: Clashing Views on Controversial Issues in Mass Media & Society. 4th ed. Ed. by Alison Alexander & Jarice Hanson. (Illus.). 368p. (C). 1996. per. 12.50 (0-697-35716-3) Dushkin Pub.

Taking Sides: Clashing Views on Controversial Issues in Race & Ethnicity. 2nd ed. Richard C. Monk. 384p. (C). 1996. per. write for info. (0-697-31294-1) Brown & Benchmark.

***Taking Sides: Clashing Views on Controversial Issues in Science, Technology, & Society.** 2nd ed. Thomas A. Easton. (C). 1997. text ed. write for info. (0-697-39275-9) Wm C Brown Pubs.

***Taking Sides: Clashing Views on Controversial Issues in Science, Technology & Society.** 2nd ed. Thomas A. Easton. (C). 1996. per. write for info. (0-697-36007-5) Wm C Brown Pubs.

***Taking Sides: Clashing Views on Controversial Legal Issues.** 7th ed. M. Ethan Katsh. (C). 1996. per. write for info. (0-697-35717-1) Wm C Brown Pubs.

***Taking Sides: Clashing Views on Controversial Moral Issues.** 5th ed. Stephen Satris. (C). 1997. text ed. write for info. (0-697-39272-4) Wm C Brown Pubs.

***Taking Sides: Clashing Views on Controversial Political Issues 9Th.** 10th ed. George McKenna & Stanley Feingold. (C). 1996. per. write for info. (0-697-35718-X) Wm C Brown Pubs.

Taking Sides: Clashing Views on Controversial Psychological Issues. 9th ed. Brent D. Slife. 384p. (C). 1996. per. write for info. (0-697-31293-3) Wm C Brown Pubs.

Taking Sides: Clashing Views on Controversial Social Issues. 6th ed. Kurt Finsterbusch & George McKenna. (C). 1990. per. write for info. (0-87967-858-5) Brown & Benchmark.

Taking Sides: Clashing Views on Controversial Social Issues. 9th ed. Kurt Finsterbusch & George McKenna. 384p. (C). 1996. per. write for info. (0-697-31295-X) Brown & Benchmark.

***Taking Sides: Clashing Views on Controversial Social Issues.** 9th ed. Kurt Finsterbusch & George Mckenna. 384p. (C). 1997. text ed. write for info. (0-697-39276-7) Wm C Brown Pubs.

Taking Sides: The Collected Social & Political Writings of Irving Layton, 1935-1977. Ed. & Intro. by Howard Aster. 244p. 1995. lib. bdg. 27.00 (0-8095-4589-6) Borgo Pr.

Taking Sides: The Fiction of John LeCarre. Tony Barley. LC 85-28434. 192p. 1986. 85.00 (0-335-15251-1, Open Univ Pr); pap. 32.00 (0-335-15252-X, Open Univ Pr) Taylor & Francis.

Taking Sides: The War at Home. rev. ed. Jerold M. Starr & Charles Di Benedetti. (Lessons of the Vietnam War Ser.). (Illus.). 32p. (C). 1991. pap. text ed. 5.00 (0-945919-07-7) Ctr Social Studies.

Taking Sides Library Index & Guide. 8th ed. 156p. (C). 1995. per. write for info. (0-697-31390-5) Brown & Benchmark.

Taking Sides Library Index & Guide. 8th ed. 156p. (C). 1995. text ed. write for info. (0-697-33492-9) Brown & Benchmark.

***Taking Sides Reference Library, 21 vols., Incl. tchr's. guide.** rev. ed. 7000p. (YA). (gr. 7 up). 1996. 389.00 (0-7172-7548-5) Grolier Educ.

Taking Soaps Seriously: The World of Guiding Light. Michael J. Intintoli. LC 83-27232. 208p. 1984. text ed. 37.50 (0-275-91738-X, C1738, Praeger Pubs) Greenwood.

Taking Society's Measure: A Personal History of Survey Research. Herbert Hyman. Ed. by Eleanor Singer. LC 90-46449. 256p. 1991. 39.95 (0-87154-395-8) Russell Sage.

***Taking Spanish Further.** Hugo. Date not set. pap. 7.95 (0-85285-273-8) Hunter NJ.

Taking Stock: A Larry McMurtry Casebook. Ed. & Intro. by Clay Reynolds. LC 88-43316. (Southwest Life & Letters Ser.). 448p. 1989. 26.95 (0-87074-291-4); pap. 15.95 (0-87074-261-2) SMU Press.

***Taking Stock: A Look at the Opportunities & Challenges Posed by Nuclear Inventories from the Cold War Era.** (Illus.). 190p. (Orig.). (C). 1997. pap. 50.00 (0-7881-3808-1) DIANE Pub.

***Taking Stock: A Soul's Journey Through Life, Death & the World of Investment.** unabridged ed. Michael R. Norwood. (Illus.). 295p. (Orig.). 1998. pap. 12.95 (0-911649-01-8) Global Pub GA.

Taking Stock: An Inventory of Who I Am & What I Want to Be. David P. Green. LC 95-71947. 128p. (Orig.). 1995. pap. 16.95 (1-886094-27-6) Chicago Spectrum.

Taking Stock: Animal Farming & the Environment. Alan B. Durning & Holly Brough. 70p. (Orig.). 1991. pap. 5.00 (1-878071-04-1) Worldwatch Inst.

Taking Stock: The North American Livestock Census. Donald E. Bixby et al. LC 93-47249. (Illus.). vii, 182p. (Orig.). 1994. pap. 16.95 (0-939923-35-1) M & W Pub Co.

Taking Stock: The Writing Process Movement in the Nineties. Ed. by Lad Tobin & Tom Newkirk. LC 94-20470. 287p. 1994. pap. text ed. 25.00 (0-86709-346-3, 0346) Boynton Cook Pubs.

Taking Stock: Tools for Teacher, Director, & Center Evaluation. Ed. by Roger Neugebauer. (Best of Exchange Ser.). (Illus.). 48p. (Orig.). (C). 1994. pap. 10.00 (0-942702-12-3) Child Care.

Taking Stock of Consequences: The Evaluation of a Dramatic Film about Teenage Pregnancy in an Educational Setting in Kenya. Richard J. Wray. 97p. 1991. text ed. 15.00 (0-936731-25-7) Devel Self Rel.

Taking Stock of Mortality Data. 79p. 1988. 18.00 (0-86688-187-5) Joint Comm Hlthcare.

Taking Students Abroad: A Complete Guide for Teachers. rev. ed. Maggie B. Cassidy. (Illus.). 176p. 1988. pap. text ed. 5.00 (0-86647-028-X) Pro Lingua.

Taking Successful Depositions in Commercial Cases. (Litigation & Administrative Practice Course Handbook, 1983-84 Ser.). 132p. 1992. pap. 35.00 (0-685-69498-4) PLI.

Taking Suffering Seriously: The Importance of Collective Human Rights. William F. Felice. (Series in Global Conflict & Peace Education). 253p. 1996. text ed. 57.50 (0-7914-3061-8) State U NY Pr.

Taking Suffering Seriously: The Importance of Collective Human Rights. William F. Felice. (SUNY Series in Global Conflict & Peace Education). 253p. 1996. pap. text ed. 19.95 (0-7914-3062-6) State U NY Pr.

Taking Tea: The Essential Guide to Brewing, Serving & Entertaining with Teas from Around the World. Andrea Israel. 144p. 1987. 19.95 (0-8021-1426-1, Grove) Grove-Atltic.

Taking Tea with Alice: Looking-Glass Tea Parties & Fanciful Victorian Teas. Diane Sedo & Dawn Gottlieb. (Illus.). 96p. 1997. 16.95 (0-446-91173-9) Warner Bks.

***Taking Tea with Clarice Cliff: A Celebration of Her Art Deco Teaware.** Leonard Griffin. (Illus.). 115p. 1996. 16.95 (1-85793-925-5, Pub. by Pavilion UK) Trafalgar.

***Taking Teaching Seriously: Meeting the Challenge of Instructional Improvement.** Michael B. Paulsen & Kenneth Feldman. Ed. by Jonathan D. Fife. LC 96-76558. (ASHE-ERIC Higher Education Reports). (Illus.). 188p. (Orig.). 1996. pap. 21.75 (1-878380-66-4) GWU Grad Schl E&HD.

***Taking Technology to Market.** Roger E. Levien. 1997. pap. text ed. 12.95 (1-56052-439-1) Crisp Pubns.

Taking Terri Mueller. Norma F. Mazer. 192p. (YA). (gr. 8 up). 1981. mass mkt. 4.50 (0-380-79004-1, Flare) Avon.

Taking the American Medical Boards Beyond the No. 2 Pencil. Zafar Y. Ibrahim. Ed. by Debra D. Richards. 51p. 1990. lib. bdg. 12.95 (0-9626615-0-3) Overseas Pub.

***Taking the Anxiety Out of Taking Tests: A Step-by-Step Guide.** Susan Johnson. LC 96-71157. 184p. (Orig.). 1997. pap. 12.95 (1-57224-068-7) New Harbinger.

***Taking the Back Road Home.** Louis D. Brodsky. LC 97-8183. 76p. 1997. spiral bd. 9.95 (1-56809-038-2) Time Being Bks.

Taking the Bible Seriously: Honest Differences about Biblical Interpretation. J. Benton White. 192p. (Orig.). 1993. pap. 13.00 (0-664-25452-7) Westminster John Knox.

Taking the Biscuit. large type ed. Faith Addis. (Non-Fiction Ser.). 320p. 1992. 25.99 (0-7089-2743-2) Ulverscroft.

Taking the Bull by the Horns: Adopting a Proactive Approach to Public Relations. New England Water Works Association Staff. 149p. 1991. student ed. 30.00 (1-881198-00-6) New Eng Water Wks.

Taking the Child's Way Home. Rob Wilkins. 224p. 1995. pap. 10.99 (0-310-20019-9) Zondervan.

Taking the Classroom into the Community: A Guidebook. Neal A. Glasgow. LC 96-15307. (1-Off Ser.). 88p. 1996. 26.95 (0-8039-6478-1) Corwin Pr.

Taking the Classroom into the Community: A Guidebook. Neal A. Glasgow. (One-Off Ser.). 88p. (C). 1996. pap. 11.95 (0-8039-6479-X) Corwin Pr.

Taking the Constitution Seriously. Walter Berns. 288p. (C). 1992. pap. text ed. 17.95 (0-8191-7970-1) U Pr of Amer.

Taking the Environment Seriously. Ed. by Roger E. Meiners & Bruce Yandle. (Political Economy Forum Ser.). 288p. (C). 1993. text ed. 57.50 (0-8476-7873-3) Rowman.

Taking the Environment Seriously. Ed. by Roger E. Meiners & Bruce Yandle. 288p. 1995. pap. 21.95 (0-8476-8054-1) Rowman.

Taking the Fear out of Changing. Dennis E. O'Grady. LC 94-28764. 1994. pap. 14.95 (1-55850-408-7) Adams Media.

Taking the Fear Out of Changing: Guidelines for Getting Through Tough Life Transitions. Dennis E. O'Grady. (Illus.). 480p. (Orig.). 1992. pap. 14.95 (0-9628476-0-7) New Insights.

Taking the Fear Out of Eating: A Nutritionists' Guide to Sensible Food Choices. Charlette Gallagher & John Allred. (Illus.). 250p. (C). 1992. pap. text ed. 16.95 (0-521-43728-8) Cambridge U Pr.

Taking the Ferry Home. Pam Conrad. LC 87-45856. 224p. (YA). (gr. 7 up). 1988. lib. bdg. 12.89 (0-06-021318-3) HarpC Child Bks.

Taking the Fifth. J. A. Jance. (J. P. Beaumont Ser.). 320p. 1987. mass mkt. 6.50 (0-380-75139-9) Avon.

Taking the First Step: Being Honest with Yourself. Laura Stamper. 14p. (J). pap. 1.75 (0-925190-03-9, F911007 C) Fairview Press.

Taking the Floor in Meetings in French As Well As in English. Benedicte Lapeyre & Pamela Sheppard. 109p. (ENG & FRE.). 1992. 39.95 (0-7859-1002-6, 2708114565) Fr & Eur.

Taking the Fruit: Modern Women's Tales of the Bible. 2nd ed. Ed. by Jane S. Zones. 107p. 1991. pap. 9.95 (0-9608054-8-6) Womans Inst-Cont Jewish Ed.

***Taking the Gate: A Journey Through Scotland.** Stephen Scobie. (Orig.). 1996. 10.95 (0-88995-155-1, Pub. by Red Deer CN) Orca Bk Pubs.

Taking the Great High Road: An Exploration & Workable Perspective of Character Building. Alan Holubesko. (Illus.). 176p. 1996. 17.95 (0-9650413-0-1); pap. 12.95 (0-9650413-1-X) A & L Pubng.

Taking the Guesswork Out of Applying the Bible see Applying the Bible

***Taking the Guilt & Fear Out of Faith.** Fred Maes. (Illus.). (Orig.). 1997. pap. write for info. (1-890462-02-0) J Francisco.

Taking the Hard Road: Life Course & Class Identity in Nineteenth-Century French & German Workers' Autobiographies. Mary J. Maynes. LC 94-27197. (Illus.). 300p. 1995. pap. text ed. 16.95 (0-8078-4497-7); lib. bdg. 39.95 (0-8078-2187-X) U of NC Pr.

Taking the Helm. Dawn Riley & Cynthia Flanagan. LC 94-47989. 1995. 24.95 (0-316-74550-2) Little.

Taking the Ice: The Mighty Ducks of Anaheim. Dean Chadwin. (Illus.). 64p. (Orig.). (J). 1994. pap. 3.95 (0-919591-33-7, Pub. by Polestar Bk Pubs CN) Orca Bk Pubs.

Taking the Initiative: Leadership Agendas in Congress & the "Contract with America" John B. Bader. LC 96-12025. (American Governance & Public Policy Ser.). 288p. (C). 1996. pap. 19.95 (0-87840-629-8); lib. bdg. 49.95 (0-87840-628-X) Georgetown U Pr.

Taking the Initiative Conference Report: A Leadership Conference for Women in Science & Engineering. Ed. by Deborah C. Fort & Penelope Kegel-Flom. LC 95-60308. 1995. 8.50 (0-9634590-4-X) Assn Women Sci.

Taking the Kids & Surviving: Family Vacations that Everyone Can Enjoy. Eileen Ogintz. LC 95-38511. 176p. 1996. pap. 10.00 (0-06-258610-6) HarpC West.

Taking the Lead: Telecourse. Intelecom Staff. (Management Ser.). 1994. student ed., pap. 25.95 (0-534-93386-6) S-W Pub.

***Taking the Lead: The United Nations & Population Assistance.** Shanti R. Conly. 68p. 1996. 8.00 (1-889735-00-0) Population Action.

Taking the Lead with PACT: Peer Education in Sexuality & Health. (Illus.). 96p. (Orig.). 1989. pap. 25.00 (1-878263-00-5) YWCA.

Taking the Limits off God. 2nd ed. James B. Richards. 96p. 1997. reprint ed. pap. 8.00 (0-924748-00-1) Impact Ministries.

Taking the Math Out of Making Patchwork Quilts. Bonnie Leman & Judy Martin. (Illus.). (Orig.). 1981. pap. 4.95 (0-9602970-3-0) Leman Pubns.

Taking the Mystery Out of Basic Trigonometry. Don Senter. Ed. by Gail H. Bickford. (Illus.). 32p. (Orig.). 1995. pap. 5.00 (0-945069-05-7) Freedom Pr Assocs.

Taking the Mystery Out of TQM. 2nd ed. Peter Capezio & Debra Morehouse. 304p. 1995. pap. 16.99 (1-56414-197-7) Career Pr Inc.

Taking the Mysticism from Mathematics. 2nd ed. Norman H. Crowhurst. 178p. (Orig.). 1981. pap. 8.95 (0-89420-223-5, 297020) Natl Book.

Taking the Name of Science in Vain. Horace J. Bridges. LC 72-86734. (Essay Index Reprint Ser.). 1977. 20.95 (0-8369-1168-7) Ayer.

Taking the Naturalistic Turn: or How Real Philosophy of Science Is Done. Werner Callebaut. (Science & Its Conceptual Foundations Ser.). (Illus.). 576p. 1993. pap. text ed. 29.95 (0-226-09187-2); lib. bdg. 85.00 (0-226-09186-4) U Ch Pr.

Taking the "Ouch" out of Headaches. Joan Miller. 1983. 24.95 incl. audio (0-9613786-0-3) J Miller.

Taking the Pain Out of Window Cleaning. John Baxter. Ed. by Lynn Bruton. (Illus.). 96p. 1992. 14.95 (0-9632123-0-3) Crystal Pr CA.

Taking the Pane Out of Window Cleaning. John Baxter. Ed. by Lynn Bruton. (Illus.). 96p. 1992. pap. 9.95 (0-9632123-1-1) Crystal Pr CA.

Taking the Path of Zen. Robert Aitken. LC 82-81475. (Illus.). 150p. (Orig.). 1982. pap. 10.00 (0-86547-080-4, North Pt Pr) FS&G.

Taking the Plunge into TQM. Albert M. Koller, Jr. 104p. 1992. pap. text ed. 10.00 (0-9634805-0-2) EThree.

Taking the Pulse of a Community: Results of the Torquay Community Health Survey Research Paper. Deanne Gaskill. (Research Monographs: No. 1). (C). 1991. pap. 24.00 (0-7300-1458-4, Pub. by Deakin Univ AT) St Mut.

Taking the Quantam Leap. rev. ed. Fred A. Wolf. LC 88-45205. 1989. pap. 18.00 (0-06-096310-7, PL) HarpC.

Taking the Quantum Leap: Using the Sinclair QL Computer. Michael De Sosa. 1985. write for info. (0-07-016578-5) McGraw.

Taking the Risk out of Democracy: Corporate Propaganda Versus Freedom & Liberty. Alex Carey & Andrew Lohrey. LC 96-20817. (History of Communication Ser.). 1997. pap. text ed. 15.95 (0-252-06616-2) U of Ill Pr.

Taking the Rules to Court. John H. Young. 352p. 1990. 60.00 (0-685-24946-8); pap. 60.00 (0-941916-50-2) ATLA Pr.

Taking the SAT I: Reasoning Test, A Guide to Taking the SAT I. (YA). (gr. 10-12). 1994. 6.00 (0-87447-069-2, 200693) College Bd.

Taking the Shield of Faith. Curtis A. Merriweather. 45p. (Orig.). 1994. pap. 3.95 (0-9623431-5-3) Faith Christ Ch.

Taking the "Sigh" Out of Science: A Handbook for Teachers & Parents of Young Children. Cynthia Lashley. (Illus.). 60p. (Orig.). 1992. spiral bd., pap. 7.95 (0-9623249-6-5) Intermountain.

Taking the Sky Out of the Box. Malacheck Constanza. (Self Realization Bks.: Bk. X). 100p. 1986. pap. 10.00 (0-938582-14-3) Sensitive Man.

Taking the Soundings on Third Avenue. Andrew X. Sarris. LC 80-14276. 64p. 1981. 14.95 (0-87951-116-8) Overlook Pr.

Taking the Soundings on Third Avenue. deluxe ed. Andrew X. Sarris. LC 80-14276. 64p. 1981. 50.00 (0-87951-119-2) Overlook Pr.

***Taking the Stage.** Playwrights Canada Press Staff. LC 94-225160. 1997. pap. text ed. 19.95 (0-88754-530-0, Pub. by Playwrights CN Pr CN) Theatre Comm.

Taking the Stand: Tips for the Expert Witness. David Tunno. (Illus.). 36p. (Orig.). 1995. pap. 1.80 (0-913875-35-X, 6121) Lawyers & Judges.

Taking the Steam Out of Wallpaper Removal. Virginia M. Yost. (Illus.). 56p. 1986. pap. 4.95 (0-938005-04-9) Rogue Wave Pub.

Taking the Strain: Families, Unemployment & the Transition to Adulthood. Susan Hutson & Richard Jenkins. 192p. 1989. 85.00 (0-335-09918-1, Open Univ Pr); pap. 32.00 (0-335-09917-3, Open Univ Pr) Taylor & Francis.

***Taking the Stress Out of Teaching.** Michael E. Bernard. 19.95 (0-85924-918-2, B114) Inst Rational-Emotive.

Taking the Train: A Tribute to Britain's Greatest Railway Photographers. Michael Baker. (Illus.). 176p. 1996. 29.95 (1-85260-409-3, Pub. by J H Haynes & Co UK) Motorbooks Intl.

Taking the Trip: A Journey Through Widowhood. Romaine Presnell. LC 96-22357. 1996. 4.95 (1-56123-095-2) Centering Corp.

Taking the University to the People: Seventy-Five Years of Cooperative Extension. Wayne D. Rasmussen. LC 88-37672. (Illus.). 310p. 1989. 34.95 (0-8138-0419-1) Iowa St U Pr.

Taking the Waters: Soil & Water Conservation among Settling Beja Nomads in Eastern Sudan. Johan A. Van Dijk. (African Studies Centre Leiden). 340p. 1995. pap. 38.95 (1-85972-162-1, Pub. by Avebury Pub UK) Ashgate Pub Co.

Taking the Waters: Spirit, Art, Sensuality. Alev L. Croutier. LC 92-15691. (Illus.). 224p. 1992. 17.98 (1-55859-219-9) Abbeville Pr.

Taking the Wheel: Women & the Coming of the Motor Age. Virginia Scharff. LC 92-15927. 230p. 1992. pap. 13.95 (0-8263-1395-7) U of NM Pr.

Taking the Word to Heart: Self & Other in an Age of Therapies. Robert C. Roberts. LC 92-34333. 1993. pap. 15.00 (0-8028-0659-7) Eerdmans.

***Taking the Word to the World.** Edwin H. Robertson. (Illus.). 352p. 1996. 22.99 (0-7852-7232-1) Nelson.

Taking the Work out of Working Out: A Revolutionary Approach for Making Exercise More Exciting. Charles R. Schroeder. 1994. pap. 9.95 (1-56561-049-0) Chronimed.

Taking the World in for Repairs. Richard Selzer. 1994. pap. 17.95 (0-87013-363-2) Mich St U Pr.

Taking Their Place: A Documentary of Women in Journalism. Maurine H. Beasley & Sheila J. Gibbons. LC 92-41011. 300p. (Orig.). (C). 1993. 51.00 (1-879383-09-8); pap. 19.95 (1-879383-10-1) Am Univ Pr.

Taking Things Apart & Puttings Things Together. John H. Woodburn. LC 76-20448. 1976. pap. 8.95 (0-685-00250-0) Am Chemical.

Taking Time. Lillian Linstromberg. LC 89-61707. (Illus.). 96p. (Orig.). 1989. pap. 7.95 (0-9623452-0-2) Oregon Coast Cmnty Col.

Taking Time: Support for People with Cancer & the People Who Care about Them. (Illus.). 68p. (Orig.). (C). 1992. pap. text ed. 20.00 (1-56806-103-X) DIANE Pub.

Taking Time for Me: How Caregivers Can Effectively Deal with Stress. Katherine L. Karr. (Golden Age Books - Perspectives on Aging Ser.). (Illus.). 179p. (Orig.). (C). 1992. 25.95 (0-87975-779-5); pap. 16.95 (0-87975-796-5) Prometheus Bks.

***Taking Time for Tea Journal.** Illus. by Sandy Clough. 128p. 1995. 8.99 (1-56507-401-7) Harvest Hse.

Taking Time Off: Profiles of Students Who Enjoyed Successful Sabbaticals from College & How You Can Do the Same. Colin Hall & Ron Lieber. LC 95-53684. 288p. 1996. pap. 12.00 (0-374-52475-0) FS&G.

Taking Time off in Israel. Fern Reiss. LC 85-1225. (Illus.). 149p. 1985. pap. 9.95 (0-915361-15-9) Hemed Bks.

Taking Time Out: Managing Employment Breaks. Ed. by Margaret Ohren. 160p. (C). 1991. pap. text ed. 65.00 (0-85292-460-7, Pub. by IPM Hse UK) St Mut.

Taking Time Out: Recreation & Play. Thomas R. Miller. Ed. by Bruce Glassman. LC 94-47412. (Our Human Family Ser.). (Illus.). 80p. (YA). (gr. 5 up). 1995. lib. bdg. 21.95 (1-56711-128-9) Blackbirch.

Taking Time to Act: A Guide to Cross-Curricular Drama. John Airs & Chris Ball. LC 94-43586. 164p. 1995. pap. 16.95 (0-435-08666-9, 08666) Heinemann.

Taking Time Together: Faith Experiences for Teens & Parents. Robert P. Stamschror. (Illus.). 56p. (Orig.). 1996. pap. 12.95 (0-88489-386-3) St Marys.

Taking Trophy Whitetails. Bob Fratzke. Ed. by Glenn Helgeland. LC 83-50905. (On Target Ser.). (Illus.). 132p. (Orig.). 1983. pap. 10.95 (0-913305-02-2) Target Comm.

Taking Trusteeship Seriously. Richard C. Turner. LC 95-16380. 1995. write for info. (1-884354-03-3) IN Univ Ctr.

***Taking up a Franchise.** 12th ed. Colin Barrow & Godfrey Golzen. (Daily Telegraph Guides Ser.). 1996. pap. 15.95 (0-7494-1836-2) Kogan Page Ltd.

Taking Up Serpents: Snake Handlers of Eastern Kentucky. David L. Kimbrough. LC 95-3593. 1995. pap. 14.95 (0-8078-4533-7); text ed. 34.95 (0-8078-2227-2) U of NC Pr.

Taking Women into the Twenty First Century: Issues Facing Pennsylvania's Women. Pennsylvania State Data Center Staff. 103p. (Orig.). 1994. pap. 25.00 (0-939667-28-2) Penn State Data Ctr.

Taking Your Back to the Future: How to Get a Pain-Free Back & Total Health with Chiropractic Care. rev. ed. W. Michael Gazdar. Ed. by Larry Wyner & Linda Wyner. (Illus.). 280p. (Orig.). (C). 1995. pap. 12.95 (0-9645301-0-4) J Muir Chirop.

***Taking Your Business Global: Your Small Business Guide to Successful International Trade.** James Wilfong & Toni Seger. LC 97-7396. 320p. (Orig.). 1997. pap. 18.99 (1-56414-275-2) Career Pr Inc.

T

Taking Your Campus for Christ. Barry St. Clair & Keith Naylor. 112p. (Orig.). (YA). 1993. student ed., pap. 5.99 (*1-56476-201-7*, 6-3201, Victor Bks) Chariot Victor.

Taking Your Medications Safely. Springhouse Publishing Company Staff. LC 95-6698. 512p. 1996. pap. 19.95 (*0-87434-824-2*) Springhouse Pub.

Taking Your Medicine: Drug Regulation in the United States. Peter Temin. LC 80-16680. (Illus.). 281p. 1980. 34.50 (*0-674-86725-4*) HUP.

Taking Your Show on the Road: A Guide for New Student Recruiters. Helen Linstrum. 49p. 1990. 25.00 (*0-89964-274-8*, 27101) Coun Adv & Supp Ed.

Takings: Private Property & the Power of Eminent Domain. Richard A. Epstein. 384p. 1985. 37.00 (*0-674-86728-9*) HUP.

Takings: Private Property & the Power of Eminent Domain. Richard A. Epstein. 384p. 1985. reprint ed. pap. 18.95 (*0-674-86729-7*) HUP.

***Takiya & Thunderheard's Life Garden.** J. Victor McGuire. (Illus.). 38p. (J). (gr. 2-4). 1997. 16.95 (*0-9623300-6-X*) Spice Life CO.

***Taklamakan.** unabridged ed. Joseph E. Murphy. (Illus.). 168p. 1997. 250.00 (*0-9646292-3-2*) Crossgar Pr.

Taktik und Witz Im Schach. Helmut Pfleger. (Praxis Schach Ser.: Bd. 8). 182p. (GER.). write for info. (*3-283-00252-5*) G Olms Pubs.

Taktika: A Manual for Ancient Warfare. J. De Voto. (Illus.). viii, 132p. (Orig.). (C). 1993. pap. text ed. 15.00 (*0-89005-517-3*) Ares.

***Taku.** Ronald L. Virden. 353p. (Orig.). 1997. mass mkt. 5.99 (*1-55237-027-5*, Pub. by Comnwlth Pub CN) Partners Pubs Grp.

Tal-Botvinnik 1960: Match for the World Championship. 4th rev. ed. Mikhail Tal. Tr. by Hanon W. Russell. 224p. (Orig.). 1996. pap. 19.95 (*1-888690-00-3*) Russell Ent.

***Tal Como Soy.** Billy Graham. 1997. 25.95 (*0-8297-0344-6*) Life Pubs Intl.

Tal Hermon: Sermon Material for Yom Kippur & Eulogy in Hebrew. P. S. Pollak. 12.00 (*0-87559-086-1*); pap. 7.50 (*0-87559-085-3*) Shalom.

Tal I Tant. Joan Brossa. (Illus.). (CAT.). 1993. bds. 250.00 (*0-614-00244-3*) Elliots Bks.

Tal I Tant. limited ed. Joan Brossa. (Ediciones Especiales y de Bibliofilo Ser.). (Illus.). (CAT.). 1993. 150.00 (*84-343-0282-9*) Elliots Bks.

Tal Vez No Sea Como Usted Pien. David Downing. 160p. (SPA.). 1990. pap. 1.50 (*0-8297-0932-0*) Life Pubs Intl.

Talanta U.S.A. Honor Issue. Christian. 320p. 1989. pap. 82.00 (*0-08-037208-2*, Pergamon Pr) Elsevier.

Talbot County: A History. Dickson J. Preston. Ed. by Norman Harrington. LC 83-40048. (Illus.). 396p. 1983. reprint ed. pap. 112.90 (*0-7837-9091-0*, 2049841) Bks Demand.

Talbot Mundy: Messenger of Destiny. Donald M. Grant. (Illus.). 1983. 20.00 (*0-937986-46-1*) D M Grant.

Talbot Odyssey. Nelson DeMille. 544p. 1991. mass mkt. 6.99 (*0-446-35858-4*) Warner Bks.

Talbot Road. deluxe limited ed. Thom Gunn. (Illus.). 16p. (Orig.). 1981. pap. 25.00 (*0-914496-05-0*) Helikon NY.

***Talbot's Box.** Thomas Kilroy. 72p. 1996. pap. 12.95 (*1-85235-198-5*) Dufour.

Talc & Pyrophyllite. (Metals & Minerals Ser.). 1994. lib. bdg. 255.95 (*0-8490-9024-5*) Gordon Pr.

Talcott Parsons. Ed. by Peter Hamilton. (Key Sociologists Ser.). 128p. 1983. pap. 8.95 (*0-85312-439-6*, NP. 3753, Pub. by Tavistock-E Horwood UK) Routledge Chapman & Hall.

***Talcott Parsons.** Peter Hamilton. (Key Sociologists Ser.). 120p. (C). 1983. pap. text ed. 12.95 (*0-415-05109-6*) Routledge.

Talcott Parsons: A Bibliography. Ed. by Joan Nordquist. (Social Theory: A Bibliographic Ser.: No. 8). 60p. (Orig.). 1987. pap. 15.00 (*0-937855-14-6*) Ref Rsch Serv.

Talcott Parsons: Critical Assessments, 4 vols., Set. Ed. by Peter Hamilton. LC 92-9971. (Critical Assessments Ser.). 1600p. (C). (gr. 13). 1992. text ed. 580.00 (*0-415-03764-6*, A7763) Routledge.

Talcott Parsons: Theorist of Modernity. Ed. by Ronald Roberston. (Theory, Culture & Society Ser.). 272p. (C). 1991. 55.00 (*0-8039-8513-4*); pap. 22.95 (*0-8039-8514-2*) Sage.

Talcott Parsons & the Capitalist Nation State: Political Sociology As a Strategic Vocation. William Buxton. 344p. 1985. pap. 17.95 (*0-8020-6531-7*) U of Toronto Pr.

Talcott Parsons' General Action Scheme. Larry Brownstein. 310p. 1982. text ed. 22.95 (*0-87073-097-5*) Schenkman Bks Inc.

Talcott Parsons on Economy & Society. Robert J. Holton & Bryan S. Turner. 288p. 1989. 59.95 (*0-7102-0746-8*, 07468, RKP); pap. 14.95 (*0-685-28275-9*, A3446, RKP) Routledge.

Talcott Parsons on Institutions & Social Evolution: Selected Writings. Talcott Parsons. Ed. by Leon H. Mayhew. LC 82-4911. (Heritage of Sociology Ser.). 368p. 1985. pap. text ed. 18.00 (*0-226-64749-8*) U Ch Pr.

Talcott Parsons on National Socialism. Intro. by Uta Gerhardt. LC 92-39625. (Social Institutions & Social Change Ser.). 364p. 1993. lib. bdg. 56.95 (*0-202-30458-2*) Aldine de Gruyter.

Talcott Pedigree in England & America from 1558-1876. S. V. Talcott. (Illus.). 316p. 1989. reprint ed. pap. 47.00 (*0-8328-1153-X*); reprint ed. lib. bdg. 55.00 (*0-8328-1152-1*) Higginson Bk Co.

Tale-Danda: A Play. Tr. by Girish Karnad. (C). 1995. 8.50 (*0-86311-529-2*, Pub. by Manohar II) S Asia.

Tale for Midnight. Frederic Prokosch. LC 76-178790. 354p. 1973. reprint ed. text ed. 38.50 (*0-8371-6281-5*, PRTM, Greenwood Pr) Greenwood.

Tale from Tangier. Dale & Sheeler. 1983. pap. text ed. 6.75 (*0-13-884545-X*) P-H.

Tale from the Crypt Class Trip. Vincent Courtney. (J). (gr. 4-7). 1996. pap. 3.99 (*0-679-88223-5*, Bullseye Bks) Random Bks Yng Read.

Tale from the Fire. Terry Braunstein. LC 95-2797. 1995. pap. 30.00 (*0-940979-30-6*) Natl Museum Women.

Tale from the Forgotten War. Harris R. Stearns. 1993. 12.95 (*0-9643621-0-4*) HRS Pubng.

Tale from the Heart: Bloodlines. Goff et al. 48p. 1992. 4.95 (*0-87135-863-8*) Marvel Entmnt.

Tale from the Heart: Temp. Natives. Goff et al. 48p. 1990. 3.95 (*0-87135-651-1*) Marvel Entmnt.

Tale Maker. Mark Harris. LC 95-30997. vii, 215p. 1995. pap. 12.00 (*0-8032-7280-4*, Bison Books) U of Nebr Pr.

Tale of a Cat: A Journal about the Life & Good Times of Your Feline Friend. Marlor Press Staff. (Illus.). 96p. 1995. pap. 8.95 (*0-943400-82-1*) Marlor Pr.

Tale of a Chinese. Xiao-Ming Chen. LC 92-91197. 176p. 1993. pap. 9.00 (*1-56002-290-6*, Univ Edtns) Aegina Pr.

Tale of a Comet & Other Stories. Helen M. White. LC 83-25086. (Illus.). ix, 273p. 1984. 16.95 (*0-87351-169-7*) Minn Hist.

Tale of a Good Cook. Alison Bundy. 32p. 4.00 (*0-945926-27-8*) Paradigm RI.

Tale of a Lonely Parish. Francis M. Crawford. (Works of Francis Marion Crawford Ser.). 1990. reprint ed. lib. bdg. 79.00 (*0-7812-2530-2*) Rprt Serv.

Tale of a Nomadic Soul. Syed A. Malik. (C). 1990. text ed. 19.50 (*81-7018-584-X*, Pub. by BR Pub II) S Asia.

Tale of a Silly Goose & Other Stories. Vicki Rogers & Sharon Stewart. (Illus.). 44p. (Orig.). (J). 1993. pap. 8.95 (*0-88865-082-5*, Pub. by Pacific Educ Pr CN) Orca Bk Pubs.

***Tale of a Tadpole.** Barbara A. Porte. LC 96-53890. (Illus.). 32p. (J). (ps-2). 1997. 15.95 (*0-531-30049-8*); lib. bdg. 16.99 (*0-531-33049-4*) Orchard Bks Watts.

Tale of a Teddy Bear. Ellen E. LeRoque. (Illus.). 28p. (Orig.). (J). (ps-2). 1985. pap. 3.95 (*0-932967-03-5*) Pacific Shoreline.

Tale of a Tiger. Robert T. Smith. LC 85-90545. (Illus.). 3624p. 1986. 20.95 (*0-317-55132-9*) Tiger Originals.

Tale of a Traveling Bag see Stichus

Tale of a Tub & Related Pieces. Jonathan Swift. Ed. by Angus Ross & David Woolley. (World's Classics Ser.). (Illus.). 192p. 1986. pap. 6.95 (*0-19-281689-6*) OUP.

Tale of Agony: The Commonwealth of Both Nations, No. III. Pawel Jasienica. Tr. by Alexander Jordan. LC 92-81175. 1992. 25.00 (*1-881284-04-2*) Am Inst Polish.

Tale of Aladdin & the Wonderful Lamp. Arabian Nights Staff. LC 91-814. (Illus.). 32p. (J). (ps-3). 1992. lib. bdg. 14.95 (*0-8234-0938-4*) Holiday.

Tale of Alain. Arnold Zimmermann. Ed. by Chris Swansen. (Illus.). 120p. (Orig.). (YA). 1983. pap. 10.00 (*0-942018-01-X*) Schoolhouse WI.

Tale of Ali Baba & the Forty Thieves: A Story from the Arabian Nights. Illus. by Will Hillenbrand. 32p. (J). (ps-3). 1996. lib. bdg. 15.95 (*0-8234-1258-X*) Holiday.

Tale of Archais. Aleister Crowley. 1973. lib. bdg. 250.00 (*0-87968-218-3*) Krishna Pr.

Tale of Bear. Helen Cooper. LC 94-21054. (Illus.). 24p. (J). (ps up). 1995. pap. 6.95 (*0-688-13990-6*) Lothrop.

Tale of Benjamin Bunny. Beatrix Potter. (Original Peter Rabbit Bks.: No.4). (J). 1987. pap. 5.95 (*0-7232-3463-9*) Warne.

Tale of Benjamin Bunny. Beatrix Potter. (Illus.). 32p. (J). (ps-3). 1994. pap. 3.99 (*0-14-054300-7*) Puffin Bks.

Tale of Benjamin Bunny. Beatrix Potter. (J). 1992. 3.99 (*0-517-07240-8*) Random Hse Value.

Tale of Benjamin Bunny. Beatrix Potter. LC 80-27468. (Illus.). 32p. (J). (gr. k-3). 1981. pap. 3.95 (*0-89375-485-4*); lib. bdg. 11.89 (*0-89375-484-6*) Troll Communs.

Tale of Benjamin Bunny. Beatrix Potter. (J). 1988. 2.99 (*0-517-65277-3*) Random Hse Value.

Tale of Benjamin Bunny. Beatrix Potter. (J). (gr. k-2). 1994. 3.99 (*0-517-10236-6*) Random Hse Value.

***Tale of Benjamin Bunny.** Beatrix Potter. (J). 1997. 3.95 (*1-57719-158-7*) GT Pubng Corp.

Tale of Benjamin Bunny. Pat R. Stewart. LC 74-78812. (Illus.). 59p. (J). (gr. 2 up). 1974. reprint ed. pap. 1.75 (*0-486-21102-9*) Dover.

Tale of Benjamin Bunny: Full-Color Storybook. Beatrix Potter & Anna Pomaska. LC 94-24672. (Little Activity Bks.). (Illus.). 32p. (Orig.). (J). 1995. pap. text ed. 1.00 (*0-486-28538-3*) Dover.

Tale of Benjamin Bunny Coloring Book. Beatrix Potter. (Illus.). (J). (gr. k-3). 1981. pap. 2.50 (*0-486-24114-9*) Dover.

Tale of Benjamin Bunny Paint with Water Book. Beatrix Potter. (Illus.). (J). (gr. 1 up). 1987. pap. 1.49 (*0-671-62986-7*, Litl Simon S&S) S&S Childrens.

Tale of Benjamin Bunny Pop Up. Beatrix Potter. (J). 1988. 3.99 (*0-517-67096-8*) Random Hse Value.

Tale of Benjamin Bunny-Sticker. Beatrix Potter. (J). 1990. pap. 2.95 (*0-671-69254-2*, Litl Simon S&S) S&S Childrens.

Tale of Boris: (A Fable of the Red-Tailed Hawk) Jane H. Stroschin. (Illus.). 32p. (J). (gr. k-6). 1991. pap. 7.00 (*1-883960-07-X*); lib. bdg. 15.00 (*1-883960-06-1*) Henry Quill.

Tale of Cats & Mice of Obeyd of Zakan. Mehdi K. Nakosteen & Obeyd E. Zakani. (Illus.). 65p. (ENG & PER.). 1988. 20.00 (*0-936347-41-4*) Iran Bks.

Tale of Christmas Mouse. 1987. pap. 2.50 (*0-8167-0035-4*) Troll Communs.

***Tale of Cinderella: Vocal Selections.** Ed. by Carol Cuellar. 48p. (Orig.). (C). 1995. pap. text ed. 14.95 (*0-89724-952-6*, PF9515) Warner Brothers.

Tale of Constantinople: Of Its Origin & Capture in the Year 1453. Nestor-Iskander. Ed. by Walter Hanak & Marios Philippides. Tr. by Marios Philippides from CHU. (Late Byzantine & Ottoman Studies: No. 5). 192p. (ENG & SLA.). 1996. text ed. 60.00 (*0-89241-503-7*) Caratzas.

Tale of Custard the Dragon. Ogden Nash. (Illus.). (J). (ps-3). 1995. 14.95 (*0-316-59880-1*) Little.

Tale of Cutter's Treasure. David L. Seidman. (Are You Afraid of the Dark Ser.). (J). (gr. 3-6). 1995. mass mkt. 3.99 (*0-671-52729-0*, Minstrel Bks) PB.

Tale of Dan De Lion. Thomas M. Disch. LC 86-19740. (Illus.). 32p. (J). (ps up). 1986. 9.95 (*0-918273-30-7*) Coffee Hse.

Tale of Don l'Orignal. Antonine Maillet. 107p. 1978. 3.95 (*0-7720-1216-4*) Genl Dist Srvs.

Tale of Duck. Helen Cooper. LC 94-24850. (Illus.). 24p. (J). (ps up). 1995. pap. 6.95 (*0-688-13991-4*) Lothrop.

***Tale of Eleventh Century Japan: Hamamatsu Chunagon Monogatari.** Thomas H. Rohlich. LC 82-61380. (Princeton Library of Asian Translations). 261p. 1983. reprint ed. pap. 74.40 (*0-608-03358-8*, 2064070) Bks Demand.

Tale of Eternity & Other Poems. Gerald Massey. 476p. 1995. reprint ed. pap. 33.00 (*1-56459-505-6*) Kessinger Pub.

Tale of Fleddy the Flog. Cyril Walmsley. (Illus.). 64p. (J). 1995. pap. 7.99 (*0-8059-3581-9*) Dorrance.

Tale of Flowering Fortunes: Annals of Japanese Aristocratic Life in the Heian Period, 2 vols., Set. Tr. by William H. McCullough & Helen C. McCullough from JPN. LC 78-66183. (Illus.). 930p. 1980. 95.00 (*0-8047-1039-2*) Stanford U Pr.

Tale of Frog. Helen Cooper. LC 94-24849. (Illus.). 24p. (J). (ps up). 1995. pap. 6.95 (*0-688-13993-0*) Lothrop.

Tale of Genji. Lady Murasaki. Tr. by Arthur Waley. 1354p. 1993. 22.00 (*0-679-42467-9*, Modern Lib) Random.

Tale of Genji. Lady Murasaki. Tr. by Edward G. Seidensticker from JPN. LC 76-13680. 1978. pap. 25.00 (*0-394-73530-7*) Knopf.

Tale of Genji. Lady Murasaki. Tr. by Arthur Waley. LC 60-52014. 1977. 16.95 (*0-394-60405-9*, Modern Lib) Random.

Tale of Genji. Murasaki Shikibu. Tr. by Edward G. Seidensticker. LC 89-40606. (Vintage Classics Ser.). 256p. 1990. pap. 13.00 (*0-679-72953-4*, Vin) Random.

Tale of Genji. Murasaki Shikibu. LC 92-52930. 1184p. 1992. 25.00 (*0-679-41738-9*, Everymans Lib) Knopf.

Tale of Genji: A Reader's Guide. William J. Puette. 196p. 1993. pap. 12.95 (*0-8048-1879-7*) C E Tuttle.

Tale of Ginger & Pickles. Beatrix Potter. (Original Peter Rabbit Books: No. 18). (J). 1987. pap. 5.95 (*0-7232-3477-9*); pap. 2.25 (*0-7232-3502-3*) Warne.

Tale of Halley's Comet: An Educational Coloring Book. Charleen C. Lyon. (Illus.). 32p. (Orig.). (J). (gr. 3-6). 1985. pap. 2.95 (*0-9614973-0-0*) Niota Pr.

Tale of Hilda Louise. Olivier Dunrea. LC 95-33511. 32p. (J). 1996. 16.00 (*0-374-37380-9*) FS&G.

Tale of Jemima Puddle-Duck. Beatrix Potter. (Original Peter Rabbit Bks.: No. 9). (Illus.). (Orig.). (J). (ps-3). 1987. pap. 5.95 (*0-7232-3468-X*); pap. 2.25 (*0-7232-3493-0*) Warne.

Tale of Jemima Puddle-Duck. Beatrix Potter. (Beatrix Potter Book & Storytape Collection). (Illus.). (Orig.). (J). (ps-3). 1989. pap. 6.95 incl. audio (*0-7232-3630-5*) Warne.

Tale of Jemima Puddle-Duck. Beatrix Potter. (Illus.). 32p. (Orig.). (J). (ps-3). 1992. pap. 3.99 (*0-14-054498-4*) Puffin Bks.

Tale of Jemima Puddle-Duck. Beatrix Potter. (Golden Deluxe Book & Cassette Ser.). (Illus.). 24p. (Orig.). (J). (ps-2). 1991. 5.98 incl. audio (*1-55886-057-6*) Smarty Pants.

Tale of Jemima Puddle-Duck. Beatrix Potter. (Giant Bks.). (Illus.). 24p. (J). 1996. pap. 18.99 (*0-7232-4231-3*) Warne.

***Tale of Jemima Puddle-Duck.** Beatrix Potter. (J). 1997. 3.95 (*1-57719-159-5*) GT Pubng Corp.

Tale of Jemima Puddle-Duck. deluxe ed. Beatrix Potter. (Illus.). 60p. (J). 1995. boxed, pap. 16.00 (*0-7232-4248-8*) Warne.

Tale of Jemima Puddle-duck. Beatrix Potter. (Illus.). 64p. (J). 1984. reprint ed. pap. 1.75 (*0-486-24634-5*) Dover.

Tale of Jemima Puddle-Duck: Full-Color Storybook. Beatrix Potter. LC 95-4653. (Illus.). 32p. (J). 1996. reprint ed. pap. text ed. 1.00 (*0-486-28821-8*) Dover.

Tale of Jemima Puddle-Duck & Other Farmyard Tales. Beatrix Potter. (Frederick Warne Picture Bks.). (Illus.). 80p. (J). (ps-3). 1987. pap. 13.00 (*0-7232-3425-6*) Warne.

Tale of Jemima Puddle-Duck in Spanish Coloring Book. Beatrix Potter & Patricia Wynne. (Little Activity Bks.). (J). 1994. pap. 1.00 (*0-486-27914-6*) Dover.

Tale of Jeremy Fisher. (Little Landoll Original Beatrix Potter Ser.). (Illus.). 32p. (J). (ps-6). Date not set. 1.29 (*1-56987-022-5*) Landoll.

***Tale of Jeremy Fisher.** Beatrix Potter & Anna Pomaska. (Illus.). (J). pap. 1.00 (*0-486-29345-9*) Dover.

Tale of Jeremy Fisher-Coloring Book. Beatrix Potter. (J). 1985. pap. 2.50 (*0-486-24964-6*) Dover.

Tale of Johnny Town-Mouse. Beatrix Potter. (Original Peter Rabbit Books: No. 13). (J). (ps-3). 1987. pap. 5.95 (*0-7232-3472-8*) Warne.

Tale of Kieu. Huynh Sanh Thong. LC 82-10979. 276p. 1987. pap. 15.00 (*0-300-04051-2*, Y-666) Yale U Pr.

Tale of Little Pig Robinson. Beatrix Potter. (Original Peter Rabbit Books: No. 19). (J). 1987. pap. 5.95 (*0-7232-3478-7*); pap. 2.25 (*0-7232-3503-1*) Warne.

Tale of Matsura: Fujiwara Teika's Experiment in Fiction. Tr. & Intro. by Wayne P. Lammers. LC 90-42197. (Michigan Monographs in Japanese Studies: No. 9). xii, 207p. 1992. 35.00 (*0-939512-48-3*) U MI Japan.

Tale of Meshka the Kvetch. Carol Chapman. LC 80-11225. (Unicorn Paperbacks Ser.). (Illus.). 32p. (J). (gr. k-3). 1989. pap. 3.95 (*0-525-44494-7*) Dutton Child Bks.

Tale of Miss Moppet. (Little Landoll Original Beatrix Potter Ser.). (J). (ps-6). Date not set. write for info. (*0-614-97965-X*) Landoll.

Tale of Mr. Jeremy Fisher. Beatrix Potter. (Original Peter Rabbit Bks.: No. 7). (J). 1987. pap. 5.95 (*0-7232-3466-3*) Warne.

Tale of Mr. Jeremy Fisher. Beatrix Potter. (Beatrix Potter Book & Storytape Collection). (J). (ps-3). 1989. pap. 6.95 incl. audio (*0-7232-3669-0*) Warne.

Tale of Mr. Jeremy Fisher. Beatrix Potter. (J). 1992. 3.99 (*0-517-07238-6*) Random Hse Value.

Tale of Mr. Jeremy Fisher. Beatrix Potter. LC 88-34668. (Illus.). 32p. (J). (ps up). 1991. pap. 14.95 (*0-88708-094-4*, Rabbit) S&S Childrens.

***Tale of Mr. Jeremy Fisher.** Beatrix Potter. (J). 1997. pap. text ed. 2.95 (*1-57719-163-3*) GT Pubng Corp.

Tale of Mr. Jeremy Fisher. Beatrix Potter. LC 74-75269. (Illus.). 59p. (J). (gr. 2-4). 1974. reprint ed. pap. 1.75 (*0-486-23066-X*) Dover.

Tale of Mr. Jeremy Fisher. Beatrix Potter. LC 92-22584. (Illus.). 64p. (J). 1992. reprint ed. 5.95 (*0-88708-253-X*, Rabbit) S&S Childrens.

Tale of Mr. Jeremy Fisher: Mini Book. Beatrix Potter. LC 92-22584. (Illus.). 64p. (J). 1992. reprint ed. Mini-bk. 9.95 incl. audio (*0-88708-252-1*, Rabbit) S&S Childrens.

Tale of Mr. Toad. Beatrix Potter. (World of Peter Rabbit & Friends Ser.). (Illus.). 24p. (J). 1996. pap. 4.99 (*0-7232-4267-4*) Warne.

Tale of Mr. Toad. Beatrix Potter. (Original Peter Rabbit Books: No. 14). (J). 1987. pap. 5.95 (*0-7232-3473-6*) Warne.

Tale of Mr. Toad. Beatrix Potter. (Illus.). (J). (ps-3). 1996. pap. 4.99 (*0-614-15584-3*) Warne.

Tale of Mrs. Tiggy-Winkle. Beatrix Potter. (Original Peter Rabbit Bks.: No. 6). (J). 1987. pap. 5.95 (*0-7232-3465-5*); pap. 2.25 (*0-7232-3490-6*) Warne.

Tale of Mrs. Tiggy-Winkle. Beatrix Potter. (Beatrix Potter Book & Storytape Collection). (Illus.). (J). (ps-3). 1989. pap. 6.95 incl. audio (*0-7232-3629-1*) Warne.

Tale of Mrs. Tiggy-Winkle. Beatrix Potter. (Golden Deluxe Book & Cassette Ser.). (Illus.). 24p. (J). (ps-2). 1991. 5.98 incl. audio (*1-55886-058-4*) Smarty Pants.

Tale of Mrs. Tiggy-Winkle & Mr. Jeremy Fisher. Beatrix Potter. (World of Peter Rabbit & Friends Ser.). (Illus.). 32p. (J). (ps-3). 1994. pap. 4.99 (*0-7232-4149-X*) Warne.

Tale of Mrs. Tittlemouse. Beatrix Potter. (Original Peter Rabbit Books: No. 11). (J). 1987. pap. 5.95 (*0-7232-3470-1*) Warne.

Tale of Mrs. Tittlemouse. Beatrix Potter. 64p. 1986. reprint ed. pap. 1.75 (*0-486-25230-2*) Dover.

Tale of Naughty Mac & Other Donkey Stories. Elisabeth D. Svendson. (Illus.). 80p. text ed. 17.95 (*1-873580-14-2*, Pub. by Whittet Bks UK) Diamond Farm Bk.

Tale of Ned & His Nose. Dorothy Potash. (Illus.). 24p. (J). (gr. k-4). 1993. lib. bdg. 13.95 (*1-879567-23-7*, Valeria Bks) Wonder Well.

Tale of Nervous Nell. Margaret Hopkins. LC 95-10286. (One Day at a Time Ser.). (Illus.). 32p. (J). (gr. k-3). 1996. mass mkt. 2.99 (*0-590-26593-8*, Cartwheel) Scholastic Inc.

Tale of Old Mortality. Walter Scott. Ed. by Douglas S. Mack. LC 93-11345. Orig. Title: Old Mortality. 522p. 1993. 45.00 (*0-231-08470-6*) Col U Pr.

Tale of One Bad Rat. Bryan Talbot. (Illus.). 136p. (YA). (gr. 7 up). 1995. pap. 14.95 (*1-56971-077-5*) Dark Horse Comics.

Tale of One City. Ed. by Ben Giladi. LC 91-606446. 1991. 32.50 (*0-88400-153-9*) Shengold.

Tale of Peter Rabbit. (Play - a - Sound Ser.). (Illus.). 24p. (J). 1993. 12.98 (*0-7853-0074-0*) Pubns Intl Ltd.

Tale of Peter Rabbit. (Little Landoll Original Beatrix Potter Ser.). (Illus.). 32p. (J). (ps-6). Date not set. 1.29 (*1-56987-021-7*) Landoll.

Tale of Peter Rabbit. Ed. by Janet L. Bolinske. LC 87-61672. (Children's Classics Ser.). (Illus.). 32p. (Orig.). (J). (gr. 1-3). 1987. pap. text ed. 4.95 (*0-88335-572-8*); spiral bd. 14.95 (*0-88335-542-6*) Milliken Pub Co.

Tale of Peter Rabbit. Golden Books Staff. (Little Golden Bks.). (Illus.). 24p. (J). (ps-2). 1995. 1.49 (*0-307-03071-7*, Golden Pr) Western Pub.

Tale of Peter Rabbit. Beatrix Potter. (J). (ps-3). 1987. pap. 5.95 (*0-7232-3460-4*); pap. 2.25 (*0-7232-3485-X*) Warne.

Tale of Peter Rabbit. Beatrix Potter. (Giant Bks.). (Illus.). 24p. (J). (ps-3). 1993. pap. 17.99 (*0-7232-4029-9*) Warne.

Tale of Peter Rabbit. Beatrix Potter. 1992. pap. 3.99 (*0-14-054295-7*) NAL-Dutton.

Tale of Peter Rabbit. Beatrix Potter. (Illus.). 32p. (J). (ps-3). 1992. pap. 3.99 (*0-14-054497-6*, Puffin) Puffin Bks.

Tale of Peter Rabbit. Beatrix Potter. LC 85-70809. (Pudgy Pal Board Bks.). (Illus.). 18p. (J). (ps). 1986. bds. 3.95 (*0-448-10224-2*, G&D) Putnam Pub Group.

Tale of Peter Rabbit. Beatrix Potter. (All Aboard Bks.). (Illus.). 32p. (J). 1991. pap. 2.95 (*0-448-40061-8*, G&D) Putnam Pub Group.

Tale of Peter Rabbit. Beatrix Potter. (J). 1992. 3.99 (*0-517-07236-X*) Random Hse Value.

Tale of Peter Rabbit. Beatrix Potter. (Easy to Read Folktales Ser.). (Illus.). 32p. (J). (gr. k-3). 1986. pap. 2.50 (*0-590-41101-2*) Scholastic Inc.

Tale of Peter Rabbit. Beatrix Potter. LC 88-11509. (Illus.). 36p. (J). (ps up). 1991. 14.95 (*0-317-89758-6*, Rabbit) S&S Childrens.

Tale of Peter Rabbit. Beatrix Potter. (Golden Deluxe Book & Cassette Ser.). (Illus.). 24p. (J). (ps-2). 1991. 5.98 incl. audio (*1-55886-055-X*) Smarty Pants.

An Asterisk (*) at the beginning of an entry indicates that the title is appearing in BIP for the first time.

Tale of Peter Rabbit. Beatrix Potter. (Rabbit Ears Storybook Classics Ser.). (Illus.). 24p. (J). (ps-3). 1993. 3.50 (0-307-12349-9, 12349, Golden Books) Western Pub.
Tale of Peter Rabbit. Beatrix Potter. LC 78-18071. (J). 1988. 2.99 (0-517-65276-5) Random Hse Value.
Tale of Peter Rabbit. Beatrix Potter. LC 78-18071. (J). (gr. k-2). 1994. 3.99 (0-517-10235-8) Random Hse Value.
Tale of Peter Rabbit. Beatrix Potter. (J). 1996. 2.99 (0-517-15989-9) Random Hse Value.
Tale of Peter Rabbit. Beatrix Potter. LC 78-18071. (David McPhail's Favorite Tales Ser.). (Illus.). 32p. (J). (ps-k). 1995. bds. 4.95 (0-590-20547-1, Cartwheel) Scholastic Inc.
Tale of Peter Rabbit. Beatrix Potter. LC 78-18071. (J). 1991. pap. 14.95 (0-88708-079-0, Rabbit) S&S Childrens.
Tale of Peter Rabbit. Beatrix Potter. LC 78-18071. (Illus.). 32p. (J). (gr. k-3). 1979. pap. 3.95 (0-89375-102-2); lib. bdg. 11.89 (0-89375-124-3) Troll Communs.
Tale of Peter Rabbit. Beatrix Potter. (Children's Classics Ser.). (Illus.). 32p. (J). 1991. 6.95 (0-8362-4908-9) Andrews & McMeel.
***Tale of Peter Rabbit.** Beatrix Potter. (J). 1997. 3.95 (1-57719-157-9) GT Pubng Corp.
Tale of Peter Rabbit. Illus. by Jody Wheeler. (Take-a-Look Bks.). 14p. (J). (ps-3). 1995. bds. 3.95 (0-307-12473-8, Golden Books) Western Pub.
Tale of Peter Rabbit. Beatrix Potter. (Illus.). 60p. (J). (gr. 1-5). 1972. reprint ed. pap. 1.75 (0-486-22827-4) Dover.
Tale of Peter Rabbit. Beatrix Potter. LC 92-36655. (Illus.). 64p. (J). 1993. reprint ed. 9.95 incl. audio (0-88708-297-1, Rabbit) S&S Childrens.
Tale of Peter Rabbit. Beatrix Potter. LC 92-36655. (Illus.). 64p. (J). 1993. reprint ed. 4.95 (0-88708-296-3, Rabbit) S&S Childrens.
Tale of Peter Rabbit. Beatrix Potter. LC 95-82094. (Wee Books for Wee Folks). (Illus.). 64p. (J). (ps-2). 1996. reprint ed. 6.95 (1-55709-412-8) Applewood.
Tale of Peter Rabbit, Set. limited ed. Beatrix Potter. (Illus.). 60p. (J). 1993. Cased set. pap. 150.00 (0-7232-4045-0) Warne.
Tale of Peter Rabbit: A Portfolio of Art Prints. limited ed. Beatrix Potter. (Illus.). 52p. 1995. boxed 950.00 (0-9627110-5-5) Battledore Ltd.
Tale of Peter Rabbit: Die Geschichte Des Peterchen Hase. Beatrix Potter. Tr. by Meike Werner. (Illus.). 64p. (Orig.). (GER.). (J). 1992. pap. 2.75 (0-486-27014-9) Dover.
Tale of Peter Rabbit: Full-Color Storybook. Beatrix Potter & Anna Pomaska. LC 94-24671. (Little Activity Bks.). (Illus.). 32p. (Orig.). (J). 1995. pap. text ed. 1.00 (0-486-28541-3) Dover.
Tale of Peter Rabbit: La Storia Del Coniglietto Pietro. Beatrix Potter. Tr. by Alessandro Vettori. (Illus.). 64p. (Orig.). (ITA.). (J). 1992. pap. 2.75 (0-486-27015-7) Dover.
Tale of Peter Rabbit & Benjamin Bunny. Beatrix Potter. (World of Peter Rabbit & Friends Ser.). (Illus.). 32p. (J). (ps-3). 1993. pap. 4.99 (0-7232-4124-4) Warne.
Tale of Peter Rabbit & Chicken Little, 2 bks. (Illus.). 40p. (J). (ps). 1989. Set. pap. 4.95 (0-448-10232-3, G&D) Putnam Pub Group.
Tale of Peter Rabbit & Other Favorite Stories, 7 vols., Set. Beatrix Potter. 447p. (J). (gr. 2 up). boxed 12.25 (0-486-23903-9) Dover.
***Tale of Peter Rabbit & 4 Other Full-Color Storybooks, 5 vols., Set.** Beatrix Potter. (Illus.). (J). pap. 8.75 (0-486-27659-7) Dover.
Tale of Peter Rabbit Coloring Book. (Illus.). (SPA.). (J). 1995. pap. 1.00 (0-486-26794-6) Dover.
Tale of Peter Rabbit Coloring Book. (Illus.). (FRE.). (J). 1995. pap. 1.00 (0-486-26793-8) Dover.
Tale of Peter Rabbit Coloring Book. Beatrix Potter. (Illus.). (J). (gr. k-3). 1976. pap. 2.50 (0-486-21711-6) Dover.
Tale of Peter Rabbit Coloring Book. Beatrix Potter. (Illus.). (J). (gr. k-3). 1986. pap. 1.00 (0-486-25160-8) Dover.
"Tale of Peter Rabbit" in French. Beatrix Potter. Tr. by Judith L. Greenberg from ENG. 64p. (Orig.). (FRE.). 1987. pap. 2.50 (0-486-25313-9) Dover.
"Tale of Peter Rabbit" in Spanish. Beatrix Potter. Tr. by Esperanza G. Saludes from ENG. 64p. (Orig.). (SPA.). 1987. pap. 2.75 (0-486-25314-7) Dover.
Tale of Peter Rabbit Pop Up. Beatrix Potter. (J). 1988. 3.99 (0-517-67098-4) Random Hse Value.
Tale of Peter Rabbit Sticker Book. Beatrix Potter. (J). 1990. pap. 3.99 (0-671-69255-0, Litl Simon S&S) S&S Childrens.
Tale of Peter Rabbit Sticker Storybook. Beatrix Potter & Anna Pomaska. (Illus.). 16p. (Orig.). (J). 1996. pap. text ed. 1.00 (0-486-29087-5) Dover.
Tale of Pig. Helen Cooper. LC 94-24848. (Illus.). 24p. (J). (ps up). 1995. pap. 6.95 (0-688-13992-2) Lothrop.
Tale of Pigling Bland. Beatrix Potter. (Original Peter Rabbit Books: No. 15). (J). 1987. pap. 5.95 (0-7232-3474-4); pap. 2.25 (0-7232-3499-X) Warne.
Tale of Pigling Bland. Beatrix Potter. (World of Peter Rabbit & Friends Ser.). (Illus.). (J). (ps-3). 1994. pap. 4.99 (0-7232-4150-3) Warne.
Tale of Poor Lovers. Vasco Pratolini. (Voices of Resistance Ser.). 368p. 1988. reprint ed. pap. 13.00 (0-85345-723-9) Monthly Rev.
Tale of Princess Charming & Her Search for the Steps to Happiness. Barry A. Ellsworth. (Illus.). 192p. (Orig.). 1992. pap. 10.95 (0-929175-03-4) Brkthrough Pub UT.
Tale of Psyche. Vincent Ferrini. 118p. (Orig.). 1991. pap. text ed. 9.00 (0-9627891-4-3) Igneus Pr.
Tale of Pumpkin Hollow. Reba W. Holt. Ed. by Currey Copple. 9p. (J). (gr. 4-5). 1995. pap. 10.95 (0-9649471-0-2) Whitson Holt.
Tale of Rabbit & Coyote. Tony Johnston. LC 92-43652. 32p. (J). (ps-3). 1994. 15.95 (0-399-22258-8, Putnam) Putnam Pub Group.
Tale of Ralph the Collier: An Alliterative Romance. Elizabeth Walsh. (American University Studies: English Language & Literature: Ser. IV, Vol. 104). 224p. (C). 1989. text ed. 40.50 (0-8204-0813-1) P Lang Pubng.
Tale of Readalot. Madelyn DiRienzo. (Illus.). 24p. (J). 1995. 3.95 (1-885110-01-4) Devers Pubng.
Tale of Ringy. Meyer Azaad. Tr. by Mohammad R. Ghanoonparvar & Diane L. Wilcox from PER. (Illus.). 24p. (Orig.). (J). (gr. 3 up). 1983. reprint ed. pap. 4.95 (0-939214-15-6) Mazda Pubs.
Tale of Sad Reality: John Richardson's Wacousta. Dennis Duffy. (Canadian Fiction Studies: No. 20). 120p. (C). 1993. pap. text ed. 14.95 (1-55022-115-9, Pub. by ECW Press CN) Genl Dist Srvs.
Tale of Samuel Whiskers. Beatrix Potter. (Original Peter Rabbit Books: No. 16). (J). 1987. pap. 5.95 (0-7232-3475-2); pap. 2.25 (0-7232-3500-7) Warne.
Tale of Samuel Whiskers. Beatrix Potter. (World of Peter Rabbit & Friends Ser.). (Illus.). 32p. (J). (ps-3). 1993. pap. 4.99 (0-7232-4142-2) Warne.
***Tale of Sinuhe & Other Ancient Egyptian Poetry 940-1640 B. C.** Richard Parkinson. (Illus.). 336p. 1997. 55.00 (0-19-814963-8) OUP.
Tale of Six Colors. Koshiro Toda. (Kindercolor Ser.). (Illus.). 44p. (J). (ps-1). 1992. 11.95 (1-881267-01-6) Intercultural.
***Tale of Squirrel Nutkin.** Beatrix Potter. (J). 1997. pap. text ed. 2.95 (1-57719-164-1) GT Pubng Corp.
Tale of Squirrel Nutkin. Beatrix Potter. (J). 1992. 3.99 (0-517-07239-4) Random Hse Value.
Tale of Squirrel Nutkin. Beatrix Potter. (Original Peter Rabbit Bks.: No. 2). (J). 1987. pap. 5.95 (0-7232-3461-2) Warne.
Tale of Squirrel Nutkin. Beatrix Potter. (Little Landoll Original Beatrix Potter Ser.). (Illus.). 32p. (J). (ps-6). Date not set. 1.29 (1-56987-020-9) Landoll.
Tale of Squirrel Nutkin. Beatrix Potter. (Illus.). 60p. (J). (gr. 1-5). 1972. reprint ed. pap. 1.75 (0-486-22828-2) Dover.
Tale of Susan Aked. (Red Stripe Ser.). 1989. pap. 4.50 (0-8216-5072-6) Carol Pub Group.
Tale of Tails. Shirley Greenway. (Illus.). 16p. (J). (ps-6). 1992. bds. 3.95 (1-879085-51-8) Whsprng Coyote Pr.
***Tale of Tails.** Vitthal A. Mills. 1995. pap. text ed. 5.00 (1-899171-30-4, Pub. by Findhorn Pr UK) Words Distrib.
Tale of Tall Toothbrush. Elayne Reiss & Rita Friedman. (J). (gr. k-1). 1978. 12.50 (0-89796-869-7) New Dimens Educ.
***Tale of Ten Cities: Immigration's Effect on the Family Environment.** Scipfo Garling & Leon Boovier. (Illus.). 64p. 1996. 10.00 (0-935776-20-6) F A I R.
Tale of the Anti-Christ. Vladimir Solovyov. 1989. reprint ed. pap. 5.95 (1-55818-162-8, Sure Fire) Holmes Pub.
Tale of the Armament of Igor, A.D. 1185, A Russian Historical Epic. Ed. by Leonard A. Magnus. 1977. lib. bdg. 59.95 (0-8490-2727-6) Gordon Pr.
Tale of the Bad Macocha & the Fable of the Underground Punkva River. Karel B. Absolon & Karla Bufkova-Hankelova. (Moravian Tales, Legends, Myths Ser.). (Illus.). 40p. (Orig.). (J). (gr. 4). 1984. pap. text ed. 12.00 (0-930329-02-3) Kabel Pubs.
***Tale of the Bad Tempered Ghost.** Mitchell. (Are You Afraid of the Dark? Ser.: No. 15). (J). 1997. mass mkt. 3.99 (0-671-01429-3) PB.
***Tale of the Body Thief.** Anne Rice. 1997. pap. 14.00 (0-345-41963-4) Ballantine.
Tale of the Body Thief. Anne O. Rice. Date not set. pap. 24.00 (0-676-50515-5) Random.
Tale of the Body Thief. Anne O. Rice. LC 92-53085. (Vampire Chronicles Ser.). 428p. 1992. 23.50 (0-394-22317-9) Knopf.
Tale of the Body Thief. Anne O. Rice. 448p. 1993. mass mkt. 6.99 (0-345-38475-X) Ballantine.
Tale of the Body Thief: The Vampire Chronicles. Anne O. Rice. LC 92-5308. 1992. 24.00 (0-679-40528-3) Knopf.
Tale of the Campaign of Igor. Tr. by Robert C. Howes. (C). 1974. pap. text ed. 3.95 (0-393-09310-7) Norton.
***Tale of the Campfire Girls.** Clayton Emery. (Are You Afraid of the Dark? Ser.). (J). (gr. 3-6). 1997. mass mkt. 3.99 (0-671-00908-7, Minstrel Bks) PB.
***Tale of the Comet.** Roland Green. (Fantastic Adventures Bks.). 1997. pap. 5.99 (0-7869-0654-5) TSR Inc.
***Tale of the Comet.** Thomas Reid. 1997. 30.00 (0-7869-0653-7) TSR Inc.
Tale of the Curious Cat. Diana G. Gallagher. (Are You Afraid of the Dark Ser.: No. 10). (J). (gr. 2-6). 1996. mass mkt. 3.99 (0-671-00081-0) PB.
Tale of the Deadly Diary. Brad Strickland. (Are You Afraid of the Dark Ser.: No. 8). (J). (gr. 4-7). 1996. pap. 3.99 (0-671-53673-7, PB Trade Paper) PB.
Tale of the Elk. W. E. Byrne. 456p. 1995. reprint ed. pap. 14.95 (0-9646197-2-5) Quarrier Pr.
Tale of the Eloquent Peasant. (Griffith Institute Ser.). 1991. pap. 30.00 (0-685-61599-5, Pub. by Aris & Phillips UK) David Brown.
Tale of the Eloquent Peasant. Parkinson. (Griffith Institute Ser.). 1991. 50.00 (0-900416-61-0, Pub. by Aris & Phillips UK) David Brown.
***Tale of the Flopsy Bunnies.** Beatrix Potter. (J). 1997. pap. text ed. 2.95 (1-57719-162-5) GT Pubng Corp.
Tale of the Flopsy Bunnies. Beatrix Potter. (Original Peter Rabbit Books: No. 10). (J). 1987. pap. 5.95 (0-7232-3469-8) Warne.
Tale of the Flopsy Bunnies & Mrs. Tittlemouse. Beatrix Potter. (World of Peter Rabbit & Friends Ser.). (Illus.). 24p. (J). (gr. k-3). 1995. pap. 4.99 (0-7232-4268-2) Warne.
Tale of the Four Dervishes of Amir Khusru. Amina Shah. 1976. 21.00 (0-900860-44-8, Pub. by Octagon Pr UK) ISHK.
Tale of the Frog Prince. Ed. by Bill Roser et al. (J). 1979. pap. 3.75 (0-87129-199-1, T48) Dramatic Pub.
***Tale of the Ghost Cruise.** Weiss. (Are You Afraid of the Dark? Ser.: No. 17). (J). 1998. mass mkt. 3.99 (0-671-01439-0) PB.
Tale of the Ghost Rider. John Vornholt. (Are You Afraid of the Dark Ser.: No. 7). (J). (gr. 4-6). 1996. pap. 3.99 (0-671-56252-5, Minstrel Bks) PB.
Tale of the Great Fruit Tree. John W. Anderson. (Illus.). 40p. (YA). 1992. 15.00 (0-9633296-0-X) Koinonia TX.
Tale of the Heike. Tr. by Helen C. McCullough from JPN. LC 87-18001. (Illus.). 504p. 1988. 69.50 (0-8047-1418-5); pap. 18.95 (0-8047-1803-2) Stanford U Pr.
Tale of the Heike, 2 Vols., Vol. 1. Edward G. Seidensticker. 391p. 1977. pap. 22.50 (0-86008-188-5, Pub. by U of Tokyo JA) Col U Pr.
Tale of the Heike, 2 Vols., Vol. 2. Edwrd G. Seidensticker. 416p. 1977. pap. 22.50 (0-86008-189-3, Pub. by U of Tokyo JA) Col U Pr.
***Tale of the Hero Who Was Exposed at Birth in Euripidean Tragedy: A Study of Motifs.** Marc Huys. (Symbolae Facultatis Litterarum Lovaniensis Series A: Vol. 20). 446p. 1995. 82.50 (90-6186-713-4, Pub. by Leuven Univ BE) Coronet Bks.
Tale of the I Ching: The Beginning of the Book of Changes. wu Wei. Ed. by Les Boston. LC 95-68199. 163p. (Orig.). 1995. pap. 6.95 (0-943015-08-1) Power Press.
Tale of the Incomparable Prince. Tshe Ring Dbang Rgyal. Tr. by Beth Newman. 240p. 1996. 25.00 (0-06-017400-5) HarpC.
***Tale of the Incomparable Prince: The Library of Tibet.** Tshe Ring Dbang Rgyal. Tr. by Beth Newman. 352p. 1997. pap. 13.00 (0-06-092784-4, PL) HarpC.
Tale of the Kind & the Unkind Girls: AA-Th 480 & Related Tales. Warren E. Roberts. LC 93-27257. (Classics in Folklore Ser.). 178p. (C). 1994. reprint ed. pap. text ed. 16.95 (0-8143-2490-8) Wayne St U Pr.
Tale of the Kite. Jacqueline Loumaye. (Child's World Library). (Illus.). 32p. (J). (gr. k-5). 1991. lib. bdg. 18.50 (0-89565-759-7) Childs World.
Tale of the Little Black Fish: Mahi Siah Kuchulu. Samad Behrangi. Tr. by Hooshang Amuzegar. LC 91-73480. (Illus.). 72p. (Orig.). (ENG & PER.). (J). 1992. pap. 8.50 (0-936347-20-1) Iran Bks.
Tale of the Mandarin Ducks. Katherine Paterson. (Illus.). (J). (gr. k-3). 1990. pap. 15.99 (0-525-67283-4, Lodestar Bks) Dutton Child Bks.
Tale of the Mandarin Ducks. Katherine Paterson. (Illus.). 40p. (J). 1995. pap. 5.99 (0-14-055739-3, Puff Unicorn) Puffin Bks.
Tale of the Mayor's Son. Gleyn Maxwell. LC 90-80810. 96p. 9000. pap. 14.95 (1-85224-098-9, Pub. by Bloodaxe Bks UK) Dufour.
Tale of the Mermaid. LeeEllen Griffith. (Illus.). 56p. 1986. pap. 9.00 (0-913346-12-8) Indep Seaport.
Tale of the Millionaire. Fisher. 1997. pap. 11.00 (0-684-80118-3, Fireside) S&S Trade.
Tale of the Mouse: The Family Book on Dying. Patricia Shelton. (Illus.). 60p. 1985. write for info. (0-318-59351-3) Sarasvati.
Tale of the Mouse's Tail. David Schaefer & Maxine Schaefer. (Illus.). 72p. (J). (gr. 3 up). 1995. 9.95 (0-9648692-1-7) Mica Pubs.
Tale of the Naked Hitchhiker: And Other True Stories. Katie Koski. (Illus.). 144p. (Orig.). 1995. pap. 12.95 (0-9649709-8-8) Local Color.
Tale of the Napkin Rabbit. A. J. Wood. LC 93-9864. (J). (gr. 3 up). 1993. 14.95 (0-307-17603-7) Western Pub.
Tale of the Next Great War, 1871-1914: Fictions of Future Warfare & Battles Still-to-Come. Ed. by I. F. Clarke. LC 95-40302. (Illus.). 396p. (FRE & GER.). (C). 1996. text ed. 39.95 (0-8156-2672-X, CLTN); pap. text ed. 17.95 (0-8156-0358-4, CLTN) Syracuse U Pr.
Tale of the Nightly Neighbors No. 4: Are You Afraid of the Dark? MacHale & Derby. (Are You Afraid of the Dark Ser.: No. 4). (J). (gr. 3-6). 1995. mass mkt. 3.99 (0-671-53445-9, PB Trade Paper) PB.
Tale of the Old Fisherman: Contemporary Urdu Short Stories. Ed. & Tr. by Muhammad U. Memon. 176p. 1991. 25.00 (0-89410-681-3, Three Contnts); pap. 11.00 (0-89410-682-1, Three Contnts) Lynne Rienner.
***Tale of the Old Maypop Tree: A Southern Folktale.** Sy Alexander. LC 96-92600. (E. Lee Harvey Collection). (Illus.). iv, 18p. (Orig.). (J). (ps-6). 1996. pap. write for info. (0-9655726-3-3) Proud Two-B Me.
Tale of the Phantom School Bus. Brad Strickland. (Are You Afraid of the Dark Ser.: No. 6). (J). (gr. 3-6). 1996. pap. 3.99 (0-671-53672-9, Pocket Books) PB.
Tale of the Pie & the Patty-Pan. Beatrix Potter. (Original Peter Rabbit Books: No. 17). (J). 1987. pap. 5.95 (0-7232-3476-0); pap. 2.25 (0-7232-3501-5) Warne.
Tale of the Purple Ants. Gale Albury. LC 95-61782. (Illus.). 20p. (Orig.). (J). (ps-8). Date not set. pap. 2.50 (0-614-13305-X) TEA Pubs.
Tale of the Restless House. John Peel. (Are You Afraid of the Dark Ser.). (J). (gr. 3-6). 1995. mass mkt. 3.99 (0-671-52547-6, Minstrel Bks) PB.
Tale of the Ring: A Kaddish. Frank Stiffel. LC 83-63000. 320p. 1984. 22.50 (0-916366-21-9) Pushcart Pr.
Tale of the Ring: A Kaddish. Frank Stiffel. 1993. pap. 15.00 (0-916366-86-3) Pushcart Pr.
Tale of the Sea Horse. (Little Golden Sound Story Bks.). (Illus.). 24p. (J). 1995. bds. 6.95 (0-307-74837-5, Golden Pr) Western Pub.
Tale of the Secret Mirror. Brad Strickland. (Are You Afraid of the Dark Ser.: No. 5). (J). (gr. 3-6). 1995. mass mkt. 3.99 (0-671-53671-0) PB.
***Tale of the Shimmering Shell.** David C. Weiss. (Are You Afraid of the Dark Ser.). (J). 1997. mass mkt. 3.99 (0-671-00392-5, Minstrel Bks) PB.
Tale of the Sinister Statues. John Peel. Ed. by Lisa Clancy. (Are You Afraid of the Dark Ser.). 128p. (Orig.). (J). (gr. 3-6). 1995. mass mkt. 3.99 (0-671-52545-X, Minstrel Bks) PB.
Tale of the Soga Brothers. Tr. by Thomas Cogan. 310p. (JPN.). 1987. 39.50 (0-86008-411-6, Pub. by U of Tokyo JA) Col U Pr.
Tale of the Tell, Archeological Studies: Archaeological Studies by Paul W. Lapp. Paul W. Lapp. Ed. by Nancy L. Lapp. LC 75-5861. (Pittsburgh Theological Monographs: No. 5). 1975. pap. 9.25 (0-915138-05-0) Pickwick.
Tale of the Tickle Bug. Jane Norman & Frank Beazley. 24p. (J). (ps-3). 1993. pap. write for info. (1-883585-03-1) Pixanne Ent.
Tale of the Tribe: Ezra Pound & the Modern Verse Epic. Michael A. Bernstein. LC 80-129. 335p. reprint ed. pap. 95.50 (0-7837-4325-4, 2044029) Bks Demand.
Tale of the Two Golden Doves. Donald F. Lippert. 64p. (Orig.). 1989. pap. 7.95 (0-925737-00-3) Pastel Pubns.
Tale of the Unicorn. Otfried Preussler. LC 88-7141. (Illus.). 32p. (J). (ps up). 1989. pap. 12.95 (0-8037-0583-2) Dial Bks Young.
Tale of the Unicorn. Otfried Preussler. (Illus.). 32p. (J). (ps up). 1992. pap. 4.99 (0-14-054568-9, Puff Pied Piper) Puffin Bks.
Tale of the Virtual Nightmare. Ted Pedersen. (Are You Afraid of the Dark Ser.: No. 9). (J). (gr. 3-6). 1996. mass mkt. 3.99 (0-671-00080-2) PB.
***Tale of the Whale: Great Adventures.** Roger Befelar. (Illus.). 24p. 1997. pap. 2.99 (0-88743-461-4) Sch Zone Pub Co.
Tale of the Whale see **Books to Learn & Live by**
Tale of the Zero Hero. John Peel. (Are You Afraid of the Dark Ser.: No. 11). (YA). 1997. mass mkt. 3.99 (0-671-00357-7) PB.
Tale of Theodore Bear. Cecile Green. LC 68-56812. (Illus.). 32p. (J). (gr. 1-2). 1968. lib. bdg. 9.95 (0-87783-038-X) Oddo.
Tale of Theodore Bear. Cecile Green. (Illus.). (J). (gr. 1-2). 1978. pap. 1.25 (0-89508-060-5) Rainbow Bks.
Tale of Thomas Mead. Pat Hutchins. LC 79-6398. (Greenwillow Read-Alone Bks.). (Illus.). 32p. (J). (gr. 1-4). 1980. lib. bdg. 15.93 (0-688-84282-8) Greenwillow.
Tale of Three Cities: Elsinore-Montreal-Tokyo. James R. Kidd. LC 74-9351. (Landmark Ser.). 1974. pap. 2.00 (0-87060-066-4, LNH 3) Syracuse U Cont Ed.
Tale of Three Cities: Labor Organization & Protest in Paterson, Passaic, & Lawrence, 1916-1921. David J. Goldberg. LC 88-15812. (Class & Culture Ser.). 275p. (C). 1989. text ed. 38.00 (0-8135-1371-5); pap. text ed. 17.00 (0-8135-1372-3) Rutgers U Pr.
***Tale of Three Cities: London, Shanghai & Hong Kong: Three Centuries of Sino-British Trade in the Decorative Arts.** (Illus.). 350p. Date not set. write for info. (0-9622588-3-0) Sothebys Pubns.
Tale of Three Cities: The 1993 Rede Lecture & Related Summit Declarations. L. M. Singhvi. 86p. (C). 1996. pap. text ed. 14.95 (0-521-57818-3) Cambridge U Pr.
Tale of Three Heads. Irina Ratushinskaya. Tr. & Intro. by Diane N. Ignashev. LC 86-25623. 128p. (ENG & RUS.). 1986. pap. 7.50 (0-938920-83-9) Hermitage.
Tale of Three Kings: A Study of Brokenness. 2nd ed. Gene Edwards. LC 92-14408. 111p. 1992. pap. 8.99 (0-8423-6908-2) Tyndale.
Tale of Three Kings: Discussion Guide. Gene Edwards. 1995. pap. 4.99 (0-8423-7153-2) Tyndale.
Tale of Three Trees. Angela E. Hunt. (Illus.). 32p. (J). (gr. 5-7). 1989. 14.95 (0-7459-1743-7) Lion USA.
***Tale of Three Wars.** Edward B. Atkeson. 400p. 1996. 29.95 (1-889927-00-7) US Army War Coll Found Pr.
Tale of Three Women: God's Call & Their Response. Aurelia R. Downey. 104p. (YA). (gr. 9-12). 1993. pap. 10.00 (0-9641602-1-8) A R Downey.
***Tale of Timmy Tiptoes.** Beatrix Potter. (J). 1997. pap. text ed. 2.95 (1-57719-161-7) GT Pubng Corp.
Tale of Timmy Tiptoes. Beatrix Potter. (Original Peter Rabbit Books: No. 12). (J). 1987. pap. 5.95 (0-7232-3471-X) Warne.
Tale of Timmy Tiptoes. Beatrix Potter. (Illus.). 64p. (J). (gr. 3 up). 1987. reprint ed. pap. 1.75 (0-486-25541-7) Dover.
Tale of Tobias. Illus. by Rachel Merriman. LC 95-4812. 32p. (J). (gr. k-3). 1996. 15.99 (1-56402-692-2) Candlewick Pr.
***Tale of Tom Kitten.** Beatrix Potter. (J). 1997. 3.95 (1-57719-160-9) GT Pubng Corp.
Tale of Tom Kitten. Beatrix Potter. (J). 1988. 2.99 (0-517-65278-1) Random Hse Value.
Tale of Tom Kitten. Beatrix Potter. (J). (gr. k-2). 1994. 3.99 (0-517-10237-4) Random Hse Value.
Tale of Tom Kitten. Beatrix Potter. (Original Peter Rabbit Bks.: No. 8). (Illus.). (J). (ps-3). 1987. pap. 5.95 (0-7232-3467-1); pap. 2.25 (0-7232-3492-2) Warne.
Tale of Tom Kitten. Beatrix Potter. LC 87-40285. (Illus.). 24p. (J). (ps up). 1990. 6.95 incl. audio (1-55782-018-X) Little.
Tale of Tom Kitten. Beatrix Potter. (Illus.). 32p. (J). (ps-3). 1994. pap. 3.99 (0-14-054296-5) Puffin Bks.
Tale of Tom Kitten. Beatrix Potter. (Illus.). 58p. (J). (gr. k up). 1983. reprint ed. pap. 1.75 (0-486-24502-0) Dover.
Tale of Tom Kitten: Full-Color Storybook. Beatrix Potter & Anna Pomaska. LC 95-4651. (Illus.). 32p. (J). 1996. reprint ed. pap. text ed. 1.00 (0-486-28853-6) Dover.
Tale of Tom Kitten & Jemima Puddle-Duck. Beatrix Potter. (World of Peter Rabbit & Friends Ser.). 1993. pap. 4.99 (0-7232-4128-7) Warne.

Tale of Tom Kitten Pop-Up. Beatrix Potter. (J). 1988. 3.99 (*0-517-67099-2*) Random Hse Value.

Tale of Troy. Roger L. Green. (Illus.). (Orig.). (J). (gr. 5-7). 1974. pap. 3.95 (*0-14-030120-8*, Puffin) Puffin Bks.

Tale of Troy. Roger L. Green. 224p. (YA). (gr. 5 up). 1995. pap. 3.99 (*0-14-036745-4*) Puffin Bks.

Tale of Tsar Saltan. Aleksandr Pushkin. LC 95-38661. (Illus.). 32p. (J). (gr. k up). 1996. pap. 16.99 (*0-8037-2001-7*) Dial Bks Young.

Tale of Two Agencies: A Comparative Analysis of the General Accounting Office & the Office of Management & Budget. Frederick C. Mosher. LC 83-10634. (Miller Center Series on the American Presidency). xxvi, 219p. 1986. pap. text ed. 12.95 (*0-8071-1305-0*) La State U Pr.

Tale of Two Bad Mice. Beatrix Potter. (Original Peter Rabbit Bks.: No. 5). (Illus.). (J). (ps-3). 1987. pap. 5.95 (*0-7232-3464-7*) Warne.

Tale of Two Bad Mice. Beatrix Potter. (J). 1992. 3.99 (*0-517-07241-6*) Random Hse Value.

Tale of Two Bad Mice. Beatrix Potter. (Silver Elm Classic Ser.). (Illus.). 32p. (J). (gr. k-3). 1992. pap. 2.99 (*0-87406-620-4*) Willowisp Pr.

***Tale of Two Bad Mice.** deluxe ed. Beatrix Potter. 1997. 16.00 (*0-614-29145-3*) Warne.

Tale of Two Bridges & the Battle for the Skies over North Vietnam. Delbert Corum et al. (USAF Southeast Asia Monograph Ser.: Monographs 1 & 2). (Illus.). 193p. 1986. reprint ed. pap. write for info. (*0-912799-26-9*) Off Air Force.

Tale of Two Brothers. Charles E. Moldenke. 60p. 1988. pap. 6.95 (*0-933121-16-4*) Black Classic.

Tale of Two Cabins. Helen H. Danforth. (Illus.). 36p. (Orig.). (J). (gr. 7 up). 1985. pap. 4.95 (*0-9614899-0-1*) Pioneer Farm.

Tale of Two Cities. (Fiction Ser.). (YA). 1993. pap. text ed. 6.50 (*0-582-08466-0*, 79830) Longman.

***Tale of Two Cities.** Dickens. Date not set. 24.95 (*0-559-35019-8*) Putnam Pub Group.

Tale of Two Cities. Charles Dickens. (Airmont Classics Ser.). (YA). (gr. 9 up). 1964. mass mkt. 4.95 (*0-8049-0021-3*, CL-21) Airmont.

Tale of Two Cities. Charles Dickens. LC 92-73542. 1993. 20.00 (*0-679-42073-8*, Everymans Lib) Knopf.

***Tale of Two Cities.** Charles Dickens. LC 95-77835. (Classroom Reading Plays Ser.). 32p. (YA). (gr. 6-12). 1995. pap. 3.95 (*0-7854-1119-4*, 40207) Am Guidance.

Tale of Two Cities. Charles Dickens. 1996. audio 22.00 (*0-553-47440-5*) Bantam.

Tale of Two Cities. Charles Dickens. 384p. (J). (gr. 7). 1960. pap. 3.95 (*0-451-52441-1*, Sig Classics) NAL-Dutton.

***Tale of Two Cities.** Charles Dickens. 1997. mass mkt. 4.95 (*0-451-52656-2*, Sig Classics) NAL-Dutton.

Tale of Two Cities. Charles Dickens. Ed. by Harry Shefter et al. 528p. mass mkt. 4.99 (*0-671-69583-5*, WSP) PB.

Tale of Two Cities. Charles Dickens. (Vintage Classics Ser.). 384p. 1990. pap. 10.00 (*0-679-72965-8*, Vin) Random.

Tale of Two Cities. Charles Dickens. 384p. (YA). 1989. pap. 2.50 (*0-8125-0506-9*) Tor Bks.

Tale of Two Cities. Charles Dickens. 1993. pap. 3.95 (*0-89375-783-7*) Troll Communs.

Tale of Two Cities. Charles Dickens. Ed. by George Woodcock. (English Library). 416p. 1970. pap. 6.95 (*0-14-043054-7*, Penguin Classics) Viking Penguin.

***Tale of Two Cities.** Charles Dickens. (Illustrated Classics Collection 2). 64p. 1994. pap. 4.95 (*0-7854-0724-3*, 40418) Am Guidance.

Tale of Two Cities. Charles Dickens. 368p. (gr. 9-12). 1989. pap. 3.95 (*0-553-21176-5*, Bantam Classics) Bantam.

Tale of Two Cities. Charles Dickens. 368p. (YA). (gr. 9-12). 1989. teacher ed. write for info. (*0-318-51005-7*, Bantam Classics) Bantam.

Tale of Two Cities. Charles Dickens. Ed. by Norman Page. 1994. pap. text ed. 4.95 (*0-460-87451-9*, Everyman's Classic Lib) C E Tuttle.

Tale of Two Cities. Charles Dickens. LC 91-58650. (Literary Classics Ser.). 256p. 1992. 5.98 (*1-56138-114-4*) Courage Bks.

Tale of Two Cities. Charles Dickens. (World's Classics Ser.). 512p. 1988. pap. 4.95 (*0-19-281771-X*) OUP.

Tale of Two Cities. Charles Dickens. LC 79-24746. (Short Classics Ser.). (Illus.). (J). (gr. 4 up). 1983. lib. bdg. 24.26 (*0-8172-1658-8*) Raintree Steck-V.

Tale of Two Cities. Charles Dickens. 1996. 17.50 (*0-679-60208-9*) Random.

Tale of Two Cities. Charles Dickens. write for info. (*0-318-58796-3*) S&S Trade.

Tale of Two Cities. Charles Dickens. 27.95 (*0-8488-0076-1*) Amereon Ltd.

Tale of Two Cities. Charles Dickens. 1993. pap. 5.25 (*0-19-585452-7*) OUP.

Tale of Two Cities. Charles Dickens. LC 95-77835. 384p. (YA). (gr. 5 up). 1996. pap. 3.99 (*0-14-037336-5*) Puffin Bks.

Tale of Two Cities. Charles Dickens. 1996. mass mkt. 5.99 (*0-671-00274-0*) PB.

***Tale of Two Cities.** Charles Dickens. Ed. by Malvina Vogel. (Great Illustrated Classics Ser.: Vol. 26). (Illus.). 240p. (J). (gr. 3-6). 1993. 9.95 (*0-86611-977-9*) Playmore Inc.

***Tale of Two Cities.** Ed. by Don Nardo. LC 97-5019. (Literary Companion Ser.). (YA). (gr. 9-12). 1997. pap. 12.96 (*1-56510-648-2*) Greenhaven.

***Tale of Two Cities.** Ed. by Don Nardo. LC 97-5019. (Literary Companion Ser.). (YA). (gr. 9-12). 1997. lib. bdg. 20.96 (*1-56510-649-0*) Greenhaven.

Tale of Two Cities. large type ed. Charles Dickens. 515p. 1996. reprint ed. lib. bdg. 24.00 (*0-939495-00-7*) North Bks.

Tale of Two Cities. large type ed. Charles Dickens. (Clear Type Classics Ser.). 485p. 1992. 23.95 (*1-85695-315-7*, Pub. by ISIS UK) Transaction Pubs.

Tale of Two Cities. Charles Dickens. 1982. reprint ed. lib. bdg. 20.95 (*0-89966-371-0*) Buccaneer Bks.

Tale of Two Cities: An Annotated Bibliography. Ruth F. Glancy. LC 92-40546. (Dickens Bibliographies Ser.: Vol. 12). 264p. 1993. text ed. 45.00 (*0-8240-7091-7*, H1339) Garland.

Tale of Two Cities: Global Change, Local Feeling & Everyy<day Life in the North of England - a Study in Manchester & Sheffield. Ian Taylor et al. LC 95-37938. 416p. (C). 1996. pap. 24.95 (*0-415-13829-9*); text ed. 75.00 (*0-415-13828-0*) Routledge.

Tale of Two Cities: Memphis Rock, New Orleans Roll. Robert Palmer. (I.S.A.M. Monographs: No. 12). (Illus.). 38p. 1979. pap. 10.00 (*0-914678-12-4*) Inst Am Music.

***Tale of Two Cities: Sodom & Gomorrah in the Old Testament, Early Jewish & Early Christian Traditions.** J. A. Loader. (Contributions to Biblical Exegesis & Theology Ser.: Vol. 1). 150p. 1990. pap. 28.50 (*90-242-5333-0*, Pub. by KOK Pharos NE) Eisenbrauns.

Tale of Two Cities: Student Activity Book. Marcia Sohl & Gerald Dackerman. (Now Age Illustrated Ser.). (Illus.). (J). (gr. 4-10). 1976. pap. 1.25 (*0-88301-196-4*) Pendulum Pr.

***Tale of Two Cities: The Dave McPherson Story.** Dave McPherson & Derek Watson. (Illus.). 192p. 1997. 34.95 (*1-85158-879-5*, Pub. by Mnstream UK) Trafalgar.

Tale of Two Cities: The Mormons-Catholics. Bill Taylor. 1981. pap. 9.50 (*0-933046-02-2*) Little Red Hen.

Tale of Two Cities see Oxford Illustrated Dickens

Tale of Two Cities - Straight. Charles Dickens. 1995. 5.25 (*0-87129-503-2*, T31) Dramatic Pub.

Tale of Two Cities & a Train: History of the Nevada County Narrow Gauge Railroad 1874-1942. Juanita K. Browne. LC 87-60181. (Illus.). viii, 216p. 1990. pap. 14.50 (*0-915641-03-8*) Nevada County Hist Society.

Tale of Two Cities (Dickens) Morrice. (Book Notes Ser.). (C). 1984. pap. 3.50 (*0-8120-3444-9*) Barron.

Tale of Two Cities Notes. James Weigel, Jr. 1988. pap. 4.50 (*0-8220-1255-3*) Cliffs.

***Tale of Two Cities Readalong.** Charles Dickens. (Illustrated Classics Collection 2). 64p. 1994. pap. 14.95 incl. audio (*0-7854-0690-5*, 40420) Am Guidance.

***Tale of Two Continents: The Life of a Physicist in a Turbulent World.** Abraham Pais. LC 96-39313. 520p. 1997. 35.00 (*0-691-01243-1*) Princeton U Pr.

Tale of Two Conventions: An Account of the Republican & Democratic National Conventions of June, 1912. Ed. by Virgil B. McNitt. LC 73-19136. (Politics & People Ser.). (Illus.). 336p. 1974. reprint ed. 25.95 (*0-405-05860-8*) Ayer.

Tale of Two Countries. Stanley Fogel. 170p. (C). 1984. pap. text ed. 14.00 (*0-920802-51-6*, Pub. by ECW Press CN) Genl Dist Srvs.

Tale of Two Courts: Judicial Settlement of Controversies Between the States of the Swiss & American Federations. William G. Rice. LC 67-20758. 149p. reprint ed. pap. 42.50 (*0-317-39658-7*, 2023718) Bks Demand.

Tale of Two Dolphins. large type ed. Horace Dobbs. (Illus.). 352p. 1988. 25.99 (*0-7089-1757-7*) Ulverscroft.

***Tale of Two Gardens: Poems from India 1952-1995.** Octavio Paz. Ed. & Tr. by Eliot Weinberger from SPA. Tr. by Elizabeth Bishop et al. from SPA. LC 96-38111. (New Directions Bibelot Ser.). 96p. 1997. pap. 8.00 (*0-8112-1349-8*, NDP841) New Directions.

Tale of Two Horses. A. F. Tschiffely. 225p. (C). 1988. 39.00 (*1-85219-045-0*, Pub. by Bishopsgate Pr Ltd UK) St Mut.

Tale of Two Industries: The Contradiction of Coal & Steel in the North East of England. Huw Beynon et al. 128p. 1991. 80.00 (*0-335-09682-4*, Open Univ Pr); pap. 27.00 (*0-335-09681-6*, Open Univ Pr) Taylor & Francis.

***Tale of Two Kingdoms.** Beatrice Ruder. 28p. (Orig.). 1997. mass mkt. 5.99 (*1-55237-297-9*, Pub. by Comnwlth Pub CN) Partners Pubs Grp.

***Tale of Two Kitties.** David Hutchinson. LC 96-71063. (Illus.). 246p. (Orig.). 1996. per. 21.00 (*0-9651412-2-5*) New Wind.

***Tale of Two Mary's.** Danny Kubat. (Orig.). 1997. mass mkt. 4.99 (*1-55197-378-2*, Pub. by Comnwlth Pub CN) Partners Pubs Grp.

Tale of Two Meetings. Julie A. Waterman. 7p. (Orig.). 1983. pap. 1.25 (*0-943334-08-X*) Carmonelle Pubns.

***Tale of Two Parties: A History of the Labour Party.** David Powell & Tony Benn. 352p. 1997. 39.95 (*0-7206-1041-9*, Pub. by P Owen Ltd UK) Dufour.

Tale of Two Princes - Eckart Zur Nieden. Adapted by Mack Thomas. 32p. (J). (ps-2). 1993. 8.99 (*0-88070-598-1*, Gold & Honey) Multnomah Pubs.

Tale of Two Rice Birds. Clare H. Meeker. (Illus.). 32p. (J). (ps up). 1994. 14.95 (*1-57061-008-8*) Sasquatch Bks.

Tale of Two Selves. Sterling G. Ellsworth. Ed. by Susan Roylance. (C). pap. 7.50 (*0-685-30413-2*) Roylance Pub.

Tale of Two Sisters. Jean Bow. 1991. 12.50 (*0-533-09395-3*) Vantage.

Tale of Two Spiders: Not for Children. E. L. Brooke. (Illus.). 104p. 1996. pap. 9.95 (*1-887922-09-1*) Orange Cty Univ Pr.

Tale of Two Tapestries. 447p. 1993. 18.95 (*0-9637148-0-5*) SILC Fnd.

Tale of Two Testaments. William Riley. LC 85-50692. 152p. (C). 1985. pap. 5.95 (*0-89622-240-3*) Twenty-Third.

Tale of Two Testaments. William Riley. 150p. 1989. pap. 22.00 (*0-86217-180-6*, Pub. by Veritas IE) St Mut.

Tale of Two Turkeys. Ellen Jackson. 32p. (J). 1995. pap. 2.50 (*0-8167-3755-X*) Troll Communs.

Tale of Two Undertakers. Alan Richardson. Ed. by William-Alan Landes. 55p. (Orig.). 1996. pap. 5.00 (*0-88734-381-3*) Players Pr.

***Tale of Two Utopia's.** Paul Berman. Date not set. pap. 13.00 (*0-393-31675-0*) Norton.

Tale of Two Utopias: The Political Journey of the Generation of 1968. Paul Berman. LC 95-25321. 352p. 1996. 24.00 (*0-393-03927-7*) Norton.

***Tale of Two Wagons & Other Chanuka Stories.** Raizy Kessler. LC 94-69038. 171p. (J). (gr. 5-9). Date not set. 12.95 (*1-56062-286-5*) CIS Comm.

***Tale of Two Zombies.** Mercer Mayer. (Pictureback Ser.). (J). 1998. pap. 3.25 (*0-679-88710-5*) Random Bks Yng Read.

Tale of Valor. Vardis Fisher. 1976. reprint ed. lib. bdg. 30.95 (*0-89190-834-X*, Rivercity Pr) Amereon Ltd.

***Tale of Valor: A Novel of the Lewis & Clark Expedition.** Vardis Fisher. 496p. 1960. pap. 2.95 (*0-614-22026-2*) Idaho Ctr Bk.

Tale of Willie Monroe. Alan Schroeder. LC 96-22493. (Illus.). (J). 1997. write for info. (*0-395-69852-9*) HM.

Tale of Woe, Vol. 127: Papyrus Pushkin. Caminos. 1997. 45.00 (*0-900416-09-2*, Pub. by Aris & Phillips UK) David Brown.

Tale-Teller Tells All. Ellen Phillips. 1990. write for info. (*0-9628226-0-4*) Cricket Papers Pr.

Tale That Wagged the Dog. Tim Kelly. 1976. 3.00 (*0-87129-544-X*, T11) Dramatic Pub.

Tale That Wags the God. James Blish. 1987. 18.00 (*0-911682-29-5*) Advent.

Tale Told by An Idiot. R. P. Noronha. 1976. 9.00 (*0-88386-933-0*) S Asia.

Tale Type & Motif Index of Early U. S. Almanacs. J. Michael Stitt & Robert K. Dodge. LC 91-15824. (Bibliographies & Indexes in American Literature Ser.: No. 14). 416p. 1991. text ed. 75.00 (*0-313-26048-6*, DHM, Greenwood Pr) Greenwood.

Tale Without a Hero & Twenty-Two Poems by Anna Axmatova. Jeanne Van Der Eng-Liedmeier. Ed. by Kees Verheul. LC 72-88218. (Dutch Studies in Russian Literature: No. 3). 141p. 1973. pap. text ed. 30.80 (*90-279-2370-1*) Mouton.

Taleb on Risk: Dynamic Hedging. Nassim Taleb. LC 96-34283. 1996. text ed. 70.00 (*0-471-15280-3*) Wiley.

Taleem-Ul-Islam, 4. M. Qaderi. (J). pap. 7.50 (*0-933511-72-8*) Kazi Pubns.

Talent. Nigel Rees. 384p. 1989. pap. 9.95 (*0-7472-3252-0*, Pub. by Headline UK) Trafalgar.

Talent & Courage: Outstanding West Virginia Women in the 1990s. Ethel O. Davie. 125p. 1992. pap. write for info. (*0-9634513-0-8*) E O Davie.

Talent & Education - Present Status & Future Directions: Conference of Gifted Children, University of Minnesota, 1958. Ed. by Ellis P. Torrance. LC 60-15896. (Modern School Practice Ser.: No. 4). 222p. reprint ed. pap. 63.30 (*0-317-28174-7*, 2055966) Bks Demand.

Talent Development: Symposium Proceedings, August 1991. Colangelo et al. 432p. 1992. pap. 20.00 (*0-89824-538-9*) Trillium Pr.

Talent Development: Theories & Practices. Jan Hansen & Steve Hoover. 356p. (C). 1995. per. 34.59 (*0-8403-9520-5*) Kendall-Hunt.

Talent Development II: Proceedings from the 1993 Henry B. & Jocelyn Wallace National Research Symposium on Talent Development. Ed. by Nicholas Colangelo et al. LC 94-35336. 1995. 26.00 (*0-910707-23-5*) Gifted Psych Pr.

Talent for Genius: The Life & Times of Oscar Levant. Sam Kashner. 1994. 28.00 (*0-679-40489-9*, Villard Bks) Random.

Talent for Murder. Carolyn Keene. Ed. by Anne Greenberg. (Nancy Drew Files Ser.: No. 75). 160p. (Orig.). (YA). (gr. 6 up). 1992. mass mkt. 3.99 (*0-671-73079-7*, Archway) PB.

Talent for Stupidity: The Psychology of the Bungler, the Incompetent, & the Ineffectual. Edmund Bergler. LC 97-9002. 250p. 1997. 32.50 (*0-8236-6345-0*) Intl Univs Pr.

Talent for Tomorrow: Life Stories of South African Servants. Suzanne Gordon. LC 82-95941. 275p. 1985. pap. text ed. 16.95 (*0-86975-243-X*, Pub. by Ravan Pr ZA) Ohio U Pr.

Talent for Trouble: The Life of Hollywood's Most Acclaimed Director, William Wyler. Jan Herman. LC 95-22432. 528p. 1996. text ed. 35.00 (*0-399-14012-3*, Putnam) Putnam Pub Group.

***Talent for Trouble: The Life of Hollywood's Most Acclaimed Director, William Wyler.** Jan Herman. LC 97-16338. (Illus.). 544p. 1997. reprint ed. pap. 16.95 (*0-306-80798-X*) Da Capo.

Talent for War. Jack McDevitt. 320p. 1989. reprint ed. mass mkt. 5.99 (*0-441-79553-6*) Ace Bks.

Talent Night. Jean D. Okimoto. LC 93-34591. 176p. (YA). (gr. 7-9). 1995. 14.95 (*0-590-47809-5*) Scholastic Inc.

Talent of T. S. Eliot. George C. Williamson. 1972. 250.00 (*0-8490-1176-0*) Gordon Pr.

Talent Opportunity Program (TOPS) U. S. A. Gymnastics - Women's National Training Camp, Birmingham, AL, May 1993. USGF Women's Elite Program Committee Staff. 29p. 1993. 24.95 incl. vhs (*1-885250-25-8*); 24.95 incl. vhs (*1-885250-24-X*); pap. 10.00 (*1-885250-23-1*) USA Gymnastics.

Talent Show. Nancy Carlson. LC 85-4122. (Illus.). 32p. (J). (ps-3). 1985. lib. bdg. 13.13 (*0-87614-284-6*, Carolrhoda) Lerner Group.

Talent, Teaching & Achievement. Ed. by John Radford. 160p. 1991. pap. 29.95 (*1-85302-111-3*) Taylor & Francis.

Talent to Annoy: Essays, Articles & Reviews 1929-1968. Nancy Mitford. Ed. by Charlotte Mosley. 232p. 1987. 16.95 (*0-8253-0429-6*) Beaufort Bks NY.

Talent-Worth Its Weight in Gold. Yvonne Reynolds. Ed. by Joanne Reynolds. LC 95-95297. (Illus.). 176p. (Orig.). 1996. pap. 12.95 (*0-9650824-0-7*) Lolot Pr.

Talented: Strategies for Developing the Talent in Every Learner. Jerry D. Flack. (Gifted Treasury Ser.). xiii, 249p. 1993. pap. text ed. 24.00 (*1-56308-127-X*) Teacher Ideas Pr.

Talented Mr. Ripley. Patricia Highsmith. LC 92-5351. 1992. pap. 11.00 (*0-679-74229-8*, Vin) Random.

Talented Teenagers: The Roots of Success & Failure. Mihaly Csikszentmihalyi et al. LC 92-38165. (Illus.). 336p. (C). 1993. text ed. 25.95 (*0-521-41578-0*) Cambridge U Pr.

Talented Teenagers: The Roots of Success & Failure. Mihaly Csikszentmihalyi et al. 320p. 1996. pap. text ed. 17.95 (*0-521-57463-3*) Cambridge U Pr.

Talented, Tired, Beautiful Feet: A Bible Study for Women. Phyllis N. Kersten & E. Louise Williams. 64p. (Orig.). 1985. pap. 3.99 (*0-570-03967-3*, 12-3002) Concordia.

Talento 7. Talento Publicacoes Staff. 1996. 65.00 (*0-8230-6508-1*) Watsn-Guptill.

Talents & Technicians: Literary Chic & the New Assembly-Line Fiction. John W. Aldridge. 160p. 1992. text ed. 18.00 (*0-684-18789-2*) S&S Trade.

***Talers of the Austrian Noble Houses.** John S. Davenport. 64p. 1988. pap. 4.00 (*1-889172-14-6*) Numismatic Intl.

Tales. Wilhelm Hauff. Tr. by S. Mendel. (Short Story Index Reprint Ser.). 1977. 23.95 (*0-8369-3404-0*) Ayer.

Tales. E. T. A. Hoffmann. Ed. & Intro. by Victor Lange. LC 82-7316. (German Library: Vol. 26). 300p. 1982. 29.50 (*0-8264-0254-2*); pap. text ed. 16.95 (*0-8264-0264-X*) Continuum.

Tales. Stephen-Paul Martin. 24p. (Orig.). 1989. pap. 4.00 (*0-945926-11-1*) Paradigm RI.

Tales. Inayat Khan. 248p. 1991. reprint ed. pap. 13.50 (*0-930872-37-1*) Omega Pubns NY.

***Tales Bk. 1: From Behind the Wire.** T. Wolfe Tone. 96p. 1996. mass mkt. 2.95 (*1-887900-14-4*) Peanut Books.

Tales about Tails. Jacqueline Mack. (Illus.). 24p. (J). (ps-1). 1985. 10.95 (*0-88625-089-7*) Durkin Hayes Pub.

Tales Alive! Ten Multicultural Folktales, with Activities. Susan Milord. LC 94-101. (Tales Alive! Ser.: No. 1). (Illus.). 127p. (Orig.). (J). (gr. k-6). 1994. pap. 15.95 (*0-913589-79-9*) Williamson Pub Co.

Tales Alive in Turkey. Warren S. Walker & Ahmet E. Uysal. LC 89-27705. xvi, 310p. (C). 1990. reprint ed. 25.00 (*0-89672-212-0*); reprint ed. pap. 13.50 (*0-89672-213-9*) Tex Tech Univ Pr.

Tales along the Appalachian Plateau. Danny Fulks. (Illus.). 128p. (Orig.). 1995. pap. 9.95 (*0-933087-38-1*) Bottom Dog Pr.

Tales Along the Grand Strand of South Carolina. Blanche W. Floyd. (Illus.). 1996. pap. 12.95 (*1-878177-08-7*) Bandit Bks.

Tales & Declarations. Bruce H. Rogers. (Dog River Review Poetry Ser.: No. 9). 32p. (Orig.). (YA). 1991. pap. 4.00 (*0-916155-13-7*) Trout Creek.

***Tales & Irreverencies of a Country Parson.** Eugene F. Todd. (Illus.). xii, 525p. (Orig.). 1997. 29.95 (*0-9654090-7-4*) Wstrn Americana.

Tales & Legends of Ancient Burma. S. W. Cocks. LC 78-67697. (Folktale Ser.). reprint ed. 34.50 (*0-404-16068-9*) AMS Pr.

Tales & Legends of Morocco. Elisa Chimenti. Tr. by Arnon Benamy. (Illus.). (J). (gr. 5 up). 1965. 10.95 (*0-8392-3049-4*) Astor-Honor.

Tales & Legends of National Origin: Or Widely Current in England from Early Times. William C. Hazlitt. LC 72-80500. 501p. 1972. reprint ed. 34.95 (*0-405-08607-5*, Pub. by Blom Pubns UK) Ayer.

Tales & Legends of the Q'anjob'al Maya. Ed. & Tr. by Fernando Penalosa. (Illus.). 178p. (Orig.). 1995. pap. 8.95 (*1-886502-03-X*) Yax Te Found.

Tales & Lores of the Mountaineers. William B. Price. 1986. reprint ed. 10.00 (*0-685-53558-4*) McClain.

Tales & Novels, 10 Vols, Set. Maria Edgeworth. LC 79-164752. reprint ed. 480.00 (*0-404-02250-2*) AMS Pr.

Tales & Novels: The Longford Edition, 10 vols., Set. Maria Edgeworth. (Anglistica & Americana Ser.: No. 31). (Illus.). 1969. reprint ed. 637.00 (*0-685-66462-7*, 05102271) G Olms Pubs.

Tales & Parables of Sri Ramakrishna. Sri Ramakrishna. 1943. pap. 5.95 (*0-87481-493-6*) Vedanta Pr.

Tales & Poems of Tonga. E. E. V. Collocott. (BMB Ser.: No. 46). 1974. reprint ed. 25.00 (*0-527-02152-0*) Periodicals Srv.

Tales & Sketches: Incl. Twice-Told Tales; Mosses from an Old Manse; The Snow Image, & Other Twice-Told Tales; A Wonder Book for Girls & Boys; Tanglewood Tales. Nathaniel Hawthorne. Ed. by Roy H. Pearce. LC 81-20760. 1493p. 1982. 35.00 (*0-940450-03-8*) Library of America.

Tales & Sketches: Twice-Told Tales; Mosses from an Old Manse; The Snow Image. Nathaniel Hawthorne. Ed. by Roy H. Pearce. (Library of America College Editions). 1181p. (C). 1996. pap. 13.95 (*1-883011-33-7*) Library of America.

Tales & Sketches from the Queen City. Benjamin Drake. (Notable American Authors Ser.). 1992. reprint ed. lib. bdg. 75.00 (*0-7812-2684-8*) Rprt Serv.

Tales & Songs of Southern Illinois: Timeless Folklore in Story & Verse. Charles Neely. 296p. 1989. reprint ed. 18.95 (*0-9623990-3-5*); reprint ed. pap. 12.95 (*0-9623990-2-7*) Crossfire Pr.

Tales & Stories by Hans Christian Andersen. Hans Christian Andersen. Tr. by Patricia Conroy & Sven H. Rossel. LC 80-50867. (Illus.). 316p. 1980. pap. 14.95 (*0-295-95936-3*) U of Wash Pr.

Tales & Tails. Mickey Hickman. Tr. & Intro. by E. J. Kirchoff. (Illus.). 264p. 1989. 25.00 (*0-8323-0501-4*) Binford Mort.

***Tales & Tails Vol. I: Stories for Students about Relevant Issues.** Sherry Leonard. 57p. (Orig.). (J). (gr. k-6). 1989. pap. 6.95 (*1-57543-014-2*) Mar Co Prods.

***Tales & Tails Vol. II: Stories for Students about Relevant Issues.** Sherry Leonard. 64p. (Orig.). (J). (gr. k-6). 1990. pap. 6.95 (*1-57543-015-0*) Mar Co Prods.

***Tales & Tails Vol. III: Stories for Students about Relevant Issues.** Sherry Leonard. 61p. (Orig.). (J). (gr. k-6). 1990. pap. 6.95 (*1-57543-016-9*) Mar Co Prods.

Tales & Tails see Story Books for We Can Read

Tales & The Raven & Other Poems. Edgar Allan Poe. LC 69-13800. 1975. pap. 4.00 (*0-675-09530-1*, Merrill Coll) P-H.

Tales & Times of Papa Keck. Robert L. Breeding. LC 84-14644. 209p. 1984. pap. 7.95 (*1-880258-01-3*) Thriftecon.

Tales & Towns of Northern New Jersey. Henry C. Beck. 357p. (Orig.). (C). 1983. reprint ed. pap. 14.95 (*0-8135-1019-8*) Rutgers U Pr.

Tales & Traditions: Storytelling in Twentieth Century American Craft. Matthew Kangas & Lloyd E. Herman. (Illus.). 96p. (C). 1993. pap. 29.95 (*0-295-97282-3*) U of Wash Pr.

Tales & Traditions of the Eskimo, with a Sketch of Their Habits, Religion, Language & Other Peculiarities. Hinrich J. Rink. LC 74-5872. (Illus.). reprint ed. 67.50 (*0-404-11681-7*) AMS Pr.

Tales & Traditions of the People of Old: Na Mo'olelo a ka Po'e Kahiko. 1993. pap. 15.95 (*0-930897-71-4*) Bishop Mus.

Tales & Transformation: Stories in Families & Family Therapy. Janine Roberts. 220p. (C). 1994. 27.00 (*0-393-70174-3*) Norton.

Tales & Treasures of California's Missions. Randall A. Reinstedt. Ed. by John Bergez. LC 92-73253. (History & Happenings of California Ser.). (Illus.). 120p. (J). (gr. 3-6). 1992. boxed 13.95 (*0-933818-24-6*) Ghost Town.

Tales & Treasures of California's Missions. Randall A. Reinstedt. LC 92-73253. (History & Happenings of California Ser.). (Illus.). 120p. (J). (gr. 3-6). 1992. pap. 10.95 (*0-933818-79-3*) Ghost Town.

Tales & Treasures of the California Gold Rush. Randall A. Reinstedt. Ed. by John Bergez. (History & Happenings of California Ser.). (Illus.). 112p. (J). (gr. 3-6). 1994. pap. 10.95 (*0-933818-80-7*); boxed 13.95 (*0-933818-28-9*) Ghost Town.

Tales As Tools: The Power of Storytelling in the Classroom. Sheila Dailey. 224p. 1994. pap. 19.95 (*1-879991-15-2*) Natl Storyting Assn.

Tales at Midnight. Hans Holzer. LC 93-85540. (Literary Classics Ser.). 176p. 1994. 5.98 (*1-56138-391-0*) Courage Bks.

Tales Before Supper. Theophile Gautier et al. Tr. by Myndart Verelst. LC 79-113271. reprint ed. 39.50 (*0-404-05506-0*) AMS Pr.

Tales Before Time. Jim Halcarz. (Illus.). 64p. (Orig.). (J). (gr. k-3). Date not set. pap. 8.95 (*0-89896-121-1*, Lindholm Pubng) Larksdale.

Tales by a Barrister, 3 vols., Set. 408p. 1986. reprint ed. lib. bdg. 150.00 (*0-89941-532-6*, 304670) W S Hein.

Tales by "A Few Good Marines" G. W. Howe. 152p. 1993. pap. 8.00 (*1-880365-11-1*) Prof Pr NC.

Tales by Moonlight. Ed. by Jessica A. Salmonson. (Illus.). 218p. 1982. 15.00 (*0-9610352-0-X*) R T Garcia.

Tales Christ Told. April O. Armstrong. LC 90-34304. 264p. 1990. reprint ed. pap. 4.95 (*0-932506-82-8*) St Bedes Pubns.

Tales, Eighteen Twelve, & Other Selected Poems. George Crabbe. Ed. by Howard Mills. LC 67-10348. 483p. reprint ed. pap. 137.70 (*0-317-20623-0*, 2024577) Bks Demand.

Tales Father Told & Pen Picture Pio Wilberforce: African American Women Writers 1910-1940 by Brown & Daniel. Gates. LC 97-13848. 1997. 25.00 (*0-7838-1427-5*, Hall Reference) Macmillan.

Tales for a Stormy Day: A Book about Good Behavior. Time-Life Books Editors. Ed. by Neil Kagan & Elizabeth Ward. (Early Learning Program Ser.). (Illus.). (J). (ps-2). 1992. write for info. (*0-8094-9307-1*); lib. bdg. write for info. (*0-8094-9308-X*) Time-Life.

Tales for a Winter's Eve. Wendy Watson. LC 87-13467. (Illus.). 32p. (J). (ps up). 1988. 13.00 (*0-374-37373-6*) FS&G.

Tales for a Winter's Eve. Wendy Watson. (Illus.). 32p. (J). (ps up). 1991. pap. 4.95 (*0-374-47419-2*) FS&G.

Tales for a Winter's Night. Arthur Conan Doyle. 207p. (Orig.). 1989. pap. 5.95 (*0-89733-309-8*) Academy Chi Pubs.

Tales for All Times. Santha Rungachary. (Nehru Library for Children). (Illus.). (J). (gr. 1-9). 1979. pap. 2.50 (*0-89744-187-7*) Auromere.

Tales for an Unknown City. Contrib. by Dan Yashinsky. 288p. (C). 1990. 44.95 (*0-7735-0786-8*, Pub. by McGill CN) U of Toronto Pr.

Tales for an Unknown City. Contrib. by Dan Yashinsky. 288p. (C). 1992. pap. 16.95 (*0-7735-0953-4*, Pub. by McGill CN) U of Toronto Pr.

Tales for Bibliophiles, Vol. 1. Ed. by Theodore W. Koch. LC 72-4406. (Short Story Index Reprint Ser.). 1977. reprint ed. 18.95 (*0-8369-4180-2*) Ayer.

Tales for Fifteen. James Fenimore Cooper. LC 59-6525. 1977. reprint ed. 50.00 (*0-8201-1247-X*) Schol Facsimiles.

Tales for Hard Times: A Story about Charles Dickens. David R. Collins. (Creative Minds Ser.). (Illus.). 64p. (J). (gr. 3-6). 1990. lib. bdg. 14.21 (*0-87614-433-4*, Carolrhoda) Lerner Group.

Tales for Heart & Mind - The Guided Experiences: A Storybook for Grownups. Silo. Tr. by Paul Tooby from SPA. (Illus.). 160p. 1993. 18.00 (*1-878977-15-6*) Latitude Pr.

Tales for Jung Folk: Original Fairytales for Persons of All Ages Dramatizing C. G. Jung's Archetypes of the Collective Unconscious. Richard Roberts. (Illus.). 120p. (Orig.). 1983. pap. 8.95 (*0-942380-01-0*); lib. bdg. 15.95 (*0-942380-02-9*) Vernal Equinox.

***Tales for Telling: Stories for Childrens Ministry, Vol. 2.** Phillip R. Legg. (Illus.). 76p. (Orig.). (J). 1996. pap. text ed. 13.50 (*0-8309-0749-1*) Herald Hse.

Tales for the Midnight Hour. Judith B. Stamper. 128p. (YA). (gr. 7-9). 1992. pap. 2.95 (*0-590-45343-2*, Point) Scholastic Inc.

Tales for the Obsessive Gay Romantic. unabridged ed. Eric Beeman. Ed. by Jim Zrimsec. LC 96-83748. (Illus.). 104p. (Orig.). 1996. pap. 9.00 (*0-9651233-0-8*) Andrsonville Pubns.

Tales for the Perfect Child. Florence P. Heide. 80p. (J). (gr. 4-7). 1991. pap. 3.99 (*0-440-40463-0*) Dell.

Tales for the Telling: Irish Folk & Fairy Stories. Edna O'Brien. (Illus.). 128p. (J). (gr. 5-8). 1996. pap. 16.95 (*1-85793-746-5*, Pub. by Pavilion UK) Trafalgar.

***Tales for the Telling: True Life Stories of Irish Scandals.** Padraic O'Farrell. 178p. 1996. pap. 13.95 (*1-898256-16-0*, Pub. by Collins Pr IE) Irish Bks Media.

Tales for Transformation. Johann Wolfgang von Goethe. Tr. by Scott Thompson from GER. 136p. (Orig.). 1987. pap. 8.95 (*0-87286-211-9*) City Lights.

***Tales for Travellers - Collection 1: 12 Unabridged Short Stories by Great Writers.** 12.95 (*1-56015-625-2*) Penton Overseas.

***Tales from a Child Enemy.** Ursula Duba. LC 96-36893. 1997. pap. 8.95 (*0-14-058787-X*) Viking Penguin.

Tales from a Duck Named Quacker: The Story Begins. Ricky Van Shelton. 24p. (J). 1992. pap. 7.00 (*0-9634257-0-6*) RVS Bks.

Tales from a Dugout. Arthur G. Empey. LC 79-101808. (Short Story Index Reprint Ser.). 1977. 20.95 (*0-8369-3196-3*) Ayer.

Tales from a Fox Hunt. Eddie Grisham. Ed. & Illus. by Dan Woodward. 19.95 (*1-882935-16-0*) Westphalia.

Tales from a Greek Island. Alexandros Papadiamantis. Tr. by Elizabeth Constantinides from GRE. LC 86-20957. 192p. 1987. 29.95 (*0-8018-3333-7*) Johns Hopkins.

Tales from a Greek Island. Alexandros Papadiamantis. 200p. (C). 1994. reprint ed. pap. text ed. 12.95 (*0-8018-4846-6*) Johns Hopkins.

Tales from a Mother-of-Pearl Casket. Anatole France. Tr. by Henri Pene Du Bois from FRE. LC 78-37542. (Short Story Index Reprint Ser.). 1977. reprint ed. 17.95 (*0-8369-4101-2*) Ayer.

Tales from a Reiki Seeker. Karen Miller. 96p. (Orig.). 1997. pap. 12.95 (*0-9630439-8-6*) Bayrock.

Tales from a Small Round Island. Joy Jobson. (Illus.). 1992. write for info. (*0-945019-33-5*) Elliot & Fitz.

Tales from a Small Tall Ship: 40 Years of Playing Boats. Bill McNaughton. LC 95-83518. (Illus.). 128p. 1996. pap. 11.95 (*0-9650320-0-0*) Acme Pack.

Tales from a Small Town. Asoke K. Bagchi. 1993. text ed. 15.95 (*81-220-0295-1*, Pub. by Konark Pubs II) Advent Bks Div.

Tales from a Tahuya Log. Effie D. Knowlton. Ed. by Joli Sandoz. LC 91-75703. 168p. 1992. 18.95 (*0-939116-32-4*) Frontier OR.

***Tales from a Tall Islander.** R. McDonald. Date not set. pap. 7.95 (*0-947962-88-3*) Dufour.

Tales from a Traveling Couch. Robert U. Akeret. LC 94-36068. 224p. 1995. 22.00 (*0-393-03779-7*) Norton.

Tales from a Troubled Land. Alan Paton. 1996. pap. 9.00 (*0-684-82584-8*) S&S Trade.

Tales from a Village School. Miss Read, pseud. LC 95-19637. (Illus.). 176p. 1995. 19.95 (*0-395-71762-0*) HM.

Tales from a Village School. large type ed. Miss Read, pseud. 226p. 1995. 24.95 (*0-7838-1441-0*, GK Hall) Thorndike Pr.

Tales from a Village School. large type unabridged ed. Miss Read, pseud. 226p. 1996. pap. 21.95 (*0-7838-1442-9*, GK Hall) Thorndike Pr.

Tales from Agrabah: Seven Original Stories of Aladdin & Jasmine. Katherine Applegate. LC 94-71484. (Illus.). 96p. (J). (gr. 1-4). 1995. 14.95 (*0-7868-3023-9*); lib. bdg. 14.89 (*0-7868-5038-8*) Disney Pr.

Tales from an Endless Summer: A Novel of the Beach. Bruce Novotny. 208p. 1996. pap. 12.00 (*0-945582-31-5*) Down the Shore Pub.

Tales from an Invisible Continent. Tony B. Milan. LC 94-72513. 110p. (Orig.). 1994. pap. 4.95 (*0-9642290-0-5*) Fly Machine.

Tales from an Irish Wake. Margaret D. Armstrong. LC 89-25798. 256p. 1990. 19.95 (*0-912526-45-9*) Lib Res.

Tales from an Urban Wilderness. Scott Holingue & Kenan Heise. (Illus.). 140p. (Orig.). 1994. 19.95 (*0-924772-25-5*) CH Bookworks.

Tales from Ancient Egypt. Tr. by George Hart from EGY. (Egypt & the Arab World). (Illus.). 48p. (Orig.). (J). (gr. 3-8). 1994. pap. 6.50 (*977-5325-15-3*, Pub. by Hoopoe Bks UA) AMIDEAST.

Tales from Arabian Nights. 1993. pap. 5.25 (*0-19-585272-9*) OUP.

Tales from Around the World. (J). 1987. 5.98 (*0-671-08502-6*) S&S Trade.

Tales from Austin. Ed. by Luis A. Ramos-Garcia. 1980. 5.95 (*0-934840-02-4*) Studia Hispanica.

Tales from Bandiland. As told by Barnabas S. Ndebe. (Liberian Research Working Papers: No. 4). (Illus.). 311p. 1974. 12.00 (*0-916712-07-9*) Arden Assocs.

Tales from Beatrix Potter. Beatrix Potter. (Picture Bks.). (Illus.). 228p. (J). (ps-3). 1986. pap. 8.95 (*0-7232-3971-1*) Warne.

Tales from Beyond the Pale. Kim Deitch. Ed. by Robert Fiore. (Illus.). 136p. (Orig.). 1989. pap. 14.95 (*0-930193-83-0*) Fantagraph Bks.

Tales from Cameroon. Rene Philombe. Tr. by Richard Bjornson from FRE. LC 84-50629. (Illus.). 136p. (C). 1984. 18.00 (*0-89410-314-8*, Three Contnts) Lynne Rienner.

Tales from Corytella: The Collected Stories of Flexmore Hudson. Flexmore Hudson. 280p. (C). 1990. 39.00 (*0-9591186-9-1*, Pub. by Pascoe Pub AT) St Mut.

Tales from Cranberryport: A New Baby in Cranberryport. Wende Devlin & Harry Devlin. LC 93-45819. (Tales from Cranberryport Ser.). 24p. (J). 1994. pap. 2.95 (*0-689-71780-6*, Aladdin Paperbacks) S&S Childrens.

Tales from Cranberryport: Cranberry Moving Day. Harry Devlin & Wende Devlin. LC 93-36279. (Tales from Cranberryport Ser.). (Illus.). 24p. (J). 1994. pap. 2.95 (*0-689-71777-6*, Mac Bks Young Read) S&S Childrens.

Tales from Cranberryport: Cranberry Trip to the Dentist. Wende Devlin & Harry Devlin. LC 93-36280. (Tales from Cranberryport Ser.). (J). 1994. pap. 2.95 (*0-689-71779-2*, Mac Bks Young Read) S&S Childrens.

Tales from Cranberryport: Maggie Has a Nightmare. Wende Devlin & Harry Devlin. LC 93-45818. 24p. (J). 1994. pap. 2.95 (*0-689-71778-4*, Aladdin Paperbacks) S&S Childrens.

Tales from Critterville. Gene Gee & Mary Gee. 1995. pap. 24.95 (*0-7880-0584-7*) CSS OH.

Tales from Crypt, 2. 48p. (J). 1995. pap. 3.50 (*0-590-25084-1*) Scholastic Inc.

Tales from Deep Space. Tod Foley. Ed. by Terry K. Amthor. (Space Master Adventure Ser.). (Illus.). 32p. (Orig.). (YA). (gr. 10-12). 1988. pap. 6.00 (*1-55806-006-5*, 9103) Iron Crown Ent Inc.

Tales from Delaware Bay: Real Life Experiences of Watermen on Delaware Bay. James M. Hanna. 100p. 1994. 4.95 (*0-9640458-2-6*) Cherokee DE.

***Tales from Dust River Gulch.** Tim Davis. LC 96-38576. (J). 1997. pap. 6.49 (*0-89084-896-3*, 102517) Bob Jones Univ Pr.

Tales from Fairyland. Illus. by Gunvor Edwards. 80p. (J). (gr. 3-5). 1994. pap. 5.95 (*0-09-913931-6*, Pub. by Hutchinson UK) Trafalgar.

Tales from Galilee. Florence DeGroat. 96p. (Orig.). (J). (gr. 4 up). 1982. pap. 4.50 (*0-87516-485-4*) DeVorss.

Tales from Gray's: Selections from Gray's Sporting Journal, 1975-1985. Ed. by Ed Gray. LC 86-83015. (Illus.). 267p. 1986. text ed. 25.00 (*0-9609842-3-2*) GSJ Press.

Tales from Greenery Street. Denis G. Mackail. LC 75-140335. (Short Story Index Reprint Ser.). 1977. 23.95 (*0-8369-3727-9*) Ayer.

Tales from Hans Christian Andersen. Mary J. Evans & Deborah Anderson. (J). (gr. k up). 1983. pap. 5.00 (*0-87602-257-3*) Anchorage.

Tales from Happyville. Martin Copilah. (J). 1994. 7.95 (*0-533-10893-4*) Vantage.

Tales from Indian Classics. Rupa Gupta. (Illus.). 136p. (J). (gr. 1-9). 1981. 7.50 (*0-89744-233-4*) Auromere.

Tales from Indian Classics, Bk. I. Savitri. (Illus.). (J). (gr. 3-9). 1979. 4.50 (*0-89744-167-2*); pap. 3.00 (*0-685-57665-5*) Auromere.

Tales from Indian Classics, Bk. II. Savitri. (Illus.). (J). (gr. 3-9). 1979. 4.50 (*0-89744-168-0*); pap. 3.00 (*0-685-57666-3*) Auromere.

Tales from Indian Classics, Bk. III. Savitri. (Illus.). (J). (gr. 3-9). 1979. 4.50 (*0-89744-169-9*); pap. 3.00 (*0-685-57667-1*) Auromere.

Tales from Indian Mythology. Rupa Gupta. (Illus.). 96p. (J). (gr. 2-8). 1982. text ed. 7.50 (*0-89744-058-7*) Auromere.

Tales from Indochina. Ed. by Marilyn Gregerson et al. LC 82-81681. 106p. 1988. fiche 8.00 (*0-88312-258-8*) Summer Instit Ling.

Tales from Inside the Iron Lung (& How I Got Out of It) Regina Woods. LC 93-47694. (Illus.). 160p. (Orig.). 1994. pap. 13.95 (*0-8122-1506-0*) U of Pa Pr.

Tales from Jackpine Bob. Bob Cary. Ed. by Susan Gustafson. (Illus.). 208p. (Orig.). 1995. pap. 12.95 (*1-57025-086-3*) Pfeifer-Hamilton.

Tales from Jalisco, Mexico. Howard T. Wheeler. LC 44-5764. (American Folklore Society Memoirs Ser.). 1974. reprint ed. 55.00 (*0-527-01087-1*) Periodicals Srv.

Tales from Jokai. 3rd ed. Mor Jokai. Tr. by R. Nisbet Bain from HUN. LC 76-163032. (Short Story Index Reprint Ser.). reprint ed. 5.37 (*0-8369-3946-8*) Ayer.

Tales from Kalidasa. H. L. Luthra. 136p. (C). 1989. 60.00 (*81-209-0228-9*, Pub. by Pitambar Pub II); pap. 35.00 (*81-209-0037-5*, Pub. by Pitambar Pub II) St Mut.

***Tales from Kathasarits.** Bhatta Somadeva. 1997. pap. 12.95 (*0-14-044698-2*, Penguin Bks) Viking Penguin.

Tales from Luristan. Ed. by Sekandar Amanolahi & Wheeler M. Thackston. (Harvard Iranian Ser.). (Illus.). 276p. 1987. pap. 19.95 (*0-674-86780-7*) HUP.

Tales from Many Lands: An Anthology of Multicultural Folk Literature. Anita Stern. 192p. (J). (gr. 7-9). 1996. pap. 16.95 (*0-8442-0855-8*, Natl Textbk) NTC Pub Grp.

Tales from Many Lands Papercrafts. Jerome C. Brown. 1991. 7.99 (*0-8224-3157-2*) Fearon Teach Aids.

Tales from Margaritaville. Jimmy Buffett. 1993. mass mkt. 5.99 (*0-449-22248-9*, Crest) Fawcett.

Tales from Margaritaville: Fictional Facts & Factual Fictions. Jimmy Buffett. 1990. pap. 12.00 (*0-449-90542-X*, Columbine) Fawcett.

Tales from Merrie England, Vol. I. Stephanie Slahor. (Orig.). (J). (gr. 3-6). 1996. pap. 5.00 (*0-88092-260-5*) Royal Fireworks.

***Tales from Mischief Mountain.** John P. Coss & Bill Coss. 68p. 1996. pap. 7.00 (*0-87012-558-3*) McClain.

Tales from Moominvalley. Tove Jansson. Tr. by Thomas Warburton from SWE. LC 95-9709. (Illus.). 192p. (J). (gr. 2-7). 1995. 16.00 (*0-374-37379-5*); pap. 4.95 (*0-374-47413-3*) FS&G.

***Tales from Morocco.** Tr. by Denys Johnson-Davies from ARA. (Tales from Egypt & the Arab World Ser.). (Illus.). 48p. (Orig.). (J). (gr. 3-8). 1995. pap. 6.50 (*977-5325-54-4*, Pub. by Hoopoe Bks UA) AMIDEAST.

Tales from My Kinderhook. John Smith. Ed. by M. L. Jones. (Orig.). 1996. pap. 6.95 (*1-882270-38-X*) Old Rugged Cross.

Tales from My Little Black Bag. John Ibberson. 160p. (Orig.). 1994. pap. 18.95 (*1-55059-093-6*) Temeron Bks.

Tales from My Mantelpiece. Ed. by Jack Haynes. 144p. (C). 1989. 85.00 (*0-7223-2345-X*, Pub. by A H S Ltd UK) St Mut.

Tales from My Teachers on the Alzheimer's Unit: Poems. Sue Silvermarie. LC 96-20487. 1996. write for info. (*0-87304-293-X*) Families Intl.

***Tales from Near & Far.** (Illus.). (J). 1997. write for info. (*0-614-29256-5*) Little Tiger.

***Tales from Old Baghdad.** Khalid Kishtainy. LC 96-44121. 1997. write for info. (*0-7103-0573-7*, Pub. by Kegan Paul Intl UK) Col U Pr.

Tales from Old Bethesda. Neal J. Conway. 208p. 1996. 23.95 (*0-9649472-1-8*) C M S MD.

Tales from Old Fiji. Lorimer Fison. LC 75-32816. reprint ed. 37.50 (*0-404-14120-X*) AMS Pr.

***Tales from Old Jerusalem.** Shlomo Z. Sonnenfeld. 14.99 (*0-89906-843-X*, TOJH) Mesorah Pubns.

***Tales from Old Jerusalem.** Shlomo Z. Sonnenfeld. (J). pap. 11.99 (*0-89906-844-8*, TOJP) Mesorah Pubns.

Tales from One Street Over. Melissa Whitcraft. 80p. (Orig.). (J). (ps-3). 1994. pap. 3.50 (*0-380-77492-5*, Camelot Young) Avon.

Tales from Open Space. Ed. by Harrison Owen. LC 95-75969. 156p. 1995. pap. 20.00 (*0-9618205-5-1*) Abbott Pub.

***Tales from Ovid: 24 Passages from the Metamorphoses.** Ted Hughes. 1997. 35.00 (*0-374-22841-8*) FS&G.

***Tales from Perrault.** Tr. by Ann Lawrence. (Illus.). 128p. 1997. pap. 11.95 (*0-19-274175-6*) OUP.

Tales from Poodles Paradise & Animal Sanctuary. Elwyn Tudor-Williams. 256p. 1994. 18.95 (*0-8059-3466-9*) Dorrance.

Tales from Ramakrishna. Swami Ramakrishna. (Illus.). 56p. (Orig.). (J). (gr. 1-5). 1975. pap. 2.95 (*0-87481-152-X*, Pub. by Advaita Ashrama II) Vedanta Pr.

Tales from Reb Nachman: Parables Told by Rabbi Nachman of Breslov. David Sears. (ArtScroll Youth Ser.). (Illus.). 32p. (J). (gr. k-6). 1987. 11.99 (*0-89906-808-1*); pap. 8.99 (*0-89906-809-X*) Mesorah Pubns.

Tales from San Diego: Short Stories about America's Finest City. Lee T. Silber. (Illus.). 128p. (Orig.). 1996. pap. 12.95 (*0-9628771-5-8*) Tales From Tropics.

Tales from Sawyerton Springs: Somewhere down the Road & across the Holler from Your Hometown. Andy Andrews. 224p. 1995. pap. 12.95 (*0-9629620-4-X*) Lightning Crown Pub.

Tales from Schroon Lake: A Visit from Rudy Beaver. Barbara Davoll. 1996. 7.99 (*0-8024-1034-0*) Moody.

Tales from Scottish Lairds. (Ghost Ser.). (Illus.). 180p. 1993. pap. 7.95 (*0-7117-0174-1*) Seven Hills Bk.

Tales from Shakespeare. (Fiction Ser.). (YA). 1993. pap. text ed. 6.50 (*0-582-08481-4*, 79832) Longman.

***Tales from Shakespeare.** Barbara Cohen. Date not set. write for info. (*0-688-09833-9*) Lothrop.

Tales from Shakespeare. Charles Lamb & Mary Lamb. (Illus.). 318p. 1995. 6.95 (*0-460-87638-4*, Everyman's Classic Lib) C E Tuttle.

Tales from Shakespeare. Charles Lamb & Mary Lamb. LC 79-89991. (Illus.). 1988. 40.00 (*0-918016-04-5*) Folger Bks.

Tales from Shakespeare. Charles Lamb & Mary Lamb. 336p. 1986. pap. 5.95 (*0-451-52391-1*, Sig Classics) NAL-Dutton.

Tales from Shakespeare. Charles Lamb & Mary Lamb. (J). (gr. 5 up). 1988. pap. 3.99 (*0-14-035088-8*, Puffin) Puffin Bks.

Tales from Shakespeare. Charles Lamb & Mary Lamb. (Puffin Classics Ser.). 346p. (J). 1995. pap. 3.99 (*0-14-036677-6*) Puffin Bks.

Tales from Shakespeare. Charles Lamb & Mary Lamb. (J). (gr. k-6). 1986. 8.98 (*0-685-16860-3*, 621568) Random Hse Value.

Tales from Shakespeare. Charles Lamb & Mary Lamb. (Children's Classics Ser.). 1988. 12.99 (*0-517-62156-8*) Random Hse Value.

Tales from Shakespeare. Charles Lamb & Mary Lamb. 1993. reprint ed. lib. bdg. 24.95 (*1-56849-117-4*) Buccaneer Bks.

Tales from Shenandoah. J. Floyd Wine. LC 89-90108. (Illus.). 92p. 1989. 11.00 (*0-9604350-7-7*); pap. 7.50 (*0-9604350-6-9*) J F Wine.

Tales from South of the Mason-Dixon Line. Lanier De Vours. LC 92-61366. 240p. 1993. pap. 7.95 (*1-55523-559-X*) Winston-Derek.

Tales from Southern Africa. A. C. Jordan. LC 76-145787. (Perspectives on Southern Africa Ser.: No. 4). (Illus.). 301p. reprint ed. pap. 85.80 (*0-685-23973-X*, 2031536) Bks Demand.

Tales from Space: The First Story. Scott M. Stoffel. LC 91-67761. 216p. 1993. pap. 10.00 (*1-56002-134-9*, Univ Edtns) Aegina Pr.

Tales from the African Plains. Anne Gatti. Ed. & Illus. by Gregory Alexander. LC 94-19747. 83p. (J). 1995. pap. 18.99 (*0-525-45282-6*) Dutton Child Bks.

***Tales from the African Plains.** Anne Gatti. Date not set. pap. 8.99 (*0-14-055751-2*) Viking Penguin.

Tales from the Arab Tribes. Charles G. Campbell. Ed. by Richard M. Dorson. LC 80-790. (Folklore of the World Ser.). (Illus.). 1981. reprint ed. lib. bdg. 25.95 (*0-405-13329-4*) Ayer.

Tales from the Arabian Nights. (Classics Ser.). 56p. (J). 3.50 (0-7214-1759-0, Ladybrd) Penguin.

Tales from the Arabian Nights. Michael B. Dixon. (Illus.). 52p. (Orig.). (J). (gr. k up). 1985. pap. 4.50 (0-88680-239-3); 5.00 (0-88680-240-7) I E Clark.

Tales from the Arabian Nights. James Riordan. LC 84-62456. (Illus.). 128p. (J). (gr. 4 up). 1985. 14.95 (1-56288-258-9) Checkerboard.

***Tales from the Archetypal World: Narrative Koans.** Velande Taylor. LC 97-90230. 230p. (Orig.). 1998. pap. 25.00 (0-9649947-4-7) WrdCraft Bks.

Tales from the Argentine. Ed. by Waldo Frank. Tr. by Anita Brenner. 1977. lib. bdg. 59.95 (0-8490-2728-4) Gordon Pr.

Tales from the Argentine. Ed. by Waldo D. Frank. Tr. by Anita Brenner from SPA. LC 78-122706. (Short Story Index Reprint Ser.). (Illus.). 1977. 19.95 (0-8369-3539-X) Ayer.

Tales from the Ark. Avril Rowlands. 160p. (J). (ps-3). 1995. pap. 4.99 (0-7459-2375-5) Lion USA.

Tales from the Bamboo Grove. Yoko K. Watkins. LC 91-38218. (Illus.). 64p. (J). (gr. 4-11). 1992. 16.00 (0-02-792525-0, Bradbury S&S) S&S Childrens.

Tales From the Bedside 2. John Wise. 104p. 1994. pap. text ed. 12.95 (0-9643043-0-9) Wise Cartoons.

Tales from the Beechy Woods: Fluff's Birthday. Gerda Neubacher. (Illus.). 32p. (J). (ps). 1983. 10.95 (0-88625-044-7) Durkin Hayes Pub.

Tales from the Bloated Goat: Early Days in Mogollon. H. A. Hoover. 64p. 1995. pap. 4.95 (0-944383-27-0) High-Lonesome.

***Tales from the Blue Archives.** Lawrence Thornton. LC 97-6896. 1998. write for info. (0-385-48010-5) Doubleday.

Tales from the Book of Morman. Blaine M. Yorgason & Brenton Yorgason. (Gospel Power Ser.). Orig. Title: The Loftier Way. 130p. (Orig.). 1991. pap. write for info. (0-929985-61-3) Jackman Pubng.

***Tales from the Brothers Grimm.** Doug Goheen. (Illus.). 40p. (J). (gr. k-8). 1997. pap. 4.00 (0-88680-441-8) I E Clark.

Tales from the Brothers Grimm. Jacob W. Grimm & Wilhelm K. Grimm. (J). 1987. 1.98 (0-671-08490-9) S&S Trade.

***Tales from the Brothers Grimm & the Sisters Weird.** Marjorie W. Sharmat. (J). 1997. pap. 3.99 (0-440-41300-1) BDD Bks Young Read.

Tales from the Brothers Grimm & the Sisters Weird. Vivian Vande Velde. LC 94-26341. (Jane Yolen Bks.). (Illus.). 196p. (YA). (gr. 5 up). 1995. 17.00 (0-15-200220-0, J Yolen Bks) HarBrace.

Tales from the Cafeteria: Spaghetti & Spooks. Louise Hawes. 160p. (Orig.). (J). (gr. 3-7). 1995. pap. 3.50 (0-380-77790-8, Camelot) Avon.

Tales from the Canadian Rockies. Ed. by Brian Patton. 304p. Date not set. pap. 19.99 (0-7710-6948-0) McCland & Stewart.

Tales from the Casting Couch. Ed. by Michael Viner & Terrie M. Frankle. 304p. 1995. pap. 19.95 (0-7871-0226-1, Dove Bks) Dove Audio.

***Tales from the Clitoris: A Female Experience of Pornography.** Ed. by Cherie Matrix & Feminists Against Censorship Staff. 128p. 1996. pap. 10.95 (1-873176-09-0, AK Pr San Fran) AK Pr Dist.

Tales from the Cloud Walking Country. Marie Campbell. LC 76-14944. (Illus.). 270p. 1976. reprint ed. text ed. 38.50 (0-8371-8607-2, CATC, Greenwood Pr) Greenwood.

Tales from the Cottage: Original Bedtime Stories from the Seven Dwarfs. Bruce Talkington. LC 94-70813. (Illus.). 96p. (J). (ps-3). 1994. 14.95 (0-7868-3008-5); lib. bdg. 14.89 (0-7868-5003-5) Disney Pr.

Tales from the Crib. Henrik Drescher. LC 93-48307. 1995. pap. 9.95 (0-15-600051-2) HarBrace.

***Tales from the Crypt.** Diehl. Date not set. pap. 19.95 (0-312-17040-8) St Martin.

Tales from the Crypt. limited ed. Diehl. 256p. 1996. 500.00 (0-312-14866-6) St Martin.

Tales from the Crypt: Demon Knight. Robert Zemeckis. 1995. mass mkt. 4.99 (0-671-52696-0) PB.

Tales From the Crypt: The Official Archives. Digby Diehl. LC 96-3078. 256p. 1996. 45.00 (0-312-14486-5) St Martin.

Tales from the Crypt, Vol 1: Introduced by the Crypt-Keeper. Illus. by Jack Davis. LC 90-23916. 96p. (Orig.). (J). (gr. 4-7). 1991. pap. 2.99 (0-679-81799-9) Random Bks Yng Read.

Tales from the Crypt, Vol. 2: Introduced by the Old Witch. Illus. by Jack Davis. LC 90-23916. 96p. (Orig.). (J). (gr. 4-7). 1991. pap. 3.99 (0-679-81800-6) Random Bks Yng Read.

Tales from the Crypt, Vol. 3: Introduced by the Vault-Keeper. Illus. by Jack Davis. LC 90-23916. 96p. (J). (gr. 4-7). 1991. pap. 3.99 (0-679-81801-4) Random Bks Yng Read.

Tales from the Cryptkeeper. Jane Manson. (Illus.). 48p. (J). (gr. 1-4). 1995. pap. 3.50 (0-590-25088-4) Scholastic Inc.

Tales from the Dark Lord. 2nd ed. John Preston. (Orig.). 1995. mass mkt. 5.95 (1-56333-323-6, Badboy) Masquerade.

Tales from the Dark Lord II. John Preston. (Orig.). 1994. mass mkt. 4.95 (1-56333-176-4, Badboy) Masquerade.

Tales from the Dena: Indian Stories from the Tanana, Koyukuk, & Yukon Rivers. Ed. by Frederica De Laguna. LC 94-41285. (Illus.). 304p. 1995. 29.95 (0-295-97429-X) U of Wash Pr.

Tales from the Doctor's Lounge. (Illus.). 239p. Date not set. pap. 15.00 (1-889249-02-5) Concorde Pubng.

Tales from the Doctor's Lounge. 2nd ed. (Illus.). 239p. Date not set. reprint ed. pap. 15.00 (1-889249-03-3) Concorde Pubng.

Tales from the Doctor's Lounge. 3rd ed. (Illus.). 239p. Date not set. reprint ed. pap. 15.00 (1-889249-04-1) Concorde Pubng.

Tales from the Dragon's Cave: Peacemaking Stories for Everyone. Arlene Williams. LC 95-61738. (Illus.). 160p. (J). (gr. 2-6). 1995. 15.95 (0-9605444-5-3) Waking Light Pr.

***Tales from the Dugout: Greatest True Baseball Stories Ever Told.** Mike Shannon. LC 97-223. 1997. write for info. (0-8092-3107-7) Contemp Bks.

***Tales from the Dugout: The Greatest True Baseball Stories Ever Told.** Mike Shannon. 1997. 18.95 (0-614-28175-X) Contemp Bks.

Tales from the Dykeside. Jorjet Harper. LC 95-52018. 200p. (Orig.). 1996. pap. 10.95 (0-934678-71-5) New Victoria Pubs.

Tales from the Edge. R. P. McMurphy. LC 95-69085. (Illus.). 100p. (Orig.). 1996. pap. 7.95 (0-9646566-0-4) Southestrn Pr.

Tales from the Empty Notebook. William Kotzwinkle. (J). (gr. 4-7). 1996. 12.95 (1-56924-792-7); pap. text ed. 5.95 (1-56924-786-2) Marlowe & Co.

Tales from the Enchanted City: Based on Tales from the Brothers Grinn (sic) L. Don Swartz. 41p. (Orig.). (J). (gr. 2-8). 1995. pap. 3.00 (1-57514-232-5, 1157) Encore Perform Pub.

Tales from the Erotic Edge: A Circlet Omnibus. Ed. by Cecilia Tan. 272p. (Orig.). 1996. pap. 15.95 (1-885865-16-3) Circlet Pr.

Tales from the Ether. Illus. by David R. Deitrick. (Space: Eighteen Eighty-Nine Ser.). 64p. (Orig.). (YA). (gr. 9-12). 1989. pap. 8.00 (1-55878-011-4) Game Designers.

Tales from the Feather Bed: Adirondack Stories & Songs. Bill Smith. 1994. pap. 12.95 (0-912678-91-7) Greenfld Rev Lit.

Tales from the Fjeld. Peter C. Asbjornsen. Tr. by George W. Dasent. LC 69-13232. (Illus.). 1972. reprint ed. 23.95 (0-405-08217-7) Ayer.

Tales from the Floating Vagabond. Lee Garvin et al. (Illus.). 96p. (Orig.). 1991. pap. write for info. (1-56038-032-2) Avalon Hill.

Tales from the Floating Vagabond: Bar Wars. (Illus.). 52p. (Orig.). 1991. pap. write for info. (1-56038-046-2) Avalon Hill.

***Tales from the Four Winds of the North.** Dale DeArmond. LC 96-79657. (Illus.). 55p. (Orig.). 1996. pap. 14.95 (0-9641998-3-1) Lapcat Pubns.

Tales from the French Folk-Lore of Missouri. Joseph M. Carriere. LC 79-128989. (Northwestern University. Humanities Ser.: No. 1). reprint ed. 32.50 (0-404-50701-8) AMS Pr.

Tales from the Gardens & Beyond. Palmer. Date not set. per. 10.95 (0-920813-09-7, Pub. by Sister Vision CN) LPC InBook.

Tales from the Gemara, Vol. I: Bernchos. Y. Weinstock. 1988. 14.99 (0-89906-812-X); pap. 11.99 (0-89906-813-8) Mesorah Pubns.

Tales from the Gemara, Vol. II: Shabbos. Y. Weinstock. Tr. by Shaindel Weinstock from HEB. (ArtScroll Youth Ser.). (Illus.). 160p. (YA). (gr. 5-12). 1989. 14.99 (0-89906-814-6); pap. 11.99 (0-89906-815-4) Mesorah Pubns.

Tales from the Gemara, Vol. III: Rosh Hashana. Y. Weinstock. 1990. 14.99 (0-89906-816-2); pap. 11.99 (0-89906-817-0) Mesorah Pubns.

Tales from the Gemara, Vol. IV: Taanis. Y. Weinstock. 1992. 14.99 (0-89906-818-9); pap. 11.99 (0-89906-819-7) Mesorah Pubns.

Tales from the Great Turtle. Ed. by Piers Anthony & Richard Gilliam. 352p. mass mkt. 5.99 (0-8125-3490-5) Tor Bks.

Tales from the Greek Drama. H. R. Jolliffe. xi, 320p. 10.00 (0-86516-013-9) Bolchazy-Carducci.

Tales from the Home Place. Shelly Corwin. (J). 1996. 14.95 (0-8050-5075-2, Bks Young Read) H Holt & Co.

Tales from the Irish Club: A Collection of Short Stories. Lester Goran. LC 95-37386. 144p. (Orig.). 1996. pap. 12.00 (0-87338-539-X) Kent St U Pr.

Tales from the Iron Triangle: Boyhood Days in the San Francisco Bay Area of the 1920's. James Polese. Ed. by Richard L. Polese. (Illus.). 96p. (Orig.). (YA). (gr. 6-12). 1995. pap. 9.95 (0-943734-12-6) Ocean Tree Bks.

Tales from the Island: Puerto Rican Stories. Ana T. Merced De Mendez. (Illus.). 60p. (J). (gr. 6-10). Date not set. write for info. (0-9627442-1-2); wbk. ed. write for info. (0-9627442-2-0) A T Merced de Mendez.

Tales from the Joint. K. Hawkeye Gross. 280p. 1995. text ed. 24.95 (0-87364-817-X) Paladin Pr.

Tales from the Jungle: The Rainforest Reader. Ed. by Daniel R. Katz & Miles Chapin. LC 94-13056. 1995. pap. 15.00 (0-517-88160-8) Crown Pub Group.

Tales from the Jungle Book. Rudyard Kipling. (Classics Ser.). (Illus.). 52p. (J). 1994. 3.50 (0-7214-1655-1, Ladybrd) Penguin.

Tales from the Jungle Book. Rudyard Kipling. (Illus.). 56p. (J). (gr. 2-4). 1996. pap. 2.99 (0-7214-5612-X, Ladybrd) Penguin.

Tales from the Jungle Book. Rudyard Kipling. LC 84-11724. (Looking Glass Library). (Illus.). 64p. (J). (gr. k-3). 1985. lib. bdg. 8.99 (0-394-96940-5) Random Bks Yng Read.

Tales from the Kingdom of Lailonia & the Key to Heaven. Leszek Kolakowski. Tr. by Agnieszka Kolakowska & Salvator Attanasio. (Illus.). 192p. 1989. 20.00 (0-226-45039-2) U Ch Pr.

***Tales from the Land of Dragons: One Thousand Years of Chinese Painting.** W. U. Tung. (Illus.). 320p. 1997. 65.00 (0-87846-439-5) Mus Fine Arts Boston.

Tales from the Land of Shadows. Christopher Hawkins. LC 93-93952. (Illus.). 64p. (Orig.). 1994. pap. 6.95 (1-56002-352-X, Univ Edtns) Aegina Pr.

***Tales from the Land of the Sufis.** Mojdeh Bayat & Mohammad A. Jamnia. 180p. 1996. pap. 12.00 (0-614-21368-1, 1211) Kazi Pubns.

Tales from the Land of the Sufis. Mojdeh Bayat & Mohammad A. Jamnia. LC 93-39137. 192p. 1994. pap. 16.00 (0-87773-955-2) Shambhala Pubns.

Tales from the Mabinogion. Tr. by Kevin Crossley-Holland & Gwyn Thomas from WEL. LC 84-14777. (Illus.). 88p. (J). (gr. 7 up). 1985. 19.95 (0-87951-987-8) Overlook Pr.

Tales from the Mabinogion. Gwyn Thomas & Kevin Crossley-Holland. (Illus.). 96p. (J). (gr. 3 up). 1996. pap. 18.95 (0-87951-637-2) Overlook Pr.

Tales from the Masnavi. Tr. by Arthur J. Arberry. 300p. (C). 1961. pap. 25.00 (0-7007-0273-3, Pub. by Curzon Pr UK) Paul & Co Pubs.

Tales from the Men's Room. Tom Caffrey. 1996. mass mkt. 5.95 (1-56333-364-3, Badboy) Masquerade.

Tales from the Mines. Geoffrey Carr. 44p. 1987. 25.00 (0-907496-45-8, Pub. by JNM Pubns UK) St Mut.

Tales from the Mos Eisley Cantina. Ed. by Kevin Anderson. (Star Wars Anthologies Ser.). 384p. (YA). 1995. mass mkt. 5.99 (0-553-56468-4) Bantam.

Tales from the Mountain. Miguel Torga. Tr. by Ivana Carlsen from POR. LC 90-53696. 160p. 1991. 21.99 (0-936609-24-9); pap. 12.99 (0-936609-23-0) QED Ft Bragg.

Tales from the New Life with Meher Baba. Eruch et al. 191p. 1976. 9.95 (0-940700-10-7); pap. 6.95 (0-940700-09-3) Meher Baba Info.

Tales from the North West. Peter James. 244p. (C). 1990. pap. 60.00 (0-86439-093-9, Pub. by Boolarong Pubns AT) St Mut.

Tales from the Opera. Anthony J. Rudel. 379p. 1985. pap. 9.95 (0-685-43051-0, Fireside) S&S Trade.

Tales from the Panchtantra. Brahm P. Gupta. 72p. (C). 1989. 50.00 (81-209-0734-5, Pub. by Pitambar Pub II); pap. text ed. 25.00 (81-209-0028-6, Pub. by Pitambar Pub II) St Mut.

***Tales from the Pewtershop.** Raymond E. Gibson. (Illus.). 125p. 1998. 15.00 (0-614-29354-5) Monadnock Pubs.

Tales from the Planet Earth. Ed. by Frederik Pohl & Elizabeth A. Hull. 1987. reprint ed. pap. 3.95 (0-312-90779-6) St Martin.

***Tales from the Plum Grove Hills.** Jesse H. Stuart. Ed. & Intro. by Charles H. Daughaday. LC 97-11659. (Illus.). 288p. (J). 1997. reprint ed. 22.00 (0-945084-62-5) J Stuart Found.

Tales from the Prairie, 3 vols., Set. Dorothy W. Creigh. Incl. Vol. 2. . LC 74-157038. 1973. pap. 6.95 (0-934858-04-7); Vol. 3. . LC 74-157038. 1976. pap. 7.95 (0-934858-05-5); Vol. 4. . LC 74-157038. 1979. pap. 9.95 (0-934858-06-3); LC 74-157038. (Illus.). reprint ed. Set pap. 6.95 (0-934858-09-8) Adams County.

Tales from the Prairie, 3 vols., Vols. 1-4. Dorothy W. Creigh. Incl. Vol. 2. . LC 74-157038. 1973. pap. 6.95 (0-934858-04-7); Vol. 3. . LC 74-157038. 1976. pap. 7.95 (0-934858-05-5); Vol. 4. . LC 74-157038. 1979. pap. 9.95 (0-934858-06-3); LC 74-157038. (Illus.). reprint ed. write for info. (0-934858-10-1); reprint ed. pap. 5.95 (0-685-00121-0); reprint ed. Set pap. 9.95 (0-685-00122-9) Adams County.

Tales from the Prince of Storytellers: Selected Short Stories. annot. ed. Robert Louis Stevenson. 250p. (Orig.). 1993. 39.95 (0-8101-1059-8); pap. 16.95 (0-8101-1084-9) Northwestern U Pr.

***Tales from the Rain Forest: Myths & Legends of the Amazonian Indians.** Ed. by Mercedes Dorson & Jeanne W. Carter. LC 97-19791. (Illus.). 96p. (J). (gr. 4-7). 1997. 16.00 (0-88001-567-5) Ecco Pr.

***Tales from the Rainforest.** Darrel Kempf & Dean Kempf. 113p. (Orig.). 1996. pap. 7.95 (0-9655927-0-7) D K & Assocs.

***Tales from the Sara Gossa Manuscript: Ten Days in the Life of Alphonse Van Worden.** Jan Potocki. Ed. by Brian Stableford. Tr. by Christine Donougher from FRE. (Dedalus European Classics Ser.). 159p. 1997. reprint ed. pap. 8.95 (0-946626-67-7, Pub. by Dedalus UK) Subterranean Co.

Tales from the Shanty. Jacqueline Deusenberry-Albert. (Orig.). 1996. pap. write for info. (1-57553-192-5) Watermrk Pr.

Tales from the Sidewalk Benches. Jimmy C. Acton. (Illus.). 103p. (Orig.). 1988. pap. 9.95 (0-943487-06-4) Sevgo Pr.

***Tales from the Skillet: 400 of the South's Best Cornbread Recipes.** David Armstrong. 400p. (Orig.). 1997. pap. text ed. 19.95 (0-9646452-8-9) Dowling Pr.

Tales from the South Pacific Islands. Anne Gittins. LC 76-5411. (Illus.). 96p. (J). (gr. 3 up). 1977. 7.95 (0-916144-02-X) Stemmer Hse.

***Tales from the South Seas.** Robert Louis Stevenson. 800p. 1997. pap. 14.95 (0-86241-643-4, Pub. by Canongate Bks UK) Interlink Pub.

Tales from the Spaceport Bar. Ed. by George H. Scithers & Darrell Schweitzer. 256p. 1987. mass mkt. 3.50 (0-380-89943-4) Avon.

Tales From the Spirit World. Virginia Hamilton. LC 90-4002. 1990. write for info. (0-15-284215-2) HarBrace.

Tales from the Springs. Sally Brinkman et al. (Illus.). 150p. (Orig.). 1994. pap. 10.00 (0-938572-07-5) Bunny Crocodile.

Tales from the Steep: John Long's Favorite Climbing Literature. Royal Robbins et al. LC 92-45869. 184p. (Orig.). 1993. pap. 11.99 (0-934802-92-0) ICS Bks.

Tales from the Storyteller's House. Thornton W. Burgess. (J). 19.95 (0-8488-0930-0) Amereon Ltd.

***Tales from the Sunday House.** Minetta A. Goyne. LC 96-31689. 148p. (Orig.). 1997. pap. 15.95 (0-87565-173-9) Tex Christian.

Tales from the Thousand & One Nights. Tr. by N. J. Dawood. 416p. 1973. pap. 11.95 (0-14-044289-8, Penguin Classics) Viking Penguin.

Tales from the U. S. Mid West. Clifton Brusso. 123p. (Orig.). 1992. pap. 4.95 (0-9633548-1-7) Iroquois Pr.

Tales from the Underground Railroad. Kate Connell. LC 92-14415. (Stories of America Ser.). (Illus.). 68p. (J). (gr. 2-5). 1992. lib. bdg. 24.26 (0-8114-7223-X) Raintree Steck-V.

Tales from the U.P.'s Copper Country. Clifton Brusso. 123p. (Orig.). 1992. pap. 4.95 (0-9633548-0-9, TXU 433 567) Iroquois Pr.

***Tales from the Workplace.** Patricia H. Latham et al. 102p. (Orig.). 1997. pap. 15.00 (1-883560-08-X) JKL Communs.

Tales from the Xinjiang Exile: Life among the Uighurs. Meng Wang. Tr. by Kang H. Jin & Li-Hua Ying from CHI. 180p. 1991. 19.95 (0-941062-57-0) Begos & Rosenberg.

***Tales from the 7,000 Isles.** Art Guillermo & NimFa Rodeheaver. LC 95-60276. (Illus.). 112p. (Orig.). 1996. pap. 16.95 (1-56550-031-8) Vis Bks Intl.

Tales from Third Street. Carol Jordan. (Illus.). 100p. 1980. pap. 3.50 (0-9605360-0-0) C Jordan.

Tales from Tiburon: An Anthology of Adventures in Seriland. Ed. by Neil B. Carmony & David E. Brown. LC 82-51171. (Illus.). 146p. (Orig.). 1983. 15.95 (0-9610126-1-7); pap. 9.95 (0-9610126-0-9) SW Nat Hist Assn.

***Tales from Time & Beyond the Stars, Vol. 1.** Alice G. Kann. (Illus.). 50p. (J). (ps-6). 1997. 16.95 (0-9654522-1-2) Metapublng.

Tales from Travelling Couch: A Psychotherapist Revisits His Most Memorable Patients. Robert Akeret. 240p. 1996. pap. 13.00 (0-393-31498-7) Norton.

Tales from Turtle Creek. Ted Browning. (Illus.). 156p. 1991. 19.95 (0-940540-04-5) Brandywine Conserv.

Tales from Two Hemispheres. Hjalmar H. Boyesen. LC 78-98563. (Short Story Index Reprint Ser.). 1977. 20.95 (0-8369-3137-8) Ayer.

Tales from Two Pockets. Karel Capek. Tr. by Norma Comrada from CZE. LC 93-42204. 352p. (Orig.). 1994. pap. 14.95 (0-945774-25-7, PG5038.C3A23) Catbird Pr.

Tales from Vagabond Hill: The Reich Stuff. Lee Garvin. (Illus.). 80p. (Orig.). 1991. pap. write for info. (1-56038-045-4) Avalon Hill.

Tales from Vivekananda. 34p. (J). 1.95 (0-614-17403-1) Vedanta Pr.

Tales from Watership Down. Richard Adams. LC 96-17047. 1996. 23.00 (0-679-45125-0) Knopf.

***Tales from Watership Down.** large type ed. Richard Adams. LC 97-16196. (Large Print Book Ser.). 1997. write for info. (1-56895-449-2) Wheeler Pub.

Tales from Well World No. 1. Jack L. Chalker. pap. write for info. (0-345-39486-0) Ballantine.

Tales from Well World No. 2. Jack L. Chalker. pap. write for info. (0-345-39485-2) Ballantine.

Tales from Wide Ruins: Jean & Bill Cousins, Traders. Jean Cousins & Bill Cousins. Ed. by Mary T. Engels. LC 96-2260. (Illus.). 264p. 1996. 29.95 (0-89672-368-2) Tex Tech Univ Pr.

***Tales from Within the Clouds: Nakhi Stories of China.** Tr. by Jaiho Cheng. LC 96-47892. (Illus.). 64p. (J). 1997. 16.95 (0-8248-1820-2, Kolowalu Bk) UH Pr.

Tales From Woolly Acres. Doris Church. (Illus.). 140p. (Orig.). 1992. pap. 10.95 (0-9627860-5-5) Lone Oak MN.

***Tales I Could Not Tell.** George Bitou. Date not set. write for info. (0-688-04409-3) Morrow.

Tales I Told My Mother. Robert Nye. 171p. 1982. pap. text ed. 12.95 (0-7145-2741-6) M Boyars Pubs.

Tales I Told My Mother. Robert Nye. 176p. 1992. 11.95 (0-7145-2954-0) M Boyars Pubs.

***Tales in Political Economy: 1874 Edition.** (Works of Henry & Millicent Garrett Fawcett). 114p. 1996. reprint ed. write for info. (1-85506-374-3) Bks Intl VA.

Tales in Pursuit of High-Quality Health Care. Ed. by Frederick Gale. LC 94-71700. 114p. (Orig.). 1994. pap. text ed. 25.00 (0-924674-29-6) Am Coll Phys Execs.

***Tales in Time: The Man Who Walked Home & Other Stories.** John Klute et al. Ed. by Peter Crowther. (Orig.). 1997. pap. 12.99 (1-56504-989-6, 10042, Borealis) White Wolf.

Tales McKlickle Told. Contrib. by Maria Illo. 44p. (J). (gr. 3 up). 1995. 10.95 incl. audio (0-9613159-5-4) Emerald Forest.

Tales Mummies Tell. Patricia Lauber. LC 83-46172. (Illus.). 128p. (J). (gr. 5-9). 1985. lib. bdg. 15.89 (0-690-04389-9, Crowell Jr Bks) HarpC Child Bks.

Tales My Father Never Told. Walter D. Edmonds. LC 94-34965. (Illus.). 220p. 1995. 24.95 (0-8156-0307-X) Syracuse U Pr.

Tales My Father Never Told. limited ed. Walter D. Edmonds. LC 94-34965. 1995. 75.00 (0-8156-2657-6) Syracuse U Pr.

Tales Mysterious & Macabre, Set. Alan Blackwood. 32.95 (0-8488-0195-4) Amereon Ltd.

Tales Mysterious & Macabre, Vol. 2. Alan Blackwood. 20.95 (0-8488-0194-6) Amereon Ltd.

Tales Never Told Around the Campfire: True Stories of Frontier America. Mark Dugan. LC 91-26183. 275p. 1992. pap. 17.95 (0-8040-0955-4) Swallow.

Tales, Now First Collected. Leigh Hunt. LC 79-178441. (Short Story Index Reprint Ser.). 1977. reprint ed. 23.95 (0-8369-4042-3) Ayer.

Tales of a Basque Grandmother. Frances Carpenter. 1976. 23.95 (0-8488-0941-6) Amereon Ltd.

Tales of a Caribbean Isle: The Dominican Republic by & for an Insider. Heinz Meder. (Illus.). 197p. 1994. pap. 14.00 (1-886254-06-0) Edic Nue Mun.

An Asterisk (*) at the beginning of an entry indicates that the title is appearing in BIP for the first time.

Tales of a Chinese Grandmother. Frances Carpenter. 293p. (J). (gr. 5-6). reprint ed. lib. bdg. 24.95 (*0-89190-481-6*, Rivercity Pr) Amereon Ltd.

Tales of a Chinese Grandmother. Frances Carpenter. 1993. reprint ed. lib. bdg. 21.95 (*1-56849-155-7*) Buccaneer Bks.

Tales of a Chinese Grandmother. Frances Carpenter. LC 72-77514. (Illus.). 302p. (J). (gr. 3-8). 1972. reprint ed. pap. 8.95 (*0-8048-1042-7*) C E Tuttle.

Tales of a Country Doctor: One Hundred Years of Health Care in Lewis County. Brandt A. Bede. LC 92-85175. 124p. (C). 1993. pap. 13.50 (*1-880222-12-4*) Red Apple Pub.

Tales of a Country Judge. Robert H. Gollmar. LC 79-65286. (Illus.). 192p. 1981. 9.95 (*0-87319-018-1*) Hallberg Pub Corp.

Tales of a Cruel Country. Charles F. Kenyon. LC 74-150546. (Short Story Index Reprint Ser.). 1977. reprint ed. 21.95 (*0-8369-3843-7*) Ayer.

Tales of a Dakota Pilot, the Way It Was, 1929-1937. F. M. Roberts. (Illus.). 112p. 1991. pap. 8.95 (*0-912746-09-2*) F M Roberts.

Tales of a Dead Kin. 93th ed. 1993. pap. text ed. 13.25 (*0-15-300375-8*, HB Juv Bks) HarBrace.

Tales of a Fledging Homestead. Joe E. Armstrong. LC 84-25389. (Illus.). 110p. (Orig.). 1985. pap. 7.95 (*0-930079-00-0*) Misty Hill Pr.

Tales of a Fourth Grade Nothing. Judy Blume. 128p. (J). (gr. k-6). 1976. mass mkt. 3.99 (*0-440-48474-X*, YB BDD) BDD Bks Young Read.

Tales of a Fourth Grade Nothing. Judy Blume. LC 70-179050. (Illus.). 128p. (J). (gr. 2-5). 1972. pap. 13.99 (*0-525-40720-0*) Dutton Child Bks.

Tales of a Fourth-Grade Nothing: A Study Guide. Garrett Christopher. Ed. by Joyce Friedland & Rikki Kessler. (Novel-Ties Ser.). (J). (gr. 2-5). 1991. pap. text ed. 15.95 (*0-88122-575-4*) Lrn Links.

Tales of a Fourth Grade Nothing: Literature Unit. Deborah Shepherd-Hayes. (Illus.). 1994. 7.95 (*1-55734-526-0*) Tchr Create Mat.

Tales of a Fourth Grade Nothing see Judy Blume

Tales of a Fourth Grade Nothing see Judy Blume Collection

Tales of a Gambling Grandma. Dayal K. Khalsa. (Dragonfly Bks.). (Illus.). 32p. (J). (ps-4). 1994. pap. 5.99 (*0-517-88262-0*, Clarkson Potter) Crown Bks Yng Read.

Tales of a Grandfather: Being Stories Taken from the History of France. Waler Scott. Ed. by William Baker & J. H. Alexander. LC 95-47959. 320p. (C). 1996. lib. bdg. 50.00 (*0-87580-208-7*) N Ill U Pr.

Tales of a Greek Island. Julia D. Dragoumis. LC 76-110184. (Short Story Index Reprint Ser.). 1977. 23.95 (*0-8369-3335-4*) Ayer.

***Tales of a Hero & the Song of Her Sword.** Dylan Brody. (YA). (gr. 7 up). 1997. pap. 7.99 (*0-88092-412-8*) Royal Fireworks.

Tales of a Korean Grandmother. Frances Carpenter. 1976. 24.95 (*0-8488-0944-0*) Amereon Ltd.

Tales of a Korean Grandmother. Frances Carpenter. LC 72-77515. (Illus.). 320p. (J). (gr. 3-8). 1972. pap. 8.95 (*0-8048-1043-5*) C E Tuttle.

Tales of a Long Night. Alfred Doblin. Tr. by Robert Kimber & Rita Kimber from GER. LC 84-18798. 486p. 1984. pap. 15.95 (*0-88064-017-0*) Fromm Intl Pub.

Tales of a Low-Rent Birder. Peter Dunne. 175p. (C). 1986. 15.95 (*0-8135-1139-9*) Rutgers U Pr.

Tales of a Low-Rent Birder. Pete Dunne. LC 93-37749. (Illus.). 176p. (C). 1994. reprint ed. pap. 10.95 (*0-292-71574-9*) U of Tex Pr.

Tales of a Magic Monastery. Theophane the Monk. LC 81-9765. (Illus.). 96p. 1981. pap. 9.95 (*0-8245-0085-7*) Crossroad NY.

Tales of a Nebraska Country Girl. Zella R. Rystrom. (Illus.). 52p. (Orig.). (YA). (gr. 6-12). 1988. pap. 4.95 (*0-936015-18-7*) Pocahontas Pr.

Tales of a New America: The Anxious Liberal's Guide to the Future. Robert B. Reich. LC 87-45915. 304p. 1988. reprint ed. pap. 13.00 (*0-394-75706-8*, Vin) Random.

Tales of a Nomad: or Sport & Strife. Charles E. Montague. LC 72-5559. (Black Heritage Library Collection). 1977. reprint ed. 21.95 (*0-8369-9144-3*) Ayer.

Tales of a Nuf in the Land of Doon. Judy F. MacKay. (Illus.). 84p. (Orig.). (J). (gr. 4-7). 1992. per. 9.95 (*1-882748-00-X*) MacKay-Langley.

Tales of a Pueblo Boy. Lawrence Vallo. LC 86-5876. (Illus.). 48p. (Orig.). (J). 1987. pap. 5.95 (*0-86534-089-7*) Sunstone Pr.

Tales of a Rambler. John Ellberg. LC 70-110185. (Short Story Index Reprint Ser.: Vol. 1). (Illus.). 1977. 21.95 (*0-8369-3336-2*) Ayer.

***Tales of a Rat-Hunting Man.** D. Brian Plummer. LC 97-5252. (Illus.). 144p. 1997. pap. 12.95 (*1-55821-595-6*) Lyons & Burford.

Tales of a Russian Grandmother. Frances Carpenter. 1976. 22.95 (*0-8488-0942-4*) Amereon Ltd.

Tales of a Seasick Doctor: Life Aboard a Mercy Ship. Christine Aroney-Sine. 224p. 1996. pap. 12.99 (*0-310-20375-9*) Zondervan.

Tales of a Shaman's Apprentice: An Ethnobotanist Searches for New Medicines in the Amazonian Rain Forest. Mark J. Plotkin. (Illus.). 352p. 1994. pap. 12.95 (*0-14-012991-X*, Penguin Bks) Viking Penguin.

Tales of a Swiss Grandmother. Frances Carpenter. 1976. 22.95 (*0-8488-0943-2*) Amereon Ltd.

***Tales of a Tail Gunner: A Memoir of Seattle & World War II.** Eddie Picardo. LC 96-77149. 254p. 1996. pap. 14.95 (*1-883697-33-6*) Hara Pub.

Tales of a Teller: An Informal Guide to a Fine Art. Morton G. Zimmerman. Ed. by Dave Johnson. (Illus.). 156p. (Orig.). 1975. pap. 19.95 (*0-9608944-0-3*, 7039104) AppleSeeds.

Tales of a Time & Place. Grace E. King. 1972. lib. bdg. 14.00 (*0-8422-8086-3*) Irvington.

Tales of a Time & Place. Grace E. King. LC 76-122593. reprint ed. 27.50 (*0-404-03690-2*) AMS Pr.

Tales of a Time & Place. Grace E. King. 1972. reprint ed. pap. text ed. 6.95 (*0-8290-0675-3*) Irvington.

Tales of a Time & Place. Grace E. King. (BCL1-PS American Literature Ser.). 303p. 1992. reprint ed. lib. bdg. 89.00 (*0-7812-6778-1*) Rprt Serv.

Tales of a Traveller. Washington Irving. LC 71-37551. (Short Story Index Reprint Ser.). 1977. reprint ed. 19.95 (*0-8369-4110-1*) Ayer.

***Tales of a Water Bailiff.** large type ed. Bob Davison. (Magna Large Print Ser.). 303p. 1996. 25.99 (*0-7505-1004-8*, Pub. by Magna Print Bks UK) Ulverscroft.

Tales of a Western Mountaineer: A Record of Mountain Experiences on the Pacific Coast. Claude E. Rusk. (American Biography Ser.). 309p. 1991. reprint ed. lib. bdg. 79.00 (*0-7812-8333-7*) Rprt Serv.

Tales of a Wilderness Trapper. Neil M. Lindsey. 66p. 1973. pap. 3.00 (*0-936622-21-0*) A R Harding Pub.

Tales of a Woodsman Vol. III: A Peek at Nature. Rodney L. Senteney. (Illus.). 104p. 1995. text ed. 12.50 (*0-9639151-2-6*) Senteney & Son.

Tales of a Woodsman, Vol. II: A Peek at Nature. Rodney L. Senteney. (Illus.). 104p. 1993. text ed. 12.00 (*0-9639151-1-8*) Senteney & Son.

Tales of a Woodsman, Vol. 1: A Peek at Nature. Rodney L. Senteney. (Illus.). 104p. 1992. text ed. 12.00 (*0-9639151-0-X*) Senteney & Son.

Tales of a 4th Grade Nothing. Ian Serraillier. 5.00 (*0-09-950401-4*) Random.

Tales of Adventure & Discovery. Mary E. Allen. (Illus.). 80p. (Orig.). (J). (gr. 1-5). 1996. pap. 9.95 (*0-9651675-0-X*) MEA Prods.

Tales of Adventurous Enterprise: Washington Irving & the Poetics of Western Expansion. Peter Antelyes. 256p. 1990. text ed. 45.00 (*0-231-06860-3*) Col U Pr.

Tales of Afghanistan. Amina Shah. 1982. 21.00 (*0-900860-94-4*, Pub. by Octagon Pr UK) ISHK.

Tales of Alaska & the Yukon. F. Oppel. 1992. 8.98 (*1-55521-119-4*) Bk Sales Inc.

Tales of Alaska's Big Bears. Jim Rearden. 238p. (Orig.). 1989. pap. 12.95 (*0-935632-83-2*) Wolfe Pub Co.

Tales of Alaska's Bush Rat Governor: The Extraordinary Autobiography of Jay Hammond, Wilderness Guide & Reluctant Politician. Jay Hammond. LC 93-49357. (Illus.). 352p. 1994. 27.95 (*0-945397-17-8*); pap. 17.95 (*0-945397-43-7*) Epicenter Pr.

Tales of All Countries, Vol. 1 First Ser. Anthony Trollope. Ed. by N. John Hall. LC 80-1879. (Selected Works of Anthony Trollope Ser.). 1981. reprint ed. lib. bdg. 38.95 (*0-405-14138-6*) Ayer.

Tales of All Countries, Vol. 2. Anthony Trollope. Ed. by N. John Hall. LC 80-1879. (Selected Works of Anthony Trollope). 1981. reprint ed. lib. bdg. 42.95 (*0-405-14139-4*) Ayer.

Tales of All Times. Mother. Orig. Title: Youth's Noble Path. (Illus.). 138p. (J). (gr. 3-8). 1983. pap. 4.95 (*0-89071-321-9*, Pub. by SAA II) Aurobindo Assn.

Tales of Alvin Maker. Orson Scott Card. 1995. boxed 14.93 (*0-8125-3662-2*) Tor Bks.

Tales of Amanda Pig. Jean Van Leeuwen. LC 82-23545. (Easy-to-Read Bks.). (Illus.). 56p. (J). (ps-3). 1983. pap. 4.95 (*0-8037-8443-0*) Dial Bks Young.

Tales of Amanda Pig Level 2, Red. Jean Van Leeuwen. LC 82-23545. (Easy-to-Read Ser.). (Illus.). (J). (gr. k-3). 1994. pap. 3.50 (*0-14-036840-X*, Puffin) Puffin Bks.

***Tales of American Buddhist.** Lenz. Date not set. write for info. (*0-312-18192-2*) St Martin.

Tales of Amherst: A Look Back. Daniel Lombardo. LC 85-23791. 140p. 1986. pap. 7.95 (*0-9616559-0-9*) Jones Lib.

Tales of an American Hobo. Charles E. Fox. LC 89-5055. (Singular Lives: The Iowa Series in North American Autobiography). 252p. 1989. 24.95 (*0-87745-251-2*) U of Iowa Pr.

Tales of an Ashanti Father. Peggy Appiah. LC 88-19059. (Night Lights Ser.). (Illus.). 160p. (J). (gr. 2-6). 1989. reprint ed. pap. 7.95 (*0-8070-8313-5*, NL4) Beacon Pr.

Tales of an Italian American Family. Joseph F. Perez. 1991. 17.95 (*0-89876-167-0*) Gardner Pr.

Tales of an Old Horsetrader: The First Hundred Years. Leroy J. Daniels. LC 87-10932. (Bur Oak Original Ser.). 247p. 1987. pap. 13.95 (*0-87745-187-7*) U of Iowa Pr.

Tales of an Uncommon Man: Uncle Ort's Keepsakes. Janice F. Britton. 296p. 1994. pap. 14.95 (*0-9643940-0-6*) Slow Loris Pr.

Tales of an Unorthodox Veterinarian. Gideon Sorokin. 204p. (Orig.). 1992. pap. 13.95 (*0-943376-57-2*) Magnes Mus.

Tales of Ancestors & Orisha. Lionel F. Scott. Ed. by Betty Goubert. (Illus.). 56p. (Orig.). (C). 1994. pap. 10.95 (*0-9638787-2-7*) Athelia-Henrietta.

Tales of Ancient Egypt. Roger L. Green. 256p. (J). 1996. pap. 3.99 (*0-14-036716-0*) Viking Penguin.

Tales of Ancient India. Tr. by J. A. Van Buitenen. LC 59-10430. 272p. 1969. pap. text ed. 14.50 (*0-226-84647-4*, P341) U Ch Pr.

Tales of Ancient Persia. Barbara L. Picard. (Oxford Myths & Legends Ser.). (Illus.). 176p. (YA). 1993. pap. 12.95 (*0-19-274154-3*) OUP.

Tales of Arizona Territory. Charles D. Lauer. LC 90-3336. (Illus.). 160p. (Orig.). 1990. pap. 6.95 (*0-914846-47-7*) Golden West Pub.

Tales of Art & Life. Henry James. LC 83-51481. (Signature Ser.). 316p. (Orig.). 1984. 14.75 (*0-912756-14-4*); pap. text ed. 6.75 (*0-912756-12-8*) Union Coll.

Tales of Arturo Vivante. Arturo Vivante. Ed. by Mary Kinzie. LC 90-30053. 256p. 1990. 24.95 (*0-935296-95-6*); pap. 15.95 (*0-935296-91-3*) Sheep Meadow.

Tales of Asgard - Raven's Banner. Roger Zelenetz & Charles Vess. (Illus.). 64p. 1985. 5.95 (*0-87135-060-2*) Marvel Entmnt.

Tales of BackWhen Ben. Johnie B. Sikes. (Tales from the BackWhen Ser.: Bk. 2). 40p. (J). 1992. pap. text ed. 3.95 (*0-9633262-2-8*) Vitamemoria.

Tales of Beatnik Glory. Ed Sanders. 1990. pap. 12.95 (*0-8065-1172-9*, Citadel Pr) Carol Pub Group.

Tales of Beaufort. Nell S. Graydon. LC 63-22685. (Illus.). 156p. (YA). (gr. 8 up). 1993. 16.95 (*0-87844-117-4*) Sandlapper Pub Co.

Tales of Belkin. Aleksandr Pushkin. Tr. by Gillon Aitken & David Budgen. 136p. 1983. 27.00 (*0-946162-04-2*) Dufour.

Tales of Belkin by A. S. Pushkin. Jan Van Der Eng et al. 1968. pap. text ed. 64.65 (*90-279-0437-5*) Mouton.

Tales of Bequia. Thomas C. Thomsen. Ed. by Eleanor Mann. (Illus.). 160p. (C). 1988. 12.95 (*0-945288-00-X*) Cross River Pr.

Tales of Big Ole. 2nd rev. ed. Samuel R. Harvey. (Illus.). 118p. (Orig.). pap. 5.00 (*0-9633798-0-1*) Harvey Pub MN.

Tales of Burning Love: A Novel. Louise Erdrich. LC 95-53315. 448p. 1996. 25.00 (*0-06-017605-9*) HarpC.

***Tales of Burning Love: A Novel.** Louise Erdrich. LC 95-53315. 464p. 1997. pap. 13.00 (*0-06-092836-0*, PL) HarpC.

***Tales of Canyonland Cowboys.** Ed. by Richard F. Negri. LC 97-4900. 320p. (Orig.). 1997. 19.95 (*0-87421-229-4*) Utah St U Pr.

***Tales of Canyonlands Cowboys.** Richard F. Negri. LC 97-4900. 1997. write for info. (*0-87421-231-6*) Utah St U Pr.

Tales of Cedar Lawn Farm. Dale Fields. (Illus.). 360p. 1982. pap. 14.95 (*0-87770-278-0*) Ye Galleon.

Tales of Change. Lloyd E. Foster. LC 89-50709. 267p. 1990. pap. 6.95 (*1-55523-241-8*) Winston-Derek.

Tales of Chekhov, 13 vols., Set. Anton P. Chekhov. Tr. by Constance Garnett from RUS. 1987. pap. 95.00 (*0-88001-175-0*) Ecco Pr.

Tales of Chekhov, 13 vols., Vol. 1, The Darling & Other Stories. Anton P. Chekhov. Tr. by Constance Garnett from RUS. 1984. Vol.1, The Darling & Other Stories. pap. 9.50 (*0-88001-038-X*) Ecco Pr.

Tales of Chekhov, 13 vols., Vol. 2, The Duel & Other Stories. Anton P. Chekhov. Tr. by Constance Garnett from RUS. 1987. pap. 9.95 (*0-88001-039-8*) Ecco Pr.

Tales of Chinatown. Sax Rohmer, pseud. LC 75-178459. (Short Story Index Reprint Ser.). 1977. reprint ed. 22.95 (*0-8369-4060-1*) Ayer.

Tales of Christian Unity: The Adventures of An Ecumenical Pilgrim. Thomas P. Ryan. LC 82-60748. 224p. 1983. pap. 9.95 (*0-8091-2502-1*) Paulist Pr.

Tales of Civilians see In the Midst of Life

Tales of Courtship by Jeremias Gotthelf. Tr. by Robert Godwin-Jones from GER. LC 84-48102. (American University Studies: Germanic Languages & Literature: Ser. I, Vol. 35). 241p. (C). 1984. text ed. 28.00 (*0-8204-0177-3*) P Lang Pubng.

Tales of Darkest America. Fenton Johnson. LC 72-178477. (Black Heritage Library Collection). 1977. reprint ed. 12.95 (*0-8369-8926-0*) Ayer.

Tales of Delight & Shame. Clyde J. Aragon. LC 95-92560. 176p. (Orig.). 1996. pap. 9.95 (*0-9648641-0-X*) Cliff Zone Bks.

Tales of Destiny. Elizabeth G. Jordan. LC 79-103522. (Short Story Index Reprint Ser.). 1977. 21.95 (*0-8369-3264-1*) Ayer.

Tales of Diverse Realities, Vol. 1: Eclectic Fantasy. Intro. by Ann Wilmer-Lasky. (Triality Presents Ser.). (Illus.). 100p. (Orig.). 1990. pap. 10.95 (*0-945152-05-1*) Skye Isle Ent.

Tales of Don L'Orignal. Antonine Maillet. 107p. 1989. pap. 5.95 (*0-7736-7234-6*) Genl Dist Srvs.

Tales of Dunstable Weir. Gwendoline Keats. LC 70-94736. (Short Story Index Reprint Ser.). 1977. 19.95 (*0-8369-3116-5*) Ayer.

Tales of E. T. A. Hoffmann. E. T. Hoffmann & Jacob Landau. Ed. by Leonard J. Kent & Elizabeth C. Knight. (Illus.). xl, 320p. 1972. pap. text ed. 12.95 (*0-226-34789-3*, P452) U Ch Pr.

***Tales of Early Fredonia.** Ellen E. Adams. (Illus.). 155p. 1997. reprint ed. lib. bdg. 24.00 (*0-8328-6144-8*) Higginson Bk Co.

Tales of Early Poland. Sigmund H. Uminski. (Illus.). 1968. 3.00 (*0-685-09288-7*) Endurance.

Tales of East & West. Sax Rohmer. 1976. 8.50 (*0-685-79490-3*) Bookfinger.

Tales of Edgar Allan Poe. Barry Moser. LC 91-3277. (Books of Wonder). (Illus.). 312p. (J). 1991. 22.00 (*0-688-07509-6*, Morrow Junior) Morrow.

Tales of Edgar Allan Poe. Edgar Allan Poe. LC 80-14064. (Short Classics Ser.). (Illus.). 48p. (J). (gr. 4 up). 1980. lib. bdg. 24.26 (*0-8172-1662-6*) Raintree Steck-V.

Tales of Edisto. rev. ed. Nell S. Graydon. LC 86-6610. (Illus.). 180p. (YA). (gr. 8 up). 1986. 16.95 (*0-87844-071-2*) Sandlapper Pub Co.

***Tales of Elijah the Prophet.** Peninnah Schram. LC 90-24914. 344p. (Orig.). 1997. pap. 24.95 (*0-7657-5991-8*) Aronson.

Tales of Elijah the Prophet. Peninnah Schram. LC 90-24914. 344p. (Orig.). 1993. reprint ed. 30.00 (*0-87668-580-7*) Aronson.

Tales of Empire: The British in the Middle East. Derek Hopwood. 256p. 1990. text ed. 49.50 (*1-85043-129-9*, Pub. by I B Tauris UK) St Martin.

Tales of Enchantment: Goal-Oriented Metaphors for Adults & Children in Therapy. Stephen R. Lankton & Carol H. Lankton. LC 89-720. 432p. 1989. text ed. 43.95 (*0-87630-504-4*) Brunner-Mazel.

Tales of Enchantment from Spain. Elsie Eells. LC 78-67706. (Folktale Ser.). (Illus.). reprint ed. 34.50 (*0-404-16079-4*) AMS Pr.

***Tales of Faith: Religion As Political Performance in Central Africa.** V. Y. Mudimbe. LC 97-10362. (Jordan Lectures in Comparative Religion: Vol. 18). 176p. 1997. 49.95 (*0-485-17418-9*, Pub. by Athlone Pr UK) Humanities.

Tales of Faith & Wonder. Hans Christian Andersen. LC 96-22429. 192p. (J). 1997. 19.99 (*0-7814-0192-5*, Chariot Bks) Chariot Victor.

Tales of Fantasy & Fact. Brander Matthews. LC 73-98586. (Short Story Index Reprint Ser.). 1977. 19.95 (*0-8369-3160-2*) Ayer.

Tales of Firenzuola. rev. ed. Intro. by Eileen Gardiner. LC 86-82698. (Illus.). 130p. 1987. pap. 11.00 (*0-934977-04-6*) Italica Pr.

Tales of Fish. Zane Grey. 1976. 22.95 (*0-8488-1029-5*) Amereon Ltd.

Tales of Four Lakes. Duane R. Lund. 1977. pap. 8.95 (*0-934860-04-1*) Adventure Pubns.

***Tales of Giant Snakes: A Historical Natural History of Anacondas & Pythons.** John C. Murphy & Robert W. Henderson. LC 96-54033. 1997. write for info. (*0-89464-995-7*) Krieger.

Tales of Glauber-Spa, 2 vols., 1. Ed. by William C. Bryant. 1972. reprint ed. lib. bdg. 26.00 (*0-8422-8012-X*) Irvington.

Tales of Glauber-Spa, 2 vols., 2. Ed. by William C. Bryant. 1972. reprint ed. lib. bdg. 26.00 (*0-8422-8013-8*) Irvington.

Tales of Gletha, the Goatlady. Roger Robbennolt. LC 91-71004. (Illus.). 160p. (Orig.). 1991. pap. 9.95 (*0-939516-14-4*) Forest Peace.

***Tales of Good & Evil, Help & Harm.** Philip P. Hallie. LC 97-3998. 224p. 1997. 24.00 (*0-06-018745-X*) HarpC.

***Tales of Grandpa & Gum Branch.** Russell Groover. Ed. by Eugene Y. Smith. (Illus.). 192p. (Orig.). 1997. per., pap. 9.95 (*0-9651232-2-7*, AC502) Ammons Communs.

Tales of Great Dragons. John K. Anderson. (Illus.). 64p. 1980. pap. 4.95 (*0-88388-075-X*) Bellerophon Bks.

Tales of Greek Heroes. Roger L. Green. (Orig.). (J). (gr. 5-7). 1989. pap. 2.99 (*0-14-035099-3*, Puffin) Puffin Bks.

Tales of Hackett's Creek. Dan Titus. (Illus.). 158p. (Orig.). 1991. pap. 9.95 (*1-878488-48-1*) Quixote Pr IA.

Tales of Henry James. Henry James. Ed. by Christof Weglin. (Critical Editions Ser.). (Orig.). (C). 1984. pap. text ed. 14.95 (*0-393-95359-9*) Norton.

Tales of Hermit Uncle John. Roger Robbennolt. LC 92-83892. (Illus.). 200p. (Orig.). 1993. pap. 9.95 (*0-939516-17-9*) Forest Peace.

Tales of Hoffman: Vocal Score. J. Offenbach. 332p. (ENG & FRE.). 1986. pap. 26.95 (*0-7935-0693-X*, 50338400) H Leonard.

Tales of Hoffman Libretto: Dialogue Met Version. J. Offenbach. (ENG & FRE.). 1986. pap. 4.95 (*0-7935-5379-2*, 50340620) H Leonard.

Tales of Hoffmann. E. T. A. Hoffmann. Tr. by R. J. Hollingdale. 416p. 1982. pap. 9.95 (*0-14-044392-4*, Penguin Classics) Viking Penguin.

Tales of Hoffmann. E. T. A. Hoffmann. 1993. reprint ed. lib. bdg. 28.95 (*1-56849-177-8*) Buccaneer Bks.

Tales of Hollywood the Bizarre. John Austin. 1992. pap. 5.50 (*1-56171-142-X*, S P I Bks) Sure Seller.

Tales of Horror & Fantasy. Ambrose Bierce. 228p. reprint ed. lib. bdg. 21.95 (*0-89190-187-6*, Rivercity Pr) Amereon Ltd.

Tales of India, Vol. 1. Daulat Panday. 114p. (J). (gr. 3-8). 1985. pap. 5.95 (*0-89071-330-8*, Pub. by SAA II) Aurobindo Assn.

Tales of India, Vol. 2. Daulat Panday. 126p. (J). (gr. 3-8). 1985. pap. 5.95 (*0-89071-331-6*, Pub. by SAA II) Aurobindo Assn.

Tales of Intrigue & Revenge. Stephen McKenna. LC 72-128738. (Short Story Index Reprint Ser.). 1977. 19.95 (*0-8369-3629-9*) Ayer.

Tales of Irish Life & Character. Anna M. Hall. LC 74-134964. (Short Story Index Reprint Ser.). 1977. 23.95 (*0-8369-3694-9*) Ayer.

Tales of Irish Life & Character. Anna M. Hall. LC 78-174395. 323p. 1972. reprint ed. 29.95 (*0-405-08592-3*, Pub. by Blom Pubns UK) Ayer.

Tales of Ise: Lyrical Episodes from Tenth-Century Japan. Tr. by Helen C. McCullough. 277p. 1968. 39.50 (*0-8047-0653-0*) Stanford U Pr.

Tales of Ivan Belkin. Aleksandr Pushkin. 16.95 (*0-8488-0111-3*) Amereon Ltd.

Tales of Japanese Justice. Saikaku Ihara. Tr. by Thomas M. Kondo & Alfred H. Marks. LC 79-2566. (Asian Studies at Hawaii: No. 24). 124p. reprint ed. pap. 35.40 (*0-8357-3563-X*, 2034639) Bks Demand.

Tales of Jedi. Veitch. 1995. 17.00 (*1-57042-138-2*) Warner Bks.

Tales of Jemima Puddle-Duck in French Coloring Book. Beatrix Potter & Patricia Wynne. (Little Activity Bks.). (J). 1994. 1.00 (*0-486-27913-8*) Dover.

Tales of Joshua. 2nd ed. Robert W. Slagle. (Illus.). 230p. (J). (gr. 3). 1994. reprint ed. 19.95 (*0-9614218-2-7*) Family Relat.

Tales of Joshua. 2nd ed. Robert W. Slagle. (Illus.). 230p. (YA). (gr. 3 up). 1994. reprint ed. pap. 11.95 (*0-9614218-1-9*) Family Relat.

Tales of Kankakee Land. Charles H. Bartlett. (Illus.). 1977. reprint ed. 7.50 (*0-915056-07-0*) Hardscrabble Bks.

Tales of Kathmandu: Folk Tales from the Himalayan Kingdom of Nepal. S. Sakya & G. Griffith. (C). 1992. 45.00 (0-7855-0216-5, Pub. by Ratna Pustak Bhandar) St Mut.

Tales of King Arthur. Thomas Malory. 1981. 24.95 (0-8052-3779-8) Schocken.

Tales of King Arthur. James Riordan. LC 81-86152. (Illus.). 128p. (J). (gr. 4-7). 1982. 14.95 (1-56288-251-1) Checkerboard.

***Tales of Knock Your Socks Off Service: Inspiring Stories of Outstanding Customer Service.** Ron Zemke & Kristin Anderson. (Illus.). 150p. 1997. pap. 16.95 (0-8144-7971-5) AMACOM.

Tales of Known Space: The Universe of Larry Niven. Larry Niven. 240p. (Orig.). 1985. mass mkt. 5.99 (0-345-33469-8, Del Rey) Ballantine.

Tales of Lonely Trails. Zane Grey. 1976. 20.95 (0-8488-0513-5) Amereon Ltd.

Tales of Lonely Trails, Vol. I. large type ed. Zane Grey. 208p. 1996. lib. bdg. 20.95 (0-7838-1897-1, GK Hall) Thorndike Pr.

***Tales of Lonely Trails, Vol. 2.** Zane Grey. 1996. pap. 20.95 (0-7838-1904-8) Thorndike Pr.

Tales of Lord Shantih. Thomas Wiloch. (Illus.). 52p. 1990. 25.00 (0-87775-225-7); pap. 12.95 (0-87775-226-5) Unicorn Pr.

Tales of Louisiana Treasure. Paul F. Serpas. 1975. 6.95 (0-87511-102-5) Claitors.

Tales of Love. Julia Kristeva. Tr. by Leon S. Roudiez from FRE. LC 86-28311. 448p. 1989. pap. text ed. 18.50 (0-231-06025-4) Col U Pr.

Tales of Love & Mystery. James C. Hogg. LC 85-73028. 216p. 8600. 19.95 (0-86241-085-1); pap. 10.95 (0-86241-103-3) Dufour.

Tales of Love & Terror: Booktalking the Classics, Old & New. Hazel Rochman. LC 86-32285. 128p. 1987. pap. text ed. 22.00 (0-8389-0463-7) ALA.

Tales of Madness. Tr. by Luigi Pirandello. (ITA.). 1984. 14.50 (0-937832-26-X) Dante U Am.

Tales of Magic & Spells. Corinne Denan. LC 79-66325. (Illus.). 48p. (J). (gr. 3-6). 1980. pap. text ed. 2.95 (0-89375-317-3) Troll Communs.

Tales of Magic Land, No. 1. Alexander Volkov. viii, 344p. (J). 1991. pap. 11.95 (0-685-49966-9) Red Branch Pr.

Tales of Mean Streets. Arthur Morrison. LC 96-42400. 175p. 1997. pap. text ed. 11.00 (0-89733-440-X) Academy Chi Pubs.

Tales of Mean Streets. Arthur Morrison. LC 78-128742. (Short Story Index Reprint Ser.). 1977. 19.95 (0-8369-3633-7) Ayer.

Tales of Men & Ghosts. Edith Wharton. 22.95 (0-8488-0665-4) Amereon Ltd.

***Tales of Mendele the Book Peddler.** S. Y. Abramovitsh. 400p. 1996. pap. 15.00 (0-8052-1013-X) Schocken.

Tales of Mendele the Book Peddler: Fishke the Lame & Benjamin the Third. S. Y. Abramovitsh. Ed. by Dan Miron & Ken Frieden. (Library of Yiddish Classics). 480p. 1996. 25.00 (0-8052-4136-1) Schocken.

Tales of Mexican California. Nunis & Harry Knill. (YA). (gr. 7-12). 1995. pap. 8.95 (0-88388-161-6) Bellerophon Bks.

Tales of Mithgar. Dennis L. McKiernan. LC 93-49356. 240p. 1994. pap. 8.95 (0-451-45430-8, ROC) NAL-Dutton.

Tales of Mithgar. Dennis L. McKiernan. 256p. 1995. mass mkt. 4.99 (0-451-45439-1, ROC) NAL-Dutton.

Tales of Mulla Nasruddin. R. Raja. (New World Literature Ser.: No. 18). (C). 1989. 18.00 (81-7018-559-9, Pub. by BR Pub II) S Asia.

Tales of My Native Town. Gabriele D'Annunzio. Tr. by Rafael Mantellini. LC 69-10065. 287p. 1968. reprint ed. text ed. 59.75 (0-8371-0056-9, DANT, Greenwood Pr) Greenwood.

Tales of My People. Sholem Asch. Tr. by Meyer Levin. LC 75-128752. (Short Story Index Reprint Ser.). 1977. 23.95 (0-8369-3609-4) Ayer.

Tales of Mysterious & Macabre, Vol. 1. Algernon Blackwood. 20.95 (0-8488-0193-8) Amereon Ltd.

Tales of Mystery & Imagination. (Fiction Ser.). (YA). 1993. pap. text ed. 6.50 (0-582-08483-0, 79831) Longman.

***Tales of Mystery & Imagination.** Tony Allan. (Library of Fantasy & Adventure). (Illus.). 96p. (J). (gr. 3 up). 1997. pap. 9.95 (0-7460-2369-3, Usborne) EDC.

***Tales of Mystery & Imagination.** Tony Allan. (Library of Fantasy & Adventure). (Illus.). 96p. (J). (gr. 3 up). 1997. lib. bdg. 17.95 (0-88110-900-2, Usborne) EDC.

Tales of Mystery & Imagination. Edgar Allan Poe. Ed. by Graham Clarke. 576p. 1993. pap. 6.95 (0-460-87342-3, Everyman's Classic Lib) C E Tuttle.

Tales of Mystery & Imagination. Edgar Allan Poe. LC 94-45648. (Illus.). (J). 1996. write for info. (1-56846-118-6) Creative Ed.

Tales of Mystery & Imagination. Edgar Allan Poe. LC 95-39315. (Illus.). (J). 1995. write for info. (0-15-200959-0) HarBrace.

Tales of Mystery & Imagination. Edgar Allan Poe. 112p. (J). 1996. 28.00 (0-15-100234-7) HarBrace.

Tales of Mystery & Imagination. Edgar Allan Poe. LC 88-40069. 304p. 1988. 25.00 (0-89296-350-6) Mysterious Pr.

Tales of Mystery & Imagination. Edgar Allan Poe. 1981. reprint ed. lib. bdg. 27.95 (0-89966-434-2) Buccaneer Bks.

Tales of Mystery & Terror. Edgar Allan Poe. 20.95 (0-8488-1127-5) Amereon Ltd.

Tales of Mystery & Terror. Edgar Allan Poe. 1995. pap. 3.99 (0-14-036720-9) Viking Penguin.

***Tales of Mystery & Terror.** Edgar Allan Poe. Ed. by Malvina Vogel. (Great Illustrated Classics Ser.: Vol. 33). (Illus.). 240p. (J). (gr. 3-6). 1994. 9.95 (0-86611-984-1) Playmore Inc.

Tales of Mystery, Suspense & the Supernatural: Ready to Use Quizzes, Projects, Activities, & Listening Lessons for Grades 4-8. Sue J. Erlenbusch. LC 94-25050. 1994. pap. 27.95 (0-87628-908-1) Ctr Appl Res.

Tales of Mystic Meaning. Reynold A. Nicholson. 200p. 1995. pap. 11.95 (1-85168-097-7) Onewrld Pubns.

***Tales of Mystic Meaning.** Tr. by Reynold A. Nicholson. 200p. 1996. pap. 11.95 (0-614-21369-X, 1459) Kazi Pubns.

Tales of Nantucket: Chronicles & Characters of America's Favorite Island. Robert F. Mooney. (Illus.). 184p. (Orig.). 1990. pap. 12.95 (0-9627851-0-5) Wesco Pub MA.

Tales of Nasr-ed-Din Khoja. Nasr Al-Din. Tr. by Henry D. Barnham from TUR. LC 77-87632. 1977. reprint ed. 32.50 (0-404-16457-9) AMS Pr.

Tales of Nationalism: Catalonia, 1939-1979. Hank Johnston. 250p. (C). 1991. text ed. 40.00 (0-8135-1705-2) Rutgers U Pr.

Tales of Natural & Unnatural Catastrophes. Patricia Highsmith. LC 89-15151. 192p. 1990. pap. 8.95 (0-87113-341-5, Atlntc Mnthly) Grove-Atltic.

Tales of Nevada, Vol. 1. Norm Nielson. Ed. by Kris Lonse. (Illus.). 230p. 1989. pap. 12.95 (0-9625020-0-6) Tales Nevada.

Tales of Nevada!, Vol. 2. Norm Nielson. Ed. by Karen Wright. (Illus.). 300p. 1990. pap. 12.95 (0-9625020-1-4) Tales Nevada.

Tales of Neveryon. Samuel R. Delany. LC 93-17848. (Return to Neveryon Ser.: Bk. 1). 264p. 1993. pap. 13.95 (0-8195-6270-X, Wesleyan Univ Pr) U Pr of New Eng.

Tales of New Cairo: Qahira Al Jadida. Naguib Mahfouz. pap. 8.95 (0-86685-150-X) Intl Bk Ctr.

Tales of New England. Sarah Orne Jewett. LC 77-110223. (Short Story Index Reprint Ser.). 1977. 18.95 (0-8369-3362-1) Ayer.

***Tales of Nokomis.** Patronella Johnston. (Illus.). 1996. pap. 10.95 (0-9641500-0-X) Nokomis Lrning.

Tales of North America: Native Americans. rev. ed. Irene Handberg. (Multicultural Education Ser.). 112p. 1995. teacher ed. write for info. (1-56831-211-3) Lrning Connect.

Tales of North America: Native Americans, Set. rev. ed. Irene Handberg. (Multicultural Education Ser.). 112p. 1995. write for info. (1-56831-201-6) Lrning Connect.

Tales of Northwest Naturalist. Jim Anderson. LC 92-13926. 1992. pap. 17.95 (0-87004-353-6) Caxton.

Tales of Old Brevard. 2nd ed. Georgiana G. Kjerulff. LC 90-61839. (Local History Ser.: Vol. 2). (Illus.). 134p. 1989. pap. 7.95 (0-9617352-2-8) Kellersberger Fund.

Tales of Old Dorset. Sean Street. 96p. 1987. 35.00 (0-905392-44-2) St Mut.

Tales of Old Florida. Frank Oppel. 1988. 8.98 (1-55521-225-5) Bk Sales Inc.

Tales of Old Hertfordshire. Doris Jones-Baker. 96p. 1987. pap. 30.00 (0-905392-82-5) St Mut.

Tales of Old Ireland. Michael O'Mara. 1994. 8.98 (0-7858-0087-5) Bk Sales Inc.

Tales of Old Ireland. Ed. by Michael O'Mara. 247p. 1994. 42.50 (1-85479-981-9, Pub. by Pan Books UK) Trans-Atl Phila.

Tales of Old Japan. A. B. Mitford. LC 66-25436. (Illus.). 430p. 1966. reprint ed. pap. 14.95 (0-8048-1160-1) C E Tuttle.

Tales of Old Kent. Alan Bignell. 96p. 1987. pap. 30.00 (0-905392-75-2) St Mut.

Tales of Old Key West. Richard Watherwax. (Illus.). 64p. (Orig.). 1990. pap. 11.95 (0-9628065-0-1) R Watherwax.

Tales of Old Lost Cabin & Parts Thereabout. 2nd ed. Mary H. Hendry. (Illus.). 129p. 1996. reprint ed. pap. 12.00 (0-9611656-1-8) Hendry Pubns.

Tales of Old Natchitoches. Elizabeth S. Mills & Gary B. Mills. (Cane River Creole Ser.: No. 3). (Illus.). 142p. 1978. reprint ed. 22.00 (0-931069-02-5) Mills Historical.

Tales of Old Oxfordshire. Cecillia Millson. 96p. 1987. pap. 30.00 (0-905392-20-5) St Mut.

***Tales of Old Sarajevo.** Isak Samokovlija et al. LC 97-17737. 1997. pap. write for info. (0-85303-331-5) Intl Spec Bk.

***Tales Of Old Sarajevo.** Isak Samokovlija et al. LC 97-17737. 1997. write for info. (0-85303-332-3) Intl Spec Bk.

Tales of Old Schenectady, Vol. 1: The Formative Years. Larry Hart. (Illus.). 207p. 1995. pap. text ed. 15.00 (0-932035-04-3) Old Dorp Bks.

Tales of Old Schenectady, Vol. 2: The Changing Scene. Larry Hart. (Illus.). 219p. (Orig.). 1994. pap. text ed. 15.00 (0-932035-05-1) Old Dorp Bks.

Tales of Old Surrey. Matthew Alexander. 96p. 1987. 30.00 (0-905392-41-8) St Mut.

Tales of Old Sussex. Lillian Candlin. 96p. 1987. 30.00 (0-905392-45-0) St Mut.

Tales of Old-Time Texas. J. Frank Dobie. (Illus.). 350p. 1984. reprint ed. pap. 12.95 (0-292-78069-9) U of Tex Pr.

Tales of Old Wiltshire. Cecilia Millson. 96p. 1987. 30.00 (0-905392-12-4) St Mut.

Tales of Oliver Pig. Jean Van Leeuwen. LC 79-4276. (Easy-to-Read Bks.). (Illus.). 64p. (J). (ps-3). 1979. pap. 4.95 (0-8037-8737-5) Dial Bks Young.

Tales of Oliver Pig. Jean Van Leeuwen. (Easy-to-Read Ser.: Level 2). (Illus.). (J). (gr. k-3). 1993. pap. 3.50 (0-14-036549-4, Puffin) Puffin Bks.

Tales of Oliver Pig: A Study Guide. Laurie Diamond. Ed. by J. Friedland & R. Kessler. (Novel-Ties Ser.). (J). (gr. 1-2). 1996. pap. text ed. 15.95 (1-56982-593-9) Lrn Links.

Tales of Oliver Pig see Los Cuentos del Cerdito Oliver

Tales of Oneida Lake. Compiled by Jack Henke. LC 93-22338. 250p. 1993. 25.00 (0-925168-14-9) North Country.

Tales of Ordinary Madness. Charles Bukowski. 1983. reprint ed. pap. 12.95 (0-87286-155-4) City Lights.

Tales of Our Coast. Samuel R. Crockett et al. LC 70-116966. (Short Story Index Reprint Ser.). (Illus.). 1977. 19.95 (0-8369-3470-9) Ayer.

Tales of Our Kinsfolk Past & Present: The Story of Our Butler Ancestry for Ten Generations, from 1602 to 1919. H. L. Butler. (Illus.). 552p. 1993. reprint ed. pap. 84.50 (0-8328-6582-6); reprint ed. lib. bdg. 94.50 (0-685-66345-0) Higginson Bk Co.

Tales of Peter Rabbit & His Friends, 2 vols. in 1. Beatrix Potter. (J). 1988. 8.99 (0-517-44901-3) Random Hse Value.

Tales of Physicists & Mathematicians. S. G. Gindikin. 200p. 1987. 43.00 (0-8176-3317-0) Birkhauser.

Tales of Pirx the Pilot. Stanislaw Lem. Tr. by Louis Iribarne. 216p. 1990. pap. 7.95 (0-15-688150-0, Harvest Bks) HarBrace.

Tales of Pocahontas County. George McNeil. 1958. pap. 5.00 (0-685-61019-5) McClain.

Tales of Political Pitfalls. Frank Sweet. (Illus.). 80p. (Orig.). (C). 1989. pap. 6.50 (0-939479-05-2) Boxes & Arrows.

Tales of Poppit. Amy Adams. 16p. (J). (gr. 1-3). 1995. pap. 10.00 (1-888166-53-3) Shining Lght.

Tales of Potosi. Bartolome Arzans de Orsua y Vela. Ed. by R. C. Padden. LC 74-6574. 243p. reprint ed. pap. 69.30 (0-7837-0367-8, 2040689) Bks Demand.

Tales of Power. Carlos Castaneda. 1991. pap. 14.00 (0-671-73252-8, WSP) PB.

Tales of Power. Carlos Castaneda. 1994. reprint ed. lib. bdg. 32.95 (1-56849-260-X) Buccaneer Bks.

Tales of Prince Samuttakote: A Buddhist Epic from Thailand. Tr. & Intro. by Thomas J. Hudak. (Monographs in International Studies, Southeast Asia Ser.: No. 90). 230p. (Orig.). (C). 1993. pap. text ed. 20.00 (0-89680-174-8) Ohio U Pr.

Tales of Princes & Princesses. 1987. 1.98 (0-671-08494-1) S&S Trade.

Tales of Punt: Somali Folktales As Retold by Abdi Abdulkadir Sheik-Abdi. Abdi Abdulkadir Sheik-Abdi. LC 93-91886. (Illus.). vii, 135p. (Orig.). 1993. pap. 11.95 (0-9638802-2-5) Dr Leisure.

Tales of Quails n' Such. Havilah Babcock. (Illus.). 248p. 1985. reprint ed. 24.95 (0-87249-441-1) U of SC Pr.

Tales of Rabbi Nachman. Martin Buber. LC 87-22906. (C). 1988. reprint ed. pap. 17.50 (0-391-03548-7) Humanities.

Tales of Rabbi Nachman of Bratslav: Retold with Commentary. Adin Steinsaltz. LC 92-33634. 352p. 1993. 30.00 (0-87668-183-6) Aronson.

Tales of Ravenloft. Brian Thomspon & TSR Inc. Staff. 320p. (Orig.). 1994. pap. 4.95 (1-56076-931-9) TSR Inc.

Tales of Real Adventures. Paul Dowswell. (Real Tales Ser.). (Illus.). 192p. (YA). (gr. 6 up). 1996. 19.95 (0-7460-2362-6, Usborne) EDC.

Tales of Real Escape. P. Dowswell. (Real Tales Ser.). (Illus.). 64p. (YA). (gr. 6 up). 1995. pap. 7.95 (0-7460-1669-7, Usborne); lib. bdg. 15.95 (0-88110-724-7, Usborne) EDC.

***Tales of Real Haunting.** Tony Allan. (Read Tales Ser.). (Illus.). 64p. (Orig.). (YA). (gr. 7 up). 1997. pap. 7.95 (0-7460-2359-6, Usborne) EDC.

Tales of Real Heroism. Paul Dowswell. (Real Tales Ser.). (Illus.). 64p. (YA). (gr. 6 up). 1996. pap. 7.95 (0-7460-2357-X, Usborne); lib. bdg. 15.95 (0-88110-849-9, Usborne) EDC.

Tales of Real Survival. Paul Dowswell. (Real Tales Ser.). (Illus.). 64p. (YA). (gr. 6 up). 1995. pap. 7.95 (0-7460-1725-1, Usborne); lib. bdg. 15.95 (0-88110-779-4, Usborne) EDC.

Tales of Reincarnation. Rosemary E. Guiley. 256p. (Orig.). 1989. mass mkt. 4.99 (0-671-66257-0) PB.

Tales of Richland, White Bluffs & Hanford 1805-1943. Martha B. Parker. (Illus.). 407p. 1987. 22.95 (0-87770-223-3) Ye Galleon.

Tales of San Francisco. Samuel Dickson. viii, 711p. (C). pap. 18.95 (0-8047-2097-5) Stanford U Pr.

Tales of San Francisco. Samuel Dickson. viii, 711p. 1955. 65.00 (0-8047-0488-0) Stanford U Pr.

Tales of Santa Barbara: From Native Story-Tellers to Sue Grafton. Ed. by Steven Gilbar & Dean Stewart. 192p. (Orig.). 1994. pap. 10.95 (1-880284-08-1) J Daniel.

Tales of Secret Egypt. Sax Rohmer. 1976. reprint ed. lib. bdg. 24.95 (0-89190-809-9) Amereon Ltd.

Tales of Sir William Wallace. Tom Scott. 120p. (C). 1989. 35.00 (0-903065-32-0, Pub. by G Wright Pub Ltd) St Mut.

Tales of Socialist Yugoslavia. Milos Acin-Kosta. Ed. & Intro. by Sandra K. Lindsay. LC 84-52846. 287p. pap. 15.00 (0-931931-15-0) Ravnogorski.

Tales of Soldiers see In the Midst of Life

Tales of Soldiers & Civilians. Ambrose Bierce. LC 70-121522. (Short Story Index Reprint Ser.). 1980. 23.95 (0-8369-3478-4) Ayer.

Tales of Soldiers & Civilians. Ambrose G. Bierce. (Principle Works of Ambrose Gwinett Bierce). 1989. reprint ed. lib. bdg. 79.00 (0-7812-1959-0) Rprt Serv.

Tales of Space & Time. H. G. Wells. LC 72-3285. (Short Story Index Reprint Ser.). 1977. reprint ed. 26.95 (0-8369-4166-7) Ayer.

***Tales of Spirit, Tales of Light: Mystical Stories for Older Children & Adults.** Arlene Williams. (Illus.). 160p. (Orig.). 1997. pap. 12.95 (0-9605444-6-1) Waking Light Pr.

***Tales of Squirrel Nutkin.** Beatrix Potter & Anna Pomaska. (Illus.). (J). pap. 1.00 (0-486-29033-6) Dover.

Tales of St. Columba. Eileen Dunlop. 136p. (J). (gr. 4 up). 1992. pap. 6.95 (1-85371-134-9, Pub. by Poolbeg Pr IE) Dufour.

Tales of St. Francis: Ancient Stories for Contemporary Times. Murray Bodo. 191p. 1992. pap. 7.95 (0-86716-195-7) St Anthony Mess Pr.

Tales of St. Patrick. Eileen Dunlop. 144p. (J). (gr. 4-7). 1996. 15.95 (0-8234-1218-0) Holiday.

Tales of Storytelling: Embedded Narrative in Modern French Fiction. Richard Shryock. LC 93-7880. (American University Studies: Romance Languages & Literature: Ser. II, Vol. 206). 148p. (C). 1994. text ed. 44.95 (0-8204-2239-8) P Lang Pubng.

Tales of Suicide. Luigi Pirandello. 1988. 11.95 (0-937832-31-6) Dante U Am.

Tales of Tahitian Waters. Zane Grey. 1976. 22.95 (0-8488-0806-1) Amereon Ltd.

Tales of Talislanta. Stephan M. Sechi et al. 206p. 1992. pap. 5.00 (1-880992-02-7) Wizards Coast.

Tales of Tango Vol. 1: The Brave Lesson. Sally Atkinson. LC 96-90338. (Illus.). 32p. (J). (ps-2). 1996. 12.95 (0-9653034-0-3) Tangos Grove.

***Tales of Teaching: Teaching & Learning with Multiple Intelligences.** (Illus.). (C). 1997. pap. text ed. write for info. (1-57110-061-X) Stenhse Pubs.

Tales of Teams...Heartwarming Memories of Hardworking Horses & Mules. Ed. by Rich Van Etten. LC 95-70190. 164p. 1995. 14.95 (0-89821-150-6, 20105) Reiman Pubns.

Tales of Tears & Laughter: Short Fiction of Medieval Japan. Tr. by Virginia Skord. LC 90-27817. (Illus.). 256p. 1991. text ed. 25.00 (0-8248-1315-4); pap. text ed. 14.95 (0-8248-1569-6) UH Pr.

***Tales of Teddy Hermann: Hermann Teddy Original.** Rolf Pistorius & Christel Pistorius. Tr. by Ingrid Taylor from GER. (Illus.). 96p. (C). 1994. 45.00 (3-8170-1015-X, Pub. by Knstvrlag Weingrtn GW) Intl Bk Import.

Tales of Temples & Tombs: A Kids-Eye View of Ancient Egypt. D. Amorosia. 64p. 1993. teacher ed., pap. 19.95 (0-7935-3605-7) H Leonard.

Tales of Tenderness & Power. Bessie Head. (African Writers Ser.). 144p. (Orig.). (C). 1990. pap. 7.95 (0-435-90579-1, 90579) Heinemann.

Tales of Terratopia: The Secret of the Dragonfly & the Daring Dino Rescue. Karla Kelly et al. (Illus.). 36p. (J). (gr. 1-6). 1993. 6.95 (1-883871-00-X) Nature Co.

***Tales of Terror.** Joseph L. French. (Illus.). 224p. 1971. 18.95 (0-8369-4080-6) Ayer.

***Tales of Terror: Scenario Ideas for Call of Cthulhu.** Ed. by Steve Hatherley. (Illus.). (Orig.). 1996. pap. 9.00 (1-887797-07-6) Tynes Cowan.

Tales of Terror: Television News & the Construction of the Terrorist Threat. Bethami A. Dobkin. LC 91-28772. (Media & Society Ser.). 144p. 1992. text ed. 47.95 (0-275-93981-2, C3981, Praeger Pubs) Greenwood.

Tales of Terror & Detection. unabridged ed. Edgar Allan Poe. (Thrift Editions Ser.). 96p. 1995. reprint ed. pap. text ed. 1.00 (0-486-28744-0) Dover.

Tales of Terror & Mystery. Arthur Conan Doyle. 1982. reprint ed. lib. bdg. 16.95 (0-89966-429-6) Buccaneer Bks.

Tales of Terror & the Supernatural. Wilkie Collins. Ed. & Intro. by Herbert Van Thal. LC 75-189974. 305p. (Orig.). 1972. pap. 6.50 (0-486-20307-7) Dover.

Tales of Terror & Titillation: A Compilation of Short Stories from the Macabre to the Erotic. Mel D. Ames. 224p. 1995. lib. bdg. 41.00 (0-8095-4896-8) Borgo Pr.

Tales of Terror & Titillation: A Compilation of Short Stories from the Macabre to the Erotic. Mel D. Ames. 224p. 1995. pap. 15.95 (0-88962-590-5) Mosaic.

Tales of Terror for the Pleasure Boater. Ed Pappalardo. LC 94-96101. 235p. (Orig.). 1994. pap. 16.95 (0-9641978-0-4) Hickory NY.

Tales of Terror from Blackwood's Magazine. Ed. by Robert Morrison & Chris Baldick. (World's Classics Ser.). 328p. 1996. pap. 11.95 (0-19-282366-3) OUP.

***Tales of the Age of Apocalypse.** Scott Lobdell. (Illus.). 48p. 1997. pap. 5.95 (0-7851-0289-2) Marvel Entmnt.

Tales of the Alimentary Canal. Richard Kent. 1976. 22.95 (0-8488-0138-5) Amereon Ltd.

Tales of the Amazon. Martin Elbl. (Illus.). 32p. (J). (gr. k-3). 1985. 10.95 (0-88625-127-3) Durkin Hayes Pub.

Tales of the American West. Neil Morris. (J). 1989. 5.99 (0-517-68024-6) Random Hse Value.

Tales of the Ancient Watering Hole, Bk. 2: Protohistoric Life on the South Plains. Eileen Johnson & David K. Dean. (Illus.). 55p. (J). (gr. 6-8). 1994. pap. 4.95 (0-9640188-0-2) Mus TX Tech.

Tales of the Anishinaubaek: Ojibway Legends. Basil H. Johnston. LC 93-94139. (Illus.). 80p. 1994. 24.95 (0-88854-407-3, Pub. by Royal Ont Mus CN) U of Toronto Pr.

Tales of the Anna Karrue. Leon B. Ward, III. (Orig.). 1988. pap. 15.00 (0-937684-25-2) Tradd St Pr.

Tales of the Apocalypse. Carl Kaiser. 500p. (Orig.). 1997. mass mkt. 6.95 (0-945969-11-2) Kohinoor Bks.

Tales of the Argonauts & Other Sketches. Bret Harte. LC 78-152943. (Short Story Index Reprint Ser.). 1977. reprint ed. 18.95 (0-8369-3802-X) Ayer.

Tales of the Austral Tropics. Ernest Favenc. Ed. by Cheryl Taylor. 197p. 1997. pap. 34.95 (0-86840-381-4, Pub. by New South Wales Univ Pr AT) Intl Spec Bk.

Tales of the Auto Graveyard. Daniel R. Fruit. LC 90-70677. 80p. (Orig.). 1990. pap. 8.00 (1-56002-019-9) Aegina Pr.

Tales of the Bark Lodges. Bertrand N. Walker. (Banner Bk.). (Illus.). 160p. 1995. pap. 14.95 (0-87805-795-1); lib. bdg. 35.00 (0-87805-794-3) U Pr of Miss.

Tales of the Batman. Ed. by Martin H. Greenberg. 560p. 1995. 9.98 (1-56731-076-1, MJF Bks) Fine Comms.

An Asterisk (*) at the beginning of an entry indicates that the title is appearing in BIP for the first time.

Tales of the Bayou Kid. Sylvia K. Escude. LC 94-90551. (Illus.). 104p. (Orig.). (YA). 1995. pap. 8.00 (1-56002-519-0, Univ Edtns) Aegina Pr.

Tales of the Big Bend. Elton Miles. LC 76-17977. (Illus.). 200p. 1995. pap. 13.95 (0-89096-360-6) Tex A&M Univ Pr.

*****Tales of the Bizarre & Unexplained: Fringe Film in Canada.** Mike Hoolboom. 1996. pap. text ed. 19.95 (1-896356-10-9, Pub. by Gutter Pr CN) Dist Art Pubs.

Tales of the Black Diamond. Richard Margopoulos. (Illus.). 80p. (Orig.). 1993. pap. 8.95 (0-9623841-9-4) Fantagor Pr.

Tales of the Brothers Grimm. Carol J. Cincereli. (Integrating Literature, Language & the Arts Ser.). 144p. (J). (gr. 1-6). teacher ed. 7.99 (0-86653-562-4, GA1160) Good Apple.

Tales of the Cakchiquels. Ed. by Larry L. Richman. 102p. 1984. 9.95 (0-941846-01-6) Centry Pub.

Tales of the Caribbean. Fritz Seyfarth. 126p. 10.95 (0-8286-0081-3) F Papy Cruising Guide.

Tales of the Chase: Hound-Dogs, Catfish & Other Pursuits Afield. M. H. Salmon. LC 91-71593. (Illus.). 209p. (Orig.). 1991. pap. 9.95 (0-944383-11-4) High-Lonesome.

Tales of the Chesapeake. George A. Townsend. LC 74-83904. (Black Heritage Library Collection). 1977. 15.95 (0-8369-8668-7) Ayer.

Tales of the Chutzper Rebbe: A Selection from the Acidic Anthology. Walter Rothschild. (Illus.). 80p. 1997. 16.50 (1-881283-12-7) Alef Design.

Tales of the City. Armistead Maupin. 371p. 1994. lib. bdg. 33.00 (0-8095-9139-1) Borgo Pr.

Tales of the City. Armistead Maupin. LC 77-11781. 384p. 1989. pap. 12.00 (0-06-096404-9) HarpC.

Tales of the City: Gift Edition. Armistead Maupin. 384p. 1996. 18.00 (0-06-018669-0) HarpC.

Tales of the City of God. Carlos G. Valles. LC 93-8938. 260p. (Orig.). 1993. pap. 12.95 (0-8294-0750-2) Loyola Pr.

Tales of the City Room. Elizabeth G. Jordan. LC 70-116958. (Short Story Index Reprint Ser.). 1977. 19.95 (0-8369-3462-8) Ayer.

Tales of the Clearwater. (Illus.). 235p. 1995. 24.00 (0-9608008-6-7) Legacy Hse.

Tales of the Clearwater. (Illus.). 235p. 1995. pap. 12.00 (0-9608008-7-5) Legacy Hse.

Tales of "the Clerk" & "the Wife of Bath" Geoffrey Chaucer. Ed. by Marion Wynne-Davies. (English Texts Ser.). 215p. (C). 1992. pap. 13.95 (0-415-00134-X, A9590) Routledge.

Tales of the Cloister. Elizabeth G. Jordan. LC 76-110204. (Short Story Index Reprint Ser.). 1977. 20.95 (0-8369-3355-9) Ayer.

*****Tales of the Clubhouse Cat: A Christmas Tale at That!** C. B. Kay. (Illus.). 122p. (J). 1996. 14.50 (0-9624875-8-9) Montpelier Pub.

Tales of the Cochiti Indians. Ruth Benedict. 1976. lib. bdg. 59.95 (0-8490-2729-2) Gordon Pr.

Tales of the Cochiti Indians. Ruth Benedict. (Bureau of American Ethnology Bulletins Ser.). 256p. 1995. lib. bdg. 89.00 (0-7812-4098-0) Rprt Serv.

Tales of the Cochiti Indians. Ruth Benedict. LC 81-16426. 270p. reprint ed. pap. 77.00 (0-318-34848-9, 2030998) Bks Demand.

Tales of the Cochiti Indians. Ruth Benedict. reprint ed. 49.00 (0-403-03705-0) Scholarly.

Tales of the Congaree. Edward C. Adams. LC 86-30912. xx, 367p. (C). 1987. 39.95 (0-8078-1709-0); pap. 17.95 (0-8078-4188-9) U of NC Pr.

Tales of the Constellations: The Myths & Legends of the Night. Marianne McDonald. 1996. 15.98 (0-8317-7277-8) Smithmark.

Tales of the Cousin. Jack B. Carmichael. (Trilogy of the Cousin Ser.). 80p. (Orig.). (YA). (gr. 12). 1992. pap. 9.95 (0-9626948-2-7) Dynamics MI.

Tales of the Cthulhu Mythos. H. P. Lovecraft et al. LC 87-17503. (Illus.). 525p. 1990. 24.95 (0-87054-159-5) Arkham.

Tales of the Dervishes. Idries Shah. 1967. 25.00 (0-900860-47-2, Pub. by Octagon Pr UK) ISHK.

Tales of the Dervishes: Teaching-Stories of the Sufi Masters over the Past Thousand Years. Idries Shah. 224p. 1993. pap. 10.00 (0-14-019358-8, Arkana) Viking Penguin.

Tales of the Diamond: Selected Gems of Baseball Fiction. Ed. by Laurence J. Hyman. (Illus.). 152p. 1996. 16.95 (0-942627-16-4) Woodford Pubng.

Tales of the Early World. Ted Hughes. (J). (gr. 4-8). 1991. 15.00 (0-374-37377-9) FS&G.

Tales of the Earth. Jake Page & Charles B. Officer. LC 92-28320. 240p. 1993. 27.50 (0-19-507785-7) OUP.

Tales of the Earth. Jake Page & Charles B. Officer. (Illus.). 246p. 1994. reprint ed. pap. 13.95 (0-19-509048-9) OUP.

Tales of the East, Vol. 1. Matthew Bennett. Ed. by Alan Dulfon & Roy Richards. (Illus.). 166p. (Orig.). 1994. pap. 9.95 (1-884295-00-2) Ananta Prnting.

Tales of the Eastern Shore. John Lewis. (Illus.). 136p. 1996. 18.95 (1-878970-02-X); pap. 11.95 (1-878970-03-8) Dyne-American.

*****Tales of the Eastern Shore.** John Lewis. (Illus.). 132p. (Orig.). 1997. 29.95 (0-9657328-0-0, 101) Cedar Tree Bks.

*****Tales of the Eastern Shore.** John Lewis. (Illus.). 132p. (Orig.). 1997. pap. 14.95 (0-9657328-1-9, 101) Cedar Tree Bks.

Tales of the Elk: And Other Stories. H. B. Davenport. 122p. 1992. reprint ed. pap. 7.95 (1-881413-01-2) Thomas In-Prints.

Tales of the Enlightened. S. Z. Kahana. Ed. by Philip S. Berg. 160p. 1987. 14.95 (0-943688-39-6); pap. 10.95 (0-943688-40-X) Res Ctr Kabbalah.

Tales of the Fairies & of the Ghost-World. Jeremiah Curtin. (Works of Jeremiah Curtin Ser.). 1990. reprint ed. lib. bdg. 79.00 (0-7812-2500-0) Rprt Serv.

Tales of the Fairies & the Ghost-World. Jeremiah Curtin. LC 75-152760. 1972. reprint ed. 23.95 (0-405-08416-1, Pub. by Blom Pubns UK) Ayer.

Tales of the Fathers of the Conservative Movement. Bernard Mandelbaum. LC 89-63758. (Illus.). 80p. 1990. pap. 7.95 (0-88400-140-7) Shengold.

Tales of the Field: On Writing Ethnography. John Van Maanen. (Chicago Guides to Writing, Editing & Publishing Ser.). xvi, 192p. 1988. lib. bdg. 30.00 (0-226-84961-9) U Ch Pr.

Tales of the Field: On Writing Ethnography. John Van Maanen. (Chicago Guides to Writing, Editing & Publishing Ser.). xvi, 192p. 1988. pap. 9.95 (0-226-84962-7) U Ch Pr.

Tales of the Fish Patrol. Jack London. (Illus.). 244p. 1982. pap. 6.95 (0-932458-07-6) Star Rover.

Tales of the Fish Patrol. Jack London. LC 72-4454. (Short Story Index Reprint Ser.). 1977. reprint ed. 24.95 (0-8369-4181-0) Ayer.

Tales of the Five Towns. Arnold Bennett. LC 74-17131. (Collected Works of Arnold Bennett: Vol. 77). 1977. reprint ed. 23.95 (0-518-19158-3) Ayer.

Tales of The Flying Mountains. Poul Anderson. 288p. (Orig.). 1984. pap. 2.95 (0-8125-3073-X) Tor Bks.

Tales of the Forgotten God, 3 vols., Set. Dan Hamilton. (Orig.). 1994. boxed 22.99 (0-8308-1670-4, 1670) InterVarsity.

Tales of the Forlorn Hope. William Moss. (Cyberpunk Ser.). (Illus.). 104p. (Orig.). 1992. pap. 10.00 (0-937279-21-8, CP3121) R Talsorian.

Tales of the Frisken Forest: The Adventures of Rusty Dusty Ripple the Rainbow Fish, Bk. I. Donald Beattle. (Illus.). 48p. 1990. 11.95 (0-929212-01-0) Donnie Corp.

Tales of the Frontier: From Lewis & Clark to the Last Roundup. Everett Dick. LC 62-14664. (Illus.). x, 390p. 1963. pap. 11.95 (0-8032-5744-9, Bison Books); text ed. 40.00 (0-8032-0038-2) U of Nebr Pr.

Tales of the Furtakers. Tom Eberhard. LC 94-90809. (Illus.). 112p. 1996. pap. 9.00 (1-56002-543-3, Univ Edtns) Aegina Pr.

Tales of the Galactic Empire. Richard G. Warga. LC 90-55262. 173p. (Orig.). 1991. pap. 8.00 (1-56002-071-7) Aegina Pr.

Tales of the Glauber Spa. William C. Bryant. (Works of William Cullen Bryant). 1989. reprint ed. lib. bdg. 79.00 (0-7812-2136-6) Rprt Serv.

*****Tales of the Golden Years of California Ocean Fishing 1900-1950.** Ed Ries. (Illus.). 128p. 1997. 24.95 (0-9657547-0-7) Frnds of LA.

*****Tales of the Golden Years of California Ocean Fishing 1900-1950.** Ed Ries. (Illus.). 128p. (Orig.). 1997. pap. 14.95 (0-9657547-1-5) Frnds of LA.

Tales of the Great Game Fish. Zane Grey. 304p. reprint ed. lib. bdg. 23.95 (0-89190-767-X, Rivercity Pr) Amereon Ltd.

Tales of the Great Lakes. F. Oppel. 1992. 8.98 (1-55521-120-8) Bk Sales Inc.

Tales of the Greek Heroes. Roger L. Green. (Puffin Classics Ser.). 240p. (J). 1995. pap. 3.99 (0-14-036683-0) Puffin Bks.

Tales of the Grizzly. Ed. by Tim Clark & Denise Casey. LC 92-81304. (Illus.). 192p. (Orig.). 1992. pap. 14.95 (0-943972-14-0) Homestead WY.

Tales of the Guadalupe Mountains. W. C. Jameson. 208p. 1995. pap. 12.95 (1-55622-396-X, Rep of TX Pr) Wordware Pub.

Tales of the Hasidim. Martin Buber. LC 90-52921. 736p. 1991. pap. 20.00 (0-8052-0995-6) Pantheon.

Tales of the Heart: Affective Approaches to Global Education. Tom Hampson & Loretta Whalen. (Orig.). 1991. pap. 19.95 (0-377-00223-2) Friendship Pr.

Tales of the Heavenly City. R'Yehoshua Leib Diskin. 112p. 1992. pap. write for info. (1-56062-133-8) CIS Comm.

Tales of the Home Folks in Peace & War. Joel C. Harris. LC 75-98573. (Short Story Index Reprint Ser.). 1977. 26.95 (0-8369-3147-5) Ayer.

Tales of the Home Folks in Peace & War. Joel C. Harris. (Notable American Authors Ser.). 1992. reprint ed. lib. bdg. 75.00 (0-7812-3020-9) Rprt Serv.

Tales of the Innovation Process. Richard Blazey. (Illus.). 1990. write for info. (1-879719-03-7) Idea Connect.

Tales of the Iron Road: My Life As King of the Hobos. Maury Graham & Robert J. Hemming. (Illus.). 222p. 1994. pap. 12.95 (1-56924-916-4) Marlowe & Co.

*****Tales of the Iroquois.** Ray Fadden. 173p. 1992. pap. 8.95 (0-614-26383-2) Purple Mnt Pr.

*****Tales of the Jedi.** (Star Wars Ser.). 25.00 (0-87431-289-2, 40082) West End Games.

Tales of the Kenduskeag. Jim Smith & Fern Stearns. 180p. 1993. pap. 15.95 (0-9638521-3-2) Bangor Beaut.

Tales of the Kingdom. David R. Mains & Karen B. Mains. (Illus.). 112p. (J). (gr. 1 up). 1983. 16.99 (0-89191-560-5) Chariot Victor.

Tales of the Knights Templar. Ed. by Katherine Kurtz. 320p. (Orig.). 1995. mass mkt. 5.99 (0-446-60138-1, Aspect) Warner Bks.

Tales of the Lance. John Terra. 1992. 20.00 (1-56076-338-8) TSR Inc.

*****Tales of the Lavender Menace.** Karla Jay. 272p. 1998. 25.00 (0-465-08364-1) Basic.

Tales of the Little Quarter. Jan Neruda. Tr. by Edith Pargeter from CZE. LC 76-49935. 296p. 1977. reprint ed. text ed. 45.00 (0-8371-9344-3, NELQ, Greenwood Pr) Greenwood.

Tales of the Living Dead. Ed. by Laurence Schorsch. (Scare Your Socks off Ser.). (Illus.). 128p. (J). (gr. 3 up). 1993. pap. 3.50 (1-56288-406-9) Checkerboard.

Tales of the Loremasters. Thomas Kane. Ed. by Terry K. Amthor & John D. Ruemmler. (Shadow World Ser.). (Illus.). 32p. (Orig.). (YA). (gr. 12). 1989. pap. 6.00 (1-55806-073-1, 6004) Iron Crown Ent Inc.

Tales of the Loremasters, Book 2. Thomas Kane. Ed. by John D. Ruemmler. (Shadow World Ser.). (Illus.). 32p. (Orig.). (YA). (gr. 12). 1989. pap. 6.00 (1-55806-034-0, 6008) Iron Crown Ent Inc.

Tales of the Lost Formicans. Congdon. 1990. pap. 5.95 (0-88145-091-X) Broadway Play.

Tales of the Lost Formicans & Other Plays. Constance Congdon. LC 93-51495. 300p. 1994. pap. 14.95 (1-55936-084-4) Theatre Comm.

Tales of the Lovecraft Mythos. Intro. by Robert M. Price. (C). 1991. 25.00 (1-878252-02-X) Fedogan & Bremer.

Tales of the Maine Coast. Noah Brooks. 1980. 8.50 (0-686-64301-1) Bookfinger.

Tales of the Malayan Coast. Rounsevelle Wildman. LC 72-90593. (Short Story Index Reprint Ser.). (Illus.). 1977. 21.95 (0-8369-3076-2) Ayer.

Tales of the Maori Bush. James Cowan. LC 75-35248. reprint ed. 49.50 (0-404-14422-5) AMS Pr.

Tales of the Marriage Bed from Medieval France, 1300-1500. R. C. Famiglietti. LC 92-60733. 1993. 34.95 (0-9633494-2-2) Picardy Pr.

Tales of the Master Race: A Novel. Marcie Hershman. LC 90-56363. 240p. 1992. pap. 11.00 (0-06-092353-9, PL) HarpC.

Tales of the Menehune. rev. ed. Mary K. Pukui & Caroline Curtis. (Illus.). 130p. (YA). (gr. 7-12). 1994. pap. 8.95 (0-87336-010-9) Kamehameha Schools.

Tales of the Middle Border. Hamlin Garland. Ed. by Joseph B. McCullough. 1991. 14.95 (0-8084-0437-7) NCUP.

Tales of the Mine Country. Eric McKeever. (Illus.). 124p. (Orig.). 1995. pap. 9.95 (0-9643905-0-7) E McKeever.

Tales of the Mississippi. rev. ed. Ray Samuel et al. LC 81-5937. (Illus.). 256p. 1992. reprint ed. pap. 14.95 (0-88289-930-9) Pelican.

*****Tales of the Mohican Country.** Lee Cavin. 1992. 7.95 (1-879377-00-4) Truax Print.

Tales of the Mysterious Traveller. Ditko. (Illus.). 1990. pap. 9.95 (0-913035-83-1) Eclipse Bks.

Tales of the Nez Perce. Donald M. Hines. (Illus.). 234p. 1984. 14.95 (0-87770-311-6) Ye Galleon.

*****Tales of the Night.** Peter Hoeg. 1998. 23.00 (0-374-27254-9) FS&G.

Tales of the Night. Sarah Wood. LC 82-61086. 188p. 1982. reprint ed. 20.00 (0-89725-025-7, 1269) Picton Pr.

Tales of the Norse Gods. As told by Barbara L. Picard. (Myths & Legends Ser.). (Illus.). 128p. (YA). 1994. pap. 12.95 (0-19-274167-5) OUP.

Tales of the North. Jack London. 1989. 7.98 (0-89009-439-X) Bk Sales Inc.

Tales of the North American Indians. Ed. by Stith Thompson. LC 66-22898. (Illus.). 416p. 1966. pap. 14.95 (0-253-20091-1, MB-91) Ind U Pr.

Tales of the North Coast. Pupils of Farr Secondary School Staff & Alan Temperley. 251p. (C). 1989. 45.00 (0-946487-18-9, Pub. by Luath Pr UK) St Mut.

Tales of the Northwest. William J. Snelling. Ed. by David Stinebeck. (Masterworks of Literature Ser.). 1975. 16.95 (0-685-53857-5); pap. 13.95 (0-8084-0418-0) NCUP.

Tales of the Occult. Ed. by Martin Greenberg & Charles G. Waugh. 354p. 1989. pap. 21.95 (0-87975-531-8) Prometheus Bks.

Tales of the Ohio Land. Jack Matthews. (Illus.). 186p. 1978. 11.95 (0-87758-011-1) Ohio Hist Soc.

Tales of the Old North Shore. Howard Sivertson. Ed. by Paul L. Hayden. LC 96-11970. (Illus.). 104p. 1996. 24.95 (0-942235-29-0) LSPC Inc.

Tales of the Old Soldiers: Nine Veterans of the First World War Remember Life & Death in the Trenches. Tom Quinn. 174p. 1995. 20.95 (1-85695-022-0, Pub. by ISIS UK) Transaction Pubs.

Tales of the Old Soldiers: Ten Veterans of the First World War Remember Life & Death in the Trenches. Tom Quinn. LC 93-2959. (Illus.). 192p. 1993. 30.00 (0-7509-0090-3, Pub. by Sutton Pubng UK) Bks Intl VA.

Tales of the Old-Timers. Frederick R. Bechdolt. 1993. reprint ed. lib. bdg. 75.00 (0-7812-5915-0) Rprt Serv.

Tales of the Old U. P. A Second Northwoods Reader. 9th ed. Cully Gage. LC 81-68104. (Illus.). 1981. pap. 10.95 (0-932212-23-9) Avery Color.

Tales of the Pacific. Jack London. 240p. 1989. pap. 10.95 (0-14-018358-2, Penguin Classics) Viking Penguin.

Tales of the Punjab. Flora A. Steel. LC 78-63222. (Folktale Ser.). reprint ed. pap. 33.00 (0-404-16159-6) AMS Pr.

Tales of the Punjab: Told by the People. Flora A. Steel. (C). 1989. 14.00 (81-206-0476-8, Pub. by Asian Educ Servs II) S Asia.

Tales of the Quintana Roo. James Tiptree, Jr. LC 85-18576. (Illus.). 112p. 1986. 11.95 (0-87054-152-8) Arkham.

Tales of the Ram. Russ Michael. 160p. (Orig.). 1989. pap. 9.95 (0-945127-04-9) Upword Pr.

Tales of the Real Gypsy. Paul Kesler. 1998. reprint ed. 40.00 (1-55888-232-4) Omnigraphics Inc.

Tales of the Red River Valley. Dorothy Crowder. LC 88-72312. (Illus.). 292p. 1988. 24.95 (0-9621196-1-X) Dorthenia Pubs.

Tales of the Resistance. David R. Mains & Karen B. Mains. (Illus.). 112p. (J). (gr. 4-7). 1986. 18.99 (0-89191-938-4) Chariot Victor.

Tales of the Restoration. David R. Mains & Karen B. Mains. LC 96-6238. (Illus.). (J). 1996. write for info. (1-55513-759-8) Cook.

*****Tales of the Revolution.** Mikhail P. Artsybashev. Tr. by Percy Pinkerton. 1972. 19.95 (0-8369-4168-3) Ayer.

Tales of the Saints Way. Beryl James. (C). 1989. text ed. 50.00 (1-85022-030-1, Pub. by Dyllansow Truran UK) St Mut.

Tales of the Samurai. James S. De Benneville. 480p. 1987. pap. 19.95 (0-7103-0233-9, 02339) Routledge Chapman & Hall.

Tales of the Scottish Highlands. Gerald Warner. (Illus.). 192p. (Orig.). 1982. pap. 6.95 (0-85683-061-5) Dufour.

Tales of the Scottish Highlands. Gerald Warner. (Illus.). 192p. (Orig.). 1982. 11.95 (0-85683-060-7) Dufour.

Tales of the Seal People: Scottish Folk Tales. Duncan Williamson. LC 92-14619. (International Folk Tale Ser.). 160p. 1992. 24.95 (1-56656-101-9); pap. 11.95 (0-940793-99-7) Interlink Pub.

Tales of the Shimmering Sky: Ten Global Folktales with Activities. Susan Milord. Ed. by Bill Jaspersohn. LC 95-47229. (Tales Alive! Ser.: Vol. 2). (Illus.). 128p. (Orig.). (J). (ps up). 1996. pap. 15.95 (1-885593-01-5) Williamson Pub Co.

Tales of the South. William G. Simms. Ed. & Intro. by Mary A. Wimsatt. 350p. 1996. pap. 17.95 (1-57003-087-1); text ed. 49.95 (1-57003-086-3) U of SC Pr.

Tales of the South Carolina Low Country. Nancy Rhyne. LC 82-9710. 112p. 1982. pap. 5.95 (0-89587-027-4) Blair.

Tales of the South Pacific. James A. Michener. 384p. 1984. mass mkt. 5.95 (0-449-20652-1, Crest) Fawcett.

Tales of the South Pacific. James A. Michener. 336p. 1987. 35.00 (0-02-584540-3) S&S Trade.

*****Tales of the South Pacific.** James A. Michener. lib. bdg. 26.95 (0-8488-2103-3) Amereon Ltd.

*****Tales of the State: Narrative in Contemporary U. S. Politics & Public Policy.** Ed. by Sanford F. Schram & Philip T. Neisser. LC 97-9878. (Illus.). 288p. 1997. 65.00 (0-8476-8502-0); pap. 22.95 (0-8476-8503-9) Rowman.

Tales of the Strange. A. A. Shelton. 51p. 1995. pap. 9.98 (1-888139-05-6) Y Morris Carib.

Tales of the Strange & Bizarre. Alan D. Maxwell, Sr. LC 95-90978. (Orig.). 1996. pap. 10.95 (0-533-11799-2) Vantage.

*****Tales of the Streets Surrounding Three Leaves.** Stephen Bean. 50p. (Orig.). 1996. pap. 6.95 (0-533-11325-3) Vantage.

Tales of the Sun: Folklore of Southern India. Ed. by Richard M. Dorson. LC 77-70604. (International Folklore Ser.). 1977. reprint ed. lib. bdg. 26.95 (0-405-10103-1) Ayer.

Tales of the Sun: Folklore of Southern India. Sastri P. Natesa & Georgiana H. Kingscote. LC 78-67728. (Folktale Ser.). reprint ed. 28.00 (0-404-16137-5) AMS Pr.

Tales of the Superstitions: Origins of the Lost Dutchman Legend. Robert Blair. LC 35-35054. 1975. 100.00 (0-910152-07-1); pap. 75.00 (0-910152-08-X) AZ Hist Foun.

*****Tales of the Tartan Army.** Ian Black. 192p. 1997. pap. 19.95 (1-85158-899-X, Pub. by Mnstream UK) Trafalgar.

Tales of the Tatras. Kazimierz P. Tetmajer. Tr. by H. E. Kennedy & Zofia Uminska from POL. LC 79-11094. (Illus.). 247p. 1979. reprint ed. text ed. 38.50 (0-313-21462-X, TETT, Greenwood Pr) Greenwood.

Tales of the Tatterman. Doven Hayes. Ed. by Roberta Munro. (Illus.). 1977. pap. 3.95 (0-918774-00-4) Fig Leaf.

Tales of the Tay. Picton Publishing Staff. (Illus.). 1987. 40.00 (0-317-90399-3, Pub. by Picton UK) St Mut.

Tales of the Texians. Dorothy T. Sinclair. LC 85-90411. (Illus.). 104p. (Orig.). (J). (gr. 4-7). 1986. 14.95 (0-9615311-0-X); pap. 9.95 (0-9615311-1-8) Sinclair Ent.

Tales of the Thumb. 2nd ed. Charles L. Severance. LC 72-86863. (Illus.). (J). (gr. 3-6). 1972. reprint ed. pap. 4.75 (0-932411-00-2) Pub Div JCS.

Tales of the Tikongs. Epeli Hauofa. LC 94-16399. (Talanoa Ser.). 104p. (C). 1994. reprint ed. pap. 9.95 (0-8248-1594-7) UH Pr.

Tales of the Tinners Way. Beryl James. (C). 1989. 50.00 (1-85022-042-5, Pub. by Dyllansow Truran UK) St Mut.

Tales of the Tongue. E. Ehrenreich & C. Kahan. 1992. pap. 11.99 (0-89906-124-9) Mesorah Pubns.

Tales of the Tongue. E. Ehrenreich & C. Kahan. 1992. 14.99 (0-89906-123-0) Mesorah Pubns.

Tales of the Town. Charles B. Davis. LC 78-167447. (Short Story Index Reprint Ser.). 1977. reprint ed. 23.95 (0-8369-3973-5) Ayer.

Tales of the U. S. Post Awful. Stephen Van Eck. LC 92-60514. 145p. 1992. pap. 4.00 (0-9632612-1-5) Wet Water.

Tales of the Uncanny & Supernatural, Vol. 1. Algernon Blackwood. 20.95 (0-8488-0196-2) Amereon Ltd.

Tales of the Uncanny & Supernatural, Vol. 2. Algernon Blackwood. 20.95 (0-8488-0197-0) Amereon Ltd.

Tales of the Unexpected. Roald Dahl. 480p. 1990. pap. 15.00 (0-679-72989-5, Publishers Media) Random.

Tales of the Unexpected. Derek Jacobi. 1995. pap. 16.95 (0-7871-0424-8, Dove Bks) Dove Audio.

Tales of the Vine. rev. ed. Wayne Jacobsen. 1995. reprint ed. pap. 9.95 (0-9647292-0-2) BodyLife Pub.

Tales of the Wandering Jew. Brian M. Stableford. (Dedalus European Fiction Classics Ser.). 384p. 1993. pap. 14.95 (0-7818-0215-6) Hippocrene Bks.

Tales of the Wandering Jew. Brian M. Stableford. 384p. 1994. pap. 14.95 (0-946626-71-5, Pub. by Dedalus Bks UK) Hippocrene Bks.

Tales of the Wars of Montrose. James Hogg. Ed. by Gillian Hughes. 311p. 1996. 49.50 (0-7486-0635-1, Pub. by Edinburgh U Pr UK) Col U Pr.

Tales of the West. F. Oppel. 1992. 7.98 (0-89009-796-8) Bk Sales Inc.

Tales of the West of Ireland. James Berry. LC 67-15940. 218p. 8900. reprint ed. pap. 12.95 (0-85105-502-8, Pub. by Colin Smythe Ltd UK) Dufour.

T

*__Tales of the Wichitas.__ Basil Moss. 224p. 1998. 25.95 (*0-89672-390-9*) Tex Tech Univ Pr.

Tales of the Wicked Witch. Hanna Kraan. Tr. by Elisabeth Koolschijn from DUT. LC 95-30924. (Illus.). 128p. (J). (gr. 2-5). 1995. 13.95 (*1-886910-04-9*) Front Str.

*__Tales of the Wicked Witch.__ Hanna Kraan. Tr. by Elisabeth Koolschijn. LC 97-13628. (J). 1997. pap. 3.99 (*0-14-038336-0*) Viking Penguin.

Tales of the Wild West: An Illustrated Collection of Adventure Stories. Intro. by Byron B. Price. LC 93-20148. (Illus.). 144p. 1993. 24.95 (*0-8478-1748-2*) Rizzoli Intl.

*__Tales of the Wild West: Western Stories.__ large type ed. Max Brand. LC 96-40347. (Circle V Western Ser.). 1997. lib. bdg. 17.95 (*1-57490-078-1*, Beeler LP Bks) T T Beeler.

Tales of the Wilderness. Boris A. Vogau. LC 72-169567. (Short Story Index Reprint Ser.). 1977. reprint ed. 19.95 (*0-8369-4030-X*) Ayer.

Tales of the Wolf. Ed. by Tim Clark & Denise Casey. (Illus.). 256p. (Orig.). 1995. pap. 14.95 (*0-943972-40-X*) Homestead WY.

Tales of the Wolf. Lawrence Sanders. 20.95 (*0-8488-0356-6*) Amereon Ltd.

Tales of the Wolf. Lawrence Sanders. 240p. 1986. mass mkt. 4.50 (*0-380-75145-3*) Avon.

Tales of the Working Girl: Wage-Earning Women in American Literature, 1890-1925. Laura Hapke. LC 92-10568. (Twayne's Literature & Society Ser.: No. 2). 192p. 1992. pap. 13.95 (*0-8057-8860-3*) Macmillan.

Tales of the Yanomami: Daily Life in the Venezuelan Forest. Jacques Lizot. (Canto Book Ser.). (Illus.). 216p. (C). 1991. pap. text ed. 11.95 (*0-521-40672-2*) Cambridge U Pr.

Tales of the 04 Ranch: Recollections of Harold J. Cook, 1887-1909. Harold J. Cook. LC 68-25320. 251p. 1968. reprint ed. pap. 71.60 (*0-8357-2536-7*, 2057157) Bks Demand.

Tales of Three Hemispheres. Lord Dunsany. LC 76-8950. (Illus.). 130p. 1976. 15.50 (*0-913896-04-7*) Owlswick Pr.

Tales of Ticasuk: Eskimo Legends & Stories. Emily I. Brown. Ed. by Jimmy Bedford & K. Fiedler Morack. LC 87-81286. 134p. 1987. lib. bdg. 15.00 (*0-912006-24-2*) U of Alaska Pr.

Tales of Ticasuk: Eskimo Legends & Stories. Emily I. Brown. LC 87-81286. (Illus.). 134p. 1990. reprint ed. pap. 8.95 (*0-912006-45-5*) U of Alaska Pr.

Tales of Tikkun: New Jewish Stories to Heal the Wounded World. Phyllis O. Berman & Arthur O. Waskow. LC 96-32547. 156p. 1996. 25.00 (*1-56821-991-1*) Aronson.

Tales of Times Now Past: Sixty-Two Stories from a Medieval Japanese Collection. Marian Ury. LC 78-66019. (Illus.). 216p. reprint ed. pap. 61.60 (*0-685-23661-7*, 2029066) Bks Demand.

Tales of Times Now Past: Sixty-Two Stories from a Medieval Japanese Collection. Marian Ury. LC 93-23945. (Michigan Classics in Japanese Studies: No. 9). xiii, 199p. 1993. reprint ed. pap. 11.95 (*0-939512-61-0*) U MI Japan.

Tales of Times Square. Josh A. Friedman. 1993. pap. 12.95 (*0-922915-17-2*) Feral Hse.

Tales of Tony Great Turtle. Roger Robbennolt. (Illus.). 160p. (Orig.). 1994. pap. 9.95 (*0-939516-27-6*) Forest Peace.

Tales of Topanga. Mary Miller. 144p. (Orig.). 1994. pap. 9.95 (*1-56474-068-4*) Fithian Pr.

Tales of Trail & Town. Bret Harte. LC 70-121562. (Short Story Index Reprint Ser.). 1977. 23.95 (*0-8369-3519-5*) Ayer.

Tales of Trickery. Kim A. Wheetley. 1981. 3.00 (*0-87129-556-3*, T53) Dramatic Pub.

Tales of Trickery from the Land of Spoof. Ed. by Alvin Schwartz. LC 85-16004. (Illus.). 87p. (J). (gr. 4 up). 1985. 14.00 (*0-374-37378-7*) FS&G.

Tales of Trickery from the Land of Spoof. Alvin Schwartz. (Sunburst Ser.). (Illus.). 88p. (J). (gr. 3 up). 1988. pap. 3.50 (*0-374-47426-5*) FS&G.

Tales of Triumph. Nugie Hancox. (Illus.). 144p. 1996. 24.95 (*1-874105-57-X*, Pub. by Veloce Pub UK) Motorbooks Intl.

Tales of Trotter Street. Shirley Hughes. LC 96-16138. (Illus.). 64p. (J). (ps up). 1997. 17.99 (*0-7636-0090-3*) Candlewick Pr.

Tales of Tutu Nene & Nele. Gale Bates. (Illus.). 36p. (J). (ps-4). 1991. 10.95 (*0-89610-193-2*) Island Heritage.

Tales of Two Cities: A Persian Memoir. Abbas Milani. (Illus.). 264p. 1996. 24.95 (*0-934211-47-7*) Mage Pubs Inc.

Tales of Two Cities: A Persian Memoir. Abbas Milani. (Illus.). 272p. 1997. reprint ed. pap. 14.00 (*1-56836-167-X*, Kodansha Globe) Kodansha.

Tales of Two City-States: The Development Progress of Hong Kong & Singapore. Theodor Geiger & Frances M. Geiger. LC 73-86119. 260p. 1979. 7.00 (*0-89068-022-1*) Natl Planning.

Tales of Two Countries. Alexander L. Kielland. Tr. by William Archer from NOR. LC 71-98580. (Short Story Index Reprint Ser.). 1977. 19.95 (*0-8369-3154-8*) Ayer.

Tales of Two Countries. Maxim Gorky. LC 70-160933. (Short Story Index Reprint Ser.). 1977. reprint ed. 18.95 (*0-8369-3912-3*) Ayer.

*__Tales of Tzaddikim.__ G. MaTov. Tr. by Shaindel Weinbach. (Illus.). (J). boxed 84.99 (*0-89906-841-3*, TA6H); boxed, pap. 56.99 (*0-89906-842-1*) Mesorah Pubns.

Tales of Tzaddikim: Bamidbar. Tr. by Shaindel Weinbach from HEB. (ArtScroll Youth Ser.). (Illus.). 320p. (YA). (gr. 7-12). 1988. 15.99 (*0-89906-831-6*); pap. 11.99 (*0-89906-832-4*) Mesorah Pubns.

Tales of Tzaddikim: Bereishis. G. Matov. Tr. by Shaindel Weinbach from HEB. (ArtScroll Youth Ser.). (Illus.). 320p. (YA). (gr. 7-12). 1987. 15.99 (*0-89906-825-1*); pap. 11.99 (*0-89906-826-X*) Mesorah Pubns.

Tales of Tzaddikim: Devarim. G. Matov. Tr. by Shaindel Weinbach. (ArtScroll Youth Ser.). (Illus.). 320p. (YA). (gr. 7-12). 1988. 15.99 (*0-89906-833-2*); pap. 11.99 (*0-89906-834-0*) Mesorah Pubns.

Tales of Tzaddikim: Sh'emos. G. Matov. Tr. by Shaindel Weinbach from HEB. (ArtScroll Youth Ser.). (Illus.). 320p. (YA). (gr. 7-12). 1988. 15.99 (*0-89906-827-8*) Mesorah Pubns.

Tales of Tzaddikim: Sh'emos. G. Matov. Tr. by Shaindel Weinbach from HEB. (ArtScroll Youth Ser.). (Illus.). 320p. (YA). (gr. 7-12). 1988. pap. 11.99 (*0-89906-828-6*) Mesorah Pubns.

Tales of Tzaddikim: Vayikra. Tr. by Shaindel Weinbach from HEB. (ArtScroll Youth Ser.). (Illus.). 320p. (YA). (gr. 7-12). 1988. 15.99 (*0-89906-829-4*); pap. 11.99 (*0-89906-830-8*) Mesorah Pubns.

*__Tales of Un-Knowing.__ Spinelli. LC 97-20435. 1997. 25.95 (*0-8147-8090-3*) NYU Pr.

Tales of Uncle Remus: The Adventures of Brer Rabbit, Vol. I. Illus. by Jerry Pinckney. LC 85-20449. (J). (ps up). 1987. pap. 18.99 (*0-8037-0271-X*); pap. 16.89 (*0-8037-0272-8*) Dial Bks Young.

*__Tales of Uncle Tompa: The Legendary Rascal of Tibet.__ Rinjing Dorje. LC 97-12947. 1997. pap. text ed. 13.95 (*1-886449-40-6*) Barrytown Ltd.

Tales of Uncle Tompa: The Legendary Rascal of Tibet. Rinjing Dorje. LC 75-18105. (Illus.). 80p. 1975. pap. 15.00 (*0-915880-02-4*) Dorje Ling.

*__Tales of Uncle Trapspringer.__ TSR Inc. Staff. 1997. pap. 5.99 (*0-7869-0775-4*) TSR Inc.

Tales of Unrest. Joseph Conrad. 1973. 250.00 (*0-87968-086-5*) Gordon Pr.

Tales of Unrest. Joseph Conrad. 1977. pap. 3.95 (*0-14-003885-X*, Penguin Bks) Viking Penguin.

Tales of Unrest. Joseph Conrad. 202p. 1991. pap. 8.95 (*0-14-018036-2*, Penguin Classics) Viking Penguin.

Tales of Vermont Ways & People. Bertha S. Dodge. LC 84-61170. (Illus.). 192p. 1984. reprint ed. pap. 14.95 (*0-933050-22-4*) New Eng Pr VT.

Tales of War. Mihail Sadoveanu. LC 61-18507. 1962. lib. bdg. 27.00 (*0-8057-5208-0*) Irvington.

Tales of Whitetails: Archibald Rutledge's Great Deer-Hunting Stories. Archibald Rutledge. Ed. by Jim Casada. LC 92-20100. 290p. 1992. 24.95 (*0-87249-860-3*) U of SC Pr.

Tales of Wild Turkey Hunting. Simon W. Everitt. (Illus.). 127p. 1984. reprint ed. 16.95 (*0-685-62741-1*) Real Turkeys Pubs.

Tales of Wisdom: One Hundred Modern Parables. Howard Schwartz. 1996. 9.99 (*0-517-14256-2*) Random Hse Value.

Tales of Witchcraft. Richard Dalby. 1994. 8.98 (*0-7858-0137-5*) Bk Sales Inc.

Tales of Wonder: Reading Level 2-3. Illus. by Holly J. Dobbs. LC 93-16083. (Timeless Tales Ser.). (J). 1993. 4.95 (*0-88336-459-X*); audio 9.95 (*0-88336-524-3*) New Readers.

*__Tales of Wonder & Magic.__ Berlie Doherty. LC 97-670. (J). 1998. write for info. (*1-56402-891-7*) Candlewick Pr.

*__Tales of Ye Merrye Woode: A Musical.__ 57p. (Orig.). (J). (gr. k-6). 1997. pap. 3.00 (*1-57514-285-6*, 4029) Encore Perform Pub.

Tales of Yesteryear. large type ed. Louis Auchincloss. LC 94-4250. 1994. lib. bdg. 22.95 (*0-7862-0235-1*) Thorndike Pr.

Tales of Yoruba Gods & Heroes. Harold Courlander. 256p. 1995. pap. 11.95 (*0-942272-40-4*) Original Pubns.

Tales of Yukaghir, Lamut & Russianized Natives of Eastern Siberia. Vladimir G. Bogoraz. LC 78-67689. (Folktale Ser.). reprint ed. 37.50 (*0-404-16057-3*) AMS Pr.

Tales on the Twisted Side, Vol 1: Fresh Blood. Intro. by Ann Wilmer-Lasky. (Triality Presents Ser.). (Illus.). 105p. (Orig.). 1989. pap. 10.95 (*0-945152-04-3*) Skye Isle Ent.

Tales Out of School. Verl C. Shoemaker. LC 95-32867. (Iowa Heritage Collection Ser.). (Illus.). 80p. (C). 1995. pap. 9.95 (*0-8138-2244-0*) Iowa St U Pr.

Tales Out of School. Benjamin Taylor. 304p. 1997. pap. 12.99 (*0-446-67269-6*) Warner Bks.

Tales Out of School: A Novel. Benjamin Taylor. LC 95-60519. 284p. 1995. 21.95 (*1-885983-04-2*) Turtle Point Pr.

Tales out of School: Selected Interviews. Robert Creeley. (Poets on Poetry Ser.). 224p. (C). 1993. pap. 13.95 (*0-472-06536-X*); text ed. 39.50 (*0-472-09536-6*) U of Mich Pr.

Tales Out of Tilt, Or Tales Out of Time, Vol. II. Regina C. Rapier. 1983. 20.00 (*0-9600584-5-1*) R C Rapier.

Tales Out of Time, Vol. 1: The Mad Compactor & Other Science Fiction Short Stories. rev. ed. Regina C. Rapier. 1995. reprint ed. 20.00 (*0-685-04205-7*) R C Rapier.

Tales Out of Trial. R. Perry Sentell, Jr. LC 94-31686. (Illus.). 80p. 1995. 11.95 (*0-89854-174-3*) U of GA Inst Govt.

Tales Out of Tulsa. Bobby Baldwin. 1984. pap. 6.95 (*0-89746-006-5*) Gambling Times.

Tales Plainly Told: The Eyewitness Narratives of Hemingway & Homer. Kathleen Morgan. (ENGL Ser.: Vol. 7). x, 90p. 1990. 44.00 (*0-938100-81-5*) Camden Hse.

Tales, Rumors, & Gossip: Exploring Contemporary Folk Literature in Grades 7-12. Gail De Vos. xx, 405p. 1996. lib. bdg. 32.00 (*1-56308-190-3*) Libs Unl.

Tales, Sketches, & Other Papers. Nathaniel Hawthorne. LC 73-37549. (Short Story Index Reprint Ser.). 1977. reprint ed. 28.95 (*0-8369-4108-X*) Ayer.

Tales, Sketches, & Other Papers: With Biographical Sketch by George Parsons Lathrop. Nathaniel Hawthorne. (Illus.). 578p. 1976. 25.00 (*0-403-02464-1*) Scholarly.

Tales, Speeches, Essays, & Sketches. Mark Twain. Ed. & Intro. by Tom Quirk. LC 94-5815. 448p. 1994. pap. 11.95 (*0-14-043417-8*, Penguin Classics) Viking Penguin.

Tales That Are, Tales That Aren't & Other Tales. Jean M. Kelty. (Illus.). 84p. (gr. 7 up). 1984. pap. 9.95 (*0-910781-01-X*) G Whittell Mem.

Tales That Dead Men Tell. J. E. Pearce. 1993. reprint ed. lib. bdg. 75.00 (*0-7812-5972-X*) Rprt Serv.

Tales the Elders Told: Ojibway Legends. Basil H. Johnston. LC 81-94102. (Illus.). 64p. 1993. 15.95 (*0-88854-261-5*) U of Toronto Pr.

*__Tales Through Time.__ 2nd rev. ed. Michael R. Collings. 100p. Date not set. pap. 15.00 (*1-886405-55-7*, Zarahemla Motets) White Crow Pr.

Tales, Tiny & Tall. Fred H. Gibson. 488p. 1995. pap. 13.50 (*0-9649383-0-8*) F H Gibson.

Tales to Be Read with Caution. Alfred Hitchcock & Eleanor Sullivan. Date not set. lib. bdg. 25.95 (*0-88411-706-5*, Aeonian Pr) Amereon Ltd.

Tales to Give You Goosebumps. R. L. Stine. 144p. (J). (gr. 4-6). 1994. pap. 11.95 (*0-590-62836-4*) Scholastic Inc.

*__Tales to Give You Goosebumps.__ R. L. Stine. (Goosebumps Special Ser.). (J). 1997. pap. text ed. 3.99 (*0-590-48993-3*) Scholastic Inc.

Tales to Scary to Tell at Camp. Tom B. Stone. (Graveyard School Ser.: No. 13). 128p. (J). (gr. 4-7). 1996. mass mkt. 3.99 (*0-553-48489-3*, Skylark BDD) BDD Bks Young Read.

Tales to Tell. Ed. by David Campbell. 88p. (C). 1989. pap. 39.00 (*0-685-66159-8*, Pub. by St Andrew UK) St Mut.

Tales to Tell. Larry G. Stenzel. 128p. (Orig.). 1979. pap. 4.50 (*0-910021-00-7*) Samuel P Co.

Tales to Tell, Vol. 2. David Campbell. 128p. 1993. pap. 24.00 (*0-685-68112-2*, Pub. by St Andrew UK) St Mut.

Tales Told at Twilight. Ruskin Bond. 166p. (J). (gr. 4-6). 1970. 1.25 (*0-88253-394-0*) Ind-US Inc.

Tales Told by Simpson. May Sinclair. LC 73-151228. (Short Story Index Reprint Ser.). 1977. reprint ed. 20.95 (*0-8369-3859-3*) Ayer.

Tales Told to the Heart. Peter Wilson. 1995. 12.95 (*0-533-11138-2*) Vantage.

Tales, Too! Tales from the Springs. Jeanne Mozier. Ed. & Intro. by Robert L. Walker. 150p. (Orig.). 1995. pap. write for info. (*0-938572-14-8*) Bunny Crocodile.

Tales Too Good To Miss. Faye Day & Annette Geistfeld. (Illus.). 44p. 1983. pap. 7.50 (*0-912773-03-0*) One Hund Twenty Creat.

Tales Too Ticklish to Tell. Berkeley Breathed. (Illus.). 128p. 1988. mass mkt. 7.95 (*0-316-10735-2*) Little.

Tales, Trails & Tommyknockers: Stories from Colorado's Past. Myriam Friggens. LC 79-84876. (Illus.). 144p. (J). (gr. 6 up). 1979. pap. 8.95 (*0-933472-01-3*) Johnson Bks.

Tales, Treasures, & Pirates of Old Monterey. Randall A. Reinstedt. LC 79-110354. (Illus.). 72p. 1976. pap. 5.95 (*0-933818-03-3*) Ghost Town.

Tales until Dawn: The World of a Cape Breton Gaelic Story-Teller. Joe N. MacNeil. Ed. by John W. Shaw. 460p. (ENG & GAE.). 1987. 70.00 (*0-7735-0559-8*, Pub. by McGill CN); pap. 24.95 (*0-7735-0560-1*, Pub. by McGill CN) U of Toronto Pr.

Tales with a Sting in Their Tails. Thomas Singleton. 1993. 8.95 (*0-533-10314-2*) Vantage.

Tales with a Twist. Greta B. Lipson. 160p. (J). (gr. 5-9). 1991. 12.99 (*0-86653-609-4*, GA1328) Good Apple.

Tales Within Tales: Apuleius Through Time. Ed. by Constance R. Wright & Julia B. Holloway. LC 91-57968. (Studies in Cultural History: No. 2). 1992. 39.50 (*0-404-64252-7*) AMS Pr.

Tales Worth Retelling: Stories from Around the World. write for info. (*0-318-58800-5*) S&S Trade.

*__Tales You Do Tell.__ Madame Billa, pseud. LC 97-67291. 50p. (Orig.). 1997. pap. 8.95 (*1-57197-069-X*) Pentland Pr.

Tales You Won't Believe. Gene S. Porter. 25.95 (*0-8488-0871-1*) Amereon Ltd.

Talespins, a Story of Early Aviation Days. Edith D. Culver. LC 85-17359. (Illus.). 148p. (Orig.). 1986. pap. 10.95 (*0-86534-073-0*) Sunstone Pr.

Taleworlds & Storyrealms. K. Galloway Young. 282p. (C). 1986. lib. bdg. 134.00 (*90-247-3415-0*, Pub. by M Nijhoff NE) Kluwer Ac.

Talfulano. Bill Rane. LC 75-27249. 104p. (Orig.). 1976. pap. 7.00 (*0-912292-39-3*) Smith.

Taliaferro - Toliver Family Records. N. W. Sherman. 242p. 1992. reprint ed. pap. 33.50 (*0-8328-2296-5*); reprint ed. lib. bdg. 43.50 (*0-8328-2295-7*) Higginson Bk Co.

Taliaferro County, Georgia: Records & Notes. Alvin M. Lunceford, Jr. LC 85-20994. (Illus.). 704p. 1987. 45.00 (*0-87152-414-7*) Reprint.

Taliaferro Family History, 1635-1899. Charles Taliaferro. 154p. 1995. reprint ed. pap. 25.00 (*0-8328-4851-4*); reprint ed. lib. bdg. 35.00 (*0-8328-4850-6*) Higginson Bk Co.

Talibah, Can We Talk? Talibah F. Modupe. Ed. by T. Munirah Harris. 111p. (Orig.). pap. 7.95 (*1-887442-00-6*) Modupe Pr.

Taliesen of the Radiant Brow: Secrets of Welsh Witchcraft. Rhuddlwm Gawr. LC 85-73754. (Illus.). 144p. (Orig.). 1989. reprint ed. 12.95 (*0-931760-44-5*, CP 10122); reprint ed. pap. 10.95 (*0-931760-22-4*) Camelot GA.

Taliesin. Stephen R. Lawhead. (Pendragon Cycle Ser.: Bk. 1). 448p. (Orig.). 1996. pap. 13.00 (*0-310-20505-0*) Zondervan.

Taliesin. Stephen R. Lawhead. (Pendragon Cycle Ser.: Bk. 1). 496p. (Orig.). 1990. reprint ed. mass mkt. 6.99 (*0-380-70613-X*, AvoNova) Avon.

Taliesin: A Masque. Richard Hovey. (Notable American Authors Ser.). 1992. reprint ed. lib. bdg. 75.00 (*0-7812-3192-2*) Rprt Serv.

Taliesin: Shamanism & the Bardic Mysteries in Britain & Ireland. John Matthews. (Illus.). 256p. 1990. pap. 13.95 (*0-04-440586-3*) Routledge Chapman & Hall.

Taliesin: Shamanism & the Bardic Mysteries in Britain & Ireland. John Matthews. (Illus.). 368p. 1991. pap. 18.00 (*1-85538-109-5*, Pub. by Aquarian Pr UK) Thorsons SF.

Taliesin Legacy: The Architecture of Frank Lloyd Wright's Apprentices. Tobias S. Guggenheimer. LC 94-47312. (Illus.). 256p. 1995. pap. 62.95 (*0-442-01879-7*) Van Nos Reinhold.

Taliesin Tradition. Emyr Humphreys. LC 89-82291. (Illus.). 256p. 1990. pap. 22.50 (*1-85411-020-9*, Pub. by Seren Bks UK) Dufour.

Taligent Commonpoint Program. Wilson. 1995. 39.95 (*0-13-454166-9*) P-H.

Taligent's Guide to Designing Programs: Well-Mannered Object-Oriented Design in C++ Taligent Inc. Staff. 144p. (C). 1994. pap. text ed. 22.95 (*0-201-40888-0*) Addison-Wesley.

Talihina Project: Survey & Testing of the Proposed Talihina Wastewater Treatment Plant Improvements, LeFlore County, Oklahoma. Robert L. Brooks. (Archeological Resource Survey Report). (Illus.). 82p. (C). 1982. pap. text ed. 5.25 (*1-881346-10-2*) Univ OK Archeol.

Talim ul-Hajj. Mahmud Ahmad Ghazanfar. 94p. (Orig.). 1985. pap. 5.99 (*1-56744-399-0*) Kazi Pubns.

*__Talion: Revenant.__ Michael A. Stackpole. 480p. 1997. mass mkt. 5.99 (*0-553-57656-9*) Bantam.

Tali's Slippers, Tova's Shoes. Yaffa Ganz. (ArtScroll Middas Ser.). (Illus.). 32p. (J). (gr. k-6). 1989. 7.99 (*0-89906-502-3*) Mesorah Pubns.

Talislanta Geographica. James Hays, Jr. et al. (Talislanta Ser.). (Illus.). 16p. (Orig.). 1992. pap. 9.95 (*1-880992-05-1*) Wizards Coast.

Talislanta Guidebook. 3rd ed. Stephan M. Sechi & Jonathan Tweet. 344p. 1992. pap. 20.00 (*1-880992-01-9*) Wizards Coast.

Talislanta Worldbook. Stephan M. Sechi. (Illus.). 184p. 1990. pap. 19.95 (*0-945849-21-4*) Wizards Coast.

Talisman. Stephen King & Peter Straub. 784p. 1987. mass mkt. 7.99 (*0-425-10533-4*) Berkley Pub.

Talisman. Stephen King & Peter Straub. LC 83-40677. 672p. 1984. pap. 32.95 (*0-670-69199-2*) Viking Penguin.

Talisman. Lynda La Plante. 698p. 1988. pap. 19.95 (*0-330-30606-5*, Pub. by Pan Books UK) Trans-Atl Phila.

Talisman. Ed. by Sam Lewis. (Earthdawn Ser.: No. 5). 288p. (Orig.). 1994. pap. 4.99 (*0-451-45389-1*, ROC) NAL-Dutton.

Talisman. Walter Scott. Ed. by W. M. Parker. 336p. 1991. pap. 7.95 (*0-460-87088-2*, Everyman's Classic Lib) C E Tuttle.

Talisman. Ganga P. Vimal. 312p. 9000. pap. 21.00 (*0-948259-57-4*, Pub. by Forest Bks UK) Dufour.

Talisman: A Collection of Nose Art. John M. Campbell & Donna Campbell. LC 92-60358. (Illus.). 256p. 1992. text ed. 49.95 (*0-88740-414-6*) Schiffer.

Talisman: Posse mit Gesang in drei Akten. Johann N. Nestroy. Ed. by Helmut Herles. 135p. (C). 1971. 15.25 (*3-11-001869-1*) De Gruyter.

Talisman Dreaming. Joseph A. Uphoff, Jr. LC 87-35145. (Halloween Ser.: No. 4). 32p. 1987. pap. text ed. 2.00 (*0-943123-03-8*) Arjuna Lib Pr.

Talisman Italian Cook Book. Ada Boni. Tr. by Mathilde La Rosa. (International Cookbook Ser.). 1997. 12.00 (*0-517-50387-5*, Harmony) Crown Pub Group.

Talisman Magic: Yantra Squares for Tantric Divination. Richard Webster. LC 95-45133. (Llewellyn's Practical Magic Ser.). (Illus.). 186p. 1995. pap. 9.95 (*1-56718-801-X*) Llewellyn Pubns.

Talisman Magick Workbook: Master Your Destiny Through the Use of Talismans. Kala Pajeon & Ketz Pajeon. LC 92-28896. (Illus.). 254p. 1992. pap. 9.95 (*0-8065-1366-7*, Citadel Pr) Carol Pub Group.

Talisman Ring. Georgette Heyer. 274p. 1993. 23.95 (*1-56723-057-1*) Yestermorrow.

Talisman Technique: A Formula for Making Two Hundred Dollars a Hour. Lane Moore. (Illus.). (Orig.). 1988. pap. text ed. 9.95 (*0-945556-00-4*) How-To Pubns.

Talismans of Shannara. Terry Brooks. 448p. 1994. mass mkt. 6.99 (*0-345-38674-4*, Del Rey) Ballantine.

*__Talismans of Shannara.__ Terry Brooks. (Shannara Ser.). 1997. pap. 6.99 (*0-345-91133-4*, Del Rey) Ballantine.

*__Taliswoman, No. 3.__ Douglas. Date not set. write for info. (*0-312-85148-0*) St Martin.

Talitha Cumi. Noel Connor. 48p. 8300. pap. 9.95 (*0-906427-53-3*, Pub. by Bloodaxe Bks UK) Dufour.

*__Talk.__ Michael Bugeja. 1997. write for info. (*1-55728-471-7*) U of Ark Pr.

*__Talk.__ Michael Bugeja. 1997. pap. write for info. (*1-55728-472-5*) U of Ark Pr.

Talk: If I Am a Musical Thinker. Benjamin Boretz. 56p. (Orig.). 1985. pap. 5.95 (*0-88268-002-1*) Station Hill Pr.

Talk: NPR's Susan Stamberg Considers All Things. Susan Stamberg. LC 93-32928. 400p. 1994. pap. 15.00 (*0-399-51873-8*, Perigee Bks) Berkley Pub.

Talk a Lot: Communication Activities for Speaking Fluency. Keith S. Folse. LC 93-60504. 180p. 1993. teacher ed. 10.95 (*0-472-08245-0*); pap. text ed. 15.95 (*0-472-08228-0*) U of Mich Pr.

Talk-A-Tivities. Richard Yorkey. 1985. text ed. 35.33 (*0-201-09911-X*) Addison-Wesley.

Talk about a Family. Eloise Greenfield. LC 77-16423. (Illus.). 64p. (J). (gr. 2-5). 1991. lib. bdg. 16.89 (*0-397-32504-5*, Lipp Jr Bks) HarpC Child Bks.

Talk about a Family. Eloise Greenfield. LC 77-16423. (Trophy Bk.). (Illus.). 64p. (J). (gr. 2-5). 1993. pap. 3.95 (*0-06-440444-7*, Trophy) HarpC Child Bks.

An Asterisk (*) at the beginning of an entry indicates that the title is appearing in BIP for the first time.

Talk about Architecture: A Century of Architectural Education at Tulane. Ed. by Bernard Lemann et al. LC 93-60383. (Illus.). 247p. 1993. 40.00 (*0-9637302-0-7*) Tulane U Archit.

Talk about Beliefs. Mark Crimmins. (Illus.). 224p. 1992. 27.50 (*0-262-03185-X*, Bradford Bks) MIT Pr.

Talk-about-Books Series: Clothes, 6 vols. Debbie Bailey. (Illus.). 14p. (J). (ps-k). 1991. Clothes. 4.95 (*1-55037-167-3*, Pub. by Annick CN) Firefly Bks Ltd.

Talk-about-Books Series: Hats, 6 vols. Debbie Bailey. (Illus.). 14p. (J). (ps-k). 1991. Hats. 4.95 (*1-55037-159-2*, Pub. by Annick CN) Firefly Bks Ltd.

Talk-about-Books Series: My Dad, 6 vols. Debbie Bailey. (Illus.). 14p. (J). (ps-k). 1991. My Dad. 4.95 (*1-55037-164-9*, Pub. by Annick CN) Firefly Bks Ltd.

Talk-about-Books Series: My Mom, 6 vols. Debbie Bailey. (Illus.). 14p. (J). (ps-k). 1991. My Mom. 4.95 (*1-55037-163-0*, Pub. by Annick CN) Firefly Bks Ltd.

Talk-about-Books Series: Shoes, 6 vols. Debbie Bailey. (Illus.). 14p. (J). (ps-k). 1991. Shoes. 4.95 (*1-55037-161-4*, Pub. by Annick CN) Firefly Bks Ltd.

Talk-about-Books Series: Toys, 6 vols. Debbie Bailey. (Illus.). 14p. (J). (ps-k). 1991. 4.95 (*1-55037-165-7*, Pub. by Annick CN) Firefly Bks Ltd.

Talk about English: How Words Travel & Change. Janet Klausner. LC 89-49116. (Illus.). 208p. (J). (gr. 5 up). 1990. 14.95 (*0-690-04831-9*) HarpC Child Bks.

Talk about Fun. Karen J. Knight & Patricia Estes. (Illus.). 1995. 27.95 (*0-937857-61-0*, 1485) Speech Bin.

Talk about Good. Lafayette Junior League Members. 450p. 1967. 11.95 (*0-935032-00-2*) Jr League Lafayette.

Talk about Good! Le Livre De la Cuisine De Lafayette. Junior League of Lafayette Staff. 450p. 17.95 (*0-935032-02-9*) Jr League Lafayette.

Talk about Good II. Lafayette Junior League Members. 9.95 (*0-935032-50-9*) Jr League Lafayette.

***Talk about It! An Integrated Approach to Bold, Dynamic Topics.** Joyce Bryan et al. (Orig.). 1997. pap. 15.95 (*0-472-08395-3*) U of Mich Pr.

***Talk about It! An Integrated Approach to Bold, Dynamic Topics.** Joyce Bryan et al. (Orig.). 1997. teacher ed., pap. 17.95 (*0-472-08396-1*) U of Mich Pr.

Talk about Problems. Thelma Paull. (C). 1990. 60.00 (*0-86431-085-4*, Pub. by Aust Council Educ Res AT) St Mut.

Talk about Trivia: One Thousand One Questions. Irene Shoenberg. Ed. by Joanne Dresner. 128p. (Orig.). 1986. pap. text ed. 15.95 (*0-582-90721-7*, 75234) Longman.

Talk about Trouble: A New Deal Portrait of Virginians in the Great Depression. Nancy J. Martin-Perdue & Charles L. Perdue, Jr. LC 95-34700. (Illus.). 544p. (C). 1996. pap. 19.95 (*0-8078-4570-1*) U of NC Pr.

Talk about Trouble: A New Deal Portrait of Virginians in the Great Depression. Nancy J. Martin-Perdue & Charles L. Perdue, Jr. LC 95-34700. (Illus.). 544p. (C). (gr. 13). 1996. 45.00 (*0-8078-2269-8*) U of NC Pr.

Talk & Social Organization. John Lee & Graham Button. 290p. 1987. 99.00 (*0-905028-75-9*, Pub. by Multilingual Matters UK); pap. 39.95 (*0-905028-74-0*, Pub. by Multilingual Matters UK) Taylor & Francis.

Talk & Social Structure. Ed. by Dierdre Boden & Don H. Zimmerman. 315p. 1991. 42.50 (*0-520-07506-4*) U CA Pr.

Talk & Taxonomy: A Methodological Comparison of Ethnosemantics & Ethnomethodology with Reference to Terms for Canadian Doctors. Peter Eglin. (Pragmatics & Beyond Ser.: Vol. 1, No. 8). x, 125p. 1980. pap. 29.00 (*90-272-2510-9*) Benjamins North Am.

Talk & Text in the Operating Room - A Study in Medical Discourse. Catherine J. Pettinari. Ed. by Roy O. Freedle. LC 88-10396. (Advances in Discourse Processes Ser.: Vol. 33). 192p. 1988. text ed. 78.50 (*0-89391-459-2*) Ablex Pub.

Talk & Toddle: A Commonsense Guide for the First Three Years. Anne M. Mueser & Lynne Liptay. 160p. 1983. pap. 7.95 (*0-312-78430-9*) St Martin.

Talk at Work: Interaction in Institutional Settings. Ed. by Paul Drew & John Heritage. (Studies in Interactional Sociolinguistics: No. 8). 490p. (C). 1993. text ed. 85.00 (*0-521-37489-8*); pap. text ed. 34.95 (*0-521-37633-5*) Cambridge U Pr.

Talk Back - Local Authority Communication with Citizens. 55p. 1995. pap. 17.00 (*0-11-886132-8*, HM61328, Pub. by Stationery Ofc UK) Bernan Associates.

Talk Before Sleep. Elizabeth Berg. 304p. 1995. mass mkt. 6.50 (*0-440-22109-9*) Dell.

***Talk Before Sleep.** Elizabeth Berg. 336p. 1997. pap. 11.95 (*0-385-31878-2*) Doubleday.

Talk Before Sleep. large type ed. Elizabeth Berg. LC 94-27102. 276p. 1994. lib. bdg. 21.95 (*0-7862-0333-1*) Thorndike Pr.

Talk Before Sleep: A Novel. Elizabeth Berg. 1994. 18.00 (*0-679-43299-X*) Random.

Talk Book: The Intimate Science of Communicating in Close Relationships. Gerald Goodman & Glenn Esterly. 432p. 1990. mass mkt. 5.99 (*0-345-36275-6*) Ballantine.

Talk Curriculum. Ed. by David Booth & Carol Thornley-Hall. 160p. 1991. pap. text ed. 20.00 (*0-435-08597-2*, 08597) Heinemann.

***Talk Dirty.** Matthias Schultheiss. (Eros Graphic Novel Ser.: No. 10). 88p. pap. 16.95 (*1-56097-208-4*) Fantagraph Bks.

Talk Dirty to Me: An Intimate Philosophy of Sex. Sallie Tisdale. 288p. 1995. reprint ed. pap. 12.95 (*0-385-46855-5*, Anchor NY) Doubleday.

Talk Does Not Cook the Rice: The Teachings of Agni Yoga, No. 2. R. H. Guru. LC 81-70390. 195p. (Orig.). 1985. pap. 8.95 (*0-87728-535-7*) Weiser.

Talk Given on a Course in Miracles: An Introduction. 5th ed. Kenneth Wapnick. LC 92-30373. 138p. 1993. pap. 5.00 (*0-933291-16-7*) Foun Miracles.

Talk Is Cheap: Declining Costs, New Competition, & Regulatory Reform in Telecommunications. Robert W. Crandall & Leonard Waverman. (Integrating National Economies: Promise & Pitfalls Ser.). 294p. (C). 1995. 42.95 (*0-8157-1608-7*); pap. 18.95 (*0-8157-1607-9*) Brookings.

Talk is Cheap: Promoting Your Business Through Word of Mouth Advertising. G. Harris & G. J. Harris. (Illus.). 136p. 1991. pap. 9.95 (*0-935047-12-3*) Americas Group.

***Talk Is Cheap: Sarcasm, Alienation & the Evolution of Language.** John Haiman. (Illus.). 240p. 1997. pap. 18.95 (*0-19-511525-2*) OUP.

***Talk Is Cheap: Sarcasm, Alienation & the Evolution of Language.** John Haiman. (Illus.). 240p. 1997. 45.00 (*0-19-511524-4*) OUP.

Talk It Out: Conflict Resolution in the Elementary Classroom. Barbara Porro. LC 96-5639. (Illus.). 148p. (Orig.). 1996. pap. 22.95 (*0-87120-262-X*, 196018) Assn Supervision.

Talk It Out! Four Steps to Managing People Problems in Your Organization. Daniel Dana. (Illus.). 248p. (Orig.). (C). 1989. pap. 13.95 (*0-87425-122-2*) HRD Press.

Talk It Up. Kevin Scoleri. (Inter Acta Ser.). (Illus.). 4p. (C). 1994. student ed., ring bd. 3.25 (*1-885702-26-4*, 741-013s, Inter Acta) WSN Pr.

Talk It Up. Kevin Scoleri. (Inter Acta Ser.). (Illus.). 6p. (C). 1994. teacher ed., ring bd. 1.25 (*1-885702-27-2*, 741-013t, Inter Acta) WSN Pr.

Talk Japanese Gambatte! Kazuhiko Nagatomo. (Illus.). 156p. 1995. pap. 19.00 (*4-7700-1932-7*) Kodansha.

Talk Japanese Gambatte! Kazuhiko Nagatomo. Ed. by Taro Hirowatari & Paul Hulbert. 1995. audio 25.00 (*4-7700-1933-5*) Kodansha.

Talk Java to Me: The Interactive Click, Listen, & Learn Guide to Java Programming. Harry McIntosh. (Illus.). 220p. (Orig.). 1996. pap. 24.99 (*1-57169-044-1*, Waite Grp Pr) Sams.

Talk Less & Say More: Vermont Proverbs. Wolfgang Mieder. LC 86-50974. (Illus.). 64p. (Orig.). 1986. pap. 6.95 (*0-933050-42-9*) New Eng Pr VT.

Talk Like a Cowboy (Poland) Reading Level 2. (Fitting In Ser.). 1993. 2.95 (*0-88336-996-6*); audio 6.95 (*0-88336-769-6*) New Readers.

Talk of Angels. Kate O'Brien. LC 95-17737. 368p. 1997. pap. 12.95 (*0-7868-6191-6*) Hyperion.

***Talk of Fame: Good Advice from Great Celebrities.** Jeffrey Zaslow. LC 97-16072. 160p. (Orig.). 1997. pap. 8.95 (*0-8362-2707-7*, Cader Bks) Andrews & McMeel.

Talk of Gin & Beer. Timothy O. Donovan. Ed. by Gwen Costa. LC 91-38017. 201p. (Orig.). 1992. pap. 13.95 (*0-87949-334-8*) Ashley Bks.

***Talk of Love.** Swidler. 1990. pap. text ed. 14.95 (*0-226-78691-9*); lib. bdg. 34.95 (*0-226-78690-0*) U Ch Pr.

Talk of the Clinic: Exploration in the Analysis of Medical & Therapeutic Discourse. Ed. by G. H. Morris & Ronald U. Chenail. (Communication Ser.). 344p. 1995. pap. 34.50 (*0-8058-1373-X*); text ed. 79.95 (*0-8058-1372-1*) L Erlbaum Assocs.

Talk of the Tide: An Oral History of Alabama Football since 1920 As Told to John Forney & Steve Townsend by the Men Who Made the Crimson Tide a Legend. John Forney & Steve Townsend. 224p. 1993. pap. 19.95 (*1-881548-03-1*) Crane Hill AL.

Talk of the Town. Beverly Barton. (Desire Ser.: No. 711). 1992. pap. 2.89 (*0-373-05711-3*, 5-05711-2) Harlequin Bks.

Talk of the Towns: Stories from Southwest Michigan. Kathryn S. Zerler. Ed. by Peggy L. Farrington. (Illus.). 262p. 1991. 15.95 (*0-9627532-1-1*) Sleeping Cat.

***Talk of the Village.** large type ed. Rebecca Shaw. (Large Print Ser.). 464p. 1997. 27.50 (*0-7089-3709-8*) Ulverscroft.

Talk on Haiku. Joseph Gustafson. 8p. (Orig.). (C). 1990. pap. 2.95 (*0-9620313-2-1*) Leicester Hill Bks.

Talk on Television: Audience Participation & Public Debate. Sonia M. Livingstone & Peter Lunt. LC 93-15440. (Communication & Society Ser.). 208p. (C). 1993. pap. 16.95 (*0-415-07738-9*) Routledge.

Talk on Television: Audience Participation & Public Debate. Sonia M. Livingstone & Peter Lunt. LC 93-15440. (Communication & Society Ser.). 208p. (C). (gr. 13). 1993. text ed. 69.95 (*0-415-07737-0*) Routledge.

Talk on the Wilde Side. Ed Cohen. 224p. (C). 1992. pap. 17.95 (*0-415-90230-4*, A4046, Routledge NY) Routledge.

Talk Radio. Edgar Sather & Catherine Sadow. (Illus.). (C). 1987. text ed. 20.00 (*0-201-16836-7*) Addison-Wesley.

Talk Sense to Yourself. Jeffrey Wragg. (C). 1990. 65.00 (*0-86431-037-4*, Pub. by Aust Council Educ Res AT); 75.00 (*0-86431-093-5*, Pub. by Aust Council Educ Res AT) St Mut.

Talk Sense to Yourself: A Guide to Cognitive Restructuring Therapy. Rian E. McMullin & Bill Casey. (Illus.). 57p. (Orig.). 1975. pap. 4.00 (*0-935205-02-0*) Counseling Res.

Talk Sense to Yourself: Language & Personal Power. Chick Moorman. 200p. 1985. 12.95 (*0-9616046-0-3*) Prsnl Power Pr.

Talk Sense to Yourself: A Guide to Cognitive Restructuring Therapy see Hablese con Sentido A Si Mismo: Una Guia de Terapia de Restructuracion Cognitiva

***Talk Sexy to the One You Love: (And Drive Each Other Wild in Bed)** Barbara Keesling. 176p. 1997. pap. 8.00 (*0-06-092802-6*, PL) HarpC.

Talk Sexy to the One You Love: And Drive Each Other Wild in Bed. Barbara Keesling. LC 95-37150. 144p. 1996. 15.00 (*0-06-017211-8*, HarpT) HarpC.

Talk Show & Entertainment Program Processes & Procedures. Robert J. Schihl. (Multiple Camera Video Ser.). 118p. 1991. pap. 32.95 (*0-240-80092-3*, Focal) Buttrwrth-Heinemann.

***Talk Show Defense.** Gross. LC 96-53529. 1997. 20.95 (*0-312-85803-5*) St Martin.

***Talk Show Selects.** rev. ed. Ed. by Mitchell P. Davis. 375p. 1996. 185.00 (*0-934333-28-9*) Broadcast Inter.

Talk Shows & Hosts on Radio: A Directory Including Show Titles & Formats, Biographical Information on Hosts, & Topic/Subject Index. 4th ed. Ed. by Annie M. Brewer. 300p. 1996. 40.00 (*0-9632341-5-3*) Whitefoord.

***Talk Small! A Guide to Effective to Small Talk.** Pete Daly. (Personal Development Ser.). 1991. pap. 12.95 (*0-7494-0617-8*) Kogan Page Ltd.

Talk Story. Mallie Moore et al. (Illus.). 115p. (Orig.). 1987. 7.95 (*0-9618620-0-9*) Bright Design.

Talk Story: An Anthology of Hawaii's Local Writers. Ed. by Eric Chock. 1978. pap. 3.95 (*0-932136-03-6*) Petronium HI.

***Talk, Talk.** Peter Sirr. 68p. 1987. pap. 11.95 (*1-85235-018-0*) Dufour.

Talk, Talk: An Ashanti Legend. Deborah M. Chocolate. LC 92-13278. (Legends of the World Ser.). (Illus.). 32p. (J). (gr. 2-5). 1992. pap. 4.95 (*0-8167-2818-6*); lib. bdg. 13.95 (*0-8167-2817-8*) Troll Communs.

Talk, Talk, Talk, Jesus. Irene Lewers & Rosellen Lewis. LC 90-61751. 112p. 1990. pap. 5.95 (*0-89221-184-9*) New Leaf.

Talk That Matters: An Introduction to Public Speaking. rev. ed. Robert A. Cocetti & Lee Snyder. 338p. (YA). (gr. 10 up). 1992. 18.00 (*1-878276-44-1*) Educ Systs Assocs Inc.

Talk That Talk: An Anthology of African-American Storytelling. Linda Goss & Marian E. Barnes. 352p. 1989. pap. 13.00 (*0-671-67168-5*, Touchstone Bks) S&S Trade.

Talk That Talk Some More! On the Cutting Room Floor. Compiled by Marian E. Barnes. LC 92-42419. 320p. 1993. 18.95 (*0-89015-895-9*) Sunbelt Media.

***Talk the Talk.** Linda Zacharias. (Illus.). 84p. (Orig.). 1996. pap. 9.95 (*0-9654387-0-8*) L Zacharias.

Talk, Thought, & Thing: The Emic Road Toward Conscious Knowledge. Kenneth L. Pike. LC 92-82114. xii, 85p. 1993. pap. 5.00 (*0-88312-610-9*); fiche 8.00 (*0-88312-582-X*) Summer Instit Ling.

Talk Thru the Bible: A Survey of a Setting & Content of Scripture. Bruce Wilkinson & Kenneth Boa. LC 83-13343. (Illus.). 544p. 1983. reprint ed. pap. 29.99 (*0-8407-5286-5*) Nelson.

Talk Time: A Method for Teaching Values to Children. Mary A. Foster. 68p. (Orig.). (C). write for info. (*0-9635784-0-5*) CA Educ Pubns.

Talk to God . . . I'll Get the Message: Black Version. Norman Geller. (Illus.). 23p. (J). (gr. 1-4). 1985. pap. 4.95 (*0-915753-08-1*) N Geller Pub.

Talk to God . . . I'll Get the Message: Catholic Version. Norman Geller. (Illus.). 23p. (J). (gr. 1-4). 1983. pap. 4.95 (*0-915753-03-0*) N Geller Pub.

Talk to God . . . I'll Get the Message: Jewish Version. Norman Geller. (Illus.). 23p. (J). (gr. 1-4). 1983. pap. 4.95 (*0-915753-02-2*) N Geller Pub.

Talk to God . . . I'll Get the Message: Protestant Version. Norman Geller. (Illus.). 23p. (J). (gr. 1-4). 1983. pap. 4.95 (*0-915753-04-9*) N Geller Pub.

Talk to God . . . I'll Get the Message: Spanish Version. Norman Geller. Tr. by Bonnie Galway from ENG. (Illus.). 23p. (J). (gr. 1-4). 1985. pap. 4.95 (*0-915753-07-3*) N Geller Pub.

Talk to Me. Sue Brearley. (Illus.). 26p. (J). (gr. 1-4). 10.95 (*0-7136-3192-9*, Pub. by A&C Black UK) Talman.

Talk to Me. Dave Burrows. 154p. (Orig.). 1992. pap. 8.99 (*1-56043-086-9*) Destiny Image.

Talk to Me: Opening up Your Silent Man. Kris Rosenberg. 192p. 1995. mass mkt. 5.50 (*0-380-72470-7*) Avon.

***Talk to Me: Stories & a Novella.** Carol Dines. (YA). (gr. 7 up). 1997. 15.95 (*0-614-28683-2*, Delacorte Pr Bks) BDD Bks Young Read.

***Talk to Me: Stories & a Novella.** Carol Dines. LC 96-43114. (J). 1997. 15.95 (*0-385-32271-2*, Delacorte Pr Bks) BDD Bks Young Read.

Talk To Me: 2,507 Questions Think, Reminisce, Reflect. Bonnie Sose. 150p. 1992. pap. 9.95 (*0-9615279-7-8*) Character Builders.

Talk to Me, Lady. Beneth P. Jones. Ed. by Wanda Sutton. 70p. (Orig.). (C). 1991. pap. 5.95 (*0-89084-584-0*, 055152) Bob Jones Univ Pr.

Talk to Me Like I'm Someone You Love: Flash Cards for Real Life. Nancy Dreyfus. 150p. 1995. pap. 7.95 (*0-89087-816-1*) Celestial Arts.

Talk to Me, Mom: Fun Ways to Teach Pre-Reading Skills Through Conversation. Leona Golden. (Illus.). 181p. 1985. spiral bd. 15.00 (*0-9616856-0-3*) Plum Grove.

Talk to Me of Love. large type ed. E. A. Webster. 1990. pap. 15.99 (*0-7089-6888-0*, Trailtree Bookshop) Ulverscroft.

Talk to the Deaf: A Manual of Approximately 1,000 Signs Used by the Deaf of North America. Lottie L. Riekehof. LC 63-17975. (Illus.). 149p. (J). (gr. k up). 1963. teacher ed. 9.95 (*0-88243-612-0*, 02-0612) Gospel Pub.

Talk to the World: A Manual for Students & Teachers of Conversational English. Edward Voeller. LC 94-75328. xx, 379p. (Orig.). 1994. pap. 16.50 (*0-9640278-5-2*) LangPower Pubns.

Talk to Win: Six Steps to a Successful Vocal Image. Lillian Glass. (Illus.). 224p. 1988. pap. 12.00 (*0-399-51386-8*, Perigee Bks) Berkley Pub.

***Talk Too Much? Who, Me?** Victor W. Doherty. (Illus.). 71p. (Orig.). 1997. pap. 7.95 (*0-9656090-0-6*) Pickled Pepper.

Talk, Trust & Feel: Keeping Codependency Out of Your Life. Melody Beattie et al. (Hazelden Recovery Bks.). 1991. mass mkt. 5.99 (*0-345-37455-X*) Ballantine.

Talk with Franciscans - 1965, Vol. 27. Eugen Rosenstock-Huessy. (Eugen Rosenstock-Huessy Lectures). 36p. pap. 20.00 incl. audio (*0-614-05400-1*); pap. 10.00 (*0-912148-46-2*); audio 10.00 (*0-614-05399-4*) Argo Bks.

Talk with Me. Lorelei Liddelow. (Illus.). 112p. (Orig.). (J). (gr. k-3). 1984. pap. 10.00 (*0-920541-97-6*) Peguis Pubs Ltd.

Talk with Me: Communication with the Multi-Handicapped Deaf. California State Department of Health Staff et al. LC 75-70066. 24.95 (*0-917002-05-9*) Joyce Media.

Talk with Me: Giving the Gift of Language & Emotional Health to the Hearing-Impaired Child. Ellyn Altman. LC 87-72929. 222p. (Orig.). 1988. pap. text ed. 19.95 (*0-88200-163-9*) Alexander Graham.

Talk with Teens about Feelings, Family, Relationships, & the Future: 50 Guided Discussions for School & Counseling Groups. Jean S. Peterson. Ed. by Pamela Espeland. LC 95-13024. 216p. (Orig.). (YA). (gr. 7-12). 1995. teacher ed., pap. 21.95 (*0-915793-88-1*) Free Spirit Pub.

Talk with Teens about Self & Stress: 50 Guided Discussions for School & Counseling Groups. Jean S. Peterson. Ed. by Pamela Espeland. LC 93-21514. 192p. (Orig.). 1993. pap. 19.95 (*0-915793-55-5*) Free Spirit Pub.

Talk with Us, Work with Us. 1986. 5.00 (*0-318-22547-6*, TR-86-4) Ed Comm States.

Talk with Your Hands, Listen with Your Eyes. Kristin Ellerbusch. LC 92-24991. (Umbrella Bks.). (Illus.). 32p. (J). (gr. 2-6). 1993. lib. bdg. 21.36 (*0-89565-974-3*) Childs World.

Talk Your Fat Off. Maye E. Keao. 150p. 1988. write for info. (*0-318-62822-8*) Keaos Enterprises.

Talk Your Way Around Europe. Shaun Dowling. 1994. pap. 7.95 (*0-8442-9602-3*, Passport Bks) NTC Pub Grp.

Talk Your Way to Success. Lilyan Wilder. (Illus.). 320p. 1991. reprint ed. pap. 11.95 (*0-9629260-1-9*) Eastside Pub.

Talk Your Way to the Top: Communication Secrets of the Ceos. Stephen R. Maloney. 1992. 19.95 (*0-13-882788-5*, Busn) P-H.

Talkable Bible Stories: Helping Your Kids Apply God's Word to Their Lives. Larry Richards. LC 91-12923. (Illus.). 256p. (J). (ps-3). 1994. reprint ed. pap. 9.99 (*0-8007-5505-7*) Revell.

Talkable Tales. Lois Muehl. (Illus.). 128p. 1993. 25.95 (*0-937857-44-0*, 1540) Speech Bin.

Talkabout - A Four Ringbinder. Ed. by R. Cordern. (C). 1988. 260.00 (*0-85950-934-6*, Pub. by S Thornes Pubs UK) St Mut.

Talkabout Animals. (Illus.). (ARA.). (J). (gr. 1-3). 1987. 4.50 (*0-86685-231-X*) Intl Bk Ctr.

Talkabout the Beach. (Illus.). (ARA.). (J). (gr. 1-3). 1987. 4.50 (*0-86685-232-8*) Intl Bk Ctr.

Talkabout the Home. (Illus.). (ARA.). (J). (gr. 1-3). 1987. 4.50 (*0-86685-233-6*) Intl Bk Ctr.

Talkative Man. R. K. Narayan. 1988. mass mkt. 5.95 (*0-14-010134-9*, Penguin Bks) Viking Penguin.

Talkative Man. R. K. Narayan. 128p. 1994. pap. 9.95 (*0-14-018546-1*, Penguin Classics) Viking Penguin.

Talkaty Talker. Molly Manley. LC 92-75858. (Illus.). 24p. (J). (ps-1). 1994. 9.95 (*1-56397-195-X*) Boyds Mills Pr.

Talked to Death. Louise Shaffer. 1996. mass mkt. 5.99 (*0-425-15407-6*) Berkley Pub.

***Talker Variability in Speech Processing.** Ed. by Keith Johnson & John W. Mullennix. LC 96-31802. (Illus.). 237p. 1997. boxed 49.95 (*0-12-386560-3*, AP Prof) Acad Pr.

Talkies. Robert Crawford. 80p. 1992. pap. 15.95 (*0-7011-3928-5*, Pub. by Chatto & Windus UK) Trafalgar.

Talkin & Testifyin: The Language of Black America. Geneva Smitherman. LC 85-22615. 298p. 1986. reprint ed. pap. 17.95 (*0-8143-1805-3*) Wayne St U Pr.

Talkin' B. A. Blues: The Life & a Couple of Deaths of Ed Teashack...etc. George Starbuck. 45p. (C). 1980. 7.50 (*0-913219-22-3*) Pym-Rand Pr.

Talkin' B. A. Blues: The Life & a Couple of Deaths of Ed Teashack...etc. limited ed. George Starbuck. 45p. (C). 1980. 10.00 (*0-913219-24-X*) Pym-Rand Pr.

***Talkin' 'Bout Bess: The Story of Aviator Bessie Coleman.** Nikki Grimes. LC 97-21978. (Illus.). (J). 1998. write for info. (*0-531-30069-2*); lib. bdg. write for info. (*0-531-33069-9*) Orchard Bks Watts.

Talkin' Dan Gable. Ed. by Stephen T. Holland. 100p. 1983. pap. 7.95 (*0-9612582-0-9*) Limerick Pubns.

Talkin Moscow Blues. Josef Skvorecky. 1990. pap. 12.95 (*0-88001-231-5*) Ecco Pr.

Talkin' Socialism: J.A. Wayland & the Role of the Press in American Radicalism, 1890-1912. Elliott Shore. LC 87-37255. (Illus.). x, 278p. 1988. 27.50 (*0-7006-0352-2*); pap. 14.95 (*0-7006-0521-5*) U Pr of KS.

Talkin' Union: The American Labor Movement see Perspectives on History Series: Part II

Talking. Richard L. Allington & Kathleen Krull. LC 80-17021. (E. G. Beginning to Learn about ... Ser.). (Illus.). 32p. (J). (ps-2). 1985. pap. 3.95 (*0-8114-8234-0*) Raintree Steck-V.

Talking. David Antin. pap. 3.50 (*0-686-09756-4*) Kulchur Foun.

Talking a Good Game: Inquiries into the Principles of Sport. Spencer K. Wertz. LC 90-53579. 276p. 1991. text ed. 28.50 (*0-87074-320-1*); pap. text ed. 14.95 (*0-87074-321-X*) SMU Press.

***Talking about a Revolution: The Politics & Practice of Feminist Teaching.** LC 96-49888. (Understanding Education & Policy Ser.). 304p. 1997. 59.50 (*1-57273-080-3*) Hampton Pr NJ.

*Talking about a Revolution: The Politics & Practice of Feminist Teaching. Cheryl L. Sattler. LC 96-49888. (Understanding Education & Policy Ser.). 304p. 1997. pap. 24.95 (1-57273-081-1) Hampton Pr NJ.

*Talking about Aphasia: Living with Loss of Language after Stroke. Susie Parr et al. LC 97-15402. 1997. write for info. (0-335-19937-2, Open Univ Pr); pap. write for info. (0-335-19936-4, Open Univ Pr) Taylor & Francis.

Talking about Books: Creating Literate Communities. Ed. by Kathy G. Short & Kathryn M. Pierce. LC 90-31126. (Illus.). 209p. (Orig.). 1990. pap. text ed. 23.50 (0-435-08526-3, 08526) Heinemann.

*Talking about Children. John Immerwahr & Janice Kamrin. (Orig.). 1995. pap. 7.50 (1-889483-02-8) Public Agenda.

Talking about Crime & Criminals: Problems & Issues in Theory Development in Criminology. Don C. Gibbons. LC 93-11980. 256p. (C). 1993. pap. text ed. 28.60 (0-13-669137-4) P-H Gen Ref & Trav.

Talking about Death: A Dialogue Between Parent & Child. 3rd ed. Earl A. Grollman. LC 89-46061. (Illus.). 128p. (J). (gr. k-4). 1991. pap. 14.00 (0-8070-2363-9) Beacon Pr.

Talking about Divorce & Separation: A Dialogue Between Parent & Child. Earl A. Grollman. LC 75-5289. (Illus.). (YA). (gr. k-4). pap. 9.95 (0-8070-2375-2, BP524) Beacon Pr.

Talking about Dreams: Dream Reports As Personal Narratives. Roger Elbourne. 320p. (C). text ed. write for info. (0-8290-1582-5) Irvington.

Talking about Films: A Discussion Guide. 2nd ed. Robert Selinske. (Illus.). 464p. (Orig.). 1988. pap. 20.00 (0-9610670-2-0) Filmquest Bks.

*Talking about Fort Collins. (Illus.). 1996. write for info. (0-8300-8027-9) Aurora News Reg.

Talking About Genesis. Bill Moyers. 112p. 1996. pap. 5.95 (0-385-48580-8, Main St Bks) Doubleday.

*Talking about Genesis: A Resource Guide. Intro. by Bill Moyers. 179p. 1996. pap. 5.95 (0-385-48582-4) Doubleday.

Talking about Grammar. R. G. Bowers et al. (YA). (gr. 9-12). 1987. pap. text ed. 13.95 (0-582-55899-9, 78323) Longman.

Talking about Jesus Today: An Introduction to the Story Behind Our Faith. William E. Reiser. LC 92-33240. 240p. 1993. pap. 11.95 (0-8091-3358-X) Paulist Pr.

Talking about Leaving: Factors Contributing to High Attrition Rates. Seymour. (C). 1996. text ed. 49.95 (0-8133-8926-7) Westview.

Talking about Literacy: Principles & Practices of Adult Literacy Education. Jane Mace. 192p. (C). 1992. pap. 17.95 (0-415-06655-7, A9638) Routledge.

Talking about Literacy: Principles & Practices of Adult Literacy Education. Jane Mace. 192p. (C). (gr. 13). 1992. text ed. 69.95 (0-415-08044-4, A9634) Routledge.

Talking about Machines: An Ethnography of a Modern Job. Julian E. Orr. LC 96-23924. (IRL Press Book/ Collection on Technology & Work). 192p. 1996. 32.50 (0-8014-3297-9) Cornell U Pr.

Talking about Machines: An Ethnography of a Modern Job. Julian E. Orr. (IRL Press Book/Collection on Technology & Work). 192p. 1996. pap. 13.95 (0-8014-8390-5) Cornell U Pr.

Talking About Mime: An Illustrated Guide. David Alberts. LC 94-18094. 120p. 1994. pap. 14.95 (0-435-08641-3, 08641) Heinemann.

*Talking about People: A Guide to Fair & Accurate Language. 3rd ed. Rosalie Maggio. Orig. Title: Dictionary of Bias-Free Usage. 336p. 1997. pap. text ed. 27.50 (1-57356-069-3) Oryx Pr.

Talking about People: A Multiple Case Study on Adult Language Acquisition. P. Broeder. (European Studies on Multilingualism: Vol. I). x, 198p. 1991. pap. 32.75 (90-265-1211-2) Swets.

Talking about People: Readings in Contemporary Cultural Anthropology. 2nd ed. Ed. by William A. Haviland & Robert J. Gordon. 296p. (C). 1995. pap. text ed. 21.95 (1-55934-524-1, 1524) Mayfield Pub.

Talking about People: Readings in Contemporary Cultural Anthropology. 2nd ed. Ed. by William A. Haviland & Robert J. Gordon. 1995. teacher ed., pap. text ed. write for info. (1-55934-525-X, 1525) Mayfield Pub.

Talking about Pianos. Corby Kummer. Ed. by William Zinsser et al. LC 81-84064. (Illus.). 80p. (Orig.). 1982. pap. write for info. (0-9607196-0-1) Steinway.

Talking about Pictures: French. Barbara Whelpton. 1987. pap. text ed. 6.75 (0-582-22465-9, 70938) Longman.

Talking about Sex. Derek C. Polonsky. 192p. 1995. 21.95 (0-88048-719-4, 8719) Am Psychiatric.

*Talking about Statistics. write for info. (0-340-52921-0, Pub. by E Arnold UK) Routledge Chapman & Hall.

Talking about Statistics: A Psychologist's Guide to Design & Analysis. Brian S. Everitt & Dale F. Hay. 130p. 1992. pap. text ed. 33.95 (0-470-21956-4) Wiley.

Talking about the U. S. A. An Active Introduction to American Culture. Janet Giannotti & Suzanne M. Szwarcewicz. LC 95-21001. 1996. pap. text ed. 15.60 (0-205-15962-1) P-H.

Talking about the War, 1939-1945: A Personal View of the War in Britain. 2nd large type ed. Anne Valery. 252p. 1993. 22.95 (1-85695-010-7, Pub. by ISIS UK) Transaction Pubs.

Talking about Tommorrow: A New Radical Politics. Ed. by Stuart Wilks. LC 93-26384. 160p. (C). 65.00 (0-7453-0792-2, Pub. by Pluto Pr UK); pap. 18.95 (0-7453-0793-0, Pub. by Pluto Pr UK) LPC InBook.

Talking about William Faulkner: Interviews with Jimmy Faulkner & Others. Sally Wolff & Floyd C. Watkins. LC 95-39359. (Southern Literary Studies). (Illus.). 240p. (C). 1996. 24.95 (0-8071-2030-8) La State U Pr.

Talking about Writing: A Guide for Tutor & Teacher Conferences. Beverly L. Clark. (Illus.). 192p. 1985. pap. text ed. 18.95 (0-472-08062-8) U of Mich Pr.

Talking Across the World: The Love Letters of Olaf Stapledon & Agnes Miller, 1913-1919. Olaf Stapledon & Agnes Miller. Ed. by Robert Crossley. LC 87-8119. (Illus.). 424p. 1987. text ed. 40.00 (0-87451-423-1) U Pr of New Eng.

Talking All Morning. Robert Bly. (Poets on Poetry Ser.). 316p. 1980. pap. 13.95 (0-472-15760-4) U of Mich Pr.

Talking American: Cultural Discourses on Donahue. Donal Carbaugh. Ed. by Brenda Dervin. LC 88-10455. (Communication & Information Science Ser.). 272p. 1988. pap. 39.50 (0-89391-477-0); text ed. 73.25 (0-89391-492-4) Ablex Pub.

Talking & Learning in Groups. Elizabeth Dunne & Neville S. Bennett. (Classroom Skills Ser.). (Illus.). 256p. (C). 1993. pap. text ed. 13.95 (0-333-55180-X, A9897) Routledge.

*Talking & Learning in Groups. Elizabeth Dunne & Neville Bennett. (Leverhulme Primary Project Classroom Skills Ser.). 57p. (C). 1993. pap. text ed. 13.95 (0-415-10931-0) Routledge.

Talking & Listening: Keys to Success with Customers & Co-Workers. 229p. 1990. pap. 34.95 (0-912857-52-8) Inst Finan Educ.

Talking & Listening Together: Couple Communication One. Elam Nunnally et al. (Illus.). 160p. (C). 1991. pap. 16.00 (0-917340-18-3) Interpersonal Comm.

Talking & Thinking: The Patterns of Behavior. David Butt. (Language Education Ser.). 120p. 1989. pap. text ed. 12.95 (0-19-437151-4) OUP.

Talking & Thinking: The Patterns of Behaviour. David Butt. 103p. (C). 1985. pap. 45.00 (0-7300-0344-2, ECS806, Pub. by Deakin Univ AT) St Mut.

Talking & Your Child: A Parents' Handbook. Clare Shaw. 145p. 1995. pap. 11.95 (0-340-57526-3, Pub. by Hodder & Stoughton Ltd UK) Trafalgar.

Talking Animals. Wilfrid D. Hambly. (Illus.). (J). 1990. 7.95 (0-87498-025-9) Assoc Pubs DC.

Talking Animals: Medieval Latin Beast Poetry, 750-1150. Jan M. Ziolkowski. LC 92-46709. (Middle Ages Ser.). 378p. (C). 1993. text ed. 41.95 (0-8122-3161-9) U of Pa Pr.

*Talking Apes & Dancing Bees: Intelligence, Emotions, & Other Marvels of the Animal Kingdom. Betsy Wyckoff. 1997. pap. text ed. 13.95 (1-886449-48-1) Barrytown Ltd.

*Talking Back: Images of Jewish Women in American Popular Culture. Ed. by Joyce Antler. LC 97-15874. (Brandeis Series in American Jewish History, Culture, & Life). (Illus.). 320p. 1997. text ed. 45.00 (0-87451-841-5) U Pr of New Eng.

*Talking Back: Images of Jewish Women in American Popular Culture. Ed. by Joyce Antler. LC 97-15874. (Brandeis Series in American Jewish History, Culture, & Life). (Illus.). 320p. 1997. pap. 21.95 (0-87451-842-3) U Pr of New Eng.

Talking Back: Thinking Feminist, Thinking Black. Bell Hooks. LC 88-42874. 184p. (Orig.). 1989. 30.00 (0-89608-353-5); pap. 14.00 (0-89608-352-7) South End Pr.

Talking Back: Toward a Latin American Feminist Literary Criticism. Debra A. Castillo. LC 91-27789. (Reading Women Writing Ser.). (Illus.). 376p. 1992. 45.00 (0-8014-2608-1); pap. 16.95 (0-8014-9912-7) Cornell U Pr.

Talking Back to Poems: A Working Guide for the Aspiring Poet. Daniel Alderson. LC 95-39441. 128p. 1996. pap. 9.95 (0-89087-795-5) Celestial Arts.

Talking Back to Prozac. Peter Breggin. 1995. mass mkt. 5.99 (0-312-95606-1) Tor Bks.

Talking Back to Prozac. Peter R. Breggin. 1994. 19.95 (0-312-11486-9, Thomas Dunne Bks) St Martin.

*Talking Back to Ritalin: What Doctor's Aren't Telling You about Today's Most Controversial Drug. Peter R. Breggin. 1998. 24.95 (1-56751-128-7) Common Courage.

*Talking Back to Ritalin: What Doctors Aren't Telling You about Today's Most Controversial Drug for Children. Peter R. Breggin. 265p. 1998. 24.95 (1-56751-129-5) Common Courage.

*Talking Back to Shakespeare. Martha T. Rozett. LC 96-28835. 224p. 1996. pap. 16.95 (0-8141-4998-7) NCTE.

Talking Back to Shakespeare. Martha T. Rozett. LC 93-45821. 1995. 35.00 (0-87413-529-X) U Delaware Pr.

Talking Birds. Alice K. Flanagan. LC 95-43801. (New True Bks.). (Illus.). 48p. (J). (gr. 2-3). 1996. lib. bdg. 19.00 (0-516-01096-4) Childrens.

Talking Birds. Alice K. Flanagan. (New True Bks.). (J). 1996. pap. 5.50 (0-516-20078-X) Childrens.

Talking Black: African, Caribbean, & Asian Lesbians Speak Out. Vakerie Mason-John. (Women on Women Ser.). 256p. 1994. pap. 14.95 (0-304-32965-7, Pub. by Cassell Pubng UK) LPC InBook.

Talking Black: African, Caribbean & Asian Lesbians Speak Out. Valerie Mason-John. (Women on Women Ser.). 256p. 1994. 55.00 (0-304-32963-0, Pub. by Cassell Pubng UK) LPC InBook.

Talking Bones. Shay Youngblood. 1994. pap. 5.00 (0-87129-298-X, T92) Dramatic Pub.

Talking Bones: The Science of Forensic Anthropology. Peggy Thomas. LC 94-44110. (Science Sourcebooks Ser.). 136p. (J). (gr. 6-9). 1995. 17.95 (0-8160-3114-2) Facts on File.

Talking Book Box B: Multiethnic (Native American, African Interest, Latin American) Poetry. Joseph Bruchac et al. Ed. by Stanley H. Barkan. Tr. by Ammiel Alcalay. (Talking Bks.). (Illus.). 92p. 1989. 50.00 incl. audio (0-89304-676-0) Cross-Cultrl NY.

*Talking Book of July: Poems. Rick Alley. 72p. 1997. pap. 12.00 (0-910055-35-1) East Wash Univ.

*Talking Book of July: Poems. Rick Alley. 72p. 1997. 23.00 (0-910055-34-3) East Wash Univ.

Talking Books: Ethnopoetics, Translation, Text. Kenneth Mendoza. LC 93-23760. (ENGL Ser.). xii, 102p. 1993. 38.95 (1-879751-78-X) Camden Hse.

Talking Cat. Ted Gibbons. (Simple Gifts - Bookcard Ser.). 8p. (Orig.). 1988. pap. text ed. 1.95 (0-929985-02-8) Jackman Pubng.

*Talking Civil Rights. Eastman. (C). Date not set. write for info. (0-8147-2197-4) NYU Pr.

Talking Clock. large type ed. Frank Gruber. (Linford Western Library). 1990. pap. 15.99 (0-7089-6846-5) Ulverscroft.

*Talking Cloth. Rhonda Mitchell. LC 96-42152. (Illus.). 32p. (J). (ps-2). 1997. 15.95 (0-531-30004-8); lib. bdg. 16.99 (0-531-33004-4) Orchard Bks Watts.

Talking Correctly for Success: A Practical Guide for Business, Professional & Social Success by Sounding "Right" James A. Fisher. 212p. (Orig.). 1996. pap. 10.95 (0-9625941-0-5) Avant Pub.

Talking Culture: Ethnography & Conversational Analysis. Michael Moerman. LC 87-14973. (Conduct & Communication Ser.). 212p. (C). 1987. pap. text ed. 19.95 (0-8122-1246-0) U of Pa Pr.

Talking Cure. Lisa Zeidner. LC 81-52502. 81p. 1982. 10.95 (0-89672-095-0); pap. 5.95 (0-89672-094-2) Tex Tech Univ Pr.

Talking Cure: A Descriptive Guide to Psychoanalysis. Joseph D. Lichtenberg. (Psychoanalytic Inquiry Bk.). 166p. (C). 1994. reprint ed. pap. 22.50 (0-88163-192-2) Analytic Pr.

Talking Cure: Essays in Psychoanalysis & Language. Ed. by Colin MacCabe. LC 79-28551. 243p. 1986. pap. 12.95 (0-312-78475-9) St Martin.

Talking Cure: Literary Representations of Psychoanalysis. Jeffrey Berman. 368p. (Orig.). (C). 1985. text ed. 44.00 (0-8147-1075-1) NYU Pr.

Talking Cure: Literary Representations of Psychoanalysis. Jeffrey Berman. 368p. (Orig.). (C). 1987. pap. text ed. 16.00 (0-8147-1091-3) NYU Pr.

*Talking Cure: The Science Behind Psychotherapy. Susan C. Vaughan. LC 96-45237. (Illus.). 224p. 1997. 24.95 (0-399-14229-0, Grosset-Putnam) Putnam Pub Group.

*Talking Cure: TV Talk Shows & Women. Jane Shattuc. LC 96-28779. 272p. (C). 1997. text ed. 55.00 (0-415-91087-0) Routledge.

*Talking Cure: TV Talk Shows And Women. Jane Shattuc. LC 96-28779. 272p. 1997. pap. 16.95 (0-415-91088-9) Routledge.

Talking Cures: A History of Western & Eastern Psychotherapies. C. Peter Bankart. (Counseling Ser.). 544p. (C). 1997. text ed. 48.95 (0-534-34383-X) Brooks-Cole.

Talking Cures: A History of Western & Eastern Psychotherapies. C. Peter Bankart. (C). 1997. teacher ed., text ed. write for info. (0-534-34384-8) Brooks-Cole.

Talking Cures: The Psychoanalyses & the Psychotherapies. Robert S. Wallerstein. LC 95-1448. 608p. 1995. 60.00 (0-300-06107-2) Yale U Pr.

Talking Data: Transcription & Coding in Discourse Research. Ed. by Jane A. Edwards & Martin D. Lampert. 336p. 1993. pap. 34.50 (0-8058-0349-1); text ed. 69.95 (0-8058-0348-3) L Erlbaum Assocs.

Talking Difference: On Gender & Language. Mary Crawford. (Gender & Psychology Ser.: Vol. 7). (Illus.). 240p. 1995. 65.00 (0-8039-8827-3); pap. 22.95 (0-8039-8828-1) Sage.

*Talking Dirt. 1997. pap. 9.99 (0-440-50788-X) Dell.

Talking Dirty: A Bawdy Compendium of Colorful Language, Humourous Insults & Wicked Jokes. Ed. by Reinhold Aman. 222p. 1994. pap. 11.95 (0-7867-0164-1) Carroll & Graf.

Talking Dirty: Slang & Expletives from Around the World. Jeremy R. Ellis. 160p. 1995. pap. 9.95 (0-614-09403-8, Citadel Pr) Carol Pub Group.

Talking Dirty: Slang, Expletives, & Curses from Around the World. Jeremy R. Ellis. 160p. 1996. pap. 10.95 (0-8065-1740-9, Citadel Pr) Carol Pub Group.

Talking Dollars & Making Sense: A Financial Planning Guide for African Americans. Brooke Stephens. LC 96-32167. (Illus.). 256p. 1996. pap. text ed. 14.95 (0-07-061389-3) McGraw.

*Talking Drum. 2nd ed. Keith Flynn. 78p. (YA). (gr. 9 up). 1996. pap. 12.00 (1-889276-00-6) Animal Sounds.

Talking Drums. Jan Bevilacqua. (Illus.). 110p. (Orig.). 1995. pap. 9.95 (1-886383-13-8) Poite OH.

Talking Drums: An African-American Quote Collection. Anita D. Diggs. LC 94-42528. 1995. 14.95 (0-312-11745-0) St Martin.

Talking Drums: An African-American Quote Collection. Compiled by Anita D. Diggs. 192p. 1996. pap. 7.95 (0-312-14138-6, Griffin) St Martin.

Talking Drums of Africa. John F. Carrington. (Illus.). 96p. 1949. 15.00 (0-317-00316-X) G Vanderstoel.

Talking Drums of Africa. John F. Carrington. LC 70-77195. (Illus.). 96p. 1969. reprint ed. text ed. 35.00 (0-8371-1292-3, CDA&, Negro U Pr) Greenwood.

Talking Earth. Jean Craighead George. LC 82-48850. (Trophy Bk.). 160p. (YA). (gr. 5 up). 1987. pap. 3.95 (0-06-440212-6, Trophy) HarpC Child Bks.

Talking Earth. Jean Craighead George. LC 82-48850. 160p. (YA). (gr. 6 up). 1983. lib. bdg. 14.89 (0-06-021976-9) HarpC Child Bks.

Talking Earth. Duncan Searl. Ed. by J. Friedland & R. Kessler. (Novel-Ties Ser.). 1993. student ed., pap. text ed. 15.95 (0-88122-903-2) Lrn Links.

Talking Earth - La Tierra Que Habla. Jean Craighead George. (SPA.). (J). 9.95 (84-204-3699-2) Santillana.

Talking Egg. Houghton Mifflin Company Staff. (Literature Experience 1993 Ser.). (J). (gr. 3). 1992. pap. 8.48 (0-395-61796-0) HM.

Talking Eggs. Robert D. San Souci. (Illus.). (J). (ps-3). 1989. pap. 15.99 (0-8037-0619-7) Dial Bks Young.

Talking Eggs. Robert D. San Souci. (J). 1989. pap. 15.89 (0-8037-0620-0) Dial Bks Young.

Talking Feet: Solo Southern Dance: Buck, Flatfoot, & Tap. Mike Seeger. (Illus.). 120p. (Orig.). 1992. pap. 12.95 (1-55643-080-9) North Atlantic.

Talking Films. Rafique Baghdadi & Rajiv Rao. (C). 1995. 34.00 (81-7223-197-0, Pub. by Indus Pub II) S Asia.

Talking Films: The Best of the Guardian Film Lectures. Andrew Britton. 266p. 1992. 29.95 (1-872180-17-5, Pub. by Fourth Estate UK) Trafalgar.

Talking from 9 to 5 - Women & Men in the Workplace: Language, Sex & Power. Deborah Tannen. 368p. 1995. reprint ed. pap. 12.50 (0-380-71783-2) Avon.

Talking from 9-5: How Women's & Men's Conversational Styles Affect Who Gets Heard. Deborah Tannen. 1994. 12.00 (0-671-50560-2) S&S Trade.

Talking Germany. Jennifer Lee. (C). 1990. pap. text ed. 32.00 (0-948032-78-2, Pub. by Rosters Ltd) St Mut.

Talking God. Tony Hillerman. 368p. 1991. mass mkt. 5.99 (0-06-109918-X, PL) HarpC.

Talking God. large type ed. Tony Hillerman. LC 89-38699. 357p. 1989. lib. bdg. 21.95 (0-89621-895-3) Thorndike Pr.

*Talking Hair: Asian Studies. Ed. by Alf Hiltebeitel & Barbara D. Miller. (Illus.). 320p. (C). 1998. text ed. 65.50 (0-7914-3741-8) State U NY Pr.

*Talking Hair: Asian Studies. Ed. by Alf Hiltebeitel & Barbara D. Miller. (Illus.). 320p. (C). 1998. pap. text ed. 21.95 (0-7914-3742-6) State U NY Pr.

Talking Head. Paolo Baciliero. Ed. by Bernd Metz. Tr. by Tom Leighton from FRE. (Illus.). 56p. (Orig.). 1990. pap. 10.95 (0-87416-105-3) Catalan Communs.

Talking Head: The Novelist & Gullain-Barre. Jimmie R. Rankin. (Literature of a Patient Response Ser.). 770p. 1994. pap. 14.95 (1-883938-14-7) Dry Bones Pr.

Talking Heads. Alan Bennett. 91p. 1992. pap. 10.95 (0-563-20622-5, BBC-Parkwest) Parkwest Pubns.

*Talking Heads: Language, Metalanguage, & Subjectivity. Benjamin Lee. LC 97-25393. 360p. 1997. text ed. 54.95 (0-8223-2006-1); pap. text ed. 18.95 (0-8223-2015-0) Duke.

*Talking Heads - Anthology. Ed. by Carol Cuellar. 112p. (Orig.). (C). 1986. pap. text ed. 16.95 (0-7692-0854-1, VF1294) Warner Brothers.

Talking Health with Dr. Brian McDonough. Ed. by Brian P. McDonough. LC 94-6020. (Health, Society, & Policy Ser.). 288p. (C). 1994. 37.95 (1-56639-207-1) Temple U Pr.

Talking Horse. Thomas A. Guthrie. LC 79-103514. (Short Story Index Reprint Ser.). 1977. 20.95 (0-8369-3256-0) Ayer.

Talking Horse: Bernard Malamud on Life & Work. Bernard Malamud. Ed. by Alan Cheuse & Nicholas Delbance. LC 95-25957. 246p. 1996. pap. 24.95 (0-231-10184-8) Col U Pr.

*Talking Horse: Bernard Malamud on Life & Work. Bernard Malamud. 1997. pap. text ed. 15.50 (0-231-10185-6) Col U Pr.

Talking Houses: Ten Lectures. Colin Ward. 142p. (Orig.). 1990. pap. 9.00 (0-900384-55-7) Left Bank.

Talking Image of Urur. Franz Hartmann. 307p. 1992. pap. 24.95 (1-56459-168-9) Kessinger Pub.

Talking in Animal. Terry Farish. LC 95-45736. 160p. (YA). (gr. 5 up). 1996. 15.00 (0-688-14671-6) Greenwillow.

Talking in Bed. Antonya Nelson. LC 95-46802. 275p. 1996. 22.95 (0-395-68678-4) HM.

Talking in Flowers: Japanese Botanical Art. Compiled by J. V. Brindle. (Illus.). 96p. 1982. pap. 15.00 (0-913196-40-1) Hunt Inst Botanical.

Talking in Tranquility: Interviews with Ted Berrigan. Ted Berrigan. Ed. by Leslie Scalapino. LC 91-71934. 208p. (C). 1991. pap. text ed. 10.50 (0-939691-05-1) Avenue B.

Talking in Tranquility: Interviews with Ted Berrigan. Ted Berrigan. LC 91-71934. 208p. 1991. 10.50 (0-614-00634-1) O Bks.

Talking Indian: Reflections on Survival & Writing. Anna L. Walters. LC 92-27211. (Illus.). 224p. (Orig.). 1992. pap. 13.95 (1-56341-021-4); lib. bdg. 26.95 (1-56341-022-2) Firebrand Bks.

Talking It Out: A Guide to Groups for Abused Women. Ginny NiCarthy et al. LC 84-23494. (New Leaf Ser.). 165p. (Orig.). 1984. pap. 12.95 (0-931188-24-5) Seal Pr WA.

*Talking It Out: A Guided-Question Approach to Problem Solving. rev. ed. Monica Gustafson & Margaret Owen. Ed. by Cindy Drolet. (Illus.). 150p. (J). 1996. pap. text ed. 34.50 (1-883315-19-0, 8001) Imaginart Pr.

Talking It Over: A Novel. Julian Barnes. LC 91-51197. 1992. pap. 12.00 (0-679-73687-5, Vin) Random.

Talking Jazz: An Oral History. expanded rev. ed. Ben Sidran. (Illus.). 560p. 1995. pap. 16.95 (0-306-80613-4) Da Capo.

Talking Justice: Six Hundred Two Ways to Build & Promote Racial Harmony. Tamera Trotter & Joycelyn Allen. Ed. by Diane Parker. LC 92-50876. 120p. 1993. pap. 6.95 (0-88247-982-2, 982) R & E Pubs.

Talking Leaves. Dumont Howard. (Illus.). 25p. (Orig.). (J). (gr. 2 up). 1989. pap. 4.50 (0-88680-304-7) I E Clark.

Talking Leaves. Ed. by Craig Lesley. 416p. 1991. reprint ed. pap. 12.95 (0-385-31272-5, Delta) Dell.

Talking Leaves: Panjandrum No. 4. Ed. by Dennis Koran & David Guss. 1975. pap. 6.95 (0-915572-33-8) Panjandrum.

Talking Like the Rain: A First Book of Poems. Ed. by Dorothy M. Kennedy. (J). (ps up). 1992. 19.95 (0-316-48889-5) Little.

T

An Asterisk (*) at the beginning of an entry indicates that the title is appearing in BIP for the first time.

Talking, Listening, Communicating: Building Interpersonal Relationships. Jeffrey S. Bormaster & Carol L. Treat. LC 82-3702. 120p. (Orig.). (C). 1982. pap. text ed. 24.00 (*0-936104-26-0*, 0072) PRO-ED.

***Talking Machine: An Illustrated Compendium, 1877-1929.** Timothy C. Fabrizio & George F. Paul. 1997. write for info. (*0-7643-0241-8*) Schiffer.

***Talking Machines.** G. Bailly et al. 524p. 1992. 175.50 (*0-444-89115-3*, North Holland) Elsevier.

Talking Man. Terry Bisson. 192p. 1987. pap. 2.95 (*0-380-75141-0*) Avon.

***Talking Mathematics: Resource Package.** Rebecca Corwin et al. 1996. pap. text ed. 450.00 (*0-435-08398-8*, 08398) Heinemann.

Talking Mathematics: Supporting Children's Voices. Rebecca B. Corwin et al. LC 95-34652. 160p. 1995. pap. text ed. 16.00 (*0-435-08377-5*, 08377) Heinemann.

Talking Music: Conversations with John Cage, Philip Glass, Laurie Anderson, & Five Generations of American Experimental Composers. William Duckworth. LC 94-41315. (Illus.). 489p. 1995. 30.00 (*0-02-870823-7*) Schirmer Bks.

Talking Mysteries: A Conversation with Tony Hillerman. Tony Hillerman & Ernie Bulow. LC 91-2467. (Illus.). 135p. 1991. 9.95 (*0-8263-1279-9*) U of NM Pr.

***Talking Nets: An Oral History of Neurocomputing.** James A. Anderson & Edward Rosenfeld. LC 97-23868. 1998. write for info. (*0-262-01167-0*) MIT Pr.

Talking of Moths. P. B. Allan. 340p. 1943. 60.00 (*0-317-07181-5*) St Mut.

Talking of Shakespeare. Ed. by John Garrett. LC 70-157334. (Select Bibliographies Reprint Ser.). 1977. reprint ed. 23.95 (*0-8369-5794-6*) Ayer.

Talking of Silence: The Sexual Harassment of Schoolgirls. Carrie M. Herbert. 208p. 1989. pap. 33.00 (*1-85000-586-9*, Falmer Pr) Taylor & Francis.

Talking of Silence: The Sexual Harassment of Schoolgirls. Carrie M. Herbert. 220p. 1989. 65.00 (*1-85000-585-0*, Falmer Pr) Taylor & Francis.

Talking of the Royal Family. Michael Billig. 272p. (Orig.). (C). (gr. 13). 1991. text ed. 85.00 (*0-415-06745-6*, A6500) Routledge.

Talking on Paper: An Anthology of Oregon Letters & Diaries. Ed. by Terence O'Donnell. (Oregon Literature Ser.: Vol. 6). (Illus.). 352p. (Orig.). 1994. pap. 21.95 (*0-87071-378-7*); text ed. 35.95 (*0-87071-377-9*) Oreg St U Pr.

Talking on the Water: Conversations about Nature & Creativity. Ed. by Jonathan White. LC 93-18402. (Illus.). 288p. (Orig.). 1994. pap. 15.00 (*0-87156-515-3*) Sierra.

Talking Peace. Jimmy Carter. (Illus.). 168p. (J). (gr. 7 up). 1993. 16.99 (*0-525-44959-0*) Dutton Child Bks.

Talking Peace. Jimmy Carter. 1996. pap. 18.99 (*0-525-45651-1*) NAL-Dutton.

Talking Peace: A Vision for the Next Generation. Jimmy Carter. 206p. (YA). (gr. 7 up). 1995. pap. 18.99 (*0-525-45517-5*) Dutton Child Bks.

Talking Peace: A Vision for the Next Generation. Jimmy Carter. (Illus.). 206p. (YA). (gr. 7 up). 1995. pap. 5.99 (*0-14-037440-X*) Puffin Bks.

Talking Philosophy: A Dictionary. A. W. Sparkes. LC 89-48900. 300p. (C). 1991. pap. 16.95 (*0-415-04223-2*, A4336) Routledge.

Talking Pictures. Ed. by P. Baker & M. Clarke. (C). 1981. teacher ed., text ed. 225.00 incl. flmstrp (*0-86158-626-3*, Pub. by S Thornes Pubs UK) St Mut.

Talking Pictures. B. Brown. 1976. lib. bdg. 69.95 (*0-8490-2730-6*) Gordon Pr.

Talking Pictures. Horton Foote. 1996. pap. 5.25 (*0-8222-1462-8*) Dramatists Play.

***Talking Pictures: Interviews with Young British Film-Makers.** Graham Jones. Ed. by Lucy Johnson. (Distributed for the British Film Institute Ser.). (Illus.). 180p. 1996. 49.95 (*0-85170-603-7*, Pub. by British Film Inst UK); pap. 17.50 (*0-85170-604-5*, Pub. by British Film Inst UK) Ind U Pr.

Talking Pictures: People Speak about the Pictures That Speak to Them. Carole Kismaric & Marvin Heiferman. LC 93-31740. (Illus.). 224p. 1994. 40.00 (*0-8118-0382-1*); pap. 24.95 (*0-8118-0376-7*) Chronicle Bks.

Talking Pictures: Screenwriters in the American Cinema. Richard Corliss. LC 72-94413. 1985. reprint ed. pap. 13.95 (*0-87951-159-1*) Overlook Pr.

Talking Pictures: The Photographs of Rudy Burckhardt, 1933-1988. Rudy Burckhardt & Simon Pettet. LC 94-19134. (Illus.). 256p. (Orig.). 1994. pap. 26.95 (*0-944072-42-9*) Zoland Bks.

Talking Pictures: With the People Who Made Them. Sylvia Shorris & Marion A. Bundy. 400p. 1994. 25.00 (*1-56584-175-1*) New Press NY.

Talking Points: A Public Policy Guide to Key Issues in Nursing & Health Care. 2nd ed. Pamela J. Maraldo et al. 132p. 1991. 19.95 (*0-88737-449-2*) Natl League Nurse.

Talking Points in Dermatology I. Ed. by Julian L. Verbov. (New Clinical Applications Dermatology Ser.). 1986. lib. bdg. 82.00 (*0-85200-939-9*) Kluwer Ac.

Talking Points in Dermatology II. Ed. by Julian L. Verbov. (New Clinical Applications Dermatology Ser.). 112p. (C). 1987. lib. bdg. 82.00 (*0-85200-689-6*) Kluwer Ac.

Talking Points in Dermatology III. Ed. by Julian L. Verbov. (New Clinical Applications Dermatology Ser.). (C). 1989. lib. bdg. 88.50 (*0-7462-0098-6*) Kluwer Ac.

Talking Points in Mathematics. Anita Straker. LC 92-32382. (Illus.). 128p. (C). 1993. pap. text ed. 18.95 (*0-521-44758-5*) Cambridge U Pr.

Talking Politics. William A. Gamson. (Illus.). 256p. (C). 1992. text ed. 59.95 (*0-521-43062-3*); pap. text ed. 19.95 (*0-521-43679-6*) Cambridge U Pr.

Talking Politics: A Psychological Framing of Views from Youth in Britain. Kum-Kum Bhavnani. (European Monographs in Social Psychology). 232p. (C). 1991. text ed. 54.95 (*0-521-38044-8*) Cambridge U Pr.

Talking Politics: A Wordbook. A. W. Sparkes. LC 93-38021. 312p. (C). (gr. 13). 1994. text ed. 69.95 (*0-415-10807-1*, B3811) Routledge.

Talking Politics: A Wordbook. A. W. Sparkes. LC 93-38021. 312p. (C). 1994. pap. 17.95 (*0-415-10808-X*, B3815) Routledge.

Talking Politics: Choosing the President in the Television Age. Liz Cunningham. LC 94-21694. 192p. 1995. text ed. 19.95 (*0-275-94187-6*, Praeger Pubs) Greenwood.

Talking Pots: Prehistoric Pottery Icons of the White Mountains of Arizona. James R. Cunkle. LC 93-9843. 1993. pap. 19.95 (*0-914846-81-7*) Golden West Pub.

***"Talking Power" The Rise of Accent as Social Symbol.** Lynda Mugglestone. (Illus.). 368p. 1997. reprint ed. pap. 26.00 (*0-19-823706-5*) OUP.

Talking Praying Mantis. Matthew Wyatt. 24p. (J). (gr. k-3). 1992. pap. 5.00 (*1-886210-00-4*) Tyketoon Yng Author.

Talking Proper: The Rise of Accent as Social Symbol. Lynda Mugglestone. (Illus.). 368p. 1995. 59.00 (*0-19-823948-3*) OUP.

***Talking Prophet Blues.** Maggie Helwig. 80p. 1989. pap. 12.95 (*0-919627-23-4*, Pub. by Quarry Pr CN) LPC InBook.

Talking Razzmatazz: Poems by Judy Ruiz. Judy Ruiz. 64p. 1991. pap. 10.95 (*0-8262-0772-3*); text ed. 18.95 (*0-8262-0771-5*) U of Mo Pr.

Talking Room. Marianne Hauser. LC 75-21557. 158p. 1976. pap. 6.95 (*0-914590-21-9*) Fiction Coll.

Talking Science: Language, Learning & Values. Jay L. Lemke. Ed. by Judith Green. (Language & Educational Processes Ser.: Vol. 1). 288p. (C). 1990. pap. 39.50 (*0-89391-566-1*); text ed. 73.25 (*0-89391-565-3*) Ablex Pub.

Talking Shop. Andrea Nash. 1992. pap. write for info. (*0-13-884503-4*) P-H.

Talking Shop: A Curriculum Sourcebook for Participatory Adult ESL. Andrea Nash et al. Ed. by Fran Keenan. (Language in Education Ser.). (Illus.). 70p. (Orig.). 1992. pap. text ed. 10.50 (*0-937354-78-3*) Delta Systems.

Talking Social Work. Cournoyer. (Social Work Ser.). Date not set. pap. 29.95 (*0-534-34305-8*) Brooks-Cole.

Talking Sociology. 2nd ed. Gary A. Fine. 300p. 1989. pap. text ed. 20.00 (*0-205-12226-4*, H22262) Allyn.

Talking Sociology. 4th ed. Gary A. Fine. LC 96-16338. 240p. 1996. pap. 22.00 (*0-205-26168-X*) Allyn.

Talking Soft Dutch. Linda McCarriston. LC 83-51718. 71p. (Orig.). 1984. 10.95 (*0-89672-116-7*); pap. 6.95 (*0-89672-115-9*) Tex Tech Univ Pr.

***Talking Sports.** Pat O'Brien. 1997. write for info. (*0-679-45975-8*, Villard Bks) Random.

Talking Stick. Carol Batdorf. 64p. 1994. reprint ed. pap. 7.95 (*0-88839-308-3*) Hancock House.

Talking Story with Nona Beamer: Stories of a Hawaiian Family. Winona D. Beamer. LC 83-70357. (Illus.). 80p. (J). (gr. 2-6). 1984. 9.95 (*0-935848-20-7*) Bess Pr.

Talking Straight. Lee Iacocca. 352p. 1989. mass mkt. 5.99 (*0-553-27805-3*) Bantam.

Talking Straight: "Dugri" Speech in Israeli "Sabra" Culture. Tamar Katriel. (Studies in the Social & Cultural Foundations of Language: No. 2). (Illus.). 176p. 1986. 47.95 (*0-521-32630-3*) Cambridge U Pr.

***Talking Tall.** Jeffery McQuain. 1998. write for info. (*0-679-45804-2*, Random Ref) Random.

Talking Texts: Innovative Recipes for Intensive Reading. R. Holme. (Pilgrims Longman Resource Bks.). (C). 1991. pap. text ed. 17.95 (*0-582-07002-3*, 79117) Longman.

Talking the Boundless Book: Art, Language, & the Book Arts. Dick Higgins et al. Ed. by Charles Alexander. (Illus.). 152p. (Orig.). 1995. pap. 15.95 (*1-879832-09-7*) MN Ctr Book Arts.

Talking Their Way into Science: Seminal Questions, Complex Theories, & Responsive Curricula. Karen Gallas. (Language & Literacy Ser.). 128p. (C). 1995. text ed. 36.00 (*0-8077-3436-5*); pap. text ed. 16.95 (*0-8077-3435-7*) Tchrs Coll.

***Talking Tidewater: Writers on the Chesapeake.** John Barth et al. 216p. (Orig.). 1996. pap. 14.95 (*0-937692-13-1*) Litrary Hse Pr.

Talking Time. Jeanette W. Stickel. 64p. 1991. pap. text ed. 14.95 (*0-937857-24-6*, 1589) Speech Bin.

Talking to Angels. Esther Watson. LC 95-30913. (Illus.). 32p. (J). 1996. 16.00 (*0-15-201077-7*) HarBrace.

Talking to Angels: A Life Spent at High Latitudes. Robert Perkins. 112p. 1996. 18.00 (*0-8070-7078-5*) Beacon Pr.

***Talking to Angels: A Life Spent at High Latitudes.** Robert Perkins. 1997. pap. 10.00 (*0-8070-7079-3*) Beacon Pr.

Talking to Cancer Patients & Their Relatives. Ann Faulkner & Peter Maguire. 200p. 1995. text ed. 62.00 (*0-19-262479-2*); pap. text ed. 27.95 (*0-19-261605-6*) OUP.

Talking to Dragons. Patricia C. Wrede. LC 92-40719. (Enchanted Forest Chronicles Ser.: Bk. 4). 272p. (YA). (gr. 7 up). 1993. 17.00 (*0-15-284247-0*, J Yolen Bks) HarBrace.

Talking to Dragons. Patricia C. Wrede. 272p. (J). (gr. 7-9). 1995. pap. 4.50 (*0-590-48475-3*) Scholastic Inc.

Talking to Ducks: Rediscovering the Joy & Meaning in Your Life. James A. Kitchens. LC 93-34919. 208p. 1994. pap. 11.00 (*0-671-87082-3*, Fireside) S&S Trade.

Talking to Faith Ringgold. Faith Ringgold et al. LC 95-23455. (J). (gr. 3 up). 1996. pap. 9.99 (*0-517-88546-8*); lib. bdg. 16.99 (*0-517-70914-7*) Crown Pub Group.

***Talking to Fireflies, Shrinking the Moon: Activities for All Ages.** Edward Duensing. (Illus.). 144p. (Orig.). 1997. pap. 15.95 (*1-55591-310-5*) Fulcrum Pub.

Talking to God: What the Bible Teaches about Prayer. Thomas L. Constable. LC 95-19658. 192p. (Orig.). (gr. 10). 1995. pap. 11.99 (*0-8010-2021-2*) Baker Bks.

***Talking to Heaven.** James Van Praagh. LC 97-24861. 1997. pap. 20.95 (*0-525-94268-8*) NAL-Dutton.

Talking to High Monks in the Snow: An Asian-American Odyssey. Lydia Minatoya. LC 91-50450. 288p. 1993. pap. 12.00 (*0-06-092372-5*, PL) HarpC.

Talking to My Body. Anna Swir. LC 96-10015. 1996. pap. 14.00 (*1-55659-108-X*) Copper Canyon.

Talking to Myself. Albert Krassner. 77p. (Orig.). 1986. pap. 4.95 (*0-912061-09-X*) Veridon Edns.

***Talking to Myself.** Phyllis Walsh & David Kopitzke. (Illus.). 1997. 10.00 (*0-9629902-4-8*) Hummngbrd WI.

Talking to Myself: A Memoir of My Times. Studs Terkel. 368p. 1995. pap. 11.95 (*1-56584-319-3*) New Press NY.

Talking to Our Brothers: Creating & Sustaining a Dynamic Men's Group. George Taylor. 100p. 1995. pap. 9.50 (*0-9644129-0-X*) Mens Comm Pub.

Talking to Parents. Donald W. Winnicott. (Illus.). 160p. 1994. pap. 10.95 (*0-201-62698-5*) Addison-Wesley.

Talking to Parents: Winnicott Helped to Bridge the Gap for Me. Donald W. Winnicott. (Illus.). 144p. 1993. 17.95 (*0-201-60893-6*) Addison-Wesley.

Talking to Strange Men. Ruth Rendell. 328p. 1988. mass mkt. 5.99 (*0-345-35174-6*) Ballantine.

Talking to Strangers. Patricia Dobler. LC 86-40046. (Brittingham Prize in Poetry Ser.). 80p. 1986. 17.95 (*0-299-10830-9*); pap. 10.95 (*0-299-10834-1*) U of Wis Pr.

Talking to Strangers: Improving American Diplomacy at Home & Abroad. Monteagle Stearns. 201p. 1996. text ed. 24.95 (*0-691-01130-3*) Princeton U Pr.

Talking to Strangers: Mediated Therapeutic Communication. Gary Gumpert & Sandra L. Fish. Ed. by Brenda Dervin. LC 89-17817. (Communication & Information Science Ser.). 272p. (C). 1989. pap. 39.50 (*0-89391-626-9*); text ed. 73.25 (*0-89391-490-8*) Ablex Pub.

***Talking to the Dead: A Novel.** Helen Dunmore. LC 96-38726. 1997. 21.95 (*0-316-19741-6*) Little.

Talking to the Dead & Other Stories. Sylvia Watanabe. LC 93-18336. 144p. 1993. pap. 11.00 (*0-385-41888-4*, Anchor NY) Doubleday.

Talking to the Earth. Gordon MacLellan. (Illus.). (Orig.). 1995. pap. 19.95 (*1-898307-43-1*) Holmes Pub.

Talking to the Ground: One Family's Journey on Horseback Across the Sacred Land of the Navajo. Douglas Preston. LC 94-46362. 288p. 1995. 24.00 (*0-684-80391-7*) S&S Trade.

Talking to the Ground: One Family's Journey on Horseback Across the Sacred Land of the Navajo. Douglas Preston. LC 95-48472. 284p. 1996. pap. 18.95 (*0-8263-1740-5*) U of NM Pr.

Talking to the Moon. John J. Mathews. LC 81-137822. (Illus.). 256p. (Orig.). 1987. pap. 12.95 (*0-8061-2083-5*) U of Okla Pr.

Talking to the Owls. Walt Franklin. (Illus.). 64p. 1984. pap. 4.00 (*0-9613465-0-7*) Great Elm.

Talking to the Sun: An Illustrated Anthology of Poems for Young People. Kenneth Koch & Kate Farrell. LC 85-15428. 112p. (J). (ps up). 1985. 24.95 (*0-8050-0144-1*, Bks Young Read) H Holt & Co.

Talking to the Top: Executive's Guide to Career-Making Presentations. Ray Anthony. LC 94-43440. 1995. text ed. 19.95 (*0-13-124470-1*) P-H.

Talking to the World: And Other Stories. Dennis Lynds. 176p. (Orig.). 1995. 18.95 (*1-880284-10-3*) J Daniel.

Talking to Virgil: A Miscellany. Wiseman. (Illus.). 262p. 1992. pap. text ed. 25.95 (*0-85989-375-8*, Pub. by Univ Exeter Pr UK) Northwestern U Pr.

Talking to You. C. MacKenzie. 3.99 (*1-871676-45-2*, Pub. by Christian Focus UK) Spring Arbor Dist.

Talking to Your Child About God: A Book for Families of All Faiths. David Heller. 224p. (Orig.). 1994. pap. 10.00 (*0-399-52128-3*, Perigee Bks) Berkley Pub.

Talking to Youth about Sexuality: A Parent's Guide. Ed. by Mike Aquilina. LC 84-62159. 64p. (Orig.). 1995. pap. 3.95 (*0-87973-716-6*, 716) Our Sunday Visitor.

Talking Together. M. Helgesen et al. (YA). 1903. pap. text ed. 12.36 (*0-582-10240-5*) Longman.

Talking Together: A Parent's Guide to the Development, Enrichment, & Problems of Speech & Language. Katherine F. Schetz & Stuart K. Cassell, Jr. LC 94-34225. (Illus.). 88p. (Orig.). 1994. pap. 9.95 (*0-936015-45-4*) Pocahontas Pr.

Talking Together: Letters of David Ignatow, 1946-1990. Gary Pacernick. LC 91-41087. (Illus.). 280p. (C). 1992. text ed. 29.95 (*0-8173-0584-X*) U of Ala Pr.

Talking Trash with Redd Foxx. Michael D. Johnson. LC 94-69408. 224p. (Orig.). pap. 7.95 (*0-9640479-2-6*) E Dalton Bks.

Talking Trash with Redd Foxx. Michael D. Johnson. 140p. (Orig.). 1995. pap. 47.70 (*0-9640479-4-2*) E Dalton Bks.

Talking Treasures. Peggy A. Griffin. (Illus.). 82p. (Orig.). (J). 1995. pap. text ed. 12.95 (*1-884056-01-6*) Scribes Pubns.

Talking Tree. 1993. pap. 5.25 (*0-19-585267-2*) OUP.

Talking Tree. Boen Hallum. (Illus.). 107p. 1981. pap. 5.95 (*0-86674-024-4*) B Hallum.

***Talking Tree.** Diane J. Omasta. (Illus.). 12p. (Orig.). (J). (gr. 1-2). 1997. pap. 5.95 (*1-55237-078-X*, Pub. by Comnwlth Pub CN) Partners Pubs Grp.

Talking Tree: Poems in Prose. Artur Lundkvist. Tr. by Diana Wormuth. 240p. 1982. 9.95 (*0-8425-2099-6*) Frnds of the Libry.

Talking Trojan: Speech & Community in the Iliad. Hilary Mackie. 208p. 1996. pap. text ed. 21.95 (*0-8476-8255-2*); lib. bdg. 52.50 (*0-8476-8254-4*) Rowman.

Talking Turkey. R. Rice. (C). 1989. text ed. 29.95 (*0-948032-38-3*, Pub. by Rosters Ltd) St Mut.

Talking Turkey: Dynamics. Deborah Tannen. pap. write for info. (*0-345-37543-2*) Ballantine.

Talking Union. Judith Stepan-Norris & Maurice Zeitlin. LC 95-9876. (Illus.). 312p. (C). 1995. 15.95 (*0-252-06489-5*); text ed. 39.95 (*0-252-02192-4*) U of Ill Pr.

Talking up a Storm: Voices of the New West. Gregory L. Morris. LC 93-46326. (Illus.). xix, 246p. 1995. pap. 12.00 (*0-8032-8224-9*, Bison Books) U of Nebr Pr.

Talking Voices: Repetition, Dialogue, & Imagery in Conversational Discourse. Deborah Tannen. (Studies in Interactional Sociolinguistics: No. 6). 256p. (C). 1989. text ed. 59.95 (*0-521-37001-9*); pap. text ed. 19.95 (*0-521-37900-8*) Cambridge U Pr.

***Talking Walls.** Margie B. Knight. Tr. by Clarita Kohen. (Illus.). 38p. (ENG & SPA.). (J). (gr. 2 up). 1995. 18.95 (*1-879600-32-3*) Pac Asia Pr.

***Talking Walls.** Margie B. Knight. Tr. by Xeng Yang. (Illus.). 38p. (J). (gr. 2 up). 1995. 18.95 (*1-879600-34-X*) Pac Asia Pr.

***Talking Walls.** Margie B. Knight. Tr. by Mory Ouk. (Illus.). 38p. (CAM.). (J). (gr. 2 up). 1995. 18.95 (*1-879600-36-6*) Pac Asia Pr.

***Talking Walls.** Margie B. Knight. Tr. by Loida S. Dupiechain. (Illus.). 38p. (ENG & TAG.). (J). (gr. 2 up). 1995. 18.95 (*1-879600-38-2*) Pac Asia Pr.

***Talking Walls.** Margie B. Knight. Tr. by Vikham Bounking & Xay Kaignavongsa. (Illus.). 38p. (ENG & LAO.). (J). (gr. 2 up). 1995. 18.95 (*1-879600-37-4*) Pac Asia Pr.

***Talking Walls.** Margie B. Knight. (Illus.). 38p. (CHI & ENG.). (J). (gr. 2 up). 1995. 18.95 (*1-879600-33-1*) Pac Asia Pr.

***Talking Walls.** Margie B. Knight. (Illus.). 38p. (ENG & KOR.). (J). (gr. 2 up). 1995. 18.95 (*1-879600-35-8*) Pac Asia Pr.

Talking Walls. Margy B. Knight. LC 91-67867. (Illus.). 40p. (J). (gr. k-8). 1992. 17.95 (*0-88448-102-6*) Tilbury Hse.

Talking Walls. Margy B. Knight. (Illus.). 40p. (J). (gr. k-8). 1995. pap. 8.95 (*0-88448-154-9*) Tilbury Hse.

***Talking Walls.** Margy B. Knight. (Illus.). 36p. (J). 1993. 19.95 (*1-55082-056-7*, Pub. by Quarry Pr CN) LPC InBook.

Talking Walls: The Stories Continue. Margy B. Knight. LC 96-15123. (Illus.). 40p. (J). (gr. 3-8). 1996. 17.95 (*0-88448-164-6*) Tilbury Hse.

Talking Walls: The Stories Continue. Margy B. Knight & Thomas V. Chan. (Illus.). 144p. (J). (gr. 3-8). 1996. teacher ed., pap. 9.95 (*0-88448-168-9*) Tilbury Hse.

***Talking Walls: The Stories Continue.** Margy B. Knight. 1997. pap. text ed. 8.95 (*0-88448-165-4*) Tilbury Hse.

Talking Walls Teacher's - Activity Guide. Margy B. Knight & Thomas V. Chan. 48p. (Orig.). 1992. Tchr.'s activity guide. teacher ed., pap. 9.95 (*0-88448-106-9*) Tilbury Hse.

Talking with African Writers: Interviews with African Poets, Playwrights & Novelists. Ed. by Jane Wilkinson. LC 91-32506. (Studies in African Literature). (Illus.). 224p. (C). 1992. pap. 17.50 (*0-435-08065-2*, 08065) Heinemann.

Talking with Angels. Tr. by Gitta Mallasz. 443p. 1995. pap. 15.95 (*3-85630-505-X*, Pub. by Daimon Pubs SZ) Continuum.

Talking with Artists. Pat Cummings. 1997. 11.95 (*0-689-81298-1*) S&S Childrens.

Talking with Artists, Vol. 2. Ed. by Pat Cummings. (J). (gr. 4 up). 1995. 19.95 (*0-689-80310-9*) Macmillan.

Talking with Artists: Conversations with Victoria Chess, Pat Cummings, Leo & Diane Dillon, Richard Egielski, Lois Ehlert, Lisa Campbell Ernst, Tom Feelings, Steven Kellogg, Jerry Pinkney, Amy Schwartz, Lane Smith, Chris Van Allsburg, & David Wiesner. Pat Cummings. LC 91-9982. (Illus.). 96p. (J). (gr. 4 up). 1992. lib. bdg. 22.00 (*0-02-724245-5*, Bradbury S&S) S&S Childrens.

Talking with Artists: Conversations with Victoria Chess, Pat Cummings, Leo & Diane Dillon, Richard Egielski, Lois Ehlert, Lisa Campbell Ernst, Tom Feelings, Steven Kellogg, Jerry Pinkney, Amy Schwartz, Lane Smith, Chris Van Allsburg, & David Wiesner. large type ed. Ed. & Compiled by Pat Cummings. 1995. 25.50 (*0-614-09611-1*, L-81885-00) Am Printing Hse.

Talking with Children. Ronald F. Reed. LC 83-9990. 123p. (Orig.). 1983. 11.95 (*0-912869-00-3*); pap. 6.95 (*0-912869-01-1*) Arden Pr.

Talking with Christ. rev. ed. Navigators Staff. (Studies in Christian Living: Bk. 3). 32p. 1981. pap. 3.00 (*0-89109-079-7*) NavPress.

Talking with Clients about Family Planning: A Guide for Health Care Providers. 102p. (Orig.). 1995. pap. text ed. 6.00 (*1-885063-11-3*) AVSC Int.

***Talking with Confidence for the Painfully Shy.** Don Gabor. LC 96-49433. 1997. pap. 12.00 (*0-517-88677-4*) Crown Pub Group.

Talking with Employees: A Guide for Managers. Marion S. Kellogg. LC 79-50242. 173p. reprint ed. pap. 49.40 (*0-685-20485-5*, 2029919) Bks Demand.

***Talking with Eve Leah Hagar Miriam.** Helen Papell. iv, 71p. (Orig.). 1996. pap. 6.00 (*1-879742-24-1*) Jewish Wom Rsce.

Talking with God. Robert A. Clark. 1994. 22.50 (*0-940168-29-4*) Boxwood.

***Talking with God.** Catherine L. Davis. LC 96-46385. 1997. write for info. (*1-56476-608-X*, Victor Bks) Chariot Victor.

Talking with God. Melanie Jongsma. (Friendship Ser.). (Illus.). 48p. (Orig.). 1993. pap. write for info. (*1-882536-21-5*, A100-0060) Bible League.

Talking with God. Lewis F. Shaffer. (Illus.). 177p. (Orig.). 1986. pap. write for info. (*0-929389-01-8*) Son Shine Ministries.

***Talking with God.** Charles Stanley. (The In Touch Study Ser.). 120p. 1997. pap. 6.99 (*0-7852-7276-3*) Nelson.

Talking with God: A Guide to Prayer. Mack B. Stokes. LC 89-33140. 160p. 1989. pap. 8.95 (*0-687-40999-3*) Abingdon.

Talking with God: A Woman's Workshop on Prayer. Glaphre. (Woman's Workshop Ser.). 160p. (Orig.). 1985. pap. 6.99 (*0-310-45301-1*, 12240P) Zondervan.

Talking with Horses. Henry Blake. (Illus.). 172p. 1991. pap. 11.95 (*0-943955-37-8*, Trafalgar Sq Pub) Trafalgar.

Talking with Ingmar Bergman. Ed. by G. William Jones. LC 83-9692. (Illus.). 132p. 1983. 24.95 (*0-87074-187-X*); pap. 12.50 (*0-87074-191-8*) SMU Press.

Talking with Kids about AIDS: Resource Manual. Jennifer Tiffany et al. (Talking with Kids about AIDS: a Program for Parents & Other Adults Who Care Ser.). (Illus.). 86p. (Orig.). 1991. pap. 6.00 (*0-9629938-0-8*) Parent AIDS.

Talking with Kids about AIDS: Resource Manual & Teaching Guide, 2 vols., Set. Jennifer Tiffany et al. (Talking with Kids about AIDS: a Program for Parents & Other Adults Who Care Ser.). (Illus.). 178p. (Orig.). 1991. 9.50 (*0-9629938-2-4*) Parent AIDS.

Talking with Kids about AIDS: Teaching Guide. Jennifer Tiffany et al. (Talking with Kids about AIDS: a Program for Parents & Other Adults Who Care Ser.). (Illus.). 92p. (Orig.). 1991. teacher ed., pap. 6.00 (*0-9629938-1-6*) Parent AIDS.

Talking with Nature: Sharing the Energies & Spirit of Trees, Plants, Birds & Earth. Michael J. Roads. Ed. by Gregory Armstrong. (Illus.). 156p. (Orig.). 1987. pap. 9.95 (*0-915811-06-5*) H J Kramer Inc.

Talking with Patients: A Self Psychological View of Creative Intuition & Analytic Discipline. Sanford Shapiro. LC 95-14483. 224p. 1995. 35.00 (*1-56821-598-3*) Aronson.

Talking with Patients: Keys to Good Communication. 3rd ed. Philip R. Myerscough & Michael J. Ford. (Oxford Medical Publications). (Illus.). 264p. (C). 1996. pap. 37.50 (*0-19-262570-5*) OUP.

Talking with Patients, Vol. 1: The Theory of Doctor-Patient Communication. Eric J. Cassell. (Illus.). 215p. 1985. pap. 12.50 (*0-262-53055-4*) MIT Pr.

Talking with Readers: Metadiscourse as Rhetorical Act. Avon Crismore. (American University Studies: Language: Ser. XIV, Vol. 17). 294p. (C). 1989. text ed. 41.95 (*0-8204-0793-3*) P Lang Pubng.

Talking with Robert Penn Warren. Ed. by Floyd C. Watkins et al. LC 89-20570. 448p. 1990. pap. 24.95 (*0-8203-1220-7*) U of Ga Pr.

Talking with Teachers. 10p. 1986. 4.00 (*0-318-22545-X*, TR-86-2) Ed Comm States.

Talking with Texas Writers: Twelve Interviews. Patrick Bennett. LC 80-5516. (Illus.). 320p. 1980. 18.95 (*0-89096-099-2*) Tex A&M Univ Pr.

Talking with the Angels. 1998. write for info. (*0-925589-30-6*) JPM Pubns.

Talking with the Clay: The Art of Pueblo Pottery. Stephen A. Trimble. LC 86-33902. (Illus.). 116p. (Orig.). 1987. pap. 15.95 (*0-933452-18-7*) Schol Am Res.

Talking with the Clay: The Art of Pueblo Pottery. Stephen A. Trimble. (Illus.). 128p. (Orig.). 1987. pap. 15.95 (*0-295-96470-7*) U of Wash Pr.

Talking with Young Children about Adoption. Mary Watkins & Susan M. Fisher. 1995. 12.00 (*0-300-06317-2*) Yale U Pr.

Talking with Your Baby: Family As the First School. Alice S. Honig & Holly E. Brophy. (Illus.). 96p. (C). 1996. pap. 9.95 (*0-8156-0355-X*, HOTWP) Syracuse U Pr.

Talking with Your Child about AIDS. Barbara Prince. LC 92-42452. (Growing Together Ser.). 1993. pap. 2.25 (*0-8298-0865-5*) Pilgrim OH.

Talking with Your Child about Change. Dallas A. Brauninger. LC 94-7202. (Growing Together Ser.). 32p. (Orig.). 1994. pap. 2.25 (*0-8298-0994-5*) Pilgrim OH.

***Talking with Your Child about Fantasy & Dreams.** Ronald W. Baard. LC 96-30144. (Growing Together Ser.). 32p. 1996. pap. 2.25 (*0-8298-1135-4*) Pilgrim OH.

Talking with Your Child about Feelings. Kathryn E. Parker. LC 90-33014. (Growing Together Ser.). (Orig.). 1990. pap. 2.25 (*0-8298-0861-2*) Pilgrim OH.

Talking with Your Child about God's Story. Hope Harle-Mould & Linda Harle-Mould. LC 92-41972. (Growing Together Ser.). 1993. pap. 2.25 (*0-8298-0955-4*) Pilgrim OH.

Talking with Your Child about Prayer. Myra B. Nagel. LC 89-39927. (Growing Together Ser.). (Orig.). 1990. pap. 2.25 (*0-8298-0845-0*) Pilgrim OH.

Talking with Your Child about Sacraments & Celebrations. Deborah A. Payden. LC 94-10150. (Growing Together Ser.). 1994. pap. 2.25 (*0-8298-1017-X*) Pilgrim OH.

Talking with Your Child about Sex: Questions & Answers for Children from Birth to Puberty. Mary S. Calderone & James W. Ramey. 162p. 1984. mass mkt. 4.99 (*0-345-31379-8*) Ballantine.

Talking with Your Child about Sexuality. R. Kenneth Ostermiller. LC 90-21702. (Growing Together Ser.). (Orig.). 1991. pap. 2.25 (*0-8298-0863-9*) Pilgrim OH.

Talking with Your Child about the Bible. Craig V. Anderson. LC 92-26093. (Growing Together Ser.). 32p. 1992. pap. 2.25 (*0-8298-0943-0*) Pilgrim OH.

Talking with Your Child about the Church Year. Roy F. Alberswerth & Deborah A. Payden. LC 92-27562. (Growing Together Ser.). 32p. 1992. pap. 2.25 (*0-8298-0864-7*) Pilgrim OH.

Talking with Your Child about the Presence of God. J. Yorke Peeler, Jr. LC 94-40774. (Growing Together Ser.). 32p. (Orig.). 1995. pap. 2.25 (*0-8298-0995-3*) Pilgrim OH.

Talking with Your Child about Worship. Sandra V. Edwards. LC 90-21210. (Growing Together Ser.). (Orig.). 1990. pap. 2.25 (*0-8298-0862-0*) Pilgrim OH.

Talking with Your Customers: What They Will Tell You about Your Business When You Ask the Right Questions. Michael J. Wing. LC 93-25197. 206p. (Orig.). 1993. pap. 19.95 (*0-7931-0516-1*, 56156001, Enter-Dearbrn) Dearborn Finan.

Talking with Your Doctor: A Guide for Older People. (Illus.). 30p. (Orig.). 1996. pap. text ed. 20.00 (*0-7881-2839-6*) DIANE Pub.

Talking with Your Kids about Love, Sex, & Dating. Barry St. Clair & Carol St. Clair. LC 93-25467. (Love/Sex/Dating Series). 184p. 1993. reprint ed. 8.99 (*1-56476-230-0*, 6-3230, Victor Bks) Chariot Victor.

Talking Work: An Oral History. Trevor Blackwell & Jeremy Seabrook. 256p. 1996. 24.95 (*0-571-14306-7*) Faber & Faber.

Talking Yellow Pages Review, 1994. Tom Maguire & Steve Smith. (Illus.). 131p. 1995. 1,295.00 (*0-88709-061-3*) Simba Info Inc.

Talking Your Roots: A Family Guide to Tape Recording & Video Taping Oral History. William P. Fletcher. LC 85-149395. 290p. (Orig.). 1985. pap. 21.95 (*0-9614867-0-8*) Talking Roots.

Talking Your Roots see Recording Your Family History

Talking Zen: By Alan Watts. Ed. by Mark Watts. 200p. (Orig.). 1994. pap. 12.95 (*0-8348-0313-5*) Weatherhill.

Talks about Art. William M. Hunt. LC 76-148797. reprint ed. 31.50 (*0-404-03448-9*) AMS Pr.

Talks & Dialogues of J. Krishnamurti. Jiddu Krishnamurti. 1983. mass mkt. 4.95 (*0-380-01573-0*, Discus) Avon.

Talks by Edmond Bordeaux Szekely. Edmond B. Szekely. 48p. 1972. pap. 3.50 (*0-89564-067-8*) IBS Intl.

Talks for Children. Ian MacLeod. 108p. (C). 1992. pap. 39.00 (*0-685-60704-6*, Pub. by St Andrew UK) St Mut.

Talks for Children. Beatrice Surtees & Ian MacLeod. 108p. (C). 1988. pap. text ed. 55.00 (*0-7152-0630-3*) St Mut.

Talks for Children. Ed. by Beatrice Surtees & Ian MacLeod. 108p. (C). 1991. pap. text ed. 39.00 (*86-15-30630-3*, Pub. by St Andrew UK) St Mut.

Talks for Girls: Finding Your True Self. Andrea Johnston. LC 96-14802. (J). 1996. pap. write for info. (*0-590-89796-9*) Scholastic Inc.

Talks for the Times. William H. Crogman. LC 78-152919. (Black Heritage Library Collection). 1977. 26.95 (*0-8369-8763-2*) Ayer.

Talks in a Free Country. William R. Inge. LC 77-167365. (Essay Index Reprint Ser.). 1977. reprint ed. 20.95 (*0-8369-2774-5*) Ayer.

Talks in a Library. Laurence Hutton. (Notable American Authors Ser.). 1992. reprint ed. lib. bdg. 75.00 (*0-7812-3322-4*) Rprt Serv.

Talks My Father Never Had with Me: Helping the Young Black Male Make It to Adulthood. Harold Davis. 236p. (Orig.). 1995. pap. text ed. 10.00 (*0-9638553-1-X*) KJAC Pubng.

Talks My Father Never Had with Me: Helping the Young Male Make It to Adulthood. Harold Davis. 207p. (Orig.). 1996. pap. text ed. 10.00 (*0-9638553-3-6*) KJAC Pubng.

Talks on Agni. Torkom Saraydarian. LC 86-722414. 1987. pap. 15.00 (*0-911794-56-5*) Aqua Educ.

Talks on Art, First and Second Series see On Painting & Drawing

Talks on Beelzebub's Tales. John G. Bennett. LC 88-3963. 195p. (Orig.). 1988. pap. 10.00 (*0-87728-680-9*) Weiser.

Talks on Mystic Christianity. Andrew Lohr. Ed. by Crafer Challgren. LC 84-90346. (Illus.). 143p. (Orig.). 1984. pap. text ed. 6.50 (*0-9613401-0-X*) Fiery Water.

Talks on Nationalism. Edward Bellamy. LC 78-102226. (Select Bibliographies Reprint Ser.). 1977. 21.95 (*0-8369-5111-5*) Ayer.

Talks on Pedagogics: An Outline of the Theory of Concentration. Francis W. Parker. LC 70-89217. (American Education: Its Men, Institutions, & Ideas. Series 1). 1978. reprint ed. 23.95 (*0-405-01456-2*) Ayer.

Talks on Poetry. Amal Kiran. 438p. 1989. 17.95 (*81-7058-173-7*) Aurobindo Assn.

Talks on the Gita. Vinoba Bhave. 241p. 1983. 15.00 (*0-934676-37-2*) Greenlf Bks.

Talks on the Origins of Public Education. Robert Levin. 1996. pap. text ed. write for info. (*0-07-037711-1*) McGraw.

Talks on the Path of Occultism Vol. 1: At the Feet of the Master. Annie Besant & Charles W. Leadbeater. 1980. 19.95 (*81-7059-160-0*) Theos Pub Hse.

Talks on the Path of Occultism Vol. 2: Voice of the Silence. Annie Besant & Charles W. Leadbeater. 1980. 17.95 (*81-7059-162-7*) Theos Pub Hse.

Talks on the Path of Occultism, Vol. 3: Light on the Path. Charles W. Leadbeater & Annie Besant. 1981. 17.95 (*0-8356-7068-6*) Theos Pub Hse.

Talks on Truth. Charles Fillmore. LC 89-50839. 1926. 7.95 (*0-87159-151-0*) Unity Bks.

***Talks to Boys: Classic Teaching on Virtues & Values.** Eleanor A. Hunter. 1996. 12.00 (*0-89109-987-5*) NavPress.

***Talks to Girls: Classic Teaching on Virtues & Values.** Eleanor A. Hunter. 1996. 12.00 (*0-89109-988-3*) NavPress.

Talks to Students on Occult Philosophy. Manly P. Hall. pap. 4.95 (*0-89314-361-8*) Philos Res.

Talks to Teachers. Ed. by David C. Berliner & Barak Rosenthine. 320p. (C). 1987. pap. text ed. write for info. (*0-07-554991-3*) McGraw.

Talks to Teachers on Psychology: And to Students on Some of Life's Ideals. William James. Ed. by Frederick Burkhardt et al. (Works of William James: No. 10). (Illus.). 386p. 1983. 37.00 (*0-674-86785-8*) HUP.

Talks to Teachers on Psychology & to Students on Some of Life's Ideals. William James. (Notable American Authors Ser.). 1992. reprint ed. lib. bdg. 75.00 (*0-7812-3475-1*) Rprt Serv.

Talks to the Children. W. Still. 4.99 (*0-906731-99-2*, Pub. by Christian Focus UK) Spring Arbor Dist.

Talks to Writers. Lafcadio Hearn. Ed. by John Erskine. LC 67-23230. (Essay Index Reprint Ser.). 1977. reprint ed. 20.95 (*0-8369-0528-8*) Ayer.

Talks with Authors. Ed. by Charles F. Madden. LC 68-10729. 256p. 1968. 5.85 (*0-8093-0300-0*) S Ill U Pr.

Talks with Great Composers: Candid Conversations with Brahms, Puccini, Strauss, & Others. Arthur M. Abell. LC 94-16762. 1994. 9.95 (*0-8065-1565-1*, Citadel Pr) Carol Pub Group.

Talks with Jonathon - Bk. I: A Guide to Transformation. Robin Miller. 156p. (Orig.). 1993. pap. 14.95 (*1-881343-04-9*) Channel One.

Talks with Mussolini. Benito Mussolini. Tr. by Eden Paul & Cedar Paul. LC 78-63699. (Studies in Fascism: Ideology & Practice). (Illus.). 256p. reprint ed. 32.00 (*0-404-16968-6*) AMS Pr.

Talks with Swami Prajnanapada. R. Srinivasan. 176p. 1910. pap. 12.95 (*1-85230-010-8*) Element MA.

Talks with Swami Vivekananda. Sharat C. Chakravarty. pap. 4.95 (*0-87481-156-2*, Pub. by Advaita Ashrama II) Vedanta Pr.

Talks with T. G. Masaryk. Karel Capek. Tr. by Michael H. Heim from CZE. LC 94-42805. 272p. (Orig.). 1995. pap. 13.95 (*0-945774-26-5*, DB2191.M38A513) Catbird Pr.

Talks with Teachers of Young Children: A Collection. Lilian G. Katz. 296p. 1995. pap. 39.50 (*1-56750-177-X*); text ed. 73.25 (*1-56750-176-1*) Ablex Pub.

Talks with the White Buffalo. Lyna Waggoner. (White Buffalo Talks Ser.: No. I). 128p. 1994. pap. 11.95 (*0-9641255-7-9*) Evolving Pr.

Talks with the White Buffalo: Tools & Techniques for Developing. Lyna Waggoner. (White Buffalo Talks Ser.: Vol. 2). 128p. 1995. pap. 10.95 (*0-9641255-2-8*) Evolving Pr.

Talkstory: Linking the Stories of Jesus with Our Individual & Collective Stories. Grant S. Lee. Ed. by Rennie Mau. 125p. (Orig.). 1989. student ed. write for info. (*0-318-66302-3*); pap. write for info. (*0-318-66301-5*); audio write for info. (*0-318-66303-1*) Media Bridge.

TalkTalk: A Children's Book Author Speaks to Grown-Ups. E. L. Konigsburg. LC 94-32341. (Illus.). 198p. (J). 1995. 29.95 (*0-689-31993-2*, Atheneum S&S) S&S Trade.

***Tall & Small.** (Get Ready...Get Set...Read! Ser.: Set 5). (J). 1996. lib. bdg. 11.95 (*1-56674-163-7*) Forest Hse.

Tall & Small. Gina C. Erickson & Kelli C. Goster. (Get Ready...Get Set...Read! Ser.). (Illus.). 24p. (J). (ps-3). 1994. pap. 3.50 (*0-8120-1840-0*) Barron.

Tall & Small: A Book about Height. Kate G. Phifer. LC 86-32401. (Illus.). 96p. (J). (gr. 5 up). 1987. 11.95 (*0-8027-6684-6*); lib. bdg. 12.85 (*0-8027-6685-4*) Walker & Co.

Tall Annie. Virginia L. Burns. LC 87-80726. (Illus.). 1987. lib. bdg. 17.50 (*0-9604726-3-0*) Enterprise Pr.

Tall Betsy & Dunce Baby: South Georgia Folktales. Mariella G. Hartsfield. LC 86-11360. (Brown Thrasher Bks.). 202p. 1991. reprint ed. pap. 12.95 (*0-8203-1332-7*) U of Ga Pr.

Tall Betsy & the Crackerbarrel Tales. Jacuqe Wheeler & Mariella G. Hartsfield. LC 93-5663. (J). 1993. pap. 6.00 (*0-88734-265-5*) Players Pr.

Tall Betsy & the Crackerbarrel Tales: Music & Lyrics. Jacuqe Wheeler & Mariella G. Hartsfield. LC 93-5663. (J). 1993. pap. 25.00 (*0-88734-036-9*) Players Pr.

Tall Birds Stalking. Michael Van Walleghen. (Poetry Ser.). 88p. (Orig.). (C). 1994. 19.95 (*0-8229-3794-8*); pap. 10.95 (*0-8229-5529-6*) U of Pittsburgh Pr.

***Tall Blondes: A Book about Giraffes.** Ed. by Lynn Sherr. LC 96-29880. (Illus.). 144p. 1997. 16.95 (*0-8362-2769-7*) Andrews & McMeel.

Tall Boys: The Rock-n-Roll Musical That Explores Teen-Age Drinking & Driving. Michael Downey. (Illus.). 68p. (Orig.). (YA). (gr. 7-12). 1990. pap. 4.50 (*0-88680-338-1*); 15.00 (*0-88680-339-X*) I E Clark.

Tall Boy's Journey. Joanna H. Kraus. (Illus.). 48p. (J). (gr. 2-5). 1992. lib. bdg. 14.96 (*0-87614-746-5*, Carolrhoda) Lerner Group.

Tall Boy's Journey. Joanna H. Kraus. (J). (gr. 2-5). 1993. pap. 5.95 (*0-87614-616-7*, Carolrhoda) Lerner Group.

Tall Brigade. Hermia Fraser. 322p. 1956. 14.95 (*0-8323-0058-6*); pap. 9.95 (*0-8323-0284-8*) Binford Mort.

Tall Building Artistically Reconsidered: The Search for a Skyscraper Style. Ada L. Huxtable. LC 92-5565. 1992. reprint ed. 15.95 (*0-520-08028-9*) U CA Pr.

***Tall Building Structures: A World View.** Ed. by Lynn S. Beedle & Dolores B. Rice. (Illus.). 488p. 1996. text ed. 45.00 (*0-939493-15-2*) Coun Tall Bldg.

Tall Building Structures: Analysis & Design. Bryan S. Stafford-Smith & Alex Coull. LC 90-13007. 537p. 1991. text ed. 150.00 (*0-471-51237-0*) Wiley.

Tall Buildings: 2000 & Beyond - Collected Papers: Fourth World Congress, Hong Kong. Council on Tall Buildings Staff. (Illus.). 800p. (C). 1991. text ed. 48.00 (*0-939493-06-3*, 903.407) Coun Tall Bldg.

Tall Buildings: 2000 & Beyond: Proceedings of Fourth World Congress, Hong Kong. Council on Tall Buildings & Urban Habitats Staff. Ed. by Dolores B. Rice. (Illus.). 1192p. (C). 1990. 60.00 (*0-939493-05-5*, 903.390) Coun Tall Bldg.

Tall Buildings in Seismic Regions: Collection of Papers. Council on Tall Buildings & Urban Habitat Staff. (Illus.). 428p. (C). 1990. pap. text ed. 20.00 (*0-939493-04-7*, 903.377) Coun Tall Bldg.

Tall Candle: the Personal Chronicle of a Yaqui Indian see Yaqui Life: The Personal Chronicle of a Yaqui Indian

***Tall Cotton.** Theron McGregor. LC 97-90014. 1997. 19.95 (*0-533-12270-8*) Vantage.

Tall, Dark Alibi. Kelsey Roberts. 1996. mass mkt. 3.75 (*0-373-22395-1*, 1-22395-7) Harlequin Bks.

Tall, Dark & Bad. Charlotte Hughes. 240p. 1996. mass mkt. 3.50 (*0-553-44524-3*, Loveswept) Bantam.

Tall, Dark, & Dangerous. Catherine Anderson. 384p. 1994. mass mkt. 5.50 (*0-06-108215-5*, Harp PBks) HarpC.

Tall, Dark & Deadly. Madeline Harper. (Intrigue Ser.). 1995. mass mkt. 3.50 (*0-373-22325-0*, 1-22325-4) Harlequin Bks.

Tall, Dark & Deadly. Carolyn Keene. Ed. by Ann Greenberg. (Nancy Drew Files Ser.: No. 66). 160p. (Orig.). (YA). (gr. 6 up). pap. 3.99 (*0-671-73070-3*, Archway) PB.

Tall, Dark, & Deadly. Francine Pascal. (Sweet Valley High Ser.: No. 126). 208p. (YA). (gr. 7 up). 1996. mass mkt. 3.99 (*0-553-56764-0*, Sweet Valley) BDD Bks Young Read.

Tall Dark Man. Anne Chamberlain. 216p. 1986. reprint ed. pap. 5.95 (*0-89733-195-8*) Academy Chi Pubs.

Tall Dark Stranger. large type ed. Joan Smith. LC 96-20472. (Large Print Bks.). 1996. 22.95 (*1-56895-347-X*) Wheeler Pub.

Tall Enough to Own the World. Berniece Rabe. LC 88-39139. 160p. (J). (gr. 5-7). 1989. lib. bdg. 21.80 (*0-531-10681-0*) Watts.

Tall Fescue. Ed. by L. P. Bush & R. C. Bucker. (Illus.). 351p. 1979. 18.75 (*0-89118-057-5*) Am Soc Agron.

Tall Houses. Elizabeth V. Hamilton & Louise F. Kerr. LC 68-59319. 1968. 5.00 (*0-937684-30-9*) Tradd St Pr.

Tall in the Saddle. Mary L. Baxter. (Desire Ser.: No. 660). 1991. pap. 2.75 (*0-373-05660-5*) Harlequin Bks.

***Tall in the Saddle: Great Lines from Classic Westerns.** Peggy Thompson. 1998. pap. text ed. 14.95 (*0-8118-1730-X*) Chronicle Bks.

Tall in the Saddle: The Long George Francis Story 1874-1920. Gary A. Wilson. LC 89-85450. (Illus.). 196p. (Orig.). 1989. pap. 12.95 (*0-937959-91-X*) High-Line Bks.

***Tall Man.** Dorothy B. Davis. (Illus.). 28p. (J). (ps-4). 1996. reprint ed. 11.95 (*0-87178-831-4*, 8314) Brethren.

Tall Man Riding. Norman A. Fox. 160p. 1988. mass mkt. 2.75 (*0-380-70294-0*) Avon.

Tall Man Riding. large type ed. Norman A. Fox. LC 91-16378. 230p. 1991. reprint ed. lib. bdg. 15.95 (*1-56054-190-3*) Thorndike Pr.

Tall Sheep: Harry Goulding, Monument Valley Trader. Samuel Moon. LC 91-50866. (Illus.). 256p. 1992. 27.95 (*0-8061-2415-6*) U of Okla Pr.

***Tall Ships.** George Quasha et al. LC 97-12548. (Gary Hill's Projective Installations Ser.). 1997. write for info. (*1-886449-54-6*) Barrytown Ltd.

***Tall Ships: An International Guide.** Thad Koza. LC 96-61174. (Illus.). 176p. 1996. 39.95 (*1-55949-313-5*) Tide-mark.

Tall Ships of Newburyport: The Montana, The Whittier, The Nearchus. George W. Goodwin. LC 89-85699. (Illus.). 72p. (Orig.). 1989. pap. 14.95 (*0-9624045-0-0*) Free Wind Pr.

Tall Ships of the Piscataqua, 1830-1877. Ray Brighton. (Portsmouth Marine Society Ser.: Vol. 15). (Illus.). 410p. 1989. 25.00 (*0-915819-14-7*, 15) Portsmouth Marine Soc.

***Tall Ships of the World.** Keith C. Wilbur. LC 96-43017. (Illustrated Living History Ser.). (Illus.). 1996. lib. bdg. 19.95 (*0-7910-4526-9*) Chelsea Hse.

Tall Ships of the World: An Illustrated Encyclopedia. C. Keith Wilbur. LC 95-46106. (Illustrated Living History Ser.). (Illus.). 112p. 1995. pap. 14.95 (*1-56440-748-9*) Globe Pequot.

Tall Ships of Today in Photographs. Frank O. Braynard. LC 93-18442. (Illus.). 128p. (Orig.). 1993. pap. 12.95 (*0-486-27163-3*) Dover.

***Tall Stacks: Celebration of America's Steamboat.** (Illus.). 1996. 26.95 (*0-9647433-1-0*) Wolf Pubng.

Tall State Revisited: A Republican Perspective. Hugh Gregg. 300p. 1993. 21.95 (*0-9637615-0-1*) Res N Hampshire.

Tall Stories. John Patience. (Happy Ending Stories Ser.). (Illus.). 32p. (J). (gr. k-6). 1991. 3.99 (*0-517-02327-X*) Random Hse Value.

Tall Stories? Reading Law & Literature. Ed. by John Morison & Christine Bell. LC 96-1351. (Applied Legal Philosophy Ser.). (Illus.). 304p. 1996. 67.95 (*1-85521-741-4*, Pub. by Dartmth Pub UK) Ashgate Pub Co.

Tall Stories about Snakes. Stephen Ray & Kathleen Murdoch. LC 93-6630. (J). 1994. pap. write for info. (*0-383-03716-6*) SRA McGraw.

Tall Story. adapted ed. Howard Nemerov. Ed. by Howard Lindsey. 1959. pap. 5.25 (*0-8222-1109-2*) Dramatists Play.

Tall Story & Other Tales. Margaret Mahy. LC 91-62222. (Illus.). 96p. (J). (gr. 3-7). 1992. lib. bdg. 15.95 (*0-689-50547-7*, McElderry) S&S Childrens.

Tall Stranger. Gillian Conoley. (Poetry Ser.). 64p. (Orig.). (C). 1991. pap. 11.95 (*0-88748-108-6*) Carnegie-Mellon.

Tall Stranger. Louis L'Amour. 128p. 1986. mass mkt. 3.99 (*0-553-28102-X*) Bantam.

Tall Tale: Junior Novelization. Adapted by Todd Strasser. LC 94-70811. (Illus.). 96p. (J). (gr. 2-6). 1995. pap. text ed. 4.95 (*0-7868-4011-0*) Disney Pr.

Tall Tale America: A Legendary History of Our Humorous Heroes. Walter Blair. (Illus.). 284p. (C). 1987. pap. 17.95 (*0-226-05596-5*) U Ch Pr.

Tall Tale in American Folklore & Literature. Carolyn S. Brown. LC 86-25125. (Illus.). 186p. 1987. 27.95 (*0-87049-529-1*); pap. 14.95 (*0-87049-671-9*) U of Tenn Pr.

Tall Tales: Reading Level 2-3. Illus. by Bill Baylis. LC 93-16084. (Timeless Tales Ser.). 1993. 4.95 (*0-88336-463-8*); audio 9.95 (*0-88336-544-8*) New Readers.

An Asterisk (*) at the beginning of an entry indicates that the title is appearing in BIP for the first time.

Tall Tales: The Glory Years of the NBA, in the Words of the Men Who Played, Coached, & Built Pro Basketball. Terry Pluto. (Illus.). 384p. 1992. 23.00 (0-671-74279-5) S&S Trade.

Tall Tales: The Glory Years of the NBA, in the Words of the Men Who Played, Coached, & Built Pro Basketball. Terry Pluto. 400p. 1994. pap. 12.00 (0-671-89937-6, Fireside) S&S Trade.

Tall Tales & Fairy Tales. Ed. by Bert Hower. (Spoofing Ser.). (Illus.). 92p. (Orig.). 1993. pap. write for info. (0-936945-22-2) Creat with Wds.

Tall Tales & Horse Shoe Nails. Wendell F. Hartt. (Illus.). 128p. (Orig.). 1994. 12.95 (1-880836-03-3) Pine Isl Pr.

Tall Tales & Short Stories: A Collection of Short Fiction. Tom Catalano. (Illus.). 176p. (Orig.). 1994. pap. 10.95 (1-882646-16-9) Wordsmith Bks.

Tall Tales & Tarnished Truths (of Nevada) Richard C. Datin. (Comstock Papers: Vol. 3). (Illus.). 50p. (Orig.). 1997. pap. 10.00 (0-9634452-1-9) R C Datin.

Tall Tales from an Island. P. A. Macnab. 245p. 1989. 35.00 (0-946487-07-3, Pub. by Luath Pr UK) St Mut.

Tall Tales from Old Smoky. C. Hodge Mathes. 252p. 1991. reprint ed. 14.95 (0-932807-59-3) Overmountain Pr.

Tall Tales from Rogue River. Hathaway Jones. LC 90-41875. (Northwest Reprints Ser.). (Illus.). 192p. 1991. reprint ed. pap. 13.95 (0-87071-512-7) Oreg St U Pr.

Tall Tales from the Land of Tall Timber. Pierre David. 1994. 12.95 (0-533-11047-5) Vantage.

Tall Tales of Davy Crockett: The Second Nashville Series of Crockett Almanacs, 1839-1841. Michael A. Lofaro. LC 86-29369. (Tennesseana Editions Ser.). (Illus.). 164p. 1987. reprint ed. 30.00 (0-87049-525-9); reprint ed. pap. 15.00 (0-87049-526-7) U of Tenn Pr.

Tall Tales of the Devil's Apron. Herbert M. Sutherland. (Illus.). 314p. 1988. reprint ed. 14.95 (0-932807-27-5) Overmountain Pr.

Tall Tales of the Mississippi. Dan Titus. (Illus.). 166p. 1995. pap. 9.95 (1-878488-72-4) Quixote Pr IA.

Tall Tales of the Rails: On the Carolina, Clinchfield & Ohio Railway. James L. Lonon. Ed. by James W. Mintz. (Illus.). 216p. 1989. 19.95 (0-932807-50-X) Overmountain Pr.

Tall Tales of the Southwest. Franklin J. Meine. 1988. reprint ed. lib. bdg. 49.00 (0-7812-0188-8) Rprt Serv.

Tall Tales of the Southwest. Franklin J. Meine. LC 78-166809. (Illus.). 1971. reprint ed. 79.00 (0-403-01424-7) Scholarly.

*Tall Tales of the United States. Patricia Cruzan. LC 96-92802. (Illus.). 38p. (Orig.). (J). (gr. 3-5). 1996. pap. 7.95 (0-9653543-1-8) Clear Creek Pubs.

*Tall Tales of the United States. Patricia Cruzan. LC 96-92802. (Illus.). 38p. (Orig.). (J). (gr. 3-5). 1997. lib. bdg. 13.95 (0-9653543-2-6) Clear Creek Pubs.

*Tall Tales over Short Fences. Mac Ashworth, Jr. LC 96-79055. 80p. 1997. 14.95 (0-8233-0512-0) Golden Quill.

Tall Tales Told in Biblical Hebrew. Irene Resnikoff & Linda Motzkin. (Illus.). 144p. (Orig.). 1994. pap. 16.95 (0-939144-20-4) EKS Pub Co.

*Tall Tales Told in Biblical Hebrew. Ethelyn Simon et al. (Illus.). 144p. (Orig.). (HEB.). 1994. pap. 59.95 incl. audio (0-939144-23-9) EKS Pub Co.

Tall Texan. large type ed. Lee Floren. (Linford Western Library). 256p. 1994. pap. 15.99 (0-7089-7498-8, Linford) Ulverscroft.

*Tall Texan: The Story of Ben Kilpatrick. Arthur Soule. (Illus.). 212p. (Orig.). 1996. pap. 14.95 (0-9655664-0-4) Traildust UT.

Tall, Thin, & Blonde. Dyan Sheldon. LC 92-53021. 176p. (YA). (gr. 6-10). 1993. 14.95 (1-56402-139-4) Candlewick Pr.

Tall, Thin, & Blonde. Dyan Sheldon. LC 92-53021. 176p. (J). (gr. 6-10). 1994. pap. 3.99 (1-56402-374-5) Candlewick Pr.

Tall Timber Short Lines, Vol. 6: B & O in Print. 9.00 (0-9616890-6-4) Tioga Pubns.

Tall Timber Tales: More Paul Bunyan Stories. Dell J. McCormick. LC 39-20778. (Illus.). (J). (gr. 4-6). 1939. 11.95 (0-87004-094-4) Caxton.

Tall Timbers Conference on Ecological Animal Control by Habitat Management: Proceedings, No. 1. Tall Timbers Research Station Staff. 250p. reprint ed. pap. 71.30 (0-685-15990-6, 2026824) Bks Demand.

Tall Timbers Conference on Ecological Animal Control by Habitat Management: Proceedings, No. 3. Tall Timbers Research Station Staff. 294p. reprint ed. pap. 83.80 (0-685-15987-6, 2026823) Bks Demand.

Tall Timbers Fire Ecology Conference Proceedings No. 11: Five in Africa April 22-23, 1971, Meeting at Auditorium, Sheraton Motor Inn, Tallahassee, FL. Tall Timbers Fire Ecology Conference Staff. 528p. reprint ed. pap. 150.50 (0-685-15978-7, 2026822) Bks Demand.

Tall Toothbrush Retires. Rita Friedman & Elaine Weimann. (Fables from the Letter People Ser.). (Illus.). 30p. (J). (ps-1). 1988. lib. bdg. 12.95 (0-89796-019-X) New Dimens Educ.

Tall Trees. Bob Von Normann. 53p. 1995. 6.95 (0-915687-12-7) FVN Corp.

Tall Trees & Far Horizons: Adventures & Discoveries of Early Botanists in America. Virginia L. Eifert. LC 70-39100. (Essay Index Reprint Ser.). (Illus.). 1977. reprint ed. 30.95 (0-8369-2686-2) Ayer.

Tall Trees Fall. Ruth E. Nelson. 194p. (Orig.). 1993. write for info. (0-9643648-0-8) R E Nelson.

Tall Trees, Tough Men. Robert E. Pike. (Illus.). 320p. 1984. reprint ed. pap. 11.95 (0-393-30185-0) Norton.

Tall Uncut. Pete Fromm. 176p. (Orig.). 1991. pap. 9.95 (0-936784-95-4) J Daniel.

Tall Woman. Wilma Dykeman. LC 62-11580. 315p. 1982. reprint ed. pap. 9.95 (0-9613859-1-X) Wakestone Bks.

Tall Wyoming. large type ed. Dan Cushman. LC 93-32758. 1994. lib. bdg. 16.95 (0-8161-5856-8) G K Hall.

Talladega College: The First Century. Maxine D. Jones & Joe M. Richardson. LC 89-32992. (Illus.). 354p. 1990. reprint ed. pap. 100.90 (0-608-01671-3, 2062327) Bks Demand.

Tallahassee: Tradition, Technology, Teamwork. James E. Turner. LC 95-17683. 144p. Date not set. pap. 24.95 (1-885352-10-7) Community Comm.

*Tallahassee Experience. Roger Rampage. 80p. 1997. pap. 5.95 (1-57502-538-8, PO1579) Morris Pubng.

Tallahassee, Florida Area Street Atlas. (Illus.). 297p. (Orig.). 1995. pap. 28.95 (1-882829-01-8) Map & Globe.

Tallahassee Higgins. Mary D. Hahn. (J). 1988. pap. 4.50 (0-380-70500-1, Camelot) Avon.

Tallahatchie County, Mississippi Will & Probate Records. Betty C. Wiltshire. 162p. (Orig.). 1996. pap. 15.00 (1-885480-07-5) Pioneer Pubng.

*Tallant for Democracy. Andrew York. 224p. 1996. 24.00 (0-7278-4959-X) Severn Hse.

*Tallchief. Dinah McCall. 384p. 1997. mass mkt. 5.99 (0-06-108444-1) HarpC.

*Tallchief for Keeps. Cait London. (Silhouette Promo Ser.). 1997. 5.99 (0-373-48337-6, 1-48337-9) Harlequin Bks.

Tallchief's Bride. Cait London. (Desire Ser.). 1996. mass mkt. 3.50 (0-373-76021-3, 1-76021-4) Silhouette.

Taller de Invenciones. Emilio D. Valcarcel. pap. write for info. (1-56758-024-6) Edit Cultl.

*Taller Internacional Sobre Ecologia y Manejo de Peces en Lagos y Embalses. 243p. (SPA.). 1986. pap. 30.00 (92-5-302465-8, FSP6758, Pub. by FAO IT) Bernan Associates.

*Taller Musical. M. Pina. (SPA.). 1.50 (0-8297-1155-4) Life Pubs Intl.

Taller Torres-Garcia: The School of the South & Its Legacy. Ed. by Mari C. Ramirez. LC 91-20731. (Illus.). 411p. 1992. 55.00 (0-292-78121-0); pap. 29.95 (0-292-78122-9) U of Tex Pr.

Taller Women: A Cautionary Tale. Lawrence Naumoff. LC 91-131. 1992. 21.95 (0-15-187991-5) HarBrace.

Taller Women: A Cautionary Tale. Lawrence Naumoff. (Harvest American Writing Ser.). 1994. pap. 10.95 (0-15-688162-4) HarBrace.

Tallest. David Armentrout. LC 96-23861. (Fascinating Facts Ser.). 1996. write for info. (1-57103-131-6) Rourke Pr.

Talleur's Basic Fly Tying. Richard W. Talleur. LC 96-12521. Orig. Title: Fly-Tyer's Primer. 1996. pap. 35.00 (1-55821-519-0) Lyons & Burford.

Talley & Son. Lanford Wilson. 1995. pap. 5.25 (0-8222-1452-0) Dramatists Play.

Talleyrand. Duff Cooper. 399p. 1932. 49.50 (0-8047-0616-6) Stanford U Pr.

Talley's Folly. Lanford Wilson. (Mermaid Dramabook Ser.). 60p. 1980. pap. 8.95 (0-374-52157-3, Noonday) FS&G.

Talley's Truth. Philip Ross. 256p. 1988. pap. 3.50 (0-8125-8784-7) Tor Bks.

*Tallgrass: A Novel of the Great Plains. Don Coldsmith. LC 96-19672. 464p. 1997. 23.95 (0-553-10632-5) Bantam.

Tallgrass Prairie. John Madson. LC 93-25835. (Illus.). 112p. 1993. 29.50 (1-56044-223-9) Falcon Pr MT.

Tallgrass Prairie Wildflowers: A Field Guide. Doug Ladd. LC 95-6990. (Nature Conservancy Bks.). (Illus.). 264p. 1995. pap. 19.95 (1-56044-299-9) Falcon Pr MT.

Tallgrass Restoration Book: For Prairies, Savannas, & Woodlands. Ed. by Stephen Packard & Cornelia F. Mutel. (C). 1996. pap. text ed. 25.00 (1-55963-320-4) Island Pr.

*Tallgrass Restoration Book: For Prairies, Savannas, & Woodlands. Ed. by Stephen Packard & Cornelia F. Mutel. 432p. (C). 1996. 50.00 (1-55963-319-0) Island Pr.

Tallien: A Brief Romance. Frederic Tuten. LC 94-12707. 152p. 1994. pap. 13.95 (0-7145-2990-7) M Boyars Pubs.

Tallie's War. large type ed. Jan Webster. 512p. 1995. 25.99 (0-7089-3267-3) Ulverscroft.

Tallinn: A Guide. (Travel Guides to the Soviet Union Ser.). (Illus.). 270p. (Orig.). 1991. 9.95 (0-87052-917-X) Hippocrene Bks.

Tallinn in 19th Century Engravings. Collets Staff. 1983. 165.00 (0-317-57465-5) St Mut.

Tallis Anthology. Thomas Tallis. (Tudor Church Music Ser.). 128p. 1992. pap. 13.95 (0-19-353410-X) OUP.

Tallis Ends & Other Tales. Don Channen. 184p. (J). 1992. pap. 9.95 (965-229-053-X, Pub. by Gefen Pub Hse IS) Gefen Bks.

Tallit see Mitzvah of the Month

Tallman Legacy. Karl L. Tallman. (Orig.). 1996. pap. write for info. (1-57553-226-3) Watermrk Pr.

Tallos de Luna: Moon Shoots. Elba R. Sanchez. (Illus.). 40p. (Orig.). (ENG & SPA.). 1992. pap. text ed. 10.95 (0-939952-12-2); lib. bdg. 280.00 (0-939952-11-4) Moving Parts.

Tallos De Luna: Moon Shoots. Elba R. Sanchez. Tr. by Robret Chiarito from SPA. (Illus.). 44p. 1992. pap. text ed. 10.95 (0-939952-20-3) Moving Parts.

Tallulah Bankhead: A Bio-Bibliography. Jeffrey L. Carrier. LC 91-24008. (Bio-Bibliographies in the Performing Arts Ser.: No. 21). 296p. 1991. text ed. 45.00 (0-313-27452-5, CTB, Greenwood Pr) Greenwood.

*Tallulah Bankhead: A Scandalous Life. David Bret. (Illus.). 280p. 1997. 31.95 (1-86105-015-1, Pub. by Robson UK) Parkwest Pubns.

Tallulah Bankhead Murder Case. large type ed. George Baxt. (General Ser.). 363p. 1989. lib. bdg. 17.95 (0-8161-4707-8, GK Hall) Thorndike Pr.

Tally of Types, with Additions by Several Hands. rev. ed. Stanley Morison. Ed. by Brooke Crutchley. LC 72-90486. (Illus.). 138p. 1973. 55.00 (0-521-20043-1) Oak Knoll.

Tallyho, Pinkerton! Steven Kellogg. LC 82-70198. (Pied Piper Bks.). (Illus.). 32p. (J). (ps-3). 1983. pap. 14.95 (0-8037-8731-6) Dial Bks Young.

Tallyho, Pinkerton! Steven Kellogg. LC 82-2341. (Pied Piper Bks.). (Illus.). 32p. (J). (ps-3). 1985. 4.95 (0-8037-0166-7) Dial Bks Young.

Tallyho Pinkerton. Steven Kellogg. (J). (gr. 4-7). 1992. pap. 5.99 (0-14-054710-X, Puffin) Puffin Bks.

Tallyman. large type ed. Bill Knox. (Linford Mystery Library). 384p. 1993. pap. 15.99 (0-7089-7388-4, Linford) Ulverscroft.

Tally's Corners. Elliot Liebow. 1968. pap. 11.95 (0-316-52514-6) Little.

Tallystick. Bryan MacMahon. 248p. 1995. pap. 12.95 (1-85371-447-X, Pub. by Poolbeg Pr IE) Dufour.

Tallystick: And Other Stories. Bryan MacMahon. 256p. 1995. 29.00 (1-85371-338-4, Pub. by Poolbeg Pr IE) Dufour.

Talmadge, Tallmadge & Talmage Genealogy, Being the Descendants of Thomas Talmadge of Lynn, Massachusetts, with an Appendix Including Other Families. A. Talmadge. (Illus.). 385p. 1989. reprint ed. pap. 58.00 (0-8328-1155-6); reprint ed. lib. bdg. 66.00 (0-8328-1154-8) Higginson Bk Co.

Talmage on Palestine: Series of Sermons. Thomas Talmage. Ed. by Moshe Davis. LC 77-70747. (America & the Holy Land Ser.). 1977. reprint ed. lib. bdg. 19.95 (0-405-10293-3) Ayer.

Talmud, 64 vols., Set. (ENG & HEB.). 995.00 (0-910218-50-1) Bennet Pub.

Talmud, Vol. 14. Adin Steinsaltz. 1996. 50.00 (0-679-44398-3) McKay.

Talmud, Vol. 15. Adin Steinsaltz. 1996. 50.00 (0-679-45222-2) McKay.

Talmud, Vol. 16. Adin Steinsaltz. Date not set. write for info. (0-679-45223-0) McKay.

Talmud: A Close Encounter. Jacob Neusner. LC 91-17994. 224p. (Orig.). 1991. pap. 15.00 (0-8006-2498-X, 1-2498, Fortress Pr) Augsburg Fortress.

Talmud: An Analytical Guide. Isaac Unterman. LC 73-148291. 351p. 1985. reprint ed. text ed. 17.95 (0-8197-0189-0); reprint ed. pap. text ed. 10.95 (0-8197-0005-3) Bloch.

Talmud: Introduction & Reader. Jacob Neusner. LC 95-39336. (South Florida Studies in the History of Judaism: No. 129). 172p. (C). 1995. pap. 39.95 (0-7885-0207-7, 240129) Scholars Pr GA.

Talmud: Law & Commentary. Harry Gersh. 64p. (YA). (gr. 9 up). 1986. pap. text ed. 6.50 (0-87441-434-2) Behrman.

Talmud: Selected Writings. Ed. by Ben Z. Bosker & Baruch M. Bosker. (Classics of Western Spirituality Ser.). 1989. 17.95 (0-8091-0430-X); pap. 14.95 (0-8091-3114-5) Paulist Pr.

Talmud: The Steinsaltz Edition: The Reference Guide. Adin Steinsaltz. (Illus.). 1990. 50.00 (0-394-57665-9) Random.

Talmud: Tractrate Bava Metzia, Vol 1, Pt. 1. Adin Steinsaltz. 1989. 40.00 (0-685-28784-X) Random.

Talmud Pt. 3: Tractate Ketubot. Adin Steinsaltz. (Steinsaltz Ser.: Vol. 9). 1993. 45.00 (0-685-70935-3) Random.

Talmud Vol. 1, Pt. 1: The Steinsaltz Edition: Bava Metzia. Adin Steinsaltz. (Illus.). 1990. 50.00 (0-394-57666-7) Random.

Talmud Vol. 2, Pt. 2: The Steinsaltz Edition: Tractate Bava Metzia. Adin Steinsaltz. 384p. 1990. 45.00 (0-394-58233-0) Random.

Talmud Vol. 3, Pt. 3: The Steinsaltz Edition: Tractate Bava Metzia. Adin Steinsaltz. 272p. 1990. 45.00 (0-394-58234-9) Random.

Talmud Vol. 4, Pt. 4: The Steinsaltz Edition: Tractate Bava Metzia. Ed. by Adin Steinsaltz. LC 89-42911. (Illus.). 384p. 1991. 45.00 (0-394-58853-3) Random.

Talmud Vol. 5: The Steinsaltz Edition: Tractate Bava Metzia, Pt. I. Adin Steinsaltz. 1992. 45.00 (0-679-41379-0) Random.

Talmud Vol. 5: The Steinsaltz Edition: Tractate Ketubot. Ed. by Adin Steinsaltz. (Illus.). 224p. 1991. 45.00 (0-679-40769-3) Random.

Talmud Vol. 6, Pt. 6: The Steinsaltz Edition: Tractate Bava Metzia. Adin Steinsaltz. 1993. 50.00 (0-679-41378-2) Random.

Talmud Vol. VII. Israel Institute Staff. 1996. 50.00 (0-679-44397-5) Random.

Talmud Vol. 8: The Steinsaltz Edition: Tractate Ketubot, Pt. II. Adin Steinsaltz. 1992. 45.00 (0-679-41632-3) Random.

Talmud Vol. 10, Pt. 4: The Steinsaltz Edition: Tractate Ketubot. Adin Steinsaltz. 1994. 45.00 (0-679-42899-2) Random.

Talmud Vol. 12: The Steinsaltz Edition: Tractate Ketubot, Pt. 5. Adin Steinsaltz & Israel Institute Staff. 1997. 50.00 (0-679-42962-X) Random.

Talmud Vol. XIII, Pt. I: The Steinsaltz Edition: Tractate Ta'anit. Adin Steinsaltz. 1995. 45.00 (0-679-42961-1) Random.

Talmud As Law Or Literature: An Analysis of David W. Halivni's Mekorot Umasorot. Irwin H. Haut. x, 83p. 1980. pap. 6.95 (0-87203-107-1) Hermon.

*Talmud Bavli Vol. I: The Schottenstein Edition - Bava Kamma. 46.99 (0-89906-704-2, TBK1) Mesorah Pubns.

*Talmud Bavli Vol. I: The Schottenstein Edition - Chullin. 46.99 (0-89906-700-X, TCH1) Mesorah Pubns.

*Talmud Bavli Vol. I: The Schottenstein Edition - Shabbos. 1996. 46.99 (0-89906-708-5, TSH1) Mesorah Pubns.

*Talmud Bavli Vol. II: The Schottenstein Edition - Zevachim. 46.99 (0-89906-748-4, TZE2) Mesorah Pubns.

*Talmud Bavli Vol. III: The Schottenstein Edition - Zevachim. 1996. 47.99 (0-89906-749-2, TZE3) Mesorah Pubns.

Talmud Bavli - Makkos: Schottenstein Edition. Ed. by Hersh GoldWurm. 1990. 46.99 (0-89906-725-5) Mesorah Pubns.

Talmud Bavli - Megillah: Schottenstein Edition. Ed. by Hersh GoldWurm. 1991. 46.99 (0-89906-728-X) Mesorah Pubns.

Talmud Bavli - Tractate Bava Metzia: Schottenstein Edition, Vol. 3. Hersh GoldWurm. 46.99 (0-89906-737-9) Mesorah Pubns.

Talmud Bavli - Tractate Beitzah: Schottenstein Edition. Ed. by Hersh GoldWurm. 1992. 46.99 (0-89906-730-1) Mesorah Pubns.

Talmud Bavli - Tractate Sanhedrin: Schottenstein Edition, Vol. 1. Ed. by Hersh Goldwurm. 1993. 46.99 (0-89906-743-3) Mesorah Pubns.

Talmud Bavli - Tractate Shevuos: Schottenstein Edition. Ed. by Y. Danziger. 1994. 46.99 (0-89906-746-8) Mesorah Pubns.

Talmud Bavli - Tractate Taanis: Schottenstein Edition. Ed. by Hersh GoldWurm. 1991. 46.99 (0-89906-729-8) Mesorah Pubns.

Talmud Bavli: Eruvin: Schottenstein Edition, Vols. 1 & 2. Ed. by Hersh Goldwurm. 1990. 46.99 (0-89906-726-3) Mesorah Pubns.

Talmud Bavli: Eruvin: Schottenstein Edition, Vols. 1 & 2. Ed. by Hersh Goldwurm. 1991. 46.99 (0-89906-727-1) Mesorah Pubns.

Talmud Bavli: Nazir: Schottenstein Edition, Vols. I & II. Ed. by Hersh Goldwurm. 1992. 46.99 (0-89906-731-X) Mesorah Pubns.

Talmud Bavli: Nazir: Schottenstein Edition, Vols. I & II. Ed. by Hersh Goldwurm. 1993. 46.99 (0-89906-732-8) Mesorah Pubns.

Talmud Bavli: Tractate Bava Basra: Schottenstein Edition, 2 vols., Set. Ed. by Hersh GoldWurm. 1992. 46.99 (0-89906-738-7) Mesorah Pubns.

Talmud Bavli: Tractate Bava Basra: Schottenstein Edition, 2 vols., Vol. 2. Ed. by Hersh GoldWurm. 1994. 46.99 (0-89906-739-5) Mesorah Pubns.

Talmud Bavli: Tractate Bava Basra: Schottenstein Edition, Vol. 3. Ed. by Hersh GoldWurm. 1994. 46.99 (0-89906-740-9) Mesorah Pubns.

Talmud Bavli: Tractate Bava Metzia: Schottenstein Edition, Vol. 1. Ed. by Hersh Goldwurm. 46.99 (0-89906-735-2) Mesorah Pubns.

Talmud Bavli: Tractate Bava Metzia: Schottenstein Edition, Vol. 2. Ed. by Hersh Goldwurm. 1993. 46.99 (0-89906-736-0) Mesorah Pubns.

Talmud Bavli: Tractate Gittin: Schottenstein Edition, Vol. 1. Ed. by Hersh GoldWurm. 1993. 46.99 (0-89906-744-1) Mesorah Pubns.

Talmud Bavli: Tractate Gittin: Schottenstein Edition, Vol. 2. Ed. by Hersh GoldWurm. 1993. 46.99 (0-89906-745-X) Mesorah Pubns.

Talmud Bavli: Tractate Kiddushin: Schottenstein Edition, Vol. I. Ed. by Hersh GoldWurm. 1992. 46.99 (0-89906-733-6) Mesorah Pubns.

Talmud Bavli: Tractate Kiddushin: Schottenstein Edition, Vol. 2. Ed. by Hersh GoldWurm. 1993. 46.99 (0-89906-734-4) Mesorah Pubns.

Talmud Bavli:Tractate Sanhedrin: Schottenstein Edition, Vol. 2. Ed. by Hersh GoldWurm. 1994. 46.99 (0-89906-742-5) Mesorah Pubns.

Talmud Bavli:Tractate Sanhedrin: Schottenstein Edition, Vol. 3. Ed. by Hersh GoldWurm. 1994. 46.99 (0-89906-747-6) Mesorah Pubns.

Talmud for Beginners Vol. 1: Prayer. Judith Z. Abrams. LC 90-1211. 232p. 1993. pap. 20.00 (1-56821-022-1) Aronson.

Talmud for Beginners Vol. 2: Text. Judith Z. Abrams. LC 90-1211. 192p. 1993. pap. 20.00 (0-87668-597-1) Aronson.

*Talmud for Beginners Vol. 3: Living in a Non-Jewish World. Judith Z. Abrams. 1997. pap. write for info. (0-7657-9967-7) Aronson.

Talmud Guides. Adin Steinsaltz. Date not set. 272.00 (0-394-23835-4) Random.

*Talmud of Babylonia: An American Translation II, Tractate Shabbat, Vol. B. Tr. by Jacob Neusner. 206p. 1992. 59.95 (1-55540-805-2, 140272) Scholars Pr GA.

Talmud of Babylonia: An American Translation: Shabbat II.A. Tr. by Jacob Neusner from HEB. LC 92-37135. (Brown Judaic Studies: No. 270). 192p. 1992. 59.95 (1-55540-797-8, 14 02 70) Scholars Pr GA.

Talmud of Babylonia: An American Translation, Tractate Hullin, No. XXX.C. Tr. by Tzvee Zahavy from HEB. (Brown Judaic Studies). 384p. 1994. 74.95 (1-55540-732-3, 140255) Scholars Pr GA.

Talmud of Babylonia: An American Translation VII Tractate Besah. Tr. by Alan J. Avery-Peck from HEB. LC 86-20237. (Brown Judaic Studies). 358p. 1986. pap. 41.95 (1-55540-054-X, 14-01-17) Scholars Pr GA.

Talmud of Babylonia: An American Translation: XI: Tractate Moed Qatan. Tr. by Jacob Neusner from HEB. LC 92-13780. (Brown Judaic Studies: No. 252). 232p. 1992. 59.95 (1-55540-725-0, 140252) Scholars Pr GA.

Talmud of Babylonia: An American Translation: XIII.A: Tractate Yebamot. Tr. by Jacob Neusner from HEB. LC 92-13781. (Brown Judaic Studies: No. 250-251). 230p. 1992. 69.95 (1-55540-722-6, 140250) Scholars Pr GA.

Talmud of Babylonia: An American Translation: XIII.B: Tractate Yebamot. Tr. by Jacob Neusner from HEB. (Brown Judaic Studies). 204p. 1992. 59.95 (1-55540-723-4, 140251) Scholars Pr GA.

Talmud of Babylonia: An American Translation: XIII.C: Tractate Yebamot. Tr. by Jacob Neusner from HEB. (Brown Judaic Studies). 223p. 1992. 69.95 (1-55540-733-1, 140256) Scholars Pr GA.

Talmud of Babylonia: An American Translation: XIII.D: Tractate Yebamot. Tr. by Jacob Neusner from HEB. (Brown Judaic Studies). 206p. 1992. 59.95 (1-55540-745-5, 140261) Scholars Pr GA.

Talmud of Babylonia: An American Translation: XIV.A: Tractate Ketubot. Tr. by Jacob Neusner from HEB. LC 92-16852. (Brown Judaic Studies). 202p. 1992. 59.95 (*1-55540-734-X*, 140257) Scholars Pr GA.

Talmud of Babylonia: An American Translation: XIV.B: Tractate Ketubot. Tr. by Jacob Neusner from HEB. (Brown Judaic Studies). 202p. 1992. 59.95 (*1-55540-735-8*, 140258) Scholars Pr GA.

Talmud of Babylonia: An American Translation: XIV.C: Tractate Ketubot. Tr. by Jacob Neusner from HEB. (Brown Judaic Studies). 213p. 1992. 59.95 (*1-55540-744-7*, 140260) Scholars Pr GA.

***Talmud of Babylonia: An American Translation XVIII, Tractate Gittin, Vol. C.** Tr. by Jacob Neusner. 186p. 1992. 59.95 (*1-55540-796-X*, 140269) Scholars Pr GA.

Talmud of Babylonia: An American Translation: XX.A: Tractate Baba Qamma. Tr. by Jacob Neusner from HEB. (Brown Judaic Studies). 221p. 1992. 59.95 (*1-55540-702-1*, 140247) Scholars Pr GA.

Talmud of Babylonia: An American Translation: XX.B: Tractate Baba Qamma. Tr. by Jacob Neusner from HEB. (Brown Judaic Studies). 248p. 1992. 59.95 (*1-55540-703-X*, 140248) Scholars Pr GA.

Talmud of Babylonia: An American Translation: XX.C: Tractate Baba Qamma. Tr. by Jacob Neusner from HEB. (Brown Judaic Studies). 238p. 1992. 59.95 (*1-55540-704-8*, 140249) Scholars Pr GA.

Talmud of Babylonia: An American Translation: XXI Tractate Bava Mesia, 4 vols., A. Tr. by Jacob Neusner from HEB. (Brown Judaic Studies). 265p. 1990. 59.95 (*1-55540-504-5*, 14 02 13) Scholars Pr GA.

Talmud of Babylonia: An American Translation: XXI Tractate Bava Mesia, 4 vols., C. Tr. by Jacob Neusner from HEB. (Brown Judaic Studies). 225p. 1990. 59.95 (*1-55540-506-1*, 14 02 15) Scholars Pr GA.

Talmud of Babylonia: An American Translation: XXI Tractate Bava Mesia, 4 vols., D. Tr. by Jacob Neusner from HEB. (Brown Judaic Studies). 237p. 1990. 59.95 (*1-55540-507-X*, 14 02 16) Scholars Pr GA.

Talmud of Babylonia: An American Translation: XXI Tractate Bava Mesia, 4 vols., Vol. B. Tr. by Jacob Neusner from HEB. (Brown Judaic Studies). 193p. 1990. Vol. 8. 59.95 (*1-55540-505-3*, 14 02 14) Scholars Pr GA.

Talmud of Babylonia: An American Translation: XXII.A: Tractate Baba Batra. Tr. by Jacob Neusner from HEB. (Brown Judaic Studies). 245p. 1992. 59.95 (*1-55540-667-X*, 140239) Scholars Pr GA.

Talmud of Babylonia: An American Translation: XXII.B: Tractate Baba Batra. Tr. by Jacob Neusner from HEB. (Brown Judaic Studies). 198p. 1992. 59.95 (*1-55540-668-8*, 140240) Scholars Pr GA.

Talmud of Babylonia: An American Translation: XXII.C: Tractate Baba Batra. Tr. by Jacob Neusner from HEB. (Brown Judaic Studies). 199p. 1992. 59.95 (*1-55540-673-4*, 140241) Scholars Pr GA.

***Talmud of Babylonia: An American Translation, XXIII Tractate Sanhedrin, Vol. C.** Tr. by Jacob Neusner. 235p. 1985. 31.95 (*0-89130-803-2*, 140087) Scholars Pr GA.

***Talmud of Babylonia: An American Translation, XXIX Tractate Menahot, Vol. B.** Tr. by Jacob Neusner. 262p. 1991. 62.95 (*1-55540-659-9*, 140236) Scholars Pr GA.

Talmud of Babylonia: An American Translation: XXVII.A: Tractate Shebuot. Tr. by Jacob Neusner from HEB. (Brown Judaic Studies). 192p. 1992. 59.95 (*1-55540-685-8*, 140242) Scholars Pr GA.

Talmud of Babylonia: An American Translation: XXVII.B: Tractate Shebuot. Tr. by Jacob Neusner from HEB. (Brown Judaic Studies). 246p. 1992. 59.95 (*1-55540-686-6*, 140243) Scholars Pr GA.

Talmud of Babylonia: An American Translation: XXVIII: Tractate Zebahim, Vol. C. Tr. by Jacob Neusner from HEB. 265p. 1991. 64.95 (*1-55540-636-X*, 14 02 34) Scholars Pr GA.

Talmud of Babylonia: An American Translation: XXVIII: Tractate Zebahim, Vol. A. Tr. by Jacob Neusner from HEB. 248p. 1991. 59.95 (*1-55540-606-8*, 14 02 31) Scholars Pr GA.

Talmud of Babylonia: An American Translation: XXX.A: Tractate Hullin. Tr. by Tzvee Zahavy from HEB. LC 92-18378. (Brown Judaic Studies: vol. 30.A, No. 253). 246p. 1992. 69.95 (*1-55540-730-7*, 140253) Scholars Pr GA.

***Talmud of Babylonia: An American Translation, XXXI Tractate Bekharot, Vol. B.** Tr. by Tzvee Zahavy. 223p. 1990. 59.95 (*1-55540-554-1*, 140220) Scholars Pr GA.

Talmud of Babylonia: An American Translation XXXV Meilah & Tamid. Tr. by Peter J. Haas from HEB. LC 86-26036. (Brown Judaic Studies). 180p. 1986. 31.95 (*1-55540-086-8*, 14-01-09) Scholars Pr GA.

***Talmud of Babylonia: An American Translation, XXXVI Tractate Niddah, Vol. B.** Tr. by Jacob Neusner. 259p. 1990. 59.95 (*1-55540-556-8*, 140222) Scholars Pr GA.

Talmud of Babylonia: Pesahim IV. A: An American Translation: Tractate Pesahim IV. A Chapter One. Jacob Neusner. (Brown Judaic Studies). 221p. 1993. 59.95 (*1-55540-826-5*, 140281) Scholars Pr GA.

Talmud of Babylonia: Pesahim IV D: An American Translation: Tractate Pesahim IV Chapters 7 & 8. Jacob Neusner. (Brown Judaic Studies). 228p. 1993. 59.95 (*1-55540-842-7*, 140284) Scholars Pr GA.

Talmud of Babylonia: Tractate Pesahim IV.C, Vol. C. Tr. by Jacob Neusner from HER. LC 93-319. (Brown Judaic Studies: No. 283). 246p. 1993. Set. 59.95 (*1-55540-833-8*, 14 02 83) Scholars Pr GA.

Talmud of Babylonia: Tractate Qiddushin XIX.A-B, A. Tr. by Jacob Neusner from HEB. LC 92-30644. (Brown Judaic Studies: Nos. 267 & 268). 210p. 1992. 59.95 (*1-55540-776-5*, 14 02 67) Scholars Pr GA.

Talmud of Babylonia: Tractate Qiddushin XIX.A-B, B. Tr. by Jacob Neusner from HEB. LC 92-30644. (Brown Judaic Studies: Nos. 267 & 268). 114p. 1992. 59.95 (*1-55540-777-3*, 14 02 68) Scholars Pr GA.

Talmud of Babylonia Vol. IX: An American Translation: Tractate Rosh Hashanah. Tr. by Alan J. Avery-Peck from HEB. LC 95-20613. (Brown Judaic Studies: Vol. 306). 510p. (C). 1995. 49.95 (*0-7885-0172-0*, 140306) Scholars Pr GA.

Talmud of Babylonia Vol. VI: Sukkah: An Academic Commentary. Jacob Neusner. (USF Academic Commentary Ser.: Series No. 6). 315p. 1994. 59.95 (*1-55540-983-0*, 243006) Scholars Pr GA.

Talmud of Babylonia Vol. XII: Hagigah: An Academic Commentary. Jacob Neusner. (USF Academic Commentary Ser.). 175p. 1994. 59.95 (*1-55540-984-9*, 243007) Scholars Pr GA.

Talmud of Babylonia Vol. XXVI: Bavli Tractate Honayot: An Academic Commentary. Jacob Neusner. (USF Academic Commentary Ser.). 155p. 1994. 59.95 (*1-55540-985-7*, 243008) Scholars Pr GA.

Talmud of Babylonia Vol. XXVII: Bavli Tractate Shebuot: An Academic Commentary. Jacob Neusner. (USF Academic Commentary Ser.). 321p. 1994. 74.95 (*1-55540-986-5*, 243009) Scholars Pr GA.

Talmud of Babylonia - An American Translation, No. XXIIIB: Sanhedrin, Ch. 4-8. (Brown Judaic Studies). 259p. 1984. 29.95 (*0-89130-801-6*, 14 00 84); pap. 22.75 (*0-89130-802-4*) Scholars Pr GA.

Talmud of Babylonia--An American Translation, No. I: Berakhot. Tr. by Jacob Neusner from HEB. (Brown Judaic Studies). 435p. 1984. 36.95 (*0-89130-808-3*, 14 00 78); pap. 31.95 (*0-89130-809-1*, 14 00 78) Scholars Pr GA.

Talmud of Babylonia--An American Translation, No. VI: Tractate Sukkah. Tr. by Jacob Neusner from HEB. (Brown Judaic Studies). 285p. 1984. 35.75 (*0-89130-786-9*, 14 00 74); pap. 23.50 (*0-89130-788-5*, 14 00 74) Scholars Pr GA.

Talmud of Babylonia--An American Translation, No. XVII: Sotah. Tr. by Jacob Nausner from HEB. (Brown Judaic Studies). 300p. 1984. 31.95 (*0-89130-777-X*, 14 00 72); pap. 23.50 (*0-89130-778-8*, 14 00 72) Scholars Pr GA.

Talmud of Babylonia--An American Translation, No. XXIIIA: Sanhedrin, Ch. 1-3. Tr. by Jacob Neusner from HEB. (Brown Judaic Studies). 1984. 25.95 (*0-89130-799-0*, 14 00 81); pap. 19.50 (*0-89130-800-8*) Scholars Pr GA.

Talmud of Babylonia--An American Translation, No. XXXII: Arakhin. Tr. by Jacob Neusner from HEB. (Brown Judaic Studies). 1984. 27.95 (*0-89130-739-7*, 14 00 63); pap. 18.25 (*0-89130-754-0*, 14 00 63) Scholars Pr GA.

Talmud of Babylonia, an Academic Commentary, Vol. XI, Moed Qatan. Jacob Neusner. LC 94-8120. (USF Academic Commentary Ser.: Vol. 1). 218p. 1994. 69.95 (*1-55540-973-3*, 243001) Scholars Pr GA.

Talmud of Babylonia, an Academic Commentary, Vol. XXXIV, Keritot. Jacob Neusner. LC 94-8120. (USF Academic Commentary Ser.: Vol. 1). 270p. 1994. 74.95 (*1-55540-972-5*, 243002) Scholars Pr GA.

***Talmud of Babylonia, an Academic Commentary: Bavli Tractate Baba Batra.** Jacob Neusner. (University of South Florida Academic Commentary Ser.: Vol. 22, Chapters 1-6). 326p. 1996. 94.95 (*0-7885-0050-3*, 243022) Scholars Pr GA.

***Talmud of Babylonia, an Academic Commentary: Bavli Tractate Baba Batra.** Jacob Neusner. (University of South Florida Academic Commentary Ser.: Vol. 22, Chapters 7-11). 412p. 1996. 104.95 (*0-7885-0283-2*, 243067) Scholars Pr GA.

***Talmud of Babylonia, an Academic Commentary: Bavli Tractate Baba Mesia.** Jacob Neusner. (University of South Florida Academic Commentary Ser.: Vol. 21, Chapters 7-11). 362p. 1996. 99.95 (*0-7885-0290-5*, 243073) Scholars Pr GA.

***Talmud of Babylonia, an Academic Commentary: Bavli Tractate Baba Mesia, A.** Jacob Neusner. (University of South Florida Academic Commentary Ser.: Vol. 21, Chapters 1-6). 408p. 1996. 104.95 (*0-7885-0049-X*, 243021) Scholars Pr GA.

***Talmud of Babylonia, an Academic Commentary: Bavli Tractate Berakhot.** Jacob Neusner. (University of South Florida Academic Commentary Ser.: Vol. 1). 562p. 1996. 129.95 (*0-7885-0056-2*, 243024) Scholars Pr GA.

***Talmud of Babylonia, an Academic Commentary: Bavli Tractate Erubin.** Jacob Neusner. (University of South Florida Academic Commentary Ser.: Vol. 3, Chapters 1-5). 322p. 1996. 94.95 (*0-7885-0086-4*, 243030) Scholars Pr GA.

***Talmud of Babylonia, an Academic Commentary: Bavli Tractate Erubin, B.** Jacob Neusner. (University of South Florida Academic Commentary Ser.: Vol. 2, Chapters 6-11). 344p. 1996. 94.95 (*0-7885-0291-3*, 243074) Scholars Pr GA.

***Talmud of Babylonia, an Academic Commentary: Bavli Tractate Gittin.** Jacob Neusner. (University of South Florida Academic Commentary Ser.: Vol. 18). 548p. 1996. 129.95 (*0-7885-0106-2*, 243035) Scholars Pr GA.

***Talmud of Babylonia, an Academic Commentary: Bavli Tractate Ketubot.** Jacob Neusner. (University of South Florida Academic Commentary Ser.: Vol. 14, Chapters 7-14). 344p. 1996. 99.95 (*0-7885-0286-7*, 243069) Scholars Pr GA.

***Talmud of Babylonia, an Academic Commentary: Bavli Tractate Ketubot, A.** Jacob Neusner. (University of South Florida Academic Commentary Ser.: Vol. 14, Chapters 1-6). 344p. 1996. 134.95 (*0-7885-0084-8*, 243028) Scholars Pr GA.

***Talmud of Babylonia, an Academic Commentary: Bavli Tractate Menahot.** Jacob Neusner. (University of South Florida Academic Commentary Ser.: Vol. 24, Chapters 1-6). 396p. 1996. 104.95 (*0-7885-0051-1*, 243023) Scholars Pr GA.

***Talmud of Babylonia, an Academic Commentary: Bavli Tractate Menahot.** Jacob Neusner. (University of South Florida Academic Commentary Ser.: Vol. 24, Chapters 7-14). 394p. 1996. 104.95 (*0-7885-0288-3*, 243071) Scholars Pr GA.

***Talmud of Babylonia, an Academic Commentary: Bavli Tractate Pesahim.** Jacob Neusner. (University of South Florida Academic Commentary Ser.: Vol. 4, Chapters 1-7). 452p. 1996. 114.95 (*0-7885-0085-6*, 243029) Scholars Pr GA.

***Talmud of Babylonia, an Academic Commentary: Bavli Tractate Pesahim, B.** Jacob Neusner. (University of South Florida Academic Commentary Ser.: Vol. 4, Chapters 8-11). 297p. 1996. 94.95 (*0-7885-0287-5*, 243070) Scholars Pr GA.

***Talmud of Babylonia, an Academic Commentary: Bavli Tractate Sanhedrin.** Jacob Neusner. (University of South Florida Academic Commentary Ser.: Vol. 23, Chapters 1-7). 382p. 1996. 99.95 (*0-7885-0058-9*, 243026) Scholars Pr GA.

***Talmud of Babylonia, an Academic Commentary: Bavli Tractate Sanhedrin.** Jacob Neusner. (University of South Florida Academic Commentary Ser.: Vol. 23, Chapters 7-12). 440p. 1996. 109.95 (*0-7885-0284-0*, 243068) Scholars Pr GA.

***Talmud of Babylonia, an Academic Commentary: Bavli Tractate Shabbat.** Jacob Neusner. (University of South Florida Academic Commentary Ser.: Vol. 2, Chapters 1-12). 476p. 1996. 109.95 (*0-7885-0088-0*, 243032) Scholars Pr GA.

***Talmud of Babylonia, an Academic Commentary: Bavli Tractate Shabbat.** Jacob Neusner. (University of South Florida Academic Commentary Ser.: Vol. 2, Chapters 12-24). 522p. 1996. 119.95 (*0-7885-0089-9*, 243033) Scholars Pr GA.

***Talmud of Babylonia, an Academic Commentary: Bavli Tractate Yebamot.** Jacob Neusner. (University of South Florida Academic Commentary Ser.: Vol. 8, Chapters 1-8). 460p. 1996. 114.95 (*0-7885-0083-X*, 243043) Scholars Pr GA.

***Talmud of Babylonia, an Academic Commentary: Bavli Tractate Yebamot.** Jacob Neusner. (University of South Florida Academic Commentary Ser.: Vol. 8, Chapters 9-17). 423p. 1996. 109.95 (*0-7885-0131-3*, 243044) Scholars Pr GA.

***Talmud of Babylonia, an Academic Commentary: Bavli Tractate Zebahim.** Jacob Neusner. (University of South Florida Academic Commentary Ser.: Vol. 28, Chapters 1-7). 418p. 1996. 109.95 (*0-7885-0035-X*, 243020) Scholars Pr GA.

***Talmud of Babylonia, an Academic Commentary: Bavli Tractate Zebahim.** Jacob Neusner. (University of South Florida Academic Commentary Ser.: Vol. 28, Chapters 8-15). 398p. 1996. 104.95 (*0-7885-0289-1*, 243072) Scholars Pr GA.

Talmud of Babylonia an Academic Commentary Vol. IV, A: A Complete Outline, the Division of Holy Things from Tractate Zebahim Through Tractate Hullin. Jacob Neusner. LC 94-36299. (USF Academic Commentary Ser.: No. 27). 327p. 1995. 99.95 (*0-7885-0053-8*, 243027) Scholars Pr GA.

Talmud of Babylonia, an Academic Commentary Vol. IA: A Complete Outline: Tractate Berakhot & the Division of Appointed Times: From Tractate Berakhot Through Tractate Pesahim. Jacob Neusner. LC 94-36299. (USF Academic Commentary Ser.). 430p. (C). 1995. 114.95 (*0-7885-0112-7*, 243039) Scholars Pr GA.

***Talmud of Babylonia, an Academic Commentary Vol. IB: A Complete Outline: Tractate Berakhot & the Division of Appointed Times from Tractate Yoma Through Tractate Hagigah.** Jacob Neusner. LC 94-36299. (USF Academic Commentary Ser.). 460p. (C). 1995. 114.95 (*0-7885-0113-5*, 243040) Scholars Pr GA.

Talmud of Babylonia, an Academic Commentary Vol. IIA: A Complete Outline: The Division of Women: From Tractate Yebamot Through Tractate Ketubot. Jacob Neusner. LC 94-36299. (USF Academic Commentary Ser.). 314p. (C). 1995. 94.95 (*0-7885-0114-3*, 243041) Scholars Pr GA.

Talmud of Babylonia, an Academic Commentary Vol. IIB: A Complete Outline: The Division of Women: From Tractate Nedarim Through Tractate Qiddushin. Jacob Neusner. LC 94-36299. (USF Academic Commentary Ser.). 382p. (C). 1995. 109.95 (*0-7885-0115-1*, 243042) Scholars Pr GA.

Talmud of Babylonia, an Academic Commentary Vol. IIIA: A Complete Outline: The Division of Damages: From Tractate Baba Qamma Through Tractate Baba Batra. Jacob Neusner. LC 94-36299. (USF Academic Commentary Ser.). 467p. (C). 1995. 114.95 (*0-7885-0087-2*, 243031) Scholars Pr GA.

Talmud of Babylonia, an Academic Commentary Vol. IIIB: A Complete Outline: The Division of Damages: From Tractate Sanhedrin Through Tractate Shebuot. Jacob Neusner. LC 94-36299. (USF Academic Commentary Ser.). 333p. (C). 1995. 99.95 (*0-7885-0111-9*, 243038) Scholars Pr GA.

Talmud of Babylonia, an Academic Commentary Vol. IVB: A Complete Outline: The Division of Holy Things: From Tractate Bekhorot Through Tractate Niddah. Jacob Neusner. LC 94-36299. (USF Academic Commentary Ser.). 437p. (C). 1995. 114.95 (*0-7885-0110-0*, 243037) Scholars Pr GA.

Talmud of Babylonia, an Academic Commentary Vol. V: Yoma. Jacob Neusner. (USF Academic Commentary Ser.: Series No. 13). 434p. 1994. 99.95 (*0-7885-0002-3*, 243013) Scholars Pr GA.

***Talmud of Babylonia, an Academic Commentary Vol. VII: Besah.** Jacob Neusner. 1995. 79.95 (*0-7885-0023-6*, 243018) Scholars Pr GA.

Talmud of Babylonia, an Academic Commentary Vol. VIII: Bavli Tractate Rosh Hashanah, No. VIII. Jacob Neusner. (USF Academic Commentary Ser.: Series No. 12). 296p. 1994. 74.95 (*0-7885-0012-0*, 243012) Scholars Pr GA.

Talmud of Babylonia, an Academic Commentary Vol. X: Bavli Tractate Megillah. Jacob Neusner. LC 94-8120. (USF Academic Commentary Ser.). 282p. (C). 1995. 74.95 (*0-7885-0025-2*, 243019) Scholars Pr GA.

***Talmud of Babylonia, an Academic Commentary Vol. XIX: Bavli Tractate Quiddushin.** Jacob Neusner. (South Florida Academic Commentary Ser.). 537p. 1996. 125.95 (*0-7885-0107-0*, 243036) Scholars Pr GA.

***Talmud of Babylonia, an Academic Commentary Vol. XV: Bavli Tractate Nedarim.** Jacob Neusner. (South Florida Academic Commentary Ser.). 335p. 1995. 89.95 (*0-7885-0095-3*, 243034) Scholars Pr GA.

Talmud of Babylonia, an Academic Commentary Vol. XVII: Sotah. Jacob Neusner. LC 94-8120. (USF Studies in the History of Judaism). 346p. 1994. 79.95 (*1-55540-978-4*, 243003) Scholars Pr GA.

Talmud of Babylonia, an Academic Commentary Vol. XX: Bavli Tractate Baba Qamma, No. XX. Jacob Neusner. (USF Academic Commentary Ser.). 666p. 1994. 139.95 (*0-7885-0004-X*, 243015) Scholars Pr GA.

Talmud of Babylonia, an Academic Commentary Vol. XXIV: Makkot, No. XXIV. Jacob Neusner. LC 94-8120. (USF Academic Commentary Ser.: Series No. 4). 162p. 1994. 59.95 (*1-55540-979-2*, 243004) Scholars Pr GA.

Talmud of Babylonia, an Academic Commentary Vol. XXV: Bavli Tractate Abodah Zarah. Jacob Neusner. LC 94-8120. (USF Academic Commentary Ser.). 410p. (C). 1995. 99.95 (*0-7885-0057-0*, 243025) Scholars Pr GA.

Talmud of Babylonia, an Academic Commentary Vol. XXX: Bavli Tractate Hullin, No. XXX. Jacob Neusner. (USF Academic Commentary Ser.). 803p. 1994. 149.95 (*0-7885-0016-3*, 243017) Scholars Pr GA.

Talmud of Babylonia, an Academic Commentary Vol. XXXI: Bavli Tractate Bekhorot, No. XXI. Jacob Neusner. (USF Academic Commentary Ser.). 359p. 1994. 89.95 (*0-7885-0005-8*, 243016) Scholars Pr GA.

***Talmud of Babylonia, an Academic Commentary Vol. XXXII: Arakhin.** Jacob Neusner. (South Florida Academic Commentary Ser.). 292p. 1994. 74.95 (*1-55540-980-6*, 243005) Scholars Pr GA.

Talmud of Babylonia, an Academic Commentary Vol. XXXVI: Bavli Tractate Niddah, No. XXXVI. Jacob Neusner. (USF Academic Commentary Ser.). 434p. 1994. 99.95 (*0-7885-0003-1*, 243014) Scholars Pr GA.

Talmud of Babylonia: An American Translation: Gittin XVIII.A & Gittin XVIII.B, Vol. A. Tr. by Jacob Neusner from HEB. LC 92-30643. (Brown Judaic Studies: Nos. 265 & 266). 199p. 1992. 59.95 (*1-55540-774-9*, 14 02 65) Scholars Pr GA.

Talmud of Babylonia: An American Translation: Gittin XVIII.A & Gittin XVIII.B, Vol. B. Tr. by Jacob Neusner from HEB. LC 92-30643. (Brown Judaic Studies: Nos. 265 & 266). 185p. 1992. 59.95 (*1-55540-775-7*, 14 02 66) Scholars Pr GA.

***Talmud of Babylonia, an American Translation: Tractate Bekharot, XXXI, Vol. A.** Tr. by Tzvee Zahavy. 189p. 1990. 54.95 (*1-55540-553-3*, 140219) Scholars Pr GA.

***Talmud of Babylonia, an American Translation: Tractate Temurah, XXXIII.** Tr. by Tzvee Zahavy. 246p. 1990. 59.95 (*1-55540-521-5*, 140218) Scholars Pr GA.

Talmud of Babylonia, an American Translation Vol. V. C. Yoma, Chapters 6-8. LC 94-28396. (Brown Judaic Studies). 276p. 1994. 61.95 (*0-7885-0009-0*, 140296) Scholars Pr GA.

Talmud of Babylonia, an American Translation Vol. V. A. Yoma. Tr. by Jacob Neusner from HEB. LC 94-28396. (Brown Judaic Studies). 196p. 1994. 59.95 (*0-7885-0007-4*, 140294) Scholars Pr GA.

Talmud of Babylonia, an American Translation Vol. V. B. Yoma, Chapters 3-5. Tr. by Jacob Neusner from HEB. LC 94-28396. (Brown Judaic Studies). 238p. 1994. 59.95 (*0-7885-0008-2*, 140295) Scholars Pr GA.

Talmud of Babylonia, an American Translation Vol. XXII.D, Chapters 7 & 8: Baba Batra. Tr. by Jacob Neusner from HEB. LC 91-14855. (Brown Judaic Studies). 256p. 1994. 64.95 (*0-7885-0021-X*, 140297) Scholars Pr GA.

Talmud of Babylonia, an American Translation Vol. XXII.E, Chapters 9 & 10: Baba Batra. Tr. by Jacob Neusner from HEB. LC 91-14855. (Brown Judaic Studies). 256p. 1994. 64.95 (*0-7885-0022-8*, 140298) Scholars Pr GA.

Talmud of Babylonia, an American Translation Vol. XXV.A: Tractate Abodah Zarah. Tr. by Jacob Neusner from HEB. (Brown Judaic Studies). 228p. 1991. 59.95 (*1-55540-594-0*, 140227) Scholars Pr GA.

Talmud of Babylonia, an American Translation Vol. XXV.B: Tractate Abodah Zarah. Tr. by Jacob Neusner from HEB. (Brown Judaic Studies). 238p. 1991. 59.95 (*1-55540-595-9*, 140228) Scholars Pr GA.

Talmud of Babylonia, an American Translation Vol. XXVIII.B: Tractate Zebahim. Tr. by Jacob Neusner from HEB. 230p. 1991. 59.95 (*1-55540-635-1*, 140233) Scholars Pr GA.

***Talmud of Babylonia, an American Translation Vol. XXIV: Tractate Makkot.** Tr. by Jacob Neusner. 213p. 1991. 59.95 (*1-55540-663-7*, 140238) Scholars Pr GA.

An Asterisk (*) at the beginning of an entry indicates that the title is appearing in BIP for the first time.

Talmud of Babylonia, an American Translation Vol. XXIX: Tractate Menahot Chapters 1-3. Tr. by Jacob Neusner from HEB. (Brown Judaic Studies). 219p. 1991. 59.95 (*1-55540-646-7*, 140235) Scholars Pr GA.

Talmud of Babylonia, an American Translation Vol. XXIX C: Tractate Menahot. Tr. by Jacob Neusner from HEB. (Brown Judaic Studies). 211p. 1991. 59.95 (*1-55540-662-9*, 140237) Scholars Pr GA.

Talmud of Babylonia, an American Translation Vol. XXXIV: Keritot. Tr. by Jacob Neusner from HEB. (Brown Judaic Studies). 226p. 1991. 59.95 (*1-55540-546-0*, 140223) Scholars Pr GA.

***Talmud of Babylonia, an American Translation XXXVI, Vol. A: Tractate Niddah.** Tr. by Jacob Neusner. 214p. 1990. 54.95 (*1-55540-555-X*, 140221) Scholars Pr GA.

Talmud of Babylonia: An American Translation: XV: Tractate Nedarim. Jacob Neusner. LC 92-25792. (American Academy of Religion Academy Ser.: Nos. 262-263). 199p. 1992. 59.95 (*1-55540-751-X*, 140262) Scholars Pr GA.

Talmud of Babylonia: An American Translation: XV: Tractate Nedarim. Tr. by Jacob Neusner from HEB. LC 92-25792. (Brown Judaic Studies: No. 262-263). 205p. 1992. 59.95 (*1-55540-752-8*, 14 02 63) Scholars Pr GA.

Talmud of Babylonia, An American Translation XXVI: Tractate Horayot. Tr. by Martin S. Jaffee from HEB. LC 87-4783. (Brown Judaic Studies). 233p. 1987. 29.95 (*1-55540-119-8*, 14-00-90) Scholars Pr GA.

Talmud of Babylonia, Erubin III.A: An American Translation: Tractate Erubin III. A-B Chapters 1 & 2. Tr. by Jacob Neusner from HEB. (Brown Judaic Studies). 229p. 1993. 59.95 (*1-55540-814-1*, 140276) Scholars Pr GA.

Talmud of Babylonia, Erubin III.B: An American Translation: Tractate Erubin III. B Chapters 3 & 4. Tr. by Jacob Neusner from HEB. (Brown Judaic Studies). 206p. 1993. 59.95 (*1-55540-815-X*, 140277) Scholars Pr GA.

Talmud of Babylonia, Erubin III.C: An American Translation: Tractate Erubin III. C Chapters 5 & 6. Tr. by Jacob Neusner from HEB. (Brown Judaic Studies). 223p. 1993. 59.95 (*1-55540-821-4*, 140278) Scholars Pr GA.

Talmud of Babylonia, Erubin III.D: An American Translation: Tractate Erubin III. D Chapters 7-10. Tr. by Jacob Neusner from HEB. (Brown Judaic Studies). 213p. 1993. 59.95 (*1-55540-822-2*, 140279) Scholars Pr GA.

Talmud of Babylonia, Hagigah XII: An American Translation: Tractate Hagigah XII. Tr. by Jacob Neusner from HEB. LC 92-247132. (Brown Judaic Studies: Vol. 280). 203p. 1993. 59.95 (*1-55540-823-0*, 14 02 80) Scholars Pr GA.

Talmud of Babylonia, Hullin XXXB: An American Translation. Tr. by Tzvee Zahavy from HEB. (Brown Judaic Studies). 189p. 1993. 69.95 (*1-55540-731-5*, 140254) Scholars Pr GA.

Talmud of Babylonia, Meilah & Tamid Vol. XXXV: An Academic Commentary. Jacob Neusner. (USF Academic Commentary Ser.). 170p. 1994. 59.95 (*1-55540-988-1*, 243011) Scholars Pr GA.

Talmud of Babylonia, Pesahim IV.B: An American Translation: Tractate Pesahim IV. B Chapters 2 & 3. Tr. by Jacob Neusner from HEB. (Brown Judaic Studies). 231p. 1993. 64.95 (*1-55540-827-3*, 140282) Scholars Pr GA.

Talmud of Babylonia, Pesahim IV.E: An American Translation: Tractate Pesahim IV. E, Chaps. 9 & 10. Tr. by Jacob Neusner from HEB. (Brown Judaic Studies). 228p. 1993. 64.95 (*1-55540-843-5*, 140285) Scholars Pr GA.

Talmud of Babylonia, Shabbat II.C: An American Translation: Tractate Shabbat II. C Chapters 7-10. Tr. by Jacob Neusner from HEB. (Brown Judaic Studies). 215p. 1993. 59.95 (*1-55540-808-7*, 140273) Scholars Pr GA.

Talmud of Babylonia, Shabbat II.D: An American Translation: Tractate Shabbat II. D Chapters 11-17. Tr. by Jacob Neusner from HEB. (Brown Judaic Studies). 230p. 1993. 59.95 (*1-55540-809-5*, 140274) Scholars Pr GA.

Talmud of Babylonia, Shabbat II.E: An American Translation: Tractate Shabbat II. E Chapters 18-24. Tr. by Jacob Neusner from HEB. (Brown Judaic Studies). 221p. 1993. 59.95 (*1-55540-812-5*, 140275) Scholars Pr GA.

Talmud of Babylonia, Temurah Vol. XXXIII: An Academic Commentary. Jacob Neusner. (USF Academic Commentary Ser.). 261p. 1994. 74.95 (*1-55540-987-3*, 243010) Scholars Pr GA.

Talmud of Jmmanuel. Tr. by J. H. Ziegler & B. L. Greene. 168p. (Orig.). 1990. pap. 15.95 (*0-926524-12-7*, Wild Flower Pr) Blue Wtr Pubng.

Talmud of the Land of Israel: A Preliminary Translation & Explanation, Vol. 6: Terumot. Ed. by Jacob Neusner. Tr. by Alan J. Avery-Peck & Martin S. Jaffee. (Chicago Studies in the History of Judaism). 582p. 1987. lib. bdg. 90.00 (*0-226-57663-9*) U Ch Pr.

Talmud of the Land of Israel: A Preliminary Translation & Explanation - Maaserot, Vol. 7. Ed. by Jacob Neusner & Martin S. Jaffee. LC 87-5852. (Chicago Studies in the History of Judaism). xii, 288p. (C). 1987. lib. bdg. 30.00 (*0-226-57664-7*) U Ch Pr.

Talmud of the Land of Israel: A Preliminary Translation & Explanation : Hagigah & Moed Qatan, Vol. 20. Ed. & Tr. by Jacob Neusner. LC 85-29037. (Chicago Studies in the History of Judaism). 256p. 1986. lib. bdg. 42.00 (*0-226-57679-5*) U Ch Pr.

Talmud of the Land of Israel: A Preliminary Translation & Explanation- Vol. 25, Gittin. Ed. by Jacob Neusner. (Chicago Studies in the History of Judaism). 280p. 1985. lib. bdg. 40.00 (*0-226-57684-1*); lib. bdg. 40.00 (*0-226-57683-3*) U Ch Pr.

Talmud of the Land of Israel: A Preliminary Translation & Explanation- Vol. 25, Gittin. Ed. & Tr. by Jacob Neusner. (Chicago Studies in the History of Judaism). 256p. 1985. lib. bdg. 37.50 (*0-226-57682-5*) U Ch Pr.

Talmud of the Land of Israel: A Preliminary Translation & Explanation, Rosh Hashanah, Vol. 16. Jacob Neusner. Tr. by Edward A. Goldman. (Chicago Studies in the History of Judaism). 136p. 1988. lib. bdg. 31.50 (*0-226-57675-2*) U Ch Pr.

Talmud of the Land of Israel: A Preliminary Translation & Explanation, Sheqalim, Ed. & Tr. by Jacob Neusner from HEB. (Chicago Studies in the History of Judaism: Vol. 15). 190p. 1990. lib. bdg. 42.00 (*0-226-57674-4*) U Ch Pr.

Talmud of the Land of Israel: A Preliminary Translation & Explanation, Sukkah, Vol. 17. Jacob Neusner. (Chicago Studies in the History of Judaism). 160p. 1988. lib. bdg. 31.50 (*0-226-57676-0*) U Ch Pr.

Talmud of the Land of Israel: A Preliminary Translation & Explanation: Vol. 19, Megillah. Ed. by Jacob Neusner. LC 86-25284. (Chicago Studies in the History of Judaism). x, 200p. (C). 1987. lib. bdg. 35.00 (*0-226-57678-7*); lib. bdg. 45.00 (*0-226-57677-9*) U Ch Pr.

Talmud of the Land of Israel: A Preliminary Translation & Explanation, Vol. 2. Ed. by Jacob Neusner. Tr. by Roger Brooks. LC 89-5136. (Chicago Studies in the History of Judaism). 364p. 1990. lib. bdg. 66.00 (*0-226-57659-0*) U Ch Pr.

Talmud of the Land of Israel: A Preliminary Translation & Explanation, Vol. 22: Ketubot. Ed. by Jacob Neusner. (Chicago Studies in the History of Judaism). 420p. 1985. lib. bdg. 59.00 (*0-226-57681-7*) U Ch Pr.

Talmud of the Land of Israel: A Preliminary Translation & Explanation, Vol. 22: Ketubot. Ed. by Jacob Neusner. Tr. by Tzvee Zahavy. (Chicago Studies in the History of Judaism). 392p. 1989. lib. bdg. 58.00 (*0-226-57658-2*) U Ch Pr.

Talmud of the Land of Israel: A Preliminary Translation & Explanation-Vol. 26, Qiddushin. Ed. & Tr. by Jacob Neusner. 252p. 1984. lib. bdg. 30.00 (*0-226-57688-4*); lib. bdg. 30.00 (*0-226-57689-2*) U Ch Pr.

Talmud of the Land of Israel: A Preliminary Translation & Explanation-Vol. 26, Qiddushin. Ed. & Tr. by Jacob Neusner. 298p. 1984. lib. bdg. 30.00 (*0-226-57687-6*) U Ch Pr.

Talmud of the Land of Israel: A Preliminary Translation & Explanation-Vol. 26, Qiddushin. Ed. & Tr. by Jacob Neusner. 278p. 1984. lib. bdg. 30.00 (*0-226-57686-8*) U Ch Pr.

Talmud of the Land of Israel: A Preliminary Translation & Explanation-Vol. 30, Baba Batra. Ed. & Tr. by Jacob Neusner. 240p. 1982. lib. bdg. 32.50 (*0-226-57693-0*); lib. bdg. 35.00 (*0-226-57694-9*) U Ch Pr.

Talmud of the Land of Israel: A Preliminary Translation & Explanation-Vol. 30, Baba Batra. Ed. & Tr. by Jacob Neusner. 302p. 1983. lib. bdg. 37.50 (*0-226-57692-2*) U Ch Pr.

Talmud of the Land of Israel: A Preliminary Translation & Explanation-Vol. 30, Baba Batra. Ed. & Tr. by Jacob Neusner. 176p. 1984. lib. bdg. 23.00 (*0-226-57695-7*) U Ch Pr.

Talmud of the Land of Israel: A Preliminary Translation & Explanation-Vol. 30, Baba Batra. Ed. & Tr. by Jacob Neusner. 224p. 1984. lib. bdg. 30.00 (*0-226-57690-6*) U Ch Pr.

Talmud of the Land of Israel: A Preliminary Translation & Explanation-Vol. 30, Baba Batra. Ed. & Tr. by Jacob Neusner. 476p. 1984. lib. bdg. 54.00 (*0-226-57691-4*) U Ch Pr.

Talmud of the Land of Israel: A Preliminary Translation & Explanation, Yoma, Vol. 14. Tr. by Jacob Neusner. (Chicago Studies in the History of Judaism). 254p. 1991. lib. bdg. 48.00 (*0-226-57673-6*) U Ch Pr.

Talmud of the Land of Israel: Yebamot. Ed. & Tr. by Jacob Neusner. LC 86-11406. (Chicago Studies in the History of Judaism). x, 528p. (C). 1987. lib. bdg. 70.00 (*0-226-57680-9*) U Ch Pr.

Talmud of the Land of Israel Vol. 5: A Preliminary Translation & Explanation: Shebiit. Ed. by Jacob Neusner. Tr. by Alan J. Avery-Peck. (Chicago Studies in the History of Judaism). 454p. 1991. lib. bdg. 75.00 (*0-226-57662-0*) U Ch Pr.

Talmud of the Land of Israel Vol. 9: A Preliminary Translation & Explanation: Hallah. Ed. by Jacob Neusner. (Chicago Studies in the History of Judaism). 166p. 1991. lib. bdg. 40.50 (*0-226-57666-3*) U Ch Pr.

Talmud of the Land of Israel Vol. 13: Yerushalmi Pesahim. Ed. by Jacob Neusner. Tr. by Baruch M. Bokser. LC 93-34781. (Chicago Studies in the History of Judaism). 658p. 1995. lib. bdg. 95.00 (*0-226-57672-8*) U Ch Pr.

Talmud of the Land of Israel Vol. I: A Complete Outline of the Second, Third, & Fourth Divisions: The Division of Appointed Times: A. Berakhot, Shabbat. Jacob Neusner. LC 95-53340. (South Florida Academic Commentary Ser.). 234p. (C). 1996. 79.95 (*0-7885-0217-4*, 243048) Scholars Pr GA.

Talmud of the Land of Israel Vol. I: A Complete Outline of the Second, Third, & Fourth Divisions: The Division of Appointed Times: B. Erubin, Yoma & Besah. Jacob Neusner. LC 95-53340. (South Florida Academic Commentary Ser.). 226p. (C). 1996. 79.95 (*0-7885-0226-3*, 243049) Scholars Pr GA.

Talmud of the Land of Israel Vol. I: A Complete Outline of the Second, Third, & Fourth Divisions: The Division of Appointed Times: C. Pesahim & Sukkah. Jacob Neusner. LC 95-53340. (South Florida Academic Commentary Ser.: Vol. 47). 203p. (C). 1996. 79.95 (*0-7885-0216-6*, 243047) Scholars Pr GA.

Talmud of the Land of Israel Vol. ID: A Complete Outline of the Second, Third, & Fourth Divisions: The Division of Appointed Time: Taanit, Megillah, Rosh Hashanah, Hagigah & Moed Qatan. Jacob Neusner. LC 95-53340. (South Florida Academic Commentary Ser.). 246p. (C). 1996. 79.95 (*0-7885-0227-1*, 243050) Scholars Pr GA.

Talmud of the Land of Israel Vol. II: A Complete Outline of the Second, Third, & Fourth Divisions: The Division of Women: A. Yebamot to Nedarim. Jacob Neusner. LC 95-18815. (South Florida Academic Commentary Ser.: Vol. 148). 323p. (C). 1996. 89.95 (*0-7885-0128-3*, 243045) Scholars Pr GA.

Talmud of the Land of Israel Vol. II: A Complete Outline of the Second, Third, & Fourth Divisions: The Division of Women: B. Nazir to Sotah. Jacob Neusner & Loren Crow. LC 95-53340. (South Florida Academic Commentary Ser.: Vol. 148). 296p. (C). 1996. 89.95 (*0-7885-0129-1*, 243046) Scholars Pr GA.

Talmud of the Land of Israel Vol. IIIA: A Complete Outline of the Second, Third, & Fourth Divisions: The Division of Damages: Baba Qamma, Baba Mesia, Baba Batra, Horayot & Niddah. Jacob Neusner. LC 96-3770. (South Florida Academic Commentary Ser.: No. 51-52). 286p. (C). 1996. 89.95 (*0-7885-0230-1*, 243051) Scholars Pr GA.

Talmud of the Land of Israel Vol. IIIB: A Complete Outline of the Second, Third, & Fourth Divisions: The Division of Damages: Sanhedrin, Makkot, Shebuot & Abodah Zarah. Jacob Neusner. LC 96-3770. (South Florida Academic Commentary Ser.). 286p. (C). 1996. 89.95 (*0-7885-0231-X*, 243052) Scholars Pr GA.

Talmud of the Land of Israel, a Preliminary Translation & Explanation, Vol. 11: Shabbat. Ed. & Tr. by Jacob Neusner. (Chicago Studies in the History of Judaism). 524p. 1991. lib. bdg. 90.00 (*0-226-57670-1*) U Ch Pr.

Talmud of the Land of Israel, a Preliminary Translation & Explanation, Vol. 12: Erubin. Ed. & Tr. by Jacob Neusner. LC 90-10963. (Chicago Studies in the History of Judaism). 324p. 1990. lib. bdg. 60.00 (*0-226-57669-8*) U Ch Pr.

Talmud of the Land of Israel, a Preliminary Translation & Explanation, Vol. 4: Kilayim. Ed. & Tr. by Irving J. Mandelbaum. LC 90-10979. (Chicago Studies in the History of Judaism). (Illus.). 450p. 1991. lib. bdg. 90.00 (*0-226-57661-2*) U Ch Pr.

Talmud of the Land of Israel, Vol. 10: A Preliminary Translation & Explanation, Orlah & Bikkurim. Ed. & Tr. by Jacob Neusner from HEB. LC 90-20468. (Chicago Studies in the History of Judaism). 238p. 1991. lib. bdg. 46.00 (*0-226-57667-1*) U Ch Pr.

Talmud of the Land of Israel, Vol. 3: Demai. Ed. by Jacob Neusner. Tr. by Richard S. Sarason. LC 93-18738. (Chicago Studies in the History of Judaism). 440p. (C). 1993. lib. bdg. 65.00 (*0-226-57660-4*) U Ch Pr.

Talmud of the Land of Israel, Vol. 8: Maaser Sheni. Ed. by Jacob Neusner. Tr. by Roger Brooks. LC 92-25277. (Chicago Studies in the History of Judaism). 240p. (HEB.). (C). 1993. lib. bdg. 46.50 (*0-226-57665-5*) U Ch Pr.

Talmud, Pt. 6: Tractate Ketubot. Adin Steinsaltz. (Steinsaltz Ser.: Vol. 6). 1993. 50.00 (*0-679-42694-9*) Random.

Talmud, Steinsaltz Edition, Reference Guide. Adin Steinsaltz. 1996. pap. 25.00 (*0-679-77367-3*) Random.

***Talmud Torah.** Jacob Neusner. 1998. 12.00 (*0-614-27558-X*) UAHC.

Talmud Torah see Mitzvah of the Month

Talmud Unmasked. Prainatis. 1979. lib. bdg. 300.00 (*0-8490-3010-2*) Gordon Pr.

Talmudic & Rabbinical Chronology. Edgar Frank. 1978. 9.95 (*0-87306-050-4*) Feldheim.

Talmudic Anthology. Samuel Spitz. Ed. by Louis I. Newman. LC 45-9682. 1978. pap. text ed. 19.95 (*0-87441-303-6*) Behrman.

Talmudic Anthology in Three Volumes, 3 vols., Set. Ed. by Jacob Neusner. LC 95-41291. (Realms of Judaism Ser.: Bd. 52). 299p. 1995. 63.95 (*3-631-47131-9*) P Lang Pubng.

Talmudic Dialectics Vol. I: Types & Forms: Tractate Berakhot & the Divisions of Appointed Times & Women. Jacob Neusner. LC 95-39335. (South Florida Studies in the History of Judaism: No. 127). 385p. (C). 1995. 99.95 (*0-7885-0205-0*, 240127) Scholars Pr GA.

Talmudic Dialectics Vol. II: Types & Forms: The Divisions of Damages & Holy Things & Tractate Niddah. Jacob Neusner. LC 95-39335. (South Florida Studies in the History of Judaism: No. 128). 348p. (C). 1995. 99.95 (*0-7885-0206-9*, 240128) Scholars Pr GA.

***Talmudic Images.** Adin Steinsaltz. LC 97-9587. 1997. write for info. (*0-7657-9960-X*) Aronson.

Talmudic Law & the Modern State. Moshe Silberg. 1973. 9.00 (*0-8381-3112-3*) USCJE.

Talmudische Archaologie, 3 Vols., Set. Samuel Krauss. Ed. by Moses Finley. LC 79-4988. (Ancient Economic History Ser.). (Illus.). (GER.). 1979. reprint ed. lib. bdg. 189.95 (*0-405-12373-6*) Ayer.

Talmudische Archaologie, 3 Vols., Vol. 1. Samuel Krauss. Ed. by Moses Finley. LC 79-4988. (Ancient Economic History Ser.). (Illus.). (GER.). 1979. reprint ed. lib. bdg. 63.95 (*0-405-12374-4*) Ayer.

Talmudische Archaologie, 3 Vols., Vol. 2. Samuel Krauss. Ed. by Moses Finley. LC 79-4988. (Ancient Economic History Ser.). (Illus.). (GER.). 1979. reprint ed. lib. bdg. 63.95 (*0-405-12375-2*) Ayer.

Talmudische Archaologie, 3 Vols., Vol. 3. Samuel Krauss. Ed. by Moses Finley. LC 79-4988. (Ancient Economic History Ser.). (Illus.). (GER.). 1979. reprint ed. lib. bdg. 63.95 (*0-405-12376-0*) Ayer.

***Talmudische Okonomie Band I: Theorie und Praxis der Nationalokonomie Palastinas Zur Zeit der Mischna und Des Thalmuds Aufgrune Talmudischer Quellen.** Arye Ben-David. xii, 488p. (GER.). 1973. write for info. (*3-487-04655-5*) G Olms Pubs.

***Talon.** Juanita Kirk. 1996. mass mkt. 4.99 (*1-55197-037-6*, Pub. by Comnwlth Pub CN) Partners Pubs Grp.

Talons. John Peel. 224p. (Orig.). (YA). (gr. 6 up). 1993. pap. 3.50 (*0-671-79405-1*, Archway) PB.

Talons: North American Birds of Prey. Millie Miller & Cyndi Nelson. (Pocket Nature Guides Ser.). (Illus.). 1989. pap. 5.95 (*1-55566-035-5*) Johnson Bks.

Talons, Beaks & Jaws. Lynn M. Stone. LC 96-8999. (Animal Weapons Ser.). 1996. write for info. (*1-57103-166-9*) Rourke Pr.

Talons of Eagles. William W. Johnstone. 1996. mass mkt. 5.99 (*0-7860-0249-2*, Pinncle Kensgtn) Kensgtn Pub Corp.

Talons of the Eagle: Dynamics of U.S.-Latin American Relations. Peter H. Smith. (Illus.). 392p. (C). 1996. 35.00 (*0-19-508303-2*) OUP.

Talons of the Eagle: Dynamics of U.S.-Latin American Relations. Peter H. Smith. (Illus.). 392p. (C). 1996. pap. text ed. 19.95 (*0-19-508304-0*) OUP.

Talons Sheathed in Fur: A Demanding Selection of Animal Poems, Predators, Prey & Prisoners. (C). 1989. 45.00 (*1-871014-03-4*, Pub. by Desk Top Bks UK) St Mut.

Talos: Crossroads of the Galaxy. Richard Pace. 371p. (Orig.). 1992. mass mkt. 5.95 (*0-9632819-0-9*) RASP Pubns.

Taltos. Steven Brust. 1988. mass mkt. 5.50 (*0-441-18200-3*) Ace Bks.

Taltos. Anne O. Rice. 480p. 1995. pap. 14.00 (*0-345-39471-2*) Ballantine.

Taltos. Anne O. Rice. 1996. mass mkt. 6.99 (*0-345-40431-9*) Ballantine.

Taltos. Anne O. Rice. 1994. 25.00 (*0-679-42573-X*) Knopf.

Taltos. limited ed. Anne O. Rice. 467p. 1994. 150.00 (*0-9631925-1-5*) B E Trice.

Taluqdari Settlement in Oudh. Raj K. Sarvadhikari. 1986. reprint ed. 18.00 (*0-8364-1582-5*, Pub. by Usha II) S Asia.

Talwar. Robert Carter. 544p. (Orig.). 1995. pap. 5.99 (*0-451-17846-7*, Onyx) NAL-Dutton.

Talwar. Robert Carter. (Orig.). 1999. pap. 25.00 (*0-525-93713-7*) NAL-Dutton.

Tam Lin. Pamela Dean. 1992. mass mkt. 4.99 (*0-8125-4450-1*) Tor Bks.

Tam Lin. Illus. by Warwick Hutton. LC 90-5571. 32p. (J). (gr. k-4). 1991. lib. bdg. 14.95 (*0-689-50505-1*, McElderry) S&S Childrens.

Tam Lin. Jane Yolen. LC 88-2280. (Illus.). 32p. (J). (gr. 1-7). 1990. 15.00 (*0-15-284261-6*) HarBrace.

Tam Na Neve Dom: Roman V Stikhakh. Gandelsman Vladimir. LC 92-42336. 140p. (Orig.). (RUS.). 1993. pap. 9.00 (*1-55779-051-5*) Hermitage.

Tam O'Shanter: A Tale. limited ed. Robert Burns. (Illus.). (C). 1989. 100.00 (*0-948473-17-7*) St Mut.

Tam O'Shanter, an American Parallel. Robert Burns & William H. Olson. 27p. (Orig.). 1995. pap. 3.50 (*0-9640210-1-3*) Jackson Harbor.

Tam O'Shanter, an American Parallel. Robert Burns & William H. Olson. (Illus.). 27p. (Orig.). 1995. 12.99 (*0-9640210-3-X*) Jackson Harbor.

***Tama Mist.** Phil Beshears. 320p. (Orig.). 1998. mass mkt. 8.99 (*1-58006-017-X*, Crusades Pr) Sovereign.

Tamagno, Il Piu Grande Fenomeno Canoro Dell'novocento: Tamagno, the Greatest Singing Phenomenon of the Nineteenth Century. Mario Corsi. Ed. by Andrew Farkas. LC 76-29931. (Opera Biographies Ser.). (Illus.). (ITA.). 1977. reprint ed. lib. bdg. 26.95 (*0-405-09673-9*) Ayer.

Tamaka de Lempicka. Laura Claridge. 1998. write for info. (*0-517-70557-5*) Random.

***Tamales.** Mark Miller. 1997. 30.00 (*0-02-861327-9*) Macmillan.

Tamalpais Trails. 3rd ed. Barry Spitz. LC 89-8739. (Illus.). 336p. 1995. pap. 16.95 (*0-9620715-0-1*) Potrero Meadow Pub.

Tamang Family Research Project. Fricke Dahal. (C). 1991. text ed. 30.00 (*0-7855-0161-4*, Pub. by Ratna Pustak Bhandar) St Mut.

Tamango: Mateo Falcone et Autres Nouvelles. Prosper Merimee. (FRE.). 1983. pap. 10.95 (*0-7859-2983-5*) Fr & Eur.

Tamar. Ann Chamberlin. 448p. 1994. pap. 5.99 (*0-8125-2370-9*) Tor Bks.

***Tamar the Tender Twig.** Illus. by Jack Adams. 256p. (Orig.). (J). 1997. pap. 9.95 (*0-9620717-3-0*) Chalet Pub Co.

***Tamara.** John Krizanc. 1997. pap. text ed. 19.95 (*0-7737-5195-5*, Pub. by Stoddart Pubng CN) Genl Dist Srvs.

***Tamara: Memoirs of St. Petersburg, Paris, Oxford & Byzantium.** Tamara T. Rice. Ed. by Elizabeth T. Rice. (Illus.). 272p. 1996. 40.00 (*0-7195-5721-6*, Pub. by John Murray UK) Trafalgar.

Tamarack Tree. Patricia Clapp. LC 86-108. 224p. (YA). (gr. 7 up). 1986. 16.00 (*0-688-02852-7*) Lothrop.

Tamarack White, Orygun Seabee in War & Peace. Robert J. White. (Illus.). 270p. (Orig.). 1990. pap. 24.00 (*0-9618390-1-5*) R J White.

Tamara's Ecstasy. Sylvie F. Sommerfield. 1982. mass mkt. 3.50 (*0-89083-998-0*, Zebra Kensgtn) Kensgtn Pub Corp.

Tamarind & Mango Woman. Opal P. Adisa. 1993. per. 11.95 (*0-920813-71-2*, Pub. by Sister Vision CN) LPC InBook.

T

An Asterisk (*) at the beginning of an entry indicates that the title is appearing in BIP for the first time.

Tamarind Lithography Workshop Inc. Catalog Raisonne, 1960-1970. Intro. by Marjorie Devon & Peter Walch. (Illus.). 284p. (Orig.). 1989. pap. 45.00 (*0-944282-08-3*) UNM Art Mus.

Tamarind Tree. Romen Basu. 227p. 1976. 7.95 (*0-317-00324-0*, Pub. by Writers Wksp II) R Basu.

Tamarindo - The Tamarind Tree: Edicion Bilingue - Bilingual Edition. Maria Vega De Febles. LC 93-72196. (Coleccion Caniqui). 170p. (Orig.). (ENG & SPA.). 1993. pap. 16.00 (*0-89729-697-4*) Ediciones.

Tamarindo Puppy. Charlotte Pomerantz. LC 79-16584. (Illus.). 32p. (J). (ps up). 1993. 14.00 (*0-688-11902-6*); lib. bdg. 13.93 (*0-688-11903-4*) Greenwillow.

***Tamarisk.** large type ed. Claire Lorrimer. (Charnwood Large Print Ser.). 688p. 1996. 27.99 (*0-7089-8903-9*) Ulverscroft.

Tamar's Revenge: La Venganza de Tamar. De Molina. Ed. by Lyon. (Hispanic Classics Ser.). 1988. 49.95 (*0-85668-323-X*, Pub. by Aris & Phillips UK); pap. 22.00 (*0-85668-324-8*, Pub. by Aris & Phillips UK) David Brown.

Tamar's Son & Other Christmas Sonnets. Esther M. Leiper. 28p. 1987. pap. 3.95 (*0-9617284-2-6*) Sand & Silk.

Tamar's Sukkah. Ellie Gellman. LC 88-23388. (Illus.). 32p. (J). (ps-2). 1988. pap. 4.95 (*0-930494-79-2*) Kar-Ben.

Tamasha & Other Stories. Mansha Yad. (C). 1993. 25.00 (*81-207-1504-7*, Pub. by Sterling Pubs II) Apt Bks.

Tamasi Monografiaja. Laszlo L. Konnyu. LC 78-74527. (Monograph of the Hungarian Town of Tamasi). (Illus.). 1979. pap. 5.00 (*0-911862-05-6*) Hungarian Rev.

Tamata & the Alliance. Bernard Moitessier. Tr. by William Rodarmor. (Illus.). 400p. 1995. 30.00 (*0-924486-77-5*) Sheridan.

Tamazight of the Ayt Ndhir. Thomas G. Penchoen. LC 73-91702. (Afroasiatic Dialects Ser.: Vol. 1). (Illus.). 122p. 1973. pap. 20.00 (*0-89003-000-6*) Undena Pubns.

Tamazight Verb Stucture: A Generative Approach. Ernest T. Abdel-Massih. LC 72-633892. (African Ser.: Vol. 2). (Orig.). 1968. pap. text ed. 19.00 (*0-87750-160-2*) Res Inst Inner Asian Studies.

Tamazine. Edwin Harrington. LC 82-80349. (Illus.). 160p. (Orig.). (J). 1992. pap. 6.60 (*0-941066-02-9*) Hillside Pr.

Tambimuttu: Bridge Between Two Worlds. Ed. by Jane Williams. LC 89-81664. (Illus.). 256p. 9000. 50.00 (*0-7206-0718-3*, Pub. by P Owen Ltd UK) Dufour.

Tambo: Life in an Andean Village. Julia Meyerson. (Illus.). 297p. 1990. pap. 16.95 (*0-292-78078-8*); text ed. 30.00 (*0-292-78077-X*) U of Tex Pr.

Tambo & Bones: A History of the American Minstrel Stage. Carl F. Wittke. LC 69-10174. 269p. 1971. reprint ed. text ed. 47.50 (*0-8371-0276-6*, WIAM, Greenwood Pr) Greenwood.

Tambopata-Candamo-Rio Health Region of Southeastern Peru: A Biological Assessment. Robin B. Foster et al. 192p. 1995. pap. text ed. 19.95 (*1-881173-09-7*) U Ch Pr.

***Tambour Work.** Yusai Fukuyama. (Illus.). 120p. 1997. 25.00 (*0-916896-88-9*) Lacis Pubns.

Tambourina's Troubles. Shen Roddie & Maureen Roffey. (Pop-Up Storybook Ser.). (Illus.). 18p. (J). (ps-1). 1995. pap. 11.95 (*0-89577-674-X*) Rdrs Dgst Yng Fam.

Tambourine! The Happy Sound. 2nd ed. Tabourot. (Illus.). 102p. 1992. pap. 18.00 (*1-881428-06-0*) Tactus Pr.

Tambourine Interweave. Rosalie Barci. 150p. 1994. 6.95 (*0-9643777-0-5*) R G Barci.

Tambours de la Pluie. Ismail Kadare. 352p. (FRE.). 1979. pap. 11.95 (*0-7859-2424-8*, 2070371425) Fr & Eur.

***Tambov Oblast: Economy, Industry, Government, Business.** 2nd rev. ed. Russian Information & Business Center, Inc. Staff. (Russian Regional Business Directories Ser.). (Illus.). 200p. 1997. pap. 99.00 (*1-57751-416-5*) Russ Info & Busn Ctr.

Tamburlaine, Parts 1 & 2 see Complete Plays

Tamburlaine, Pt. I & Its Audience. Frank B. Fieler. LC 62-62580. (University of Florida Humanities Monographs: No. 8). 87p. reprint ed. pap. 25.00 (*0-7837-4989-9*, 2044656) Bks Demand.

Tamburlaine, Pt. 1 see Six Elizabethan Plays

Tamburlaine the Great. Christopher Marlowe. Ed. by J. S. Cunningham. LC 81-47596. (Revels Plays Ser.). 354p. (C). 1981. text ed. 34.50 (*0-8018-2669-1*) Johns Hopkins.

Tamburlaine the Great, 2 pts. Christopher Marlowe. Ed. by V. M. Ellis-Fermor. LC 66-23027. (Works & Life of Christopher Marlowe Ser.: Vol. 2). 321p. 1966. reprint ed. 50.00 (*0-87752-192-1*) Gordian.

Tamburlaine the Great, Parts I & II. Christopher Marlowe. Ed. by John D. Jump. LC 67-10666. (Regents Renaissance Drama Ser.). xxvi, 205p. (C). 1967. pap. text ed. 7.95 (*0-8032-5271-4*, Bison Books) U of Nebr Pr.

Tame Algebras & Integral Quadratic Forms. Claus M. Ringel. (Lecture Notes in Mathematics Ser.: Vol. 1099). xiii, 376p. 1985. 49.95 (*0-387-13905-2*) Spr-Verlag.

Tame Game: One Hundred Twenty-Eight Deer & Elk Recipes to Tame Your Wild Game. Steven H. Broom. LC 92-81420. (Illus.). 137p. (Orig.). 1992. pap. 14.95 (*0-9632946-0-1*) Teven Pr.

Tame My Wild Heart. Sylvie F. Sommerfield. 1984. mass mkt. 3.95 (*0-8217-1351-5*, Zebra Kensgtn) Kensgtn Pub Corp.

Tame That Phone! Controlling the Tyranny of the Telephone. Polly Bird. 192p. 1994. pap. 45.00 (*0-273-60330-2*, Pub. by Pitman Pubng UK) St Mut.

Tame the Wild Heart. F. Rosanne Bittner. 432p. 1996. mass mkt. 5.99 (*0-553-56996-1*, Fanfare) Bantam.

Tame the Wild Heart. Ellen T. Marsh. 448p. 1988. mass mkt. 3.95 (*0-380-75219-0*) Avon.

Tame the Wild Stallion. Jeanne Williams. LC 84-16257. (Chaparral Bks.). (Illus.). 182p. (J). (gr. 4 up). 1985. 14.95 (*0-87565-002-3*); pap. 8.95 (*0-87565-009-0*) Tex Christian.

***Tame the Wild Wind.** Roseanne Bittner. 1996. mass mkt. 5.99 (*0-614-20500-X*) Bantam.

Tame the Wildest Heart. Parris A. Bonds. 304p. 1994. mass mkt. 5.50 (*0-06-108178-7*, Harp PBks) HarpC.

Tame the Wind. Katherine Kilgore. 336p. 1993. mass mkt. 4.50 (*0-06-108182-5*, Harp PBks) HarpC.

Tame the Yeast Beast! Self-Help for Yeast Infections. Celina Poy-Wing. (All Women's Health in the 90s Ser.). (Illus.). 80p. (Orig.). 1994. pap. 4.95 (*0-9638783-0-1*) All Womens Hlth.

Tame Your Fears & Transform Them into Faith, Confidence & Action. Carol Kent. LC 93-33347. 216p. (Orig.). 1993. pap. 12.00 (*0-89109-760-0*) NavPress.

Tame Your Fears Discussion Guide. Carol Kent. LC 93-33347. 216p. (Orig.). 1993. pap. 6.00 (*0-89109-761-9*) NavPress.

***Tame Your Tongue! Learn English Using the Bible, Vol. 1.** Rosa M. Mosley. (Illus.). vii, 123p. (Orig.). 1997. pap. text ed. 25.00 (*0-9657229-0-2*) ROSAL Intl.

***Tamed Power: Germany in Europe.** Ed. by Peter J. Katzenstein. 328p. 1997. 49.95 (*0-8014-3429-7*) Cornell U Pr.

***Tamed Power: Germany in Europe.** Ed. by Peter J. Katzenstein. 328p. 1997. pap. 19.95 (*0-8014-8449-9*) Cornell U Pr.

Tamer of the Wild. large type ed. Max Brand. LC 95-30741. (Western Ser.). 381p. 1995. 19.95 (*0-7862-0529-6*) Thorndike Pr.

Tamerlane. Edward D. Sokol. 1977. 25.00 (*0-87291-093-8*) Coronado Pr.

Tamerlane. Dennis Wepman. (World Leaders - Past & Present Ser.). (Illus.). 112p. (YA). (gr. 5 up). 1987. lib. bdg. 19.95 (*0-87754-442-5*) Chelsea Hse.

Tamerlane the Earth Shaker. Harold Lamb. 1976. 26.95 (*0-8488-1072-4*) Amereon Ltd.

***Tamerlane's Tableware: A New Approach to Chinoiserie Ceramics of Fifteenth & Sixteenth Century Iran.** Ed. by Lisa Golombek et al. LC 96-35772. (Islamic Art & Architecture Ser.: Vol. 6). (Illus.). 296p. 1996. 65.00 (*1-56859-043-1*) Mazda Pubs.

Tami Knight Returns. Tami Knight. (Illus.). 36p. 1993. pap. 5.50 (*0-89732-117-0*) Menasha Ridge.

Tamieion Ton Tes Kaines Diathekes Lexeon. Carl H. Bruder. lii, 885p. 1975. reprint ed. 230.00 (*3-487-05894-4*) G Olms Pubs.

Tamika & the Wisdom Rings. Camille Yarbrough. LC 93-39477. (First Stepping Stone Bks.). (Illus.). 112p. (Orig.). (J). (gr. 1-4). 1995. pap. 3.99 (*0-679-82749-8*) Random Bks Yng Read.

Tamil. R. E. Asher. (Descriptive Grammars Ser.). 280p. 1986. 72.50 (*0-415-03682-8*) Routledge.

Tamil Asylum Diaspora: Sri Lankan Migration, Settlement & Politics in Switzerland. Christopher McDowell. LC 96-18377. (Refugee & Forced Migration Studies: Vol. 1). (Illus.). 288p. 1996. 59.95 (*1-57181-917-7*) Berghahn Bks.

Tamil-English Comprehensive Dictionary. 3rd rev. ed. M. Winslow. 974p. (ENG & TAM.). 1987. 34.75 (*81-206-0001-0*) IBD Ltd.

Tamil-English Dictionary. P. Percival. 297p. (ENG & TAM.). 1993. 21.95 (*0-7859-9810-1*) Fr & Eur.

Tamil-English Dictionary. Pillay. 731p. 1988. 24.50 (*81-206-0437-7*) IBD Ltd.

Tamil-English Dictionary. Pillay. 731p. (ENG & TAM.). 1988. 19.95 (*0-7859-7525-X*, 8120604377) Fr & Eur.

Tamil-English Dictionary. Miron Winslow. Ed. by Kalus L. Janert. xvi, 976p. 1978. reprint ed. text ed. 97.50 (*3-515-02703-3*) Coronet Bks.

Tamil for Beginners, 2 pts. Kausalya Hart. Incl. Pt. 1. Reading & Writing Pt. II. LC 92-42763. (Illus.). 160p. (Orig.). 1992. pap. text ed. 12.50 (*0-944613-18-7*); Pt. 2. Grammar Pt. I: Reading & Writing, a Textbook. LC 92-42763. 202p. 1992. pap. 12.50 (*0-944613-17-9*); LC 92-42763. 1992. Set pap. text ed. 20.00 (*0-614-16664-0*) UC Berkeley Ctrs SE Asia.

Tamil-French Dictionary: Vocabulaire Tamoul-Francais. M. Lap. (FRE & TAM.). 1984. 24.95 (*0-8288-1727-8*, F109490) Fr & Eur.

Tamil Literature. M. S. Pillai. (C). 1995. 24.00 (*81-206-0955-7*, Pub. by Asian Educ Servs II) S Asia.

Tamil Love Poetry & Poetics. Takanobu Takahashi. LC 94-48200. (Indological Library: Vol. 9). 1995. 95.25 (*90-04-10042-3*) E J Brill.

Tamil Nadu. Raghubir Singh. (Illus.). 144p. 1996. 45.00 (*1-881616-66-5*) Dist Art Pubs.

Tamil Nadu Economy. C. R. Kurien & Guhan. (C). 1988. 11.50 (*81-204-0321-5*, Pub. by Oxford IBH II) S Asia.

Tamil National Question & the Indo-Sri Lanka Accord. Ed. by N. Seevaratnam. ix, 246p. 1989. text ed. 27.95 (*81-220-0138-6*, Pub. by Konark Pubs Pvt Ltd II) Advent Bks Div.

Tamil Nedu Integrated Nutrition Program: A Review of the Project with Special Emphasis on the Monitoring & Information System. CFNPP Staff & Meera Shekar. (Working Papers). (C). 1991. pap. text ed. 7.00 (*1-56401-114-3*) Cornell Food.

Tamil Newspaper Reader. Sowhagyalakshmi Vaidyanathan & John D. Murphy. LC 89-85772. 434p. (ENG & TAM.). 1990. 49.00 (*0-931745-60-8*) Dunwoody Pr.

Tamil Newspaper Reader. Contrib. by Sowhagyalakshmi Vaidyanathan. (ENG & TAM.). 1990. audio 20.00 (*0-931745-61-6*) Dunwoody Pr.

Tamil Prose Reader. G. U. Pope. 124p. 1982. 19.00 (*0-88431-874-5*) IBD Ltd.

Tamil Prose Reader. G. U. Pope. 132p. 1986. reprint ed. 12.50 (*0-8364-1679-1*, Pub. by Abhinav II) S Asia.

Tamil Revivalism in the 1930's. Eugene F. Irschick. 372p. 1986. 32.00 (*0-8364-1918-9*, Pub. by Manohar II) S Asia.

Tamil Short Stories. Ka Naa Subramanyam. 202p. 1980. 9.50 (*0-685-21571-7*) Asia Bk Corp.

Tamil-Sinhalese Ethnic Conflict in Sri Lanka: A Case Study in Efforts to Negotiate a Settlement, 1983-1988. Marshall R. Singer. (Pew Case Studies in International Affairs). 50p. (C). 1994. pap. text ed. 3.50 (*1-56927-416-9*) Geo U Inst Dplmcy.

Tamil Studies. Srinivasa Aiyangar. (Illus.). 428p. 1986. reprint ed. 22.00 (*0-8364-1714-3*, Pub. by Abhinav II) S Asia.

Tamil Veda: Pillan's Interpretation of the Tiruvaymoli. John Carman & Vasudha Narayanan. 342p. 1989. pap. text ed. 24.00 (*0-226-09306-9*); lib. bdg. 60.00 (*0-226-09305-0*) U Ch Pr.

Tamil Veda of Tiruvalluvar see Sacred Kural

Tamilee Webb's Original Rubber Band Workout. Tamilee Webb. LC 85-40987. (Illus.). 144p. 1986. pap. 11.95 (*0-89480-056-6*, 1056) Workman Pub.

Tamilee Webb's Step Up Fitness Workout. Tamilee Webb. LC 94-18268. (Illus.). 160p. (Orig.). 1995. pap. 11.95 (*1-56305-491-4*, 3491) Workman Pub.

Taming. Jude Deveraux. Ed. by Linda Morrow. 1991. mass mkt. 5.99 (*0-671-74383-X*) PB.

Taming. large type ed. Jude Deveraux. (General Ser.). 382p. 1990. lib. bdg. 20.95 (*0-8161-4937-2*, GK Hall) Thorndike Pr.

Taming a Sea-Horse. Robert B. Parker, Jr. 250p. 1987. mass mkt. 6.50 (*0-440-18841-5*, Sey Lawr) Dell.

Taming a Tartar see Modern Mephistopheles

Taming a Tycoon. Leigh Michaels. (Romance Ser.). 1995. mass mkt. 2.99 (*0-373-03367-2*, 1-03367-9) Harlequin Bks.

Taming a Tycoon. large type ed. Leigh Michaels. 288p. 1996. 19.95 (*0-263-14669-3*, Thorndike Lrg Prnt) Thorndike Pr.

Taming Ancient Rivers of Greece. Jack Moore. 337p. 1981. 75.00 (*0-9507476-0-2*) St Mut.

Taming & Training African Grey Parrots. Risa Teitler. (Illus.). 96p. 1989. 9.95 (*0-86622-757-1*, KW-025) TFH Pubns.

Taming & Training Amazon Parrots. Risa Teitler. 1989. 9.95 (*0-86622-952-3*, KW-039) TFH Pubns.

Taming & Training Cockatiels. Risa Teitler. (Illus.). 128p. 1995. 9.95 (*0-7938-0585-6*, KW001) TFH Pubns.

Taming & Training Cockatoos. Risa Teitler. (Illus.). 96p. 1989. 9.95 (*0-86622-779-2*, KW-071) TFH Pubns.

Taming & Training Conures. Risa Teitler. (Illus.). 96p. 1981. 9.95 (*0-87666-842-2*, KW-139) TFH Pubns.

Taming & Training Lovebirds. Risa Teitler. 1989. 9.95 (*0-86622-986-8*, KW-038) TFH Pubns.

Taming & Training Your First Budgerigar. Risa Teitler. (Illus.). 96p. 1989. 9.95 (*0-86622-759-8*, KW-070) TFH Pubns.

Taming Armageddon? Revising the U. S. Russian Nuclear Relationship. Ed. by Alexei G. Arbatov & Steven E. Miller. (CSIA Studies in International Security: No. 8). (Illus.). 350p. 1997. 39.95 (*0-262-01149-2*) MIT Pr.

Taming Armageddon? Revising the U.S. - Russian Nuclear Relationship. Ed. by Alexei G. Arbatov & Steven E. Miller. (CSIA Studies in International Security: No. 8). (Illus.). 350p. 1997. pap. 17.95 (*0-262-51085-5*) MIT Pr.

Taming Asthma & Allergy by Controlling Your Environment: A Guide for Patients. Robert A. Wood. LC 94-79901. (Illus.). 164p. (Orig.). 1995. 14.95 (*0-9643272-0-1*) A & AFOA.

Taming C Plus Plus: Pattern Classes & Persistence for Large Projects. Jiri Soukup. (C). 1994. 48.50 (*0-201-52826-6*) Addison-Wesley.

Taming Charlotte. Linda Lael Miller. Ed. by Linda Marrow. 352p. 1993. mass mkt. 5.99 (*0-671-73754-6*, Pocket Star Bks) PB.

Taming City Hall: Rightsizing for Results. Gerald Seals. LC 94-30644. 1995. 29.95 (*1-55815-338-1*) ICS Pr.

Taming Democracy: Models of Political Rhetoric in Classical Athens. Harvey Yunis. LC 95-36535. (Rhetoric & Society Ser.). 336p. 1996. 49.95 (*0-8014-2770-3*); pap. 19.95 (*0-8014-8358-1*) Cornell U Pr.

Taming Eliza. Barbara Hazard. 1996. pap. 4.99 (*0-451-18203-0*, Sig) NAL-Dutton.

Taming Fire. (Voyages of Discovery Ser.). (Illus.). 48p. (J). (gr. 4-6). 1994. 19.95 (*0-590-47637-8*) Scholastic Inc.

Taming Jenna. Charlene Raddon. 416p. 1994. mass mkt. 4.50 (*0-8217-4604-9*, Zebra Kensgtn) Kensgtn Pub Corp.

Taming Kate. Eugenia Riley. 384p. (Orig.). 1992. mass mkt. 4.50 (*0-380-76475-X*) Avon.

Taming More Dragons: Another Collection of Creative Relaxation Activities for Home & School. Martha Belknap. (Illus.). 48p. 1994. pap. 9.00 (*0-9643459-1-9*) M Belknap.

Taming New Guinea. Charles A. Monckton. LC 75-35143. (Illus.). reprint ed. 28.50 (*0-404-14159-5*) AMS Pr.

Taming of Amelia. Maura Seger. (Historical Ser.). 1993. mass mkt. 3.99 (*0-373-28759-3*, 1-28759-8) Harlequin Bks.

Taming of Chance. Ian Hacking. 300p. (C). 1990. pap. text ed. 18.95 (*0-521-38884-8*) Cambridge U Pr.

Taming of Chance. Ian Hacking. 300p. (C). 1990. text ed. 59.95 (*0-521-38014-6*) Cambridge U Pr.

***Taming of Democracy: The Conservative Party 1880-1924.** Jeremy Smith. 128p. 1997. pap. 14.95 (*0-7083-1402-3*, Pub. by Univ Wales Pr UK) Paul & Co Pubs.

***Taming of Democracy: The Conservative Party 1880-1924.** Jeremy Smith. 128p. 1997. 35.00 (*0-7083-1434-1*, Pub. by Univ Wales Pr UK) Paul & Co Pubs.

Taming of Evolution: The Persistence of Non-Evolutionary Views in the Study of Humans. Davydd J. Greenwood. LC 84-45147. (Illus.). 232p. 1984. 39.95 (*0-8014-1743-0*) Cornell U Pr.

***Taming of Reid Donovan.** Pappano. 1997. mass mkt. 3.99 (*0-373-07824-2*) Harlequin Bks.

Taming of Roberta Parsley. Carol Gorman. LC 93-38312. (I Witness Ser.). (Illus.). 96p. (Orig.). (J). (gr. 4-7). 1994. pap. 4.99 (*0-570-04628-9*, 12-3209) Concordia.

Taming of Romanticism: European Literature & the Age of the Biedermeier. Virgil Nemoianu. (Studies in Comparative Literature: No. 37). 320p. 1984. 37.00 (*0-674-86802-1*) HUP.

Taming of Solitude: Separation Anxiety in Psychoanalysis. Jean-Michel Quinodoz. LC 93-9866. (New Library of Psychoanalysis: Vol. 20). 208p. (C). 1993. pap. 22.95 (*0-415-09154-3*); text ed. 69.95 (*0-415-09153-5*) Routledge.

Taming of the C. A. N. D. Y. Monster. rev. ed. Vicki Lansky. 156p. 1988. reprint ed. pap. 7.95 (*0-916773-07-8*); reprint ed. lib. bdg. 7.95 (*0-916773-08-6*) Book Peddlers.

Taming of the Frontier. Ed. by Duncan Aikman. LC 67-26711. (Essay Index Reprint Ser.). 1980. 31.95 (*0-8369-0141-X*) Ayer.

Taming of the Nations: A Study of the Cultural Bases of International Policy. F. S. Northrop. LC 86-28587. xvi, 362p. (C). 1987. reprint ed. 30.00 (*0-918024-45-5*); reprint ed. pap. 16.00 (*0-918024-46-3*) Ox Bow.

Taming of the Samurai: Honorific Individualism & the Making of Modern Japan. Eiko Ikegami. LC 94-36784. (Illus.). 448p. 1995. text ed. 45.00 (*0-674-86808-0*, IKETAM) HUP.

***Taming of the Samurai: Honorific Individualism & the Making of Modern Japan.** Eiko Ikegami. 1997. pap. text ed. 18.95 (*0-674-86809-9*) HUP.

Taming of the Screw: Several Million Homeowner's Problems. Dave Barry. LC 83-11205. (Illus.). 96p. (Orig.). 1983. pap. 8.95 (*0-87857-484-0*, 10-197-1) Rodale Pr Inc.

Taming of the Shrew. (Book Notes Ser.). 1985. pap. 3.95 (*0-8120-3544-5*) Barron.

Taming of the Shrew. Adapted by Charlotte Brown. (Illus.). 32p. (J). (gr. 5 up). 1987. pap. 3.25 (*0-88680-276-8*) I E Clark.

Taming of the Shrew. Dolan. 1996. pap. text ed. 6.00 (*0-312-10836-2*) St Martin.

***Taming of the Shrew.** Ed. by Roma Gill. (Oxford School Shakespeare Ser.). (C). 1994. text ed. 10.72 (*0-669-40354-7*) HM College Div.

Taming of the Shrew. Graham Holderness. 1991. text ed. 22.95 (*0-7190-2738-1*, Pub. by Manchester Univ Pr UK) St Martin.

Taming of the Shrew. Holt. (YA). 1989. student ed., pap. 10.50 (*0-03-032394-0*) HR&W Schl Div.

Taming of the Shrew. William Shakespeare. Ed. by Robert R. Heilman. 1966. pap. 3.95 (*0-451-52126-9*, Sig Classics) NAL-Dutton.

Taming of the Shrew. William Shakespeare. (BBC Television Plays Ser.). 1980. pap. 3.95 (*0-563-17873-6*, Pub. by BBC UK) Parkwest Pubns.

***Taming of the Shrew.** William Shakespeare. (English Text Ser.). 1981. pap. 9.95 (*0-415-02703-9*) Routledge.

Taming of the Shrew. William Shakespeare. Ed. by Brian Morris. LC 81-16785. 1981. text ed. 45.00 (*0-416-47580-9*, NO. 3590) Routledge Chapman & Hall.

Taming of the Shrew. William Shakespeare. Ed. by Brian Morris. LC 81-16785. 1982. pap. 8.95 (*0-416-17800-6*, NO. 3589) Routledge Chapman & Hall.

Taming of the Shrew. William Shakespeare. 320p. 1996. pap. 9.95 (*0-312-14203-X*) St Martin.

Taming of the Shrew. William Shakespeare. Ed. by Richard Hosley. (Pelican Shakespeare Ser.). 144p. 1964. pap. 4.95 (*0-14-071425-1*, Pelican Bks) Viking Penguin.

***Taming of the Shrew.** William Shakespeare. (Illustrated Classics Shakespeare Collection). 64p. 1994. pap. 4.95 (*0-7854-0812-6*, 40618) Am Guidance.

Taming of the Shrew. William Shakespeare. (Classics Ser.). 160p. 1988. 3.95 (*0-553-21306-7*, Bantam Classics) Bantam.

Taming of the Shrew. William Shakespeare. Ed. by Ann Thompson. (New Cambridge Shakespeare Ser.). (Illus.). 204p. 1984. text ed. 39.95 (*0-521-22195-1*); pap. text ed. 10.95 (*0-521-29388-X*) Cambridge U Pr.

Taming of the Shrew. William Shakespeare. Ed. by Michael Fynes-Clinton & Perry Mills. (Cambridge School Shakespeare Ser.). (Illus.). 192p. (YA). (gr. 5 up). 1992. pap. text ed. 7.95 (*0-521-42505-0*) Cambridge U Pr.

Taming of the Shrew. William Shakespeare & Luella E. McMahon. 1969. 3.00 (*0-87129-555-5*, T12) Dramatic Pub.

Taming of the Shrew. William Shakespeare. Ed. by H. J. Oliver. (Oxford English Text Ser.). 254p. 1982. 58.00 (*0-19-812907-6*) OUP.

Taming of the Shrew. William Shakespeare. Ed. by H. J. Oliver. (Oxford English Text Ser.). 254p. 1984. pap. 7.95 (*0-19-281440-0*) OUP.

Taming of the Shrew. William Shakespeare. Ed. by Paul Werstine & Barbara A. Mowat. (New Folger Library). 1992. pap. 3.99 (*0-671-72289-1*, Folger Lib) PB.

Taming of the Shrew. William Shakespeare. Ed. by G. R. Hibbard. (New Penguin Shakespeare Ser.). 256p. 1981. pap. 5.95 (*0-14-070710-7*, Penguin Classics) Viking Penguin.

Taming of the Shrew. William Shakespeare. Ed. by Stevie Davies. (Penguin Critical Studies). 128p. 1995. pap. 8.95 (*0-14-077271-5*, Penguin Bks) Viking Penguin.

***Taming of the Shrew.** William Shakespeare. LC 97-6768. (Thrift Editions Ser.). 1997. pap. write for info. (*0-486-29765-9*) Dover.

An Asterisk (*) at the beginning of an entry indicates that the title is appearing in BIP for the first time.

*__Taming of the Shrew.__ William Shakespeare. (English Ser.). (C). Date not set. pap. 9.95 (0-17-443534-7) Wadsworth Pub.

Taming of the Shrew. large type ed. William Shakespeare. 1992. pap. 24.95 (0-7089-4508-2, Trail West Pubs) Ulverscroft.

Taming of the Shrew. rev. ed. William Shakespeare. Ed. by Roma Gill. (Oxford School Shakespeare Ser.). (Illus.). 144p. (YA). (gr. 9-11). 1993. pap. 7.50 (0-19-831976-2) OUP.

*__Taming of the Shrew.__ 3rd ed. William Shakespeare. (English Ser.). (C). Date not set. text ed. 45.00 (0-17-443567-3) Wadsworth Pub.

Taming of the Shrew. LC 79-133743. (Tudor Facsimile Texts. Old English Plays Ser.: No. 69). reprint ed. 49.50 (0-404-53369-8) AMS Pr.

Taming of the Shrew: A Comparative Study of Oral & Literary Versions. Jan H. Brunvand. LC 90-39612. (Folklore Library: Vol. 5). 298p. 1991. text ed. 64.00 (0-8240-7149-2, 1289) Garland.

Taming of the Shrew: A Play Packet to Accompany Elementary, My Dear Shakespeare. Barbara Engen & Joy Campbell. (Illus.). 36p. 1989. teacher ed. 8.95 (0-922947-03-1) Mkt Masters.

Taming of the Shrew: An Annotated Bibliography, Vol. 21. Nancy L. Harvey. LC 94-6493. (Shakespeare Criticism Ser.). 328p. 1994. text ed. 52.00 (0-8240-8892-1, H523) Garland.

Taming of the Shrew for Young People. William Shakespeare. Ed. by Diane Davidson. LC 86-5934. (Shakespeare for Young People Ser.: Vol. 3). (Illus.). 64p. (J). (gr. 5-8). 1986. pap. 5.95 (0-934048-20-7) Swan Books.

Taming of the Shrew Notes. L. L. Hillegass. (Cliffs Notes Ser.). 1971. pap. 3.75 (0-8220-0081-4) Cliffs.

*__Taming of the Shrew Readalong.__ William Shakespeare. (Illustrated Classics Shakespeare Collection). 64p. 1994. pap. 14.95 incl. audio (0-7854-0828-2, 40620) Am Guidance.

Taming of the Text: Explorations in Language, Literature & Culture. Ed. by Willie Van Peer. 328p. (C). 1988. lib. bdg. 59.95 (0-415-01309-7) Routledge.

Taming of the Troops: Social Control in the United States Army. Lawrence B. Radine. LC 76-5262. (Contributions in Sociology Ser.: No. 22). 276p. (Orig.). 1977. text ed. 59.95 (0-8371-8911-X, RTT/, Greenwood Pr) Greenwood.

*__Taming of the True.__ Neil Tennant. (Illus.). 480p. 1997. 49.95 (0-19-823717-0) OUP.

Taming of the West: Age of the Gunfighter. Joseph G. Rosa. (Illus.). 192p. 1993. 24.95 (0-8317-0381-4) North South Trader.

Taming of the Wilderness in Northern New York: Wm. C. Pierrepont's 1826 Journal. Inez B. McConnell. (The/Piereepont Journals). 86p. 1993. pap. 10.00 (1-886303-03-7) Write to Print.

Taming of Tofu. Kerri B. Williamson. (Cookbook Ser.). 111p. 1991. pap. 9.99 (0-8163-1027-0) Pacific Pr Pub Assn.

Taming Our Monkey Mind: Insight, Detachment, Identity. Phyllis Krystal. LC 93-42842. 187p. (Orig.). 1994. pap. 12.95 (0-87728-793-7) Weiser.

Taming Paper Tiger. 2nd ed. Barbara Hemphill. LC 96-39192. 1997. pap. 13.00 (0-8129-2836-9) Random.

Taming Philippine Headhunters: A Study of Government & of Cultural Change in Northern Luzon. Felix M. Keesing. LC 77-86953. (Ethnology-South East Asia Ser.). (Illus.). (C). 1984. reprint ed. 31.50 (0-404-16747-0) AMS Pr.

Taming the Atom. Von. 1995. pap. 15.00 (0-679-76534-4) Random.

Taming the Atom. Hans C. Von Baeyer. 1992. 23.00 (0-679-40039-7) Random.

Taming the Atom: Facing the Future with Nuclear Power. fac. ed. Ian M. Blair. LC 83-124844. (Illus.). 257p. 1983. reprint ed. pap. 73.30 (0-7837-7993-3, 2047749) Bks Demand.

Taming the Bear: How to Invest in Stocks Without Getting Eaten Alive. Thomas D. Saler. LC 93-42696. (Business Book). (Illus.). 240p. 1994. pap. 12.95 (1-56440-368-8) Globe Pequot.

Taming the Beast: An Alternative Twelve-Step Process of Regeneration from Addictions. Henry Herlong & Rita Herlong. LC 94-96623. 544p. (Orig.). 1995. pap. 26.00 (0-9643802-3-4) Beast Haven.

Taming the Blue. Marge Van Galder. 106p. 11.95 (0-614-13202-9, 21-13563) EAA Aviation.

Taming the Buck. William Pettus Buck. 1979. 1.98 (0-934530-02-5) Buck Pub.

Taming the Bureaucracy: Muscles, Prayers & Other Strategies. W. T. Gormley, Jr. 256p. 1989. text ed. 39.50 (0-691-07806-8) Princeton U Pr.

*__Taming the Chaos: English Poetic Diction Theory Since the Renaissance.__ Emerson R. Marks. 432p. (C). 1998. text ed. 39.95 (0-8143-2698-6) Wayne St U Pr.

Taming the Criminal: Adventures in Penology. John L. Gillin. LC 69-14927. (Criminology, Law Enforcement, & Social Problems Ser.: No. 71). (Illus.). 1969. reprint ed. 22.00 (0-87585-071-5) Patterson Smith.

Taming the Diet Dragon: Using Language & Imagery for Weight Control & Body Transformation. 2nd ed. Constance C. Kirk. LC 92-727. 256p. 1994. mass mkt. 4.99 (1-56718-383-2) Llewellyn Pubns.

*__Taming the Donkeyphant.__ Betty J. Erb. LC 96-86702. 64p. (Orig.). 1996. pap. 7.95 (1-56167-340-4) Am Literary Pr.

Taming the Dragon: Transforming Economic Institutions in the Face of Global Change, Vol. 5. Carlo C. Jaeger. (International Studies in Global Change). 320p. 1994. text ed. 48.00 (2-88124-638-9); pap. text ed. 20.00 (2-88124-637-0) Gordon & Breach.

Taming the Dragon - Module One: Learning to Benefit from Feelings. Helen L. Webster & Lorraine Parker. (Illus.). 240p. 1994. teacher ed., spiral bd. 21.95 (1-55059-078-2, Pub. by Detselig CN) Temeron Bks.

Taming the Dragon in Your Child: Solutions for Breaking the Cycle of Family Anger. Meg Eastman & Sydney C. Rozen. 227p. 1994. pap. text ed. 15.95 (0-471-59405-9) Wiley.

*__Taming the Dragon in Your Child: Solutions for Breaking the Cycle of Family Anger.__ Meg Eastman. 1997. pap. text ed. 5.99 (0-471-17692-3) Wiley.

Taming the Dragons: Real Help for Real School Problems. Susan Setley. Ed. by Judith S. Wright. LC 94-92425. (Illus.). (Orig.). 1995. pap. 23.00 (1-886243-04-2) Starfish Pubng.

Taming the Ego. Adnan Sarhan. 88p. 1991. pap. 5.00 (1-884328-03-2) Sufi Fnd Amer.

*__Taming the Electronic Babysitter: A Guide to Children's Videos for Parents & Caregivers.__ LC 96-52614. 1997. write for info. (1-57895-005-8) Bridge Resources.

Taming the Future: A Revolutionary Breakthrough in Scientific Forecasting. (Illus.). 1991. write for info. (1-880014-01-7) Contextured Web.

Taming the Great South Land: A History of the Conquest of Nature in Australia. William J. Lines. 1992. 32.50 (0-520-07830-6) U CA Pr.

Taming the HP 3000, Vol. 1: Over 101 Ways to Monitor, Manage, & Maximize System Performance on the Hewlett-Packard 3000. Robert A. Lund. LC 87-92025. 142p. (Orig.). (C). 1990. pap. text ed. 49.95 (0-945325-01-0) Perf Pr OR.

Taming the HP 3000, Vol. 2: The Theory & Practice of Successful Performance Management for Hewlett-Packard HP 3000 Computer Systems. Robert A. Lund. LC 87-92025. 282p. (C). 1992. text ed. 99.95 (0-945325-02-9); pap. text ed. 79.95 (0-945325-03-7) Perf Pr OR.

Taming the IEP: A Handbook for Parents, 6 packets. David O. Krantz. 44p. (Orig.). 1996. pap. 25.00 (1-57035-066-3, 80TAME) Sopris.

Taming the Land. unabridged ed. VeraLee Wiggins. (Young Reader's Christian Library). (Illus.). 224p. (J). (gr. 3-7). 1996. pap. text ed. 1.39 (1-55748-774-X) Barbour & Co.

Taming the Lawyers. Ken Menendez. 305p. 1996. pap. 19.95 (1-56343-133-5) Merritt Pub.

Taming the Lions in Your Life. Les Morgan. LC 91-58677. 160p. (Orig.). (YA). (gr. 8-12). 1992. pap. 6.99 (0-87509-479-1) Chr Pubns.

Taming the Lions in Your Life: Here's a Hero - Daniel. 3rd ed. Douglass B. Wright et al. 677p. 1992. text ed. 150.00 (1-878698-07-9) Atlantic Law.

Taming the Marketing Jungle: Marketing When Your Creativity Is High, & Your Budget Is Low. Silvana Clark. LC 94-78210. 112p. (Orig.). 1994. pap. 6.95 (1-883697-78-6) Hara Pub.

Taming the Money Monster. Ron Blue. LC 93-10563. 1993. pap. 9.99 (1-56179-168-7) Focus Family.

Taming the Monkey Mind. Thubten Chodron. 198p. 1995. pap. 9.95 (1-871948-55-X) Heian Intl.

Taming the Nueces Strip: The Story of McNelly's Rangers. George Durham. (Illus.). 198p. 1962. pap. 9.95 (0-292-78048-6) U of Tex Pr.

Taming the Office Tiger: The Complete Guide to Getting Organized at Work. Barbara Hemphill. 170p. 1995. pap. 13.00 (0-8129-2712-5, Times Business) Kiplinger Bks.

Taming the Prince: The Ambivalence of Modern Executive Power. Harvey C. Mansfield, Jr. 310p. 1989. 32.95 (0-02-919980-8, Free Press) Free Pr.

Taming the Prince: The Ambivalence of Modern Executive Power. Harvey C. Mansfield, Jr. LC 92-31982. 384p. 1993. reprint ed. pap. 16.95 (0-8018-4589-0) Johns Hopkins.

*__Taming the Recess Jungle.__ Carol Gray. 33p. (Orig.). 1993. pap. 8.95 (1-885477-21-X) Fut Horizons.

*__Taming the Scorpion: Preparing American Business for the Third Millennium.__ William C. Jeffries. 336p. Date not set. pap. 25.00 (1-57087-287-2) Prof Pr NC.

Taming the Star Runner. S. E. Hinton. 192p. (YA). (gr. 7 up). 1989. mass mkt. 4.50 (0-440-20479-8, LLL BDD) BDD Bks Young Read.

*__Taming the Storm: The Life & Times of Judge Frank M. Johnson, Jr. & the South's Fight over Civil Rights.__ unabridged ed. Jack Bass. 470p. 1993. write for info. (0-614-19145-9) Hurricane Hse.

Taming the System: The Control of Discretion in Criminal Justice, 1950-1990. Samuel E. Walker. 224p. 1993. 39.95 (0-19-507820-9) OUP.

Taming the Taildragger. 5th ed. John F. Ball. 107p. 1994. pap. 9.95 (0-929214-06-4, Goldstr Enter) Goldstar Enterprises.

Taming the Tiger: Tibetan Teachings on Right Conduct, Mindfulness & Universal Compassion. Akong T. Rinpoche. (Illus.). 188p. 1996. pap. 12.95 (0-89281-569-8) Inner Tradit.

Taming the Tornado Tube: 50 Weird & Wacky Things to Do with a Tornado Tube. Steve Spangler. (Illus.). 96p. (Orig.). (J). (gr. 3-8). 1995. pap. text ed. 9.95 (0-9649353-1-7) Wren Pubng.

*__Taming the Tyrant.__ Dean Schuyler. LC 97-20532. 1998. 32.00 (0-393-70257-X) Norton.

*__Taming the Vernacular: From Dialect to Written Standard Language.__ Jenny Cheshire & Dieter Stein. LC 97-8801. 1997. write for info. (0-582-29808-3); pap. write for info. (0-582-29809-1) Longman.

Taming the Wild Man. Camp. 1995. pap. 3.50 (0-373-16598-6) Harlequin Bks.

Taming the Wild Mushroom: A Culinary Guide to Market Foraging. Arleen R. Bessette & Alan E. Bessette. LC 92-32991. (Illus.). 125p. (Orig.). 1993. 24.95 (0-292-70798-3) U of Tex Pr.

*__Taming the Wild Mushroom: A Culinary Guide to Market Foraging.__ Arleen R. Bessette & Alan E. Bessette. (Illus.). 125p. (Orig.). 1997. pap. 16.95 (0-292-70856-4) U of Tex Pr.

Taming the Wild Pendulum. Judith L. Powell & Tag Powell. Ed. by Yvonne Fawcett. LC 94-11030. (Illus.). 208p. (Orig.). 1995. pap. 19.95 (1-56087-057-5) Top Mtn Pub.

Taming the Wild Tube: A Family's Guide to Television & Video. Robert L. Schrag. LC 89-35663. (Illus.). 181p. 1990. reprint ed. pap. 51.60 (0-608-00200-3, 2060983) Bks Demand.

Taming the Wind of Desire: Psychology, Medicine, & Aesthetics in Malay Shamanistic Performance. Carol Laderman. LC 90-38031. (Comparative Studies of Health Systems & Medical Care: Vol. 29). (Illus.). 386p. 1991. 45.00 (0-520-06916-1); pap. 16.95 (0-520-08258-3) U CA Pr.

Taming the Wolf. Simmons. 1995. mass mkt. 4.50 (0-373-28884-0) Harlequin Bks.

Taming the Wolf: Full Moon Meditations. Steve Hounsome. (Illus.). 168p. (Orig.). 1995. pap. 19.95 (1-898307-37-7) Holmes Pub.

Taming the Yellow River - Silt & Floods: Proceedings of a Bilateral Seminar on Problems in the Lower Reaches of the Yellow River, China. Ed. by Lucien M. Brush et al. (C). 1989. lib. bdg. 348.50 (0-7923-0416-0) Kluwer Ac.

Taming Your Dragons: A Collection of Creative Relaxation Activities for Home & School. Martha Belknap. (Illus.). 44p. 1994. pap. 9.00 (0-9643459-0-0) M Belknap.

*__Taming Your Ego.__ Wayne Dyer. mass mkt. write for info. (0-06-109268-1, Harp PBks) HarpC.

Taming Your Gremlin: A Guide to Enjoying Yourself. Richard D. Carson. LC 86-45310. (Illus.). 128p. 1986. reprint ed. pap. 11.00 (0-06-096102-3, PL/6102, PL) HarpC.

Taming Your Personal Finances with Quicken 4 for Windows. Sharon Crawford. LC 94-61358. 285p. 1994. pap. 16.99 (0-7821-1610-8) Sybex.

Taminy. Maya K. Bohnhoff. (Fantasy Ser.). 416p. 1993. mass mkt. 4.99 (0-671-72174-7) Baen Bks.

Tammany Hall. Morris R. Werner. LC 69-14145. 586p. 1970. reprint ed. text ed. 38.50 (0-8371-0746-6, WETH, Greenwood Pr) Greenwood.

Tammany Hall & the New Immigrants: The Progressive Years. Thomas M. Henderson. LC 76-6347. (Irish Americans Ser.). (Illus.). 1976. 26.95 (0-405-09341-1) Ayer.

Tammarnlit (Mistakes) Inuit Relocation in the Eastern Arctic, 1939-63. Frank Tester & Peter Kulchyski. 421p. 1994. pap. 24.95 (0-7748-0494-7, Pub. by U BC Pr) U of Wash Pr.

Tammuz & Ishtar. Stephen H. Langdon. LC 78-72750. (Ancient Mesopotamian Texts & Studies). reprint ed. 34.50 (0-404-18193-7) AMS Pr.

*__Tammy & Her Family of Dolls.__ John Axe. (Illus.). 128p. 1996. pap. 14.95 (0-87588-433-4, H4857) Hobby Hse.

Tammy Turtle: A Tale of Saving Sea Turtles. Suzanne Tate. LC 91-67275. (Suzanne Tate's Nature Ser.: No. 11). (Illus.). 28p. (Orig.). (J). (gr. k-4). 1991. pap. 3.95 (1-878405-05-5) Nags Head Art.

Tammy Wynette Southern Cookbook. Tammy Wynette. LC 89-16112. (Illus.). 224p. 1990. 17.95 (0-88289-734-9) Pelican.

Tammy's Smile. Sharon Otis & Lois Walker. (Illus.). (Orig.). (J). (ps-7). 1985. student ed. 6.00 (0-9617737-0-7) Total Lrn.

*__Tamoanchan, Tlalocan: Places of Mist.__ Alfredo L. Austin. Tr. by Thelma Ortiz De Montellano & Bernard R. Ortiz De Montellano. LC 96-53289. (Mesoamerican Worlds Ser.). (Illus.). 440p. 1997. 49.95 (0-87081-445-1) Univ Pr Colo.

Tamotzu in Haiku. Harriet Kimbro. LC 77-10844. (Illus.). 1977. pap. 4.95 (0-913270-78-4) Sunstone Pr.

*__Tamoxifen: A Guide for Clinicians & Patients.__ Ed. by V. Craig Jordan. 200p. 1996. write for info. (0-9641823-4-3) PRR.

Tamoxifen: Beyond the Antiestrogen. Ed. by John A. Kellen. 392p. 1996. 94.50 (0-8176-3842-3); write for info. (3-7643-3842-3) Birkhauser.

*__Tamoxifen: Index of New Information Involving Health Dangers, Risks, Adverse Reactions & Body Damage Treatments with Authors, Subjects & References.__ Jackson J. Tiller. 150p. 1996. 47.50 (0-7883-1232-4); pap. 44.50 (0-7883-1233-2) ABBE Pubs Assn.

*__Tamoxifen: Index of New Information with Authors, Subjects, Research Categories & References.__ Jackson J. Tiller. 150p. 1996. 47.50 (0-7883-1230-8); pap. 44.50 (0-7883-1231-6) ABBE Pubs Assn.

Tamoxifen & Breast Cancer. Michael W. DeGregorio & Valerie J. Wiebe. LC 93-43148. (Illus.). 136p. (C). 1994. 27.50 (0-300-05907-8); pap. 12.00 (0-300-05992-2) Yale U Pr.

Tamoxifen, Molecular Basis of Use in Cancer Treatment & Prevention. Helen Wiseman. LC 94-18163. 250p. 1994. text ed. 59.95 (0-471-94316-9) Wiley.

Tamoxifen Papers. Hazel Cunningham. (Orig.). 1995. pap. 9.95 (0-9643829-2-X) Blue-Green Delta.

Tampa: A Pictorial History. Hampton Dunn. Ed. by Nancy Morgan. LC 85-4450. (Portrait of American Cities Ser.). (Illus.). 224p. 1985. pap. 14.95 (0-89865-409-2) Donning Co.

Tampa Bay - Days of Long Ago. 3rd ed. Kenneth W. Mulder. Ed. by Sandra Mulder. (Illus.). 24p. 1990. 5.00 (1-889034-02-9) Mulder Ent.

Tampa Bay Buccaneers. Bob Italia. LC 95-36979. (Inside the NFL Ser.). (J). 1996. lib. bdg. 15.98 (1-56239-529-7) Abdo & Dghtrs.

Tampa Bay Buccaneers. Richard Rambeck. (NFL Today Ser.). (Illus.). 48p. (J). (gr. 4-12). 1991. lib. bdg. 14.95 (0-88682-385-4) Creative Ed.

Tampa Bay Buccaneers. 2nd rev. ed. Michael Goodman. (NFL Today Ser.). (Illus.). 32p. (J). (gr. 4-8). 1996. lib. bdg. 14.95 (0-88682-808-2) Creative Ed.

Tampa Bay Lightning. Jeff Babineau. LC 94-4305. (NHL Today Ser.). 32p. (J). (gr. 3 up). 1995. lib. bdg. 15.95 (0-88682-688-8) Creative Ed.

Tampa Dine-a-Mate. 256p. 1994. pap. 25.00 (1-57393-010-5) Dine-A-Mate.

*__Tampa Dine-a-Mate Book.__ 256p. 1996. pap. text ed. 30.00 (1-57393-062-8) Dine-A-Mate.

Tampa Treasures. Junior League of Tampa, Inc., Staff. (Illus.). 340p. 1992. 19.95 (0-9609556-2-3) Jr Leag Tampa.

*__Tampa Triangle Dead Zone.__ Bill Miller & Mary F. Miller. LC 96-35590. (Illus.). 208p. 1996. reprint ed. pap. 14.95 (0-9624019-7-8) Ticket Adventure.

Tamper Resistant Packaging: What's Ahead? Business Communications Co., Inc. Staff. 194p. 1984. pap. 1,500.00 (0-89336-394-4, GB-067) BCC.

Tampons & Other Catamenial Receptors. M. H. Gutcho. LC 79-84431. (Chemical Technology Review Ser.: No. 129). (Illus.). 294p. 1979. 39.00 (0-8155-0753-4) Noyes.

Tam's Slipper: A Story from Vietnam. Janet Palazzo-Craig. (First-Start Legends Ser.). (Illus.). 32p. (Orig.). (J). (gr. k-2). 1997. pap. 4.95 (0-8167-4000-3) Troll Communs.

Tamsen Donner: A Woman's Journey. Ruth Whitman. LC 77-90508. 75p. 1977. pap. 9.95 (0-914086-20-0) Alicejamesbooks.

*__Tamworth, New Hampshire Narrative.__ Marjorie G. Harkness. (Illus.). 336p. 1996. reprint ed. lib. bdg. 42.50 (0-8328-5211-2) Higginson Bk Co.

Tan & Sandy Silence. John D. MacDonald. 1996. mass mkt. 5.99 (0-449-22476-7, Crest) Fawcett.

Tan & Sandy Silence. John D. MacDonald. 256p. 1986. mass mkt. 4.95 (0-449-13250-1) Fawcett.

*__Tan Can.__ (Get Ready...Get Set...Read! Ser.: Set 2). (J). lib. bdg. 11.95 (1-56674-137-8) Forest Hse.

Tan Can. Gina C. Erickson & Kelli C. Foster. (Get Ready... Get Set...Read! Ser.). (Illus.). 24p. (J). 1992. pap. 3.50 (0-8120-4856-3) Barron.

Tan Chanteuse. Carole B. Weatherford. (Harperprints Chapbook Ser.). 24p. 1995. 5.00 (1-883314-04-6) NC Writers Network.

Tan-Gun & To-San of Tae Kwon Do Hyung. Jhoon Rhee. LC 71-150320. (Korean Arts Ser.). (Illus.). 1971. pap. text ed. 16.95 (0-89750-001-6, 106) Ohara Pubns.

Tan Kah-Kee: The Making of an Overseas Chinese Legend. C. F. Fong. 444p. 1990. text ed. 18.00 (0-9625118-3-8); pap. text ed. 15.00 (0-9625118-4-6) World Scientific Pub.

*__Tan Phu: Special Forces Team A-23 in Combat.__ Leigh Wade. 1997. mass mkt. 5.99 (0-8041-1616-4) Ivy Books.

Tan Solo Hombres. Pedro Lain Entralgo. (Nueva Austral Ser.: Vol. 250). (SPA.). 1991. pap. text ed. 24.95 (84-239-7250-X) Elliots Bks.

Tan Ssu-Tung, 1865-1898: Life & Thought of a Reformer. Luke S. Kwong. (Sinica Leidensia Ser.: Vol. 36). 1996. 97.00 (90-04-10471-2) E J Brill.

Tan Student Activity Book. Debbie Strayer & Susan S. Simpson. (Learning Language Arts Through Literature Ser.). 171p. 1992. 16.00 (1-880892-28-6) Com Sense FL.

Tan Vat. William G. Merrick. LC 93-83571. 124p. (Orig.). 1992. pap. 8.50 (0-9635951-0-5) Piedmont Coll.

Tan Your Hide: Home Tanning Leathers & Furs. Phyllis Hobson. LC 77-2593. (Illus.). 144p. 1977. pap. 9.95 (0-88266-101-9, Garden Way Pub) Storey Comm Inc.

Tana & the Artist Lady: Adventure Stories from Highlights. Highlights for Children Editors. 96p. (J). 1996. pap. text ed. 3.95 (1-56397-587-4) Boyds Mills Pr.

Tana Hoban's Red, Blue, Yellow Shoe. Tana Hoban. (Illus.). 8p. (J). (ps up). 1994. pap. 3.95 (0-688-13492-0, Tupelo Bks) Morrow.

Tana Hoban's What Is It? Tana Hoban. (Illus.). 8p. (J). (ps up). 1994. pap. 3.95 (0-688-13493-9, Tupelo Bks) Morrow.

Tanagrafiguren: Untersuchengen zur hellenistischen Kunst und Geschichte. Gerhard Kleiner. (Illus.). 368p. 1983. 152.35 (3-11-008982-3) De Gruyter.

Tanagran Studies, No. I: Sources & Documents on Tanagra in Boiotia. Duane Roller. (McGill University Monographs in Classical Archaeology & History: Vol. 9.1). xii, 173p. 1989. 50.00 (90-5063-030-8, Pub. by Gieben NE) Benjamins North Am.

Tanagran Studies, No. II: The Prosopography of Tanagra in Boiotia. Duane Roller. (McGill University Monographs in Classical Archaeology & History: Vol. 9.2). 122p. 1989. 47.00 (90-5063-031-6, Pub. by Gieben NE) Benjamins North Am.

Tanah Air Kita: A Book of the Country & People of Indonesia. 2nd ed. Niels A. Douwes Dekker. LC 77-86970. reprint ed. 46.00 (0-404-16705-5) AMS Pr.

Tanaina Tales from Alaska. Bill Vaudrin. LC 69-16717. (Civilization of the American Indian Ser.: Vol. 96). 133p. 1981. pap. 10.95 (0-8061-1414-2) U of Okla Pr.

*__Tanaiste.__ Don T. Phelan. 1994. mass mkt. 5.99 (1-896320-33-3, Pub. by Comnwlth Pub CN) Partners Pubs Grp.

Tanala, a Hill Tribe of Madagascar. Ralph Linton. (Chicago Field Museum of Natural History Fieldiana Anthropology Ser.). 1974. 40.00 (0-527-01882-1) Periodicals Srv.

Tanana Basin. Alaska Geographic Staff. Ed. by Penny Rennick. LC 72-92087. (Alaska Geographic Ser.: Vol. 16, No. 3). (Illus.). 96p. (Orig.). 1989. pap. 19.95 (0-88240-190-4) Alaska Geog Soc.

*__Tanana Valley Railroad: The Gold Dust Line - Alaska.__ Nicholas Deely. 161p. 1996. pap. text ed. 50.00 (0-9648669-1-9) Denali Desgns.

Tanaquil: The Hardest Thing of All. deluxe ed. Donald Windham. 1972. 250.00 (0-917366-02-6) S Campbell.

T

Tanar of Pellucidar. Edgar Rice Burroughs. 256p. 1990. mass mkt. 3.95 (0-345-36670-0, Del Rey) Ballantine.

Tancheng-Lujiang Wrench Fault System. Ed. by Jiawei Xu. LC 92-10287. 245p. 1993. text ed. 215.00 (0-471-93332-5) Wiley.

Tancook Schooners: An Island & It's Boats. Wayne M. O'Leary. (Illus.). 304p. 1994. pap. 17.95 (0-7735-1206-3, Pub. by McGill CN) U of Toronto Pr.

Tancook Schooners: An Island & It's Boats. Wayne M. O'Leary. (Illus.). 304p. 1994. 49.95 (0-7735-1172-5, Pub. by McGill CN) U of Toronto Pr.

Tancook Whalers: Origins, Rediscovery & Revival. Robert C. Post. LC 85-63457. (Illus.). 113p. (Orig.). 1986. pap. 15.00 (0-937410-05-5) ME Maritime Mus.

Tancred: A Study of His Career & Work. Robert L. Nicholson. LC 79-29847. reprint ed. 29.50 (0-404-15425-5) AMS Pr.

Tancred: Or, the New Crusade. Benjamin Disraeli. LC 79-98811. 487p. 1971. reprint ed. text ed. 35.00 (0-8371-3072-7, BATA, Greenwood Pr) Greenwood.

Tancred & Gismund. Robert Wilmot et al. LC 70-133765. (Tudor Facsimile Texts. Old English Plays Ser.: No. 60). reprint ed. 59.50 (0-404-53360-4) AMS Pr.

Tancredi, 2 vols. Gioachino Rossini. Ed. by Philip Gossett. Tr. by Bruno Cagli et al. from ITA. (Works of Gioachino Rossini Ser.). 1164p. 1986. One vol. pap., 200 p. lib. bdg. 301.00 (0-226-72838-2, 718382) U Ch Pr.

Tancreds Andre Campra see Chefs-d'Oeuvres Classiques de l'Opera Francais

***Tandem.** Nelson U. K. Staff. 1988. student ed., pap. text ed. write for info. (0-17-555847-7) Addison-Wesley.

Tandem Book. Angel Rodriguez & Carla Black. (Illus.). 154p. (Orig.). 1997. pap. 14.95 (0-924272-03-1) Info Net Pub.

Tandem Canoeing on Quietwater. Lou Glaros. (Nuts-n-Bolts Guides Ser.). (Illus.). 32p. (Orig.). 1995. pap. 4.95 (0-89732-168-5) Menasha Ridge.

Tandem Mass Spectrometry. Ed. by Fred W. McLafferty. LC 83-10528. (Wiley-Interscience Publications). 526p. reprint ed. pap. 150.00 (0-7837-2401-2, 2040086) Bks Demand.

Tandem Organic Reactions. Tse-Lok Ho. LC 92-10637. 512p. 1992. text ed. 99.95 (0-471-57022-2) Wiley.

***Tandem Plus.** Read & Matthews. 1992. pap. text ed. write for info. (0-17-555880-9) Addison-Wesley.

Tandem Press: Five Years of Collaboration & Experimentation. Andrew Stevens. (Illus.). 116p. 1994. pap. 24.95 (0-932900-35-6) Elvejhem Mus.

***Tandem Techniques.** Raymond P. Scott. LC 96-42339. (Separation Science Ser.). 1997. audio write for info. (0-471-96760-2) Wiley.

Tandem Times: A Bicycle Journey Around the World. Kathryn A. Robinson et al. LC 95-81894. (Illus.). 410p. (Orig.). 1996. pap. 22.95 (0-9650232-0-6) Inst Med Econ.

Tandia. Courtney. 1992. write for info. (0-316-15828-3) Little.

***Tandia.** Courtney. 1992. 5.99 (0-316-15840-2) Little.

Tandis que J'Agonise. William Faulkner. (FRE.). 1973. pap. 10.95 (0-7859-2299-7, 2070363074) Fr & Eur.

T&T Clark Story. J. A. Dempster. 352p. (C). 1989. text ed. 39.00 (1-872795-09-9, Pub. by Pentland Pr UK) St Mut.

Tandy's Money Machine: How Charles Tandy Built Radio Shack into the World's Largest Electronics. Irvin Farman. 1993. 19.95 (0-916371-12-3) Mobium Pr.

Tang Code: General Principles, Vol. I. Tr. by Wallace Johnson from CHI. LC 78-51172. (Studies in East Asian Law). 336p. 1979. text ed. 55.00 (0-691-09239-7) Princeton U Pr.

Tang Dynasty Stories. Tr. by Xianyi Yang & Gladys Yang from CHI. 149p. (Orig.). 1986. pap. 6.95 (0-8351-1602-6) China Bks.

Tang Poet-Monk Chiao-Jan. Thomas P. Nielson. 64p. 1972. pap. 6.00 (0-939252-01-5) ASU Ctr Asian.

Tang Soo (Soo Bahk) Do Moo Duk Kwan: Green Belt Instructional Guide. Hwang Kee & H. C. Hwang. Ed. & Illus. by Tom Wasylyk. 160p. 1993. vinyl bd. write for info. (0-9631358-4-8) H Kee.

Tang Soo (Soo Bahk) Do, Moo Duk Kwan: Instructional Guide. Hwang Kee & H. C. Hwang. Ed. & Illus. by Tom Wasylyk. 592p. 1994. text ed. write for info. (0-9631358-6-4) H Kee.

Tang Soo (Soo Bahk) Do Moo Duk Kwan: Orange Belt, Instructional Guide. Hwang Kee & H. C. Hwang. Ed. & Illus. by Tom Wasylyk. 152p. 1993. vinyl bd. write for info. (0-9631358-3-X) H Kee.

Tang Soo (Soo Bahk) Do Moo Duk Kwan: Red Belt Instructional Guide. Hwang Kee & H. C. Hwang. Ed. & Illus. by Tom Wasylyk. 160p. 1993. vinyl bd. write for info. (0-9631358-5-6) H Kee.

Tang Soo (Soo Bohk) Do Moo Duk Kwan: White Belt International Guide. Kwang Kee & H. C. Hwang. Ed. & Illus. by Tom Wasylyk. 120p. 1993. vinyl bd. write for info. (0-9631358-2-1) H Kee.

Tang Transformation Texts: A Study of the Buddhist Contribution to the Rise of Vernacular Fiction & Drama in China. Victor H. Mair. LC 88-37893. (Harvard-Yenching Institute Monographs: No. 28). 300p. 1989. 28.00 (0-674-86815-3) HUP.

Tanganyika: Preplanning. Fred G. Burke. LC 65-25989. (National Planning Ser.: No. 3). 138p. reprint ed. pap. 39.40 (0-317-28737-0, 2020396) Bks Demand.

Tanganyika under International Mandate, 1919-1946. Peter A. Dumbuya. (C). 1995. lib. bdg. 42.50 (0-7618-0063-8) U Pr of Amer.

Tangent & Cotangent Bundles: Differential Geometry. Kentaro Yano & Shigeru Ishihara. LC 72-91438. (Pure & Applied Mathematics Ser.: 16). 448p. reprint ed. pap. 127.70 (0-317-07841-0, 2055025) Bks Demand.

Tangent Factor. Lawrence Sanders. 288p. 1986. mass mkt. 6.99 (0-425-10062-6) Berkley Pub.

Tangent Objective. Lawrence Sanders. 352p. 1987. mass mkt. 6.99 (0-425-10331-5) Berkley Pub.

Tangents. Miguelanxo Prado. Tr. by Robert Legault from SPA. (Illus.). 48p. 1996. 16.95 (1-56163-148-5, Comics Lit) NBM.

Tangents & Secants of Algebraic Varieties. F. L. Zak. LC 93-17502. (Translations of Mathematical Monographs: Vol. 127). 164p. 1993. 96.00 (0-8218-4585-3, MMONO/127) Am Math.

***Tangerine.** Edward Bloor. LC 96-34182. (J). 1997. 17.00 (0-15-201246-X) HarBrace.

Tangerine. Edward Delaunay. 1993. pap. 5.95 (1-56201-008-5, 115) Blue Moon Bks.

***Tangerine Bear.** Betty Paraskevas. LC 96-70884. (Michael di Capua Bks.). (Illus.). 32p. (J). (ps up). 1997. 14.95 (0-06-205146-6); lib. bdg. 14.89 (0-06-205147-4) HarpC Child Bks.

Tangerine Green. James W. Demarest. LC 94-90742. 304p. (Orig.). 1996. pap. 10.00 (1-56002-529-8, Univ Edtns) Aegina Pr.

Tangerine Tree. Regina Hanson. LC 93-40530. (Illus.). (J). 1995. 14.95 (0-395-68963-5, Clarion Bks) HM.

Tangible Evidence. Deanne C. Siemer. Date not set. pap. write for info. (1-55681-482-8) Natl Inst Trial Ad.

Tangible Personal Property: Assessment & Taxation. Robert M. Clatanoff. (Bibliographic Ser.). 20p. 1982. 9.00 (0-88329-112-6) IAAO.

Tangible Visions: Northwest Coast Indian Shamanism & Its Art. Allen Wardwell. LC 95-24157. (Illus.). 336p. 1996. 85.00 (1-885254-16-4) Monacelli Pr.

Tangible Word. France Theoret. Tr. by Barbara Godard from FRE. 162p. 1991. pap. 12.00 (0-920717-56-X) SPD-Small Pr Dist.

***Tangier & All That.** Hugh A. Harter. (Illus.). 1993. reprint ed. pap. 12.00 (1-57889-018-7) Passeggiata.

Tangle. Meg E. Atkins. (Iris Ser.). 224p. 1988. 18.95 (0-7145-2877-3) M Boyars Pubs.

Tangle Box. Terry Brooks. 352p. 1995. reprint ed. mass mkt. 6.99 (0-345-38700-7, Del Rey) Ballantine.

***Tangle of Octopuses: Plus Cuttlefish, Nautilus & a Giant Squid or Two.** Vicki Leon. LC 97-10935. (Close up Ser.). 1998. write for info. (0-382-39726-6) Silver Burdett Pr.

***Tangle of Octopuses: Plus Cuttlefish, Nautilus & a Giant Squid or Two.** Vicki Leon. LC 97-10935. (Close up Ser.). (J). 1998. pap. write for info. (0-382-39727-4) Silver Burdett Pr.

Tangle Town. Kurt Cyrus. LC 96-24269. (J). 1997. write for info. (0-374-37384-1) FS&G.

***Tanglebird.** Bernard Lodge. LC 96-31030. (J). 1997. 14.95 (0-395-84543-2) HM.

Tangled. Mary Balogh. 384p. (Orig.). 1994. pap. 4.99 (0-451-40452-1, Topaz) NAL-Dutton.

Tangled Destinies. Sara Wood. (Presents Ser.). 1996. mass mkt. 3.25 (0-373-11790-6, 1-11790-2) Harlequin Bks.

Tangled Dreams. Julie Tetel. 352p. (Orig.). 1989. mass mkt. 3.95 (0-445-20640-3, Mysterious Paperbk) Warner Bks.

Tangled Emotions. Billie J. Longstreth et al. 357p. 1989. 12.95 (0-317-99837-4); pap. 4.95 (0-317-99838-2) Shamrock Pubns.

Tangled Fire of William Faulkner. William Van O'Connor. LC 68-22386. 191p. 1968. reprint ed. 45.00 (0-87752-078-X) Gordian.

Tangled Fortunes. Margaret Mahy. LC 93-32202. (Cousins Quartet Ser.: Bk. 4). 112p. (J). 1994. 14.95 (0-385-32066-3) Delacorte.

Tangled Fortunes. Margaret Mahy. (Cousins Quartet Ser.: Bk. 4). 112p. (J). 1996. pap. 3.99 (0-440-41163-7) Dell.

Tangled Garden. David Crawford. LC 93-28929. 1995. pap. 6.00 (0-88734-276-0) Players Pr.

Tangled Garden. large type ed. Elizabeth Coleman. 320p. 1989. 25.99 (0-7089-1991-X) Ulverscroft.

Tangled Garden. large type ed. Patricia Lawson. 608p. 1986. 27.99 (0-7089-8357-X) Ulverscroft.

Tangled Garden: Memories of My Girlhood. Elizabeth Coleman. 192p. 1989. 24.95 (0-575-04187-0, Pub. by V Gollancz UK) Trafalgar.

Tangled Hair: Love Poems of Yosano Akiko. Yosano Akiko. Tr. by Dennis Maloney & Hide Oshiro. (Illus.). 1986. pap. 7.50 (0-934834-05-9) White Pine.

Tangled Hair: Selected Tanka from Midaregami. Akiko Yosano. Tr. by Sanford Goldstein & Seishi Shinoda from JPN. LC 87-50164. Orig. Title: Midaregami. 166p. (Orig.). 1987. pap. 11.95 (0-8048-1522-4) C E Tuttle.

Tangled Hearts. Phoebe Conn. 512p. 1993. mass mkt. 4.50 (0-8217-4400-3, Zebra Kensgtn) Kensgtn Pub Corp.

Tangled Hierarchies: Teachers As Professionals & the Management of Schools. Joseph B. Shedd & Samuel B. Bacharach. LC 90-26937. (Education-Higher Education Ser.). 254p. text ed. 29.95 (1-55542-342-6) Jossey-Bass.

***Tangled in the Tinsel: A Look at Christmas Through Sketches & Monologues for All.** 86p. 1986. 8.99 (0-8341-9369-8) Lillenas.

***Tangled June: A Dave Garrett Mystery.** Neil Albert. LC 97-1350. 246p. 1997. 20.95 (0-8027-3305-0) Walker & Co.

***Tangled Knot of Murder.** C. F. Roe. 1996. pap. 5.50 (0-451-19079-3, Sig) NAL-Dutton.

Tangled Lies. Anne Stuart. (Men Made in America Ser.). 1994. mass mkt. 3.59 (0-373-45161-X, 1-45161-6) Harlequin Bks.

Tangled Lives. Margot Dalton. 1996. pap. 5.50 (0-614-07831-8, 1-66047-1, Mira Bks) Harlequin Bks.

Tangled Lives. Margot Dalton. 1996. mass mkt. 5.50 (1-55166-047-4, Mira Bks) Harlequin Bks.

***Tangled Lives.** John B. Jones. 1997. pap. text ed. 13.95 (1-879360-48-9) Noble Pr.

Tangled Lives. Joann Ross. (Temptation Ser.: No. 345). 1991. pap. 2.95 (0-373-25445-8) Harlequin Bks.

Tangled Loyalties: The Life & Times of Ilya Ehrenburg. Joshua Rubenstein. LC 95-36588. 482p. 1996. 35.00 (0-465-08386-2) Basic.

Tangled Memories: The Vietnam War, the AIDS Epidemic, & the Politics of Remembering. Marita Sturken. LC 96-12609. 358p. 1997. 45.00 (0-520-08653-8); pap. 16.95 (0-520-20620-7) U CA Pr.

Tangled Roots. Taffy Cannon. 320p. 1995. 19.95 (0-7867-0137-4) Carroll & Graf.

Tangled Roots. Taffy Cannon. 1996. mass mkt. 5.99 (0-449-22390-6) Fawcett.

Tangled Roots. large type ed. Mary Williams. 431p. 1992. 25.99 (0-7505-0242-8) Ulverscroft.

***Tangled Sheets: Stories & Poems of Lesbian Lust.** Ed. by Rosamund Elwin & Karen X. Tulchinsky. 224p. pap. 12.95 (0-88961-207-2, Pub. by Wmns Pr CN) LPC InBook.

Tangled Tale. Lewis Carroll. LC 74-82735. 1975. 15.00 (0-89388-181-3) Okpaku Communications.

***Tangled Tassels: Tales of Academe.** Richard M. Eastman. LC 96-78453. 192p. (Orig.). 1997. pap. 17.95 (1-878044-27-3) Mayhaven Pub.

***Tangled Threads.** large type ed. Susanne McCarthy. (Magna Large Print Ser.). 256p. 1996. 25.99 (0-7505-1015-3, Pub. by Magna Print Bks UK) Ulverscroft.

Tangled Tongue: Living with a Stutter. Jock A. Carlisle. LC 86-8029. 272p. 1986. pap. 9.95 (0-201-11243-4) Addison-Wesley.

Tangled up in Blue. Larry Duplechan. 272p. 1990. pap. 8.95 (0-312-05167-0) St Martin.

***Tangled up in Blue.** Marcia Evanick. (Loveswept Ser.: No. 818). 240p. 1997. mass mkt. 3.50 (0-553-44562-6, Loveswept) Bantam.

***Tangled up in School: Politics, Space, Bodies, & Signs in the Educational Process.** Jan Nespor. LC 97-1959. (Sociocultural, Political, & Historical Studies in Education). 304p. 1997. pap. write for info. (0-8058-2653-X); text ed. write for info. (0-8058-2652-1) L Erlbaum Assocs.

Tangled Vines. Janet Dailey. 448p. 1993. mass mkt. 5.99 (0-316-17163-8) Little.

***Tangled Vines.** Diane Noble. 1998. pap. 8.99 (1-57673-219-3) Multnomah Pubs.

Tangled Vines. Mary J. Roberts. LC 86-21683. 252p. 1987. 16.95 (0-916515-16-8) Mercury Hse Inc.

Tangled Vines: A Novel. large type ed. Janet Dailey. LC 92-10351. 1992. Large print ed. 24.95 (0-316-17158-1) Little.

Tangled Vines: New Edition. Ed. by Lyn Lifshin. 1992. pap. 9.95 (0-15-688166-7, Harvest Bks) HarBrace.

Tangled Vows. Rebecca York. (Intrigue Ser.). 1994. mass mkt. 2.99 (0-373-22289-0, 1-22289-2) Harlequin Bks.

Tangled Web. Nicholas Blake. 224p. 1987. 3.50 (0-88184-292-3) Carroll & Graf.

Tangled Web. Cecil Day-Lewis. 1976. 19.95 (0-8488-0977-7) Amereon Ltd.

Tangled Web. Barbara Hazard. 224p. 1981. pap. 1.95 (0-449-50177-9, Coventry) Fawcett.

***Tangled Web.** B. J. Hoff. LC 96-27246. (Daybreak Mysteries Ser.). 1997. pap. 8.99 (0-8423-7194-X) Tyndale.

Tangled Web. Ed. by Christina Krayer. (YA). (gr. 7-12). 1994. pap. write for info. (1-882869-10-9) Varsity Read Servs.

Tangled Web. Judith Michael. Ed. by Julie Rubenstein. 1995. pap. 6.50 (0-671-52548-4) PB.

Tangled Web. Judith Michael. 1995. pap. 6.99 (0-671-53288-X) PB.

Tangled Web. Lucy Maud Montgomery. 1976. 25.95 (0-8488-0722-7) Amereon Ltd.

Tangled Web. Lucy Maud Montgomery. 272p. (J). 1989. mass mkt. 3.99 (0-7704-2245-4) Bantam.

***Tangled Web.** Pan Pantziarka. (Crime & Passion Ser.). (Orig.). 1997. mass mkt. 5.95 (0-7535-0156-2, Pub. by Virgin Pub UK) London Brdge.

Tangled Web. Cathy G. Thacker. (American Romance Ser.: No. 423). 1992. mass mkt. 3.29 (0-373-16423-8) Harlequin Bks.

Tangled Web. large type ed. Julia Ashwell. 352p. 1995. 25.99 (0-7089-3343-2) Ulverscroft.

Tangled Web. large type ed. Judith Michael. LC 95-2007. (Large Print Bks.). 1995. 25.95 (1-56895-201-5) Wheeler Pub.

Tangled Web: Legacy of Auto Pioneer, John F. Dodge. Jean M. Pitrone & George J. Nosis. 336p. 1989. 19.95 (0-910977-05-4) Avenue Pub.

Tangled Web: The Long Awaited Sequel to Deceptions. Judith Michael. 464p. 1994. 23.00 (0-671-79879-0) S&S Trade.

***Tangled Web of Worship.** George A. McCabe. 100p. 1996. pap. 12.95 (0-929529-07-3) Vision Ministry Pr.

Tangled Web They Weave: Truth, Falsity, & Advertisers. Ivan L. Preston. LC 93-39166. 236p. 1994. 22.50 (0-299-14190-X) U of Wis Pr.

Tangled Web They Weave: Truth, Falsity, & Advertisers. Ivan L. Preston. LC 93-39166. 236p. 1996. pap. 12.95 (0-299-14194-2) U of Wis Pr.

Tangled Webb. Eloise McGraw. LC 92-27911. 160p. (YA). (gr. 5 up). 1993. lib. bdg. 13.95 (0-689-50573-6, McElderry) S&S Childrens.

Tangled Webb. E. B. Wight. 1981. 30.00 (0-686-87220-7, Pub. by A H S Ltd UK) St Mut.

***Tangled Webs.** TSR Inc. Staff. 1997. pap. 5.99 (0-7869-0698-7) TSR Inc.

Tangled Webs: Indians & the Law in Canada's Pacific Coast Fisheries. Dianne Newell. (Illus.). 288p. 1993. 40.00 (0-8020-0547-0); pap. 18.95 (0-8020-7746-3) U of Toronto Pr.

Tangled Webs: The U. S. in Greece 1947-1967. Yiannis P. Roubatis. LC 87-60390. 228p. (Orig.). 1987. 25.00 (0-317-64511-0); pap. 12.00 (0-918618-34-7) Pella Pub.

Tangled Wing: Biological Constraints on the Human Spirit. Melvin Konner. LC 81-47464. 560p. 1990. pap. 22.50 (0-8050-1327-X, Owl) H Holt & Co.

Tangles of the Mind: A Journey Through Alzheimer's. Elizabeth Stewart. LC 90-86289. 106p. (Orig.). 1991. pap. 8.50 (0-9628589-1-9) Elderberry Pr.

Tangletalk. W. Nikola-Lisa. (J). 1997. pap. 14.99 (0-525-45399-7) NAL-Dutton.

Tanglewood Tales. Nathaniel Hawthorne. (Airmont Classics Ser.). (Illus.). (J). (gr. 7 up). 1968. mass mkt. 2.50 (0-8049-0175-9, CL-175) Airmont.

Tanglewood Tales. large type ed. Nathaniel Hawthorne. 226p. 1991. 19.95 (1-85089-403-5, Pub. by ISIS UK) Transaction Pubs.

Tanglewood Tales. Nathaniel Hawthorne. 225p. 1990. reprint ed. lib. bdg. 22.95 (0-89966-737-6) Buccaneer Bks.

Tanglewood Tales for Girls & Boys. Nathaniel Hawthorne. (Notable American Authors Ser.). (J). 1992. reprint ed. lib. bdg. 75.00 (0-7812-3046-2) Rprt Serv.

Tanglewood's Secret. Patricia M. St. John. (Patricia St. John Bks.). (J). (gr. 5-8). 1951. mass mkt. 5.99 (0-8024-0007-8) Moody.

Tango. Earl Atkinson. (Ballroom Dance Ser.). 1986. lib. bdg. 250.00 (0-8490-3634-8) Gordon Pr.

Tango. Earl Atkinson. (Ballroom Dance Ser.). 1983. lib. bdg. 250.00 (0-87700-490-0) Revisionist Pr.

Tango. Simon Collier et al. LC 95-60478. (Illus.). 208p. 1995. 40.00 (0-500-01671-2) Thames Hudson.

***Tango.** Alan Judd. Date not set. write for info. (0-688-09254-3) Morrow.

***Tango.** Evelyne Pieller. (Illus.). 110p. 1997. 35.00 (1-55670-597-2) Stewart Tabori & Chang.

Tango: A Bibliography: Books, History, People, Words. Oscar De Buenosaires. (Book's Fingerprints Ser.: No. 7). (Illus.). 108p. (Orig.). 1991. pap. 13.00 (0-929928-08-3) Fog Pubns.

***Tango! The Dance, the Song, the Story.** Simon Collier et al. LC 95-6078. (Illus.). 208p. 1997. pap. 29.95 (0-500-27979-9) Thames Hudson.

Tango & How to Dance It. Gladys B. Crozier. (Ballroom Dance Ser.). 1986. lib. bdg. 79.95 (0-8490-3476-0) Gordon Pr.

Tango & Other up to Date Dances. J. S. Hopkins. (Ballroom Dance Ser.). 1985. lib. bdg. 79.95 (0-87700-659-8) Revisionist Pr.

Tango & Other Up to Date Dances. J. S. Hopkins. (Ballroom Dance Ser.). 1986. lib. bdg. 79.95 (0-8490-3331-4) Gordon Pr.

Tango & Rumba. Frank Veloz & Yolanda Veloz. (Ballroom Dance Ser.). 1986. lib. bdg. 79.95 (0-8490-3383-7) Gordon Pr.

Tango & Rumba. Yolanda Veloz & Frank Veloz. (Ballroom Dance Ser.). 1985. lib. bdg. 250.00 (0-87700-718-7) Revisionist Pr.

Tango & the Political Economy of Passion. Marta E. Savigliano. LC 94-32610. (Institutional Structures of Feeling Ser.). (C). 1994. pap. text ed. 25.00 (0-8133-1638-3) Westview.

Tango Argentino. Paul Bottomer. 1996. 12.95 (1-85967-216-7, Lorenz Bks) Anness Pub.

Tango Argentino: A Guide. (Ballroom Dance Ser.). 1991. lib. bdg. 75.00 (0-8490-5180-0) Gordon Pr.

Tango Argentino: A History of the Tango. Lucy Gordon. (Ballroom Dance Ser.). 1986. lib. bdg. 99.95 (0-8490-3471-X) Gordon Pr.

Tango Argentino: Technique & Figures. (Ballroom Dance Ser.). 1991. lib. bdg. 79.95 (0-685-49804-2) Gordon Pr.

Tango Around the Horn: The World War II Voyage of America's Last Large Sailing Ship. enl. rev. ed. Lawrence Barber. (Illus.). 256p. 1991. pap. 13.95 (1-880827-01-8) OR Maritime Ctr & Mus.

Tango Attitude. (Ballroom Dance Ser.). 1986. lib. bdg. 79.95 (0-8490-3403-5) Gordon Pr.

Tango Attitude. (Ballroom Dance Ser.). 1985. lib. bdg. 74.50 (0-87700-798-5) Revisionist Pr.

Tango Briefing. Adam Hall. 336p. 1993. mass mkt. 4.50 (0-06-100530-4, Harp PBks) HarpC.

Tango Made Easy. (Ballroom Dance Ser.). 1985. lib. bdg. 79.95 (0-87700-674-1) Revisionist Pr.

Tango Player. Christopher Hein. Tr. by Philip Boehm from GER. 224p. 1992. 20.00 (0-374-27252-2) FS&G.

Tango Player. Christoph Hein. Tr. by Philip Boehm from GER. LC 93-47923. (Writings from an Unbound Europe). 224p. (C). 1994. reprint ed. pap. 13.95 (0-8101-1116-0) Northwestern U Pr.

Tango Rond De Jambe for Intermediate Classes. 1985. lib. bdg. 74.00 (0-87700-797-7) Revisionist Pr.

Tango Rond de Jambe for Intermediate Classes. (Ballroom Dance Ser.). 1986. lib. bdg. 79.95 (0-8490-3402-7) Gordon Pr.

***Tangos a los Maestros.** Mario Broeders. 106p. 1996. 20.00 (0-9654944-1-1) Music Pub NY.

Tango's Baby. Martin Waddell. LC 95-13827. 207p. (YA). (gr. 9-12). 1995. 16.95 (1-56402-615-9) Candlewick Pr.

***Tangram.** (Discovery Box Ser.). 32p. (J). (gr. 1-5). 1997. 11.95 (0-590-92672-1) Scholastic Inc.

***Tangram: The Ancient Chinese Puzzle.** Joost Elffers & Michael Schuyt. 1997. write for info. (1-55670-581-6) Stewart Tabori & Chang.

***Tangram Activities.** Jo E. Moore. (Mathematics Ser.). (Illus.). 32p. (J). (gr. 4-6). 1997. teacher ed., pap. 2.95 (1-55799-469-2, 4071) Evan-Moor Corp.

Tangram Diary. Clara E. Clark. (Illus.). 64p. (Orig.). (J). (gr. 3-6). 1980. pap. 6.95 (0-934734-05-4) Construct Educ.

Tangram Geometry in Metric. Juanita Brownlee. Ed. by Mary Laycock. (Illus.). 64p. (Orig.). (J). (gr. 5-10). 1975. pap. 8.50 (0-918932-43-2, AA-1407) Activity Resources.

Tangram Treasury, Bk. C. Jan Fair. 48p. (J). (gr. 5-10). 1987. pap. text ed. 8.95 (0-914040-55-3) Cuisenaire.

An Asterisk (*) at the beginning of an entry indicates that the title is appearing in BIP for the first time.

Tangram Treasury, Bk. A. Jan Fair. 48p. (J). (gr. 1-4). 1987. pap. text ed. 8.95 (0-914040-53-7) Cuisenaire.

Tangram Treasury, Bk. B. Jan Fair. 48p. (J). (gr. 3-6). 1987. pap. text ed. 8.95 (0-914040-54-5) Cuisenaire.

Tangrams. John Millington. 1993. pap. 6.95 (0-906212-56-1, Pub. by Tarquin UK) Parkwest Pubns.

Tangrams. Frank Nichols. (J). 1989. pap. 3.99 (0-85953-050-7) Childs Play.

Tangrams: Three Hundred & Thirty Puzzles. Ronald C. Read. 1978. pap. 3.95 (0-486-21483-4) Dover.

***Tangrams ABC Kit.** Johnston. (Illus.). pap. 3.50 (0-486-23853-9) Dover.

Tangweera: Life & Adventures among Gentle Savages. C. Napier Bell. (Illus.). 352p. 1989. 25.00 (0-292-78066-4); pap. 14.95 (0-292-78103-2) U of Tex Pr.

Tania-Concert Band Score. Edward Weiss. 136p. reprint ed. pap. 38.80 (0-317-10078-5, 2002892) Bks Demand.

***Tania y Sus Amigos - Tanya Thinker & the Gizmo Gang.** (Early Learning Program Ser.). (Illus.). 64p. (SPA.). (J). (gr. k-2). 16.95 (0-7835-3516-3) Time-Life.

Tania's Trolls. Lisa W. Peters. 64p. (J). (gr. 3). 1992. pap. 2.99 (0-380-71444-2, Camelot Young) Avon.

Taniguchi Symposia on Brain Sciences No. 18: Emotion, Memory & Behavior: Studies on Human & Nonhuman Primates. Ed. by Teruo Nakajima & Taketoshi Ono. (Taniguchi Symposia on Brain Sciences Ser.: No. 18). 1995. 95.00 (0-8493-7777-3, JS7777) CRC Pr.

Tanith see Wolf-Woman

Tanjore Maharatta: Principality in Southern India, The Land of Chola, The Eden of the South. William Hickey. 1988. reprint ed. 25.00 (81-206-0302-8, Pub. by Asian Educ Servs II) S Asia.

Tank Aces. Zumbro. 1997. mass mkt. 6.50 (0-671-53612-5) PB.

Tank Action from the Great War to the Gulf. George Forty. (Illus.). 320p. 1995. 39.95 (0-7509-0479-8, Pub. by Sutton Pubng UK) Bks Intl VA.

Tank & Mechanized Infantry Battalion Task Force. 1991. lib. bdg. 79.95 (0-8490-4074-4) Gordon Pr.

Tank & Mechanized Infantry Company Team. 1991. lib. bdg. 79.95 (0-8490-4077-9) Gordon Pr.

***Tank Barge Fire Fighting Manual.** J. S. Glantz & W. D. Kline. (Illus.). 133p. (Orig.). 1997. pap. 9.95 (0-9647051-2-5) One River Pr.

Tank Battalions of the U. S. Army. James A. Sawicki. LC 82-6069. (Illus.). 427p. 1983. 25.00 (0-9602404-5-4) Wyvern.

Tank Cars. John Henderson. LC 92-97130. (Classic Freight Cars Ser.: Vol. 2). (Illus.). 64p. (Orig.). 1992. pap. text ed. 23.95 (0-9629037-9-5) H & M Prods.

***Tank Cleaning Safety Code.** Institute of Petroleum (Great Britain) Staff. LC 89-9068. Date not set. write for info. (0-471-92430-X) Wiley.

***Tank Cleaning Safety Code.** 2nd ed. Institute of Petroleum Staff. LC 96-30617. (Institute of Petroleum Model Code of Safe Practice in the Petroleum Industry Ser.). 1996. write for info. (0-471-97096-4) Wiley.

Tank Commanders: Knights of the Modern Age. George Forty. (MBI Rights Ser.). (Illus.). 256p. 1993. 14.98 (0-87938-720-3) Motorbooks Intl.

Tank Container Market. ICHCA-Cargo Systems Editors. (C). 1991. text ed. 200.00 (0-907499-74-0, Pub. by Cargo Systs UK) St Mut.

Tank Corps Honours & Awards, 1916-1919. enl. ed. 402p. (C). 1987. 42.00 (0-317-90458-2, Pub. by Picton UK) St Mut.

Tank Destroyers. Turner Publishing Company Staff. LC 90-70690. 144p. 1991. 48.00 (0-938021-93-1) Turner Pub KY.

Tank Girl Collection. Alan Martin & Jamie Hewlett. (Illus.). 136p. 1993. pap. 17.95 (1-56971-082-1) Dark Horse Comics.

Tank Girl Movie Adaptation. Peter Milligan & A. Young. (Illus.). 64p. 1995. pap. 5.95 (1-56389-219-7, Vertigo) DC Comics.

Tank Girl 2. Alan Martin. (Illus.). 128p. 1995. pap. 17.95 (1-56971-107-0) Dark Horse Comics.

Tank Gunnery. 1991. lib. bdg. 79.95 (0-8490-4172-4) Gordon Pr.

***Tank Hill.** Flora B. Adams. (Illus.). 87p. (Orig.). (J). (gr. 3-8). 1998. mass mkt. 6.99 (1-889501-29-8, Blue Jean) Sovereign.

***Tank Killing: Anti-Tank Warfare by Men & Machines.** Ian Hogg. LC 96-38871. (Illus.). 288p. 1997. 22.95 (1-885119-40-2) Sarpedon.

***Tank Lords.** David Drake. 464p. 1997. mass mkt. 6.99 (0-671-87794-1) Baen Bks.

Tank of Serpents. large type ed. James Leasor. 528p. 1987. 25.99 (0-7089-1712-7) Ulverscroft.

Tank Sergeant. Ralph Zumbro. 1988. pap. 3.95 (0-317-67551-6) PB.

***Tank Tracks: The 9th Battalion Royal Tank Regiment at War 1940-1945.** Peter Beale. (Illus.). 256p. (Orig.). 1997. pap. 19.95 (0-7509-1519-6, Pub. by Sutton Pubng UK) Bks Intl VA.

Tank Twins: East End Brothers in Arms 1943-45. Stephen Dyson. (Illus.). 224p. 1994. 39.50 (0-85052-274-9, Pub. by L Cooper Bks UK) Trans-Atl Phila.

Tank Vehicles for Flammable & Combustible Liquids. National Fire Protection Association Staff. 1990. 16.75 (0-317-63417-8, 385-90) Natl Fire Prot.

Tank War: 1939-1945. Janusz Piekalkiewicz. Tr. by Jan Van Heurck from GER. (Illus.). 332p. 1986. 19.95 (0-918678-08-0) Natl Hist Soc.

Tank Wars Central Front: NATO vs Warsaw Pact. Steven J. Zaloga. (Elite Ser.: No. 26). (Illus.). 64p. pap. 12.95 (0-85045-904-4, 9426, Pub. by Osprey UK) Stackpole.

Tankas from the Koelz Collection: Museum of Anthropology, University of Michigan. rev. ed. Carolyn Copeland. (Michigan Papers on South & Southeast Asia: No. 18). (Illus.). 100p. (Orig.). (C). 1986. pap. 17.95 (0-89148-018-8) Ctr S&SE Asian.

Tanker. Joanne Barkan. (Truckin' Board Bks.). (J). 1996. bds. 4.99 (0-689-81150-0) S&S Childrens.

Tanker Handbook for Deck Officers. C. Baptist. (Illus.). (C). 1987. 140.00 (0-85174-386-2, Pub. by Brwn Son Ferg) St Mut.

Tanker Handbook for Deck Officers. 7th ed. C. Baptist. (Illus.). 200p. 1993. text ed. 95.00 (0-85174-587-3) Sheridan.

Tanker Operations: A Handbook for the Ship's Officer. 3rd ed. G. S. Marton. LC 92-8997. (Illus.). 328p. 1992. text ed. 35.00 (0-87033-432-8) Cornell Maritime.

Tanker Performance & Cost: Measurement, Analysis & Management. Ernest Gannett. LC 73-80638. 117p. 1969. text ed. 8.50 (0-87033-122-1) Cornell Maritime.

Tanker Register, 1988. 28th ed. 400p. 1988. 285.00 (0-8002-4218-1) Taylor & Francis.

Tanker Safety Guide (Chemicals) ICS Staff. (C). 1990. 270.00 (0-948691-50-6, Pub. by Witherby & Co UK) St Mut.

Tanker Safety Guide (Liquefied Gas) ICS Staff. 1978. 950.00 (0-906270-01-4, Pub. by Witherby & Co UK) St Mut.

Tanker Safety Guide (Liquefied Gas) ICS Staff. (C). 1991. 220.00 (1-85609-000-0, Pub. by Witherby & Co UK) St Mut.

***Tanker Safety Guide (Liquefied) Gas.** ICS Staff. 1996. pap. 444.00 (0-906270-03-0, Pub. by Witherby & Co UK) St Mut.

Tanker Spills: Prevention by Design. National Research Council, Committee on Vision Staff. 384p. 1991. text ed. 39.95 (0-309-04377-8) Natl Acad Pr.

Tanker Wars: The Assault on Commercial Shipping during the Iran-Iraq Crisis 1980-1988. Martin S. Navias & Edward Hooton. 256p. 1996. text ed. 110.00 (1-86064-032-X) St Martin.

Tankerman - All Grades: Revised Edition "E" Ed. by Richard A. Block. (Illus.). 526p. (Orig.). 1991. pap. 55.00 (1-879778-05-X, BK-106) Marine Educ.

Tankermen. Margo Lanagan. 160p. (J). (gr. 5-9). 1993. pap. 6.95 (1-86373-253-5, Pub. by Allen & Unwin Aust Pty AT) IPG Chicago.

Tankers & Tanker Terminals: A Bibliography for the Natural Gas Industry, 1960-1974. 146p. 1975. pap. 10.00 (0-318-12718-0, X50275) Am Gas Assn.

Tankers Full of Trouble: The Perilous Journey of Alaskan Crude. Eric Nalder. LC 93-31198. 293p. 1994. 24.00 (0-8021-1458-X, Grove) Grove-Atltic.

***Tanks.** Chelsea House Publishers Staff. (Concise Collection). 1997. 15.95 (1-85627-748-8) Chelsea Hse.

***Tanks.** Ian Harvey & Richard Chasemore. (Illus.). (J). pap. 8.99 (0-590-24940-1) Scholastic Inc.

Tanks. Ian V. Hogg. LC 84-9650. (Modern Military Techniques Ser.). (Illus.). 48p. (YA). (gr. 5 up). 1985. pap. 4.95 (0-8225-9507-9, Lerner Publctns); lib. bdg. 17.50 (0-8225-1378-1, Lerner Publctns) Lerner Group.

***Tanks: Main Battle Tanks & Light Tanks.** Marsh Gelbart. Ed. by James Marchington. (Modern Military Equipment Ser.). (Illus.). 160p. 1996. 28.95 (1-85753-168-X, Pub. by Brasseys UK) Brasseys Inc.

Tanks: The History of the Royal Tank Regiment & Its Predecessors, 1914-1915, 2 vols., Set. Basil H. Liddell-Hart. 1980. reprint ed. 49.95 (0-89201-079-7) Zenger Pub.

Tanks: Vietnam Stories. John Mort. LC 85-73391. 88p. 1986. pap. 8.95 (0-933532-55-5) BkMk.

Tanks: World War II Fighting Armour. George Forty. (Illus.). 208p. 1995. 29.95 (1-85532-532-2, Pub. by Osprey Pubng Ltd UK) Motorbooks Intl.

Tanks & Trenches: First Hand Accounts of Tank Warfare in the First World War. David Fletcher. (Illus.). 224p. 1995. 29.95 (0-7509-0346-5, Pub. by Sutton Pubng UK) Bks Intl VA.

Tanks & Vessels. Multimedia Development Services Staff. (Plant Fundamentals Ser.). (Illus.). 68p. (Orig.). 1995. student ed. 30.00 (1-57431-008-9) Tech Trng Systs.

Tanks & Vessels Vol., Vol. III, Module I. Multimedia Development Services Staff. (Plant Fundamentals Ser.). (Illus.). (Orig.). 1995. teacher ed. 65.00 (1-57431-048-8) Tech Trng Systs.

***Tanks at War.** Peter Darman. 1996. 13.98 (0-7603-0275-8) Motorbooks Intl.

Tank's Choice. E.J. Davis. 1995. 4.99 (1-85792-102-X, Pub. by Christian Focus UK) Spring Arbor Dist.

***Tanks for the Memories: An Oral History of the 712th Tank Battalion from World War II.** (Illus.). 211p. 1994. pap. 13.95 (0-9640611-0-4) Chi Chi Pr.

Tanks for the Memories: Flotation Tank Talks. E. J. Gold & John C. Lilly. LC 95-38869. (Illus.). (Orig.). 1996. pap. 12.50 (0-89556-071-2) Gateways Bks & Tapes.

Tanks of World War II. Restyn & Buffeteaut. (Jane's Gem Ser.). (Illus.). 144p. (Orig.). 1995. pap. 8.00 (0-00-470847-4, PL) HarpC.

***Tanks of World War Two.** Jean Restayn. 1996. 37.95 (2-908182-38-6, Zenith Aviation) Motorbooks Intl.

Tanks, Vessels & Other Components. Resource Systems International Staff. 1982. pap. text ed. 15.00 (0-8359-7538-X, Reston) P-H.

Tannenbaum. Hans Christian Andersen. (Illus.). (GER.). (J). 14.95 (3-314-00515-6) North-South Bks NYC.

Tannenbaum Collection of Miniatures. Bruce Weber. LC 82-81935. (Illus.). 32p. 1982. pap. 4.00 (0-943411-15-7) Norton Gal Art.

Tannenberg: Clash of Empires. Dennis E. Showalter. LC 90-1088. viii, 419p. (C). 1991. lib. bdg. 42.50 (0-208-02252-X, Archon Bks) Shoe String.

Tanner Lecture on Human Values, Vol. 13. Ed. by Grethe B. Peterson. (Tanner Lectures). 1992. 30.00 (0-87480-406-X) U of Utah Pr.

Tanner Lectures on Human Values. Ed. by Grethe B. Peterson. (Tanner Lectures: Vol. 15). 400p. (C). 1994. 30.00 (0-87480-450-7) U of Utah Pr.

Tanner Lectures on Human Values, Vol. 1. Sterling M. McMurrin. LC 81-641369. 268p. reprint ed. pap. 76.40 (0-685-20458-8, 2029851) Bks Demand.

Tanner Lectures on Human Values, Vol. VIII. Ed. by Sterling M. McMurrin. 333p. (C). 1988. text ed. 30.00 (0-87480-302-0) U of Utah Pr.

Tanner Lectures on Human Values, Vol. IX: 1988. Ed. by Grethe B. Peterson. 320p. 1988. 30.00 (0-87480-326-8) U of Utah Pr.

Tanner Lectures on Human Values, Vol. X. Ed. by Grethe B. Peterson. (Tanner Lectures). 300p. (C). 1989. text ed. 30.00 (0-87480-318-7) U of Utah Pr.

Tanner Lectures on Human Values, Vol. XI. Ed. by Grethe B. Peterson. (Tanner Lectures). 500p. 1990. lib. bdg. 30.00 (0-87480-340-3) U of Utah Pr.

Tanner Lectures on Human Values, Vol. XII. Ed. by Grethe B. Peterson. 250p. 1991. lib. bdg. 30.00 (0-87480-350-0) U of Utah Pr.

Tanner Lectures on Human Values, Vol. 14. Ed. by Grethe B. Peterson. (Tanner Lectures). 320p. (C). 1993. text ed. 30.00 (0-87480-418-3) U of Utah Pr.

Tanner Lectures on Human Values, Vol. 16. Ed. by Grethe B. Peterson. (Tanner Lecture Ser.). 360p. 1995. text ed. 30.00 (0-87480-476-0) U of Utah Pr.

Tanner Lectures on Human Values, Vol. 17. Ed. by Grethe B. Peterson. 320p. (C). 1996. text ed. 30.00 (0-87480-505-8) U of Utah Pr.

***Tanner Lectures on Human Values, Vol. 18.** Ed. by Grethe B. Peterson. 320p. 1997. 30.00 (0-87480-543-0) U of Utah Pr.

Tanner Lectures on Human Values, Vol. II: 1981. George J. Stigler et al. 272p. 1981. 30.00 (0-87480-193-1) U of Utah Pr.

Tanner Lectures on Human Values, Vol. IV: 1983. Ed. by Sterling M. McMurrin. 300p. 1983. 30.00 (0-87480-216-4) U of Utah Pr.

Tanner Lectures on Human Values, Vol. V: 1984. Ed. by Sterling M. McMurrin. 220p. 1984. 30.00 (0-87480-234-2) U of Utah Pr.

Tanner Lectures on Human Values, Vol. VI: 1985. Ed. by Sterling M. McMurrin. 300p. 1985. 30.00 (0-87480-243-1) U of Utah Pr.

Tanner Lectures on Human Values, Vol. VII: 1986. Ed. by Sterling M. McMurrin. 288p. 1986. 30.00 (0-87480-259-8) U of Utah Pr.

Tanner Letters: A Pioneer Saga of Swan River & Tasmania 1831-1845. Compiled by Pamela Statham. (Illus.). xxix, 226p. pap. 7.95 (0-85564-192-4, Pub. by Univ of West Aust Pr AT) Intl Spec Bk.

Tanneries & the Environment: A Technical Guide. 119p. 1991. 25.00 (92-807-1276-4) UN.

Tanners. Leonard E. Fisher. LC 66-10136. (Illus.). 48p. (J). (gr. 3 up). 1986. pap. 5.95 (0-87923-609-4) Godine.

Tannersville Circuit Church Records. Kim P. Kimler. 160p. 1994. pap. 14.95 (1-55856-162-5) Closson Pr.

Tannhaeuser Legende. Dietz-Ruediger Moser. (Fabula Supplement Ser.: Vol. 4). (C). 1977. 80.00 (3-11-005957-6) De Gruyter.

Tannhauser. Richard Wagner. Ed. by Nicholas John. (English National Opera Guide Series: Bilingual Libretto, Articles: No. 39). (Illus.). 96p. (Orig.). 1988. pap. 9.95 (0-7145-4147-8) Riverrun NY.

Tannhauser: A Story of All Time. Aleister Crowley. 1973. lib. bdg. 250.00 (0-87968-215-9) Krishna Pr.

Tannhauser & the Mountain of Venus: A Study in the Legend of the Germanic Paradise. P. S. Barto. 1977. lib. bdg. 59.95 (0-685-01975-6) Gordon Pr.

Tannhauser in Full Score. Richard Wagner. (Music Scores & Music to Play Ser.). 576p. 1984. pap. 18.95 (0-486-24649-3) Dover.

Tanning Materials (Gerbstoffe) see Rohstoffe des Pflanzenreichs

Tanning of Hides & Skins. (Technical Memorandum, Technology Ser.: No. 1). xii, 229p. (Orig.). 1989. pap. 24.75 (92-2-102904-2) Intl Labour Office.

Tannisho: A Resource for Modern Living. Alfred Bloom. LC 80-39523. 112p. (Orig.). (C). 1981. pap. 8.95 (0-938474-00-6) Buddhist Study.

Tannisho: A Shin Buddhist Classic. rev. ed. Taitetsu Unno. LC 84-22987. 73p. (Orig.). 1996. pap. 12.95 (0-938474-04-9) Buddhist Study.

Tannisho: A Shin Buddhist Classic. 2nd rev. ed. Taitetsu Unno. LC 96-12400. 102p. (JPN.). 1996. pap. 8.95 (0-938474-18-9) Buddhist Study.

Tannisho: A Tract Deploring Heresies of Faith. Ed. by Kosho Ko-nyo Otani. 101p. 1991. 31.50 (0-914910-99-X) Buddhist Bks.

Tannisho - Passages Deploring Deviations Rennyo Shonin Ofumi: The Letters of Rennyo. Numata Center for Buddhist Translation & Research Staff. Ed. by Hanayama Shoyu et al. Tr. by Bando Shojun & Harold Stewart from CHI. LC 95-73152. (BDK English Tripitaka Ser.: Vols. 105-II & 106-I). 261p. (C). 1996. 30.00 (1-886439-03-6) Numata Ctr.

Tano & Binti: Two Chimpanzees Return to the Wild. Linda DaVolls. LC 93-25403. (Illus.). (J). (gr. k-3). 1994. 14.95 (0-395-68701-2, Clarion Bks) HM.

Tano Festa Eighteen Poems, 1956-1986. Ed. by Paola Igliori. Tr. by George Scrivani & Paolo Morante. Orig. Title: ITA. (Illus.). 96p. (Orig.). 1993. pap. 15.00 (0-9625119-7-8) Inanout Pr.

Tanoan-Egyptian Djed Festival Stone: Thothmes III's Expedition to America, c. 1475 B.C. William R. Lyne. (Illus.). 50p. (YA). 1997. pap. 8.00 (0-9637467-3-1) Creatopia Prods.

Tanques: Tanks. Norman S. Barrett. (Illus.). 32p. (SPA.). (J). (gr. k-4). 1991. lib. bdg. 18.60 (0-531-07922-8) Watts.

Tansu: Traditional Japanese Cabinetry. Ty Heineken & Kiyoko Heineken. LC 81-3032. (Illus.). 264p. 1981. 65.00 (0-8348-0162-0) Weatherhill.

Tansy. large type ed. Maureen Peters. 288p. 1995. 25.99 (0-7089-3227-4) Ulverscroft.

Tanta: Two Introductory Constitutions to Justinian's Digest. Tammo Wallinga. x, 158p. (Orig.). 1989. pap. 36.00 (90-6980-031-4, Pub. by Egbert Forsten NE) Benjamins North Am.

Tanta Teva & the Magic Booth. Joel L. Grishaver. LC 93-13193. (Illus.). (J). (gr. 3-5). 1993. pap. 5.95 (1-881283-00-3) Alef Design.

Tantalizing Thai Cuisine. Vinita Lawler. LC 93-78019. 208p. (Orig.). 1993. pap. 12.95 (1-878044-10-9) Mayhaven Pub.

Tantalizing Tingles: A Discography of Early Ragtime, Jazz, & Novelty Syncopated Piano. LC 94-45220. 296p. 1995. text ed. 69.50 (0-313-29240-X) Greenwood.

***Tantalizing Tomatoes: Smart Tips & Tasty Picks for Gardeners Everywhere.** Ed. by Karan Cutler. (Illus.). 1997. pap. 9.95 (1-889538-00-0) Bklyn Botanic.

***Tantalum.** Ed. by E. Chen et al. (Illus.). 493p. 1996. 140.00 (0-87339-330-9, 3309) Minerals Metals.

Tantalum: Physico-Chemical Properties of Its Compounds & Alloys. (Atomic Energy Review Ser.: No. 3). (Illus.). 133p. (Orig.). 1973. pap. 19.00 (92-0-149072-0, IAER3, Pub. by IAEA AU) Bernan Associates.

Tantalum & Niobium. George L. Miller. (Metallurgy of the Rarer Metals Ser.: 6). 789p. reprint ed. pap. 180.00 (0-317-41849-1, 2025734) Bks Demand.

Tantalus. Catherine Arley. 1982. pap. 5.25 (0-8222-1110-6) Dramatists Play.

Tante Jeanne. Georges Simenon. (FRE.). 1991. pap. 11.95 (0-7859-3244-5, 2266045202) Fr & Eur.

Tante Martine. Henri Bosco. 318p. (FRE.). 1990. pap. 11.95 (0-7859-2239-3, 207038229X) Fr & Eur.

Tanto: Japanese Knives & Knife Fighting. Russell Maynard. LC 86-50440. 160p. (Orig.). 1986. pap. 7.95 (0-86568-078-7, 110) Unique Pubns.

Tantra: A Handbook for Spiritual Lovers. Jivan Swann. Ed. by Christine Westley. (Illus.). 32p. (J). 1989. pap. 6.00 (0-9622052-1-4) Turtle Prints.

Tantra: Hedonism in Indian Culture. Prem Saran. (C). 1994. 16.00 (81-246-0012-0, Pub. by DK Pubs Dist II) S Asia.

Tantra: Occultism & Spirituality. Pranab Bandyopadhyay. (C). 1994. 18.00 (0-8364-2893-5, Pub. by Firma KLM II) S Asia.

Tantra: The Art of Conscious Loving. Charles Muir & Caroline Muir. LC 88-7854. (Illus.). 144p. 1989. pap. 12.95 (0-916515-86-9) Mercury Hse Inc.

Tantra: The Cult of the Feminine. rev. ed. Andre Van Lysebeth. LC 95-17217. (Illus.). 408p. 1995. 30.00 (0-87728-845-3) Weiser.

Tantra: The Indian Cult of Ecstasy. Philip Rawson. (Art & Imagination Ser.). (Illus.). 1984. pap. 15.95 (0-500-81001-X) Thames Hudson.

Tantra: The Supreme Understanding Discourses of the Tantric Way of Tilopa's Song of Mahamudra. Osho. Ed. by Ma Prem Maneesha. (Tantra Ser.). 263p. 1991. 17.95 (3-89338-109-0, Pub. by Rebel Hse GW) Osho America.

Tantra: The Yoga of Sex. Omar Garrison. 1983. pap. 12.00 (0-517-54948-4, Harmony) Crown Pub Group.

Tantra - The Way of Action: A Practical Guide to Its Teachings & Techniques. rev. ed. Francis King. 160p. 1990. pap. 10.95 (0-89281-274-5) Inner Tradit.

Tantra & Popular Religion in Tibet. Ed. by Geoffrey Samuel et al. (C). 1994. text ed. 28.00 (81-85689-68-7, Pub. by Popular Prakashan II) S Asia.

Tantra Experience. Osho. 1994. pap. 13.95 (1-85230-597-5) Element MA.

Tantra in Bengal. S. C. Banerji. (C). 1992. reprint ed. 29.50 (81-85425-63-9, Pub. by Manohar II) S Asia.

Tantra in Tibet. Dalai Lama et al. LC 87-16561. 96p. (Orig.). 1987. pap. 14.95 (0-937938-49-1) Snow Lion Pubns.

Tantra of Svayambhu Vidyapada: Commentary of Sadyojyoti. Ed. & Tr. by Pierre-Sylvain Filliozat. (C). 1994. 22.00 (81-208-1125-9, Pub. by Motilal Banarsidass II) S Asia.

Tantra of the Beloved. M. Virochana Khalsa. LC 95-83266. (Illus.). 600p. (Orig.). 1996. pap. 21.95 (0-9598048-9-7, TOTB) Bks Light Pub.

Tantra of the Great Liberation. Arthur Avalon. Tr. by John Woodroffe from SAN. (Illus.). 509p. 1913. pap. 9.95 (0-486-20150-3) Dover.

Tantra Spirituality & Sex. Osho. Ed. by Swami D. Anutoshen. LC 94-7836. (Introduction to the Teachings of Osho Ser.). 160p. 1994. pap. 9.95 (0-918963-03-6) Osho America.

Tantra Vidya. Oscar M. Hinze. (C). 1989. 14.50 (81-208-0524-0, Pub. by Motilal Banarsidass II) S Asia.

Tantra Without Tears. Christopher S. Hyatt & S. Jason B;acl. LC 96-62336. (Illus.). 192p. (Orig.). 1997. pap. 14.95 (1-56184-060-2) New Falcon Pubns.

Tantra Yoga. Nik Douglas. 1971. 24.00 (0-685-40172-3, Pub. by Munshiram Manoharial II) S Asia.

Tantraloka of Abhinav Gupta, 8 vols., Set. Abhina Gupta. Ed. by R. C. Swivedi & Navjivan Rastogi. (C). 1987. 125.00 (81-208-0240-3, Pub. by Motilal Banarsidass II) S Asia.

Tantraraja Tantra. Arthur Avalon, pseud. & Lakshmana Shastri. 740p. (SAN.). (C). 1982. text ed. 52.00 (0-89744-238-5) Auromere.

Tantraraja Tantra. Arthur Avalon. (C). 1981. 22.00 (0-8364-2356-9, Pub. by Motilal Banarsidass II) S Asia.

Tantras. Richard Awlinson. LC 88-51724. (Forgotten Realms Avatar Trilogy Ser.: Bk. 2). 352p. (Orig.). 1989. pap. 5.99 (0-88038-748-3) TSR Inc.

T

An Asterisk (*) at the beginning of an entry indicates that the title is appearing in BIP for the first time.

Tantras: Their Philosophy & Occult Secrets with Critical Intro & Index. D. N. Bose. 1992. 14.00 (*0-8364-2868-4*, Pub. by Eastern Bk Linkers II) S Asia.

Tantrasara see Hindu Religion & Iconology According to the Tantrasara

Tantri Reliefs on Ancient Javanese Qandi. Marijke J. Klokke. (KITLV Verhandelingen Ser.: No. 153). (Illus.). ii, 312p. (Orig.). 1993. pap. 44.00 (*90-6718-054-8*, Pub. by KITLV Pr NE) Cellar.

Tantric Art & Meditation: The Tendai Tradition. Michael R. Saso. (Illus.). 112p. 1990. pap. text ed. 16.00 (*0-8248-1363-4*) UH Pr.

Tantric Distinction: An Introduction to Tibetan Buddhism. Jeffrey Hopkins. Ed. by Anne C. Klein. 176p. (Orig.). (C). 1984. pap. 8.95 (*0-86171-023-1*) Wisdom MA.

Tantric Doctrine of Immaculate Conception. Elizabeth Sharpe. 1994. pap. text ed. 8.95 (*1-55818-302-7*, Oriental Classics) Holmes Pub.

Tantric Grounds & Paths: How to Enter, Progress on, & Complete the Vajrayana Path. Geshe Kelsang Gyatso. (Illus.). 280p. 1994. 24.95 (*0-948006-34-X*, Pub. by Tharpa Pubns UK) ACCESS Pubs Network.

Tantric Massage: An Illustrated Manual for Meditative Sexuality. Kenneth R. Stubbs. (Illus.). 112p. (Orig.). 1993. pap. 18.95 (*0-939263-09-2*) Secret Garden.

Tantric Mysticism of Tibet. John Blofeld. 256p. 1992. reprint ed. pap. 13.95 (*0-14-019336-7*, Arkana) Viking Penguin.

Tantric Numerology, Bk. 2. rev. ed. Guruchander S. Khalsa. Ed. by Gurujivan K. Khalsa. 128p. 1993. pap. 14.95 (*0-9636752-1-4*) Radiant Lght.

Tantric Path of Purification: The Yoga Method of Heruka Vajrasattva, Including Complete Retreat Instructions. Lama T. Yeshe. Ed. by Nicholas Ribush. LC 94-30513. 344p. (Orig.). 1994. pap. 15.00 (*0-86171-020-7*) Wisdom MA.

Tantric Poetry of Kukai. Tr. by Morgan Gibson & Hiroshi Murakami. 1985. pap. 7.00 (*0-934834-67-9*) White Pine.

Tantric Practice in Nying-Ma. Khetsun S. Rinbochay. Ed. by Jeffery Hopkins & Anne C. Klein. LC 86-3762. 90p. (Orig.). 1983. pap. 14.95 (*0-937938-14-9*) Snow Lion Pubns.

***Tantric Quest: An Encounter with Absolute Love.** Daniel Odier. 192p. 1997. pap. 12.95 (*0-89281-620-1*) Inner Tradit.

Tantric Ritual of Japan. Richard K. Payne. (C). 1991. 90.00 (*81-85179-76-X*, Pub. by Aditya Prakashan II) S Asia.

Tantric Sex. rev. ed. E. J. Gold & Cybele Gold. LC 88-2551. Orig. Title: Beyond Sex. (Illus.). 192p. 1988. reprint ed. pap. 12.95 (*0-917879-02-3*) Peak Skill.

***Tantric Sexuality: A Beginner's Guide.** Richard Craze. 96p. 1997. pap. 11.95 (*0-340-68349-X*, Pub. by Headway UK) Trafalgar.

Tantric Tarot. Keith Morgan. (Orig.). 1995. pap. 8.95 (*0-614-16788-4*, Pub. by Mandrake Pr UK) Holmes Pub.

Tantric Traditions. enl. rev. ed. Agehananda Bharati. (C). 1993. 38.00 (*81-7075-022-9*, Pub. by Hindustan IA) S Asia.

Tantric Transformation. Osho. 1994. pap. 13.95 (*1-85230-596-7*) Element MA.

***Tantric Visions of the Divine Feminine: The Ten Mahavidyas.** David R. Kinsley. LC 96-27331. (Illus.). 1997. 45.00 (*0-520-20498-0*); pap. 16.95 (*0-520-20499-9*) U CA Pr.

Tantric Way: Art-Science-Ritual. Ajit Mookerjee & Madhu Khanna. LC 88-51353. (Illus.). 350p. (Orig.). 1989. pap. 16.95 (*0-500-27088-0*) Thames Hudson.

Tantric Yoga: The Royal Path to Raising Kundalini Power. Gavin Frost & Yvonne Frost. LC 89-9128. (Illus.). 308p. (Orig.). (HIN.). 1989. pap. text ed. 14.95 (*0-87728-692-2*) Weiser.

Tantric Yoga & the Wisdom Goddesses. David Frawley. 258p. 1994. pap. 16.95 (*1-878423-17-7*) Morson Pub.

Tantric Yoga Techniques. R. Chander. (Illus.). 173p. 1979. 12.95 (*0-318-36401-8*) Asia Bk Corp.

Tantrum. Kathryn Lasky. LC 92-3701. (Illus.). 32p. (J). (ps-1). 1993. lib. bdg. 13.95 (*0-02-751661-X*, Mac Bks Young Read) S&S Childrens.

***Tantrum Tabatha.** (Little Monsters Ser.). (J). 1997. write for info. (*0-614-21790-3*, Pub. by Splash UK) Assoc Pubs Grp.

Tantrums: Secrets to Calming the Storm. Ann LaForge. 96p. 1996. mass mkt. 5.99 (*0-671-88039-X*) PB.

Tantsuiushchii David. Elena Shvarts. LC 83-63002. (Russica Poetry Ser.: No. 6). 120p. (Orig.). 1985. pap. 9.95 (*0-89830-085-1*) Russica Pubs.

Tantzor. Paul-Loup Sulitzer. 1993. pap. 17.95 (*0-7859-3175-9*, 2253062324) Fr & Eur.

Tanuma Okitsugu, 1719-1788: Forerunner of Modern Japan. Whitney J. Hall. LC 82-981. (Harvard-Yenching Institute Monograph: No. 14). xii, 208p. 1982. reprint ed. text ed. 55.00 (*0-313-23369-1*, HATA, Greenwood Pr) Greenwood.

Tanya & Emily in a Dance for Two. Patricia L. Gauch. LC 93-5354. (Illus.). 40p. (J). (ps-3). 1994. lib. bdg. 15.95 (*0-399-22688-5*, Philomel Bks) Putnam Pub Group.

Tanya & the Green-Eyed Monster. Jonathan Sherwood. (Illus.). 40p. (J). (gr. k-4). 1993. 14.95 (*1-56844-002-2*) Enchante Pub.

Tanya & the Green-Eyed Monster: Jealousy. 2nd rev. ed. Jonathan Sherwood. Ed. by Gudrun Hoy & Bobi Martin. (Emotional Literacy Ser.). (Illus.). 40p. (J). (gr. k-5). 1996. 14.95 (*1-56844-102-9*) Enchante Pub.

Tanya & the Magic Wardrobe. Gauch, Patricia L. Gauch. LC 96-22012. (J). 1997. 15.95 (*0-399-22940-X*, Philomel Bks) Putnam Pub Group.

Tanya & the Tobo Man: A Story for Children Entering Therapy. Lesley Koplow. LC 92-56875. (Books to Help Children Ser.). (Illus.). (J). 1993. lib. bdg. 18.60 (*0-8368-0936-X*) Gareth Stevens Inc.

Tanya & the Tobo Man: A Story for Children Entering Therapy. Lesley Koplow. LC 91-85. (Illus.). 32p. (ENG & SPA.). (J). (ps-4). 1991. 16.95 (*0-945354-34-7*); pap. 8.95 (*0-945354-33-9*) Magination Pr.

Tanya Marcuse: Photographs. Faye Hirsch. (Illus.). 8p. (Orig.). 1993. pap. 5.00 (*0-9626731-4-5*) Yoshii Gallery.

Tanya Steps Out: A Book of Magical Moving Pictures. Patricia L. Gauch. (Illus.). 10p. (J). (ps-2). 1996. 13.95 (*0-399-22936-1*, Philomel Bks) Putnam Pub Group.

Tanya Talks about Chemical Dependence in the Family. Teresa M. Schmidt. (Building Trust, Making Friends Ser.). 232p. (J). (gr. 6-8). 1991. pap. 59.95 (*1-56246-020-X*, P164) Johnsn Inst.

Tanya Tinker & the Gizmo Gang: A Lift-the-Flap Book about How Things Work. LC 92-20859. (Early Learning Program Ser.). (J). 1992. write for info. (*0-8094-9315-2*); lib. bdg. write for info. (*0-8094-9316-0*) Time-Life.

Tanya Tucker Story. Ace Collins. 1995. mass mkt. 4.99 (*0-312-95614-2*) Tor Bks.

Tanya's Big Green Dream. Linda Glaser. LC 93-9968. (Illus.). 48p. (J). (gr. 1-4). 1994. lib. bdg. 13.95 (*0-02-735994-8*, Mac Bks Young Read) S&S Childrens.

Tanya's Daddy. 1995. pap. 8.95 (*0-86543-457-3*) Africa World.

Tanya's Reunion. Valerie Flournoy. LC 94-13067. (J). 1995. pap. 15.89 (*0-8037-1605-2*) Dial Bks Young.

Tanya's Reunion. Valerie Flournoy. LC 94-13067. (Illus.). (J). (ps-3). 1995. pap. 15.99 (*0-8037-1604-4*) Dial Bks Young.

Tanz in der Antike. Fritz Weege. (Volkskundliche Quellen, Reihe V Ser.). 196p. 1976. reprint ed. write for info. (*3-487-05968-1*) G Olms Pubs.

***Tanzania.** (Cultures of The World Ser.: Group 16). (Illus.). 128p. (YA). (gr. 5 up). 1998. lib. bdg. 25.00 (*0-7614-0809-6*) Marshall Cavendish.

Tanzania. Lisa Asch. (Passport's Regional Guides of Africa Ser.). (Illus.). 192p. 1997. pap. 19.95 (*0-8442-8962-0*, Passport Bks) NTC Pub Grp.

Tanzania. Ettagale Blauer & Jason Laure. LC 93-35495. (Enchantment of the World Ser.). (Illus.). 128p. (J). (gr. 5-8). 1994. lib. bdg. 30.00 (*0-516-02622-4*) Childrens.

Tanzania. Dona Bretherick. Ed. by Dale E. Gough. (OIES Country Guide Ser.). (C). 1995. 24.00 (*0-929851-31-5*) Am Assn Coll Registrars.

Tanzania. Darch Colin. (World Bibliographical Ser.). 1996. lib. bdg. 105.00 (*1-85109-219-6*) ABC-CLIO.

Tanzania. Compiled by Colin Darch. (World Bibliographical Ser.: No. 54). 316p. 1985. lib. bdg. 65.00 (*0-903450-91-7*) ABC-CLIO.

Tanzania. Patricia E. McCulla. (Let's Visit Places & Peoples of the World Ser.). (Illus.). 112p. (J). (gr. 5 up). 1989. lib. bdg. 19.95 (*1-55546-784-9*) Chelsea Hse.

Tanzania. Ed. by Tom Pelnar & Valerie Weber. LC 88-42890. (Children of the World Ser.). (Illus.). 64p. (J). (gr. 5-6). 1989. lib. bdg. 23.93 (*1-55532-210-7*) Gareth Stevens Inc.

Tanzania: Agriculture. International Bank for Reconstruction & Development Staff. (Country Study). 286p. 1995. 15.95 (*0-8213-3101-9*, 13101) World Bank.

Tanzania: An African Experiment. Rodger Yeager. (Nations of Contemporary Africa Ser.). (Illus.). 136p. 1983. pap. text ed. 18.95 (*0-86531-694-5*) Westview.

Tanzania: An African Experiment. 2nd ed. Rodger Yeager. 191p. (C). 1991. pap. text ed. 21.50 (*0-8133-8344-7*) Westview.

Tanzania: Party Transformation & Economic Development. enl. ed. Henry Bienen. LC 71-104098. (Center of International Studies). 1970. 65.00 (*0-691-03063-4*) Princeton U Pr.

***Tanzania: Party Transformation & Economic Development.** Henry Bienen. LC 71-104098. 537p. 1970. reprint ed. pap. 153.10 (*0-608-03328-6*, 2064040) Bks Demand.

Tanzania: Travel Guide. Globe Pequot Press Staff. 1996. pap. text ed. 9.95 (*1-85368-424-4*) Globe Pequot.

Tanzania & Nyerere: A Study of Ujamaa & Nationhood. William R. Duggan & John R. Civille. LC 76-18121. 298p. reprint ed. pap. 85.00 (*0-8357-7044-3*, 2033542) Bks Demand.

Tanzania in Pictures. Department of Geography, Lerner Publications. (Visual Geography Ser.). (Illus.). 64p. (YA). (gr. 5 up). 1989. lib. bdg. 19.95 (*0-8225-1838-4*, Lerner Publctns) Lerner Group.

***Tanzania on Tuesday: Writing by Women Traveling Abroad.** Ed. by Alan Davis & Michael White. 350p. (Orig.). 1997. pap. 19.95 (*0-89823-179-5*) New Rivers Pr.

Tanzanian Doctor. Leader Stirling. LC 78-316167. 154p. reprint ed. pap. 43.90 (*0-317-26454-0*, 2023860) Bks Demand.

Tanzanian Economy: Income Distribution & Economic Growth. Enos S. Bukuku. LC 90-24562. 240p. 1992. text ed. 59.95 (*0-275-93812-3*, C3812, Praeger Pubs) Greenwood.

Tanzanian Peasantry: Economy in Crisis. P. G. Forster & S. Maghimbi. 300p. 1992. 72.95 (*1-85628-155-8*, Pub. by Avebury Pub UK) Ashgate Pub Co.

Tanzanian Peasantry: Further Studies. Peter Forster. 368p. 1995. 72.95 (*1-85628-493-X*, Pub. by Avebury Pub UK) Ashgate Pub Co.

Tanzania's Financial Experience in the Post-War Period. Charles S. Kimei. (Studia Oeconomica Upsaliensia: No. 13). 252p. (Orig.). 1987. pap. 45.50 (*91-554-2080-X*, Pub. by Uppsala Univ Acta Univ Uppsaliensis SW) Coronet Bks.

Tao. Ed. by Robert Adkinson. LC 96-60180. (Sacred Symbols Ser.). (Illus.). 80p. 1996. 10.00 (*0-500-06024-X*) Thames Hudson.

Tao: The Chinese Philosophy of Time & Change. Philip Rawson & Laszlo Legeza. (Art & Imagination Ser.). (Illus.). 1984. pap. 14.95 (*0-500-81002-8*) Thames Hudson.

Tao: The Golden Gate, Vol. 1. Rajneesh Osho Staff. Ed. by Ma P. Asha. LC 84-42615. (Tao Ser.). 336p. (Orig.). 1984. pap. 4.95 (*0-88050-646-6*) Osho America.

Tao: The Golden Gate, Vol. 2. Rajneesh Osho Staff. Ed. by Swami K. Prabhu. LC 84-42615. (Tao Ser.). 304p. (Orig.). 1985. pap. 4.95 (*0-88050-647-4*) Osho America.

Tao: The Three Treasures, Vol. I. 2nd ed. Rajneesh Osho Staff. Ed. by Ma P. Veena. LC 83-10910. (Tao Ser.). 336p. (Orig.). 1983. reprint ed. pap. 4.95 (*0-88050-650-4*) Osho America.

Tao: The Watercourse Way. Alan Watts & Al Chung-Liang Huang. LC 76-4762. 1977. pap. 10.00 (*0-394-73311-8*) Pantheon.

Tao & Dharma: Chinese Medicine & Ayurveda. Robert Svoboda & Arnie Lade. LC 95-80859. 160p. (Orig.). 1995. pap. 12.95 (*0-914955-21-7*) Lotus Pr WI.

Tao & Longevity: Mind Body Transformation. Wen Kuan Chu & Huai-Chin Nan. LC 82-60164. 195p. (Orig.). 1984. pap. 9.95 (*0-87728-542-X*) Weiser.

Tao & Method: A Reasoned Approach to the Tao Te Ching. Michael LaFargue. LC 93-50081. (SUNY Series in Chinese Philosophy & Culture). 642p. (C). 1994. text ed. 74.50 (*0-7914-1601-1*) State U NY Pr.

Tao & Mother Goose. Robert Carter. LC 87-40524. (Illus.). 190p. (Orig.). 1988. pap. 10.00 (*0-8356-0631-7*, Quest) Theos Pub Hse.

Tao & Tai Chi Kung. Robert C. Sohn. 152p. 1989. pap. 14.95 (*0-89281-217-6*, Destiny Bks) Inner Tradit.

Tao & the Art of System Administration. Brendan P. Kehoe. 1994. pap. text ed. 24.00 (*0-13-099938-5*) P-H.

Tao & the Daimon. Robert C. Neville. LC 82-5888. 281p. 1983. text ed. 59.50 (*0-87395-661-3*); pap. text ed. 19.95 (*0-87395-662-1*) State U NY Pr.

Tao & the Logos: Literary Hermeneutics, East & West. Longxi Zhang. LC 91-37126. (Post-Contemporary Interventions Ser.). 258p. 1992. text ed. 39.95 (*0-8223-1211-5*); pap. text ed. 17.95 (*0-8223-1218-2*) Duke.

Tao & the Tree of Life: Alchemical & Sexual Mysteries of the East & West. Eric Yudelove. LC 95-47291. (Illus.). 256p. 1996. pap. 14.95 (*1-56718-250-X*) Llewellyn Pubns.

Tao at Work: On Leading & Following. Stanley M. Herman. LC 94-5609. (Management Ser.). 142p. 17.00 (*1-55542-709-X*) Jossey-Bass.

***Tao-Bible.** M. L. Smock. LC 96-95420. xii, 122p. (Orig.). 1997. pap. 12.95 (*0-9656705-0-3*, 1-97 06 01) Juniper Sun.

Tao-Billy. Kirk Judd. (Illus.). 56p. (Orig.). 1996. pap. 6.95 (*1-881692-12-4*) Trillium WV.

***TAO Cards.** Alexis Brimberry et al. x, 104p. (Orig.). (CHI & ENG.). 1996. spiral bd. 29.99 (*1-889890-00-6*) Prods of Purpose.

Tao Ching. Stephen Mitchell. pap. 8.00 (*0-685-51784-5*, PL) HarpC.

Tao Ching. Ed. by Stephen Mitchell. 1989. boxed write for info. (*0-318-66674-X*, HarpT) HarpC.

Tao, Eastern Wisdom: To Know & Not Be Know. Kiyoko Heineken. LC 92-42256. (Eastern Wisdom Ser.). 64p. 1993. 9.95 (*0-8118-0420-8*) Chronicle Bks.

TAO en Francais: Transcription Assistee par Ordinateur. Claire L. Yelle. (Illus.). 111p. (Orig.). (FRE.). (C). 1989. pap. 25.00 (*0-685-31726-9*); pap. text ed. 25.00 (*0-685-31727-7*) Stenograph Corp.

Tao Is Silent. Raymond M. Smullyan. LC 76-62939. (Orig.). 1977. pap. 13.00 (*0-06-067469-5*, RD 206) Harper SF.

Tao Magic: The Secret Language of Diagrams & Calligraphy. Laszlo Legeza. LC 86-51463. (Illus.). 167p. 1987. pap. 10.95 (*0-500-27062-7*) Thames Hudson.

Tao of AppleScript: BMUG's Guide to Macintosh Scripting. 2nd ed. Derrick Schneider et al. (Illus.). 300p. 1994. 29.95 (*1-56830-115-4*) Hayden.

Tao of Architecture. A. I. Chang. 80p. 1981. pap. text ed. 9.95 (*0-691-00330-0*) Princeton U Pr.

Tao of Balanced Diet: Secrets of a Thin & Healthy Body. Stephen T. Chang. LC 86-897. (Illus.). 200p. 1987. 18.95 (*0-942196-05-8*) Tao Pub.

Tao of Being: A Think & Do Workbook. Ray Grigg. LC 88-12885. 212p. (Orig.). 1989. pap. 16.95 (*0-89334-115-0*) Humanics Ltd.

Tao of Being: A Think & Do Workbook. Ray Grigg. LC 88-12885. (Illus.). 194p. (Orig.). 1992. lib. bdg. 26.95 (*0-89334-202-5*, 202-5) Humanics Ltd.

Tao of Bioenergetics: East - West. George A. Katchmer. Ed. by James O'Leary. (Illus.). 232p. (Orig.). 1993. pap. 16.95 (*0-940871-28-9*, B018) YMAA Pubn.

Tao of Chaos: DNA & the I Ching Unlocking the Code of the Universe. Katya Walter. 288p. 1996. pap. 9.95 (*1-85230-806-0*) Element MA.

Tao of Chaos: Essence & the Enneagram. Stephen H. Wolinsky. LC 94-33697. (Illus.). 213p. (Orig.). 1994. pap. 16.95 (*1-883647-02-9*, Bramble Bks) Bramble Co.

Tao of Chaos: Merging East & West. Katya Walter. Ed. by Terry Sherrell. (Illus.). 206p. (ENG & GER.). 1994. pap. 17.95 (*1-884178-17-0*) Kairos Ctr.

Tao of Ch'i: Healing with the Unseen Life Force. Mark D. Mincolla. (Illus.). 52p. (Orig.). (YA). 1995. pap. 14.95 (*0-9632811-1-9*) Pennyroyal Pr.

Tao of Chinese Landscape Painting: Principles & Methods. Wucius Wong. (Illus.). 144p. 1990. 29.95 (*0-8306-9010-7*, 50010, Design Pr) TAB Bks.

***Tao of Ching of Lao Tzu.** Tr. by Brian B. Walker. 1996. pap. 8.95 (*0-614-20793-2*, Griffin) St Martin.

***Tao of Coaching: Motivating Your Employees to Become All-Star Managers.** Max Landsberg. LC 97-19284. 200p. 1997. 22.95 (*1-888232-34-X*) Knowldge Exchange.

Tao of Conversation. Michael Kahn. LC 95-69487. 160p. (Orig.). 1995. pap. 12.95 (*1-57224-028-8*) New Harbinger.

Tao of Delphi: The Programmer's Path to Advanced Delphi Development. Blake Watson. 544p. 1996. pap. 39.95 incl. disk (*0-201-48927-9*) Addison-Wesley.

***Tao of Dying: A Guide to Caring.** Doug Smith. (Illus.). 163p. 1995. per. 12.50 (*0-9628363-9-7*) Caring Pub.

Tao of Fully Feeling: Harvesting Forgiveness Out of Blame. Pete Walker. LC 94-96296. 286p. 1995. 12.00 (*0-9642996-0-7*) Azure Coyote.

Tao of Golf. Leland T. Lewis. 1995. pap. 11.95 (*1-56875-096-X*) R & E Pubs.

***Tao of Gung Fu.** Bruce Lee. (Bruce Lee Library). 1997. pap. text ed. 14.95 (*0-8048-3110-6*) C E Tuttle.

Tao of Healing: Meditations for Body & Spirit. Haven Trevino. LC 92-44807. 96p. (Orig.). 1993. pap. 10.95 (*1-880032-18-X*) New Wrld Lib.

***TAO of Health & Longevity.** Liu Da. 1997. pap. text ed. 10.95 (*1-56924-718-8*) Marlowe & Co.

Tao of Health & Longevity. Da Liv. 1994. pap. 9.95 (*1-56924-900-8*) Marlowe & Co.

Tao of Health, Sex, & Longevity: A Modern Practical Guide to the Ancient Way. Daniel P. Reid. 416p. 1989. pap. 14.00 (*0-671-64811-X*, Fireside) S&S Trade.

Tao of I Ching: Way to Divination. Tsung Jou. 414p. 1986. 24.95 (*0-8048-1423-6*) C E Tuttle.

***Tao of Immunology: A Revolutionary New Understanding of Our Body's Defenses.** Marc Lappe. 1997. 27.95 (*0-306-45626-5*) Plenum.

Tao of Inner Peace. Diane Dreher. LC 90-55632. Orig. Title: The Tao of Peace. 320p. 1991. reprint ed. pap. 13.00 (*0-06-097375-7*, PL) HarpC.

***Tao of Islam.** Sachiko Murata. 400p. 1996. pap. 22.95 (*0-614-21396-7*, 1215) Kazi Pubns.

Tao of Islam: A Sourcebook on Gender Relationships in Islamic Thought. Sachiko Murata. LC 91-2610. 397p. (C). 1992. text ed. 64.50 (*0-7914-0913-9*); pap. text ed. 21.95 (*0-7914-0914-7*) State U NY Pr.

Tao of Jeet Kune Do. Bruce Lee. LC 75-13803. (Specialties Ser.). (Illus.). 1975. pap. 14.50 (*0-89750-048-2*, 401, Wehman) Ohara Pubns.

Tao of Jesus: A Book of Days for the Natural Year. Compiled by John B. Butcher. LC 94-6371. 448p. 1994. pap. 14.00 (*0-06-061188-X*) Harper SF.

***Tao of Jesus: An Exercise in Inter-Traditional Understanding.** Joseph A. Loya et al. 160p. 1998. 9.95 (*0-8091-3764-X*) Paulist Pr.

Tao of Jung: The Way of Integrity. David Rosen. 256p. 1996. pap. 21.95 (*0-670-86069-7*) Viking Penguin.

***Tao of Jung: The Way of Integrity.** David H. Rosen. 1997. pap. 10.95 (*0-14-019502-5*) Viking Penguin.

Tao of Kiteflying: The Dynamics of Tethered Flight. Harm Van Veen. LC 96-293. (Illus.). 56p. (Orig.). 1996. pap. 12.95 (*0-937315-01-X*) Aeolus Pr.

Tao of Leadership: Lao Tzu's Tao Te Ching Adapted for a New Age. John Heider. LC 84-19750. (Illus.). 170p. 1985. lib. bdg. 26.95 (*0-89334-194-0*, 194-0) Humanics Ltd.

Tao of Leadership: Lao Tzu's Tao te Ching Adapted for a New Age. John Heider. LC 84-19750. 170p. (Orig.). 1985. reprint ed. pap. 16.95 (*0-89334-079-0*) Humanics Ltd.

Tao of Learning. Pamela Metz. LC 93-1945. 176p. 1994. pap. 16.95 (*0-89334-222-X*) Humanics Ltd.

Tao of Learning: Lao Tzu's Tao Te Ching Adapted for a New Age. Pamela K. Metz. LC 93-1945. (Illus.). 160p. 1994. lib. bdg. 26.95 (*0-89334-243-2*, 2432052) Humanics Ltd.

Tao of Love. Cheng Heng. Tr. by Reina De Wit from FRE. (Illus.). 178p. 1995. 14.95 (*1-56924-817-6*) Marlowe & Co.

Tao of Love & Sex: The Ancient Chinese Way to Ecstasy. Jolan Chang. 136p. 1991. pap. 15.95 (*0-14-019338-3*, Arkana) Viking Penguin.

Tao of Management: An Age Old Study for New Age Managers. Bob Messing. LC 88-12913. (Illus.). 148p. 1989. lib. bdg. 26.95 (*0-89334-199-1*, 199-1) Humanics Ltd.

Tao of Mao Tse-Tung. Martin J. O'Malley. 1977. pap. 1.00 (*0-9606610-1-8*) M J O'Malley.

Tao of Meditation: Way to Enlightenment. Tsung Jou. 176p. 1984. 17.95 (*0-8048-1465-1*) C E Tuttle.

Tao of Meow. Waldo JaPussy. 162p. 1990. pap. 14.50 (*0-89804-800-1*, Enthea Pr) Ariel GA.

***Tao of Motherhood.** 2nd rev. ed. Vimala McClure. LC 96-47177. (Illus.). 176p. (Orig.). 1997. pap. 12.95 (*1-57731-014-4*) New Wrld Lib.

Tao of Muhammad Ali. Davis Miller. LC 96-10891. 320p. 1996. 22.00 (*0-446-51946-4*) Warner Bks.

***Tao of Music: Sound Psychology.** John Ortiz. LC 97-9196. 384p. (Orig.). 1997. pap. 19.95 (*1-57863-008-8*) Weiser.

Tao of Natural Breathing: For Health, Well-Being & Inner Growth. Dennis Lewis. LC 96-75684. (Illus.). 208p. (Orig.). 1996. pap. 17.95 (*0-9651611-0-2*) Mtn Wind.

Tao of Negotiation. Joel Edelman. LC 92-56236. 384p. 1994. pap. 12.00 (*0-88730-702-7*) Harper Busn.

Tao of Nutrition. expanded ed. Maoshing Ni & Cathy McNease. LC 93-7783. 264p. 1993. pap. 14.95 (*0-937064-66-1*) SevenStar Comm.

Tao of Objects. 2nd ed. Gary Entsminger. 1995. pap. 27.95 (*1-55851-412-0*, M&T Books) H Holt & Co.

***Tao of Parenting.** Greta Nagel. 1998. pap. write for info. (*1-55611-531-8*) D I Fine.

Tao of Peace see Tao of Inner Peace

Tao of Personal Leadership. Diane Dreher. LC 95-38547. 304p. 1996. 21.00 (*0-88730-792-2*, HarpT) HarpC.

***Tao of Personal Leadership.** Diane Dreher & Lao Tzu. 224p. 1997. pap. 12.50 (*0-88730-837-6*) Harper Busn.

An Asterisk (*) at the beginning of an entry indicates that the title is appearing in BIP for the first time.

Tao of Philosophy: The Edited Transcripts. Alan Watts. LC 95-22261. (The Alan Watts "Love of Wisdom" Library). 1995. 16.95 (*0-8048-3052-5*) C E Tuttle.

Tao of Physics: An Exploration of the Parallels Between Modern Physics & Eastern Mysticism. 3rd rev. ed. Fritjof Capra. LC 91-52520. (Illus.). 368p. 1991. pap. 14.00 (*0-87773-594-8*) Shambhala Pubns.

Tao of Politics see Book of Leadership & Strategy: Lessons of the Chinese Masters

Tao of Pooh. Benjamin Hoff. 1982. pap. 19.95 (*0-525-24458-1*, Dutton) NAL-Dutton.

Tao of Pooh. Benjamin Hoff. 1987. 1.50 (*0-416-46960-4*) Routledge Chapman & Hall.

Tao of Pooh. Benjamin Hoff. (Illus.). 158p. 1983. pap. 11.95 (*0-14-006747-7*, Penguin Bks) Viking Penguin.

Tao of Pooh & The Te of Piglet. Benjamin Hoff. (Illus.). 1994. pap. 23.90 (*0-14-095144-X*, Penguin Bks) Viking Penguin.

Tao of Pooh & The Te of Piglet Boxed Set. Benjamin Hoff. (Illus.). 272p. 1992. pap. 34.95 (*0-525-48609-7*, Dutton) NAL-Dutton.

Tao of Power. R. L. Wing. LC 85-10210. (Illus.). 192p. 1986. pap. 18.50 (*0-385-19637-7*, Dolp) Doubleday.

Tao of Programming. Geoffrey James. LC 86-18635. (Illus.). 176p. 1987. pap. 9.95 (*0-931137-07-1*) Infobooks.

Tao of Psychology: Synchronicity & the Self. Jean S. Bolen. LC 79-1778. 1982. pap. 12.00 (*0-06-250081-3*) Harper SF.

***Tao of Recovery: A Quiet Path to Wholeness.** Jim McGregor. (Illus.). 169p. 1997. lib. bdg. 26.95 (*0-89334-267-X*, Humanics Trade) Humanics Ltd.

***Tao of Recovery: Lao Tzu's Tao Te Ching Adapted for a New Age.** James MacGregor. LC 97-5279. (Illus.). 172p. (Orig.). 1997. pap. 16.95 (*0-89334-249-1*, Humanics Trade) Humanics Ltd.

Tao of Relationships. Ray Grigg. LC 87-22643. 254p. (Orig.). 1988. pap. 18.95 (*0-89334-104-5*) Humanics Ltd.

Tao of Relationships. Ray Grigg. 256p. 1989. mass mkt. 6.50 (*0-553-28043-0*) Bantam.

Tao of Relationships: A Balancing of Man & Woman. Ray Grigg. LC 87-22643. (Illus.). 254p. 1988. lib. bdg. 28.95 (*0-89334-200-9*, 200-9) Humanics Ltd.

Tao of Sailing: A Bamboo Way of Life. Ray Grigg. LC 90-30317. (Illus.). 176p. 1995. lib. bdg. 26.95 (*0-89334-201-7*, 2107028) Humanics Ltd.

Tao of Sailing: Lao Tzu's Tao Te Ching Adapted for a New Age. Ray Grigg. LC 90-30317. (Illus.). 170p. (Orig.). 1990. pap. 16.95 (*0-89334-138-X*) Humanics Ltd.

***Tao of Sales: Timeless Principles for Positive Partnerships.** E. Thomas Behr. 176p. 1997. pap. 21.95 (*1-86204-058-3*) Element MA.

Tao of Science: An Essay on Western Knowledge & Eastern Wisdom. Ralph G. Siu. (Illus.). 1964. pap. 12.00 (*0-262-69004-7*) MIT Pr.

Tao of Sex. 2nd ed. Howard S. Levy & Akira Ishihara. (Illus.). 241p. 1989. pap. 14.95 (*0-941255-44-1*) Integral Pub.

Tao of Sexology: The Book of Infinite Wisdom. Stephen T. Chang. Orig. Title: Tao of Sexology. (Illus.). 224p. 1986. 22.95 (*0-942196-03-1*) Tao Pub.

Tao of Sexology see Tao of Sexology: The Book of Infinite Wisdom

Tao of Sexual Massage. Stephen Russell & Jurgen Kolb. (Illus.). 192p. (Orig.). 1992. pap. 15.00 (*0-671-78089-1*, Fireside) S&S Trade.

Tao of Spirit. John-Roger. 169p. 1995. 15.00 (*0-914829-33-5*) Mandeville LA.

***TAO of Spirit: Inspiring Thoughts to Live By.** John-Roger. 1997. 9.00 (*0-914829-41-6*) Mandeville LA.

***Tao of Sports.** Bob Mitchell. LC 96-49859. 100p. (Orig.). 1997. pap. 11.95 (*1-883319-56-0*) Frog Ltd CA.

***Tao of Success.** Sang H. Kim. 160p. (Orig.). 1998. pap. 12.95 (*1-880336-14-6*) Turtle CT.

Tao of Surfing: Finding Depth at Low Tide. Michael A. Allen. LC 96-15408. (Illus.). 152p. (Orig.). 1997. pap. 12.95 (*1-56825-057-6*) Rainbow Books.

Tao of Symbols. James N. Powell. LC 82-5383. 1982. pap. 13.45 (*0-688-01354-6*, Quill) Morrow.

Tao of Tai-Chi Chuan: Way to Rejuvenation. Tsung H. Jou. Ed. by Shoshana Shapiro. (Illus.). 286p. (Orig.). 1981. pap. 19.95 (*0-8048-1357-4*) C E Tuttle.

Tao of Teaching: The Special Meaning of the Tao Te Ching As Related to the Art of Teaching. Greta K. Nagel. LC 94-71108. 240p. 1994. pap. 12.95 (*1-55611-415-X*) D I Fine.

Tao of Teaching: The Teaching Experience. Gerald A. Walford & Gerald E. Walford. (C). 1995. pap. text ed. 8.95 (*0-89641-241-5*) American Pr.

Tao of Teams: A Guide to Team Success. Cresencio Torres. LC 94-1880. (Illus.). 192p. 1994. pap. 12.95 (*0-89384-258-3*, Pfffr & Co) Jossey-Bass.

Tao of the Cross & the Oxherding Parable. rev. ed. Frederick Franck. (Illus.). 62p. (Orig.). 1996. pap. 9.99 (*0-88092-222-2*) Royal Fireworks.

***Tao of the Goddess Vol. 1: Spirituality & Selfhood.** Joan R. Tarpley. (Illus.). 131p. (Orig.). 1996. pap. 10.00 (*0-9655213-0-3*) Lemurian Connections.

***Tao of the Goddess Vol. II: Spirituality & Intimacy.** Date not set. per. 11.00 (*0-9655213-1-1*) Lemurian Connections.

Tao of the Loving Couple: True Liberation Through the Tao. Jolan Chang. 136p. 1991. pap. 15.95 (*0-14-019339-1*, Arkana) Viking Penguin.

Tao of the Tao Te Ching: A Translation & Commentary. Michael LaFargue. LC 91-18284. (SUNY Series in Chinese Philosophy & Culture). 270p. 1992. pap. 16.95 (*0-7914-0986-4*) State U NY Pr.

Tao of Tribute Money: The Truth Lies Beyond the Paradox. George A. Rapanos. LC 92-75845. (Philosophy-Metaphysics-Religion-Mysticism Ser.). 233p. 1994. pap. 9.95 (*0-9634591-1-2*) Avensblume Pr.

Tao of Voice. Stephen C. Cheng. 208p. 1991. pap. 14.95 (*0-89281-260-5*, Destiny Bks) Inner Tradit.

***Tao of Womanhood.** Diane Dreher. Date not set. write for info. (*0-688-15114-0*) Morrow.

Tao of Women. Pamela K. Metz & Jacqueline L. Tobin. (Illus.). 192p. (Orig.). 1995. pap. 16.95 (*0-89334-237-8*, 2378X35); lib. bdg. 26.95 (*0-89334-245-9*, 2459X35) Humanics Ltd.

Tao of Zen. Ray Grigg. LC 94-7736. (Tuttle Library of Enlightenment). 256p. 1994. 14.95 (*0-8048-1988-2*) C E Tuttle.

***Tao Passages: The Way Home.** Dorien Israel. LC 96-90769. 104p. (Orig.). 1996. pap. 14.95 (*1-879473-04-6*) Willow Way.

Tao Qian & the Chinese Poetic Tradition: The Quest for Cultural Identity. Charles Y. Kwong. LC 94-39652. (Michigan Monographs in Chinese Studies: No. 66). 1994. text ed. 50.00 (*0-89264-108-8*); pap. text ed. 25.00 (*0-89264-109-6*) Ctr Chinese Studies.

Tao-Sheng's Commentary on the Lotus Sutra: A Study & Translation. Young-ho Kim. LC 89-4629. (SUNY Series in Buddhist Studies). 374p. 1990. text ed. 64.50 (*0-7914-0227-4*) State U NY Pr.

Tao-Sheng's Commentary on the Lotus Sutra: A Study & Translation. Young-ho Kim. LC 89-4629. (SUNY Series in Buddhist Studies). 374p. 1990. pap. text ed. 21.95 (*0-7914-0228-2*) State U NY Pr.

Tao Shiatsu: Life Medicine for the Twenty-First Century. Ryokyu Endo. (Illus.). 192p. 1994. pap. 19.00 (*0-87040-940-9*) Japan Pubns USA.

Tao-Te Ching. Gia-Fu Feng. 1997. pap. 18.00 (*0-679-77619-2*) Random.

Tao Te Ching. Lao-Tzu. Tr. by Stephen Addiss & Stanley Lombardo. LC 93-21939. (Hackett Classics Ser.). (Illus.). 128p. (Orig.). (C). 1993. pap. text ed. 6.95 (*0-87220-232-1*); lib. bdg. 27.95 (*0-87220-233-X*) Hackett Pub.

Tao Te Ching. Darrell T. Liu. 1988. pap. 10.95 (*0-14-019060-0*, Penguin Bks) Viking Penguin.

Tao Te Ching. Stephen Mitchell. 1991. pap. 79.50 (*0-06-092133-1*, PL) HarpC.

Tao Te Ching. Chu Ta-kao. 1990. pap. 9.95 (*0-04-299012-2*) Routledge Chapman & Hall.

Tao Te Ching. Lao Tse. 1994. 15.00 (*0-679-43316-3*) Random.

Tao Te Ching. Lao Tsu. Tr. by Gia-fu Feng & Jane English. LC 89-45146. 1989. pap. 7.00 (*0-679-72434-6*) Random.

Tao Te Ching. Lao Tza. Tr. & Intro. by D. C. Lau. (Classics Ser.). 192p. 1964. pap. 7.95 (*0-14-044131-X*, Penguin Classics) Viking Penguin.

Tao Te Ching. Lao Tzu. 24.95 (*0-8488-1496-7*) Amereon Ltd.

Tao Te Ching. Lao Tzu. LC 88-45123. 1988. 22.00 (*0-06-016001-2*, HarpT) HarpC.

Tao Te Ching. Lao Tzu. Ed. by Feng Gia-Fu. Tr. by Jane English. 1972. pap. 16.00 (*0-394-71833-X*, V-833, Vin) Random.

Tao Te Ching. Lao Tzu. Ed. by Gia-Fu Feng. Tr. by Jane English. 1989. pap. 7.95 (*0-317-99637-1*, Vin) Random.

Tao Te Ching. 2nd ed. Tr. by Ch'u Ta-Kao. (Unwin Paperbacks Ser.). (Illus.). 128p. 1982. pap. 9.95 (*0-04-299011-4*) Routledge Chapman & Hall.

Tao Te Ching. Lao Tzu. 190p. 1987. reprint ed. lib. bdg. 23.95 (*0-89966-610-8*) Buccaneer Bks.

Tao Te Ching, Liber CLXVII. rev. ed. Lao-Tsu, pseud. Tr. by Aleister Crowley from CHI. LC 95-22270. (Illus.). 175p. 1995. pap. 12.95 (*0-87728-846-1*) Weiser.

Tao Te Ching: A New Approach - Backward down the Path. Jerry O. Dalton. 192p. 1996. mass mkt. 5.99 (*0-380-72560-6*) Avon.

Tao Te Ching: A New English Version. Tr. by Stephen Mitchell from CHI. LC 88-45123. 128p. 1988. 15.95 (*0-318-35603-1*, HarpT) HarpC.

Tao Te Ching: A New English Version. Stephen Mitchell. 144p. 1992. pap. 6.50 (*0-06-081245-1*, PL) HarpC.

Tao Te Ching: A New English Version. Stephen Mitchell. LC 88-45123. 144p. 1991. reprint ed. pap. 10.00 (*0-06-091608-7*, PL) HarpC.

Tao Te Ching: A New Translation with Commentary. Ellen M. Chen. 274p. 1989. pap. 12.95 (*1-55778-238-5*) Paragon Hse.

Tao Te Ching: A New Translation with Commentary. Ellen M. Chen. 274p. 1989. 24.95 (*1-55778-083-8*) Paragon Hse.

Tao Te Ching: About the Way of Nature & Its Powers. Lao Tzu. Tr. by Thomas H. Miles. LC 91-46362. (Illus.). 176p. (Orig.). pap. 8.95 (*0-89529-506-7*) Avery Pub.

***Tao Te Ching: An Active Edition.** Lao Tsu. (Illus.). 160p. (Orig.). 1996. pap. 10.00 (*1-889543-03-9*) Beachchair Pr.

Tao Te Ching: An Illustrated Journey. Lao Tzu. LC 93-39655. (Illus.). 104p. 1994. 12.95 (*0-8212-2075-6*) Bulfinch Pr.

Tao Te Ching: Backward Down the Path. Jerry O. Dalton. LC 93-1946. (Illus.). 176p. 1994. pap. 16.95 (*0-89334-223-8*) Humanics Ltd.

Tao Te Ching: Backward down the Path - a New Approach. Jerry O. Dalton. LC 93-1946. (Illus.). 208p. 1995. lib. bdg. 26.95 (*0-89334-231-9*, 2319053) Humanics Ltd.

Tao Te Ching: The Classic Book of Integrity & the Way. Lao Tzu. 192p. 1990. pap. 11.95 (*0-553-34935-X*) Bantam.

Tao Te Ching of Lao Tzu. Lao Tzu. 112p. 1996. pap. 9.95 (*0-312-14744-9*) St Martin.

Tao Teh Chin: The Taoists' New Library. Lao Tze. Ed. & Tr. by Shi F. Hwang from CHI. LC 91-65888. (Illus.). 100p. (Orig.). (C). 1991. 9.95 (*0-9629633-0-5*); pap. 3.95 (*0-9629633-2-1*) Taoism Pub.

Tao Teh Ching. Hua-Ching Ni. Tr. by Mark Sanchez-Piltz & Olga V. Barrero. 112p. (Orig.). (SPA.). 1995. pap. 8.95 (*0-937064-92-0*) SevenStar Comm.

Tao Teh Ching. Lao Tzu. Tr. by John C. Wu. LC 90-52692. (Pocket Classics Ser.). 96p. 1990. pap. 6.00 (*0-87773-542-5*) Shambhala Pubns.

Tao Teh Ching. Lao Tzu. Tr. by John C. Wu from CHI. LC 89-33467. 184p. 1989. reprint ed. pap. 11.00 (*0-87773-388-0*) Shambhala Pubns.

Tao Teh King. Tr. by Isabella Mears. 1983. pap. 9.95 (*0-7229-0300-6*) Theos Pub Hse.

Tao Teh King: Interpreted As Nature & Intelligence. 2nd rev. ed. Archie J. Bahm & Lao Tzu. LC 96-13670. 128p. (Orig.). (CHI.). 1997. reprint ed. pap. 12.95 (*0-87573-040-X*) Jain Pub Co.

Tao-Teh-King see Inner Life

Tao-Teh-King by Lao Tzu. 2nd ed. Archie J. Bahm. LC 58-9331. 130p. 1992. pap. 9.00 (*0-911714-20-0*, World Bks) Bahm.

Tao the Subtle Universal Law & the Integral Way of Life. 2nd ed. Hua-Ching Ni. LC 93-12497. 208p. 1995. reprint ed. pap. 12.95 (*0-937064-65-3*) SevenStar Comm.

Tao to Earth: Michael's Guide to Relationships & Growth. Jose Stevens. (Illus.). 348p. (Orig.). 1994. reprint ed. pap. 12.95 (*1-879181-14-2*) Bear & Co.

T'ao Yuan-ming: His Works & Their Meaning, 2 Vols., Set. A. R. Davis. LC 82-22092. (Cambridge Studies in Chinese History, Literature & Institutions). 320p. 1984. 144.00 (*0-521-25347-0*) Cambridge U Pr.

Tao Yuan-ming (AD 365-427) His Works & Their Meaning, Vol. 1. Albert R. Davis. LC 84-104289. 279p. 1983. reprint ed. pap. 79.60 (*0-608-02387-6*, 2063029) Bks Demand.

Tao Yuan-ming (AD 365-427) His Works & Their Meaning, Vol. 2. Albert R. Davis. LC 84-104289. 229p. 1983. reprint ed. pap. 65.30 (*0-608-02388-4*, 2063029) Bks Demand.

Taoism. Stephen F. Brown. (World Religions Ser.). (Illus.). 128p. (YA). (gr. 7-12). 1992. bds. 17.95 (*0-8160-2448-0*) Facts on File.

***Taoism: Growth of a Religion.** Isabelle Robinet & Phyllis Brooks. LC 96-30127. 1996. write for info. (*0-8047-2838-0*); pap. write for info. (*0-8047-2839-9*) Stanford U Pr.

Taoism: The Magic, the Mysticism. Julius Evola. Ed. by J. D. Holmes. Tr. & Intro. by Guido Stucco. (Orig.). 1993. pap. 6.95 (*1-55818-227-6*, Oriental Classics) Holmes Pub.

Taoism: The Parting of the Way. Holmes H. Welch. Orig. Title: Parting of the Way. 1966. pap. 13.00 (*0-8070-5973-0*) Beacon Pr.

Taoism: The Road to Immortality. John Blofeld. LC 77-90882. 195p. 1979. pap. 16.00 (*0-87773-116-0*) Shambhala Pubns.

Taoism: The Road to Immortality. John Blofeld. 1979. pap. 16.00 (*0-394-73582-X*) Shambhala Pubns.

Taoism & the Rite of Cosmic Renewal. 2nd ed. Michael R. Saso. LC 89-5687. (Illus.). 152p. 1990. pap. text ed. 20.00 (*0-87422-054-8*) Wash St U Pr.

***Taoist Astrology: A Handbook of the Authentic Chinese Tradition.** Susan Levitt & Jean Tang. LC 97-10330. 224p. 1997. pap. 14.95 (*0-89281-606-6*) Inner Tradit.

Taoist Body. Kristofer Schipper. Tr. by Karen C. Duval from FRE. LC 93-28999. 1993. pap. 15.00 (*0-520-08224-9*) U CA Pr.

Taoist Classic: Chuang-Tzu. Chuang-Tzu. Tr. by Fung Yu-Lan from CHI. 150p. (C). 1989. text ed. 16.95 (*0-8351-1970-X*) China Bks.

***Taoist Classic: The Book of Lao Zi.** Ren Jiyu. 104p. 1993. 16.95 (*7-119-01571-0*, Pub. by Foreign Lang CH) China Bks.

Taoist Cookbook: Eighty-One Recipes with 81 Meditations of Lao-Tzu. Michael R. Saso. (Illus.). 224p. (Orig.). 1994. pap. 16.95 (*0-8048-3037-1*) C E Tuttle.

Taoist Experience: An Anthology. Ed. by Livia Kohn. LC 92-32933. (SUNY Series in Chinese Philosophy & Culture). 391p. (C). 1993. pap. 21.95 (*0-7914-1580-5*); text ed. 64.50 (*0-7914-1579-1*) State U NY Pr.

Taoist Health Exercise Book. Liu Da. 1994. pap. 10.95 (*1-56924-901-6*) Marlowe & Co.

Taoist I Ching. Tr. by Thomas Cleary from CHI. LC 85-27890. 332p. 1986. pap. 18.00 (*0-87773-352-X*) Shambhala Pubns.

Taoist I Ching. Liu I-Ming. Tr. by Thomas Cleary. LC 85-27890. 333p. 1986. pap. 18.00 (*0-394-74387-3*) Shambhala Pubns.

Taoist Inner View of the Universe & the Immortal Realm. Hua-Ching Ni. LC 79-92389. (Illus.). 218p. (Orig.). 1979. pap. text ed. 14.95 (*0-937064-02-5*) SevenStar Comm.

Taoist Meditation: The Mao-shan Tradition of Great Purity. Isabelle Robinet. Tr. by Julian F. Pas & Norman J. Girardot from FRE. LC 92-23086. (SUNY Series in Chinese Philosophy & Culture). (Illus.). 285p. (C). 1993. pap. text ed. 21.95 (*0-7914-1360-8*) State U NY Pr.

Taoist Meditation & Longevity Techniques. Ed. by Livia Kohn. LC 89-806. (Michigan Monographs in Chinese Studies: No. 61). (Illus.). 384p. (C). 1989. pap. text ed. 25.00 (*0-89264-085-5*) Ctr Chinese Studies.

Taoist Mystical Philosophy: The Scripture of Western Ascension. Livia Kohn. LC 90-34598. (SUNY Series in Chinese Philosophy & Culture). 361p. (C). 1991. text ed. 64.50 (*0-7914-0542-7*); pap. text ed. 21.95 (*0-7914-0543-5*) State U NY Pr.

Taoist Ritual & Popular Cults in Southeast China. Kenneth Dean. LC 92-21047. (Illus.). 320p. (C). 1993. text ed. 55.00 (*0-691-07417-8*) Princeton U Pr.

Taoist Ritual & Popular Cults of Southeast China. Kenneth Dean. 308p. (C). 1993. pap. text ed. 16.95 (*0-691-04473-2*) Princeton U Pr.

Taoist Secrets of Love: Cultivating Male Sexual Energy. Mantak Chia. 300p. 1984. pap. 14.95 (*0-943358-19-1*) Aurora Press.

Taoist Texts. Frederic H. Balfour. 1973. lib. bdg. 250.00 (*0-87968-191-8*) Krishna Pr.

Taoist Tradition in Chinese Thought. Yao-yu Wu. Ed. by Gary Seaman. LC 91-72077. (Ethnographics Monographs: No. 4). (Illus.). 250p. (Orig.). 1991. pap. 15.00 (*1-878986-03-1*) Ethnogphics Pr.

Taoist Ways to Transform Stress into Vitality: The Inner Smile - Six Healing Sounds. Mantak Chia. LC 85-81656. (Illus.). 146p. (Orig.). 1986. pap. 9.95 (*0-935621-00-8*) Heal Tao Bks.

Taoist Yoga. Charles Luk. LC 83-60831. 224p. 1973. pap. 11.00 (*0-87728-067-3*) Weiser.

Taormina. 2nd ed. Wilhelm Von Gloeden. (Illus.). 112p. 1991. reprint ed. pap. 40.00 (*0-942642-43-0*) Twelvetrees Pr.

Taos Area, NM. Ed. by Trails Illustrated Staff. (Illus.). 1994. 8.99 (*1-56695-001-5*) Trails Illustrated.

Taos Art Colony House & Studio: A Stand up Paper Model. Bunny Huffman. 1992. pap. 17.50 (*0-89013-240-2*) Museum NM Pr.

Taos Crescent. Phillips Kloss. LC 91-8593. 76p. (Orig.). 1991. pap. 10.95 (*0-86534-165-6*) Sunstone Pr.

Taos Guide. rev. ed. Kathryn Johnson. LC 83-4900. (Illus.). 64p. (Orig.). 1993. pap. 6.95 (*0-86534-026-9*) Sunstone Pr.

Taos Indians & the Battle for Blue Lake. R. C. Gordon-McCutchan. LC 90-61680. (Illus.). 256p. (Orig.). 1991. 25.95 (*1-878610-12-0*) Red Crane Bks.

Taos Indians & the Battle for Blue Lake. rev. ed. 1995. pap. 14.95 (*1-878610-57-0*) Red Crane Bks.

Taos Landmarks & Legends. Bill Hemp. LC 95-60832. (Illus.). 144p. (Orig.). 1995. 34.95 (*0-944482-41-4*); 150.00 (*0-944482-42-2*); pap. 19.95 (*0-944482-40-6*) Except Bks NM.

Taos Moderns: Art of the New. David L. Witt. LC 92-10213. (Illus.). 136p. 1992. 37.50 (*1-878610-16-3*); pap. 25.00 (*1-878610-17-1*) Red Crane Bks.

Taos Pueblo: A Walk Through Time. John J. Bodine. LC 77-73460. (Illus.). 64p. (Orig.). 1996. pap. 6.95 (*1-887896-00-7*) Treas Chest Bks.

Taos Pueblo & Its Sacred Blue Lake. Marcia Keegan. LC 91-72482. (Illus.). 64p. 1992. 14.95 (*0-940666-12-X*) Clear Light.

Taos Recipe: A Cookbook of Recipes from Taos, New Mexico Restaurants. Joan Stromquist & Carl Stromquist. (Illus.). 192p. (Orig.). 1990. pap. 12.95 (*0-9622807-1-2*) Tierra Pubns.

Taos Tales. unabridged ed. Elsie C. Parsons. LC 95-45565. 192p. 1996. reprint ed. pap. text ed. 7.95 (*0-486-28974-5*) Dover.

Taos Trappers: The Fur Trade in the Far Southwest, 1540-1846. David J. Weber. LC 75-145508. (Illus.). 280p. 1980. pap. 15.95 (*0-8061-1702-8*) U of Okla Pr.

Tap! The Greatest Tap Dance Stars & Their Stories, 1900-1955. 2nd rev. ed. Rusty E. Frank. (Illus.). 342p. 1995. reprint ed. pap. 19.95 (*0-306-80635-5*) Da Capo.

Tap along with Tommy, 3 vols., 1. Tommy Sutton. Ed. by Georgia Dreger. LC 86-90550. (Illus.). 486p. 1986. write for info. (*0-9617568-1-0*) T Sutton.

Tap along with Tommy, 3 vols., 2. Tommy Sutton. Ed. by Georgia Dreger. LC 86-90550. (Illus.). 486p. 1986. write for info. (*0-9617568-2-9*) T Sutton.

Tap along with Tommy, 3 vols., 3. Tommy Sutton. Ed. by Georgia Dreger. LC 86-90550. (Illus.). 486p. 1986. write for info. (*0-9617568-3-7*) T Sutton.

Tap along with Tommy, 3 vols., Set. Tommy Sutton. Ed. by Georgia Dreger. LC 86-90550. (Illus.). 486p. 1986. 49.95 (*0-9617568-0-2*) T Sutton.

***Tap Clap & Sing! Note-Reading Activity Book, Vol. 1.** Peggy Wise. 60p. 1986. pap. text ed. 5.95 (*0-9616794-0-9*) Summy-Birchard.

Tap Clap & Sing! Note-Reading Activity Book, Vol. 2. Peggy Wise. (Illus.). 48p. 1991. student ed., pap. text ed. 5.95 (*0-9616794-1-7*) Summy-Birchard.

Tap Dance (A Dictionary in Labanotation) Sheila Marion. Ed. by Cook et al. (Illus.). 60p. (Orig.). 1986. pap. text ed. 20.00 (*0-9602002-5-8*) Ray Cook.

***Tap Dance Dictionary.** Mark Knowles. 288p. 1997. lib. bdg. 55.00 (*0-7864-0352-7*) McFarland & Co.

Tap Dancer. B. Barrow. pap. 28.95 (*0-7156-2416-4*, Pub. by Duckworth UK) Focus Pub-R Pullins.

***Tap Dancing.** Tracy Maurer. LC 97-8392. (Let's Dance Ser.). (J). 1997. write for info. (*1-57103-172-3*) Rourke Pr.

Tap Dancing at a Glance. Jimmy Ormonde. LC 96-85686. (Illus.). 96p. (Orig.). 1996. reprint ed. pap. 9.95 (*1-55709-435-7*) Applewood.

Tap Dancing for Big Mom. Roseann Lloyd. 1990. pap. 4.50 (*0-89823-073-X*) New Rivers Pr.

Tap Dancing for the Relatives. Richard Michelson. LC 85-9166. (University of Central Florida Contemporary Poetry Ser.). 69p. 1985. 14.95 (*0-8130-0827-1*) U Press Fla.

Tap-Dancing Lizard: Three Hundred Thirty-Seven Fanciful Charts for the Adventurous Knitter. Catherine Cartwright-Jones & Roy Jones. (Illus.). 176p. (Orig.). 1992. pap. 18.95 (*0-934026-78-5*) Interweave.

***Tap Dancing on Ice: The Life & Times of a Nevada Gaming Pioneer.** Jack R. Douglass & William A. Douglass. (Illus.). xvi, 255p. 1996. 21.95 (*1-56475-373-5*) U NV Oral Hist.

TAP Services Guide. 150p. 1995. pap. 75.00 (*0-11-330839-6*, HM08396, Pub. by Stationery Ofc UK) Bernan Associates.

TAP Systems Guide. HMSO Staff. 172p. 1995. pap. 75.00 (*0-11-330840-X*, HM0840X, Pub. by Stationery Ofc UK) Bernan Associates.

Tap, Tap. David Martin. LC 93-38838. 1995. 20.00 (*0-679-41055-4*) Random.

***Tap, Tap.** David Martin. 1996. mass mkt. 6.99 (*0-614-20521-2*, St Martins Paperbacks) St Martin.

Tap Tap. David Martin. 1996. mass mkt. 6.99 (*0-312-95835-8*) Tor Bks.

Tap-Tap. Karen L. Williams. LC 93-13006. (Illus.). (J). (gr. 1-4). 1994. 14.95 (*0-395-65617-6*, Clarion Bks) HM.

Tap-Tap. Karen L. Williams. 1996. pap. 8.95 (*0-395-72087-7*, Clarion Bks) HM.

Tap-Tap. Karen Lynn Williams. LC 93-13006. 1995. pap. 5.95 (*0-395-72086-9*, Clarion Bks) HM.

Tap the Deck. Tanis Knight & Larry Lewin. Ed. by Herbert J. Hrebic. (Writing Program Ser.). (Illus.). (Orig.). (J). (gr. 5-6). 1985. text ed. 9.10 (*0-933282-18-4*); pap. text ed. 6.00 (*0-933282-17-6*) Stack the Deck.

Tap the Hidden Wealth in Your Business. Lawrence W. Tuller. 224p. 1991. 29.95 (*0-8306-8708-4*, 3708, Liberty Hall Pr); pap. 16.95 (*0-8306-1400-1*, Liberty Hall Pr) TAB Bks.

Tap Water & the Dynamics of Good Health. Robert A. Gegan. 84p. (Orig.). 1986. pap. text ed. 3.95 (*0-940062-03-8*) Consumer Info Pubns.

Tapa in Tonga. Wendy Arbeit. (Illus.). 32p. (Orig.). 1995. pap. text ed. 9.00 (*0-8248-1727-3*) Palm Frond Prods.

Tapa Samples from Polynesia. Robert D. Craig & Vernice W. Pere. 1980. pap. 4.50 (*0-939154-06-4*) Inst Polynesian.

Tapamveni: The Rock Art Galleries of Petrified Forest & Beyond. Photos by Ekkehart Malotki. LC 94-17796. (Illus.). 194p. 1994. pap. 29.95 (*0-945695-05-5*) Petrified Forest Mus Assn.

Tapas. Harper Collins Staff. (Little Appetiser Library). 64p. 1994. 9.00 (*0-207-18605-7*, Pub. by Angus & Robertson AT) HarpC.

Tapas. Adrian Linssen. 1995. 6.98 (*0-7858-0491-9*) Bk Sales Inc.

***Tapas.** Smithmark Staff. (Creative Cooking Library). 1996. 12.98 (*0-7651-9877-0*) Smithmark.

Tapas. Ann Walker & Larry Walker. LC 94-508. (Illus.). 112p. 1994. 14.95 (*0-8118-0331-7*) Chronicle Bks.

Tapas: The Little Dishes of Spain. Penelope Casas. LC 85-40160. (Illus.). 256p. (Orig.). 1985. pap. 18.00 (*0-394-74235-4*) Knopf.

Tape Automated Bonding. Business Communications Co., Inc. Staff. 154p. 1987. pap. 1,950.00 (*0-89336-615-3*, GB-104) BCC.

Tape for the Turn of the Year. A. R. Ammons. 216p. 1994. pap. 11.00 (*0-393-31204-6*) Norton.

Tape for the Turn of the Year. A. R. Ammons. 96p. 1993. 21.00 (*0-393-03553-0*) Norton.

Tape Reading & Market Tactics. Humphrey B. Neill. LC 73-115001. 224p. 1970. reprint ed. pap. 17.00 (*0-87034-074-3*) Fraser Pub Co.

Tape-Recorded Interview: A Manual for Field Workers in Folklore & Oral History. Edward D. Ives. LC 79-20527. 144p. 1980. 20.00 (*0-87049-257-8*); pap. text ed. 10.00 (*0-87049-291-8*) U of Tenn Pr.

Tape-Recorded Interview: A Manual for Field Workers in Folklore & Oral History. 2nd ed. Edward D. Ives. LC 94-18757. (Illus.). 128p. (C). 1995. pap. text ed. 9.95 (*0-87049-878-9*) U of Tenn Pr.

Tape Recording Local History. David Haines. 1977. 2.50 (*0-913714-17-8*) Legacy Books.

Tape Recording Made Easy: A Programmed Primer. 1983. 3.75 (*0-9601006-3-6*) G T Yeamans.

Tape-Recording Your Church's History. Ronald A. Tonks. Ed. by Charles W. Deweese. (Resource Kit for Your Church's History Ser.). 8p. 1984. pap. 0.60 (*0-939804-17-4*) Hist Comm S Baptist.

Tape 2 see Orientation in American English

Tape 2 see Orientation in Business English

Tape 3 see Hablemos en Espanol

Tape 3 see Orientation in American English

Tape 3 see Orientation in Business English

Tape 3 see SR French: Parlons Francais

Tapebook 1 see Hablemos en Espanol

Tapebook 1 see Orientation in American English

Tapebook 1 see SR Italian: Lo Dica in Italiano

Tapebook 2 see Hablemos en Espanol

Tapebook 2 see Orientation in American English

Tapebook 3 see Orientation in American English

Tapebook 4 see Orientation in American English

Tapeless Sound Recording. Francis Rumsey. (Illus.). 195p. 1990. pap. 32.95 (*0-240-51297-9*) Buttrwrth-Heinemann.

Tapenum's Day: A Day in the Life of a Wampanoag Indian Boy. Kate Waters. LC 94-36060. (Illus.). 40p. (J). (gr. 2-4). 1996. 16.95 (*0-590-20237-5*) Scholastic Inc.

Tapenum's Day: A Wampanoag Indian Boy in Pilgrim Times. Kate Waters. (Illus.). (J). (gr. 2-4). 1996. 16.95 (*0-614-15760-9*) Scholastic Inc.

***Tapered Roller Bearing for Enclosed Gear Drive Applications.** P. L. Haager & Charles A. Moyer. (Technical Papers). 1964. pap. text ed. 30.00 (*1-55589-368-6*) AGMA.

Tapes of the Night Sky: A Guided Tour of the Stars. Sherwood Harrington. Ed. by Andrew Fraknoi. (Illus.). 60p. 1995. pap. 24.95 incl. audio (*0-937707-17-1*, QA 102) Astron Soc Pacific.

Tapes of the River Delta. Peter Cunningham. 352p. 1996. 23.95 (*0-312-14051-7*) St Martin.

Tapescript Nuevas Dimensiones. 2nd ed. Hendrickson. (College Spanish Ser.). 1992. pap. 21.95 (*0-8384-2331-0*) Wadsworth Pub.

Tapestries. Faye Winstead. 1996. pap. 8.95 (*1-884570-55-0*) Research Triangle.

Tapestries: An Anthology. Ed. by Kathy Ice. LC 95-9986. (Magic: The Gathering Ser.). 304p. 1995. pap. 12.00 (*0-06-105308-2*) HarpC.

Tapestries: An Anthology. Kathy Ice. (Magic: The Gathering Ser.). 384p. 1996. mass mkt. 5.99 (*0-06-105428-3*, Harp PBks) HarpC.

***Tapestries: Stories of Women in the Bible.** Ruth Sanderson. LC 97-6319. 1998. write for info. (*0-316-77093-0*) Little.

Tapestries for the Courts of Federico II, Ercole, & Ferrante Gonzaga, 1522-63. Clifford M. Brown & Guy Delmarcel. LC 95-25130. (College Art Association Monograph on the Fine Arts Ser.: Vol. LII). (Illus.). 232p. 1996. text ed. 50.00 (*0-295-97513-X*) U of Wash Pr.

Tapestries in Sand: The Spirit of Indian Sandpainting. rev. ed. David Villasenor. (Illus.). 112p. 1966. pap. 8.95 (*0-911010-22-X*) Naturegraph.

Tapestries of Europe & Colonial Peru in the Museum of Fine Arts, Boston. Adolph S. Cavallo. LC 67-17672. 1968p. 1968. boxed 17.50 (*0-87846-015-2*) Mus Fine Arts Boston.

Tapestries of Hope, Threads of Love: The Arpillera Movement in Chile, 1974-1994. Marjorie Agosin & Celeste Kostopulos-Cooperman. LC 95-32448. (Illus.). 160p. (C). 1996. 70.00 (*0-8263-1691-3*) U of NM Pr.

Tapestries of Hope, Threads of Love: The Arpillera Movement in Chile, 1974-1994. Marjorie Agosin. Tr. by Celeste Kostopulos-Cooperman. LC 95-32448. (Illus.). 160p. (C). 1996. pap. 39.95 (*0-8263-1692-1*) U of NM Pr.

Tapestries of Life: Poems for Sermons, Meditations, Bulletins & Newsletters. 64p. (Orig.). 1993. pap. text ed. 5.95 (*0-687-03616-X*) Abingdon.

Tapestries of Life: Women's Work, Women's Consciousness, & the Meaning of Daily Experience. Bettina Aptheker. LC 88-26715. 312p. 1989. pap. 17.95 (*0-87023-659-8*) U of Mass Pr.

Tapestries of the Lowlands. Heinrich Gobel. Tr. by Robert West. LC 73-79046. (Illus.). 1974. reprint ed. lib. bdg. 75.00 (*0-87817-132-0*) Hacker.

Tapestry. 1996. pap. 2.99 (*0-8217-5485-8*) Kensgtn Pub Corp.

Tapestry. Sally Cheney. (Historical Ser.). 1993. mass mkt. 3.99 (*0-373-28792-5*, 1-28792-9) Harlequin Bks.

Tapestry. Barty Phillips. (Illus.). 240p. (C). 1994. 55.00 (*0-7148-2920-X*, Pub. by Phaidon Press UK) Chronicle Bks.

Tapestry. Belva Plain. 560p. 1989. mass mkt. 6.99 (*0-440-20271-X*) Dell.

Tapestry. James M. Rose & Barbara W. Brown. (Illus.). 163p. (Orig.). 1979. pap. 4.95 (*0-9607744-2-4*) New London County.

Tapestry. Maura Seger. 352p. 1993. mass mkt. 5.50 (*0-06-108018-7*, Harp PBks) HarpC.

Tapestry, Vol. III. Ed. by Urania Fung. (Illus.). 230p. (Orig.). (YA). (gr. 9-12). 1994. write for info. (*0-9636974-2-0*) Lamar HS.

Tapestry: An Anthology of Poetry & Short Stories by Four Generations of One Family. Illus. & Pref. by Helen J. Sherry. 145p. 1989. pap. 9.95 (*0-922273-01-4*) Chocho Bks.

Tapestry: Directed Journaling for Life Weavers. Patsy R. Booth. 172p. 1994. pap. 12.95 (*1-884393-02-0*) Cedar Tree.

Tapestry Cats. Ann Turnbull. (Illus.). (J). 1992. 14.95 (*0-316-85626-6*) Little.

Tapestry Cats & Dogs: Twenty-five Complete Projects. Amanda Davidson. (Illus.). 128p. 1995. 24.95 (*0-7153-0167-5*, Pub. by D & C Pub UK) Sterling.

Tapestry Crochet. Carol V. Norton. 1991. pap. 17.95 (*0-932394-15-9*) Dos Tejedoras.

Tapestry for Mother. rev. ed. Jean Hutchinson. (Illus.). 141p. 1995. spiral bd., pap. 26.95 (*0-9648008-0-2*) ArtReach Pubs.

Tapestry Grammar: A Reference for Learners of English. Alice H. Deakins. (College ESL Ser.). 1994. pap. 26.95 (*0-8384-4122-X*) Heinle & Heinle.

Tapestry Handbook: An Illustrated Manual of Traditional Techniques. Carol K. Russell. Ed. by Carol Taylor. (Illus.). 180p. 1990. 26.95 (*0-937274-54-2*) Lark Books.

Tapestry in Question: The Poetry of Jeffrey Stephen. Jeffrey Stephen. LC 94-92078. 92p. (Orig.). 1994. pap. 6.95 (*0-9640900-0-7*) Tapestry Pubns.

Tapestry Loom Techniques: A Guide to Exploration on the Two Harness Loom. Jules Kliot. 1974. pap. 8.00 (*0-916896-04-8*) Lacis Pubns.

Tapestry of Caring: Education as Nurturance. Ed. by A. Renee Prillaman et al. LC 93-46343. 224p. 1994. pap. 39.50 (*1-56750-075-7*); text ed. 73.25 (*0-89391-971-3*) Ablex Pub.

Tapestry of Courage. Mary A. Welch. LC 92-81192. 236p. (Orig.). 1992. 14.95 (*0-9632509-0-6*); pap. 9.95 (*0-9632509-1-4*) Blue & Gold.

Tapestry of Culture. 4th ed. Abraham Rosman & Paula G. Rubel. 1992. text ed. write for info. (*0-07-053718-6*) McGraw.

Tapestry of Culture: An Introduction to Cultural Anthropology. 5th ed. Abraham Rosman & Paula G. Rubel. LC 94-9412. 1994. pap. text ed. 24.00 (*0-07-053955-3*) McGraw.

***Tapestry of Culture: An Introduction to Cultural Anthropology.** 6th ed. Abraham Rosman & Paula G. Rubel. LC 97-25978. 1997. write for info. (*0-07-054000-4*) McGraw.

Tapestry of Dreams. Nina Beaumont. (Historical Ser.). 1995. mass mkt. 4.50 (*0-373-28878-6*, 1-28878-6) Harlequin Bks.

Tapestry of Early Christian Discourse: Rhetoric, Society, & Ideology. Vernon K. Robbins. 296p. (C). 1996. pap. 19.95 (*0-415-13998-8*); text ed. 65.00 (*0-415-13997-X*) Routledge.

Tapestry of Fate. Nina Beaumont. 1994. mass mkt. 3.99 (*0-373-28846-8*, 1-28846-3) Harlequin Bks.

Tapestry of Fear. large type ed. Margaret A. Pemberton. (Dales Large Print Ser.). 268p. 1995. pap. 17.99 (*1-85389-492-3*, Dales) Ulverscroft.

Tapestry of Hope. Alice Kern. (Illus.). 165p. (Orig.). (C). reprint ed. pap. text ed. 12.00 (*0-9644994-0-1*) A L Kern.

Tapestry of Impressions. George G. Guerin. (Orig.). 1996. pap. write for info. (*1-57553-275-1*) Watermrk Pr.

Tapestry of Language Learning. Robin C. Scarcella. 1992. pap. 26.95 (*0-8384-2359-0*) Heinle & Heinle.

Tapestry of Life. Nancy Huston Cox Clifton. (Illus.). 72p. 1995. per., pap. 11.00 (*0-8059-3623-8*) Dorrance.

Tapestry of Life. Nancy Cole. LC HB-13. Date not set. 14.99 (*1-56292-013-8*) Honor Bks OK.

Tapestry of Life. Timothy D. Naegele. (Illus.). 1400p. 1990. write for info. (*0-9625131-7-2*) Sotweed Pr.

Tapestry of Life Bk. 2: Devotions for the Unique Woman. Nancy C. Cole. 272p. Date not set. 14.99 (*1-56292-286-6*) Honor Bks OK.

Tapestry of Lions. Jennifer Roberson. (Chronicles of the Cheysuli Ser.: Bk. 8). 464p. (Orig.). 1992. mass mkt. 5.99 (*0-88677-524-8*) DAW Bks.

Tapestry of Morning. Susan English. Ed. by Don D. Wilson. 24p. (Orig.). 1991. pap. 4.00 (*1-880286-06-8*) Singular Speech Pr.

Tapestry of Murders. P. C. Doherty. 256p. 1996. 21.95 (*0-312-14052-5*) St Martin.

Tapestry of Murders. large type ed. P. C. Doherty. 416p. 1996. 25.99 (*0-7089-3446-3*) Ulverscroft.

Tapestry of Orbits. Desmond G. King-Hele. LC 92-11674. (Illus.). 248p. (C). 1992. text ed. 69.95 (*0-521-39323-X*) Cambridge U Pr.

***Tapestry of Praise.** 44p. 1986. 7.99 (*0-8341-9340-X*) Lillenas.

Tapestry of Praise. Ed. by Evonne Neuenschwander et al. 1986. 8.99 (*0-685-68291-9*, MB-566) Lillenas.

Tapestry of Reading: Introducing Literary Genres, Grades 4-6. Terry Z. McDermid. (Illus.). 130p. (Orig.). 1994. pap. 10.95 (*0-673-36090-3*, GoodYrBooks) Addson-Wesley Educ.

Tapestry of Saint Joseph: "Chronological History of St. Joseph & His Apostle, Blessed Brother Andre" Susan T. Stein. LC 91-71601. (Illus.). 240p. 1991. 14.95 (*0-9629293-0-1*) Apostle PA.

Tapestry of Service, No. 1: The Evolution of Nursing in Australia. Bartz Schultz. (Illus.). 440p. 1991. text ed. write for info. (*0-443-02719-6*) Churchill.

***Tapestry of Spies.** Stephen Hunter. 1997. mass mkt. 6.99 (*0-440-22185-4*) Dell.

Tapestry of Tales: Family Chronicle from Indiana Homestead to Florida Everglades, 1893-1991. Daisy S. Kurtz. LC 91-60803. 221p. 1991. pap. 12.50 (*0-9629264-0-X*) M E Kurtz.

Tapestry of the Boar. Nigel Tranter. 320p. 1993. 27.00 (*0-340-60106-X*, Pub. by H & S UK) Trafalgar.

Tapestry of the Boar. large type ed. Nigel Tranter. 1995. 25.99 (*0-7089-3340-8*) Ulverscroft.

Tapestry of the Gods: Psychological Transformation & the Seven Rays, 2 vols., Vol. I. Michael D. Robbins. 400p. (Orig.). 1988. pap. write for info. (*0-9621869-0-2*) Univ Seven Rays Pub.

Tapestry of the Gods: Psychological Transformation & the Seven Rays, 2 vols., Vol. II. Michael D. Robbins. 400p. (Orig.). 1988. pap. write for info. (*0-9621869-1-0*) Univ Seven Rays Pub.

Tapestry of the Gods: Psychological Transformation & the Seven Rays, 2 vols., Vols. I-II. Michael D. Robbins. LC 88-51065. 1207p. (Orig.). 1996. Set. pap. 65.00 (*0-9621869-2-9*) Univ Seven Rays Pub.

***Tapestry of the Law: Scotland, Legal Culture & Legal Theory.** Elspeth Attwooll. LC 96-48834. (Law & Philosophy Library). 270p. (C). 1996. lib. bdg. 120.00 (*0-7923-4310-7*) Kluwer Ac.

Tapestry of Thought, Vol. 1. Antonia B. Laird. LC 95-179006. 72p. 1995. 13.95 (*0-8233-0504-X*) Golden Quill.

Tapestry of Thoughts. Ed. by Nicole Walstrum. 1996. 69.95 (*1-57553-064-3*) Watermrk Pr.

Tapestry of Words. Charles J. Palmer & Jacqueline Palmer. LC 93-73453. (Illus.). 240p. 1993. 49.00 (*1-881808-04-1*) Creat Arts & Sci.

Tapestry, the Mirror of Civilization. Phyllis Ackerman. LC 74-108123. reprint ed. 45.00 (*0-404-00279-X*) AMS Pr.

Tapestry Two. Archer M. Huntington. 1952. 5.00 (*0-87535-070-4*) Hispanic Soc.

Tapestry, Vol. I: A Multicultural Volume. Ed. by Bernice D. Reid. 200p. 1992. pap. 12.00 (*0-9636974-0-4*) Lamar HS.

Tapestry, Vol. II: A Multicultural Volume. 2nd ed. Ed. by Bernice D. Reid et al. (Illus.). 253p. 1993. pap. 15.00 (*0-9636974-1-2*) Lamar HS.

Tapestry Weaving: A Comprehensive Study Guide. Nancy Harvey. LC 90-56139. (Illus.). 208p. (Orig.). 1991. pap. 19.95 (*0-934026-64-5*) Interweave.

***Tapeten Beruhmter Kunstler: Von Durer Bis Warhol.** Marilyn O. Hapgood. Tr. by C. W. Auffhammer. (Illus.). 272p. (ENG & GER.). (C). 1992. 143.00 (*3-8170-2025-2*, Pub. by Knstvrlag Weingrtn GW) Intl Bk Import.

Tapetum: Cytology, Function, Biochemistry & Evolution. Ed. by M. Hesse et al. 200p. 1993. 149.95 (*0-387-82486-3*) Spr-Verlag.

Taphonomy: A Bibliographic Guide to the Literature. Ed. by Christopher P. Koch. 67p. 1989. pap. 17.00 (*0-912933-05-4*) Ctr Study First Am.

Taphonomy: Releasing the Information Found in the Fossil Record. Ed. by D. Briggs & P. Allison. (Topics in Geobiology Ser.: Vol. 9). (Illus.). 420p. 1991. 110.00 (*0-306-43876-3*, Plenum Pr) Plenum.

Taphonomy & Paleoecology of the Christensen Bog Mastodon Bone Bed, Hancock County, Indiana. Russell W. Graham et al. (Reports of Investigations Ser.: No. 38). (Illus.). 29p. (Orig.). 1983. pap. 4.00 (*0-89792-097-X*) Ill St Museum.

Taphonomy of Rampithecus Wickeri at Fort Ternan, Kenya. Pat Shipman. (Museum Briefs Ser.: No. 26). (Illus.). v, 37p. 1982. pap. 2.00 (*0-913134-26-0*) Mus Anthro MO.

Taphonomy, Sedimentology, & Genesis of Plant Fossil Deposit Types in Lettenkohle (Lower Keuper) & Schilfsandstein (Middle Keuper) in Lower Franconia (Germany) Detlef Mader. 164p. 1995. 23.95 (*0-8204-2813-2*) P Lang Pubng.

***Tapices Literarios: Stories for Building Language Skills & Cultural Awareness.** Glynis S. Cowell & Joan F. Turner. 1996. pap. text ed. write for info. (*0-07-912039-3*) McGraw.

Tapies. Carmen Gimenez et al. (Illus.). 232p. 1995. 75.00 (*0-8109-6881-9*) Abrams.

Tapies: The Graphic Work, 1947-1978, 2 vols., Set. Mariuccia Galfetti. 474p. 1984. 350.00 (*1-55660-117-4*) A Wofsy Fine Arts.

Tapies, Vol. 3: The Complete Works, 1969-1975. Anna Agusti et al. LC 88-42714. (Illus.). 550p. 1992. 275.00 (*0-8478-1442-4*) Rizzoli Intl.

Tapies. Vol. 4: The Complete Works, 1976-1981. Anna Agusti et al. LC 88-42714. (Illus.). 500p. 1997. 275.00 (*0-8478-1829-2*) Rizzoli Intl.

Tapies y la Nueva Cultura. Lluis Permanyer. (Grandes Monografias). (Illus.). 216p. (SPA.). 1993. 350.00 (*84-343-0470-8*) Elliots Bks.

Taping Techniques: Principles & Practice. Ed. by Rose MacDonald. (Illus.). 263p. 1994. pap. 115.00 (*0-7506-0577-4*) Buttrwrth-Heinemann.

Tapio, Master of the Forest. Astrud Ivask. Ed. by Stanley H. Barkan. Tr. by Inara Cedrins. (Review Chapbook Ser.: No. 14: Latvian Poetry 1). 40p. (ENG & LAV.). 1991. 15.00 (*0-89304-865-8*); pap. 5.00 (*0-89304-866-6*) Cross-Cultrl NY.

Tapio, Master of the Forest: Mini Book. Astrud Ivask. Ed. by Stanley H. Barkan. Tr. by Inara Cedrins. (Review Chapbook Ser.: No. 14: Latvian Poetry 1). 40p. (ENG & LAV.). 1991. 15.00 (*0-89304-867-4*); pap. 5.00 (*0-89304-868-2*) Cross-Cultrl NY.

Tapioca for Tea. large type ed. Sarah A. Shears. 1978. 15.95 (*0-7089-0105-0*) Ulverscroft.

Tapiola Sound. Erkki Pohjola & Matti Tuomisto. 204p. 1993. pap. text ed. 24.95 (*1-884598-00-5*) Walton Music.

Tapisseries. Charles Peguy. (Poesie Ser.). (FRE.). pap. 7.95 (*2-07-030214-8*) Schoenhof.

Tapiz de Abuela. Omar S. Castaneda. Tr. by Aida E. Marcuse. LC 93-38628. (Illus.). 32p. (SPA.). (J). (ps-4). 1994. 14.95 (*1-880000-08-3*); pap. 5.95 (*1-880000-11-3*) Lee & Low Bks.

***Tapiz de Verdades de Juan.** Arthur B. Walton. Ed. by Richard Meyer. (Adult Sunday School Ser.). 104p. (SPA.). 1991. 3.95 (*1-879892-27-8*) Editorial Bautista.

Tappan School, a History Book: The Story of a School in Ravenna, Ohio, U. S. A. Lois F. Lewis. (Illus.). 28p. (Orig.). (J). (gr. 5). 1989. pap. text ed. write for info. (*0-9620136-1-7*) L F Lewis.

Tappan Three Hundred Years: 1686-1986. Wilfred B. Talman et al. Ed. by Firth H. Fabend. (Illus.). 200p. (Orig.). 1989. pap. 18.00 (*0-317-93771-5*); text ed. 30.00 (*0-317-93770-7*) Tappan Hist Soc.

Tappan Three Hundred Years, Sixteen Eighty-Six to Nineteen Eighty-Six. Wilfred B. Talman et al. Ed. by Firth H. Fabend. (Illus.). 200p. 1989. 30.00 (*0-9621969-0-8*); pap. 18.00 (*0-9621969-1-6*) Tappan Hist Soc.

Tappan Zee Dress: Plain & Fancy, 1780-1930. Anne R. Adams. (Illus.). 40p. 1984. pap. 2.00 (*0-911183-20-5*) Rockland County Hist.

Tappan's Burro. Zane Grey. 224p. 1993. mass mkt. 3.99 (*0-06-100588-6*, Harp PBks) HarpC.

Tappan's Burro & Other Stories. large type ed. Zane Grey. 1996. 18.95 (*0-7862-0581-4*) Thorndike Pr.

TAPPI Annual Meeting, 1992: Georgia World Congress Center, Atlanta, GA, March 2-4. Technical Association of the Pulp & Paper Industry Staff. (TAPPI Proceedings Ser.). reprint ed. pap. 111.80 (*0-7837-2780-1*, 2043172) Bks Demand.

***TAPPI Applications in Wet End Chemistry: The Portland Hilton, Portland, OR, November 10-12, 1993.** Technical Association of the Pulp & Paper Industry Staff. (TAPPI Course Notes Ser.). 199p. 1993. reprint ed. pap. 56.80 (*0-608-03301-4*, 2082397) Bks Demand.

TAPPI Career Planning Manual: Career Development for Technical Professionals in the Pulp, Paper, & Allied Industries. Technical Association of the Pulp & Paper Industry Staff. 115p. reprint ed. pap. 32.80 (*0-317-30113-6*, 2025298) Bks Demand.

TAPPI High Barrier Packaging Seminar, 1985: Marriott Hilton Head Hotel, Hilton Head, SC, April 1. Technical Association of the Pulp & Paper Industry Staff. 24p. reprint ed. pap. 25.00 (*0-317-26880-5*, 2025296) Bks Demand.

***TAPPI Introduction to Wet End Chemistry: The Portland Hilton, Portland, OR, November 8-10, 1993.** Technical Association of the Pulp & Paper Industry Staff. (TAPPI Course Notes Ser.). 531p. 1993. reprint ed. pap. 151.40 (*0-608-03302-2*, 2082398) Bks Demand.

TAPPI Ninety: Georgia World Congress Center, Atlanta, GA, March 5-8, 1990. Technical Association of the Pulp & Paper Industry Staff. (TAPPI Proceedings Ser.). (Illus.). 253p. reprint ed. pap. 72.20 (*0-8357-3839-6*, 2036565) Bks Demand.

T

An Asterisk (*) at the beginning of an entry indicates that the title is appearing in BIP for the first time.

***TAPPI Paper Machine Rebuild Seminar, 1994: March 2-4, Hyatt Regency Atlanta, Atlanta, GA.** Technical Association of the Pulp & Paper Industry Staff. (TAPPI Course Notes Ser.). (Illus.). 211p. reprint ed. pap. 60.20 (*0-608-05356-2*, 2082404) Bks Demand.

***TAPPI Paper Properties, 1994: What, How, & Why Short Course: Sheraton Colony Square, Atlanta, GA, June 12-15.** Technical Association of the Pulp & Paper Industry Staff. (TAPPI Course Notes Ser.). (Illus.). 200p. pap. 57.00 (*0-608-05371-6*, 2082421) Bks Demand.

TAPPI Technical Information Sheets, 1989, 3 vols., Vol. 1. Technical Association of the Pulp & Paper Industry Staff. (Illus.). 358p. reprint ed. pap. 93.10 (*0-8357-4299-7*, 2037098) Bks Demand.

TAPPI Technical Information Sheets, 1989, 3 vols., Vol. 2. Technical Association of the Pulp & Paper Industry Staff. (Illus.). 454p. reprint ed. pap. 118.10 (*0-8357-4300-4*) Bks Demand.

TAPPI Technical Information Sheets, 1989, 3 vols., Vol. 3. Technical Association of the Pulp & Paper Industry Staff. (Illus.). 340p. reprint ed. pap. 88.40 (*0-8357-4301-2*) Bks Demand.

TAPPI Test Methods, Nineteen Eighty-Nine, 2 vols., Vol. 1. Technical Association of the Pulp & Paper Industry Staff. LC 89-656192. (Illus.). 706p. reprint ed. pap. 160.00 (*0-8357-4297-0*, 2037097) Bks Demand.

TAPPI Test Methods, Nineteen Eighty-Nine, 2 vols., Vol. 2. Technical Association of the Pulp & Paper Industry Staff. LC 89-656192. (Illus.). 418p. reprint ed. pap. 119.20 (*0-8357-4298-9*) Bks Demand.

TAPPI 1995-1996 Technical Information Sheets. annuals (Illus.). 1368p. 1995. pap. 134.00 (*0-89852-483-0*, 0108T195) TAPPI.

Tapping Creativity. Mescon Group Staff. (GC - Principles of Management Ser.). 1996. suppl. ed., text ed. 14.95 (*0-538-84932-0*); suppl. ed., text ed. 23.95 (*0-538-84933-9*) S-W Pub.

Tapping Federal Technology: Inventions, Expertise & Facilities. 220p. (Orig.). (C). 1994. pap. text ed. 50.00 (*0-7881-0524-8*) DIANE Pub.

Tapping Hidden Power. Ed. by Robert Somerville. (Journey Through the Mind & Body Ser.). (Illus.). 144p. 17.95 (*0-7835-1052-7*); lib. bdg. 17.99 (*0-7835-1053-5*) Time-Life.

Tapping into Prosperity: The Universal Path to Success. Ruth Drury. Ed. by Gene N. Levine. 222p. (Orig.). 1992. pap. 18.95 (*0-9631383-0-8*) Prosperity Times.

***Tapping Potential: Achieving What You Want with the Abilities You Already Have.** Kenneth J. Lodi. 162p. 1995. pap. 15.95 (*0-9646523-0-7*) Am Correctional.

Tapping Potential: Issues in Human Resource Management. 87p. 1991. pap. 31.00 (*0-913359-64-5*) APPA VA.

Tapping Techniques. (Four Bass Superchops Ser.). 1992. pap. 12.95 incl. audio (*0-7935-1037-6*, 00660312) H Leonard.

Tapping Techniques. (Four Bass Superchops Ser.). 1992. pap. 14.95 incl. audio compact disk (*0-7935-1038-4*, 00660313) H Leonard.

Tapping the Charcoal. large type ed. Ed. & Intro. by Kenneth Jernigan. (Kernel Bk.: No. 9). (Illus.). 96p. (Orig.). 1995. pap. 3.00 (*1-885218-03-6*) Natl Fed Blind.

Tapping the Earth's Natural Heat. Wendall A. Duffield et al. (Illus.). 63p. (Orig.). (C). 1995. pap. text ed. 20.00 (*0-7881-1922-2*) DIANE Pub.

Tapping the Earth's Natural Heat. Wendell A. Duffield et al. (Orig.). 1994. write for info. (*0-615-00032-0*) US Geol Survey.

Tapping the Government Grapevine: The User Friendly Guide to U. S. Government Information Sources. 2nd ed. Judith S. Robinson. LC 92-40201. (Illus.). 240p. 1993. pap. 34.50 (*0-89774-712-7*) Oryx Pr.

***Tapping the Government Grapevine: The User-Friendly Guide to U. S. Government Information Sources.** 3rd ed. Judith S. Robinson. (Illus.). 288p. 1997. pap. text ed. 34.50 (*1-57356-024-3*) Oryx Pr.

Tapping the Human Spirit: Managers Tell How to Build a Caring & Productive Workplace. Terri R. Hoyland. Ed. by Sarah Lindberg. (Illus.). 218p. 1995. 14.95 (*1-883794-32-3*) InnerSources.

Tapping the Potential: Discovering Congregations' Role in Building Assets in Youth. Eugene C. Roehlkepartain & Glenn A. Seefeldt. (Everyone's an Asset-Builder Ser.). 1995. pap. 4.50 (*1-57482-329-9*) Search Inst.

Tapping the Power Within: A Path to Self-Empowerment for Black Women. Iyanla Vanzant. (Illus.). 128p. (Orig.). 1992. pap. 10.00 (*0-86316-140-5*) Writers & Readers.

Tapping the Vein, Bk. 1. Clive Barker. (Illus.). 64p. 1989. pap. 6.95 (*0-913035-92-0*) Eclipse Bks.

Tapping the Vein, Bk. 2. Clive Barker. (Illus.). 64p. 1989. pap. 6.95 (*0-913035-93-9*) Eclipse Bks.

Tapping the Vein, Bk. 3. Clive Barker. (Illus.). 1990. pap. 6.95 (*1-56060-029-2*) Eclipse Bks.

Tapping the Vein, Bk. 4. Clive Barker. (Illus.). 1990. pap. 7.95 (*1-56060-030-6*) Eclipse Bks.

Tapping the Wisdom Within: A Guide to Joyous Living. Stephanie Noble. LC 93-79753. 240p. (Orig.). 1994. pap. 10.95 (*0-9638088-3-4*) Inside Out Bks.

Tapping the Zero Point Energy. (Nikola Tesla Ser.). 1991. lib. bdg. 79.95 (*0-8490-4329-8*) Gordon Pr.

Tapping the Zero-Point Energy. Moray B. King. (Illus.). 170p. (Orig.). 1989. pap. text ed. 9.95 (*0-9623356-0-6*) Paraclete Pub.

Tapping This Stone, No. 19. Jane Schapiro. 72p. (Orig.). 1995. pap. 10.00 (*0-931846-47-1*) Wash Writers Pub.

***Tapping Through.** Jacqueline Burks-Shiver. Ed. by Eileen Allman. 30p. 1996. pap. 5.95 (*0-9654212-1-X*) Burks-Shiver.

Tapping Your Own Resources: A Decision-Maker's Guide for Small Town Drinking Water. National Center for Small Communities Staff. 1993. write for info. (*0-925532-09-6*) Natl Assn Town & Twps.

TAPPI's First Seventy-Five Years, 1915-1990: From Distinguished Past to Dynamic Future. Shawn Sudia-Skehan. (Illus.). 104p. reprint ed. pap. 27.10 (*0-8357-3930-9*, 2036665) Bks Demand.

TAPPI'S First Seventy-Five Years, 1990. 100p. 1990. 30.00 (*0-89852-054-1*, 0102B054) TAPPI.

Tapply, No. 2. Tapply. 1995. 20.00 (*1-883402-31-X*) S&S Trade.

Tappus Event. Geraldo Guirty. 1994. 15.95 (*0-533-10760-1*) Vantage.

Taproots: Underlying Principles of Milton Erickson's Therapy & Hypnosis. William H. O'Hanlon. (Professional Bks.). 1987. 22.95 (*0-393-70031-3*) Norton.

Taps at Reveille. F. Scott Fitzgerald. 352p. 1976. 45.00 (*0-684-14742-4*) S&S Trade.

Taps for a Jim Crow Army: Letters from Black Soldiers in World War II. Compiled by Phillip McGuire. LC 93-1718. 320p. 1993. reprint ed. 35.00 (*0-8131-1851-4*); reprint ed. pap. 19.00 (*0-8131-0822-5*) U Pr of Ky.

Taps for Private Tussie. Jesse H. Stuart. LC 91-62582. (Illus.). 255p. 1992. reprint ed. 22.00 (*0-945084-24-2*) J Stuart Found.

Taps for Space. Aaron Rosen. LC 80-52194. 79p. (Orig.). 1980. pap. 7.95 (*0-935296-16-6*) Sheep Meadow.

Taps Moratorium. Donald G. Smock. 5p. 1996. pap. 0.99 (*1-888923-00-8*) Poetic License.

TAPS Test of Auditory-Perceptual Skills. Morrison F. Gardner. 75p. (Orig.). 1985. teacher ed., pap. 16.95 (*0-931421-06-3*); teacher ed. 54.50 (*0-931421-07-1*) Psychol Educ Pubns.

TAPSOFT Eighty-Nine, Vol. 2. Fernando Orejas & J. Diaz. (Lecture Notes in Computer Science Ser.). x, 389p. 1989. 45.00 (*0-387-50940-2*) Spr-Verlag.

TAPSOFT Eighty-Nine, Vol. 1. Fernando Orejas & J. Diaz. (Lecture Notes in Computer Science Ser.: Vol. 351). x, 383p. 1989. 45.00 (*0-387-50939-9*) Spr-Verlag.

TAPSOFT, Eighty-Seven: Proceedings of the International Advanced Seminar on Foundations, Vol. 1. Ed. by H. Ehrig et al. (Lecture Notes in Computer Science Ser.: Vol. 249). xiv, 289p. 1987. pap. 39.00 (*0-387-17660-8*) Spr-Verlag.

TAPSOFT Eighty-Seven--Proceedings of the International: Advanced Seminar on Foundations, Vol. 2. Ed. by H. Ehrig et al. (Lecture Notes in Computer Science Ser.: Vol. 250). xiv, 336p. 1987. pap. 39.00 (*0-387-17611-X*) Spr-Verlag.

TAPSOFT Ninety-One Vol. 1: Proceedings of the International Joint Conference on Theory & Practice of Software Development Brighton, U. K., April 8-12, 1991: Colloquium on Trees in Algebra & Programming (CAAP '91) Ed. by S. Abramsky & T. S. Maillbaum. (Lecture Notes in Computer Science Ser.: Vol. 493). viii, 455p. 1991. 57.00 (*0-387-53982-4*) Spr-Verlag.

TAPSOFT Ninety-One Vol. 2: Proceedings of the Internatioanl Joint Conference on Theory & Practice of Software Development Brighton, U. K., April 8-12, 1991: Advances in Distributed Computing (ADC) & Colloquium on Combining Paradigms for Software Development (CCPSD) Ed. by S. Abramsky & T. S. Maillbaum. (Lecture Notes in Computer Science Ser.: Vol. 494). viii, 482p. 1991. 57.00 (*0-387-53981-6*) Spr-Verlag.

TAPSOFT '93 - Theory & Practice of Software Development: Proceedings of the Fourth International Joint Conference CAAP-FASE, Orsay, France, April 13-17, 1993. Ed. by M. C. Gaudel & Jean-Pierre Jouannaud. LC 93-10178. (Lecture Notes in Computer Science Ser.: Vol. 668). 1993. Acid-free paper. 108.95 (*0-387-56610-4*) Spr-Verlag.

TAPSOFT '95: Theory & Practice of Software Development: Proceedings of the 6th International Joint Conference CAAP/FASE, Held at Aarhus, Denmark, May 22-26, 1995. Sixth International Joint Conference on Theory & Practice of Software Development Staff et al. Ed. by Peter D. Mosses et al. LC 95-15959. (Lecture Notes in Computer Science Ser.: Vol. 915). 1995. write for info. (*0-387-59293-8*) Spr-Verlag.

TAPSOFT '95: Theory & Practice of Software Development: Proceedings of the 6th International Joint Conference CAAP/FASE, Held at Aarhus, Denmark, May 22-26, 1995. Sixth International Joint Conference on Theory & Practice of Software Development Staff et al. Ed. by Peter D. Mosses et al. LC 95-15959. (Lecture Notes in Computer Science Ser.: Vol. 915). 810p. 1995. 117.00 (*3-540-59293-8*) Spr-Verlag.

Tapta-Marga: Asceticism & Initiation in Vedic India. Walter O. Kaelber. LC 88-15917. 204p. 1989. text ed. 64.50 (*0-88706-813-8*); pap. text ed. 21.95 (*0-88706-814-6*) State U NY Pr.

Taquigrafia Gregg, Primer Curso. John R. Gregg. 1974. text ed. 19.75 (*0-07-024620-3*) McGraw.

Taquigrafia Gregg, Segundo Curso: Edicion Diamante. John R. Gregg. (SPA.). 1970. text ed. 23.50 (*0-07-024621-1*) McGraw.

Taquisara. Francis M. Crawford. (Works of Francis Marion Crawford Ser.). 1990. reprint ed. lib. bdg. 79.00 (*0-7812-2547-7*) Rprt Serv.

Tar-Aiym Krang. Alan Dean Foster. 251p. 1981. mass mkt. 5.99 (*0-345-30280-X*, Del Rey) Ballantine.

Tar-Aiym Krang. Alan Dean Foster. (Flinx & Pip Novels Ser.). 1995. reprint ed. mass mkt. 5.99 (*0-345-90857-0*, Del Rey) Ballantine.

Tar Baby. Jerome Charyn. LC 94-25163. (Illus.). 243p. 1995. pap. 10.95 (*1-56478-078-3*) Dalkey Arch.

Tar Baby. Toni Morrison. LC 80-22821. 320p. 1981. 26.00 (*0-394-42329-1*) Knopf.

Tar Baby. Toni Morrison. LC 87-15238. 352p. 1987. pap. 7.95 (*0-452-26012-4*, Z5326, Plume); pap. 10.95 (*0-452-26479-0*, Plume) NAL-Dutton.

Tar Baby. Toni Morrison. 1993. pap. 5.99 (*0-451-18238-3*, Sig) NAL-Dutton.

"Tar Baby" Option: American Policy Toward Southern Rhodesia. Anthony Lake. LC 76-2455. 316p. 1976. text ed. 49.50 (*0-231-04066-0*) Col U Pr.

Tar Beach. Richard Elman. (New American Fiction Ser.: No. 23). 276p. (Orig.). 1991. pap. 12.95 (*1-55713-117-1*) Sun & Moon CA.

Tar Beach. Faith Riggold. 1996. pap. 6.99 (*0-517-88544-1*) Random Hse Value.

Tar Beach. Faith Ringgold. LC 90-40410. (Illus.). 32p. (J). (ps-3). 1991. 18.00 (*0-517-58030-6*); lib. bdg. 18.99 (*0-517-58031-4*) Crown Bks Yng Read.

Tar Beach. Faith Ringgold. (Book & Doll Packages Ser.). (Illus.). 32p. (J). (ps-4). 1994. 16.00 (*0-517-59961-9*) Crown Bks Yng Read.

Tar Beach. Faith Ringold. Date not set. mass mkt. 5.99 (*0-517-58984-2*) Random Hse Value.

Tar Heel Angler: Fresh Water Game Fishing in North Carolina. Buck Paysour. LC 91-71000. (Illus.). 180p. 1991. pap. 13.95 (*1-878086-03-0*) Down Home NC.

Tar Heel Editor. Josephus Daniels. LC 74-2840. (Illus.). 544p. 1974. reprint ed. text ed. 85.00 (*0-8371-7440-6*, DATH, Greenwood Pr) Greenwood.

Tar Heel Ghosts. John Harden. LC 54-13061. (Illus.). xiv, 178p. 1980. reprint ed. 16.95 (*0-8078-0660-9*); reprint ed. pap. 9.95 (*0-8078-4069-6*) U of NC Pr.

Tar Heel Laughter. Ed. by Richard Walser. LC 73-15568. (Illus.). xvi, 310p. 1983. pap. 12.95 (*0-8078-4115-3*) U of NC Pr.

Tar Heel, North Carolina Football. Ken Rappoport. LC 76-19968. (College Sports Bks.). (Illus.). 1980. 10.95 (*0-87397-029-2*, Strode Pubs) Circle Bk Service.

Tar Heel Politics: Myths & Realities. Paul Luebke. LC 89-14677. xiv, 238p. (C). 1990. pap. 12.95 (*0-8078-4271-0*) U of NC Pr.

Tar Heel Tales. Henry E. Bryant. LC 72-6511. (Black Heritage Library Collection). 1977. reprint ed. 23.95 (*0-8369-9162-1*) Ayer.

Tar Heel Tombstones: And the Tales They Tell. Henry King. Ed. by Jerry Bledsoe. LC 90-60344. (Illus.). 188p. (Orig.). 1990. pap. 9.95 (*0-9624255-2-4*) Down Home NC.

Tar Heels Cooking for Ronald's Kids. Ed. by Jean Durham et al. (Illus.). 184p. 1988. 13.95 (*0-9620949-0-0*) R McDonald Hse.

***Tar Heels Handbook: Stories, Stats & Stuff about UNC Basketball.** Tom Harris. (Illus.). 160p. (Orig.). 1996. pap. 9.95 (*1-880652-81-1*) Wichita Eagle.

Tar Hell Trivia: Tantalizing Tidbits from a Basketball Powerhouse. Chip Alexander & Dane Huffman. Ed. by Jim Wilson. LC 91-67942. (Illus.). 192p. (Orig.). 1991. pap. 9.95 (*1-880123-02-9*) Village Sports.

Tar Pit. Tor Seidler. LC 87-74338. (Michael di Capua Bks.). 160p. (J). 1987. 14.00 (*0-374-37383-3*) FS&G.

Tar Pit. Tor Seidler. (Michael di Capua Bks.). 160p. (J). 1991. pap. 3.95 (*0-374-47452-4*) FS&G.

Tar Sand & Oil Upgrading Technology. Ed. by Stuart S. Shis & Michael C. Oballa. LC 91-14676. (Symposium Ser.). 115p. (Orig.). 1991. pap. 25.00 (*0-8169-0547-9*, S282) Am Inst Chem Eng.

Tara: A Maharatta Tale. Meadows Taylor. 534p. 1986. reprint ed. 22.00 (*0-8364-1735-6*, Pub. by Abhinav II) S Asia.

Tara: A Mahratta Tale, 3 vols. in 2. Philip M. Taylor. LC 79-8206. reprint ed. Set. 84.50 (*0-404-62137-6*) AMS Pr.

Tara: The Supreme Goddess. Pushpendra Kumar. (C). 1992. text ed. 80.00 (*81-217-0063-9*, Pub. by Bharatiya Vidya Bhavan II) S Asia.

***Tara & Michelle: The Road to Gold.** Wendy Daly. (J). 1998. pap. 3.99 (*0-679-88930-2*); lib. bdg. 11.99 (*0-679-98930-7*) Random Bks Yng Read.

Tara Lane. Shama Futehally. (C). 1993. 14.00 (*0-86311-404-0*, Pub. by Ravi Dayal II) S Asia.

***Tara Lipinski Triumph on Ice.** Tara Lipinski. 1997. 15.95 (*0-553-09775-X*) Bantam.

Tara of the Twilight. Lin Carter. (Orig.). 1979. mass mkt. 2.25 (*0-89083-428-8*, Zebra Kensgtn) Kensgtn Pub Corp.

Tara Revisited: Women, War, & the Plantation Legend. Catherine Clinton. LC 94-39218. (Illus.). 240p. 1996. 27.50 (*1-55859-491-4*) Abbeville Pr.

Tara Revisited: Women, War, & the Plantation Legend. Catherine Clinton. (Illus.). 240p. 1997. pap. 16.95 (*0-7892-0159-3*) Abbeville Pr.

Tarabas. Joseph Roth. Tr. by Winifred Katzin from GER. LC 86-31239. 280p. 1987. reprint ed. 18.95 (*0-87951-275-X*) Overlook Pr.

Tarabas: A Guest on Earth. Joseph Roth. 280p. 1989. Tusk. pap. 10.95 (*0-87951-299-7*) Overlook Pr.

Tarahumar of Mexico: Their Environment & Material Culture. Campbell W. Pennington. LC 64-1645. 299p. reprint ed. pap. 85.30 (*0-317-30111-X*, 2025281) Bks Demand.

***Tarahumara: Where Night Is the Day of the Moon.** 2nd ed. Bernard L. Fontana. LC 96-29939. (Illus.). 160p. 1997. reprint ed. pap. 19.95 (*0-8165-1706-1*) U of Ariz Pr.

Tarahumara of the Sierra Madre: Survivors on the Canyon's Edge. 2nd rev. ed. John G. Kennedy. Ed. & Illus. by Wendy Utsuki. 301p. 1996. pap. 17.95 (*0-9647877-3-3*) Asilomar Pr.
This book describes the life of the Tarahumara Indians living in the remote Copper Canyon country of Mexico. Crushed by the Spaniards in the 17th century, they retreated to distant canyons, where by isolating themselves, they were able to preserve their ancient culture. The author lived in a community of non-Christian Tarahumara, the most isolated members of the tribe. He discusses their close adaptation to the rugged environment, their unique curing ceremonies, the activities of their shamans & sorcerers, the cooperative work parties which involve the institutionalized drinking of maize beer, & the 100 mile foot races for which the Tarahumara are famous. Travelers to Copper Canyon country can enrich their experience through this account of the natives of this spectacular area. Armchair travelers & long distance runners will also enjoy the book. It also makes an interesting supplementary text for college courses in the social sciences, cultural or social anthropology, Indians of Mesoamerica, cultural ecology, social organization, etc. For ordering information contact: ASILOMAR PRESS, 1199 Forest Avenue, #321, Pacific Grove, CA 93950. ***Publisher Provided Annotation.***

Tarahumaras. Antonin Artaud. (Folio Essais Ser.: No. 52). 217p. (FRE.). 1963. 9.95 (*2-07-032402-8*) Schoenhof.

Taran Wanderer. Lloyd Alexander. 272p. (J). (gr. k-6). 1969. pap. 4.99 (*0-440-48483-9*, YB BDD) BDD Bks Young Read.

Taran Wanderer. Lloyd Alexander. 272p. (YA). (gr. 5-9). 1980. pap. 3.50 (*0-440-98483-1*, LLL BDD) BDD Bks Young Read.

Taran Wanderer. Lloyd Alexander. LC 67-10230. 256p. (J). (gr. 4-6). 1967. 16.95 (*0-8050-1113-7*, Bks Young Read) H Holt & Co.

Taranathas's History of Buddhism in India. Ed. by Debiprasad Chattopadhyay. 1990. reprint ed. 29.50 (*81-208-0696-4*, Pub. by Motilal Banarsidass II) S Asia.

Taranta Rheumatic Fever. 2nd ed. 1989. pap. text ed. write for info. (*0-7462-0104-4*) Kluwer Ac.

Tarantasse Journey Through Eastern Russia in the Autumn of 1856. William Spottiswoode. LC 70-115586. (Russia Observed Ser., No. 1). 1970. reprint ed. 20.95 (*0-405-03063-0*) Ayer.

Tarantella: Avagy Utazasok a Pokhalon (Egy Pszichoanalizis Tortenete) Janos Makkay. 63p. (Orig.). 1985. pap. 15.00 (*0-933104-21-9*) Jupiter Pr.

Tarantella: For Men's Chorus & Piano Four Hands. E. Carter. 40p. 1986. pap. 8.95 (*0-7935-3023-7*) H Leonard.

***Tarantino A-Z: The Films of Quentin Tarantino.** Alan Barnes & Marcus Hearn. (Illus.). 192p. 1996. pap. 22.95 (*0-7134-7990-6*, Pub. by Batsford UK) Trafalgar.

Taranto 1940: Prelude to Pearl Harbor. A. J. Smithers. (Illus.). 160p. 1996. 26.95 (*1-55750-878-X*) Naval Inst Pr.

Tarantula. James E. Gerholdt. LC 95-13010. (Spiders Ser.). (J). (gr. k-3). 1995. lib. bdg. 13.99 (*1-56239-506-8*) Abdo & Dghtrs.

Tarantula. Labonte. (Remarkable Animals Ser.). 60p. (J). 1995. pap. 5.95 (*0-382-39235-3*, Dillon Silver Burdett) Silver Burdett Pr.

Tarantula. Gail LaBonte. (Remarkable Animals Ser.). (Illus.). 60p. (J). (gr. 3 up). 1991. lib. bdg. 13.95 (*0-87518-452-9*, Dillon Silver Burdett) Silver Burdett Pr.

Tarantula: Poems. Bob Dylan. 160p. 1993. pap. 12.95 (*0-312-10554-1*) St Martin.

***Tarantula in My Purse: And 172 Other Wild Pets.** Jean C. George. LC 95-54151. (Trophy Book Ser.). (Illus.). 144p. (J). (gr. 3-7). 1997. pap. 4.50 (*0-06-446201-3*, Trophy) HarpC Child Bks.

Tarantula in My Purse: And 172 Other Wild Pets. Jean Craighead George. LC 95-54151. (Illus.). 134p. (J). (gr. 3-7). 1996. 14.95 (*0-06-023626-4*); lib. bdg. 14.89 (*0-06-023627-2*) HarpC Child Bks.

Tarantula Shoes. Tom Birdseye. 96p. (J). (gr. 3-7). 1995. 14.95 (*0-8234-1179-6*) Holiday.

Tarantula Shoes. Tom Birdseye. 144p. (J). (gr. 3-7). 1996. pap. 3.99 (*0-14-037955-X*, Puffin) Puffin Bks.

Tarantula Stone. large type ed. Philip Caveney. 528p. 1986. 27.99 (*0-7089-8362-6*) Ulverscroft.

***Tarantula Toes.** Beverly Lewis. (Cul-De-Sac Kids Ser.: No. 13). (J). 1997. pap. 3.99 (*1-55661-984-7*) Bethany Hse.

Tarantulas. John Browning. (Illus.). 128p. 1989. 9.95 (*0-86622-833-0*, KW-075) TFH Pubns.

Tarantulas. L. Martin. (Spider Discovery Library). (Illus.). 24p. (J). (gr. k-5). 1988. lib. bdg. 11.94 (*0-86592-967-X*); lib. bdg. 8.95 (*0-685-58302-3*) Rourke Corp.

***Tarantulas.** Emily McAuliffe. LC 97-8342. (Dangerous Creatures Ser.). (J). 1998. write for info. (*1-56065-621-2*) Capstone Pr.

Tarantulas. Peter Murray. (Nature Bks.). 32p. (J). (gr. 2-6). 1993. lib. bdg. 22.79 (*1-56766-060-6*) Childs World.

***Tarantulas.** Conrad J. Storad. LC 97-5141. (Early Bird Nature Books Ser.). (Illus.). (J). 1997. write for info. (*0-8225-3024-4*) Lerner Group.

Tarantulas: A Complete Introduction. Al David. (Complete Introduction to...Ser.). (Illus.). 95p. (Orig.). 1987. pap. 8.95 (*0-86622-353-3*, CO-024S) TFH Pubns.

Tarantulas: In Nature & As Pets. Laurie Perrero & Louis Perrero. (Illus.). 1979. pap. 2.95 (*0-89317-029-1*) Windward Pub.

Tarantulas & Other Arachnids. Samuel D. Marshall. LC 96-11352. (Complete Pet Owner's Manual Ser.). (Illus.). 1996. pap. 6.95 (*0-8120-9315-1*) Barron.

Tarantulas & Scorpions. W. Rankin. (Illus.). 96p. 1995. pap. text ed. 9.95 (*0-7938-0259-8*, RE124) TFH Pubns.

Tarantulas Are Spiders. Norman I. Platnick. LC 95-18644. (J). 1995. pap. write for info. (*1-57255-038-4*) Mondo Pubng.

Tarantulas As a New Pet. B. Reger. (Illus.). 64p. 1995. pap. 6.95 (*0-7938-0082-X*, TU029) TFH Pubns.

Tarantulas on the Lifebuoy. Thomas Lux. 22p. 1983. pap. 2.50 (*0-9604740-4-8*) Ampersand RI.

Tarantulas Today. Andreas Tinter. (Illus.). 64p. 1996. 12.95 (*0-7938-0113-3*, WW015) TFH Pubns.

Tarare. Antonio Salieri. Ed. by Gustave Lefevre & Arthur Pougin. (Chefs-d'oeuvre classiques de l'opera francaise Ser.: Vol. 40). (Illus.). 466p. (FRE.). 1970. reprint ed. pap. 40.00 (*0-8450-1140-5*) Broude.

Taras: Its History & Coinage. George Brauer, Jr. (Illus.). xii, 231p. (C). 1986. lib. bdg. 55.00 (*0-89241-377-8*) Caratzas.

Tara's Angels: One Family's Extraordinary Journey of Courage & Healing. Kirk Moore. Ed. by Nancy Carleton. LC 95-46941. 180p. 1996. 16.00 (*0-915811-67-7*) H J Kramer Inc.

Taras Boulba (Ed. Aucouturier) Nikolai V. Gogol. 250p. (FRE.). 1991. pap. 10.95 (*0-7859-2616-X*, 2070383830) Fr & Eur.

Taras Bulba. Nikolai V. Gogol. reprint ed. lib. bdg. 17.95 (*0-88411-138-5*) Buccaneer Bks.

Taras Bulba. Nikolai V. Gogol. 1990. reprint ed. lib. bdg. 13.95 (*0-89968-509-9*) Buccaneer Bks.

Tara's Child: Woman of Mystery. Susan Kearney. (Harlequin Intrigue Ser.: No. 340). 1995. mass mkt. 3.50 (*0-373-22340-4*) Harlequin Bks.

Tara's Coloring Book. Illus. by Andy Weber & Nigel Wellings. (Orig.). 1979. pap. 9.95 (*0-86171-002-9*) Wisdom MA.

***Tara's Consort.** Margareta Waterman. 32p. 1997. pap. write for info. (*1-878888-27-7*) Nine Muses.

Tara's Healing. Janice H. Giles. 1976. 22.95 (*0-8488-0503-8*) Amereon Ltd.

Tara's Healing. Janice H. Giles. 256p. 1994. 28.00 (*0-8131-1886-7*); pap. 15.00 (*0-8131-0832-2*) U Pr of Ky.

Taras Shevchenko: A Life. Pavlo Zaitsev. Tr. by George S. Luckyj. 1988. 37.50 (*0-8020-3450-0*) U of Toronto Pr.

Tarascan Civilization: A Late Prehispanic Cultural System. Shirley Gorenstein & Helen P. Pollard. (Publications in Anthropology: No. 28). (Illus.). 199p. 1983. pap. 12.75 (*0-935462-19-8*) VUPA.

Tarascan Suffixes of Locative Space: Meaning & Morphotactics. Paul Friedrich. (Language Science Monographs: Vol. 9). (Orig.). 1971. pap. text ed. 23.50 (*0-87750-159-9*) Res Inst Inner Asian Studies.

Tarasoff & Beyond: Legal & Clinical Considerations in the Treatment of Life-Endangering Patients. rev. ed. Leon VandeCreek & Samuel Knapp. LC 93-6607. (Practitioner's Resource Ser.). 72p. 1993. pap. 15.20 (*0-943158-91-5*, TABBP, Prof Resc Pr) Pro Resource.

***Tarasov: Autobiography of Hockey's Coaching Legend.** Anatoly Tarasov. 1997. pap. text ed. 19.95 (*1-882180-74-7*) Griffin CA.

Tarass Boulba. Nikolai V. Gogol. (FRE.). 1996. pap. 5.95 (*2-87714-322-8*, Pub. by Bookking Intl FR) Distribks Inc.

Taratuta & Still Life with Pipe. Jose Donoso. 1994. pap. 8.95 (*0-393-31164-3*) Norton.

Taratuta & Still Life with Pipe: Two Novellas. Jose Donoso. Tr. by Gregory Rabassa from SPA. LC 92-10529. 160p. 1993. 17.95 (*0-393-03436-4*) Norton.

Tarawa: The Story of a Battle. Robert Sherrod. LC 73-84464. (Illus.). 215p. (C). 1986. reprint ed. pap. 7.95 (*0-934841-14-4*) Adm Nimitz Foun.

Tarbells Teacher Guide, 95-96. William P. Barker. 1995. teacher ed., pap. 14.95 (*0-7814-5125-6*, 18234) Cook.

***Tarbell's Teachers Guide 1996-1997.** William Barker. 1996. pap. text ed. 8.99 (*0-7814-5186-8*) Cook.

***Tardemah: The Creation of Man According to an Ancient Hebraic Source.** Morris Frank. Ed. by Robert M. Hoffstein. 118p. 1978. 12.95 (*0-913002-02-X*) Tsimtsum Hse.

Tardive Dyskinesia. Ed. by H. Haag et al. LC 91-35360. (WHO Expert Series on Neuroscience: Vol. 2). (Illus.). 124p. 1992. text ed. 29.00 (*0-88937-086-9*) Hogrefe & Huber Pubs.

Tardive Dyskinesia: Biological Mechanisms & Clinical Aspects. Ed. by Marion E. Wolf & Aron D. Mosnaim. LC 88-14590. (Progress in Psychiatry Ser.: No. 13). 290p. 1988. text ed. 35.00 (*0-88048-176-5*, 8176) Am Psychiatric.

Tardive Dyskinesia: Report of the American Psychiatric Association Task Force on Late Neurological Effects of Antipsychotic Drugs. American Psychiatric Association Staff. LC 80-137799. (Task Force Report: No. 18). 211p. reprint ed. pap. 60.20 (*0-8357-2805-6*, 2036169) Bks Demand.

Tardive Dyskinesia & Affective Disorders. Ed. by George Gardos & Daniel E. Casey. LC 84-6166. (Clinical Insights Ser.). 85p. reprint ed. pap. 25.00 (*0-8357-7820-7*, 2036192) Bks Demand.

Tardive Dyskinesia & Neuroleptics: From Dogma to Reason. Ed. by Daniel E. Casey & George Gardos. LC 86-10749. (Clinical Insights Ser.). 125p. reprint ed. pap. 35.70 (*0-8357-2809-9*, 2036225) Bks Demand.

Tarek. Lisa Kaaki. (Illus.). 66p. 1989. pap. 6.50 (*0-89259-083-1*) Am Trust Pubns.

Tarendol. Rene Barjavel. 512p. (FRE.). 1972. pap. 11.95 (*0-7859-1707-1*, 2070361691) Fr & Eur.

Tarentiner Goldschmuck in Berlin. Formigli et al. (Winckelmannsprogramm der Archaologischen Gesellschaft zu Berlin Ser.: No. 130-131). (Illus.). 100p. (C). 1990. lib. bdg. 57.70 (*3-11-012583-8*) De Gruyter.

Tares & the Good Grain or the Kingdom of Man at the Hour of Reckoning. Tage Lindbom. Tr. by Alvin Moore from FRE. LC 83-944. 161p. 1983. pap. 11.95 (*0-86554-079-9*, MUP/H069) Mercer Univ Pr.

Target: Competent Staff-Competency-Based Inservice Training for Child Welfare. Ronald C. Hughes & Judith S. Rycus. 1990. pap. 10.95 (*0-87868-395-X*, 3950) Child Welfare.

Target: Hero. David Matalon. Ed. by Robert Bell. (Champions Adventure Ser.). (Illus.). 32p. (Orig.). (YA). (gr. 10-12). 1988. pap. 6.00 (*1-55806-004-9*, 34) Iron Crown Ent Inc.

Target: Pearl Harbor. Michael Slackman. LC 90-30063. (Illus.). p. 1990. 24.95 (*0-8248-1123-2*) UH Pr.

Target: Pearl Harbor. Michael Slackman. LC 90-30063. (Illus.). 336p. 1991. reprint ed. pap. 14.95 (*0-8248-1378-2*) UH Pr.

Target: Point Zero. Mack Maloney. 384p. 1996. mass mkt. 4.99 (*0-7860-0299-9*, Pinncle Kensgtn) Kensgtn Pub Corp.

***Target: Pornography.** Timothy Sable. 115p. (Orig.). (YA). (gr. 7-12). 1996. pap. 6.95 (*1-57515-091-3*) PPI Pubng.

Target: Prime Time: Advocacy Groups & the Struggle over Entertainment Television. Kathryn C. Montgomery. (Communication & Society Ser.). (Illus.). 288p. 1990. reprint ed. pap. 9.95 (*0-19-506320-1*) OUP.

***Target: Selected Poems.** Manolis Anagnostakis. Tr. by Kimon Friar. LC 80-81164. 135p. (Orig.). (ENG & GRE.). 1980. pap. text ed. 9.00 (*0-918618-16-9*) Pella Pub.

Target: Subic Bay. Mack Tanner. 320p. 1992. mass mkt. 4.50 (*0-8217-3936-0*, Zebra Kensgtn) Kensgtn Pub Corp.

Target: Techniques for Aphasia Rehabilitation - Generating Effective Treatment. Robert Goldfarb & Mary J. Santo Pietro. 400p. 1994. text ed. 45.00 (*0-937857-50-5*, 1434) Speech Bin.

***Target: The Antimicrobial Reference Guide to Effective Treatment.** David Aucoin. (Illus.). 161p. (Orig.). 1994. pap. 85.00 (*1-889750-04-2*); disk 35.00 (*1-889750-05-0*) Nrth Amer Compendiums.

Target: Tokyo. Laurence Cortesi. 1983. mass mkt. 3.25 (*0-685-07872-8*, Zebra Kensgtn) Kensgtn Pub Corp.

***Target: UCAS.** FASA Corporation Staff. 1997. pap. text ed. 15.00 (*1-55560-314-9*) FASA Corp.

Target Adaptive Matched Illumination Radar. G. T. Gjessing. Ed. by James R. Wait et al. (Electromagnetic Waves Ser.). 1986. 84.00 (*0-86341-057-X*, EW022) Inst Elect Eng.

Target Akai-I Refuse to Die. Todd Shields. 460p. 1995. pap. 9.00 (*0-9645379-0-7*) Studio Ronin.

Target America: Terrorism in the U. S. Today. Yossef Bodansky. 1993. pap. 5.99 (*1-56171-269-8*, S P I Bks) Sure Seller.

Target Assays for Modern Herbicides & Related Phytotoxic Compounds. Ed. by Peter Boger & Gerhard Sandmann. LC 92-26381. 320p. 1992. 110.00 (*0-87371-539-X*, QK753, CRC Reprint) Franklin.

Target Costing. Shahid L. Ansari et al. 32p. (C). 1996. 7.50 (*0-256-23779-4*) Irwin.

***Target Costing: The Next Frontier in Strategic Cost Management: A CAM-I CMS Model for Profit Planning & Cost Management.** Shahid L. Ansari & Jan Bell. LC 96-31814. 240p. 1996. text ed. 50.00 (*0-7863-1053-7*) Irwin Prof Pubng.

***Target Costing & Value Engineering.** Robin Cooper & Regine Slagmulder. LC 97-15146. (Strategies in Confrontational Cost Management Ser.). (Illus.). 400p. 1997. 50.00 (*1-56327-172-9*) Prod Press.

Target Delta V. James Good. (Sub Wars Ser.: No. 1). (Orig.). 1981. mass mkt. 2.50 (*0-89083-892-5*, Zebra Kensgtn) Kensgtn Pub Corp.

Target Earth! John Bunyan. LC 82-61244. (Victorian Children's Classics Ser.). 178p. 1982. pap. 5.95 (*0-88270-536-9*) Bridge-Logos.

Target Earth! Asteroid Collisions Past & Future. Jon S. Erickson. (Illus.). 176p. (J). (gr. 7 up). 1991. 23.95 (*0-8306-8673-8*, 3673) McGraw-Hill Prof.

Target Earth! Asteroid Collisions Past & Future. Jon S. Erickson. (Illus.). 176p. (YA). (gr. 7 up). 1991. pap. 14.95 (*0-8306-7673-2*) TAB Bks.

Target Editing: Quick VanWrite Revisions Energize Business Writing. Linda B. Vanderwold. Ed. by Jim Donovan. LC 94-90019. (Illus.). 160p. (Orig.). 1995. pap. 29.95 (*0-9639282-0-1*) VanWrite Pubs.

Target Fluency: Leading Edge Foreign Language Teaching Techniques. Michael Hager. (Illus.). 100p. (Orig.). 1996. pap. 9.95 (*1-55552-068-5*) Metamorphous Pr.

Target for Murder. J. F. Trainor. 288p. 1993. mass mkt. 3.99 (*0-8217-4069-5*, Zebra Kensgtn) Kensgtn Pub Corp.

Target for Terror. Carolyn Keene. (Nancy Drew Hardy Boys Super Mystery Ser.: No. 24). (YA). 1995. mass mkt. 3.99 (*0-671-88462-X*, Archway) PB.

Target Hitler: The Plots to Kill Adolf Hitler. James P. Duffy & Vincent L. Ricci. LC 92-15695. 248p. 1992. text ed. 29.95 (*0-275-94037-3*, C4037, Praeger Pubs) Greenwood.

Target Industry Studies for Alleghany Highlands. 1989. 10.45 (*0-685-61062-4*) U VA Ctr Pub Serv.

Target Industry Studies for Eastern Shore. 1989. 10.45 (*0-685-61063-2*) U VA Ctr Pub Serv.

Target Industry Studies for Northern Neck. 1989. 10.45 (*0-685-61064-0*) U VA Ctr Pub Serv.

Target Industry Studies for Southside. 1989. 10.45 (*0-685-61065-9*) U VA Ctr Pub Serv.

Target Industry Studies for Southwest Virginia. 1987. 10.45 (*0-685-61066-7*) U VA Ctr Pub Serv.

Target Industry Studies Methodology for Studies. 1989. 10.45 (*0-685-61067-5*) U VA Ctr Pub Serv.

***Target Language, Collaborative Learning & Autonomy.** Ernesto Macaro. LC 96-33004. (Modern Languages in Practice Ser.). 220p. 1997. 79.00 (*1-85359-369-9*, Pub. by Multilingual Matters UK); pap. 29.95 (*1-85359-368-0*, Pub. by Multilingual Matters UK) Taylor & Francis.

Target Marketer's Guide on Canada. Daniel F. Huck & Kirk A. Sauber. Ed. by Denise L. Almond & Tanya H. Charlick. (Illus.). 520p. (C). 1989. 295.00 (*0-9624786-0-1*); 675.00 incl. disk (*0-685-30844-8*); disk 495.00 (*0-685-30845-6*) Intl Inst Mktg.

Target Marketing for the Small Business: Researching, Reaching & Retaining Your Target Market. Linda Pinson & Jerry A. Jinnett. LC 93-9086. 176p. (Orig.). 1993. pap. 19.95 (*0-936894-51-2*) Upstart Pub.

Target Marketing for the Small Business: Researching, Reaching & Retaining Your Target Market. 2nd ed. Linda Pinson & Jerry A. Jinnett. 176p. (Orig.). 1996. pap. 22.95 (*1-57410-027-0*, 6100-3702) Upstart Pub.

Target Marketing's Guide to Direct Marketing Creative Services. Denny Hatch. 300p. 1995. pap. text ed. 195.00 (*0-912920-40-8*) North Am Pub Co.

Target Marketing's Guide to Direct Marketing Creative Services: Writers--Designers--Consultants Direct Mail, Space, Telemarketing, Television, Radio. Denison Hatch. 228p. (Orig.). 1996. pap. 195.00 (*0-912920-47-5*) Whos Mailing What.

Target Marketing's Guide to Direct Marketing Suppliers. Ed. by Nancy D. Smith. 376p. 1995. pap. 95.00 (*0-912920-19-X*) North Am Pub Co.

Target of Health in Ethiopia: A Holistic Reader in Applied Anthropology. Ed. by Simon D. Messing. 285p. 1973. text ed. 34.50 (*0-8422-5074-3*); pap. text ed. 16.95 (*0-8422-0261-7*) Irvington.

Target of Opportunity. (Destroyer Ser.). 1995. mass mkt. 4.99 (*0-373-63213-4*, 1-63213-2) Harlequin Bks.

Target of Opportunity. Justine Davis. (Intimate Moments Ser.). 1993. mass mkt. 3.50 (*0-373-07506-5*, 5-07506-4) Silhouette.

Target of Penicillin: The Murein Sacculus of Bacterial Cell Walls, Architecture & Growth. Ed. by R. Hakenbeck et al. LC 83-15215. xxviii, 664p. 1983. 173.10 (*3-11-009705-2*) De Gruyter.

Target on Gold: Goal Setting for Swimmers & Other Kinds of People. Keith Bell. LC 83-80199. (Illus.). 80p. 1980. pap. 8.95 (*0-945609-02-7*) Keel Pubns.

Target Organ & the Toxic Process. Ed. by P. L. Chambers et al. (Archives of Toxicology Ser.: Suppl. 12). (Illus.). 465p. 1988. 182.00 (*0-387-18512-7*) Spr-Verlag.

Target Organ File see Handbook of Identified Carcinogens & Noncarcinogens: Carcinogenicity-Mutagenicity Database

Target Organ Pathology: A Basic Text. J. A. Turton & J. Hoosen. 350p. 1996. 110.00 (*0-7484-0156-3*); pap. 39.95 (*0-7484-0157-1*) Taylor & Francis.

Target Organ Toxicity, 2 vols. Gerald M. Cohen. 1986. Set. 339.90 (*0-8493-5769-1*, RA1211) CRC Pr.

Target Organ Toxicity, 2 vols., Vol. I. Gerald M. Cohen. 272p. 1986. 206.00 (*0-8493-5775-6*) CRC Pr.

Target Organ Toxicity, 2 vols., Vol. 2. Gerald M. Cohen. 288p. 1986. 206.00 (*0-8493-5776-4*) CRC Pr.

Target Populations. Marc Kaminsky. 50p. (Orig.). 1991. pap. 5.00 (*0-9622390-2-X*) Central Park.

***Target Practice.** Rex Stout & John Buchan. 320p. 1998. mass mkt. 5.95 (*0-7867-0496-9*) Carroll & Graf.

Target Rabaul. John Darby. (McLeane's Rangers Ser.: No. 2). 1983. mass mkt. 2.50 (*0-685-07874-4*, Zebra Kensgtn) Kensgtn Pub Corp.

Target Receptors for Anxiolytics & Hypnotics: From Molecular Pharmacology to Therapeutics. Ed. by J. Mendlewicz & Giorgio Racagni. (International Academy for Biomedical & Drug Research Ser.: Vol. 3). (Illus.). vi, 162p. 1992. 152.25 (*3-8055-5602-0*) S Karger.

Target Rifle in Australia. J. E. Corcoran. (Illus.). 223p. 1995. 40.00 (*1-884849-17-2*) R&R Bks.

Target Setting for Basic Needs: The Operation of Selected Government Services. Ed. by M. D. Leonor & P. J. Richards. vii, 130p. 1982. 22.50 (*92-2-102946-8*) Intl Labour Office.

Target Sites for Herbicide Action. Ed. by R. C. Kirkwood. (Topics in Applied Chemistry Ser.). (Illus.). 350p. 1991. 95.00 (*0-306-43846-1*, Plenum Pr) Plenum.

Target Sites of Fungicide Action. D. W. Wolframkoeller. 320p. 1991. 243.95 (*0-8493-6855-3*, SB733) CRC Pr.

Target Sites of Herbicide Action. Ed. by Peter H. Boger & Gerhard Sandmann. 304p. 1989. 250.00 (*0-8493-4985-0*, QK753) CRC Pr.

Target Sixteen Hundred. David B. Charnay. 1980. 10.00 (*0-8184-0290-3*) Carol Pub Group.

***Target Source.** 610p. 1996. pap. 695.00 (*0-9654255-0-9*) Target Source.

Target Stealth. Jack Merek. LC 88-40095. 352p. 1990. mass mkt. 4.95 (*0-446-34843-0*) Warner Bks.

Target Success: How You Can Become a Successful Entrepreneur - Regardless of Your Background. Don Dwyer. 228p. (Orig.). 1993. pap. 5.95 (*1-55850-245-9*) Adams Media.

Target Tennis: Learning to Play Tennis Using Tennis Court Trainer. Amby Dexter. LC 92-70292. (Illus.). 94p. 1992. pap. 30.00 (*1-881123-01-4*) The Catacombs.

Target Terrorism: Providing Protective Services. Richard W. Kobetz & H. H. Cooper. 1978. text ed. 12.75 (*0-88269-050-7*) Intl Assn Chiefs Police.

Target: The U. S. Asian Market: A Practical Guide to Doing Business. Angi Ma Wong. LC 93-83449. (Illus.). 224p. (Orig.). 1993. pap. 27.50 (*0-9635906-9-3*) Pacific Herit.

Target Two Thousand: Defence Industry Spinoffs for the 21st Century. Intro. by John Lessels. (Illus.). 253p. (Orig.). 1992. pap. 57.75 (*0-85825-572-3*) Accents Pubns.

Target Westminster. B. M. Gill. 200p. 1996. pap. 8.95 (*0-340-61766-7*, Pub. by H & S UK) Trafalgar.

Target Westminster. large type ed. B. M. Gill. 1993. 39.95 (*0-7066-1010-5*, Pub. by Remploy Pr CN) St Mut.

Target Zone. Patrick F. Rogers. (Omega Ser.). 1993. mass mkt. 3.50 (*0-373-63209-6*, 1-63209-0) Harlequin Bks.

Target 5. Colin Forbes. 270p. 1984. pap. 13.95 (*0-330-24023-4*, Pub. by Pan Books UK) Trans-Atl Phila.

Targeted: The Anatomy of an Animal Rights Attack. Lorenz O. Lutherer & Margaret S. Simon. LC 92-32505. 1993. 19.95 (*0-8061-2492-X*) U of Okla Pr.

***Targeted Credit Programs & Rural Poverty in Bangladesh.** Shahidur K. Khandker & Osman H. Chowdhury. (Discussion Papers: No. 336). 62p. 1996. 7.95 (*0-8213-3706-8*, 13706) World Bank.

Targeted Drug Delivery. Ed. by R. I. Juliano et al. (Handbook of Experimental Pharmacology Ser.: Vol. 100). (Illus.). 400p. 1991. 275.00 (*0-387-52843-1*) Spr-Verlag.

Targeted Fund Raising: Defining & Refining Your Development Strategy. Judith E. Nichols. LC 91-77217. 229p. 1991. 40.00 (*0-944496-29-6*) Precept Pr.

***Targeted Inactivation ("Knock-Out") of the Mouse Genes Coding for the Alpha-2-Macroglobulin & for the A2M Receptor Associated Protein.** Lieve. (Acta Biomedica Lovaniensia Ser.: No. 123). (Illus.). 137p. (Orig.). 1996. pap. 43.50 (*90-6186-728-2*, Pub. by Leuven Univ BE) Coronet Bks.

Targeted Public Relations: How to Get Thousands of Dollars of Free Publicity for Your Product, Service, Organization, or Idea. Robert W. Bly. 224p. 1993. 22.50 (*0-8050-1975-8*) H Holt & Co.

Targeted Secondary Recovery of Hydrocarbons from Barrier-Bar & Tidal-Channel Facies, Jackson Group, Prado Field, South Texas. S. J. Seni & S. J. Choh. (Geological Circular Ser.: No. GC 94-2). (Illus.). 47p. 1994. pap. 5.00 (*0-614-06202-0*) Bur Econ Geology.

Targeted Selling. Mike Godfrey. LC 95-22515. 1995. write for info. (*0-7248-1199-0*) P-H.

Targeted Selling. Mike Godfrey. 1995. pap. 20.95 (*0-13-456799-4*) P-H.

Targeted Therapeutic Systems. Tyle & Ram. (Targeted Diagnosis & Therapy Ser.: Vol. 3). 408p. 1989. 190.00 (*0-8247-8181-3*) Dekker.

***Targeting Autism: What We Know, Don't Know & Can Do to Help Young Children with Autism.** Shirley Cohen. 1998. pap. text ed. 14.95 (*0-520-21309-2*) U CA Pr.

Targeting Economic Incentives for Environmental Protection. Albert L. Nichols. (Regulation of Economic Activity Ser.). (Illus.). 248p. 1984. 30.00 (*0-262-14036-5*) MIT Pr.

Targeting Families: Marketing to & Through the New Family Structures. Robert Boutilier. LC 93-71268. 160p. 1993. pap. 29.95 (*0-936889-23-3*) American Demo.

***Targeting Families: Marketing to & Through the New Family Structures.** Sarah E. Hutchinson & Stacey Sawyer. 1993. per. 29.95 (*0-07-413187-7*) Irwin.

Targeting for Success: A Guide to New Techniques for Measurement & Analysis in Database & Direct Marketing. John Ozimek. LC 93-10242. (Marketing for Professionals Ser.). 1993. write for info. (*0-07-707766-0*) McGraw.

Targeting Fraud: Uncovering & Deterring Fraud in Financial Institutions. 2nd rev. ed. Benton E. Gup. (C). 1994. text ed. 47.50 (*1-55738-740-0*) Irwin Prof Pubng.

***Targeting Guns.** Gary Kleck. (Social Institutions & Social Change Ser.). 400p. 1997. pap. text ed. 24.95 (*0-202-30569-4*) Aldine de Gruyter.

Targeting Hygiene. Highfield Publications Staff. (C). 1989. 65.00 (*0-89771-806-2*, Pub. by Highfield Pubns UK) St Mut.

***Targeting Inflation: The Effects of Monetary Policy on the CPI & Its Housing Component.** Dimitri B. Papadimitriou & L. Randall Wray. (Illus.). 54p. (Orig.). 1996. pap. 3.00 (*0-941276-18-X*) Bard Coll Pubns.

Targeting Intelligible Speech: A Phonological Approach to Remediation. 2nd ed. Barbara W. Hodson & Elaine P. Paden. LC 90-5424. (Illus.). 190p. (C). 1991. pap. text ed. 27.00 (*0-89079-405-7*, 1582) PRO-ED.

Targeting of Drugs 4: Advances in System Constructs. Ed. by George H. Poste et al. LC 94-41747. (NATO ASI Ser.: Series A, Life Sciences: Vol. 273). 200p. 1995. 75.00 (*0-306-44910-2*, Plenum Pr) Plenum.

Targeting of Drugs with Synthetic Systems. Ed. by George H. Poste et al. LC 86-16891. (NATO ASI Series A, Life Sciences: Vol. 113). 308p. 1986. 75.00 (*0-306-42377-4*, Plenum Pr) Plenum.

Targeting of Drugs 1: Anatomical & Physiological Considerations. Ed. by George H. Poste & Gregory Gregoriadis. LC 88-28892. (Illus.). 230p. 1988. 79.50 (*0-306-43023-1*, Plenum Pr) Plenum.

Targeting of Drugs 2: Optimization Strategies. Ed. by Gregory Gregoriadis et al. LC 90-14327. (NATO ASI Series A, Life Sciences: Vol. 199). (Illus.). 180p. 1990. 75.00 (*0-306-43739-2*, Plenum Pr) Plenum.

Targeting of Drugs 3: The Challenge of Peptides & Proteins. Ed. by George H. Poste et al. (NATO ASI Series A, Life Sciences: Vol. 238). (Illus.). 124p. (C). 1993. 69.50 (*0-306-44400-3*, Plenum Pr) Plenum.

***Targeting of Drugs 5, Strategies for Oligonucleotide & Gene Delivery in Therapy Vol. 5: Proceedings of a NATO ASI Held in Cape Sounion, Greece, June 24-July 5, 1995.** Ed. by Gregory Gregoriadis & Brenda McCormack. (NATO ASI Series A: Vol. 290). 206p. 1997. 125.00 (*0-306-45504-8*) Plenum.

Targeting Students' Science Misconceptions: Physical Science Activities Using the Conceptual Change Model. Joseph Stepans. (Illus.). 224p. (Orig.). (C). 1994. pap. text ed. 21.95 (*1-885041-00-4*) Idea Factory.

***Targeting the Adult Student.** Norman C. Tognazzini. (Illus.). 8p. (Orig.). 1995. pap. 2.50 (*0-9626591-6-9*, PO316) Energeia Pub.

Targeting the Computer: Government Support & International Competition. Kenneth Flamm. LC 87-11706. 266p. 1987. 36.95 (*0-8157-2852-2*); pap. 16.95 (*0-8157-2851-4*) Brookings.

Targeting the Foreign Direct Investor: Strategic Motivation, Investment Size, & Developing Country Investment-Attraction Packages. Edward J. Coyne, Sr. LC 95-37845. 224p. (C). 1995. lib. bdg. 85.00 (*0-7923-9638-3*) Kluwer Ac.

Targeting the Job You Want: For Job Hunters, Career Changers, Consultants & Freelancers. Kate Wendleton. (Illus.). 256p. 1996. pap. 15.00 (*0-944054-08-0*) Five Oclock.

***Targeting the Job You Want: For Job Hunters, Career Changers, Consultants & Freelancers.** 2nd ed. Kate Wendleton. (The Five O'Clock Club Ser.). 1997. pap. text ed. 15.00 (*0-944054-11-0*) Five Oclock.

Targeting the Message: A Receiver-Centered Process for Public Relations Writing. William Thompson. LC 95-34685. 480p. (Orig.). (C). 1996. pap. text ed. 38.95 (*0-8013-0748-1*) Longman.

Targeting the Over-55 Client: Your Guide to Today's Fastest Growing Market. John Tuccillo et al. 182p. (Orig.). 1995. pap. 25.95 (*0-7931-1318-0*, 1913-3201, Real Estate Ed) Dearborn Finan.

Targeting the Trendsetting Consumer: How to Market Your Product or Service to Influential Buyers. Irma Zandl & Richard Leonard. 225p. 1991. text ed. 30.00 (*1-55623-478-3*) Irwin Prof Pubng.

Targeting Tomorrow: Washington's Economy Adjusts to the '90s. League of Women Voters Education Fund Staff. 42p. 1991. pap. text ed. 4.95 (*1-878170-02-3*) LWV WA.

***Targeting Transitions: Marketing to Consumers During Life Changes.** Sarah E. Hutchinson & Stacey Sawyer. 1994. per. 29.95 (*0-07-413189-3*) Irwin.

Targeting Transitions: Marketing to Consumers During Life Changes. Paula Mergenhagen. LC 93-73829. 253p. (Orig.). 1994. 39.95 (*0-936889-29-2*); pap. 29.95 (*0-936889-30-6*) American Demo.

Targeting Wellness: The Core. Janet H. Shirreffs et al. 1992. text ed. write for info. (*0-07-037575-5*) McGraw.

Targeting Your Market: Characteristics of the SLA Membership. Special Libraries Association Staff. 66p. 1992. reprint ed. pap. 25.00 (*0-608-00758-7*, 2061556) Bks Demand.

Targeting Youth: Child Labor, Tobacco & Kids, School Tracking. Ed. & Intro. by Pat Arnow. (Southern Exposure Ser.). (Illus.). 64p. (Orig.). (C). 1995. pap. 5.00 (*0-943810-65-5*) Inst Southern Studies.

***Targets & Backgrounds: Characterization & Representation III.** Ed. by Wendell R. Watkins & Dieter Clement. 43p. 1997. pap. 80.00 (*0-8194-2477-3*) SPIE.

Targets & Goals. Concept by L. Ron Hubbard. 48p. 1994. pap. 4.00 (*0-88404-924-8*) Bridge Pubns Inc.

Targets & Indicators: A Blueprint for the International Coordination of Economic Policy. Marcus Miller & John Williamson. LC 87-22724. (Policy Analyses in International Economics Ser.: No. 22). 108p. (Orig.). (C). 1987. pap. 10.00 (*0-88132-051-X*) Inst Intl Eco.

Targets & Syntactic Change. John Haiman. LC 73-87535. (Janua Linguarum, Ser. Minor: No. 186). 156p. (Orig.). 1974. pap. text ed. 26.95 (*90-279-2703-0*) Mouton.

Targets for Health for All Two Thousand: Targets in Support of the European Regional Strategy for Health for All. 201p. 1985. pap. text ed. 18.00 (*92-890-1034-7*) World Health.

Targets for Research in Library Education. Ed. by Harold Borko. LC 72-9923. 253p. reprint ed. pap. 72.20 (*0-317-26362-5*, 2024223) Bks Demand.

Targets of Opportunity. Joe Weber. 352p. 1994. mass mkt. 6.50 (*0-515-11246-1*) Jove Pubns.

Targets of Violence & Aggression. Ed. by R. Baenninger. (Advances in Psychology Ser.: No. 76). 476p. 1991. 196. 50 (*0-444-88483-1*, North Holland) Elsevier.

TARGETSMART: Database Marketing for the Small Business. Claudio Marcus & Jay Newburg. LC 96-35404. (Successful Business Library). (Illus.). 200p. (Orig.). 1996. pap. 19.95 (*1-55571-384-X*) Oasis Pr OR.

***Targett.** Robert J. Randisi. 176p. 1997. reprint ed. mass mkt. 3.99 (*0-8439-4337-8*, Leisure Bks) Dorchester Pub Co.

***Targhee Trails.** Rebecca Woods. (Illus.). 256p. 1997. pap. 14.95 (*0-9642423-3-8*) Whte Willow.

Targilon for Haschalas Chumash: A Chumash Workbook for Beginners. Shnayer Weinberg. (Illus.). 130p. (Orig.). (J). pap. text ed. 8.00 (*1-878895-00-1*, A135) Torah Umesorah.

Targilon Hasefer Chelek Rishon, Pt. 1. Kalman Bachrach. 42p. (HEB.). (J). (gr. 1). 1950. student ed. 2.25 (*1-878530-11-9*) K Bachrach Co.

Targilon Hasefer Chelek Sheini, Pt. 2. Kalman Bachrach. 76p. (HEB.). (J). (gr. 1). 1949. student ed. 2.25 (*1-878530-12-7*) K Bachrach Co.

Targilon Hasefer Chelek Shlishi, Pt. 3. Kalman Bachrach. 60p. (HEB.). (J). (gr. 3). 1953. student ed. 2.25 (*1-878530-13-5*) K Bachrach Co.

Targilon l'Sefer Shoftim. A. Weinhaus. Ed. by Yaakov Fruchter. 60p. (Orig.). (HEB.). 1994. pap. text ed. 5.50 (*1-878895-09-5*, A390) Torah Umesorah.

Targilon Olami Sefer Rishon, Bk. 1. Kalman Bachrach. 54p. (HEB.). (J). (gr. 2). 1936. student ed. 2.00 (*1-878530-17-8*) K Bachrach Co.

Targilon Olami Sefer Sheini, Bk. 2. Kalman Bachrach. 54p. (HEB.). (J). (gr. 3-4). 1936. student ed. 2.00 (*1-878530-18-6*) K Bachrach Co.

Targilon Olami Sefer Shlishi, Bk. 3. Kalman Bachrach. 60p. (HEB.). (J). (gr. 4-6). 1939. student ed. 2.00 (*1-878530-19-4*) K Bachrach Co.

Targilon Shmuel Aleph. Solomon Skaist. 53p. (J). (gr. 5-6). pap. 3.00 (*0-318-13639-2*) Board Jewish Educ.

Targu Neofiti 1: Genesis. Martin McNamara. (Aramaic Bible Ser.: No. 1A). 256p. (Orig.). 1992. 65.00 (*0-8146-5476-2*) Liturgical Pr.

Targum Jonathan of the Former Prophets. Daniel J. Harrington & Anthony J. Saldarini. (Aramaic Bible (The Targums) Ser.: Vol. 10). 320p. (Orig.). 1987. 89.95 (*0-8146-5479-7*) Liturgical Pr.

Targum Jonathan to the Prophets. Pinkos Churgin. LC 78-63558. (Yale Oriental Series: Researches: No. 14). reprint ed. 32.50 (*0-404-60284-3*) AMS Pr.

Targum Neofiti Vol. 5A: Deuteronomy. Martin McNamara. LC 96-22805. (Aramaic Bible (The Targums) Ser.). 200p. (Orig.). 1997. pap. text ed. 79.95 (*0-8146-5484-3*, M Glazier) Liturgical Pr.

Targum Neofiti One - Exodus: Targum Pseudo Jonathan: Exodus. Tr. & Intro. by Martin McNamara. LC 94-2487. (Aramaic Bible Ser.: Vol. 2). 344p. (Orig.). 1994. 79.95 (*0-8146-5477-0*, M Glazier) Liturgical Pr.

Targum Neophyti One: A Textual Study: Leviticus, Numbers, Deuteronomy, Vol. 2. B. Barry Levy. LC 86-11117. (Brown Classics in Judaica Ser.). 396p. (Orig.). (C). 1987. pap. text ed. 32.00 (*0-8191-6314-7*, Studies in Judaism); lib. bdg. 56.50 (*0-8191-6313-9*, Studies in Judaism) U Pr of Amer.

Targum of Jeremiah. Robert Hayward. (Aramaic Bible (The Targums) Ser.: Vol. 12). 206p. 1987. 79.95 (*0-8146-5481-9*) Liturgical Pr.

Targum of Judges. Willem F. Smelik. (Oudtestamentische Studien: Vol. 36). 1995. 180.00 (*90-04-10365-1*) E J Brill.

Targum of Neofiti 1 & Pseudo-Jonathan: Leviticus. McNamara et al. (Aramaic Bible Ser.: No. 3). 264p. (Orig.). 1995. 79.95 (*0-8146-5478-9*, M Glazier) Liturgical Pr.

Targum of the Minor Prophets. Kevin Cathcart & Robert Gordon. (Aramaic Bible Ser.: Vol. 14). 259p. 1989. 65. 00 (*0-8146-5489-4*) Liturgical Pr.

Targum Onkelos on Deuteronomy. Israel Drazin. 1981. 59. 50 (*0-87068-755-7*) Ktav.

Targum Onkelos on Exodus. Nathan Aviezer & Israel Drazin. 1990. 15.95 (*0-88125-328-6*) Ktav.

Targum Onkelos on Exodus. Israel Drazin. 1990. 59.50 (*0-88125-342-1*) Ktav.

Targum Onkelos to Deuteronomy. Tr. by Bernard Grossfeld. LC 86-45349. (Aramaic Bible Ser.: Vol. 9). 126p. (C). 1988. text ed. 47.95 (*0-8146-5488-6*) Liturgical Pr.

Targum Onkelos to Exodus. Tr. by Bernard Grossfeld. LC 88-45083. (Aramaic Bible Ser.: Vol. 7). 120p. (C). 1988. text ed. 45.95 (*0-8146-5486-X*) Liturgical Pr.

Targum Onkelos to Genesis. M. Aberbach & B. Grossfeld. 45.00 (*0-87068-339-X*) Ktav.

Targum Onkelos to Genesis. Tr. by Bernard Grossfeld. LC 86-45349. (Aramaic Bible Ser.: Vol. 6). 193p. (C). 1988. text ed. 49.95 (*0-8146-5485-1*) Liturgical Pr.

Targum Onkelos to Leviticus: An English Translation of the Text with Analysis & Commentary. Israel Drazin. LC 93-34042. 1993. 59.50 (*0-88125-470-3*) Ktav.

Targum Onkelos to Leviticus & Numbers. Tr. by Bernard Grossfeld. LC 88-45359. (Aramaic Bible Ser.: Vol. 8). 171p. (C). 1988. text ed. 47.95 (*0-8146-5487-8*) Liturgical Pr.

***Targum Pseudo - Jonathan: Deuteronomy, Vol. 5B.** Ernest G. Clarke. 128p. Date not set. 79.95 (*0-8146-5863-6*) Liturgical Pr.

Targum Pseudo-Jonathan: Genesis. Michael Maher. (Aramaic Bible Ser.: No. 1B). 256p. (Orig.). 1992. 65.00 (*0-8146-5492-4*) Liturgical Pr.

Targum Pseudo-Jonathan of the Pentateuch. E. G. Clarke. 1983. 150.00 (*0-88125-015-5*) Ktav.

Targum Sheni to the Book of Esther: A Critical Edition Based on Ms. Sassoon 282 with Critical Apparatus. Bernard Grossfeld. (Illus.). 425p. (ARC.). 1994. 49.95 (*0-87203-142-X*) Hermon.

Targum Studies, Vol. 1: Textual & Contextual Studies in the Pentateuchal Targums. Ed. by Paul V. McCracken-Flesher. (USF Studies in the History of Judaism). 155p. 1992. 59.95 (*1-55540-754-4*, 240055) Scholars Pr GA.

Targumic & Cognate Studies: Essays in Honour of Martin McNamara. Ed. by Kevin J. Cathcart & Michael J. Maher. (JSOTS Ser.: No. 230). 255p. 1996. 49.00 (*1-85075-632-5*, Pub. by Sheffield Acad UK) CUP Services.

Targumic Manuscripts in the Cambridge Genizah Collections. Michael L. Klein. (Library Genizah Ser.: No. 8). (Illus.). 180p. (C). 1992. text ed. 125.00 (*0-521-42076-8*) Cambridge U Pr.

Targums Neofiti 1 & Pseudo-Jonathan: Numbers. Martin McNamara & Ernst Clarke. (Aramaic Bible Ser.: Vol. 4). 352p. (Orig.). 1995. 79.95 (*0-8146-5483-5*, M Glazier) Liturgical Pr.

Targums of Job, Proverbs, & Qohelet. Celine Mangan et al. (Aramaic Bible Ser.: No. 15). 256p. 1991. text ed. 65.00 (*0-8146-5490-8*) Liturgical Pr.

Targums of Ruth & Chronicles. D. R. Beattie & J. S. McIvor. (Aramaic Bible Ser.: Vol. 19). 270p. (Orig.). 1993. 79.95 (*0-8146-5455-X*, M Glazier) Liturgical Pr.

Targun Neophyti One: A Textual Study: Introduction, Genesis, Exodus. B. Barry Levy. LC 86-11117. (Studies in Judaism). 470p. (Orig.). (C). 1986. pap. text ed. 35.50 (*0-8191-5465-2*, Studies in Judaism) U Pr of Amer.

Tarheel Hilarities: A Collection of Humor by Warren Dixon, Jr. LC 95-90674. 192p. (Orig.). 1995. pap. 11.95 (*0-9648321-0-0*) Five Hawks Pr.

Tarheel Tailgating: A Recipe Guide to North Carolina Tailgating. Illus. by Dorothy Wells. 128p. 1995. pap. 8.95 (*1-885623-08-9*) Owl Bay Pubs.

Tarheel Tales. Adapted by Tom Behm. 35p. (Orig.). (J). 1991. Playscript. pap. 5.00 (*0-87602-292-1*) Anchorage.

Tariacuri's Legacy: The Prehispanic Tarascan State. Helen P. Pollard. LC 92-37080. (Civilization of the American Indian Ser.: Vol. 209). 1993. 39.95 (*0-8061-2497-0*) U of Okla Pr.

Tariff & Science Policies: Applications of a Model of Nationalism. Donald J. Daly & S. Globerman. LC 76-24911. (Ontario Economic Council Research Studies: No. 4). 135p. reprint ed. pap. 38.50 (*0-8357-4021-8*, 2036712) Bks Demand.

Tariff Commission: Its History, Activities & Organization. Joshua Bernhardt. LC 72-3018. (Brookings Institution. Institute for Government Research. Service Monographs of the U. S. Government: No. 5). reprint ed. 21.50 (*0-404-57105-0*) AMS Pr.

***Tariff Determination in the General Equilibrium of a Political Economy: A Bargain Theoretic Approach to Policy Modelling.** Hom Moorti Pant. (Illus.). 260p. 1997. text ed. 63.95 (*1-85972-547-3*, Pub. by Ashgate UK) Ashgate Pub Co.

Tariff Examiner. Jack Rudman. (Career Examination Ser.: C-828). 1994. pap. 27.95 (*0-8373-0828-3*) Nat Learn.

Tariff Idea. W. M. Curtiss. LC 96-85396. 81p. 1996. reprint ed. pap. 2.95 (*0-910614-46-6*) Foun Econ Ed.

Tariff Levels & the Economic Unity of Europe: An Examination of Tariff Policy Export Movements & the Economic Integration of Europe 1913-1931. Heinrich Liepmann. Tr. by H. Stenning from GER. LC 79-12741. (Studies in International Economics: No. 3). (Illus.). 424p. 1980. reprint ed. lib. bdg. 49.50 (*0-87991-852-7*) Porcupine Pr.

Tariff of Syria, 1919 to 1932. Norman Burns. LC 76-180328. (Mid-East Studies). reprint ed. 42.50 (*0-404-56234-5*) AMS Pr.

Tariff on Iron & Steel. Abraham Berglund & Phillip G. Wright. (Brookings Institution Reprint Ser.). reprint ed. lib. bdg. 36.50 (*0-697-00151-2*) Irvington.

Tariff, Politics, & American Foreign Policy, 1874-1901. Tom E. Terrill. LC 72-140921. (Contributions in American History Ser.: No. 31). 306p. 1973. text ed. 65. 00 (*0-8371-5819-2*, TTP/, Greenwood Pr) Greenwood.

Tariff Preferences in Mediterranean Diplomacy. Alfred Tovias. LC 77-12265. 1978. text ed. 29.95 (*0-312-78550-X*) St Martin.

Tariff Problem. 4th ed. William J. Ashley. LC 68-30515. (Reprints of Economic Classics Ser.). xxxiv, 269p. 1968. reprint ed. 39.50 (*0-678-00433-1*) Kelley.

Tariff Problem in China. Chin Chu. LC 68-56650. (Columbia University. Studies in the Social Sciences: No. 169). reprint ed. 37.50 (*0-404-51169-4*) AMS Pr.

Tariff Question: Confronting Industrialism in the Gilded Age. Joanne Reitano. LC 93-5313. 190p. 1994. 28.50 (*0-271-01035-5*) Pa St U Pr.

Tariff Reform Movement in Great Britain, 1881-1895. Benjamin H. Brown. reprint ed. 12.50 (*0-404-01119-5*) AMS Pr.

Tariffs: A Study in Method. Theodore E. Gregory. LC 68-20038. (Reprints of Economic Classics Ser.). xv, 518p. 1968. reprint ed. 49.50 (*0-678-00420-X*) Kelley.

Tariffs: The Case for Protectionism. Lewis E. Lloyd. 9.50 (*0-8159-6902-3*) Devin.

Tariffs & Growth: Some Illustrations from the World Economy, 1850-1940. Forrest Capie. LC 93-35901. 1994. text ed. 59.95 (*0-7190-3937-1*, Pub. by Manchester Univ Pr UK); text ed. 16.95 (*0-7190-3938-X*, Pub. by Manchester Univ Pr UK) St Martin.

Tariffs, Quotas, & Trade: The Politics of Protectionism. Walter Adams et al. LC 78-66267. 330p. 1979. pap. text ed. 24.95 (*0-917616-34-0*) Transaction Pubs.

***Tariffs, Trade & European Integration, 1947-57: From Study Group to Common Market.** Wendy A. Brusse. LC 96-39531. 1997. text ed. write for info. (*0-312-16518-8*) St Martin.

Tarih. Ed. by William Brinner. (Papers in Near Eastern Studies: Vol. 2). xi, 233p. 1992. pap. text ed. 17.50 (*0-685-65025-1*, Ctr Judaic Studies) Eisenbrauns.

Tarih: A Volume of Occasional Papers in Near Eastern Studies, Vol. 1. Ed. by Leon Nemoy & Vera B. Moreen. 129p. 1990. pap. text ed. 17.50 (*0-685-57085-1*, Ctr Judaic Studies) Eisenbrauns.

Tarikh al-Qada' fi al-Islam. Muhammad Al-Zuhayli. 592p. 1995. 16.95 (*1-57547-198-1*) Dar Al-Fikr.

Tarikh-I-Mubarakshahi. Tr. by Henry Beveridge. 1990. 10. 00 (*81-85418-55-1*, Pub. by Low Price II) S Asia.

Tarikh Ulama' Dimashq fi Qarn al-Rabi Ashar al-Hijri, 3 vols., Set. Nizar Abazah & M. Muti Al-Hafiz. 1986. 47. 95 (*1-57547-164-7*) Dar Al-Fikr.

Tarikh Ulama' Dimashq fi Qarn al-Rabi Ashar al-Hijri, Vol. 1. Nizar Abazah & M. Muti Al-Hafiz. 1986. write for info. (*1-57547-165-5*) Dar Al-Fikr.

Tarikh Ulama' Dimashq fi Qarn al-Rabi Ashar al-Hijri, Vol. 2. Nizar Abazah & M. Muti Al-Hafiz. 1986. write for info. (*1-57547-166-3*) Dar Al-Fikr.

Tarikh Ulama' Dimashq fi Qarn al-Rabi Ashar al-Hijri, Vol. 3. Nizar Abazah & M. Muti Al-Hafiz. 1986. write for info. (*1-57547-167-1*) Dar Al-Fikr.

Tarjaman-ul-Quran, 3 vols. A. K. Azad. Set. 60.00 (*0-933511-73-6*) Kazi Pubns.

Tarjaman-ul-Quran, 3 vols., 1. A. K. Azad. 16.50 (*1-56744-205-6*) Kazi Pubns.

Tarjaman-ul-Quran, 3 vols., 2. A. K. Azad. 20.00 (*1-56744-207-2*) Kazi Pubns.

Tarjaman-ul-Quran, 3 vols., 3. A. K. Azad. 20.00 (*1-56744-208-0*) Kazi Pubns.

Tarjei Vesaas. Kenneth C. Chapman. LC 78-110715. (Twayne's World Authors Ser.). 1970. lib. bdg. 17.95 (*0-8057-2948-8*) Irvington.

Tarka the Otter: His Joyful Water-Life & Death in the Country of the Two Rivers. Henry Williamson. LC 90-55169. (Concord Library). (Illus.). 276p. (J). 1990. reprint ed. pap. 12.00 (*0-8070-8507-3*) Beacon Pr.

Tarkay. Illus. by Itzchak Tarkay. LC 91-67878. 160p. 1992. 50.00 (*0-8048-1799-5*) C E Tuttle.

***Tarkhoff (Nicolas)** Gaston Diehl. (Illus.). 306p. (FRE.). 1982. 125.00 (*1-55660-281-2*) A Wofsy Fine Arts.

Tarkovsky: Cinema As Poetry. Maya Turovskaya. Tr. by Natasha Ward. (Illus.). 208p. 1990. 19.95 (*0-571-14709-7*) Faber & Faber.

Tarleton Blackwell: The Greatest Show of Hogs. Catherine L. O'Hara. (Illus.). 44p. (Orig.). 1993. pap. 12.00 (*0-915577-25-9*) Taft Museum.

***Tarleton Freshman Writer, Vol. 6.** Ed. by Tarleton. (C). 1996. text ed. 13.50 (*0-673-67611-0*) Addison-Wesley.

Tarlton Law Library Annual Report: 1988-1989. 59p. 1989. 15.00 (*0-935630-36-8*) U of Tex Tarlton Law Lib.

Tarlton Law Library Annual Report: 1990-91. 38p. 1991. 17.50 (*0-935630-41-4*) U of Tex Tarlton Law Lib.

Tarlton Law Library Annual Report: 1991-92. 35p. 1993. 17.50 (*0-935630-43-0*) U of Tex Tarlton Law Lib.

Tarlton Law Library Annual Report 1989-1990. (Illus.). 33p. 1991. 15.00 (*0-935630-37-6*) U of Tex Tarlton Law Lib.

Tarlton Law Library Triennial Report, 1985-88. 62p. (Orig.). 1988. pap. 14.00 (*0-935630-25-2*) U of Tex Tarlton Law Lib.

Tarlton Law Library Users' Guide. 8p. 1989. 5.00 (*0-935630-32-5*) U of Tex Tarlton Law Lib.

Tarlton's Jests & News Out of Purgatory, with a Life by J. O. Halliwell. Tarlton. LC 71-131503. reprint ed. 34.00 (*0-404-07943-1*) AMS Pr.

Tarnefell. large type ed. Mary Williams. 368p. (C). 1996. 25.99 (*0-7089-3457-9*) Ulverscroft.

Tarnish on the Golden Years. Nona K. Carver. LC 94-94371. 124p. 1994. pap. 12.95 (*0-9641195-0-1*) Carver Cntry.

Tarnished Angel. Jennifer Lee. 448p. 1993. mass mkt. 5.50 (*0-06-100559-2*, Harp PBks) HarpC.

Tarnished Badge. Will Camp. 1990. mass mkt. 2.95 (*1-55817-390-0*, Pinncle Kensgtn) Kensgtn Pub Corp.

Tarnished Badge. Ralph L. Smith. LC 74-3852. (Criminal Justice in America Ser.). 1974. reprint ed. 23.95 (*0-405-06167-6*) Ayer.

Tarnished Blue. William Heffernan. 384p. (Orig.). 1995. mass mkt., pap. 5.99 (*0-451-18295-2*, Onyx) NAL-Dutton.

Tarnished Dreams. Larry Hancock & Michael Cherkas. (Silent Invasion Ser.: No. 3). 80p. (Orig.). 1989. pap. 9.95 (*0-918348-66-8*) NBM.

Tarnished Expansion: The Alaska Scandal, the Press, & Congress, 1867-1871. Paul S. Holbo. LC 82-17513. 164p. 1983. text ed. 22.00 (*0-87049-380-9*) U of Tenn Pr.

Tarnished Expansion: The Alaska Scandal, the Press & Congress, 1867-1871. Paul S. Holbo. LC 82-17513. 167p. reprint ed. pap. 47.60 (*0-608-00933-4*, 2061727) Bks Demand.

Tarnished Gold. V. C. Andrews. 1996. mass mkt., pap. 6.99 (*0-671-87321-0*) PB.

Tarnished Gold. V. C. Andrews. Ed. by Linda Marrow. 320p. 1996. 23.00 (*0-671-87576-0*, PB Hardcover) PB.

Tarnished Gold. large type ed. V. C. Andrews. LC 96-17810. (Large Print Bks.). 1996. 26.95 (*1-56895-338-0*) Wheeler Pub.

Tarnished Gold: Prejudice During the California Gold Rush. Winifred S. Hill. 106p. (Orig.). 1996. text ed. 69.95 (*1-57309-023-9*); pap. text ed. 49.95 (*1-57309-022-0*) Intl Scholars.

Tarnished Gold: The Record Industry Revisited. R. Serge Denisoff. 350p. 1986. 29.95 (*0-88738-618-0*) Transaction Pubs.

Tarnished Hearts. Raine Cantrell. 348p. (Orig.). 1994. pap. 4.99 (*0-451-40442-4*, Topaz) NAL-Dutton.

Tarnished Hero: A Sam Sharpstein Novel. Steve W. Berman. LC 87-92175. 1989. 17.95 (*0-87212-214-X*) Libra.

***Tarnished Icons.** Stuart M. Kaminsky. 1997. mass mkt. 5.99 (*0-8041-1289-4*) Ivy Books.

Tarnished Knight. William C. Stump. (Illus.). 346p. 1984. 14.95 (*0-9613487-0-4*) W C Stump.

Tarnished Lady. Sandra Hill. 300p. (Orig.). 1995. mass mkt., pap. text ed. 4.99 (*0-8439-3834-X*) Dorchester Pub Co.

Tarnished Phoenix. large type ed. James Melville. (Adventure Suspense Ser.). 432p. 1992. 25.99 (*0-7089-2666-5*) Ulverscroft.

Tarnished Rainbow. large type ed. Jocelyn Day. (Romance Ser.). 352p. 1993. 25.99 (*0-7089-2950-8*) Ulverscroft.

Tarnished Rings. Jim Hawkins. 266p. 1993. pap. 9.99 (*1-56043-522-4*) Destiny Image.

Tarnished Shield. John J. Delamer. 208p. (Orig.). 1995. pap. 12.95 (*1-56474-156-7*) Fithian Pr.

Tarnished Silver - After the Photo Boom: Essays on Photography & Related Matters 1979-1989. A. D. Coleman. LC 95-80903. (Illus.). 224p. (Orig.). 1996. pap. 20.00 (*1-877675-20-2*) Midmarch Arts-WAN.

Tarnished Star. large type ed. Gil Harmon. (Linford Western Library). 1991. pap. 15.99 (*0-7089-7039-7*) Ulverscroft.

Tarnished Victory. Rosemary Joyce. (Dream Girls Ser.: No. 3). 160p. (J). (gr. 4-7). 1994. pap. 4.50 (*1-56171-317-1*, S P I Bks) Sure Seller.

Tarnished Vision: Crime & Community Action in the Inner City. David Robins. LC 92-22144. 160p. 1993. 45.00 (*0-19-825751-1*); pap. 16.95 (*0-19-825816-X*) OUP.

An Asterisk (*) at the beginning of an entry indicates that the title is appearing in BIP for the first time.

Tarnished Warrior, Major General James Wilkinson. James R. Jacobs. 1977. 36.95 (0-8369-6943-X, 7824) Ayer.

Tarnsman of Gor. John Norman. 1996. mass mkt. 6.95 (1-56333-486-0) Masquerade.

Taro Classico. Stuart R. Kaplan. Tr. by Maio Miranda from ENG. (Illus.). 224p. (Orig.). (POR.). pap. 10.95 (0-88079-251-5) US Games Syst.

Tarocchi. Stuart R. Kaplan. (Illus.). 240p. (ITA.). 1979. 10.95 (0-88079-256-6) US Games Syst.

Taroleywick: A Century of Iowa Farming. Henry C. Taylor. LC 70-103840. 144p. reprint ed. pap. 41.10 (0-317-55556-1, 2029623) Bks Demand.

TAROsolution(TM) A Complete Guide to Interpreting the Tarot. Edmund J. Sullivan. (Illus.). 50p. (Orig.). 1994. pap. 15.00 (1-885794-08-8) E Haga Pub.

Tarot. Ed. by Robert Adkinson. LC 95-60473. (Sacred Symbols Ser.). (Illus.). 80p. 1995. 160.00 (0-500-06021-5) Thames Hudson.

Tarot. Piers Anthony. 1987. pap. 9.95 (0-441-79841-1) Ace Bks.

Tarot. David V. Barrett. LC 95-12890. (Predictions Library). (Illus.). 64p. 1995. 8.95 (0-7894-0306-4, 6-70512) DK Pub Inc.

Tarot. Alfred Douglas. 1992. pap. 10.95 (0-14-019239-5, Viking) Viking Penguin.

Tarot. Cynthia Giles. 1994. 21.95 (1-56924-932-6) Marlowe & Co.

Tarot. Cynthia Giles. 1996. pap. 12.00 (0-684-81883-3) S&S Trade.

Tarot. E. Grey et al. 1991. boxed 25.95 (0-451-92510-6) NAL-Dutton.

Tarot. Stuart R. Kaplan. Tr. by Burkhardt Kiegeland from ENG. (Illus.). 256p. (Orig.). (GER.). 1984. pap. 10.95 (0-88079-252-3) US Games Syst.

***Tarot.** Pamela Lloyd. 96p. 1996. 12.99 (1-57215-208-7, JG1207) World Pubns.

Tarot. S. L. Mathers. 1973. 59.95 (0-8490-1177-9) Gordon Pr.

Tarot. Joseph Maxwell. Tr. by Ivor C. Powell from FRE. 224p. (Orig.). pap. 26.95 (0-8464-4297-3) Beekman Pubs.

Tarot. Joseph Maxwell. 190p. 1988. pap. 17.95 (0-85207-206-6, Pub. by C W Daniel UK) Natl Bk Netwk.

Tarot. Kenneth D. Newman. 160p. 1983. pap. 9.95 (0-615-00937-9) Weiser.

Tarot. Nancy Shavick. 1988. pap. 4.50 (0-425-11263-2, Berkley Trade) Berkley Pub.

Tarot. abr. ed. Robert Adkinson. (Sacred Symbols Ser.). 80p. 1995. 10.00 (0-500-06019-3) Thames Hudson.

Tarot: A Key to the Wisdom of the Ages. rev. ed. Paul F. Case. 213p. reprint ed. 18.00 (0-938002-08-2) Builders of Adytum.

Tarot: A New Handbook for the Apprentice. Eileen Connolly. LC 79-15303. (Illus.). 254p. 1979. pap. 14.95 (0-87877-045-3) Newcastle Pub.

Tarot: A New Handbook for the Apprentice. rev. ed. Eileen Connolly. 254p. 1990. pap. 14.95 (0-87877-162-X) Newcastle Pub.

Tarot: A Short Treatise on Reading Cards. rev. ed. S. L. Mathers. LC 71-17150. (Illus.). 96p. 1969. pap. 5.95 (0-87728-754-6) Weiser.

Tarot: A Universal Language. Beatrex Quntanna. (Illus.). 96p. (Orig.). 1989. pap. 14.95 (0-9625292-0-6) Art Ala Carte Pub.

Tarot: An Essay. Manly P. Hall. pap. 6.95 (0-89314-382-0) Philos Res.

Tarot: History, Mystery & Lore. Cynthia Giles. LC 94-16157. 254p. 1994. reprint ed. write for info. (0-671-89101-4, Fireside) S&S Trade.

***Tarot: It's in the Cards!** Ariel Books Staff. LC 96-85927. 80p. 1997. 4.95 (0-8362-2653-4, Arie Bks) Andrews & McMeel.

Tarot: Mirror of the Soul. Gerd Ziegler. LC 87-34087. (Illus.). 203p. (Orig.). 1988. pap. 9.95 (0-87728-683-3) Weiser.

***Tarot: Plus Deck.** Joanna Swinnerton. 1996. 9.98 (0-7651-9692-1) Smithmark.

Tarot: Spanish Language Edition of Tarot Classic. Stuart R. Kaplan. (Illus.). 256p. 1982. pap. 10.95 (0-88079-255-8) US Games Syst.

Tarot: The First Handbook for the Master. Eileen Connolly. Ed. by Gina Wisiroglo. (Illus.). 320p. (Orig.). 1996. pap. 18.95 (0-87877-235-9) Newcastle Pub.

Tarot: The Handbook for the Journeyman. Eileen Connolly. LC 87-31995. xiii, 193p. 1987. lib. bdg. 35.00 (0-8095-6124-7) Borgo Pr.

Tarot: The Origins, Meaning & Uses of the Cards. Alfred Douglas. 1973. mass mkt. 6.95 (0-14-003737-3, Penguin Bks) Viking Penguin.

Tarot: The Path to Wisdom. rev. ed. Joseph D. D'Agostino. LC 94-36189. (Illus.). 188p. 1994. pap. 9.95 (0-87728-819-4) Weiser.

***Tarot Abecedarian: The Treasure House of Images.** A. R. Naylor. (Illus.). 160p. 1997. 24.95 (1-872736-52-1, Pub. by Mandrake Pr UK) Holmes Pub.

Tarot & Astrology. Muriel B. Hasbrouck. 304p. (Orig.). 1987. pap. 10.95 (0-89281-121-8, Destiny Bks) Inner Tradit.

Tarot & Individuation: Correspondence with Cabala & Alchemy. Irene Gad. LC 93-42844. (Illus.). 512p. (Orig.). 1994. pap. 21.95 (0-89254-026-5) Nicolas-Hays.

Tarot & the Tree of Life: Finding Everyday Wisdom in the Minor Arcana. Isabel Kliegman. LC 97-47. (Illus.). 304p. 1997. pap. 14.00 (0-8356-0747-X, Quest) Theos Pub Hse.

Tarot & Transformation. Lynn M. Buess. LC 73-77608. (Illus.). 1977. reprint ed. pap. 8.95 (0-87516-238-X) DeVorss.

Tarot & You. 1995. 19.99 (0-517-15930-9) Random Hse Value.

Tarot As a Tool for Personal Growth: The "Getting There from Here" Spreads. Anna Jedrziewski. (Illus.). viii, 110p. (Orig.). 1996. pap. 12.95 (0-9650816-0-5) Inanna Wrks.

Tarot As a Tool for Personal Growth: The Numerology Spreads. Anna Jedrziewski. (Illus.). xii, 112p. (Orig.). 1996. pap. 12.95 (0-9650816-1-3) Inanna Wrks.

***Tarot As a Tool for Personal Growth Vol. 3: The Sacred Geometry Spreads.** Anna Jedrziewski. (Illus.). xii, 120p. (Orig.). 1997. pap. 12.95 (0-9650816-2-1) Inanna Wrks.

***Tarot As a Way of Life: A Jungian Approach to the Tarot.** Karen Hamaker-Zondag. LC 97-1920. (Illus.). 288p. (Orig.). 1997. pap. 16.95 (0-87728-878-X) Weiser.

***Tarot Basics.** Evelin Burger & Johannes Fiebig. LC 96-48607. 1997. write for info. (0-8069-9503-3) Sterling Pubng.

Tarot Book: Basic Instruction for Reading Cards. Jana Riley. LC 91-29396. (Illus.). 188p. (Orig.). 1992. pap. 11.95 (0-87728-723-6) Weiser.

Tarot Card Combinations. Dorothy Kelly. LC 95-15314. (Illus.). 368p. (Orig.). 1995. pap. 16.95 (0-87728-829-1) Weiser.

Tarot Card Symbology. 3rd rev. ed. Max F. Long. Ed. by E. Otha Wingo. (Illus.). 1983. pap. 10.00 (0-910764-07-7) Huna Res Inc.

Tarot Cards for Fun & Fortune Telling. Stuart R. Kaplan. LC 71-119490. (Illus.). 96p. 1970. pap. 5.95 (0-913866-02-4) US Games Syst.

***Tarot Celebrations: Honoring the Inner Voice.** Geraldine Amaral & Nancy B. Cunningham. LC 97-18744. (Illus.). 176p. (Orig.). 1997. pap. 16.95 (1-57863-014-2) Weiser.

Tarot Classic. Stuart R. Kaplan. LC 74-183028. (Illus.). 240p. 1972. pap. 9.95 (0-913866-17-2) US Games Syst.

Tarot Constellations: Patterns of Personal Destiny. Mary K. Greer. 192p. 1987. pap. 14.95 (0-87877-128-X) Newcastle Pub.

Tarot Dictionary & Compendium. Jana Riley. LC 95-8713. (Illus.). 175p. 1995. pap. text ed. 14.95 (0-87728-821-6) Weiser.

Tarot Divination. Aleister Crowley. 72p. 1976. pap. 4.95 (0-87728-347-8) Weiser.

Tarot Fantastic. Ed. by Martin H. Greenberg & Lawrence Schimel. 1997. pap. 5.99 (0-88677-729-1) DAW Bks.

Tarot for Beginners. Kristyna Arcarti. (Headway Guide for Beginners Ser.). (Illus.). 89p. 1995. pap. 11.95 (0-340-59550-7, Pub. by Headway UK) Trafalgar.

Tarot for Beginners: An Easy Guide to Understanding & Interpreting the Tarot. P. Scott Hollander. LC 94-43321. (Illus.). 384p. 1995. pap. 12.95 (1-56718-363-8) Llewellyn Pubns.

Tarot for Beginners: How to Read the Tarot. Dayle Schear. (Orig.). 1996. pap. 19.95 incl. vhs (0-931892-93-7) B Dolphin Pub.

Tarot for Cats. Regen Dennis. 64p. 1996. 14.95 (0-02-860828-3) Macmillan.

Tarot for Every Day: Ideas & Activities for Bringing Tarot Wisdom into Your Daily Life. Cait Johnson. LC 94-67634. (Illus.). 148p. (Orig.). 1994. pap. 14.95 (1-885482-00-0) Shawangunk Pr.

Tarot for Lovers. E. W. Neville. Ed. by Julie Lockhart. LC 87-62096. (Illus.). 252p. (Orig.). 1987. pap. 14.95 (0-914918-75-3, Whitford Pr) Schiffer.

Tarot for Relationships. Jocelyn Almond. 176p. 1990. pap. 11.00 (0-85030-850-X, Pub. by Aquarian Pr UK) Thorsons SF.

***Tarot for Relationships: A Practical Guide to Understanding Love & Sex from Tarot Reading.** Jocelyn Almond. pap. 15.00 (0-7225-3276-8) Thorsons SF.

Tarot for the Beginner: A Simple & Easy Step-by-Step Guide to Reading the Tarot Cards in One Hour or Less. Dayle Schear. LC 94-10402. (Illus.). 64p. (Orig.). 1994. pap. 6.95 (0-931892-92-9) B Dolphin Pub.

***Tarot for the New Age.** 29.95 (0-9615079-5-0) Merrill-West Pub.

***Tarot for the New Age, Vol. 2.** 29.95 (0-9615079-6-9) Merrill-West Pub.

Tarot for Today's Woman. Cassandra Eason. 160p. 1995. pap. 7.95 (0-572-01812-6, Pub. by Foulsham UK) Assoc Pubs Grp.

Tarot for Your Self: A Workbook for Personal Transformation. Mary K. Greer. (Illus.). 267p. 1984. pap. 14.95 (0-87877-077-1) Newcastle Pub.

Tarot for Your Self: A Workbook for Personal Transformation. Mary K. Greer. LC 84-21620. (Illus.). xiii, 253p. 1984. reprint ed. lib. bdg. 45.00 (0-89370-677-9) Borgo Pr.

Tarot Games: Forty-Five Playful Ways to Explore Tarot Cards Together. Cait Johnson & Maura D. Shaw. LC 93-48283. 128p. 1994. pap. 14.00 (0-06-250964-0) Harper SF.

Tarot Guide to Love & Relationships. Nancy Shavick. 160p. (Orig.). 1993. mass mkt. 4.99 (0-425-13583-7) Berkley Pub.

Tarot Gypsy Tales: Definitive Resource on the Cards. Carol J. Rose. LC 89-92413. (Illus.). 300p. (C). 1990. 59.00 (1-878490-50-8); lib. bdg. 69.00 (1-878490-51-6) Rosehips Ink.

Tarot Gypsy Trips: Emerald Secrets of a Road Scholar. Carol J. Rose. 1995. 49.00 (1-878490-64-8); lib. bdg. 59.00 (1-878490-65-6) Rosehips Ink.

Tarot Handbook. Hajo Banzhaf. LC 93-60077. (Illus.). 184p. 1993. pap. 17.95 (0-88079-511-5) US Games Syst.

***Tarot Handbook: Practical Applications of Ancient Visual Symbols.** rev. ed. Angeles Arrien. 320p. 1997. 22.95 (0-87477-895-6, Tarcher Putnam) Putnam Pub Group.

Tarot II: The Handbook for the Journeyman. Eileen Connolly. 288p. (Orig.). 1988. pap. 14.95 (0-87877-124-7) Newcastle Pub.

Tarot in Action: An Introduction to Simple & More Complex Tarot Spreads. Sasha Fenton. (Illus.). 240p. (Orig.). 1989. pap. 7.95 (0-85030-525-X, Pub. by Aquarian Pr UK) Thorsons SF.

Tarot in Ten Minutes: A New Way of Reading the Cards & Yourself. R. T. Kaser. (Illus.). 368p. (Orig.). 1992. pap. 12.00 (0-380-76689-2) Avon.

***Tarot Kit - Golden Dawn Magical.** Cicero. 1996. pap. 34.95 (1-56718-134-1, 112770T) Llewellyn Pubns.

Tarot Lays. (Salamander Ser.: No. 2). (Illus.). 31p. 1993. reprint ed. pap. 3.95 (1-56640-592-0) Pomegranate Calif.

Tarot Made Easy. Nancy Garen. 368p. 1989. pap. 15.00 (0-671-67087-5, Fireside) S&S Trade.

Tarot Mirrors: Reflections of Personal Meaning. Mary K. Greer. 221p. 1988. pap. 14.95 (0-87877-131-X) Newcastle Pub.

Tarot Mirrors: Reflections of Personal Meaning. Mary K. Greer. LC 88-34114. (Illus.). xv, 206p. (C). 1988. reprint ed. lib. bdg. 45.00 (0-8095-6131-X) Borgo Pr.

Tarot of Ceremonial Magick. Lon Du Quette & Constance Du Quette. 38p. 1995. pap. 15.00 (0-88079-728-2) US Games Syst.

Tarot of Ceremonial Magick: A Pictorial Synthesis of Three Great Pillars of Magick. Lon M. Duquette. LC 95-14649. 304p. 1995. pap. 14.95 (0-87728-764-3) Weiser.

Tarot of Cornelius Agrippa. Frederick Morgan. LC 77-94782. (Illus.). 50p. (Orig.). 1978. pap. 75.00 (0-915298-11-2) Hudson Rev.

Tarot of Love Book. Wulfing Von Rohr & Gayan S. Winter. LC 91-66319. (Illus.). 176p. 1992. pap. 9.95 (0-88079-521-2) US Games Syst.

Tarot of the Bohemians. Papus. 385p. 1978. pap. 7.00 (0-87980-158-1) Wilshire.

Tarot of the Cat People. Kay Kuykendall. LC 90-71242. (Illus.). 188p. 1991. pap. 9.95 (0-88079-420-8) US Games Syst.

Tarot of the Magi. Carlyle A. Pushong. 112p. 1994. pap. 10.95 (0-87877-192-1) Newcastle Pub.

Tarot of the Magicians. Oswald Wirth. LC 85-51592. 195p. (Orig.). 1986. pap. 14.95 (0-87728-656-6) Weiser.

Tarot of the Magicians. Oswald Wirth. LC 85-51592. (Illus.). 224p. (Orig.). 1990. pap. 14.95 (0-88079-301-5) US Games Syst.

Tarot of the Orishas. Zolrak. LC 94-34942. (Illus.). 300p. (ENG & SPA.). 1994. pap. 14.95 (1-56718-844-3) Llewellyn Pubns.

Tarot of the Orishas Kit. Zolrak. 300p. 1994. reprint ed. boxed 29.95 (1-56718-842-7) Llewellyn Pubns.

Tarot of the Soul: How to Uncover the Secret Wisdom of Your Soul Using Regular Playing Cards. Belinda Atkinson. 88p. 1995. pap. 8.95 (0-926524-32-1) Swan Raven.

Tarot of the Spirit. Pamela Eakins. LC 90-23600. (Illus.). 188p. (Orig.). 1992. pap. 22.95 (0-87728-730-9) Weiser.

Tarot of the Spirit Set, Set. Pamela Eakins. (Illus.). 188p. (Orig.). 1994. pap. 34.95 (0-87728-763-5) Weiser.

Tarot of the Witches Book. Stuart R. Kaplan. LC 73-80526. (Illus.). 96p. 1981. pap. 4.95 (0-913866-40-7) US Games Syst.

Tarot Pack: The Traditional Tarot System Reinterpreted for the Modern World. Adam Fronteras. (Illus.). 128p. 1996. boxed 24.95 (1-55670-504-2) Stewart Tabori & Chang.

Tarot Path to Self-Development. Micheline Stuart. (Illus.). 128p. 1996. pap. 6.00 (1-57062-132-2) Shambhala Pubns.

Tarot Plain & Simple. Anthony Louis. LC 96-30422. (Illus.). 288p. (Orig.). 1996. pap. 14.95 (1-56718-400-6, K-400-6) Llewellyn Pubns.

Tarot Poems. Stephen Dunstan. 56p. 8000. pap. 9.95 (0-906427-10-X, Pub. by Bloodaxe Bks UK) Dufour.

***Tarot Practitioner's Handbook.** Dale W. Emme. (Illus.). 265p. (Orig.). 1997. pap. 24.95 (1-889529-11-7) Two Feathers.

Tarot Reader. Nancy Shavick. 1991. mass mkt. 4.99 (0-425-12736-2) Berkley Pub.

Tarot Revealed: A Modern Guide to Reading the Tarot Cards. Eden Gray. 1969. pap. 5.99 (0-451-15673-0, AE1965, Sig) NAL-Dutton.

Tarot Revelations. 2nd ed. Joseph Campbell & Richard Roberts. LC 81-66684. (Illus.). 308p. 1982. pap. 10.95 (0-942380-00-2) Vernal Equinox.

***Tarot Says Beware.** Betsy Byars. (J). 1997. pap. 3.99 (0-14-036997-X) Viking Penguin.

Tarot Says Beware. Betsy C. Byars. LC 95-12334. (Herculeah Jones Mystery Ser.). (J). 1995. pap. 13.99 (0-670-85575-8, Viking) Viking Penguin.

Tarot Shows the Path. Rolla Nordic. 132p. 1989. 8.95 (0-939708-25-6) Magickal Childe.

Tarot Spells. Janina Renee. LC 89-77199. (New Age Tarot Ser.). (Illus.). 275p. (Orig.). 1990. pap. 12.95 (0-87542-670-0) Llewellyn Pubns.

Tarot Tales. Caitlin Mathews & Rachel Pollack. 1996. mass mkt. 5.99 (0-441-00352-4) Ace Bks.

Tarot Tool Kit. Carl Japikse. 1990. Incl. Exploring the Tarot, Aquarian Tarot Deck, pad of 100 worksheets. pap. 33.00 (0-89804-044-2) Ariel GA.

Tarot 2000: Lifting the Veil of Illusion, Incls. 72 cards. Carla Parks-Flack. (Illus.). 201p. 1995. text ed. 24.95 (1-885499-52-3) Angelight.

Tarot Unveiled: The Method to Its Magic. Laura E. Clarson. LC 89-83840. (Illus.). 144p. (Orig.). 1984. pap. 10.00 (0-88079-356-2) US Games Syst.

Tarot Workbook: Understanding & Using Tarot Symbolism. rev. ed. Emily Peach. (Workbook Ser.). (Illus.). 256p. (Orig.). 1985. pap. 14.95 (0-85030-390-7) Sterling.

Tarotmania. Woudhuysen. 1995. pap. 7.95 (0-316-85247-3) Little.

Tarpaulin Muster. John Masefield. LC 73-132120. (Short Story Index Reprint Ser.). 1977. 17.95 (0-8369-3677-9) Ayer.

Tarpleywick: A Century of Iowa Farming. Henry C. Taylor. LC 90-4874. (Iowa Heritage Collection). (Illus.). 144p. 1990. reprint ed. pap. 9.95 (0-8138-1959-8) Iowa St U Pr.

Tarpon Book: A Complete Angler's Guide. Frank Sargeant. LC 91-76442. (Inshore Ser.). (Illus.). 160p. (Orig.). 1991. pap. 11.95 (0-936513-16-0) Larsens Outdoor.

***Tarpon Quest.** John Cole. 128p. 1997. reprint ed. pap. 14.95 (1-55821-622-7) Lyons & Burford.

Tarquin Globe. Gerald Jenkins & Magdalen Bear. (Illus.). 32p. (Orig.). (J). (gr. 4-6). 1991. pap. 7.95 (0-906212-55-3, Pub. by Tarquin UK) Parkwest Pubns.

Tarquin Starglobe. Gerald Jenkins & Magdalen Bear. (Illus.). 32p. (Orig.). (J). (gr. 4-6). 1991. pap. 7.95 (0-906212-60-X, Pub. by Tarquin UK) Parkwest Pubns.

Tarr: The Nineteen Eighteen Version. Afterword by Wyndham Lewis. LC 89-29842. (Illus.). 430p. (C). 1990. reprint ed. 25.00 (0-87685-785-3); reprint ed. pap. 17.50 (0-87685-784-5) Black Sparrow.

Tarrant Trains Gun Dogs: Humane Way to Get Top Results. Bill Tarrant. LC 88-26774. (Illus.). 224p. 1989. 18.95 (0-8117-1723-2) Stackpole.

Tarrasch French Guimard Variation. Eric Schiller. 92p. (Orig.). 1991. pap. 7.95 (0-945470-02-9) Chess Ent.

Tarrington Chase. Sylvia Thorpe. 1980. pap. 1.75 (0-449-50055-1, Coventry) Fawcett.

Tarrisbroke Hall. large type ed. Cresswell. 1995. 25.99 (0-7089-3373-4) Ulverscroft.

Tarry Flynn. Patrick Kavanagh. 12.50 (0-8159-6903-1) Devin.

Tarry Flynn. Patrick Kavanagh & P. J. O'Connor. Ed. by John Nemo. (Abbey Theatre Ser.). 1977. pap. 2.50 (0-912262-40-0) Proscenium.

Tarryall Mountains - Cheesman Res, CO. rev. ed. Ed. by Trails Illustrated Staff. (Illus.). 1994. 8.99 (0-925873-26-8) Trails Illustrated.

Tarrying with the Negative: Kant, Hegel, & the Critique of Ideology. Slavoj Zizek. LC 93-17366. (Post-Contemporary Interventions Ser.). 304p. 1993. pap. 17.95 (0-8223-1395-2); text ed. 39.95 (0-8223-1362-6) Duke.

Tarrytown, NY 1929 to 1945. Historical Briefs, Inc. Staff. Ed. by Thomas Antonucci & Michael Antonucci. 176p. 1994. pap. 14.95 (0-89677-057-5) Hist Briefs.

Tarski Symposium: Proceedings of the Symposium in Pure Mathematics, University of California, Berkeley, June 1971. Ed. by L. Henkin. LC 74-8666. (Proceedings of Symposia in Pure Mathematics Ser.: Vol. 25). 498p. 1974. reprint ed. pap. 61.00 (0-8218-1425-7, PSPUM/25) Am Math.

Tarski's World: IBM-Compatible Windows Version 4.0. Jon Barwise & John Etchemendy. LC 93-30042. (CSLI Lecture Notes Ser.: No. 45). 1993. pap. 21.95 (1-881526-28-3) CSLI.

Tarski's World: Version 4.0 for the Macintosh. Jon Barwise & John Etchemendy. LC 93-30034. (CSLI Lecture Notes Ser.: No. 25). 1993. pap. 21.95 (1-881526-27-5) CSLI.

Tarski's World 3.0, Including the Macintosh Program. Jon Barwise & John Etchemendy. LC 91-8756. (Center for the Study of Language & Information-Lecture Notes Ser.: No. 25). 111p. (Orig.). (C). 1991. pap. 19.50 (0-937073-67-9) CSLI.

Tart Tales: Elegant Erotic Stories. Carolyn Banks. 160p. 1993. 18.95 (0-88184-863-8) Carroll & Graf.

Tart Tales: Elegant Erotic Stories. Carolyn Banks. 224p. 1994. pap. 8.95 (0-7867-0079-3) Carroll & Graf.

Tart Tales: Elegant Erotic Stories. Carolyn Banks. 1995. 6.98 (0-7858-0466-8) Bk Sales Inc.

Tartan: The Highland Habit. Hugh Cheape. (Illus.). 96p. 1995. pap. 14.95 (0-948636-70-X, 6238, Pub. by Natl Mus Scotland UK) A Schwartz & Co.

Tartan: The Highland Textile. James D. Scarlett. (Illus.). 216p. 1983. 39.95 (0-85683-120-4, Pub. by Shepheard-Walwyn Pubs UK) Paul & Co Pubs.

Tartan Conspiracy. large type ed. Richard Grindal. LC 94-7339. 311p. 1994. lib. bdg. 17.95 (0-8161-5984-X, GK Hall) Thorndike Pr.

Tartan for Me! Suggested Tartans for Scottish, Scotch-Irish, Irish, & North American Surnames with Lists of Clan, Family, & District Tartans. 6th expanded ed. Philip D. Smith. (Orig.). 1995. pap. text ed. 20.00 (0-7884-0137-8) Heritage Bk.

Tartan Sell. Jonathan Gash. 240p. 1987. pap. 3.95 (0-14-009745-7, Penguin Bks) Viking Penguin.

Tartan Tiger. Jean B. Smith. (Illus.). (Orig.). (J). (gr. 7 up). 1986. pap. 8.00 (0-935827-00-5) Tartan Tiger.

Tartan Weavers' Guide. Will Scarlett. 1985. 16.95 (0-85683-078-X) Robin & Russ.

Tartans: The Facts & Myths. (Illus.). 32p. 1993. pap. 3.95 (0-7117-0341-8) Seven Hills Bk.

***Tartans of Scotland.** Herbert E. Nass. LC 72-190274. 1997. pap. text ed. 5.95 (0-7188-1930-6, Lutterworth-Parkwest) Parkwest Pubns.

***Tartanware: Souvenirs from Scotland.** H. R. H. Princess Ira Von Furstenberg. (Illus.). 72p. 1997. 19.95 (1-85793-514-4, Pub. by Pavilion UK) Trafalgar.

Tartar Steppe. Dino Buzzati. Tr. by Stuart Hood. 224p. 1995. pap. 13.95 (0-87923-992-1) Godine.

Tartarin de Tarascon. Alphonse Daudet. (Coll. Prestige). 1965. 27.95 (0-685-11580-1) Fr & Eur.

Tartarin de Tarascon. Alphonse Daudet. (Illus.). 228p. (FRE.). 1991. pap. 14.95 (0-7859-4669-1) Fr & Eur.

Tartarin de Tarascon. Alphonse Daudet. (Folio Ser.: No. 1824). (FRE.). pap. 7.95 (2-07-037824-1) Schoenhof.

***Tartarin de Tarascon.** unabridged ed. Alphonse Daudet. (FRE.). Date not set. reprint ed. pap. 6.95 (2-87714-338-4, Pub. by Bookking Intl FR) Distribks Inc.

Tartarin sur les Alpes. Alphonse Daudet. 8.95 (0-686-55601-1) Fr & Eur.

Tarte a la Creme - Comedy & Gastronomy in Moliere's Theater. Ronald W. Tobin. 200p. 1990. text ed. 45.00 (0-8142-0493-7) Ohio St U Pr.

Tartuffe. Moliere & Noyce Burleson. 1994. 3.95 (0-87129-422-2, T61) Dramatic Pub.

Tartuffe. Moliere. Tr. by Richard Wilbur. 1988. pap. 5.25 (0-8222-1111-4) Dramatists Play.

Tartuffe. Moliere. (ENG & FRE.). 1992. pap. 10.95 (0-7859-3240-2, 2266043218) Fr & Eur.

***Tartuffe.** Moliere. Tr. by Richard Wilbur. (ENG & FRE.). 1997. 25.00 (0-614-29407-X) HarBrace.

Tartuffe. Moliere. Tr. by Richard Wilbur. LC 63-17778. 164p. 1968. reprint ed. pap. 7.00 (0-15-688180-2, Harvest Bks) HarBrace.

***Tartuffe: A Comedy in Five Acts, 1669.** Moliere & Richard Wilbur. LC 96-47083. 1997. write for info. (0-15-100281-9) HarBrace.

Tartuffe: Acting Edition. Moliere. Tr. by Robert W. Hartle. 1965. pap. 4.95 (0-672-60275-X, LLA87, Bobbs) Macmillan.

Tartuffe: Acting Edition. Moliere. (Seventeenth Century French Drama). 1967. write for info. (0-318-54371-0) McGraw.

Tartuffe: Don Juan; Le Misanthrope. Moliere. (FRE.). 1973. pap. 11.95 (0-7859-2872-3) Fr & Eur.

Tartuffe see Misanthrope & Other Plays

Tartuffe see Misanthrope & Tartuffe

Tartuffe - Dom Juan. unabridged ed. Moliere. (FRE.). pap. 5.95 (2-87714-197-7, Pub. by Bookking Intl FR) Distribks Inc.

Tartuffe: Acting Edition see Seventeenth Century French Drama

Tartuffe & Other Plays. Moliere. (Signet Classics Ser.). 1960. mass mkt. 6.95 (0-451-52454-3, Sig Classics) NAL-Dutton.

Tartuffe & Other Plays: Ridiculous Precieuses, School for Husbands, School for Wives, Critique for the School for Wives, Versailles Impromptu, Don Juan. Moliere. Tr. by Donald M. Frame. 1960. pap. 3.50 (0-451-52011-4, CE1566, Sig Classics) NAL-Dutton.

Tartuffe. Don Juan. Le Misanthrope. Moliere. (Folio Ser.: No. 332). (FRE.). pap. 9.95 (2-07-036332-5) Schoenhof.

Tartuffe Libretto. K. Mechem. 52p. 1994. pap. 5.95 (0-7935-3476-3) H Leonard.

Tartuffe, Misanthrope & the Bourgeois Gentleman Notes. Denis M. Calandra & James L. Roberts. 1982. pap. 4.25 (0-8220-1265-0) Cliffs.

Tartuffe ou L'Imposteur. Moliere. Ed. by Daniel R. Martin. (Illus.). 141p. 1989. 10.95 (1-878417-21-5) Hestia Pr.

Tartuffe/The Sisterhood. Tr. & Adapted by Ranjit Bolt. 128p. 1989. pap. 12.95 (0-948230-50-9, Pub. by Absolute Classics UK) Theatre Comm.

TaRYaG: A Study of the Tradition That the Written Torah Contains 613 Mitzvot. Abraham H. Rabinowitz. LC 96-22408. 240p. 1996. 25.00 (1-56821-449-9) Aronson.

***Tarzan.** Edgar Rice Burroughs. (Two-in-One Ser.: Nos. 13 & 14). 1997. mass mkt. 6.99 (0-345-41349-0, Del Rey) Ballantine.

***Tarzan.** San Souci. (J). 1999. 14.89 (0-7868-2334-8) Hyperion.

***Tarzan.** Edgar Rice Burroughs & Robert Blaisdell. LC 96-49011. (Children's Thrift Classics Ser.). (Illus.). 96p. (J). 1997. reprint ed. pap. text ed. 1.00 (0-486-29530-3) Dover.

Tarzan: The Epic Adventures. R. A. Salvatore. 256p. 1996. pap. 10.00 (0-345-40810-1) Ballantine.

***Tarzan: The Epic Adventures.** R. A. Salvatore. 1997. mass mkt. 5.99 (0-345-41295-8, Del Rey) Ballantine.

***Tarzan: The Epic Adventures.** R. A. Salvatore. 1997. mass mkt. 5.99 (0-614-27739-6, Del Rey) Ballantine.

Tarzan: The Land That Time Forgot. unabridged ed. Russ Manning. (Illus.). 112p. (Orig.). (YA). (gr. 9 up). 1996. pap. 12.95 (1-56971-151-8) Dark Horse Comics.

Tarzan: The Lost Adventure. limited ed. Edgar Rice Burroughs & Joe R. Lansdale. (Illus.). 208p. (YA). (gr. 7 up). 1996. 99.95 (1-56971-128-3) Dark Horse Comics.

***Tarzan: The Lost Adventures.** Edgar R. Burroughs & Joe R. Landsdale. 1997. mass mkt. 5.99 (0-614-27738-8, Del Rey) Ballantine.

***Tarzan: The Lost Adventures.** Edgar Rice Burroughs & Joe R. Landsda. 1997. mass mkt. 5.99 (0-345-41273-7, Del Rey) Ballantine.

Tarzan Bk. 1: The Lost Adventure. limited ed. Edgar Rice Burroughs & Joe R. Lansdale. (Illus.). 208p. 1996. 19.95 (1-56971-083-X) Dark Horse Comics.

Tarzan & Shane Meet the Toad. limited ed. Gerald Locklin et al. 1975. 4.00 (0-917554-01-9) Maelstrom.

Tarzan & the Forbidden City. Edgar Rice Burroughs. 176p. 1980. mass mkt. 4.50 (0-345-29106-9, Del Rey) Ballantine.

Tarzan & the Leopard Man. Edgar Rice Burroughs. 1986. mass mkt. 4.99 (0-345-33828-6, Del Rey) Ballantine.

Tarzan & the Lion Men. Edgar Rice Burroughs. 192p. 1980. mass mkt. 2.95 (0-345-28988-9, Del Rey) Ballantine.

Tarzan & Tradition: Classical Myth in Popular Literature. Erling B. Holtsmark. LC 80-1023. (Contributions to the Study of Popular Culture Ser.: No. 1). (Illus.). xv, 196p. 1981. text ed. 49.95 (0-313-22530-3, HOT/, Greenwood Pr) Greenwood.

Tarzan Can - Not Return to Africa But I Can: Tarzan. Kalamu Y. Salaam. 200p. 1996. 20.00 (0-9649795-0-0); pap. 10.00 (0-9649795-1-9) Visions Three-Thousand.

Tarzan, Lord of the Jungle, No. 11. Edgar Rice Burroughs. 190p. 1984. mass mkt. 4.99 (0-345-32455-2, Del Rey) Ballantine.

***Tarzan, Lord of the Jungle/Tarzan & the Lost Empire.** Edgar Rice Burroughs. 1997. mass mkt. 5.99 (0-345-41347-4, Del Rey) Ballantine.

Tarzan, No. 19: Tarzan's Quest. Edgar Rice Burroughs. 178p. 1980. mass mkt. 4.99 (0-345-29562-5, Del Rey) Ballantine.

Tarzan of the Apes. Edgar Rice Burroughs. 22.95 (0-8488-1257-3) Amereon Ltd.

Tarzan of the Apes. Edgar Rice Burroughs. 228p. (YA). 1990. mass mkt. 3.95 (0-451-52423-3, Sig Classics) NAL-Dutton.

Tarzan of the Apes. Edgar Rice Burroughs. 320p. 1990. pap. 8.95 (0-14-018464-3, Penguin Classics) Viking Penguin.

***Tarzan of the Apes.** Edgar Rice Burroughs. 1997. pap. 6.95 (0-7871-1454-5, Dove Bks) Dove Audio.

Tarzan of the Apes. Harold Woods & Geraldine Woods. LC 81-19873. (Step-up Adventures Ser.: No. 4). (Illus.). 96p. (J). (gr. 2-7). 1982. pap. 3.99 (0-394-85089-0) Random Bks Yng Read.

Tarzan of the Apes. large type ed. Edgar Rice Burroughs. 1994. lib. bdg. 21.95 (0-7838-1160-8, GK Hall) Thorndike Pr.

Tarzan of the Apes. Edgar Rice Burroughs. 1976. reprint ed. lib. bdg. 23.95 (0-89966-046-0) Buccaneer Bks.

***Tarzan of the Apes.** Edgar Rice Burroughs. LC 96-53315. (Thrift Editions Ser.). 224p. 1997. reprint ed. pap. text ed. 2.00 (0-486-29570-2) Dover.

Tarzan of the Apes, No. 1. Edgar Rice Burroughs. (Tarzan Ser.). 246p. 1984. mass mkt. 4.99 (0-345-31977-X, Del Rey) Ballantine.

***Tarzan the Classics: Tarzan & the Jewels of Opar, Jungle Tales of Tarzan.** Edgar Rice Burroughs. (Tarzan Ser.). 1997. mass mkt. 5.99 (0-345-40831-4) Ballantine.

Tarzan the Terrible, No. 8. Edgar Rice Burroughs. 190p. 1985. mass mkt. 3.99 (0-345-32392-0, Del Rey) Ballantine.

Tarzan the Untamed, No. 7. Edgar Rice Burroughs. 254p. 1984. mass mkt. 4.99 (0-345-32391-2, Del Rey) Ballantine.

***Tarzan (1931-1933)** Hal Foster. LC 93-84318. (Illus.). 128p. 1997. pap. 24.95 (1-56163-178-7, Flying Buttress Class) NBM.

***Tarzan (1933-1935)** Hal Foster. (Illus.). 128p. 1997. pap. 24.95 (1-56163-186-8, Flying Buttress Class) NBM.

***Tarzan (1935-1937)** Hal Foster. (Illus.). 128p. 1997. pap. 24.95 (1-56163-187-6, Flying Buttress Class) NBM.

***Tarzan (1937-1939)** Burne Hogarth. (Illus.). 128p. 1998. pap. 24.95 (1-56163-188-4, Flying Buttress Class) NBM.

Tarzan 2 in 1, Nos. 3 & 4. Edgar Rice Burroughs. 1996. mass mkt. 5.99 (0-345-40830-6, Del Rey) Ballantine.

***Tarzan 2 in 1, Nos. 7 & 8.** Edgar Rice Burroughs. 1997. mass mkt. 5.99 (0-345-40832-2, Del Rey) Ballantine.

***Tarzan 2-in-1, Nos. 9 & 10.** Edgar Rice Burroughs. 1997. mass mkt. 5.99 (0-345-41348-2, Del Rey) Ballantine.

Tarzan 3-in-1. Edgar Rice Burroughs. 1996. mass mkt. write for info. (0-345-40647-8) Ballantine.

T'As Pas de Veine, Charlie Brown. Charles M. Schulz. (Peanuts Ser.). (FRE.). (J). 1985. 4.95 (0-8288-4525-5) Fr & Eur.

Tasaday Controversy: Assessing the Evidence. Ed. by Thomas N. Headland. LC 92-25352. 1992. write for info. (0-913167-51-7) Am Anthro Assn.

Taschen Lexikon Sicherheit der Informationstechnik. H. Pohl. 184p. (ENG & GER.). 1989. pap. 95.00 (0-8288-3883-6, F120960) Fr & Eur.

Taschenbuch Der Geholzverwendung see Pocket Guide to Choosing Woody Ornamentals

Taschenbuch der Vornamen. 144p. (GER.). 1978. pap. 8.00 (3-581-66210-8) Langenscheidt.

Taschenbuch Fuer Pilzfreunde. 10th ed. Bruno Hennig. (Illus.). 215p. 1987. text ed. 9.95 (3-334-00124-5) Lubrecht & Cramer.

Taschenlexikon der Logistik. F. Linden. 130p. (ENG & GER.). 1991. pap. 95.00 (0-8288-3882-8, F112511) Fr & Eur.

Taschenlexikon Elektronik, Funktechnik: Pocket Dictionary of Electronics & Radio. 320p. (GER.). 1974. 24.95 (0-8288-6213-3, M-7630) Fr & Eur.

Taschenlexikon Technik. Gerhard Butzmann. (GER.). 1993. 59.95 (0-7859-8501-8, 3816909728) Fr & Eur.

Taschenwoerterbuch der Botanischen Pflanzennamem. 2nd ed. F. Boerner. 435p. (GER.). 1966. 75.00 (0-8288-6728-3, M7631) Fr & Eur.

Taschenwoerterbuch des Fremdenverkehrs. W. Friedrich. 187p. (ENG & GER.). 1970. Dictionary of Tourism. 24. 95 (0-8288-6553-1, M-7632) Fr & Eur.

Taschenwoerterbuch Eisen und Stahl: Pocket Dictionary of Iron & Steel. H. L. Freeman. 600p. (ENG & GER.). 1966. 24.95 (0-8288-6729-1, M-7634) Fr & Eur.

Taschenwoerterbuch Kraftfahrzeugtechnik. Henry G. Freeman. 384p. (ENG & GER.). 1980. 59.95 (0-8288-0043-X, M7635) Fr & Eur.

Taschenworterbuch der Katalanischen und Deutschen Sprache, 2 vols. Eberhard Vogel. cx, 1147p. reprint ed. write for info. (0-318-71643-7) G Olms Pubs.

Taschenworterbuch der Praktische Buroautomation. P. Hellermann. 84p. (ENG & GER.). 1989. pap. 59.95 (0-8288-3884-4, F101270) Fr & Eur.

Taschworterbuch der Personalarbeit. H. Blaeser. 120p. (ENG & GER.). 1989. pap. 95.00 (0-8288-3881-X, F93160) Fr & Eur.

Tascosa: Historic Site in the Texas Panhandle. 2nd rev. ed. Pauline D. Robertson & R. L. Robertson. (Illus.). 72p. 1995. pap. 6.95 (0-942376-15-3) Paramount TX.

Tascosa Gun: The Story of Jim East. large type ed. Gene Shelton. LC 93-20594. (Texas Legends Ser.: Vol. 4). 1993. lib. bdg. 16.95 (1-56054-793-6) Thorndike Pr.

Tasek Bera: The Ecology of a Freshwater Swamp. J. I. Furtado & S. Mori. 1982. lib. bdg. 216.50 (90-6193-100-2) Kluwer Ac.

Tasha. John W. Benton. 176p. (Orig.). (J). 1994. pap. 3.50 (0-9635411-2-9) J Benton Bks.

Tasha Tudor Cookbook: Recipes & Reminiscences from Corgi Cottage. Tasha Tudor. LC 93-16438. (Illus.). 1993. 24.95 (0-316-85531-6) Little.

Tasha Tudor Favorite. Tasha Tudor. 1986. pap. 9.95 (0-679-20985-9) McKay.

Tasha Tudor's Garden. Photos by Richard Brown. LC 94-7886. (Illus.). 1994. 35.00 (0-395-43609-5) HM.

Tasha Tudor's Heirloom Crafts. Tovah Martin. LC 95-18605. (Illus.). 160p. 1995. 35.00 (0-395-73527-0) HM.

Tasha What Time Is It? Tunde Dada. (Illus.). 17p. (J). (gr. k-3). 1995. write for info. (1-882920-02-3) Tunde Dada-Hse.

Tasha's Witch. Natalie J. Prior. (Storybridge Ser.). 96p. (J). (gr. 4-7). 1995. pap. 9.95 (0-7022-2793-5, Pub. by Univ Queensland Pr AT) Intl Spec Bk.

Tashi. Anna Fienberg & Barbara Fienberg. 64p. (J). (gr. 1-4). 1996. pap. text ed. 4.95 (1-86373-806-1) IPG Chicago.

***Tashi & the Ghosts.** Anna Fienberg & Barbara Fienberg. (Illus.). 64p. (Orig.). (J). (gr. 1-4). 1997. pap. 4.95 (1-86448-090-4, Pub. by Allen & Unwin Aust Pty AT) IPG Chicago.

Tashi & the Giants. Anna Fienberg & Barbara Fienberg. 64p. (J). (gr. 1-4). 1996. pap. text ed. 4.95 (1-86373-945-9) IPG Chicago.

Tashlich. Avrohom C. Feuer. (ArtScroll Mesorah Ser.). 64p. 1979. pap. 2.99 (0-89906-159-1) Mesorah Pubns.

Task. Jack Collom. (Illus.). 53p. 1996. 7.00 (1-887997-06-7) Baksun Bks.

Task Ahead. Indira Gandhi. 137p. 1984. 24.95 (0-318-36642-8) Asia Bk Corp.

***Task Analysis: An Occupational Performance Approach.** Diane Watson. (Illus.). 460p. (Orig.). (C). 1997. pap. text ed. 35.00 (1-56900-065-4) Am Occup Therapy.

Task & Language Learning: Integrating Theory & Practice. Ed. by Graham Crookes & Susan M. Gass. LC 92-46197. (Multilingual Matters Ser.). 169p. 1993. 79.00 (1-85359-185-8, Pub. by Multilingual Matters UK); pap. 29.00 (1-85359-184-X, Pub. by Multilingual Matters UK) Taylor & Francis.

Task & Organization. Ed. by Eric J. Miller. LC 75-12606. (Wiley Series on Individuals, Groups & Organizations). 397p. reprint ed. pap. 113.20 (0-318-35028-9, 2030928) Bks Demand.

Task, & Selected Other Poems. Ed. by James Sambrook. LC 94-4019. (Annotated Texts Ser.). 336p. (C). 1994. text ed. 71.95 (0-582-08728-7, 76865, Pub. by Longman UK) Longman.

Task, & Selected Other Poems. Ed. by James Sambrook. LC 94-4019. (Annotated Texts Ser.). 336p. (C). 1995. pap. text ed. 32.95 (0-582-08727-9, 76864, Pub. by Longman UK) Longman.

Task Buster. Walnut Creek CD-ROM Staff. 1996. pap. text ed. 39.95 incl. cd-rom (1-57176-132-2) Walnut Creek.

Task-Centered Casework. William J. Reid & Laura Epstein. LC 72-4931. 350p. (C). 1972. text ed. 37.50 (0-231-03466-0) Col U Pr.

Task-Centered Practice. William J. Reid & Laura Epstein. LC 76-28177. 1977. text ed. 37.50 (0-231-04072-5) Col U Pr.

Task-Centered Social Work. Mark Doel & Peter Marsh. 144p. 1992. pap. text ed. 24.95 (1-85742-070-5, Pub. by Arena UK) Ashgate Pub Co.

Task Design: An Integrative Approach. Ricky W. Griffin. LC 81-18316. (Scott, Foresman Series in Management & Organizations). 253p. reprint ed. pap. 72.20 (0-7837-4056-5, 2043889) Bks Demand.

Task-Directed Sensor Fusion & Planning: A Computational Approach. Gregory D. Hager. (C). 1990. lib. bdg. 93.50 (0-7923-9108-X) Kluwer Ac.

Task for Diogenes: A Satire. Francis Neilson. 1971. 250.00 (0-87700-017-4) Revisionist Pr.

Task Force. Mike Dunn. 480p. (Orig.). 1992. mass mkt. 4.99 (0-380-76373-7) Avon.

Task Force Blue. Richard Marcinko & John Weisman. Ed. by Judith Regan & Paul McCarthy. (Rogue Warrior Ser.). 480p. 1993. mass mkt. 6.99 (0-671-79593-7, Pocket Star Bks) PB.

Task Force Blue. Richard Marcinko & John Weisman. Ed. by Paul McCarthy. (Rogue Warrior Ser.). 336p. 1996. 23.00 (0-671-79958-4, PB Hardcover) PB.

***Task Force Blue.** Richard Marcinko. (Rogue Warrior Ser.). 1997. mass mkt. 6.99 (0-671-89672-5) PB.

***Task Force Blue, Green Team, Red Cell, Rogue Warrior.** Richard Marcinko. (Rogue Warrior Ser.). 1997. mass mkt. write for info. (0-671-85552-2) PB.

Task Force on Drugs & the Courts. (Illus.). 61p. (Orig.). (C). 1993. pap. text ed. 20.00 (1-56806-824-7) DIANE Pub.

Task Force on Education for Children with Disabilities: Final Report. 51p. (Orig.). (C). 1994. pap. text ed. 25. 00 (0-7881-1441-7) DIANE Pub.

Task Force on Sexual Predators: Final Report to the Minnesota Legislature. 90p. (Orig.). (C). 1995. pap. text ed. 25.00 (0-7881-2010-7) DIANE Pub.

Task Force Report: The Courts. United States Task Force on the Administration of Justice. LC 77-28367. (Illus.). x, 178p. 1978. reprint ed. text ed. 59.75 (0-313-20225-7, USTF, Greenwood Pr) Greenwood.

Task Force Report: The Police. President's Commission on Law Enforcement & Administration of Justice. LC 73-154585. (Police in America Ser.). 1979. reprint ed. 29.95 (0-405-03383-4) Ayer.

Task Force Report on Clinician Safety. American Psychiatric Association Staff. LC 93-10489. 35p. 1993. pap. text ed. 3.00 (0-89042-244-3, 2244) Am Psychiatric.

Task Force Report on Innovative Models of Mental Health Services for Children, Adolescents, & Their Families: A Special Issue of the "Journal of Clinical Child Psychology", Vol. 23, Suppl., 1994. Ed. by Scott W. Henggeler. 64p. 1995. pap. 20.00 (0-8058-9952-9) L Erlbaum Assocs.

Task Force Study of Ritual Crime to the Governor & the General Assembly of Virginia. 61p. (Orig.). (C). 1994. pap. text ed. 20.00 (0-7881-0344-X) DIANE Pub.

Task Groups in the Social Services. Marian Fatout & Steven R. Rose. (Sourcebooks for the Human Services Ser.). 200p. 1995. text ed. 39.95 (0-8039-5449-2); pap. text ed. 18.95 (0-8039-5450-6) Sage.

Task Maths 4. Ball. (Um - International Math Ser.). 1991. teacher ed., text ed. 72.95 (0-538-62781-6) S-W Pub.

Task Math's 4-Teacher Resource. 2nd ed. Ball. (UM - International Math Ser.). 1991. 30.95 (0-17-431428-0) S-W Pub.

Task Maths 5. Ball. (Um - International Math Ser.). 1991. 72.95 (0-538-62769-7) S-W Pub.

Task of Gestalt Psychology. Wolfgang Kohler. LC 69-17397. (Princeton Paperback Ser.). (Illus.). 172p. reprint ed. pap. 49.10 (0-8357-7045-1, 2033378) Bks Demand.

Task of Interpretation: Quarter 5. Bill Patterson. (Growing Christian Disciples Ser.). 126p. 1989. student ed. 3.95 (1-56794-022-6, C2285); teacher ed. 4.95 (1-56794-023-4, C2285T); teacher ed. 4.95 (1-56794-024-2, C2286) Star Bible.

Task of Old Testament Theology: Essays. Rolf P. Knierim. LC 95-20781. 1995. pap. 40.00 (0-8028-0715-1) Eerdmans.

Task of Post-Contemporary Education: Essays in Behalf of a Human Future. Kenneth D. Benne. 256p. (C). 1990. pap. text ed. 19.95 (0-8077-3012-2) Tchrs Coll.

Task of the Church & the Role of Its Members. Bruce Reed. pap. 5.95 (1-56699-097-1, OD69) Alban Inst.

***Task of Truth: Essays on Karl Jaspers's Idea of the University.** Ed. by Gregory J. Walters. LC 95-42196. 167p. 1996. pap. 42.95 (0-8204-2941-4, 68729) P Lang Pubng.

Task of Universities in a Changing World. Ed. by Stephen D. Kertesz. LC 75-14819. (International Studies of the Committee on International Relations, University of Notre Dame). 525p. 1971. reprint ed. pap. 149.70 (0-608-00886-9, 2061680) Bks Demand.

Task-Oriented Team Development. Irwin M. Rubin et al. (Illus.). 1978. ring bd. 85.00 (0-07-054196-5) McGraw.

Task Reading. Evelyn Davies et al. (Illus.). 128p. (C). 1990. pap. text ed. 13.95 (0-521-35810-8) Cambridge U Pr.

Task Strategies: An Empirical Approach to Clinical Social Work. William J. Reid. (Illus.). 320p. 1992. text ed. 37. 50 (0-231-07550-2) Col U Pr.

Tasker Street. Mark Halliday. LC 91-41031. 88p. (C). 1992. pap. 9.95 (0-87023-777-2); lib. bdg. 20.00 (0-87023-776-4) U of Mass Pr.

***Taskmaster.** Mary Murchison. 1996. mass mkt. 4.99 (1-55197-113-5, Pub. by Comnwlth Pub CN) Partners Pubs Grp.

Tasks Ahead: Speeches of Mrs. Gandhi. Indira Ghandi. 1984. text ed. 17.50 (0-685-14061-X) Coronet Bks.

Tasks & Masks: Themes & Styles of African Literature. Lewis Nkosi. LC 82-107343. 212p. reprint ed. pap. 60. 50 (0-685-20311-5, 2030350) Bks Demand.

Tasks, Errors & Mental Models. Ed. by L. P. Goodstein et al. 300p. 1988. 115.00 (0-85066-401-2) Taylor & Francis.

Tasks for Independent Language Learning. Ed. by David Gardner & Lindsay Miller. LC 96-60327. 300p. (Orig.). 1996. pap. 24.95 (0-939791-65-X) Tchrs Eng Spkrs.

Tasks for Language Teachers: A Resource Book for Training & Development. Martin Parrott. LC 92-34467. (Teacher Training & Development Ser.). 256p. (C). 1993. text ed. 52.95 (0-521-41648-5); pap. text ed. 26.95 (0-521-42666-9) Cambridge U Pr.

Tasks for Today: A Daily Job Planner. 100p. 1995. pap. 3.98 (0-88290-528-7, 1057) Horizon Utah.

Tasks in a Pedagogical Context: Integrating Theory & Practice. Ed. by Graham Crookes & Susan M. Gass. LC 92-45646. 163p. 1993. 79.00 (1-85359-187-4, Pub. by Multilingual Matters UK); pap. 29.00 (1-85359-186-6, Pub. by Multilingual Matters UK) Taylor & Francis.

Tasks of Business Credit Personnel. Credit Research Foundation Staff. 14p. 1985. 40.00 (0-939050-40-4) Credit Res NYS.

Tasks of Emotional Development. Haskel Cohen & Geraldine R. Weil. LC 75-42572. 359p. reprint ed. 35.00 (0-916598-02-0); reprint ed. teacher ed., pap. 12.00 (0-317-00903-6); reprint ed. 25.00 (0-317-00904-4) T E D Assocs.

Tasks of Mourning No. 1. Vickie Kaczmarek. 12p. 1993. pap. text ed. 4.00 (1-882472-11-X) Comm Grief Ctr.

Tasks of Survival (Poems 1970-1990) Allan Johnston. LC 93-44182. 64p. 1996. pap. 12.95 (0-7734-0034-6, Mellen Poetry Pr) E Mellen.

Tasks Required of Automotive Service Industry Technicians in the Year 2000. 42p. 1993. 15.00 (1-56091-369-X, SP-976) Soc Auto Engineers.

Tasks to Jobs: Developing a Modular System of Training for Hotel Occupations. (Hotel & Tourism Management Ser.: No. 3). 302p. 1991. text ed. 27.00 (92-2-102148-3) Intl Labour Office.

Tasmania. John Chapman & Monica Chapman. (Illus.). 304p. 1996. pap. 14.95 (0-86442-384-5) Lonely Planet.

***Tasmania.** I. Kepars. (World Bibliographical Ser.: Vol. 194). 164p. 1997. 56.50 (1-85109-273-0) ABC-CLIO.

***Tasmania: A Guide.** 2nd ed. Sally Odgers & Darrel Odgers. (Illus.). 240p. 1997. pap. 15.95 (0-86417-842-5, Pub. by Kangaroo Pr AT) Seven Hills Bk.

Tasmanian Devil. Tom Demichael. (Look & Find Ser.). (Illus.). 24p. (J). (ps-6). 1996. lib. bdg. 13.95 (1-56674-126-2, HTS Bks) Forest Hse.

T

Tasmanian Devil. Pauline Reilly. (Picture Roo Bks.). (Illus.). 32p. (Orig.). (J). 1993. pap. 6.95 (0-86417-207-9, Pub. by Kangaroo Pr AT) Seven Hills Bk.

Tasmanian Devil: On Location. Kathy Darling. LC 91-27561. (Illus.). 40p. (J). (gr. 2 up). 1992. 16.00 (0-688-09726-X); lib. bdg. 15.93 (0-688-09727-8) Lothrop.

Tasmanian Devils. Lynn M. Stone. (Australian Animals Discovery Library). (Illus.). 24p. (J). (gr. k-5). 1990. lib. bdg. 11.94 (0-86593-056-2); lib. bdg. 8.95 (0-685-36373-2) Rourke Corp.

Taso: Trabajador de la Cana. Sidney W. Mintz. LC 88-82494. 321p. 1988. pap. 12.25 (0-940238-73-X) Ediciones Huracan.

TASP - Texas Academic Skills Program. rev. ed. Research & Education Association Staff. 528p. 1995. pap. text ed. 18.95 (0-87891-893-0) Res & Educ.

TASP Preparation Guide: Texas Academic Skills Program. 2nd ed. Jerry Bobrow et al. (Cliffs Test Preparation Ser.). (Orig.). 1994. student ed., pap. 8.95 (0-8220-2072-6) Cliffs.

Tass Is Authorized to Announce... Julian Semyonov. 384p. 1988. mass mkt. 4.50 (0-380-70569-9) Avon.

Tass Is Authorized to Announce. Juliann Semyonov. 350p. 22.95 (0-88962-359-7) Mosaic.

Tassa. 16p. (J). 1994. pap. 8.95 (0-9641021-0-2) E Nordley.

Tassajara Bread Book. Edward E. Brown. (Orig.). 1974. pap. 5.95 (0-394-73003-8) Random.

Tassajara Bread Book. 25th anniversary ed. Edward E. Brown. (Illus.). 160p. 1995. pap. 12.00 (1-57062-089-X) Shambhala Pubns.

Tassajara Cooking. Edward E. Brown. 1974. pap. 8.95 (0-394-70949-7) Random.

Tassajara Cooking. Edward E. Brown. LC 85-8185. 1986. pap. 17.00 (0-87773-344-9) Shambhala Pubns.

Tassajara Recipe Book: Favorites of the Guest Season. Edward E. Brown. LC 84-23576. (Illus.). 160p. (Orig.). 1985. pap. 17.00 (0-87773-308-2); pap. 17.00 (0-394-73520-X) Shambhala Pubns.

Tassels: The Fanciful Embellishment. Nancy Welch. LC 91-34630. (Illus.). 144p. 1992. 26.95 (0-937274-53-4) Lark Books.

***Tassels: The Fanciful Embellishment.** Nancy Welch. 160p. 1997. pap. 18.95 (1-887374-23-X) Lark Books.

***Tassels Book: An Inspirational Guide to Tassels & Tassel-Making, with over 40 Practical Projects.** Anna Crutchley. (Illus.). 160p. 1996. 27.50 (1-85967-222-1, Lorenz Bks) Anness Pub.

***Tassels, Tiebacks & Trimmings & How to Use Them.** Elizabeth Valenti. 1997. pap. 19.95 (0-8019-8937-X) Chilton.

Tassie Terms: A Glossary of Tasmanian Words. Maureen Brooks & Joan Ritchie. (Illus.). 224p. (C). 1996. pap. text ed. 29.95 (0-19-553812-9) OUP.

Tasso: Aminta. Ed. by Sarah D'Alberti. (C). 1967. pap. 7.95 (0-913298-21-2) S F Vanni.

Tasso & His Times. William Boulting. LC 68-24953. (World History Ser.: No. 48). 1969. reprint ed. lib. bdg. 75.00 (0-8383-0915-1) M S G Haskell Hse.

Tasso & Milton: The Problem of the Christian Epic. Judith A. Kates. LC 82-71268. 184p. 1983. 29.50 (0-8387-5046-X) Bucknell U Pr.

Tasso's Dialogues: A Selection, with the "Discourse on the Art of the Dialogue" Torquato Tasso. Tr. by Carnes Lord & Dain A. Trafton. LC 81-12937. (Biblioteca Italiana Ser.: No. 4). 288p. 1983. pap. 12.00 (0-520-04985-3) U CA Pr.

Taste. Illus. by Francisco Arredondo. (Five Senses of the Animal World Ser.). (J). 1996. lib. bdg. 15.95 (0-7910-3493-3) Chelsea Hse.

***Taste.** Sue Hurwitz. LC 96-29959. (Library of the Five Senses (Plus the Sixth Sense)). (J). 1997. write for info. (0-8239-5052-2) Rosen Group.

Taste. J. M. Parramon & J. J. Puig. (Five Senses Ser.). (Illus.). 32p. (J). (ps). 1985. pap. 6.95 (0-8120-3566-6); Span. ed. pap. 6.95 (0-8120-3608-5) Barron.

***Taste.** Maria Rius et al. (Five Senses Ser.). (J). 1985. 6.95 (0-8120-5739-2) Barron.

***Taste.** David Rosengarten. 1997. write for info. (0-375-50011-1) Random.

Taste. Mandy Suhr. LC 93-44191. (Illus.). (J). (ps-1). 1994. lib. bdg. 14.21 (0-87614-836-4, Carolrhoda) Lerner Group.

***Taste & Criticism in the Eighteenth Century.** H. A. Needham. (Illus.). 231p. Date not set. 19.95 (0-8369-5035-6) Ayer.

Taste & Ideology in Seventeenth-Century France. Michael Moriarty. (Cambridge Studies in French: No. 25). 244p. (C). 1989. text ed. 69.95 (0-521-30686-8) Cambridge U Pr.

Taste & Know, Vol. 1. Moshe Sternbuch. 124p. 1990. 12.00 (0-940118-62-9) Moznaim.

Taste & Odor in Drinking Water Supplies, Phases 1-2. 378p. 1989. pap. 46.00 (0-89867-467-0, 90542) Am Water Wks Assn.

Taste-&-Odor Problems Associated with Chlorine Dioxide. 168p. 1991. pap. 47.00 (0-89867-578-2, 90589) Am Water Wks Assn.

Taste & Odour in Waters & Aquatic Organisms. Ed. by P. E. Persson et al. (Water Science & Technology Ser.: No. 15). (Illus.). 340p. 1983. pap. 91.00 (0-08-029713-7, Pergamon Pr) Elsevier.

Taste & Other Tales. (Fiction Ser.). (YA). 1993. pap. text ed. 6.50 (0-582-08478-4, 79833) Longman.

Taste & Power: Furnishing Modern France. Leora Auslander. LC 95-715. (Studies on the History of Society & Culture: Vol. 24). (Illus.). 526p. (C). 1996. 40.00 (0-520-08894-8) U CA Pr.

Taste & See: A Personal Guide to the Spiritual Life. rev. ed. William O. Paulsell. 128p. 1992. pap. 9.99 (0-8272-3629-8) Chalice Pr.

Taste & See: Allergy Relief Cooking. Penny King. 254p. 1992. pap. 11.95 (1-878726-21-8) Fam Hlth Pubns.

Taste & See: Awakening Our Spiritual Senses. Tim Dearborn. LC 96-16318. 137p. (Orig.). 1996. pap. 9.99 (0-8308-1985-1, 1985) InterVarsity.

Taste & See: Prayer Services for Gatherings of Faith. Jacqueline S. Bergan & S. Marie Schwan. Ed. by Carl Koch. (Illus.). 109p. 1996. pap. 7.95 (0-88489-377-4) St Marys.

Taste & See: Prayer Services for Gatherings of Faith. Jacqueline S. Bergan & S. Marie Schwan. Ed. by Carl Koch. (Illus.). 109p. 1996. spiral bd. 9.95 (0-88489-391-X) St Marys.

Taste & Smell. Brenda Walpole. LC 96-6957. (See for Yourself Ser.). (Illus.). (J). 1996. lib. bdg. 21.40 (0-8172-4215-5) Raintree Steck-V.

Taste & Smell Disorders. Allen M. Seiden. LC 96-23875. (Rhinology & Sinusology Ser.). 1996. 69.00 (0-86577-533-8) Thieme Med Pubs.

Taste & the Antique: The Lure of Classical Sculpture 1500-1900. Francis Haskell & Nicholas Penny. LC 80-24951. (Illus.). 1982. pap. 22.50 (0-300-02913-6, Y-438) Yale U Pr.

Taste & Tour of Dallas. Candy Coleman. (Illus.). 112p. (Orig.). 1986. spiral bd. 7.95 (0-943768-08-X) C Coleman.

Taste California: A Sampling of the Golden State. Ed. by Marcy Monteith. (Illus.). 150p. (Orig.). 1993. pap. text ed. 11.95 (0-9638619-0-5) CA Dietetic.

Taste Chemistry. Robert S. Shallenberger. LC 92-11271. 613p. 1993. 215.99 (0-7514-0150-1, Pub. by Blackie Acad & Prof UK) Routledge Chapman & Hall.

Taste Divine: Indian Vegetarian Cooking the Natural Way. Vanamali. LC 92-30764. 132p. 1992. pap. 16.95 (0-7914-1188-5) State U NY Pr.

Taste Divine: Indian Vegetarian Cooking the Natural Way. Vanamali. LC 92-30764. 132p. 1993. text ed. 49.50 (0-7914-1187-7) State U NY Pr.

Taste, Experience, & Feeding. Ed. by Elizabeth D. Capaldi & Terry L. Powley. 275p. (C). 1993. pap. text ed. 19.95 (1-55798-235-X) Am Psychol.

Taste for A. L. L. Seasons: A Collection of Recipes from the Associated Ladies for David Lipscomb University. Associated Ladies for Lipscomb Staff. 272p. 1994. 18.00 (0-9642809-0-6) Assoc Ladies.

Taste for All Seasons: A Celebration of American Food. David P. Larousse. LC 89-24688. (Illus.). 192p. 1990. 24.95 (1-55832-020-2) Harvard Common Pr.

Taste for Angels: Neapolitan Painting in North America, 1650-1750. John T. Spike et al. LC 87-50866. (Illus.). 355p. (Orig.). 1987. pap. 25.00 (0-89467-046-8) Yale Art Gallery.

Taste for Beauty. Eric Rohmer. Tr. by Carol Volk. (Cambridge Studies in Film). (Illus.). 207p. (C). 1990. pap. text ed. 19.95 (0-521-38592-X) Cambridge U Pr.

Taste for Beer. Stephen Beaumont. LC 95-11078. 256p. 1995. pap. 14.95 (0-88266-907-9, Garden Way Pub) Storey Comm Inc.

Taste for Books, 2 bks. R. Thompson et al. (C). 1988. write for info. (0-318-65626-4) St Mut.

Taste for Books, 2 bks., 1. R. Thompson et al. (C). 1988. 30.00 (0-7157-2125-9) St Mut.

Taste for Books, 2 bks., 2. R. Thompson et al. (C). 1988. 30.00 (0-7157-2126-7) St Mut.

***Taste for Burning.** Bannister. 1997. mass mkt. 4.99 (0-373-26259-0) Harlequin Bks.

Taste for Burning. Jo Bannister. 208p. 1995. 19.95 (0-312-13191-7) St Martin.

Taste for Burning. large type ed. Jo Bannister. 364p. 1996. pap. 20.95 (0-7862-0526-1) Thorndike Pr.

Taste for Comfort: A Scenic Tour of Pacific Northwest Inns with Selected Recipes. Anita Stewart. (Illus.). 160p. 1993. 24.95 (0-9634294-0-X) C&D Pub OR.

Taste for Death. P. D. James. 512p. 1987. mass mkt. 6.50 (0-446-32352-7) Warner Bks.

***Taste for Death.** large type ed. Peter O'Donnell. (Large Print Ser.). 528p. 1997. 27.50 (0-7089-3672-5) Ulverscroft.

***Taste for Empire & Glory: Studies in British Overseas Expansion, 1600-1800.** Philip Lawson et al. LC 96-37233. (Collected Studies: No. CS563). 320p. 1997. text ed. 89.95 (0-86078-636-6, Pub. by Variorum UK) Ashgate Pub Co.

Taste for Health: Low-Fat, Low-Cholesterol Recipes. 160p. 1989. spiral bd. 5.95 (0-941016-64-1) Penfield.

Taste for Language: A Recipe for Second Language Acquisition. Mary J. Ervin. LC 88-92521. (Illus.). 194p. 1988. 18.50 (0-685-24436-9) Melt Pot Pr.

Taste for Language: A Recipe for Second Language Acquisition. 3rd rev. ed. Mary J. Ervin. LC 88-92521. (Illus.). 194p. (SPA.). 1988. reprint ed. teacher ed., pap. text ed. 14.95 (0-9621272-0-5) Gessler Pub Co.

Taste for Living: Take-Away Thoughts for the Weekdays of the Year. Liam Hickey. 160p. (Orig.). 1992. pap. 9.95 (1-85607-006-9, Pub. by Columba Pr IE) Twenty-Third.

Taste for Love: Romantic Meals for Two. Elizabeth M. Harbison & Mary McGowan. 1996. 12.99 (0-517-14792-0, Wings Books) Random.

Taste for Murder. Claudia Bishop. 240p. (Orig.). 1994. pap. text ed. 5.99 (0-425-14350-3, Prime Crime) Berkley Pub.

Taste for Noah. Susan R. Topek. LC 92-39384. (Illus.). (J). (gr. k up). 1993. 12.95 (0-929371-39-9); pap. 4.95 (0-929371-40-2) Kar-Ben.

***Taste for Pop: Pop Art, Gender & Consumer Culture.** Cecile Whiting. LC 96-49965. (Cambridge Studies in American Visual Culture). (Illus.). 336p. (C). 1997. 50.00 (0-521-45004-7) Cambridge U Pr.

Taste for Sailing. John Lewis. 240p. 1990. 48.00 (0-86138-077-0, Pub. by T Dalton UK) St Mut.

Taste for Terror. Franklin W. Dixon. Ed. by Ruth Ashby. (HBCF Ser.: No. 94). 160p. (Orig.). (J). (gr. 6 up). 1994. pap. 3.99 (0-671-88205-8, Archway) PB.

Taste for the Beautiful: Zairian Art from the Hampton University Museum. David A. Binkley. (Illus.). 116p. 1993. pap. 24.95 (0-9616982-6-8); text ed. 40.00 (0-9616982-7-6) Hampton Univ Muse.

Taste for the Classics. Patrick Kavanaugh. LC 93-2593. 1993. 16.95 (0-917143-29-9) Sparrow TN.

Taste for Things That Are True: Essays & Talks by a Pupil of G. I. Gurdjieff. Henri Tracol. 1994. pap. 14.95 (1-85230-468-5) Element MA.

Taste for Treason. Ora Mendels. 1990. 17.95 (1-55972-047-6, Birch Ln Pr) Carol Pub Group.

Taste for Treason. Ora Mendels. 273p. 1993. reprint ed. pap. 5.50 (1-56171-197-7, S P I Bks) Sure Seller.

Taste from Back Home. Barbara Wortham. LC 82-62529. (Illus.). 330p. 1983. pap. 12.95 (0-915216-79-5) Marathon Intl Bk.

***Taste from the Mediterranean.** Nawja Bedoun. 106p. (Orig.). Date not set. pap. 12.95 (0-910119-54-6) SOCO Pubns.

Taste Missouri Wine Country. Tom April. 150p. 1991. spiral bd. 11.95 (0-9631456-0-6) MO River Trad.

Taste of a Rain Forest. Pranab Chatterjee. (Redbird Ser.). 1976. 4.80 (0-89253-137-1); lib. bdg. 10.00 (0-89253-121-5) Ind-US Inc.

Taste of Africa. Dorinda Hafner. LC 92-30158. 1993. 24.95 (0-89815-522-3) Ten Speed Pr.

Taste of Africa. Dorinda Hafner. 144p. 1994. pap. 16.95 (0-89815-660-2) Ten Speed Pr.

***Taste of Africa: An African Cookbook.** Tebereh Inquai. 1997. write for info. (0-86543-308-9) Africa World.

Taste of Africa: The African Cookbook. Tebereh Inquai. LC 97-19418. 1995. pap. text ed. 14.95 (0-86543-309-7) Africa World.

Taste of Africa: 70 Easy-to-Cook Recipes from an Undiscovered Cuisine. Rosamund Grant. (Creative Cooking Library). 1995. 10.98 (0-8317-7893-8) Smithmark.

Taste of Almost Heaven. (Illus.). 330p. 1987. pap. text ed. 12.95 (0-685-22508-9) Monongalia Arts.

Taste of Ancient Rome. Ilaria G. Giacosa. Tr. by Anna Herklotz. LC 91-44601. (Illus.). 224p. (C). 1992. 29.95 (0-226-29030-1) U Ch Pr.

Taste of Ancient Rome. Ilaria G. Giacosa. Tr. by Anna Herklotz. xii, 244p. (C). 1994. pap. 16.95 (0-226-29032-8) U Ch Pr.

Taste of Ashes. Howard Browne. 221p. 1988. pap. 7.95 (0-89366-277-1) Ultramarine Pub.

***Taste of Ashes.** John Evans. Date not set. pap. write for info. (0-688-04793-9, Quill) Morrow.

***Taste of Ashes.** Edward Gillen. 96p. 1997. pap. 10.00 (0-8059-4193-2) Dorrance.

Taste of Asia. Louis Segaloff. 64p. 1992. pap. 5.95 (1-881455-03-3) Atoll Pr.

Taste of Australia: Bathers Pavilion Cookbook. Victoria Alexander. 144p. 1995. 24.95 (0-89815-756-0) Ten Speed Pr.

Taste of Blackberries. Doris B. Smith. LC 72-7558. (Illus.). 64p. (J). (gr. 3-6). 1973. lib. bdg. 13.89 (0-690-80512-8, Crowell Jr Bks) HarpC Child Bks.

Taste of Blackberries. Doris B. Smith. LC 88-45077. (Trophy Bk.). (Illus.). 64p. (J). (gr. 3-6). 1992. reprint ed. pap. 3.95 (0-06-440238-X, Trophy) HarpC Child Bks.

Taste of Blackberries: A Study Guide. Marcia Tretler. (Novel-Ties Ser.). 1988. student ed., teacher ed., pap. text ed. 15.95 (0-88122-071-X) Lrn Links.

Taste of Blood: Spirit Possession in Brazilian Candomble. Jim Wafer. LC 90-28641. (Contemporary Ethnography Ser.). (Illus.). 256p. (C). 1991. text ed. 36.95 (0-8122-3061-2); pap. text ed. 16.95 (0-8122-1341-6) U of Pa Pr.

Taste of Boston. Gillian Drake. 7.50 (0-9609814-6-2) Pineapple Pubns.

Taste of Bountiful Ohio: Favorite Recipes from Ohio's Favorite Cookbook. Susan Failor. (Illus.). 64p. (Orig.). 1995. pap. 5.95 (0-911861-11-4) Gabriels Horn.

Taste of Buffalo Cookbook: Tenth Birthday Cookbook. Ed. by Peg Ehrenreid. (Illus.). 265p. (Orig.). 1994. pap. write for info. (0-9641880-0-7) Kaleido Events.

Taste of Burgundy. Julian More. (Illus.). 160p. 1993. 14.98 (1-55859-464-7) Abbeville Pr.

Taste of Chai. Temple Emanu-El Sisterhood Staff. Ed. & Pref. by Lynne Thrope. (Illus.). 340p. (Orig.). 1994. pap. 14.50 (0-9643768-0-6) Temple Emanu-El.

Taste of Chateau Elan, Vol. 1. Chateau Elan Staff. 224p. 1995. 21.95 (0-9649347-0-1) Chateau Elan.

***Taste of China.** Ken Hom & John Swannell. (Illus.). 192p. 1997. pap. 24.95 (1-85793-924-7, Pub. by Pavilion UK) Trafalgar.

Taste of China. Deh-ta Hsiung. (Illus.). 96p. 1995. 12.98 (0-8317-8735-X) Smithmark.

Taste of Cleveland: Favorite Family Recipes from Greater Cleveland. Ed. by Shirley Fetherolf. LC 92-62389. 172p. (Orig.). 1992. pap. 10.95 (0-9634831-0-2) Rabbit Hill HFP.

***Taste of Colombia.** 1997. 50.00 (958-9138-98-5) St Martin.

Taste of Columbus II. Beth Chilcoat & David Chilcoat. (Illus.). 128p. (Orig.). 1982. pap. 8.95 (0-9608710-1-2) Corban Prods.

***Taste of Corruption.** Timothy Burns. 467p. (Orig.). 1997. mass mkt. 5.99 (1-55197-965-9, Pub. by Comnwlth Pub CN) Partners Pubs Grp.

Taste of Country Cooking. Edna Lewis. 1976. 24.95 (0-394-48311-1); pap. 21.00 (0-394-73215-4) Knopf.

Taste of Cuba: Recipes from the Cuban-American Community. Linette Creen. (Illus.). 336p. 1994. pap. 12.95 (0-452-27089-8, Plume) NAL-Dutton.

Taste of Curry. Louis Segaloff. 64p. 1992. pap. 5.95 (1-881455-01-7) Atoll Pr.

***Taste of Death.** large type ed. Richard Grayson. (Linford Mystery Large Print Ser.). 336p. 1997. pap. 16.99 (0-7089-5109-0, Linford) Ulverscroft.

Taste of Dorset. Larren Wood. LC 94-60195. (Orig.). 1994. pap. 11.95 (0-9636546-1-6) Woodstock North.

Taste of Earth & Other Legends of Vietnam. Thich Nhat Hanh. Tr. & Intro. by Mobi Warren. LC 93-24083. (Illus.). 120p. (Orig.). 1993. pap. 14.00 (0-938077-66-X) Parallax Pr.

Taste of English: Nutrition Workbook for Adult ESL Students - Student Workbook. Association of Farmworker Opportunity Programs Staff. 126p. 1994. write for info. (1-886567-04-2) Assn Farmwrker.

Taste of English: Nutrition Workbook for Adult ESL Students - Teacher's Manual. Association of Farmworker Opportunity Programs Staff. 74p. 1994. write for info. (1-886567-05-0) Assn Farmwrker.

Taste of Essex: Food & Recipes of Essex Through the Ages. Lynn Pewsey. LC 93-40448. 1994. 15.00 (0-88734-902-1) Players Pr.

***Taste of Ethiopia: The Other Good Food.** 2nd rev. ed. Webayehu Tsegaye & Tamiru Degefa. (Illus.). 144p. 1996. pap. 19.95 (0-9654626-6-8) Merkato Pub.

Taste of Ethnographic Things: The Senses in Anthropology. Paul Stoller. LC 89-33670. (Contemporary Ethnography Ser.). (Illus.). 200p. (C). 1989. text ed. 36.50 (0-8122-8186-1); pap. text ed. 16.95 (0-8122-1292-4) U of Pa Pr.

Taste of Evil. large type ed. Patricia Matthews. LC 93-42206. 1994. lib. bdg. 21.95 (1-56054-334-5) Thorndike Pr.

***Taste of Fire.** Hannah Howell. 448p. 1997. mass mkt. 5.99 (0-8217-5804-7, Zebra Kensgtn) Kensgtn Pub Corp.

Taste of France. Robert Freson. LC 83-6709. (Illus.). 288p. 1983. 50.00 (0-941434-36-2); pap. 24.95 (1-55670-369-4) Stewart Tabori & Chang.

Taste of Freedom. Sangharakshita. 96p. (Orig.). 1990. pap. 6.95 (0-904766-42-X, Pub. by Windhorse UK) Windhorse Pubns.

Taste of Freedom. N. A. Woychuk. (Spiritual Life Ser.: Memory Bk. 1). (Illus.). 164p. (Orig.). 1981. pap. 3.00 (1-880960-16-8) Script Memory Fl.

Taste of Freedom: The ICU in Rural South Africa 1924-1930. Helen Bradford. LC 87-10451. 448p. 1988. text ed. 48.00 (0-300-03873-9) Yale U Pr.

Taste of Georgia. Junior Service League Staff. 1983. pap. 11.95 (0-9611002-0-6) Newnan JSL.

Taste of Goa: Illustrated Guide to Goan Cooking. Suchitra K. Misra. (C). 1992. pap. 14.00 (81-7023-208-2, Pub. by Allied II) S Asia.

***Taste of God's Love.** Marilyn G. Stonestreet. 96p. (Orig.). 1996. pap. 9.95 (1-883893-63-1) WinePress Pub.

***Taste of Greece.** Joanna Farrow. (Creative Cooking Library Ser.). 1997. 12.98 (0-7651-9555-0) Smithmark.

Taste of Hawaii: New Cooking from the Crossroads of the Pacific. Jean-Marie Josselin. LC 91-37797. (Illus.). 224p. 1992. 35.00 (1-55670-191-8) Stewart Tabori & Chang.

Taste of Heaven. Barbara Benedict. 416p. 1993. mass mkt. 4.50 (0-8217-4303-1, Zebra Kensgtn) Kensgtn Pub Corp.

Taste of Heaven. Alexis Harrington. 352p. 1996. mass mkt., pap. 5.50 (0-451-40653-2, Topaz) NAL-Dutton.

Taste of Heaven & Earth: A Zen Approach to Cooking & Eating with 150 Satisfying Vegetarian Recipes. Bettina Vitell. LC 93-56253. (Illus.). 256p. (Orig.). 1993. pap. 16.00 (0-06-096934-2, PL) HarpC.

Taste of Herbs. Geraldene Holt. (Illus.). 96p. 1995. 22.95 (1-85029-500-X, Pub. by Conran Octopus UK) Trafalgar.

Taste of Heritage. 1996. 25.00 (0-02-860382-6) Macmillan.

***Taste of Hidden Things: Images of the Sufi Path.** Sara Sviri. LC 97-13608. (Orig.). 1997. pap. 12.95 (0-9634574-8-9) Golden Sufi Ctr.

***Taste of Home Recipe Book.** Reiman Publications Staff. 1996. 12.95 (0-89821-178-6) Reiman Pubns.

Taste of Home Recipe Book. Ed. by Julie Schnittka. LC 94-61368. 116p. 1995. 12.95 (0-89821-133-6, 19550) Reiman Pubns.

Taste of Home Recipe Book. 2nd ed. Julie Schnittka & Reiman Publications Staff. LC 95-72659. 112p. Date not set. 12.95 (0-89821-157-3) Reiman Pubns.

Taste of Homecoming: Traditional Cooking from the Heartland of the South. Daisy King. LC 89-10745. 223p. 1989. pap. 12.95 (1-55853-039-8) Rutledge Hill Pr.

Taste of Home's Down-Home Diabetic Cookbook. Reiman Publications Staff. Ed. by Julie Schnittka. LC 95-71713. 320p. Date not set. 16.95 (0-89821-153-0, 22102) Reiman Pubns.

Taste of Honey. Shelagh Delaney. LC 59-8206. 87p. (Orig.). 1989. pap. 8.95 (0-8021-3185-9, Grove) Grove-Atltic.

Taste of Honey. Stephanie Mittman. 368p. 1995. mass mkt. 4.50 (0-06-108394-1, Harp PBks) HarpC.

Taste of Honey. Hilaire Walden. 1995. 14.98 (0-7858-0349-1) Bk Sales Inc.

Taste of Hunterdon. Hunterdon Medical Center Auxiliary Staff. (Illus.). 263p. 1993. 12.95 (0-9638475-0-3) Hunterdon Med.

Taste of India. Madhur Jaffrey. LC 85-72598. (Illus.). 256p. 1988. pap. 26.00 (0-689-70726-6, Pub. by Ctrl Bur voor Schimmel NE) Macmillan.

Taste of India. Bibi I. Kaur. 1985. pap. 9.95 (0-89509-051-1) KRI Pubns.

Taste of Indochina. Jan Castorina & Dimitra Stais. LC 96-302. (Illus.). 160p. 1996. 18.95 (0-8120-6602-2) Barron.

***Taste of Indonesia: Over 70 Aromatic Dishes from the Spice Islands of Bali, Java, Sumara.** Sallie Morris. 1996. 12.98 (0-8317-7402-9) Smithmark.

An Asterisk (*) at the beginning of an entry indicates that the title is appearing in BIP for the first time.

Taste of Ireland: In Food & Pictures. Theodora Fitzgibbon. (Illus.). 120p. 1995. pap. 19.95 (*0-297-83348-0*, Weidenfeld) Trafalgar.

Taste of Israel: A Mediterranean Feast. Avi Ganor. 1993. 19.98 (*0-88365-844-5*) Galahad Bks.

Taste of Italy. Antonio Carluccio. 1986. 24.95 (*0-316-12858-9*) Little.

***Taste of Italy, Vol. 42.** (Collector's Ser.). (Illus.). 64p. (Orig.). 1996. pap. 3.95 (*0-942320-55-7*) Am Cooking.

Taste of Jackson Hole. Christine Goodman. 267p. 1991. pap. text ed. 17.95 (*0-9633566-0-7*) C Goodman.

***Taste of Japan.** Masaji Ko. (Creative Cooking Library Ser.). 1997. 12.98 (*0-7651-9557-7*) Smithmark.

Taste of Japan. Donald Richie. Ed. by Tsuizaki & Pocknell. (Illus.). 112p. 1993. pap. 18.00 (*4-7700-1707-3*) Kodansha.

Taste of Kentucky. Janet A. Anderson. LC 86-9197. (Illus.). 112p. 1986. 15.00 (*0-8131-1580-9*) U Pr of Ky.

Taste of Lebanon: Cooking Today the Lebanese Way. Mary Salloum. LC 88-596. (Illus.). 190p. 1992. pap. 14.95 (*0-940793-90-3*) Interlink Pub.

Taste of Lemon. Jane Oxley. 1994. 8.95 (*0-533-10874-8*) Vantage.

Taste of Life. Rexella Van Impe. (Illus.). 104p. (Orig.). 1995. pap. 5.00 (*1-884137-78-4*) J Van Impe.

Taste of Louisiana: Cajun - Creole Recipes. 2nd ed. Effie McDaniel. Ed. by Theresa Millang. 163p. 1989. write for info. (*0-9624584-0-6*) id Pub.

Taste of Love: Recipes from Romance. Leigh Michaels. 190p. (Orig.). 1995. pap. 12.95 (*0-9641275-1-2*) PBL Ltd.

Taste of Madras: A South Indian Cookbook. Rani Kingman. LC 95-49065. (Illus.). 160p. 1996. 35.00 (*1-56656-195-7*); pap. 17.95 (*1-56656-196-5*) Interlink Pub.

***Taste of Malta.** Claudia Caruana. 1997. 19.95 (*0-614-27972-0*) Hippocrene Bks.

***Taste of Man.** Slavenka Drakulic. 1997. pap. 10.95 (*0-14-026622-4*) Viking Penguin.

Taste of Maryland. Carol Strohecker. (Illus.). 96p. 1984. pap. 5.00 (*0-911886-28-1*) Walters Art.

Taste of Memories from Columbus Park, Vol. III: Recipes, Memories & Photographs of the Old West Side Neighborhood in Kenosha, Wisconsin. Intro. by Catherine T. Murray. LC 91-91350. (Illus.). 535p. (Orig.). 1992. spiral bd. 19.95 (*0-9626346-2-X*) Greenbush Remembered.

Taste of Memories from the Old "Bush" Recipes, Memories & Photographs of the Old Greenbush Neighborhood, Vol. I. LC 88-17637. 410p. 1988. spiral bd. 17.00 (*0-9626346-0-3*) Greenbush Remembered.

Taste of Memories from the Old "Bush", Vol. II: Recipes, Memories & Photographs of the Old Greenbush Neighborhood. Catherine T. Murray. LC 88-176375. (Illus.). 554p. (Orig.). 1990. spiral bd. 18.50 (*0-9626346-1-1*) Greenbush Remembered.

Taste of Mexico. Patricia Quintana. Ed. by Marilyn Wilkinson. LC 86-5817. (Illus.). 304p. 1986. 50.00 (*0-941434-89-3*) Stewart Tabori & Chang.

Taste of Mexico. Patricia Quintana. LC 86-5817. (Illus.). 304p. 1993. pap. 24.95 (*1-55670-326-0*) Stewart Tabori & Chang.

***Taste of Mexico: 70 Fiery & Flavourful Recipes from South of the Border.** Elisabeth L. Ortiz. (Creative Cooking Library). 1996. 12.98 (*0-7651-9875-4*) Smithmark.

Taste of Mexico with Jozi Maldonado. 280p. 1994. pap. 17.95 (*0-9642308-0-1*) Castaway.

Taste of Milwaukee. Friends of the Museum, Inc. Staff. Ed. by Mary Garity. (Illus.). 200p. 1983. 9.95 (*0-913965-00-6*) Friends Mus Inc.

***Taste of Morocco.** Robert Carrier. 224p. 1997. pap. 19.95 (*0-7522-1039-4*, Pub. by Boxtree UK) Trafalgar.

Taste of My Own Medicine: When the Doctor Is the Patient. Edward E. Rosenbaum. LC 87-43218. 192p. 1988. 16.95 (*0-394-56282-8*) Random.

***Taste of Nature: Edible Plants of the Southwest & How To Prepare Them.** Kahanah Farnsworth. LC 96-35789. 1997. pap. 15.95 (*0-941270-93-9*) Ancient City Pr.

Taste of New England. Junior League of Worcester Staff. 1993. 16.95 (*0-9637509-0-9*) Jr Leag Worcester.

Taste of New Money. Judith Fearon. Ed. by M. L. Jones. (Orig.). 1996. pap. 8.95 (*1-882270-33-9*) Old Rugged Cross.

Taste of New Wine. Keith Miller. LC 93-82109. 128p. 1993. pap. 8.95 (*1-55725-059-6*); audio 14.95 (*1-55725-061-8*) Paraclete MA.

Taste of New York: Signature Dishes of the Best Restaurants. Karen G. Zahler. LC 93-176. (Illus.). 1993. 35.00 (*0-201-62208-4*) Addison-Wesley.

Taste of Newport. Gillian Drake. 7.50 (*0-9609814-1-1*) Pineapple Pubns.

Taste of Noodles. Louis Segaloff. 64p. 1992. pap. 5.95 (*1-881455-02-5*) Atoll Pr.

***Taste of Nostalgia.** Allen Weiss. (Illus.). 208p. 1997. pap. 15.00 (*1-882791-05-3*) Dist Art Pubs.

Taste of Nova Scotia Cookbook. Charles Lief & Heather MacKenzie. (Illus.). (Orig.). 1986. pap. 16.95 (*1-55013-527-9*, Pub. by Key Porter Bks CN) Firefly Bks Ltd.

Taste of Old Cuba. O'Higgins. LC 94-10684. 320p. 1994. 25.00 (*0-06-016964-8*, HarpT) HarpC.

Taste of Olde York. Yorkville Historical Society Staff. (Illus.). 255p. (Orig.). 1986. pap. 7.00 (*0-912081-03-1*) Delmar Co.

Taste of Oregon. Ed. by Junior League of Eugene Staff. (Illus.). 382p. 1980. reprint ed. spiral bd. 17.95 (*0-9607976-0-2*) Jr League Eugene.

Taste of Paisley: A Community Cookbook from Paisley, Oregon. 2nd ed. JoAnn Solheim. (Illus.). 184p. 1994. spiral bd. write for info. (*1-57502-129-3*) Morris Pubng.

Taste of Palestine: Menus & Memories. Aziz Shihab. LC 92-75657. (Illus.). 120p. (Orig.). 1993. pap. 10.95 (*0-931722-93-4*) Corona Pub.

Taste of Paradise. Louis Segaloff. 64p. 1992. pap. 5.95 (*1-881455-00-9*) Atoll Pr.

Taste of Philippines. K. Mitchell. (Illus.). 40p. 1979. 5.95 (*0-318-36280-5*) Asia Bk Corp.

Taste of Poetry...Chicago Style: An Anthology by Poets & Patrons Club of Chicago. Poets & Patrons Club Members Staff. 140p. 1996. pap. 9.95 (*1-887312-03-X*) P Gangas.

Taste of Power. Elaine Brown. (Illus.). 528p. 1994. pap. 14.95 (*0-385-47107-6*, Anchor NY) Doubleday.

***Taste of Prairie Life: Recipes, Remedies, Reminiscings.** Loaun W. Vaad. LC 96-90357. (Illus.). 224p. (Orig.). 1996. spiral bd., pap. 12.95 (*0-9652586-3-7*, Buffalo Grass) Vaads.

Taste of Proof. large type ed. Bill Knox. 1978. 25.99 (*0-7089-0154-9*) Ulverscroft.

Taste of Provence. Carey More & Julian More. (Illus.). 160p. 1991. pap. 24.95 (*1-85145-528-0*, Pub. by Pavilion UK) Trafalgar.

Taste of Provence: Classic Recipes from the South of France. Leslie Forbes. (Illus.). 160p. 1991. pap. 16.95 (*0-87701-826-X*) Chronicle Bks.

***Taste of Provence: The Columbe D'Or at Saint Paul de Vence.** Martine Buchet. (Illus.). 146p. 1996. 40.00 (*2-908228-47-5*) St Martin.

Taste of Puerto Rico. Yvonne Ortiz. 1997. pap. 13.95 (*0-452-27548-2*, Plume) NAL-Dutton.

Taste of Puerto Rico: Traditional & New Dishes from the Puerto Rican Community. Yvonne Ortiz. LC 93-46165. 320p. 1994. pap. 23.95 (*0-525-93812-5*) NAL-Dutton.

Taste of Quality: Favorite Recipes from the Merillat Kitchens of America. Ruth Seighman. 1980. write for info. (*0-937304-01-8*) Rand Partners.

***Taste of Red Leaves.** Steve Dreben. (Illus.). 40p. (Orig.). (J). (gr. 1-5). 1997. pap. 8.99 (*1-55197-997-7*, Pub. by Comnwlth Pub CN) Partners Pubs Grp.

Taste of Revenge. Kazuo Koike. 1996. pap. 19.95 (*1-56931-076-9*) Viz Commns Inc.

Taste of Revenge, Vol. 1: Crying Freeman, Graphic Novel. Kazuo Koike. Ed. by Seiji Horibuchi. Tr. by Satoru Fujii from JPN. (Illus.). 184p. 1992. pap. 14.95 (*0-929279-89-1*) Viz Commns Inc.

Taste of Revenge, Vol. 2: Crying Freeman, Graphic Novel. Kazuo Koike. Ed. by Seiji Horibuchi. Tr. by Satoru Fujii from JPN. (Illus.). 184p. 1993. pap. 14.95 (*0-929279-90-5*) Viz Commns Inc.

Taste of Revenge, Vol. 3: Crying Freeman, Graphic Novel. Kazuo Koike. Ed. by Seiji Horibuchi. Tr. by Satoru Fujii from JPN. (Illus.). 184p. 1993. pap. 14.95 (*0-929279-91-3*) Viz Commns Inc.

***Taste of Romania.** Nicolae Klepper. LC 97-9783. (Original Cookbook Ser.). 150p. 1997. 22.50 (*0-7818-0523-6*) Hippocrene Bks.

Taste of Salt: A Story of Modern Haiti. Frances Temple. (Trophy Bk.). 192p. (YA). (gr. 7 up). 1994. pap. 4.50 (*0-06-447136-5*, Trophy) HarpC Child Bks.

Taste of Salt: A Story of Modern Haiti. Frances Temple. LC 92-6716. 192p. (YA). (gr. 7 up). 1992. 16.95 (*0-531-05459-4*); lib. bdg. 17.99 (*0-531-08609-7*) Orchard Bks Watts.

Taste of Shabbos, The Complete Cookbook. Compiled by Aish Hatorah Women's Organization Staff. 1987. 19.95 (*0-87306-426-7*) Feldheim.

Taste of Smoke. Marion Dane Bauer. 112p. (J). 1995. pap. 3.99 (*0-440-41034-7*) Dell.

Taste of Smoke. Marion Dane Bauer. LC 92-32585. (YA). (gr. 5 up). 1993. 14.95 (*0-395-64341-4*, Clarion Bks) HM.

Taste of Smoke: Stories about Africa. Stacy J. Tuthill. 200p. 1995. pap. 12.00 (*0-9637290-1-2*) East Coast Bks.

Taste of South Carolina. Palmetto Cabinet Staff. LC 85-14573. (Illus.). 345p. 1985. reprint ed. spiral bd. 16.95 (*0-87844-064-X*) Sandlapper Pub Co.

Taste of Spain: Traditional Spanish Recipes & Their Origins. Camilla Jessel. (Illus.). 160p. 1991. 27.95 (*0-312-06478-0*) St Martin.

Taste of Summer. Claudia Nice. 96p. 1990. pap. text ed. 9.50 (*1-56770-223-6*) S Scheewe Pubns.

Taste of Tampa. Junior League of Tampa, Inc. Staff. 184p. 1983. pap. 9.95 (*0-9609556-1-5*) Jr Leag Tampa.

Taste of Texas Ranching. Tom Bryant. 1994. pap. 15.95 (*1-884374-05-0*) Border Bks.

Taste of Texas Ranching: Cowboys & Cooks. Joel Bernstein & Tom Bryant. (Illus.). 256p. (Orig.). 1995. pap. 18.95 (*0-89672-348-8*) Tex Tech Univ Pr.

Taste of Texas Ranching: Recipe Postcards. Tom Bryant & Joel Bernstein. (Illus.). 30p. (Orig.). 1996. pap. 9.95 (*0-89672-367-4*) Tex Tech Univ Pr.

Taste of Thailand. Vatcharin Bhumichitr. LC 92-44582. (Illus.). 224p. 1993. pap. 15.00 (*0-02-009130-3*) Macmillan.

***Taste of Thailand: 70 Easy-to-Cook Authentic Recipes from an Exciting Exotic Cuisine.** Kit Chan. (Creative Cooking Library). 1996. 12.98 (*0-7651-9878-9*) Smithmark.

Taste of the Aegean. Andy Harris & Terry Harris. (Illus.). 152p. 1992. 27.50 (*1-55859-361-6*) Abbeville Pr.

Taste of the Caribbean: 70 Simple-to-Cook Recipes from This Tropical Cuisine. Rosamund Grant. 1995. 10.98 (*0-8317-7892-X*) Smithmark.

***Taste of the Country.** Reiman Publications Staff. 1994. 12.95 (*0-89821-180-8*) Reiman Pubns.

Taste of the Country. Ed. by Jean Van Dyke. LC 88-61945. 100p. 1988. spiral bd. 9.95 (*0-89821-086-0*, 3018) Reiman Pubns.

***Taste of the Country.** 2nd ed. Reiman Publications Staff. 1994. 12.95 (*0-89821-181-6*) Reiman Pubns.

***Taste of the Country.** 3rd ed. Reiman Publications Staff. 1994. 12.95 (*0-89821-182-4*) Reiman Pubns.

Taste of the Country. 4th ed. Ed. by Linda Piepenbrink. LC 91-62226. 100p. 1991. pap. 9.95 (*0-89821-094-1*, 6662) Reiman Pubns.

***Taste of the Country.** 4th ed. Reiman Publications Staff. 1994. 12.95 (*0-89821-183-2*) Reiman Pubns.

***Taste of the Country.** 5th ed. Reiman Publications Staff. 1995. 12.95 (*0-89821-184-0*) Reiman Pubns.

***Taste of the Country.** 6th ed. Reiman Publications Staff. 1995. 12.95 (*0-89821-185-9*) Reiman Pubns.

***Taste of the Country.** 7th ed. Reiman Publications Staff. 1996. 12.95 (*0-89821-186-7*) Reiman Pubns.

***Taste of the Country.** 8th ed. Reiman Publications Staff. 1996. 12.95 (*0-89821-191-3*) Reiman Pubns.

Taste of the Country. 8th ed. Ed. by Julie Schnittka. LC 95-67305. 100p. 1995. pap. 9.95 (*0-89821-144-1*, 19955) Reiman Pubns.

Taste of the Country. 9th ed. Ed. by Julie Schnittka. LC 95-73093. 112p. Date not set. pap. write for info. (*0-89821-158-1*) Reiman Pubns.

Taste of the Country: A Collection of Calvin Beale's Writings. Calvin L. Beale. Ed. by Peter A. Morrison. LC 87-43183. 320p. 1990. lib. bdg. 32.50 (*0-271-00631-5*) Pa St U Pr.

Taste of the Country Five. 5th ed. Ed. by Linda Piepenbrink. LC 92-60968. 100p. 1992. pap. 9.95 (*0-89821-098-4*, 11566) Reiman Pubns.

Taste of the Country Seven. 7th ed. Ed. by Julie Schnittka. LC 94-66234. 100p. 1994. pap. 9.95 (*0-89821-120-4*, 18847) Reiman Pubns.

Taste of the Country Six. 6th ed. Ed. by Nancy Mack & Linda Piepenbrink. LC 93-84018. 100p. 1993. pap. 9.95 (*0-89821-105-0*, 12280) Reiman Pubns.

Taste of the Country Three. 3rd ed. Ed. by Jean Van Dyke. LC 90-62428. 100p. 1990. pap. 9.95 (*0-89821-091-7*, 6362) Reiman Pubns.

Taste of the Country Two. 2nd ed. Ed. by Jean Van Dyke. LC 89-61837. 100p. 1989. pap. 9.95 (*0-89821-089-5*, 5301) Reiman Pubns.

Taste of the East. Deh-ta Hsiung et al. (Illus.). 256p. 1995. 19.98 (*0-8317-2743-8*) Smithmark.

Taste of the Exotic. Louis Segaloff. 64p. 1992. pap. 5.95 (*1-881455-05-X*) Atoll Pr.

Taste of the Good Life. Richard Briers & Ann Briers. (Illus.). 256p. 1996. 35.00 (*1-85793-583-7*, Pub. by Pavilion UK) Trafalgar.

Taste of the Gulf Coast. Jessie Tirsch. LC 96-51129. 1997. 25.00 (*0-02-860356-7*) Macmillan.

***Taste of the Gulf Coast.** Jessie Tirsch. 1997. 25.00 (*0-614-27974-7*) Mac Pub USA.

Taste of the Holidays. Dot Gibson. 96p. 1988. pap. 3.95 (*0-941162-07-9*) D Gibson.

Taste of the Knife. 4th ed. Marnie Walsh. Ed. by Tom Trusky. LC 76-15877. (Ahsahta Press Modern & Contemporary Poets of the West Ser.). 64p. 1976. pap. 6.95 (*0-916272-03-6*) Ahsahta Pr.

Taste of the Lake. Lake of the Ozarks General Hospital Auxiliary Staff. LC 93-70696. 1993. write for info. (*0-87197-369-3*) Favorite Recipes.

***Taste of the Mediterranean.** Diana Vowles. 1996. 15.98 (*0-7858-0559-1*) Bk Sales Inc.

Taste of the Mediterranean: 150 Authentic Recipes from the Cuisines of the Sun: Italy, Greece... Joanna Farrow. 256p. 1996. 32.50 (*1-85967-244-2*, Lorenz Bks) Anness Pub.

Taste of the Middle East. (Creative Cooking Library). 1996. 12.98 (*0-8317-7405-3*) Smithmark.

Taste of the Mountains Cooking School Cookbook. Steven Raichlen. 1986. pap. write for info. (*0-671-54429-2*) S&S Trade.

Taste of the Pacific. Susan Parkinson et al. (Illus.). 112p. 1995. pap. 16.95 (*0-8248-1791-5*) UH Pr.

Taste of the Past: Early Foodways of the Albemarle Region, 1585-1830. Ed. by James C. Jordan. (Illus.). 60p. 1991. pap. write for info. (*0-9624332-1-7*) Mus Albemarle.

Taste of the Pineapple: Essays on C.S. Lewis as Reader, Critic, & Imaginative Writer. Ed. by Bruce L. Edwards. 264p. 1988. 36.95 (*0-87972-407-2*); pap. 17.95 (*0-87972-406-4*) Bowling Green Univ Popular Press.

***Taste of the Sea.** Mayflower Culinary Editors. (The Everyday Chef Ser.). 1997. pap. text ed. 5.99 (*1-58029-011-6*) Everywhere Pr.

***Taste of the Sea.** Rick Stein. (Illus.). 224p. (Orig.). 1997. reprint ed. pap. 18.95 (*0-912333-48-0*) BB&T Inc.

Taste of the South. Compiled by Alabama Gas Corporation Staff. (Illus.). 192p. 1994. 16.95 (*1-878561-27-8*) Seacoast AL.

Taste of the South. Ed. by J. Baldwin Wakeland et al. (Illus.). 430p. 1984. 17.95 (*0-9608552-1-1*) Sym League.

Taste of the States: A Food History of America. Hilde G. Lee. 1992. 45.00 (*0-943231-56-6*) Howell Pr VA.

***Taste of the Sun: Over 50 Quick & Healthy Recipes from the Mediterranean.** Joanna Farrow. 1997. 12.98 (*0-7651-9389-2*) Smithmark.

Taste of the Territory: The Flair & Flavor of Oklahoma! Photos by Jerry Poppenhouse. (Illus.). 270p. 1996. spiral bd. 18.95 (*0-9648976-0-1*) Serv Leag Bartlesville.

***Taste of the Town: A Collection of Recipes from News Channel 5's Talk of the Town.** (Illus.). 192p. 1996. 15.95 (*0-9654961-0-4*) Landmark TV Tenn Inc.

Taste of the Treasure Coast. Yacht & Country Club Staff. (Illus.). 325p. 1990. 16.95 (*0-9626849-0-2*) Yacht Ctry Club.

***Taste of the Triangle: A Guide to the Finer Restaurants of Raleigh, Durham, Cary & Chapel Hill with Recipes.** Juli Brown. (Illus.). 200p. (Orig.). 1997. pap. 14.95 (*1-878086-56-1*) Down Home NC.

Taste of the Tropics: Traditional & Innovative Cooking from the Pacific & Caribbean. Jay Solomon. (Illus.). 200p. (Orig.). 1992. pap. 10.95 (*0-89594-533-9*) Crossing Pr.

Taste of the Valley. Ed. by Alice Powell & Hazel McAroy. (Illus.). 300p. 1988. write for info. (*0-318-64734-6*) St John Don Bosco Ch.

***Taste of the Wild.** Blanche P. Garrett. pap. 12.95 (*0-88862-127-2*, Pub. by J Lorimer CN) Formac Dist Ltd.

Taste of the Wild. Louis Segaloff. 64p. 1992. pap. 5.95 (*1-881455-04-1*) Atoll Pr.

Taste of the Wild. Edelene Wood. (Illus.). 160p. 1990. 13.95 (*0-910042-59-4*); pap. 9.95 (*0-910042-65-9*) Allegheny.

Taste of Time, 1842-1992: One Hundred Fifty Years of Good Cooking Made Easy for Today's Kitchens. Judy Loughrin. Ed. by Ce C. Patterson. LC 92-81893. (Illus.). 224p. (Orig.). 1992. pap. text ed. 14.95 (*0-9632981-2-7*) Lucky Canyon.

Taste of Toronto Ohio, That Is. Ed. by James Walker et al. LC 94-60570. 360p. 1994. pap. 14.95 (*0-9643221-1-0*) Toronto HS.

Taste of Tradition: Old World Wisconsin Cooking. Old World Wisconsin Staff. Ed. & Pref. by Carolyn Larson. (Illus.). 208p. (Orig.). 1988. 12.50 (*0-9620365-0-1*) Friends Old World WI.

***Taste of Tradition: The Story of a Family Business 1950-1996.** Patrick Beaver. (Illus.). 220p. 1997. 49.95 (*0-485-11510-7*, Pub. by Athlone Pr UK) Humanities.

Taste of Treason. large type ed. Arthur Maling. 416p. 1985. 25.99 (*0-7089-1338-5*) Ulverscroft.

Taste of Tuscany. John D. Meis. (Illus.). 160p. 1993. 27.50 (*1-55859-466-3*) Abbeville Pr.

Taste of Tuskegee: Traditional Recipes & Fond Remembrances from Alabama's Renowned Tuskegee Institute. Carolyn Q. Tillery. (Illus.). 280p. 1996. 18.95 (*1-55972-325-4*, Birch Ln Pr) Carol Pub Group.

Taste of Victory. Sandy Dengler. LC 89-18075. (Australian Destiny Ser.: Vol. 3). 272p. (Orig.). 1989. pap. 8.99 (*1-55661-085-8*) Bethany Hse.

Taste of War: Soldiering in World War II. Alfred De Grazia. 490p. 1992. pap. 22.00 (*0-685-59571-4*) Metron Pubns.

Taste of Water. Arthur Von Wisenberger. (Illus.). 32p. (Orig.). 1996. pap. 4.95 (*0-9624574-1-8*) Best Cellar Bks.

Taste of Water: Christianity Through Taoist-Buddhist Eyes. Chwen J. Lee & Thomas G. Hand. 270p. 1990. pap. 11.95 (*0-8091-3149-8*) Paulist Pr.

Taste of Wine. Jilly Goolden. 1995. pap. 6.95 (*0-563-36993-0*, BBC-Parkwest) Parkwest Pubns.

Taste of Wine: The Art & Science of Wine Appreciation. 2nd ed. Emile Peynaud. LC 96-24181. 1996. text ed. 54.95 (*0-471-11376-X*) Wiley.

***Taste of Wine: The Art & Science of Wine Appreciation.** Emile Peynaud. Tr. by Michael Schuster from FRE. (Illus.). 260p. 1996. reprint ed. 39.95 (*0-932664-64-4*, 940E) Wine Appreciation.

Taste, Olfaction & the Central Nervous System: A Festschrift in Honor of Carl Pfaffmann. Ed. by Donald W. Pfaff. LC 84-43054. 346p. 1985. 29.95 (*0-87470-039-6*) Rockefeller.

Taste the Good Life. Assistance League of Omaha Members. 282p. 1992. 16.95 (*0-9632957-0-5*) Assist Lgue Omaha.

Taste the Good Life: Nebraska Cookbook. Morris. 1992. ring bd., pap. 10.95 (*0-9631249-0-0*, Cookbks by Morris) Morris Pubng.

Taste the Seasons. Ed. by Linda Brandt. LC 85-51259. (Illus.). 136p. 1985. 18.95 (*0-9615260-0-9*) Woodside-Atherton.

Taste Today: The Role of Appreciation in Consumerism & Design. Peter Lloyd Jones. (Illus.). 318p. 1991. 86.50 (*0-08-040251-8*, Pergamon Pr) Elsevier.

Taste vs. Fat: Rating the Low-Fat & Fat-Free Foods: How to Save Money, Time, & Your Taste Buds by Knowing Which Brand-Name Products Rate the Highest on Taste & Nutrition. Elaine Moquette-Magee. 210p. (Orig.). 1997. pap. 12.95 (*1-56561-109-8*) Chronimed.

Taste Without Waist. Service League of Hickory, NC, Inc. Staff. 64p. (Orig.). 1993. pap. 4.95 (*0-9611356-1-1*) Serv Leag Hickory.

Tasteful Interlude: American Interiors Through the Camera's Eye, 1860-1917. 2nd enl. rev. ed. William Seale. LC 95-46053. (American Association for State & Local History Book Ser.). (Illus.). 288p. 1982. reprint ed. pap. 19.95 (*0-7619-9134-4*) AltaMira Pr.

Tasteful Tennis: Team Tennis Cuisine & Counsel. Jane Finkbeiner & Martha Williamson. LC 90-82933. (Illus.). 256p. (Orig.). 1991. spiral bd. 14.95 (*0-9627221-0-3*) Bolder Bks FL.

Tasteful Traditions. Ed. by Jerry Burge. LC 88-63950. 350p. (Orig.). 1989. pap. 10.00 (*0-685-27870-0*) MS Ext Homemakers.

Tastefully Oregon. Oregon Dietetic Association Staff. (Illus.). 277p. (Orig.). 1996. pap. write for info. (*0-9650697-0-2*) Oregon Dietetic.

Tastefully Yours. Lynette Arceneaux et al. 1993. 2.95 (*0-9637140-0-7*) Tstefully Yours.

Tastemakers. Steven Watson. write for info. (*0-679-44139-5*) Random.

Tastemakers. Russell Lynes. LC 82-25116. (Illus.). xiv, 362p. (C). 1983. reprint ed. text ed. 67.50 (*0-313-23843-X*, LYTA, Greenwood Pr) Greenwood.

Tastemakers: The Development of American Popular Taste. Russell Lynes. (Illus.). 384p. 1980. reprint ed. pap. 8.95 (*0-486-23993-4*) Dover.

Tastes & Tales: Jewish Cookery for Young People with Tales from Around the World. Malvina W. Liebman. (Illus.). 200p. (Orig.). 1986. spiral bd. 8.95 (*0-930029-02-X*) Central Agency.

Tastes & Tales from Texas. Peg Hein. 1984. pap. 12.95 (*0-9613881-0-2*) Hein & Assocs.

Tastes & Tales of Erie, Pennsylvania. Nancy C. Cocke. 184p. 1995. reprint ed. spiral bd. 12.95 (0-9644737-0-4) N C Cocke.

Tastes & Traditions: The Sam Houston Heritage Cookbook. Study Club of Huntsville Staff. 1992. 16.00 (0-9634159-0-5) Study Club.

Tastes in Plaid. 16.95 (0-9626558-2-1) Alamance Cnty Hist Mus.

Tastes of Aspen. Jill Sheeley. (Illus.). 200p. 1988. 14.95 (0-9609108-1-6) Courtney Pr.

Tastes of Montana, No. 1. Joy Brown. 128p. 1994. pap. text ed. 12.50 (0-9644206-0-0) Jaybee Pubns.

Tastes of Paradise: A Social History of Spices, Stimulants, & Intoxicants. Wolfgang Schivelbusch. Tr. by David Jacobson from GER. LC 92-50603. 1993. pap. 13.00 (0-679-74438-X, Vin) Random.

Tastes of Tuscany: Treasured Family Recipes & Vignettes from the Heartland of Italy. Liana G. Figone. LC 91-16950. (Illus.). 320p. 1992. spiral bd. 19.95 (0-931892-24-4) B Dolphin Pub.

Tastes of Wales. Gilli Davies. (Illus.). 136p. 1991. pap. 9.95 (0-563-36043-7, BBC-Parkwest) Parkwest Pubns.

***Tastes That Teach: And Other Devotional Object Lessons.** Marilynn M. Moe. (Illus.). 49p. (YA). (gr. 6 up). 1997. 14.95 (1-884816-03-7) M M Moe.

***TasteTour Collection: Fine Wines of the World, 6 vols.** Ronn Wiegand & Brenda Boblitt. Incl. Chardonnay TasteTour Vol. 1, No. 1: World's Greatest Dry White Wine. (Illus.). 6p. 1996. pap. 12.95 (1-889578-00-2, TT001); Cabernet Sauvignon TasteTour Vol. 1, No. 2: King of Red Wines. (Illus.). 6p. 1996. pap. 12.95 (1-889578-01-0, TT002); Pinot Noir TasteTour Vol. 1, No. 3: Queen of Red Wines. (Illus.). 6p. 1996. pap. 12.95 (1-889578-02-9, TT003); Merlot TasteTour Vol. 1, No. 4: Generous Noble Red Wines. 6p. 1996. pap. 12.95 (1-889578-03-7, TT004); Sauvignon Blanc TasteTour Vol. 1, No. 5: White Wines of Distinction. (Illus.). 6p. 1996. pap. 12.95 (1-889578-04-5, TT005); Tastetour Collection: Fine Wines of the World Vol. 1, Nos. 1-6: Chardonnay, Cabenet Sauvignon, Pinot Noir, Merlot, Sauvignon Blanc, Zinfandel. (Illus.). 36p. 1996. pap. 74.95 (1-889578-06-1, TT006); 74.95 (0-614-19221-8, TT007) TasteTour Pub.

Tastetour Collection: Fine Wines of the World, Vol. 1, Nos. 1-6, Chardonnay, Cabenet Sauvignon, Pinot Noir, Merlot, Sauvignon Blanc, Zinfandel see TasteTour Collection: Fine Wines of the World

Tasting. Kathie B. Smith & Victoria Crenson. LC 87-5884. (Question Bks.). (Illus.). 24p. (J). (gr. k-3). 1988. lib. bdg. 11.89 (0-8167-1014-7) Troll Communs.

Tasting & Smelling. Nigel Snell. (Senses Ser.). (Illus.). 32p. (J). (gr. k-2). 1991. 10.95 (0-237-60258-X, Pub. by Evans Bros Ltd UK) Trafalgar.

***Tasting & Smelling.** 2nd ed. Ed. by Edward C. Carterette et al. LC 97-22352. (Handbook of Perception & Cognition Ser.). (Illus.). 256p. 1997. boxed 75.00 (0-12-161958-3, AP Prof) Acad Pr.

Tasting Food, Tasting Freedom: Excursions into Eating, Culture, & the Past. Sidney W. Mintz. 176p. 1996. 22.00 (0-8070-4628-0) Beacon Pr.

***Tasting Food, Tasting Freedom: Excursions into Eating, Power, & the Past.** Sidney W. Mintz. LC 95-47569. 176p. 1997. reprint ed. pap. 11.00 (0-8070-4629-9) Beacon Pr.

Tasting Gold: A Goldmine of Recipes from Nevada County's Best Restaurants. Susan Wolbarst. 156p. 1992. pap. 12.95 (0-9634425-0-3) S Wolbarst.

Tasting It. David MacArthur. (Illus.). 104p. (Orig.). 1984. pap. 9.95 (0-9612674-0-2) Wine Country.

Tasting Life Twice: Lesbian Literary Fiction by New American Writers. Ed. by Ellen Levy. LC 94-47010. (Orig.). 1995. pap. 12.00 (0-380-78123-9) Avon.

Tasting Paradise: Restaurants & Recipes of the Hawaiian Islands. Karen Bacon. 201p. 1995. pap. 14.95 (0-9644327-0-6) Coastal Images.

Tasting Paris. James Salter. Date not set. 18.00 (0-88001-445-8) Norton.

Tasting the Dish: Rabbinic Rhetorics of Sexuality. Michael L. Satlow. LC 95-38540. (Brown Judaic Studies: Vol. 303). 370p. (C). 1995. 44.95 (0-7885-0159-3, 140303) Scholars Pr GA.

Tasting Things. Allan Fowler. LC 90-21647. (Rookie Read-about Science Ser.). (Illus.). 32p. (J). (ps-2). 1991. pap. 3.95 (0-516-44911-7); lib. bdg. 17.30 (0-516-04911-9) Childrens.

Tasting Things Big Book. Allan Fowler. (Rookie Read-about Science Big Bks.). (Illus.). 32p. (J). (ps-2). 1991. pap. 32.40 (0-516-49471-6) Childrens.

***Tasty Bytes: Best-of-the-Internet Vegetarian Recipes.** Ed. by Cynthia Holzapfel. LC 96-46752. 144p. (Orig.). 1997. pap. 9.95 (1-57067-037-4) Book Pub Co.

Tasty Economical Cookbook, Vol. 2. M. R. Muhaiyaddeen. (Illus.). 166p. 1983. spiral bd. 6.00 (0-914390-22-8) Fellowship Pr PA.

Tasty Holiday Gifts. 1993. 19.95 (0-942237-21-8) Leisure AR.

Tasty Imitations: A Practical Guide to Meat Substitutes: TVP Recipes. Barbara G. Salsbury. LC 74-78024. (Illus.). 76p. 1973. pap. 7.98 (0-88290-025-0) Horizon Utah.

Tasty Poems. (J). write for info. (0-19-276133-1) OUP.

Tasty Recipes & Cherished Memories. Mary L. Carson. 1989. 5.95 (0-941620-40-9) Carson Ent.

Tasty Taters: Potato Cook Book. Ed. by Judith Bosley. (Illus.). 100p. (Orig.). 1989. pap. 8.50 (0-930809-03-3) Kitch Cupbd Cookbks.

Tasty Tidbits-Easy Appetizers & Hors D'Oeuvres. Ed. by Elaine M. Myers. 48p. 1993. pap. 7.20 (0-944943-38-1, 21328-1) Current Inc.

Tasty Way to Die. large type ed. Janet Lawrence. 464p. 1992. 25.99 (0-7089-2613-4) Ulverscroft.

Tat Tvam Asi - That Thou Art: The Path of Fire According to Asparsa-Yoga. Raphael. xiii, 122p. 1992. 12.95 (1-881338-20-7) Nataraj Bks.

Tata: A Voice from the Rio Puerco. Ed. by Nasario Garcia. LC 94-8241. (Historical Society of New Mexico Publications). (Illus.). 240p. 1994. 39.95 (0-8263-1519-4) U of NM Pr.

Tata: A Voice from the Rio Puerco. Ed. by Nasario Garcia. LC 94-8241. (Historical Society of New Mexico Publications). (Illus.). 240p. 1994. pap. 10.95 (0-8263-1520-8) U of NM Pr.

Tata Lecture Notes on Theta Functions, Vol. 1. David Mumford. (Progress in Mathematics Ser.: Vol.43). 220p. 1994. 40.50 (0-8176-3109-7) Birkhauser.

Tata Lecture Notes on Theta Functions, Vol. 2. David Mumford. (Progress in Mathematics Ser.: Vol.43). 200p. 1993. 42.50 (0-8176-3110-0) Birkhauser.

Tata Lectures on Theta III. D. Mumford et al. (Progress in Mathematics Ser.: Vol. 97). vii, 202p. 1991. 55.00 (0-8176-3440-1) Spr-Verlag.

Tatar English, English Tatar Concise Dictionary. Sergey Shakhmayev. 400p. (Orig.). 1994. pap. 11.95 (0-7818-0250-4) Hippocrene Bks.

Tatarische Etymologische Studien, No. II. Ed. by Arpad Berta. (Studia Uralo-altaica Ser.: Vol. 30). 283p. (Orig.). (GER.). 1988. pap. 58.00 (0-685-33595-X, Pub. by Attila Josef Univ HU) Benjamins North Am.

Tatars of Crimea: Their Struggle for Survival. Ed. by Edward Allworth. LC 87-33186. (Central Asia Book Ser.). (Illus.). xv, 396p. (C). 1988. text ed. 62.95 (0-8223-0758-8) Duke.

***Tatars of the Crimea: Return to the Homeland.** 2nd enl. rev. ed. Ed. by Edward Allworth. LC 97-19110. 384p. 1997. text ed. 55.95 (0-8223-1985-3); pap. text ed. 19.95 (0-8223-1994-2) Duke.

***Tatarstan Republic: Economy, Industry, Government, Business.** 2nd rev. ed. Russian Information & Business Center, Inc. Staff. (Russian Regional Business Directories Ser.). (Illus.). 200p. 1997. pap. 99.00 (1-57751-368-1) Russ Info & Busn Ctr.

***Tate: A Centenary History.** Frances Spalding. (Illus.). 272p. 1997. 50.00 (1-85437-231-9, Pub. by Tate Gallery UK) U of Wash Pr.

***Tate Cookbook.** Paul King et al. (Illus.). 128p. 1997. 29.95 (1-85437-191-6, Pub. by Tate Gallery UK) U of Wash Pr.

Tate Gallery St. Ives: The Building. David Shalev & Michael Tooby. (Illus.). 48p. (C). 1996. pap. 19.95 (1-85437-161-4, Pub. by Tate Gallery UK) U of Wash Pr.

Tate Williams: Reminiscences of a Son of Eureka Pioneers, a Reno Civic Leader, & Manager of the Nevada Retail Merchants Association. Intro. by Mary E. Glass. 65p. 1967. lib. bdg. 26.50 (1-56475-043-4); fiche write for info. (1-56475-044-2) U NV Oral Hist.

Tatemae & Honne: Good Form & Real Intention in Japanese Business Culture. Mitsubishi Corporation Staff. 225p. 1988. 24.95 (0-02-921591-9, Free Press) Free Pr.

***Taters of the Ozarks.** Deanna L. Harris. (Illus.). 76p. (Orig.). (J). 1997. pap. 5.00 (1-57502-415-2, P01283) Morris Pubng.

Tathagata Akshobhya & the Vajra Kula. Achyutanand Jh. (C). 1992. 68.50 (81-85821-01-1, Pub. by Aditya Prakashan II) S Asia.

Tathagata Akshobhya & the Vajra Kula: Studies in the Iconography of the Akshobhya Family. Achyutanand Jha. (Illus.). xxi, 150p. 1993. 39.95 (1-881338-36-3) Nataraj Bks.

Tatham Mound. Piers Anthony. 528p. 1992. mass mkt. 5.99 (0-380-71309-8) Avon.

Tatiani Oratio ad Graecos/Theophili Antiocheni ad Autolycum. Ed. by Miroslav Marcovich. (Patristische Texte und Studien: Vols. 43-44). (GRE.). (C). 1995. lib. bdg. 160.00 (3-11-014406-9) De Gruyter.

Tatian's Diatessaron: Its Creation, Dissemination, Significance, & History in Scholarship. William L. Petersen. LC 94-2883. (Supplements to Vigiliae Christianae Ser.: Vol. 25). 1994. 148.00 (90-04-09469-5) E J Brill.

Tatl'ahwt'aenn Nenn' The Headwaters People's Country. Ed. by James Kari et al. LC 85-72828. (Illus.). x, 219p. 1986. pap. 10.00 (1-55500-000-2) Alaska Native.

Tatler, 4 vols. Richard Steele & Joseph Addison. Ed. by George A. Aitken. (Anglistica & Americana Ser.: No. 100). 1734p. 1970. reprint ed. set. 193.70 (0-685-66222-5, 05103147) G Olms Pubs.

Tatler, 3 vols., Vol. 1. Richard Steele. Ed. by Donald F. Bond. 632p. 1987. 150.00 (0-19-812484-8) OUP.

Tatler, 3 vols., Vol. 2. Richard Steele. Ed. by Donald F. Bond. 560p. 1987. 140.00 (0-19-818533-2) OUP.

Tatler, 3 vols., Vol. 3. Richard Steele. Ed. by Donald F. Bond. 584p. 1987. 140.00 (0-19-818534-0) OUP.

Tatler & the Spectator. Addison. Date not set. text ed. 35.00 (0-312-16371-1) St Martin.

***Tatlin.** Ed. by Larissa A. Shadowa. Tr. by Hannelore Schmor-weichenhain from RUS. 569p. (GER.). (C). 1987. 118.00 (3-8170-2010-4, Pub. by Knstvrlag Weingrtn GW) Intl Bk Import.

Tatlin. O. Zhadova. (C). 1990. 400.00 (0-685-34340-5, Pub. by Collets) St Mut.

***Tatlin: Six Stories.** Guy Davenport. LC 81-48197. (Illus.). 271p. 1982. reprint ed. pap. 77.30 (0-608-04050-9, 2064786) Bks Demand.

Tatlin & the Russian Avant-Garde. C. Milner. (C). 1990. pap. 150.00 (0-685-34339-1, Pub. by Collets) St Mut.

***Tatnuck Bookseller's Totally Irreverent Cookbook.** Jack Corey & Larry Abramoff. 128p. (Orig.). 1997. pap. 6.99 (1-886284-07-5, Tatnuck) Databks.

Tator Tales: A Guide to Substance Abuse Prevention for Youth & Adults. Christine R. Gibson & J. Michael Hargrave. (Illus.). (Orig.). (J). (gr. 4-8). 1989. pap. write for info. (0-318-65796-1) Tator Enterprises.

Tator Tales: A Story & Activity Book on Handling Peer Pressure. Christine R. Gibson & J. Michael Hargrave. (Illus.). 51p. (J). (gr. 3-5). 1988. pap. 6.95 (0-9624285-0-7) Tator Enterprises.

Tator Tales: Cool Spuds Avoid Drugs, a Story & Activity Book on Substance Abuse Prevention. J. Michael Hargrave & Christine R. Gibson. (Illus.). 96p. (Orig.). (J). (gr. 4-8). 1990. pap. 8.95 (0-9624285-1-5) Tator Enterprises.

Tatsinda. Elizabeth Enright. Ed. by Allyn Johnston. (Illus.). 72p. (J). (ps-5). 1991. 17.00 (0-15-284280-2) HarBrace.

***Tatsinda.** Elizabeth Enright. (Illus.). 66p. (J). 4.98 (0-8317-0010-6) Smithmark.

Tatsuo Takayama. Tatsuo Takayama. LC 87-81683. (Illus.). 182p. 1988. 150.00 (0-87011-846-3) Kodansha.

***Tattawaprakasham, Vol. III.** K. Padmanabha Menon. 109p. 1997. pap. text ed. 17.00 (0-914793-23-3) Advaita Pubs.

***Tattawaprakasham, Vol. III.** K. Padmanabha Menon. 109p. 1997. text ed. 23.00 (0-914793-24-1) Advaita Pubs.

Tatted Baby Gift Set. JoAnn Stearns. 7p. 1990. pap. 4.95 (1-888837-02-0) Silver Shuttle.

Tatted Christening Set. JoAnn Stearns. 11p. 1990. pap. 4.95 (1-888837-04-7) Silver Shuttle.

Tatted Christmas Balls. JoAnn Stearns. 5p. 1990. pap. 4.95 (1-888837-06-3) Silver Shuttle.

Tatted Christmas Ornaments. JoAnn Stearns. 10p. 1990. pap. 4.95 (1-888837-05-5) Silver Shuttle.

Tatted Flowering Vines. JoAnn Stearns. 3p. 1990. pap. 3.95 (1-888837-03-9) Silver Shuttle.

Tatted Hearts. Jacquelyn Smyers. (Illus.). (Orig.). pap. write for info. (0-9615130-1-2) Very Idea.

Tatted Laces. JoAnn Stearns. 5p. 1990. pap. 3.95 (1-888837-01-2) Silver Shuttle.

Tatted Snowflakes. Vida Sunderman. (Illus.). 32p. (Orig.). 1994. pap. text ed. 3.50 (0-486-28303-8) Dover.

***Tattenhoe & Westbury Two Deserted Medieval Settlements in Milton Keynes.** Roberto Ivens et al. (Buckinghamshire Archaeological Society Monograph Ser.: No. 8). (Illus.). 505p. 1995. pap. 62.00 (0-949003-00-X, Pub. by Oxbow Bks UK) David Brown.

***Tatter Tails.** Patricia Edwards. (Illus.). 24p. 1997. pap. 7.00 (0-8059-4124-X) Dorrance.

Tattercoats. Margaret Greaves. LC 90-6919. (Illus.). 32p. (J). (ps-2). 1990. 13.95 (0-517-58026-8) Crown Bks Yng Read.

Tattered Banners: Labor, Conflict, & Corporatism in Postcommunist Russia. Walter D. Connor. 1996. text ed. 69.00 (0-8133-2911-6) Westview.

Tattered Banners: Labor, Conflict, & Corporatism in Postcommunist Russia. Walter D. Connor. (C). 1996. pap. text ed. 21.00 (0-8133-2912-4) Westview.

Tattered Loving. Angela Wells. (Presents Ser.: No. 462). 1992. pap. 2.89 (0-373-11462-1, 1-11462-8) Harlequin Bks.

Tattered Pages. Gyeorgos C. Hatonn. (The Phoenix Journals). 228p. 1993. pap. 6.00 (1-56935-009-4) Phoenix Source.

Tattered Tom. Horatio Alger, Jr. (Works of Horatio Alger Jr.). 1989. reprint ed. lib. bdg. 79.00 (0-7812-1710-5) Rprt Serv.

***Tattered Trust: Is There Hope for Your Denomination?** Lyle E. Schaller. LC 96-32846. (Ministry for the Third Millennium Ser.). 144p. 1997. pap. 12.95 (0-687-05740-X) Abingdon.

Tatterhood & Other Tales. Ed. & Intro. by Ethel J. Phelps. LC 78-9352. (Illus.). 192p. (Orig.). (J). (gr. 1 up). 1978. pap. 9.95 (0-912670-50-9) Feminist Pr.

Tatterhood & the Hobgoblins. Retold by Lauren Mills. (Illus.). 32p. (J). (ps-3). 1996. pap. text ed. 5.95 (0-316-57334-5) Little.

Tatterhood & the Hobgoblins: A Norwegian Folktale, Vol. 1. Retold by Lauren Mills. (Illus.). (J). (ps-3). 1993. 15.95 (0-316-57406-6) Little.

***Tatter's Treasure Chest.** Mary C. Waldrep. (Illus.). pap. 5.95 (0-486-26355-X) Dover.

Tattersall the Legend. Edward R. Watson & Dennis Newlyn. (Illus.). 256p. (Orig.). 1991. pap. 14.95 (0-9627653-1-7) Witness Prods.

Tatti Wattles: A Love Story. Rachel Rosenthal. (Illus.). 64p. 1997. 20.00 (0-9646426-9-7, 620242) Smart Art Pr.

Tatting. Cathy Bryant. (Illus.). 128p. 1992. 34.95 (0-7134-6554-9, Pub. by Batsford UK) Trafalgar.

Tatting. Elgiva Nicholls. (Knitting, Crocheting, Tatting Ser.). 144p. 1984. reprint ed. pap. 4.95 (0-486-24612-4) Dover.

Tatting: Designs from Victorian Lace Craft. 2nd ed. Ed. by Jules Kliot & Kaethe Kliot. 96p. 1994. pap. 10.00 (0-916896-59-5) Lacis Pubns.

Tatting: Patterns & Designs. Gun Blomqvist & Elwy Persson. 1990. 18.75 (0-8446-6392-1) Peter Smith.

***Tatting Butterflies.** Teri Dusenbury. (Illus.). 32p. (Orig.). 1997. pap. text ed. 3.95 (0-486-29665-2) Dover.

Tatting Doilies & Edgings. Rita Weiss. (Illus.). 50p. (Orig.). 1980. pap. 3.50 (0-486-24051-7) Dover.

Tatting Goes West. JoAnn Stearns. 8p. 1995. pap. 3.95 (1-888837-09-8) Silver Shuttle.

Tatting Hearts. Teri Dusenbury. LC 94-17257. (Needlework Ser.). (Illus.). 32p. (Orig.). 1994. pap. 3.50 (0-486-28071-3) Dover.

Tatting Patterns. Julia E. Sanders. 1978. pap. 2.95 (0-486-23554-8) Dover.

***Tatting Patterns & Designs.** Gun Blomqvist & Elwy Persson. (Illus.). pap. 5.95 (0-486-25813-0) Dover.

Tatting with Anne Orr. Anne Orr. (J). 1989. pap. 2.50 (0-486-25982-X) Dover.

Tatting with Visual Patterns. Mary Konior. 1992. 30.00 (0-916896-42-0) Lacis Pubns.

Tattle-Tales of Cupid. Paul L. Ford. LC 70-94720. (Short Story Index Reprint Ser.). 1977. 19.95 (0-8369-3099-1) Ayer.

Tattle Tales of Cupid. Paul L. Ford. (Notable American Authors Ser.). 1992. reprint ed. lib. bdg. 75.00 (0-7812-2875-1) Rprt Serv.

***Tattles on the Terrace.** Paddy Murphy. 705p. (Orig.). 1997. mass mkt. 5.99 (1-55197-781-8, Pub. by Comnwlth Pub CN) Partners Pubs Grp.

Tattletale Sparkie. Lucy A. Conley. (J). (gr. 3 up). 1983. 7.70 (0-318-01337-1) Rod & Staff.

Tattletale Tongue. Barbara Davoll. (J). 1990. 8.99 (0-89693-537-X, 6-1537, Victor Bks) Chariot Victor.

Tattletale Tongue. Barbara Davoll. (J). 1990. audio 11.99 (0-89693-138-2, 3-2138, Victor Bks) Chariot Victor.

Tattlin' Madeline. Carol Cummings. (Learn with Me Ser.). (Illus.). 24p. (Orig.). (J). (ps-3). 1991. pap. 4.99 (0-9614574-4-9) Teaching WA.

Tattoo. Dale Banks. 352p. 1995. mass mkt. 4.99 (0-7860-0169-0, Pinncle Kensgtn) Kensgtn Pub Corp.

***Tattoo.** Anthony Britto. LC 96-45540. 1997. 24.95 (0-312-15220-5) Thomas Dunne Bks.

Tattoo. Intro. by Jack Cady & Colleen McElroy. 1978. pap. 6.25 (0-931594-01-4) Circinatum Pr.

***Tattoo.** Lauri Emswiler. 240p. (Orig.). 1998. mass mkt. 7.99 (1-58006-001-3, Appaloosa) Sovereign.

Tattoo. Earl Thompson. 704p. 1991. pap. 6.95 (0-88184-727-5) Carroll & Graf.

***Tattoo.** Earl Thompson. 6.95 (0-7867-0727-5) Carroll & Graf.

Tattoo Book: Fantasy. (J). 1996. pap. 5.99 (0-689-80926-3, S&S Bks Young Read) S&S Childrens.

Tattoo Book: Monsters. (J). 1996. pap. 5.99 (0-689-80927-1, S&S Bks Young Read) S&S Childrens.

Tattoo Book of Days: Past, Present & Future. Lyle Tuttle. Ed. by William Demichele. (Illus.). 64p. 1996. pap. 20.00 (0-9631708-4-8) Proteus NY.

Tattoo Buyer's Guide: A Complete & Candid Guide to Getting a Great Tattoo. Paul Schwartz. (Illus.). 57p. (Orig.). 1993. pap. 6.95 (0-9635778-0-8) Alter Ego Pr.

Tattoo Flash. Donald E. Hardy. (Illus.). 74p. (Orig.). 1990. pap. text ed. 80.00 (0-945367-06-6) Hardy Marks Pubns.

***Tattoo Murder Case.** Akimitsu Takagi. 1997. 22.00 (1-56947-108-8) Soho Press.

Tattoo of Death. Raymond A. Montgomery. (Choose Your Own Adventure Ser.: No. 159). 128p. (J). (gr. 4-7). 1995. pap. 3.50 (0-553-56616-4) Bantam.

Tattoo the Wicked Cross. Floyd Salas. LC 81-80895. 352p. 1982. 22.00 (0-933256-26-4); pap. text ed. 16.00 (0-933256-27-2) Second Chance.

Tattoo, Torture, Mutilation, & Adornment: The Denaturalization of the Body in Culture & Text. Ed. by Frances E. Mascia-Lees & Patricia Sharpe. LC 91-21296. (SUNY Series, The Body in Culture, History, & Religion). 172p. 1992. text ed. 59.50 (0-7914-1065-X); pap. text ed. 21.95 (0-7914-1066-8) State U NY Pr.

Tattoo You ! Barbara Klunder. (Illus.). 24p. (J). (gr. k up). 1996. pap. 7.95 (0-8431-7993-7) Price Stern Sloan.

***Tattoo You: Aquarius.** Ladybird Books Staff. Date not set. pap. 4.99 (0-7214-5734-7, Ladybrd) Penguin.

***Tattoo You: Aries.** Ladybird Books Staff. Date not set. pap. 4.99 (0-7214-5724-X, Ladybrd) Penguin.

***Tattoo You: Cancer.** Ladybird Books Staff. Date not set. pap. 4.99 (0-7214-5727-4, Ladybrd) Penguin.

***Tattoo You: Capricorn.** Ladybird Books Staff. Date not set. pap. 4.99 (0-7214-5733-9, Ladybrd) Penguin.

***Tattoo You: Gemini.** Ladybird Books Staff. Date not set. pap. 4.99 (0-7214-5726-6, Ladybrd) Penguin.

***Tattoo You: Leo.** Ladybird Books Staff. Date not set. pap. 4.99 (0-7214-5728-2, Ladybrd) Penguin.

***Tattoo You: Libra.** Ladybird Books Staff. Date not set. pap. 4.99 (0-7214-5730-4, Ladybrd) Penguin.

***Tattoo You: Pisces.** Joan Powers. Date not set. pap. 4.99 (0-7214-5735-5, Ladybrd) Penguin.

***Tattoo You: Sagittarius.** Ladybird Books Staff. Date not set. pap. 4.99 (0-7214-5732-0, Ladybrd) Penguin.

***Tattoo You: Scorpio.** Ladybird Books Staff. Date not set. pap. 4.99 (0-7214-5731-2, Ladybrd) Penguin.

***Tattoo You: Taurus.** Ladybird Books Staff. Date not set. pap. 4.99 (0-7214-5725-8, Ladybrd) Penguin.

***Tattoo You: Virgo.** Ladybird Books Staff. Date not set. pap. 4.99 (0-7214-5729-0, Ladybrd) Penguin.

Tattoo'd with Attitude. Steve Bonge. (Illus.). 128p. 1995. pap. 19.95 (0-86369-935-9, Pub. by Virgin Pub UK) London Brdge.

Tattooed Cat: Where Cats & Tattoos Meet. Steven Wood. (Illus.). 96p. (Orig.). 1993. pap. 12.95 (0-9610330-6-1) J Tabler-Bks.

Tattooed Countess. Carl Van Vechten. LC 77-78307. 296p. reprint ed. 37.50 (0-404-15127-2) AMS Pr.

Tattooed Countess. Carl Van Vechten. LC 87-19237. (Bur Oak Bk.). 320p. 1987. reprint ed. pap. 12.95 (0-87745-186-9) U of Iowa Pr.

Tattooed Desert. Richard Shelton. LC 76-134489. (Pitt Poetry Ser.). 82p. reprint ed. pap. 25.00 (0-8357-9761-9, 2015446) Bks Demand.

Tattooed Heart of the Drunken Sailor. Ivan Arguelles. 26p. (Orig.). 1983. pap. 4.00 (0-941160-07-6) Ghost Pony Pr.

Tattooed in the Cradle: The Healing Journey from Family to Spiritual Wholeness. Lamont R. Satterly. 300p. (Orig.). 1993. pap. 11.95 (0-9636686-0-9) Search Fnd.

Tattooed Innocent & the Raunchy Grandmother: An Adult Fairy Tale, Quite Grim. Robert F. Cline. LC 81-69430. 192p. (Orig.). 1983. pap. 7.95 (0-9607082-0-0) Argos House.

Tattooed Loverboy & Other Drawings. Paul LeChien. (Illus.). 62p. (Orig.). 1992. pap. 25.00 (1-873741-03-0, Pub. by Millvres Bks UK) LPC InBook.

An Asterisk (*) at the beginning of an entry indicates that the title is appearing in BIP for the first time.

Tattooed Man. large type ed. T. C. Jacobs. 1971. 25.99 (*0-85456-078-5*) Ulverscroft.

Tattooed Map: A Novel. Barbara Hodgson. LC 94-40729. (Illus.). 120p. 1995. 17.95 (*0-8118-0817-3*) Chronicle Bks.

Tattooed on Their Tongues: A Journey Through the Backrooms of American Music. Colin Escott. 256p. 1996. 25.00 (*0-02-870679-X*) Schirmer Bks.

Tattooed Torah. Marvell Ginsburg. (Illus.). 32p. (J). (gr. k-3). 1994. 10.95 (*0-8074-0252-4*, 104030) UAHC.

***Tattooed Woman.** Carolyn E. Campbell. 128p. (Orig.). 1996. pap. 11.95 (*1-888219-05-X*) Pearl Edit.

Tattooed Women. Chris Wroblewski. (Illus.). 128p. 1992. pap. 19.95 (*0-86369-524-8*, Pub. by W H Allen UK) Carol Pub Group.

Tattooing A to Z: A Guide to Successful Tattooing. Huck Spaulding. (Illus.). 141p. 1988. 45.00 (*0-929719-00-X*) Spaulding & Rogers.

Tattooing in the Marquesas. Willowdean C. Handy. (BMB Ser.). 1974. reprint ed. 25.00 (*0-527-02104-0*) Periodicals Srv.

Tattooists. Albert L. Morse. Ed. by John A. Walsh. (Illus.). 1977. 100.00 (*0-918320-01-1*) A L Morse.

***Tattoos.** Ariel Books Staff. 1996. 4.95 (*0-8362-1523-0*, Arie Bks) Andrews & McMeel.

Tattva-Sandarbha: Sacred India's Philosophy of Ecstasy. B. V. Tripurari. 120p. 1996. 19.95 (*1-886069-12-3*) Clarion Call.

Tattvabindu by Vacaspatimisra with Tattvavibhavana by Rsiputra Paramesvara. Ed. by V. A. Sastri. 1991. 36.00 (*81-7013-091-3*, Pub. by Navrang) S Asia.

Tattvarthadhigama Sutra (A Treatise on the Essential Principles of Jainism) Umasvati. Ed. & Intro. by J. L. Jaini. LC 73-3836. (Sacred Books of the Jainas: No. 2). reprint ed. 41.25 (*0-404-57702-4*) AMS Pr.

Tattvasangraha with the Commentary of Kamalashila, 2 vols. Shantaraksita. Tr. by Ganganath Jha. 1986. reprint ed. Set. 100.00 (*0-685-35379-6*, Pub. by Motilal Banarsidass II) S Asia.

Tattvasangraha with the Commentary of Kamalashila, 2 vols., Vol. 1 xi. Shantaraksita. Tr. by Ganganath Jha. 740p. 1986. reprint ed. write for info. (*81-208-0059-1*, Pub. by Motilal Banarsidass II) S Asia.

Tattvasangraha with the Commentary of Kamalashila, 2 vols., Vol. 2 xi. Shantaraksita. Tr. by Ganganath Jha. 741p. 1986. reprint ed. write for info. (*81-208-0060-5*, Pub. by Motilal Banarsidass II) S Asia.

***Tattwaprakasham.** K. Padmanabha Menon. 149p. 1997. pap. text ed. 18.00 (*0-914793-19-5*) Advaita Pubs.

***Tattwaprakasham.** K. Padmanabha Menon. 149p. 1997. text ed. 25.00 (*0-914793-20-9*) Advaita Pubs.

***Tattwaprakasham, Vol. II.** K. Padmanabha Menon. 99p. 1997. pap. text ed. 16.00 (*0-914793-21-7*) Advaita Pubs.

***Tattwaprakasham, Vol. II.** K. Padmanabha Menon. 99p. 1997. text ed. 22.00 (*0-914793-22-5*) Advaita Pubs.

Tattybogle. Sandra Horn. (Illus.). 32p. (J). 1995. 13.95 (*0-86264-596-4*, Pub. by Anderson Pr UK) London Bridge.

***Tatyana's Golden Doe: A Musical.** Kate Paxton. (Orig.). (J). 1998. pap. 5.50 (*0-87602-363-4*) Anchorage.

Tau: Its Origin & Symbolic Use in Royal Arch Masonry. J. Cooper Malcolm. 1990. pap. 6.95 (*1-55818-173-3*, Sure Fire) Holmes Pub.

Tau Lepton Physics: Proceedings of the Second International Workshop. K. K. Gan. 588p. 1993. text ed. 130.00 (*981-02-1289-5*) World Scientific Pub.

TAU-P: A Plane Wave Approach to the Analysis of Seismic Data. Ed. by Paul L. Stoffa. (C). 1989. lib. bdg. 154.50 (*0-7923-0038-6*) Kluwer Ac.

Tauberian Theorems for Generalized Functions. V. S. Vladimirov et al. (C). 1988. lib. bdg. 167.00 (*90-277-2383-4*) Kluwer Ac.

Tauberian Theory & Its Applications. Ed. by A. G. Postnikov. LC 80-23821. (Proceedings of the Steklov Institute of Mathematics Ser.: No. 144). 138p. 1980. pap. 47.00 (*0-8218-3048-1*, STEKLO/144) Am Math.

Tauchnitz International Editions in English 1841-1955: A Bibliographical History. William B. Todd & Ann Bowden. LC 88-4332. (Illus.). 1088p. 1988. 75.00 (*0-914930-12-5*, 28583) Biblio Soc Am.

Taught by the Spirit. Ron Auch. LC 90-64184. 232p. (Orig.). 1991. pap. 8.95 (*0-89221-191-1*) New Leaf.

Taught Not Caught. Deakin University Press Staff. 128p. (C). 1986. 75.00 (*0-7300-0403-1*, Pub. by Deakin Univ AT) St Mut.

Taulbee's International Pocket Companion: International GLPs in Parallel. Ed. by Stephanie M. Taulbee & Robert S. DeWoskin. 118p. 1994. pap. 29.00 (*0-935184-86-4*) Interpharm.

Taulbee's Pocket Companion: U. S. FDA & EPA GLPs in Parallel. Ed. by Stephanie M. Taulbee & Robert S. DeWoskin. 1993. pap. 29.00 (*0-935184-87-2*) Interpharm.

***Tauler.** Deutschen Akademie der Wissenschaften Staff & Ferdinand Vetter. (Deutsche Texte des Mittelalters Ser.: Band XI). xx, 518p. (GER.). 1968. write for info. (*3-296-17211-4*, Pub. by Weidmann GW) Lubrecht & Cramer.

Taungya: Forest Plantations with Agriculture in Southeast Asia. Carl F. Jordan et al. 168p. 1992. 60.00 (*0-85198-801-6*) CAB Intl.

Taunton's Fine Homebuilding Index: Issues 1-85. 204p. 1994. pap. 14.95 (*1-56158-074-0*) Taunton.

***Taunton's Fine Woodworking Index: Issues 1-120.** Harriet Hodges. LC 97-3607. 272p. 1997. 12.95 (*1-56158-215-8*) Taunton.

TAUP 91: Proceedings of the Second International Workshop on Theoretical & Phenomenological Aspects of Underground Physics, Toledo, Spain, 9-13 September 1991. Ed. by A. Morales et al. LC 92-25597. 1992. 207.00 (*0-444-89769-0*, North Holland) Elsevier.

Taureau Blanc. Francois-Marie De Voltaire. Ed. by Rene Pomeau. 171p. (FRE.). 1957. pap. 12.95 (*0-7859-5516-X*) Fr & Eur.

Taurhievel Domain Sourcebook. D. Maxwell & S. Miller. 1996. 7.95 (*0-7869-0398-8*) TSR Inc.

Taurine: Nutritional Value & Mechanisms of Action. Ed. by J. B. Lombardini et al. (Advances in Experimental Medicine & Biology Ser.: Vol. 315). (Illus.). 402p. (C). 1992. 120.00 (*0-306-44224-8*, Plenum Pr) Plenum.

Taurine & the Heart. Ed. by H. Iwata et al. (Developments in Cardiovascular Medicine Ser.). 192p. 1988. lib. bdg. 116.00 (*0-89838-396-X*) Kluwer Ac.

Taurine in Health & Disease. Ed. by Ryan Huxtable & D. Michalk. (Advances in Experimental Medicine & Biology Ser.). (Illus.). 444p. 1994. 120.00 (*0-306-44812-2*, Plenum Pr) Plenum.

***Taurine 2: Basic & Clinical Aspects.** International Society for Neurochemistry Staff. Ed. by Ryan J. Huxtable et al. LC 96-32064. (Advances in Experimental Medicine & Biology Ser.: Vol. 403). 650p. 1996. 139.50 (*0-306-45385-1*) Plenum.

Tauris Directory of Russia & the Republics: A Who's Who of the New Elite. Ed. by Lennard Geron. 700p. 1992. text ed. 185.00 (*0-685-66182-2*, Pub. by I B Tauris UK) St Martin.

Tauris Soviet Directory: The Elite of the U. S. S. R. Today. Ed. by Alex Pravda. 700p. 1990. text ed. 185.00 (*1-85043-090-X*) St Martin.

Tauro: Astro-Numerogia. Michael J. Kurban. Tr. by Loretta H. Kurban from ENG. LC 86-91268. (Illus.). (Orig.). (SPA.). 1992. pap. 8.00 (*0-938863-46-0*) Libra Press Chi.

Tauromaquia A-Z: Diccionario Enciclopedico de la Historia, la Tecnica, del Arte, 2 vols. M. Ortiz Blasco. 1614p. (SPA.). 1993. 425.00 (*0-7859-9235-9*) Fr & Eur.

Tauromaquia A-Z: Diccionario Enciclopedico de la Historia la Tecnica y la Cultura Del Arte Del Toreo, 2 vols., Set. M. Ortiz Blasco. (Illus.). 1614p. (SPA.). 1993. 450.00 (*84-239-5888-4*) Elliots Bks.

Tauromaquia & the Bulls of Bordeaux. Francisco Goya. LC 69-15666. (Illus.). 1969. pap. 9.95 (*0-486-22342-6*) Dover.

Taurus. (Super Horoscopes, 1995 Ser.). 256p. 1994. pap. text ed. 4.99 (*0-7865-0027-1*) Diamond.

Taurus. (Total Horoscopes, 1995 Ser.). 272p. 1994. pap. text ed. 4.50 (*0-515-11412-X*) Jove Pubns.

Taurus. (Love Signs Library). 64p. 1996. 8.95 (*0-7894-1090-7*) DK Pub Inc.

***Taurus.** (Parker's Love Signs Ser.). 1996. 8.95 (*0-614-20710-X*) DK Pub Inc.

***Taurus.** (Astrology Journals). (Illus.). 80p. 1997. pap. 6.50 (*1-55670-569-7*) Stewart Tabori & Chang.

***Taurus.** (Fisher-Price Little People Coloring & Activity Ser.). (Illus.). 24p. 1997. pap. write for info. (*1-56144-961-X*, Honey Bear Bks) Modern Pub NYC.

***Taurus.** Ariel Books Staff. (Tiny Tomes Ser.). 128p. 1997. 3.95 (*0-8362-2672-0*, Arie Bks) Andrews & McMeel.

***Taurus.** Berkley Publishing Staff. (Berkley Super Horoscopes Ser.). 256p. 1997. pap. 6.99 (*0-425-15887-X*) Berkley Pub.

Taurus. Lucille Callard. (Astro-Pups: Your Sign, Your Dogs Ser.). (Illus.). 60p. 1991. pap. 9.95 (*1-881038-01-7*) Penzance Pr.

***Taurus.** Jove Publications Incorporated, Staff. (Total Horoscopes Ser.). 272p. 1997. mass mkt. 5.99 (*0-515-12109-6*) Jove Pubns.

Taurus. Derek Parker & Julia Parker. LC 92-52785. (Sun & Moon Signs Library). (Illus.). 64p. 1992. 8.95 (*1-56458-085-7*) DK Pub Inc.

Taurus. Kathleen Paul. (Sun Sign Ser.). 40p. (J). (gr. 4). 1989. lib. bdg. 13.95 (*0-88682-257-2*) Creative Ed.

***Taurus: A Little Book of Zodiac Wisdom, a Pop-Up Book.** Running Press Staff. (Zodiac Wisdom Ser.). 1997. 4.95 (*0-7624-0032-3*) Running Pr.

Taurus: Astro-Numerology. 2nd ed. Michael J. Kurban. (Illus.). 50p. 1991. pap. 8.00 (*0-938863-10-X*) Libra Press Chi.

Taurus: Little Birth Sign. 1994. 4.95 (*0-8362-3079-5*) Andrews & McMeel.

***Taurus: Old Moore's Horoscopes & Astral Diaries.** W. Foulsham & Co. Staff. 1997. pap. text ed. 5.95 (*0-572-02352-9*, Pub. by W Foulsham UK) Trans-Atl Phila.

***Taurus: Your Sun-&-Moon Guide to Love & Life.** Ariel Books Staff. 374p. (Orig.). 1997. pap. 5.95 (*0-8362-3566-5*, Arie Bks) Andrews & McMeel.

Taurus Gun. Lauran Paine. 192p. 1989. 18.95 (*0-8027-4086-3*) Walker & Co.

Taurus Method. 2nd ed. Michael Chisholm. 1985. 75.00 (*0-930233-08-5*) Windsor.

Taurus Rising. Douglas M. Baker. (Esoteric Astrology: The Rising Signs Ser.). 1978. pap. 7.50 (*0-906006-30-9*, Pub. by Baker Pubns UK) New Leaf Dist.

Taurus Sun Sign. Douglas M. Baker. (Astrological Sun Sign Ser.). 1972. pap. 5.50 (*0-906006-18-X*, Pub. by Baker Pubns UK) New Leaf Dist.

Taurus 1994 Purse Book. 1994. mass mkt. 1.25 (*0-440-60221-1*) Dell.

Taurus 1995 Love Signs. 1995. mass mkt. 1.29 (*0-440-22121-8*) Dell.

Taurus 1995 Purse Book. 1994. mass mkt. 0.99 (*0-440-60230-0*) Dell.

Taurus 1996 Purse Book. 1995. mass mkt. 1.19 (*0-440-60247-5*) Dell.

Taurus 97. Sydney Omarr. 1996. pap. 4.99 (*0-451-18838-1*, Sig) NAL-Dutton.

Tausend Redensarten Deutsch. R. Quinalt & Langenscheidt Editorial Staff. 248p. 1981. 20.00 (*3-468-43112-0*) Langenscheidt.

Tausend und Einen Nacht Noch Nicht Ubersetzte Mahrchen, Erzahlungen und Anekdoten, 3 vols. Joseph F. Von Hammer-Purgstall. (Volkskundliche Quellen Ser.: No. III). lvi, 1116p. 1976. reprint ed. Set. write for info. (*3-487-06097-3*) G Olms Pubs.

Tausug: Violence & Law in a Philippine Moslem Society. Thomas M. Kiefer. (Illus.). 150p. (C). 1986. reprint ed. pap. text ed. 9.95 (*0-88133-242-9*) Waveland Pr.

Tau'Tevu. N. Whallen. (Orig.). 1996. mass mkt. 5.95 (*1-56333-426-7*) Masquerade.

Tavern in a Box. Dale Zaklad. (Illus.). 118p. 1986. teacher ed. 250.00 (*0-9616415-3-3*) Fraunces Tavern.

Tavern in the Town. Margaret Shea. (American Autobiography Ser.). 215p. 1995. reprint ed. lib. bdg. 79.00 (*0-7812-8636-0*) Rprt Serv.

Tavern in the Town: Early Inns & Taverns of Ontario. Margaret McBurney & Mary Byers. (Illus.). 259p. 1987. 35.00 (*0-8020-5732-2*) U of Toronto Pr.

Tavern Lamps Are Burning: Literary Journeys Through Six Regions & Four Centuries of New York. rev. ed. Ed. by Carl Carmer. (Illus.). xx, 567p. 1996. reprint ed. 35.00 (*0-8232-1697-7*); reprint ed. pap. 19.95 (*0-8232-1698-5*) Fordham.

Tavern on the Green Cookbook. L. Warner & M. Hodgson. Date not set. write for info. (*0-517-70498-6*) Random.

Tavern Signs of America: History--Complement to Tavern Signs of America Catalog Series. Helene Smith. Ed. by George Swetnam. LC 88-62557. (Illus.). 112p. (Orig.). 1989. pap. 19.95 (*0-945437-02-1*) MacDonald-Sward.

Tavern Signs of America Catalog: Complement to Tavern Signs of America History. Helene Smith. Ed. by George Swetnam. LC 87-91280. (Illus.). 52p. (Orig.). 1988. pap. 17.95 (*0-945437-01-3*) MacDonald-Sward.

Tavern Tales. Alvin Roberts. LC 91-77387. 78p. 1993. pap. 7.00 (*1-56002-143-8*) Aegina Pr.

Tavernacle Sermons: Prose Poems. Mather T. Schneider. 126p. (Orig.). 1996. pap. 10.00 (*0-9652195-0-X*) OBanan Pr.

Taverner Novels: Armed with Madness & Death of Felicity Taverner. Mary Butts. LC 91-32693. (Recovered Classics Ser.). 384p. (Orig.). 1992. 25.00 (*0-929701-17-8*); pap. 15.00 (*0-929701-18-6*) McPherson & Co.

Taverns of Cumberland County Pennsylvania 1750-1840. Merri Lou Schaumann. (Illus.). 200p. 34.95 (*0-9638923-1-2*) Cumberlnd Cnty Hist.

Tavi Bear & the Musical Alphabet. Effie A. Harris. (Illus.). 20p. (Orig.). (J). 1993. pap. write for info. (*1-56167-149-5*) Am Literary Pr.

Taviani: Poetry of the Italian Landscape. Riccardo Ferrucci. 1996. 39.95 (*88-7301-052-0*) Natl Bk Netwk.

***Tawdry Place of Salvation: The Art of Jane Bowles.** Ed. by Jennie Skerl. LC 96-43454. 240p. 1997. 34.95 (*0-8093-2100-9*) S Ill U Pr.

***Tawdry Place of Salvation: The Art of Jane Bowles.** Jennie Skerl. LC 96-43454. 1997. pap. write for info. (*0-8093-2121-1*) Southern Illinois Univ at Edwardsville.

Tawhid: Its Implications for Thought & Life. rev. ed. Isma'il Raji al Faruqi. (Issues of Islamic Thought Ser.: No. 3). 367p. (Orig.). 1991. pap. text ed. 8.95 (*0-912463-80-5*) IIIT VA.

Tawhid: Its Implications for Thought & Life. 2nd rev. ed. Isma'il Raji al Faruqi. (Issues of Islamic Thought Ser.: No. 3). 367p. (Orig.). 1991. text ed. 15.00 (*0-912463-79-1*) IIIT VA.

***Tawhid & Science: Essays on the History & Philosophy of Islamic Science.** Osman Bakar. 266p. 1996. pap. 18.00 (*0-614-21612-5*, 1217) Kazi Pubns.

Tawil al-Ahadith. Shah Waliyullah. 105p. (C). 1985. pap. text ed. 10.50 (*1-56744-400-8*) Kazi Pubns.

Tawny Gold Man. Amii Lorin. 256p. 1993. mass mkt., pap. text ed. 4.99 (*0-505-51919-4*, Love Spell) Dorchester Pub Co.

Tawny Scrawny Lion. Golden Books Staff. (Little Golden Bks.). (Illus.). 24p. (J). (ps-2). 1995. 1.49 (*0-307-02168-8*, Golden Pr) Western Pub.

Tax: One Payment. Little. 1995. 1,595.00 (*0-316-52807-2*) Little.

Tax Abatement. Gary Conley. Ed. by Stephanie Sampson. 12p. (Orig.). 1982. pap. 9.00 (*0-317-04833-3*) Natl Coun Econ Dev.

Tax Accounting, 2 vols. Durkwood Alkire. 1982. Updates. ring bd. write for info. (*0-8205-1703-8*) Bender.

Tax Accounting for Small Business: How to Prepare Tax Form 1040C. Joseph Gelb. (Illus.). 32p. (Orig.). 1996. pap. 14.95 (*0-9631289-7-3*) Career Advan.

Tax Accounting Methods: Characteristics, Adoptions, Changes. Davenport. 592p. 1988. 45.00 (*0-685-67039-2*, 5260) Commerce.

Tax Act: Investment Strategies after the New Tax Act. Martin M. Shenkman. 289p. 1994. pap. text ed. 14.95 (*0-471-01699-3*) Wiley.

***Tax Administration: Audit Trends & Results for Individual Taxpayers.** (Illus.). 34p. (Orig.). (C). 1996. pap. 25.00 (*0-7881-3612-7*) DIANE Pub.

Tax Administration: Compliance Measures & Audits of Large Corporations Need Improvement. (Illus.). 201p. (Orig.). (C). 1995. pap. text ed. 40.00 (*0-7881-1703-3*) DIANE Pub.

***Tax Administration: Compliance Measures & Audits of Large Corporations Need Improvement.** (Illus.). 202p. 1994. pap. text ed. 60.00 (*1-57979-129-8*) BPI Info Servs.

Tax Administration: IRS Can Strengthen Its Efforts to See That Taxpayers Are Treated Properly. (Illus.). 59p. (Orig.). (C). 1995. pap. text ed. 20.00 (*0-7881-2236-3*) DIANE Pub.

Tax Administration: IRS' Efforts to Improve Corporate Compliance. (Illus.). 40p. (Orig.). (C). 1993. pap. text ed. 20.00 (*1-56806-961-8*) DIANE Pub.

***Tax Administration: IRS' Partnership Compliance Activities Could Be Improved.** Ralph Block & Rodney Hobbs. (Illus.). 33p. (C). 1996. reprint ed. pap. 20.00 (*0-7881-3273-3*) DIANE Pub.

Tax Administration: State Tax Administrators' Views on Delinquent Tax Collection Methods. (Illus.). 54p. (Orig.). (C). 1995. pap. text ed. 20.00 (*0-7881-2297-5*) DIANE Pub.

***Tax Administration: State Tax Administrators' Views on Delinquent Tax Collection Methods.** (Illus.). 54p. 1994. pap. text ed. 30.00 (*1-57979-090-9*) BPI Info Servs.

***Tax Administration: Trends for Certain IRS Programs.** (Illus.). 130p. (C). 1996. reprint ed. pap. 30.00 (*0-7881-3416-7*) DIANE Pub.

Tax Advisory Board Roundtable Discussion: A First Look at Clinton's Tax Proposals. 48p. 1993. pap. 10.00 (*0-685-67040-6*, 5413) Commerce.

Tax & Business Planning of Limited Liability Companies. Carter G. Bishop & Daniel S. Kleinberger. 1993. ring bd. 175.00 (*0-685-69541-7*, TBUS) Warren Gorham & Lamont.

***Tax & EC Harmonization.** Lier. 1993. pap. text ed. 71.00 (*90-6544-709-1*) Kluwer Ac.

Tax & Financial Planning for Medical Practitioners. 3rd ed. Nigel Eastaway & Stephen Burwood. 252p. 1993. pap. text ed. 80.00 (*0-406-00897-3*, UK) MICHIE.

Tax & Financial Planning for Professional Partnerships. 3rd ed. Nigel Eastaway & Brian Gilligan. 329p. 1994. pap. text ed. 66.00 (*0-406-02303-4*, UK) MICHIE.

Tax & Financial Planning for the Elderly. 97th ed. Jurinski. 1997. pap. text ed. 79.00 (*0-15-601911-6*) HarBrace.

Tax & Financial Planning Strategies in Divorce. 2nd ed. Bruce L. Richman. 1996. 125.00 (*0-471-13975-0*) Wiley.

Tax & Interest Tables, 1988-89. Rodney Nelson-Jones & Graeme Nuttall. (Illus.). 80p. (C). 1988. 100.00 (*1-85190-047-0*, Pub. by Fourmat Pub UK) St Mut.

Tax & Legal Aspects see **Asset Protection Strategies**

Tax & Marriage. Anne Mccaffrey. 1995. 125.00 (*0-316-55336-0*) Little.

Tax & Remuneration Strategies. Ian Luder & Patricia Mock. 275p. 1994. boxed 154.00 (*0-406-02801-X*, UK) MICHIE.

Tax & the Farmer. Shaw & Sons Ltd. Staff. 1988. 100.00 (*0-7219-1160-9*, Pub. by Scientific UK) St Mut.

Tax-Appraisal Strategy: What You Don't Know Can Hurt You. J. Willis Judkins, Sr. LC 95-90779. (Orig.). 1996. pap. 11.95 (*0-533-11707-0*) Vantage.

Tax Aspects of California Partnerships - Forming, Dissolving, Terminating: April 1994 Update. L. Randolph Harris et al. Ed. by Cherri Allison. LC 83-72279. 170p. 1994. pap. text ed. 40.00 (*0-88124-729-4*, TX-37748) Cont Ed Bar-CA.

Tax Aspects of Divorce & Separation. Robert S. Taft. LC 83-26825. 1984. ring bd. 90.00 (*0-318-01110-7*) NY Law Pub.

Tax Aspects of Forming & Operating Closely Held Corporations. J. Clifton Fleming, Jr. LC 83-20291. (Tax & Estate Planning Ser.). 700p. 1984. text ed. 135.00 (*0-07-021298-8*) Shepards.

Tax Aspects of Litigation & Settlements. Sandy Kasten & Brad Seligman. 1989. 130.00 (*0-685-30643-7*) Clark Boardman Callaghan.

Tax Aspects of Marital Dissolution. Harold G. Wren et al. 1992. 125.00 (*0-685-14400-3*) Clark Boardman Callaghan.

Tax Aspects of Marital Dissolution. annuals Harold G. Wren et al. 1992. suppl. ed. write for info. (*0-318-61036-1*) Clark Boardman Callaghan.

Tax Aspects of Property & Casualty Risk Management. Keith C. Kakacek & Adams. 128p. (Orig.). 1987. pap. 15.00 (*0-318-33150-0*, 5268) Commerce.

Tax Aspects of Real Estate Investments: A Practical Guide for Structuring Real Estate Transactions, 2 vols. Peter M. Fass et al. (Taxation Ser.). 1987. Set. ring bd. 240.00 (*0-87632-576-2*, RC) Clark Boardman Callaghan.

Tax Audit Guide. 1991. lib. bdg. 250.00 (*0-8490-4454-5*) Gordon Pr.

Tax Audit Guidelines-A Self-Study Course: Continuing Professional Education Credits-Self Study Course-Worth 12 CPE Credits. 216p. 1995. pap. 81.35 (*1-57402-322-5*) Athena Info Mgt.

Tax Audit Guidelines for Individuals, Partnerships, Estates & Trusts, & Corporations: Internal Revenue Manual (4233) 75p. 1995. pap. 27.50 (*1-57402-317-9*) Athena Info Mgt.

Tax Audit Guidelines for Internal Revenue Examiners: As Issued by the Internal Revenue Service, April 23, 1985. United States Internal Revenue Service Staff. LC 85-236068. (Illus.). 1985. 8.00 (*0-13-884768-1*) P-H.

Tax Audit Guidelines for Internal Revenue Examiners: Internal Revenue Manual (4231) 188p. 1995. pap. 49.93 (*1-57402-314-4*) Athena Info Mgt.

Tax Audit Manual. 2nd ed. B. A. Palkhivala. (C). 1989. 460.00 (*0-685-36450-X*) St Mut.

Tax Auditor. Jack Rudman. (Career Examination Ser.: C-2313). 1994. reprint ed. pap. 29.95 (*0-8373-2313-4*) Nat Learn.

Tax Avoidance, Tax Evasion. International Fiscal Association Staff. LC 83-214098. 644p. 1983. 91.00 (*90-6544-123-9*) Kluwer Law Tax Pubs.

Tax Avoidance thru Interest-Free Loans see **Tax Savings thru Interest-Free Loans**

Tax Base Sharing. Douglas Harbit. Ed. by Michael Segel. 12p. (Orig.). 1976. pap. 8.00 (*0-317-04921-6*) Natl Coun Econ Dev.

Tax Base Sharing: Local Response to Fiscal Federalism. Paul Smith. (Land Policy Roundtable Case Studies: No. 303). 45p. 1979. reprint ed. pap. 25.00 (*0-608-02089-3*, 2062742) Bks Demand.

Tax Basis Revocable Trust: New Concepts in Estate Planning - Analysis with Forms. Paul Fletcher. LC 93-5064. 467p. 1993. ring bd. 210.00 (0-9637464-0-5) Clovercroft-Twigmore.

Tax Benefits. Ferguson. 1995. 47.50 (0-316-27926-9) Little.

Tax Benefits for Homeowners. 32p. 1993. pap. 6.50 (0-685-67041-4, 5419) Commerce.

Tax Break: How to Reduce the Taxes on Your Home. Troy J. Larkin. Ed. by Lois Graviet. 100p. (Orig.). 1992. pap. 29.95 (0-9632424-0-7) CITTA.

Tax Burden on Indian Agriculture. Ved P. Gandhi. LC 66-15721. (Illus.). 260p. 1966. pap. 5.00 (0-915506-06-8) Harvard Law Intl Tax.

Tax Burdens in American Agriculture: An Intersectoral Comparison. Charles A. Sisson. LC 81-8206. (Illus.). 162p. 1982. reprint ed. pap. 46.20 (0-608-00129-5, 2060910) Bks Demand.

Tax Calendar, 1993. 32p. 1992. pap. write for info. (0-318-71659-3, 4700) Commerce.

Tax Cashier. Jack Rudman. (Career Examination Ser.: C-2573). 1994. pap. 19.95 (0-8373-2573-0) Nat Learn.

Tax Challenge Casebook. Hoffman. Date not set. pap. text ed. write for info. (0-314-06042-1) West Pub.

Tax Changes & Modernization in the Textile Industry. Thomas M. Stanback, Jr. (Fiscal Studies Ser.: No. 13). 135p. 1969. reprint ed. 35.10 (0-87014-483-9) Natl Bur Econ Res.

Tax Cheating: Hide & Seek with the IRS. Mark Siegel & Barry Wolfson. 162p. (Orig.). 1988. pap. 7.95 (0-945165-01-3) Blue Sky Pr Inc.

Tax Collector. Jack Rudman. (Career Examination Ser.: C-801). 1994. pap. 23.95 (0-8373-0801-1) Nat Learn.

Tax Companion, 1995. 1995. pap. 18.95 (0-7931-0980-9, 5606-0195, R & R Newkirk) Dearborn Finan.

Tax Compliance Agent. Jack Rudman. (Career Examination Ser.: C-2122). 1994. reprint ed. pap. 27.95 (0-8373-2122-0) Nat Learn.

Tax Compliance Agent (Spanish Speaking) Jack Rudman. (Career Examination Ser.: C-2123). 1994. reprint ed. pap. 29.95 (0-8373-2123-9) Nat Learn.

Tax Compliance Representative. Jack Rudman. (Career Examination Ser.: C-2997). 1994. pap. 27.95 (0-8373-2997-3) Nat Learn.

Tax Consequences of Foreign Exchange Gains & Losses, No. 3. OECD Staff. (Issues in International Taxation Ser.). 71p. (Orig.). 1988. pap. 22.00 (92-64-13124-8) OECD.

Tax Consequences of International Acquisitions and Business Combinations, Vol. LXXVIIb. International Fiscal Association Staff. 660p. 1992. pap. 84.00 (90-6544-619-2) Kluwer Law Tax Pubs.

Tax Consequences of Marriage, Separation, & Divorce. 3rd ed. Lowell S. Thomas, Jr. 224p. 1986. suppl. ed. 107.00 (0-8318-0452-1, B452/B579) Am Law Inst.

Tax Consequences of Marriage, Separation & Divorce Supplement. Lowell S. Thomas, Jr. 30p. 1987. pap. 31.00 (0-8318-0579-X, B579) Am Law Inst.

Tax Consequences of Pension Provision for the Internationally Transferred Employee. (IFA Congress Seminar Ser.: Vol. 13b). 62p. 1990. pap. 32.00 (90-6544-438-6) Kluwer Law Tax Pubs.

***Tax Considerations for the Real Estate Professional.** Randall S. Van Reken. (C). 1997. pap. text ed. 6.00 (0-13-677379-6) P-H.

Tax Considerations in the Organization of a Small Business. 32p. 1983. 2.00 (0-686-89047-7, 88470-0) P-H.

***Tax Considerations of Real Estate Ownership.** Randall S. Van Reken. 64p. (C). 1997. write for info. (0-614-24133-2) Gorsuch Scarisbrick.

Tax Coordination in the European Community. Sijbren Cnossen & Erasmus Universiteit Rotterdam, Faculteit der Ecinomische Wetenschappen. LC 86-18526. (International Taxation Ser.: No. 7). 387p. 1987. 147.00 (90-6544-272-3) Kluwer Law Tax Pubs.

Tax Court. ring bd. write for info. (0-318-57353-9) P-H.

Tax Court Litigation: Practice and Procedure. Nina J. Crimm. 848p. 1992. ring bd. 145.00 (0-316-16109-8) Little.

Tax Court Practice. 7th ed. Marshall W. Taylor & Karen J. Simonson. Ed. by Marc J. Winter & Brian J. Seery. LC 90-55395. 394p. 1990. text ed. 57.50 (0-8318-0527-7, B527) Am Law Inst.

Tax Court Practice. 8th ed. Marshall W. Taylor et al. LC 92-56142. 413p. 1993. text ed. 115.00 (0-8318-0667-2, B667) Am Law Inst.

Tax Credits & Intergovernmental Fiscal Relations. James A. Maxwell. LC 86-22731. 216p. 1987. reprint ed. text ed. 59.75 (0-313-25279-3, MATX, Greenwood Pr) Greenwood.

Tax Credits for Charitable Contributions: Alternatives, Projections & Comparisons. James P. Angelini et al. 1996. pap. text ed. write for info. (1-886320-01-2) BHIFPPR.

Tax Credits for Low Income Housing. 9th ed. Joseph Guggenheim. 396p. 1996. pap. 66.00 (0-941239-06-3); suppl. ed., ring bd. 175.00 (0-941239-07-1) Simon Pubns.

Tax-Cutting Tactics for Investors: Legal Loopholes for the 1990s. Denise Lamaute. 220p. 1989. 22.95 (0-8306-4048-7, Liberty Hse); pap. 14.95 (0-8306-3048-1, Liberty Hse) TAB Bks.

Tax Decade, 1981-1990. Eugene C. Steuerle. 266p. (Orig.). (C). 1992. pap. text ed. 14.95 (0-87766-523-0); lib. bdg. 60.00 (0-87766-522-2) Urban Inst.

Tax Deductions for Job-Related Moving Expenses. 32p. 1992. pap. 6.00 (0-318-35095-5, 4772) Commerce.

Tax-Deferred Exchanges of Real Estate Investments. Charles W. McMullen. LC 81-3041. (Real Estate For Professional Practitioners Ser.). 100p. 1981. reprint ed. pap. 28.50 (0-7837-3456-5, 2057782) Bks Demand.

Tax-Deferred Real Estate Exchanges. Owen T. Smith & Alvin L. Arnold. LC 92-7637. (Real Estate Practice Library). 360p. 1992. text ed. 130.00 (0-471-54976-2) Wiley.

Tax-Deferred Real Estate Exchanges. Owen T. Smith & Alvin L. Arnold. (Real Estate Practice Library). 61p. 1993. pap. text ed. 50.00 (0-471-30401-8) Wiley.

Tax-Effective Structuring of Foreign Investment in U. S. Real Estate. 180.00 (1-85271-172-8, Pub. by IBC Finan Pubng UK) IBC Pubns.

Tax Efficient Foreign Exchange Management. Ed. by John Chown. LC 89-10884. 284p. 1990. text ed. 69.50 (0-89930-541-5, DTE/, Quorum Bks) Greenwood.

Tax, Estate & Financial Planning for the Elderly. John J. Regan. 1982. Updates. ring bd. write for info. (0-8205-1289-3) Bender.

Tax, Estate & Financial Planning for the Elderly-Forms & Practice, Vol. 1. Bender Editorial Staff. 1991. write for info. (0-8205-1774-7) Bender.

Tax Evasion: An Experimental Approach. Paul Webley et al. (European Monographs in Social Psychology). (Illus.). 206p. (C). 1991. text ed. 64.95 (0-521-37459-6) Cambridge U Pr.

Tax Examiner. Jack Rudman. (Career Examination Ser.: C-802). 1994. pap. 27.95 (0-8373-0802-X) Nat Learn.

Tax Examiner Trainee. Jack Rudman. (Career Examination Ser.: C-803). 1994. pap. 23.95 (0-8373-0803-8) Nat Learn.

Tax Examples, 1 vol. John C. Wisdom. (Tax Ser.). 1993. 125.00 (0-685-68845-3) Clark Boardman Callaghan.

Tax Executive: 1951-1996, Vols. 4-48. Bound set. 2,080.00 (0-8377-9157-X) Rothman.

Tax-Exempt Bonds: Retirement Center Bonds Were Risky & Benefited Moderate-Income Elderly. (Illus.). 69p. (Orig.). (C). 1993. pap. text ed. 25.00 (1-56806-445-4) DIANE Pub.

Tax-Exempt Charitable Organizations. 2nd ed. Paul E. Treusch & Norman A. Sugarman. LC 83-70067. 726p. 1983. 54.50 (0-8318-0429-7, B429) Am Law Inst.

Tax-Exempt Charitable Organizations. 3rd ed. Paul E. Treusch. 706p. 1988. text ed. 105.00 (0-8318-0511-0, B511) Am Law Inst.

Tax Exempt Financing. (Tax Law & Estate Planning Ser.). 503p. 1992. pap. text ed. 70.00 (0-685-56935-7, J4-3657) PLI.

***Tax-Exempt Financing for Health Care Organizations.** Steven B. Kite. (BNA's Health Law & Business Ser.: No. 1100). 1996. 125.00 (1-55871-341-7) BNA.

Tax Exempt Financing 1995. (Tax Law & Estate Planning Course Handbook Ser.). 576p. 1995. pap. 99.00 (0-685-65539-3, J4-3675) PLI.

Tax-Exempt Organizations. ring bd. write for info. (0-318-57368-7) P-H.

Tax-Exempt Organizations. E. C. Lashbrooke, Jr. LC 84-22253. xi, 364p. 1985. text ed. 69.50 (0-89930-083-9, LTE/, Quorum Bks) Greenwood.

Tax-Exempt Organizations: Information on Selected Types of Organizations. (Illus.). 72p. (Orig.). (C). 1995. pap. text ed. 25.00 (0-7881-2045-X) DIANE Pub.

Tax-Exempt Securities & the Surtax. Charles O. Hardy. (Brookings Institution Reprint Ser.). reprint ed. lib. bdg. 34.00 (0-697-00158-X) Irvington.

***Tax-Exempt Status of Health Care Organizations.** Bernadette M. Broccolo & Kathleen M. Niles. (BNA's Health Law & Business Ser.: No. 1900). 1996. 125.00 (1-55871-340-9) BNA.

Tax Expenditures. Stanley S. Surrey & Paul R. McDaniel. (Illus.). 320p. 1985. 37.00 (0-674-86832-3) HUP.

Tax Expenditures: A Critical Appraisal. Norman B. Ture. 20p. 1990. pap. 6.95 (0-614-04372-7) IRET.

***Tax Expenditures: Recent Experiences.** OECD Staff. 108p. (Orig.). 1996. pap. 39.00 (92-64-14879-5, Pub. by Org for Econ FR) OECD.

***Tax Facts 96/97.** (Small Business Ser.). 1996. pap. 14.95 (0-7494-2024-3) Kogan Page Ltd.

Tax Fairness: Myths & Reality. Gary Robbins & Aldona Robbins. 1991. pap. 10.00 (0-943802-63-6, 160) Natl Ctr Pol.

***Tax Fairness for the Elderly: Eliminating the Social Security Earnings Penalty.** Stephen J. Entin. 11p. 1995. pap. 5.00 (1-56808-064-6, BG137) Natl Ctr Pol.

Tax Foundation Research Library Collection. Date not set. write for info. (1-57588-368-6, 307130) W S Hein.

Tax Fraud: Audits, Investigations, Prosecutions, 2 vols. Robert S. Fink & Stuart E. Abrams. 1980. Updates. ring bd. write for info. (0-8205-1305-9) Bender.

Tax Fraud & Evasion. 5th ed. Harry G. Balter. 920p. 1982. Cumulative Suppls., semi-annual. suppl. ed. 150.00 (0-88262-796-1, TFE) Warren Gorham & Lamont.

Tax Fraud & Evasion, No. 1. 5th ed. Harry G. Balter. 920p. 1991. Supplement, 1991-1. suppl. ed. 66.50 (0-7913-0836-7) Warren Gorham & Lamont.

Tax Fraud & Evasion, No. 2. 5th ed. Harry G. Balter. 920p. 1991. Supplement, 1991-2. suppl. ed. 150.00 (0-7913-0967-3) Warren Gorham & Lamont.

Tax Fraud & Evasion: Money Laundering, Asset Forfeiture, Sentencing Guidelines. Ian M. Comisky & Lawrence S. Feld. 1056p. 1994. 150.00 (0-7913-2033-2) Warren Gorham & Lamont.

Tax Fraud & Evasion: The War Stories. Donald W. MacPherson. 250p. (Orig.). 1989. pap. 17.95 (0-9617124-6-5) Winning St Paul.

Tax Fraud & Money Laundering. Richard A. Westin et al. LC 93-77771. 730p. 1993. pap. 68.00 (0-916081-33-8) J Marshall Pub Co.

Tax Gap: Many Actions Taken, but a Cohesive Compliance Strategy Needed. (Illus.). 87p. (Orig.). (C). 1995. pap. text ed. 20.00 (0-7881-2241-X) DIANE Pub.

Tax Guide Controller's Edition: (1996) RIA In-House Professional Staff. 2008p. (Orig.). 1995. pap. text ed. 195.00 (0-7811-0119-0) Res Inst Am.

Tax Guide for Buying & Selling a Business. Stanley Hagendorf & Wayne Hagendorf. 1994. 150.00 (1-878337-37-8) Knowles Law.

Tax Guide for Buying & Selling a Business. 6th ed. Stanley Hagendorf. LC 85-25667. 289p. 1986. text ed. 39.95 (0-13-885005-4, Busn) P-H.

Tax Guide for College Teachers, 1985. Allen Bernstein. 400p. 1984. pap. 18.95 (0-916018-27-X) Acad Info Serv.

Tax Guide for College Teachers, 1986. Allen Bernstein. 416p. 1985. pap. 19.95 (0-916018-30-X) Acad Info Serv.

Tax Guide for College Teachers 1988. Allen Bernstein. 21.95 (0-916018-36-9) Acad Info Serv.

Tax Guide for College Teachers, 1994. 500p. 1993. pap. text ed. 29.00 (0-916018-50-4) Acad Info Serv.

Tax Guide for College Teachers, 1994. rev. ed. Academic Information Service, Inc. Staff. 500p. 1992. pap. text ed. 28.00 (0-916018-48-2) Acad Info Serv.

Tax Guide for Engineers, 1994. 475p. 1993. pap. text ed. 30.00 (0-916018-49-0) Acad Info Serv.

Tax Guide for Engineers, 1994. Academic Information Service, Inc. Staff. 496p. (C). 1992. pap. text ed. 30.00 (0-916018-47-4) Acad Info Serv.

Tax Guide for Professionals. 64p. 1993. pap. 12.95 (0-685-67042-2, 5443) Commerce.

Tax Guide for Residential Real Estate. Michael P. Sampson. 296p. (Orig.). 1987. pap. 25.00 (0-13-884801-7, Busn) P-H.

Tax Guide for Residential Real Estate: The Complete Tax Handbook for Homeowners & Investors. rev. ed. Michael P. Sampson. LC 92-81587. 335p. 1992. pap. 16.95 (0-9633058-0-8) Conted Media.

Tax Guide for Salespersons. 96p. 1993. pap. 12.95 (0-685-67043-0, 5445) Commerce.

Tax Guide 1994-95: The Professional's Complete Guide to Taxation in Ireland. 1544p. write for info. (1-85475-661-3, IE) MICHIE.

Tax Handbook 1992-93. E. Danziger & E. M. Stack. 711p. 1992. pap. 48.00 (0-614-05468-0, SA); pap. 48.00 (0-614-05480-X, SA) MICHIE.

Tax Harmonization in the European Community. Ed. by George F. Kopits. (Occasional Paper Ser.: No. 94). 85p. 1992. pap. 15.00 (1-55775-225-7) Intl Monetary.

***Tax Havens.** 1996. 315.00 (0-614-25442-6, M727) Econ Intel.

Tax Havens. Anthony Ginsberg. 1991. 34.95 (0-13-886649-X) P-H.

Tax Havens: How to Bank, Invest, & Do Business Offshore & Tax Free. Hoyt L. Barber. 1993. text ed. 24.95 (0-07-003659-4) McGraw.

Tax Havens: What They Are & What They Can Do for the Shrewd Investor. Adam Starchild. LC 79-19657. 255p. reprint ed. pap. 72.70 (0-8357-4131-1, AU00402) Bks Demand.

Tax Havens & Investment Incentives to Industry. W. Wahi. (C). 1988. 285.00 (0-685-27889-1) St Mut.

Tax Havens Encyclopaedia. Barry Spitz. U.K. ring bd. 280.00 (0-406-38226-3, U.K.) MICHIE.

Tax Havens for Corporations. Adam Starchild. LC 79-9325. 188p. reprint ed. pap. 53.60 (0-8357-4132-X, AU00403) Bks Demand.

Tax Havens of the World, 3 vols. Walter H. Diamond & Dorothy B. Diamond. 1974. Looseleaf updates avail. ring bd. write for info. (0-8205-1722-4) Bender.

Tax Heaven or Hell: A Guide to the Tax Consequences of Your Retirement Relocation. R. Alan Fox & Eve G. Evans. LC 96-60037. 132p. 1996. pap. 11.95 (0-9644216-5-8) Vacation Pubns.

Tax Help for the Self-Employed. write for info. (0-318-57733-X) P-H.

Tax Ideas, 3 vols. write for info. (0-318-61660-2) P-H.

Tax Ideas Especially for the Professional. 46p. 1982. 4.25 (0-685-07391-2, 88497-3) P-H.

***Tax in North Africa.** Bernardi. 1994. pap. text ed. 50.50 (90-6544-779-2) Kluwer Ac.

Tax Incentives & Capital Spending: Proceedings of Brookings Conference on the Effects of Tax Policy on Investment, Brooking Institution, 1967. Brookings Conference on the Effects of Tax Policy on Investment, Brooking Institution, 1967. Ed. by Gary Fromm. LC 79-115225. (Brookings Institution Staff Paper Ser.). 319p. reprint ed. pap. 91.00 (0-317-20832-2, 2025379) Bks Demand.

Tax Incentives & Economic Growth. Barry P. Bosworth. LC 84-9625. 208p. 1984. 34.95 (0-8157-1036-4); pap. 14.95 (0-8157-1035-6) Brookings.

Tax Incentives & Investment Behavior. Manju Agarwal. (C). 1988. 175.00 (0-685-36457-7) St Mut.

Tax Incentives for Industry in Less Developed Countries. Jack Heller & Kenneth M. Kauffman. LC 63-19475. (Illus.). 300p. (Orig.). 1963. pap. 7.00 (0-915506-20-3) Harvard Law Intl Tax.

Tax Incidence: A Selected Bibliography. Heather Barrera. (CPL Bibliographies Ser.: No. 109). 67p. 1983. 10.00 (0-86602-109-4, Sage Prdcls Pr) Sage.

Tax Increment Financing. Douglas Harbit. 8p. (Orig.). 1975. pap. 8.00 (0-317-05497-X) Natl Coun Econ Dev.

Tax Increment Financing in Illinois: A Legislative Issue for the 89th General Assembly. Kent D. Redfield. Ed. by Steve Sandstrom. (Legislative Issues Ser.). (Illus.). 1995. pap. 10.00 (1-884203-01-9) Taxpayers Fed.

***Tax Increment Financing (in Minnesota)** James Noble & Roger Brooks. (Illus.). 100p. (Orig.). (C). 1997. pap. text ed. 30.00 (0-7881-4150-3) DIANE Pub.

Tax Inspector. Peter Carey. LC 92-56375. 1993. pap. 13.00 (0-679-73598-4, Vin) Random.

Tax Institute, University of Southern California: Major Tax Planning, 1948-1993, 45 vols., Set. Bound set. 4,160.00 (0-8377-9158-8) Rothman.

Tax Issues in Bankruptcy: Complete Planning & Practice Guide. rev. ed. 1994. ring bd. 195.00 (1-55645-020-6, 500003) Busn Legal Reports.

Tax Justice: Social & Moral Aspects of American Tax Policy. Ronald Pasquariello. LC 85-3250. (Illus.). 132p. (Orig.). 1985. pap. text ed. 14.00 (0-8191-4607-2); lib. bdg. 41.00 (0-8191-4606-4) U Pr of Amer.

Tax Law. Ed. by Frans J. Vanistendael. 1991. ring bd. write for info. (0-318-68487-X) Kluwer Law Tax Pubs.

Tax Law. Ed. by Patricia D. White. LC 94-21391. (C). 1995. 125.00 (0-8147-9279-0) NYU Pr.

Tax Law, 2 vols., Set. Patricia D. White. Ed. by Tom D. Campbell. (International Library of Essays in Law & Legal Theory). 500p. (C). 1995. 250.00 (0-8147-9281-2) NYU Pr.

Tax Law, Vol. 2. White. (C). 1995. 125.00 (0-8147-9280-4) NYU Pr.

Tax Law & Estate Planning Series, 1992-1993, 20 vols. 1993. Set. pap. 695.00 (0-685-69499-2) PLI.

Tax Law Conference Supplemental Materials, 11th Annual. 48p. 1987. pap. text ed. 25.00 (1-56986-188-9) Federal Bar.

Tax Law Conference Supplemental Materials, 16th Annual (1992) 154p. 1992. pap. text ed. 25.00 (1-56986-194-3) Federal Bar.

Tax Law Conference, 10th Annual. 558p. 1986. pap. text ed. 15.00 (1-56986-186-2) Federal Bar.

Tax Law Conference, 11th Annual. 80p. 1987. pap. text ed. 25.00 (1-56986-187-0) Federal Bar.

Tax Law Conference, 12th Annual. 282p. 1988. pap. text ed. 10.00 (1-56986-189-7) Federal Bar.

Tax Law Conference, 13th Annual. 247p. 1989. pap. text ed. 10.00 (1-56986-190-0) Federal Bar.

Tax Law Conference, 14th Annual. 508p. 1990. pap. text ed. 15.00 (1-56986-191-9) Federal Bar.

Tax Law Conference, 15th Annual. 238p. 1991. pap. text ed. 10.00 (1-56986-192-7) Federal Bar.

Tax Law Conference, 16th Annual (1992) 387p. 1992. pap. text ed. 45.00 (1-56986-193-5) Federal Bar.

Tax Law Conference, 17th Annual (1993) 525p. 1993. pap. text ed. 45.00 (1-56986-222-2) Federal Bar.

Tax Law Conference, 18th Annual (1994) 310p. (Orig.). 1994. 75.00 (1-56986-239-7) Federal Bar.

Tax Law Conference, 19th Annual (1995) 685p. 1995. pap. 75.00 (1-56986-259-1) Federal Bar.

Tax Law Conference, 6th Annual. 192p. 1982. pap. text ed. 15.00 (1-56986-182-X) Federal Bar.

Tax Law Conference, 7th Annual. 334p. 1983. pap. text ed. 15.00 (1-56986-183-8) Federal Bar.

Tax Law Conference, 8th Annual. 257p. 1984. pap. text ed. 10.00 (1-56986-184-6) Federal Bar.

***Tax Law Design & Drafting, Vol. 1.** Ed. by Victor Thuronyi. LC 96-34672. 526p. pap. 150.00 (0-608-04848-8, 2065507) Bks Demand.

***Tax Law Design & Drafting, Vol. I.** Victor T. Thuronyi. 1996. 25.00 (1-55775-587-6) Intl Monetary.

Tax Law of Charitable Giving. B. R. Hopkins et al. 166p. 1994. suppl. ed., pap. 45.00 (0-471-30526-X) Wiley.

Tax Law of Charitable Giving. Bruce R. Hopkins. (Nonprofit Law, Finance, & Management Ser.). 760p. 1993. text ed. 125.00 (0-471-55527-4) Wiley.

Tax Law of Charitable Giving: 1996-1997 Cumulative Supplement. Bruce R. Hopkins. 1996. pap. text ed. 60.00 (0-471-16619-7) Wiley.

***Tax Law of Colleges & Universities.** Bertrand M. Harding. LC 97-11011. (Nonprofit Law, Finance & Management Ser.). 384p. 1997. 125.00 (0-471-15939-5) Wiley.

Tax Law of the State of New York: As of December, 1992. 1040p. 1993. pap. 45.00 (0-685-67080-5, 5460) Commerce.

Tax Law Review. Ed. by Graduate Tax Faculty of NYU School of Law Staff. 110.00 (0-685-69576-X, TLRE) Warren Gorham & Lamont.

Tax Law Review: 1945-1994/95, 50 vols., Set. Bound set. 2,660.00 (0-8377-9159-6) Rothman.

Tax Laws of Kuwait. Tr. by N. H. Karam. 50p. 1986. pap. text ed. 30.00 (0-86010-140-1) G & T Inc.

Tax Lawyer: 1947-1995/96, 49 vols., Set. Bound set. 1,975.00 (0-8377-9160-X) Rothman.

Tax Lawyer Fifteen Year Cumulative Index, Vols.21-35. 61p. 1983. pap. 20.00 (0-685-42950-4, 547-0041) Amer Bar Assn.

***Tax Legislation: Explanation, 1996.** 276p. 1996. pap. 22.50 (0-614-26821-4, 21596BLS04) Commerce.

***Tax Legislation: Highlights, 1996.** 48p. 1996. pap. 7.00 (0-614-26822-2, 21596BLS03) Commerce.

***Tax Legislation: Law & Explanation, 1996.** 720p. 1996. pap. 32.50 (0-614-26823-0, 21996BLS01) Commerce.

Tax Legislative Process Conference (1995) 124p. 1994. 35.00 (1-56986-254-0) Federal Bar.

Tax Literature: 1995. Crimm. 1995. suppl. ed. 105.00 (0-316-16106-3) Little.

Tax Loopholes: Everything the Law Allows. rev. ed. Boardroom's Experts & Editors Staff. LC 86-30967. 352p. 1996. 59.00 (0-614-14887-1) Boardroom.

Tax Management - U. S. Income. Tax Management, Inc. Staff. 1959. 1,867.00 (1-55871-094-9) BNA.

Tax Management Compensation Planning. Tax Management, Inc. Staff. 1973. 879.00 (1-55871-092-2) BNA.

Tax Management Estates, Gifts, & Trusts. Tax Management, Inc. Staff. 1967. 902.00 (1-55871-093-0) BNA.

Tax Map Technician. Jack Rudman. (Career Examination Ser.: C-3199). 1994. pap. 29.95 (0-8373-3199-4) Nat Learn.

Tax on Luxuries in Hotels in U. P. Vijay Malik. 40p. 1975. 60.00 (0-317-54595-7) St Mut.

Tax on Luxuries in Hotels in U. P. 2nd ed. Vijay Malik. (C). 1991. 95.00 (0-685-39629-0) St Mut.

Tax on Value Added. Clara K. Sullivan. LC 65-14322. 109p. 1965. text ed. 57.50 (0-231-02807-5) Col U Pr.

An Asterisk (*) at the beginning of an entry indicates that the title is appearing in BIP for the first time.

Tax Options & Strategies: A State-by-State Guide for People with Disabilities, Senior Citizens, Veterans, & Their Families. Bruce E. Bondo. 111p. 1995. pap. 29.95 (*0-939957-79-5*) Demos Vermande.

Tax Options & Strategies for People with Disabilities. 2nd rev. ed. Steven B. Mendelsohn. 312p. (Orig.). 1996. pap. 29.95 (*0-939957-85-X*) Demos Vermande.

Tax Penalties: The Complete Guide to Penalties under the Internal Revenue Code, 1992-1993. P. White & Consuelo M. Ohanesian. 1992. pap. 49.95 (*0-942061-29-2*, Financial Sourcebks) Sourcebks.

Tax Penalties & Interest Handbook, 1990-1991. Howard Davidoff & David A. Minars. 1991. suppl. ed., ring bd. 40.00 (*0-318-68638-4*) MICHIE.

Tax Penalties & Interest Handbook, 1990-1991. David A. Minars & Howard Davidoff. 340p. 1990. ring bd. 80.00 (*0-88063-748-X*) MICHIE.

Tax Penalties, 1991: The Complete Guide to Penalties Under the Internal Revenue Code. Pauline White & Consuelo M. Ohanesian. 388p. 1991. pap. 49.95 (*0-942061-19-5*, Financial Sourcebks); boxed 89.95 (*0-942061-20-9*, Financial Sourcebks) Sourcebks.

Tax Philosophers: Two Hundred Years of Thought in Great Britain & the United States. Harold M. Groves. Ed. by Donald J. Curran. LC 74-5901. 168p. 1975. 32.50 (*0-299-06660-6*) U of Wis Pr.

Tax Planning: Strategy Tactics, Decisions & Actions. 4th ed. Richard R. Sylvester. 1980. 24.95 (*0-932010-21-0*) PhD Pub.

Tax Planning & Compliance for Tax-Exempt Organizations: Forms, Checklists, & Procedures. 2nd ed. J. Blazek. 126p. 1994. suppl. ed., text ed. 45.00 (*0-471-30528-6*) Wiley.

Tax Planning & Compliance for Tax-Exempt Organizations: Forms, Checklists, Procedures. 2nd rev. ed. Jody Blazek. (Nonprofit Law, Finance, & Management Ser.). 736p. 1993. text ed. 130.00 (*0-471-58499-1*) Wiley.

Tax Planning & Corporate Responsibilities of Boardmembers: Perspectives for Companies in Germany, The Netherlands, Spain & the United Kingdom. Ed. by Harrie L. Van Mens & Wiggin Group Staff. LC 95-36817. 1995. write for info. (*90-411-0114-4*) Kluwer Law Tax Pubs.

Tax Planning & Preparation for Horse Owners 1995. Tony Winter & Sue E. Marder. (Illus.). 129p. 1992. pap. 17.95 (*0-914327-47-X*) Breakthrgh NY.

Tax Planning & Preparation Made Easy for the Self-Employed. Gregory L. Dent & Jeffrey E. Johnson. 224p. 1995. pap. text ed. 15.95 (*0-471-11493-6*) Wiley.

Tax Planning for Closely Held Corporations, 1989. 184p. 1989. 50.00 (*0-685-69500-X*) PLI.

Tax Planning for Corporate Acquisitions. George Brode, Jr. (Illus.). 770p. 1995. suppl. ed., pap. text ed. 87.00 (*1-884673-04-X*) Brode Pubns.

*__Tax Planning for Corporate Acquisitions.__ 2nd ed. George Brode, Jr. (Illus.). 1200p. 1997. 245.00 (*1-884673-07-4*) Brode Pubns.

Tax Planning for Corporate Acquisitions: (With Current Supplement) George Brode, Jr. (Illus.). 1995. 175.00 (*1-884673-03-1*) Brode Pubns.

Tax Planning for Corporate Joint Ventures, Partnerships & Other Strategic Alliances 1995, 2 vols., Set. (Tax Law & Estate Planning Course Handbook Ser.). 1704p. 1994. pap. 149.00 (*0-614-17274-8*, J4-3679) PLI.

Tax Planning for Corporations & Shareholders: Forms. Zolman Cavitch. 1985. Looseleaf updates avail. ring bd. write for info. (*0-8205-1430-6*) Bender.

Tax Planning for Different Categories of Assessees. R. K. Agarwal. (C). 1989. 120.00 (*0-685-36456-9*) St Mut.

Tax Planning for Different Tax Payers. R. K. Agarwal. (C). 1990. 90.00 (*0-89771-283-8*) St Mut.

Tax Planning for Disposition of Business Interest. 2nd ed. Indoe Ness. 704p. Supplemented semi-annually. suppl. ed. 160.00 (*0-7913-0627-5*); suppl. ed. 48.00 (*0-7913-0932-0*); suppl. ed. 50.75 (*0-685-51110-3*) Warren Gorham & Lamont.

Tax Planning for Executive Compensation, 2 vols. Harvey L. Frutkin. 1983. Updates available. ring bd. write for info. (*0-8205-1451-9*) Bender.

Tax Planning for Family Wealth Transfers. 2nd ed. Howard M. Zaritsky. 864p. Supplemented semi-annually. suppl. ed. 140.00 (*0-7913-0886-3*); suppl. ed. 43.50 (*0-685-51111-1*); suppl. ed. write for info. (*0-318-68840-9*) Warren Gorham & Lamont.

Tax Planning for Foreign Investors in the United States. Adam Starchild & Paul D. Brundage. 160p. 38.00 (*90-6544-109-3*) Kluwer Ac.

Tax Planning for Groups of Companies. 2nd ed. M. B. Squires. 1991. 130.00 (*0-406-50590-X*, U.K.) MICHIE.

Tax Planning for Highly Compensated Individuals. 2nd ed. Robert E. Madden. 816p. 1989. Supplemented semi-annually. suppl. ed. 160.00 (*0-7913-0210-5*); suppl. ed. 45.75 (*0-7913-0902-9*); suppl. ed. 48.50 (*0-685-32298-X*) Warren Gorham & Lamont.

Tax Planning for Industrial Collaborations. Ed. by K. V. Iyer. (C). 1988. 80.00 (*0-685-36453-4*) St Mut.

Tax Planning for Investors: The 90's Guide to Securities & Commodities Investments. Jack Crestol & Herman M. Schneider. 296p. 1993. 35.00 (*0-318-37891-4*, 4906) Commerce.

Tax Planning for Real Estate Transactions, 2 vols. Stefan Tucker. 1990. Set. 240.00 (*0-318-41448-1*) Clark Boardman Callaghan.

Tax Planning for Real Estate Transactions. Robert M. Weiss & Robert E. Dallman. LC 83-4487. 368p. 1983. 39.95 (*0-13-885095-X*) P-H.

Tax Planning for Retirement. William P. Streng. 928p. 1989. suppl. ed. 51.25 (*0-685-44812-6*) Warren Gorham & Lamont.

Tax Planning for Retirement. annuals William P. Streng. 928p. 1989. Supplemented annually. suppl. ed. 140.00 (*0-7913-0246-6*) Warren Gorham & Lamont.

Tax Planning for S Corporations. Richard Robinson & Arthur Weiss. 1988. write for info. (*0-8205-1496-9*) Bender.

Tax Planning for Securities & Options Transactions. Auster. 248p. 1988. pap. 19.50 (*0-685-67044-9*, 5192) Commerce.

Tax Planning for the Alternative Minimum Tax. Lance W. Rook. 1989. Updates available. ring bd. write for info. (*0-8205-1694-5*) Bender.

Tax Planning for the Salaried Employees. R. Palat Raghu. (C). 1990. 55.00 (*0-89771-259-5*) St Mut.

Tax Planning in Divorce Settlements. Robert W. McGee. LC 86-133322. 64p. write for info. (*0-13-778846-0*) P-H.

Tax Planning of Real Estate. 7th ed. Paul E. Anderson. LC 77-77507. 242p. 1977. suppl. ed., pap. 5.00 (*0-8318-0438-6*, B438/B430) Am Law Inst.

Tax Planning on the Microcomputer. John O. Everett & Thomas W. McNinch. 160p. (C). 1988. pap. text ed. 12.00 (*0-15-535294-6*) Dryden Pr.

Tax Planning Strategies, 2 vols. Lewis D. Solomon. 1990. 210.00 (*0-685-34491-6*) Clark Boardman Callaghan.

Tax Planning Through Trusts & Wills. 2nd ed. R. N. Lakhotia. (C). 1988. 60.00 (*0-685-27884-0*) St Mut.

Tax Planning under Direct Taxes. S. Shuklendra & G. Ghura. (C). 1990. 238.00 (*0-89771-262-5*) St Mut.

Tax Planning with Life Insurance. Howard M. Zaritsky & Stephen F. Leimberg. 1995. 79.95 (*0-615-00557-8*) Warren Gorham & Lamont.

Tax Planning with Life Insurance: Analysis with Forms. Howard M. Zaritsky & Stephen F. Leimberg. 1992. ring bd. 130.00 incl. disk (*0-685-69553-0*, TPLI) Warren Gorham & Lamont.

Tax Planning with Life Insurance: Executive Edition. Howard M. Zaritsky. 832p. 1994. 79.95 (*0-7913-1311-5*) Warren Gorham & Lamont.

Tax Policy: An Introduction & Survey of the Principal Debates. Stephen G. Utz. LC 93-9795. 260p. 1993. pap. 19.50 (*0-314-01930-8*) West Pub.

*__Tax Policy: Analysis of Certain Potential Effects of Extending Federal Income Taxation to Puerto Rico.__ (Illus.). 58p. (Orig.). (C). 1996. pap. 25.00 (*0-7881-3597-X*) DIANE Pub.

Tax Policy: Experience with the Corporate Alternative Minimum Tax. (Illus.). 75p. (Orig.). (C). 1995. pap. text ed. 30.00 (*0-7881-1813-7*) DIANE Pub.

*__Tax Policy: Experience with the Corporation Alternative Minimum Tax (AMT)__ (Illus.). 76p. 1994. pap. text ed. 40.00 (*1-57979-130-1*) BPI Info Servs.

Tax Policy: Health Insurance Tax Credit Participation Rate Was Low. (Illus.). 43p. (Orig.). (C). 1995. pap. text ed. 20.00 (*0-7881-2216-9*) DIANE Pub.

*__Tax Policy: Health Insurance Tax Credit Participation Rate Was Low.__ (Illus.). 44p. 1994. pap. text ed. 30.00 (*1-57979-091-7*) BPI Info Servs.

Tax Policy: Many Factors Contributed to the Growth in Home Equity Financing in the 1980s. (Illus.). 78p. (Orig.). (C). 1995. reprint ed. pap. text ed. 20.00 (*0-7881-0857-3*) DIANE Pub.

Tax Policy: Pharmaceutical Industry's Use of the Research Tax Credit. (Illus.). 38p. (Orig.). (C). 1995. pap. text ed. 20.00 (*0-7881-2089-1*) DIANE Pub.

*__Tax Policy: Pharmaceutical Industry's Use of the Research Tax Credit.__ (Illus.). 38p. 1994. pap. text ed. 30.00 (*1-57979-092-5*) BPI Info Servs.

Tax Policy: Proposals for Direct Tax Reform. Ed. by Malcolm S. Adiseshiah. (C). 1987. 14.00 (*81-7062-028-7*, Pub. by Lancer II) S Asia.

Tax Policy: Tax Expenditures Deserve More Scrutiny. (Illus.). 135p. (Orig.). (C). 1995. pap. text ed. 30.00 (*0-7881-1695-9*) DIANE Pub.

*__Tax Policy: Tax Expenditures Deserve More Scrutiny.__ (Illus.). 136p. 1994. pap. text ed. 40.00 (*1-57979-131-X*) BPI Info Servs.

Tax Policy: Value-Added Tax: Administrative Costs Vary with Complexity & Number of Businesses. (Illus.). 159p. (Orig.). (C). 1995. reprint ed. pap. text ed. 35.00 (*0-7881-0403-9*) DIANE Pub.

Tax Policy: 1988 & 1989 Company Effective Tax Rates Higher Than in Prior Years. (Illus.). 80p. (Orig.). (C). 1993. pap. text ed. 25.00 (*1-56806-953-7*) DIANE Pub.

Tax Policy & Administration: California Taxes on Multinational Corporations & Related Federal Issues. (Illus.). 61p. (Orig.). (C). 1996. pap. text ed. 20.00 (*0-7881-2942-2*) DIANE Pub.

Tax Policy & Administration: Improvements for More Effective Tax-Exempt Bond Oversight. 81p. (Orig.). (C). 1993. pap. text ed. 30.00 (*0-7881-0093-9*) DIANE Pub.

*__Tax Policy & Administration: Review of Studies of the Effectiveness of the Research Tax Credit.__ 26p. (Orig.). (C). 1996. pap. 25.00 (*0-7881-3637-2*) DIANE Pub.

Tax Policy & Economic Development. Richard M. Bird. LC 91-16243. (Studies in Development). 264p. 1991. text ed. 48.50 (*0-8018-4223-9*); pap. text ed. 18.95 (*0-8018-4265-4*) Johns Hopkins.

Tax Policy & Economic Growth. 150p. 1995. pap. text ed. 25.00 (*1-884032-03-6*) Am Coun Capital.

Tax Policy & Housing. Ed. by Michael Lea. (Contemporary Studies in Economic & Financial Analysis: Vol. 54). 1989. 73.25 (*0-89232-602-6*) Jai Pr.

Tax Policy & the Economy. Ed. by James M. Poterba. (Tax Policy & the Economy Ser.: Vol. 7). (Illus.). 200p. 1993. 30.00 (*0-262-16135-4*) MIT Pr.

Tax Policy & the Economy. Ed. by James M. Poterba. (Tax Policy & the Economy Ser.: Vol. 7). (Illus.). 200p. 1993. pap. 15.00 (*0-262-66081-4*) MIT Pr.

Tax Policy & the Economy. Ed. by James M. Poterba. (Tax Policy & the Economy Ser.: Vol. 8). (Illus.). 200p. 1994. 30.00 (*0-262-16143-5*); pap. 15.00 (*0-262-66091-1*) MIT Pr.

Tax Policy & the Economy. Ed. by James M. Poterba. (Tax Policy & the Economy Ser.: Vol. 9). 350p. 1995. 30.00 (*0-262-16153-2*); pap. 15.00 (*0-262-66095-4*) MIT Pr.

Tax Policy & the Economy. Ed. by James M. Poterba. (Tax Policy & the Economy Ser.: Vol. 10). 200p. 1996. 30.00 (*0-262-16161-3*) MIT Pr.

Tax Policy & the Economy, 2. Ed. by Lawrence H. Summers. 200p. (Orig.). 1988. 30.00 (*0-262-19272-1*); pap. 15.00 (*0-262-69121-3*) MIT Pr.

Tax Policy & the Economy, 3. Ed. by Lawrence H. Summers. 200p. (Orig.). 1989. 30.00 (*0-262-19279-9*); pap. 15.00 (*0-262-69129-9*) MIT Pr.

*__Tax Policy & the Economy, No. 11.__ Ed. by James M. Poterba. (Illus.). 200p. 1997. 30.00 (*0-262-16167-2*) MIT Pr.

*__Tax Policy & the Economy, No. 11.__ Ed. by James M. Poterba. (Illus.). 200p. 1997. pap. 15.00 (*0-262-66104-7*) MIT Pr.

Tax Policy & the Economy, Vol. 1. Ed. by Lawrence H. Summers. 200p. (Orig.). 1987. pap. 15.00 (*0-262-69115-9*) MIT Pr.

Tax Policy & the Economy, Vol. 4. Ed. by Lawrence H. Summers. (Orig.). (C). 1990. pap. 15.00 (*0-262-69140-X*) MIT Pr.

Tax Policy & the Economy, Vol. 5. Ed. by David F. Bradford. 200p. 1991. 30.00 (*0-262-02295-8*); pap. 15.00 (*0-262-52158-X*) MIT Pr.

Tax Policy & the Economy, Vol. 6. Ed. by James M. Poterba. (Illus.). 200p. 1992. 30.00 (*0-262-16130-3*); pap. 15.00 (*0-262-66077-6*) MIT Pr.

Tax Policy & the Economy, Vol. 10. Ed. by James M. Poterba. (Tax Policy & the Economy Ser.: Vol. 10). (Illus.). 200p. (C). 1996. pap. 15.00 (*0-262-66098-9*) MIT Pr.

Tax Policy for Economic Growth in the 1990s. 190p. (Orig.). 1994. pap. text ed. 25.00 (*1-884032-01-X*) Am Coun Capital.

Tax Policy in Developing Countries. Ed. by Javad Khalilzadeh-Shirazi & Anwar Shah. (Symposium Ser.). 276p. 1992. 27.95 (*0-8213-1990-6*, 11990) World Bank.

Tax Policy in Small Open Economies. Ed. by Torben M. Andersen et al. LC 94-41026. 196p. 1995. pap. text ed. 33.95 (*0-631-19443-6*) Blackwell Pubs.

Tax Policy in Sub-Saharan Africa: A Framework for Analysis. Zmarak Shalizi & Lyn Squire. (Policy & Research Ser.: No. 2). 34p. 1989. 6.95 (*0-8213-1165-4*, 11165) World Bank.

Tax Policy in the United States: A Selective Bibliography with Annotations 1960-1984. Ed. by Howard A. Hood. 752p. (C). 1985. ring bd. write for info. (*0-935449-00-0*) A Q M Law Lib.

Tax Policy Lessons for LDCs & Eastern Europe. Charles E. McLure, Jr. 1992. pap. 5.00 (*1-55815-194-X*) ICS Pr.

Tax Policy Towards the National Heritage: Proceedings of a Seminar held in Venice, 1983, during the 37th Congress of the International Fiscal Association. Ed. by International Fiscal Association Staff. LC 84-4426. (IFA Congress Seminar Ser.: No. 8). 1984. 44.00 (*90-6544-178-6*) Kluwer Law Tax Pubs.

Tax Politics: How They Make You Pay & What You Can Do About It. Robert M. Brandon et al. 297p. 1976. 6.95 (*0-394-49847-X*) Tax Reform Res.

Tax Politics: Testbank. 5th ed. James W. Lamare. Date not set. suppl. ed., teacher ed., pap. text ed. write for info. (*0-314-03265-7*) West Pub.

Tax Practice Guides & Checklists, 1990. American Institute of Certified Public Accountants Staff. 330p. reprint ed. pap. 94.10 (*0-7837-1923-X*, 2042134) Bks Demand.

Tax Practice Guides & Checklists, 1991. American Institute of Certified Public Accountants Staff. 310p. reprint ed. pap. 88.40 (*0-7837-6698-X*, 2046322) Bks Demand.

Tax Practice Guides & Checklists, 1992. American Institute of Certified Public Accountants Staff. 338p. reprint ed. pap. 96.40 (*0-7837-6699-8*, 2046323) Bks Demand.

Tax Practice Guides & Checklists, 1993. American Institute of Certified Public Accountants Staff. 386p. 1993. pap. 110.10 (*0-7837-8475-9*, 2049280) Bks Demand.

Tax Practice Handbook. Frank M. Burke & Buford Berry. LC 85-16899. 436p. 1985. text ed. 39.95 (*0-13-884735-5*) P-H.

Tax Practice Management. annuals William H. Behrenfeld & Robert J. Ranweiler. 640p. 159.50 (*0-87051-079-7*) Am Inst CPA.

Tax Practice Management: Client Servicing. William L. Raby & Burgess J. Raby. ring bd. write for info. (*0-318-61973-3*) P-H.

Tax Practitioner: Tax Research, Ethical & Legal Standards, IRS Practice & Procedure, 1990 Edition. Denzil Y. Causey, Jr. & Frances M. McNair. LC 89-48021. 320p. 1990. lib. bdg. 59.95 (*0-930001-03-6*) Accountants Pr.

Tax Practitioner's Diary, 1994-95. 1994. pap. 16.50 (*0-406-03655-1*) MICHIE.

Tax Preparer's Marketing Guide: More New Clients Every Year. 2nd rev. ed. Mitch Paioff. (Illus.). 92p. 1996. pap. 29.98 (*0-614-14933-9*) Anderson Laser.

Tax Problems of the Liquidation of Corporations. (Cahiers de Droit Fiscal International Ser.: Vol. LXXIIb). 526p. 1987. pap. 96.00 (*90-6544-309-6*) Kluwer Law Tax Pubs.

Tax Procedure & Tax Fraud: Cases & Materials. 3rd ed. Marvin J. Garbis et al. (American Casebook Ser.). 921p. (C). 1992. text ed. 57.00 (*0-314-89561-2*) West Pub.

Tax Procedure & Tax Fraud in a Nutshell. Patricia T. Morgan. (Nutshell Ser.). 400p. 1991. reprint ed. pap. 18.00 (*0-314-73300-0*) West Pub.

Tax Procedure Digest. 1980. text ed. 130.00 (*0-685-69561-1*, TPD) Warren Gorham & Lamont.

Tax Process & Fraud. 2nd ed. Morgan. (Nutshell Ser.). Date not set. pap. text ed. write for info. (*0-314-06586-5*) West Pub.

Tax Processing Manager. Jack Rudman. (Career Examination Ser.: C-3173). 1994. pap. 34.95 (*0-8373-3173-0*) Nat Learn.

Tax Processing Specialist. (Career Examination Ser.: C-3771). pap. 34.95 (*0-8373-3771-2*) Nat Learn.

Tax Progressivity & Income Inequality. Ed. by Joel Slemrod. LC 93-32410. 1994. write for info. (*0-521-46127-8*) Cambridge U Pr.

Tax Progressivity & Income Inequality. Ed. by Joel Slemrod. (Illus.). 384p. (C). 1994. text ed. 44.95 (*0-521-46543-5*) Cambridge U Pr.

*__Tax Progressivity & Income Inequality.__ Ed. by Joel Slemrod. 375p. 1996. pap. text ed. 19.95 (*0-521-58776-X*) Cambridge U Pr.

*__Tax Protestor's Handbook.__ Max. 50p. (Orig.). 1997. pap. 30.00 (*0-922070-44-X*) M Tecton Pub.

Tax Questions & Answers 1994. I. G. Wallschutzky & G. L. Payne. 1993. pap. 51.00 (*0-409-30950-8*, Austral) MICHIE.

Tax Racket: Government Extortion from A to Z. Martin L. Gross. 321p. 1995. pap. 12.00 (*0-345-38778-3*) Ballantine.

Tax Rates in Virginia's Cities, Counties & Selected Towns, 1991. Albert Spengler. 1991. pap. 18.81 (*0-318-04162-6*) U VA Ctr Pub Serv.

Tax Rates, Tax Revenues & Economic Growth. Gerald W. Scully. 1991. pap. 10.00 (*0-943802-62-8*, 159) Natl Ctr Pol.

Tax Record Book. B. J. Worth. 1991. ring bd. 21.99 (*0-529-06990-3*) World Publng.

Tax Records: Common Source with Uncommon Value. Arlene H. Eakle. 1978. pap. text ed. 10.50 (*0-940764-14-8*) Genealog Inst.

Tax Records for Washington County, Arkansas, Real Estate & Personal Property, 1890. Lois N. Miller. 317p. 1990. 42.50 (*1-878193-16-3*); pap. 34.00 (*1-878193-17-1*) L N Miller Geog Pubns.

Tax Reform: A Strategic Issues Brief. Date not set. pap. 40.00 (*0-939900-46-7*) Soc Human Resc Mgmt.

Tax Reform Act of 1986. LC 86-72465. 352p. 1986. pap. 37.00 (*0-8318-0573-0*, B573) Am Law Inst.

Tax Reform Act of 1986, 2 vols. (Tax Management Portfolio Ser.: No. 986). 1987. 100.00 (*1-55871-096-5*) BNA.

T

*__Tax Reform Act of 1986 & Its Impact on the Real Estate Industry.__ Marilyn L. Hankel. 31p. 1993. pap. 10.00 (*0-86602-300-3*, Sage Prdcls Pr) Sage.

Tax Reform & Real Estate. Ed. by James R. Follain. (Illus.). 246p. (Orig.). 1986. pap. text ed. 32.00 (*0-87766-396-3*) Urban Inst.

Tax Reform & the Cost of Capital: An International Comparison. Ed. by Dale W. Jorgenson & Ralph Landau. 420p. 1993. 52.95 (*0-8157-4716-0*); pap. 24.95 (*0-8157-4715-2*) Brookings.

Tax Reform & the U. S. Economy. Joseph A. Pechman. LC 87-70178. (Dialogues on Public Policy Ser.). 108p. 1987. pap. 10.95 (*0-8157-6959-8*) Brookings.

Tax Reform for a Productive Economy: CED Statement on National Policy. (CED Statement on National Policy Ser.). 29p. 1985. pap. 5.00 (*0-87186-081-3*) Comm Econ Dev.

Tax Reform in Developing Countries. Ed. by Malcolm Gillis. LC 88-36859. (Fiscal Reform in the Developing World Ser.). ix, 545p. (C). 1989. text ed. 79.95 (*0-8223-0874-6*); pap. text ed. 29.95 (*0-8223-0898-3*) Duke.

Tax Reform in Disequilibrium Economies. Serge Wibaut. (Illus.). 150p. 1989. 44.95 (*0-521-35588-5*) Cambridge U Pr.

Tax Reform in Eighteenth-Century Lombardy. Daniel M. Klang. (East European Monographs: No. 27). 110p. 1977. text ed. 47.00 (*0-914710-20-6*) East Eur Monographs.

Tax Reform, Spending Reform, & Party Realignment. Aaron Wildavsky. 1987. pap. 1.00 (*1-55614-129-7*) U of SD Gov Res Bur.

Tax Reform, 1969: A Legislative History of the Tax Reform Act of 1969, 25 vols., Set. Ed. by Bernard D. Reams, Jr. LC 91-71948. 27000p. 1991. lib. bdg. 2,250.00 (*0-89941-762-0*, 306130) W S Hein.

Tax Reform 1971: A Legislative History of the Revenue Act of 1971, 6 vols., Set. Ed. by Bernard D. Reams, Jr. LC 95-80021. 1996. 595.00 (*0-89941-988-7*, 307530) W S Hein.

Tax Reform 1975: A Legislative History of the Tax Reduction Act of 1975 Public Law No. 94-12, 8 Vols., Set. Ed. by Bernard D. Reams, Jr. 9324p. 1995. 825.00 (*0-89941-984-4*, 307390) W S Hein.

Tax Reform, 1976: A Legislative History of the Tax Reform Act of 1976 (Public Law 94-455), 17 vols. Ed. by Bernard D. Reams, Jr. & Emelyn B. House. 1992. Set. 1,525.00 (*0-89941-773-6*, 307020) W S Hein.

Tax Reform 1978: A Legislative History of the Revenue Act of 1978. Ed. by Bernard D. Reams, Jr. LC 78-72018. 1982. fiche 348.00 (*0-89941-565-2*, 301801) W S Hein.

Tax Reform 1980: A Legislative History of Public Law 96-613, 3 vols., Set. Ed. by Bernard D. Reams, Jr. LC 95-78418. 3464p. 1995. 295.00 (*1-57588-280-9*, 307960) W S Hein.

Tax Reform 1984: The Law, Reports, Hearings, Debates & Related Documents, 20 vols. Ed. by Bernard D. Reams, Jr. LC 85-45437. 1985. fiche 515.00 (*0-89941-669-1*, 303931) W S Hein.

Tax Reform 1986: A Legislative History of the Tax Reform Act of 1986, 64 vols. Bernard D. Reams, Jr. & Margaret H. McDermott. 1987. lib. bdg. 3,985.00 (*0-89941-621-7*, 305450) W S Hein.

An Asterisk (*) at the beginning of an entry indicates that the title is appearing in BIP for the first time.

Tax Reform 1988: A Legislative History of the Technical & Miscellaneous Revenue Act of 1988 Public Law No. 100-647, 30 vols., Set. Ed. by Bernard D. Reams, Jr. LC 94-79748. 1994. 2,595.00 (*0-89941-886-4*, 307310) W S Hein.

*__Tax Reform's "Third Rail" Mortgage Interest.__ Bruce Barlett. 9p. 1996. pap. 5.00 (*1-56808-070-0*, BG139) Natl Ctr Pol.

Tax Regulations Specialist. (Career Examination Ser.: C-3755). pap. 29.95 (*0-8373-3755-0*) Nat Learn.

Tax Regulatory Update 1993: Tax Strategies for Corporate Acquisitions, Dispositions, Financings, Joint Ventures, Reorganizations, & Restructurings. (Tax Law & Estate Planning Course Handbook Ser.: Vol. 337). 548p. 1993. 70.00 (*0-685-69745-2*, J4-3667) PLI.

Tax Relations Among Governmental Units. Tax Policy League Staff. LC 77-74959. (American Federalism-the Urban Dimension Ser.). 1978. reprint ed. lib. bdg. 21.95 (*0-405-10502-9*) Ayer.

Tax Relief. Henry Bloch & Michael Shook. (Illus.). 128p. 1995. pap. 6.95 (*0-8362-0556-1*) Andrews & McMeel.

*__Tax Religions, Foundations, Unions, Charities, Etc.__ Max. 50p. (Orig.). 1997. pap. 30.00 (*0-922070-75-X*) M Tecton Pub.

Tax Reports: Live & Leading Cases 1875-1985. O. P. Wylie. 1987. boxed 1,100.00 (*0-86205-283-1*, U.K.) MICHIE.

*__Tax Research: IRS Has Made Progress but Major Challenges Remain.__ (Illus.). 66p. (Orig.). (C). 1996. pap. 25.00 (*0-7881-3480-9*) DIANE Pub.

Tax Research Techniques. 2nd ed. Ray M. Sommerfeld & G. Fred Streuling. LC 81-176005. (Tax Study Ser.: No. 5). (Illus.). 249p. reprint ed. pap. 71.00 (*0-8357-6733-7*, 2035386) Bks Demand.

Tax Research Techniques. 3rd rev. ed. Ray M. Sommerfeld et al. LC 89-8910. (Studies in Federal Taxation: No. 5). 278p. reprint ed. pap. 79.30 (*0-7837-6637-8*, 2046229) Bks Demand.

Tax Research Techniques. 4th ed. Robert L. Gardner & Dave N. Stewart. LC 93-454. 1993. 35.75 (*0-87051-133-5*) Am Inst CPA.

Tax Return Practice Problems for Corporations, S Corporations, & Partnerships, 1991. 6th ed. Marguerite R. Hutton & Thomas Dalton. 184p. (C). 1992. text ed. 19.95 (*0-256-11272-X*, 35-2650-06) Irwin.

Tax Return Preparer's Liability. Jules Ritholz & Barry London. LC 85-147123. 25.00 (*0-13-885252-9*) P-H.

Tax Revolt. Alvin Rabushka & Pauline Ryan. (Publication Ser.: No. 270). 272p. 1982. 6.78 (*0-8179-7701-5*) Hoover Inst Pr.

Tax Revolt: Something for Nothing in California. David O. Sears & Jack Citrin. LC 81-20049. (Illus.). 304p. 1982. 36.00 (*0-674-86835-8*) HUP.

Tax Revolt: Something for Nothing in California. enl. ed. David O. Sears & Jack Citrin. LC 84-25233. 304p. 1985. pap. 15.95 (*0-674-86836-6*) HUP.

Tax Revolt: The Battle for the Constitution. Martin A. Larson. LC 84-14219. 304p. 1985. 16.95 (*0-8159-6922-8*) Devin.

Tax Sales Manual 1983-84. Russell A. Morse, Jr. (Mining District Record Ser.). 8p. 1983. pap. 25.00 (*0-943714-00-1*) Cmdrs-Rusty's.

Tax Sales Manual, 1984-85. Russell A. Morse, Jr. 32p. 1984. pap. 17.50 (*0-943714-01-X*) Cmdrs-Rusty's.

Tax Savers. Incl. . 5.95 (*0-685-17256-2*); . 5.95 (*0-685-17257-0*); . 5.95 (*0-685-17258-9*); . 5.95 (*0-685-17259-7*); 1986. write for info. (*0-318-61428-6*, Sunset) Sunset Bks Inc.

Tax Saving Ideas for Retirees. 48p. 1982. 3.50 (*0-685-07417-X*, 88670-5) P-H.

Tax Saving Plans for the Self-Employed: Reflecting the Technical & Miscellaneous Revenue Act of 1988. 80p. pap. 5.00 (*0-318-33213-2*, 4956) Commerce.

*__Tax Savings Strategy Guide.__ Ernst & Young Staff. pap. text ed. write for info. (*0-471-95282-6*) Wiley.

Tax Savings thru Interest-Free Loans. rev. ed. Harry G. Gordon. Orig. Title: Tax Avoidance thru Interest-Free Loans. 162p. (Orig.). (C). 1981. reprint ed. pap. 19.95 (*0-9612184-0-1*) H G Gordon.

Tax Savvy for Small Business. Fred S. Steingold. (Illus.). 320p. 1996. pap. 26.95 (*0-87337-262-X*) Nolo Pr.

*__Tax Savvy for Small Business.__ 2nd rev. ed. Frederick W. Daily. LC 96-39243. (Illus.). 302p. (Orig.). 1997. pap. 26.95 (*0-87337-372-3*) Nolo Pr.

Tax Secrets of the Wealthy. Irving L. Blackman & Brian T. Whitlock. (Special Report Ser.). 1995. ring bd. 367.00 (*0-916181-38-3*) Blackman Kallick Bartelstein.

Tax Shelter Opportunities in Real Estate. Executive Reports Corporation Editorial Staff. 1978. 89.50 (*0-13-885269-3*) Exec Reports.

Tax Sheltered Opportunities for the Owner of a Closely-Held Business. Executive Reports Corporation Editorial Staff. 1981. 119.50 (*0-13-886507-8*) Exec Reports.

Tax Shelters: The Basics. Andersen, Arthur & Co. Staff. LC 82-74373. (Illus.). iii, 147p. 1985. 15.95 (*0-318-11685-5*) A Andersen.

Tax Shelters & Tax-Free Income for Everyone, Vol. 1. 4th ed. William C. Drollinger. LC 81-125456. 1981. 21.95 (*0-914244-04-3*) Epic Pubns.

Tax Shelters & Tax-Free Income for Everyone, Vol II. 4th ed. William C. Drollinger & William C. Jr. Drollinger. LC 81-125456. 1981. 24.95 (*0-914244-06-X*) Epic Pubns.

Tax Shelters & Tax-Free Income for Everyone: Special Edition. William C. Drollinger. LC 81-125456. 1981. 14.95 (*0-914244-08-6*) Epic Pubns.

Tax Shelters for the Middle Class. R. Westin. 1982. text ed. 95.00 (*0-07-069484-2*) McGraw.

Tax Shelters in Executive Compensation. Executive Reports Corporation Editorial Staff. 1979. 89.50 (*0-13-886721-6*) Exec Reports.

*__Tax Specific Term Structures of Interest Rates: Evidence from the United Kingdom Government Bond Market.__ Andrew Derry & Mahmood Pradhan. (Bank of England, Working Paper Ser.: Vol. 11). 29p. reprint ed. pap. 25.00 (*0-608-05320-1*, 2065858) Bks Demand.

Tax Strategies: Making the Right Decision. 2nd ed. Auster. 312p. 1988. 37.50 (*0-685-67804-0*, 5273) Commerce.

Tax Strategies for Corporate Acquisitions, Dispositions, Financings, Joint Ventures, Reorganizations, & Restructurings, 5 vols. (Tax Law & Estate Planning Ser.). 4893p. 1991. Set. pap. text ed. 50.00 (*0-685-59338-X*, J4-3652) PLI.

Tax Strategies for Corporate Acquisitions, Dispositions, Spin-Offs, Joint Ventures & Other Strategic Alliances, Financings, Reorganizations & Restructurings 1994, 9 vols., Set. (Tax Law & Estate Planning Course Handbook Ser.). 9512p. 1994. pap. 220.00 (*0-685-65538-5*, J4-3672) PLI.

Tax Strategies for Corporate Acquisitions, Dispositions, Spin-Offs, Joint Ventures, Financings, Reorganizations & Restructurings 1995, 10 vols., Set. (Tax Law & Estate Planning Course Handbook Ser.). Date not set. pap. 299.00 (*0-614-17278-0*, J4-3678) PLI.

Tax Strategy for Physicians. 3rd ed. Lawrence Farber. 300p. 1986. 35.95 (*0-87489-387-9*) Med Econ.

*__Tax Systems Modernization: Management & Technical Weaknesses Must Be Corrected If Modernization Is to Succeeed.__ Rona B. Stillman. (Illus.). 64p. (C). 1996. reprint ed. pap. 25.00 (*0-7881-3596-1*) DIANE Pub.

*__Tax Table Handbook, 1997 Edition.__ 832p. 1996. pap. 29.50 (*0-614-26824-9*, 16996BLS01) Commerce.

Tax Tactics for Small Business: Pay Less Taxes Legally. Ed. by Dale L. Flesher. 100p. (Orig.). 1980. pap. 4.00 (*0-938004-06-9*) U MS Bus Econ.

Tax Technician. Jack Rudman. (Career Examination Ser.: C-2370). 1994. pap. 27.95 (*0-8373-2370-3*) Nat Learn.

Tax Technician Trainee. Jack Rudman. (Career Examination Ser.: C-214). 1994. pap. 23.95 (*0-8373-0214-5*) Nat Learn.

Tax Techniques for Foundations & Other Exempt Organizations, 7 vols. Stanley S. Weithorn. 1979. Updates available. ring bd. write for info. (*0-8205-1807-7*) Bender.

*__Tax Time.__ Tana Reiff. LC 94-79115. (That's Life Ser.: Bk. 7). 96p. 1994. pap. 4.95 (*0-7854-1092-9*, 40707); audio 10.95 (*0-7854-1101-1*, 40717) Am Guidance.

Tax Tips & Strategies: Income Tax Hints Every Taxpayer Should Know, 1994. 2nd ed. Larry F. Meyers. (Illus.). 1993. pap. 14.95 (*0-9639166-0-2*) L Meyers Pubng.

Tax Tips & Strategies: 1995 Edition. Larry F. Meyers. (Illus.). 160p. 1995. pap. 13.95 (*0-9639166-1-0*) L Meyers Pubng.

Tax Tips for Horse Owners. Thomas A. Davis. 16p. 1997. 10.00 (*0-317-04924-0*) Am Horse Coun.

Tax Tips for Professionals. Prentice Hall Editorial Staff. LC 85-154863. 4.25 (*0-13-884973-0*) P-H.

Tax Tips for the Small Business Owner & Professional, 1989. General Business Services, Inc. Staff. (Illus.). 200p. 1988. 8.95 (*0-923716-01-7*) Genl Busn Servs.

Tax Tips for Writers. 2nd ed. Elizabeth Klungness. 1996. pap. text ed. 8.95 (*0-910431-02-7*) Tower Ent.

Tax Treaties. ring bd. write for info. (*0-318-57366-0*) P-H.

Tax Treaties Between Developed & Developing Countries: Eighth Report. 23p. 1980. 5.00 (*92-1-159025-6*, E.80. XVI.1) UN.

Tax Treatment of Computer Software. (Cahiers de Droit Fiscal International Ser.: Vol. LXXIIIb). 580p. 1988. pap. 100.00 (*90-6544-363-0*) Kluwer Law Tax Pubs.

Tax Treatment of Employment-Based Health Insurance. Leonard Burman. (Illus.). 59p. (Orig.). (C). 1994. pap. text ed. 30.00 (*0-7881-1090-X*) DIANE Pub.

Tax Treatment of Financial Instruments: A Survey to France, Germany, The Netherlands & the United Kingdom. Ed. by Cyrille David et al. LC 93-42437. (Series on International Taxation: Vol. 14). 1993. write for info. (*90-6544-666-4*) Kluwer Law Tax Pubs.

Tax Treatment of Fringe Benefits. Stephen A. Woodbury & Wei-Jang Huang. LC 91-6792. 178p. 1991. text ed. 25.00 (*0-88099-107-0*); pap. text ed. 15.00 (*0-88099-108-9*) W E Upjohn.

Tax Treatment of Inside Buildup in Life Insurance Products. Michael A. Schuyler. 41p. 1994. pap. 6.95 (*0-614-04375-1*) IRET.

Tax Treatment of Interest in International Economic Transactions. (Cahiers de Droit Fiscal International Ser.: Vol. LXVIIa). 662p. 1982. pap. 109.00 (*90-6544-060-7*) Kluwer Law Tax Pubs.

Tax Treaty Networks: 1988-1989 Edition. J. S. Phillips. 712, xxiip. 1988. text ed. 189.00 (*2-88316-000-7*) Gordon & Breach.

Tax Treaty Networks, 1991. 2nd ed. John S. Phillips. 882, xviip. 1991. text ed. 293.00 (*2-88316-003-1*) Gordon & Breach.

Tax Tricks. 4th ed. David Coleman. LC 90-86067. (For the Proprietor Ser.). 1995. pap. 20.00 (*0-930726-10-3*) Concept Pub.

Tax Warranties & Indemnities. 2nd ed. Tony Ring & John Clark. 180p. 1990. boxed 120.00 (*0-614-05553-9*, UK) MICHIE.

Tax Warranties & Indemnities (with Precedents) 2nd ed. Tony Ring & John Clark. 1990. U. K. 120.00 (*0-406-51166-7*, U.K.) MICHIE.

Tax We Need. 2nd rev. ed. Tertius Chandler. 103p. 1980. pap. 6.00 (*0-9603872-3-4*) Gutenberg.

Tax Wise Money Strategies: Protect Yourself from the Highest Taxes in History. Robert C. Carlson. (Illus.). 208p. 1995. pap. 14.95 (*0-7867-0165-X*) Carroll & Graf.

Tax-Wise Ways to Handle Retirement Benefits in Marital Split-Ups. 32p. 1983. 2.30 (*0-685-07418-8*) P-H.

Tax-Wise Ways to Sell Your House. Prentice Hall Editorial Staff. 30p. 1984. 2.75 (*0-685-08926-6*, 88679-6) P-H.

Tax Without Tears for Economic Independence & National Integration. V. Sathe. 1994. write for info. (*81-224-0676-9*, Pub. by Wiley Estrn II) Franklin.

Taxable & Business Income. Dan T. Smith & J. Keith Butters. (Fiscal Studies: No. 2). 367p. 1949. reprint ed. 29.95 (*0-87014-118-X*) Ayer.

Taxable & Business Income. Ed. by Dan T. Smith & J. Keith Butters. LC 50-5132. (National Bureau of Economic Research, Fiscal Studies: No. 2). 368p. reprint ed. pap. 104.90 (*0-7837-4523-0*, 2005978) Bks Demand.

Taxable & Tax-Free Corporate Mergers, Acquisitions & LBO'S. Samuel C. Thompson Jr. (American Casebook Ser.). 430p. 1994. pap. 32.00 (*0-314-03547-8*) West Pub.

Taxable Sales, 1990: An Analysis of Current & Past Taxable Sales for Virginia Localities. (Electronic Bulletin Board Ser.). 1991. 6.50 (*0-685-49113-7*) U VA Ctr Pub Serv.

Taxables in the City of Philadelphia. Hannah B. Roach. (Special Publications: No. 4). 41p. 1990. reprint ed. pap. 6.00 (*1-887099-03-4*) Geneal Soc Pa.

Taxane Anticancer Agents Vol. 583: Basic Science & Current Status. Ed. by Gunda I. Georg et al. LC 94-37226. (Symposium Ser.: No. 583). (Illus.). 368p. 1994. 99.95 (*0-8412-3073-0*) Am Chemical.

Taxation. Thomas Docherty. 176p. 1994. pap. 33.00 (*0-273-60732-4*, Pub. by Pitman Pubng UK) St Mut.

Taxation. Charles Hirsch. LC 92-5198. (Good Citizenship Ser.). (Illus.). 48p. (J). (gr. 5-6). 1992. lib. bdg. 24.26 (*0-8114-7356-2*) Raintree Steck-V.

Taxation: Adaptable to Courses to Bittker, Clark & McCouch's Casenotes on Estate & Gift Taxation. Casebooks Publishing Co., Inc. Staff. Ed. by Norman S. Goldenberg et al. (Legal Briefs Ser.). 1996. pap. write for info. (*0-87457-128-6*, 1217) Casenotes Pub.

Taxation: Adaptable to Courses Utilizing Andrew's Casebook on Basic Federal Income Taxation. Casenotes Publishing Co., Inc. Staff. Ed. by Norman S. Goldenberg et al. (Legal Briefs Ser.). 1991. pap. write for info. (*0-87457-126-X*, 1215) Casenotes Pub.

Taxation: Adaptable to Courses Utilizing Freeland, Lind & Stephens' Casebook on Fundamentals of Federal Income Taxation. Casenotes Publishing Co., Inc. Staff. Ed. by Norman S. Goldenberg et al. (Legal Briefs Ser.). 1996. pap. write for info. (*0-87457-129-4*, 1212) Casenotes Pub.

Taxation: Adaptable to Courses Utilizing Graetz's Schenk's Casebook on Federal Income Taxation. Casenotes Publishing Co., Inc. Staff. Ed. by Norman S. Goldenberg et al. (Legal Briefs Ser.). 1995. pap. write for info. (*0-87457-130-8*, 1211) Casenotes Pub.

Taxation: Adaptable to Courses Utilizing Kahn & Waggoner's Casebook on Basic Federal Taxation of Gifts, Trusts, & Estates. Casenotes Publishing Co., Inc. Staff. Ed. by Norman S. Goldenberg & Peter Tenen. (Legal Briefs Ser.). 1982. pap. write for info. (*0-87457-131-6*, 1214) Casenotes Pub.

Taxation: Adaptable to Courses Utilizing Klein, Bankman, Bittker & Stone's Casebook on Federal Income Taxation. Casenotes Publishing Co., Inc. Staff. Ed. by Norman S. Goldenberg et al. (Legal Briefs Ser.). 1993. pap. write for info. (*0-87457-127-8*, 1210) Casenotes Pub.

Taxation: Adaptable to Courses Utilizing Lind, Schwarz, Lathrope & Rosenberg's Casebook on Fundamentals of Corporate Taxation. Casenotes Publishing Co., Inc. Staff. Ed. by Norman S. Goldenberg & Peter Tenen. (Legal Briefs Ser.). (Orig.). 1991. pap. text ed. write for info. (*0-87457-150-2*, 1218) Casenotes Pub.

Taxation: Adaptable to Courses Utilizing Surrey, Warren, McDaniel & Gutman's Casebook on Federal Wealth Transfer Taxation. Casenotes Publishing Co., Inc. Staff. Ed. by Peter Tenen et al. (Legal Briefs Ser.). 1982. pap. write for info. (*0-87457-133-2*, 1213) Casenotes Pub.

Taxation: Managing the Small Business, Vol. 16. Cliff Headford. 36p. 1995. 8.95 (*0-644-45508-X*, Pub. by AGPS Pr AT) Intl Spec Bk.

Taxation: The People's Business. Andrew W. Mellon. LC 73-2521. (Big Business; Economic Power in a Free Society Ser.). 1973. reprint ed. 19.95 (*0-405-05101-8*) Ayer.

Taxation & Accounting for Financial Instruments. Andrew Boynton et al. 408p. 1995. 140.00 (*1-873446-08-X*, Pub. by IFR Pub UK) Am Educ Systs.

Taxation & Benefit Reform in Central & Eastern Europe. Ed. by David M. Newbery. 217p. (C). 1995. pap. 24.95 (*1-898128-19-7*) Brookings.

Taxation & Confiscation. Intro. by Hans F. Sennholz. (Freeman Classics Ser.). iv, 206p. (Orig.). 1993. pap. 14.95 (*0-910614-89-X*) Foun Econ Ed.

Taxation & Democracy: Swedish, British, & American Approaches to Financing the Modern State. Sven Steinmo. 1996. pap. 17.00 (*0-300-06721-6*) Yale U Pr.

Taxation & Development: Lessons from Colombian Experience. Richard M. Bird. LC 77-89965. 294p. reprint ed. pap. 83.80 (*0-7837-4447-1*, 2057977) Bks Demand.

Taxation & Economic Development: A Blueprint for Tax Reform in Ohio. Ed. by Roy Bahl. 1995. 44.95 (*1-57477-015-2*) Battelle.

Taxation & Economic Development: A Conference in Hungary. Michael Wasylenko et al. (International Socioeconomic Research Ser.). 321p. (HUN.). (C). 1988. pap. text ed. 20.00 (*0-940191-10-5*) Univ TN Ctr Bus Econ.

Taxation & Economic Development: Twelve Critical Studies. Ed. by J. F. Toye. (Twelve Critical Studies Ser.). 299p. 1978. 35.00 (*0-7146-3016-0*, Pub. by F Cass Pubs UK); pap. 17.50 (*0-7146-4028-X*, Pub. by F Cass Pubs UK) Intl Spec Bk.

Taxation & Economic Development among Pacific Asian Countries. Ed. by Richard A. Musgrave et al. 290p. (C). 1994. text ed. 83.50 (*0-8133-8751-5*) Westview.

Taxation & Economic Performance. W. Kurt Hauser. LC 96-7834. (Essays in Public Policy Ser.: No. 68). 1996. pap. 5.00 (*0-8179-5732-4*) Hoover Inst Pr.

Taxation & Fiscal Federalism: Essays in Honour of Russell Mathews. G. Brennan et al. 320p. 1988. 20.00 (*0-08-034401-1*, Pergamon Pr) Elsevier.

Taxation & Foreign Currency: Supplement One, 1973-1981. Donald R. Ravenscroft. LC 81-19391. 233p. 1982. pap. 30.00 (*0-915506-25-4*) Harvard Law Intl Tax.

Taxation & Foreign Currency: The Income Tax Consequences of Foreign Exchange Transactions & Exchange Rate Fluctuations. Donald R. Ravenscroft. LC 72-81277. (Illus.). 888p. 1973. 50.00 (*0-915506-15-7*) Harvard Law Intl Tax.

Taxation & Household Saving. OECD Staff. 308p. (Orig.). 1994. pap. 60.00 (*92-64-14251-7*) OECD.

Taxation & Household Savings: Country Surveys. OECD Staff. 212p. (Orig.). 1994. pap. 24.00 (*92-64-04265-2*) OECD.

Taxation & Human Rights. (IFA Congress Seminar Ser.: Vol. XII). 92p. 1988. pap. 45.00 (*90-6544-384-3*) Kluwer Law Tax Pubs.

Taxation & International Capital Flows: A Symposium of OECD & Non-OECD Countries, June, 1990. OECD Staff. 283p. (Orig.). 1990. pap. 36.00 (*92-64-13426-3*) OECD.

Taxation & Investment Flows: An Exchange of Experiences Between the OECD & the Dynamic Asian Economies. OECD Staff. 264p. (Orig.). 1994. pap. 45.00 (*92-64-14309-2*) OECD.

Taxation & Liberty. Anwar M. Shaikh. 442p. (C). 1988. 125.00 (*0-9513349-0-5*) St Mut.

Taxation & Public Goods: A Welfare-Economic Critique of Tax Policy Analysis. Herbert Kiesling. 400p. (C). 1992. text ed. 65.00 (*0-472-10346-6*) U of Mich Pr.

Taxation & Small Businesses. OECD Staff & Mark Robson. 126p. (Orig.). 1994. pap. 20.00 (*92-64-14093-X*, 23-94-02-1) OECD.

Taxation & the Community's Internal Market. Alex J. Easson. LC 92-44634. (European Community Law Ser.: Vol. 6). 220p. (C). 1993. text ed. 90.00 (*0-485-70010-7*, Pub. by Athlone Pr UK) Humanities.

Taxation & the Deficit Economy: Fiscal Policy & Capital Formation in the United States. Ed. by Dwight R. Lee. LC 85-63549. (Illus.). 554p. (C). 1986. 34.95 (*0-936488-13-1*); pap. 15.95 (*0-936488-03-4*) PRIPP.

Taxation Aspects of Currency Fluctuations. 2nd ed. Jill C. Pagan. 1991. 150.00 (*0-406-50886-0*, U.K.) MICHIE.

*__Taxation by Litigation: The Economics of Civil Justice Reform in Massachusetts.__ David G. Tuerck. Date not set. pap. text ed. write for info. (*1-886320-03-9*) BHIFPPR.

Taxation for Accountants. 110.00 (*0-685-69569-7*, TXAC) Warren Gorham & Lamont.

Taxation for Accountants: 1966-1996, 57 vols., Set. Bound set. 2,707.50 (*0-8377-9161-8*) Rothman.

Taxation for Engineering & Technical Consultants. Marc J. Lane. LC 80-12065. 182p. reprint ed. pap. 51.90 (*0-317-07941-7*, 2055530) Bks Demand.

Taxation for Environmental Protection: A Multinational Study. Sanford Gaines et al. LC 91-10310. 256p. 1991. text ed. 69.50 (*0-89930-575-X*, WTB/, Quorum Bks) Greenwood.

Taxation for Executors & Trustees. 7th ed. Anthony R. Mellows. 1993. U.K. pap. 101.00 (*0-406-62401-1*, U.K.) MICHIE.

Taxation for Lawyers. 110.00 (*0-685-69575-1*, TXLW) Warren Gorham & Lamont.

Taxation for Lawyers: 1972-1995/96, 24 vols., Set. Bound set. 1,560.00 (*0-8377-9162-6*) Rothman.

Taxation for Small Manufacturers. Marc J. Lane. LC 80-11621. 174p. reprint ed. pap. 49.60 (*0-317-07945-X*, 2055532) Bks Demand.

Taxation for the Computer Industry. Marc J. Lane. LC 80-12070. 189p. reprint ed. pap. 53.90 (*0-317-07943-3*, 2055531) Bks Demand.

Taxation, Housing Markets & the Markets for Building Land. B. Gutting. (Microeconomic Studies). viii, 138p. 1988. 44.00 (*0-387-18381-7*) Spr-Verlag.

Taxation in an Integrating World. Vito Tanzi. LC 94-27337. (Integrating National Economies: Promise & Pitfalls Ser.). 168p. (C). 1994. 34.95 (*0-8157-8298-5*); pap. 14.95 (*0-8157-8297-7*) Brookings.

Taxation in Ancient India. Kunwar Prasad. 1987. 21.00 (*0-317-89531-1*, Pub. by Mittal II) S Asia.

Taxation in Canada: 1995-1996 Edition. 2nd ed. Janet Denhamer. 560p. (C). 1995. per. 44.95 (*0-256-17503-9*) Irwin.

Taxation in Centrally Planned Economies. P. T. Wanless. LC 85-2118. 176p. 1985. text ed. 32.50 (*0-312-78633-6*) St Martin.

Taxation in Developing Countries. rev. ed. Ed. by Richard M. Bird & Oliver S. Oldman. LC 89-28367. (Studies in Development). 550p. 1990. pap. text ed. 29.95 (*0-8018-3944-0*) Johns Hopkins.

Taxation in Developing Countries. 4th rev. ed. Ed. by Richard M. Bird & Oliver S. Oldman. LC 89-28367. (Studies in Development). 550p. 1990. text ed. 69.50 (*0-8018-3943-2*) Johns Hopkins.

Taxation in Egypt from Augustus to Diocletian. Sherman L. Wallace. LC 69-14134. 512p. 1969. reprint ed. text ed. 79.50 (*0-8371-1049-1*, WATE, Greenwood Pr) Greenwood.

Taxation in OECD Countries. OECD Staff. 116p. (Orig.). 1993. pap. 36.00 (*92-64-13815-3*) OECD.

An Asterisk (*) at the beginning of an entry indicates that the title is appearing in BIP for the first time.

Taxation in Sub-Saharan Africa: Pt. I: Tax Policy & Administration in Sub-Saharan Africa & Pt. II: A Statistical Evaluation of Taxation in Sub-Saharan Africa. Carlos A. Aguirre et al. (Occasional Paper Ser.: No. 8). 73p. 1981. pap. 5.00 (*1-55775-081-5*) Intl Monetary.

Taxation in the Global Economy. Ed. by Assaf Razin & Joel Slemrod. LC 90-30262. (National Bureau of Economic Research Project Report Ser.). (Illus.). ix, 454p. 1991. pap. text ed. 23.00 (*0-226-70592-7*) U Ch Pr.

Taxation in the Global Economy. Ed. by Assaf Razin & Joel Slemrod. LC 90-30262. (National Bureau of Economic Research Project Report Ser.). (Illus.). 453p. reprint ed. pap. 129.20 (*0-7837-4095-6*, 2057916) Bks Demand.

Taxation in the Netherlands. Gerrit T. Spenke. 150p. 1995. lib. bdg. 70.00 (*90-6544-871-3*) Kluwer Ac.

Taxation in the Netherlands. 2nd ed. Gerrit T. Spenke. 154p. 1992. 55.00 (*90-6544-599-4*) Kluwer Law Tax Pubs.

Taxation in the People's Republic of China. Jinyan Li. LC 90-19994. 208p. 1991. text ed. 59.95 (*0-275-93688-0*, C3688, Praeger Pubs) Greenwood.

Taxation in the Republic of Ireland 1995-96. Glyn Saunders. 400p. 1995. pap. 225.00 (*0-614-09732-0*, Pub. by Tolley Pubng UK) St Mut.

Taxation in the Soviet Union. Michael A. Newcity. LC 85-19359. 406p. 1986. text ed. 59.95 (*0-275-92005-4*, C2005, Praeger Pubs) Greenwood.

Taxation in the U. S. A. & Europe - Theory & Practice: Proceedings of a Conference Held by the Confederation of European Economic Associations at Amsterdam, the Netherlands, 1991. Ed. by Anthonie Knoester. LC 93-7664. (Confederation of European Economic Associations Conference Volumes Ser.). 1993. text ed. 79.95 (*0-312-09989-4*) St Martin.

Taxation in the United States 1789-1816. Henry C. Adams. LC 78-63745. (Johns Hopkins University. Studies in the Social Sciences. Thirtieth Ser. 1912: 5-6). reprint ed. 37.50 (*0-404-61015-3*) AMS Pr.

Taxation, Inflation, & Interest Rates. Ed. by Vito Tanzi. xxiv, 247p. 1984. 20.00 (*0-939934-32-9*); pap. 15.00 (*0-939934-33-7*) Intl Monetary.

Taxation, Inflation, & Interest Rates. Ed. by Vito Tanzi. 271p. reprint ed. pap. 77.30 (*0-317-26530-X*, 2023981) Bks Demand.

Taxation Law. Martin Dubler. (LBC Nutshell Ser.). 120p. 1995. pap. 14.95 (*0-455-21324-0*, Pub. by Law Bk Co AT) Gaunt.

***Taxation Law in Australia.** 4th ed. Geoffrey Lehmann & Cynthia Coleman. 1417p. 1996. pap. 96.00 (*0-455-21407-7*, Pub. by Law Bk Co AT) Gaunt.

Taxation Laws of Australia, 14 vols., Set. 7,365.00 (*0-333-31482-4*, Austral) MICHIE.

Taxation of American Railroads: A Policy Analysis. Dennis L. Thompson. LC 79-6194. (Contributions in Economics & Economic History Ser.: No. 34). (Illus.). 248p. 1981. text ed. 55.00 (*0-313-22248-7*, TTR/, Greenwood Pr) Greenwood.

Taxation of Banks & Banking Operations. Tony Angel & David Greenhaigh. 1995. boxed write for info. (*0-406-00735-7*, UK) MICHIE.

Taxation of Branches & Subsidiaries in Western Europe, Canada & the U. S. A. S. N. Frommel. 121p. 1975. pap. text ed. 16.75 (*90-200-0429-8*) Rothman.

Taxation of Business by American State & Local Governments. Steven D. Gold. (Legislative Finance Papers: No. 53). 22p. 1986. pap. 6.25 (*1-55516-053-0*, 5101-53) Natl Conf State Legis.

Taxation of Business Entities, C Corporations, Partnerships & S Corporations: Teacher's Manual. Samuel C. Thompson, Jr. (American Casebook Ser.). 239p. 1994. pap. text ed. write for info. (*0-314-04401-9*) West Pub.

Taxation of Business Property: Is Uniformity Still a Valid Norm? Ed. by John H. Bowman. LC 94-2983. 224p. 1995. text ed. 57.95 (*0-275-94310-0*, Praeger Pubs) Greenwood.

Taxation of Capital Income. Alan J. Auerbach. (Economic Studies: No. 153). 136p. 1983. 20.00 (*0-674-86845-5*) HUP.

Taxation of Companies & Company Reconstructions. 6th ed. Richard Bramwell et al. 1994. 240.00 (*0-421-52030-2*, Pub. by Sweet & Maxwll UK) Gaunt.

Taxation of Companies & Corporate Investors. John Prebble. 64p. 1984. pap. 29.00 (*0-409-70142-4*, NZ) MICHIE.

Taxation of Corporate Joint Ventures. 2nd ed. Nigel Doran. 193p. 1996. 134.00 (*0-406-07916-1*) MICHIE.

Taxation of Corporate Liquidations. Robert W. Wood. 1987. ring bd. 160.00 (*0-685-69544-1*, TCLQ) Warren Gorham & Lamont.

Taxation of Corporations & Partnerships. 4th ed. Douglas A. Kahn & Jeffrey S. Lehman. (Hornbook Ser.). 1070p. 1994. write for info. (*0-556-77577-5*) West Pub.

Taxation of Corporations & Shareholders. Martin Norr. 226p. 1982. 42.00 (*90-6544-015-1*) Kluwer Ac.

Taxation of Corporations & Their Shareholders. David J. Shakow. (University Casebook Ser.). 408p. 1991. text ed. 31.50 (*0-88277-872-2*) Foundation Pr.

Taxation of Corporations & Their Shareholders. David J. Shakow. (University Casebook Ser.). 71p. (C). 1991. teacher ed., pap. text ed. write for info. (*0-88277-955-9*) Foundation Pr.

Taxation of Corporations & Their Shareholders, 1993. David J. Shakow. (University Casebook Ser.). 123p. 1994. suppl. ed., pap. text ed. 8.50 (*1-56662-124-0*) Foundation Pr.

Taxation of Corporations in Massachusetts. Harry G. Friedman. LC 76-76678. (Columbia University. Studies in the Social Sciences: No. 74). reprint ed. 27.50 (*0-404-51074-4*) AMS Pr.

***Taxation of Corporations, Partnerships & Their Owners.** 2nd ed. David J. Shakow. LC 97-13315. (University Casebook Ser.). 1997. write for info. (*1-56662-465-7*) Foundation Pr.

Taxation of Credit Unions. Albert E. Burger & Gregory J. Lypny. 68p. 1991. pap. 40.00 (*1-880572-01-X*) Filene Res.

***Taxation of Cross Border Income.** Vogel. 1994. pap. text ed. 17.50 (*90-6544-803-9*) Kluwer Ac.

Taxation of Cross Border Leasing, Vol. 525a. International Fiscal Association Staff. (Cahiers de Droit Fiscal International Ser.). 698p. 1990. pap. 103.00 (*90-6544-471-8*) Kluwer Law Tax Pubs.

Taxation of Damage Awards & Settlement Payments. Robert W. Wood. 500p. 1991. text ed. 129.00 (*0-9629404-0-2*) Tax Inst CA.

Taxation of Distributions from Qualified Plans. Dianne Bennett et al. 1991. text ed. 150.00 (*0-685-69577-8*, TADI) Warren Gorham & Lamont.

Taxation of Dividends & Corporate Distributions. Daniel Scheidner. 1000p. 195.00 (*0-614-05345-5*) Warren Gorham & Lamont.

Taxation of Domestic Shareholders on Undistributed Income of Foreign corporate Affiliates: Objectives, Techniques & Consequenses. (IFA Congress Seminar Ser.: Vol. XIa). 114p. 1987. pap. 42.00 (*90-6544-334-7*) Kluwer Law Tax Pubs.

Taxation of Estates: The Law in Ireland. J. M. O'Callaghan. 1993. pap. text ed. 91.00 (*1-85475-621-4*, IE) MICHIE.

***Taxation of Estates, Gifts & Trusts.** Regis W. Campfield et al. LC 97-2351. (American Casebook Ser.). 863p. 1997. text ed. write for info. (*0-314-21204-3*) West Pub.

Taxation of Farmers & Landowners. 5th ed. Oliver Stanley. 1993. pap. 90.00 (*0-406-02133-3*) MICHIE.

Taxation of Financial Institutions, 3 vols. Henry W. Schmidt et al. 1983. Looseleaf updates avail. ring bd. write for info. (*0-8205-1752-6*) Bender.

Taxation of Financial Instruments. Reuven S. Avi-Yonah et al. (Tax Law Ser.). ring bd. write for info. (*0-614-96289-7*) Clark Boardman Callaghan.

Taxation of Financial Services under a Consumption Tax. Peter R. Merrill. (AEI Studies in Tax Reform). 50p. (Orig.). 1997. pap. 9.95 (*0-8447-7072-8*, AEI Pr) Am Enterprise.

Taxation of Financially Distressed Businesses, 1 vol. David B. Newman. LC 93-9101. (Tax Ser.). 1993. 120.00 (*0-685-67256-5*) Clark Boardman Callaghan.

Taxation of Fringe Benefits. OECD Staff. 104p. (Orig.). 1988. pap. 13.20 (*92-64-13054-3*) OECD.

Taxation of Health & Welfare Benefits. Walter W. Miller. 1000p. 1995. 150.00 (*0-7913-2085-5*) Warren Gorham & Lamont.

Taxation of Hospitals & Health Care Organizations. Douglas M. Mancino. 1200p. 1995. 345.00 (*0-7913-2512-1*) Warren Gorham & Lamont.

Taxation of Income from Business & Capital in Colombia: Fiscal Reform in the Developing World. Charles E. McLure, Jr. et al. LC 89-11832. 422p. 1990. text ed. 74.95 (*0-8223-0925-4*) Duke.

Taxation of Income from Capital. Ed. by Arnold C. Harberger & Martin J. Bailey. LC 68-31834. (Studies of Government Finance). 349p. reprint ed. pap. 99.50 (*0-317-28361-8*, 2022558) Bks Demand.

Taxation of Income from Foreign Investments: A Tax Study of Developing Countries. Kibuta Ongwamuhana. 156p. 1991. pap. 40.00 (*90-6544-542-0*) Kluwer Law Tax Pubs.

Taxation of Individual Income. Burke & Friel. 1992. teacher ed. write for info. (*0-8205-0422-X*) Bender.

***Taxation of Individual Income.** 4th ed. J. Martin Burke & Michael K. Friel. LC 97-24840. (Contemporary Casebook Ser.). 1997. write for info. (*0-8205-2889-7*) Bender.

Taxation of Individuals & Companies. 6th ed. E. M. Stack & M. Cronje. 542p. 1992. pap. 70.00 (*0-614-05469-9*, SA) MICHIE.

Taxation of Insurance Business. 3rd ed. J. S. MacLeod & A. R. Levitt. 356p. 1992. boxed 175.00 (*0-406-50882-8*, U.K.) MICHIE.

Taxation of Intellectual Property. Anthony Pickford. 400p. 1993. pap. text ed. 100.00 (*0-406-01538-4*, UK) MICHIE.

Taxation of Intellectual Property: Tax Planning Guide. Marvin Petry. 1985. Looseleaf updates available. ring bd. write for info. (*0-8205-1688-0*) Bender.

Taxation of Intercompany Transactions in Selected Countries in Europe & the U. S. A. Ed. by Peat, Marwick, Mitchell & Co. Staff. 119p. 1979. pap. 16.00 (*90-200-0589-8*) Kluwer Ac.

Taxation of International Entertainers & Athletes: All the World's a Stage. Daniel Sandler. LC 95-40068. (Chartered Institute of Taxation Ser.: Vol. 1). 1995. write for info. (*90-411-0118-7*) Kluwer Law Tax Pubs.

Taxation of International Portfolio Investment. Donald J. Brean et al. 115p. 1991. pap. text ed. 20.00 (*0-88645-123-X*, Pub. by Inst Res Pub CN) Ashgate Pub Co.

***Taxation of International Transactions.** Charles H. Gustafson et al. (American Casebook Ser.). 921p. (C). 1996. text ed. write for info. (*0-314-20465-2*) West Pub.

Taxation of International Transactions: Code & Regulations Selected Sections, 1991-1992. 1624p. 1991. pap. 45.00 (*0-685-67805-9*, 4891) Commerce.

***Taxation of International Transactions Cases & Materials, Teacher's Manual to Accompany.** Charles H. Gustafson et al. (American Casebook Ser.). 330p. 1997. pap. text ed. write for info. (*0-314-22522-6*) West Pub.

Taxation of Investments. Lewis D. Solomon. LC 87-1288. write for info. (*0-15-004430-5*) P-H.

Taxation of Land Transactions. 4th ed. Jeffrey Price. 482p. 1994. pap. text ed. 110.00 (*0-406-62410-0*, UK) MICHIE.

***Taxation of Limited Liability Companies.** David J. Cartano. 500p. (Orig.). 1997. pap. text ed. 48.00 (*0-9658184-0-3*) Internet Pubns.

***Taxation of Lloyd's Underwriters.** 4th ed. K. S. Carmichael & P. H. Wolstenholme. 1994. write for info. (*0-406-01138-9*, UK) MICHIE.

Taxation of Mineral Enterprises. Otto. (International Energy & Resources Law & Policy Ser.). 1995. lib. bdg. 141.00 (*1-85966-105-X*) Kluwer Ac.

Taxation of Mineral Resources. Robert F. Conrad & R. Bryce Hool. LC 80-8392. 127p. reprint ed. pap. 36.20 (*0-7837-3261-9*, 2043280) Bks Demand.

Taxation of Mining Operations. Peter C. Maxfield. 1981. write for info. (*0-8205-1418-7*, 418) Bender.

Taxation of Multinational Corporations. Ed. by Joel Slemrod. LC 96-20103. 168p. (C). 1996. lib. bdg. 99.95 (*0-7923-9719-3*) Kluwer Ac.

Taxation of Nonrenewable Resources. Albert M. Church. LC 80-8784. 349p. reprint ed. pap. 99.50 (*0-7837-3260-0*, 2043279) Bks Demand.

Taxation of Partnerships, 1987-1991, 2 vols. John Bonn. Set. 240.00 (*0-685-24503-9*) Clark Boardman Callaghan.

Taxation of Passive Activities. write for info. (*0-318-66951-X*) P-H.

Taxation of Payments to Non-Residents for Independent Personal Services. (Cahiers de Droit Fiscal International Ser.: Vol. LXVIIb). 472p. 1982. pap. 100.00 (*90-6544-061-5*) Kluwer Law Tax Pubs.

Taxation of Personal Wealth. Alan A. Tait. LC 67-12992. (Illus.). 248p. reprint ed. pap. 70.70 (*0-8357-3564-8*, 2034464) Bks Demand.

Taxation of Productive Consumption in Developing Countries. Carl S. Shoup. 37p. 1989. pap. 6.95 (*1-55815-048-X*) ICS Pr.

Taxation of Property & Casualty Insurance Companies. Ernst & Young. 450p. 1996. text ed. 199.95 (*0-471-13030-3*) Wiley.

Taxation of Public Utilities. Herman Gonzalez & William A. Erken. 1992. write for info. (*0-8205-1761-5*) Bender.

Taxation of Real Estate Transactions, 2 vols. 2nd ed. Sanford M. Guerin. 1768p. 1988. text ed. 195.00 (*0-07-025101-0*) Shepards.

Taxation of Securities Transactions. Martin L. Fried. 1971. write for info. (*0-8205-1729-1*) Bender.

***Taxation of Small Business Enterprise: Individual Partnership & Corporation.** Philip F. Postlewaite. (American Casebook Ser.). 150p. 1996. teacher ed., pap. text ed. write for info. (*0-314-21812-2*) West Pub.

Taxation of Sole Proprietors. rev. ed. James A. Fellows. LC 96-21536. 220p. (Orig.). 1996. pap. text ed. 28.00 (*1-881934-18-7*) Unicorn Res.

Taxation of Specialized Industries: The Entertainment Industry. Schuyler M. Moore. Ed. by Silva & Cooley. 1995. 520.00 (*0-7913-2313-7*) Warren Gorham & Lamont.

Taxation of the Closely-Held Corporation. 4th ed. Theodore Ness & Eugene L. Vogel. 1991. Cumulative supplements, semi-annual. suppl. ed. 160.00 (*0-685-45578-5*, TCHC) Warren Gorham & Lamont.

Taxation of the Closely Held Corporation. 5th ed. Theodore Ness & Eugene L. Vogel. 1991. text ed. 160.00 (*0-685-69545-X*, TCHC) Warren Gorham & Lamont.

Taxation of the Family. 3rd ed. O. P. Wylie. 296p. 1993. pap. 70.00 (*0-406-02197-X*, U.K.) MICHIE.

Taxation of the Income Arising from the International Seabed. Ed. by International Fiscal Association Staff. (IFA Congress Seminar Ser.: Vol. VI). 160p. 1982. 49.00 (*90-6544-059-3*) Kluwer Law Tax Pubs.

Taxation of the Shipping Industry. 2nd ed. Richard E. Madigan. LC 82-7470. 108p. 1982. text ed. 20.00 (*0-87033-292-9*) Cornell Maritime.

Taxation of the United Kingdom. Charles F. Arrowood. (Works of Charles Flinn Arrowood). vi, 180p. 1985. reprint ed. lib. bdg. 39.00 (*0-685-10502-4*) Rprt Serv.

Taxation of Trusts: The Law in Ireland. J. M. O'Callaghan. 1993. pap. text ed. 91.00 (*1-85475-616-8*, IE) MICHIE.

Taxation of U. K. Corporate Investment in the U. S. A. Dicker. Ed. by W. Burke. 1988. 120.00 (*0-406-50173-4*, UK) MICHIE.

Taxation of U. S. Corporations Doing Business Abroad: U. S. Rules & Competitiveness Issues. Price Waterhouse LLP Staff. LC 95-83617. 101p. (Orig.). 1996. pap. 35.00 (*1-885065-06-X*, 096-05) Finan Exec.

Taxation of Urban Property in Less Developed Countries. Ed. by Roy W. Bahl. LC 78-65018. (Publications of the Committee on Taxation, Resources & Economic Development: Vol. 10). 299p. 1979. reprint ed. pap. 85.30 (*0-608-01973-9*, 2062628) Bks Demand.

Taxation of 401(K) & Other Salary Reduction Plans. Paul L. Behing. 800p. 1994. 145.00 (*0-7913-1979-2*) Warren Gorham & Lamont.

Taxation on Non-Residents. V. P. Verma. (C). 1989. 200.00 (*0-685-27888-3*) St Mut.

Taxation Policies & Financial Decisions. S. N. Mittal. (C). 1988. 200.00 (*0-685-36451-8*) St Mut.

Taxation, Poverty, & Income Distribution. Ed. by John Creedy. 272p. 1994. 80.00 (*1-85278-913-1*) E Elgar.

Taxation Questions. Clifford J. Mancer. vii, 122p. 1990. pap. 21.00 (*0-455-21005-5*, Pub. by Law Bk Co AT) Gaunt.

Taxation, Technology & the User Cost of Capital. Ed. by E. Biorn. (Contributions to Economic Analysis Ser.: No. 182). 325p. 1989. 120.75 (*0-444-87490-9*, North Holland) Elsevier.

Taxation Treatment of Compensation & Damages. Graham Chase. 264p. 1994. boxed 150.00 (*0-406-02305-0*, UK) MICHIE.

Taxation 1995. P. G. Rowes. 528p. 1995. pap. 59.95 (*1-85805-126-6*, Pub. by DP Publns UK) St Mut.

Tax/Benefit Position of Production Workers 1991-1994. 264p. (Orig.). (ENG & FRE.). 1995. pap. 54.00 (*92-64-04613-5*, Pub. by Org for Econ FR) OECD.

Taxe sur la Valeur Ajoutee et les Prestations de Services Internationalee: Etude de Droit Compare et de Droit Communautaire. Francois Kaiser. 234p. 1982. 33.00 (*90-6544-029-1*) Kluwer Ac.

Taxed to Death: Mystery Jigsaw Puzzle Thriller. John Lutz. (Bepuzzled Ser.). (Orig.). 1996. pap. 21.00 (*1-57561-007-8*, 00517TTD) Bepuzzled.

***Taxed to Death: The Book Lowell Weicker Didn't Write.** Jane Twain. LC 96-60766. 163p. (Orig.). 1996. pap. 10.40 (*0-9653014-3-5*) TWISI Pr.

Taxes - Burden or Blessing? Stanley Booth-Clibborn. (C). 1990. pap. 24.00 (*0-85305-298-0*, Pub. by J Arthur Ltd UK) St Mut.

Taxes Acts: Income, Corporation & Capital Gains Tax 1995, 7 vols. H. M. S. O. Staff. 1995. pap. text ed. 185.00 (*0-11-641422-7*, HM414227, Pub. by Stationery Ofc UK) Bernan Associates.

***Taxes Acts: Income, Corporation & Capital Gains Tax, 1996, 6 vols.** HMSO Staff. 1996. pap. 215.00 (*0-11-641427-8*, HM14278, Pub. by Stationery Ofc UK) Bernan Associates.

Taxes & Business Strategy: A Planning Approach. Myron S. Scholes & Mark A. Wolfson. 640p. 1991. text ed. 93.00 (*0-13-885740-7*, 110701) P-H.

Taxes & Capital Formation. Intro. by Martin Feldstein. LC 87-5898. (Illus.). xii, 130p. (C). 1987. 21.95 (*0-226-24079-7*) U Ch Pr.

***Taxes & Pensions - What the Matrimonial Lawyer Needs to Know.** 384p. 1993. 30.00 (*0-614-26692-0*, 19358) NYS Bar.

***Taxes & Pensions - What the Matrimonial Lawyer Needs to Know.** 384p. 1993. 92.00 incl. audio (*0-614-26693-9*, 29358) NYS Bar.

***Taxes & Pensions - What the Matrimonial Lawyer Needs to Know.** 384p. 1993. 175.00 incl. vhs (*0-614-26694-7*, 39358) NYS Bar.

Taxes & People in Israel. Harold C. Wilkenfeld. LC 72-76562. (Harvard Law School International Tax Program Ser.). (Illus.). 327p. 1973. 32.00 (*0-674-86850-1*) HUP.

Taxes & Social Contributions 1982-1993. Eurostat Staff. 187p. 1995. pap. 20.00 (*92-827-4383-7*, CA-89-95-5433AC, Pub. by Europ Com UK) Bernan Associates.

***Taxes & Social Contributions 1983-1994.** Eurostat Staff. 187p. 1996. pap. 25.00 (*92-827-7599-2*, CA96-96-869-3AC, Pub. by Europ Com UK) Bernan Associates.

Taxes & State Power: Political Instability in Bolivia, 1900-1950. Carmenza Gallo. 200p. 1991. 44.95 (*0-87722-800-0*) Temple U Pr.

Taxes & Tax Harmonization in Central America. Virginia G. Watkin. LC 67-26564. (Illus.). 534p. (Orig.). 1967. pap. 15.00 (*0-915506-07-6*) Harvard Law Intl Tax.

Taxes & the Professional Corporation. LC 86-70188. 40p. 1986. pap. 19.95 (*0-89707-220-0*, 515-0048-01) Amer Bar Assn.

Taxes & Wealth of a Nation. Dublin. 1996. 23.00 (*0-02-874024-6*) Free Pr.

Taxes & Wealth of a Nation. Dublin. 1997. 23.00 (*0-684-82724-7*) Free Pr.

Taxes Are Devilish Things. Francis Neilson. 1979. lib. bdg. 79.95 (*0-685-96638-0*) Revisionist Pr.

Taxes, Current Pronouncements, & Updated CMA Questions: 1987-1988. Grant W. Newton. (Illus.). 238p. 1987. 19.95 (*0-918937-15-9*) Malibu Pub.

Taxes, Deficits & the Current Recession. Gary Robbins & Aldona Robbins. 1991. pap. 10.00 (*0-943802-59-8*, 156) Natl Ctr Pol.

***Taxes for Busy People, 1998.** Robert Cooke. 1997. pap. text ed. 14.95 (*0-07-012557-0*) McGraw.

Taxes for Dummies: 1996 Edition. Eric Tyson. 1995. pap. 14.99 (*1-56884-394-1*) IDG Bks.

***Taxes for Dummies: 1997 Edition.** Eric Tyson. 1996. pap. 14.99 (*0-7645-5016-0*) IDG Bks.

Taxes for Dummies, 1995 Edition. Eric Tyson & David J. Silverman. 384p. 1994. pap. 14.99 (*1-56884-220-1*) IDG Bks.

***Taxes for Dummies, 1998 Edition.** Eric Tyson. 1997. pap. 14.99 (*0-7645-5069-1*) IDG Bks.

Taxes in Paradise: Developing Basic Income Tax Concepts. Richard L. Haight. (Illus.). xi, 198p. (Orig.). (C). 1990. pap. text ed. 12.50 (*0-8377-0713-7*) Rothman.

Taxes, Loans & Inflation: How the Nation's Wealth Becomes Misallocated. Eugene C. Steuerle. LC 84-45980. (Studies of Government Finance). 205p. 1985. 31.95 (*0-8157-8134-2*); pap. 12.95 (*0-8157-8133-4*) Brookings.

***Taxes on Business.** Kevin Armstrong. (Business Basics Ser.). 1994. pap. 12.95 (*0-7494-1122-8*) Kogan Page Ltd.

Taxes on Knowledge in America: Exactions on the Press from Colonial Times to the Present. Randall P. Bezanson. LC 93-44447. 336p. (C). 1994. text ed. 46.95 (*0-8122-3212-7*) U of Pa Pr.

Taxes, Subsidies & Competitiveness Internationally. John Mutti. LC 81-86163. (Committee on Changing International Realities Ser.). 76p. 1982. pap. 7.00 (*0-89068-062-0*) Natl Planning.

***Taxi.** Homeshaw. 1991. pap. text ed. write for info. (*0-17-556660-7*) Addison-Wesley.

Taxi. Christina Oxenberg. (Illus.). 208p. 1988. 14.95 (*0-7043-2517-9*, Pub. by Quartet UK) Interlink Pub.

Taxi: A Book of City Words. Betsy Maestro. LC 88-22867. (Illus.). (J). (ps-2). 1989. 14.95 (*0-89919-528-8*, Clarion Bks) HM.

T

Taxi: A Book of City Words. Betsy Maestro. LC 88-22867. (Illus.). (J). (ps-3). 1990. reprint ed. pap. 6.95 (*0-395-54811-X*, Clarion Bks) HM.

Taxi: Poem of Love in Transit. Adriano Espinola. Tr. by Charles A. Perrone from POR. LC 90-3042. (Library of World Literature in Translation: Vol. 21). (Illus.). 106p. 1993. text ed. 15.00 (*0-8240-0038-2*) Garland.

Taxi: The Harry Chapin Story. Peter M. Coan. 1990. pap. 14.95 (*0-8184-0513-9*) Carol Pub Group.

Taxi: The Official Fan's Guide. Frank Lovece & Jules Franco. LC 95-26387. (Illus.). 288p. 1996. pap. 17.95 (*0-8065-1801-4*, Citadel Pr) Carol Pub Group.

Taxi & Limosine Inspector. Jack Rudman. (Career Examination Ser.: C-2552). 1994. pap. 23.95 (*0-8373-2552-8*) Nat Learn.

Taxi Cat & Huey. Gen LeRoy. LC 90-27383. (Illus.). 144p. (J). (gr. 3-7). 1992. lib. bdg. 14.89 (*0-06-021769-3*) HarpC Child Bks.

Taxi-Dance Hall: A Sociological Study in Commercialized Recreation & City Life. Paul G. Cressey. LC 69-16236. (Criminology, Law Enforcement, & Social Problems Ser.: No. 76). (Illus.). 1969. reprint ed. 12.00 (*0-87585-076-6*) Patterson Smith.

Taxi Dog Christmas. Debra Barracca & Sal Barracca. LC 91-44953. (Illus.). 40p. (J). (ps-3). 1994. pap. 14.99 (*0-8037-1360-6*); pap. 14.89 (*0-8037-1361-4*) Dial Bks Young.

Taxi Driver. Paul Schrader. (Illus.). 91p. (Orig.). 1990. pap. 12.95 (*0-571-14464-0*) Faber & Faber.

Taxi Driver Wisdom. Photos by Joanna Dugan. LC 95-22085. 176p. 1996. 14.95 (*0-8118-1165-4*) Chronicle Bks.

Taxi Driving As a Profession: How to Do It Profitably. 1991. lib. bdg. 62.95 (*0-8490-4798-6*) Gordon Pr.

Taxi Driving Made Simple: How to Do It Profitably, Pleasurably & Professionally. Michael Santee. LC 89-6087. (Illus.). 252p. (Orig.). 1989. pap. 16.95 (*0-9622021-1-8*) Round Robin Pr.

Taxi from Hell: Confessions of a Russian Hack. Vladimir Lobas. LC 91-5680. 304p. 1992. pap. 12.00 (*0-939149-86-9*) Soho Press.

Taxi Mauve. Michel Deon. 160p. (FRE.). 1992. pap. 11.95 (*0-7859-2183-4*, 2070385108) Fr & Eur.

Taxi Navigator: A Novella. Richard Mosher. 144p. (J). (gr. 3-7). 1996. 15.95 (*0-399-23104-8*, Philomel Bks) Putnam Pub Group.

***Taxi! Taxi!** Cari Best. LC 96-21108. (Illus.). 32p. (J). (ps-3). 1997. pap. 6.95 (*0-531-07084-0*) Orchard Bks Watts.

Taxi That Hurried. Lucy S. Mitchell et al. (Little Golden Bks.). (Illus.). 24p. (J). (ps). 1992. write for info. (*0-307-00144-X*, 312-09, Golden Pr) Western Pub.

Taxi, the Harry Chapin Story. Peter Coan. LC 85-9125. 1987. 22.95 (*0-87949-262-7*) Ashley Bks.

Taxicab: An Urban Transportation Survivor. Gorman Gilbert & Robert E. Samuels. LC 82-2726. (Illus.). 214p. reprint ed. pap. 61.00 (*0-7837-2470-5*, 2042623) Bks Demand.

Taxicab Geometry: An Adventure in Non-Euclidean Geometry. Eugene Krause. 88p. 1986. reprint ed. pap. 3.95 (*0-486-25202-7*) Dover.

Taxicabs. (Research Record Ser.: No. 1103). 48p. 1986. 8.20 (*0-309-04124-4*) Transport Res Bd.

Taxicabs: Audit Technique Guides. (IRS Tax Audit Information Ser.). 24p. 1994. pap. 13.00 (*1-57402-108-7*) Athena Info Mgt.

Taxidermist's Journal: A Collection of True-Life Hunting & Fishing Stories. Brian E. McGray. Ed. by Meredith A. McGray. (Illus.). 108p. (Orig.). 1996. per., pap. 11.95 (*1-886975-02-7*) Goose Hse Pubns.

Taxidermy Color or the Dummy's Guide to Speedy Airbrush Coloring. Gerald O. Schaefer. (Illus.). 55p. 1985. student ed. 8.95 (*0-9614928-0-5*) Schaefer Studios.

Taxidermy Guide. 3rd ed. Russell Tinsley. 1990. pap. 14.95 (*0-88317-156-2*) Stoeger Pub Co.

Taxila: An Illustrated Account of Archaeological Excavations, 1913-1934, 3 vols. John Marshall. 1977. reprint ed. Set. 90.00 (*0-8364-0022-4*, Pub. by Motilal Banarsidass II) S Asia.

Taxing Agricultural Land in Developing Countries. Richard M. Bird. LC 73-77991. (Harvard Law School International Tax Program Ser.). 384p. 1974. 37.00 (*0-674-86855-2*) HUP.

Taxing America. Ed. by Karen B. Brown & Mary L. Fellows. 340p. (C). 1997. 65.00 (*0-8147-2648-8*); pap. 24.95 (*0-8147-2661-5*) NYU Pr.

Taxing & Spending: Issues of Process. Bruce G. Doern et al. 184p. 1995. pap. 22.50 (*0-8020-7194-5*) U of Toronto Pr.

Taxing & Spending Policy. Ed. by Larry Wade & Warren J. Samuels. 1980. pap. 15.00 (*0-918592-41-0*) Pol Studies.

Taxing Bads by Taxing Goods: Pollution Control with Presumptive Charges. Gunnar S. Eskeland & Shantayanan Devarajan. LC 95-49782. 72p. 1996. 10.95 (*0-8213-3457-3*) World Bank.

Taxing California Property, 1988-1989, 2 vols. Kenneth A. Ehrman & Sean Flavin. Set. 160.00 (*0-8321-0052-8*) Bancroft Whitney Co.

Taxing Capital Gains. Gary Robbins. 1989. pap. 10.00 (*0-943802-46-6*, 143) Natl Ctr Pol.

Taxing Choice: The Political Economy of Fiscal Discrimination. Ed. by William Shughart, II. LC 97-13662. 392p. 1997. text ed. 39.95 (*1-56000-303-0*); pap. text ed. 19.95 (*1-56000-931-4*) Transaction Pubs.

Taxing Choices. Timothy J. Conlan et al. 275p. 1989. 21.95 (*0-87187-480-6*) Congr Quarterly.

Taxing Consumption. OECD Staff. 288p. (Orig.). 1988. pap. text ed. 37.50 (*92-64-13160-4*, 23-88-09-1) OECD.

Taxing Consumption in a Global Economy. Harry Grubert & T. Scott Newlon. (AEI Studies in Tax Reform). 50p. (Orig.). 1997. pap. 9.95 (*0-8447-7069-8*, AEI Pr) Am Enterprise.

Taxing Energy: Oil Severance Taxation & the Economy. Robert Deacon et al. LC 89-15390. (Independent Institute Ser.). 176p. 1990. 43.95 (*0-8419-1179-7*) Holmes & Meier.

Taxing Heaven's Storehouse: Horses, Bureaucrats, & the Destruction of the Sichuan Tea Industry, 1074-1224. Paul J. Smith. (Harvard-Yenching Institute Monographs: Vol. 32). 489p. (C). 1991. 32.00 (*0-674-40641-9*) HUP.

***Taxing International Business: Emerging Trends in APEC & OECD Economies.** Ed. by Richard Vann. 148p. (Orig.). 1997. pap. 28.00 (*92-64-15455-8*, 23-97-02-1, Pub. by Org for Econ FR) OECD.

Taxing Multinational Corporations. Ed. by Martin Feldstein et al. LC 95-2789. (National Bureau of Economic Research Project Reports). 124p. 1995. 21.50 (*0-226-24094-0*) U Ch Pr.

Taxing Ourselves: A Citizens Guide to the Great Debate over Tax Reform. Joel Slemrod et al. LC 96-15005. (Illus.). 304p. 1996. 25.00 (*0-262-19375-2*) MIT Pr.

Taxing Profits in a Global Economy: Domestic & International Issues. OECD Staff. 470p. (Orig.). 1992. pap. 84.00 (*92-64-13596-0*) OECD.

Taxing Women. McCaffery. LC 96-30188. 1997. 29.95 (*0-226-55557-7*) U Ch Pr.

Taxis De la Marne. Jean Dutourd. 224p. (FRE.). 1973. pap. 11.95 (*0-7859-1767-5*, 2070365069) Fr & Eur.

Taxman Commeth! A Simulation Game Designed to Help You Avoid Small Business I. R. S. Problems. Karl Grube. (Illus.). 56p. (Orig.). 1996. pap. 24.00 (*0-614-13432-3*, 030941) Games By Grube.

Taxol: Science & Applications. Ed. by Matthew Suffness. 448p. 1995. 136.95 (*0-8493-8382-X*, 8382) CRC Pr.

Taxonomia y la Revolucion en las Ciencias Biologicas. rev. ed. (Serie de Biologia: No. 3). (SPA.). 1980. pap. 3.50 (*0-8270-6050-5*) OAS.

Taxonomic Analysis of Avian Faunal Remains from Three Archaeological Sites in Marina Del Rey, Los Angeles County, California, Vol. 30. Joan C. Brown. (Archives of California Prehistory Ser.: Vol. 30). 72p. (Orig.). (C). 1989. pap. text ed. 7.15 (*1-55567-068-7*) Coyote Press.

Taxonomic & Nomenclatural Study of the Genus Amanita Section Amanita for North America. D. T. Jenkins. (Bibliotheca Mycologica Ser.: No. 57). (Illus.). 1977. lib. bdg. 48.00 (*3-7682-1132-0*) Lubrecht & Cramer.

***Taxonomic Aspects of African Economic Botany.** Ed. by Gunther Kunkel. (Illus.). 250p. 1979. pap. 22.00 (*0-614-21725-3*, Pub. by Royal Botnic Grdns UK) Balogh.

***Taxonomic Atlas of the Benthic Fauna of the Santa Maria Basin & Western Santa Barbaa Channel Vol. 2: The Porifera.** rev. ed. Karen D. Green & Gerald J. Bakus. Ed. by James A. Blake & Paul H. Scott. LC 96-72236. (Illus.). iv, 87p. 1996. pap. 15.00 (*0-936494-22-0*) Santa B Museum.

***Taxonomic Atlas of the Benthic Fauna of the Santa Maria Basin & Western Santa Barbara Channel Vol. 1: Introduction, Benthic Ecology, Platyhelminthes, & Nemertea.** Ed. by James A. Blake & Andrew Lissner. LC 94-68651. (Illus.). viii, 132p. (Orig.). 1993. pap. 34.00 (*0-936494-06-9*) Santa B Museum.

***Taxonomic Atlas of the Benthic Fauna of the Santa Maria Basin & Western Santa Barbara Channel Vol. 2: The Porifera.** Karen D. Green & Gerald J. Bakus. Ed. by James A. Blake et al. LC 94-68651. (Illus.). iv, 82p. (Orig.). 1994. pap. 15.00 (*0-936494-07-7*) Santa B Museum.

***Taxonomic Atlas of the Benthic Fauna of the Santa Maria Basin & Western Santa Barbara Channel Vol. 4, Pt. 1: The Annelida: Oligochaeta & Polychaeta: Phyllodocida (Phyllodocidae to Paralacydoniidae)** Ed. by James A. Blake & Brigitte Hilbig. LC 94-68651. (Illus.). xviii, 377p. (Orig.). 1994. pap. 36.00 (*0-936494-09-3*) Santa B Museum.

***Taxonomic Atlas of the Benthic Fauna of the Santa Maria Basin & Western Santa Barbara Channel Vol. 5, Pt. 2: The Annelida: Polychaeta: Phyllodocida (Syllidae & Scale-Bearing Families), Amphinomida, & Eunicida.** Ed. by James A. Blake et al. LC 94-68651. (Illus.). viii, 378p. (Orig.). 1995. pap. 34.00 (*0-936494-10-7*) Santa B Museum.

***Taxonomic Atlas of the Benthic Fauna of the Santa Maria Basin & Western Santa Barbara Channel Vol. 6, Pt. 3: The Annelida: Polychaeta: Orbiniidae to Cossuridae.** Ed. by James A. Blake et al. LC 94-68651. (Illus.). vii, 418p. (Orig.). 1996. pap. 39.00 (*0-936494-11-5*) Santa B Museum.

***Taxonomic Atlas of the Benthic Fauna of the Santa Maria Basin & Western Santa Barbara Channel Vol. 9, Pt. 2: The Mollusca: the Gastropoda.** James H. McLean & Terrence M. Gosliner. Ed. by Paul H. Scott et al. LC 94-68651. (Illus.). vii, 228p. (Orig.). 1996. pap. 39.00 (*0-936494-14-X*) Santa B Museum.

***Taxonomic Atlas of the Benthic Fauna of the Santa Maria Basin & Western Santa Barbara Channel Vol. 10, Pt. 1: The Arthropoda - the Pychnogonida - the Crustacea - the Pecapoda.** Ed. by James A. Blake & Paul H. Scott. (Illus.). 151p. (Orig.). 1997. pap. write for info. (*0-936494-15-8*) Santa B Museum.

***Taxonomic Atlas of the Benthic Fauna of the Santa Maria Basin & Western Santa Barbara Channel Vol. 11, Pt. 2: The Crustacea - the Isopoda, Lumacea & Tanaidacea.** Ed. by James A. Blake & Paul H. Scott. LC 94-68651. (Illus.). 278p. (Orig.). 1997. pap. 34.00 (*0-936494-16-6*) Santa B Museum.

***Taxonomic Atlas of the Benthic Fauna of the Santa Maria Basin & Western Santa Barbara Channel Vol. 12, Pt. 3: The Crustacea: the Amphipoda.** Ed. by James A. Blake et al. LC 94-68651. (Illus.). xiv, 251p. (Orig.). 1995. pap. 28.00 (*0-936494-17-4*) Santa B Museum.

***Taxonomic Atlas of the Benthic Fauna of the Santa Maria Basin & Western Santa Barbara Channel Vol. 13: The Bryozoa.** Dorothy F. Soule et al. Ed. by James A. Blake et al. LC 94-68651. (Illus.). 344p. (Orig.). 1995. pap. 34.00 (*0-936494-18-2*) Santa B Museum.

***Taxonomic Atlas of the Benthil Fauna of the Santa Maria Basin & Western Santa Barbara Channel Vol. 14: Miscellaneous Taxa.** Ed. by James A. Blake et al. (Illus.). 305p. (Orig.). 1996. pap. 36.00 (*0-936494-19-0*) Santa B Museum.

Taxonomic Catalog of the Ant Subfamilies Aneuretinae & Dolichoderinae. Steven O. Shattuck. LC 93-37066. (Publications in Entomology: No. 112). 1994. 27.00 (*0-520-09787-4*) U CA Pr.

Taxonomic Investigations in the Genera Perityle & Laphamia (Compositae) W. E. Niles. (Memoirs Ser.: Vol. 21 (1)). (Illus.). 82p. 1970. pap. 10.00 (*0-89327-070-9*) NY Botanical.

Taxonomic Keys to the Common Animals of the North Central States. 4th ed. Samuel Eddy et al. 1982. spiral bd. write for info. (*0-8087-2210-7*) Burgess MN Intl.

Taxonomic Literature: A Selective Guide to Botanical Publications & Collections with Dates, Commentaries & Types. F. A. Stafleu & R. S. Cowan. (Sti-Vuy Ser.: Vol. 6). 926p. 1986. lib. bdg. 250.00 (*90-313-0714-9*) Lubrecht & Cramer.

Taxonomic Literature: A Selective Guide to Botanical Publications & Collections with Dates, Commentaries & Types, 7 vols., Set. 2nd ed. F. A. Stafleu & R. S. Cowan. 6250p. 1988. lib. bdg. 1,650.00 (*90-313-0224-4*) Lubrecht & Cramer.

Taxonomic Monograph of the Genus Aglaia Lour (Meliaceae) Meliaceae. C. M. Pannell. (Kew Bulletin Additional Ser.: No. 16). (Illus.). 384p. 1997. pap. 99.00 (*0-11-250067-6*, HM00676, Pub. by Statnry Ofc UK) Seven Hills Bk.

Taxonomic Notes on the Species, Figured by H. B. Brady in His Report on the Foraminifera ...During the Years 1873-1876. Reginald W. Barker. LC 62-6771. (Society of Economic Paleontologists & Mineralogists, Special Publication Ser.: No. 9). 262p. reprint ed. pap. 74.70 (*0-317-27163-6*, 2024735) Bks Demand.

Taxonomic, Pt. 1, Cupressaceae to Poaceae see Alpine Flora of New Guinea

Taxonomic, Pt. 2, Winteraceae to Polygonaceae see Alpine Flora of New Guinea

Taxonomic, Pt. 3, Fagaceae to Asteraceae see Alpine Flora of New Guinea

Taxonomic Relationships of Diomma Engler ex Harms see Memoirs of the New York Botanical Garden: No. 10(2)

Taxonomic Review of the Pallid Bat: Antrozous Pallidus (Le Conte) Chester O. Martin & David J. Schmidly. (Special Publications: No. 18). (Illus.). 48p. 1982. pap. 7.00 (*0-89672-097-7*) Tex Tech Univ Pr.

Taxonomic Review of the Southern Andean Marsupial Frogs (Hylidae Gastrotheca) William E. Duellman & Thomas H. Fritts. (Occasional Papers: No. 9). 37p. 1972. pap. 1.00 (*0-686-80344-2*) U KS Nat Hist Mus.

Taxonomic Revision of Nearctic Endasys Foerster 1868: Hymenoptera: Ichneumonidae, Gelinae. John C. Luhman. LC 89-20636. (Publications in Entomology: Vol. 109). (Illus.). 198p. 1991. pap. 30.00 (*0-520-09757-2*) U CA Pr.

Taxonomic Revision of the American Species of Cladophora (Chlorophyceae) in the North Atlantic Ocean & Their Geographic Distribution. C. Van den Hoek. (Oceans & Their Geographic Distribution Ser.). 236p. pap. 68.75 (*0-444-85541-6*) Elsevier.

Taxonomic Revision of the Castilleja viscidula Group. Noel H. Holmgren. (Memoirs Ser.: Vol. 21 (4)). (Illus.). 63p. 1971. pap. 8.50 (*0-89327-073-3*) NY Botanical.

Taxonomic Revision of the Genus Entorrhiza C. Weber (Ustilaginales) J. M. Fineran. (Nova Hedwigia Ser.). (Illus.). 1979. pap. text ed. 15.00 (*3-7682-1211-4*) Lubrecht & Cramer.

***Taxonomic Revision of the Genus Haplophyllum (Rutaceae)** C. C. Townsend. (Illus.). 336p. 1986. pap. 50.00 (*0-9504876-5-1*, Pub. by Royal Botnic Grdns UK) Balogh.

Taxonomic Revision of the Genus Macrolobium (Leguminosae-Caesalpinioideae) see Memoirs of the New York Botanical Garden: No. 8(4)

Taxonomic Revision of the Genus Persea (Lauraceae) in the Western Hemisphere. L. E. Kopp. (Memoirs Ser.: Vol. 14 (1)). (Illus.). 117p. 1966. pap. 10.00 (*0-89327-049-0*) NY Botanical.

Taxonomic Revision of the Moss Families Hookeriaceae & Hypopterygiaceae in Malaya. Haji Mohamed & Harold Robinson. LC 91-4223. (Smithsonian Contributions to Botany Ser.: No. 80). (Illus.). 48p. reprint ed. pap. 25.00 (*0-7837-1890-X*, 2042094) Bks Demand.

Taxonomic Revision of the Section Sideritis (Genus Sideritis) (Labiatae) Comcepcion Obon De Castro & D. R. Nunez. (Phanerogamarum Monographiae: Tomus XXI, Vol. 22). (Illus.). 640p. 1994. pap. 209.95 (*3-443-78003-2*, Pub. by Cramer-Borntraeger GW) Lubrecht & Cramer.

Taxonomic Revision of the Superspecific Groups of the Cretaceous & Cenozoic Tellinidae. Freydoun Afshar. LC 72-98019. (Geological Society of America, Memoir Ser.: No. 119). 231p. reprint ed. pap. 65.90 (*0-317-28386-3*, 2025467) Bks Demand.

Taxonomic Studies in the Genus Heterococcus (Tribophyceae, Tribonematales, Heteropediaceae) A Combined Cultural & Electron Microscopy Study. Gijsbert M. Lokhorst. (Cryptogamic Studies: Vol. 3). (Illus.). 256p. 1992. pap. 112.00 (*1-56081-346-6*) G F Verlag.

Taxonomic Studies of the Encyrtidae with the Descriptions of New Species & a New Genus (Hymenoptera, Chalcidoidea) Gordon Gordh & V. A. Trjapitzin. LC 81-1327. (University of California Publications in Social Welfare: No. 93). (Illus.). 70p. reprint ed. pap. 25.00 (*0-685-24004-5*, 2031589) Bks Demand.

Taxonomic Studies on Lac Insects of India. R. K. Varshney. (Oriental Insects Monographs: No. 5). 1976. pap. 30.00 (*1-877711-15-2*) Assoc Pubs FL.

Taxonomic Study of the Ranunculus Hispidus Michaux Complex in the Western Hemisphere. Thomas Duncan. LC 80-10493. (University of California Publications in Social Welfare: No. 77). (Illus.). 131p. reprint ed. pap. 37.40 (*0-685-23798-2*, 2032898) Bks Demand.

Taxonomic Synopsis of the Asopine Pentatomids of the Western Hemisphere. D. Thomas. (Thomas Say Monographs: Vol. 16). (Illus.). 156p. 1992. 40.00 (*0-614-05651-9*, TS16) Entomol Soc.

***Taxonomic Systems & Distribution of the Genus Rhododendrom.** Fang Ming-yuan. (CHI & LAT.). 1993. pap. 118.00 (*0-7855-0533-4*, Pub. by Wanhai Books CH) St Mut.

Taxonomical Revision of the Garovaglioideae (Pterobryaceae, Musci) H. J. During. (Bryophytorum Bibliotheca Ser.: No. 12). (Illus.). 1977. lib. bdg. 48.00 (*3-7682-1161-4*) Lubrecht & Cramer.

Taxonomies of the School Library Media Program. David V. Loertscher. xvi, 336p. 1988. pap. text ed. 26.50 (*0-87287-662-4*) Libs Unl.

Taxonomisch-Pflanzengeographische Monographie der Gattung Bovista. H. Kreisel. 1967. 80.00 (*3-7682-5425-9*) Lubrecht & Cramer.

Taxonomist's Glossary of Genitalia in Insects. Ed. by S. L. Tuxen. 1970. text ed. 35.00 (*0-934454-76-0*) Lubrecht & Cramer.

Taxonomy, Anatomy, Reproduction see Primatology: Proceedings of the International Congress, 3rd, Zurich, 1970

Taxonomy & Behavioral Science: Comparative Performance of Grouping Methods. Juan E. Mezzich & Herbert Solomon. (Quantitative Studies in Social Relations). 1980. text ed. 94.00 (*0-12-493340-8*) Acad Pr.

***Taxonomy & Biogeography of West African Beach Ostracods.** Ed. by L. Witte. (Verhandelingen der Koninklijke Nederlandse Akademie van Wetenschappen, Afd. Natuurkunde Ser.: No. 39). 84p. 1993. pap. text ed. 30.00 (*0-444-85764-8*) Elsevier.

Taxonomy & Classification of the Subfamily Lamiinae: Tribes Parmenini Through Acanthoderini. Earle G. Linsley & John A. Chemsak. (Publications in Entomology: Vol. 102). 1985. pap. 28.00 (*0-520-09690-8*) U CA Pr.

Taxonomy & Distribution of the Marine Calanoid Copepod Family Euchaetidae. Ed. by Taisoo Park. LC 94-28941. 1995. pap. text ed. 26.00 (*0-520-09802-1*) U CA Pr.

Taxonomy & Distribution of the Stomioid Fish Genus Eustomias: Melanostomiidae, I: Subgenus Nominostomias. LC 83-600023. (Smithsonian Contributions to Zoology Ser.: No. 380). 144p. reprint ed. pap. 41.10 (*0-317-29925-5*, 2021730) Bks Demand.

Taxonomy & Distribution of the Stomioid Fish Genus Eustomias (Melanostomiidae) Pt. 2: Biradiostamies, New Subgenus. Janet R. Gomon & Robert H. Gibbs, Jr. LC 84-600383. (Smithsonian Contributions to Zoology Ser.: No. 409). 62p. reprint ed. pap. 25.00 (*0-317-42008-9*, 2025685) Bks Demand.

Taxonomy & Identification of Steamer-Ducks: Anatidae: Tachyeres. Bradley C. Livezey & Philip S. Humphrey. (Monographs: No. 8). 210p. 1992. pap. 14.95 (*0-89338-042-3*) U KS Nat Hist Mus.

Taxonomy & Pathology of Venturia Species. A. Sivanesan. (Bibliotheca Mycologica Ser.: No. 59). 1977. lib. bdg. 32.00 (*3-7682-1167-3*) Lubrecht & Cramer.

Taxonomy, Distribution, & Phylogeny of the Cymatiid Gastropods Argobuccinum, Fusitriton, Mediargo & Priene, No. 254 see Bulletins of American Paleontology: Vol. 56

Taxonomy for Texture Description & Identification. A. R. Rao. Ed. by R. C. Jain. (Perception Engineering Ser.). (Illus.). 208p. 1990. 59.95 (*0-387-97302-8*) Spr-Verlag.

Taxonomy in Europe: Final Report of the European Science Research Council's Ad Hoc Group on Biological Recording Systematics & Taxonomy. Ed. by Vernon H. Heywood & R. B. Clark. (European Science Research Council Review Ser.: Vol. 17). 170p. 1982. pap. 18.50 (*0-444-86363-X*, North Holland) Elsevier.

Taxonomy, Morphology & Ecology of Recent Ostracoda. J. W. Neale. 1969. 60.00 (*0-934454-77-9*) Lubrecht & Cramer.

Taxonomy of Agastache Section Brittonastrum (Lamiaceae-Nepeteae) Roger W. Sanders. Ed. by Christiane Anderson. LC 86-22278. (Systematic Botany Monographs: Vol. 15). (Illus.). 92p. (Orig.). 1987. pap. 11.00 (*0-912861-15-0*) Am Soc Plant.

Taxonomy of Amauroderma (Basidiomycetes, Polyporaceae) Joao S. Furtado. LC 81-11126. (Memoirs Ser.: Vol. 34). (Illus.). 109p. 1981. pap. 13.00 (*0-89327-234-5*) NY Botanical.

Taxonomy of Behavioral Objectives & Social Readiness Program. 2nd rev. ed. Ron Talarico & Francella Hewitt. (Illus.). 700p. 1993. 89.95 (*0-9635238-0-5*) Prtlnd Habilitat.

Taxonomy of Communication Media. Rudy Bretz. LC 72-125874. (Illus.). 192p. 1971. 34.95 (*0-87778-012-9*) Educ Tech Pubns.

An Asterisk (*) at the beginning of an entry indicates that the title is appearing in BIP for the first time.

Taxonomy of Complaya, Elaphandra, Iogeton, Jefea, Wamalchitamia, Wedelia, Zexmenia, & Zyzyxia (Compositae- Heliantheae-Ecliptinae) John L. Strother. Ed. by Christiane Anderson. (Systematic Botany Monographs: Vol. 33). (Illus.). 111p. 1991. Smyth-sewn, acid-free paper. pap. 14.50 (*0-912861-33-9*) Am Soc Plant.

Taxonomy of Cyperus (Cyperaceae) in Costa Rica & Panama. Gordon C. Tucker. Ed. by Christiane Anderson. LC 83-7144. (Systematic Botany Monographs: Vol. 2). (Illus.). 85p. 1983. pap. 11.00 (*0-912861-02-9*) Am Soc Plant.

***Taxonomy of Economic Seaweeds: With Reference to Some Pacific Species, Vol. VI.** Ed. by Isabella Abbott. (Illus.). 175p. (Orig.). 1997. pap. text ed. 10.00 (*1-888691-04-2*, T-040) U CA Calif Sea.

Taxonomy of Educational Objectives: Handbook 1: Cognitive Domain. Benjamin S. Bloom et al. LC 64-12369. (C). 1984. reprint ed. pap. text ed. 39.50 (*0-582-28010-9*, 71079) Longman.

Taxonomy of Educational Objectives: Handbook 2: Affective Domain. David R. Krathwohl et al. (C). 1984. pap. text ed. 39.95 (*0-582-28239-X*, 71284) Longman.

Taxonomy of Eupatorium Section Verticillata (Asteraceae) E. Lamont. (Memoirs of the New York Botanical Garden Ser.: Vol. 72). (Illus.). 67p. 1995. pap. 14.00 (*0-89327-391-0*) NY Botanical.

Taxonomy of Human Services: A Conceptual Framework with Standardized Terminology & Definitions for the Field. 3rd rev. ed. Georgia Sales. LC 94-76274. 768p. 1994. reprint ed. 200.00 (*0-938371-02-9*) Info Referral Fed.

Taxonomy of North American Epicauta: Coleoptera: Meloidae: With a Revision of the Nominate Subgenus & a Survey of Courtship Behavior. John D. Pinto. (Publications in Entomology: Vol. 110). 448p. (C). 1991. pap. 50.00 (*0-520-09764-5*) U CA Pr.

Taxonomy of Polygonum Section Echinocaulon (Polygonaceae) C. Park. LC 88-5361. (Memoirs Ser.: Vol. 47). (Illus.). 82p. (C). 1988. pap. text ed. 19.00 (*0-89327-329-5*) NY Botanical.

Taxonomy of Saxifraga (Saxifragaceae) Section Boraphila Subsection Integrifoliae in Western North America: Patrick E. Elvander. Revision of The Genus Heuchera (Saxifragaceae) in Eastern North America. Elizabeth F. Wells. Ed. by Christiane Anderson. LC 84-393. (Systematic Botany Monographs: Vol. 3). (Illus.). 122p. (Orig.). 1984. pap. 16.00 (*0-912861-03-7*) Am Soc Plant.

Taxonomy of Specimens of the Pennsylvanian-Age Marattialean Fern Psaronius from Ohio & Illinois. James E. Mickle. (Scientific Papers: Vol. XIX). (Illus.). vii, 64p. (Orig.). 1984. pap. 5.00 (*0-89792-101-1*) Ill St Museum.

Taxonomy of the Bruchidae (Coleoptera) of Northwest India Pt. 2: Larvae; A Catalogue of the Ephemeroptera of the Indian Subregion, 2 suppls., Combined Vol. (Oriental Insects Monographs: Nos. 8 & 9). 1978. Combined Volume. pap. 30.00 (*1-877711-18-7*) Assoc Pubs FL.

Taxonomy of the Flowering Plants. A. M. Johnson. (Illus.). 1977. reprint ed. lib. bdg. 120.00 (*3-7682-1169-X*) Lubrecht & Cramer.

Taxonomy of the Genus Phytophtora. C. M. Tucker. (Illus.). 1967. reprint ed. 36.00 (*3-7682-0515-0*) Lubrecht & Cramer.

Taxonomy of the Indian Myxomycetes. T. N. Lakhanpal & K. G. Mukerji. (Bibliotheca Mycologica Ser.: No. 78). (Illus.). 532p. 1981. lib. bdg. 112.00 (*3-7682-1287-4*) Lubrecht & Cramer.

Taxonomy of the Subgenus Pterodes, Genus Luzula see Memoirs of the New York Botanical Garden: No. 10(5)

Taxonomy of Thelypteris Subgenus Steiropteris, Including Glaphyropteris (Pteridophyta) Alan R. Smith. LC 78-62882. (University of California Publications in Botany: No. 76). 52p. 1980. pap. 25.00 (*0-7837-8428-7*, 2049230) Bks Demand.

Taxonomy of Visual Processes. William R. Uttal. LC 80-18262. (Illus.). 1119p. reprint ed. pap. 180.00 (*0-7837-5185-0*, 2044918) Bks Demand.

Taxonomy of West African Flowering Plants. Omotoye Olorode. (Illus.). 176p. 1984. text ed. 25.95 (*0-582-64429-1*) Longman.

Taxonomy, Phylogeny & Zoogeography of Beetles & Ants. Ed. by George E. Ball. (Entomologica Ser.). 1985. lib. bdg. 304.00 (*90-6193-511-3*) Kluwer Ac.

Taxonomy, Systematics, & Zoogeography of Hypsibarbus, a New Genus of Large Barbs (Pisces, Cyprinidae) from the Rivers of Southeastern Asia. Walter J. Rainboth. LC 96-13759. (Publications in Zoology: Vol. 129). (Illus.). 214p. (C). 1996. pap. 23.00 (*0-520-09809-9*) U CA Pr.

***Taxpayer Bill of Rights 2 - Law & Explanation.** 120p. 1996. 19.00 (*0-614-26825-7*) Commerce.

Taxpayer Compliance, Vol. 1. Ed. by Jeffrey A. Roth et al. LC 88-36250. (Law in Social Context Ser.). 414p. 1989. Vol. I: An Agenda for Research, 414p. text ed. 49.50 (*0-8122-8182-9*) U of Pa Pr.

Taxpayer Compliance, Vol. 2. Ed. by Jeffrey A. Roth et al. LC 88-36250. (Law in Social Context Ser.). 282p. 1989. Vol. II: Social Science Perspectives, 282p. text ed. 47.50 (*0-8122-8150-0*) U of Pa Pr.

Taxpayer, Dragonslayer: The Consumer's Guide to Solving IRS Problems. Sal Olimpio. Ed. by Jim Donovan. 280p. 1995. pap. 17.95 (*1-880925-06-0*) Equitable Media.

Taxpayer Service Representative. Jack Rudman. (Career Examination Ser.: C-833). 1994. pap. 27.95 (*0-8373-0833-X*) Nat Learn.

Taxpayers' Bill of Rights. 1992. lib. bdg. 65.95 (*0-8490-5264-5*) Gordon Pr.

Taxpayers in Revolt: Tax Resistance During the Great Depression. David T. Beito. LC 88-26032. 232p. 1989. reprint ed. pap. 66.20 (*0-7837-9016-3*, 2049768) Bks Demand.

Taxpayer's Manifesto. Daniel J. Hushek. 192p. 1992. pap. 12.95 (*0-9634442-0-4*) Plainfld Pub.

Taxpayers of Medieval Gloucestershire. E. Peter Franklin. 192p. (C). 1993. text ed. 80.00 (*0-86299-980-4*, Pub. by Sutton Pubng UK) Bks Intl VA.

Taxpayers, Payers Guide to Revolt: Perspectives on the Taxpayers Revolt. Robert J. Dworak. LC 80-135. 272p. 1980. text ed. 59.95 (*0-275-90473-3*, C0473, Praeger Pubs) Greenwood.

Taxpayers Rights & Obligations: A Survey of the Legal Situation in OECD Countries. OECD Staff. 105p. (Orig.). 1990. pap. 21.00 (*92-64-13390-9*) OECD.

Taxpayer's Tea Party. Chuck Asay. 1994. pap. 4.99 (*0-671-87627-9*) S&S Trade.

Taxpayers' Ultimate Defense Manual: Nine Devastating Weapons Against I.R.S. Abuse. Daniel J. Pilla. Ed. by David M. Engstrom. 224p. (Orig.). 1989. 29.95 (*0-9617124-7-3*) Winning St Paul.

Taxpayer's Vehicle Log. Ed. by Turner, W. J., & Associates, Inc. Staff. 64p. (Orig.). 1984. pap. text ed. 2.95 (*0-936537-01-9*) Metro WI.

***Taxpoint.** 2nd ed. Everett. (Income Tax Ser.). 1998. 104.95 (*0-538-88243-3*) S-W Pub.

***Tay John.** Howard Ohagan. 1996. pap. text ed. 6.95 (*0-7710-9850-2*) McClland & Stewart.

Tay John & the Cyclical Quest. Ella Tanner. 170p. (C). 1990. text ed. 25.00 (*1-55022-130-2*, Pub. by ECW Press CN); pap. text ed. 15.00 (*1-55022-132-9*, Pub. by ECW Press CN) Genl Dist Srvs.

Tayeb Salih's "Season of Migration to the North" A Casebook. Mona T. Amyuni. 174p. (Orig.). 1986. pap. text ed. 18.00 (*0-8156-6075-8*, Am U Beirut) Syracuse U Pr.

Taylor. Vivian A. Velasco. (J). (gr. 1-5). 1995. 11.95 (*0-533-11556-6*) Vantage.

Taylor: Family History of Anthony Taylor. H. M. Taylor. 530p. 1991. reprint ed. pap. 79.50 (*0-8328-2180-2*); reprint ed. lib. bdg. 89.50 (*0-8328-2179-9*) Higginson Bk Co.

Taylor - A Friendly Heritage along the Delaware: The Taylors of Washington Crossing & Some Allied Families in Bucks County. Arthur E. Bye. (Illus.). 258p. 1994. reprint ed. pap. 35.00 (*0-8328-4508-6*); reprint ed. lib. bdg. 45.00 (*0-8328-4507-8*) Higginson Bk Co.

Taylor, a Friendly Heritage along the Delaware: The Taylors of Washington Crossing & Some Allied Families in Bucks County. Arthur E. Bye. (Illus.). 258p. 1994. reprint ed. pap. 35.00 (*0-8328-4244-3*); reprint ed. lib. bdg. 45.00 (*0-8328-4243-5*) Higginson Bk Co.

Taylor, Anthony Taylor of Hampton, NH: Additions, Supplement to 1935 Edition. H. M. Taylor. (Illus.). 134p. 1991. reprint ed. pap. 23.50 (*0-8328-1731-7*); reprint ed. lib. bdg. 33.50 (*0-8328-1730-9*) Higginson Bk Co.

Taylor, Fillmore, Pierce, & Buchanan. Richard Steins. LC 95-43545. (Complete History of Our Presidents Ser.: Vol. 4). (J). 1996. write for info. (*0-86593-408-8*) Rourke Corp.

Taylor Made. Elise Title. 1992. mass mkt. 2.99 (*0-373-25524-1*, 1-25524-9) Harlequin Bks.

Taylor Made: The Best of Bee Talk. Richard Taylor. Ed. by Kim Flottum. (Illus.). 200p. 1988. 9.95 (*0-936028-00-9*) A I Root.

Taylor Made Piano. Billy Taylor. 266p. (C). 1982. per. write for info. (*0-697-09959-8*) Brown & Benchmark.

Taylor-Made Tales. Samuel W. Taylor. 214p. (Orig.). 1994. pap. 7.95 (*1-56236-216-X*) Aspen Bks.

Taylor-Moore Lodge. Suzanne Taylor-Moore. 1981. pap. 3.50 (*0-938758-10-1*) MTM Pub Co.

Taylor Streit's No Nonsense Guide to Fly Fishing in New Mexico. Taylor Streit. Ed. by David Banks. (Illus.). 77p. (Orig.). 1996. pap. 14.95 (*0-9637256-6-1*) D Comm.

Taylor to Lacey - the Long Road: Memories of Jessie Kinnear Kenton. Jessie K. Kenton. 150p. 1993. pap. text ed. 12.00 (*1-881908-05-4*) PanPress.

Taylor Trading Technique. George D. Taylor. (Illus.). 160p. 1994. reprint ed. pap. 25.00 (*0-934380-24-4*, 195-A) Traders Pr.

Taylor Twinkle Finds a Home: A Christmas Story for All Seasons. Kathy A. Long. 32p. (J). (gr. k-4). 1994. pap. 5.00 (*0-9642063-0-7*) Best Frnds.

Taylor University the First 150 Years. 2nd rev. ed. William C. Ringenberg. (Illus.). 272p. 1996. 25.00 (*0-9621187-2-9*) Taylor Univ.

***Taylor University the First 150 Years.** 2nd rev. ed. William C. Ringenberg. 272p. 1996. pap. 15.00 (*0-9621187-3-7*) Taylor Univ.

Taylor Weekend Guide to Birds & Butterflies. Thomas. 128p. 1997. pap. 12.95 (*0-395-81372-7*) HM.

Taylor Weekend Guide to Lawns. Thomas. 128p. 1997. pap. 12.95 (*0-395-81369-7*) HM.

Taylor Weekend Guide to Pests. Thomas. 128p. 1997. pap. 12.95 (*0-395-81370-0*) HM.

Taylor Weekend Guide to Window Boxes. Thomas. LC 96-44020. 128p. 1997. pap. 12.95 (*0-395-81371-9*) HM.

Taylorcraft Story. Chet Peek. (Illus.). 220p. 1993. pap. text ed. 24.95 (*0-943691-08-7*) Aviation Heritage.

Taylorcraft Story. Chet Peek. (Illus.). 236p. 1995. pap. 24.95 (*1-886196-01-X*) Three Peaks.

Taylored Lives: Narrative Productions in the Age of Taylor, Veblen, & Ford. Martha Banta. LC 92-38609. (Illus.). 464p. (C). 1993. 37.50 (*0-226-03701-0*) U Ch Pr.

Taylored Lives: Narrative Productions in the Age of Taylor, Veblen, & Ford. Martha Banta. LC 92-38609. (Illus.). 446p. (C). 1995. pap. text ed. 18.95 (*0-226-03702-9*) U Ch Pr.

***Tayloring Shop: Essays on the Poetry of Edward Taylor in Honor of Thomas M. & Virginia L. Davis.** Edward Taylor et al. LC 96-36754. 1997. write for info. (*0-87413-623-7*) U Delaware Pr.

Taylorism Transformed: Scientific Management Theory since 1945. Stephen P. Waring. LC 91-11027. xiv, 288p. (C). 1994. pap. text ed. 15.95 (*0-8078-4469-1*) U of NC Pr.

Taylor's Ark. Jody L. Nye. 288p. (Orig.). 1993. mass mkt. 4.99 (*0-441-79974-4*) Ace Bks.

***Taylor's Dictionary for Gardeners.** Frances Tenenbaum. 1997. 25.00 (*0-395-87606-0*) HM.

***Taylor's Formula.** Riestra. 1995. pap. 35.95 (*0-582-27781-7*, Pub. by Longman UK) Longman.

***Taylor's Gardening Dictionary.** Frances Tenenbaum. LC 97-23701. 1997. write for info. (*0-03-958760-6*) Houghton Lib.

Taylor's Guide to Annuals. rev. ed. Norman Taylor. Ed. by Gordon P. DeWolf, Jr. LC 85-30496. (Taylor's Guides to Gardening Ser.). 479p. 1986. pap. 19.95 (*0-395-40447-9*) HM.

Taylor's Guide to Antique Shops in Illinois & Southern Wisconsin. 28th rev. ed. Irene Taylor. (Illus.). 256p. 1996. per., pap. 4.95 (*1-888312-00-9*) Moonlight IL.

Taylor's Guide to Bulbs. rev. ed. Norman Taylor. Ed. by Gordon P. DeWolf, Jr. LC 85-30508. (Taylor's Guides to Gardening Ser.). 463p. 1986. pap. 19.95 (*0-395-40449-5*) HM.

Taylor's Guide to Container Gardening. Ed. by Roger Holmes & Frances Tenenbaum. LC 94-46216. (Taylor's Guides to Gardening Ser.). (Illus.). 416p. 1995. pap. 19.95 (*0-395-69829-4*) HM.

Taylor's Guide to Fruits & Berries. Ed. by Roger Holmes & Frances Tenenbaum. (Illus.). 400p. 1996. pap. 19.95 (*0-395-71086-3*) HM.

Taylor's Guide to Garden Design. (Taylor's Guides to Gardening Ser.). (Illus.). 480p. 1988. pap. 19.95 (*0-395-46784-5*) HM.

Taylor's Guide to Garden Techniques. (Taylor's Guides to Gardening Ser.). (Illus.). 448p. 1991. pap. 19.95 (*0-395-56403-4*) HM.

Taylor's Guide to Gardening in the South. Ed. by Rita Buchanan & Frances Tenenbaum. (Taylor's Regional Guides to Gardening Ser.). (Illus.). 450p. 1992. pap. 19.95 (*0-395-59681-5*) HM.

Taylor's Guide to Gardening in the Southwest & Southern California. Ed. by Roger Holmes & Frances Tenenbaum. (Taylor's Regional Guides to Gardening Ser.). (Illus.). 450p. 1992. pap. 19.95 (*0-395-59680-7*) HM.

Taylor's Guide to Gardening with Perennials for Sun. Norman Taylor. LC 88-46140. (Taylor's Pocket Guides to Gardening Ser.: Vol. 2). (Illus.). 128p. 1989. pap. 5.95 (*0-395-51020-1*) HM.

Taylor's Guide to Ground Covers, Vines & Grasses. Taylor's Guide Staff. (Illus.). 496p. (Orig.). 1987. pap. 19.95 (*0-395-43094-1*) HM.

Taylor's Guide to Heirloom Vegetables. Ben Watson. Ed. by Frances Tenenbaum. (Illus.). 350p. 1996. pap. 19.95 (*0-395-70818-4*) HM.

Taylor's Guide to Herbs. Ed. by Rita Buchanan & Frances Tenenbaum. LC 94-44241. (Taylor's Guides to Gardening Ser.). (Illus.). 464p. 1995. pap. 19.95 (*0-395-68081-6*) HM.

Taylor's Guide to House Plants. Norman Taylor. 1987. pap. 19.95 (*0-395-43091-7*) HM.

Taylor's Guide To Houseplants. Gordon P. DeWolf, Jr. (Illus.). 480p. 1987. pap. 14.95 (*0-317-53568-4*) HM.

Taylor's Guide to Natural Gardening. Ed. by Roger Holmes & Frances Tenenbaum. LC 92-16334. (Taylor's Guides to Gardening Ser.). (Illus.). 528p. 1993. pap. 19.95 (*0-395-60729-9*) HM.

Taylor's Guide to Orchids. Ed. by Judy White. LC 95-44963. (Guides to Gardening Ser.). (Illus.). 400p. 1996. pap. 19.95 (*0-395-67726-2*) HM.

***Taylor's Guide to Ornamental Grasses.** Roger Holmes. LC 96-38427. (Taylor's Guides to Gardening Ser.). 1996. pap. 19.95 (*0-395-79761-6*) HM.

Taylor's Guide to Perennials. rev. ed. Norman Taylor. Ed. by Gordon P. DeWolf, Jr. LC 85-30495. (Taylor's Guides to Gardening Ser.). 479p. 1986. pap. 19.95 (*0-395-40448-7*) HM.

Taylor's Guide to Roses. rev. ed. Ed. by Peter Schneider. LC 94-2023. (Taylor's Guides to Gardening Ser.). 451p. 1995. pap. 19.95 (*0-395-69459-0*) HM.

Taylor's Guide to Seashore Gardening. Ed. by Frances Tenenbaum. LC 95-48906. (Taylor's Guides to Gardening Ser.). (Illus.). 400p. 1996. pap. 19.95 (*0-395-73532-7*) HM.

Taylor's Guide to Shade Gardening. Ed. by Frances Tenenbaum. LC 93-17635. (Taylor's Guides to Gardening Ser.). 512p. 1994. pap. 19.95 (*0-395-65165-4*) HM.

Taylor's Guide to Shrubs. Taylor's Guide Staff. (Illus.). 480p. 1987. pap. 19.95 (*0-395-43093-3*) HM.

Taylor's Guide to Specialty Nurseries. Ed. by Barbara J. Barton & Frances Tenenbaum. LC 92-30802. (Taylor's Guides to Gardening Ser.). (Illus.). 352p. 1993. pap. 16.95 (*0-395-60836-8*) HM.

Taylor's Guide to Trees. (Taylor's Guides to Gardening Ser.). (Illus.). 1988. pap. 19.95 (*0-395-46783-7*) HM.

Taylor's Guide to Trees, Vol. 9. 1988. write for info. (*0-318-63747-2*) Chanticleer.

Taylor's Guide To Vegetables & Herbs. Gordon P. DeWolf, Jr. (Illus.). 480p. (Orig.). 1987. pap. 19.95 (*0-395-43092-5*) HM.

Taylor's Guide to Water-Saving Gardening. Norman Taylor. LC 89-71750. (Taylor's Guides to Gardening Ser.: Vol. 11). (Illus.). (Orig.). 1990. pap. 19.95 (*0-395-54422-X*) HM.

Taylors Gut: In the Delaware State. Dudley C. Lunt. (Illus.). 320p. 1986. reprint ed. pap. 8.95 (*0-912608-30-7*) Mid Atlantic.

Taylor's Master Guide to Gardening. Ed. by Frances Tenenbaum et al. LC 93-48865. (Illus.). 1994. 60.00 (*0-395-64995-1*) HM.

Taylor's Pocket Guide to Ground Covers for Sun. Ann Reilly. Ed. by Ann Whitman. LC 89-85028. (Taylor's Guides to Gardening Ser.: Vol. 9). (Illus.). (Orig.). 1990. pap. 5.95 (*0-395-52249-8*) HM.

Taylor's Pocket Guide to Herbs & Edible Flowers. Ann Reilly. Ed. by Amy Hughes. LC 89-85027. (Taylor's Guides to Gardening Ser.: Vol. 8). (Illus.). 1990. pap. 5.95 (*0-395-52246-3*) HM.

Taylor's Pocket Guide to Modern Roses. Norman Taylor. LC 88-46144. (Taylor's Pocket Guides to Gardening Ser.: Vol. 6). (Illus.). 128p. 1989. pap. 5.95 (*0-395-51017-1*) HM.

Taylor's Pocket Guide to Perennials for Shade. Ann Reilly. Ed. by Ann Whitman. LC 88-46141. (Taylor's Guides to Gardening Ser.: Vol. 1). (Illus.). (Orig.). 1989. pap. 5.95 (*0-395-51019-8*) HM.

***Taylor's Weekend: Small Garden.** Morris. 1998. pap. write for info. (*0-395-86643-X*) HM.

***Taylor's Weekend Gardening Guide to Backyard Building Projects.** David Tenenbaum. 1997. pap. 12.95 (*0-395-83812-6*) HM.

***Taylor's Weekend Gardening Guide to Indoor Gardens: Designing & Planting the Interior Landscape.** Tovah Martin. 1997. pap. 12.95 (*0-395-82944-5*) HM.

***Taylor's Weekend Gardening Guide to Plants for Problem Places: Easy Species for Difficult Garden.** Linda Yang. LC 97-22929. 1997. pap. 12.95 (*0-395-82762-0*) HM.

***Taylor's Weekend Guide to Easy Practical Pruning: Techniques for Training Trees, Shrubs, Vines...** Barbara Ellis. LC 97-1775. 1997. pap. 12.95 (*0-395-81591-6*) HM.

***Taylor's Weekend Guide to Water Gardens: How to Plan & Plant a Backyard Pool.** Charles Thomas. LC 97-10468. 1997. pap. 12.95 (*0-395-81590-8*) HM.

Taylorvision. Edmund E. Taylor. LC 84-51960. (Illus.). 64p. (Orig.). 1984. pap. text ed. 3.98 (*0-9613839-0-9*) TEL Pr.

***Taymyrskiy Autonomous Okrug: Economy, Industry, Government, Business.** 2nd rev. ed. Russian Information & Business Center, Inc. Staff. (Russian Regional Business Directories Ser.). (Illus.). 200p. 1997. pap. 99.00 (*1-57751-429-7*) Russ Info & Busn Ctr.

Tayniye Zapiski: Eighteen Thirty Six-Eighteen Thirty Seven Godov. Aleksandr Pushkin. LC 86-90457. 104p. (RUS.). 1986. reprint ed. pap. 5.00 (*0-916201-02-3*) M I P Co.

Tazewell & Allied Families Scrapbooks, 9 vols. Anthologies on the Tazewell, Goode, Bradford, Parks, Walke, Waller, Littleton, Jackson, etc. Families. Intro. by Calvert W. Tazewell. LC 90-81464. 1300p. (Orig.). 1990. pap. write for info. (*1-878515-00-4*) W S Dawson.

Tazewell & Florida: Libraries, Civil Defense & a 5,000,000 Dollar Bargain. Ed. by Calvert W. Tazewell. LC 92-74109. 60p. (Orig.). 1993. pap. 8.00 (*1-878515-76-4*) W S Dawson.

Tazewell County. Louise Leslie. (Illus.). 794p. 1995. reprint ed. 34.95 (*1-57072-031-2*) Overmountain Pr.

Tazewell Scrapbook: Lawyers & Such. Ed. by Calvert W. Tazewell. LC 90-80456. (Tazewell & Allied Families Scrapbooks Ser.: Vol. 1). 120p. (Orig.). 1991. pap. write for info. (*1-878515-01-2*) W S Dawson.

Taz's Gross Riddles. Illus. by J. T. McKingey. (Looney Tunes Joke Bks.). 96p. (J). (gr. 1-4). 1995. pap. 3.50 (*0-307-13177-7*, Golden Pr) Western Pub.

TB Compliance Manual for Healthcare Providers. W. H. Heaton. 200p. 1994. ring bd. 99.00 (*1-881057-75-5*) Heaton Pubns.

***TBA.** unabridged ed. TBA. (Stonewall Chapbook Competition Ser.). 30p. (Orig.). 1997. mass mkt. 8.00 (*0-932616-60-7*) Brick Hse Bks.

TBD Devastator in Action. Al Adcock. (Aircraft in Action Ser.). (Illus.). 50p. (Orig.). 1989. pap. 7.95 (*0-89747-231-4*, 1097) Squad Sig Pubns.

TBI Annual Research Index. Charles M. Arokiasamy et al. 400p. (Orig.). 1993. Set. pap. 29.95 (*1-878205-01-3*) GR Press.

TBI Tool Kit. Linda J. Courtney. Ed. by Pamela G. Burns. 224p. (Orig.). 1994. pap. 24.95 (*1-882855-07-8*) HDI Pubs.

TBM - TBF Avenger in Action. Charles Scrivner. (Aircraft in Action Ser.). (Illus.). 50p. 1987. pap. 7.95 (*0-89747-197-0*, 1082) Squad Sig Pubns.

Tchaadaev. Arkady Rovner & Victoria Andreyeva. 76p. (Orig.). (RUS.). 1989. pap. 10.00 (*0-922792-05-4*) Gnosis Pr.

Tchaikovsky. (Dent Master Musicians Ser.). (Illus.). (C). pap. write for info. (*0-19-816474-2*) OUP.

Tchaikovsky. David Nice. LC 95-3359. (Compact Companions Ser.). 1995. 17.50 (*0-684-81357-2*) S&S Trade.

Tchaikovsky. Ann Rachlin. (Famous Children Ser.). (Illus.). 24p. (J). (gr. k-3). 1993. pap. 5.95 (*0-8120-1545-2*) Barron.

Tchaikovsky. Todtri Productions Staff. (Great Composers Ser.). 1996. 10.98 (*0-8317-3589-9*) Smithmark.

Tchaikovsky. Herbert Weinstock. LC 80-15059. (Music Reprint Ser.). 1980. reprint ed. 42.50 (*0-306-76040-1*) Da Capo.

Tchaikovsky: A Biography. Anthony Holden. (Illus.). 576p. 1996. 35.00 (*0-679-42006-1*) Random.

Tchaikovsky: His Life & Works with Extracts from His Writings and the Diary of His Tour Abroad in 1888. Rosa H. Newmarch. LC 69-14011. 232p. 1969. reprint ed. text ed. 55.00 (*0-8371-1116-1*, NETC, Greenwood Pr) Greenwood.

T

Tchaikovsky: His Life & Works, with Extracts from His Writings, & the Diary of His Tour Abroad in 1888. Rosa H. Newmarch. LC 68-25298. (Studies in Music: No. 42). 1968. reprint ed. lib. bdg. 75.00 (*0-8383-0310-2*) M S G Haskell Hse.

Tchaikovsky: His Life & Works, with Extracts from His Writings, & the Diary of His Tour Abroad in 1888. Rosa H. Newmarch. 232p. 1990. reprint ed. lib. bdg. 69.00 (*0-7812-0775-4*, 10093) Rprt Serv.

Tchaikovsky: Music Book Index. Gerald E. Abraham. 144p. 1993. reprint ed. lib. bdg. 69.00 (*0-7812-9626-9*) Rprt Serv.

Tchaikovsky: Orchestral Works. Eric Blom. 51p. 1990. reprint ed. lib. bdg. 59.00 (*0-7812-9162-3*) Rprt Serv.

Tchaikovsky: Quest for the Inner Man. Alexander Poznansky. 679p. 1991. 39.95 (*0-02-871885-2*) Schirmer Bks.

Tchaikovsky: The Ballet Suites. David Foil. (Black Dog Music Library). 48p. 1995. 9.98 incl. audio compact disk (*1-884822-39-8*) Blck Dog & Leventhal.

Tchaikovsky: The Final Years, 1885-1983. David B. Brown. 544p. 1992. 40.00 (*0-393-03099-7*) Norton.

Tchaikovsky: The Quest for the Inner Man. Alexander Poznansky. 679p. 1993. 20.00 (*0-02-871886-0*) Schirmer Bks.

Tchaikovsky Ballet Music. John Warrack. (BBC Music Guides Ser.). 72p. 1996. 2.95 (*0-563-12860-7*, BB 11134, BBC-Parkwest) Parkwest Pubns.

Tchaikovsky Discovers America. Esther Kalman. LC 94-29739. (Illus.). 48p. (J). (gr. k-3). 1995. 15.95 (*0-531-06894-3*) Orchard Bks Watts.

Tchaikovsky Remembered. David Brown. (Illus.). 248p. 1994. 24.95 (*0-931340-65-9*, Amadeus Pr); pap. 12.95 (*0-931340-66-7*, Amadeus Pr) Timber.

Tchaikovsky Very Best for Piano. Ed. by John L. Haag. (Illus.). 144p. (Orig.). 1995. pap. 14.95 (*0-614-14366-7*, 07-2031) Creat Cncpts.

Tchaikovsky's Last Days: A Documentary Study. Alexander Poznansky. LC 96-13332. (Illus.). 224p. 1996. 29.95 (*0-19-816596-X*, Clarendon Pr) OUP.

Tchaikovsky's Musical Style. Henry Zajaczkowski. LC 87-19029. (Russian Music Studies: No. 19). 257p. reprint ed. pap. 73.30 (*0-8357-1806-9*, 2070639) Bks Demand.

Tchelitchew: Paintings, Drawings. James T. Soby. LC 77-169319. (Museum of Modern Art Publications in Reprint). (Illus.). 100p. 1972. reprint ed. 21.95 (*0-405-01577-1*) Ayer.

T

Tchipayuk: or The Way of the Wolf. Ronald Lavallee. Tr. by Patricia Claxton. 400p. 1994. pap. 21.95 (*0-88922-338-6*) Genl Dist Srvs.

Tchula Period in the Mid-South & Lower Mississippi Valley. Ed. by David H. Dye & Ronald C. Brister. LC 86-620005. (Mississippi Department of Archives & History Archaeological Reports: No.17). (Illus.). 138p. (Orig.). 1986. pap. text ed. 5.00 (*0-938896-48-2*) Mississippi Archives.

TCI Manual of Concrete Inspection. 8th ed. ACI Committee Staff. 200p. 1992. 69.50 (*0-685-62675-X*, SP-2(92)BOW6) ACI.

***TCI/TK Tools.** Mark Harrison. (Illus.). 900p. (Orig.). 1997. pap. 49.95 (*1-56592-218-2*) OReilly & Assocs.

TCL & the TK Toolkit. John K. Ousterhout. (C). 1994. pap. text ed. 38.95 (*0-201-63337-X*) Addison-Wesley.

TCL & TK Reference Manual. John K. Ousterhout. 600p. 1996. pap. write for info. (*0-201-63443-0*) Addison-Wesley.

***TCL/TK for Dummies.** Tim Webster. 1997. pap. 29.99 (*0-7645-0152-6*) IDG Bks.

***TCL/TK Unleashed.** Red Hat Press Staff. 1100p. 1997. 49.99 (*0-672-31143-7*) Sams.

TCL/TK Workshop Proceedings, Toronto, Ontario, Canada. 288p. 1995. pap. text ed. 34.00 (*1-880446-72-3*) USENIX Assn.

TCN Guide to Professional Practice in Clinical Neuropsychology. Ed. by Kenneth Adams & Byron P. Rourke. vi, 234p. 1992. 56.00 (*90-265-1242-2*); pap. 29.95 (*90-265-1243-0*) Swets.

TCO SE an Archaeology Study of the Bedrock Mortar-Petroglyph at AMA 14, Near Volcano, California, No. 8. Louis A. Payen & David S. Boloyan. (Publications of the Department of Parks & Recreation: No. 8). (Illus.). 46p. (C). 1963. reprint ed. pap. text ed. 4.35 (*1-55567-460-7*) Coyote Press.

Tcoy, City of Seattle. 5th ed. Donald M. Vickery. 1994. pap. write for info. (*0-201-40781-7*) Addison-Wesley.

TCP Invariance & Charge Quantization: Anti-Hydrogen & the Fifth Dimension. Ian McCrimmon. (C). 1992. pap. 25.00 (*0-9514698-8-6*, Pub. by Cosmatom UK) St Mut.

TCP/IP. Ease Tech Staff. 1994. pap. 14.95 (*0-13-123787-X*) P-H.

TCP/IP & NFS: Internetworking in a Unix Environment. Michael Santifaller. (C). 1991. pap. text ed. 39.75 (*0-201-54432-6*) Addison-Wesley.

TCP/IP & ONC NFS: Internetworking in a Unix Environment. 2nd ed. Michael Santifaller. (C). 1994. text ed. 39.75 (*0-201-42275-1*) Addison-Wesley.

TCP/IP & Related Protocols. 2nd ed. Ulysses D. Black. 1995. text ed. 50.00 (*0-07-005560-2*) McGraw.

***TCP-IP & Related Protocols: Includes IPV6, Frame Relay & Aim.** 3rd ed. Uyless Black. 1997. text ed. 44.95 (*0-07-913282-0*) McGraw.

TCP/IP Applications & Protocols. Computer Technology Research Corp. Staff. LC 95-15398. (Illus.). 248p. (Orig.). 1995. pap. 280.00 (*1-56607-951-9*) Comput Tech Res.

TCP/IP for the Internet: The Complete Buyer's Guide to Micro-Based TCP-IP Software. Marshall Breeding. 185p. 1995. pap. 24.95 (*0-88736-980-4*) Mecklermedia.

TCP/IP Illustrated Vol. 1: The Protocols. W. Richard Stevens. (C). 1994. text ed. 55.95 (*0-201-63346-9*) Addison-Wesley.

TCP/IP Networking: Architecture, Administration & Programming. James Martin & Joe Leben. 400p. 1994. text ed. 57.00 (*0-13-642232-2*) P-H.

***TCP-IP Networks: Performance Analysis & Fine Tuning.** Uday Pabrai. (McGraw Hill Series on Computer Communication). 1997. pap. text ed. 44.95 incl. cd-rom (*0-07-913624-9*) McGraw.

TCP/IP: Running a Successful Network. K. Washburn. LC 93-9661. (Data Communications & Networks Ser.). (C). 1993. pap. text ed. 48.95 (*0-201-62765-5*) Addison-Wesley.

TCP/ICP Illustrated, Vol. 3. Richard Stevens. (C). 1996. text ed. 39.95 (*0-201-63495-3*) Addison-Wesley.

TCP/IP: Architecture, Protocols, & Implementation. 2nd ed. Sidnie Feit. LC 96-18758. (Illus.). 464p. 1996. pap. text ed. 55.00 (*0-07-021389-5*) McGraw.

TCP/IP Vol. III: ATT TLI Version. Douglas E. Cower & David L. Stevens. 528p. (C). 1993. text ed. 61.00 (*0-13-474230-3*) P-H.

TCP/IP Addressing: Designing & Optimizing Your IP Addressing Scheme. Norman B. Graham. (Illus.). 322p. 1996. pap. 24.95 (*0-12-294630-8*) Acad Pr.

***TCP/IP Administrators.** Craig Zacker. (Infraworld Networking Ser.). 1997. pap. 39.99 (*0-7645-3158-1*) IDG Bks.

TCP/IP Applications Programming for OS/2: With Applications for Presentation Manager. Steve Gutz. 1996. 47.00 incl. disk (*0-13-261249-6*) P-H.

***TCP/IP Blueprints.** Martin Bligh. 500p. 1997. 39.99 (*0-672-31055-4*) Sams.

***TCP/IP Clearly Explained.** Peter Loshin. LC 96-48637. (Illus.). 419p. 1997. pap. 29.95 (*0-12-455835-6*, AP Prof) Acad Pr.

TCP/IP Companion: A Guide for the Common User. Martin R. Arick. 272p. 1993. pap. text ed. 29.95 (*0-471-55631-9*, GD4663) Wiley.

***TCP/IP Explained.** Philip Miller. LC 96-41116. 518p. 1996. pap. 39.95 (*1-55558-166-8*) Buttrwrth-Heinemann.

TCP/IP for Dummies. M. Wilensky. 400p. 1995. pap. 19.99 (*1-56884-241-4*) IDG Bks.

***TCP/IP for Dummies.** 2nd ed. Marshall Wilensky. (Illus.). 432p. (Orig.). 1997. pap. 24.99 (*0-7645-0063-5*) IDG Bks.

TCP/IP Illustrated Vol. 2: The Implementation. Gary R. Wright & W. Richard Stevens. (Professional Computing Ser.). 1120p. (C). 1995. text ed. 55.95 (*0-201-63354-X*) Addison-Wesley.

***TCP/IP Internetworking: A Hands on Guide to Understanding the TCP/IP Suite of Protocols.** Paul Simoneau. LC 97-20199. (Illus.). 452p. 1997. pap. text ed., pap. 54.95 incl. cd-rom (*0-07-912640-5*) McGraw.

TCP/IP Network Administration. Craig Hunt. (Nutshell Handbook Ser.). (Illus.). 502p. (Orig.). 1992. pap. 32.95 (*0-937175-82-X*) OReilly & Assocs.

***TCP/IP Networking.** 2nd rev. ed. Craig Hunt. Ed. by Gigi Estabrook. (Orig.). 1997. pap. write for info. (*1-56592-322-7*) OReilly & Assocs.

TCP/IP Networking Protocol Source Code Secrets. Lynne G. Jolitz & William F. Jolitz. (Operating System Source Code Secrets Ser.: Vol. 4). 525p. 1997. 44.95 (*1-57398-007-2*) Peer-to-Peer Communications.

***TCP/IP Over ATM: A No-Nonsense Networking Guide.** Berry Kercheval. (C). 1997. pap. text ed. 36.00 (*0-13-768599-8*) P-H.

***TCP/IP Primer for the AS/400: The Essential Guide to AS/400 TCP/IP Concepts, Configuration & Use.** Jim Hoopes et al. (Illus.). 390p. (Orig.). 1996. pap. 99.00 (*1-883884-33-0*) Midrange Comput.

TCP/IP Strategies. Joel Synder. 1996. pap. 29.99 (*1-56884-845-5*) IDG Bks.

TCP/IP Survival Guide. Timothy Parker. 880p. 1996. 55.00 (*0-672-30603-4*) Sams.

TCP/IP Tutorial & Technical Overview. Eamon Murphy. 608p. (C). 1995. pap. text ed. 52.00 (*0-13-460858-5*) P-H.

***TCP/IP Unleashed.** 2nd ed. Timothy Parker et al. 900p. 1997. 59.99 (*0-672-31112-7*) Sams.

***TCP/IP Unleashed: MCSE Edition.** Timothy Parker. 1997. 65.00 (*0-672-31185-2*) Mac Comp Pub.

***TDDUP (Till Death Do Us Part)** Clarence J. Rockey. 157p. (Orig.). 1997. mass mkt. 4.99 (*1-55197-575-0*, Pub. by Comnwlth Pub CN) Partners Pubs Grp.

TDP Support Guide. ITD TVU. (Trainer Development Programme Managemen & Design 8 Ser.). 1994. pap. text ed. write for info. (*0-08-042172-5*, Pergamon Pr) Elsevier.

TDP-1 Fossil Fueled Plants see ASME Standard Number TWDPS-1: Recommended Practices for the Prevention of Water Damage to Steam Turbines Used for Electric Power Generation

TDR vs Gravimetric: A Comparison of Soil Moisture Determination Methods. Tony H. Rojas. (University of Michigan Reports: No. 030613-1-T). 15p. reprint ed. pap. 25.00 (*0-7837-6780-3*, 2046610) Bks Demand.

Te Alabare. Carlos Jimenez. 120p. (SPA.). 1990. pap. 3.79 (*1-56063-109-0*, 498407) Editorial Unilit.

***Te Amo Por Que Somos Differentes!** Tim La Haye. (SPA.). 10.95 (*0-8297-1989-X*) Life Pubs Intl.

Te Asustan? Criaturas Espeluznantes. Sneed B. Collard, III. LC 93-41497. (Illus.). 32p. (Orig.). (SPA.). (J). (ps-4). 1993. pap. 6.95 (*0-88106-423-8*); lib. bdg. 15.88 (*0-88106-643-5*) Charlesbridge Pub.

Te Canto Mi Corazon. Oscar R. Benitez. 120p. 1992. pap. 7.95 (*1-881619-01-X*) Edit Encuentro.

***Te Canto Mi Corazon.** 6th ed. Oscar R. Benitez. 120p. (SPA.). 1997. pap. 8.99 (*1-890701-02-5*) La Mancha.

Te Dejo el Mar. Carmen Riera. Tr. & Intro. by Luisa Cotoner. (Nueva Austral Ser.: Vol. 211). (SPA.). 1991. pap. text ed. 24.95 (*84-239-7211-9*) Elliots Bks.

Te Fais Pas de Bile, Charlie Brown. Charles M. Schulz. (Peanuts Ser.). (FRE.). (J). 1985. 4.95 (*0-8288-4523-9*) Fr & Eur.

***Te Gustaria Conocer a Jesus? - Would You Like to Know Jesus?** Reeves. (SPA.). (J). write for info. (*1-56063-739-0*) Editorial Unilit.

***TE Holt Modern Health.** J. Otto. 1987. pap. text ed. 81.00 (*0-03-010134-4*) HR&W Schl Div.

Te Iwi Maori: A New Zealand Population Past, Present & Projected. Ian Pool. (Illus.). 224p. 1991. 19.95 (*1-86940-049-6*, Pub. by Auckland Univ NZ) Paul & Co Pubs.

***Te Kingitanga: Selected Essays from the Dictionary of New Zealand Biography.** Intro. by Angela Ballara. (Illus.). 136p. 1997. pap. 19.95 (*1-86940-202-2*, Pub. by Auckland Univ NZ) Paul & Co Pubs.

TE Linde's Operative Gynecology. 8th ed. Ed. by John A. Rock & John D. Thompson. LC 96-4875. 1,680p. 1996. text ed. 139.00 (*0-397-51399-2*) Lppncott-Raven.

Te Lo Prometo. Marion Dane Bauer. (SPA.). 1996. pap. text ed. 9.75 (*84-279-3190-5*) Lectorum Pubns.

Te Mamae Me Te Aroha - The Pain & the Love: A History of the Kai Tahu Whanui in Otago, 1844-1994. Bill Dacker. 104p. 1994. pap. 29.95 (*0-908569-89-0*, Pub. by U Otago Pr NZ) Intl Spec Bk.

Te Matatiki: Contemporary Maori Words. Maori Language Commission. 300p. 1996. pap. 19.95 (*0-19-558341-8*) OUP.

Te of Piglet. Benjamin Hoff. (Illus.). 224p. 1992. pap. 16.00 (*0-525-93496-0*, Dutton) NAL-Dutton.

Te of Piglet. large type ed. Benjamin Hoff. 1993. 10.95 (*1-56895-012-8*) Wheeler Pub.

Te of Piglet. Benjamin Hoff. (Illus.). 272p. 1993. reprint ed. pap. 11.95 (*0-14-023016-5*, Penguin Bks) Viking Penguin.

Te Presento a La Orquesta. Ann Hayes. Tr. by Alma F. Ada. (Illus.). 32p. (SPA.). (J). (ps-3). 1995. pap. 6.00 (*0-15-200275-8*, Voyager Bks) HarBrace.

***Te Tendre en el Cielo - I'll Hold You in Heaven.** Jack W. Hayford. 155p. (SPA.). 1995. write for info. (*1-56063-744-7*) Editorial Unilit.

Te Toca a Ti. Patricia Lennon & Douglas Moore. (Aiming for Proficiency Ser.). (Illus.). 160p. (Orig.). (SPA.). 1990. student ed. 14.95 (*1-879279-04-5*, TX 3-018-188) Proficiency Pr.

Te Vas a Desnucar, Charlie Brown. Charles M. Schulz. (FRE.). 1972. pap. 1.50 (*0-03-086659-6*) H Holt & Co.

Te Y Tu: Special Adaptation. Holt. (SPA.). 1989. suppl. ed., pap. text ed. 10.00 (*0-03-021389-4*) HR&W Schl Div.

Tea. Bro Halff. 44p. 1987. pap. 12.95 (*1-885238-00-2*) Simpler Gifts.

Tea. Bro Halff. 44p. 1987. 24.95 (*1-885238-01-0*) Simpler Gifts.

Tea. deluxe ed. George Tysh. (Burning Deck Poetry Ser.). 1979. pap. 15.00 (*0-930900-69-3*) Burning Deck.

Tea: Cultivation to Consumption. Ed. by K. C. Willson & M. N. Clifford. (Illus.). 704p. (gr. 13). 1991. text ed. 190.50 (*0-412-33850-5*) Chapman & Hall.

Tea: Delectables for All Seasons. Maryjo Koch. LC 94-30914. 1995. 15.00 (*0-00-255480-1*) Harper SF.

***Tea: Essence of the Leaf.** Sara Slavin et al. LC 97-17999. 1998. write for info. (*0-8118-1632-X*) Chronicle Bks.

Tea: The Gentle Brew. David R. Richards. 44p. 1985. pap. text ed. 9.95 (*0-9614431-0-3*) D R Richards.

***Tea & Scandal.** large type ed. Joan Smith. LC 96-43644. (Romance Ser.). 213p. 1996. lib. bdg. 21.95 (*0-7862-0918-6*) Thorndike Pr.

Tea & Scones: And So Much More. Aubrey Franklin. 110p. 1991. 19.98 (*0-9632840-0-2*); pap. 9.50 (*0-9632840-1-0*) Sheringham Hall.

Tea & Sects. Samuel E. Churchill-Taylor. 64p. (Orig.). 1975. pap. 3.95 (*0-938758-01-2*) MTM Pub Co.

Tea & Sympathy see Best American Plays: Fourth Series, 1952-1957

Tea & Tea Drinking. Arthur Reade. (Illus.). 174p. 1985. reprint ed. pap. 15.95 (*0-936253-00-2*) Attic Pr Discoveries.

***Tea & Teatime Recipes.** Maggie Stuckey. LC 97-13174. 1997. pap. write for info. (*0-88266-720-3*, Storey Pub) Storey Comm Inc.

Tea at Miss Cranston's: A Century of Glasgow Memories. Anna Blair. (Illus.). 224p. (Orig.). 1984. pap. 7.95 (*0-85683-081-X*, Pub. by Shepheard-Walwyn Pubs UK) Paul & Co Pubs.

Tea at Miss Cranston's: A Century of Glasgow Memories. 2nd large type ed. Anna Blair. 288p. (Orig.). 1993. 23.95 (*1-85695-326-2*, Pub. by ISIS UK) Transaction Pubs.

Tea at Miss Jean's. Bishpham Page. LC 91-65465. (Illus.). 28p. (Orig.). (J). (gr. 2 up). 1991. pap. 8.95 (*0-9628129-1-9*) R Rinehart.

Tea Book. Dawn L. Campbell. LC 94-31638. (Illus.). 256p. 1995. 16.95 (*1-56554-074-3*) Pelican.

Tea Book: A Gourmet Guide to Buying, Brewing, & Cooking. Sarah Perry. Ed. by Bill LeBlond. LC 92-38967. (Illus.). 96p. 1993. pap. 12.95 (*0-8118-0336-8*) Chronicle Bks.

Tea Breads & Coffeecakes. Elizabeth Alston. LC 90-55523. (Illus.). 112p. 1991. 13.00 (*0-06-016149-3*, HarpT) HarpC.

***Tea Break.** Groves. Date not set. pap. text ed. write for info. (*0-582-18297-2*, Pub. by Longman UK) Longman.

***Tea, C, D&C/Cycles Interrupted.** Amy Wilson. (Illus.). 36p. 1994. pap. 10.00 (*0-614-18190-9*) Visual Studies.

***Tea Caddies.** Noel Riley. (Antique Pocket Guides Ser.). 1997. pap. text ed. 6.95 (*0-7188-2598-5*, Lutterworth-Parkwest) Parkwest Pubns.

Tea Caddies. Noel Riley. (Antique Pocket Guides Ser.). (Illus.). 64p. 1985. pap. 6.95 (*0-911403-25-6*) Seven Hills Bk.

Tea Clippers: Their History & Development 1833-1875. David R. MacGregor. LC 82-61670. (Illus.). 255p. 1982. 36.95 (*0-87021-884-0*) Naval Inst Pr.

***Tea Companion.** Macmillan Publishing Satff. 1997. 22.00 (*0-02-861727-4*) Macmillan.

Tea-Cup Reading & the Art of Fortune Telling by Tea-Leaves. 94p. 1968. reprint ed. spiral bd. 7.00 (*0-7873-1282-7*) Hlth Research.

***Tea Cup Tales.** 2nd rev. ed. Margaret L. McWhorter. Ed. by Summer Andrecht. 100p. 1997. pap. 9.95 (*0-941903-23-0*) Ransom Hill.

Tea Economy of India. T. Chiranjeevi. (C). 1994. 24.00 (*0-614-13260-6*) S Asia.

Tea Economy of India. T. Chiranjeevi. (C). 1995. 22.00 (*81-7033-243-5*, Pub. by Rawat II) S Asia.

Tea Etiquette for Guests. Shoshitsu Sen Staff. (Illus.). 118p. 1994. pap. 69.95 (*4-473-01294-8*) Bks Nippan.

Tea for All Seasons. Mary P. Hampton. (Illus.). 96p. 1997. 15.99 (*0-310-96912-3*) Zondervan.

***Tea for All Seasons: Celebrating Tea, Art, & Music at the Elmwood Inn.** Shelley Richardson & Bruce Richardson. (Illus.). 116p. 1996. 19.95 (*1-889937-00-2*) Crescent Hill Bks.

Tea for Two: Taking Time for Friends. (Cherished Moments Ser.). (Illus.). 1994. 9.99 (*1-57051-035-0*) Brownlow Pub Co.

***Tea Fungus Kombucha: The Natural Remedy & Its Significance in Cases of Cancer & Other Metabolic Diseases.** R. Fasching. (Illus.). 87p. (FRE & GER.). 25.00 (*3-85068-231-5*, Pub. by Ennsthaler GW) Am Educ Systs.

Tea in China: The History of China's National Drink. John C. Evans. LC 91-23428. (Contributions to the Study of World History Ser.: No. 33). 184p. 1992. text ed. 45.00 (*0-313-28049-5*, ETC, Greenwood Pr) Greenwood.

Tea in Japan: Essays on the History of Chanoyu. Ed. by Paul Varley & Kumakura Isao. LC 89-4659. (Illus.). 344p. (C). 1989. reprint ed. pap. text ed. 18.00 (*0-8248-1717-6*) UH Pr.

Tea in the East. Carole Manchester. LC 95-47841. 1996. 23.00 (*0-688-13243-X*) Morrow.

Tea in the Harem. Charef Mehdi. Tr. by Ed Emery from FRE. 160p. (Orig.). 1991. 13.95 (*1-85242-151-7*) Serpents Tail.

Tea Industry in India. Sibranjan R. Misra. 1986. 24.00 (*81-7024-015-8*, Pub. by Ashish II) S Asia.

Tea Ingredient Centerpiece Recipe Book. Cookbook Consortium Staff. 1992. ring bd. 19.95 (*0-318-04324-6*) Prosperity & Profits.

Tea Island: A Perfect Little Gem: The Story of a Lake George Island. rev. ed. Trip Sinnott. LC 93-71743. (Illus.). 64p. (Orig.). 1993. pap. 7.95 (*1-883551-01-3*) Attic Studio Pub.

Tea Leaf Reading. William W. Hewitt. LC 89-38754. (New Age Ser.). (Illus.). 240p. (Orig.). 1989. mass mkt. 3.95 (*0-87542-308-6*) Llewellyn Pubns.

***Tea Leaves.** Louise C. Barden. (Harperprints Chapbook Ser.). 24p. (Orig.). 1996. pap. 5.00 (*1-883314-06-2*) NC Writers Network.

Tea Leaves. Compiled by Nancy Stutzman. 1990. pap. 5.25 (*0-87813-531-6*) Christian Light.

Tea Leaves. Francis S. Drake. (Notable American Authors Ser.). 1992. reprint ed. lib. bdg. 75.00 (*0-7812-2691-0*) Rprt Serv.

Tea Life, Tea Mind. Soshitsu Sen. LC 79-10763. (Illus.). 96p. 1979. pap. 12.50 (*0-8348-0142-6*) Weatherhill.

Tea Lover's Companion: The Ultimate Connoisseur's Guide to Buying, Brewing, & Enjoying Tea. James N. Pratt. Ed. by Diana Rosen. (Illus.). 176p. 1995. 15.95 (*1-55972-323-8*, Birch Ln Pr) Carol Pub Group.

***Tea Parties.** Ellen Easton. 64p. 1996. 20.00 (*1-890406-00-7*) Red Wagon Pr.

***Tea Party.** Illus. by Laurie Montgomery. 198p. 1996. 14.95 (*0-938577-11-5*) St Johns Pub.

Tea Party & The Basement: Two Plays. Harold Pinter. 1969. pap. 5.25 (*0-8222-1115-7*) Dramatists Play.

Tea Party Book. Lucille R. Penner. LC 91-52093. (Illus.). 48p. (J). (ps-4). 1993. 12.95 (*0-679-82440-5*) Random Bks Yng Read.

Tea Party Book & Miniature China Tea Set. Lucille R. Penner. (Illus.). (J). 1995. 14.99 (*0-679-87005-9*) Random.

Tea Party for Two. Michelle Poploff. LC 96-8329. (J). 1997. write for info. (*0-385-32260-7*); pap. write for info. (*0-440-41334-6*) Delacorte.

Tea Party Puzzle. Illus. by Tony Linsell. (Squeaky Surprise Ser.). 14p. (J). 1996. bds. 7.99 (*1-57584-002-2*) Rdrs Dgst Yng Fam.

***Tea Party Time: Romantic Quilts & Tasty Tidbits.** Nancy J. Martin. (Illus.). 64p. pap. text ed. 8.95 (*0-486-29472-2*) Dover.

Tea Party to Independence: The Third Phase of the American Revolution, 1773-1776. Peter D. Thomas. 368p. 1991. 75.00 (*0-19-820142-7*) OUP.

Tea Planter's Bride. Rosemary Rogers. 416p. (Orig.). 1995. mass mkt. 6.50 (*0-380-76477-6*) Avon.

***Tea Rituals.** Tomislav Padreka. Date not set. write for info. (*0-688-15808-0*) Morrow.

Tea-Shop in Limehouse. Thomas Burke. LC 77-103499. (Short Story Index Reprint Ser.). 1977. 20.95 (*0-8369-3241-2*) Ayer.

Tea-Table Miscellany: Or, a Collection of Choice Songs, Scots & English. 12th ed. Allan Ramsay. LC 73-144572. reprint ed. 41.50 (*0-404-08687-X*) AMS Pr.

Tea Taste in Japanese Art. Sherman E. Lee. LC 74-27416. (Asia Society Ser.). (Illus.). 1976. reprint ed. lib. bdg. 31.95 (*0-405-06565-5*) Ayer.

Tea Time. M. Dalton King. LC 92-53689. (Miniature Editions Ser.). (Illus.). 120p. 1992. 4.95 (*1-56138-152-7*) Running Pr.

Tea-Time at the Inn. Gail Greco. LC 91-23461. (Illus.). 224p. 1991. 24.95 (*1-55853-120-3*) Rutledge Hill Pr.

Tea Time at the Masters: A Collection of Recipes. Junior League of Augusta, Georgia, Inc. Staff. 292p. 1977. 9.95 (*0-918544-38-6*) JL Augusta.

Tea Time Friends. Brownlow. (Easelette Miniatures Ser.). (Illus.). 1995. spiral bd. 4.99 (*1-57051-048-2*) Brownlow Pub Co.

***Tea Time Journeys.** Gail Greco. LC 97-583. (Illus.). 128p. 1997. 12.95 (*1-55853-473-3*) Rutledge Hill Pr.

Tea Time with God. Honor Books Staff. (Quiet Moments with God Ser.). 208p. Date not set. 14.99 (*1-56292-033-2*) Honor Bks OK.

Tea-Totalers. Helen Forelle. Ed. by Janet Leih. 25p. (Orig.). 1990. spiral bd. 4.00 (*1-877649-08-2*) Tesseract SD.

Tea-Totally Dead. Jacqueline Girdner. 1994. pap. 4.99 (*0-425-14210-8*) Berkley Pub.

***Tea Travels.** 2nd rev. ed. Ellen Easton. Orig. Title: The Afternoon Tea Guide by Ellen Easton. 133p. 1997. pap. 16.00 (*1-890406-01-5*) Red Wagon Pr.

Tea Tree Oil. Susan Drury. 111p. 1991. pap. 7.95 (*0-85207-238-4*, Pub. by C W Daniel UK) Natl Bk Netwk.

Tea Tree Oil. 3rd ed. Susan Drury. 88p. pap. 11.95 (*0-8464-4299-X*) Beekman Pubs.

***Tea Tree Oil: The New Guide to One of Nature's Most Remarkable Gifts.** Julia Lawless. 96p. 1995. pap. 7.00 (*0-7225-3032-3*) Thorsons SF.

Tea with Adella Dine Crow. Valerie H. Damon. Ed. by Dave Damon. LC 88-92261. (Illus.). 32p. (J). (ps-5). 1990. 9.95 (*0-932356-15-X*) Star Pubns MO.

Tea with Mr. Timothy. 2nd large type ed. Geoffrey Morgan. (Illus.). 111p. (J). 1993. 18.95 (*1-85695-300-9*, Pub. by ISIS UK) Transaction Pubs.

***Tea with Pasty Clairmont.** Patsy Clairmont. LC 97-16862. 1997. 14.99 (*1-56955-039-5*) Servant.

Teabags from England: Frontier Stories. Ed. by David Wilde. (Sun Also Sets Ser.). (Orig.). 1993. pap. 12.95 (*0-9625472-8-X*) Wilde Pub.

TEACCS Codex. Fred P. Abitia. 300p. 1990. 112.00 (*1-880944-00-6*); pap. 49.50 (*1-880944-01-4*) Atabichron.

Teach! Plain Talk about Teaching. Leo A. Meyer. 124p. (Orig.). 1992. text ed. 18.95 (*0-88069-014-3*) L A Meyer.

Teach - Practice - Apply: The TPA Instructional Model, K-8. Judy Reinhartz & Daniel Van Cleef. 112p. 1986. pap. 10.95 (*0-8106-1830-3*) NEA.

Teach a Beginning Reader with Common Sense & a Cookie Sheet: A Guide for Parents. Melisa Buchanan. (Illus.). 96p. (Orig.). 1990. pap. write for info. (*1-879129-00-0*) Oak Plantation.

Teach a Child to Read with Children's Books: Combining Story Reading, Phonics, & Writing to Promote Reading Success. Mark B. Thogmartin. Ed. by Eleanor C. MacFarlane. (Illus.). 216p. 1996. pap. 19.95 (*1-883790-20-4*, 109-1633, EDINFO Pr) Grayson Bernard Pubs.

***Teach a Child to Read with Children's Books: Combining Story Reading, Phonics, & Writing to Promote Reading Success.** 2nd ed. Mark B. Thogmartin. LC 97-21001. 1997. pap. write for info. (*1-883790-25-5*) Grayson Bernard Pubs.

***Teach American English Around the World, Vol. 1.** Thomas A. Kane et al. Ed. by Cheryl DeJong. 216p. (Orig.). 1997. pap. 19.95 (*1-888811-06-4*, 110) Abbot Pr.

Teach an Adult to Read: Tutor Training Workbook. Susan G. Paull. Ed. by Betty Ringo. 40p. 1987. 6.95 (*0-910475-36-9*) KET.

***Teach & Learn Across Culture.** Carmen Mercado. Ed. by David M. Fetterman. (Studies in Education & Culture). 250p. Date not set. text ed. 37.50 (*0-8153-0914-7*) Garland.

Teach & Learn Elementary Social Studies. 5th ed. Ellis. 1994. text ed. 66.00 (*0-205-15768-8*) P-H.

Teach & Reach Students with Attention Deficit Disorders. rev. ed. Nancy L. Eisenberg & Pamela H. Esser. (Educator's Handbook & Resource Guide Ser.). (Illus.). 200p. 1994. teacher ed. 19.95 (*0-9630847-0-4*) Multigrowth.

Teach & Reach Students with Attention Deficit Disorders. 2nd ed. Nancy L. Eisenberg & Pamela H. Esser. (Educator's Handbook & Resource Guide Ser.). 1997. teacher ed. 23.95 (*0-9630847-1-2*) Multigrowth.

Handbook & resource guide for parents & educators of ADD students preschool through high school. This easy-to-use, comprehensive reference covers all aspects of ADD students' functioning (academic, social, emotional, behavioral) in the classroom. Promotes understanding of the ADD student & the crucial role of the educator with guidelines to facilitate the effectiveness of the educator's teaching skills & utilization of the school's resources. Includes characteristics of ADD & manifestations in the classroom & information regarding diagnosis & treatment including use of medications. Detailed, specific, innovative, effective teaching techniques & academic modifications in addition to homework strategies, building self-esteem, stimulating motivation, using grades more effectively, increasing organizational skills, & behavior modification are described. Chapters include developing effective, cooperative home-school relationships & education laws which protect the ADD student. There are numerous time-saving forms & worksheets suitable for copying. Authors are professionals, have conducted numerous teacher in-service workshops & are the parents of ADD students. To order, send $19.95 plus $3.00 for postage & handling to MultiGrowth Resources, 12345 Jones Rd., #101, Houston, TX 77070, 713-890-5334. ***Publisher Provided Annotation.***

Teach at Your Own Risk. Diana M. Shead. Ed. by Judy Williams. 260p. 21.95 (*0-9644236-1-8*) Fmly & Frnds.

***Teach Children.** Edward DeBono. 1997. pap. 24.95 (*0-7871-1234-8*, Dove Bks) Dove Audio.

Teach Children to Sew: Video & Manual. Winky Cherry. (Illus.). 112p. pap. 29.95 incl. vhs (*0-935278-33-8*) Palmer-Pletsch.

Teach Creatively Working Words. Vivian. 1995. pap. text ed. 33.50 (*0-205-19949-6*) Allyn.

Teach Dynamic Truths. C. S. Lovett. 1973. teacher ed., pap. 7.95 (*0-938148-14-1*) Prsnl Christianity.

Teach English: A Training Course for Teachers. Adrian Doff. (Illus.). 294p. 1988. teacher ed., pap. text ed. 19.95 (*0-521-34864-1*); teacher ed., pap. text ed. 15.95 (*0-521-34863-3*) Cambridge U Pr.

Teach Every Child to Read Creatively Via Learning Circuits: Primary Curriculum Guide for Language Arts. Elinor L. Brown. 1990. pap. 9.75 (*0-685-28045-4*) Midwest Pub NE.

Teach for Transfer. Madeline C. Hunter. LC 95-11690. 104p. 1971. pap. 11.95 (*0-8039-6322-X*) Corwin Pr.

***Teach Interactive Science Technology.** Lowe. Date not set. pap. text ed. write for info. (*0-582-87310-X*, Pub. by Longman UK) Longman.

Teach Masters, Profiles: A Language Skill. Workman. (EC - HS Communication/Engl Ser.). 1995. 71.95 (*0-538-62785-9*) S-W Pub.

Teach Me about God: Includes Special Tips to Help Parents Explain Big Truths to Small Children. Linda J. Sattgast. 150p. (J). (ps). 1993. 9.99 (*0-945564-64-3*, Gold & Honey) Multnomah Pubs.

Teach Me about Jesus. Linda J. Sattgast. 160p. (J). (ps-2). 1994. 9.99 (*0-88070-635-X*, Gold & Honey) Multnomah Pubs.

Teach Me Chinese: A Musical Journey Through the Day. Judy Mahoney. (Teach Me More...Ser.). (Illus.). 20p. (Orig.). (CHI & ENG.). (J). (ps-6). 1996. pap. 12.95 incl. audio (*0-934633-84-3*) Teach Me.

Teach Me English: A Musical Journey Through the Day. Judy Mahoney. (Illus.). 31p. 1993. teacher ed., pap. 6.50 (*0-934633-25-8*) Teach Me.

Teach Me English: A Musical Journey Through the Day. Judy Mahoney. (Illus.). 20p. (J). (ps-6). 1993. pap. 12.95 incl. audio (*0-934633-60-6*) Teach Me.

Teach Me Even More French: 21 Songs to Sing & a Story about Pen Pals. Judy Mahoney. (Teach Me Even More...Ser.). (Illus.). 24p. (Orig.). (ENG & FRE.). (J). (gr. 2-6). 1996. pap. 15.95 incl. audio compact disk (*0-934633-98-3*) Teach Me.

Teach Me Even More French: 21 Songs to Sing & a Story about Pen Pals, Clam-Shell Case. Judy Mahoney. (Illus.). 24p. (Orig.). (ENG & FRE.). (J). (gr. 2-6). 1996. pap. 14.95 incl. audio (*0-934633-72-X*) Teach Me.

Teach Me Even More Spanish: 21 Songs to Sing with Pen Pals. Judy Mahoney. Ed. by Virginia See. (Teach Me Even More...Ser.). (Illus.). 24p. (Orig.). (ENG & SPA.). (J). (gr. 2-6). 1995. pap. 14.95 incl. audio (*0-934633-69-X*) Teach Me.

Teach Me Even More Spanish: 21 Songs to Sing with Pen Pals. Judy Mahoney. (Illus.). 24p. (Orig.). (ENG & SPA.). (J). (gr. 2-6). 1995. boxed, pap. 14.95 incl. audio (*0-934633-67-3*) Teach Me.

Teach Me Even More Spanish: 21 Songs to Sing with Pen Pals. Judy Mahoney. Ed. by Virginia See. (Teach Me Even More...Ser.). (Illus.). 24p. (Orig.). (ENG & SPA.). (J). (gr. 2-6). 1996. pap. 15.95 incl. audio compact disk (*0-934633-97-5*) Teach Me.

Teach Me Even More Spanish CD Book Box. Judy Mahoney. (Teach Me More...Ser.). (Illus.). 24p. (ENG & SPA.). (J). (gr. 2-6). 1996. boxed, pap. 15.95 incl. audio compact disk (*0-934633-89-4*) Teach Me.

Teach Me French: A Musical Journey Through the Day. rev. ed. Judy Mahoney. (Illus.). 20p. (ENG & FRE.). (J). (ps-6). 1989. pap. 12.95 incl. audio (*0-934633-02-9*) Teach Me.

Teach Me French: A Musical Journey Through the Day. rev. ed. Judy Mahoney. Ed. by Virginia See. 32p. (FRE.). 1994. teacher ed., pap. 6.50 (*0-934633-26-6*) Teach Me.

Teach Me French - A Musical Journey through the Day. Judy Mahoney. (Teach Me More...Ser.). (Illus.). 20p. (ENG & FRE.). (J). (ps-6). 1996. pap. 14.95 incl. audio compact disk (*0-934633-94-0*) Teach Me.

Teach Me French Book Box. Judy R. Mahony. (Illus.). 20p. (ENG & FRE.). (J). (ps-6). 1994. boxed, pap. 14.95 incl. audio (*0-934633-00-2*) Teach Me.

Teach Me French CD Book Box. Judy Mahoney. (Teach Me More...Ser.). (Illus.). 20p. (ENG & FRE.). (J). (ps-6). 1996. boxed, pap. 14.95 incl. audio compact disk (*0-934633-86-X*) Teach Me.

Teach Me German: A Musical Journey Through the Day. rev. ed. Judy Mahoney. (Illus.). 20p. (ENG & GER.). (J). (ps-6). 1985. pap. 12.95 incl. audio (*0-934633-07-X*) Teach Me.

Teach Me German: A Musical Journey Through the Day. rev. ed. Judy Mahoney. Ed. by Virginia See. 31p. 1996. teacher ed., pap. 6.50 (*0-934633-27-4*) Teach Me.

Teach Me Hebrew: A Musical Journey Through the Day. Judy Mahoney. Tr. by Shelly Horowitz. 18p. 1991. teacher ed., pap. 6.50 (*0-934633-28-2*) Teach Me.

Teach Me Hebrew: A Musical Journey Through the Day. Judy Mahoney. Tr. by Shelly Horowitz. (Illus.). 20p. (ENG & HEB.). (J). (ps-6). 1991. pap. 12.95 incl. audio (*0-934633-54-1*) Teach Me.

Teach Me How to Cry. Patricia Joudry. 1955. pap. 5.25 (*0-8222-1113-0*) Dramatists Play.

Teach Me How to Pray. Mary D. Thayer. (Illus.). 1984. 9.95 (*0-911346-08-2*) Christianica.

Teach Me, I'm Yours. Joan Bramsch. LC 79-88155. (Illus.). 1979. spiral bd. 12.95 (*0-934334-00-5*) Libty Comm Hse.

Teach Me Italian: A Musical Journey Through the Day. Judy Mahoney. Tr. by Maria C. Grifoni. (Illus.). 20p. 1992. teacher ed., pap. 6.50 (*0-934633-29-0*) Teach Me.

Teach Me Italian: A Musical Journey Through the Day. Judy Mahoney. Tr. by Maria C. Grifoni. (Illus.). 20p. (ENG & ITA.). (J). (ps-6). 1992. pap. 12.95 incl. audio (*0-934633-57-6*) Teach Me.

Teach Me Japanese: A Musical Journey Through the Day. Judy Mahoney. Tr. by Naomi Satoh. (Illus.). 20p. (ENG & JPN.). (J). (ps-6). 1990. pap. 12.95 incl. audio (*0-934633-17-7*) Teach Me.

Teach Me Japanese: A Musical Journey Through the Day. rev. ed. Judy Mahoney. Ed. by Virginia See. Tr. by Naomi Satoh. (Illus.). 29p. 1996. teacher ed., pap. 6.50 (*0-934633-30-4*) Teach Me.

***Teach Me Language: A Language Manual for Children with Autism, Asperger's Syndrome & Related Developmental Disorders.** Sabrina Freeman & Lorelei Dahe. (Illus.). 410p. 1996. 59.95 (*0-9657565-0-5*, TML-1) SKF Bks.

***Teach Me Lord That I May Teach: What We Learned Homeschooling the Kids.** Barbara Smith & Douglas Smith. (Illus.). 128p. 1995. reprint ed. pap. 8.95 (*1-878140-06-X*) Phys Dis Servs.

***Teach Me More Chinese: A Musical Journey Through the Year.** Judy Mahoney. (Teach Me More...Ser.). (Illus.). 24p. (Orig.). (CHI & ENG.). (J). (ps-6). 1997. boxed, pap. 13.95 incl. audio (*0-934633-48-7*) Teach Me.

Teach Me More English: A Musical Journey Through the Year. Judy Mahoney. (Illus.). 20p. (Orig.). (J). (ps-6). 1994. pap. 13.95 (*0-934633-66-5*) Teach Me.

Teach Me More English: A Musical Journey Through the Year. Virginia See. (Illus.). 37p. (Orig.). 1994. teacher ed., pap. text ed. 6.95 (*0-934633-38-X*) Teach Me.

Teach Me More French: A Musical Journey Through the Year. Judy Mahoney. (Illus.). 35p. (ENG & FRE.). (J). (ps-6). 1989. pap. 13.95 incl. audio (*0-934633-11-8*) Teach Me.

Teach Me More French: A Musical Journey Through the Year. rev. ed. Judy Mahoney. Ed. by Virginia See. 20p. 1994. teacher ed., pap. 6.95 (*0-934633-33-9*) Teach Me.

Teach Me More French - A Musical Journey Through the Year. Judy Mahoney. (Teach Me More...Ser.). (Illus.). 20p. (ENG & FRE.). (J). (ps-6). 1996. pap. 15.95 incl. audio compact disk (*0-934633-96-7*) Teach Me.

Teach Me More French Book Box. Judy Mahoney. (Illus.). 20p. (Orig.). (J). (ps-6). 1995. boxed, pap. 14.95 incl. audio (*0-934633-10-X*) Teach Me.

Teach Me More French CD Book Box. Judy Mahoney. (Teach Me More...Ser.). (Illus.). 20p. (ENG & FRE.). (J). (ps-6). 1996. boxed, pap. 15.95 incl. audio compact disk (*0-934633-88-6*) Teach Me.

Teach Me More German: A Musical Journey Through the Year. Judy Mahoney. (Illus.). 20p. (GER.). (J). (ps-6). 1990. pap. 13.95 incl. audio (*0-934633-23-1*) Teach Me.

Teach Me More German: A Musical Journey Through the Year. rev. ed. Judy Mahoney. Ed. by Virginia See. 36p. (GER.). 1994. teacher ed., pap. 6.95 (*0-934633-34-7*) Teach Me.

Teach Me More Italian: A Musical Journey Through the Year. Judy Mahoney. Tr. by Maria C. Grifoni. 31p. (Orig.). 1993. teacher ed., pap. 6.95 (*0-934633-35-5*) Teach Me.

Teach Me More Italian: A Musical Journey Through the Year. Judy Mahoney. Tr. by Maria Grifoni. (Illus.). 20p. (Orig.). (J). (ps-6). 1993. pap. 13.95 incl. audio (*0-934633-63-0*) Teach Me.

Teach Me More Japanese: A Musical Journey Through the Year. Judy Mahoney. Tr. by Naomi Satoh. (Illus.). 20p. (JPN.). (J). (ps-6). 1991. pap. 13.95 incl. audio (*0-934633-20-7*) Teach Me.

Teach Me More Japanese: A Musical Journey Through the Year. rev. ed. Judy Mahoney. Ed. by Virginia See. Tr. by Naomi Satoh. 35p. (JPN.). 1994. teacher ed., pap. 6.95 (*0-934633-36-3*) Teach Me.

Teach Me More Russian - A Musical Journey Through the Year. Judy Mahoney. (Illus.). 20p. (Orig.). (J). (ps-6). 1997. pap. 13.95 incl. audio (*0-934633-78-9*) Teach Me.

Teach Me More Spanish: A Musical Journey Through the Year. Judy Mahoney. (Illus.). 20p. (J). (ps-6). 1989. pap. 13.95 incl. audio (*0-934633-14-2*) Teach Me.

Teach Me More Spanish: A Musical Journey Through the Year. Judy Mahoney. (Teach Me More... Ser.). (Illus.). 20p. (ENG & SPA.). (J). (ps-6). 1996. pap. 15.95 incl. audio compact disk (*0-934633-95-9*) Teach Me.

Teach Me More Spanish: A Musical Journey Through the Year. rev. ed. Judy Mahoney. Ed. by Virginia See. 35p. 1996. teacher ed., pap. 6.95 (*0-934633-37-1*) Teach Me.

Teach Me More Spanish Book Box. Judy Mahoney. (Illus.). 20p. (Orig.). (J). (ps-6). 1995. boxed, pap. 14.95 incl. audio (*0-934633-13-4*) Teach Me.

Teach Me More Spanish CD Book Box. Judy Mahoney. (Teach Me More...Ser.). (Illus.). 20p. (ENG & SPA.). (J). (ps-6). 1996. boxed, pap. 15.95 incl. audio compact disk (*0-934633-87-8*) Teach Me.

Teach Me Now. 80p. (J). (ps). 1982. 6.99 (*0-685-30468-X*) CEF Press.

Teach Me Now Vol. 2: About Myself & My Savior. Betty Johnson. (Illus.). 90p. (J). (ps). 1982. pap. text ed. 27.99 (*1-55976-109-1*) CEF Press.

Teach Me Now 1. 80p. (J). (ps). 1981. 6.99 (*0-685-17899-4*) CEF Press.

Teach Me Now 3. 80p. (J). (ps). 1983. 6.99 (*0-685-17902-8*) CEF Press.

Teach Me Now 4. 80p. (J). (ps). 1984. 6.99 (*0-685-17903-6*) CEF Press.

Teach Me Russian: A Musical Journey Through the Day. Judy Mahoney. Tr. by Sasha Gybin. 19p. (Orig.). 1991. teacher ed., pap. 6.50 (*0-934633-31-2*) Teach Me.

Teach Me Russian: A Musical Journey Through the Day. Judy Mahoney. Tr. by Sasha Gybin. 20p. (Orig.). (ENG & RUS.). (J). (ps-6). 1991. pap. 12.95 incl. audio (*0-934633-51-7*) Teach Me.

Teach Me Spanish. Judy Mahoney. (Teach Me More...Ser.). (Illus.). 20p. (ENG & SPA.). (J). (ps-6). 1996. pap. 14.95 incl. audio compact disk (*0-934633-93-2*) Teach Me.

Teach Me Spanish. rev. ed. Judy Mahoney. (Teach Me More...Ser.). (Illus.). 20p. (SPA.). (J). (ps-6). 1989. pap. 12.95 incl. audio (*0-934633-05-3*) Teach Me.

Teach Me Spanish. rev. ed. Judy Mahoney. Ed. by Virginia See. (Teach Me More...Ser.). 32p. 1994. teacher ed., pap. 6.50 (*0-934633-32-0*) Teach Me.

Teach Me Spanish Book Box. Judy Mahoney. (Illus.). 20p. (SPA.). (J). (ps-6). 1994. boxed, pap. 14.95 incl. audio (*0-934633-03-7*) Teach Me.

Teach Me Spanish CD Book Box. Judy Mahoney. (Teach Me More...Ser.). (Illus.). 20p. (ENG & SPA.). (J). (ps-6). 1996. boxed, pap. 14.95 incl. audio compact disk (*0-934633-85-1*) Teach Me.

Teach Me Sports Baseball: Join the Fun by Learning the Game! Barry Dreayer. Ed. by Colby Allerton. (Teach Me Sports Ser.). (Illus.). 128p. (Orig.). 1994. pap. 7.99 (*1-881649-34-2*) Genl Pub Grp.

Teach Me Sports Basketball: Join the Fun by Learning the Game! Barry Dreayer. 1994. pap. 7.99 (*1-881649-33-4*) Genl Pub Grp.

Teach Me Sports Football: Join the Fun by Learning the Game! Barry Dreayer. Ed. by Colby Allerton. (Teach Me Sports Ser.). (Illus.). 128p. 1995. pap. 7.99 (*1-881649-37-7*) Genl Pub Grp.

Teach Me Sports Hockey: Join the Fun by Learning the Game! Barry Dreayer. 1994. pap. 7.99 (*1-881649-35-0*) Genl Pub Grp.

Teach Me Sports Soccer: Join the Fun by Learning the Game. Barry Dreayer. Ed. by Colby Allerton. (Teach Me Sports Ser.). (Illus.). 128p. (Orig.). 1994. pap. 7.99 (*1-881649-36-9*) Genl Pub Grp.

Teach Me the Way. Lori M. Poe. LC 91-92913. 131p. pap. 19.95 (*0-9624804-7-9*) Place Light.

Teach Me to Fly, Vol. 1. Suzanne Grenell. (Illus.). 80p. 1993. pap. 7.50 (*0-9637632-8-8*) Wings As Eagles.

Teach Me to Kill. Stephen Sawicki. 1991. mass mkt. 4.99 (*0-380-76649-3*) Avon.

Teach Me to Play: A First Book of Bridge. Jude Goodwin & Don Ellison. (J). (gr. 3-9). 1988. pap. 10.95 (*0-944705-01-4*); lib. bdg. 10.95 (*0-944705-03-0*) Pando Pubns.

Teach Me to Play Piano: Preliminary Book for the Earliest Beginner. H. Kasschau. 48p. 1986. pap. 6.95 (*0-7935-5294-X*, 50329420) H Leonard.

Teach Me to Pray. William E. Sangster. 1959. pap. 4.95 (*0-8358-0125-X*) Upper Room Bks.

Teach Me to Pray. large type ed. Gabe Huck. (Large Print Inspirational Ser.). 160p. 1986. pap. 8.95 (*0-8027-2567-8*) Walker & Co.

Teach Me to Pray - I'm Falling Asleep. Richard D. Gazowsky. 102p. (Orig.). (C). 1989. pap. 5.95 (*0-317-93315-9*) Voice Pentecost Pub.

Teach Me to Walk in the Light. Allan K. Burgess. 1995. pap. 8.95 (*1-57008-180-8*) Bookcraft Inc.

Teach Me Tomorrow. Walter A. Coole et al. 39p. (Orig.). 1986. pap. text ed. 4.00 (*0-926725-04-1*) Scaramouche.

Teach Me Your Ways (the Pentateuch) Kay Arthur. (International Inductive Study Ser.). 1994. pap. 6.99 (*1-56507-204-9*) Harvest Hse.

Teach More--Faster! A Programmed Book. Madeline C. Hunter. LC 95-6573. 1967. pap. 11.95 (*0-8039-6318-1*) Corwin Pr.

Teach My People. Vincent M. Walsh. 104p. 1983. pap. 4.00 (*0-943374-06-5*) Key of David.

Teach On: Teaching Strategies for Reading & Writing Workshops. David Hornsby et al. LC 93-16625. 64p. 1993. pap. text ed. 16.50 (*0-435-08790-8*, 08790) Heinemann.

Teach Only Love: The Seven Principles of Attitudinal Healing. Gerald G. Jampolsky. 128p. 1984. pap. 10.95 (*0-553-34367-X*) Bantam.

Teach Our Children Well: Bringing K-12 Education into the 21st Century. Robert C. Calfee & Cynthia L. Patrick. Ed. by Bruce Goldman. (Portable Stanford Bks.). (Illus.). 234p. (Orig.). 1995. pap. 14.95 (*0-916318-55-9*) Stanford Alumni Assn.

Teach Physical Education. Jacqueline Williams & Kay Williamson. 128p. (C). 1995. per., pap. text ed. 25.14 (*0-7872-0949-X*) Kendall-Hunt.

***Teach Primary Drama.** 2nd ed. Longman Publishing Staff. Date not set. pap. text ed. write for info. (*0-582-87491-2*, Pub. by Longman UK) Longman.

Teach Smarter, Not Harder. Sharon Rybak. 128p. (J). (gr. k-6). 1991. 12.99 (*0-86653-620-5*, GA1339) Good Apple.

***Teach Someone to Read: A Step-by-Step Guide for Literacy Tutors.** Nadine Rosenthal. 204p. 1987. spiral bd. 17.55 (*0-8224-5834-9*) Fearon Teach Aids.

Teach Someone to Read! An Effective How-to Method for Basic Reading & Literacy Programs. Michael W. Nunn. (Orig.). 1986. pap. text ed. 12.00 (*0-910609-13-6*) Gifted Educ Pr.

An Asterisk (*) at the beginning of an entry indicates that the title is appearing in BIP for the first time.

Teach Soul-Winning. C. S. Lovett. 1962. teacher ed., pap. 4.95 (*0-938148-12-5*) Prsnl Christianity.

Teach Speech. Loretta B. Minn. 64p. (J). (gr. 3-7). 1982. 6.99 (*0-86653-058-4*, GA 418) Good Apple.

Teach-Stat for Statistics Educators: Statistics: a Key to Better Mathematics. University of North Carolina Mathematics & Science Education Network Staff. Ed. by Joan Gideon. (Teach-Stat Ser.). 141p. (Orig.). 1995. teacher ed. 18.95 (*1-57232-144-X*, DS21439) Seymour Pubns.

Teach-Stat for Teachers: Professional Development Manual: Statistics: A Key to Better Mathematics. University of North Carolina Mathematics & Science Education Network Staff. Ed. by Joan Gideon. (Teach-Stat Ser.). 372p. (Orig.). 1996. teacher ed. 32.00 (*0-86651-950-5*, DS21407) Seymour Pubns.

Teach-State Activities: Statistics Investigations for Grades 1-3. University of North Carolina Mathematics & Science Education Network Staff. Ed. by Joan Gideon. (Teach-Stat Ser.). (Illus.). 111p. (Orig.). (J). (gr. 1-3). 1996. teacher ed., pap. 14.95 (*0-86651-951-3*, 21408) Seymour Pubns.

Teach-State Activities: Statistics Investigations for Grades 3-6. University of North Carolina Mathematics & Science Education Network Staff. Ed. by Joan Gideon. (Teach-Stat Ser.). (Illus.). 111p. (Orig.). (J). (gr. 1-3). 1996. teacher ed., pap. 14.95 (*0-86651-952-1*, 21409) Seymour Pubns.

Teach, Teacher. abr. ed. Luanna C. Blagrove. (Illus.). 1988. 24.95 (*0-939776-42-1*) Blagrove Pubns.

Teach the Mind, Touch the Spirit: A Guide to Focused Field Trips. Helen H. Voris et al. (Illus.). 90p. (Orig.). 1986. pap. write for info. (*0-914868-09-8*) Field Mus.

Teach Them about Satan. C. S. Lovett. 1970. teacher ed., pap. 7.45 (*0-938148-26-5*) Prsnl Christianity.

Teach Them Good Customs: Colonial Indian Education & Acculturation in the Andes. Robert D. Wood. LC 85-50096. 142p. (Orig.). 1986. pap. 20.00 (*0-911437-17-7*) Labyrinthos.

Teach Them Thinking: Mental Menus for 24 Thinking Skills. Robin Fogarty & James Bellanca. (Illus.). 144p. (Orig.). 1986. pap. text ed. 23.95 (*0-932935-03-6*) IRI-SkyLght.

Teach Them to Be Happy. Robert A. Sullo. LC 89-61056. (Illus.). 100p. (Orig.). 1989. pap. text ed. 12.00 (*0-944337-04-X*, 04X) New View Pubns.

Teach Thinking by Discussion. D. Bligh. 1986. 44.00 (*1-85059-004-4*, Open Univ Pr) Taylor & Francis.

Teach Those Things Most Plain & Precious. Rick Simons. (LDS Resource Ser.). 60p. 1994. pap. text ed. 8.95 (*1-886046-31-X*) Dovetail Pr.

Teach to Reach: Over 300 Strategies, Tips, & Helpful Hints for Teachers of All Grades. Craig Mitchell. Ed. by Pamala Espeland. LC 96-7812. (Free Spirited Classroom Ser.). 200p. (Orig.). 1996. pap. 9.95 (*1-57542-010-4*) Free Spirit Pub.

Teach Us, Amelia Bedelia. Amelia Parish. (Hello Reader! Ser.). (Illus.). 56p. (J). (gr. 2-3). 1995. pap. 3.99 (*0-590-53773-3*, Cartwheel) Scholastic Inc.

Teach Us, Amelia Bedelia. Peggy Parish. LC 76-22663. (Greenwillow Read-Alone Bks.). (Illus.). 56p. (J). (gr. 1-4). 1977. 16.00 (*0-688-80069-6*); lib. bdg. 15.93 (*0-688-84069-8*) Greenwillow.

Teach Us, Amelia Bedelia. Peggy Parish. (Illus.). 64p. (J). (gr. k-3). 1987. pap. 2.95 (*0-590-43345-8*) Scholastic Inc.

Teach Us to Laugh at Porcupines: A Collection of Contemporary Prayers. Jerry D. Johnson. 120p. (Orig.). 1994. pap. 8.95 (*1-885473-05-2*) Wood NBarnes.

Teach Us to Laugh at Porcupines: A Collection of Contemporary Prayers, Pulpit Ed. Jerry D. Johnson. 120p. (Orig.). 1994. spiral bd. 9.95 (*1-885473-06-0*) Wood NBarnes.

Teach Us to Number Our Days: Inspirational Thoughts on Wisdom & Aging. Steven McFadden. 1996. pap. 11.95 (*1-85230-803-6*) Element MA.

Teach Us to Outgrow Our Madness. Kenzaburo Oe. Tr. by John Nathan from JPN. LC 76-54582. 261p. 1977. pap. 11.00 (*0-8021-5185-X*, Grove) Grove-Atltic.

Teach Us to Pray. Ed. by Francis A. Eigo. LC 96-5597. 1996. write for info. (*0-87723-064-1*) Villanova U Pr.

Teach Us to Pray. Ed. by Thomas Jones & Sheila Jones. (Daily Power Ser.). 145p. 1995. pap. 6.99 (*1-884553-54-0*) Discipleshp.

Teach Us to Pray. St. Paul Publications Staff. (C). 1988. 35.00 (*0-85439-151-7*, Pub. by St Paul Pubns UK) St Mut.

***Teach Us to Pray.** 20th ed. Charles Fillmore & Cora Fillmore. 224p. 1997. reprint ed. 11.95 (*0-87159-203-7*, 47) Unity Bks.

Teach Us to Pray: A Cowley Classic. Andre Louf. LC 92-5949. 115p. 1992. pap. 8.95 (*1-56101-058-8*) Cowley Pubns.

Teach Us to Pray: Overcoming Obstacles in Daily Prayer. Bradley Hanson. LC 09-2468. 112p. (Orig.). 1990. pap. 9.99 (*0-8066-2468-X*, 9-2468) Augsburg Fortress.

Teach Us to Pray: Prayer in the Bible & the World. Ed. by D. A. Carson. (World Evangelical Fellowship Ser.). 352p. (Orig.). 1989. pap. 14.99 (*0-8010-2537-0*) Baker Bks.

Teach Us to Pray: The Disciples Request Cast Anew. Fred C. Lofton. 96p. 1983. pap. 4.00 (*0-89191-751-9*) Prog Bapt Pub.

***Teach Us to Pray (Ensine - Nos a Orar)** Ed. by Thomas Jones & Sheila Jones. Tr. by Thais Neves. 144p. (Orig.). (POR.). 1996. pap. 6.99 (*1-884553-96-6*) Discipleshp.

Teach with Discipline. Ed. by William P. McLemore. LC 93-5605. 148p. (Orig.). (C). 1993. pap. text ed. 26.00 (*0-8191-9265-1*) U Pr of Amer.

Teach Witnessing. C. S. Lovett. 1966. teacher ed., pap. 7.95 (*0-938148-09-5*) Prsnl Christianity.

Teach Ye Diligently. rev. ed. Boyd K. Packer. LC 75-22704. x, 388p. 1991. reprint ed. pap. 12.95 (*0-87579-476-9*) Deseret Bk.

Teach Your Baby to Sleep Through the Night. Charles E. Schaefer & Michael R. Petronko. 1988. pap. 3.95 (*0-451-15608-0*, Sig) NAL-Dutton.

Teach Your Baby to Swim. Bonnie Prudden. LC 73-79534. (Illus.). 1978. pap. text ed. 12.95 (*0-9602146-0-7*) Bonnie Prudden.

Teach Your Cat to Read, 2 bks., Set. Chronicle Staff. (Illus.). 1994. boxed 12.95 (*0-8118-0789-4*) Chronicle Bks.

Teach Your Chicken to Fly. Trevor Weekes. 36p. (Orig.). 1995. pap. 9.95 (*0-89815-740-4*) Ten Speed Pr.

Teach Your Child How to Think. Edward De Bono. LC 93-6473. 320p. 1993. pap. 22.00 (*0-670-83013-5*, Viking) Viking Penguin.

Teach Your Child How to Think. Edward De Bono. 320p. 1994. pap. 11.95 (*0-14-023830-1*, Penguin Bks) Viking Penguin.

Teach Your Child Math: Making Math Fun for the Both of You. Arthur Benjamin & Michael B. Shermer. (Illus.). 168p. (Orig.). 1991. pap. 10.95 (*0-929923-32-4*) Lowell Hse.

Teach Your Child Math: Making Math Fun for the Both of You. Arthur Benjamin & Michael B. Shermer. 192p. 1996. pap. 16.00 (*1-56565-481-1*) Lowell Hse.

Teach Your Child Science. Michael B. Shermer. 168p. 1995. pap. 12.95 (*1-56565-347-5*) Lowell Hse.

Teach Your Child Science: Making Science Fun for the Both of You. Michael B. Shermer. Ed. by Janice Gallagher. (Illus.). 168p. 1989. pap. 9.95 (*0-929923-08-1*, Legcy) Lowell Hse.

Teach Your Child the Consequences of Crime. Clifton M. Kelly & Sherman P. Wantz. LC 82-81035. (Illus.). 200p. (Orig.). 1982. pap. 6.95 (*0-943328-00-4*) Highlands Pub.

Teach Your Child to Behave: Disciplining with Love from 2 to 8 Years. Charles E. Schaefer & Theresa F. DiGeronimo. (Illus.). 240p. 1991. pap. 11.95 (*0-452-26574-6*, Plume) NAL-Dutton.

Teach Your Child to Draw: Bringing Out Your Child's Talents & Appreciation for Art. Mia Johnson. (Illus.). 160p. (Orig.). 1990. pap. 12.95 (*0-929923-25-1*) Lowell Hse.

Teach Your Child to Read in One Hundred Easy Lessons. Siegfried Engleman et al. 396p. 1986. pap. 17.95 (*0-671-63198-5*) S&S Trade.

Teach Your Child to Read in Sixty Days. Sidney Ledson. 1994. 12.95 (*0-7737-5445-8*) Genl Dist Srvs.

Teach Your Child to Talk to God. Todd Temple. 1994. 7.98 (*0-88486-096-5*) Arrowood Pr.

Teach Your Child with Games. Gretchen Buchenholz. Ed. by Manon Tingue. 128p. 1984. pap. 8.95 (*0-685-08792-1*, Fireside) S&S Trade.

***Teach Your Children Values: 95 Things Parents Can Do!** Sharon V. Andrews & Cynthia D. Ali. LC 97-4571. (Illus.). 136p. (Orig.). 1997. pap. 12.95 (*1-883790-24-7*, EDINFO Pr) Grayson Bernard Pubs.

***Teach Your Children Well.** Choon Tan & Veronika Meduna. 119p. (Orig.). 1996. pap. 19.95 (*0-908812-51-5*, Pub. by Canterbury Univ NZ) Aubrey Bks.

Teach Your Dog to Behave: Simple Solutions to over 300 Common Dog Behavior Problems from A to Z. Bashkim Dibra & Elizabeth Randolph. 400p. 1994. pap. 5.99 (*0-451-17926-9*, Sig) NAL-Dutton.

Teach Your Dog to Behave see Simple Solutions to the Most Common Dog Problems

Teach Your Kids about Music: An Activity Handbook for Parents & Teachers Using Children's Literature. Ruby Chroninger. LC 93-8081. 176p. (Orig.). 1994. 22.95 (*0-8027-1280-0*); pap. 12.95 (*0-8027-7410-5*) Walker & Co.

Teach Your Kids Computers! Alan Smukler. (Illus.). 120p. (Orig.). 1996. pap. 14.95 (*0-9652253-4-8*) Three Point.

***Teach Your Oracle Database Administration in 21 Days.** Ed Whalen. 1997. 39.99 (*0-672-31159-3*) Macmillan.

Teach Your Self Machine Piecing & Quilting. Debra Wagner. LC 91-58292. (Illus.). 192p. 1992. pap. 19.95 (*0-8019-8189-1*) Chilton.

Teach Yourself. . . Pagemaker 5.0 for the MAC. David Browne. 1993. pap. 21.95 (*1-55828-246-7*) MIS Press.

Teach Yourself. . . Pagemaker 5.0 for Windows. David Browne. 1993. pap. 21.95 (*1-55828-245-9*) MIS Press.

Teach Yourself. . . Windows NT. Hayagriva Rao. 1995. pap. 21.95 (*1-55828-269-6*) MIS Press.

Teach Yourself. . . Wordperfect 6.0. Kris Jamsa. 1995. pap. 24.95 incl. disk (*1-55828-249-1*) MIS Press.

Teach Yourself ... CorelDraw! 2nd ed. A. Frank Iritz. 1992. pap. 21.95 (*1-55828-235-5*) MIS Press.

Teach Yourself ... UNIX. 2nd ed. Kevin Reichard. 1992. pap. 22.95 (*1-55828-239-4*) MIS Press.

Teach Yourself Access 2 in 14 Days. 2nd ed. Paul Cassel. 704p. 1994. pap. text ed. 24.95 (*0-672-30488-0*) Sams.

Teach Yourself Access 95 in 14 Days. 3rd ed. Paul Cassel. (Illus.). 720p. 1995. 29.99 (*0-672-30792-8*) Sams.

***Teach Yourself Access 97 for Windows.** Charles Siegel. LC 96-50404. 1996. pap. text ed. 24.95 (*1-55828-526-1*) MIS Press.

***Teach Yourself Access 97 in Fourteen Days.** 4th ed. Paul Cassel. 750p. 1996. 29.99 (*0-672-30969-6*) Sams.

***Teach Yourself Access 97 in 24 Hours.** Timm Buchanan et al. 384p. 1997. 19.99 (*0-672-31027-9*) Mac Comp Pub.

***Teach Yourself Access 97 Visually.** Maran Graphics Staff. (Teach Yourself Ser.). 1997. pap. 29.99 (*0-7645-6026-3*) IDG Bks.

***Teach Yourself Access 97 Visually.** Ruth Maran. 320p. (Orig.). 1997. pap. write for info. (*0-614-26343-3*) IDG Bks.

***Teach Yourself Active Server Pages in 14 Days.** Sanjaya Hettiwa. 500p. 1997. 39.99 (*1-57521-330-3*) Sams.

Teach Yourself Active Web Database Programming in 21 Days. Dina Fleet et al. 700p. 1997. 39.99 (*1-57521-139-4*) Mac Comp Pub.

Teach Yourself Active X Programming in 21 Days. Sams Development Group Staff. 600p. 1996. pap. text ed. 39.99 incl. audio compact disk (*1-57521-163-7*, SamsNet Bks) Sams.

***Teach Yourself Activex Controls with Visual C++ in 14 Days.** Vincent Mayfield. 900p. Date not set. pap. text ed. 39.99 incl. cd-rom (*1-57521-294-3*, SamsNet Bks) Sams.

***Teach Yourself Activex Programming with Visual Basic in 21 Days.** Keith Brophy & Tim Koets. 800p. 1997. 39.99 (*1-57521-245-5*) Mac Comp Pub.

***Teach Yourself ActiveX Programming with Visual J++ in 21 Days.** Keith Brophy & Tim Koets. 700p. 1997. 39.99 (*1-57521-246-3*) Mac Comp Pub.

Teach Yourself Adobe Illustrator. Tom Reed. (Illus.). 1995. pap. 21.95 (*1-55828-435-4*) MIS Press.

Teach Yourself Advanced Bass. Clive Harrison. (Illus.). 64p. 1984. pap. 11.95 (*0-949785-10-5*, AM35106) Music Sales.

Teach Yourself Advanced C in 21 Days. Bradley Jones. 878p. 1994. pap. text ed. 34.95 (*0-672-30471-6*) Sams.

***Teach Yourself Advanced Java in 21 Days.** Scott Williams. 1997. 35.00 (*1-57521-331-1*) Sams.

Teach Yourself Afrikaans. Helena Van Schalwyk. (Teach Yourself Ser.). 1992. 19.95 (*0-8288-8300-9*) Fr & Eur.

Teach Yourself Afrikaans: A Complete Course for Beginners. Helena Van Schalkwyk. 244p. (AFR & ENG.). 1993. pap. 14.95 (*0-8442-3750-7*, Teach Yourslf) NTC Pub Grp.

Teach Yourself Algebra. P. Abbott. (Teach Yourself Ser.). 1980. 9.95 (*0-679-10386-4*) McKay.

Teach Yourself Algebra. P. Abbott. 342p. 1995. pap. 10.95 (*0-8442-3904-6*, Teach Yourslf) NTC Pub Grp.

Teach Yourself Algebra. 2nd rev. ed. P. Abbott & Hugh Neill. 336p. 1996. pap. 11.95 (*0-8442-3117-7*) NTC Pub Grp.

***Teach Yourself America Online in 24 Hours.** Bob Temple. (Teach Yourself Ser.). 1997. 19.99 (*1-57521-327-3*, SamsNet Bks) Sams.

Teach Yourself Ancient Greek. Gavin Betts & Alan Henry. 352p. 1994. pap. 16.95 (*0-8442-3786-8*, Teach Yourslf) NTC Pub Grp.

Teach Yourself ANSI C++ in 21 Days: Premiere Edition. Jesse Liberty & J. Mark Hord. 880p. 1996. 39.99 (*0-672-30887-8*) Sams.

Teach Yourself Apple BASIC. Peter M. Mears. 192p. 1983. spiral bd. write for info. (*0-318-57868-9*) Addison-Wesley.

Teach Yourself Arabic. S. Ali. 9.50 (*0-935782-17-6*) Kazi Pubns.

Teach Yourself Arabic. Arthur S. Ritton. (Teach Yourself Ser.). 1979. pap. 9.95 (*0-679-10164-0*) McKay.

Teach Yourself Arabic. J. R. Smart. (Teach Yourself Ser.). 1992. 15.95 (*0-8288-8301-7*); 45.00 incl. audio (*0-8288-8302-5*) Fr & Eur.

Teach Yourself Arabic: Quick & Easy. Teach Yourself Staff. (Teach Yourself Ser.). 1992. 12.95 (*0-8288-8304-1*); 29.95 incl. audio (*0-8288-8305-X*) Fr & Eur.

Teach Yourself Arabic Phrase Book. 1980. pap. 5.95 (*0-679-10550-6*) McKay.

Teach Yourself Arabic Phrasebook. A. Khouri et al. (Teach Yourself Ser.). 1992. 12.95 (*0-8288-8303-3*) Fr & Eur.

Teach Yourself Archery. rev. ed. Margherita E. Richardson. (Illus.). 1980. pap. 4.95 (*0-679-12000-9*) McKay.

Teach Yourself Arithmetic: Decimalized & Metricated. L. C. Pascoe. (Teach Yourself Ser.). 1972. pap. 5.95 (*0-679-10452-6*) McKay.

Teach Yourself Aromatherapy. Denise W. Brown. 192p. 1996. pap. 9.95 (*0-8442-3102-9*) NTC Pub Grp.

Teach Yourself Assembler. Mark Goodwin. 1991. pap. 34.95 incl. disk (*1-55828-063-4*) MIS Press.

Teach Yourself Assembler. 2nd ed. Mark Goodwin. 1993. pap. 29.95 (*1-55828-329-3*) MIS Press.

Teach Yourself Astrology. Jeff Mayo. (Teach Yourself Ser.). (Orig.). 1980. pap. 6.95 (*0-679-12001-7*) McKay.

Teach Yourself Astrology. Jeff Mayo. 182p. (Orig.). 1995. pap. 7.95 (*0-8442-3906-2*, Teach Yourslf) NTC Pub Grp.

Teach Yourself Astrology. Jeff Mayo. 182p. (Orig.). 1996. pap. 9.95 (*0-8442-3916-X*) NTC Pub Grp.

Teach Yourself Astronomy. D. S. Evans. (Teach Yourself Ser.). 1978. pap. 6.95 (*0-679-10416-X*) McKay.

Teach Yourself Backgammon. Robin Clay. (Teach Yourself Ser.). (Illus.). 1978. pap. 3.95 (*0-679-10241-8*) McKay.

Teach Yourself Backgammon. Robin Clay. 176p. 1994. pap. 7.95 (*0-8442-3907-0*, Teach Yourslf) NTC Pub Grp.

Teach Yourself Ballet. Woodward. (Teach Yourself Ser.). 1977. 7.95 (*0-679-10518-2*) McKay.

Teach Yourself Basic French. 1990. pap. 8.95 (*0-679-72770-1*) McKay.

Teach Yourself Basic German. 1990. pap. 7.95 (*0-679-72760-4*) McKay.

Teach Yourself Basic Spanish. 1990. pap. 7.95 (*0-679-72740-X*) McKay.

Teach Yourself Beginner's Chinese. Liz Scurfield & Lianyi Song. (CHI.). 1996. pap. 9.95 (*0-8442-3710-8*) NTC Pub Grp.

Teach Yourself Beginner's French. Catrine Carpenter. 240p. (ENG & FRE.). 1995. pap. 6.95 (*0-8442-3767-1*, Teach Yourslf) NTC Pub Grp.

Teach Yourself Beginner's German. Rosi McNab. 224p. (ENG & GER.). 1995. pap. 6.95 (*0-8442-3778-7*, Teach Yourslf) NTC Pub Grp.

Teach Yourself Beginner's Italian. Vittoria Bowles. 224p. (ENG & ITA.). 1995. pap. 6.95 (*0-8442-3801-5*, Teach Yourslf) NTC Pub Grp.

Teach Yourself Beginner's Japanese. Helen Gilhooly. (Teach Yourself Ser.). 256p. (Orig.). (ENG & JPN.). 1996. pap. 8.95 (*0-8442-3708-6*, Teach Yourslf) NTC Pub Grp.

Teach Yourself Beginner's Japanese Audio Pack. 240p. (JPN.). 1996. pap. 17.95 incl. audio (*0-8442-3611-X*) NTC Pub Grp.

Teach Yourself Beginner's Portuguese. Sue Tyson-Ward. 240p. (POR.). 1996. pap. 9.95 (*0-8442-3714-0*) NTC Pub Grp.

Teach Yourself Beginner's Russian. Rachel Farmer. (Teach Yourself Ser.). 240p. (Orig.). (RUS.). 1996. pap. 8.95 (*0-8442-3681-0*, Teach Yourslf) NTC Pub Grp.

Teach Yourself Beginner's Spanish. Mark Stacey & Angela Gonzalez-Hevia. 208p. 1995. pap. 6.95 (*0-8442-3828-7*, Teach Yourslf) NTC Pub Grp.

Teach Yourself Bengali. William Radice. (BEN & ENG.). 1993. pap. 18.95 (*0-7859-1052-2*, 0-340-552573); pap. 29.95 incl. audio (*0-7859-1058-1*, 0-340-56489X) Fr & Eur.

Teach Yourself Bengali: A Complete Course for Beginners. William Radice. 384p. 1995. pap. 16.95 (*0-8442-3752-3*, Teach Yourslf) NTC Pub Grp.

Teach Yourself Bengali Audio Pack. William Radice. 1995. pap. 25.95 incl. audio (*0-8442-3851-1*, Teach Yourslf) NTC Pub Grp.

Teach Yourself Better Chess. William Hartston. 160p. 1996. pap. 7.95 (*0-8442-3933-X*) NTC Pub Grp.

Teach Yourself Biblical Hebrew. R. K. Harrison. 224p. 1995. pap. 11.95 (*0-8442-3793-0*, Teach Yourslf) NTC Pub Grp.

Teach Yourself Biblical Hebrew. Roland K. Harrison. (Teach Yourself Ser.). 1979. 10.00 (*0-679-10180-2*) McKay.

Teach Yourself Biology. J. R. Hall. (Teach Yourself Ser.). 1980. pap. 6.95 (*0-679-10388-0*) McKay.

Teach Yourself Bluegrass Banjo, EFS182. Tony Trischka. (Illus.). 64p. 1979. pap. 11.95 (*0-8256-2182-8*, AM21593) Music Sales.

Teach Yourself Bluegrass Fiddle, EFS183. Matt Glaser. (Illus.). 64p. pap. 11.95 (*0-8256-2183-6*, AM21619) Music Sales.

Teach Yourself Bluegrass Guitar, EFS184. Russ Barenberg. (Illus.). 64p. pap. 11.95 (*0-8256-2184-4*, AM21627) Music Sales.

Teach Yourself Bluegrass Mandolin. Andy Statman. (Illus.). 64p. 1978. pap. 11.95 (*0-8256-2185-2*) Music Sales.

Teach Yourself Book-Keeping. D. Cousins. (Teach Yourself Ser.). 1978. pap. 7.95 (*0-679-10455-0*) McKay.

***Teach Yourself Borland C++ Builder in 21 Days.** Kent Reisdorph & Ken Henderson. 800p. 1997. 39.99 (*0-672-31020-1*) Mac Comp Pub.

Teach Yourself Borland C Plus Plus 5 in 21 Days. 3rd ed. Craig Arnush. (Illus.). 864p. (Orig.). 1996. 39.99 (*0-672-30756-1*) Sams.

Teach Yourself Botany. John H. Elliott. (Teach Yourself Ser.). 1978. 4.95 (*0-679-10390-2*) McKay.

Teach Yourself Bulgarian. Michael Holman & Mira Kovatcheva. (BUL & ENG.). 1993. pap. 18.95 (*0-7859-1055-7*, 0-340-561777); pap. 29.95 incl. audio (*0-7859-1054-9*, 0-340-561769) Fr & Eur.

Teach Yourself Bulgarian: A Complete Course for Beginners. Michael Holman & Mira Kovatcheva. 352p. 1995. pap. 14.95 (*0-8442-3753-1*, Teach Yourslf) NTC Pub Grp.

Teach Yourself Bulgarian Audio Pack. Michael Holman & Mira Kovatcheva. (Orig.). 1995. pap. 25.95 incl. audio (*0-8442-3853-8*, Teach Yourslf) NTC Pub Grp.

Teach Yourself Business French. 1990. 9.95 (*0-679-72790-6*) McKay.

Teach Yourself Business Russian: A Complete Course for Beginners. Olga Bridges et al. 320p. 1995. pap. 14.95 (*0-8442-3784-1*, Teach Yourslf) NTC Pub Grp.

Teach Yourself Business Russian Audio Pack. Olga Bridges et al. (Orig.). 1995. pap. 24.95 incl. audio (*0-8442-3876-7*, Teach Yourslf) NTC Pub Grp.

Teach Yourself Business Spanish. 1990. pap. 8.95 (*0-679-72780-9*) McKay.

Teach Yourself C++ 2nd ed. Herbert Schildt. 608p. 1994. pap. text ed. 24.95 (*0-07-882025-1*) McGraw.

***Teach Yourself C.** 3rd ed. Herbert Schildt. 1997. pap. text ed. 27.99 (*0-07-882311-0*) Osborne-McGraw.

***Teach Yourself C++** 3rd ed. Herbert Schildt. (Illus.). 656p. 1997. pap. 27.99 (*0-07-882392-7*, Oracle Press) Osborne-McGraw.

***Teach Yourself C++ in 24 Hours.** Jesse Liberty. 450p. 1997. 24.99 (*0-672-31067-8*) Sams.

***Teach Yourself C in 24 Hours.** Sams Development Group Staff. 400p. 1997. 24.99 (*0-672-31068-6*) Sams.

***Teach Yourself C++ in 21 Days.** 2nd ed. Jesse Liberty. 800p. 1997. 29.99 (*0-672-31070-8*) Sams.

***Teach Yourself C in 21 Days.** 4th ed. Brad Jones & Peter Aitken. 800p. 1997. 29.99 (*0-672-31069-4*) Sams.

Teach Yourself C Plus Plus. 2nd ed. Alan Stevens. 1991. pap. 34.95 incl. disk (*1-55828-176-2*) MIS Press.

Teach Yourself C Plus Plus. 4th ed. Alan Stevens. 1995. pap. 29.95 (*1-55828-406-0*) MIS Press.

***Teach Yourself C++** 5th ed. Al Stevens. LC 97-23417. 1997. pap. text ed. 29.95 incl. cd-rom (*1-55828-552-0*) MIS Press.

Teach Yourself.... C Plus Plus (C + +) 2nd ed. Charles Siegal. 1993. 21.95 (*1-55828-252-1*) MIS Press.

Teach Yourself C Plus Plus in 21 Days. Jesse Liberty. (Illus.). 815p. (Orig.). 1994. pap. 29.99 (*0-672-30541-0*) Sams.

Teach Yourself C Programming in 21 Days: Premier Edition. Brad Jones & Peter Aitken. (Illus.). 798p. (Orig.). 1995. 35.00 (*0-672-30736-7*) Sams.

Teach Yourself C, Second Edition. 2nd ed. Herbert Schildt. 688p. 1994. pap. text ed. 24.95 (*0-07-882011-1*) Osborne-McGraw.

An Asterisk (*) at the beginning of an entry indicates that the title is appearing in BIP for the first time.

Teach Yourself Calculus. P. Abbott. (Teach Yourself Ser.). 1976. 10.95 (*0-679-10391-0*) McKay.
Teach Yourself Calculus. P. Abbott. 380p. 1995. pap. 14.95 (*0-8442-3911-9*, Teach Yourslf) NTC Pub Grp.
Teach Yourself Cantonese. R. Bruce. (Teach Yourself Ser.). 1979. 9.95 (*0-679-10208-6*) McKay.
Teach Yourself Cantonese. R. Bruce. (Teach Yourself Ser.). 1992. 15.95 (*0-8288-8306-8*) Fr & Eur.
Teach Yourself Cantonese: A Complete Course for Beginners. R. Bruce. 240p. 1994. pap. 12.95 (*0-8442-3756-6*, Teach Yourslf) NTC Pub Grp.
Teach Yourself Cantonese: A Complete Course for Beginners. 2nd ed. Hugh Baker & Hanson Ho. (Teach Yourself Ser.). (CHI.). 1996. pap. text ed. 12.95 (*0-8442-3892-9*, Teach Yourslf) NTC Pub Grp.
Teach Yourself Cantonese Complete Course Audio Pack. 2nd rev. ed. 320p. 1996. pap. 21.95 incl. audio (*0-8442-3897-X*) NTC Pub Grp.
Teach Yourself Card Games for One. (Teach Yourself Bks.). 1980. pap. 6.95 (*0-679-10352-X*) McKay.
Teach Yourself Card Games for Two. K. Parlett. (Teach Yourself Ser.). 1980. pap. 7.95 (*0-679-12054-8*) McKay.
Teach Yourself Catalan. Alan Yates. (Teach Yourself Bks.). 1979. pap. 10.95 (*0-679-10231-0*) McKay.
Teach Yourself Catalan. Alan Yates. (Teach Yourself Ser.). 1992. 14.95 (*0-8288-8307-6*) Fr & Eur.
Teach Yourself Catalan: A Complete Course for Beginners. Alan Yates. 400p. 1994. pap. 16.95 (*0-8442-3755-8*, Teach Yourslf) NTC Pub Grp.
Teach Yourself CGI Programming with Perl in a Week. Reuven Lerner & Hylton. (Illus.). 544p. (Orig.). 1995. pap. 39.99 (*1-57521-009-6*, SamsNet Bks) Sams.
***Teach Yourself CGI Programming with Perl 5 in a Week.** 2nd ed. Eric Herrmann. 600p. 1996. pap. text ed. 39.99 incl. cd-rom (*1-57521-196-3*, SamsNet Bks) Sams.
Teach Yourself Chemistry. 1990. pap. 9.95 (*0-679-72750-7*) McKay.
Teach Yourself Chemistry. John S. Clarke. 1979. 5.95 (*0-679-12055-6*) McKay.
Teach Yourself Chess. Gerald Abrahams. (Teach Yourself Ser.). 1980. pap. 8.95 (*0-679-10354-6*) McKay.
Teach Yourself Chinese. Elizabeth Scurfield. (Teach Yourself Ser.). 1992. 23.95 (*0-8288-8308-4*); 49.95 incl. audio (*0-8288-8309-2*) Fr & Eur.
Teach Yourself Chinese. H. R. Williamson. (Teach Yourself Ser.). 1979. pap. 6.95 (*0-679-10209-4*) McKay.
Teach Yourself Chinese: A Complete Course for Beginners. Elizabeth Scurfield. 346p. (CHI & ENG.). 1995. pap. 15.95 (*0-8442-3757-4*, Teach Yourslf) NTC Pub Grp.
Teach Yourself Chinese Audio Pack. Elizabeth Scurfield. 1995. pap. 19.95 incl. audio (*0-8442-3854-6*, Teach Yourslf) NTC Pub Grp.
Teach Yourself Christianity. John Young. 192p. 1996. pap. 12.95 (*0-8442-3116-9*) NTC Pub Grp.
***Teach Yourself Christmas Gifts under $10.** Leisure Arts Staff. 1997. 19.95 (*1-57486-063-1*) Oxmoor Hse.
Teach Yourself Cloth Dollmaking: Simple Techniques & Patterns for Dolls & Doll Clothes. Jodie Davis. 1995. 24.95 (*1-56799-188-2*, Friedman-Fairfax); pap. 14.95 (*1-56799-159-9*, Friedman-Fairfax) M Friedman Pub Grp Inc.
Teach Yourself COBOL in 21 Days. Mo Budlong. 1150p. 1994. pap. text ed. 34.95 (*0-672-30469-4*) Sams.
***Teach yourself COBOL in 21 Days.** 2nd ed. Mo Budlong. 1200p. 1997. 39.99 (*0-672-31137-2*) Sams.
Teach Yourself Codes & Ciphers. F. Higenbottam. (Teach Yourself Ser.). 1980. pap. 3.95 (*0-679-10356-2*) McKay.
Teach Yourself Colloquial Arabic. T. F. Mitchell. (Teach Yourself Ser.). 1979. 6.95 (*0-679-10165-9*) McKay.
Teach Yourself Computer Based Systems. 1983. pap. write for info. (*0-318-57103-X*) Macmillan.
Teach Yourself Computer Based Systems. Race. (Teach Yourself Ser.). pap. 7.95 (*0-685-03265-5*) McKay.
Teach Yourself Computer Programming: FORTRAN. 1983. pap. write for info. (*0-318-57102-1*) Macmillan.
Teach Yourself Computer Programming: MSX Basic. (Teach Yourself Bks.). 1986. pap. 6.95 (*0-679-10540-9*) McKay.
Teach Yourself Computer Programming - FORTRAN. A. S. Radford. (Teach Yourself Ser.). 1975. pap. 5.95 (*0-685-03266-3*) McKay.
Teach Yourself Computer Programming in BASIC. L. R. Carter & E. Huzan. (Teach Yourself Ser.). 174p. 1981. pap. 5.95 (*0-679-10535-2*) McKay.
Teach Yourself Computer Programming in COBOL. 1983. pap. 7.95 (*0-679-10259-0*) McKay.
Teach Yourself Computer Programming in Pascal. D. Lightfood. 1984. pap. 8.95 (*0-679-10539-5*) McKay.
Teach Yourself Computer Programming with the Commodore 64. L. R. Carter & E. Huzan. 192p. 1983. pap. 6.95 (*0-679-10538-7*) McKay.
Teach Yourself Computers & the Internet Visually. Ruth Maran. 1996. pap. 29.99 (*0-7645-6002-6*) IDG Bks.
Teach Yourself Copywriting. Jonathan Gabay. 224p. 1996. pap. 14.95 (*0-8442-4012-5*) NTC Pub Grp.
***Teach Yourself Corel Wordperfect 8 for Windows.** Jan Weingarten. LC 97-23421. 1997. pap. text ed. 24.95 (*1-55828-573-3*) MIS Press.
Teach Yourself CorelDRAW. Webster. 1991. pap. 19.95 (*1-55828-123-1*) MIS Press.
Teach Yourself Creative Writing. (Teach Yourself Bks.). 1981. pap. 6.95 (*0-679-10260-4*) McKay.
Teach Yourself Creative Writing. Dianne Doubtfire. 144p. 1994. pap. 8.95 (*0-8442-3762-0*, Teach Yourslf) NTC Pub Grp.
Teach Yourself Creative Writing. 2nd rev. ed. Diane Doubtfire. 160p. 1996. pap. 10.95 (*0-8442-4011-7*) NTC Pub Grp.
Teach Yourself Critical Path Analysis. Lang. (Teach Yourself Ser.). 1977. pap. 6.95 (*0-679-10504-2*) McKay.
Teach Yourself Crochet. Jean Kinmond. (Teach Yourself Bks.). (Orig.). 1980. pap. 4.95 (*0-679-12057-2*) McKay.
Teach Yourself Czech. W. R. Lee & Z. Lee. (Teach Yourself Ser.). 1979. 10.95 (*0-679-10211-6*) McKay.
Teach Yourself Czech. W. Rand & Z. Lee. (Teach Yourself Ser.). 1992. 19.95 (*0-8288-8310-6*) Fr & Eur.
Teach Yourself Czech. David Short. 272p. 1995. pap. 14.95 (*0-8442-3758-2*, Teach Yourslf) NTC Pub Grp.
Teach Yourself Czech Audio Pack. David Short. 1995. 25.95 incl. audio (*0-8442-3855-4*, Teach Yourslf) NTC Pub Grp.
Teach Yourself Dancing. Imperial Society of Teachers of Dancing Staff. (Teach Yourself Ser.). 1978. pap. 7.95 (*0-679-10244-2*) McKay.
Teach Yourself Dancing. Imperial Society of Teachers of Dancing Staff. (Ballroom Dance Ser.). 1986. lib. bdg. 79.95 (*0-8490-3260-1*) Gordon Pr.
Teach Yourself Dancing. Imperial Society of Teachers of Dancing Staff. (Ballroom Dance Ser.). 1985. lib. bdg. 74.95 (*0-87700-852-3*) Revisionist Pr.
Teach Yourself Danish. H. A. Koefoed. (Teach Yourself Ser.). 1979. 9.95 (*0-679-10212-4*) McKay.
Teach Yourself Danish. H. A. Koefoed. (Teach Yourself Ser.). 1992. 19.95 (*0-8288-8311-4*) Fr & Eur.
Teach Yourself Danish Complete Course. 2nd ed. Bente Elsworth. (Teach Yourself Ser.). (DAN.). 1996. pap. 14.95 (*0-8442-3744-2*, Teach Yourslf) NTC Pub Grp.
Teach Yourself Dart Player's Handbook. George Hakim. 1979. 3.50 (*0-679-12076-9*) McKay.
***Teach Yourself Database Development with Oracle in 21 Days.** David Lockman. (Teach Yourself Ser.). 1997. 49.99 (*0-672-31078-3*) Sams.
Teach Yourself Database Programming with Delphi in 21 Days. Nathan Gurewich & Ori Gurewich. (Illus.). 608p. (Orig.). 1995. 39.99 (*0-672-30851-7*) Sams.
Teach Yourself Database Programming with JDBC in 21 Days. Ashton Hobbs. 600p. 1997. 39.99 (*1-57521-123-8*) Mac Comp Pub.
***Teach Yourself Database Programming with Visual Basic in 21 Days.** 2nd ed. Michael Amundsen & Curtis Smith. 1000p. 1997. 45.00 (*0-672-31018-X*) Mac Comp Pub.
Teach Yourself Database Programming with Visual Basic 4 in 21 Days. Michael Amundsen & Curtis Smith. (Illus.). 888p. (Orig.). 1995. 39.99 (*0-672-30832-0*) Sams.
***Teach Yourself Database Programming with Visual J++ in 14 Days.** John Fronckowiak et al. 750p. 1997. 39.99 (*1-57521-262-5*) Mac Comp Pub.
Teach Yourself dBASE III Plus. Pierre-Jean Charra & Marie-Jose Meys. Tr. by EDIDACOM Staff from FRE. 171p. ring bd. 69.95 incl. disk (*0-317-90950-9*) Tutorland.
Teach Yourself dBASE 5 for Windows. Charles Siegel. 1994. pap. 21.95 (*1-55828-231-9*) MIS Press.
Teach Yourself Decision-Aiding Software. Stuart S. Nagel & Lisa A. Bievenue. LC 92-11135. 318p. (Orig.). (C). 1992. lib. bdg. 47.50 (*0-8191-8738-0*) U Pr of Amer.
***Teach Yourself Delphi.** 3rd ed. Devra Hall. (Teach Yourself Ser.). 1997. pap. text ed. 29.95 (*1-55828-555-5*) MIS Press.
Teach Yourself Delphi 2 in 21 Days. 2nd ed. Dan Osier. (Illus.). 736p. 1996. 35.00 (*0-672-30863-0*) Sams.
***Teach Yourself Delphi 3 in 14 Days.** Osier & Batson. 1997. 29.99 (*0-672-31074-0*) Mac Comp Pub.
***Teach Yourself Delphi 3 in 14 Days.** 3rd ed. Dan Osier. 1997. 29.99 (*0-672-31114-3*) Sams.
***Teach Yourself Digital Photography in 14 Days.** Carla Rose. (Teach Yourself Ser.). 1997. pap. text ed. 39.99 (*1-56830-405-6*) Hayden.
***Teach Yourself Director 6 in 21 Days.** David Berger. 400p. 1997. 39.99 (*1-56830-409-9*) Hayden.
***Teach Yourself Divining.** Richard Foord. (Orig.). 1997. pap. write for info. (*1-898307-73-3*, Pub. by Capall Bann Pubng UK) Holmes Pub.
Teach Yourself Dutch. H. Koolhoven. (Teach Yourself Ser.). pap. 6.95 (*0-679-10213-2*) McKay.
Teach Yourself Dutch. H. Koolhoven. (Teach Yourself Ser.). 1992. 15.95 (*0-8288-8312-2*) Fr & Eur.
Teach Yourself Dutch: A Complete Course for Beginners. 2nd ed. 296p. (DUT & ENG.). 1995. pap. (*0-8442-3760-4*, Teach Yourslf) NTC Pub Grp.
Teach Yourself Dutch: A Complete Course for Beginners. 2nd ed. Lesley Gilbert & Gerdi Quist. 296p. (Orig.). 1995. pap. 14.95 (*0-8442-3886-4*, Teach Yourslf) NTC Pub Grp.
Teach Yourself Dutch Dictionary. Peter King & Margaret King. (Teach Yourself Ser.). 1992. 15.95 (*0-8288-8313-0*) Fr & Eur.
***Teach Yourself Dynamic HTML in a Week.** John Jung & Derrick Woolworth. 500p. 1997. 39.99 (*1-57521-335-4*) Sams.
Teach Yourself Electricity. C. W. Wilman. (Teach Yourself Ser.). 1980. pap. 4.95 (*0-679-10395-3*) McKay.
Teach Yourself Electricity & Electronics. Stan Gibilisco. 1993. text ed. 39.95 (*0-07-023563-5*); pap. text ed. 29.95 (*0-07-023564-3*) McGraw.
***Teach Yourself Electricity & Electronics.** 2nd ed. Stan Gibilisco. 1997. text ed. 49.95 (*0-07-024578-9*); pap. text ed. write for info. (*0-07-024579-7*) McGraw.
Teach Yourself Electricty & Electronics. Stan Gibilisco. LC 92-41312. 1993. text ed. 28.95 (*0-8306-4134-3*); pap. text ed. 24.95 (*0-8306-4133-5*) McGraw-Hill Prof.
Teach Yourself Electronic Computers. F. L. Westwater & D. H. Joyce. (Teach Yourself Ser.). 1979. pap. 3.50 (*0-679-10382-1*) McKay.
Teach Yourself Electronics. (Teach Yourself Bks.). 1979. 8.95 (*0-679-10396-1*) McKay.
Teach Yourself Elementary Logic. (Teach Yourself Bks.). 1981. pap. 5.95 (*0-679-10534-4*) McKay.
Teach Yourself English Grammar. Gordon S. Humphries. (Teach Yourself Ser.). 1980. pap. 8.95 (*0-679-10166-7*) McKay.
Teach Yourself Esperanto. John Cresswell & John Hartley. (Teach Yourself Ser.). 1980. pap. 9.95 (*0-679-10167-5*) McKay.
Teach Yourself Esperanto. John Cresswell. (Teach Yourself Ser.). 1992. 14.95 (*0-8288-8314-9*); 45.00 incl. audio (*0-8288-8315-7*) Fr & Eur.
Teach Yourself Esperanto Dictionary. J. C. Wells. (Teach Yourself Ser.). (ESP.). 1974. pap. 9.95 (*0-679-10205-1*) McKay.
Teach Yourself Essential Accounting. 2nd ed. Robert H. Anthony. (C). 1996. 37.95 (*0-201-82382-9*) Addison-Wesley.
Teach Yourself Essential Accounting Version 5.0. 2nd ed. Robert N. Anthony. (C). 1996. 37.95 (*0-201-82381-0*) Addison-Wesley.
Teach Yourself Essentials of Accounting on the IBM PC. Robert N. Anthony. 80p. 1983. write for info. incl. disk (*0-201-15328-9*) Addison-Wesley.
Teach Yourself Everyday French. N. Scarlyn Wilson. (Teach Yourself Ser.). 1979. 10.00 (*0-679-10168-3*) McKay.
Teach Yourself Everyday Spanish. L. D. Collier. (Teach Yourself Ser.). 1979. 10.00 (*0-679-10169-1*) McKay.
Teach Yourself Excel PC. Pierre-Jean Charra. 224p. 1989. ring bd. 89.95 incl. disk (*0-929533-07-0*) Tutorland.
Teach Yourself Excel Programming with Visual Basic for Applications in 21 Days. 2nd ed. Matthew Harris. (Illus.). 992p. 1995. 35.00 (*0-672-30782-0*) Sams.
Teach Yourself Excel 4.0 for Windows. Susan Rothenberg. 1992. pap. 19.95 (*1-55828-208-4*) MIS Press.
***Teach Yourself Excel 97 for Windows.** John Weingarten. LC 96-50403. 1996. pap. text ed. 24.95 (*1-55828-523-7*) MIS Press.
Teach Yourself FileMaker Pro. Jan L. Harrington. 1994. pap. 24.95 (*1-55828-369-2*) MIS Press.
Teach Yourself Finnish. Terttu Leney. (ENG & FIN.). 1993. pap. 29.95 incl. audio (*0-7859-1053-0*, 0-340-561734) Fr & Eur.
Teach Yourself Finnish. Arthur H. Whitney. (Teach Yourself Ser.). pap. 7.95 (*0-679-10170-5*) McKay.
Teach Yourself Finnish. Arthur H. Whitney. (Teach Yourself Ser.). 1992. 14.95 (*0-8288-8316-5*) Fr & Eur.
Teach Yourself First French. N. Scarlyn Wilson. (Teach Yourself Ser.). 1969. pap. 4.95 (*0-679-10215-9*) McKay.
Teach Yourself First German. L. Stringer. (Teach Yourself Ser.). 1966. pap. 4.95 (*0-679-10171-3*) McKay.
Teach Yourself Fortune Telling: Palmistry, the Crystal Ball, Tea Leaves, the Tarot. Rachel Pollack. (Illus.). 144p. 1986. pap. 10.95 (*0-8050-0125-5*, Owl) H Holt & Co.
Teach Yourself FoxPro 3 for Windows. Nelson King. 1995. pap. 27.95 (*1-55828-397-8*) MIS Press.
Teach Yourself French. J. Adams & N. Scarlyn Wilson. (Teach Yourself Ser.). pap. 7.95 (*0-679-10172-1*) McKay.
Teach Yourself French. Gaella Graham. (Teach Yourself Ser.). 1992. 14.99 (*0-8288-8317-3*); 37.95 incl. audio (*0-8288-8320-3*) Fr & Eur.
Teach Yourself French. Gaella Graham. (ENG & FRE.). 1993. pap. 39.95 incl. cd-rom (*0-7859-1067-0*, 0-340-586702) Fr & Eur.
Teach Yourself French: A Complete Course for Beginners. Gaelle Graham. 312p. (ENG & FRE.). 1995. pap. 7.95 (*0-8442-3769-8*, Teach Yourslf) NTC Pub Grp.
Teach Yourself French: Essential Grammar. Seymour Resnick. (Teach Yourself Ser.). 1992. 14.95 (*0-8288-8326-2*) Fr & Eur.
Teach Yourself French: Quick & Easy. Teach Yourself Staff. (Teach Yourself Ser.). 1992. 12.95 (*0-8288-8330-0*); 29.95 incl. audio (*0-8288-8332-7*) Fr & Eur.
Teach Yourself French: Quick & Easy Dictionary. Holtkamp & Whitlam. (Teach Yourself Ser.). 1992. 9.95 (*0-8288-8331-9*) Fr & Eur.
Teach Yourself French Audio Pack. Gaelle Graham. 1995. pap. 17.95 incl. audio (*0-8442-3860-0*, Teach Yourslf) NTC Pub Grp.
Teach Yourself French, Basic. Jean-Claude Arragon. (Teach Yourself Ser.). 1992. 12.95 (*0-8288-8321-1*) Fr & Eur.
Teach Yourself French, Beginner's. Catrine Carpenter. (Teach Yourself Ser.). 1992. 13.95 (*0-8288-8322-X*); 33.95 incl. audio (*0-8288-8323-8*) Fr & Eur.
Teach Yourself French Business. Barbara Coultras. (Teach Yourself Ser.). 1992. 19.95 (*0-8288-8324-6*); 45.00 incl. audio (*0-8288-8325-4*) Fr & Eur.
Teach Yourself French Dictionary. Teach Yourself Staff. (Teach Yourself Ser.). 1992. 12.95 (*0-8288-8318-1*) Fr & Eur.
Teach Yourself French, Everyday. N. Scarlyn Wilson. (Teach Yourself Ser.). 1992. 12.95 (*0-8288-8327-0*) Fr & Eur.
Teach Yourself French, Further. R. Olorenshaw. (Teach Yourself Ser.). 1992. 15.95 (*0-8288-8328-9*); 45.00 incl. audio (*0-8288-8329-7*) Fr & Eur.
Teach Yourself French Grammar. Jean-Claude Arragon. (Teach Yourself Ser.). 1992. 19.95 (*0-8288-8319-X*, M14756) Fr & Eur.
Teach Yourself French Grammar. Edward S. Jenkins. (Teach Yourself Ser.). pap. 5.95 (*0-679-10173-X*) McKay.
Teach Yourself French Grammar: A Modern Guide. Jean-Claude Arragon. 278p. 1995. pap. 7.95 (*0-8442-3772-8*, Teach Yourslf) NTC Pub Grp.
Teach Yourself French Verbs. Therese Weston. 224p. 1995. pap. 6.95 (*0-8442-3634-9*, Teach Yourslf) NTC Pub Grp.
Teach Yourself French Vocabulary. Nelly Moysan. (Teach Yourself Ser.). 256p. (Orig.). (ENG & FRE.). 1996. pap. 7.95 (*0-8442-3984-4*, Teach Yourslf) NTC Pub Grp.
Teach Yourself Fretless Bass. David C. Gross. (Illus.). 80p. 1985. pap. 11.95 (*0-8256-2347-2*, AM38662) Music Sales.
Teach Yourself Further French. (FRE.). 1996. pap. 19.95 incl. audio (*0-8442-3884-8*, Teach Yourslf) NTC Pub Grp.
Teach Yourself Gaelic. Roderick Mackinnon. (Teach Yourself Ser.). 1979. 11.95 (*0-679-10217-5*) McKay.
Teach Yourself Gaelic. Roderick Mackinnon. (Teach Yourself Ser.). 1992. 15.95 (*0-8288-8333-5*) Fr & Eur.
Teach Yourself Gaelic. Boyd Robertson & Iain Taylor. 336p. 1995. pap. 14.95 (*0-8442-3776-0*, Teach Yourslf) NTC Pub Grp.
Teach Yourself Gaelic Complete Course. (GAE.). 1996. pap. 24.95 incl. audio (*0-8442-3861-9*, Teach Yourslf) NTC Pub Grp.
Teach Yourself Game-Programming in 21 Days. Andre Lamothe. 948p. 1994. pap. 39.99 incl. cd-rom (*0-672-30562-3*) Sams.
Teach Yourself Geometry. P. Abbott. (Teach Yourself Ser.). 1976. 10.95 (*0-679-10398-8*) McKay.
Teach Yourself German. J. Adams et al. (Teach Yourself Ser.). 1978. 10.00 (*0-679-10174-8*) McKay.
Teach Yourself German. Paul Coggle. (Teach Yourself Ser.). 1992. 14.95 (*0-8288-8336-X*); 37.95 incl. audio (*0-8288-8338-6*) Fr & Eur.
Teach Yourself German. Paul Coggle. (ENG & GER.). 1993. pap. 39.95 incl. cd-rom (*0-7859-1066-2*, 0-340-586699) Fr & Eur.
Teach Yourself German: A Complete Course for Beginners. Paul Coggle. 334p. (ENG & GER.). 1994. pap. 7.95 (*0-8442-3779-5*, Teach Yourslf) NTC Pub Grp.
Teach Yourself German: Quick & Easy. Teach Yourself Staff. (Teach Yourself Ser.). 1992. 12.95 (*0-8288-8342-4*); 29.95 incl. audio (*0-8288-8344-0*) Fr & Eur.
Teach Yourself German: Quick & Easy Dictionary. Holtkamp & Whitlam. (Teach Yourself Ser.). 1992. 9.95 (*0-8288-8343-2*) Fr & Eur.
Teach Yourself German Audio Pack. Paul Coggle. 1995. pap. 17.95 incl. audio (*0-8442-3862-7*, Teach Yourslf) NTC Pub Grp.
Teach Yourself German, Basic. Norman Paxton. (Teach Yourself Ser.). 1992. 12.95 (*0-8288-8339-4*) Fr & Eur.
Teach Yourself German, Beginner's. Rosi McNab. (Teach Yourself Ser.). 1992. 13.95 (*0-8288-8340-8*); 33.95 incl. audio (*0-8288-8341-6*) Fr & Eur.
Teach Yourself German Business. Andrew Castley & Debbie Wagener. (Teach Yourself Ser.). 1992. 19.95 (*0-8288-8334-3*); 45.00 incl. audio (*0-8288-8345-9*) Fr & Eur.
Teach Yourself German Dictionary. (Teach Yourself Bks.). pap. 6.95 (*0-679-10246-9*) McKay.
Teach Yourself German Essential Grammar. Guy Stern. (Teach Yourself Ser.). 1992. 14.95 (*0-8288-8335-1*) Fr & Eur.
Teach Yourself German, Further. Paul Coggle. (ENG & GER.). 1993. pap. 29.95 (*0-7859-1064-6*, 0-340-585420) Fr & Eur.
Teach Yourself German Grammar. Norman Paxton. (Teach Yourself Ser.). 1992. 15.95 (*0-8288-8337-8*) Fr & Eur.
Teach Yourself German Grammar. P. G. Wilson. (Teach Yourself Ser.). 1979. 8.95 (*0-679-10175-6*) McKay.
Teach Yourself German Grammar: A Modern Guide. Norman Paxlox. 166p. (ENG & GER.). 1995. pap. 7.95 (*0-8442-3781-7*, Teach Yourslf) NTC Pub Grp.
Teach Yourself German Phrase Book. Hamilton. (Teach Yourself Ser.). 1980. 3.95 (*0-679-10176-4*) McKay.
Teach Yourself German Verbs. Sylvia Robertson. 224p. 1994. pap. 6.95 (*0-8442-3635-7*, Teach Yourslf) NTC Pub Grp.
Teach Yourself German Vocabulary. Susan Fiedler. (Teach Yourself Ser.). 256p. (Orig.). (ENG & GER.). 1996. pap. 7.95 (*0-8442-3985-2*, Teach Yourslf) NTC Pub Grp.
***Teach Yourself Golf.** 2nd ed. Bernard Gallacher. 1997. pap. text ed. 9.95 (*0-8442-3051-0*) NTC Pub Grp.
Teach Yourself Good English. G. H. Thornton & Katheleen Baron. (Teach Yourself Ser.). pap. 3.95 (*0-679-10177-2*) McKay.
***Teach Yourself Great Web Design in a Week.** Anne-Rae Vasquez-Patterson & Paul Chow. 400p. 1997. 49.99 (*1-57521-253-6*) Mac Comp Pub.
Teach Yourself Greek. F. K. Smith & T. W. Melluish. (Teach Yourself Ser.). pap. 7.95 (*0-679-10178-0*) McKay.
Teach Yourself Greek: New Testament. D. F. Hudson. (Teach Yourself Ser.). 1992. 19.95 (*0-8288-8349-1*) Fr & Eur.
Teach Yourself Greek: Quick & Easy. Teach Yourself Staff. (Teach Yourself Ser.). 1992. 12.95 (*0-8288-8350-5*); 29.95 incl. audio (*0-8288-8351-3*) Fr & Eur.
Teach Yourself Greek, Ancient: Complete Course. Gavin G. Betts & Alan Henry. (Teach Yourself Ser.). 1992. 29.95 (*0-8288-8346-7*) Fr & Eur.
Teach Yourself Greek, Ancient: Foundation Course. F. Kinchin Smith & T. W. Melluish. (Teach Yourself Ser.). 1992. 29.95 (*0-8288-8347-5*) Fr & Eur.
Teach Yourself Greek Complete Course. Aristarhos Matsukus. 320p. (GRE.). 1996. pap. 14.95 (*0-8442-3705-1*) NTC Pub Grp.
Teach Yourself Greek, Modern. S. A. Sofronious. (Teach Yourself Ser.). 1992. 15.95 (*0-8288-8348-3*) Fr & Eur.
Teach Yourself Greek Phrase Book. 1980. pap. 3.95 (*0-679-10700-2*) McKay.
Teach Yourself Guitar. Dale Fradd. (Teach Yourself Ser.). 1975. pap. 7.95 (*0-679-10365-1*) McKay.
Teach Yourself Guitar. Dale Fradd. 120p. 1995. pap. 7.95 (*0-8442-3922-4*, Teach Yourslf) NTC Pub Grp.
Teach Yourself Guitar. Harry Taussig. (Illus.). 150p. pap. 15.95 (*0-8256-0010-3*, OK62356, Oak) Music Sales.

Teach Yourself Guitar with Chord Diagrams, Photos & Tablature. F. Jester. 48p. 1986. pap. 5.95 (*0-7935-3753-3*, 50394210) H Leonard.

Teach Yourself Gujarati: A Complete Course for Beginners. Rachel Dwyer. 256p. (GUJ.). 1995. pap. 16.95 (*0-8442-3775-2*, Teach Yourslf) NTC Pub Grp.

Teach Yourself Gujarati Complete Course Audio Pack. Rachel Dwyer. (Teach Yourself Ser.). (Orig.). (GUJ.). 1996. pap. 25.95 incl. audio (*0-8442-3877-5*, Teach Yourslf) NTC Pub Grp.

Teach Yourself Hausa. C. H. Craft & Anthony H. Kirk-Greene. 416p. 1995. pap. 17.95 (*0-8442-3791-4*, Teach Yourslf) NTC Pub Grp.

Teach Yourself Hausa. Charles H. Kraft & Anthony H. Kirk-Greene. (Teach Yourself Ser.). 1973. pap. 9.95 (*0-679-10179-9*) McKay.

Teach Yourself Hausa. Charles H. Kraft & Anthony H. Kirk-Greene. (Teach Yourself Ser.). 1992. 15.95 (*0-8288-8352-1*) Fr & Eur.

Teach Yourself Healthy Eating for Babies & Children. Mary Whiting & Tom Lobstein. 196p. 1996. pap. 10.95 (*0-8442-3725-6*) NTC Pub Grp.

Teach Yourself Hebrew, Biblical. R. K. Harrisson. (Teach Yourself Ser.). 1992. 14.95 (*0-8288-8353-X*) Fr & Eur.

Teach Yourself Herbs. Susie White. (Illus.). 192p. 1995. pap. 7.95 (*0-8442-3928-3*, Teach Yourslf) NTC Pub Grp.

Teach Yourself Hindi. Mohini Rao. (Language Bks.). 207p. (C). 1989. pap. 8.95 (*0-87052-831-9*) Hippocrene Bks.

Teach Yourself Hindi. R. Snell. 1991. 13.00 (*0-679-40190-3*) McKay.

Teach Yourself Hindi. R. Snell & B. Weightman. (Teach Yourself Ser.). 1992. 19.95 (*0-8288-8354-8*); 45.00 incl. audio (*0-8288-8355-6*) Fr & Eur.

Teach Yourself Hindi: A Complete Course for Beginners. Simon Weightman. 302p. 1995. pap. 14.95 (*0-8442-3795-7*, Teach Yourslf) NTC Pub Grp.

Teach Yourself Hindi Audio Pack. Simon Weightman. 1995. pap. 24.95 incl. audio (*0-8442-3863-5*, Teach Yourslf) NTC Pub Grp.

Teach Yourself House Repairs. T. Wilkins. (Teach Yourself Ser.). 1978. pap. 3.95 (*0-679-10471-2*) McKay.

***Teach Yourself How to Become a Webmaster in 14 Days.** Michael Norton. 450p. 1997. 39.99 (*1-57521-228-5*) Mac Comp Pub.

***Teach Yourself HTML in 24 Hours.** Dick Oliver. 300p. 1997. 19.99 (*1-57521-235-8*) Mac Comp Pub.

Teach Yourself Human Anatomy & Physiology. David Le Vay. (Teach Yourself Ser.). 1978. pap. 10.95 (*0-679-10399-6*) McKay.

Teach Yourself Human Anatomy & Physiology. David Le Vay. 384p. 1995. pap. 12.95 (*0-8442-3924-0*, Teach Yourslf) NTC Pub Grp.

Teach Yourself Hungarian. Zsu Z. Pontifex. (ENG & HUN.). 1993. pap. 18.95 (*0-7859-1056-5*, 0-340-562862); pap. 29.95 incl. audio (*0-7859-1057-3*, 0-340-562889) Fr & Eur.

Teach Yourself HyperCard. Dominique Vannier. 170p. 1989. ring bd. 79.95 incl. disk (*0-929533-08-9*) Tutorland.

Teach Yourself Icelandic. P. J. Glendening. (Teach Yourself Ser.). 1979. 10.00 (*0-679-10181-0*) McKay.

Teach Yourself Icelandic. P. J. Glendening. (Teach Yourself Ser.). 1992. 14.95 (*0-8288-8356-4*) Fr & Eur.

Teach Yourself Icelandic: A Complete Course for Beginners. P. J. T. Glendening. 208p. 1995. pap. 16.95 (*0-8442-3797-3*, Teach Yourslf) NTC Pub Grp.

***Teach Yourself Illustrator in 21 Days.** Mordy Golding. (Teach Yourself Ser.). 1997. 39.99 (*1-56830-410-2*) Hayden.

Teach Yourself Indonesian. John B. Kwee. (Teach Yourself Ser.). 1980. 11.95 (*0-679-10182-9*) McKay.

Teach Yourself Indonesian. John B. Kwee. (Teach Yourself Ser.). 1992. 14.95 (*0-8288-8357-2*) Fr & Eur.

Teach Yourself Indonesian: A Complete Course for Beginners. John B. Kwee. 192p. 1994. pap. 12.95 (*0-8442-3798-1*, Teach Yourslf) NTC Pub Grp.

***Teach Yourself Informix in 21 Days.** 1997. 49.99 (*0-672-31124-0*) Mac Comp Pub.

Teach Yourself Internet Game Programming with Java in 21 Days. Michael Morrison. 456p. 1996. 39.99 (*1-57521-148-3*) Mac Comp Pub.

***Teach Yourself IntraBuilder in 21 Days.** Paul Mahar et al. 600p. 1997. 39.99 (*1-57521-224-2*) Mac Comp Pub.

Teach Yourself Irish. Myles Dillon & D. O. Croinin. (Teach Yourself Ser.). 1979. pap. 5.95 (*0-679-10183-7*) McKay.

Teach Yourself Irish. Myles Dillon & Connacha O'Croinin. (Teach Yourself Ser.). 1992. 15.95 (*0-8288-8358-0*) Fr & Eur.

Teach Yourself Irish. Diarmuid O'Se & Joe Sheils. (ENG & IRI.). 1993. pap. 18.95 (*0-7859-1059-X*, 0-340-564903); pap. 29.95 incl. audio (*0-7859-1060-3*, 0-340-56492-X) Fr & Eur.

Teach Yourself Irish: A Complete Course for Beginners. Myles Dillion & Donncha O'Croinin. 256p. 1995. pap. 9.95 (*0-8442-3800-7*, Teach Yourslf) NTC Pub Grp.

Teach Yourself Irish Audio Pack. Myles Dillion & Donncha O. Croinin. 1995. pap. 25.95 incl. audio (*0-8442-3865-1*, Teach Yourslf) NTC Pub Grp.

***Teach Yourself ISAPI in 21 Days.** S. Scott Zimmerman. 500p. Date not set. 39.99 (*1-57521-220-X*) Mac Comp Pub.

Teach Yourself Islamic Ideology. Dar Rah Haqq. Tr. by Laleh Bakhtiar from PER. 1989. pap. text ed. 6.70 (*1-871031-11-7*) Abjad Bk.

Teach Yourself Italian. Kathleen Speight. (Teach Yourself Ser.). 1978. 10.00 (*0-679-10184-5*) McKay.

Teach Yourself Italian. Lydia Vellacio & Maurice Elston. (Teach Yourself Ser.). 1992. 14.95 (*0-8288-8359-9*); 37.95 incl. audio (*0-8288-8361-0*) Fr & Eur.

Teach Yourself Italian: A Complete Course for Beginners. Lydia Vellaccio & Maurice Elston. 336p. (ENG & ITA.). 1995. pap. 7.95 (*0-8442-3802-3*, Teach Yourslf) NTC Pub Grp.

Teach Yourself Italian: Beginner's Book. Victoria Bowles. (Teach Yourself Ser.). 1992. 13.95 (*0-8288-8362-9*); 33.95 incl. audio (*0-8288-8363-7*) Fr & Eur.

Teach Yourself Italian: Essential Grammar. Olga Ragusa. (Teach Yourself Ser.). 1992. 14.95 (*0-8288-8364-5*) Fr & Eur.

Teach Yourself Italian: Quick & Easy. Teach Yourself Staff. (Teach Yourself Ser.). 1992. 12.95 (*0-8288-8365-3*); 29.95 incl. audio (*0-8288-8367-X*) Fr & Eur.

Teach Yourself Italian: Quick & Easy Dictionary. Holtkamp & Whitlam. (Teach Yourself Ser.). 1992. 9.95 (*0-8288-8366-1*) Fr & Eur.

Teach Yourself Italian Audio Pack, Set 2. Lydia Vellaccio & Maurice Elston. 1995. pap. 17.95 incl. audio (*0-8442-3867-8*, Teach Yourslf) NTC Pub Grp.

Teach Yourself Italian Grammar. Anna Proudfoot. (Teach Yourself Ser.). 1992. 15.95 (*0-8288-8360-2*) Fr & Eur.

Teach Yourself Italian Grammar: A Modern Guide. Anna Proudfoot. 192p. (ENG & ITA.). 1995. pap. 7.95 (*0-8442-3803-1*, Teach Yourslf) NTC Pub Grp.

Teach Yourself Italian Phrase Book. (Teach Yourself Ser.). 1976. 3.95 (*0-679-10236-1*) McKay.

Teach Yourself Italian Verbs. Maria Morris. 224p. 1995. pap. 6.95 (*0-8442-3637-3*, Teach Yourslf) NTC Pub Grp.

Teach Yourself Italian Vocabulary. Vittoria B. Protej. (Teach Yourself Ser.). 256p. (Orig.). (ENG & ITA.). 1996. pap. 7.95 (*0-8442-3987-9*, Teach Yourslf) NTC Pub Grp.

Teach Yourself Japanese. H. Ballhatchet & Stefan Kaiser. (Teach Yourself Ser.). 1992. 15.95 (*0-8288-8368-8*); 45.00 incl. audio (*0-8288-8370-X*) Fr & Eur.

Teach Yourself Japanese. C. J. Dunn & S. Yanoda. (Teach Yourself Ser.). 1979. 9.95 (*0-679-10185-3*) McKay.

Teach Yourself Japanese: A Complete Course for Beginners. H. Ballhatchet & S. Kaiser. 348p. (ENG & JPN.). 1994. pap. 9.95 (*0-8442-3807-4*, Teach Yourslf) NTC Pub Grp.

Teach Yourself Japanese: Quick & Easy. Teach Yourself Staff. (Teach Yourself Ser.). 1992. 12.95 (*0-8288-8372-6*); 29.95 incl. audio (*0-8288-8373-4*) Fr & Eur.

Teach Yourself Japanese Audio Pack, Set 2. H. Ballhatchet & S. Kaiser. 1995. pap. 17.95 incl. audio (*0-8442-3868-6*, Teach Yourslf) NTC Pub Grp.

Teach Yourself Japanese Business. Michael Jenkins & Lynne Strugnell. (Teach Yourself Ser.). 1992. 19.95 (*0-8288-8369-6*); 45.00 incl. audio (*0-8288-8371-8*) Fr & Eur.

***Teach Yourself Java for Macintosh in 21 Days.** Laura Lemay. 1996. 40.00 (*1-56830-292-4*) Hayden.

***Teach Yourself Java Reference in 21 Days: Professional Edition.** Laura Lemay & Michael Morrison. 1296p. 1996. 59.99 (*1-57521-183-1*) Mac Comp Pub.

Teach Yourself Java 1.1 in 21 Days. 2nd ed. Laura Lemay & Charles L. Perkins. Date not set. 39.99 (*1-57521-142-4*) Mac Comp Pub.

***Teach Yourself Java 1.1 Programming in 24 Hours.** Rogers Cadenhead. 350p. 1997. 24.99 (*1-57521-270-6*) Mac Comp Pub.

***Teach Yourself JavaBeans in 21 Days.** Donald Doherty. (Teach Yourself Ser.). 1997. 39.99 (*1-57521-316-8*, SamsNet Bks) Sams.

Teach Yourself Javain Cafe in 21 Days. Dan Joshi. 648p. 1996. pap. text ed. 39.99 incl. cd-rom (*1-57521-157-2*, SamsNet Bks) Sams.

Teach Yourself JavaScript in a Week. Arman Danesh. 576p. 1996. pap. text ed. 39.99 incl. cd-rom (*1-57521-073-8*, SamsNet Bks) Sams.

***Teach Yourself Javascript 1.1 in a Week.** 2nd ed. Arman Danesh. 600p. 1996. pap. text ed. 39.99 incl. cd-rom (*1-57521-195-5*, SamsNet Bks) Sams.

***Teach Yourself Javascript 1.2 in a Week.** 3rd ed. Arman Danesh. 1997. 39.99 (*1-57521-304-4*, SamsNet Bks) Sams.

Teach Yourself Jazz. John Chilton. 1979. 6.95 (*0-679-12225-7*) McKay.

Teach Yourself JBuilder in 21 Days. Susan Charlesworth. 700p. 1997. pap. text ed. 39.99 incl. cd-rom (*1-57521-104-1*, SamsNet Bks) Sams.

Teach Yourself Karate. Steve Arneil & Liam Keaveny. 192p. 1995. pap. 9.95 (*0-8442-3927-5*, Teach Yourslf) NTC Pub Grp.

Teach Yourself Keyboard Playing & Improvisation, Vol. 1. Jack Weaton & Peter Alexander. Orig. Title: Touch Sensitivity. 126p. (C). 1987. pap. 21.95 (*0-939067-33-1*) Alexander Pub.

Teach Yourself Keyboard Playing & Improvisation, Vol. 2. Jack Wheaton & Peter L. Alexander. (Illus.). 141p. (C). 1988. pap. text ed. 23.95 (*0-939067-34-X*) Alexander Pub.

Teach Yourself Latin. Gavin G. Betts. (Teach Yourself Ser.). 1992. 15.95 (*0-8288-8374-2*) Fr & Eur.

Teach Yourself Latin. F. K. Smith. (Teach Yourself Ser.). 1979. pap. 10.95 (*0-679-10186-1*) McKay.

Teach Yourself Latin: A Complete Course for Beginners. G. G. Betts. 362p. (ENG & LAT.). 1995. pap. 12.95 (*0-8442-3811-2*, Teach Yourslf) NTC Pub Grp.

Teach Yourself Latin Dictionary. A. Wilson. (Teach Yourself Ser.). (LAT.). 1974. pap. 6.95 (*0-679-10204-3*) McKay.

Teach Yourself Latin Dictionary. A. Wilson. (Teach Yourself Ser.). 1992. 12.95 (*0-8288-8375-0*) Fr & Eur.

Teach Yourself Lead Guitar. Steve Tarshis. 64p. pap. 11.95 (*0-8256-2200-X*, AM21643) Music Sales.

Teach Yourself Lead Guitar. Steve Tarshis. 1981. pap. 11.95 (*0-8256-2234-4*) Music Sales.

Teach Yourself Linguistics. (Teach Yourself Bks.). pap. 9.95 (*0-679-10258-2*) McKay.

Teach Yourself Lip Reading. Olive M. Wyatt. (Illus.). 172p. 1974. 31.95 (*0-398-02128-7*); pap. 19.95 (*0-398-06505-5*) C C Thomas.

Teach Yourself Living Mandarin Vol. 1: Beginner's Course, 4 cass., Set. Sarah Lu. 236p. 1988. pap. 69.95 incl. audio (*0-582-99910-3*) Cheng & Tsui.

Teach Yourself Living Mandarin Vol. 2: Lower Intermediate Course, 2 cass., Set. Sarah Lu. 182p. 1994. pap. 69.95 incl. audio (*962-00-0071-4*) Cheng & Tsui.

Teach Yourself Living Welsh. John T. Bowan & P. Jones. (Teach Yourself Ser.). 1978. 11.95 (*0-679-10825-4*) McKay.

***Teach Yourself Lotus Notes 4.5.** Bill Kreisle. LC 96-38080. 1997. pap. text ed. 24.95 (*1-55828-529-6*) MIS Press.

***Teach Yourself Lotus Notes 4.5 in 14 Days.** Don Child. 1997. 29.99 (*0-672-31080-5*) Sams.

***Teach Yourself Lotus Notes 4.5 in 24 Hours.** Don Child. (Teach Yourself Ser.). 1997. 19.99 (*0-672-31126-7*) Sams.

Teach Yourself Lotus 1-2-3 for Windows. Jacky Royall & David Royall. 212p. 1994. pap. 11.95 (*0-8442-3959-3*, Teach Yourslf) NTC Pub Grp.

Teach Yourself Lotus 1-2-3 for Windows 95. Andrew Sussman. LC 96-43450. 1996. pap. 24.95 (*1-55828-489-3*) MIS Press.

Teach Yourself Lotus 1-2-3 5.0 for Windows. Meredith Fein & Andrew Sussman. LC 94-35042. 486p. 1994. pap. 21.95 (*1-55828-400-1*) MIS Press.

***Teach Yourself Lotusscript 3.1 for Notes 4.5: With Disk.** Bill Kreisle. 1997. pap. text ed. 29.95 (*1-55828-560-1*) MIS Press.

Teach Yourself Machine Embroidery: Easy Decorative Stitching Using Any Sewing Machine. Susan Rock. LC 96-17853. (Illus.). 1996. pap. 19.95 (*0-8019-8522-6*) Chilton.

***Teach Yourself Macintosh in 24 Hours.** Hayden Books Staff. (Teach Yourself Ser.). 1997. pap. text ed. 19.99 (*1-56830-408-0*) Hayden.

Teach Yourself Magic Tricks. John Wade. (Illus.). 96p. 1994. pap. 5.95 (*0-8442-3930-5*, Teach Yourslf) NTC Pub Grp.

Teach Yourself Malay. Geoffrey L. Lewis. (Teach Yourself Ser.). 1980. pap. 6.95 (*0-679-10187-X*) McKay.

Teach Yourself Maltese. J. Aquilina. 240p. 1995. pap. 14.95 (*0-8442-3697-7*, Teach Yourslf) NTC Pub Grp.

Teach Yourself Management Accounting. Brian Murphy. (Teach Yourself Ser.). 1978. pap. 3.95 (*0-679-10477-1*) McKay.

Teach Yourself Mandarin Chinese. Elizabeth Scurfield. 1991. 13.00 (*0-679-40180-6*) Random.

Teach Yourself Manual for Drawing & Painting. (Teach Yourself Bks.). 1978. 10.95 (*0-679-12300-8*) McKay.

***Teach Yourself Marketing on the Web in a Week.** Rick Tracewell. 1997. 39.99 (*1-57521-291-9*, SamsNet Bks) Sams.

Teach Yourself Meditation. James Hewitt. 200p. 1995. pap. 9.95 (*0-8442-3899-6*, Teach Yourslf) NTC Pub Grp.

Teach Yourself Micro-Electronics & Micro-Computers. 1983. pap. write for info. (*0-679-10254-X*) Macmillan.

Teach Yourself Microsoft Excel 1.5. Pierre-Jean Charra. 171p. 1989. ring bd. 79.95 incl. disk (*0-929533-09-7*) Tutorland.

***Teach Yourself Microsoft Excel 97 in 24 Hours.** Lois Patterson. (Teach Yourself Ser.). 400p. 1997. pap. text ed. 19.99 (*0-672-31116-X*) Sams.

***Teach Yourself Microsoft FrontPage in a Week.** Peter Kent. 500p. 1997. 39.99 (*1-57521-225-0*) Mac Comp Pub.

***Teach Yourself Microsoft Internet Explorer in 24 Hours.** John San Fillipo. 300p. 1997. 19.99 (*1-57521-233-1*) Mac Comp Pub.

***Teach Yourself Microsoft Internet Explorer 4.** Kevin Reichard. 1997. pap. text ed. 24.95 (*1-55828-572-5*) MIS Press.

***Teach Yourself Microsoft Office 97 in 24 Hours.** Greg M. Perry. 450p. 1996. 19.99 (*0-672-31009-0*) Mac Comp Pub.

***Teach Yourself Microsoft Outlook 97 in 24 Hours.** Brian Proffitt & Kim Spilker. 400p. 1997. 19.99 (*0-672-31044-9*) Mac Comp Pub.

***Teach Yourself Microsoft Powerpoint 97 in 24 Hours.** Alexandria Haddad. (Teach Yourself Ser.). 1997. 19.99 (*0-672-31117-8*) Sams.

Teach Yourself Microsoft Visual InterDev in 21 Days. Jane G. Reh. 600p. 1997. 39.99 (*1-57521-093-2*) Mac Comp Pub.

***Teach Yourself Microsoft Visual Studio 97 in 21 Days.** Paul Kimmel. (Teach Yourself Ser.). 1997. 39.99 (*0-672-31125-9*) Sams.

Teach Yourself Microsoft Windows 2 & Windows 386. Jacques Albert. 197p. 1989. ring bd. 79.95 incl. disk (*0-929533-12-7*) Tutorland.

Teach Yourself Microsoft Word 4 for IBM PC, PS - Compatibles. Pierre-Jean Charra. Tr. by EDIDACOM Staff from FRE. 252p. 1988. ring bd. 89.95 incl. disk (*0-317-90949-5*) Tutorland.

***Teach Yourself Microsoft Word 97 in 24 Hours.** Linda Jones. (Teach Yourself Ser.). 1997. pap. text ed. 19.99 (*0-672-31115-1*) Sams.

Teach Yourself Modern Dancing. Bernard Stetson. (Ballroom Dance Ser.). 1985. lib. bdg. 79.95 (*0-8490-3251-2*) Gordon Pr.

Teach Yourself Modern Greek. S. A. Sofronious. 240p. 1994. pap. 10.95 (*0-8442-3788-4*, Teach Yourslf) NTC Pub Grp.

Teach Yourself Modern Greek. S. A. Sofronious. (Teach Yourself Ser.). pap. 6.95 (*0-679-10189-6*) McKay.

Teach Yourself Modern Persian. J. Male. (Teach Yourself Ser.). 1979. pap. 8.95 (*0-679-10220-5*) McKay.

Teach Yourself Modern Persian: A Complete Course for Beginners. John Mace. 272p. 1995. pap. 14.95 (*0-8442-3815-5*, Teach Yourslf) NTC Pub Grp.

Teach Yourself More German. Sydney W. Wells. (Teach Yourself Ser.). 1979. pap. 4.95 (*0-679-10190-X*) McKay.

***Teach Yourself More Java 1.1 in 21 Days.** Laura Lemay. 1997. 39.99 (*1-57521-347-8*) Sams.

***Teach Yourself More Visual BASIC in 21 Days.** Nathan Gurewich & Ori Gurewich. 1000p. 1997. pap. text ed. 39.99 incl. cd-rom (*0-672-31062-7*) Sams.

***Teach Yourself More Visual C++ 5 in 21 Days.** Nathan Gurewich. (Teach Yourself Ser.). 1997. pap. text ed. 39.99 (*0-672-31132-1*) Sams.

Teach Yourself More Web Publishing with HTML in a Week. Laura Lemay. (Illus.). 480p. 1995. pap. 29.99 (*1-57521-005-3*, SamsNet Bks) Sams.

***Teach Yourself MS Exchange Server: MCSE Exam Preparation G.** Erica Elam. 1997. 75.00 (*0-672-31182-8*) Mac Comp Pub.

***Teach Yourself MS Frontpage in 24 Hours.** Denise Tyler. 1997. 19.99 (*1-57521-342-7*) Sams.

***Teach Yourself MS Frontpage 98 in a Week.** Donald Dougherty. 1997. 29.99 (*1-57521-350-8*) Sams.

Teach Yourself Multimedia. Signe Hoffos & Jim Ayre. 160p. 1995. pap. 11.95 (*0-8442-3967-4*, Teach Yourslf) NTC Pub Grp.

Teach Yourself Music. King C. Palmer. 256p. 1995. pap. 9.95 (*0-8442-3934-8*, Teach Yourslf) NTC Pub Grp.

Teach Yourself Mythology. Ros Jay. 192p. 1996. pap. 10.95 (*0-8442-3129-0*) NTC Pub Grp.

Teach Yourself Nepali. Karunakar Baidya. 105p. (C). 1986. 40.00 (*0-89771-083-5*, Pub. by Ratna Pustak Bhandar) St Mut.

Teach Yourself Nepali. Karunakar Baidya. 1991. 30.00 (*0-7855-0288-2*, Pub. by Ratna Pustak Bhandar) St Mut.

***Teach Yourself Netscape Communicator.** Kevin Reichard. LC 97-20211. 1997. pap. text ed. 24.95 (*1-55828-541-5*) MIS Press.

***Teach Yourself Netscape Communicator Visually.** Maran Graphics Staff. (Teach Yourself Ser.). 1997. pap. 29.99 (*0-7645-6028-X*) IDG Bks.

***Teach Yourself Netscape Communicator 4 in 24 Hours.** Galen Grimes. 350p. 1997. 24.99 (*1-57521-227-7*) Mac Comp Pub.

Teach Yourself Netscape 2 Web Publishing in a Week. Wes Tatters. 672p. 1996. pap. text ed. 39.99 incl. cd-rom (*1-57521-068-1*, SamsNet Bks) Sams.

Teach Yourself Netscape 4 Web Publishing in a Week. 2nd ed. Wes Tatters. 1600p. 1997. 39.99 (*1-57521-165-3*, SamsNet Bks) Sams.

***Teach Yourself Networking Essentials: MCSE Exam G.** Robin Burk. 1998. 75.00 (*0-672-31175-5*) Mac Comp Pub.

***Teach Yourself Networking in 24 Hours.** Greg Newman. 500p. 1997. 19.99 (*0-672-31145-3*) Sams.

***Teach Yourself Networking Visually.** Maran Graphics Staff. 1997. pap. 29.99 (*0-7645-6023-9*) IDG Bks.

Teach Yourself New Era Shorthand. (Teach Yourself Bks.). pap. 7.95 (*0-679-12325-3*) McKay.

Teach Yourself New Testament. David Stone. 192p. 1996. pap. 12.95 (*0-8442-3115-0*) NTC Pub Grp.

Teach Yourself New Testament Greek. D. F. Hudson. 1979. pap. 6.95 (*0-685-03268-X*) McKay.

Teach Yourself New Testament Greek. D. F. Hudson. 192p. 1994. pap. 14.95 (*0-8442-3789-2*) NTC Pub Grp.

Teach Yourself New Testament Greek. Ian Macnair. LC 94-45016. 512p. 1995. student ed., pap. 16.99 (*0-8407-1151-4*) Nelson.

Teach Yourself Norwegian. Ingvald Marm & Alf Sommerfelt. (Teach Yourself Ser.). 1992. 19.95 (*0-8288-8376-9*) Fr & Eur.

Teach Yourself Norwegian. Alf Sommerfelt. (Teach Yourself Ser.). pap. 7.95 (*0-679-10221-3*) McKay.

Teach Yourself Norwegian: A Complete Course for Beginners. Ingvald Marm & Alf Sommerfelt. 304p. 1995. pap. 15.95 (*0-8442-3814-7*, Teach Yourslf) NTC Pub Grp.

***Teach Yourself Object-Oriented Programming with Vb 5.1 21 Days.** John Conley. 1997. 39.99 (*0-672-31203-4*) Macmillan.

Teach Yourself ODBC Programming in 21 Days. Bill Whiting & Osborne. 480p. 1995. 29.99 (*0-672-30609-3*) Sams.

Teach Yourself Office Management. P. W. Betts. (Teach Yourself Ser.). 1980. pap. 4.95 (*0-679-10383-X*) McKay.

***Teach Yourself Office 97 Electronic Starter Kit.** Publishing Sams. 1997. boxed, pap. text ed. 39.99 incl. cd-rom (*0-672-31098-8*) Sams.

***Teach Yourself Office 97 for Windows.** Patrick Burns. LC 96-29918. 1997. pap. text ed. 24.95 (*1-55828-530-X*) MIS Press.

***Teach Yourself Office 97 Visually.** Maran Graphics Staff. 1997. pap. 29.99 (*0-7645-6018-2*) IDG Bks.

Teach Yourself Old Testament. Gordon McConville. 192p. 1996. pap. 12.95 (*0-8442-3114-2*) NTC Pub Grp.

Teach Yourself Organization & Methods. R. G. Breadmore. (Teach Yourself Ser.). 1976. 4.95 (*0-679-10509-3*) McKay.

Teach Yourself Origami. Robert Harbin. (Illus.). 192p. 1994. pap. 8.95 (*0-8442-3935-6*, Teach Yourslf) NTC Pub Grp.

Teach Yourself Paradox 5 for Windows. Charles Siegel. LC 94-22466. 1994. pap. 21.95 (*1-55828-359-5*) MIS Press.

Teach Yourself Pascal. 2nd ed. Mark Goodwin. 1993. pap. 29.95 (*1-55828-328-5*) MIS Press.

***Teach Yourself Perfect Office in 24 Hours.** Alexandria Haddad. 1997. 19.99 (*0-672-31151-8*) Mac Comp Pub.

***Teach Yourself PERL in 21 Days.** 2nd ed. David Till. 1000p. 1997. 49.99 (*0-672-31061-9*) Sams.

An Asterisk (*) at the beginning of an entry indicates that the title is appearing in BIP for the first time.

*Teach Yourself Perl 5 for Windows NT in 21 Days. David Till & Tony Zhang. 900p. 1997. 39.99 (0-672-31047-3) Mac Comp Pub.

Teach Yourself Perl 5 in 21 Days. 2nd ed. David Till. 912p. 1996. 39.99 (0-672-30894-0) Sams.

Teach Yourself Persian, Modern. John Mace. (Teach Yourself Ser.). 1992. 14.95 (0-685-63252-0) Fr & Eur.

Teach Yourself Photography. Reg Meson. (Illus.). 224p. (Orig.). 1995. pap. 9.95 (0-8442-3937-2, Teach Yourslf) NTC Pub Grp.

*Teach Yourself Photoshop in 14 Days. Harry St. Ours. 1997. 39.99 (1-56830-403-X) Hayden.

*Teach Yourself Photoshop in 24 Hours. Hayden Development Staff. 350p. 1997. 19.99 (1-56830-425-0) Hayden.

*Teach Yourself Photoshop 4.0 for Mac & Windows. Clay Andres. LC 97-7184. 1997. pap. text ed. 29.95 (1-55828-532-6) MIS Press.

Teach Yourself Physics. D. Bryant. (Teach Yourself Ser.). 1979. 9.95 (0-679-10406-2) McKay.

Teach Yourself Piano. King C. Palmer. (Teach Yourself Ser.). 1974. pap. 7.95 (0-679-10256-6) McKay.

Teach Yourself Piano. King C. Palmer. 152p. 1995. pap. 7.95 (0-8442-3936-4, Teach Yourslf) NTC Pub Grp.

Teach Yourself Piano & Other Keyboard Instruments for Beginners. D. Bennett. 48p. 1986. pap. 5.95 (0-7935-2859-3, 50394370) H Leonard.

Teach Yourself Piano Audio Pack. King C. Palmer. 1995. pap. 17.95 incl. audio (0-8442-3973-9, Teach Yourslf) NTC Pub Grp.

*Teach Yourself PL/SQL in 21 Days. Jonathan Merrick. (Teach Yourself Ser.). 1997. 39.99 (0-672-31123-2) Sams.

Teach Yourself Polish. Corbridge & M. Patkaniowska. (Teach Yourself Ser.). 1992. 15.95 (0-8288-8378-5) Fr & Eur.

Teach Yourself Polish. M. Corbridge-Patkaniowska. (Teach Yourself Ser.). 1974. pap. 7.95 (0-679-10232-9) McKay.

Teach Yourself Polish: A Complete Course for Beginners. M. Corbridge-Patkaniowska. 300p. (ENG & POL.). 1995. pap. 12.95 (0-8442-3816-3, Teach Yourslf) NTC Pub Grp.

Teach Yourself Polish Complete Course. 2nd rev. ed. Nigel Gotteri & Joanna Gray. 300p. (POL.). 1996. pap. 12.95 (0-8442-3704-3) NTC Pub Grp.

Teach Yourself Politics. Peter Joyce. 320p. 1997. pap. 12.95 (0-614-16989-5) NTC Pub Grp.

*Teach Yourself Politics. Peter Joyce. 1997. pap. 12.95 (0-8442-3109-6) NTC Pub Grp.

Teach Yourself Portuguese. J. W. Barker. (Teach Yourself Ser.). pap. 6.95 (0-679-10193-4) McKay.

Teach Yourself Portuguese. Manuela Cook. (Teach Yourself Ser.). 1992. 14.95 (0-8288-8379-3) Fr & Eur.

Teach Yourself Portuguese: Quick & Easy. Manuela Cook. (Teach Yourself Ser.). 1992. 12.95 (0-8288-8382-3); 29.95 incl. audio (0-8288-8381-5) Fr & Eur.

Teach Yourself Portuguese Pack. Manuela Cook. (Teach Yourself Ser.). 1992. 37.95 (0-8288-8380-7) Fr & Eur.

Teach Yourself PowerBuilder 4 in 14 Days. Judah Holstein et al. (Illus.). 672p. (Orig.). 1995. 25.00 (0-672-30676-X) Sams.

*Teach Yourself Powerbuilder 6 in 21 Days. 2nd ed. Judah Holstein. 1997. pap. text ed. 39.99 (0-672-31087-2) Sams.

*Teach Yourself PowerPoint 97. Tom Badgett. LC 96-54902. 1997. pap. text ed. 24.95 (1-55828-522-9) MIS Press.

Teach Yourself QBASIC. Chuck Butkus. 1991. 39.90 incl. disk (1-55828-175-4); disk 19.95 (1-55828-177-0) MIS Press.

Teach Yourself QBASIC. 2nd ed. Chuck Butkus. 1994. pap. 24.95 (1-55828-341-2) MIS Press.

Teach Yourself QBasic in Twenty-One Days. Namir C. Shammas. 806p. 1993. 24.95 (0-672-30324-8) Sams.

*Teach Yourself QuarkXpress in 14 Days. Al Gibbs. 400p. 1997. pap. text ed. 39.99 incl. cd-rom (1-56830-411-0) Hayden.

Teach Yourself Quattro Pro for Windows. David Royall. 224p. 1995. pap. 11.95 (0-8442-3949-6, Teach Yourslf) NTC Pub Grp.

Teach Yourself Quattro Pro 6.0 for Windows. Christopher Van Buren, pseud. 1994. pap. 21.95 (1-55828-401-X) MIS Press.

Teach Yourself Quattro 5.0 for DOS. Bill Kling. 1993. pap. 21.95 (1-55828-331-5) H Holt & Co.

Teach Yourself Reflexology. Chris Stormer. 192p. 1996. pap. 9.95 (0-8442-3726-4) NTC Pub Grp.

Teach Yourself Relaxation. James Hewitt. 200p. 1995. pap. 9.95 (0-8442-3939-9, Teach Yourslf) NTC Pub Grp.

Teach Yourself REXX in 21 Days. William F. Schindler. (Illus.). 527p. (Orig.). 1994. 29.99 (0-672-30529-1) Sams.

Teach Yourself Rhythm Guitar. Mark Michaels. 64p. pap. 11.95 (0-8256-2201-8, AM21650) Music Sales.

Teach Yourself Rock Bass. David Gross. 64p. pap. 11.95 (0-8256-2202-6, AM21668) Music Sales.

Teach Yourself Rock Drums. Mike Finkelstein. 80p. pap. 11.95 (0-8256-2211-5, AM25180) Music Sales.

Teach Yourself Rock Piano. Jeff Gutcheon. 72p. pap. 11.95 (0-8256-2207-7, AM25172) Music Sales.

Teach Yourself Romanian. Denis Deletant & Yvonne Alexandrescu. (Teach Yourself Ser.). 1992. 19.95 (0-8288-8383-1); 45.00 incl. audio (0-8288-8384-X) Fr & Eur.

Teach Yourself Romanian. M. Murrell. (Teach Yourself Ser.). 1972. pap. 8.95 (0-679-10222-1) McKay.

Teach Yourself Russian. M. Fourman. (Teach Yourself Ser.). pap. 8.95 (0-679-10223-X) McKay.

Teach Yourself Russian. K. V. Mayorova. 318p. (C). 1988. 19.95 incl. audio (0-8285-3927-8) Firebird NY.

Teach Yourself Russian. Daphne M. West. (Teach Yourself Ser.). 1992. 15.95 (0-8288-8385-8); 45.00 incl. audio (0-8288-8386-6) Fr & Eur.

Teach Yourself Russian: A Complete Course for Beginners. Daphne M. West. 334p. (ENG & RUS.). 1994. pap. 12.95 (0-8442-3823-6, Teach Yourslf) NTC Pub Grp.

Teach Yourself Russian: Quick & Easy. Teach Yourself Staff. (Teach Yourself Ser.). 1992. 12.95 (0-8288-8387-4); 29.95 incl. audio (0-8288-8388-2) Fr & Eur.

Teach Yourself Russian Audio Pack. Daphne M. West. 1995. 19.95 incl. audio (0-8442-3871-6, Teach Yourslf) NTC Pub Grp.

Teach Yourself Russian Complete Course. 2nd ed. Daphne M. West. (Teach Yourself Ser.). 334p. (ENG & RUS.). 1996. pap. 12.95 (0-8442-3703-5, Teach Yourslf) NTC Pub Grp.

Teach Yourself Russian Complete Course Audio Pack. 2nd rev. ed. 320p. (RUS.). 1996. pap. 19.95 incl. audio (0-8442-3706-X) NTC Pub Grp.

Teach Yourself Sanskrit. (Teach Yourself Ser.). 1976. pap. 10.95 (0-679-10238-8) McKay.

Teach Yourself Sanskrit. Michael Coulson. (Teach Yourself Ser.). 1992. 25.95 (0-8288-8389-0) Fr & Eur.

Teach Yourself Sanskrit: A Complete Course for Beginners. Michael Coulson. 544p. (ENG & SAN.). 1995. pap. 17.95 (0-8442-3825-2, Teach Yourslf) NTC Pub Grp.

Teach Yourself Screenwriting. Raymond G. Frensham. 320p. 1996. pap. 12.95 (0-8442-3111-8) NTC Pub Grp.

Teach Yourself Serbo-Croat. Vera Javarek & Miroslava Sudjic. (Teach Yourself Ser.). pap. 6.95 (0-679-10195-0) McKay.

Teach Yourself Serbo-Croat. Vera Javarek & Miroslava Sudjic. (Teach Yourself Ser.). 1992. 14.95 (0-8288-8390-4) Fr & Eur.

Teach Yourself Serbo-Croat. David Norris. (ENG & SER.). 1993. pap. 18.95 (0-7859-1062-X, 0-340-568038); pap. 29.95 incl. audio (0-7859-1063-8, 0-340-568046) Fr & Eur.

Teach Yourself Serbo-Croat: A Complete Course for Beginners. David Norris. 272p. 1995. pap. 12.95 (0-8442-3826-0, Teach Yourslf) NTC Pub Grp.

Teach Yourself Serbo-Croat Audio Pack. David Norris. (Orig.). 1995. pap. text ed. 25.95 incl. audio (0-8442-3872-4, Teach Yourslf) NTC Pub Grp.

*Teach Yourself Server-Side Database Programming with ADO & OLE DB in 21 Days. John Fronckowiak. (Teach Yourself Ser.). 1997. 39.99 (0-672-31083-X) Sams.

Teach Yourself Snooker. John Spencer. Ed. by Clive Everton. 160p. 1995. pap. 7.95 (0-8442-3940-2, Teach Yourslf) NTC Pub Grp.

Teach Yourself Spanish. Juan K. Ibarra. (Teach Yourself Ser.). 1992. 19.95 (0-8288-8391-2); 45.00 incl. audio (0-8288-8394-7) Fr & Eur.

Teach Yourself Spanish. Juan Kattan-Ibarra. (ENG & SPA.). 1993. pap. 39.95 incl. cd-rom (0-7859-1065-4, 0-340-586680) Fr & Eur.

Teach Yourself Spanish. N. Scarlyn Wilson. (Teach Yourself Ser.). 1980. pap. 8.95 (0-679-10197-7) McKay.

Teach Yourself Spanish: A Complete Course for Beginners. Juan Kattan-Ibarra. 314p. 1995. pap. 7.95 (0-8442-3829-5, Teach Yourslf) NTC Pub Grp.

Teach Yourself Spanish: Essential Grammar. Seymour Resnick. (Teach Yourself Ser.). 1992. 12.95 (0-8288-8397-1) Fr & Eur.

Teach Yourself Spanish: Quick & Easy. Teach Yourself Staff. (Teach Yourself Ser.). 1992. 12.95 (0-8288-8400-5); 29.95 incl. audio (0-8288-8401-3) Fr & Eur.

Teach Yourself Spanish: Quick & Easy Dictionary. Holtkamp & Whitlam. (Teach Yourself Ser.). 1992. 9.95 (0-8288-8399-8) Fr & Eur.

Teach Yourself Spanish Audio Pack. Juan Kattan-Ibarra. 1995. pap. 17.95 incl. audio (0-8442-3873-2, Teach Yourslf) NTC Pub Grp.

Teach Yourself Spanish, Basic. Juan K. Ibarra. (Teach Yourself Ser.). 1992. 12.95 (0-8288-8402-1) Fr & Eur.

Teach Yourself Spanish, Beginner's. Mark Stacey & Angela Gonzalez-Hevia. (Teach Yourself Ser.). 1992. 13.95 (0-8288-8395-5); 33.95 incl. audio (0-8288-8396-3) Fr & Eur.

Teach Yourself Spanish Dictionary. Margaret H. Raventos. (Teach Yourself Ser.). (SPA.). 1974. pap. 9.95 (0-679-10230-2) McKay.

Teach Yourself Spanish, Everyday. L. D. Collier. (Teach Yourself Ser.). 1992. 10.95 (0-8288-8398-X) Fr & Eur.

Teach Yourself Spanish, Further. Juan Kattan-Ibarra. (ENG & SPA.). 1993. pap. 29.95 (0-7859-1061-1, 0-340-565829) Fr & Eur.

Teach Yourself Spanish Grammar. Juan K. Ibarra. (Teach Yourself Ser.). 1992. 15.95 (0-8288-8393-9) Fr & Eur.

Teach Yourself Spanish Grammar. Juan K. Ibarra. 1991. pap. 10.00 (0-679-73620-4) Random.

Teach Yourself Spanish Grammar: A Modern Guide. Juan Kattan-Ibarra. 224p. (ENG & SPA.). 1995. pap. 7.95 (0-8442-3831-7, Teach Yourslf) NTC Pub Grp.

Teach Yourself Spanish Phrase Book. Coleman & Newton. (Teach Yourself Ser.). 1976. pap. 3.95 (0-679-10237-X) McKay.

Teach Yourself Spanish Verbs. Maria Hollis. 224p. 1995. pap. 6.95 (0-8442-3636-5, Teach Yourslf) NTC Pub Grp.

Teach Yourself Spanish Vocabulary. Pilar C. Lopez. (Teach Yourself Ser.). 256p. (Orig.). (SPA.). 1996. pap. 7.95 (0-8442-3986-0, Teach Yourslf) NTC Pub Grp.

Teach Yourself SQL in 14 Days. Jeff Perkins & Bryan Morgan. (Illus.). 408p. (Orig.). 1995. 29.99 (0-672-30855-X) Sams.

*Teach Yourself SQL in 21 Days. Jeff Perkins. 1997. 39.99 (0-672-31110-0) Sams.

Teach Yourself Sunsoft Java Workshop in 21 Days. Laura Lemay. 656p. 1996. pap. text ed. 39.99 incl. cd-rom (1-57521-159-9, SamsNet Bks) Sams.

Teach Yourself Swahili. D. V. Perrott. (Teach Yourself Ser.). 1979. pap. 6.95 (0-679-10225-6) McKay.

Teach Yourself Swahili. D. V. Perrott. (Teach Yourself Ser.). 1992. 15.95 (0-8288-8404-8) Fr & Eur.

Teach Yourself Swahili: A Complete Course for Beginners. D. V. Perrott. 224p. 1995. pap. 14.95 (0-8442-3837-6, Teach Yourslf) NTC Pub Grp.

Teach Yourself Swahili Complete Course. 2nd rev. ed. Joan Russell. 320p. (SWA.). 1996. pap. 14.95 (0-8442-3709-4) NTC Pub Grp.

Teach Yourself Swahili Dictionary. D. V. Perrot. (Teach Yourself Ser.). (SWA.). 1978. 10.00 (0-679-10015-6) McKay.

Teach Yourself Swahili Dictionary. D. V. Perrott. (Teach Yourself Ser.). 1992. 15.95 (0-8288-8405-6) Fr & Eur.

Teach Yourself Swedish. R. J. McClean. (Teach Yourself Ser.). 1978. 10.95 (0-679-10226-4) McKay.

Teach Yourself Swedish. R. J. McClean. (Teach Yourself Ser.). 1992. 15.95 (0-8288-8406-4) Fr & Eur.

Teach Yourself Swedish. 2nd ed. R. J. McClean. 322p. (ENG & SWE.). 1995. pap. 14.95 (0-8442-3702-7, Teach Yourslf) NTC Pub Grp.

Teach Yourself Swedish Audio Pack: A Complete Course for Beginners. 2nd ed. R. J. McClean. 322p. 1994. pap. 14.95 incl. audio (0-8442-3839-2, Teach Yourslf) NTC Pub Grp.

Teach Yourself Swedish Complete Course Audio Pack. Vera Croghan. (Teach Yourself Ser.). (Orig.). (SWE.). 1996. pap. 24.95 incl. audio (0-8442-3983-6, Teach Yourslf) NTC Pub Grp.

Teach Yourself Tarot. Terry Donaldson. (Illus.). 1995. pap. 11.00 (1-85538-431-0) Thorsons SF.

Teach Yourself TCP-IP in 14 Days. Timothy Parker. 464p. 1994. 29.99 (0-672-30549-6) Sams.

*Teach Yourself TCP/IP: MCSE Exam Preparation Guide. Robin Burk. 1997. 75.00 (0-672-31167-4) Mac Comp Pub.

Teach Yourself Technical Drawing. 1980. 8.95 (0-679-12476-4) McKay.

Teach Yourself Teddy Bear Making: Simple Techniques & Patterns for Teddy Bears. Jodie Davis. 1996. 24.95 (1-56799-256-0, Friedman-Fairfax) M Friedman Pub Grp Inc.

Teach Yourself Thai: A Complete Course for Beginners. David Smyth. 320p. (ENG & THA.). 1995. pap. 15.95 (0-8442-3782-5, Teach Yourslf) NTC Pub Grp.

Teach Yourself Thai Complete Course Audio Pack. (Teach Yourself Ser.). (Orig.). (THA.). 1996. pap. 25.95 incl. audio (0-8442-3878-3, Teach Yourslf) NTC Pub Grp.

Teach Yourself the Cinema. Keith Reader. 1979. pap. 4.95 (0-679-12056-4) McKay.

Teach Yourself the Internet. Mac Bride. 214p. 1996. pap. 9.95 (0-8442-3700-0, M3700-0, NTC Busn Bks) NTC Pub Grp.

Teach Yourself the Internet: Around the World in 21 Days. 2nd ed. Neil Randall. (Illus.). 668p. (Orig.). 1995. 25.00 (0-672-30735-9) Sams.

*Teach Yourself the Internet in 24 Hours. Noel Estabrook. 300p. 1997. 19.99 (1-57521-236-6) Mac Comp Pub.

*Teach Yourself the Internet in 24 Hours. Bob Temple. 1997. 24.99 (1-57521-348-6) Sams.

Teach Yourself the Pocket Calculator. L. R. Carter & E. Huzan. 1979. 4.95 (0-679-12375-X) McKay.

Teach Yourself the UNIX C Shell in 14 Days. David Ennis & James Armstrong. 494p. 1994. 29.99 (0-672-30540-2) Sams.

Teach Yourself to Cook. Evelyn White & Jessie R. Watson. 1974. lib. bdg. 69.95 (0-685-51371-8) Revisionist Pr.

*Teach Yourself to Create a Home Page in 24 Hours. Rogers Cadenhead. (Teach Yourself Ser.). 1997. 24.99 (1-57521-325-7, SamsNet Bks) Sams.

Teach Yourself to Dream: A Practical Guide to Unleashing the Power of the Subconscious Mind. David Fontana. LC 96-18546. 1997. pap. 14.95 (0-8118-1628-1) Chronicle Bks.

*Teach Yourself to Make Angels & Fairies: Simple Techniques & Patterns for Cloth Dolls & Their Clothes. Jodie Davis. LC 96-28957. (Jodie Davis Needle Arts School Ser.). (Illus.). 128p. 1996. 24.95 (1-56799-370-2, Friedman-Fairfax) M Friedman Pub Grp Inc.

*Teach Yourself to Make Soft Toys. Jodie Davis. LC 96-35748. (Jodie Davis Needle Arts School Ser.). 1997. write for info. (1-56799-399-0, Friedman-Fairfax) M Friedman Pub Grp Inc.

Teach Yourself to Play the Folk Harp. Sylvia Woods. 80p. 1982. pap. 9.95 (0-9602990-3-3) Woods Mus Bks.

Teach Yourself to Read Hebrew. 2nd rev. ed. Ethelyn Simon & Joseph Anderson. 104p. 1985. pap. 9.95 (0-939144-11-5) EKS Pub Co.

*Teach Yourself to Read Hebrew. 2nd rev. ed. Ethelyn Simon & Joseph Anderson. 104p. 1985. pap. 31.95 incl. audio (0-939144-22-0) EKS Pub Co.

Teach Yourself to Swim: The Racing Strokes. Lucille Griffin. (Illus.). 73p. (Orig.). 1985. pap. 10.00 (0-9615520-0-X) Gap Mountain.

*Teach Yourself to Think. Edward DeBono. 1997. 25.00 (0-7810-7107-0, Dove Bks) Dove Audio.

Teach Yourself to Write Irresistible Fund Raising Letters. Conrad Squires. LC 93-83402. 215p. 1993. pap. 50.00 (0-944496-38-5) Precept Pr.

Teach Yourself Torchon Lace: Six Basic Lessons in Bobbin Lace with Workcards. Eunice Arnold. 1980. pap. 15.00 (0-903585-08-1) Robin & Russ.

*Teach Yourself Transact SQL in 21 Days. David Solomon & Ben McEwan. 500p. 1997. 39.99 (0-672-31045-7) Mac Comp Pub.

Teach Yourself Trigonometry. P. Abbott. (Teach Yourself Ser.). 1979. 9.95 (0-679-10409-7) McKay.

Teach Yourself Trigonometry. P. Abbott. 194p. 1995. pap. 10.95 (0-8442-3943-7, Teach Yourslf) NTC Pub Grp.

Teach Yourself Turbo C Plus Plus 4.5 for Windows in 21 Days. Craig Arnush. (Illus.). 768p. (Orig.). 1995. 29.99 (0-672-30727-8) Sams.

Teach Yourself Turkish. Geoffrey L. Lewis. (Teach Yourself Ser.). 1979. pap. 5.95 (0-679-10200-0) McKay.

Teach Yourself Turkish. Geoffrey L. Lewis. (Teach Yourself Ser.). 1992. 15.95 (0-8288-8407-2); 45.00 incl. audio (0-8288-8408-0) Fr & Eur.

Teach Yourself Turkish: A Complete Course for Beginners. Geoffrey L. Lewis. 224p. 1994. pap. 13.95 (0-8442-3840-6, Teach Yourslf) NTC Pub Grp.

Teach Yourself Turkish: Quick & Easy. Necdet Teymur. (Teach Yourself Ser.). 1992. 12.95 (0-8288-8409-9); 29.95 incl. audio (0-8288-8410-2) Fr & Eur.

Teach Yourself Turkish Complete Course. 2nd rev. ed. Asuman C. Pollard & David Pollard. 320p. (TUR.). 1997. pap. 14.95 (0-8442-3715-9) NTC Pub Grp.

Teach Yourself Typing. (Teach Yourself Bks.). 1979. pap. 7.95 (0-679-12475-6) McKay.

Teach Yourself Ukrainian Complete Course. Jame Dingley & Olena Bekh. 320p. (UKR.). 1996. pap. 14.95 (0-8442-3680-2) NTC Pub Grp.

Teach Yourself Understanding Medicine. Paul Whiteman. 234p. 1996. pap. 12.95 (0-8442-3995-X) NTC Pub Grp.

Teach Yourself UNIX. Ashley & Fernandez. 1989. 24.95 (1-55828-017-0) MIS Press.

Teach Yourself... UNIX. 3rd ed. Kevin Reichard & Eric F. Johnson. 380p. 1995. pap. text ed. 24.95 (1-55828-418-4) MIS Press.

Teach Yourself UNIX in a Week. Dave Taylor. 800p. 1994. pap. text ed. 28.00 (0-672-30464-3) Sams.

*Teach Yourself UNIX in 24 Hours. Dave Taylor. 1997. 19.99 (0-672-31107-0) Sams.

*Teach Yourself Vb 5. Gurewich. 1997. 59.99 (0-672-31176-3) Mac Comp Pub.

*Teach Yourself Vb5 in 21 Days. 1997. 75.00 (0-672-31197-6) Mac Comp Pub.

Teach Yourself Vietnamese Complete Course. Dana Healy. 320p. (VIE.). 1997. pap. 14.95 (0-8442-3707-8) NTC Pub Grp.

Teach Yourself Visual Basic. Bob Albrecht et al. (Illus.). 512p. 1995. pap. text ed. 24.95 (0-07-882078-2) McGraw.

Teach Yourself Visual Basic for Applications in 21 Days. Namir C. Shammas. 909p. 1994. 29.99 (0-672-30447-3) Sams.

*Teach Yourself Visual Basic for Applications in 21 Days. 3rd ed. Matthew Harris. 1000p. 1997. 39.99 (0-672-31016-3) Mac Comp Pub.

*Teach Yourself Visual Basic in 14 Days. 4th ed. Nathan Gurewich & Ori Gurewich. 1997. pap. 39.99 (0-614-28483-X, Sams Sftwre) MCP SW Interactive.

Teach Yourself Visual Basic in 21 Days. 4th ed. Nathan Gurewich & Ori Gurewich. 1000p. 1997. 29.99 (0-672-30978-5) Mac Comp Pub.

Teach Yourself Visual Basic 3 in 21 Days: Bestseller Edition. Nathan Gurewich & Ori Gurewich. (Illus.). 1024p. (Orig.). 1995. 35.00 (0-672-30715-4) Sams.

Teach Yourself Visual Basic 4 in 21 Days. 2nd ed. Nathan Gurewich & Ori Gurewich. (Illus.). 944p. (Orig.). 1995. 29.99 (0-672-30620-4) Sams.

*Teach Yourself Visual Basic 5. John Socha. LC 97-2629. 1997. pap. text ed. 29.95 incl. disk (1-55828-547-4) MIS Press.

*Teach Yourself Visual Basic 5 in 24 Hours. Vilas Ekbote. 450p. 1997. pap. text ed. 19.99 incl. cd-rom (0-672-31064-3) Sams.

*Teach Yourself Visual C++ David A. Holzgang. LC 97-20210. (Teach Yourself Ser.). 1997. pap. text ed. 29.95 (1-55828-554-7) MIS Press.

*Teach Yourself Visual C++ 5 in 21 Days. 1997. 75.00 (0-672-31194-1) Mac Comp Pub.

*Teach Yourself Visual CafO in 21 Days. Mike Cohn. 700p. 1997. 39.99 (1-57521-303-6, SamsNet Bks) Sams.

*Teach Yourself Visual C++5 in 21 Days. 4th ed. Nathan Gurewich & Ori Gurewich. 799p. 1997. 35.00 (0-672-31014-7) Mac Comp Pub.

Teach Yourself Visual dBASE 5.5 Programming in 21 Days. Nathan Gurewich & Ori Gurewich. (Illus.). 592p. (Orig.). 1995. 29.99 (0-672-30673-5) Sams.

Teach Yourself Visual Foxpro 3.0 for the Mac. Nelson King. 1996. pap. 29.95 (1-55828-496-6) MIS Press.

*Teach Yourself Visual Foxpro 5.0 for Windows. Nelson King. LC 96-47695. 1997. pap. text ed. 29.95 incl. disk (1-55828-519-9) MIS Press.

Teach Yourself Visual J++ in 21 Days. Sams Development Group Staff. 500p. 1996. pap. text ed. 39.99 incl. cd-rom (1-57521-158-0, SamsNet Bks) Sams.

*Teach Yourself Visual J++ in 21 Days. 2nd ed. Laura Lemay & Patrick Winters. 500p. 1997. 39.99 (1-57521-244-7) Mac Comp Pub.

*Teach Yourself Visual Javascript in 21 Days. Danny Goodman. 1997. 39.99 (1-57521-345-1) Sams.

*Teach Yourself Visual Sourcesafe in 21 Days. Mike Amundsen. 1997. 29.99 (1-57521-332-X) Sams.

*Teach Yourself Visualization. Pauline Wills. 1997. pap. 9.95 (0-8442-3120-7) NTC Pub Grp.

*Teach Yourself VRML 2.0 in 21 Days. Jeffrey Sonstein. 500p. 1997. pap. text ed. 39.99 incl. cd-rom (1-57521-193-9, SamsNet Bks) Sams.

Teach Yourself Weather. Ralph Hardy. 192p. 1996. pap. 9.95 (0-8442-3727-2) NTC Pub Grp.

*Teach Yourself Web Publishing with HTML in a Week. 4th ed. Laura LeMay. 600p. 1997. 29.99 (1-57521-336-2) Sams.

*Teach Yourself Web Publishing with HTML in 14 Days. 4th ed. Laura Lemay. 1100p. 1997. 59.99 (1-57521-305-2, SamsNet Bks) Sams.

Teach Yourself Web Publishing with HTML in 14 Days: Premier Edition. 2nd ed. Laura Lemay & Samsnet Publishing Staff. (Illus.). (Orig.). 1995. pap. 39.99 (*1-57521-014-2*, SamsNet Bks) Sams.

Teach Yourself Web Publishing with HTML 3.0 in 14 Days: Premier. 2nd ed. Laura Lemay. 1104p. 1996. 59.99 incl. cd-rom (*1-57521-096-7*, SamsNet Bks) Sams.

***Teach Yourself Web Publishing with HTML 3.2 in a Week.** 3rd ed. Laura Lemay. (Illus.). 600p. 1997. pap. 29.99 (*1-57521-192-0*, SamsNet Bks) Sams.

***Teach Yourself Web Publishing with Microsoft Office 97 in a Week.** Michael Larson. 500p. 1997. 39.99 (*1-57521-232-3*) Mac Comp Pub.

Teach Yourself Welding. C. G. Brainbridge. (Teach Yourself Ser.). 192p. 1981. pap. 6.95 (*0-679-10495-X*) McKay.

Teach Yourself Welsh. Jones T. Rhys. (Teach Yourself Ser.). 1992. 15.95 (*0-8288-8411-0*, 828884110); 45.00 incl. audio (*0-8288-8413-7*) Fr & Eur.

Teach Yourself Welsh: A Complete Course for Beginners. Jones T. Rhys. 334p. (ENG & WEL.). 1995. pap. 14.95 (*0-8442-3841-4*, Teach Yourslf) NTC Pub Grp.

Teach Yourself Welsh Audio Pack. Jones T. Rhys. 1995. pap. 24.95 incl. audio (*0-8442-3874-0*, Teach Yourslf) NTC Pub Grp.

Teach Yourself Welsh Dictionary. Edwin Lewis. (Teach Yourself Ser.). 1992. 15.95 (*0-8288-8412-9*) Fr & Eur.

Teach Yourself Windows. 2nd ed. Alan Stevens. 1992. pap. 19.95 (*1-55828-193-2*) MIS Press.

***Teach Yourself Windows CE in 24 Hours.** David Hayden. 250p. 1997. 19.99 (*0-672-31065-1*) Sams.

***Teach Yourself Windows NT: MCSE Exam Preparation Guide.** David Schaer. 1997. 75.00 (*0-672-31128-3*) Sams.

***Teach Yourself Windows NT Workstation.** 1997. 75.00 (*0-672-31192-5*) Macmillan.

***Teach Yourself Windows NT Workstation in 24 Hours.** Martin Kenley. 400p. 1997. 19.99 (*0-672-31011-2*) Mac Comp Pub.

***Teach Yourself Windows NT 4 Server 4 in 14 Days.** Peter Davis & Barry Lewis. 700p. 1997. 35.00 (*0-672-31019-8*) Mac Comp Pub.

***Teach Yourself Windows NT 4.0 Workstation.** Aaron Hoffmeyer. LC 97-10395. 1997. pap. text ed. 24.95 (*1-55828-533-4*) MIS Press.

Teach Yourself Windows 3.1. Stephen D. Saxon. 224p. 1995. pap. 11.95 (*0-8442-3645-4*, Teach Yourslf) NTC Pub Grp.

***Teach Yourself Windows 95.** 3rd ed. Alan Stevens. LC 97-19173. 1997. pap. text ed. 24.95 (*1-55828-543-1*) MIS Press.

***Teach Yourself Windows 95: MCSE Exam Preparation Guide.** Todd Gagorik. 1997. 75.00 (*0-672-31183-6*) Mac Comp Pub.

***Teach Yourself Windows 95 Electronic Starter Kit.** Publishing Sams. Date not set. boxed, pap. text ed. 39.99 incl. cd-rom (*0-672-31099-6*) Sams.

Teach Yourself Windows 95 in 24 Hours. Greg M. Perry. (Illus.). 560p. 1995. pap. text ed. 25.00 (*0-672-30504-6*) Sams.

***Teach Yourself Windows 95 in 24 Hours.** 2nd ed. Greg M. Perry. 550p. 1997. 19.99 (*0-672-31006-6*) Mac Comp Pub.

Teach Yourself Windows 95 Visually. Ruth Maran. 1996. pap. 29.99 (*0-7645-6001-8*) IDG Bks.

***Teach Yourself Windows 97 Visually.** Maran Graphics Staff. 1997. pap. 29.99 (*0-7645-6025-5*) IDG Bks.

Teach Yourself Wine Appreciation. Andrew Durkin & John Cousins. 192p. 1995. pap. text ed. 7.95 (*0-8442-3644-6*, Teach Yourslf) NTC Pub Grp.

Teach Yourself Women's Studies. Joy Magezis. 192p. 1996. pap. 10.95 (*0-8442-3113-4*) NTC Pub Grp.

Teach Yourself Word for Windows. Chris Watson. 224p. (Orig.). 1995. pap. 11.95 (*0-8442-3975-5*, Teach Yourslf) NTC Pub Grp.

Teach Yourself Word 3.0. Philippe Mathieu. 189p. 1989. ring bd. 79.95 incl. disk (*0-929533-10-0*) Tutorland.

Teach Yourself Word 5 for the Macintosh. Stephen Kahn. 1992. pap. 24.95 (*1-55828-194-0*) MIS Press.

Teach Yourself Word 6.0 for DOS. Joan Bannan. 1993. pap. 21.95 incl. disk (*1-55828-312-9*) MIS Press.

Teach Yourself Word 6.0 for the Mac. Stephen Kahn. LC 94-32294. 1994. pap. 24.95 incl. disk (*1-55828-371-4*) MIS Press.

***Teach Yourself Word 97.** Jan Weingarten. LC 96-40499. 1997. pap. text ed. 24.95 (*1-55828-524-5*) MIS Press.

Teach Yourself WordPerfect for Windows 95. Jan Weingarten. 640p. 1996. pap. 24.95 incl. disk (*1-55828-478-8*) MIS Press.

Teach Yourself WordPerfect 5.0 Module I & II. Laurent Buisseret. 158p. 1989. ring bd. 69.95 incl. disk (*0-929533-13-5*) Tutorland.

Teach Yourself WordPerfect 5.1. rev. ed. Robert Krumm. 1990. pap. 19.95 (*1-55828-048-0*) MIS Press.

Teach Yourself... Works 3 for Windows. Judi N. Fernandez. 1993. pap. 21.95 (*1-55828-311-0*) MIS Press.

Teach Yourself Writing Poetry. Date not set. pap. 10.95 (*0-8442-3947-X*) NTC Pub Grp.

Teach Yourself Yoga. James Hewitt. (Illus.). 176p. 1995. pap. 7.95 (*0-8442-3945-3*, Teach Yourslf) NTC Pub Grp.

Teach Yourself Yorruba. E. C. Rowlands. (Teach Yourself Ser.). 1992. 15.95 (*0-8288-8414-5*) Fr & Eur.

Teach Yourself Yoruba. E. C. Rowlands. (Teach Yourself Ser.). 1979. 10.95 (*0-679-10224-8*) McKay.

Teach Yourself Yoruba: A Complete Course for Beginners. E. C. Rowlands. 288p. 1994. pap. 14.95 (*0-8442-3843-0*, Teach Yourslf) NTC Pub Grp.

Teach Yourself Zen: A Way of Life. Christmas Humphreys. 208p. 1995. pap. 7.95 (*0-8442-3946-1*, Teach Yourslf) NTC Pub Grp.

Teach Yourself Zulu. Arnett Wilkes & Nicholas Nkosi. 320p. (ZUL.). 1996. pap. 17.95 (*0-8442-3701-9*, Teach Yourslf) NTC Pub Grp.

Teach Yourself Zulu Complete Course Audio Pack. Nicholas Nkosi. (Teach Yourself Ser.). (Orig.). (ZUL.). 1996. pap. 27.95 incl. audio (*0-8442-3687-X*, Teach Yourslf) NTC Pub Grp.

Teach Yourself 1-2-3: Includes Versions 2.2 & 3.0. Robert Williams. 1990. pap. 19.95 (*1-55828-049-9*) MIS Press.

Teach Yourself...Access for Windows 95. Charles Siegel. 1995. pap. 24.95 incl. disk (*1-55828-441-9*) MIS Press.

Teach Yourself...AutoCad 13. John Gibb. 372p. 1994. pap. 27.95 (*1-55828-405-2*) MIS Press.

Teach Yourself...CorelDRAW! 6.0. Dawn Erdos. 1995. pap. 24.95 (*1-55828-454-0*) MIS Press.

Teach Yourself...Delphi 2. 2nd abr. ed. Devra Hall. 450p. 1996. pap. 29.95 incl. disk (*1-55828-457-5*) MIS Press.

Teach Yourself...Excel for Windows 95. John Weingarten. 1995. pap. 24.95 incl. disk (*1-55828-443-5*) MIS Press.

Teach Yourself...Freelance Graphics 96. Jan Weingarten & Katherine MacDonald. 416p. 1996. pap. 24.95 (*1-55828-389-7*) MIS Press.

Teach Yourself...Microsoft Project for Windows 95. Nelson King. 1996. pap. 27.95 incl. disk (*1-55828-433-8*) MIS Press.

Teach Yourself...Microsoft Publisher 3. Devra Hall. LC 95-26025. 1995. pap. 21.95 (*1-55828-466-4*) MIS Press.

Teach Yourself...Netscape Navigator 2. Kevin Reichard. LC 96-15534. 352p. 1996. pap. 21.95 (*1-55828-471-0*) MIS Press.

Teach Yourself...PageMaker 6 for the Macintosh. David Browne & David D. Busch. 480p. 1996. pap. 24.95 (*1-55828-476-1*) MIS Press.

Teach Yourself...PageMaker 6 for Windows. David Browne. 480p. 1996. pap. 24.95 (*1-55828-419-2*) MIS Press.

Teach Yourself...Pascal-with Disk. Mark Goodwin. 1990. 29.95 (*1-55828-055-3*) MIS Press.

Teach Yourself...PhotoShop 3.0 for the Mac. Karen Winters & David D. Busch. 425p. 1994. pap. 27.95 incl. disk (*1-55828-402-8*) MIS Press.

Teach Yourself...PowerBuilder 5. David McClanahan. LC 96-46896. 450p. 1996. pap. 29.95 incl. disk (*1-55828-474-5*) MIS Press.

Teach Yourself...PowerPoint for Windows 95. Tom Badgett. 1995. pap. 24.95 (*1-55828-442-7*) MIS Press.

Teach Yourself...Visual Basic 4.0 for Windows 95. John Socha & Devra Hall. 1995. pap. 27.95 incl. disk (*1-55828-399-4*) MIS Press.

Teach Yourself...Visual C Plus Plus 4.0. David A. Holzgang. 640p. 1996. pap. 29.95 (*1-55828-475-3*) MIS Press.

Teach Yourself...Windows 95. 2nd ed. Alan Stevens. 1995. pap. 21.95 (*1-55828-383-8*) MIS Press.

***Teach Yourself...Windows 95.** 3rd ed. Al Stevens. 1997. pap. 24.95 (*0-614-28501-1*) MIS Press.

Teach Yourself...Word for Windows 95. Colin Bay. 1995. pap. 24.95 incl. disk (*1-55828-444-3*) MIS Press.

Teach Yourself...Word Pro 96. June Reeder. 416p. 1996. pap. 24.95 incl. disk (*1-55828-473-7*) MIS Press.

Teach Yourself...WordPerfect 6.1 for Windows. Jan Weingarten. LC 94-45640. (Teach Yourself Ser.). 1995. 24.95 incl. disk (*1-55828-425-7*) MIS Press.

Teach Yourself...Works for Windows 95. Judi N. Fernandez. 1995. pap. 21.95 (*1-55828-453-2*) MIS Press.

***Teach Youself Visual Age for Java in 21 Days.** Chamberlain & Mark Ryan. 1997. 39.99 (*1-57521-359-1*) Sams.

Teachable Moments: The Art of Teaching in Primary Schools. Peter Woods & Bob Jeffrey. 160p. 1996. 79.00 (*0-335-19374-9*, Open Univ Pr); pap. 24.95 (*0-335-19373-0*, Open Univ Pr) Taylor & Francis.

Teachable Spirit: Recovering the Teaching Office in the Church. Richard R. Osmer. 340p. (Orig.). 1990. pap. 22.00 (*0-664-25079-3*) Westminster John Knox.

Teacher. Sylvia Ashton-Warner. 224p. 1986. pap. 9.95 (*0-671-61768-0*, Touchstone Bks) S&S Trade.

Teacher. Kira Daniel. LC 88-10041. (What's It Like to Be a. ..Ser.). (Illus.). 32p. (J). (gr. k-3). 1997. pap. 3.95 (*0-8167-1431-2*) Troll Communs.

Teacher. Mark Dunster. 15p. (Orig.). 1985. pap. 4.00 (*0-89642-127-9*) Linden Pubs.

Teacher. Jack Rudman. (Career Examination Ser.: C-2267). 1994. reprint ed. pap. 27.95 (*0-8373-2267-7*) Nat Learn.

Teacher: A New Definition & Model for Development. Helen B. Regan et al. 118p. (Orig.). 1992. pap. 21.95 (*1-56602-048-4*) Research Better.

Teacher: An Existential Approach to the Bible. Zvi Kolitz. LC 95-7776. 234p. 1995. pap. 25.00 (*1-56821-547-9*) Aronson.

Teacher: Anne Sullivan Macy. Helen A. Keller. LC 84-25274. (Illus.). vi, 247p. 1985. reprint ed. text ed. 59.75 (*0-313-24738-2*, KETE, Greenwood Pr) Greenwood.

Teacher: Eleven Aspects of the Guru Rinpoche. (Salamander Ser.: No. 1). (Illus.). 23p. 1993. reprint ed. pap. 3.95 (*1-56640-591-2*) Pomegranate Calif.

Teacher: Theory & Practice in Education. rev. ed. Allen Pearosn. LC 88-92216. 200p. 1989. pap. text ed. 30.00 (*0-9620940-0-5*, A2713) Routledge Chapman & Hall.

***Teacher: Theory & Practice in Teacher Education.** Allen Pearson. (Philosophy of Education Research Library). 224p. (C). 1989. text ed. 39.95 (*0-415-90088-3*) Routledge.

Teacher: Twenty-Five Years Later. Lawrence J. Babin. 1981. pap. 3.00 (*0-912492-26-0*) Pyquag.

Teacher Absence & Leave Regulations: Some Basic Facts & Principles Related to Temporary Absence of Teachers for Use in Formulating Valid Absence Regulations. William D. Kuhlmann. LC 70-176939. (Columbia University. Teachers College. Contributions to Education Ser.: No. 564). reprint ed. 37.50 (*0-404-55564-0*) AMS Pr.

***Teacher Activism in the 1990s.** Ed. by Susan Robertson & Harry Smaller. (Our Schools/Our Selves Ser.). pap. 19. 95 (*1-55028-538-6*, Pub. by J Lorimer CN) Formac Dist Ltd.

Teacher Affects Eternity. Smallwood & Stewart. (Illus.). 96p. 1995. 15.00 (*0-8362-4246-7*) Andrews & McMeel.

Teacher Agency & Curriculum Making in the Classroom. Cynthia L. Paris. LC 92-34554. 176p. (C). 1993. pap. text ed. 18.95 (*0-8077-3225-7*) Tchrs Coll.

Teacher Aide Handbook. Michael Perl. 64p. (C). 1994. teacher ed. 10.44 (*0-8403-8288-X*) Kendall-Hunt.

Teacher Aide in the Instructional Team. Don A. Welty & Dorothy R. Welty. (Illus.). 1976. text ed. 30.95 (*0-07-069263-7*) McGraw.

Teacher & Child. Haim G. Ginott. 256p. 1976. mass mkt. 4.95 (*0-380-00323-6*) Avon.

Teacher & Child. Haim G. Ginott. 320p. 1993. pap. 10.00 (*0-02-013974-8*) Macmillan.

Teacher & Christian Belief. Ninian Smart. 208p. 1966. 8.00 (*0-227-67703-X*) Attic Pr.

Teacher & Education in Emerging Indian Society. C. L. Anand et al. 358p. 1983. 16.95 (*0-318-36832-3*) Asia Bk Corp.

Teacher & Friend: Memoirs of an Education Officer in Colonial Africa. John C. Clarke. (Illus.). 07p. (Orig.). 1993. pap. 15.00 (*0-9639288-0-5*) Allies Behav.

Teacher & Religion. F. H. Hilliard. 191p. 1963. 8.50 (*0-227-67675-0*) Attic Pr.

Teacher & Student Insect Identification Guide. Gary A. Dunn. (YES Special Publication Ser.: No. 6). 54p. 1991. pap. text ed. 6.95 (*1-884256-09-0*) Yng Entomol.

Teacher & the Machine. Philip W. Jackson. LC 68-12729. (Horace Mann Lecture Ser.). 102p. reprint ed. 29.10 (*0-8357-9762-7*, 2017870) Bks Demand.

Teacher & the Needs of Society in Evolution. Edmanuel J. King. 1971. write for info. (*0-318-55233-7*, Pub. by Pergamon Repr UK) Franklin.

Teacher Appraisal. Jan Lokan & Phillip McKenzie. (C). 1990. 65.00 (*0-86431-045-5*, Pub. by Aust Council Educ Res AT) St Mut.

Teacher Appraisal: A Guide to Training. 2nd ed. Cyril Poster & Doreen Poster. LC 93-16582. 256p. (C). 1993. pap. 24.95 (*0-415-09577-8*, B2445) Routledge.

Teacher Appraisal: A Practical Guide for Schools. Mel West & Rob Bollington. 112p. (Orig.). 1990. pap. 23.00 (*0-8464-4335-X*) Beekman Pubs.

Teacher Appraisal Observed. Edward C. Wragg et al. LC 95-25984. 224p. (C). 1996. text ed. 65.00 (*0-415-12580-4*); pap. text ed. 22.95 (*0-415-12581-2*) Routledge.

Teacher As Actor. Woods & Burns. 208p. (C). 1991. pap. text ed. 19.89 (*0-8403-7217-5*) Kendall-Hunt.

Teacher As Counselor: Developing the Helping Skills You Need. Jeffrey A. Kottler & Ellen Kottler. LC 92-42781. (New Survival Skills for Teachers Ser.). 112p. 1993. pap. 11.95 (*0-8039-6050-6*) Corwin Pr.

Teacher As Decision Maker: Real-Life Cases to Hone Your People Skills. Dale L. Brubaker & Lawrence H. Simon. LC 93-13917. 200p. 1993. 47.95 (*0-8039-6081-6*); pap. 21.95 (*0-8039-6082-4*) Corwin Pr.

Teacher As Expert: A Theoretical & Historical Examination. Robert Welker. LC 90-49368. (SUNY Series, The Philosophy of Education). 183p. (C). 1991. pap. text ed. 21.95 (*0-7914-0798-5*) State U NY Pr.

Teacher As Expert: A Theoretical & Historical Examination. Robert Welker. LC 90-49368. (SUNY Series, The Philosophy of Education). 183p. (C). 1992. text ed. 64.50 (*0-7914-0797-7*) State U NY Pr.

Teacher As Facilitator. Joe Wittmer & Robert D. Myrick. 224p. (Orig.). (C). 1989. pap. text ed. 9.95 (*0-932796-27-3*) Ed Media Corp.

***Teacher As Helper Training Manual.** William L. Fibkins. 248p. 1997. ring bd. 120.00 (*0-89390-411-2*) Resource Pubns.

Teacher As Inventor see Inventive Teaching: The Heart of the Small School

Teacher As Minister: Weekly Plan Book. Robert J. Kealey. 208p. 1991. 4.80 (*1-55833-073-9*) Natl Cath Educ.

Teacher As World Citizen: A Scenario of the 21st Century. Theodore Brawick. (Education Futures Ser.: No. 5). 1976. 12.95 (*0-88280-042-6*); pap. 12.95 (*0-88280-043-4*) ETC Pubns.

Teacher Assessment: Report of the Commission on Teacher Assessment. Ed. by Edelfelt Johnson. LC 87-33447. 1988. pap. 6.85 (*0-685-41081-1*) Assn Tchr Ed.

Teacher Beware: A Legal Primer for the Classroom Teacher. Alex J. Proudfoot & Lawrence Hutchings. 391p. (Orig.). (C). 1988. pap. text ed. 23.95 (*0-920490-82-4*) Temeron Bks.

Teacher Burnout in the Public Schools: Structural Causes & Consequences for Children. Ed. by Anthony G. Dworkin. LC 86-5713. (SUNY Series, Educational Leadership). 241p. (C). 1986. pap. text ed. 24.95 (*0-88706-349-7*) State U NY Pr.

Teacher Burnout in the Public Schools: Structural Causes & Consequences for Children. Ed. by Anthony G. Dworkin. LC 86-5713. (SUNY Series, Educational Leadership). 241p. (C). 1986. text ed. 74.50 (*0-88706-348-9*) State U NY Pr.

Teacher Careers: Crisis & Continuities. Patricia J. Sikes et al. (Issues in Education & Training Ser.: Vol. 5). 225p. 1985. 55.00 (*1-85000-066-2*, Falmer Pr); pap. 33.00 (*1-85000-067-0*, Falmer Pr) Taylor & Francis.

Teacher Centers: What Place in Education. Ed. by Sharon Feiman. (Orig.). 1980. pap. 1.50 (*0-686-29035-6*) U Chi Ctr Policy.

Teacher Certification in Ohio & a Proposed Plan of Reconstruction. Frank B. Dilley. LC 73-176720. (Columbia University. Teachers College. Contributions to Education Ser.: No. 630). reprint ed. 37.50 (*0-404-55630-2*) AMS Pr.

Teacher Certification Tests. 3rd ed. Elna M. Dimock. LC 92-31173. 1993. pap. 14.00 (*0-671-86526-9*, Arco) Macmillan Gen Ref.

***Teacher Certification Tests: The Only Guide to the State-Developed Teacher-Licensing Exams!** 4th ed. Elna M. Dimock. 288p. 1996. pap. 14.95 (*0-02-861314-7*, Arco) Macmillan Gen Ref.

Teacher Change & the Staff Development Process. Ed. by Virginia Richardson. 240p. (C). 1994. text ed. 40.00 (*0-8077-3361-X*); pap. text ed. 18.95 (*0-8077-3360-1*) Tchrs Coll.

Teacher, Child & Waldorf Education. Willi Aeppli. Tr. by Angelika V. Ritscher from GER. 1987. pap. 3.50 (*0-88010-166-0*) Anthroposophic.

Teacher-Child Partnership: The Negotiating Classroom. John Ingram & Norman Worrall. 144p. 1993. pap. 21.95 (*1-85346-232-2*, Pub. by D Fulton UK) Taylor & Francis.

Teacher-Clinician Planbook & Guide to the Development of Speech Skills. Daniel Ling. LC 77-93949. 1978. pap. text ed. 10.50 (*0-88200-116-7*, A2092) Alexander Graham.

Teacher Cognition. Johnson. (Teaching Methods Ser.). 1999. pap. 18.95 (*0-8384-6690-7*) Wadsworth Pub.

Teacher Cognition in Language Teaching: Beliefs, Decision-Making & Classroom Practice. Devon Woods. (Applied Linguistics Ser.). (Illus.). 320p. (C). 1996. text ed. 52.95 (*0-521-49700-0*); pap. text ed. 20.95 (*0-521-49788-4*) Cambridge U Pr.

Teacher Compensation & Motivation. Ed. by Larry Frase. LC 91-58005. 605p. 1991. 39.95 (*0-87762-813-0*) Technomic.

***Teacher Connections.** Carolyn J. Brown. (Illus.). 80p. 1995. spiral bd. 25.00 (*1-890891-04-5*) Breakthrough Inc.

Teacher Creature. Betsy Haynes. (Bone Chillers Ser.: No. 6). 144p. (J). 1995. mass mkt. 3.99 (*0-06-106314-2*, Harp PBks) HarpC.

Teacher-Curriculum Encounter: Freeing Teachers from the Tyranny of Texts. Miriam Ben-Peretz. LC 89-28867. (SUNY Series in Curriculum Issues & Inquiries). 152p. 1990. text ed. 74.50 (*0-7914-0375-0*) State U NY Pr.

Teacher-Curriculum Encounter: Freeing Teachers from the Tyranny of Texts. Miriam Ben-Peretz. LC 89-28867. (SUNY Series in Curriculum Issues & Inquiries). 152p. 1991. pap. text ed. 24.95 (*0-7914-0376-9*) State U NY Pr.

Teacher Development: A Model from Science Education. Beverly Bell & John Gilbert. LC 95-7255. 224p. 1995. 72.00 (*0-7507-0426-8*, Falmer Pr); pap. 24.95 (*0-7507-0427-6*, Falmer Pr) Taylor & Francis.

Teacher Development: Induction, Renewal & Redirection. Peter Burke. LC 86-29357. 225p. 1987. 65.00 (*1-85000-143-X*, Falmer Pr); pap. 33.00 (*1-85000-144-8*, Falmer Pr) Taylor & Francis.

Teacher Development & Educational Change. Ed. by Michael G. Fullan & Andy Hargreaves. 224p. 1992. 85. 00 (*0-7507-0010-6*, Falmer Pr); pap. 32.50 (*0-7507-0011-4*, Falmer Pr) Taylor & Francis.

Teacher Development & the Struggle for Authenticity: Professional Growth & Restructuring in the Context of Change. Peter Grimmett & Jonathan Neufeld. (Series on School Reform). 264p. (C). 1994. text ed. 46.00 (*0-8077-3351-2*); pap. text ed. 21.95 (*0-8077-3350-4*) Tchrs Coll.

Teacher Education. Ed. by J. T. Voorbach & L. G. Prick. (Selecta Reeks Ser.: Vol. 39). vi, 236p. 1985. 12.75 (*90-6472-052-5*) Taylor & Francis.

Teacher Education, No. 2. Ed. by J. T. Voorbach & L. G. Prick. (Selecta Reeks Ser.: Vol. 40). ii, 236p. 1986. 20.00 (*90-6472-068-1*) Taylor & Francis.

Teacher Education, No. 3. Ed. by J. T. Voorbach & L. G. Prick. (Selecta Reeks Ser.: Vol. 41). iv, 326p. 1987. 24. 50 (*90-6472-100-9*) Taylor & Francis.

Teacher Education, No. 4. Ed. by J. T. Voorbach & L. G. Prick. (Selecta Reeks Ser.: Vol. 42). 248p. 1988. 24.00 (*90-6472-126-2*) Taylor & Francis.

Teacher Education: Role-Playing & Analogies to Art. Ed. by Ayers Bagley. (Occasional Papers: No. 7). 1975. pap. 3.00 (*0-933669-10-0*) Soc Profs Ed.

Teacher Education: Today & in the Year 2001. R. P. Singh. 200p. (C). 1992. 35.00 (*81-207-1394-X*) Apt Bks.

***Teacher Education & Human Rights.** Ed. by Audrey Osler & Hugh Starkey. 192p. 1996. pap. 25.95 (*1-85346-406-6*, Pub. by D Fulton UK) Taylor & Francis.

***Teacher Education & School Partnerships.** Ed. by Mary I. Fuller & Anthony J. Rosie. LC 97-12635. (Mellen Studies in Education: No. 31). 172p. 1997. text ed. 79. 95 (*0-7734-8638-0*) E Mellen.

Teacher Education & the Revival of Civic Learning. R. Freeman Butts. (DeGarmo Lectures: No. 7). 1982. 3.00 (*0-933669-31-3*) Soc Profs Ed.

Teacher Education & the Social Conditions of Schooling. Daniel P. Liston & Kenneth M. Zeichner. (Critical Social Thought Ser.). 288p. (C). 1991. pap. 16.95 (*0-415-90233-9*, A5174, Routledge NY) Routledge.

Teacher Education As Actor Training. Ed. by Ayers Bagley. (Occasional Papers: No. 3). 1974. pap. 3.00 (*0-933669-06-2*) Soc Profs Ed.

Teacher Education As Transformation: A Psychological Perspective. C. T. Diamond. (Developing Teachers & Teaching Ser.). 144p. 1991. 85.00 (*0-335-09255-1*, Open Univ Pr); pap. 32.00 (*0-335-09254-3*, Open Univ Pr) Taylor & Francis.

Teacher Education Evaluation. Ed. by William J. Gephart & Jerry B. Ayers. (C). 1988. lib. bdg. 59.50 (*0-89838-270-X*) Kluwer Ac.

An Asterisk (*) at the beginning of an entry indicates that the title is appearing in BIP for the first time.

*__Teacher Education for LSP.__ Ron Howard & Gillian Brown. LC 96-33012. 220p. 1996. 79.00 (*1-85359-364-8*, Pub. by Multilingual Matters UK); pap. 29.95 (*1-85359-363-X*, Pub. by Multilingual Matters UK) Taylor & Francis.

Teacher Education for Special Needs in Europe. Ed. by Peter Mittler & Patrick Daunt. (Cassell Education Ser.). (Illus.). 176p. 1996. 90.00 (*0-304-33405-7*); pap. 23.00 (*0-304-33406-5*) Cassell.

*__Teacher Education for the Arts Disciplines: Issues Raised by the National Standards for Arts Education.__ 16p. 1996. pap. 1.25 (*1-56545-096-5*, 1609) Music Ed Natl.

Teacher Education for the Environment: European Perspectives. Ed. by Walter L. Filho & Kathryn O'Loan. 150p. (Orig.). 1996. pap. 35.00 (*1-85070-772-3*) Prthnon Pub.

Teacher Education for the Future. William Van Til et al. (NSCTE Monographs). 1968. 3.00 (*0-933669-01-1*) Soc Profs Ed.

Teacher Education in America: A Documentary History. Ed. by Merle L. Borrowman. LC 65-17004. 264p. reprint ed. 75.30 (*0-8357-9609-4*, 2016925) Bks Demand.

*__Teacher Education in America: Reform Agendas for the 21st Century.__ Christopher J. Lucas. LC 96-35421. 1997. text ed. 39.95 (*0-312-16444-0*) St Martin.

Teacher Education in Industrialized Nations: Issues in Changing Social Contexts. Ed. by Nobuo K. Shimahara & Ivan Z. Holowinsky. LC 94-30393. (Reference Books in International Education, Vol. 27, Reference Library of Social Science: Vol. 30). 327p. 1995. text ed. 54.00 (*0-8153-1458-2*, SS917) Garland.

Teacher Education in Nepal: Historical & Comprehensive. Kedar N. Shrestha. 55p. 1980. 6.00 (*0-318-12886-1*, 34) Am-Nepal Ed.

Teacher Education in Plural Societies: An International Review. Ed. by Maurice Craft. LC 95-47193. 177p. 1996. 69.95 (*0-7507-0519-1*, Falmer Pr); pap. 24.95 (*0-7507-0520-5*, Falmer Pr) Taylor & Francis.

*__Teacher Education in the Asia-Pacific Region: Systems, Tensions, & Prospects.__ Paul Morris & John Williamson. Ed. by Edward R. Beauchamp. (Reference Books in International Education). 350p. 1998. text ed. 52.00 (*0-8153-1856-1*) Garland.

Teacher Education in the Sixth Five-Year Plan. Kedar N. Shrestha. 57p. 1979. 6.00 (*0-318-12887-X*, 32) Am-Nepal Ed.

Teacher Education in the United States: The Responsibility Gap: A Report. Study Commission on Undergraduate Education & the Education of Teachers Staff. LC 75-34710. 262p. reprint ed. pap. 74.70 (*0-7837-1828-4*, 2042028) Bks Demand.

Teacher Education Pipeline: SCDE Enrollments by Race-Ethnicity. 1988. 7.00 (*0-89333-055-8*) AACTE.

Teacher Education Pipeline II. 1991. 10.00 (*0-89333-078-7*) AACTE.

Teacher Education Pipeline Three: SCDE Enrollments by Race, Ethnicity, & Gender. 1994. 15.00 (*0-89333-117-1*) AACTE.

Teacher Education Policy: Narratives, Stories, & Cases. Ed. by Hendrik D. Gideonse. LC 91-23032. (SUNY Series, Frontiers in Education). 349p. (C). 1992. text ed. 64.50 (*0-7914-1055-2*); pap. text ed. 21.95 (*0-7914-1056-0*) State U NY Pr.

Teacher Education Policy: Some Issues Arising from Research & Practice. Ed. by Rob McBride. 304p. 1996. 72.95 (*0-7507-0487-X*, Falmer Pr); pap. 29.95 (*0-7507-0488-8*, Falmer Pr) Taylor & Francis.

Teacher Education Policy in the States. 1993. 25.00 (*0-89333-112-0*) AACTE.

Teacher Education Policy in the States: A 50-State Survey of Legislative & Administrative Actions. 1994. 25.00 (*0-89333-121-X*) AACTE.

Teacher Education Policy in the States: A 50-State Survey of Legislative & Administrative Actions. 1994. 25.00 (*0-89333-128-7*) AACTE.

*__Teacher Education Reform in Russia: Hope & Reality.__ Delbert Long & Roberta Long. Ed. by Edward R. Beauchamp. (Reference Books on International Education). Date not set. text ed. 52.50 (*0-8153-1604-6*) Garland.

Teacher Education Seven: Research & Developments on Teacher Education in the Netherlands. Ed. by J. T. Voorbach et al. viii, 192p. 1992. pap. 31.25 (*90-265-1251-1*) Swets.

Teacher Education Six: Research & Developments on Teacher Education in the Netherlands. Ed. by J. T. Voorbach & L. G. Prick. viii, 184p. 1990. pap. 28.00 (*90-265-1130-2*) Swets.

Teacher Educator's Handbook: Building a Knowledge Base for the Preparation of Teachers. Ed. by Frank B. Murray. (Education Ser.). 763p. text ed. 75.00 (*0-7879-0121-0*) Jossey-Bass.

Teacher Effectiveness & Reading Instruction. Richard D. Robinson. LC 91-31023. (Illus.). 100p. (Orig.). (C). 1991. pap. text ed. 14.95 (*0-927516-25-X*) ERIC-REC.

Teacher Effectiveness Training. Thomas Gordon. 1975. 13.95 (*0-88326-080-8*, Wyden) McKay.

Teacher Evaluation: A Color & Activity Book. Bill Allen et al. LC 76-21433. (Mandala Series in Education). (Illus.). reprint ed. pap. write for info. (*0-8290-2148-5*) Irvington.

Teacher Evaluation: A Comprehensive Guide to New Directions & Practices. Kenneth D. Peterson. (Illus.). 320p. 1995. pap. 29.95 (*0-8039-6244-4*) Corwin Pr.

Teacher Evaluation: Educative Alternatives. Ed. by Andrew Gitlin & John Smyth. (Contemporary Analysis in Education Ser.). 220p. 1989. 65.00 (*1-85000-522-2*, Falmer Pr); pap. 31.00 (*1-85000-523-0*, Falmer Pr) Taylor & Francis.

Teacher Evaluation: Guide to Effective Practice. Anthony J. Shinkfield & Daniel L. Stufflebeam. LC 95-14669. (Evaluation in Education & Human Services Ser.). 424p. (C). 1995. lib. bdg. 115.00 (*0-7923-9581-6*) Kluwer Ac.

Teacher Evaluation: Guide to Effective Practice. Anthony J. Shinkfield. (Evaluation in Education & Human Services Ser.). 424p. (C). 1996. pap. text ed. 49.95 (*0-7923-9674-X*) Kluwer Ac.

Teacher Evaluation: Improvement, Accountability, & Effective Learning. Milbrey McLaughlin & R. Scott Pfeiffer. 176p. (C). 1988. pap. text ed. 17.95 (*0-8077-2890-X*) Tchrs Coll.

Teacher Evaluation: Six Prescriptions for Success. W. James Popham et al. LC 88-19308. 173p. (Orig.). 1988. pap. 14.95 (*0-87120-153-4*, 611-88048) Assn Supervision.

Teacher Evaluation & Merit Pay: An Annotated Bibliography. Compiled by Elizabeth L. Karnes & Donald D. Black. LC 85-27226. (Bibliographies & Indexes in Education Ser.: No. 2). 403p. 1986. text ed. 75.00 (*0-313-24557-6*, KTE/, Greenwood Pr) Greenwood.

Teacher Evaluation Handbook. Renfro C. Manning. 224p. 1988. 27.95 (*0-13-888389-0*) P-H.

Teacher Evaluation Policy: From Accountability to Professional Development. Ed. by Daniel L. Duke. LC 95-11832. (SUNY Series, Educational Leadership). 203p. 1995. text ed. 57.50 (*0-7914-2791-9*) State U NY Pr.

Teacher Evaluation Policy: From Accountability to Professional Development. Ed. by Daniel L. Duke. LC 95-11832. (SUNY Series, Educational Leadership). 203p. (C). 1995. pap. text ed. 18.95 (*0-7914-2792-7*) State U NY Pr.

Teacher Expectancies. Ed. by Jerome B. Dusek et al. (Psychology of Teaching & Instruction Ser.). 408p. (C). 1985. 79.95 (*0-89859-443-X*) L Erlbaum Assocs.

Teacher Expectations & Low-Achieving Students. Barbara Smey-Richman. 45p. 1989. pap. 10.95 (*1-56602-029-8*) Research Better.

Teacher Facilitator: A Doable Journal for Professional Self-Development. Marilyn Gerstner-Horvath. Ed. by Jane H. Combs. (Illus.). 100p. 1991. student ed. 7.95 (*0-9625440-1-9*) Longmuir Jones Pub.

Teacher Fellowships, Scholarships & Awards. Jackie Ferguson. 1994. spiral bd. 39.00 (*1-56925-021-9*, TFSA) Capitol Publns.

Teacher from Outer Space. Justine Korman. LC 93-24846. (Illus.). 32p. (J). (gr. 1-4). 1993. pap. text ed. 3.50 (*0-8167-3181-0*) Troll Communs.

Teacher from the Black Lagoon. Mike Thaler. 32p. (J). (gr. 1-4). 1989. pap. 2.99 (*0-590-41962-5*) Scholastic Inc.

Teacher Guide & Poem: The Courtship of Miles Standish, The Puritan Pastoral, by Henry Wadsworth Longfellow: For Use in Principle Approach Teaching & Learning of America's Christian History Literature. Elizabeth L. Youmans. (Illus.). 96p. (Orig.). 1994. pap. 13.00 (*0-912498-13-5*) F A C E.

Teacher Guide to "Learn How to Learn" Study Skills. rev. ed. Herman Ohme. Ed. by Jean Ohme. (Illus.). 24p. 1989. pap. 5.00 (*0-936047-02-X*) CA Educ Plan.

Teacher Handbook for Sequencing Math Skills: Grades K-4. (Illus.). 1979. pap. 3.95 (*0-934734-03-8*) Construct Educ.

Teacher Handbook for Symbol Communications Technique (SCT) rev. ed. Alfred W. Munzert. 8p. pap. write for info. (*0-917292-30-8*) H-U Public.

Teacher Idea Book for Reading Today & Tomorrow Level 1. Beck. (Reading Ser.). 1989. teacher ed., pap. 39.75 (*0-15-718271-1*) HB Schl Dept.

Teacher Idea Book for Reading Today & Tomorrow Level 7-8. Beck. (Reading Ser.). 1989. teacher ed., pap. 39.75 (*0-15-718301-7*) HB Schl Dept.

Teacher Idea Book for Reading Today & Tomorrow Level 11. Beck. (Reading Ser.). 1989. teacher ed., pap. 39.75 (*0-15-718321-1*) HB Schl Dept.

Teacher Immortal: The Enduring Influence Of Wilson C. Morris. 120p. 1985. pap. 10.00 (*0-318-17674-2*) Sigma Tau Gamma.

Teacher in America. Jacques Barzun. LC 80-82370. 496p. 1981. reprint ed. 14.00 (*0-913966-78-9*); reprint ed. pap. 6.00 (*0-913966-79-7*) Liberty Fund.

Teacher in America. Jacques Barzun. 328p. (C). 1986. reprint ed. pap. text ed. 28.50 (*0-8191-5447-4*) U Pr of Amer.

Teacher in International Law. Manfred Lachs. 1982. lib. bdg. 120.00 (*90-247-2566-6*) Kluwer Ac.

Teacher in International Law: Teachings & Teaching. 2nd rev. ed. Manfred Lachs. LC 86-2540. 1986. pap. text ed. 75.50 (*90-247-3313-8*) Kluwer Ac.

Teacher in the Catholic School. 2nd ed. Francis Raftery. 61p. 1988. 6.00 (*1-55833-014-3*) Natl Cath Educ.

*__Teacher, Inc. A Private-Practice Option for Educators.__ Janet R. Beales. (Illus.). 24p. (Orig.). 1995. pap. 5.00 (*0-9647703-0-X*, S95-05) Mackinac Ctr Public Pol.

Teacher Induction. Ed. by Judy Reinhartz. 128p. 1989. pap. 14.95 (*0-8106-3003-6*) NEA.

Teacher Induction & Mentoring: School-Based Collaborative Programs. Ed. by Gary P. DeBolt & Greta Marine-Dershimer. (SUNY Series, Educational Leadership). 203p. 1992. pap. text ed. 21.95 (*0-7914-1136-2*) State U NY Pr.

Teacher Induction & Mentoring: School-Based Collaborative Programs. Ed. by Gary P. DeBolt. (SUNY Series, Educational Leadership). 203p. 1992. text ed. 64.50 (*0-7914-1135-4*) State U NY Pr.

Teacher Is a Special Person. Illus. by Jenny Faw. (Hardcover Personals Ser.). 64p. 1996. 6.99 (*0-88088-686-2*) Peter Pauper.

Teacher Is Better Than Two Books. Linda Conway. 168p. (Orig.). 1992. pap. 5.95 (*1-56245-055-7*) Great Quotations.

Teacher Is Many Things. Earl Pullias & James D. Young. LC 68-14612. 314p. reprint ed. pap. 89.50 (*0-8357-6671-3*, 2056849) Bks Demand.

Teacher Is the Key: A Practical Guide for Teaching the Adolescent with Learning Disabilities. Ken Weber. 166p. 1983. pap. 14.95 (*0-89108-117-8*) Love Pub Co.

Teacher Job Satisfaction: An Annotated Bibliography & Guide to Research. Paula Lester. Ed. by Joseph M. McCarthy. LC 88-9768. (Bibliographies in Contemporary Education Ser.: Vol. 7). 362p. 1988. text ed. 59.00 (*0-8240-8922-7*) Garland.

Teacher Jokes. Gary Chmielewski. LC 86-17773. (Smile-a-While Ser.). (Illus.). (J). (gr. 2-3). 1986. 13.27 (*0-86592-688-3*); 9.95 (*0-685-58365-1*) Rourke Corp.

Teacher Jokes. Viki Woodworth. (Funny Side up Ser.). (Illus.). 32p. (J). (gr. 1-4). 1991. lib. bdg. 19.93 (*0-89565-725-2*) Childs World.

Teacher, Kids, & LOGO. Carolyn Green & Christi Jaeger. (Illus.). 160p. 1984. pap. 19.95 (*0-9612226-0-3*) Educomp Pubns.

Teacher Learning: New Policies, New Practices. Ed. by Milbrey W. McLaughlin & Ida Oberman. (Series on School Reform). 264p. (C). 1996. text ed. 51.00 (*0-8077-3495-0*); pap. text ed. 23.95 (*0-8077-3494-2*) Tchrs Coll.

Teacher Learning in Language Teaching. Ed. by Donald A. Freeman & Jack C. Richards. (Language Teaching Library). (Illus.). 378p. (C). 1996. text ed. 49.95 (*0-521-55121-8*); pap. text ed. 22.95 (*0-521-55907-3*) Cambridge U Pr.

Teacher Liability. John D. Williams. (Changing Behavior Through Understanding Ser.). 20p. (Orig.). (C). 1991. pap. text ed. 2.95 (*1-56456-050-3*) W Gladden Found.

Teacher Liability in School-Shop Accidents. rev. ed. Denis J. Kigin. LC 82-61688. 1983. pap. 7.50 (*0-911168-51-6*) Prakken.

Teacher Lore: Learning from Our Own Experience. Ed. by William H. Schubert & William C. Ayers. 164p. (Orig.). (C). 1992. pap. text ed. 26.50 (*0-8013-0796-1*, 78850) Longman.

Teacher-Made Aids for Elementary School Mathematics, Vol. 2: Readings from the Arithmetic Teacher. Ed. by Carole J. Reesink. LC 73-21581. (Illus.). 185p. 1985. pap. 12.00 (*0-87353-225-2*) NCTM.

Teacher-Made Games. 1980. 15.00 (*0-939418-00-2*) Ferguson-Florissant.

Teacher-Manager Systems: Think & Learn & Grow While Nurturing the Human Spirit. Irvine H. Millgate. (Illus.). 412p. 1991. 24.00 (*0-938919-05-9*) Six Lights.

Teacher Manual for Touch-Type Your Computer in Four Hours & Touch 'n Type. Gwen Fouche. 62p. 1990. pap. text ed. 10.00 (*1-56243-008-4*, KP-TM) DDC Pub.

Teacher My Stomach Hurts! A Guide to Student Health Complaints. Daniel D. Stuhlman & Arnold G. Brody. (Teachers Education Ser.: No. 1). (Orig.). 1980. pap. 1.25 (*0-934402-04-3*) BYLS Pr.

Teacher of Advertising & Lettering. D. M. Campana. (Illus.). 8.00 (*0-939608-29-4*) Campana Art.

Teacher of Animal Painting. D. M. Campana. (Illus.). 6.95 (*0-939608-14-6*) Campana Art.

Teacher of Brain Injured Children: A Discussion of the Bases for Competency. Ed. by William M. Cruickshank. LC 66-20050. (Special Education & Rehabilitation Monograph Ser.: No. 7). (C). 1966. 17.95 (*0-8156-2096-9*) Syracuse U Pr.

Teacher of China Painting. D. M. Campana. (Illus.). 9.95 (*0-939608-00-6*) Campana Art.

Teacher of Dante, & Other Studies in Italian Literature. Nathan H. Dole. LC 67-26733. (Essay Index Reprint Ser.). 1977. 18.95 (*0-8369-0383-8*) Ayer.

Teacher of Drawing. D. M. Campana. (Illus.). 12.00 (*0-939608-13-8*) Campana Art.

Teacher of Flower & Fruit Painting. D. M. Campana. (Illus.). 14.95 (*0-939608-03-0*) Campana Art.

Teacher of His Heart. Norbert Nguyen-Van-Khanh. (Franciscan Pathways Ser.). 253p. 1994. pap. 15.00 (*1-57659-066-6*) Franciscan Inst.

Teacher of Jesso-Craft. D. M. Campana. (Illus.). 5.50 (*0-939608-21-9*) Campana Art.

Teacher of Linoleum Block Painting. D. M. Campana. 3.50 (*0-939608-25-1*) Campana Art.

Teacher of Oil Painting. D. M. Campana. (Illus.). 6.60 (*0-939608-07-3*) Campana Art.

Teacher of Pastel Painting. D. M. Campana. (Illus.). 8.45 (*0-939608-09-X*) Campana Art.

Teacher of Picture Frame Finishing. A. M. Campana. (Illus.). 12.95 (*0-939608-12-X*) Campana Art.

Teacher of Pottery, Clay Modeling, Casting, Sculpturing, Wood Carving. D. M. Campana. (Illus.). 5.40 (*0-939608-10-3*) Campana Art.

Teacher of Pottery Made at Home. D. M. Campana. (Illus.). 6.00 (*0-939608-11-1*) Campana Art.

Teacher of Rose Painting. D. M. Campana. (Illus.). 10.95 (*0-939608-01-4*) Campana Art.

Teacher of Textile Painting. D. M. Campana. (Illus.). 3.50 (*0-939608-15-4*) Campana Art.

*__Teacher of the Heart: A Self Health Journey.__ Ed. by Carrie Chesnic. LC 97-72310. (Illus.). 240p. (Orig.). 1997. pap. 24.00 (*1-887747-08-7*) Legendary Pub.

Teacher of the Year. Joe David. LC 96-85521. 196p. 1996. pap. 9.95 (*0-939360-03-9*) Bks for All Times.

Teacher of Water Color Painting. D. M. Campana. (Illus.). 7.60 (*0-939608-08-1*) Campana Art.

Teacher, Oh Teacher. Jerry Patterson. 180p. 1988. pap. 8.95 (*0-89697-300-X*) Intl Univ Pr.

Teacher on Roller Skates & Other School Riddles. David A. Adler. LC 89-1929. (Illus.). 64p. (J). (gr. 1-4). 1989. lib. bdg. 13.95 (*0-8234-0775-6*) Holiday.

Teacher on the Wards. large type ed. Margaret Lovell. (Linford Romance Library). 272p. 1993. pap. 15.99 (*0-7089-7471-6*, Trailtree Bookshop) Ulverscroft.

Teacher-Parent Partnerships Handbook. Ed. by Ellen Meyers. (Illus.). 64p. 1989. pap. 10.95 (*0-939229-02-1*) Teachers Ntwrk.

Teacher-Parent Partnerships to Enhance School Success in Early Childhood Education. Kevin J. Swick. 144p. 1991. pap. 15.95 (*0-8106-0363-2*) NEA.

Teacher-Parent Relationships. Jeannette G. Stone. LC 87-62636. 40p. 1987. pap. 3.50 (*0-935989-10-2*, NAEYC #226) Natl Assn Child Ed.

*__Teacher Pay & Teacher Quality.__ Dale Ballou & Michael J. Podgursky. LC 96-39941. (C). 1997. pap. text ed. 15.00 (*0-88099-176-3*) W E Upjohn.

*__Teacher Pay & Teacher Quality.__ Dale Ballou & Michael Podgursky. LC 96-39941. (C). 1997. text ed. 25.00 (*0-88099-177-1*) W E Upjohn.

Teacher Personal Theorizing: Connecting Curriculum, Practice, Theory, & Research. Ed. by E. Wayne Ross et al. LC 91-27209. (SUNY Series, Teacher Preparation & Development). 324p. (C). 1992. text ed. 64.50 (*0-7914-1125-7*); pap. text ed. 21.95 (*0-7914-1126-5*) State U NY Pr.

Teacher Planning Guide, Units 1 & 2. (Networks Ser.). (J). (gr. 1). 1991. 27.50 (*0-88106-702-4*, N112) Charlesbridge Pub.

Teacher Planning Guide, Units 3 & 4. (Networks Ser.). (J). (gr. 1). 1991. 27.50 (*0-88106-719-9*, N132) Charlesbridge Pub.

Teacher Planning Guide, Units 5 & 6. (Networks Ser.). (J). (gr. 2). 1991. 27.50 (*0-88106-740-7*, N212) Charlesbridge Pub.

Teacher Planning Guide, Units 7 & 8. (Networks Ser.). (J). (gr. 2). 1991. 27.50 (*0-88106-754-7*, N232) Charlesbridge Pub.

Teacher Planning Guide, Units 9 & 10. (Networks Ser.). (J). (gr. 3). 1991. 27.50 (*0-88106-771-7*, N312) Charlesbridge Pub.

Teacher Planning Guide, Units 11 & 12. (Networks Ser.). (J). (gr. 3). 1991. 27.50 (*0-88106-785-7*, N332) Charlesbridge Pub.

Teacher Pleaser: 10,000 Instant Activities for the Jewish Classroom. Marji Gold-Vukson. LC 91-70051. (Illus.). 104p. (Orig.). 1991. pap. text ed. 16.50 (*0-86705-025-X*) A R E Pub.

Teacher Politics: The Influence of Unions. Maurice R. Berube. LC 87-29546. (Contributions to the Study of Education Ser.: No. 26). 192p. 1988. text ed. 49.95 (*0-313-25685-3*, BTH/, Greenwood Pr) Greenwood.

Teacher Portfolio: A Strategy for Professional Development & Evaluation. James E. Green & Sheryl O. Smyser. LC 95-61713. 150p. 1995. pap. text ed. 29.95 (*1-56676-371-1*) Technomic.

Teacher Portfolios: Literacy Artifacts & Themes. Rogers & Danielson. LC 96-28883. 1996. pap. text ed. 27.50 (*0-435-08881-5*) Heinemann.

Teacher Preparation for Early Childhood Education. Ed. by Roy Evans & Olivia N. Saracho. LC 92-23011. (Special Aspects of Education Ser.: Vol. 15). 248p. 1993. text ed. 58.00 (*2-88124-882-9*) Gordon & Breach.

*__Teacher Preparation for Health Education.__ (Technical Report Ser.: No. 193). 19p. 1960. pap. text ed. 5.00 (*92-4-120193-2*) World Health.

Teacher Professional Development: A Multiple Perspective Approach. Ed. by Lya Kremer-Hayon et al. LC 92-27542. xii, 320p. 1992. pap. 48.75 (*90-265-1295-3*) Swets.

Teacher Renewal: Professional Issues, Personal Choices. Ed. by Francis S. Bolin & Judith McConnell-Falk. 240p. (C). 1986. pap. 19.95 (*0-8077-2822-5*) Tchrs Coll.

Teacher Research: From Promise to Power. Leslie Patterson et al. LC 90-36504. 123p. (Orig.). (C). 1991. pap. text ed. 12.95 (*1-878450-09-3*) R Owen Pubs.

Teacher Research & Educational Reform. Ed. by Sandra Hollingsworth & Hugh Sackett. 294p. 1994. 28.00 (*0-226-60163-3*) U Ch Pr.

*__Teacher Research & School Improvement: Opening Doors from the Inside.__ Rob Halsall. LC 97-23229. 1997. write for info. (*0-335-19953-4*, Open Univ Pr); pap. write for info. (*0-335-19952-6*, Open Univ Pr) Taylor & Francis.

Teacher Research & Special Educational Needs. Ed. by Graham Vulliamy & Rosemary Webb. 208p. 1992. pap. 29.95 (*1-85346-187-3*, Pub. by D Fulton UK) Taylor & Francis.

Teacher Research & Urban Literacy Education: Lessons & Conversations in a Feminist Key. Sandra Hollingsworth et al. LC 93-48148. 272p. (C). 1994. text ed. 48.00 (*0-8077-3364-4*); pap. text ed. 25.95 (*0-8077-3363-6*) Tchrs Coll.

Teacher Resource Book for HBJ & Holt: Level 1-3. Harcourt Brace Staff. 1986. teacher ed. 56.25 (*0-15-395655-0*) HB Schl Dept.

Teacher Resource Kit. L. Petersen. 1992. 14.95 (*0-7935-1230-1*, 00860100) H Leonard.

Teacher Retirement System of Texas: Survey of Annuitants & State Teacher Retirement Systems. Contrib. by Lodis Rhodes. (Policy Research Project Report: No. 79). 75p. 1986. pap. 8.00 (*0-89940-683-1*) LBJ Sch Pub Aff.

Teacher Self-Assessment: A Means for Improving Classroom Instruction. Gerald D. Bailey. 72p. 1985. pap. 7.95 (*0-8106-1687-4*) NEA.

Teacher Self-Evaluation: Teachers in Their Own Mirror-Aspects of Self-Evaluation. Lya H. Kremer. LC 93-1614. (Evaluation in Education & Human Services Ser.). 1993. lib. bdg. 93.00 (*0-7923-9366-X*) Kluwer Ac.

*__Teacher Self-Evaluation Tool Kit.__ Peter W. Airasian & Arlen R. Gullickson. (Illus.). 96p. 1996. 39.95 (*0-8039-6516-8*); pap. 19.95 (*0-8039-6517-6*) Corwin Pr.

Teacher Skills & Strategies. Peter Woods. 232p. 1990. 75.00 (1-85000-732-2, Falmer Pr); pap. 33.00 (1-85000-733-0, Falmer Pr) Taylor & Francis.

*Teacher Smart! 125 Tested Techniques for Classroom Management & Control. George Watson. 256p. 1996. pap. 28.50 (0-87628-913-8) Ctr Appl Res.

Teacher Smart! 125 Tested Techniques for Classroom Management & Control. George Watson. 256p. 1996. spiral bd. 28.95 (0-87628-910-3) P-H.

Teacher Socialisation: The Individual in the System. Ed. by Jennifer Nias. 151p. (C). 1986. 60.00 (0-7300-0399-X, Pub. by Deakin Univ AT) St Mut.

Teacher Stories: Teaching Archetypes Revealed by Analysis. Marguerite H. Nelson. 122p. (Orig.). 1993. pap. text ed. 10.40 (0-911168-86-9) Prakken.

Teacher Supervision That Works: A Guide for University Supervisors. Debra J. Anderson et al. LC 91-39696. 184p. 1992. text ed. 42.95 (0-275-94264-3, C4264, Praeger Pubs) Greenwood.

Teacher Supply & Teacher Quality: Issues for the 1990s. Ed. by Gerald Grace & Martin Lawn. 100p. 1991. 59.00 (1-85359-156-4, Pub. by Multilingual Matters UK); pap. 19.95 (1-85359-155-6, Pub. by Multilingual Matters UK) Taylor & Francis.

Teacher Supply, Demand, & Quality: Policy Issues, Models, & Data Bases. National Research Council Staff. Ed. by Erling E. Boe & Dorothy M. Gifford. LC 92-50735. 344p. (C). 1992. pap. text ed. 44.00 (0-309-04792-7) Natl Acad Pr.

Teacher Survey NEA Report: Computers in the Classroom. National Education Association of the United States Staff. 98p. reprint ed. pap. 28.00 (0-317-55509-X, 2029543) Bks Demand.

Teacher Survey on Safe, Disciplined, & Drug-Free Schools. 51p. (Orig.). (C). 1993. pap. text ed. 20.00 (0-7881-0166-8) DIANE Pub.

Teacher Survival Training Guide. Marvin Silverman. 95p. (Orig.). 1989. pap. write for info. (0-318-65280-3) AFE&I.

*Teacher Talk. Eldridge. LC 97-19607. 1997. pap. text ed. 24.95 (0-205-26762-9) P-H.

Teacher Talk: Notes from the Teacher. ICB Staff. (Love Notes Ser.). (Illus.). 112p. (Orig.). (J). (ps-5). 1995. per., pap. 5.95 (1-57102-052-7, Ideals Child) Hambleton-Hill.

Teacher Talk: What It Really Means. Chick Moorman & Nancy Moorman-Weber. 160p. 1989. pap. 12.95 (0-9616046-2-X) Prsnl Power Pr.

*Teacher, Teacher. Elma Solo. (Illus.). 201p. (Orig.). 1995. pap. 11.99 (0-9654708-0-6) E Solo.

Teacher, Teacher! Did You Know... Jo A. Spiceland. 1995. pap. text ed. 12.95 (0-913383-39-2) McClanahan Pub.

Teacher-Tested Timesavers. Imogene Forte. (Illus.). 128p. 1989. pap. text ed. 10.95 (0-86530-066-6, IP 166-3) Incentive Pubns.

Teacher, the Children Are Here: A Guide for Teachers of the Elementary Grades. Diane Appleman & Johanna McClear. (Illus.). 180p. (Orig.). 1988. pap. 9.95 (0-673-38001-7, GoodYrBooks) Addson-Wesley Educ.

Teacher Thinking & Professional Action. Ed. by J. Lowyck & C. Clark. (Studia Paedagogica: No. 9). 418p. (Orig.). 1989. pap. 63.50 (90-6186-349-X, Pub. by Leuven Univ BE) Coronet Bks.

Teacher Thinking & the Case Method: Theory & Future Directions. Amy R. McAninch. LC 93-18207. 160p. (C). 1993. text ed. 23.00 (0-8077-3243-5) Tchrs Coll.

Teacher Thinking in Cultural Contexts. Ed. by Francisco A. Rios. LC 95-51310. (SUNY Series, the Social Context of Education). 400p. 1996. text ed. 59.50 (0-7914-2881-8); pap. text ed. 19.95 (0-7914-2882-6) State U NY Pr.

Teacher Time-Savers. Stevan Krajnjan. 80p. 1996. teacher ed. 10.99 (1-56417-847-1, GA1554) Good Apple.

Teacher to Teacher: Strategies for the Elementary Classroom. Ed. by Mary W. Olson & Susan P. Homan. 256p. 1993. pap. 24.95 (0-87207-382-3) Intl Reading.

*Teacher to Teacher: The Power of Questioning in Teaching & Learning. Eleanor Duckworth & Experienced Teachers Group Staff. 290p. (Orig.). 1997. pap. text ed. 19.95 (0-8077-3652-X) Tchrs Coll.

*Teacher to Teacher: The Power of Questioning in Teaching & Learning. Eleanor Duckworth & Experienced Teachers Group Staff. 290p. 1997. text ed. 42.00 (0-8077-3653-8) Tchrs Coll.

Teacher Today. Organization for Economic Cooperation & Development Staff. 140p. (Orig.). 1991. pap. 20.00 (92-64-13413-1) OECD.

Teacher Trainer Handbook: Professional Development Workshops. Ed. by Jerold M. Starr. 134p. 1994. pap. text ed. 29.95 (0-945919-20-4) Ctr Social Studies.

*Teacher Training: Status & Participants' Views of Delta Teachers Academy. 21p. (Orig.). (C). 1996. pap. 20.00 (0-7881-3105-2) DIANE Pub.

Teacher Training Manual - Cosmetology. Jacob J. Yahm. (Cosmetology Ser.). 1977. teacher ed., wbk. ed. 22.95 (0-87350-441-0) Van Nos Reinhold.

Teacher-Training Program for Ohio. Alonzo F. Myers. LC 70-177049. (Columbia University. Teachers College. Contributions to Education Ser.: No. 266). reprint ed. 37.50 (0-404-55266-8) AMS Pr.

Teacher Tricks. 2nd ed. Douglas L. Simmons. 32p. (C). 1991. pap. text ed. 4.00 (0-9627728-2-8) Brite-Idea.

Teacher Trouble. Paul Hutchens. (Sugar Creek Gang Ser.: Vol. 9). (J). (gr. 2-7). 1970. mass mkt., pap. 3.99 (0-8024-4811-9) Moody.

*Teacher Trouble. Paul Hutchens. (Sugar Creek Gang Ser.: No. 11). (J). 1997. mass mkt. 4.99 (0-8024-7015-7) Moody.

Teacher Trouble. Linda J. Singleton. (My Sister, the Ghost Ser.: No. 3). 128p. (Orig.). (J). 1996. pap. 3.50 (0-380-77895-5, Camelot) Avon.

Teacher Turnover in the Cities & Villages of New York State. Willard S. Elsbree. LC 75-176750. (Columbia University. Teachers College. Contributions to Education Ser.: No. 300). reprint ed. 37.50 (0-404-55300-1) AMS Pr.

Teacher Unions & TQE: Building Quality Labor Relations. William A. Streshly & Todd A. DeMitchell. LC 94-386. (Total Quality Education for the World's Best Schools Ser.: Vol. 6). 120p. 1994. pap. 18.00 (0-8039-6090-5) Corwin Pr.

Teacher Views on Language Arts Instruction. Ed. by June R. Gilstad. 63p. (Orig.). 1988. pap. 5.50 (0-939132-03-6) Hermione Hse.

Teacher Who Came to Rivertown: A Case Study. Ed. by Judith Kleinfeld. (Teaching Cases in Cross-Cultural Education Ser.). 64p. (C). 1989. pap. text ed. 7.50 (1-877962-08-2) Univ AK Ctr CCS.

Teacher Who Couldn't Read. John Corcoran & C. C. Carlson. LC 94-9250. 1994. 15.99 (1-56179-249-7); audio 15.99 (1-56179-250-0) Focus Family.

*Teacher with an Attitude: Only You Prevent Education! David Blomstrom. Ed. by Jay Lane. LC 96-94827. (Illus.). 324p. (Orig.). 1996. pap. 15.95 (0-9646777-1-7) Geobopological.

Teacher Zone. Kimberly Chambers. Ed. by Patrick Caton. 365p. 1996. 6.50 (1-56245-235-5) Great Quotations.

Teachers. Charles Hodge. 195p. (Orig.). 1991. pap. write for info. (0-945441-05-3) Res Pubns AR.

Teachers. Herbert I. Kavet. 48p. 1993. 8.95 (0-88032-365-5) Ivory Tower Pub.

Teachers: A Survival Guide for the Grown-up in the Classroom. Norma Peterson. 144p. 1985. mass mkt. 6.95 (0-452-25741-7, Plume) NAL-Dutton.

Teachers: A to Z. Jean Johnson. (Walker's Community Helpers Ser.). (Illus.). (J). (gr. 1-3). 1987. 11.95 (0-8027-6676-5); lib. bdg. 12.85 (0-8027-6677-3) Walker & Co.

Teachers: A Tribute. (Little Gift Bks.). (Illus.). 80p. 1996. 4.95 (0-8362-1056-5) Andrews & McMeel.

Teachers: Economic Growth & Society. Ed. by Mary Frank. LC 84-6621. (Journal of Children in Contemporary Society: Vol. 16, Nos. 3-4). 185p. 1984. text ed. 44.95 (0-86656-286-9) Haworth Pr.

*Teachers: Talking Out of School. Catherine Collins & Douglas Frantz. 260p. 3.98 (0-8317-7060-0) Smithmark.

Teachers: The Culture & Politics of Work. Ed. by Martin Lawn & G. Grace. 225p. 1987. 60.00 (1-85000-216-9, Falmer Pr); pap. 33.00 (1-85000-217-7, Falmer Pr) Taylor & Francis.

Teachers: The Missing Voice in Education. Marilyn M. Cohn & Robert B. Kottkamp. LC 92-14008. (SUNY Series, Teacher Preparation & Development). 358p. (C). 1992. pap. 24.95 (0-7914-1342-X) State U NY Pr.

Teachers: The Missing Voice in Education. Marilyn M. Cohn & Robert B. Kottkamp. LC 92-14008. (SUNY Series, Teacher Preparation & Development). 358p. (C). 1992. text ed. 74.50 (0-7914-1341-1) State U NY Pr.

Teachers - Their World & Their Work: Implications for School Improvement. Ann Lieberman & Lynne Miller. 160p. (C). 1991. reprint ed. pap. text ed. 14.95 (0-8077-3165-X) Tchrs Coll.

Teacher's A-B-C's. L. Kim Jones. LC 91-90285. 64p. 1991. 8.95 (0-9629476-0-1) L K Jones.

Teachers Across Texas. Katz. Date not set. pap. text ed. write for info. (0-314-04628-3) West Pub.

Teacher's Activity. 1993. pap. 12.95 (0-590-49010-9) Scholastic Inc.

Teacher's Aid: Research Notekeeping & Analysis of Evidence. Arlene H. Eakle. 77p. 1988. pap. 48.00 incl. trans. (0-940764-40-7) Genealog Inst.

Teacher's Almanac: The Professional Teacher's Handbook. Pat Woodward. LC 96-53318. 192p. 1997. pap. 15.00 (1-56565-468-4) Lowell Hse.

Teacher's Almanac, 1988-89. Ed. by Sherwood Harris & Lorna B. Harris. LC 87-647888. 320p. reprint ed. pap. 91.20 (0-8357-3492-7, 2039751) Bks Demand.

Teachers & Crisis: Urban School Reform & Teachers' Work Culture. Dennis Carlson. 320p. (Orig.). 1992. pap. 15.95 (0-685-50333-X, A4269, Routledge NY) Routledge.

Teachers & Crisis: Urban School Reform & Teachers' Work Culture. Dennis Carlson. (Critical Social Thought Ser.). 320p. (C). 1992. pap. 16.95 (0-415-90270-3) Routledge Chapman & Hall.

Teachers & Educators. Harlow G. Unger. LC 94-8628. (American Profiles Ser.). 144p. (J). 1994. 17.95 (0-8160-2990-3) Facts on File.

Teachers & Goals 2000: Leading the Journey Toward High Standards for All Students. Kirk Winters. (Illus.). 75p. (Orig.). (C). 1996. pap. text ed. 25.00 (0-7881-2619-9) DIANE Pub.

Teachers & Librarians Working Together: To Make Students Lifelong Library Users. Barbara H. Sorrow. LC 91-52837. (Illus.). 144p. 1991. pap. 24.95 (0-89950-649-6) McFarland & Co.

Teachers & Machines: The Classroom Use of Technology Since 1920. Larry Cuban. 144p. (C). 1985. pap. text ed. 14.95 (0-8077-2792-X) Tchrs Coll.

Teachers & Mentors: Profiles of Distinguished Twentieth-Century Professors of Education. Ed. by Craig Kridel et al. LC 95-47074. (Source Books on Education: Vol. 48). 312p. 1996. text ed. 50.00 (0-8153-1746-8, SS969) Garland.

Teachers & Nuclear Energy. OECD Staff. 312p. (Orig.). (ENG & FRE.). 1994. pap. 42.00 (92-64-04036-6) OECD.

Teachers & Politics in France: A Pressure Group Study of the Federation de l'Education Nationale. James M. Clark. LC 67-13494. 215p. reprint ed. pap. 61.30 (0-8357-3981-3, 2036679) Bks Demand.

Teachers & Politics in Japan. Donald R. Thurston. LC 72-6525. (Studies of the East Asian Institute, Columbia University). 183p. 1973. text ed. 32.50 (0-691-07553-0) Princeton U Pr.

*Teachers & Research: Language Learning in the Classroom. Ed. by Gay Su Pinnell & Myna L. Matlin. LC 89-15276. 189p. 1989. reprint ed. pap. 53.90 (0-608-03470-3, 2064180) Bks Demand.

Teachers & Research in Action. Ed. by Carol Livingston & Shari Castle. 104p. 1989. pap. 10.95 (0-8106-3004-4) NEA.

Teachers & Scholars: A Memoir of Berkeley in Depression & War. Robert A. Nisbet. 224p. (C). 1992. 39.95 (1-56000-034-1) Transaction Pubs.

*Teachers & Special Educational Needs. 2nd ed. Hinson. 1991. text ed. write for info. (0-582-08673-6, Pub. by Longman UK) Longman.

Teachers & Students Thought Processes. Ed. by Amer. 1990. 15.95 (0-02-897008-X) Macmillan.

Teachers & Teacher Education: Essays on the National Education Goals. Ed. by Marilyn J. Guy. 1993. 20.00 (0-89333-103-1) AACTE.

Teachers & Teacher Education in Developing Countries. Linda A. Dove. 320p. 1986. 45.00 (0-7099-0886-5, Pub. by Croom Helm UK) Routledge Chapman & Hall.

*Teachers & Teacher Education in the United States: Perspectives from Members of the Japanese-United States Teacher Education Consortium: A Special Issue of the "Peabody Journal of Education" Ed. by Allen D. Glenn. 236p. 1997. pap. write for info. (0-8058-9873-5) L Erlbaum Assocs.

Teachers & Teaching: From Classroom to Reflection. Ed. by Tom Russell & Hugh Munby. 224p. 1992. 80.00 (0-7507-0020-3, Falmer Pr); pap. 29.00 (0-7507-0021-1, Falmer Pr) Taylor & Francis.

Teachers & Teaching in the Developing World. Val D. Rust & Per Dalin. LC 89-27603. (Reference Books in International Education: Vol. 8). 398p. 1990. reprint ed. text ed. 63.00 (0-8240-3532-1) Garland.

Teachers & Technology: Making the Connection. (Illus.). 292p. (Orig.). (C). 1995. pap. text ed. 40.00 (0-7881-2503-6) DIANE Pub.

Teachers & Technology: Making the Connection. 1996. lib. bdg. 250.99 (0-8490-6894-0) Gordon Pr.

Teachers & Technology: Staff Development for Tomorrow's Schools. Ed. by Bobby Goodson & Anne Ward. 184p. (Orig.). 1991. pap. text ed. 35.00 (0-88364-161-5) Natl Sch Boards.

Teachers & Television. Ernest Chaot et al. 256p. 1987. text ed. 49.50 (0-7099-4819-0, Pub. by Croom Helm UK) Routledge Chapman & Hall.

Teachers & Testing. David A. Goslin. LC 67-25912. 202p. 1967. 24.95 (0-87154-358-3) Russell Sage.

Teachers & Texts: A Political Economy of Class & Gender Relations in Education. Michael W. Apple. 259p. (C). 1988. pap. 12.95 (0-415-90074-3, Routledge NY) Routledge.

Teachers & the Economy. Gerald Burke. 132p. (C). 1985. 59.00 (0-7300-0373-6, Pub. by Deakin Univ AT) St Mut.

Teachers & the Law. 4th ed. Louis Fischer et al. LC 94-2952. 480p. (C). 1995. pap. text ed. 39.95 (0-8013-1271-X) Longman.

Teachers & the Politics of Gender 1850-1914: A Study of Scottish & English Education. Helen Corr. 1995. text ed. 29.50 (0-7130-0173-9, Pub. by Woburn Pr UK); text ed. write for info. (0-7130-4013-0, Pub. by Woburn Pr UK) Intl Spec Bk.

Teachers & Their Workplace: Commitment, Performance, & Productivity. Ed. by Pedro Reyes. LC 90-32183. 320p. 1990. 49.95 (0-8039-3688-5, 36885) Corwin Pr.

Teachers & Their Workplace: Commitment, Performance, & Productivity. Ed. by Pedro Reyes. (Focus Editions Ser.: Vol. 122). (Illus.). 320p. (C). 1990. pap. 24.95 (0-8039-3689-3) Corwin Pr.

Teachers & Trainers in Vocational Training Vol. 1: Germany, Spain, France, & U. K. European Commission Staff. 190p. 1995. pap. 14.00 (92-827-4081-1, HX-88-95-961ENC, Pub. by Europ Com UK) Bernan Associates.

Teachers & Writers Guide to Frederick Douglass. Ed. & Pref. by Wesley Brown. (Illus.). 128p. (Orig.). 1995. pap. 11.95 (0-915924-46-3) Tchrs & Writers Coll.

Teachers & Writers Guide to Walt Whitman. Ed. by Ron Padgett. (Illus.). 224p. (Orig.). 1991. pap. 13.95 (0-915924-36-6) Tchrs & Writers Coll.

Teachers & Writers Handbook of Poetic Forms. Ed. by Ron Padgett. 230p. (J). 1987. 22.95 (0-915924-24-2); pap. 13.95 (0-915924-23-4) Tchrs & Writers Coll.

Teachers & Writers Magazine: An Index of the First 22 Years. Elizabeth Fox et al. 48p. (Orig.). 1990. pap. 8.95 (0-915924-18-8) Tchrs & Writers Coll.

Teacher's Answer Key to Accompany Legal Research & Citation Student Library Exercises. Larry L. Teply. (American Casebook Ser.). 1044p. (C). 1992. pap. text ed. write for info. (0-314-01049-1) West Pub.

Teacher's Appreciation Book of Wit & Wisdom. Compiled by Anna Trimiew. 96p. 1996. mass mkt. 5.99 (0-87788-802-7) Shaw Pubs.

Teachers Are First Class. Anthony P. Witham. 366p. 1994. spiral bd., pap. 8.95 (1-56245-045-X) Great Quotations.

Teachers Are Researchers: Reflection & Action. Ed. by Leslie Patterson et al. 248p. 1993. pap. 27.95 (0-87207-748-9) Intl Reading.

Teachers As Agents of Change: A New Look at School Improvement. Allan A. Glatthorn. LC 92-26974. (School Restructuring Ser.). 208p. 1993. pap. 16.95 (0-8106-1853-2) NEA.

Teachers As Collaborative Learners: Challenging Dominant Forms of Supervision. John Smyth. (Developing Teachers & Teaching Ser.). 160p. 1991. 90.00 (0-335-09588-7, Open Univ Pr); pap. 32.00 (0-335-09587-9, Open Univ Pr) Taylor & Francis.

Teachers As Course Developers. Ed. by Kathleen Graves. (Cambridge Language Education Ser.). 240p. (C). 1996. text ed. 44.95 (0-521-49722-1); pap. text ed. 17.95 (0-521-49768-X) Cambridge U Pr.

*Teachers As Cultural Workers: Letters to Those Who Dare Teach. Paulo Freire. (Edge: Critical Studies in Education Theory Ser.). 1997. text ed. 22.95 (0-8133-2304-5) Westview.

Teachers As Curriculum Planners: Narratives of Experience. F. Michael Connelly & Jean D. Clandinin. 240p. (C). 1988. text ed. 32.95 (0-8077-2907-8); pap. text ed. 18.95 (0-8077-2906-X) Tchrs Coll.

Teachers As Intellectuals: Toward a Critical Pedagogy of Learning. Henry A. Giroux. LC 88-10433. (Critical Studies in Education). 288p. 1988. text ed. 55.00 (0-89789-157-0, Bergin & Garvey); pap. text ed. 16.95 (0-89789-156-2, Bergin & Garvey) Greenwood.

Teachers as Leaders: Evolving Roles. Carol Livingston. 176p. 1992. pap. 15.95 (0-8106-1848-6) NEA.

Teachers as Learners: Exemplary Teachers' Perception of Personal & Professional Development. Vivienne Collinson. LC 94-3924. 175p. 1994. 64.95 (1-880921-79-0); pap. 44.95 (1-880921-78-2) Austin & Winfield.

Teachers as Mentors: A Practical Guide. Ed. by Barbara Field & Terry Field. LC 93-47532. 180p. 1994. 75.00 (0-7507-0316-4, Falmer Pr); pap. 29.00 (0-7507-0317-2, Falmer Pr) Taylor & Francis.

Teachers as Researchers: Qualitative Inquiry As a Path to Empowerment. Ed. by Joe L. Kincheloe. (Falmer Press Teachers' Library). 210p. 1991. 55.00 (1-85000-853-1, Falmer Pr); pap. 24.00 (1-85000-854-X, Falmer Pr) Taylor & Francis.

Teachers As Writers. Ed. by George T. Kurian. 339p. 1989. 24.95 (0-914746-26-X) G Kurian.

Teachers at Work: Achieving Success In Our Schools. Susan M. Johnson. LC 89-49694. 416p. 1991. pap. 20.00 (0-465-08363-3) Basic.

Teacher's Bag of Tricks. Patty Nelson. (Illus.). 80p. (J). (gr. 2-6). 1986. pap. text ed. 9.95 (0-86530-132-8) Incentive Pubns.

Teacher's Bible Commentary. Ed. by Hobbs & H. Franklin Paschall. LC 75-189505. 1972. 39.99 (0-8054-1116-X, 4211-16) Broadman.

Teacher's Big Book of Fun. Arnold B. Kanter & Wendy Kanter. (Illus.). 96p. 1996. pap. 9.95 (0-8092-3161-1) Contemp Bks.

Teacher's Book of English Verbs. Sheehan. 1996. pap. text ed. 5.00 (0-13-320227-5) P-H.

Teacher's Book of Lists. Joyce Senn. 1996. pap. 10.95 (0-590-93100-8) Scholastic Inc.

Teacher's Book of Lists. 2nd ed. Sheila Madsen & Bette Gould. (Illus.). 336p. (J). (gr. k-6). 1994. pap. 19.95 (0-673-36074-1, GoodYrBooks) Addson-Wesley Educ.

Teacher's Book of Wit: Quips, Quotes, & Anecdotes to Make Learning More Fun. Mark Orlman. LC 95-61631. 96p. (Orig.). 1996. pap. 8.95 (0-9634699-7-5) Wise Owl Bks & Mus.

Teacher's Book Walk Through. Read. 1990. pap. write for info. (0-395-56840-4) HM.

Teacher's Book Walk Through: Level 3. Houghton Mifflin Company Staff. 1990. pap. write for info. (0-395-56847-1) HM.

Teachers Can Be Fired! The Quest for Quality. Hans A. Andrews. 286p. 1995. 38.95 (0-8126-9280-2); pap. 18.95 (0-8126-9281-0) Open Court.

*Teachers' Career & Promotional Patterns: A Sociological Analysis. Ed. by Robert Maclean. 284p. 1992. 85.00 (0-7507-0000-9, Falmer Pr); pap. 33.00 (0-7507-0001-7, Falmer Pr) Taylor & Francis.

Teacher's Career & Promotional Patterns: A Sociological Analysis. Ed. by Rupert Maclean. 284p. 1991. 55.00 (0-685-50669-X, Falmer Pr); pap. 25.00 (0-685-50670-3, Falmer Pr) Taylor & Francis.

Teacher's Choice. Sandy Terrell & Frank White. (Illus.). 192p. (J). (gr. 4-9). 1992. student ed. 15.99 (0-86653-691-4, 1425) Good Apple.

Teacher's Classroom Companion: A Handbook for Primary Teachers. Mary H. Coons. LC 92-85215. (Illus.). 320p. (Orig.). (J). (ps-3). 1993. per. 24.95 (0-9634938-0-9) Teachers Handbk.

Teachers College Follow-up Service: Its Factors & Development in an Unsupervised Service Area. Effie G. Bathurst. LC 79-176542. (Columbia University. Teachers College. Contributions to Education Ser.: No. 478). reprint ed. 37.50 (0-404-55478-4) AMS Pr.

Teacher's Commentary. Lawrence O. Richards. 1200p. 1987. text ed. 41.99 (0-89693-810-7, 6-2810, Victor Bks) Chariot Victor.

Teacher's Communication Resource Book. P. Susan Mamchak & Steven R. Mamchak. LC 85-16730. 233p. 1986. pap. text ed. 22.95 (0-13-888355-6, Busn) P-H.

*Teacher's Computer Book: Forty Student Projects to Use with Your Classroom Software. Patricia M. Shillingburg et al. LC 86-30130. (Computers & Education Ser.). 160p. 1987. reprint ed. pap. 45.60 (0-608-02757-X, 2063820) Bks Demand.

Teachers, Computers, & Curriculum: Microcomputers in the Classroom. 2nd ed. Paul Geisert & Mynga K. Futrell. LC 94-31004. 1994. pap. text ed. 49.00 (0-205-15627-4) Allyn.

Teachers, Computers & Kids: Recipes for Success in Early Childhood Settings. Suzy Crowe & Elaine Penney. LC 95-79414. (Kids & Computers Ser.). 200p. 1995. ring bd. 24.95 (1-887899-00-6) Bit-By-Bit.

An Asterisk (*) at the beginning of an entry indicates that the title is appearing in BIP for the first time.

Teachers Constructing the Future. Kevin Harris. LC 93-21333. 1994. write for info. (*0-7507-0300-8*, Falmer Pr); pap. write for info. (*0-7507-0301-6*, Falmer Pr) Taylor & Francis.

***Teacher's Daybook: One-A-Day Language Lessons - People at Work.** Lake Editors. LC 95-80019. 192p. 1995. teacher ed., spiral bd. 49.50 (*0-7854-0831-2*, 40271) Am Guidance.

Teacher's Delight. Claudia L. Boysen. (Illus.). 366p. 1992. spiral bd. write for info. (*1-879127-17-2*) Lighten Up Enter.

Teacher's Delights Gift Pack. Date not set. spiral bd. write for info. (*1-879127-39-3*) Lighten Up Enter.

Teacher's Dependency Load. Theresa P. Pyle. LC 79-177172. (Columbia University. Teachers College. Contributions to Education Ser.: No. 782). reprint ed. 37.50 (*0-404-55782-1*) AMS Pr.

Teachers Develop Teachers Research: Papers on Classroom Research & Teacher Development. Ed. by Julian Edge & Keith Richards. LC 94-33271. 197p. 1994. pap. text ed. 26.00 (*0-435-24056-0*, 24056) Heinemann.

Teacher's Dictation Library, 2 pts. Roberta Thomas. 1974. audio 229.95 (*0-89420-212-X*, 139000); audio 289.95 (*0-89420-213-8*, 139300) Natl Book.

Teacher's Dictation Library, 2 pts., Pt. 1. Roberta Thomas. 1974. pap. text ed. 25.95 (*0-89420-064-X*, 139555) Natl Book.

Teacher's Dictation Library, 2 pts., Pt. 2. Roberta Thomas. 1974. pap. text ed. 25.95 (*0-89420-065-8*, 139666) Natl Book.

Teachers Dictation Manual. Allen I. McHose. (Eastman School of Music Ser.). 26.95 (*0-89197-437-7*); pap. text ed. 12.95 (*0-89197-960-3*) Irvington.

Teachers, Discourses, & Authority in the Postmodern Composition Classroom. Xin L. Gale. LC 95-10268. 201p. 1996. text ed. 54.50 (*0-7914-2765-X*); pap. text ed. 17.95 (*0-7914-2766-8*) State U NY Pr.

Teachers Doing Research: Practical Possibilities. Ed. by Gail Burnaford et al. 216p. 1996. pap. 15.95 (*0-8058-2254-2*) L Erlbaum Assocs.

Teacher's Encyclopedia of Behavior Management: 100 Problems/500 Plans. Randall S. Sprick & Lisa M. Howard. (Library: Management, Motivation, & Discipline Ser.). (Illus.). 892p. 1995. pap. text ed. 39.50 (*1-57035-031-0*, 65ENC) Sopris.

Teacher's End. Margery Allingham. 216p. 1993. 18.95 (*1-56723-018-0*) Yestermorrow.

Teachers' Everyday Use of Imagination & Intuition: In Pursuit of the Elusive Image. Virginia M. Jagla. LC 93-42684. (SUNY Series, Teacher Preparation & Development). 218p. (C). 1994. text ed. 57.50 (*0-7914-2097-3*); pap. text ed. 18.95 (*0-7914-2098-1*) State U NY Pr.

Teachers' Favorite Books for Kids. 104p. 1994. pap. 8.00 (*0-87207-389-0*) Intl Reading.

***Teacher's File for Key Stage Three.** 64p. 1995. pap. text ed. 14.95 (*0-521-43888-8*) Cambridge U Pr.

***Teacher's Footbook.** Bronwen Loveday. 1988. pap. text ed. write for info. (*0-582-65992-2*, Pub. by Longman UK) Longman.

Teachers for Our Nation's Schools. John I. Goodlad. LC 90-53090. (Education-Higher Education Ser.). 453p. 1990. text ed. 36.95 (*1-55542-270-5*) Jossey-Bass.

Teachers for Our Nation's Schools. John I. Goodlad. LC 90-53090. (Education-Higher Education Ser.). 454p. reprint ed. pap. 18.95 (*1-55542-663-8*) Jossey-Bass.

Teachers for the New Millennium: Aligning Teacher Development, National Goals, & High Standards for All Students. Ed. by Leonard Kaplan & Roy A. Edelfelt. LC 96-19928. (1-Off Ser.). (Illus.). 240p. 1996. 54.95 (*0-8039-6468-4*); pap. 24.95 (*0-8039-6469-2*) Corwin Pr.

Teacher's Friend. Ella J. Anderson. 1970. pap. 3.10 (*0-87813-905-2*) Christian Light.

Teacher's Friend "Note"book: A Complete Record Keeping System for Teachers to Send Notes Home to Parents. Karen Sevaly & Harry Truax. Ed. by Janet Lovelady. (Illus.). 112p. (Orig.). (J). (ps-8). 1989. Ps-8. pap. 9.95 (*0-943263-12-3*, TF-1401) Teachers Friend Pubns.

Teachers, Gender & Careers. Ed. by Sandra Acker. 250p. 1989. 70.00 (*1-85000-426-9*, Falmer Pr); pap. 32.00 (*1-85000-427-7*, Falmer Pr) Taylor & Francis.

Teacher's Gold Mine II: More Ideas & Activities for Creative Teaching. Dorothy Michener & Beverly Muschlitz. (Illus.). 160p. (Orig.). 1992. pap. text ed. 14.95 (*0-86530-150-6*, 83-9) Incentive Pubns.

Teachers Guide. (Crayola Creativity Ser.). (Illus.). 32p. 1988. 25.00 (*0-86696-213-1*) Binney & Smith.

Teacher's Guide. Marilyn Kile & Kristin Baird. (BodyRights: a DUSO Approach to Preventing Sexual Abuse of Children Ser.). 1986. pap. text ed. 29.95 (*0-88671-174-6*, 7201) Am Guidance.

Teacher's Guide: Classroom Activities for Grades 7-12, A Supplement to The Athabaskans: People of the Boreal Forest. 39p. 1983. pap. 4.00 (*0-685-53779-X*) U Alaska Museum.

Teacher's Guide: Family Issues, Community Issues, Work Issues. Linda Ribaudo & Darlyne Walker. LC 94-5516. (Today's World Ser.). 1994. 10.95 (*1-56420-067-1*) New Readers.

Teacher's Guide: Famous People of Asian Ancestry. Barbara J. Marvis. 48p. 1994. teacher ed., pap. 11.95 (*1-883845-15-7*) M Lane Pubs.

Teacher's Guide: Friends Old & New; My Wonderful World. Linda Swears. Ed. by Sandra Reichenbach. (Growing with Kindermusik Ser.). (Illus.). 170p. (Orig.). 1994. pap. 45.00 (*0-945613-23-7*) Kindermusik Intl.

Teacher's Guide: Music & My Favorite Things; Music & My Animal Friends. Linda Swears & Lorna L. Heyge. Ed. by Kathleen Roulston. (Kindermusik Beginnings Ser.). (Illus.). 126p. (Orig.). 1990. pap. 45.00 (*0-945613-22-9*) Kindermusik Intl.

Teacher's Guide: Music & My Favorite Things; Music & My Animal Friends. Linda Swears & Lorna L. Heyge. Ed. by Kathleen Roulston. (Kindermusik in the Early Years Ser.). (Illus.). 126p. (Orig.). 1994. pap. 45.00 (*0-945613-29-6*) Kindermusik Intl.

Teacher's Guide: Music for Me; Me & My World. Linda Swears & Lorna L. Heyge. Ed. by Kathleen Roulston. (Kindermusik in the Early Years Ser.). (Illus.). 126p. (Orig.). 1994. pap. 45.00 (*0-945613-28-8*) Kindermusik Intl.

Teacher's Guide: Music for Me; Music & My World. Linda Swears & Lorna L. Heyge. Ed. by Kathleen Roulston. (Kindermusik Beginnings Ser.). (Illus.). 126p. (Orig.). 1990. pap. 45.00 (*0-945613-21-0*) Kindermusik Intl.

Teacher's Guide for Advocacy: Using the "Action Kit for Music Education" to Build Community Support. Music Educators National Conference Staff. 48p. (Orig.). (C). 1992. pap. 13.25 (*1-56545-016-7*, 1614) Music Ed Natl.

Teacher's Guide for Beginning Yoga. 2nd ed. Vijayendra Pratap. LC 87-91956. (Illus.). 122p. 1991. pap. 9.95 (*0-944731-00-7*) Sky Fnd.

Teacher's Guide for Children Who Survived the Holocaust. Ed. by Avivah Benamy & Yaffa Eliach. (Education Ser.). (Illus.). 47p. (Orig.). 1988. teacher ed., pap. text ed. 4.95 (*0-9609970-6-7*) Mus Jew Heritage.

***Teachers Guide for First Books: Indians of the Americas, Vol. 1.** Sharon Spencer. 52p. (J). (gr. 4-6). 1995. teacher ed., pap. 4.95 (*0-531-20114-7*) Watts.

***Teachers Guide for First Books: Indians of the Americas, Vol. 2.** Sharon Spencer. 52p. (J). (gr. 4-6). 1995. teacher ed., pap. 4.95 (*0-531-20116-3*) Watts.

Teacher's Guide for Four Seasons Series. Elaine W. Good. (Illus.). 24p. 1995. teacher ed., pap. text ed. 3.95 (*1-56148-152-1*) Good Bks PA.

Teacher's Guide for Graphics for Engineers, No. 1. James H. Earle. 44p. 1984. reprint ed. suppl. ed. 3.50 (*0-932702-72-4*) Creative Texas.

Teacher's Guide for My Values, My Choices. Dorothy L. Williams. (Values & Choices Ser.). 36p. 1991. pap. text ed. 5.00 (*1-57482-211-X*) Search Inst.

Teacher's Guide for Reuben & the Fire. Compiled by Lois E. Lahman. (Illus.). 24p. 1995. teacher ed., pap. 3.95 (*1-56148-140-8*) Good Bks PA.

Teacher's Guide for the First Hebrew Primer. rev. ed. Irene Resnikoff & Ethelyn Simon. 64p. (Orig.). (C). 1992. pap. text ed. 8.95 (*0-939144-17-4*) EKS Pub Co.

Teacher's Guide for Uncle Noel's Fun Fables. Polly Renshaw & Ann Levens. (Illus.). 52p. 1991. student ed. 5.95 (*0-9630734-1-9*) Aesop Systs.

Teacher's Guide to a History of the United States. 32p. 1984. teacher ed. 3.00 (*0-941342-05-0*, 1027) Entry Pub.

***Teacher's Guide to a Jerusalem Mystery.** Aaron Frankel. (Illus.). 24p. (Orig.). 1997. teacher ed., pap. 15.00 (*0-8074-0638-4*, 208046) UAHC.

Teacher's Guide to A Quetzalcoatl Tale of Chocolate, Incl. student work sheets. Illus. by Lynn Castle. 48p. (ENG & SPA.). 8.99 (*0-86653-957-3*, FE0957) Fearon Teach Aids.

Teacher's Guide to A Quetzalcoatl Tale of Corn, Incl. student work sheets. Illus. by Lynn Castle. 48p. (ENG & SPA.). teacher ed. 8.99 (*0-86653-963-8*, FE0963) Good Apple.

Teacher's Guide to Aki & the Banner of Names. Atsuko G. Lolling. (Orig.). 1991. pap. 5.95 (*0-377-00221-6*) Friendship Pr.

Teacher's Guide to Analytic Perception, No. 1. Reuven Feuerstein & Mildred B. Hoffman. (IE Teacher's Guides Ser.). (Illus.). 144p. (Orig.). 1995. pap. 24.95 (*0-932935-97-4*, OTMS13) IRI-SkyLght.

Teacher's Guide to Assessment. Ed. by D. Frith & H. G. Macintosh. (C). 1987. text ed. 45.00 (*0-85950-708-4*, Pub. by S Thornes Pubs UK) St Mut.

Teacher's Guide to Assessment. D. Frith & H. G. Macintosh. 284p. (C). 1988. 70.00 (*0-85950-517-0*, Pub. by S Thornes Pubs UK) St Mut.

Teacher's Guide to Bakk'aatugh Ts'uhuniy: Stories We Live By. Chad Thompson & Helen F. Thompson. vi, 133p. (Orig.). 1989. pap. 8.00 (*1-55500-032-0*) Alaska Native.

Teacher's Guide to Behavioral Interventions: Intervention Strategies for Behavior Problems in the Educational Environment. Kathy K. Wunderlich. 291p. (Orig.). 1988. pap. 26.00 (*1-878372-13-0*) Hawthorne Educ Servs.

Teacher's Guide to Beyond O.K. Win Wenger. (Psychegenic Library of Experiential Protocols). 36p. (Orig.). 1985. pap. 2.00 (*0-931865-05-0*) Psychegenics.

Teacher's Guide to Categorization, No. 1. Reuven Feuerstein & Mildred B. Hoffman. (IE Teacher's Guides Ser.). (Illus.). 112p. (Orig.). 1995. pap. 19.95 (*1-57517-007-8*, OTMS21) IRI-SkyLght.

Teacher's Guide to Choices & Other Stories from the Caribbean. Doris L. Willis. 1993. pap. 5.95 (*0-377-00258-5*) Friendship Pr.

Teacher's Guide to Classroom Management. Daniel L. Duke & Adrienne M. Mekel. 160p. (C). 1984. pap. text ed. write for info. (*0-07-554253-6*) McGraw.

Teacher's Guide to Classroom Management. Elbert M. Hoppenstedt. 268p. 1991. pap. 34.95 (*0-398-06153-X*) C C Thomas.

Teacher's Guide to Classroom Management. Elbert M. Hoppenstedt. 268p. (C). 1991. text ed. 45.95 (*0-398-05718-4*) C C Thomas.

Teacher's Guide to Classroom Research. 2nd ed. David Hopkins. LC 93-16193. 1993. 23.00 (*0-335-19065-0*, Open Univ Pr) Taylor & Francis.

***Teacher's Guide to Cognitive Type Theory & Learning Style.** Carolyn Mamchur. LC 96-45842. (Illus.). 132p. (Orig.). 1996. pap. 22.95 (*0-87120-278-6*, 196275) Assn Supervision.

Teacher's Guide to Comparisons, No. 1. Reuven Feuerstein & Mildred B. Hoffman. (IE Teacher's Guides Ser.). (Illus.). 96p. (Orig.). 1995. pap. 19.95 (*0-932935-98-2*, OTMS14) IRI-SkyLght.

Teacher's Guide to Creating Portfolios for Success in School, Work, & Life. Martin Kimeldorf. (Illus.). 72p. (Orig.). 1994. teacher ed., pap. 12.95 (*0-915793-74-1*) Free Spirit Pub.

Teacher's Guide to Cyberspace. Ed. by Ellen Meyers & Paul McIsaac. (Illus.). 86p. (Orig.). 1996. pap. 19.95 (*0-939229-08-0*) Teachers Ntwrk.

Teacher's Guide to Dancing Threads: Community Dances from Africa to Zuni. 1995. 4.00 (*1-881020-22-3*) KET.

Teacher's Guide to Education Law. Michael Imber & Tyll van Geel. LC 94-33801. 1995. pap. text ed. write for info. (*0-07-031525-6*) McGraw.

Teacher's Guide to Elementary School Physical Education. Norman A. Cochran et al. 496p. (C). 1993. ring bd. 30.39 (*0-8403-9113-7*) Kendall-Hunt.

Teacher's Guide to Eureka! Gordon J. Murray. (Creative Art Ser.). 1995. teacher ed. write for info. (*1-887662-00-6*) Kent St Univ.

Teacher's Guide to Exciting Writing, Successful Speaking: Activities to Make Language Come Alive in the Classroom. Martin Kimeldorf. Ed. by Pamela Espeland. (Free Spirited Classroom Ser.). (Illus.). 112p. (Orig.). 1994. pap. text ed. 19.95 (*0-915793-67-9*) Free Spirit Pub.

Teacher's Guide to Family Relations, No. 1. Reuven Feuerstein & Mildred B. Hoffman. (IE Teacher's Guides Ser.). (Illus.). 128p. (Orig.). 1995. pap. 21.95 (*1-57517-001-9*, OTMS22) IRI-SkyLght.

Teacher's Guide to Folklife Resources for K-12 Classrooms. Ed. by Peter T. Bartis et al. LC 94-14147. (Publications of the American Folklife Center: No. 19). 1994. write for info. (*0-8444-0814-X*) Lib Congress.

Teacher's Guide to Helping Young Children Grow. Erna Furman. LC 87-3197. v, 83p. 1987. teacher ed. 24.95 (*0-8236-6367-1*, BN 06367) Intl Univs Pr.

Teacher's Guide to Holding Steady. Stephen Schwandt. 32p. (Orig.). 1996. teacher ed., pap. 10.95 (*0-915793-95-4*) Free Spirit Pub.

Teacher's Guide to Illustrations, No. 1. Reuven Feuerstein & Mildred B. Hoffman. (IE Teacher Guides Ser.). (Illus.). 112p. (Orig.). 1995. pap. 19.95 (*1-57517-008-6*, OTMS25) IRI-SkyLght.

Teacher's Guide to Including Students with Disabilities in Regular Physical Education. Martin H. Block. LC 93-38428. 288p. 1994. reprint ed. pap. 38.00 (*1-55766-156-1*) P H Brookes.

Teacher's Guide to Instructions, No. 1. Reuven Feuerstein & Mildred B. Hoffman. (IE Teacher Guides Ser.). (Illus.). 144p. (Orig.). 1996. pap. 27.95 (*1-57517-051-5*, OTMS31) IRI-SkyLght.

Teacher's Guide to It's All in Your Head. Susan L. Barrett. Ed. by Pamela Espeland. 52p. (Orig.). 1992. pap. 6.95 (*0-915793-46-6*) Free Spirit Pub.

Teachers Guide to Jewish Holidays: Teacher's Guide. Robert Goodman. LC 83-70197. 224p. 1983. pap. text ed. 22.50 (*0-86705-036-5*) A R E Pub.

Teacher's Guide to Kidspeak. Robert S. Littlefield & Jane A. Ball. (Illus.). 24p. (C). 1991. pap. text ed. 8.95 (*1-879340-09-7*, K0110) Kidspeak.

Teacher's Guide to Learning Styles; A Companion to the Student's Guide: Personal Exploration & Practical Applications. 2nd rev. ed. Kathleen A. Butler. (Illus.). 94p. 1995. teacher ed., pap. text ed. 16.95 (*0-945852-08-8*) Learners Dimension.

***Teachers Guide to Lifetimes.** Bruce Malnor. 48p. (J). (gr. 4-8). 1997. pap. text ed. 7.95 (*1-883220-60-2*) Dawn CA.

Teacher's Guide to Numerical Progressions, No. 1. Reuven Feuerstein & Mildred B. Hoffman. (IE Teacher Guides Ser.). (Illus.). 160p. (Orig.). 1995. pap. 27.95 (*0-932935-99-0*, OTMS24) IRI-SkyLght.

Teacher's Guide to Organization of Dots, No. 1. Reuven Feuerstein & Mildred B. Hoffman. (IE Teacher's Guides Ser.). (Illus.). 176p. (Orig.). 1995. pap. 29.95 (*0-932935-87-7*, OTMS11) IRI-SkyLght.

Teacher's Guide to Orientation in Space, No. 1. Reuven Feuerstein & Mildred B. Hoffman. (Instrumental Enrichment Level I). (Illus.). 96p. (Orig.). 1995. pap. 19.95 (*0-932935-96-6*, OTMS12) IRI-SkyLght.

Teacher's Guide to Orientation in Space II. Reuven Feuerstein & Mildred B. Hoffman. (IE Teacher Guides: Level III). (Illus.). 112p. (Orig.). Date not set. pap. 23.95 (*1-57517-048-5*, OTMS35) IRI-SkyLght.

Teachers Guide to Overseas Teaching: A Complete & Comprehensive Guide of English-Language Schools & Colleges Overseas. 3rd rev. ed. Louis A. Bajkai. LC 77-81788. (Illus.). 192p. 1983. pap. 19.95 (*0-9601550-2-3*) Friends World Teach.

Teacher's Guide to Pearl Makers. Doris Willis. (Illus.). 64p. (Orig.). (J). 1989. pap. 5.95 (*0-377-00194-5*) Friendship Pr.

Teacher's Guide to Performance-Based Learning & Assessment. K. Michael Hibbard et al. LC 96-9979. 294p. (Orig.). 1996. pap. 29.95 (*0-87120-261-1*, 196021) Assn Supervision.

Teacher's Guide to Representation Stencil Design, No. 1. Reuven Feuerstein & Mildred B. Hoffman. (IE Teacher Guides Ser.). (Illus.). 144p. (Orig.). 1996. pap. 31.95 (*1-57517-052-3*, OTMS34) IRI-SkyLght.

Teachers Guide to Silly Trivia Books. Carole Marsh. (Books for Teachers). (Illus.). (Orig.). 1994. teacher ed., pap. 19.95 (*0-935326-91-X*) Gallopade Pub Group.

Teacher's Guide to Special Needs: A Positive Response to the 1981 Education Act. Jonathan Solity & Edward Raybould. 128p. 1988. 80.00 (*0-335-15843-9*, Open Univ Pr); pap. 24.00 (*0-335-15842-0*, Open Univ Pr) Taylor & Francis.

Teacher's Guide to Stick Up for Yourself: A 10-Part Course in Self-Esteem & Assertiveness for Kids. Gerri Johnson et al. 128p. (Orig.). 1991. teacher ed., pap. 16.95 (*0-915793-31-8*) Free Spirit Pub.

Teacher's Guide to Students Shopping for a Better World. Ed. by William Coplin et al. (Illus.). 84p. (Orig.). 1993. pap. text ed. 25.00 (*0-936826-40-1*) PS Assocs Croton.

***Teachers Guide to Surviving after High School: Overcoming Lifes Hurdles.** Arthur J. Heine. 1996. pap. text ed. 19.95 (*0-9628376-2-8*) J-Mart Pr.

Teacher's Guide to Syllogisms, No. 1. Reuven Feuerstein & Mildred B. Hoffman. (IE Teacher Guides Ser.). (Illus.). 160p. (Orig.). 1996. pap. 31.95 (*1-57517-050-7*, OTMS33) IRI-SkyLght.

Teachers' Guide to Teaching Art. Mitchell Terry. 1989. 20.00 (*0-931510-14-7*) Hi Willow.

Teacher's Guide to Teaching BASIC in the Elementary Schools. Elaine David. 1982. 5.95 (*0-318-01731-8*) E David Assoc.

Teacher's Guide to Temporal Relations, No. 1. Reuven Feuerstein & Mildred B. Hoffman. (IE Teacher Guides Ser.). (Illus.). 160p. (Orig.). 1995. pap. 27.95 (*1-57517-000-0*, OTMS23) IRI-SkyLght.

Teachers' Guide to the Commodore Computer: BASIC Programming & Classroom Applications. Susan E. Thrall & Fred A. Springer. LC 84-4737. (Illus.). 135p. reprint ed. pap. 38.50 (*0-8357-8398-7*, 2034672) Bks Demand.

Teacher's Guide to the Constitution. Susan English. Ed. by David Steinecker. 96p. (Orig.). 1987. spiral bd. 16.00 (*0-941342-17-4*) Entry Pub.

Teacher's Guide to the Depositional Environments on San Salvador Island, Bahamas. Gene Hinman. 61p. (Orig.). (C). 1994. pap. text ed. 10.00 (*0-935909-54-0*) Bahamian.

Teacher's Guide to the Government Series. Lynne Glasner & Marilyn Thypin. 32p. (gr. 7-12). 1984. teacher ed. 3.00 (*0-941342-12-3*, 1044) Entry Pub.

Teacher's Guide to the Great American West. Monica Michell. (Illus.). 24p. (Orig.). 1985. pap. 4.95 (*0-935213-09-0*) A M Huntington Art.

***Teacher's Guide to the Information Highway.** LC 96-47998. 1996. 20.00 (*0-13-621558-0*) P-H.

Teacher's Guide to the Institute of Texan Cultures. 2nd ed. Barbara Stanush. (Illus.). 70p. 1985. ring bd. 2.95 (*0-86701-023-1*) U of Tex Inst Tex Culture.

Teacher's Guide to the Last Goodie. Stephen Schwandt. 40p. (YA). (gr. 9 up). 1995. teacher ed., pap. 10.95 (*0-915793-84-9*) Free Spirit Pub.

Teacher's Guide to the Perspectives on History Series. JoAnne W. Deitch. (Illus.). 100p. (Orig.). 1996. ring bd. 25.00 (*1-878668-72-2*) Disc Enter Ltd.

Teacher's Guide to the Psychology of Learning. Michael J. Howe. 254p. 1994. pap. 25.95 (*0-631-13578-2*) Blackwell Pubs.

Teacher's Guide to the Special Educational Needs of Blind & Visually Handicapped Children. Ed. by Sally Mangold. LC 82-4025. 164p. 1982. pap. 24.95 (*0-89128-108-8*) Am Foun Blind.

Teacher's Guide to the U. S. Department of Education. 3rd ed. Terry K. Dozier. 140p. (C). 1996. teacher ed., pap. text ed. 25.00 (*0-7881-2618-0*) DIANE Pub.

Teacher's Guide to Transitive Relations, No. 1. Reuven Feuerstein & Mildred B. Hoffman. (IE Teacher Guides Ser.). (Illus.). 128p. (Orig.). 1996. pap. 24.95 (*1-57517-024-8*, OTMS32) IRI-SkyLght.

Teacher's Guide to United for a Better World. Carol F. Krau. 48p. (Orig.). 1995. teacher ed. 5.95 (*0-377-00296-8*) Friendship Pr.

Teacher's Guide to Your Limitless Inventing Machine. Win Wenger. (Psychegenic Library of Experiential Protocols). 50p. (Orig.). 1986. pap. text ed. 4.00 (*0-931865-08-5*) Psychegenics.

Teacher's Guide Year One. rev. ed. Lorna L. Heyge & Audrey Sillick. Ed. by Kathleen Roulston. (Kindermusik for the Young Child Ser.). (Illus.). 120p. (Orig.). 1994. pap. 45.00 (*0-945613-01-6*) Kindermusik Intl.

Teacher's Guide Year Two. Lorna L. Heyge & Audrey Sillick. Ed. by Kathleen Roulston. (Kindermusik for the Young Child Ser.). (Illus.). 130p. (Orig.). 1988. pap. 45.00 (*0-945613-04-0*) Kindermusik Intl.

Teacher's Handbook. Glisan & Shrum. 1993. pap. 32.95 (*0-8384-4061-4*) Heinle & Heinle.

Teacher's Handbook - Self Esteem. Shaun Hains. Ed. by Diane Parker. LC 92-50909. 60p. 1993. spiral bd. 7.95 (*0-88247-971-7*) R & E Pubs.

Teacher's Handbook for a Functional Behavior-Based Curriculum: Communicable Models & Guides for Classroom Use. Sidney J. Drumheller. LC 72-933. 138p. 1972. pap. 24.95 (*0-87778-036-6*) Educ Tech Pubns.

***Teacher's Handbook of Children's Games: A Guide to Developing Perceptual-Motor Skills.** Marian J. Wirth. 272p. 1996. pap. 16.95 (*0-13-234139-5*) P-H.

***Teacher's Handbook of Multicultural Games Children Play.** Ed. & Illus. by Shannon Murphy. 155p. 1996. teacher ed., per. 21.00 (*0-9630608-9-9*) R Dean Pr.

Teacher's Handbook on Diagnosis & Remediation in Reading. 2nd ed. Eldon E. Ekwall. 496p. 1986. pap. 45.95 (*0-205-08595-4*, H85954) Allyn.

***Teacher's Handbook to Cultural Diversity: Families & the Special Education System.** Beth Harry. 56p. (Orig.). 1996. pap. text ed. 9.95 (*0-8077-3611-2*) Tchrs Coll.

Teachers Handbook to Elementary Social Studies: An Inductive Approach. 2nd ed. Hilda Taba. 1971. pap. text ed. 20.75 (*0-201-07426-5*) Addison-Wesley.

Teacher's Handbook to Susan B. Anthony & Justice for All. Jennifer Spungin. 50p. (Orig.). 1993. ring bd. 19.95 (*1-884281-00-1*) Verbal Images Pr.

An Asterisk (*) at the beginning of an entry indicates that the title is appearing in BIP for the first time.

***Teacher's Handbook to Susan B. Anthony & Justice for All.** Jennifer Spungin. 50p. 1994. ring bd. 10.95 (*1-884281-14-1*) Verbal Images Pr.

Teacher's Handbook to the Longman Latin Readers. Ed. by Gilbert Lawall. 1988. pap. text ed. 13.95 (*0-582-36770-0*, 72542) Longman.

***Teachers Have 9 Lives.** Aaron Hall. 242p. (Orig.). 1997. mass mkt. 4.99 (*1-55197-698-6*, Pub. by Comnwlth Pub CN) Partners Pubs Grp.

***Teachers Help People Learn.** Carol Greene. LC 97-2303. (J). 1997. lib. bdg. write for info. (*1-56766-404-0*) Childs World.

Teachers Helping Teachers: Peer Observation & Assistance. Marvin E. Willerman et al. LC 91-2221. 200p. 1991. text ed. 45.00 (*0-275-93884-0*, C3884, Praeger Pubs) Greenwood.

Teacher's Holiday Helper. Lynn Brisson. Ed. by Sherri Y. Lewis. (Illus.). 96p. (Orig.). 1990. pap. text ed. 9.95 (*0-86530-172-7*, 190-9) Incentive Pubns.

Teacher's Idea Book for Reading Today & Tomorrow. Beck. 1989. teacher ed., pap. 45.75 (*0-15-718391-2*) HB Schl Dept.

Teacher's Idea Book 1: Daily Planning Around the Key Experiences. Michelle Graves. LC 88-35794. 87p. 1989. pap. text ed. 19.95 (*0-931114-80-2*) High-Scope.

***Teacher's Idea Book 2: Planning Around Children's Interests.** M. Graves. (Illus.). 171p. 1996. pap. 25.95 (*1-57379-019-2*) High-Scope.

***Teachers Ideas Book.** Thomas-Cochran. (What a Wonderful World 2 Ser.). 1992. pap. text ed. write for info. (*0-582-90977-5*, Pub. by Longman UK) Longman.

Teachers in Control: Cracking the Code. Martin Powell & Jonathan Solity. 183p. (C). 1990. pap. text ed. 22.95 (*0-415-03668-2*, A4654) Routledge.

Teachers in Developing Countries: A Survey of Employment Conditions. (Illus.). viii, 167p. (Orig.). 1991. pap. 20.25 (*92-2-106441-7*) Intl Labour Office.

Teachers in Developing Countries: Improving Effectiveness & Managing Costs. Ed. by Joseph P. Farrell & Joao B. Oliveira. (EDI Seminar Ser.). 224p. 1993. 11.95 (*0-8213-1792-X*, 11792) World Bank.

Teachers in Germany in the Sixteenth Century: Conditions in Protestant Elementary & Secondary Schools. Charles L. Robbins. LC 74-177195. (Columbia University. Teachers College. Contributions to Education Ser.: No. 52). reprint ed. 37.50 (*0-404-55052-5*) AMS Pr.

Teachers in New Careers: Stories for Successful Transitions. Frances Bastress. LC 84-12647. 240p. 1984. 13.50 (*0-910328-40-4*) Sulzburger & Graham Pub.

Teacher's Inspirations. Ed. by Mac Anderson. 78p. (Orig.). 1990. pap. 7.95 (*0-931089-95-6*) Great Quotations.

Teacher's Introduction to Composition in the Rhetorical Tradition. W. Ross Winterowd & Jack Blum. 129p. 1994. 12.95 (*0-8141-5024-1*) NCTE.

Teacher's Introduction to Philosophical Hermeneutics. Timothy W. Crusius. 105p. 1992. pap. 10.95 (*0-8141-5016-0*) NCTE.

***Teacher's Introduction to Postmodernism.** Ray Linn. (Teacher's Introduction Ser.). 153p. 1996. pap. 12.95 (*0-8141-5009-8*) NCTE.

Teacher's Introduction to Reader-Response Theories. Richard Beach. LC 92-38891. (Teacher's Introduction Ser.). 209p. 1993. pap. 12.95 (*0-8141-5018-7*) NCTE.

Teachers Investigate Their Work: An Introduction to the Methods of Action Research. Herbert Altrichter et al. LC 92-45851. (Investigating Schooling Ser.). (Illus.). 256p. (C). 1993. pap. 18.95 (*0-415-09357-0*, B2451) Routledge.

Teachers, Language & Learning. Ed. by John Hickman & Keith Kimberley. 176p. 1989. pap. 17.95 (*0-415-00089-0*) Routledge.

Teachers' Lesson Plan Book Series. 1994. pap. write for info. (*0-8373-7950-4*) Nat Learn.

Teachers License Examination Passbook Series. Jack Rudman. (Entire Ser.). 1994. pap. write for info. (*0-8373-8000-6*) Nat Learn.

***Teacher's Links: Science Links.** Ait. (Applied Science Ser.). 1998. pap. 100.95 (*0-538-67842-9*) S-W Pub.

Teacher's Little Book of Wisdom. Bob Algozzine. LC 95-15940. 160p. 1995. 5.95 (*1-57034-017-X*) ICS Bks.

***Teacher's Little Instruction Book.** Homer Adams. 1997. pap. text ed. 5.99 (*1-57757-005-7*) Honor Bks OK.

Teachers' Lives & Careers. Ed. by Stephen J. Ball & Ivor F. Goodson. LC 85-4562. (Issues in Education & Training Ser.: Vol. 3). 247p. 1985. pap. 30.00 (*1-85000-029-8*, Falmer Pr) Taylor & Francis.

Teachers Managing Stress & Preventing Burnout: The Professional Health Solution. Yvonne Gold & Robert A. Roth. LC 92-39817. 220p. 1993. 75.00 (*0-7507-0158-7*, Falmer Pr); pap. 25.00 (*0-7507-0159-5*, Falmer Pr) Taylor & Francis.

Teacher's Manual: Companion to Gleason H. Ledyard's Topical Study Outlines. Gleason H. Ledyard. 80p. 1975. pap. text ed. 5.00 (*0-913201-18-9*) Christian Lit.

Teacher's Manual: The SUM Program Curriculum in Medical Transcription. 2nd rev. ed. Linda C. Campbell & Susan M. Turley. 177p. 1992. pap. 95.00 (*0-934385-53-X*) Hlth Prof Inst.

Teacher's Manual see Deutsch Konkret, Level 1

Teacher's Manual see Deutsch Konkret, Level 2

Teachers Manual see Philosophy for Young Thinkers Program

Teacher's Manual for Business Planning. 2nd ed. Franklin A. Gevurtz. (University Casebook Ser.). 153p. 1995. teacher ed., pap. text ed. write for info. (*1-56662-323-5*) Foundation Pr.

Teacher's Manual for Cases & Materials on Evidence. 8th ed. Jon R. Waltz. (University Casebook Ser.). 382p. 1995. pap. text ed. write for info. (*1-56662-322-7*) Foundation Pr.

***Teacher's Manual for Cases & Problems on Remedies.** 2nd ed. Elaine W. Shoben & William M. Tabb. (University Casebook Ser.). 373p. 1996. teacher ed., pap. text ed. write for info. (*1-56662-438-X*) Foundation Pr.

Teacher's Manual for Fundamentals of Modern Real Property Law. 3rd ed. Edward H. Rabin & Roberta R. Kwall. (University Casebook Ser.). 1992. pap. text ed. write for info. (*1-56662-002-3*) Foundation Pr.

Teacher's Manual for Legal Ethics. Deborah L. Rhode. (University Casebook Ser.). 118p. 1995. teacher ed., pap. text ed. write for info. (*1-56662-283-2*) Foundation Pr.

Teachers Manual for Materials on Legislation: Political Language & the Political Process. William D. Popkin. (University Casebook Ser.). 179p. 1993. pap. text ed. write for info. (*1-56662-070-8*) Foundation Pr.

Teacher's Manual for Parent & Community Involvement. Larry E. Decker et al. 96p. (Orig.). 1996. teacher ed., pap. text ed. 17.95 (*0-930388-13-5*) Comm Collaborators.

Teacher's Manual for Product Liability Problems: 1995 Edition for Use in Conjunction with Products Liability & Safety, Cases & Materials. 2nd ed. Paul A. LeBel. (University Casebook Ser.). 241p. 1995. teacher ed., pap. text ed. write for info. (*1-56662-263-8*) Foundation Pr.

***Teacher's Manual for Use with Cases & Materials on Tort Law & Alternatives.** 6th ed. Marc A. Franklin & Robert L. Rabin. (University Casebook Ser.). 234p. 1996. teacher ed., pap. text ed. write for info. (*1-56662-440-1*) Foundation Pr.

Teacher's Manual for Use with Insurance Law & Regulation. 2nd ed. Kenneth S. Abraham. (University Casebook Ser.). Date not set. teacher ed., pap. text ed. write for info. (*0-614-07457-6*) Foundation Pr.

Teacher's Manual for Writing & Analysis in the Law. Helene S. Shapo et al. 163p. 1995. teacher ed., pap. text ed. write for info. (*1-56662-282-4*) Foundation Pr.

Teacher's Manual for 1995 Supplement to Fundamentals of Modern Real Property. 3rd ed. Roberta R. Kwall. (University Casebook Ser.). 79p. 1995. pap. text ed. write for info. (*1-56662-306-5*) Foundation Pr.

Teacher's Manual to Accompany Administrative Law: The American Public Law System, Cases & Materials. 3rd ed. Jerry L. Mashaw et al. 271p. 1993. pap. text ed. write for info. (*0-318-70372-6*) West Pub.

***Teacher's Manual to Accompany California Legal Ethics.** 2nd ed. Richard C. Wydick & Rex R. Perschbacher. (American Casebook Ser.). 260p. 1997. pap. text ed. write for info. (*0-314-22699-0*) West Pub.

***Teacher's Manual to Accompany Cases & Materials on Bankruptcy.** 3rd ed. James J. White & Raymond T. Nimmer. (American Casebook Ser.). 180p. 1996. teacher ed., pap. text ed. write for info. (*0-314-20616-7*) West Pub.

Teacher's Manual to Accompany Cases & Materials on Decedents' Estates & Trusts. 8th ed. Neill H. Alford, Jr. & Joel C. Dobris. (University Casebook Ser.). 229p. 1993. pap. text ed. write for info. (*1-56662-138-0*) Foundation Pr.

Teacher's Manual to Accompany Course Materials on Commercial Paper & Modern Payment Systems. Steve H. Nickles et al. (American Casebook Ser.). 146p. 1993. pap. text ed. write for info. (*0-314-03587-7*) West Pub.

Teacher's Manual to Accompany Criminal Justice: Introductory Cases & Materials. 5th ed. Candace McCoy. 300p. 1993. pap. text ed. write for info. (*1-56662-127-5*) Foundation Pr.

***Teacher's Manual to Accompany Employment Discrimination Law, Cases & Materials.** 2nd ed. Mack A. Player et al. (American Casebook Ser.). 370p. 1997. pap. text ed. write for info. (*0-314-22697-4*) West Pub.

Teacher's Manual to Accompany Family Law. David Westfall. (American Casebook Ser.). 83p. 1993. pap. text ed. write for info. (*0-314-03581-8*) West Pub.

Teacher's Manual to Accompany Kids & the Law. John Gilchrist & Nancy Canfield. 41p. 1994. pap. 5.95 (*0-945896-06-9*) Pro Se Pub.

Teacher's Manual to Accompany Problems & Materials on Professional Responsibility. 6th ed. Thomas D. Morgan & Ronald D. Rotunda. (University Casebook Ser.). 340p. 1995. teacher ed., pap. text ed. write for info. (*1-56662-264-6*) Foundation Pr.

***Teacher's Manual to Accompany Problems in Legal Ethics.** 4th ed. Mortimer D. Schwartz et al. (American Casebook Ser.). 240p. 1997. teacher ed., pap. text ed. write for info. (*0-314-22700-8*) West Pub.

***Teachers' Manual to Accompany Readings & Materials on Tax Policy.** Philip D. Oliver & Fred W. Peel, Jr. (University Casebook Ser.). 1996. teacher ed., pap. text ed. write for info. (*1-56662-435-5*) Foundation Pr.

Teacher's Manual to Accompany Tax Policy: An Introduction & Survey of the Principal Debates. Stephen G. Utz. 28p. 1993. pap. text ed. write for info. (*0-314-02693-2*) West Pub.

Teacher's Manual to Accompany the Criminal Process: Prosecution & Defense Functions. Harry I. Subin et al. 115p. 1993. pap. text ed. write for info. (*0-314-02183-3*) West Pub.

Teacher's Manual to Accompany the First Amendment & the Fifth Estate, Regulation of Electronic Mass Media. 3rd ed. T. Barton Carter et al. 104p. 1993. pap. text ed. write for info. (*1-56662-129-1*) Foundation Pr.

Teacher's Manual to Accompany Torts & Compensation. 2nd ed. Dan B. Dobbs. (American Casebook Ser.). 1050p. 1993. pap. text ed. write for info. (*0-314-02651-7*) West Pub.

Teacher's Manual to Accounting Issues of Lawyers, Teaching Materials. 4th ed. Ted J. Fiflis. (American Casebook Ser.). 121p. (C). 1991. pap. text ed. write for info. (*0-314-92200-8*) West Pub.

Teacher's Manual to Pension & Employee Benefit Law. Bruce A. Wolk & John H. Langbein. (University Casebook Ser.). 208p. 1995. teacher ed., pap. text ed. write for info. (*1-56662-275-1*) Foundation Pr.

Teacher's Manual to the Law & Ethics of Lawyering. 2nd ed. Geoffrey C. Hazard, Jr. et al. (University Casebook Ser.). 292p. 1993. pap. text ed. write for info. (*1-56662-150-X*) Foundation Pr.

Teacher's Marks & Objective Tests As Indices of School Adjustment. Frances Sobel. LC 71-177757. (Columbia University. Teachers College. Contributions to Education Ser.: No. 674). reprint ed. 37.50 (*0-404-55674-4*) AMS Pr.

***Teacher's Mentor: Tips to Accelerate Your Expertise in the Classroom.** Sharon Gentry. 100p. (Orig.). 1997. pap. 9.95 (*0-9657868-0-3*) DYNO Teach.

Teacher's Messages for Report Cards. rev. ed. 1991. 7.99 (*0-8224-6777-1*) Fearon Teach Aids.

Teacher's Messages for Report Cards: English - Spanish Edition. 1991. 10.99 (*0-86653-997-2*) Fearon Teach Aids.

Teacher's Messages for Report Cards: French Edition. 1991. 7.99 (*0-86653-996-4*) Fearon Teach Aids.

Teacher's Night Before Christmas. Sue Carabine. (Illus.). 60p. 1996. 5.95 (*0-87905-764-5*, Peregrine Smith) Gibbs Smith Pub.

Teacher's Notes for Criminal Law: Cases, Comments, Questions. 5th ed. Lloyd L. Weinreb. (University Casebook Ser.). 99p. 1993. pap. text ed. write for info. (*1-56662-126-7*) Foundation Pr.

Teachers of Emerson. John S. Harrison. LC 80-2536. reprint ed. 37.00 (*0-404-19262-9*) AMS Pr.

Teachers of Emerson. John S. Harrison. LC 68-715. 1970. reprint ed. 75.00 (*0-8383-0566-0*) M S G Haskell Hse.

Teachers of History. Ed. by Henry S. Hughes. LC 75-142644. (Essay Index Reprint Ser.). 1977. 23.95 (*0-8369-2164-X*) Ayer.

Teachers of Mathematics: Some Aspects of Professional Life. Ed. by Hilary Shuard & Douglas Quadling. 158p. (C). 1980. pap. 28.00 (*0-06-318175-4*, Pub. by P Chapman Pub UK) St Mut.

Teachers of My Youth: An American Jewish Experience. Israel Scheffler. (Philosophy & Education Ser.: Vol. 5). 216p. 1995. pap. text ed. 43.50 (*0-7923-3236-9*, Pub. by Klwr Acad Pubs NE); lib. bdg. 102.00 (*0-7923-3232-6*, Pub. by Klwr Acad Pubs NE) Kluwer Ac.

Teachers of the Inner Chambers: Women & Culture in Seventeenth-Century China. Dorothy Ko. LC 94-1166. xviii, 396p. 1994. 45.00 (*0-8047-2358-3*); pap. 16.95 (*0-8047-2359-1*) Stanford U Pr.

Teachers on Trial: Values, Standards, & Equity in Judging Conduct & Competence. James A. Gross. LC 88-13673. (ILR Paperback Ser.: No. 20). 128p. 1988. pap. 12.95 (*0-87546-142-5*, ILR Press) Cornell U Pr.

Teacher's Participant's Packet. Merle B. Karnes. (PT-GT for Parents & Teachers of Gifted & Talented Children Ser.). 1987. 22.95 (*0-88671-237-8*, 5058) Am Guidance.

Teacher's Pest. Candice F. Ransom. (Illus.). 64p. (Orig.). (J). (gr. 1-4). 1996. pap. 3.95 (*0-8167-4017-8*) Troll Communs.

Teacher's Pet. Richie T. Cusick. 224p. (Orig.). (YA). (gr. 7-9). 1990. pap. 3.50 (*0-590-43114-5*) Scholastic Inc.

Teacher's Pet. Terrance Dicks. (Adventures of Goliath Ser.). (Illus.). 52p. (J). (gr. 2-5). 1992. pap. 3.50 (*0-8120-4820-2*) Barron.

***Teacher's Pet.** Joanna Hurwitz. (J). Date not set. lib. bdg. write for info. (*0-688-07507-X*, Morrow Junior) Morrow.

Teacher's Pet. Johanna Hurwitz. 128p. (J). (gr. 2-5). 1989. pap. 2.99 (*0-590-42031-3*, Apple Paperbacks) Scholastic Inc.

Teacher's Pet. Johanna Hurwitz. LC 87-24003. (Illus.). 128p. (J). (gr. 2-5). 1988. 16.00 (*0-688-07506-1*, Morrow Junior) Morrow.

Teacher's Pet. Ann M. Martin. (Kids in Ms. Colman's Class Ser.: No. 1). 96p. (J). 1995. pap. 2.99 (*0-590-26215-7*) Scholastic Inc.

Teacher's Pet. Francine Pascal. (Sweet Valley Twins Ser.: No. 2). 112p. (Orig.). (J). 1986. pap. 3.50 (*0-553-15656-X*) Bantam.

Teacher's Pet. Sheryl Prenzlau. (B. Y. Times Kid Sisters Ser.: No. 6). (Illus.). 115p. (Orig.). (J). (gr. 4-7). Date not set. pap. 7.95 (*1-56871-025-9*) Targum Pr.

Teacher's Pet. Linda Schwartz. (Teacher Time-Savers Ser.). 192p. (J). (gr. 3-6). 1983. 15.95 (*0-88160-097-0*, LW 240) Learning Wks.

Teacher's Pet. large type ed. Jamie Suzanne. (Sweet Valley Twins Ser.: No. 2). 103p. (YA). (gr. 7-12). 1990. reprint ed. 9.95 (*1-55905-065-9*) Grey Castle.

Teacher's Pet: Notes on Children, Teaching, & Discipline. Deborah E. Jones. Ed. by Stanley C. Coy. (Illus.). 38p. (Orig.). 1993. pap. 7.95 (*1-881459-06-3*) Eagle Pr SC.

Teacher's Pet Projects: A Pet Education Program. Phil Arkow. Ed. by Jonna Gress. (Illus.). 14p. (Orig.). 1993. teacher ed., bds. 16.20 (*0-944943-22-5*, 20554-8) Current Inc.

Teacher's Petit Piaget. C. M. Charles. LC 74-83219. 1974. pap. 5.99 (*0-8224-6780-1*) Fearon Teach Aids.

Teacher's Pets, Troublemakers, & Nobodies: Black Children in Elementary School. Helen Gouldner. LC 78-53660. (Contributions in Afro-American & African Studies: No. 41). (Illus.). 152p. 1978. text ed. 45.00 (*0-313-20417-9*, GOE/, Greenwood Pr) Greenwood.

Teacher's Plan Book Plus, No. 4. Lee Canter. (Illus.). 104p. 1992. student ed. 6.95 (*0-939007-44-4*) Lee Canter & Assocs.

Teachers Plan Book Plus, Vol. 5. 1996. pap. 6.95 (*1-57271-010-1*) Lee Canter & Assocs.

Teacher's Planbook Plus, No. 1. Lee Canter. (Illus.). 1994. student ed. 6.95 (*0-939007-17-7*) Lee Canter & Assocs.

Teacher's Planbook Plus, No. 2. Lee Canter. (Illus.). 104p. 1987. student ed. 6.95 (*0-939007-18-5*) Lee Canter & Assocs.

Teacher's Planning Guide for Fitness & Nutrition: The Winning Combination. 3rd ed. Jane Buch. Ed. by Tate Bard. LC 84-51951. (My School Ser.). (Illus.). 160p. (YA). (gr. 7-12). 1993. student ed., pap. 7.60 (*0-914127-46-2*) Univ Class.

Teacher's Planning Guide for Fitness & Nutrition: The Winning Combination. 3rd rev. ed. Jane Buch. Ed. by Tate Bard. LC 84-51951. (Illus.). 160p. 1994. 18.27 (*0-914127-18-7*) Univ Class.

Teacher's Portfolio of Library Skills: Lessons & Activities. Hilda K. Weisburg & Ruth Toor. LC 85-14921. 326p. 1985. spiral bd. 27.95 (*0-87628-799-2*) Ctr Appl Res.

Teacher's Post Office. Lee Canter. (Illus.). 64p. 1988. student ed. 7.95 (*0-939007-11-8*) Lee Canter & Assocs.

Teacher's Practical Philosophy: A Treatise of Education As a Species of Conduct. George T. Ladd. LC 75-3228. reprint ed. 32.50 (*0-404-59226-0*) AMS Pr.

***Teacher's Prayerbook: To Know & Love Your Students.** Ginger Farry. 1997. pap. text ed. 4.95 (*0-89622-727-8*) Twenty-Third.

Teachers, Preachers, Non-Believers: A Social History of Black Zimbabwean Writing. Flora V. Wild. (New Perspectives on African Literature Ser.: No. 6). 226p. 1993. 75.00 (*1-873836-15-5*, Pub. by H Zell Pubs UK) Bowker-Saur.

Teachers! Prepare Your Students for Mathematics SAT I: Methods & Problem-Solving Strategies. Alfred S. Posamentier & Stephen Krulik. LC 96-5312. 128p. 1996. teacher ed. 49.95 (*0-8039-6481-1*); teacher ed., pap. 19.95 (*0-8039-6416-1*) Corwin Pr.

Teachers' Problem Solving: A Casebook of Award-Winning Teaching Cases. Ed. by James M. Cooper. LC 94-12554. 1994. pap. text ed. 20.00 (*0-205-15203-1*) Allyn.

Teachers Professional Development. Phillip Hughes. (C). 1990. 70.00 (*0-86431-071-4*, Pub. by Aust Council Educ Res AT) St Mut.

Teachers Professional Knowledge Landscapes. Ed. by Jean Clandinin & F. Michael Connelly. (Advances in Contemporary Educational Thought Ser.). 192p. (C). 1995. pap. text ed. 17.95 (*0-8077-3418-7*) Tchrs Coll.

Teachers Professional Knowledge Landscapes. Ed. by Jean Clandinin & F. Michael Connelly. (Advances in Contemporary Educational Thought Ser.). 192p. (C). 1995. text ed. 40.00 (*0-8077-3419-5*) Tchrs Coll.

Teachers' Professional Learning. Ed. by James Calderhead. 225p. 1988. 65.00 (*1-85000-388-2*, Falmer Pr); pap. 30.00 (*1-85000-389-0*, Falmer Pr) Taylor & Francis.

Teachers' Professional Lives. Ed. by Ivor F. Goodson & Andy Hargreaves. LC 96-480. (New Prospects Ser.: No. 3). 256p. 1996. 69.95 (*0-7507-0513-2*, Falmer Pr); pap. 24.95 (*0-7507-0514-0*, Falmer Pr) Taylor & Francis.

Teachers' Professional Responsibilities. Frances Spackman. 128p. 1991. pap. 21.00 (*1-85346-162-8*, Pub. by D Fulton UK) Taylor & Francis.

***Teacher's Project Guide to the Internet.** Kevin Crotchett. LC 97-4068. 1997. pap. text ed. write for info. (*0-435-07104-1*, 07104) Heinemann.

Teachers, Pupils & Behavior: A Managerial Approach. John McGuiness. Ed. by Ron Best & Peter J. Lang. (Studies in Pastoral Care, Personal & Social Education). (Illus.). 176p. 1994. text ed. 70.00 (*0-304-32784-0*); pap. text ed. 24.95 (*0-304-32785-9*) Cassell.

Teachers, Pupils & Primary Schooling. Ed. by Paul Croll. (Education Ser.). (Illus.). 176p. 1996. text ed. 65.00 (*0-304-33660-2*) Cassell.

***Teachers, Pupils & Primary Schooling.** Ed. by Paul Croll. (Education Ser.). (Illus.). 176p. 1996. pap. 23.95 (*0-304-33659-9*) Cassell.

Teacher's Quick Library Guide. 2nd rev. ed. 1990. pap. 15.00 (*0-943932-28-9*) Petervin Pr.

***Teachers' Reading/Teachers' Lives.** Mary K. Rummel & Elizabeth P. Quintero. LC 96-36918. (SUNY Series, Urban Voices, Urban Visions). 224p. (C). 1997. text ed. 57.50 (*0-7914-3485-0*) State U NY Pr.

***Teachers Reproducible Classroom Coloring Book.** Standard Publishing Staff. 1997. pap. text ed. 6.99 (*0-7847-0605-0*) Standard Pub.

Teacher's Resource Book Math Unlimited 1991: Grade K. 1991. teacher ed., pap. text ed. 84.25 (*0-15-351579-1*) HB Schl Dept.

Teacher's Resource Book Math Unlimited 1991: Grade 1. 1991. teacher ed., pap. text ed. 149.50 (*0-15-351580-5*) HB Schl Dept.

Teacher's Resource Book Math Unlimited 1991: Grade 2. 1991. teacher ed., pap. text ed. 149.50 (*0-15-351581-3*) HB Schl Dept.

Teacher's Resource Book Math Unlimited 1991: Grade 3. 1991. teacher ed., pap. text ed. 149.50 (*0-15-351582-1*) HB Schl Dept.

Teacher's Resource Guide. Mary E. Soley et al. 400p. (Orig.). 1987. pap. 19.95 (*0-87124-115-3*) Foreign Policy.

Teacher's Resource Guide to Accompany Basic Blueprint Reading & Sketching. 6th ed. C. Thomas Olivo & Thomas P. Olivo. 154p. 1993. teacher ed. 24.50 (*0-8273-5921-7*) Delmar.

Teacher's Resource Guide to Accompany the Science of Animal Agriculture. Ray V. Herren. 351p. 1994. teacher ed. 89.95 (*0-8273-6114-9*) Delmar.

Teacher's Resource Manual. rev. ed. Ralph McCoy. Ed. by Ellen Gruszewski & Sandra Sladkey. (H. I. S. Songs for Children Ser.). (Illus.). 45p. 1994. teacher ed., pap. 7.95 (*1-885819-04-8*) His Songs.

Teacher's Resource Manual for Structured Pacing in Chemistry Education (SPICE) Teachers Resource Manual. Hines Stone et al. 432p. 1994. ring bd. 49.90 (*0-8403-4199-7*) Kendall-Hunt.

An Asterisk (*) at the beginning of an entry indicates that the title is appearing in BIP for the first time.

Teacher's Resource Package for the Advanced Placement Computer Science A Examination. Bruce Presley & Tim Corica. 1988. ring bd. 53.25 (*0-931717-20-5*) Lawrenceville Pr.

Teachers' Retirement System Information Representative. Jack Rudman. (Career Examination Ser.: C-3482). 1994. pap. 29.95 (*0-8373-3482-9*) Nat Learn.

Teacher's Sampler. Lillie Pope et al. (Illus.). 96p. (Orig.). 1973. pap. text ed. 9.95 (*0-87594-194-X*, 2565) Book-Lab.

Teachers, Schools, & Society. 3rd ed. David M. Sadker & Myra P. Sadker. 1993. student ed., pap. text ed. write for info. (*0-07-054951-6*) McGraw.

Teachers, Schools, & Society. 3rd ed. Myra P. Sadker & David M. Sadker. LC 93-8343. 1993. text ed. write for info. (*0-07-054922-2*) McGraw.

Teachers, Schools, & Society. 4th ed. Myra P. Sadker & David M. Sadker. LC 96-26269. 1996. text ed. write for info. (*0-07-057784-6*) McGraw.

Teacher's Science Companion: Resources & Activities in Science & Math. Phyllis J. Perry. LC 93-43620. pap. 14.95 (*0-07-049519-X*) McGraw-Hill Prof.

Teacher's Science Companion: Resources & Activities in Science & Math. Phyllis J. Perry. LC 93-43620. 1994. text ed. 24.95 (*0-07-049518-1*) McGraw-Hill Prof.

***Teacher's Selection: Anthology of Eleventh Grade Poetry: 1996 Edition.** 157p. 1996. 16.95 (*1-883931-08-8*) Anthology Poetry.

***Teacher's Selection: Anthology of Eleventh Grade Poetry: 1997 Edition.** 158p. 1997. 16.95 (*1-883931-11-8*) Anthology Poetry.

***Teacher's Selection: Anthology of Fifth Grade Poetry: 1996 Edition.** 157p. 1996. 16.95 (*1-883931-07-X*) Anthology Poetry.

***Teacher's Selection: Anthology of Fifth Grade Poetry: 1997 Edition.** 158p. 1997. 16.95 (*1-883931-10-X*) Anthology Poetry.

Teacher's Shadow. J. Kevin Haugh. 1993. pap. 4.95 (*0-89137-142-7*) Quality Pubns.

Teacher's Stories. Ed. by David Thomas. LC 94-45444. 1995. 79.00 (*0-335-19255-6*, Open Univ Pr); pap. 24.95 (*0-335-19254-8*, Open Univ Pr) Taylor & Francis.

Teachers' Stories: From Personal Narrative to Professional Insight. Mary R. Jalango & Joan P. Isenberg. (Education Ser.). 295p. 29.95 (*0-7879-0048-6*) Jossey-Bass.

Teacher's Stories: Reflections on High School Writers. Joyce Lott. LC 93-43816. 168p. (J). 1994. pap. text ed. 20.00 (*0-86709-331-5*, 0331) Boynton Cook Pubs.

***Teachers' Stress.** (C). 1996. text ed. 65.00 (*0-415-09483-6*) Routledge.

***Teacher's Stress & Success: (Black & White Edition)** large type ed. Thomas S. Parish & James R. Necessary. (Illus.). 76p. 1995. 9.95 (*1-888487-01-1*) KD Ent.

***Teacher's Stress & Success: (Color Edition)** large type ed. Thomas S. Parish & James R. Necessary. (Illus.). 76p. 1995. pap. 19.95 (*1-888487-02-X*) KD Ent.

Teachers, Students Activities Are Newsmakers. Previti Campbell. 2.00 (*0-318-19220-9*) Quill & Scroll.

Teacher's Supplement to Genesis the Student's Guide Pt. 1. Louis Newman. pap. 2.95 (*0-8381-0403-7*) USCJE.

Teacher's Survival Guide. C. Arthur Peterson. 1985. pap. 9.95 (*0-452-26399-9*, Plume) NAL-Dutton.

Teachers Talk. John Godar. LC 89-80781. 300p. 1990. 19.95 (*0-944435-08-4*) Glenbridge Pub.

Teachers Talk. John Godar. LC 89-80781. 300p. 1991. pap. 14.95 (*0-944435-16-5*) Glenbridge Pub.

Teachers Talk about Teaching: Coping with Change in Turbulent Times. Ed. by Judith Bell. LC 94-25719. 128p. 1995. pap. 19.95 (*0-335-19174-6*) Open Univ TX.

Teachers! Teachers! Teachers! A Cartoon Collection. Ed. by S. Gross. LC 95-35781. (Illus.). 112p. 1995. 9.95 (*0-8092-3347-9*) Contemp Bks.

Teachers, Teaching & Control in Physical Education. John Evans. 1988. pap. 29.00 (*1-85000-411-0*, Falmer Pr) Taylor & Francis.

Teachers, Teaching & Control in Physical Education. John Evans. 250p. 1988. 53.00 (*1-85000-410-2*, Falmer Pr) Taylor & Francis.

Teachers, Teaching, & Teacher Education. Ed. by Margo Okazawa-Rey et al. LC 87-80233. (Reprint Ser.: No. 19). 488p. 1987. pap. 19.95 (*0-916690-21-0*) Harvard Educ Rev.

Teachers Thinking, Teachers Knowing: Reflections on Literacy & Language Education. Ed. by Timothy Shanahan. LC 94-29237. 203p. (Orig.). 1994. pap. 18.95 (*0-8141-5013-6*) NCTE.

Teacher's Time Management Survival Kit: Ready-To-Use Techniques & Materials. Susan Mamchak & Steven R. Mamchak. LC 93-3737. 1993. write for info. (*0-13-014374-X*) P-H.

Teachers Today: A Guide to Surviving Creatively. Mary Z. McGrath. LC 95-9037. (Illus.). 128p. 1995. 40.00 (*0-8039-6336-X*); pap. 18.00 (*0-8039-6229-0*) Corwin Pr.

***Teacher's Tole to China.** Virginia McLean. 1997. 6.50 (*0-614-29856-3*) Redbird.

***Teacher's Tole to Italy.** Virginia McLean. 1997. teacher ed. 6.50 (*1-885870-02-7*) Redbird.

***Teacher's Tole to Kenya.** Virginia McLean. 1997. teacher ed. 6.50 (*1-885870-01-9*) Redbird.

***Teacher's Tote to China.** Virginia McLean. 1997. teacher ed. 6.50 (*1-885870-00-0*) Redbird.

Teacher's Treasury: Of Ideas, Activities, & Projects to Perk up Primary Programs. Imogene Forte. (Illus.). 160p. (Orig.). 1990. pap. text ed. 14.95 (*0-86530-067-4*, IP 191-2) Incentive Pubns.

Teacher's Treasury of Quotations. Bernard E. Farber. LC 84-43218. 384p. 1985. lib. bdg. 43.50 (*0-89950-150-8*) McFarland & Co.

***Teachers Tricks of Trade.** Gwilliams. 1991. pap. text ed. write for info. (*0-582-04695-5*, Pub. by Longman UK) Longman.

Teachers under Pressure: Stress in the Teaching Profession. Cary Cooper & Cheryl Travers. LC 95-9587. 248p. (C). 1995. pap. text ed. 34.95 (*0-415-09484-4*) Routledge.

***Teachers' Unions: How the NEA & AFT Suffocate Reform, Waste Teachers' Money, & Hold Students & Parents Hostage to Politics.** Myron Lieberman. LC 97-2982. 1997. 25.00 (*0-684-84282-3*) Free Pr.

Teachers, Unions & Change: A Comparative Study. Dorothy K. Jessup. 256p. 1985. text ed. 59.95 (*0-275-90122-X*, C0122, Praeger Pubs) Greenwood.

Teachers Version. (Crayola Creativity Ser.). (Illus.). 32p. 1988. 125.00 (*0-86696-217-4*) Binney & Smith.

Teacher's Voice: A History of Teaching in Twentieth Century America. Ed. by Richard J. Altenbaugh. 227p. 1992. 80.00 (*1-85000-960-0*, Falmer Pr); pap. 29.00 (*1-85000-961-9*, Falmer Pr) Taylor & Francis.

Teachers' Voices: Portfolios in the Classroom. Ed. by Mary A. Smith & Miriam Ylvisaker. 184p. (C). 1993. pap. text ed. 12.50 (*1-883920-07-8*) Nat Writing Proj.

Teachers' Voices for School Change. Andrew Gitlin. 256p. (C). 1992. text ed. 48.00 (*0-8077-3181-1*); pap. text ed. 20.95 (*0-8077-3180-3*) Tchrs Coll.

Teachers' Voices, Teachers' Wisdom: Seven Adventurous Teachers Think Aloud. Nancy Kreinberg & Harriet Nathan. (Equals Ser.). (Illus.). 164p. (Orig.). 1991. pap. 11.00 (*0-912511-55-9*) Lawrence Science.

Teacher's Way: The Role of the Teacher in Today's Classroom. Anne Forester & Margaret Reinhard. (Illus.). 352p. (Orig.). 1994. teacher ed., pap. 20.00 (*1-895411-67-X*) Peguis Pubs Ltd.

Teachers Who Lead: The Rhetoric of Reform & the Realities of Practice. Patricia Wasley. (Series on School Reform). 224p. (C). 1991. text ed. 42.00 (*0-8077-3104-8*); pap. text ed. 17.95 (*0-8077-3103-X*) Tchrs Coll.

Teachers Who Teach Teachers: Reflections on Teacher Education. Ed. by Tom Russell & Fred Korthagen. LC 95-16665. 202p. 1995. 64.00 (*0-7507-0465-9*, Falmer Pr); pap. write for info. (*0-7507-0466-7*, Falmer Pr) Taylor & Francis.

Teachers Who Touch Lives: Methods of the Masters. Philip L. Barlow. 200p. 1988. 13.98 (*0-88290-334-9*) Horizon Utah.

Teacher's Window into the Child's Mind: And Papers from the Institute for Neuro-Physiological Psychology. Sally Goddard. (Illus.). 144p. (C). 1996. pap. 19.95 (*0-9615332-5-0*) Fern Ridge Pr.

Teachers Without Goals, Students Without Purposes. Henry J. Perkinson. LC 92-26491. 1992. pap. text ed. write for info. (*0-07-049372-3*) McGraw.

Teacher's Word Book of the Twenty Thousand Words Found Most Frequently & Widely in General Reading for Children & Young People. rev. ed. Edward L. Thorndike. 1998. reprint ed. 48.00 (*1-55888-233-2*) Omnigraphics Inc.

Teacher's Work. R. W. Connell. 212p. (C). 1985. text ed. 29.95 (*0-86861-752-0*, Pub. by Allen Unwin AT); pap. text ed. 14.95 (*0-86861-760-1*, Pub. by Allen Unwin AT) Paul & Co Pubs.

Teacher's Work: Individuals, Colleagues, & Contexts. Ed. by Judith W. Little & Milbrey W. McLaughlin. LC 92-34794. (Series on School Reform). 208p. (C). 1993. text ed. 39.00 (*0-8077-3229-X*); pap. text ed. 17.95 (*0-8077-3228-1*) Tchrs Coll.

Teachers' Workplace: The Organizational Context of Schooling. Susan J. Rosenholtz. (Research on Teaching Ser.). 256p. (C). 1991. pap. text ed. 19.95 (*0-8077-3149-8*) Tchrs Coll.

Teacher's Workshop in a Book! Sylvia F. Harding. (Illus.). 128p. (Orig.). (J). (gr. k-4). 1992. student ed., pap. 10.95 (*0-923979-00-X*) Harding Hse Pubns.

Teachers, Writers, Celebrities: The Intellectuals of Modern France. Regis Debray. Tr. by David Macey from FRE. 251p. 1985. pap. text ed. 14.95 (*0-86091-039-3*, A1144, Pub. by Verso UK) Routledge Chapman & Hall.

Teacher's Year-Timer: A Complete Organizer for Teachers. Lyvita Reese. 1996. spiral bd. 19.95 (*1-889003-01-8*) LRW Publns.

Teaching. (Opportunities in...Ser.). 160p. 1994. 13.95 (*0-8442-4420-1*, VGM Career Bks) NTC Pub Grp.

Teaching. (Opportunities in...Ser.). 160p. 1996. pap. 10.95 (*0-8442-4422-8*, VGM Career Bks) NTC Pub Grp.

Teaching. Marjorie Eberts & Margaret Gisler. LC 93-47956. 96p. (YA). (gr. 9-12). 1994. 13.95 (*0-8442-4362-0*, VGM Career Bks) NTC Pub Grp.

Teaching. David J. Hargreaves. 1991. 63.00 (*0-335-09578-X*, Open Univ Pr); pap. 23.00 (*0-335-09577-1*, Open Univ Pr) Taylor & Francis.

Teaching: A Beacon unto Our Educational Path, Yet, a Thankless Task. J. L. Thomas, pseud. (Illus.). 82p. 1985. text ed. 10.95 (*0-935243-00-3*) Thomas Ent.

Teaching: An Introduction. D. Cecil Clark & Beverly R. Cutler. 466p. (C). 1990. pap. text ed. 32.00 (*0-15-586597-8*) HB Coll Pubs.

Teaching: An Introduction. Daniel L. Duke. 1990. text ed. write for info. (*0-07-557193-5*) McGraw.

Teaching: Bearing the Torch. Pamela J. Farris. 512p. (C). 1995. per. write for info. (*0-697-22527-5*) Brown & Benchmark.

Teaching: Bearing the Torch. Pamela J. Farris. 512p. (C). 1995. student ed., per. write for info. (*0-697-22584-4*) Brown & Benchmark.

Teaching: Making Sense of an Uncertain Craft. Joseph P. McDonald. (Professional Development & Practice Ser.). 160p. (C). 1992. text ed. 15.95 (*0-8077-3168-4*); pap. text ed. 15.95 (*0-8077-3167-6*) Tchrs Coll.

Teaching: Strategies for Student-Centered Curriculum. Lang. (C). 1994. pap. text ed. 47.75 (*0-03-922866-5*) HB Coll Pubs.

Teaching: The Way of the Master: A Handbook for the Martial Artist. Sang H. Kim. 145p. 1991. pap. 19.95 (*1-880336-00-6*) Turtle Pr.

Teaching: Theory into Practice. Allan C. Ornstein. LC 94-27202. 1994. pap. text ed. 52.00 (*0-205-15778-5*) Allyn.

***Teaching - Pure & Simple: One Way of Looking at Teaching.** 200p. (Orig.). 1997. pap. 12.95 (*0-9658138-0-0*) J Beaman.

Teaching--Actions, Methods, Views, Progress, Stress & Burn-Out: Index of New Information with Authors, Subjects, & References. Mickey K. Zaharis. LC 96-12662. 1996. 47.50 (*0-7883-1018-6*); pap. 44.50 (*0-7883-1019-4*) ABBE Pubs Assn.

Teaching a Child to Read. Bill Kirtland. Ed. by Wendy S. Kolsen. (Illus.). 44p. (Orig.). (J). (gr. k-6). 1995. pap. 7.99 (*1-885101-13-9*) Writers Pr Srv.

Teaching a Child to Read. Nancy L. Roser. 514p. (C). 1979. text ed. 38.75 (*0-15-586650-8*) HB Coll Pubs.

Teaching a "New Canon"? Students, Teachers & Texts in the College Literature Classroom. Ed. by Bruce A. Goebel & James C. Hall. LC 95-8711. 259p. 1995. 25.95 (*0-8141-5191-4*) NCTE.

Teaching a Non-Spontaneous Learner for Threes & Fours. rev. ed. 1992. 1.00 (*0-939418-45-2*) Ferguson-Florissant.

Teaching a Psychology of People: Resources for Gender & Sociocultural Awareness. Ed. by Phyllis Bronstein & Kathryn Quina. LC 88-16715. 220p. 1988. pap. 29.95 (*1-55798-039-X*) Am Psychol.

Teaching a Psychology of People: Resources for Gender & Sociocultural Awareness. 7th ed. American Psychological Association Staff. 220p. (C). 1994. boxed write for info. (*0-697-27869-7*) Brown & Benchmark.

Teaching a Psychology of People Vol. 3: Resources for Gender & Sociocultural Awareness. 7th ed. American Psychological Association Staff. 384p. (C). 1994. write for info. (*0-697-27872-7*) Brown & Benchmark.

Teaching a Stone to Talk. Annie Dillard. LC 82-45720. 1988. pap. 12.00 (*0-06-091541-2*, PL) HarpC.

Teaching a Young Actor: How to Train Children of All Ages for Success in Movies, TV, & Commercials. Renee Harmon. 224p. (Orig.). 1994. pap. 14.95 (*0-8027-7423-7*) Walker & Co.

Teaching about Africa: A Continent of Complexities. Ronald Byrnes et al. 1994. ring bd. 39.95 incl. sl. (*0-943804-88-4*) U of Denver Teach.

Teaching about AIDS: Lesson Plans for Elementary & High School. Eileen P. Flynn. LC 87-63005. (Illus.). 96p. 1988. teacher ed., pap. 8.95 (*1-55612-113-X*) Sheed & Ward MO.

Teaching about American Indians in Connecticut. (Ethnic Studies Bulletins: No. 7). 17p. 1982. 2.00 (*0-685-05160-9*) I N Thut World Educ Ctr.

Teaching about Conflict: Nothern Ireland. Jacquelyn S. Johnson. (Illus.). 145p. (gr. 7-12). 1983. pap. 8.95 (*0-943804-36-1*) U of Denver Teach.

Teaching about Cultural Awareness. rev. ed. Gary R. Smith & George G. Otero. (Illus.). 225p. (gr. 4-12). 1994. pap. 26.95 (*0-943804-18-3*) U of Denver Teach.

Teaching about Cultural Awareness with Student Handouts in Spanish. George G. Otero & Gary R. Smith. Tr. by Ann L. Espinosa & Ismael E. Espinosa. (Illus.). 235p. (gr. 4-12). 1982. pap. 8.50 (*0-943804-26-4*) U of Denver Teach.

Teaching about Diversity: Latin America; with Student Handouts in Spanish. Kenneth A. Switzer & Charlotte A. Redden. Tr. by Ann L. Espinosa & Ismael E. Jacome. (Illus.). 175p. (Orig.). (gr. 9-12). 1982. pap. 6.00 (*0-943804-27-2*) U of Denver Teach.

Teaching about Energy: Nineteen Eighty-Four to Nineteen Eighty-Five Supplement. John Lord et al. (Energy Eighty Ser.). 280p. 1985. pap. 10.00 (*0-934653-05-4*) Enterprise Educ.

Teaching about Ethnic Heritage. rev. ed. George G. Otero & Gary R. Smith. (Illus.). 147p. (Orig.). (gr. k-12). 1977. pap. 15.95 (*0-943804-06-X*) U of Denver Teach.

Teaching about Europe. Margaret Shennan. (Council of Europe Ser.). 300p. 1992. text ed. 60.00 (*0-304-32292-X*); pap. text ed. 24.95 (*0-304-32288-1*) Cassell.

Teaching about Food & Hunger. 2nd ed. Gary Smith & George G. Otero. (Illus.). 124p. (Orig.). 1989. pap. 24.95 (*0-943804-67-1*) U of Denver Teach.

Teaching about Global Issues: Population, Health, Hunger, Culture, Environment. Ed. by Hazel S. Greenberg. 110p. 1993. ring bd. 25.00 (*0-614-02986-4*) Amer Forum.

Teaching about International Conflict & Peace. Ed. by Merry M. Merryfield & Richard C. Remy. LC 94-13643. (SUNY Series, Theory, Research, & Practice in Social Education). 374p. (C). 1995. pap. text ed. 21.95 (*0-7914-2374-3*) State U NY Pr.

Teaching about International Conflict & Peace. Ed. by Merry M. Merryfield & Richard C. Remy. LC 94-13643. (SUNY Series, Theory, Research, & Practice in Social Education). 374p. (C). 1995. text ed. 64.50 (*0-7914-2373-5*) State U NY Pr.

***Teaching about Islam & Muslims in the Public School Classroom: A Handbook for Educators.** 114p. 1996. pap. 8.00 (*0-614-21538-2*, 1380) Kazi Pubns.

Teaching about Job Hazards: A Guide for Workers & Their Health Providers. Nina Wallerstein & Harriet Rubenstein. 141p. 1993. pap. 20.00 (*0-87553-209-8*, 008) Am Pub Health.

Teaching about Law & Cultures: Japan, Southeast Asia (Hmong), & Mexico. Barbara Miller et al. (Illus.). (Orig.). 1992. pap. 21.95 (*0-89994-366-7*) Soc Sci Ed.

Teaching about Moshiach. (Shlichus Ser.). 174p. 1994. reprint ed. 12.50 (*0-8266-0396-3*, Neshei Chabad) Kehot Pubn Soc.

Teaching about Native Americans. Karen D. Harvey et al. LC 90-61482. (Bulletin Ser.: No. 84). 82p. 1990. pap. 12.95 (*0-87986-059-6*) Nat Coun Soc Studies.

Teaching about Nonprofit Boards: A Resource Kit for Academics, Consultants, Trainers, & Other Teachers. (Nonprofit Governance Ser.: No. 45). 29p. (Orig.). (C). 1990. bds. 20.00 (*0-925299-07-3*) Natl Ctr Nonprofit.

Teaching about Palestine. 35p. 1990. write for info. (*92-1-100437-3*, 90.I.13) UN.

Teaching about Population Growth. George G. Otero. (Illus.). (gr. 6-12). 1983. pap. 7.50 (*0-943804-01-9*) U of Denver Teach.

Teaching about Population Issues. George G. Otero. (Illus.). 81p. (gr. 6-12). 1983. pap. 7.50 (*0-943804-02-7*) U of Denver Teach.

Teaching about Religion in the Public Schools. Charles R. Kniker. LC 84-62994. (Fastback Ser.: No. 224). 50p. (Orig.). 1985. pap. 3.00 (*0-87367-224-0*) Phi Delta Kappa.

Teaching about Sexual Abuse. Pat Huggins. (ASSIST Program, Affective/Social Skills Ser.). (Illus.). 72p. 1991. teacher ed., pap. text ed. 15.00 (*0-944584-32-2*, 18SA) Sopris.

Teaching about Sexuality & HIV: Principles & Methods for Effective Education. Evonne Hedgepeth & Joan Helmich. LC 96-13431. 293p. (C). 1996. 55.00 (*0-8147-3515-0*) NYU Pr.

Teaching about Sexuality & HIV: Principles & Methods for Effective Education. Evonne Hedgepeth & Joan Helmich. (C). 1996. pap. 20.00 (*0-8147-3535-5*) NYU Pr.

Teaching about Stress. Donald A. Tubesing. 62p. (Orig.). 1989. pap. text ed. 14.95 (*0-938586-32-7*) Whole Person.

Teaching about Substance Abuse: A Resource Manual for Faculty Development. 1992. lib. bdg. 79.95 (*0-8490-8825-9*) Gordon Pr.

Teaching about Substance Abuse: A Resource Manual for Faculty Development. rev. ed. Stephen P. Flynn et al. 45p. (C). 1995. pap. text ed. 20.00 (*0-7881-2580-X*) DIANE Pub.

***Teaching About the Adolescent.** John McKinney et al. (Michigan State University Series on Children, Youth, & Families). 400p. 1998. text ed. 60.00 (*0-8153-1981-9*) Garland.

Teaching about the Constitution. Ed. by Clair W. Keller & Denny L. Schillings. LC 87-61298. (Bulletin Ser.: No. 80). (Orig.). 1987. pap. text ed. 9.95 (*0-87986-055-3*) Nat Coun Soc Studies.

Teaching about the Consumer & the Global Marketplace. Ed. by Bruce Koranski. (Illus.). 219p. (Orig.). (gr. 4-12). 1990. pap. 16.95 (*0-943804-17-5*) U of Denver Teach.

Teaching about the Former Soviet Union. rev. ed. Louise Cadwell et al. (Illus.). 189p. 39.95 (*0-943804-73-6*) U of Denver Teach.

Teaching about the Future: Tools, Topics, & Issues. Barbara Miller et al. (Illus.). 176p. (Orig.). 1987. pap. 8.50 (*0-89994-311-X*) Soc Sci Ed.

Teaching about the History & Nature of Science & Technology: Teacher's Resource Guide. SSEC Staff & BSCS Staff. (Illus.). 167p. (Orig.). 1996. pap. text ed. 21.95 (*0-89994-386-1*) Soc Sci Ed.

Teaching about Values: A Practical Approach. Graham Haydon. LC 96-931. (Studies in Pastoral Care, & Personal & Social Education). 192p. 1996. pap. 21.95 (*0-304-33560-6*); text ed. 65.00 (*0-304-33559-2*) Cassell.

Teaching Abroad 1988-91. 250p. 1988. pap. 21.95 (*0-87206-158-2*, 1582E) Inst Intl Educ.

Teaching Academic Subjects to Diverse Learners: What Teachers Need to Know. Ed. by Mary M. Kennedy. 312p. (C). 1991. text ed. 33.00 (*0-8077-3089-0*) Tchrs Coll.

Teaching Across Cultures in the University ESL Program (1986) Patricia Byrd. 149p. 1986. pap. text ed. 15.00 (*0-912207-17-5*) NAFSA Washington.

Teaching Adolescents with Learning Disabilities: Strategies & Methods. 2nd ed. Donald D. Deshler et al. LC 95-75399. 656p. 1995. 54.00 (*0-89108-241-7*) Love Pub Co.

Teaching Adolescents with Mild Disabilities. Olsen & Jennifer M. Platt. (Special Education Ser.). 448p. (C). 1997. pap. 45.95 (*0-534-21006-6*) Brooks-Cole.

Teaching Adults. (Training by Design Ser.). 1994. 12.00 (*1-56420-039-6*, 2039-6) New Readers.

Teaching Adults. Alan Roger. 224p. 1986. pap. 24.00 (*0-335-15234-1*, Open Univ Pr) Taylor & Francis.

Teaching Adults. 2nd ed. Adam Rogers. LC 96-10731. 249p. 1996. 69.95 (*0-335-19687-X*, Open Univ Pr) Taylor & Francis.

Teaching Adults. 2nd ed. Alan Rogers. LC 96-10731. 224p. 1996. pap. 21.95 (*0-335-19623-3*, Open Univ Pr) Taylor & Francis.

Teaching Adults: An Active Learning Approach. Elizabeth Jones. LC 85-63557. 155p. 1986. pap. 6.00 (*0-912674-96-2*, NAEYC #205) Natl Assn Child Ed.

Teaching Adults-for a Change. Gene VanNote. 104p. 1981. pap. 5.99 (*0-8341-0720-1*) Beacon Hill.

***Teaching Adults Improvement Skills in the Workplace.** Raymond W. Meliza. (Illus.). 24p. 1996. pap. 3.50 (*1-884241-38-7*, SPSO319) Energeia Pub.

Teaching Adults with Confidence. 32p. 1984. teacher ed. 4.50 (*0-910566-44-5*) Evang Trg Assn.

Teaching Adults with Confidence. Paul E. Loth. 48p. 1984. pap. 4.25 (*0-910566-43-7*) Evang Trg Assn.

Teaching Adults with Learning Disabilities. Dale R. Jordan. LC 95-13766. (Professional Practices in Adult Education & Human Resource Development Ser.). (Illus.). 160p. (C). 1996. 21.50 (*0-89464-910-8*) Krieger.

T

Teaching Advanced Composition: Why & How. Ed. by Katherine H. Adams & John L. Adams. LC 90-35967. 289p. (Orig.). (gr. 13). 1990. pap. text ed. 23.00 (*0-86709-260-2*, 0260) Boynton Cook Pubs.

Teaching Advanced Skills to At-Risk Students: Views from Research & Practice. Ed. by Barbara Means et al. LC 91-21683. (Education-Higher Education Ser.). 317p. text ed. 32.95 (*1-55542-393-0*) Jossey-Bass.

Teaching African-American History: 1992. rev. ed. Robert L. Harris, Jr. Ed. by Nell I. Painter & Antonio Rios-Bustamante. LC 92-71867. (Diversity Within America Essay Ser.). 96p. (C). 1992. pap. 8.00 (*0-87229-066-2*) Am Hist Assn.

***Teaching African American Literature: Theory & Practice.** Ed. by Marianna W. Davis & Maryemma Graham. (Transforming Teaching). 256p. 1997. pap. 18.95 (*0-415-91696-8*, Routledge NY) Routledge.

***Teaching African American Literature: Theory & Practice.** Ed. by Marianna W. Davis & Maryemma Graham. (Transforming Teaching Ser.). 256p. (C). 1997. text ed. 65.00 (*0-415-91695-X*, Routledge NY) Routledge.

Teaching Against the Grain: Texts for a Pedagogy of Possibility. Roger I. Simon. LC 91-35246. (Critical Studies in Education & Culture). 192p. 1992. text ed. 52.95 (*0-89789-207-0*, H207, Bergin & Garvey); pap. text ed. 16.95 (*0-89789-206-2*, G206, Bergin & Garvey) Greenwood.

Teaching Age-Appropriate Purposeful Skills: An Orientation & Mobility Curriculum for Students with Visual Impairments. 2nd ed. Rona L. Pogrund et al. 1995. pap. 45.00 (*1-880366-18-5*) TSBVI.

Teaching AIDS. Douglas Tonks. LC 95-30105. 224p. (C). (gr. 13 up). 1995. text ed. 49.95 (*0-415-90874-4*) Routledge.

Teaching AIDS. Douglas Tonks. LC 95-30105. 224p. 1995. pap. 16.95 (*0-415-90875-2*) Routledge.

Teaching AIDS. rev. ed. Marcia Quackenbush & Pamela Sargent. 164p. 1988. pap. text ed. 19.95 (*0-941816-41-9*); pap. text ed. 21.95 (*1-56071-029-2*) ETR Assocs.

Teaching Aids & Techniques see Language Classroom

Teaching Aids & Techniques: The Secondary School Language Laboratory see Language Learner

Teaching Aids for Blind & Visually Limited Children. Barbara Dorward & Natalie C. Barraga. 142p. reprint ed. pap. 40.50 (*0-7837-0140-3*, 2040429) Bks Demand.

Teaching Aids for Home Care Nurses. Springhouse Publishing Company Staff. 320p. 1995. ring bd., pap. 34.95 (*0-87434-831-5*) Springhouse Pub.

Teaching All the Children to Read: Concentrated Language Encounter Techniques. Richard Walker, Jr. et al. LC 92-8566. 1992. 80.00 (*0-335-15729-7*, Open Univ Pr); pap. 27.50 (*0-335-15728-9*, Open Univ Pr) Taylor & Francis.

Teaching All the Children to Write. Ed. by James L. Collins. 100p. 1983. pap. text ed. 7.00 (*0-930348-10-9*) NY St Eng Coun.

Teaching American English Pronounciations. 1992. 13.95 (*0-19-432815-5*) OUP.

Teaching American Ethnic Literatures: Nineteen Essays. Ed. by John R. Maitino & David R. Peck. 384p. (Orig.). (C). 1996. pap. 22.50 (*0-8263-1686-7*) U of NM Pr.

Teaching American Indian History. Terry P. Wilson. Ed. by Antonio Rios-Bustamante & Nell I. Painter. (Diversity Within America Ser.). 66p. 1993. pap. 8.00 (*0-87229-069-7*) Am Hist Assn.

Teaching American Indian Students. Ed. by Jon Reyhner. LC 92-54136. (Illus.). 344p. 1994. pap. 14.95 (*0-8061-2674-4*) U of Okla Pr.

Teaching & Acquisition of South Asian Languages. Ed. by Vijay Gambhir. LC 95-33261. (Illus.). 256p. 1996. text ed. 29.95 (*0-8122-3328-X*) U of Pa Pr.

Teaching & Addresses on Christian Science. Edward A. Kimball. 380p. (C). 1991. reprint ed. pap. 14.95 (*0-930227-15-8*) Bookmark CA.

***Teaching & Advocacy.** Ed. by Denny Taylor et al. (Illus.). 256p. (Orig.). (C). 1997. pap. text ed. 22.50 (*1-57110-045-8*) Stenhse Pubs.

***Teaching & Assessing Intercultural Communicative Competence.** Michael Byram. LC 97-6559. 1997. write for info. (*1-85359-378-8*, Pub. by Multilingual Matters UK); pap. write for info. (*1-85359-377-X*, Pub. by Multilingual Matters UK) Taylor & Francis.

***Teaching & Assessing Nurses: A Handbook for Preceptors.** Robert Oliver & Colin Endersby. (Illus.). 166p. 1994. pap. write for info. (*0-7020-1720-5*, Pub. by W B Saunders UK) Saunders.

Teaching & Assessing of Mathematical Problem Solving. Ed. by Randall I. Charles & Edward A. Silver. (Research Agenda for Mathematics Education Ser.: Vol. 3). 296p. 1989. text ed. 59.95 (*0-8058-0355-6*) L Erlbaum Assocs.

***Teaching & Assessing Phonics: Why, What, When, How.** Jeanne S. Chall & Helen M. Popp. Ed. by Jen Noon. (Orig.). 1996. pap. text ed. 16.00 (*0-8388-2314-9*) Ed Pub Serv.

Teaching & Assessing Writing: Recent Advances in Understanding, Evaluating, & Improving Student Performance. Edward M. White. LC 84-43036. (Higher & Adult Education Ser.). 328p. 1985. text ed. 36.95 (*0-87589-641-3*) Jossey-Bass.

Teaching & Assessing Writing: Recent Advances in Understanding, Evaluating, & Improving Student Performance. 2nd exp. rev. ed. Edward M. White. LC 93-43200. (Higher & Adult Education Ser.). 355p. text ed. 34.95 (*1-55542-619-0*) Jossey-Bass.

Teaching & Counseling Gifted & Talented Adolescents: An International Learning Style Perspective. Ed. by Roberta M. Milgram et al. LC 92-35348. 296p. 1993. text ed. 59.95 (*0-275-93640-6*, C3640, Praeger Pubs) Greenwood.

Teaching & Development: A Soviet Investigation. Leonid V. Zankov et al. Ed. by Beatrice B. Szekely. Tr. by Arlo Schultz. LC 77-82338. (Illus.). 304p. (Orig.). reprint ed. pap. 86.70 (*0-685-23748-6*, 2032789) Bks Demand.

Teaching & Development of Hindi. Ed. by S. R. Sharma. (C). 1993. 36.00 (*81-7041-785-6*, Pub. by Anmol II) S Asia.

Teaching & Development of Marathi: Encyclopaedia of Teaching Languages in India Series. Ed. by S. R. Sharma. (Encyclopaedia of Teaching Languages in India). (C). 1993. 36.00 (*81-7041-788-0*, Pub. by Anmol II) S Asia.

Teaching & Development of Punjabi. Ed. by S. R. Sharma. (C). 1993. 34.00 (*81-7041-790-2*, Pub. by Anmol II) S Asia.

Teaching & Development of Sanskrit. Ed. by S. R. Sharma. (C). 1993. 28.00 (*81-7041-791-0*, Pub. by Anmol II) S Asia.

Teaching & Development of Urdu: Encyclopaedia of Teaching Languages in India Series. Ed. by S. R. Sharma. (Encyclopaedia of Teaching Languages in India). (C). 1993. 42.00 (*81-7041-795-3*, Pub. by Anmol II) S Asia.

Teaching & Directing: The Basic Communications Course. Lawrence W. Hugenberg. 336p. 1992. per. 16.75 (*0-8403-8228-6*) Kendall-Hunt.

Teaching & Directing Forensics. Michael D. Bartanen. LC 93-31147. 1993. pap. text ed. 30.95 (*0-89787-348-3*) Gorsuch Scarisbrick.

***Teaching & Education for a New Europe: A Challenge for the Countries of the European Union.** Bryan T. Peck. (Illus.). 137p. (C). 1996. lib. bdg. 59.00 (*1-56072-386-6*) Nova Sci Pubs.

Teaching & Interactive Methods: With Cases, Simulations & Games. Hans E. Klein. (Illus.). 600p. 1995. 50.00 (*1-877868-07-8*) WACRA.

***Teaching & Its Predicaments.** David T. Hansen. Ed. by Nicholas C. Burbules. LC 97-22269. (C). 1997. pap. text ed. 19.95 (*0-8133-2864-0*) Westview.

***Teaching & Its Predicaments.** David T. Hansen. Ed. by Nicholas C. Burbules. LC 97-22269. (C). 1997. text ed. 60.00 (*0-8133-2863-2*) Westview.

***Teaching & Joy.** Robert Sornson & James Scott. LC 97-4642. 1997. pap. 16.95 (*0-87120-271-9*) Assn Supervision.

Teaching & Learning. Ed. by Donald Vandenberg. LC 69-17365. (Readings in the Philosophy of Education Ser.). 309p. reprint ed. pap. 88.10 (*0-317-41924-2*, 2025920) Bks Demand.

Teaching & Learning: A Guide for Therapists. Sally French et al. LC 93-44789. (Skills for Practice Ser.). (Illus.). 120p. 1994. pap. 30.00 (*0-7506-0617-7*) Buttrwrth-Heinemann.

Teaching & Learning: A Problem-Solving Focus. Ed. by Frances R. Curcio. (Illus.). 116p. 1987. pap. 13.50 (*0-87353-240-6*) NCTM.

Teaching & Learning about Science & Society. John M. Ziman. LC 80-40326. (Illus.). 148p. 1980. text ed. 34.95 (*0-521-23221-X*) Cambridge U Pr.

Teaching & Learning America's Christian History: The Principle Approach. Rosalie J. Slater. LC 65-26334. 414p. 1993. lib. bdg. 35.00 (*0-912498-02-1*) F A C E.

Teaching & Learning Basic Skills: A Guide for Adult Basic Education & Developmental Education Programs. Mark H. Rossman et al. LC 83-9118. 188p. reprint ed. pap. 53.60 (*0-7837-3885-4*, 2043733) Bks Demand.

Teaching & Learning Computer Programming: Multiple Research Perspectives. Ed. by Richard E. Mayer. 336p. 1988. 59.95 (*0-8058-0073-5*) L Erlbaum Assocs.

***Teaching & Learning Early Number.** Ian Thompson. LC 96-49718. 1997. pap. write for info. (*0-335-19851-1*, Open Univ Pr); lib. bdg. write for info. (*0-335-19852-X*, Open Univ Pr) Taylor & Francis.

Teaching & Learning Elementary & Middle School Mathematics. 3rd ed. Cruickshan & Linda J. Sheffield. 456p. (C). 1995. pap. text ed. 57.00 (*0-02-326113-7*, Macmillan Coll) P-H.

***Teaching & Learning Elementary Social Studies.** 6th ed. Arthur K. Ellis. LC 97-8999. 1997. 50.67 (*0-205-26763-7*) Allyn.

Teaching & Learning English As a Foreign Language. Charles C. Fries. (Orig.). 1945. pap. 19.95 (*0-472-08347-3*) U of Mich Pr.

Teaching & Learning English Worldwide. Ed. by James N. Britton et al. 356p. 1990. 99.00 (*1-85359-065-7*, Pub. by Multilingual Matters UK); pap. 39.95 (*1-85359-064-9*, Pub. by Multilingual Matters UK) Taylor & Francis.

Teaching & Learning Formal Methods. Ed. by C. Neville Dean & Michael Hinchey. (International Series in Formal Methods). (Illus.). 272p. 1996. text ed. 49.95 (*0-12-349040-5*) Acad Pr.

Teaching & Learning Geography. Michael Williams & Daniella Tilbury. LC 96-22402. 336p. (C). 1997. pap. text ed. write for info. (*0-415-14244-X*) Routledge.

Teaching & Learning Grammar. Jeremy Harmer. (Keys to Language Teaching Ser.). (C). 1987. pap. text ed. 20.67 (*0-582-74623-X*, 78336) Longman.

Teaching & Learning Grammar. Allison Taylor. 1994. pap. 35.00 (*1-85234-554-3*, Pub. by Stanley Thornes UK) Trans-Atl Phila.

***Teaching & Learning History in Elementary School.** Jere E. Brophy & Bruce A. Van Sledright. LC 96-52833. 304p. (C). 1997. text ed. 56.00 (*0-8077-3608-2*); pap. text ed. 27.95 (*0-8077-3607-4*) Tchrs Coll.

Teaching & Learning in a Diverse World: Multicultural Education for Young Children. Patricia G. Ramsey. (Early Childhood Education Ser.). (C). 1986. pap. text ed. 17.95 (*0-8077-2828-4*) Tchrs Coll.

Teaching & Learning in a Microelectronic Age. Harold G. Shane. LC 86-63343. 90p. (Orig.). 1987. pap. 9.00 (*0-87367-434-0*) Phi Delta Kappa.

Teaching & Learning in Changing Times. Ed. & Intro. by Martin Hughes. (Illus.). 256p. (C). 1995. 52.95 (*0-631-19277-8*); pap. 23.95 (*0-631-19278-6*) Blackwell Pubs.

Teaching & Learning in Communities of Faith: Empowering Adults Through Religious Education. Linda J. Vogel. LC 91-21686. (Higher & Adult Education Ser.). 239p. text ed. 32.95 (*1-55542-390-6*) Jossey-Bass.

Teaching & Learning in Further & Adult Education. Les Walklin. 300p. (Orig.). (C). 1990. 75.00 (*0-7487-0145-1*, Pub. by Stanley Thornes UK); 60.00 (*0-7478-0145-2*, Pub. by Stanley Thornes UK) Trans-Atl Phila.

***Teaching & Learning in Further Education.** Prue Huddlestone & Lorna Unwin. LC 96-50041. 224p. (C). 1997. pap. text ed. 19.95 (*0-415-12017-9*) Routledge.

Teaching & Learning in History. Ed. by Gaea Leinhardt & Isabel L. Beck. 280p. 1994. text ed. 59.95 (*0-8058-1245-8*) L Erlbaum Assocs.

Teaching & Learning in Japan. Ed. by Thomas P. Rohlen & Gerald K. LeTendre. (Illus.). 350p. (C). 1996. text ed. 49.95 (*0-521-49587-3*) Cambridge U Pr.

Teaching & Learning in Logo-Based Environments: Proceedings of the Eurologo '89 Conference, Gent, Belgium, 1989. Ed. by G. Schuyten & M. Valcke. (Frontiers in Artificial Intelligence & Applications Ser.: Vol. 6). 268p. (gr. 12). 1990. pap. 70.00 (*90-5199-024-3*, Pub. by IOS Pr NE) IOS Press.

Teaching & Learning in Physical Education: A Social Psychological Perspective. Gordon L. Underwood. 225p. 1989. 70.00 (*1-85000-422-6*, Falmer Pr); pap. 35.00 (*1-85000-423-4*, Falmer Pr) Taylor & Francis.

Teaching & Learning in Schools of Nursing. H. Heidgerken. 705p. (C). 1991. 75.00 (*81-7002-031-X*, Pub. by Himalayan Bks II) St Mut.

Teaching & Learning in the Early Years. David Whitebread. LC 96-2574. 384p. (C). 1996. pap. 22.95 (*0-415-13532-X*) Routledge.

***Teaching & Learning in the Elementary School: Focus on Curriculum.** Judy Reinhartz & Don M. Beach. LC 96-33011. 1996. 48.00 (*0-02-399285-9*, Merrill Pub Co) Macmillan.

Teaching & Learning in the Middle Grades. K. Denise Muth & Donna E. Alvermann. 448p. (C). 1992. text ed. 62.00 (*0-205-13302-9*) Allyn.

Teaching & Learning in the Middle Level School. Harvey A. Allen et al. LC 92-31113. 464p. (C). 1993. text ed. 69.00 (*0-675-21347-9*, Merrill Coll) P-H.

Teaching & Learning in the Primary School. Ed. by Andrew Pollard & Jill Bourne. LC 93-5056. 272p. (C). 1993. pap. text ed. 18.95 (*0-415-10258-8*) Routledge.

Teaching-&-Learning Language-&-Culture. Michael Byram & Carol Morgan. LC 93-30783. (Multilingual Matters Ser.: No. 100). 228p. 1994. 79.00 (*1-85359-212-9*, Pub. by Multilingual Matters UK); pap. 29.95 (*1-85359-211-0*, Pub. by Multilingual Matters UK) Taylor & Francis.

Teaching & Learning Languages. Earl W. Stevick. 220p. 1982. pap. text ed. 18.95 (*0-521-28201-2*) Cambridge U Pr.

***Teaching & Learning Mathematical Modelling.** S. K. Houston et al. 320p. 1997. 65.00 (*1-898563-29-2*, Pub. by Albion Pubng UK) Paul & Co Pubs.

Teaching & Learning Mathematical Problem Solving: Multiple Research Perspectives. Ed. by Edward S. Silver. (Problem Solving Ser.). 469p. (C). 1985. 69.95 (*0-89859-681-5*); pap. 45.00 (*0-89859-759-5*) L Erlbaum Assocs.

Teaching & Learning Mathematics. Peter Dean. (Illus.). 265p. 1982. text ed. 25.00 (*0-7130-0168-2*, Pub. by Woburn Pr UK) Intl Spec Bk.

Teaching & Learning Mathematics. Peter Dean. (Illus.). 265p. 1982. pap. text ed. 12.50 (*0-7130-4007-6*, Pub. by Woburn Pr UK) Intl Spec Bk.

Teaching & Learning Mathematics in Context. T. Breiteig et al. 250p. 1994. text ed. 72.00 (*0-13-031006-9*) P-H.

Teaching & Learning Mathematics in the 1990s: 1990 Yearbook. Ed. by Thomas J. Cooney. LC 89-14410. (Illus.). 248p. 1990. 22.00 (*0-87353-285-6*) NCTM.

Teaching & Learning Mathematics 11-16. John Costello. 256p. (C). 1992. pap. text ed. 22.95 (*0-415-04988-1*, A5449) Routledge.

Teaching & Learning of Psychoanalysis: Selected Papers of Joan Fleming, M.D. Ed. by Stanley Weiss. LC 86-14910. (Guilford Psychoanalysis Ser.). 216p. 1986. lib. bdg. 31.50 (*0-89862-326-X*) Guilford Pr.

Teaching & Learning of Psychotherapy. rev. ed. Robert S. Wallerstein & Rudolf Ekstein. LC 70-184442. 277p. 1972. 49.00 (*0-8236-6363-9*) Intl Univs Pr.

***Teaching & Learning Personality Assessment.** Ed. by Leonard Handler & Mark J. Hilsenroth. 430p. 1997. write for info. (*0-8058-2332-8*) L Erlbaum Assocs.

Teaching & Learning Primary Science. 2nd ed. Wynne Harlen. LC 93-9685. 1993. 29.00 (*1-85396-185-X*, Pub. by Paul Chapman UK) Taylor & Francis.

***Teaching & Learning Science: Critical & Alternative Views.** Anita Roychoudhury. Ed. by Joe Kincheloe & Shirley R. Steinberg. (Critical Education Practice Ser.). 300p. Date not set. text ed. 45.00 (*0-8153-1726-3*); pap. text ed. 18.95 (*0-8153-2327-1*) Garland.

Teaching & Learning Secondary Social Studies. Albert Ellis et al. (C). 1991. text ed. 64.50 (*0-673-38599-X*) Addson-Wesley Educ.

Teaching & Learning Signing Exact English: An Idea Book. Gerilee Gustason. 470p. (Orig.). 1983. pap. 39.95 (*0-916708-08-X*) Modern Signs.

Teaching & Learning Technology. Ed. by Robert McCormick et al. LC 92-37018. 1992. 32.00 (*0-201-63169-5*) Addison-Wesley.

Teaching & Learning Through Discussion: The Theory, Research & Practice of the Discussion Method. Ed. by William W. Wilen. (Illus.). 226p. 1990. pap. 31.95 (*0-398-06497-0*) C C Thomas.

Teaching & Learning Through Topic Work. Rosemary Webb. 224p. 1994. 60.00 (*1-85000-958-9*, Falmer Pr); pap. 24.95 (*1-85000-959-7*, Falmer Pr) Taylor & Francis.

Teaching & Learning Vocabulary. Daryl Nation. 1990. pap. 26.95 (*0-8384-2863-0*) Heinle & Heinle.

Teaching & Learning Vocabulary. Linda L. Taylor. 96p. (C). 1990. pap. 18.25 (*0-13-895301-5*) P-H.

Teaching & Learning with Cases: Promoting Active Learning in Agriculture, Food & Natural Resource Education. Ed. & Intro. by Scott M. Swinton. (Illus.). 238p. (Orig.). 1995. pap. 14.00 (*1-56525-009-5*) MSU Ext.

Teaching & Learning with Computers: A Guide for College Faculty & Administrators. Barry Heermann. LC 87-46331. (Higher & Adult Education Ser.). 261p. text ed. 36.95 (*1-55542-084-2*) Jossey-Bass.

***Teaching & Learning with Multimedia.** Janet Collins & Michael Hammond. 224p. (C). 1998. pap. text ed. 21.95 (*0-415-14897-9*, Routledge NY) Routledge.

Teaching & Learning with Robots. Ed. by Colin Terry & Peter Thomas. 256p. 1987. lib. bdg. 57.50 (*0-7099-4318-0*, Pub. by Croom Helm UK) Routledge Chapman & Hall.

Teaching & Mainstreaming Autistic Children. Peter Knoblock. LC 81-84572. 360p. (C). 1982. pap. text ed. 29.95 (*0-89108-111-9*) Love Pub Co.

Teaching & Managing: Inseparable Activities in Schools. Cyril Wilkinson & Ernie Cave. 224p. 1987. lib. bdg. 52.50 (*0-7099-3693-1*, Pub. by Croom Helm UK) Routledge Chapman & Hall.

Teaching & Mastery of Language. Aelita K. Markova. Ed. by Beatrice B. Szekely. Tr. by Michel Vale. LC 78-65595. 293p. reprint ed. pap. 83.60 (*0-317-41987-0*, 2026124) Bks Demand.

***Teaching & Performing: Ideas for Energizing Your Classes.** Suzanne Burgoyne et al. LC 96-46235. (Orig.). 1996. pap. 24.95 (*0-912150-44-0*) Magna Pubns.

Teaching & Performing Renaissance Choral Music: A Guide for Conductors & Performers. Francis R. Poe. LC 93-23597. 227p. 1994. 37.50 (*0-8108-2778-6*); pap. 25.00 (*0-8108-2886-3*) Scarecrow.

Teaching & Reaching: Junior Resources. Sally E. Stuart. 1983. pap. 2.99 (*0-87162-285-8*, D5702) Warner Pr.

Teaching & Reaching: Primary Resources. Sally E. Stuart. 1983. pap. 2.99 (*0-87162-284-X*, D5701) Warner Pr.

Teaching & Religious Imagination: An Essay in the Theology of Teaching. Maria Harris. LC 90-55780. 1991. pap. 14.00 (*0-06-063840-0*) Harper SF.

***Teaching & Research in the University.** Lewis Pyenson. (Publications of the Graduate School, University of Southwestern Louisiana: Vol. 2). (Illus.). 90p. (Orig.). (C). 1996. pap. 10.00 (*1-889911-00-3*) U SW LA Grad.

Teaching & Researching Language in African Classrooms. Ed. by Casmir M. Rubagumya. LC 93-29931. (Multilingual Matters Ser.: Vol. 98). 214p. 1994. 79.00 (*1-85359-200-5*, Pub. by Multilingual Matters UK); pap. 29.95 (*1-85359-199-8*, Pub. by Multilingual Matters UK) Taylor & Francis.

Teaching & Stress. Ed. by Martin Cole & Stephen Walker. 224p. 1989. 90.00 (*0-335-09548-8*, Open Univ Pr); pap. 32.00 (*0-335-09547-X*, Open Univ Pr) Taylor & Francis.

Teaching & Talking with Deaf Children. David Wood et al. 199p. 1992. pap. text ed. 39.95 (*0-471-93327-9*) Wiley.

Teaching & Technology: The Impact of Unlimited Information Access on Classroom Teaching. Frwd. by Evan I. Farber. 152p. 1991. pap. 25.00 (*0-87650-293-1*) Pierian.

Teaching & Testimony: Rigoberta Menchu & the North American Classroom. Ed. by Allen Carey-Webb & Stephen Benz. LC 96-592. (SUNY Series, Interruptions). 391p. 1996. text ed. 71.50 (*0-7914-3013-8*); pap. text ed. 24.95 (*0-7914-3014-6*) State U NY Pr.

***Teaching & the Art of Successful Classroom Management: A How-To Guidebook for Teachers in Secondary Schools.** Harvey Kraut. LC 96-83576. Orig. Title: A Primer for Beginning Teachers in Secondary Schools. 128p. (Orig.). 1997. pap. 18.95 (*0-8106-2004-9*, 2004-9) NEA.

Teaching & the Art of Successful Classroom Management: A How-to-Guidebook for Teachers in Secondary Schools. 2nd rev. ed. Harvey Kraut. LC 96-83576. (Illus.). 144p. 1996. pap. text ed. 16.95 (*0-9640602-2-1*) Aysa Pubng.

Teaching & the Case Method. 3rd ed. Louis B. Barnes et al. 1994. text ed. 35.00 (*0-07-103601-6*) McGraw.

Teaching & the Case Method. 3rd ed. Louis B. Barnes et al. 1994. pap. text ed. 16.00 (*0-07-103602-4*) McGraw.

Teaching & the Case Method: Text, Cases, & Readings. 3rd ed. Louis B. Barnes et al. LC 94-766. 352p. 1994. 35.00 (*0-87584-403-0*) Harvard Busn.

Teaching & the Unconscious Mind. J. C. Hill. LC 78-141661. 176p. 1971. 30.00 (*0-8236-6365-5*) Intl Univs Pr.

Teaching & Thinking about Curriculum: Critical Inquiries. Ed. by Jim Sears & J. Dan Marshall. 320p. (C). 1990. pap. text ed. 21.95 (*0-8077-2968-X*) Tchrs Coll.

***Teaching & Training on the Internet.** Abigail Hubbard. 220p. 1998. pap. 40.00 (*0-88415-846-2*, 5846) Gulf Pub.

Teaching & Worship of the Liberal Catholic Church. Edmund W. Sheehan. Ed. by William H. Pitkin. (Illus.). 1978. pap. 2.90 (*0-918980-07-0*) St Alban Pr.

Teaching & Writing Popular Fiction: Horror, Adventure, Mystery & Romance in the American Classroom. Karen M. Hubert. (Illus.). 236p. (Orig.). 1976. pap. 13.95 (*0-915924-04-8*) Tchrs & Writers Coll.

Teaching & You: Committing, Preparing, & Succeeding. Jack M. Evans & Martha M. Brueckner. 256p. (C). 1991. pap. text ed. 47.00 (*0-205-13248-0*) Allyn.

An Asterisk (*) at the beginning of an entry indicates that the title is appearing in BIP for the first time.

Teaching Anthropology. Ed. by P. C. Rice. (Special Issues of the Anthropology & Education Quarterly Ser.: Vol. 16, No. 4). 1985. 7.50 (*0-317-66347-X*) Am Anthro Assn.

Teaching Apprentice Program in Language & Literature. Ed. by Joseph Gibaldi et al. LC 81-1159. (Options for Teaching Ser.: No. 4). ix, 133p. (Orig.). 1981. pap. 19.75 (*0-87352-303-2*, J203) Modern Lang.

Teaching Approaches in Music Theory: An Overview of Pedagogical Philosophies. Michael R. Rogers. LC 83-10167. 236p. 1984. 29.95 (*0-8093-1147-X*) S Ill U Pr.

Teaching Archaeology in Schools. James Dyer. 1989. pap. 25.00 (*0-85263-622-9*, Pub. by Shire UK) St Mut.

Teaching Art, Complete Kit 1-3. Laura H. Chapman. (J). (gr. 1-3). 1989. Grades 1-3. 135.50 (*0-87192-200-2*) Davis Mass.

Teaching Art, Complete Kit 4-6. Laura H. Chapman. (J). (gr. 4-6). 1989. Grades 4-6. 135.50 (*0-87192-199-5*) Davis Mass.

Teaching Art: Academies & Schools from Vasari to Albers. Carl Goldstein. (Illus.). 352p. (C). 1996. text ed. 74.95 (*0-521-48099-X*) Cambridge U Pr.

Teaching Art & So On. Edmund B. Feldman. 27p. (Orig.). 1994. pap. text ed. 7.00 (*0-937652-84-9*, 252) Natl Art Ed.

Teaching Art in Elementary School. Sharon L. House. 16.00 (*0-536-58316-1*) Ginn Pr.

Teaching Art in the Elementary School: Enhancing Visual Perception. Phil H. Rueschoff & M. Evelyn Swartz. LC 78-75641. (Illus.). 345p. reprint ed. pap. 98.40 (*0-317-10362-8*, 2055518) Bks Demand.

Teaching Art the Easy Way: A Complete Art Curriculum for Grades K-3. Marcy U. Effinger. (Illus.). 152p. 1993. teacher ed., spiral bd. 19.95 (*0-9633334-6-1*) Rainbow Artist.

Teaching Art the Easy Way: A Complete Art Curriculumm & Textbook for Grades 4 - 8. Marcy Uphoff Effinger. (Illus.). 184p. (Orig.). 1992. pap. 19.95 (*0-9633334-7-X*) Rainbow Artist.

Teaching Art to the Deaf. Linda K. Kingsley. 1974. lib. bdg. 250.00 (*0-8490-1179-5*) Gordon Pr.

Teaching Art to Young Children. Rob Barnes. LC 86-8032. (Illus.). 215p. (C). 1987. pap. text ed. 19.95 (*0-415-07891-1*, Routledge NY) Routledge.

Teaching Art to Young Children Four to Nine. Rob Barnes. (Illus.). 176p. (C). 1987. pap. text ed. 19.95 (*0-04-371097-2*) Routledge Chapman & Hall.

Teaching As a Lively Art. Marjorie Spock. 145p. 1988. reprint ed. pap. 12.95 (*0-88010-127-X*) Anthroposophic.

***Teaching As a Seductive Activity: The English Teacher As School Reformer.** Denny Wolfe & Joseph C. Antinarella. LC 97-3436. (Orig.). 1997. pap. text ed. 18.50 (*0-86709-420-6*, 0420) Boynton Cook Pubs.

Teaching As Communication. Bob Hodge. LC 93-3899. 1993. pap. text ed. write for info. (*0-582-07222-0*) Longman.

Teaching as Decision Making. Georgia Langer. (C). 1996. pap. text ed. write for info. (*0-8013-1560-3*) Addison-Wesley.

Teaching as Decision Making. Georgia Langer. (C). 1996. pap. text ed. write for info. (*0-8013-1561-1*) Addison-Wesley.

Teaching As Decision Making. Georgea Sparking-Langer. (C). 1996. pap. text ed. write for info. (*0-8013-1278-7*) Addison-Wesley.

***Teaching As Decision Making.** 3rd ed. Marvin Pasch. (C). 1998. text ed. write for info. (*0-8013-1864-5*) Addison-Wesley.

Teaching As Decision-Making: Successful Practices for the Elementary Teacher. 2nd ed. Marvin Pasch et al. LC 94-27769. 373p. (C). 1995. pap. text ed. 41.95 (*0-8013-1431-3*) Longman.

Teaching As Enhancing Human Effectiveness. Ed. by Erskine S. Dottin & Lynne D. Miller. LC 94-17669. 98p. (Orig.). (C). 1994. reprint ed. pap. text ed. 19.50 (*0-8191-9576-6*) U Pr of Amer.

Teaching As Jesus Taught. Roy B. Zuck. LC 95-4024. 368p. (Orig.). (C). 1995. pap. 19.99 (*0-8010-9940-4*) Baker Bks.

Teaching As Leading: Profiles of Excellence on the Open-Door College. George A. Baker, III et al. 300p. 1990. 34.00 (*0-87117-199-6*, 1211) Am Assn Comm Coll.

Teaching As Learning: An Action Research Approach. Jean McNiff. LC 92-32095. 128p. (C). 1993. pap. 17.95 (*0-415-08390-7*, B0179) Routledge.

Teaching As Learning: An Action Research Approach. Jean McNiff. LC 92-32095. 128p. (C). (gr. 13). 1993. text ed. 69.95 (*0-415-08980-8*, B0175) Routledge.

***Teaching as Paul Taught.** Roy B. Zuck. 272p. (C). Date not set. pap. 19.99 (*0-8010-2159-6*) Baker Bks.

Teaching As Story Telling: An Alternative Approach to Teaching & Curriculum in the Elementary School. Kieran Egan. viii, 132p. 1989. pap. text ed. 8.95 (*0-226-19032-3*); lib. bdg. 24.95 (*0-226-19031-5*) U Ch Pr.

Teaching As Though Students Mattered. Ed. by Joseph Katz. LC 84-82380. (New Directions for Teaching & Learning Ser.: No. TL 21). (Orig.). 1985. pap. 19.00 (*0-87589-771-1*) Jossey-Bass.

***Teaching Asian American History.** Gary Y. Okihiro. Ed. by Nell I. Painter & Antonio Rios-Bustamante. (Teaching Diversity Ser.). 72p. (Orig.). 1997. pap. 8.00 (*0-87229-077-8*) Am Hist Assn.

***Teaching Asian American Women's History.** Shirley Hune. Ed. by Nell I. Painter & Antonio Rios-Bustamante. (Teaching Diversity Ser.). 72p. (Orig.). 1997. pap. 8.00 (*0-87229-079-4*) Am Hist Assn.

Teaching ASL As a Second-Foreign Language: Proceedings of National Symposium on Sign Language Research & Teaching. Ed. by Frank Caccamise et al. 240p. (Orig.). (C). 1982. pap. text ed. 4.95 (*0-913072-49-4*) Natl Assn Deaf.

Teaching Assistant. Jack Rudman. (Career Examination Ser.: C-2845). 1994. pap. 23.95 (*0-8373-2845-4*) Nat Learn.

Teaching Assistant Training in the 1990s. Ed. by Jody D. Nyquist et al. LC 85-644763. (New Directions for Teaching & Learning Ser.: No. TL 39). 1989. 19.00 (*1-55542-858-4*) Jossey-Bass.

***Teaching at a Distance with the Merging Technologies: An Instructional Systems Approach.** Thomas E. Cyrs. Ed. & Des. by Eugenia D. Conway. (Illus.). 300p. (Orig.). 1997. pap. text ed. 48.00 (*0-9628477-3-9*) NM State U CED.

Teaching At-Risk & Inner-City Students. Kevin Angulski. LC 93-73960. 150p. (Orig.). 1994. pap. 12.95 (*0-9638899-0-7*) DSD Pubns.

Teaching Atlas of Breast Ultrasound. 2nd ed. Wolfgang Leucht & Dagmar Leucht. LC 95-39577. (Illus.). 250p. 1996. text ed. 95.00 (*0-86577-572-9*) Thieme Med Pubs.

***Teaching Atlas of Hand Radiology: A Self-Assessment Text.** S. Gilani & B. K. Wignall. (Illus.). 213p. 1995. pap. write for info. (*0-7020-1731-0*, Pub. by W B Saunders UK) Saunders.

Teaching Atlas of Mammography. 2nd rev. ed. Lazzlo Tabar & Peter B. Dean. (Illus.). 328p. 1985. 140.00 (*0-86577-198-7*) Thieme Med Pubs.

Teaching Atlas of Thoracic Radiology. Sebastian Lange & Paul Stark. LC 92-49323. 1993. 99.00 (*0-86577-467-6*) Thieme Med Pubs.

Teaching Atlas of Urologic Radiology. Sebastian Lange. LC 94-35149. (Illus.). 300p. (ENG.). 1994. 99.00 (*0-86577-540-0*) Thieme Med Pubs.

Teaching Authority in the Early Church. Robert B. Eno. Ed. by Thomas Halton. LC 83-83253. (Message of the Fathers of the Church Ser.: Vol. 14). 168p. 1984. pap. 11.95 (*0-8146-5325-1*) Liturgical Pr.

***Teaching Ballet Technique.** Gayle Kassing & Danielle Jay. (Illus.). (Orig.). (C). 1997. pap. text ed. write for info. (*0-87322-997-5*, BKAS0997) Human Kinetics.

Teaching Bankers see Creative Approaches to Teaching Adults

Teaching Basic Aquatics . . . Especially to Those Who Have Difficulty Learning. Marlene M. Donahue-Gandy. LC 84-71097. (Illus.). 104p. (Orig.). 1984. pap. 10.00 (*0-9613514-0-3*) M M Donahue-Gandy.

Teaching Basic Ceramics. Alberta Meitin. LC 90-63281. 54p. 1990. pap. text ed. 4.95 (*0-916809-45-5*) Scott Pubns MI.

Teaching Basic Guitar Skills to Special Learners: A Data-Based Approach. 2nd rev. ed. Robert M. Krout. 1983. spiral bd. 16.00 (*0-918812-31-3*, ST 156) MMB Music.

Teaching Basic Gymnastics: A Coeducational Approach. 3rd ed. Phyllis S. Cooper & Milan Trnka. LC 93-7874. 320p. (C). 1993. pap. text ed. 49.00 (*0-02-324701-0*, Macmillan Coll) P-H.

Teaching Basic Jumping. Martin Diggle. 141p. (C). 1990. pap. 30.00 (*0-85131-481-3*, Pub. by J A Allen & Co UK) St Mut.

Teaching Basic Skills in College: A Guide to Objectives, Skills Assessment, Course Content, Teaching Methods, Support Services, & Administration. Alice S. Trillin et al. LC 79-92469. 349p. reprint ed. pap. 99.50 (*0-8357-4694-1*, 2052349) Bks Demand.

Teaching Basic Skills Through Home Economics. Ed. by Sandra W. Miller & Charlotte R. Tulloch. 75p. (C). 1989. pap. text ed. 8.00 (*0-911365-29-X*, A261-08474) Family & Consumer Sci Educ.

Teaching Basic Skills Through Literature, Language Arts. Owens. (Illus.). 144p. (J). (gr. 1-3). 1995. wbk. ed., pap. text ed. 12.95 (*1-55734-792-1*) Tchr Create Mat.

Teaching Basics: Adult. Daryl Dale. (Illus.). 80p. (Orig.). 1985. pap. 3.50 (*0-87509-369-8*) Chr Pubns.

Teaching Basics: Junior. Daryl Dale. (Illus.). 73p. (Orig.). 1985. pap. 3.50 (*0-87509-359-0*) Chr Pubns.

Teaching Basics: Preschool. Mavis Weidman. Ed. by Daryl Dale. (Illus.). 78p. (Orig.). 1985. pap. 3.50 (*0-87509-370-1*) Chr Pubns.

Teaching Basics: Primary. Daryl Dale. (Illus.). 77p. (Orig.). 1985. pap. 3.50 (*0-87509-363-9*) Chr Pubns.

Teaching Basics: Youth. Daryl Dale. (Illus.). 80p. (Orig.). 1985. pap. 3.50 (*0-87509-364-7*) Chr Pubns.

Teaching Basis Riding. Ed. by Anne Lewis. 93p. (C). 1990. pap. 21.00 (*0-85131-460-0*, Pub. by J A Allen & Co UK) St Mut.

Teaching Basketball. N. Sue Whiddon & Howard Reynolds. (Illus.). 131p. (C). 1991. reprint ed. pap. text ed. 12.50 (*0-88133-581-9*) Waveland Pr.

***Teaching, Bearing the Torch.** Pamela J. Farris. 36p. (C). 1996. teacher ed., per. write for info. (*0-697-35645-0*) Wm C Brown Pubs.

Teaching Behavior to Infants & Toddlers: A Manual for Caregivers & Parents. Bernice Stewart & Julie S. Vargas. (Illus.). 268p. 1990. pap. 32.95 (*0-398-06444-X*) C C Thomas.

Teaching Behavior to Infants & Toddlers: A Manual for Caregivers & Parents. Bernice Stewart & Julie S. Vargas. (Illus.). 268p. (C). 1990. text ed. 49.95 (*0-398-05638-2*) C C Thomas.

Teaching Behavioral Self-Control to Students. Edward Workman. LC 82-435. (Illus.). 120p. (Orig.). (C). 1982. pap. text ed. 19.00 (*0-936104-23-6*, 0071) PRO-ED.

Teaching Behavioral Self-Control to Students. 2nd ed. Edward A. Workman & Alan M. Katz. LC 94-33599. 1995. 21.00 (*0-89079-617-3*) PRO-ED.

Teaching Behaviorally Disordered Students: Preferred Practices. Daniel P. Morgan & William R. Jenson. 480p. (C). 1990. text ed. 77.00 (*0-675-20543-3*, Merrill Coll) P-H.

Teaching Better Riding. Werner Habermann. 77p. (C). 1990. pap. 21.00 (*0-85131-355-8*, Pub. by J A Allen & Co UK) St Mut.

***Teaching Bible in the Classroom.** Robert J. Walker. (Illus.). 220p. 1997. lib. bdg. 19.95 (*0-9642553-3-2*) In His Name.

Teaching Bibliographic Skills in History: A Sourcebook for Historians & Librarians. Ed. by Charles D'Aniello. LC 92-8833. 392p. 1993. text ed. 65.00 (*0-313-25266-1*, DTB, Greenwood Pr) Greenwood.

Teaching Bilingual Children: Anthology Dealing with Key Issues & Practical Problems in Bilingual Education. Ed. by Arthur Tobier. 54p. 1974. pap. 2.00 (*0-918374-17-0*) City Coll Wk.

Teaching Billy to Cook: Recipes & Life at Georgia Grille. Karen Hilliard. (Illus.). 64p. 1994. 18.00 (*0-9644697-0-7*) Montgmry Pub.

Teaching Black Children to Read. Ed. by Joan C. Baratz & Roger W. Shuy. LC 72-3760. (Urban Language Ser.: No. 4). 233p. reprint ed. pap. 66.50 (*0-8357-3342-4*, 2039570) Bks Demand.

Teaching Boating Safety. YMCA of The U.S.A. Staff. (Illus.). 64p. 1989. pap. text ed. 6.00 (*0-87322-225-3*, LYMC5001, YMCA USA) Human Kinetics.

Teaching Brass: A Resource Manual. Wayne Bailey et al. 192p. (C). 1992. text ed. write for info. (*0-07-003266-1*) McGraw.

Teaching Bridge: How to Do It Better. Caroline Sydnor. LC 78-104076. (Illus.). 217p. (Orig.). 1988. pap. 15.00 (*0-318-41049-4*) C Sydnor.

***Teaching Buddy Skills to Preschoolers.** Kristine M. English. LC 97-2471. (Innovations Ser.). 1997. write for info. (*0-940898-45-4*) Am Assn Mental.

Teaching Business Communication. Max L. Waters & Don Leonard. (Rapid Reader Ser.: No. 6). (Illus.). 44p. (C). 1985. pap. text ed. 8.00 (*0-9603064-4-7*) Delta Pi Epsilon.

Teaching Business Ethics in the U. K., U. S. A. & Europe: A Comparative Study. Jack Mahoney. LC 90-635. 224p. (C). 1990. text ed. 49.95 (*0-485-11399-6*, Pub. by Athlone Pr UK) Humanities.

Teaching Business Studies. David Needham et al. LC 92-20520. 1992. 15.99 (*0-07-707602-8*) McGraw.

***Teaching Cases from Annals of Oncology.** R. L. Souhami. 196p. 1997. lib. bdg. 99.00 (*0-7923-4373-5*) Kluwer Ac.

Teaching Cases from Annals of Oncology. Robert L. Souhami. LC 96-21996. 1997. pap. text ed. 47.00 (*0-7923-4117-1*) Kluwer Ac.

Teaching Catholic Family Values: A Parent Handbook. Ann Gallagher et al. (Grade School Chastity - Project Genesis Ser.). (Illus.). 96p. (Orig.). (YA). (gr. 5 up). 1996. pap. text ed. write for info. (*1-885845-22-7*) Leaflet Missal.

Teaching Chemistry with Toys: Activities for Grades K-9. Terrific Science Press Staff. LC 95-2028. 1995. pap. text ed. 19.95 (*0-07-064722-4*) McGraw.

Teaching Children. C. H. Spurgen. 1981. mass mkt. 1.00 (*1-56186-344-0*) Pilgrim Pubns.

Teaching Children: A Curriculum Guide to What Children Need to Know at Each Grade Level Through Sixth Grade. Diane Lopez. LC 87-71895. 299p. 1988. pap. 12.99 (*0-89107-489-9*) Crossway Bks.

Teaching Children about Food: A Teaching & Activities Guide. Christine Berman & Jacki Fromer. (Illus.). 96p. (Orig.). 1991. pap. 8.95 (*0-923521-15-1*) Bull Pub.

Teaching Children about Life & Earth Science: Ideas & Activities Every Teacher & Parent Can Use. Elaine Levenson. LC 93-40784. 1994. pap. text ed. 16.95 (*0-07-037655-7*) McGraw.

Teaching Children about Prayer. Judy G. Smith. 25p. (Orig.). (J). (gr. 4-6). 1988. pap. 6.95 (*0-940754-56-8*) Ed Ministries.

Teaching Children about Science: Ideas & Activities Every Teacher & Parent Can Use. Elaine Levenson. LC 93-34326. 1994. pap. text ed. 16.95 (*0-07-037619-0*) McGraw-Hill Prof.

Teaching Children about Science Ideas & Activities Teachers & Parents Can Use. Elaine Levenson. 1993. pap. text ed. write for info. (*0-8306-4598-5*) TAB Bks.

Teaching Children about Technology. Scobey. (Tech & Industrial Education Ser.). 1993. teacher ed. 14.95 (*0-8273-5310-3*); text ed. 47.95 (*0-8273-5308-1*) Delmar.

Teaching Children & Adolescents with Special Needs. 2nd ed. Judy L. Olson & Jennifer M. Platt. 448p. (C). 1995. pap. text ed. 49.00 (*0-13-432899-X*) P-H.

Teaching Children & Youth with Behavior Disorders. 2nd ed. Thomas M. Shea & Anne M. Bauer. (Illus.). 400p. 1986. text ed. 75.00 (*0-13-891888-0*) P-H.

Teaching Children Art. Hobbs & Rush. 1997. pap. text ed. 48.00 (*0-13-104159-2*) P-H.

Teaching Children Charity. Linda Eyre & Richard Eyre. LC 85-27468. (Illus.). 270p. 1986. 9.95 (*0-87579-024-0*) Deseret Bk.

***Teaching Children Christian Values.** 272p. 1998. write for info. (*1-56476-695-0*, Victor Bks) Chariot Victor.

***Teaching Children Dance.** Theresa M. Purcell. 136p. 1994. pap. text ed. 29.95 (*0-87322-705-0*, AMTP0308) Human Kinetics.

Teaching Children Dance: Becoming a Master Teacher. Theresa Purcell. (Illus.). 136p. 1994. pap. text ed. 15.00 (*0-87322-479-5*, BPUR0479) Human Kinetics.

***Teaching Children English: An Activity-Based Training Course Book.** 288p. 1995. text ed. 47.95 (*0-521-42015-6*) Cambridge U Pr.

***Teaching Children Fitness.** Thomas Ratliffe & Larraine M. Ratliffe. 128p. 1994. pap. text ed. 29.95 incl. vhs (*0-87322-707-7*, AMTP0309) Human Kinetics.

Teaching Children Fitness: Becoming a Master Teacher. Thomas Ratliffe & Laraine M. Ratliffe. LC 93-42449. (Illus.). 128p. 1994. pap. text ed. 15.00 (*0-87322-478-7*, BRAT0478) Human Kinetics.

***Teaching Children Games.** David E. Belka. 144p. 1994. pap. text ed. 29.95 incl. vhs (*0-87322-701-8*, AMTP0306) Human Kinetics.

Teaching Children Games: Becoming a Master Teacher. David E. Belka. LC 93-30702. (Illus.). 144p. 1994. pap. text ed. 15.00 (*0-87322-481-7*, BBEL0481) Human Kinetics.

***Teaching Children Gymnastics.** Peter H. Werner. 160p. 1994. pap. text ed. 29.95 incl. vhs (*0-87322-709-3*, AMTP0310) Human Kinetics.

Teaching Children Gymnastics: Becoming a Master Teacher. Peter Werner. LC 93-21409. (Illus.). 160p. 1994. pap. text ed. 15.00 (*0-87322-477-9*, BWER0477) Human Kinetics.

Teaching Children How to Succeed. Bruce W. Tuckman. 20p. 1995. 2.95 (*1-56456-093-7*) W Gladden Found.

Teaching Children in Multicultural Classrooms. De Melendez. LC 96-23105. (Early Childhood Education Ser.). 416p. 1996. 41.50 (*0-8273-7275-2*) Delmar.

Teaching Children in Multicultural Classrooms. Demelendez. (Early Childhood Education Ser.). 64p. 1996. teacher ed., pap. 10.00 (*0-8273-7276-0*) Delmar.

Teaching Children in the Laboratory. Joan Solomon. 156p. 1980. 25.00 (*0-7099-2304-X*, Pub. by Croom Helm UK); pap. 9.00 (*0-7099-2305-8*, Pub. by Croom Helm UK) Routledge Chapman & Hall.

***Teaching Children Movement Concepts.** Craig A. Buschner. 160p. 1994. pap. text ed. 29.95 incl. vhs (*0-87322-703-4*, ATMP0307) Human Kinetics.

Teaching Children Movement Concepts & Skills: Becoming a Master Teacher. Craig A. Buschner. LC 93-33577. (Illus.). 160p. 1994. pap. text ed. 15.00 (*0-87322-480-9*, BBUS0480) Human Kinetics.

Teaching Children Music: Fundamentals of Music & Method. 3rd ed. Grant Newman. 400p. (C). 1988. spiral bd. write for info. (*0-697-03644-8*) Brown & Benchmark.

Teaching Children Music: Fundamentals of Music & Method. 3rd ed. Grant Newman. 400p. (C). 1989. student ed., per. write for info. (*0-697-03652-9*) Brown & Benchmark.

Teaching Children Music: Fundamentals of Music & Method. 4th ed. Grant Newman. 400p. (C). 1994. spiral bd. write for info. (*0-697-12540-8*) Brown & Benchmark.

Teaching Children Music: Fundamentals of Music & Method. 4th ed. Grant Newman. 80p. (C). 1995. student ed., per. write for info. (*0-697-12541-6*) Brown & Benchmark.

Teaching Children Physical Education: Becoming a Master Teacher. George Graham. LC 91-25520. (Illus.). 192p. (Orig.). 1992. pap. text ed. 22.00 (*0-87322-340-3*, BGRA0340) Human Kinetics.

Teaching Children Responsibility: Children & Jobs. rev. ed. Linda Dastrup. (Illus.). 15p. 1986. student ed. 5.95 (*0-9621898-0-4*) Creative Changes.

Teaching Children Science. Joseph Abruscato. (Illus.). 544p. (C). 1982. write for info. (*0-13-891754-X*) P-H.

Teaching Children Science: A Discovery Approach. 4th ed. Joseph Abruscato. LC 95-23052. 1995. text ed. 63.67 (*0-205-16807-8*) Allyn.

Teaching Children Self-Discipline...at Home & at School. Thomas Gordon. 1989. 17.95 (*0-8129-1780-4*, Times Bks) Random.

Teaching Children Self-Esteem. Anne R. Smith. LC 93-41915. (Illus.). 294p. 1994. spiral bd. 29.95 (*0-7734-1976-4*) E Mellen.

Teaching Children Tennis the Vic Braden Way. Vic Braden & Bill Bruns. (Sports Illustrated Book). (Illus.). 1982. 17.45 (*0-316-10512-0*) Little.

Teaching Children the Love of Missionary Work. Marc S. Garrison & Bruce L. Olsen. 93p. (Orig.). 1990. pap. 7.95 (*1-56236-151-1*) Aspen Bks.

Teaching Children to be Leaders. Anthony V. Manzo. (C). 1994. teacher ed., pap. text ed. 33.75 (*0-15-502399-3*) HB Coll Pubs.

Teaching Children to Be Literate: A Reflective Approach. Anthony V. Manzo & Ula C. Manzo. (Illus.). 640p. (C). 1994. write for info. (*0-15-300560-2*) HB Coll Pubs.

Teaching Children to Care: Management in the Responsive Classroom. Ruth S. Charney. LC 91-68573. (Illus.). 304p. (Orig.). 1992. pap. 22.50 (*0-9618636-1-7*) NE Found Child.

***Teaching Children to Focus: An Interview with Marianne Thompson.** Edwin M. McMahon & Peter A. Campbell. 20p. 1996. 2.00 (*1-55612-505-4*, LL1505) Sheed & Ward MO.

Teaching Children to Love: Eighty Games & Fun Activities for Raising Balanced Children in Unbalanced Times. Lew Childre. Ed. by Sara H. Paddison. LC HQ769. C482. 200p. 1996. pap. text ed. 16.95 (*1-879052-26-1*) Planetary Pubns.

Teaching Children to Paint. Karla Cikanova. 128p. (J). (gr. 3-7). 1993. text ed. 22.50 (*976-8097-39-6*) Gordon & Breach.

Teaching Children to Pray. Keith Wooden. 112p. 1992. pap. 10.99 (*0-310-54481-5*) Zondervan.

Teaching Children to Read. 3rd ed. Lillian Gray. LC 63-11837. 458p. reprint ed. pap. 130.60 (*0-317-07747-3*, 2012543) Bks Demand.

Teaching Children to Read: From Basals to Books. 2nd ed. Robert B. Cooter, Jr. & Ray D. Reutzel. LC 95-16834. 1995. text ed. 63.00 (*0-02-399573-4*, Macmillan Coll) P-H.

Teaching Children to Read & Write: Becoming an Influential Teacher. Robert B. Ruddell & Martha R. Ruddell. LC 94-24036. 1994. text ed. 62.00 (*0-205-13788-1*) Allyn.

Teaching Children to Read Art. Joyce Renshaw. Ed. by Ken Renshaw. (Illus.). 115p. (Orig.). 1992. pap. 16.50 (*0-9616620-8-5*) Constellation Pr.

Teaching Children to Summarize in Fifth Grade History. Chester O. Newlun. LC 75-177120. (Columbia University. Teachers College. Contributions to Education Ser.: No. 404). (C). reprint ed. 37.50 (*0-404-55404-0*) AMS Pr.

***Teaching Children to Think.** Robert Fisher. 272p. (Orig.). 1990. pap. 47.50 (*0-7487-2235-1*, Pub. by Stanley Thornes UK) Trans-Atl Phila.

Teaching Children to Write K-8. Robert L. Hillerich. LC 85-3588. 290p. 1985. 18.95 (*0-13-891805-8*, Busn) P-H.

Teaching Children with Autism: Strategies for Initiating Positive Interactions & Improving Learning Opportunities. Robert L. Koegel. Ed. by Lynn K. Koegel. LC 94-45943. 272p. 1995. pap. 32.00 (*1-55766-180-4*) P H Brookes.

Teaching Children with Autism: Strategies to Enhance Communication & Socialization. Kathleen Ann Quill. 336p. 1996. pap. 29.95 (*0-8273-6269-2*) Delmar.

Teaching Children with Confidence. 32p. 1983. teacher ed. 4.50 (*0-910566-40-2*) Evang Trg Assn.

Teaching Children with Confidence. David Jenkins. 48p. 1983. ring bd. 4.25 (*0-910566-39-9*) Evang Trg Assn.

Teaching Children with Diversity. Churton & Cranston. LC 97-17563. 1996. pap. text ed. 44.00 (*0-205-18344-1*) P-H.

Teaching Children with Severe Behavior-Communication Disorders. Betty Van Witsen. LC 77-10483. (Teachers College Series in Special Education). (Illus.). 159p. reprint ed. pap. 45.40 (*0-8357-8341-3*, 2034165) Bks Demand.

Teaching Children with Severe Learning Difficulties: The Practise of Practice. Ed. by Christina Tilstone & Rosemary Siddles. 160p. 1991. pap. 29.95 (*1-85346-171-7*, Pub. by D Fulton UK) Taylor & Francis.

Teaching Children with Visual Impairments. Tony Best. (Children with Special Needs Ser.). 160p. 1991. 90.00 (*0-335-15990-7*, Open Univ Pr); pap. 32.00 (*0-335-15989-3*, Open Univ Pr) Taylor & Francis.

Teaching Children's Literature. Geoff Fenwick. (Illus.). 208p. (Orig.). 1990. pap. 32.95 (*0-8464-1444-9*) Beekman Pubs.

Teaching Children's Literature. Glenn E. Sadler. LC 92-3112. (Options for Teaching Ser.: No. 11). ix, 257p. 1992. pap. 19.75 (*0-87352-367-9*, J211P); lib. bdg. 37.50 (*0-87352-366-0*, J211C) Modern Lang.

Teaching Children's Literature: A Resource Guide, with a Directory of Courses. Anne H. Lundin & Carol W. Cubberley. LC 94-32679. 363p. 1995. lib. bdg. 42.50 (*0-89950-990-8*) McFarland & Co.

Teaching China's Lost Generation. Barlow & Lowe. 1987. reprint ed. 8.95 (*0-8351-1818-5*) China Bks.

Teaching Choral Concepts: Simple Lesson Plans & Teaching Aids for In-Rehearsal Choir Instruction. Duane S. Crowther. LC 79-89356. (Illus.). 447p. 1979. 39.98 (*0-88290-119-2*) Horizon Utah.

Teaching Choral Music. Don L. Collins. 448p. 1993. text ed. 45.00 (*0-13-891490-7*) P-H.

Teaching Choral Music: A Course of Study. Ed. by Charles Hoffer et al. 64p. (Orig.). (C). 1991. teacher ed. 18.25 (*1-56545-002-7*, 1601) Music Ed Natl.

Teaching Choral Sight Reading. Jack Boyd. LC 75-12658. 209p. 1981. reprint ed. pap. text ed. 16.95 (*0-916656-17-9*, MFBK 17) Mark Foster Mus.

Teaching Christian Children about Judaism. Deborah J. Levine. LC 94-48369. 64p. (Orig.). (J). 1995. pap. 18.00 incl. audio (*1-56854-076-0*, TCCAJ) Liturgy Tr Pubns.

Teaching Christian Values. Lucie W. Barber. LC 83-22981. 250p. (Orig.). (C). 1984. pap. 2.95 (*0-89135-041-1*) Religious Educ.

Teaching Christianity, Vol. I/11. Augustine, Saint. Ed. by John E. Rotelle. Tr. by Edmund Hill from LAT. (Works of St. Augustine: No. I/18). 248p. (Orig.). 1996. pap. 19.95 (*1-56548-049-X*) New City.

Teaching Christianity, Vol. I/11. St. Augustine. Ed. by John E. Rotelle. Tr. by Edmund Hill from LAT. (Works of St. Augustine). 248p. (Orig.). 1996. 29.95 (*1-56548-048-1*) New City.

Teaching Church. 2nd ed. L. T. Johnson & Edward A. Buchanan. (Enabling Ser.). (Illus.). 95p. (Orig.). 1984. pap. 3.95 (*0-935797-00-9*) Harvest IL.

Teaching Church: Active in Mission. Paul Gehris & Kathy Gehris. 80p. 1987. pap. 8.00 (*0-8170-1080-7*) Judson.

Teaching Church: Moving Christian Education to Center Stage. Eugene C. Roehlkepartain. LC 92-41987. 208p. (Orig.). 1993. pap. 13.95 (*0-687-41083-5*) Abingdon.

Teaching Church at Work: A Manual for the Board of Christian Education. rev. ed. Ed. by Kenneth D. Blazier & Linda R. Isham. LC 93-31239. 88p. 1993. pap. 11.00 (*0-8170-1191-9*) Judson.

Teaching Classical Ballet. John White. (Illus.). 240p. (C). 1996. 49.95 (*0-8130-1394-1*); pap. 24.95 (*0-8130-1395-X*) U Press Fla.

Teaching Clinical Decison Making: A Handbook for Instructors. Ed. by Randall D. Cebul & Lawrence H. Beck. LC 85-3532. 192p. 1985. text ed. 37.50 (*0-275-91333-3*, C1333, Praeger Pubs) Greenwood.

Teaching Clinical Nursing. 2nd ed. Ed. by Susan J. Hinchliff. LC 85-32550. (Illus.). 296p. (Orig.). (C). 1986. pap. 30.00 (*0-443-02845-1*) Churchill.

Teaching, Coaching, & Learning Tennis: An Annotated Bibliography. Dennis J. Phillips. LC 89-10534. 190p. 1989. 19.50 (*0-8108-2254-7*) Scarecrow.

***Teaching Cognitive Concepts Through Psychomotor Activities.** John Helion & Frank Fry. 168p. (C). 1996. pap. text ed. 25.40 (*0-7872-2834-6*) Kendall-Hunt.

Teaching College: Collected Readings for the New Instructor. Rose A. Neff & Maryellen G. Weimer. 146p. 1990. pap. 21.95 (*0-912150-12-2*) Magna Pubns.

Teaching College Freshmen. Bette L. Erickson & Diane W. Strommer. LC 90-46069. (Higher & Adult Education Ser.). 269p. text ed. 31.95 (*1-55542-310-8*) Jossey-Bass.

***Teaching College Writing.** Maggy Smith. pap. write for info. (*0-205-17506-6*) Allyn.

Teaching Communication. Graeme Burton & Richard Dimbleby. 272p. (C). 1990. pap. text ed. 18.95 (*0-415-03063-3*, A4002) Routledge.

Teaching Communication: Theory, Research & Methods. Ed. by J. A. Daly et al. 520p. (C). 1990. pap. 45.00 (*0-8058-0162-6*); text ed. 125.00 (*0-8058-0645-8*) L Erlbaum Assocs.

Teaching Communication & Reading Skills in the Content Areas. Dorothy G. Hennings. 125p. (Orig.). 1982. pap. 9.00 (*0-87367-780-3*) Phi Delta Kappa.

Teaching Composition: Ten Bibliographical Essays. Gary Tate. LC 76-629. 316p. 1976. reprint ed. pap. 90.10 (*0-608-00736-6*, 2061512) Bks Demand.

Teaching Composition: Twelve Bibliographical Essays. 2nd rev. ed. Ed. by Gary Tate. LC 86-40376. 434p. 1987. pap. text ed. 16.95 (*0-87565-069-4*) Tex Christian.

Teaching Composition Around the Pacific Rim: Politics & Pedagogy. Ed. by Mark N. Brock & Larry Walters. LC 92-13741. 1992. 79.00 (*1-85359-161-0*, Pub. by Multilingual Matters UK); pap. 29.95 (*1-85359-160-2*, Pub. by Multilingual Matters UK) Taylor & Francis.

Teaching Comprehensive Medical Care: A Psychological Study of a Change in Medical Education. Kenneth Hammond. (Commonwealth Fund Publications). 664p. (C). 1959. 49.95 (*0-674-86910-9*) HUP.

Teaching Computer Applications. Carol A. Lundgren et al. (Illus.). 66p. (Orig.). (C). 1996. pap. text ed. 12.00 (*1-881530-01-9*) Delta Pi Epsilon.

Teaching Computers to Teach. 2nd ed. Esther R. Steinberg. 248p. 1992. pap. 27.50 (*0-8058-0779-9*); text ed. 49.95 (*0-8058-0778-0*) L Erlbaum Assocs.

Teaching Computers to Teach. 2nd ed. Esther R. Steinberg. 200p. (C). 1992. Apple II. disk 24.95 (*1-56321-051-7*) L Erlbaum Assocs.

Teaching Concepts: An Instructional Design Guide. 2nd ed. M. David Merrill et al. LC 92-15348. (Illus.). 232p. 1992. 37.95 (*0-87778-247-4*) Educ Tech Pubns.

Teaching Conflict Resolution & Peace Education. rev. ed. Ed. by Frank A. Stone. 56p. 1982. 5.00 (*0-317-65387-3*) I N Thut World Educ Ctr.

Teaching Conflict Resolution Skills. Barbara S. Fritz. (For Parents Only Ser.). 16p. 1994. 1.95 (*1-56688-196-X*) Bur For At-Risk.

Teaching Conflict Resolution Through Children's Literature. William J. Kreidler. 1994. pap. 14.95 (*0-590-49747-2*) Scholastic Inc.

***Teaching Consultation Process Sourcebook.** Susan Edington & Cathy Hunt. (Faculty Development Ser.). 176p. (Orig.). 1996. pap. 18.95 (*0-913507-76-8*) New Forums.

Teaching Consumer Education. David Graf. (Rapid Reader Ser.: No. 2). (Illus.). 59p. (C). 1977. pap. text ed. 5.00 (*0-9603064-0-4*) Delta Pi Epsilon.

Teaching Contemporary Theory to Undergraduates. Ed. by Dianne F. Sadoff & William E. Cain. (Options for Teaching Ser.: No. 12). vi, 271p. (Orig.). 1994. pap. 19.75 (*0-87352-369-5*, J212P); lib. bdg. 37.50 (*0-87352-368-7*, J212C) Modern Lang.

Teaching Content: ESL Strategies for Classroom Teachers. rev. ed. Frank Gonzales. 52p. (Orig.). 1995. pap. text ed. 8.50 (*1-878550-56-X*) Inter Dev Res Assn.

Teaching Content Areas. Harold L. Herber & Joan Nelson-Herber. 1991. 25.00 (*0-13-892712-X*, 710112) P-H.

Teaching Content Reading & Writing. Martha R. Ruddell. LC 92-31127. 1993. text ed. 58.00 (*0-205-14003-3*) Allyn.

Teaching Content Reading & Writing. 2nd ed. Ruddell. 480p. 1996. 58.00 (*0-205-26563-4*) Allyn.

Teaching Content Through Reading: A Human Experience. E. Coston Frederick. (Illus.). 214p. (Orig.). (C). 1983. pap. text ed., spiral bd. 29.95 (*0-398-04901-7*) C C Thomas.

Teaching Cooperation Skills. 2nd ed. Pat Huggins. (ASSIST Program, Affective/Social Skills Ser.). (Illus.). 342p. 1994. teacher ed., pap. text ed. 30.00 (*1-57035-005-1*, 18CO) Sopris.

Teaching Cooperative Learning in the Classroom. David W. Johnson et al. LC 94-36938. 1994. pap. 16.95 (*0-87120-239-5*) Assn Supervision.

***Teaching Creation Science in Public Schools.** Gish. pap. 4.95 (*0-932766-36-6*, Inst Creation) Master Bks.

Teaching Creative Behavior. Doris J. Shallcross. 168p. 1985. reprint ed. pap. 14.95 (*0-943456-07-X*) Bearly Ltd.

Teaching Creative Writing. Melissa Donovan. 144p. (J). (gr. 3-8). 1990. 13.99 (*0-86653-559-4*, GA1156) Good Apple.

Teaching Creative Writing: Theory & Practice. Ed. by Moira Monteith & Robert Miles. 192p. 1992. 90.00 (*0-335-15685-1*, Open Univ Pr); pap. 32.00 (*0-335-15684-3*, Open Univ Pr) Taylor & Francis.

Teaching Creatively: Learning Through Discovery. Byron G. Massialas & Jack Zevin. LC 81-19375. 270p. 1983. pap. 19.50 (*0-89874-437-7*) Krieger.

Teaching Creatively by Working the Word: Language, Music, & Movement. Susan A. Katz & Judith A. Thomas. 320p. 1992. text ed. 55.00 (*0-13-963950-0*) P-H.

Teaching Creatively with Video: A Guide for Health Professionals. Jane Westberg & Hilliard Jason. LC 93-43777. (Medical Education Ser.: Vol. 18). 256p. 1994. 36.95 (*0-8261-8360-3*) Springer Pub.

***Teaching Criminal Justice Ethics: Strategic Issues.** John Kleinig & Margaret L. Smith. LC 97-72026. 250p. (C). 1997. pap. text ed. 19.95 (*0-87084-831-3*) Anderson Pub Co.

Teaching Critical Reading with Children's Literature. Nancy Polette. (Illus.). 128p. (J). (gr. 4-9). 1988. pap. 12.95 (*0-913839-73-6*) Pieces of Lrning.

Teaching Critical Thinking. Grace E. Grant. LC 87-29289. 148p. 1988. text ed. 49.95 (*0-275-92749-0*, C2749, Praeger Pubs) Greenwood.

Teaching Critical Thinking. John E. McPeck et al. (Philosophy of Education Research Library). 176p. (C). (gr. 13). 1990. text ed. 39.95 (*0-415-90225-8*, A4032, Routledge NY) Routledge.

Teaching Critical Thinking Skills. Joseph P. Hester. LC 93-73552. 225p. (C). 1994. pap. text ed. 14.95 (*0-89089-563-5*) Carolina Acad Pr.

Teaching Critical Thinking Skills in Biology. 20.00 (*0-941212-13-0*) Natl Assn Bio Tchrs.

Teaching Culture. H. Ned Seelye. 1992. pap. text ed. 22.60 (*0-8442-9328-8*, Natl Textbk) NTC Pub Grp.

Teaching Culture: Strategies for Intercultural Communication. 3rd ed. H. Ned Seelye. 1994. pap. text ed. 25.95 (*0-8442-9329-6*) NTC Pub Grp.

Teaching Dance to Senior Adults. Liz Lerman. (Illus.). 190p. 1984. pap. text ed. 18.95 (*0-398-06641-8*) C C Thomas.

Teaching Dance to Senior Adults. Liz Lerman. (Illus.). 190p. (C). 1984. text ed. 31.95 (*0-398-04903-3*) C C Thomas.

Teaching Decision Making to Adolescents. Ed. by J. Baron. 352p. (C). 1991. text ed. 69.95 (*0-8058-0497-8*) L Erlbaum Assocs.

Teaching Decoding in Holistic Classrooms. J. Lloyd Eldredge. (Illus.). 288p. (C). 1995. pap. text ed. 24.00 (*0-02-332230-6*, Macmillan Coll) P-H.

Teaching Democracy: A Professor's Journal. John A. Minahan. 220p. 1993. 20.00 (*1-883285-01-1*) Delphinium.

Teaching Democracy by Being Democratic. Ed. by Theodore L. Becker & Richard A. Couto. LC 96-20930. (Transformational Politics & Political Science Ser.). 200p. 1996. text ed. 59.95 (*0-275-95552-4*, Praeger Pubs); pap. text ed. 18.95 (*0-275-95553-2*, Praeger Pubs) Greenwood.

Teaching Demography: A Summary Handlist of Universities & Other Institutions, Vol. I. 97p. 1986. 14.50 (*92-1-123101-9*, E.85.II.H.2) UN.

Teaching Demography: Details of Curricula & Related Matters in Universities & Other Institutions Teaching Demography, Vol. II. 99p. 1986. 13.00 (*92-1-123102-7*, E.85.II.H.3) UN.

Teaching Design & Technology. John Eggleston. (Developing Science & Technology Education Ser.). 100p. 1992. 80.00 (*0-335-09874-6*, Open Univ Pr); pap. 27.00 (*0-335-09869-X*, Open Univ Pr) Taylor & Francis.

Teaching Design & Technology. 2nd ed. John Eggleston. LC 95-22127. (Developing Science & Technology Education Ser.). 132p. 1995. 85.00 (*0-335-19577-6*, Open Univ Pr); pap. write for info. (*0-335-19502-4*, Open Univ Pr) Taylor & Francis.

Teaching Design & Technology in the Primary School. Tina Jarvis. LC 92-45849. 192p. (C). 1993. pap. text ed. 15.95 (*0-415-07228-X*, B2322, Routledge NY) Routledge.

Teaching Design in Electrical Engineering. Ed. by John G. Webster. 81p. (C). pap. text ed. 12.00 (*0-87942-414-1*) Inst Electrical.

Teaching Developmental Gymnastics: Skills to Take Through Life. Garland O'Quinn, Jr. & E. Jessica Hickman. (Illus.). 224p. 1990. 39.95 (*0-292-78101-6*); pap. 24.95 (*0-292-78104-0*) U of Tex Pr.

Teaching Developmentally. Fay Gang. 112p. 10.00 (*0-87879-402-6*) Acad Therapy.

Teaching Developmentally Disabled Children: The Me Book. O. Ivar Lovaas. LC 80-26047. 264p. 1981. pap. 32.00 (*0-936104-78-3*, 1213) PRO-ED.

Teaching Discipline: A Positive Approach for Educational Development. 3rd ed. Charles H. Madsen, Jr. & Clifford K. Madsen. 318p. (C). 1981. pap. text ed. 28.95 (*0-89892-053-1*) Contemp Pub Co of Raleigh.

Teaching Disturbed & Disturbing Students: An Integrative Approach. Paul Zionts. LC 84-22328. 281p. 1985. pap. 28.00 (*0-936104-48-1*, 1291) PRO-ED.

Teaching Disturbed & Disturbing Students: An Integrative Approach. 2nd ed. Paul Zionts. LC 94-45437. 300p. (C). 1995. pap. text ed. 34.00 (*0-89079-623-8*, 6959) PRO-ED.

Teaching Diverse Populations: Formulating a Knowledge Base. Ed. by Etta R. Hollins et al. LC 93-18084. (SUNY Series, the Social Context of Education). 289p. (C). 1994. pap. text ed. 19.95 (*0-7914-1722-0*) State U NY Pr.

Teaching Diverse Populations: Formulating a Knowledge Base. Ed. by Etta R. Hollins et al. LC 93-18084. (SUNY Series, The Social Context of Education). 289p. (C). 1994. text ed. 59.50 (*0-7914-1721-2*) State U NY Pr.

***Teaching Diversity: Listening to the Soul, Speaking from the Heart.** Joan V. Gallos & V. Jean Ramsey. LC 96-32707. (Higher & Adult Education Ser.). 1996. write for info. (*0-7879-0325-6*) Jossey-Bass.

Teaching Dog Obedience Classes: A Manual for Instructors. Joachim J. Volhard & Gail T. Fisher. LC 85-27172. (Illus.). 384p. 1986. pap. 32.95 (*0-87605-765-2*) Howell Bk.

Teaching Drama to Young Children. Mem Fox. LC 86-14858. 118p. 1986. pap. 17.95 (*0-435-08265-5*, 08625) Heinemann.

Teaching Drawing from Art. Brent Wilson et al. LC 86-72605. (Illus.). 192p. 1987. 25.50 (*0-87192-188-X*) Davis Mass.

Teaching Driver Education to the Physically Disabled: A Sample Course. Edward C. Colverd et al. LC 78-62053. (Driver Education Ser.). (Illus.). 54p. (C). 1978. 5.00 (*0-686-38805-4*) Human Res Ctr.

Teaching During Rounds: A Handbook for Attending Physicians & Residents. Donn Weinholtz & Janine Edwards. 152p. (Orig.). 1992. pap. text ed. 16.95 (*0-8018-4351-0*) Johns Hopkins.

Teaching Early Childhood Math. Bernard. (C). 1996. pap. text ed. write for info. (*0-15-500871-4*) HB Coll Pubs.

Teaching Early Literacy Guide. AIT-WI Education Communication Board Staff. 200p. (Orig.). 1996. pap. text ed. write for info. (*0-7842-0806-9*) Agency Instr Tech.

***Teaching Earth Science Through Movement.** Helen Landalf. LC 97-11379. 128p. (Orig.). 1997. pap. 19.95 (*1-57525-108-6*) Smith & Kraus.

Teaching Economics: Content & Strategies. Ronald A. Banaszak. 1983. pap. text ed. 22.00 (*0-201-11012-1*) Addison-Wesley.

Teaching Edition for Student Study Guide for Biological Science: An Ecological Approach. 7th ed. BSCS Staff. 208p. 1994. per. 27.90 (*0-8403-5867-9*) Kendall-Hunt.

Teaching, Education, Culture & Information As Means of Eliminating Racial Discrimination. Implementation of the International Convention on the Elimination of All Forms of Racial Discrimination Article 7. 30p. 1985. pap. text ed. 5.00 (*92-1-154045-3*, E.85.XIV.3) UN.

Teaching Educational Politics & Policy. Ed. by Donald H. Layton & Jay D. Scribner. 102p. 1989. 4.50 (*0-922971-04-8*) Univ Council Educ Admin.

Teaching Educational Psychology: A Special Issue of Educational Psychologist. Ed. by Phyllis C. Blumenfeld & Linda Anderson. 88p. 1996. pap. 20.00 (*0-8058-9920-0*) L Erlbaum Assocs.

Teaching Effective Listening: A Practical Guide for the High School Classroom. Carolyn G. Coakley. (Illus.). 1993. text ed. 39.95 (*1-877936-01-4*) SPECTRA Inc.

Teaching Effectiveness: Its Meaning, Assessment & Improvement. Ed. by Madan Mohan & Ronald E. Hull. LC 75-14090. 326p. 1975. 39.95 (*0-87778-084-6*) Educ Tech Pubns.

Teaching Eighteenth-Century Poetry. Ed. by Christopher Fox. LC 86-47851. (Studies in the Eighteenth Century: No. 12). 1990. 49.00 (*0-404-63512-1*) AMS Pr.

Teaching Electronic Communication: Technology for the Digital Age. Ed. by Marie E. Flatley. 38p. (Orig.). 1996. pap. text ed. 12.00 (*1-881530-02-7*) Delta Pi Epsilon.

***Teaching Electronic Information Literacy: A How-To-Do-It Manual.** Donald A. Barclay. LC 95-31401. 179p. (Orig.). 1995. pap. 60.00 incl. disk (*1-55570-299-6*) Neal-Schuman.

Teaching Electronic Information Literacy: A How-To-Do-It Manual. Ed. by Donald A. Barclay. LC 95-31401. (Illus.). 179p. (Orig.). 1995. pap. 45.00 (*1-55570-186-8*) Neal-Schuman.

***Teaching Electronic Literacy: A Concepts-Based Approach for School Library Media Specialists.** Kathleen W. Craver. LC 96-53844. (Greenwood Professional Guides in School Librarianship Ser.). 1997. text ed. write for info. (*0-313-30220-0*, Greenwood Pr) Greenwood.

Teaching Elementary Health Science. 2nd ed. Walter D. Sorochan & Stephen J. Bender. LC 78-62551. (Health Education Ser.). (Illus.). 1979. text ed. write for info. (*0-201-07492-3*) Addison-Wesley.

Teaching Elementary Language Arts: An Integrated Approach. 5th ed. Dorothy Rubin. LC 94-11078. 1994. pap. text ed. 58.00 (*0-205-15979-6*) Allyn.

Teaching Elementary Mathematics: Research Based Material. Thomas R. Post. 496p. (C). 1988. pap. text ed. 45.00 (*0-205-11076-2*, H10762) Allyn.

Teaching Elementary Mathematics in a Technological Age. James H. Wiebe. (Orig.). (C). 1988. pap. text ed. 40.00 (*0-89787-520-6*) Gorsuch Scarisbrick.

Teaching Elementary Physical Education. Robert P. Pangarazi. LC 96-24587. 1996. pap. 22.95 (*0-205-19362-5*) P-H.

Teaching Elementary Reading: Principles & Strategies. 4th ed. Robert Karlin & Andrea R. Karlin. 480p. (C). 1987. text ed. 40.00 (*0-15-588004-7*) HB Coll Pubs.

Teaching Elementary School Health. 3rd ed. Stephen J. Bender & Walter D. Sorochan. 576p. 1989. 45.00 (*0-86720-411-7*) Jones & Bartlett.

Teaching Elementary School Health. 3rd ed. Stephen J. Bender & Walter D. Sorochan. 576p. 1989. teacher ed., pap. 10.00 (*0-86720-424-9*) Jones & Bartlett.

Teaching Elementary School Math. Juraschek & Silverman. (Education Ser.). Date not set. text ed. 43.95 (*0-534-13362-2*) Wadsworth Pub.

Teaching Elementary School Math. 6th ed. C. Alan Riedesel & Schwartz. 1996. pap. text ed. 59.00 (*0-205-15223-6*) Allyn.

Teaching Elementary School Music. Eileen Rexroad. 320p. (C). 1992. pap. text ed. 53.00 (*0-13-039983-3*) P-H.

Teaching Elementary Science. 6th ed. William K. Esler & Mary K. Esler. 601p. (C). 1993. text ed. 44.75 (*0-534-17700-X*) Wadsworth Pub.

Teaching Elementary Science. 7th ed. William K. Esler & Mary K. Esler. LC 95-4753. (C). 1996. text ed. 64.95 (*0-534-50511-2*) Wadsworth Pub.

Teaching Elementary Students Through Their Individual Learning Styles: A Practical Approach. Rita S. Dunn & Kenneth J. Dunn. 464p. (C). 1992. text ed. 57.00 (*0-205-13221-9*, Longwood Div) Allyn.

Teaching Emotionally Disturbed. Jack Rudman. (National Teacher Examination Ser.: NT-43). 1994. pap. 23.95 (*0-8373-8453-2*) Nat Learn.

T

An Asterisk (*) at the beginning of an entry indicates that the title is appearing in BIP for the first time.

Teaching EMS: An Educator's Guide to Improved Instruction. Catherine A. Parvensky. 000384p. (gr. 13). 1995. pap. text ed. 35.95 (*0-8151-6611-7*) Mosby Yr Bk.

Teaching Engineering. Phillip C. Wankat & Frank S. Oreovicz. LC 92-37689. 1993. pap. text ed. write for info. (*0-07-068154-6*) McGraw.

Teaching Engineering: A Beginner's Guide. Madhu S. Gupta. LC 87-22543. 288p. 1987. 29.95 (*0-87942-234-3*, PCO2238) Inst Electrical.

Teaching-Engineering, Science, Mathematics. abr. ed. Hugh H. Skilling. LC 76-47476. 128p. 1977. reprint ed. pap. text ed. 8.50 (*0-88275-461-0*) Krieger.

Teaching English. Ed. by Susan Brindley. LC 93-23077. 240p. (C). 1993. pap. text ed. 16.95 (*0-415-10251-0*) Routledge.

Teaching English. David Martin. 1977. pap. 1.80 (*0-686-32333-5*) Rod & Staff.

Teaching English Abroad. 3rd ed. 368p. 1997. pap. 16.95 (*1-85458-160-0*, Pub. by Vacation-Work UK) Petersons.

Teaching English As a Foreign Language. 2nd ed. Ed. by Geoffrey Broughtn et al. (Education Bks.). 256p. 1981. 24.50 (*0-7100-0642-X*, RKP) Routledge.

Teaching English As a Foreign Language. 2nd ed. Roger D. Wilde et al. 256p. (C). 1993. pap. text ed. 15.95 (*0-415-05882-1*, B3746) Routledge.

Teaching English As a Second Language. C. Paul Verghese. vi, 121p. (C). 1989. text ed. 18.95 (*81-207-0941-1*, Pub. by Sterling Pubs II) Apt Bks.

Teaching English As a Second Language: A Classified Bibliography. Yao Shen & Ruth H. Crymes. LC 65-20583. 122p. reprint ed. pap. 34.80 (*0-7837-3981-8*, 2043811) Bks Demand.

Teaching English as a Second Language: A Resource Guide. Angela L. Carrasquillo. LC 93-41180. (Source Books on Education: Vol. 41). 240p. 1994. text ed. 40.00 (*0-8153-0821-3*, SS750) Garland.

***Teaching English As a Second Language 98/99.** Inez A. Heath & Cheryl Serrano. (Annual Ser.). (Illus.). 256p. Date not set. pap. text ed. 11.75 (*0-07-027620-X*) Dushkin Pub.

Teaching English As a Second or Foreign Language. 2nd ed. Ed. by Marianne Celce-Murcia. 1991. pap. 31.95 (*0-8384-2860-6*) Heinle & Heinle.

Teaching English Creatively. 2nd ed. John H. Bushman & Kay P. Bushman. LC 94-7069. (Illus.). 254p. (C). 1994. text ed. 47.95 (*0-398-05911-X*) C C Thomas.

Teaching English in Asia: Finding a Job & Doing It Well. Galen H. Valle. LC 94-74933. 250p. (Orig.). 1995. pap. text ed. 19.95 (*1-881896-11-0*) Pacific View Pr.

Teaching English in Eastern & Central Europe: Finding Work, Teaching & Living in Europe. Robert Lynes. 304p. 1995. pap. 14.95 (*0-8442-0876-0*, Passport Bks) NTC Pub Grp.

Teaching English in Italy. Martin Penner. 224p. (Orig.). 1996. pap. 14.95 (*0-8442-0878-7*, Passport Bks) NTC Pub Grp.

Teaching English in Japan: Finding Work, Teaching & Living in Japan. Jerry O'Sullivan. 228p. 1995. pap. 14.95 (*0-8442-0875-2*) NTC Pub Grp.

Teaching English in Middle & Secondary Schools. 2nd ed. Rhoda J. Maxwell & Mary Meiser. 416p. (C). 1996. pap. text ed. 46.00 (*0-13-461666-9*) P-H.

Teaching English in South-East Asia. Jerry O'Sullivan & Nuala O'Sullivan. 272p. (Orig.). 1996. pap. 14.95 (*0-8442-0877-9*, Passport Bks) NTC Pub Grp.

Teaching English Naturally Module 1. S. Bunch. 1983. text ed. 160.88 (*0-201-19281-0*) Addison-Wesley.

Teaching English Naturally Module 2. S. Bunch. 1983. text ed. 160.88 (*0-201-19282-9*) Addison-Wesley.

Teaching English Naturally Module 3. S. Bunch. 1983. text ed. 156.20 (*0-201-19283-7*) Addison-Wesley.

Teaching English Overseas. 1992. 13.95 (*0-19-432814-7*) OUP.

Teaching English Pronunciation. J. Kenworthy. (Handbooks for Language Teachers Ser.). 1987. pap. text ed. 28.26 (*0-582-74621-3*, 74763) Longman.

Teaching English So It Matters: Creating Curriculum for & with High School Students. Deborah Stern. (Illus.). 368p. 1995. pap. 29.95 (*0-8039-6183-9*) Corwin Pr.

Teaching English Through Action. Bertha E. Segal-Cook. 1995. teacher ed. 17.99 (*0-938395-35-1*) B Segal.

Teaching English Through Action: Student Profile Cards (Continuum) Bertha E. Segal-Cook. 2p. 1989. reprint ed. teacher ed. 9.99 (*0-938395-01-7*) B Segal.

Teaching English to Children. W. Scott & L. Ytreberg. (Keys to Language Teaching Ser.). (C). 1991. pap. text ed. 20.67 (*0-582-74606-X*, 79114) Longman.

Teaching English to Speakers of ESD, ESL & EFL. Sheilah A. Bobo & Pearl M. Thompson. 216p. (C). 1990. lib. bdg. 49.00 (*0-8191-7868-3*) U Pr of Amer.

Teaching English to Speakers of Other Languages: Substance & Technique. Betty W. Robinett. LC 78-11448. 335p. reprint ed. pap. 95.50 (*0-8357-3334-3*, 2039559) Bks Demand.

Teaching Environmental Literature: Materials, Methods, Resources. Ed. by Frederick O. Waage. LC 84-27179. (Options for Teaching Ser.: No. 7). xvi, 191p. 1985. 37.50 (*0-87352-308-3*); pap. 19.75 (*0-87352-309-1*, J207P) Modern Lang.

Teaching ESL - Speaking, Reading, Writing. Bertha E. Segal-Cook. 106p. (J). (gr. 4-12). 1995. 13.99 (*0-938395-37-8*) B Segal.

Teaching Ethics: An Interdisciplinary Approach. Robert B. Ashmore & William C. Starr. LC 94-78564. 241p. 1994. 8.00 (*0-87462-997-7*) Marquette.

***Teaching Ethics & Values in Public Administration Programs: Innovations, Strategies, & Issues.** Ed. by James S. Bowman & Donald C. Menzel. (Series in Public Administration). 336p. (C). 1997. pap. text ed. 21.95 (*0-7914-3510-5*) State U NY Pr.

***Teaching Ethics & Values in Public Administration Programs: Innovations, Strategies, & Issues.** Ed. by James S. Bowman & Donald C. Menzel. (SUNY Series in Public Administration). 336p. (C). 1997. text ed. 65.50 (*0-7914-3509-1*) State U NY Pr.

Teaching Ethics in Journalism Education. Clifford G. Christians & Catherine L. Covert. LC 80-10426. (Teaching of Ethics Ser.). 71p. 1980. pap. 4.00 (*0-916558-08-8*) Hastings Ctr.

Teaching Ethnic & Gender Awareness: Methods & Materials for the Elementary School. 2nd ed. Edith W. King. 224p. 1989. per. 21.99 (*0-8403-5610-2*) Kendall-Hunt.

***Teaching Every Child Every Day: Integrated Learning in Diverse Classrooms.** Ed. by Karen R. Harris et al. (Advances in Teaching & Learning Ser.). 224p. 1997. pap. text ed. 19.95 (*1-57129-040-0*) Brookline Bks.

***Teaching Evolution & the Nature of Science.** 72p. 1997. pap. 14.95 (*0-309-06364-7*) Natl Acad Pr.

Teaching Evolution in Public Schools: A Comparison of Evolution & Special Creation see Creation vs. Evolution: A Comparison

Teaching Examples: Ideas for Music Educators. Ed. by Paul Lehman. 142p. (Orig.). (C). 1994. pap. 27.50 (*1-56545-041-8*, 1620) Music Ed Natl.

Teaching Exceptional Children & Youth in the Regular Classroom. Terry Cicchelli & Claire Ashby-Davis. 368p. (Orig.). 1986. text ed. 39.95 (*0-8156-2341-0*); pap. text ed. 16.95 (*0-8156-2342-9*) Syracuse U Pr.

Teaching Exceptional Students in Your Classroom. Anne M. Bauer & Thomas M. Shea. 384p. 1988. text ed. 72.00 (*0-205-11886-0*, H1886-4) Allyn.

Teaching Factories: A Strategy for World Class Manufacturing Application & Education Networks. Mary A. Roe et al. 208p. 1993. pap. 16.95 (*1-887406-01-8*) ICTwo Inst.

***Teaching Family Child Care Record Keeping & Tax Preparation: A Curriculum for Trainers.** Tom Copeland. 1997. pap. text ed. 25.95 (*0-934140-91-X*) Redleaf Pr.

Teaching Family Medicine in Medical School: A Companion to Predoctoral Education in Family Medicine. David E. Swee. Ed. by STFM & AAFP Staff. 271p. 1991. 25.00 (*0-942295-23-4*) Soc Tchrs Fam Med.

Teaching Family Policy: A Handbook of Course Syllabi, Teaching Strategies & Resources. Ed. by Denise Skinner & Elaine Anderson. (Orig.). (C). 1993. pap. 23.95 (*0-916174-41-7*) Natl Coun Family.

Teaching Family Reunification: A Sourcebook. Anthony N. Maluccio et al. 1994. 24.95 (*0-87868-511-1*) Child Welfare.

Teaching Family Therapy. Ros Draper et al. 262p. 1992. pap. text ed. 32.50 (*1-85575-021-X*, Pub. by Karnac Bks UK) Brunner-Mazel.

Teaching Fieldwork to Educational Researchers: A Symposium. (Special Issues of the Anthropology & Education Quarterly Ser.: Vol. 14, No. 3). 1983. 7.50 (*0-317-66342-9*) Am Anthro Assn.

Teaching First Aid & Emergency Care Resource Book. Alton L. Thygerson. 96p. (Orig.). 1988. pap. text ed. 37.50 (*0-86720-096-0*) Jones & Bartlett.

***Teaching Folk Dance: Successful Steps.** LC 96-48038. 728p. 1997. 49.95 (*1-57379-008-7*) High-Scope.

Teaching Food Technology in Secondary School. Marion Rutland. (Roehampton Teaching Studies). 144p. 1996. pap. 24.95 (*1-85346-426-0*, Pub. by D Fulton UK) Taylor & Francis.

Teaching for a Lifetime: Nutrition Education for Young Children. Barbara J. Mayfield. 70p. 1994. 45.95 incl. vhs (*1-883983-25-8*) Noteworthy Creat.

Teaching for Better Learning: A Guide for Teachers of Primary Health Care Staff. 2nd ed. F. R. Abbatt. vii, 190p. (ENG, FRE & SPA.). 1992. pap. text ed. 41.00 (*92-4-154442-2*, 1150377) World Health.

Teaching for Change: Addressing Issues of Difference in the College Classroom. Ed. by Kathryn Geismar & Guitele Nicoleau. (Reprint Ser.: No. 25). 224p. (Orig.). 1993. pap. 17.95 (*0-916690-27-X*) Harvard Educ Rev.

Teaching for Changed Attitudes & Values. J. B. Ruud. LC 71-187577. (C). 1971. pap. 2.00 (*0-911365-00-1*, A261-08378) Family & Consumer Sci Educ.

Teaching for Christian Hearts, Souls, & Minds. Locke E. Bowman. 118p. 1990. 7.95 (*0-06-060981-8*) Morehouse Pub.

Teaching for Commitment: Liberal Education, Indoctrination, & Christian Nurture. Elmer J. Thiessen. 344p. 1993. 49.95 (*0-7735-0998-4*, Pub. by McGill CN); pap. 17.95 (*0-7735-1162-8*, Pub. by McGill CN) U of Toronto Pr.

Teaching for Competence. Howard J. Sullivan & Norman Higgins. LC 82-19584. 112p. 1983. pap. 12.95 (*0-8077-2725-3*) Tchrs Coll.

Teaching for Creative Endeavor: Bold New Venture. Ed. by William B. Michael. LC 76-6603. reprint ed. 45.00 (*0-404-15292-9*) AMS Pr.

Teaching for Decision. Richard L. Dresselhaus. LC 89-80210. (Sunday School Staff Training Ser.). 126p. 1989. pap. 2.95 (*0-88243-620-1*, 02-0620) Gospel Pub.

Teaching for Diversity. Ed. by Laura L. Border & Nancy V. Chism. LC 85-644763. (New Directions for Teaching & Learning Ser.: No. TL 49). 100p. 1992. 19.00 (*1-55542-763-4*) Jossey-Bass.

***Teaching for Diversity & Social Justice: A Sourcebook for Teachers & Trainers.** Maurianne Adams et al. LC 96-37658. 288p. (C). 1997. pap. write for info. (*0-415-91057-9*) Routledge.

***Teaching for Diversity & Social Justice: A Sourcebook for Teachers & Trainers.** Maurianne Adams et al. LC 96-37658. 288p. (C). 1997. text ed. write for info. (*0-415-91056-0*) Routledge.

Teaching for Faith: A Guide for Teachers of Adult Classes. Richard R. Osmer. 224p. (Orig.). 1992. pap. 17.00 (*0-664-25217-6*) Westminster John Knox.

Teaching for Health. Lyn Coutts & Leslie Hardy. 1995. write for info. (*0-443-04126-1*) Churchill.

Teaching for Learning. Ed. by John Biggs. (C). 1990. 100.00 (*0-86431-080-3*, Pub. by Aust Council Educ Res AT) St Mut.

Teaching for Learning Success: Practical Strategies & Materials for Everyday Use. Gloria Frender. Ed. by Leslie Britt. (Illus.). 304p. (Orig.). 1994. pap. text ed. 21.95 (*0-86530-280-4*) Incentive Pubns.

Teaching for Life. Ivan Herald & David Mendez. 56p. (Orig.). 1989. pap. 4.50 (*1-56428-014-4*) Logos Intl Pub.

Teaching for Life-Changing Learning. Peggy Payne. (Christian Education Ministries Ser.). 94p. (Orig.). 1984. pap. 3.95 (*0-89367-092-8*) Light & Life Comm.

Teaching for Meaning in High-Poverty Classrooms. Michael Knapp et al. LC 94-46779. 256p. (C). 1995. text ed. 44.00 (*0-8077-3424-1*); pap. text ed. 21.95 (*0-8077-3423-3*) Tchrs Coll.

***Teaching for Moral Growth - a Guide for the Christian Community: Teachers, Parents & Pastors.** 416p. 1993. pap. 16.99 (*0-8010-5746-9*, Bridgept Bks) Baker Bks.

Teaching for Outcomes in Elementary Physical Education: A Guide for Curriculum & Assessment. Christine J. Hopple. LC 94-10391. (Illus.). 232p. 1994. spiral bd. 28.00 (*0-87322-712-3*, BHOP0712) Human Kinetics.

Teaching for Proficiency Handbook. V. Galloway. (Spanish K-12 Ser.). (Illus.). 56p. 1989. pap. text ed. 14.25 (*0-201-52192-X*) Addison-Wesley.

Teaching for Reconciliation: Foundations & Practice of Christian Educational Ministry. Ronald Habermas & Klaus Issler. LC 92-25728. 424p. (C). 1992. text ed. 29.99 (*0-8010-4367-0*) Baker Bks.

Teaching for Results. rev. ed. Findley B. Edge. LC 94-21873. 248p. 1995. 24.99 (*0-8054-1094-5*, 4210-94) Broadman.

Teaching for "Self-Directed" Living & Learning in Students - How to Help Students Get in Charge of Their Lives: "Self-Directed" Living & Learning. R. C. Bradley. LC 90-85800. 224p. (YA). 1991. text ed. 19.95 (*0-9628624-0-1*) Bassi Bk.

Teaching for Spiritual Growth. Perry G. Downs. 224p. 1994. 22.99 (*0-310-59370-0*) Zondervan.

Teaching for Success: Strengthening Child-Centered Classrooms. Ed. by Jim Grant. 336p. Date not set. teacher ed., pap. 24.95 (*1-884548-02-4*, Crystal Spgs) Soc Dev Educ.

Teaching for the Two-Sided Mind: A Guide to Right Brain-Left Brain Education. Linda V. Williams. (Illus.). 213p. 1983. pap. 7.95 (*0-13-892547-X*) P-H.

Teaching for the Two-Sided Mind: A Guide to Right Brain-Left Brain Education. Linda V. Williams. 214p. 1986. pap. 11.00 (*0-671-62239-0*, Touchstone Bks) S&S Trade.

Teaching for Thinking. Ed. by James W. Keefe & Herbert J. Walberg. 140p. (Orig.). (C). 1992. pap. 15.00 (*0-88210-265-6*) Natl Assn Principals.

Teaching for Thinking. Louise C. Spear-Swerling. LC 96-20123. (Psychology in the Classroom Ser.). 200p. (Orig.). 1996. pap. text ed. 17.95 (*1-55798-375-5*) Am Psychol.

Teaching for Thinking: Theory, Strategies, & Activities for the Classroom. 2nd ed. Arnold Rothstein et al. 240p. (C). 1986. pap. 18.95 (*0-8077-2814-4*) Tchrs Coll.

Teaching for Thoughtfulness: Classroom Strategies to Enhance Intellectual Development. 2nd rev. ed. John Barell. LC 94-27770. 349p. (C). 1995. pap. text ed. 37.50 (*0-8013-1302-3*) Longman.

Teaching for Transfer: Fostering Generalization in Learning. Ed. by Anne McKeough et al. 256p. 1995. text ed. 49.95 (*0-8058-1309-8*) L Erlbaum Assocs.

Teaching for Transformation: A Comprehensive Handbook for Teachers of Christian Home Groups. Chester M. Wright & David A. Huston. (Illus.). 260p. 1991. ring bd. 24.95 (*0-932345-06-9*) Antioch Publishes.

***Teaching for Understanding.** Tina Blythe. 1997. wbk. ed., pap. 27.95 (*0-7879-0993-9*) Jossey-Bass.

Teaching for Understanding: Challenges for Policy & Practice. Ed. by David Cohen et al. LC 92-35498. (Education-Higher Education Ser.). 312p. text ed. 34.95 (*1-55542-515-1*) Jossey-Bass.

***Teaching for Understanding: Linking Theory with Practice.** Martha S. Wiske. LC 97-17571. 1997. 29.95 (*0-7879-1002-3*) Jossey-Bass.

Teaching for Workplace Success. Audrey B. Champagne. 22p. 1986. 3.00 (*0-318-22211-6*, OC113) Ctr Educ Trng Employ.

Teaching Foreign Language: Speaking, Reading, Writing. 5th ed. Bertha E. Segal-Cook. (J). (ps-12). 1995. 13.99 (*0-938395-34-3*) B Segal.

Teaching Foreign Language Skills. rev. ed. Wilga M. Rivers. LC 80-24993. 576p. (C). 1981. reprint ed. pap. text ed. 24.95 (*0-226-72097-7*) U Ch Pr.

Teaching Foreign Languages in Schools: The Silent Way. Caleb Gattegno. 144p. 1972. pap. text ed. 8.95 (*0-87825-046-8*) Ed Solutions.

Teaching Four-Year-Olds. Carol B. Hillman. LC 88-61775. 104p. (Orig.). 1989. pap. 9.00 (*0-87367-799-4*) Phi Delta Kappa.

Teaching French. Wilga M. Rivers. 412p. (C). 1988. 180.00 (*0-8442-1265-2*, Pub. by S Thornes Pubs UK) St Mut.

Teaching French. Ed. by Ann Swarbick. LC 93-1712. 192p. (C). 1993. pap. text ed. 17.95 (*0-415-10255-3*) Routledge.

Teaching Friendship Skills: Intermediate Version. Pat Huggins. (ASSIST Program, Affective/Social Skills Ser.). (Illus.). 476p. 1993. teacher ed., pap. text ed. 37.50 (*0-944584-70-5*, 18FSI) Sopris.

Teaching Friendship Skills: Primary Version. Pat Huggins. (ASSIST Program, Affective/Social Skills Ser.). (Illus.). 540p. 1993. teacher ed., pap. text ed. 37.50 (*0-944584-69-1*, 18FSP) Sopris.

Teaching from a Multicultural Perspective: Focus on International Film. Robert Singer et al. 60p. (Orig.). 1992. pap. write for info. (*0-918537-03-7*) Justin Bks.

Teaching from a Scriptural Viewpoint. Richard Grunze. 51p. (Orig.). 1993. pap. 4.99 (*0-8100-0159-4*, 07N0745) Northwest Pub.

Teaching from Cupboards & Closets: Integrated Learning Activities for Young Children, Ages 2-6. Moira D. Green. (Illus.). 224p. (Orig.). 1994. pap. 14.95 (*0-673-36011-3*, GoodYrBooks) Addson-Wesley Educ.

Teaching from Research Knowledge. Bellon. 1991. pap. text ed. 38.20 (*0-675-20639-1*, Merrill Coll) P-H.

Teaching from the Heart. Jerold W. Apps. LC 95-37271. (Professional Practices in Adult Education & Human Resource Development Ser.). 140p. (C). 1996. 21.50 (*0-89464-940-X*) Krieger.

Teaching from the Heart: Theology & Educational Method. Mary E. Moore. LC 91-17972. 246p. 1991. pap. 18.00 (*0-8006-2497-1*, 1-2497, Fortress Pr) Augsburg Fortress.

Teaching Function Nursing Practition. 4th ed. Margaret L. Pohl. 176p. (C). 1981. per. write for info. (*0-697-05546-9*) Wm C Brown Pubs.

***Teaching Gender in U. S. History.** Karen Anderson. Ed. by Nell I. Painter & Antonio Rios-Bustamante. (Teaching Diversity Ser.). 72p. 1997. pap. 8.00 (*0-87229-078-6*) Am Hist Assn.

Teaching Genealogy. Nancy E. Carlberg. (Illus.). 340p. (Orig.). 1988. pap. 25.00 (*0-944878-07-5*) Carlberg Pr.

Teaching Genealogy. Arlene H. Eakle. 32p. 1989. pap. write for info. (*0-940764-32-6*) Genealog Inst.

Teaching General Business. Betty J. Brown. (Rapid Reader Ser.: No. 1). (Illus.). 34p. (C). 1977. pap. text ed. 5.00 (*0-9603064-6-3*) Delta Pi Epsilon.

Teaching General Chemistry: A Materials Science Companion. Arthur B. Ellis et al. LC 93-29739. 554p. 1993. pap. 29.95 (*0-8412-2725-X*) Am Chemical.

Teaching General Music: A Course of Study. Intro. by Donald Corbett. (Illus.). 40p. (C). 1991. teacher ed. 13.25 (*0-940796-98-8*, 1602) Music Ed Natl.

Teaching General Semantics. 2nd ed. Ed. by Mary Morain. LC 75-108193. 142p. 1977. reprint ed. pap. text ed. 10.00 (*0-918970-04-0*) Intl Gen Semantics.

Teaching Genocide Awareness in Multicultural Education. (Ethnic Studies Bulletins: No. 6). 24p. 1982. 2.00 (*0-918158-65-6*) I N Thut World Educ Ctr.

Teaching Genre. Tara McCarthy. (J). 1996. pap. 14.95 (*0-590-60345-0*) Scholastic Inc.

Teaching Geography in the Disciplines. James B. Binko & Gloria A. Neubert. LC 96-67180. (Fastback Ser.: No. 400). 64p. (Orig.). 1996. pap. 3.00 (*0-87367-600-9*) Phi Delta Kappa.

Teaching German. Ed. by Wilga M. Rivers et al. 412p. (C). 1988. 160.00 (*0-8442-2401-4*, Pub. by S Thornes Pubs UK) St Mut.

Teaching German in America: Prolegomena to a History. Ed. by David Benseler et al. (Monatshefte Occasional Ser.: Vol. 7). 320p. (C). 1988. text ed. 25.00 (*0-299-97022-1*); pap. text ed. 14.00 (*0-299-97023-X*) U of Wis Pr.

Teaching Gerontology. Ed. by Verle Waters. 192p. 1991. 25.95 (*0-88737-527-8*) Natl League Nurse.

Teaching Giants to Dance. Rosbeth Kinter. 1989. write for info. (*0-318-65456-3*) S&S Trade.

Teaching Gifted & Talented Learners in Regular Classrooms. Roberta M. Milgram. (Illus.). 316p. 1989. pap. 39.95 (*0-398-06290-0*) C C Thomas.

Teaching Gifted & Talented Learners in Regular Classrooms. Roberta M. Milgram. (Illus.). 316p. (C). 1989. text ed. 62.95 (*0-398-05557-2*) C C Thomas.

Teaching Gifted Kids in the Regular Classroom: Strategies & Techniques Every Teacher Can Use to Meet the Academic Needs of the Gifted & Talented. Susan Winebrenner. Ed. by Pamela Espeland. LC 92-20926. 168p. (Orig.). 1992. pap. 21.95 (*0-915793-47-4*) Free Spirit Pub.

Teaching Global Awareness with Simulations & Games. Steven L. Lamy et al. (Illus.). 245p. (Orig.). (YA). (gr. 6-12). 1992. pap. text ed. 29.95 (*0-943804-15-9*) U of Denver Teach.

Teaching Global Development: A Curriculum Guide. Ed. by William Savitt. LC 93-24718. 1993. text ed. 40.50 (*0-268-01882-0*); pap. text ed. 21.00 (*0-268-01883-9*) U of Notre Dame Pr.

Teaching Godly Play: The Sunday Morning Handbook. Jerome W. Berryman. 144p. 1995. pap. 14.95 (*0-687-08651-5*) Abingdon.

Teaching Grammar in Context. Constance Weaver. LC 95-50512. 287p. 1996. pap. text ed. 25.00 (*0-86709-375-7*, 0375) Boynton Cook Pubs.

Teaching Grammar of Thai: Phasa Thai Rian Sanuk Chang. 2nd ed. William Kuo. LC 92-44749. 500p. 1992. pap. 23.50 (*0-944613-15-2*) UC Berkeley Ctrs SE Asia.

Teaching Group Dynamics: Process & Practices. Nina W. Brown. LC 92-16144. 176p. 1992. text ed. 42.95 (*0-275-94380-1*, C4380, Praeger Pubs) Greenwood.

Teaching Guide for Book "Your Name Is Renee" Teresa M. Morretta & Ruth K. Hartz. 16p. 1995. spiral bd. 9.95 (*1-879418-20-7*) Biddle Pub.

Teaching Guide for Indian Literature, 2 vols., Set. Diana Campbell. 69p. (gr. 6 up). 1983. 16.00 (*0-685-42638-6*) Rough Rock Pr.

Teaching Guide for Lincoln: A Photobiography. Brian A. Haggerty. Ed. by Lois Fowkes & Bev Dana. (Nurturing Intelligences Ser.). (Illus.). 144p. (Orig.). 1995. teacher ed., pap. 14.95 (*0-201-49059-5*) Supplementary Div.

T

Teaching Guide for Mildred Taylor's "Roll of Thunder, Hear Me Cry" Brian A. Haggerty. Ed. by Lois Fowkes & Jean Nattkemper. (Nurturing Intelligences Core Literature Ser.). (Illus.). 148p. (Orig.). 1995. pap. 18.75 (0-201-49403-5) Addison-Wesley.

Teaching Guide for Suzanne Tate's Nature Series. Ed. by Suzanne Tate & Susan Maloney. LC 94-69560. (Illus.). 108p. (Orig.). 1994. pap. text ed. 12.95 (1-878405-11-X) Nags Head Art.

*__Teaching Guide for Suzanne Tate's Nature Series, Bks. 17 & 18.__ Ed. by Suzanne Tate & Susan Maloney. (Illus.). 16p. (Orig.). 1996. pap. 2.95 (1-878405-15-2) Nags Head Art.

Teaching Guide Imagery & Music: An Experiential - Didactic Approach. Marilyn F. Clark & Linda H. Keiser. 214p. 1989. teacher ed. 100.00 (0-944135-00-5) Archedigm Pubns.

Teaching Guide to "Island of the Blue Dolphins" Mary Spicer. (Discovering Literature Ser.). (Illus.). 80p. (Orig.). 1996. wbk. ed., pap. text ed. 5.95 (0-931993-79-2, GP-079) Garlic Pr OR.

Teaching Guide to "Mrs. Frisby & the Rats of Nimh" Mary Spicer. (Discovering Literature Ser.). (Illus.). 80p. (Orig.). 1996. wbk. ed., pap. text ed. 5.95 (0-931993-78-4, GP-078) Garlic Pr OR.

Teaching Guide to "My Side of the Mountain" Mary Spicer. (Discovering Literature Ser.). (Illus.). 80p. (Orig.). 1996. wbk. ed., pap. text ed. 5.95 (0-931993-76-8, GP-076) Garlic Pr OR.

Teaching Guide to Preventing Adolescent Sexual Abuse. Joan Krebill & Julie Taylor. 187p. 1988. pap. text ed. 29.95 (0-941816-50-8) ETR Assocs.

Teaching Guide to "Where the Red Fern Grows" Mary Spicer. (Discovering Literature Ser.). (Illus.). 80p. (Orig.). 1996. wbk. ed., pap. text ed. 5.95 (0-931993-77-6, GP-077) Garlic Pr OR.

Teaching Guides for 50 Young Adult Novels see Teaching Guides for 50 Young Adult Novels & Tests for 250 Young Adult Novels

*__Teaching Guides for 50 Young Adult Novels & Tests for 250 Young Adult Novels, 2 vols.__ Roberta G. Shipley. Incl. Tests for 250 Young Adult Novels. LC 94-36771. 272p. (Orig.). 1995. pap. 29.95 (1-55570-192-2); Teaching Guides for 50 Young Adult Novels. LC 95-36534. 150p. (Orig.). 1995. teacher ed., pap. 29.95 (1-55570-193-0); 50.00 (1-55570-301-1) Neal-Schuman.

Teaching Gymnastics. 2nd ed. Harriet R. Lihs. 150p. (Orig.). 1994. pap. text ed. 11.95 (0-89641-226-1) American Pr.

*__Teaching Gymnastics.__ 2nd ed. Mauldon. 1989. pap. text ed. write for info. (0-582-02950-3, Pub. by Longman UK) Longman.

Teaching Hair Coloring: A Step-by-Step Guide to Building Props. Andre Nizetich. LC 92-35110. 1992. pap. 21.95 (1-56253-072-0) Milady Pub.

Teaching Hamlet & Henry IV, Pt. 1. Ed. by Peggy O'Brien & Jane Rosenman. (Shakespeare Set Free Ser.). 272p. (Orig.). 1994. pap. 18.00 (0-671-76048-3, WSP) PB.

Teaching Hand Papermaking: A Classroom Guide. GLoria Z. Smith. LC 94-93961. (Illus.). 192p. (Orig.). 1995. teacher ed. 24.95 (0-9644582-0-9) Zpaperpr.

Teaching Handicapped Students Study Skills. 2nd ed. John J. Hoover. LC 87-83122. 77p. 1988. pap. text ed. 8.50 (0-940059-03-7) Hamilton Pubns.

Teaching Hard, Teaching Soft. Colin Corder. 200p. 1990. text ed. 54.95 (0-566-02865-4, Pub. by Gower UK) Ashgate Pub Co.

Teaching Health & Science from a Feminist Perspective: A Practical Guide. Sue V. Rosser. (Athene Ser.). (Illus.). 200p. 1986. 36.50 (0-08-033135-1, Pergamon Pr); pap. 19.95 (0-08-033997-2, Pergamon Pr) Elsevier.

Teaching Health Conservation. Jack Rudman. (National Teacher Examination Ser.: NT-23). 1994. pap. 23.95 (0-8373-8433-8) Nat Learn.

Teaching Health Law: A Guide on Health Law for Health Services Administration. Ed. by Arnold J. Rosoff & David F. Bergwall. 1986. pap. text ed. 12.95 (0-910591-01-6) AUPHA Pr.

*__Teaching Health Related Exercise at Key Stages 1 & 2.__ Jo Harris & Jill P. Elbourn. LC 96-48338. (Illus.). 168p. 1997. pap. text ed. 19.00 (0-87322-666-6, BHAR0666) Human Kinetics.

*__Teaching Health Science: Elementary & Middle School.__ 4th ed. Stephen J. Bender. LC 96-36806. 1996. write for info. (0-7637-0256-0) Jones & Bartlett.

Teaching Health Statistics: Twenty Lesson & Seminar Outlines. Ed. by Stephen K. Lwanga & Cho-Yook Tye. 230p. (ARA, FRE & SPA.). 1986. pap. text ed. 39.00 (92-4-156090-8, 1150261) World Health.

Teaching Hearing Handicapped. Jack Rudman. (National Teacher Examination Ser.: NT-28). 1994. pap. 23.95 (0-8373-8438-9) Nat Learn.

Teaching Hearing-Impaired Children in Regular Classrooms. Peter M. Blackwell. (Language in Education: Theory & Practice Ser.: No. 54). 55p. reprint ed. pap. 25.00 (0-8357-3353-X, 2039588) Bks Demand.

Teaching Hearts & Minds: College Students Reflect on the Vietnam War in Literature. Barry M. Kroll. LC 91-2868. 216p. (C). 1992. 24.95 (0-8093-1748-6) S Ill U Pr.

Teaching Helping Skills to Middle School Students: Program Leader's Guide. Robert D. Myrick & Don L. Sorenson. LC 92-70804. (Illus.). 128p. (Orig.). (J). (gr. 6-8). 1992. teacher ed., pap. 8.95 (0-932796-41-9) Ed Media Corp.

Teaching Helps in First Corinthians. Richard P. Belcher. (Ministry Helps Ser.). 58p. 1993. reprint ed. pap. 6.95 (1-883265-04-5) Richbarry Pr.

Teaching Helps in First Peter. Richard P. Belcher. (Minstry Helps Ser.). 76p. 1993. reprint ed. pap. 6.95 (1-883265-05-3) Richbarry Pr.

Teaching Helps in Psalms. Richard P. Belcher. (Ministry Helps Ser.). 53p. 1993. reprint ed. pap. 6.95 (1-883265-02-9) Richbarry Pr.

Teaching History: A Reader. Ed. by Hilary Bourdillon. LC 93-10714. 192p. (C). 1993. pap. text ed. 16.95 (0-415-10256-1) Routledge.

Teaching History: Suggested Themes of the Curriculum in Waldorf Schools. Christoph Lindenberg. Tr. by Peter Luborsky from GER. 204p. (Orig.). 1989. pap. text ed. 10.00 (0-9623978-0-6) Assn Waldorf Schls.

Teaching History in the Elementary School. John D. Hoge & Claudia Crump. 95p. (Orig.). 1988. pap. 8.00 (0-941339-05-X) Ind U SSDC.

Teaching History in the New Europe. John Slater. (Council of Europe Ser.). 176p. 1995. pap. 21.00 (0-304-32777-8) Cassell.

Teaching History Primary Evidence. Keith Andreetti. 128p. 1993. pap. 22.00 (1-85346-183-0, Pub. by D Fulton UK) Taylor & Francis.

Teaching History to Gifted Students: An In-Depth Instructional Resource for Secondary Level Programs. Andrew Flaxman. (Humanities Publications). 1989. 12.00 (0-910609-20-9) Gifted Educ Pr.

Teaching History with a Computer: A Complete Guide for College Professors. James B. Schick. LC 89-13883. 251p. 1990. pap. text ed. 31.95 (0-925065-32-3) Lyceum IL.

Teaching History with Film & Television. John E. O'Connor. (Discussions on Teaching Ser.: No. 2). 86p. 1987. pap. 6.00 (0-87229-040-9) Am Hist Assn.

Teaching Home School. Eliza Hainstock. 1978. pap. 11.95 (0-452-26403-0, Plume) NAL-Dutton.

Teaching Hospital: Evolution & Contemporary Issues. Ed. by John H. Knowles. LC 66-21338. (Illus.). 152p. reprint ed. pap. 43.40 (0-7837-4163-4, 2059011) Bks Demand.

Teaching House. Elizabeth S. McKinnon. Ed. by Jean Warren & Kathleen Cubley. LC 95-60511. (Learning Everywhere Ser.). (Illus.). 128p. (Orig.). (J). (ps). 1996. pap. 6.95 (1-57029-068-7, 2801, Totline Bks) Warren Pub Hse.

Teaching How to Work in Groups. Ed. by Gerald M. Phillips & Brenda Dervin. LC 90-867. (Communication & Information Science Ser.). 272p. (C). 1990. pap. 39.50 (0-89391-730-3); text ed. 73.25 (0-89391-690-0) Ablex Pub.

Teaching Human Rights. David A. Shiman. (Illus.). 1993. pap. 29.95 (0-943804-79-5) U of Denver Teach.

Teaching Human Sexuality in Caribbean Schools: A Teachers Handbook. Allison Lewis et al. Ed. by Rene Jaimes. (Illus.). 306p. (Orig.). pap. 15.00 (0-916683-07-9) Intl Plan Parent.

Teaching Humane Education: Animal Welfare Issue, Vol. I. Intro. by Henrietta Howard-Moineau. (Illus.). 162p. (Orig.). 1983. pap. 10.00 (0-318-01114-X) Hampshre Pr.

Teaching Humanities in the Microelectronic Age. Anthony Adams & Esnor Jones. 128p. 1983. pap. 25.00 (0-335-10196-8, Open Univ Pr) Taylor & Francis.

Teaching Hydrologic Application: Computer Programs for Water Resources with Computer Programs. J. K. Koelliker & Geoff W. Kite. LC 90-84901. 154p. (Orig.). 1996. reprint ed. pap. 40.00 (0-918334-69-1) WRP.

Teaching Ideas II: A Collection of Successful Classroom Strategies. Ed. by Lynne Tatlock & Steven Trobisch. 32p. (Orig.). (YA). (gr. 7-12). 1994. pap. text ed. 6.00 (0-942017-20-X) Amer Assn Teach German.

Teaching Improvement Practices: Successful Strategies for Higher Education. Wright, Alan W., & Associates Staff. 424p. (C). 1995. text ed. 42.95 (1-882982-06-1) Anker Pub.

Teaching in a Diverse Society. Herbert Grossman. LC 94-759. 1994. pap. text ed. 48.00 (0-205-16247-9) Allyn.

Teaching in a New Era. Allan C. Ornstein. 1976. pap. text ed. 6.80 (0-87563-110-X) Stipes.

Teaching in a Plural Society. 2nd ed. Garcia. (C). 1991. pap. text ed. 40.50 (0-06-042237-8) Addson-Wesley Educ.

Teaching in America. George S. Morrison. 592p. 1996. 46.00 (0-205-15253-8) Allyn.

Teaching in America: The Common Ground. 2nd ed. Yale-New Haven Teachers Institute Staff. 135p. (C). 1985. pap. 8.95 (0-87447-192-3) College Bd.

Teaching in College: A Resource for College Teachers. rev. ed. Donald Greive & Bill W. Frye. 296p. (C). 1994. pap. text ed. 24.95 (0-940017-18-0) Info Tec OH.

Teaching in Content Areas: Reading, Writing & Reasoning. Harold L. Herber & Joan N. Herber. 448p. (C). 1992. pap. text ed. 58.00 (0-205-14158-7, H41585) Allyn.

Teaching in Further Education: An Outline of Principles & Practice. L. B. Curzon. 400p. 1990. pap. text ed. 24.95 (0-304-31961-9) Cassell.

*__Teaching in Laboratories.__ David Boud et al. 208p. 1986. pap. 15.99 (0-335-15609-6, Open Univ Pr) Taylor & Francis.

Teaching in Laboratories. David Bound et al. LC 86-1443. 208p. 1986. pap. 29.95 (0-85059-109-0, Open Univ Pr) Taylor & Francis.

Teaching in Nursing Practice. 2nd ed. Nancy I. Whitman & Barbara A. Graham. Ed. by Carol J. Gleit & Marlyn D. Boyd. (Illus.). 300p. (C). 1992. pap. text ed. 37.95 (0-8385-8824-7, A8824-3) Appleton & Lange.

Teaching in Practice: How Professionals Can Work Effectively with Clients, Patients, & Colleagues. Andy Farquharson. LC 95-17001. (Psychology Ser.). 309p. text ed. 30.95 (0-7879-0128-8) Jossey-Bass.

Teaching in the Block: Strategies for Engaging Active Learners. Ed. by Robert L. Canady & Michael D. Rettig. LC 96-12419. (Illus.). 300p. 1996. 41.95 (1-883001-23-4) Eye On Educ.

*__Teaching in the Community: Preparing Nurses for the 21st Century.__ M. Elaine Tagliareni & Barbara Marckx. LC 97-11195. 1997. write for info. (0-88737-726-2) Natl League Nurse.

Teaching in the Diverse Classroom: Learner-Centered Activities That Work. Tonya Huber-Bowen. 200p. 1993. 19.95 (1-879639-28-9) Natl Educ Serv.

Teaching in the Health Related Professions. Steven B. Dowd. LC 96-14014. 292p. 1996. per. 29.95 (0-89089-732-8) Carolina Acad Pr.

Teaching in the Information Age: The Role of Educational Technology. Ed. by Michael J. Albright & David L. Graf. LC 85-644763. (New Directions for Teaching & Learning Ser.: No. TL 51). 100p. 1992. 19.00 (1-55542-744-8) Jossey-Bass.

Teaching in the Key of Life. Mimi B. Chenfeld. LC 93-85701. (Illus.). 84p. (Orig.). 1993. pap. text ed. 5.00 (0-935989-57-9, 315) Natl Assn Child Ed.

Teaching in the Middle & Secondary Schools. 5th ed. Ed. by Joseph F. Callahan et al. LC 94-16330. 608p. (C). 1994. pap. text ed. 48.00 (0-02-318272-5, Macmillan Coll) P-H.

*__Teaching in the Middle & Secondary Schools.__ 6th ed. Joseph F. Callahan et al. LC 97-14079. 1997. 50.00 (0-13-621004-X, Merrill Coll) P-H.

Teaching in the Multicultural Classroom. Helen R. Roberts et al. (Survival Skills for Scholars Ser.: Vol. 12). 128p. 1994. 35.00 (0-8039-5613-4); pap. 15.94 (0-8039-5614-2) Sage.

Teaching in the North: Gender Tales. Ed. by Judith Kleinfeld et al. (Teaching Cases in Cross-Cultural Education Ser.: No. 10). 124p. (Orig.). (C). 1992. pap. text ed. 12.00 (1-877962-25-2) Univ AK Ctr CCS.

Teaching in the Outdoors. 4th ed. Donald R. Hammerman et al. (Illus.). xviii, 286p. 1994. pap. text ed. 23.95 (0-8134-3009-7) Interstate.

*__Teaching in the Primary Classroom: A Learning Relationship.__ Neil Kitson & Roger Merry. LC 96-31848. 208p. (C). 1997. pap. text ed. write for info. (0-415-14814-6) Routledge.

Teaching in the Primary School. Maurice Galton. 208p. (Orig.). 1990. pap. 32.95 (0-8464-1446-5) Beekman Pubs.

Teaching in the Real World. Robert Simola. (Illus.). 200p. 1996. pap. text ed. 21.50 (1-56308-393-0) Teacher Ideas Pr.

Teaching in the Secondary School. Robert S. Griffin. 264p. (C). 1993. pap. 24.50 (0-8058-0979-1); text ed. 59.95 (0-8058-0978-3) L Erlbaum Assocs.

*__Teaching in the Secondary School: An Introduction.__ 4th ed. David G. Armstrong et al. LC 97-3421. 1997. 46.00 (0-13-496498-5) P-H.

Teaching in the Secondary Schools. William Rieck. 224p. (C). 1996. per., pap. text ed. 41.94 (0-7872-2317-4) Kendall-Hunt.

Teaching in the Small College: Issues & Applications. Ed. by Richard A. Wright & John A. Burden. LC 85-24850. (Contributions to the Study of Education Ser.: No. 17). (Illus.). 198p. 1986. text ed. 49.95 (0-313-24662-9, WTC/, Greenwood Pr) Greenwood.

Teaching in the Universities: No One Way. Ed. by Edward F. Sheffield. 264p. 1974. 34.95 (0-7735-0193-2, Pub. by McGill CN) U of Toronto Pr.

Teaching in the Universities: No One Way. Ed. by Edward F. Sheffield. LC 74-75974. 266p. (ENG & FRE.). reprint ed. pap. 75.90 (0-7837-6925-3, 2046754) Bks Demand.

Teaching in the 90's. McDonald & Russel. (C). 1994. text ed. 7.95 (0-06-502222-X) Addson-Wesley Educ.

Teaching in Wartime China: A Photo-Memoir, 1937-1939. Edward V. Gulick. LC 93-21344. (Illus.). 296p. (C). 1995. 32.50 (0-87023-912-0) U of Mass Pr.

Teaching in Your Own Write see Case for Socially Functional Art Culture & Education

Teaching Individuals with Physical & Multiple Disabilities. 3rd ed. June L. Bigge. 560p. (C). 1990. text ed. 71.00 (0-675-21017-8, Merrill Coll) P-H.

Teaching Inductively: Lesson Plans for English Teachers. Jerry Sullivan. 50p. (C). 1992. pap. 10.00 (0-933990-09-X) Canterbury Pr.

Teaching Industrial Education: Principles & Practices. Robert Andrews & E. E. Ericson. 1976. pap. text ed. 15.40 (0-02-665790-2) Glencoe.

*__Teaching Infants.__ Trevor Kerry & Janice Tollitt. 184p. (Orig.). 1987. pap. 43.50 (0-7487-2234-3, Pub. by Stanley Thornes UK) Trans-Atl Phila.

Teaching Infants & Preschoolers with Disabilities. 2nd ed. Donald B. Bailey, Jr. & Mark Wolery-Allegheny. (Illus.). 592p. (C). 1992. text ed. 64.00 (0-675-21390-8, Merrill Coll) P-H.

Teaching Information Literacy on Campus: A How-to-Do-It Manual for Librarians. Hannelore B. Rader & Trish Ridgeway. (How-to-Do-It Ser.). 150p. 1993. 39.95 (1-55570-109-4) Neal-Schuman.

Teaching Information Literacy Using Electronic Resources for Grades K-6. Ed. by Linworth Publishing, Inc. Staff & Linda Skeele. LC 96-2050. (Professional Growth Ser.). 240p. 1996. ring bd. 39.95 (0-938865-44-7) Linworth Pub.

Teaching Information Literacy Using Electronic Resources for Grades 6-12. Ed. by Linworth Publishing, Inc. Staff. LC 96-16511. (Professional Growth Ser.). 250p. 1996. ring bd. 39.95 (0-938865-45-5) Linworth Pub.

Teaching Information Retrieval & Evaluation Skills to Education Students & Practioners: A Casebook of Applications. Ed. by Patricia O. Libutti & Bonnie Gratch. 152p. (Orig.). (C). 1995. pap. 26.50 (0-8389-7813-4) Assn Coll & Res Libs.

Teaching Information Skills: A Review of the Research & Its Impact on Education. Rick Rogers. LC 93-33414. (British Library Research Ser.). 240p. 1994. 50.00 (1-85739-054-7) Bowker-Saur.

*__Teaching Information Skills in Schools.__ James E. Herring. 144p. 1996. pap. 40.00 (1-85604-176-X, LAP176X, Pub. by Library Association UK) Bernan Associates.

*__Teaching Integrated Language Arts.__ Ed. by Fredericks. (C). 1997. text ed. 53.50 (0-673-98557-1) Addison-Wesley.

Teaching Interactive Skills in Health Care. Ann Faulkner. LC 93-36308. 128p. 1993. pap. 31.75 (1-56593-227-7, 0573) Singular Publishing.

*__Teaching International Affairs with Cases: Cross-National Perspectives.__ Karen A. Mingst & Katsuhiko Mori. LC 96-48452. (C). 1997. text ed. 55.00 (0-8133-9014-1) Westview.

Teaching International Politics in High School. Ed. by Raymond English. LC 89-1250. (Illus.). 171p. (C). 1989. pap. text ed. 20.75 (0-89633-138-5); lib. bdg. 39.75 (0-89633-137-7) Ethics & Public Policy.

Teaching Interpersonal Skills: A Handbook of Experiential Learning for Health Professionals. Philip Burnard. Ed. by Jo Campling. (Therapy in Practice Ser.: No. 10). 204p. 1990. pap. 23.00 (0-412-34590-0, A4190) Chapman & Hall.

Teaching Introductory Physics. Arnold B. Arons. LC 96-16838. 816p. 1996. text ed. 62.95 (0-471-13707-3) Wiley.

Teaching Introductory Physics: A Sourcebook. Clifford E. Swartz. LC 96-17141. (Illus.). 848p. 1996. 75.00 (1-56396-320-5) Am Inst Physics.

*__Teaching Introductory Psychology: Survival Tips from the Experts.__ Ed. by Robert J. Sternberg. LC 97-3870. (Illus.). 224p. 1997. pap. text ed. 24.95 (1-55798-417-4, 4316860) Am Psychol.

Teaching Is Communicating: Nonverbal Language in the Classroom. Charles W. Galloway. LC 74-17909. 1970. pap. 2.50 (0-685-41082-X) Assn Tchr Ed.

Teaching Is Touching Tomorrow: A Changing Picture Book. Mary Engelbreit. (Main Street Gift Bks.). (Illus.). 10p. 1996. 6.95 (0-8362-0945-1) Andrews & McMeel.

Teaching Jack & Jill Right vs. Wrong in the Homes & Schools, Vol. 1. Harry S. Dent. 150p. (Orig.). 1996. pap. write for info. (0-9652786-0-3) Laity Alive.

*__Teaching Jazz: A Course of Study.__ International Association of Jazz Educators Curriculum Committee. 76p. (Orig.). 1996. pap. 18.25 (1-56545-102-3, 1607) Music Ed Natl.

Teaching Jewish Civilization: A Global Approach to Higher Education. Ed. by Moshe Davis. 400p. (C). 1995. 50.00 (0-8147-1866-3) NYU Pr.

Teaching Jewish Civilization: A Global Approach to Higher Education. Ed. by Moshe Davis. 400p. (C). 1995. pap. 20.00 (0-8147-1867-1) NYU Pr.

*__Teaching Jewish Lifecycle: Traditions & Activities.__ Barbara B. Kadden & Bruce Kadden. LC 97-71022. 180p. 1997. per. 24.50 (0-86705-040-3) A R E Pub.

Teaching Job Seeking Skills. Ed. by William H. Burke. (Professional Series on Traumatic Brain Injury: Vol. 16). 100p. (Orig.). 1988. pap. 9.50 (1-882855-23-X) HDI Pubs.

*__Teaching Jumping.__ Jane H. Brown. LC 97-471. (Illus.). 208p. (Orig.). 1997. pap. 32.95 (0-632-04127-7) Blackwell Sci.

Teaching Junior High. Carol E. Miller. 1980. pap. 3.50 (0-915374-23-4) Rapids Christian.

Teaching Keyboarding. rev. ed. Gary N. McLean. 69p. (C). 1995. pap. text ed. 12.00 (1-881530-00-0) Delta Pi Epsilon.

Teaching Kids About Birds: A Special Publication from Bird Watcher's Digest. Eirik A. T. Blom. Ed. by William Thompson, III & Mary B. Bowers. (Illus.). 32p. (Orig.). 1996. pap. write for info. (1-880241-09-9) Bird Watchers.

Teaching Kids about How AIDS Works. Marcia Quackenbush & David Schonfeld. (J). (gr. k-3). 1995. 25.00 (1-56071-377-1) ETR Assocs.

Teaching Kids about How AIDS Works. Marcia Quackenbush & David Schonfeld. (J). (gr. 4-6). 1995. 25.00 (1-56071-378-X) ETR Assocs.

Teaching Kids to Care. 1993. pap. 14.95 (0-590-49039-7) Scholastic Inc.

Teaching Kids to Care: Exploring Values Through Literature & Inquiry. Sharon V. Andrews. LC 94-19040. 236p. (Orig.). 1994. pap. 19.95 (0-927516-41-1) Grayson Bernard Pubs.

Teaching Kids to Learn: An Integrated Study Skills Curriculum for Grades 5-7. John Seaman. 168p. (Orig.). 1996. pap. text ed. 17.50 (1-57035-071-X, 86KIDS) Sopris.

Teaching Kids to Love the Earth. Marina Herman et al. LC 90-62852. (Illus.). 192p. 1991. pap. 14.95 (0-938586-42-4) Pfeifer-Hamilton.

Teaching Kids to Sing. Kenneth H. Phillips. (Illus.). 392p. 1992. 39.00 (0-02-871795-3) Schirmer Bks.

Teaching Kids to Sing: Exercise & Vocalize Cards. Kenneth H. Phillips. (C). 1994. 60.00 (0-02-871804-6) Schirmer Bks.

Teaching Kids to Sing: Level 1. Kenneth H. Phillips. 1994. 34.00 (0-02-871797-X) Schirmer Bks.

Teaching Kids to Spell. J. Richard Gentry & Jean W. Gillet. LC 92-24371. 136p. 1992. pap. text ed. 17.50 (0-435-08760-6, 08760) Heinemann.

Teaching Kids with Learning Difficulties in the Regular Classroom: Strategies & Techniques Every Teacher Can Use to Challenge & Motivate Struggling Students. Susan Winebrenner. Ed. by Pamela Espeland. 248p. 1996. pap. 27.95 (1-57542-004-X) Free Spirit Pub.

Teaching Kindergarten: A Developmentally Appropriate Approach. Bonnie B. Walmsley et al. LC 92-8496. 128p. (C). 1993. pap. text ed. 16.50 (0-435-08715-0, 08715) Heinemann.

An Asterisk (*) at the beginning of an entry indicates that the title is appearing in BIP for the first time.

Teaching Kindergarten: A Theme-Centered Curriculum. Bonnie B. Walmsley et al. LC 92-21466. 470p. 1992. 195.00 (*0-435-08719-3*, 08719) Heinemann.

Teaching Knowledge & Intelligent Tutoring. Ed. by Peter Goodyear. 432p. 1991. pap. 42.50 (*0-89391-629-3*); text ed. 82.50 (*0-89391-628-5*) Ablex Pub.

Teaching Language & Literacy: Preschool Through the Elementary Grades. James Christie et al. LC 96-14141. 1996. write for info. (*0-06-501852-4*) Addson-Wesley Educ.

***Teaching Language & Literacy: Preschool through the Elementary Grades.** James F. Christie. (C). 1997. text ed. 33.50 (*0-673-98553-9*, GoodYrBooks) Addson-Wesley Educ.

Teaching Language & Literature in Elementary Classrooms: A Resource Book for Professional Development. Marcia Popp. LC 95-49925. 512p. 1996. pap. 37.50 (*0-8058-2253-4*) L Erlbaum Assocs.

Teaching Language & Literature in Elementary Classrooms: A Resource Book for Professional Development. Marcia Popp. 432p. 1996. pap. 45.00 (*0-8058-8021-6*) L Erlbaum Assocs.

Teaching Language Arts. 2nd ed. Collins-Block. LC 96-43559. 576p. 1997. pap. 46.67 (*0-205-26080-2*) Allyn.

Teaching Language Arts. 2nd ed. Carole Cox. 1996. text ed. 65.00 (*0-205-17488-4*) Allyn.

Teaching Language Arts: An Integrated Approach. Suzanne I. Barchers. Ed. by Jucha. LC 93-36299. 530p. (C). 1993. text ed. 54.25 (*0-314-02503-0*) West Pub.

Teaching Language Arts Creatively. 2nd ed. Mimi B. Chenfeld. 417p. (C). 1987. pap. text ed. 20.75 (*0-15-588806-4*) HB Coll Pubs.

Teaching Language Arts to Children. Karel Rose. 510p. (C). 1982. text ed. 40.00 (*0-15-588808-0*) HB Coll Pubs.

Teaching Language As Communication. H. G. Widdowson. 1978. pap. text ed. 15.50 (*0-19-437077-1*) OUP.

Teaching Language-Disabled Children: A Communication Games Intervention. Susan Conant et al. LC 83-27303. 185p. 1983. pap. 17.95 (*0-914797-38-7*) Brookline Bks.

Teaching Language-Disabled Children: A Communication Games Intervention. Susan Conant et al. LC 83-27303. 185p. 1987. 22.95 (*0-914797-04-2*) Brookline Bks.

Teaching Language in Context. 2nd ed. Ommagio-Hadley. 1993. pap. 37.95 (*0-8384-4067-3*) Heinle & Heinle.

Teaching Language in Context. 2nd ed. Ommagio-Hadley. 1993. student ed., pap. 19.95 (*0-8384-4068-1*) Heinle & Heinle.

Teaching Language Learning: In-Service Training for Communicative Teaching & Self-Directed Learning in English As a Foreign Language. Rigmor Erikson. (Goteborg Studies in Educational Sciences: No. 92). xii, 218p. 1993. pap. 67.50 (*91-7346-265-9*, Pub. by Acta U Gothenburg SW) Coronet Bks.

Teaching Language, Learning Culture. Richard M. Swiderski. LC 92-42904. 248p. 1993. text ed. 59.95 (*0-89789-326-3*, H326, Bergin & Garvey) Greenwood.

Teaching Language Through Literature. Paul Simpson. (English, Language & Education Ser.). 128p. 1995. pap. 24.95 (*0-335-15797-1*) Taylor & Francis.

Teaching Language with Pictures. Jane J. Giddan & Norman S. Giddan. (Illus.). 232p. 1984. pap. text ed. 23.95 (*0-398-06635-3*) C C Thomas.

Teaching Language with Pictures. Jane J. Giddan & Norman S. Giddan. (Illus.). 232p. (C). 1984. text ed. 38.95 (*0-398-04972-6*) C C Thomas.

Teaching Languages: A Way & Ways. Earl W. Stevick. 320p. (Orig.). (C). 1980. pap. 28.95 (*0-8384-3092-9*, Newbury) Heinle & Heinle.

Teaching Languages in College. Wilga M. Rivers. 448p. 1993. pap. 29.95 (*0-8442-9364-4*, NTC Busn Bks) NTC Pub Grp.

Teaching Large Classes Well. Ed. by Maryellen G. Weimer. LC 85-644763. (New Directions for Teaching & Learning Ser.: No. TL 32). 1987. 19.00 (*1-55542-934-3*) Jossey-Bass.

***Teaching Law & Gospel.** William E Fischer. LC 95-71848. 92p. 1996. pap. 6.50 (*0-8100-0575-1*, 12N1764) Northwest Pub.

***Teaching Leadership: Essays in Theory & Practice.** Ed. by Peter S. Temes. (American University Studies XIV: Vol. 40). 216p. (C). 1996. pap. text ed. 29.95 (*0-8204-2862-0*) P Lang Pubng.

Teaching Learners with Mild Disabilities: Integrating Research & Practice. Ruth L. Meese. LC 93-28274. 474p. 1994. pap. 50.95 (*0-534-21102-X*) Brooks-Cole.

Teaching, Learning & Communication. rev. ed. P. J. Hills. (New Patterns of Learning Ser.). 128p. 1987. 39.50 (*0-7099-4707-0*, Pub. by Croom Helm UK) Routledge Chapman & Hall.

Teaching Learning Disabled. Jack Rudman. (National Teacher Examination Ser.: NT-44). 1994. pap. 23.95 (*0-8373-8454-0*) Nat Learn.

Teaching Learning Strategies to Adolescents & Adults with Learning Disabilities. David G. Scanlon et al. LC 94-41597. 1996. pap. 26.00 (*0-89079-650-5*, 6960) PRO-ED.

Teaching-Learning System for Business Education. Estelle L. Popham et al. 1975. text ed. 31.75 (*0-07-050504-7*) McGraw.

Teaching-Learning Unit. Harold F. Rahmlow. Ed. by Danny G. Langdon. LC 77-25107. (Instructional Design Library). (Illus.). 88p. 1978. 27.95 (*0-87778-122-2*) Educ Tech Pubns.

Teaching Library Skills in Grades K Through 6: A How-to-Do-It Manual for School & Public Librarians. Catharyn Roach & JoAnne Moore. (How-to-Do-It Ser.). 157p. 1993. 35.00 (*1-55570-126-4*) Neal-Schuman.

Teaching Library Skills in Middle & High School: A How-to-Do-It Manual for School & Public Librarians. Linda J. Garrett & JoAnne Moore. (How-to-Do-It Ser.). 192p. 1993. 35.00 (*1-55570-125-6*) Neal-Schuman.

Teaching Library Use: A Guide for Library Instruction. James Rice, Jr. LC 80-21337. (Contributions in Librarianship & Information Science Ser.: No. 37). (Illus.). 216p. 1981. text ed. 45.00 (*0-313-21485-9*, RTL/, Greenwood Pr) Greenwood.

Teaching Library Use Competence: Bridging the Gap from High School to College. Ed. by Carolyn A. Kirkendall. LC 82-62645. (Library Orientation Ser.: No. 13). 242p. 1982. 25.00 (*0-87650-145-5*) Pierian.

***Teaching Lifelong Leisure Activities.** John P. Bennett et al. (Illus.). 200p. (C). 1997. pap. text ed. 21.95 (*0-614-24492-7*) American Pr.

Teaching Like the Master: Developing Christlike Ideals in Teaching. D. Cecil Clark. LC 94-23087. 1994. pap. 8.95 (*1-55503-745-3*) Covenant Comms.

Teaching Linguistically Handicapped Children. Mildred F. Berry. 1980. text ed. write for info. (*0-13-893545-9*) P-H.

Teaching Listening Comprehension. Penny Ur. (Cambridge Handbooks for Language Teachers Ser.). 173p. 1984. pap. text ed. 16.95 (*0-521-28781-2*) Cambridge U Pr.

Teaching Literature: A Collection of Essays on Theory & Practice. Compiled by Lee A. Jacobus. 1995. pap. text ed. 22.60 (*0-13-455123-0*) P-H.

Teaching Literature: What Is Needed Now. Ed. by James Engell & David D. Perkins. LC 88-11029. (English Studies: No. 15). 208p. 1988. 20.00 (*0-674-86970-2*); pap. 9.95 (*0-674-86971-0*) HUP.

Teaching Literature: Writers & Teachers Talking Interviews. Ed. by Judy Kravis. 264p. Date not set. 35.00 (*1-85918-025-6*, Pub. by Cork Univ IE) Intl Spec Bk.

Teaching Literature: Writers & Teachers Talking Interviews. Ed. by Judy Kravis. 264p. 1996. pap. 18.00 (*1-85918-026-4*, Pub. by Cork Univ IE) Intl Spec Bk.

Teaching Literature & Other Arts. Ed. by Jean-Pierre Barricelli et al. LC 89-13829. (Options for Teaching Ser.: No. 10). vi, 183p. 1990. lib. bdg. 19.75 (*0-87352-364-4*, J210C) Modern Lang.

Teaching Literature by Women Authors. Carolyn S. McGowen. Ed. by Warren W. Lewis. LC 93-34695. 224p. (Orig.). 1993. pap. 16.95 (*0-927516-38-1*, EDINFO Pr) ERIC-REC.

Teaching Literature for Admission to College with Advanced Standing see Language Classroom

Teaching Literature for Examinations. Robert Protherough. LC 86-754. (English, Language & Education Ser.). 160p. 1986. pap. 27.00 (*0-335-15076-4*, Open Univ Pr) Taylor & Francis.

Teaching Literature in Grades Seven Through Nine. Ed. by Edward B. Jenkinson & Jane S. Hawley. LC 67-63019. (English Curriculum Study Ser.). 316p. reprint ed. 90.10 (*0-8357-9244-7*, 2015823) Bks Demand.

Teaching Literature in High School: The Novel. LC 95-40689. (Standards Consensus Ser.). 212p. (Orig.). 1995. teacher ed., pap. 12.95 (*0-8141-5282-1*) NCTE.

Teaching Literature in Middle School: Fiction. LC 95-49420. (Standards Consensus Ser.). 115p. 1996. pap. 12.95 (*0-8141-5285-6*) NCTE.

Teaching Literature in the Elementary Grades: A Thematic Approach. F. Moss. 304p. (C). 1996. pap. text ed. 29.95 (*0-926842-55-2*) CG Pubs Inc.

Teaching Literature in the Secondary School. Richard W. Beach & James D. Marshall. 571p. (C). 1990. text ed. 33.25 (*0-15-589104-9*) HB Coll Pubs.

Teaching Literature Inductively. 2nd ed. Jerry Sullivan & John Hurley. 225p. (Orig.). (C). 1995. pap. 20.00 (*0-933990-05-7*) Canterbury Pr.

***Teaching Lives: Essays & Stories.** Wendy Bishop. (Illus.). 1997. pap. text ed. 19.95 (*0-87421-224-3*) Utah St U Pr.

***Teaching Low Achieving & Disadvantaged Students.** 2nd ed. Charles Hargis. LC 96-39494. 202p. 1997. pap. text ed. 36.95 (*0-398-06698-1*) C C Thomas.

Teaching Macbeth (& More) Better Planning, Better Learning. Dan Flickstein. LC 95-50182. 192p. 1996. 44.95 (*0-8039-6390-4*); pap. 19.95 (*0-8039-6391-2*) Corwin Pr.

Teaching Main Idea Comprehension. Ed. by James F. Baumann. LC 85-23185. 286p. reprint ed. pap. 81.60 (*0-7837-1237-5*, 2041374) Bks Demand.

***Teaching Mainstreamed, Diverse & At-Risk Students in the General Education Classroom.** Sharon Vaughn et al. LC 96-28482. 576p. 1996. pap. 49.00 (*0-205-19954-2*) Allyn.

Teaching Mainstreamed Students. 2nd ed. T. M. Stephens et al. 370p. 1988. 184.00 (*0-08-035836-5*, Pub. by Pergamon Repr UK) Franklin.

Teaching Mainstreamed Students see Teaching Special Learners in the General Education Classroom: Methods & Techniques

Teaching Makes a Difference. 2nd ed. Carol Cummings. (Illus.). 224p. (C). 1990. reprint ed. pap. text ed. 8.95 (*0-9614574-1-4*) Teaching WA.

Teaching Malcolm X: Popular Culture & Literacy. Ed. by Theresa Perry. 224p. (C). (gr. 13). 1995. text ed. 62.95 (*0-415-91154-0*, B4925, Routledge NY) Routledge.

Teaching Malcolm X: Popular Culture & Literacy. Ed. by Theresa Perry. 224p. (gr. 13). 1995. pap. 16.95 (*0-415-91155-9*, B4929, Routledge NY) Routledge.

Teaching Manual for Tutor-Librarians. David Finn et al. LC 79-313583. (Illus.). 183p. reprint ed. pap. 52.20 (*0-7837-5327-6*, 2045066) Bks Demand.

Teaching Marketplace: Make Money with Freelance Teaching, Corporate Trainings, & on the Lecture Circuit. Bart Brodsky & Janet Geis. (Illus.). 176p. (Orig.). 1991. pap. 14.95 (*0-9628464-0-6*) Cmnty Resc Inst.

Teaching Martial Arts. Tony Gummerson. (Illus.). 160p. 1992. pap. 19.95 (*0-7136-3399-9*, Pub. by A&C Black UK) Talman.

***Teaching Martial Arts: The Way of the Master.** 2nd rev. ed. Sang H. Kim. LC 97-595. (Illus.). 208p. 1997. pap. 19.95 (*1-880336-15-4*) Turtle CT.

Teaching Mass Communication: A Guide to Better Instruction. Ed. by Michael D. Murray & Anthony J. Ferri. LC 91-28831. 288p. 1992. text ed. 55.00 (*0-275-94156-6*, C4156, Praeger Pubs) Greenwood.

Teaching Materials & Cases on Commercial Transactions. 2nd ed. J. R. Peden. 560p. 1983. 69.00 (*0-409-49364-3*, AT) MICHIE.

Teaching Materials on Estate Planning. Gerry W. Beyer. LC 95-1066. (American Casebook Ser.). 763p. (C). 1995. 45.00 (*0-314-05619-X*) West Pub.

Teaching Mathematics. Ed. by Michelle Selinger. LC 93-19457. 224p. (C). 1993. pap. text ed. 16.95 (*0-415-10252-9*) Routledge.

Teaching Mathematics: A Source Book for Aids, Activities, & Strategies. Max A. Sobel & Evan M. Maletsky. (Illus.). 288p. (C). 1975. pap. text ed. write for info. (*0-13-894121-1*) P-H.

Teaching Mathematics: A Sourcebook of Aids, Activities, & Strategies. 2nd ed. Max A. Sobel & Evan M. Maletsky. (Illus.). 240p. (C). 1987. text ed. 67.95 (*0-13-894155-6*); pap. text ed. 34.95 (*0-13-894148-3*) P-H.

Teaching Mathematics: Strategies in Mathematics, Vol. II. Tepper G. Gill et al. 35p. (Orig.). 1987. pap. 3.50 (*0-941001-01-6*) Inst Indep Educ.

Teaching Mathematics: Toward a Sound Alternative. Brent Davis. Ed. by Joe Kincheloe. LC 96-1697. (Critical Education Practice Ser.: Vol. 7). 254p. 1996. text ed. 47.00 (*0-8153-2297-6*) Garland.

Teaching Mathematics: Toward a Sound Alternative. Brent Davis. Ed. by Joe Kincheloe. LC 96-1697. (Critical Education Practice Ser.: Vol. 7). 360p. 1996. pap. text ed. 21.95 (*0-8153-2298-4*) Garland.

Teaching Mathematics - A Tantalising Enterprise: On the Nature of Mathematics & Mathematics Teaching. Neil A. Pateman. (C). 1989. 44.00 (*0-7300-0630-1*, Pub. by Deakin Univ AT) St Mut.

Teaching Mathematics & Art. Lesley Jones. 160p. 1994. pap. 75.00 (*0-7487-0456-6*, Pub. by Stanley Thornes UK) Trans-Atl Phila.

Teaching Mathematics in Grades K-8: Research Based Methods. 2nd ed. Judith S. Zawojewski. 576p. (C). 1991. text ed. 67.00 (*0-205-13414-9*) Allyn.

Teaching Mathematics in the Elementary School. David Fuys & Rosamond Tischler. (C). 1979. text ed. 53.50 (*0-673-39152-3*) Addson-Wesley Educ.

Teaching Mathematics in the Elementary School. Clyde G. Corle. LC 64-13943. 395p. reprint ed. pap. 112.60 (*0-317-08697-9*, 2012479) Bks Demand.

Teaching Mathematics Through Children's Art. Doug Williams. LC 94-36399. 116p. 1995. pap. text ed. 16.50 (*0-435-08368-6*, 08368) Heinemann.

Teaching Mathematics to Adults: Returning to Study. Gail Fitzsimons. 74p. (C). 1995. pap. 39.00 (*0-7300-2079-7*, Pub. by Deakin Univ AT) St Mut.

Teaching Mathematics to Children. 2nd ed. Graham. (C). 1995. teacher ed. write for info. (*0-06-502358-7*) Addson-Wesley Educ.

Teaching Mathematics to Children. 2nd ed. Robert J. Sovchik. LC 94-37623. (Illus.). 592p. (C). 1996. text ed. 53.95 (*0-06-502357-9*) Addson-Wesley Educ.

Teaching Mathematics to Children with Special Needs. Carol A. Thornton. 1983. text ed. 26.00 (*0-201-07728-0*) Addison-Wesley.

Teaching Mathematics to Students with Learning Disabilities. 3rd ed. Nancy S. Bley & Carol A. Thornton. LC 94-6988. (Illus.). 510p. (C). 1994. pap. text ed. 38.00 (*0-89079-603-3*, 6783) PRO-ED.

Teaching Mathematics to Young Children. 3rd ed. Dennis Thyer & John Maggs. 336p. 1991. pap. text ed. 24.95 (*0-304-32291-1*) Cassell.

Teaching Mathematics, Vol. 1: Culture, Motivation, History & Classroom Management. Edwin J. Nichols et al. Ed. by Oswald M. Ratteray. (Illus.). 48p. (Orig.). 1986. pap. 3.50 (*0-941001-00-8*) Inst Indep Educ.

Teaching Mathematics with Manipulatives: A Resource of Activities for K-12 Teacher. Mark A. Spikell. LC 92-19589. 1992. pap. text ed. 42.95 (*0-205-13993-0*, Longwood Div) Allyn.

***Teaching Mathematics with Pentablocks.** Sheldon Berman. 112p. (YA). (gr. 9-12). 1997. pap. text ed. 12.95 (*1-57452-024-5*) Cuisenaire.

Teaching Maths to Slow Learners, 8-12. Derek Haylock. 176p. 1991. pap. 29.95 (*1-85396-151-5*, Pub. by P Chapman Pub UK) Taylor & Francis.

Teaching Matters. Pica & Barnes. 1990. pap. 26.95 (*0-8384-2788-X*) Heinle & Heinle.

Teaching Media in the Primary School. Adrian Emerson. Ed. by Cedric Cullingford. (Children, Teachers & Learning Ser.). 144p. 1993. text ed. 70.00 (*0-304-32416-7*); pap. text ed. 22.00 (*0-304-32435-3*) Cassell.

Teaching Medical Transcription: Meeting the Challenges of the 90s! 52p. 1993. pap. 195.00 incl. vhs (*0-934385-58-0*) Hlth Prof Inst.

***Teaching Medicine in the Community: A Guide for Undergraduate Education.** Ed. by C. Whitehouse et al. (Oxford General Practice Ser.: No. 38). (Illus.). 240p. 1997. pap. 69.50 (*0-19-262653-1*) OUP.

Teaching Memory Improvement to Adults. rev. ed. Janet Fogler & Lynn Stern. LC 93-36784. 128p. 1994. pap. 29.95 (*0-8018-4769-9*) Johns Hopkins.

Teaching Method for Brain-Injured & Hyperactive Children: A Demonstration-Pilot Study. William Cruickshank. LC 81-6255. (Syracuse University Special Education & Rehabilitation Monograph Ser.: No. 6). (Illus.). xxi, 576p. 1981. reprint ed. text ed. 95.00 (*0-313-23071-4*, CRTC) Greenwood.

Teaching Methods Cases for Teacher Problem Solving. Rita A. Silverman. 1993. pap. text ed. write for info. (*0-07-057662-9*); pap. text ed. write for info. (*0-07-057663-7*) McGraw.

***Teaching Methods for Today's Schools: Collaboration & Inclusion.** John Scott Hewit & Kathleen S. Whittier. LC 96-41529. 400p. 1997. pap. 48.00 (*0-205-15413-1*) Allyn.

Teaching Microscopy, Vol. 52. John G. Dedy. (Illus.). 1994. 45.00 (*0-904962-14-8*) Microscope Pubns.

Teaching Microwave Cooking: A Basic Technique Course Guide. Millie Delahunty. (Illus.). 114p. (Orig.). 1989. pap. text ed. 18.95 (*0-932243-12-6*) Microwave Cuisine.

Teaching Middle & Secondary School Math. 2nd ed. Cangelosi. 457p. (C). 1995. pap. text ed. 62.00 (*0-13-439233-7*) P-H.

Teaching Middle Grades to Use Process Writing Skills: Strategies, Techniques, & Activities. Marilyn Seguin et al. Ed. by Leslie Britt. (Illus.). 80p. (Orig.). 1994. pap. text ed. 9.95 (*0-86530-299-5*) Incentive Pubns.

***Teaching Middle School Physical Education.** Bonnie S. Mohnsen. LC 96-39066. (Illus.). 360p. (Orig.). 1997. pap. text ed. 27.00 (*0-88011-513-0*, BMOH0513) Human Kinetics.

Teaching Minister. Clark M. Williamson & Ronald J. Allen. 168p. (Orig.). 1991. pap. 14.00 (*0-664-25174-9*) Westminster John Knox.

Teaching Ministry of the Church: Integrating Biblical with Truth & Contemporary Application. Ed. by Daryl Eldridge. LC 94-34202. 336p. 1995. 34.99 (*0-8054-1087-2*, 4210-87) Broadman.

Teaching Ministry of the Diocesan Bishop: A Pastoral Reflection. Committee on Doctrine Staff. 28p. (Orig.). (C). 1992. pap. 2.95 (*1-55586-484-8*) US Catholic.

Teaching Minorities More Effectively: A Model for Educators. Thomas J. Brown. 82p. (Orig.). (C). 1987. lib. bdg. 33.00 (*0-8191-5662-0*) U Pr of Amer.

Teaching Minorities to Play the Corporate Language Game. Henry H. Parker & Marilyn I. Crist. 51p. (Orig.). 1996. pap. 15.00 (*1-889271-20-9*) Nat Res Ctr.

Teaching Mitzvot: Concepts, Values, & Activities. Barbara B. Kadden & Bruce Kadden. LC 88-70869. 175p. 1988. pap. text ed. 22.50 (*0-86705-021-7*) A R E Pub.

Teaching Mixed Media to Children. Karla Cikanova. (Illus.). 128p. (J). (gr. 3-7). 1995. text ed. 22.50 (*976-641-004-6*, Pub. by Craftsman Hse VB) Gordon & Breach.

Teaching Models in Education of the Gifted. C. June Maker. LC 82-1692. (Illus.). 475p. 1982. 39.00 (*0-89079-186-4*, 2066) PRO-ED.

Teaching Models in Education of the Gifted. 2nd ed. C. June Maker & Aleene B. Nielson. (C). 1994. text ed. 41.00 (*0-89079-609-2*, 6802) PRO-ED.

Teaching Modern Ideas of Biology. O. Roger Anderson. LC 73-185961. (Studies in Science Education). 251p. reprint ed. pap. 71.60 (*0-317-41944-7*, 2025987) Bks Demand.

Teaching Modern Physics. Ed. by K. Luchner et al. 500p. (C). 1989. text ed. 55.00 (*9971-5-0923-7*); pap. text ed. 33.00 (*9971-5-0960-1*) World Scientific Pub.

Teaching Modern Science. 7th ed. Arthur A. Carin. LC 96-26853. 400p. (C). 1996. pap. text ed. 46.00 (*0-13-457060-X*) P-H.

Teaching Monolingual Classes. David Atkinson. LC 92-26630. (Keys to Language Teaching Ser.). 1993. 17.95 (*0-582-06110-5*, 79900) Longman.

Teaching Montessori in the Home: The Pre-School Years. Elizabeth G. Hainstock. 1976. mass mkt. 4.50 (*0-452-25418-3*, Z5418, Plume) NAL-Dutton.

***Teaching Montessori in the Home: The Preschool Years.** Elizabeth G. Hainstock & Lee Davis. LC 97-11024. 1997. pap. 11.95 (*0-452-27909-7*, Plume) NAL-Dutton.

Teaching Montessori in the Home: The School Years. Elizabeth G. Hainstock. 1976. pap. 11.95 (*0-452-26268-2*, Plume) NAL-Dutton.

Teaching Montessori in the Home: The School Years. Elizabeth G. Hainstock. (Illus.). 192p. 1989. mass mkt. 6.95 (*0-452-26178-3*, Plume) NAL-Dutton.

***Teaching Montessori in the Home: The School Years.** Elizabeth G. Hainstock & Lee Davis. LC 97-11025. 1997. pap. 11.95 (*0-452-27910-0*, Plume) NAL-Dutton.

Teaching Moral & Spiritual Values. Langdon & Stout. 1979. 7.95 (*0-933062-02-8*) R H Sommer.

Teaching Movement & Dance: A Sequential Approach to Rhythmic Movement. 3rd ed. Phyllis S. Weikart. 416p. (C). 1989. pap. text ed. 29.95 (*0-929816-03-X*) High-Scope.

Teaching Movement & Dance: Intermediate Folk Dance. Phyllis S. Weikart. 300p. (Orig.). 1984. pap. 25.95 (*0-931114-30-6*) High-Scope.

Teaching Multicultural Literature in Grades K-8. Ed. by Violet J. Harris. 296p. 1992. text ed. 38.95 (*0-926842-13-7*) CG Pubs Inc.

Teaching Multicultural Literature in Grades K-8. Ed. by Violet J. Harris. 302p. 1993. pap. text ed. 28.95 (*0-926842-30-7*) CG Pubs Inc.

Teaching Multilingual Classrooms. Hernandez. LC 96-21265. 1996. pap. text ed. 27.00 (*0-675-21358-4*, Merrill Coll) P-H.

Teaching Music. James P. O'Brien. 362p. (C). 1983. pap. text ed. 34.00 (*0-03-057718-7*) HB Coll Pubs.

Teaching Music. Ed. by Gary Spruce. LC 95-46063. 288p. (C). 1996. pap. 22.95 (*0-415-13367-X*) Routledge.

Teaching Music. 2nd ed. 1997. 30.00 (*0-02-864596-0*) Macmillan.

Teaching Music: Managing the Successful Music Program. Darwin E. Walker. 302p. (C). 1989. 32.00 (*0-02-872721-5*) Schirmer Bks.

Teaching Music: The Human Experience. Shirley S. Mullins. 115p. (Orig.). 1985. pap. text ed. 9.95 (*0-9616262-0-8*) Media Servs.

Teaching Music Effectively in the Elementary School. Lois Choksy. 320p. 1991. pap. text ed. 54.00 (*0-13-892704-9*) P-H.

Teaching Music in Small Churches. Marilyn J. Keiser. (Hymnal Studies: 3). 64p. 1983. pap. 7.95 (*0-89869-102-8*) Church Pub Inc.

Teaching Music in the Elementary Classroom. Charles R. Hoffer & Marjorie L. Hoffer. 384p. (C). 1982. pap. text ed. 26.75 (*0-15-588809-9*) HB Coll Pubs.

Teaching Music in the Elementary Classroom. 2nd ed. Charles R. Hoffer & Marjorie L. Hoffer. 325p. 1987. text ed. 18.00 (*0-685-20272-0*) HB Coll Pubs.

Teaching Music in the Primary School. Ed. by Joanna Glover et al. LC 92-17096. (Children, Teachers & Learning Ser.). 208p. 1993. text ed. 70.00 (*0-304-32598-8*); pap. text ed. 22.50 (*0-304-32578-3*) Cassell.

Teaching Music in the Secondary Schools. 4th ed. Charles R. Hoffer. 399p. (C). 1991. text ed. 48.95 (*0-534-14136-6*) Wadsworth Pub.

Teaching Music in Today's Secondary Schools: A Creative Approach to Contemporary Music Education. 2nd ed. Malcolm E. Bessom et al. 400p. (C). 1980. text ed. 33.25 (*0-03-021556-0*) HB Coll Pubs.

Teaching Music in Twentieth-Century America. Lois Choksy et al. (Illus.). 400p. (C). 1985. text ed. 64.00 (*0-13-892662-X*) P-H.

***Teaching Music Through Performance in Band.** Richard B. Miles & Larry Blocher. LC 96-38981. 1996. write for info. (*0-941050-93-9*) GIA Pubns.

Teaching Music with a Multicultural Approach. William M. Anderson. (Illus.). 104p. (Orig.). (C). 1991. pap. text ed. 18.00 (*0-940796-91-0*, 1048) Music Ed Natl.

***Teaching Music with Technology.** Thomas E. Rudolph. LC 96-42093. (Illus.). 320p. (Orig.). (C). 1996. pap. 19.95 (*0-941050-92-0*, G3866) GIA Pubns.

Teaching My Daughter to Mulch: Gardening Meditations. Donna E. Schaper. LC 95-75760. 105p. (Orig.). 1995. pap. 10.95 (*1-886172-19-6*) Ash Grove Pr.

Teaching Myself. 1994. 14.95 (*0-19-437188-3*) OUP.

Teaching Nation: Prospects for Teachers in the European Community. Guy Neave. 180p. 1992. text ed. 79.25 (*0-08-041381-1*, Pergamon Pr) Elsevier.

Teaching Native American. Hap Gilliland. 304p. 1995. per., pap. text ed. 21.95 (*0-7872-0955-4*) Kendall-Hunt.

Teaching Natural Birth: Deciding to Teach & Establishing Your Own Successful Business. Jan H. Whitcomb. LC 93-94258. (Illus.). 258p. (Orig.). 1994. pap. 21.95 (*0-9639280-7-4*) Thornwood Grdns.

Teaching Nature in Cities & Towns. Sonia W. Vogl & Robert L. Vogl. (Illus.). 102p. 1985. pap. text ed. 9.95 (*0-8134-2458-5*, 2458) Interstate.

Teaching Non-Western Studies: A Handbook of Materials & Methods. Stephen Guild et al. 139p. (Orig.). (C). 1972. pap. 5.00 (*0-932288-02-2*) Ctr Intl Ed U of MA.

Teaching Notes for Cases on International Technology Transfer. Richard D. Robinson. (Illus.). 107p. (Orig.). (C). 1988. pap. text ed. 15.00 (*0-317-93295-0*) Hamlin Pubns.

***Teaching Notes to Accompany Studies in Contract.** 5th ed. Richard E. Speidel & Ian Ayres. (University Casebook Ser.). 349p. 1997. pap. text ed. write for info. (*1-56662-548-3*) Foundation Pr.

Teaching Nursing. Sandra DeYoung. Ed. by Debra Hunter. 288p. (C). 1990. pap. text ed. 32.25 (*0-201-09265-4*) Addison-Wesley.

Teaching Nursing: A Self-Instructional Handbook. 2nd ed. C. Ewan & R. White. (Illus.). 208p. 1996. pap. 39.95 (*1-56593-431-8*, 1100) Singular Publishing.

***Teaching Nursing Home: A New Approach to Geriatric Research, Education, & Clinical Care.** Ed. by Edward L. Schneider et al. LC 84-42863. 383p. 1985. reprint ed. pap. 109.20 (*0-608-03447-9*, 2064148) Bks Demand.

Teaching Nursing in the Neighborhoods: The Northeastern University Model. Ed. by Peggy Matteson. (Teaching of Nursing Ser.). (Illus.). 256p. 1995. 34.95 (*0-8261-9100-2*) Springer Pub.

Teaching Nutrition. Joanne P. Nestor & Judith A. Glotzer. 302p. 1981. pap. text ed. 20.00 (*0-89011-559-1*) Abt Bks.

Teaching Nutrition. 2nd ed. Ercel S. Eppright et al. LC 63-24032. 357p. reprint ed. pap. 101.80 (*0-317-28207-7*, 2022764) Bks Demand.

Teaching Nutrition: A Review of Programs & Research. Ed. by Joanne P. Nestor & Judith A. Glotzer. 302p. 1984. reprint ed. pap. text ed. 27.00 (*0-8191-4115-1*) U Pr of Amer.

***Teaching Obedience Classes & Seminars.** Joel M. McMains. LC 96-49090. (Illus.). 256p. 1996. 27.95 (*0-87605-470-X*) Howell Bk.

Teaching Occupational Home Economics. Terrass & Comfort. 1979. 18.20 (*0-02-665800-3*) Glencoe.

Teaching of Addai. Tr. by George Howard. LC 81-5802. (Society of Biblical Literature Texts & Translations Ser.). 117p. (C). 1981. pap. 20.95 (*0-89130-490-8*, 06 02 16) Scholars Pr GA.

Teaching of African Literature. rev. ed. Ed. by Thomas Hale & Richard Priebe. LC 85-50380. (African Literature Association Annuals Ser.: No. 2). 200p. 1989. reprint ed. 24.00 (*0-89410-472-1*); reprint ed. pap. 14.00 (*0-89410-473-X*) Cornell AS&RC.

Teaching of Animal Welfare, Pt. 1: (Veterinary & Agricultural Degree Courses) UFAW Staff. (C). 1988. 35.00 (*0-900767-53-7*) St Mut.

Teaching of Animal Welfare, Pt. 11: (Ond & HND Agricultural College Courses) UFAW Staff. (C). 1988. 40.00 (*0-900767-54-5*) St Mut.

Teaching of Anthropology: Problems, Issues, & Religions. Conrad P. Kozzak et al. LC 96-19790. 380p. (Orig.). (C). 1996. text ed. 38.00 (*1-55934-711-2*) Mayfield Pub.

Teaching of Arabic As a Foreign Language. Raja T. Nasr. 123p. (ARA.). 1975. pap. 12.95 (*0-86685-047-3*, LDL0473, Pub. by Librairie du Liban FR) Intl Bk Ctr.

Teaching of Arabic As a Foreign Language: Issues & Directions. Mahmoud Al-Batal et al. LC 95-22101. (Al-Arabiyya Monograph Ser.: No. 2). 359p. 1995. 30.00 (*0-9621530-9-5*) AM Assn Teach.

Teaching of Arithmetic & the Waldorf School Plan. Herman Von Baravalle. 1991. pap. 6.95 (*0-945803-14-1*) R Steiner Col Pubns.

Teaching of Astronomy: Proceedings of the 105th Colloquium of the International Astronomical Union. Ed. by Jay M. Pasachoff & John R. Percy. 445p. (C). 1992. pap. text ed. 36.95 (*0-521-42966-8*) Cambridge U Pr.

Teaching of Banking Service: Impact & Implications. 206p. 1994. 27.50 (*92-1-104424-3*, E.94.II.A.4) UN.

Teaching of Business Communication II. Ed. by G. H. Douglas. 292p. 1987. pap. 9.95 (*0-931874-18-1*) Assn Busn Comm.

Teaching of Calvin: A Modern Interpretation. Adam M. Hunter. LC 83-45618. reprint ed. 37.50 (*0-404-19836-8*) AMS Pr.

Teaching of Christ. G. Campbell Morgan. 344p. 1982. 16.99 (*0-8007-0395-2*) Revell.

Teaching of Christ: A Catholic Catechism for Adults. 3rd rev. ed. Donald W. Wuerl et al. LC 75-34852. 600p. 1991. pap. 12.95 (*0-87973-850-2*, 850) Our Sunday Visitor.

Teaching of Christ: A Catholic Catechism for Adults. 4th ed. Donald W. Wuerl et al. 1995. pap. 16.95 (*0-87973-665-8*, 665) Our Sunday Visitor.

Teaching of Classical & Modern Foreign Languages: Common Areas & Problems see Language Learner

Teaching of Classical Ballet. Lawson. 1985. 19.95 (*0-87830-143-7*) Routledge Chapman & Hall.

Teaching of Classical Ballet. Joan Lawson. LC 73-83997. (Illus.). 1974. 19.95 (*0-87830-583-1*, Thtre Arts Bks) Routledge.

Teaching of Classical Cultures see Culture in Language & Learning

Teaching of Classical Subjects in English. Ed. by Clarence A. Forbes. 98p. (ENG, GRE & LAT.). 5.10 (*0-939507-12-9*, B301) Amer Classical.

Teaching of Development Economics. Kurt Martin. Ed. by John Knapp. 238p. 1967. 30.00 (*0-7146-1014-3*, Pub. by F Cass Pubs UK) Intl Spec Bk.

Teaching of Drama in the Primary School. Brian Wooland. LC 92-28989. (Effective Teacher Ser.). 1993. pap. text ed. write for info. (*0-582-08906-9*) Longman.

Teaching of Dynamic Psychiatry: A Reappraisal of the Goals & Techniques in the Teaching of Psychoanalytic Psychiatry. Ed. by Grete L. Bibring. LC 67-27426. 277p. 1968. 38.50 (*0-8236-6380-9*) Intl Univs Pr.

Teaching of Elementary Problem Solving in Engineering & Related Fields. Ed. by James L. Lubkin. 198p. 1980. 10.00 (*0-318-13172-2*) Am Soc Eng Ed.

Teaching of English: From the Sixteenth Century to 1870. Ian Michael. (Illus.). 600p. 1987. text ed. 95.00 (*0-521-24196-0*) Cambridge U Pr.

Teaching of English: 76th Yearbook, Part I. Ed. by James R. Squire. LC 76-44918. (National Society for the Study of Education Publication Ser.). (Illus.). 384p. 1977. lib. bdg. 12.00 (*0-226-60122-6*) U Ch Pr.

***Teaching of English As an International Language.** Wingard. 1991. pap. text ed. write for info. (*0-17-556497-3*) Addison-Wesley.

Teaching of English at the University of Iowa Vol. I: The First Hundred Years 1861-1961. John C. Gerber. 196p. pap. 15.00 (*0-944266-21-5*) Maecenas Pr.

Teaching of English Suffixes. Edward L. Thorndike. LC 78-177713. (Columbia University. Teachers College. Contributions to Education Ser.: No. 847). reprint ed. 37.50 (*0-404-55847-X*) AMS Pr.

Teaching of Ethics in Higher Education: A Report by the Hastings Center. Ed. by Daniel Callahan. LC 80-10294. (Teaching of Ethics Ser.). 103p. 1980. pap. 5.00 (*0-916558-09-6*) Hastings Ctr.

Teaching of Ethnic Dance. Anatol M. Joukowsky. LC 79-7768. (Dance Ser.). (Illus.). 1980. reprint ed. lib. bdg. 24.95 (*0-8369-9296-2*) Ayer.

***Teaching of Genetics in the Undergraduate Medical Curriculum & in Postgraduate Training.** (Technical Report Ser.: No. 238). 19p. 1962. pap. text ed. 3.00 (*92-4-120238-6*) World Health.

Teaching of Grammar in Late Medieval England: An Edition with Commentary, of Oxford Lincoln College MS Latin 130. Cynthia R. Bland. (Medieval Texts & Studies: No. 6). 235p. 1991. text ed. 32.00 (*0-937191-16-7*) Colleagues Pr Inc.

Teaching of History. 2nd rev. ed. S. K. Kochhar. xiii, 386p. 1984. text ed. 25.00 (*0-86590-425-1*, Pub. by Sterling Pubs II) Apt Bks.

Teaching of History: Implementing the National Curriculum. Hilary Cooper. (Studies in Primary Education Ser.). 160p. 1992. pap. 29.95 (*1-85346-186-5*, Pub. by D Fulton UK) Taylor & Francis.

Teaching of History in English Schools. Olive E. Shropshire. LC 70-177789. (Columbia University. Teachers College. Contributions to Education Ser.: No. 617). reprint ed. 37.50 (*0-404-55671-X*) AMS Pr.

Teaching of History in Primary Schools: Implementing the Revised National Curriculum. 2nd ed. Hilary Cooper. 208p. 1995. pap. 25.95 (*1-85346-403-1*, Pub. by D Fulton UK) Taylor & Francis.

Teaching of Home Science. 2nd rev. ed. R. R. Das & Binita Ray. 146p. 1990. text ed. 25.00 (*81-207-0064-3*, Pub. by Sterling Pubs II) Apt Bks.

Teaching of Human Sexuality in Schools for Health Professionals. J. Burton et al. (Public Health Papers: No. 57). 1974. pap. text ed. 5.00 (*92-4-130057-4*, 1110057) World Health.

***Teaching of Immunology in the Medical Curriculum: Report of a WHO Expert Committee, 1967.** (Technical Report Ser.: No. 358). 0046p. 1967. pap. text ed. 5.00 (*92-4-120358-7*, 1100358) World Health.

Teaching of Instrumental Music. 2nd ed. Richard J. Colwell & Thomas Goolsby. 432p. 1991. text ed. 62.00 (*0-13-892688-3*, 650801) P-H.

Teaching of Islam. M. Ahmad. 208p. 1984. 150.00 (*1-85077-020-4*, Pub. by Darf Pubs Ltd UK) St Mut.

Teaching of Italian in the United States: A Documentary History. Joseph G. Fucilla. LC 74-17929. 304p. 1975. reprint ed. 21.95 (*0-405-06401-2*) Ayer.

***Teaching of Jean De Reszke.** Dale V. Gilliand. Ed. by Edward V. Foreman. (Twentieth Century Masterworks on Singing Ser.: Vol. VII). 1993. pap. 12.50 (*1-887117-03-2*) Pro musica pr.

***Teaching of Jesus.** Lawrence G. Lovasik. (Saint Joseph Picture Bks.). (Illus.). 1978. pap. 1.25 (*0-89942-302-7*, 302-00) Catholic Bk Pub.

Teaching of Judaica in American Universities: Proceedings. Leon A. Jick. 1970. 15.00 (*0-87068-127-3*) Ktav.

Teaching of Legal Research. Christopher G. Wren & Jill R. Wren. 54p. 1988. teacher ed. 4.00 (*0-916951-19-7*) Adams & Ambrose.

Teaching of Literature see Foreign Language Teachers & Tests

Teaching of Mathematical Modeling & Applications. Mogens Niss et al. (Mathematics & Its Applications Ser.). 426p. 1991. 89.00 (*0-13-892068-0*, 540301) P-H.

Teaching of Mathematics. 3rd enl. rev. ed. Kulbir Singh Sidhu. 395p. 1990. text ed. 35.00 (*81-207-0098-8*, Pub. by Sterling Pubs II) Apt Bks.

Teaching of Music. Gowri Kuppuswamy & H. Hariharan. 88p. 1980. 13.95 (*0-940500-57-4*, Pub. by Sterling II) Asia Bk Corp.

Teaching of Non-Fiction in Elementary & Secondary Classrooms: Essays by Milton Meltzer. Milton Meltzer. Ed. by Wendy Saul. (Language & Literacy Ser.). 216p. (C). 1994. text ed. 40.00 (*0-8077-3378-4*); pap. text ed. 18.95 (*0-8077-3377-6*) Tchrs Coll.

Teaching of Organizational Behavior Across Discipline & National Boundaries: A Role for Information Technology. Ed. by Alma M. Whiteley. LC 96-19855. (Journal of Teaching in International Business: Vol. 7, No. 4). 113p. 1996. 24.95 (*1-56024-739-8*, Intl Busn Pr) Haworth Pr.

Teaching of Physical Skills. Annie Clement & Betty G. Hartman. 368p. (C). 1994. per. write for info. (*0-697-14802-5*) Brown & Benchmark.

Teaching of Poetry: European Perspectives. Ed. by Linda Thompson. (Education Ser.). (Illus.). 112p. 1996. pap. 17.95 (*0-304-32878-2*, Pub. by Cassell UK) Cassell.

Teaching of Practical Statistics. C. W. Anderson & R. M. Loynes. LC 87-8238. (Probability & Mathematical Ser.). 199p. 1987. text ed. 225.00 (*0-471-91572-6*) Wiley.

Teaching of Psychology: Method, Content, & Context. Ed. by John Radford & David Rose. LC 79-40824. 380p. reprint ed. pap. 108.30 (*0-8357-7046-X*, 2033621) Bks Demand.

Teaching of Psychosomatic Medicine & Consultation-Liaison Psychiatry. Adam J. Krakowski. (Bibliotheca Psychiatrica Ser.: No. 159). 1979. pap. 66.50 (*3-8055-2955-4*) S Karger.

Teaching of Public Health in Europe. J. D. Cottrell et al. (Monograph Ser.: No. 58). 246p. 1969. pap. text ed. 36.00 (*92-4-140058-7*, 1140058) World Health.

Teaching of Reading. 6th ed. Martha Dallmann et al. LC 81-20010. 456p. (C). 1982. text ed. 42.75 (*0-03-059884-2*) HB Coll Pubs.

Teaching of Reading: An International View. William S. Gray. LC 58-6579. (Burton Lectures: 1956). 38p. 1957. 5.95 (*0-674-87001-8*) HUP.

***Teaching of Reading: The Development of Literacy in the Early Years of School.** Jeni Riley. 160p. 1996. pap. 24.95 (*1-85396-307-0*, Pub. by Paul Chapman UK) Taylor & Francis.

Teaching of Reading see Foreign Languages: Reading, Literature, Requirements

Teaching of Reading in English As a Second Language Among Disadvantaged Students in Puerto Rico. Melendez Winifred. 1976. lib. bdg. 250.00 (*0-8490-2731-4*) Gordon Pr.

Teaching of Responsibility. B. E. Rollin. 1983. 20.00 (*0-317-43863-8*) St Mut.

Teaching of Science. Wynne Harlen. (Studies in Primary Education Ser.). 160p. 1991. pap. 29.95 (*1-85346-154-7*, Pub. by D Fulton UK) Taylor & Francis.

Teaching of Science in Normal Schools & Teachers Colleges. Alice M. Van De Voort. LC 75-177679. (Columbia University. Teachers College. Contributions to Education Ser.: No. 287). reprint ed. 37.50 (*0-404-55287-0*) AMS Pr.

Teaching of Science in Primary Schools. 2nd ed. Wynne Harlen. 240p. 1996. pap. text ed. 24.95 (*1-85346-398-1*, Pub. by D Fulton UK) Taylor & Francis.

Teaching of Secondary School Mathematics. National Council of Teachers of Mathematics Staff. LC 27-7119. (National Council of Teachers of Mathematics Yearbook Ser.: 33rd). 441p. reprint ed. pap. 125.70 (*0-685-15850-0*, 2027058) Bks Demand.

Teaching of Slavic Cultures see Culture in Language & Learning

Teaching of Soccer: A Working Manual for Youth Coaches. Simon Whitehead. Ed. by Jim Hoehn. (Illus.). 128p. (Orig.). (C). 1987. spiral bd. 9.95 (*0-9622202-0-5*); per. 9.95 (*0-317-93542-9*) Edctnl Sports.

Teaching of Social Studies. S. K. Kochar. 376p. 1983. text ed. 22.50 (*0-86590-114-7*, Pub. by Sterling Pubs II) Apt Bks.

Teaching of Social Studies in India. P. K. Khasnavis. 1983. 12.50 (*0-8364-1054-8*, Pub. by Abhinav II) S Asia.

Teaching of Speech. George S. Haycock. 302p. reprint ed. pap. 86.10 (*0-7837-1250-2*, 2041387) Bks Demand.

Teaching of Tennyson. John Oates. 1972. 59.95 (*0-8490-1181-7*) Gordon Pr.

Teaching of Tennyson. John Oates. LC 72-3619. (Studies in Tennyson: No. 27). 1972. reprint ed. lib. bdg. 64.95 (*0-8383-1583-6*) M S G Haskell Hse.

Teaching of the Decorative Arts see Encyclopedie Des Arts Decoratifs et Industriels Modernes

Teaching of the Early Church on the Use of Wine & Strong Drink. Irving W. Raymond. LC 79-120207. (Columbia University. Studies in the Social Sciences: No. 286). reprint ed. 20.00 (*0-404-51286-0*) AMS Pr.

Teaching of the Prophets: Statements of the LDS Leaders on Contemporary Issues. R. Clayston Brough. 1993. 14.98 (*0-88290-461-2*, 1010) Horizon Utah.

Teaching of the Qura'an. H. V. Stanton. 144p. 1987. 190.00 (*1-85077-157-X*, Pub. by Darf Pubs Ltd UK) St Mut.

Teaching of the Qur'An, with an Account of Its Growth & Subject Index. H. U. Stanton. LC 74-90040. 1969. reprint ed. 34.00 (*0-8196-0253-1*) Biblo.

Teaching of Thinking. Ray Nickerson et al. 400p. (C). 1985. text ed. 49.95 (*0-89859-539-8*) L Erlbaum Assocs.

Teaching of Values: Caring & Appreciation. James L. Jarrett. LC 91-20584. 272p. (C). (gr. 13). 1991. pap. 22.95 (*0-415-05288-2*, A5444) Routledge.

Teaching of Vimalakirti. Tr. by E. Lamotte & S. Boin from SAN. (C). 1976. 76.50 (*0-86013-077-0*, Pub. by Pali Text) Wisdom MA.

Teaching of Western European Cultures see Culture in Language & Learning

Teaching of Wordsworth. Derek Colville. (American University Studies: English Language & Literature: Ser. IV, Vol. 7). 128p. (Orig.). 1984. pap. text ed. 12.55 (*0-8204-0077-7*) P Lang Pubng.

Teaching of World History. Gerald Leinwand. LC 77-95099. (National Council for the Social Studies Bulletin: No. 54). 96p. reprint ed. pap. 27.40 (*0-685-16452-7*, 2052194) Bks Demand.

Teaching of Writing. Ed. by Anthony R. Petrosky & David Bartholomae. LC 85-62666. (Eighty-Fifth Yearbook of the National Society for the Study of Education Ser.: Pt. 2). x, 222p. 1989. pap. text ed. 11.95 (*0-226-59949-3*, Natl Soc Stud Educ) U Ch Pr.

Teaching of Writing see Language Teacher

Teaching off the Wall. Elaine Prizzi & Jeanne Hoffman. LC 80-81836. (J). (gr. 2-5). 1981. pap. 9.99 (*0-8224-6830-1*) Fearon Teach Aids.

***Teaching Offside! A Soccer Manual for Coaches & Players.** 2nd rev. ed. Tony Walters. Ed. by Bob Evans. (Illus.). 28p. 1997. pap. text ed. 4.50 (*1-889424-02-1*, B-0109) Yth Sports.

***Teaching On-Line: Internet Research, Conversation & Composition.** 2nd ed. Fowler. (C). 1998. pap. text ed. write for info. (*0-321-01957-1*) Addison-Wesley Educ.

Teaching on Solid Ground: Using Scholarship to Improve Practice. Ed. by Robert J. Menges & Maryellen G. Weimer. (Higher & Adult Education Ser.). 422p. text ed. 34.95 (*0-7879-0133-4*) Jossey-Bass.

Teaching on the Crest of the Third Wave: Proceedings CELA 84. Council of Educators in Landscape Architecture Staff. 471p. reprint ed. pap. 134.30 (*0-317-26816-3*, 2023482) Bks Demand.

Teaching on TV & Video. Ralph Ayers. LC 94-41466. (Engineer's Guide to Business Ser.: Vol. 6). 1994. 19.95 (*0-7803-2246-0*, DG106) Inst Electrical.

Teaching Opportunities in the Middle East & North Africa. Amideast. Ed. by Susan Gibbs et al. 232p. (Orig.). 1987. pap. 14.95 (*0-913957-03-8*) AMIDEAST.

Teaching Oral English. Donn Byrne. (Handbooks for Language Teachers Ser.). 1976. pap. text ed. 21.95 (*0-582-74620-5*, 74762) Longman.

***Teaching Orienteering.** 2nd ed. McNeill et al. 160p. 1997. pap. text ed. write for info. (*0-614-31000-8*) Human Kinetics.

***Teaching Orienteering.** 2nd ed. Carol McNeill et al. LC 97-17531. 1997. write for info. (*0-88011-804-0*) Human Kinetics.

Teaching Orthopedically Handicapped. (National Teacher Examination Ser.: NT-25). pap. 23.95 (*0-8373-8435-4*) Nat Learn.

Teaching Our Babies to Read: A Guide for African American Parents. Jannah Al-Uqdah. LC 93-90748. 64p. (Orig.). 1993. pap. 4.00 (*0-9638046-0-X*) Al-Uqdah Ent.

Teaching Our Children to Read: The Role of Skills in a Comprehensive Reading Program. Bill Honig. LC 95-41752. (Illus.). 160p. 1996. 42.95 (*0-8039-6404-8*); pap. 18.95 (*0-8039-6405-6*) Corwin Pr.

Teaching Our Tomorrows. 2nd ed. Spice I Teachers Staff. LC 86-72006. 155p. 1987. teacher ed. 15.00 (*1-879953-00-5*) CRD Law-Related.

Teaching Painting in the Primary School. Keith Gentle. Ed. by Cedric Cullingford. (Children, Teachers & Learning Ser.). 144p. 1993. text ed. 70.00 (*0-304-32564-3*); pap. text ed. 22.50 (*0-304-32566-X*) Cassell.

Teaching Parents of Young Children: A Curriculum in 12 Sessions. Laura L. Wetzel. LC 95-47023. 150p. (Orig.). 1996. pap. text ed. 16.95 (*0-87868-570-7*, Child-Family Pr) Child Welfare.

Teaching Parents to Teach: Education for the Handicapped. Ed. by David L. Lillie. (First Chance Ser.). (Illus.). 1976. pap. 9.95 (*0-8027-7262-5*) Walker & Co.

An Asterisk (*) at the beginning of an entry indicates that the title is appearing in BIP for the first time.

Teaching Patient Education Skills: A Curriculum for Residents. Marion F. Fass et al. 200p. 1983. 5.00 (*0-942295-14-5*) Soc Tchrs Fam Med.

Teaching Patients with Acute Conditions. Springhouse Publishing Company Staff. (Illus.). 604p. 1992. pap. 32.95 (*0-87434-496-4*) Springhouse Pub.

Teaching Patients with Chronic Conditions. Springhouse Publishing Company Staff. (Illus.). 663p. 1992. pap. 32.95 (*0-87434-497-2*) Springhouse Pub.

Teaching Patients with Low Literacy Skills. 2nd ed. Cecilia C. Doak et al. LC 95-11640. 224p. 1995. pap. text ed. 26.95 (*0-397-55161-4*) Lppncott-Raven.

Teaching Peace: How to Raise Children in Harmony Without Prejudice, Fear or Violence. Jan Arnow. LC 95-8712. 1995. pap. 12.00 (*0-399-52155-0*, Perigee Bks) Berkley Pub.

Teaching Peace: Toward Cultural Selflessness. Thomas J. Lasley. LC 93-43730. 216p. 1994. text ed. 52.95 (*0-89789-371-9*, Bergin & Garvey) Greenwood.

Teaching Peace Songbook & Teacher's Guide. Kathy Grammer & Red Grammer. (J). (ps-6). 1993. 13.00 (*1-886146-00-4*) Red Note Recs.

Teaching People to Love Themselves: A Leader's Handbook of Theory & Technique for Self-Esteem & Affirmation. 2nd rev. ed. Dov Peretz Elkins. LC 78-61670. 1978. pap. 22.00 (*0-918834-06-6*) Growth Assoc.

Teaching People to Speak Well: Training & Remediation of Communication Reticence. Lynne Kelly et al. Ed. by Gary L. Kreps. LC 95-23134. (Speech Communication Association Applied Communication Ser.). 336p. (C). 1995. text ed. 69.50 (*1-881303-50-0*); pap. text ed. 26.50 (*1-881303-51-9*) Hampton Pr NJ.

Teaching Percussion. Gary D. Cook. 418p. 1988. pap. 36.00 (*0-02-870190-9*) Schirmer Bks.

Teaching Percussion. 2nd ed. Cook. LC 96-31697. 1996. 40.00 (*0-02-870191-7*) Macmillan.

Teaching Personality with Gracefulness: The Transmission of Japanese Cultural Values Through Japanese Dance Theatre. Barbara Sellers-Young. LC 92-41782. 1993. 52.00 (*0-8191-9014-4*); pap. 27.50 (*0-8191-9015-2*) U Pr of Amer.

*__Teaching Persons with a Brain Injury: What to Expect.__ 2nd rev. ed. Tampa General Rehabilitation Center Staff. (Coping Ser.: Vol. 5). 64p. 1996. pap. 9.50 (*1-882855-51-5*) HDI Pubs.

Teaching Persons with Mental Retardation: A Model for Curriculum Development & Teaching. Richard B. Dever & Dennis R. Knapczyk. 496p. (C). 1996. per. write for info. (*0-697-20559-2*) Brown & Benchmark.

Teaching Persons with Severe Disabilities. David L. Westling & Lise Fox. 544p. (C). 1995. text ed. 66.00 (*0-02-426581-0*, Macmillan Coll) P-H.

Teaching Philosophy to Gifted Students: A Secondary Level Course of Study for Teachers & Administrators. James LoGiudice. 1985. 12.00 (*0-910609-09-8*) Gifted Educ Pr.

Teaching Phonics & Other Word Attack Skills. Thomas G. Gunning. 240p. (C). 1988. pap. text ed. 32.95 (*0-398-05486-X*) C C Thomas.

Teaching Photography: A Guide for Teaching Photography to Yourself or to a Class. Gary Twesten & Dwight Guerrant. (Illus.). 389p. 1983. 30.00 (*0-9602428-1-3*) G Twesten.

Teaching Physical Education. 4th ed. Muska Mosston & Sara Ashworth. 288p. (C). 1993. pap. text ed. 48.00 (*0-02-384183-4*, Macmillan Coll) P-H.

Teaching Physical Education: A Guide for Mentors & Students. Anne Williams. (Quality in Secondary Schools & Colleges Ser.). 128p. 1996. pap. 24.95 (*1-85346-427-9*, Pub. by D Fulton UK) Taylor & Francis.

Teaching Physical Science Through Children's Literature: 20 Complete Lessons For Elementary Grades. Terrific Science Press Staff. (Illus.). 256p. (J). (gr. 1-4). 1996. teacher ed., pap. text ed. 17.95 (*0-07-064723-2*, Lrng Triangle) McGraw-Hill Prof.

Teaching Physical Sciences in Secondary Schools. 2nd rev. ed. S. K. Gupta. 232p. (C). 1985. text ed. 25.00 (*0-86590-422-7*, Pub. by Sterling Pubs II) Apt Bks.

Teaching Physics Safely: Some Practical Guidelines in Seven Areas of Common Concern in Physics Classrooms. 4th ed. Richard W. Peterson. 30p. 1979. reprint ed. 13.00 (*0-917853-87-3*, OP19) Am Assn Physics.

Teaching Physics with Toys: Activities for Grades K-9. Teffiric Science Press Staff. LC 95-2022. 1995. pap. text ed. 19.95 (*0-07-064721-6*) McGraw.

Teaching Piano: A Comprehensive Guide & Reference Book for the Instructor, 2 vols. Denes Agay. (Illus.). 702p. pap. 24.95 (*0-8256-8039-5*, YK30054, Yorktown Mus) Omnibus NY.

Teaching Piano: Synthesis of Mind, Ear & Body. Max W. Camp. 224p. (Orig.). (C). 1992. 39.95 (*0-88284-526-8*, 6518); pap. 24.95 (*0-88284-527-6*, 6032) Alfred Pub.

Teaching Pieces for Classic Guitar. Walt Lawry. 1993. 9.95 (*1-56222-304-6*, 94703) Mel Bay.

*__Teaching Pigs to Sing.__ Cordelia Strube. 288p. (Orig.). 1997. pap. 15.00 (*0-00-648098-5*) HarperColl Wrld.

Teaching Plans for International Finance, Transactions, Policy, & Regulation. 2nd ed. Hal S. Scott & Philip A. Wellons. (University Casebook Ser.). 297p. 1995. pap. text ed. write for info. (*1-56662-321-9*) Foundation Pr.

*__Teaching Plans for International Finance, Transactions, Policy, & Regulation.__ 3rd ed. Hal S. Scott & Philip A. Wellons. (University Casebook Ser.). 309p. 1996. pap. text ed. write for info. (*1-56662-431-2*) Foundation Pr.

Teaching Poetry. 120p. 1993. pap. 15.95 (*0-590-49419-8*) Scholastic Inc.

Teaching Poetry to Children. David Greenberg. (Illus.). 74p. (Orig.). (C). 1978. pap. 8.95 (*0-87678-068-0*) PSU CE Pr.

Teaching Policy Briefs. 16p. 1992. 4.50 (*0-317-05345-0*) NASBE.

Teaching Policy Studies. William Coplin. (C). 1978. pap. 15.00 (*0-918592-26-7*) Pol Studies.

Teaching Portfolio: A Practical Guide to Improved Performance & Promotion/Tenure Decisions. Peter Seldin. 112p. (Orig.). (C). 1991. pap. 15.95 (*0-9627042-1-0*) Anker Pub.

*__Teaching Portfolio: A Practical Guide to Improved Performance & Promotion/Tenure Decisions.__ 2nd ed. Peter Seldin. 284p. (Orig.). (C). 1997. 24.95 (*1-882982-15-0*) Anker Pub.

Teaching Power of Dreams: Using Your Dreams to Change Your Life. Brad Steiger & Sherry H. Steiger. LC 89-52097. 230p. (C). 1990. pap. 14.95 (*0-924608-04-8*, Whitford Pr) Schiffer.

Teaching Practical Communication Skills. Kathleen Dyer & Stephen C. Lune. Ed. by Diane Browder. LC 96-8706. (Innovations Ser.). (Illus.). 30p. (Orig.). 1996. pap. 21.95 (*0-940898-42-X*) Am Assn Mental.

Teaching Practical Intelligence: What Research Tells Us. Tina Blythe et al. (What Research Tells Us Ser.). 16p. 1995. pap. 1.50 (*0-912099-31-3*) Kappa Delta Pi.

Teaching Practical Social Work. 3rd ed. Hazel Danbury. 124p. 1994. 76.95 (*1-85742-160-4*, Pub. by Arena UK) Ashgate Pub Co.

*__Teaching Practice: A Guide for Early Years.__ Rosemary Perry. 240p. (C). 1997. pap. text ed. write for info. (*0-415-14882-0*) Routledge.

Teaching Practice Handbook. Roger Gower & Steve Walters. 188p. (Orig.). (C). 1983. pap. text ed. 23.50 (*0-435-28995-0*, 28995) Heinemann.

Teaching Prayer in the Classroom. Delia Helverson. (Griggs Educational Resources Ser.). 1989. pap. 10.95 (*0-687-41100-9*) Abingdon.

Teaching Preschool Language Arts. Lawrence J. Foster et al. (Illus.). 272p. 1982. pap. text ed. 12.95 (*0-8425-1933-5*) Frnds of the Libry.

Teaching Preschool Math: Foundations & Activities. Anthony C. Maffei & Patricia Buckley. LC 79-27448. 176p. 1980. 26.95 (*0-87705-492-4*) Human Sci Pr.

Teaching Preschoolers. Barbara Hanna & Jane T. Hoover. 1980. pap. 4.95 (*0-89137-608-9*) Quality Pubns.

Teaching Preschoolers: It Looks Like This ... in Pictures. Jeannette G. Stone. LC 90-62661. (Illus.). 62p. (Orig.). 1990. pap. 5.00 (*0-935989-38-2*, NAEYC #305) Natl Assn Child Ed.

Teaching Preschoolers: Preparing Preschoolers, Projects for Preschoolers, 2 bks., Set. Suzan W. Allen & Karen H. Talbot. 1994. pap. 33.98 (*0-88290-463-9*) Horizon Utah.

Teaching Preschoolers in the Christian Community. rev. ed. Phoebe M. Anderson. LC 94-6910. (Illus.). 288p. 1994. pap. 19.95 (*0-8298-0922-8*) Pilgrim OH.

Teaching Preschoolers with Confidence. 32p. 1983. teacher ed. 4.50 (*0-910566-38-0*) Evang Trg Assn.

Teaching Preschoolers with Confidence. Robert E. Clark. 48p. 1983. pap. 4.25 (*0-910566-37-2*) Evang Trg Assn.

Teaching Primaries. Diane Mauck & Janet Jenkins. 1983. pap. 4.95 (*0-89137-610-0*); student ed., pap. 3.95 (*0-89137-612-7*) Quality Pubns.

Teaching Primary English: The State of the Art. Ed. by David Wray & Jane Medwell. LC 93-19887. 1994. pap. write for info. (*0-415-08670-1*) Routledge.

Teaching Primary English: The State of the Art. Ed. by David Wray & Jane Medwell. LC 93-19887. 224p. (C). (gr. 13). 1994. text ed. 69.95 (*0-415-08669-8*) Routledge.

*__Teaching Primary Math.__ Kalejaive. Date not set. pap. text ed. write for info. (*0-582-77925-1*, Pub. by Longman UK) Longman.

*__Teaching Primary Science.__ B. Young. Date not set. pap. text ed. write for info. (*0-582-65016-X*, Pub. by Longman UK) Longman.

Teaching Principles & Practices. (National Teacher Examination Ser.: NC-3). pap. 23.95 (*0-8373-8403-6*) Nat Learn.

Teaching Problem-Solving. John A. Ross & Florence J. Maynes. LC 82-207857. (Informal Ser.: No. 43). (Illus.). 216p. reprint ed. pap. 61.60 (*0-7837-0553-0*, 2040894) Bks Demand.

Teaching Problem Solving in Vocational Education. Rebecca Soden. LC 93-39846. 224p. (C). 1994. pap. 16.95 (*0-415-09246-9*, B0801, Routledge NY) Routledge.

Teaching Problem Solving in Vocational Education. Rebecca Soden. LC 93-39846. 224p. (C). (gr. 13). 1994. text ed. 62.95 (*0-415-09245-0*, B0797, Routledge NY) Routledge.

Teaching Problem-Solving Strategies. Daniel T. Dolan. 1983. pap. text ed. 18.35 (*0-201-10231-5*) Addison-Wesley.

Teaching Problem Students. Jere Brophy. LC 96-19772. 466p. 1996. lib. bdg. 40.00 (*1-57230-144-9*, 0144) Guilford Pr.

Teaching Process Writing with Computers. rev. ed. Randy Boone. 200p. 1991. 17.95 (*0-924667-93-1*) Intl Society Tech Educ.

Teaching Program in Psychiatry, Vol. 2. Peter G. Beckett et al. LC 67-64750. 278p. pap. 79.30 (*0-318-39789-7*, 2033191) Bks Demand.

Teaching Pronunciation: A Course for Teachers of English to Speakers of Other Languages. Marianne Celce-Murcia et al. LC 96-20132. (Illus.). 384p. (C). 1996. text ed. 54.95 (*0-521-40504-1*); pap. text ed. 24.95 (*0-521-40694-3*) Cambridge U Pr.

Teaching Pronunciation: A Course for Teachers of English to Speakers of Other Languages. Marianne C. Murcia et al. LC 96-20132. (C). 1996. digital audio 13.95 (*0-521-40695-1*) Cambridge U Pr.

Teaching Pronunciation: Focus on English Rhythm & Intonation. Rita Wong. (Language in Education Ser.). 60p. 1987. pap. text ed. 13.00 (*0-13-895095-4*) P-H.

Teaching Prose: A Guide for Writing Instructors. Fredric V. Bogel & Katherine K. Gottschalk. LC 87-20364. (Orig.). (C). 1988. pap. text ed. 22.95 (*0-393-95654-7*) Norton.

Teaching Psychology: A Handbook Reading from Teaching of Psychology. Ed. by J. Hartley & W. J. McKeachie. 240p. (C). 1989. pap. 36.00 (*0-8058-0608-3*) L Erlbaum Assocs.

Teaching Psychology in America: A History. Ed. by Antonio E. Puente et al. 578p. 1992. text ed. 39.95 (*1-55798-181-7*); pap. text ed. 36.95 (*1-55798-183-3*) Am Psychol.

Teaching Public Policy: Theory, Research, & Practice. Ed. by Peter J. Bergerson. LC 90-43371. (Contributions in Political Science Ser.: No. 268). 240p. 1991. text ed. 55.00 (*0-313-27636-6*, BTD/, Greenwood Pr) Greenwood.

Teaching Public Policy & Administration. Ed. by Peter J. Bergerson. (Orig.). 1989. pap. 15.00 (*0-944285-09-0*) Pol Studies.

Teaching Quality Assurance & Cost Containment in Health Care: A Faculty Guide. John W. Williamson et al. LC 82-48071. (Jossey-Bass Series in Higher Education). 382p. reprint ed. pap. 108.90 (*0-7837-2528-0*, 2042687) Bks Demand.

Teaching Racquetball: Steps to Success. Stan Kittleson. LC 93-15754. (Steps to Success Activity Ser.). (Illus.). 160p. 1993. pap. text ed. 19.95 (*0-87322-533-3*, PKIT0533) Human Kinetics.

Teaching Reading: A Global Approach. rev. ed. George G. Otero, Jr. & Carol Moeller. (Illus.). 191p. (Orig.). (gr. 6-12). 1994. pap. 26.95 (*0-943804-30-2*) U of Denver Teach.

Teaching Reading: A Practicum Approach to Elementary Reading. Timothy R. Blair et al. (Illus.). 224p. (Orig.). (C). 1992. pap. text ed. 22.75 (*0-03-051558-0*) HB Coll Pubs.

Teaching Reading: Diagnosis, Direct Instruction Practice. 2nd ed. William H. Rupley & Timothy R. Blair. 256p. (C). 1990. pap. text ed. 41.00 (*0-675-20891-2*, Merrill Coll) P-H.

Teaching Reading: Language, Letters & Thought. Sara Brody. 402p. (Orig.). (C). 1994. pap. text ed. 29.00 (*1-886042-12-8*) Larc Pubg.

Teaching Reading: Problems & Solutions. American Association of School Administrators Staff. (Critical Issues Report Ser.). 65p. (Orig.). 1990. pap. 14.95 (*0-87652-155-3*, 021-00274) Am Assn Sch Admin.

*__Teaching Reading & Literature, Grades 4-6.__ National Council of Teachers of English Staff. LC 96-17940. (Standards Consensus Ser.). 93p. 1996. 12.95 (*0-8141-5189-2*) NCTE.

*__Teaching Reading & Literature in the Early Elementary Grades.__ National Council of Teachers of English Staff. (Standards Consensus Ser.). 108p. 1997. 12.95 (*0-8141-5193-0*) NCTE.

Teaching Reading & Study Skills in Content Areas. Dorothy Rubin. (C). 1983. text ed. 42.75 (*0-03-060473-7*) HB Coll Pubs.

Teaching Reading & Study Strategies at the College Level. Ed. by Rona F. Flippo & David C. Caverly. LC 90-45739. 361p. 1991. reprint ed. pap. 102.90 (*0-608-00504-5*, 2061324) Bks Demand.

Teaching Reading & Writing in Spanish in the Bilingual Classroom. Freeman. LC 96-30430. 1997. pap. text ed. 28.50 (*0-435-07231-5*, 07231) Heinemann.

*__Teaching Reading & Writing in the Elementary Grades.__ 2nd ed. John F. Savage. LC 97-8708. 496p. (C). 1997. per. write for info. (*0-697-24437-7*) Wm C Brown Pubs.

Teaching Reading & Writing Together: The Classroom Connection. Carl B. Smith & Karin L. Dahl. LC 84-2522. 206p. (Orig.). reprint ed. pap. 58.80 (*0-7837-3892-7*, 2043740) Bks Demand.

Teaching Reading at Home: A Supplement to Romalda Spalding's The Writing Road to Reading. Wanda K. Sanseri. 112p. 1991. reprint ed. student ed., pap. 19.95 (*1-880045-00-1*) Back Home Indust.

Teaching Reading Comprehension. T. H. Caerney. 1990. 80.00 (*0-335-09268-3*, Open Univ Pr); pap. 23.00 (*0-335-09267-5*, Open Univ Pr) Taylor & Francis.

Teaching Reading Comprehension: A Ten Step Program. Clair J. Fullerton. LC 82-61478. 125p. (Orig.). (C). 1985. pap. 14.95 (*0-88247-719-6*) R & E Pubs.

Teaching Reading Comprehension Processes. 2nd ed. Judith W. Irwin. 240p. (C). 1990. pap. text ed. 42.00 (*0-13-892738-3*) P-H.

Teaching Reading for the Twenty-First Century: Breaking the Paradigms of the Past. 2nd ed. Arnold Burron. (Illus.). 168p. 1993. teacher ed., pap. text ed. 22.50 (*0-944584-67-5*, 34TEACH21) Sopris.

Teaching Reading in Elementary Classrooms. 2nd ed. Rebecca Barr. LC 96-20145. (C). 1997. text ed. 39.50 (*0-8013-1677-4*) Addison-Wesley.

Teaching Reading in Elementary Classrooms: Developing Independent Readers. Rebecca Barr & Barbara Johnson. 500p. (C). 1991. text ed. 55.50 (*0-8013-0173-4*, 75832) Longman.

Teaching Reading in High School: Improving Reading in Content Areas. 3rd ed. Robert Karlin. LC 76-48523. 1977. 19.95 (*0-672-61402-2*, Bobbs) Macmillan.

Teaching Reading in the Content Areas: Developing Content Literacy for All Students. Robert B. Cooter, Jr. & E. Sutton Flynt. 448p. (C). 1996. pap. text ed. 53.00 (*0-02-324711-8*, Macmillan Coll) P-H.

Teaching Reading in the Elementary Classroom. John W. Miller & Michael McKenna. (C). 1988. text ed. 40.00 (*0-89787-521-4*) Gorsuch Scarisbrick.

Teaching Reading in the Elementary Grades. Marvin L. Klein et al. 540p. 1991. text ed. 62.00 (*0-205-12846-7*, H28467) Allyn.

Teaching Reading in the Elementary Schools. 2nd ed. Eldon E. Ekwall. 512p. (C). 1990. text ed. 81.00 (*0-675-21059-3*, Merrill Coll) P-H.

Teaching Reading in the Secondary School. Lucy Fuchs. LC 86-63883. (Fastback Ser.: No. 251). 50p. 1987. pap. 3.00 (*0-87367-251-8*) Phi Delta Kappa.

Teaching Reading in the Social Studies. John P. Lunstrum & Bob L. Taylor. LC 78-17205. 98p. reprint ed. pap. 28.00 (*0-8357-2628-2*, 2040116) Bks Demand.

Teaching Reading in the Social Studies: A Global Approach for K-5. rev. ed. Mary C. Gold. (Illus.). 106p. (Orig.). (J). (gr. k-5). 1991. pap. 21.95 (*0-943804-29-9*) U of Denver Teach.

*__Teaching Reading in Today's Elementary Schools, 6 Vols.__ 6th ed. Paul C. Burns et al. 672p. (C). 1995. text ed. 59.96 (*0-395-75293-0*) HM.

*__Teaching Reading in Today's Elementary Schools, 6 Vols.__ 6th ed. Paul C. Burns et al. (C). 1995. teacher ed., text ed. 11.96 (*0-395-75294-9*) HM.

Teaching Reading Skills in a Foreign Language. Christine Nuttall. 282p. 1996. pap. text ed. 29.50 (*0-435-24057-9*) Heinemann.

Teaching Reading Skills Through the Newspaper. 2nd ed. Arnold B. Cheyney. LC 84-10884. (IRA Reading Aids Ser.). 58p. reprint ed. pap. 25.00 (*0-8357-2639-8*, 2040127) Bks Demand.

Teaching Reading Skills Through the Newspaper. 3rd ed. Arnold B. Cheyney. 64p. 1992. pap. 8.95 (*0-87207-236-3*) Intl Reading.

Teaching Reading, Thinking, Study Skills in Content Classrooms. 3rd ed. Marian J. Tonjes & Miles V. Zintz. 500p. (C). 1993. per. write for info. (*0-697-22372-8*) Brown & Benchmark.

Teaching Reading Through the Arts. Ed. by John E. Cowen. LC 82-12755. 118p. reprint ed. pap. 33.70 (*0-8357-2635-5*, 2040123) Bks Demand.

Teaching Reading to Children with Down Syndrome: A Guide for Parents & Teachers. Patricia L. Oelwein. (Topics in Down Syndrome Ser.). (Illus.). 392p. (Orig.). (C). 1995. pap. 16.95 (*0-933149-55-7*) Woodbine House.

Teaching Reading to Deaf Children. Beatrice O. Hart. LC 78-50668. 1978. pap. text ed. 12.95 (*0-88200-117-5*, C1119) Alexander Graham.

Teaching Reading to Disabled & Handicapped Learners. Harold D. Love & Freddie W. Litton. LC 94-3917. (Illus.). 260p. 1994. pap. 35.95 (*0-398-06248-X*) C C Thomas.

Teaching Reading to Disabled & Handicapped Learners. Harold D. Love & Freddie W. Litton. LC 94-3917. (Illus.). 260p. (C). 1994. text ed. 51.95 (*0-398-05909-8*) C C Thomas.

T

Teaching Reading to Every Child. 3rd ed. David Lapp & James Flood. 720p. (C). 1991. text ed. 82.00 (*0-02-367630-2*, Macmillan Coll) P-H.

Teaching Reading to Handicapped Children. Charles H. Hargis. LC 81-84574. 272p. (C). 1982. text ed. 24.95 (*0-89108-113-5*) Love Pub Co.

Teaching Reading to High-Risk Learners: A Unified Perspective. Ed. by Karen D. Wood & Bob Algozzine. LC 93-27345. 1993. text ed. 34.50 (*0-205-14582-5*) Allyn.

Teaching Reading Using Literature. John F. Savage. 480p. (C). 1993. text ed. write for info. (*0-697-17193-0*) Brown & Benchmark.

Teaching Reading Vocabulary. 2nd ed. Dale D. Johnson & P. David Pearson. 224p. (C). 1984. pap. text ed. 25.50 (*0-03-062778-8*) HB Coll Pubs.

*__Teaching Reading with Children's Literature.__ Cox & Zarrillo. 1997. pap. text ed. 56.00 (*0-13-640012-4*) P-H.

Teaching Reading with Children's Literature. Carole Cox & James Zarrillo. LC 92-29993. 448p. (C). 1992. text ed. 73.00 (*0-02-325335-5*, Macmillan Coll) P-H.

Teaching Reading with Literature: Case Studies to Action Plans. Gail E. Tompkins & Lea M. McGee. LC 92-22203. 512p. (C). 1992. pap. text ed. 36.00 (*0-675-21303-7*, Merrill Coll) P-H.

*__Teaching Reading, Writing & Spelling: All You Need to Succeed.__ Virginia Talbot. LC 97-4609. 240p. 1997. 69.95 (*0-8039-6591-5*); pap. 29.95 (*0-8039-6592-3*) Corwin Pr.

Teaching Reasoning Skills in Schools & Homes: A Gamebook of Methods. David S. Goodman & Phyllis F. Goodman. 98p. 1991. pap. 16.95 (*0-398-06355-9*) C C Thomas.

Teaching Reasoning Skills in Schools & Homes: A Gamebook of Methods. David S. Goodman & Phyllis F. Goodman. 98p. (C). 1991. text ed. 26.95 (*0-398-05727-3*) C C Thomas.

Teaching Religion in a Catholic Secondary School. James J. DiGiacomo. (Keynote Ser.). 70p. (Orig.). 1989. pap. 6.00 (*1-55833-033-X*) Natl Cath Educ.

Teaching Religion with Confidence & Joy. Greg Dues. LC 87-51568. 96p. (Orig.). 1988. pap. 4.95 (*0-89622-359-0*) Twenty-Third.

Teaching, Research, & Community Service - Paradigms for Success in the 1990's: Proceedings. Council of Educators in Landscape Architecture Staff. Ed. by Joanne M. Westphal. (CELA Conference Proceedings Ser.: No. 1). 188p. reprint ed. pap. 53.60 (*0-7837-1135-2*, 2041665) Bks Demand.

Teaching Research Curriculum for Moderately & Severely Handicapped: Gross & Fine Motor. H. D. Fredericks et al. (Illus.). 264p. 1980. pap. 37.95 (*0-398-04035-4*) C C Thomas.

Teaching Research Curriculum for Moderately & Severely Handicapped: Self-Help & Cognitive. H. D. Fredericks et al. (Illus.). 280p. 1980. pap. 38.95 (*0-398-04034-6*) C C Thomas.

Teaching Resources Math Plus. 1994. teacher ed., text ed. 30.75 (*0-15-301912-3*) H Holt & Co.

Teaching Resources Math Plus. 1994. teacher ed., text ed. 30.75 (*0-15-301913-1*) H Holt & Co.

Teaching Resources Math Plus. 1994. teacher ed., text ed. 30.75 (*0-15-301914-X*) H Holt & Co.

Teaching Resources Math Plus. 1994. teacher ed., text ed. 30.75 (*0-15-301915-8*) H Holt & Co.

Teaching Resources Math Plus. 1994. teacher ed., text ed. 30.75 (*0-15-301916-6*) H Holt & Co.

Teaching Resources Math Plus. 1994. teacher ed., text ed. 30.75 (*0-15-301917-4*) H Holt & Co.

Teaching Responsible Homework Habits Grades 1-3. Lee Canter. (Illus.). 64p. 1993. student ed. 7.95 (*0-939007-54-1*) Lee Canter & Assocs.

Teaching Responsible Homework Habits Grades 4-6. Lee Canter. (Illus.). 64p. 1993. student ed. 7.95 (*0-939007-55-X*) Lee Canter & Assocs.

Teaching Responsible Homework Habits Grades 6-8. Lee Canter. (Illus.). 64p. 1993. student ed. 7.95 (*0-939007-56-8*) Lee Canter & Assocs.

Teaching Role of the School Media Specialist. Kay E. Vandergrift. LC 78-27401. (School Media Center: Focus on Trends & Issues Ser.: No. 3). 64p. reprint ed. pap. 25.00 (*0-317-27977-7*, 2025607) Bks Demand.

Teaching Russian Through Action. Bertha E. Cook. Tr. by Aidar Galeev. (Orig.). (RUS.). 1994. teacher ed., pap. 17.99 (*0-938395-33-5*) B Segal.

***Teaching Safe Horsemanship: A Guide to English & Western Instruction.** Jan Dawson. LC 97-648. 144p. 1997. 29.95 (*0-88266-972-9*) Storey Comm Inc.

Teaching Safety in the Elementary School. Daniel Della-Giustina & Charles P. Yost. (Illus.). (Orig.). 1991. pap. text ed. 5.00 (*0-88314-519-7*) AAHPERD.

Teaching Sanity in an Insane World: The Unholy Trio, 3 pts. Michael J. Carluccio. (Illus.). 255p. 1990. Set. pap. 10.00 (*1-878032-01-1*) Clear Thinking.

Teaching Sanity in an Insane World: The Unholy Trio, Pt. 1. Michael J. Carluccio. (Illus.). 81p. 1989. pap. 4.00 (*0-685-36279-5*) Clear Thinking.

Teaching Sanity in an Insane World: The Unholy Trio, Pt. 2. Michael J. Carluccio. (Illus.). 80p. 1989. pap. 4.00 (*1-878032-03-8*) Clear Thinking.

Teaching School. rev. ed. Eric W. Johnson. 1987. pap. 16.00 (*0-934338-62-0*) NAIS.

Teaching School: Points Picked Up. Eric W. Johnson. 160p. 1993. reprint ed. pap. 17.95 (*0-9636513-1-5*) Assn Ind Sch.

Teaching School Chemistry. UNESCO Staff. 302p. 1987. text ed. 35.00 (*81-207-0595-5*, Pub. by Sterling Pubs II) Apt Bks.

Teaching, Schools & Society. Ed. by Evelina O. Miranda & Romula Magsino. 444p. 1990. 100.00 (*1-85000-687-3*, Falmer Pr); pap. 38.00 (*1-85000-688-1*, Falmer Pr) Taylor & Francis.

Teaching Science. Ed. by Jenny Frost. LC 93-48381. (Illus.). 178p. 1995. 39.50 (*0-7130-0185-2*, Pub. by Woburn Pr UK); pap. 19.50 (*0-7130-4015-7*, Pub. by Woburn Pr UK) Intl Spec Bk.

Teaching Science. Ed. by Ralph Levinson. LC 93-17467. 192p. (C). 1993. pap. text ed. 15.95 (*0-415-10253-7*) Routledge.

Teaching Science: A Guide for College & Professional School Instructors. Barbara Gastel. LC 90-7075. (Illus.). 144p. 1990. pap. 16.95 (*0-89774-524-8*) Oryx Pr.

Teaching Science & Health from a Feminist Perspective: A Practical Guide. Sue V. Rosser. (Athene Ser.). 256p. (C). 1986. pap. text ed. 19.95 (*0-8077-6223-7*) Tchrs Coll.

Teaching Science As Inquiry. Steven J. Rakow. LC 86-61751. (Fastback Ser.: No. 246). 50p. (Orig.). 1986. pap. 3.00 (*0-87367-246-1*) Phi Delta Kappa.

Teaching Science for All Children. 2nd ed. Martin & Sexton. LC 96-19152. 640p. 1996. 61.00 (*0-205-19585-7*) Allyn.

Teaching Science in a Climate of Controversy: A View from the American Scientific Affiliation. rev. ed. Committee for Integrity in Science Education Staff. 48p. 1993. 7.00 (*1-881479-00-5*) Am Sci Affil.

Teaching Science in a Multicultural World. Elizabeth R. Offutt. 184p. 1996. 14.99 (*0-86653-866-6*, FE3866) Fearon Teach Aids.

***Teaching Science in the Elementary School.** Ed. by Hammerich. (C). 1998. text ed. write for info. (*0-321-01334-4*); teacher ed., text ed. write for info. (*0-321-40357-6*) Addson-Wesley Educ.

Teaching Science Process Skills. Joyce Ramig et al. 192p. teacher ed. 15.99 (*0-86653-835-6*, GA1526) Good Apple.

Teaching Science, Technology & Society. Joan Solomon. LC 92-8255. (Developing Science & Technology Education Ser.). 1993. 80.00 (*0-335-09953-X*, Open Univ Pr); pap. 23.00 (*0-335-09952-1*, Open Univ Pr) Taylor & Francis.

***Teaching Science Through Discovery.** 8th ed. Arthur A. Carin. LC 96-27830. 1996. pap. 62.00 (*0-13-234089-5*, Merrill Pub Co) Macmillan.

Teaching Science to Children. 2nd ed. Mary D. Iatridis. LC 92-28047. (Source Books on Education: Vol. 35). 216p. 1993. text ed. 35.00 (*0-8153-0090-5*, SS747) Garland.

***Teaching Science to Children.** Lazer Goldberg. LC 96-53258. 160p. 1997. reprint ed. pap. text ed. 6.95 (*0-486-29600-8*) Dover.

Teaching Science to Children: An Inquiry Approach. 4th ed. Alfred E. Friedl. LC 96-18502. 1996. pap. text ed. write for info. (*0-07-022459-5*) McGraw.

Teaching Science to Children: An Integrated Approach. 3rd ed. Alfred E. Friedl. 1995. pap. text ed. write for info. (*0-07-022455-2*) McGraw.

Teaching Science to Language Minority Students: Theory & Practice. Judith W. Rosenthal. LC 95-6554. (Bilingual Education & Bilingualism Ser.: Vol. 3). 1995. 69.00 (*1-85359-273-0*, Pub. by Multilingual Matters UK); pap. 24.00 (*1-85359-272-2*, Pub. by Multilingual Matters UK) Taylor & Francis.

Teaching Science with Everyday Things. Victor E. Schmidt & Verne N. Rockcastle. 1995. 16.95 (*1-881431-57-6*, 2010) AIMS Educ Fnd.

Teaching Scripture from an African-American Perspective. Joseph V. Crockett. LC 90-82978. 104p. 1990. pap. 7.95 (*0-88177-086-8*, DR086) Discipleship Res.

Teaching Second Language Reading for Academic Purposes. David Eskey et al. (A-W Second Language Professional Library). (C). 1986. spiral bd. 26.03 (*0-201-11668-5*) Addison-Wesley.

Teaching Secondary English. David Curtis. LC 92-8564. 1992. 27.50 (*0-335-15758-0*, Open Univ Pr) Taylor & Francis.

***Teaching Secondary English.** Ed. by Glatthorn. (C). 1998. text ed. write for info. (*0-321-01000-0*) Addson-Wesley Educ.

Teaching Secondary English. John J. De Boer. LC 76-100155. 427p. 1970. reprint ed. text ed. 65.00 (*0-8371-3426-9*, DETS, Greenwood Pr) Greenwood.

Teaching Secondary English: Readings & Applications. Daniel Sheridan. 432p. (C). 1993. pap. text ed. 36.50 (*0-8013-0791-0*, 78845) Longman.

Teaching Secondary English Literature. Knoeller. 1996. pap. text ed. 29.00 (*0-205-17485-X*) Allyn.

Teaching Secondary School Mathematics. 4th ed. Alfred S. Posamentier. 1995. pap. text ed. 68.00 (*0-02-396262-3*, Macmillan Coll) P-H.

Teaching Secondary School Students Through Their Individual Learning Styles: Practical Approaches for Grades 7-12. Rita S. Dunn & Kenneth J. Dunn. 464p. (C). 1993. text ed. 57.00 (*0-205-13308-8*) Allyn.

Teaching Secondary Students with Mild Learning & Behavior Problems: Methods, Materials, Strategies. 2nd ed. Lowell F. Masters et al. LC 92-30450. (Illus.). 360p. (C). 1992. text ed. 39.00 (*0-89079-570-3*, 2073) PRO-ED.

Teaching Secrets: The Technology in Social Work Education. Ed. by Ruth R. Middleman & Gale G. Wood. LC 91-27072. (Journal of Teaching in Social Work: Vol. 5, No. 2). (Illus.). 138p. 1992. 39.95 (*1-56024-213-2*) Haworth Pr.

Teaching Secrets: The Technology in Social Work Education. Ed. by Ruth R. Middleman & Gale G. Wood. LC 91-27072. 138p. 1996. pap. 19.95 (*0-7890-6045-0*) Haworth Pr.

***Teaching Self-Control: A Curriculum for Responsible Behavior.** Martin Henley. 190p. 1997. pap. 25.00 (*1-879639-45-9*) Natl Educ Serv.

Teaching Self-Defense: Steps to Success. Joan M. Nelson. LC 93-31620. (Illus.). 160p. 1994. pap. text ed. 19.95 (*0-87322-620-8*, PNEL0620) Human Kinetics.

***Teaching Self-Determination to Students with Disabilities: Basic Skills for Successful Transition.** Michael L. Wehmeyer et al. LC 97-22271. 1997. write for info. (*1-55766-302-5*) P H Brookes.

Teaching Self-management Strategies to Adolescents. K. Richard Young et al. 120p. 1991. teacher ed., pap. text ed. 19.50 (*0-944584-35-7*, 32SELF) Sopris.

***Teaching Self-Management to Elementary Students with Developmental Disabilities.** Margaret E. King-Sears & Stephanie L. Carpenter. 1997. write for info. (*0-940898-48-9*) Am Assn Mental.

Teaching Seminar with Milton H. Erickson. Ed. by Jeffrey K. Zeig. LC 80-23804. 349p. 1985. text ed. 35.95 (*0-87630-247-9*) Brunner-Mazel.

Teaching Sermon. Ronald Allen. 160p. (Orig.). 1995. pap. 12.95 (*0-687-37522-3*) Abingdon.

***Teaching Shakespeare.** Rex Gibson. (School Shakespeare Ser.). 240p. (C). 1997. pap. write for info. (*0-521-57788-8*) Cambridge U Pr.

Teaching Shakespeare. Ed. by Walter Edens et al. LC 77-71979. 360p. reprint ed. pap. 102.60 (*0-8357-4676-3*, 2037623) Bks Demand.

***Teaching Shakespeare into the Twenty-First Century.** Ed. by Ronald E. Salomone & James E. Davis. LC 97-23373. 280p. 1997. pap. 24.95 (*0-8214-1203-5*) Ohio U Pr.

Teaching Shakespeare to Gifted Students: An Examination of the Sensibility of Genius. Michael E. Walters. (J). (gr. 6-12). 1990. 12.00 (*0-910609-22-5*) Gifted Educ Pr.

Teaching Shakespeare Today: Practical Approaches & Productive Strategies. Ed. by James E. Davis & Ronald E. Salomone. 300p. (Orig.). 1993. pap. 19.95 (*0-8141-5296-1*) NCTE.

***Teaching Shakespeare with Film & Television: A Guide.** H. R. Coursen. LC 96-49732. 200p. 1997. text ed. 49.95 (*0-313-30066-6*, Greenwood Pr) Greenwood.

Teaching Shira is More Than Clapping Hands see Kadima Kesher Series

Teaching Shooting Sports to Persons with Disabilities. Ed. by Robin Taylor et al. LC 93-49380. (Illus.). 104p. 1994. lib. bdg. 11.95 (*0-916682-66-8*) Outdoor Empire.

Teaching Side-Saddle. Janet MacDonald. 100p. (C). 1990. pap. 24.00 (*0-85131-556-9*, Pub. by J A Allen & Co UK) St Mut.

Teaching Sign Language to Chimpanzees. Ed. by R. Allen Gardner et al. LC 88-18863. 324p. 1989. text ed. 64.50 (*0-88706-965-7*); pap. text ed. 21.95 (*0-88706-966-5*) State U NY Pr.

Teaching Singing. John C. Burgin. LC 72-10594. 290p. 1973. 27.50 (*0-8108-0565-0*) Scarecrow.

***Teaching Skills for Academis Success.** 11th ed. West Publishing Company Editorial Staff. (CA - Career Development Ser.). (C). 1994. pap. write for info. (*0-314-04697-6*) West Pub.

***Teaching Slides for Respiratory Disease: Principles of Patient Care.** 2nd ed. Robert L. Wilkins & James R. Dexter. 1997. 40.00 (*0-8036-0264-2*) Davis Co.

Teaching Snacks: Teaching Concepts at Snack Time. Gayle Bittinger. Ed. by Kathleen Cubley. (Illus.). 48p. (Orig.). (J). (ps-1). 1994. pap. 6.95 (*0-911019-82-0*, WPH 1603) Warren Pub Hse.

Teaching Soccer: Tactics, Skills & Drills of the Most Popular Ball Game in the World. John Hayward. LC 76-24434. (Illus.). 1976. pap. 2.95 (*0-917252-01-2*) Per Ardua.

Teaching Social Change: A Group Approach. Norman E. Zinberg et al. LC 75-26746. 264p. reprint ed. pap. 75.30 (*0-317-42064-X*, 2025884) Bks Demand.

Teaching Social Competence: A Practical Approach for Improving Social Skills in Students at Risk. Dennis R. Knapczyk. (Special Education Ser.). 448p. 1996. pap. 48.95 (*0-534-33894-1*) Brooks-Cole.

Teaching Social Education & Communication. C. Butterworth & M. McDonald. (C). 1985. 115.00 (*0-685-39378-X*, Pub. by S Thornes Pubs UK) St Mut.

Teaching Social Skills to Children. Ed. by Gwendolyn Cartledge & JoAnne F. Milburn. (General Psychology Ser.). 1980. 40.00 (*0-08-024654-0*, Pergamon Pr); pap. text ed. 12.00 (*0-08-024653-2*, Pergamon Pr) Elsevier.

Teaching Social Skills to Children & Youth: Innovative Approaches. 3rd ed. Ed. by Gwendolyn Cartledge & JoAnne F. Milburn. 1994. text ed. 49.95 (*0-205-16073-5*); pap. text ed. 39.50 (*0-205-16507-9*) Allyn.

Teaching Social Skills to Hearing-Impaired Students. Richard G. Stoker. (Centennial Celebration Ser.). 203p. (Orig.). 1990. pap. text ed. 21.95 (*0-88200-169-8*) Alexander Graham.

Teaching Social Skills to Youths: A Curriculum for Child-Care Providers. rev. ed. Tom Dowd & Jeff Tierney. 284p. (C). 1992. pap. 29.95 (*0-938510-30-4*, 45-006) Boys Town Pr.

Teaching Social Studies: Handbook of Trends, Issues, & Implications for the Future. Ed. by Gerald L. Wilson et al. LC 92-17837. 312p. 1993. text ed. 59.95 (*0-313-27881-4*, WTG, Greenwood Pr) Greenwood.

Teaching Social Studies in Middle & Secondary Schools. 2nd ed. Peter H. Martorella. 433p. (C). 1995. text ed. 70.00 (*0-13-442070-5*) P-H.

Teaching Social Studies in the Middle & Senior High School. Wayne Mahood et al. 416p. (C). 1990. text ed. 70.00 (*0-675-21253-7*, Merrill Coll) P-H.

Teaching Social Work Practice: A Programme of Exercises & Activities Towards the Practice Teaching Award. Mark Doel. 222p. (Orig.). 1996. pap. 42.95 (*1-85742-327-5*, Pub. by Arena UK) Ashgate Pub Co.

Teaching Social Work Research: Alternative Programs & Strategies. Ed. by Robert W. Weinbach & Allen Rubin. 1980. 6.60 (*0-318-35373-3*) Coun Soc Wk Ed.

Teaching Sociology: The Quest for Excellence. Ed. by Frederick L. Campbell et al. LC 84-1107. 256p. 1984. lib. bdg. 37.95 (*0-8304-1097-X*) Nelson-Hall.

Teaching Sociology of Aging: Syllabi and Materials. D. Harris. 300p. 1986. 16.00 (*0-317-36344-1*) Am Sociological.

Teaching Softball: Steps to Success. Diane L. Potter & Gretchen A. Brockmeyer. LC 88-36782. (Steps to Success Activity Ser.). (Illus.). 256p. (Orig.). 1989. pap. text ed. 19.95 (*0-88011-359-6*, PPOT0359) Human Kinetics.

Teaching Spanish. Milton M. Azevdo et al. 412p. (C). 1988. 170.00 (*0-8442-7605-7*, Pub. by S Thornes Pubs UK) St Mut.

Teaching Spanish-Speaking Children. Loyd S. Tireman. Ed. by Carlos E. Cortes. LC 76-1591. (Chicano Heritage Ser.). 1977. reprint ed. 15.95 (*0-405-09526-0*) Ayer.

Teaching Spanish Speech Sounds: Drills for Articulation Therapy. Larry J. Mattes & George Santiago. (Illus.). 122p. 1985. pap. text ed. 18.50 (*0-930951-02-6*) Acad Comm.

Teaching Spanish to the Native Spanish Speaker see Sensitivity in the Foreign Language Classroom

Teaching Special Learners in the General Education Classroom: Methods & Techniques. 2nd rev. ed. Kathleen M. McCoy. Orig. Title: Teaching Mainstreamed Students. 496p. 1995. text ed. 49.95 (*0-89108-238-7*) Love Pub Co.

Teaching Special Needs: Strategies & Activities for Children in the Primary Classroom. Sylvia McNamara & Gill Moreton. 96p. 1993. pap. 25.00 (*1-85346-247-0*, Pub. by D Fulton UK) Taylor & Francis.

Teaching Special Students in the Mainstream. 4th ed. Rena B. Lewis & Donald H. Doorlag. LC 94-3463. 1994. pap. text ed. 50.00 (*0-02-370502-7*, Macmillan Coll) P-H.

Teaching Speech for the Stage: A Manual for Classroom Instruction. Evangeline Machlin. 1980. pap. 4.95 (*0-87830-573-4*, Thtre Arts Bks) Routledge.

Teaching Speech Handicapped. Jack Rudman. (National Teacher Examination Ser.: NT-26). 1994. pap. 23.95 (*0-8373-8436-2*) Nat Learn.

Teaching Speech to Hearing-Impaired Infants & Children: Zero to Three Years. Dene Stovall. (Illus.). 102p. (C). 1982. spiral bd., pap. 22.95 (*0-398-04680-8*) C C Thomas.

Teaching Spelling, 2 Vols. Henderson. (C). 1995. pap. 30.76 (*0-395-78074-8*) HM.

Teaching Spelling, 2 Vols. 2nd ed. Henderson. (C). 1989. pap. 41.56 (*0-395-52297-8*) HM.

Teaching Spelling: A Practical Resource. Faye Bolton & Diane Snowball. LC 93-8989. 120p. (YA). 1993. pap. text ed. 19.50 (*0-435-08802-5*, 08802) Heinemann.

Teaching Spelling Through Writing. Patricia J. Hagerty. (Illus.). vii, 58p. 1994. pap. text ed. 12.00 (*1-56308-132-6*) Teacher Ideas Pr.

Teaching Sport Skills Study Guide. American Coaching Effectiveness Program Staff & Daniel M. Corcos. LC 87-19687. (Illus.). 224p. 1988. Three-ring notebook, 224 pgs. ring bd. 3.00 (*0-87322-021-8*, ACEP0205) Human Kinetics.

***Teaching Sports Concepts & Skills: A Tactical Games Approach.** Linda L. Griffin et al. LC 97-2387. (Illus.). 176p. (Orig.). 1997. pap. text ed. 19.00 (*0-88011-478-9*, BGRI0478) Human Kinetics.

Teaching Sports Medicine & Recreation to Family Practice Residents. Ed. by Society for Teachers of Family Medicine, Task Force on the Family in Family Medicine Staff. 122p. 1981. 5.00 (*0-942295-15-3*) Soc Tchrs Fam Med.

Teaching Standard English in the Inner City. Ed. by Ralph W. Fasold & Roger W. Shuy. LC 72-120748. (Urban Language Ser.: No. 6). 161p. reprint ed. pap. 45.90 (*0-8357-3346-7*, 2039579) Bks Demand.

Teaching State Government. Allan O. Kownslar. 1980. text ed. 13.20 (*0-07-035411-1*) McGraw.

***Teaching Statistical Concepts.** Hawkins. 1992. pap. text ed. write for info. (*0-582-06820-7*, Pub. by Longman UK) Longman.

Teaching Statistics & Probability: 1981 Yearbook. Ed. by Albert P. Shulte. LC 81-1679. (Illus.). 246p. 1981. 22.00 (*0-87353-170-1*) NCTM.

Teaching Stories. Judy Logan. LC 93-91529. 110p. 1993. pap. text ed. 11.95 (*0-9636822-0-2*) J Logan.

***Teaching Stories.** Judy Logan. LC 97-25761. 176p. 1997. 17.00 (*1-56836-195-5*) Kodansha.

Teaching Strategies: A Guide to Better Instruction. 4th ed. Donald C. Orlich et al. 400p. (Orig.). (C). 1994. pap. text ed. 48.36 (*0-669-34960-7*) HM College Div.

***Teaching Strategies: A Guide to Better Instruction.** 4th ed. Donald C. Orlich et al. (Orig.). (C). 1994. teacher ed., text ed. 2.66 (*0-669-34961-5*) HM College Div.

Teaching Strategies & Techniques for Adjunct Faculty. Donald E. Greive. 32p. 1986. pap. 5.95 (*0-940017-14-8*) Info Tec OH.

Teaching Strategies for Social Studies. James Banks. 1996. text ed. write for info. (*0-8013-1165-9*) Addison-Wesley.

Teaching Strategies for the Social Studies: Inquiry, Valuing & Decision-Making. 4th ed. James A. Banks & Ambrose A. Clegg, Jr. LC 84-14388. 505p. (C). 1990. text ed. 55.50 (*0-8013-0472-5*, 78302) Longman.

Teaching Strategies of Soccer. Michael Sutliff. 1995. pap. text ed. 23.00 (*0-205-15968-0*) Allyn.

***Teaching Strategies to Facilitate Learning.** Cathleen T. Love et al. 1995. 8.00 (*0-911365-36-2*, A261-08486) Family & Consumer Sci Educ.

Teaching Strategy Ethnic Studies. 6th ed. Cherry A. Banks. 574p. 1996. pap. 48.00 (*0-205-18940-7*) Allyn.

Teaching Stress Management & Relaxation Skills: An Instructor's Guide. John D. Curtis et al. (Illus.). 280p. 1985. text ed. 26.50 (*0-9611456-2-5*, Coulee Press) Adastra Pub.

Teaching Stress Management Skills: A Manual for Beginning & Experienced Teachers. Frances K. Wiggins & Suni Petersen. (Illus.). 167p. (Orig.). (C). 1986. pap. text ed. 16.95 (*0-942937-01-5*) Rivijon Pr.

Teaching Stress Management Skills, 1989: For Beginning & Experienced Teachers. rev. ed. Frances K. Wiggins & Suni Petersen. 171p. (C). 1989. pap. text ed. 16.95 (*0-942937-04-X*) Rivijon Pr.

Teaching Stringed Instruments: A Course of Study. Intro. by Donald L. Corbett. (Illus.). 32p. (Orig.). (C). 1991. teacher ed. 13.25 (*0-940796-99-6*, 1604) Music Ed Natl.

Teaching Stringed Instruments in Classes. Elizabeth Green. 104p. 1987. 19.75 (*0-89917-507-4*) Am String Tchrs.

Teaching Strings: Technique & Pedagogy. 2nd ed. Robert H. Klotman. 270p. 1996. 35.00 (*0-02-864579-0*) Schirmer Bks.

Teaching Structured Programming in Secondary Schools. Pat McIntyre. LC 88-37600. 232p. 1991. lib. bdg. 29.50 (*0-89464-360-6*) Krieger.

***Teaching Students about Death: A Comprehensive Resource for Educators & Parents.** Robert G. Stevenson. LC 95-20266. 256p. 1996. pap. text ed. 22.95 (*0-914783-50-5*) Charles.

Teaching Students in Clinical Settings. Stengelhofen. 244p. 1992. pap. 44.75 (*1-56593-119-X*, 0422) Singular Publishing.

Teaching Students in Inclusive Settings. Bradley & King Sears Staff. 384p. 1996. pap. 42.00 (*0-205-16703-9*) Allyn.

Teaching Students Strategies for Survival in a Dysfunctional Environment: Discussion Guidebook for "Does Anyone Hear Our Cries for Help?" Berite Ryan Synowiec. (Successful Living Ser.). 50p. 1994. pap. text ed. 34.95 (*1-885335-04-0*) Positive Support.

Teaching Students Through Their Individual Learning Styles: A Practical Approach. Kenneth J. Dunn & Rita S. Dunn. (Illus.). 1978. text ed. 78.00 (*0-87909-808-2*, R80821, Reston) P-H.

***Teaching Students to Be Peacemakers.** 3rd rev. ed. David W. Johnson & Roger T. Johnson. (Illus.). 382p. 1995. pap. text ed. 25.00 (*0-939603-22-5*) Interaction Bk Co.

Teaching Students to Get Along: Reducing Conflict & Increasing Corporation in K-6 Classrooms. Lee Canter & Katia Peterson. 166p. 1995. pap. text ed. 14.95 (*0-939007-99-1*) Lee Canter & Assocs.

Teaching Students to Learn. Graham Gibbs. 111p. 1981. pap. 29.00 (*0-335-10033-3*, Open Univ Pr) Taylor & Francis.

Teaching Students to Read. James Flood & Diane K. Lapp. xxiv, 642p. (C). 1985. pap. text ed. 64.00 (*0-02-367660-4*, Macmillan Coll) P-H.

Teaching Students to Read Through Their Individual Learning Styles. rev. ed. Marie Carbo et al. (Illus.). 384p. (C). 1986. text ed. 39.95 (*0-8359-7517-7*, Reston) P-H.

An Asterisk (*) at the beginning of an entry indicates that the title is appearing in BIP for the first time.

Teaching Students to Teach Themselves. Crawford W. Lindsey, Jr. 148p. 1988. pap. 27.95 (*0-89397-315-7*) Nichols Pub.

Teaching Students to Think. John Langrehr. 122p. 1988. Manual 122 p. teacher ed. 21.95 (*1-879639-12-2*) Natl Educ Serv.

Teaching Students to Think Critically: A Guide for Faculty in All Disciplines. Chet Meyers. LC 86-45627. (Higher Education Ser.). 146p. 1986. text ed. 26.95 (*1-55542-011-7*) Jossey-Bass.

Teaching Students to Write. 2nd ed. Beth S. Neman. 624p. (C). 1995. pap. text ed. 25.95 (*0-19-506428-3*) OUP.

Teaching Students Ways to Remember: Strategies for Learning Mnemonically. Margo A. Mastropieri & Thomas E. Scruggs. (Cognitive Strategy Training Ser.). 132p. 1990. pap. text ed. 21.95 (*0-914797-67-0*) Brookline Bks.

Teaching Students with Behavior Disorders: Techniques for Classroom Instruction. 2nd ed. Patricia A. Gallagher. LC 87-83465. 406p. 1995. pap. text ed. 34.95 (*0-89108-242-5*) Love Pub Co.

Teaching Students with Behavioral Disorders: Basic Questions & Answers. Tim Lewis et al. 37p. 1991. pap. text ed. 9.75 (*0-86586-205-2*, P337) Coun Exc Child.

Teaching Students with Language & Communication Disabilities. S. Jay Kuder. LC 96-24905. 1996. 56.00 (*0-205-15694-0*) P-H.

Teaching Students with Learning & Behavior Problems. 3rd ed. Diane P. Rivera & Deborah D. Smith. LC 96-26089. 448p. 1996. pap. 62.00 (*0-205-16448-X*) Allyn.

Teaching Students with Learning & Behavior Problems. 5th ed. Donald D. Hammill & Nettie R. Bartel. LC 90-30795. (Illus.). 598p. 1990. 39.00 (*0-205-12537-9*, 1500) PRO-ED.

Teaching Students with Learning & Behavior Problems: Managing Mild-to-Moderate Difficulties in Resource & Inclusive Settings. 6th ed. Donald D. Hammill & Nettie R. Bartel. LC 94-15554. (Illus.). 596p. (C). 1994. text ed. 44.00 (*0-89079-610-6*, 6816) PRO-ED.

Teaching Students with Learning Disabilities: Strategies for Success. Ed. by Karen A. Waldron. (Illus.). 172p. (Orig.). (C). 1992. pap. text ed. 24.95 (*1-879105-40-3*, 0275) Singular Publishing.

Teaching Students with Learning Problems. 4th ed. Cecil D. Mercer & Ann R. Mercer. LC 92-21059. 720p. (C). 1992. pap. text ed. 70.00 (*0-02-380561-7*, Macmillan Coll) P-H.

***Teaching Students with Learning Problems.** 5th ed. Ann R. Mercer. LC 97-15652. (C). 1997. pap. text ed. 60.00 (*0-13-490228-9*) P-H.

Teaching Students with Learning Problems to Use Study Skills: A Teacher's Guide. John J. Hoover & James R. Patton. LC 94-24964. 1995. 26.00 (*0-89079-662-9*) PRO-ED.

Teaching Students with Mental Retardation: A Life Goal Curriculum Planning Approach. Glen E. Thomas. LC 95-46387. 597p. (C). 1996. text ed. 54.00 (*0-02-420240-1*, Macmillan Coll) P-H.

Teaching Students with Mild & Moderate Learning Problems. John J. Langone. 472p. 1990. pap. text ed. 44.00 (*0-205-12362-7*, H23625) Allyn.

Teaching Students with Mild Disabilities. William N. Bender. LC 95-37933. 1996. pap. text ed. 64.00 (*0-13-892720-0*) Allyn.

Teaching Students with Mild Disabilities. Sabornie & Debettencourt. 464p. (C). 1996. pap. text ed. 48.00 (*0-02-404991-3*, Macmillan Coll) P-H.

Teaching Students with Moderate-Severe Disabilities, Including Autism: Strategies for Second Language Learners in Inclusive Settings. 2nd ed. Elva Duran. LC 96-23691. Orig. Title: Teaching the Moderately & Severely Handicapped Student & Autistic Adolescent. 416p. 1996. text ed. 75.95 (*0-398-06700-7*) C C Thomas.

Teaching Students with Moderate-Severe Disabilities, Including Autism: Strategies for Second Language Learners in Inclusive Settings. 2nd ed. Elva Duran. LC 96-23691. Orig. Title: Teaching the Moderately & Severely Handicapped Student & Autistic Adolescent. 416p. 1996. pap. text ed. 55.95 (*0-398-06701-5*) C C Thomas.

Teaching Students with Moderate to Severe Disabilities: Use of Response Prompting Strategies. Mark Wolery-Allegheny et al. 252p. (Orig.). (C). 1992. pap. text ed. 40.95 (*0-8013-0491-1*, 78343) Longman.

Teaching Students with Severe Emotional & Learning Impairments. Ellen Browning. 331p. 1983. text ed. 37.95 (*0-205-07677-7*, H76771) Allyn.

Teaching Students with Special Needs in Inclusive Settings. Tom E. Smith. LC 94-34735. 1994. text ed. 51.00 (*0-205-14653-8*) Allyn.

Teaching Students with Visual & Multiple Impairments: A Resource Guide. Millie Smith & Nancy Levack. LC 96-2922. 1996. pap. 40.00 (*1-880366-20-7*) TSBVI.

***Teaching Study Skills & Strategies in Grades 4-8.** Charles T. Mangrum et al. LC 97-13470. 1997. 24.95 (*0-205-19879-1*) Allyn.

Teaching Study Strategies to Students with Learning Disabilities. Stephen S. Strichart & Charles T. Mangrum, II. LC 92-33136. 400p. 1992. pap. text ed. 29.95 (*0-205-13992-2*, Longwood Div) Allyn.

Teaching Styles & Pupil Progress. Neville S. Bennett. 203p. 1976. 24.00 (*0-674-87095-6*) HUP.

Teaching Styles As Related to Student Achievement. 2nd ed. David Silvernail. 40p. 1986. pap. 3.95 (*0-8106-1069-8*) NEA.

Teaching Subjects. Harris. LC 96-31844. 160p. (C). 1996. pap. text ed. 22.40 (*0-13-515800-1*) P-H.

Teaching Sunday School. Brian Forster. 1984. pap. 3.99 (*0-85234-191-1*, Pub. by Evangelical Pr) Presby & Reformed.

Teaching Suzuki Cello: A Manual for Teachers & Parents. Charlene Wilson. (Illus.). 128p. 1980. pap. 7.95 (*0-87297-052-3*) Diablo.

Teaching Systemic Thinking. David Campbell et al. 88p. 1992. pap. text ed. 21.95 (*1-85575-015-5*, Pub. by Karnac Bks UK) Brunner-Mazel.

Teaching Taas Success. Clarkson Wests. Date not set. 8.25 (*0-314-04613-5*) West Pub.

Teaching Talk: Strategies for Production & Assessment. Gillian Brown et al. (Illus.). 192p. 1985. pap. 19.95 (*0-521-31942-0*) Cambridge U Pr.

Teaching Tank Discovery Book. David R. Burgess & Paul J. Reinbold. (Illus.). 112p. (C). 1992. lab manual ed., spiral bd. 21.95 (*0-9633907-0-8*) Captivation.

***Teaching Tank Discovery Book.** David R. Burgess & Gordon Corbett. 102p. (J). (gr. k up). 1996. teacher ed. 21.95 (*0-9633907-1-6*) Captivation.

Teaching Teachers to Teach: A Basic Manual for Church Teachers. Donald L. Griggs. (Griggs Educational Resources Ser.). 1980. reprint ed. pap. 11.95 (*0-687-41120-3*) Abingdon.

Teaching Team Sports: A Coeducational Approach. Joan A. Philipp & Jerry D. Wilkerson. LC 89-7533. (Illus.). 320p. (C). 1990. pap. text ed. 30.00 (*0-87322-259-8*, BPHI0259) Human Kinetics.

Teaching Techniques. LC 84-129711. 90p. 1983. teacher ed., ring bd. 19.95 (*0-910566-23-2*) Evang Trg Assn.

Teaching Techniques. rev. ed. Clarence H. Benson. LC 84-129711. 96p. 1983. pap. text ed. 8.95 (*0-910566-05-4*) Evang Trg Assn.

Teaching Techniques. rev. ed. Eric Parkinson. Ed. by Connie Doyle. (Design & Make Ser.). (Illus.). 45p. (J). (gr. 3-6). reprint ed. 9.99 (*1-884461-05-0*) NES Arnold.

Teaching Techniques & Insights for Instrumental Music Educators. Joseph L. Casey. LC 91-76805. 476p. 1991. 39.50 (*0-941050-28-9*, G-3723) GIA Pubns.

Teaching Techniques in the Radiologic Sciences. Steven B. Dowd & Stephen F. Hulse. (Illus.). 200p. (Orig.). (C). 1996. pap. text ed. write for info. (*1-886800-01-4*) Am Soc Radiologic Techns.

Teaching Techniques of Jesus. Herman H. Horne. LC 64-16634. 224p. 1971. pap. 7.99 (*0-8254-2804-1*) Kregel.

Teaching Technologies in Libraries. Linda B. MacDonald et al. (Professional Librarian Ser.). 198p. (C). 1990. 40.00 (*0-8161-1906-6*, Hall Reference); 30.00 (*0-8161-1907-4*, Hall Reference) Macmillan.

Teaching Technology. Ed. by Frank Banks. LC 93-17206. 192p. (C). 1993. pap. 18.95 (*0-415-10254-5*) Routledge.

Teaching Technology for College Teachers. E. G. Vedanayagam. 200p. (C). 1988. text ed. 30.00 (*81-207-0751-6*, Pub. by Sterling Pubs II) Apt Bks.

Teaching Technology from a Feminist Perspective: A Practical Guide. Joan Rothschild. (Athene Ser.). 200p. 1988. 36.50 (*0-08-034234-5*, Pergamon Pr); pap. 17.95 (*0-08-034233-7*, Pergamon Pr) Elsevier.

Teaching Technology from a Feminist Perspective: A Practical Guide. Joan Rothschild. (Athene Ser.). 178p. (C). 1988. text ed. 36.50 (*0-8077-6263-6*); pap. text ed. 18.95 (*0-8077-6214-8*) Tchrs Coll.

Teaching Teenage Girls. Ed. by Sherlie Rowe. 1987. pap. 6.25 (*0-89137-808-1*) Quality Pubns.

Teaching Teenagers: Model Activity Sequences for Humanistic Language Learning. H. Puchta & M. Schratz. (Pilgrims Resource Bks.). 135p. 1993. pap. text ed. 21.32 (*0-582-03763-8*, 79897) Longman.

Teaching Teenagers & Living to Tell about It: Gifted Students & Other Creatures in the Regular Classroom. Pamela Everly. (Gifted Treasury Ser.). (Illus.). xiv, 211p. 1992. pap. text ed. 23.00 (*0-87287-894-5*) Teacher Ideas Pr.

Teaching Tefilah: Insights & Activities on Jewish Prayer. Bruce Kadden & Barbara B. Kadden. LC 94-70561. 152p. (Orig.). 1994. pap. text ed. 22.50 (*0-86705-032-2*) A R E Pub.

Teaching Ten to Fourteen Year Olds. Chris Stevenson. 338p. (Orig.). (C). 1992. pap. text ed. 42.95 (*0-8013-0363-X*, 78140) Longman.

Teaching Tennis the USTA Way. Lawrence Tabak. 224p. (C). 1991. per. write for info. (*0-697-11394-9*) Brown & Benchmark.

***Teaching Tenses.** Aitken. 1992. pap. text ed. write for info. (*0-17-555920-1*) Addison-Wesley.

Teaching Terriffic Two's & Other Toddlers. Terry Graham. LC 87-31201. (Illus.). 200p. (Orig.). 1988. pap. 17.95 (*0-89334-106-1*) Humanics Ltd.

Teaching Terrific Two's & Other Toddlers. Terry L. Graham & Linda Camp. LC 87-31201. (Illus.). 200p. 1988. lib. bdg. 27.95 (*0-89334-172-X*, 172-X) Humanics Ltd.

Teaching Test Taking Skills: Helping Students Show What They Know. Margo Mastropieri & Thomas E. Scruggs. Ed. by Michael Pressley. (Cognitive Strategy Training Ser.). 139p. 1992. pap. text ed. 21.95 (*0-914797-76-X*) Brookline Bks.

Teaching Texas History: An All-Level Resource Guide. rev. ed. David C. De Boe et al. vii, 153p. 1990. reprint ed. pap. text ed. 7.00 (*0-87611-091-X*) Tex St Hist Assn.

Teaching That Makes a Difference. Ronald G. Held. LC 91-76515. 128p. 1992. pap. 2.95 (*0-88243-664-3*, 02-0664) Gospel Pub.

Teaching the Adult Bible Class. Chris Willerton. 1982. 3.95 (*0-89137-609-7*) Quality Pubns.

Teaching the Ancient World. Ed. by Douglas Astolfi. LC 82-10831. (Scholars Press General Ser.). 194p. (C). 1983. pap. 16.95 (*0-89130-590-4*, 00 03 05) Scholars Pr GA.

Teaching the Argument in Writing. Richard Fulkerson. LC 96-6295. (Illus.). 184p. 1996. pap. 19.95 (*0-8141-0190-9*) NCTE.

Teaching the Baha'i Faith: Extracts from the Writings of Baha'u'llah, Abdu'l-Baha, Shoghi Effendi & the Universal House of Justice. Compiled by Universal House of Justice Staff. 256p. 1995. pap. 9.95 (*0-909991-68-5*) Bahai.

Teaching the Baha'i Faith: Spirit in Action. Nathan Rutstein. 192p. 1984. 10.95 (*0-85398-175-2*); pap. 9.50 (*0-85398-176-0*) G Ronald Pub.

Teaching the Basic Skills in English: The Role of Spelling, Punctuation & Grammar in Secondary English. Don Smedley. (Teaching Secondary English Ser.). 182p. (C). 1984. pap. text ed. 10.95 (*0-416-34150-0*, NO. 3865) Routledge Chapman & Hall.

Teaching the Bible Creatively to Young People. Bill McNabb & Steve Mabry. 192p. 1990. pap. 10.99 (*0-310-52921-2*) Zondervan.

Teaching the Bible to Adults & Youth. rev. ed. Dick Murray. LC 93-20102. 176p. 1993. Alk. paper. 12.95 (*0-687-41084-3*) Abingdon.

Teaching the Bible to Adults & Youth: Korean Edition. Dick Murray. 176p. 1995. pap. 12.50 (*0-687-00785-2*) Abingdon.

Teaching the Bible with Puppets. Jeanne S. Fogle. LC 89-50563. (Illus.). 80p. (J). 1989. teacher ed. 9.95 (*0-89622-405-8*) Twenty-Third.

Teaching the Bilingual Special Education Student. Ed. by Angela Carrasquillo et al. LC 90-37630. (Second Language Learning Ser.). 240p. (C). 1990. pap. 39.50 (*0-89391-712-5*); text ed. 73.25 (*0-89391-623-4*) Ablex Pub.

***Teaching the Cat to Water-Ski.** Robertson. (Clipper Fiction Ser.). 1991. pap. text ed. write for info. (*0-582-87516-1*, Pub. by Longman UK) Longman.

Teaching the Child Rider. Pamela Roberts. 1987. 7.50 (*0-87556-302-3*) Saifer.

Teaching the Child Rider. Pamela Roberts. 102p. (C). 1990. pap. 21.00 (*0-85131-195-4*, Pub. by J A Allen & Co UK) St Mut.

***Teaching the Child under Six.** 4th ed. James L. Hymes, Jr. 194p. (C). 1997. reprint ed. pap. text ed. 16.95 (*0-940139-37-5*) Consortium RI.

Teaching the Conflicts: Gerald Graff, Curricular Reform, & the Culture Wars. Ed. by William E. Cain. LC 93-29157. (Wellesley Studies in Critical Theory: Vol. 2). 280p. 1993. text ed. 46.00 (*0-8153-1466-3*, H1782) Garland.

Teaching the Developmentally Handicapped Communicative Gesturing: A How-to-Do Book. Pieter C. Duker. (Modern Approaches to the Diagnosis & Instruction of Multi-Handicapped Children Ser.: Vol. 22). viii, 160p. 1989. 40.75 (*90-265-0940-5*) Swets.

Teaching the Disadvantaged: New Curriculum Approaches. Joseph O. Loretan. LC 66-15325. (Illus.). 256p. reprint ed. 73.00 (*0-8357-9610-8*, 2016939) Bks Demand.

Teaching the Disadvantaged Adult. Curtis Ulmer. Ed. by Robert A. Luke. LC 74-85759. 100p. 1969. reprint ed. pap. text ed. 3.00 (*0-7510-1062-6*) A A A C E.

Teaching the Dyslexic Child. Anita Griffiths. LC 78-12875. 1978. pap. 10.00 (*0-87879-205-8*) Acad Therapy.

***Teaching the Early Years: Birth-5 Years; Foundations & Activities.** Theresa M. Hauck & Anthony C. Maffei. (Illus.). 198p. (Orig.). (C). 1997. spiral bd. 33.45 (*0-9634429-9-6*) AM Educ Pub.

Teaching the Educable Mentally Retarded. Robert A. Sedlak & Denise M. Sedlak. LC 84-16344. (SUNY Series in Special Education). (Illus.). 334p. 1985. text ed. 64.50 (*0-88706-055-2*); pap. text ed. 21.95 (*0-88706-056-0*) State U NY Pr.

Teaching the Elementary School Chorus. Linda Swears. LC 84-16656. 209p. 1985. text ed. 24.95 (*0-13-892514-3*, Busn) P-H.

Teaching the Elephant to Dance: Empowering Change in Your Organization. James A. Belasco. 1990. 20.00 (*0-517-57478-0*, Crown) Crown Pub Group.

Teaching the Elephant to Dance: The Manager's Guide to Empowering Change. James A. Belasco. 288p. 1991. reprint ed. pap. 12.95 (*0-452-26629-7*, Plume) NAL-Dutton.

Teaching the English Language. John H. Bushman. (Illus.). 156p. (C). 1988. pap. text ed. 28.95 (*0-398-05466-5*) C C Thomas.

***Teaching the Folk Guitar: A Step by Step Method for Group Instruction.** Phil Johnson. (Illus.). 256p. (Orig.). 1997. pap. 34.95 (*0-9657323-0-4*) Euphoria Falls.

Teaching the Folktale Plays: An Instructional Guide. Martha Mutz. (Illus.). 57p. (Orig.). 1996. pap. 8.00 (*1-889397-21-0*, 021) Curiosity Canyon.

Teaching the Fun of Physics. Janice P. VanCleave. (Illus.). 224p. 1985. 14.95 (*0-13-892423-6*) P-H.

Teaching the Gifted & Talented in the Elementary Classroom. Mary J. Heimberger. 80p. 1991. pap. 9.95 (*0-8106-0735-2*) NEA.

Teaching the Gifted & Talented in the English Classroom. William W. West. 48p. 1985. pap. 7.95 (*0-8106-0734-4*) NEA.

Teaching the Gifted & Talented in the Middle School. Jill D. Wright. 64p. 1983. pap. 9.95 (*0-8106-0745-X*) NEA.

Teaching the Gifted & Talented in the Science Classroom. 2nd ed. William D. Romey & Mary L. Hibert. 64p. 1988. pap. 8.95 (*0-8106-0748-4*) NEA.

Teaching the Gifted & Talented in the Social Studies Classroom. Paul D. Plowman. 56p. 1980. pap. 6.95 (*0-8106-0737-9*) NEA.

Teaching the Gifted Child. 4th ed. James J. Gallgher & Shelagh A. Gallagher. LC 93-36642. 1994. text ed. 72.00 (*0-205-14828-X*) Allyn.

Teaching the Helping Skills: A Field Instructor's Guide. 2nd ed. Lawrence Shulman. (Orig.). 1993. pap. text ed. 11.00 (*0-87293-036-X*) Coun Soc Wk Ed.

Teaching the Helping Skills: A Field Instructor's Guide. Lawrence Shulman. LC 83-60456. 68p. reprint ed. pap. 25.00 (*0-7837-1435-1*, 2041812) Bks Demand.

Teaching the History of Medicine at a Medical Center. Jerome J. Bylebyl. LC 82-148. 200p. 1982. 30.00 (*0-8018-2799-X*) Johns Hopkins.

Teaching the Humanities. Ed. by Peter Gordon. (Education Ser.). 1991. text ed. 37.00 (*0-7130-0180-1*, Pub. by Woburn Pr UK); pap. text ed. 22.00 (*0-7130-4017-3*, Pub. by Woburn Pr UK) Intl Spec Bk.

Teaching-The Imperiled Profession. Daniel L. Duke. LC 83-18181. 174p. 1984. text ed. 59.50 (*0-87395-788-1*); pap. text ed. 19.95 (*0-87395-789-X*) State U NY Pr.

Teaching the Infant with Down Syndrome: A Guide for Parents & Professionals. 2nd ed. Marci J. Hanson. LC 85-28213. Orig. Title: Teaching Your Down's Syndrome Infant. (Illus.). 288p. 1987. pap. text ed. 27.00 (*0-89079-103-1*, 1392) PRO-ED.

Teaching the Integrated Language Arts. Shane Templeton. (C). 1990. text ed. 61.96 (*0-395-48154-6*) HM Soft Schl Col Div.

Teaching the Integrated Language Arts: Process & Practice. Anthony D. Fredericks et al. LC 95-25902. 1996. write for info. (*0-06-501510-X*) Addson-Wesley Educ.

Teaching the Introductory Course in Religious Studies: A Sourcebook. Ed. by Mark Juergensmeyer. 318p. 1991. pap. 34.95 (*1-55540-599-1*, 000115) Scholars Pr GA.

Teaching the Introductory Public Relations Course: Communication Perspective. James S. Measell. Ed. by Warren W. Lewis. LC 90-14056. (Illus.). 85p. (C). 1990. pap. 9.50 (*0-927516-20-9*) ERIC-REC.

Teaching the Learning Disabled & Emotionally Disturbed Child. Madge E. Shelby. (Illus.). 120p. (Orig.). 1979. pap. text ed. 4.50 (*0-935648-00-3*) Halldin Pub.

Teaching the Library Research Process. 2nd ed. Carol C. Kuhlthau. LC 94-1982. (Illus.). 206p. 1994. 39.50 (*0-8108-2723-9*) Scarecrow.

Teaching the Linguistically Diverse. Judy J. Schwartz. (Monographs). (C). 1980. text ed. 7.00 (*0-930348-08-7*) NY St Eng Coun.

Teaching the Majority: Breaking the Gender Barrier in Science, Mathematics, & Engineering. Sue V. Rosser. (Athene Ser.). 272p. (C). 1995. pap. text ed. 22.95 (*0-8077-6276-8*) Tchrs Coll.

Teaching the Majority: Breaking the Gender Barrier in Science, Mathematics, & Engineering. Sue V. Rosser. (Athene Ser.). 272p. (C). 1995. text ed. 50.00 (*0-8077-6277-6*) Tchrs Coll.

Teaching the Mature Rider. Martin Diggle. 125p. (C). 1990. pap. 30.00 (*0-85131-553-4*, Pub. by J A Allen & Co UK) St Mut.

Teaching the Meaning of Church Ordinances to Children. Terri Breeden. (Orig.). 1986. pap. 6.95 (*0-89265-097-4*) Randall Hse.

***Teaching the Mechanical Art of Song.** Celeste R. Watson. Ed. by Edward V. Foreman. (Twentieth Century Masterworks on Singing Ser.: Vol. VI). 1975. pap. 10.00 (*1-887117-07-5*) Pro musica pr.

Teaching the Media. 2nd ed. Len Masterman. (Comedia Bk.). 220p. (C). 1988. pap. 17.95 (*0-415-03974-6*, A4918) Routledge.

***Teaching the Media: International Perspectives.** Ed. by Andrew Hart. 350p. 1998. write for info. (*0-8058-2476-6*) L Erlbaum Assocs.

***Teaching the Media: International Perspectives.** Ed. by Andrew Hart. 350p. 1998. pap. write for info. (*0-8058-2477-4*) L Erlbaum Assocs.

Teaching the Mental Aspects of Baseball: A Coach's Handbook. Al Figone. 240p. 1991. pap. write for info. (*0-697-12767-2*) Brown & Benchmark.

Teaching the Mentally Retarded Child: Enlarged to Survey All Trainable Retardates & Their Social Needs. 2nd ed. Natalie Perry. LC 73-20246. 750p. 1974. text ed. 55.00 (*0-231-03652-3*) Col U Pr.

Teaching the Mentally Retarded Student. Richard L. Luftig. 1986. text ed. 46.00 (*0-205-10262-X*, H02629) Allyn.

Teaching the Middle Ages. Ed. by Robert V. Graybill et al. 160p. (Orig.). pap. 6.95 (*0-942912-00-4*) Smart.

Teaching the Middle Ages II. Ed. by Robert V. Graybill et al. 170p. (Orig.). pap. 6.95 (*0-942912-01-2*) Smart.

***Teaching the Millennium.** Craig A. Munsart & Christine M. Izmirian. LC 97-2952. (Illus.). 192p. (Orig.). (J). (gr. 4-8). 1997. pap. text ed. 17.95 (*1-55591-284-2*) Fulcrum Pub.

Teaching the Moderately & Severely Handicapped, Vol. I. 2nd ed. Michael Bender et al. LC 84-22861. (Illus.). 280p. 1985. pap. 30.00 (*0-936104-52-X*, 1293) PRO-ED.

Teaching the Moderately & Severely Handicapped, Vol. II. 2nd ed. Michael Bender et al. LC 84-22861. (Illus.). 352p. 1985. pap. 32.00 (*0-936104-53-8*, 1294) PRO-ED.

Teaching the Moderately & Severely Handicapped, Vol. III. Michael Bender et al. LC 79-46596. 272p. 1976. pap. text ed. 29.00 (*0-936104-54-6*, 1111) PRO-ED.

Teaching the Moderately & Severely Handicapped Student & Autistic Adolescent see Teaching Students with Moderate-Severe Disabilities, Including Autism: Strategies for Second Language Learners in Inclusive Settings

Teaching the Music of Six Different Cultures. rev. ed. Luvenia A. George. LC 87-16060. (Illus.). 256p. (C). 1988. pap. 14.95 (*0-937203-06-8*); pap. 21.50 incl. audio (*0-937203-27-0*) World Music Pr.

Teaching the Music Tree: A Handbook for Teachers. Frances Clark & Louise Goss. (Frances Clark Library for Piano Students). 24p. 1973. pap. text ed. 5.95 (*0-87487-124-7*) Summy-Birchard.

Teaching the New Basic Skills: Principles for Educating Children to Thrive in a Changing Economy. Frank Levy. 272p. 1996. 24.00 (*0-684-82739-5*) Free Pr.

T

Teaching the New Library: A How-to-Do-It Manual for Planning & Designing Instructional Programs. Michael Blake et al. LC 96-43647. (How-to-Do-It Manuals Ser.). 171p. 1996. pap. 45.00 (*1-55570-214-7*) Neal-Schuman.

Teaching the Non-English-Speaking Child: Grades K-2. Mary Ashworth & Patricia Wakefield. (Language in Education: Theory & Practice Ser.: No. 45). 60p. reprint ed. pap. 25.00 (*0-8357-3345-9*, 2039578) Bks Demand.

Teaching the Novel. Becky Alano. Ed. by Mary Morgan. (Teaching Resources in the ERIC Database (TRIED) Ser.). 1989. pap. 14.95 (*0-927516-06-3*) ERIC-REC.

Teaching the Old Testament in English Classes. James S. Ackerman et al. LC 72-93907. (Indiana University English Curriculum Study Ser.). 511p. reprint ed. pap. 145.70 (*0-685-23874-1*, 2056691) Bks Demand.

Teaching the Online Catalog User. Ed. by Carolyn A. Kirkendall. (Library Orientation Ser.: No. 16). 256p. 1988. pap. 35.00 (*0-87650-250-8*) Pierian.

Teaching the Postmodern. Brenda Marshall. 224p. (C). 1991. pap. 17.95 (*0-415-90455-2*, A5885, Routledge NY) Routledge.

Teaching the Practice of Nursing. 3rd ed. J. M. Mellish. 1991. pap. 40.00 (*0-409-11154-6*) Buttrwrth-Heinemann.

Teaching the Process of Thinking, k-12. Kenneth R. Chuska. LC 86-61753. (Fastback Ser.: No. 244). 50p. 1986. pap. 3.00 (*0-87367-244-5*) Phi Delta Kappa.

Teaching the Research Paper: From Theory to Practice, from Research to Writing. Ed. by James E. Ford. LC 94-17407. (Illus.). 325p. 1995. 39.50 (*0-8108-2910-X*) Scarecrow.

Teaching the Scans Competencies. (Illus.). 123p. (Orig.). (C). 1994. pap. text ed. 30.00 (*0-7881-0597-3*) DIANE Pub.

Teaching the Scriptures: A Study Guide for Bible Students & Teachers. 6th rev. ed. Russell D. Robinson. (Illus.). 220p. 1993. pap. text ed. 19.95 (*1-877837-11-3*) Bible Study Pr.

Teaching the Severely Handicapped, 2 vols., Set. Ed. by Norris G. Haring & Louis J. Brown. LC 76-25992. (Illus.). 1977. 84.50 (*0-685-02028-2*, Grune) Saunders.

Teaching the Severely Handicapped, 2 vols., Vol. 1. Ed. by Norris G. Haring & Louis J. Brown. LC 76-25992. (Illus.). 320p. 1976. text ed. 45.00 (*0-8089-0945-2*, 791901, Grune) Saunders.

Teaching the Severely Handicapped, 2 vols., Vol. 2. Ed. by Norris G. Haring & Louis J. Brown. LC 76-25992. (Illus.). 224p. 1977. text ed. 52.50 (*0-8089-0980-0*, 791902, Grune) Saunders.

Teaching the Severely Handicapped Child: Basic Skills for the Developmentally Disabled. Robert M. Browning. 292p. 1980. text ed. 37.95 (*0-205-06877-4*, H68778) Allyn.

Teaching the Short Story: A Guide to Using Stories from Around the World. Ed. by Bonnie H. Neumann & Helen M. McDonnell. 302p. 1996. pap. 21.95 (*0-8141-1947-6*) NCTE.

***Teaching the Short Story Curriculum Guide.** C. D. Buchanan. (Classic Short Stories Ser.). 64p. 1994. pap. 19.95 (*0-7854-0618-2*, 40101) Am Guidance.

Teaching the Sick: A Manual of Occupational Therapy & Re-Education. George E. Barton. Ed. by William R. Phillips & Janet Rosenberg. LC 79-6895. (Physically Handicapped in Society Ser.). (Illus.). 1980. reprint ed. lib. bdg. 19.95 (*0-405-13106-2*) Ayer.

Teaching the Sixties: An In-Depth, Interactive, Interdisciplinary Approach. Brooke Workman. 221p. (Orig.). 1992. pap. 15.95 (*0-8141-5236-8*) NCTE.

Teaching the Skills of Conflict Resolution: Activities & Strategies for Counseling & Teaching. David Cowan et al. (Illus.). 186p. 1992. pap. text ed. 19.95 (*1-56499-009-5*) Innerchoice Pub.

Teaching the Social Sciences & History in Secondary Schools: A Methods Book. Social Science Education Consortium, Inc. Staff. LC 95-12893. 1996. text ed. 59.95 (*0-534-26526-X*) Wadsworth Pub.

Teaching the Spanish-Speaking Child: A Practical Guide. Jo Ann Crandall et al. 74p. (Orig.). 1989. pap. text ed. 8.00 (*0-13-895707-X*) P-H.

***Teaching the Spoken Language: An Approach Based on the Analysis of Conversational English.** 176p. 1984. pap. text ed. 17.95 (*0-521-27384-6*) Cambridge U Pr.

Teaching the Spoken Language: An Approach Based on the Analysis of Conversational English. Gillian Brown & George Yule. 162p. 1984. digital audio 17.95 (*0-521-25378-0*) Cambridge U Pr.

Teaching the Student with Spina Bifida. Ed. by Fern L. Rowley-Kelly & Donald H. Reigel. 496p. (Orig.). (C). 1992. pap. text ed. 40.00 (*1-55766-064-6*); vhs 49.00 (*1-55766-109-X*) P H Brookes.

***Teaching the Teachers: The History of Jordanhill College of Education 1828-1993.** Margaret M. Harrison & Willis B. Marker. 240p. 1996. pap. 45.00 (*0-85976-436-2*, Pub. by J Donald UK) St Mut.

Teaching the Ten Themes of Social Studies. Frank Schaffer Publications, Inc. Staff. (Middle School Bks.). (Illus.). 1996. wbk. ed. 12.95 (*0-7647-0011-1*, FS-10187) Schaffer Pubns.

Teaching the Three R's Through Movement Experiences. Anne G. Gilbert. LC 76-19465. 304p. (C). 1986. pap. text ed. 40.00 (*0-02-342800-7*, Macmillan Coll) P-H.

Teaching the Tiger: A Handbook for Individuals Involved in the Education of Students with Attention Deficit Disorders, Tourette Syndrome or Obsessive-Compulsive Disorders. Marilyn P. Dornbush & Sheryl K. Pruitt. LC 95-2018. (Illus.). 200p. 1995. pap. 35.00 (*1-878267-34-5*) Hope Pr CA.

Teaching the Tough Ones. Danni Odom-Winn & Dianne E. Dunagan. Ed. by Rosalie Dow. (Illus.). 118p. 1991. pap. 14.95 (*0-7925-3213-9*, B305) Ed Activities.

Teaching the Unconventional Child. Randy L. Comfort. LC 92-10118. xi, 162p. (Orig.). 1992. pap. text ed. 21.50 (*0-87287-941-0*) Teacher Ideas Pr.

Teaching the Universe of Discourse. James Moffett. LC 87-27816. 215p. (C). 1982. pap. text ed. 21.50 (*0-86709-181-9*, 0181) Boynton Cook Pubs.

Teaching the Visually Limited Child see Teaching Visually Impaired Children

***Teaching the Whole Class.** 4th ed. Betty L. Leaver. LC 97-21131. 256p. 1997. 65.95 (*0-8039-6645-8*) Sage.

***Teaching the Whole Class.** 4th ed. Betty L. Leaver. LC 97-21131. 256p. 1997. pap. 27.95 (*0-8039-6646-6*) Sage.

Teaching the Word of Truth. Donald G. Barnhouse. 1958. reprint ed. pap. 20.00 (*0-8028-1610-X*) Eerdmans.

Teaching the World's Children: ESL for Ages Three to Seven. Mary Ashworth. (Pippin Teachers Library). 96p. 1994. pap. text ed. 14.50 (*0-88751-062-0*, 00761) Heinemann.

Teaching the Writing Process in High School. LC 95-40688. (Standards Consensus Ser.). (Illus.). 142p. (Orig.). 1995. teacher ed., pap. 12.95 (*0-8141-5286-4*) NCTE.

Teaching the Young Child with Motor Delays: A Guide for Parents & Professionals. Marci J. Hanson & Susan R. Harris. LC 85-25827. 228p. (Orig.). 1986. pap. text ed. 27.00 (*0-936104-91-0*, 1366) PRO-ED.

Teaching Theatre Through Poetry & Vice-Versa: An Approach to the Essence of Performing Theatre. Rod Martin & C. Michael Perry. (Theatre Book Ser.). 26p. 1993. pap. 3.00 (*1-57514-007-1*, 5013) Encore Perform Pub.

Teaching Them to Read. 5th ed. Dolores Durkin. 1989. text ed. 45.00 (*0-205-11706-6*, H17064) Allyn.

Teaching Them to Read. 6th ed. Dolores Durkin. LC 92-17718. 1992. text ed. 61.00 (*0-205-13915-9*) Allyn.

Teaching Thermodynamics. Ed. by Jeffery D. Lewins. 538p. 1986. 125.00 (*0-306-42207-7*, Plenum Pr) Plenum.

Teaching Thinking. 1996. pap. 12.95 (*0-590-49171-7*) Scholastic Inc.

Teaching Thinking. Edward De Bono. 1990. 25.00 (*0-317-90562-7*) Intl Ctr Creat Think.

Teaching Thinking. Edward De Bono. (Illus.). 272p. 1992. pap. 11.95 (*0-14-013785-8*, Penguin Bks) Viking Penguin.

Teaching Thinking: A Survey of Programmes in Education. 2nd ed. M. J. Coles & W. D. Robinson. 120p. 1989. pap. 17.95 (*1-85399-277-1*, Pub. by Brstl Class Pr UK) Focus Pub-R Pullins.

Teaching Thinking: An Agenda for the 21st Century. Ed. by John N. Mangieri & Cathy Collins. 352p. (C). 1992. text ed. 69.95 (*0-8058-0867-1*) L Erlbaum Assocs.

Teaching Thinking: Issues & Approaches. Swartz & Perkins. 280p. 1995. pap. 27.50 (*0-89455-378-X*) Crit Think Bks.

Teaching Thinking Across the Grades: Ideas, Activities, & Resources. Iris M. Tiedt et al. 340p. 1989. pap. text ed. 35.95 (*0-205-11729-5*, H1729-6) Allyn.

Teaching Thinking & Reasoning Skills. Robert A. Pauker. Ed. by Ben Brodinsky. (Critical Issues Report Ser.). 80p. (Orig.). 1987. pap. text ed. 13.95 (*0-87652-112-X*, 021-00175) Am Assn Sch Admin.

Teaching Thinking Skills. Joan B. Baron & Robert J. Sternberg. LC 86-4776. (Psychology Ser.). (Illus.). 295p. (C). 1995. pap. text ed. 19.95 (*0-7167-1791-3*) W H Freeman.

Teaching Thinking Skills: A Handbook for Secondary Teachers. Barry Beyer. 320p. 1991. pap. text ed. 31.50 (*0-205-12797-5*, H27972, Longwood Div) Allyn.

Teaching Thinking Skills: Mathematics. Marcia Heiman et al. 48p. 1987. pap. 7.95 (*0-8106-0678-X*); pap. 7.95 (*0-8106-0203-2*) NEA.

Teaching Thinking Skills: Science. Ronald Narode et al. 48p. 1987. pap. 7.95 (*0-8106-0202-4*) NEA.

Teaching Thinking Skills: Theory & Practice. Joyce N. French & Carol Rhoder. LC 91-17257. (Source Books on Education: Vol. 28). 488p. 1992. text ed. 65.00 (*0-8240-4843-1*, 511) Garland.

Teaching Thinking Skills with Databases - AppleWorks Version. Jim Watson. 213p. 1988. School site license. teacher ed. 35.00 incl. disk (*0-924667-49-4*) Intl Society Tech Educ.

Teaching Thinking Skills with Databases - FrEdBase Version. Jim Watson. 213p. 1988. School site license. teacher ed. 35.00 incl. disk (*0-924667-54-0*) Intl Society Tech Educ.

Teaching Thinking Skills with Databases Macintosh Version. Jim Watson. 200p. 1991. teacher ed. 35.00 (*0-924667-78-8*) Intl Society Tech Educ.

Teaching Thinking Through Effective Questioning. 2nd ed. Francis P. Hunkins. (Illus.). 320p. (YA). (gr. 8-12). 1994. text ed. 44.95 (*0-926842-41-2*) CG Pubs Inc.

Teaching Threes Specific Skills. 1977. 3.00 (*0-939418-22-3*) Ferguson-Florissant.

***Teaching Through Inquiry: Basic Skills Assessment Program: Science.** (Illus.). 45p. (C). 1996. reprint ed. pap. 25.00 (*0-7881-2699-7*) DIANE Pub.

Teaching Through Modality Strengths: Concepts & Practices. Walter B. Barbe & Raymond H. Swassing. LC 79-66953. (C). 1979. 12.95 (*0-88309-100-3*) Zaner-Bloser.

Teaching Through Play: Teachers Thinking & Classroom Practice. Neville Bennett et al. LC 96-19875. 160p. 1996. 74.00 (*0-335-19733-7*, Open Univ Pr); pap. 20.95 (*0-335-19732-9*, Open Univ Pr) Taylor & Francis.

Teaching Through Projects: Creating Effective Learning Environments. Heidi Goodrich et al. Ed. by Lois Fowkes. (Illus.). 124p. (Orig.). 1995. pap. text ed. 24.95 (*0-201-49507-4*) Addison-Wesley.

Teaching Through Radio & Television. rev. ed. William B. Levenson & Edward Stasheff. LC 72-92303. 560p. 1969. reprint ed. text ed. 38.50 (*0-8371-2414-X*, LERT, Greenwood Pr) Greenwood.

Teaching Through Text: A Content Literacy Approach to Content Area Reading. Michael C. McKenna & Richard D. Robinson. LC 92-27870. 366p. (C). 1993. pap. text ed. 52.95 (*0-8013-0584-5*, 79560) Longman.

Teaching Through Text: A Content Literacy Approach to Content Area Reading. 2nd ed. Michael C. McKenna & Richard D. Robinson. LC 96-10446. (C). 1997. text ed. 48.95 (*0-8013-1648-0*) Longman.

Teaching Through Themes. Scholastic Books Staff. 1991. pap. 15.95 (*0-590-49129-6*) Scholastic Inc.

***Teaching Tips: Strategies, Research, & Theory for College & University Teachers.** 9th ed. Robert J. Menges. 444p. (C). 1994. pap. text ed. 23.56 (*0-669-19434-4*) HM College Div.

***Teaching Tips & Effective Strategies for Weekend Islamic Schools.** Mohammed Ismail. 126p. 1996. pap. 6.50 (*0-614-21539-0*, 1221) Kazi Pubns.

***Teaching Tips for Adolescent Catechesis.** Richard J. Reichert & Michael Westenberg. 109p. 1996. teacher ed., spiral bd. 14.95 (*0-87973-344-6*) Our Sunday Visitor.

Teaching Tips for Cosmetology. Linnea M. Lindquist. 24p. (C). 1981. pap. text ed. 16.00 (*0-314-63395-2*) West Pub.

***Teaching Tips for Early Childhood Religious Education.** Joan E. Plum & Paul S. Plum. 224p. 1996. teacher ed., spiral bd. 14.95 (*0-87973-345-4*) Our Sunday Visitor.

Teaching Tips for Religion Teachers Grades 4-8. Richard J. Reichert. 160p. 1989. spiral bd. 9.95 (*0-87973-365-9*, 365) Our Sunday Visitor.

Teaching to Change Lives. Howard Hendricks & Garnet Pike. 1991. teacher ed., pap. 12.95 (*0-911866-17-5*) LifeSprings Res.

Teaching to Change Lives. Howard Hendricks. 156p. 1996. pap. 10.99 (*0-88070-969-3*, Multnomah Bks) Multnomah Pubs.

Teaching to Diversity. Mary Meyers. 144p. 1994. pap. text ed. 24.72 (*0-201-55547-6*) Addison-Wesley.

Teaching to Diversity: Teaching & Learning in the Multi-Ethnic Classroom. Mary Meyers. LC 94-137. 1994. write for info. (*0-7725-1958-7*) Addison-Wesley.

Teaching to Learn: A Direction for Education. Guy Claxton. 176p. 1990. text ed. 60.00 (*0-304-31904-X*); pap. text ed. 18.95 (*0-304-31903-1*) Cassell.

Teaching to Observe: The Counselor As Teacher. Jay E. Adams. 140p. (Orig.). 1996. pap. 8.95 (*0-9643556-8-X*) Timeless Texts.

Teaching to the Heart: An Affective Approach to Literacy Instruction. 2nd ed. Nancy L. Cecil. 153p. (Orig.). (C). 1992. pap. text ed. 13.95 (*1-879215-13-6*) Sheffield WI.

Teaching to Transgress: Education As the Practice of Freedom. Bell Hooks. 200p. (gr. 13). 1994. pap. 15.95 (*0-415-90808-6*, B2862) Routledge.

***Teaching to Wonder: Responding to Poetry in the Secondary Classroom.** Carl Leggo. 160p. (Orig.). 1997. pap. 19.95 (*1-895766-31-1*, Pub. by Pacific Educ Pr CN) Orca Bk Pubs.

***Teaching to Wonder: Spiritual Growth Through Imagination & Movement.** Judy G. Smith. 96p. 1997. pap. 12.95 (*1-57438-011-7*, 5198) Ed Ministries.

Teaching Today: A Practical Guide. Geoffrey Petty. 384p. (C). 1993. 60.00 (*0-7487-1697-1*, Pub. by Stanley Thornes UK) Trans-Atl Phila.

Teaching Today: An Introduction to Education. 5th ed. David G. Armstrong & Kenneth T. Henson. LC 96-20386. 426p. (C). 1996. text ed. 60.00 (*0-13-382177-3*) P-H.

Teaching Today's Health. 4th ed. David Anspaugh & Gene Ezell. (Illus.). 672p. (C). 1994. text ed. 54.00 (*0-02-303570-6*, Macmillan Coll) P-H.

***Teaching Today's Health.** 5th ed. Anspaugh & Ezell. 1997. text ed. 48.67 (*0-205-27413-7*) P-H.

Teaching Today's Health in Middle & Secondary Schools. David Anspaugh & Gene Ezell. LC 93-30752. 544p. (C). 1993. text ed. 58.00 (*0-02-303562-5*, Macmillan Coll) P-H.

***Teaching Today's Youth: The Victory & the Challenge.** Mark A. Simone. (Accent Teacher Training Ser.). 192p. 1996. pap. 9.99 (*0-89636-329-5*) Accent CO.

Teaching Toddlers. Carol E. Miller. 1971. pap. 3.50 (*0-915374-22-6*, 22-6) Rapids Christian.

Teaching Toddlers the Bible. V. Gilbert Beers. LC 93-19696. (Toddlers Ser.). (Illus.). 120p. 1993. pap. 5.99 (*1-56476-155-X*, 6-3155, Victor Bks) Chariot Victor.

***Teaching Tolerance.** Sara Bullard. 1997. pap. 11.95 (*0-385-47265-X*) Doubleday.

Teaching Tolerance: Raising Open-Minded, Empathetic Children. Sara Bullard. LC 95-36045. 256p. 1996. 21.95 (*0-385-47264-1*) Doubleday.

***Teaching Tools.** Barbara Acello. (Illus.). 220p. (Orig.). (C). 1997. pap. text ed. write for info. (*1-56930-074-7*) Skidmore Roth Pub.

***Teaching Tools for the 21st Century.** Carolyn Coil. (Illus.). 184p. (Orig.). 1997. teacher ed., pap. 18.95 (*1-880505-55-X*, CLC0200) Pieces of Lrning.

Teaching Torah: A Treasury of Activities & Insights. Sorel G. Loeb & Barbara B. Kadden. LC 84-70318. 300p. 1984. pap. text ed. 22.50 (*0-86705-013-6*) A R E Pub.

Teaching Torts: A Teacher's Guide to Studies in American Tort Law. Vincent R. Johnson & Alan Gunn. 388p. (Orig.). 1995. pap. text ed. 32.50 (*0-89089-013-7*, JOHNSONTM) Carolina Acad Pr.

Teaching Toward Tomorrow: A Music Teacher's Primer for Using Electronic Keyboards, Computers, & MIDI in the Studio. Sam Holland. Ed. by Helen S. Tarchalski. LC 93-71723. (Illus.). 115p. (Orig.). 1993. pap. text ed. 24.95 (*0-9639311-0-5*) Debut Music.

Teaching Town. Elizabeth S. McKinnon. Ed. by Jean Warren & Kathleen Cubley. LC 95-60512. (Learning Everywhere Ser.). (Illus.). 128p. (Orig.). (J). (ps). 1996. pap. 6.95 (*1-57029-069-5*, 2802, Totline Bks) Warren Pub Hse.

***Teaching TQM/CQI Concepts in 20 Minute Sessions.** Marianne Dolson & Nancy E. Fritch. (Illus.). 324p. 1996. pap. text ed. 74.95 (*1-880610-76-0*) PRO-ACT Pub.

Teaching Transcultural Care: A Guide for Teachers of Nursing & Health Care. Paula McGee. LC 92-22885. 1992. 38.25 (*1-56593-065-7*, 0379) Singular Publishing.

Teaching Translation & Interpreting: Training, Talent & Experience. Ed. by Cay Dollerup & Anne Loddegaard. LC 91-47538. vii, 344p. 1992. 83.00 (*1-55619-453-6*); pap. 29.95 (*1-55619-456-0*) Benjamins North Am.

Teaching Translation & Interpreting 2: Insights, Aims, Visions. Ed. by Cay Dollerup & Annette Lindegaard. LC 94-10141. (Benjamins Translation Library: Vol. 5). 1994. 69.00 (*1-55619-682-2*) Benjamins North Am.

Teaching Translation & Interpreting 3: New Horizons, Papers from the Third Language International Conference, Elsinore, Denmark 9-11 June 1995. Ed. by Cay Dollerup & Vibeke Appel. LC 96-20500. (Benjamins Translation Library: Vol. 16). viii, 338p. 1996. lib. bdg. 69.00 (*1-55619-698-9*) Benjamins North Am.

Teaching Translation from Spanish to English: Worlds Beyond Words. Allison B. Lonsdale. 288p. 1995. pap. 30.00 (*0-7766-0399-X*) Paul & Co Pubs.

Teaching Travel: A Handbook for the Educator. Claudine Dervaes. 356p. 1996. 39.95 (*0-933143-08-7*) Solitaire Pub.

Teaching Trips. Elizabeth S. McKinnon. Ed. by Jean Warren & Kathleen Cubley. LC 95-60513. (Learning Everywhere Ser.). (Illus.). 128p. (Orig.). (J). (ps). 1996. pap. 6.95 (*1-57029-070-9*, 2803, Totline Bks) Warren Pub Hse.

Teaching Troubled & Troublesome Adolescents. Jane Lovey. 128p. 1992. pap. 24.95 (*1-85346-194-6*, Pub. by D Fulton UK) Taylor & Francis.

Teaching Troubled Children: A Case Study in Effective Classroom Practice. Joseph Cambone. 224p. (C). 1994. text ed. 39.00 (*0-8077-3304-0*); pap. text ed. 18.95 (*0-8077-3303-2*) Tchrs Coll.

Teaching Tumbling. Phillip Ward. LC 96-21955. (Illus.). 152p. (Orig.). 1996. pap. text ed. 18.00 (*0-87322-497-3*, BWAR0497) Human Kinetics.

Teaching U. S. History in the Elementary School: An Interdisciplinary Approach. Ed. by Laurel R. Singleton et al. 195p. 1993. pap. 21.95 (*0-89994-365-9*) Soc Sci Ed.

Teaching under Pressure: Looking at Primary Teachers' Stress. Anne Cockburn. LC 95-50707. (Illus.). 176p. 1995. 69.95 (*0-7507-0503-5*, Falmer Pr); pap. 24.95 (*0-7507-0504-3*, Falmer Pr) Taylor & Francis.

Teaching Undergraduates: Essays from the Lilly Endowment Workshop on Liberal Arts. Ed. by Bruce A. Kimball. (Contemporary Issues in Philosophy Ser.). 215p. (C). 1988. text ed. 33.95 (*0-87975-489-3*) Prometheus Bks.

Teaching Units for the Giant Book of Theme Patterns. Jean Stangl. 1992. pap. 10.99 (*0-86653-966-2*) Fearon Teach Aids.

Teaching Values: An Idea Book for Teachers & Parents. Gary A. Davis. LC 95-90783. 305p. 1996. pap. 21.95 (*1-888115-02-5*) Westwood Pubng.

***Teaching Values: Reaching Kids.** Linda Schwartz. (Illus.). 224p. (Orig.). (J). (gr. 4-6). 1997. pap. 21.95 (*0-88160-299-X*, LW369) Learning Wks.

Teaching Values & Ethics: Problems & Solutions. Kristen Amundson. LC 91-71672. (Critical Issues Report Ser.: No. 24). 64p. 1991. pap. 14.95 (*0-87652-162-6*, 021-00326) Am Assn Sch Admin.

Teaching Values in College. Richard L. Morrill. LC 80-8003. (Jossey-Bass Series in Higher Education). 191p. reprint ed. pap. 54.50 (*0-8357-4692-5*, 2052347) Bks Demand.

Teaching Values in the Literature Classroom: A Debate in Print. Bernard Suhor & Charles Suhor. LC 92-10117. 1992. 16.95 (*0-927516-32-2*) ERIC-REC.

Teaching Vermont's Heritage: Proceedings of the Second Working Conference on Vermont's Heritage for Teachers. Ed. by Marshall True et al. (Illus.). 160p. (Orig.). 1984. pap. text ed. 7.00 (*0-944277-11-X*, V47) U VT Ctr Rsch VT.

Teaching Visually Handicapped. Jack Rudman. (National Teacher Examination Ser.: NT-27). 1994. pap. 23.95 (*0-8373-8437-0*) Nat Learn.

Teaching Visually Impaired Children. 2nd ed. Virginia E. Bishop. LC 96-1751. Orig. Title: Teaching the Visually Limited Child. (Illus.). 274p. 1996. 48.95 (*0-398-06595-0*); pap. 33.95 (*0-398-06596-9*) C C Thomas.

Teaching Vocabulary in All Classrooms. Camille Blachowicz & Peter Fisher. 1995. pap. text ed. 25.00 (*0-02-310172-5*, Macmillan Coll) P-H.

Teaching Vocabulary to Improve Reading Comprehension. William E. Nagy. 52p. 1988. pap. 8.25 (*0-87207-151-0*) Intl Reading.

Teaching Voice. Stephanie Martin & Lyn Darnley. (Illus.). 160p. (Orig.). 1996. pap. 39.95 (*1-56593-790-2*, 1542) Singular Publishing.

Teaching Wallace Stevens: Practical Essays. Ed. by John N. Serio & Bobby J. Leggett. LC 93-8866. (Tennessee Studies in Literature: Vol. 35). 336p. (C). 1994. text ed. 32.95 (*0-87049-817-7*) U of Tenn Pr.

Teaching Well & Liking It: Motivating Faculty to Teach Effectively. James L. Bess. 448p. 1996. text ed. 39.95 (*0-8018-5364-8*) Johns Hopkins.

An Asterisk (*) at the beginning of an entry indicates that the title is appearing in BIP for the first time.

Teaching What We Do: Essays by Amherst College Faculty. Ed. by Richard Todd & Douglas C. Wilson. 264p. (C). 1993. 16.50 (*0-87023-843-4*) U of Mass Pr.

Teaching What You're Not: Identity Politics in Higher Education. Ed. by Katherine J. Mayberry. (C). 1996. pap. 19.95 (*0-8147-5547-X*) NYU Pr.

Teaching What You're Not: Identity Politics in Higher Education. Ed. by Katherine J. Mayberry. 380p. (C). 1996. 55.00 (*0-8147-5531-3*) NYU Pr.

Teaching Wind & Percussion Instruments: A Choral Course of Study. Ed. by Donald L. Corbett et al. 72p. (Orig.). (C). 1991. teacher ed. 18.25 (*1-56545-004-3*, 1603) Music Ed Natl.

Teaching with a Multicultural Perspective: A Practical Guide. Leonard Davidman & Patricia Davidman. LC 92-38387. 288p. (C). 1994. pap. text ed. 31.95 (*0-8013-0835-6*, 78902) Longman.

Teaching with a Multicultural Perspective: A Practical Guide. 2nd ed. Leonard Davidman & Patricia T. Davidman. LC 96-10445. (C). 1997. pap. text ed. 30.50 (*0-8013-1748-7*) Longman.

Teaching with Authority: A Theology of the Magisterium in the Church. Richard R. Gaillardetz. LC 96-36775. (Theology & Life Ser.: Vol. 4). 232p. (Orig.). 1997. pap. text ed. 24.95 (*0-8146-5529-7*, M Glazier) Liturgical Pr.

Teaching with Authority: Miracles & Christology in the Gospel of Mark. Edwin K. Broadhead. (JSNT Supplement Ser.: No. 74). 220p. (C). 1992. 56.50 (*1-85075-366-0*, Pub. by Sheffield Acad UK) CUP Services.

Teaching with Bible Games: "Kid-Tested" Contests to Make Christian Education Fun. Ed Dunlop. Ed. by Rhonda Wray. LC 93-16857. (Illus.). 224p. (Orig.). 1993. pap. 10.95 (*0-916260-94-1*, B108) Meriwether Pub.

Teaching with Caldecott Books. Scholastic Books Staff. 180p. 1996. pap. 15.95 (*0-590-49079-6*) Scholastic Inc.

Teaching with Charisma: A Teaching Styles Overview. Lloyd Duck. (Illus.). 315p. (C). 1994. pap. text ed. 19.95 (*0-9639874-5-3*) Chatelaine.

Teaching with Children's Books: Paths to Literature-Based Instruction. Ed. by Marilou Sorensen & Barbara Lehman. 270p. (Orig.). (C). 1995. pap. 19.95 (*0-8141-5292-9*) NCTE.

Teaching with Documents. National Archives Staff. LC 89-12602. (Illus.). 225p. (C). 1989. pap. 15.00 (*0-911333-79-7*, 200047) National Archives & Recs.

Teaching with Eggs. Alfred De Vito. (Illus.). 70p. (Orig.). (J). (gr. 3-8). 1982. pap. write for info. (*0-942034-00-7*) Creat Ventures IN.

Teaching with God's Heart for the World, Vol. 2. Ann Dunagan. (Illus.). 256p. (Orig.). 1995. ring bd. 49.95 (*0-9645420-1-3*) Fam Mission.

Teaching with Heart: Making Healthy Connections with Students. Judith A. Deiro. LC 95-50203. (Illus.). 248p. 1996. 51.95 (*0-8039-6344-0*); pap. 23.95 (*0-8039-6345-9*) Corwin Pr.

Teaching with Historic Places: A Series of Lesson Plans Produced by the National Park Service & the National Trust for Historic Preservation. Fay D. Metcalf. LC 92-32149. 1992. write for info. (*0-89133-229-4*) Natl Trust Hist Pres.

***Teaching with Issues Across the Curriculum, Instructor's Manual: Reading, Writing, Research.** Dolores LaGuardia & Hans P. Guth. 302p. (Orig.). 1997. pap. text ed. write for info. (*1-55934-571-3*, 1571) Mayfield Pub.

Teaching with LOGO. Daniel Watt & Molly Watt. 1985. write for info. (*0-318-60129-X*) Addison-Wesley.

Teaching with Logo: Building Blocks for Learning. Daniel Watt. 1986. text ed. 15.00 (*0-201-08112-1*) Addison-Wesley.

***Teaching with Love: A Feminist Approach to Early Childhood Education.** Lisa Goldstein. (Rethinking Childhood Ser.: No. 1). 200p. (C). 1997. pap. 29.95 (*0-8204-3481-7*) P Lang Pubng.

Teaching with Love & Logic: Taking Control of the Classroom. Jim Fay & David Funk. LC 95-14613. 440p. (C). 1995. 29.95 (*0-944634-29-X*, Love & Logic Pr) Cline-Fay Inst.

Teaching with Manipulatives: Middle School Investigations. Rosamond Welchman-Tischler. 120p. (J). (gr. 5-8). 1994. pap. 12.95 (*0-938587-75-7*) Cuisenaire.

Teaching with Newbery Books. Chris Broadman-Moen. 96p. (J). Date not set. pap. 12.95 (*0-590-49415-5*) Scholastic Inc.

Teaching with Power. Grant Von Harrison. (Missionary Success Ser.). 23p. 1990. pap. text ed. 2.95 (*0-685-35554-3*) Jackman Pubng.

Teaching with Quotes. Alfred De Vito. (Illus.). 162p. (Orig.). 1983. pap. 14.95 (*0-942034-01-5*) Creat Ventures IN.

Teaching with Shakespeare: Critics in the Classroom. Ed. by Bruce McIver & Ruth Stevenson. LC 92-59966. 1994. 41.50 (*0-87413-491-9*) U Delaware Pr.

Teaching with Spiritual Power. Jerry A. Wilson. 1995. pap. 10.95 (*1-57008-223-5*) Bookcraft Inc.

Teaching with Spiritual Power: The Relationship That Makes All the Difference. rev. ed. Roy B. Zuck. LC 92-39334. 1993. pap. 9.99 (*0-8254-4066-1*) Kregel.

Teaching with "Student Math Notes" Ed. by Evan M. Maletsky. (Illus.). 123p. 1987. pap. 14.50 (*0-87353-244-9*) NCTM.

Teaching with "Student Math Notes" Vol. 2. Ed. by Evan M. Maletsky. (Illus.). 128p. (Orig.). 1993. pap. text ed. 14.50 (*0-87353-369-0*) NCTM.

Teaching with Style. Bruce Wilkinson. Ed. by William M. Kruidenier. (Applied Principles of Learning Curriculum Ser.). (Illus.). 96p. 1994. teacher ed., wbk. ed. write for info. (*0-9612142-9-5*) Walk Thru the Bible.

Teaching with Style: A Practical Guide to Enhancing Learning by Understanding Teaching & Learning Styles. Anthony F. Grasha & Laurie Richlin. (Curriculum for Change Ser.: Vol. 2). 386p. 1996. 47.00 (*0-9645071-1-0*) Allnce Pub.

Teaching with Style: Observations, Reflections, & Assignments. Carole L. France. 98p. 1995. pap. text ed. 16.95 (*0-945852-05-3*) Learners Dimension.

Teaching with Technology. Desberg & Fisher. 1994. 49.00 (*0-205-16252-5*) Allyn.

Teaching with Technology. Edwards & M. D. Roblyer. 503p. (C). 1996. pap. text ed. 50.00 (*0-02-402608-5*, Macmillan Coll) P-H.

***Teaching with Technology.** Ed. by Karen Gutloff. (Teacher-to-Teacher Ser.). 96p. (Orig.). 1997. pap. 12.95 (*0-8106-2912-7*, 2912-7) NEA.

***Teaching with Technology: Creating Student-Centered Classrooms.** Judith Sandholtz et al. LC 96-34755. 1996. pap. 18.95 (*0-8077-3586-8*) Tchrs Coll.

***Teaching with Technology: Creating Student-Centered Classrooms.** Judith Sandholtz et al. LC 96-34755. 208p. (C). 1996. text ed. 42.00 (*0-8077-3587-6*) Tchrs Coll.

Teaching with Texts: Preparaing & Choosing Textual Materials. Douglas Newton. 130p. (Orig.). 1990. pap. text ed. 32.95 (*0-8464-1451-1*) Beekman Pubs.

***Teaching with the Internet: Lessons from the Classroom.** Donald J. Leu, Jr. & Deborah D. Leu. (Illus.). 214p. (Orig.). (J). (gr. k-8). 1997. teacher ed., pap. text ed. 24.95 (*0-926842-59-5*) CG Pubs Inc.

Teaching with the Internet: Putting Teachers Before Technology. Douglas R. Steen et al. (Illus.). 334p. 1995. pap. 16.95 (*0-945264-19-4*) Resolution Busn Pr.

Teaching with the Norton Anthology of American Literature: A Guide for Instructors. 4th ed. Marjorie Pryse. LC 93-48016. (C). 1994. pap. text ed. write for info. (*0-393-96463-9*) Norton.

Teaching with the Norton Anthology of World Masterpieces. 6th expanded ed. Ed. by Patricia M. Spacks et al. (C). 1995. teacher ed., pap. text ed. write for info. (*0-393-96364-0*) Norton.

Teaching with Toys: Making Your Own Educational Toys. Sally Goldberg. LC 81-16435. (Illus.). 103p. reprint ed. pap. 29.40 (*0-7837-4714-4*, 2059066) Bks Demand.

Teaching with Variety. Arlo Moehlenpah & Jane Moehlenpah. LC 90-43007. (Illus.). 184p. (Orig.). 1990. pap. 7.99 (*0-932581-67-6*) Word Aflame.

Teaching with Video: Techniques & Activities with Family Album, U. S. A. Alison M. Rice. LC 92-5414. 1992. 12.95 (*0-02-881250-6*) Macmillan.

Teaching with Writing: An Interdisciplinary Workshop Approach. Toby Fulwiler. LC 86-14732. 158p. (Orig.). 1986. pap. text ed. 21.50 (*0-86709-055-3*, 0055) Boynton Cook Pubs.

Teaching Within the Rhythms of the Semester. Donna K. Duffy & Janet W. Jones. LC 94-41810. (Higher & Adult Education Ser.). 281p. text ed. 32.95 (*0-7879-0073-7*) Jossey-Bass.

Teaching Without Tears. R. L. Bowley. 204p. 1973. pap. 17.95 (*0-8464-0909-7*) Beekman Pubs.

Teaching Without Tears: The Classroom Teachers Survival Book. rev. ed. Charles O. Preece. LC 88-80829. 124p. (C). 1988. pap. 8.95 (*0-9619349-3-X*) C O Preece.

Teaching Women: Feminism & English Studies. Ed. by Ann Thompson & Helen Wilcox. LC 88-12946. (Cultural Politics Ser.). 176p. 1989. 49.95 (*0-7190-2603-2*, Pub. by Manchester Univ Pr UK) St Martin.

Teaching Women's Literature from a Regional Perspective. Ed. by Leonore Hoffman & Deborah Rosenfelt. LC 82-211. xii, 213p. 1982. lib. bdg. 19.75 (*0-87352-334-2*, B814C) Modern Lang.

Teaching Woodwings. Dietz. LC 97-17928. 1997. 39.00 (*0-02-864569-3*, Hall Reference) Macmillan.

Teaching Word Recognition Skills. 5th rev. ed. Lee A. Rinsky. 1993. spiral bd. 29.95 (*0-89787-535-4*) Gorsuch Scarisbrick.

***Teaching Word Recognition Skills.** 6th ed. Rinsky. (C). 1997. pap. text ed. 37.33 (*0-13-776865-6*) P-H.

Teaching Word Recognition Skills. 6th ed. Lee A. Rinsky. LC 96-41592. 224p. (C). 1996. spiral bd. write for info. (*0-89787-541-9*) Gorsuch Scarisbrick.

Teaching Workplace Skills: Creative Ways to Teach Students the Skills Employers Want. Linda Koffel. LC 93-44413. 304p. 1994. 27.50 (*0-88415-076-3*) Gulf Pub.

Teaching World History: A Resource Book. Ed. by Heidi Roupp. LC 96-23391. (Sources & Studies in World History Ser.). 288p. (C). (gr. 13). 1996. text ed. 62.95 (*1-56324-419-5*) M E Sharpe.

Teaching World History: A Resource Book. Ed. by Heidi Roupp. LC 96-23391. (Sources & Studies in World History Ser.). 288p. (C). (gr. 13). 1996. pap. text ed. 29.95 (*1-56324-420-9*) M E Sharpe.

Teaching World Studies: An Introduction to Global Perspectives in the Curriculum. Ed. by David Hicks & Charles Townley. LC 81-20750. (Illus.). 230p. reprint ed. pap. 65.60 (*0-8357-6587-3*, 2035982) Bks Demand.

Teaching Worlds. Strang. 1993. 30.00 (*0-205-13818-7*) P-H.

Teaching Writing: A Systematic Approach. Colin Peacock. 160p. (Orig.). 1986. pap. 19.95 (*0-7099-4028-9*, Pub. by Croom Helm UK) Routledge Chapman & Hall.

Teaching Writing: A Workshop Approach. Adele Fiderer. 112p. 1993. pap. 14.95 (*0-590-49202-0*) Scholastic Inc.

Teaching Writing: Balancing Process & Product. 2nd ed. Gail E. Tompkins. 448p. (C). 1993. pap. text ed. 36.00 (*0-02-420843-4*, Macmillan Coll) P-H.

Teaching Writing: Integrating Theories. George Hillocks, Jr. (Language & Literacy Ser.). 264p. (C). 1995. text ed. 41.00 (*0-8077-3434-9*); pap. text ed. 18.95 (*0-8077-3433-0*) Tchrs Coll.

Teaching Writing: Pedagogy, Gender, & Equity. Ed. by Cynthia Caywood & Gillian R. Overing. LC 86-14520. 238p. 1986. pap. text ed. 24.95 (*0-88706-353-5*) State U NY Pr.

Teaching Writing: Pedagogy, Gender, & Equity. Ed. by Cynthia Caywood & Gillian R. Overing. LC 86-14520. 238p. 1986. text ed. 67.50 (*0-88706-352-7*) State U NY Pr.

Teaching Writing As a Second Language. Alice S. Horning. LC 86-13043. (Studies in Writing & Rhetoric). 99p. (Orig.). 1986. pap. text ed. 12.95 (*0-8093-1327-8*) S Ill U Pr.

Teaching Writing As Thinking. Florence F. Pritchard. 395p. (C). 1994. pap. text ed. 34.95 (*0-9636011-4-8*) Shore Educ.

Teaching-Writing-As-Thinking Strategy Masters: Reproducible Handouts to Guide the Thinking - Writing Process in Grades 4-14. Florence F. Pritchard. 68p. (Orig.). (C). 1994. student ed. 19.95 (*0-9636011-1-3*) Shore Educ.

Teaching Writing in All Disciplines. Ed. by C. Williams Griffin. LC 81-48585. (New Directions for Teaching & Learning Ser.: No. TL 12). 1982. 19.00 (*0-87589-926-9*) Jossey-Bass.

Teaching Writing in the Content Areas: Elementary School. Stephen N. Tchudi & Susan J. Tchudi. 64p. 1983. pap. 8.95 (*0-8106-0776-X*) NEA.

Teaching Writing in the Content Areas: Middle School-Junior High School. Stephen N. Tchudi & Margie C. Huerta. 64p. 1983. pap. 8.95 (*0-8106-0777-8*) NEA.

Teaching Writing in the Content Areas: Senior High School. Stephen N. Tchudi & Joanne M. Yates. 80p. 1983. pap. 9.95 (*0-8106-0778-6*) NEA.

Teaching Writing Manual. rev. ed. Evelyn Rothstein & Diane Gess. (Illus.). 170p. 1987. pap. text ed. 17.95 (*0-913935-39-5*) ERA-CCR.

Teaching Writing Mechanics with Concept Attainment: A Guide for Teaching Grammar, Punctuation, Spelling & Capitalization. Florence F. Pritchard. 101p. (Orig.). (C). 1994. pap. text ed. 19.95 (*0-9636011-2-1*) Shore Educ.

Teaching Writing Skills. Ed. by Christine J. Dillon. (Illus.). 35p. 1993. pap. text ed. 4.95 (*0-913717-24-X*) Hewitt Res Fnd.

Teaching Writing Skills: A Global Approach. rev. ed. John Benegar. (Illus.). 189p. (Orig.). (gr. 6-12). 1987. pap. 26.95 (*0-943804-31-0*) U of Denver Teach.

Teaching Writing That Works. Macklin Smith & Eric S. Rabkin. LC 90-39360. 224p. (C). 1990. pap. text ed. 16.95 (*0-472-06443-6*) U of Mich Pr.

Teaching Writing to Adults. NYS Ed. Dept. Staff. 1990. text ed. 175.00 (*0-8273-4510-0*) S-W Pub.

Teaching Writing to Adults: Strategies & Concepts for Improving Learner Performance. Robert F. Sommer. LC 89-45603. (Higher & Adult Education-Management Ser.). 276p. text ed. 34.95 (*1-55542-172-5*) Jossey-Bass.

Teaching Written Expression: The Phelps Sentence Guide Program. Tricia Phelps & Diana Phelps-Terasaki. 112p. 1980. pap. text ed. 15.00 (*0-87879-248-1*); 10.00 (*0-87879-290-2*) Acad Therapy.

Teaching You about Animals with Stories That Rhyme. Story Rhyme Staff. (Illus.). 22p. 1996. ring bd. 7.95 (*1-56820-152-4*) Story Time.

Teaching You about Bartering with Stories That Rhyme. Story Rhyme Staff. (Illus.). 21p. 1996. ring bd. 7.95 (*1-56820-153-2*) Story Time.

Teaching You about Butterflies with Stories That Rhyme. Story Rhyme Staff. (Illus.). 26p. 1996. ring bd. 7.95 (*1-56820-147-8*) Story Time.

Teaching You about Fish with Stories That Rhyme. Story Rhyme Staff. (Illus.). 32p. 1996. ring bd. 7.95 (*1-56820-146-X*) Story Time.

Teaching You about Mushrooms with Stories That Rhyme. Story Rhyme Staff. (Illus.). 21p. 1996. ring bd. 7.95 (*1-56820-145-1*) Story Time.

***Teaching You about Plants, Animals, Science & More with Stories That Rhyme.** A. Doyle. (Illus.). 65p. (Orig.). (YA). (gr. 4-10). 1997. ring bd. 25.95 (*1-56820-188-5*) Story Time.

Teaching You about Recycling with Stories That Rhyme. Story Rhyme Staff. (Illus.). 32p. 1996. ring bd. 7.95 (*1-56820-151-6*) Story Time.

Teaching You about Sea Shells w. h Stories That Rhyme. Story Rhyme Staff. (Illus.). 26p. 1996. ring bd. 7.95 (*1-56820-144-3*) Story Time.

Teaching You about Weather with Stories That Rhyme. Story Rhyme Staff. (Illus.). 20p. 1996. ring bd. 7.95 (*1-56820-148-6*) Story Time.

Teaching You Black History with Stories That Rhyme. Story Rhyme Staff. (Illus.). 22p. 1996. ring bd. 7.95 (*1-56820-149-4*) Story Time.

Teaching You Science with Stories That Rhyme. Story Rhyme Staff. (Illus.). 35p. 1996. ring bd. 7.95 (*1-56820-150-8*) Story Time.

Teaching Young Adult Literature: Sharing the Connection. Jean E. Brown & Elaine C. Stephens. LC 94-35183. 320p. 1995. text ed. 27.95 (*0-534-19938-0*) Wadsworth Pub.

Teaching Young Children: A Guide for the Beginning Teacher. Dianne Jurek. 192p. (J). pap. 15.99 (*0-86653-911-5*, FE0911) Fearon Teach Aids.

Teaching Young Children: Infancy to Grade 3. Suzanne L. Krogh. 1993. teacher ed., pap. text ed. write for info. (*0-07-035709-9*) McGraw.

Teaching Young Children Effective Listening Skills. Charlotte G. Garman & J. Frederick Garman. 20p. 1992. 2.95 (*1-56456-072-4*, 271) W Gladden Found.

Teaching Young Children in Violent Times: Building a Peaceable Classroom. Diane Levin. 194p. 1996. per., pap. text ed. 16.95 (*0-7872-2220-8*) Kendall-Hunt.

Teaching Young Children in Violent Times: Building a Peaceable Classroom Environment. Diane E. Levin. (Illus.). 176p. 1994. pap. 16.95 (*0-86571-316-2*); lib. bdg. 44.95 (*0-86571-315-4*) New Soc Pubs.

Teaching Young Children Through Their Individual Learning Styles: Practical Approaches for Grades K-2. Rita S. Dunn et al. LC 93-13944. 1993. text ed. 55.50 (*0-205-15271-6*, H52715, Longwood Div) Allyn.

Teaching Young Children to Care: Thirty-Seven Activities for Developing Concern for Others. Dorothy A. Dixon. LC 90-70417. (Illus.). 88p. (Orig.). (J). (gr. k-3). 1990. pap. 9.95 (*0-89622-437-6*) Twenty-Third.

Teaching Young Children to Care: Thirty-Seven Activities for Developing Self-Esteem. Dorothy A. Dixon. LC 90-70418. 88p. (Orig.). (J). (gr. k-3). 1990. pap. 9.95 (*0-89622-436-8*) Twenty-Third.

***Teaching Young Children to Read.** rev. ed. Wood Smethurst. 192p. 1997. pap. 16.95 (*1-57129-048-6*) Brookline Bks.

Teaching Young Children Using Themes, Ages 2-6. Marjorie J. Kostelnik et al. 1991. pap. 29.95 (*0-673-46057-6*, GoodYrBooks) Addson-Wesley Educ.

Teaching Young Children with Behavioral Disorders. Mary K. Zabel. 23p. 1991. pap. text ed. 9.75 (*0-86586-200-1*, P341) Coun Exc Child.

Teaching Young Dancers: Muscular Coordination in Classical Ballet. Joan Lawson. LC 75-15369. (Illus.). 1975. 19.95 (*0-87830-144-5*, Thtre Arts Bks) Routledge.

***Teaching Young Gifted Children in the Regular Classroom: Identifying, Nurturing, & Challenging Ages 4-9.** Joan F. Smutny et al. LC 96-46737. 272p. (Orig.). 1997. pap. 29.95 (*1-57542-017-1*) Free Spirit Pub.

Teaching Young Playwrights. Gerald Chapman. Ed. by Lisa Barnett. LC 90-44760. 129p. (Orig.). 1990. pap. 15.95 (*0-435-08212-4*, 08212) Heinemann.

***Teaching Your Child Creativity: A Playskool Guide.** Child Development Experts of Playskool. 220p. (Orig.). 1997. pap. 14.95 (*0-89526-434-X*) Regnery Pub.

Teaching Your Child God's Love for the World Vol. 1: A Social Studies/Mission Unit Study Guide. Ed. by Karen Randau. (Illus.). 160p. 1996. ring bd. 29.99 (*0-939989-00-X*) Food for Hungry Inc.

***Teaching Your Child How to Pray.** Rick Osborne. 1997. pap. 10.99 (*0-8024-8489-1*) Moody.

Teaching Your Child Responsibility. Diane T. Rubins. (For Parents Only Ser.). 16p. 1994. 1.95 (*1-56688-192-7*) Bur For At-Risk.

Teaching Your Child the Language of Social Success. Marshall Duke et al. 192p. (Orig.). 1996. pap. 14.95 (*1-56145-126-6*) Peachtree Pubs.

Teaching Your Child the Value of Friendship. Diane T. Rubins. (For Parents Only Ser.). 16p. 1994. 1.95 (*1-56688-194-3*) Bur For At-Risk.

Teaching Your Child to Appreciate Diversity. Diane T. Rubins. (For Parents Only Ser.). 16p. 1994. 1.95 (*1-56688-195-1*) Bur For At-Risk.

Teaching Your Child to Be Home Alone. Earl A. Grollman & Gerri L. Sweder. 132p. pap. 12.95 (*0-02-912751-3*, Free Press) Free Pr.

Teaching Your Child to Listen. 1979. 6.00 (*0-939418-19-3*) Ferguson-Florissant.

Teaching Your Child to Make Smart Choices. Barbara S. Fritz. (For Parents Only Ser.). 16p. 1994. 1.95 (*1-56688-191-9*) Bur For At-Risk.

Teaching Your Child to Read. 1980. 4.00 (*0-939418-13-4*) Ferguson-Florissant.

Teaching Your Child to Read. Ann Fusco & Anne Russo. (Illus.). 116p. (Orig.). 1982. pap. 12.00 (*0-9607368-0-8*) Leprechaun Pr.

Teaching Your Child to Read for the Fun of It. Patricia C. Beall. LC 88-82067. (Illus.). 105p. (Orig.). 1989. pap. 10.95 (*0-9621138-0-8*) Hand Pub.

***Teaching Your Child to Write: How Parents Can Encourage Writing Skills for Success in School, Work, & Life.** Cheri Fuller. 192p. 1997. pap. 12.00 (*0-425-15983-3*, Berkley Trade) Berkley Pub.

Teaching Your Children about God. David J. Wolpe. 1994. pap. 12.00 (*0-06-097647-0*, HarpT) HarpC.

***Teaching Your Children Christian Values.** (On Main Street Ser.). 64p. 1996. 49.99 incl. vhs (*0-570-09620-0*, 20-2843) Concordia.

Teaching Your Children Joy. Linda Eyre. 224p. 1994. pap. 11.00 (*0-671-88725-4*) S&S Trade.

***Teaching Your Children Life Skills.** Deborah Carroll. (Orig.). 1997. pap. 12.00 (*0-614-28118-0*) Berkley Pub.

***Teaching Your Children Life Skills: (While Having a Life of Your Own)** Deborah Carroll. 176p. 1997. pap. 12.00 (*0-425-15303-7*, Berkley Trade) Berkley Pub.

Teaching Your Children Responsibility. Linda Eyre & Richard Eyre. 256p. 1994. pap. 11.00 (*0-671-88716-5*, Fireside) S&S Trade.

Teaching Your Children to Read Using the Book of Mormon. Grant Von Harrison. (Illus.). 412p. 1994. 24.95 (*1-56509-070-5*) Grandin Bk Co.

Teaching Your Children to Tell Themselves the Truth: Helping Children Before Misbeliefs Become Deeply Entrenched. William Backus & Candace Backus. 176p. (Orig.). 1992. pap. 8.99 (*1-55661-279-6*) Bethany Hse.

Teaching Your Children Values. Linda Eyre & Richard Eyre. 256p. (Orig.). 1993. pap. 11.00 (*0-671-76966-9*, Fireside) S&S Trade.

Teaching Your Down's Syndrome Infant see **Teaching the Infant with Down Syndrome: A Guide for Parents & Professionals**

Teaching Your Horse Tricks (for Fun & Profit) Jonnie Stinson. Ed. by Roy A. Gregory. (Illus.). 1978. 15.00 (*0-9620709-0-4*) Blue Bonnet.

Teaching Your Kids the Truth about Consequences: Helping Them Make the Connection Between Choices & Results. Daniel Hahn. LC 95-25840. 256p. (Orig.). 1995. pap. 9.99 (*1-55661-680-5*) Bethany Hse.

Teaching Your Kids to Care: How to Discover & Develop the Spirit of Charity in Your Children. Deborah Spaide. (Illus.). 304p. 1995. pap. 9.95 (0-8065-1637-2, Citadel Pr) Carol Pub Group.

Teaching Your Occupation to Others. Bott. 1987. pap. text ed. 27.50 (0-13-894023-1) P-H.

Teaching Your Occupation to Others: A Guide to Surviving the First Year. Paul A. Bott. 1986. pap. text ed. 9.95 (0-935920-40-4, Ntl Pubs Blck) P-H.

*Teaching Your Occupation to Others: A Guide to Surviving the First Year. 2nd ed. Paul A. Bott. LC 97-1295. 1997. 34.00 (0-205-27101-4) Allyn.

Teaching Youth. Larry Richards. 156p. 1982. pap. 7.99 (0-8341-0776-7) Beacon Hill.

Teaching Youth about Conflict & War. William A. Nesbitt & Norman Abramowitz. Ed. by Charles Bloomstein. LC 73-75291. (Teaching Social Studies in an Age of Crisis: No. 5). 112p. reprint ed. pap. 32.00 (0-317-08320-1, 2005099) Bks Demand.

Teaching Youth with Confidence. 32p. 1983. teacher ed. 4.50 (0-910566-42-9) Evang Trg Assn.

Teaching Youth with Confidence. Bill Bynum. 48p. 1983. pap. 4.25 (0-910566-41-0) Evang Trg Assn.

Teaching 10 to 14 Year Olds. 2nd ed. Christopher Stevenson. (C). 1998. pap. text ed. write for info. (0-8013-1582-4) Addison-Wesley.

*Teaching/Learning Anti-Racism: A Developmental Approach. Carol B. Phillips & Louise Derman-Sparks. LC 97-18761. 342p. (Orig.). 1997. pap. 17.95 (0-8077-3637-6) Tchrs Coll.

*Teaching/Learning Anti-Racism: A Developmental Approach. Carol B. Phillips & Louise Derman-Sparks. LC 97-18761. 342p. 1997. 40.00 (0-8077-3638-4) Tchrs Coll.

Teaching/Learning Enterprise: Miami-Dade Community College's Blueprint for Change. Vincent Napoli & Mardee S. Jenrette. 216p. (C). 1994. text ed. 31.95 (0-9627042-8-8) Anker Pub.

Teachings. David Fisher. (Illus.). 40p. pap. 4.95 (0-918510-01-5); lib. bdg. 9.95 (0-918510-02-3) Monday Bks.

Teachings. deluxe ed. David Fisher. (Illus.). 40p. 10.95 (0-686-96877-8) Monday Bks.

Teachings: Drawn from African-American Spirituals. Aminah B. Robinson. LC 92-18614. 1992. pap. 12.95 (0-15-688247-7) HarBrace.

Teachings Around the Sacred Wheel. Lynn A. Andrews. LC 89-45524. 156p. 1989. pap. 13.00 (0-06-250022-8) Harper SF.

Teachings for the Fourth Density Aquarian, 4 vols. Chief Little Summer & Warm Night Rain. (Illus.). (Orig.). 1991. Set. pap. write for info. (1-880440-00-8) Piqua Pr.

Teachings for the Fourth Density Aquarian, Vol. 1. Chief Little Summer & Warm Night Rain. (Illus.). 320p. (Orig.). 1991. 17.95 (1-880440-01-6) Piqua Pr.

Teachings for the Fourth Density Aquarian, Vol. 2: The Teachings. Chief Little Summer & Warm Night Rain. (Illus.). 440p. (Orig.). 1992. 18.95 (1-880440-04-0) Piqua Pr.

Teachings from the American Earth: Indian Religion & Philosophy. Ed. by Dennis Tedlock & Barbara Tedlock. 304p. 1992. pap. 11.95 (0-87140-146-0) Liveright.

Teachings from the Angelic Messenger Cards. Meredith L. Young-Sowers. (Illus.). 288p. 1996. 18.95 (1-883478-05-7) Stillpoint.

*Teachings from the Wordly Philosophy. Robert Heilbroner. 368p. (Orig.). 1997. pap. 14.95 (0-393-31607-6) Norton.

Teachings from the Worldly Philosophy. Robert Heilbroner. LC 95-37470. 352p. 1996. 27.50 (0-393-03919-6) Norton.

Teaching's Next Generation. Recruiting New Teachers, Inc. Staff. (Illus.). 160p. 1993. 9.95 (1-884139-01-9) Recruit New Tchrs.

Teachings of a Buddhist Monk. Ajahn Sumedho. 96p. 1995. pap. 10.95 (0-946672-23-7, Pub. by Buddhist Pub UK) Assoc Pubs Grp.

Teachings of Bhagavad Gita. Laxmi N. Chaturvedi. (Religion & Philosophy Ser.). 383p. 1991. 19.95 (81-207-1272-2) L N Chaturvedi.

Teachings of Both Bible & Holy Qur'an As Taught by, The Most Honorable Elijah Muhammad Messenger of Allah (God) Master Fard Muhammad, Bk. I. Ed. by Atiyah Majied. (Illus.). 359p. 1995. pap. 15.95 (1-56411-078-8) Untd Bros & Sis.

Teachings of Carl Schmitts. Meier. 1997. 29.95 (0-226-51890-6) U Ch Pr.

Teachings of Christian Science. John H. Gerstner. 32p. (gr. 10). 1978. pap. 3.99 (0-8010-3717-4) Baker Bks.

Teachings of Dante. Charles A. Dinsmore. (Select Bibliographies Reprint Ser.). 1977. 19.95 (0-8369-5521-8) Ayer.

Teachings of Don Carlos: Practical Applications of the Works of Carlos Castaneda. Victor Sanchez. Tr. by Robert Nelson from SPA. 276p. 1995. pap. 12.95 (1-879181-23-1) Bear & Co.

Teachings of Don Juan. Carlos Castaneda. 1990. pap. 14.00 (0-671-72791-5, WSP) PB.

Teachings of Don Juan: A Yaqui Way of Knowledge. Carlos Castaneda. LC 68-17303. 1968. 35.00 (0-520-00217-2); pap. 14.95 (0-520-02258-0) U CA Pr.

Teachings of Don Von: A Turnkey Way of Knowledge. Tom Abellera. LC 92-96956. (Illus.). 211p. (Orig.). 1992. pap. write for info. (0-9633942-0-7) Stochos Bks.

Teachings of Don Von: A Turnkey Way of Knowledge. Tom Abellera. (Illus.). 244p. (Orig.). 1994. write for info. (0-9633942-1-5) Stochos Bks.

Teachings of Ezra Taft Benson. Ezra T. Benson. 1988. 18.95 (0-88494-639-8) Bookcraft Inc.

Teachings of George Albert Smith. Robert McIntosh & Susan McIntosh. 1996. 14.95 (1-57008-235-9) Bookcraft Inc.

Teachings of Grandfather Fox. Leonard Nathan. LC 76-57990. 49p. 1976. 3.50 (0-87886-079-7, Greenfld Rev Pr) Greenfld Rev Lit.

Teachings of Gurdjieff: A Pupil's Journey. C. S. Nott. (Illus.). 248p. 1991. pap. 10.95 (0-14-019156-9, Arkana) Viking Penguin.

Teachings of H. Verlan Andersen. Hans V. Andersen, Jr. LC 95-70913. 450p. 1996. text ed. 29.95 (0-9644552-2-6) SunRise Pbl.

Teachings of Hafiz. Gertrude Bell. 1979. 18.00 (0-900860-63-4, Pub. by Octagon Pr UK) ISHK.

Teachings of Harold B. Lee. Clyde Williams. 1996. 24.95 (1-57008-234-0) Bookcraft Inc.

Teachings of Hasidism. Joseph Dan. 1983. pap. text ed. 14.95 (0-87441-223-4) Behrman.

*Teachings of Howard W. Hunter. Clyde Williams. 1997. 15.95 (0-614-30574-8) Bookcraft Inc.

Teachings of Islam. Ahmad Hazrat. 1987. pap. 3.95 (0-913321-34-6) Ahmadiyya Anjuman.

Teachings of Islam (Tablighi Nisab) M. Zakeriyya. 1987. 19.95 (0-933511-09-4) Kazi Pubns.

Teachings of Jehovah's Witnesses. John H. Gerstner. 32p. (gr. 10). 1978. pap. 3.99 (0-8010-3718-2) Baker Bks.

Teachings of Jesus: A Dialogue Between an Indian Mystic & a Group of Christian Fundamentalists. Ed. by David C. Lane. (Jewels of India Ser.). 50p. 1992. pap. 2.00 (1-56543-005-0) Mt SA Coll Philos.

Teachings of Jesus in John: New International Version Bible Scripture Quotes. (Teachings of Jesus Picture Bks.). (Illus.). 64p. 1994. 15.99 (1-56476-255-6, 6-3255, Victor Bks) Chariot Victor.

Teachings of Jesus in Luke: New International Version Bible Scripture Quotes. (Teachings of Jesus Picture Bks.). (Illus.). 64p. 1994. 15.99 (1-56476-254-8, 6-3254, Victor Bks) Chariot Victor.

Teachings of Jesus in Matthew: New International Version Bible Scripture Quotes. (Teachings of Jesus Picture Bks.). (Illus.). 64p. 1994. 15.99 (1-56476-253-X, 6-3253, Victor Bks) Chariot Victor.

*Teachings of Joseph Smith. Larry E. Dahl & Donald Q. Cannon. 1997. 27.95 (1-57008-311-8) Bookcraft Inc.

Teachings of Kirpal Singh, 3 vols. in 1. 2nd ed. Kirpal Singh. (Illus.). 480p. (C). 1989. reprint ed. pap. 11.00 (0-942735-33-1) Ruhani Satsang.

Teachings of Kirpal Singh: Three Volumes Complete in One Book. 2nd ed. Kirpal Singh. LC 81-51513. (Illus.). 506p. (Orig.). 1982. pap. 13.00 (0-918224-13-6) S K Pubns.

Teachings of Lord Caitanya. Bhaktivedanta S. Prabhupada. 1990. 17.95 (0-912776-07-2) Bhaktivedanta.

*Teachings of Lord Caitanya. Bhaktivedanta S. Prabhupada. (Illus.). 440p. 19.95 (0-902677-01-2) Bhaktivedanta.

*Teachings of Lorenzo Snow: Collector's Edition. Clyde Williams. 1996. 13.95 (1-57008-288-X) Bookcraft Inc.

Teachings of Maimonides. Jacob S. Minkin. LC 87-70737. 448p. 1997. pap. 24.95 (1-56821-039-6) Aronson.

Teachings of Michio Kushi. Michio Kushi. (Illus.). 160p. (Orig.). 1993. pap. 12.95 (0-9628528-9-9) One Peaceful World.

Teachings of Mormonism. John H. Gerstner. 32p. (gr. 10). 1978. pap. 3.99 (0-8010-3719-0) Baker Bks.

*Teachings of Mother Wit. Henry J. Carter. LC 96-92386. (Illus.). 98p. (Orig.). 1996. pap. 14.00 (0-7880-0691-6) CSS OH.

Teachings of Nature. Adolf Hungry Wolf. (Illus.). 94p. 1992. pap. 8.95 (0-913990-75-2) Book Pub Co.

Teachings of Nature in the Kingdom of Grace. Charles H. Spurgeon. 1976. mass mkt. 8.00 (1-56186-323-8) Pilgrim Pubns.

Teachings of Oscar Camille, 2 vols., Vol. 1. Paul E. Napora. LC 96-8154. 160p. 1996. pap. 12.95 (0-931892-36-8) B Dolphin Pub.

Teachings of Oscar Camille, 2 vols., Vol. 2. Paul E. Napora. LC 96-8154. 144p. 1996. pap. 12.95 (0-931892-37-6) B Dolphin Pub.

Teachings of Oscar Camille, Vols. 1 & 2. Paul E. Napora. Ed. by Gwen Costa. LC 91-32254. 1992. 21.95 (0-87949-354-2); 21.95 (0-87949-362-3) Ashley Bks.

*Teachings of Our Prophet: A Selection of Ahadith for Children. 2nd ed. Abidullah Ghazi & Tasneema Ghazi. 84p. (J). (gr. 1-3). 1991. reprint ed. pap. text ed. 6.00 (1-56316-159-1) Iqra Intl Ed Fdtn.

Teachings of Padmasambhava. Herbert Guenther. LC 96-18308. (Indological Library). 255p. 1996. 77.00 (90-04-10542-5) E J Brill.

Teachings of "Pastor" Russell. 68p. 1988. reprint ed. pap. 2.95 (1-883858-42-9) Witness CA.

Teachings of Patriots & Statesmen: Or, the 'Founders of the Republic' on Slavery. Ezra B. Chase. LC 72-83941. (Black Heritage Library Collection). 1977. 24.95 (0-8369-8535-4) Ayer.

Teachings of Ramana Maharshi. 2nd rev. ed. Ed. by Arthur Osborne. 208p. 1996. reprint ed. pap. 12.95 (0-87728-897-6) Weiser.

Teachings of Rizal see Filipinos Fight for Freedom

*Teachings of Rumi. Jalal A. Rumi. Tr. by E. H. Whinfield. 330p. 1996. 39.95 (0-614-21370-3, 1223) Kazi Pubns.

Teachings of Rumi: The Masnaui. Jalaludin Rumi. Tr. by E. H. Whinfield. 1994. pap. 15.00 (0-86304-067-5, Pub. by Octagon Pr UK) ISHK.

*Teachings of Sathya Sai Baba. Sai B. Sathya. Date not set. pap. 2.00 (0-614-19091-6, BW-195) Sathya Sai Bk Ctr.

Teachings of Seventh-Day Adventism. John H. Gerstner. 30p. (gr. 10). 1978. pap. 3.99 (0-8010-3720-4) Baker Bks.

Teachings of Spencer W. Kimball. Edward L. Kimball. 1962. 17.95 (0-88494-472-7) Bookcraft Inc.

Teachings of Sri Ramakrishna. Sri Ramakrishna. 344p. (C). 1934. pap. 4.95 (0-87481-133-3, Pub. by Advaita Ashrama II) Vedanta Pr.

Teachings of Sri Sarada Devi: The Holy Mother. Sarada Devi. 175p. 1996. pap. 4.95 (81-7120-624-7, Pub. by Ramakrishna Math II) Vedanta Pr.

Teachings of Sri Satya Sai Baba. Ed. by Roy E. Davis. 3.95 (0-87707-232-9) CSA Pr.

Teachings of St. John Cassian. John Cassian. pap. 5.95 (0-89981-102-7) Eastern Orthodox.

Teachings of Swami Vivekananda. Swami Vivekananda. 298p. (C). 1971. pap. 4.95 (0-87481-134-1, Pub. by Advaita Ashrama II) Vedanta Pr.

Teachings of Taoist Master Chuang. Michael R. Saso. LC 76-58919. (Illus.). 331p. reprint ed. pap. 94.40 (0-8357-8342-1, 2033880) Bks Demand.

Teachings of the Angel of North America Bk. 1: How to Save Your Soul & Your Society. Patricia A. Meyer. 160p. 1996. pap. 10.95 (0-9646601-0-5) Oaklea Pr.

Teachings of the Buddha. Ed. by Jack Kornfield & Gil Fronsdal. LC 92-56457. (Orig.). (C). 1993. pap. 6.00 (0-87773-860-2, Sham Pocket Class) Shambhala Pubns.

Teachings of the Buddha. expanded rev. ed. Ed. by Jack Kornfield & Gil Fronsdal. LC 95-17227. 160p. (Orig.). 1996. pap. 12.00 (1-57062-124-1) Shambhala Pubns.

*Teachings of the Christian Mystics. Andrew Harvey. LC 97-22297. 1998. pap. 10.00 (1-57062-343-0) Shambhala Pubns.

Teachings of the Compassionate Buddha. Ed. by Edwin A. Burtt. (Orig.). 1955. pap. 6.99 (0-451-62711-3, Ment) NAL-Dutton.

Teachings of the Essenes. Edmond B. Szekely. 174p. 1978. pap. 7.00 (0-85207-141-8, Pub. by C W Daniel UK) Natl Bk Netwk.

Teachings of the Essenes from Enoch to the Dead Sea Scrolls. Tr. by Edmond Szekely. (Illus.). 96p. pap. 10.95 (0-8464-4298-1) Beekman Pubs.

Teachings of the Essenes from Enoch to the Dead Sea Scrolls. Edmond B. Szekely. (Illus.). 112p. 1981. pap. 5.95 (0-89564-006-6) IBS Intl.

Teachings of the Fathers of the Musar Movement. Lester Eckman. LC 86-63759. 194p. 1990. 18.95 (0-88400-139-3) Shengold.

Teachings of the Great Mystics. Karl Pruter. LC 85-13306. 118p. 1985. reprint ed. pap. 17.00 (0-912134-00-3); reprint ed. lib. bdg. 27.00 (0-89370-595-0) Borgo Pr.

Teachings of the Jewish Sages: A New Rendering of Ancient Rabbinic Wisdom. Rami M. Shapiro. LC 94-20922. 1995. 16.00 (0-517-79966-9, Bell Tower) Crown Pub Group.

Teachings of the Masters. R. Swinburne Clymer. 256p. 1952. 8.95 (0-932785-46-8) Philos Pub.

Teachings of the Prophet Joseph Smith. Joseph F. Smith. LC 90-220999. 437p. 1989. pap. 12.95 (0-87579-243-X) Deseret Bk.

*Teachings of the Qur'an Vol. 2: Islamic Morals & Manners. unabridged ed. Abidullah Ghazi & Tasneema Ghazi. Ed. by Noura Durkee & Khwaja M. Hassan. LC 92-248962. 94p. (Orig.). (J). (gr. 4-6). 1995. pap. text ed. 9.00 (1-56316-104-4) Iqra Intl Ed Fdtn.

*Teachings of the Qur'an Vol. 3: Human Community, Muslim Community, & Social Action. unabridged ed. Abidullah Ghazi & Tasneema Ghazi. Ed. by Suhaib Ghazi. LC 92-248962. 79p. (J). (gr. 3-8). 1996. pap. text ed. 8.00 (1-56316-113-3) Iqra Intl Ed Fdtn.

*Teachings of the Qur'an Workbook Vol. 1: Islam, the Qur'an, 'Iman, & Arkan. unabridged ed. Tasneema Ghazi. Ed. by Fadel Abdallah. (Illus.). 95p. (Orig.). (J). (gr. 1-3). 1995. pap. 6.00 (1-56316-111-7) Iqra Intl Ed Fdtn.

*Teachings of the Tao: Readings from the Taoist Spiritual Tradition. Tr. & Selected by Eva Wong. LC 96-9728. (Illus.). 176p. (Orig.). 1997. pap. 10.00 (1-57062-245-0) Shambhala Pubns.

Teachings of the Temple, 3 vols. Ed. by Temple of the People Publications Staff. 1985. 30.00 (0-933797-08-7) Halcyon Bk.

Teachings of the Temple, 3 vols., Vol. 1. Ed. by Temple of the People Publications Staff. 661p. 1985. 14.00 (0-933797-03-6) Halcyon Bk.

Teachings of the Temple, 3 vols., Vol. 2. Ed. by Temple of the People Publications Staff. 400p. 1985. 14.00 (0-933797-04-4) Halcyon Bk.

Teachings of the Temple, 3 vols., Vol. 3. Ed. by Temple of the People Publications Staff. 400p. 1985. 14.00 (0-933797-05-2) Halcyon Bk.

*Teachings of the Winged Disk. Phaedron Stone. (Illus.). 224p. (Orig.). 1997. pap. 14.95 (0-9637498-3-8, Belfry) Toad Hall PA.

Teachings of Tibetan Yoga. Garma C. Chang. 128p. 1974. reprint ed. pap. 3.45 (0-8065-0460-9, Citadel Pr) Carol Pub Group.

Teachings of Tibetan Yoga: An Introduction to the Spiritual, Mental, & Physical Exercises of the Tibetan Religion. annot. ed. Tr. & Anno. by Garma C. Chang. 128p. 1993. pap. 9.95 (0-8065-1453-1, Citadel Pr) Carol Pub Group.

*Teachings of Yoga. George Feuerstein. LC 97-7507. 1997. pap. 12.00 (1-57062-318-X) Shambhala Pubns.

*Teachings of Zen. Thomas Cleary. LC 97-23349. 1998. pap. 10.00 (1-57062-338-4) Shambhala Pubns.

Teachings on Living Things & Protection Dolls. Naomi Albright. 80p. 1992. spiral bd. 16.95 (1-882218-05-1) Blue Star Pubs.

Teachings on Love. Thich Nhat Hanh. Tr. by Mobi Warren from VIE. LC 97-153. 128p. (Orig.). 1997. 18.00 (0-938077-96-1) Parallax Pr.

Teachings on the Nature of Mind. Ole Nydahl. (Illus.). 40p. (Orig.). 1993. pap. 5.00 (0-931892-58-9) B Dolphin Pub.

Teachings Styles & Learning. D. Solomon et al. 1963. 2.50 (0-87060-035-4, REP 127) Syracuse U Cont Ed.

Teacup Full of Roses. Sharin B. Mathis. Date not set. pap. 1.75 (0-590-03178-3) Scholastic Inc.

Teacup Full of Roses. Sharon B. Mathis. (Novels Ser.). (J). (gr. 7). 1987. pap. 4.99 (0-14-032328-7, Puffin) Puffin Bks.

Teacup Tales: Folklore of the Hudson Valley. Pauline Hommell. 99p. 1992. reprint ed. pap. 11.95 (0-910746-99-0, TT01) Hope Farm.

Teagle of Jersey Standard. Bennett H. Wall & George S. Gibb. LC 73-94124. (Center for Business History Studies). 1974. 12.00 (0-686-11154-0) Tulane Univ.

Teahouse of the August Moon. adapted ed. Vern Sneider. 1957. pap. 5.25 (0-8222-1114-9) Dramatists Play.

Teak see Novella Box

*Teakwood Cross. Harry Mileaf. 1996. mass mkt. 5.99 (1-55197-028-7, Pub. by Comnwlth Pub CN) Partners Pubs Grp.

Teakwood Decks. Chris A. Barker. (Illus.). 775p. 15.00 (0-9609382-1-4) Susquehanna.

Tealeaf Oracles. Maureen Freer. 68p. (C). 1990. pap. 30.00 (0-908175-38-8, Pub. by Boolarong Pubns AT) St Mut.

Team: On & Off the Set. Joy D. Cain. 96p. (J). 1993. pap. 3.50 (0-553-56455-2) Bantam.

Team see Phonics Is My Way Series

Team Approach to Audiologic Assessment: A Module for Training Personnel Serving Families of Deaf & Hard of Hearing Infants & Young Children. Ed. by Valerie Schuyler. (Early Intervention Ser.). 48p. (C). 1993. ring bd. 89.00 incl. vhs (0-9618297-9-6) Infant Hearing Resc.

Team Architecture: The Manager's Guide to Designing Effective Work Teams. Francis L. Ulschak & Sharon M. Snowantle. LC 94-44916. 178p. 1995. pap. 30.00 (1-56793-023-9, 0953) Health Admin Pr.

Team Barriers: Actions for Overcoming the Barriers to Empowerment, Involvement, & High-Performance. Ann Harper & Bob Harper. (Illus.). 240p. (Orig.). (C). 1996. reprint ed. pap. 34.95 (1-880859-03-3) MW Corp.

Team Baseball Card Checklist, No. 7. Jeff Fritsch. 1995. pap. 13.95 (0-937424-78-1) Edgewater.

Team Baseballs. Mark Baker. LC 91-76401. (Illus.). 544p. 1992. pap. 19.95 (0-87341-185-4, BL01) Krause Pubns.

Team-Based Health Care Organizations: Blueprint for Success. Jo Manion et al. LC 96-19770. 380p. 1996. 49.00 (0-8342-0782-6) Aspen Pub.

Team Based Organizations: Developing a Successful Team Environment. James H. Shonk. 200p. 1992. text ed. 42.50 (1-55623-703-0) Irwin Prof Pubng.

*Team-Based Organizations: Developing a Successful Team Environment. James H. Shonk. LC 96-35525. 208p. 1996. per. 18.95 (0-7863-1124-X) Irwin Prof Pubng.

Team-Based Problem Solver. Joan P. Klubnik & Penny F. Greenwood. LC 94-1191. 240p. 1994. text ed. 35.00 (0-7863-0187-2) Irwin Prof Pubng.

*Team-Based Project Management. James P. Lewis. 256p. 1997. 55.00 (0-8144-0364-6) AMACOM.

Team-Based Strategic Planning: A Complete Guide to Structuring, Facilitating & Implementing the Process. C. Davis Fogg. 368p. 1994. 65.00 (0-8144-5127-6) AMACOM.

Team Behavior Board for Groups of 2 to 6. Michael Martin. Ed. by Steven Harris & Nancy Brower. (Illus.). 23p. (Orig.). 1989. pap. text ed. 15.95 (0-9621191-0-5) Behavior Products.

Team-Building. Eric Skopec & Dayle M. Smith. LC 96-45996. (Practical Executive Ser.). (Illus.). 192p. 1997. pap. 14.95 (0-8442-2982-2, NTC Busn Bks) NTC Pub Grp.

Team Building. Rod Storey. 202p. (C). 1989. ring bd. 285.00 (0-85171-087-5, Pub. by IPM Hse UK) St Mut.

Team Building. Tebow. 1997. 19.95 (1-56253-333-9) Milady Pub.

Team-Building. James Vaughan. (Illus.). 28p. (Orig.). 1996. pap. 15.00 (0-936390-05-0, Lrning Tools) Dialog Pr.

*Team Building. Graham Willcocks & Steve Morris. (Business Success Ser.). 1997. pap. 6.95 (0-614-28139-3) Barron.

*Team Building. 2nd ed. Robert B. Maddux. (Better Management Skills Ser.). 1994. pap. 12.95 (0-7494-1411-1) Kogan Page Ltd.

Team Building: A Practical Guide for Trainers. Neil Clark. LC 94-4259. (McGraw-Hill Training Ser.). 1994. pap. text ed. 24.95 (0-07-707846-2) McGraw.

Team Building: A Structured Learning Approach. Peter Mears & Frank Voehl. (Illus.). 192p. (C). 1994. pap. 24.95 (1-884015-15-8) St Lucie Pr.

Team Building: An Exercise in Leadership. Robert Maddux. 70p. (Orig.). 1988. 7.95 (0-318-33263-9, 116) Am Bartenders.

Team Building: An Exercise in Leadership. rev. ed. Robert B. Maddux. Ed. by Michael G. Crisp. LC 91-77080. (Fifty-Minute Ser.). (Illus.). 77p. (Orig.). 1992. pap. 10.95 (1-56052-118-X) Crisp Pubns.

Team Building: ASTD Trainer's Sourcebook. C. Torres. 1996. pap. text ed. 34.95 (0-07-053435-7) McGraw.

Team Building: Blueprints for Productivity & Satisfaction. Ed. by W. Brendan Reddy & Kaleel Jamison. 225p. (Orig.). 1988. pap. text ed. 19.00 (0-9610392-5-6) NTL Inst.

Team Building: Current Issues & New Alternatives. 3rd ed. William G. Dyer. (Illus.). 176p. (C). 1995. pap. text ed. 26.95 (0-201-62882-1) Addison-Wesley.

Team Building: Issues & Alternatives. 2nd ed. William G. Dyer. LC 86-20635. (Organization Development Ser.). 160p. (C). 1987. pap. text ed. 26.95 (0-201-18037-5) Addison-Wesley.

Team Building Book: How to Build Your Staff into a High Performance Team. Michael P. O'Connor & Becky Erickson. 250p. (Orig.). 1992. pap. 23.95 (0-9629366-3-4) Old Stone Pub.

Team-Building for Diverse Work Groups: A Practical Guide to High-Performance & Diverse Teams. Selma Myers. (Workplace Diversity Ser.). (Illus.). 120p. 1995. pap. 12.95 (*1-883553-68-7*) R Chang Assocs.

Team Building for School Change: Equipping Teachers for New Roles. Gene I. Maeroff. LC 93-19983. (Series on School Reform). 192p. (C). 1993. text ed. 36.00 (*0-8077-3268-0*); pap. text ed. 17.95 (*0-8077-3267-2*) Tchrs Coll.

Team Building for the Future: Beyond the Basics. Robin Elledge & Steve Phillips. LC 94-65257. 364p. 1994. ring bd. 79.95 (*0-88390-380-6*, Pfffr & Co) Jossey-Bass.

Team Building Instructor's Manual: A Structured Learning Approach. Peter Mears. (Illus.). 120p. (C). 1994. spiral bd. 49.95 (*1-884015-14-X*) St Lucie Pr.

Team Building Lesson Plan. John W. Sisson, Jr. Ed. by American Correctional Association Staff. 299p. 1994. pap. 370.00 (*1-56991-014-6*, 178) Am Correctional.

Team-Building Skills: Trainer's Guide. Ralph Lewis. LC 94-13300. (One-Day Workshop Ser.). 1995. text ed. 110.00 (*0-07-040831-9*) McGraw.

Team-Building Source Book. Steven L. Phillips & Robin L. Elledge. LC 89-5094. 208p. (Orig.). 1989. ring bd. 79.95 (*0-88390-232-X*, Pfffr & Co) Jossey-Bass.

Team Building Through Physical Challenges. Donald R. Glover & Daniel W. Midura. (Illus.). 160p. 1992. pap. 16.95 (*0-87322-359-4*, BGLO0359) Human Kinetics.

Team Building Tool Kit: Tips, Tactics, & Rules for Effective Workplace Teams. Deborah Harrington-Mackin. 176p. 1993. pap. 17.95 (*0-8144-7826-3*) AMACOM.

Team Coach: Vital New Skills for Supervisors & Managers in a Team Environment. Donna Deeprose. LC 95-638. 176p. (Orig.). 1995. pap. 17.95 (*0-8144-7859-X*) AMACOM.

Team Decision Making see Team Decision Making Techniques: A Practical Guide to Successful Team Outcomes

Team Decision Making Techniques: A Practical Guide to Successful Team Outcomes. P. Keith Kelly. (High Performance Team Ser.). Orig. Title: Team Decision Making. (Illus.). 120p. 1994. pap. 12.95 (*1-883553-27-X*) R Chang Assocs.

Team Doc. Rollie Perkins. 1996. 18.95 (*0-533-11612-0*) Vantage.

Team Earth: Advanced ABC Environmental Coloring Book, No. 1. Stephen Pysz. (Illus.). 56p. (J). (gr. k-1). 1991. pap. text ed. 2.95 (*0-9630186-7-1*) Team Earth.

Team Earth: Show You Care, No. 2. Stephen Pysz. Ed. by Sarah Patton. (Illus.). 32p. (J). (gr. 2-5). 1992. student ed., pap. text ed. 2.95 (*0-9630186-1-2*) Team Earth.

Team Effectiveness & Decision Making in Organizations. Richard A. Guzzo et al. LC 94-41296. (Management, Social & Behavioral Sciences Ser.). 440p. lib. bdg. 39.95 (*1-55542-641-7*) Jossey-Bass.

Team Entrepreneurship. Alex Stewart. 184p. 1989. text ed. 44.00 (*0-8039-3493-9*); pap. text ed. 19.95 (*0-8039-3494-7*) Sage.

Team Evangelism. Larry A. Gilbert. Ed. by Cindy G. Spear. LC 94-180208. (C). 1991. pap. 8.95 (*0-941005-35-6*); Team Mate application bklt. 2.95 (*0-941005-28-3*) Chrch Grwth VA.

Team Evangelism, 1. Larry A. Gilbert. Ed. by Cindy G. Spear. (C). 1991. student ed., ring bd. 99.95 incl. audio (*0-941005-39-9*) Chrch Grwth VA.

Team Evangelism, 2. Larry A. Gilbert. Ed. by Cindy G. Spear. (C). 1991. ring bd. write for info. (*0-941005-40-2*) Chrch Grwth VA.

Team Evangelism, Set. Larry A. Gilbert. Ed. by Cindy G. Spear. 1991. 99.95 (*1-57052-019-4*) Chrch Grwth VA.

Team Evangelism for Youth. Cindy G. Spear. (Illus.). 26p. 1995. ring bd. 59.95 incl. vhs (*1-57052-046-1*) Chrch Grwth VA.

Team Facilitator's Handbook. Council for Continuous Improvement Staff. (Illus.). 119p. 1992. pap. text ed. 20.00 (*0-527-91702-8*, 917028) Qual Resc.

Team Fitness: A How-to Manual for Building a Winning Work Team. Meg Hartzler & Jane E. Henry. LC 93-48626. (Illus.). 245p. 1994. pap. 32.00 (*0-87389-269-0*, H0825) ASQC Qual Pr.

Team Football & Basketball Card Checklist, No. 2. Jeff Fritsch. (Sport Americana Ser.). 160p. 1993. pap. 12.95 (*0-937424-67-6*) Edgewater.

Team Games for Trainers. Carolyn Nilson. LC 93-3369. 322p. 1993. pap. text ed. 24.95 (*0-07-046588-6*) McGraw.

Team Handball: Skills, Strategies & Training. Baha M. Hamil & James D. LaPoint. (Illus.). 139p. 1994. pap. text ed. 14.95 (*0-945483-23-6*) E Bowers Pub.

Team Handball: Steps to Success. Reita E. Clanton & Mary P. Dwight. LC 96-15149. (Steps to Success Activity Ser.). 168p. (Orig.). 1996. pap. 15.95 (*0-87322-411-6*, PCLA0411) Human Kinetics.

***Team Handbook.** 2nd ed. Barbara J. Streibel et al. (Illus.). 336p. 1996. pap. 39.00 (*1-884731-11-2*) Joiner Assoc.

Team Handbook: How to Use Teams to Improve Quality. Peter R. Scholtes. Ed. by Sue Reynard. (Illus.). 336p. (Orig.). 1988. 39.00 (*0-9622264-0-8*) Joiner Assoc.

Team Handbook for Educators: How to Use Teams to Improve Quality. Peter R. Scholtes et al. (Illus.). 330p. (Orig.). 1994. pap. 39.00 (*0-9622264-9-1*) Joiner Assoc.

Team Interaction Skills. Dennis E. Coates. 48p. 1994. pap. text ed. 18.00 (*1-886713-04-9*) Perform Support Systs.

Team Investigation of Child Sexual Abuse: The Uneasy Alliance. Donna Pence & Charles Wilson. (Interpersonal Violence: the Practice Ser.: Vol. 6). 176p. 1994. 46.00 (*0-8039-5169-8*); pap. 19.95 (*0-8039-5170-1*) Sage.

Team Language Learning for French, Spanish & German. Libyan Labiosa-Cassone. Ed. by Diana Rose. (Illus.). (Orig.). 1991. student ed., pap. 199.00 incl. vhs (*0-685-54740-X*, Pub. by Accel Lrn Sys UK) Acclrtd Learn.

***Team Launch.** Ingrid Bens. Ed. by Michael Goldman. 165p. (Orig.). 1997. pap. text ed. 39.00 (*1-890416-01-0*) Participative Dyn.

***Team Launch - Member Handbook.** Ingrid Bens. Ed. by Michael Goldman. 160p. (Orig.). 1997. pap. text ed. 39.00 (*1-890416-02-9*) Participative Dyn.

***Team Leader Idea-a-Day Guide.** Susan F. Woodring & Drea Zigarmi. (Illus.). 300p. (Orig.). 1997. pap. 29.95 (*0-85013-295-9*) Dartnell Corp.

Team Leader's Handbook. Council for Continuous Improvement Staff. (Illus.). 148p. 1992. pap. text ed. 20.00 (*0-527-91701-X*, 91701X) Qual Resc.

Team Leader's Problem Solver. Clay Carr. LC 95-39795. 350p. 1995. 39.95 (*0-13-409970-2*); pap. 14.95 (*0-13-409962-1*) P-H.

Team Leader's Survival Guide. Jeanne Wilson & Jill George. (Illus.). 289p. 1995. wbk. ed. 49.95 (*0-9623483-2-5*) Dev Dimensions.

***Team Leadership.** David Kolb. (Illus.). 66p. 1996. wbk. ed., ring bd. write for info. (*1-57740-057-7*, ILW032) Intl LrningWrk.

***Team Leadership.** David C. Kolb. (Illus.). 120p. (Orig.). 1996. pap. write for info. (*1-57740-055-0*, ILW019) Intl LrningWrk.

Team Leadership: Developing Great Leaders Through the Eight Laws of Leadership. Elmer L. Towns. 91p. 1992. teacher ed., ring bd. 89.95 incl. audio (*0-941005-59-3*) Chrch Grwth VA.

***Team Leadership: School Boards at Work.** Michael Rosenberger. LC 96-62020. 185p. 1997. pap. text ed. 34.95 (*1-56676-526-9*) Technomic.

***Team Leadership: Training Package.** David Kolb & Barbara Singer. (Illus.). 144p. 1996. ring bd. write for info. (*1-57740-056-9*, ILW031) Intl LrningWrk.

***Team Leadership in Christian Ministry: Using Multiple Gifts to Build a Unified Vision.** Kenneth O. Gangel. 480p. 1997. 29.99 (*0-8024-9016-6*) Moody.

Team Leadership Skills. Dennis E. Coates. 76p. 1994. pap. text ed. 18.00 (*1-886713-00-6*) Perform Support Systs.

Team Leading. (Open Learning for Supervisory Management). 1986. pap. text ed. 19.50 (*0-08-033972-7*, Pergamon Pr) Elsevier.

Team Leading. (Open Learning for Supervisory Management). 1986. pap. text ed. 19.50 (*0-08-070010-1*, Pergamon Pr) Elsevier.

Team Leading. 2nd ed. (Open Learning Super Ser.). 1991. pap. text ed. 26.00 (*0-08-041522-9*, Pergamon Pr) Elsevier.

Team Lotus: The Indianapolis Years. Andrew Ferguson. (Illus.). 224p. 1996. 39.95 (*1-85260-491-3*, Pub. by J H Haynes & Co UK) Motorbooks Intl.

Team Management: Creating Systems & Skills for a Team-Based Organization. 2nd ed. Jennifer Howard & Lawrence Miller. (Illus.). 328p. 1994. student ed., spiral bd. 49.95 (*0-9629679-3-9*) Miller Howard Cnslt.

Team Member Handbook for Teamwork. Price Pritchett. 60p. (Orig.). 1992. pap. 5.95 (*0-944002-11-0*) Pritchett Assocs.

Team Member's Handbook. Council for Continuous Improvement Staff. (Illus.). 113p. 1992. pap. text ed. 20.00 (*0-527-91700-1*, 917001) Qual Resc.

***Team Member's Survival Guide.** Jill A. George & Jeanne M. Wilson. (Illus.). 200p. 1997. pap. text ed. 24.95 (*0-07-024566-5*) McGraw.

***Team Memory Jogger: A Pocket Guide for Team Members.** Joiner Associates, Inc. Staff. (Illus.). 164p. 1995. spiral bd. 7.95 (*1-879364-51-4*, 1050E) GOAL-QPC.

Team Memory Jogger: A Pocket Guide for Team Members. Joiner Assocs., Inc. Staff & Goal/QPC Staff. Ed. by Sue Reynard. (Illus.). 176p. (Orig.). 1995. pap. 7.95 (*1-884731-10-4*) Joiner Assoc.

Team Ministry. Dick Iverson & Ray Grant. (Illus.). 152p. 1984. pap. 9.95 (*0-914936-61-1*) BT Pub.

Team Ministry: A Guide to Spiritual Gifts & Lay Involvement. 2nd ed. Larry A. Gilbert. LC 94-166345. 194p. 1987. pap. 9.95 (*0-941005-00-3*); student ed., pap. 1.95 (*0-941005-02-X*); student ed., ring bd. 99.95 incl. audio (*0-941005-04-6*) Chrch Grwth VA.

***Team Ministry: A Workbook for Getting Things Done.** Steven Schey. 112p. 1996. pap. 14.95 (*0-687-01719-X*) Abingdon.

***Team Ministry for Youth: A Guide to Gift Discovery & Involvement in Ministry.** Cindy G. Spear. (Illus.). 27p. 1996. wbk. ed., ring bd. 59.95 incl. audio (*1-57052-054-2*) Chrch Grwth VA.

Team Organization: An Enduring Competitive Advantage. Dean R. Tjosvold. LC 90-12600. (Series in Industrial & Organizational Psychology). 249p. 1992. pap. text ed. 60.00 (*0-471-93483-6*) Wiley.

Team Organization: Promise - Practices & Possibilities. Thomas O. Erb & Nancy M. Doda. 128p. 1989. pap. 12.95 (*0-8106-3075-3*) NEA.

Team Penning. Phil Livingston. (Illus.). 144p. 1991. 12.95 (*0-911647-24-4*) Western Horseman.

Team Performance: Creating & Sustaining Results. David Sibbet. (Illus.). 180p. 1994. pap. 125.00 (*1-879502-09-7*) Grove Cnslts.

Team Physician's Handbook. Ed. by Michael Walsh & Guy L. Shelton. LC 90-82905. (Illus.). 680p. (Orig.). 1990. pap. text ed. 60.00 (*1-56053-001-4*) Hanley & Belfus.

Team Physician's Handbook. 2nd rev. ed. Ed. by Morris B. Mellion et al. LC 96-45304. (Illus.). 680p. 1996. pap. text ed. 52.00 (*1-56053-174-6*) Hanley & Belfus.

Team Picture. Dean Hughes. (J). (gr. 3-7). 1996. 16.00 (*0-689-31924-X*, Atheneum Bks Young) S&S Childrens.

Team Planning for Educational Leaders. Rima Miller. 79p. 1987. pap. 21.95 (*1-56602-017-4*) Research Better.

Team Play. Bonnie Bryant. (Saddle Club Ser.: No. 15). 144p. (J). (gr. 4-7). 1991. 3.99 (*0-553-15862-7*) Bantam.

Team Play Polo. William G. Langdon, Jr. LC 93-206527. (Illus.). 128p. 1985. spiral bd. 29.95 (*1-883714-01-X*) Langdon Ent.

Team Player. (Kaleidoscope Ser.: Set B). 1993. 2.95 (*0-88336-279-1*) New Readers.

Team Player: A Practical Guide to Team Membership. Michael D. Maginn. LC 93-5. 112p. 1993. per. 10.00 (*1-55623-880-0*) Irwin Prof Pubng.

Team Players & Teamwork: The New Competitive Business Strategy. Glenn M. Parker. LC 90-53093. (Business & Management Ser.). 202p. 26.00 (*1-55542-257-8*) Jossey-Bass.

Team Players & Teamwork: The New Competitive Business Strategy. Glenn M. Parker. (The Management Ser.). 210p. (Orig.). 1996. pap. 16.50 (*0-7879-0185-7*) Jossey-Bass.

***Team-Power: How to Build & Grow Successful Teams.** Jim Temme. Ed. by Kelly Scanlon. LC 96-68230. (Lifelong Learning Library). (Illus.). 242p. 1996. pap. 18.95 (*1-878542-93-1*, 17-0002) SkillPath Pubns.

Team Power: Making Library Meetings Work. Ed. by Barbara I. Dewey & Sheila D. Creth. LC 93-1075. 130p. 1993. pap. text ed. 25.00 (*0-8389-0616-8*) ALA.

Team Problem Solving. rev. ed. Sandy Pokras. Ed. by Michael Crisp & Francine L. Ruvolo. LC 94-72611. (Fifty-Minute Ser.). (Illus.). 132p. 1994. pap. 10.95 (*1-56052-314-X*) Crisp Pubns.

Team Process: A Handbook for Teachers. 3rd enl. ed. Elliot Y. Merenbloom. 168p. (C). 1991. pap. text ed. 18.00 (*1-56090-054-7*) Natl Middle Schl.

Team Processes Module 5: Managing for the Future. Ancona et al. (GI - Organizational Behavior Ser.). 1996. text ed. 6.95 (*0-538-85879-6*) S-W Pub.

Team Processes, Training, & Performance: A Special Issue of "Military Psychology", Vol. 7, No. 2, 1995. Ed. by Eduardo Salas et al. 72p. 1995. pap. 20.00 (*0-8058-9946-4*) L Erlbaum Assocs.

Team ReConstruction: High Velocity Moves for Repairing Work Groups Rocked by Change. Price Pritchett & Ron Pound. 24p. (Orig.). 1992. pap. 5.95 (*0-944002-10-2*) Pritchett Assocs.

Team Roles at Work. Meredith Belbin. 160p. 1993. 32.95 (*0-7506-0925-7*) Buttrwrth-Heinemann.

Team Roles at Work. Meredith Belbin. 160p. 1996. pap. 34.95 (*0-7506-2675-5*) Buttrwrth-Heinemann.

Team Roping. Leo Camarillo. Tr. by Randy Witte. (Illus.). 144p. (Orig.). 1982. pap. 12.95 (*0-911647-00-7*) Western Horseman.

Team Science: Organizing Classroom Experiments That Develop Group Skills, Grades 4-8. Marilyn F. Coffin. LC 95-47823. 1995. pap. 20.00 (*1-56976-013-6*) Zephyr Pr AZ.

Team Selling. Sheila Kessler. LC 90-85529. 1990. pap. 19.95 (*1-879404-13-3*) Cmpetitive Edge.

Team Spirit. Susan Sollins et al. LC 90-84214. (Illus.). 60p. 1990. 19.00 (*0-916365-30-1*) Ind Curators.

***Team Spirituality: A Guide for Staff & Church.** William Carter. LC 96-32278. 160p. 1997. pap. 12.95 (*0-687-01604-5*) Abingdon.

Team Startup: Creating Gameplans for Success. David Sibbet. (Illus.). 82p. 1995. pap. 45.00 (*1-879502-20-8*) Grove Cnslts.

Team Stealth: F-117. Photos by Randy Jolly. (Illus.). 96p. (Orig.). 1992. pap. 17.95 (*0-933424-45-0*) Specialty Pr.

Team Strategy: How to Structure & Lead an Ephesians Four Church. Larry A. Gilbert. Ed. by Cindy G. Spear. 58p. 1996. teacher ed., wbk. ed., pap. text ed. 129.95 incl. vhs (*1-57052-050-X*) Chrch Grwth VA.

Team Talk. Anne Donnellon. 1996. text ed. 24.95 (*0-07-103634-2*) McGraw.

Team Talk: The Power of Language in Team Dynamics. Anne Donnellon. LC 95-36810. 320p. (C). 1996. 24.95 (*0-87584-619-X*) Harvard Busn.

Team Teaching. Northern Nevada Writing Project Teacher Researcher Group Staff. 120p. (Orig.). (C). 1996. pap. text ed. 12.50 (*1-57110-040-7*) Stenhse Pubs.

Team Teaching: Bold New Venture. Ed. by David W. Beggs, 3rd. LC 64-17456. (Bold New Venture Ser). (Illus.). 192p. reprint ed. 54.80 (*0-8357-9245-5*, 2015810) Bks Demand.

***Team That Could'nt Lose, 57 Vols., Vol. 55.** Matt Christopher. (Matt Christopher Sports Classics Ser.). 1997. pap. text ed. 3.95 (*0-316-14167-4*) Little.

Team That Jack Built. Paul Rowan. (Illus.). 192p. 1995. 29.95 (*1-85158-670-9*, Pub. by Mnstream UK) Trafalgar.

Team Think: 72 Ways to Make Good, Smart, Quick Decisions In Any Meeting. Ava S. Butler. (Illus.). 224p. 1996. pap. text ed. 14.95 (*0-07-009433-0*) McGraw.

Team Think: 72 Ways to Make Good, Smart, Quick Decisions in Any Meeting. Ava S. Butler. (Illus.). 224p. 1996. text ed. 29.95 (*0-07-009432-2*) McGraw.

Team Tonka Saves the Day. Marilyn Bollinger. (Magic Touch Talking Bks.). (Illus.). 22p. (J). (ps-2). 1996. 19.99 (*1-888208-06-6*) Hasbro.

Team Toyota: Transplanting the Toyota Culture to the Camry Plant in Kentucky. Terry L. Besser. LC 96-11692. (SUNY Series in the Sociology of Work). 199p. (C). 1996. text ed. 44.50 (*0-7914-3145-2*); pap. text ed. 14.95 (*0-7914-3146-0*) State U NY Pr.

Team Trainer: Winning Tools & Tactics for a Successful Workout. William I. Gorden et al. 240p. 1995. per. 35.00 (*0-7863-0511-8*) Irwin Prof Pubng.

Team Training: From Startup to High Performance. Carl L. Harshman & Steve Phillips. LC 95-4747. 1996. text ed. 99.95 (*0-07-912220-5*); pap. text ed. 39.95 (*0-07-026925-4*) McGraw.

Team Traps: Survival Stories & Lessons from Team Disasters, Mishaps & Other Near-Death Experiences. Steven R. Rayner. 256p. 1995. 25.00 (*0-939246-79-1*) Wiley.

Team Traps: Survival Stories and Lessons from Team Disasters, Near-Misses, Mishaps and Other Near-Death Experiences. Stephen R. Rayner. LC 95-49752. 256p. 1996. text ed. 24.95 (*0-471-13285-3*) Wiley.

Team Turbo-Training Facilitator's Kit. Lawrence Holpp. 1997. text ed. 149.00 (*0-07-029593-X*) McGraw.

Team U. S. A. 1996 Scrapbook. (J). 1996. mass mkt. 4.50 (*0-590-89661-X*) Scholastic Inc.

Team up for Excellence. Allen Mackay. (Illus.). 220p. 1993. pap. 29.95 (*0-19-558268-3*) OUP.

***Team Work.** Dandi MacKall. (Career Skills Library). (Illus.). 128p. (YA). (gr. 9-12). 1997. write for info. (*0-89434-212-6*) Ferguson.

Team Work see Career Skills Library

Team Yankee. Harold Coyle. 352p. 1988. pap. text ed. 6.99 (*0-425-11042-7*) Berkley Pub.

Team Zebra: How 1500 Partners Revitalized Eastman Kodak's Black & White Film-Making Flow. Stephen J. Frangos. 226p. 1995. text ed. 27.95 (*0-471-13187-3*) Wiley.

Team Zebra: How 1500 Partners Revitalized Eastman Kodak's Black & White Film-Making Flow. Stephen R. Frangos & Stephen J. Bennett. LC 93-60668. 226p. 1993. 22.00 (*0-939246-38-4*) Wiley.

Team Zebra: How 1500 Partners Revitalized Eastman Kodak's Black & White Film-Making Flow. Ed. by Steve Frangos & Stephen Bennett. 256p. 1993. 60.00 (*0-614-04101-5*, Pub. by Pitman Pubng UK) St Mut.

Team Zebra: How 1500 Partners Revitalized Eastman Kodak's Black & White Film-Making Flow. Stephen J. Frankos. 256p. 1996. pap. text ed. 17.95 (*0-471-14739-7*) Wiley.

TeamBook: 27 Exercises for Enhancing Work Groups. John E. Jones & William L. Bearley. 125p. (Orig.). 1994. ring bd. 80.00 (*0-925652-18-0*) Orgn Design & Dev.

Teambuilding. (Leadership Ser.). 63p. (Orig.). 1989. pap. 9.95 (*1-55852-030-9*) Natl Pr Pubns.

***Teambuilding.** Laurie Kagan et al. (Illus.). 178p. 1997. pap. text ed. 25.00 (*1-879097-41-9*) Kagan Cooperative.

Teambuilding: A Self Directed Approach to Improving Work Teams. Glenn H. Varney. 1985. pap. 12.00 (*0-318-04728-4*) Mgmt Advisory Assoc Inc.

***Teambuilding & Total Quality: A Guidebook to TQM Success.** Gene H. Milas. LC 97-13900. (Illus.). 240p. 1997. 29.95 (*0-89806-173-3*, MILTQM) Eng Mgmt Pr.

Teambuilding Strategy. Mike Woodcock & Dave Francis. 200p. 1994. 49.95 (*0-566-07496-6*, Pub. by Gower UK) Ashgate Pub Co.

Teambuilt. 1992. 19.95 (*0-942361-54-7*) MasterMedia Pub.

Teambuilt: Making Teamwork Work. Mark Sanborn. 1994. pap. 12.95 (*0-942361-94-6*) MasterMedia Pub.

***Teamguides: A Self-Directed System for Teams.** Brad Humphrey. 1997. 89.95 (*0-7879-1101-1*, Pfffr & Co) Jossey-Bass.

***Teamguides Pocket Coach.** Brad Humphrey. 1997. pap. 19.95 (*0-7879-1102-X*, Pfffr & Co) Jossey-Bass.

Teaming by Design: Real Teams for Real People. Donna Mcintosh-Fletcher. 192p. 1995. text ed. 24.95 (*0-7863-0536-3*) Irwin Prof Pubng.

Teaming for Tomorrow: A Mentoring Program That Introduces Girls to a World of Career Choices. Joyce A. Richards et al. (Illus.). 36p. (YA). (gr. 9-12). 1996. ring bd. 25.00 (*0-9651432-0-1*) Girl Scout Coun.

Teaming Up: Making the Transition to a Self-Directed, Team-Based Organization. Darrell W. Ray & Howard Bronstein. LC 94-33604. 1995. text ed. 24.95 (*0-07-051646-4*) McGraw.

***Teaming Up: Shared Leadership in Youth Ministry.** Ginny W. Holderness & Robert Hay. LC 97-1730. 216p. (Orig.). 1997. pap. 16.00 (*0-664-25624-4*) Westminster John Knox.

Teaming Up: The Small-Business Guide to Collaborating with Others to Boost Your Earnings & Expand Your Horizons. Paul Edwards et al. LC 96-33515. (Working from Home Ser.). 416p. (Orig.). 1997. pap. 13.95 (*0-87477-842-5*, Tarcher Putnam) Putnam Pub Group.

***Teaming up for Excellence.** LC 96-95159. (Illus.). xi, 289p. 1997. 36.95 (*1-890062-00-6*) R V Armstrong.

Teaming up for the Nineties. Collins & Doorley. 1990. 45.00 (*1-55623-430-9*) Irwin Prof Pubng.

Teaming up for the '90s: A Guide to International Joint Ventures & Strategic Alliances, Braxton Association Special Edition. Timothy Collins & Thomas Doorley. 1994. 45.00 (*0-7863-0359-X*) Irwin Prof Pubng.

Teammates. Peter Golenbock. (Illus.). 32p. (J). (gr. 1-4). 1990. 16.00 (*0-15-200603-6*, Gulliver Bks) HarBrace.

Teammates. Peter Golenbock. LC 89-3816. (Illus.). 32p. (J). (gr. 1-4). 1992. pap. 6.00 (*0-15-284286-1*, Gulliver Bks) HarBrace.

***Teammates.** Hughes. (J). Date not set. mass mkt. 3.99 (*0-689-81942-0*) S&S Childrens.

Teammates. Walker & Barry W. Enoch. 1996. mass mkt. 5.99 (*0-671-56830-2*) PB.

***Teammates, Vol. 3.** Marilyn Kaye. (After School Club Ser.). (J). 1997. pap. 3.50 (*0-671-51028-2*, Minstrel Bks) PB.

Teammates: Home Team Book. Ruth L. Perle. Ed. by Evelyn J. Bergstrom. (Arista TeamMates Ser.). (Illus.). (J). (ps). 1977. pap. text ed. 4.25 (*0-89796-862-X*) New Dimens Educ.

***Teammates: John Stockton & Karl Malone.** Bob Schnakenberg. LC 97-19765. (J). 1998. lib. bdg. write for info. (*0-7613-0300-6*) Millbrook Pr.

***Teammates Book 1.** Hughes. (J). Date not set. pap. 14.00 (*0-689-81924-2*); mass mkt. 3.99 (*0-689-81933-1*) S&S Childrens.

T

***Teammates Book 2.** Hughes. (J). Date not set. pap. 14.00 (*0-689-81925-0*) S&S Childrens.

***Teammates Book 2.** Hughes. (J). Date not set. mass mkt. 3.99 (*0-689-81934-X*) S&S Childrens.

***Teammates Book 3.** Hughes. (J). Date not set. pap. 14.00 (*0-689-81926-9*) S&S Childrens.

***Teammates Book 3.** Hughes. (J). Date not set. mass mkt. 3.99 (*0-689-81936-6*) S&S Childrens.

***Teammates Book 4.** Hughes. (J). Date not set. pap. 14.00 (*0-689-81927-7*) S&S Childrens.

***Teammates Book 4.** Hughes. (J). Date not set. mass mkt. 3.99 (*0-689-81937-4*) S&S Childrens.

***Teammates Book 5.** Hughes. (J). Date not set. pap. 14.00 (*0-689-81928-5*) S&S Childrens.

***Teammates Book 5.** Hughes. (J). Date not set. mass mkt. 3.99 (*0-689-81938-2*) S&S Childrens.

***Teammates Book 6.** Hughes. (J). Date not set. pap. 14.00 (*0-689-81929-3*) S&S Childrens.

***Teammates Book 6.** Hughes. (J). Date not set. mass mkt. 3.99 (*0-689-81939-0*) S&S Childrens.

***Teammates Book 7.** Hughes. (J). Date not set. pap. 14.00 (*0-689-81930-7*) S&S Childrens.

***Teammates Book 7.** Hughes. (J). Date not set. mass mkt. 3.99 (*0-689-81940-4*) S&S Childrens.

***Teammates Book 8.** Hughes. (J). Date not set. pap. 14.00 (*0-689-81931-5*) S&S Childrens.

***Teammates Book 8.** Hughes. (J). Date not set. mass mkt. 3.99 (*0-689-81941-2*) S&S Childrens.

***Teammates Book 9.** Hughes. (J). Date not set. pap. 14.00 (*0-689-81932-3*) S&S Childrens.

Teammates School Team Book. Ruth L. Perle. Ed. by Evelyn J. Bergstrom. (Arista TeamMates Ser.). (Illus.). (J). (ps). 1977. pap. text ed. 4.25 (*0-89796-861-1*) New Dimens Educ.

TeamNet Factor: Bringing the Power of Boundary Crossing into the Heart of Your Business. Jessica Lipnack & Jeffrey Stamps. 400p. 1995. text ed. 29.95 (*0-471-13188-1*) Wiley.

TeamNet Factor: Bringing the Power of Boundary-Crossing Teams into the Heart of Your Business. Jessica Lipnack & Jeffrey Stamps. LC 92-85207. 256p. 1993. 27.50 (*0-939246-34-1*) Wiley.

TeamPower. Richard R. Pieper. LC 88-92255. 70p. (Orig.). (C). 1989. pap. 30.00 (*0-9621149-0-1*) PPC Inc.

Teampower: Increasing Productivity & Profitability with Self-Managed Organizations. Clay Carr. 1992. text ed. 21.95 (*0-13-892761-8*, Busn) P-H.

Teams: A Game to Develop Group Skills. Stephen D. Platt et al. 1988. 129.95 (*0-566-02735-6*, Pub. by Gower UK) Ashgate Pub Co.

Teams: Structure, Process, Culture, & Politics. Eileen K. Aranda. 250p. (C). 1996. pap. text ed. 24.67 (*0-13-494584-0*) P-H.

Teams: Their Training & Performance. Ed. by Robert W. Swezey & Eduardo Salas. 432p. (C). 1992. pap. 49.50 (*0-89391-942-X*); text ed. 82.50 (*0-89391-852-0*) Ablex Pub.

Teams: Who Needs Them & Why? Ronald J. Recardo et al. (Illus.). 224p. 1996. 39.95 (*0-88415-852-7*, 5852) Gulf Pub.

Teams a Management Approach for Cities & Counties. Marsiea Dahlgren & Linda Young. 72p. 1994. pap. 29.95 (*1-882403-13-4*) The Innovation Grps.

Teams & Techniques: For World Class Improvement. Thomas R. King. (Illus.). 104p. 1996. text ed. 28.00 (*0-9652622-0-0*) T R King.

Teams & Techniques Workbook: For World Class Improvement. Thomas R. King. (Illus.). 186p. 1996. wbk. ed., pap. 24.00 (*0-9652622-1-9*) T R King.

Teams & Technology: Fulfilling the Promise of the New Organization. Don Mankin et al. LC 95-35767. 320p. (C). 1996. 29.95 (*0-87584-399-9*) Harvard Busn.

Teams & Technology: Fulfilling the Promise of the New Organization. Don Mankin & Susan G. Cohen. 1996. text ed. 29.95 (*0-07-103674-1*) McGraw.

Teams & TQM. A. Aune. (C). 1994. 150.00 (*0-946655-66-9*, Pub. by Stanley Thornes UK) Trans-Atl Phila.

***Teams at the Top: Unleashing the Potential of Both Teams & Individual Leaders.** Harvard Business School Press Staff. 1997. text ed. 24.95 (*0-07-105061-2*) McGraw.

***Teams at the Top: Unleashing the Potential of Both Teams & Individual Leaders.** Jon R. Katzenbach. 240p. 1997. 24.95 (*0-87584-789-7*, HBS Pr) Harvard Busn.

Teams at Work: Seven Keys to Success. Suzanne W. Zoglio. Ed. by Susan Kidney. LC 93-94078. (Illus.). 144p. 1993. pap. 19.95 (*0-941668-04-5*) Tower Hill Pr.

Teams-Games-Tournament: The Team Learning Approach. David L. DeVries et al. Ed. by Danny G. Langdon. LC 79-26378. (Instructional Design Library). 104p. 1980. 27.95 (*0-87778-157-5*) Educ Tech Pubns.

Teams in Education: Creating an Integrated Approach. Jerome S. Arcaro. 120p. (Orig.). 1995. pap. text ed. 29.95 (*1-884015-52-2*) St Lucie Pr.

Teams in Government: A Handbook for Team-Based Organizations. Jerry W. Koehler & Joseph M. Pankowski. (Illus.). 175p. (Orig.). 1996. pap. 32.95 (*1-57444-016-0*) St Lucie Pr.

Teams in Organizations Module 6: Managing for the Future. Ancona et al. (GI - Organizational Behavior Ser.). 1996. text ed. 7.95 (*0-538-85880-X*) S-W Pub.

***Teams in Trouble.** Ingrid Bens. Ed. by Michael Goldman. 180p. (Orig.). 1997. pap. text ed. 39.00 (*1-890416-03-7*) Participative Dyn.

Teams, Markets, & Systems: Business Innovation & Information Technology. Claudio U. Ciborra. LC 92-23172. (Illus.). 264p. (C). 1993. text ed. 49.95 (*0-521-40463-0*) Cambridge U Pr.

Teams, Markets & Systems: Business Innovation & Information Technology. Claudio U. Ciborra. 260p. 1996. pap. text ed. 19.95 (*0-521-57465-X*) Cambridge U Pr.

TEAMS, Together Each Achieves More Success: How to Develop Peak Performance Teams for World-Class Results. James Lundy. 222p. 1994. pap. 15.95 (*0-85013-228-2*) Dartnell Corp.

TEAMS Together Each Achieves More Success: How to Develop Peak Performance Teams for World-Class Results. Jim Lundy. 222p. 1992. 20.50 (*0-85013-207-X*, TE7607) Dartnell Corp.

Teamster Bureaucracy. Farrell Dobbs. LC 76-52771. (Illus.). 304p. 1977. reprint ed. pap. 18.95 (*0-913460-53-2*); reprint ed. lib. bdg. 55.00 (*0-913460-52-4*) Pathfinder NY.

Teamster Politics. Farrell Dobbs. LC 75-17324. (Illus.). 256p. 1975. reprint ed. pap. 17.95 (*0-913460-39-7*); reprint ed. lib. bdg. 50.00 (*0-913460-38-9*) Pathfinder NY.

Teamster Power. Farrell Dobbs. LC 73-78115. 255p. 1973. reprint ed. pap. 17.95 (*0-913460-21-4*); reprint ed. lib. bdg. 50.00 (*0-913460-20-6*) Pathfinder NY.

Teamster Rank & File. Samuel Friedman. LC 82-9510. 320p. 1982. text ed. 49.50 (*0-231-05372-X*) Col U Pr.

***Teamster Rank & File Legal Defense Handbook.** Ellis Boal. 312p. 1984. pap. 8.00 (*0-614-29601-3*) Assn Union Demo.

Teamster Rebellion. Farrell Dobbs. LC 78-186690. (Illus.). 218p. 1972. reprint ed. pap. 16.95 (*0-913460-03-6*); reprint ed. lib. bdg. 45.00 (*0-913460-02-8*) Pathfinder NY.

Teamthink: Using the Sports Connection to Develop, Motivate, & Manage a Winning Business Team. Don Martin. Ed. by Renee Martin. LC 93-47185. 320p. 1994. pap. 12.95 (*0-452-27213-0*, Plume) NAL-Dutton.

TeamView 360: Evaluating Team Performance. Advanced Teamware Staff. LC 94-67190. (Illus.). 220p. 1994. ring bd. 49.95 (*0-88390-449-7*, Pfffr & Co) Jossey-Bass.

***Teamwork.** Lydia Kelley & Stew Nordensson. Ed. by Stewart Gellman. (Illus.). 1997. spiral bd. write for info. (*0-9656216-0-X*) Top Dog.

Teamwork: Involving People in Quality & Productivity Improvement. Charles A. Aubrey, II & Patricia K. Felkins. 180p. 1988. pap. text ed. 21.50 (*0-527-91626-9*, 916269) Qual Resc.

Teamwork: Joint Labor-Management Programs in America. Ed. by Jerome M. Rosow. 199p. 1986. 27.50 (*0-08-032799-0*) Work in Amer.

Teamwork: Parents & Professionals. Ed. by Fred P. Orelove & Howard Garner. Date not set. 16.95 (*0-87868-602-9*) Child Welfare.

***Teamwork: We Have Met the Enemy & They Are Us.** Matt M. Starcevich & Steven J. Stowell. (Illus.). 147p. 1991. 19.95 (*0-916095-40-1*) Ctr Mgmt Org.

Teamwork: What Must Go Right - What Can Go Wrong. Carl E. Larson & Frank M. LaFasto. (Series in Interpersonal Communication). 152p. (C). 1989. text ed. 48.00 (*0-8039-3289-8*); pap. text ed. 23.50 (*0-8039-3290-1*) Sage.

Teamwork Advantage: An Inside Look at Japanese Product & Technology Development. Jeffrey L. Funk. (Illus.). 508p. 1992. 50.00 (*0-915299-69-0*) Prod Press.

Teamwork & Team Sabotage. Alyce P. Cornyn-Selby. Orig. Title: Whatever Happened to Teamwork?. 84p. 1994. pap. text ed. 8.95 (*0-941383-22-9*) Beynch Pr.

Teamwork & the Bottom Line: Groups Make a Difference. Ned Rosen. (Series in Applied Psychology). 240p. 1989. pap. text ed. 27.50 (*0-8058-0461-7*) L Erlbaum Assocs.

Teamwork & the Bottom Line: Groups Make a Difference. Ned Rosen. 240p. 1989. 49.95 (*0-8058-0459-5*) L Erlbaum Assocs.

Teamwork Discipleship Guides Series, 2 vols., Set. Dale Larsen & Sandy Larsen. (Orig.). 1993. wbk. ed., pap. 9.98 (*0-8308-1125-7*, 1125) InterVarsity.

Teamwork for Customers: Building Organizations That Take Pride in Serving. Dean R. Tjosvold. LC 92-28015. (Management Ser.). 200p. text ed. 28.95 (*1-55542-491-0*) Jossey-Bass.

Teamwork for Preventive Care. Nigel Bruce. LC 80-41095. (Social Policy Research Monograph Ser.: No. 1). 261p. reprint ed. pap. 74.40 (*0-8357-7047-8*, 2033330) Bks Demand.

Teamwork for Primary & Shared Care. 2nd ed. Peter Pritchard & James Pritchard. (Practical Guides for General Practice Ser.). (Illus.). 136p. 1994. pap. text ed. 26.95 (*0-19-262527-6*) OUP.

***Teamwork from Start to Finish: 10 Steps to Results.** Fran Rees. LC 97-4606. 1997. write for info. (*0-7879-1061-9*, Pfffr & Co) Jossey-Bass.

Teamwork in Human Services: Models & Applications Across the Life Span. Howard Glenn Garner & Frank P. Orelove. 224p. 1994. pap. 35.00 (*0-7506-9519-6*) Buttrwrth-Heinemann.

Teamwork in Neurology. Nieuwenhuis. 208p. 1993. pap. 46.95 (*1-56593-121-1*, 0433) Singular Publishing.

***Teamwork in the Classroom: A Student Guide to Collaborative Learning.** Donna Foster & Curtis Miles. 30p. (Orig.). 1995. pap. text ed. 9.95 (*0-943202-52-3*) H & H Pub.

Teamwork Models & Experience in Education & Child Care. Ed. by Howard G. Garner. LC 94-32869. 1995. text ed. 46.95 (*0-205-13783-0*, Longwood Div) Allyn.

Teamwork Through Flexible Leadership: A How-to-Guide for Conducting Business in a Changing Work Environment. Rex P. Gatto. LC 91-73602. 212p. (Orig.). 1992. pap. text ed. 11.95 (*0-945997-21-3*, Gardner Pr) GTA Pr.

Teamwork Through Time Management: New Time Management Methods for Everyone in Your Organization. R. Alec Mackenzie. 257p. 1991. pap. 23.95 (*0-85013-182-0*) Dartnell Corp.

Teanaway Country. Mary Sutliff. LC 79-66697. (Illus.). (Orig.). 1980. pap. 5.95 (*0-913140-39-2*) Signpost Bk Pub.

Teape...A Genealogy. 110p. 1983. pap. 5.95 (*0-317-68202-4*) J H Day Pub.

Teapot Dome: Oil & Politics in the 1920's. Burl Noggle. LC 80-15396. (Illus.). ix, 234p. 1980. reprint ed. text ed. 59.75 (*0-313-22601-6*, NOTD, Greenwood Pr) Greenwood.

Teapot Treasury. Richard W. Luckin. (Illus.). 152p. 1987. 19.95 (*0-685-59604-4*) RK Pub.

Teapots. Paul Tippett. (Christie's Collectibles Ser.). 1996. 12.95 (*0-614-96828-3*) Bulfinch Pr.

Tear & a Smile. Kahlil Gibran. (Illus.). 1950. 24.50 (*0-394-44804-9*) Knopf.

Tear & a Star. Darshan Singh. LC 82-61430. (Illus.). 164p. 1986. 12.95 (*0-918224-21-7*); pap. 7.00 (*0-918224-20-9*) S K Pubns.

Tear Drops of Love. Eduardo L. Digirolamo. 1978. 15.00 (*0-931138-03-5*) Maiden Bks.

***Tear Here. Rachel Gladstone-Gelman. (Illus.). 36p. 1997. 3.50 (*0-9657408-1-1*) Third Rail NY. A chapbook of poems of gritty disclosure, by Rachel Gladstone-Gelman. "These short poems are deceptively simple. Linger over them & begin to see things. Like the darkness that inhabits some of the best of these."--Tom Hansen, Lunar Offensive Press. 36pp. $4.50. ISBN 0-9657408-1-1. Also available from Third Rail Press, GENTLE ON THE HEART, poems of calm exploration, by Rachel Gladstone-Gelman. 32pp. $4.00. ISBN 0-9657408-0-3. Prices include shipping. P.O. Box 350098, Brooklyn, NY 11235. Other poems at http://www.escape.com/~pinata.**

Publisher Provided Annotation.

***Tear This Heart Out.** Angeles Mastretta. Tr. by Margaret Peden. LC 96-39816. 304p. 1997. pap. 12.00 (*1-57322-602-5*, Riverhd Trade) Berkley Pub.

***Tear This Heart Out.** Angeles Mastretta. 1997. pap. 12.00 (*0-614-27266-1*, Riverhd Trade) Berkley Pub.

Tearaways: Stories to Make You Think Twice. Robin Klein. 144p. (YA). (gr. 5-9). 1991. pap. 12.95 (*0-670-83212-X*) Viking Child Bks.

Teardrops & Laughter, 3 vols. Ed. by Carolyn E. Cardwell. (Illus.). 250p. (Orig.). 1984. Set. pap. write for info. (*0-916395-10-3*) Hieroglyphics.

Teardrops & Laughter, 3 vols., 1. Ed. by Carolyn E. Cardwell. (Illus.). 250p. (Orig.). 1984. pap. 10.95 (*0-916395-01-4*, TD-1) Hieroglyphics.

Teardrops & Laughter, 3 vols., 2. Ed. by Carolyn E. Cardwell. (Illus.). 250p. (Orig.). 1984. pap. 8.45 (*0-916395-04-9*, TD-2) Hieroglyphics.

Teardrops & Laughter, 3 vols., Vol. 3. Ed. by Carolyn E. Cardwell. (Illus.). 250p. (Orig.). 1985. pap. 8.45 (*0-916395-07-3*, TD-3) Hieroglyphics.

Teardrops & Silicon. Emshock. (Illus.). 1978. 2.97 (*0-9603504-0-3*) Vongrutnorv Og.

Teardrops in Sand. Sam Sax. Ed. by Margaret E. Burton. LC 87-6149. (Illus.). 96p. (Orig.). 1987. pap. 9.95 (*0-938310-07-0*) Volunteer Pubns.

Teares for the Death of Alexander, Earle of Dunfermeling, Lord Chancellar of Scotland. John Lyon. LC 79-172760. (Bannatyne Club, Edinburgh. Publications: No. 4). reprint ed. 29.50 (*0-404-52704-3*) AMS Pr.

Tearing Away the Veils: The Financiers Who Control the World. F. Coty. 1987. lib. bdg. 79.95 (*0-8490-3948-7*) Gordon Pr.

Tearing Away the Veils of International Finance. Francois Coty. 1979. lib. bdg. 69.95 (*0-8490-3011-0*) Gordon Pr.

Tearing Down Strongholds. rev. ed. Richard A. Webster. LC 93-1449. 368p. 1993. reprint ed. pap. 16.95 (*0-87808-240-9*, WCL240-9) William Carey Lib.

Tearing Down the Color Bar: A Documentary History & Analysis of the Brotherhood of Sleeping Car Porters. Joseph F. Wilson. (Illus.). 396p. 1989. text ed. 63.00 (*0-231-06478-0*) Col U Pr.

Tearing Down the Walls: An Adult Woman's Guide to Educational Financial Aid. Christine Payne. 195p. (Orig.). (C). 1993. pap. text ed. write for info. (*0-9635930-0-5*) Bibury Court.

***Tearing the Silence: On Being German in America.** Ursula Hegi. 1997. 24.00 (*0-684-82996-7*) S&S Trade.

Tearoom Trade: Impersonal Sex in Public Places. rev. ed. Laud Humphreys. LC 74-22642. 253p. 1975. pap. text ed. 26.95 (*0-202-30283-0*); lib. bdg. 43.95 (*0-202-30282-2*) Aldine de Gruyter.

Tears. Mark C. Taylor. LC 89-4228. (SUNY Series, Intersections). 263p. 1989. text ed. 59.50 (*0-7914-0102-2*); pap. text ed. 19.95 (*0-7914-0103-0*) State U NY Pr.

Tears. John Tholen. 92p. 1991. 7.95 (*0-9630926-1-8*) Tholen Enter.

***Tears: A Key to a Remedy.** Peter Van Oosterum. 1997. pap. text ed. 10.95 (*1-85398-103-6*, Pub. by Ashgrove UK) Words Distrib.

Tears: From a Father's Eyes. Steven L. Rogers. 126p. (Orig.). 1996. pap. 6.95 (*1-57502-099-8*) Morris Pubng.

Tears & Laughter. Ed. by A. J. Born. 192p. 1990. 10.00 (*0-945242-13-1*) Shri Ram Chandra.

Tears & Laughter. Kahlil Gibran. 1993. 4.98 (*1-55521-895-4*) Bk Sales Inc.

Tears & Laughter. Kahlil Gibran. 96p. 1984. pap. 5.95 (*0-8065-0903-1*, Citadel Pr) Carol Pub Group.

***Tears & Laughter: A Couple of Dozen Dog Stories.** Gene Hill. (Illus.). 176p. 1996. reprint ed. 25.00 (*0-924357-67-3*, 21280-A) Countrysport Pr.

Tears & Laughter of a Man's Soul. James Kavanaugh. LC 90-62061. (Illus.). 29p. 1991. 15.95 (*1-878995-08-1*) S J Nash Pub.

***Tears & Laughter of a Man's Soul.** James Kavanaugh. 29p. 1996. pap. 9.95 (*1-878995-41-3*) S J Nash Pub.

Tears & Rage: The Nursing Crisis in America. Jane Schweitzer. LC 95-80226. (Illus.). 244p. (Orig.). 1996. pap. 18.95 (*1-883422-05-1*) Adams-Blake.

Tears & Saints. E. M. Cioran. Tr. by Ilinca Zarifopol-Johnston. LC 95-8428. 154p. 1995. 18.95 (*0-226-10672-1*) U Ch Pr.

Tears & Stone. Donita Simpson. 1971. pap. 6.50 (*0-685-99409-0*) Peace Ways.

***Tears & Triumphs.** Valentine Dmitriev. Ed. by Elizabeth Lake. (Illus.). 219p. (Orig.). 1997. pap. 22.00 (*0-89716-715-5*, A10057) P B Pubng.

Tears & Turmoil No. 11: Order. Joanne C. Eakin. (Illus.). 110p. 1996. pap. text ed. 10.95 (*0-9636780-9-4*) C M Bartels.

Tears Before the Rain: An Oral History of the Fall of South Vietnam. Larry Engelmann. (Illus.). 408p. 1990. 22.95 (*0-19-505386-9*) OUP.

***Tears Before the Rain: An Oral History of the Fall of South Vietnam.** Larry Engelmann. LC 97-21949. (Illus.). 417p. 1997. reprint ed. pap. 15.95 (*0-306-80789-0*) Da Capo.

***Tears Flow, Ice Melts, Spring Comes! A Soul Blossoms.** Calla M. Binet. 200p. (Orig.). 1997. pap. 14.00 (*1-889245-03-8*) Glden Reed.

Tears for Ashan. D. Marie. LC 88-63766. (Illus.). 32p. (J). (ps-3). 1989. 11.95 (*0-9621681-0-6*) Creative Pr Works.

***Tears for the Smaller Dragon.** Jean Livingston. (Jaffray Collection of Missionary Portraits: No. 18). 1997. pap. 8.99 (*0-87509-703-0*) Chr Pubns.

Tears from My Heart. Ester B. Williams. LC 90-70572. 60p. 1990. 5.95 (*1-55523-347-3*) Winston-Derek.

***Tears from My Heart: A Memorial to Lost Works.** Amy Marschak. (Illus.). 44p. (Orig.). 1997. pap. 8.00 (*0-9653298-2-8*) Human Theatre.

Tears from the Cross. Embree J. De Witt. 1995. 13.95 (*0-533-11486-1*) Vantage.

Tears in Heaven, Good for Me & Other Top Hits, No. 403. 64p. 1992. pap. 6.95 (*0-7935-1493-2*, 00102236) H Leonard.

Tears in Heaven, Good for Me & Other Top Hits, No. 403. 64p. 1992. pap. 5.95 (*0-7935-1492-4*, 00243124) H Leonard.

Tears in Heaven, Save the Best for Last & Other Top Hits: Easy Piano. (Easy Play Ser.). 64p. 1992. pap. 7.95 (*0-7935-1648-X*, 00222553) H Leonard.

Tears in My Horseradish. Robert F. Karolevitz. LC 83-63001. (Illus.). 138p. (Orig.). 1983. pap. 7.95 (*0-940161-01-X*) Dakota Homestead Pub.

Tears in Teardrop Island. M. V. Alagappan. 103p. 1985. text ed. 15.00 (*0-86590-593-2*, Pub. by Sterling Pubs II) Apt Bks.

Tears in the Lion's Heart. Margaret O'Connor. Ed. by Bev Balliett. LC 88-84155. 292p. (Orig.). 1989. pap. 7.95 (*0-317-93748-0*) Po Kuan Pr.

***Tears in the Snow: A True Story of Love, Courage & Danger.** Arnie Wilson. 1997. 27.50 (*1-85782-154-8*, Pub. by Blake Publng UK) Seven Hills Bk.

Tears Like Rain. Connie Mason. 448p. (Orig.). 1994. mass mkt., pap. text ed. 5.99 (*0-8439-3629-0*, Leisure Bks) Dorchester Pub Co.

***Tears Like Rain.** Connie Mason. 448p. (Orig.). 1996. mass mkt. 5.99 (*0-8439-4039-5*, Leisure Bks) Dorchester Pub Co.

Tears, Love & Laughter: The Story of the Cajuns & Their Music. 4th rev. ed. Pierre V. Daigle. 160p. 1987. pap. 9.95 (*0-9614245-1-6*) Swallow Pubns.

Tears of a Clown: Mask - What Do They Really Hide? rev. ed. Otis T. McMillan. 96p. 1996. pap. 6.00 (*1-57502-138-2*) Morris Pubng.

Tears of a Tiger. Sharon Draper. LC 94-10278. (J). (gr. 7 up). 1994. 16.00 (*0-689-31878-2*, Atheneum S&S) S&S Trade.

Tears of a Tiger. Sharon M. Draper. (J). 1996. 3.95 (*0-689-80698-1*) S&S Childrens.

Tears of Eros. Georges Bataille. Tr. by Peter Connor from FRE. (Illus.). 208p. (Orig.). 1989. pap. 14.95 (*0-87286-222-4*) City Lights.

Tears of Fire. Nelle McFather. 448p. (Orig.). 1994. mass mkt., pap. text ed. 4.99 (*0-505-51932-1*, Love Spell) Dorchester Pub Co.

Tears of Glass: Shattering of a Daughter's Heart. Patricia Diener & Gail Peterson. 85p. (Orig.). 1994. pap. text ed. 14.95 (*0-9643323-0-2*) P Diener.

Tears of Gold. Laurie McBain. 576p. 1979. mass mkt. 5.50 (*0-380-41475-9*) Avon.

***Tears of Internment: The Indian History of Fox Island & the Puget Sound Indian War.** Cecelia S. Carpenter. LC 96-96300. (Illus.). 102p. (Orig.). 1996. pap. 11.00 (*0-9616969-2-3*) Tahoma Pubns.

Tears of Jade. Leigh Riker. 384p. 1993. mass mkt. 4.99 (*0-06-108047-0*, Harp PBks) HarpC.

Tears of Lady Meng: A Parable of People's Political Theology. Choan-Seng Song. LC 82-2295. (Illus.). 79p. (Orig.). reprint ed. pap. 25.00 (*0-8357-7048-6*, 2033543) Bks Demand.

Tears of My Sister, the Prisoner's Song, the One-Armed Man, the Land of the Astronauts. Horton Foote. 1993. pap. 5.25 (*0-8222-1357-5*) Dramatists Play.

Tears of Narcissus: Melancholia & Masculinity in Early Modern Writing. Lynn Enterline. x, 429p. 1995. 49.50 (*0-8047-2397-4*) Stanford U Pr.

An Asterisk (*) at the beginning of an entry indicates that the title is appearing in BIP for the first time.

Tears of the Crocodile: From Rio to Reality in the Developing World. Neil Middleton et al. LC 93-5266. 228p. (C). pap. 19.95 (*0-7453-0765-5*, Pub. by Pluto Pr UK) LPC InBook.
Tears of the Crocodile: From Rio to Reality in the Developing World. Neil Middleton et al. LC 93-5266. 228p. (C). 70.00 (*0-7453-0764-7*, Pub. by Pluto Pr UK) LPC InBook.
Tears of the Dead: The Social Biography of an African Family. Richard P. Werbner. LC 91-62225. (Illus.). 224p. (Orig.). (C). 1992. pap. text ed. 19.95 (*1-56098-150-4*) Smithsonian.
Tears of the Heart. Lauran Paine. LC 95-31058. 1996. write for info. (*0-7838-1410-0*, GK Hall) Thorndike Pr.
Tears of the Heart. large type ed. Lauran Paine. (Western Ser.). 286p. 1996. 18.95 (*0-7862-0806-6*, Thorndike Lrg Prnt) Thorndike Pr.
Tears of the Heart: A Western Story. Lauran Paine. (Five-Star Western Ser.). 176p. 1995. 16.95 (*0-7862-0511-3*) Thorndike Pr.
Tears of the Heliads. Collets. 169p. 1991. 150.00 (*0-89771-892-5*, Pub. by Collets) St Mut.
Tears of the Inquisition. Paul Little. (Orig.). 1993. mass mkt. 4.95 (*1-56333-146-2*) Masquerade.
***Tears of the Lotus: Accounts of Tibetan Resistance to the Chinese Invasion, 1950-1962.** Roger E. McCarthy. LC 97-6131. 312p. 1997. lib. bdg. 48.50 (*0-7864-0331-4*) McFarland & Co.
Tears of the Madonna. George Herman. 288p. 1996. 22.95 (*0-7867-0243-5*) Carroll & Graf.
Tears of the Moon. Jeanne Nickson. 464p. 1992. mass mkt., pap. text ed. 4.50 (*0-8439-3328-3*) Dorchester Pub Co.
Tears of the Prophets. Roe Halper. (Illus.). 104p. (Orig.). 1975. 18.00 (*0-916326-01-2*) Bayberry Pr.
Tears of the Rose. B. J. James. (Desire Ser.: No. 709). 1992. pap. 2.89 (*0-373-05709-1*, 5-05709-6) Harlequin Bks.
Tears of the Shaman. Rebecca Daniels. (Intimate Moments Ser.). 1995. mass mkt. 3.75 (*0-373-07654-1*, 1-07654-6) Silhouette.
Tears of the Singers. Melinda M. Snodgrass. (Star Trek Ser.: No. 19). 1989. mass mkt. 5.50 (*0-671-69654-8*, Pocket Star Bks) PB.
Tears of the Sun. Al Lacy. (Journeys of the Stranger Ser.). 320p. 1995. pap. 9.99 (*0-88070-838-7*, Multnomah Bks) Multnomah Pubs.
Tears of Things. Ralph M. McInerny. LC 96-19917. 1996. write for info. (*0-03-214746-5*) St Martin.
Tears of Things Vol. 1: A Father Dowling Mystery. Ralph McInerny. 368p. 1996. 24.95 (*0-312-14746-5*) St Martin.
Tears of Time. Nancy Asire. 336p. (Orig.). 1993. mass mkt. 4.99 (*0-671-72191-7*) Baen Bks.
***Tears of Yesterday.** Baxter. 1998. mass mkt. 5.50 (*1-55166-417-8*) Harlequin Bks.
Tears Often Shed. Gandevia. 1979. 28.00 (*0-08-023159-4*, Pergamon Pr) Elsevier.
Tears on the Wind. unabridged ed. Alma G. Stenger. Ed. by Vicki Lloyd. (Illus.). 300p. (Orig.). 1997. per. 14.95 (*1-886364-01-X*) Rabeth Pub Co.
***Tears Throughout Time.** Boris Vukov. (Illus.). 146p. (Orig.). 1997. pap. 12.00 (*0-9657106-3-7*) Zona Incerta.
Teaser & the Firecat. (J). pap. 1.95 (*0-590-04793-0*) Scholastic Inc.
Teasers, Twisters, & Stumpers: A Bookful of Tricky Torah Riddles. Yaffa Ganz. 1990. 11.95 (*0-87306-517-4*) Feldheim.
Teasing: Innocent Fun or Sadistic Malice? Linda S. Feinberg. 256p. 1996. pap. 13.95 (*0-88282-145-8*) New Horizon NJ.
Teat: The Saga of an American Frontiersman. Theodore A. Gould. Ed. by Lana Davis. 325p. 1987. 17.95 (*0-685-25054-7*) World Promos.
Teater's Knoll: Frank Lloyd Wright's Idaho Legacy. LC 87-61042. 188p. 1987. 42.50 (*0-87359-046-5*) Northwood Univ.
***Teatime.** (Country Friends Ser.). (Illus.). 31p. pap. 6.95 (*1-888052-06-6*) Gooseberry Patch.
Teatime Cookbook. Steffi Berne. LC 94-2125. (Illus.). 1995. 25.00 (*0-679-42144-0*, Villard Bks) Random.
***Teatime in the Northwest: The Northwest's Best Tea Rooms & Recipes for Tasty Tea Treats.** Sharon Foster-Lewis & Ken Foster-Lewis. (Illus.). 224p. (Orig.). 1996. pap. 14.95 (*0-9617699-6-3*) Speed Graphics.
***Teatime with Emma Buttersnap.** Tate. 1998. 15.95 (*0-8050-5476-6*) H Holt & Co.
Teatr I-III. Mikhail A. Kuzmin. Ed. by A. Timofeev. (Modern Russian Literature & Culture, Studies & Texts: Vol. 30). (Illus.). 425p. (Orig.). (RUS.). Date not set. pap. 25.00 (*0-933884-94-X*) Berkeley Slavic.
Teatr IV. Mikhail A. Kuzmin. Ed. by A. Timofeev. (Modern Russian Literature & Culture, Studies & Texts: Vol. 31). (Illus.). 418p. (Orig.). (RUS.). Date not set. pap. 25.00 (*0-933884-95-8*) Berkeley Slavic.
Teatri 1827-1831, 2 vols., Set. Ed. by H. Robert Cohen. (Repertoire International de la Presse Musicale Ser.). (ITA.). 1992. lib. bdg. 240.00 (*0-8357-2209-0*) Univ Microfilms.
Teatro. Clarisa Bell. (This Is Entertainment Ser.). (Illus.). 24p. (SPA.). (J). (gr. 2-6). 1992. lib. bdg. 9.95 (*1-56492-056-9*) Laredo.
Teatro. Carlos Felipe. LC 87-62801. 633p. (SPA.). 1988. pap. 50.00 (*0-89295-044-7*) Society Sp & Sp-Am.
Teatro. Ricardo Salvat. 152p. (SPA.). 1983. pap. 7.00 (*84-85859-56-1*, 2113) Ediciones Norte.
Teatro. Ignacio Sanchez Mejias. Ed. by Antonio Gallego Morell. (Nueva Austral Ser.: Vol. 47). (SPA.). 1991. pap. text ed. 24.95 (*84-239-1847-5*) Elliots Bks.
Teatro: Big Book. Clarisa Bell. (This Is Entertainment Ser.). (Illus.). 24p. (Orig.). (SPA.). (J). (gr. 2-6). 1992. pap. 19.95 (*1-56492-057-7*) Laredo.
Teatro! Hispanic Plays for Young People. Angel Vigil. 220p. 1996. pap. text ed. 25.00 (*1-56308-371-X*) Teacher Ideas Pr.
Teatro: Un Color Para Este Miedo. El Mar De Cada Dia. Donde Esta La Luz. El Hombre Inmaculado. Ramon Ferreira. LC 92-73983. (Coleccion Teatro). (Illus.). 224p. (Orig.). (SPA.). 1993. pap. 19.00 (*0-89729-655-9*) Ediciones.
Teatro: 5 Autores Cubanos. Maria I. Fornes et al. LC 95-699901. (Theater Collection: Vol. I). 277p. (SPA.). 1995. pap. 14.00 (*0-9625127-5-3*) Ollantay Pr.
Teatro Absurdo de Jose Triana. Ramiro Fernandez-Fernandez. LC 95-67524. 94p. 1995. pap. text ed. 25.00 (*0-89295-080-3*) Society Sp & Sp-Am.
***Teatro Alegorico de Muguel (Daniel Levi) de Barrios.** Ed. by Julia R. Lieberman. (Ediciones Criticas Ser.: Vol. 5). 234p. (Orig.). (SPA.). 1996. pap. 17.00 (*0-936388-68-4*) Juan de la Cuesta.
Teatro Brasileiro Contemporaneo. rev. ed. Ed. by Wilson Martins & Seymour Menton. LC 77-2753. (gr. 11-12). 1978. reprint ed. pap. text ed. 19.95 (*0-89197-640-X*) Irvington.
Teatro Bufo (Robame un Billoncito, Apertura, Orangutan, Punk y Punk y Colegram) Fernando Arrabal. Ed. by Francisco Torres Monreal. (Nueva Austral Ser.: No. 18). (SPA.). 1991. pap. text ed. 24.95 (*84-239-1818-1*) Elliots Bks.
Teatro Campesino: Theater in the Chicano Movement. Yolanda Broyles-Gonzalez. LC 94-935. (Illus.). 304p. (C). 1994. pap. 17.95 (*0-292-70801-7*); text ed. 37.50 (*0-292-72082-3*) U of Tex Pr.
Teatro Cervantes de Alcala de Henares: 1602-1866: Estudio y Documentos. Miguel A. Marin et al. (Fuentes Ser.: No. 18). (Illus.). 390p. (C). 1990. 53.00 (*0-7293-0310-1*, Pub. by Tamesis Bks Ltd UK) Boydell & Brewer.
Teatro Completo. Ed. by Egon Wolff. LC 89-64396. 659p. 1990. pap. 50.00 (*0-89295-058-7*) Society Sp & Sp-Am.
Teatro de Max Aub. Estela R. Lopez. LC 76-46372. (UPREX, Teatro y Cine Ser.: No. 52). 200p. (Orig.). 1976. pap. text ed. 1.50 (*0-8477-0052-6*) U of PR Pr.
Teatro de Nuestra America: Un Proyecto Continental, 1959-1989. Marina Pianca. (Series Towards a Social History of Hispanic & Luso-Brazilian Literatures). 408p. (Orig.). (C). 1990. pap. 14.95 (*1-877660-05-1*) IFTSOIL.
***Teatro Del Gonzaga Al Tempo Di Isabella D'Este.** Mauda Bregoli-Russo. (Studies in Italian Culture: No. 21). 144p. (ITA.). (C). 1997. text ed. 36.95 (*0-8204-3124-9*) P Lang Pubng.
Teatro Del Mexico Colonial: Epoca Misionera. Jerry M. Williams. LC 91-39543. (Iberica Ser.: Vol. 4). 162p. (C). 1993. text ed. 57.95 (*0-8204-7792-3*) P Lang Pubng.
Teatro en Alicante, 1901-1910: Cartelera y Estudio. Francisco R. Boyd-Swan. (Fuentes Ser.: Vol. 23). (Illus.). 440p. (C). 1994. pap. 54.00 (*1-85566-036-9*, Pub. by Tamesis Bks Ltd UK) Boydell & Brewer.
Teatro en America Latina: Religion, Politica & Cultura, desde Cortes Hasta la Decada de los 80. Adam Versenyi. 342p. (SPA.). (C). 1996. pap. text ed. 16.95 (*0-521-47850-2*) Cambridge U Pr.
***Teatro en Badajoz, 1860-1886.** Ed. by Angel S. Munoz. (Fuentes Para la Historia del Teatro en Espana, Series C: Vol. 28). 360p. (SPA.). 1997. 63.00 (*1-85566-055-5*, Pub. by Tamesis Bks Ltd UK) Boydell & Brewer.
Teatro en la Espana del Siglo XIX. David T. Gies. 540p. (SPA.). (C). 1996. pap. text ed. 19.95 (*0-521-47836-7*) Cambridge U Pr.
Teatro en Puerto Rico: Notas Para Su Historia. 2nd ed. Antonio Saez. (UPREX, Teatro y Cine Ser.: No.6). 134p. (C). 1972. pap. 1.50 (*0-8477-0006-2*) U of PR Pr.
Teatro Espanol E Iberoamericano En Madrid (1962-1991) Juan Molla. LC 92-64365. 204p. 1993. pap. 40.00 (*0-89295-070-6*) Society Sp & Sp-Am.
Teatro Hispano! Three Major New York Companies. rev. ed. Elisa De La Roche. LC 95-14987. (Studies in American Popular History & Culture). 220p. 1995. text ed. 62.00 (*0-8153-1986-X*) Garland.
Teatro Medieval. Ed. by Ana M. Pellitero. (Nueva Austral Ser.: No. 157). (SPA.). 1991. pap. text ed. 24.95 (*84-239-1957-9*) Elliots Bks.
Teatro Mexicano En Ciernes 1922-1938. Guillermo Schmidhuber. LC 91-39544. (Taft & University of Cincinnati Series in Latin American & Hispanic American Theater: Vol. 1). 223p. (C). 1993. text ed. 50.95 (*0-8204-1757-2*) P Lang Pubng.
***Teatro Palaciego en Madrid: 1586-1707 Vol. 2: Documentos y Estudio.** Ed. by Margaret R. Greer & J. E. Varey. (Fuentes Historia Teatral Ser.: Vol. 29). 300p. (SPA.). 1997. 53.00 (*1-85566-050-4*, Pub. by Tamesis Bks Ltd UK) Boydell & Brewer.
Teatro, Prosa, Poesia. Althea C. Reynolds & Argentina Brunetti. (Illus.). 160p. 1982. pap. text ed. 27.50 (*0-915838-12-5*) Anma Libri.
Teatro Renacentista. Ed. by Alfredo Hermenegilda. (Nueva Austral Ser.: No. 171). (SPA.). 1991. pap. text ed. 24.95 (*84-239-1971-4*) Elliots Bks.
Teatro y Practicas Escenicas II: La Comedia. Ed. by Jose L. Valles. 392p. 1986. pap. 35.00 (*0-7293-0242-3*, Pub. by Tamesis Bks Ltd UK) Boydell & Brewer.
Teatros y Comedias en Madrid 1600-1650: Estudio y Documentos. Ed. by J. E. Varey & N. D. Shergold. (Fuentes Ser.: No. 3). 195p. (SPA.). (C). 1971. pap. 35.00 (*0-900411-21-X*, Pub. by Tamesis Bks Ltd UK) Boydell & Brewer.
Teatros y Comedias en Madrid 1651-1655: Estudio y Documentos. Ed. by J. E. Varey & N. D. Shergold. (Fuentes Ser.: No. 4). 258p. (Orig.). (SPA.). (C). 1973. pap. 35.00 (*0-900411-55-4*, Pub. by Tamesis Bks Ltd UK) Boydell & Brewer.
Teatros y Comedias en Madrid 1666-1687: Estudio y Documentos. Ed. by J. E. Varey & N. D. Shergold. (Fuentes Ser.: No. 5). 206p. (SPA.). (C). 1974. pap. 35.00 (*0-900411-89-9*, Pub. by Tamesis Bks Ltd UK) Boydell & Brewer.
Teatros y Comedias en Madrid 1688-1699: Estudio y Documentos. N. D. Shergold & J. E. Varey. (Fuentes Ser.: No. 6). 319p. (SPA.). (C). 1979. pap. 35.00 (*0-7293-0064-1*, Pub. by Tamesis Bks Ltd UK) Boydell & Brewer.
Teatros y Comedias en Madrid 1699-1719: Estudio y Documentos. Ed. by N. D. Shergold & J. E. Varey. (Fuentes Ser.: Vol. XI). 222p. (SPA.). 1986. pap. 35.00 (*0-7293-0241-5*, Pub. by Tamesis Bks Ltd UK) Boydell & Brewer.
Teatros y Comedias en Madrid 1719-1744: Estudios y Documentos. Ed. by J. E. Varey et al. (Fuentes Ser.: No. XII). 384p. (SPA.). (C). 1994. 53.00 (*1-85566-010-5*, Pub. by Tamesis Bks Ltd UK) Boydell & Brewer.
Teatros y Vida Teatral del Siglo de Oro a Traves las Fuentes Documentales. Ed. by Luciano G. Lorenzo & J. E. Varey. (Monagrafias A Ser.: No. 145). (C). 1992. pap. 35.00 (*1-85566-007-5*, Pub. by Tamesis Bks Ltd UK) Boydell & Brewer.
***Teatros y Vida Teatral en Badajoz, 1601-1699.** Ed. by Fernando M. Alvarez. (Fuentes Para la Historia del Teatro en Espana, Series C: Vol. 27). 325p. (SPA.). 1997. 53.00 (*1-85566-054-7*, Pub. by Tamesis Bks Ltd UK) Boydell & Brewer.
Teatros y Vida Teatral en Tudela: 1563-1750. Maria T. Bonis. (Fuentes Ser.: No. XVII). (Illus.). 224p. (SPA.). 1991. pap. 53.00 (*1-85566-003-2*, Pub. by Tamesis Bks Ltd UK) Boydell & Brewer.
Tebaldi: The Voice of an Angel. Carlamaria Casanova. Tr. by Connie De Caro. (Great Voices Ser.). (Illus.). 265p. 1995. 35.00 (*1-880909-40-5*) Baskerville.
Tebaldo ed Isolina. Francesco Morlacchi. (Italian Opera Ser., 1810-1840: Vol. 24). 260p. 1990. text ed. 30.00 (*0-8240-6573-5*) Garland.
Tebe Sonati Iran: Traditional Medicine of Iran. Shah Maghsoud Sadegh Angha. LC 83-80800. 519p. (PER.). 1983. 75.00 (*0-910735-45-X*) MTO Printing & Pubn Ctr.
Tebi Mayramoud. Antranig Antreassian. LC 89-91382. (ARM.). 1989. write for info. (*0-936893-05-2*) Baikar.
TEC Course - Interconnections: Bridges & Routers. Joseph Passafiume. 1992. write for info. (*0-201-41887-8*) Addison-Wesley.
TEC Course - Software Project Management. Richard Fairley. 1990. write for info. (*0-201-41871-1*) Addison-Wesley.
TEC Course - Software Requirements Analysis & Specification Workshop. Patrick Loy. 1990. write for info. (*0-201-41872-X*) Addison-Wesley.
TEC Course - Structure Analysis & Design for Real-Time. Patrick Loy. 1990. write for info. (*0-201-41873-8*) Addison-Wesley.
TEC Course-Advanced C++ Workshop. Vilot Michael. 1991. write for info. (*0-201-41899-1*) Addison-Wesley.
TEC Course-Advanced C Workshop: Algorithms & Data Structures. David Prosser. 1990. write for info. (*0-201-41891-6*) Addison-Wesley.
TEC Course Advanced-UNIX Programming. Richard Stevens. 1992. write for info. (*0-201-41889-4*) Addison-Wesley.
TEC Course-C++ Workshop for Non-C Programmers. Tom Cargill. 1991. write for info. (*0-201-41898-3*) Addison-Wesley.
TEC Course-Computer Architecture. Max Vasilatos. 1990. write for info. (*0-201-41883-5*) Addison-Wesley.
TEC Course-Data Communications. William Stallings. 1990. write for info. (*0-201-41881-9*) Addison-Wesley.
TEC Course-Database Design: Relational, Distributed, & Object-Oriented Concepts. Edgar Codd. 1991. write for info. (*0-201-41876-2*) Addison-Wesley.
TEC Course-Local Area Networks. William Stallings. 1990. write for info. (*0-201-41882-7*) Addison-Wesley.
TEC Course Management Technologies. Yemini Yechiam. 1991. write for info. (*0-201-41880-0*) Addison-Wesley.
TEC Course-Microsoft Windows Programming. Alan Feuer. 1991. write for info. (*0-201-41896-7*) Addison-Wesley.
TEC Course-Multi-Vendor Networking. Stuart Wecker. 1991. write for info. (*0-201-41884-3*) Addison-Wesley.
TEC Course-Network Management Technologies. Alan Feuer. 1993. write for info. (*0-201-41879-7*) Addison-Wesley.
TEC Course-Object Oriented Analysis & Design. Michael Vilot. 1991. write for info. (*0-201-41877-0*) Addison-Wesley.
TEC Course-Software Design Methods, Tools & Techniques. James Bouhana. 1991. write for info. (*0-201-41874-6*) Addison-Wesley.
TEC Course-Software Quality Assurance: Control, Metrics & Testing. Pat Hurst. 1991. write for info. (*0-201-41875-4*) Addison-Wesley.
TEC Course-UNIX Network Programming. William Versteeg. 1992. write for info. (*0-201-41888-6*) Addison-Wesley.
TEC UNIX System Administration. Evi Nemeth. 1991. pap. write for info. (*0-201-41895-9*) Addison-Wesley.
TEC X Windows. Wayne Dykson. 1991. pap. write for info. (*0-201-41897-5*) Addison-Wesley.
TEC-1994 Revised Courses. Hendrickson. 1994. write for info. (*0-201-41800-2*) Addison-Wesley.
TEC-1994 Train the Trainer. 1994. write for info. (*0-201-41810-X*) Addison-Wesley.
Tech Activities Sampler. Harms. (Tech & Industrial Education Ser.). 1989. text ed. 10.00 (*0-8273-3235-1*) Delmar.
Tech & Theory of Periodontal Instrumentation. Perry et al. (Illus.). 432p. 1990. pap. text ed. 50.00 (*0-7216-2734-X*) Saunders.
Tech & Tools Book: A Guide to the Technologies Women Are Using Worldwide. Ed. by J. Sandler & R. Sandhu. 200p. (Orig.). 1986. pap. 20.95 (*0-946688-17-6*, Pub. by Intermed Tech UK) Women Ink.
Tech Book. Classic Chevy International Staff. 1994. 59.95 (*0-9641464-0-1*) Classic Chevy.
Tech Challenges: A Collection of Technology Education Activity Masters-Design Solutions Manual. Kenneth L. Smith. 36p. 1994. teacher ed. 14.00 (*0-8273-6981-6*) Delmar.
***Tech Decisions: The Hottest Tech Prep Careers.** Joseph A. Despres. 1997. 20.00 (*1-878172-48-4*, 397TDB) Wintergrn-Orchard Hse.
***Tech Girl's Internet Adventures.** Girl Tech Staff. 260p. 1997. pap. 19.99 (*0-7645-3046-1*) IDG Bks.
***Tech Girl's Internet Adventures.** Janese Swanson & Linda Halnnen. 260p. (Orig.). 1997. pap. write for info. (*0-614-26258-5*) IDG Bks.
Tech-Heaven. Linda Nagata. 368p. (Orig.). 1995. mass mkt., pap. 4.99 (*0-553-56926-0*, Spectra) Bantam.
Tech Intell Vol. 2: World War II U. S. Army Technical Intelligence Reports & Summaries. Ed. by Jeffrey D. McKaughan. (Tech Intell Ser.). (Illus.). 132p. pap. 13.95 (*0-9648793-0-1*) Darlington Prods.
Tech-Master for Refrigerators & Freezers, Vol. 13: 1966 Through 1970 Reference Manual. Barnee Schollnick. (Illus.). 377p. (Orig.). 1990. pap. 40.00 (*1-56302-036-X*, 7550-2) R Longhurst.
Tech-Master for Refrigerators & Freezers, Vol. 14: 1971 Through 1975 Reference Manual. Woody Wooldridge. (Illus.). 331p. (Orig.). 1990. pap. 40.00 (*1-56302-039-4*, 7550-3) R Longhurst.
Tech-Master for Refrigerators & Freezers, Vol. 15: 1976 Through 1981 Reference Manual. Barnee Schollnick. Ed. by Woody Wooldridge. (Illus.). 378p. (Orig.). 1990. pap. 40.00 (*1-56302-042-4*, 7550-4) R Longhurst.
Tech Prep - Associate Degree: A Win Win Experience. Dan Hull. 1991. 32.50 (*1-55502-392-4*) CORD Commns.
Tech Prep-Associate Degree: A Win Win Experience. Dan Hull & Dale Parnell. (Illus.). (Orig.). 1991. pap. 19.50 (*1-55502-430-0*) CORD Commns.
Tech Prep Bridge: Preparing Adult Students to Enter a Two-Year Degree Program. Center for Occupational Research & Development Staff. (Illus.). 1993. pap. text ed. write for info. (*1-55502-518-8*) CORD Commns.
***Tech Prep Career Programs: A Practical Guide to Preparing Students for High-Tech, High Skill, High Wage Opportunities.** rev. ed. Carol Fagan & Dan Lumley. LC 96-25388. (Illus.). 144p. 1997. 54.95 (*0-8039-6510-9*); pap. 24.95 (*0-8039-6511-7*) Corwin Pr.
Tech Prep Education: A Total Quality Approach. Charles J. Law. LC 93-60982. 250p. 1993. pap. text ed. 39.95 (*1-56676-086-0*) Technomic.
Tech Prep Handbook: A Guide to 2+2 Articulation Agreements & More. Marcia Dier. LC 75-20074. 1994. 14.95 (*0-912486-69-4*) Finney Co.
***Tech Team: Student Technology Assistants.** Erica Peto et al. (Professional Growth Ser.). 1997. pap. text ed. write for info. (*0-938865-60-9*) Linworth Pub.
Tech Tips. Ed. by Hugh H. Milligan. (Illus.). 176p. (Orig.). 1993. teacher ed. write for info. (*0-9635225-0-7*) Jensen Intercep.
Tech Vocabulary-Vocabulaire Anglais-Francais de la Haute Technologie. C. Lassure. 223p. (ENG & FRE.). 1991. pap. 39.95 (*0-7859-7150-5*) Fr & Eur.
Tech Writing Game: A Comprehensive Career Guide for Aspiring Technical Writers. Janet Van Wicklen. 256p. 1992. 22.95 (*0-8160-2607-6*) Facts on File.
***Teche!** Jess R. DeHart. 480p. (Orig.). 1996. pap. 9.95 (*0-913861-01-4*) Hamlet Hse.
Techgnosis. Erik Davis. 1997. write for info. (*0-517-70415-3*, Harmony) Crown Pub Group.
***Techie Freelancing: Careers in Theatre & Business.** J. L. Dolice. (Illus.). 200p. (Orig.). 1997. pap. 29.95 (*0-935901-06-X*) Dolice Graphics.
Techknowledge Newsletter. Hill. (Tech & Industrial Education Ser.). 1995. 72.95 (*0-8273-6883-6*) Delmar.
Techknowledge Reference Series. Holodnick. (TP - Technology Education Ser.). (J). (gr. k-12). 1996. teacher ed. 82.95 (*0-538-64480-X*) S-W Pub.
Techman of the Twenties. Patricia G. Johnson. LC 90-50124. (Illus.). 117p. (Orig.). 1991. 15.00 (*0-9614765-9-1*) Walpa Pub.
TechNails: Extensions, Wraps, & Nail Art. Tammy Bigan. (Illus.). 160p. (C). 1991. pap. 31.95 (*0-87350-382-1*) Milady Pub.
Technetium Ninety-Nine-M: Generators, Chemistry, & Preparation of Radiopharmaceuticals. Ed. by W. C. Eckelman. (Illus.). 168p. 1983. pap. 28.00 (*0-08-029144-9*, Pergamon Pr) Elsevier.
Technic Companion. Nancy Bachus & Denes Agay. (Illus.). 80p. 1990. pap. 19.95 (*0-8256-1122-9*, YK20600, Yorktown Mus); pap. 7.95 (*0-8256-8081-6*, YK20600, Yorktown Mus) Music Sales.
Technic Control One Resource Guide. Tom Barrowman et al. Ed. by Cathy Helgoe & Tom Lough. (Illus.). 416p. (YA). (gr. 6-12). 1991. text ed. 75.00 (*0-914831-74-7*, 959) Lego Dacta.
Technic Time, Pt. A. Louise Goss & Marion McArtot. (Frances Clark Library for Piano Students). 48p. (Orig.). (J). (gr. k-6). 1974. pap. text ed. 6.95 (*0-87487-189-1*) Summy-Birchard.
Technic Time, Part B. (Frances Clark Library for Piano Students). (J). (gr. k-6). 1955. pap. text ed. 6.95 (*0-87487-190-5*) Summy-Birchard.
Technic Treasury: YPL, No. 8B. Ed. by Carole Flatau. 32p. (Orig.). 1994. pap. 5.95 (*0-89724-353-6*, DA0024) Warner Brothers.

Technical. P.A.R. Staff. 64p. (C). 1988. 10.55 (*0-89702-080-4*) Irwin.

Technical Advances in AIDS Research in the Human Nervous System: Proceedings of a NIH Workshop Held in Washington, D. C., October 4-5, 1993. Ed. by Eugene O. Major et al. 360p. 1995. 95.00 (*0-306-45000-3*) Plenum.

Technical Advances in Biofilm Reactors. Ed. by J. Bernard. (Water Science & Technology Ser.: No. 22). (Illus.). 510p. 1990. pap. 190.25 (*0-08-040170-8*, Pergamon Pr) Elsevier.

Technical Advances in Biomedical Physics. Ed. by Philip P. Dendy. 1984. lib. bdg. 159.50 (*90-247-2934-3*) Kluwer Ac.

Technical Aid in Science & Engineering. Jack Rudman. (Career Examination Ser.: C-829). 1994. pap. 29.95 (*0-8373-0829-1*) Nat Learn.

Technical Aide. Jack Rudman. (Career Examination Ser.: C-1514). 1994. pap. 27.95 (*0-8373-1514-X*) Nat Learn.

Technical Aids to Teaching Higher Education. 3rd ed. Collin F. Page & John Kitching. 92p. 1981. pap. 32.00 (*0-900868-49-X*, Open Univ Pr) Taylor & Francis.

Technical Analysis. Jack D. Schwager & Steven C. Turner. 208p. 1995. student ed., pap. 30.00 (*0-471-12354-4*) Wiley.

Technical Analysis. Jack D. Schwager. LC 95-43790. 424p. 1995. text ed. 65.00 (*0-471-02051-6*) Wiley.

Technical Analysis. P. Michael Smyrk. 192p. 1996. 125.00 (*1-85573-157-6*, Pub. by Woodhead Pubng UK) Am Educ Systs.

Technical Analysis: A Personal Seminar. New York Institute of Finance Staff. 1989. pap. 21.95 (*0-13-898370-4*) NY Inst Finance.

Technical Analysis & Options Strategies. Kenneth H. Shaleen. 325p. 1992. text ed. 55.00 (*1-55738-407-X*) Irwin Prof Pubng.

***Technical Analysis Applications in the Global Currency Markets.** Cornelius Luca. LC 97-11241. 1997. 69.95 (*0-13-494055-5*) P-H.

Technical Analysis Course: A Winning Program for Investors & Traders. rev. ed. Thomas A. Meyers. 1993. text ed. 47.50 (*1-55738-523-8*) Irwin Prof Pubng.

Technical Analysis Explained: The Successful Investor's Guide to Spotting Investment Trends & Turning Points. 3rd ed. Martin J. Pring. 544p. 1991. text ed. 49.95 (*0-07-051042-3*) McGraw.

Technical Analysis from A to Z: Covers Every Trading Tool from the Absolute Breadth Index. Steven B. Achelis. 1994. text ed. 29.95 (*1-55738-816-4*) Irwin Prof Pubng.

Technical Analysis in the Options Market: The Effective Use of Computerized Trading Systems. Richard Hexton. (Market Place Book Ser.). 240p. 1994. text ed. 55.00 (*0-471-08489-1*) Wiley.

Technical Analysis of Stock Trends. 6th ed. Robert D. Edwards & John Magee. (Illus.). 1992. 75.00 (*0-13-904343-8*, Busn) Magee.

***Technical Analysis of Stock Trends.** 7th ed. Robert D. Edwards & John Magee. LC 97-7190. 704p. 1997. 75.00 (*0-8144-0373-5*) AMACOM.

***Technical Analysis of Stock Trends.** 7th rev. ed. Robert D. Edwards & John Magee. Ed. by Richard J. McDermott. (Illus.). 792p. 1997. 75.00 (*0-910944-04-0*) Magee.

Technical Analysis of Stocks & Commodities, Vol. 7. Ed. by Jack K. Hutson. LC 86-50575. (Illus.). 490p. (Orig.). 1990. pap. text ed. 59.95 (*0-938773-07-0*) Tech Analysis.

Technical Analysis of Stocks & Commodities, Vol. 8. Ed. by Jack K. Hutson. 607p. (Orig.). 1991. pap. 59.95 (*0-938773-08-9*) Tech Analysis.

Technical Analysis of Stocks & Commodities, Vol. 9. Ed. & Intro. by Jack K. Hutson. 608p. (Orig.). 1992. reprint ed. pap. 59.95 (*0-938773-09-7*) Tech Analysis.

Technical Analysis of Stocks & Commodities, Vol. 10. Intro. by Jack K. Hutson. 668p. (Orig.). 1993. reprint ed. pap. 59.95 (*0-938773-11-9*) Tech Analysis.

Technical Analysis of Stocks & Commodities, Vol. 11. Ed. by Jack K. Hutson. LC 86-50575. 648p. (Orig.). 1994. pap. 59.95 (*0-938773-12-7*) Tech Analysis.

Technical Analysis of Stocks & Commodities, Vol. 12. Ed. by Jack K. Hutson. LC 86-50575. (Illus.). 686p. (Orig.). 1995. pap. 59.95 (*0-938773-13-5*) Tech Analysis.

Technical Analysis of Stocks & Commodities, Vol. 13. Ed. by Jack K. Hutson. LC 86-50575. (Illus.). 686p. (Orig.). 1995. pap. 59.95 (*0-938773-14-3*) Tech Analysis.

***Technical Analysis of Stocks & Commodities, Vol. 14.** Ed. by Jack K. Hutson. LC 86-50575. (Illus.). 696p. (Orig.). 1996. pap. 59.95 (*0-938773-16-X*) Tech Analysis.

Technical Analysis of Stocks & Commodities: Intelligent Trading, Vol. 4. Ed. by Jack K. Hutson. LC 86-50575. (Illus.). 364p. (Orig.). (C). 1989. pap. 49.95 (*0-938773-03-8*) Tech Analysis.

Technical Analysis of Stocks & Commodities: Investment Techniques, Vol. 2. Ed. by Jack K Hutson. LC 86-50575. (Illus.). 224p. (Orig.). 1987. pap. 34.95 (*0-938773-01-1*) Tech Analysis.

Technical Analysis of Stocks & Commodities: Market Timing, Vol. 6. Ed. by Jack K. Hutson. LC 86-50575. (Illus.). 484p. (Orig.). (C). 1989. pap. text ed. 59.95 (*0-938773-05-4*) Tech Analysis.

Technical Analysis of Stocks & Commodities: Profitable Trading Methods, Vol. 1. Ed. by Jack K. Hutson. LC 86-50575. (Illus.). 192p. (Orig.). (C). 1986. pap. 29.95 (*0-938773-00-3*) Tech Analysis.

Technical Analysis of Stocks & Commodities: Successful Speculation, Vol. 3. Ed. by Jack K. Hutson. LC 86-50575. (Illus.). 272p. (Orig.). (C). 1988. pap. 39.95 (*0-938773-02-X*) Tech Analysis.

Technical Analysis of Stocks & Commodities: Trading Strategies, Vol. 5. Ed. by Jack K. Hutson. LC 86-50575. (Illus.). 387p. (Orig.). (C). 1988. pap. 49.95 (*0-938773-04-6*) Tech Analysis.

Technical Analysis of Stocks, Options & Futures: Advanced Trading Systems & Techniques. William F. Eng. 1996. text ed. 55.00 (*1-55738-803-2*) Irwin Prof Pubng.

Technical Analysis of Stocks, Options & Futures: Advanced Trading Systems & Techniques. Willliam F. Eng. 475p. 1988. text ed. 60.00 (*1-55738-003-1*) Irwin Prof Pubng.

Technical Analysis of the Futures Markets: A Comprehensive Guide to Trading Methods & Applications. John J. Murphy. 555p. 54.95 (*0-13-898008-X*) NY Inst Finance.

Technical Analysis of the Futures Markets: Study Guide. John J. Murphy. LC 87-10991. (Illus.). 160p. (Orig.). 1987. pap. text ed. 27.95 (*0-13-858747-7*) NY Inst Finance.

Technical & Biological Components of Marrow Transplantation. Ed. by C. Dean Buckner. LC 95-1584. (Cancer Treatment & Research Ser.: Vol. 76). 400p. (C). 1995. lib. bdg. 215.00 (*0-7923-3394-2*) Kluwer Ac.

Technical & Critical Vocabulary of Philosophy: Vocabulaire Technique et Critique de la Philosophie. 13th ed. A. Lelande. 1323p. (FRE.). 1980. 150.00 (*0-8288-2274-3*, F18440) Fr & Eur.

Technical & Economic Aspects of Measures to Reduce Water Pollution Caused by Disazinphos-Ethyl (No. 5) Azinphos-Methyl (No. 6) Fenthion (No. 81) European Communities Staff. 87p. 1994. pap. 20.00 (*92-826-7132-1*, CR-81-93-600ENC, Pub. by Europ Com UK) Bernan Associates.

Technical & Economic Study on Reduction, Based on Best Available Technology. European Communities Staff. 244p. 1994. pap. 55.00 (*92-826-7131-3*, CR-81-43-599ENC, Pub. by Europ Com UK) Bernan Associates.

Technical & Economical Comparison of Conventional & Continuous Casting & Rolling Methods for the Production of Cold-Rolled Aluminum Strip: Information Sheets Issued by the DGM Casting Division, Committee on Continuous Casting with Moving Molds. Ed. by DGM Continuous Casting Division Staff. 48p. (Orig.). 1992. ring bd. 35.00 (*3-88355-175-9*, Pub. by DGM Metallurgy Info GW) IR Pubns.

***Technical & Managerial Guidelines for Vasectomy Services.** WHO Staff. 135p. 1988. 22.00 (*92-4-154218-7*) World Health.

Technical & Marketing Issues Impacting the Fire Safety of Electrical, Electronic & Composite Applications: Fire Retardant Chemicals Association, October 1991 Conference. 252p. 1992. pap. 149.95 (*0-87762-927-7*) Technomic.

Technical & Professional Assistant. Jack Rudman. (Career Examination Ser.: C-805). 1994. pap. 29.95 (*0-8373-0805-4*) Nat Learn.

***Technical & Strategy Management.** Dodgson. Date not set. pap. text ed. write for info. (*0-582-05057-X*) Addison-Wesley.

Technical & Vocational Education in the United Kingdom: A Bibliographical Survey (UNESCO) R. C. Benge. (Education Studies & Documents: No. 27). 1974. reprint ed. pap. 25.00 (*0-8115-1351-3*) Periodicals Srv.

Technical & Vocational Education in the U.S.A. A Bibliographical Survey (UNESCO) (Education Studies & Documents: No. 36). 1974. reprint ed. pap. 25.00 (*0-8115-1360-2*) Periodicals Srv.

Technical & Vocational Education in the U.S.S.R. A Bibliographical Survey (UNESCO) M. I. Movsovic. (Education Studies & Documents: No. 30). 1974. reprint ed. pap. 25.00 (*0-8115-1354-8*) Periodicals Srv.

Technical Approach to Glass. M. B. Volf. (Glass Science & Technology Ser.: No. 10). 392p. 1990. 197.75 (*0-444-98805-X*) Elsevier.

Technical Aspects of Data Communication. Digital Press Staff & John McNamara. (Networking Ser.). (Illus.). 383p. (Orig.). 1988. pap. 38.95 (*1-55558-111-0*, EY-M741E, Digital DEC) Buttrwrth-Heinemann.

***Technical Assessment of Switched Reluctance Drives for Application in Electric & Hybrid Vehicles (Oct. 1995)** (Electric Vehicle Information Ser.: Vol. 12). 102p. 1996. pap. 65.00 (*0-89934-297-3*, BT056); lib. bdg. 115.00 (*0-89934-298-1*, BT956) Bus Tech Bks.

Technical Assistance: Theory & Guidelines. Sidney C. Sufrin. LC 66-29623. 126p. reprint ed. pap. 36.00 (*0-685-10926-7*, 2022379) Bks Demand.

Technical Assistance Manual on the Employment Provisions (Title 1) of the Americans with Disabilities Act. 125p. (Orig.). (C). 1993. pap. text ed. 40.00 (*1-56806-228-1*) DIANE Pub.

Technical Assistance Packet: Enrollment Forms. 1988. 14.50 (*0-318-41984-X*) Am Prepaid.

Technical Assistance Packet: Legal Service Provider Agreements. 1986. 14.50 (*0-317-65827-1*, 2-018) Am Prepaid.

Technical Assistance Packet: Marketing Materials. 1988. 14.50 (*0-318-41983-1*) Am Prepaid.

Technical Assistance Packet: Prepaid Legal Service Plan Description. 1987. 14.50 (*0-317-65829-8*, 2-019) Am Prepaid.

Technical Assistance Packet: Prepaid Legal Service Plans for Credit Unions. 1988. 14.50 (*0-318-41982-3*) Am Prepaid.

Technical Assistant. Jack Rudman. (Career Examination Ser.: C-1515). 1994. pap. 27.95 (*0-8373-1515-8*) Nat Learn.

Technical Automotive Dictionary: Russian-English-German-French-Bulgarian. deluxe ed. G. Sikora. 624p. (BUL, ENG, FRE, GER & RUS.). 1977. 95.00 (*0-8288-5520-X*, M9828) Fr & Eur.

Technical Bases for Yucca Mountain Standards. National Research Council Staff. Ed. by Committee on Technical Bases for Yucca Mountain Standards. 222p. (Orig.). (C). 1995. pap. text ed. 39.00 (*0-309-05289-0*) Natl Acad Pr.

Technical Basis for Legislation on Irradiated Food: A Report of the Joint FAO-IAEA-WHO Expert Committee. Joint FAO-IAEA-WHO Expert Committee, Rome, 1964. (Technical Report Ser.: No. 316). 56p. (ENG, FRE, RUS & SPA.). 1966. pap. text ed. 5.00 (*92-4-120316-1*, 1100316) World Health.

Technical Basis for Peace: Third International Seminar on Nuclear War. W. S. Newman & S. Stipcich. (Science & Culture Ser.). 400p. 1992. text ed. 121.00 (*981-02-1186-4*) World Scientific Pub.

Technical Book Buyer's Guide. 2nd ed. Ed. by Gilbert T. Lopez. (Illus.). 400p. (Orig.). 1991. pap. text ed. 14.95 (*1-880072-00-9*) Utd Techbook.

Technical Book Buyer's Guide. 2nd ed. Gilbert T. Lopez & Tom Cloney. (Illus.). 370p. (Orig.). 1994. pap. text ed. 19.95 (*1-880072-01-7*) Utd Techbook.

Technical Bulletins: 1944-1974, Vol. 3. Association of Operative Millers Staff. 1975. 25.00 (*0-686-00376-4*) AG Pr.

Technical Bulletins: 1944-1975, Vol. 4. Association of Operative Millers Staff. 1977. 25.00 (*0-686-00375-6*) AG Pr.

Technical Bulletins of Dianetics & Scientology, 18 vols., Set. Incl. Vol. 1. 1950-52. L. Ron Hubbard. 1991. 175.00 (*0-88404-472-6*); Vol. 2. 1953-54. 1991. 175.00 (*0-88404-473-4*); Vol. 3. 1955-56. L. Ron Hubbard. 1991. 175.00 (*0-88404-474-2*); Vol. 4. 1957-58. 1991. 175.00 (*0-88404-475-0*); Vol. 5. 1959-60. LC 70-649588. 175.00 (*0-88404-476-9*); Vol. 6. 1961-62. 1991. 175.00 (*0-88404-478-5*); Vol. 7. 1963-65. L. Ron Hubbard. 1991. 175.00 (*0-88404-477-7*); Vol. 8. 1966-69. L. Ron Hubbard. 1991. 175.00 (*0-88404-479-3*); Vol. 9. 1970-71. L. Ron Hubbard. 1991. 175.00 (*0-88404-480-7*); Vol. 10. 1972-76. L. Ron Hubbard. 1991. 175.00 (*0-88404-481-5*); Vol. 11. 1977-79. L. Ron Hubbard. 1991. 175.00 (*0-88404-701-6*); Vol. 12. 1980-84. L. Ron Hubbard. 1991. 175.00 (*0-88404-702-4*); Vol. 13. 1985-91. L. Ron Hubbard. 1991. 175.00 (*0-88404-703-2*); Index. 1991. 175.00 (*0-88404-708-3*); Subj. Vol. 1. Case Supervisor, Basic Auditing Auditor Admin. L. Ron Hubbard. 1991. 175.00 (*0-88404-697-4*); Subj. Vol. 2. Technical Series. L. Ron Hubbard. 1991. 175.00 (*0-88404-698-2*); Subj. Vol. 3. Auditing Rundowns. L. Ron Hubbard. 1991. 175.00 (*0-88404-699-0*); Subj. Vol. 4. Processes & Lists. L. Ron Hubbard. 1991. 175.00 (*0-88404-700-8*); 1991. 1,382.63 (*0-685-04188-3*) Bridge Pubns Inc.

Technical C Plus Plus Using Turbo. Andrew C. Staugaard. 530p. 1994. pap. text ed. 66.00 (*0-13-042888-4*) P-H.

Technical Calculus. Paul Calter. 432p. 1987. text ed. 65.00 (*0-13-898149-3*) P-H.

Technical Calculus. 2nd ed. Dale R. Ewen & Michael A. Topper. (Illus.). 656p. (C). 1986. text ed. 89.00 (*0-13-898164-7*) P-H.

***Technical Calculus.** 3rd ed. Dale Ewen et al. LC 97-24466. 1998. write for info. (*0-13-673690-4*) P-H.

Technical Calculus with Analytic Geometry. Peterson. (Trade/Tech Math Ser.). 1997. text ed. 54.95 (*0-8273-7415-1*) Delmar.

Technical Calculus with Analytic Geometry. Peterson. (Trade/Tech Math Ser.). 1998. teacher ed., text ed. 20.00 (*0-8273-7416-X*); student ed., text ed. 22.00 (*0-8273-7417-8*) Delmar.

Technical Calculus with Analytic Geometry. unabridged ed. Judith L. Gersting. LC 92-34100. (Illus.). 501p. 1992. reprint ed. pap. text ed. 13.95 (*0-486-67343-X*) Dover.

Technical Calculus with Analytic Geometry. 3rd ed. Peter K. Kuhfittig. LC 93-11823. 1994. text ed. 80.95 (*0-534-21852-0*) Brooks-Cole.

Technical Calculus with Analytic Geometry. 3rd ed. Peter K. Kuhfittig. (Mathematics Ser.). 1994. student ed., pap. 24.95 (*0-534-21853-9*) Brooks-Cole.

Technical Calculus with Analytic Geometry. 3rd ed. Allyn J. Washington. (Illus.). 450p. (C). 1986. teacher ed. 9.95 (*0-8053-9513-X*); text ed. 58.25 (*0-8053-9512-1*); student ed., pap. text ed. 10.75 (*0-8053-9514-8*) Addison-Wesley.

Technical Careers Test. Jack Rudman. (Career Examination Ser.: C-804). 1994. pap. 27.95 (*0-8373-0804-6*) Nat Learn.

Technical Challenges & Opportunities of a United Europe. Ed. by Michael Steinberg. (C). 1990. text ed. 54.50 (*0-389-20900-7*) B&N Imports.

Technical Change & American Enterprise. J. Herbert Holloman. LC 74-19049. 52p. 1974. 1.50 (*0-89068-013-2*) Natl Planning.

Technical Change & Economic Growth: An Empirical Analysis of the EEC. George Korres. (Perspectives on Europe Ser.). 320p. 1996. 76.95 (*1-85972-280-6*, Pub. by Avebury Pub UK) Ashgate Pub Co.

Technical Change & Economic Theory. Ed. by Giovanni Dosi et al. 656p. 1988. text ed. 79.00 (*0-86187-949-X*) St Martin.

Technical Change & Economic Theory. Ed. by Giovanni Dosi et al. 656p. 1990. text ed. 32.50 (*0-86187-894-9*) St Martin.

Technical Change & the World Economy: Convergence & Divergence in Technology Strategies. Ed. by John Hagedoorn. 256p. 1995. 80.00 (*1-85898-089-5*) E Elgar.

Technical Change, Human Capital, & Spillovers in United States Agriculture, 1949-1985. rev. ed. Klaus W. Deininger. LC 95-31442. (Studies on Industrial Productivity). (Illus.). 172p. 1995. text ed. 50.00 (*0-8153-2139-2*) Garland.

Technical Change, Relative Prices, & Environmental Resource Evaluation. Vincent K. Smith. LC 74-6840. 117p. reprint ed. pap. 33.40 (*0-317-26482-6*, 2023816) Bks Demand.

Technical Choice Innovation & Economic Growth: Essays on American & British Experience in the Nineteenth Century. Paul A. David. LC 74-76583. 344p. reprint ed. pap. 98.10 (*0-317-26014-6*, 2024448) Bks Demand.

Technical Co-Operation Among Developing Countries. Ed. by T. Jamal & A. Jain. 1989. 28.50 (*0-86132-244-4*, Pub. by Popular Prakashan II) S Asia.

Technical Co-Operation in Africa, New Directions. 336p. 1991. 17.50 (*92-1-126022-1*, 91.III.B.4) UN.

Technical Co-Operation in Latin-American Agriculture. Arthur T. Mosher. LC 75-26310. (World Food Supply Ser.). (Illus.). 1976. reprint ed. 40.95 (*0-405-07788-2*) Ayer.

Technical College Physics. 2nd ed. Jerry D. Wilson. 640p. (C). 1987. student ed., pap. text ed. 36.00 (*0-03-011957-X*) SCP.

Technical College Physics. 3rd ed. Wilson. (C). 1992. suppl. ed., teacher ed., pap. text ed. 47.75 (*0-03-074591-8*) HB Coll Pubs.

Technical College Physics. 3rd ed. Wilson. (C). 1992. student ed., pap. text ed. 20.75 (*0-03-074586-1*) HB Coll Pubs.

Technical College Physics. 3rd ed. Jerry D. Wilson. 752p. (C). 1992. text ed. 53.25 (*0-03-073898-9*) SCP.

Technical Communication. Norbert Elliot. (C). 1997. pap. text ed. write for info. (*0-8053-6344-0*) Addison-Wesley.

Technical Communication. Mary M. Lay. LC 94-29205. 784p. (C). 1994. text ed. 56.75 (*0-256-11985-6*) Irwin.

***Technical Communication.** Sauer. (C). Date not set. pap. write for info. (*0-395-68428-5*); pap. write for info. (*0-395-68429-3*) HM.

Technical Communication. 2nd ed. Rebecca E. Burnett. 668p. (C). 1990. pap. 39.95 (*0-534-12426-7*) Wadsworth Pub.

***Technical Communication.** 2nd ed. Lay-Wahlstrom. 1997. text ed. 45.40 (*0-256-22058-1*) McGraw.

Technical Communication. 3rd ed. Rebecca E. Burnett. 680p. 1994. pap. 41.00 (*0-534-19932-1*) Wadsworth Pub.

Technical Communication. 4th ed. Rebecca E. Burnett. LC 96-44283. (Freshman English/Advanced Writing Ser.). (C). 1997. pap. text ed. 53.95 (*0-534-51605-X*) Wadsworth Pub.

Technical Communication. 4th ed. Michael H. Markel. 1995. teacher ed., pap. text ed. 5.00 (*0-312-11518-0*) St Martin.

Technical Communication. 4th ed. Michael H. Markel. 1995. pap. text ed. 39.90 (*0-312-11519-9*) St Martin.

***Technical Communication.** 5th ed. Markel. Date not set. pap. text ed. 38.00 (*0-312-17087-4*) St Martin.

Technical Communication: A Guided Approach. June Dostal & Deborah St. Vincent. LC 95-35122. 1995. text ed. write for info. (*0-314-06935-6*) West Pub.

Technical Communication: A Practical Guide. Joseph P. Dagher. (Illus.). 1978. pap. text ed. write for info. (*0-13-898247-3*) P-H.

Technical Communication: An Outline. Thomas L. Warren. (Quality Paperback Ser.: No. 332). 148p. 1978. pap. 7.95 (*0-8226-0332-2*) Littlefield.

Technical Communication: Problems & Solutions. Fox. (C). 1994. text ed. 49.50 (*0-06-042173-8*) Addson-Wesley Educ.

Technical Communication: The Practical Craft. 3rd ed. Maris Roze. LC 96-5164. 362p. (C). 1996. pap. text ed. 40.00 (*0-13-455874-X*) P-H.

Technical Communication & Ethics. R. John Brockmann & Fern Rook. (Anthology Ser.). 126p. 1989. per. 30.00 (*0-914548-56-5*, 132-89) Soc Tech Comm.

Technical Communication & Its Application. Jerome N. Borowick. LC 95-35883. 425p. (C). 1995. text ed. 47.00 (*0-13-199275-9*) P-H.

Technical Communication at Work. Collins. (C). 1994. teacher ed., pap. text ed. 33.75 (*0-15-500854-4*) HB Coll Pubs.

Technical Communication at Work. C. Edward Collins & Deborah S. Bosley. LC 93-80815. (Illus.). 380p. (Orig.). (C). 1994. pap. text ed. 41.00 (*0-15-500853-6*) HB Coll Pubs.

***Technical Communication in the Global Community.** Andrews. (C). 1900. pap. text ed. 48.00 (*0-13-103060-4*) P-H.

Technical Communication Topics, Activities, & Portfolio Builders - A Collection by Professional Communicators. Ed. by Clark Germann & Trudy Israel. 109p. (Orig.). 1990. pap. 18.95 (*0-941775-08-9*) Finesse Pub.

Technical Communications. Center for Occupational Research & Development Staff. (High Technology Ser.). (Illus.). 228p. (C). 1985. pap. text ed. 25.00 (*1-55502-164-6*) CORD Commns.

Technical Communications for Engineers. Scott Evans. (C). 1997. pap. text ed. write for info. (*0-8053-6390-4*) Addison-Wesley.

Technical Communicator's Handbook of Technology Transfer. Hyman Olken. 14p. 1980. pap. 12.50 (*0-934818-01-0*) Olken Pubns.

Technical Conference on Dry Bean Research: Proceedings. Food Processors Institute Staff. 65p. (Orig.). (C). 1985. pap. text ed. 10.00 (*0-937774-14-6*) Food Processors.

Technical Consideration in Choosing Mass Deacidification Processes. Peter Sparks. 22p. 1990. pap. 10.00 (*1-887334-01-7*) Comm Preserv & Access.

Technical Control for the Modern Pianist: Finger Exercises Used by Members of the Piano Teachers Congress of N.Y., Inc. Piano Teachers Congress Members. Ed. by Albert De Vito. LC 78-95128. 1978. pap. 9.95 (*0-934286-11-6*) Kenyon.

Technical Coordinator. Jack Rudman. (Career Examination Ser.: C-3614). 1994. pap. 34.95 (*0-8373-3614-7*) Nat Learn.

Technical Criteria for the Selection of Woodworking Machines. 400p. 1992. 25.00 (*92-1-106257-8*, 91.III.E.6) UN.

T

Technical Data Financial Markets Almanac 1995. (Financial Management Ser.). 1996. pap. 86.95 (*0-538-85782-X*) S-W Pub.

Technical Data on Telephone Security Devices & Equipment. abr. ed. Ed. by Michael P. Jones. (Illus.). 38p. 1984. pap. text ed. 6.00 (*0-89904-080-2*) Crumb Elbow Pub.

Technical Demography. R. Ramakumar. (C). 1987. pap. 9.50 (*0-85226-743-6*) S Asia.

Technical Description of New Features in STATISTICA 5.0. (Illus.). 32p. (C). 1995. pap. text ed. write for info. (*1-884233-36-8*) StatSoft.

Technical Descriptive Geometry. 2nd ed. B. Leighton Wellman. 1957. text ed. write for info. (*0-07-069234-3*) McGraw.

Technical Descriptive Geometry: Problem Layouts for Technical Descriptive Geometry. 2nd ed. B. Leighton Wellman. (Classic Textbook Ser.). 1957. pap. text ed. write for info. (*0-07-069237-8*) McGraw.

Technical Design Graphics Problem Solver. rev. ed. Ed. by Research & Education Association Staff. LC 81-86648. (Illus.). 960p. (Orig.). 1994. pap. 23.95 (*0-87891-534-6*) Res & Educ.

Technical Development of Air Cargo ULD's, Onboard Handling & Restraint Systems. 35p. 1993. 12.00 (*1-56091-386-X*, SP-978) Soc Auto Engineers.

Technical Development of Television. Ed. by Christopher H. Sterling & George Shiers. LC 75-23902. (Historical Studies in Telecommunications). 1979. reprint ed. 59.95 (*0-405-07761-0*) Ayer.

Technical Diagnostics. Ed. by K. Havrilla & T. Kemeny. (Illus.). 298p. (C). 1988. text ed. 125.00 (*0-941743-41-1*) Nova Sci Pubs.

Technical Dictionary: Diccionario Tecnico: Suplemento, Vol. 2. deluxe ed. Herman Mink. 384p. (GER & SPA.). 1981. 59.95 (*0-8288-4437-2*, S50270) Fr & Eur.

Technical Dictionary: English-French-German-Arabic. A. M. Abd-El-Wahed. 297p. 1981. 29.95 (*0-7859-6880-6*, 3361000297) Fr & Eur.

Technical Dictionary: French-English, English-French. 7th rev. ed. F. Cusset. 434p. (ENG & FRE.). 1967. 175.00 (*0-7859-7146-7*) Fr & Eur.

Technical Dictionary: Tietotekniikan Sanasto. L. E. Bjork et al. 59p. (FIN.). 1984. 29.95 (*0-8288-1367-1*, F24070) Fr & Eur.

***Technical Dictionary, English-German.** Langenscheidt Editorial Staff. (ENG & GER.). 1996. 250.00 (*0-7859-9385-1*) Fr & Eur.

Technical Dictionary English-Slovene. 1137p. (ENG & SLV.). 1975. 150.00 (*0-8288-5946-9*, M9891) Fr & Eur.

Technical Dictionary for the Shoe Industry: Woerterbuch der Schuhtechnik. Gerhard Knebel. 303p. (ENG & GER.). 1969. pap. 95.00 (*0-8288-6730-5*, M-7641) Fr & Eur.

Technical Dictionary for Weaponry. Gustav Sybertz. (ENG & GER.). 1969. pap. 24.95 (*0-8288-6615-5*, M-7642) Fr & Eur.

Technical Dictionary of Aeronautics. H. DeMaison. 671p. (ENG, FRE & SPA.). 1978. 85.00 (*2-85608-007-3*) IBD Ltd.

Technical Dictionary of Agricultural Machinery & Equipment. J. Baudel. 1400p. (ENG, FRE, GER, ITA, POR & SPA.). 1989. 185.00 (*2-85608-034-0*) IBD Ltd.

Technical Dictionary of Automotive Engineering: French & English. F. L. Wyhlidal. 1867p. (ENG & FRE.). 1982. 250.00 (*0-8288-8056-5*, M9877) Fr & Eur.

Technical Dictionary of Automotive Engineering: German & English. F. L. Wyhlidal. 529p. (ENG & GER.). 1974. pap. 350.00 (*0-8288-8055-7*, M15467) Fr & Eur.

***Technical Dictionary of Automotive Engineering: German/English - English/German.** F. L. Wyhlidal. 2145p. (ENG & GER.). 1991. 395.00 (*0-7859-9291-X*) Fr & Eur.

***Technical Dictionary of Automotive Engineering: German/English-English/German.** F. L. Wyhlidal. 2145p. (ENG & GER.). 1991. 395.00 (*0-7859-9281-2*) Fr & Eur.

Technical Dictionary of Computer Science: Hardware-Software. Georges A. Nania. 808p. (ENG, FRE, ITA, POR & SPA.). 1983. 119.00 (*2-903988-01-3*) IBD Ltd.

Technical Dictionary of High Polymers: English, French, German, Russian. W. Dawydoff. 960p. 1969. 385.00 (*0-08-013112-3*, Pergamon Pr) Elsevier.

Technical Dictionary of Library & Information Science. Ed. by Marta Stiefel Ayala et al. LC 92-43348. 680p. (Reference Library of Social Science: Vol. 815). 680p. (ENG & SPA.). 1993. text ed. 110.00 (*0-8153-0655-5*, SS815) Garland.

Technical Dictionary of Machine Tools & Foundry. 6th ed. J. C. Von Rosen. 560p. (ENG, FIN, FRE, GER, GRE, ITA, POR, RUS, SER, SPA, SWE & TUR.). 1982. 70.00 (*91-85026-29-8*) IBD Ltd.

Technical Dictionary of Mechanics, Metallurgy, Hydraulics. Ed. by Michel Feutry et al. 400p. (ENG, FRE & GER.). 1976. Supplemental Spanish Index, 400pp., 1976. suppl. ed. 44.50 (*2-85608-001-4*) IBD Ltd.

Technical Dictionary of Mechanics, Metallurgy, Hydraulics. Ed. by Michel Feutry et al. 750p. (ENG, FRE & GER.). 1976. 65.00 (*2-85608-000-6*) IBD Ltd.

Technical Dictionary of Mechanics, Metallurgy, Hydraulics. Ed. by Michel Feutry et al. 380p. (ENG, FRE & GER.). 1981. Supplemental Portugese Index, 380pp., 1981. suppl. ed. 40.00 (*2-85608-014-6*) IBD Ltd.

Technical Dictionary of Plastic Materials. W. V. Titow. LC 97-24521. 1997. pap. write for info. (*0-08-041891-0*, Pergamon Pr) Elsevier.

Technical Dictionary of Printing. W. Muller. 1020p. (C). 1981. 195.00 (*0-685-37160-3*, Pub. by Collets) St Mut.

Technical Dictionary of Printing Technique. I. Shawaki & A. Rashwan. 420p. (C). 1981. 90.00 (*0-89771-923-9*, Pub. by Collets) St Mut.

Technical Dictionary of Printing Technique. Ed. by I. Shawaki & A. Rashwan. 420p. (C). 1981. 100.00 (*0-685-37159-X*, Pub. by Collets) St Mut.

Technical Dictionary of Printing Technique. Ismail Shawki. 292p. (ARA, ENG, FRE & GER.). 1981. 39.95 (*0-8288-0694-2*, M 15401) Fr & Eur.

Technical Dictionary of Production Engineering, 2 vols., Vol. 1: English-German. Rudolph Walther. 856p. 1972. 228.00 (*0-08-016959-7*, Pub. by Pergamon Repr UK) Franklin.

Technical Dictionary of Production Engineering, 2 vols., Vol. 2: German-English. Rudolph Walther. 856p. 1972. Vol 2: German-English. 148.00 (*0-08-016960-0*, Pub. by Pergamon Repr UK) Franklin.

Technical Dictionary of Railroads: Technik-Woerterbuch Eisenbahn. Adolf Dannehl. 400p. (ENG, FRE, GER & RUS.). 1983. 125.00 (*0-8288-2373-1*, M15065) Fr & Eur.

Technical Dictionary of Springs. Syndicat National des Fabricants de Ressorts Staff. 110p. (ENG, FRE, GER & SPA.). 1978. 28.00 (*2-85608-006-5*) IBD Ltd.

Technical Dictionary of Water Management. I. Nagy & A. Kertai. 516p. (C). 1988. 100.00 (*0-569-09157-8*, Pub. by Collets) St Mut.

Technical Dictionary of Woodworking: French Definitions Plus Index with Appendix of Technical Terms in French-German-English-Spanish-Dutch-Italian-Swedish. T. Moirant. 350p. 1986. pap. 75.00 (*2-85608-021-9*) IBD Ltd.

Technical Dictionary, Swedish-English, English-Swedish. E. Engstrom. 176p. (ENG & SWE.). 1990. pap. 45.00 (*0-7859-7147-5*) Fr & Eur.

Technical Difficulties: African-American Notes on the State of the Union. June Jordan. 240p. 1994. pap. 12.00 (*0-679-74762-1*, Villard Bks) Random.

Technical Digest of 1994 Solid State Sensors & Actuators Workshop. Transducer Research Foundation Staff. LC 94-60019. (Solid State Sensors & Actuators Workshop Ser.). 250p. 1994. pap. 75.00 (*0-9640024-0-X*) Transducer Res.

Technical Diving. Meduno. 288p. 1993. pap. 29.95 (*0-8016-7478-6*) Mosby Yr Bk.

Technical Division Four of the Organization Executive Course see Organization Executive Course

Technical Drafting. William P. Spence & Atkins. (gr. 9-12). 1980. 12.68 (*0-02-665820-8*); text ed. 26.40 (*0-02-665810-0*) Glencoe.

Technical Drawing. Dennis Maguire & Colin Simmons. (Illus.). 256p. 1994. pap. 9.95 (*0-8442-3942-9*, Teach Yourslf) NTC Pub Grp.

Technical Drawing. Kenneth Stibolt. Date not set. wbk. ed., pap. text ed. 28.00 (*0-314-04277-6*) West Pub.

Technical Drawing. 3rd ed. David L. Goetsch et al. LC 93-2026. 941p. 1994. text ed. 65.95 (*0-8273-6285-4*) Delmar.

Technical Drawing. 10th ed. Frederick E. Giesecke. LC 96-37161. 1050p. (C). 1996. text ed. 80.00 (*0-13-461971-4*) P-H.

Technical Drawing, Ser. 3, Problems. 9th ed. Henry C. Spencer. 208p. (C). 1991. Problems, Ser. 3. pap. text ed. 36.20 (*0-02-414630-7*, Macmillan Coll) P-H.

Technical Drawing: Fund CAD Des Solutions Manual. 2nd ed. David Goetsch. 1989. teacher ed., pap. 16.00 (*0-8273-3283-1*) Delmar.

Technical Drawing: Instructor's Resource Guide. 3rd ed. Goetsch et al. 672p. 1994. teacher ed., text ed. 45.00 (*0-8273-6511-X*) Delmar.

Technical Drawing & Design. David L. Goetsch & John A. Nelson. 950p. 1986. teacher ed. 16.00 (*0-8273-2230-5*) Delmar.

Technical Drawing & Design. L. Gary Lamit. Ed. by Conty. LC 92-43902. 1184p. (C). 1993. text ed. 76.75 (*0-314-01264-8*) West Pub.

Technical Drawing & Design. Louis G. Lamit. Date not set. student ed., pap. text ed. write for info. (*0-314-02913-3*) West Pub.

Technical Drawing & Design. 2nd ed. David L. Goetsch. 1989. text ed. 62.95 (*0-8273-3280-7*) Delmar.

Technical Drawing & Graphics. Jack Rudman. (Dantes Subject Standardized Tests Ser.: DANTES-36). 1994. pap. 23.95 (*0-8373-6636-4*) Nat Learn.

Technical Drawing Problems. George K. Stegman & Jerry Jenkins. (Sea Power: Naval Vessels Weapon Systems & Technology Ser.: Series 4). 224p. (C). 1986. pap. text ed. 37.20 (*0-02-416330-9*, Macmillan Coll) P-H.

Technical Drawing with AutoCAD Release 10: A Teaching Tutorial - with Problems. Leendert Kersten. 391p. 1989. pap. 32.95 (*0-912855-75-4*) E Bowers Pub.

Technical Drawing Workbook. James Luckow. (Illus.). 208p. (C). 1994. pap. text ed. 21.50 (*0-201-62330-7*) Addison-Wesley.

Technical Drawing Workbook. 3rd ed. David L. Goetsch et al. 159p. 1994. pap. 25.95 (*0-8273-6512-8*) Delmar.

Technical Drawings: Fundamentals of CAD Design. 2nd ed. Goetsch. (C). 1989. teacher ed., pap. text ed. 16.00 (*0-8273-3281-5*) Delmar.

Technical Drawings: Fundamentals of CAD Design. 2nd ed. Goetsch. (C). 1989. wbk. ed., pap. text ed. 25.95 (*0-8273-3282-3*) Delmar.

Technical-Economical Dictionary for Business Purposes. B. Bajic. 1700p. (CRO, ENG, FRE, GER & SER.). 1973. 150.00 (*0-8288-6332-6*, M9689) Fr & Eur.

Technical Editing. Joseph C. Mancuso. 208p. 1991. text ed. 33.00 (*0-13-898503-0*, 640704) P-H.

Technical Editing. Joseph C. Mancuso. 191p. 1994. 39.95 (*0-9643750-0-1*) Training Edge.

Technical Editing. Carolyn D. Rude. 430p. (C). 1991. text ed. 48.95 (*0-534-15000-4*) Wadsworth Pub.

***Technical Editing.** 2nd ed. Rude. 1997. pap. 40.00 (*0-205-20032-X*) P-H.

Technical Editing: A Workbook & Glossary. Anne Eisenberg. (Illus.). 320p. (C). 1992. pap. text ed. 23.95 (*0-19-506306-6*) OUP.

Technical Editing: Basic Theory & Practice. Charles F. Kemnitz. 148p. 1994. pap. text ed. 30.00 (*0-914548-75-1*, 151-94) Soc Tech Comm.

Technical Editing: The Practical Guide for Editors & Writers. Judith Tarutz. LC 92-11644. (Illus.). 490p. 1992. pap. 30.95 (*0-201-56356-8*) Addison-Wesley.

Technical Editor's Handbook: A Desk Guide for All Processors of Scientific or Engineering Copy. rev. ed. George Freedman & Deborah A. Freedman. LC 94-3172. (Illus.). 592p. 1994. reprint ed. pap. 14.95 (*0-486-28009-8*) Dover.

Technical Education in the Arab States (UNESCO) Mohammed K. Harby et al. (Education Studies & Documents: No. 53). 1974. reprint ed. pap. 25.00 (*0-8115-1377-7*) Periodicals Srv.

Technical Elite. Jay M. Gould. LC 66-15566. (Illus.). 178p. 1966. 29.50 (*0-678-00131-6*) Kelley.

***Technical Engineering Training Series, 7 vols.** Incl. Pumping System Analysis. Multimedia Development Services Staff. (Illus.). (Orig.). 1996. pap. 125.00 (*1-57431-081-X*); Centrifugal Pumps. Multimedia Development Services Staff. (Illus.). (Orig.). 1996. pap. 125.00 (*1-57431-082-8*); Positive Displacement Pumps. Multimedia Development Services Staff. (Illus.). (Orig.). 1996. pap. 125.00 (*1-57431-083-6*); Hydraulics. Multimedia Development Services Staff. (Illus.). (Orig.). 1996. pap. 125.00 (*1-57431-084-4*); Fractionation. Multimedia Development Staff. (Illus.). (Orig.). 1996. pap. 125.00 (*1-57431-085-2*); Tower & Tray Design. Multimedia Development Services Staff. (Illus.). (Orig.). 1996. pap. 125.00 (*1-57431-086-0*); Thermodynamics & Physical Properties. Multimedia Development Services Staff. (Illus.). (Orig.). 1996. pap. 125.00 (*1-57431-087-9*); 700.00 (*1-57431-080-1*) Tech Trng Systs.

Technical English. 6th ed. Pickett & Ann A. Laster. (C). 1993. 45.50 (*0-06-500278-4*) Addson-Wesley Educ.

Technical English: Writing, Reading and Speaking. 7th ed. Pickett & Ann A. Laster. 880p. (C). 1996. teacher ed., pap. text ed. write for info. (*0-673-99795-2*) Addson-Wesley Educ.

Technical English: Writing, Reading & Speaking. 7th ed. Nell A. Pickett & Ann A. Laster. 704p. (C). 1996. text ed. 49.50 (*0-673-99794-4*) Addson-Wesley Educ.

Technical English for German-Speaking Engineers. 8th ed. H. G. Freeman. 376p. (ENG & GER.). 1983. 96.75 (*3-590-85012-4*, Pub. by Cornelsen) IBD Ltd.

***Technical English for Industry.** Yates Fitzpatr. 1988. pap. text ed. write for info. (*0-582-85276-5*, Pub. by Longman UK) Longman.

Technical Evaluations in Government Contracting: A Complete Guide. Peter S. Cole. 254p. (Orig.). 1995. pap. 85.00 (*1-56726-032-2*, B568) Holbrook & Kellogg.

Technical Excellence in a Global Economy: 1992 IES Proceedings. 38th Annual Technical Meeting, 2 vols. LC 62-38584. 1992. Set. 175.00 (*1-877862-13-4*) Inst Environ Sci.

Technical Excellence in a Global Economy: 1992 IES Proceedings. 38th Annual Technical Meeting, Vol. 1. LC 62-38584. 529p. 1992. 100.00 (*1-877862-14-2*) Inst Environ Sci.

Technical Excellence in a Global Economy: 1992 IES Proceedings. 38th Annual Technical Meeting, Vol. 2. LC 62-38584. 1992. 100.00 (*1-877862-15-0*) Inst Environ Sci.

Technical Exercises & Variations. write for info. (*0-7935-3855-6*, 50482271) H Leonard.

Technical Exercises Jazz for Intermediate to Professional Muscian. 19.95 (*0-7935-5598-1*, 00841047) H Leonard.

Technical Explanatory Dictionary: Construction Industry Building Mechanization. V. Zoltanka & Gy Sebestyen. 456p. (ENG, FRE, GER, HUN & RUS.). 1986. 65.00 (*0-8288-1340-X*, F10023) Fr & Eur.

Technical Explanatory Dictionary: Meteorology. R. Czelnai & D. Szepesi. 456p. (ENG, FRE, GER, HUN & RUS.). 1986. 75.00 (*0-8288-1475-9*, F10024) Fr & Eur.

Technical Extracts. Aleister Crowley. (Orig.). 1993. pap. 6.95 (*1-55818-266-7*) Holmes Pub.

Technical Factors in the Treatment of the Severely Disturbed Patient. Ed. by Peter Giovacchini & L. Bryce Boyer. LC 81-20587. 544p. 1982. 50.00 (*0-87668-630-7*) Aronson.

***Technical Forestry Education: Design & Implementation.** 133p. 1984. 17.00 (*92-5-102080-9*, F2630, Pub. by FAO IT) Bernan Associates.

***Technical Fouls.** John K. Jacobson. (Interventions Ser.). (C). 1998. pap. text ed. 18.95 (*0-8133-1999-4*) Westview.

***Technical Fouls: Democracy & Technological Change.** John K. Jacobson. 1998. text ed. 49.00 (*0-8133-1998-6*) Westview.

Technical Foundations of Client-Server Systems. Carl Hall. 219p. 1994. pap. text ed. 42.95 (*0-471-06086-0*) Wiley.

Technical Framework for Life-Cycle Assessment. Ed. by James A. Fava et al. 134p. 1991. text ed. 35.00 (*1-880611-00-7*) SETAC.

Technical Freehand Drawing & Sketching. K. Knowlton et al. 1976. text ed. 36.95 (*0-07-035207-0*) McGraw.

Technical Graphics. E. T. Boyer et al. 1072p. 1991. wbk. ed., text ed. 59.50 (*0-471-55578-9*) Wiley.

Technical Graphics: Electronics Worktext. 2nd ed. Edward Maruggi. 464p. (C). 1990. pap. text ed. 44.20 (*0-675-21378-9*, Merrill Coll) P-H.

Technical Graphics: Graphic Software. Edwin T. Boyer et al. 768p. (C). 1991. text ed. 59.50 (*0-471-53371-8*) Wiley.

Technical Graphics Communication. Gary R. Bertoline et al. LC 95-1599. (Graphics Ser.). 1336p. (C). 1995. text ed. 72.95 (*0-256-11417-X*) Irwin.

***Technical Graphics Communication.** 2nd ed. Bertoline. 1997. pap. text ed. write for info. (*0-256-26668-9*) McGraw.

***Technical Graphics Communication.** 2nd ed. Gary R. Bertoline et al. 1152p. (C). 1996. text ed. 69.95 (*0-256-22981-3*) Irwin.

Technical Graphics Communication & Autocad. Leonard O. Nasman et al. (C). 1995. 98.20 (*0-256-19305-3*) Irwin.

Technical Graphics Communication Chapter 16. Gary R. Bertoline. (C). 1995. pap. text ed. 1.50 (*0-256-20452-7*) Irwin.

Technical Greek-English & English-Greek Dictionary. Papanikolau. 684p. (ENG & GRE.). 1990. 150.00 (*0-7859-9052-6*) Fr & Eur.

Technical Guidance for Hazards Analysis...The Workbook. Peter R. Jensen. 89p. (C). 1991. student ed. 14.95 (*0-9630429-1-2*) Quark Mgmt.

Technical Guidance Manual for Silver Discharges. Water Environment Federation Staff. 1994. write for info. (*1-881369-97-8*) Water Environ.

Technical Guide for Reviewing Prime Farmland Restoration Plans in the Midwest. Russell Boulding. (Illus.). 1984. pap. 5.00 (*0-943724-07-4*) Illinois South.

Technical Guide to Alternative Fuels. McGlinchy. (Automotive Technology Ser.). 1996. pap. 36.95 (*0-8273-7170-5*) Van Nos Reinhold.

Technical Guide to Automotive Emission Systems: Education Version. Carley. (Automotive Technology Ser.). 1994. pap. 34.95 (*0-8273-7135-7*) Van Nos Reinhold.

Technical Guide to Program Controllers. 3rd ed. Cox. (Electrical Trades Ser.). 144p. 1995. lab manual ed., text ed. 20.50 (*0-8273-7151-9*) Delmar.

Technical Guide to Program Controllers. 3rd ed. Richard Cox. (Electrical Trades Ser.). 32p. 1996. teacher ed. 16.00 (*0-8273-6239-0*) Delmar.

Technical Guidelines for Field Variety Trials. Elena Rossello & Fernandez De Gorostiza. (Plant Production & Protection Papers: No. 75). 126p. 1993. pap. 17.00 (*92-5-102486-3*, F24863, Pub. by FAO IT) Bernan Associates.

***Technical Guidelines for Mushroom Growing in the Tropics.** 170p. 1990. 20.00 (*92-5-103026-X*, F026X, Pub. by FAO IT) Bernan Associates.

Technical Guidelines for Pharmaceuticals in the European Economic Community. Ed. by Duilio Poggiolini. LC 83-9580. 73p. 1983. reprint ed. pap. 25.00 (*0-608-00650-5*, 2061238) Bks Demand.

Technical Handbook for Coaches & Judges (Women's) United States Gymnastics Federation Staff. 98p. 1993. pap. 15.00 (*1-885250-10-X*) USA Gymnastics.

Technical Handbook on Symbiotic Nitrogen Fixation Legume Rhizobium 1993. 162p. 1994. 17.00 (*92-5-103199-1*, F31991, Pub. by FAO IT) Bernan Associates.

Technical History of the Motorcar. T. P. Newcomb & R. T. Spurr. (Illus.). 430p. 1989. 53.00 (*0-85274-074-3*) IOP Pub.

Technical Illustration. James D. Bethune. LC 82-8529. 237p. (C). 1983. write for info. (*0-471-05308-2*) P-H.

Technical Illustration. James H. Earle. (gr. 12 up). 1978. 8.95 (*0-932702-65-1*) Creative Texas.

Technical Illustration. 3rd ed. T. A. Thomas. (Illus.). 1978. text ed. 40.95 (*0-07-064228-1*) McGraw.

Technical Illustration & Graphics. Jan Mracek. (Illus.). 352p. (C). 1983. 34.00 (*0-685-05866-2*) P-H.

Technical Information Retrieval Techniques. Kaiser & Roan. 1991. 13.95 (*0-536-58004-9*) Ginn Pr.

Technical Innovations in Blow Molding: 10th Annual High Performance Blow Molding Conference, October 12-13, 1994. Society of Plastics Engineers Staff. (Illus.). 328p. 1994. reprint ed. pap. 93.50 (*0-7837-9703-6*, 2060434) Bks Demand.

Technical Instruction. IAP, Inc. Staff. LC 92-25664. 209p. (C). 1981. pap. 9.95 (*0-89100-183-2*, EA-183-2) IAP.

Technical Instructions for the Safe Transport of Dangerous Goods by Air, 1987-88. Dangerous Goods Panel of Air Navigations Commissions of ICAO & Commission of ICAO Staff. 535p. 1986. 40.00 (*0-940394-21-9*) Labelmaster.

Technical Instructions for the Safe Transport of Dangerous Goods by Air 1989-90. Dangerous Goods Panel of Air Navigations Commissions of ICAO. (Illus.). 535p. 1988. 42.00 (*0-940394-28-6*) Labelmaster.

Technical Introduction to Digital Video. Charles A. Poynton. LC 95-38474. 352p. 1996. text ed. 42.95 (*0-471-12253-X*) Wiley.

Technical Introduction to the Macintosh Family. Apple Computer, Inc. Staff. (Illus.). 160p. 1987. pap. 19.95 (*0-201-17765-X*) Addison-Wesley.

Technical Introduction to the Macintosh Family. 2nd ed. Apple Computer, Inc. Staff. 1992. pap. 26.95 (*0-201-62215-7*) Addison-Wesley.

Technical Knowledge in American Culture: Science, Technology, & Medicine since the Early 1800s. Ed. by Hamilton Cravens et al. LC 95-19084. (History of American Science & Technology Ser.). 280p. (Orig.). (FRE & GER.). (C). 1996. pap. text ed. 24.95 (*0-8173-0793-1*) U of Ala Pr.

***Technical Laboratory Management.** ring bd. 250.00 (*0-614-20205-1*, SC15-L) Natl Comm Clin Lab Stds.

Technical Magnetic Resonance Imaging. Michael G. Aquilia & John A. Markisz. 320p. 1996. pap. text ed. 35.00 (*0-8385-8836-0*, A8836-7) Appleton & Lange.

Technical Manager's Handbook: A Survival Guide. Melvin Silverman. LC 95-45287. 505p. (gr. 13). 1996. pap. text ed. 44.95 (*0-412-99121-7*) Chapman & Hall.

***Technical Manual.** 12th rev. ed. Ed. by Virginia Vengelen-Tyler. (Illus.). 752p. 1996. 94.00 (*1-56395-062-6*, PC97-TM9612) Am Assn Blood.

T

Technical Manual & Dictionary of Classical Ballet. 3rd rev. ed. Gail Grant. (Illus.). 160p. (C). 1982. reprint ed. pap. 3.95 (*0-486-21843-0*) Dover.

Technical Manual for Church Planters. Dwayne Ruth-Heffelbower. Ed. by Melba Martin et al. (Illus.). 80p. 1989. pap. 5.00 (*0-317-93801-0*) MB Missions.

Technical Manual for the Biologist. (Illus.). 169p. 1993. pap. 24.95 (*0-940168-24-3*) Boxwood.

Technical Manual of Anesthesiology: An Introduction. James E. Heavner et al. 176p. 1989. text ed. 37.00 (*0-88167-515-6*, 1988) Lppncott-Raven.

Technical Manual of Deep Wholistic Bodywork: Postural Integration. Jack W. Painter. 203p. 1987. pap. 22.00 (*0-938405-05-5*) Bodymind Bks.

Technical Manual to Accompany Automotive Technology. Jack Erjavec. 1991. pap. 24.95 (*0-8273-4145-8*) Delmar.

Technical Manual, 1997. American Association of Textile Chemists & Colorists Staff. LC 54-34349. 429p. 1996. write for info. (*0-685-57400-8*) AATCC.

Technical Math. 3rd ed. Smith. LC 95-18917. 720p. (C). 1996. text ed. 42.95 (*0-8273-6807-0*) Delmar.

Technical Math. 4th ed. Austin. (C). 1988. teacher ed., pap. text ed. 34.00 (*0-03-013232-0*) HB Coll Pubs.

Technical Math with Calculus. Linda Davis. 1136p. (C). 1990. write for info. (*0-675-20965-X*, Merrill Coll); pap. text ed. 20.00 (*0-675-20964-1*, Merrill Coll) P-H.

Technical Math with Calculus. Eleanor H. Ninestein. (C). 1991. text ed. 60.00 (*0-673-18748-9*) Addson-Wesley Educ.

Technical Math with Calculus. Eleanor H. Ninestein. (C). 1991. 18.50 (*0-673-46458-X*) Addson-Wesley Educ.

Technical Math with Calculus. Radford & Anthony Vavra. (Physics Ser.). 1986. text ed. 62.50 (*0-8273-3870-8*) Delmar.

Technical Mathematics. Paul Calter. (Illus.). 688p. (C). 1983. write for info. (*0-13-598714-8*) P-H.

Technical Mathematics. Linda Davis. 816p. (C). 1990. text ed. 75.00 (*0-675-20338-4*, Merrill Coll) P-H.

Technical Mathematics. Linda Davis. 816p. (C). 1990. pap. text ed. 21.00 (*0-675-20966-8*, Merrill Coll) P-H.

Technical Mathematics. Robert Donovan. 584p. 1995. text ed. 79.00 (*0-13-440694-X*) P-H.

Technical Mathematics. Eleanor H. Ninestein. (C). 1991. text ed. 56.50 (*0-673-18747-0*); student ed. write for info. (*0-318-68849-2*) Addson-Wesley Educ.

Technical Mathematics. John C. Peterson. LC 92-32234. 846p. 1994. text ed. 49.95 (*0-8273-4575-5*) Delmar.

Technical Mathematics. Jack Rudman. (Dantes Subject Standardized Tests Ser.: DANTES-37). 1994. pap. 23.95 (*0-8373-6637-2*) Nat Learn.

Technical Mathematics. 2nd ed. Paul Calter. 800p. (C). 1989. Casebound. text ed. 80.00 (*0-13-902883-8*) P-H.

Technical Mathematics. 2nd ed. Peterson. (Trade/Tech Math Ser.). 1997. lab manual ed. 26.50 (*0-8273-7238-8*) Delmar.

Technical Mathematics. 2nd ed. Peterson. (Nursing Education Ser.). 1997. teacher ed. 69.95 (*0-8273-7239-6*) Delmar.

Technical Mathematics. 2nd ed. John Peterson. LC 95-13517. 928p. 1996. text ed. 49.95 (*0-8273-7236-1*) Delmar.

Technical Mathematics. 3rd ed. Paul Calter. (C). 1995. text ed. 75.00 (*0-13-898883-8*) P-H.

Technical Mathematics. 3rd ed. Harold S. Rice & Raymond M. Knight. 1973. text ed. 35.95 (*0-07-052200-6*) McGraw.

Technical Mathematics. 3rd ed. Smith. (Trade/Tech Math Ser.). 683p. 1995. text ed. 44.95 (*0-8273-6808-9*) Delmar.

Technical Mathematics. 4th ed. Jacqueline Austin et al. 728p. (C). 1988. pap. text ed. 47.00 (*0-03-013233-9*) SCP.

Technical Mathematics & Technical Mathematics with Calculus: Solutions Manual. John C. Peterson & Alan Herweyer. 647p. 1994. pap. text ed. 31.50 (*0-8273-4582-8*) Delmar.

Technical Mathematics Computer Program. Peterson. (Physics Ser.). 1994. 10.00 (*0-8273-6503-9*) Delmar.

Technical Mathematics I. Thomas J. McHale & Paul T. Witzke. 704p. (C). 1988. pap. text ed. 49.50 (*0-201-15408-0*) Addison-Wesley.

Technical Mathematics II. Thomas J. McHale & Paul T. Witzke. (Illus.). 704p. (C). 1988. pap. text ed. 49.50 (*0-201-15409-9*) Addison-Wesley.

Technical Mathematics with Calculus. John C. Peterson. LC 92-32757. 1342p. 1994. text ed. 54.95 (*0-8273-4577-1*) Delmar.

Technical Mathematics with Calculus. 2nd ed. Peterson. (Trade/Tech Math Ser.). 1997. student ed. 18.95 (*0-8273-7237-X*) Delmar.

Technical Mathematics with Calculus. 2nd ed. John C. Peterson. LC 95-13516. 1376p. 1996. text ed. 54.95 (*0-8273-7243-4*) Delmar.

Technical Mathematics with Calculus. 3rd ed. Paul Calter. (C). 1995. text ed. 82.00 (*0-13-898875-7*) P-H.

Technical Mathematics with Calculus. 3rd ed. Harold S. Rice & Raymond M. Knight. (Illus.). 704p. (C). 1975. text ed. 42.95 (*0-07-052205-7*) McGraw.

Technical Mathematics with Calculus CTB. Peterson. (Physics Ser.). 1994. 49.95 (*0-8273-6507-1*) Delmar.

Technical, Medical, & Educational Problems of Acute Care: Proceedings of the International Symposium on Acute Care, 4th, November, 1975. International Symposium on Acute Care Staff. Ed. by B. M. Tavares. (Current Topics in Critical Care Medicine Ser.: Vol. 2). (Illus.). 200p. 1977. 39.25 (*3-8055-2374-2*) S Karger.

Technical Metals. Harold V. Johnson. (gr. 9-12). 1981. student ed., teacher ed. 2.00 (*0-02-665880-1*); teacher ed. 2.64 (*0-02-665860-7*); text ed. 26.00 (*0-02-665850-X*); student ed. 7.60 (*0-02-665870-4*) Glencoe.

Technical Mineralogy & Petrography: An Introduction to Materials Technology, 2 vols. A. Szymanski. (Materials Science Monographs: No. 43). 950p. 1989. Set. 495.75 (*0-444-98991-9*, North Holland) Elsevier.

Technical Needs: Nonwovens for Medical-Surgical & Consumer Uses. LC 86-50647. 236p. 1986. 37.00 (*0-89852-049-5*, 0102B049) TAPPI.

Technical Office Protocol: User's Group Summary, December 3-4, 1985, Bellevue, WA - Sponsored by MAP User's Group of SME. TOP Users' Group, Meeting (1st: 1985: Bellevue, WA) Staff. LC 86-60239. (Illus.). 312p. reprint ed. pap. 89.00 (*0-8357-6477-X*, 2035848) Bks Demand.

Technical Options for the Advanced Liquid Metal Reactor. (Illus.). 56p. (Orig.). (C). 1994. pap. text ed. 25.00 (*0-7881-1038-1*) DIANE Pub.

Technical Papers, Annual Convention, 1990: Countdown to the 21st Century. 1990. pap. write for info. (*0-944426-68-9*) ASP & RS.

Technical Papers, Annual Convention, 1990: Countdown to the 21st Century, 1. 1990. pap. 5.00 (*0-944426-69-7*) ASP & RS.

Technical Papers, Annual Convention, 1990: Countdown to the 21st Century, 2. 1990. pap. 5.00 (*0-944426-70-0*) ASP & RS.

Technical Papers, Annual Convention, 1990: Countdown to the 21st Century, 3. 1990. pap. 5.00 (*0-944426-71-9*) ASP & RS.

Technical Papers, Annual Convention, 1990: Countdown to the 21st Century, 5. 1990. pap. 5.00 (*0-944426-73-5*) ASP & RS.

Technical Papers, Annual Convention, 1990: Countdown to the 21st Century, Vol. 4. 1990. pap. 5.00 (*0-944426-72-7*) ASP & RS.

Technical Papers, Annual Convention, 1991, 5 vols. 1885p. 1991. pap. write for info. (*0-944426-43-3*) ASP & RS.

Technical Papers, Annual Convention, 1991, 5 vols., 1. 1885p. 1991. 10.00 (*0-944426-39-5*) ASP & RS.

Technical Papers, Annual Convention, 1991, 5 vols., 2. 1885p. 1991. 10.00 (*0-944426-40-9*) ASP & RS.

Technical Papers, Annual Convention, 1991, 5 vols., 3. 1885p. 1991. 10.00 (*0-944426-41-7*) ASP & RS.

Technical Papers, Annual Convention, 1991, 5 vols., 4. 1885p. 1991. 10.00 (*0-944426-42-5*) ASP & RS.

Technical Papers, Annual Convention, 1991, 5 vols., Set. 1885p. 1991. write for info. (*0-944426-38-7*) ASP & RS.

Technical Papers, Fall Convention. 506p. 1991. 10.00 (*0-944426-78-6*) ASP & RS.

Technical Papers, Fall Convention, 1989: From Compass to Computer, 2 vols., 2. 630p. 1989. write for info. (*0-944426-59-X*) ASP & RS.

Technical Papers, 1989 Annual Convention: Agenda for the '90s, 5 vols., 5. 1512p. 1989. write for info. (*0-944426-54-9*) ASP & RS.

Technical Papers, 1992 Annual Convention, 2 vols. 875p. 1992. Set. write for info. (*0-944426-79-4*) ASP & RS.

Technical Papers, 1992 Annual Convention, 2 vols., 1. 875p. 1992. 10.00 (*0-944426-81-6*) ASP & RS.

Technical Papers, 1992 Annual Convention, 2 vols., 2. 875p. 1992. 10.00 (*0-944426-80-8*) ASP & RS.

Technical Papers, 1993 Annual Convention, 3 vols., Set. 1354p. 1993. pap. 25.00 (*0-944426-93-X*) ASP & RS.

Technical Papers, 1993 Annual Convention, Vol. 1. 1354p. 1993. pap. write for info. (*0-944426-94-8*) ASP & RS.

Technical Papers, 1993 Annual Convention, Vol. 2. 1354p. 1993. pap. write for info. (*0-944426-95-6*) ASP & RS.

Technical Papers, 1993 Annual Convention, Vol. 3. 1354p. 1993. pap. write for info. (*0-944426-96-4*) ASP & RS.

Technical Papers, 1994 Annual Convention, 2 vols., Set. 1142p. 1994. write for info. (*1-57083-007-X*) ASP & RS.

Technical Papers, 1994 Annual Convention Vol. 1. 1994. 30.00 (*1-57083-005-3*) ASP & RS.

Technical Papers, 1994 Annual Convention Vol. 2. 1994. 30.00 (*1-57083-006-1*) ASP & RS.

Technical Pascal. Andrew C. Staugaard, Jr. 384p. 1988. pap. text ed. 21.75 (*0-317-62009-6*) P-H.

Technical Pen. Gary Simmons. (Illus.). 144p. 1992. pap. 24.95 (*0-8230-5227-3*, Watsn-Guptill) Watsn-Guptill.

Technical Physics. Granet. (Physics Ser.). 1995. text ed. 59.95 (*0-8273-6004-5*) Delmar.

Technical Physics. Erwin Selleck. 768p. 1991. text ed. 56.95 (*0-8273-4607-7*) Delmar.

Technical Physics. 4th ed. F. Bueche. 704p. 1994. text ed. 47.50 (*0-471-52462-X*) Wiley.

Technical Physics Laboratory Manual. Olan E. Kruse et al. (C). 1971. reprint ed. student ed., pap. 12.00 (*0-934786-07-0*) G Davis.

Technical Pocket Dictionary, English-German. 2nd ed. Henry G. Freeman. (ENG & GER.). English-German. 35.95 (*3-19-006213-7*) Adlers Foreign Bks.

Technical Pocket Dictionary, German-English. 2nd ed. Henry G. Freeman. (ENG & GER.). German-English. 35.95 (*3-19-006212-9*) Adlers Foreign Bks.

Technical Presentation Skills: A Practical Guide for Better Speaking. rev. ed. Steve Mandel. Ed. by W. Philip Gerould. LC 93-74052. (Fifty-Minute Ser.). (Illus.). 94p. (Orig.). 1994. pap. 10.95 (*1-56052-263-1*) Crisp Pubns.

Technical Presentation Workbook: Winning Strategies for Effective Public Speaking. Richard L. Sullivan & Jerry L. Wircenski. 278p. 1996. wbk. ed., spiral bd. 29.95 (*0-7918-0040-7*, 800407) ASME Pr.

Technical Principles, Design, & Safety of Joint Implants. Ed. by Gottfried H. Buchhorn & Hans-Georg Willert. LC 92-1425. (Illus.). 550p. 1994. 159.00 (*0-88937-090-7*) Hogrefe & Huber Pubs.

Technical Principles of Building for Safety: Technical Principles & Details of Low-Cost, Hazard-Resistant Construction. Andrew Coburn et al. (Building for Safety Ser.). 120p. (Orig.). 1994. pap. 15.50 (*1-85339-182-4*, Pub. by Intermed Tech UK) Women Ink.

Technical Problems in the Verification of a Ban on Space Weapons. (Disarmament Topical Papers: No. 17). 104p. Date not set. pap. 23.00 (*92-9045-080-0*, E.GV.93.0.12) UN.

Technical Production Handbook: A Guide for Performing Arts Presenting Organizations & Touring Companies. rev. ed. Kay Barrell. Ed. by Mimi McKell. LC 90-50991. (Illus.). 56p. 1991. pap. 7.50 (*0-9611710-6-5*) Western States.

Technical Progress & Agricultural Depression. Eugen Altschul & Frederick Strauss. (NBER Bulletin Ser.: No. 67). 1937. reprint ed. 20.00 (*0-685-61185-X*) Natl Bur Econ Res.

Technical Rationale Behind CSC-STD-003-85: Guidance for Applying the Department of Defense Trusted Computer System Evaluation on Criteria in Specific Environments. (Illus.). 41p. (Orig.). (C). 1995. pap. text ed. 20.00 (*0-7881-2207-X*) DIANE Pub.

Technical Reader: Readings in Technical, Business, & Scientific Communication. 2nd ed. Cox Anderson. 384p. (C). 1984. pap. text ed. 21.50 (*0-03-062396-0*) HB Coll Pubs.

Technical Readout 2750. FASA Staff. (BattleTech Ser.). (Illus.). 126p. 1989. pap. 12.00 (*1-55560-089-1*, 8613) FASA Corp.

Technical Readout 3025. FASA Staff. (BattleTech Ser.). (Illus.). 198p. 1986. pap. 15.00 (*0-931787-84-X*, 8603) FASA Corp.

Technical Readout 3026. FASA Staff. (BattleTech Ser.). (Illus.). 126p. 1987. pap. 15.00 (*0-931787-32-7*, 8606) FASA Corp.

Technical Readout 3050: The Return of Kerensky. FASA Staff. (BattleTech Ser.). (Illus.). 240p. 1989. pap. 18.00 (*1-55560-090-5*, 8614) FASA Corp.

Technical Readout 3055. FASA Staff. (BattleTech Ser.). (Illus.). 168p. 1992. pap. 15.00 (*1-55560-164-2*, 8619) FASA Corp.

Technical Readout 3057. FASA Staff. (BattleTech Ser.). (Illus.). 128p. 1994. pap. 18.00 (*1-55560-234-7*, 8620) FASA Corp.

Technical Reference Book on Valves for Control of Fluids. 2nd ed. BVMA Staff. 1966. 156.00 (*0-08-012268-X*, Pub. by Pergamon Repr UK) Franklin.

***Technical Reference Handbook.** 3rd ed. E. P. Rasis. (Illus.). 220p. 1991. 23.96 (*0-8269-3452-8*) Am Technical.

Technical Regulations, Vol. 2: Meteorological Service for International Air Navigation. World Meteorological Organization Staff. (WMO Ser.: No. 49). (Illus.). 1992. ring bd. 60.00 (*92-63-15049-4*, Pub. by Wrld Meteorological SZ); 22.00 (*0-685-37800-4*, Pub. by Wrld Meteorological SZ) Am Meteorological.

Technical Regulations, Vol. 3: Hydrology. World Meteorological Organization Staff. (WMO Ser.: No. 49). 1988. ring bd. 59.00 (*92-63-14049-9*, Pub. by Wrld Meteorological SZ); suppl. ed. write for info. (*0-318-68019-X*, Pub. by Wrld Meteorological SZ); 22.00 (*0-685-37801-2*, Pub. by Wrld Meteorological SZ) Am Meteorological.

Technical Report, No. 5. Y. John Wang & Yie W. Chien. (Sterile Pharmaceutical Packaging Compatibility & Stability Ser.). 137p. 1984. pap. 35.00 (*0-939459-04-3*) PDA.

Technical Report, No. 7. PDA Task Force on Depyrogenation Staff. (Depyrogenation Ser.). 116p. 1985. pap. 35.00 (*0-939459-06-X*) PDA.

Technical Report: The Treatment of Acute Exacerbations of Asthma in Children. 28p. 1994. pap. 17.95 (*0-910761-54-X*) Am Acad Pediat.

Technical Report - Practice Parameter: The Management of Hyperbilirubinemia in Healthy Newborns. 66p. 1994. pap. 17.95 (*0-910761-69-8*) Am Acad Pediat.

Technical Report for Human Sexuality: Values & Choices. Michael J. Donahue. (Values & Choices Ser.). 122p. 1987. pap. 25.00 (*1-57482-215-2*) Search Inst.

Technical Report of the NAEP 1992 Trial State Assessment Program in Reading. Eugene G. Johnson et al. (Illus.). 316p. (Orig.). (C). 1995. pap. text ed. 40.00 (*0-7881-1919-2*) DIANE Pub.

Technical Report Standards: How to Prepare & Write Effective Technical Reports. Lawrence R. Harvill & Thomas L. Kraft. LC 77-70964. (Illus.). (C). 1979. pap. 14.95 (*0-89491-004-3*) Weber Systems.

Technical Report Writing. Steven E. Pauley. (C). 1995. pap. 27.96 (*0-395-72176-8*) HM.

Technical Report Writing, 6 Vols. Riordan. (C). 1995. pap. 41.96 (*0-395-73052-X*) HM.

Technical Report Writing, 6 Vols. Riordan. (C). 1995. suppl. ed., teacher ed., pap. 11.96 (*0-395-73053-8*) HM.

Technical Report Writing. 2nd ed. James W. Souther & Myron L. White. LC 84-15474. 104p. (C). 1984. reprint ed. lib. bdg. 24.50 (*0-89874-786-4*) Krieger.

Technical Risk Management. Jack V. Michaels. 1996. text ed. 71.00 (*0-13-155756-4*) P-H.

Technical Secretary: Terminology & Transcription. Dorothy Adams & Margaret A. Kurtz. (Diamond Jubilee Ser.). 1967. text ed. 38.75 (*0-07-000320-3*) McGraw.

Technical Series see Technical Bulletins of Dianetics & Scientology

Technical Services in Libraries. Maurice F. Tauber. LC 54-10328. (Columbia Library Service Studies: No. 7). 1954. text ed. 86.00 (*0-231-02054-6*) Col U Pr.

Technical Services in Libraries: Systems & Applications, Vol. 25. Ed. by Thomas W. Leonhardt. LC 91-43729. (Foundations in Library & Information Science: Vol. 25). 279p. 1991. 73.25 (*1-55938-214-7*) Jai Pr.

Technical Services in the Medium-Sized Library. Sheila S. Intner & Josephine R. Fang. LC 91-18311. xxii, 189p. (C). 1991. lib. bdg. 35.00 (*0-208-02173-6*, Lib Prof Pubns) Shoe String.

Technical Services Management, 1965-1990: A Quarter Century of Change & a Look to the Future: Fetschrift for Kathryn Luther Henderson. Ed. by Linda C. Smith & Ruth C. Carter. LC 95-20463. (Illus.). 370p. (C). 1995. lib. bdg. 49.95 (*1-56024-960-9*) Haworth Pr.

Technical Shop Mathematics. 2nd ed. John G. Anderson. LC 82-11847. (Illus.). 500p. (C). 1983. 25.95 (*0-8311-1145-3*) Indus Pr.

Technical Sketching. 2nd ed. Dale H. Besterfield & Robert E. O'Hagan. 300p. 1989. pap. text ed. 45.00 (*0-13-901935-9*) P-H.

***Technical Sketching for Engineers, Technologists & Technicians.** 3rd ed. Dale H. Besterfield & Robert E. O'Hagan. LC 97-14321. 1998. 40.00 (*0-13-472572-7*) P-H.

Technical Skills for Alpine Skiing. Ellen P. Foster. 142p. 1995. pap. 15.95 (*0-9647390-2-X*) Turning Pt Ski Found.

***Technical Solutions to Alternative Transportation Problems.** 1996. 55.00 (*1-56091-840-3*, SP-1189) Soc Auto Engineers.

Technical Speaker's Guide: Designing & Delivering Business & Professional Presentations. Beverly C. Quinn. (Illus.). 200p. 1997. 29.95 (*0-9628765-2-6*) Typhoon Pr.

Technical Standards: An Introduction for Librarians. 2nd ed. Walt Crawford. (Professional Librarian Ser.). 220p. 1991. 45.00 (*0-8161-1950-3*, Hall Reference); 30.00 (*0-8161-1951-1*, Hall Reference) Macmillan.

Technical Statics & Strength of Material. 2nd ed. Thrower. (Mechanical Technology Ser.). 1986. text ed. 68.95 (*0-8273-3918-6*) Delmar.

Technical Studies for Beginning Cello. Craig Duncan. (Building Excellence Ser.). 1993. 4.95 (*1-56222-213-9*, 94599) Mel Bay.

Technical Studies for Beginning Clarinet: Level 1. Norman Heim. (Building Excellence Ser.). 1993. 4.95 (*1-56222-165-5*, 94547) Mel Bay.

Technical Studies for Beginning Saxophone: Level 1. Mike Buerk. (Building Excellence Ser.). 1993. 4.95 (*1-56222-216-3*, 94588) Mel Bay.

Technical Studies for Beginning Viola. Craig Duncan. (Building Excellence Ser.). 1993. 4.95 (*1-56222-214-7*, 94598) Mel Bay.

Technical Studies for Beginning Violin. Craig Duncan. (Building Excellence Ser.). 1993. 4.95 (*1-56222-164-7*, 94559) Mel Bay.

Technical Studies for the Cornet. Herbert L. Clarke. 53p. 1934. pap. 10.50 (*0-8258-0158-3*, 02280) Fischer Inc NY.

Technical Studies for Violin, Op. 92, Pt. 1. Hans Sitt. (Carl Fischer Music Library: No. L500). 1932. pap. 6.95 (*0-8258-0151-6*, L500) Fischer Inc NY.

Technical Support Aide. Jack Rudman. (Career Examination Ser.: C-2476). 1994. pap. 29.95 (*0-8373-2476-9*) Nat Learn.

Technical Terms in Plastics Engineering. Annemarie Wittfoht. 356p. (DUT, ENG, FRE, GER & SPA.). 1976. 158.25 (*0-444-99846-2*) Elsevier.

Technical Terms in Plastics Engineering. Annemarie Wittfoht. 324p. (DUT, ENG, FRE, GER, ITA & SPA.). 1975. 195.00 (*0-8288-9197-4*, M8184); 195.00 (*0-8288-9300-4*, M8184) Fr & Eur.

Technical Tips. Michele Bousquet. 204p. 1996. pap. 129.95 incl. disk (*0-534-95126-0*) Delmar.

Technical Tips: 3D Studio Tips & Tricks. Michele Bousquet. (3D Studio Tips & Tricks Ser.). 240p. 1994. pap. 31.50 (*0-8273-7013-X*) Delmar.

Technical Tips on Hand Surgery. Ed. by Morton L. Kasdan et al. 350p. 1994. text ed. 69.00 (*1-56053-020-0*) Hanley & Belfus.

Technical, Trade & Business School Data Handbook - Midwest Regional Edition. 5th ed. Ed. by Susan Weddle. 600p. 1991. pap. 45.00 (*1-878172-31-X*) Wintergrn-Orchard Hse.

Technical, Trade & Business School Data Handbook - Northeast Regional Edition. 5th ed. Ed. by Susan Weddle. 600p. 1991. pap. 45.00 (*1-878172-29-8*) Wintergrn-Orchard Hse.

Technical, Trade & Business School Data Handbook - Southeast Regional Edition. 5th ed. Ed. by Susan Weddle. 600p. 1991. pap. 45.00 (*1-878172-30-1*) Wintergrn-Orchard Hse.

Technical, Trade & Business School Data Handbook - West Regional Edition. 5th ed. Ed. by Susan Weddle. 600p. 1991. pap. 45.00 (*1-878172-32-8*) Wintergrn-Orchard Hse.

Technical, Trade & Business School Data Handbook, 1994-96: National Edition, 4 vols. 5th ed. Ed. by Mary G. Lynch & Don Beattie. 2950p. (Orig.). 1994. pap. 150.00 (*1-878172-28-X*) Wintergrn-Orchard Hse.

Technical Traders Guide to Computer Analysis of the Futures Market. Charles LeBeau & David W. Lucas. 312p. 1991. text ed. 70.00 (*1-55623-468-6*) Irwin Prof Pubng.

***Technical Traffic Accident Investigators' Handbook: A Level 3 Reference, Training & Investigation Manual.** 2nd ed. R. W. Rivers. LC 96-47758. (Illus.). 504p. (Orig.). 1997. text ed. 86.95 (*0-398-06696-5*) C C Thomas.

***Technical Traffic Accident Investigators' Handbook: A Level 3 Reference, Training & Investigation Manual.** 2nd ed. R. W. Rivers. LC 96-47758. (Illus.). 504p. (Orig.). 1997. pap. text ed. 66.95 (*0-398-06697-3*) C C Thomas.

Technical Trainer's Source Book. Pfeiffer & Co Staff. LC 91-25508. (Illus.). 400p. 1992. ring bd. 99.95 (*0-88390-298-2*, Pfffr & Cc) Jossey-Bass.

Technical Transformation of Agriculture in Communist China. Leslie T. Kuo. LC 73-181867. (Special Studies in International Economics & Development). 1971. 39.50 (*0-275-28276-7*) Irvington.

An Asterisk (*) at the beginning of an entry indicates that the title is appearing in BIP for the first time.

Technical Trends & Strategic Policy. Sidney D. Drell & Thomas H. Johnson. (Occasional Paper of Center for International Security & Arms Control, Stanford University Ser.). 41p. (Orig.). 1988. pap. 9.00 (0-935371-18-4) CFISAC.

Technical Variants. Hanon & A. Lindquist. 32p. (Orig.). (J). (gr. k-12). 1929. pap. text ed. 5.95 (0-87487-657-5) Summy-Birchard.

Technical Veterinary Dictionary. Wolfgang Lindeke. 185p. (ENG, GER, RUS & SLV.). 1972. 95.00 (0-8288-6421-7, M-9894) Fr & Eur.

Technical Victory: Battles in Writing. Roberta M. Humble. (Illus.). 475p. (C). 1989. pap. text ed. 32.95 (0-940139-14-6) Consortium RI.

Technical Vocabulary of Life Insurance: Vocabulaire Technique des Assurances sur la Vie, Vol. 1, French-English. Louis-Paul Beguin et al. 309p. (ENG & FRE.). 1990. pap. 14.95 (0-8288-4843-2, M9244) Fr & Eur.

Technical Vocabulary of Life Insurance, English-French Vocabulary. Louis-Paul Beguin. 135p. (ENG & FRE.). 1990. pap. 29.95 (0-8288-4844-0, M9245) Fr & Eur.

Technical Vocabulary of Tobacco: Vocabulaire Technique du Tabac. CILF Staff. 320p. (ENG, FRE & GER.). 1982. pap. 49.95 (0-8288-0761-2, M14591) Fr & Eur.

Technical Woodworking. 2nd ed. Chris H. Groneman & E. R. Glazener. 1975. text ed. 34.44 (0-07-024964-4) McGraw.

***Technical Workshop on Sediments.** 148p. 1993. pap. 9.95 (0-614-30384-2, PR4) Terrene Inst.

***Technical Writer's Freelancing Guide.** Peter Kent. 1997. 16.95 (0-02-861883-1) Macmillan.

***Technical Writer's Guide.** Robert McGraw. Ed. by Jane D. Guthrie & Kelly Scanlon. LC 95-72618. 134p. (Orig.). 1996. pap. 15.95 (1-57294-012-3, 13-0007) SkillPath Pubns.

Technical Writers' Guide: Fifteen Hundred Verbs & Usages, Set. 1140p. 1985. boxed 170.00 (0-317-89472-2, Inter Am U Pr) Taylor & Francis.

Technical Writer's Handbook. Ed. by Harry E. Chandler. 418p. 1983. 20.00 (0-87170-151-0, 6028) ASM.

Technical Writer's Handbook. Matt Young. 241p. 1989. text ed. 24.50 (0-935702-60-1) Univ Sci Bks.

Technical Writing. Francis B. Emerson. LC 85-80764. 560p. 1987. teacher ed. 2.36 (0-318-36890-0); pap. text ed. 29.56 (0-318-36889-7) HM.

Technical Writing. William Pfeiffer. 1991. pap. write for info. (0-675-21221-9, Merrill Coll) P-H.

Technical Writing. Jack Rudman. (Dantes Subject Standardized Tests Ser.: DANTES-43). 1994. pap. 23.95 (0-8373-6643-7) Nat Learn.

Technical Writing. 2nd ed. Gerson. 480p. (C). 1996. pap. text ed. 47.00 (0-13-190810-3) P-H.

Technical Writing. 3rd ed. Anderson. (C). 1995. teacher ed., pap. text ed. 33.75 (0-15-502325-X) HB Coll Pubs.

***Technical Writing.** 4th ed. Anderson. (C). 1998. pap. text ed. write for info. (0-15-508309-0) HB Coll Pubs.

***Technical Writing.** 5th ed. Brusaw. Date not set. wbk. ed., pap. text ed. write for info. (0-312-15288-4) St Martin.

Technical Writing. 5th ed. Gordon Mills & John Walter. 576p. (C). 1986. text ed. 32.00 (0-03-062019-8) HB Coll Pubs.

Technical Writing. 6th ed. John M. Lannon. (C). 1993. pap. 33.00 (0-673-52294-6) Addson-Wesley Educ.

Technical Writing. 7th ed. John M. Lannon. LC 96-19525. (C). 1997. text ed. 46.50 (0-673-52472-8) Addson-Wesley Educ.

Technical Writing: A Bibliography. Sarojini Balachandran. 1977. pap. 3.90 (0-931874-07-6) Assn Busn Comm.

Technical Writing: A Handbook of Examples & Exercises. rev. ed. Brenda R. Sims. 204p. (Orig.). (C). 1995. student ed., pap. 14.95 (0-929398-19-X) UNTX Pr.

Technical Writing: A Practical Approach. Turner. (C). 1984. teacher ed. write for info. (0-8359-7547-9, Reston) P-H.

Technical Writing: A Practical Approach. 3rd ed. William S. Pfeiffer. LC 95-52175. 1996. pap. text ed. 52.00 (0-13-455339-X) P-H.

Technical Writing: A Reader-Centered Approach. 2nd ed. Paul V. Anderson. 848p. (C). 1990. pap. text ed. 34.75 (0-15-589682-2) HB Coll Pubs.

Technical Writing: A Reader-Centered Approach. 3rd ed. Paul V. Anderson. (Illus.). 800p. (C). 1994. pap. text ed. write for info. (0-15-501185-5) HB Coll Pubs.

Technical Writing: A Theoretical Basis. Fillmer Hevener, Jr. (Illus.). 128p. (C). 1992. pap. text ed. 12.95 (0-940139-25-1) Consortium RI.

Technical Writing: Contexts, Audiences, & Communities. Carolyn R. Boiarsky. LC 92-35635. 652p. 1992. pap. text ed. 48.00 (0-205-13932-9) Allyn.

Technical Writing: Method Application & Management. Philbin. (Technical Communications Ser.). 1988. pap. 35.95 (0-8273-2685-8) Delmar.

Technical Writing: Method Application & Management. Philbin. (Technical Communications Ser.). 1989. teacher ed., pap. 10.00 (0-8273-2686-6) Delmar.

Technical Writing: Principles, Strategies, & Readings. 3rd ed. Diana C. Reep. LC 96-12470. 604p. 1996. pap. text ed. 46.00 (0-205-26077-2) Allyn.

Technical Writing: Theory & Practice. Ed. by Bertie E. Fearing & W. Keats Sparrow. LC 89-12477. vii, 176p. 1989. pap. 19.75 (0-87352-181-1, J306P); lib. bdg. 37.50 (0-87352-180-3, J306C) Modern Lang.

Technical Writing & Communication. Ed. by Carole M. Mablekos. 174p. 1988. 510.00 incl. audio (0-8412-1484-0, A3); teacher ed. 39.00 (0-8412-1501-4) Am Chemical.

Technical Writing & Professional Communication. 2nd ed. Leslie A. Olsen. 1991. pap. text ed. write for info. (0-07-047823-6) McGraw.

Technical Writing & Professional Communication for Non-Native Speakers. 2nd ed. Thomas N. Huckin. 1991. pap. text ed. write for info. (0-07-030825-X) McGraw.

Technical Writing & Speaking: An Introduction. Joan Van Emden & Jennifer Easteal. LC 96-22751. 1996. pap. write for info. (0-07-709027-6) McGraw.

Technical Writing for Industry. Larry Riney. 288p. 1989. boxed 29.00 (0-13-901828-X) P-H.

Technical Writing for Private Industry: The A to Z of O & M Manuals. Edward Von Koenigseck et al. 164p. 1991. 24.50 (0-89464-363-0) Krieger.

Technical Writing for Social Scientists. John S. Harris & Reed H. Blake. LC 75-20129. 128p. 1976. 29.95 (0-911012-39-7) Nelson-Hall.

***Technical Writing for Success.** Mehlich. 1997. text ed. 27.95 (0-538-68296-5) S-W Pub.

Technical Writing for Success: A School-to-Work Approach. S. Mehlich & D. Smith-Worthington. (EC - HS Communication/Engl Ser.). 448p. 1997. text ed. 27.95 (0-538-63673-4) S-W Pub.

Technical Writing for Technicians: How to Build a Career As a Hardware Technical Writer. Warren R. Freeman. LC 94-90876. (Illus.). 160p. (Orig.). (C). 1995. pap. text ed. 19.95 (0-9644739-0-9) Contemax Pub.

***Technical Writing Guide Non-National.** 3rd ed. Anderson. (C). 1995. lab manual ed. write for info. (0-15-502326-8) HB Coll Pubs.

***Technical Writing Handbook.** Voss. (C). Date not set. pap. write for info. (0-669-33991-1) HM.

Technical Writing in a Corporate Culture: A Study of the Nature of Information. Christine Barabas. Ed. by Marcia Farr. LC 90-32194. (Writing Research Ser.: Vol. 18). 272p. (C). 1990. pap. 39.50 (0-89391-664-1); text ed. 73.25 (0-89391-603-X) Ablex Pub.

Technical Writing in the Corporate World. H. Estrin & N. Elliot. LC 89-81249. (Fifty-Minute Ser.). (Illus.). 78p. (Orig.). 1990. pap. 10.95 (1-56052-004-3) Crisp Pubns.

***Technical Writing Style.** Jones. 1997. pap. text ed. 36.00 (0-205-19722-1) P-H.

Technical Writing Workbook. Sally T. Taylor. 236p. (C). 1996. per., pap. text ed. 19.89 (0-7872-2075-2) Kendall-Hunt.

Technically-Write! Communicating in a Technological Era. 4th ed. Ronald S. Blicq. 432p. (C). 1993. pap. text ed. 53.00 (0-13-904434-5) P-H.

Technician As Writer: Preparing Technical Reports. Ingrid Brunner et al. (C). 1980. pap. text ed. 63.00 (0-02-315950-2, Macmillan Coll) P-H.

Technician Class License Manual. 1993. pap. 6.00 (0-87259-418-1) Am Radio.

Technician Class Radio Amateur: FCC Test Manual. Martin Schwartz. LC 89-83307. 96p. 1993. pap. 5.95 (0-912146-27-3, 28-01) Ameco.

Technician Exam Review Guide. 1995. pap. 9.95 (0-87259-515-3) Am Radio.

***Technician Mathematics.** 2nd ed. J. O. Bird. 1994. pap. 20.95 (0-582-23424-7, Pub. by Longman UK); pap. 25.95 (0-582-23425-5, Pub. by Longman UK) Longman.

***Technician Maths 1.** Bird. 1996. pap. write for info. (0-582-23426-3, Pub. by Longman UK) Longman.

***Technician No-Code Plus: FCC License Preparation For Elements 2 & 3A Novice & Technician Class Theory.** 3rd rev. ed. Gordon West. Ed. by Pete Trotter & Gerald Luecke. (Illus.). 320p. 1997. pap. 12.95 (0-945053-16-9) Master Pubng.

Technician Physics, Level 2. Eric Deeson. (Longman Technician Series, Mathematics & Sciences). 284p. reprint ed. pap. 81.00 (0-8357-2978-8, 2039240) Bks Demand.

***Technician Science.** Bolton. 1988. pap. text ed. write for info. (0-582-01656-8, Pub. by Longman UK) Longman.

Technicians ECG Analyzer. Burdick Corporation Staff. 1973. pap. 5.40 (0-13-898610-X) P-H.

Technicians Guide Fiber Optics. 2nd ed. Sterling. (Tech & Industrial Education Ser.). 1995. pap. 45.95 (0-8273-7427-5) Van Nos Reinhold.

Technician's Guide to Advanced Automotive Emissions Systems. Rick Escalambre. LC 94-46450. 248p. 1996. pap. 26.95 (0-8273-7154-3) Delmar.

Technician's Guide to Anti-Lock Brake Systems. Jack Erjavec. LC 95-45145. (Automotive Technology Ser.). 176p. 1996. pap. 24.95 (0-8273-7504-2) Delmar.

Technician's Guide to ASE Advanced Engine Performance L1 Test. Mike Stubblefield. LC 95-22838. (Automotive Technology Ser.). 176p. 1996. pap. 20.95 (0-8273-7248-5) Delmar.

Technician's Guide to Auto Emission Systems. Larry Carley. LC 94-22901. 352p. 1994. student ed., pap. 37.50 (0-8273-7048-2) Delmar.

Technician's Guide to Certification. Richard Jazwin. LC 93-49565. 1994. pap. 19.95 (0-912524-88-X) Busn News.

***Technician's Guide to Electronic Communications.** Frederick L. Gould. LC 97-8074. (Illus.). 320p. 1997. text ed. 52.95 (0-07-024536-3); pap. text ed. 27.95 (0-07-024537-1) McGraw.

Technician's Guide to Fiber Optics. Donald J. Sterling, Jr. LC 86-32988. 288p. (C). 1987. teacher ed. 10.00 (0-8273-2613-0) Delmar.

***Technicians Guide to Fiber Optics.** Donald J. Sterling, Jr. 33.95 (0-614-18439-8, B040006) Info Gatekeepers.

Technician's Guide to Fiber Optics. 2nd ed. Sterling. (Electronics Technology Ser.). 1993. pap. 14.00 (0-8273-6133-5) Delmar.

Technician's Guide to Fiber Optics: Instructor's Guide. 2nd ed. Donald J. Sterling, Jr. 26p. 1993. teacher ed. 21.00 (0-8273-5836-9) Delmar.

Technician's Guide to HVAC Systems. Gary K. Skimin. LC 95-17261. 1995. text ed. 40.00 (0-07-057914-8) McGraw.

Technician's Guide to Industrial Electronics: How to Troubleshoot & Repair Automated Equipment. Robert S. Carrow. LC 95-3240. 1995. text ed. 45.00 (0-07-011273-8) McGraw-Hill Prof.

Technicians Guide to Programmable Controllers. 2nd ed. Richard A. Cox. (C). 1988. teacher ed., pap. 15.00 (0-8273-2831-1) Delmar.

Technicians Guide to Programmable Controllers. 2nd ed. Richard A. Cox. (C). 1989. pap. 31.95 (0-8273-2830-3) Delmar.

Technician's Guide to Programmable Controllers. 3rd ed. Richard A. Cox. LC 94-24400. 320p. 1994. pap. 35.00 (0-8273-6238-2) Delmar.

Technician's Guide to Refrigeration Systems. John A. Corinchock. LC 96-42366. 1996. text ed. 49.95 (0-07-013159-7) McGraw.

Technicians Guide to Servicing Two-Way FM Radio. Daniel K. Neely. (Illus.). 1978. 14.95 (0-13-898635-5, Parker Publishing Co) P-H.

Technician's Guidebook to EMI - RFI. William H. Taylor. (Illus.). 416p. 1997. text ed. 45.00 (0-07-063298-7) McGraw.

***Technician's Handbook to Fiber Optics/CATV.** (Fiber Optics for the CATV Industry Reprint Ser.: Vol. III). 29.95 (0-614-18461-4, 133ZAC) Info Gatekeepers.

Technicians of Ecstasy: Shamanism & the Modern Artist. Mark Levy. LC 93-14704. (Illus.). 360p. (Orig.). 1993. pap. 14.95 (0-9626184-4-6) Bramble Co.

Technicians of the Finite: The Rise & Decline of the Schizophrenic in American Thought, 1840-1960. S. P. Fullinwider. LC 81-23771. (Contributions in Medical History Ser.: No. 9). ix, 253p. 1982. text ed. 55.00 (0-313-23021-8, FFI/) Greenwood.

Technicians of the Sacred: A Range of Poetries from Africa, America, Asia, Europe & Oceania. rev. ed. Ed. by Jerome Rothenberg. LC 84-16276. 1985. pap. 17.95 (0-520-04912-8) U CA Pr.

Technicolor Movies: The History of Dye Transfer Printing. Richard W. Haines. LC 92-56648. (Illus.). 168p. 1993. lib. bdg. 28.50 (0-89950-856-1) McFarland & Co.

Technicolor Time Machine. Harry Harrison. 256p. 1991. pap. 3.95 (0-8125-1607-9) Tor Bks.

Technics & Architecture: The Development of Materials & Systems for Buildings. Cecil D. Elliott. (Illus.). 480p. 1992. 75.00 (0-262-05045-5) MIT Pr.

Technics & Architecture: The Development of Materials & Systems for Buildings. Cecil D. Elliott. (Illus.). 480p. 1994. 29.95 (0-262-55024-5) MIT Pr.

Technics & Civilization. Lewis Mumford. LC 63-19641. (Illus.). 495p. 1963. pap. 22.00 (0-15-688254-X, Harvest Bks) HarBrace.

Technics Learning Course: Music Made Easy. 1993. pap. text ed. 15.95 (0-7935-5608-2, 00287051) H Leonard.

Technics of the Organ. Edwin Evans. 140p. 1991. reprint ed. text ed. 69.00 (0-7812-9325-1) Rprt Serv.

Technik der Antike und des Mittelalters. Franz M. Feldhaus. (Documenta Technica, Reihe 1 Ser.). xi, 442p. 1985. reprint ed. write for info. (3-487-04038-7) G Olms Pubs.

Technik und Ihre Sprachliche Darstellung. Erhard Eydam. (Studien Zu Sprache und Technik Ser.: Bd. 4). 289p. (GER.). 1992. write for info. (3-487-09630-7) G Olms Pubs.

Technik-Woerterbuch der Geowissenschaften: English-German. 3rd ed. Adolf Watznauer. 388p. (ENG & GER.). 1987. 135.00 (0-7859-8517-4, 3861170264) Fr & Eur.

***Techniken des Betrachters Sehen und Moderne Im 19. Jahrhundert.** Jonathan Crary. (GER.). 1996. text ed. 37.00 (3-364-00359-9) Gordon & Breach.

***Technikwissenschaften.** Wolfgang Konig. (Technik Interdisziplinar Ser.). 1996. text ed. 85.00 (3-7186-5791-0, Harwood Acad Pubs); pap. text ed. 48.00 (3-7186-5755-4, Harwood Acad Pubs) Gordon & Breach.

Technimanagement: Empowering the Organization by Liberating Your People. David B. Brown. 1995. 36.95 (0-13-180811-7) P-H.

Technique. Jacques Pepin. 1989. pap. 25.00 (0-671-70711-6) S&S Trade.

Technique & Aesthetics in the Design of Tall Buildings. Ed. by David Billington & Myron Goldsmith. (Illus.). 100p. (C). 1986. text ed. 25.00 (0-939493-01-2) Coun Tall Bldg.

Technique & Design of Cluny Lace. L. Paulis. Tr. by M. Rutgers. 1984. 16.50 (0-903585-18-9) Robin & Russ.

Technique & Enlightment: Limits of Instrumental Reason. Ian H. Angus. LC 83-27363. (Current Continental Research Ser.). 172p. (Orig.). 1984. pap. text ed. 20.50 (0-8191-3816-9); lib. bdg. 45.00 (0-8191-3815-0) U Pr of Amer.

Technique & Interpretation on the Harpsichord & Clavichord. Richard Troeger. LC 85-42830. (Illus.). 272p. 1987. 39.95 (0-253-35835-3); pap. 17.50 (0-253-20408-9, MB-408) Ind U Pr.

***Technique & Interpretation on the Harpsichord & Clavichord.** Richard Troeger. LC 85-42830. (Illus.). 268p. pap. 76.40 (0-608-05046-6, 2059707) Bks Demand.

Technique & Practice of Intensive Psychotherapy. Richard D. Chessick. LC 84-45011. 392p. 1983. 40.00 (0-87668-657-9) Aronson.

Technique & Practice of Listening in Intensive Psychotherapy. Richard D. Chessick. LC 89-104. 296p. 1992. reprint ed. pap. 30.00 (0-87668-300-6) Aronson.

Technique & Practice of Object Relations Family Therapy. Samuel Slipp. LC 87-33463. 336p. 1993. pap. 35.00 (1-56821-075-2) Aronson.

Technique & Practice of Object Relations Family Therapy. Samuel Slipp. LC 87-33463. 336p. 1992. reprint ed. 40.00 (0-87668-996-9) Aronson.

Technique & Practice of Psychoanalysis, Vol. I. Ralph R. Greenson. LC 67-15417. 452p. 1967. 65.00 (0-8236-6420-1) Intl Univs Pr.

Technique & Practice of Psychoanalysis, Vol. 2: A Memorial Volume to Ralph R. Greenson. Ed. by Alan Sugarman et al. (Monograph Series of the Ralph R. Greenson Memorial Library of the San Diego Psychoanalytic Institute & Society). 520p. (C). 1992. 65.00 (0-8236-6421-X) Intl Univs Pr.

Technique & Spirit of Fugue: An Historical Study. George Oldroyd. LC 85-27089. viii, 228p. 1986. reprint ed. text ed. 59.75 (0-313-25052-9, OLTS, Greenwood Pr) Greenwood.

Technique & Style in Choral Singing. George Howerton. 201p. (Orig.). 1957. pap. 15.00 (0-8258-0007-2, 03867) Fischer Inc NY.

Technique & Theory see Developments in the Rorschach Technique

Technique & Tradition in Beckett's Trilogy of Novels. Gonul Pultar. LC 96-6281. 194p. 1996. lib. bdg. 42.00 (0-7618-0306-8) U Pr of Amer.

Technique Anglaise: Current Trends in British Art. Andrew Renton. LC 91-65285. (Illus.). 224p. (Orig.). 1991. pap. 19.95 (0-500-97396-2) Thames Hudson.

Technique Dances: Early Intermediate Piano Solos. K. Glaser. 40p. 1993. pap. 7.95 (0-7935-2021-5, 00290401) H Leonard.

Technique de Construction du Violon. Harry S. Wake. Tr. by Marcel Rotman from ENG. (Illus.). 114p. (Orig.). (FRE.). (C). 1986. pap. 23.50 (0-9607048-7-6) H S Wake.

Technique Development for Flute. Dona Gilliam & Mizzy McCaskill. 1993. 4.95 (1-56222-228-7, 94544) Mel Bay.

Technique, Discourse, & Consciousness: An Introduction to the Philosophy of Jacques Ellul. David Lovekin. LC 89-85467. 256p. 1991. 42.50 (0-934223-01-7) Lehigh Univ Pr.

Technique for Appraising Certain Observable Behavior of Children in Science in Elementary Schools. Joe Y. West. LC 71-177651. (Columbia University. Teachers College. Contributions to Education Ser.: No. 728). (C). reprint ed. 37.50 (0-404-55728-7) AMS Pr.

Technique for Computer Use: Software Education, Basics: Bridging Vocational & Academic Skills - Targeted Teaching Techniques. 1987. 7.50 (0-317-03917-2, SP300ED) Ctr Educ Trng Employ.

Technique for Computing the Amount of New Aid Required for State Equalization Programs. Eugene S. Lawler. LC 77-176981. (Columbia University. Teachers College. Contributions to Education Ser.: No. 547). reprint ed. 37.50 (0-404-55547-0) AMS Pr.

Technique for Developing Content for a Professional Course in Science for Teachers in Elementary Schools. Florence G. Billig. (Columbia University. Teachers College. Contributions to Education Ser.: No. 397). reprint ed. 37.50 (0-404-55397-4) AMS Pr.

Technique for Evaluating Interviewer Performance: A Manual for Coding & Analyzing Interviewer Behavior from Tape Recordings of Household Interviews. Charles F. Cannell et al. LC 74-620203. 138p. 1975. pap. 10.00 (0-87944-174-7) Inst Soc Res.

Technique for Evaluating Interviewer Performance: A Manual for Coding & Analyzing Interviewer Behavior from Tape Recordings of Household Interviews. Charles F. Cannell et al. LC 75-320702. 144p. reprint ed. pap. 41.10 (0-7837-5242-3, 2044976) Bks Demand.

Technique for Indentifying Textual Errors & Its Application to the Sources of Music by Thomas Tallis. Penelope R. Rapson. 832p. 1989. text ed. 20.00 (0-8240-2023-5) Garland.

Technique for Individualization: The Academic Development Plan, Basics: Bridging Vocational & Academic Skills - Targeting Teaching Techniques. National Center for Research in Vocational Education Staff. 1987. 9.95 (0-317-03918-0, SP300EE) Ctr Educ Trng Employ.

Technique for Management: Time for Learning, Basics: Bridging Vocational & Academic Skills - Targeted Teaching Techniques. National Center for Research in Vocational Education Staff. 1987. 7.50 (0-317-03919-9, SP300EB) Ctr Educ Trng Employ.

Technique for Remediation: Peer Tutoring with Audiocassette, Basics: Bridging Vocational & Academic Skills - Targeted Teaching Techniques. National Center for Research in Vocational Education Staff. 1987. 13.95 (0-317-03920-2, SP300EC) Ctr Educ Trng Employ.

Technique for the Experimental Investigation of Associative Interference in Artificial Linguistics. Erwin A. Esper. (LM Ser.: No. 1). 1925. pap. 25.00 (0-527-00805-2) Periodicals Srv.

Technique in Chess. 2nd ed. Gerald Abrahams. 216p. 1973. reprint ed. pap. 5.95 (0-486-22953-X) Dover.

Technique in Fiction. Robie Macauley & George Lanning. 288p. 1990. pap. 10.95 (0-312-05168-9) St Martin.

Technique in Singing: A Program for Singers & Teachers. Richard W. Harpster. 137p. (Orig.). 1984. 17.00 (0-02-870350-2) Schirmer Bks.

Technique in the Tales of Henry James. Krishna B. Vaid. LC 64-22723. 297p. 1964. reprint ed. pap. 84.70 (0-7837-4132-4, 2057955) Bks Demand.

Technique in Transition. Ed. by Robert J. Langs. LC 78-65121. 744p. 1978. 60.00 (0-87668-349-9) Aronson.

Technique Melodies: Early Elementary Piano. K. Glaser. 32p. 1993. pap. 6.95 (0-7935-2019-3, 00290399) H Leonard.

Technique of Analytical Psychotherapy. Wilhelm Stekel. (C). Date not set. text ed. 8.95 (0-87140-836-8) Liveright.

Technique of Audio Post-Production in Video & Film. Tim Amyes. (Illus.). 216p. 1990. pap. 32.95 (0-240-51363-0, Focal) Buttrwrth-Heinemann.

Technique of Ballroom Dancing. Guy Howard. (Ballroom Dance Ser.). 1986. lib. bdg. 79.95 (*0-8490-3332-2*) Gordon Pr.

Technique of Ballroom Dancing. Guy Howard. (Ballroom Dance Ser.). 1985. lib. bdg. 78.00 (*0-87700-665-2*) Revisionist Pr.

***Technique of Bobbin Lace.** Pamela Nottingham. (Illus.). pap. 16.95 (*0-486-29205-3*) Dover.

Technique of Borislov-Musatov's Paintings. O. I. Kochik. 234p. 1980. 66.00 (*0-317-57466-3*) St Mut.

Technique of Breeding Better Dogs. rev. ed. Dieter Fleig. LC 95-47419. (Illus.). 192p. 1996. 27.95 (*0-87605-789-X*) Howell Bk.

Technique of Bruges Flower Lace. J. E. Rombach-De Kievid. (Illus.). 144p. 1995. 34.95 (*0-7134-7329-0*, Pub. by Batsford UK) Trafalgar.

Technique of Canon. Hugo Norden. 1982. pap. 19.95 (*0-8283-1839-5*) Branden Pub Co.

Technique of Child Psychoanalysis: Discussions with Anna Freud. Joseph Sandler et al. 287p. 1986. pap. 15.95 (*0-674-87101-4*) HUP.

Technique of Controversy: Principles of Dynamic Logic. B. B. Bogoslovsky. 1977. lib. bdg. 59.95 (*0-8490-1180-9*) Gordon Pr.

Technique of Copperplate Calligraphy: A Manual & Model Book of the Pointed Pen Method. Gordon Turner. (Illus.). 48p. (Orig.). 1987. pap. 3.50 (*0-486-25512-3*) Dover.

Technique of Decorative Stained Glass. Paul S. Casciani. 1989. pap. 8.95 (*0-486-26157-3*) Dover.

Technique of Effective Prayer. Eugene E. Whitworth. 50p. 1988. 2.00 (*0-944155-06-5*) Grt Western Univ.

Technique of Etching. Maxime Lalanne. Tr. by S. R. Koehler from FRE. Orig. Title: The Treatise. (Illus.). 120p. 1982. reprint ed. pap. 4.95 (*0-486-24182-3*) Dover.

Technique of Executive Control. Erwin H. Schell, Jr. Ed. by Alfred D. Chandler. LC 79-7554. (History of Management Thought & Practice Ser.). 1980. reprint ed. lib. bdg. 17.95 (*0-405-12340-X*) Ayer.

Technique of Feminist Psychoanalytic Psychotherapy. Charlotte Prozan. LC 93-20278. 584p. 1993. 50.00 (*0-87668-268-9*) Aronson.

Technique of Film & Video Editing. Ken Dancyger. 332p. 1993. pap. 32.95 (*0-240-80048-6*, Focal) Buttrwrth-Heinemann.

Technique of Film & Video Editing: Theory & Practice. 2nd ed. Ken Dancyger. LC 96-30880. (Illus.). 384p. 1996. pap. 32.95 (*0-240-80255-1*, Focal) Buttrwrth-Heinemann.

Technique of Film Editing. Karel Reisz. 1995. pap. text ed. 39.95 (*0-240-51437-8*, Focal) Buttrwrth-Heinemann.

Technique of Honiton Lace. Elsie Luxton. (Illus.). 168p. 1979. 13.50 (*0-8231-5051-8*) Robin & Russ.

Technique of Icon Painting. Guillem Ramos-Poqui. (Illus.). 80p. 1995. pap. 17.95 (*0-8192-1624-0*) Morehouse Pub.

Technique of Inner Action: The Soul of a Performer's Work. Bill Bruehl. LC 95-16495. 97p. 1995. pap. 14.95 (*0-435-08687-1*, 08687) Heinemann.

Technique of Judo. Shinzo Takagaki. 15.95 (*0-685-38456-X*) Wehman.

Technique of Latin Dancing. Walter Laird. (Ballroom Dance Ser.). 1984. lib. bdg. 79.95 (*0-87700-510-9*) Revisionist Pr.

Technique of Lighting for Television & Film. 3rd ed. Gerald Millerson. (Library of Communication Techniques Ser.). 466p. 1991. 59.95 (*0-240-51299-5*, Focal) Buttrwrth-Heinemann.

Technique of Lymphography & Principles of Interpretation. Hans Kuisk. LC 74-96986. (Illus.). 342p. 1971. 21.25 (*0-87527-046-8*) Green.

Technique of Modern Jazz Theory. Frank Leanza. (Illus.). 94p. (C). 1993. pap. 17.95 (*0-934687-06-4*) Crystal Pubs.

Technique of Motor Racing. Piero Taruffi. LC 60-1662. (Illus.). 125p. (YA). (gr. 9 up). 1989. 25.95 (*0-8376-0228-9*) Bentley.

Technique of My Musical Language. Oliver Messiaen. 1987. reprint ed. lib. bdg. 39.00 (*0-685-14827-0*) Rprt Serv.

Technique of North American Indian Beadwork. Monte Smith. LC 83-82002. (Illus.). 104p. 1983. per. 10.95 (*0-943604-02-8*, BOO/02) Eagles View.

Technique of Orchestration. 5th ed. Kent Kennan & Adler. LC 96-43040. 432p. (C). 1996. text ed. 48.00 (*0-13-466327-6*) P-H.

Technique of Piano Playing. J. Gat. 283p. (C). 1988. 85.00 (*0-569-08419-9*, Pub. by Collets) St Mut.

Technique of Piano Playing. 5th ed. Jozsef Gat. Tr. by Istvan Kleszky. (Illus.). 283p. 1989. 21.95 (*0-912483-28-8*) Pro-Am Music.

Technique of Porcupine Quill Decoration among the Indians of North America. William C. Orchard. Ed. by Monte Smith. (Illus.). 88p. 1982. reprint ed. per. 9.95 (*0-943604-00-1*, BOO/01) Eagles View.

Technique of Pseudodifferential Operators. H. O. Cordes. (London Mathematical Society Lecture Note Ser.: No. 202). 390p. (C). 1995. pap. text ed. 38.95 (*0-521-37864-8*) Cambridge U Pr.

Technique of Psychiatric Self Help. Gordon R. Forrer. LC 75-42601. 1975. 12.95 (*0-87212-039-2*) Libra.

Technique of Psychoanalysis. rev. ed. Edward Glover. 404p. 1968. 60.00 (*0-8236-6400-7*) Intl Univs Pr.

Technique of Psychoanalytic Psychotherapy, Vol. 1: The Initial Contact, Theoretical Framework, Understanding the Patient's Communications, the Therapist's Interventions. Robert J. Langs. LC 72-96542. 672p. 1973. 55.00 (*0-87668-104-6*) Aronson.

Technique of Psychoanalytic Psychotherapy, Vol. 2: The Patient's Responses to Intervention, the Patient-Therapist Relationship, the Phases of Psychotherapy. Robert J. Langs. LC 72-96542. 544p. 1974. 50.00 (*0-87668-105-4*) Aronson.

Technique of Psychotherapy, 2 vols., Set. 4th rev. ed. Lewis R. Wolberg. LC 94-74284. 1568p. 1995. 150.00 (*1-56821-498-7*) Aronson.

Technique of Safe & Vault Manipulation. 1986. lib. bdg. 150.00 (*0-8490-3577-5*) Gordon Pr.

Technique of Special Effects Cinematography. 4th ed. Raymond Fielding. 472p. 1985. 74.95 (*0-240-51234-0*, Focal) Buttrwrth-Heinemann.

Technique of Special Effects in Television. 2nd ed. Bernard Wilkie. (Illus.). 282p. 1994. pap. 39.95 (*0-240-51361-4*, Focal) Buttrwrth-Heinemann.

Technique of Systems & Procedures. H. John Ross. (Illus.). 19.50 (*0-911056-01-7*) Office Res.

Technique of T. S. Eliot. Thomas R. Rees. LC 72-94500. (De Proprietatibus Litterarum, Ser. Practica: No. 39). (Illus.). 397p. (Orig.). 1974. pap. text ed. 53.10 (*90-279-3190-9*) Mouton.

Technique of Television Production. 12th ed. Gerald Millerson. (Illus.). 566p. (Orig.). 1990. pap. 59.95 (*0-240-51289-8*, Focal) Buttrwrth-Heinemann.

Technique of the Disciple. 4th ed. Raymond Andrea. LC 36-35. 168p. 1935. pap. 12.95 (*0-912057-12-2*, 501870) RO AMORC.

Technique of the Drama. Gustav Freytag. Tr. by Elias J. MacEwan. LC 68-57962. 236p. 1972. reprint ed. 23.95 (*0-405-08534-6*, Pub. by Blom Pubns UK) Ayer.

Technique of the Master. 12th ed. Raymond Andrea. LC 35-11449. 174p. 1932. pap. 12.95 (*0-912057-10-6*, 501680) RO AMORC.

Technique of the Neurologic Examination: A Programmed Text. 4th ed. William DeMeyer. LC 93-25996. (Illus.). 553p. 1993. pap. text ed. 39.00 (*0-07-016353-7*) McGraw-Hill HPD.

Technique of the Novel. Carl H. Grabo. LC 64-8178. 325p. 1964. reprint ed. 45.00 (*0-87752-046-1*) Gordian.

Technique of the Professional Make-up Artist. rev. ed. Vincent J. Kehoe. (Illus.). 290p. 1995. pap. 47.95 (*0-240-80217-9*, Focal) Buttrwrth-Heinemann.

Technique of the Saxophone Vol. 1: Scale Studies. J. Viola. 176p. 1986. per. 12.95 (*0-7935-5409-8*, 50449820) H Leonard.

Technique of the Saxophone Vol. 2: Chord Studies. J. Viola. 176p. 1986. per. 12.95 (*0-7935-5412-8*, 50449830) H Leonard.

Technique of the Saxophone Vol. 3: Rhythm Studies. J. Viola. 132p. 1986. per. 12.95 (*0-7935-5428-4*, 50449840) H Leonard.

Technique of the Spiritual Life. 2nd ed. Clara M. Codd. 1963. 7.50 (*0-8356-7090-2*) Theos Pub Hse.

Technique of Total Hip Arthroplasty. Hugh U. Cameron. 409p. (C). (gr. 13). 1991. text ed. 115.00 (*0-8016-0825-2*) Mosby Yr Bk.

Technique of Total Knee Arthroplasty. Krackow. (Illus.). 464p. (C). (gr. 13). 1990. text ed. 121.00 (*0-8016-2733-8*) Mosby Yr Bk.

Technique of Violin Making. rev. ed. Harry S. Wake. LC 81-166772. (Illus.). 114p. (Orig.). 1994. pap. 23.00 (*0-9607048-0-9*) H S Wake.

Technique Orchestration. 5th ed. Kent Kennan. 1996. wbk. ed., pap. text ed. 18.00 (*0-13-495755-5*) P-H.

Technique Studies for Beginning Trumpet. William Bay. (Building Excellence Ser.). 1993. 4.95 (*1-56222-306-2*, 94708) Mel Bay.

Technique Tunes: Elementary Piano Solos. K. Glaser. 24p. 1993. pap. 6.95 (*0-7935-2020-7*, 00290400) H Leonard.

Techniques. Ed. by George W. Zobrist. LC 89-37022. (Progress in Computer Aided VLSI Design Ser.: Vol. 2). 336p. (C). 1990. text ed. 82.50 (*0-89391-539-4*) Ablex Pub.

***Techniques: Le Cordon Bleu.** Le Cordon Bleu Staff. Date not set. write for info. (*0-688-15206-6*) Morrow.

Techniques & Applications of Fast Reactions in Solution. Ed. by W. J. Gettins & E. Wyn-Jones. (NATO Advanced Study Institutes Series C, Mathematical & Physical Sciences: No. 50). 1979. lib. bdg. 146.00 (*90-277-1022-8*) Kluwer Ac.

Techniques & Applications of Path Integration. L. S. Schulman. LC 80-19129. 359p. 1981. text ed. 112.00 (*0-471-76450-7*) Wiley.

Techniques & Applications of Path Integration. L. S. Schulman. LC 80-19129. (Wiley Classics Library Editions Ser.). 1996. pap. text ed. 38.95 (*0-471-16610-3*, Wiley-Interscience) Wiley.

Techniques & Applications of Thin Layer Chromatography. Ed. by Joseph C. Touchstone & Joseph Sherma. LC 84-11924. 395p. 1985. text ed. 170.00 (*0-471-88017-5*) Wiley.

Techniques & Approaches in Forest Tree Ecophysiology. Lassoie & Hinckle. 616p. 1991. 340.00 (*0-8493-6866-9*, QK938) CRC Pr.

Techniques & Assumptions in Jewish Exegesis before 70 C.E. David I. Brewer. xiii, 299p. 1992. 155.00 (*3-16-145803-6*, Pub. by J C B Mohr GW) Coronet Bks.

Techniques & Concepts of High-Energy Physics, No. IV. Ed. by Thomas Ferbel. LC 87-21293. (NATO ASI Series B, Physics: Vol. 164). (Illus.). 600p. 1987. 135.00 (*0-306-42688-9*, Plenum Pr) Plenum.

Techniques & Concepts of High-Energy Physics, No. V. Ed. by Thomas Ferbel. LC 89-22990. (NATO ASI Series B, Physics: Vol. 204). (Illus.). 512p. 1990. 125.00 (*0-306-43371-0*, Plenum Pr) Plenum.

Techniques & Concepts of High-Energy Physics, No. VI. Ed. by Thomas Ferbel. (NATO ASI Series B, Physics: Vol. 275). (Illus.). 468p. 1991. 125.00 (*0-306-44043-1*, Plenum Pr) Plenum.

Techniques & Concepts of High Energy Physics VII. Ed. by Thomas Ferbel. (NATO ASI Series B, Physics: Vol. 322). (Illus.). 266p. (C). 1994. 85.00 (*0-306-44674-X*, Plenum Pr) Plenum.

Techniques & Concepts of High-Energy Physics VIII No. 8: Proceedings, NATO Advanced Study Institute on Techniques & Concepts of High-Energy Physics, 6th, St. Croix, V.I., 1995. Ed. by Thomas Ferbel. LC 95-46484. (NATO ASI Series B: Vol. 351). 438p. 1995. 125.00 (*0-306-45182-4*, QC793) Plenum.

***Techniques & Experiments for Advanced Organic Laboratory.** Charles M. Garner. pap. text ed. write for info. (*0-471-17045-3*) Wiley.

Techniques & Experiments for Organic Chemistry. 5th ed. Addison Ault. (Illus.). 541p. (C). 1994. reprint ed. text ed. 53.95 (*0-88133-803-6*) Waveland Pr.

***Techniques & Experiments for Organic Chemistry.** 6th ed. Addison Ault. LC 97-1814. 1997. 54.00 (*0-935702-76-8*) Univ Sci Bks.

Techniques & Experiments in Organic Chemistry. 2nd ed. Ed. by Leon B. Gortler & Robert C. Tripp. (Illus.). 224p. (C). 1979. student ed. 16.95 (*0-89529-016-2*) Avery Pub.

Techniques & Experiments in Organic Chemistry. 5th ed. Ault. 1986. teacher ed. write for info. (*0-318-61511-8*, H87539) P-H.

Techniques & Guidelines for Social Work Practice. 4th ed. Bradford Sheafor. 1996. text ed. 55.00 (*0-205-19177-0*) Allyn.

Techniques & Management of Personnel Thermoluminescence Dosimetry Services: Based on the Lectures Given During the Eurocourse Techniques & Management of Thermoluminescence Dosimetry Held at the Joint Research Centre, Ispra, Italy, October 19-23, 1992. Ed. by Martin Oberhofer. 446p. (C). 1993. lib. bdg. 200.00 (*0-7923-2436-6*) Kluwer Ac.

Techniques & Materials in Biology. 2nd ed. Marjorie P. Behringer. LC 88-39702. 636p. (C). 1989. lib. bdg. 57.50 (*0-89464-350-9*) Krieger.

***Techniques & Materials of Tonal Music.** 5th ed. Thomas Benjamin et al. (Music Ser.). (C). 1997. text ed. 53.95 (*0-534-52623-3*) Wadsworth Pub.

Techniques & Materials of Tonal Music: With an Introduction to Twentieth-Century Techniques. 4th ed. Thomas Benjamin et al. 282p. (C). 1992. text ed. 53.95 (*0-534-16680-6*) Wadsworth Pub.

Techniques & Mechanisms in Electrochemistry. P. A. Christensen & A. Hemnett. LC 93-11366. 1993. pap. write for info. (*0-7514-0129-3*, Pub. by Blackie Acad & Prof UK) Routledge Chapman & Hall.

Techniques & Mechanisms in Gas Sensing. Ed. by P. T. Moseley et al. (Sensors Ser.). (Illus.). 408p. 1991. 156.00 (*0-7503-0074-4*) IOP Pub.

Techniques & Methods of Ethnobotany. David R. Given & Warwick Harris. 1994. 25.00 (*0-85092-405-7*, Pub. by Manaaki Whenua NZ) Balogh.

Techniques & Methods of Organic & Organometallic Chemistry, Vol. 1. Ed. by Donald B. Denney. LC 69-20008. 242p. reprint ed. pap. 69.00 (*0-685-16337-7*, 2027123) Bks Demand.

Techniques & Methods of Polymer Evaluation, Vol. 1: Thermal Analysis. Ed. by Philip E. Slade, Jr. & Lloyd T. Jenkins. LC 66-19038. 263p. reprint ed. pap. 75.00 (*0-685-16237-0*, 2027110) Bks Demand.

Techniques & New Developments in Photosynthesis Research. Ed. by J. Barber & R. Malkin. (NATO ASI Series A, Life Sciences: Vol. 168). (Illus.). 622p. 1989. 155.00 (*0-306-43220-X*, Plenum Pr) Plenum.

Techniques & Normal Platelet Kinetics see Platelet Kinetics & Imaging

Techniques & Practice of Chromatography. Raymond P. Scott. LC 95-7466. (Chromatographic Science Ser.: Vol. 70). 416p. 1995. 85.00 (*0-8247-9460-5*) Dekker.

Techniques & Principles in Language Teaching. Diane Larsen-Freeman. (Techniques in Teaching English As a Second Language Ser.). 142p. 1986. pap. 11.50 (*0-19-434133-X*) OUP.

Techniques & Problems of Theory Construction in Sociology. Jerald Hage. LC 72-6447. (Illus.). 255p. reprint ed. pap. 72.70 (*0-317-08645-6*, 2020263) Bks Demand.

Techniques & Strategies for Effective Small Business Management. Harvey C. Krentzman et al. LC 79-52715. 1982. 22.95 (*0-8359-7542-8*, Reston) P-H.

Techniques & Topics in Flow Measurement. Contrib. by Frank E. Jones. LC 95-16808. 176p. 1995. 49.95 (*0-8493-2475-0*, 2475) CRC Pr.

Techniques d'Analyse et de Controle Dans les Industries Agro-Alimentaires see Microbiological Control for Foods & Agricultural Products

Techniques for Ablation of Benign & Malignant Prostate Tissue. Ed. by Joseph A. Smith, Jr. & Douglas F. Milam. LC 95-47709. (Topics in Clinical Urology Ser.). (Illus.). 256p. 1996. 87.95 (*0-89640-305-X*) Igaku-Shoin.

***Techniques for Analyzing Food Aroma.** Ed. by Ray Marsili. LC 96-36593. (Food Science & Technology Ser.: Vol. 79). 400p. 1996. 150.00 (*0-8247-9788-4*) Dekker.

Techniques for Better Communication. Mescon Group Staff. (Performance Through Participation Ser.). 90p. 1996. text ed. 14.95 (*0-538-84940-1*); teacher ed., text ed. 23.95 (*0-538-84941-X*) S-W Pub.

Techniques for Burglar Alarm Bypassing. (Criminology Ser.). 1992. lib. bdg. 88.00 (*0-8490-8755-4*) Gordon Pr.

Techniques for Business Process Redesign: Tying It All Together. Lynn C. Kubeck. LC 94-40076. 286p. 1995. pap. text ed. 39.95 (*0-471-05295-7*) Wiley.

Techniques for Capital Expenditure Analysis. Thorne. (Cost Engineering-A Series of Reference Books & Textbooks: Vol. 24). 336p. 1995. 145.00 (*0-8247-9084-7*) Dekker.

Techniques for Casual Clothes. Threads Magazine Editors. Ed. by Christine Timmons. LC 93-32087. (Illus.). 96p. 1994. pap. 15.95 (*1-56158-071-6*, 070199) Taunton.

Techniques for Characterization of Electrodes & Electrochemical Processes. J. Robert Selman. (Electrochemical Society Ser.). 800p. 1991. text ed. 194.00 (*0-471-82499-2*) Wiley.

Techniques for Classroom Interaction. Donn Byrne. (Keys to Language Teaching Ser.). (C). 1987. pap. text ed. 20.67 (*0-582-74627-2*, 78335) Longman.

Techniques for Computer Graphics. Ed. by D. F. Rogers & R. A. Earnshaw. (Illus.). 590p. 1987. 107.95 (*0-387-96492-4*) Spr-Verlag.

Techniques for Concrete Removal & Bar Cleaning on Bridge Rehabilitation Projects. Michael C. Vorster et al. 121p. (Orig.). (C). 1992. pap. text ed. 15.00 (*0-309-05256-4*, SHRP-S-336) SHRP.

Techniques for Construction Network Scheduling. James D. Stevens. (Illus.). 256p. 1990. text ed. write for info. (*0-07-061291-9*) McGraw.

Techniques for Corrosion Measurement. Ed. by A. Bronson & G. W. Warren. (Illus.). 276p. 1992. 59.00 (*1-877914-47-9*) NACE Intl.

Techniques for Desert Reclamation. Ed. by Andrew S. Goudie. LC 90-30302. 271p. 1990. text ed. 150.00 (*0-471-92179-3*) Wiley.

Techniques for Determining Probabilities of Geologic Events & Processes. Ed. by Regina L. Hunter & C. John Mann. (International Association for Mathematical Geology: Studies in Mathematical Geology: No. 4). (Illus.). 304p. 1992. 60.00 (*0-19-507498-X*) OUP.

Techniques for Engineering Genes. (BIOTOL Ser.). 278p. 1993. pap. 46.95 (*0-7506-0556-1*) Buttrwrth-Heinemann.

Techniques for Evaluating & Improving Instruction. Ed. by Lawrence M. Aleamoni. LC 85-644763. (New Directions for Teaching & Learning Ser.: No. 31). 1987. 19.00 (*1-55542-935-1*) Jossey-Bass.

Techniques for Evaluating Insect Resistance in Crop Plants. C. Michael Smith et al. 336p. 1993. 89.95 (*0-87371-856-9*, L856) Lewis Pubs.

Techniques for Evaluation of Marginal Field Development. D. Plouwden & C. Worthington. 1989. 125.00 (*90-6314-532-2*, Pub. by Lorne & MacLean Marine) St Mut.

Techniques for Evaluation of Marginal Field Development. Ed. by D. Plowden & C. Worthington. (C). 1989. 125.00 (*0-89771-742-2*, Pub. by Lorne & MacLean Marine) St Mut.

Techniques for Geographers: Book One. Liebenberg. 160p. 1987. pap. 24.95 (*0-409-11147-3*) Buttrwrth-Heinemann.

Techniques for Health & Wholeness. Betty Bethards. 108p. 1985. pap. 11.95 (*0-918915-17-1*) Inner Light Found.

Techniques for Image Processing & Classification in Remote Sensing. Robert A. Schowengerdt. LC 83-11769. 272p. 1983. text ed. 80.00 (*0-12-628980-8*) Acad Pr.

Techniques for Including Musical Examples in Theses & Dissertations: A Handbook. Dwight D. Gatwood. LC 70-18258. (Illus.). 37p. (Orig.). 1970. pap. 12.00 (*0-934082-09-X*) Theodore Front.

Techniques for Industrial Pollution Prevention. Michael R. Overcash. 203p. 1986. 10.00 (*0-317-05673-5*, P89004HAZ); 10.00 (*0-317-05691-3*, P93002WAT) Assn Bay Area.

Techniques for Industrial Pollution Prevention. Michael R. Overcash. (Illus.). 200p. 1986. 124.00 (*0-87371-071-1*, TD897, CRC Reprint) Franklin.

Techniques for Laser Remote Sensing of the Environment, Vol. 3. T. Kobayashi. Ed. by F. Becker. (Remote Sensing Reviews Ser.: Vol. 3, No. 1). 57p. 1987. pap. text ed. 64.00 (*3-7186-0421-3*) Gordon & Breach.

Techniques for Long-Term Protection of Steel Structures: Proceedings of SSPC Symposium, Feb. 1986. Ed. by Bernard R. Appleman & J. G. Busse. (Illus.). 238p. 1986. pap. text ed. 40.00 (*0-938477-23-4*, SSPC 86-01) SSPC.

Techniques for Managing Verbally & Physically Aggressive Students. Beverley Johns & Valerie Carr. LC 95-75400. 168p. 1995. pap. 19.95 (*0-89108-240-9*) Love Pub Co.

Techniques for Marbleizing Paper. Gabriele Grunebaum. (Illus.). 32p. (Orig.). 1992. pap. 2.95 (*0-486-27156-0*) Dover.

Techniques for Measuring Indoor Air Quality. John E. Yocom & Sharon M. McCarthy. LC 91-9385. (Principles & Techniques in the Environmental Sciences Ser.: No. 1958). 228p. 1991. text ed. 140.00 (*0-471-90728-6*) Wiley.

***Techniques for Minimally Invasive Direct Coronary Artery Bypass Surgery.** Robert W. Emery. LC 97-7042. 1997. write for info. (*1-56053-218-1*) Hanley & Belfus.

Techniques for Modern Aquaculture: Proceedings Aquacultural Engineering Conference, June 1993. LC 93-71584. 605p. 1993. pap. 42.00 (*0-929355-40-7*, P0293) Am Soc Ag Eng.

Techniques for Multiobjective Decision Making in Systems Management: Advances in Industrial Engineering, No. 2. Ferenc Szidarovszky et al. 506p. 1986. 212.50 (*0-444-42592-6*) Elsevier.

Techniques for Mycorrhizal Research. Ed. by D. J. Read et al. (Methods in Microbiology Ser.: Vols. 23 & 24). (Illus.). 960p. 1994. 63.00 (*0-12-521490-1*) Acad Pr.

Techniques for Nuclear & Particle Physics Experiments: A How-to Approach. William R. Leo. LC 92-7633. 1992. write for info. (*3-540-17386-2*) Spr-Verlag.

Techniques for Nuclear & Particle Physics Experiments: A How-To Approach. 2nd rev. ed. William R. Leo. LC 93-38494. 1996. 64.95 (*0-387-57280-5*) Spr-Verlag.

Techniques for Nuclear & Particle Physics Experiments: A How-To Approach. William R. Leo. (Illus.). xvi, 368p. 1992. reprint ed. pap. 49.50 (*0-387-17386-2*) Spr-Verlag.

Techniques for Nurses: A Comprehensive Clinical Approach. Barbara Kozier & Glenora L. Erb. 1982. text ed. write for info. (*0-201-03911-7*) Addison-Wesley.

Techniques for Observing Normal Child Behavior. Nancy T. Carbonara. LC 61-9991. 32p. 1961. pap. 3.95 (*0-8229-5043-X*) U of Pittsburgh Pr.

***Techniques for Planning & Producing Instructional Media.** Mary Tipton. 152p. (C). 1996. pap. text ed., spiral bd. 24.15 (*0-7872-2771-4*) Kendall-Hunt.

T

An Asterisk (*) at the beginning of an entry indicates that the title is appearing in BIP for the first time.

Techniques for Pollination Biologists. Carol A. Kearns & David W. Inouye. 1993. pap. 29.95 (*0-87081-281-5*) Univ Pr Colo.

Techniques for Porcelain Laminate Veneers. Michio Haga & Akira Nakazawa. LC 90-56163. (Dental Technique Ser.: Vol. 1). (Illus.). 46p. (Orig.). 1995. reprint ed. pap. 30.00 (*0-912791-91-8*) Ishiyaku Euro.

Techniques for Problem Solving. Mescon Group Staff. (GC - Principles of Management). 1995. teacher ed., text ed. 25.95 (*0-538-85039-6*) S-W Pub.

Techniques for Project Appraisal under Uncertainty. Shlomo Reutlinger. LC 74-94827. (World Bank Staff Occasional Papers: No. 10). (Illus.). 109p. (Orig.). reprint ed. pap. 31.10 (*0-7837-5385-3*, 2045149) Bks Demand.

Techniques for Rapid Assessment of Seismic Vulnerability. Ed. by Charles Scawthorn. (Sessions Proceedings Ser.). 116p. 1986. 16.00 (*0-87262-552-4*) Am Soc Civil Eng.

***Techniques for Reducing Pesticide Use: Economic & Environmental Benefits.** David Pimentel. LC 96-27169. 1997. text ed. 90.00 (*0-471-96838-2*) Wiley.

***Techniques for Semen Evaluation, Semen Storage, & Fertility Determination.** M. R. Bakst & H. C. Cecil. (Illus.). 98p. (Orig.). 1997. lab manual ed., pap. text ed. 12.00 (*0-9649811-1-4*) Poultry Sci.

Techniques for Starting & Maintaining an FHA - Hero Chapter. V. L. Clark et al. 1988. pap. 6.00 (*0-911365-28-1*, A261-08472) Family & Consumer Sci Educ.

Techniques for Teachers: A Guide for Nonnative Speakers of English. Ann Wennerstrom. (Illus.). 240p. 1991. pap. text ed. 19.95 (*0-472-08148-9*) U of Mich Pr.

Techniques for Teaching Conservation Education. Robert E. Brown & G. W. Mouser. LC 64-24115. 120p. reprint ed. 34.20 (*0-8357-9054-1*, 2013323) Bks Demand.

Techniques for Teaching in a Medical Transcription Program. Carolee Sormunen. Ed. by American Association for Medical Transcription (AAMT) Staff. 20p. (Orig.). 1988. pap. text ed. 15.00 (*0-935229-03-5*) Am Assoc Med.

Techniques for Teaching Music in the Schools. Victor M. Fink. LC 94-30534. 112p. (Orig.). 1995. pap. 7.95 (*0-942963-53-9*) Distinctive Pub.

Techniques for Teaching Thinking. Costa & Lowery. 120p. 1995. pap. 13.95 (*0-89455-379-8*) Crit Think Bks.

Techniques for Teaching Thinking, 3 vols., Set. Costa & Lowery. 1995. pap. 45.00 (*0-89455-389-5*) Crit Think Bks.

Techniques for Technical Communicators. Carol M. Barnum & Saul Carliner. LC 92-10660. (Illus.). 384p. (Orig.). (C). 1992. pap. text ed. 49.00 (*0-02-306095-6*, Macmillan Coll) P-H.

Techniques for the Analysis & Modelling of Enzyme Kinetic Mechanisms. Chan F. Lam. LC 81-188222. (Medical Computing Ser.: No. 4). (Illus.). 412p. reprint ed. pap. 117.50 (*0-8357-7049-4*, 2033343) Bks Demand.

Techniques for the Analysis of Complex Genomes. Ed. by Rakesh Anand. (Illus.). 256p. 1992. 55.00 (*0-12-057620-1*) Acad Pr.

Techniques for the Automated Optimization of HPLC Separations. fac. ed. John C. Berridge. LC 85-12485. (Illus.). 215p. 1985. pap. 61.30 (*0-7837-7664-0*, 2047417) Bks Demand.

Techniques for the Collection & Reporting of Data on Community Water Supply: Proceedings of the WHO Scientific Group, Geneva, 1971. WHO Staff. (Technical Report Ser.: No. 490). 1972. pap. text ed. 3.00 (*92-4-120490-7*, 1100490) World Health.

***Techniques for the Genetic Analysis of Brain & Behavior.** D. Goldowitz et al. (Techniques in the Behavioral & Neural Sciences Ser.: Vol. 8). xiv, 530p. 1992. 314.50 (*0-444-81249-0*); pap. 153.25 (*0-444-89682-1*) Elsevier.

Techniques for the Rapid Detection of Plant Pathogens. Ed. by J. M. Duncan & Lesley Torrance. (Illus.). 256p. 1991. 125.00 (*0-632-03066-6*) Blackwell Sci.

Techniques for the Solidification of High-Level Waste. (Technical Reports: No. 176). (Illus.). 1978. pap. 35.00 (*92-0-125077-0*, IDC176, Pub. by IAEA AU) Bernan Associates.

Techniques for the Study of Ion-Molecule Reactions. Ed. by Arnold Weissberger. (Weissberger Techniques of Chemistry Ser.). 652p. 1988. text ed. 199.00 (*0-471-84812-3*) Wiley.

Techniques for Three D Machine Perception: Machine Intelligence & Pattern Recognition, Vol. 3. Ed. by Azriel Rosenfeld. 320p. 1986. 68.75 (*0-444-87901-3*, North Holland) Elsevier.

Techniques for Wildlife Habitat Management of Wetlands. Neil F. Payne. 250p. 1992. pap. text ed. 34.95 (*0-07-048956-4*) McGraw.

Techniques for Wildlife Investigations: Design and Analysis of Capture Data. John R. Skalski & Douglas S. Robson. (Illus.). 237p. 1992. text ed. 59.00 (*0-12-647675-6*) Acad Pr.

Techniques Handbook for Specialized Industries: Auto Dealers. 18p. 1995. pap. 13.00 (*1-57402-311-X*) Athena Info Mgt.

Techniques Handbook for Specialized Industries: Construction: Internal Revenue Manual (4232.7) 140p. 1995. pap. 47.00 (*1-57402-313-6*) Athena Info Mgt.

Techniques Handbook for Specialized Industries: Timber: Internal Revenue Manual (4232.4) 41p. 1995. pap. 18.00 (*1-57402-312-8*) Athena Info Mgt.

***Techniques Healthy Cooking.** (Culinary Arts Ser.). 1997. pap. 34.95 (*0-442-02555-6*) Van Nos Reinhold.

Techniques in Abdominal Surgery. Philippe Detrie. Tr. by Richard R. Pryer from FRE. LC 73-593870. 127p. reprint ed. pap. 36.20 (*0-317-26196-7*, 2052070) Bks Demand.

***Techniques in Adlerian Psychology.** Jon Carlson & Steven Slavik. LC 97-8530. 1997. pap. write for info. (*1-56032-555-0*) Hemisp Pub.

Techniques in Apoptosis: A User's Guide. T. G. Cotter & S. J. Martin. (Illus.). 333p. (Orig.). (C). 1996. text ed. 89.50 (*1-85578-076-3*, Pub. by Portland Pr Ltd UK) Ashgate Pub Co.

Techniques in Applied Microbiology. B. Sikyta. (Progress in Industrial Mircobiology Ser.: Vol. 31). 436p. 1995. 301.25 (*0-444-98666-9*) Elsevier.

Techniques in Aquatic Toxicology. Gary K. Ostrander. LC 96-6037. (Illus.). 704p. 1996. 79.95 (*1-56670-149-X*, L1149) Lewis Pubs.

Techniques in Biocompatibility Testing, 2 vols. David F. Williams. 1986. Set. 359.00 (*0-8493-6627-5*, R857) CRC Pr.

Techniques in Biocompatibility Testing, Vol. I. David F. Williams. 216p. 1986. write for info. (*0-318-61367-0*) CRC Pr.

Techniques in Biocompatibility Testing, Vol. II. David F. Williams. 240p. 1986. write for info. (*0-318-61368-9*) CRC Pr.

Techniques in Cell Cycle Analysis. Ed. by Joe W. Gray & Zbigniew Darzynkiewicz. LC 86-16114. (Biological Methods Ser.). 304p. 1987. 89.50 (*0-89603-097-0*) Humana.

Techniques in Clinical Capillary Microscopy. Ed. by F. Mahler et al. (Mikrozirkulation in Forschung und Klinik; Progress in Applied Microcirculation Ser.: Vol. 11). (Illus.). xii, 152p. 1986. pap. 63.25 (*3-8055-4327-1*) S Karger.

Techniques in Clinical Electrophysiology of Vision. G. Niemeyer & Charles H. Huber. 1982. lib. bdg. 275.00 (*90-6193-727-2*) Kluwer Ac.

Techniques in Clinical Nursing. 3rd ed. Barbara Kozier & Glenora L. Erb. Ed. by Debra Hunter. 745p. (C). 1989. pap. text ed. 48.50 (*0-201-12945-0*) Addison-Wesley.

Techniques in Clinical Nursing. 4th ed. Barbara Kozier. (C). 1993. pap. text ed. 49.5050.95 (*0-8053-5950-8*) Benjamin-Cummings.

Techniques in Clinical Nursing: A Nursing Process Approach. 2nd ed. Barbara Kozier & Glenora L. Erb. (Illus.). 1000p. 1986. student ed. write for info. (*0-201-11759-2*, Health Sci); pap. text ed. 37.75 (*0-201-11755-X*, Health Sci) Addison-Wesley.

Techniques in College Reading. 2nd ed. James Schiavone. 240p. 1993. per. 29.34 (*0-8403-8902-7*) Kendall-Hunt.

Techniques in Comparative Respiratory Physiology. Ed. by E. R. Bridges & P. J. Butler. (Society for Experimental Biology Seminar Ser.: No. 37). 368p. (C). 1989. text ed. 80.00 (*0-521-34568-5*) Cambridge U Pr.

Techniques in Computational Learning. Thornton. (ITCP-UK Computer Science Ser.). (C). 1992. pap. 41.95 (*0-412-40430-3*) Van Nos Reinhold.

Techniques in Computational Learning. C. J. Thornton. 1992. pap. 39.95 (*0-442-31574-0*) Chapman & Hall.

Techniques in Consumer Science. William C. Kleinelp, Jr. et al. (Illus.). 154p. 1992. student ed. 18.95 (*0-685-57459-8*); text ed. 29.95 (*0-929941-14-4*); pap. text ed. 23.95 (*0-685-57458-X*) Wood River Pubns.

Techniques in Consumer Science. 2nd ed. Kleinelp Staff. 1994. 23.95 (*0-929941-16-0*) Wood River Pubns.

Techniques in Data Communications. Ralph Glasgal. LC 82-74128. (Illus.). 221p. reprint ed. pap. 63.00 (*0-8357-4232-6*, 2037019) Bks Demand.

Techniques in Diagnostic Human Biochemical Genetics: A Laboratory Manual. Ed. by Frits A. Hommes. LC 90-12423. 646p. 1990. text ed. 210.00 (*0-471-56818-X*); pap. text ed. 119.95 (*0-471-56076-6*) Wiley.

Techniques in Diagnostic Imaging. 3rd ed. P. Armstrong & M. L. Wastie. (Illus.). 456p. 1992. 65.00 (*0-632-03093-3*) Blackwell Sci.

Techniques in Diagnostic Imaging. 3rd ed. Ed. by G. H. Whitehouse & B. S. Worthington. LC 95-8217. 1996. 135.00 (*0-86542-808-5*) Blackwell Sci.

Techniques in Diagnostic Pathology, Vol. 2: ELISA Techniques - New Developments & Practical Applications in a Broad Field. Ed. by Gillian R. Bullock et al. (Illus.). 176p. 1991. text ed. 79.00 (*0-12-681912-2*) Acad Pr.

Techniques in Electrochemistry, Corrosion & Metal Finishing: A Handbook. Ed. by Anselm T. Kuhn. LC 86-26769. 585p. reprint ed. pap. 166.80 (*0-7837-6387-5*, 2046100) Bks Demand.

Techniques in Experimental High Energy Physics. Thomas Ferbel. 608p. 1987. 52.95 (*0-201-11487-9*, Adv Bk Prog) Addison-Wesley.

Techniques in Extracorporeal Circulation. 3rd ed. Ed. by Philip H. Kay. (Illus.). 380p. 1992. text ed. 155.00 (*0-7506-1391-2*) Buttrwrth-Heinemann.

Techniques in Fish Immunology. Ed. by J. S. Stolen et al. LC 89-92807. (Fish Immunology Technical Communications Ser.). (Illus.). 200p. (C). 1994. Set. write for info. (*0-9625505-4-X*) SOS Pubns NJ.

Techniques in Fish Immunology, Vol. 1. 2nd ed. Ed. by J. S. Stolen et al. LC 89-92807. (Fish Immunology Technical Communications Ser.). (Illus.). 200p. (C). 1993. student ed. 70.00 (*0-9625505-0-7*) SOS Pubns NJ.

Techniques in Fish Immunology, Vol. 2. Ed. by J. S. Stolen et al. LC 89-92807. (Fish Immunology Technical Communications Ser.). (Illus.). 200p. (C). 1992. student ed. 70.00 (*0-9625505-3-1*) SOS Pubns NJ.

Techniques in Fish Immunology, Vol. 3. Ed. by J. S. Stolen et al. LC 89-92807. (Fish Immunology Technical Communications Ser.). (Illus.). 200p. (C). 1994. student ed. 70.00 (*0-9625505-7-4*) SOS Pubns NJ.

Techniques in Fish Immunology, Vol. 4: Aquatic Invertebrates. Ed. by J. S. Stolen et al. LC 89-92807. (Fish Immunology Technical Communications Ser.). (Illus.). 200p. (C). 1995. Vol. 4, winter 1994, lab manual. student ed. 70.00 (*0-9625505-8-2*) SOS Pubns NJ.

***Techniques in Fracture Surgery.** Tornetta. 1250p. (C). 1999. text ed. 199.00 (*0-8151-3666-8*) Mosby Yr Bk.

***Techniques in Free Radical Research.** M. C. Symons et al. (Laboratory Techniques in Biochemistry & Molecular Biology Ser.: Vol. 22). 292p. 1991. 182.25 (*0-444-81304-7*); pap. 48.25 (*0-444-81314-4*) Elsevier.

Techniques in General Thoracic Surgery. R. Maurice Hood. (Illus.). 378p. 1985. text ed. 93.00 (*0-7216-1137-0*) Saunders.

Techniques in General Thoracic Surgery. 2nd ed. R. Maurice Hood. (Illus.). 310p. 1993. pap. text ed. 58.00 (*0-8121-1546-5*) Williams & Wilkins.

***Techniques in Glycobiology.** Ed. by Townsend & Hotchkiss. LC 97-1913. 648p. 1997. 65.00 (*0-8247-9822-8*) Dekker.

Techniques in Hand Surgery. Ed. by William F. Blair & Curtis M. Steyers. LC 95-7309. 1199p. 1996. 225.00 (*0-683-00842-0*) Williams & Wilkins.

Techniques in Hemodynamic Monitoring. 5th ed. Elaine K. Daily. 492p. (C). (gr. 13). 1994. pap. text ed. 34.95 (*0-8016-7260-0*) Mosby Yr Bk.

Techniques in HIV Research. Ed. by Anna Aldovini & Bruce D. Walker. (Illus.). 304p. 1993. pap. text ed. 65.00 (*0-7167-7006-7*) OUP.

***Techniques in Human Geography.** James M. Lindsay. LC 97-7185. (Contemporary Human Geography Ser.). 192p. (C). 1997. pap. write for info. (*0-415-15476-6*); text ed. write for info. (*0-415-15475-8*) Routledge.

***Techniques in Human Geography.** Guy M. Robinson. text ed. 65.00 (*0-471-96231-7*); pap. text ed. 47.95 (*0-471-96232-5*) Wiley.

Techniques in Immunocytochemistry, Vol. 1. Gillian R. Bullock. Ed. by Peter Petrusz. 1982. text ed. 99.00 (*0-12-140401-3*) Acad Pr.

Techniques in Immunocytochemistry, Vol. 1. Gillian R. Bullock. Ed. by Peter Petrusz. 306p. 1986. pap. text ed. 55.00 (*0-12-140404-8*) Acad Pr.

Techniques in Immunocytochemistry, Vol. 2. Gillian R. Bullock. Ed. by Peter Petrusz. 290p. 1986. pap. text ed. 55.00 (*0-12-140405-6*) Acad Pr.

Techniques in Immunocytochemistry, Vol. 3. Gillian R. Bullock & Peter Petrusz. 1985. text ed. 99.00 (*0-12-140403-X*) Acad Pr.

Techniques in Immunocytochemistry, Vol. 3. Gillian R. Bullock. Ed. by Peter Petrusz. 241p. 1988. reprint ed. pap. text ed. 55.00 (*0-12-140406-4*) Acad Pr.

Techniques in Immunocytochemistry, Vol. 4. Gillian R. Bullock. Ed. by Peter Petrusz. 400p. 1989. text ed. 99.00 (*0-12-140407-2*) Acad Pr.

Techniques in Large Animal Surgery. A. Simon Turner & C. Wayne McIlwraith. LC 88-13377. (Illus.). 381p. 1988. text ed. 70.00 (*0-8121-1177-X*) Williams & Wilkins.

***Techniques in Liver Surgery.** Ed. by Alighieri Mazziotti & Antonio Cavallari. (Greenwich Medical Media Ser.). (Illus.). 226p. 1997. 125.00 (*1-900151-25-1*) OUP.

***Techniques in Microbial Ecology.** Ed. by Robert S. Burlage et al. (Illus.). 432p. (Orig.). 1997. pap. 65.00 (*0-19-509223-6*) OUP.

Techniques in Molecular Medicine. F. Hildebrandt. 1995. 58.00 (*0-387-57129-9*) Spr-Verlag.

Techniques in Organic Reaction Kinetics. Petr Zuman & Ramesh C. Patel. LC 91-42643. 352p. (C). 1992. reprint ed. lib. bdg. 69.50 (*0-89464-686-9*) Krieger.

Techniques in Orthopaedic Surgery. D. Evans. (Illus.). 480p. 1993. 235.00 (*0-632-02511-5*) Blackwell Sci.

Techniques in Pheremone Research. Ed. by H. E. Hummel & T. A. Miller. (Experimental Entomology Ser.). (Illus.). 450p. 1984. 186.95 (*0-387-90919-2*) Spr-Verlag.

Techniques in Photomorphogenesis. Ed. by Harold Smith & Martin G. Holmes. (Biological Techniques Ser.). 1984. text ed. 159.00 (*0-12-652990-6*) Acad Pr.

Techniques in Programming Logic: With an Introduction to BASIC & FORTRAN. Myrtle I. Jonas. LC 91-73456. (Illus.). 454p. (C). 1993. pap. text ed. 48.00 (*0-9635298-0-3*) Capitol Pr.

Techniques in Protein Chemistry. Ed. by Ruth H. Angeletti. (Illus.). 640p. 1993. 59.95 (*0-12-058758-0*) Acad Pr.

Techniques in Protein Chemistry, Vol. 7. Ed. by Daniel R. Marshak. (Illus.). 533p. 1996. 55.00 (*0-12-473556-8*); text ed. 110.00 (*0-12-473555-X*) Acad Pr.

Techniques in Protein Chemistry Two. Ed. by Joseph J. Villafranca. (Illus.). 579p. 1991. 69.00 (*0-12-721957-9*) Acad Pr.

Techniques in Protein Chemistry V. Ed. by John W. Crabb. (Illus.). 1994. spiral bd. 59.00 (*0-12-194711-4*) Acad Pr.

Techniques in Protein Chemistry VI. John W. Crabb. (Illus.). 585p. 1995. pap. text ed. 55.00 (*0-12-194713-0*) Acad Pr.

Techniques in Protein Chemistry VI. Ed. by John W. Crabb. (Illus.). 585p. 1995. text ed. 110.00 (*0-12-194712-2*) Acad Pr.

***Techniques in Protein Chemistry VIII.** Ed. by Daniel R. Marshak. (Illus.). 872p. 1997. boxed 130.00 (*0-12-473557-6*, AP Prof) Acad Pr.

***Techniques in Protein Chemistry VIII.** Ed. by Daniel R. Marshak. (Illus.). 872p. 1997. pap. 75.00 (*0-12-473558-4*, AP Prof) Acad Pr.

Techniques in Protein Modification. Roger L. Lundblad. LC 94-11646. 304p. 1994. 52.95 (*0-8493-2606-0*, 2606) CRC Pr.

Techniques in Psychophysiology. Ed. by Irene Martin & Peter H. Venables. LC 79-42925. (Illus.). 711p. reprint ed. pap. 180.00 (*0-685-23760-5*, 2032834) Bks Demand.

***Techniques in Rheological Measurement.** Ed. by Collyer. (Illus.). 360p. (C). (gr. 13 up). 1993. text ed. 128.95 (*0-412-53490-8*, Chap & Hall NY) Chapman & Hall.

Techniques in Sedimentology. M. Tucker. 1988. pap. 62.95 (*0-632-01372-9*) Blackwell Sci.

Techniques in Skin Surgery. Ervin H. Epstein & Ervin Epstein, Jr. LC 79-11457. 213p. reprint ed. pap. 60.80 (*0-685-24137-8*, 2056681) Bks Demand.

Techniques in Somatic Cell Genetics. Ed. by Jerry W. Shay. LC 82-9848. (Illus.). 568p. 1982. 85.00 (*0-306-41040-0*, Plenum Pr) Plenum.

Techniques in Spinal Fusion & Stabilization. Ed. by Setti S. Rengachary et al. (Illus.). 408p. 1994. 129.00 (*0-86577-523-0*) Thieme Med Pubs.

Techniques in Teaching Reading. 1994. 11.50 (*0-19-434134-8*) OUP.

Techniques in Teaching Vocabulary. Virginia F. Allen. (Teaching Techniques in English as a Second or Foreign Language Ser.). (Illus.). (Orig.). (C). 1983. pap. 11.50 (*0-19-434130-5*) OUP.

Techniques in Teaching Writing. Ann Raimes. (Techniques in Teaching English As a Second Language Ser.). (Illus.). 176p. (Orig.). (C). 1983. pap. text ed. 11.50 (*0-19-434131-3*) OUP.

Techniques in Testing. Harold S. Madsen. (Techniques in Teaching English As a Second Language Ser.). (Illus.). (C). 1983. pap. text ed. 11.50 (*0-19-434132-1*) OUP.

Techniques in the Clinical Supervision of Teachers. 2nd ed. Keith A. Acheson & Meredith D. Gall. (Illus.). 226p. (C). 1987. pap. text ed. 18.36 (*0-582-28563-1*, 71591) Longman.

Techniques in the Clinical Supervision of Teachers. 4th ed. Keith A. Acheson. LC 96-20130. (C). 1997. pap. text ed. 37.50 (*0-8013-1509-3*) Addison-Wesley.

Techniques in the Clinical Supervision of Teachers: Preservice & Inservice Applications. 3rd ed. Keith A. Acheson & Meredith D. Gall. 336p. (C). 1992. pap. text ed. 38.95 (*0-8013-0469-5*, 78299) Longman.

Techniques in the Management of Gallstone Disease. A. Darzi et al. 272p. 1995. 135.00 (*0-632-03675-3*) Blackwell Sci.

Techniques in Therapeutic Arthroscopy. J. Serge Parisien. 392p. 1993. text ed. 152.50 (*0-7817-0054-X*) Lppncott-Raven.

Techniques in Therapeutic Arthroscopy. J. Serge Parisien. 392p. 1994. sl. 500.00 (*0-7817-0055-8*) Lppncott-Raven.

Techniques in Therapeutic Endoscopy. Jerome D. Waye et al. (Illus.). 160p. 1987. text ed. 135.00 (*0-03-012793-9*) Saunders.

Techniques of Abdominal Vascular Sonography. Marsha M. Neumyer & Brian L. Thiele. 1996. vhs 125.00 (*0-941022-32-3*) Davies Pubng.

Techniques of Abdominal Vascular Sonography. Marsha M. Neumyer & Brian L. Thiele. 1998. text ed. write for info. (*0-941022-27-7*) Davies Pubng.

Techniques of Admissible Recursion Theory. C. T. Chong. (Lecture Notes in Mathematics Ser.: Vol. 1106). ix, 214p. 1985. 37.95 (*0-387-13902-8*) Spr-Verlag.

Techniques of Applied Quantum Mechanics. fac. ed. John P. Killingbeck. LC 76-356269. 240p. 1975. reprint ed. pap. 68.40 (*0-7837-8012-5*, 2047768) Bks Demand.

Techniques of Arterial Surgery. John J. Bergan & James S. Yao. (Illus.). 447p. 1989. text ed. 162.00 (*0-7216-3297-1*) Saunders.

Techniques of Astral Projection. Douglas M. Baker. 1978. pap. 12.50 (*0-906006-89-9*, Pub. by Baker Pubns UK) New Leaf Dist.

Techniques of Basketry. Virginia I. Harvey. LC 86-19057. (Illus.). 132p. 1986. pap. 17.95 (*0-295-96415-4*) U of Wash Pr.

Techniques of Beading Earrings. Deon DeLange. Ed. by Monte Smith. LC 83-82121. (Illus.). 76p. (Orig.). 1984. per. 8.95 (*0-943604-03-6*, BOO/03) Eagles View.

Techniques of Biocompatibility Testing. D. Williams. LC 85-21354. (Biocompatibility Ser.: Vol. 1). 216p. 1986. 123.00 (*0-8493-6615-1*, CRC Reprint) Franklin.

Techniques of Biocompatibility Testing. D. Williams. LC 85-21354. (Biocompatibility Ser.: Vol. 2). 240p. 1986. 135.00 (*0-8493-6616-X*, CRC Reprint) Franklin.

Techniques of Brief Psychotherapy. Walter V. Flegenheimer. LC 82-13891. 224p. 1993. pap. 27.50 (*1-56821-095-7*) Aronson.

Techniques of Burglar Alarm Bypassing. Wayne B. Yeager. LC 90-6262. (Illus.). 112p. (Orig.). 1990. pap. 14.95 (*1-55950-032-8*, 52050) Loompanics.

Techniques of Casino Surveillance. Marcia A. McDowell. (Illus.). 196p. (C). 1995. pap. text ed. 32.50 (*0-9648090-0-1*) Cndlelight Bks.

Techniques of Cerebrovascular Sonography. Jean Primozich & D. E. Strandness. text ed. write for info. (*0-941022-30-7*); vhs write for info. (*0-941022-33-1*) Davies Pubng.

Techniques of Chemistry Vol. 16: Separations by Centrifugal Phenomena. Hsien-Wen Hsu et al. Ed. by Arnold Weissberger & B. W. Rossiter. LC 81-4991. (Techniques of Chemistry Ser.: Vol. 16). 484p. 1981. 78.50 (*0-471-05564-6*) Krieger.

Techniques of Chemistry - Physical Methods of Chemistry Vol. 1, Pt. 03D: X-Ray, Nuclear, Male. Bryant W. Rossiter. LC 45-8533. 720p. 1972. 71.00 (*0-471-92733-3*) Krieger.

Techniques of Chemistry Molecular Design of Electrode Surfaces. Royce W. Murray. LC 91-25499. (Techniques of Chemistry Ser.: Vol. 22). 448p. 1992. text ed. 198.00 (*0-471-55773-0*) Wiley.

Techniques of Chemistry, Organic Solvents: Physical Properties & Methods of Purification, Vol. 2. 4th ed. Theodore Sakano et al. LC 86-15698. (Techniques of Chemistry Ser.). 1325p. 1986. text ed. 250.00 (*0-471-08467-0*) Wiley.

Techniques of Child Therapy: Psychodynamic Strategies. Morton Chethik. LC 88-24384. 276p. 1989. lib. bdg. 33.95 (*0-89862-745-1*) Guilford Pr.

Techniques of Chinese Painting. Wu Yangmu. 192p. 1991. pap. 21.95 (*0-941533-89-1*) New Amsterdam Bks.

Techniques of Chinese Paintng. Wu Yangmu. (Illus.). 192p. (C). 1990. 30.00 (0-941533-88-3) New Amsterdam Bks.

Techniques of Circuit Analysis. Geoffrey W. Carter & A. Richardson. LC 79-183222. 556p. reprint ed. pap. 158.50 (0-685-20629-7, 2030584) Bks Demand.

Techniques of Code Drafting: The Lively Art of Personal Weaving Drafts. Harry P. Linder. LC 83-72938. (Illus.). 140p. (Orig.). 1983. 16.95 (0-915113-00-7) Bizarre Butterfly.

Techniques of Combined Gas Chromatography-Mass Spectrometry: Applications in Organic Analysis. William McFadden. LC 87-35344. 482p. (C). 1988. reprint ed. lib. bdg. 70.00 (0-89464-280-4) Krieger.

Techniques of Communism. Louis F. Budenz. LC 76-46068. (Anti-Movements in America Ser.). 1977. reprint ed. lib. bdg. 27.95 (0-405-09942-8) Ayer.

Techniques of Creative Thinking. Robert P. Crawford. LC 54-6456. 287p. 1964. reprint ed. pap. 19.00 (0-87034-010-7) Fraser Pub Co.

Techniques of Creative Wood Carving. 2nd ed. Ian Norbury. LC 94-5579. 160p. 1994. reprint ed. pap. 19.95 (0-941936-29-5) Linden Pub Fresno.

Techniques of Crime Scene Investigation. Barry A. Fisher. LC 95-881. (Series in Forensic & Police Science). 552p. 1992. 57.95 (0-8493-9506-2) CRC Pr.

Techniques of Crime Scene Investigation. 3rd ed. Barry A. Fisher. 1992. 44.50 (0-444-01636-8, HV8073) CRC Pr.

Techniques of Demographic Analysis. K. B. Pathak & F. Ram. (Illus.). 1992. 40.00 (81-7040-418-5, Pub. by Himalaya II) Apt Bks.

Techniques of Description: Spoken & Written Discourse. Ed. by John M. Sinclair et al. LC 92-27981. 304p. (C). (gr. 13). 1993. text ed. 69.95 (0-415-08805-4, B0322, Routledge NY) Routledge.

Techniques of Differential Topology in Relativity. Roger Penrose. (CBMS-NSF Regional Conference Ser.: No. 7). viii, 72p. (Orig.). 1972. reprint ed. pap. text ed. 15.50 (0-89871-005-7) Soc Indus-Appl Math.

Techniques of Drawing. Howard Simon. (Illus.). 140p. 1972. pap. 7.95 (0-486-21578-4) Dover.

Techniques of Effective Telephone Communication. 2nd rev. ed. (Communication Ser.). 124p. 1989. pap. 9.95 (1-55852-148-8) Natl Pr Pubns.

Techniques of Electron Microscopy, Diffraction, & Microprobe Analysis. American Society for Testing & Materials Staff. (American Society for Testing & Materials: No. 372). 95p. reprint ed. pap. 27.10 (0-317-09550-1, 2000730) Bks Demand.

Techniques of Environmental Systems Analysis. Richard H. Pantell. LC 76-98. (Illus.). 201p. 1976. reprint ed. pap. 57.30 (0-7837-3524-3, 2057859) Bks Demand.

Techniques of Estimating School Equipment Costs. Arthur K. Loomis. LC 70-177010. (Columbia University. Teachers College. Contributions to Education Ser.: No. 208). reprint ed. 37.50 (0-404-55208-0) AMS Pr.

Techniques of Event History Modeling: New Approaches to Casual Analysis. Hans-Peter Blossfeld & Gotz Rohwer. LC 95-23513. 304p. 1995. 59.95 (0-8058-1959-2); pap. 32.50 (0-8058-1960-6) L Erlbaum Assocs.

Techniques of Extension of Analytic Objects. Siu. (Lecture Notes in Pure & Applied Mathematics Ser.: Vol. 8). 272p. 1974. 130.00 (0-8247-6168-5) Dekker.

Techniques of Family Therapy. David S. Freeman. LC 80-69669. 368p. 1981. 40.00 (0-87668-431-2) Aronson.

Techniques of Family Therapy. Jay Haley & Lynn Hoffman. LC 94-72313. 494p. 1995. pap. 40.00 (1-56821-329-8) Aronson.

Techniques of Fashion Earrings. Deon DeLange. Ed. by Denise Knight. LC 94-72283. (Illus.). 64p. (Orig.). 1995. per. 9.95 (0-943604-44-3, BOO/37) Eagles View.

Techniques of Fashion Merchandising. 1968. teacher ed. 5.00 (0-672-96043-5, Bobbs); pap. 9.90 (0-672-96042-7, Bobbs) Macmillan.

Techniques of Financial Analysis. 7th ed. Erich A. Helfert. 528p. (C). 1990. pap. text ed. 34.95 (0-256-07926-9) Irwin.

Techniques of Financial Analysis. 8th ed. Erich A. Helfert. LC 93-31832. 624p. (C). 1993. per. 31.25 (0-256-12025-0) Irwin Prof Pubng.

Techniques of Financial Analysis: A Modern Approach. 9th ed. Erich Helfert. 448p. (C). 1996. per. 31.25 (0-256-14611-X) Irwin.

Techniques of Financial Analysis: A Modern Approach. 9th ed. Erich A. Helfert. LC 96-20988. 448p. 1996. per. 37.50 (0-7863-1120-7) Irwin Prof Pubng.

Techniques of Financial Analysis: A Practical Guide to Managing & Measuring Business Performance. 7th ed. Erich A. Helfert. 42p. 1994. 55.00 (0-7863-0260-7) Irwin Prof Pubng.

Techniques of Financial Analysis: A Practical Guide to Managing & Measuring Business Performance. 8th ed. Erich A. Helfert. 1995. text ed. 55.00 (0-7863-0262-3) Irwin Prof Pubng.

Techniques of Financial Analysis: A Practical Guide to Managing & Measuring Business Practices. 8th ed. Erich Helfert. 624p. 1993. per. 35.00 (0-7863-0246-1) Irwin Prof Pubng.

Techniques of Flavonoid Identification. K. R. Markham. (Biological Techniques Ser.). 1982. text ed. 69.00 (0-12-472680-1) Acad Pr.

***Techniques of Flowsheeting.** William H. Bennett & Hank Archuleta. 34p. (Orig.). (YA). (gr. 7-12). 1990. pap. text ed. write for info. (1-889510-28-9) Chmpionship Debate.

Techniques of Fund-Raising. Daniel L. Conrad. 1974. 25.00 (0-8184-0169-9) Carol Pub Group.

Techniques of Harassment: How the Underdog Gets Justice. Victor Santoro. (Illus.). 168p. 1984. 19.95 (0-87364-298-8) Paladin Pr.

Techniques of High Magic: A Guide to Self-Empowerment. Francis King. 228p. 1991. pap. 12.95 (0-89281-350-4) Inner Tradit.

Techniques of Income Property Appraisal. Jeffrey D. Fisher & Robert S. Martin. LC 94-33749. 155p. 1995. pap. 29.95 (0-7931-1071-8, 1521-0301, Real Estate Ed) Dearborn Finan.

Techniques of Indian Embroidery. Anne Morrell. 144p. 1995. pap. 18.95 (1-883010-08-X) Interweave.

Techniques of Instruction. Roger James. Ed. by Billie Taylor. LC 95-2231. 176p. 1995. 48.95 (0-566-07550-4, Pub. by Gower UK) Ashgate Pub Co.

Techniques of Jewelry Illustration & Color Rendering. (Illus.). 180p. write for info. (0-9644193-0-0) Du-Matt.

Techniques of Joint Effort: The Vocational Academic Approach with Audiocassette, Basics: Bridging Vocational & Academic Skills - Targeted Teaching Techniques. National Center for Research in Vocational Education Staff. 1987. 13.95 (0-317-03916-4, SP300EA) Ctr Educ Trng Employ.

***Techniques of Kiln-Formed Glass.** Keith Cummings. (Illus.). 192p. 1997. 49.95 (0-8122-3402-2) U of Pa Pr.

Techniques of Ladies' Hairdressing of the 19th Century. Mark Campbell & A. Mallemont. Ed. by Jules Kliot & Kaethe Kliot. (Illus.). 144p. 1996. pap. 16.00 (0-916896-71-4, LA24) Lacis Pubns.

Techniques of Legal Investigation. 3rd ed. Anthony M. Golec. LC 95-4260. (Illus.). 580p. (C). 1995. text ed. 74.95 (0-398-06515-2) C C Thomas.

Techniques of Master Gem Polishing: A Comprehensive Overview of the Techniques, Tools & Knowledge Required to Apply a Fine Polish on All Types of Gemstones. Gerald L. Wykoff. (Illus.). 310p. 1994. pap. 24.50 (0-9607892-9-4) Adamas Pubs.

***Techniques of Medical Litigation: A Professional's Handbook for Plaintiffs, Defendants, & Medical Consultants.** Randine A. Lewis. LC 96-3250. 320p. 1997. text ed. 75.00 (1-56720-088-5, Quorum Bks) Greenwood.

Techniques of Melt Crystallization. Gilbert J. Sloan & Andrew R. McGhie. (Weissberger Techniques of Chemistry Ser.). 532p. 1988. text ed. 199.00 (0-471-07875-1) Wiley.

Techniques of Microscale Organic Chemistry. Dana W. Mayo et al. LC 91-4412. 285p. 1991. Net. pap. text ed. 23.50 (0-471-62192-7) Wiley.

Techniques of Military Instruction. (Military Science Ser.). 1989. lib. bdg. 79.95 (0-8490-3972-X) Gordon Pr.

Techniques of Modern Orchestral Conducting. 2nd enl. rev. ed. Benjamin Grosbayne. LC 78-184105. (Illus.). 381p. 1973. reprint ed. pap. 108.90 (0-7837-4153-7, 2059001) Bks Demand.

Techniques of Modern Structural Geology, Vol. 1. John G. Ramsay & Martin Huber. 1984. text ed. 121.00 (0-12-576901-6); pap. text ed. 55.00 (0-12-576921-0) Acad Pr.

Techniques of Modern Structural Geology: Folds & Fractures, Vol. 2. John G. Ramsay & Martin Huber. 400p. 1987. pap. text ed. 55.00 (0-12-576922-9) Acad Pr.

Techniques of Monetary Control. Joseph Aschheim. LC 61-7804. (Illus.). 176p. reprint ed. pap. 50.20 (0-685-23917-9, 2032987) Bks Demand.

Techniques of Natural Light Photography. Jim Zuckerman. LC 95-34728. (Illus.). 144p. (Orig.). 1996. pap. 27.99 (0-89879-716-0, Wrtrs Digest Bks) F & W Pubns Inc.

Techniques of Neutralization: A Theory of Delinquency. Gresham M. Sykes & David Matza. (Reprint Series in Sociology). (C). 1993. reprint ed. pap. text ed. 1.00 (0-8290-2627-4, S-288) Irvington.

Techniques of Observation & Learning Retention: A Handbook for the Policeman & the Lawyer. Louis F. Basinger. (Illus.). 88p. 1973. spiral bd., pap. 19.95 (0-398-02935-0) C C Thomas.

Techniques of Painting Miniatures. Sue Burton. (Illus.). 141p. 1996. 35.00 (0-7134-7459-9, Pub. by Batsford UK) Trafalgar.

Techniques of Patient-Oriented Research. Ed. by Perrie M. Adams & Charles Y. Pak. LC 93-4602. 224p. 1993. text ed. 49.50 (0-7817-0107-4) Lppncott-Raven.

Techniques of Pendulum Dowsing: Step by Step Method for Use of the Pendulum in Dowsing. Bill Cox. (Illus.). 38p. 1977. 6.00 (0-88234-006-9) Life Understanding.

Techniques of Peripheral Arterial Sonography. Ruth Cato & Jonathan B. Towne. text ed. write for info. (0-941022-31-5); vhs write for info. (0-941022-34-X) Davies Pubng.

Techniques of Photojournalism. Milton Feinberg. LC 73-96959. 291p. reprint ed. pap. 83.00 (0-317-10701-1, 2013630) Bks Demand.

Techniques of Plant Cytogenetics. Joseph Jahier. 192p. 1996. lib. bdg. 48.00 (1-886106-57-6) Science Pubs.

Techniques of Polymer Syntheses & Characterization. Dietrich Braun & Harald Cherdron. LC 79-148168. 296p. reprint ed. pap. 84.40 (0-317-08665-0, 2011967) Bks Demand.

Techniques of Pressworking Sheet Metal: An Engineering Approach to Die Design. 2nd ed. Donald F. Eary & Edward A. Reed. 1974. text ed. 69.80 (0-13-900696-6) P-H.

Techniques of Privatization of State-Owned Enterprises, Vol. I: Methods & Implementation. Charles Vuylsteke. 196p. 1988. 20.00 (0-8213-1111-5, 11111) World Bank.

Techniques of Privatization of State-Owned Enterprises, Vol. II: Selected Country Case Studies. Helen Nankani. (Technical Paper Ser.: No. 89). 168p. 1988. 10.95 (0-8213-1112-3, 11112) World Bank.

Techniques of Problem Solving. Steven Krantz. LC 96-23878. 465p. 1996. 29.00 (0-8218-0619-X, TPS) Am Math.

Techniques of Program System Maintenance. 2nd ed. Girish Parikh. LC 87-36023. 483p. reprint ed. pap. 137.70 (0-7837-4065-4, 2044015) Bks Demand.

Techniques of Prolog Programming with Implementation of Logical Negation & Quantified Goals. T. U. Van Le. 624p. 1992. pap. text ed. 31.00 (0-471-57175-X) Wiley.

Techniques of Pulse-Code Modulation in Communication Networks. George C. Hartley et al. LC 67-15307. (IEE Monograph Ser.: No. 1). 116p. reprint ed. pap. 33.10 (0-8357-7050-8, 2033457) Bks Demand.

Techniques of Quantitative Fire Hazard Analysis: Proceedings, Annual Symposium, 1985. E. K. Budnick et al. 140p. 1986. 45.00 (0-318-22359-7) Society Fire Protect.

Techniques of Radar Reflectivity Measurement. Ed. by Nicholas C. Currie. LC 83-72777. (Illus.). 540p. reprint ed. pap. 153.90 (0-8357-7924-6, 2036350) Bks Demand.

Techniques of Regional Anesthesia. D. Bruce Scott. (Illus.). 224p. 1989. text ed. 105.00 (0-8385-8844-1, A8844-1) Appleton & Lange.

Techniques of Regional Anesthesia. 2nd ed. Scott. 1995. pap. text ed. 89.95 (0-8385-8846-8) P-H.

***Techniques of Reporting & Writing.** Starr. 1996. pap. text ed. write for info. (0-07-061045-2) McGraw.

Techniques of Rug Weaving. Peter Collingwood. LC 68-24486. (Illus.). 480p. 1987. 60.00 (0-8230-5200-1, Watsn-Guptill) Watsn-Guptill.

Techniques of Safecracking. (Criminology Ser.). 1992. lib. bdg. 88.95 (0-8490-8754-6) Gordon Pr.

Techniques of Safecracking. Wayne B. Yeager. LC 90-63304. (Illus.). 88p. (Orig.). 1990. pap. 12.95 (1-55950-052-2, 52054) Loompanics.

Techniques of Safety Management: A Systems Approach. 3rd ed. Daniel C. Petersen. (Illus.). 414p. 1989. text ed. 39.50 (0-913690-14-7) Aloray.

Techniques of Satire: The Case of Saltykov-Shchedrin. Emil A. Draitser. LC 93-43693. (Humor Research Ser.: No. 2). xiii, 213p. (C). 1994. lib. bdg. 83.10 (3-11-012624-9) Mouton.

Techniques of Semigroup Theory. Peter M. Higgins. (Illus.). 320p. 1992. 79.00 (0-19-853577-5) OUP.

Techniques of Solubilization of Drugs. Samuel H. Yalkowsky. LC 81-15262. (Drugs & the Pharmaceutical Sciences Ser.: No. 12). 240p. reprint ed. pap. 68.40 (0-7837-2205-2, 2052455) Bks Demand.

***Techniques of Soul Alignment: The Rays, the Subtle Bodies, & the Use of Keywords.** Kurt Abraham. 125p. (Orig.). 1997. pap. write for info. (0-9609002-6-8) Lampus Pr.

Techniques of Spiral Work: A Practical Guide to the Craft of Making Twists by Hand. Stuart Mortimer. LC 95-34339. (Illus.). 176p. 1996. pap. 24.95 (0-941936-34-1) Linden Pub Fresno.

Techniques of Staircase Construction. Willibald Mannes. (Illus.). 112p. (gr. 13). 1986. text ed. 60.95 (0-442-26086-5) Chapman & Hall.

Techniques of Stuttering Therapy. Richard J. Ham. 448p. 1986. text ed. write for info. (0-13-901844-1) P-H.

Techniques of Subversion in Modern Literature: Transgression, Abjection, & the Carnivalesque. M. Keith Booker. 352p. (C). 1991. lib. bdg. 49.95 (0-8130-1065-9) U Press Fla.

Techniques of Successful Delegation. (Leadership Ser.). 52p. (Orig.). 1988. pap. 9.95 (1-55852-019-8) Natl Pr Pubns.

Techniques of Surface & Colloid Chemistry & Physics, Vol. 1. Ed. by Robert J. Good et al. LC 71-184201. (Illus.). 264p. reprint ed. pap. 75.30 (0-685-23662-5, 2027998) Bks Demand.

Techniques of Surveillance & Undercover Operations. 1995. lib. bdg. 260.75 (0-8490-7402-9) Gordon Pr.

Techniques of Swing-Rod Dowsing: Step-by-Step Method for Use of the Pendulum in Dowsing. Bill Cox. (Illus.). 38p. 1977. 6.00 (0-88234-007-7) Life Understanding.

***Techniques of Tablet Weaving.** 2nd rev. ed. Peter Collingwood. 1996. reprint ed. pap. 35.00 (1-56659-056-6) Robin & Russ.

Techniques of Teaching Blind Children. M. N. Mani. 1993. text ed. 27.50 (81-207-1393-1, Pub. by Sterling Pubs II) Apt Bks.

***Techniques of Teaching in a Letter to Maya: What Is Bahai?** Mahendranath Gooljar. 50p. (Orig.). 1997. pap. 8.95 (0-533-12066-7) Vantage.

Techniques of the Artists of the American West. Peggy Samuels et al. 1991. 29.98 (1-55521-662-5) Bk Sales Inc.

Techniques of the Boundary Element Method. Zafrany El. 300p. 1993. 70.00 (0-13-898511-1) P-H.

Techniques of the Contemporary Composer. Cope. 1997. 32.00 (0-02-864737-8) Mac Lib Ref.

Techniques of the Impressionists. Athea Callen. 1993. 17.98 (0-89009-545-0) Bk Sales Inc.

Techniques of the Observer: On Vision & Modernity in the Nineteenth Century. Johnathan Crary. (Illus.). 200p. 1990. 30.00 (0-262-03169-8) MIT Pr.

Techniques of the Observer: On Vision & Modernity in the Nineteenth Century. Jonathan Crary. (Illus.). 184p. 1992. reprint ed. pap. 14.95 (0-262-53107-0) MIT Pr.

Techniques of the Professional Pickpocket. Wayne B. Yeager. LC 90-62934. (Illus.). 80p. (Orig.). 1990. pap. 12.95 (1-55950-046-8, 40068) Loompanics.

Techniques of the Selling Writer. Dwight V. Swain. LC 73-7419. 336p. 1981. pap. 16.95 (0-8061-1191-7) U of Okla Pr.

Techniques of the World's Greatest Paintings. Waldemas Januezczak. 1993. 17.98 (0-89009-368-7) Bk Sales Inc.

Techniques of Training. 3rd rev. ed. Leslie Rae. LC 94-47426. 1995. pap. 28.95 (0-566-07629-2, Pub. by Gower UK) Ashgate Pub Co.

Techniques of Translation: Chaucer's Boece. Tim W. Machan. LC 85-524. 163p. (C). 1985. 29.95 (0-937664-68-5) Pilgrim Bks OK.

Techniques of Transport Planning. Vol. 1: Pricing & Project Evaluation. Ed. by John R. Meyer. LC 79-108833. (Transport Research Program Ser.). 343p. 1971. 17.95 (0-8157-5690-9) Brookings.

Techniques of Transport Planning. Vol. 2: Systems Analysis & Simulation Models, Transport Research Program. Ed. by John R. Meyer. LC 79-108833. 1971. 22.95 (0-8157-5040-4) Brookings.

Techniques of Treasury Debt Management. Tilford C. Gaines. LC 62-11849. 1962. 12.95 (0-02-911050-5, Free Press) Free Pr.

Techniques of Trout Fishing & Fly Tying. enl. ed. George Harvey. (Illus.). 140p. 1990. reprint ed. pap. 16.95 (1-55821-074-1) Lyons & Burford.

Techniques of Twentieth-Century Composition: A Guide to the Materials of Modern Music. 3rd ed. Leon Dallin. 304p. (C). 1974. per. write for info. (0-697-03614-6) Brown & Benchmark.

Techniques of Vacuum Ultraviolet Spectroscopy. James A. Samson. LC 67-19780. 1990. reprint ed. 75.00 (0-918626-15-3) VUV Assocs.

Techniques of Venous Imaging. Steven R. Talbot & Mark A. Oliver. LC 91-31486. (Illus.). 220p. 1992. text ed. 79.00 (0-941022-22-6) Davies Pubng.

Techniques of Veterinary Radiography. 5th ed. Ed. by Joe P. Morgan. LC 92-41342. (Venture Series in Veterinary Medicine). (Illus.). 496p. (C). 1993. pap. text ed. 69.95 (0-8138-1727-7) Iowa St U Pr.

Techniques of Wood Sculpture. David Orchard. (Illus.). 144p. 1994. 27.50 (0-7134-7262-6, Pub. by Batsford UK) Trafalgar.

Techniques of Working with Resistance. Ed. by Donald Milman & George Goldman. LC 85-18653. 417p. 1986. 50.00 (0-87668-616-1) Aronson.

Techniques of Writing. Burgess. (C). 1995. pap. 6.76 (0-395-73787-7) HM.

Techniques of Writing Business Letters, Memos, & Reports. 2nd rev. ed. Courtland L. Bovee. LC 77-92913. 96p. (C). 1989. reprint ed. pap. text ed. write for info. (0-935732-15-2) Roxbury Pub Co.

Techniques, Technology & Training in the Manufacture of Men's Clothing. 51p. 1970. 20.00 (0-318-13705-4) Clothing Mfrs.

***Techniques to Assess the Corrosion Activity of Steel Reinforced Concrete Structures, STP1276.** 2nd ed. Ed. by Neal S. Berke et al. LC 96-35303. (Illus.). 200p. 1996. pap. text ed. 39.00 (0-8031-2009-5, 04-012760-07) ASTM.

Techniques to Improve Your Writing Skills. (Communication Ser.). 48p. (Orig.). 1989. pap. 9.95 (1-55852-025-2) Natl Pr Pubns.

Techniques to Technology: A French Historiography of Technology. Ed. by Sabyasachi Bhattacharya & Pietro Redondi. Tr. by Radha Sharma et al. from FRE. 1990. text ed. 30.00 (0-86311-061-4, Pub. by Orient Longman Ltd II) Apt Bks.

Techniques Used in Bioproduct Analysis. 302p. 1992. pap. 42.95 (0-7506-1501-X) Buttrwrth-Heinemann.

Techniques Used in Nepalese Image Making. Y. Akita. (C). 1991. text ed. 60.00 (0-685-64810-9, Pub. by Ratna Pustak Bhandar) St Mut.

Techniques with a Thirty-Six Inch Baton: Modern Methods Made Easy. George M. Pekar & Timothy N. Oettmeier. (Illus.). 82p. (C). 1983. 16.95 (0-398-04751-0) C C Thomas.

Technisch Engels Woordenboek: Dutch-English, English-Dutch. H. Jansonius. 555p. (DUT & ENG.). 1976. 195.00 (0-7859-7148-3) Fr & Eur.

Technisch Wissenschaftliches Taschenwoerterbuch. 6th ed. 408p. (GER.). 1990. 75.00 (0-7859-0951-6, M-7643) Fr & Eur.

Technische Uebersetzinb - English. Theo Franck. 210p. (ENG & GER.). 1980. 49.95 (0-8288-2107-0, M5043) Fr & Eur.

Technisches Deutschfuer Auslaender: Technical German for Foreigners. Jaroslav Strasak. (GER.). 1969. 29.95 (0-8288-6616-3, M-7644) Fr & Eur.

Technisches Taschenwoerterbuch. A. Grunwald-Beyer. 533p. (FRE & GER.). 25.00 (3-87749-013-1, M-7646); 59.95 (0-8288-7793-9, M15051) Fr & Eur.

Technisches Taschenwoerterbuch. A. Kroeger-Jannetti. 804p. (GER & SPA.). 75.00 (3-87749-012-3, M-7645); 75.00 (0-8288-7829-3, M7645) Fr & Eur.

Technisches Woerterbuch, Vol. 1. Antonin Kucera. (GER & RUS.). 1966. 75.00 (0-8288-6731-3, M-7654, Pub. by O Brandstetter Verlag GW) Fr & Eur.

Technisches Woerterbuch, Vol. 1. A. Naxerova. (CZE & GER.). 1970. 89.95 (0-8288-6554-X, M-7649, Pub. by O Brandstetter Verlag GW) Fr & Eur.

Technisches Woerterbuch, Vol. 2. Antonin Kucera. 464p. (GER & RUS.). 1966. 85.00 (0-8288-6732-1, M-7655) Fr & Eur.

Technisches Woerterbuch, Vol. 2. A. Naxerova. (CZE & GER.). 1972. 89.95 (0-8288-6422-5, M-7650, Pub. by O Brandstetter Verlag GW) Fr & Eur.

Technisches Woerterbuch: Serbocroatian & German Technical Dictionary, 2 vols. Ulatko Dabac. (CRO, GER & SER.). 1969. 195.00 (0-8288-6617-1, M7653) Fr & Eur.

Techniseasonal Commodity Trading. Everet Beckner. 1984. 65.00 (0-930233-22-0) Windsor.

Techno-Crazed: The Businessperson's Guide to Controlling Technology - Before It Controls You. Michael Finley. LC 95-18847. 212p. (Orig.). 1995. pap. 14.95 (1-56079-570-0, Petersons Pacesetter) Petersons.

Techno-Diplomacy: U. S.-Soviet Confrontations in Science & Technology. G. E. Schweitzer. LC 89-8787. (Illus.). 320p. 1989. 22.95 (0-306-43289-7, Plenum Pr) Plenum.

An Asterisk (*) at the beginning of an entry indicates that the title is appearing in BIP for the first time.

***Techno-Economic Aspects of Measures to Reduce Water Pollution in Small & Medium-Sized Enterprises.** 165p. 1996. pap. 40.00 (*92-827-5580-0*, CR92-95-861-ENC, Pub. by Europ Com UK) Bernan Associates.

***Techno-Economic Study on the Reduction Measures Based on Best Available Technology: Final Report 1, Sept. 1993.** 138p. 1996. pap. 35.00 (*92-827-5579-7*, CR92-95-998-ENC, Pub. by Europ Com UK) Bernan Associates.

Techno Lab: How Science Is Changing Entertainment. Robert Sheely & Carol Anderson. LC 94-24894. (Science Lab Ser.). (Illus.). 64p. (J). (gr. 4-8). 1995. lib. bdg. 13.95 (*1-881889-63-7*) Silver Moon.

Techno Lab see Police Lab; Sports Lab; Entertainment Lab

Techno-Nationalism & Techno-Globalism: Conflict & Cooperation. Sylvia Ostry & Richard R. Nelson. (Integrating National Economies Ser.). 160p. (C). 1995. 34.95 (*0-8157-6674-2*); pap. 14.95 (*0-8157-6673-4*) Brookings.

Techno-Security in an Age of Globalization: Perspectives from the Pacific Rim. Ed. by Denis F. Simon. LC 95-52836. 256p. (C). 1996. pap. text ed. 24.95 (*1-56324-673-2*, East Gate Bk) M E Sharpe.

Techno-Security in an Age of Globalization: Perspectives from the Pacific Rim. Ed. by Denis F. Simon. LC 95-52836. 256p. (C). (gr. 13). 1996. text ed. 62.95 (*1-56324-672-4*, East Gate Bk) M E Sharpe.

***Techno Style: Graphics, Fashion, Culture.** Ed. by Martin Pesch & Markus Weisbeck. (Illus.). 132p. (ENG & GER.). 1996. pap. 39.95 (*3-283-00290-8*) Gingko Press.

***Techno Textiles.** Sarah E. Braddock & Marie O'Mahony. LC 97-60247. 192p. 1997. 50.00 (*0-500-23740-9*) Thames Hudson.

Techno-Tyrannical Society - Rasta Prophesy: Babylon's Genocidal Plan to Enslave Humanity. Ricardo A. Scott & Giancarlo T. Scott. (R.A.S.P.E.C.T-1/Reggae Education). (Illus.). 100p. (Orig.). Date not set. pap. write for info. (*1-883427-56-8*) Crnerstone GA.

Techno Vision: An Executive's Survival Guide to Understanding & Managing Information. Charles B. Wang. 1994. text ed. 19.95 (*0-07-068155-4*) McGraw.

***Technoart - The Chromapark Issue.** Ed. by Alfred M. Jones. (Localizer 1.1 Ser.). (Illus.). 80p. (Orig.). Date not set. pap. 19.99 (*3-931126-01-3*, Pub. by Die Gestalten GW) Consort Bk Sales.

Technobabble. John A. Barry. 250p. 1991. 27.50 (*0-262-02333-4*) MIT Pr.

Technobabble. John A. Barry. (Illus.). 288p. (C). 1993. pap. 13.50 (*0-262-52182-2*) MIT Pr.

TechnoBrands: How to Create & Use "Brand Identity" to Market, Advertise & Sell Technology Products. Chuck Pettis. LC 94-31044. (Illus.). 208p. 1994. 26.95 (*0-8144-0243-7*) AMACOM.

Technocracy: New World Order. White Wolf Staff & Brian Campbell. (Mage Ser.). 72p. 1995. per., pap. 10.00 (*1-56504-423-1*, 4203(4423)) White Wolf.

Technocracy: Progenitors. M.S. Human Genetics Staff & Judith McLaughlin. (Mage Ser.). 1994. 10.00 (*1-56504-111-9*, 4201) White Wolf.

Technocracy: Technological Social Design. Ed. by Technocracy Inc. Staff. (Illus.). 76p. (Orig.). 1975. pap. 3.00 (*0-686-28500-X*) Technocracy.

Technocracy: Void Engineers. Judith McLaughlin et al. (Mage Ser.). (Illus.). 72p. (Orig.). 1996. pap. text ed. 10.00 (*1-56504-424-X*, 4204) White Wolf.

Technocracy & Development in the Philippines. Roman Dubsky. 276p. (C). 1994. pap. text ed. 15.00 (*971-542-016-8*, Pub. by U of Philippines Pr PH) UH Pr.

Technocracy & the Politics of Expertise: Managerial & Policy Perspectives. Frank Fischer. (Illus.). 384p. (C). 1989. 17.95 (*0-8039-3379-7*) Sage.

Technocracy at Work. Beverly H. Burris. LC 92-24052. (SUNY Series, the New Inequalities). 243p. (C). 1993. text ed. 64.50 (*0-7914-1495-7*); pap. text ed. 21.95 (*0-7914-1496-5*) State U NY Pr.

Technocracy vs. Democracy: The Comparative Politics of International Airports. Elliot J. Feldman & Jerome Milch. LC 81-17671. (Illus.). 299p. (C). 1981. text ed. 39.95 (*0-86569-063-4*, Auburn Hse) Greenwood.

***Technocrary: Syndicate.** Mark Cenczyk. (Mage). (Illus.). (Orig.). 1997. pap. 10.00 (*1-56504-421-5*, 4206) White Wolf.

Technocrat: Biography of a Boffin. W. E. Oulton. 1995. 15.95 (*0-533-11221-4*) Vantage.

Technocratic Illusion: A Study of Managerial Power in Italy. Flavia Derossi. Tr. by Susan LaBello. LC 81-14341. (Illus.). 247p. reprint ed. pap. 70.40 (*0-685-23736-2*, 2032777) Bks Demand.

Technocratic Socialism: The Soviet Union in the Advanced Industrial Era. Erik P. Hoffmann & Robbin F. Laird. LC 85-4553. (Duke Press Policy Studies). (Illus.). ix, 229p. 1985. 41.95 (*0-8223-0644-1*); pap. text ed. 16.95 (*0-8223-0692-1*) Duke.

Technocrats: Prophets of Automation. Henry Elsner. LC 67-14522. (Men & Movements Ser.). 270p. reprint ed. pap. 77.00 (*0-317-52019-9*, 2027413) Bks Demand.

Technocrats & Nuclear Politics: The Influence of Professional Experts in Policy-Making. Andrew Massey. 200p. 1988. text ed. 53.95 (*0-566-05644-5*, Pub. by Dartmth Pub UK) Ashgate Pub Co.

Technoculture. Constance Penley & Andrew Ross. (Cultural Politics Ser.: Vol. 3). (Illus.). 312p. (C). 1991. pap. 17.95 (*0-8166-1932-8*); text ed. 39.95 (*0-8166-1930-1*) U of Minn Pr.

Technodemocratic Economic Theory: From Capitalism & Socialism to Democracy. Reza Rezazadeh. LC 91-70823. 359p. (C). 1992. lib. bdg. 20.00 (*0-9629032-0-5*) Etarnalist.

Technofollies. Phil Patton. 1996. 24.95 (*0-8050-3319-X*) H Holt & Co.

Technofundamental Trading: A Revolutionary Approach to Combining Technical & Fundamental. Phil Gotthelf. 1994. text ed. 45.00 (*1-55738-541-6*) Irwin Prof Pubng.

Technohistory: Using the History of American Technology in Interdisciplinary Research. Ed. by Chris H. Gray. LC 94-36684. 296p. (Orig.). (C). 1996. pap. 24.50 (*0-89464-853-5*) Krieger.

Technoid Marxism: Walter Benjamin & "Overpowering Conformism" Esther Leslie. (C). 1996. 45.00 (*1-899438-25-4*, Pub. by Porcupine Bks UK); pap. 22.50 (*1-899438-23-8*, Pub. by Porcupine Bks UK) Humanities.

Technological Acceleration & the Great Depression. Joseph P. Waters. Ed. by Stuart Bruchey. LC 76-45122. (Nineteen Seventy-Seven Dissertations Ser.). (Illus.). 1977. lib. bdg. 28.95 (*0-405-09933-9*) Ayer.

Technological Advance in an Expanding Economy: Its Impact on a Cross-Section of the Labor Force. Eva Mueller et al. LC 71-627965. 266p. reprint ed. pap. 75.90 (*0-685-23663-3*, 2029137) Bks Demand.

Technological Advance in Japan's Building Design & Construction Industry. Anthony C. Webster. LC 93-50713. 1994. pap. 26.00 (*0-87262-932-5*) Am Soc Civil Eng.

Technological Advances in Health Sciences & the Moral & Theological Implications. Ed. by R. Borghgraef & R. Schotsmans. 90p. (Orig.). 1993. pap. 27.50 (*90-6186-579-4*, Pub. by Leuven Univ BE) Coronet Bks.

Technological Advances in Improved & Alternative Sources of Lipids. Ed. by B. S. Kamel & Y. S. Kakuda. LC 93-28697. 1994. 119.00 (*0-7514-0001-7*, Pub. by Blackie Acad & Prof UK) Routledge Chapman & Hall.

Technological Alterations to Motion Pictures & Other Audiovisual Works: Colorization, Panning, Scanning, Time Compression, 3 vols. 1991. Set. lib. bdg. 475.95 (*0-8490-4384-0*) Gordon Pr.

Technological & Economic Origins of the Information Society. 1991. lib. bdg. 75.00 (*0-8490-4630-0*) Gordon Pr.

Technological & Market Innovation: Strategies for Product & Company Development. Harry Nystrom. LC 89-29727. 307p. 1993. pap. text ed. 55.00 (*0-471-93466-6*) Wiley.

Technological & Social Factors in Long Term Fluctuations. Ed. by M. Di Matteo et al. (Lecture Notes in Economics & Mathematical Systems Ser.: Vol. 321). ix, 442p. 1989. 61.95 (*0-387-50663-2*) Spr-Verlag.

Technological Application of Immunochemicals. BIOTOL Staff. (BIOTOL Ser.). 1994. pap. 52.95 (*0-7506-0508-1*) Buttrwrth-Heinemann.

Technological Applications of Biocatalysts. (BIOTOL Ser.). 378p. 1994. pap. 49.95 (*0-7506-0506-5*) Buttrwrth-Heinemann.

Technological Applications of Dispersions. McKay. LC 93-50099. (Surfactant Science Ser.: Vol. 52). 576p. 1994. 220.00 (*0-8247-9180-0*) Dekker.

Technological Aspects of the Mechanical Behavior of Polymers. Ed. by Raymond F. Boyer. LC 74-181576. (Applied Polymer Symposia Ser.: No. 24). 121p. reprint ed. 34.50 (*0-8357-9378-8*, 2007371) Bks Demand.

Technological Behaviour of Public Enterprises in Developing Countries. Ed. by Jeffrey James. 256p. 1989. 49.95 (*0-415-02650-4*, A3447) Routledge.

Technological Breakthrough in Agriculture. K. Siva Prasad. (C). 1987. 17.50 (*81-85076-15-4*, Pub. by Chugh Pubns II) S Asia.

Technological Capabilities & Learning in African Enterprises. Tyler Biggs et al. LC 95-17540. (Technical Papers Ser.: No. 288). 250p. 1996. 14.95 (*0-8213-3318-6*, 13318) World Bank.

***Technological Capabilities in Developing Countries: Industrial Biotechnology in Mexico.** Ruby Gonsen. LC 97-22118. 1997. write for info. (*0-312-17735-6*) St Martin.

Technological Capability in the Informal Sector: Metal Manufacturing in Developing Countries. International Labour Office Staff. Ed. by C. Maldonado & S. V. Sethuraman. (WEP Study Ser.). v, 235p. (Orig.). 1992. pap. 31.50 (*92-2-106468-9*) Intl Labour Office.

Technological Challenge in the Asia-Pacific Economy. Ed. by Hadi Soesastro & Mari Pangestu. 392p. 1991. pap. text ed. 34.95 (*0-04-442229-6*, Pub. by Allen Unwin AT) Paul & Co Pubs.

Technological Change: Its Impact on Man & Society. Emmanuel G. Mesthene. LC 76-106960. (Harvard Studies in Technology & Society). 127p. reprint ed. pap. 36.20 (*0-7837-3851-X*, 2043673) Bks Demand.

Technological Change: Methods & Themes in the History of Technology. Ed. by Robert Fox. (Studies in the History of Science, Technology & Medicine Ser.). 325p. 1996. text ed. 54.00 (*3-7186-5792-9*, Harwood Acad Pubs) Gordon & Breach.

Technological Change: The Role of Scientists & Engineers. Derek Bosworth et al. 149p. 1992. 63.95 (*1-85628-322-4*, Pub. by Avebury Pub UK) Ashgate Pub Co.

Technological Change: The Tripartite Response, 1982-1985. Intro. by Hady Sarfati & Margaret Cove. 355p. 1985. pap. 27.00 (*92-2-105162-5*) Intl Labour Office.

Technological Change & Agrarian Structure: A Study of Bangladesh (WEP Study) Iftikhar Ahmed. xiii, 136p. (Orig.). 1981. pap. 13.50 (*92-2-102543-8*) Intl Labour Office.

Technological Change & Co-Determination in Sweden. Ake Sandburg et al. (Labor & Social Change Ser.). 352p. (C). 1992. 59.95 (*0-87722-918-X*) Temple U Pr.

Technological Change & Company Strategies. Ed. by Rod Coombs et al. (Economic & Social Analysis of Technology Ser.). (Illus.). 255p. 1992. pap. text ed. 51.00 (*0-12-187582-2*) Acad Pr.

Technological Change & Development: Puerto Rico's Technological Leap. Sandor Boyson. (International Development Studies Series St. Mary's University Halifax, Canada: No. 2). (Illus.). xiii, 425p. 1993. 32.00 (*81-7024-553-2*, Pub. by Ashish Pub Hse II) Nataraj Bks.

Technological Change & Employment: Innovation in the German Economy. Ronald Schettkat. xxii, 384p. (C). 1990. lib. bdg. 84.95 (*3-11-012427-0*) De Gruyter.

Technological Change & Labour Relations. Muneto Ozaki et al. xiv, 205p. 1992. pap. 27.00 (*92-2-107753-5*) Intl Labour Office.

Technological Change & Management. Ed. by David W. Ewing. LC 78-125645. 160p. 1970. 10.00 (*0-674-87230-4*) HUP.

Technological Change & Productivity Growth. Albert N. Link. (Fundamentals of Pure & Applied Economics Ser.: Vol. 13). 78, viiip. 1987. pap. text ed. 37.00 (*3-7186-0347-0*) Gordon & Breach.

Technological Change & Rural Development in Poor Countries: Neglected Issues. Ed. by Kartik C. Roy & Cal M. Clark. 192p. 1995. 21.00 (*0-19-563583-3*) OUP.

Technological Change & Skills Development. Elaine Bernard. 162p. (C). 1991. 60.00 (*0-7300-1251-4*, Pub. by Deakin Univ AT) St Mut.

Technological Change & the British Iron Industry, 1700-1870. Charles K. Hyde. LC 76-45901. 300p. reprint ed. pap. 85.50 (*0-7837-6776-5*, 2046606) Bks Demand.

Technological Change & the City. Ed. by Patrick N. Troy. 202p. 1995. pap. 35.00 (*1-86287-184-1*, Pub. by Federation Pr AU) Gaunt.

***Technological Change & the Rural Environment.** Ed. by Philip Lowe et al. (Critical Perspectives on Rural Change Ser.). s202p. 1995. text ed. 95.00 (*0-471-95928-6*, GE11) Wiley.

Technological Change & the Rural Environment, Vol. 2. 208p. (C). 1990. 110.00 (*1-85346-112-1*, Pub. by D Fulton Pubs UK) St Mut.

Technological Change & the Rural Environment, Vol. 2. Ed. by Terry Marsden et al. (Critical Perspectives on Rural Change Ser.). 224p. (C). 1990. 79.00 (*0-8464-1518-6*) Beekman Pubs.

Technological Change & United States Energy Consumption, 1939-1954. Alan M. Strout. Ed. by Stuart Bruchey. LC 78-22753. (Energy in the American Economy Ser.). (Illus.). 1979. lib. bdg. 28.95 (*0-405-12017-6*) Ayer.

Technological Change & Women's Work Experience: Alternative Methodological Perspectives. Barbara S. Burnell. LC 92-38705. 224p. 1993. text ed. 52.95 (*0-89789-292-5*, H292, Bergin & Garvey) Greenwood.

Technological Change & Workers' Movements. Ed. by Melvyn Dubofsky. LC 85-2173. (Explorations in the World-Economy Ser.: No. 4). 272p. reprint ed. pap. 77.60 (*0-8357-8458-4*, 2034723) Bks Demand.

Technological Change at Work. Ian McLoughlin & Jon Clark. 224p. 1988. 90.00 (*0-335-15417-4*, Open Univ Pr); pap. 32.00 (*0-335-15416-6*, Open Univ Pr) Taylor & Francis.

Technological Change at Work. 2nd ed. Ian McLoughlin & Jon Clark. LC 93-27839. 1994. pap. 13.99 (*0-335-19009-X*, Open Univ Pr) Taylor & Francis.

Technological Change, Development & the Environment: Socio-Economic Perspectives. Ed. by Clement A. Tisdell & P. Maitra. 288p. 1988. lib. bdg. 62.50 (*0-415-00447-0*) Routledge.

Technological Change, Economic Development & Space. Ed. by Cristoforo S. Bertuglia et al. LC 95-24292. (Advances in Spatial Science Ser.). (Illus.). 354p. 1995. 117.00 (*3-540-59288-1*) Spr-Verlag.

Technological Change in a Spatial Context: Theory, Empirical Evidence & Policy. Ed. by E. Ciciotti et al. (Illus.). xi, 400p. 1990. 107.95 (*0-387-52948-9*) Spr-Verlag.

Technological Change in China. Richard Conroy. 276p. (Orig.). 1992. pap. 54.00 (*92-64-13652-5*) OECD.

Technological Change in Printing & Publishing. Lowell H. Hattery & George P. Bush. LC 77-176224. 275p. 1973. 23.75 (*0-87671-503-X*) Lomond.

Technological Change in the American Cotton Spinning Industry, 1790-1836. Robert R. MacMurray. Ed. by Stuart Bruchey. LC 76-39835. (Nineteen Seventy-Seven Dissertations Ser.). (Illus.). 1977. lib. bdg. 62.95 (*0-405-09915-0*) Ayer.

Technological Change in the Chavez Pass Region, North-Central Arizona. Ed. by Gary Brown. LC 90-84767. (Anthropological Research Papers: No. 41). (Illus.). xiv, 226p. 1990. pap. 20.00 (*0-936249-06-4*) AZ Univ ARP.

Technological Change in the Information Economy. Peter Monk. 256p. 1992. 54.00 (*0-86187-713-6*) St Martin.

Technological Change in the Workplace: Health Impacts for Workers. Ed. by Marianne Brown & John Froines. 1993. 18.50 (*0-89215-180-3*) U Cal LA Indus Rel.

Technological Change, Rationalisation & Industrial Relations. Ed. by Otto Jacobi et al. LC 85-2166. 320p. 1986. text ed. 39.95 (*0-312-78878-9*) St Martin.

Technological Change, Work Organisation & Pay: Lessons from Asia. (Labour-Management Relations Ser.: No. 68). xvi, 218p. (Orig.). 1988. pap. 22.50 (*92-2-106324-0*) Intl Labour Office.

Technological Changes & the Law: A Reader. Otto G. Gara & Bruce A. Naegeli. LC 79-92276. 925p. 1980. 45.00 (*0-89941-037-5*, 300400) W S Hein.

Technological Choice in the Indian Environment. Ed. by Vinod Vyasulu. 351p. 1980. 44.95 (*0-940500-59-0*, Pub. by Sterling II) Asia Bk Corp.

Technological Choices: Arbitraries in Technology from the Neolithic to Modern High Technology. Ed. by Pierre Lemonnier. LC 92-23310. (Material Cultures Ser.). (Illus.). 320p. (C). (gr. 13). 1993. text ed. 85.00 (*0-415-07331-6*, B0311) Routledge.

Technological Collaboration: The Dynamics of Cooperation in Industrial Innovation. Ed. by Rob Coombs et al. LC 95-18024. 256p. 1996. 80.00 (*1-85898-235-9*) E Elgar.

Technological Collaboration for Europe's Survival: The Information Technology Research Programmes of the 1980s. Vassiliki N. Koutrakou. 320p. 1995. 68.95 (*1-85628-842-0*, Pub. by Avebury Pub UK) Ashgate Pub Co.

Technological Collaboration in Industry: Strategy, Policy & Internationalization in Innovation. Mark Dodgson. LC 91-44793. 240p. (C). 1993. pap. 16.95 (*0-415-05941-0*, Pub. by Intl Thomson Busn UK) Inter Thomson.

Technological Collaboration in Industry: Strategy, Policy & Internationalization in Innovation. Mark Dodgson. LC 92-26293. (Illus.). 240p. (C). 1993. 65.00 (*0-415-08230-7*, A9939) Routledge.

Technological Competition & Interdependence: A Search for Policy in the United States, West Germany, & Japan. Gunter Heiduk & Kozo Yamamura. LC 89-28169. 282p. (C). 1991. text ed. 35.00 (*0-295-96931-8*) U of Wash Pr.

Technological Competition & Trade in the Experimentally Organized Economy. Gunnar Eliasson. 118p. (Orig.). 1987. pap. text ed. 40.00 (*91-7204-294-X*, Pub. by Industriens SW) Coronet Bks.

Technological Competition in Global Industries: Marketing & Planning Strategies for American Industry. David T. Methe. LC 90-8908. 248p. 1990. text ed. 55.00 (*0-89930-480-X*, MTG/, Quorum Bks) Greenwood.

Technological Competitiveness: Contemporary & Historical Perspectives on the Electrical, Electronics, & Computer Industries. Intro. by Bill Aspray. LC 92-30772. (Illus.). 384p. (C). 1993. text ed. 49.95 (*0-7803-0427-6*, PC0324-4) Inst Electrical.

Technological Competitiveness of Japanese Multinationals: The European Dimension. Robert Peace & Marina Papanastassiou. LC 96-4456. (Thames Essays Ser.). (Illus.). (C). 1995. 39.50 (*0-472-10728-3*) U of Mich Pr.

Technological Decisions & Democracy: European Experiments in Public Participation. Dorothy Welkin. LC 77-9133. 112p. reprint ed. pap. 32.00 (*0-317-10754-2*, 2021937) Bks Demand.

Technological Democracy: Bureaucracy & Citizenry in the German Energy Debate. Carol J. Hager. (Social History, Popular Culture, & Politics in Germany Ser.). 200p. 1995. text ed. 44.50 (*0-472-10553-1*) U of Mich Pr.

Technological Development: The Historical Experience. Raymond Vernon. (EDI Seminar Paper Ser.: No. 39). 48p. 1989. 6.95 (*0-8213-1162-X*, 11162) World Bank.

Technological Development & Pollution Abatement: A Study of How Enterprises Are Finding Alternatives to Chlorofluorocarbons. Kulsum Ahmed. LC 94-23780. (Technical Papers: No. 271). 66p. 1995. 6.95 (*0-8213-3120-5*, 13120) World Bank.

Technological Development & Science in the Industrial Age: New Perspectives on the Science-Technology Relationship. Ed. by Peter Kroes & Martijn Bakker. LC 92-1611. (Boston Studies in the Philosophy of Science: Vol. 144). 284p. 1992. lib. bdg. 137.50 (*0-7923-1898-6*, Pub. by Klwr Acad Pubs NE) Kluwer Ac.

Technological Development in China, India & Japan: Cross-Cultural Perspectives. Erik Baark & Andrew Jamison. LC 85-22199. 172p. 1986. text ed. 39.95 (*0-312-78794-4*) St Martin.

Technological Development, Society & State. Ed. by W. H. Schnell. 300p. (C). 1991. text ed. 89.00 (*981-02-0682-8*) World Scientific Pub.

Technological Developments & Trends in Pediatric Radiology. Ed. by H. J. Kaufmann. (Progress in Pediatric Radiology Ser.: Vol. 7). (Illus.). 1979. 133.00 (*3-8055-2953-8*) S Karger.

Technological Developments in Drugs & Pharmaceutical Industry in India. Husain Ahmad. (C). 1988. 32.00 (*81-7013-004-2*, Pub. by Navrang) S Asia.

Technological Developments of Earthquake-Resistant Structures: Report of the Expert Committe on Advanced Technology for Building Structures 1987. Japan Building Center Staff. (Illus.). 494p. (C). 1994. text ed. 95.00 (*90-6191-935-5*, Pub. by A A Balkema NE) Ashgate Pub Co.

Technological Dictionary of Agricultural Equipment/Machinery. Hatier. 1295p. (ENG, FRE, GER, ITA, POR & SPA.). 1990. 295.00 (*0-7859-9961-2*) Fr & Eur.

Technological Dictionary of Telecommunications: English - French - German. Jens P. Rehahn. 480p. (ENG, FRE & GER.). 1992. lib. bdg. 275.00 (*0-7859-3657-2*, 3761170426) Fr & Eur.

Technological Diffusion & the Computer Revolution: The UK Experience. Paul Stoneman. LC 75-12136. (University of Cambridge, Dept. of Applied Economics, Occasional Papers: No. 25). (Illus.). 231p. reprint ed. pap. 65.90 (*0-685-20573-8*, 2030623) Bks Demand.

Technological Diffusion in the Hospital Sector. Louise B. Russell & Carol S. Burke. LC 75-37308. 240p. 1976. 8.00 (*0-89068-007-8*) Natl Planning.

Technological Dynamism in Industrial Districts: An Alternative Approach to Industrialization in Developing Countries? 346p. 1994. 35.00 (*92-1-112337-2*) UN.

Technological Education - Technological Style (ICOHTEC XVII International Congress, Berkeley, Calif.) Ed. by Melvin Kranzberg. 1986. 15.00 (*0-911302-59-X*) San Francisco Pr.

Technological Engineering Dictionary German-Serbocroatian. Ed. by S. Radic. 495p. (CRO, GER & SER.). 1981. 95.00 (*0-8288-4678-2*, M9687) Fr & Eur.

Technological Evolution, Variety, & the Economy. Pier P. Saviotti. LC 95-32858. (Illus.). 240p. (C). 1996. text ed. 80.00 (*1-85278-774-0*) E Elgar.

Technological Exchange - the US-Japanese Experience: Proceedings of a Japan-America Society of Washington Symposium, Washington, D.C., 1981. 132p. 1982. pap. 8.00 (*0-317-01144-8*) Japan-Am Soc.

*__Technological Failures: An Encyclopedia.__ Susan D. Herring. Date not set. text ed. 100.00 (*0-8153-0052-2*) Garland.

Technological Forecasting: A Practical Approach. Marvin J. Cetron. 346, xxxp. (C). 1969. text ed. 189.00 (*0-677-02140-2*) Gordon & Breach.

Technological Frontiers & Foreign Relations. Ed. by Anne G. Keatley. LC 85-61129. (Illus.). 314p. reprint ed. pap. 89.50 (*0-8357-4266-0*, 2037062) Bks Demand.

Technological Hazards. Ed. by Donald J. Zeigler et al. LC 83-22356. (Resource Publications in Geography). 90p. (C). 1983. pap. 15.00 (*0-89291-173-5*) Assn Am Geographers.

Technological History of Motion Pictures & Television: An Anthology from the Pages of "The Journal of the Society of Motion Pictures & Television Engineers" Intro. by Raymond Fielding. 1979. pap. 16.00 (*0-520-05064-9*) U CA Pr.

Technological Impact of Surfaces: Relationship to Forming, Welding, & Painting: Proceedings of a Conference, 14-15 April 1981, Dearborn, MI. American Society for Metals Staff. LC 81-69527. (Materials-Metalworking Technology Ser.). (Illus.). 367p. reprint ed. pap. 104.60 (*0-318-39726-9*, 2033085) Bks Demand.

Technological Infrastructure Policy: An International Perspective. Ed. by Morris Teubal et al. LC 95-45765. (Economics of Science, Technology & Innovation Ser.: No. 7). 388p. (C). 1996. lib. bdg. 133.00 (*0-7923-3835-9*) Kluwer Ac.

Technological Injury: The Effect of Technological Advances on Environment Life & Society. Ed. by J. Rose. 244p. 1969. pap. 63.00 (*0-677-13645-5*) Gordon & Breach.

*__Technological Innovation: Oversights & Foresights.__ Ed. by Raghu Garud et al. (Illus.). 384p. (C). 1997. text ed. 54.95 (*0-521-55299-0*) Cambridge U Pr.

Technological Innovation: Strategies for a New Partnership. Ed. by D. O. Gray et al. 334p. 1986. 152.50 (*0-444-70033-1*, North Holland) Elsevier.

Technological Innovation: The R & D Work Environment. Augustus Abbey. LC 82-4883. (Research for Business Decisions Ser.: No. 49). 140p. reprint ed. pap. 39.90 (*0-685-20860-5*, 2070123) Bks Demand.

Technological Innovation & the Decorative Arts. Hagley Museum Staff. (Illus.). 80p. 1973. pap. 1.50 (*0-914650-05-X*) Hagley Museum.

Technological Innovation & the Decorative Arts Catalog: An Exhibition at the Hagley Museum Co-Sponsored by the Henry Francis Du Pont Winterthur Museum. Ed. by Ian M. Quimby & Polly A. Earl. (Illus.). 80p. 1984. reprint ed. pap. text ed. 16.95 (*0-8139-0569-9*) U Pr of Va.

Technological Innovation & the Great Depression. Rick Szostak. LC 95-19901. 367p. (C). 1995. text ed. 69.00 (*0-8133-8941-0*) Westview.

Technological Innovation & Third World Multinationals. Paz E. Tolentino. LC 92-5426. 416p. (C). (gr. 13). 1993. text ed. 85.00 (*0-415-04807-9*, A7668) Routledge.

Technological Innovation in the '80s. Ed. by James S. Coles. LC 84-2072. 1984. 12.95 (*0-13-902123-X*); pap. 6.95 (*0-13-902115-9*) Am Assembly.

Technological Innovations in Libraries, 1860-1960: An Anecdotal History. Klaus Musmann. LC 93-18143. (Contributions in Librarianship & Information Science Ser.: No. 73). 272p. 1993. text ed. 59.95 (*0-313-28015-0*, MTV, Greenwood Pr) Greenwood.

*__Technological Innovations, Industrial Evolution, & Economic Growth.__ Sanjaya Panth. LC 97-22274. (Studies on Industrial Productivity). 1997. write for info. (*0-8153-2784-6*) Garland.

Technological Innovations, Multinational Corporations & the New International Competitiveness: The Case of Intermediate Countries, Vol. 2. Ed. by Jose Molero. 336p. 1996. text ed. 59.00 (*3-7186-5685-X*, Harwood Acad Pubs) Gordon & Breach.

Technological Lag: Diffusion of Electrical Technology in England, 1879-1914. A. J. Millard. (Modern European History Ser.). 264p. 1987. text ed. 15.00 (*0-8240-7823-3*) Garland.

Technological Lag & Intellectual Background: Problems of Transition in East Central Europe. Ed. by Janos Kovacs. (Illus.). 400p. 1995. text ed. 62.95 (*1-85521-642-6*, Pub. by Dartmth Pub UK) Ashgate Pub Co.

Technological Literacy & the Curriculum. John Beynon & Hughie Mackay. 224p. 1992. 80.00 (*1-85000-985-6*, Falmer Pr); pap. 29.00 (*1-85000-986-4*, Falmer Pr) Taylor & Francis.

Technological Marketplace: Supply & Demand for Scientists & Engineers. 3rd ed. 50p. 1985. 25.00 (*0-318-16455-8*) Comm Prof Sci & Tech.

Technological Mechanics of Porous Bodies. B. Druyanov. LC 92-33960. (Illus.). 200p. 1993. 65.00 (*0-19-856364-7*, Old Oregon Bk Store) OUP.

Technological Muse. Susan Fillin-Yeh. (Illus.). 96p. 1990. 14.95 (*0-915171-19-8*) Katonah Gal.

Technological Parameters in Agricultural Production Function. Sita R. Singh. 1986. 17.00 (*81-7024-026-3*, Pub. by Ashish II) S Asia.

Technological Perspectives on Behavioral Change. Michael B. Schiffer. LC 92-5383. (Culture & Technology Ser.). 168p. 1992. 33.50 (*0-8165-1195-0*) U of Ariz Pr.

Technological Powers & the Person: Nuclear Energy & Reproduction Technology: Proceedings of the 1983 Bishops' Workshop. Ed. by Michael McDonough et al. LC 84-1933. (Illus.). 500p. (Orig.). 1983. pap. 15.95 (*0-935372-12-1*) Pope John Ctr.

Technological Principles Flow Line & Automated Production, 2 vols., Set. F. Demyanyuk & O. Blunn. LC 61-9176. 1963. 405.00 (*0-08-009902-5*, Pub. by Pergamon Repr UK) Franklin.

Technological Progress, Factor Endowments, & International Agricultural Trade. Joseph C. Salvacruz. LC 95-16726. (Foreign Economic Policy of the United States Ser.). (Illus.). 178p. 1995. text ed. 58.00 (*0-8153-1934-7*) Garland.

Technological Reshaping of Metropolitan America. 1996. lib. bdg. 255.95 (*0-8490-5998-4*) Gordon Pr.

*__Technological Reshaping of Metropolitan America.__ 1997. lib. bdg. 250.99 (*0-8490-6184-9*) Gordon Pr.

Technological Risk. H. W. Lewis. 368p. 1992. pap. 12.95 (*0-393-30829-4*) Norton.

Technological Risk Assessment. Paolo F. Ricci et al. 1984. lib. bdg. 133.00 (*90-247-2961-0*) Kluwer Ac.

Technological Shortcuts to Social Change. Amitai Etzioni & Richard Remp. LC 72-83834. 236p. 1973. 22.50 (*0-87154-236-6*) Russell Sage.

Technological Society. Jacques Ellul. 1967. pap. 11.00 (*0-394-70390-1*, V390, Vin) Random.

Technological Specialization of Advanced Countries: A Report to the EEC on International Science & Technology Activities. Daniele Archibugi & Mario Pianta. LC 92-8629. 1992. lib. bdg. 109.50 (*0-7923-1750-5*) Kluwer Ac.

*__Technological Substitution in Circuit Equipment for Local Telecommunications.__ Lawrence K. Vanston. 170p. 1989. pap. 45.00 (*0-614-18123-2*) Tech Futures.

*__Technological Substitution in Transmission Facilities for Local Telecommunications.__ Lawrence K. Vanston & Ralph C. Lenz. 350p. 1988. pap. 45.00 (*0-614-18121-6*) Tech Futures.

Technological Support for Work Group Collaboration. Ed. by M. H. Olson. (John Seely Brown Ser.). 208p. 1988. 29.95 (*0-8058-0304-1*) L Erlbaum Assocs.

*__Technological Systems.__ Carlsson. LC 97-16536. 1997. text ed. write for info. (*0-7923-9940-4*) Kluwer Ac.

Technological Systems & Economic Performance: The Case of Factory Automation. Ed. by Bo Carlsson. LC 95-14924. (Economics of Science, Technology & Innovation Ser.: Vol. 5). 512p. (C). 1995. lib. bdg. 99.00 (*0-7923-3512-0*) Kluwer Ac.

Technological Terrorism. Richard C. Clark. 1980. 10.00 (*0-8159-6915-5*) Devin.

Technological Trajectories & the Human Environment. Rockefeller University Staff et al. Ed. by Jessee H. Ausubel & H. Dale Langford. LC 96-48427. 230p. (C). 1997. text ed. 42.95 (*0-309-05133-9*) Natl Acad Pr.

Technological Tranformation, Vol. 5. Ed. by Surendra J. Patel. (Technological Transformation in the Third World Ser.). 304p. 1995. 63.95 (*1-85628-612-6*, Pub. by Avebury Pub UK) Ashgate Pub Co.

Technological Transformation: Contextual & Conceptual Implications. Ed. by Edmund F. Byrne & Joseph C. Pitt. 325p. (C). 1989. pap. text ed. 57.00 (*90-277-2827-5*, D Reidel); lib. bdg. 154.50 (*90-277-2826-7*, D Reidel) Kluwer Ac.

Technological Transformation in the Third World: Strategies & Prospects. M. R. Bhagavan. LC 88-2682. 128p. (C). 1990. pap. 17.50 (*0-86232-813-6*, Pub. by Zed Bks Ltd UK); text ed. 49.95 (*0-86232-812-8*, Pub. by Zed Bks Ltd UK) Humanities.

Technological Transformation in the Third World Vol. 4: Developed Countries. Ed. by Surendra J. Patel. (Technological Transformation in the Third World Ser.: Vol. 4). 310p. 1993. 59.95 (*1-85628-472-7*, Pub. by Avebury Pub UK) Ashgate Pub Co.

Technological Transformation in the Third World - Asia, Vol. 1. Ed. by Surendra J. Patel. (Technological Transformation in the Third World Ser.). 344p. 1993. 67.95 (*1-85628-469-7*, Pub. by Avebury Pub UK) Ashgate Pub Co.

Technological Transformation in the Third World Series Vol. 3: Latin America. Ed. by Surendra J. Patel. 346p. 1993. 67.95 (*1-85628-471-9*, Pub. by Avebury Pub UK) Ashgate Pub Co.

*__Technological Transformation of China.__ (Illus.). 216p. 1990. pap. text ed. 45.00 (*1-57979-176-X*) BPI Info Servs.

Technological Transformation of China. T. David McDonald. (Illus.). 221p. 1990. per. 5.50 (*0-16-001720-3*, S/N 008-020-01172-0) USGPO.

*__Technological Transformation of China.__ T. David McDonald. (Illus.). 191p. (Orig.). 1996. pap. 30.00 (*0-7881-3062-5*) DIANE Pub.

Technological Transformation of Japan from the Seventeenth to the Twenty-First Century. Tessa Morris-Suzuki. LC 94-10310. (Illus.). 328p. (C). 1994. pap. text ed. 19.95 (*0-521-42492-5*) Cambridge U Pr.

Technological Transformation of Japan from the Seventeenth to the Twenty-First Century. Tessa Morris-Suzuki. LC 94-10310. (Illus.). 328p. (C). 1995. text ed. 59.95 (*0-521-41463-6*) Cambridge U Pr.

Technological Transformation of Rural India. Ed. by Amulya K. Reddy & Ajit S. Bhalla. LC 93-29554. 192p. 1994. text ed. 49.95 (*0-312-09595-3*) St Martin.

Technological Transistion in Cartography. Mark S. Monmonier. LC 84-40499. (Illus.). 304p. 1985. text ed. 25.00 (*0-299-10070-7*) U of Wis Pr.

Technological Treason. Ed. by Anthony C. Sutton. 31p. (Orig.). 1983. pap. 12.95 (*0-914981-08-0*) Res Pubns AZ.

Technological Trends & National Policy, Including the Social Implications of New Inventions: National Resources Committee, Report of the Subcommittee on Technology. Congress, 75th, 1st Session, House Document No. 360. LC 72-5084. (Technology & Society Ser.). (Illus.). 398p. 1972. reprint ed. 33.95 (*0-405-04732-0*) Ayer.

Technological Unemployment & Structural Unemployment Debates. Gregory R. Woirol. LC 95-41691. (Contributions in Economics & Economic History Ser.: No. 173). 224p. 1996. text ed. 57.95 (*0-313-29892-0*, Greenwood Pr) Greenwood.

Technological Woman: Interfacing with Tomorrow. Ed. by Jan Zimmerman. LC 82-14033. 304p. 1983. text ed. 65.00 (*0-275-91730-4*, C1730, Praeger Pubs) Greenwood.

Technologie de la Pierre de Taille. P. Noel. 376p. (FRE.). 1968. 49.95 (*0-686-56777-3*, M-6429) Fr & Eur.

*__Technologie des Fromages au Lait de Dromadaire (Camelus Dromedarius)__ 125p. (FRE.). 1993. 12.00 (*92-5-203154-5*, Pub. by FAO IT) Bernan Associates.

Technologie und Terminologie der Gewerbe und Kunste bei Griechen und Romern, 4 Vols. Hugo Blumner. Ed. by Moses Finley. LC 79-4963. (Ancient Economic History Ser.). (Illus.). (GER.). 1979. reprint ed. Set. lib. bdg. 117.95 (*0-405-12350-7*) Ayer.

Technologie und Terminologie der Gewerbe und Kunste Bei Griechen und Romern, 4 vols., Set. Hugo Blumner. xxxix, 1732p. 1969. reprint ed. write for info. (*0-318-70727-6*) G Olms Pubs.

Technologie und Terminologie der Gewerbe und Kunste bei Griechen und Romern, 4 Vols., Vol. 1. Hugo Blumner. Ed. by Moses Finley. LC 79-4963. (Ancient Economic History Ser.). (Illus.). (GER.). 1979. reprint ed. 40.95 (*0-405-12351-5*) Ayer.

Technologie und Terminologie der Gewerbe und Kunste bei Griechen und Romern, 4 Vols., Vol. 2. Hugo Blumner. Ed. by Moses Finley. LC 79-4963. (Ancient Economic History Ser.). (Illus.). (GER.). 1979. reprint ed. 40.95 (*0-405-12352-3*) Ayer.

Technologie und Terminologie der Gewerbe und Kunste bei Griechen und Romern, 4 Vols., Vol. 3. Hugo Blumner. Ed. by Moses Finley. LC 79-4963. (Ancient Economic History Ser.). (Illus.). (GER.). 1979. reprint ed. 40.95 (*0-405-12484-8*) Ayer.

Technologie und Terminologie der Gewerbe und Kunste bei Griechen und Romern, 4 Vols., Vol. 4. Hugo Blumner. Ed. by Moses Finley. LC 79-4963. (Ancient Economic History Ser.). (Illus.). (GER.). 1979. reprint ed. 40.95 (*0-405-12485-6*) Ayer.

Technologies for a Greenhouse Constrained Society. 928p. 1992. 110.00 (*0-87371-797-X*, L797) Lewis Pubs.

Technologies for Advanced Land Combat: Proceedings of a Conference Held 17-18 April, 1995, Orlando, Florida. Ed. by Gerald R. Lane et al. LC 95-9816. (Critical Reviews of Optical Science & Technology Ser.: Vol. 59). 1995. pap. 66.00 (*0-8194-1851-X*) SPIE.

Technologies for Cleaner Production & Products: Towards Technological Transformation for Sustainable Development. OECD Staff. 96p. (Orig.). 1995. pap. 30.00 (*92-64-14473-0*, Pub. by Org for Econ FR) OECD.

Technologies for Detection of DNA Damage & Mutations. Ed. by Gerd P. Pfeifer. LC 96-22324. (Illus.). 440p. (C). 1996. 95.00 (*0-306-45237-5*, Plenum Pr) Plenum.

Technologies for Economic Development. P. D. Malgavkar. (C). 1987. 18.00 (*81-204-0158-1*, Pub. by Oxford IBH II) S Asia.

Technologies for Environmental Cleanup - Soil & Groundwater: Based on the Lectures Given During the Eurocourse on Technologies for Environmental Cleanup: Soil & Groundwater Held at the Joint Research Centre, Ispra, Italy, 21-25 September 1992. Ed. by A. Avogadro. (Eurocourses: Environmental Management Ser.). 480p. (C). 1993. lib. bdg. 192.50 (*0-7923-2145-6*) Kluwer Ac.

Technologies for Environmental Cleanup Toxic & Hazardous Waste Management: Based on the Lectures Given During the Eurocourse on Technologies for Environmental Cleanup - Toxic & Hazardous Waste Management, Held at the Joint Research Centre, Ispra, Italy, September 13-17, 1993. Ed. by A. Avogadro & R. C. Ragaini. LC 94-7724. (Eurocourses: Environmental Management Ser.: Vol. 2). 268p. (C). 1994. lib. bdg. 137.50 (*0-7923-2776-4*) Kluwer Ac.

Technologies for Management of Hazardous Waste. Business Communications Co., Inc. Staff. 394p. 1992. 2,550.00 (*0-89336-827-X*, C-059R) BCC.

Technologies for Occupant Protection Assessment. (Special Publications). 154p. 1996. pap. 61.00 (*1-56091-804-7*, SP-1174) Soc Auto Engineers.

Technologies for Prehistoric & Historic Preservation. Office of Technology Assessment Staff. LC 87-3304. 210p. 1988. reprint ed. lib. bdg. 27.50 (*0-89464-219-7*) Krieger.

Technologies for Protecting the Ozone Layer: Catalogue for Flexible & Rigid Foams. 1994. 24.00 (*92-807-1430-9*) UN.

Technologies for Protecting the Ozone Layer: Catalogue for Specialized Solvent Uses. 1994. 17.00 (*92-807-1429-5*) UN.

Technologies for Rainfed Agriculture in Mediterranean Climates: A Review of World Bank Experiences. Peter A. Oram & Cornelis De Haan. LC 95-37034. (World Bank Technical Paper Ser.: No. 300). 192p. 1996. 10.95 (*0-8213-3433-6*) World Bank.

Technologies for Sustainable Agriculture in the Tropics: Proceedings of an International Symposia Sponsored by Division A-6 of the American Society of Agronomy in San Antonio, TX, & Denver, CO, 1990 & 1991 Respectively. Ed. by Gary A. Peterson et al. LC 93-21161. (Special Publications: No. 56). 1993. write for info. (*0-89118-118-0*) Am Soc Agron.

*__Technologies for Synthetic Environments: Hardware-in-the-Loop Testing II.__ Robert L. Munner. 36p. 1997. pap. 69.00 (*0-8194-2499-4*) SPIE.

Technologies for Understanding & Preventing Substance Abuse & Addiction. (Illus.). 250p. (Orig.). 1996. pap. text ed. 40.00 (*0-7881-2786-1*) DIANE Pub.

Technologies for Upgrading Existing or Designing New Drinking Water Treatment Facilities. U. S. EPA, Center for Environmental Research Information, Office of Drinking Water Staff. 209p. 1991. pap. 49.95 (*0-87762-824-6*) Technomic.

*__Technologies for Wireless Computing.__ Robert W. Brodersen. Ed. by Anantha P. Chandrakasan. LC 96-35750. 200p. (C). 1996. lib. bdg. 110.00 (*0-7923-9785-1*) Kluwer Ac.

Technologies in the Laboratory Handling of Motion Picture & Other Long Films: Proceedings: Two Day Tutorial Seminar Co-Sponsored by the Society of Motion Picture & Television Engineers. Society of Photographic Scientists & Engineers Staff. Ed. by Frank P. Clark. LC 79-24494. 232p. reprint ed. pap. 66.20 (*0-317-42051-8*, 2025701) Bks Demand.

Technologies in Vascular Surgery. Yao. 1991. text ed. 172.00 (*0-7216-4429-5*) Saunders.

Technologies of Control: The New Interactive Media for the Home. Kevin G. Wilson. LC 87-40378. (Studies in Communication & Society). 208p. (C). 1988. text ed. 37.50 (*0-299-11370-1*); pap. text ed. 15.25 (*0-299-11374-4*) U of Wis Pr.

Technologies of Freedom. Ithiel de Sola Pool. 312p. 1984. pap. 15.95 (*0-674-87233-9*) Belknap Pr.

Technologies of Gender: Essays on Theory, Film & Fiction. Teresa De Lauretis. LC 86-46317. (Theories of Representation & Difference Ser.). 166p. 1987. 27.50 (*0-253-35853-1*); pap. 9.95 (*0-253-20441-0*, MB-441) Ind U Pr.

Technologies of Light. Ed. by E. U. Kotte et al. (Illus.). ix, 144p. 1988. 72.95 (*0-387-50458-3*) Spr-Verlag.

Technologies of Manned Space Systems. A. C. Bond & M. A. Faget. 122p. 1965. text ed. 194.00 (*0-677-01250-0*) Gordon & Breach.

Technologies of Power. Majid Tehranian. Ed. by Brenda Dervin. LC 89-18080. (Communication & Information Science Ser.). 272p. (C). 1990. pap. 39.50 (*0-89391-634-X*); text ed. 73.25 (*0-89391-280-8*) Ablex Pub.

*__Technologies of Seeing: Photography, Cinematography & Television.__ Brian Winston. (Distributed for the British Film Institute Ser.). 176p. 1996. 49.95 (*0-85170-601-0*, Pub. by British Film Inst UK); pap. 24.95 (*0-85170-602-9*, Pub. by British Film Inst UK) Ind U Pr.

Technologies of the Gendered Body: Reading Cyborg Women. Anne Balsamo. LC 95-22648. (Illus.). 232p. 1995. text ed. 49.95 (*0-8223-1686-2*); pap. text ed. 17.95 (*0-8223-1698-6*) Duke.

Technologies of the Self: A Seminar with Michel Foucault. Ed. by Luther H. Martin et al. LC 87-10756. 176p. (Orig.). (C). 1988. pap. 13.95 (*0-87023-593-1*) U of Mass Pr.

Technologies Related to Participatory Forestry in Tropical & Subtropical Countries. Eric Tamale et al. (Technical Paper Ser.: No. 299). 64p. 1996. 7.95 (*0-8213-3399-2*, 13999) World Bank.

Technologies to Sustain Tropical Forest Resources & Biological Diversity. 1992. lib. bdg. 255.95 (*0-8490-5617-9*) Gordon Pr.

Technologies Underlying Weapons of Mass Destruction. 1994. lib. bdg. 256.95 (*0-8490-5799-X*) Gordon Pr.

Technologies Without Boundaries: On Telecommunications in a Global Age. Ithiel De Sola Pool. 352p. 1990. text ed. 33.95 (*0-674-87263-0*) HUP.

Technologisches Woerterbuch. Egon Von Bahder. (GER & RUS.). 1970. 135.00 (*0-8288-6555-8*, M-7656) Fr & Eur.

Technologisches Woerterbuch Franzoisisch. Martin Pabst. 550p. (FRE & GER.). 1971. 175.00 (*0-8288-6482-9*, M-7662) Fr & Eur.

Technologisches Woerterbuch Franzoisisch. 3rd deluxe ed. Kurt Stellhorn. (FRE & GER.). 1965. 86.00 (*0-8288-6755-0*, M-7660) Fr & Eur.

Technologisches Woerterbuch Spanisch. deluxe ed. Werner Hacke. 564p. (GER & SPA.). 1967. 160.00 (*0-8288-6692-9*, M-7664) Fr & Eur.

Technology. (Library of Science). (Illus.). 112p. (J). (gr. 4-9). 1989. 18.95 (*1-85435-073-0*) Marshall Cavendish.

Technology. Roger Bridgman. LC 94-34859. (Eyewitness Science Ser.). (Illus.). 64p. (J). (gr. 3 up). 1995. 15.95 (*1-56458-883-1*) DK Pub Inc.

Technology. Donald Cardwell. 1994. pap. 18.95 (*0-393-31192-9*) Norton.

Technology. Neil Postman. 1992. 21.00 (*0-685-51846-9*) Knopf.

Technology. Brad Thode & Terry Thode. LC 92-23972. 435p. 1993. text ed. 36.95 (*0-8273-5098-8*) S-W Pub.

Technology. Brad Thode & Terry Thode. 1993. pap. 152.95 (*0-8273-6401-6*) S-W Pub.

Technology. annot. ed. Susan K. Baumann. Date not set. teacher ed., text ed. write for info. (*0-314-09713-9*) West Pub.

Technology. annot. ed. Brad Thode & Terry Thode. 435p. 1994. teacher ed., text ed. 34.95 (*0-8273-5516-5*) S-W Pub.

*__Technology.__ 2nd ed. Brad Thode. Date not set. text ed. 35.95 (*0-538-67624-8*) S-W Pub.

Technology: A Reign of Benevolence & Destruction. Ed. by Fred A. Olsen. LC 73-16385. 1974. 29.50 (*0-8422-5130-8*) Irvington.

*__Technology: Creating High Impact Learning Environments.__ Mercedes Fisher. 232p. (C). 1996. per., pap. text ed. 27.30 (*0-7872-2567-3*) Kendall-Hunt.

Technology: Philosophical & Social Aspects. Joseph Agassi. 288p. 1985. lib. bdg. 122.00 (*90-277-2044-4*, D Reidel) Kluwer Ac.

Technology: Report of the Project 2061 Phase I Technology Panel. James R. Johnson. 32p. 1989. 7.50 (*0-87168-347-4*, 89-06S) AAAS.

T

An Asterisk (*) at the beginning of an entry indicates that the title is appearing in BIP for the first time.

Technology: Shaping Our World. John Gradwell et al. LC 95-12533. 281p. 1996. 33.28 (*1-56637-217-8*) Goodheart.

***Technology: Teacher's Resource Guide.** 2nd ed. Brad Thode. Date not set. teacher ed., text ed. 79.95 (*0-538-67640-X*) S-W Pub.

Technology: The Law of Exploitation & Transfer. Mark S. Anderson. 1995. boxed write for info. (*0-406-01304-7*, UK) MICHIE.

Technology Vol. 4: (Incl. 1993-1994 Supplement) Ed. by Eleanor C. Goldstein. (Resources Ser.). 1995. suppl. ed. 76.00 (*0-89777-182-6*) Sirs Inc.

Technology see Ideas & Investigations in Science: Physical Science

Technology - Systems Approach. J. Myerson. (C). 1989. 60. 00 (*0-09-173089-9*, Pub. by S Thornes Pubs UK) St Mut.

Technology Absorption in Indian Industry. Ashok V. Desai. (C). 1988. pap. 21.00 (*81-224-0051-5*) S Asia.

Technology Acquisition under Alternative Arrangements with Transnational Corporations: Selected Industrial Case Studies in Thailand. (UNCTC Current Studies A: No. 6). 55p. 1987. 7.50 (*92-1-104208-9*, E.87.II.A.14) UN.

***Technology Across the Curriculum: Activities & Ideas.** Marilyn J. Bazeli & James L. Heintz. LC 96-45459. 190p. 1997. teacher ed., lib. bdg. 24.50 (*1-56308-444-9*) Libs Unl.

Technology Activities. Harms. (Tech & Industrial Education Ser.). 1988. teacher ed., pap. 15.00 (*0-8273-3241-6*) Delmar.

Technology Activity Guide (for LWT) Hacker. (Tech & Industrial Education Ser.). 1992. pap. 10.95 (*0-8273-5142-9*) Delmar.

Technology Advisory Council: A Vehicle for Improving Our Schools. Tackett Austin et al. (Illus.). 152p. 1993. pap. text ed. 17.95 (*1-56484-026-3*) Intl Society Tech Educ.

Technology Against Terrorism: Structuring Security. (Illus.). 142p. (Orig.). (C). 1994. pap. text ed. 40.00 (*0-7881-0389-X*) DIANE Pub.

Technology Against Terrorism: The Federal Effort. (Illus.). 106p. (Orig.). (C). 1992. pap. text ed. 30.00 (*0-941375-57-9*) DIANE Pub.

Technology Age Classroom. Terence R. Cannings & LeRoy Finkel. LC 92-22963. 1992. 35.95 (*0-938661-44-2*) Franklin Beedle.

Technology & Adult Learning: A Selected Bibliography. Adele F. Bane & Amy C. Lear. LC 93-38477. (Educational Technology Selected Bibliography Ser.: Vol. 11). 55p. 1994. pap. 24.95 (*0-87778-273-3*) Educ Tech Pubns.

Technology & Aging in America. 1991. lib. bdg. 79.95 (*0-8490-4943-1*) Gordon Pr.

Technology & Aging in America: Health, Life Science, Employment, Housing, Public Service & International Aspects. 1991. lib. bdg. 75.95 (*0-8490-4973-3*) Gordon Pr.

Technology & Agricultural Development in Pre-War Japan. Penelope Francks. LC 82-20306. 352p. 1984. 55.00 (*0-300-02927-6*) Yale U Pr.

Technology & American Competitiveness. Ed. by Dianne Rahm & W. Henry Lambright. (Orig.). 1989. pap. 15.00 (*0-944285-12-0*) Pol Studies.

Technology & American Economic Growth. Nathan Rosenberg. LC 76-52621. 214p. (C). 1977. reprint ed. pap. text ed. 22.95 (*0-87332-104-9*) M E Sharpe.

***Technology & American History.** Stephen H. Cutcliffe & Terry S. Reynolds. LC 97-5925. 1997. pap. text ed. 18. 95 (*0-226-71028-9*); lib. bdg. 35.00 (*0-226-71027-0*) U Ch Pr.

Technology & American Society: A History. Gary Cross & Rick Szostak. LC 94-5332. 352p. 1994. pap. text ed. 31. 40 (*0-13-898644-4*) P-H.

Technology & Applications of Closed-Cell Foams (Seminar Notes) 150p. 1989. ring bd. 99.95 (*0-87762-737-1*) Technomic.

***Technology & Applications of Single-Electron Tunneling Devices.** Erick H. Visscher. (Illus.). vi, 90p. (Orig.). 1996. pap. 44.50 (*90-407-1381-2*, Pub. by Delft U Pr NE) Coronet Bks.

Technology & Applied Sciences Dictionary Vol. 2: German - English. 5th ed. Rudolf Walther. 1056p. (ENG & GER.). 1992. 250.00 (*0-8288-0636-5*, M7593) Fr & Eur.

Technology & Assessment of Safety-Critical Systems: Proceedings of the Second Safety-Critical Systems Symposium, Birmingham, UK, 8-10 February 1994. Ed. by Felix Redmill & Tom Anderson. LC 93-50853. 1994. 78.95 (*0-387-19859-8*) Spr-Verlag.

Technology & Biochemistry of Wine, 2 vols. J. Farkas. 744p. 1988. text ed. 418.00 (*2-88124-070-4*) Gordon & Breach.

Technology & Capital Formation. Ed. by Dale W. Jorgenson & Ralph Landau. 544p. 1989. 47.50 (*0-262-10039-8*) MIT Pr.

Technology & Chapter One Solutions for Catholic School Participation Considerations. Ed. by Frederick H. Brigham, Jr. 28p. 1993. pap. text ed. 9.30 (*1-55833-099-2*) Natl Cath Educ.

Technology & Choice: Readings from Technology & Culture. Ed. by Marcel C. LaFollette & Jeffrey K. Stine. (Illus.). 352p. 1991. pap. 19.50 (*0-226-46777-5*) U Ch Pr.

Technology & Choice: Readings from Technology & Culture. Ed. by Marcel C. LaFollette & Jeffrey K. Stine. (Illus.). 352p. 1991. lib. bdg. 40.50 (*0-226-46776-7*) U Ch Pr.

Technology & Civility: The Skill Revolution in Politics. Heinz Eulau. LC 76-48483. (Publication Ser.: No. 167). 1977. pap. 5.95 (*0-8179-6672-2*) Hoover Inst Pr.

Technology & Competition in the Brazilian Computer Industry. Paulo B. Tigre. LC 82-21487. 250p. 1983. text ed. 35.00 (*0-312-78787-1*) St Martin.

Technology & Competition in the International Telecommunications Industry. David Charles et al. 200p. 1992. 54.00 (*0-86187-993-7*) St Martin.

Technology & Competitiveness: The Case of Brazilian & Indian Machine Tools. Jan P. Wogart et al. LC 93-7508. (Illus.). 156p. (C). 1993. 32.00 (*0-8039-9120-7*) Sage.

Technology & Contemporary Life. Ed. by Paul T. Durbin. 328p. (C). 1987. pap. text ed. 56.50 (*90-277-2571-3*, D Reidel); lib. bdg. 139.00 (*90-277-2570-5*, D Reidel) Kluwer Ac.

Technology & Copyright: Annotated Bibliography & Source Materials. Ed. by George P. Bush. LC 72-87129. 454p. 1972. 28.50 (*0-912338-03-2*); pap. 14.50 (*0-685-03093-8*); fiche 9.50 (*0-912338-04-0*) Lomond.

Technology & Copyright: Sources & Materials. rev. ed. Ed. by George P. Bush & Robert Dreyfuss. 552p. 1979. fiche 15.50 (*0-912338-18-0*) Lomond.

Technology & Copyright: Sources & Materials. 2nd rev. ed. Ed. by George P. Bush & Robert Dreyfuss. 552p. 1979. 32.50 (*0-912338-17-2*) Lomond.

Technology & Copyright Law: A Guidebook for the Library, Research, & Teaching Professions. Arlene Bielefield & Lawrence Cheeseman. LC 96-48255. 213p. 1997. pap. 49.95 (*1-55570-267-8*) Neal-Schuman.

Technology & Creativity. Subrata Dasgupta. (Illus.). 256p. 1996. 25.00 (*0-19-509688-6*) OUP.

Technology & Culture: A Historical Romance. Barry M. Katz. (Portable Stanford Bks.). 156p. (Orig.). 1990. pap. 12.95 (*0-916318-45-1*) Stanford Alumni Assn.

Technology & Developing Countries. Ed. by Richard Heeks. 306p. 1995. 39.50 (*0-7146-4613-X*, Pub. by F Cass Pubs UK); pap. 22.50 (*0-7146-4139-1*, Pub. by F Cass Pubs UK) Intl Spec Bk.

Technology & Developing Country Agriculture: The Impact of Economic Reform. OECD Staff. 136p. (Orig.). 1993. pap. 24.00 (*92-64-13931-1*) OECD.

Technology & Developing Economics: The Impact of Eastern European vs Western Technology Transfer. Zeinab A. Karake. LC 89-36698. 144p. 1990. text ed. 49.95 (*0-275-93431-4*, C3431, Praeger Pubs) Greenwood.

Technology & Development. Ed. by Konenigsber. 332p. 1981. pap. 39.00 (*0-08-028146-X*, Pergamon Pr) Elsevier.

Technology & Development in the Third Industrial Revolution. Ed. by Charles Cooper & Raphael Kaplinsky. 113p. 1990. text ed. 35.00 (*0-7146-3389-5*, Pub. by F Cass Pubs UK) Intl Spec Bk.

Technology & Development Public Policy & Managerial Issues. Dhirendra K. Vajpeyi. (C). 1991. 29.50 (*0-685-50010-1*, Pub. by Rawat II) S Asia.

Technology & Economic Crises: A Special Issue of the Journal History & Technology, Vol. 1, Nos. 3-4. D. Woronoff & J. C. Guedon. 100p. 1984. pap. text ed. 47. 00 (*3-7186-0286-5*) Gordon & Breach.

Technology & Economic Development. Ed. by Robert McGowan & Edward J. Ottensmeyer. 192p. (Orig.). 1987. pap. 15.00 (*0-918592-91-7*) Pol Studies.

***Technology & Economic Development.** 2nd ed. Edward J. Malecki. (C). 1997. pap. text ed. 23.95 (*0-582-27723-X*, Pub. by Longman UK) Longman.

Technology & Economic Development: The Dynamics of Local, Regional & National Change. Edward J. Malecki. (C). 1991. pap. text ed. 54.50 (*0-582-01758-0*) Addison-Wesley.

Technology & Economic Performance: Organizing the Executive Branch for a Stronger National Technology Base. Carnegie Commission on Science, Technology, & Government Staff & B. R. Inman. 58p. 1993. reprint ed. pap. write for info. (*1-881054-15-2*) Carnegie Comm Sci.

Technology & Economics. National Academy of Engineering Staff. 140p. 1991. pap. text ed. 19.00 (*0-309-04397-2*) Natl Acad Pr.

Technology & Education: Articles from Educational Technology Magazine. Ed. by Lawrence Lipsitz. LC 79-125873. 192p. 1971. 29.95 (*0-87778-011-0*) Educ Tech Pubns.

Technology & Education: Policy Implementation - Evaluation. LC 81-81832. 372p. 1981. 20.00 (*0-317-36894-X*); 18.00 (*0-317-36895-8*) Assn Ed Comm Tech.

Technology & Education: Policy, Implementation, Evaluation-Proceedings of the National Conference on Technology & Education, January 26-28, 1981. National Conference on Technology & Education Staff. 340p. 1981. lib. bdg. 20.00 (*0-318-03015-2*) Inst Educ Lead.

Technology & Education Reform: The Reality Behind the Promise. Ed. by Barbara Means. LC 93-45336. (Education Ser.). 256p. text ed. 29.95 (*1-55542-625-5*) Jossey-Bass.

***Technology & Employment: Innovation & Growth in the U. S. Economy.** Ed. by Richard M. Cyert & David C. Mowery. LC 87-42807. (Illus.). 239p. 1987. reprint ed. pap. 68.20 (*0-608-04257-9*, 2065012) Bks Demand.

Technology & Employment Effects: Interim Report. National Research Council (U. S.), Panel on Alternative Policies Affecting the Prevention of Alcohol Abuse & Alcoholism Staff. 160p. reprint ed. pap. 45.60 (*0-8357-7687-5*, 2036038) Bks Demand.

Technology & Employment in Footwear Manufacturing: A Study Prepared for the International Labour Office Within the Framework of the World Employment Programme. Gerard K. Boon. LC 80-50458. 232p. 1980. lib. bdg. 91.00 (*90-286-0170-8*) Kluwer Ac.

Technology & Employment in Industry: A Case Study Approach. enl. rev. ed. Amartya K. Sen. xviii, 436p. 1985. 40.50 (*92-2-103969-2*) Intl Labour Office.

Technology & Employment in Industry: A Case Study Approach. 3rd enl. rev. ed. Amartya K. Sen. xviii, 436p. 1985. pap. 33.75 (*92-2-103970-6*) Intl Labour Office.

Technology & Enterprise Development: Ghana under Structural Adjustment. Sanjaya Lall et al. LC 93-47038. 1994. text ed. 75.00 (*0-312-12149-0*) St Martin.

Technology & Environment. National Academy of Engineering Staff. Ed. by Jesse H. Ausubel & Hedy E. Slodevich. 236p. (C). 1991. pap. text ed. 25.95 (*0-309-04426-X*) Natl Acad Pr.

***Technology & Equipment Suppliers, 1995.** (Telecom Power-2000 Ser.: Vol. 2). 1995. 2,495.00 (*0-614-18333-2*, IGIC-88) Info Gatekeepers.

Technology & European Overseas Enterprise: Diffusion, Adaption & Adoption. Ed. by Michael Adas. LC 95-44267. (Expanding World Ser.: Vol. 7). 464p. 1996. 134. 95 (*0-86078-525-4*, Pub. by Variorum UK) Ashgate Pub Co.

***Technology & Gender: Fabrics of Power in Late Imperial China.** Francesca Bray. LC 96-28828. (Illus.). 1997. 50. 00 (*0-520-20685-1*); pap. 19.95 (*0-520-20861-7*) U CA Pr.

Technology & Global Competition: The Challenge for Newly Industrialising Economies. Dieter Ernst & David O'Connor. Ed. by OECD Staff. (Development Centre Studies). 172p. (Orig.). 1989. pap. 21.00 (*92-64-13279-1*) OECD.

Technology & Governance in the 1990s: Proceedings. 55p. (Orig.). (C). 1993. pap. text ed. 20.00 (*0-7881-0048-3*) DIANE Pub.

Technology & Health Care in an Era of Limits. Institute of Medicine Staff. Ed. by Annetine C. Gelijns. LC 92-22704. (Medical Innovation at the Crossroads Ser.: Vol. 3). 296p. (Orig.). (C). 1992. pap. text ed. 36.00 (*0-309-04695-5*) Natl Acad Pr.

***Technology & Higher Education.** Ed. by Linda Enghagen. (Excellence in the Academy Ser.). 208p. (Orig.). 1997. pap. 19.95 (*0-8106-2682-9*, 2682-9) NEA.

Technology & Human Communication. Ed. by Noel Williams & Peter Hartley. 1991. text ed. 57.50 (*0-86187-766-7*) St Martin.

Technology & Human Fulfillment. George W. Thompson, Jr. LC 85-6039. (Orig.). 1985. pap. text ed. 22.00 (*0-8191-4679-X*) U Pr of Amer.

Technology & Human Productivity: Challenges for the Future. Ed. by John W. Murphy & John T. Pardeck. LC 85-23237. 256p. 1986. text ed. 59.95 (*0-89930-194-0*, PTH/, Quorum Bks) Greenwood.

Technology & Human Service Delivery: Challenges & a Critical Perspective. Ed. by John T. Pardeck. LC 88-2794. (Computers in Human Services Ser.: Vol. 3, Nos. 1-2). (Illus.). 161p. 1988. text ed. 39.95 (*0-86656-731-3*) Haworth Pr.

Technology & Human Values in American Civilization: A Guide to Information Sources. Ed. by Stephen H. Cutcliffe et al. (American Government & History Information Guide Ser.: Vol. 9). 728p. 1980. 68.00 (*0-8103-1475-4*) Gale.

Technology & Humanism: Some Exploratory Essays for Our Times. William G. Carleton. LC 70-112601. 300p. 1970. 24.95 (*0-8265-1154-6*) Vanderbilt U Pr.

Technology & Industrial Development in Japan: Building Capabilities by Learning, Innovation & Public Policy. Hiroyuki Odagiri & Akira Goto. LC 96-571. (Japan Business & Economics Ser.). (Illus.). 328p. 1996. 75.00 (*0-19-828802-6*, Clarendon Pr) OUP.

Technology & Industrial Growth in Pre-War Japan: The Mitsubishi Nagasaki Shipyard 1884-1934. Yukiko Fukasaku. LC 91-46065. (Nissan Institute Japanese Studies). 208p. (C). 1992. text ed. 69.95 (*0-415-06552-6*, A7519) Routledge.

***Technology & Industrial Performance: Technology Diffusion, Productivity, Employment & Skills, International Competitiveness.** OECD Staff. 200p. (Orig.). 1997. pap. 50.00 (*92-64-15355-1*, 92-96-10-1, Pub. by Org for Econ FR) OECD.

Technology & Industrial Progress: The Foundations of Economic Growth. G. N. Von Tunzelmann. LC 95-10745. 560p. 1995. 95.00 (*1-85898-174-3*) E Elgar.

Technology & Industry. Ed. by Jan Hult & Bengt Nystrom. LC 92-13610. 1992. 40.00 (*0-88135-151-2*, Sci Hist); pap. 15.00 (*0-88135-150-4*, Sci Hist) Watson Pub Intl.

Technology & Infertility: Clinical Psychosocial, Legal, & Ethical Aspects. Machelle M. Seibel. (Illus.). 440p. 1993. 80.00 (*0-387-97793-7*) Spr-Verlag.

Technology & Information Services: Challenges for the 1990s. Carol L. Anderson & Robert Hauptman. LC 92-40228. (Information Management, Policies & Services Ser.). 242p. 1993. pap. 39.50 (*1-56750-021-8*); text ed. 73.25 (*1-56750-020-X*) Ablex Pub.

Technology & Information Transfer: A Survey of Practice in Industrial Organizations. Richard S. Rosenbloom & Francis W. Wolek. LC 70-119550. 190p. reprint ed. pap. 54.20 (*0-317-10820-4*, 2002225) Bks Demand.

***Technology & Infrastructure: Brighton, U. K.** 150.00 (*0-614-26564-9*, E95TAI) Info Gatekeepers.

Technology & Innovation in the International Economy. Ed. by Charles Cooper. 256p. 1994. 75.00 (*1-85898-027-5*) E Elgar.

Technology & Institutional Response: Papers Presented to a Joint Session of the American Military Institute at the Duquesne History Forum, Pittsburgh, Pennsylvania, 1 November 1972. 132p. 1975. pap. text ed. 24.95 (*0-89126-007-2*) MA-AH Pub.

Technology & International Affairs. Joseph S. Szyliowicz. LC 81-13985. 302p. 1981. text ed. 65.00 (*0-275-90727-9*, C0727, Praeger Pubs) Greenwood.

Technology & International Relations. Ed. by Otto Hieronymi. 200p. 1987. text ed. 39.95 (*0-312-78933-5*) St Martin.

Technology & International Trade. Ed. by Jan Fagerberg et al. LC 96-26477. 256p. 1997. 80.00 (*1-85898-528-5*) E Elgar.

Technology & Investment: Crucial Issues for the 1990s. Enrico Delaco & Erik Hornell. 1991. text ed. 59.00 (*0-86187-170-7*) St Martin.

Technology & Investment: The Prewar Japanese Chemical Industry. Barbara Molony. LC 89-48815. (East Asian Monographs: No. 145). 396p. 1990. 32.00 (*0-674-87260-6*) HUP.

Technology & Justice. George P. Grant. LC 86-51455. 144p. 1986. pap. 10.50 (*0-268-01863-4*) U of Notre Dame Pr.

Technology & Labor: Study of the Human Problems of Labor Saving. Elliot D. Smith & Richmond C. Nyman. Ed. by Leon Stein. LC 77-70533. 1977. reprint ed. lib. bdg. 26.95 (*0-405-10201-1*) Ayer.

Technology & Language Testing. Ed. by Charles W. Stansfield. 188p. 1986. pap. 12.50 (*0-939791-08-0*) Tchrs Eng Spkrs.

Technology & Management. Ed. by Ray Wild. 288p. 1990. 36.95 (*0-89397-363-7*) Nichols Pub.

***Technology & Management in Library & Information Services.** F. W. Lancaster & Beth Sandore. 1997. 39.50 (*0-87845-099-8*) U of Ill Grad Sch.

Technology & Manufacture of Ammonia. Samuel Strelzoff. LC 87-21385. 308p. (C). 1988. reprint ed. lib. bdg. 99.50 (*0-89464-250-2*) Krieger.

Technology & Material Life of Central India: (From Chalcolithic Period to Mauryan Period) R. A. Sharma. (C). 1991. text ed. 90.00 (*0-8364-2806-4*, Pub. by Agam Kala Prakashan) S Asia.

Technology & Media: Instructional Applications. Fred A. Teague et al. 352p. (C). 1995. spiral bd. 34.59 (*0-8403-8438-6*) Kendall-Hunt.

Technology & Music Teaching & Learning. Robin S. Stevens. 74p. 1994. 40.00 (*0-7300-1794-X*, Pub. by Deakin Univ AT) St Mut.

Technology & National Competitiveness: Oligopoly, Technological Innovation, & International Competition. Ed. by Jorge Niosi. 304p. (C). 1991. pap. text ed. 24.95 (*0-7735-0859-7*, Pub. by McGill CN) U of Toronto Pr.

Technology & Operations Management. Bowen et al. (GF - Production & Operations Management Ser.). Date not set. text ed. 49.95 (*0-538-85577-0*) S-W Pub.

Technology & Organizations. Lee S. Sproull & Assoc. Staff et al. LC 89-26993. (Management Ser.). 303p. text ed. 32.95 (*1-55542-209-8*) Jossey-Bass.

Technology & Physics of Molecular Beam Epitaxy. Ed. by M. G. Dowsett & E. H. Parker. 680p. 1985. 140.00 (*0-306-41860-6*, Plenum Pr) Plenum.

Technology & Planned Organizational Change. James C. Taylor. LC 78-161549. 151p. 1971. 12.00 (*0-87944-003-1*) Inst Soc Res.

Technology & Politics. Ed. by Michael E. Kraft & Norman J. Vig. LC 88-3841. xv, 358p. (C). 1988. text ed. 65.95 (*0-8223-0838-X*); pap. text ed. 23.95 (*0-8223-0846-0*) Duke.

Technology & Power. 1989. 53.95 (*0-387-97082-7*) Spr-Verlag.

Technology & Power in the Early American Cotton Industry: James Montgomery, the Second Edition of His "Cotton Manufacture" (1840) & the 'Justitia' Controversy about Relative Power Costs. David J. Jeremy. LC 87-73044. (Memoirs Ser.: Vol. 189). (Illus.). 400p. (C). 1990. 38.00 (*0-87169-189-2*, M189-JED) Am Philos.

***Technology & Privacy.** Philip E. Agre & Marc Rotenberg. (Illus.). 280p. 1997. pap. 25.00 (*0-262-01162-X*) MIT Pr.

Technology & Productivity: The Challenge for Economic Policy. OECD Staff. 588p. (Orig.). 1991. pap. 129.00 (*92-64-13549-9*) OECD.

***Technology & Public Policy: Meeting Society's 21st Century Needs.** unabridged ed. John Diebold. (Papers & Speeches of John Diebold: Vol. 7). (Illus.). 192p. (Orig.). 1997. pap. 12.95 (*0-9658066-0-X*) Mngmnt Science.

Technology & Responsibility. Ed. by Paul T. Durbin. (Philosophy & Technology Ser.: No. 3). 404p. (C). 1987. lib. bdg. 139.00 (*90-277-2415-6*, D Reidel) Kluwer Ac.

Technology & Responsibility. Ed. by Paul T. Durbin. (Philosophy & Technology Ser.: No. 3). 404p. 1989. pap. text ed. 55.00 (*90-277-2416-4*) Kluwer Ac.

Technology & Responsibility: Essays Presented on the Occasion of the Centenary of the College of Engineering & Applied Science, University of Colorado, Boulder. Ed. by Athanasios Moulakis. LC 93-61149. (Illus.). 155p. 1993. 17.00 (*0-918714-39-7*) Intl Res Ctr Energy.

Technology & Science in Industrializing Nations 1500-1914. Eric D. Brose. (Control of Nature Ser.). (C). 1997. 39. 95 (*0-391-03973-3*); pap. 12.50 (*0-391-03974-1*) Humanities.

Technology & Sector Choice in Economic Development. Gerard K. Boon. 324p. 1978. lib. bdg. 80.50 (*90-286-0068-X*) Kluwer Ac.

Technology & Social Change. 2nd ed. Ed. by H. Russell Bernard & Pertti J. Pelto. (Illus.). 393p. 1987. pap. text ed. 15.95 (*0-88133-261-5*) Waveland Pr.

Technology & Social Complexity. Maurice N. Richter, Jr. LC 82-5683. 120p. 1983. text ed. 64.50 (*0-87395-644-3*); pap. text ed. 21.95 (*0-87395-645-1*) State U NY Pr.

Technology & Social Progress. Ed. by Philip K. Eckman. (Science & Technology Ser.: Vol. 18). (Illus.). 1969. 20. 00 (*0-87703-046-4*) Univelt Inc.

Technology & Society, 53 bks. Ed. by Daniel J. Boorstin. 1972. reprint ed. Set. 1,502.50 (*0-405-04680-4*) Ayer.

Technology & Society in Twentieth Century America: An Anthology. Randall E. Stross. 273p. (C). 1989. pap. 29. 95 (*0-534-10927-6*) Wadsworth Pub.

Technology & Strategic Forces. Brent Scowcroft. (CISA Working Papers: No. 54). 27p. (Orig.). 1986. pap. 15.00 (*0-86682-069-8*) Ctr Intl Relations.

Technology & Strategy: Conceptual Models & Diagnostics. Richard A. Goodman & Michael W. Lawless. (Illus.). 368p. 1994. 39.95 (*0-19-507949-3*) OUP.

Technology & Structural Unemployment: Reemploying Displaced Adults. 1992. lib. bdg. 288.95 (*0-8490-5480-X*) Gordon Pr.

Technology & Teacher: Education Annual, 1992. Ed. by Regan Carey et al. (Illus.). 656p. (Orig.). 1992. pap. 45.00 (*1-880094-03-7*) Assn Advan Comput Educ.

Technology & Teacher Education Annual 1991. Ed. by Regan Carey et al. (Illus.). 372p. (Orig.). 1991. pap. 45.00 (*1-880094-00-2*) Assn Advan Comput Educ.

Technology & Teacher Education Annual 1993. Ed. by Regan Carey et al. (Illus.). 756p. (Orig.). 1993. teacher ed., spiral bd. 45.00 (*1-880094-05-3*) Assn Advan Comput Educ.

Technology & Teacher Education Annual 1994. Ed. by Jerry Willis et al. (Illus.). 812p. (Orig.). 1994. teacher ed., pap. 45.00 (*1-880094-11-8*) Assn Advan Comput Educ.

***Technology & Teaching.** Ed. by Les Lloyd. LC 96-45083. 366p. 1997. 42.50 (*1-57387-014-5*) Info Today Inc.

Technology & Teaching: Class Studies on the Use of Computers, Networks, & Multimedia in the Classroom. Ed. by Les Lloyd. (Supplement to Computers in Libraries Ser.: No. 62). Orig. Title: Integrating Technology into the Curriculum. 200p. 1995. pap. 49.50 (*0-88736-867-0*) Info Today Inc.

Technology & Terrorism. Ed. by Paul Wilkinson. LC 93-28481. (Illus.). 153p. 1994. text ed. 37.50 (*0-7146-4552-4*, Pub. by F Cass Pubs UK) Intl Spec Bk.

Technology & the American Economic Transition: Choices for the Future. (Orig.). 1992. lib. bdg. 250.00 (*0-8490-8787-2*) Gordon Pr.

Technology & the Character of Contemporary Life: A Philosophical Inquiry. Albert Borgmann. LC 84-8639. viii, 312p. 1987. pap. text ed. 17.95 (*0-226-06629-0*) U Ch Pr.

Technology & the Civil Future in Space. Ed. by Leonard A. Harris. LC 57-43769. (Science & Technology Ser.: Vol. 73). (Illus.). 246p. 1989. pap. text ed. 35.00 (*0-87703-302-1*); lib. bdg. 50.00 (*0-87703-301-3*) Univelt Inc.

Technology & the Dynamics of Specialization in Open Economies. Michael Stolpe. (C). 1996. 82.50 (*0-472-10763-1*) U of Mich Pr.

Technology & the Economy: The Key Relationships - TEP Programme. OECD Staff. 328p. (Orig.). 1992. pap. 60.00 (*92-64-13622-3*) OECD.

Technology & the Future. 6th ed. Ed. by Albert H. Teich. LC 92-50024. 385p. (C). 1992. pap. text ed. 18.00 (*0-312-06747-X*) St Martin.

***Technology & the Future.** 7th ed. Albert H. Teich. 1996. pap. text ed. 20.00 (*0-312-11612-8*) St Martin.

Technology & the Future of Europe: Competition & the Global Environment in the 1990s. Ed. by Christopher Freeman et al. 508p. 1992. text ed. 69.00 (*0-86187-075-1*) St Martin.

Technology & the Future of Schooling in America. Ed. by Stephen T. Kerr. (Ninety-Fifth Yearbook of the National Society for the Study of Education Ser.: Pt. 2). 275p. 1996. 28.00 (*0-226-43193-2*) U Ch Pr.

Technology & the Future of Work. Ed. by Paul S. Adler. (Illus.). 352p. 1992. 45.00 (*0-19-507171-9*) OUP.

Technology & the Future Strategic Environment. Kenneth B. Moss. 194p. 1992. pap. text ed. 18.75 (*0-943875-24-2*) W Wilson Ctr Pr.

Technology & the Healing of the Earth. Thomas Berry. (Teilhard Studies: No. 14). 1985. 3.50 (*0-89012-043-9*) Am Teilhard.

***Technology & the Hospitality Industry.** Williams & Karen Hall. (C). 1997. pap. text ed. 19.95 (*0-13-634296-5*) P-H.

Technology & the Human Prospect. Macleod. (C). 1992. text ed. 59.00 (*0-86187-530-3*) St Martin.

Technology & the Lifeworld: From Garden to Earth. Don Ihde. LC 89-45472. (Indiana Series in the Philosophy of Technology). (Illus.). 240p. 1990. 35.00 (*0-253-32900-0*); pap. 15.95 (*0-253-20560-3*, MB-560) Ind U Pr.

***Technology & the New Diplomacy: The Creation & Control of EC Industrial Policy for Semiconductors.** Thomas C. Lawton. (Illus.). 292p. 1997. text ed. 68.95 (*1-85972-523-6*, Pub. by Ashgate UK) Ashgate Pub Co.

Technology & the Organisation of Work. C. R. Littler. 1992. pap. 45.00 (*0-7300-1309-X*, Pub. by Deakin Univ AT) St Mut.

Technology & the Politics of Knowledge. Ed. by Andrew Feenberg & Alastair Hannay. LC 94-27789. (Philosophy of Technology Ser.). 304p. 1995. pap. 15.95 (*0-253-20940-4*) Ind U Pr.

Technology & the Politics of Knowledge. Ed. by Andrew Feenberg & Alastair Hannay. LC 94-27789. (Philosophy of Technology Ser.). 1995. 35.00 (*0-253-32154-9*) Ind U Pr.

Technology & the Proliferation of Nuclear Weapons. Richard Kokoski. (SIPRI Publication). 384p. 1996. 55.00 (*0-19-829170-1*) OUP.

Technology & the Pursuit of Economic Growth. David C. Mowery & Nathan Rosenberg. 338p. (C). 1989. text ed. 54.95 (*0-521-38033-2*) Cambridge U Pr.

Technology & the Pursuit of Economic Growth. David C. Mowery & Nathan Rosenberg. 352p. (C). 1991. pap. text ed. 18.95 (*0-521-38936-4*) Cambridge U Pr.

Technology & the Raj: Western Technology & Technical Transfers to India, 1700-1947. Ed. by Roy MacLeod & Deepak Kumar. (Theory, Culture & Society Ser.: Vol. 31). 340p. (C). 1995. 32.00 (*0-8039-9237-8*) AltaMira Pr.

Technology & the Rise of the Networked City in Europe & America. Ed. by Joel A. Tarr & Gabriel Dupuy. LC 87-27787. (Technology & Urban Growth Ser.). (Illus.). 360p. (C). 1988. 37.95 (*0-87722-540-0*) Temple U Pr.

Technology & the Rural Community: The Social Impact. Ed. by M. J. Campbell. LC 87-30345. Orig. Title: New Technology & Rural Development. 432p. 1989. lib. bdg. 55.00 (*0-7099-4864-6*, Pub. by Croom Helm UK) Routledge Chapman & Hall.

Technology & the Transformation of White Color Work. Ed. by Robert E. Kraut. 296p. 1987. text ed. 59.95 (*0-89859-633-5*) L Erlbaum Assocs.

Technology & the Tyranny of Export Controls: Whisper Who Dares. Stuart MacDodnald. 256p. 1990. text ed. 59.95 (*0-312-04085-7*) St Martin.

***Technology & the Vision of Socialism.** unabridged ed. Donald C. Wellington. 105p. 1997. 100.00 (*0-9629480-2-0*) Evelin Pr.

Technology & the Wealth of Nations. Ed. by Nathan Rosenberg et al. 464p. (C). 1992. 52.50 (*0-8047-2082-7*); pap. 17.95 (*0-8047-2083-5*) Stanford U Pr.

Technology & the Wealth of Nations: The Dynamics of Constructed Advantage. Ed. by D. Foray & C. Freeman. LC 92-27953. 1993. write for info. (*1-85567-082-8*) St Martin.

Technology & the Welfare State: The Development of Health Care in Britain & America. Stephen Uttley. 192p. (C). 1991. pap. text ed. 19.95 (*0-04-445841-X*, A8150) Routledge Chapman & Hall.

Technology & the Welfare State: The Development of Health Care in Britain & America. Stephen Uttley. 192p. (C). 1992. text ed. 64.00 (*0-04-445840-1*, A8149) Routledge Chapman & Hall.

***Technology & the West: A Historical Anthology from Technology & Culture.** Terry S. Reynolds & Stephen H. Cutcliffe. LC 97-5926. 1997. pap. text ed. 18.95 (*0-226-71034-3*); lib. bdg. 35.00 (*0-226-71033-5*) U Ch Pr.

Technology & Transformation in the American Electric Utility Industry. Richard Hirsh. (Illus.). 288p. (C). 1989. text ed. 59.95 (*0-521-36478-7*) Cambridge U Pr.

Technology & Transformation of Schools. Lewis J. Perelman. 274p. (Orig.). 1987. pap. 35.00 (*0-88364-168-2*) Natl Sch Boards.

Technology & Transition: A Survey of Biotechnology in Russia, Ukraine & the Baltic States. Anthony Rimington. LC 92-20948. 384p. 1992. text ed. 79.50 (*0-89930-804-X*, Q804, Quorum Bks) Greenwood.

Technology & Transition: The Maghreb at the Crossroads. Ed. by Girma Zawdie & Abdelkadar Djeflat. LC 96-19696. 216p. (C). 1996. text ed. 37.50 (*0-7146-4745-4*, Pub. by F Cass Pubs UK); pap. text ed. 18.50 (*0-7146-4303-3*, Pub. by F Cass Pubs UK) Intl Spec Bk.

Technology & U. S. Competitiveness: An Institutional Focus. Ed. by W. Henry Lambright & Dianne Rahm. LC 92-8845. (Contributions in Economics & Economic History Ser.: No. 139). 200p. 1992. text ed. 49.95 (*0-313-28560-8*, LRH, Greenwood Pr) Greenwood.

Technology & U. S. Government Information. pap. 5.00 (*0-918006-13-9*) ARL.

Technology & Union Survival: A Study of the Printing Industry. Daniel T. Scott. LC 87-2334. 204p. 1987. text ed. 49.95 (*0-275-92680-X*, C2680, Praeger Pubs) Greenwood.

Technology & Use of Synthetic Oligomers. Uster. 1995. write for info. (*0-8493-4955-9*) CRC Pr.

Technology & Utopian Thought. Mulford Q. Sibley. LC 72-88752. (Critical Issues in Political Science Ser.). 63p. (C). reprint ed. pap. 25.00 (*0-8357-9055-X*, 2013326) Bks Demand.

***Technology & Values.** Ed. by Kristin Shrader-Frechette & Laura Westra. 356p. 1997. 69.50 (*0-8476-8630-2*) Rowman.

***Technology & Values.** Ed. by Kristin Shrader-Frechette & Laura Westra. 356p. 1997. pap. 26.95 (*0-8476-8631-0*) Rowman.

Technology & War: From 2000 B.C. to the Present. rev. ed. Martin L. Van Creveld. (Illus.). 304p. 1991. pap. 17.95 (*0-02-933153-6*, Free Press) Free Pr.

Technology & Women's Voices Keeping in Touch. Ed. by Cheris Kramarae. 256p. (C). 1988. pap. text ed. 13.95 (*0-7102-0679-8*, RKP) Routledge.

Technology & Work in Canada. Ed. by Scott Bennett. LC 90-31082. (Canadian Studies: Vol. 8). 324p. 1990. lib. bdg. 99.95 (*0-88946-213-5*) E Mellen.

Technology & Writing: Readings in the Psychology of Written Communication. Ed. by James Hartley. 200p. 1992. 62.00 (*1-85302-097-4*) Taylor & Francis.

Technology & You. David L. Goetsch & John A. Nelson. LC 86-19751. 384p. 1987. teacher ed. 10.00 (*0-8273-2663-7*); text ed. 32.95 (*0-8273-2662-9*) Delmar.

Technology Applications Report: The Strategic Defense Initiative. (Illus.). 79p. (Orig.). (C). 1993. pap. text ed. 25.00 (*1-56806-646-5*) DIANE Pub.

Technology As a Social & Political Phenomenon. Philip L. Bereano. LC 76-18723. 554p. reprint ed. pap. 157.90 (*0-318-34745-8*, 2032004) Bks Demand.

Technology As Freedom: The New Deal & the Electrical Modernization of the American Home. Ronald C. Tobey. (Illus.). 367p. (C). 1996. 35.00 (*0-520-20421-2*) U CA Pr.

Technology As Symptom & Dream. Robert Romanyshyn. (Illus.). 320p. 1989. 45.00 (*0-415-00786-0*, A3877) Routledge.

Technology As Symptom & Dream. Robert Romanyshyn. (Illus.). 320p. 1989. pap. 16.95 (*0-415-00787-9*, A3881) Routledge.

Technology As Translation Strategy. Ed. by Muriel Vasconcellos. (American Translators Association Scholarly Monograph Ser.: Vol. 2). viii, 248p. 1988. lib. bdg. 45.00 (*0-614-16448-6*) Benjamins North Am.

Technology Assessment, 2 vols., Set. Ed. by Eva L. Baker & Harold F. O'Neil. 1994. pap. 50.00 (*0-8058-1709-5*) L Erlbaum Assocs.

Technology Assessment, 2 vols., Vol. I. Ed. by Eva L. Baker & Harold F. O'Neil. 272p. 1994. 59.95 (*0-8058-1246-6*); pap. 36.00 (*0-8058-1247-4*) L Erlbaum Assocs.

Technology Assessment, 2 vols., Vol. II. Ed. by Eva L. Baker & Harold F. O'Neil. 296p. 1994. 59.95 (*0-8058-1248-2*) L Erlbaum Assocs.

Technology Assessment, 2 vols., Vol. II. Ed. by Eva L. Baker & Harold F. O'Neil. 296p. 1994. pap. 36.00 (*0-8058-1249-0*) L Erlbaum Assocs.

Technology Assessment: A Feminist Perspective. Janine M. Morgall. LC 93-9447. (Labor & Social Change Ser.). 288p. 1993. 49.95 (*1-56639-090-7*); pap. 19.95 (*1-56639-091-5*) Temple U Pr.

Technology Assessment & Development. Ed. by Mangalam Srinivisan. LC 82-3795. 288p. 1982. text ed. 65.00 (*0-275-90908-5*, C0908, Praeger Pubs) Greenwood.

Technology Assessment & Development - ATAS Bulletin, No. 4. 89p. 1987. 15.00 (*92-1-104195-3*, E.87.II.A.1) UN.

Technology Assessment & Health Care: From Theory to Practice. Ed. by Joshua Shemer & Tore Schersten. 234p. (Orig.). (C). 1995. 60.00 (*965-229-122-6*, Pub. by Gefen Pub Hse IS) Gefen Bks.

Technology Assessment & New Kidney Stone Treatment Methods. Ed. by Finn Kamper-Jorgensen et al. (Commission of the European Communities Health Services Research Ser.: No. 4). (Illus.). 208p. 1988. 49.95 (*0-19-261649-8*) OUP.

Technology Assessment for State & Local Government: A Guide to Decision Making. Lawrence P. O'Keefe. LC 82-71314. 222p. reprint ed. pap. 63.30 (*0-317-26718-3*, 2023520) Bks Demand.

Technology Assessment for Water Supplies. Evan Vlachos & David W. Hendricks. LC 76-19871. 1977. 35.00 (*0-918334-13-6*) WRP.

Technology Assessment Process: A Strategic Framework for Managing Technical Innovation. Blake L. White. LC 88-3101. 177p. 1988. text ed. 55.00 (*0-89930-318-8*, WTA/, Quorum Bks) Greenwood.

Technology Assessments: Index of New Information with Authors, Subjects, & Bibliography. American Health Research Institute Staff. LC 94-30989. 1994. 44.50 (*0-7883-0412-7*); pap. 39.50 (*0-7883-0413-5*) ABBE Pubs Assn.

Technology Assessments in Health Sciences. American Health Research Institute Staff. 150p. 1990. 44.50 (*1-55914-110-7*); pap. 39.50 (*1-55914-111-5*) ABBE Pubs Assn.

Technology Assessments of Advanced Energy Storage Systems for Electric & Hybrid Electric Vehicles. Abacus Technology Corporation Staff. (Electric Vehicle Information Ser.: Vol. VIII). (Illus.). 115p. 1996. pap. 75.00 (*0-89934-255-8*, BT035) Bus Tech Bks.

Technology Assessments of Advanced Energy Storage Systems for Electric & Hybrid Electric Vehicles, Vol. 8. Abacus Technology Corporation Staff. (Electric Vehicle Information Ser.). (Illus.). 115p. 1996. lib. bdg. 125.00 (*0-89934-256-6*, BT935) Bus Tech Bks.

Technology Assisted Teaching Techniques. Janie Duncan. (Language Resource Handbook Ser.: No. 5). (Illus.). 112p. 1987. pap. text ed. 12.00 (*0-86647-022-0*) Pro Lingua.

Technology at Work: A Survey of Technology. Daggett & Williams. (GB - Basic Business Ser.). 1987. text ed. 34.95 (*0-538-16300-3*) S-W Pub.

***Technology-Based Firms in the Innovation Process: Management, Financing & Regional Networks.** Ed. by K. Koschatzky. (Technology, Innovation & Policy Ser.: Vol. 5). (Illus.). xii, 290p. 1997. pap. 73.00 (*3-7908-1021-5*) Spr-Verlag.

Technology-Based Learning: A Handbook for Principals & Technology Leaders. Tweed W. Ross & Gearld D. Bailey. LC 94-12518. (Illus.). 192p. 1995. 29.95 (*0-590-49626-3*) Scholastic Inc.

***Technology-Based Learning: A Handbook for Principals & Technology Leaders.** 2nd rev. ed. Tweed W. Ross, Jr. & Gerald D. Bailey. LC 96-78481. (Illus.). 208p. 1996. pap. 29.95 (*1-57517-074-4*, 1468) IRI-SkyLght.

Technology-Based Learning Environments: Psychological & Educational Foundations. Ed. by S. Vosinadou et al. (NATO ASI Series F: Computer & Systems Sciences). 336p. 1995. 79.00 (*0-387-58253-3*) Spr-Verlag.

Technology-Based Learning Environments: Psychological & Educational Foundations. Ed. by Stella Vosniadou & Erik De Corte. LC 94-42229. (NATO ASI Series F: Computer & Systems Science: Vol. 137). 1994. write for info. (*3-540-58253-3*) Spr-Verlag.

***Technology-Based Training.** Serge Ravet & Maureen Laute. LC 97-17796. 1997. pap. 39.95 (*0-88415-866-7*, 5866) Gulf Pub.

***Technology Based Training: A Comprehensive Guide to All New Digital Training Media for Trainers.** Contrib. by Serge Ravet. 224p. 1996. 59.95 (*0-7494-1975-X*, Falmer Pr) Taylor & Francis.

***Technology Benchmarks: Printer's Use & Assessment of Printing & Imaging Technology.** 174p. 1996. 129.00 (*0-614-25548-1*, 00BT44536) Print Indus Am.

Technology, Bureaucracy, & Healing in America: A Postmodern Paradigm. Roger J. Bulger. LC 88-20597. 141p. 1988. text ed. 19.95 (*0-87745-219-9*) U of Iowa Pr.

Technology Bytes! Randy Glasbergen. Ed. by Cliff Carle. 1996. pap. 5.95 (*1-57644-014-1*) CCC Pubns.

Technology CAD: Computer Simulation of IC Processes & Devices. Robert W. Dutton & Zhiping Yu. LC 93-20663. (International Engineering & Computer Science Ser.: No. 243). 400p. (C). 1993. lib. bdg. 105.50 (*0-7923-9379-1*) Kluwer Ac.

Technology CAD Systems. Ed. by F. Fasching et al. LC 93-20890. 1993. 93.95 (*0-387-82505-3*) Spr-Verlag.

Technology Century: 100 Years of ESD - The Engineering Society 1895-1995. Ed. by Mike Davis & David Tell. (Illus.). 262p. 1995. text ed. 25.00 (*1-56378-022-4*) ESD.

Technology Challenges Activity Masters. Kenneth L. Smith. LC 93-38087. 1994. 64.95 (*0-8273-6541-1*) S-W Pub.

Technology Change in Less Developed Countries: A Guide to Selected Literature. Patricia Hill et al. (Bibliographies in Technology & Social Change Ser.: No. 5). 350p. (Orig.). (C). 1989. pap. 24.00 (*0-945271-12-3*) ISU-CIKARD.

Technology Choice & Change in Developing Countries: Internal & External Constraints. Ed. by Barbara A. Lucas & Stephen Freedman. (Illus.). 155p. 1983. 70.00 (*0-907567-32-0*, Tycooly Pub); pap. 40.00 (*0-907567-33-9*, Tycooly Pub) Weidner & Sons.

Technology Choice in Developing Countries: The Textile & Pulp & Paper Industries. Michel A. Amsalem. (Illus.). 224p. 1983. 32.50 (*0-262-01072-0*) MIT Pr.

Technology Common to Aero & Marine Engineering. Ed. by Society for Underwater Technology Staff. (C). 1988. lib. bdg. 188.00 (*1-85333-054-X*, Pub. by Graham & Trotman UK) Kluwer Ac.

Technology Companies & Global Markets: Programs, Policies & Strategies to Accelerate Innovation & Entrepreneurship. Ed. by David V. Gibson. (International Series on Technical Innovation & Entrepreneurship). 240p. (C). 1990. lib. bdg. 59.00 (*0-8476-7643-9*) Rowman.

***Technology, Competitiveness & Radical Policy Change: The Case of Brazil.** Jorg Meyer-Stamer & Deutsches Institut fur Entwicklungspolitik Staff. LC 97-8178. (GDI Book Ser.). 1997. write for info. (*0-7146-4379-3*, Pub. by F Cass Pubs UK) Intl Spec Bk.

Technology, Computers F&TE Special Needs Learner. John R. Ray & Kathleen Warden. LC 94-6812. 224p. 1995. pap. 31.50 (*0-8273-6476-8*) Delmar.

Technology Control, Competition & National Security: Conflict & Consensus. Ed. by Bernard L. Seward. LC 86-24999. 334p. (Orig.). (C). 1987. pap. text ed. 29.00 (*0-8191-5736-8*, Ctr for Law & Natl Security) U Pr of Amer.

Technology Coordinator. David G. Moursund. (Illus.). 192p. 1992. pap. text ed. 23.95 (*1-56484-015-8*) Intl Society Tech Educ.

***Technology, Culture & Competitiveness: Change & the World Political Economy.** Michael Talalay et al. LC 96-43248. 272p. (C). 1997. pap. write for info. (*0-415-14255-5*); text ed. write for info. (*0-415-14254-7*) Routledge.

Technology, Culture & Development: The Experience of the Soviet Model. Ed. & Intro. by James P. Scanlan. LC 91-22611. 200p. (gr. 13). 1992. text ed. 67.95 (*0-87332-891-4*); pap. text ed. 30.95 (*0-87332-892-2*) M E Sharpe.

Technology, Development & Global Environmental Issues. Ed. by William J. Makofske & Eric F. Karlin. LC 94-12437. 352p. (C). 1995. text ed. 18.95 (*0-673-99181-4*) Addson-Wesley Educ.

***Technology Development & Transfer: The Transactional & Legal Environment.** Alan S. Gutterman & Jacob N. Erlich. LC 96-46717. 224p. 1997. text ed. 65.00 (*1-56720-021-4*, Quorum Bks) Greenwood.

Technology Development Goals for Automotive Fuel Cell Power Systems (Aug.-94) Directed Technologies, Inc. Staff. (Fuel Cells Information Ser.: Vol. VIII). (Illus.). 185p. 1996. lib. bdg. 125.00 (*0-89934-264-7*, BT939) Bus Tech Bks.

Technology Dictionary of the Armed Forces. Ibeas F. Franco. 121p. (ENG & SPA.). 1983. 12.95 (*0-8288-1910-6*) Fr & Eur.

Technology Diffusion: Federal Programs & Procedures. Granville W. Hough. LC 73-88035. 406p. 1975. 44.00 (*0-912338-05-9*); fiche 12.50 (*0-912338-06-7*) Lomond.

Technology Diffusion, Productivity Employment & Phase Shifts in Developing Economies. Ohkawa Kazushi & Katsuo Otsuka. 291p. 1994. 59.50 (*0-86008-506-6*, Pub. by U of Tokyo JA) Col U Pr.

Technology Directory: Business Resource Directory, High-Technology Manufacturing & Development Version 6.0. Ed. & Frwd. by Bruce E. Ahern. 1996. 59.95 (*1-885062-03-6*) Tech Directory.

Technology Directory: 1995 San Diego County Edition. Ed. & Frwd. by Bruce E. Ahern. (Version 5.0 Ser.). 1995. spiral bd. 59.95 (*1-885062-01-X*) Tech Directory.

Technology-Driven Corporate Alliances: A Legal Guide for Executives. Alan S. Gutterman. LC 93-49032. 304p. 1994. text ed. 65.00 (*0-89930-843-0*, Quorum Bks) Greenwood.

Technology, Duality, & Foreign Trade: The GNP Function Approach to Modeling Imports & Exports. Ulrich Kohli. (Studies In International Trade Policy). 400p. 1991. text ed. 72.50 (*0-472-10253-2*) U of Mich Pr.

Technology, Economic Growth & the Labour Process. Phil Blackburn et al. LC 84-22849. 272p. 1985. text ed. 35.00 (*0-312-79001-5*) St Martin.

Technology Edge: Opportunities for America in World Competition. Gerard K. O'Neill. 299p. 1983. pap. 9.95 (*0-671-44766-1*) SSIP.

Technology Education: Industrial Arts in Transition, A Review & Synthesis of the Research. 4th ed. David L. McCory. 69p. 1987. 7.00 (*0-318-35275-3*, IN 325) Ctr Educ Trng Employ.

An Asterisk (*) at the beginning of an entry indicates that the title is appearing in BIP for the first time.

Technology, Education & Productivity. Zvi Grilliches. LC 94-16093. (Occassional Papers: No. 18). 1994. pap. 9.95 (*1-55815-256-3*) ICS Pr.

Technology Education in School & Industry: Emerging Didactics for Human Resource Development. Ed. by D. Blandow & M. Dyrenfurth. (NATO ASI Series F: Computer & Systems Science: Vol. 135). 367p. 1994. 93.95 (*0-387-58250-9*) Spr-Verlag.

Technology Education in the Classroom: Understanding the Designed World. Senta A. Raizen et al. LC 95-33950. (Educational Ser.). 279p. text ed. 32.95 (*0-7879-0178-4*) Jossey-Bass.

Technology Education, Innovation, & Management: Proceedings of WOCATE Conference. Ed. by K. Langer et al. LC 95-30836. 336p. 1995. 79.00 (*3-540-60018-3*) Spr-Verlag.

***Technology, Energy, & Development: The South Korean Tansition.** LC 96-48224. 176p. 1997. 70.00 (*1-85898-593-5*) E Elgar.

Technology Enriched Schools: Nine Case Studies with Reflections. Ed. by Gerrit Carleer. (Illus.). 145p. 1992. pap. text ed. 23.95 (*1-56484-017-4*) Intl Society Tech Educ.

Technology, Environment & Human Values. Ian G. Barbour. LC 80-12330. 344p. 1980. text ed. 27.95 (*0-275-90448-2*, C0448, Praeger Pubs); pap. text ed. 24.95 (*0-275-91483-6*, B1483, Praeger Pubs) Greenwood.

Technology Exchange: A Guide to Successful Cooperative Research & Development Partnerships. Ed. by John Lesko & Michael Irish. LC 94-40083. 188p. 1995. pap. text ed. 29.95 (*0-935470-86-7*) Battelle.

***Technology Exchange in the Information Age: A Guide to Successful Cooperative R&D Partnerships.** 2nd ed. Rev. by John Lesko et al. 1997. pap. text ed. 29.95 (*1-57477-037-3*) Battelle.

Technology Explosion in Medical Science: Implications for the Health Care Industry & the Public (1981-2001) Ed. by James Gay & Barbara S. Jacobs. (Health Care Administration Monographs: Vol. 2). 176p. 1983. text ed. 14.95 (*0-88331-205-0*) Luce.

Technology Factor in International Trade. Ed. by Raymond Vernon. (Universities-National Bureau Conference Ser.: No. 22). 503p. 1970. text ed. 130.80 (*0-87014-208-9*) Natl Bur Econ Res.

Technology Factor in International Trade. Ed. by Raymond Vernon. LC 73-99130. (Universities-National Bureau Conference Ser.: No. 22). 503p. reprint ed. pap. 143.40 (*0-8357-7583-6*, 2056904) Bks Demand.

Technology, Farm Output & Employment in a Tribal Region. R. N. Tripathy. (C). 1988. 22.50 (*81-7099-055-6*, Pub. by Mittal II) S Asia.

Technology for a Sustainable Future: A Framework for Action. 1996. lib. bdg. 253.95 (*0-8490-6004-4*) Gordon Pr.

***Technology for All Americans: Rational & Structure for the Study of Technology.** Technology for All Americans Project Staff. (Illus.). (Orig.). 1996. pap. text ed. 10.00 (*1-887101-01-2*) Intl Tech Educ.

Technology for America's Economic Growth: A New Direction to Build Economic Strength. 1994. lib. bdg. 250.00 (*0-8490-9036-9*) Gordon Pr.

Technology for America's Economic Growth, a New Direction to Build Economic Strength. William J. Clinton & Albert J. Gore, Jr. 36p. (Orig.). (C). 1993. pap. text ed. 25.00 (*0-7881-0129-3*) DIANE Pub.

***Technology for Diverse Learners.** Ed. by Karen Gutloff. (Teacher-to-Teacher Bks.). 96p. (Orig.). 1997. pap. 12.95 (*0-8106-2908-9*, 2908-9) NEA.

Technology for Inclusion. 3rd ed. Male. LC 96-41904. 224p. 1996. pap. 46.00 (*0-205-19654-3*) Allyn.

Technology for Liberation. W. Riedjik. 250p. (Orig.). 1986. pap. text ed. 29.50 (*90-6275-244-6*, Pub. by Delft U Pr NE) Coronet Bks.

Technology for Premium Quality Castings: Proceedings of a Symposium Sponsored by the TMS Solidification Committee & Held at the TMS Annual Meeting in Denver, Colorado, February 24-27, 1987. Metallurgical Society of AIME Staff. Ed. by E. Dunn & D. R. Durham. LC 87-43112. 187p. reprint ed. pap. 53.30 (*0-7837-5645-3*, 2052497) Bks Demand.

Technology for Production & Decision Making. 3rd ed. Clark & Dale H. Klooster. (DC - Introduction to Computing Ser.). 1996. wbk. ed., pap. 16.95 (*0-538-64988-7*) S-W Pub.

Technology for Productivity & Decision Making. 3rd ed. Clark & Dale H. Klooster. (DC - Introduction to Computing Ser.). 1996. text ed. 47.95 (*0-538-64986-0*) S-W Pub.

***Technology for Productivity & Decision-Making: A Brief Course.** 3rd ed. James F. Clark et al. LC 96-43281. 1998. 19.95 (*0-538-67526-8*) S-W Pub.

***Technology for Real Estate Practitioners.** Ron Rothenberg. 64p. (C). 1997. write for info. (*0-614-24130-8*) Gorsuch Scarisbrick.

Technology for Rural Development: Proceedings of the Second Asia Conference, Kuala Lumpur, Malaysia, December 4-7, 1985. Ed. by S. Radhakrishna et al. 728p. 1988. text ed. 93.00 (*9971-5-0285-2*) World Scientific Pub.

Technology for Small Spacecraft. National Research Council, Panel on Small Spacecraft Technology Staff. 156p. (Orig.). (C). 1994. pap. text ed. 27.00 (*0-309-05075-8*) Natl Acad Pr.

***Technology for Students with Disabilities: A Decision Maker's Resource Guide.** 106p. (Orig.). 1997. pap. 25.00 (*0-88364-207-7*) Natl Sch Boards.

***Technology for Students with Learning Disabilities: Educational Applications.** Kyle Higgins & Randall Boone. LC 96-48422. 1997. 49.00 (*0-89079-716-1*) PRO-ED.

Technology for Teachers. Roger P. Volker & Michael Simonson. 144p. (C). 1995. spiral bd. 29.34 (*0-8403-8474-2*) Kendall-Hunt.

Technology for Teams: Enhancing Productivity in Networked Organizations. Susanna Opper & Henry Fersko-Weiss. (Illus.). 181p. 1992. pap. 35.95 (*0-442-23928-9*) Van Nos Reinhold.

Technology for Technology Education. Ed. by Robert McCormick et al. LC 92-36800. 1992. write for info. (*0-201-63168-7*) Addison-Wesley.

Technology for Test-Item Writing. Gale Roid & Tom Haladyna. (Educational Technology Ser.). 1981. text ed. 57.00 (*0-12-593250-2*) Acad Pr.

Technology for the Automotive Trade, Vol. 1: Basic Information. H. Gerschler. (C). 1987. pap. 10.00 (*81-224-0138-4*) S Asia.

Technology for the Common Good. Joel Yudken et al. Ed. by Julia Sweig. 192p. (Orig.). 1993. pap. 12.95 (*0-89758-047-8*) Inst Policy Stud.

Technology for the Nineties. Ed. by M. K. Au-Yang. LC 93-70159. 1131p. 1993. pap. 200.00 (*0-7918-0684-7*) ASME.

***Technology for the Real Estate Professional.** Ronald S. Rothenberg. (C). 1997. pap. text ed. 6.00 (*0-13-677445-8*) P-H.

Technology for Tomorrow: A Survey of Technology. Daggett & Williams. (GB - Basic Business Ser.). 1985. text ed. 35.95 (*0-538-16250-3*) S-W Pub.

Technology for U. S. Industry from Department of Energy Laboratories: Near-Term Technology Opportunities. Intro. by William Happer. 52p. (Orig.). (C). 1993. pap. text ed. 20.00 (*1-56806-201-X*) DIANE Pub.

Technology for Water Supply & Sanitation Developing Countries. (Technical Report Ser.: No. 742). 38p. 1987. pap. text ed. 7.00 (*92-4-120742-6*, 1100742) World Health.

***Technology for Waterborne Coatings, Vol. 663.** J. E. Glass & American Chemical Society Staff. LC 97-5741. (ACS Symposium Ser.). 1997. write for info. (*0-8412-3501-5*) Am Chemical.

Technology Forecast Assessments. Commission on Engineering & Technical Systems Staff. (Star 21: Strategic Technologies for the Army in the Twenty-First Century Ser.: Vol. 2). 600p. 1992. pap. 59.00 (*0-309-04637-8*) World Scientific Pub.

***Technology Forecasting: An Aid to Effective Technology Management.** John H. Vanston. 59p. 1988. pap. 45.00 (*1-884154-03-4*) Tech Futures.

Technology Fountainheads: The Management Challenge of R&D Consortia. E. Raymond Corey. 192p. 1996. 29.95 (*0-87584-723-4*) Harvard Busn.

***Technology Fountainheads: The Management Challenge of R&D Consortia.** E. Raymond Corey. 1996. text ed. 29.95 (*0-07-103843-4*) McGraw.

Technology Gamble: Informatics & Public Policy - a Study of Technological Choice. Cees J. Hamelink. Ed. by Brenda Dervin. LC 88-16632. (Communication & Information Science Ser.). 136p. 1988. text ed. 73.25 (*0-89391-478-9*) Ablex Pub.

Technology Gauntlet: Meeting the Challenges of Workplace Computing. Margaret Kilduff. 1995. pap. 25.95 (*0-201-63359-0*) Addison-Wesley.

***Technology, Globalisation & Economic Performance.** Ed. by Daniele Archibugi & Jonathan Michie. 312p. (C). 1997. text ed. 59.95 (*0-521-55392-X*); pap. text ed. 19.95 (*0-521-55642-2*) Cambridge U Pr.

***Technology Guide to Accounting Software: A Handbook for Evaluating Vendor Applications.** Stewart McKie. LC 97-4605. 200p. (Orig.). 1997. pap. 59.00 (*1-882419-55-3*, Duke Pr) Duke Commns Intl.

***Technology, Guilds, & Early English Drama.** Clifford Davidson. LC 96-32689. (Early Drama, Art & Music Monograph). 1996. write for info. (*1-879288-79-6*); write for info. (*1-879288-80-X*) Medieval Inst.

Technology-Humanism or Nihilism: A Critical Analysis of the Philosophical Basis & Practice of Modern Technology. Gregory H. Davis. LC 81-40178. 304p. (Orig.). 1981. pap. text ed. 24.00 (*0-8191-1777-3*) U Pr of Amer.

Technology Impact: Potential Directions for Laboratory Medicine. Intro. by David B. Goodman. (Annals Ser.: Vol. 428). 334p. 1984. pap. 64.00 (*0-89766-251-2*); lib. bdg. 64.00 (*0-89766-250-4*) NY Acad Sci.

Technology in a Changing World: The Technology - Economy Programme. OECD Staff. 157p. (Orig.). 1992. pap. 42.00 (*92-64-13598-7*) OECD.

Technology in Action. Sally Morgan & Adrian Morgan. (Designs in Science Ser.). (Illus.). 48p. (YA). (gr. 5-9). 1994. 14.95 (*0-8160-3126-6*) Facts on File.

***Technology in America.** 2nd ed. Marcus. (C). 1998. pap. text ed. 23.25 (*0-15-505531-3*) HB Coll Pubs.

Technology in America: A Brief History. Alan I. Marcus & Howard P. Segal. 380p. (C). 1989. pap. text ed. 16.00 (*0-15-589762-4*) HB Coll Pubs.

Technology in America: A History of Individuals & Ideas. 2nd ed. Ed. by Carroll W. Pursell, Jr. (Illus.). 300p. 1990. pap. 16.00 (*0-262-66067-9*) MIT Pr.

Technology in American Water Development. Edward A. Ackerman & George O. Lof. LC 59-10066. 788p. reprint ed. pap. 180.00 (*0-7837-3147-7*, 2042839) Bks Demand.

Technology in Ancient & Medieval India. Ed. by Aniruddha Roy. 170p. 1986. 46.00 (*81-85055-95-5*, Pub. by Minerva II) S Asia.

Technology in Banking: Creating Value & Destroying Profits. Thomas D. Steiner & Diogo B. Teixeira. 300p. 1990. text ed. 60.00 (*1-55623-150-4*) Irwin Prof Pubng.

Technology in Calculus: A Sourcebook of Activities. Thomas P. Dick & Charles M. Patton. 200p. 1992. pap. 35.95 (*0-534-93081-6*) PWS Pubs.

Technology in Clothing Manufacture. 2nd ed. Harold Carr & Barbara Latham. LC 93-25907. (Illus.). 288p. 1994. pap. 29.95 (*0-632-03748-2*, Pub. by Blckwell Sci Pubns UK) Blackwell Sci.

Technology in Early Intervention. Ed. by James A. Blackman. LC 94-39482. (Infants & Young Children Ser.). 240p. 1995. pap. 30.00 (*0-8342-0649-8*) Aspen Pub.

Technology in Education: Looking Toward 2020. Raymond Nickerson & Philip Zodhiates. 352p. (C). 1988. pap. 36.00 (*0-8058-0297-5*); text ed. 69.95 (*0-8058-0214-2*) L Erlbaum Assocs.

Technology in Education & Training: Planning & Management. 302p. 1984. 25.00 (*0-317-36882-6*) Assn Ed Comm Tech.

Technology in Hospitals: Medical Advances & Their Diffusion. Louise B. Russell. LC 79-10737. (Studies in Social Economics). 180p. 1979. 34.95 (*0-8157-7630-6*); pap. 14.95 (*0-8157-7629-2*) Brookings.

Technology in Human Communication. Ed. by Noel Williams & Peter Hartley. 224p. 1992. pap. text ed. 19.50 (*0-86187-767-5*) St Martin.

Technology in Industrial America: Records of the Committee on Science & the Arts of the Franklin Institute, 1824-1900: A Guide. A. Michael McMahon & Stephanie A. Morris. LC 77-77872. 1977. 40.00 (*0-8420-2123-X*) Scholarly Res Inc.

Technology in Instruction: Standards for College & University Learning Resources Programs. 2nd ed. Richard A. Cornell. 112p. 1988. pap. 13.95 (*0-89240-045-5*) Assn Ed Comm Tech.

Technology in Mental Health Care Delivery Systems. Ed. by J. Sidowski et al. LC 79-21126. (Illus.). 336p. 1980. text ed. 73.25 (*0-89391-023-6*) Ablex Pub.

Technology in News. Pierce. Date not set. pap. text ed. write for info. (*0-314-06018-9*) West Pub.

Technology in Nonformal Education. David R. Evans. (Issues in Nonformal Education Ser.: No. 2). 36p. (Orig.). (C). 1977. pap. 3.00 (*0-932288-38-3*) Ctr Intl Ed U of MA.

Technology in Paper Industry. V. Podder. 586p. 1990. 200.00 (*81-209-0004-9*, Pub. by Pitambar Pub II) St Mut.

Technology in People Services: Research, Theory, & Applications. Ed. by Charles Guzetta et al. LC 92-47278. (Computers in Human Services Ser.: Vol. 9, Nos. 1-4). (Illus.). 504p. 1993. lib. bdg. 89.95 (*1-56024-456-9*) Haworth Pr.

Technology in School: A Handbook of Practical Approaches & Ideas. John Cave. (Education Bks.). (Illus.). 160p. (C). 1986. pap. text ed. 12.95 (*0-7102-0732-8*, RKP) Routledge.

Technology in Schools. Ed. by Anita Cross & Robert McCormick. LC 86-12607. (Exploring Curriculum Ser.). 320p. 1986. 90.00 (*0-335-15237-6*, Open Univ Pr); pap. 32.00 (*0-335-15236-8*, Open Univ Pr) Taylor & Francis.

Technology in Services: Policies for Growth, Trade, & Employment. 256p. 1988. 34.95 (*0-309-03895-2*) Natl Acad Pr.

Technology in Services: Policies for Growth, Trade, & Employment. National Academy of Engineering Staff. Ed. by Bruce R. Guile & James B. Quinn. 256p. 1988. pap. 24.95 (*0-309-03887-1*) Natl Acad Pr.

Technology in Student Affairs: Issues, Applications, & Trends. Ed. by John L. Baier & Thomas S. Strong. LC 93-23439. 296p. (Orig.). 1994. pap. text ed. 32.50 (*1-883485-03-7*); lib. bdg. 57.50 (*1-883485-02-9*) Am Coll Personnel.

Technology in the Classroom, Vol. 1. Ed. by Gary Froelich. (Illus.). 94p. 1992. pap. 13.00 (*0-912843-32-2*, 9392) COMAP Inc.

Technology in the Classroom, Vol. 2. Ed. by Gary Froelich. (Illus.). 102p. 1993. pap. 13.00 (*0-912843-35-7*, 9393) COMAP Inc.

***Technology in the Classroom: A Collection of Articles.** Ed. by Tom King. LC 97-70720. (Illus.). 128p. (Orig.). 1997. pap. 22.95 (*1-57517-038-8*, 1501) IRI-SkyLght.

Technology in the Classroom: Communication Module. 147p. 1992. pap. text ed. 40.00 (*0-910329-70-2*, 0111671) Am Speech Lang Hearing.

Technology in the Classroom: Education Module. 176p. 1992. pap. text ed. 40.00 (*0-910329-71-0*, 0111672) Am Speech Lang Hearing.

Technology in the Classroom: Listening & Hearing Module. 42p. 1992. pap. text ed. 29.00 (*0-910329-72-9*, 0111673) Am Speech Lang Hearing.

Technology in the Classroom: Positioning, Access, & Mobility Module. 57p. 1992. pap. text ed. 35.00 (*0-910329-69-9*, 0111670) Am Speech Lang Hearing.

Technology in the Courtroom (1994) 121p. 1994. 20.00 (*1-56986-249-4*) Federal Bar.

Technology in the Garden: Research Parks & Regional Economic Development. 264p. 1991. 15.95 (*0-317-05042-7*) Natl Coun Econ Dev.

Technology in the Garden: Research Parks & Regional Economic Development. Michael I. Luger & Harvey A. Goldstein. LC 91-50255. (Illus.). xxii, 242p. (C). 1991. 49.95 (*0-8078-2000-8*); pap. 16.95 (*0-8078-4345-8*) U of NC Pr.

Technology in the Hospital: Transforming Patient Care in the Early Twentieth Century. Joel D. Howell. (Illus.). 352p. 1996. reprint ed. pap. text ed. 16.95 (*0-8018-5501-2*) Johns Hopkins.

Technology in the Modern Corporation: A Strategic Perspective. Ed. by M. Horwitch. (Technology in Society Ser.). (Illus.). 200p. 1986. 19.50 (*0-685-14280-9*, Pergamon Pr) Elsevier.

Technology in the Music Classroom. Robert A. Carpenter. 76p. (Orig.). 1991. pap. 8.95 (*0-88284-493-8*, 4700) Alfred Pub.

Technology in the Pacific Century: Trade, Security & Competitiveness. Ed. by S. C. Pu & Steven McCoy-Thompson. (US-Asia Institute National Leadership Conference Ser.: No. 6). (Illus.). 224p. (C). 1989. pap. 35.00 (*0-9621762-0-6*) US-Asia Inst.

Technology in the Schools: Equity & Funding. Ed. by John C. Arch. 56p. 1986. pap. 6.95 (*0-8106-1535-5*) NEA.

***Technology in the Time of Ancient Egypt.** Judith Crosher. LC 97-13922. (J). 1998. write for info. (*0-8172-4875-7*) Raintree Steck-V.

***Technology in the Time of Ancient Greece.** Judith Crosher. LC 97-19067. (J). 1998. write for info. (*0-8172-4877-3*) Raintree Steck-V.

***Technology in the Time of Ancient Rome.** Robert Snedden. LC 97-13924. (J). 1998. write for info. (*0-8172-4876-5*) Raintree Steck-V.

***Technology in the Time of the Aztecs.** Nina Morgan. LC 97-19066. (J). 1998. write for info. (*0-8172-4878-1*) Raintree Steck-V.

Technology in the Western Political Tradition. Ed. by Arthur M. Melzer et al. 352p. 1993. 39.95 (*0-8014-2724-X*); pap. 16.95 (*0-8014-8006-X*) Cornell U Pr.

***Technology in the 20th Century.** Dana Graves. (In the 20th Century Ser.). (Illus.). 144p. (YA). (gr. 7 up). 1996. pap. 9.95 (*0-912517-25-5*) Bluewood Bks.

***Technology in the 21st Century.** 222p. 1997. pap. 46.00 (*90-5199-315-3*) IOS Press.

Technology in Today's Schools. fac. ed. Ed. by Cynthia L. Warger. LC 90-36344. 211p. 1990. reprint ed. pap. 60.20 (*0-608-01035-9*, 2082511) Bks Demand.

Technology in Trucking. American Trucking Assns. Staff. (Illus.). 1995. pap. 72.00 (*0-88711-289-7*) Am Trucking Assns.

Technology in Vedic Literature. Prem Sagar Chaturvedi. (C). 1993. 58.00 (*81-85016-38-0*, Pub. by Bks & Bks II) S Asia.

Technology in Working Order: Studies of Work, Interaction, & Technology. Ed. by Graham Button. LC 92-10514. (Illus.). 240p. (C). 1992. text ed. 89.95 (*0-415-06839-8*, A6921) Routledge.

Technology in World Civilization: A Thousand-Year History. Arnold Pacey. (Illus.). 200p. 1990. 27.50 (*0-262-16117-6*) MIT Pr.

Technology in World Civilization: A Thousand-Year History. Arnold Pacey. (Illus.). 256p. 1991. pap. 13.50 (*0-262-66072-5*) MIT Pr.

Technology in Your World. 2nd ed. Michael Hacker & Robert Barden. 448p. 1992. teacher ed. 12.00 (*0-8273-4426-0*) S-W Pub.

Technology in Your World. 3rd ed. Hacker. (TP - Technology Education Ser.). (J). (gr. k-12). 1998. text ed. 38.95 (*0-538-65823-1*) S-W Pub.

Technology in Your World. 3rd ed. Hacker. (TP - Technology Education Ser.). (J). (gr. k-12). 1998. teacher ed., text ed. 47.95 (*0-538-65824-X*) S-W Pub.

Technology in Your World. 3rd ed. Hacker. (TP - Technology Education Ser.). (J). (gr. k-12). 1998. wbk. ed., pap. 24.95 (*0-538-65825-8*) S-W Pub.

Technology in Your World, Resource Bk. 2nd ed. Michael Hacker & Robert Barden. 448p. 1992. teacher ed. 54.95 (*0-8273-5249-2*) S-W Pub.

Technology in Your World, Testbank. 2nd ed. Michael Hacker & Robert Barden. 1991. teacher ed. 115.95 incl. disk (*0-8273-5768-0*) S-W Pub.

Technology (Industrial Arts) Education. Jack Rudman. (National Teacher Examination Ser.: NT-5). 1994. pap. 23.95 (*0-8373-8415-X*) Nat Learn.

Technology, Industry & Trade: The Levant vs. Europe, 1250-1500. Eliyahu Ashtor. Ed. by Benjamin Z. Kedar. (Collected Studies: No. CS372). 350p. 1992. 94.95 (*0-86078-323-5*, Pub. by Variorum UK) Ashgate Pub Co.

Technology Infrastructure & Competitive Position. Gregory Tassey. 336p. (C). 1992. lib. bdg. 103.00 (*0-7923-9232-9*) Kluwer Ac.

***Technology, Infrastructure, WDM Networks.** 330p. 1996. pap. 89.00 (*90-5199-277-7*) IOS Press.

***Technology, Innovation & Competitiveness.** Ed. by Jeremy Howells & Jonathan Michie. LC 97-5357. 240p. 1997. 80.00 (*1-85898-428-9*) E Elgar.

***Technology Innovation & Enterprise: The European Experience.** Dylan Jones-Evans & Magnus Klofsten. LC 97-7760. 1997. text ed. 75.00 (*0-312-17546-9*) St Martin.

Technology, Innovation, & Regional Economic Development: Encouraging High-Technology Development. 1992. lib. bdg. 255.95 (*0-8490-5479-6*) Gordon Pr.

Technology, Institutions & Government Policies. Ed. by Jeffrey James & Susumu Watanabe. LC 84-17955. 320p. 1985. text ed. 35.00 (*0-312-79006-6*) St Martin.

***Technology Integration: Making Critical Choices in a Dynamic World.** Harvard Business School Press Staff. 1997. text ed. 35.00 (*0-07-105063-9*) McGraw.

***Technology Integration: Making Critical Choices in a Dynamic World.** Marco Iansiti. LC 97-13996. 1997. write for info. (*0-87584-787-0*) Harvard Busn.

Technology, Investment & Trade. Ed. by K. Uno. 443p. 1991. 125.00 (*0-444-01615-5*) P-H.

Technology Laser Discs. Brad Thode. (Tech & Industrial Education Ser.). 1995. teacher ed., pap. 14.00 (*0-8273-7138-1*) Delmar.

Technology, Law, & the Working Environment. rev. ed. Nicholas A. Ashford & Charles C. Caldart. LC 96-21826. 650p. 1995. pap. text ed. 39.95 (*1-55963-446-4*) Island Pr.

***Technology Leaders: How America's Most Profitable High-Tech Companies Innovate Their Way to Success.** Peter S. Cohan. LC 97-11674. (Business & Management Ser.). 1997. write for info. (*0-7879-1072-4*) Jossey-Bass.

T

An Asterisk (*) at the beginning of an entry indicates that the title is appearing in BIP for the first time.

Technology Licensing. (Patents, Copyrights, Trademarks, & Literary Property Ser.). 408p. 1989. 70.00 (*0-685-69503-4*) PLI.

Technology Licensing & Litigation. (Litigation & Administrative Practice Course Handbook, 1983-84 Ser.). 445p. 1989. 50.00 (*0-685-69502-6*) PLI.

Technology Licensing & Litigation 1992. (Patents, Copyrights, Trademarks, & Literary Property Ser.). 441p. 1992. pap. text ed. 70.00 (*0-685-56911-X*, G4-3880) PLI.

Technology Licensing & Litigation 1995. (Patents, Copyrights, Trademarks, & Literary Property Ser.). 560p. 1995. pap. 99.00 (*0-685-65517-2*, G4-3938) PLI.

Technology Licensing & Litigation 1996. (Patents, Copyrights, Trademarks, & Literary Property Course Handbook, 1994-95 Ser.). Date not set. pap. 99.00 (*0-614-17250-0*, G4-3967) PLI.

Technology Licensing & Litigation, 89. (Patents, Copyrights, Trademarks, & Literary Property Ser.). 505p. 1989. 70.00 (*0-685-69501-8*) PLI.

Technology Licensing Strategies. Ed. by Russell L. Parr & Patrick H. Sullivan. LC 95-53195. (Intellectual Property Library). 1996. text ed. 65.00 (*0-471-13081-8*) Wiley.

Technology Licensing to Distant Markets: Interaction Between Sweden & Indian Firms. Carl G. Thunman. (Acta Universitatis Upsaliensis Ser.: No. 28). 184p. (Orig.). 1988. pap. 41.00 (*91-554-2276-4*, Pub. by Uppsala Univ Acta Univ Uppsaliensis SW) Coronet Bks.

Technology Life Cycles & Human Resources. Patricia M. Flynn. 248p. (C). 1992. reprint ed. pap. text ed. 29.00 (*0-8191-8504-3*) U Pr of Amer.

Technology Link to Economic Development: Past Lessons & Future Imperatives. Susan U. Raymond et al. LC 96-20393. (Annals of the New York Academy of Sciences Ser.). 1996. pap. 110.00 (*1-57331-043-3*) NY Acad Sci.

Technology Link to Economic Development: Past Lessons &Future Imperatives. Susan U. Raymond et al. LC 96-20393. (Annals of the New York Academy of Sciences Ser.). 1996. write for info. (*1-57331-042-5*) NY Acad Sci.

Technology Making a Difference: The Peakview Elementary School Study. Brent G. Wilson et al. (Illus.). 230p. 1995. 7.50 (*0-937597-39-2*) ERIC Clear.

Technology Management. Robert Goldscheider. LC 88-4956. 1988. ring bd. 140.00 (*0-87632-591-6*) Clark Boardman Callaghan.

Technology Management: Applications for Corporate Markets & Military Missions. George K. Chacko. LC 88-12029. 213p. 1988. text ed. 49.95 (*0-275-92941-8*, C2941, Praeger Pubs) Greenwood.

Technology Management: Case Studies in Innovation. Ed. by Robert Szakonyi. 1992. text ed. 134.00 (*0-685-69683-9*, TMAN) Warren Gorham & Lamont.

Technology Management: Licensing & Protection for Computers in the World Market. Michael D. Rostoker. 267p. 1993. 29.95 (*0-9639750-0-5*) Cap Info Assocs.

Technology Management & Corporate Strategies: A Tricontinental Perspective. Ed. by Jose Allouche & Gerard Pogorel. 368p. 1995. text ed. 145.75 (*0-444-82173-2*, North Holland) Elsevier.

Technology Management & International Business: The Internationalization of R&D Technology. Ed. by Ove Granstrand et al. LC 91-45187. 254p. 1992. text ed. 85.00 (*0-471-93425-9*) Wiley.

Technology, Management & Marketing. Ove Granstrand. LC 82-16804. 300p. 1982. text ed. 32.50 (*0-312-79007-4*) St Martin.

Technology Management & Public Policy in the European Union. Ed. by William Cannell & Ben Dankbaar. (Illus.). 200p. 1996. 55.00 (*0-19-829028-4*) OUP.

Technology Management Combo. Robert Szakonri. 928p. 1993. 175.00 (*0-7913-1127-9*) Warren Gorham & Lamont.

Technology Management in Decentralized Firm. Albert H. Rubenstein. LC 88-20875. (Engineering Management Ser.). 476p. 1989. text ed. 84.95 (*0-471-61024-0*) Wiley.

Technology Management in Organizations. Urs E. Gattiker. (Illus.). 336p. (C). 1990. 48.00 (*0-8039-3607-9*); pap. 22.50 (*0-8039-3608-7*) Sage.

Technology Management in Organizations. Urs E. Gattiker. LC 90-8227. (Illus.). 339p. 1990. reprint ed. pap. 96.70 (*0-608-01717-5*, 2062372) Bks Demand.

***Technology, Market Structure, & Internationalization: Issues & Policies for Developing Countries.** Nagesh Kumar & N. S. Siddharthan. LC 97-7415. 192p. (C). 1998. text ed. write for info. (*0-415-16925-9*) Routledge.

Technology Markets & Export Controls in the 1990s. Ed. by David M. Kemme. 175p. (C). 1991. text ed. 32.00 (*0-8147-4617-9*) NYU Pr.

Technology Maze in Wholesale Distribution. Arthur Andersen & Co. Staff. 205p. 1991. pap. 160.00 (*0-614-02665-2*) Natl Assn Wholesale Dists.

Technology-Mediated Communication. Ed. by Urs E. Gattiker & Rosemarie S. Stollenmaier. LC 92-5545. (Technological Innovation & Human Resources Ser.: No. 3). viii, 325p. 1992. lib. bdg. 120.00 (*3-11-013419-5*) De Gruyter.

Technology of Artificial Lift Methods, 6 vol. set. Kermit E. Brown. Incl. Vol. 1. . 487p. 1977. 125.95 (*0-87814-031-X*); Vol. 2A. . 736p. 1980. 125.95 (*0-87814-119-7*); Vol. 2B. . 616p. 1980. 125.95 (*0-87814-133-2*); Vol. 3A. . 1087p. 1980. 125.95 (*0-87814-137-5*, P4244); Vol. 3B. . 1152p. 1980. 125.95 (*0-87814-138-3*, P4245); Vol. 4. . 474p. 1984. 125.95 (*0-87814-252-5*, P4345); 675.95 (*0-685-06893-5*, P4378) PennWell Bks.

Technology of Biological Processes, Safety in Biotechnology, Applied Genetic Engineering. Ed. by D. Behrens. (Dechema Biotechnology Conferences Ser.: Vol. 1). 496p. 1989. pap. text ed. 170.00 (*3-527-27821-4*, VCH); 150.00 (*0-685-56080-5*, VCH) Wiley.

***Technology of Biscuits, Crackers & Cookies.** 2nd ed. Duncan Manley. 476p. 1991. text ed. 199.95 (*1-85573-280-7*) Technomic.

***Technology of Breadmaking.** Cauvain. (Illus.). 448p. 1997. text ed. write for info. (*0-7514-0345-8*, Pub. by Blackie Acad & Prof UK) Routledge Chapman & Hall.

Technology of Breath-Alcohol Analysis. 1995. lib. bdg. 251.95 (*0-8490-6835-5*) Gordon Pr.

***Technology of Building Defects.** Hinks & Cook. (Illus.). 200p. (Orig.). 1997. text ed. 64.50 (*0-419-19770-2*, E & FN Spon); pap. text ed. 34.00 (*0-419-19780-X*, E & FN Spon) Routledge Chapman & Hall.

Technology of Carbon & Graphite Fiber Composites. 1996. lib. bdg. 350.95 (*0-8490-8298-6*) Gordon Pr.

Technology of Carbon & Graphite Fiber Composites. John Delmonte. LC 86-20820. 464p. 1987. reprint ed. lib. bdg. 49.50 (*0-89874-981-6*) Krieger.

Technology of Cereals: An Introduction for Students of Food Science & Agriculture. N. L. Kent. LC 75-6654. (Illus.). 200p. 1983. pap. text ed. 26.00 (*0-08-029800-1*, Pergamon Pr) Elsevier.

Technology of Cereals: An Introduction for Students of Food Science & Agriculture. 3rd ed. N. L. Kent. LC 75-6654. (Illus.). 200p. 1983. text ed. 47.00 (*0-08-029801-X*, Pergamon Pr) Elsevier.

Technology of Cereals: An Introduction for Students of Food Science & Agriculture. 4th ed. N. L. Kent & A. D. Evers. LC 93-6996. 250p. (C). 1994. text ed. 49.95 (*0-08-040833-8*, Prgamon Press); pap. text ed. 49.95 (*0-08-040834-6*, Prgamon Press) Buttrwrth-Heinemann.

Technology of Chemistry & Physics. Gauger. (Tech & Industrial Education Ser.). 1992. pap. 22.95 (*0-8273-4617-4*) Delmar.

Technology of Communication. W. J. Haynie. (TP - Technology Education Ser.). 1996. text ed. 30.95 (*0-538-64475-3*) S-W Pub.

Technology of Communication: Drawing, Photographic & Optical Systems, Print & Electronic Media. W. J. Haynie, III & Richard E. Peterson. LC 94-18582. 1994. write for info. (*0-8273-6714-7*) Delmar.

Technology of Continuously Annealed Cold-Rolled Sheet Steel: Proceedings of a Symposium Held at the TMS-AIME Fall Meeting in Detroit, MI, September 17-18, 1984. Metallurgical Society of AIME Staff. Ed. by R. Pradhan. LC 85-4776. (Conference Proceedings Ser.). 471p. reprint ed. pap. 134.30 (*0-8357-2520-0*, 2052400) Bks Demand.

Technology of Controlled Thermonuclear Fusion Experiments & the Engineering Aspects of Fusion Reactors: Proceedings. Ed. by E. Linn Draper, Jr. LC 74-600044. (AEC Symposium Ser.). 1040p. 1974. pap. 34.25 (*0-87079-221-0*, CONF-721111); fiche 9.00 (*0-87079-222-9*, CONF-721111) DOE.

Technology of Corn Wet Milling & Associated Processes. Paul H. Blanchard. LC 92-14173. (Industrial Chemistry Library: Vol. 4). 536p. 1992. 313.00 (*0-444-88255-3*) Elsevier.

***Technology of Dairy Products.** Ed. by R. Early. xiii, 306p. 1992. 125.00 (*1-56081-547-7*, VCH) Wiley.

Technology of Diabetes Care: Converging Medical & Psychosocial Perspectives. C. Bradley. x, 224p. 1991. text ed. 95.00 (*3-7186-5084-3*, Harwood Acad Pubs) Gordon & Breach.

Technology of Drafting. Edward Maruggi. 1990. wbk. ed., pap. text ed. 37.33 (*0-675-21234-0*, Merrill Coll) P-H.

***Technology of Ecological Building: Basic Principles & Measures, Examples & Ideas.** Klaus Daniels. 1997. write for info. (*0-8176-5461-5*) Birkhauser.

***Technology of Ecological Building: Basic Principles, Examples & Ideas.** Klaus Daniels. LC 97-13752. (Illus.). 304p. 1997. 69.50 (*3-7643-5461-5*) Birkhauser.

Technology of Electrical Measurements. Ed. by L. Schnell. (Series in Measurement Science & Technology). 409p. 1993. text ed. 105.00 (*0-471-93435-6*) Wiley.

Technology of Environmental Pollution Control. 2nd ed. Esber I. Shaheen. 576p. 1992. 94.95 (*0-87814-367-X*) PennWell Bks.

Technology of Extrusion Cooking. Frame. 1994. text ed. 99.95 (*0-442-30865-5*) Van Nos Reinhold.

Technology of Extrusion Cooking. Ed. by N. D. Frame. LC 93-21259. 1994. write for info. (*0-7514-0090-4*, Pub. by Blackie Acad & Prof UK) Routledge Chapman & Hall.

Technology of Fluid Power. Reeves. (Mechanical Technology Ser.). 480p. 1996. text ed. 51.95 (*0-8273-6664-7*) Delmar.

Technology of Fluid Power. Reeves. (Mechanical Technology Ser.). 1997. teacher ed. 14.00 (*0-8273-6665-5*) Van Nos Reinhold.

Technology of Fluid Power. Reeves. (Mechanical Technology Ser.). 1995. lab manual ed. 15.95 (*0-8273-6666-3*) Van Nos Reinhold.

Technology of Fluid Power. William W. Reeves. (Illus.). 320p. (C). 1987. text ed. 45.00 (*0-8359-7525-8*) P-H.

Technology of Food Product Development. Samuel A. Matz. 300p. 1993. 79.00 (*0-942849-11-6*) Pan Tech Intl.

***Technology of Glass & Ceramics.** J. Hlavac. (Glass Science & Technology Ser.: Vol. 4). 432p. 1983. 203.25 (*0-444-99688-5*) Elsevier.

Technology of Hybrid Rice Production. Yuan Long-Ping & Fu Xi-Qin. 94p. 1995. pap. 12.00 (*92-5-103613-6*) Food & Agriculture Organization of.

Technology of Hypermedia Learning Environment: Instructional Design & Integration. Piet A. Kommers et al. LC 96-8898. 300p. 1996. text ed. 69.95 (*0-8058-1828-6*); pap. text ed. 24.50 (*0-8058-1829-4*) L Erlbaum Assocs.

Technology of Industrial Materials. Hercules C. Kazanas et al. 1979. pap. 22.00 (*0-02-665900-X*) Glencoe.

Technology of Industrial Plant Layout & Material Handling. Fred E. Meyers. 1993. text ed. 52.00 (*0-13-904426-4*) P-H.

Technology of Killing: A Military & Political History of Anti-Personnel Weapons. Eric Prokosh. 256p. (C). 1995. pap. 19.95 (*1-85649-358-X*, Pub. by Zed Bks Ltd UK); text ed. 55.00 (*1-85649-357-1*, Pub. by Zed Bks Ltd UK) Humanities.

Technology of Love. Lynn Emanuel. (Illus.). 1988. pap. 27.50 (*0-318-41024-9*) Abattoir.

Technology of Machine Tools. 3rd ed. Joseph E. Amand et al. 672p. 1984. text ed. 40.95 (*0-07-035425-1*) McGraw.

Technology of Machine Tools. 4th ed. Stephen F. Krar & James W. Oswald. 1989. text ed. 32.76 (*0-07-035563-0*) McGraw.

Technology of Machine Tools. 8th ed. Steve F. Krar & Albert F. Check. LC 96-5183. 1996. write for info. (*0-02-803071-0*) Glencoe.

Technology of Machining Systems. M. Mullick & B. Bhattacharyya. (C). 1989. 50.00 (*0-89771-381-8*, Pub. by Current Dist II) St Mut.

Technology of Metallurgy. William K. Dalton. LC 92-43577. 463p. (C). 1993. text ed. 81.00 (*0-02-326900-6*, Macmillan Coll) P-H.

Technology of Our Times. Ed. by F. Su. 236p. 1990. 15.00 (*0-8194-0472-1*, PM04) SPIE.

***Technology of Paper Recycling.** Ed. by Mckinney. (Illus.). 416p. 1994. text ed. 136.95 (*0-7514-0017-3*, Pub. by Blackie Acad & Prof UK) Routledge Chapman & Hall.

Technology of Plastic Waste Processing. 194p. 1992. 2,450.00 (*0-89336-897-0*, P-132) BCC.

Technology of Political Control. 2nd ed. Carol Ackroyd. (C). pap. 19.95 (*0-86104-307-3*, Pub. by Pluto Pr UK) LPC InBook.

Technology of Portland Cement & Blended Cements. H. N. Banerjea. 154p. 1980. 15.95 (*0-318-37338-6*) Asia Bk Corp.

Technology of Proximal Probe Lithography. Ed. by Christie Marrian. LC 93-8684. (Institutes for Advanced Optical Technologies Ser.: Vol. IS 10). 1993. pap. 30.00 (*0-8194-1233-3*) SPIE.

Technology of Proximal Probe Lithography. Ed. by Christie Marrian. LC 93-8684. (Institutes for Advanced Optical Technologies Ser.: Vol. IS 10/HC). 1993. 30.00 (*0-8194-1232-5*) SPIE.

Technology of Reduced-Additive Foods. Ed. by Jim Smith. LC 92-43545. 1993. write for info. (*0-7514-0002-5*, Pub. by Blackie Acad & Prof UK) Routledge Chapman & Hall.

Technology of Skilled Processes: Assembling & Dismantling. Ed. by City & Guilds Staff. (C). 1987. 60.00 (*0-85973-023-9*, Pub. by S Thornes Pubs UK) St Mut.

Technology of Skilled Processes: Fabrication. Stanley Thornes. (C). 1987. 50.00 (*0-85973-025-5*, Pub. by S Thornes Pubs UK) St Mut.

Technology of Skilled Processes: Forming. Stanley Thornes. (C). 1986. 50.00 (*0-85973-042-5*, Pub. by S Thornes Pubs UK) St Mut.

Technology of Skilled Processes: Fusion Welding. Stanley Thornes. (C). 1987. 65.00 (*0-85973-019-0*, Pub. by S Thornes Pubs UK) St Mut.

Technology of Skilled Processes: Interpreting Drawing, Specs., Data. Stanley Thornes. (C). 1986. 80.00 (*0-85973-017-4*, Pub. by S Thornes Pubs UK) St Mut.

Technology of Skilled Processes: Joining. Stanley Thornes. (C). 1987. 65.00 (*0-85973-021-2*, Pub. by S Thornes Pubs UK) St Mut.

Technology of Skilled Processes: Measuring & Marking out. Stanley Thornes. (C). 1986. 60.00 (*0-85973-015-8*, Pub. by S Thornes Pubs UK) St Mut.

Technology of Skilled Processes: Observing Safe Practice. City & Guilds Staff. (C). 1984. 35.00 (*0-85973-008-5*, Pub. by S Thornes Pubs UK) St Mut.

Technology of Skilled Processes: Power Transmission. Stanley Thornes. (C). 1987. 50.00 (*0-85973-027-1*, Pub. by S Thornes Pubs UK) St Mut.

Technology of Skilled Processes: Soft Soldering & Brazing. Stanley Thornes. (C). 1987. 50.00 (*0-85973-029-8*, Pub. by S Thornes Pubs UK) St Mut.

Technology of Skilled Processes: Workholding & Toolholding. Stanley Thornes. (C). 1986. 50.00 (*0-85973-016-6*, Pub. by S Thornes Pubs UK) St Mut.

Technology of Study. Concept by L. Ron Hubbard. 48p. 1994. pap. 4.00 (*0-88404-908-6*) Bridge Pubns Inc.

Technology of Teaching Elementary School Science in the 21st Century. R. M. Kalra. (C). 1995. 14.00 (*81-207-1648-5*, Pub. by Sterling Plns Pvt II) S Asia.

Technology of Text: Principles for Structuring, Designing, & Displaying, Vol. 2. Ed. by David H. Jonassen. LC 81-22167. 442p. 1985. text ed. 49.95 (*0-87778-191-5*) Educ Tech Pubns.

Technology of Text: Principles for Structuring, Designing, & Displaying Text, Vol. 1. Ed. by David H. Jonassen. LC 81-22167. (Illus.). 500p. 1982. 49.95 (*0-87778-182-6*) Educ Tech Pubns.

***Technology of Textile Properties.** 3rd ed. M. A. Taylor. 1990. pap. 31.00 (*0-901762-82-2*, Pub. by Textile Inst UK) St Mut.

Technology of the Inorganic Azides see Energetic Materials

Technology of the Metal Trade. Hans Appold et al. (C). 1987. pap. 16.00 (*81-224-0029-9*) S Asia.

Technology of Thermoforming. James L. Throne. LC 96-24175. 1996. write for info. (*1-56990-198-8*) Hanser-Gardner.

***Technology of Transition: Science & Technology Policies for Transition Countries.** Ed. by David A. Dyker. (Illus.). 336p. 1997. 68.00 (*1-85866-050-5*); pap. 29.95 (*1-85866-051-3*) OUP.

***Technology of Underground Liquid Storage Tank Systems.** John P. Hartmann. text ed. 79.95 (*0-471-15412-1*) Wiley.

***Technology of Vitamins in Food.** Ed. by Berry Ottaway. (Illus.). 280p. 1992. text ed. 168.95 (*0-7514-0092-0*, Pub. by Blackie Acad & Prof UK) Routledge Chapman & Hall.

Technology of Vitamins in Food. Ottaway. 1994. text ed. 99.95 (*0-442-30864-7*) Van Nos Reinhold.

Technology of Wood Bonding: Principles in Practice. Alan A. Marra. (Structural Engineering Ser.). (Illus.). 608p. (gr. 13). 1992. text ed. 72.95 (*0-442-00797-3*) Chapman & Hall.

Technology, Open Learning, & Distance Education. A. Tony Bates. LC 94-44835. (Studies in Distance Education). 280p. (C). 1995. pap. 19.95 (*0-415-12799-8*) Routledge.

Technology, Open Learning, & Distance Education. A. Tony Bates. LC 94-44835. (Studies in Distance Education). 280p. (C). (gr. 13). 1995. text ed. 62.95 (*0-415-11682-1*) Routledge.

Technology Opportunities: Researching Emerging & Critical Technologies. Washington Researchers Publishing Staff. LC 86-51629. 467p. (Orig.). 1994. pap. 275.00 (*1-56365-030-4*) Wash Res.

Technology Options & Economic Policy for Dryland Agriculture. Ed. by N. S. Jodha. (C). 1989. 43.50 (*81-7022-225-7*, Pub. by Concept II) S Asia.

Technology Options for Electricity Generation: Economic & Environmental Factors. Hadi Dowlatabadi & Michael A. Toman. LC 91-6324. 87p. 1991. pap. 12.95 (*0-915707-58-6*) Resources Future.

***Technology, Organization, & Competitiveness: Perspectives on Industrial & Corporate Change.** Ed. by David Teece & Giovanni Dosi. 354p. 1997. pap. 24.95 (*0-19-829096-9*) OUP.

***Technology, Organization, & Competitiveness: Perspectives on Industrial & Corporate Change.** Ed. by David Teece & Giovanni Dosi. 354p. 1997. 85.00 (*0-19-829098-5*) OUP.

Technology, Organization, & Economic Structure: Essays in Honor of Prof. Isamu Yamada. Ed. by R. Sato & Martin J. Beckmann. (Lecture Notes in Economics & Mathematical Systems Ser.: Vol. 210). (Illus.). 195p. 1983. 34.00 (*0-387-11998-1*) Spr-Verlag.

Technology, Pessimism, & Postmodernism. Howard P. Segal. LC 93-23651. (Sociology of the Sciences Yearbook Ser.). 224p. (C). 1994. lib. bdg. 126.00 (*0-7923-2630-X*, Pub. by Klwr Acad Pubs NE) Kluwer Ac.

Technology, Pessimism, & Postmodernism. Howard P. Segal. LC 95-8315. 224p. (Orig.). 1995. pap. 14.95 (*0-87023-977-5*) U of Mass Pr.

***Technology Planning.** Steve Baule. LC 96-33499. (Professional Growth Ser.). 107p. 1996. pap. 29.95 (*0-938865-55-2*) Linworth Pub.

Technology Planning & Management Handbook: A Guide for School District Educational Technology Leaders. Philip J. Brody. LC 95-6388. 178p. 1995. pap. 37.95 (*0-87778-287-3*) Educ Tech Pubns.

Technology, Planning & Self-Reliant Development: A Latin American View. Francisco R. Sagasti. LC 78-26010. (Praeger Special Studies). 202p. 1979. text ed. 55.00 (*0-275-90416-4*, C0416, Praeger Pubs) Greenwood.

Technology Policies for Development & Selected Issues for Action. 267p. 1988. pap. 32.00 (*92-1-112247-3*, 88.II.D.7) UN.

Technology Policy: Towards an Integration of Social & Ecological Concerns. Ed. by Georg Aichholzer & Gerd Schienstock. LC 93-37994. (Studies in Organization: No. 52). xiv, 418p. (C). 1994. lib. bdg. 94.95 (*3-11-013677-5*) De Gruyter.

Technology Policy & America's Future. Steven M. Irwin. LC 93-952. 224p. 1993. text ed. 39.95 (*0-312-09961-4*) St Martin.

Technology Policy & Critical Technologies: A Summary of Recent Reports. Mary E. Mogee. 50p. (Orig.). (C). 1993. pap. text ed. 20.00 (*0-7881-0031-9*) DIANE Pub.

Technology Policy & Development: A Third World Perspective. Ed. by Pradip K. Ghosh. LC 83-22771. (International Development Resource Bks.: No. 3). (Illus.). xv, 593p. 1984. text ed. 89.50 (*0-313-24139-2*, GTE/, Greenwood Pr) Greenwood.

Technology Policy & Economic Performance: Lessons from Japan. Christopher Freeman. 150p. 1987. text ed. 39.00 (*0-86187-928-7*) St Martin.

Technology Policy for Small Developing Countries. David J. Forsyth. LC 90-31551. 206p. 1990. text ed. 65.00 (*0-312-04663-4*) St Martin.

Technology Pork Barrel. Roger G. Noll. 400p. 1991. 44.95 (*0-8157-1508-0*); pap. 19.95 (*0-8157-1507-2*) Brookings.

Technology Pricing: From Principles to Strategy. Francis Bidault. Tr. by Brian Page & Peter Sherwood. LC 88-18156. 300p. 1989. text ed. 55.00 (*0-312-02391-X*) St Martin.

***Technology Projects for the Classroom.** Allan Kaufman & Jim Flowers. LC 96-69775. (Illus.). 136p. (Orig.). (YA). (gr. 6 up). 1996. teacher ed. 2.00 (*0-911168-93-1*); pap. text ed. 14.95 (*0-911168-92-3*) Prakken.

Technology, R&D, & the Economy. Ed. by Bruce L. Smith & Claude E. Barfield. 222p. 1996. 38.95 (*0-8157-7986-0*); pap. 16.95 (*0-8157-7985-2*) Brookings.

Technology, Reading, & Lanaguage Arts. Jerry W. Willis et al. 1996. pap. text ed. 28.00 (*0-205-16286-X*) Allyn.

Technology Reference Series: Introduction Set. Holodnick & Campbell. (TP - Technology Education Ser.). 1996. 73.95 (*0-538-65235-7*) S-W Pub.

Technology, Regions, & Policy. Ed. by John Rees. 336p. (C). 1986. 59.50 (*0-8476-7409-6*, R7409) Rowman.

Technology Responses to Global Environmental Challenges. OECD Staff. 974p. (Orig.). 1994. pap. 100.00 (*92-64-14072-7*) OECD.

An Asterisk (*) at the beginning of an entry indicates that the title is appearing in BIP for the first time.

Technology, Scholarship, & the Humanities: The Implications of Electronic Information. 44p. 1993. write for info. (0-9632792-1-1) Am Coun Lrnd Soc.

Technology Schools Initiative: 1992-93. HMSO Staff. 60p. 1994. pap. 13.00 (0-11-350038-6, HM00386, Pub. by Stationery Ofc UK) Bernan Associates.

Technology Staff Development Programs: A Leadership Sourcebook for School Administrators. Gerald D. Bailey & Dan Lumley. LC 93-29341. 1995. 39.95 (0-590-49220-9, 1731b25 1994) Scholastic Inc.

Technology Strategies & Management in Large Corporations. Granstrand & Sjolander. 200p. 1996. text ed. 70.00 (0-471-95358-X) Wiley.

*__Technology Strategies of Best Practice Credit Unions: Today, the Near Future, & the Far Future.__ Albert E. Burger et al. 183p. 1997. pap. 40.00 (1-880572-28-1) Filene Res.

Technology Systems. R. Thomas Wright. 480p. 1996. 38.60 (1-56637-263-1) Goodheart.

Technology Teaching & Learning Science. Karen E. Reynolds & Barba. 256p. 1996. pap. 26.00 (0-205-16287-8) Allyn.

Technology, the Economy & Education. Ed. by Peter Watkins. 125p. (C). 1985. 48.00 (0-7300-0332-9, Pub. by Deakin Univ AT) St Mut.

Technology, the Economy, & Society: The American Experience. Ed. by Joel Colton & Stuart Bruchey. LC 86-24475. 304p. 1987. text ed. 55.00 (0-231-05964-7) Col U Pr.

Technology, the Environment, & Social Change: Papers of the 38th Annual Meeting of the Seminar on the Acquisition of Latin American Library Materials. Ed. by Patricia Noble. 467p. (Orig.). (C). 1995. pap. 55.00 (0-917617-49-5) SALALM.

Technology, the University, & the Community. Ed. by George Bugliarello & H. A. Simon. 1976. 230.00 (0-08-017872-3, Pub. by Pergamon Repr UK) Franklin.

Technology, Time & the Conversations of Modernity. Lorenzo C. Simpson. LC 94-19289. 256p. (C). 1994. pap. 17.95 (0-415-90772-1, B0559, Routledge NY); text ed. 59.95 (0-415-90771-3, B0555, Routledge NY) Routledge.

Technology Today & Tomorrow. 2nd ed. James E. Fales. 27.99 (0-02-677103-9) Glencoe.

Technology, Tradition, & the State in Africa. John R. Goody. LC 79-24375. 96p. reprint ed. pap. 27.40 (0-685-20551-7, 2030597) Bks Demand.

*__Technology Transfer.__ Campbell. 1900. pap. text ed. 145.00 (90-6544-609-5) Kluwer Ac.

Technology Transfer: A Communication Perspective. Ed. by Frederick Williams & David V. Gibson. (Focus Editions Ser.: Vol. 122). (Illus.). 320p. (C). 1990. 44.00 (0-8039-3740-7); pap. 22.95 (0-8039-3741-5) Sage.

Technology Transfer: A Communication Perspective. Ed. by Frederick Williams & David V. Gibson. LC 90-8778. 302p. 1990. reprint ed. pap. 86.10 (0-608-01535-0, 2059579) Bks Demand.

Technology Transfer: A Realistic Approach. Silvere Seurat. LC 78-62608. (Illus.). 184p. reprint ed. pap. 52.50 (0-685-23783-4, 2032869) Bks Demand.

Technology Transfer: A Unit Report from the Energy Task Force of the Urban Cosortium. 80p. 1981. 15.00 (0-318-17348-4, DG/81-305) Pub Tech Inc.

Technology Transfer: An Executive Guide. R. Duane Hall. LC 87-4954. write for info. (0-394-55325-X) Random.

Technology Transfer: Barriers Limit Royalty Sharing's Effectiveness. (Illus.). 128p. (Orig.). (C). 1993. pap. text ed. 50.00 (1-56806-651-1) DIANE Pub.

Technology Transfer: Federal Efforts to Enhance the Competitiveness of Small Manufacturers. 52p. (Orig.). (C). 1993. pap. text ed. 25.00 (1-56806-540-X) DIANE Pub.

Technology Transfer: Geographic, Economic, Cultural & Technical Dimensions. Ed. by A. Coskun Samli. LC 84-16113. (Illus.). xviii, 296p. 1985. text ed. 59.95 (0-89930-057-X, SBK/, Quorum Bks) Greenwood.

Technology Transfer: How to Make It Work, a Management Handbook. Hyman Olken. 92p. 1972. pap. 7.00 (0-934818-00-2) Olken Pubns.

Technology Transfer: Law & Practice in Latin America. International Law & Practice Section. 360p. 1980. 12.00 (0-685-14374-0, 521-0028) Amer Bar Assn.

Technology Transfer: Making the Most of Your Intellectual Property. Neil F. Sullivan. (Illus.). 240p. (C). 1996. text ed. 69.95 (0-521-46066-2); pap. text ed. 25.95 (0-521-46616-4) Cambridge U Pr.

Technology Transfer: National SAMPE Technical Conference, 13th, Mount Airy Lodge, Mount Pocono, Pennsylvania, October 13-15, 1981. National SAMPE Technical Conference Staff. LC 82-103085. (National SAMPE Technical Conference Ser.: No. 13). 711p. reprint ed. pap. 180.00 (0-7837-1289-8, 2041430) Bks Demand.

Technology Transfer: New Issues, New Analysis. Ed. by Alan W. Heston & Howard Pack. (Annals of the American Academy of Political & Social Science Ser.: Vol. 458). 322p. 1981. 26.00 (0-8039-1707-4); pap. 17.00 (0-8039-1706-6) Sage.

Technology Transfer: Options for Sustainable Development. 1994. 35.00 (92-1-104428-6) UN.

Technology Transfer: Scandinavian Industrialization & Economic Growth. Ed. by Kristine Bruland. 424p. 1992. 19.95 (0-85496-605-6) Berg Pubs.

Technology Transfer: The Role of the Sci-Tech Librarian. Ed. by Cynthia A. Steinke. (Science & Technology Libraries: Vol. 11, No. 2). (Illus.). 168p. 1990. text ed. 39.95 (1-56024-116-0) Haworth Pr.

Technology Transfer & Business Enterprise. Ed. by David J. Jeremy. (International Library of Critical Writings in Business History: Vol. 9). 712p. 1994. 225.00 (1-85278-727-9) E Elgar.

Technology Transfer & East-West Relations. Ed. by Mark E. Schaffer. LC 84-40373. 288p. 1985. text ed. 45.00 (0-312-79016-3) St Martin.

Technology Transfer & Economic Development. James Breagy. Ed. by Jenny Murphy. 72p. (Orig.). 1990. pap. 22.50 (0-317-04804-X) Natl Coun Econ Dev.

Technology Transfer & Foreign Trade: The Case of Japan, 1950 to 1966. rev. ed. Yoshihiro Tsurumi. Ed. by Stuart Bruchey. LC 80-600. (Multinational Corporations Ser.). (Illus.). 1981. lib. bdg. 31.95 (0-405-13390-1) Ayer.

Technology Transfer & International Law. Peter Nanyenya-Takirambudde. LC 79-23571. 190p. 1980. text ed. 36.95 (0-275-90529-2, C0529, Praeger Pubs) Greenwood.

Technology Transfer & Management in Export Processing Zones. Ed. by Richard L. Bolin. 127p. 1990. pap. 40.00 (0-945951-05-1) Flagstaff Inst.

*__Technology Transfer & Public Policy.__ Ed. by Yong S. Lee. LC 97-1699. 1997. text ed. write for info. (1-56720-084-2, Quorum Bks) Greenwood.

Technology Transfer & Public Policy: Preparing for the Twenty-First Century. Ed. by Yong S. Lee. 236p. (Orig.). 1994. pap. 15.00 (0-944285-38-4) Pol Studies.

Technology Transfer & the University. Gary W. Matkin. (ACE-Oryx Series on Higher Education). (Illus.). 352p. 1990. 29.95 (0-02-897263-5, ACE-Oryx) Oryx Pr.

Technology Transfer by Multinationals, Pts. I & II. (C). 1988. 90.00 (0-8364-2341-0, Pub. by Ashish II) S Asia.

*__Technology Transfer in a Global Community: 28th International SAMPE Technical Conference, Westin Hotel, Seattle, Washington, November 4-7, 1996.__ Ed. by John Hoggatt et al. (International SAMPE Technical Conference Ser.: No. 28). (Illus.). 1414p. pap. 298.00 (0-608-04966-2, 2065545) Bks Demand.

Technology Transfer in Consortia & Strategic Alliances. Ed. by David V. Gibson & Raymond W. Smilor. 360p. (C). 1992. 59.50 (0-8476-7717-6) Rowman.

Technology Transfer in Europe. John Bessant. 224p. (C). (gr. 13). 1996. text ed. 65.00 (0-415-08231-5, B4414) Routledge.

Technology Transfer in Europe. David Charles & Jeremy Howells. (Illus.). 256p. 1992. text ed. 54.00 (1-85293-160-4) St Martin.

Technology Transfer in Export Processing Zones the Semiconductor Industry in Malaysia. Ed. by Mark Lester. (Contemporary Studies in Economic & Financial Analysis: Vol. 47). 1989. 73.25 (0-89232-429-5) Jai Pr.

Technology Transfer in Fibres, Textile & Apparel. Gerard K. Boon. 600p. 1981. lib. bdg. 235.50 (90-286-0520-7) Kluwer Ac.

Technology Transfer in Industrialized Countries. Ed. by S. Gee. 464p. 1979. lib. bdg. 93.00 (90-286-0038-8) Kluwer Ac.

Technology Transfer in International Business. Ed. by Tamir Agmon & Mary A. Von Glinow. (Research Book from the International Business School & Research Program Ser.). (Illus.). 304p. 1991. 42.00 (0-19-506235-3) OUP.

Technology Transfer in Rural Industries: Cases & Analysis. T. K. Moulik & P. Purushotham. 1986. 18.50 (0-86132-124-3, Pub. by Popular Prakashan II) S Asia.

Technology Transfer in the Developing World: The Case of the Chile Foundation. Frank Meissner. LC 87-36127. 177p. 1988. text ed. 49.95 (0-275-92926-4, C2926, Praeger Pubs) Greenwood.

Technology Transfer in the Peoples' Republic of China: Law & Practice. Richard J. Goossen. LC 86-33343. 1987. lib. bdg. 103.00 (90-247-3442-8) Kluwer Ac.

Technology Transfer in U. S. Aeronautics: U. S. Government Support of the U. S. Commercial Aircraft Industry. 105p. (Orig.). (C). 1992. pap. text ed. 40.00 (0-941375-71-4) DIANE Pub.

Technology Transfer Law: The Export Administration Acts of the United States, 1969-1985 Federal Laws, Legislative Histories, &..., 15 vols. in 33 bks. Bernard D. Reams, Jr. 1986. reprint ed. Set. 1,750.00 (0-89941-437-0, 303790) W S Hein.

*__Technology Transfer of Plant Biotechnology.__ Ed. by Peter M. Gresshoff. LC 96-48232. (Current Topics in Plant Molecular Biology Ser.). 240p. 1996. 69.95 (0-8493-8265-3) CRC Pr.

Technology Transfer Out of Germany After 1945. Burghard Ciesla & Matthias Judt. (Studies in the History of Science, Technology & Medicine Ser.). 1996. text ed. 45.00 (3-7186-5822-4) Gordon & Breach.

*__Technology Transfer Regulation & the EC Competition Rules.__ Valentine Korah. 220p. 1997. 115.00 (0-19-826243-4) OUP.

Technology Transfer Report: Who's Doing What with What. 304p. 1992. 1,250.00 (0-89336-975-6, GB-153) BCC.

*__Technology Transfer Research, Progress & Results: Index of New Information.__ Science & Life Consultants Association Staff. 170p. (Orig.). 1997. 47.50 (0-7883-1440-8); pap. 44.50 (0-7883-1441-6) ABBE Pubs Assn.

*__Technology Transfer System: Inventions - Marketing - Licensing - Patenting - Setting - Practice - Management - Policy.__ Albert E. Muir. LC 97-93356. xiii, 241p. 1997. 24.95 (0-9657597-6-8) Latham Bk Pub.

Technology Transfer Systems in the United States & Germany: Lessons & Perspectives. National Academy Press Staff. 150p. 1996. pap. text ed. 30.00 (0-309-05530-X) Natl Acad Pr.

*__Technology Transfer to China Through Foreign Direct Investment.__ Ping Lan. 260p. 1996. text ed. 59.95 (1-85972-205-9, Pub. by Avebury Pub UK) Ashgate Pub Co.

Technology Transfer to Developing Countries: The Case of the Fertilizer Industry. Ingo I. Walter. LC 80-82478. (Contemporary Studies in Economic & Financial Analysis: Vol. 27). 181p. 1981. 73.25 (0-89232-160-1) Jai Pr.

Technology Transfer to Developing Nations. Intro. by I. Crambari. (Illus.). 198p. (C). 1995. pap. text ed. write for info. (1-885778-04-X) Seaburn.

Technology Transfer, Working for Collaboration Commerce, & Competitiveness: Report of the Advisory Committee on Development & Transfer of Biotechnology. Advisory Committee on Development & Transfer of Biotechnology Staff. 68p. (Orig.). 1994. pap. write for info. (0-945597-29-0) NC Biotech Ctr.

Technology Trap. Timothy Garden. 148p. 1989. 32.00 (0-08-036710-0, Pub. by Brasseys UK) Brasseys Inc.

Technology Trendlines: Technology Success Stories from Today's Visionaries. Jessica Keyes. 448p. 1995. text ed. 36.95 (0-442-02022-8) Van Nos Reinhold.

Technology Trends in the Golf Industry. unabridged ed. (NGF Info Pacs Ser.). (Illus.). 100p. (Orig.). 1995. pap. 45.00 (1-57701-026-4) Natl Golf.

Technology Utilization Ideas for the 70's & Beyond: Proceedings of the Governor Rockefeller Symposium, Winrock, Arkansas, October 1970. Ed. by Fred W. Forbes & Paul Dergarabedian. (Science & Technology Ser.: Vol. 26). 1971. 30.00 incl. fiche (0-87703-057-X) Univelt Inc.

Technology Vectors: National SAMPE Symposium & Exhibition, 29th, MGM Grand Hotel, Reno, Nevada, April 3-5, 1984. National SAMPE Symposium & Exhibition Staff. LC 84-215021. (Science of Advanced Materials & Process Enginnering Ser.: No. 29). 1638p. reprint ed. pap. 180.00 (0-7837-1282-0, 2041423) Bks Demand.

Technology Venturing: American Innovation & Risk-Taking. Ed. by Eugene B. Konecci & Robert L. Kuhn. LC 85-12192. 272p. 1985. text ed. 59.95 (0-275-90211-0, C0211, Praeger Pubs) Greenwood.

Technology, Vol. 3: (Incl. 1988-1992 Supplements) Ed. by Eleanor C. Goldstein. (Social Issues Resources Ser.). 1993. 95.00 (0-89777-092-7) Sirs Inc.

*__Technology, War & Fascism.__ Herbert Marcuse & Douglas Kellner. LC 97-14885. (Collected Papers of Herbert Marcuse). 1998. write for info. (0-415-13780-2) Routledge.

Technology, Women, & Farming Systems. Heather Baser. (Studies in Technology & Social Change: No. 5). 26p. (Orig.). (C). 1988. pap. 4.00 (0-945271-08-5) ISU-CIKARD.

Technology, Workers, & Wages: An International Review. Ed. by Bronwyn Hall et al. 275p. (C). 1997. 39.95 (0-309-05528-8) Natl Acad Pr.

Technology, World Politics, & American Policy. Victor Basiuk. LC 76-51841. (Institute of War & Peace Studies). 409p. 1977. 64.00 (0-231-04154-3) Col U Pr.

Technology 2000: Technology Transfer Conference: Jet Propulsion Laboratory (JPL) Papers. (Illus.). 64p. (Orig.). (C). 1993. pap. text ed. 20.00 (1-56806-203-6) DIANE Pub.

Technology 2001: The Future of Computing & Communications. Ed. by Derek Leebaert. (Illus.). 416p. 1992. reprint ed. pap. 17.95 (0-262-62084-7) MIT Pr.

Technology's Challenge to Science Education: Cathedral, Quarry, or Company Store? David Layton. LC 92-30287. (Developing Science & Technology Education Ser.). 1993. 82.00 (0-335-09959-9, Open Univ Pr); pap. 25.00 (0-335-09958-0, Open Univ Pr) Taylor & Francis.

Technology's Crucible. James Martin. (Illus.). 192p. 1986. pap. 17.50 (0-13-902024-1) P-H.

Technology's Harvest: Feeding a Growing World Population. Gunther P. Eschenbrenner & Robert H. Multhaup. LC 96-15591. (Illus.). 288p. 1996. 35.00 (0-88415-867-5, 5867) Gulf Pub.

Technology's New Horizons: Conversations with Japanese Scientists. Ed. by Hiroaki Yanagida. 200p. 1995. text ed. 35.00 (0-19-856514-3) OUP.

Technology's Past: America's Industrial Revolution & the People Who Delivered the Goods. Dennis Karwatka. LC 95-72938. (Illus.). 272p. (Orig.). 1996. pap. 24.95 (0-911168-91-5) Prakken.

Technology's School Supplement 3: The Challenge to Philosophy. Leonard J. Waks. Ed. by Carl Mitcham. 280p. 1995. 73.25 (1-55938-956-7) Jai Pr.

Technology's Storytellers: Reweaving the Human Fabric. John M. Staudenmaier. 350p. 1985. 42.50 (0-262-19237-3) MIT Pr.

Technology's Storytellers: Reweaving the Human Fabric. John M. Staudenmaier. 350p. 1989. pap. 14.95 (0-262-69135-3) MIT Pr.

*__Technomancer's Toybox.__ White Wolf Staff. 1998. pap. 15.00 (1-56504-420-7) White Wolf.

*__Technophobe.__ Godin, Seth, Productions Staff. 1996. pap. 9.95 (0-7871-1159-7, Dove Bks) Dove Audio.

Technopoles of the World: Making of 21st Century Industrial Complexes. Manuel Castells. (Illus.). 320p. (C). 1994. pap. 19.95 (0-415-10015-1, Routledge NY) Routledge.

Technopolis: High-Technology Industry & Regional Development in Southern California. Allen J. Scott. LC 93-3137. 1993. 35.00 (0-520-08189-7) U CA Pr.

Technopolis Phenomenon: Smart Cities, Fast Systems, Global Networks. Ed. by David V. Gibson et al. LC 92-10225. (International Series on Technical Innovation & Entrepreneurship). 380p. (C). 1992. text ed. 59.50 (0-8476-7758-3) Rowman.

Technopols: Freeing Politics & Markets in Latin America in the 1990s. Ed. by Jorge I. Dominguez. LC 96-12003. (Illus.). 352p. 1996. 55.00 (0-271-01613-2); pap. 18.95 (0-271-01614-0) Pa St U Pr.

Technopoly. Jim McBurney. Ed. by Mae Kraven. (Technology Education Ser.). (Illus.). 96p. (J). (gr. 4-5). 1991. text ed. 19.95 (0-9629471-0-5) J McBurney.

Technopoly. Neil Postman. 1992. pap. 22.00 (0-394-58272-1) Knopf.

Technopoly: The Surrender of Culture to Technology. Neil Postman. LC 92-50584. 1993. pap. 12.00 (0-679-74540-8, Vin) Random.

*__Technoscience.__ Berland. 1997. pap. 19.50 (0-85315-825-8) NYU Pr.

Technoscience & Cyberculture: A Cultural Study. Ed. by Stanley Aronowitz et al. LC 95-22528. 288p. (C). (gr. 13). 1995. text ed. 74.95 (0-415-91175-3, C0241, Routledge NY) Routledge.

Technoscience & Cyberculture: A Cultural Study. Ed. by Stanley Aronowitz et al. LC 95-22528. 328p. 1995. pap. 18.95 (0-415-91176-1, C0244, Routledge NY) Routledge.

Technoscience Worlds. David Turnbull. 61p. (C). 1995. pap. 28.00 (0-7300-1306-5, Pub. by Deakin Univ AT) St Mut.

*__Technoscientific Angst: Ethics & Responsibility.__ Raphael Sassower. LC 97-20529. 1997. write for info. (0-8166-2956-0); pap. write for info. (0-8166-2957-9) U of Minn Pr.

Technoscientific Imaginaries: Conversations, Profiles, & Memoirs. Ed. by George E. Marcus. 570p. 1995. pap. text ed. 22.50 (0-226-50444-1); lib. bdg. 65.00 (0-226-50443-3) U Ch Pr.

TechnoSelling: How to Use Today's Technology to Increase Your Sales. Ed Callaghan & Peter W. Nauert. 288p. 1995. 24.95 (0-9645225-0-0) Lone Str Pub.

Technosex: Cyber Age Erotica. Ed. by Cecilia Tan. (Illus.). 96p. (Orig.). 1993. pap. 7.95 (0-9633970-5-2) Circlet Pr.

*__Technoshock: Combatting Stress at Work & Home in the 90's & Beyond.__ Michael Cohn. 124p. 1996. per., pap. text ed. 15.00 (0-7872-2807-9) Kendall-Hunt.

*__TechnoStress: Coping with Technology @ Work @ Home @ Play.__ Michelle M. Weil & Larry D. Rosen. LC 97-16114. 224p. 1997. 22.95 (0-471-17709-1) Wiley.

Technotouch: The Journey to Twenty First Century Success. Marlene B. Brown. LC 92-90740. 112p. 1994. pap. text ed. 14.95 (1-56728-015-3) Sunrise Pl.

Technotrends: How to Use Technology to Go Beyond Your Competition. Daniel Burns. LC 92-56234. 400p. 1993. pap. 15.00 (0-88730-700-0) Harper Busn.

*__Technovision II: Every Executive's Guide to Understanding & Mastering Technology & the Internet.__ Charles B. Wang. 1997. text ed. 19.95 (0-07-068169-4) McGraw.

Techpro: Information Processing/Keyboarding Simulation. Abramson. (TA - Typing/Keyboarding Ser.). 1993. pap. 21.95 (0-538-61725-X) S-W Pub.

Techtransfer & CRADA with Federal Laboratories. Som R. Soni. LC 94-70347. 1994. pap. text ed. 29.95 (0-9640110-0-X) AdTech Systs.

Techwise: Wise Protocols for X-Ray Technologists. Ricardo A. Scott. (Illus.). 120p. (Orig.). (C). write for info. (1-883427-17-7) Crnerstone GA.

Tecicas e Ideas para Eiupar Su Taller. Cy DeCosse Incorporated Staff. (Black & Decker Home Improvement Library). 1994. 16.95 (0-86573-737-1) Cowles Creative.

Teckla. Steven Brust. 224p. 1987. mass mkt. 4.99 (0-441-79977-9) Ace Bks.

*__Tecnazene.__ (Environmental Health Criteria Ser.: No. 42). 23p. 1984. pap. text ed. 11.00 (92-4-154182-2, 1160042) World Health.

*__Tecnazene Health & Safety Guide.__ WHO Staff. (Health & Safety Guides: No. 12). 28p. 1988. 5.00 (92-4-154336-1) World Health.

Tecnica. J. A. Lopez. (SPA.). 7.95 (84-241-5628-5) E Torres & Sons.

*__Tecnicas Cruciales de Marketing: Marketing & Mastering Your Small Business.__ Gloria Green & Jeffrey Williams. 240p. (Orig.). (SPA.). 1997. pap. 19.95 (0-7931-2714-9, 1700-1101, Upstart) Dearborn Finan.

Tecnicas De Comunicacion Oral Para Estudiantes De Vocacional Tecnica: Metodo Basado En la Practica De Estas Tecnicas Para Lograr Su Perfeccionamiento. Cathy S. Mester & Robert T. Tauber. Tr. by Francisco J. Tellez & Nanette De Paoli de Sales from ENG. 160p. (Orig.). (SPA.). 1992. pap. text ed. 10.75 (0-911168-83-4) Prakken.

Tecnicas Mecanograficas Modernas. 3rd ed. J. Q. Gorbea. 240p. 1979. text ed. 21.96 (0-07-023791-3) McGraw.

Tecnicas Medico-Quirurgicas en Situaciones de Aislamiento. Ed. by Jean Rigal. (Medecins Sand Frontieres - Hatier Ser.). 172p. (SPA.). 1989. vinyl bd. 23.95 (2-218-02165-X) Hatier Pub.

Tecnicas Quirurgicas de Base. Ed. by Jean Rigal. (Medesins Sans Frontieres - Hatier Ser.). 207p. (SPA.). 1992. vinyl bd. 23.95 (2-218-02346-6) Hatier Pub.

*__Tecnologia de la Leche.__ Aurelio Revilla. (Orig.). (SPA.). (C). 1996. pap. text ed. write for info. (0-614-24435-8) Escuela Agricola.

Tecnologia de los Composites-Plasticos Reforzados. Walter Michaeli et al. 182p. (C). 1992. pap. text ed. write for info. (1-56990-171-6) Hanser-Gardner.

Tecnologia Farmaceutica Industrial. Rodolfo S. Escabi. LC 76-46412. 356p. (Orig.). (SPA.). 1977. pap. 8.00 (0-8477-2321-6) U of PR Pr.

Tecnologias Para el Cero Defectos: Inspecciones En la Fuente & el Sistema Poka-Yoke. Shigeo Shingo. (Illus.). 299p. (Orig.). (SPA.). 1990. pap. 65.00 (84-87022-97-9) Prod Press.

TECO: Art Pottery of the Prairie School. Sharon S. Darling & Richard Zakin. (Illus.). 192p. 1989. 39.95 (0-614-04811-7) Erie Art Mus.

T

An Asterisk (*) at the beginning of an entry indicates that the title is appearing in BIP for the first time.

Tectonic & Eustatic Controls on Sedimentary Cycles. Ed. by J. M. Dennison & F. R. Ettensohn. (Concepts in Sedimentology & Paleontology Ser.: No. 4). (Illus.). 264p. 1994. pap. text ed. 45.00 (*1-56576-017-4*) SEPM.

Tectonic & Geologic Evolution of Southeast Asian Seas & Islands, Pt. 1. Ed. by D. E. Hayes. (Geophysical Monograph Ser.: Vol. 23). 334p. 1980. 32.00 (*0-87590-023-2*) Am Geophysical.

Tectonic & Geologic Evolution of Southeast Asian Seas & Islands, Pt. 2. Ed. by D. E. Hayes. (Geophysical Monograph Ser.: Vol. 27). 396p. 1983. 42.00 (*0-87590-053-4*) Am Geophysical.

Tectonic & Metamorphic Investigations of Kumaon-Garhwal Himachal Lesser Himalaya. I. C. Pandey. Ed. by P. S. Saklani. (Current Trends in Geology Ser.: Vol. 13). (Illus.). 179p. 1991. 65.00 (*1-55528-240-7*, Messers Today & Tomorrow) Scholarly Pubns.

***Tectonic Boundary Conditions for Climate Reconstructions.** Ed. by Thomas J. Crowley & Kevin C. Burke. (Oxford Monographs on Geology & Geophysics). (Illus.). 288p. 1998. 75.00 (*0-19-511245-8*) OUP.

Tectonic Controls & Signatures in Sedimentary Successions. Ed. by L. E. Frostick & R. J. Steel. LC 93-7590. 528p. 1994. 95.00 (*0-632-03745-8*) Blackwell Sci.

Tectonic, Depositional, & Paleoecological History of Early Mesozoic Rift Basins, Eastern North America, No. T351. Ed. by Olsen. (IGC Field Trip Guidebooks Ser.). 184p. 1989. 35.00 (*0-87590-658-3*) Am Geophysical.

Tectonic Evolution of a Forearc Terrane, Southern Scotia Ridge, Antarctica. Ian W. Dalziel. (Special Papers: No. 200). (Illus.). 38p. 1985. pap. 2.00 (*0-8137-2200-4*) Geol Soc.

Tectonic Evolution of Asia. Ed. by An Yin & Mark Harrison. LC 95-20092. (World & Regional Geology Ser.: No. 8). (Illus.). 600p. (C). 1996. text ed. 200.00 (*0-521-48049-3*) Cambridge U Pr.

Tectonic Evolution of Northern California. Ed. by Blake. (IGC Field Trip Guidebooks Ser.). 80p. 1989. 21.00 (*0-87590-614-1*, T108) Am Geophysical.

Tectonic Evolution of Southeast Asia. Ed. by R. Hall & D. J. Blundell. (Geological Society Special Publication: Series 106). (Illus.). xiv, 566p. 1996. 132.00 (*1-897799-52-7*, 344, Pub. by Geol Soc Pub Hse UK) AAPG.

Tectonic Evolution of the North Sea Rifts. Ed. by D. J. Blundell & A. D. Gibbs. (Illus.). 290p. 1991. 125.00 (*0-19-854595-9*) OUP.

Tectonic Evolution of the Tethyan Region. Ed. by A. M. Sengor. (C). 1989. lib. bdg. 291.00 (*0-7923-0067-X*) Kluwer Ac.

***Tectonic Evolution of the Uinta Mountains: Palinspastic Restoration of a Structural Cross Section along Longitude 109 Degrees 15', Utah.** Donald S. Stone. (Miscellaneous Publication of the Utah Geological Survey Ser.: Vol. 93-8). (Illus.). 19p. (Orig.). 1993. pap. 6.00 (*1-55791-326-9*, MP93-8) Utah Geological Survey.

Tectonic Geology of the Himalaya. Ed. by P. S. Saklani. (Current Trends in Geology Ser.: Vol. I). 340p. 1978. 50.00 (*0-88065-187-3*, Messers Today & Tomorrow) Scholarly Pubns.

Tectonic History of the Bering Sea & the Evolution of Tertiary Strike-Slip Basins of the Bering Shelf. D. M. Worrall. (Special Papers: No. 257). (Illus.). 126p. 1991. pap. 22.00 (*0-8137-2257-8*) Geol Soc.

Tectonic Influence on Sedimentation, Early Cretaceous, East Flank Powder River Basin, Wyoming & South Dakota. T. L. Davis et al. Ed. by J. H. Goldberg & Jon W. Raese. LC 82-17894. (Colorado School of Mines Quarterly Ser.: Vol. 77, No. 4). (Illus.). 61p. 1983. pap. text ed. 12.00 (*0-686-82131-9*) Colo Sch Mines.

***Tectonic, Magmatic, Hydrothermal & Biological Segmentation at Mid-Ocean Ridges.** C. L. Walker. (Geological Society Special Publication Ser.: No. 118). (Illus.). vi, 266p. 1996. 108.00 (*1-897799-72-1*, 359, Pub. by Geol Soc Pub Hse UK) AAPG.

Tectonic Setting of Faulted Tertiary Strata Associated with the Catalina Core Complex in Southern Arizona. W. R. Dickinson. (Special Papers: No. 264). (Illus.). 120p. 1991. pap. 18.00 (*0-8137-2264-0*) Geol Soc.

Tectonic Stresses in the Alpine-Mediterranean Region: Proceedings. Adrian E. Scheidegger. (Rock Mechanics Ser.: Suppl. 9). (Illus.). 270p. 1980. 103.95 (*0-387-81578-3*) Spr-Verlag.

***Tectonic Uplift & Climate Change.** Ed. by W. F. Ruddiman. 458p. (C). 1997. write for info. (*0-306-45642-7*, Plenum Pr) Plenum.

Tectonics. Eldridge M. Moores & Robert J. Twiss. LC 95-10975. 415p. (C). 1996. text ed. 59.95 (*0-7167-2437-5*) W H Freeman.

Tectonics: A Selection of Papers. Ed. by J. F. Dewey et al. 150p. 1981. pap. 25.00 (*0-08-028742-5*, Pergamon Pr) Elsevier.

Tectonics: Proceedings of the 27th International Geological Congress, Vol. 7. International Geological Congress Staff. 392p. 1984. lib. bdg. 112.00 (*90-6764-016-6*, Pub. by VSP NE) Coronet Bks.

Tectonics & Geophysics of Continental Rifts. Ed. by Ivar B. Ramberg & Else-Ragnhild Neumann. (NATO Advanced Study Institute Ser.: No. 37). 1978. lib. bdg. 112.00 (*90-277-0867-3*) Kluwer Ac.

Tectonics & Sedimentation: Based on a Symposium Sponsored by the Society of Economic Paleontologists & Mineralogists: Papers. Ed. by William R. Dickinson. LC 75-302534. (Society of Economic Paleontologists & Mineralogists, Special Publication Ser.: No. 22). (Illus.). 210p. reprint ed. pap. 59.90 (*0-8357-6634-9*, 2035287) Bks Demand.

Tectonics & Sedimentation along Faults of the San Andreas System. Ed. by David W. Andersen & Michael J. Rymer. (Illus.). 120p. (Orig.). 1983. pap. 6.00 (*1-878861-42-5*) Pac Section SEPM.

Tectonics & Sedimentation along the California Margin. Ed. by James K. Crouch & Steven B. Bachman. (Illus.). 188p. (Orig.). 1984. pap. 7.00 (*1-878861-34-4*) Pac Section SEPM.

Tectonics & Seismic Sequence Stratigraphy. Ed. by G. D. Williams & A. Dobb. (Geological Society Special Publications: No. 71). (Illus.). viii, 226p. (C). 1993. 75.00 (*0-903317-87-7*, 284, Pub. by Geol Soc Pub Hse UK) AAPG.

Tectonics of China. Chen Guoda. (International Academic Publishers Ser.). (Illus.). 266p. 1989. 81.00 (*0-08-037033-0*, Pergamon Pr) Elsevier.

Tectonics of Circum-Pacific Continental Margins: Proceedings of the 28th International Geology Congress, July 1989. Ed. by Jean Aubouin & Jacques Bourgois. (Illus.). 243p. 1990. 110.00 (*90-6764-132-4*, Pub. by VSP NE) Coronet Bks.

Tectonics of Sedimentary Basis. C. Busby. 1995. pap. 69.95 (*0-86542-245-1*) Blackwell Sci.

Tectonics of the Eastern Part of the Cordilleran Orogenic Belt, Chihuahua, New Mexico, & Arizona. Ed. by Drewes. (IGC Field Trip Guidebooks Ser.). 88p. 1989. 21.00 (*0-87590-589-7*, T121) Am Geophysical.

Tectonics of the Potwar Plateau Region & the Development of Syntaxes, Punjab, Pakistan. Harald Drewes. LC 95-7440. (Bulletin Ser.: Vol. 2126). 1996. write for info. (*0-615-00642-6*) US Geol Survey.

Tectonics of the Scotia Arc, Antarctica, No. T180. Ed. by Dalziel. (IGC Field Trip Guidebooks Ser.). 216p. 1989. 35.00 (*0-87590-550-1*) Am Geophysical.

Tectonics of the Southern Central Andes: Structure & Evolution of an Active Continental Margin. Ed. by Klaus-Joachim Reutter et al. LC 93-15961. 1994. 238.95 (*0-387-55232-4*) Spr-Verlag.

Tectonics of the Virginia Blue Ridge & Piedmont. Ed. by Glover. (IGC Field Trip Guidebooks Ser.). 64p. 1989. 21.00 (*0-87590-655-9*, T363) Am Geophysical.

Tectonics of the Western Himalayas. Ed. by L. L. Malinconico, Jr. & R. J. Lillie. (Special Papers: No. 232). (Illus.). 300p. 1989. pap. 20.00 (*0-8137-2232-2*) Geol Soc.

Tectonics, Sedimentation & Palaeoceanography of the North Atlantic Region. G. B. Shimmield. (Geological Society Special Publication Ser.: No. 90). (Illus.). 312p. 1995. 100.00 (*1-897799-27-6*, 331, Pub. by Geol Soc Pub Hse UK) AAPG.

Tectonics, Sedimentation, & Petroleum Potential, Northern Denver Basin, Colorado, Wyoming, and Nebraska. Stephen A. Sonnenberg et al. Ed. by Jon W. Raese. LC 81-17980. (Colorado School of Mines Quarterly Ser.: Vol. 76, No. 2). (Illus.). 45p. 1981. pap. text ed. 10.00 (*0-686-46973-9*) Colo Sch Mines.

Tectonofractography. D. Bahat. (Illus.). xviii, 354p. 1991. 260.95 (*0-387-53281-1*) Spr-Verlag.

Tectonostratigraphic Evolution of the Central & East European Orogens. Ed. by R. D. Dallmeyer et al. 1995. write for info. (*3-540-55472-6*) Spr-Verlag.

Tectonostratigraphic Terranes & Tectonic Evolution of Mexico. Ed. by R. L. Sedlock et al. LC 93-3196. (Special Papers: No. 278). 1993. pap. 24.38 (*0-8137-2278-0*) Geol Soc.

Tectonostratigraphic Terranes in the Northern Appalachians. Ed. by Zen. (IGC Field Trip Guidebooks Ser.). 80p. 1989. 21.00 (*0-87590-560-9*, T359) Am Geophysical.

Tectonostratigraphic Terranes of the Circum- Pacific Region. Ed. by David G. Howell. (Earth Science Ser.: Vol. 1). (Illus.). 602p. 1985. 10.00 (*0-933687-00-1*, 826-28) Circum-Pacific.

Tecumseh. Mark Dunster. 1979. pap. 4.00 (*0-89642-053-1*) Linden Pubs.

Tecumseh. Allan W. Eckert. 1992. pap. 8.95 (*1-56060-140-X*) Eclipse Bks.

Tecumseh. Zachary Kent. LC 92-8217. (Cornerstones of Freedom Ser.). (Illus.). 32p. (J). (gr. 3-6). 1992. lib. bdg. 18.00 (*0-516-06660-9*) Childrens.

Tecumseh. Zachary Kent. LC 92-8217. (Cornerstones of Freedom Ser.). (Illus.). 32p. (J). (gr. 3-6). 1993. pap. 4.95 (*0-516-46660-7*) Childrens.

Tecumseh. Russell Shorto. Ed. by Nancy Furstinger. (Alvin Josephy's Biography of the American Indians Ser.). (Illus.). 136p. (J). (gr. 5-7). 1989. pap. 7.95 (*0-382-09758-0*, Silver Pr NJ); lib. bdg. 12.95 (*0-382-09569-3*, Silver Pr NJ) Silver Burdett Pr.

Tecumseh! Graphic Novel. Allan W. Eckert. 1992. pap. 9.95 (*1-56060-157-4*) Eclipse Bks.

Tecumseh: One Nation for His People. Gina Ingoglia. LC 92-56162. (Disney's American Frontier Ser.: Bk. 11). (Illus.). 80p. (Orig.). (J). (gr. 1-4). 1993. pap. 3.50 (*1-56282-489-9*) Disney Pr.

***Tecumseh & His Brothers.** Sugden. 1997. 35.00 (*0-8050-4138-9*) St Martin.

Tecumseh & the Quest for Indian Leadership. R. David Edmunds. (Library of American Biography). (C). 1984. text ed. 16.95 (*0-673-39336-4*) Addson-Wesley Educ.

Tecumseh & the Quest for Indian Leadership. R. David Edmunds. (Library of American Biography). 232p. reprint ed. pap. 15.95 (*1-886746-31-1*, 93476) Talman.

Tecumseh L-Head Engine Repair Manual. 1994. pap. 12.95 (*0-89287-617-4*, H105) Intertec Pub.

Tecumseh, Leader. D. L. Birchfield. (Illus.). (J). (gr. 1-4). 1995. pap. 4.95 (*0-8136-5768-7*); lib. bdg. 10.60 (*0-8136-5762-8*) Modern Curr.

Tecumseh, Matsushita, & Refrigeration Compression Subsidies in Singapore. Michael Ryan et al. (Pew Case Studies in International Affairs). 50p. (C). 1995. pap. text ed. 3.50 (*1-56927-716-8*, GU Schl Foreign) Geo U Inst Dplmcy.

Tecumseh, Oklahoma: An Illustrated History of Its First Century. Phil Cannon & Glenn DaleCarter. (Illus.). 115p. 1991. write for info. (*0-934188-36-X*) Evans Pubns.

Tecumseh: Shawnee Rebel see North American Indians of Achievement

Tecumseh, Shawnee War Chief. Jane Fleischer. LC 78-18046. (Illus.). 48p. (J). (gr. 4-6). 1979. pap. 3.50 (*0-89375-143-X*); lib. bdg. 11.89 (*0-89375-153-7*) Troll Communs.

Tecumseh's Last Stand. John Sugden. LC 85-40480. (Illus.). 288p. 1990. pap. 14.95 (*0-8061-2242-0*) U of Okla Pr.

Tecumseh's Trail: The Appalachian Trail, Then & Now. Carl Bradfield. (Illus.). 137p. (Orig.). (YA). (gr. 8-12). pap. write for info. (*0-9632319-3-6*) ASDA Pub.

Teczowa Nowina: Czyliwprowadzemie do Evangelii Wienxzem. Jeazy Cichowlas. LC 93-74281. 300p. 1994. pap. write for info. (*0-9639577-3-2*) J Cichowlas.

Ted: A Personal Memoir of Ted Berrigan. Ron Padgett. 1993. pap. 10.00 (*0-935724-60-5*) Figures.

Ted & Dolly Fairytale Flight. Richard Fowler. (Slot Bks.). (Illus.). 24p. (J). (ps-3). 1984. 10.95 (*0-88110-190-7*) EDC.

Ted & Dolly's Magic Carpet Ride. Richard Fowler. (Slot Bks.). 24p. (J). (ps-1). 1984. 10.95 (*0-88110-155-9*) EDC.

Ted & Dolly's Submarine. R. Fowler. (Slot Bks.). (Illus.). 20p. (J). 1991. text ed. 10.95 (*0-88110-569-4*, Usborne) EDC.

***Ted Andrews Gift Set.** Ted Andrews. (Illus.). (Orig.). 1996. pap. 13.89 (*1-56718-893-1*) Llewellyn Pubns.

Ted Bear's Magic Swing. Dianne Baker. LC 91-65819. (Illus.). 32p. (J). (gr. 1-3). 1997. 12.95 (*0-87159-162-6*) Unity Bks.

Ted Berrigan: Selected Poems. Ted Berrigan. LC 93-28191. 160p. (Orig.). 1994. pap. 12.50 (*0-14-058699-7*, Penguin Bks) Viking Penguin.

Ted Bundy: Conversations with a Killer. Stephen G. Michaud & Hugh Aynesworth. 1990. pap. 5.99 (*0-451-16355-9*, Sig) NAL-Dutton.

Ted Bundy: The Deliberate Stranger. Richard Larsen. 1990. mass mkt. 5.50 (*0-671-72866-0*) PB.

Ted Dexter: Test Match Career. Spellmount Ltd. Publishers Staff. (C). 1986. 75.00 (*1-871876-30-3*, Pub. by Spellmount UK) St Mut.

Ted "Double Duty" Radcliffe: 36 Years of Pitching & Catching in Baseball's Negro Leagues. Kyle McNary. (Illus.). 288p. (Orig.). (C). 1994. pap. 14.95 (*0-9642002-0-1*) K McNary.

***Ted Hughes.** Paul Bentley. LC 97-20600. (Studies in Twentieth-Century Literature). 1998. write for info. (*0-582-22776-3*); pap. write for info. (*0-582-22775-5*) Longman.

Ted Hughes. Dennis Walder. (Open Guides to Literature Ser.). 128p. 1987. 75.00 (*0-335-15113-2*, Open Univ Pr); pap. 22.00 (*0-335-15112-4*, Open Univ Pr) Taylor & Francis.

Ted Hughes: A Bibliography, 1946-1980. S. Tabor & Keith Sagar. 274p. 1983. text ed. 110.00 (*0-7201-1654-6*, Mansell Pub) Cassell.

Ted Hughes: The Unaccommodated Universe (with Selected Critical Writings by Ted Hughes & Two Interviews) Ekbert Faas. LC 79-27434. 250p. (Orig.). 1980. pap. 12.50 (*0-87685-459-5*) Black Sparrow.

Ted Hughes As Shepherd of Being. Craig Robinson. 240p. 1989. text ed. 39.95 (*0-312-03202-1*) St Martin.

Ted Hunt - Yes I Can. 44p. 1989. student ed., per. 3.00 (*0-8187-0117-X*) Harlo Press.

Ted Kennedy Jr. He Faced His Challenge. Patricia S. Martin. (Reaching Your Goal Bks.). (Illus.). 24p. (J). (gr. 1-4). 1987. 10.95 (*0-685-58129-2*); lib. bdg. 14.60 (*0-86592-174-1*) Rourke Corp.

Ted Kid Lewis: His Life & Times. Morton Lewis. (Illus.). 273p. 1992. 24.95 (*0-86051-644-X*, Robson-Parkwest) Parkwest Pubns.

Ted McRoberts: North Country Marshal. Gene Medaris. (Illus.). 224p. 1986. 29.95 (*0-937708-04-6*) Great Northwest.

Ted McRoberts: North Country Marshal. Gene Medaris. 224p. 1987. pap. 19.95 (*0-937708-06-2*) Great Northwest.

Ted Nicholas Small Business Course. Ted Nicholas. 327p. (Orig.). 1993. pap. 29.95 (*0-7931-0725-3*, 5615-6901, Enter-Dearbrn) Dearborn Finan.

Ted Sennett's On Screen/Off Screen Film Guide. Ted Sennett. 1992. pap. 16.95 (*0-13-900630-3*) P-H.

Ted Turner. David M. Fischer. LC 92-44761. (Biographies: Pioneers Ser.). (J). 1993. 19.93 (*0-86625-496-X*); 14.95 (*0-685-66547-X*) Rourke Pubns.

***Ted Turner: It Ain't As Easy As It Looks.** rev. ed. Porter Bibb. LC 97-23805. (Illus.). 512p. 1997. pap. 20.00 (*1-55566-203-X*) Johnson Bks.

Ted Turner: Television's Triumphant Tiger. Rebecca Stefoff. Ed. by Richard G. Young. LC 91-32774. (Wizards of Business Ser.). (Illus.). 64p. (J). (gr. 4-8). 1992. lib. bdg. 17.26 (*1-56074-024-8*) Garrett Ed Corp.

Ted Williams. Rick Wolff. (Baseball Legends Ser.). (Illus.). 64p. (J). (gr. 3 up). 1994. lib. bdg. 15.95 (*0-7910-1194-1*) Chelsea Hse.

Ted Williams: A Portrait in Words & Pictures. Dick Johnson & Glenn Stout. (Illus.). 224p. 1991. 24.95 (*0-8027-1140-5*) Walker & Co.

Ted Williams: A Portrait in Words & Pictures. Dick Johnson & Glenn Stout. (Illus.). 224p. 1994. reprint ed. pap. 12.95 (*0-8027-7434-2*) Walker & Co.

***Ted Williams: A Tribute.** Jim Prime & Bill Nowlin. (Illus.). 320p. 1997. 29.95 (*1-57028-138-6*) Masters Pr IN.

Ted Williams' Hit List: The Ultimate Ranking of Baseball's Greatest Hitters. Ted Williams & Jim Prime. (Illus.). 256p. 1996. 19.95 (*1-57028-078-9*) Masters Pr IN.

Teddies & Machines. Maude Salinger. (J). (ps). 1996. pap. 3.99 (*0-525-45401-2*) Dutton Child Bks.

Teddies & Trucks. Suzanne Haldane & Maude Salinger. Ed. by Maude Salinger. (J). (ps). 1996. pap. 3.99 (*0-525-45400-4*) Dutton Child Bks.

Teddie's Tasty Temptations: A Collection of Fine Recipes from the Teddie Kossof Salon & Spa. 1995. 14.95 (*0-615-00814-3*) Crohns & Colitis.

***Teddy & Louis.** Wendy L. Jones. 1996. mass mkt. 4.99 (*1-55197-050-3*, Pub. by Comnwlth Pub CN) Partners Pubs Grp.

***Teddy & the Beanstalk.** Sue Inman. (Illus.). 24p. (J). (ps-3). 1997. 4.98 (*1-85854-604-4*) Brimax Bks.

Teddy & the Duckling. M. Rogers. (Read to Me Ser.). 10p. (J). 1995. bds. 3.98 (*1-85854-244-8*) Brimax Bks.

Teddy & the Frog. M. Rogers. (Read to Me Ser.). 10p. (J). 1995. bds. 3.98 (*1-85854-247-2*) Brimax Bks.

***Teddy & the Ghost.** Sue Inman. (Illus.). 24p. (J). (ps-3). 1997. 4.98 (*1-85854-548-X*) Brimax Bks.

Teddy & the Mice. M. Rogers. (Read to Me Ser.). 10p. (J). 1995. bds. 3.98 (*1-85854-246-4*) Brimax Bks.

Teddy & the Puppy. M. Rogers. (Read to Me Ser.). 10p. (J). 1995. bds. 3.98 (*1-85854-245-6*) Brimax Bks.

Teddy at the Farm. Gill Davies. (My Big Little Fat Bks.). (Illus.). 20p. (J). (ps). 1996. bds. 3.49 (*1-85854-401-7*) Brimax Bks.

Teddy at the Park. Illus. by Jenny Tulip. 12p. (J). (ps). 1996. bds. 4.98 (*1-85854-495-5*) Brimax Bks.

***Teddy Bear - Tales & Patterns.** Linda Mullins. (Orig.). 1997. pap. 19.95 (*0-87588-492-X*, 5315) Hobby Hse.

Teddy Bear ABC. (J). write for info. (*0-7894-0325-0*, 5-70676) DK Pub Inc.

Teddy Bear ABC. Laura R. Johnson. LC 91-18207. (Illus.). 64p. (J). (ps-2). 1992. 12.00 (*0-671-74979-X*, Green Tiger S&S) S&S Childrens.

Teddy Bear & Friends Price Guide. 4th ed. Linda Mullins. 192p. 1992. pap. 12.95 (*0-87588-399-0*) Hobby Hse.

Teddy Bear Artist Postcards. Ho Phi Le. 30p. 1995. pap. 6.95 (*0-87588-436-9*) Hobby Hse.

Teddy Bear Bandit. Cynthia Powell. 1994. 17.95 (*0-8034-9086-0*, 094524) Bouregy.

Teddy Bear Bedtime Stories. Cass Hollander. (Storytime Bks.). (Illus.). 24p. (J). (ps-2). 1992. pap. 1.29 (*1-56293-115-6*) McClanahan Bk.

Teddy Bear Birthday Book. Joanna Isles. 1992. 9.99 (*1-85145-695-3*, Pavilion Bks) Viking Penguin.

***Teddy Bear Book.** Ariel Books Staff. 1996. 4.95 (*0-8362-1524-9*, Arie Bks) Andrews & McMeel.

Teddy Bear Book. Lucille R. Penner. LC 96-2645. (Illus.). (J). 1997. 14.99 (*0-679-88091-7*) Random.

Teddy Bear Book. Maureen Stanford & Amanda O'Neill. (Illus.). 156p. 1995. write for info. (*1-57215-054-8*) World Pubns.

Teddy Bear Book of Days. Sara Ball. (Illus.). (J). (gr. 4-12). 1992. 16.00 (*1-56021-185-7*) W J Fantasy.

Teddy Bear Carving with Kelley Stadelman. Kelley Stadelman. LC 95-36311. 64p. (YA). (gr. 10). 1996. pap. 12.95 (*0-88740-890-7*) Schiffer.

Teddy Bear Christmas. Sue Dreamer. LC 91-77714. (Illus.). 10p. (J). (ps-1). 1992. bds. 7.95 (*1-56397-121-6*) Boyds Mills Pr.

Teddy Bear Circus. Che Rudko. (Little Look-In Bks.). (Illus.). 20p. (J). (ps). 1994. bds. 2.95 (*0-307-16710-0*, Golden Books) Western Pub.

Teddy Bear Companion, Vol. I. Dee Hockenberry. LC 95-13998. 208p. 1995. pap. 14.95 (*0-86573-968-4*) Cowles Creative.

Teddy Bear Companion, Vol. II. Dee Hockenberry. LC 95-13998. 208p. 1995. pap. 14.95 (*0-86573-969-2*) Cowles Creative.

Teddy Bear Company: Economics for Kids. Carole Marsh. (Quantum Leap Ser.). (Illus.). (J). (gr. 4-8). 1994. 29.95 (*0-935326-16-2*) Gallopade Pub Group.

Teddy Bear Connection Color-Me Calendar. Judy Frye. (J). 1992. write for info. (*0-9632316-1-8*) Teddy Bear Connect.

Teddy Bear-Cut & Use Stencils. Theodore Menten. (J). 1983. pap. 5.95 (*0-486-24595-0*) Dover.

Teddy Bear Encyclopedia. Pauline Cockrill. LC 93-18274. (Illus.). 240p. 1993. 34.95 (*1-56458-302-3*) DK Pub Inc.

Teddy Bear Express! A Phonological Development Program. N. J. Bonsangue & S. G. Flatley. LC 93-78926. 1994. pap. 24.95 (*0-89108-232-8*, 9308) Love Pub Co.

Teddy Bear Farmer. Joan Worthington & Phoebe Worthington. (J). (ps-1). pap. 2.95 (*0-317-62188-2*, Puffin) Puffin Bks.

Teddy Bear Figurines Price Guide. Jesse Murray. (Illus.). 144p. 1996. pap. 19.95 (*0-87588-448-2*) Hobby Hse.

Teddy Bear for Sale. Gail Herman. LC 95-10283. (Hello Reader! Ser.). (Illus.). 32p. (J). (ps-1). 1996. pap. 3.50 (*0-590-25943-1*, Cartwheel) Scholastic Inc.

Teddy Bear Habit. James L. Collier. (J). (gr. 5-9). 1990. 16.00 (*0-8446-6191-0*) Peter Smith.

Teddy Bear Heir. Elda Minger. (American Romance Ser.). 1994. mass mkt. 3.50 (*0-373-16531-5*, 1-6531-5) Harlequin Bks.

Teddy Bear Journal: An Illustrated Notebook. (Illus.). 96p. 1996. pap. 5.95 (*1-56138-698-7*) Running Pr.

Teddy Bear Junction: Stop Here for Fine Collector Bears. Phyllis Consentino. (Illus.). 104p. (Orig.). (YA). 1985. pap. 10.95 (*0-935855-00-9*) T B J Pubns.

Teddy Bear Kit. Alicia Merrett. (Illus.). 48p. 1994. 19.95 (*0-312-11119-3*) St Martin.

***Teddy Bear Knits, Bk. II.** 1995. write for info. (*0-614-28553-4*) B Lampen Knit.

Teddy Bear Lane: Christmas Remembered. (J). 1996. 9.00 (*0-679-86560-8*) Random.

An Asterisk (*) at the beginning of an entry indicates that the title is appearing in BIP for the first time.

Teddy Bear Magic: Making Adorable Teddy Bears from Anita Louise's Bearlace Cottage. Anita L. Crane. LC 94-23433. (Illus.). 144p. 1995. 27.95 (*0-8069-0992-7*, Chapelle) Sterling.

Teddy Bear Mystery, Vol. 3. Hilda Stahl. (Elizabeth Gail Ser.: Vol. 3). (J). 1988. pap. 5.99 (*0-8423-0741-9*) Tyndale.

Teddy Bear Number Book: A Bilingual Book. Margaret K. Garaway. Tr. by Maria R. Cartes. (Illus.). 32p. (ENG & SPA.). (J). (ps-4). 1995. 14.95 (*0-9638851-3-8*); pap. 7.95 (*0-9638851-4-6*) Old Hogan Pubng.

Teddy Bear Paper Dolls. Crystal Collins. (J). 1983. pap. 3.95 (*0-486-24550-0*) Dover.

Teddy Bear Play House. (J). (ps). 1995. pap. text ed. 4.95 (*0-307-08053-6*, Golden Pr) Western Pub.

Teddy Bear Punch Out Stencils. Theodore Menten. (J). 1985. pap. 3.95 (*0-486-24832-1*) Dover.

Teddy Bear Quotations. Ed. by Helen Exley. (Quotations Bks.). (Illus.). 60p. 1990. 8.00 (*1-85015-054-0*) Exley Giftbooks.

***Teddy Bear Say-a-Picture Storybook.** Jenny Tulip. (J). 1996. 9.98 (*0-7651-9650-6*) Smithmark.

Teddy Bear Sourcebook: For Collectors & Artists. Ed. by Argie Manolis. (Illus.). 356p. (Orig.). 1995. pap. 18.99 (*1-55870-386-1*, Betrwy Bks) F & W Pubns Inc.

Teddy Bear Sticker Paper Doll. Theodore Menten. (Illus.). (J). (gr. k-3). 1991. pap. 1.00 (*0-486-26235-9*) Dover.

Teddy Bear Stickers & Seals. Theodore Menten. 1985. 3.50 (*0-486-24928-X*) Dover.

Teddy Bear Stories. large type ed. 1995. 25.99 (*0-7089-3303-3*) Ulverscroft.

Teddy Bear Stories for Grown-Ups. Ed. by Catherine Taylor. 256p. 1994. pap. 14.95 (*1-55591-192-7*) Fulcrum Pub.

***Teddy Bear Tales.** Dorothy Grimes. (J). 1997. 8.95 (*0-533-12299-6*) Vantage.

Teddy Bear Tales: The Lost Teddy Bear Tales Children's Stories. Harry J. Jacobson. 70p. 1995. lib. bdg. 4.95 (*0-9649561-0-1*) H J Jacobson.

Teddy Bear Tears. Aylesworth. (J). 1997. 16.00 (*0-689-31776-X*, Atheneum Bks Young) S&S Childrens.

***Teddy Bear, Teddy Bear.** Michael Hague. (J). 1997. pap. 6.95 (*0-688-15251-1*, Tupelo Bks) Morrow.

Teddy Bear, Teddy Bear. Illus. by Tracey Moroney. (My First Nursery Rhyme Books Ser.). 12p. (J). (ps). 1995. 3.99 (*0-88705-843-4*, Wshng Well Bks) Joshua Morris.

Teddy Bear, Teddy Bear: A Classic Action Rhyme. Illus. by Michael Hague. LC 92-17997. 32p. (J). (ps up). 1993. 14.00 (*0-688-10671-4*, Morrow Junior); lib. bdg. 13.93 (*0-688-12085-7*, Morrow Junior) Morrow.

Teddy Bear, Teddy Bear Big Book. Illus. by Sheila Somerville. (J). (ps-2). 1988. pap. text ed. 14.00 (*0-922053-04-9*) N Edge Res.

Teddy Bear That Prowled at Night. Deihl. (J). 1998. pap. 7.95 (*0-671-75188-3*, S&S Bks Young Read) S&S Childrens.

Teddy Bear That Prowled at Night. Edna G. Deihl. (Illus.). 24p. (J). (gr. k-3). 1991. reprint ed. pap. 7.95 (*0-88138-079-2*, Green Tiger S&S) S&S Childrens.

***Teddy Bear Too-Too.** Martha Lee Brannock. (Illus.). 25p. (J). (ps up). 1995. pap. write for info. (*1-85863-352-4*) M Sanders Ent.

Teddy Bear Treasures: Making Movable Wooden Toys. Alan Bridgewater & Gill Bridgewater. LC 92-41248. 1993. 14.60 (*0-8306-2168-7*) McGraw-Hill Prof.

Teddy Bear Tree. Barbara Dillon. Ed. by Patricia MacDonald. (Illus.). 80p. (J). (gr. 3-5). 1990. reprint ed. pap. 2.95 (*0-671-68432-9*, Minstrel Bks) PB.

Teddy Bear Trilogy. deluxe ed. Jayne Elliott. Ed. & Illus. by Eileen Cummings. 18p. (J). 1988. 22.00 (*0-926272-00-4*) E C Pr.

Teddy Bear Twins Paper Dolls. Ming-Ju Sun. (Illus.). (J). (gr. k-3). 1994. pap. 2.95 (*0-486-28130-2*) Dover.

Teddy Bear Under the Bed. Molly Wigand. (J). 1996. 3.99 (*0-689-80852-6*) S&S Trade.

Teddy Bear Who Couldn't Do Anything. Dina Anastasio. (S Eight Hundred Ninety-Seven Ser.). (Illus.). 24p. (J). 1993. 2.95 (*0-7214-3511-4*, Ladybrd) Penguin.

***Teddy Bears.** (Sense of History Ser.). Date not set. pap. text ed. write for info. (*0-582-04017-5*, Pub. by Longman UK) Longman.

***Teddy Bears.** Ariel Books Staff. 1996. 3.95 (*0-8362-0997-4*, Arie Bks) Andrews & McMeel.

***Teddy Bears.** Debbie Bliss. LC 97-16671. 1997. pap. 18.95 (*0-312-17042-4*) St Martin.

***Teddy Bears.** Arlene Erlbach. LC 96-45021. (Household History Ser.). (J). 1997. write for info. (*1-57505-019-6*, Carolrhoda) Lerner Group.

***Teddy Bears.** Debbie Hansen. Ed. by Patrick Caton. LC 96-78971. (Illus.). 68p. 1997. 6.50 (*1-56245-276-2*) Great Quotations.

***Teddy Bears.** Jeannie Kants. (Illus.). 48p. 3.98 (*0-8317-2109-X*) Smithmark.

Teddy Bears. Judy Sparrow. (Illus.). 48p. 1995. 6.98 (*0-8317-3382-9*) Smithmark.

Teddy Bears. Robert S. Young. LC 92-4347. (Collectibles Ser.). (Illus.). 64p. (YA). (gr. 5 up). 1992. lib. bdg. 13.95 (*0-87518-520-7*, Dillon Silver Burdett) Silver Burdett Pr.

Teddy Bears: A Celebration. Mary Hillier. 96p. (J). (gr. k up). 1985. 14.95 (*0-8253-0298-6*) Beaufort Bks NY.

Teddy Bears: A Celebration in Words & Paintings. Helen Exley. (Words & Paintings Ser.). (Illus.). 60p. 1993. 8.00 (*1-85015-332-9*) Exley Giftbooks.

Teddy Bears: A Complete Guide to History, Collecting & Care. Sue Pearson & Dottie Ayers. LC 95-11517. (Illus.). 192p. 1995. 19.95 (*0-02-860417-2*) Macmillan.

Teddy Bears: An Anthology of Verse & Prose. Smithmark Staff. 1995. 6.98 (*0-8317-3833-2*) Smithmark.

Teddy Bears: Facts, Trivia, & Interesting Stories. John E. Dunn. 1995. pap. 5.95 (*0-9645218-4-9*) Hipp-Daniel.

***Teddy Bears: Images of Love.** Ho Thi Le. (Illus.). 1997. 14.95 (*0-87588-498-9*, H5583) Hobby Hse.

***Teddy Bears: Very First Picture Book.** Nicola Tuxworth. (Illus.). 20p. (J). (ps). 1997. 3.95 (*1-85967-509-3*, Lorenz Bks) Anness Pub.

***Teddy Bears - Scripture Journal.** Bargain Books Staff. (Scripture Journal). 128p. 1997. 4.97 (*1-57748-112-7*) Barbour & Co.

***Teddy Bears' Adventures.** Smithmark Staff. (J). 1997. 7.98 (*0-7651-9344-2*) Smithmark.

Teddy Bears & How to Make Them. Margaret Hutchings. LC 76-70049. (Illus.). 1978. pap. 12.95 (*0-486-23487-8*) Dover.

Teddy Bears & Soft Toys. Pauline Cockrill. 1989. pap. 25.00 (*0-85263-968-6*, Pub. by Shire UK) St Mut.

Teddy Bears & Steiff Animals. Margaret F. Mandel. (Illus.). 288p. 1993. pap. 9.95 (*0-89145-267-2*) Collector Bks.

Teddy Bears & Steiff Animals, Second Series. Margaret Mandel. (Illus.). 200p. 1996. pap. 19.95 (*0-89145-356-3*, 1817) Collector Bks.

Teddy Bears & Toys: Playtime Memories in Counted Cross-Stitch. Annette Bradshaw & Gwyn Franson. 1984. 5.98 (*0-88290-264-4*) Horizon Utah.

Teddy Bears, Annalee Animals. Margaret Mandel. 1996. 19.95 (*0-89145-419-5*) Collector Bks.

Teddy Bear's Annual Report. Carole Marsh. (Quantum Leap Ser.). (Illus.). (J). (gr. 4-8). 1994. 29.95 (*0-935326-26-X*) Gallopade Pub Group.

Teddy Bears at School: An Activities Handbook for Teachers of Young Children. Arlene Steen & Martha L. Lane. (Illus.). 224p. (J). (ps-3). 1986. pap. 16.95 (*0-89334-092-8*) Humanics Ltd.

Teddy Bears at School: An Activities Handbook for Teachers of Young Children. Arleen Steen & Martha Lane. (Illus.). 224p. 1986. reprint ed. lib. bdg. 26.95 (*0-89334-227-0*, 2270X23) Humanics Ltd.

Teddy Bear's Christmas. (J). (gr. k-2). 1996. pap. 2.95 (*0-8167-2191-2*) Troll Communs.

***Teddy Bear's Christmas.** Illus. by Linda Worrall. (Toddlers' First Stories Ser.). 12p. (J). (ps up). 1997. bds. 2.98 (*1-85854-748-2*) Brimax Bks.

Teddy Bears' Christmas: A Pop-up Book. Mary Engelbreit. (Illus.). 8p. (J). (ps-3). 1994. 4.95 (*0-8362-3091-4*) Andrews & McMeel.

Teddy Bears Cure a Cold. Susanna Gretz. (Illus.). 32p. (J). (ps-2). 1986. pap. 4.99 (*0-590-43495-0*) Scholastic Inc.

Teddy Bears' Jamboree. (J). 1994. pap. 12.98 (*1-879496-41-0*) Lightyear Entrtnmnt.

Teddy Bear's Life, As Told by One. Isabel Martin. (Illus.). (J). (gr. 3-5). 1996. 7.95 (*0-533-11682-1*) Vantage.

Teddy Bears Past & Present, Vol. II. Linda Mullins. (Illus.). 256p. 1991. 25.00 (*0-87588-384-2*) Hobby Hse.

Teddy Bears Past & Present Collector's Edition, Vol. I. Linda Mullins. (Illus.). 305p. 1986. 29.95 (*0-87588-264-1*, 3120) Hobby Hse.

Teddy Bear's Picnic. (J). 1993. pap. 12.98 (*1-879496-40-2*) Lightyear Entrtnmnt.

Teddy Bears' Picnic. Jerry Garcia & Dave Grisman. (Illus.). 32p. (J). (ps-3). 1996. 14.95 incl. audio (*0-06-027302-X*) HarpC Child Bks.

Teddy Bears' Picnic. Jimmy Kennedy. LC 86-32111. (Illus.). 32p. (J). (ps-2). 1987. bds. 6.95 (*0-685-67547-5*) P Bedrick Bks.

Teddy Bears' Picnic. Jimmy Kennedy. LC 86-32111. (Illus.). 32p. (J). 1990. pap. 6.95 (*0-87226-424-6*) P Bedrick Bks.

Teddy Bears' Picnic. Jimmy Kennedy. LC 91-24944. (Illus.). 40p. (J). (ps-2). 1991. 14.00 (*0-671-75589-7*, Green Tiger S&S); 15.95 incl. lp (*0-671-74903-X*, Green Tiger S&S) S&S Childrens.

***Teddy Bears Picnic.** Jimmy Kennedy. 1997. pap. text ed. 5.95 (*0-8050-5349-2*) H Holt & Co.

Teddy Bear's Scrapbook. 2nd ed. Deborah Howe & James Howe. LC 93-20919. (Illus.). 80p. (J). (gr. 3-7). 1994. reprint ed. pap. 3.95 (*0-689-71812-8*, Aladdin Paperbacks) S&S Childrens.

Teddy Bears Stay Indoors. Susanna Gretz. LC 86-19511. (Illus.). 32p. (J). (gr. k-3). 1987. lib. bdg. 13.95 (*0-02-738150-1*, Four Winds Pr) S&S Childrens.

Teddy Bears Take the Train. Susanna Gretz. LC 87-8572. (Illus.). 32p. (J). (gr. k-3). 1988. lib. bdg. 13.95 (*0-02-738170-6*, Four Winds Pr) S&S Childrens.

Teddy Bear's Wardrobe. 6.98 (*0-317-38608-5*) Gick.

Teddy Beddy Bear's Bedtime Songs & Poems. Illus. by Judy Blankenship. LC 84-4837. (Pictureback Ser.). 32p. (J). (ps). 1984. pap. 2.25 (*0-394-86826-9*) Random Bks Yng Read.

Teddy Berlitz French ll. Berlitz. 1996. pap. 19.95 incl. audio (*0-689-71817-9*, Aladdin Paperbacks) S&S Childrens.

Teddy Book. (Illus.). (J). (ps). 1992. 9.00 (*1-56021-186-5*) W J Fantasy.

***Teddy Book.** Fantasy, W. J., Inc. Staff. 1992. 3.75 (*1-56021-115-6*) W J Fantasy.

Teddy in the House. Lucy Cousins. LC 91-71821. (Illus.). 8p. (J). (ps). 1992. 5.95 (*1-56402-030-4*) Candlewick Pr.

Teddy Is First. (My Big Little Fat Bks.). 20p. (J). 1994. bds. 2.98 (*0-86112-991-1*) Brimax Bks.

Teddy Kollek: Builder of Jerusalem. Abraham Rabinovich. LC 95-15871. (Young Biography Ser.). (Orig.). (J). 1995. 14.95 (*0-8276-0559-5*) JPS Phila.

Teddy Kollek: Builder of Jerusalem. Abraham Rabinovich. LC 95-15871. 130p. (Orig.). (J). (gr. 3-8). 1996. pap. 9.95 (*0-8276-0561-7*) JPS Phila.

Teddy Lover's Address Book. rev. ed. Helen Exley. (Mini Address Bks.). (Illus.). 64p. 7.50 (*1-85015-427-9*) Exley Giftbooks.

Teddy on Time. Michael J. Pellowski. LC 85-14127. (Illus.). 48p. (Orig.). (J). (gr. 1-3). 1996. pap. 3.95 (*0-8167-0583-6*) Troll Communs.

Teddy Roosevelt: Young Rough Rider. Edd W. Parks. LC 89-37819. (Childhood of Famous Americans Ser.). (Illus.). 192p. (J). (gr. 2-6). 1989. reprint ed. pap. 4.95 (*0-689-71349-5*, Aladdin Paperbacks) S&S Childrens.

***Teddy Roosevelt at San Juan: The Making of a President.** Peggy Samuels & Harold Samuels. LC 97-9903. (Texas A&M/Military History Ser.). (Illus.). 384p. 1997. 39.95 (*0-89096-771-7*) Texas A&M Univ.

Teddy Roosevelt, Rough Rider. Louis Sabin. LC 85-1090. (Illus.). 48p. (J). (gr. 4-6). 1986. pap. 3.95 (*0-8167-0556-9*); lib. bdg. 12.95 (*0-8167-0555-0*) Troll Communs.

***Teddy Roosevelt's Elk.** Brenda Z. Guiberson. LC 96-52144. (J). 1996. 15.95 (*0-8050-4296-2*) H Holt & Co.

Teddy Ruxpin Lullabies II. Ken Forsse. (Teddy Ruxpin Adventure Ser.). (Illus.). 26p. (J). (ps). 1988. Incl. pre-programmed audiocassette. 21.00 incl. audio (*0-934323-68-2*) Alchemy Comms.

Teddy Ruxpin's Lullabies. Ken Forsse. (Teddy Ruxpin Adventure Ser.). (Illus.). 26p. (J). (ps). 1985. 9.95 incl. audio (*0-934323-01-1*) Alchemy Comms.

Teddy Tales: Bears Repeating, Too! Terry Michaud. (Illus.). 112p. 1989. 19.95 (*0-87588-349-4*) Hobby Hse.

***Teddy Tells Time.** Keith Faulkner. Date not set. 9.95 (*1-57719-091-2*) GT Pubng Corp.

Teddy the Better-Than-New Bear. Nancy H. Lecourt. (Sunshine Ser.). 32p. (J). 1993. pap. 0.97 (*0-8163-1116-1*) Pacific Pr Pub Assn.

Teddy! Where Are You? Ralph Steadman. (Illus.). 32p. (J). 1996. 12.95 (*0-86264-484-4*, Pub. by Anderson Pr UK) London Brdge.

Teddy Wilson Talks Jazz: The Autobiography of Teddy Wilson. Ed. by Humphrey Van Loo & Ari Ligthart. (Bayou Press Ser.). (Illus.). 192p. 1996. 27.95 (*0-304-33610-6*) Cassell.

Teddybears Eat Out. Sage Gretz. (J). 7.95 (*0-7136-3293-3*, 92833, Pub. by A&C Black UK) Talman.

Teddybears in the Swim. Sage Gretz. (J). 7.95 (*0-7136-3290-9*, 92835, Pub. by A&C Black UK) Talman.

Teddybears in Trouble. Gretz. (J). 7.95 (*0-7136-3292-5*, 92836, Pub. by A&C Black UK) Talman.

Teddybears on Stage. Sage Gretz. (J). 7.95 (*0-7136-3291-7*, 92834, Pub. by A&C Black UK) Talman.

***Teddy's Bed.** Illus. by Jenny Tulip. (My Big Little Fat Bks.). 20p. (J). (ps up). 1997. bds. 3.49 (*1-85854-636-2*) Brimax Bks.

Teddy's Book Train, 5 bks., Set. Illus. by Margaret Stevens. 18p. (J). 1995. bds. 21.95 (*1-85479-732-8*, Pub. by M OMara UK) Assoc Pubs Grp.

***Teddy's Busy Day.** Lone Morton. LC 96-53361. (J). 1998. pap. 12.99 (*0-8037-2283-4*) Dial Bks Young.

***Teddy's Christmas: Pop-Up Book with Mini X-Mas Card.** Pete Bowman. (Illus.). 24p. (J). (ps up). 1997. pap. 14.95 (*0-7868-0345-2*) Hyprn Child.

Teddy's Christmas Cut-Out. Amanda Davidson. 16p. (J). (gr. 4-7). 1990. pap. 2.50 (*0-8167-2197-1*) Troll Communs.

Teddy's Countdown to Christmas. Amanda Davidson. 16p. (J). (gr. 4-7). 1990. pap. 2.50 (*0-8167-2198-X*) Troll Communs.

Teddy's Day. Illus. by Marie-Anne Didierjean. 6p. (J). (ps). 1993. 16.99 (*1-881445-18-6*) Sandvik Pub.

Teddy's Day: A Huggable Cloth Book. JTG of Nashville Staff. (J). (ps). 1994. pap. 16.95 (*1-884832-02-4*) JTG Nashville.

Teddy's Day in the Forest. Brenda Eldrid. (Storytime Bks.). (Illus.). 24p. (J). (ps-2). 1993. pap. text ed. 1.29 (*1-56293-341-8*) McClanahan Bk.

Teddy's Easter Basket. Barbara James. (J). 1997. pap. 2.95 (*0-8167-2072-X*, PT076) Troll Communs.

Teddy's First Christmas. Amanda Davidson. LC 82-82092. (Illus.). 24p. (J). (ps-2). 1982. 7.95 (*0-03-062616-1*, Bks Young Read) H Holt & Co.

Teddy's Friends. Michelle Cartlidge. LC 91-58758. (Illus.). 24p. (J). (ps). 1992. 5.95 (*1-56402-077-0*) Candlewick Pr.

***Teddy's Lost Toy.** Sue Inman. (Illus.). 24p. (J). (ps-3). 1997. 4.98 (*1-85854-605-2*) Brimax Bks.

***Teddy's Shadow.** Sue Inman. (Illus.). 24p. (J). (ps-3). 1997. 4.98 (*1-85854-606-0*) Brimax Bks.

Teddy's Tail. Illus. by Peter Rutherford. (You Can Read It Ser.). 24p. (J). (ps-1). 1996. 3.49 (*1-85854-469-6*) Brimax Bks.

Teddy's Toyshop. Reader's Digest Editors. (J). 1996. boxed 17.99 (*0-88705-960-0*) Rdrs Dgst Yng Fam.

***Teddys Traumwelt: So Leben Alte Steiff-Teddybaren.** Rolf Pistorius & Christel Pistorius. (Illus.). 128p. (GER.). (C). 1993. 67.00 (*3-8170-1011-7*, Pub. by Knstvrlag Weingrtn GW) Intl Bk Import.

Tedium & the Software Process. Bruce I. Blum. (Information Systems Ser.). 296p. 1989. 35.00 (*0-262-02294-X*) MIT Pr.

Tee-Ga's Story: A Cougar's Autobiography. Jim Swayne & Ot-Ne-We Swayne. (Illus.). 105p. 1986. pap. 10.00 (*0-9608008-3-2*) Legacy Hse.

TEE in Japan: A Realistic Vision: the Feasibility of Theological Education by Extension for Churches in Japan. W. Frederic Sprunger. LC 81-7739. (Illus.). 472p. (Orig.). 1981. pap. 15.95 (*0-87808-434-7*) William Carey Lib.

***Tee-Making Connections 1-'96 Version.** McCloskey. (Adult Esl Ser.). 1996. pap. 29.95 (*0-8384-7001-7*) Heinle & Heinle.

Tee-New Secondary French, Level 3. Bragger. (Miscellaneous/Catalogs Ser.). 1998. text ed. 52.95 (*0-8384-7301-6*) Heinle & Heinle.

Tee-ology: 18 Inspirational Lessons for Golfers. John Freeman. 144p. 1996. 12.99 (*0-7852-7677-7*) Nelson.

***Tee Times.** Burnett. 1997. 25.00 (*0-684-83128-7*) S&S Trade.

Tee Times: The Golfer's Daily Companion. Edward Frei. Ed. by Patrick Caton. 366p. 1996. 6.50 (*1-56245-269-X*) Great Quotations.

***Tee-Up Michigan Golf Guides 1996: North Edition.** Anneliese Morris. 1996. pap. 8.95 (*1-879152-03-7*) Unicorn Grap Commns.

***Tee-Up Michigan Golf Guides 1996: Southeast Edition.** Anneliese Morris. 1996. pap. 8.95 (*1-879152-04-5*) Unicorn Grap Commns.

***Tee-Up Michigan Golf Guides 1996: Southwest Edition.** Anneliese Morris. 1996. pap. 8.95 (*1-879152-05-3*) Unicorn Grap Commns.

***Teebaumol Hausapotheke.** Cynthia B. Olsen. Ed. by Christopher S. Gerlach. Tr. by Christopher Baker. (Illus.). 121p. (Orig.). (GER.). 1994. pap. write for info. (*3-89385-138-0*) Kali Pr.

Teebox Hawaii Golf Guide: The Comprehensive Source for Playing Golf in Hawaii. Stephan Harper. (Illus.). 160p. (Orig.). 1994. pap. 12.95 (*1-883415-01-2*) Teebox.

Teed Off! The Modern Guide to Golf. Tom Carey. (Illus.). 112p. (Orig.). 1995. pap. 7.95 (*1-877590-92-4*) DE Pr IL.

Teed Stories. Jeff Danziger. LC 88-30789. (Illus.). 116p. (Orig.). 1988. pap. 7.95 (*0-933050-60-7*) New Eng Pr VT.

Teeing Off in Central Ohio. Carl Japikse. 128p. 1991. pap. 14.95 (*0-89804-809-5*, Enthea Pr) Ariel GA.

Teeing off to the Green: Using Golf As a Business Tool. Judy Anderson. 224p. (Orig.). 1995. per., pap. 14.95 (*0-7872-1105-2*) Kendall-Hunt.

***Teen Addiction.** Marti Heuer. 1997. pap. 11.00 (*0-345-42014-4*) Ballantine.

Teen Addiction. Ed. by Paul A. Winters. LC 96-42911. (Current Controversies Ser.). 170p. (J). (gr. 5-12). 1997. pap. 12.96 (*1-56510-535-4*); lib. bdg. 20.96 (*1-56510-536-2*) Greenhaven.

Teen-Age Dance Book. B. White. (Ballroom Dance Ser.). 1986. lib. bdg. 79.95 (*0-8490-3379-9*) Gordon Pr.

Teen-Age Dance Book. B. White. (Ballroom Dance Ser.). 1985. lib. bdg. 79.95 (*0-87700-711-X*) Revisionist Pr.

Teen-Aged Dope Slaves & Reform School Girls. (Illus.). 1990. pap. 9.95 (*0-913035-79-3*) Eclipse Bks.

Teen-Agers at Work. Yvette Dogin. 64p. (YA). (gr. 8 up). 1988. pap. text ed. 3.75 (*0-88323-244-8*, 164) Pendergrass Pub.

Teen-agers in the Bible. Ernest L. Green. 16p. 1980. 1.00 (*0-89814-049-8*) Grace Publns.

***Teen Alcoholism.** Hayley R. Mitchell. (Overview Series). (Illus.). (J). (gr. 4-12). 1997. lib. bdg. 17.96 (*1-56006-514-1*) Lucent Bks.

Teen Alcoholism. Nancy Nielsen. LC 90-66. (Overview Ser.). (Illus.). 96p. (J). (gr. 5-8). 1990. lib. bdg. 17.96 (*1-56006-121-9*) Lucent Bks.

Teen Angels No. 6: Love Without End. Cherie Bennett & Jeff Gottesfeld. (Teen Angels Ser.: No. 6). 144p. (Orig.). (YA). 1996. mass mkt. 3.99 (*0-380-78579-X*, Flare) Avon.

***Teen Angst.** James Mantooth. (Tanbark Ser.). 24p. (Orig.). 1997. pap. 6.00 (*1-887853-13-8*) Radiolarian.

Teen Angst: A Treasury of '50s Romance. Intro. by Tom Mason & Jim Korkis. (Illus.). 154p. 1990. pap. 14.95 (*0-944735-35-5*) Malibu Comics Ent.

Teen Assemblies, Retreats & Prayer Services: Prayer Experiences for Teen Assemblies & Retreats. Greg Dues. LC 93-60027. 96p. (Orig.). 1993. pap. 9.95 (*0-89622-561-5*) Twenty-Third.

***Teen Choices.** (YA). 1996. write for info. (*5-900522-07-5*, Chariot Bks) Chariot Victor.

Teen Conflicts. Ed. by Evelyn Bachelor et al. (Illus.). 240p. (Orig.). (YA). (gr. 8 up). 1972. 9.95 (*0-87297-006-X*); pap. 7.95 (*0-87297-007-8*) Diablo.

Teen Counseling. Bedinger. 272p. (C). 1992. per. 28.29 (*0-8403-8193-X*) Kendall-Hunt.

***Teen Crime: A Growing Problem.** Jeffrey A. Margolis. LC 96-53650. (Issues in Focus Ser.). (Illus.). 112p. (YA). (gr. 6 up). 1997. lib. bdg. 18.95 (*0-89490-910-X*) Enslow Pubs.

Teen Crime Crisis: Societal Consensus Required. Edward L. Correll, Sr. LC 96-90051. 1996. 11.95 (*0-533-11862-X*) Vantage.

Teen Dads: Rights, Responsibilities & Joys. Jeanne W. Lindsay. 28p. (Orig.). (YA). (gr. 7 up). 1993. teacher ed., pap. 2.50 (*0-930934-80-6*); student ed., wbk. ed., pap. 2.50 (*0-930934-79-2*) Morning Glory.

Teen Dads: Rights, Responsibilities & Joys. Jeanne W. Lindsay. (Illus.). 192p. (Orig.). (YA). (gr. 7 up). 1993. 15.95 (*0-930934-77-6*); pap. 9.95 (*0-930934-78-4*) Morning Glory.

***Teen Drug Abuse.** Wendy Mass. (Overview Series). (Illus.). (J). (gr. 4-12). 1997. lib. bdg. 17.96 (*1-56006-196-0*) Lucent Bks.

Teen Esteem. 366p. (Orig.). (YA). (gr. 6-12). 1992. spiral bd. 7.00 (*1-882835-09-3*) STA-Kris.

Teen Esteem. Sarah Radcliff. 194p. (YA). 1992. 16.95 (*0-944070-80-9*) Targum Pr.

Teen Esteem: A Self-Direction Manual for Young Adults. Pat Palmer & Melissa A. Froehner. LC 89-39305. 128p. (Orig.). 1989. pap. 7.95 (*0-915166-66-6*) Impact Pubs CA.

Teen Families & Welfare Dependency in California: Background Briefing Report with Seminar Presentations. Diane Levitt. 137p. 1994. pap. 15.00 (*0-929722-83-3*) CA State Library Fndtn.

Teen Fathers. Paul S. Lang & Susan S. Lang. (Changing Family Ser.). 128p. (YA). (gr. 9-12). 1995. lib. bdg. 22.70 (*0-531-11216-0*) Watts.

***Teen Fathers.** Gail B. Stewart. (Other America Ser.). (Illus.). (J). (gr. 4-12). 1997. lib. bdg. 17.96 (*1-56006-575-3*) Lucent Bks.

***Teen Genreflecting.** Diana T. Herald. LC 96-29139. 120p. 1997. lib. bdg. 23.50 (*1-56308-287-X*) Libs Unl.

T

An Asterisk (*) at the beginning of an entry indicates that the title is appearing in BIP for the first time.

***Teen Glory.** Peter Regan. Date not set. pap. 8.95 (*0-947962-78-6*) Dufour.

Teen Guide. 6th ed. Valerie M. Chamberlain et al. Ed. by Martha O'Neill. (Illus.). 528p. (YA). 1985. text ed. 30.00 (*0-07-007842-4*); pap. text ed. 11.68 (*0-07-007831-9*) McGraw.

Teen Guide. 7th ed. Valerie M. Chamberlain. 544p. 1989. text ed. 30.80 (*0-07-007847-5*) McGraw.

Teen Guide Job Search: Ten Easy Steps to Your Future. Donald L. Wilkes & Viola Hamilton-Wilkes. (Illus.). 112p. (YA). (gr. 10-12). 1991. pap. 10.95 (*0-9628787-1-5*) JEM Job Educ.

Teen Guide to Homemaking. 4th ed. J. H. Brinkley et al. 1976. text ed. 33.88 (*0-07-007840-8*) McGraw.

Teen Guide to Homemaking. 5th ed. Valerie M. Chamberlain. 1982. text ed. 31.08 (*0-07-007843-2*) McGraw.

Teen Health the Natural Way. Yaakov Berman. (Illus.). 176p. (YA). (gr. 7-11). 1995. pap. 10.95 (*0-943706-52-1*) Pitspopany.

Teen Idol. Kate Daniel. 224p. (YA). 1992. mass mkt. 3.50 (*0-06-106779-2*, Harp PBks) HarpC.

Teen Interviews. Marina Budhos. 1996. write for info. (*0-8050-5113-9*, Bks Young Read) H Holt & Co.

***Teen Issues, 6 vols.** (Illus.). (YA). (gr. 6 up). 1997. lib. bdg. 113.70 (*0-89490-887-1*) Enslow Pubs.

Teen Issues Student Workbook. 2nd rev. ed. Monte Elchoness. LC 86-737. 168p. 1989. pap. 6.95 (*0-936781-05-X*) Monroe Pr.

Teen Legal Rights: A Guide for the 90s. Kathleen A. Hempelman. LC 93-37509. 256p. 1994. text ed. 39.95 (*0-313-28760-0*, Greenwood Pr) Greenwood.

Teen Living. Prentice. 23.06 (*0-13-903964-3*) P-H.

Teen Manners--Why Bother: Showing You Care Helps Others to Like you. Sarah Fletcher. (Illus.). 64p. (YA). (gr. 7-12). 1987. pap. 3.99 (*0-570-04449-9*, 12-3060) Concordia.

Teen Model Mystery. Carolyn Keene. (Illus.). (YA). (gr. 3-6). 1995. pap. 3.99 (*0-671-87208-7*, Minstrel Bks) PB.

***Teen Moms: The Pain & the Promise.** Evelyn Lerman. LC 97-20134. (Illus.). 192p. 1997. 21.95 (*1-885356-24-2*) Morning Glory.

***Teen Moms: The Pain & the Promise.** Evelyn Lerman. LC 97-20134. (Illus.). 192p. (Orig.). 1997. pap. 14.95 (*1-885356-25-0*) Morning Glory.

Teen Mothers. Gail B. Stewart. LC 95-40340. (Other America Ser.). (Illus.). 112p. (J). (gr. 5-12). 1996. lib. bdg. 17.96 (*1-56006-332-7*) Lucent Bks.

Teen Mothers: Citizens or Dependents? Ruth Horowitz. 290p. 1994. 32.95 (*0-226-35378-8*) U Ch Pr.

Teen Mothers: Citizens or Dependents? Ruth Horowitz. 290p. (C). 1996. reprint ed. pap. 14.95 (*0-226-35379-6*) U Ch Pr.

Teen Mothers & the Revolving Welfare Door. Kathleen M. Harris. LC 96-36157. (Women in the Political Economy Ser.). 224p. (C). 1996. 39.95 (*1-56639-499-6*) Temple U Pr.

***Teen Power: A Treasury of Solid Gold Advice for Today's Teens.** Kevin Wanzer. 1997. pap. text ed. 11.95 (*0-9651447-0-4*) ChesPress.

Teen Prayer Services: Twenty Themes for Reflection. S. Kevin Regan. LC 92-81797. 80p. (Orig.). 1992. pap. 9.95 (*0-89622-520-8*) Twenty-Third.

Teen Pregnancy. Judy Berlfein. LC 92-9673. (Overview Ser.). (Illus.). 112p. (J). (gr. 5-8). 1992. lib. bdg. 17.96 (*1-56006-130-8*) Lucent Bks.

Teen Pregnancy: A Special Issue of Families in Society. 64p. 1993. pap. 8.00 (*0-87304-268-9*) Families Intl.

Teen Pregnancy: Impact on the Schools. Ed. by Roberta Weiner. LC 86-83248. 94p. (Orig.). (C). 1987. 29.95 (*0-937925-03-9*, TPPP) Capitol VA.

Teen Pregnancy: Why Are Kids Having Babies? Laurie Rozakis. (Issues of Our Time Ser.). (Illus.). 64p. (J). (gr. 5-8). 1993. lib. bdg. 15.98 (*0-8050-2569-3*) TFC Bks NY.

Teen Pregnancy & Parenting. Annette U. Rickel. 225p. 1989. 48.95 (*0-89116-808-7*); pap. 29.95 (*0-89116-908-3*) Hemisp Pub.

Teen Pregnancy & Parenting Handbook. Patricia G. Mathes & Beverly J. Irby. LC 92-85264. 440p. (Orig.). (YA). 1993. pap. text ed. 19.95 (*0-87822-333-9*, 4660) Res Press.

Teen Pregnancy & Parenting Handbook: Discussion Guide. Patricia G. Mathes & Beverly J. Irby. LC 92-85263. 64p. (Orig.). 1993. spiral bd. 6.95 (*0-87822-334-7*, 4661) Res Press.

Teen Pregnancy Challenge, Bk. 2, Programs for Kids. Jeanne W. Lindsay & Sharon Rodine. LC 89-14491. (Illus.). 256p. (Orig.). 1989. 19.95 (*0-930934-39-3*); pap. 14.95 (*0-930934-38-5*) Morning Glory.

Teen Pregnancy in California: Effective Prevention Strategies: Background Briefing Report with Seminar Presentations. Ed. by M. Anne Powell. 168p. 1994. pap. 15.00 (*0-929722-82-5*) CA State Library Fndtn.

***Teen Prostitution.** Ruth Dean & Melissa Thompson. (Overview Series). (Illus.). (J). (gr. 4-12). 1997. lib. bdg. 17.96 (*1-56006-512-5*) Lucent Bks.

Teen Prostitution. Joan J. Johnson. LC 92-15231. (Illus.). 112p. (YA). (gr. 9-12). 1992. lib. bdg. 22.70 (*0-531-11099-0*) Watts.

Teen Runaways. Gail B. Stewart. LC 96-17209. (Other America Ser.). (Illus.). 112p. (YA). 1996. lib. bdg. 17.96 (*1-56006-336-X*) Lucent Bks.

Teen Satanism: Redeeming the Devil's Children. Greg Reid. 32p. (Orig.). 1990. pap. 10.00 (*1-877858-04-8*, TS-RDC) Amer Focus Pub.

Teen Scene: Personal Stories for Students Who Are Beginning to Read. Kamla D. Koch et al. (Illus.). 139p. 1987. teacher ed., pap. 6.95 (*0-916591-08-5*); pap. text ed. 8.95 (*0-916591-07-7*) Linmore Pub.

Teen Self-Esteem: A Common Sense Path to a Happy & Successful Life. Charles L. Van House, Sr. & Sarah M. Swoszowski. 213p. (Orig.). (YA). (gr. 7-12). 1995. pap. 9.95 (*0-9635745-7-4*) Life Lines Pr.

Teen Self-Steam Pocket Coach: Exploring Life's Puzzles & Developing Personal Strength, 2 wkbks., Set. Mary S. Moore. LC 94-92393. (YA). (gr. 6-12). 1994. pap. text ed. 11.95 (*1-885574-01-0*) Courage Press.

Teen Sexuality. Don Nardo. LC 96-8696. (Overview Ser.). (Illus.). (J). (gr. 4-12). 1996. lib. bdg. 17.96 (*1-56006-189-8*) Lucent Bks.

Teen Smoking: Understanding the Risks. Daniel McMillan. LC 96-36323. (Issues in Focus Ser.). (Illus.). 128p. (YA). (gr. 6 up). 1997. lib. bdg. 18.95 (*0-89490-722-0*) Enslow Pubs.

Teen Spirit. Sprague. 1996. pap. 16.00 (*0-684-83356-5*) S&S Trade.

Teen Stress: Stories to Guide You. William L. Coleman. LC 94-33427. 112p. (J). (gr. 4-7). 1994. pap. 5.99 (*0-8066-2732-8*, Augsburg) Augsburg Fortress.

Teen Styles. Beverly Getschel. (C). 1998. 26.95 (*1-56253-337-1*) Delmar.

Teen Suicide. Judith Galas. LC 93-11081. (Overview Ser.). 100p. (J). 1994. lib. bdg. 17.96 (*1-56006-148-0*) Lucent Bks.

Teen Suicide. rev. ed. Nancy Merritt. 1996. pap. 0.50 (*0-89230-237-2*) Do It Now.

Teen Suicide: Is It Too Painful to Grow Up? Eleanor Ayer. (Issues of Our Time Ser.). (Illus.). 64p. (J). (gr. 5-8). 1993. lib. bdg. 15.98 (*0-8050-2573-1*) TFC Bks NY.

Teen Suicide: Too Young to Die. Cynthia Copeland Lewis. LC 93-25010. (Issues in Focus Ser.). (Illus.). 128p. (YA). (gr. 6 up). 1994. lib. bdg. 18.95 (*0-89490-433-7*) Enslow Pubs.

Teen Suicide see Life Issues - Group 3

Teen Tips: A Practical Guide for Parents with Kids 11-19. Tom McMahon. 288p. (J). 1996. pap. 12.00 (*0-671-89106-5*) PB.

Teen to Teen. Ruth H. Smith. 1984. pap. 3.95 (*0-89137-813-8*) Quality Pubns.

Teen to Teen: Responding to Peers in Crisis. Robert P. Stamschror. (Illus.). 104p. (Orig.). (YA). 1996. pap. 22.95 (*0-88489-353-7*) St Marys.

Teen Troubles: How to Keep Them from Becoming Tragedies. Carolyn M. Wesson. 1988. 17.95 (*0-8027-1011-5*); pap. 11.95 (*0-8027-7310-9*) Walker & Co.

***Teen Violence.** William Goodwin. (Overview Series). (Illus.). (J). (gr. 4-12). 1997. lib. bdg. 17.96 (*1-56006-511-7*) Lucent Bks.

Teen Violence. Susan S. Lang. (Violence in America Ser.). (Illus.). 144p. (YA). (gr. 9-12). 1994. lib. bdg. 22.00 (*0-531-11202-0*) Watts.

Teen Violence: Out of Control. David E. Newton. LC 95-6943. (Issues in Focus Ser.). (Illus.). 112p. (YA). (gr. 6 up). 1995. lib. bdg. 18.95 (*0-89490-506-6*) Enslow Pubs.

Teenage Addicts Can Recover: Treating the Addict, Not the Age. Shelly Marshall. 176p. 1992. pap. 12.95 (*1-880197-02-2*) Gylantic Pub.

Teenage Alcoholism & Substance. John Bartimole. 1994. pap. 6.95 (*0-8119-0724-4*) LIFETIME.

Teenage Alcoholism & Substance Abuse: Causes, Cures & Consequences. John Bartimole & Carmella Bartimole. (Illus.). 160p. (Orig.). 1986. pap. 6.95 (*0-936320-18-4*, Compact Books) LIFETIME.

Teenage & Pregnant: What You Can Do. Herma Silverstein. (Illus.). (YA). (gr. 7 up). 1989. pap. 5.95 (*0-671-65222-2*, Julian Messner) Silver Burdett Pr.

Teenage Bodybuilding. Ed Gaut. LC 95-61393. (Illus.). 140p. (Orig.). Date not set. pap. 19.95 (*0-9640945-2-5*) Pierpoint-Martin.

Teenage Book of Manners...Please! Fred Hartley. (YA). 1991. pap. 6.97 (*1-55748-246-2*) Barbour & Co.

Teenage Book of Manners...Please! Fred Hartley. (YA). 6.97 (*1-55748-245-4*) Barbour & Co.

Teenage Competition: A Survival Guide. Susan Cohen & Daniel Cohen. LC 86-24307. 144p. (J). (gr. 7 up). 1986. 13.95 (*0-87131-487-8*) M Evans.

***Teenage Confidential: An Illustrated History of the American Teen.** Michael Barson. (Illus.). 1998. pap. text ed. 16.95 (*0-8118-1584-6*) Chronicle Bks.

Teenage Conflicts. David W. Felder. LC 95-90513. 110p. (YA). (gr. 7-12). 1995. 24.95 (*0-910959-16-1*, B&G 16H); teacher ed. 44.95 (*0-910959-36-6*, B&G 16T) Wellington Pr.

Teenage Couples - Expectations & Reality: Teens' Views on Living Together, Roles, Work, Children, Jealousy, & Partner Abuse. Jeanne W. Lindsay. LC 95-46209. (Illus.). 192p. (Orig.). (YA). (gr. 9 up). 1996. 21.95 (*0-930934-99-7*); pap. 14.95 (*0-930934-98-9*) Morning Glory.

Teenage Couples: Caring, Commitment & Change: How to Build a Relationship That Lasts. Jeanne W. Lindsay. (Teenage Couples Ser.). 36p. (Orig.). (YA). (gr. 7 up). 1995. student ed., wbk. ed., pap. 2.50 (*0-930934-96-2*) Morning Glory.

Teenage Couples: Caring, Commitment & Change: How to Build a Relationship That Lasts. Jeanne W. Lindsay. LC 94-37983. (Teenage Couples Ser.). (Illus.). 208p. (Orig.). (YA). (gr. 7 up). 1996. pap. 9.95 (*0-930934-93-8*) Morning Glory.

Teenage Couples: Caring, Commitment & Change: How to Build a Relationship That Lasts. Jeanne W, Lindsay. LC 94-37983. (Teenage Couples Ser.). (Illus.). 208p. (Orig.). (YA). (gr. 7 up). 1996. 15.95 (*0-930934-92-X*) Morning Glory.

Teenage Couples: Coping with Reality: Dealing with Money, In-Laws, Babies & Other Details of Daily Life. Jeanne W. Lindsay. (Teenage Couples Ser.). 32p. (Orig.). (YA). (gr. 7 up). 1995. student ed., wbk. ed., pap. 2.50 (*0-930934-88-1*) Morning Glory.

Teenage Couples: Coping with Reality: Dealing with Money, In-Laws, Babies & Other Details of Daily Life. Jeanne W. Lindsay. LC 94-36860. (Teenage Couples Ser.). (Illus.). 188p. (Orig.). 1996. pap. 9.95 (*0-930934-86-5*) Morning Glory.

Teenage Couples: Coping with Reality: Dealing with Money, In-Laws, Babies & Other Details of Daily Life. Jeanne W. Lindsay. LC 94-36860. (Teenage Couples Ser.). (Illus.). 188p. (Orig.). (YA). (gr. 7 up). 1996. 15.95 (*0-930934-87-3*) Morning Glory.

Teenage Couples Series Curriculum Guide. Jeanne W. Lindsay. (Teenage Couples Ser.). 136p. 1995. pap. 19.95 (*0-930934-89-X*) Morning Glory.

Teenage Depression & Suicide. John A. Chiles. (Encyclopedia of Psychoactive Drugs Ser.: No. 1). (Illus.). (YA). (gr. 7 up). 1992. lib. bdg. 19.95 (*0-87754-771-8*) Chelsea Hse.

Teenage Drinking. Elaine Landau. LC 94-40. (Issues in Focus Ser.). (Illus.). 104p. (YA). (gr. 6 up). 1994. lib. bdg. 18.95 (*0-89490-575-9*) Enslow Pubs.

Teenage Drug Abuse: One Hundred Most Commonly Asked Questions about Adolescent Substance Abuse. Ronald J. Gaetano & James J. Masterson. 110p. (Orig.). 1989. pap. write for info. (*0-9621620-0-0*) Union Hosp Found.

Teenage Drug Abusers: One Hundred Most Commonly Asked Questions about Adolescent Substance Abuse. Ronald J. Gaetano & James J. Masterson. 128p. (YA). (gr. 9 up). 1988. write for info. (*0-318-64424-X*) Union Hosp Found.

***Teenage Expectations: The Real Parent's Guide to the Terrible Teens.** Terry L. Bilsky & Jill Weber. (Illus.). 48p. 1997. 10.95 (*0-8362-2898-7*) Andrews & McMeel.

Teenage Fathers. Karen Gravelle. LC 91-2967. (YA). 1992. pap. 5.95 (*0-671-72851-2*, Julian Messner) Silver Burdett Pr.

Teenage Fathers. Bryan E. Robinson. LC 86-45896. 173p. (C). pap. 12.95 (*0-669-14587-4*, Lexington) Jossey-Bass.

Teenage Genius. 95th ed. HB Staff. (J). (gr. 6). 1995. text ed., lib. bdg., pap. text ed. 10.25 (*0-15-305233-3*) HB Coll Pubs.

Teenage Girls: A Parent's Survival Manual. Lauren K. Ayers. LC 93-48386. 240p. (Orig.). 1994. pap. 17.95 (*0-8245-1356-8*) Crossroad NY.

Teenage Health Care. Gail B. Slap & Martha M. Jablow. Ed. by Paul McCarthy. (Orig.). 1994. pap. 14.00 (*0-671-75412-2*) PB.

***Teenage Liberation Handbook: How to Quit School & Get a Real Life & Education.** Grace Llewellyn. LC 97-19785. 1997. pap. 9.95 (*1-86204-104-0*) Element MA.

Teenage Liberation Handbook: How to Quit School & Get a Real Life & Education. Grace Llewellyn. 401p. (YA). (gr. 7-12). 1991. pap. 14.95 (*0-9629591-0-3*) Lowry Hse.

Teenage Mambo. (Ballroom Dance Ser.). 1986. lib. bdg. 79.95 (*0-8490-3400-0*) Gordon Pr.

Teenage Mambo. (Ballroom Dance Ser.). 1985. lib. bdg. 44.00 (*0-87700-794-2*) Revisionist Pr.

Teenage Mambo, No. 2. (Ballroom Dance Ser.). 1986. lib. bdg. 79.95 (*0-8490-3404-3*) Gordon Pr.

Teenage Mambo, No. 2. (Ballroom Dance Ser.). 1985. lib. bdg. 74.00 (*0-87700-792-6*) Revisionist Pr.

Teenage Marriages: A Demographic Analysis. John R. Weeks. LC 76-5330. (Studies in Population & Urban Demography: No. 2). (Illus.). 192p. (Orig.). 1976. text ed. 49.95 (*0-8371-8898-9*, WTM/, Greenwood Pr) Greenwood.

Teenage Money Making Guide. Ed. by Allan H. Smith. LC 84-90126. (Illus.). 281p. (Orig.). (J). (ps-12). 1984. pap. 10.00 (*0-931113-00-8*) Success Publ.

Teenage Mothers: Their Experience, Strength, & Hope. Andre Beauchamp. Tr. by Rosemarie Fisher from FRE. LC 90-38476. (Illus.). 96p. (Orig.). (YA). (gr. 7-12). 1990. reprint ed. pap. 8.95 (*0-89390-180-6*) Resource Pubns.

Teenage Mouth. Roger Karshner. 64p. (Orig.). (YA). (gr. 8-12). 1991. pap. 8.95 (*0-940669-17-X*, D-12) Dramaline Pubns.

Teenage Mutant Ninja Turtles, 5 vols. (J). (gr. 4-7). 1990. boxed 14.75 (*0-440-36030-7*) Dell.

Teenage Mutant Ninja Turtles. Bob Italia. Ed. by Rosemary Wallner. LC 91-73051. (Behind the Creation of Ser.). (J). 1991. lib. bdg. 13.95 (*1-56239-050-3*) Abdo & Dghtrs.

***Teenage Mutant Ninja Turtles: A New Beginning.** Gary Carlson. (Illus.). 112p. 1997. pap. 9.95 (*1-887279-56-3*) Image Comics.

Teenage Mutant Ninja Turtles Adventures. Erick Wujcik. Ed. by Alex Marciniszyn. (Teenage Mutant Ninja Turtles RPG Adventures Ser.). (Illus.). 48p. (Orig.). (YA). (gr. 8 up). 1986. pap. 7.95 (*0-916211-16-9*, 504) Palladium Bks.

Teenage Mutant Ninja Turtles & Other Strangeness. Erick Wujcik. Ed. by Alex Marciniszyn et al. (Illus.). 112p. (Orig.). (YA). (gr. 8 up). 1985. pap. 11.95 (*0-916211-14-2*, 502) Palladium Bks.

Teenage Mutant Ninja Turtles Exposed. Joan H. Robie. 80p. 1991. pap. 5.95 (*0-914984-31-4*) Starburst.

Teenage Mutant Ninja Turtles Guide to the Universe. Erick Wujcik. Ed. by Alex Marciniszyn & Florence Siembieda. (Teenage Mutant Ninja Turtles RPG Adventures Ser.). (Illus.). 48p. (Orig.). (YA). (gr. 8 up). 1987. pap. 7.95 (*0-916211-25-8*, 506) Palladium Bks.

Teenage Mutant Ninja Turtles Pizza Party: A Step 1 Book - Preschool-Grade 1. Eleanor Hudson. LC 90-53243. (Step into Reading Bks.). (Illus.). 32p. (Orig.). (J). (ps-1). 1991. pap. 3.99 (*0-679-81452-3*); lib. bdg. 7.99 (*0-679-91452-8*) Random Bks Yng Read.

Teenage Mutant Ninja Turtles Totally Awesome Activity Book. Shelley Greene. (Illus.). 96p. (J). (gr. 1-5). 1990. pap. 3.95 (*0-679-81108-7*) Random Bks Yng Read.

***Teenage Mystique: A Guide for Concerned Adults.** James H. Humphrey. LC 96-90584. 144p. (Orig.). 1997. pap. 9.95 (*1-56002-692-8*, Univ Edtns) Aegina Pr.

***Teenage New Jersey, 1941-1975.** Ed. by Kathryn Grover. LC 97-15355. (Illus.). 136p. 1997. pap. 19.00 (*0-911020-31-4*) NJ Hist Soc.

Teenage of Insanity: Raising Your Teenager Without Raising Your Blood Pressure. Sherrie Weaver. Ed. by Patrick Caton. 168p. (Orig.). 1996. pap. 5.95 (*1-56245-228-2*) Great Quotations.

Teenage Parents. John Glore. (Family Ser.). (Illus.). 64p. (YA). (gr. 7 up). 1990. lib. bdg. 17.27 (*0-86593-080-5*); lib. bdg. 12.95 (*0-685-36299-X*) Rourke Corp.

Teenage Pregnancy. Charlotte G. Garman & Waln K. Brown. 20p. 1989. 2.95 (*1-56456-040-6*, 213) W Gladden Found.

***Teenage Pregnancy.** Ed. by Stephen P. Thompson. LC 96-48031. (Opposing Viewpoints Ser.). (Illus.). (YA). (gr. 5-12). 1997. pap. 12.96 (*1-56510-561-3*) Greenhaven.

***Teenage Pregnancy.** Ed. by Stephen P. Thompson. LC 96-48031. (Opposing Viewpoints Ser.). (Illus.). (YA). (gr. 5-12). 1997. lib. bdg. 20.96 (*1-56510-562-1*) Greenhaven.

Teenage Pregnancy. rev. ed. Cathryn Jakobson. (Think Ser.). 160p. (YA). (gr. 7 up). 1993. pap. 9.95 (*0-8027-7372-9*); lib. bdg. 15.85 (*0-8027-8128-4*) Walker & Co.

Teenage Pregnancy: A New Beginning. Linda Barr & Catherine P. Monserrat. (Illus.). 112p. (YA). (gr. 6-12). 1996. pap. 15.95 (*0-945886-12-8*) New Futures.

Teenage Pregnancy: A New Beginning. rev. ed. Linda Barr & Catherine P. Monserrat. (Illus.). 60p. (YA). (gr. 6-12). 1996. student ed. 4.95 (*0-945886-13-6*) New Futures.

Teenage Pregnancy: A Research Guide to Programs & Services. Patrice A. Gillotti. LC 87-30153. (Legal Research Guides Ser.: Vol. 4). 44p. 1987. lib. bdg. 30.00 (*0-89941-586-5*, 305400) W S Hein.

Teenage Pregnancy: Developing Strategies for Change in the Twenty-First Century. Ed. by Dionne J. Jones. 175p. 1989. 21.95 (*0-88738-818-3*) Transaction Pubs.

Teenage Pregnancy see Life Issues - Group 1

Teenage Pregnancy & Poverty: The Economic Realities, 8 vols. Barbara Miller. LC 96-40416. (Teen Pregnancy Prevention Library). (Illus.). 64p. (YA). (gr. 7-12). 1997. lib. bdg. 16.95 (*0-8239-2249-9*) Rosen Group.

Teenage Q & A Book. Josh McDowell & Bill Jones. 160p. 1990. pap. 9.99 (*0-8499-3232-7*) Word Pub.

Teenage Refugees from Bosnia-Herzegovina Speak Out. Compiled by Valerie Tekavec. LC 94-40369. (In Their Own Voices Ser.). (Illus.). 64p. (YA). (gr. 7-12). 1995. lib. bdg. 15.95 (*0-8239-1843-2*) Rosen Group.

Teenage Refugees from Cambodia Speak Out. Stephanie St. Pierre. LC 94-41411. (In Their Own Voices Ser.). (Illus.). 64p. (YA). (gr. 7-12). 1995. lib. bdg. 15.95 (*0-8239-1848-3*) Rosen Group.

Teenage Refugees from China Speak Out. Compiled by Colleen She. LC 94-40368. (In Their Own Voices Ser.). (Illus.). 64p. (YA). (gr. 7-12). 1995. lib. bdg. 15.95 (*0-8239-1847-5*) Rosen Group.

Teenage Refugees from Eastern Europe Speak Out. Carl Rollyson. (In Their Own Voices Ser.). (Illus.). 64p. (YA). (gr. 7-12). 1997. lib. bdg. 15.95 (*0-8239-2437-8*, D2437-8) Rosen Group.

Teenage Refugees from Ethiopia Speak Out. Ladena Schapper. (In Their Own Voices Ser.). (Illus.). 64p. (YA). (gr. 7-12). 1997. lib. bdg. 15.95 (*0-8239-2438-6*, D2438-6) Rosen Group.

Teenage Refugees from Guatemala Speak Out. Gerald Hadden. (In Their Own Voices Ser.). (Illus.). 64p. (YA). (gr. 7-12). 1997. lib. bdg. 15.95 (*0-8239-2439-4*, D2439-4) Rosen Group.

Teenage Refugees from Haiti Speak Out. Compiled by Valerie Tekavec. LC 94-40367. (In Their Own Voices Ser.). (Illus.). 64p. (YA). (gr. 7-12). 1995. lib. bdg. 15.95 (*0-8239-1844-0*) Rosen Group.

Teenage Refugees from India Speak Out. Rupa Viswanath. (In Their Own Voices Ser.). (Illus.). 64p. (YA). (gr. 7-12). 1997. lib. bdg. 15.95 (*0-8239-2440-8*, D2440-8) Rosen Group.

Teenage Refugees from Iran Speak Out. Gina Strazzabosco. LC 94-41372. (In Their Own Voices Ser.). (Illus.). 64p. (YA). (gr. 7-12). 1995. lib. bdg. 15.95 (*0-8239-1845-9*) Rosen Group.

Teenage Refugees from Mexico Speak Out. Gerald Hadden. (In Their Own Voices Ser.). (Illus.). 64p. (YA). (gr. 7-12). 1997. lib. bdg. 15.95 (*0-8239-2441-6*, D2441-6) Rosen Group.

Teenage Refugees from Nicaragua Speak Out. K. Melissa Cerar. LC 94-23653. (In Their Own Voices Ser.). (Illus.). 64p. (YA). (gr. 7-12). 1995. lib. bdg. 15.95 (*0-8239-1849-1*) Rosen Group.

Teenage Refugees from Russia Speak Out. Tatyana Zemenova. LC 94-23654. (In Their Own Voices Ser.). (Illus.). 64p. (YA). (gr. 7-12). 1995. lib. bdg. 15.95 (*0-8239-1846-7*) Rosen Group.

Teenage Refugees from Rwanda Speak Out. Aimable Twagilimana. (In Their Own Voices Ser.). (Illus.). 64p. (YA). (gr. 7-12). 1997. lib. bdg. 15.95 (*0-8239-2443-2*, D2443-2) Rosen Group.

Teenage Refugees from Somalia Speak Out. Ikram Hussein. (In Their Own Voices Ser.). (Illus.). 64p. (YA). (gr. 7-12). 1997. lib. bdg. 15.95 (*0-8239-2444-0*, D2444-0) Rosen Group.

Teenage Refugees from Vietnam Speak Out. Compiled by Kenneth Wapner. LC 94-40370. (In Their Own Voices Ser.). (Illus.). 64p. (YA). (gr. 7-12). 1995. lib. bdg. 15.95 (*0-8239-1842-4*) Rosen Group.

Teenage Religion & Values. Leslie Francis & William K. Kay. 1995. pap. 15.95 (*0-85244-282-3*, Pub. by Gracewing UK) Morehouse Pub.

An Asterisk (*) at the beginning of an entry indicates that the title is appearing in BIP for the first time.

***Teenage Rider's Handbook: A Guide for Buying, Training Showing & Selling Your Horse.** (Illus.). 187p. (Orig.). (YA). (gr. 8 up). 1997. pap. 14.95 (0-614-29848-2) Sterling Hse.

***Teenage Rider's Handbook: A Guide for Buying, Training, Showing & Selling Your Horse.** Barbara J. Deworken. 1997. pap. 14.95 (1-56315-046-8) Sterling Hse.

***Teenage Roadhogs: What the Driver's Manuals Don't Teach You.** Michael Schein. (Orig.). 1997. pap. 12.95 (0-614-28106-7) Mac Pub USA.

***Teenage Roadhogs: What the Driver's Manuals Don't Teach You!** Michael Schein. 160p. 1997. pap. 12.95 (0-02-861731-2, Alpha Ref) Macmillan Gen Ref.

Teenage Romance. Alan Edwards. (Orig.). 1996. pap. 11.95 (0-533-11744-5) Vantage.

Teenage Sexuality: Opposing Viewpoints. Ed. by Karin L. Swisher et al. LC 93-30962. (Opposing Viewpoints Ser.). (Illus.). 240p. (YA). (gr. 10 up). 1994. pap. text ed. 12.96 (1-56510-102-2); lib. bdg. 20.96 (1-56510-103-0) Greenhaven.

Teenage Sexuality see Life Issues - Group 2

Teenage Shitkicker Shout. Al Blair. 4p. 1990. pap. 3.95 (0-930366-31-X) Northcountry Pub.

Teenage Soldiers-Adult Wars: From the Barracks to the Battlefield. Yitzhak Ben-Ner et al. (World Issues Ser.: Vol. 1). (Illus.). (YA). (gr. 7-12). 1991. pap. 8.95 (0-8239-1305-8); lib. bdg. 16.95 (0-8239-1304-X) Rosen Group.

Teenage Spaceblob Love. Al Blair. 6p. 1990. pap. 3.95 (0-930366-43-3) Northcountry Pub.

Teenage Street Gangs: Differences, Membership & Intervention. unabridged ed. Fred A. Clark. Ed. by Lee S. Curry. (Illus.). 186p. (Orig.). 1996. pap. text ed. 39.95 (0-9651587-0-5) Clarco Ent.

Teenage Stress: How to Cope in a Complex World. Eileen Van Wie. LC 87-7742. (Illus.). 224p. (J). (gr. 6 up). 1988. pap. 6.95 (0-671-65980-4, Julian Messner) Silver Burdett Pr.

Teenage Stress: Understanding the Tensions You Feel at Home, at School & among Your Friends. Daniel Cohen & Susan Cohen. LC 83-16477. 160p. (J). (gr. 5 up). 1984. 13.95 (0-87131-423-1) M Evans.

Teenage Survival Book: The Complete Revised, Updated Edition of You. Sol Gordon. 150p. 1981. pap. 18.00 (0-8129-0972-0, Times Bks) Random.

***Teenage Survival Guide.** Patricia Sternberg. (J). Date not set. write for info. (0-688-04280-5); lib. bdg. write for info. (0-688-04281-3) Lothrop.

Teenage Survival Manual: A Safe Landing Place for Kaimbaze Kids. 4th rev. ed. H. Samm Coombs. LC 95-7970. (Illus.). 240p. (Orig.). (YA). (gr. 9-12). 1996. pap. 13.95 (1-879904-16-0) Halo Bks.

***Teenage Survival Manual: A Safe Landing Place for Kaimbaze Kids.** 5th rev. ed. Samm Coombs & Moore. LC 97-21273. (Illus.). 272p. (Orig.). (YA). (gr. 9-12). 1997. pap. 14.95 (1-879904-18-7) Halo Bks.

Teenage Tenderness. Ed. by Elmer Morgan & Don Tudor. 115p. (Orig.). 1991. pap. 6.95 (1-56794-013-7, C2274) Star Bible.

Teenage Violence: A Deadly Trend. Eileen S. Roggenthen. 111p. 1992. pap. 6.95 (1-57515-015-8) PPI Pubng.

Teenage World: Adolescents' Self-Image in Ten Countries. Daniel Offer et al. LC 88-4127. (Illus.). 288p. 1988. 49.50 (0-306-42747-8, Plenum Med Bk) Plenum.

Teenager Who Dared Obey God. Louise S. Murphy. 97p. (Orig.). (YA). 1985. pap. text ed. 3.95 (0-937580-44-9) LeSEA Pub Co.

Teenagers. J. M. Parramon et al. (Family Ser.). 32p. (J). (gr. 3-5). 1987. Eng. ed. pap. 3.95 (0-8120-3851-7) Barron.

Teenagers. J. M. Parramon et al. (Family Ser.). 32p. (SPA.). (J). (gr. 3-5). 1987. Span. ed.: Los Jovenes. pap. 6.95 (0-8120-3855-X) Barron.

Teenagers: A Bewildered Parent's Guide. Elizabeth Caldwell. 176p. (Orig.). 1996. pap. 11.95 (0-9624945-0-X) Silvercat Pubns.

Teenagers: An American History. Grace Palladino. (Illus.). 304p. 1996. 25.00 (0-465-00767-8) Basic.

***Teenagers: An American History.** Grace Palladino. (Illus.). 304p. 1997. pap. 14.00 (0-465-00766-X) Basic.

Teenagers & AIDS in America. Ed. by J. Stango. (Illus.). 227p. (C). 1994. lib. bdg. 59.00 (1-56072-178-2) Nova Sci Pubs.

Teenagers & Alcohol: When Saying No Isn't Enough. Roger E. Vogler & Wayne R. Bartz. LC 91-38965. 160p. 1992. pap. 16.95 (0-914783-57-2) Charles.

Teenagers & Compulsive Gambling. Edward F. Dolan. LC 93-31956. (Teen Issues Ser.). (Illus.). 112p. (YA). (gr. 9-12). 1994. lib. bdg. 22.70 (0-531-11100-8) Watts.

Teenagers & Parents: Ten Steps for a Better Relationship. 3rd rev. ed. Roger W. McIntire. Ed. by Eileen Haavik et al. (Illus.). 264p. (Orig.). 1996. pap. 11.95 (0-9640558-6-4) Summit Crossrds.

Teenagers & Peer Pressure. Stephen D. Willeford & Ruth H. Smith. 1984. pap. 4.50 (0-89137-809-X) Quality Pubns.

Teenagers & Stress. Nancy O. Wilson. 103p. (YA). (gr. 7-12). 1990. pap. 6.95 (1-57515-002-6) PPI Pubng.

***Teenagers Are People Too: A Communication Kit for Parents & Teens.** Stephanie Roth-Nelson. 1996. 22.95 (0-942097-36-X) Ctr Adolescent.

Teenagers Are Temporary. Charles L. Allen. (Heartgifts Ser.). 156p. 1993. pap. 2.99 (1-55748-347-7) Barbour & Co.

Teenagers Come & Pray! Celebrating Milestones, Memorials, & Holy Days. Michael D. Ausperk. LC 94-61851. 110p. (Orig.). 1995. pap. 12.95 (0-89622-642-5) Twenty-Third.

Teenagers, Drugs, & Growing Up. Gary DuDell. (Illus.). 170p. (Orig.). 1990. pap. 9.95 (0-9627553-0-3) C E Mendez Found.

Teenagers Face to Face with Bereavement. Karen Gravelle & Charles Haskins. Ed. by Jane Steltenpohl. 128p. (YA). (gr. 7 up). 1989. pap. 5.95 (0-671-65975-8, Julian Messner) Silver Burdett Pr.

Teenagers, Graybeards & 4-F's. Harrington E. Crissey, Jr. Incl. Vol. 2. American League. (Illus.). 179p. 1982. pap. 11.00 (0-9608878-1-4); Set. Set pap. write for info. (0-9608878-2-2) H E Crissey.

Teenager's Guide How to Manipulate Your Way to Happiness: Thirty-Seven Easy Steps in the Care & Feeding of Your Parents. 2nd ed. Kevin M. Denny. LC 92-81556. (Illus.). 240p. (Orig.). (YA). (gr. 8-12). 1995. pap. 12.95 (0-9633108-0-1) Warthog Pub.

***Teenagers Guide to A. D. D. Understanding & Treating Attention Disorders Through the Teenage Years.** Antony Amen. 1996. pap. text ed. 29.95 (1-886554-05-6) MindWrks.

Teenager's Guide to Study, Travel, & Adventure Abroad. Council on International Educational Exchange Staff. 288p. 1988. pap. 9.95 (0-312-02296-4) St Martin.

Teenagers Guide to Study, 91-92. Ciee. 1991. pap. 11.95 (0-312-05282-0) St Martin.

Teenager's Guide to the Law. Gabrielle J. Posner. 384p. 1995. pap. 18.00 (1-874241-00-7, Pub. by Cavendish UK) Gaunt.

***Teenager's Guide to the Real World.** Marshall Brain. LC 97-93314. (Illus.). 368p. (Orig.). (YA). 1997. pap. 19.95 (0-9657430-3-9) BYG Pub.

Teenagers in War. C. Gibson. (C). 1989. pap. 30.00 (0-7223-2373-5, Pub. by A H S Ltd UK) St Mut.

Teenager's One Minute Bible. Michael D. Murdock. Ed. by Joy A. Loy. 365p. (Orig.). (YA). 1991. pap. text ed. 5.95 (1-56394-003-5) Wisdom Intl.

Teenagers Pray. William A. Kramer. LC 55-12193. 82p. (YA). (gr. 8-12). 1967. 6.99 (0-570-03018-8, 06-1054) Concordia.

Teenagers Pray. large type ed. William J. Kraemer. spiral bd. write for info. (0-318-66324-4) LBW.

Teenagers Preparing for the Real World: The Inside Scoop That You Won't Learn in School. Chad Foster. 132p. (Orig.). (YA). (gr. 7-10). 1995. pap. 10.95 (0-9644456-0-3) Rising Books.

Teenagers Role in the Family Structure. Recco Richardson. Ed. by Tanya C. Stokes. 117p. (Orig.). 1991. pap. 8.00 (0-9627849-7-4) Temperance Pub Hse.

Teenagers Talk about Adoption. Marion Crook. 128p. (Orig.). 1987. pap. 12.95 (0-920053-67-X, Pub. by NC Press CN) U of Toronto Pr.

Teenagers Talk about Adoption. Marion Crook. 116p. (Orig.). (YA). (gr. 6 up). 1990. pap. 10.95 (1-55021-047-5, Pub. by NC Press CN) U of Toronto Pr.

Teenagers Talk about Grief. June C. Kolf. 64p. (Orig.). (YA). 1990. pap. 5.99 (0-8010-5292-0) Baker Bks.

Teenagers Talk about School. Elaine Landau. Ed. by Jane Steltenpohl. LC 88-23065. 120p. (YA). (gr. 7 up). 1989. pap. 5.95 (0-671-68148-6, Julian Messner) Silver Burdett Pr.

Teenagers Talk about Suicide. Marion Crook. (Teenagers Talk about...Ser.). 128p. (YA). (gr. 7-12). 1988. pap. 12.95 (1-55021-013-0, Pub. by NC Press CN) U of Toronto Pr.

Teenagers, Teachers, & Mathematics. David A. Thomas. 372p. (C). 1991. pap. text ed. 36.95 (0-205-13194-8, Longwood Div) Allyn.

Teenagers Themselves. Ed. by Howard Spanogla. LC 83-26568. (Illus.). 272p. (J). (gr. 9-12). 1985. 16.95 (0-915361-04-3); pap. 9.95 (0-915361-33-7, 09734-X) Hemed Bks.

Teenagers with ADD: A Parents' Guide. Chris A. Dendy. 350p. (Orig.). 1995. pap. 18.95 (0-933149-69-7) Woodbine House.

Teendreams & Our Own People. David Edgar. (Methuen Modern Plays Ser.). 160p. (C). 1988. pap. 9.95 (0-413-16890-5, A0281) Heinemann.

Teenie Tennis: A Love Game. Marceil Whitney. 72p. (Orig.). (J). (ps up). 1991. pap. write for info. (0-9629089-0-8) ATS Pub.

Teenie Tennis: A Progressive Teaching Method for Teaching Young Juniors. Marceil Whitney. (Orig.). 1991. teacher ed. write for info. (0-9629089-1-6) ATS Pub.

Teens: A Fresh Look. Anne Pedersen. Ed. by Mothering Magazine Staff. (Illus.). 240p. (Orig.). 1991. pap. 10.95 (0-945465-54-8) Mothering Magazine.

Teens: The Power to Obtain Wealth. Elizabeth Harris-Charity. Ed. by Samuel Tanguma et al. (Illus.). 25p. (YA). (gr. 7 up). 1990. reprint ed. pap. 5.95 (0-9651866-1-X) Youth Corp.

***Teens & Depression.** Gail B. Stewart. (Other America Ser.). (Illus.). (J). (gr. 4-12). 1997. lib. bdg. 17.96 (1-56006-577-X) Lucent Bks.

Teens & Gambling: Who Wins? Patricia Haddock. LC 95-39273. (Issues in Focus Ser.). (Illus.). 112p. (YA). (gr. 6 up). 1996. lib. bdg. 18.95 (0-89490-719-0) Enslow Pubs.

Teens & the Death Penalty. Elaine Landau. LC 91-23351. (Issues in Focus Ser.). 112p. (YA). (gr. 6 up). 1992. lib. bdg. 18.95 (0-89490-297-0) Enslow Pubs.

Teens & Trust: Building Bridges in Jewish Education. Steven Bayar & Francine Hirschman. LC 93-18138. 1993. 12.95 (0-933873-76-X) Torah Aura.

Teens Are Nondivorceable: A Workbook for Divorced Parents & Their Children (Ages 12-18) Sara Bonkowski. LC 90-62137. (Illus.). 160p. (Orig.). 1990. pap. 7.95 (0-915388-36-7, 179) ACTA Pubns.

***Teens As Parents of Babies & Toddlers.** 2nd rev. ed. Jennifer Birckmayer et al. 222p. 1997. ring bd. 25.00 (1-57753-095-0, 321TP) Corn Coop Ext.

Teens at Risk: How to Recognize & Prevent Adolescent Suicide. Kevin Leehey. 144p. (Orig.). 1991. pap. 8.95 (0-929162-25-0) PIA Pr.

Teen's Clinic: A First AId Kit for the Teen Years. Dave Ray. 308p. 1996. student ed., ring bd. 49.95 (1-57326-021-5) Core Ministries.

***Teens Community Project.** Nicel. (HA - Social Studies). Date not set. pap. write for info. (0-314-22323-1) S-W Pub.

***Teens, Crime & the Community.** 3rd ed. Nicel. (HA - Social Studies). (C). 1997. text ed. write for info. (0-314-20560-8) West Pub.

Teens Face to Face with Chronic Illness. Suzanne LeVert. LC 92-45819. (YA). 1993. pap. 7.95 (0-671-74541-7, Julian Messner) Silver Burdett Pr.

Teens' Favorite Books: Young Adults' Choices, 1987-1992. International Reading Association Staff. LC 93-122737. 87p. 1992. reprint ed. pap. 25.00 (0-608-01420-6, 2062183) Bks Demand.

***Teens Fight Adult Corruption.** R. A. Scott. 352p. (Orig.). 1997. 14.95 (0-9637645-2-7) Allon Pub.

Teen's Guide to Business: The Secret to a Successful Enterprise. Linda Menzies. (YA). 1992. pap. 7.95 (0-942361-50-4) MasterMedia Pub.

Teen's Guide to Business: The Secrets to a Successful Enterprise. large type ed. Linda Menzies et al. LC 93-30254. (Teen Scene Ser.). (YA). (gr. 9-12). 1993. pap. 15.95 (0-7862-0061-8) Thorndike Pr.

***Teen's Guide to Getting Published: The Young Writer's Publishing Handbook.** Danielle Dunn & Jessica Dunn. 83p. Date not set. pap. 14.95 (1-882664-22-1) Prufrock Pr.

Teen's Guide to Going Vegetarian. Judy Krizmanic. (Illus.). 240p. (YA). (gr. 7 up). 1994. pap. 8.95 (0-14-036589-3) Puffin Bks.

Teen's Guide to Going Vegetarian. Judy Krizmanic. (Illus.). 240p. (YA). (gr. 7 up). 1994. pap. 14.99 (0-670-85114-0) Viking Child Bks.

Teens in Drama Ministry. Tim D. Miller. (Drama Topics Ser.). 1994. 8.99 (0-8341-9129-6, MP-514) Lillenas.

Teens in Prison. Gail B. Stewart. LC 96-44687. (Other America Ser.). (Illus.). 112p. (YA). 1996. lib. bdg. 17.96 (1-56006-338-6) Lucent Bks.

Teens in the 90's. Esther P. Davis. 179p. (YA). (gr. 7-12). 1992. pap. 6.95 (1-57515-058-1) PPI Pubng.

Teens in Two Worlds: How to Live in the World Without the World Living in You. Mike Cope & Robert Oglesby, Jr. (Illus.). 156p. 1989. pap. 6.99 (0-89225-347-9) Gospel Advocate.

Teens Parenting - Discipline from Birth to Three: How to Prevent & Deal with Discipline Problems with Babies & Toddlers. Jeanne W. Lindsay & Sally McCullough. LC 91-3711. (Teens Parenting Ser.). (Illus.). 192p. (Orig.). (YA). (gr. 6 up). 1991. 15.95 (0-930934-55-5); pap. 9.95 (0-930934-54-7); student ed., wbk. ed., pap. 2.50 (0-930934-66-0) Morning Glory.

Teens Parenting - The Challenge of Toddlers: Parenting Your Child from One to Three. Jeanne W. Lindsay. LC 91-30316. (Teens Parenting Ser.). (Illus.). 192p. (Orig.). 1991. 15.95 (0-930934-59-8); pap. 9.95 (0-930934-58-X); student ed., wbk. ed., pap. 2.50 (0-930934-65-2) Morning Glory.

Teens Parenting - Your Baby's First Year: A How-to-Parent Book Especially for Teenage Parents. rev. ed. Jeanne W. Lindsay. LC 91-21513. (Teens Parenting Ser.). (Illus.). 192p. (J). (gr. 6 up). 1991. 15.95 (0-930934-53-9); pap. 9.95 (0-930934-52-0) Morning Glory.

Teens Parenting - Your Baby's First Year: A How-to-Parent Book Especially for Teenage Parents. rev. ed. Jeanne W. Lindsay. LC 91-21513. (Teens Parenting Ser.). 48p. (YA). (gr. 6 up). 1991. student ed., wbk. ed., pap. 2.50 (0-930934-64-4) Morning Glory.

Teens Parenting - Your Pregnancy & Newborn Journey: How to Take Care of Yourself & Your Newborn When You're a Pregnant Teen. Jeanne W. Lindsay & Jean Brunelli. LC 91-3712. (Teens Parenting Ser.). (Illus.). 192p. (Orig.). (YA). (gr. 6 up). 1991. 15.95 (0-930934-51-2); pap. 9.95 (0-930934-50-4); student ed., wbk. ed., pap. 2.50 (0-930934-60-1) Morning Glory.

Teens Parenting - Your Pregnancy & Newborn Journey (Easier Reading) How to Take Care of Yourself & Your Newborn When You're a Pregnant Teen - Easy Reading Edition. Jeanne W. Lindsay & Jean Brunelli. LC 91-3712. 24p. (Orig.). (YA). (gr. 6 up). 1992. teacher ed., pap. 2.50 (0-930934-68-7); student ed., wbk. ed., pap. 2.50 (0-930934-63-6); text ed. 15.95 (0-930934-62-8); pap. text ed. 9.95 (0-930934-61-X) Morning Glory.

Teens, Sex & Happiness. Karl Duff. 140p. (Orig.). 1994. pap. 7.99 (1-56043-131-8) Destiny Image.

***Teens' Solutions Workbook.** Lawrence Shapiro. 74p. (YA). (gr. 6-12). 1996. pap. 19.95 (1-882732-62-6) Ctr Applied Psy.

Teens with AIDS Speak Out. Mary Kittredge. (YA). (gr. 7 up). 1992. lib. bdg. 8.95 (0-671-74543-3, Julian Messner) Silver Burdett Pr.

Teens with AIDS Speak Out. large type ed. Mary Kittredge. LC 93-6878. 161p. (J). 1993. Alk. paper. pap. 16.95 (1-56054-691-3) Thorndike Pr.

Teens with Physical Disabilities: Real-Life Stories of Meeting the Challenge. Glenn A. Cheney. LC 94-3603. (Issues in Focus Ser.). (Illus.). 112p. (YA). (gr. 6 up). 1995. lib. bdg. 18.95 (0-89490-625-9) Enslow Pubs.

***Teens with Single Parents: Why Me?** Margaret A. Shultz. LC 96-39439. (Teen Issues Ser.). 128p. (YA). (gr. 6 up). 1997. lib. bdg. 18.95 (0-89490-913-4) Enslow Pubs.

Teens with Talent: Developing the Potential of the Bright, Brighter & Brightest. Ellie Schatz & Nancy Schuster. Ed. by Elinor Katz. (Professional Development Ser.). (Illus.). 100p. (Orig.). 1996. pap. 15.45 (0-9638228-8-8) Open Space Comn.

***Teenscenes: Theatre Peer Educator Training Project on Relationship Violence & Racism.** unabridged ed. Bronwyn Rucker. Ed. by Rick Russo. 43p. (Orig.). 1994. pap. 5.00 (0-9657394-0-6) Meltdown Inc.

Teenspeak: A Bewildered Parent's Guide to Teenagers. Linda Meyer. LC 94-21338. 144p. 1994. pap. 8.95 (1-56079-338-4) Petersons.

***Teeny Books 1.** Playskool Staff. (J). 1998. pap. 3.99 (0-525-45818-2) NAL-Dutton.

***Teeny Books 2.** Playskool Staff. (J). 1998. pap. 3.99 (0-525-45819-0) NAL-Dutton.

***Teeny Books 3.** Playskool Staff. (J). 1998. pap. 4.99 (0-525-45820-4) NAL-Dutton.

***Teeny Books 4.** Playskool Staff. 1998. pap. 4.99 (0-525-45821-2) Viking Penguin.

***Teeny Mouse Plays with Shapes.** (Early Learning Ser.). (Illus.). 12p. (J). (ps). 1996. bds. write for info. (0-614-19519-5, 6088, Golden Books) Western Pub.

***Teeny Rain's Adventure.** Hyon McDaniel. (Illus.). 20p. (Orig.). (J). (gr. 1-2). 1997. pap. 8.99 (1-55197-840-7, Pub. by Comnwlth Pub CN) Partners Pubs Grp.

Teeny, Tiny Baby. Amy Schwartz. LC 93-4876. (Illus.). 32p. (J). (ps-1). 1994. 15.95 (0-531-06818-8); lib. bdg. 16.99 (0-531-08668-2) Orchard Bks Watts.

Teeny Tiny Farm-Chucky Shape Book. Katherine Ross. LC 91-50647. (J). (ps). 1992. 3.25 (0-679-83069-3) Random Bks Yng Read.

***Teeny Tiny Ghost.** Kay Winters. LC 96-24061. (Illus.). 32p. (J). (ps-3). 1997. 14.95 (0-06-025479-3); lib. bdg. 14.89 (0-06-025684-2) HarpC Child Bks.

Teeny Tiny Ghost. Kay Winters. LC 96-24061. 1998. write for info. (0-06-027358-5); lib. bdg. write for info. (0-06-027359-3) HarpC.

Teeny Tiny Monster. (J). 1996. 8.99 (0-679-87413-5) Random.

***Teeny Tiny Tales.** Helen Bramos et al. Tr. & Illus. by Ann S. Bramos. 77p. (Orig.). (J). (ps-7). 1996. pap. 8.00 (0-9635333-4-7) A S Bramos.

***Teeny Tiny Teacher.** Stephanie Calmenson. LC 97-23070. (Illus.). (J). 1998. write for info. (0-590-37123-1) Scholastic Inc.

***Teeny Tiny, the Snowflake: Learns to Obey His Parents.** Judy Berryhill. (Illus.). 38p. (Orig.). (J). (ps-6). 1996. pap. 5.95 (0-9653872-0-8) Hartford Publns.

Teeny Tiny Tots. pap. 5.98 (0-317-38605-0) Gick.

Teeny Tiny Voice. David M. Polakiewicz & Stephanie Mellen. (Illus.). 52p. (Orig.). 1992. pap. 7.95 (1-878040-08-1) Meltec.

***Teeny-Tiny Witch.** Mary Hogan. (J). 1997. 3.50 (1-57719-218-4) GT Pubng Corp.

Teeny Tiny Woman. Illus. by R. W. Alley. LC 86-485. (Step into Reading Bks.). 32p. (J). (ps-1). 1986. pap. 3.99 (0-394-88320-9); lib. bdg. 11.99 (0-394-98320-3) Random Bks Yng Read.

Teeny Tiny Woman. Paul Galdone. LC 84-4311. (Illus.). 32p. (J). (ps-3). 1984. 14.95 (0-89919-270-X, Pub. by Clarion II) HM.

Teeny Tiny Woman. Paul Galdone. LC 84-4311. (Illus.). 32p. (J). (ps-3). 1986. pap. 5.95 (0-89919-463-X, Pub. by Clarion II) HM.

Teeny Tiny Woman. Paul Galdone. (Illus.). (J). 1993. Incl. cassette. 8.95 incl. audio (0-395-52602-7, Clarion Bks) HM.

Teeny Tiny Woman. Harriet Ziefert. Date not set. pap. 3.99 (0-14-055541-2) NAL-Dutton.

Teeny Tiny Woman: An Old English Ghost Tale. Barbara Seuling. (Illus.). (J). (gr. k-3). 1978. pap. 4.99 (0-14-050266-1, Puffin) Puffin Bks.

Teeny Tiny Woman Level 2, Red. Harriet Ziefert. (Illus.). (J). (gr. k-3). 1995. pap. 3.50 (0-14-037625-9) Puffin Bks.

Teeny Tiny Yarmulka. Aydel Lebovics. (Illus.). 32p. (J). 1982. reprint ed. 10.00 (0-8266-0360-2, Merkos LInyonei Chinuch) Kehot Pubn Soc.

Teeny Weeny. Walter Swan. Ed. by Deloris Swan. (Illus.). 16p. (Orig.). (J). (ps). 1989. pap. 1.50 (0-927176-01-7) Swan Enterp.

Teeny Weeny Zucchinis. Judy Delton. (Pee Wee Scouts Ser.: No. 27). (Illus.). 96p. (Orig.). (J). (gr. 1-4). 1995. pap. 3.50 (0-440-40978-0, YB BDD) BDD Bks Young Read.

Teeny Witch & Christmas Magic. Liz Matthews. LC 90-11206. (Teeny Witch Ser.). (Illus.). 48p. (J). (gr. k-1). 1991. pap. 3.50 (0-8167-2271-4) Troll Communs.

Teeny Witch & the Great Halloween Ride. Liz Matthews. LC 90-11207. (Teeny Witch Ser.). (Illus.). 48p. (J). (gr. k-1). 1991. pap. 3.50 (0-8167-2275-7) Troll Communs.

Teeny Witch & the Perfect Valentine. Liz Matthews. LC 90-11204. (Teeny Witch Ser.). (Illus.). 48p. (J). (gr. k-1). 1996. pap. 3.95 (0-8167-2281-1) Troll Communs.

Teeny Witch & the Terrible Twins. Liz Matthews. LC 90-11139. (Illus.). 48p. (J). (gr. k-1). 1997. pap. 3.50 (0-8167-2267-6) Troll Communs.

Teeny Witch & the Tricky Easter Bunny. Liz Matthews. LC 90-11205. (Teeny Witch Ser.). (Illus.). 48p. (J). (gr. k-1). 1997. pap. 3.50 (0-8167-2273-0) Troll Communs.

Teeny Witch Goes on Vacation. Liz Matthews. LC 90-11141. (Teeny Witch Ser.). (Illus.). 48p. (J). (gr. k-1). 1997. pap. 3.50 (0-8167-2279-X) Troll Communs.

Teeny Witch Goes to School. Liz Matthews. LC 90-11208. (Teeny Witch Ser.). (Illus.). 48p. (J). (gr. k-1). 1991. pap. 3.95 (0-8167-2277-3) Troll Communs.

Teeny Witch Goes to the Library. Liz Matthews. LC 90-11140. (Illus.). 48p. (J). (gr. k-1). 1997. pap. 3.50 (0-8167-2269-2) Troll Communs.

Teepee Book, Pts. 1 & 2. John M. Carroll. 1976. 74.50 (0-914074-10-5, J M C & Co) Amereon Ltd.

***Teetering on the Brink of Climbing: The Ugliest Stuff Yet.** Tami Knight. (Illus.). 24p. (Orig.). 1996. pap. 6.95 (0-89732-221-5) Menasha Ridge.

Teeth. Simon Hillson. (Manuals in Archaeology Ser.). (Illus.). 376p. (C). 1990. pap. text ed. 42.95 (*0-521-38671-3*) Cambridge U Pr.

Teeth. Jacqueline Maloy. (Real Readers Ser.: Level Blue). (Illus.). 32p. (J). (gr. 1-4). 1989. lib. bdg. 21.40 (*0-8172-3520-5*) Raintree Steck-V.

Teeth. Jacqueline Maloy. (Real Readers Ser.: Level Blue). (Illus.). 32p. (J). (gr. 1-4). 1989. pap. 4.95 (*0-8114-6722-8*) Raintree Steck-V.

Teeth. Ed. by A. Oksche & L. Vollrath. (Handbook of Microscopic Anatomy Ser.: Vol. V/6). (Illus.). 605p. 1988. 464.00 (*0-387-19331-6*) Spr-Verlag.

Teeth: Form, Function & Evolution. Ed. by Bjorn Kurten. LC 81-10210. 456p. 1982. text ed. 92.50 (*0-231-05202-2*) Col U Pr.

Teeth & Claws. Lynn M. Stone. LC 96-8996. (Animal Weapons Ser.). 1996. write for info. (*1-57103-165-0*) Rourke Pr.

Teeth & Tusks. Theresa Greenaway. LC 94-3496. (Head to Tail Ser.). (Illus.). (J). (gr. 1 up). 1995. lib. bdg. 24.26 (*0-8114-8269-3*) Raintree Steck-V.

***Teeth Are Smiling: The Persistance of Racism in Multicultural Australia.** Ed E. Vasta & Stephen Castles. 232p. 1997. pap. text ed. 24.95 (*1-86448-055-6*, Pub. by Allen Unwin AT) Paul & Co Pubs.

Teeth of Mordor. Terry K. Amthor. Ed. by Peter C. Fenlon, Jr. (Fortresses of Middle Earth Ser.). 32p. (YA). (gr. 10-12). 1988. pap. 6.00 (*0-915795-96-5*, 8202) Iron Crown Ent Inc.

Teeth of the Tiger. Maurice LeBlanc. 490p. 1980. reprint ed. lib. bdg. 17.95 (*0-89968-204-9*, Lghtyr Pr) Buccaneer Bks.

Teeth, Tusks & Fangs. Roger Dievart. Tr. by Vicki Bogard from FRE. LC 90-50778. (Young Discovery Library). (Illus.). 38p. (J). (gr. k-5). 1991. 5.95 (*0-944589-35-9*, 359) Young Discovery Lib.

Teetoncey. Theodore Taylor. (Illus.). 160p. (J). (gr. 3-7). 1991. pap. 3.99 (*0-380-71024-2*, Camelot) Avon.

Teetoncey & Ben O'Neal. Theodore Taylor. (Illus.). 192p. (J). (gr. 5-7). 1991. pap. 3.99 (*0-380-71025-0*, Camelot) Avon.

Teetotalism, Eighteen Forty-Two (Temperence) 25p. 1984. reprint ed. pap. text ed. 12.50 (*0-87556-380-5*) Saifer.

Tefilin: A Chassidic Discourse. Nathan. Ed. & Tr. by Avraham Greenbaum from HEB. (Illus.). 96p. 1989. pap. text ed. 7.00 (*0-930213-38-6*) Breslov Res Inst.

***Tefillin: The Inside Story.** Moshe Emanuel. 461p. 1995. 22.95 (*1-56871-090-9*) Targum Pr.

Tegafur-Ftorafur. Ed. by N. I. Perevodchikova et al. (Beitraege zur Onkologie, Contributions to Oncology Ser.: Vol. 14). (Illus.). viii, 146p. 1983. pap. 37.00 (*3-8055-3653-4*) S Karger.

Teged. Aron Kibedi Varga. LC 73-88423. (HUN.). 1973. pap. 4.00 (*0-911050-42-6*) Occidental.

Tegne. Richard La Plante. 1995. write for info. (*0-615-00544-6*) Tor Bks.

Tegne: Warlord of Zendow. Richard La Plante. LC 95-34765. 352p. 1995. 23.95 (*0-312-85977-5*) Tor Bks.

Tegne Vol. 1: Soul Warrior. Richard La Plante. 1996. mass mkt. 5.99 (*0-8125-5270-9*) Tor Bks.

Tegotomono: Music for Japanese Koto. Bonnie C. Wade. LC 75-5265. (Contributions in Intercultural & Comparative Studies: No. 2). 379p. 1976. text ed. 79.50 (*0-8371-8908-X*, WAT/, Greenwood Pr) Greenwood.

10 Habits for Effective Ministry: A Guide for Life-Giving Pastors. Lowell O. Erdahl. LC 96-20562. 1996. pap. 11.99 (*0-8066-2990-8*, Augsburg) Augsburg Fortress.

Tehachapi: Railroading on a Desert Mountain. Steve Schmollinger. (Illus.). 160p. 45.00 (*1-55046-063-3*, Pub. by Boston Mills Pr CN) Genl Dist Srvs.

Tehanu. Ursula K. Le Guin. 288p. 1991. mass mkt. 6.50 (*0-553-28873-3*, Spectra) Bantam.

Tehanu: The Last Book of Earthsea. Ursula K. Le Guin. LC 89-32780. 240p. (J). (ps up). 1990. lib. bdg. 16.95 (*0-689-31595-3*, Atheneum Bks Young) S&S Childrens.

Teheran Operation: The Rescue of Jewish Children from the Nazis. Devora Omer. Tr. by Riva Rubin from HEB. 426p. 29.95 (*0-910250-18-9*); pap. 15.95 (*0-910250-19-7*, 01-1300-18) Bnai Brith Intl.

Tehidy & the Bassets. Michael Tangye. (C). 1989. 35.00 (*0-907566-97-9*, Pub. by Dyllansow Truran UK) St Mut.

Tehillim, 5 vols. Shmuel Yerushalmi. Tr. by Zvi Faier from HEB. (Book of Tehilim Ser.). 1991. 90.00 (*0-940118-38-6*) Moznaim.

Tehillim: Psalms, 2 vols. A. C. Feuer. 1985. 64.99 (*0-89906-064-1*) Mesorah Pubns.

Tehillim Treasury. Avrohm C. Fever. 1993. 17.99 (*0-89906-434-5*) Mesorah Pubns.

Tehillim Treasury. Avrohom C. Fever. 1993. 20.99 (*0-89906-433-7*) Mesorah Pubns.

***Tehiyyat Ha-Metim: The Resurrection of the Dead in the Palestinian Targums of the Pentateuch & Parallel Traditions in Classical Rabbinic Literature.** Harry Sysling. (Texte und Studien zum Antiken Judentum: No. 57). 329p. 1996. 172.50 (*3-16-146583-0*, Pub. by J C B Mohr GW) Coronet Bks.

Tehran-Yalta-Potsdam: The Soviet Protocols. Ed. by Robert Beitzell. (Russian Ser.: Vol. 17). 35.00 (*0-87569-013-0*) Academic Intl.

***Tehuantepec Jungle: A Memoir.** Walter W. Dalquest. 175p. 1996. 19.95 (*0-915323-10-9*) Midwestern St U Pr.

Teichm Uller Theory in Riemannian Geometry. Anthony J. Tromba. LC 92-12778. (Lectures in Mathemtics ETH Zurich Ser.). 224p. 1992. 34.50 (*0-8176-2735-9*) Birkhauser.

Teifi: Scenery & Antiquities of a Welsh River. Richard J. Colyer. 94p. (C). 1987. text ed. 30.00 (*0-86383-435-3*, Pub. by Gomer Pr UK) St Mut.

***Teiidae's.** large type ed. Erik Stoops. Ed. by Graphic Arts & Production Staff. (Young Explorer Series I: Vol. 6). (Illus.). 32p. (J). (gr. 3-7). 1997. lib. bdg. 12.95 (*1-890475-05-X*) Faulkners Pub.

Teilhard & Mendel: Contrasts & Parallels. Edward O. Dodson. (Teilhard Studies: No. 12). 1984. pap. 3.50 (*0-89012-039-0*) Am Teilhard.

Teilhard & Prigogine. James F. Salmon. (Teilhard Studies: No. 16). 1986. 3.50 (*0-89012-045-5*) Am Teilhard.

Teilhard de Chardin: A Short Biography. John Grim & Mary E. Grim. (Teilhard Studies: No. 11). 1984. pap. 3.50 (*0-89012-038-2*) Am Teilhard.

Teilhard de Chardin: An Analysis & Assessment. David G. Jones. LC 70-127933. 72p. reprint ed. pap. 25.00 (*0-317-08998-6*, 2012937) Bks Demand.

Teilhard de Chardin: In Quest of the Perfection of Man. Ed. by Joseph L. Alioto et al. LC 72-9596. 290p. 1973. 36.50 (*0-8386-1258-X*) Fairleigh Dickinson.

***Teilhard de Chardin & the Piltdown Hoax.** Winifred McCulloch. (Teilhard Studies: No. 33). 1996. write for info. (*0-89012-075-7*) Am Teilhard.

Teilhard de Chardin's Biological Ideas. Alexander Wolsky. (Teilhard Studies: No. 4). 1981. 3.50 (*0-89012-027-7*) Am Teilhard.

Teilhard de Chardin's Vision of the Future. Francis Neilson. 1979. lib. bdg. 250.00 (*0-685-96640-2*) Revisionist Pr.

Teilhard, Evil & Providence. Thomas M. King. (Teilhard Studies: No. 21). 1989. 3.50 (*0-89012-058-7*) Am Teilhard.

Teilhard in the Ecological Age. Thomas Berry. (Teilhard Studies: No. 7). 1982. 3.50 (*0-89012-032-3*) Am Teilhard.

Teilhard, Scripture, & Revelation: Teilhard de Chardin's Reinterpretation of Pauline Themes. Richard W. Kropf. LC 73-20907. 352p. 1980. 40.00 (*0-8386-1481-7*) Fairleigh Dickinson.

Teilhard, Taoism, & Western Thought. Allerd Stikker. (Teilhard Studies: No. 15). 1986. 3.50 (*0-89012-044-7*) Am Teilhard.

Teilhardian Synthesis, Lamarckism, & Orthogenesis. Edward O. Dodson. (Teilhard Studies: No. 29). 1993. pap. 3.50 (*0-89012-072-2*) Am Teilhard.

Teilhardism & the New Religion: A Thorough Analysis of the Teachings of Pierre Teilhard de Chardin. Wolfgang Smith. LC 87-50749. 248p. (Orig.). 1991. pap. 13.00 (*0-89555-315-5*) TAN Bks Pubs.

Teilhards Unity of Knowledge. Thomas M. King. (Teilhard Studies: No. 9). 1983. pap. 3.50 (*0-89012-035-8*) Am Teilhard.

Teilhard's Vision of the Past: The Making of a Method. Robert J. O'Connell. LC 82-71279. x, 205p. 1982. 30.00 (*0-8232-1090-1*) Fordham.

Teilhard's Vision of the Past: The Making of a Method. Robert J. O'Connell. LC 82-71279. x, 205p. 1982. pap. 15.00 (*0-8232-1091-X*) Fordham.

Teilnahme und Spiegelung: Festschrift fuer Horst Ruediger. Ed. by Erwin Koppen & Beda Allemann. viii, 680p. (GER.). (C). 1975. 311.55 (*3-11-004013-1*) De Gruyter.

Teitotekniikan Artikkelisanakirja. S. Peltonen. 276p. (FIN.). 1985. 195.00 (*0-8288-1368-X*, M 356) Fr & Eur.

***Tejano Community, 1836-1900.** Arnoldo De Leon. LC 97-16564. (Illus.). 304p. 1997. pap. 14.95 (*0-87074-419-4*) SMU Press.

Tejano Journey, 1770-1850. Ed. by Gerald E. Poyo. (Illus.). 208p. 1996. 24.95 (*0-292-76570-3*) U of Tex Pr.

Tejano Origins in Eighteenth-Century San Antonio. Ed. by Gerald E. Poyo & Gilberto M. Hinojosa. (Illus.). 222p. (Orig.). 1991. 19.95 (*0-292-71138-7*) U of Tex Pr.

Tejano Origins in Eighteenth-Century San Antonio. Gerald E. Poyo. 1995. pap. 13.95 (*0-292-76566-5*) U of Tex Pr.

Tejano Religion & Ethnicity: San Antonio, 1821-1860. Timothy M. Matovina. 176p. 1995. 24.95 (*0-292-75170-2*) U of Tex Pr.

Tejanos & Texas under the Mexican Flag, 1821-1836. Andres Tijerina. LC 93-40484. (Centennial Series of the Association of Former Students: Vol. 54). (Illus.). 184p. 1994. pap. 15.95 (*0-89096-606-0*) Tex A&M Univ Pr.

Tejanos & the Numbers Game: A Socio-Historical Interpretation from the Federal Censuses, 1850-1900. Arnoldo De Leon & Kenneth L. Stewart. LC 88-20773. 130p. 1989. 24.95 (*0-8263-1118-0*) U of NM Pr.

Tek Kill. William Shatner. 304p. 1996. 22.95 (*0-399-14202-9*, Putnam) Putnam Pub Group.

***Tek Kill.** William Shatner. 1997. mass mkt. write for info. (*0-441-00489-X*) Ace Bks.

TEK Money. William Shatner. LC 95-8686. 288p. 1995. 21.95 (*0-399-14109-X*, Ace-Putnam) Putnam Pub Group.

***Tek Money.** William Shatner. 1996. mass mkt. 5.99 (*0-441-00390-7*) Ace Bks.

***Tek Net.** William Shatner. LC 97-5398. 1997. write for info. (*0-399-14339-4*) Putnam Pub Group.

Tek Power. William Shatner. 304p. (Orig.). 1995. mass mkt. 5.99 (*0-441-00289-7*) Ace Bks.

Tek Secret. William Shatner. 304p. (Orig.). 1994. mass mkt. 5.99 (*0-441-00119-X*) Ace Bks.

Tek Vengeance. William Shatner. 304p. 1993. mass mkt. 5.99 (*0-441-80012-2*) Ace Bks.

***Tekhelet: The Renaissance of a Mitzvah.** Alfred S. Cohen. LC 96-41810. 1996. write for info. (*0-88125-577-7*) Yeshiva Univ Pr.

Tekiah: Poems by Richard Chess. Richard Chess. LC 94-9199. (Contemporary Poetry Ser.). 88p. 1994. pap. 14.95 (*0-8203-1678-4*) U of Ga Pr.

Tekken Official Strategy Guide. BradyGAMES Staff. (Illus.). 153p. (Orig.). 1995. 9.99 (*1-56686-441-0*) Brady Pub.

***Tekken 1 & 2 Survival Guide.** Zach Meston. (Gaming Mastery Ser.). (Illus.). 160p. (Orig.). 1996. pap. 12.95 (*1-884364-47-0*) Sandwich Islands.

Tekken 2. Brady Computer Books Staff. 96p. 1996. 9.99 (*1-56686-539-5*) Brady Pub.

***Tekken 2 Unauthorized.** PCS Staff. 128p. 1996. pap. 12.99 (*0-7615-0584-9*) Prima Pub.

***Tekken 3.** Prima Publishing Staff. 1997. pap. 12.99 (*0-7615-1185-7*) Prima Pub.

Tekko & the White Man. Alie Vogelaar-Van Amersvoort. Tr. by Alice Ekema from DUT. (Tekko Ser.: No. 1). (Illus.). 106p. (Orig.). 1993. pap. 6.90 (*0-921100-47-7*) Inhtce Pubns.

Tekko the Fugitive. Alie Vogelaar-Van Amersfoort. Tr. by Jean Van Brugge from DUT. LC 95-32014. (Tekko Ser.: No. 2). (Illus.). 93p. (Orig.). 1995. pap. 6.90 (*0-921100-74-4*) Inhtce Pubns.

Tekla & the Lion. Elaine M. Stone. LC 90-71366. (Illus.). 44p. (J). (gr. 3-6). 1991. pap. 7.95 (*1-55523-388-0*) Winston-Derek.

Teklab. William Shatner. 320p. 1993. mass mkt. 5.99 (*0-441-80011-4*) Ace Bks.

TekLords. William Shatner. 1992. mass mkt. 5.99 (*0-441-80010-6*) Ace Bks.

TekLords. William Shatner. 1991. 15.95 (*0-671-73951-4*) S&S Audio.

Teknologi Kampungan: A Compendium of Indonesian Indigenous Technologies. Craig Thorburn. Ed. by Ken Darrow & Bill Stanley. (Illus.). 154p. 1982. pap. 5.00 (*0-917704-16-9*) Volunteers Asia Pr.

Tekonwatonti: Molly Brant, Poems of War, 1735-1795. Maurice Kenny. 1992. pap. 12.00 (*1-877727-20-2*) White Pine.

Tektite. Forrest B. Johnson. Ed. by Chiaki Takeuchi. 280p. 1989. 19.95 (*1-882032-03-9*) Thousand Autumns Pr.

Tekwar, 3 vols. William Shatner. 1993. pap. 16.50 (*0-441-00003-7*) Ace Bks.

Tekwar. deluxe ed. William Shatner. 1989. boxed 75.00 (*0-932096-50-6*) Phantasia Pr.

Tel Anafa I, i (Text) & ii (Plates) Final Report on Ten Years of Excavation at a Hellenistic & Roman Settlement in Northern Israel. Sharon C. Herbert. (JRA Supplementary Ser.: No. 10, Pt. 1). (Illus.). 561p. 1994. 129.00 (*1-887829-10-5*) Jour Roman Arch.

***Tel Anafa II Pt. I: The Hellenistic & Roman Pottery: The Plain Wares - The Fine Wares.** Andrea Berlin & Kathleen W. Slane. Ed. by Sharon C. Herbert. (JRA Supplementary Ser.: Vol. 10, Pt. 2). (Illus.). 592p. 1997. 89.50 (*1-887829-98-9*) Jour Roman Arch.

***Tel Aviv Modern Architecture 1930-1939.** Photos by Irmel Kamp-Bandau. (Illus.). 252p. 1996. 65.00 (*3-8030-2820-5*, 620642, Pub. by Ernst Wasmuth GW) Dist Art Pubs.

Tel Aviv Review, No. 1. Ed. by Gabriel Moked. 360p. 1988. pap. 21.95 (*0-8223-0873-8*) Duke.

Tel Aviv Review Three. Ed. by Gabriel Moked. 450p. 1991. pap. 21.95 (*0-8223-1120-8*) Duke.

Tel Aviv Review Two. Ed. by Gabriel Moked. 450p. (Orig.). (C). 1989. pap. 21.95 (*0-685-74190-7*) Duke.

Tel-Ed Conference Proceedings, 1993: Global Connections. Ed. by David Foster & Deborah V. Jolly. (Illus.). 330p. 1993. pap. text ed. 20.00 (*0-685-72761-0*) Intl Society Tech Educ.

Tel el Kebir 1882. Don Featherstone. (Campaign Ser.). (Illus.). 96p. 1993. pap. 14.95 (*1-85532-333-8*, 9526, Pub. by Osprey UK) Stackpole.

Tel Quel, 2 vols., 1. Paul Valery. (Idees Ser.). (FRE.). pap. 8.95 (*2-07-035240-4*) Schoenhof.

Tel Quel, 2 vols., 2. Paul Valery. (Idees Ser.). (FRE.). pap. 8.95 (*2-07-035241-2*) Schoenhof.

Tel Quel, 2 vols., Set. Paul Valery. (Idees Ser.). (FRE.). pap. write for info. (*0-685-36627-8*) Schoenhof.

Tel quel see Oeuvres

***Tel Quel Reader.** Patrick Ffrench & Roland-Fran C. Lack. LC 97-21264. 1998. write for info. (*0-415-15713-7*) Routledge.

***Tel Quel Reader.** Patrick Ffrench & Roland-Fran Lack. LC 97-21264. 1998. pap. write for info. (*0-415-15714-5*) Routledge.

Tel Quel, Vol. 1: Choses Vues, Moralites, Litterature. Paul Valery. (FRE.). 1971. pap. 10.95 (*0-7859-2839-1*) Fr & Eur.

Tel Quel, Vol. 2: Rhumbs, Autre Rhumbs, Analecta. Paul Valery. (FRE.). 1971. pap. 10.95 (*0-7859-2840-5*) Fr & Eur.

Tel Qu'en Lui-Meme. Georges Duhamel. 1973. 8.95 (*0-686-55197-4*) Fr & Eur.

Tel Qu'en Lui-Meme. Georges Duhamel. (Vie et Aventures De Salavin Ser.: Vol. II). (FRE.). 1973. pap. 10.95 (*0-7859-1730-6*, 2070363198) Fr & Eur.

Tela Charlottae. E. B. White. Tr. by Bernice Fox. LC 90-55691. (Illus.). 256p. (LAT.). (J). (gr. 2 up). 1991. 18.95 (*0-06-026401-2*) HarpC Child Bks.

Tela de Arana: Edicion Critica de Dr. Argimiro Ruano, PhD. Eugenio M. Hostos. LC 92-81238. 320p. 1992. pap. 14.95 (*1-881375-00-5*) Libreria Univ.

Telah Speaks! Partana Vegan. 47p. 1961. reprint ed. spiral bd. 3.50 (*0-7873-1299-1*) Hlth Research.

Telaranas de Carlota - Charlotte's Web. E. B. White. 1996. pap. text ed. 9.50 (*84-279-3388-6*) Lectorum Pubns.

Telco-Video: Competitive Issues & Broadcast Industry Directions. Marcia DeSonne. 29p. 1989. 30.00 (*0-89324-078-8*) Natl Assn Broadcasters.

***Telcom Policy & Infrastructure.** (China Telecom-2000 Ser.: Vol. 1). 1995. 2,995.00 (*0-614-18323-5*, IGIC-01) Info Gatekeepers.

Telcos in Interactive Services. Karen Burka & Ben De la Cruz. (Illus.). 225p. 1996. 1,095.00 (*0-88709-114-8*) Simba Info Inc.

***Tele: A History of the Belfast Telegraph.** Malcolm Brodie. 300p. 9500. pap. 33.00 (*0-85640-547-7*, Pub. by Blackstaff Pr IE) Dufour.

Tele-Advising: Therapeutic Discourse in American Television. Mimi White. LC 92-53623. xii, 218p. (C). 1992. text ed. 32.50 (*0-8078-2055-5*); pap. text ed. 11.95 (*0-8078-4390-3*) U of NC Pr.

Tele-Learning: From Television to the World Wide Web & Beyond. Betty Collis. 400p. 1996. pap. 39.95 (*1-85032-157-4*) ITCP.

Tele-ology: Studies in Television. John Hartley. LC 91-17312. 240p. (C). 1992. pap. 16.95 (*0-415-06818-5*, A6717) Routledge.

Tele Operating System: CD: Console Display. Ken Berry. 1989. pap. 40.00 (*0-317-93703-0*) Crosby Assocs.

Tele Operating System: FS: File System. Ken Berry. 1989. pap. 40.00 (*0-317-93704-9*) Crosby Assocs.

Tele Operating System: SK: System Kernel. Ken Berry. (Orig.). 1989. pap. 50.00 (*0-317-93705-7*) Crosby Assocs.

Tele Operating System: XS: Index System. Ken Berry. 1989. pap. 50.00 (*0-317-93706-5*) Crosby Assocs.

***Tele-Stress: Relief for Call Center Stress Syndrome.** Steve Coscia. 96p. 1996. 12.95 (*0-936648-90-2*, P50005) Flatiron Pubng.

Telebanking, Teleshopping & the Law. Ed. by Y. Poullet & G. P. Vandenberghe. (Computer - Law Ser.: Vol. 1). 402p. 1988. pap. 104.00 (*90-6544-349-5*) Kluwer Law Tax Pubs.

Telecabulary, No. 2. rev. ed. Tom Smith. LC 73-85629. (Specialized Ser.). (Illus.). 104p. 1987. pap. text ed. 12.95 (*1-56016-018-7*) ABC TeleTraining.

Telechelic Polymers: Synthesis & Applications. Ed. by Eric J. Goethals. 368p. 1988. 311.00 (*0-8493-6764-6*, QD382) CRC Pr.

Telecity: Information Technology & Its Impact on City Form. Tarik A. Fathy. LC 91-443. 176p. 1991. text ed. 45.00 (*0-275-93814-X*, C3814, Praeger Pubs) Greenwood.

Teleclass Teaching: A Resource Guide. 2nd ed. Thomas E. Cyrs & Frank A. Smith. (Illus.). 368p. (C). 1990. pap. text ed. 38.00 (*0-9628477-0-4*) NM State U CED.

Telecollaboration in Foreign Language Learning: Proceedings of the Hawaii Symposium. Ed. by Mark Warschauer. (Technical Report Ser.: No. 12). 1996. pap. text ed. 20.00 (*0-8248-1867-9*) Sec Lang Tching.

Telecom Basics. Jack L. Dempsey. LC 87-83662. 104p. 1988. 19.95 (*0-917845-07-2*) Intertec IL.

***Telecom Business Opportunities: The Entrepreneur's Guide to Making Money in the Telecommunications Revolution.** Steven Rosenbush. 336p. (Orig.). 1997. pap. 24.95 (*1-890154-04-0*) Aegis Pub Grp.

***Telecom Deregulation & Yellow Pages, 1996.** Natalie Schwartz & Karen Blakely. (Illus.). 112p. 1996. 1,995.00 (*0-88709-098-2*) Simba Info Inc.

Telecom Distribution Channel Analysis: Complex Issues, Trends & Channel Definitions Clarified. Market Intelligence Staff. 377p. 1992. 995.00 (*1-56753-415-5*) Frost & Sullivan.

***Telecom Glossary: Understanding Telecommunications Technology.** Marc Robins. 96p. (Orig.). 1997. pap. 9.95 (*1-890154-02-4*) Aegis Pub Grp.

Telecom Industry Advertising & Marketing Forecast, 1997. Dan Hanover & Peter Breen. (Illus.). 270p. 1996. 1,695.00 (*0-88709-094-X*) Simba Info Inc.

***Telecom Industry Advertising & Marketing Forecast, 1997.** Dan Hanover & Peter Breen. (Illus.). 270p. 1996. write for info. (*0-88709-136-9*) Simba Info Inc.

***Telecom Made Easy: Money-Saving, Profit-Building Solutions for Home Businesses, Telecommuters & Small Organizations.** 3rd ed. June Langhoff. 384p. (Orig.). 1997. pap. 19.95 (*0-9632790-7-6*) Aegis Pub Grp.

***Telecom Marketplace: A Guide to Over 1,000 Information Sources.** William H. Wilson. 1997. write for info. (*0-86587-583-9*) Gov Insts.

***Telecom Policy & Infrastructure, 1995, Vol. 1.** 2,995.00 (*0-614-26461-8*) Info Gatekeepers.

***Telecom Power-2000: Reports, Newsletters, & Consulting Services.** 1994. 12,000.00 (*0-614-18337-5*, IGIC-002) Info Gatekeepers.

Telecom Regatta: EC Ninety-Two & Beyond. Ed. by Craig A. Johnson et al. (International Communications Report Ser.). 331p. (Orig.). 1993. pap. text ed. 10.00 (*0-89206-226-6*) CSI Studies.

Telecom Sourcebook, 1993. Market Intelligence Staff. 1993. 545.00 (*1-56753-594-1*) Frost & Sullivan.

Telecom Sourcebook 1996 Edition. Frost & Sullivan Staff. 500p. 1996. write for info. (*0-7889-0480-9*, 2836) Frost & Sullivan.

Telecom 2000: Forecasts of U. S. Telecommunications Demand. IGIC, Inc. Staff. 200p. (Orig.). 1993. pap. 1,995.00 (*0-918435-79-X*, IGIC-26) Info Gatekeepers.

Telecommuncations Directory 1995-96: An International Guide to Organizations, Systems & Services Concerned with the Interactive Electronic Transmission of Voice, Image & Data. 7th ed. John Krol. (Electronic Information Ser.). 1152p. 1994. 340.00 (*0-8103-9125-2*) Gale.

Telecommunicating Typesetters. Michael L. Kleper. (Illus.). 1982. pap. 10.00 (*0-930904-02-8*) Graphic Dimensions.

Telecommunication: New Signposts to Old Roads. Ed. by Paul Slaa & Franca Klaver. LC 92-53261. (European Communication Policy Research Ser.). 187p. (gr. 12). 1992. pap. 75.00 (*90-5199-089-8*, Pub. by IOS Pr NE) IOS Press.

Telecommunication - Limits to Deregulation. Ed. by M. Christoffersen & A. Henten. LC 93-77462. (European Communication Policy Research Ser.). 200p. (gr. 12). 1993. pap. 78.00 (*90-5199-128-2*, Pub. by IOS Pr NE) IOS Press.

An Asterisk (*) at the beginning of an entry indicates that the title is appearing in BIP for the first time.

Telecommunication Access Networks: Technology & Service Trends: Proceedings of the IX International Symposium on Subscriber Loops & Services (ISSLS 91), Amsterdam, the Netherlands, 22-26 April 1991. Ed. by W. Lemstra. 440p. 1991. 159.50 (*0-444-89050-5*, North Holland) Elsevier.

Telecommunication & Control - TELECON '84: Proceedings, IASTED Symposium, Halkidiki, Greece, August 27-30, 1984. Ed. by G. V. Bafas. 498p. 1984. 120.00 (*0-88986-072-6*, 075) Acta Pr.

Telecommunication & Control - TELECON '85: Proceedings, IASTED Symposium, Rio de Janeiro, Brazil, December 10-13, 1985. Ed. by J. A. Felippe de Souza. 361p. 1985. 70.00 (*0-88986-092-0*, 095) Acta Pr.

Telecommunication Demand Modelling: An Integrated View. A. De Fontenay et al. (Contributions to Economic Analysis Ser.: Vol. 187). 480p. 1990. 176.75 (*0-444-88539-0*) Elsevier.

Telecommunication Economics & International Regulatory Policy: An Annotated Bibliography. Compiled by Marcellus S. Snow & Meheroo Jusawalla. LC 86-12130. (Bibliographies & Indexes in Economics & Economic History Ser.: No. 4). 230p. 1986. text ed. 69.50 (*0-313-25370-6*, SWT/) Greenwood.

***Telecommunication for Business in Africa.** 250p. Date not set. pap. 73.00 (*90-5199-348-X*) IOS Press.

Telecommunication for the Executive. Ronald R. Thomas. 180p. 1984. 22.50 (*0-89433-233-3*) Petrocelli.

Telecommunication in Transition. M. Carpentier et al. 176p. 1992. pap. text ed. 54.95 (*0-471-93190-X*) Wiley.

Telecommunication Networks. Fraidoon Mazda. (Telecommunication Ser.). (Illus.). 314p. 1996. pap. 28.95 (*0-240-51454-8*, Focal) Buttrwrth-Heinemann.

Telecommunication Networks. Ed. by John E. Flood. LC 76-358907. (IEE Telecommunications Ser.: Vol. 1). (Illus.). 449p. reprint ed. pap. 128.00 (*0-685-23331-6*, 2032257) Bks Demand.

Telecommunication Networks: Protocols & Design. John D. Spragins et al. (Electrical Engineering Ser.). (Illus.). 768p. (C). 1991. text ed. 70.95 (*0-201-09290-5*) Addison-Wesley.

Telecommunication Networks: Protocols, Modeling & Analysis. Mischa Schwartz. (Illus.). 575p. (C). 1987. text ed. 73.25 (*0-201-16423-X*) Addison-Wesley.

Telecommunication Networks & Services. J. Van Duuren et al. LC 92-7233. (C). 1992. pap. text ed. 37.25 (*0-201-56542-0*) Addison-Wesley.

Telecommunication Policy for the Information Age: From Monopoly to Competition. Gerald W. Brock. LC 94-3911. (Illus.). 336p. 1994. text ed. 45.00 (*0-674-87277-0*, BROTEP) HUP.

Telecommunication Policy for the 90s. 2nd ed. Walter G. Bolter. 464p. (C). (gr. 13). 1998. text ed. 82.95 (*1-56324-918-9*) M E Sharpe.

Telecommunication System Engineering. 3rd ed. Roger L. Freeman. LC 96-10943. (Telecommunications & Signal Processing Ser.). 800p. 1996. text ed. 94.95 (*0-471-13302-7*) Wiley.

Telecommunication Systems Engineering. Marvin K. Simon & William C. Lindsey. (Illus.). 592p. reprint ed. pap. 14.95 (*0-486-66838-X*) Dover.

Telecommunication Transmission Handbook. 3rd ed. Roger L. Freeman. LC 91-14668. (Series in Telecommunications). 1040p. 1991. text ed. 112.00 (*0-471-51816-6*) Wiley.

***Telecommunication Transmission Handbook.** 4th ed. Roger L. Freeman. LC 97-20305. 1120p. 1998. text ed. 125.00 (*0-471-24018-4*) Wiley.

Telecommunication Transmission Principles. Fraidoon Mazda. (Telecommunication Ser.). (Illus.). 342p. 1996. pap. 28.95 (*0-240-51452-1*, Focal) Buttrwrth-Heinemann.

Telecommunication Transmission Systems: Microwave, Fiber Optic, Mobile Cellular Radio, Data, & Digital Multiplexing. Robert G. Winch. LC 92-26723. 560p. 1993. text ed. 70.00i (*0-07-070964-5*) McGraw.

Telecommunication Wiring. Clyde N. Herrick & C. Lee McKim. 272p. 1991. text ed. 51.00 (*0-13-151531-4*) P-H.

***Telecommunication Wiring.** 2nd ed. Herrick. 1997. text ed. 35.00 (*0-13-632845-8*) P-H.

***Telecommunications.** Central Office of Info. (Aspects of Britain Ser.). (Illus.). 90p. 1994. pap. 12.00 (*0-11-701784-1*, Pub. by Stationery Ofc UK) Seven Hills Bk.

***Telecommunications.** Chris Oxlade. LC 96-46005. (20th Century Inventions Ser.). (J). 1997. 24.26 (*0-8172-4813-7*) Raintree Steck-V.

Telecommunications. Arnold Rosen. 304p. (C). 1987. text ed. 39.00 (*0-15-589815-9*) Dryden Pr.

Telecommunications. Schrum & Berenfeld. LC 96-37335. 256p. 1997. pap. 34.00 (*0-205-19801-5*) Allyn.

Telecommunications. Wayne Tomasi. 1988. lab manual ed., pap. text ed. 20.00 (*0-13-902636-3*) P-H.

Telecommunications. 2nd ed. Warren Hioki. 1994. lab manual ed., pap. text ed. 39.00 (*0-13-133604-5*) P-H.

Telecommunications. 2nd ed. Warren Hioki. LC 94-26757. 501p. (C). 1995. text ed. 82.00 (*0-13-123878-7*) P-H.

***Telecommunications.** 3rd ed. Hioki. LC 97-18006. 1998. text ed. 78.00 (*0-13-632043-0*) P-H.

Telecommunications, 33 vols, Set. (Illus.). 14902p. 1974. 1,109.50 (*0-405-06030-0*) Ayer.

Telecommunications: A Bridge to the 21st Century: Program on International Economics & Politics, Honolulu, HI, USA. Ed. by Meheroo Jussawalla. 380p. 1995. 136.50 (*0-444-82325-5*) Elsevier.

Telecommunications: A Handbook for Educators. Reza Azarmsa. LC 92-28454. (Source Books on Education: Vol. 30). 320p. 1993. text ed. 52.00 (*0-8153-0743-8*, SS849) Garland.

Telecommunications: A Short Course. Dennis P. Curtin. 1992. pap. text ed. 14.00 (*0-13-902735-1*, 180301) P-H.

Telecommunications: A Text-Lab Manual. 2nd ed. Morris Tischler. 240p. 1989. teacher ed. (*0-07-064795-X*); pap. write for info. (*0-07-064794-1*) McGraw.

Telecommunications: An Interdisciplinary Survey. Ed. by Leonard Lewin. LC 78-26665. (Illus.). 722p. reprint ed. pap. 180.00 (*0-8357-7923-8*, 2036349) Bks Demand.

Telecommunications: An Interdisciplinary Text. Ed. by Leonard Lewin. LC 84-70225. (Illus.). 709p. reprint ed. pap. 180.00 (*0-7837-1188-3*, 2041718) Bks Demand.

Telecommunications: An Introduction to Electronic Media. 4th ed. Lynne S. Gross. 520p. (C). 1991. student ed., per. write for info. (*0-697-14448-8*); per. write for info. (*0-697-08647-X*) Brown & Benchmark.

Telecommunications: An Introduction to Electronic Media. 5th ed. Lynne S. Gross. 480p. (C). 1994. per. write for info. (*0-697-20138-4*) Brown & Benchmark.

Telecommunications: An Introduction to Electronic Media. 6th ed. Lynne S. Gross. 520p. (C). 1996. per. write for info. (*0-697-28883-8*) Brown & Benchmark.

***Telecommunications: An Introduction to Electronic Media.** 7th ed. Gross. 1998. pap. text ed. 31.00 (*0-697-35506-3*) McGraw.

***Telecommunications: Competitive Impact of Restructuring the International Satellige Organizations.** (Illus.). 40p. (Orig.). (C). 1996. pap. 25.00 (*0-7881-3614-3*) DIANE Pub.

Telecommunications: Concpets & Applications. C. Thomas Olivo & Cubbler. (DF - Computer Applications Ser.). 1992. pap. 20.95 (*0-538-60360-7*) S-W Pub.

***Telecommunications: Costs Reported by Federal Organizations for Fiscal Year 1995.** (Illus.). 70p. (Orig.). (C). 1996. pap. 25.00 (*0-7881-3466-3*) DIANE Pub.

***Telecommunications: Detecting & Deterring Fraud.** David W. McNamee. Ed. by Lee A. Campbell. 1993. pap. 200.00 (*0-89413-300-4*, A6061) Inst Inter Aud.

Telecommunications: Economics & Regulations. James M. Herring & Gerald C. Gross. LC 74-4686. (Telecommunications Ser.). 558p. 1974. reprint ed. 38.95 (*0-405-06050-5*) Ayer.

Telecommunications: Exploring Competition. Howard Williams & Mark Borman. LC 94-78816. (European Communication Policy Research Ser.). 146p. (gr. 12). 1994. 68.00 (*90-5199-192-4*) IOS Press.

Telecommunications: Fact Book & Illustrated Dictionary. Ahmed S. Kahn. 200p. 1992. pap. 35.95 (*0-8273-4615-8*) Delmar.

Telecommunications: Financial Information on Sixteen Telephone & Cable Companies. (Illus.). 51p. (Orig.). (C). 1994. pap. text ed. 25.00 (*0-7881-1327-5*) DIANE Pub.

***Telecommunications: Financial Information on 16 Telephone & Cable Companies.** (Illus.). 36p. 1994. pap. text ed. 45.00 (*1-57979-093-3*) BPI Info Servs.

Telecommunications: From Telegraphs to Modems. Christopher Lampton. LC 90-48230. (Venture Bks.). (Illus.). 112p. (J). (gr. 7-9). 1991. lib. bdg. 22.00 (*0-531-12527-0*) Watts.

***Telecommunications: FTS 2000 Cost Comparison.** (Illus.). 61p. (Orig.). (C). 1996. pap. 30.00 (*0-7881-3396-9*) DIANE Pub.

***Telecommunications: Glossary of Telecommunications Terms.** 400p. 1997. pap. text ed. 69.00 (*0-86587-580-4*) Gov Insts.

Telecommunications: Index of New Information with Authors, Subjects & References. Hovis J. Larsen. 1994. 47.50 (*1-55914-994-9*); pap. 44.50 (*1-55914-995-7*) ABBE Pubs Assn.

***Telecommunications: Index of New Information with Authors, Subjects & References.** Hovis J. Larsen. 183p. 1997. 49.50 (*0-7883-1614-1*) ABBE Pubs Assn.

***Telecommunications: Index of New Information with Authors, Subjects & References.** Hovis J. Larsen. 183p. 1997. pap. 39.50 (*0-7883-1615-X*) ABBE Pubs Assn.

Telecommunications: Initiatives Taken by Three States to Promote Increased Access & Investment. (Illus.). 50p. (Orig.). (C). 1996. pap. text ed. 25.00 (*0-7881-2866-3*) DIANE Pub.

Telecommunications: Lab Pack. Irene Danziger & Paula Weinberger. Ed. by Bonnie Schroeder & Catherine Doheny. (Illus.). 99.95 (*1-56177-097-3*, L394-4); disk 15.95 (*1-56177-096-5*, D394-4) CES Compu-Tech.

Telecommunications: Lab Pack. Irene Danziger & Paula Weinberger. Ed. by Catherine Doheny & Bonnie Schroeder. (Illus.). student ed., teacher ed. 99.95 incl. disk (*1-56177-049-3*, L194-4); Apple II 15.95 (*1-56177-048-5*, D194-4) CES Compu-Tech.

***Telecommunications: New Dynamics & Driving Forces.** Ed. by A. Bianchi & G. Richeri. LC 96-7508. (European Communication Policy Research Ser.). 135p. (YA). (gr. 12 up). 1996. pap. 72.00 (*90-5199-256-4*, 256-4) IOS Press.

Telecommunications: Planning for the Future. (Special Report Ser.). 160p. 1996. pap. 45.00 (*0-87326-116-X*) Intl City-Cnty Mgt.

Telecommunications: Present Status & Future Trends. Robert F. Linfield. LC 94-31267. (Advanced Computing & Telecommunications Ser.). (Illus.). 169p. 1995. 42.00 (*0-8155-1368-2*) Noyes.

***Telecommunications: Restructuring Work & Employment Relations Worldwide.** Ed. by Harry C. Katz. LC 96-32042. 1996. 49.95 (*0-8014-3286-3*) Cornell U Pr.

Telecommunications: Restructuring Work & Employment Relations Worldwide. Ed. by Harry C. Katz. (IRL Press Book/Cornell International Reports: No. 32). (Illus.). 393p. 1996. 49.95 (*0-614-16952-6*); pap. 19.95 (*0-8014-8361-1*) Cornell U Pr.

Telecommunications: Status of Research on the Safety of Cellular Telephones. (Illus.). 40p. (Orig.). (C). 1995. pap. text ed. 20.00 (*0-7881-1690-8*) DIANE Pub.

***Telecommunications: Status of Research on the Safety of Cellular Telephones.** (Illus.). 40p. 1994. pap. text ed. 40.00 (*1-57979-094-1*) BPI Info Servs.

Telecommunications: Systems & Applications. Robert Hendricks et al. 248p. 1993. pap. text ed. 24.95 (*1-56118-579-5*) Paradigm MN.

Telecommunications: Systems & Applications. Robert Hendricks et al. 128p. 1993. teacher ed., pap. text ed. 9.95 (*1-56118-580-9*) Paradigm MN.

Telecommunications: The Next American Revolution. Ed. by Karen Glass. 52p. (Orig.). 1994. pap. text ed. 15.00 (*1-55877-192-1*) Natl Governor.

***Telecommunications: Today's Ten Most Critical Telecommunications Technologies.** Computer Technology Research Corp. Staff. LC 96-38036. (Illus.). 200p. (Orig.). 1997. pap. 285.00 (*1-56607-981-0*) Comput Tech Res.

Telecommunications: World Bank Experience & Strategy. Bjorn Wellenius et al. (Discussion Paper Ser.: Vol. 192). 36p. 1993. 6.95 (*0-8213-2391-1*, 12391) World Bank.

Telecommunications - Physics Now! H. G. McGill. (C). 1988. text ed. 50.00 (*0-09-182277-7*, Pub. by S Thornes Pubs UK) St Mut.

Telecommunications Access & Public Policy. Allan Baughcum & Gerald Faulhaber. Ed. by Melvin J. Voigt. LC 84-6233. (Communication & Information Science Ser.). 300p. 1984. text ed. 45.00 (*0-89391-259-X*) Ablex Pub.

Telecommunications Act Handbook: A Complete Reference for Business. Ronald K. Machtley et al. Ed. by Leon Knaver. LC 96-24661. 640p. 1996. text ed. 89.00 (*0-86587-545-6*) Gov Insts.

***Telecommunications Act of 1996: Public Law 104-104, February 8, 1996.** 106p. (Orig.). (C). 1997. pap. text ed. 40.00 (*0-7881-3757-3*) DIANE Pub.

Telecommunications Act, 1984. R. N. Hamilton. 320p. (C). 1984. text ed. 135.00 (*0-85406-242-4*, Pub. by Surveyors Pubns) St Mut.

***Telecommunications Aerial Service Wire.** 35.00 (*0-614-18721-4*, S-89-648-1993) Insulated Cable.

Telecommunications Aide. Jack Rudman. (Career Examination Ser.: C-2877). 1994. pap. 23.95 (*0-8373-2877-2*) Nat Learn.

Telecommunications Alternative Regulation Plans. 108p. 1992. 22.00 (*0-317-04710-8*) NARUC.

Telecommunications America: Markets Without Boundaries. Manley R. Irwin. LC 83-9448. (Illus.). xiv, 147p. 1984. text ed. 55.00 (*0-89930-029-4*, IIS/, Quorum Bks) Greenwood.

Telecommunications Analyst. Jack Rudman. (Career Examination Ser.: C-3000). 1994. pap. 29.95 (*0-8373-3000-9*) Nat Learn.

Telecommunications Analyst Trainee. Jack Rudman. (Career Examination Ser.: C-3483). 1994. pap. 27.95 (*0-8373-3483-7*) Nat Learn.

Telecommunications & Broadcasting: Convergence or Collision? 288p. (Orig.). 1992. pap. 60.00 (*92-64-13764-5*) OECD.

Telecommunications & Development in Africa. M. Werner. LC 94-76400. 134p. 1994. pap. 69.50 (*90-5199-169-X*) IOS Press.

***Telecommunications & Development in China.** Ed. by Paul Lee. LC 97-20064. (Hampton Press Communication Ser.). 288p. (Orig.). 1997. text ed. 59.50 (*1-57273-060-9*); pap. text ed. 26.50 (*1-57273-061-7*) Hampton Pr NJ.

Telecommunications & Developmentally Disabled People: Evaluations of Audio Conferencing, Personal Computers, Computers Conferencing, & Electronic Mail. Robert Johansen et al. 235p. 1981. 15.00 (*0-318-19195-4*, R-50) Inst Future.

Telecommunications & Economic Development. 2nd ed. Bjorn Wellenius et al. (World Bank Ser.). 486p. (C). 1994. pap. text ed. 29.95 (*0-8018-4665-X*) Johns Hopkins.

Telecommunications & Economic Development: The State & Local Role. Robert H. Wilson. (Working Paper Ser.: No. 53). 36p. 1989. pap. 5.00 (*0-89940-534-7*) LBJ Sch Pub Aff.

Telecommunications & Education: Surfing & the Art of Change. Gloria Frazier & Deneen Frazier. Ed. by Anne Ward. (ITTE Technology Leadership Network Special Report Ser.). (Illus.). 124p. (Orig.). 1994. teacher ed., pap. 35.00 (*0-88364-187-9*) Natl Sch Boards.

***Telecommunications & Energy in Systemic Transformation: International Dynamics, Deregulation & Adjustment in Network Industries.** Paul J. Welfens & George K. Yarrow. LC 96-41582. (Illus.). 483p. 1996. 129.50 (*3-540-61586-5*) Spr-Verlag.

***Telecommunications & Enterprise Networks Glossary of Acronyms & Terms.** 39.95 (*0-614-18423-1*) Info Gatekeepers.

Telecommunications & Geography. Aharon Kellerman. LC 93-14953. 224p. 1993. text ed. 59.95 (*0-470-22034-1*) Halsted Pr.

Telecommunications & Geography. Aharon Kellerman. 230p. 1993. text ed. 88.00 (*0-471-94432-7*) Wiley.

Telecommunications & Networking. Udo W. Pooch et al. (Illus.). 400p. 1991. 69.95 (*0-8493-7172-4*, T) CRC Pr.

Telecommunications & Networking Glossary. George S. Machovec. (LITA Guides Ser.: No. 3). 68p. 1990. pap. 18.00 (*0-8389-7476-7*) ALA.

***Telecommunications & Networks.** K. M. Hussain. 1997. pap. text ed. 47.95 (*0-7506-2339-X*) Buttrwrth-Heinemann.

Telecommunications & Pacific Development: Alternatives for the Next Decade. Dan J. Wedemeyer. (Studies in Telecommunication: No. 11). 666p. 1989. 230.75 (*0-444-87118-7*, North Holland) Elsevier.

Telecommunications & Policy: The Decentralised Alternative. Andrew C. Davies. 290p. 1993. 49.00 (*1-85567-144-1*, Pub. by Pntr Pubs UK) Bks Intl VA.

Telecommunications & Rural Development: A Study of Private & Public Sector Innovation. Ed. by Jurgen Schmandt et al. LC 91-10178. 272p. 1991. text ed. 59.95 (*0-275-93951-0*, C3951, Praeger Pubs) Greenwood.

Telecommunications & Rural Economic Development. Kenneth Poole. Ed. by Jenny Murphy. 60p. (Orig.). 1991. pap. 22.50 (*0-317-04801-5*) Natl Coun Econ Dev.

***Telecommunications & Space Journal: Law - Economics - Public Policy, 1996, Vol. 3, 1996.** Ed. by Lucien Rapp. 368p. 1996. 69.95 (*0-8058-2328-X*) L Erlbaum Assocs.

Telecommunications & Space Journal 1995. Ed. by Lucien Rapp. 360p. 1995. 72.00 (*0-8058-2327-1*) L Erlbaum Assocs.

Telecommunications & Teleconferencing in Education & Training: A Selected Bibliography. Alexander J. Romiszowski & Bonnie Gratch. LC 95-6110. (Educational Technology Selected Bibliography Ser.: Vol. 13). 63p. 1995. pap. 24.95 (*0-87778-281-4*) Educ Tech Pubns.

Telecommunications & the City: Electronic Spaces, Urban Places. Stephen Graham & Simon Marvin. LC 95-21880. 336p. (C). 1996. pap. 22.95 (*0-415-11903-0*); text ed. 74.95 (*0-415-11902-2*) Routledge.

Telecommunications & the Computer. 3rd ed. James Martin & Simon Grant. 640p. 1990. text ed. 76.00 (*0-13-902644-4*) P-H.

Telecommunications & the Internet. Levy. (DF-Computer Applications Ser.). 1997. teacher ed., pap. 20.95 (*0-538-67250-1*); teacher ed., pap. 14.95 (*0-538-67251-X*) S-W Pub.

Telecommunications Applications: An Introduction to Designing Solutions to Meet Telecommunication Needs. Helen Parisi. Ed. by Maureen Doyle et al. (Illus.). 182p. (Orig.). (C). 1989. pap. text ed. 32.00 (*0-9625818-1-X*, 105-1) A G Comns Systs.

***Telecommunications Basics.** Travis Russell. LC 97-17358. (Telecommunications Ser.). (Illus.). 416p. 1997. text ed. 44.95 (*0-07-057695-5*) McGraw.

***Telecommunications Cable, Filled Polyolefin Insulated, Copper Conductor.** 40.00 (*0-614-18716-8*, S-84-608-1994) Insulated Cable.

***Telecommunications Cables: Design, Manufacture, & Installation.** LC 97-1820. 1997. write for info. (*0-471-97410-2*) Wiley.

Telecommunications Circuit Design. Patrick D. Van Der Puije. LC 91-34097. (Series in Telecommunications: No. 1794). 368p. 1992. text ed. 94.95 (*0-471-50777-6*) Wiley.

Telecommunications Circuits Data Book. Ed. by Texas Instruments Engineering Staff. (Illus.). 640p. (Orig.). 1991. pap. 11.95 (*0-318-41772-3*) Tex Instr Inc.

Telecommunications Competition: The Last Ten Miles. Ingo Vogelsang & Bridget M. Mitchell. (AEI Studies in Telecommunication Regulation). (Illus.). 210p. 1996. 35.00 (*0-262-22050-4*) MIT Pr.

***Telecommunications Competition & Universal Service: The Essential Tradeoffs.** unabridged ed. P. H. Longstaff. 45p. (Orig.). 1996. pap. text ed. write for info. (*1-879716-32-1*, P-96-2) Ctr Info Policy.

Telecommunications: Concepts, Development & Management. Mary M. Blyth & W. John Blyth. 352p. (C). 1985. teacher ed. write for info. (*0-672-97992-6*); text ed. write for info. (*0-672-97991-8*) Macmillan.

Telecommunications Cost & Call Management. (Illus.). 648p. 1982. ring bd. 461.00 (*0-318-23151-4*) Faulkner Tech Reports.

Telecommunications Curriculum Guide. Center for Occupational Research & Development Staff. 76p. 1988. pap. text ed. 20.00 (*1-55502-283-9*) CORD Commns.

Telecommunications Demand in Theory & Practice. rev. ed. Lester D. Taylor. LC 93-14522. 424p. (C). 1994. lib. bdg. 158.50 (*0-7923-2389-0*) Kluwer Ac.

Telecommunications Deregulation: Market Power & Cost Allocation Issues. Ed. by John R. Allison & Dennis L. Thomas. LC 90-32725. 304p. 1990. text ed. 59.95 (*0-89930-572-5*, ATA, Quorum Bks) Greenwood.

Telecommunications Deregulation Sourcebook. Stuart N. Brotman. 225p. 1987. text ed. 10.00 (*0-89006-205-6*) Artech Hse.

Telecommunications Deregulation Sourcebook. Ed. by Stuart N. Brotman. LC 87-1012. (Artech House Telecommunications Library). 355p. 1987. reprint ed. pap. 101.20 (*0-608-00212-7*, 2060995) Bks Demand.

Telecommunications Development: The Case of Africa. L. Kwabena Riverson. 130p. (C). 1995. lib. bdg. 38.00 (*0-8191-9315-1*) U Pr of Amer.

Telecommunications Directory, 1992-93. 5th ed. John Krol. 1991. 310.00 (*0-8103-7747-0*) Gale.

Telecommunications Directory 1994-95. 6th ed. John Krol. 1993. 340.00 (*0-8103-7748-9*) Gale.

Telecommunications Directory 1996-97. 8th ed. John Krol. 1996. 360.00 (*0-7876-0097-0*) Gale.

***Telecommunications Directory 1998: An International Guide to Organizations, Systems, & Services Concerned with the Interactive Electronic Transmission of Voice, Image, & Data.** 9th ed. Ed. by Pare. 1000p. 1997. 360.00 (*0-7876-1632-X*, 00156970) Gale.

Telecommunications Engineering. 3rd ed. J. Dunlop. 1994. pap. 34.00 (*0-412-56270-7*, Blackie & Son-Chapman NY) Routledge Chapman & Hall.

Telecommunications Engineer's Reference Book. F. F. Mazda. (Illus.). 1000p. 1993. 130.00 (*0-7506-1162-6*) Buttrwrth-Heinemann.

T

Telecommunications Equipment: Changing Markets & Rate Structures. OECD Staff. (Information Computer Communications Policy Ser.: No. 24). 78p. (Orig.). 1991. pap. 19.00 (92-64-13553-7) OECD.

Telecommunications Equipment: Industry & Trade Summary. Lori H. Brown. (Illus.). 51p. (Orig.). (C). 1994. pap. text ed. 25.00 (0-7881-1557-X) DIANE Pub.

Telecommunications Export Guide: A Directory of International Trade Data & Resources. 3rd ed. MultiMedia Telecommunications Association Staff. 210p. 1993. pap. 103.00 (0-940919-31-1) MultiMedia Telecomm.

Telecommunications for Europe, 1992, Vol. 1: CEC Sources. Ed. by H. Ungerer et al. (European Communication Policy Research Ser.). 488p. 1989. pap. 90.00 (90-5199-012-X, Pub. by IOS Pr NE) IOS Press.

Telecommunications for Europe, 1992, Vol. 2: CEC Sources. Ed. by H. Ungerer et al. (European Communication Policy Research Ser.). 730p. (gr. 12). 1991. 150.00 (90-5199-047-2, Pub. by IOS Pr NE) IOS Press.

***Telecommunications for Europe 1995, Vol. 3.** LC 95-7833. (YA). (gr. 12 up). 1995. 140.00 (90-5199-228-9, 228-9) IOS Press.

Telecommunications for Information Management & Transfer: Proceedings of the First International Conference Held at Leicester Polytechnic, April 1987. Ed. by Mel Collier. 200p. 1988. text ed. 49.95 (0-566-05551-1, Pub. by Gower UK) Ashgate Pub Co.

Telecommunications for Information Specialties. Larry Leoin. (Library, Information, & Computer Science Ser.: No. 11). (Illus.). 180p. (Orig.). 1989. pap. 15.00 (1-55653-075-7) OCLC Online Comp.

Telecommunications for Learning. Ed. by Educational Technology Magazine Staff. LC 90-41902. (Anthology Ser.: Vol. 3). (Illus.). 202p. 1991. 34.95 (0-87778-225-3) Educ Tech Pubns.

Telecommunications for Library Management. Richard W. Boss. LC 84-26140. (Professional Librarian Ser.). 184p. 1985. 45.00 (0-86729-126-5, Hall Reference) Macmillan.

Telecommunications for Managers. 3rd rev. ed. Stanford H. Rowe, II. LC 94-19934. Orig. Title: Business Telcommunications. 720p. 1994. text ed. 82.00 (0-02-404114-9, Macmillan Coll) P-H.

***Telecommunications for Television/Advanced Television: Forecasts of Markets & Technologies.** Lawrence K. Vanston et al. 144p. 1992. pap. 45.00 (0-614-18105-4) Tech Futures.

Telecommunications Free Trade Zones: Crafting a Model for Local Exchange Competition. Terrence L. Barnich et al. 53p. (Orig.). (C). 1994. pap. text ed. 25.00 (0-7881-0366-0) DIANE Pub.

Telecommunications Glossary. 283p. (ENG, FRE, GER, NOR & SWE.). 1980. pap. 75.00 (0-8288-0191-6, M 14053) Fr & Eur.

Telecommunications Guide: Model License Agreement Language & Lease Language. 50p. (Orig.). 1995. pap. 79.00 (0-943130-14-X) Build Own & Man.

Telecommunications in Asia: Policy, Planning & Development. Ed. by John Ure. 285p. (Orig.). (C). 1995. pap. 37.50 (962-209-383-3, Pub. by Hong Kong Univ Pr HK) Coronet Bks.

Telecommunications in Business: Strategy & Application. John J. Vargo & Ray Hunt. 576p. (C). 1995. text ed. 64.50 (0-256-19787-3) Irwin.

Telecommunications in Canada. Robert Babe. 392p. 1989. 55.00 (0-8020-5831-0); pap. 25.95 (0-8020-6738-7) U of Toronto Pr.

Telecommunications in Europe. Eli Noam. (Communication & Society Ser.). (Illus.). 496p. 1992. 69.00 (0-19-507052-6, 819) OUP.

Telecommunications in Germany: An Economic Perspective. G. Pfeiffer & B. Wieland. (Illus.). viii, 199p. 1990. 56.00 (0-387-52360-X) Spr-Verlag.

Telecommunications in Health Care. H. U. Brown. 112p. 1982. 69.00 (0-8493-5588-5, R118, CRC Reprint) Franklin.

***Telecommunications in Latin America.** Ed. by Eli Noam. LC 96-36073. 320p. 1997. 65.00 (0-19-510200-2) OUP.

Telecommunications in the Age of Information: How to Improve the International Competitiveness of the United States & the Quality of the Life of U. S. Citizens & Business. 1992. lib. bdg. 279.95 (0-8490-8838-0) Gordon Pr.

Telecommunications in the Age of Information: The NTIA Infrastructure Report. (Illus.). 365p. (C). 1994. reprint ed. pap. text ed. 45.00 (0-7881-1462-X) DIANE Pub.

Telecommunications in the Classroom. Chris Clark et al. 74p. 1989. teacher ed. 10.00 (1-56484-006-9) Intl Society Tech Educ.

Telecommunications in the Pacific Basin: An Evolutionary Approach. Ed. by Eli M. Noam et al. LC 92-46617. (Communication & Society Ser.). 544p. 1994. 59.00 (0-19-508421-7) OUP.

Telecommunications in the U. S. Trends & Policies. Ed. by Leonard Lewin. LC 81-67809. (Illus.). 487p. reprint ed. pap. 138.80 (0-8357-4190-7, 2036968) Bks Demand.

Telecommunications in the Year 2000. Ed. by Indu B. Singh. LC 82-13800. (Communication & Information Science Ser.). 304p. 1983. 59.50 (0-89391-137-2) Ablex Pub.

Telecommunications in the 1990s. Marshall. 1995. 39.95 (0-8161-1974-0) G K Hall.

Telecommunications in Transition: Policies, Services & Technologies in the European Economic Community. Ed. by Charles Steinfield et al. (Illus.). 320p. (C). 1993. text ed. 48.00 (0-8039-4606-6); pap. text ed. 23.95 (0-8039-4607-4) Sage.

***Telecommunications in Western Asia.** Ed. by Eli Noam. (Illus.). 256p. 1997. 55.00 (0-19-510202-9) OUP.

Telecommunications Industry. 1994. write for info. (1-879087-31-6) Assn I M&R.

Telecommunications Industry. E. Sciberras & B. D. Payne. 1987. 45.00 (0-912289-71-6) St James Pr.

Telecommunications Industry: The Dynamics of Market Structure. Gerald W. Brock. LC 80-25299. (Economic Studies: No. 151). (Illus.). 348p. (C). 1981. 24.95 (0-674-87285-1) HUP.

Telecommunications Industry in Japan. Business Communications Co., Inc. Staff. 120p. 1986. pap. 1,950.00 (0-89336-469-X, G-099) BCC.

***Telecommunications Industustry.** Sciberras. 1986. pap. text ed. write for info. (0-582-90208-8, Pub. by Longman UK) Longman.

Telecommunications Information Millenium: A Vision & Plan for the Global Information Society. R. Heldman. LC 95-8324. 1995. pap. text ed. 24.95 (0-07-028106-8) McGraw.

Telecommunications, KLT & Relativity. Claudio Maccone. Ed. by Richard A. Blade. (Textbooks in Science & Mathematics Ser.). (Illus.). x, 238p. (Orig.). (C). 1994. pap. 35.00 (1-880930-04-8) IPI Pr.

Telecommunications Law. David Gillies & J. W. Marshall. boxed write for info. (0-406-02096-5, UK) MICHIE.

Telecommunications Law. Kellogg. 1995. suppl. ed. 95.00 (0-316-48678-7) Little.

Telecommunications Law & Policy. Thomas G. Krattenmaker. LC 94-73843. 644p. (C). 1995. boxed 75.00 (0-89089-828-6) Carolina Acad Pr.

***Telecommunications Law & Policy.** Thomas G. Krattenmaker. 185p. (C). 1996. suppl. ed., pap. text ed. 15.00 (0-89089-018-8) Carolina Acad Pr.

Telecommunications Law in Europe. 3rd rev. ed. Ed. by J. Scherer. LC 95-13743. 1995. pap. text ed. 91.25 (90-411-0028-8) Kluwer Ac.

***Telecommunications Local Networks.** Ed. by Ritchie & Stern. (BT Telecommunications Ser.). 321p. 1992. text ed. 114.50 (0-412-45810-1, Chap & Hall NY) Chapman & Hall.

Telecommunications Local Networks. Ed. by W. Ritchie & V. Stern. 500p. 1992. 79.95 (0-442-30883-3) Chapman & Hall.

Telecommunications Making Sense Out of New Technology & New Legislation. Deborah K. Conrad et al. Ed. by J. L. Divilbiss. (Clinic on Library Applications of Data Processing, Proceedings: 1977). 1985. text ed. 10.00 (0-87845-072-6) U of Ill Grad Sch.

Telecommunications Management: Broadcasting-Cable & the New Technologies. 2nd ed. Barry L. Sherman. LC 94-11082. (McGraw-Hill Series in Mass Communication). 1994. text ed. write for info. (0-07-056698-4) McGraw.

Telecommunications Management, Control, & Audit. Bernard K. Plagman & Anne O'Loughlin. 207p. 1988. pap. text ed. 45.00 (0-89413-181-8, A776) Inst Inter Aud.

Telecommunications Management for the Data Processing Executive: A Decision-Maker's Guide to Systems Planning & Implementation. Milburn D. Smith, III. LC 87-2520. 208p. 1987. text ed. 65.00 (0-89930-110-X, LOT/, Quorum Bks) Greenwood.

Telecommunications Market Opportunities in China. Contrib. by Jianguo Liu. 187p. 1995. 2,650.00 (1-56965-072-1, G-188) BCC.

Telecommunications Market Review & Forecast. Damin Luo. 279p. 1991. pap. 595.00 (0-940919-27-3, 200) MultiMedia Telecomm.

Telecommunications Market Sourcebook '95. Market Intelligence Staff. 298p. 1995. 595.00 (0-7889-0217-2, 2827-63) Frost & Sullivan.

Telecommunications, Mass Media, & Democracy: The Battle for the Control of U. S. Broadcasting, 1928-1935. Robert W. McChesney. 416p. 1995. reprint ed. pap. 18.95 (0-19-509394-1) OUP.

Telecommunications Measurements, Analysis, & Instrumentation. Kamilo Feher. (Illus.). 448p. 1986. text ed. 97.00 (0-13-902404-2) P-H.

Telecommunications Network Architecture in the Former Soviet Union, Vol. II. Leonid Balanvskiy et al. (Foreign Technology Assessment Ser.). xviii, 155p. (Orig.). 1994. pap. 200.00 (1-881874-10-9) Global Cnslts.

Telecommunications Network Design Algorithms. Aaron Kershenbaum. 1993. text ed. write for info. (0-07-034228-8) McGraw.

Telecommunications Network Management into the 21st Century: Techniques, Standards, Technologies, & Applications. Ed. by Salah Aidarous & Thomas Plevyak. LC 93-41040. 1994. 59.95 (0-7803-1013-6, PC03624) Inst Electrical.

Telecommunications, Networking, & Internet Glossary. George S. Machovec. LC 93-31054. (LITA Monographs: No. 4). 124p. 1993. pap. 18.00 (0-8389-7697-2) Lib Info Tech.

Telecommunications Networks: Issues & Trends. Ed. by M. E. Jacob. 179p. 1986. pap. 28.50 (0-313-25783-3); text ed. 49.95 (0-313-25782-5) Greenwood.

Telecommunications Networks & Services. 2nd ed. J. Van Duuren. (C). 1997. pap. text ed. 29.95 (0-201-87754-6) Addison-Wesley.

Telecommunications on the Mac. Steven Taylor. 1992. pap. 19.95 (1-55828-209-2) MIS Press.

Telecommunications Outside Plant - U.S. Markets, Customers, & Competitors: 1994-1999 Analysis & Forecasts. Kimberly McGowan. 258p. 1994. pap. text ed. 2,400.00 (1-878218-49-2) World Info Tech.

Telecommunications Outside Plant Products - U. S. Markets, End-Users & Competitors: 1991-1996 Analysis. Timothy W. Archdeacon. (Illus.). 260p. 1992. pap. text ed. 2,400.00 (1-878218-25-5) World Info Tech.

***Telecommunications Outside Plant Products, Copper vs. Fiber - U. S. Markets, Customers, & Competitors: 1997-2000 Analysis & Forecasts.** Kimberly O'Brien. 78p. 1997. pap. text ed. 2,400.00 (1-878218-74-3) World Info Tech.

***Telecommunications Policies for Sub-Saharan Africa.** Mohammad A. Mustafa et al. (Discussion Papers: No. 353). 90p. 1997. 7.95 (0-8213-3851-X, 13851) World Bank.

***Telecommunications Policy: Have Regulators Dialed the Wrong Number?** Ed. by Donald L. Alexander. LC 97-9181. 1997. text ed. write for info. (0-275-95855-8, Praeger Pubs) Greenwood.

Telecommunications Policy & Economic Development: The New State Role. Ed. by Jurgen Schmandt et al. LC 89-16148. 317p. 1989. text ed. 59.95 (0-275-93399-7, C3399, Praeger Pubs) Greenwood.

Telecommunications Policy & Regulation, 1991: The Year Ahead, Congress, the FCC & Judge Greene's Court, 2 vols. R. Clark Wodlow & Richard E. Wiley. (Patents, Copyrights, Trademarks, & Literary Property Ser.). 1506p. 1991. pap. text ed. 30.00 (0-685-56907-1, G4-3874) PLI.

Telecommunications Policy & Regulation 1994. (Patents, Copyrights, Trademarks, & Literary Property Ser.). 328p. 1994. pap. 99.00 (0-685-65515-6, G4-3930) PLI.

Telecommunications Policy & Regulation 1995. (Patents, Copyrights, Trademarks, & Literary Property Course Handbook, 1994-95 Ser.). Date not set. pap. 99.00 (0-614-17232-2, G4-3937) PLI.

Telecommunications Policy & the Citizen: Public Interest Prespectives on the Communications Act Rewrite. Ed. by Timothy R. Haight. 296p. 1979. pap. 19.95 (0-03-054136-0, Praeger Pubs); text ed. 59.95 (0-275-90359-1, C0359, Praeger Pubs) Greenwood.

Telecommunications Policy for the 1990s & Beyond: New Markets, Technology, & Global Competitive Trends. Walter G. Bolter et al. LC 89-10803. 456p. (gr. 13). 1990. text ed. 90.95 (0-87332-586-9) M E Sharpe.

Telecommunications Policy, High Definition Television, & U. S. Competitiveness. Robert Cohen & Kenneth Donow. LC 89-80758. 50p. 1989. 12.00 (0-944826-10-5) Economic Policy Inst.

Telecommunications Policy Yearbook 1981. Ed. by Jorge R. Schement et al. LC 81-22648. 332p. 1982. text ed. 65.00 (0-275-90897-6, C0897, Praeger Pubs) Greenwood.

Telecommunications Politics: Ownership & Control of the Information Highway in Developing Countries. Ed. by Bella Mody et al. (LEA's Telecommunications Ser.). 360p. 1995. 69.95 (0-8058-1752-2) L Erlbaum Assocs.

Telecommunications Politics: Ownership & Control of the Information Highway in Developing Countries. Ed. by Bella Mody et al. (LEA's Telecommunications Ser.). 360p. 1995. pap. 34.50 (0-8058-1753-0) L Erlbaum Assocs.

Telecommunications Pricing: Theory & Practice. Ingo Vogelsang & Bridget M. Mitchell. (Illus.). 324p. (C). 1991. text ed. 59.95 (0-521-41667-1); pap. text ed. 20.95 (0-521-42678-2) Cambridge U Pr.

Telecommunications Primer. Graham Langley. 192p. (C). 1990. pap. text ed. 125.00 (0-273-03187-2, Pub. by Pitman Pubng UK) St Mut.

Telecommunications Primer. 4th ed. Graham Langley & John Ronayne. 240p. 1993. pap. 42.50 (0-273-60157-1, Pub. by Pitman Pub Ltd UK) Trans-Atl Phila.

Telecommunications Primer: Signals, Building Blocks & Networks. E. Bryan Carne. LC 95-16021. 1995. text ed. 62.00 (0-13-206129-5) P-H.

***Telecommunications Primer: Signals, Building Clocks, & Networks.** E. Bryan Carne. (Handbook Ser.). 624p. 1996. 59.00 (0-13-490426-5, PC5670) P-H.

***Telecommunications Principles.** 2nd ed. O'Reilly. (Tutorial Guides in Electronic Engineering Ser.). (Illus.). 168p. (Orig.). (C). (gr. 13 up). 1992. pap. text ed. 41.95 (0-412-43700-7, Chap & Hall NY) Chapman & Hall.

***Telecommunications Qualification Test (TQT)** Jack Rudman. (Career Examination Ser.: Vol. C-3820). 1997. pap. 27.95 (0-8373-3820-4) Nat Learn.

***Telecommunications Regulation in the Netherlands.** Peter V. Eijsvoogel. LC 97-5685. (Loeff Legal Ser.). 1997. pap. write for info. (90-411-0371-6) Kluwer Law Tax Pubs.

Telecommunications Regulatory Monitor. David A. Irwin. LC 87-114898. 1984. 3.97 (0-934960-19-4) Phillips Business.

Telecommunications Research Resources: An Annotated Guide. James K. Bracken & Christopher H. Sterling. (LEA's Telecommunications Ser.). 184p. 1995. pap. 19.95 (0-8058-1887-1); text ed. 36.00 (0-8058-1886-3) L Erlbaum Assocs.

Telecommunications' Retail Opportunities, No. G-133. Business Communications Co., Inc. Staff. 178p. 1991. 1,950.00 (0-89336-824-5) BCC.

Telecommunications Revolution. (C). 1998. text ed. write for info. (0-201-63397-3) Addison-Wesley.

Telecommunications Revolution: Past, Present & Future. Ed. by Harvey M. Sapolsky & Rhonda J. Crane. LC 91-26477. 304p. (C). (gr. 13 up). 1991. text ed. 52.95 (0-415-06771-5, Routledge NY) Routledge.

Telecommunications Revolution in Korea. James F. Larson. (Illus.). 360p. 1995. 59.00 (0-19-586785-8) OUP.

Telecommunications Sector Reform in Asia: Toward a New Pragmatism. Peter L. Smith & Gregory Staple. (Discussion Paper Ser.: No. 232). 128p. 1994. 7.95 (0-8213-2760-7, 12760) World Bank.

***Telecommunications Security Guidelines for Telecommunications Management Network.** John Kimmins et al. 37p. 1996. reprint ed. pap. 20.00 (0-7881-3317-9) DIANE Pub.

Telecommunications Source Book, 1993. MultiMedia Telecommunications Association Staff. 208p. 1993. pap. 53.00 (0-940919-28-1) MultiMedia Telecomm.

Telecommunications Specialist. Jack Rudman. (Career Examination Ser.: C-3410). 1994. pap. 27.95 (0-8373-3410-1) Nat Learn.

Telecommunications Strategy for Economic Development. William H. Read & Jan L. Youtie. LC 95-40582. 176p. 1996. text ed. 55.00 (0-275-95415-3, Praeger Pubs) Greenwood.

Telecommunications Switching. J. Gordon Pearce. LC 80-20586. (Applications of Communications Theory Ser.). 348p. 1981. 75.00 (0-306-40584-9, Plenum Pr) Plenum.

Telecommunications Switching, Traffic & Networks. J. E. Flood. LC 94-29046. 352p. 1995. pap. text ed. 68.00 (0-13-033309-3) P-H.

Telecommunications System Guide. (Illus.). 878p. 1982. ring bd. 461.00 (0-685-18834-5) Faulkner Tech Reports.

Telecommunications Systems. (Illus.). 1986. pap. 20.25 (0-685-54122-3, 297-86) Natl Fire Prot.

Telecommunications Systems & Applications. Fraidoon Mazda. (Telecommunication Ser.). (Illus.). 350p. 1996. pap. 28.95 (0-240-51453-X, Focal) Buttrwrth-Heinemann.

***Telecommunications Systems & Services.** 2nd ed. 1985. 270.00 (0-8103-1697-8, 00007120, Gale Res Intl) Gale.

Telecommunications Systems & Services Directory. 3rd ed. Ed. by John Krol. LC 83-11628. 1987. 285.00 (0-8103-2345-1) Gale.

Telecommunications Systems & Services Directory. 4th ed. Ed. by John Krol. 1989. 295.00 (0-8103-2241-2) Gale.

***Telecommunications Take-Off in Transition Countries.** Ed. by Karl-Ernst Schenk et al. 272p. 1997. 63.95 (1-85972-572-4, Pub. by Avebury Pub UK) Ashgate Pub Co.

Telecommunications Technician. Jack Rudman. (Career Examination Ser.: C-3411). 1994. pap. 27.95 (0-8373-3411-X) Nat Learn.

Telecommunications Technologies & Applications. Computer Technology Research Corp., Staff. (Illus.). 196p. (Orig.). 1995. 260.00 (1-56607-953-5) Comput Tech Res.

Telecommunications Technology Handbook. Daniel Minoli. (Artech House Telecommunications Library). 680p. 1991. 89.00 (0-89006-425-3, C1425) Artech Hse.

Telecommunications Terms. International Telecommunications Union Staff. 179p. (ENG, FRE & SPA.). 1981. pap. 295.00 (0-8288-0189-4, F52930) Fr & Eur.

Telecommunications Test Equipment - U. S. Markets & Opportunities: 1991-1996 Analysis. Ely S. Lurin. (Illus.). 220p. 1992. pap. text ed. 1,900.00 (1-878218-26-3) World Info Tech.

Telecommunications Test Equipment - U.S. Markets & Opportunities: 1993-1998 Analysis & Forecasts. Ely S. Lurin. 250p. 1994. pap. text ed. 1,900.00 (1-878218-47-6) World Info Tech.

Telecommunications Transmission Engineering, 3 vols., Set. 3rd ed. Bellcore & Bell Operating Companies, Technical Personnel Staff. LC 90-62180. (Illus.). 824p. (C). 1990. text ed. 399.00 (1-878108-04-2) Bellcore.

Telecommunications Transmission Engineering, 3 vols., Vol. 1: Principles. 3rd ed. Bellcore & Bell Operating Companies, Technical Personnel Staff. LC 90-62180. (Illus.). 824p. (C). 1990. text ed. 195.00 (1-878108-01-8) Bellcore.

Telecommunications Transmission Engineering, 3 vols., Vol. 2: Facilities. 3rd ed. Bellcore & Bell Operating Companies, Technical Personnel Staff. LC 90-62180. (Illus.). 824p. (C). 1990. text ed. 195.00 (1-878108-02-6) Bellcore.

Telecommunications Transmission Engineering, 3 vols., Vol. 3: Networks & Services. 3rd ed. Bellcore & Bell Operating Companies, Technical Personnel Staff. LC 90-62180. (Illus.). 824p. (C). 1990. text ed. 195.00 (1-878108-03-4) Bellcore.

Telecommunications Type Approval: Policies & Procedures for Market Access. OECD Staff. (Information Computer Communications Policy Ser.: No. 27). 166p. (Orig.). 1992. pap. 37.00 (92-64-13615-0) OECD.

Telecommunications Using ProComm & ProComm Plus Made Easy. Michele Woggon. LC 94-28044. (C). 1995. pap. text ed. 36.80 (0-13-148412-5) P-H.

Telecommunications, Values & the Public Interest. Ed. by Sven B. Lundstedt & Brenda Dervin. LC 90-999. (Communication & Information Science Ser.). 320p. (C). 1990. pap. 39.50 (0-89391-733-8); text ed. 73.25 (0-89391-693-5) Ablex Pub.

Telecommunications Wiring for Commercial Buildings: A Practical Guide. Elliot M. Gilbert & John G. Nellist. LC 96-6748. 224p. 1996. pap. 59.95 (0-7803-1114-0, PC4671) Inst Electrical.

Telecommute! How You, Too, Can Make the Virtual Office a Reality. Lisa Shaw. LC 96-1326. 224p. 1996. pap. text ed. 14.95 (0-471-11820-6) Wiley.

Telecommuter's Advisor: Working in the Fast Lane. June Langhoff. LC 95-83159. (Illus.). 240p. (Orig.). 1996. pap. 14.95 (0-9632790-5-X) Aegis Pub Grp.

Telecommuters Guide to Electronic Products. Nolan. 1997. 79.00 (0-7876-1032-1) Gale.

Telecommuter's Handbook: How to Earn a Living Without Going to the Office. 2nd ed. Brad Schepp. LC 95-18231. 1995. pap. text ed. 12.95 (0-07-057102-3) McGraw.

Telecommuters, the Workforce of the Twenty-First Century: An Annotated Bibliography. Teri R. Switzer. LC 96-23195. 192p. 1996. 34.00 (0-8108-3210-0) Scarecrow.

Telecommuting. Osman Eldib & Daniel Minoli. LC 94-49213. 1995. 67.00 (0-89006-738-4) Artech Hse.

An Asterisk (*) at the beginning of an entry indicates that the title is appearing in BIP for the first time.

Telecommuting: A Manager's Guide to Flexible Work Arrangement. Joel Kugelmass. 232p. 25.00 (*0-02-917691-3*, Free Press) Free Pr.

Telecommuting: How to Make It Work for You & Your Company. Gilbert E. Gordon & Marcia M. Kelly. 233p. 1986. 29.95 (*0-13-902339-9*, Busn) P-H.

***Telecommuting: The Employer's & Employee's Decision-Making Process.** rev. ed. Adriana Bernardino. LC 96-36710. (Studies on Industrial Productivity). (Illus.). 178p. 1996. text ed. 46.00 (*0-8153-2723-4*) Garland.

Telecommuting: The Organizational & Behavioral Effects of Working at Home. Reagan M. Ramsower. Ed. by Richard Farmer. LC 84-28095. (Research for Business Decisions Ser.: No. 75). 208p. reprint ed. 59.00 (*0-8357-1628-7*, 2070413) Bks Demand.

Telecommuting: The Ride of the Future. Ed. by Pamela Martin. 100p. (Orig.). (C). 1992. pap. text ed. 20.00 (*0-941375-93-5*) DIANE Pub.

Telecommuting: Work Strategies for the Information Organization. Thomas B. Cross & Marjorie B. Raizman. 225p. 1986. 32.50 (*0-87094-645-5*) Irwin Prof Pubng.

Telecommuting in the Twin Cities Metropolitan Area: A Report to the Minnesota Legislature. 104p. (Orig.). (C). 1995. pap. text ed. 25.00 (*0-7881-2392-0*) DIANE Pub.

Telecommuting Pluses & Pitfalls. Brenda B. Thompson. 56p. 1996. spiral bd. 47.00 (*0-925773-30-1*) M Lee Smith.

Telecommuting Problems. Christena E. Nippert-Eng. 1995. 19.95 (*0-226-58652-9*) U Ch Pr.

Telecompetition: The Free Market Road to the Information Highway. Lawrence D. Gasman. 230p. 1993. 24.95 (*1-882577-08-6*); pap. 14.95 (*1-882577-09-4*) Cato Inst.

***Telecoms for Older People & People with Disabilities in Europe: Preparing for the Information Society.** 250p. Date not set. 78.00 (*90-5199-346-3*) IOS Press.

Teleconferencing. Ed. by Dennis Bodson & Richard Schaphorst. LC 89-15540. (Illus.). 360p. 1989. text ed. 49.95 (*0-87942-252-1*, PC02444) Inst Electrical.

Teleconnections Linking Worldwide Climate Anomalies. Ed. by Michael H. Glantz et al. (Illus.). 300p. (C). 1991. 69.95 (*0-521-36475-2*) Cambridge U Pr.

***Telecourse: Living with Health.** Dallas County Community College Staff. 1993. student ed., pap. text ed. write for info. (*0-07-015187-3*) McGraw.

***Telecourse, Contemporary.** 6th ed. Boone. (C). 1997. student ed., pap. text ed. 26.75 (*0-03-019029-0*) HB Coll Pubs.

***Telecourse Cycles of Life Biology.** Starr & Robertson. (Biology Ser.). (C). 1997. lab manual ed., pap. 27.95 (*0-534-50459-0*) Wadsworth Pub.

Telecourse (Faculty Version) Moore & McCabe. 1995. student ed. write for info. (*0-7167-2457-X*) W H Freeman.

***Telecourse for America in Perspective: U. S. History Sience 1877.** 2nd ed. By Alfers. (C). 1994. pap. text ed. 27.95 (*0-673-99048-6*) Addison-Wesley.

Telecourse Guide. 3rd ed. Comap. 1995. write for info. (*0-7167-2530-4*) W H Freeman.

***Telecourse Study Guide "By The Numbers" Business Math.** 7th ed. Southern. (C). 1990. pap. text ed. 33.95 (*0-673-46351-6*) Addison-Wesley.

Telecourse Study Guide for the New Literacy: An Introduction to Computers. 2nd ed. Marilyn Bohl. 331p. (C). 1990. pap. text ed. 36.40 (*0-02-311888-1*, Macmillan Coll) P-H.

Telecourse Study Guide II: Executive, Legislative & Judicial. 3rd ed. DCCCD (Lee) Staff. 320p. (C). 1994. per. 18.84 (*0-8403-8442-4*) Kendall-Hunt.

Telecourse Study Guide, No. 1: People, Parties, & Politics. 3rd ed. DCCCD (Lee) Staff. 320p. (C). 1994. per. 16.74 (*0-8403-8441-6*) Kendall-Hunt.

Telecourse Study Guide to Government by Consent: A Texas Perspective. DCCCD (Forshee) Staff. 320p. (C). 1995. per. 19.89 (*0-8403-8440-8*) Kendall-Hunt.

Telecult Power: The Amazing New Way to Psychic & Occult Wonders. Reese P. Dubin. (Illus.). 1986. 16.95 (*0-13-902437-9*, Reward) P-H.

Teledemocracy: Can Technology Protect Democracy? F. Christopher Arterton. LC 86-17447. (Sage Library of Social Research: No. 165). 224p. 1987. reprint ed. pap. 63.90 (*0-608-01486-9*, 2059530) Bks Demand.

***Teledetection Satellitaire & Pecheries Thonieres Oceaniques.** 155p. (FRE.). 1989. 20.00 (*92-5-202825-0*, Pub. by FAO IT) Bernan Associates.

Telefon. Johannes Beeck et al. (Illus.). 50p. (GER.). (YA). (gr. 7 up). 1990. Incls. cass. tape. 22.00 incl. audio (*0-939990-70-9*) Intl Linguistics.

TeleGeography 1995: Global Telecommunications Traffic Statistics & Commentary Annual. Ed. by Gregory C. Staple. 168p. 1995. pap. write for info. (*1-886142-03-3*) TeleGeography.

TeleGeography 1994: Global Telecommunications Traffic Statistics & Commentary Annual. Ed. by Gregory C. Staple. 180p. 1994. pap. write for info. (*1-886142-01-7*) TeleGeography.

***TeleGeography 100: A Graphical Guide to the World's Leading Information Companies.** Ed. by Gregory C. Staple. (Illus.). 240p. (Orig.). 1996. pap. write for info. (*1-886142-06-8*) TeleGeography.

TeleGeography 1993: Global Telecommunications Traffic Statistics & Commentary Annual. Ed. by Gregory C. Staple. 168p. 1993. pap. write for info. (*1-886142-00-9*) TeleGeography.

***TeleGeography 1996/97: Global Telecommunications Traffic Statistics & Commentary.** Ed. by Gregory C. Staple. (Illus.). 170p. (Orig.). 1996. pap. write for info. (*1-886142-08-4*) TeleGeography.

***TeleGeography 1997/98: Global Telecommunications Traffic Statistics & Commentary.** Ed. by Gregory C. Staple. (Illus.). 170p. (Orig.). 1997. pap. write for info. (*1-886142-10-6*) TeleGeography.

Telegram & Other Gram Rhymes for All Occasions: Any Occasion, That Occasion & Most Occasions. Biblio Press Staff. 15p. pap. text ed. 27.95 (*0-939476-12-6*) Prosperity & Profits.

Telegram from Marcel Duchamp. David Prowler. LC 90-91685. (Illus.). (Orig.). 1990. pap. 15.00 (*0-9628062-1-8*) Ready Made Pr.

Telegrams from the Soul: Peter Altenberg & the Culture of Fin-de-Siecle Vienna. Andrew Barker. (GERM Ser.). xx, 260p. 1996. 55.95 (*1-57113-079-9*) Camden Hse.

Telegraph: A History of Morse's Invention & Its Predecessors in the United States. Lewis Coe. LC 92-53597. (Illus.). 192p. 1993. lib. bdg. 28.50 (*0-89950-736-0*) McFarland & Co.

Telegraph Avenue Then. Jennifer Stone. 53p. (Orig.). 1992. pap. 9.95 (*0-916147-21-5*) Regent Pr.

Telegraph Boy. Horatio Alger, Jr. (Works of Horatio Alger Jr.). 1989. reprint ed. lib. bdg. 79.00 (*0-685-27551-5*) Rprt Serv.

Telegraph in America: Its Founders, Promoters & Noted Men. James D. Reid. LC 74-7493. (Telecommunications Ser.). (Illus.). 926p. 1974. reprint ed. 69.95 (*0-405-06056-4*) Ayer.

Telegu Chodas of Kanduru: History, Art & Architecture. G. Stayanarayan Rao. 1987. 34.00 (*0-8364-2205-8*, New Era Bks) S Asia.

***Teleguide: A Structured Approach: Living Well Telecourse.** Cindy Hanawalt-Squires et al. 272p. (C). 1997. spiral bd. write for info. (*0-697-28997-4*) Wm C Brown Pubs.

***Telekommunikation in Mittelosteuropa: Die Reform der Festnetzkommunikation in Polen, Tschechien & Ungarn.** Henrik Probdorf. (Illus.). xvi, 207p. (GER.). 1996. 51.95 (*3-631-30205-3*) P Lang Pubng.

Teleliteracy: Taking Television Seriously. David Bianculli. LC 91-34941. (Illus.). 332p. 1992. 27.50 (*0-8264-0535-5*) Continuum.

Telemachus. Francois Fenelon. Ed. by Patrick Riley. Tr. by Patrick Wiley from FRE. LC 93-44349. (Texts in the History of Political Thought Ser.). 400p. (C). 1994. text ed. 59.95 (*0-521-45042-X*); pap. text ed. 19.95 (*0-521-45662-2*) Cambridge U Pr.

Telemachus Clay. Lewis J. Carlino. 114p. 1964. 14.95 (*0-910278-12-1*) Boulevard.

Telemachus Clay. Lewis J. Carlino. LC 64-17945. 1963. pap. 5.25 (*0-8222-1116-5*) Dramatists Play.

Telemanage Your Customers: A System for Telephone Account Management. Merlin Stone et al. 160p. 1990. text ed. 89.95 (*0-566-02903-0*, Pub. by Gower UK) Ashgate Pub Co.

Telemanagement: How to Select & Manage Your Business Telephone System. John Fuhrman. 250p. 1986. 39.95 (*0-13-902529-4*, Busn) P-H.

Telemanagement Systems, Software, & Services Market: Who's Winning, Who's Losing, & Why. Market Intelligence Staff. 303p. (Orig.). 1992. 1,495.00 (*1-56753-044-3*) Frost & Sullivan.

Telemarketer's Handbook: Professional Tactics & Strategies for Instant Results. Darlene Maciuba-Koppel. 192p. 1994. lib. bdg. 35.00 (*0-8095-7624-4*) Borgo Pr.

Telemarketing: Applications & Opportunities. Lloyd Finch & Vivyan Finch. Ed. by Philip Gerould. LC 94-68576. (Fifty-Minute Ser.). (Illus.). 110p. (Orig.). 1995. pap. 10.95 (*1-56052-307-7*) Crisp Pubns.

Telemarketing: Setting up for Success. Michael R. Burns. 200p. 1987. 22.00 (*0-936840-10-2*) Tech Marketing.

Telemarketing at Home - Finding Opportunities Workbook. rev. ed. Carrol, Frieda, Research Division Staff. 1991. ring bd. 25.95 (*0-317-04091-X*, Pub. by Frieda Carrol) Prosperity & Profits.

Telemarketing Basics: A Practical Guide for Professional Results. Julie Freestone & Janet Brusse. Ed. by Michael G. Crisp. LC 88-72249. (Fifty-Minute Ser.). (Illus.). 63p. (Orig.). 1989. pap. 10.95 (*0-931961-60-2*) Crisp Pubns.

Telemarketing Buyers Guide, 1991, Vol. 9. Ed. by Technology Marketing Corporation Staff. 1990. pap. text ed. 20.00 (*0-685-51898-1*) Tech Marketing.

Telemarketing Course & Workbook. Arnold A. DeLuca. (Illus.). 138p. 1985. pap. 34.50 (*1-878666-09-6*) Dynamo Inc.

Telemarketing Encyclopedia: Word Mapping Edition with Script Presentations. rev. ed. 1991. ring bd. 79.95 (*0-939476-79-7*, Biblio Pr) Prosperity & Profits.

Telemarketing Essentials for the Executive: What You Need to Know Before You Start a Telemarketing Call Center. Clarence R. Smith. Ed. by Telemarketing Magazine Editorial Staff. (Illus.). 40p. (Orig.). 1993. pap. 9.95 (*0-936840-11-0*) Tech Marketing.

Telemarketing Factomatic. Peggy M. Fielding & Gary Drummond. 528p. 1991. ring bd. 59.95 (*0-13-921990-0*, 150201) P-H.

Telemarketing for Business: A Guide to Building Your Own Telemarketing Operation. Eugene B. Kordahl. LC 83-19064. 324p. ring bd. 79.95 (*0-13-902313-5*, Busn) P-H.

***Telemarketing for Non-Telemarketers.** Gary Goodman. (Illus.). 200p. 1997. pap. 16.95 (*0-85013-298-3*) Dartnell Corp.

Telemarketing in Action: A Handbook of Marketing & Sales Applications. Michael Stevens. LC 95-7968. 1995. 24.95 (*0-07-707863-2*) McGraw.

Telemarketing Skills Training Manual. Sandra Ambrose & Daniel Hellmuth. 384p. 1990. spiral bd. 59.95 (*0-13-902677-0*) P-H.

Telemarketing Tactics: Techniques that Work in the Real World. Michael Stevens. (Pitman Marketing Ser.). (Illus.). 320p. 1995. pap. 19.95 (*0-273-61688-9*) Pitman Publng.

Telemarketing, Telephone Sales & Telephone Soliciting wth Telemarketing Script Presentations. rev. ed. 1991. ring bd. 29.95 (*0-911569-04-9*) Prosperity & Profits.

***Telemarketing, Telephone Soliciting & Telephone Sales: At Home Opportunities.** 1991. 31.95 (*1-890928-21-6*) F Carrol.

Telemarketing's One Hundred Do's & Dont's. Telemarketing Magazine Staff. 160p. 1986. 20.00 (*0-936840-09-9*) Tech Marketing.

Telematic Society: A Challenge for Tomorrow. James Martin. (Illus.). 256p. (C). 1981. 35.95 (*0-13-902460-3*) P-H.

Telematics: Communication Networks & Office Systems. Joe Ettinger. (C). 1989. pap. text ed. write for info. (*0-201-18044-8*) Addison-Wesley.

Telematics: Transportation & Spatial Development. Ed. by Hans M. Soekkha et al. 354p. 1990. 137.50 (*90-6764-125-1*, Pub. by VSP NE) Coronet Bks.

Telematics & Government. Dan Schiller. LC 82-1795. (Communication & Information Science Ser.). 256p. 1982. text ed. 73.25 (*0-89391-106-2*) Ablex Pub.

Telematics & Government. Daniel Schiller. LC 82-1795. (Communication & Information Science Ser.). 256p. 1982. pap. 24.95 (*0-89391-129-1*) Ablex Pub.

Telematics & Transport Behaviour. Peter Nijkamp et al. LC 96-14883. (Advances in Spatial Science Ser.). 227p. 1996. 99.00 (*3-540-60919-9*) Spr-Verlag.

Telematics for Education & Training. Held & Kugemann. LC 95-79592. (gr. 12). 1995. 102.00 (*90-5199-223-8*) IOS Press.

Telematics for Flexible & Distance Learning (DELTA) Final Report. (Illus.). 90p. (Orig.). (C). 1995. pap. text ed. 40.00 (*0-7881-2454-4*) DIANE Pub.

Telematics for Health: The Role of Telehealth & Telemedicine in Homes & Communities. Eroc Verbprgj. LC 94-38840. 1995. pap. 32.95 (*1-85775-023-3*, Radcliffe Med Pr) Scovill Paterson.

Telematics for Health, Global Information Society & D-Count. M. Sosa. LC 95-76268. (Studies in Health Technology & Informatics). 487p. (gr. 12). 1995. 92.00 (*90-5199-226-2*) IOS Press.

Telematics in Goods Transport: ECMT Round Table 78. OECD Staff. 115p. (Orig.). 1989. pap. 17.00 (*92-821-1140-7*) OECD.

Telematics in Medicine. J. S. Duisterhout et al. 1991. 152.50 (*0-444-89015-7*) Elsevier.

Telematics in Primary Care. J. DeMaeseneer & L. Beolchi. LC 94-73421. (Studies in Health Technology & Informatics: Vol. 20). 250p. (gr. 12). 1995. 70.00 (*90-5199-209-2*) IOS Press.

Telemedicine: A Guide to Assessing Telecommunications for Health Care. Institute of Medicine Staff. Ed. by Marilyn J. Field. 288p. (C). 1996. text ed. 39.95 (*0-309-05531-8*) Natl Acad Pr.

Telemedicine: Past, Present, Future: Bibliography. January 1966 Through March 1995. 123p. (Orig.). (C). 1995. pap. text ed. 30.00 (*0-7881-2019-0*) DIANE Pub.

***Telemedicine: Theory & Practice.** Ed. by Rashid L. Bashshur et al. LC 96-36746. (Illus.). 454p. 1996. text ed. 89.95 (*0-398-06731-7*); pap. text ed. 69.95 (*0-398-06732-5*) C C Thomas.

Telemedicine: What the Future Holds When You're Ill. Maryann Karinch. LC 94-66757. 288p. 1994. 23.95 (*0-88282-130-X*); pap. 13.95 (*0-88282-131-8*) New Horizon NJ.

***Telemedicine Primer: Understanding the Issues.** Jim Reid. LC 96-94441. xi, 294p. (Orig.). 1996. spiral bd. 75.00 (*0-9653045-0-7*) Innvtve Med.

***Telemedicine Sourcebook 1998.** Ed. by Gwendolyn Segre. 496p. (Orig.). 1997. pap. text ed. 265.00 (*1-57987-002-3*) Faulkner & Gray.

Telemetric Studies of Vertebrates. Ed. by C. L. Cheeseman & R. B. Mitson. (Symposia of the Zoological Society of London Ser.: No. 49). 1982. text ed. 164.00 (*0-12-613349-2*) Acad Pr.

Telemetric Systems Specialist. Jack Rudman. (Career Examination Ser.: C-1940). 1994. pap. 34.95 (*0-8373-1940-4*) Nat Learn.

Telemetry System Architecture. 3rd ed. O. J. Strock & E. M. Rueger. LC 95-47371. 1995. 68.00 (*1-55617-537-X*) ISA.

Telemetry Systems Design. Frank Carden. LC 95-19077. 256p. 1995. 79.00 (*0-89006-800-3*) Artech Hse.

Teleny. 1992. mass mkt. 4.95 (*1-56333-020-2*, Badboy) Masquerade.

Teleny: Novel Attributed to Oscar Wilde. Intro. by Winston Leyland. 184p. 1984. reprint ed. pap. 7.95 (*0-917342-33-X*); reprint ed. lib. bdg. 25.00 (*0-917342-32-1*) Gay Sunshine.

***Teleological Language in the Life Sciences.** Lowell Nissen. LC 97-7424. 192p. 1997. 52.50 (*0-8476-8693-0*) Rowman.

***Teleological Language in the Life Sciences.** Lowell Nissen. LC 97-7424. 192p. 1997. pap. 21.95 (*0-8476-8694-9*) Rowman.

***Teleologie und die Krisis der Principien.** Martin Zubiria. (Philosophische Texte und Studien: Vol. 39). ix, 234p. (GER.). 1995. write for info. (*3-487-10040-1*) G Olms Pubs.

Teleologies in Husserlian Phenomenology. Ed. by Anna-Teresa Tymieniecka. (Analecta Husserliana Ser.: No. IX). 501p. 1979. lib. bdg. 117.50 (*90-277-0981-5*, D Reidel) Kluwer Ac.

Teleology Revisited & Other Essays in the Philosophy & History of Science. Ernest Nagel. LC 78-1437. 368p. 1982. pap. text ed. 19.50 (*0-231-04505-0*) Col U Pr.

Teleoperated Robotics in Hostile Environments. Society of Manufacturing Engineers Staff. Ed. by Martin D. Kuban. 230p. 1985. 42.00 (*0-87263-185-0*) SME.

Teleoperation: Numerical Simulation & Experimental Validation. Ed. by Marc C. Becquet. (C). 1992. lib. bdg. 126.00 (*0-7923-1584-7*) Kluwer Ac.

Telepathic Impressions: A Review & Report of Thirty-Five New Cases. Ian Stevenson. LC 73-135114. 218p. reprint ed. pap. 62.20 (*0-8357-3480-3*, 2039739) Bks Demand.

Telepaths Don't Need Safewords: And Other Stories. Cecilia Tan. 49p. 1992. pap. 2.95 (*0-9633970-0-1*) Circlet Pr.

Telepathy. 10p. 1993. reprint ed. spiral bd. 3.00 (*0-7873-0947-8*) Hlth Research.

Telepathy. Sidney A. Weltmer. 82p. 1959. reprint ed. spiral bd. 8.50 (*0-7873-0036-5*) Hlth Research.

Telepathy: Its Theory, Facts, & Proof (1910) William W. Atkinson. 94p. 1996. pap. 14.95 (*1-56459-732-6*) Kessinger Pub.

Telepathy: What It Is & How It Is Done. R. Dimsdale Stocker. 24p. 1960. reprint ed. spiral bd. 4.50 (*0-7873-0847-1*) Hlth Research.

Telepathy & the Etheric Vehicle. Alice A. Bailey. LC 50-11465. 1950. 21.00 (*0-85330-016-X*) Lucis.

Telepathy & the Etheric Vehicle. Alice A. Bailey. LC 50-11465. 1971. pap. 11.00 (*0-85330-116-6*) Lucis.

Telepathy, Its Theory, Facts & Proof. William W. Atkinson. 94p. 1993. reprint ed. spiral bd. 5.50 (*0-7873-0053-5*) Hlth Research.

Telephone. (Illus.). (ARA.). (J). (gr. 5-12). 1987. 4.50 (*0-86685-236-0*) Intl Bk Ctr.

Telephone. Chukovsky. 1977. 11.25 (*0-440-08532-2*) Delacorte.

Telephone. Kornei Chukovsky. Tr. & Adapted by Jamey Gambrell. LC 96-18718. (Illus.). (J). Date not set. lib. bdg. 15.88 (*1-55858-481-1*) North-South Bks NYC.

Telephone. Kornei Chukovsky. Tr. & Adapted by Jamey Gambrell. LC 96-18718. (Illus.). (J). (gr. k-3). Date not set. 15.95 (*1-55858-480-3*) North-South Bks NYC.

Telephone. Amy Stone. (Inventors & Inventions Ser.). 64p. (J). (gr. 4-7). 1995. lib. bdg. 17.95 (*0-7614-0065-6*, Benchmark NY) Marshall Cavendish.

Telephone. Harris Winitz. (All about Language Ser.). (Illus.). 50p. (Orig.). (YA). (gr. 7 up). 1987. pap. text ed. 22.00 incl. audio (*0-939990-50-4*) Intl Linguistics.

Telephone: An Historical Anthology. Ed. by Christopher H. Sterling & George Shiers. LC 75-23899. (Historical Studies in Telecommunications). (Illus.). 1979. reprint ed. 59.95 (*0-405-07758-0*) Ayer.

Telephone: Techniques & Technology. Bonnie R. White. 1994. pap. 15.95 (*0-538-60528-6*) S-W Pub.

Telephone: Uses & Abuses. Moira D. Reynolds & Gina Strazzabosco. LC 93-25717. (Lifeskills Library). (Illus.). 48p. (YA). (gr. 7-12). 1993. lib. bdg. 14.95 (*0-8239-1608-1*) Rosen Group.

Telephone Ability Battery (TAB) Jack Rudman. (Career Examination Ser.: C-3371). 1994. pap. 23.95 (*0-8373-3371-7*) Nat Learn.

***Telephone Address Books.** Platinum Press Staff. 128p. 1996. 5.95 (*1-879582-24-4*) Platinum Pr.

Telephone & Its Several Inventors: A History. Lewis Coe. LC 95-13651. (Illus.). 240p. 1995. lib. bdg. 28.50 (*0-7864-0138-9*) McFarland & Co.

Telephone & Peripheral Systems for Law Firms. ALA Staff. 112p. 1993. per. 75.00 (*0-8403-8582-X*) Kendall-Hunt.

Telephone & Reception Skills. Stanley Thornes. (C). 1985. 50.00 (*0-85950-223-6*, Pub. by S Thornes Pubs UK) St Mut.

Telephone & Telephone Exchanges: Their Invention & Development. John E. Kingsbury. LC 72-5057. (Technology & Society Ser.). (Illus.). 580p. 1978. reprint ed. 44.95 (*0-405-04709-6*) Ayer.

Telephone & Time Management: Making It a Tool & Not a Tyrant. Dru Scott. Ed. by Michael G. Crisp. LC 88-70489. (Fifty-Minute Ser.). (Illus.). 71p. (Orig.). 1988. pap. 10.95 (*0-931961-53-X*) Crisp Pubns.

***Telephone Answering As a Home Business.** rev. ed. 1991. 25.95 (*1-890928-22-4*) F Carrol.

Telephone Applications of Fiber Optics. rev. ed. IGIC, Inc. Staff. (Fiber Optics Reprint Ser.: Vol. 16). (Illus.). 277p. 1994. pap. 75.00 (*1-56851-065-9*) Info Gatekeepers.

Telephone Between Worlds. James Crenshaw. 233p. 1996. reprint ed. pap. 12.95 (*0-87516-692-X*) DeVorss.

Telephone Book. Ed Friedman. Ed. by Maureen Owen & Barbara Barg. LC 79-12379. (Illus.). (Orig.). 1979. pap. 6.00 (*0-916382-20-6*) Telephone Bks.

Telephone Book: Technology, Schizophrenia, Electric Speech. Avital Ronell. LC 88-27960. (Illus.). xviii, 466p. 1989. text ed. 50.00 (*0-8032-3876-2*); pap. text ed. 27.50 (*0-8032-8938-3*, Bison Books) U of Nebr Pr.

Telephone Bypass. Business Communications Co., Inc. Staff. 126p. 1989. pap. 1,750.00 (*0-89336-520-3*, G-097) BCC.

Telephone Cable Maintainer. Jack Rudman. (Career Examination Ser.: C-830). 1994. pap. 23.95 (*0-8373-0830-5*) Nat Learn.

Telephone Collecting: Seven Decades of Design. Kate E. Dooner. LC 92-63107. (Illus.). 128p. (Orig.). 1993. pap. 24.95 (*0-88740-489-8*) Schiffer.

Telephone Collection Guide. rev. ed. 1989. pap. text ed. 7.95 (*0-88711-019-3*) Am Trucking Assns.

Telephone Collector's Fly-up Answers: What to Do & Say No Matter What Excuse They Offer, 4 vols. Jane K. Cleland. 80p. 1989. Set. 118.00 (*1-877680-00-1*) Tiger Pr.

Telephone Communication in the Information Age. Roberta Mantus & Roberta Moore. LC 95-37276. 168p. 1996. 20.95 (*0-538-71514-6*) S-W Pub.

Telephone Communications. Moore. (General Business & Business Education Ser.). 1995. teacher ed. 10.00 (*0-8273-6359-1*); pap. 18.60 (*0-8273-6358-3*) Delmar.

Telephone Companies in Paradise: A Case Study in Telecommunications Deregulation. Milton L. Mueller. 250p. (C). 1993. text ed. 44.95 (*1-56000-103-8*) Transaction Pubs.

Telephone Company & Cable Television Competition. Stuart N. Brotman. (Telecommunications Library). (Illus.). 532p. 1990. pap. write for info. (*0-89006-461-X*) Artech Hse.

Telephone Company Repairman Poems. Barbara Moraff. LC 82-19275. (Illus.). 17p. (Orig.). 1983. pap. 15.00 (*0-915124-75-0*, Toothpaste) Coffee Hse.

Telephone Company Test. Margaret Ehrlich. 160p. 1991. pap. 12.95 (*0-13-904244-X*, Arco) Macmillan Gen Ref.

Telephone Connection. Rebecca Smith. 1981. pap. 1.75 (*0-686-37154-2*) Eldridge Pub.

Telephone Conversation. Robert Hopper. LC 91-34116. (Illus.). 264p. 1992. 21.50 (*0-253-32846-2*); pap. 8.95 (*0-253-20724-X*, MB-724) Ind U Pr.

*__Telephone Cordage & Cord Sets.__ 30.00 (*0-614-18720-6*, S-88-626-1993) Insulated Cable.

*__Telephone Counseling Desk Guide: Solution Focused Telephone Counseling Guide.__ 2nd rev. ed. Fred E. Waddell. 28p. 1995. spiral bd. 19.95 (*0-9615923-8-9*) Genesis Finan Srvs.

Telephone Courtesy & Customer Service. 2nd rev. ed. Lloyd Finch. Ed. by Michael G. Crisp. LC 90-82869. (Fifty-Minute Ser.). (Illus.). 68p. 1990. pap. 10.95 (*1-56052-064-7*) Crisp Pubns.

Telephone Eavesdropping & Detection. Charles L. Taylor & Richard J. Udovich. Ed. & Illus. by Terry R. Cross. 500p. (C). 1989. 189.00 (*0-9625466-0-7*) Taylor Hill Pub Co.

*__Telephone Enterprise: The Evolution of the Bell System's Horizontal Structure, 1876-1909.__ Robert W. Garnet. LC 84-43080. (Johns Hopkins AT&T Series in Telephone History). 238p. 1985. reprint ed. pap. 67.90 (*0-608-03730-3*, 2064555) Bks Demand.

Telephone Fund Raising. Jonathan A. Segal & Janet B. Allen. (Nonprofit Management & Finance Ser.). 210p. 1986. 42.50 (*0-306-42340-5*, Plenum Pr) Plenum.

Telephone Health Assessment: Documentation Tablet. Sandra M. Simonsen. 000001p. (C). (gr. 13). 1995. 4.95 (*0-8151-8532-4*) Mosby Yr Bk.

Telephone Health Assessment: Guidelines for Practice. Sandra M. Simonsen. LC 95-9442. 56p. (C). (gr. 13). 1995. 32.95 (*0-8151-8024-1*) Mosby Yr Bk.

T

Telephone Inspector. Jack Rudman. (Career Examination Ser.: C-3599). 1994. pap. 27.95 (*0-8373-3599-X*) Nat Learn.

Telephone Lines & Offices Converted to Equal Access. 53p. (Orig.). (C). 1994. pap. text ed. 30.00 (*0-7881-1420-4*) DIANE Pub.

Telephone Maintainer. Jack Rudman. (Career Examination Ser.: C-807). 1994. pap. 23.95 (*0-8373-0807-0*) Nat Learn.

Telephone Maintenance: The Barter Way - Possibilities Workbook. rev. ed. 60p. 1992. ring bd. 28.95 (*0-911617-53-1*) Prosperity & Profits.

Telephone Marketing Techniques. Murray Roman. LC 78-32000. (AMA Management Briefing Ser.). 34p. reprint ed. pap. 25.00 (*0-317-09567-6*, 2051565) Bks Demand.

Telephone Mastery: Skills for Business Productivity. Mary Pekas. (C). 1990. teacher ed. 8.00 (*1-56118-020-3*) Paradigm MN.

Telephone Medicine: Triage & Training - A Handbook for Primary Care Health Professionals. Katz. (Illus.). 222p. (C). 1990. spiral bd. 27.95 (*0-8036-5228-3*) Davis Co.

Telephone Murders. large type ed. James A. Pattinson. (Linford Mystery Library). 336p. 1996. pap. 15.99 (*0-7089-7875-4*, Linford) Ulverscroft.

Telephone Nursing: The Process. Sandra Matherly & Shannon Hodges. Ed. by Janice Pramik. 132p. (Orig.). (C). 1990. pap. text ed. 44.00 (*0-933948-23-9*, 2550) Ctr Res Ambulatory.

Telephone Operator. Jack Rudman. (Career Examination Ser.: C-806). 1994. pap. 19.95 (*0-8373-0806-2*) Nat Learn.

Telephone Phrase Practice for Business: Basic Phone Answering. Gary S. Green. LC 93-31196. 1993. pap. text ed. 14.40 (*0-13-083080-1*) P-H.

Telephone Poles & Other Poems. John Updike. 1963. 19.95 (*0-394-40457-2*) Knopf.

*__Telephone Power!__ Lloyd C. Finch. 1996. pap. 24.95 incl. audio (*1-56052-404-9*) Crisp Pubns.

*__Telephone Power!__ Lloyd C. Finch. 1996. pap. 149.00 incl. audio, vhs (*1-56052-406-5*) Crisp Pubns.

Telephone Repair & Operations - A Locating Services Workbook. rev. ed. Data Notes Publishing Staff. LC 83-90725. 25p. 1996. ring bd. 29.95 (*0-911569-64-2*) Prosperity & Profits.

Telephone Repair Illustrated. Stephen J. Bigelow. LC 92-32381. 1993. write for info. (*0-8306-4033-9*); pap. 17.95 (*0-8306-4034-7*) McGraw-Hill Prof.

Telephone Repair Illustrated. Stephen J. Bigelow. 1993. text ed. 27.95 (*0-07-005238-7*) McGraw-Hill Prof.

Telephone Repair Illustrated. Stephen J. Bigelow. 1993. pap. text ed. 18.95 (*0-07-005239-5*) McGraw-Hill Prof.

Telephone Repair Service & Recycling Possibilities: A How to Find or Locate Workbook. rev. ed. Center for Self-Sufficiency, Research Division Staff. 1996. ring bd. 24.95 (*0-910811-40-7*) Ctr Self Suff.

Telephone Sales Management & Motivation Made Easy: With 50 Sales Contests You Can Use Immediately! Valerie Sloane & Theresa A. Jackson. LC 95-83888. 161p. (Orig.). 1996. pap. 19.95 (*1-881081-04-4*, TMEZ) Busn By Phone.

Telephone Service Quality Handbook. 180p. 1992. 30.00 (*0-317-04711-6*) NARUC.

Telephone Services Directory. Ed. by Marilyn Stern et al. 248p. 1983. 170.00 (*0-8103-1542-4*) Gale.

Telephone Services Supervisor. Jack Rudman. (Career Examination Ser.: C-2586). 1994. pap. 27.95 (*0-8373-2586-2*) Nat Learn.

Telephone Set Circuits. James B. Eppes. (ABC Pocket Guide for the Field Ser.). (Illus.). 29p. 1981. pap. 6.95 (*1-56016-032-2*) ABC TeleTraining.

Telephone Skills. Leebov. (gr. 13). 1995. 5.95 (*0-8151-5316-3*) Mosby Yr Bk.

Telephone Skills from A to Z: The Telephone "Doctor" Phone Book. Nancy J. Friedman. Ed. by Carol Henry. LC 94-68081. (Fifty-Minute Ser.). (Illus.). 106p. (Orig.). 1994. pap. 10.95 (*1-56052-301-8*) Crisp Pubns.

Telephone Strategies: A Technical & Practical Guide for Hard-of-Hearing People. Diane L. Castle. (Illus.). 55p. 1988. 6.50 (*0-935473-04-1*) SHHH.

Telephone Survey Methodology. Robert M. Groves et al. LC 88-20559. 581p. 1988. text ed. 99.95 (*0-471-62218-4*) Wiley.

Telephone Survey Methods: Sampling, Selection & Supervision. 2nd ed. Paul J. Lavrakas. (Applied Social Research Methods Ser.). (Illus.). 160p. 1993. 39.95 (*0-8039-5306-2*); pap. 17.95 (*0-8039-5307-0*) Sage.

Telephone Systems of the Continent of Europe, 1895, 2 Vols. A. R. Bennett. LC 74-4666. (Telecommunications Ser.). 395p. 1974. reprint ed. 40.95 (*0-405-06033-5*) Ayer.

Telephone Tag. Sherry Shahan. 112p. (J). (gr. 3-7). 1996. mass mkt. 3.50 (*0-553-48305-6*, Skylark BDD) BDD Bks Young Read.

Telephone Tag. Sherry Shahan. (J). 1996. pap. 3.50 (*0-440-41304-4*) BDD Bks Young Read.

Telephone Techniques. Dorothy A. Neal. 1989. pap. 8.70 (*0-07-046156-2*) McGraw.

Telephone Terrific! Facts, Fun & One Hundred Three How-to Tips for Phone Success. David Dee. 172p. 1994. pap. 10.95 (*0-85013-226-6*) Dartnell Corp.

Telephone, the Microphone, & the Phonograph. Theodore A. Du Moncel. LC 74-4673. (Telecommunications Ser.). (Illus.). 282p. 1974. reprint ed. 25.95 (*0-405-06039-4*) Ayer.

Telephone, the Or l'Amour a 'Trois Vocal Score. Gian-Carlo Menotti. 56p. (ENG & FRE.). 1986. pap. 11.95 (*0-7935-5370-9*, 50337660) H Leonard.

Telephone Theory, Principles & Practice. rev. ed. Frank E. Lee. LC 73-85629. (ABC of the Telephone Ser.: Vol. 1). (Illus.). 148p. (C). 1988. pap. text ed. 16.95 (*1-56016-000-4*) ABC TeleTraining.

Telephone Time: A First Book of Telephone Do's & Don'ts. Ellen Weiss. LC 86-42560. (Pictureback Ser.). (Illus.). 32p. (J). (gr. k-3). 1986. lib. bdg. 5.99 (*0-394-98252-5*) Random Bks Yng Read.

Telephone Tips That Sell! 501 How-To Ideas & Affirmations to Help You Get More Business by Phone. Art Sobczak. LC 95-83972. 165p. (Orig.). 1996. pap. 14.95 (*1-881081-05-2*, 501B) Busn By Phone.

Telephone Tongues: A "Rap" Around the World. Shelby Tayler. LC 94-77488. (Illus.). 112p. (Orig.). 1995. pap. 6.95 (*0-9640783-7-6*) Hands on Books.

Telephone Triage: Theory, Practice, & Protocol Development. Sheila Q. Wheeler & Judith H. Windt. LC 92-18437. 1993. text ed. 32.50 (*0-8273-4991-2*) Delmar.

Telephone Triage & Advice Protocol Manual. Lomax. 1996. 163.00 (*0-8342-0779-6*) Aspen Pub.

Telephone Triage & Management: A Nursing Process Approach. Reba McGear & Jo P. Simms. (Illus.). 174p. 1988. Book & Tape. 49.00 (*0-7216-2406-5*) Saunders.

Telephone Triage Card Deck. Shea & Carter-Ward. 150p. 1995. 25.95 (*0-8273-6719-8*) Delmar.

Telephone Triage Card Deck. Shea. (C). 1994. teacher ed., pap. text ed. 14.00 (*0-8273-7171-3*) Delmar.

Telephone Triage for the Family Practice Physician's Office. Upper Valley Family Care Staff. 93p. 1993. ring bd. 94.95 (*0-9653057-0-8*, 87443) Upper Valley Fmly.

Telephone Triage for the Family Practice Physician's Office. 2nd rev. ed. Upper Valley Family Care Staff. 102p. 1993. ring bd. 94.95 (*0-9653057-1-6*) Upper Valley Fmly.

*__Telephone Triage Protocols for Adults 18 Years & Older.__ Sheila Q. Wheeler. LC 97-25103. (Telephone Triage Protocols for Pediatric & Adult Populations Ser.). 1997. write for info. (*0-8342-0980-2*) Aspen Pub.

*__Telephone Triage Protocols for Infants & Children: Birth to 6 Years.__ Sheila Q. Wheeler. LC 97-4387. (Telephone Triage Protocols for Pediatric & Adult Populations Ser.). 1997. write for info. (*0-8342-0982-9*) Aspen Pub.

Telephone Triage Protocols for Nurses. Julie Briggs. LC 96-39097. 416p. 1997. spiral bd. 36.95 (*0-397-55410-9*, Lippnctt) Lppncott-Raven.

Telephone Triage Protocols for Primary Care Centers. 2nd ed. Dale Woodke. Ed. by Jane A. Miller. (Quality Primary Care Ser.). 1994. pap. text ed. 96.00 (*1-884742-02-5*) Clarian Hlth.

*__Telephone Triage Protocols for School-Age Children, 6 to 18 Years.__ Sheila Q. Wheeler. LC 97-25102. (Telephone Triage Protocols for Pediatric & Adult Populations Ser.). 1997. write for info. (*0-8342-0981-0*) Aspen Pub.

Telephone Voice Transmission Standards & Measurement. Winston Gaylor. 240p. 1989. text ed. 30.00 (*0-13-902776-9*) P-H.

Telephones: Antique to Modern. Kate Dooner. LC 91-67008. (Illus.). 176p. 1992. pap. 29.95 (*0-88740-386-7*) Schiffer.

Telephones & Answering Machines. Gene B. Williams. 1993. pap. text ed. 9.95 (*0-07-070592-5*) McGraw.

Telephones Are Better Than Men Because: Or Whatever Women Would Say If They Dared. Karen Rostoker-Gruber. (Illus.). 80p. 1996. pap. 5.95 (*1-56352-343-4*) Longstreet Pr Inc.

Telephones, Televisions, & Toilets: How They Work - What Can Go Wrong. Melvin Berger & Gilda Berger. LC 92-18198. (Discovery Readers Ser.). (Illus.). 48p. (J). (gr. k-4). 1993. per., pap. 4.50 (*0-8249-8608-3*, Ideals Child); lib. bdg. 12.00 (*0-8249-8645-8*, Ideals Child) Hambleton-Hill.

Telephones, Words over Wires. Marcus Webb. LC 92-11400. (Encyclopedia of Discovery & Invention Ser.). (Illus.). 96p. (J). (gr. 5-8). 1992. lib. bdg. 18.96 (*1-56006-219-3*) Lucent Bks.

TelephonesTwo. 2nd ed. (ABC Pocket Guide for the Field Ser.). 92p. (C). 1987. pap. text ed. 6.95 (*1-56016-031-4*) ABC TeleTraining.

Telephoning in English. B. J. Naterop & R. Revel. 1987. Cassette. pap. 32.95 (*0-521-26429-4*); pap. text ed. 13.95 (*0-521-26975-X*) Cambridge U Pr.

Telephony: Today & Tomorrow. Dimitris N. Chorafas. (Illus.). 272p. 1984. 33.95 (*0-13-902700-9*) P-H.

Telephony for Computer Professionals. Jane Laino. write for info. (*0-936648-49-X*) Flatiron Pubng.

Telephony for Network Mechanics. Michael D. Odell. 1996. pap. 26.95 (*0-201-65620-5*) Addison-Wesley.

Telephony for Network Mechanics. Mike O'Dell. (C). 1997. pap. text ed. write for info. (*0-201-85620-4*) Addison-Wesley.

*__Telephoto Lens Photography.__ Rob Sheppard. 1997. pap. text ed. 17.95 (*0-936262-53-2*) Amherst Media.

Telepledge: The Complete Guide to Mail-Phone Fund Raising. Louis A. Schultz. 203p. 1986. write for info. (*0-914756-03-6*, 600003) Taft Group.

Teleportation! A Practical Guide for the Metaphysical Traveler. Jessica Severn. LC 95-38954. (Illus.). 1996. pap. 14.95 (*1-884695-42-6*) Wrds of Wizdom.

*__Teleportation! Journal: Recording Your Visits to Magical Destinies.__ Gwen Totterdale & Jessica Severn. Ed. by Leslie Weld. (Illus.). 177p. (Orig.). 1996. pap. 14.95 (*1-884695-35-3*) Wrds of Wizdom.

Telepower, Planning & Society: Crisis in Communication. Melville C. Branch. LC 94-15882. 216p. 1994. text ed. 55.00 (*0-275-94599-5*, Praeger Pubs) Greenwood.

Teleprocessing Network Organization. James Martin. 1969. 38.00 (*0-13-902452-2*) P-H.

Teleprospecting: Warming up the Cold Call to Increase Your Income. Lou E. Davis. 1992. 21.95 (*0-13-140252-8*) P-H.

Telepsychics: The Magic Power of Perfect Living. Joseph Murphy. LC 73-6775. 230p. 1988. reprint ed. pap. 11.00 (*0-87516-598-2*) DeVorss.

Telerobotics, Automation, & Human Supervisory Control. Thomas B. Sheridan. (Illus.). 416p. 1992. 47.50 (*0-262-19316-7*) MIT Pr.

Telesales Script Presentations Directory. Data Notes Publishing Staff. 100p. (Orig.). (C). 1991. ring bd. 59.95 (*0-911569-91-X*) Prosperity & Profits.

Telescience: Scientific Communication in the Information Age. Ed. by Murray Aborn. (Annals Ser.: Vol. 495). 1988. 26.00 (*0-8039-2937-4*); pap. 17.00 (*0-8039-2938-2*) Sage.

Telescope. Carter. (J). 1996. 15.00 (*0-671-87310-5*, S&S Bks Young Read) S&S Childrens.

Telescope & Techniques: An Introduction to Practical Astronomy. Chris Kitchin. (Practical Astronomy Ser.). 216p. 1995. 24.95 (*0-387-19898-9*) Spr-Verlag.

Telescope Making for Beginners. Roy Worvill. 79p. 1984. 70.00 (*0-900707-80-1*) St Mut.

Telescope Making (1905) Paul N. Hasluck. (Illus.). 160p. 1983. pap. 15.00 (*0-87556-498-4*) Saifer.

Telescope Optics - Evaluation & Design. Rutten & Van Venrooij. 1988. 24.95 (*0-943396-18-2*) Willmann-Bell.

Telescope Power: Fantastic Activities & Easy Projects for Young Astronomers. Gregory L. Matloff. LC 92-39602. 128p. (Orig.). 1993. pap. text ed. 12.95 (*0-471-58039-2*) Wiley.

Telescopes: Searching the Heavens. Deborah Hitzeroth. LC 91-16711. (Encyclopedia of Discovery & Invention Ser.). (Illus.). 96p. (J). (gr. 5-8). 1991. lib. bdg. 18.96 (*1-56006-209-6*) Lucent Bks.

Telescopes Level 8: HBJ Reading 1987. Early. (J). 1987. student ed., pap. 32.50 (*0-15-330509-6*) HB Schl Dept.

Telescopes & Techniques: An Introduction to Practical Astronomy. Christopher R. Kitchin. LC 95-10169. 1997. 24.95 (*3-540-19898-9*) Spr-Verlag.

Telescopes, Tides, & Tactics: A Galilean Dialogue about the "Starry Messenger" & Systems of the World. Stillman Drake. LC 82-24790. 256p. 1983. 27.00 (*0-226-16231-1*) U Ch Pr.

Telescreen & Radiographic Examination of the Urinary Transport. E. Hajos. 116p. (C). 1978. 40.00 (*963-05-1507-5*, Pub. by Akad Kiado HU) St Mut.

Telesearch: Direct Dial to the Best Job of Your Life. John Truitt. LC 82-15714. (Illus.). 134p. reprint ed. pap. 38.20 (*0-8357-5602-5*, 2035244) Bks Demand.

Teleselling: A Self-Teaching Guide. 2nd rev. ed. James D. Poterfield. LC 95-38849. Orig. Title: Selling on the Phone. 176p. 1996. pap. text ed. 16.95 (*0-471-11567-3*) Wiley.

TeleSelling: High Performance Business-to-Business Phone. Phillip E. Mahfood. 225p. 1993. reprint ed. per. 16.95 (*1-55738-500-9*) Irwin Prof Pubng.

*__Teleselling Techniques That Close the Sale.__ Flyn L. Penoyer. LC 97-5372. 192p. (Orig.). 1997. pap. 19.95 (*0-8144-7939-1*) AMACOM.

Teleservices & Multimedia Communications: Second International COST 237 Workshop, Copenhagen, Denmark, November, 1995 Proceedings. Ed. by D. Hutchison et al. LC 96-14775. (Lecture Notes in Computer Science Ser.: Vol. 1052). 277p. 1996. pap. 49.00 (*3-540-61028-6*) Spr-Verlag.

Telesthesia. Frances Dyson & Douglas Kahn. (Illus.). 24p. (Orig.). 1991. pap. 5.00 (*0-930495-12-8*) San Fran Art Inst.

Teleteaching: Proceedings of the IFIP TC3 Third Teleteaching Conference. Ed. by Gordon Davies & Brian Samways. LC 93-8819. (IFIP Transactions Ser.: Vol 29). 960p. 1993. pap. 204.50 (*0-444-81585-6*, North Holland) Elsevier.

Teletechniques: An Instructional Model for Interactive Teleconferencing. Lorne A. Parker & Mavis K. Monson. Ed. by Danny G. Langdon. LC 79-24442. (Instructional Design Library). 108p. 1980. 27.95 (*0-87778-158-3*) Educ Tech Pubns.

Teletexte. Ciccione & Meyer. 1992. 14.95 (*0-8384-3667-6*) Heinle & Heinle.

Teletexte. Ciccione & Meyer. 1992. pap. 39.95 (*0-8384-3666-8*) Heinle & Heinle.

Teletexte. Ciccione. (College French Ser.). 1992. teacher ed., pap. 21.95 (*0-8384-3884-9*) Heinle & Heinle.

Teletexte. Ciccione. (College French Ser.). 1992. suppl. ed., pap. 6.95 (*0-8384-3672-2*) Heinle & Heinle.

Teletexte. Ciccione & Meyer. 1992. student ed., pap. 33.95 (*0-8384-3669-2*) Heinle & Heinle.

Teletheory: Grammatology in the Age of Video. Gregory L. Luper. 256p. 1989. 45.00 (*0-415-90120-0*, A3232, Routledge NY); pap. 14.95 (*0-415-90121-9*, A3236, Routledge NY) Routledge.

*__Teletherapy: Present & Future.__ Raul Urtasun et al. 817p. 1996. text ed. 90.00 (*1-888340-03-7*) AAPM.

Teletraffic: Theory & Applications. Haruo Akimaru & Konosuke Kawashima. LC 92-21122. (Telecommunications Networks & Computer Systems Ser.). 1993. 78.95 (*0-387-19805-9*) Spr-Verlag.

Teletraffic & Data Traffic in a Period of Change: Proc. of the 13th Congress, Copenhagen, Denmark, 19-26 June, 1991. Ed. by A. A. Jensen & Villy B. Iversen. (Studies in Telecommunication: Vol. 14). 1034p. 1991. 301.25 (*0-444-88666-4*, North Holland) Elsevier.

Teletraffic & Datatraffic: Socio-Economic Aspects: ITC-13: International Teletraffic Congress, 13th, Copenhagen, Denmark, 1991. LC 92-3009. (North-Holland Studies in Telecommunication: Vol. 17). 540p. 1992. 187.50 (*0-444-89389-X*, TK5101, North Holland) Elsevier.

Teletraffic Concepts in Corporate Communications. Robert W. Lawson. (Traffic Ser.). (Illus.). 220p. 1989. pap. 39.95 (*1-56016-042-X*) ABC TeleTraining.

*__Teletraffic Contributions for the Information Age: Proceedings of the 15th International Teletraffic Congress-ITC-15, Washington, D. C., U. S. A., 22-27 June, 1977.__ Ramaswami, V., Teletraffic Congress Staff & P. E. Wirth. LC 97-20195. (Teletraffic Science & Engineering Ser.). 1997. write for info. (*0-444-82598-3*) Elsevier.

Teletraffic Science for New Cost-Effective Systems, Networks & Services: Proceedings of the 12th International Teletraffic Congress, Torino, Italy, 1-8 June, 1988. Ed. by M. Bonatti. (Studies in Telecommunication: No. 12). 1598p. 1989. 326.25 (*0-444-87355-4*, North Holland) Elsevier.

Teletraffic Technologies in ATM Networks. Hiroshi Saito. LC 93-39252. 1994. 69.00 (*0-89006-622-1*) Artech Hse.

Teletypewriter Circuits & Equipment: Fundamentals. 1991. lib. bdg. 76.00 (*0-8490-4114-7*) Gordon Pr.

Teletypist. Jack Rudman. (Career Examination Ser.: C-831). 1994. pap. 23.95 (*0-8373-0831-3*) Nat Learn.

Televangelism & American Culture: The Business of Popular Religion. Quentin J. Schultze. LC 90-49378. 264p. (gr. 10). 1995. reprint ed. pap. 14.99 (*0-8010-5303-X*) Baker Bks.

Televangelism Reconsidered: Ritual in Search for Human Community. Bobby C. Alexander. LC 94-19987. (AAR Reflection & Theory in the Study of Religion Ser.: No. 68). 216p. 1994. 39.95 (*1-55540-906-7*, 010068); pap. 24.95 (*1-55540-907-5*, 010068) Scholars Pr GA.

Televised Legislatures: Political Information Technology & Public Choice. W. Mark Crain. (C). 1988. lib. bdg. 57.00 (*0-89838-262-9*) Kluwer Ac.

Televised Medicine Advertising & Children. Thomas S. Robertson et al. LC 79-4280. 192p. 1979. text ed. 49.95 (*0-275-90413-X*, C0413, Praeger Pubs) Greenwood.

Televised Presidential Debates: Advocacy in Contemporary America. Susan A. Hellweg et al. LC 91-28176. (Praeger Series in Political Communication). 192p. 1992. text ed. 59.95 (*0-275-93621-X*, C3621, Praeger Pubs); pap. text ed. 15.95 (*0-275-93622-8*, B3622, Praeger Pubs) Greenwood.

Televised Presidential Debates & Public Policy. Sidney Kraus. (LEA's Communication Ser.). 192p. 1988. pap. 22.50 (*0-8058-0008-5*) L Erlbaum Assocs.

Televising Democracies. Ed. by Bob Franklin. 288p. (C). 1992. pap. text ed. 22.95 (*0-415-07022-8*, A6643) Routledge.

Televising the Performing Arts: Interviews with Merrill Brockway, Kirk Browning, & Roger Englander. Brian G. Rose. LC 92-10677. (Contributions to the Study of Music & Dance Ser.: No. 29). 216p. 1992. text ed. 47.95 (*0-313-28617-5*, RTR/, Greenwood Pr) Greenwood.

Television. (Illus.). (ARA.). (J). (gr. 5-12). 1987. 4.50 (*0-86685-237-9*) Intl Bk Ctr.

Television. B. Balcziak. (Communication: Today & Tomorrow Ser.). (Illus.). 48p. (J). (gr. 4-8). 1989. lib. bdg. 17.27 (*0-86592-059-1*); lib. bdg. 12.95 (*0-685-58628-6*) Rourke Corp.

Television. George Coulter & Shirley Coulter. LC 95-51374. (You Make It Work Ser.). (J). 1996. write for info. (*0-86625-583-4*) Rourke Pubns.

Television. R. Gee & Les Inglis. (Young Scientist Ser.). (Illus.). 32p. (J). (gr. 3-9). 1992. pap. 6.95 (*0-7460-1057-5*); lib. bdg. 14.95 (*0-88110-586-4*) EDC.

Television. Random House Staff. (J). 1996. write for info. (*0-679-87193-4*) Random Bks Yng Read.

Television. Janet Riehecky. (Inventors & Inventions Ser.). 64p. (J). (gr. 3-5). 1996. lib. bdg. 17.95 (*0-7614-0045-1*, Benchmark NY) Marshall Cavendish.

An Asterisk (*) at the beginning of an entry indicates that the title is appearing in BIP for the first time.

Television. Michael Winship. LC 87-42662. (Illus.). 416p. 1988. 19.95 (*0-394-56401-4*) Random.

Television: A Challenge to the Psychoanalytic Establishment. Jacques Lacan. 1990. 24.95 (*0-393-02496-2*) Norton.

Television: A Struggle for Power. Frank Waldrop & Joseph Borkin. LC 72-161140. (History of Broadcasting: Radio to Television Ser.). 1976. reprint ed. 24.95 (*0-405-03561-6*) Ayer.

Television: A World Survey. UNESCO Staff. LC 72-4684. (International Propaganda & Communications Ser.). 235p. 1972. reprint ed. 18.95 (*0-405-04768-1*) Ayer.

Television: An International History. Ed. by Anthony Smith. (Illus.). 480p. 1995. 55.00 (*0-19-811999-2*) OUP.

Television: Careers in Television. Jessica Vitkus-Weeks. LC 93-446. (Now Hiring Ser.). (Illus.). 48p. (J). (gr. 5-6). 1994. lib. bdg. 14.95 (*0-89686-783-8*, Crstwood Hse) Silver Burdett Pr.

Television: Critical Methods & Applications. Jeremy G. Butler. 369p. 1994. pap. 37.95 (*0-534-16686-5*) Wadsworth Pub.

Television: Identifying Propaganda Techniques. Carol O'Sullivan. LC 90-3785. (Opposing Viewpoints Juniors Ser.). (Illus.). 36p. 1990. lib. bdg. 12.96 (*0-89908-606-3*) Greenhaven.

Television: Policy & Culture. Richard L. Collins. 256p. (C). 1992. pap. 19.95 (*0-04-445766-9*); text ed. 62.95 (*0-04-445765-0*) Routledge Chapman & Hall.

Television: Technology & Cultural Form. Raymond Williams. LC 92-50297. (Illus.). 192p. 1992. pap. 14.95 (*0-8195-6259-9*, Wesleyan Univ Pr) U Pr of New Eng.

Television: The Critical View. 5th ed. Ed. by Horace Newcomb. 512p. (C). 1994. pap. text ed. 22.95 (*0-19-508528-0*) OUP.

Television: What's Behind What You See. Carter Merbreier & Linda C. Riley. LC 95-13605. (Illus.). 40p. (J). (gr. 3-5). 1995. 16.00 (*0-374-37388-4*) FS&G.

Television, a Danger for the Individual. J. Schootemeijer. Ed. by De Rozekruis Pers Staff. (Orig.). 1986. pap. 2.50 (*90-70196-44-1*) Rosycross Pr.

Television Access & Political Power: The Networks, the Presidency & The "Loyal Opposition" Joe S. Foote. LC 89-29763. (Praeger Series in Political Communication). 240p. 1990. text ed. 55.00 (*0-275-93438-1*, C3438, Greenwood Pr) Greenwood.

Television Advertising & Televangelism: Discourse Analysis of Persuasive Language. Rosemarie Schmidt & Joseph F. Kess. LC 87-15812. (Pragmatics & Beyond Ser.: No. VII-5). vi, 88p. (C). 1986. 33.00 (*1-55619-006-9*) Benjamins North Am.

Television Aesthetics: Perceptual, Cognitive & Compositional Bases. Nikos Metallinos. (L E A's Communication Ser.). 250p. 1996. 69.95 (*0-8058-1221-0*); pap. text ed. 29.95 (*0-8058-2218-6*) L Erlbaum Assocs.

***Television, AIDS & Risk: A Cultural Studies Approach to Health Communication.** John Tulloch & Deborah Lupton. 256p. 1997. pap. 29.95 (*1-86448-224-9*, Pub. by Allen Unwin AT) Paul & Co Pubs.

Television & Adult Education. Ed. by Robert Hilliard. 160p. 1985. 18.95 (*0-87073-241-2*) Schenkman Bks Inc.

Television & Aggression: An Experimental Field Study. Seymour Feshbach & Roger D. Singer. LC 70-138457. (Jossey-Bass Behavioral Science Ser.). 204p. reprint ed. pap. 58.20 (*0-317-26063-4*, 2023777) Bks Demand.

Television & America's Children: A Crisis of Neglect. Edward L. Palmer. (Communication & Society Ser.). 224p. 1990. reprint ed. pap. 8.95 (*0-19-506321-X*) OUP.

***Television & Cable Factbook, Vol. 65.** Ed. by Michael Taliaferro. iv, 762p. (Orig.). 1997. pap. 495.00 (*1-57696-004-8*) Warren Pub Inc.

***Television & Cable Factbook: Cable, Vol. 65.** Ed. by Michael Taliaferro. ii, 192p. (Orig.). 1997. pap. 495.00 (*1-57696-007-2*) Warren Pub Inc.

***Television & Cable Factbook: Services Volume.** Ed. by Michael Taliaferro. 617p. (Orig.). 1997. pap. 495.00 (*1-57696-005-6*) Warren Pub Inc.

***Television & Cable Factbook: Stations, Vol. 65.** Ed. by Michael Taliaferro. i, 953p. (Orig.). 1997. pap. 495.00 (*1-57696-006-4*) Warren Pub Inc.

Television & Cable Factbook Cable & Services Volume No. 60: 1992 Edition. 60th rev. ed. Warren Publishing, Inc. Staff. Ed. by Albert Warren. (Illus.). 2000p. 1992. 375.00 (*0-911486-58-5*) Warren Pub Inc.

Television & Cable Factbook, Cable Volume Vol. 61: 1993 Edition. rev. ed. Warren Publishing, Inc. Staff. Ed. by Albert Warren. (Illus.). 2100p. 1993. Cable Systems, 2100p. write for info. (*0-911486-66-6*) Warren Pub Inc.

Television & Cable Factbook, No. 61: 1993 Edition, 3 vols. rev. ed. Warren Publishing, Inc. Staff. Ed. by Albert Warren. (Illus.). 1993. Set. 395.00 (*0-911486-64-X*) Warren Pub Inc.

Television & Cable Factbook, Services Volume Vol. 61: 1993 Edition. rev. ed. Warren Publishing, Inc. Staff. Ed. by Albert Warren. (Illus.). 1993. Services, 600p. write for info. (*0-911486-67-4*) Warren Pub Inc.

Television & Cable Factbook, Station Volumes Vol. 61: 1993 Edition. rev. ed. Warren Publishing, Inc. Staff. Ed. by Albert Warren. (Illus.). 1993. TV Stations, 1900p. write for info. (*0-911486-65-8*) Warren Pub Inc.

Television & Cable Factbook, Vol. One: Stations, 1992 Edition. 60th rev. ed. Warren Publishing, Inc. Staff. Ed. by Albert Warren. (Illus.). 1800p. 1991. 375.00 (*0-911486-57-7*) Warren Pub Inc.

Television & Cable Factbook, 1991: Cable Volume, 2 vols. Warren Publishing, Inc. Staff. Ed. by Albert Warren. (Illus.). 4600p. 1991. reprint ed. Set. write for info. (*0-911486-46-1*) Warren Pub Inc.

Television & Cable Factbook, 1991: Services, 2 vols., Vol. II. Warren Publishing, Inc. Staff. Ed. by Albert Warren. (Illus.). 4600p. 1991. reprint ed. write for info. (*0-911486-48-8*) Warren Pub Inc.

Television & Cable Factbook, 1991: Stations Volume, 2 vols., Vol. I. Warren Publishing, Inc. Staff. Ed. by Albert Warren. (Illus.). 4600p. 1991. reprint ed. write for info. (*0-911486-47-X*) Warren Pub Inc.

Television & Cable Factbook, 1994, 3 vols. rev. ed. Warren Publishing, Inc. Staff. Ed. by Michael Taliaferro. (Illus.). 1994. Set, 5000p. 405.00 (*0-911486-75-5*) Warren Pub Inc.

Television & Cable Factbook, 1994, 3 vols., Cable System Vol. rev. ed. Warren Publishing, Inc. Staff. Ed. by Michael Taliaferro. (Illus.). 200p. 1994. write for info. (*0-911486-77-1*) Warren Pub Inc.

Television & Cable Factbook, 1994, 3 vols., Services Vol. rev. ed. Warren Publishing, Inc. Staff. Ed. by Michael Taliaferro. (Illus.). 1500p. 1994. write for info. (*0-911486-78-X*) Warren Pub Inc.

Television & Cable Factbook, 1994, 3 vols., Stations Vol. rev. ed. Warren Publishing, Inc. Staff. Ed. by Michael Taliaferro. (Illus.). 1500p. 1994. write for info. (*0-911486-76-3*) Warren Pub Inc.

Television & Cable Factbook, 1995 Vol. 63, 3 vols., Set. rev. ed. Warren Publishing, Inc. Staff. Ed. by Michael Taliaferro. (Illus.). 5000p. 1995. 425.00 (*0-911486-86-0*) Warren Pub Inc.

Television & Cable Factbook, 1995 Vol. 63: Cable Systems Volume. rev. ed. Warren Publishing, Inc. Staff. Ed. by Michael Taliaferro. (Illus.). 2000p. 1995. write for info. (*0-911486-88-7*) Warren Pub Inc.

Television & Cable Factbook, 1995 Vol. 63: Services Volume. rev. ed. Warren Publishing, Inc. Staff. Ed. by Michael Taliaferro. (Illus.). 1500p. 1995. write for info. (*0-911486-89-5*) Warren Pub Inc.

Television & Cable Factbook, 1995 Vol. 63: Stations Volume. rev. ed. Warren Publishing, Inc. Staff. Ed. by Michael Taliaferro. (Illus.). 1500p. 1995. write for info. (*0-911486-87-9*) Warren Pub Inc.

Television & Cable Factbook, 1996, 3 vols. Incl. Vol. 1 Services. Warren Publishing, Inc. Staff. Ed. by Michael Taliferro. 580p. 1996. pap. Not sold separately (*0-911486-98-4*); Vol. 2 TV Stations. Ed. by Michael Taliferro. 2000p. 1996. pap. Not sold separately (*0-911486-99-2*); Vol. 3 Cable Systems. Ed. by Michael Taliferro. 2230p. 1996. pap. Not sold separately (*1-57696-000-5*); 1996. 455.00 (*0-911486-97-6*) Warren Pub Inc.

Television & Child Development. Judith Van Evra. (Comunication Textbook Ser.). 248p. (C). 1990. pap. 34.50 (*0-8058-0858-2*); text ed. 69.95 (*0-8058-0575-3*) L Erlbaum Assocs.

***Television & Child Development.** Judith Van Evra. (Communication Ser.). 248p. 1998. write for info. (*0-8058-2800-1*) L Erlbaum Assocs.

***Television & Child Development.** Judith Van Evra. (Communication Ser.). 248p. 1998. pap. write for info. (*0-8058-2801-X*) L Erlbaum Assocs.

Television & Children: A Special Medium for a Special Audience. Aim'ee Dorr. LC 85-19675. (Sage Commtext Ser.: No. 14). 160p. 1986. reprint ed. pap. 45.60 (*0-608-01487-7*, 2059531) Bks Demand.

Television & Children: Program Evaluation, Comprehension, & Impact. Brian R. Clifford et al. (Communication Ser.). 264p. 1995. text ed. 59.95 (*0-8058-1682-8*) L Erlbaum Assocs.

Television & Children: Program Evaluation, Comprehension, & Impact. Ed. by Brian R. Clifford et al. (LEA's Communication Ser.). 264p. 1995. text ed. 27.50 (*0-8058-1683-6*) L Erlbaum Assocs.

Television & Delinquency. James D. Halloran et al. LC 71-517136. (Great Britain Television Research Committee Working Paper Ser.: No. 3). 222p. reprint ed. pap. 63.30 (*0-317-28256-5*, 2022636) Bks Demand.

Television & Education. Ed. by Chester M. Pierce. LC 77-94473. (Sage Contemporary Social Science Issues Ser.: No. 44). 104p. reprint ed. pap. 29.70 (*0-317-08983-8*, 2021940) Bks Demand.

Television & Ethics: A Bibliography. Thomas Cooper. 300p. 1988. 55.00 (*0-8161-8966-8*, Hall Reference) Macmillan.

***Television & Ethnic Minorities: Producers' Perspectives: A Study of BBC In-House & Independent Producers of Minority Ethnic Programmes.** Simon Cottle. 246p. 1997. 55.95 (*0-614-25489-2*, Pub. by Avebury Pub UK) Ashgate Pub Co.

Television & Everyday Life. Roger Silverstone. 272p. (C). 1994. pap. 16.95 (*0-415-01647-9*) Routledge.

Television & Everyday Life. Roger Silverstone. LC 93-32143. 272p. (C). (gr. 13). 1994. text ed. 79.95 (*0-415-01646-0*, Routledge NY) Routledge.

Television & It's Audience. Patrick Barwise & Andrew Ehrenberg. 224p. (C). 1989. text ed. 39.95 (*0-8039-8154-6*); pap. text ed. 16.95 (*0-8039-8155-4*) Sage.

Television & National Sport: The U. S. & Britain. Joan M. Chandler. (Sport & Society Ser.). 264p. 1988. text ed. 27.50 (*0-252-01516-9*) U of Ill Pr.

Television & National Sport: The United States & Britain. fac. ed. Joan M. Chandler. LC 87-35709. (Sport & Society Ser.). 259p. 1988. pap. 73.90 (*0-7837-7612-8*, 2047364) Bks Demand.

Television & Nuclear Power: Making the Public Mind. Mallory Wober. Ed. by Brenda Dervin. (Communication & Information Science Ser.). 320p. (C). 1992. pap. 39.50 (*0-89391-836-9*); text ed. 78.50 (*0-89391-676-5*) Ablex Pub.

Television & Political Advertising, 2 vols. F. Biocca. (Communication Ser.). (C). 1991. Set. text ed. 90.00 (*0-8058-1101-X*) L Erlbaum Assocs.

Television & Political Advertising, Vol. I. F. Biocca. (Communication Ser.). 376p. (C). 1991. Vol. 1: Psychological Processes, 344p. text ed. 79.95 (*0-8058-0655-5*) L Erlbaum Assocs.

Television & Political Advertising, Vol. II. F. Biocca. (Communication Ser.). 280p. (C). 1991. Vol. 2: Signs, Codes & Images, 328p. text ed. 59.95 (*0-8058-0662-8*) L Erlbaum Assocs.

Television & Popular Culture in India: A Study of the Mahabharat. Ananda Mitra. LC 93-27379. 1993. 28.50 (*0-8039-9134-7*) Sage.

Television & Radio: 1973 & 1974 Supplement: Forms Bk. II. Joseph Taubman. LC 74-189328. 60.00 (*0-318-00775-4*) Law Arts.

Television & Radio in the United Kingdom. Burton Paulu. LC 80-20870. 490p. reprint ed. pap. 139.70 (*0-7837-2927-8*, 2057527) Bks Demand.

Television & Screen Writing: From Concept to Contract. 3rd ed. Richard A. Blum. (Illus.). 272p. 1995. pap. 28.95 (*0-240-80194-6*, Focal) Buttrwrth-Heinemann.

Television & Social Behavior: Beyond Violence & Children: A Report of the Committee on Television & Social Behavior Social Science Research Council. Ed. by Stephen B. Withey & Ronald P. Abeles. LC 79-29684. 366p. 1980. reprint ed. pap. 104.40 (*0-608-00471-5*, 2061290) Bks Demand.

Television & Social Control. Mallory Wober & Barrie Gunter. LC 87-18763. 250p. 1988. text ed. 39.95 (*0-312-01305-1*) St Martin.

Television & Society. Nicholas Abercrombie. (Illus.). 240p. (C). 1996. text ed. 57.95 (*0-7456-1435-3*, Pub. by Polity Pr UK); pap. text ed. 23.95 (*0-7456-1436-1*, Pub. by Polity Pr UK) Blackwell Pubs.

Television & Sponsorship. Bianca Ford & James Ford. LC 93-8959. 256p. 1993. pap. 62.95 (*0-240-51356-8*, Focal) Buttrwrth-Heinemann.

Television & the Aggressive Child: A Cross National Comparison. Ed. by L. R. Huesmann & L. D. Eron. (Zillman-Bryant Ser.). 328p. (C). 1986. text ed. 59.95 (*0-89859-754-4*) L Erlbaum Assocs.

Television & the American Child. George Comstock & Hae J. Paik. (Illus.). 386p. 1991. text ed. 42.00 (*0-12-183575-8*) Acad Pr.

Television & the American Family. Ed. by Jennings Bryant. (Communication Ser.). 392p. (C). 1990. text ed. 89.95 (*0-8058-0116-2*) L Erlbaum Assocs.

Television & the Child: An Empirical Study of the Effect of Television on the Young. Hilde T. Himmelweit et al. LC 59-197. 543p. reprint ed. pap. 154.80 (*0-317-29717-1*, 2019716) Bks Demand.

Television & the Classroom Reading Program: If You Can't Beat 'em Join 'em. George J. Becker. LC 73-89304. (Reading Aids Ser.). 32p. reprint ed. pap. 25.00 (*0-685-15888-8*, 2026792) Bks Demand.

Television & the Crisis of Democracy. Douglas M. Kellner. (Interventions: Theory & Contemporary Politics Ser.). 287p. (C). 1990. pap. text ed. 24.00 (*0-8133-0549-7*) Westview.

Television & the Drama of Crime. Richard Sparks. (New Directions in Criminology Ser.). 192p. 1992. 85.00 (*0-335-09328-0*, Open Univ Pr); pap. 27.50 (*0-335-09327-2*, Open Univ Pr) Taylor & Francis.

Television & the Exceptional Child: A Forgotten Audience. Joyce N. Sprafkin et al. (Communication Ser.). 248p. 1992. pap. 24.50 (*0-8058-0788-8*); text ed. 49.95 (*0-8058-0787-X*) L Erlbaum Assocs.

***Television & the Household.** Duncan Petrie. 1995. pap. text ed. 16.95 (*0-85170-504-9*, Pub. by British Film Inst UK) Ind U Pr.

Television & the Lives of Our Children: A Manual for Teachers & Parents. Gloria M. DeGaetano. (Illus.). 128p. 1993. pap. text ed. 10.95 (*0-9638737-0-9*) Train Thought.

Television & the News: A Critical Appraisal. Harry J. Skornia. LC 68-8629. (Paperbounds Ser.: No. PB-13). 1974. reprint ed. pap. 3.95 (*0-87015-209-2*) Pacific Bks.

Television & the Performing Arts: A Handbook & Reference Guide to American Cultural Programming. Brian G. Rose. LC 85-14655. 291p. 1986. text ed. 55.00 (*0-313-24159-7*, RTV/, Greenwood Pr) Greenwood.

Television & the Public Interest: Vulnerable Values in West European Broadcasting. Ed. by Jay G. Blumler. 240p. (C). 1992. 69.95 (*0-8039-8649-1*); pap. 25.95 (*0-8039-8650-5*) Sage.

Television & the Public Sphere: Citizenship, Democracy & the Media. Peter Dahlgren. (Media, Culture & Society Ser.: Vol. 10). 208p. 1995. 65.00 (*0-8039-8922-9*); pap. 21.95 (*0-8039-8923-7*) Sage.

Television & the Quality of Life: How Viewing Shapes Everyday Experiences. Ed. by Robert Kubey & M. Csikszentmihalyi. (Volume in the Communication Ser.). 296p. (C). 1990. pap. 36.00 (*0-8058-0708-X*); text ed. 59.95 (*0-8058-0552-4*) L Erlbaum Assocs.

Television & the Red Menace: The Video Road to Vietnam. J. Fred MacDonald. LC 84-18302. 277p. 1985. text ed. 55.00 (*0-275-90141-6*, C0141, Praeger Pubs); pap. text ed. 19.95 (*0-275-91807-6*, B1807, Praeger Pubs) Greenwood.

Television & the Remote Control: Grazing on a Vast Wasteland. Bellamy & Walker. LC 96-14086. (Communication Ser.). 192p. 1996. lib. bdg. 30.00 (*1-57230-085-X*) Guilford Pr.

***Television & Today's Families.** Nancy O. Wilson. (Orig.). 1996. pap. 6.95 (*1-57515-098-0*) PPI Pubng.

Television & Video. Shonan F. Noronha. (Opportunities in... Ser.). 128p. 1993. pap. 7.95 (*0-8442-8682-6*, VGM Career Bks) NTC Pub Grp.

Television & Video. Shonan F. Noronha. (Opportunities in... Ser.). 60p. 1995. 13.95 (*0-8442-4090-7*) NTC Pub Grp.

Television & Video. Shonan F. Noronha. (Opportunities in... Ser.). 160p. 1995. pap. 10.95 (*0-8442-4091-5*) NTC Pub Grp.

Television & Video Engineer's Reference Book. Kenneth G. Jackson & Boris Townsend. (Illus.). 772p. 1991. 79.95 (*0-7506-1021-2*) Buttrwrth-Heinemann.

Television & Video Engineer's Reference Book. Kenneth G. Jackson & Boris Townsend. (Illus.). 876p. 1994. pap. 79.95 (*0-7506-1953-8*) Buttrwrth-Heinemann.

Television & Video Systems. Charles Buscombe. 450p. 1990. text ed. 84.00 (*0-13-903014-X*) P-H.

Television & Women's Culture: The Politics of the Popular. Mary E. Brown. 244p. (C). 1990. pap. 19.95 (*0-86819-222-8*) Aubrey Bks.

Television & Women's Culture: The Politics of the Popular. Ed. by Mary E. Brown. (Communication & Human Values Ser.: Vol. 7). (Illus.). 256p. (C). 1990. 52.00 (*0-8039-8228-3*); pap. 24.95 (*0-8039-8229-1*) Sage.

Television & Youth: Twenty-Five Years of Research & Controversy. John P. Murray. 278p. (Orig.). 1980. pap. text ed. 10.00 (*0-938510-00-2*, 010-TV) Boys Town Pr.

Television As an Instrument of Terror. Arthur A. Berger. LC 78-55942. 214p. 1979. 21.95 (*0-87855-708-3*) Transaction Pubs.

Television at Crossroads. Andrea Branzi. 1995. 45.00 (*1-85490-425-6*) Academy Ed UK.

Television Audience: Patterns of Viewing. A. Ehrenberg et al. 250p. 1986. text ed. 68.95 (*0-566-05083-8*, Pub. by Avebury Pub UK) Ashgate Pub Co.

Television, Audiences, & Cultural Studies. David Morley. LC 92-10404. 272p. (C). (gr. 13). 1992. pap. 16.95 (*0-415-05445-1*, A7921) Routledge.

Television Careers: A Guide to Breaking & Entering. Linda G. Farris. LC 95-75581. 232p. (Orig.). 1995. pap. 14.95 (*0-9638673-1-8*) Buy The Book.

Television Cartoon Shows: An Illustrated Encyclopedia, 1949 Through 1993. Hal Erickson. LC 94-23878. (Illus.). 671p. 1995. lib. bdg. 75.00 (*0-7864-0029-3*) McFarland & Co.

Television Character & Story Facts: Over 110,000 Details from 1,008 Shows, 1945-1992. Vincent Terrace. LC 92-51095. (Illus.). 557p. 1993. lib. bdg. 62.50 (*0-89950-891-X*) McFarland & Co.

Television Comedy Series: An Episode Guide to 153 TV Sitcoms in Syndication. Joel Eisner & David Krinsky. LC 83-42901. (Illus.). 880p. 1984. lib. bdg. 82.00 (*0-89950-088-9*) McFarland & Co.

Television Commercial Processes & Procedures. Robert J. Schihl. (Multiple Camera Video Ser.). 136p. 1991. pap. 32.95 (*0-240-80098-2*) Buttrwrth-Heinemann.

Television Continuum - 1967 to 2017. Ed. by Jeffrey Friedman. 228p. 1991. pap. 35.00 (*0-940690-18-7*) Soc Motion Pic & TV Engrs.

Television Coverage of International Affairs. Ed. by William C. Adams. LC 81-15054. (Communication & Information Science Ser.). 272p. 1982. text ed. 73.25 (*0-89391-103-8*) Ablex Pub.

Television Coverage of the Middle East. Ed. by William C. Adams. LC 81-15049. (Communication & Information Science Ser.). 168p. 1981. text ed. 73.25 (*0-89391-083-X*) Ablex Pub.

Television Coverage of the 1980 Presidential Campaign. Ed. by William C. Adams. LC 83-3768. (Communication & Information Science Ser.). 196p. 1983. text ed. 73.25 (*0-89391-104-6*) Ablex Pub.

Television Critical Viewing Skills: A Survey & Evaluation of Major Media Literacy Projects in the U. S. & Selected Countries. Ed. by J. A. Brown. (Communication Ser.). 392p. (C). 1991. pap. 39.95 (*0-8058-0974-0*); text ed. 69.95 (*0-8058-0786-1*) L Erlbaum Assocs.

Television Criticism: Approaches & Applications. Leah R. Vande Berg & Lawrence A. Wenner. 496p. (Orig.). (C). 1991. pap. text ed. 31.50 (*0-8013-0580-2*, 78506) Longman.

Television Criticism: Reading, Writing, & Analysis. 2nd ed. Kimberley K. Massey & Stanley Baran. 408p. (C). 1996. per., pap. text ed. 47.19 (*0-7872-2474-X*) Kendall-Hunt.

Television Culture: Popular Pleasures & Politics. John Fiske. (Studies in Communication). 400p. 1988. 42.50 (*0-415-04284-4*) Routledge.

Television Culture: Popular Pleasures & Politics. John Fiske. (Studies in Communication). 400p. (C). 1988. pap. 13.95 (*0-415-03934-7*) Routledge.

Television Culture & Women's Lives: Thirtysomething & the Contradictions of Gender. Margaret J. Heide. LC 94-41723. (Feminist Cultural Studies, the Media, & Political Culture). 192p. 1995. text ed. 29.95 (*0-8122-3253-4*) U of Pa Pr.

Television Culture & Women's Lives: Thirtysomething & the Contradictions of Gender. Margaret J. Heide. LC 94-41723. (Feminist Cultural Studies, the Media, & Political Culture). 192p. 1995. pap. 13.95 (*0-8122-1534-6*) U of Pa Pr.

Television Detective Shows of the 1970s: Credits, Storylines & Episode Guides for 109 Series. David Martindale. LC 90-53508. (Illus.). 576p. 1991. lib. bdg. 62.50 (*0-89950-557-0*) McFarland & Co.

Television Directing. Harold R. Hickman. 1991. text ed. write for info. (*0-07-028719-8*) McGraw.

Television Directors Guide. 2nd ed. Lynne Naylor. 1994. 40.00 (*0-943728-59-2*) Lone Eagle Pub.

***Television Directors Guide.** 3rd ed. Ed. by Lynne Naylor. 350p. 1996. pap. 45.00 (*0-943728-76-2*) Lone Eagle Pub.

Television Drama: Agency, Audience & Myth. John Tulloch. 288p. (C). 1990. pap. text ed. 17.95 (*0-415-01649-5*, A3841) Routledge.

Television Drama Programming: A Comprehensive Chronicle, 1975-1980. Larry J. Gianakos. LC 81-5319. 471p. 1981. 42.50 (*0-8108-1438-2*) Scarecrow.

An Asterisk (*) at the beginning of an entry indicates that the title is appearing in BIP for the first time.

Television Drama Series Programming: A Comprehensive Chronicle, 1980-1982. Larry J. Gianakos. LC 83-3388. 686p. 1983. 59.50 (*0-8108-1626-1*) Scarecrow.

Television Drama Series Programming: A Comprehensive Chronicle, 1982-1984. Larry J. Gianakos. LC 85-30428. 838p. 1987. 74.50 (*0-8108-1876-0*) Scarecrow.

Television Drama Series Programming: A Comprehensive Chronicle, 1984-1986. Larry J. Gianakos. LC 92-27808. 717p. 1992. 74.50 (*0-8108-2601-1*) Scarecrow.

Television Electronics: Theory & Servicing. 8th ed. Milton S. Kiver & M. Kaufman. 768p. 1983. text ed. 68.00 (*0-8273-1328-4*) Delmar.

Television Engineering. Arvind M. Dhake. (Illus.). 1986. pap. text ed. 27.50 (*0-07-096389-4*) McGraw.

Television Engineering: Proceedings of the International Television Conference, London, 1962. International Television Conference Staff. LC 65-56108. (Institution of Electrical Engineers Conference Report Ser.: No. 5). 592p. reprint ed. pap. 168.80 (*0-317-10164-1*, 2050325) Bks Demand.

Television Engineering Handbook: Featuring HDTV Systems. rev. ed. K. Blair Benson. 1992. text ed. 99.50 (*0-07-004788-X*) McGraw.

Television, Ethnicity, & Cultural Change. Marie Gillespie. LC 94-22627. (Comedia Ser.). 256p. (YA). (gr. 8-12). 1995. pap. 18.95 (*0-415-09675-8*, C0147); text ed. 49.95 (*0-415-09674-X*, C0146) Routledge.

Television Experience: What Children See. Mariann P. Winick & Charles Winick. LC 78-19670. (People & Communication Ser.: No. 6). 215p. reprint ed. pap. 61.30 (*0-8357-4867-7*, 2037799) Bks Demand.

Television Field Production & Reporting. 2nd ed. Frederick Shook. 400p. (C). 1996. pap. text ed. 39.95 (*0-8013-1604-9*, 76967) Longman.

Television Form & Public Address. John Corner. 224p. 1995. text ed. 59.95 (*0-340-62538-4*, Pub. by E Arnld UK); text ed. 18.95 (*0-340-56753-8*, Pub. by E Arnld UK) St Martin.

Television Fraud: The History & Implications of the Quiz Show Scandals. Ed. by Kent Anderson. LC 77-94755. (Contributions in American Studies: No. 39). 226p. 1979. text ed. 29.95 (*0-313-20321-0*, ATF/, Greenwood Pr) Greenwood.

Television Frequency Allocation Policy in the United States. John M. Kittross. Ed. by Christopher H. Sterling. LC 78-21723. (Dissertations in Broadcasting Ser.). 1980. lib. bdg. 40.95 (*0-405-11762-0*) Ayer.

Television Fundamentals. John Watkinson. (Illus.). 320p. 1996. pap. 37.95 (*0-240-51411-4*, Focal) Buttrwrth-Heinemann.

Television Gray Market. Henry L. Eisenson. LC 92-75120. (Electronic Underground Ser.: Vol. 2). (Illus.). 160p. (Orig.). 1993. pap. 23.75 (*1-56866-037-5*) Index Pub Grp.

Television Guest Stars: An Illustrated Career Chronicle for 678 Performers of the Sixties & Seventies. Jack Ward. LC 92-51009. (Illus.). 598p. 1993. lib. bdg. 75.00 (*0-89950-807-3*) McFarland & Co.

***Television Handbook.** Patricia Holland. (Media Practice Ser.). 304p. (C). 1997. pap. 22.95 (*0-415-12732-7*); text ed. 69.95 (*0-415-12731-9*) Routledge.

Television Horror Movie Hosts: 68 Vampires, Mad Scientists & Other Denizens of the Late-Night Airwaves Examined & Interviewed, Vol. 1. Elena M. Watson. LC 91-52642. (Illus.). 256p. 1991. lib. bdg. 32.50 (*0-89950-570-8*) McFarland & Co.

***Television IC Data Files.** Edwards. 240p. 1996. pap. 29.95 (*0-7506-2899-5*) Buttrwrth-Heinemann.

Television Image Quality. Ed. by Jeffrey B. Friedman. 377p. 1984. pap. 35.00 (*0-940690-09-8*) Soc Motion Pic & TV Engrs.

Television, Imagination & Aggression: A Study of Preschoolers. Jerome L. Singer & Dorothy G. Singer. LC 80-36810. 224p. 1981. text ed. 39.95 (*0-89859-060-4*) L Erlbaum Assocs.

Television in America. 2nd ed. George Comstock. (CommText Ser.: Vol. 1). 237p. (C). 1991. text ed. 37.00 (*0-8039-3338-X*); pap. text ed. 16.95 (*0-8039-3339-8*) Sage.

***Television in America.** George A. Comstock. LC 91-25358. (Sage Commtext Ser.: Vol. 1). 160p. 1991. reprint ed. pap. 45.60 (*0-608-03496-7*, 2064211) Bks Demand.

***Television in America: Local Station History from Across the Nation.** Ed. by Michael D. Murray & Donald G. Godfrey. 416p. (C). 1996. text ed. 42.95 (*0-8138-2969-0*) Iowa St U Pr.

Television in Europe. Eli M. Noam. (Communication & Society Ser.). (Illus.). 408p. 1992. 55.00 (*0-19-506942-0*) OUP.

***Television in India: Changes & Challenges.** Gopal Saksena. (C). 1996. 25.00 (*0-7069-9969-X*, Pub. by Vikas II) S Asia.

Television in Society. Arthur A. Berger. 224p. 1986. 34.95 (*0-88738-109-X*) Transaction Pubs.

Television in the Lives of Our Children. Wilbur L. Schramm et al. vii, 324p. 1961. 47.50 (*0-8047-0062-1*); pap. 15.95 (*0-8047-0064-8*) Stanford U Pr.

Television Industry: A Historical Dictionary. Anthony Slide. LC 91-4363. 392p. 1991. text ed. 65.00 (*0-313-25634-9*, STV, Greenwood Pr) Greenwood.

Television Interviews, 1951-1955: A Catalog of Longines Chronoscope Interviews in the National Archives. Compiled by Sarah L. Shamley. LC 90-5772. 108p. 1991. 25.00 (*0-911333-82-7*, 100042) National Archives & Recs.

Television Magick. Temple of Psychick Youth Staff. 24p. (Orig.). 1994. pap. 5.00 (*1-871744-80-6*, Pub. by Temple Pr UK) AK Pr Dist.

Television Measurement Techniques. Leslie E. Weaver. LC 78-112330. (Institution of Electrical Engineers Monograph Ser.: No. 9). 530p. reprint ed. pap. 151.10 (*0-317-09175-1*, 2017591) Bks Demand.

Television-Merging Multiple Technologies. Ed. by Carol King. 436p. 1990. pap. 35.00 (*0-940690-17-9*) Soc Motion Pic & TV Engrs.

***Television Microprocessor IC Data Files.** J. Edwards. 1997. pap. text ed. 28.95 (*0-7506-3335-2*) Buttrwrth-Heinemann.

***Television Musicals: Plots Critiques, Casts & Credits for 222 Shows Written for & Presented on Television, 1944-1996.** Joan Baxter. LC 97-13655. (Illus.). 192p. 1997. lib. bdg. 45.00 (*0-7864-0286-5*) McFarland & Co.

Television Myth & the American Mind. 2nd ed. Hal Himmelstein. LC 93-43796. 432p. 1994. text ed. 65.00 (*0-275-93156-0*, Praeger Pubs); pap. text ed. 24.95 (*0-275-93157-9*, Praeger Pubs) Greenwood.

Television Network Daytime & Late-Night Programming, 1959-1989. Mitchell E. Shapiro. LC 90-52508. 282p. 1990. lib. bdg. 43.50 (*0-89950-526-0*) McFarland & Co.

Television Network News: Issues in Content Research. Ed. by William Adams & Fay Schreibman. LC 78-64489. 1978. 6.50 (*0-932768-00-8*) CTS-GWU.

Television Network Prime-Time Programming, 1948-1988. Mitchell E. Shapiro. LC 89-45006. 763p. 1989. lib. bdg. 58.50 (*0-89950-412-4*) McFarland & Co.

Television News. 3rd ed. Ivor Yorke. 224p. 1995. pap. 39.95 (*0-240-51372-X*, Focal) Buttrwrth-Heinemann.

Television News: Whose Bias? Martin Harrison. 408p. 1987. reprint ed. pap. 24.95 (*0-946967-05-9*) Transaction Pubs.

Television News Anchors: An Anthology of Profiles of the Major Figures & Issues in United States Network Reporting. Ed. by Thomas Fensch. LC 92-50940. (Illus.). 320p. 1993. lib. bdg. 41.50 (*0-89950-769-7*) McFarland & Co.

***Television News & the Elderly: Broadcast Managers' Attitudes Toward Older Adults.** rev. ed. Michael L. Hilt. LC 96-36711. (Studies on the Elderly in America). (Illus.). 135p. 1996. text ed. 45.00 (*0-8153-2627-0*) Garland.

Television News & the New Technology. 3rd ed. Charles F. Cremer. 1996. pap. text ed. 28.25 (*0-07-013530-4*) McGraw.

Television News Interview. Akiba A. Cohen. LC 87-13025. (Sage Context Ser.: No. 18). 160p. reprint ed. pap. 45.60 (*0-7837-6716-1*, 2046343) Bks Demand.

Television Newswriting: Captivating an Audience. Frederick Shook. LC 93-7796. 336p. (C). 1994. pap. text ed. 41.95 (*0-8013-0686-8*, 78692) Longman.

Television PA's Handbook. 2nd ed. Avril Rowlands. LC 93-3718. 224p. 1993. pap. 36.95 (*0-240-51353-3*, Focal) Buttrwrth-Heinemann.

Television Performance: News & Information. William Hawes. (Electronic Media Guide Ser.). 104p. 1991. pap. 19.95 (*0-240-80056-7*, Focal) Buttrwrth-Heinemann.

Television Picture Tubes & Other Cathode-Ray Tubes: Industry & Trade Summary. John Kitzmiller. (Illus.). 20p. (Orig.). (C). 1995. pap. text ed. 20.00 (*0-7881-2100-6*) DIANE Pub.

Television Plays. Philip Ward. (Dramascripts Ser.: Vol. 8). 1976. pap. 4.95 (*0-902675-45-1*) Oleander Pr.

Television Plays, 1965-1984. Tom Stoppard. 1994. pap. 11.95 (*0-571-16570-2*) Faber & Faber.

Television, Politics, & the Transition to Democracy in Latin America. Ed. by Thomas E. Skidmore. LC 92-37345. (Woodrow Wilson Center Press Ser.). 168p. 1993. 25.00 (*0-943875-44-7*) Johns Hopkins.

Television Producers. Jeremy Tunstall. LC 93-7178. (Communication & Society Ser.). (Illus.). 240p. (C). 1993. pap. 16.95 (*0-415-09472-0*) Routledge.

Television Producers. Jeremy Tunstall. LC 93-7178. (Communication & Society Ser.). (Illus.). 240p. (C). (gr. 13). 1993. text ed. 69.95 (*0-415-09471-2*, B2568) Routledge.

Television Production. Dan Baker & Bill Weisgerber. Ed. by James E. Duane. LC 80-23479. (Instructional Media Library: Vol. 15). (Illus.). 112p. 1981. 27.95 (*0-87778-175-3*) Educ Tech Pubns.

Television Production. Ron Whittaker. LC 92-16005. 579p. (C). 1992. text ed. 57.95 (*1-55934-020-7*, 1020) Mayfield Pub.

Television Production: A Classroom Approach. Keith Kyker & Christopher Curchy. (Illus.). xvi, 378p. 1993. teacher ed., pap. text ed. 28.50 (*1-56308-101-6*); vhs 35.00 (*1-56308-107-5*) Libs Unl.

Television Production: A Classroom Approach, Bk. 1. Keith Kyker & Christopher Curchy. (Illus.). iv, 121p. 1993. Beginning, 175p. student ed., pap. text ed. 15.00 (*1-56308-108-3*) Libs Unl.

Television Production: A Classroom Approach, Bk. 2. Keith Kyker & Christopher Curchy. (Illus.). iv, 137p. 1993. Advanced, 175p. student ed., pap. text ed. 14.50 (*1-56308-161-X*) Libs Unl.

Television Production: An Introduction. 2nd ed. Donald L. MacRae. (Illus.). 1982. pap. 17.95 (*0-458-93930-7*, 6508) Routledge Chapman & Hall.

Television Production: Disciplines & Techniques. 5th ed. Thomas D. Burrows et al. 528p. (C). 1991. per. write for info. (*0-697-12917-9*) Brown & Benchmark.

Television Production: Disciplines & Techniques. 6th ed. Thomas D. Burrows et al. 464p. (C). 1994. per. write for info. (*0-697-20131-7*) Brown & Benchmark.

***Television Production Equipment: An Educator's Survival Guide to Equipment & Setup.** Christopher Curchy & Keith Kyker. LC 97-24477. 1997. write for info. (*1-56308-582-8*) Libs Unl.

Television Production for Elementary & Middle Schools. Keith Kyker & Christopher Curchy. (Illus.). xiv, 211p. 1994. pap. text ed. 24.00 (*1-56308-186-5*) Libs Unl.

Television Production Handbook. 5th ed. Herbert Zettl. 647p. (C). 1992. text ed. 51.75 (*0-534-14826-3*) Wadsworth Pub.

Television Production Handbook. 6th ed. Herbert Zettl. (Radio/TV/Film Ser.). (Illus.). 672p. (C). 1997. text ed. 74.95 (*0-534-26058-6*) Wadsworth Pub.

Television Production Handbook. 6th ed. Herbert Zettl. 672p. 1996. 64.95 (*0-8199-6649-5*) Wadsworth Pub.

Television Production, Instructor's Manual. Ron Whittaker. LC 92-16005. (C). 1992. teacher ed., pap. text ed. write for info. (*1-55934-191-2*, 1191) Mayfield Pub.

Television Production Workbook. 4th rev. ed. Herbert Zettl. 213p. (C). 1985. pap. 14.95 (*0-534-03542-6*) Wadsworth Pub.

Television Production Workbook. 5th ed. Herbert Zettl. 190p. (C). 1992. pap. 14.00 (*0-534-14827-1*) Wadsworth Pub.

Television Program Master Index: Access to Critical & Historical Information on 1002 Shows in 341 Books. Charles V. Dintrone. LC 96-11763. 143p. 1996. lib. bdg. 36.50 (*0-7864-0150-8*) McFarland & Co.

Television-Radio Age Communications Coursebook. Scott H. Robb. 1981. 29.00 (*0-686-12160-0*); ring bd. 16.50 (*0-686-12159-7*) CRI.

Television Research: A Directory of Conceptual Categories, Topic Suggestions & Selected Sources. Ronald L. Jacobson. LC 94-44118. 144p. 1995. pap. 32.50 (*0-7864-0033-1*) McFarland & Co.

Television Series Regulars of the Fifties & Sixties in Interview. Dina-Marie Kulzer. LC 91-51229. (Illus.). 224p. 1992. lib. bdg. 34.50 (*0-89950-722-0*) McFarland & Co.

Television Series Revivals: Sequels or Remakes of Cancelled Shows. Lee Goldberg. LC 92-51008. (Illus.). 208p. 1993. lib. bdg. 32.50 (*0-89950-772-7*) McFarland & Co.

Television Servicing. Jack Rudman. (Dantes Subject Standardized Tests Ser.: DANTES-38). 1994. pap. 23.95 (*0-8373-6638-0*) Nat Learn.

Television, Sex Roles & Children: A Developmental Social Psychological Account. Kevin Durkin. LC 85-13629. 160p. 1985. pap. 27.00 (*0-335-15068-3*, Open Univ Pr) Taylor & Francis.

Television Sherlock Holmes. Peter Haining. 1991. pap. 19.95 (*1-85227-398-4*, Pub. by W H Allen UK) Carol Pub Group.

Television Specials: 3201 Entertainment Spectaculars, 1939 Through 1993. Vincent Terrace. LC 94-7225. (Illus.). 557p. 1995. lib. bdg. 55.00 (*0-89950-966-5*) McFarland & Co.

Television Station Operations & Management. Robert L. Hilliard. (Illus.). 264p. 1989. 42.95 (*0-240-80027-3*, Focal) Buttrwrth-Heinemann.

Television Studies: Textual Analysis. Ed. by Gary Burns & Robert J. Thompson. LC 88-23170. (Media & Society Ser.). 268p. 1989. text ed. 59.95 (*0-275-92745-8*, C2745, Praeger Pubs) Greenwood.

***Television Studies Book.** Geraghty. Date not set. text ed. write for info. (*0-340-66231-X*); text ed. 59.95 (*0-340-66232-8*) St Martin.

Television Sweetheart. large type ed. Eileen Barry. (Linford Romance Library). 327p. 1984. pap. 15.99 (*0-7089-6012-X*) Ulverscroft.

Television Symptom Diagnosis. Richard W. Tinnell. 1977. teacher ed. write for info. (*0-672-97618-8*); student ed. write for info. (*0-672-97617-X*) Macmillan.

Television, Tabloid & Tears: Fassbinder & Popular Culture. Jane Shattuc. LC 94-30357. 1994. pap. text ed. 19.95 (*0-8166-2455-0*) U of Minn Pr.

Television Technology: A Look Toward the 21st Century. Ed. by Jeffrey B. Friedman. 224p. 1987. pap. 35.00 (*0-940690-13-6*) Soc Motion Pic & TV Engrs.

Television Technology: Fundamentals & Future Prospects. A. Michael Noll. (Telecommunications Management Library). 200p. 1988. text ed. 33.00 (*0-89006-332-X*) Artech Hse.

Television Technology in the Eighties. 240p. 1981. 30.00 (*0-318-16594-5*) Soc Motion Pic & TV Engrs.

Television Technology in Transition. Ed. by Jeffrey Friedman. 376p. 1988. pap. 35.00 (*0-940690-14-4*) Soc Motion Pic & TV Engrs.

Television, the Book & the Classroom: A Seminar Cosponsored by the Center for the Book in the Library of Congress & the U. S. Office of Education & Held at the Library of Congress on April 26-27, 1978. LC 78-23543. 128p. 4.95 (*0-8444-0303-2*) Lib Congress.

Television, the Public Sphere, & National Identity. Monroe E. Price. 312p. 1996. 65.00 (*0-19-818362-3*); pap. 24.95 (*0-19-818338-0*) OUP.

Television Theme Recordings: An Illustrated Discography, 1951-1994. Steve Gelfand. LC 91-61882. (Illus.). 352p. 1994. lib. bdg. 75.00 (*1-56075-021-9*) Popular Culture.

Television Times: A Reader. John Corner & Sylvia Harvey. 256p. 1996. text ed. 18.95 (*0-340-65233-0*, Pub. by E Arnld UK) St Martin.

Television Times: A Reader. John Corner & Sylvia Harvey. 256p. 1996. text ed. 49.95 (*0-340-65234-9*, Pub. by E Arnld UK) St Martin.

***Television Today & Tomorrow: It Won't Be What You Think.** Gene F. Jankowski & David C. Fuchs. (Illus.). 256p. 1996. reprint ed. pap. 12.95 (*0-19-511129-X*) OUP.

Television Viewers Guide to World Cup Soccer '94. Tim Guelker. (Illus.). 149p. (Orig.). (SPA.). 1994. pap. 6.95 (*0-9639593-0-1*) H P Merchand.

Television Viewing Related to Aggressive & Prosocial Behaviour. O. Wiegman et al. (Selecta Reeks Ser.: Vol. 36). xii, 192p. 1986. 20.00 (*90-6472-095-9*) Taylor & Francis.

Television Violence: A Guide to the Literature. Ed. by P. T. Kelly. 237p. (C). 1996. lib. bdg. 69.00 (*1-56072-299-1*) Nova Sci Pubs.

Television Wars: Local Effects of Competition Between Multinational Telecommunication Corporations. Peter B. Seel. Ed. by Victoria Cuffel. (MacArthur Scholar Series, Occasional Paper: No. 18). 59p. (Orig.). 1993. pap. 3.50 (*1-881157-21-0*) In Ctr Global.

Television Weathercasting: A History. Robert Henson. LC 89-43696. (Illus.). 205p. 1990. lib. bdg. 38.50 (*0-89950-492-2*) McFarland & Co.

***Television Western Players of the Fifties: A Biographical Encyclopedia of All Regular Cast Members in Western Series, 1949 Through 1959.** Everett Aaker. LC 97-13647. (Illus.). 736p. 1997. boxed 85.00 (*0-7864-0284-9*) McFarland & Co.

Television Westerns: Major & Minor Series, 1946-1978. Richard West. LC 87-42525. (Illus.). 168p. 1987. lib. bdg. 29.95 (*0-89950-252-0*) McFarland & Co.

***Television Westerns Episode Guide, 1949-1996: All United States Series, 1949-1996.** Harris M. Lentz, III. LC 97-10085. (All United States Ser.). 560p. 1997. boxed 95.00 (*0-7864-0377-2*) McFarland & Co.

Television Writer's Guide. 4th ed. Lynne Naylor. 1995. pap. text ed. 50.00 (*0-943728-75-4*) Lone Eagle Pub.

***Television Writers Guide.** 5th ed. Ed. by Lynne Naylor. 608p. 1997. pap. 55.00 (*0-943728-86-X*) Lone Eagle Pub.

Television y la Educacion. Fundacion Angel Ramos, Inc. LC 91-73368. (Illus.). 103p. (Orig.). (C). 1991. pap. text ed. 7.00 (*0-9622522-8-X*) Editorial Academica.

Television You Watch. Richard H. Turner. 48p. 1988. pap. text ed. 5.00 (*0-8428-2259-3*) Cambridge Bk.

TeleVisionaries: In Their Own Words, Public Television's Founders Tell How It All Began. Jim Robertson. LC 92-62246. (Illus.). 280p. 1992. 29.95 (*0-9627974-8-0*) Tabby Hse Bks.

Televisionaries: The Red Army Faction Story, 1963-1993. Tom Vague. (Illus.). 112p. (Orig.). 1994. pap. 6.95 (*1-873176-47-3*, AK Pr San Fran) AK Pr Dist.

Television's Guardians: The FCC & the Politics of Programming, 1958-1967. James L. Baughman. LC 84-13178. 328p. (C). 1985. text ed. 37.00 (*0-87049-448-1*) U of Tenn Pr.

***Television's Guardians: The FCC & the Politics of Programming, 1958-1967.** James L. Baughman. LC 84-13178. (Illus.). 328p. pap. 93.50 (*0-608-05199-3*, 2065736) Bks Demand.

Television's Imageable Influences: The Self-Perceptions of Young African Americans. Camille O. Cosby. LC 94-9258. (Illus.). 192p. 1994. reprint ed. 27.95 (*0-8191-9521-9*) U Pr of Amer.

Television's Private Eye. Robert Larka. Ed. by Christopher H. Sterling. LC 78-21724. (Dissertations in Broadcasting Ser.). (Illus.). 1980. lib. bdg. 23.95 (*0-405-11763-9*) Ayer.

Television's Second Golden Age: From Hill Street Blues to ER. Robert J. Thompson. (Illus.). 224p. 1996. 27.50 (*0-8264-0901-6*) Continuum.

***Television's Second Golden Age: From Hill Street Blues to ER.** Robert J. Thompson. (Television Ser.). 225p. 1997. pap. 16.95 (*0-8156-0504-8*) Syracuse U Pr.

Television's Window on the World: International Affairs Coverage on the U. S. Networks. James Larson. Ed. by Melvin J. Voigt. LC 84-15859. (Communication & Information Science Ser.). 224p. 1984. pap. 39.50 (*0-89391-312-X*); text ed. 73.25 (*0-89391-142-9*) Ablex Pub.

***Televison Receivers.** Ibrahim. 1992. pap. text ed. write for info. (*0-582-08617-5*, Pub. by Longman UK) Longman.

Televisuality: Performing Style in American Television. John T. Caldwell. LC 94-39017. (Communication, Media & Culture Ser.). (Illus.). 475p. 1995. text ed. 55.00 (*0-8135-2163-7*); pap. text ed. 20.00 (*0-8135-2164-5*) Rutgers U Pr.

Televote: Expanding Citizen Participation in the Quantum Age. Christa D. Slayton. LC 91-16687. 240p. 1991. text ed. 55.00 (*0-275-93836-0*, C3836, Praeger Pubs) Greenwood.

***Telewars in the States: Telecommunications Issues in a New Era of Competition.** Bonnett. 1996. pap. 22.95 (*0-8058-2822-2*) L Erlbaum Assocs.

Telewars in the States: Telecommunications Issues in a New Era of Competition. Thomas W. Bonnett. LC 96-28061. 1996. pap. 22.95 (*0-934842-16-7*) CSPA.

***Telework: Penetration, Potential & Practice.** Ed. by Korte & Wynne. LC 96-7508. 310p. (YA). (gr. 12 up). 1996. 98.00 (*90-5199-255-6*, 255-6) IOS Press.

Telework: Present Situation & Future Development of a New Form of Work Organization. Ed. by Werner B. Korte et al. 254p. 1988. 163.00 (*0-444-70355-1*, North Holland) Elsevier.

Telework: The Human Resource Implications. John Stanworth & Celia Stanworth. 144p. (C). 1991. 95.00 (*0-85292-465-8*, Pub. by IPM Hse UK) St Mut.

Telework, 1990. (Conditions of Work Digest Ser.: Vol. 9, No. 1). vii, 251p. (Orig.). 1990. pap. 36.00 (*92-2-107277-0*) Intl Labour Office.

Teleworkbook for Government by Consent. Steve Dedeaux & Bryan Reece. 110p. (C). 1996. 8.00 (*1-888271-00-0*) Wstrn Custom.

Teleworkbook for Sociological Imagination. Steve Dedeaux & Bryan Reece. 110p. 1996. 8.00 (*1-888271-01-9*) Wstrn Custom.

***Teleworking: In Brief.** Mike Johnson. LC 97-8474. 1997. write for info. (*0-7506-2875-8*) Buttrwrth-Heinemann.

***Teleworking & Telelearning: Perspectives from the Pacific.** Ed. by L. S. Harms & Frank S. Sabado. 258p. 1991. pap. 55.00 (*0-614-31036-9*) Pac Telecom.

An Asterisk (*) at the beginning of an entry indicates that the title is appearing in BIP for the first time.

Teleworking Explained. Ed. by M. Gary et al. LC 93-26459. 289p. 1993. text ed. 70.00 (*0-471-93975-7*) Wiley.

Telex English. Palstra. 64p. (C). 1990. pap. text ed. 10.00 (*0-13-902826-9*) P-H.

***Telex Iran.** Photos by Gilles Peress. (Illus.). 102p. 1996. 58.00 (*3-931141-36-5*, 620301, Pub. by Scalo Pubs) Dist Art Pubs.

Telfair County, Georgia. Pioneer Historical Society Staff. (Illus.). 574p. 1988. 50.00 (*0-88107-114-5*) Curtis Media.

Tell a Story. (Sesame Street Ser.: No. 19). (J). 1989. 1.49 (*0-553-18402-4*) Bantam.

Tell a Story (Big Book), Unit 2. (Networks Ser.). 1991. 19.50 (*0-88106-709-1*, N120) Charlesbridge Pub.

Tell & Draw Animal Cut-outs. 3rd ed. Margaret J. Olson. (J). (gr. k-2). 1963. pap. 4.00 (*0-934876-15-0*) Creative Storytime.

Tell & Draw Paper Bag Puppet Book. 2nd ed. Margaret J. Oldfield. (Illus.). (J). (gr. k-2). 1978. pap. 6.95 (*0-934876-16-9*) Creative Storytime.

Tell & Draw Paper Cut-Outs. Margaret J. Oldfield. (Illus.). (Orig.). (J). (gr. k-2). 1988. pap. 4.00 (*0-934876-23-1*, 23) Creative Storytime.

Tell & Draw Stories. Margaret J. Olson. (Illus.). (J). (ps-3). 1963. pap. 6.95 (*0-934876-01-0*); lib. bdg. 11.95 (*0-934876-05-3*) Creative Storytime.

Tell El-Amarna Tablets, 2 vols., Set. Ed. by Samuel A. Mercer & Frank H. Hallock. LC 78-72764. (Ancient Mesopotamian Texts & Studies). (Illus.). 942p. 1983. reprint ed. 145.00 (*0-404-18216-X*) AMS Pr.

Tell El-Amarna Tablets in the British Museum with Auto-Type Facsimiles. LC 78-72765. (Ancient Mesopotamian Texts & Studies). reprint ed. 49.50 (*0-404-18219-4*) AMS Pr.

Tell El-Hesi Field Manual. Jeffrey A. Blakely & Lawrence E. Toombs. LC 80-21724. (Joint Archaeological Expedition to Tell El-Hesi Ser.: Vol. 1). xix, 134p. (C). 1980. text ed. 20.00 (*0-89757-205-X*); pap. text ed. 15.00 (*0-89757-203-3*) Am Sch Orient Res.

Tell el-Hesi, Vol. 4-Phase One: The Site & the Expedition. Pref. by Bruce T. Dahlberg. (American Schools of Oriental Research Excavation Reports). (Illus.). 212p. (C). 1989. text ed. write for info. (*0-918401-01-1*) U Wake Forest.

***Tell el Mazar Vol. I: Cemetery A, Analysis of Iron IIC Jordan Valley Site.** Khair Yassine. (Illus.). xxv, 195p. 1984. 25.00 (*0-614-23980-X*) U PA Mus Pubns.

Tell Es-Sa'Idiyeh: Excavations on the Tell, 1964-1966. James B. Pritchard. (University Museum Monographs: No. 60). (Illus.). 216p. (ARA & ENG.). 1985. text ed. 60.00 (*0-934718-60-1*) U PA Mus Pubns.

Tell Freedom. Peter Abrahams. 311p. 1982. 12.95 (*0-571-11777-5*) Faber & Faber.

Tell It All: The Story of a Life's Experience in Mormonism: An Autobiography. Fanny Stenhouse. (American Biography Ser.). 633p. 1991. reprint ed. lib. bdg. 109.00 (*0-7812-8363-9*) Rprt Serv.

Tell It by Heart: Women & the Healing Power of Story. Erica H. Meade. 285p. 1995. 38.95 (*0-8126-9301-9*); pap. 17.95 (*0-8126-9302-7*) Open Court.

Tell It Like It Is: Straight Talk about Sex. Annamaria Formichella et al. 240p. (Orig.). 1991. pap. 7.95 (*0-380-75813-X*) Avon.

Tell It Like It Is: Tough Choices for Today's Teens. Ellen Frankel & Sarah Levine. (YA). 1995. write for info. (*0-88125-522-X*) Ktav.

Tell It! Manual: The Complete Program for Evaluating Library Performance. Douglas L. Zweizig et al. LC 95-26323. (Illus.). 272p. 1996. pap. 30.00 (*0-8389-0679-6*, 0-6796-2045) ALA.

Tell It Slant: The Christian Gospel & Its Communication. John Tinsley. LC 89-40805. 450p. 1990. text ed. 39.95 (*1-55605-136-0*); pap. text ed. 29.95 (*1-55605-135-2*) Wyndham Hall.

Tell It to Sweeney: The Informal History of the New York Daily News. John Chapman. LC 77-8991. (Illus.). 288p. 1977. reprint ed. text ed. 59.75 (*0-8371-9724-4*, CHTS, Greenwood Pr) Greenwood.

Tell It to the Dead: Memories of a War. Donald Kirk. LC 95-53180. (Illus.). 306p. (C). (gr. 13). 1996. 58.95 (*1-56324-717-8*, East Gate Bk); pap. 20.95 (*1-56324-718-6*, East Gate Bk) M E Sharpe.

Tell It to the World: A Guide to International Public Relations. Burton M. Halpern. 152p. 1992. 14.95 (*0-317-06102-X*, Pub. by Gefen Pub Hse IS) Gefen Bks.

Tell It to Washington. League of Women Voters Education Fund Staff. 24p. 1993. 2.75 (*0-89959-361-5*, 349) LWVUS.

***Tell It to Women: An Epic Drama for Women.** Osonye T. Onwueme. LC 97-450. (African American Life Ser.). 176p. (Orig.). 1997. pap. text ed. 18.95 (*0-8143-2649-8*) Wayne St U Pr.

Tell It Well: Communicating the Gospel Across Cultures. J. T. Seamands. 236p. (Orig.). 1981. pap. 11.99 (*0-8341-0684-1*) Beacon Hill.

Tell It with Style. Helen T. Boursier. 168p. (Orig.). 1995. pap. 9.99 (*0-8308-1639-9*, 1639, Saltshaker Bk) InterVarsity.

***Tell MacArthur to Wait.** rev. ed. Ralph E. Hibbs. LC 97-20936. (Illus.). 250p. 1996. 35.00 (*1-56216-039-7*); pap. 19.00 (*1-56216-040-0*) Systems Co.

***Tell Me.** Theodore Meth. 70p. (Orig.). 1996. pap. write for info. (*1-57502-309-1*) Morris Pubng.

Tell Me: Children, Reading, & Talk. Aidan Chambers. 128p. (C). 1996. pap. text ed. 10.00 (*1-57110-030-X*) Stenhse Pubs.

Tell Me - No More Secrets, No More Lies: Life As an Adoptee. Ginni D. Snodgrass. Tr. by I. R. Jacobsen from ENG. (Illus.). 150p. (Orig.). 1990. pap. 10.95 (*0-9620410-3-3*) GS Enterprise.

Tell Me a Bible Story. Doris Willis. LC 90-22423. (Bible Board Book Ser.). (J). 1991. pap. 1.19 (*0-687-03126-5*) Abingdon.

Tell Me a Fairy Tale: A Parent's Guide to Telling Magical & Mythical Fairy Tales. Bill Adler, Jr. LC 94-29891. 224p. (Orig.). 1995. pap. 11.95 (*0-452-27174-6*, Plume) NAL-Dutton.

Tell Me a Mitzi. Lore Segal. LC 69-14980. (Illus.). 40p. (J). (ps-3). 1982. 17.00 (*0-374-37392-2*) FS&G.

Tell Me a Mitzi. Lore Segal. LC 69-14980. (Illus.). 40p. (J). (ps-3). 1991. pap. 5.95 (*0-374-47502-4*) FS&G.

Tell me a Mitzi. Lore Segal & Harriet Pincus. (J). pap. 7.50 (*0-590-20039-9*) Scholastic Inc.

Tell Me a Mitzvah: Little & Big Ways to Repair the World. Danny Siegel. LC 93-7552. (Illus.). 64p. (Orig.). (J). (gr. 2-6). 1993. pap. 7.95 (*0-929371-78-X*) Kar-Ben.

Tell Me a Prayer. Nathaniel Noble. LC 91-65162. 51p. 1991. pap. 5.95 (*1-55523-424-0*) Winston-Derek.

Tell Me a Riddle. Tillie Olsen. 128p. 1971. pap. 10.95 (*0-385-29010-1*, Delta) Dell.

Tell Me a Riddle. Tillie Olsen. 1984. 21.75 (*0-8446-6090-6*) Peter Smith.

Tell Me a Riddle. Tillie Olsen. Ed. by Deborah S. Rosenfelt. (Women Writers: Texts & Contexts Ser.). 200p. (C). 1995. text ed. 38.00 (*0-8135-2136-X*); pap. text ed. 14.00 (*0-8135-2137-8*) Rutgers U Pr.

Tell Me a Season. Mary M. Siddals. LC 96-23313. (J). 1997. 12.95 (*0-395-71021-9*) HM.

Tell Me a Story! Kathy M. Littlefield & Robert S. Littlefield. (Illus.). 32p. (Orig.). (J). (gr. 3-6). 1989. pap. text ed. 8.95 (*1-879340-02-X*, K0103) Kidspeak.

Tell Me a Story. Ruth B. McDougall. LC 85-17214. (Illus.). 152p. (Orig.). 1985. pap. 7.95 (*0-89407-070-3*) Strawberry Hill.

***Tell Me a Story.** Joseph J. Sollish. 338p. (Orig.). 1997. mass mkt. 4.99 (*1-55197-991-8*, Pub. by Comnwlth Pub CN) Partners Pubs Grp.

Tell Me a Story. Katharine B. Rondthaler. (Illus.). 64p. (J). (ps-5). 1992. reprint ed. pap. 4.00 (*1-878422-06-5*) Moravian Ch in Amer.

Tell Me a Story. Walt Disney Productions Staff. (Walt Disney's Fun-to-Learn Library Ser.: Vol. 18). (Illus.). 44p. (J). (gr. 1-6). 1983. reprint ed. 3.49 (*1-885222-09-2*) Advance Pubs.

Tell Me a Story: Creating Bedtime Stories Your Children Will Dream On. Chase Collins. 160p. 1992. pap. 8.95 (*0-395-61211-X*) HM.

Tell Me a Story: Narrative & Intelligence. Roger C. Schank. 264p. (C). 1995. pap. text ed. 16.95 (*0-8101-1313-9*) Northwestern U Pr.

Tell Me a Story at Christmas: Heartwarming Stories from Around the World. Ed. by Kathryn Deering. 220p. (Orig.). 1996. 16.99 (*0-89283-987-2*, Vine Bks) Servant.

Tell Me a Story, Dad. Virginia Ferguson & Peter Durkin. LC 93-6629. (J). 1994. write for info. (*0-383-03717-4*) SRA McGraw.

Tell Me a Story, Mama. Angela Johnson. LC 88-17917. (Illus.). 32p. (J). (ps-1). 1989. 15.95 (*0-531-05794-1*); lib. bdg. 16.99 (*0-531-08394-2*) Orchard Bks Watts.

Tell Me a Story, Mama. Angela Johnson. LC 88-17917. (Illus.). 32p. (J). (ps-1). 1992. pap. 6.95 (*0-531-07032-8*) Orchard Bks Watts.

Tell Me a Story, Nana! Bedtime Fantasy Tales. Peg Garner-Cheadle. 102p. (J). (gr. 3-6). 1995. pap. 10.00 (*0-9649249-0-0*) Heather Hill MA.

Tell Me a Story, Sing Me a Song: A Texas Chronicle. William A. Owens. 336p. 1983. pap. 17.95 (*0-292-78056-7*) U of Tex Pr.

Tell Me a Tale. James McEachin. LC 95-38666. 256p. 1996. 18.95 (*0-89141-584-X*, Lyford Bks) Presidio Pr.

Tell Me a Tale: A Book about Storytelling. Joseph Bruchac. LC 96-21697. 1997. 16.00 (*0-15-201221-4*) HarBrace.

***Tell Me a Tale: A Book about Storytelling.** Joseph Bruchac. (YA). (gr. 5 up). 1997. 16.00 (*0-614-28819-3*) HarBrace.

***Tell Me a Tale: A Novel of the Old South.** James McEachin. 288p. 1997. mass mkt. 6.99 (*0-425-15689-3*) Berkley Pub.

Tell Me a Texas Story. June R. Welch. 220p. 1991. 17.95 (*0-912854-16-2*) Yellow Rose Pr.

***Tell Me a Toy Riddle: Haunted House.** (J). 1997. write for info. (*0-614-29215-8*) NAL-Dutton.

***Tell Me a Toy Riddle: Sneak-&-Peek Book.** Playskool Staff. Orig. Title: Sliding Surprise. (J). 1997. pap. 7.99 (*0-525-45817-4*) Dutton Child Bks.

Tell Me a Trudy. Lore Segal. LC 77-24123. (Illus.). 40p. (J). (ps-3). 1977. 15.00 (*0-374-37395-7*) FS&G.

Tell Me a Trudy. Lore Segal. (Illus.). (J). (ps up). 1989. pap. 4.95 (*0-374-47504-0*) FS&G.

Tell Me about God. Aza Baxter. (Cosmology Ser.). 16p. (YA). (gr. 7 up). 1995. pap. 3.00 (*0-9643205-2-5*) Intuitive Psy.

Tell Me about God: Simple Studies in the Doctrine of God for Children. Susan Harding. (Illus.). 64p. (J). (ps-4). 1985. pap. 7.99 (*0-85151-510-X*) Banner of Truth.

Tell Me about God: 12 Lessons, Vol. 1. Lois J. Haas. (Tiny Steps of Faith Ser.). (J). (ps). 1966. 3.50 (*0-86508-012-7*); 1.75 (*0-86508-013-5*) BCM Pubn.

Tell Me about God: 12 Lessons, Vol. 1. Lois J. Haas. (Tiny Steps of Faith Ser.). (J). (ps). 1994. 14.95 (*0-86508-011-9*) BCM Pubn.

Tell Me about God for Self Study & Teaching. Aza Baxter. (Cosmology Ser.). 16p. 1995. pap. 3.00 (*0-9643205-3-3*) Intuitive Psy.

***Tell Me about Heaven, I Think I'm Forgetting.** Janet Clowes. LC 96-38764. (Illus.). 32p. (J). 1998. 14.95 (*1-57102-100-0*, Ideals Child) Hambleton-Hill.

Tell Me about It! Laluzerne & Tsuk. 1993. audio 28.95 (*0-8384-3609-9*) Heinle & Heinle.

Tell Me about It! Laluzerne & Tsuk. 1993. pap. 21.95 (*0-8384-3608-0*) Heinle & Heinle.

Tell Me about It! Laluzerne & Tsuk. 1993. teacher ed., pap. 9.95 (*0-8384-4202-1*) Heinle & Heinle.

Tell Me about Jesus: 16 Lessons, Vol. 2. Lois J. Haas. (Tiny Steps of Faith Ser.). (J). (ps). 1967. 14.95 (*0-86508-014-3*); 3.50 (*0-86508-015-1*); 1.75 (*0-86508-016-X*) BCM Pubn.

Tell Me About Nature Dictionary. Querida L. Pearce. (J). 1990. 5.99 (*0-517-03567-7*) Random Hse Value.

Tell Me about Prayer: Prayer Guide for Children, Grade 1-3. Kathryn Kizer. Ed. by Karen Gross. 64p. (Orig.). (J). (gr. 1-3). 1993. pap. 4.95 (*1-56309-067-8*, New Hope) Womans Mission Union.

***Tell Me about Your Day.** Robin Stiles. LC 95-90737. (Illus.). 72p. (J). 1996. pap. 8.00 (*1-56002-613-8*, Univ Edtns) Aegina Pr.

***Tell Me Again: The Cry of the Children.** Patricia Morgan. (Illus.). 144p. 1996. 15.99 (*1-56043-174-1*) Destiny Image.

Tell Me Again: The Cry of the Children. Patricia Morgan. (Illus.). 144p. 1996. pap. 10.99 (*1-56043-180-6*) Destiny Image.

Tell Me Again About the Night I Was Born. Jamie L. Curtis. LC 95-5412. (Illus.). 40p. (J). (ps-3). 1996. 14.95 (*0-06-024528-X*); lib. bdg. 14.89 (*0-06-024529-8*) HarpC Child Bks.

Tell Me Again How the White Heron Rises & Flies Across the Nacreous River at Twilight Toward the Distant Islands. Hayden Carruth. LC 89-31603. 96p. 1989. pap. 8.95 (*0-8112-1104-5*, NDP677) New Directions.

Tell Me All That You Know: The Unauthorized Grateful Dead Trivia Book. Brian A. Folker. 1996. pap. 6.99 (*0-7860-0265-4*) Kensgtn Pub Corp.

Tell Me Another: Storytelling & Reading Aloud at Home, at School, & in the Community. Bob Barton. LC 86-18406. 160p. (Orig.). 1986. pap. 12.95 (*0-435-08231-0*, 08231) Heinemann.

Tell Me Another Tale. 1993. pap. 8.95 (*0-87162-649-7*, D4202) Warner Pr.

Tell Me, Dark. Ed. by Karen Berger. (Illus.). 80p. 1993. pap. 14.95 (*1-56389-088-7*, Vertigo) DC Comics.

Tell Me Doctor: About Prenatal Care. American BookWorks Corporation Staff. (Illus.). 96p. (Orig.). 1989. pap. 4.95 (*0-317-94000-7*) Amer Bookworks.

Tell Me Doctor: About Prenatal Care. American Bookworks Corporation Staff. 1991. pap. 4.95 (*0-9622813-0-1*) Amer Bookworks.

Tell Me Everything. Carolyn Coman. (YA). 1993. 15.00 (*0-374-37390-6*) FS&G.

Tell Me Everything. Carolyn Coman. 160p. (YA). 1995. 3.95 (*0-374-47506-7*) FS&G.

Tell Me How Long the Train's Been Gone. James Baldwin. 384p. 1986. mass mkt. 6.50 (*0-440-38581-4*, LE) Dell.

Tell Me How to Please God: 16 Lessons, Vol. 4. Lois J. Haas. (Tiny Steps of Faith Ser.). (J). (ps). 1974. 14.95 (*0-86508-020-8*); 3.50 (*0-86508-021-6*); 1.75 (*0-86508-022-4*) BCM Pubn.

Tell Me How to Trust God: 16 Lessons, Vol. 3. Lois J. Haas. (Tiny Steps of Faith Ser.). (J). (ps). 1970. 14.95 (*0-86508-017-8*); 3.50 (*0-86508-018-6*); 1.75 (*0-86508-019-4*) BCM Pubn.

Tell Me If I've Stopped. David Greenberger. (Illus.). 179p. (Orig.). 1995. pap. 14.95 (*0-9517012-3-1*, Pub. by Sun Tavern Flds UK) AK Pr Dist.

Tell Me if the Lovers Are Losers. Cynthia Voigt. LC 81-8079. 256p. (YA). (gr. 7 up). 1982. lib. bdg. 17.00 (*0-689-30911-2*, Atheneum Bks Young) S&S Childrens.

Tell Me If the Lovers Are Losers. Cynthia Voigt. 241p. 1987. mass mkt. 4.50 (*0-449-70235-9*) Fawcett.

Tell Me I'm Here: One Family's Experience of Schizophrenia. Anne Deveson. (Illus.). 288p. (Orig.). 1992. pap. 10.00 (*0-14-017339-0*, Penguin Bks) Viking Penguin.

***Tell Me Lies.** Crusie. Date not set. write for info. (*0-312-17940-5*) St Martin.

Tell Me Lies about Vietnam: Cultural Battles for the Meaning of the War. Alf Louvre & Jeffrey Walsh. 224p. 1989. 90.00 (*0-335-15594-4*, Open Univ Pr); pap. 34.00 (*0-335-15593-6*, Open Univ Pr) Taylor & Francis.

Tell Me More. Elbaum & Peam. 1989. pap. 22.95 (*0-8384-2951-3*) Heinle & Heinle.

Tell Me More. Larry King. 1992. mass mkt. 4.99 (*0-312-92690-1*) St Martin.

Tell Me More. large type ed. Larry King. 1991. 27.99 (*0-7089-8612-9*, Trail West Pubs) Ulverscroft.

Tell Me More: A Cookbook Spiced with Cajun Tradition & Food Memories. Junior League of Lafayette Staff. (Illus.). 200p. 1993. 15.95 (*0-935032-25-8*) Jr League Lafayette.

Tell Me More Ancestor Stories, Grandma. Diana J. Dennett. (Illus.). 16p. (Orig.). 1992. pap. 5.95 (*1-877809-75-6*) Park Pl Pubns.

Tell Me No Lies. Micheal Cecilione. 1996. pap. 5.99 (*1-57566-061-X*) Kensgtn Pub Corp.

Tell Me No Lies. Elizabeth Lowell. 1996. mass mkt. 5.99 (*1-55166-096-2*, 1-66096-8, Mira Bks) Harlequin Bks.

Tell Me No Lies. Patricia Rosemoor. (Intrigue Ser.). 1996. mass mkt. 3.75 (*0-373-22386-2*, 1-22386-6) Harlequin Bks.

***Tell Me No Lies, Vol. 845.** Jill Shalvis. (Loveswept Ser.). 1997. mass mkt. 3.50 (*0-553-44600-2*) Bantam.

Tell Me No Secrets. Joy Felding. 4.98 (*0-8317-8649-3*) Smithmark.

Tell Me No Secrets. Joy Fielding. 416p. 1994. mass mkt. 5.99 (*0-380-72122-8*) Avon.

Tell Me No Secrets. large type ed. Marlene McFadden. (Dales Large Print Ser.). 1995. pap. 17.99 (*1-85389-553-9*, Dales) Ulverscroft.

Tell Me of a Land That's Fair: An Historical Essay in Celebration of the 250th Anniversary of the Formation of Frederick County, Virginia (1738-1988) James V. Hutton, Jr. 52p. (Orig.). 1988. pap. 5.00 (*0-935931-37-6*) Borgo Pr.

Tell Me of a Land That's Fair: An Historical Essay in Celebration of the 250th Anniversary of the Formation of Frederick County, Virginia (1738-1988) James V. Hutton, Jr. 52p. (Orig.). (C). 1988. reprint ed. lib. bdg. 25.00 (*0-8095-8217-1*) Borgo Pr.

Tell Me One Good Thing: Bedtime Stories. Richard Thompson. (Illus.). 48p. (J). (ps-3). 1992. pap. 7.95 (*1-55037-212-2*, Pub. by Annick CN); lib. bdg. 15.95 (*1-55037-215-7*, Pub. by Annick CN) Firefly Bks Ltd.

Tell Me, Papa: A Family Book for Children's Questions about Death & Funerals. Joy Johnson & Marvin Johnson. (Illus.). 24p. (Orig.). (J). (gr. 2-7). 1978. reprint ed. pap. 3.95 (*1-56123-011-1*) Centering Corp.

Tell Me Papa: Tell Me about Funerals. Joy Johnson & Marvin Johnson. 1980. bds. 8.95 (*0-930194-02-0*) Ctr Thanatology.

Tell Me Some More. Crosby N. Bonsall & Fritz Siebel. LC 61-5773. (Harper I Can Read Bk.). (Illus.). 64p. (J). (ps-3). 13.89 (*0-06-020601-2*, 133507) HarpC Child Bks.

Tell Me That You Love Me, Junie Moon. Marjorie B. Kellogg. 1972. pap. 5.00 (*0-87129-324-2*, T15) Dramatic Pub.

Tell Me That You Love Me, Junie Moon. Marjorie B. Kellogg. 224p. (YA). 1993. pap. 3.95 (*0-374-47510-5*) FS&G.

Tell Me That You Love Me, Junie Moon. Marjorie B. Kellogg. 1996. 17.75 (*0-8446-6820-6*) Peter Smith.

Tell Me the Bible. Joelle Chabert et al. 110p. (Orig.). 1991. 14.95 (*0-8146-2064-7*) Liturgical Pr.

Tell Me the Promises. Joni E. Tada. (Illus.). 48p. (J). 1996. 15.99 (*0-89107-904-1*) Crossway Bks.

Tell Me the Secrets. Max Lucado. LC 93-25957. (Illus.). 48p. (J). 1993. 15.99 (*0-89107-730-8*) Crossway Bks.

Tell Me the Stories of Jesus. Andy Holmes. (J). (ps-3). 1992. 5.99 (*0-929216-59-8*) KindrVision.

***Tell Me the Stories of Jesus: The Parables for Children.** Carole Essenmacher & Nancy Regensburger. 147p. 1996. pap. 19.95 (*1-877871-99-0*, 5501) Ed Ministries.

Tell Me the Story. Max Lucado. LC 92-26963. (Illus.). 48p. 1992. 15.99 (*0-89107-679-4*) Crossway Bks.

Tell Me the Tale. Merle Strege. 1991. pap. 8.95 (*0-87162-989-5*, D4200) Warner Pr.

Tell Me the Time. (First Bks.: No. S808-3). (Illus.). (J). (ps). 3.95 (*0-7214-5054-7*, Ladybrd) Penguin.

Tell Me the Truth. Carolyn Keene. (Nancy Drew on Campus Ser.: No. 4). (J). (gr. 8 up). 1995. mass mkt. 3.99 (*0-671-52745-2*) PB.

***Tell Me the Truth: God's Truths for Eternity.** Joni Eareckson Tada. (Illus.). 486p. (J). 1997. 15.99 (*0-89107-946-7*) Crossway Bks.

***Tell Me the Truth about Love.** W. H. Auden. Date not set. 1.99 (*0-517-17582-7*) Random Hse Value.

Tell Me the Truth about Love: Ten Poems. W. H. Auden. 1994. pap. 6.00 (*0-679-75782-1*, Vin) Random.

Tell Me the Way It Was ... Robert S. Littlefield & Jane A. Ball. (Illus.). 32p. (Orig.). (J). (gr. 3-6). 1990. pap. text ed. 8.95 (*1-879340-07-0*, K0108) Kidspeak.

Tell Me What You Like: An Alison Kaine Mystery. Kate Allen. LC 92-47054. (Orig.). 1993. pap. 9.95 (*0-934678-48-0*) New Victoria Pubs.

***Tell Me When to Look! Modern Horror Films from The Curse of Frankenstein to Today.** John McCarty. 256p. 1997. pap. 19.95 (*0-8065-1849-9*, Citadel Pr) Carol Pub Group.

Tell Me Who You Are. R. G. Des Dixon. 1995. pap. 16.95 (*1-55022-231-7*) LPC InBook.

***Tell Me Who Your Friend Is: An Armenian Folktale.** Alidz Agbabian. (Illus.). 32p. (Orig.). (J). (ps-2). 1996. pap. 12.00 (*0-9655507-0-2*) Dziludzar.

Tell Me Why: Answering Tough Questions about the Faith. Ronda D. Chervin & Joseph K. Pollard. LC 94-66026. 160p. (Orig.). 1994. pap. 8.95 (*0-87973-647-X*, 647) Our Sunday Visitor.

Tell Me Why: Beatles. Tim Riley. 1989. pap. 15.00 (*0-679-72198-3*, Vin) Random.

Tell Me Your Best Thing. Anna G. Hines. (Illus.). 128p. (J). (gr. 2-5). 1994. pap. 3.99 (*0-14-036447-1*) Puffin Bks.

Tell My Horse. Zora Neale Hurston. LC 89-45673. 304p. 1990. pap. 13.00 (*0-06-091649-4*, PL) HarpC.

Tell My Horse: Voodoo & Life in Haiti & Jamaica. Zora Neale Hurston. 326p. (C). 1990. reprint ed. lib. bdg. 35.00 (*0-8095-9020-4*) Borgo Pr.

Tell My Priests: The Words of Our Lord to Priests about His Mercy As Revealed to Sr. Faustina Kowalska. George W. Kosicki. 123p. 1992. 4.95 (*0-940535-50-5*, UP150) Franciscan U Pr.

Tell My Priests: Words of Our Lord to Priests about His Mercy As Revealed to Sister Faustina Kowalska. Ed. by Marians of the Immaculate Conception Staff. LC 87-62982. 112p. 1988. pap. text ed. write for info. (*0-944203-08-6*) Marian Pr.

Tell Newt to Shut Up: Prize Winning Washington Post Journalists Reveal How Reality Gagged The... David Maraniss & Michael Weisskopf. 218p. 1996. pap. 10.00 (*0-684-83293-3*, Touchstone Bks) S&S Trade.

Tell No Man. Adela R. St. Johns. 1994. lib. bdg. 32.95 (*1-56849-378-9*) Buccaneer Bks.

Tell No One Who You Are: The Hidden Childhood of Regine Miller. Walter Buchignani. LC 92-80412. 185p. (J). (gr. 5-8). 1994. 17.95 (*0-88776-286-7*) Tundra Bks.

Tell No One Who You Are: The Hidden Childhood of Regine Miller. Walter Buchignani. LC 92-80412. (Illus.). 185p. (YA). (gr. 7 up). 1996. reprint ed. pap. 9.95 (*0-88776-303-0*) Tundra Bks.

T

Tell Pharaoh. Loften Mitchell. 1987. pap. 5.95 (0-88145-048-0) Broadway Play.

Tell Rubeidheh. Killick. (Archaeological Reports Ser.: Vol. 2). 1989. pap. 75.00 (0-85668-431-7, Pub. by Aris & Phillips UK) David Brown.

***Tell Sabi Abyad - the Late Neolithic Settlement: Report on the Excavations of the University of Amsterdam (1988) & the National Museum of Antiquities Leiden (1991-1993) in Syria.** Ed. by Peter M. Akkermans. 556p. 1996. 139.50 (90-6258-078-5, Pub. by Netherlands Inst NE) Eisenbrauns.

Tell-Tale Article: A Critical Approach to Modern Poetry. George R. Hamilton. LC 72-3494. (Essay Index Reprint Ser.). 1977. reprint ed. 15.95 (0-8369-2906-3) Ayer.

Tell-Tale Heart. Edgar Allan Poe. (Creative's Classics Ser.). (Illus.). 32p. (YA). (gr. 9 up). 1980. lib. bdg. 13.95 (0-87191-772-6) Creative Ed.

Tell-Tale Heart. Edgar Allan Poe. Ed. by Raymond Harris. (Classics Ser.). (Illus.). 48p. (YA). (gr. 6-12). 1982. teacher ed. 7.32 (0-89061-263-3, 469); pap. text ed. 5.99 (0-89061-262-5, 467); audio 17.96 (0-89061-264-1, 468) Jamestown Pubs.

Tell-Tale Heart. rev. ed. Edgar Allan Poe. (Read-Along Radio Dramas Ser.). (YA). (gr. 6-12). 1993. reprint ed. boxed 35.00 (1-878298-04-6) Balance Pub.

Tell-Tale Heart & Other Writings. Edgar Allan Poe. 432p. (gr. 7-12). 1983. pap. 4.95 (0-553-21228-1, Bantam Classics) Bantam.

***Tell-Tale Tallulah.** (Little Monsters Ser.). (J). 1997. write for info. (0-614-21791-1, Pub. by Splash UK) Assoc Pubs Grp.

***Tell the Children the Truth.** Leonard Lucas. 46p. Date not set. pap. 10.00 (0-9654173-0-1) Chi-Town Polyrhythm.

Tell the People: Talks with James Yen About the Mass Education Movement. Pearl S. Buck. 141p. 1984. reprint ed. pap. 5.00 (0-318-14582-0) Intl Inst Rural.

Tell the Secret: Sharing the Secret of Abuse Is the Beginning of Healing. 2nd ed. Irie L. Session. 70p. pap. 10.00 (0-9641655-0-3) Tell The Secret.

Tell the Time. (Ready to Learn Ser.: No. S813-1). (J). 1989. pap. 1.95 (0-7214-5181-0, Ladybrd) Penguin.

Tell the Time at the Farm. Illus. by Stephanie Ryder. (Clock Books Ser.). 12p. (J). (ps-1). 1996. bds. 5.98 (1-85854-378-9) Brimax Bks.

Tell the Time with Benji. (J). (ps). 1983. bds. 5.50 (0-904494-49-7) Borden.

Tell the Time with Teddy. (J). (ps). 1995. bds. 5.98 (1-85854-263-4) Brimax Bks.

Tell the Time with Thomas. Christopher Awdry. LC 91-67877. (Illus.). 32p. (J). (ps-3). 1993. 8.99 (0-679-83461-3) Random Bks Yng Read.

Tell the Truth. 2nd ed. Will Metzger. LC 83-25304. 191p. (Orig.). 1984. pap. 11.99 (0-87784-934-X, 934) InterVarsity.

Tell The World. Severn Suzuki. 32p. 1993. pap. 10.95 (0-385-25422-9) Doubleday.

Tell the World: What Happened in China & Why. Liu Binyan et al. LC 89-43171. 1989. 18.95 (0-394-58370-1) Pantheon.

Tell Them from Me. Lesley Gow & Andrew McPherson. 137p. 1980. text ed. 25.00 (0-08-025738-0, Pergamon Pr); pap. text ed. 13.00 (0-08-025739-9, Pergamon Pr) Elsevier.

Tell Them I Am Coming: Jesus Told Me To... Richard E. Eby. LC 80-41. 160p. 1984. reprint ed. mass mkt. 4.99 (0-8007-8496-0, Spire) Revell.

Tell Them I Love Them. Joyce Meyer. 52p. (Orig.). 1988. pap. 3.00 (0-944834-00-0) Life Word-Meyer Ministries.

Tell Them I Love Them. Joyce Meyer. 80p. 1995. mass mkt. 3.99 (0-89274-783-8, HH-783) Harrison Hse.

Tell Them to Me. Ed. by Gwyn Filby. (C). 1990. pap. 40.00 (0-85305-280-8, Pub. by J Arthur Ltd UK) St Mut.

***Tell Them We Are Rising.** Ruth W. Hayre & Alexis Moore. LC 97-1492. 1997. text ed. 24.95 (0-471-12679-9) Wiley.

Tell Them We Remember: The Story of the Holocaust with Images from the United States Holocaust Memorial Museum. Susan D. Backrach. LC 93-40090. (YA). (gr. 5 up). 1994. 21.95 (0-316-69264-6); pap. 12.95 (0-316-07484-5) Little.

Tell Them Who I Am: The Lives of Homeless Women. Elliot Liebow. 339p. 1993. 27.95 (0-02-919095-9, Free Press) Free Pr.

Tell Them Who I Am: The Lives of Homeless Women. Elliot Liebow. 368p. 1995. pap. 11.95 (0-14-024137-X, Penguin Bks) Viking Penguin.

Tell Time with Thomas. (J). (gr. 2 up). 1993. 107.88 (0-679-86107-6) Random Bks Yng Read.

Tell Toqaan: A Syrian Village. Louise E. Sweet. (Anthropological Papers: No. 14). (Illus.). 1960. pap. 1.00 (0-932206-20-4) U Mich Mus Anthro.

Tell-Trothes New Yeares Gift, & the Passionate Morrice, 1593: John Lane's Tom Tell-Trothe's Message, & His Pens Complaint, 1600: Thomas Powell's Tom of All Trades, 1631: The Glass of Godly Love (by John Rogers?), 1596. Ed. by F. J. Furnivall. (New Shakespeare Society, London, Ser.: Ser. 6, Nos. 2-3). 1974. reprint ed. pap. 70.00 (0-8115-0243-0) Periodicals Srv.

Tell Us a Story. Allan Ahlberg. LC 95-67159. (Illus.). 32p. (Orig.). (J). 1996. pap. 4.99 (1-56402-574-8) Candlewick Pr.

***Tell Us Another.** George F. Brooks. 44p. 1970. 6.60 (3-296-50100-2, Pub. by Weidmann GW) Lubrecht & Cramer.

Tell Us of the Morning: The Parables of Christ. Benjamin H. Skyles. (Illus.). 162p. (Orig.). 1991. pap. 11.95 (0-9631268-0-6) St Peters Episcopal.

Tell Us Our Names: Story Theology from an Asian Perspective. Choan-Seng Song. LC 84-5139. 224p. (Orig.). reprint ed. pap. 63.90 (0-7837-6410-3, 2046390) Bks Demand.

Tell You What I'll Do see Henry Cecil Reprint Series

Tell Your Secret. Fran Lance & Pat King. 128p. 1986. reprint ed. pap. 6.95 (0-89221-142-3) New Leaf.

Tellable Cracker Tales. Annette J. Bruce. LC 95-41668. (Illus.). 96p. (Orig.). 1996. 14.95 (1-56164-100-6); pap. 8.95 (1-56164-094-8) Pineapple Pr.

***Teller & Tale in Joyce's Fiction: Oscillating Perspectives.** John P. Riquelme. LC 82-7805. 288p. 1983. reprint ed. pap. 82.10 (0-608-03745-1, 2064570) Bks Demand.

Teller & the Tale: Aspects of the Short Story. Ed. by Wendell M. Aycock. LC 81-52254. (Proceedings of the Comparative Literature Symposium Ser.: Vol. 13). 156p. (C). 1982. pap. 12.00 (0-89672-100-0) Tex Tech Univ Pr.

***Teller Handbook: Everything a Teller Needs to Know to Succeed.** 6th ed. Joan German-Grapes. LC 97-3302. 1997. pap. text ed. 21.95 (0-7863-1216-5) Irwin Prof Pubng.

Teller of Hawaiian Tales. Eric Knudsen. 272p. 1987. reprint ed. mass mkt. 4.95 (0-935180-33-8) Mutual Pub HI.

Teller of Tales. William J. Brooke. LC 93-43421. 176p. (YA). (gr. 5 up). 1994. 15.00 (0-06-023399-0); lib. bdg. 14.89 (0-06-023400-8) HarpC Child Bks.

Teller of Tales. William J. Brooke. LC 93-43421. (Trophy Bk.). 176p. (J). (gr. 3-7). 1995. pap. 5.95 (0-06-440511-7, Trophy) HarpC Child Bks.

Teller of Tales: In Search of Robert Louis Stevenson. Hunter Davies. (Literary Roads Ser.). (Illus.). 352p. (Orig.). 1996. 40.00 (1-56656-205-8); pap. 16.00 (1-56656-204-X) Interlink Pub.

***Teller Operations.** 12th ed. 120p. 1996. pap. 34.95 (0-912857-78-1, TE 7622) Inst Finan Educ.

Tellerium in Organic Synthesis. Ed. by Nicola Petragnani. (Best Synthetic Methods Ser.). 248p. 1994. text ed. 73.00 (0-12-552810-8) Acad Pr.

Tellers of the Word. John Navone & Thomas Cooper. 1981. 23.00 (0-317-01341-6); pap. 14.00 (0-317-03298-4) Haymkt-Doyma.

Teller's Tales: Short Stories. Sherwood Anderson. LC 83-80751. (Signature Ser.). 229p. (Orig.). (C). 1983. pap. text ed. 5.95 (0-912756-08-X) Union Coll.

Tellico Archaeology: 12,000 Years of Native American History. rev. ed. Jefferson Chapman. LC 94-18737. (Illus.). 164p. (C). 1995. pap. text ed. 14.95 (0-87049-871-1) U of Tenn Pr.

Tellin' It Like It Is: An African-Centered Christian Interpretation of Black Life & Issues. Richard D. Bullard. (Illus.). 160p. (Orig.). 1995. pap. 10.00 (0-9652135-0-1) Vision Impact.

Telling. Marilyn Reynolds. 186p. (Orig.). 1989. pap. 6.95 (0-929848-01-2) Peace Ventures Pr.

***Telling.** Marion Winik. Date not set. 3.99 (0-517-17603-3) Random Hse Value.

Telling. Marion Winik. 1995. pap. 10.00 (0-679-75522-5, Vin) Random.

Telling. rev. ed. Marilyn Reynolds. LC 95-39149. 160p. (Orig.). (YA). (gr. 7-12). 1996. reprint ed. pap. 8.95 (1-885356-03-X) Morning Glory.

Telling. rev. ed. Marilyn Reynolds. LC 95-39149. 160p. (Orig.). (YA). (gr. 7 up). 1996. reprint ed. 15.95 (1-885356-04-8) Morning Glory.

Telling: A Loving Hagadah for Passover (Non-Sexist, Yet Traditional) Judaism: Fast & Feast. rev. ed. Dov Ben-Khayyim. (Illus.). 48p. (ENG & HEB.). 1984. pap. 5.00 (0-9612500-0-3) Rakhamim Pubns.

Telling America's Story: Teaching American History Through Children's Literature. Thomas McGowan & Meredith McGowan. (Illus.). 116p. (Orig.). 1989. pap. text ed. 17.95 (0-931205-41-7) Jenson Pubns.

***Telling & Remembering: A Century of American Jewish Poetry.** Ed. by Steven J. Rubin. LC 97-19292. 480p. 1997. 27.50 (0-8070-6838-1) Beacon Pr.

Telling & Retelling: Quotation in Biblical Narrative. George W. Savran. LC 85-45315. (Indiana Studies in Biblical Literature). 170p. 1988. reprint ed. pap. 49.40 (0-7837-3726-2, 2057904) Bks Demand.

***Telling Complexions: The Nineteenth-Century English Novel & the Blush.** Mary A. O'Farrell. LC 96-38211. (Illus.). 192p. 1997. pap. text ed. 16.95 (0-8223-1895-4); lib. bdg. 49.95 (0-8223-1903-9) Duke.

Telling Distance: Conversations with the American Desert. Bruce Berger. LC 89-33144. (Illus.). 243p. 1990. 19.95 (0-932576-74-5) Breitenbush Bks.

***Telling Distance: Conversations with the American Desert.** Bruce Berger. LC 96-44304. 1997. pap. 19.95 (0-8165-1677-4) U of Ariz Pr.

Telling Each Other the Truth. William Backus. LC 85-20003. 192p. (Orig.). 1989. pap. 8.99 (0-87123-852-7) Bethany Hse.

Telling Educator's Lives: Intellectual Biography in Educational Studies. Frank A. Stone. (Multicultural Research Guides Ser.). 25p. 1983. 2.50 (0-685-09446-4) I N Thut World Educ Ctr.

Telling Facts: History & Narration in Psychoanalysis. Ed. by Joseph H. Smith & Humphrey Morris. (Psychiatry & the Humanities Ser.: Vol. 13). 336p. 1992. text ed. 52.00 (0-8018-4305-7) Johns Hopkins.

***Telling Flesh: Substance of the Corporeal.** Vicki Kirby. LC 97-9790. 224p. (C). 1997. text ed. 59.95 (0-415-91030-7, Routledge NY) Routledge.

***Telling Flesh: Substance of the Corporeal.** Vicky Kirby. LC 97-9790. 224p. (C). 1997. pap. 16.95 (0-415-91029-3, Routledge NY) Routledge.

Telling Fortunes by Cards. Cecily Kent. 1982. pap. 5.95 (0-87877-055-0) Newcastle Pub.

Telling Fortunes by Cards. Mohammed Ali. Ed. by Carleton B. Case. 159p. 1972. reprint ed. spiral bd. 7.50 (0-7873-1277-0) Hlth Research.

Telling Glances: Voyeurism in the French Novel. Dorothy Kelly. LC 91-48336. 260p. (C). 1992. text ed. 50.00 (0-8135-1845-8); pap. text ed. 18.00 (0-8135-1846-6) Rutgers U Pr.

Telling God's Story: Bible, Church & Narrative Theology. Gerard Loughlin. (Illus.). 280p. (C). 1996. text ed. 54.95 (0-521-43285-5) Cambridge U Pr.

Telling Identities: The California Testimonios. Rosaura Sanchez. 1995. text ed. 49.95 (0-8166-2558-1); pap. text ed. 19.95 (0-8166-2559-X) U of Minn Pr.

Telling Image: Explorations in the Emblem. Ed. by Ayers Bagley et al. LC 92-16981. (Studies in the Emblem: No. 12). 1993. 76.50 (0-404-63712-4) AMS Pr.

Telling Isn't Tattling. Kathryn M. Hammerseng. (Illus.). 32p. (Orig.). (J). (ps-4). 1995. pap. 5.95 (1-884734-06-5); lib. bdg. 15.95 (1-884734-07-3) Parenting Pr.

Telling It: Story & Script Development for Canadian Film & Television. Ed. by Anne Frank. 288p. 1996. pap. 22.95 (0-385-25584-5) Doubleday.

Telling It: Women & Language Across Cultures. Telling It Bk Collective Staff. 1990. pap. 14.95 (0-88974-027-5, Pub. by Press Gang CN) LPC InBook.

Telling It Again & Again: Repetition in Literature & Film. Bruce F. Kawin. 196p. (C). 1989. reprint ed. pap. text ed. 17.50 (0-87081-176-2) Univ Pr Colo.

Telling It All: A Legal Guide to the Exercise of Free Speech. Harold W. Fuson, Jr. 128p. 1995. pap. 8.95 (0-8362-7025-8) Andrews & McMeel.

Telling It Like It Is. Roy S. Martin. LC 92-59946. 169p. 1993. 7.95 (1-55523-568-9) Winston-Derek.

Telling It Like It Is. rev. ed. Mike Dante. (Orig.). 1996. pap. 9.95 (0-533-11669-4) Vantage.

Telling It Like It Is: Reflections of a Not So Radical Feminist. Elayne Clift. 198p. (Orig.). 1991. pap. 14.95 (1-879198-00-2) Knwldg Ideas & Trnds.

Telling It Like It Isn't: A Tiptoe Approach to Communications - A Dilbert Little Book. Scott Adams. (Illus.). 1996. 4.95 (0-8362-1324-6) Andrews & McMeel.

Telling It My Way. Tammy F. Messner & David Rudnitsky. 256p. 1996. 22.95 (0-679-44515-3, Villard Bks) Random.

Telling Jews about Jesus. Paul Morris. 1994. pap. 8.99 (0-85234-532-1, Pub. by Evangelical Pr) Presby & Reformed.

Telling Lies. Wendy Hornsby. (Maggie MacGowen Mystery Ser.). 272p. 1993. pap. 5.99 (0-451-40380-0, Onyx) NAL-Dutton.

Telling Lies: Clues to Deceit in the Marketplace, Politics & Marriage. Paul Ekman. 1993. 23.50 (0-8446-6688-2) Peter Smith.

Telling Lies: Clues to Deceit in the Marketplace, Politics, & Marriage. Paul Ekman. (Orig.). (C). 1991. pap. text ed. 8.95 (0-393-96213-X) Norton.

Telling Lies: Clues to Deceit in the Marketplace, Politics, & Marriage. Paul Ekman. 336p. (Orig.). 1992. pap. 13.95 (0-393-30872-3) Norton.

Telling Lies for Fun & Profit: A Manual for Fiction Writers. Lawrence Block. LC 93-33749. 1994. reprint ed. pap. 10.00 (0-688-13228-6, Quill) Morrow.

Telling Lies in Modern American Autobiography. Timothy D. Adams. LC 89-35380. xvi, 206p. (C). 1990. 29.95 (0-8078-1888-7) U of NC Pr.

Telling Lives in Science: Essays on Scientific Biography. Ed. by Michael Shortland & Richard R. Yeo. (Illus.). 304p. (C). 1996. text ed. 80.00 (0-521-43323-1) Cambridge U Pr.

Telling Lives, Telling Histories: Autobiography & Historical Imagination in Modern Indonesia. Ed. by Susan Rodgers. LC 94-30282. 1995. 20.00 (0-520-08547-7); pap. text ed. 55.00 (0-520-08546-9) U CA Pr.

Telling Maya Tales. Gossen. 256p. (C). 1997. pap. 18.95 (0-415-91467-1, Routledge NY); text ed. 59.95 (0-415-91466-3, Routledge NY) Routledge.

Telling Memories among Southern Women: Domestic Workers & Their Employers in the Segregated South. Susan Tucker. LC 88-9437. (Illus.). xi, 279p. 1988. 24.95 (0-8071-1440-5) La State U Pr.

Telling Memories among Southern Women: Domestic Workers & Their Employers in the Segregated South. Susan Tucker. LC 88-9437. (Illus.). 1990. pap. 14.00 (0-8052-0953-0) Schocken.

Telling Moments: Fifteen Gay Monologues. Robert Reinhart. (Acting Ser.). 96p. 1994. pap. 8.95 (1-55783-163-7) Applause Theatre Bk Pubs.

***Telling My Love Lies.** Keath Fraser. 224p. 1996. pap. 16.95 (0-88984-179-9, Pub. by Porcupines Quill CN) Genl Dist Srvs.

Telling New Lies: Seven Essays in Fiction, Past & Present. Melvyn New. 256p. (C). 1992. lib. bdg. 39.95 (0-8130-1120-5) U Press Fla.

Telling of the World: Native American Stories & Art. Ed. by W. S. Penn. (Illus.). 240p. 1996. 45.00 (1-55670-488-7) Stewart Tabori & Chang.

Telling Our Selves: Ethnicity & Discourse in Southwestern Alaska. Chase Hensel. (Oxford Studies in Anthropological Linguistics: 5). 192p. 1996. 49.95 (0-19-509476-X) OUP.

Telling Our Selves: Ethnicity & Discourse in Southwestern Alaska. Chase Hensel. (Oxford Studies in Anthropological Linguistics: 5). 192p. 1996. pap. 24.95 (0-19-509477-8) OUP.

Telling Our Tales, Stories & Storytelling for All Ages. Jeanette Ross. 216p. (J). 1994. pap. 20.00 (1-55896-280-8, Skinner Hse Bks) Unitarian Univ.

Telling People What to Think: Early Eighteenth-Century Periodicals from the Review to the Rambler. Ed. by J. A. Downie & Thomas N. Corns. LC 92-36615. 1992. 35.00 (0-7146-4508-7, Pub. by F Cass Pubs UK) Intl Spec Bk.

Telling Queen Michal's Story: An Experiment in Comparative Interpretation. Clines. (JSOT Supplement Ser.: No. 119). 220p. (C). 1991. 50.00 (1-85075-301-6, Pub. by Sheffield Acad UK) CUP Services.

Telling Rhythm: Body & Meaning in Poetry. Amittai F. Aviram. 324p. 1994. text ed. 39.50 (0-472-10513-2) U of Mich Pr.

Telling Right from Wrong: What Is Moral, What Is Immoral & What Is Neither One Nor the Other. Timothy J. Cooney. 158p. 1985. 29.95 (0-87975-297-1) Prometheus Bks.

Telling Ripe from Hype in Multimedia: The Ecstasy & the Agony. Anthony G. Oettinger. 32p. (Orig.). 1994. pap. text ed. write for info. (1-879716-14-3, I-94-2) Ctr Info Policy.

Telling Secrets. Frederick Buechner. LC 90-41770. 128p. 1992. reprint ed. pap. 12.00 (0-06-060936-2) Harper SF.

Telling Sexual Stories: Power, Change, & Social Worlds. Ken Plummer. LC 94-1215. 288p. (gr. 13). 1994. pap. 17.95 (0-415-10296-0, B4405) Routledge.

Telling Sexual Stories: Power, Change, & Social Worlds. Ken Plummer. LC 94-1215. 288p. (C). (gr. 13). 1994. text ed. 62.95 (0-415-10295-2, B4401) Routledge.

Telling Silence: Russian Frame Narratives of Renunciation. Charles Isenberg. (Studies in Russian Literature & Theory). 200p. 1993. 39.95 (0-8101-1108-X) Northwestern U Pr.

***Telling Stories.** Joyce Oates. LC 97-22548. (C). 1997. pap. 27.95 (0-393-97176-7) Norton.

Telling Stories. Valerie Windsor. 1996. mass mkt. 5.99 (0-614-14514-7, Reed Trade) Buttrwrth-Heinemann.

Telling Stories: A Theoretical Analysis of Narrative Fiction. Steven Cohan & Linda M. Shires. (New Accents Ser.). 224p. 1988. text ed. 55.00 (0-415-01386-0) Routledge.

Telling Stories: A Theoretical Analysis of Narrative Fiction. Steven Cohan & Linda M. Shires. (New Accents Ser.). 224p. (C). 1988. pap. 12.95 (0-415-01387-9) Routledge.

Telling Stories: Postmodernism, Free Will, & the Invalidation of Narrative. Michael Roemer. 386p. (C). 1995. pap. text ed. 22.95 (0-8476-8042-8); lib. bdg. 39.95 (0-8476-8041-X) Rowman.

Telling Stories: Studies in Honour of Ulrich Broich on the Occasion of His 60th Birthday. Ed. by Elmar Lehmann & Bernd Lenz. LC 92-12496. 1992. 76.00 (90-6032-334-3) Benjamins North Am.

Telling Stories, Compelling Stories. William J. Bausch. LC 90-71137. 200p. (Orig.). 1991. pap. 9.95 (0-89622-456-2) Twenty-Third.

Telling Stories to Children. Sylvia Ziskind. LC 75-42003. 162p. 1976. 25.00 (0-8242-0588-X) Wilson.

Telling Stories, Writing Lives: A Handbook for Beginning Adult Writers. Bird Stasz & Matthew D. Adams. LC 92-36801. 1993. pap. text ed. 6.50 (0-13-501123-X) P-H.

***Telling Stories/Taking Risks: Journalism Writing at the Century's Edge.** Alice Klement & Carolyn Matalene. (Mass Communication Ser.). (C). 1997. pap. text ed. 20.95 (0-534-52272-6) Wadsworth Pub.

***Telling Tails.** Allan Fowler. LC 97-23299. (Rookie Read-About Ser.). (J). 1998. write for info. (0-516-20803-9) Childrens.

Telling Tales: A Book about Story & Storytelling. Joseph Bruchac. LC 96-21697. (J). 1997. pap. write for info. (0-15-201268-0) HarBrace.

Telling Tales: And Other New One-Act Plays. Ed. by Eric Lane. 350p. (Orig.). 1993. pap. 15.95 (0-14-048237-7, Penguin Bks) Viking Penguin.

Telling Tales: How to Produce a Book of Stories by Parents & Their Children. Jan Goethel. (Illus.). 92p. (Orig.). 1995. pap. text ed. 12.95 (1-885474-10-5) Chipp Valley.

***Telling Tales: How to Use Stories to Help Your Children Overcome Their Problems.** Arthur Rowshan. 1997. pap. 10.95 (1-85168-139-6) Onewrld Pubns.

Telling Tales: Nineteenth-Century Narrative Painting from the Collection of the Pennsylvania Academy of the Fine Arts. Susan Danly. (Illus.). 100p. (Orig.). (C). 1991. pap. 22.50 (0-943836-15-8) Am Fed Arts.

***Telling Tales: Paradise Illustrated & a Faust Book.** D. J. Enright. LC 97-4450. 96p. 1998. pap. 13.95 (0-19-288029-2) OUP.

***Telling Tales: Perspectives on the Short Story.** Mary Rohrberger. Ed. by Barbara Lounsberry & Susan Lohafer. (Contributions to the Study of World Literature: Vol. 88). 1998. text ed. write for info. (0-313-30396-7, Greenwood Pr) Greenwood.

Telling Tales: The Hysteric's Seducton in Fiction & Theory. Katherine Cummings. LC 90-41802. 320p. 1991. 39.50 (0-8047-1825-3) Stanford U Pr.

Telling Tales: The Pedagogy & Promise of African American Literature for Youth. Dianne A. Johnson. LC 90-36777. (Contributions in Afro-American & African Studies: No. 139). 184p. 1990. text ed. 45.00 (0-313-27206-9, JCS/, Greenwood Pr) Greenwood.

Telling Tales of the Unexpected: The Organization of Factual Discourse. Robin Wooffitt. (C). 1992. text ed. 64.50 (0-389-20985-6) B&N Imports.

Telling Tales Teacher's Guide. 2nd ed. Marylou Awiakta et al. (Telling Tales TV Ser.). 84p. 1991. pap. 3.50 (0-910475-53-9) KET.

Telling Tears in the English Renaissance. Marjory E. Lange. LC 95-53245. (Studies in the History of Christian Thought, 0081-8607: Vol. 70). 1996. 96.50 (90-04-10517-4) E J Brill.

T

An Asterisk (*) at the beginning of an entry indicates that the title is appearing in BIP for the first time.

Telling the American Story: A Structural & Cultural Analysis of Conversational Storytelling. Livia Polanyi. LC 84-24196. (Language & Being Ser.). 160p. 1985. text ed. 73.25 (*0-89391-041-4*) Ablex Pub.

***Telling the Barn Swallow: Poets on the Poetry of Maxine Kumin.** Emily Grosholz. LC 96-24250. 214p. 1997. 29.95 (*0-87451-784-2*) U Pr of New Eng.

Telling the Beads. M. Montgomery. 80p. 1994. write for info. (*0-932616-50-X*) Brick Hse Bks.

***Telling the Bees.** John Ennis. 100p. 1995. 18.95 (*1-873790-78-3*) Dufour.

***Telling the Bees.** John Ennis. 100p. 9500. pap. 11.95 (*1-873790-77-5*) Dufour.

Telling the Churches' Stories: Ecumenical Perspectives on Writing Christian History. Ed. by Timothy J. Wengert & Charles W. Brockwell, Jr. 160p. 1995. pap. 15.00 (*0-8028-0556-6*) Eerdmans.

Telling the News Is Not Enough: An Editor's Challenge to Journalism. Davis Merritt. (Communication Ser.). 144p. 1995. pap. 17.50 (*0-8058-1983-5*); text ed. 36.00 (*0-8058-1982-7*) L Erlbaum Assocs.

Telling the Next Generation: The Educational Development in North American Calvinist Christian Schools. Harro W. Van Brummelen. (Illus.). 332p. (Orig.). (C). 1986. pap. text ed. 28.50 (*0-8191-5308-7*, Inst Christ Stud); lib. bdg. 52.00 (*0-8191-5307-9*, Inst Christ Stud) U Pr of Amer.

Telling the Old, Old Story: The Art of Narrative Preaching. David L. Larsen. LC 94-42394. 320p. (Orig.). 1995. pap. 14.99 (*0-89107-836-3*) Crossway Bks.

Telling the Other: The Question of Value in Modern & Postcolonial Writing. Patrick McGee. LC 91-48247. 232p. 1992. 42.50 (*0-8014-2749-5*); pap. 15.95 (*0-8014-8027-2*) Cornell U Pr.

Telling the Story: Evangelism in Black Churches. James O. Stallings. 128p. 1988. pap. 11.00 (*0-8170-1124-2*) Judson.

Telling the Success Story: Acclaiming & Disclaiming Discourse. Pamela J. Benoit. LC 96-47391. (SUNY Series in Speech Communication). 207p. (C). 1997. text ed. 39.50 (*0-7914-3317-X*); pap. text ed. 12.95 (*0-7914-3318-8*) State U NY Pr.

Telling the Tale: A Tribute to Elie Wiesel on the Occasion of His 65th Birthday: Essays, Reflections & Poems. Ed. by Harry J. Cargas. 169p. 1993. 22.95 (*1-56809-006-4*); pap. 14.95 (*1-56809-007-2*) Time Being Bks.

***Telling the Tales of Painting.** Jonathan Lasker. 1994. 55.00 (*3-89322-564-1*, Pub. by Edition Cantz GW) Dist Art Pubs.

Telling the Truth. Lynne V. Cheney. 256p. 1996. pap. 12.00 (*0-684-82534-1*) S&S Trade.

Telling the Truth. Shelly Nielsen. Ed. by Rosemary Wallner. LC 91-73046. (Values Matter Ser.). (J). 1992. lib. bdg. 14.98 (*1-56239-062-7*) Abdo & Dghtrs.

Telling the Truth: Growing Up to Intimacy & Freedom. Brad Blanton. 300p. 1991. 24.95 (*0-9630921-0-3*) Sparrowhawk.

Telling the Truth: How to Revitalize Christian Journalism. Marvin N. Olasky. LC 95-42467. 320p. (Orig.). 1996. pap. 20.00 (*0-89107-885-1*) Crossway Bks.

Telling the Truth: The Gospel As Tragedy, Comedy & Fairy Tale. Frederick Buechner. LC 77-7839. 1977. 18.00 (*0-06-061156-1*) Harper SF.

Telling the Truth: Why Our Schools, Culture & Country Have Stopped Making Sense & What We Can Do About It. Lynne V. Cheney. 256p. 1995. 23.00 (*0-684-81101-4*, S&S) S&S Trade.

***Telling the Truth about America's Public Schools.** Kristen Amundson. 20p. (Orig.). 1996. pap. 5.00 (*0-87652-224-X*, 021-0580) Am Assn Sch Admin.

Telling the Truth about History. Joyce Appleby et al. 1994. 25.00 (*0-393-03615-4*, Norton Paperbks) Norton.

Telling the Truth about History. Joyce Appleby et al. 336p. 1995. pap. 13.95 (*0-393-31286-0*, Norton Paperbks) Norton.

Telling the Truth to Troubled People. William Backus. LC 84-28413. 256p. (Orig.). 1985. pap. 9.99 (*0-87123-811-X*) Bethany Hse.

Telling the Untold Story: How Investigative Reporters Are Changing the Craft of Biography. Steve Weinberg. 264p. 1992. 34.95 (*0-8262-0873-8*) U of Mo Pr.

Telling the Whole Story. Robert McGregor & Marion Meiers. (C). 1990. 75.00 (*0-86431-082-X*, Pub. by Aust Council Educ Res AT) St Mut.

Telling Their Stories: Puerto Rican Women & Abortion. Jean P. Peterman. 112p. (C). 1996. text ed. 47.00 (*0-8133-8991-7*) Westview.

***Telling Things: Poems.** Michael J. Rosen. LC 96-28800. 1997. 22.00 (*0-15-100240-1*); pap. write for info. (*0-15-600482-8*) HarBrace.

***Telling Time.** Jo E. Moore. (Mathematics Ser.). (Illus.). 32p. (J). (gr. 2-3). 1997. teacher ed., pap. 2.95 (*1-55799-455-2*, 4057) Evan-Moor Corp.

Telling Time. Earl Ockenga & Walt Rucker. (Elementary Mathematics Ser.). (Illus.). 16p. (J). (gr. 1). 1990. pap. text ed. 1.25 (*1-56281-120-7*, M120) Extra Eds.

Telling Time. Austin Wright. 264p. 1995. 21.00 (*1-880909-36-7*) Baskerville.

Telling Time: Angels, Ancestors, & Stories. Nancy Willard. LC 93-16390. 240p. (J). (gr. 4-7). 1993. pap. 13.00 (*0-15-693130-3*, Harvest Bks) HarBrace.

Telling Time: Clocks, Diaries, & English Diurnal Form, 1660-1785. Stuart Sherman. 296p. 1997. pap. text ed. 19.95 (*0-226-75277-1*); lib. bdg. 60.00 (*0-226-75276-3*) U Ch Pr.

Telling Time: Levi-Strauss, Ford, Lessing, Benjamin, De Man, Wordworth, Rilke. Carol Jacobs. 271p. 1993. text ed. 38.50 (*0-8018-4477-0*) Johns Hopkins.

***Telling Time with Big Mama Cat.** Dan Harper. LC 97-18952. (Illus.). (J). 1998. write for info. (*0-15-201738-0*) HarBrace.

Telling Time with Goofy see Walt Disney's Read & Grow Library

Telling Travels: Selected Writings by Nineteenth-Century American Women Abroad. Ed. & Intro. by Mary S. Schriber. LC 94-28678. (Illus.). 336p. (Orig.). 1994. lib. bdg. 35.00 (*0-87580-195-1*) N Ill U Pr.

Telling Travels: Selected Writings by Nineteenth-Century American Women Abroad. Ed. & Intro. by Mary S. Schriber. LC 94-28678. (Illus.). 336p. (Orig.). 1994. pap. 18.50 (*0-87580-561-2*) N Ill U Pr.

Telling Triple: Essays, Poems, & Stories. Antonio Allego. 136p. (Orig.). 1986. pap. 7.50 (*971-10-0281-7*, Pub. by New Day Pub PH) Cellar.

Telling Without Talking: Art As a Window into the World of Multiple Personality. Barry M. Cohen & Carol T. Cox. (Illus.). 320p. (C). 1995. 45.00 (*0-393-70196-4*) Norton.

Telling Without Telling: A Clinical Guide to Screening Children's Art Productions. Linda Peterson et al. LC 95-67176. (Illus.). 144p. 1995. pap. 39.95 (*0-9645604-0-2*) Drawing Conclusions.

Telling Women's Lives: The New Biography. Linda Wagner-Martin. LC 93-42403. (Illus.). 201p. (C). 1994. 35.00 (*0-8135-2092-4*) Rutgers U Pr.

Telling Women's Lives: The New Biography. Linda Wagner-Martin. LC 93-42403. (Illus.). 201p. (C). 1996. pap. 16.95 (*0-8135-2375-3*) Rutgers U Pr.

Telling Writing. 4th ed. Ken Macrorie. LC 84-29296. 300p. (YA). (gr. 10). 1985. pap. text ed. 21.50 (*0-86709-153-3*, 0153) Boynton Cook Pubs.

Telling Your Own Stories: A Resource for Family Storytelling, Classroom Story Creation, & Personal Journaling. Donald Davis. (American Storytelling Ser.). 96p. 1993. pap. 10.00 (*0-87483-235-7*) August Hse.

Telling Your Story see Your Mythic Journey: Finding Meaning in Your Life Through Writing & Storytelling

Telling Yourself the Truth. William Backus & Marie Chapian. LC 80-10136. 192p. (Orig.). 1980. pap. 8.99 (*0-87123-562-5*) Bethany Hse.

Telling Yourself the Truth. William Backus & Marie Chapian. LC 80-10136. 48p. (Orig.). 1981. student ed. 4.99 (*0-87123-567-6*) Bethany Hse.

Tellington Touch: A Breakthrough Technique to Train & Care for Your Favorite Animal. Linda Tellington-Jones & Sybil Taylor. (Illus.). 304p. 1995. pap. 12.95 (*0-14-011728-8*, Penguin Bks) Viking Penguin.

***Tells of Cutezar.** Jo Bower. 147p. (Orig.). 1997. mass mkt. 4.99 (*1-55237-112-3*, Pub. by Comnwlth Pub CN) Partners Pubs Grp.

Telltale Hearts: The Origins & Impact of the Vietnam Antiwar Movement. Adam Garfinkle. LC 94-39655. 384p. 1995. 24.95 (*0-312-12520-8*) St Martin.

Telltale Hearts: The Origins and Impact of the Vietnam Antiwar Movement. Adam Garfinkle. 1997. pap. 16.95 (*0-312-16363-0*) St Martin.

Telltale Lilac Bush & Other West Virginia Ghost Tales. Ruth A. Musick. LC 64-14000. (Illus.). 208p. 1965. reprint ed. pap. 12.95 (*0-8131-0136-0*) U Pr of Ky.

Telltale Trees: What the Tree You Draw Reveals about You. Ethel Johnson. (Illus.). 91p. (Orig.). pap. write for info. (*0-9613738-0-6*) Maple Terrace.

Telltale Turkey Caper. Georgette Livingston. LC 96-96148. 192p. 1996. 17.95 (*0-8034-9203-0*) Bouregy.

Telluranes: Synthesis, Structure & Reactivity. Alexander Senning. (Sulfur Reports: Vol. 8, Pt. 2). 43p. 1988. pap. text ed. 58.00 (*3-7186-4834-2*) Gordon & Breach.

Telluride. Rose Weber. (Illus.). pap. 4.50 (*0-936564-10-5*) Little London.

Telluride: A Novel. Susan C. Schofield. LC 93-1072. 344p. 1993. 18.95 (*0-945575-96-3*) Algonquin Bks.

Telluride: A Novel. large type ed. Susan C. Schofield. LC 93-40528. 1994. lib. bdg. 20.95 (*0-7862-0156-8*) Thorndike Pr.

Telluride: From Pick to Powder. Richard L. Fetter. LC 77-87369. (Illus.). 1979. pap. 9.95 (*0-87004-265-3*) Caxton.

Telluride Hiking Guide. Susan Kees. 1992. pap. 11.95 (*0-943727-14-6*) Wayfinder Pr.

***Telluride Mountain Almanac: A Book about Life in the Colorado Rockies.** Elisabeth Gick & Chandler T. Tamulonis. (Illus.). 120p. 1997. pap. 12.95 (*0-9658503-0-7*) Sylvan Books.

Telluride, Pandora & the Mines Above. Russ Collman & Dell A. McCoy. (RGS Story Ser.: Vol. 2). (Illus.). 496p. 1992. 68.00 (*0-913582-49-2*, 0223) Sundance.

Telluride Story. David Lavender. 68p. (Orig.). 1987. pap. 19.95 (*0-9608764-6-4*) Wayfinder Pr.

Tellurides: A Mountain Biking Guide to Telluride Colorado. Dave Rich. 1994. pap. 11.95 (*0-943727-18-9*) Wayfinder Pr.

Tellurium-Containing Heterocycles, Vol. 53. Michael R. Detty & Marie B. O'Regan. (Chemistry of Heterocyclic Compounds, a Series of Monographs: Vol. 53). 511p. 1994. text ed. 250.00 (*0-471-63395-X*) Wiley.

Telomere. David Kipling. (Illus.). 240p. 1995. 75.00 (*0-19-963467-X*); pap. 40.00 (*0-19-963600-1*) OUP.

Telomeres. Ed. by Elizabeth H. Blackburn & Carol W. Greider. LC 95-69539. (Monographs: Vol.). (Illus.). 396p. 1995. 80.00 (*0-87969-457-2*) Cold Spring Harbor.

Telosgedanke in Den Dramen Des Aischylos. Ulrich Fischer. (Spudasmata Ser.: Bd. 6). 175p. (GER.). 1965. write for info. (*3-487-00978-1*) G Olms Pubs.

Telugu-English Dictionary. P. Sankaranarayan. (ENG & TEL.). 1986. 35.00 (*0-8288-1150-4*, F 10800) Fr & Eur.

Telugu-English Dictionary. 2nd ed. Charles P. Brown. 1416p. (C). 1985. reprint ed. 34.00 (*0-88431-052-3*) IBD Ltd.

Telugu English Dictionary. C. P. Brown. 1424p. 1986. reprint ed. 32.00 (*0-8364-1690-2*, Pub. by Usha II) S Asia.

Telugu-English Dictionary. C. P. Brown. (ENG & TEL.). 1986. reprint ed. 59.95 (*0-8288-1149-0*, M15174) Fr & Eur.

Telugu English Dictionary. P. Sankaranarayana. 1380p. 1986. reprint ed. 20.00 (*0-8364-1695-3*, Pub. by Usha II) S Asia.

Telugu Verbal Bases: A Comparative & Descriptive Study. Bhadriraju Krishnamurti. LC 61-63422. (California University Publications in Linguistics: Vol. 24). 533p. reprint ed. pap. 152.00 (*0-317-10155-2*, 2011682) Bks Demand.

Tem T Tchaas: Egyptian Proverbs. Abhaya A. Muata. 160p. 1993. pap. 9.95 (*1-884564-00-3*) Cruzian Mystic.

Tema de la Soledad En la Narrativa de Soledad Puertolas. Marguerite D. Intemann. LC 93-47113. 240p. 1994. 89.95 (*0-7734-2293-5*, Mellen Univ Pr) E Mellen.

Tema de Nuestro Tiempo. Jose Ortega y Gasset. (Nueva Austral Ser.: Vol. 28). (SPA.). 1991. pap. text ed. 24.95 (*84-239-1828-9*) Elliots Bks.

TEMA Five: Trace Elements in Man & Animals. C. F. Mills et al. 977p. (C). 1985. text ed. 108.00 (*0-85198-533-5*) CAB Intl.

Temagami. Michael Barnes. (Illus.). 88p. 1995. pap. 15.95 (*1-55046-031-5*) Genl Dist Srvs.

Temagami. Jim Flosdorf. 48p. 1985. 6.95 (*0-920806-52-X*, Pub. by Penumbra Pr CN) U of Toronto Pr.

Temagami Experience: Recreation, Resources & Aboriginal Rights in the Northern Ontario Wilderness. Bruce W. Hodgins & Jamie Benidickson. 378p. 1989. 45.00 (*0-8020-5800-0*); pap. 20.95 (*0-8020-6713-1*) U of Toronto Pr.

Temalpakh: Cahuilla Indian Knowledge & Usage of Plants. Lowell J. Bean & Katherine S. Saubel. LC 72-85815. 1972. pap. 16.00 (*0-939046-24-5*) Malki Mus Pr.

Temari: How to Make Japanese Thread Balls. Diana Vandervoort. (Illus.). 122p. (Orig.). 1991. pap. 18.00 (*0-87040-881-X*) Japan Pubns USA.

Temari Traditions: More Techniques for Japanese Thread Balls. Diana Vandervoort. (Illus.). 96p. 1995. pap. text ed. 17.00 (*0-87040-949-2*) Japan Pubns USA.

Temari Treasures: Japanese Thread Balls & More. Diana Vandervoort. (Illus.). 122p. (Orig.). 1996. pap. 18.00 (*0-87040-983-2*) Kodansha.

Temas Basicos de Dibujo see Drawing Basic Subjects

***Temas Candentes de la Biblia - Controversial Issues of the Bible.** Fernandez. 148p. (SPA.). 1995. write for info. (*0-7899-0105-6*) Editorial Unilit.

Temas de Isaias. Ronald Youngblood. Orig. Title: Themes from Isaiah. 132p. (SPA.). 1987. pap. 1.50 (*0-8297-0896-0*) Life Pubs Intl.

Temas Gramaticales. Lenard Studerus. LC 89-27396. 244p. (Orig.). (SPA.). (C). 1990. pap. text ed. 18.00 (*0-8191-7643-5*) U Pr of Amer.

Temas y Dialogos. 5th ed. David F. Altabe. (Illus.). 288p. (SPA.). (C). 1988. pap. text ed. 23.50 (*0-03-007543-2*) HB Coll Pubs.

Tematica E Struttura Dell'Eneide di Virgilio. E. Coleiro. 148p. (Orig.). (ITA.). 1983. pap. 24.00 (*90-6032-245-2*, Pub. by B R Gruener NE) Benjamins North Am.

Tematica Narrativa de Severo Sarduy: De Donde Son Los Cantantes. Jose Sanchez-Boudy. LC 77-78252. (Coleccion Polymita). 102p. (Orig.). (SPA.). 1985. pap. 10.00 (*0-89729-257-X*) Ediciones.

***Temenos: A Review Devoted to the Arts of the Imagination, Vol. 4.** Ed. by Kathleen Raine & Brian Keeble. (Illus.). 216p. (Orig.). 1983. pap. 22.95 (*0-900588-90-X*, Pub. by Temenos UK) S Perennis.

***Temenos: A Review Devoted to the Arts of the Imagination, Vol. 5.** Ed. by Kathleen Raine & Brian Keeble. (Illus.). 296p. (Orig.). 1984. pap. 22.95 (*0-900588-91-8*, Pub. by Temenos UK) S Perennis.

***Temenos: A Review Devoted to the Arts of the Imagination, Vol. 6.** Ed. by Kathleen Raine & Brian Keeble. (Illus.). 304p. (Orig.). 1985. pap. 22.95 (*0-900588-92-6*, Pub. by Temenos UK) S Perennis.

***Temenos: A Review Devoted to the Arts of the Imagination, Vol. 7.** Ed. by Kathleen Raine & Brian Keeble. (Illus.). 335p. (Orig.). 1986. pap. 22.95 (*0-900588-93-4*, Pub. by Temenos UK) S Perennis.

***Temenos: A Review Devoted to the Arts of the Imagination, Vol. 8.** Ed. by Kathleen Raine & Brian Keeble. (Illus.). 294p. (Orig.). 1987. pap. 22.95 (*0-900588-94-2*, Pub. by Temenos UK) S Perennis.

***Temenos: A Review Devoted to the Arts of the Imagination, Vol. 9.** Ed. by Kathleen Raine & Brian Keeble. (Illus.). 308p. (Orig.). 1988. pap. 22.95 (*0-900588-95-0*, Pub. by Temenos UK) S Perennis.

***Temenos: A Review Devoted to the Arts of the Imagination, Vol. 10.** Ed. by Kathleen Raine & Brian Keeble. (Illus.). 306p. (Orig.). 1989. pap. 22.95 (*0-900588-96-9*, Pub. by Temenos UK) S Perennis.

***Temenos: A Review Devoted to the Arts of the Imagination, Vol. 11.** Ed. by Kathleen Raine & Brian Keeble. (Illus.). 304p. (Orig.). 1990. pap. 22.95 (*0-900588-97-7*, Pub. by Temenos UK) S Perennis.

***Temenos: A Review Devoted to the Arts of the Imagination, Vol. 12.** Ed. by Kathleen Raine & Brian Keeble. (Illus.). 267p. (Orig.). 1991. pap. 22.95 (*0-900588-98-5*, Pub. by Temenos UK) S Perennis.

***Temenos: A Review Devoted to the Arts of the Imagination, Vol. 13.** Ed. by Kathleen Raine & Brian Keeble. (Illus.). 296p. (Orig.). 1992. pap. 22.95 (*0-900588-99-3*, Pub. by Temenos UK) S Perennis.

Temeraire. Daniel Boulanger. (FRE.). 1984. pap. 10.95 (*0-7859-1985-6*, 2070375250) Fr & Eur.

Temistocle. Ed. by Ernest Warburton. (Johann Christian Bach Ser.). 700p. 1988. text ed. 195.00 (*0-8240-6056-3*) Garland.

Temmoku: A Study of Pottery & Tea Aesthetics. F. Bleicher & W. C. Hu. write for info. (*0-89344-032-9*) Ars Ceramica.

Temoigner. (FRE.). 1989. 3.95 (*0-86508-381-9*) BCM Pubn.

Temoins de l Homme: La Condition Humaine dans la Litterature Contemporaine. Pierre-Henri Simon. (Cahiers de la Fondat. Nat. Sc. Polit. Ser.). pap. 8.75 (*0-685-36580-8*) Fr & Eur.

Temoins du Monde Francais. Ed. by Adrien Therio & James F. Burks. LC 68-12127. (Illus.). (Orig.). (FRE.). (YA). (gr. 9 up). 1968. pap. text ed. 9.95 (*0-89197-446-6*) Irvington.

Temor: Enfermedad de Nuestra Decada. Kenneth Nichols. (Serie Guia - Pocket Guide Ser.). 120p. (SPA.). 1990. pap. 2.49 (*1-56063-035-3*, 498061) Editorial Unilit.

Temores Familiares. Jerry Schreur & Jack Schreur. 168p. (SPA.). 1995. pap. 7.99 (*0-8254-1666-3*, Edit Portavoz) Kregel.

Temp: How to Survive & Thrive in the World of Temporary Employment. Deborahann Smith. LC 93-28072. 144p. (Orig.). 1994. pap. 9.00 (*0-87773-934-X*, 934) Shambhala Pubns.

T.E.M.P. - Temporary Employment Management Portfolio. Jean B. Hill. 52p. (Orig.). (SPA.). 1995. mass mkt. 2.99 (*1-888620-03-X*) Common Snse PA.

Temp by Choice. Diane Thrailkill. 224p. (Orig.). 1994. pap. 10.95 (*1-56414-122-5*) Career Pr Inc.

Temp FM-EM, Nos. 1-9. Phillip E. Areeda. 1991. 40.00 (*0-316-05079-2*) Little.

Temp FM/EM. Areeda. 1994. lib. bdg. 45.00 (*0-316-05017-2*) Little.

***Temp Survival Guide: How to Prosper As an Economic Nomad of the Nineties.** Brian Hassett. 1996. pap. text ed. 11.95 (*0-8065-1843-X*, Citadel Pr) Carol Pub Group.

Temp Track: Make One of the Hottest Job Trends of the 90s Work for You. Peggy O. Justice. LC 93-5877. 208p. (Orig.). 1993. pap. 12.95 (*1-56079-254-X*) Petersons.

Tempe: A Portrait in Color. Michel F. Sarda. LC 93-71292. 144p. 1993. 45.00 (*0-927015-06-4*) Bridgewood Pr.

Tempe & Her Horse: A Story of Revolutionary Times. Susan Knauss. LC 96-69276. (Illus.). 96p. (Orig.). (J). (gr. 3-5). 1996. pap. 9.95 (*1-884570-56-9*) Research Triangle.

Tempeh & Tempeh Products - Bibliography & Sourcebook, 1815-1993: Detailed Information of 616 Published Documents, 432 Commercial Tempeh Products, 216 Original Interviews & Overviews, 247 Unpublished & Archival Documents. Ed. by Akiko Aoyagi. 435p. (Orig.). 1993. spiral bd. 109.00 (*0-933332-82-3*) Soyfoods Center.

Tempeh Cookbook. Dorothy R. Bates. LC 89-35499. (Illus.). 96p. (Orig.). 1989. pap. 10.95 (*0-913990-65-5*) Book Pub Co.

Tempeh Primer. 2nd ed. Robin Clute & Sigrid Andersen. (Illus.). 64p. pap. 3.95 (*0-685-43000-6*) Creat Arts Bk.

Tempeh Production: A Craft & Technical Manual. William Shurtleff & Akiko Aoyagi. LC 85-304441. (Soyfoods Production Ser.: No. 3). (Illus.). 176p. 1986. pap. 39.95 (*0-933332-23-8*) Soyfoods Center.

Tempel und Heiligtuemer im alten Mesopotamien: Typologie, Morphologie und Geschichte. Ernst Heinrich. (Illus.). 1982. 215.40 (*3-11-008531-3*) De Gruyter.

Tempel Von Jerusalem. Konrad Rupprecht. (Beiheft 144 zur Zeitschrift fuer die Alttestamentliche Wissenschaft Ser.). (C). 1976. text ed. 60.80 (*3-11-006619-X*) De Gruyter.

Tempel von Paestum, 2 pts. Friedrich Krauss. (Denkmaeler Antiker Architektur Ser.: Vol. 9, Pt. 1, Fascicule 1). (Illus.). 97p. (GER.). (C). 1978. reprint ed. 134.65 (*3-11-002237-0*) De Gruyter.

Temper. Lawrence H. Conrad. LC 74-22774. (Labor Movement in Fiction & Non-Fiction Ser.). reprint ed. 34.50 (*0-404-58414-4*) AMS Pr.

Temper Embrittlement of Alloy Steels: A Symposium Presented at the Seventy-Fourth Annual Meeting, American Society for Testing & Materials. American Society for Testing & Materials Staff. LC 73-185535. (American Society for Testing & Materials Special Technical Publication Ser.: No. 499). 141p. reprint ed. pap. 40.20 (*0-317-10341-5*, 2015504) Bks Demand.

Temper Lines in Japanese Swords. rev. ed. Hawley. 1991. pap. 6.95 (*0-910704-47-3*) Hawley.

Temper of John Dryden. Thomas H. Fujimura. Ed. by Robert McHenry. (Studies in Literature, 1500-1800: Vol. 4). xxx, 245p. 1993. 44.95 (*0-937191-25-6*) Colleagues Pr Inc.

Temper of Our Time. Eric Hoffer. (Illus.). 154p. 1992. reprint ed. lib. bdg. 21.95 (*0-89966-909-3*) Buccaneer Bks.

Temper of Shakespeare's Thought. William G. Zeeveld. LC 74-75869. 282p. reprint ed. pap. 80.40 (*0-8357-8343-X*, 2033934) Bks Demand.

Temper of the Seventeenth Century in English Literature. Clark Lectures, 1902-1903. Barrett Wendell. LC 67-26794. (Essay Index Reprint Ser.). 1977. 21.95 (*0-8369-0980-1*) Ayer.

Temper of Victorian Belief: Studies in the Religious Novels of Pater, Kingsley, & Newman. David A. Downes. LC 76-147189. 159p. 1972. 29.50 (*0-8290-0209-X*) Irvington.

Temper of Wisdom. Lynn Abbey. 1992. mass mkt. 4.99 (*0-446-36226-3*, Aspect) Warner Bks.

Temper Tantrum Book. Edna M. Preston & Rainey Bennett. (Picture Puffins Ser.). (Illus.). (J). (ps-3). 1976. pap. 4.99 (*0-14-050181-9*, Puffin) Puffin Bks.

Temper Your Child's Tantrums. abr. ed. James Dobson. (Pocket Guides Ser.). 80p. 1986. pap. 3.99 (*0-8423-6994-5*) Tyndale.

Tempera. Isidro Sanchez. (I Draw, I Paint Ser.). (J). (gr. 4-7). 1992. pap. 7.95 (*0-8120-1373-5*) Barron.

T

An Asterisk (*) at the beginning of an entry indicates that the title is appearing in BIP for the first time.

Temperament: Early Developing Personality Traits. Arnold H. Buss & Robert Plomin. 200p. (C). 1984. text ed. 39.95 (*0-89859-415-4*) L Erlbaum Assocs.

Temperament: Individual Differences at the Inteface of Biology & Behavior. Ed. by John E. Bates & Theodore D. Wachs. (Illus.). 362p. 1994. text ed. 39.95 (*1-55798-222-8*) Am Psychol.

Temperament: Theory & Practice. Stella Chess & Alexander Thomas. LC 96-28525. (Basic Principles into Practice Ser.: Vol. 12). 224p. 1996. pap. 24.95 (*0-87630-835-3*) Brunner-Mazel.

Temperament & Behavior Disorders in Children. Alexander Thomas et al. LC 68-13025. 309p. (C). 1968. text ed. 52.00 (*0-8147-0415-8*) NYU Pr.

Temperament & Character Inventory: A Guide to Its Development & Use. R. D. Wetzel. 184p. text ed. write for info. (*0-9642917-0-3*); pap. text ed. write for info. (*0-9642917-1-1*) Wash U Ctr Psychobiol.

Temperament & Character of the Arabs. Sania Hamady. LC 60-9942. 285p. 1960. 29.50 (*0-8290-0210-3*) Irvington.

Temperament & Child Psychopathology. William T. Garrison & Felton J. Earls. (Developmental Clinical Psychology & Psychiatry Ser.: Vol. 12). 160p. 1987. text ed. 39.95 (*0-8039-2296-5*); pap. text ed. 17.95 (*0-8039-2297-3*) Sage.

Temperament & Eating Characteristics. Albert Mehrabian. (Illus.). 150p. 1987. 85.95 (*0-387-96510-6*) Spr-Verlag.

Temperament, Character & Personality: Biobehavioral Concepts in Science, Art, & Social Psychology. P. V. Simonov & P. M. Ershov. (Monographs Psychobiology Ser.). iv, 166p. 1991. text ed. 118.00 (*2-88124-443-2*) Gordon & Breach.

Temperament Discussed. Ed. by Geldolph A. Kohnstamm. x, 200p. 1986. pap. 26.50 (*90-265-0783-6*) Swets.

Temperament in Childhood. Ed. by Geldolph A. Kohnstamm et al. 641p. 1990. text ed. 130.00 (*0-471-91692-7*) Wiley.

Temperament in Childhood. Ed. by Geldolph A. Kohnstamm et al. 660p. 1995. pap. text ed. 65.00 (*0-471-95583-3*) Wiley.

Temperament in Clinical Practice. Stella Chess & Thomas. LC 85-17733. 1995. pap. text ed. 19.95 (*0-89862-813-X*, 2813) Guilford Pr.

Temperament in Clinical Practice. Stella Chess & Alexander Thomas. LC 85-17733. 333p. reprint ed. pap. 95.00 (*0-7837-3880-3*, 2043728) Bks Demand.

Temperament of Generations: Fifty Years of Meanjin. Ed. by Jenny Lee et al. 400p. 1990. pap. 29.95 (*0-522-84448-0*, Pub. by Melbourne Univ Pr AT) Paul & Co Pubs.

***Temperament Tools: Working with Your Child's Inborn Traits.** Helen Neville. 1997. 19.95 (*1-884734-35-9*); pap. text ed. 13.95 (*1-884734-34-0*) Parenting Pr.

Temperamental Bases of Behavior. Ed. by Jan Strelau. x, 210p. 1985. pap. 38.75 (*90-265-0598-1*) Swets.

Temperamental Journeys: Essays on the Modern Literature of Travel. Ed. by Michael Kowalewski. LC 91-26602. 376p. 1992. pap. 22.00 (*0-8203-1431-5*) U of Ga Pr.

Temperamentos Controlados. Tim La Haye. 125p. (SPA.). 1986. pap. 3.99 (*0-8423-6254-1*, 490212) Editorial Unilit.

***Temperamentos Transformados.** Tim La Haye. 160p. (SPA.). 1986. pap. write for info. (*0-614-27142-8*) Editorial Unilit.

Temperamentos Transformados. Tim LaHaye. (SPA.). 1986. 3.99 (*0-8423-6255-X*, 490213) Editorial Unilit.

TemperaMysticism: Exploding the Temperament Theory. Shirley A. Miller. 176p. 1991. pap. 8.95 (*0-914984-30-6*) Starburst.

Temperance. Ellen G. White. 1949. 12.99 (*0-8163-0151-4*, 20100-4) Pacific Pr Pub Assn.

Temperance: A Tract for the Times. Aleister Crowley. 1993. reprint ed. pap. 7.95 (*1-55818-256-X*) Holmes Pub.

Temperance & Prohibition Papers, 1830-1933: Guide to the Microfilm Edition. Ed. by Randall C. Jimerson et al. 380p. 1977. pap. 69.00 (*0-89887-186-7*) Chadwyck-Healey.

Temperance Selections. Ed. by John H. Bechtel. LC 71-116393. (Granger Index Reprint Ser.). 1977. 17.95 (*0-8369-6134-X*) Ayer.

***Temperate Agroforestry Systems.** A. M. Gordon & S. M. Newman. 288p. 1997. pap. 45.00 (*0-85199-147-5*) CAB Intl.

Temperate & Polar Zonobiomes of Northern Eurasia. H. Walter & S. W. Breckle. (Ecological Systems of the Geobiosphere Ser.: Vol. 3). (Illus.). 590p. 1989. 240.95 (*0-387-15029-3*) Spr-Verlag.

Temperate Broad-Leaved Evergreen Forests. Ed. by J. D. Ovington. (Ecosystems of the World Ser.: Vol. 10). 242p. 1983. 182.25 (*0-444-42091-6*, I-399-83) Elsevier.

Temperate Chile: A Progressive Spain. W. Anderson Smith. 1976. lib. bdg. 59.95 (*0-8490-2732-2*) Gordon Pr.

***Temperate Climates.** Keith Lye. LC 96-31162. (The World's Climate Ser.). (J). 1997. lib. bdg. 24.26 (*0-8172-4827-7*) Raintree Steck-V.

Temperate Deciduous Forest. April P. Sayre. (Exploring Earth's Biomes Ser.). (Illus.). 64p. (J). (gr. 5-8). 1994. lib. bdg. 15.98 (*0-8050-2828-5*) TFC Bks NY.

***Temperate Deciduous Forests.** E. Rohrig & B. Ulrich. (Ecosystems of the World Ser.: Vol. 7). 636p. 1991. 329.75 (*0-444-88599-4*) Elsevier.

Temperate Deserts & Semi-Deserts. Ed. by N. E. West. (Ecosystems of the World Ser.: Vol. 5). 522p. 1983. 363.75 (*0-444-41931-4*, I-483-82) Elsevier.

***Temperate Forage Legumes.** John Frame et al. LC 97-22229. 1997. write for info. (*0-85199-214-5*) CAB Intl.

Temperate Forest. Lorenzo Fornasari et al. LC 96-22407. (Deep Green Planet Ser.). (J). 1997. lib. bdg. 24.26 (*0-8172-4312-7*) Raintree Steck-V.

Temperate Forest. Elizabeth Kaplan. LC 95-4065. (Biomes of the World Ser.). 64p. (J). (gr. 4-6). 1995. lib. bdg. 17.95 (*0-7614-0082-6*, Benchmark NY) Marshall Cavendish.

Temperate Forest Mammals. Elaine Landau. LC 96-3889. (True Bk.). (Illus.). 48p. (J). 1996. lib. bdg. 19.00 (*0-516-20043-7*) Childrens.

***Temperate Forest Mammals.** Elaine Landau. (True Bks.). 48p. (J). 1997. pap. 6.95 (*0-516-26115-0*) Childrens.

Temperate Forests. Basil Booth. Ed. by Nancy Furstinger. (Our World Ser.). (Illus.). 48p. (J). (gr. 5-8). 1989. lib. bdg. 12.95 (*0-382-09791-2*) Silver Burdett Pr.

Temperate Forests. L. Stone. (Ecozones Ser.). (Illus.). 48p. (J). (gr. 4-8). 1989. 11.95 (*0-685-58574-3*); lib. bdg. 15.94 (*0-86592-439-2*) Rourke Corp.

Temperate Fruit. Ed. by B. B. Beattie et al. (Postharvest Diseases of Horticultural Produce Ser.: Vol. 1). (Illus.). 84p. 1990. pap. 35.00 (*0-643-05051-5*, Pub. by CSIRO AT) Aubrey Bks.

***Temperate Fruit Crops in Warm Climates.** Erez. (Illus.). 368p. (C). 1997. text ed. write for info. (*0-412-63290-X*, Chap & Hall NY) Chapman & Hall.

Temperate Palaeohydrology: Fluvial Processes in the Temperate Zone During the Last 15000 Years. Ed. by L. Starkel et al. LC 90-35945. 548p. 1991. text ed. 300.00 (*0-471-92212-9*) Wiley.

Temperate Pastures: Their Production, Use & Management. Ed. by J. L. Wheeler et al. 1987. 95.00 (*0-643-04773-5*, Pub. by CSIRO AT) Aubrey Bks.

Temperate Zone Pomology. 3rd ed. Melvin N. Westwood. LC 92-6821. (Illus.). 548p. 1993. text ed. 65.00 (*0-88192-253-6*) Timber.

Temperature. Brenda Walpole. LC 95-21854. (Measure up with Science Ser.). (Illus.). (J). 1995. lib. bdg. 18.60 (*0-8368-1363-4*) Gareth Stevens Inc.

Temperature. 2nd ed. T. J. Quinn. (Monographs in Physical Measurement). (Illus.). 495p. 1991. text ed. 129.00 (*0-12-569681-7*) Acad Pr.

Temperature: Its Measurement & Control in Science & Industry, Pt. 3 Biology & Medicine. American Institute of Physics Staff. Ed. by Charles M. Herzfeld. LC 62-19138. 696p. 1972. reprint ed. 49.50 (*0-88275-058-5*, (K)VN) Krieger.

Temperature: Its Measurement & Control in Science & Industry, Vol. 3, Pt. 2: Applied Methods & Instruments. American Institute of Physics Staff. Ed. by Charles M. Herzfeld. LC 62-19138. 1108p. 1972. reprint ed. Pt. 2 Applied Methods & Instruments. 79.50 (*0-88275-059-3*, (K)VN) Krieger.

Temperature: Its Measurement & Control in Science & Industry, 3 pts., Vol. 4. Incl. Pt. 1. Basic Methods, Scales & Fixed Points, Radiation. Ed. by H. Preston-Thomas et al. LC 62-19138. pap. 160.00 (*0-685-73698-9*); Pt. 2. Resistance, Electronic & Magnetic Thermometry: Controls & Calibration; Bridges. Ed. by L. G. Rubin et al. LC 62-19138. pap. 160.00 (*0-685-73699-7*); Pt. 3. Thermocouples, Biology & Medicine, Geophysics & Space. Ed. by D. I. Finch et al. LC 62-19138. pap. 160.00 (*0-685-73700-4*); LC 62-19138. reprint ed. Set pap. write for info. (*0-318-59253-3*, 2052133) Bks Demand.

Temperature: Its Measurement & Control in Science & Industry, Proceedings of the Sixth International Symposium, Washington, DC, March 15, 1982. Ed. by James F. Schooley. LC 62-19138. 1472p. 1982. 150.00 (*0-88318-403-6*) Am Inst Physics.

Temperature Adaptation of Biological Membranes. Ed. by A. R. Cossins. (Portland Press Proceedings Ser.: Vol. 7). (Illus.). 240p. (C). 1994. text ed. 110.50 (*1-85578-062-3*, Pub. by Portland Pr Ltd UK) Ashgate Pub Co.

Temperature & Animal Cells. Ed. by K. Bowler & B. J. Fuller. (Society for Experimental Biology Symposia Ser.: No. 41). 460p. 1987. 70.00 (*0-948601-08-6*) Portland FL.

Temperature & Environmental Effects on the Testis. Ed. by A. W. Zorgniotti. LC 90-14362. (Advances in Experimental Medicine & Biology Ser.: Vol. 286). (Illus.). 348p. 1991. 95.00 (*0-306-43834-8*, Plenum Pr) Plenum.

Temperature & Life. H. Precht et al. LC 73-13495. (Illus.). 779p. 1973. 98.00 (*0-387-06441-9*) Spr-Verlag.

Temperature & Racism: John Bull, Johnny Reb, & the Good Templars. David M. Fahey. LC 96-12156. (Illus.). 232p. (C). 1996. text ed. 39.95 (*0-8131-1984-7*) U Pr of Ky.

Temperature Biology of Animals. A. R. Cossins & K. Bowler. 300p. 1987. text ed. 57.50 (*0-412-15900-7*) Chapman & Hall.

Temperature Calibration of Water Baths, Instruments & Temperature Sensors. 2nd ed. (Approved Standard Ser.). 1990. 75.00 (*1-56238-075-3*, I2-A2) Natl Comm Clin Lab Stds.

Temperature Control Principles for Process Engineers: A Guidebook for Chemical, Bio-Chemical, & Polymer Process Engineers Who Design Temperature Control Systems. Ed. by Eugene P. Dougherty. LC 93-34840. 288p. (C). 1993. text ed. write for info. (*1-56990-152-X*) Hanser-Gardner.

Temperature Controlled Storage & Distribution Buyers Guide. FMJ Intl. Publ. Ltd. Staff. (C). 1989. 295.00 (*0-685-36819-X*, Pub. by Fuel Metallurgical Jrnl UK) St Mut.

Temperature Effect on Concrete - STP 858. Ed. by Tarun R. Naik. LC 84-70335. (Illus.). 180p. 1985. text ed. 28.00 (*0-8031-0435-9*, 04-858000-07) ASTM.

Temperature Measurement. Bela G. Liptak. LC 92-56586. 128p. 1993. pap. 29.95 (*0-8019-8385-1*) Chilton.

Temperature Measurement. L. Michalski et al. LC 90-35320. (Series in Measurement Science & Technology: No. 1824). 514p. 1991. text ed. 210.00 (*0-471-92229-3*) Wiley.

***Temperature Measurement: Technology & Standards.** INSPEC Staff. 85.00 (*0-614-18485-1*, 135P19) Info Gatekeepers.

Temperature Measurement see 1997 Annual Book of ASTM Standards: General Methods & Instrumentation, Section 14

Temperature Measurement & Control. J. R. Leigh. (Control Engineering Ser.: No. 33). 208p. 1988. 77.00 (*0-86341-111-8*, CE033) Inst Elect Eng.

Temperature Measurement in Industry. Ernest C. Magison. 176p. 1990. text ed. 60.00 (*1-55617-208-7*, A208-7) ISA.

Temperature Measurement Thermocouples: An ANSI Approved Standard MC96.1. rev. ed. 47p. 1982. pap. text ed. 40.00 (*0-87664-708-5*, 1708-5) ISA.

***Temperature Measurements: Technology & Standards.** Physics & Engineering Communities Database Staff. 85.00 (*0-614-18489-4*, 135P26) Info Gatekeepers.

Temperature Measurements in Seeded Air & Nitrogen Plasmas. H. N. Olsen et al. LC 79-131016. 133p. 1970. 19.00 (*0-403-04524-X*) Scholarly.

Temperature-Programmed Reduction for Solid Materials Characterization. Jones & McNicol. (Chemical Industries Ser.: Vol. 24). 216p. 1986. 125.00 (*0-8247-7583-X*) Dekker.

Temperature Regulation. S. A. Richards & P. S. Fielden. LC 73-77794. (Wykeham Science Ser.: No. 27). 212p. (C). 1973. pap. 18.00 (*0-8448-1335-4*, Crane Russak) Taylor & Francis.

Temperature Regulation: Recent Physiological & Pharmacological Advances. Ed. by A. S. Milton. LC 93-50550. (Advances in Pharmacological Sciences Ser.). xii, 376p. 1994. 119.50 (*0-8176-2992-0*) Birkhauser.

Temperature Regulation & Drug Action: Proceedings of the Pharmacology of Thermoregulation Symposium, 2nd, Paris, 1974. Pharmacology of Thermoregulation symposium Staff. Ed. by Edward Schonbaum & P. Lommax. 450p. 1975. 119.25 (*3-8055-1756-4*) S Karger.

Temperature Relations in Animals & Man. Werner Nachtigall. (BIONA Report Ser.: No. 4). 229p. 1986. pap. 19.00 (*0-89574-226-8*, Pub. by G Fischer Verlag GW) Lubrecht & Cramer.

Temperature-Salinity Analysis of World Ocean Waters. O. I. Mamayev. (Oceanography Ser.: Vol. 11). 374p. 1975. 133.50 (*0-444-41251-4*) Elsevier.

Temperature, Salinity & Density of the Surface Waters of the Atlantic Ocean Vol. 5: Scientific Results of the German Atlantic Expedition of the Research Vessel "Meteor", 1925-1927, Atlas, Vol. 5. Gunther Bohnecke. Tr. by N. P. Date from GER. (Illus.). 172p. 1992. 115.00 (*90-5410-238-1*, Pub. by A A Balkema NE) Ashgate Pub Co.

Temperature Sensors. Richard K. Miller & Terri C. Walker. LC 88-72188. (Survey on Technology & Markets Ser.: No. 30). 50p. 1989. pap. text ed. 200.00 (*1-55865-098-9*) Future Tech Surveys.

Temperatures Rising. Sandra Brown. 256p. 1993. mass mkt. 5.99 (*0-553-56045-X*) Bantam.

Temperatures Very Low & Very High. Mark W. Zemansky. 144p. 1981. reprint ed. pap. 4.95 (*0-486-24072-X*) Dover.

Tempered Iron. Steve Sherman. 192p. 1989. 18.95 (*0-8027-4100-2*) Walker & Co.

Tempering. Howard S. Buck. LC 70-144708. (Yale Series of Younger Poets: No. 1). reprint ed. 18.00 (*0-404-53801-0*) AMS Pr.

Tempering Blaze. Sally Laity & Dianna Crawford. LC 94-23236. (Freedom's Holy Light Ser.: Vol. 3). 1995. pap. 10.99 (*0-8423-6902-3*) Tyndale.

Tempering of T. S. Eliot. John J. Soldo. Ed. by A. Walton Litz. LC 83-9115. (Studies in Modern Literature: No. 33). 207p. reprint ed. pap. 59.00 (*0-8357-1488-8*, 2070333) Bks Demand.

Temperley-Lieb Recoupling Theory & Invariants of 3-Manifolds. Louis H. Kaufmann. 312p. 1994. text ed. 55.00 (*0-691-03641-1*); pap. text ed. 24.95 (*0-691-03640-3*) Princeton U Pr.

Tempest. Arden. 1985. pap. 8.95 (*0-416-10190-9*) Routledge Chapman & Hall.

Tempest. Aime Cesaire. LC 74-82723. 1974. 5.95 (*0-89388-174-0*); pap. 2.95 (*0-89388-175-9*) Okpaku Communications.

Tempest. Sandra DuBay. 480p. (Orig.). 1989. mass mkt., pap. text ed. 4.50 (*0-8439-2719-4*) Dorchester Pub Co.

Tempest. Ed. by Alan Durband. (Shakespeare Made Easy Ser.). 288p. 1985. pap. 6.95 (*0-8120-3603-4*) Barron.

Tempest. Forman. (Book Notes Ser.). (C). 1986. pap. 2.95 (*0-8120-3545-3*) Barron.

Tempest. Northrop Frye. (New Penguin Shakespeare Ser.). 192p. 1981. pap. 5.50 (*0-14-070713-1*, Penguin Classics) Viking Penguin.

Tempest. Catherine Hart. 400p. (Orig.). 1991. mass mkt. 4.95 (*0-380-76005-3*) Avon.

Tempest. Illus. by Eric Kincaid. 32p. (J). (gr. 2-4). 1996. 8.00 (*1-85854-270-7*) Brimax Bks.

***Tempest.** Ed. by Sidney Lamb. 1996. student ed., pap. text ed. 6.95 (*0-8220-1441-6*) Cliffs.

Tempest. Ed. by Bernard Lott. (New Swan Shakespeare Ser.). 1900. pap. text ed. 2.95 (*0-582-74500-4*, TG7013) Longman.

***Tempest.** Marianna Mayer. (J). Date not set. write for info. (*0-688-14061-0*, Morrow Junior); lib. bdg. write for info. (*0-688-14062-9*, Morrow Junior) Morrow.

Tempest. M.H. Publications Staff. 165p. 1990. 175.00 (*1-872680-08-9*, Pub. by M H Pubns UK) St Mut.

Tempest. Arthur Moore. (Orig.). 1979. mass mkt. 2.50 (*0-89083-521-7*, Zebra Kensgtn) Kensgtn Pub Corp.

Tempest. James R. Neal. LC 93-93905. 112p. (Orig.). 1994. pap. 7.00 (*1-56002-344-9*) Aegina Pr.

Tempest. Laura Parker. 416p. 1997. mass mkt. 4.99 (*0-8217-5550-1*, Zebra Kensgtn) Kensgtn Pub Corp.

Tempest. Ed. by A. L. Rowse. LC 84-5070. (Contemporary Shakespeare Ser.: Vol. I). 104p. (Orig.). (C). 1984. pap. text ed. 3.45 (*0-8191-3899-1*) U Pr of Amer.

Tempest. William Shakespeare. Ed. by John Andrews. (Everyman Shakespeare Ser.). 256p. 1994. pap. 3.95 (*0-460-87455-1*, Everyman's Classic Lib) C E Tuttle.

Tempest. William Shakespeare. Ed. by Robert Langbaum. 1964. pap. 3.95 (*0-451-52125-0*, Sig Classics) NAL-Dutton.

Tempest. William Shakespeare. Ed. by Northrop Frye. (Pelican Shakespeare Ser.). 120p. 1959. pap. 3.95 (*0-14-071415-4*, Pelican Bks) Viking Penguin.

Tempest. William Shakespeare. Ed. by John R. Brown. (Shakespeare Library). 192p. 1996. pap. 7.95 (*1-55783-182-3*) Applause Theatre Bk Pubs.

***Tempest.** William Shakespeare & Neil Freeman. LC 97-9574. (Applause Shakespeare Library). 1997. pap. write for info. (*1-55783-295-1*) Applause Theatre Bk Pubs.

Tempest. William Shakespeare. (Classics Ser.). 160p. 1988. 3.95 (*0-553-21307-5*, Bantam Classics) Bantam.

Tempest. William Shakespeare. 40p. (J). 1996. pap. 6.99 (*0-440-41297-8*) Dell.

Tempest. William Shakespeare. (Illustrated Classics Shakespeare Collection). 64p. 1994. pap. 3.60 (*1-56103-685-4*) Moonbeam Pubns.

Tempest. William Shakespeare. Ed. by Stephen Orgel. (Oxford Shakespeare Ser.). 264p. 1987. pap. 6.95 (*0-19-281450-8*) OUP.

Tempest. William Shakespeare. Ed. by Paul Werstine & Barbara A. Mowat. (New Folger Library). 1994. pap. 3.99 (*0-671-72290-5*, Folger Lib) PB.

***Tempest.** William Shakespeare. (English Ser.). (C). Date not set. pap. 9.95 (*0-17-443535-5*) Wadsworth Pub.

Tempest. William Shakespeare. LC 94-33357. 32p. (J). (gr. 3 up). 1996. 16.95 (*0-399-22764-4*, Philomel Bks) Putnam Pub Group.

Tempest. William Shakespeare. Ed. by Rex Gibson. (Shakespeare Ser.). (Illus.). 176p. (C). 1995. pap. text ed. 7.95 (*0-521-47903-7*) Cambridge U Pr.

Tempest. William Shakespeare. Date not set. write for info. (*0-517-15119-7*) Random Hse Value.

Tempest. William Shakespeare. (Applause Shakespeare Library). 1996. pap. 7.95 (*0-614-97673-1*) Applause NY.

Tempest. William Shakespeare. (BBC Television Plays Ser.). 1980. pap. 4.95 (*0-563-17777-2*, Pub. by BBC UK) Parkwest Pubns.

Tempest. Eric J. Siry. (Wallet-Size Classics Ser.: No. 1). (Illus.). 16p. (Orig.). 1993. 2.95 (*1-884304-00-1*) Eric Siry.

Tempest. Nigel Wood. LC 94-19659. write for info. (*0-335-15689-4*) Taylor & Francis.

Tempest. Ed. by Nigel Wood. (Theory in Practice Ser.). 197p. 1994. pap. 19.95 (*0-335-15688-6*, Open Univ Pr) Taylor & Francis.

***Tempest.** Wright. (Deep Space Nine Ser.: No. 19). 1997. mass mkt. 5.99 (*0-671-00227-9*, Star Trek) PB.

Tempest. large type ed. William Shakespeare. (Charnwood Large Print Ser.). 1991. pap. 24.95 (*0-7089-4538-4*, Charnwood) Ulverscroft.

Tempest. rev. ed. Aime Cesaire. Tr. by Richard Miller from FRE. LC 92-63019. 72p. (Orig.). 1993. pap. 8.95 (*0-913745-40-5*) Ubu Repertory.

***Tempest.** 3rd ed. William Shakespeare. (English Ser.). (C). Date not set. text ed. 45.00 (*0-17-443568-1*) Wadsworth Pub.

Tempest. 6th ed. William Shakespeare. Ed. by Frank Kermode. (Arden Shakespeare Ser.). 1958. reprint ed. pap. 9.95 (*0-415-02704-7*, NO. 2491) Routledge.

Tempest: A Play Packet to Accompany Elementary, My Dear Shakespeare. Barbara Engen & Joy Campbell. (Illus.). 39p. 1992. 8.95 (*0-922947-06-6*) Mkt Masters.

Tempest: A Screenplay. Paul Mazursky & Leon Capetanos. LC 82-81975. (Illus.). 1982. pap. 8.95 (*0-933826-41-9*) PAJ Pubns.

***Tempest: An Annotated Bibliography.** Michelle Holley. Ed. by William Godshalk. (Garland Shakespeare Bibliographies Ser.). 600p. Date not set. text ed. 80.00 (*0-8153-0828-0*) Garland.

Tempest: HBJ Shakespeare 1989. William Shakespeare. Ed. by Patenaude. 1990. student ed., pap. 12.00 (*0-7747-1359-3*) HB Schl Dept.

Tempest: Original Text & Modern Verse. William Shakespeare. Ed. by Alan Durband. (Shakespeare Made Easy Ser.). (Orig.). 1995. pap. 16.95 (*0-7487-0379-9*, Pub. by Stanley Thornes UK) Trans-Atl Phila.

Tempest: Piano Vocal Score. L. Hoiby. 328p. 1992. pap. 40.00 (*0-7935-0630-1*) H Leonard.

Tempest see Shakespearean Adaptations

Tempest & After. Ed. by Stanley Wells. (Shakespeare Survey Ser.: No. 43). (Illus.). 320p. (C). 1991. text ed. 69.95 (*0-521-39529-1*) Cambridge U Pr.

Tempest & Shipwreck in Dutch & Flemish Art: Convention, Rhetoric, & Interpretation. Lawrence O. Goedde. LC 86-43030. 272p. 1989. 45.00 (*0-271-00487-8*) Pa St U Pr.

***Tempest at Stonehaven.** Grace Johnson. LC 97-12400. (Scottish Shores Ser.). 1997. pap. write for info. (*0-8423-6250-9*) Tyndale.

Tempest Complete Study Guide. Sidney Lamb. 1965. pap. 6.95 (*0-8220-1440-8*) Cliffs.

Tempest, Flute, & Oz: Essays on the Future. Frederick Turner. 192p. 1991. 19.95 (*0-89255-159-3*) Persea Bks.

Tempest in a Teapot: The Falkland Islands War. R. Reginald & Jeffrey M. Elliot. LC 83-8807. (Stokvis Studies in Historical Chronology & Thought: No. 3). (Illus.). 173p. 1983. pap. 21.00 (*0-89370-267-6*); lib. bdg. 31.00 (*0-89370-167-X*) Borgo Pr.

Tempest in Eden. Sandra Brown. 240p. 1996. mass mkt. 6.50 (*0-446-36431-2*, Warner Vision) Warner Bks.

***Tempest in Time.** Eugenia Riley. 448p. (Orig.). 1996. mass mkt. 5.50 (*0-505-52154-7*) Dorchester Pub Co.

An Asterisk (*) at the beginning of an entry indicates that the title is appearing in BIP for the first time.

Tempest in Venice. John Sampson. LC 86-50056. 268p. 1986. 8.95 (0-9613075-2-8) Thornfield Pr.

Tempest Notes. L. L. Hillegass. (Cliffs Notes Ser.). 1971. pap. 3.95 (0-8220-0083-0) Cliffs.

Tempest of Clemenza: A Novel. Glenda Adams. LC 96-18116. 312p. 1996. 22.95 (0-571-19897-X) Faber & Faber.

Tempest of Stars: Selected Poems. Jean Cocteau. Tr. by Jeremy Reed from FRE. (Illus.). 137p. 9300. pap. 22.00 (1-870612-12-4, Pub. by Enitha Pr UK) Dufour.

Tempest over Mexico: A Personal Chronicle. Rosa E. King. LC 71-111721. (American Imperialism: Viewpoints of United States Foreign Policy, 1898-1941 Ser.). 1970. reprint ed. 20.95 (0-405-02031-7) Ayer.

Tempest Pilot. C. J. Sheddan. (Illus.). 192p. 1993. 29.95 (0-948817-70-4, Pub. by Grub St Pubns UK) Seven Hills Bk.

***Tempest Readalong.** William Shakespeare. (Illustrated Classics Shakespeare Collection). 64p. (YA). (gr. 6-12). 1994. pap. 14.95 incl. audio (0-7854-0829-0, 40623) Am Guidance.

Tempest Tossed. Buffy St. John. (Orig.). 1995. pap. 6.95 (0-9626783-1-7) Buffed Computer.

Tempest Tost. Robertson Davies. 784p. 1980. pap. 11.95 (0-14-016792-7, Penguin Bks); mass mkt. 4.95 (0-14-005431-6, Penguin Bks) Viking Penguin.

***Tempest-Tost: Refugees, Race, & the Dilemma of Diversity.** Peter I. Rose. LC 96-38822. 288p. 1997. 30.00 (0-19-510070-0) OUP.

Tempest Within: Account of East Pakistan. D. Moraes. 102p. 1971. 8.95 (0-318-37274-6) Asia Bk Corp.

Tempestad en un Vaso de Agua. Marie-Francine Hebert. (Primeros Lectores Ser.). (Illus.). 60p. (SPA.). (YA). (gr. 5 up). 1994. pap. 5.95 (958-07-0076-1) Firefly Bks Ltd.

Tempests into Rainbows: Managing Turbulence. Robben W. Fleming. LC 95-46711. (C). 1995. 24.95 (0-472-10674-0) U of Mich Pr.

Tempestuous: Opal's Story. Jude Watson. (Brides of Wildcat County Ser.). (J). 1996. pap. 5.99 (0-689-81023-7) S&S Trade.

Tempestuous Petticoat: The Story of an Invincible Edwardian. Clare Leighton. 272p. 1984. reprint ed. pap. 10.00 (0-89733-099-4) Academy Chi Pubs.

Tempestuous Reunion. Lynne Graham. (Presents Ser.). 1993. pap. 2.89 (0-373-11551-2, 1-11551-8) Harlequin Bks.

Tempestuous Sands. large type ed. Helen McCabe. (Linford Romance Library). 1995. pap. 15.99 (0-7089-7795-2, Linford) Ulverscroft.

***Tempestuous Shore.** large type ed. Clare Benedict. (Dales Large Print Ser.). (Illus.). 220p. 1996. pap. 17.99 (1-85389-613-6) Ulverscroft.

Tempete. Rene Barjavel. 277p. (FRE.). 1985. pap. 10.95 (0-7859-2022-6, 2070376966) Fr & Eur.

Tempete. Aime Cesaire. 1975. pap. 10.95 (0-8288-9087-0) Fr & Eur.

***Tempete dans une Verre D'eau.** Marie-Francine Hebert. (Novels in the Premier Roman Ser.). 64p. (FRE.). (J). (gr. 2-5). 1996. pap. 7.95 (2-89021-109-6, Pub. by Les Editions CN) Firefly Bks Ltd.

Tempete sur Douarnenez. Henri Queffelec. (FRE.). 1973. pap. 10.95 (0-7859-4006-5) Fr & Eur.

Tempi Moderni. Anna C. Burney. 204p. (ITA.). (C). 1982. pap. text ed. 22.75 (0-03-059557-6) HB Coll Pubs.

***Tempietto del Clitunno Near Spoleto.** Judson J. Emerick. LC 97-7729. 1998. write for info. (0-271-01728-7) Pa St U Pr.

***Temping, Freelancing, & Entrepreneurial Opportunities.** Kaplan Staff. LC 97-3406. 1997. 15.00 (0-684-83756-0) S&S Trade.

Templa Graphics: A Generic Graphical Editor for the Macintosh. Sharam Hekmatpour. 184p. 1991. boxed 55.00 (0-13-904160-5, 220106) P-H.

Templar Orders in Freemasonry. Arthur E. Waite. 1991. pap. 4.95 (1-55818-133-4, Sure Fire) Holmes Pub.

Templario: And Excerpts from Other Operas. Otto Nicolai. (Italian Opera 1810-1840 Ser.: Vol. 26). 280p. 1991. text ed. 40.00 (0-8240-6575-1) Garland.

Templars: Knights of God. Edward Burman. 208p. 1987. pap. 12.95 (0-89281-221-4) Inner Tradit.

Templars, Hospitallers & Teutonic Knights: Images of the Military Orders, 1128-1291. Helen Nicholson. 208p. 1993. text ed. 59.00 (0-7185-1411-4) St Martin.

Templars, Hospitallers & Teutonic Knights: The Image of the Military Orders, 1128-1291. Helen Nicholson. 224p. 1995. pap. 24.95 (0-7185-2277-X, Pub. by Leicester Univ Pr) St Martin.

Template-Free Quilts & Borders. Trudie Hughes. Ed. by Liz McGehee. LC 89-20677. (Illus.). 96p. (Orig.). 1990. pap. 17.95 (0-943574-64-1, B111) That Patchwork.

***Template-Free Stars.** Jo Parrott. (Illus.). 64p. pap. text ed. 7.95 (0-486-29473-0) Dover.

Template-Makers of the Paris Basin: Toichological Techniques for Identifying the Pioneers of the Gothic Movement. John James. (Illus.). 256p. 1989. 79.00 (0-7316-4520-0) Boydell & Brewer.

Template Polymerization & Copolymerization. Polowinski. 1994. write for info. (0-8493-6778-6) CRC Pr.

Template Software to Accompany Financial Accounting, Macintosh. 7th ed. Ernest I. Hanson et al. (C). 1993. 25.75 (0-03-097472-0) Dryden Pr.

Template Software to Accompany Principles of Accounting, Macintosh. 6th ed. Ernest I. Hanson et al. (C). 1993. 20.75 (0-03-097404-6) Dryden Pr.

Templates for the Solution of Linear Systems: Building Blocks for Iterative Methods. Richard Barrett et al. (Miscellaneous Titles in Applied Mathematics Ser.: No. 43). xvii, 124p. 1993. pap. 19.00 (0-89871-328-5) Soc Indus-Appl Math.

Temple. George Dennison. 194p. 1994. 19.50 (1-883642-22-1) Steerforth Pr.

Temple. Janet Hamill. Ed. by Maureen Owen. LC 80-16515. (Illus.). 33p. (Orig.). 1981. pap. 6.00 (0-916382-22-2) Telephone Bks.

Temple. John M. Lundquist. LC 92-62138. (Art & Imagination Ser.). (Illus.). 96p. 1993. pap. 15.95 (0-500-81040-0) Thames Hudson.

Temple. Laurie S. Monsees. LC 93-20854. 1994. 60.00 (0-8309-0648-7) Herald Hse.

Temple: Concerning Diseases of the Brain & Nerves. Andrew J. Davis. 487p. 1972. reprint ed. spiral bd. 24.50 (0-7873-0250-3) Hlth Research.

Temple: Its Ministry & Services. Alfred Edersheim. 332p. 1994. pap. 12.95 (1-56563-006-8) Hendrickson MA.

Temple: Its Ministry & Services. Alfred Edersheim. 332p. 1994. 19.95 (1-56563-136-6) Hendrickson MA.

***Temple: Its Ministry & Services As They Were at the Time of Jesus Christ.** rev. ed. Alfred Edersheim. Ed. by John J. Bimson. LC 96-41024. (Illus.). 256p. 1997. 24.99 (0-8254-2509-3) Kregel.

Temple: Its Symbolism & Meaning Then & Now. Joshua Berman. LC 95-5211. 280p. 1996. 30.00 (1-56821-415-4) Aronson.

Temple: Sacred Poems & Private Ejaculations. 6th ed. George Herbert. LC 72-5489. (Select Bibliographies Reprint Ser.). 1977. reprint ed. 20.95 (0-8369-6915-4) Ayer.

Temple: Some Temple Pedigrees. L. D. Temple. (Illus.). 316p. 1991. reprint ed. pap. 47.50 (0-8328-2182-9); reprint ed. lib. bdg. 57.50 (0-8328-2181-0) Higginson Bk Co.

Temple & a Priest to the Temple. George Herbert. (BCL1-PR English Literature Ser.). 304p. 1992. reprint ed. lib. bdg. 89.00 (0-7812-7364-1) Rprt Serv.

Temple & Contemplation. Henry Corbin. Tr. by Philip Sherrard & Liadain Sherrard. (Illus.). 390p. (C). 1986. text ed. 65.00 (0-7103-0129-4); pap. text ed. 17.95 (0-7103-0130-8) Routledge Chapman & Hall.

Temple & Cosmos. Hugh Nibley. LC 91-33320. (Collected Works of Hugh Nibley: Vol. 12). 597p. 1992. 24.95 (0-87579-523-4) Deseret Bk.

Temple, & Other Poems. Tr. by Arthur Waley. LC 78-70137. reprint ed. 31.50 (0-404-17407-8) AMS Pr.

Temple & the Lodge. Michael Baigent & Richard Leigh. (Illus.). 324p. 1991. pap. 13.95 (1-55970-126-9) Arcade Pub Inc.

Temple and the Lodge. Michael. Baigent. 1990. mass mkt. 8.99 (0-552-13596-8) Bantam.

Temple & the Teahouse in Japan. Werner Blaser. 180p. (ENG & GER.). 1988. 132.00 (0-8176-1963-1) Birkhauser.

Temple Arts of Kerala. Ronald M. Bernier. (Illus.). 258p. 1982. 99.00 (0-940500-79-5) Asia Bk Corp.

Temple Arts of Kerala: A South Indian Tradition. Ronald M. Berner. 272p. 1985. 100.00 (0-317-52158-6, Pub. by S Chand II) St Mut.

Temple at Ayia Irini: The Statues. Miriam E. Caskey. LC 85-15713. (Keos Ser.: Vol. 2, Pt. 1). (Illus.). xxviii, 130p. 1986. 45.00 (0-87661-702-X) Am Sch Athens.

Temple aux Miroirs. Alain Robbe-Grillet & Irina Ionesco. 50.00 (0-686-54740-3) Fr & Eur.

Temple Beyond Time: Mount Moriah - From Solomon's Temple to Christian & Islamic Shrines. rev. ed. Herbert A. Klein. Ed. by Joseph Simon. LC 86-90357. (Illus.). 192p. (ps-12). 1986. reprint ed. 27.50 (0-934710-14-7) J Simon.

Temple Bombing. Melissa F. Greene. 502p. 1996. 25.00 (0-201-62206-8) Addison-Wesley.

***Temple Bombing.** Melissa F. Greene. 1997. pap. 14.00 (0-449-90809-7) Fawcett.

Temple Cat. Andrew Clements. LC 94-44082. (Illus.). 32p. (J). (gr. k-3). 1996. 14.95 (0-395-69842-1, Clarion Bks) HM.

Temple Cat. Andrew Clements. (J). 16.00 (0-689-80248-X, Aladdin Paperbacks) S&S Childrens.

Temple Culture of South India. V. Parameswaran Pillai. 1986. 40.00 (0-317-53516-1, Pub. by Manohar II) S Asia.

Temple Documents of the Third Dynasty of Ur from Umma. Ed. by George G. Hackman. LC 78-63524. (Babylonian Inscriptions in the Collection of James B. Nies Ser.: No. 5). reprint ed. 28.50 (0-404-60135-9) AMS Pr.

Temple Dogs. Warren Murphy & Molly Cochran. 416p. 1989. 18.95 (0-318-40988-7) NAL-Dutton.

Temple Doors Edition, Vol. 1. Maia C. Shamayyim. 350p. 1993. spiral bd. 46.00 (1-888420-10-3) Johannine Grove.

Temple Doors Edition, Vol. 2. Maia C. Shamayyim. Ed. by Simeon Nartoomid. (Illus.). Date not set. spiral bd. write for info. (1-888420-19-7) Johannine Grove.

Temple du Gout. Francois-Marie De Voltaire. 203p. (FRE.). 1953. pap. 13.95 (0-7859-5517-8) Fr & Eur.

Temple du Soleil. Herge. (Illus.). (FRE.). (J). (gr. 7-9). 19.95 (0-8288-5078-X) Fr & Eur.

Temple Dusk: Zen Haiku. Mitsu Suzuki. Tr. by Kazuaki Tanahashi & Gregory A. Wood from JPN. LC 92-8673. 175p. 1992. 12.00 (0-938077-48-1) Parallax Pr.

Temple Entry Movement & the Sivakasi Riots. B. Sobhanan. 1986. 11.00 (0-8364-1856-5, Pub. by Heritage IA) S Asia.

Temple Flowers. J. P. Vaswani & Jyoti Mirchandani. 182p. 1986. text ed. 25.00 (0-317-43153-6, Pub. by Chopmen Singapore SI) Advent Bks Div.

Temple for Byzantium: The Discovery & Excavation of a Palace Church in Istanbul. Martin Harrison. 160p. 1989. text ed. write for info. (0-905203-82-8) Gordon & Breach.

Temple Foundations: Essays on an Emerging Concept. Richard A. Brown. 150p. (Orig.). 1991. pap. 12.00 (0-8309-0589-8) Herald Hse.

Temple Gateways in South India: The Architecture & Iconography of Cidambaram Gopuras. James C. Harle. (Illus.). 217p. (C). 1995. reprint ed. 67.50 (81-215-0666-2, Pub. by M Manoharial II) Coronet Bks.

Temple Greek & Latin Classics, 5 Vols, Set. Ed. by G. Lowes Dickinson & H. O. Meredeth. reprint ed. 120.00 (0-404-07900-8) AMS Pr.

Temple Household Horseback: Rugs of the Tibetan Plateau. Diana K. Myers et al. LC 84-52139. (Illus.). 112p. 1984. pap. 27.50 (0-87405-024-3) Textile Mus.

Temple, Household, Horseback: Rugs of the Tibetan Plateau. Diana K. Myers et al. (Illus.). 112p. 1984. pap. 27.50 (0-295-96979-2) U of Wash Pr.

Temple in Andhradesa. A. Surya Kumari. (C). 1988. 50.00 (81-212-0230-2, Pub. by Gian Publng Hse II) S Asia.

Temple in History & Prophecy. T. Hugh Moreton. 40p. (Orig.). 1992. pap. 2.50 (1-879366-37-7) Hearthstone OK.

Temple in Man: Sacred Architecture & the Perfect Man. R. A. Schwaller De Lubicz. Tr. by Robert Lawlor & Deborah Lawlor from FRE. LC 81-13374. (Illus.). 136p. 1981. reprint ed. pap. 10.95 (0-89281-021-1) Inner Tradit.

Temple in Nimes. limited ed. James Wright. (Metacom Limited Edition Ser.: No. 5). 28p. 1982. 25.00 (0-911381-04-X) Metacom Pr.

Temple in Society. Ed. by Michael V. Fox. LC 88-3979. vi, 138p. (C). 1988. text ed. 25.00 (0-931464-38-2) Eisenbrauns.

Temple in the House: Finding the Sacred in Everyday Architecture. Anthony Lawlor. LC 94-6985. (Illus.). 256p. 1994. 17.95 (0-87477-777-1, Tarcher Putnam) Putnam Pub Group.

Temple-Inland Inc. A Report on the Company's Environmental Policies & Practices. (Illus.). 34p. (C). 1994. reprint ed. pap. text ed. 250.00 (0-7881-0969-3, Coun on Econ) DIANE Pub.

Temple Israel of Tallahassee, Florida: 1937-1987. Claire B. Levenson. 96p. 1987. text ed. 6.95 (0-9616000-1-2) Peninsular Pub Co.

Temple, Its Ministry & Services. Alfred Edersheim. 1950. pap. 10.00 (0-8028-8133-5) Eerdmans.

***Temple Lectures Pts. 1 & 2: Religion of the Stars; Evolutionism.** Olney H. Richmond. Ed. & Pref. by Iain McLaren-Owens. (Astro-Cards Reprints Ser.). (Illus.). 263p. 1996. reprint ed. pap. text ed. 22.00 (1-885500-14-9, AR9) Astro-Cards.

Temple Lectures of the Order of the Magi. Olney H. Richmond. reprint ed. spiral bd. 11.00 (0-7873-0718-1) Hlth Research.

Temple Lectures of the Order of the Magi (1892) Olney H. Richmond. 270p. 1996. pap. 21.00 (1-56459-801-2) Kessinger Pub.

Temple Magic: Building the Personal Temple: Gateway to Inner Worlds. William Gray. LC 88-45184. (High Magick Ser.). (Illus.). 288p. (Orig.). 1988. pap. 7.95 (0-87542-274-8) Llewellyn Pubns.

Temple Messages. Ed. by Temple of the People Publications Staff. (Illus.). 183p. 1983. 14.00 (0-933797-07-9) Halcyon Bk.

***Temple Not Made with Hands.** Walter C. Lanyon. 184p. (Orig.). 1983. pap. 8.00 (1-889870-00-5) Union Life.

Temple of Apollo Bassitas Vol. 1: The Architecture. Frederick A. Cooper & Nancy J. Kelly. (Illus.). 430p. 1996. 110.00 (0-87661-946-4) Am Sch Athens.

Temple of Apollo Bassitas Vol. 2: The Sculpture. Brian C. Madigan. LC 92-23979. (Illus.). 144p. 1992. 50.00 (0-87661-947-2) Am Sch Athens.

Temple of Apollo Bassitas Vol. 3: Photographs for Vol. 1: Notebook of Baron Haller Von Hallerstein; & Inventory of Blocks. Frederick A. Cooper. (Illus.). 480p. 1996. 90.00 (0-87661-948-0) Am Sch Athens.

Temple of Apollo Bassitas Vol. 4: Maps, Plans & Other Drawings. Frederick A. Cooper. LC 92-23979. (Illus.). 68p. 1992. 80.00 (0-87661-949-9) Am Sch Athens.

Temple of Baseball. Ed. by Richard Grossinger. (Io Ser.: No. 34). (Illus.). 268p. (Orig.). 1985. 27.50 (0-938190-44-X); pap. 12.95 (0-938190-43-1) North Atlantic.

***Temple of Beastmen.** 1990. 28.00 (1-55878-027-0) Game Designers.

Temple of Chausatha-Yogini at Bheraghat. R. K. Sharma. (Illus.). 184p. 1978. 60.00 (0-318-36260-0) Asia Bk Corp.

Temple of Confessions: Mexican Beasts & Living Santos. Guillermo Gomez-Pena. (Illus.). 144p. 1996. audio compact disk 12.95 (1-57687-005-7, 620252, pwerHse Bks) pwerHse Cultrl.

Temple of Confessions: Mexican Beasts & Living Santos. Guillermo Gomez-Pena & Roberto Sifuentes. (Illus.). 144p. 1997. 29.95 incl. audio compact disk (1-57687-004-9, 620251, pwerHse Bks) pwerHse Cultrl.

Temple of Confessions: Mexican Beasts & Living Santos. limited ed. Guillermo Gomez-Pena. (Illus.). 144p. 1997. boxed 150.00 (1-57687-006-5, 620253, pwerHse Bks) pwerHse Cultrl.

Temple of Dawn. Yukio Mishima. LC 89-40557. 1990. pap. 14.00 (0-679-72242-4, Vin) Random.

Temple of Death. David Cook. 1983. 5.50 (0-394-53166-3) Random.

***Temple of Doom.** (Indiana Jones Roleplaying Game Ser.). 25.00 (0-87431-435-6, 45008) West End Games.

Temple of Glory. Stan R. Abbott. 236p. (Orig.). 1986. pap. 5.95 (0-915545-01-2) S R Abbott Mini.

Temple of God. Annalee Skarin. 224p. 1995. reprint ed. pap. 6.95 (0-87516-093-X) DeVorss.

Temple of Hashem: Futuristic Rebuilding of the Temple. Haym Y. Becker. 1997. text ed. write for info. (965-229-156-0) Gefen Bks.

Temple of Hibis in el Khargeh Oasis: Metropolitan Museum of Art Egyptian Expedition Publications, 2 Vols. Herbert E. Winlock et al. LC 76-168414. (Illus.). 298p. 1973. reprint ed. 35.95 (0-405-02252-2) Ayer.

Temple of Jerusalem. Andre Parrot. Tr. by Beatrice E. Hooke from FRE. LC 85-8037. (Studies in Biblical Archaeology: No. 5). (Illus.). 112p. 1985. reprint ed. text ed. 38.50 (0-313-24224-0, PATJ, Greenwood Pr) Greenwood.

Temple of Jesus: His Sacrificial Program Within a Cultural History of Sacrifice. Bruce Chilton. 224p. 1992. 34.50 (0-271-00824-5) Pa St U Pr.

Temple of Khonsu: Vol. 2, Scenes & Inscriptions in the Court & the First Hypostyle Hall. Epigraphic Survey Staff. LC 80-82999. (Oriental Institute Publications: No. 103). 1981. pap. 115.00 (0-918986-29-X) Orient Inst.

Temple of Khonsu, Vol. 1: Scenes of King Herihor in the Court with Translations of Texts. Epigraphic Survey Staff. LC 78-59119. (Oriental Institute Publications: No. 100). (Illus.). 1979. 110.00 (0-918986-20-6) Orientl Inst Pr IT.

Temple of Liberty: Building the Capitol for a New Nation. Pamela Scott. (Illus.). 176p. 1995. 48.00 (0-19-509857-9); pap. 21.95 (0-19-509858-7) OUP.

Temple of Limestone: A History of Boehms Chapel - 1791-1991. Abram W. Sangrey. (Illus.). 175p. 1991. pap. 12.00 (0-9623805-1-2) A W Sangrey.

Temple of Love. large type ed. Dorothy Osborne. (Linford Romance Library). 304p. 1987. pap. 8.95 (0-7089-6379-X, Linford) Ulverscroft.

Temple of Man, 2 vols. R. A. Schwaller De Lubicz. Tr. by Deborah Lawlor & Robert Lawlor. LC 97-21877. (Illus.). 1024p. 1997. boxed 100.00 (0-89281-570-1) Inner Tradit.

Temple of Memories: History, Power, & Morality in a Chinese Village. Jun Jing. LC 96-15406. 1996. write for info. (0-8047-2756-2) Stanford U Pr.

Temple of Momus: Mitchell's Olympic Theatre. David L. Rinear. LC 85-22077. (Illus.). 237p. 1987. 29.50 (0-8108-1850-7) Scarecrow.

Temple of Muktesvara at Caudadanapura: A Little-Known 12th-13th Century Temple in Dharwar District, Karnataka. Vasundhara Villiozat. (C). 1995. 65.00 (81-7017-327-2, Pub. by Abhinav II) S Asia.

Temple of My Familiar. Alice Walker. LC 96-42427. 1997. pap. 14.00 (0-671-00376-3) PB.

Temple of My Familiar. large type ed. Alice Walker. 1990. reprint ed. lib. bdg. 12.95 (0-89621-937-2) Thorndike Pr.

Temple of My Familiar. Alice Walker. Ed. by Julie Rubenstein. 432p. 1990. reprint ed. pap. 6.99 (0-671-68399-3) PB.

T

Temple of Poseidon. Oscar Broneer. LC 73-61010. (Isthmia Ser.: Vol. 1). (Illus.). xiv, 188p. 1971. 35.00 (0-87661-931-6) Am Sch Athens.

Temple of Rec Stalek. (Torg Ser.). 64p. 12.00 (0-87431-334-1, 20572) West End Games.

Temple of Solomon. Kevin J. Conner. (Illus.). 270p. 1988. pap. 11.95 (0-914936-96-4) BT Pub.

Temple of Solomon the King. Aleister Crowley. LC 92-64419. (Illus.). 704p. (Orig.). 1997. pap. 24.95 (1-56184-049-1) New Falcon Pubns.

Temple of Sulis Minerva at Bath Vol. I: The Site. Barry Cunliffe & Peter Davenport. (Illus.). 210p. 1985. 49.98 (0-947816-07-0, Pub. by Oxford Univ Comm Arch UK) David Brown.

Temple of Sulis Minerva at Bath Vol. II: The Finds from the Sacred Spring. Ed. by Barry Cunliffe. (Illus.). 362p. 1988. not sold separately (0-947816-16-X, Pub. by Oxford Univ Comm Arch UK) David Brown.

Temple of the Cosmos: The Ancient Egyptian Experience of the Sacred. Jeremy Naydler. 224p. 1995. pap. 19.95 (0-89281-555-8) Inner Tradit.

Temple of the Golden Pavilion. Yukio Mishima. 1994. pap. 12.00 (0-679-75270-6) Random.

Temple of the Living Earth. Nicole Christine. 126p. 1995. pap. write for info. (0-9647306-0-X) Earth Song Pubns.

***Temple of the Lord: And Other Stories.** William A. Meninger. LC 97-23225. 1997. pap. text ed. 12.95 (0-8264-1062-6) Continuum.

Temple of the Mind: Education & Literary Taste in Seventeenth-Century England. John R. Mulder. LC 79-79059. 1969. 27.50 (0-672-53602-1) Irvington.

Temple of the Muses: An SPQR Mystery. John M. Roberts. 224p. (Orig.). 1992. mass mkt. 4.50 (0-380-76629-9) Avon.

Temple of the Rosy Cross: The Soul Its Powers & Migrations. F. B. Dowd. 244p. 1994. reprint ed. pap. 17.95 (1-56459-445-9) Kessinger Pub.

Temple of the Rosy Cross: The Soul, Its Powers, Migrations & Transmigrations. 3rd ed. F. B. Dowd. 167p. 1993. reprint ed. spiral bd. 11.00 (0-7873-0292-9) Hlth Research.

Temple of the Warriors: The Adventure of Exploring & Restoring a Masterpiece of Native American Architecture in the Ruined City of Chichen Itza, Yucatan. Earl H. Morris. LC 76-64764. (Illus.). reprint ed. 55.00 (0-404-15871-4) AMS Pr.

Temple of the Warriors at Chichen Itza, Yucatan, 2 vols., Set. Earl H. Morris et al. LC 77-11511. (Carnegie Institution of Washington. Publications: No. 406). reprint ed. 104.50 (0-404-16280-0) AMS Pr.

***Temple of the Winged Lions, Petra, Jordan 1973-1990.** Philip C. Hammond. Ed. by Lin J. Hammond. LC 96-92584. (Illus.). xxi, 237p. (Orig.). 1996. pap. 40.00 (0-9653721-0-3) Petra Pub AZ.

Temple of Tone. George A. Audsley. LC 79-108119. (BCL Ser.: No. 1). (Illus.). 1970. reprint ed. lib. bdg. 37.50 (0-404-00417-2) AMS Pr.

Temple of Tone: A Disquisition on the Scientific & Artistic Tonal Appointment & Control of Concert-Room, Church, & Theater Organs. George A. Audsley. 1990. reprint ed. lib. bdg. 75.00 (*0-7812-9109-7*) Rprt Serv.

Temple of Topaz, Vol. 5. Frank W. Boreham. LC 93-37844. (Life Verses Ser.: No. 5). 272p. 1994. pap. 9.99 (*0-8254-2166-7*) Kregel.

***Temple of Winds.** Goodkind. Date not set. 26.95 (*0-312-89053-2*) St Martin.

Temple of Zeus at Nemea. rev. ed. Charles K. Williams. LC 67-102135. (Illus.). xvii, 149p. 1966. 40.00 (*0-87661-921-9*) Am Sch Athens.

Temple on the River. Jacques Hebert. LC 67-30119. 175p. reprint ed. pap. 49.90 (*0-317-28419-3*, 2022301) Bks Demand.

Temple Organization in a Chinese Village. Gary Seaman. (Asian Folklore & Social Life Monographs: No. 101). 173p. 1981. 20.00 (*0-89986-332-6*) Oriental Bk Store.

Temple Poems. Richard O'Connell. 1985. pap. 6.00 (*0-317-38870-3*) Atlantis Edns.

Temple Propaganda: The Purpose & Character of 2 Maccabees. Robert Doran. LC 81-10084. (Catholic Biblical Quarterly Monographs: No. 12). ix, 124p. 1981. pap. 4.50 (*0-915170-11-6*) Catholic Bibl Assn.

Temple Reflections. Paul F. Schmidt. LC 80-80346. (Illus.). 112p. 1980. 16.00 (*0-912998-04-0*); pap. 8.00 (*0-912998-05-9*) Hummingbird.

Temple Scroll. Johann Maier. (Journal for the Study of the Old Testament Supplement Ser.: No. 34). 147p. pap. 14.95 (*1-85075-004-1*, Pub. by Sheffield Acad UK) CUP Services.

Temple Scroll: The Old Covenant Meets the New World Order in Modern Jerusalem. Danger & Intrigue Follow When an Ancient Text Reveals Plans to Rebuild the City of God. Stephen P. Adams. 1996. pap. 10.99 (*0-8024-3702-8*) Moody.

Temple Scroll & the Bible: The Methodology of MQT. Dwight D. Swanson. (Studies on the Texts of the Desert of Judah: No. 14). 300p. 1993. 85.25 (*90-04-09849-6*, NLG125) E J Brill.

Temple Scroll Studies. George J. Brooke. (Journal for the Study of the Pseudepigrapha Supplement Ser.: No. 7). 299p. 60.00 (*1-85075-200-1*, Pub. by Sheffield Acad UK) CUP Services.

Temple Sholom Presents ... Great Tastes. Temple Sholom Cookbook Committee Staff. 282p. 1993. pap. 15.95 (*0-9636007-0-2*) Temple Sholom.

Temple Slave. Robert Patrick. 1994. pap. 12.95 (*1-56333-191-8*, R Kasak Bks) Masquerade.

Temple Tiger. Jim Corbett. 210p. 1991. reprint ed. lib. bdg. 19.95 (*0-89966-799-6*) Buccaneer Bks.

Temple Tiger & More Man Eaters of Kumaon. Jim Corbett. 190p. 1989. pap. 8.95 (*0-19-562257-X*) OUP.

Temple, Tomb & Dwelling: Egyptian Antiquities from the Harer Family Trust Collection. Gerry D. Scott, III. LC 91-39824. (Illus.). 207p. (Orig.). 1992. per. 50.00 (*0-945486-08-1*) CSU SBRVFAM.

Temple Towns of Tamil Nadu. Ed. by George Michell. (Illus.). (C). 1993. 68.00 (*81-85026-21-1*, Pub. by Marg) S Asia.

Temple Treasury: The Judaica Collection of Congregation Emanu-El of the City of New York. Cissy Grossman et al. LC 87-73301. (Illus.). 256p. 1989. 50.00 (*1-55595-036-1*) Hudson Hills.

Temple Wilderness: The Nature of Spirituality. (Illus.). 160p. 1996. 29.50 (*1-57223-051-7*, 0517) Idyll Arbor.

Templeman on Marine Insurance: Its Principles & Practice. 6th ed. R. J. Lambeth. 628p. 1986. text ed. 89.50 (*0-273-02537-6*) Sheridan.

Temples & Idol Worship. Panduranga R. Malyala. 4.99 (*0-938924-02-8*) Sri Shirdi Sai.

Temples & Temple-Service in Ancient Israel: An Inquiry into Biblical Cult Phenomena & the Historical Setting of the Priestly School. Menahem Haran. LC 83-16479. xviii, 394p. 1985. reprint ed. text ed. 29.50 (*0-931464-18-8*) Eisenbrauns.

Temples, Churches & Mosques of Turkey. James Steele. 220p. 1993. 65.00 (*0-7103-0354-8*, A3928) Routledge Chapman & Hall.

Temples, Kings & Peasants: Perceptions of South India's Past. George Spencer. 1987. 27.00 (*0-8364-2277-5*, New Era Bks) S Asia.

***Temples of Ancient Egypt.** Ed. by Byron F. Shafer. LC 97-23851. (Illus.). 352p. 1997. 42.50 (*0-8014-3399-1*) Cornell U Pr.

Temples of Bankura District. David McCutchion. 12.00 (*0-89253-673-X*); text ed. 6.75 (*0-89253-674-8*) Ind-US Inc.

Temples of Bhitargaon. Mohammad Zaheer. (Illus.). 184p. 1981. 75.00 (*0-318-36253-8*) Asia Bk Corp.

Temples of Cahokia Lords: Preston Holder's 1955-1956 Excavations of Kunnemann Mound. Timothy R. Pauketat et al. LC 93-13529. (Memoirs Ser.: No. 26). 1993. pap. 28.00 (*0-915703-33-5*) U Mich Mus Anthro.

Temples of Convenience. Lucinda Lambton. 160p. 1996. 24.95 (*0-312-14191-2*) St Martin.

Temples of Cuddapah District. A. Gurumurthi. 1990. 29.00 (*0-685-40058-1*, Pub. by New Era) S Asia.

Temples of Delight. Barbara Trapido. LC 91-16023. 311p. 1993. pap. 11.95 (*0-8021-3322-3*, Grove) Grove-Atltic.

Temples of Himachal Pradesh. Shanti L. Nagar. (C). 1990. 120.00 (*81-85179-48-4*, Pub. by Aditya Prakashan II) S Asia.

Temples of India, Set, Vols. 1 & 2. Krishna Deva. (C). 1995. text ed. 195.00 (*81-7305-054-6*, Pub. by Aryan Bks Intl II) S Asia.

Temples of Justice: County Courthouses in Nevada. Ronald M. James. LC 93-37575. (Wilbur S. Shepperson Series in History & Humanities). (Illus.). 216p. (C). 1994. 31.95 (*0-87417-239-X*) U of Nev Pr.

Temples of Kyoto. Donald Richie. 1995. 29.95 (*0-8048-2032-5*) C E Tuttle.

Temples of Mammon: The Architecture of Banking. John Booker. (Illus.). 361p. 1991. 70.00 (*0-7486-0198-8*, Pub. by Edinburgh U Pr UK) Col U Pr.

Temples of Midnapur. G. Santra. 1980. 24.00 (*0-8364-0595-1*, Pub. by Mukhopadhyaya II) S Asia.

Temples of Nepal. Ronald M. Bernier. 204p. 1985. 45.00 (*0-317-52159-4*, Pub. by S Chand II) St Mut.

Temples of Nepal: An Introductory Survey. Ronald M. Bernier. (Illus.). 247p. 1970. text ed. 27.50 (*0-685-43589-X*) Coronet Bks.

Temples of South India: A Study of Hindu, Jain & Buddhist Monuments of the Deccan. J. Ramaniah. (C). 1989. 52.00 (*81-7022-223-0*, Pub. by Concept II) S Asia.

Temples of the Ancient World: Ritual & Symbolism. Ed. by Donald W. Parry. LC 93-36629. xxiv, 805p. 1994. 29.95 (*0-87579-811-X*) Deseret Bk.

Temples of the Most High. deluxe ed. N. B. Lundwall. 1993. Collector's ed. 11.95 (*0-88494-875-7*) Bookcraft Inc.

Temples of Vrindaban. R. K. Das. 1990. 94.00 (*81-85067-47-3*, Pub. by Sundeep II) S Asia.

Temples of Western Tibet & Their Artistic Symbolism III-I: Monstaries of Spiti & Kunavar. Giuseppe Tucci. (C). 1989. 78.00 (*0-685-33287-X*, Pub. by Aditya Prakashan II) S Asia.

Temples of Western Tibet & Their Artistic Symbolism III-2: Monastery of Tsaparang. Giuseppe Tucci. (C). 1989. 92.00 (*81-85179-23-9*, Pub. by Aditya Prakashan II) S Asia.

***Temple's Prize.** Castle. 1997. mass mkt. 4.99 (*0-373-28994-4*) Harlequin Bks.

***Temples, Religion & Politics in the Roman Republic.** Eric M. Orlin. (Mnemosyne, Supplements Ser.: Vol. 164). 184p. (ENG & GRE.). 1996. 67.75 (*90-04-10708-8*) E J Brill.

Temples, Tombs & Hieroglyphs: A Popular History of Ancient Egypt. Barbara Mertz. LC 89-17911. (Illus.). 336p. 1990. pap. 15.95 (*0-87226-223-5*) P Bedrick Bks.

Templet Development for the Pipe Trades. Raymond P. Jones. LC 63-22021. (Illus.). 166p. (C). 1963. pap. 31.00 (*0-8273-0077-8*) Delmar.

***Templeton Touch.** William Proctor. 1997. 14.95 (*0-385-18302-X*) Templeton Fnd.

Templins of Tennessee. Ronald R. Templin. LC 89-50470. (Illus.). 196p. (Orig.). 1989. pap. 47.00 (*0-9622502-1-X*) R R Templin.

***Templo de los Ultimos Dias.** Thomas Ice. (Profecia Ser.). (SPA.). 1997. pap. 2.99 (*0-8254-1341-9*, Edit Portavoz) Kregel.

Templo del Sol. Herge. (Illus.). 62p. (SPA.). (J). 19.95 (*0-8288-5079-8*) Fr & Eur.

Templo del Sol. Herge. (Illus.). 62p. (ITA.). (J). pap. 19.95 (*0-8288-5080-1*) Fr & Eur.

Templum Amicitiae. William A. Horbury. 75.00 (*1-85075-273-7*, Pub. by Sheffield Acad UK) CUP Services.

Templum Musicum: Or the Musical Synopsis see **Monuments of Music & Music Literature in Facsimile**

Templus Multiplan. Professional Computer Staff. 1985. 79.95 (*0-13-903048-4*) P-H.

Templus Supercalculus. Professional Computer Staff. 1985. 79.95 (*0-13-903089-1*) P-H.

Templus Visicalc I. Professional Computer Staff. 1985. 79.95 (*0-13-903105-7*) P-H.

***Tempnapping: Saga & Solution: A Guide to Protecting Your Company.** A. Bernard Frechtman. 200p. 1997. text ed. 149.00 (*0-9638629-8-7*) Twin Pleasures.

Tempo. Al Geiberger. Ed. by Sally Peters. (Golf Digest Ser.). (Illus.). 160p. 1992. reprint ed. pap. 13.00 (*0-671-72316-2*) S&S Trade.

***Tempo, No. 1.** Evelyne Berard. (Illus.). 223p. (FRE.). 1996. pap. text ed. 23.95 (*2-278-04423-0*, Pub. by Edns Didier FR) Hatier Pub.

***Tempo, No. 1.** Evelyne Berard. (Illus.). (FRE.). 1996. vhs 102.95 (*2-278-04513-X*, Pub. by Edns Didier FR) Hatier Pub.

***Tempo, No. 2.** Evelyne Berard. (Illus.). (FRE.). 1997. pap. text ed. 24.95 (*2-278-04427-3*, Pub. by Edns Didier FR) Hatier Pub.

TEMPO: A Unified Treatment of Binding Time & Parameter Passing Concepts in Programming Languages. N. D. Jones & S. S. Muchnick. (Lecture Notes in Computer Science Ser.: Vol. 66). 1978. 14.00 (*0-387-09085-1*) Spr-Verlag.

Tempo & Mode in Evolution. George G. Simpson. LC 83-23132. (Columbia Biological Ser.). 256p. 1984. reprint ed. pap. text ed. 25.00 (*0-231-05847-0*) Col U Pr.

Tempo & Mode in Evolution: Genetics & Paleontology 50 Years After Simpson. National Academy of Sciences Staff. Ed. by Walter Fitch & Francisco J. Ayala. (Orig.). (C). 1995. text ed. 49.95 (*0-309-05191-6*) Natl Acad Pr.

Tempo Di Colombo: The Times of Columbus. Alfonso Aiello. 28p. 1992. pap. text ed. 10.95 (*0-9634106-9-5*) A Aiello.

Tempo ed Essere Nell'Autunno del Medioeve: Il "De Tempore" di Nicola di Strasburgo e il Dibattito Sulla Natura ed il Senso del Tempo Agli Inizi del XIV Secolo. Tiziana Suarez-Nani. (Bochumer Studien zur Philosophie Ser.). xxiv, 250p. (ITA.). 1989. 35.00 (*90-6032-298-3*, Pub. by B R Gruener NE) Benjamins North Am.

Tempo Indications of Mozart. Jean-Pierre Marty. LC 87-29571. 416p. (C). 1989. text ed. 50.00 (*0-300-03852-6*) Yale U Pr.

Tempo Luggage Inc. Simulation with Narrative. 4th ed. Swanson & Ross. (Accounting - First Year Ser.). 1988. 20.95 (*0-538-02479-8*) S-W Pub.

Tempo Notation in Renaissance Spain. Charles Jacobs. (Wissenschaftliche Abhandlungen-Musicological Studies: Vol. 8). 121p. 1966. lib. bdg. 27.00 (*0-912024-78-X*) Inst Mediaeval Mus.

Tempo of Modern Life. James T. Adams. LC 74-121444. (Essay Index Reprint Ser.). 1977. 23.95 (*0-8369-1691-3*) Ayer.

Tempomandibular Joint Problems. 1996. lib. bdg. 250.96 (*0-8490-5881-3*) Gordon Pr.

Tempomatic IV: A Management Simulation. 3rd ed. Charles R. Scott, III & Alonzo J. Strickland. 128p. 1983. Computer center manual & various computer systems. student ed. write for info. incl. disk (*0-318-57689-9*) HM.

Tempora. Dieling et al. 70p. 1989. 13.00 (*3-324-00510-8*) Langenscheidt.

Temporal. Jose Corrales. 50p. (SPA.). 1993. pap. text ed. 3.95 (*1-885901-09-7*) Presbyters Peartree.

Temporal. Jose M. Garcia. LC 86-82542. 58p. (Orig.). 1986. pap. 3.50 (*0-943722-13-6*) Gavea-Brown.

Temporal & Areal Relationships in Central California Archaeology, Pt. 1. fac. ed. Richard K. Bearsley. (Reports of the University of California Archaeological Survey: No. 24). (Illus.). 91p. 1954. reprint ed. pap. 8.10 (*1-55567-344-9*) Coyote Press.

Temporal & Areal Relationships in Central California Archaeology, Pt. 2. fac. ed. R. K. Beardeley. (Reports of the University of California Archaeological Survey: No. 25). 79p. 1954. reprint ed. pap. 7.15 (*1-55567-345-7*) Coyote Press.

Temporal & Causal Conjunctions in Ancient Greek. Albert Rijksbaron. xvi, 240p. 1976. pap. 64.00 (*90-256-0674-1*, Pub. by A M Hakkert NE) Benjamins North Am.

***Temporal & Spatial Agricultural Development in the Sudan.** 98p. 1989. 9.00 (*92-5-102771-4*, Pub. by FAO IT) Bernan Associates.

Temporal & Spatial Patterns in Carbonate Platforms. Gianni Galli. LC 93-8317. (Lecture Notes in Earth Sciences Ser.: Vol. 46). 1993. 114.95 (*0-387-56231-1*) Spr-Verlag.

Temporal & Spatial Patterns of Vegetation Dynamics. Ed. by J. Miles et al. (Advances in Vegetation Science Ser.). (C). 1989. lib. bdg. 220.50 (*0-7923-0103-X*) Kluwer Ac.

Temporal & Spatial Regulations. 1988. 170.95 (*0-387-82046-9*) Spr-Verlag.

Temporal & Spiritual Conquest of Ceylon, 6 bks. in 2 vols. Fernao De Queyroz. LC 71-153629. reprint ed. 155.00 (*0-404-09630-1*) AMS Pr.

Temporal & Spiritual Conquest of Ceylon: Sixteenth & Seventeenth Century Account of Ceylon, 3 vols., Set. Tr. by S. C. Perera from POR. (C). 1992. reprint ed. 105.00 (*81-206-0764-3*, Pub. by Asian Educ Servs II) S Asia.

Temporal Assessment of Diagnostic Materials from the Pinon Canyon Maneuver Site: Towards the Development of a Cultural Chronology for Southeastern Colorado. Christopher R. Lintz & Jane L. Anderson. (Memoir Ser.: No. 4). 475p. 1989. pap. text ed. 15.00 (*1-888400-01-3*) Colo Archaeol.

Temporal Bone Malignancy: Anatomy, Pathology, & Treatment. Kathryn Evans et al. LC 94-23526. (SIPac Ser.). 1994. write for info. (*0-615-00383-4*) Amer Acad Oto Surg.

Temporal Bone Malignancy: Anatomy, Pathology, & Treatment. John Rutka et al. LC 94-23526. (Illus.). 73p. (Orig.). (C). 1994. pap. text ed. 25.00 (*1-56772-016-1*) AAO-HNS.

Temporal Codes for Memories: Issues & Problems. B. J. Underwood. 176p. 1977. 29.95 (*0-89859-142-2*) L Erlbaum Assocs.

Temporal Coding in the Brain. Ed. by G. Buzsaki et al. LC 94-12945. (Research & Perspectives in Neurosciences Ser.). 1994. 99.00 (*0-387-58074-3*) Spr-Verlag.

***Temporal Databases.** Richard Snodgrass & Christian Jensen. 416p. (C). 1999. text ed. 59.95 (*1-55860-435-9*) Morgan Kaufmann.

Temporal Databases: Theory, Design, & Implementation. Abdullah U. Tansel et al. LC 93-25. (Series on Database Systems & Applications). 500p. (C). 1993. 61.25 (*0-8053-2413-5*) Benjamin-Cummings.

Temporal Dimensions of Development Administration. Ed. by Dwight Waldo et al. LC 73-97215. (Comparative Administration Group Ser.). 328p. reprint ed. pap. 93.50 (*0-317-27297-7*, 2023465) Bks Demand.

Temporal Disorder in Human Oscillatory Systems. Ed. by L. Rensing & M. C. Mackey. (Synergetics Ser.: Vol. 36). (Illus.). 270p. 1987. 79.95 (*0-387-17765-5*) Spr-Verlag.

Temporal Information Processing in the Nervous System: Special Reference to Dyslexia & Dysphasia. Ed. by Paula Tallal et al. LC 93-17625. (Annals Ser.: Vol. 682). 1993. Alk. paper. write for info. (*0-89766-785-9*); Alk. paper. write for info. (*0-89766-786-7*) NY Acad Sci.

***Temporal Lobe & Limbic System.** Pierre Gloor. (Illus.). 832p. 1997. 135.00 (*0-19-509272-4*) OUP.

Temporal Lobe Epilepsy, Mania & Schizophrenia & the Limbic System. Ed. by W. P. Koella & M. R. Trimble. (Advances in Biological Psychiatry Ser.: Vol. 8). (Illus.). x, 166p. 1982. pap. 63.25 (*3-8055-3494-9*) S Karger.

Temporal Lobe Epilepsy, 1948 to 1986. Christopher Ounsted et al. (Clinics in Developmental Medicine Ser.: No. 103). 129p. 1991. text ed. 49.95 (*0-521-41220-X*) Cambridge U Pr.

Temporal Lobe Epilepsy 1948-1986. Christopher Ounsted et al. (Clinics in Developmental Medicine Ser.: No. 103). (Illus.). 129p. (C). 1987. text ed. 49.50 (*0-685-41924-X*, Pub. by Mc Keith Pr UK) Cambridge U Pr.

Temporal Lobes & the Limbic System. Ed. by Michael R. Trimble & Tom G. Bolwig. 300p. 1992. 85.00 (*1-871816-14-9*, Pub. by Wrightson Biomed UK) Taylor & Francis.

Temporal Logic: From Ancient Ideas to Artificial Intelligence. Peter Ohrstrom & Per F. Hasle. LC 95-22191. (Studies in Linguistics & Philosophy: Vol. 57). 424p. (C). 1995. lib. bdg. 99.00 (*0-7923-3586-4*, Pub. by Klwr Acad Pubs NE) Kluwer Ac.

Temporal Logic: Mathematical Foundations & Conputational Aspects. Dov M. Gabbay & Mark Reynolds. (Illus.). 656p. 1994. 98.00 (*0-19-853769-7*) OUP.

Temporal Logic: Proceedings of the First International Conference, ICTL '94, Bonn, Germany, July 11-14, 1994, 827. Dov M. Gabbay & Hans J. Ohlbach. (Lecture Notes in Computer Science-Artificial Intelligence). 545p. 1994. 79.95 (*0-387-58241-X*) Spr-Verlag.

Temporal Logic: Proceedings of the First International Conference, ICTL '94, Bonn, Germany, July 11-14, 1994. Ed. by Dov M. Gabbay & Hans J. Ohlbach. LC 94-3449. (Lecture Notes in Computer Science: Lecture Note in Artificial Intelligence). 1994. write for info. (*3-540-58241-X*) Spr-Verlag.

Temporal Logic for Real Time Systems. Jonathan S. Ostroff. LC 89-4012. 209p. 1989. text ed. 150.00 (*0-471-92402-4*) Wiley.

Temporal Logic in Specification. Ed. by B. Banieqbal et al. (Lecture Notes in Computer Science Ser.: Vol. 398). vi, 448p. 1989. 54.00 (*0-387-51803-7*) Spr-Verlag.

Temporal Logic of Programs. Fred Kroger. (EATCS Monographs on Theoretical Computer Science: Vol. 8). 160p. 1987. 62.95 (*0-387-17030-8*) Spr-Verlag.

Temporal Logic of Reactive Systems Vol. 1: Specification. Zohar Manna & Amir Pnueli. (Illus.). 392p. 1991. 65.95 (*0-387-97664-7*) Spr-Verlag.

Temporal Logics & Their Application. Ed. by Antony Galton. 244p. 1988. text ed. 78.00 (*0-12-274060-2*) Acad Pr.

Temporal Man: The Meaning & Uses of Social Time. Robert H. Lauer. LC 81-11917. 192p. 1981. text ed. 49.95 (*0-275-90666-3*, C0666, Praeger Pubs) Greenwood.

Temporal Order. Ed. by L. Rensing & N. I. Jaeger. (Synergetics Ser.: Vol. 29). (Illus.). ix, 325p. 1985. 80.95 (*0-387-15274-1*) Spr-Verlag.

Temporal Processes in Beethoven's Music. D. B. Greene. (Monographs on Musicology: Vol. 2). 192p. 1982. text ed. 49.00 (*0-677-05600-1*) Gordon & Breach.

Temporal Relations & Temporal Becoming: A Defense of a Russellian Theory of Time. L. Nathan Oaklander. 250p. (Orig.). (C). 1984. pap. text ed. 22.50 (*0-8191-4150-X*); lib. bdg. 48.00 (*0-8191-4149-6*) U Pr of Amer.

Temporal Representation & Reasoning, 3rd Workshop On: Time 96. LC 96-83327. 223p. 1996. pap. text ed. 60.00 (*0-8186-7528-4*, PR07528) IEEE Comp Soc.

***Temporal Representation & Reasoning, 4th Workshop.** LC 97-71303. 240p. 1997. pap. 60.00 (*0-8186-7937-9*) IEEE Comp Soc.

Temporal Sequence in the Perception of Speech. Warren H. Fay. (Janua Linguarum, Ser. Minor: No. 45). (Orig.). 1966. pap. text ed. 26.15 (*90-279-0579-7*) Mouton.

Temporal Variables in Speech: Studies in Honour of Frieda Golman-Eisler. Hans W. Dechert & Manfred Raupach. (Janua Linguarum, Series Major: No. 86). 370p. 1980. 69.25 (*90-279-7946-4*) Mouton.

Temporal Variations of the Cardiovascular Systems. Ed. by T. F. Schmidt & B. T. Engel. (Illus.). 432p. 1992. 163.00 (*0-387-54776-2*) Spr-Verlag.

Temporal Verification of Reactive Systems: Safety. Zohar Manna & Amir Pnueli. LC 95-5442. 1995. 65.95 (*0-387-94459-1*) Spr-Verlag.

Temporalite romanesque chez Stendhal "L'Echafaudage de la Batisse" Charles J. Stivale. LC 88-63131. 210p. (FRE.). 1989. lib. bdg. 27.95 (*0-917786-71-8*) Summa Pubns.

Temporalizing Space: The Triumphant Strategies of Piero della Francesca. Albert S. Cook. LC 91-43126. (Literature & the Visual Arts Ser.: Vol. 8). 232p. (C). 1992. text ed. 47.95 (*0-8204-1865-X*) P Lang Pubng.

Temporally Distributed Symptoms in Technical Diagnosis. K. Nokel. Ed. by Joerg H. Siekmann. (Lecture Notes in Artificial Intelligence Ser.: Vol. 517). ix, 164p. 1991. 31.00 (*0-387-54316-3*) Spr-Verlag.

Temporarily Hers. Susan Meier. 1995. mass mkt. 2.99 (*0-373-19109-X*, 1-19109-7) Silhouette.

Temporarily Possessed: The Semi-Permanent Collection. Ed. by Brian Goldfarb et al. LC 95-69870. (Illus.). 176p. (Orig.). 1995. pap. 19.95 (*0-915557-78-9*) New Mus Contemp Art.

Temporarily Yours, Vol. I. Wendy Perkins. (Illus.). 112p. (Orig.). (C). 1989. pap. 11.95 (*0-9622980-3-4*) Permanently Collectible.

Temporary Agency. Rachel Pollack. 202p. 1995. pap. 10.95 (*0-87951-602-X*) Overlook Pr.

Temporary Arrangement. Shannon Waverly. (Romance Ser.). 1993. pap. 2.89 (*0-373-03259-5*, 1-03259-8) Harlequin Bks.

Temporary Betrothal. Dorothy Mack. (Regency Romance Ser.). 224p. (Orig.). 1995. mass mkt. 3.99 (*0-451-18469-6*, Sig) NAL-Dutton.

Temporary Bride. Glenna Finley. 208p. (Orig.). 1993. pap. 3.99 (*0-451-17744-4*, Sig) NAL-Dutton.

Temporary Bride. Julie Tetel. (Regency Romance Ser.). 1993. mass mkt. 2.99 (*0-373-31205-9*, 1-31205-7) Harlequin Bks.

Temporary Cardiac Assist with an Axial Pump System. Ed. by W. Flameng. 88p. 1992. pap. 39.00 (*0-387-91413-7*) Spr-Verlag.

Temporary Child: A Foster Care Survivor's Story. Edward J. Benzola & Neva Beach. LC 93-84352. 144p. 1993. 18.95 (*1-883359-02-3*); pap. 12.95 (*1-883359-03-1*) Real People CA.

*Temporary Cycles or Volatile Trends? Economic Fluctuations in 21 OECD Countries. Gabriel Sterne & Tamimi Bayoumi. (Bank of England, Working Paper Ser.: Vol. 13). (Illus.). 50p. reprint ed. pap. 25.00 (0-608-05321-X, 2065859) Bks Demand.
Temporary Dentistry. Michael J. Segerdal. (Illus.). 122p. 1994. student ed. write for info. (1-883558-03-4) PIBL.
Temporary Equilibrium: Selected Readings. Ed. by Jean-Michel Grandmont. (Economic Theory, Econometrics & Mathematical Economics Ser.). 485p. (Orig.). 1988. pap. text ed. 62.00 (0-12-295146-8) Acad Pr.
Temporary Family. Sally T. Hayes. (Intimate Moments Ser.). 1996. mass mkt. 3.99 (0-373-07738-6, 1-07738-7) Silhouette.
Temporary Groom: Hawke's Way. Joan Johnston. (Desire Ser.). 1996. mass mkt. 3.50 (0-373-76004-3, 1-76004-0) Silhouette.
Temporary Guide, No. 1: For the Secretary. Kathleen A. Kurtz. (Temporary Guide for Managers Ser.: No. 2). 40p. 1992. pap. text ed. 9.95 (1-882768-02-7) Queue Pub.
Temporary Help Services: Possibilities for Home Businesses, School & College Placements, Community Job Services, Seminar Workshop Workbook. Bibliotheca Press Staff. 125p. 1993. ring bd. 39.95 (0-939476-97-5, Biblio Pr) Prosperity & Profits.
Temporary Homeland. Alison H. Deming. 224p. 1996. pap. 12.00 (0-312-14428-8) St Martin.
Temporary Homelands. Alison H. Deming. LC 93-41676. 224p. 1994. 18.00 (1-56279-062-5) Mercury Hse Inc.
Temporary Husband. Barbara Allister. (Regency Romance Ser.). 224p. 1987. pap. 3.99 (0-451-14745-6, Sig) NAL-Dutton.
Temporary Husband. Day LeClaire. 1996. mass mkt. 3.25 (0-373-03433-4, 1-03433-9) Harlequin Bks.
Temporary Husband. Val Whisenand. (Romance Ser.: No. 1165). 1996. mass mkt. 3.25 (0-373-19165-0, 1-19165-9) Silhouette.
*Temporary Husband. large type ed. Day Leclaire. (Fairytale Weddings Trilogy Ser.). 1996. mass mkt. 3.25 (0-373-15679-0) Harlequin Bks.
Temporary Insanity. S. M. Richardson. LC 96-90013. (Orig.). 1996. pap. 10.00 (0-533-11861-1) Vantage.
*Temporary Marriage. Leann Harris. 1997. mass mkt. 3.99 (0-373-07821-8, 1-07821-1) Silhouette.
Temporary Measures. Leigh Michaels. (Romance Ser.: No. 3160). 1991. pap. 2.79 (0-373-03160-2) Harlequin Bks.
Temporary Sanity. Thomas Glynn. LC 76-4765. 166p. 1976. pap. 6.95 (0-914590-29-4) Fiction Coll.
*Temporary Sanity: Managing Today's Flexible Workforce. Shannon VanNostrand & Marsha Brekke. 1997. pap. 19.95 (0-9655172-4-1) SOCAA Pub.
Temporary Structures in Construction Operations. Ed. by Robert T. Ratay. 156p. 1987. 17.00 (0-87262-592-3) Am Soc Civil Eng.
Temporary Systems: Professional Development, Manpower Utilization, Task Effectiveness, & Innovation. Richard A. Goodman. LC 81-15902. 204p. 1981. text ed. 49.95 (0-275-90635-3, C0635, Praeger Pubs) Greenwood.
Temporary Texan. Heather Allison. (Romance Ser.). 1996. mass mkt. 3.25 (0-373-03421-0, 1-03421-4) Harlequin Bks.
Temporary Work. Heidi Hartmann & June Lapidus. 55p. 1989. pap. 15.00 (0-685-29941-4) Inst Womens Policy Rsch.
Temporary Work & Labour Law of the European Community & Member States. Ed. by Roger Blanpain. LC 92-45138. 1993. 57.00 (90-6544-682-6) Kluwer Law Tax Pubs.
Temporary Work in Modern Society, Pt. 3. International Institute for Temporary Work Staff. 1979. lib. bdg. 26.00 (90-312-0088-3) Kluwer Ac.
Temporary Worker in the Nuclear Power Industry: An Equity Analysis. Mary H. Melville. LC 81-65590. (CENTED Monographs: No. 1). (Illus.). 70p. 1981. pap. text ed. 5.00 (0-939436-00-0) Ctr Tech Environ.
*Temporary Workers or Future Citizens? Japanese & U. S. Migration Policies. Myron Weiner & Tadashi Hanami. LC 97-12526. 1997. 50.00 (0-8147-9326-6) NYU Pr.
Temporary Works: Their Role in Construction. J. R. Illingworth. 296p. 1987. 79.00 (0-7277-0393-5) Am Soc Civil Eng.
Temporomandibular Disorders. 2nd ed. Ed. by Steven L. Kraus. LC 94-5632. (Clinics in Physical Therapy Ser.). 486p. 1994. 59.95 (0-443-08924-8) Churchill.
Temporomandibular Disorders: Guidelines for Classification, Assessment, & Management. 2nd ed. American Academy of Orofacial Pain Staff. Ed. by Charles McNeil. LC 92-37493. (Illus.). 144p. 1993. pap. text ed. 20.00 (0-86715-253-2) Quint Pub Co.
Temporomandibular Disorders & Related Pain Conditions. Barry J. Sessle. LC 95-3084. (Progress in Pain Research & Management Ser.: Vol. 4). (Illus.). 506p. 1995. 67.00 (0-931092-09-4, PPRM4) Intl Assn Study Pain.
Temporomandibular Joint: A Biological Basis for Clinical Practice. 4th ed. Sarnet & Laskin. (Illus.). 576p. 1991. text ed. 127.00 (0-7216-7928-5) Saunders.
Temporomandibular Joint & Masticatory Muscle Disorders. George A. Zarb. 624p. (C). (gr. 13). 1995. 142.00 (0-8151-9861-2) Mosby Yr Bk.
Temporomandibular Joint & Related Orofacial Disorders. Francis M. Bush & M. Franklin Dolwick. LC 94-33796. (Illus.). 416p. 1994. text ed. 69.50 (0-397-50982-0) Lppncott-Raven.
Temporomandibular Joint Dysfunction: The Essentials. R. G. Jagger et al. 240p. 1995. pap. text ed. 37.50 (0-7236-1015-0) Buttrwrth-Heinemann.
Temps, Ce Grand Sculpteur. Marguerite Yourcenar. 239p. (FRE.). 1991. 10.95 (0-7859-0461-1, 2070326543) Fr & Eur.
Temps d'Aimer (Les Boussardels, IV) Philippe Heriat. (FRE.). 1973. pap. 11.95 (0-7859-2321-7, 2070364607) Fr & Eur.
Temps de Amours. Marcel Pagnol. (Souvenirs d'Enfance Ser.: No. 4). (FRE.). 1988. pap. 13.95 (0-7859-3334-4, 2877060535) Fr & Eur.
Temps De Anais, un Noel De Maigret, Maigret Au Picratt's, Maigret En Meuble, une Vie Comme Neuve, Maigret et la Grande Perche, Marie Qui Louche, Miagret Lognon et les Gangsters. Georges Simenon. (FRE.). 1988. 49.95 (0-7859-0479-4, 2258023564) Fr & Eur.
Temps de la Confidence: Jean de Boschere et Andre Suares. Monique Fol. LC 89-13950. (American University Studies: Romance Languages & Literature: Ser. II, Vol. 136). 170p. (FRE.). (C). 1990. lib. bdg. 32.95 (0-8204-1210-4) P Lang Pubng.
Temps de Parents. Vitia Hessel. 544p. (FRE.). 1973. pap. 11.95 (0-7859-2311-X, 2070363821) Fr & Eur.
Temps des Secrets. Marcel Pagnol. (Souvenirs d'Enfance Ser.: No. 3). (FRE.). 1988. pap. 13.95 (0-7859-3327-1, 2877060527) Fr & Eur.
Temps des Secrets see Souvenirs d'Enfance
Temps des Verbes. 2nd ed. Marcel Lacarra. 96p. (FRE.). 1984. pap. 19.95 (0-8288-3355-9, 2801105260) Fr & Eur.
Temps Difficile. Charles Dickens. 435p. (FRE.). 1985. pap. 16.95 (0-7859-2011-0, 2070376478) Fr & Eur.
Temps du SIDA - AIDS Zeit. (Illus.). 208p. (FRE & GER.). 1991. pap. 45.00 (3-7165-0442-4, Pub. by Parkett Pubs SZ) Dist Art Pubs.
Temps du SIDA - AIDS Zeit. (Illus.). 208p. 1992. pap. 25.00 (3-907509-15-3, Pub. by Parkett Verlag AG SZ) Dist Art Pubs.
Temps Retrouve. Marcel Proust. (Folio Ser.: No. 2203). 442p. (FRE.). 1987. pap. 10.95 (2-07-038293-1) Schoenhof.
Temps Retrouve, Bk. 8: A la Recherche du Temps Perdu. Marcel Proust. (FRE.). 1990. pap. 16.95 (0-8288-3766-X, F128080) Fr & Eur.
Temps Sauvages. Joseph Kessel. 180p. (FRE.). 1979. pap. 10.95 (0-7859-2409-4, 2070370720) Fr & Eur.
Temps, une Ville, une Reforme: La Reformation a Strasbourg. Marc Lienhard. 310p. 1990. text ed. 98.95 (0-86078-268-9, Pub. by Variorum UK) Ashgate Pub Co.
Temps Universel. unabridged ed. Tr. by Margie Mounier. LC 95-72719. (Illus.). 36p. (Orig.). (FRE.). 1995. pap. 15.00 (1-888457-00-7) Photo Do Not Bend.
Temps Uoulu see Our Share of Time
Tempt a Lady. Susan Weldon. 384p. (Orig.). 1994. mass mkt. 4.50 (0-380-77738-X) Avon.
Tempt Me Not. Eve Byron. (Orig.). 1995. mass mkt. 4.99 (0-380-77624-3) Avon.
Tempt Me Not. Susan Napier. (Presents Ser.). 1993. pap. 2.89 (0-373-11531-8, 1-11531-0) Harlequin Bks.
Tempt My Heart Cookbook. Mary Taylor. 1990. 11.95 (0-934860-64-5) Adventure Pubns.
Temptation. Cynthia Blair. 1994. mass mkt. 5.99 (0-345-37129-1) Ballantine.
Temptation. Dietrich Bonhoeffer. 1965. write for info. (0-318-54207-2) Macmillan.
Temptation. Jane E. Harrison. 400p. (Orig.). 1993. mass mkt., pap. text ed. 4.99 (0-505-51906-2, Love Spell) Dorchester Pub Co.
Temptation. Catherine Hart. 400p. (Orig.). 1992. mass mkt. 4.99 (0-380-76006-1) Avon.
Temptation. Vaclav Havel. Tr. by Marie Winn from CZE. LC 88-13939. 112p. 1989. pap. 9.95 (0-8021-3100-X, Grove) Grove-Atltic.
Temptation. Donna Hill. 320p. 1994. mass mkt. 4.99 (0-7860-0070-8, Pinncle Kensgtn) Kensgtn Pub Corp.
Temptation. M. Mercedes. LC 95-90796. (Orig.). 1996. pap. 8.50 (0-533-11711-9) Vantage.
Temptation. Wolff Ryp. (Midnight Secrets Ser.: No. 01). (YA). 1996. pap. 3.50 (0-8167-3542-5) Troll Communs.
*Temptation. Hiroyuki Utatane. (MangErotica Ser.). 88p. 1996. pap. 14.95 (1-56097-225-4) Fantagraph Bks.
Temptation. Sherryl Woods. 320p. 1996. mass mkt. 4.99 (0-8217-5508-0, Zebra Kensgtn) Kensgtn Pub Corp.
Temptation. large type ed. Catherine Hart. LC 92-32529. (General Ser.). (Orig.). 1993. lib. bdg. 22.95 (0-8161-5463-5, GK Hall) Thorndike Pr.
*Temptation. 3rd ed. Diogenis Allen. Orig. Title: Between Two Worlds. xi, 155p. 1996. reprint ed. pap. 9.95 (0-9653625-0-7) Caroline Pr.
Temptation & Discernment. Segundo Galilea. Tr. by Stephen-Joseph Ross from SPA. LC 96-11205. 80p. (Orig.). 1996. pap. 8.95 (0-935216-57-X) ICS Pubns.
Temptation & the Passion: The Markan Sotenology. 2nd ed. Ernest Best. (Society for New Testament Studies Monographs: No. 2). 300p. (C). 1990. text ed. 75.00 (0-521-38360-9) Cambridge U Pr.
Temptation Beat It! Let Go & Let God. Michael J. Duseau, Sr. 96p. (Orig.). 1989. pap. write for info. (0-318-65834-8) Word Power Pub.
Temptation Game. deluxe ed. John Gardner. 45.00 (0-686-78138-4) New London Pr.
Temptation of Aaron Campbell. Lisa Samson. (Highlanders Ser.). (Orig.). 1996. pap. 9.99 (1-56507-390-8) Harvest Hse.
Temptation of Christ. John Bale. LC 74-133636. (Tudor Facsimile Texts. Old English Plays Ser.: No. 22). reprint ed. 59.50 (0-404-53322-1) AMS Pr.
Temptation of Homo Europaeus. Victor Neumann. LC 93-73007. (East European Monographs: No. CCCLXXXIV). 269p. 1994. 41.00 (0-88033-281-6) East Eur Monographs.
Temptation of Jesus in Early Christianity. Jeffrey B. Gibson. (Journal for the Study of the New Testament, Supplement Ser.: Vol. 112). 370p. 65.00 (1-85075-539-6) CUP Services.
Temptation of Saint Anthony. Gustave Flaubert. LC 78-6700. 1978. reprint ed. 17.50 (0-86527-312-X) Fertig.
Temptation of Saint Anthony by Odilon Redon. Frank A. Trapp et al. (Mead Museum Monographs: Vol. 2). (Illus.). 30p. (Orig.). 1980. pap. 2.00 (0-914337-02-5) Mead Art Mus.
Temptation of Saint Redon: Biography, Ideology & Style in the Noirs of Odilon Redon. Stephen Eisenman. LC 91-47200. (Illus.). 310p. 1992. 60.00 (0-226-19548-1) U Ch Pr.
Temptation of St. Anthony. Gustave Flaubery. Tr. & Intro. by Kitty Mrosovsky. (Classics Ser.). 304p. 1983. pap. 9.95 (0-14-044410-6, Penguin Classics) Viking Penguin.
Temptation of the West. Andre Malraux. Tr. by Robert Hollander. 136p. 1991. pap. 12.95 (0-226-50291-0) U Ch Pr.
Temptation Tenth Anniversary. 1994. write for info. (0-373-15258-2, 1-15258-6) Harlequin Bks.
Temptation Texas Style! Annette Broadrick. 1994. mass mkt. 2.99 (0-373-05883-7, 1-05883-3) Harlequin Bks.
Temptation to Exist. E. M. Cioran. Tr. by Richard Howard from FRE. LC 86-6692. 224p. 1986. 17.95 (0-8050-0002-X) Seaver Bks.
Temptation to Forget: Racism, Anti-Semitism, Neo-Nazism. Franco Ferrarotti. LC 94-22026. (Contributions in Sociology Ser.: Vol. 110). 200p. 1994. text ed. 49.95 (0-313-29443-7, Greenwood Pr) Greenwood.
Temptations. LC 97-5278. (YA). 1997. pap. 8.95 (0-7910-2588-8) Chelsea Hse.
Temptations. LC 97-5278. (YA). 1997. lib. bdg. 19.95 (0-7910-2587-X) Chelsea Hse.
Temptations. Susan Blackwood & Anne Dilworth. 398p. 1986. 14.95 (0-9617154-0-5) Presby Day Schl.
Temptations. Junior League of Lansing Staff. LC 83-83367. (Illus.). 345p. 1984. 14.95 (0-9611858-0-5) Jr League Lansing.
Temptations. Jessica March. 1989. mass mkt. 4.95 (0-446-35226-8) Warner Bks.
Temptations: A Book of Short Stories. David Pinski. Tr. by Isaac Goldberg from YID. LC 74-163045. (Short Story Index Reprint Ser.). 1977. reprint ed. 23.95 (0-8369-3959-X) Ayer.
Temptations: Sex & Selling in the Department Store. Gail Reekle. (Illus.). 240p. 1993. pap. text ed. 19.95 (1-86373-342-6, Pub. by Allen Unwin AT) Paul & Co Pubs.
Temptation's Darling. Joanna Jordan. 368p. 1988. pap. 3.95 (0-380-75527-0) Avon.
Temptations Families Face: Breaking Patterns That Keep Us Apart. Tom L. Eisenman. LC 95-48957. 222p. 1996. 17.99 (0-8308-1688-7, 1688, Saltshaker Bk) InterVarsity.
Temptations for the Theology of Liberation. Bonaventure Kloppenberg. (Synthesis Ser.). 1974. pap. 1.00 (0-8199-0362-0, Frncscn Herld) Franciscan Pr.
Temptations from Ancrene Wisse, Vol. 1. Yoko Wada. 256p. (Orig.). (C). 1995. pap. 45.00 (0-85991-451-8) Boydell & Brewer.
Temptation's Kiss. Lisa Bingham. Ed. by Carolyn Tolley. 336p. (Orig.). 1992. mass mkt. 4.99 (0-671-74564-6) PB.
*Temptation's Kiss. Sandra Brown. 256p. 1998. pap. 6.50 (0-446-36430-4, Warner Vision) Warner Bks.
*Temptations Men Face. Tom Eisenman. (SPA.). 7.95 (0-8297-0308-X) Life Pubs Intl.
Temptations Men Face. Tom L. Eisenman. LC 90-30478. 252p. 1991. reprint ed. pap. 11.99 (0-8308-1379-9, 1379, Saltshaker Bk) InterVarsity.
Temptations of a Superpower. Ronald Steel. LC 94-40791. (The Joanna Jackson Goldman Memorial Lecture on American Civilization & Government). 156p. 1995. 18.95 (0-674-87340-8, STETEM) HUP.
Temptations of a Superpower. Ronald Steel. 160p. 1996. pap. 10.95 (0-674-87341-6) HUP.
*Temptations of Big Bear. Rudy Wiebe. 1996. pap. text ed. 7.95 (0-7710-3454-7) McCland & Stewart.
Temptations of Cremorne. 256p. (Orig.). 1993. mass mkt. 6.99 (0-515-11252-6) Jove Pubns.
*Temptations of Emile Cioran. William Kluback & Michael Finkenthal. (American University Studies II: No. 221). 240p. (C). 1997. text ed. 43.95 (0-8204-3104-4) P Lang Pubng.
Temptations of Evolutionary Ethics. Paul L. Farber. LC 94-5507. 1994. 35.00 (0-520-08773-9) U CA Pr.
Temptations of Jesus. Howard Thurman. LC 78-74718. 1979. reprint ed. pap. 4.95 (0-913408-47-6) Friends United.
Temptations of Jesus: An Illustrated Bible Passage for Young Children. Alice Meyer. LC 93-60713. (Illus.). 40p. (Orig.). (J). (ps-4). 1996. pap. 12.95 incl. audio (1-879099-08-X) Thy Word.
Temptations of Jesus: Six Dramas for Lent. Curt M. Joseph. LC 92-32271. 1992. pap. 5.95 (1-55673-562-6) CSS OH.
Temptations of St. Ed & Brother S. Frank Bergon. Frank Bergon. LC 93-17053. (Western Literature Ser.). 320p. 1993. 22.00 (0-87417-226-8) U of Nev Pr.
*Temptations Women Face. Mary E. Ashcroft. (SPA.). 7.95 (0-8297-1845-1) Life Pubs Intl.
Temptations Women Face. Mary E. Ashcroft. LC 91-14233. 213p. 1993. reprint ed. pap. 10.99 (0-8308-1320-9, 1320, Saltshaker Bk) InterVarsity.
Tempted. Laurel Ames. (Historical Ser.). 1996. mass mkt. 4.99 (0-373-28938-3, 1-28938-8) Harlequin Bks.
Tempted. Virginia Henley. 528p. 1993. mass mkt. 4.99 (0-440-20625-1) Dell.
Tempted by Happiness: Kazantzakis Post-Christian Christ. Peter Bien. LC 83-63552. 1984. pap. 3.00 (0-87574-253-X) Pendle Hill.
Tempted to Love. large type ed. Barbara Cartland. (Magna Large Print Ser.). 240p. 1996. 25.99 (0-7505-0906-6, Pub. by Magna Print Bks UK) Ulverscroft.
Tempted Women. Carol Botwin. LC 93-28822. 1994. 22.00 (0-688-11646-9) Morrow.
Tempter's Voice: Language & the Fall in Medieval Literature. Eric Jager. (Illus.). 352p. 1993. 45.00 (0-8014-2753-3) Cornell U Pr.
Tempting: (Secret Fantasies) Lisa Harris. (Temptation Ser.). 1995. mass mkt. 3.25 (0-373-25634-5, 1-25634-6) Harlequin Bks.
Tempting Faith. Susan Mallery. (Intimate Moments Ser.). 1994. mass mkt. 3.50 (0-373-07554-5, 5-07554-4) Silhouette.
Tempting Fate. Jaclyn Reding. 384p. 1995. 4.99 (0-451-40558-7, Topaz) NAL-Dutton.
Tempting Fate. Nora Roberts. (NR Flowers Ser.: No. 13). 1992. mass mkt. 3.59 (0-373-51013-6) Silhouette.
Tempting Fate. Joann Ross. (Mira Bks.). 1996. pap. 5.50 (1-55166-157-8, 1-66157-8, Mira Bks) Harlequin Bks.
*Tempting Fate: An Experimental Test Pilot's Story. Bob Rahn. 1997. 22.95 (0-933424-81-7) Specialty Pr.
Tempting Fortune. Jo Beverley. 448p. 1995. mass mkt. 4.99 (0-8217-4858-0, Zebra Kensgtn) Kensgtn Pub Corp.
Tempting Fortune: The Way Business Really Works. Fred Meredith. Ed. by David Piper. 144p. 1995. lib. bdg. 39.00 (0-8095-4862-3) Borgo Pr.
Tempting Fortune: The Way Business Really Works. Fred Meredith. Ed. by David Piper. 144p. pap. 14.95 (0-88962-571-9) Mosaic.
Tempting Harriet. Mary Balogh. 224p. (Orig.). 1994. pap. 3.99 (0-451-17952-8, Sig) NAL-Dutton.
Tempting Jake. Molly Liholm. (Temptation Ser.). 1995. mass mkt. 3.25 (0-373-25652-3, 1-25652-8) Harlequin Bks.
*Tempting Kate. Deborah Simmons. (Historical Ser.: No. 371). 1997. pap. 4.99 (0-373-28971-5, 1-28971-9) Harlequin Bks.
Tempting Letters: Letters from an Experienced Demon to a Novice. B. Koppany, III. LC 95-68354. 176p. 1995. 27.00 (0-9639422-1-2) Striking Impress.
Tempting Miss. Janice Bennett. 1989. mass mkt. 3.95 (0-8217-2849-0, Zebra Kensgtn) Kensgtn Pub Corp.
Tempting Miss Prissy. Sharon Ihle. 336p. (Orig.). 1996. mass mkt. 5.50 (0-06-108400-X, Harp PBks) HarpC.
Tempting of Audra Grey. Tricia Padgett. (Destiny Ser.). 159p. 1992. pap. 2.97 (0-8163-1069-6) Pacific Pr Pub Assn.
Tempting of Julia. Maura Seger. 1994. mass mkt. 3.99 (0-373-28844-1, 1-28844-8) Harlequin Bks.
Tempting of Pescara. Conrad F. Meyer. Tr. by C. Bell. LC 75-4902. 184p. 1975. reprint ed. 35.00 (0-86527-313-8) Fertig.
Tempting Tess. Joyce Adams. 352p. 1997. mass mkt. 4.99 (0-8217-5539-0, Zebra Kensgtn) Kensgtn Pub Corp.
Temptress. Jude Deveraux. Ed. by Linda Morrow. 1991. pap. 6.99 (0-671-74384-8) PB.
*Tempus in Nummis Vol. 1: History & Fundamentals of Dating in Numismatics. James O. Sweeny & Robert Turfboer. 176p. 1992. 40.00 (1-889172-16-2); pap. 30.00 (1-889172-15-4) Numismatic Intl.
*Tempus in Nummis Vol. 2: The Romantic Story of Time Themes in Numismatics. James O. Sweeny & Robert Turfboer. 254p. 1992. 50.00 (1-889172-18-9); pap. 40.00 (1-889172-17-0) Numismatic Intl.
Tempus Interludium, Vol. 1. Ernest L. Norman. (Illus.). 290p. 1978. 16.00 (0-932642-09-8) Unarius Acad Sci.
Tempus Interludium, Vol. 2. Ernest L. Norman. Ed. by Ruth E. Norman. 224p. 1982. 16.00 (0-932642-48-9) Unarius Acad Sci.
Tempus Invictus. rev. ed. Ernest L. Norman. (Illus.). 496p. 1968. 17.00 (0-932642-08-X) Unarius Acad Sci.
Tempus Procedium. Ernest L. Norman. (Illus.). 480p. 1968. 17.00 (0-932642-07-1) Unarius Acad Sci.
TEMSITE. Marlin Kemmerer. 153p. (Orig.). 1988. pap. 5.95 (0-9620321-0-7) TEMSITE.
Temurah, 1 vol. (ENG & HEB.). 15.00 (0-910218-84-6) Bennet Pub.
*Ten Acres Enough: The Small Farm Dream Is Possible. 2nd ed. Edmund Morris. Ed. by L. R. Miller. 264p. reprint ed. pap. 11.95 (1-885210-02-7) Small Farmers.
*Ten Acres Enough: The Small Farm Dream Is Possible. 2nd ed. Edmund Morris. Ed. by L. R. Miller. 264p. reprint ed. 19.95 (1-885210-03-5) Small Farmers.
10 Amazing Secrets to Financial Success: How to Unleash the Power of Your Financial Dreams, Increase Prosperity, & Avoid Money Mistakes. Ronald Silich. 183p. (Orig.). 1997. pap. 9.95 (0-9647005-1-4) Tax & Finan.
Ten American History Plays for the Classroom. Sarah J. Glassock. 1996. pap. text ed. 12.95 (0-590-59931-3) Scholastic Inc.
Ten American Painters. William H. Gerdts et al. (Illus.). 188p. 1990. pap. 45.00 (0-945936-07-9) Spanierman Gallery.
Ten Americans. John Caldwell. (Illus.). 32p. (Orig.). 1987. pap. 5.95 (0-88039-016-6) Mus Art Carnegie.
*Ten Ancient Scrolls for Success: From the Greatest Salesman in the World. Og Mandino. 108p. 1997. 9.95 (0-8119-0856-9) LIFETIME.
Ten & a Kid. Sadie R. Weilerstein. LC 61-12600. (Illus.). 186p. (J). (gr. 3 up). 1973. reprint ed. 8.95 (0-8276-0009-7) JPS Phila.
Ten & Twenty-Two: A Journey Through the Paths of Wisdom. Michael Jacobs. LC 97-12626. (Illus.). 144p. 1997. write for info. (1-56821-988-1) Aronson.
Ten Apples up on Top. Theodore Le Sieg. LC 61-7068. (Illus.). 72p. (J). (gr. 1-2). 1961. lib. bdg. 11.99 (0-394-90019-7) Beginner.
Ten Apples up on Top. Theodore Le Sieg. LC 61-7068. (Illus.). 72p. (J). (gr. 1-2). 1961. 7.99 (0-394-80019-2) Beginner.
Ten Applications of Graph Theory. Hansjoachim Walther. 1985. lib. bdg. 107.50 (90-277-1599-8) Kluwer Ac.

Ten Artists - Ten Visions: 1989. Rachel R. Lafo. LC 89-51080. (Orig.). 1989. bds. 6.00 (0-945506-03-1) DeCordova Mus.

***10 Artists/10 Visions: 1994.** Rachel R. Lafo & Sara R. Roberts. LC 94-72173. (Orig.). Date not set. pap. write for info. (0-945506-16-3) DeCordova Mus.

Ten at Night. Laurie Sheck. 1989. 18.95 (0-394-57765-5) Knopf.

Ten Basic Math Skills with Geometry. James Streeter. 1991. pap. 31.95 (0-07-062629-4) McGraw.

Ten Basic Responsibilities of Nonprofit Boards. rev. ed. Richard T. Ingram. (Nonprofit Governance Ser.: No. 01). 22p. (Orig.). (C). 1996. pap. text ed. 12.00 (0-925299-00-6) Natl Ctr Nonprofit.

Ten Basic Rules for Better Living. Manly P. Hall. pap. 4.95 (0-89314-362-6) Philos Res.

10 Basic Steps Toward Christian Maturity: Leader's Guide. Bill Bright. Ed. by Don Tanner et al. (Illus.). 552p. (Orig.). 1994. pap. text ed. 14.99 (1-56399-028-8) NewLife Pubns.

Ten Basics of Business Etiquette. Meridian Education Corporation Staff. (Illus.). 4p. (Orig.). 1993. student ed., pap. 1.00 (1-56191-276-X, 11123); teacher ed., pap. 2.83 (1-56191-275-1, 11124) Meridian Educ.

Ten Beads Tall. Pam Adams. LC 90-1964. (Bead Frame Ser.). (J). 1989. 11.95 (0-85953-242-9) Childs Play.

***Ten Beads Tall.** Pam Adams. (Bead Frame Ser.). (FRE.). (J). 1989. 11.99 (0-85953-456-1) Childs Play.

Ten Bears Go Marching: A Pop-Up Book. John Richardson. LC 95-81181. 24p. (J). 1996. 13.95 (0-7868-0266-9) Hyprn Child.

Ten Bears in a Bed. Illus. by John Richardson. LC 91-26501. 22p. (J). (ps-k). 1992. 13.95 (1-56282-157-1) Hyprn Child.

Ten Bears in My Bed: A Goodnight Countdown. Stanley Mack. LC 74-151. (Illus.). 32p. (J). (ps-1). 1974. lib. bdg. 11.99 (0-394-92902-0) Pantheon.

***10 Bears in My Bed: A Goodnight Countdown.** Stanley Mack. (Illus.). (J). (ps-1). 11.99 (0-394-82902-6, 594388) Pantheon.

Ten Beethoven Sonatas for Piano & Violin. Joseph Szigeti. Ed. by Paul Rolland. 1993. reprint ed. 12.00 (1-883026-01-6) Am String Tchrs.

Ten Best Casino Bets. 2nd rev. ed. Henry J. Tamburin. LC 93-83953. 82p. (Orig.). 1993. pap. 3.95 (0-912177-07-1) Res Serv Unltd.

Ten Best Ideas for Reading. Edward Fry. 1991. pap. 19.95 (0-201-25141-8) Addison-Wesley.

Ten Best Jewish Children's Stories. Daniel Sperber & Chana Sperber. (Illus.). 48p. (J). (gr. 1-4). 1995. 16.95 (0-943706-58-0) Pitspopany.

Ten Best Object Lessons. (Illus.). 5p. (J). (gr. k-6). 1956. pap. text ed. 1.25 (1-55976-146-6) CEF Press.

Ten Best of Everything in Albuquerque. Elizabeth Thornton et al. (Illus.). 190p. (Orig.). pap. 12.00 (1-878776-01-0) Adobe Pub NM.

Ten Best of Everything in Martha's Vineyard. Elizabeth Thornton. (Illus.). 195p. (Orig.). pap. 12.00 (1-878776-03-7) Adobe Pub NM.

Ten Best of Everything in Nantucket. Elizabeth Thornton. (Illus.). 195p. (Orig.). pap. 12.00 (1-878776-02-9) Adobe Pub NM.

Ten Best of Everything in Santa Barbara. Elizabeth Thornton. 195p. (Orig.). pap. 12.00 (1-878776-04-5) Adobe Pub NM.

Ten Best of Everything in Santa Fe. Elizabeth Thornton. (Illus.). 208p. (Orig.). 1996. pap. 14.95 (1-878776-00-2) Adobe Pub NM.

Ten Best Opportunities for Starting a Home Business Today. New Careers Center, Inc. Staff & Reed Glenn. 244p. (Orig.). 1993. pap. 14.95 (0-911781-10-2) Live Oak Pubns.

Ten Bible People Like Me Workbook. Jamie Buckingham. 109p. (Orig.). 1988. student ed. 6.95 (0-941478-98-X) Paraclete MA.

Ten Black Dots. Donald Crews. LC 85-14871. (Illus.). 32p. (J). (ps up). 1995. pap. 4.95 (0-688-13574-9, Mulberry) Morrow.

Ten Black Dots. rev. ed. Donald Crews. LC 85-14871. (Illus.). 32p. (J). (ps-3). 1986. 16.00 (0-688-06067-6); lib. bdg. 15.93 (0-688-06068-4) Greenwillow.

Ten Books of Architecture: The 1755 Leoni Edition. Leon B. Alberti. 480p. 1986. pap. 14.95 (0-486-25239-6) Dover.

Ten Books on Architecture. Vitruvius. Tr. by Morris H. Morgan. (Illus.). pap. text ed. 8.95 (0-486-20645-9) Dover.

Ten British Pictures, 1740-1840. Robert R. Wark. LC 74-169905. (Illus.). 151p. 1971. reprint ed. pap. 43.10 (0-608-00232-1, 2060734) Bks Demand.

10X10: Ten Women - Ten Prints. Robert D. Schildgen. (Illus.). 30p. (Orig.). 1995. pap. 10.00 (0-942744-04-7) Berkeley Art.

Ten Cats Have Hats. Jean Marzollo. 24p. (J). (ps). 1994. 6.95 (0-590-20656-7) Scholastic Inc.

***Ten Centuries of Manuscripts in the Huntington Library.** Herbert C. Schulz et al. (Huntington Library Publications). (Illus.). 95p. 1982. reprint ed. pap. 27.10 (0-608-03174-7, 2063627) Bks Demand.

Ten Centuries of Spanish Poetry: An Anthology in English Verse with Original Texts, from the Eleventh Century to the Generation of 1898. Ed. by Eleanor L. Turnbull. LC 72-5469. 468p. reprint ed. pap. 133.40 (0-685-20480-4, 2029913) Bks Demand.

Ten Centuries That Shaped the West: Greek & Roman Art in Texas Collections. Herbert Hofmann. LC 71-131999. (Illus.). 1970. 24.95 (0-914412-18-3) Inst for the Arts.

Ten Challenges. D. Len Felder. 1997. 25.00 (0-517-70505-2) Random.

***Ten Challenges.** Leonard Felder. 1998. pap. write for info. (0-609-80180-5, Crown) Crown Pub Group.

10 Challenges of a Worldchanger. Ron Luce. LC 95-37405. 228p. (YA). 1995. pap. 7.99 (0-7852-7575-4) Nelson.

Ten Children's Pieces, Opus 27, Bk. 2. D. Kabalevsky. 24p. 1985. pap. 4.95 (0-7935-2277-3, 00123068) H Leonard.

Ten Christians: By Their Deeds You Shall Know Them. Boniface Hanley. LC 79-53836. (Illus.). 272p. (Orig.). 1979. pap. 8.95 (0-87793-183-6) Ave Maria.

Ten Christmas Sheep. Nancy W. Carlstrom. LC 96-21212. (Illus.). 6p. (J). 1996. 13.00 (0-8028-5137-1) Eerdmans.

Ten Classical Myths. Barbara Brothers & Deborah Neyrohr. 23p. (Orig.). (LAT.). 1992. spiral bd. 1.65 (0-939507-34-X, B733) Amer Classical.

Ten Colloquies Erasmus. Craig R. Thompson. 208p. (C). 1957. pap. text ed. 14.80 (0-02-420620-2, Macmillan Coll) P-H.

***Ten Command Words: For the Believer in Christ.** Tom Smith. 20p. (Orig.). 1997. pap. 2.50 (1-880573-39-3) Grace WI.

Ten Commandments. (Bible Stories Ser.: No. S846-13). (J). 1989. boxed 3.95 (0-7214-5262-0, Ladybrd) Penguin.

Ten Commandments. Inos Biffi. LC 93-39147. (My First Catechism Ser.). (Illus.). 30p. (J). 1994. 12.00 (0-8028-3758-1) Eerdmans.

Ten Commandments. K. Cavanagh. (J). Date not set. pap. text ed. 1.25 (0-88271-205-5) Regina Pr.

Ten Commandments. Patricia S. Daniels. Ed. by Jean Crawford. LC 96-15330. (Family Time Bible Stories Ser.). (Illus.). 32p. (J). 1996. write for info. (0-7835-4631-9) Time-Life.

Ten Commandments. Charles F. Degner. 48p. (Orig.). 1987. pap. 3.50 (0-8100-0266-3, 22N0801) Northwest Pub.

Ten Commandments. Emmet Fox. LC 92-54664. 1993. pap. 12.00 (0-06-250307-3) Harper SF.

Ten Commandments. LeRoy Lawson. 161p. (Orig.). 1991. 12.99 (0-89900-403-2) College Pr Pub.

***10 Commandments.** Roberta Letwenko & Edward Letwenko. (Jeremy the Bible Bookworm Ser.). (Illus.). 32p. (J). 3.95 (0-614-22064-5) Regina Pr.

Ten Commandments. Lawrence G. Lovasik. (Saint Joseph Picture Bks.). (Illus.). (J). (gr. 1-6). 1978. pap. 1.25 (0-89942-287-X, 287-00) Catholic Bk Pub.

***Ten Commandments.** Lawrence G. Lovasik. (Saint Joseph Beginner Ser.). (Illus.). (J). 1993. 3.25 (0-89942-222-5, 222/22) Catholic Bk Pub.

***Ten Commandments.** J. D. McClatchy. 1998. write for info. (0-375-40137-7); pap. write for info. (0-375-70134-6) Knopf.

***Ten Commandments.** Norbert C. Oesch. LC 96-28876. (Expository Sermon Series). 1997. 12.99 (0-570-04878-8, 12-3301) Concordia.

***Ten Commandments.** Rob Suggs. (LifeGuide Bible Studies). 64p. 1997. pap. 4.99 (0-8308-1084-6, 1084) InterVarsity.

Ten Commandments. Lester Sumrall. 51p. (C). 1978. pap. text ed. 10.00 (0-937580-50-3) LeSEA Pub Co.

Ten Commandments. Lois Veals. 2.99 (1-871676-17-7, Pub. by Christian Focus UK) Spring Arbor Dist.

Ten Commandments. Ed. by Tom Wakefield. 1993. pap. 13.99 (1-85242-232-7) Serpents Tail.

Ten Commandments. Arthur W. Pink. 80p. (gr. 10). 1995. reprint ed. pap. 6.99 (0-8010-7140-2) Baker Bks.

Ten Commandments. Thomas Watson. 245p. 1990. reprint ed. pap. 14.99 (0-85151-146-5) Banner of Truth.

Ten Commandments. Thomas Watson. 245p. 1995. reprint ed. 21.99 (0-85151-681-5) Banner of Truth.

Ten Commandments: A Series of Sermons. Theodore Pitcairn. 70p. 1964. pap. 3.75 (1-883270-05-7) Swedenborg Assn.

Ten Commandments: An Illustrated Bible Passage for Young Children. Ed. by David Meyer & Alice Meyer. LC 90-71557. (Illus.). 40p. (Orig.). (J). (ps-4). 1991. pap. 12.95 incl. audio (1-879099-02-0) Thy Word.

Ten Commandments: God's Rules for Living. Stuart Briscoe. (Fisherman Bible Studyguide Ser.). 80p. 1995. pap. 4.99 (0-87788-803-5) Shaw Pubs.

Ten Commandments: Learning about God's Law. Gloria A. Truitt. LC 56-1398. (Concept Books for Children). (J). (gr. 1 up). 1983. pap. 3.99 (0-570-08527-6, 56-1398) Concordia.

***Ten Commandments: Manual for the Christian Life.** J. Douma. Tr. by Nelson Kloosterman from DUT. 424p. 1996. pap. 24.99 (0-87552-237-8) Presby & Reformed.

Ten Commandments: Playing by the Rules. rev. ed. Stuart Briscoe. (Foundations of the Faith Ser.). 224p. 1993. pap. 8.99 (0-87788-805-1) Shaw Pubs.

Ten Commandments: Sounds of Love from Sinai. Alfred A. McBride. 158p. 1990. pap. 6.95 (0-86716-109-4) St Anthony Mess Pr.

Ten Commandments: Text & Activity Book. Nancy Karkowsky. (J). (gr. 3-4). pap. 6.50 (0-87441-477-6) Behrman.

Ten Commandments: The Enduring Power of Cecil B. DeMille's Epic Movie. Lisa Mitchell. (Illus.). 200p. Date not set. write for info. (1-887322-05-1); pap. write for info. (1-887322-06-X) Emprise NY.

Ten Commandments: Then & Now. Jim Lewis. LC 84-50912. 95p. (Orig.). 1984. pap. 5.95 (0-942482-07-7) Unity Church Denver.

Ten Commandments: Youth & Adult Student. Carol E. Miller. 1971. pap. 1.00 (0-915374-45-5) Rapids Christian.

Ten Commandments: Youth & Adult Teacher. Carol E. Miller. 1991. pap. 2.50 (0-915374-37-4) Rapids Christian.

10 Commandments & Christian Community. Jay W. Marshall. LC 95-24084. 128p. (Orig.). 1996. pap. 8.99 (0-8361-9027-0) Herald Pr.

***Ten Commandments & Human Rights.** Walter Harrelson. 240p. (Orig.). 1997. pap. text ed. 19.95 (0-86554-542-1) Mercer Univ Pr.

Ten Commandments & the Sermon on the Mount. Rudolf Steiner. Tr. by Frieda Solomon from GER. 44p. 1978. pap. 3.95 (0-910142-79-3) Anthroposophic.

Ten Commandments for Children. W. Murphy. (J). (ps-3). Date not set. pap. text ed. 1.95 (0-88271-159-8) Regina Pr.

Ten Commandments for Children. H. J. Richards. 28p. (J). pap. 2.95 (0-8146-1801-4) Liturgical Pr.

Ten Commandments for Children. Lois Rock. 32p. (J). (ps-3). 1995. 8.99 (0-7459-3055-7) Lion USA.

Ten Commandments for Grandparents: A Wise & Witty Handbook for Today's Grandmas & Grandpas. Caryl W. Krueger. 192p. 1991. pap. 12.95 (0-687-41237-4) Abingdon.

Ten Commandments for Husbands. Benny Bristow. 1986. pap. 6.25 (0-89137-623-2) Quality Pubns.

Ten Commandments for Now. Stephen M. Crotts. LC 87-62893. 1988. pap. text ed. 3.00 (0-932050-34-4) New Puritan.

Ten Commandments for Public Speakers. Stephen D. Gladis. 144p. 1990. pap. 10.95 (0-87425-146-X) HRD Press.

***Ten Commandments for Success: Unlocking Principles of Prosperous Personal, Business, & Family Living from the Life of Moses.** Robert I. Winer. 180p. 1997. pap. 12.95 (0-9655180-0-0) Gesher Pub.

Ten Commandments for Teaching: A Teacher's View. Ray Reyes. 48p. 1991. pap. 8.95 (0-8106-1539-8) NEA.

Ten Commandments for Wives. Benny Bristow. 1983. pap. 6.25 (0-89137-430-2) Quality Pubns.

Ten Commandments in History & Tradition. Ed. by B. Segal. Tr. by G. Levi from HEB. xv, 453p. 1990. text ed. 35.00 (965-223-724-8, Pub. by Magnes Press IS) Eisenbrauns.

Ten Commandments in the Animal World: Some Startling Revelations of the Behavior of the Wild Animals, Direct from the Note-Book of a Famous Naturalist. Ernest T. Seton. 78p. (YA). 1994. pap. 12.95 (1-885529-05-8) Stevens Pub.

Ten Commandments in the Year 2000 Pt. 1. Claudio Apfel. 176p. 1994. pap. 11.95 (0-89716-519-5) P B Pubng.

Ten Commandments in Today's World. George Drew. 48p. (Orig.). 1979. pap. 7.95 (0-940754-00-2) Ed Ministries.

Ten Commandments of Business & How to Break Them. William Fromm. 1992. pap. 7.95 (0-425-13216-1, Berkley Trade) Berkley Pub.

Ten Commandments of God. Albert J. Shamon. LC 95-74801. 70p. (Orig.). 1995. pap. 3.50 (1-877678-37-6) Riehle Found.

Ten Commandments of God & the Lord's Prayer. Abd-ru-shin. LC BV4655.A2313. 102p. 1995. pap. 9.00 (1-57461-004-X) Grail Found Pr.

Ten Commandments of God & the Lord's Prayer. Abd-ru-shin. LC BV4655.A2313 1995. 84p. 1995. 14.00 (1-57461-007-4) Grail Found Pr.

***Ten Commandments of Good Writing.** Jessica P. Morrell. (Illus.). 8p. (Orig.). 1995. pap. 2.50 (1-884241-55-7, SPS0317) Energeia Pub.

***Ten Commandments of Highly Successful Leaders: Leadership in Challenging Times.** Tim L. Holman. (Illus.). 70p. (Orig.). 1997. pap. 5.00 (1-57502-398-9, PO1238) Morris Pubng.

Ten Commandments of Hinduism: A Quest & a Find. V. Krishnamurthy. (C). 1994. 18.00 (81-224-0628-9, Pub. by Wiley Estrn II) Franklin.

Ten Commandments of Love. Joan Hutson. LC 95-7071. (Illus.). 32p. (J). (gr. k-3). 1996. 5.95 (0-8198-7382-9) Pauline Bks.

***Ten Commandments of Office Etiquette: Being All You Were Hired to Be.** unabridged ed. Don M. Icenogle. 71p. (Orig.). 1996. mass mkt. 9.95 (0-9655597-0-X) Herta Pub & Distrib.

10 Commandments of Pleasure. Susan Block. 144p. 1996. 18.95 (0-312-14429-6) St Martin.

Ten Commandments of Pleasure: Erotic Keys to the Best Sex of Your Life. Susan Block. 1996. 16.95 (0-614-97012-1) St Martin.

Ten Commandments of Systemic Reform. Vaclav Klaus. (Orig.). 1993. pap. text ed. write for info. (1-56708-094-4) Grp of Thirty.

Ten Commandments of Tennis. Russell Warner. (Orig.). 1995. pap. 7.95 (0-9640706-5-0) Cock-a-Hoop.

Ten Commandments of the Law of God. Santiago Martinez. Tr. by Maria L. Martinez from SPA. LC 95-72817. 80p. (Orig.). 1996. pap. text ed. 4.95 (1-882972-63-5) Queenship Pub.

Ten Commandments of the Workplace & How to Break Them Every Day. Perry Pascarella. 144p. 1996. 15.99 (0-310-20713-4) Zondervan.

Ten Commandments: Revelation at Sinai see Torah Anthology: Meam Lo'ez

Ten Commandments Yesterday & Today. James B. Coffman. pap. 4.50 (0-88027-094-2) Firm Foun Pub.

***Ten Commandments/The Beattitudes.** Ed. by David Meyer & Alice Meyer. 16p. (Orig.). 1997. pap. 12.95 (1-879099-26-8) Thy Word.

Ten Commands of Christian Parenting. David E. Miller. (Illus.). 182p. (Orig.). 1996. pap. 8.95 (1-883928-15-X) Longwood.

Ten Common Inferences: Oscar-The Big Escape for Use with IBM-PC, Pt. 2. California State University Staff. 1984. 49.95 (0-07-831015-6) McGraw.

Ten Contemporary Polish Stories. Ed. by Edmund Ordon. LC 74-2842. 252p. 1974. reprint ed. text ed. 47.50 (0-8371-7436-8, ORPS, Greenwood Pr) Greenwood.

Ten Coptic Legal Texts: Metropolitan Museum of Art, Department of Egyptian Art Publications, Vol. 2. A. Arthur Schiller. LC 71-168410. (Metropolitan Museum of Art Publications in Reprint). (Illus.). 126p. 1973. reprint ed. 24.95 (0-405-02246-8) Ayer.

***Ten Corps in Korea, 1950.** Shelby L. Stanton. LC 89-8835. 1996. pap. text ed. 16.95 (0-89141-603-X) Presidio Pr.

Ten Crazy Caterpillars. Judy Tuer. LC 92-30672. (Voyages Ser.). (Illus.). (J). 1993. 2.50 (0-383-03658-5) SRA McGraw.

***Ten Creepiest Creatures in America.** Allan Zullo. (J). 1997. pap. 2.95 (0-8167-4288-X) Troll Communs.

***Ten Creepiest Places in America.** George E. Lyon. 1997. pap. 2.95 (0-8167-4221-9) Troll Communs.

10 Critical Keys for Highly Effective Mormon Families. Phillip Kunz & William Dyer. 205p. 1994. pap. 10.95 (1-55517-155-9) CFI Dist.

***Ten Critical Success Factors for Integrated Delivery Systems.** Peter R. Kongstvedt. 1996. 29.00 (0-8342-0858-X, 20858) Aspen Pub.

Ten-Day Checklist of the Birds of Trinidad & Tobago. William L. Murphy. 10p. (Orig.). (C). 1994. 3.00 (0-941475-03-4) Peregrine Enter.

***10-Day Fully Financed Wealth System Guide.** 9th ed. Tyler G. Hicks. 100p. 1998. pap. 10.00 (1-56150-236-7) Intl Wealth.

10-Day Fully Financed Wealth System Guide. 8th ed. Tyler G. Hicks. 100p. 1996. pap. 10.00 (1-56150-186-7) Intl Wealth.

Ten Day MBA: A Step-by-Step Guide to Mastering the Skills Taught in America's Top Business... Steven Silbiger. 1994. pap. 12.00 (0-688-13788-1, Quill) Morrow.

Ten-Day MBA: A Step-by-Step Guide to Mastering the Skills Taught in America's Top Business Schools. Steven Silbiger. 1993. 23.00 (0-688-12317-1) Morrow.

Ten Days in Canaan. R. Michael Henegar. 313p. (Orig.). 1993. pap. 9.99 (1-881379-05-1) Samaritan Pr.

Ten Days in the Light of 'Akka. rev. ed. Julia M. Grundy. LC 79-12177. 107p. 1979. pap. 8.95 (0-87743-131-0, 332-040) Bahai.

Ten Days of Infamy. Malcolm Decker. LC 68-20204. (Illus.). 1969. reprint ed. 19.95 (0-405-00053-7) Ayer.

Ten Days That Shook the World. John Reed. 1982. lib. bdg. 75.00 (0-8490-3225-3) Gordon Pr.

Ten Days That Shook the World. John Reed. LC 67-27252. (Illus.). 445p. (C). 1989. pap. 6.95 (0-7178-0200-0) Intl Pubs Co.

Ten Days That Shook the World. John Reed. 368p. 1990. pap. 10.95 (0-14-018293-4, 612, Penguin Classics) Viking Penguin.

Ten Days That Shook the World. John Reed. 1992. reprint ed. lib. bdg. 21.95 (0-89968-271-5, Lghtyr Pr) Buccaneer Bks.

***Ten Days That Shook the World: Illustrated Edition.** John Reed. (Illus.). 288p. 1997. 35.95 (0-7509-1646-X, Pub. by Sutton Pubng UK) Bks Intl VA.

***Ten Days That Shook World.** Reed. LC 97-14782. 1997. text ed. 35.00 (0-312-17711-9) St Martin.

Ten Days to a Great New Life. William E. Edwards. 1976. pap. 3.00 (0-87980-159-X) Wilshire.

Ten Days to Destiny. G. C. Kiriakopoulos. 352p. 1986. mass mkt. 3.95 (0-380-70102-2) Avon.

***Ten Days to Destiny: The Battle for Crete, 1941.** George Kiriakopoulos. LC 97-22956. (Illus.). 375p. (Orig.). 1997. reprint ed. pap. 19.95 (0-917653-49-1) Hellenic Coll Pr.

Ten Days to Self-Esteem! David D. Burns. LC 92-42449. 1993. pap. 12.95 (0-688-09455-4) Morrow.

Ten Days to Self-Esteem: Leader's Manual. David D. Burns. LC 92-38209. 1993. pap. 23.00 (0-688-12708-8) Morrow.

Ten Decisive Battles of Christianity. Frank S. Mead. LC 72-117823. (Essay Index Reprint Ser.). 1977. 18.95 (0-8369-1812-6) Ayer.

Ten Degrees Cooler Inside. Aimee Grunberger. LC 93-144505. 24p. (Orig.). 1992. pap. 4.95 (1-880743-01-9) Dead Metaphor.

Ten Dharma Realms Are Not Beyond a Single Thought. 2nd ed. Hsuan Hua. Ed. & Tr. by Buddhist Text Translation Society Staff. LC 96-19701. Orig. Title: Shih Fa Chieh Pu li i Nian Hsin. 143p. (CHI & ENG.). 1996. pap. write for info. (0-88139-503-X) Buddhist Text.

Ten Dharma Realms Are Not Beyond a Single Thought. Tripitaka Master Hua. Tr. by Buddhist Text Translation Society from CHI. (Illus.). 72p. (Orig.). 1976. reprint ed. pap. 4.00 (0-917512-12-X) Buddhist Text.

Ten Dinner Parties for Two. Frances Bissell. LC 89-32090. (Ten Menus Ser.). (Illus.). 128p. 1989. Cookery Book. 19.95 (0-940793-30-X) Interlink Pub.

***Ten Disciplines to Growing You.** J. Kuhn & M. Mullins. 1997. write for info. (0-8129-2920-9, Times Bks) Random.

Ten Diversions for the Young Pianist. A. Tansman. 16p. 1986. pap. 4.95 (0-7935-3915-3) H Leonard.

***Ten Dogs in the Window.** Claire Masurel. (Illus.). (J). 1997. 15.95 (0-614-29275-1) North-South Bks NYC.

***Ten Dogs in the Window: A Countdown Book.** Claire Masurel. LC 97-20945. 1997. write for info. (1-55858-754-3) North South Trader.

***Ten Dogs in the Window: A Countdown Book.** Claire Masurel. LC 97-20945. (J). 1997. write for info. (1-55858-755-1) North South Trader.

Ten Doreset Mysteries, County Murders & Mysteries. Roger Guttridge. (C). 1989. 45.00 (1-85455-012-8, Pub. by Ensign Pubns & Print UK) St Mut.

Ten Dumbest Mistakes Smart People Make & How to Avoid Them: Simple & Sure Techniques for Gaining Greater Control of Your Life. Arthur Freeman & Rose DeWolf. LC 91-50440. 288p. 1993. reprint ed. pap. 12.50 (0-06-092199-4, PL) HarpC.

Ten Early Poems. Harold Pinter. (C). 1990. 35.00 (0-906887-50-X, Pub. by Greville Pr UK) St Mut.

Ten Early Songs for Middle Voice & Piano. S. Barber. 32p. 1994. pap. 8.95 (0-7935-3709-6) H Leonard.

An Asterisk (*) at the beginning of an entry indicates that the title is appearing in BIP for the first time.

Ten Easy Steps: To a Great Looking Saltwater & Reef Aquarium. Albert J. Thiel. (Illus.). 240p. (Orig.). pap. write for info. (*0-945777-07-8*) Aardvark Pr.

***Ten Easy Steps to Effective Writing Skills.** Alice P. Franklin. (Illus.). 225p. (Orig.). (C). 1997. pap. text ed. 29.95 (*1-890870-01-3*) Comn Opport.

Ten Educators from Japan: A Japanese Perspective. Ed. by Benjamin C. Duke. (Illus.). 200p. 1990. 42.50 (*0-86008-442-6*, Pub. by U of Tokyo JA) Col U Pr.

Ten-Eight: A Cop's Honest Look at Life on the Street. Officer X. LC 94-68989. 240p. (Orig.). 1994. pap. 14.95 (*0-935878-13-0*) Calibre Pr.

***Ten Eighteenth-Century Voluntaries.** John Bennett et al. Ed. by Gwilym Beechey. (Recent Researches in Music of the Baroque Era Ser.: Vol. RRB6). (Illus.). xiii, 97p. 1969. pap. 38.40 (*0-89579-016-5*) A-R Eds.

Ten, Ekrane Suzibus: Amerikos Lietuviu Kinematografija, 1909-1979. Raimundas M. Lapas. LC 81-69029. (Illus.). 386p. (ENG & LIT.). 19.95 (*0-941618-00-5*) Baltic Cinema.

Ten English Farces. Ed. by Leo Hughes & A. H. Scouten. LC 79-132135. (Play Anthology Reprint Ser.). 1977. 17.95 (*0-8369-8212-6*) Ayer.

Ten Essays on Zionism & Judaism. Achad Ha-am, pseud. LC 73-2202. (Jewish People; History, Religion, Literature Ser.). 1979. reprint ed. 29.95 (*0-405-05267-7*) Ayer.

***Ten Essential Foods.** Lalitha Thomas. LC 97-1005. 400p. (Orig.). 1997. pap. 16.95 (*0-934252-74-2*) Hohm Pr.

Ten Essential Herbs: Everyone's Handbook to Health. 2nd rev. ed. Lalitha Thomas. LC 92-54953. (Illus.). 400p. (C). 1995. pap. 16.95 (*0-934252-48-3*) Hohm Pr.

Ten Essentials for Travel in the Outdoors. (Illus.). 36p. pap. 2.95 (*0-89886-374-0*) Mountaineers.

Ten Ever-Lovin' Years with Pogo. Walt Kelly. 1976. 27.95 (*0-8488-1556-4*) Amereon Ltd.

Ten Faces of the Universe. Hoyle. 1977. pap. 11.95 (*0-7167-0383-1*) W H Freeman.

Ten Famous Plays. John Galsworthy. LC 75-41108. (BCL Ser.: II). 1976. reprint ed. 41.75 (*0-404-14749-6*) AMS Pr.

Ten Fat Hens. Intervisual Books Staff. (J). 1997. pap. 3.99 (*0-679-88376-2*) Random.

***10 Fatal Dating Mistakes That Men & Women Commit: How to Avoid Them.** Lila Gruzen. 1997. pap. text ed. 14.95 (*1-882180-87-9*) Griffin CA.

Ten Favorite French Stories. Joseph S. Galland. (FRE.). 1985. pap. text ed. 9.95 (*0-89197-962-X*) Irvington.

Ten Favorite Hawaiian Songs for Ukulele Groups: A Group Leader's Manual. Hideo M. Kimura. 60p. 1989. pap. text ed. 10.95 (*0-917822-23-4*) Heedays.

10 Feet Tall & Bulletproof: The Travis Tritt Story. Travis Tritt & Michael Bane. 224p. 1995. mass mkt. 5.99 (*0-446-60231-0*) Warner Bks.

***Ten Fingers for God: The Life & Work of Dr. Paul Brand.** Dorothy C. Wilson. 1996. pap. text ed. 9.95 (*0-9643137-0-7*) P Brand Pubng.

10 First Steps for the New Christian. Woodrow M. Kroll. 1992. 2.50 (*0-8474-0877-9*) Back to Bible.

Ten Flashing Fireflies. Philemon Sturges. LC 94-38572. (Illus.). 32p. (J). (ps-3). Date not set. 15.95 (*1-55858-420-X*); lib. bdg. 15.88 (*1-55858-421-8*) North-South Bks NYC.

***Ten Flashing Fireflies.** Philemon Sturges. (Illus.). 32p. (J). (gr. k-2). 1997. pap. 6.95 (*1-55858-674-1*) North-South Bks NYC.

Ten Flemish Poems. Tr. by Manfred Wolf. 1972. pap. 5.00 (*0-685-27793-3*) Twowindows Pr.

Ten Folk Dances in Labanotation. Fred Berk & Lucy Venable. i, 32p. (C). 1959. audio 15.00 (*0-685-08568-6*) Dance Notation.

Ten Folk Dances in Labanotation. Fred Berk & Lucy Venable. (Illus.). 32p. (C). 1959. pap. text ed. 7.95 (*0-932582-09-5*, Pub. by Dance Bks UK) Princeton Bk Co.

Ten Foolish Things Christians Do to Stunt Their Growth. Tom Allen. LC 96-84983. 1996. pap. 9.99 (*0-87509-674-3*) Chr Pubns.

Ten-Foot Chain. Achmed Abdullah et al. LC 73-116924. (Short Story Index Reprint Ser.). 1977. 16.95 (*0-8369-3426-1*) Ayer.

Ten Foot Square Hut & Tales of Heike. Tr. by A. L. Sadler. LC 72-157261. (Illus.). 298p. 1971. reprint ed. pap. 12.95 (*0-8048-0879-1*) C E Tuttle.

Ten Foot Square Hut & Tales of the Heike. Chomei Kamo. Ed. by Arthur L. Sadler. LC 71-98844. 271p. 1970. reprint ed. text ed. 55.00 (*0-8371-3114-6*, KATF, Greenwood Pr) Greenwood.

Ten for Dinner. Bogart. (J). 1989. 19.95 (*0-590-73173-4*) Scholastic Inc.

Ten Forty Handbook, Incl. Suppl. Julian Block. 550p. 1989. Incl. 64 pg. suppl. 23.50 (*0-13-903535-4*, Busn) P-H.

Ten-Forty Handbook: 1988 Special New Tax Law Edition. Julian Block & Alan S. Robinson. 550p. 1987. 21.50 (*0-13-903709-8*) P-H.

Ten-Forty Handbook, 1985: How to Prepare Income Tax Returns. Martin E. Holbrook. 538p. 1984. 21.00 (*0-13-903659-8*) P-H.

Ten Forty Preparation: 1994 Edition. Sidney Kess et al. 480p. (Orig.). 1994. pap. 40.00 (*0-8080-0004-7*) Commerce.

***1040 Preparation - 1997 Edition.** 480p. 1996. pap. 37.50 (*0-614-26826-5*, 13496BLS02) Commerce.

Ten Forty Preparation, 1993. Eisenberg et al. 480p. 1993. pap. 35.00 (*0-685-67047-3*, 4769) Commerce.

Ten-Forty Reference Series. Jeff Ward. 1996. ring bd. write for info. (*0-9652986-0-4*) Aquarian Pr CA.

Ten Four-Part Motets for the Church's Year. Giovanni P. Palestrina. Tr. by Alec Harman. 112p. (ENG & LAT.). 1985. 24.95 (*0-19-353332-4*) OUP.

Ten (Fun) Things to Do Before You Die. Karol Jackowski. LC 89-84558. 112p. (Orig.). 1989. pap. 6.95 (*0-87793-409-6*) Ave Maria.

Ten Furry Monsters. (Parents Magazine Press Read-Aloud Library). (J). 1994. lib. bdg. 17.27 (*0-8368-0989-0*) Gareth Stevens Inc.

Ten Furry Monsters. Stephanie Calmenson. LC 84-4998. (Illus.). 48p. (J). (ps-3). 1984. 5.95 (*0-8193-1128-6*) Parents.

Ten Gates: The Kong-An Teaching of Zen Master Seung Sahn. Ed. by Stan Lombardo & Dennis Duermeier. (Illus.). 96p. (Orig.). 1987. pap. 11.95 (*0-942795-01-6*) Primary Point Pr.

***Ten Generations of Myers in America.** George Alford & Verna B. Alford. 996p. 1996. write for info. (*0-9654355-0-4*) Fmly History.

10 Geographic Ideas That Changed the World. Ed. by Susan E. Hanson. LC 96-18123. (Illus.). 280p. (C). 1997. text ed. 55.00 (*0-8135-2356-7*); pap. text ed. 20.00 (*0-8135-2357-5*) Rutgers U Pr.

Ten Golden Keys to Your Abundance. Rod Parsley. 190p. (Orig.). 1995. pap. 9.99 (*1-880244-20-9*) Wrld Harvest Church.

Ten Golden Keys to Your Abundance Study Guide. Ed. by Rod Parsley. 57p. 1995. pap. 10.00 (*1-880244-19-5*) Wrld Harvest Church.

10 Golden Rules for Financial Success: Riches I've Gathered from Legendary Mutual Fund Manager Sir John M. Templeton. Gary D. Moore. 224p. 1996. 18.99 (*0-310-20693-6*) Zondervan.

Ten Good Reasons to Be a Catholic: A Teenager's Guide to the Church. Jim Auer. LC 87-80988. (YA). (gr. 7-12). 1987. pap. 3.95 (*0-89243-271-3*) Liguori Pubns.

Ten Good Rules. Susan R. Topek. LC 91-32109. (Illus.). 24p. (J). (ps-1). 1992. 12.95 (*0-929371-30-5*); pap. 5.95 (*0-929371-28-3*) Kar-Ben.

Ten Gospel Favorites for Piano Solo. Darrell Archer. 7.95 (*0-87166-695-2*, 93958) Mel Bay.

Ten Grand. George G. Gilman. 1989. pap. 3.50 (*1-55817-223-8*) Kensgtn Pub Corp.

Ten Grandmothers. Alice Marriott. LC 45-1584. (Civilization of the American Indian Ser.: Vol. 26). 306p. 1983. pap. 14.95 (*0-8061-1825-3*) U of Okla Pr.

Ten Great Critical Ones. Witness Lee. 64p. 2.00 (*0-87083-937-3*) Living Stream Ministry.

Ten Great English Novelists. Valerie G. Myer. LC 89-77771. 160p. 1990. text ed. 39.95 (*0-312-03564-0*) St Martin.

***Ten Great Ideas from Church History: A Decision-Maker's Guide to Shaping Your Church.** Mark Shaw. LC 96-46370. 237p. (Orig.). 1997. pap. 12.99 (*0-8308-1681-X*, 1681) InterVarsity.

10 Great Jewish Children's Stories. Chaya Burstein. (Ten Jewish Children's Stories Ser.: Vol. 1). (Illus.). 48p. (J). (ps-3). 1994. 14.95 (*965-483-005-1*) Pitspopany.

Ten Great Works of Plato. Robert P. Wolff. 480p. 1969. pap. 6.99 (*0-451-62577-3*, Ment) NAL-Dutton.

Ten Great Years: Statistics of the Economic & Cultural Achievements of the People's Republic of China. Kuo Chia T'ung Chi Chii & Peoples Republic of China Staff. LC 72-38054. (China Classic & Contemporary Works in Reprint Ser.). 1995. reprint ed. 39.50 (*0-404-56908-0*) AMS Pr.

Ten Greatest Christmas Movies Ever Made: Fun Facts, Quizzes, & Behind-the-Scenes Trivia about Your Holiday Favorites! Edward Wilkins. 104p. (Orig.). 1993. pap. 7.95 (*0-9637195-1-3*, Kingsley Pr) Anton Enterprises.

Ten Greatest Gifts I Give My Children. Steven W. Vannoy. 1994. pap. 12.00 (*0-671-50227-1*, Fireside) S&S Trade.

Ten Greatest Gifts I Give My Children: Parenting from the Heart. Steven W. Vannoy. LC 93-93979. 251p. (Orig.). 1993. pap. 14.95 (*0-9637226-1-1*, Fireside) S&S Trade.

Ten Greek Plays in Contemporary Translations. Incl. Prometheus Bound. Aeschylus. LC 57-59175. (*0-318-53437-1*); Agamemnon. Aeschylus. LC 57-59175. (*0-318-53438-X*); Antigone. Sophocles. LC 57-59175. (*0-318-53439-8*); Oedipus Rex. Sophocles. LC 57-59175. (*0-318-53440-1*); Philoctetes. Sophocles. LC 57-59175. (*0-318-53441-X*); Alcestis. Euripides. LC 57-59175. (*0-318-53442-8*); Suppliants. Euripides. LC 57-59175. 1972. (*0-318-53443-6*); Andromache. Euripides. LC 57-59175. (*0-318-53444-4*); Bacchae. Euripides. LC 57-59175. (*0-318-53445-2*); Lysistrata. Aristophanes. LC 57-59175. (*0-318-53446-0*); LC 57-59175. (YA). (gr. 9-p). 1972. pap. 11.56 (*0-395-05117-7*, RivEd) HM.

Ten Greek Popes. Dennis Michelis. 1987. pap. 6.95 (*0-937032-54-9*) Light&Life Pub Co MN.

Ten Green Monsters: A Lift-the-Flap-&-See-Them-Fall Book. Gus Clarke. (Lift-the-Flap-&-See-Them-Fall-Book Ser.). (Illus.). 28p. (J). (ps-3). 1994. 10.95 (*0-307-17605-3*) Western Pub.

***Ten Habits of Naturally Slim People: And How to Make Them Part of Your Life.** Jill H. Podjasek. LC 97-6713. 1997. 19.95 (*0-8092-3177-8*) Contemp Bks.

Ten Hispano-Arabic Strophic Songs in the Modern Oral Tradition: Music & Texts. Benjamin M. Liu & James T. Monroe. (Publications in Modern Philology: Vol. 125). (Illus.). 101p. 1990. pap. 15.00 (*0-520-09751-3*) U CA Pr.

Ten-Hour Job Search Training Mini Course for Vocational-Occupational Skills Program. Lawrence E. Barlow. 14p. (Orig.). 1985. 1.75 (*0-940150-03-4*) Voc Career Assess.

Ten Hours' Labor: Religion, Reform, & Gender in Early New England. Teresa A. Murphy. LC 91-55534. 248p. 1992. 35.00 (*0-8014-2683-9*) Cornell U Pr.

Ten Hours Movement in Eighteen Thirty-One & Eighteen Thirty-Two. 1974. 23.95 (*0-405-04439-9*) Ayer.

***Ten Houses: Enrique Browne.** Oscar R. Ojeda. (Orig.). Date not set. pap. 19.99 (*1-56496-391-8*) Rockport Pubs.

Ten in a Bed. Allan Ahlberg. (Illus.). 112p. (J). (gr. 2-6). 1991. pap. 3.99 (*0-14-032531-X*, Puffin) Puffin Bks.

Ten in the Bed. (Little Golden Sound Story Bks.). (Illus.). 24p. (J). (ps up). 1992. 6.95 (*0-307-74812-X*, 64812, Golden Pr) Western Pub.

Ten-Inch Diagonal. Mark Sonnenfeld. 40p. pap. 3.00 (*0-9632820-7-7*) M Sonnenfeld.

10 Incredible Mistakes Made at Gettysburg: A Review of the Battle & How Blunders by the Generals Shaped the Outcome. Harris Mullen. (Illus.). 32p. (Orig.). 1995. pap. text ed. 5.95 (*0-9646629-0-6*) High Water Pr.

Ten Indians. Madison Smartt Bell. 264p. 1996. 23.00 (*0-679-44246-4*) McKay.

***Ten Indians.** Madison Smartt Bell. 1997. pap. 12.95 (*0-14-026846-4*) Viking Penguin.

Ten International Short Stories: For ESL Students. Raja T. Nasr. LC 94-48840. (Illus.). 62p. (C). 1995. reprint ed. pap. text ed. 14.50 (*0-8191-9865-X*) U Pr of Amer.

Ten Is the Age of Darkness: The Black Bildungsroman. Geta LeSeur. 248p. 1995. text ed. 34.95 (*0-8262-1011-2*) U of Mo Pr.

Ten-Key Adding Machine: Student Guide. Marvin W. Hempel. 1970. pap. text ed. 6.95 (*0-89420-056-9*, 126600); audio 143.05 (*0-89420-187-5*, 156700) Natl Book.

Ten Key Events from the Bible. (Bible Basics for Adults Ser.). 64p. 1996. teacher ed., pap. 5.95 (*0-8066-2326-8*, 15-7393, Augsburg) Augsburg Fortress.

Ten Key Events from the Bible: Bible Basics for Adults. Prod. by Augsburg Fortress Staff. 1996. student ed., pap. 4.25 (*0-8066-2325-X*, 15-7392, Augsburg) Augsburg Fortress.

Ten Key Events in Jesus' Life. (Bible Basics for Adults Ser.). 64p. 1996. teacher ed., pap. 5.95 (*0-8066-2328-4*, 15-7395, Augsburg) Augsburg Fortress.

Ten Key Events in Jesus' Life. Prod. by Augsburg Fortress Staff. (Bible Basics for Adults Ser.). 1996. student ed., pap. 4.25 (*0-8066-2327-6*, 15-7394, Augsburg) Augsburg Fortress.

Ten Key Passages from the Bible. (Bible Basics for Adults Ser.). 64p. 1996. teacher ed., pap. 5.95 (*0-8066-2330-6*, 15-7397, Augsburg) Augsburg Fortress.

Ten Key Passages from the Bible. Prod. by Augsburg Fortress Staff. (Bible Basics for Adults Ser.). 1996. student ed., pap. 4.25 (*0-8066-2329-2*, 15-7396, Augsburg) Augsburg Fortress.

Ten Key People from the Bible. Prod. by Augsburg Fortress Staff. (Bible Basics for Adults Ser.). 64p. 1996. teacher ed., pap. 5.95 (*0-8066-2324-1*, 15-7391, Augsburg) Augsburg Fortress.

Ten Key People from the Bible. Augsburg Fortress Staff. (Bible Basics for Adults Ser.). 1996. student ed., pap. text ed. 4.25 (*0-8066-2323-3*, 15-7390) Augsburg Fortress.

Ten-Key Skill Builder. William R. Pasewark. (KH - Office Machines Ser.). 1992. pap. 11.95 (*0-538-61410-2*) S-W Pub.

Ten-Key Skill Builder for Computers. William R. Pasewark & Todd Knowlton. (J). 1995. pap. 13.95 (*0-538-62919-3*) S-W Pub.

Ten-Key Skill Builder for Computers. William R. Pasewark. (Office Procedures Ser.). 1996. pap. 98.95 (*0-538-62920-7*) S-W Pub.

Ten-Key Touch System on Modern Calculators. Gilbert Eckern & Walter Hardin. 128p. 1989. student ed. 14.95 (*0-89863-132-7*) Star Pub CA.

Ten Keys to Dynamic Customer Relations. Gregory H. Sorensen. 78p. 1988. 8.98 (*0-88290-329-2*) Horizon Utah.

***Ten Keys to Helping Your Child Grow up with Diabetes.** Tim Wysocki. LC 96-37470. 1997. pap. write for info. (*0-945448-74-0*) Am Diabetes.

Ten Keys to Sales & Financial Success for Small Business. Ron Torrence. (Illus.). 180p. (Orig.). 1994. pap. write for info. (*1-885364-02-4*) Wave Communs.

Ten Keys to Understanding People. Henry C. Smith & James J. Mullin. LC 87-80562. (Self-Paced Program for Improving Relationships Ser.). (Orig.). 1987. pap. 8.95 (*0-942027-00-0*) Lantern Hill Pr.

Ten Keys to Writing Success. Donald E. Bower. LC 87-60072. 160p. (Orig.). 1987. pap. 10.95 (*0-88100-057-4*) Natl Writ Pr.

Ten Kids, No Pets. Ann M. Martin. LC 87-25206. 184p. (J). (gr. 3-7). 1988. 15.95 (*0-8234-0691-1*) Holiday.

Ten Kids No Pets. Ann M. Martin. 176p. (J). (gr. 4-6). 1990. pap. 3.50 (*0-590-43620-1*) Scholastic Inc.

Ten Knights in a Bar Room: Missing in Action in the Southwest Pacific, 1943. Michael J. Cundiff. LC 89-48526. (Illus.). 132p. 1990. reprint ed. pap. 37.70 (*0-608-00020-5*, 2060786) Bks Demand.

Ten Late Breakfasts. Alexandra Carlier. LC 88-21935. (Ten Menus Ser.). (Illus.). 128p. 1989. Cookery Book. 19.95 (*0-940793-24-5*) Interlink Pub.

Ten Latin Schooltexts of the Later Middle Ages: Translated Selections. Ed. by Ian Thomson & Louis Perraud. LC 90-13491. (Medieval Studies: Vol. 6). 376p. 1990. lib. bdg. 99.95 (*0-88946-124-4*) E Mellen.

Ten Laws of Lasting Love. Paul P. Pearsall. LC 92-42016. 352p. 1993. 22.00 (*0-671-76798-4*) S&S Trade.

Ten Laws of Lasting Love. Paul P. Pearsall. 336p. 1995. pap. 11.00 (*0-380-72307-7*) Avon.

***10 Lb. Penalty.** Dick Francis. 320p. 1997. 24.95 (*0-399-14302-5*) Putnam Pub Group.

Ten Lectures on Art. Edward J. Poynter. 1977. 17.95 (*0-8369-7325-9*, 8118) Ayer.

Ten Lectures on Operator Algebras. William B. Arveson. LC 84-9222. (CBMS Regional Conference Series in Mathematics: No. 55). 93p. 1984. reprint ed. pap. 22.00 (*0-8218-0705-6*, CBMS/55) Am Math.

Ten Lectures on the Interface Between Analytic Number Theory & Harmonic Analysis. Hugh L. Montgomery. LC 94-26864. (CBMS Regional Conference Mathematics Ser.: No. 84). 1994. pap. 44.00 (*0-8218-0737-4*, CBMS/84) Am Math.

Ten Lectures on the Probabilistic Method. 2nd ed. Joel H. Spencer. LC 93-40332. (CBMS-NSF Regional Conference Series in Applied Mathematics: No. 64). x, 88p. 1993. pap. 19.75 (*0-89871-325-0*) Soc Indus-Appl Math.

Ten Lectures on Theories of the Dance. Drid Williams. LC 89-27028. (Illus.). 441p. 1991. 45.00 (*0-8108-2219-9*) Scarecrow.

Ten Lectures on Wavelets. I. Daubechies. LC 92-13201. (CBMS-NSF Regional Conference Series in Applied Mathematics: No. 61). xix, 357p. 1992. pap. text ed. 43.75 (*0-89871-274-2*) Soc Indus-Appl Math.

Ten Lessons: An Introduction to Black History. 2nd ed. Mba Mbulu. Ed. by Bomani Sekou. 230p. 1993. reprint ed. pap. 12.00 (*1-883885-06-X*) ASET Pubns.

Ten Lessons in Chinese Cooking. Florence Lee & H. Lee. 1989. 18.95 (*0-930878-62-0*) Hollym Intl.

Ten Lessons in Japanese Cooking. Florence C. Lee. (Illus.). 80p. 1996. 16.95 (*1-56591-061-3*, Pub. by Hollym Bks SK) Weatherhill.

Ten Lessons in Seven Universal Rays. Mae R. Wilson-Ludlam. 75p. 1984. 11.00 (*0-86690-275-9*, W2534-014) Am Fed Astrologers.

Ten Lessons of the Energy Crisis. Morris Goran. LC 80-130511. 1980. 19.80 (*0-915250-35-7*) Environ Design.

Ten Letter-Writers. Lyn L. Irvine. LC 68-16942. (Essay Index Reprint Ser.). 1977. 19.95 (*0-8369-0560-1*) Ayer.

Ten Little Animals. Laura J. Coats. LC 89-37768. (Illus.). 32p. (J). (ps-1). 1990. lib. bdg. 14.00 incl. 5.25 hd (*0-02-719054-4*, Mac Bks Young Read) S&S Childrens.

Ten Little Ballerinas. Illus. by Joan Holub. (Jewel Sticker Stories Ser.). 24p. (Orig.). (J). (ps-2). 1996. pap. 3.95 (*0-448-41491-0*, G&D) Putnam Pub Group.

Ten Little Bunnies. Lisa Bassett. LC 92-37986. (Illus.). (J). (gr. 2 up). 1993. 4.99 (*0-517-08154-7*) Random Hse Value.

Ten Little Bunnies. Nurit Karlin. (J). (ps-3). 1994. pap. 4.95 (*0-671-88601-0*, Litl Simon S&S) S&S Childrens.

Ten Little Chicks in the Farmyard. 1983. 5.50 (*0-904494-07-1*, Brimax Bks) Borden.

Ten Little Circus Mice. Bob Beeson. (Illus.). 32p. (J). (ps-1). 1993. 11.95 (*0-8249-8616-4*, Ideals Child) Hambleton-Hill.

Ten Little Crocodiles. Colin West. LC 93-44027. (J). 1995. pap. 4.99 (*1-56402-463-6*) Candlewick Pr.

Ten Little Dinosaurs. Pattie L. Schnetzler. LC 96-15125. (Illus.). 28p. (J). 1996. 15.95 (*0-939251-74-4*) Accord CO.

***Ten Little Ducklings.** Illus. by Jenny Tulip. (Interactive Ser.). 12p. (J). (ps). Date not set. bds. 4.98 (*1-85854-590-0*) Brimax Bks.

Ten Little Ducks. Franklin Hammond. (J). 1989. 19.95 (*0-590-73338-9*) Scholastic Inc.

***Ten Little Ducks.** Franklin Hammond. (Illus.). (FRE.). (J). pap. 5.99 (*0-590-74161-6*) Scholastic Inc.

Ten Little Hippos: A Counting Book. Bobette McCarthy. LC 91-17175. (Illus.). 32p. (J). (ps-2). 1992. lib. bdg. 13.95 (*0-02-765445-1*, Bradbury S&S) S&S Childrens.

***Ten Little Kittens.** Illus. by Fiona Redmond. 20p. (J). (ps). 1997. bds. 5.98 (*1-85854-589-7*) Brimax Bks.

Ten Little Mice. Joyce Dunbar. (Illus.). 32p. (J). (ps-1). 1990. 14.00 (*0-15-200601-X*, Gulliver Bks) HarBrace.

Ten Little Mice. Joyce Dunbar. (Illus.). 32p. (J). (ps-1). 1992. pap. 22.00 (*0-15-284614-X*, Gulliver Bks) HarBrace.

Ten Little Mice. large type ed. Joyce Dunbar. LC 89-36463. (Illus.). 32p. (J). (ps-1). 1995. pap. 5.00 (*0-15-200770-9*, Gulliver Bks) HarBrace.

Ten Little Monsters. (J). 1995. 8.99 (*0-679-87414-3*) Random.

Ten Little Motor Cars. 1983. 5.50 (*0-904494-80-2*, Brimax Bks) Borden.

Ten Little Puppy Dogs. Illus. by Lisa McCue. LC 86-63577. (Chunky Bks.). 28p. (J). (ps). 1987. 3.99 (*0-394-89149-X*) Random Bks Yng Read.

Ten Little Pussy Cats. Jill Leman. (Illus.). 32p. (J). (gr. 1-4). 1996. 11.95 (*0-575-05979-6*, Pub. by V Gollancz UK) Trafalgar.

Ten Little Rabbits. Virginia Grossman. (Illus.). 32p. (J). (ps-1). 13.95 (*0-87701-552-X*) Chronicle Bks.

Ten Little Rabbits. Virginia Grossman. 40p. (J). (ps-3). 1995. pap. 6.95 (*0-8118-1057-7*) Chronicle Bks.

Ten Little Teddies. Lucy Su. LC 93-24148. 24p. (J). (ps up). 1994. pap. 3.99 (*1-56402-251-X*) Candlewick Pr.

10 Little Whitepeople. Beverly Slapin & Annie Esposito. (Illus.). (Orig.). (YA). (gr. 9 up). 1995. pap. 5.00 (*0-9625175-4-2*) Oyate.

Ten Lives of the Buddha: Siamese Temple Paintings & Jataka Tales. Elizabeth Wray et al. LC 96-9424. 156p. 1996. pap. 22.95 (*0-8348-0374-7*) Weatherhill.

Ten Lords A-Leaping. Ruth D. Edwards. LC 96-5213. 272p. 1996. 21.95 (*0-312-14430-X*) St Martin.

***Ten Lords A-Leaping.** large type ed. Ruth D. Edwards. (Ulverscroft Large Print Ser.). 432p. 1997. 27.50 (*0-7089-3718-7*) Ulverscroft.

Ten "Lost" Plays. Eugene O'Neill. 320p. 1995. pap. text ed. 8.95 (*0-486-28367-4*) Dover.

Ten Love Poems. Ed. by Robert Bly. 1981. pap. 3.50 (*0-915408-24-4*) Ally Pr.

Ten Luminous Emanations, Vol. 1. rev. ed. R. Yehuda Ashlag. 160p. 1991. write for info. (*0-318-70380-7*) Res Ctr Kabbalah.

Ten Luminous Emanations, Vol. 2. R. Yehuda Ashlag. Ed. by Philip S. Berg. 208p. 1972. 11.95 (*0-943688-09-4*); pap. 11.95 (*0-943688-25-6*) Res Ctr Kabbalah.

Ten Luminous Emanations, Vol. 3. R. Yehuda Ashlag. Ed. by Philip S. Berg. 256p. 1991. write for info. (*0-943688-90-6*); pap. write for info. (*0-943688-91-4*) Res Ctr Kabbalah.

Ten Luminous Emanations, Vol. 4. R. Yehuda Ashlag. Ed. by Philip S. Berg. 256p. 1992. write for info. (*0-924457-57-0*); pap. write for info. (*0-924457-58-9*) Res Ctr Kabbalah.

Ten Luminous Emanations I. R. Yehuda Ashlag. Ed. by Philip S. Berg. 224p. (SPA.). 1994. pap. write for info. (*0-318-70262-2*) Res Ctr Kabbalah.

Ten Luminous Emanations I. rev. ed. R. Yehuda Ashlag. Ed. by Philip S. Berg. 15p. 1993. pap. 10.95 (*0-924457-91-0*) Res Ctr Kabbalah.

Ten Luminous Emanations II. R. Yehuda Ashlag. Ed. by Philip S. Berg. 224p. (SPA.). 1994. pap. write for info. (*0-318-70263-0*) Res Ctr Kabbalah.

Ten Madrigals. Claudio Monteverdi. Ed. by Denis Stevens. 106p. 1979. pap. 22.95 (*0-19-343676-0*) OUP.

Ten Madrigals for Mixed Voices. Luca Marenzio. Ed. by Denis Arnold. 84p. 1985. 18.95 (*0-19-343675-2*) OUP.

Ten Major Causes of Death & Disease in America: How to Beat Them. expanded ed. Dorie Erickson. 200p. (Orig.). 1997. spiral bd., pap. 29.95 (*0-937242-15-2*) Scandia Pubs.

10 Man Q the Golden Robot: Adult Picture Book. Avonelle Kelsey. (Picture Book-Philosophy). (Illus.). 200p. 45.00 (*1-885351-05-4*, 10) Cheval Intl.

Ten Marks of a False Minister. Bayless Conley. 48p. 1991. pap. text ed. write for info. (*0-9638534-1-4*) Cottonwood Chr.

Ten Master Historians. Lionel M. Angus-Butterworth. LC 69-18919. (Essay Index Reprint Ser.). 1977. 18.95 (*0-8369-0000-6*) Ayer.

***Ten Memorable People of Western Electric at 555 Union Blvd, (Allentown, PA.)** George Allerton. 30p. (Orig.). 1997. pap. 1.00 (*0-945620-06-3*) Associated Specialties.

***Ten Men Dead: The Story of the 1981 Irish Hunger Strike.** David Beresford. 1997. pap. text ed. 12.00 (*0-87113-702-X*, Atlntc Mnthly) Grove-Atltic.

Ten Men of Minnesota & American Foreign Policy, 1898-1968. Barbara Stuhler. LC 73-15967. (Public Affairs Center Publications). (Illus.). xii, 263p. 1973. 8.95 (*0-87351-080-1*) Minn Hist.

Ten Men on a Ladder. Craig Macaulay. (J). (ps). 1993. lib. bdg. 14.95 (*1-55037-341-2*, Pub. by Annick CN) Firefly Bks Ltd.

Ten Men on a Ladder. Craig Macaulay. (Illus.). (J). (ps up). 1996. pap. 4.95 (*1-55037-340-4*, Pub. by Annick CN) Firefly Bks Ltd.

Ten-Meter FM for the Radio Amateur. Dave Ingram. (Illus.). 140p. (Orig.). 1980. 9.95 (*0-8306-9933-3*, 1189H) McGraw-Hill Prof.

Ten Mile Day: The Building of the Transcontinental Railroad. Mary A. Fraser. LC 92-3007. (Illus.). 40p. (J). (gr. 3-7). 1993. 15.95 (*0-8050-1902-2*, Bks Young Read) H Holt & Co.

Ten Mile Day: The Building of the Transcontinental Railroad. Mary A. Fraser. (Illus.). 40p. (J). (gr. 3-7). 1996. pap. 6.95 (*0-8050-4703-4*) H Holt & Co.

***Ten Million Steps.** Paul Reese. 226p. 1994. 12.95 (*0-915297-20-5*) Cedarwinds.

Ten Minute Addresses. Melissinos. 1994. pap. 4.00 (*0-88053-356-0*, S411) Macoy Pub.

10-Minute Card Games. William A. Moss. LC 95-22505. (Illus.). 96p. 1995. pap. 4.95 (*0-8069-3847-1*) Sterling.

Ten Minute Cure for the Common Cold: A Natural Approach. James F. Dorobiala. Ed. by Kerry A. Martinez. LC 87-18114. 160p. (Orig.). 1988. 24.95 (*0-944346-01-4*); pap. 9.95 (*0-944346-02-2*) Sun Eagle Pub.

10 Minute Detective: 25 Scene of the Crime Mystery Puzzles. Christopher Golden. LC 97-17227. 96p. 1997. per., pap. 12.00 (*0-7615-0700-0*) Prima Pub.

10-Minute Devotions for Youth Groups. J. B. Collingsworth. (Illus.). 90p. (Orig.). 1989. pap. 12.99 (*0-931529-85-9*) Group Pub.

***Ten Minute Ecologist.** Janovy. Date not set. 17.95 (*0-312-17043-2*) St Martin.

***Ten-Minute Editing Skillbuilders.** Murray Suid. (Illus.). 96p. (Orig.). (J). (gr. 3-6). 1996. pap. 11.95 (*1-878279-98-X*, MM2027) Monday Morning Bks.

Ten Minute Field Trips. Helen R. Russell. (Illus.). 176p. 1991. pap. text ed. 16.95 (*0-87355-098-6*) Natl Sci Tchrs.

***Ten-Minute Grammar Grabbers.** Murray Suid. (Illus.). 96p. (Orig.). (J). (gr. 3-6). 1996. pap. 11.95 (*1-878279-99-8*, MM2028) Monday Morning Bks.

10 Minute Guide for Paying for College. Bill Van Dusen. 144p. 1996. 10.95 (*0-02-860614-0*) Macmillan.

Ten Minute Guide Microsoft Office Bundle. Que Development Group Staff. 1993. 39.42 (*1-56761-231-8*, Alpha Ref) Macmillan Gen Ref.

10 Minute Guide to Schedule. Sherry Kinkoph. (Illus.). 192p. (Orig.). 1995. 12.99 (*0-7897-0568-0*) Que.

10 Minute Guide to Access for Windows 95. Faithe Wempen. (Illus.). 178p. (Orig.). 1995. 12.99 (*0-7897-0555-9*) Que.

***10 Minute Guide to Access 97.** Faithe Wempen. 208p. Date not set. pap. 14.99 (*0-7897-1022-6*) Mac Comp Pub.

***10 Minute GUide To Accounting.** Wayne Label. 1997. pap. text ed. 10.95 (*0-02-861407-0*) Macmillan.

10 Minute Guide to ACT! for Windows. Shelley O'Hara. (Illus.). 166p. (Orig.). 1994. 10.99 (*1-56761-539-2*, Alpha Ref) Macmillan Gen Ref.

***10 Minute GUide to ActiveX Control Pad.** Richard Irving. 192p. 1997. 14.99 (*0-7897-1070-6*) Mac Comp Pub.

10 Minute Guide to America Online. John Pivovarnick. 208p. 1997. 14.99 (*0-7897-0929-5*) Mac Comp Pub.

Ten Minute Guide to AmiPro 3. Jennifer Flynn. (Ten Minute Guides Ser.). (Illus.). 164p. (Orig.). 1992. 10.95 (*0-672-30048-6*, Alpha Ref) Macmillan Gen Ref.

10 Minute Guide to Annual Reports & Prospectuses. Eric Gelb. 144p. 1996. 10.95 (*0-02-861116-0*) Macmillan.

10 Minute Guide to Applying to Graduate School. Ellen Lichtenstein. 1997. 10.95 (*0-02-861192-6*, Arco) Macmillan Gen Ref.

Ten Minute Guide to Approach. Robert Mullen. 160p. 1994. 10.99 (*1-56761-407-8*, Alpha Ref) Macmillan Gen Ref.

10 Minute Guide to Approach for Windows 95. Shelley O'Hara. (Illus.). (Orig.). Date not set. pap. 12.99 (*0-614-10396-7*) Que.

Ten Minute Guide to Approach for Windows 95. Shelley O'Hara. 174p. 1995. 12.99 (*0-7897-0647-4*) Que.

10 Minute Guide to Beating Debt. Susan Abentrod. 144p. 1996. 10.95 (*0-02-861115-2*) Macmillan.

10 Minute Guide to Building Your Vocabulary. Ellen Lichtenstein. 1997. 10.95 (*0-02-861158-6*, Arco) Macmillan Gen Ref.

***10 Minute Guide To Business Communication.** Raymond M. Olderman. (10 Minute Guides). 1997. pap. 10.95 (*0-02-861600-6*) Macmillan.

***10 Minute Guide to Business Research on the Net.** Que Development Group Staff. 208p. 1997. 14.99 (*0-7897-1170-2*) Mac Comp Pub.

10 Minute Guide to Buying & Selling Your Home. 1996. 10.95 (*0-02-861286-8*) Macmillan.

Ten Minute Guide to CC: Mail Release 6. Sue Plumley. 192p. 1996. pap. text ed. 14.99 (*0-7897-0853-1*) Que.

***Ten Minute Guide to CC: Mail Release 7.** Sue Plumley. 208p. 1996. pap. text ed. 14.99 (*0-7897-0994-5*) Que.

10 Minute Guide to cc: Mail with cc: Mail Mobile. Kate Miller. 176p. (Orig.). 1994. 10.99 (*1-56761-587-2*, Alpha Ref) Macmillan Gen Ref.

10 Minute Guide to cc: Mail with cc: Mail Mobile. rev. ed. Kate Miller. (Illus.). 161p. (Orig.). 1995. 9.99 (*0-7897-0458-7*, Alpha Ref) Macmillan Gen Ref.

***10 Minute Guide to CC: Mail 8.** Elaine Marmel. 1997. 14.99 (*0-7897-1311-X*) Que.

10 Minute Guide to cc: Mail with cc: Mobile. Kate Miller. (Illus.). (Orig.). 1995. pap. text ed. 10.99 (*0-614-07357-X*, Alpha Ref) Macmillan Gen Ref.

Ten Minute Guide to CompuServe. Phillip Reed. 168p. 1994. 10.99 (*1-56761-427-2*, Alpha Ref) Macmillan Gen Ref.

***10 Minute Guide to Estate Planning.** Steven Maple. 1997. pap. text ed. 10.95 (*0-02-861749-5*) Macmillan.

Ten Minute Guide to Excel for Windows 95. Alpha Research Division Staff. (Illus.). 178p. 1995. 12.99 (*0-7897-0373-4*, Alpha Ref) Macmillan Gen Ref.

***10 Minute Guide to Excel 97.** Jennifer Fulton. 224p. 1996. 14.99 (*0-7897-1020-X*) Mac Comp Pub.

Ten Minute Guide to Excel 5. Joe Kraynak. 166p. 1993. 12.99 (*1-56761-321-7*, Alpha Ref) Macmillan Gen Ref.

Ten Minute Guide to Freelance for Windows 2. J. Christen. (Ten Minute Guides Ser.). (Illus.). 160p. (Orig.). 1993. 10.95 (*1-56761-182-6*, Alpha Ref) Macmillan Gen Ref.

10 Minute Guide to Freelance Graphics for Windows 95. Que Development Group Staff. (Illus.). 180p. (Orig.). 1995. 12.99 (*0-7897-0554-0*) Que.

10 Minute Guide to Getting into College. O'Neal Turner. 144p. 1996. 10.95 (*0-02-860616-7*) Macmillan.

10 Minute Guide to H. T. M. L. Tim Evans. (Illus.). 208p. (Orig.). 1995. 14.99 (*0-7897-0541-9*) Que.

***10 Minute Guide to Household Budgeting.** Tracy Loungo. 1997. 10.95 (*0-02-861442-9*) Macmillan.

***Ten Minute Guide to HTML.** 2nd ed. Tim Evans. 240p. 1996. pap. text ed. 14.99 (*0-7897-0965-1*) Que.

***10 Minute Guide to HTML Style Sheets.** Que Development Group Staff. 192p. 1997. 14.99 (*0-7897-1034-X*) Mac Comp Pub.

***10 Minute Guide to InterNotes Web Navigator.** Jane Calabria. 208p. 1996. 14.99 (*0-7897-0941-4*) Mac Comp Pub.

10 Minute Guide to Intranets. MBR Consultants, Inc. Staff. 208p. 1996. 14.99 (*0-7897-0855-8*) Mac Comp Pub.

***10 Minute Guide to Leadership.** Andrew J. Dubrin. (10 Minute Guides). 1997. pap. 10.95 (*0-02-861406-2*) Macmillan.

10 Minute Guide to Lotus Notes: New Edition. Kate Miller. (Illus.). 193p. (Orig.). 1996. 14.99 (*1-56761-582-1*, Alpha Ref) Macmillan Gen Ref.

Ten Minute Guide to Lotus Notes for Windows. Kate M. Barnes. (Ten Minute Guides Ser.). (Illus.). 164p. (Orig.). 1993. 10.95 (*1-56761-176-1*, Alpha Ref) Macmillan Gen Ref.

***10 Minute Guide to Lotus Notes 4.5.** Sue Plumley. 208p. 1997. 14.99 (*0-7897-0945-7*) Mac Comp Pub.

***10 Minute Guide to Lotus Notes Mail 4.5.** Jane Calabria. 1997. pap. 14.99 (*0-7897-0974-0*) Que.

10 Minute Guide to Lotus Organizer. Jennifer Fulton. (Illus.). 138p. (Orig.). 1995. 10.99 (*1-56761-580-5*, Alpha Ref) Macmillan Gen Ref.

10 Minute Guide to Lotus Organizer for Windows 95. Jennifer Fulton. (Illus.). 208p. (Orig.). 1996. 14.99 (*0-7897-0560-5*) Que.

Ten Minute Guide to Lotus 1-2-3 for Windows. Peter Aitken. (Ten Minute Guides Ser.). (Illus.). 166p. 1993. 10.95 (*1-56761-034-X*, Alpha Ref) Macmillan Gen Ref.

Ten Minute Guide to Memory Management. 2nd ed. Jennifer Flynn. (Ten Minute Guides Ser.). (Illus.). 164p. 1993. 10.95 (*1-56761-235-0*, Alpha Ref) Macmillan Gen Ref.

Ten Minute Guide to Microsoft Access. 2nd ed. Carl Townsend. 160p. (Orig.). 1994. 12.99 (*1-56761-450-7*, Alpha Ref) Macmillan Gen Ref.

10 Minute Guide to Microsoft Exchange. Gabrielle Nemes. (Illus.). 208p. (Orig.). 1996. 14.99 (*0-7897-0677-6*) Que.

***10 Minute Guide to Microsoft Exchange 5.0.** Scott Warner. 240p. 1997. 14.99 (*0-7897-1310-1*) Que.

Ten Minute Guide to Microsoft Exchange 4.0. Gabrielle Nemes. 208p. 1996. 14.99 (*0-7897-0897-3*) Que.

10 Minute Guide to Microsoft Internet Explorer. J. Michael Roach. (Illus.). 191p. (Orig.). 1995. 14.99 (*0-7897-0628-8*) Que.

***10 Minute Guide to Microsoft Internet Explorer.** Matthew Brown. 208p. 1997. 14.99 (*0-7897-1081-1*) Mac Comp Pub.

Ten Minute Guide to Microsoft Mail. Jennifer Flynn. 147p. 1992. 10.95 (*1-56761-128-1*, Alpha Ref) Macmillan Gen Ref.

10 Minute Guide to Microsoft Mail for Windows 95. 2nd ed. Que Development Group Staff. (Illus.). 192p. (Orig.). 1995. pap. 12.99 (*0-7897-0553-2*) Que.

***10 Minute Guide to Motivating People.** Marshall J. Cook. 1997. 10.95 (*0-02-861738-X*) Macmillan.

Ten Minute Guide to MS-DOS 6.2. Jennifer Fulton. 166p. 1993. 10.95 (*1-56761-416-7*, Alpha Ref) Macmillan Gen Ref.

10 Minute Guide to Mutual Funds. Werner Renberg. (Best-Selling Ser.). 144p. 1996. pap. 10.95 (*0-02-861284-1*) Macmillan.

***10 Minute Guide to Negotiating.** Neil Shister. 1997. pap. text ed. 10.95 (*0-02-861615-4*) Macmillan.

***10 Minute Guide to Netscape Communicator.** Sherry Kinkoph & Galen Grimes. 208p. 1997. 14.99 (*0-7897-0984-8*) Mac Comp Pub.

10 Minute Guide to Netscape for Windows. Galen Grimes. (Illus.). 146p. (Orig.). 1995. 14.99 (*0-7897-0570-2*) Que.

10 Minute Guide to Netscape for the Mac. Noel Estabrook. (Illus.). 159p. (Orig.). 1995. 14.99 (*0-7897-0569-9*) Que.

10 Minute Guide to Netscape for X-Windows. Tim Evans. (Illus.). 180p. (Orig.). 1995. 14.99 (*0-7897-0571-0*) Que.

10 Minute Guide to Novell Groupwise. Kate Miller. (Illus.). 176p. (Orig.). 1994. pap. 12.99 (*1-56761-474-4*) Que.

Ten Minute Guide to Novell Groupwise. 2nd ed. Que Development Group Staff. 208p. 1996. 14.99 (*0-7897-0726-8*) Que.

Ten Minute Guide to 1-2-3 for Windows 95. Peter Aitken. (Illus.). 208p. (Orig.). 1997. 14.99 (*0-7897-0372-6*, Alpha Ref) Macmillan Gen Ref.

10 Minute Guide to OS-2 Warp. Jennifer Fulton. (Illus.). 176p. (Orig.). 1995. 12.99 (*1-56761-650-X*, Alpha Ref) Macmillan Gen Ref.

***10 Minute Guide to Outlook 97.** Sue Plumley. 192p. 1996. 14.99 (*0-7897-1018-8*) Mac Comp Pub.

10 Minute Guide to Paying for Graduate School. Ellen Lichtenstein. 1997. 10.95 (*0-02-861165-9*, Arco) Macmillan Gen Ref.

Ten Minute Guide to PC Computing. Joe Kraynak. 162p. 1994. 10.99 (*1-56761-512-0*, Alpha Ref) Macmillan Gen Ref.

***10 Minute Guide to Personal Computers.** Sue Plumley. 1997. 14.99 (*0-7897-1269-5*) Que.

10 Minute Guide to Personal Finance for Newlyweds. Stewart H. Welch, 3rd. 144p. 1996. 10.95 (*0-02-861118-7*) Macmillan.

***10 Minute Guide to Planning.** Edwin E. Bobrow. 1997. pap. text ed. 10.95 (*0-02-861818-1*) Macmillan.

Ten Minute Guide to Powerpoint: New Edition. Joe Kraynak. 1994. 12.99 (*1-56761-423-X*, Alpha Ref) Macmillan Gen Ref.

10 Minute Guide to PowerPoint for Windows 95. Joe Kraynak & Faithe Wempen. (Illus.). 192p. (Orig.). 1995. 12.99 (*0-7897-0549-4*) Que.

***10 Minute Guide to PowerPoint 97.** Faithe Wempen. 208p. 1996. 14.99 (*0-7897-1021-8*) Mac Comp Pub.

Ten Minute Guide to Quattro Pro. Joe Kraynak. (Ten Minute Guides Ser.). (Illus.). 160p. (Orig.). 1993. pap. 10.95 (*1-56761-144-3*, Alpha Ref) Macmillan Gen Ref.

Ten Minute Guide to Quattro Pro for Windows, Release 6.0. Joe Kraynak. 164p. 1994. 10.99 (*1-56761-536-8*, Alpha Ref) Macmillan Gen Ref.

10 Minute Guide to Retirement for Women. Kerry Hannon. 144p. 1996. 10.95 (*0-02-861179-9*) Macmillan.

10 Minute Guide to Retirement Planning under 40. Mark Battersby. 1997. 10.95 (*0-02-861180-2*) Macmillan.

10 Minute Guide to Retirement Planning over 40. Mark Battersby. 1997. 10.95 (*0-02-861181-0*) Macmillan.

Ten Minute Guide to SAP R/3. Deanna Wright. 192p. 1997. 14.99 (*0-7897-0898-1*) Que.

10 Minute Guide to Smart Borrowing. Barbara Hetzer. 1996. 10.95 (*0-02-861178-0*) Macmillan.

***10 Minute Guide to Teams & Teamwork.** John Woods. 1997. 10.95 (*0-02-861739-8*) Macmillan.

Ten Minute Guide to the Internet. Peter Kent. 162p. 1994. 9.99 (*1-56761-428-0*, Alpha Ref) Macmillan Gen Ref.

Ten Minute Guide to the Internet & the Web. 2nd ed. Galen Grimes. 208p. 1996. pap. text ed. 14.99 (*0-7897-0909-0*) Que.

***10 Minute Guide to the Internet & World Wide Web.** 3rd ed. Galen Grimes. 1997. 14.99 (*0-7897-1405-1*) Que.

10 Minute Guide to the Internet with Windows 95. Galen Grimes. (Illus.). 188p. (Orig.). 1995. 14.99 (*0-7897-0663-6*) Que.

***10 Minute Guide to Time Management.** John Woods. 1997. pap. text ed. 10.95 (*0-02-862045-3*) Macmillan.

***Ten Minute Guide to Travel Planning on the Net.** Que Development Group, Staff. 208p. 1997. 14.99 (*0-7897-1218-0*) Que.

10 Minute Guide to Upping Your SAT Scores. Lisa Bartl. 144p. 1996. 10.95 (*0-02-860617-5*) Macmillan.

10 Minute Guide to Windows NT Workstation 4.0. Sue Plumley. 208p. 1996. 14.99 (*0-7897-0870-1*) Mac Comp Pub.

Ten Minute Guide to Windows NT 3.51 Workstation. Sue Plumley. 196p. 1996. pap. 14.99 (*0-7897-0746-2*) Que.

10 Minute Guide to Windows 95. Trudi Reisner. (Illus.). 180p. (Orig.). 1995. 12.99 (*1-56761-515-5*, Alpha Ref) Macmillan Gen Ref.

***10 Minute Guide to Windows 95.** 2nd ed. Sue Plumley. 208p. 1998. 14.99 (*0-7897-1160-5*) Que.

10 Minute Guide to WinFax Pro. 2nd ed. Joe Kraynak. (Illus.). 192p. (Orig.). 1995. pap. 12.99 (*0-7897-0376-9*) Que.

Ten Minute Guide to WinFaxPro. 2nd ed. Joe Kraynak. 160p. 10.99 (*1-56761-613-5*, Alpha Ref) Macmillan Gen Ref.

Ten-Minute Guide to Word for Windows 2. Sams Development Group Staff. (Ten Minute Guide Ser.). (Illus.). 160p. (Orig.). 1991. 10.95 (*0-672-30044-3*) Sams.

Ten Minute Guide to Word for Windows 6. 2nd ed. Peter Aitken. 148p. 1993. 12.99 (*1-56761-345-4*, Alpha Ref) Macmillan Gen Ref.

Ten Minute Guide to Word for Windows 95. Peter Aitken. (Illus.). 175p. (Orig.). 1995. 12.99 (*0-7897-0379-3*, Alpha Ref) Macmillan Gen Ref.

***10 Minute Guide to Word 97.** Peter Aitken. 208p. 1996. 14.99 (*0-7897-1019-6*) Mac Comp Pub.

10 Minute Guide to Word Pro. Jennifer Fulton. (Illus.). 190p. (Orig.). 1995. 10.99 (*1-56761-310-1*) Que.

10 Minute Guide to WordPerfect for Windows 95. Que Development Group Staff. (Illus.). 208p. (Orig.). 1996. 14.99 (*0-7897-0454-4*) Que.

10 Minute Guide to WordPerfect 6.1 for Windows. Jennifer Fulton. (Illus.). 160p. (Orig.). 1994. 10.99 (*1-56761-541-4*, Alpha Ref) Macmillan Gen Ref.

Ten Minute Guide to WordPerfect 5.1. Katherine Murray & Doug Sabotin. 160p. 1991. 10.95 (*0-672-22808-4*, Alpha Ref) Macmillan Gen Ref.

Ten Minute Guide to WordPerfect 6. Joe Kraynak. (Ten Minute Guides Ser.). (Illus.). 147p. (Orig.). 1993. 10.95 (*1-56761-021-8*, Alpha Ref) Macmillan Gen Ref.

10 Minute Guide to WordPro 96 Edition for Windows 95. Jennifer Fulton. (Illus.). 182p. (Orig.). 1995. 12.99 (*0-7897-0552-4*) Que.

10 Minute Guide to 1-2-3 for Windows, Release 5.0. Peter Aitken. 166p. 1994. 10.99 (*1-56761-484-1*, Alpha Ref) Macmillan Gen Ref.

10 Minute Guide to 401(K) Plans. Paul Katzeff. 144p. 1996. 10.95 (*0-02-861117-9*) Macmillan.

***Ten-Minute Marketing.** Patricia Brenna. 131p. 1997. pap. 48.00 (*1-885750-03-X*, MM97) Visions Communs.

***10 Minute Math Mind-Stretchers: Quick Problems & Activities to Help Reinforce Essential Math Skills.** Professional Books Staff. (J). 1997. pap. text ed. 14.95 (*0-590-86563-3*) Scholastic Inc.

***Ten-Minute Mysteries Basic Set, 10 bks.** (J). 1994. teacher ed., pap. 49.95 (*0-7854-0839-8*, 40750) Am Guidance.

***Ten-Minute Mysteries Classroom Library, 30 bks.** (J). 1994. teacher ed., pap. 79.95 (*0-7854-0838-X*, 40781) Am Guidance.

***Ten-Minute Mysteries Readalongs Basic Set, 10 bks.** 1994. teacher ed., pap. 129.95 incl. audio (*0-7854-0600-X*, 40782) Am Guidance.

***Ten-Minute Real World Math.** Scott McMorrow. (Ten-Minute Ser.). (Illus.). 96p. (Orig.). (J). (gr. 3-6). 1997. pap. 11.95 (*1-57612-021-X*, MM2041) Monday Morning Bks.

***Ten-Minute Real World Reading.** Murray Suid. (Ten-Minute Ser.). (Illus.). 96p. (Orig.). (J). (gr. 3-6). 1997. pap. 11.95 (*1-57612-022-8*, MM2042) Monday Morning Bks.

***Ten-Minute Real World Science.** Murray Suid & Scott McMorrow. (Ten-Minute Ser.). (Illus.). 96p. (Orig.). (J). (gr. 3-6). 1997. pap. 11.95 (*1-57612-020-1*, MM2040) Monday Morning Bks.

***Ten-Minute Real World Writing.** Murray Suid. (Ten-Minute Ser.). (Illus.). 96p. (Orig.). (J). (gr. 3-6). 1996. pap. 11.95 (*1-57612-000-7*, MM2029) Monday Morning Bks.

Ten Minute Romances. Abigail Sommers et al. 157p. 1995. spiral bd. 6.95 (*1-888038-05-5*) Rubenesque.

***10-Minute Shopper.** Martin Sloane. 1995. pap. 4.99 (*0-425-14575-1*) Berkley Pub.

Ten Minute Stories. Algernon Blackwood. LC 72-103495. (Short Story Index Reprint Ser.). 1977. 20.95 (*0-8369-3237-4*) Ayer.

Ten Minute Team: Ten Steps to Building High Performing Teams. 2nd ed. Thomas Isgar. 120p. 1993. pap. text ed. 14.95 (*0-9623464-1-1*) Seluera Pr.

Ten-Minute Terrors: A Collection of Scary Stories. Anne B. Fowler. LC 95-9468. 128p. (J). (gr. 5-7). 1995. pap. 4.95 (*1-56565-321-1*) Lowell Hse.

Ten-Minute Theatre. David S. Raine. 57p. 1994. pap. 5.25 (*0-87129-431-1*, T17) Dramatic Pub.

Ten-Minute Thinking Tie-Ins. Murray Suid & Wanda Lincoln. (Illus.). 128p. (J). (gr. 2-6). 1992. pap. 11.95 (*1-878279-39-4*, MM 1956) Monday Morning Bks.

***Ten-Minute Thrillers Basic Set, 10 bks.** (YA). (gr. 6-12). 1995. pap. 49.95 (*0-7854-1060-0*, 40792) Am Guidance.

***Ten-Minute Thrillers Classroom Library, 10 bks.** (YA). (gr. 6-12). 1995. pap. 79.95 (*0-7854-1059-7*, 40793) Am Guidance.

***Ten-Minute Thrillers Readalong Basic Set, 10 bks. & cassettes.** 32p. 1995. pap. 129.95 incl. audio (*0-7854-1061-9*, 40794) Am Guidance.

Ten-Minute Vegetarian Cook Book. Phyllis Avery. (Illus.). 144p. (Orig.). 1992. pap. 11.95 (*1-880598-74-4*) P Avery.

Ten Minute Whole Language Warm-Ups. Murray Suid & Wanda Lincoln. (Illus.). 128p. (J). (gr. 2-6). 1992. teacher ed., pap. 11.95 (*1-878279-38-6*, MM 1955) Monday Morning Bks.

Ten Minutes Ahead of the Rest of the World. 2nd rev. ed. Sue D. Lowe et al. LC 81-81534. (Illus.). 308p. 1982. reprint ed. 30.00 (*0-9607742-0-3*) Milford Hist Soc.

An Asterisk (*) at the beginning of an entry indicates that the title is appearing in BIP for the first time.

***Ten Minutes Till Bed.** Peggy Rathmann. (J). Date not set. 15.95 (0-399-23103-X) Putnam Pub Group.

Ten Minutes till Christmas. Roger Clark. 21p. 1996. pap. 3.00 (0-87129-706-X, TA4) Dramatic Pub.

10 Minutes to Massive Arms. Manfred Hoeberi et al. Ed. by Jo Ellen Krumm. (Illus.). 84p. (Orig.). 1994. pap. 9.95 (1-885096-03-8) Little-Wolff.

Ten Minutes to MS-DOS Word Perfect, WordStar, Lotus BASIC. Clifford W. Lazar. (Illus.). 210p. 1989. teacher ed. 24.95 (0-685-30761-1, TM01); pap. 24.95 (0-685-30759-X, TM01); pap. text ed. 24.95 (0-685-30760-3, TM01); lib. bdg. 29.95 (0-9624618-0-6, TM01) Systems Express.

Ten Minutes to MS-DOS, WordPerfect, WordStar, Lotus, BASIC. Clifford W. Lazar. (Illus.). 210p. 1989. pap. 24. 95 (0-685-29337-8, TM01); pap. text ed. 24.95 (0-685-29338-6, TM01); lib. bdg. 24.95 (0-685-29336-X, TM01) Systems Express.

Ten Miracles of Jesus Workbook. Jamie Buckingham. 95p. (Orig.). 1988. student ed. 6.95 (0-941478-96-3) Paraclete MA.

***Ten Modern Arab Poets.** Desmond O'Grady. 72p. 9200. pap. 11.95 (1-873790-04-X) Dufour.

Ten Modern Masters: An Anthology of the Short Story. 3rd ed. Robert G. Davis. 583p. (C). 1972. pap. text ed. 20.00 (0-15-590281-4); pap. text ed. 2.00 (0-15-590282-2) HB Coll Pubs.

Ten Modern Poets. Rica Brenner. LC 68-22091. (Essay Index Reprint Ser.). 1977. 20.95 (0-8369-0249-1) Ayer.

Ten Monsters in Bed. Rozanne L. Williams. (Emergent Reader Bks.). 16p. (Orig.). (J). (gr. k-2). 1995. 2.49 (0-916119-90-4) Creat Teach Pr.

Ten Monsters in Bed. Rozanne L. Williams. (Emergent Reader Big Bks.). (Illus.). 16p. (Orig.). (J). (gr. k-2). 1996. pap. 11.98 (1-57471-109-1) Creat Teach Pr.

***Ten-Month Year.** Laura Hume. LC 96-90829. (Orig.). 1997. pap. 14.95 (0-533-12179-5) Vantage.

Ten Months among the Tents of the Tuski. William H. Hooper. LC 74-5847. (Illus.). reprint ed. 69.50 (0-404-11652-3) AMS Pr.

Ten More Aesthetic Realism Essays. Eli Siegel. 37p. 1979. pap. 3.50 (0-911492-23-2) Aesthetic Realism.

***Ten More Tales of the Great Lakes.** Skip Gillham. (Great Lakes Marine History Ser.). (Illus.). 72p. pap. 10.95 (0-919549-18-7, Pub. by Riverbank Trade CN) Partners Pubs Grp.

***Ten Most Troublesome Teenage Problems: And How to Solve Them.** Lawrence Bauman & Robert Riche. LC 96-51713. 240p. 1997. 19.95 (1-55972-396-3, Birch Ln Pr) Carol Pub Group.

Ten Most Wanted List: Ten Things You Must Do to Get the Job You Really Want. Jerry Roemisch. 33p. (Orig.). 1993. pap. 4.95 (1-883439-00-0) Jericho Pr.

Ten Most Wanted Men. Paul H. Dunn. 1966. 10.95 (0-88494-150-7) Bookcraft Inc.

Ten Myths about Higher Taxes. Alvin Rabushka. LC 93-30446. (Essays in Public Policy Ser.: No. 43). 1993. pap. 5.00 (0-8179-5482-1) Hoover Inst Pr.

Ten Myths That Damage a Woman's Confidence. Patricia Holt. 272p. 1995. pap. 9.99 (1-55661-379-2) Bethany Hse.

Ten Natural Laws of Successful Time & Life Management: Proven Strategies for Increased Productivity & Inner Peace. Hyrum W. Smith. LC 92-51037. 240p. 1994. 21. 95 (0-446-51741-0) Warner Bks.

Ten Natural Laws of Successful Time & Life Management: Proven Strategies for Increased Productivity & Inner Peace. Hyrum W. Smith. LC 92-51037. 240p. 1995. pap. 12.99 (0-446-67064-2) Warner Bks.

Ten Nequdoth of the Torah. Butin. 1969. 15.00 (0-87068-043-9) Ktav.

Ten New England Leaders. Williston Walker. LC 76-83445. (Religion in America, Ser.). 1974. reprint ed. 30.95 (0-405-00278-5) Ayer.

Ten Nights in a Barroom & What I Saw There. Timothy S. Arthur. (Works of Timothy Shay Arthur). 1989. reprint ed. lib. bdg. 79.00 (0-7812-1802-0) Rprt Serv.

Ten, Nine, Eight. Molly Bang. LC 81-20106. (Illus.). 24p. (J). (ps-1). 1983. 16.00 (0-688-00906-9); lib. bdg. 15.93 (0-688-00907-7) Greenwillow.

Ten, Nine, Eight. Molly Bang. (J). 1989. 19.95 (0-590-73313-3) Scholastic Inc.

Ten, Nine, Eight. Molly Bang. LC 81-20106. (Illus.). 24p. (J). (ps up). 1991. reprint ed. pap. 4.95 (0-688-10480-0, Mulberry) Morrow.

Ten, Nine, Eight (Bang) Molly Band. (J). 1996. pap. 6.95 (0-688-14901-4, Tupelo Bks) Greenwillow.

Ten Nocturnes for Piano. M. Valenti. 32p. 1986. pap. 9.95 (0-7935-4080-1) H Leonard.

Ten North-East Poets. Ed. by Neil Astley. 104p. 8000. pap. 12.95 (0-906427-13-4, Pub. by Bloodaxe Bks UK) Dufour.

Ten North Frederick. John O'Hara. 408p. 1985. pap. 4.50 (0-88184-173-0) Carroll & Graf.

Ten Northeast Poets: An Anthology. Ed. by L. W. Wheeler. 184p. 1985. text ed. 22.95 (0-08-032430-4, Pub. by Aberdeen U Pr); pap. text ed. 12.00 (0-08-032431-2, Pub. by Aberdeen U Pr) Macmillan.

Ten Novels & Their Authors. W. Somerset Maugham. 301p. 1978. 6.95 (0-330-25497-9) Academy Chi Pubs.

Ten O'Clock Club. Carol B. York. 128p. (J). (gr. 4-7). 1985. 2.95 (0-590-33475-1) Scholastic Inc.

Ten O'Clock Scholar. Lewis Banci & Milburn Smith. 1969. pap. 5.25 (0-8222-1117-3) Dramatists Play.

Ten on a Train. John O'Leary. (J). 1995. pap. 5.99 (0-14-037527-9, Viking) Viking Penguin.

Ten on Ten. Atwan. 1992. teacher ed., pap. text ed. 5.00 (0-312-06844-1) St Martin.

***Ten on Ten, Vol. 1.** Atwan. Date not set. pap. text ed. write for info. (0-312-10337-9) St Martin.

Ten on Ten: Major Essayists on Recurring Themes. Robert Atwan. LC 91-61137. 528p. (Orig.). (C). 1992. pap. text ed. 23.50 (0-312-06236-2) St Martin.

***Ten Ounce Siesta.** Norman Partridge. 1998. mass mkt. write for info. (0-425-16143-9, Prime Crime) Berkley Pub.

Ten Out of Bed. Penny Dale. LC 92-46116. (Illus.). 32p. (J). (ps up). 1994. 14.95 (1-56402-322-2) Candlewick Pr.

Ten Out of Bed. Penny Dale. LC 92-46116. (Illus.). 32p. (J). 1996. reprint ed. pap. 5.99 (1-56402-834-8) Candlewick Pr.

***Ten Oxherding Poems.** John Gohorry. (Illus.). 28p. (Orig.). 1996. pap. 25.00 (0-930126-52-1) Typographeum.

Ten Papers in Analysis. M. S. Budjanu et al. LC 73-16013. (Translations Ser.: Series 2, Vol. 102). 252p. 1973. 58.00 (0-8218-3052-X, TRANS2/102) Am Math.

Ten Papers in Analysis. Ed. by V. Zmorovich et al. LC 86-20550. (Translations Ser.: Series 2, Vol. 131). 120p. 1986. text ed. 57.00 (0-8218-3106-2, TRANS2/131) Am Math.

Ten Papers on Algebra & Functional Analysis. N. D. Filippov et al. LC 51-5559. (Translations Ser.: Series 2, Vol. 96). 254p. 1970. 44.00 (0-8218-1796-5, TRANS2/96) Am Math.

Ten Papers on Analysis. B. F. Bylov et al. LC 51-5559. (Translations Ser.: Series 2, Vol. 74). 260p. 1968. 49.00 (0-8218-1774-4, TRANS2/74) Am Math.

Ten Papers on Complex Analysis. Incl. Elliptic Boundary Value Problems. LC 83-25744. 268p. 1984. 102.00 (0-8218-3082-1, TRANS2-123); Vol. 124. Fifteen Papers on Functional Analysis. LC 83-25744. 183p. 1984. 82.00 (0-8218-3085-6, TRANS2-124); LC 83-25744. (Translations Ser.: No. 2-122). 226p. 1984. Set text ed. 74.00 (0-8218-3081-3, TRANS 2-122) Am Math.

Ten Papers on Differential Equations & Functional Analysis. A. D. Aleksandrov et al. LC 51-5559. (Translations Ser.: Series 2, Vol. 68). 264p. 1968. 49.00 (0-8218-1768-X, TRANS2/68) Am Math.

Ten Papers on Functional Analysis & Measure Theory. L. M. Abramov et al. LC 51-5559. (Translations Ser.: Series 2, Vol. 49). 268p. 1966. 35.00 (0-8218-1749-3, TRANS2/49) Am Math.

Ten Papers on Topology. P. S. Aleksandrov et al. LC 51-5559. (Translations Ser.: Series 2, Vol. 30). 358p. 1963. 42.00 (0-8218-1730-2, TRANS2/30) Am Math.

Ten Papers Translated from the Russian. M. B. Abalovich et al. LC 89-371. (Translations Ser.: Series 2, Vol. 142). 121p. 1989. 62.00 (0-8218-3122-4, TRANS2/142) Am Math.

Ten Parables of Jesus Workbook. Jamie Buckingham. 109p. (Orig.). 1988. student ed. 6.95 (0-941478-97-1) Paraclete MA.

10 Patterns for Carving Whales. Brian Gilmore. LC 95-22367. (Illus.). 48p. (Orig.). 1995. pap. 12.95 (0-88740-855-9) Schiffer.

***Ten Peaches Things about Georgia.** Linda Crockem. 12p. (J). Date not set. 14.99 (1-887637-06-0) First Bk Prodns.

10% Low-Fat Cookbook: 200 Tantalizing Recipes with No More Than 10% Calories from Fat. Miriam Jacobs. 176p. 1997. 17.95 (0-88266-855-2); pap. 12.95 (0-88266-944-3) Storey Comm Inc.

Ten Percent Revue. Tom W. Weinberg. 39p. 1989. pap. text ed. 5.95 (0-685-28074-8) New Mus Theater Lib.

***Ten Percent Solution.** Charles Kipps. Date not set. write for info. (0-688-08647-0) Morrow.

Ten Percent Solution: Your Key to Financial Security. Ed Blitz. 180p. 1988. pap. 12.95 (0-8306-3023-6, 30023, Liberty Hse) TAB Bks.

Ten Percent Solution for a Healthy Life: How to Eliminate Virtually All Risk of Heart Disease & Cancer. Raymond Kurzweil. LC 92-19993. 320p. 1993. 20.00 (0-517-59106-5, Crown) Crown Pub Group.

Ten Percent Solution for a Healthy Life: How to Reduce Fat in Your Diet... Raymond Kurzweil. 1995. pap. 13. 00 (0-517-88301-5) Crown Pub Group.

Ten Personal Studies. Wilfrid P. Ward. LC 73-107742. (Essay Index Reprint Ser.). 1977. 23.95 (0-8369-1584-4) Ayer.

Ten Philosophical Mistakes. Mortimer J. Adler. 200p. 1987. pap. 7.95 (0-02-064120-6) Macmillan.

Ten Physical Applications of Spectral Zeta Functions, Vol. XIV. Emilio Elizalde. Ed. by W. Beiglbock et al. LC 95-37505. (Lecture Notes in Physics Ser.: No. 35). 228p. 1995. 49.95 (3-540-60230-5) Spr-Verlag.

Ten Pieces Bassoon & Piano: Opus 37 No. 5. L. Moyse. 32p. 1991. pap. 9.95 (0-7935-0640-9, 50481111) H Leonard.

Ten Pieces Clarinet & Piano: Opus 37 No. 3. L. Moyse. 32p. 1991. pap. 8.95 (0-7935-0641-7, 50481110) H Leonard.

Ten Pieces for Five Viols. Bela Bartok. Ed. by David Goldstein. (Contemporary Consort Ser.: No. 21). 32p. 1992. pap. text ed. 12.00 (1-56571-066-5, CC021) PRB Prods.

Ten Pieces for Flute & Piano. L. Moyse. 32p. 1991. pap. 8.95 (0-7935-0643-3, 50481279) H Leonard.

Ten Pieces for Horn & Piano: Opus 37 No. 4. L. Moyse. 24p. 1991. pap. 8.95 (0-7935-0642-5, 50481109) H Leonard.

Ten Pieces for Oboe & Piano: Opus 37 No. 3. L. Moyse. 24p. 1991. pap. 8.95 (0-7935-0639-5, 50481112) H Leonard.

***Ten Pillars of Buddhism.** Sangharakshita. 98p. 1997. pap. 11.95 (1-899579-21-4) Windhorse Pubns.

Ten Pillars of Buddhism. 3rd ed. Sangharakshita. 128p. 1996. pap. 8.95 (0-904766-39-X) Windhorse Pubns.

Ten Pink Piglets: Garth Pig's Wall Song. Mary Rayner. (Illus.). 24p. (J). (ps-1). 1994. 5.99 (0-685-70795-4) Dutton Child Bks.

Ten Plagues of Egypt. Shoshana Lepon. Ed. by Neva Goldstein-Alpern. (Illus.). 32p. (J). (gr. k-4). 1988. 11.95 (0-910818-77-0); pap. 8.95 (0-910818-76-2) Judaica Pr.

Ten Plays. Alfred De Musset. Tr. by R. Pellissier & M. Dey from FRE. LC 87-7426. 506p. 1987. reprint ed. lib. bdg. 49.50 (0-86527-358-8) Fertig.

Ten Plays of Euripides. Incl. Alcestis. Euripides. Ed. by Moses Hadas & John H. McLean. 1984. (0-318-51006-5); Andromache. Euripides. Ed. by Moses Hadas & John H. McLean. 1984. (0-318-51007-3); Bacchants. Euripides. Ed. by Moses Hadas & John H. McLean. 1984. (0-318-51008-1); Electra. (0-318-51009-X); Hippolytus. Euripides. Ed. by Moses Hadas & John H. McLean. 1984. (0-318-51010-3); Ion. (0-318-51011-1); Iphigenia among the Taurians. Euripides. Ed. by Moses Hadas & John H. McLean. 1984. (0-318-51012-X); Iphigenia at Aulis. Euripides. Ed. by Moses Hadas & John H. McLean. 1984. (0-318-51013-8); Medea. (0-318-51014-6); Trojan Women. Euripides. Ed. by Moses Hadas & John H. McLean. 1984. (0-318-51015-4); 384p. (Orig.). (gr. 11-12). 1984. mass mkt. 6.50 (0-553-21363-6, Bantam Classics) Bantam.

Ten Plus: Women with Long-Term Sobriety Talk About Life, Love, Family, Work, & Money. Sylvia Cary. LC 92-26570. 276p. 1993. 22.95 (1-56565-004-2) Lowell Hse.

Ten Plus One. Ed McBain. 272p. 1982. pap. 4.50 (0-451-16367-2, Sig) NAL-Dutton.

Ten Plus One. Ed McBain. 1989. pap. 2.95 (0-451-14598-4) NAL-Dutton.

Ten Plus Ten: Contemporary Soviet & American Painters. John E. Bowlt. 1989. 39.95 (0-8109-1668-1) Abrams.

Ten Plus Ten: Contemporary Soviet & American Painters. Genrikh P. Popov et al. LC 89-80354. (Illus.). 176p. (Orig.). (ENG & RUS.). 1989. pap. write for info. (0-929865-03-0) Mod Art Mus Ft Worth.

Ten Poems. Nessie Dunsmuir. (C). 1990. 35.00 (0-906887-27-5, Pub. by Greville Pr UK) St Mut.

Ten Poems & Lyrics by Mao Tse-tung. Mao Tse-tung. Tr. by Wang Hui-Ming. LC 74-21248. 72p. 1975. 15.00 (0-87023-178-2); pap. 9.95 (0-87023-182-0) U of Mass Pr.

Ten Poems of Issa. Robert Bly. (Illus.). 1992. pap. 6.00 (0-912449-41-1) Floating Island.

***Ten Point: Deer Camp in the Mississippi Delta.** Alan Huffman. LC 97-1236. (Illus.). 144p. 1997. 35.00 (1-57806-000-1) U Pr of Miss.

Ten Ponds: Adirondack Mountain Poetry. Chuck Gibson. LC 95-68731. (Illus.). 94p. (Orig.). 1995. pap. 14.95 (0-9646605-0-4) Panther Mtn.

Ten Pound Immigrants. Reginald T. Appleyard. 192p. 1988. 60.00 (1-85283-220-7, Pub. by Boxtree Ltd UK) St Mut.

***10 Power Principles for Christian Service: Ministry Dynamics for a New Century.** Warren W. Wiersbe & David W. Wiersbe. LC 97-6648. 160p. (Orig.). 1997. pap. 9.99 (0-8010-9029-6) Baker Bks.

Ten Practical Tips for Business & Economic Reporting in Developing Economies. rev. ed. Paul Hemp. 58p. reprint ed. pap. text ed. 7.50 (0-614-07031-7) Intl Ctr Journal.

Ten Practical Tips for Environmental Reporting. Peter Nelson. 57p. pap. text ed. 7.50 (0-9626584-6-4) Intl Ctr Journal.

Ten Precisionist Artists: Annotated Bibliographies. Ed. by David L. Henderson. LC 92-14511. (Art Reference Collection: No. 14). 384p. 1992. text ed. 59.95 (0-313-27664-1, HTP, Greenwood Pr) Greenwood.

Ten Presidents & the Press. Ed. by Kenneth W. Thompson. LC 82-20293. (American Presidents & the Press Ser.). 128p. (Orig.). 1983. pap. text ed. 15.00 (0-8191-2878-3) U Pr of Amer.

Ten Principal Upanishads. Tr. by Shri Patanjali & William Butler Yeats. 160p. (Orig.). 1970. pap. 11.95 (0-571-09363-9) Faber & Faber.

Ten Principal Upanishads. A. Wade. 1972. 300.00 (0-8490-1183-3) Gordon Pr.

Ten Principles of a Happy Marriage. Selwyn Hughes. 1992. pap. 4.99 (0-551-00947-0) Zondervan.

Ten Principles on Raising Chinese-American Teens. Evelyn Lee. (Illus.). 69p. (Orig.). 1988. student ed., pap. 10.65 (0-9621298-0-1); 7.50 (0-9621298-1-X) Chinatown Youth Ctr.

Ten Problems of Consciousness: A Representational Theory of the Phenomenal Mind. Michael Tye. LC 95-19301. (Representation & Mind Ser.). 248p. 1995. 32.50 (0-262-20103-8, Bradford Bks) MIT Pr.

***Ten Problems of Consciousness: A Representational Theory of the Phenomenal Mind.** Michael Tye. (Bradford/Representation & Mind Ser.). (Illus.). 264p. 1996. reprint ed. pap. 15.00 (0-262-70064-6, Bradford Bks) MIT Pr.

Ten Progressive Etudes for the Marimba. Raynor Carroll. 16p. 1996. pap. text ed. 6.00 (0-9650322-1-3) Batterie Music.

***Ten Queens & Portraits of Women of Power.** Milton Meltzer. 1997. pap. 20.00 (0-525-45643-0) Dutton Child Bks.

Ten Questions: A Sociological Perspective. Joel M. Charon. 254p. (C). 1992. pap. 15.95 (0-534-16050-6) Wadsworth Pub.

Ten Questions: A Sociological Perspective. 2nd ed. Joel M. Charon. LC 94-16174. 269p. 1995. pap. 21.95 (0-534-23814-9) Wadsworth Pub.

Ten Questions on Prayer. Gerald Heard. LC 51-10133. (Orig.). 1951. pap. 3.00 (0-87574-058-8) Pendle Hill.

Ten Radical Priests. Ed. by Gerard Moran. 220p. 1996. 45. 00 (1-85182-249-6, Pub. by Four Cts Pr IE); pap. 25.00 (1-85182-281-X, Pub. by Four Cts Pr IE) Intl Spec Bk.

***10 Real SATs.** 600p. 1997. pap. 17.95 (0-87447-567-8) College Bd.

Ten Red Rods. Timothy J. Thompson. LC 80-83135. (Illus.). 16p. (Orig.). (J). (ps-1). 1980. pap. text ed. 3.50 (0-915676-02-8) Ed Sys Pub.

Ten Rules for Investing. James L. Fraser. LC 64-20192. 1964. pap. 5.00 (0-87034-030-1) Fraser Pub Co.

***Ten Rules of High Performance Living: The 10 Rules to Living a Vibrant Life.** Barnet Meltzer. 192p. (Orig.). 1997. pap. 14.95 (1-57071-208-5) Sourcebks.

Ten Sacred Songs see Music of the Moravians in America from the Archives of the Moravian Church at Bethlehem Pa.

Ten Sails in the Sunrise. Allan Campbell. 200p. 1986. 14. 95 (0-317-39595-5) C I L Inc.

Ten Seasons: New York Theatre in the Seventies. Samuel L. Leiter. LC 86-369. (Contributions in Drama & Theatre Studies). 257p. 1986. text ed. 55.00 (0-313-24994-6, LTS/, Greenwood Pr) Greenwood.

Ten-Second Business Forms. 3rd ed. Robert L. Adams. 208p. 1993. pap. 10.95 (1-55850-307-2) Adams Media.

Ten Second Message. Dan McKinnon. 130p. 1994. pap. 9.95 (0-941437-04-3) House Hits.

Ten-Second Rainshowers: Poems by Young People. Illus. by Virginia Halstead. LC 95-1071. 124p. (YA). (gr. 3 up). 1996. 16.00 (0-689-80113-0, S&S Bks Young Read) S&S Childrens.

Ten Seconds. Louis Edwards. 166p. 1991. pap. 8.95 (1-55597-150-4) Graywolf.

Ten Secrets for a Successful Family: A Perfect 10 for Homes That Win. Adrian Rogers. LC 95-52024. 224p. 1996. 17.99 (0-89107-883-5) Crossway Bks.

Ten Secrets of Abundant Happiness. Adam J. Jackson. 144p. 1996. mass mkt. 5.99 (0-06-104421-0, Harp PBks) HarpC.

Ten Secrets of Abundant Health. Adam J. Jackson. 144p. 1996. mass mkt. 5.99 (0-06-104424-5, Harp PBks) HarpC.

Ten Secrets of Abundant Love. Adam J. Jackson. 144p. 1996. mass mkt. 5.99 (0-06-104422-9, Harp PBks) HarpC.

Ten Secrets of Abundant Wealth. Adam J. Jackson. 128p. 1996. mass mkt. 5.99 (0-06-104423-7, Harp PBks) HarpC.

Ten Secrets of Highly Successful Women. Kathleen Remington. Ed. & Illus. by Tim White. 220p. 1994. pap. 59.95 (1-887126-92-9) Natl Bus Bur.

10 Secrets of Marketing Success: How to Jump Start Your Marketing. Rick Crandall. 460p. 1997. pap. 19.95 (0-9644294-4-6) Select Pr.

Ten Sermons on the Second Advent. E. W. Bullinger. LC 95-24908. 144p. 1996. pap. 7.99 (0-8254-2162-4, Kregel Class) Kregel.

Ten Sevens. Charles Lee. LC 82-15771. 80p. 1983. 12.50 (0-915180-23-5) Harrowood Bks.

Ten-Shun: The Making of a Soldier. John W. Logan. Ed. by Linda A. Bird. 216p. (Orig.). 1995. pap. 16.95 (1-878151-04-5) J & J Bks NY.

Ten Signs of Faith. Hassan Kazemi. Ed. by Helen Graves. LC 85-51959. 154p. 1986. 6.95 (1-55523-012-1) Winston-Derek.

***Ten Sisters: A True Story.** Alfred et al. (Illus.). 288p. 1997. 24.95 (1-878044-49-4) Mayhaven Pub.

Ten Sixty-Six: The Year of the Conquest. David Howarth. 208p. 1981. pap. 11.95 (0-14-005850-8, Penguin Bks) Viking Penguin.

Ten Sixty-Six & All That. Walter C. Sellar. (Illus.). 160p. 1993. reprint ed. 33.00 (0-7509-0083-0, Pub. by Sutton Pubng UK) Bks Intl VA.

Ten Skills of Highly Effective Principals. June H. Schmieder & Donald Cairns. 134p. 1996. 29.95 (1-56676-381-9, 763819) Technomic.

Ten Sly Piranhas: A Counting Story in Reverse (A Tale of Wickedness - & Worse!) William Wise. LC 91-33704. (Illus.). 32p. (J). (ps-3). 1993. pap. 14.99 (0-8037-1200-6); lib. bdg. 13.89 (0-8037-1201-4) Dial Bks Young.

Ten Small Tales. Celia B. Lottridge. LC 92-2878. (Illus.). 64p. (J). (gr. k-4). 1994. lib. bdg. 15.95 (0-689-50568-X, McElderry) S&S Childrens.

***Ten Smart Moves Women Make to Succeed in Love & Life.** Dianna Booher. 1997. 14.99 (1-57757-016-2) Honor Bks OK.

Ten Sonatas for Piano. Alexander Scriabin. 208p. 1985. per. 14.95 (0-7935-2279-X, 00120090) H Leonard.

Ten Spikes to the Rail. John R. Twohy. (Illus.). 211p. (Orig.). 17.50 (0-9610240-0-3); pap. 10.00 (0-9610240-1-1) Goat Rock.

Ten Standard Turns: Cross Turns, Spot Turns, Pivots, Twinkles. 1985. lib. bdg. 76.00 (0-87700-796-9) Revisionist Pr.

Ten Steps. 1994. pap. 17.95 (0-7871-0182-6, Dove Bks) Dove Audio.

Ten Steps. 3rd ed. Brookes. 1995. teacher ed., pap. text ed. 6.00 (0-13-460015-0) P-H.

Ten Steps: Controlled Composition for Beginning & Intermediate Language Development. rev. ed. Gay Brookes & Jean Withrow. Ed. by Helen Munch. 72p. (YA). (gr. 7-12). 1988. teacher ed. 4.65 (0-13-904111-7) Alemany Pr.

Ten Steps: Controlled Composition for Beginning & Intermediate Language Development. 2nd rev. ed. Gay Brookes & Jean Withrow. Ed. by Helen Munch. 72p. (gr. 7-12). 1988. pap. text ed. 6.25 (0-88084-253-9) Alemany Pub.

Ten Steps: Controlled Composition for Language Development. 3rd ed. Brookes & Withrow. (Illus.). 64p. 1995. pap. 8.75 (0-13-456989-X) P-H.

Ten Steps Dynamic Presentation. Wayne E. Page. 276p. (C). 1995. pap. 15.69 (0-7872-1544-9) Kendall-Hunt.

Ten Steps for Preventing Student Relapse. Thomas J. Shiltz. (Illus.). 174p. 1992. pap. text ed. 29.95 (0-9618023-2-4) Community Rec Pr.

Ten Steps in Writing the Research Paper. 5th ed. Roberta H. Markman & Marie L. Waddell. 160p. (C). 1994. pap. 9.95 (0-8120-1868-0) Barron.

Ten Steps to a Better Essay, Pt. I. Michael Zeitsoff. 256p. (C). 1993. per. 31.44 (0-8403-8564-1) Kendall-Hunt.

Ten Steps to a Better Essay, Pt. II. Michael Zeitsoff. 256p. (C). 1993. per. 37.74 (0-8403-8976-0) Kendall-Hunt.

Ten Steps to a Learning Organization. Peter Kline & Bernard Saunders. LC 93-28065. 1993. 29.95 (0-915556-24-3); pap. 15.95 (0-915556-23-5) Great Ocean.

Ten Steps to Advancing College Reading Skills. 2nd ed. John Langan. 496p. (C). 1993. pap. text ed. 16.00 (0-944210-56-2) Townsend NJ.

Ten Steps to Behavioral Research. Thomas E. Whalen. LC 89-5460. 288p. (Orig.). (C). 1989. pap. text ed. 21.00 (0-8191-7395-9); lib. bdg. 38.00 (0-8191-7394-0) U Pr of Amer.

***Ten Steps to Better Staff Training.** Cathryn Harvey & Diane Howard. 1995. pap. 23.00 (0-902789-99-6, Pub. by Natl Inst Soc Work) St Mut.

Ten Steps to Breaking the Two Hundred Barrier. Bill M. Sullivan. 96p. 1987. pap. 6.99 (0-8341-1223-X) Beacon Hill.

Ten Steps to Building College Reading Skills, Form A. 2nd ed. John Langan. 430p. (C). 1993. pap. text ed. 16.00 (0-944210-58-9) Townsend NJ.

Ten Steps to Building College Reading Skills, Form B. 2nd ed. Bill Broderick. 1994. pap. text ed. 16.00 (0-944210-67-8, Form B) Townsend NJ.

Ten Steps to Connecting with Your Customers: How to Ask the Right Questions, Get the Right Answers & Make the Right Sale. Bill Bethel. 262p. 1995. 28.95 (0-85013-201-0) Dartnell Corp.

Ten Steps to Empowerment: A Common-Sense Guide to Managing People. Diane Tracy. 192p. 1992. pap. 12.00 (0-688-11279-X, Quill) Morrow.

Ten Steps to Ending Illegal Immigration. Ed. by Scipio Garling. (Illus.). 81p. 1995. pap. 10.00 (0-935775-16-8) F A I R.

Ten Steps to Financial Freedom. Alfred Herron. 103p. (Orig.). 1988. 8.95 (0-317-94053-8) Galloway Herron.

***Ten Steps to Financial Freedom: For You, Your Family, & Your Country.** Robert H. Schuller & Paul D. Dunn. 160p. 1997. pap. 6.95 (1-55853-533-0) Rutledge Hill Pr.

Ten Steps to Financial Health. Malcolm Newell. 139p. 1995. pap. 17.95 (0-949142-32-8, Pub. by Stirling Pr AT) Intl Spec Bk.

***10 Steps to Financial Success: A Beginner's Guide to Saving & Investing.** W. Patrick Naylor. 272p. 1997. pap. text ed. 17.95 (0-471-17533-1) Wiley.

Ten Steps to Home Ownership. Ilyce R. Glink. 1996. pap. 14.00 (0-614-12598-7) Random.

Ten Steps to Improving College Reading Skills. 2nd ed. John Langan. (C). 1992. pap. text ed. 16.00 (0-944210-52-X) Townsend NJ.

10 Steps to Marketing Artwork. Sue Viders & Steve Doherty. 30p. 1994. pap. 4.95 (0-942011-12-0) S Viders.

10 Steps to Realtime Writing. Beverly L. Ritter. (Realtime Machine Shorthand Ser.). 272p. (C). 1993. pap. text ed. 43.25 (0-938643-34-7) Stenotype Educ.

10 Steps to Realtime Writing Package. Beverly L. Ritter. (Realtime Machine Shorthand Ser.). 271p. (C). 1993. pap. text ed. 82.00 incl. audio (0-938643-45-2) Stenotype Educ.

Ten Steps to Self-Fulfillment. Robert G. Chaney. LC 93-70705. 256p. 1993. pap. 15.95 (0-918936-28-4) Astara.

Ten Steps to Successful Retirement. James H. Hutchinson. Ed. by Lydia L. Hutchinson. (Illus.). 140p. (Orig.). 1989. pap. write for info. (0-9622301-0-3) J H Hutchinson.

Ten Steps to Winning: A Professional Method for Selecting Winners. Danny Holmes. 144p. 1988. pap. 9.95 (0-89709-172-8) Liberty Pub.

Ten Steps Toward Saving America. Jack W. Hayford. 96p. (Orig.). 1994. pap. text ed. 3.95 (0-916847-16-0) Living Way.

Ten Stories for Children. Nelle A. Hardegrove. (Illus.). 10p. (Orig.). (J). (gr. 1-5). 1987. pap. text ed. 7.95 (0-9619227-3-7) N A Hardegrove.

Ten Strategies for Preaching in a Multi Media Culture. Thomas H. Troeger. 144p. (Orig.). 1996. pap. 12.95 (0-687-00701-1) Abingdon.

***Ten Stupid Things Men Do to Mess Up Their Lives.** Laura C. Schlessinger. LC 97-23121. 1997. 22.00 (0-06-017308-4) HarpC.

Ten Stupid Things Women Do to Mess up Their Lives. Laura C. Schlessinger. 256p. 1995. pap. 10.00 (0-06-097649-7, PL) HarpC.

Ten Stupid Things Women Do to Mess up Their Lives. Laura C. Schlessinger. 1996. pap. 10.00 (0-614-13230-4, PL) HarpC.

***Ten Suns: A Chinese Legend.** Eric A. Kimmel. LC 96-30044. (Illus.). 1998. lib. bdg. write for info. (0-8234-1317-9) Holiday.

Ten Sure-Fire Confidence Builders from God: A Study in 1 John 3: 1 - 4: 6. Edward A. Friess. 120p. 1996. pap. 12.00 (0-9643297-6-X) E A Friess.

Ten Sure-Fire Confidence Builders from God: A Study in 1 John 3: 1 - 4: 6. large type ed. Edward A. Friess. 136p. 1996. spiral bd. 12.95 (0-9643297-5-1, 96-96990) E A Friess.

Ten Talents in the American Theatre. Ed. by David H. Stevens. LC 76-20514. 299p. 1976. reprint ed. text ed. 59.75 (0-8371-8996-9, STTA, Greenwood Pr) Greenwood.

Ten Talents Natural Foods Vegetarian Cookbook: Natural Foods Vegetarian Cookbook & Health Manual. rev. ed. Frank J. Hurd & Rosalie Hurd. LC 85-90936. 1985. ring bd. 9.95 (0-9603532-1-6) Ten Talents.

Ten Talents Natural Foods Vegetarian Cookbook: Natural Foods Vegetarian Cookbook & Health Manual. rev. ed. Frank J. Hurd & Rosalie Hurd. LC 85-90936. 1996. spiral bd. 21.95 (0-9603532-4-0) Ten Talents.

Ten Tales. Francois Coppee. Ed. by Walter Learned. LC 76-86140. (Short Story Index Reprint Ser.). (Illus.). 1977. 19.95 (0-8369-3044-4) Ayer.

Ten Tales. deluxe ed. Neal Barrett, Jr. et al. 185p. 1994. 100.00 (0-9640454-9-4) J Cahill Pubng.

Ten Tales Tall & True. Alasdair Gray. LC 93-40980. 1994. 19.95 (0-15-100090-5) HarBrace.

Ten Tales Tall & True. Alasdair Gray. (Illus.). 176p. 1995. pap. 11.00 (0-15-600196-9) HarBrace.

Ten Tall Oaktrees. Richard Edwards. LC 92-41771. (Illus.). 32p. (J). (ps up). 1993. 15.00 (0-688-04620-7, Tambourine Bks); lib. bdg. 14.93 (0-688-04621-5, Tambourine Bks) Morrow.

Ten Tall Soldiers. Robison. 1995. 4.98 (0-8317-2271-1) Smithmark.

Ten Tall Tales. E. J. Bird. LC 84-12086. (Carolrhoda Good Time Library). (Illus.). 56p. (J). (gr. 2-6). 1984. lib. bdg. 14.95 (0-87614-267-6, Carolrhoda) Lerner Group.

***Ten Teddies.** Illus. by Linda Worrall. (My Big Little Fat Bks.). 20p. (J). (ps up). 1997. bds. 3.49 (1-85854-690-7) Brimax Bks.

***Ten Terrible Dinosaurs.** Paul Stickland. (J). 1997. 13.99 (0-525-45905-7) Dutton Child Bks.

Ten Tests of Abraham. Shoshana Lepon. (Judaica Bible Series for Young Children). (Illus.). 32p. (Orig.). (J). (gr. k-4). 1986. pap. 7.95 (0-910818-67-3) Judaica Pr.

***Ten Things Every Parent Needs to Know: A Guide for New Parents & Everyone Else Who Cares about Children.** Kim Paleg. LC 96-71154. 628p. (Orig.). 1997. pap. 12.95 (1-57224-065-2) New Harbinger.

Ten Things Parents Must Teach Their Children: And Learn for Themselves. Edith Schaeffer. 224p. (YA). (gr. 10). 1994. reprint ed. pap. 12.99 (0-8010-8373-7, Ravens Ridge) Baker Bks.

Ten Things Parents Should Know about Drug & Alcohol Abuse. Jep Hostetler. LC 91-70664. 128p. 1991. pap. 9.95 (1-56148-013-4) Good Bks PA.

Ten Things Your Teen Will Thank You for Someday. William L. Coleman. 176p. 1992. pap. 8.99 (1-55661-249-4) Bethany Hse.

Ten Thousand. Harold Coyle. Ed. by Paul McCarthy. xvi, 592p. 1994. reprint ed. pap. 6.99 (0-671-88565-0) PB.

Ten Thousand - A Dictionary of New Chinese-English-Chinese. C. H. Lo. 474p. (CHI & ENG.). 1980. 25.00 (0-8288-1606-9, M9266) Fr & Eur.

Ten Thousand a Year, 3 vols. in 2, Set. Samuel Warren. LC 79-8215. reprint ed. 84.50 (0-404-62163-5) AMS Pr.

***Ten Thousand Angels.** 1983. pap. 1.20 (0-8341-9198-9) Lillenas.

Ten Thousand Baby Names. Bruce Lansky. LC 85-717. 144p. 1985. pap. 3.50 (0-88166-067-1) Meadowbrook.

10,000 Baskets: Based on "Assembly Line," a Short Story by B. Traven. Lonnie B. Hewitt & Penny Bernal. LC 94-33731. (Spotlight Ser.). 1994. text ed. 4.00 (0-07-028589-6) McGraw.

Ten Thousand Commandments: A Story of the Antitrust Laws. Harold M. Fleming. LC 75-172211. (Right Wing Individualist Tradition in America Ser.). 1972. reprint ed. 18.95 (0-405-00420-6) Ayer.

Ten Thousand Day War: Vietnam 1945-1975. Michael MacLear. 384p. 1982. pap. 10.95 (0-380-60970-3) Avon.

Ten Thousand Days. Kenneth Royce. 256p. 1984. pap. 3.50 (0-88184-082-3) Carroll & Graf.

Ten Thousand Days. large type ed. Kenneth Royce. 464p. 1984. 25.99 (0-7089-1175-7) Ulverscroft.

Ten Thousand Days Has Our Youth, Vol. 1. Stephen McNamee. LC 86-42964. 328p. 1987. 17.75 (0-930950-03-8); pap. 10.75 (0-930950-04-6) Nopoly Pr.

$10,000 Trivia Challenge. Henry Hook. 1995. pap. 14.00 (0-8129-2607-2) Random.

Ten Thousand Dollars of Publicity for Your Small Business: How to Work with the Media to Sell Your Product. John C. Vita. 225p. 1989. 29.95 (0-685-30129-X) Rose Bks IL.

Ten Thousand Dollars Per Month as a Private Investigator. John R. Rose. 264p. (Orig.). 1992. pap. 29.95 (1-881170-02-0) Rose Pub OR.

Ten Thousand Dreams & Their Traditional Meanings. Foulsham Staff. 150p. 1995. pap. 13.95 (0-572-02144-5, Pub. by W Foulsham UK) Trans-Atl Phila.

Ten Thousand Dreams Interpreted. G. Hindman Miller. 1988. 9.99 (0-517-65834-8) Random Hse Value.

10,000 Dreams Interpreted: A Complete Guide to the Meaning of Your Dreams. 617p. (Orig.). 1995. pap. 12.95 (0-85091-461-2, Pub. by Lothian Pub AT) Seven Hills Bk.

Ten Thousand French Words. William Rowlinson. LC 94-9758. (Paperback Reference Ser.). 336p. 1994. reprint ed. pap. 7.95 (0-19-282895-9) OUP.

Ten Thousand Garden Questions. Marjorie J. Dietz. 1994. 19.99 (0-517-12226-X) Random Hse Value.

Ten Thousand German Words. William Rowlinson. LC 93-45641. (Paperback Reference Ser.). 320p. 1994. pap. 7.95 (0-19-283095-3) OUP.

Ten Thousand German Words. William Rowlinson. LC 93-45641. (Paperback Reference Ser.). 320p. 1994. 6.95 (0-19-211686-X) OUP.

Ten Thousand Goddam Cattle: A History of the American Cowboy in Song, Story & Verse. limited rev. ed. Katie Lee. (Illus.). 257p. 1985. reprint ed. pap. 25.00 (0-934573-68-9) Katyd Bks & Music.

10,000 Ideas for Term Papers, Projects, Reports & Speeches. 4th ed. Kathryn Lamm. 448p. 1995. 12.95 (0-02-860560-8) Macmillan.

Ten Thousand Ideas for Term Papers, Projects, Reports & Speeches. 3rd ed. Kathryn Lamm. 1994. pap. 11.00 (0-13-904228-8) P-H.

10,000 Illustrations from the Bible: For Pastors, Teachers, Students, Speakers, & Writers. Charles Little. 640p. (C). 1991. pap. 29.99 (0-8010-5606-3) Baker Bks.

Ten Thousand in Thrace: An Archaeological & Historical Commentary on Xenophon's Anabis, Bks. VI.iii-vi-VII. Jan P. Stronk. (Amsterdam Classical Monographs: No. 2). xiv, 338p. 1995. lib. bdg. 100.00 (90-5063-396-X, Pub. by Gieben NE) Benjamins North Am.

Ten Thousand Jokes, Toasts & Stories. Ed. by Lewis Copeland. LC 66-737. 1040p. 1956. 22.95 (0-385-00163-0) Doubleday.

Ten Thousand Leaves: A Translation of the Man'yoshu, Japan's Premier Anthology of Classical Poetry, Vol. 1. English Man'yoshu. LC 80-8561. (Princeton Library of Asian Translations). (Illus.). 418p. 1987. reprint ed. pap. 119.20 (0-7837-8176-8, 2047881) Bks Demand.

Ten Thousand Leaves: Love Poems from the Manyoshu. Tr. by Harold Wright from JPN. LC 78-65436. (Illus.). 96p. 1986. 14.95 (0-87951-214-8) Overlook Pr.

Ten Thousand Leaves: Love Poems from the Manyoshu. Tr. by Harold Wright. 96p. 1988. pap. 8.95 (0-87951-240-7) Overlook Pr.

Ten Thousand Legal Words. Margaret A. Kurtz et al. 1971. text ed. 10.96 (0-07-035669-6) McGraw.

Ten Thousand Maniacs: Anthology. (Illus.). 130p. 1993. pap. 21.95 (0-8256-1359-0, AM91243) Music Sales.

***10,000 Maniacs: MTV Unplugged.** Date not set. 19.95 (0-614-22084-X, AM 91729) Music Sales.

***10,000 Maniacs: MTV Unplugged.** 96p. 1997. 19.95 (0-8256-1381-7, AM 91729) Music Sales.

***10,000 Maniacs: Our Time in Eden.** 88p. 1997. pap. 15.95 (0-8256-1350-7, AM 91046) Music Sales.

Ten Thousand Medical Words, Spelled & Divided for Quick Reference. Edward E. Byers. 128p. 1972. text ed. 10.24 (0-07-009503-5) McGraw.

Ten Thousand Miles on a Bicycle. rev. ed. Karl Kron, pseud. LC 82-23120. 911p. 1982. 21.95 (0-9610060-0-5) E Rosenblatt.

Ten Thousand Miles with a Dog Sled. Hudson Stuck. (Illus.). 452p. 1988. pap. 14.95 (0-935632-66-2) Wolfe Pub Co.

Ten Thousand Miles with a Dog Sled. Hudson Stuck. LC 87-35192. (Illus.). xxxii, 516p. 1988. reprint ed. pap. 12.95 (0-8032-9185-X, Bison Books) U of Nebr Pr.

***10,000 Names for Your Baby.** 1997. mass mkt. 5.99 (0-440-22336-9) Dell.

10,001 Titillating Tidbits of Avian Trivia. Frank S. Todd. 630p. (C). 1994. pap. 24.95 (0-934797-08-0) Ibis Pub CA.

***10,000 Superstitions You Really Need.** rev. ed. Ed. by William Carroll. 350p. (Orig.). 1997. pap. 24.95 (0-910390-56-8, Coda Pubns) Auto Bk.

Ten Thousand Things to Praise God For. Jan Dargatz. LC 92-46559. 1993. pap. 7.99 (0-8407-9656-0) Nelson.

Ten Thousand Tons by Christmas: A Comprehensive Story of Flying the Hump in W. W. II by an Officer Who Was There. Edwin L. White. LC 77-72751. (Illus.). 256p. 1975. 7.95 (0-912760-05-2) Valkyrie Pub Hse.

***Ten Thousand Whispers: A Guide to Conscious Creation.** Lynda M. Dahl. LC 96-39535. 208p. (Orig.). 1995. pap. 13.95 (1-889964-06-9) Woodbridge Grp.

Ten Thousand Wonderful Things. Edmund F. King. 1974. 59.95 (0-8490-1184-1) Gordon Pr.

Ten Thousand Years in the Suburbs. Jack Zimmerman. 1994. 25.00 (0-941702-38-3); pap. 9.95 (0-941702-36-7) Lake View Pr.

***Ten Time Bombs: Defusing the Most Explosive Pressures Teenagers Face.** Ron Hutchcraft. LC 97-15024. 160p. (YA). 1997. pap. 9.99 (0-310-20808-4) Zondervan.

Ten Times More Beautiful: The Rebuilding of Vietnam. Kathleen Gough. LC 78-14890. 277p. 1978. 22.50 (0-85345-464-7) Monthly Rev.

Ten Times More Beautiful: The Rebuilding of Vietnam. Kathleen E. Aberle. LC 78-14890. 275p. reprint ed. pap. 78.40 (0-7837-3923-0, 2043771) Bks Demand.

Ten Tiny Fingers, Nine Tiny Toes. Sue Townsend. (Methuen Modern Plays Ser.). 56p. (C). 1991. pap. 9.95 (0-413-61760-2, A0502, Pub. by Methuen UK) Heinemann.

***Ten Tiny Monsters.** Sheila W. Samton. LC 96-47355. (J). 1997. write for info. (0-517-70941-4); write for info. (0-517-70942-2) Crown Pub Group.

Ten Tiny Tales, Bk. 1. Robert Haiduck. 87p. (J). (gr. 1-8). 1990. write for info. (0-9627661-0-0) Tiny Tales.

Ten Tiny Turtles: A Crazy Counting Book. Paul Cherrill. LC 94-19904. (Illus.). 32p. (J). (ps-2). 1995. 14.95 (0-395-71250-5) Ticknor & Flds Bks Yng Read.

***10-5 NE-1?** Jerry Cooper. 24p. (Orig.). 1996. pap. 3.95 (1-889419-12-5) J Cooper.

Ten to Grow on: Teaching the Ten Commandments to Today's Child. Sandra Klaus. 112p. 1992. pap. 10.99 (0-310-54061-5) Zondervan.

Ten to Seventeen February Afternoons. Lawrence E. Keith. (Orig.). 1977. pap. 4.00 (0-932222-00-5) Sunrise Tortoise.

Ten Tools for Quality. Richard Chang. LC 94-70860. (AMI How-to Ser.). 115p. (Orig.). 1994. per. 12.95 (1-884926-24-X) Amer Media.

Ten Tools of Language-Written. 2nd ed. Ann N. Black et al. (Illus.). 166p. (J). (gr. 11-12). 1982. pap. text ed. 12.60 (0-910513-00-7) Mayfield Printing.

Ten Tools of Language-Written: Revised Edition II, Form B. rev. ed. E. R. Black et al. (Illus.). 166p. (C). 1983. pap. text ed. 12.60 (0-910513-01-5) Mayfield Printing.

Ten Top Hits for Easy Piano. (Easy Play Ser.). 56p. 1993. pap. 7.95 (0-7935-2776-7, 00222567) H Leonard.

***Ten Top Sales Techniques for Small Firms.** Neil Jonson. (Small Business Ser.). 1995. pap. 14.95 (0-7494-1837-0) Kogan Page Ltd.

Ten Top Short Stories of 1994, No. 7. 96p. (Orig.). 1994. pap. 11.95 (1-56167-167-3) Am Literary Pr.

Ten Top Stories. Ed. by David A. Sohn. 176p. (Orig.). 1985. mass mkt. 5.99 (0-553-26979-8) Bantam.

Ten Tough Trips: Montana Writers & the West. William W. Bevis. LC 89-77570. 248p. 1990. 24.95 (0-295-96941-5) U of Wash Pr.

***Ten Toughest Sales Calls.** John MacMillan. (Marketing & Sales Ser.). 1994. pap. 16.95 (0-7494-1278-X) Kogan Page Ltd.

Ten Traditional Jewish Children's Stories. Gloria Goldreich. (Illus.). 48p. (J). (gr. 1-4). 1996. 16.95 (0-943706-69-6) Pitspopany.

Ten Treats for Ginger. Amye Rosenberg. (Sticker Bks.). (Illus.). 24p. (J). (ps-1). 1992. pap. 2.95 (0-671-75511-0, Litl Simon S&S) S&S Childrens.

***Ten True Loves: Finding the Soul in Love Relationships.** Alex T. Quenk & Naomi L. Quenk. LC 97-15324. 240p. 1997. pap. 16.95 (0-89106-107-X, 7760) Davies-Black.

Ten Tunes for Ten Fingers. Robert Donahue. 24p. 1988. pap. 6.95 (0-938170-09-0) Wimbledon Music.

Ten-Twelve Monastery Road. William A. Meninger. (Illus.). 120p. (Orig.). 1989. pap. 5.95 (0-932506-73-9) St Bedes Pubns.

Ten-Twenty-Thirty Minutes to Sew. Nancy L. Zieman. 160p. 1992. 29.99 (0-8487-1118-1); pap. 19.99 (0-8487-1129-7) Oxmoor Hse.

***Sew Easy Embellishments.** Nancy L. Zieman. LC 97-66727. 1997. pap. 19.95 (0-8487-1605-1) Oxmoor Hse.

Ten Vineyard Lunches. Richard Olney. LC 88-21936. (Ten Menus Ser.). (Illus.). 128p. 1988. Cookery Book. 19.95 (0-940793-23-7) Interlink Pub.

Ten Visits: Brief Accounts of Visits to All Ten Japanese American Relocation Centers of World War II. Frank Iritani & Joanne Iritani. (Illus.). 60p. 1994. pap. text ed. 15.95 (0-934609-02-0) JACP Inc.

Ten Waltzes by J. Strauss. Gail Smith. 9.95 (0-7866-0097-7, 95219) Mel Bay.

***Ten Waltzes by Johann Strauss, Jr. for Solo.** Gail Smith. 24.95 incl. audio compact disk (0-7866-1232-0, 95219CDP); 18.95 incl. audio (0-7866-1406-4, 95219P); audio 9.98 (0-7866-0437-9, 95219C); audio compact disk 15.98 (0-7866-0519-7, 95219CD) Mel Bay.

Ten Ways Christians Maintain Confident Fellowshipping with the Father, His Son Jesus Christ & His Church: A Study in 1 John 1: 1 - 2: 29. Edward A. Friess. 109p. 1996. pap. 12.00 (0-9643297-4-3) E A Friess.

Ten Ways Christians Maintain Confident Fellowshipping with the Father, His Son Jesus Christ & His Church: A Study in 1 John 1: 1 - 2: 29. large type ed. Edward A. Friess. LC 95-96206. 131p. 1996. spiral bd. 12.95 (0-9643297-2-7) E A Friess.

Ten Ways to a Better Iowa: A Strategic Plan for State Government. James Strohman. 90p. (Orig.). 1994. pap. write for info. (1-885591-09-8) Morris Pubng.

Ten Ways to Become Rich. James L. Fraser. LC 67-18101. (Illus.). 1967. pap. 5.00 (0-87034-031-X) Fraser Pub Co.

Ten Ways to Get into the New Testament: A Teenager's Guide. Jim Auer. LC 90-64270. 80p. (Orig.). (YA). (gr. 9-12). 1991. pap. text ed. 2.95 (0-89243-342-6) Liguori Pubns.

Ten Ways to Lobby Your Representatives from Home. Daniel P. Moriarty. 1979. pap. 2.00 (0-933968-03-5) D Moriarty.

Ten Ways to Lose Ten Pounds in Two Weeks. Susie Tompkins. 153p. 1993. reprint ed. pap. 4.50 (1-56171-213-2, S P I Bks) Sure Seller.

Ten Ways to Meet God: Spirituality for Teens. Jim Auer. LC 88-83574. 64p. (YA). (gr. 7-12). 1989. pap. 3.95 (0-89243-299-3) Liguori Pubns.

Ten Ways to Wreck a Date. Minstrel Books Staff. (Full House Stephanie Ser.: No. 15). (J). (gr. 3-6). 1996. pap. 3.99 (0-671-53548-X, Minstrel Bks) PB.

Ten Ways You Can Earn One Million Dollars This Year. Charles R. Whitlock & R. Dwane Krumme. 1988. pap. 8.95 (0-943631-01-7) Princeton Pr Pub.

Ten Wedding Solos: High Voice. 1995. pap. 19.95 incl. audio compact disk (0-7935-4097-6, 00740004) H Leonard.

Ten Week Garden. Cary Scher. LC 73-76848. (Illus.). 407p. 1973. pap. 20.00 (0-87110-101-7) Ultramarine Pub.

***Ten Weeks.** Yolanda Deshannon. 165p. (Orig.). (J). (gr. 7-10). 1997. pap. 5.00 (1-884429-04-1) Frst Choice.

Ten Who Left: People Who Left the Church & Why. Fred Cornforth & Tim Lale. LC 95-36786. 1995. pap. 8.99 (0-8163-1298-2) Pacific Pr Pub Assn.

***Ten Women.** Photos by Peter Lindbergh. (Illus.). 120p. 1996. 35.00 (3-8238-1416-8) te Neues.

Ten Women: Political Pioneers. Carol J. Perry. 96p. (YA). (gr. 5 up). 1994. pap. 2.99 (0-87406-642-5) Willowisp Pr.

10 Women of Mystery. Ed. by Earl F. Bargainnier. LC 80-85393. 1981. 22.95 (0-87972-172-3); pap. 11.95 (0-87972-173-1) Bowling Green Univ Popular Press.

Ten Women Poets of Greece. Dino Siotis. 1982. pap. 6.00 (0-918034-11-6, Pub. by Wire Pr) SPD-Small Pr Dist.

***10 Wooden Boats You Can Build: For Sail, Motor, Paddle & Oar.** Ed. by Peter H. Spectre. 1996. pap. text ed. 24.95 (0-07-060030-9) McGraw.

10 Wooden Boats You Can Build: For Sail, Motor, Paddle & Oar. Ed. by Peter H. Spectre. (Wooden Boat Ser.). 191p. 1995. pap. 24.95 (0-937822-34-5) WoodenBoat Pubns.

Ten Word Book Series, 10 bks., Set. Bob Reese et al. (Illus.). (J). (gr. k-1). 1979. pap. 39.50 (0-89868-077-8, Read Res) ARO Pub.

An Asterisk (*) at the beginning of an entry indicates that the title is appearing in BIP for the first time.

Ten Word Book Series, 4 bks., Set. Bob Reese & Pam Preece-Sandoval. (Illus.). (J). (gr. k-3). 1994. pap. 15.80 (*0-89868-274-6*, Read Res); lib. bdg. 99.50 (*0-89868-273-8*, Read Res) ARO Pub.

Ten Words of Freedom: An Introduction to the Faith of Israel. LC 75-139344. 240p. reprint ed. pap. 68.40 (*0-685-15418-1*, 2026879) Bks Demand.

Ten Words of Power: A New Age Interpretation of the Ten Commandments. Marc E. Jones. (Illus.). 105p. 1987. 10.00 (*0-87878-019-X*) Sabian Pub.

Ten Words That Will Change Your Life. Ervin Seale. LC 54-6796. 188p. 1992. reprint ed. pap. 9.95 (*0-87516-651-2*) DeVorss.

Ten Yatzachi Zapotec Folktales No. 4: Folklore Texts in Mexican Indian Languages. Inez Butler. (Language Data, Amerindian Ser.: No. 13). (Orig.). pap. write for info. (*0-88312-711-3*); fiche write for info. (*1-55671-987-6*) Summer Instit Ling.

Ten Year Harvest: Third Decennial Reader 1966-1976. Ed. by Louis Harap. 286p. (Orig.). 1977. 3.50 (*0-9618122-1-4*) AFPOJS.

Ten Year Index: Mental & Physical Disability Law Reporter. ABA, Commission on the Mentally Disabled. 232p. 1987. pap. 65.00 (*0-685-21546-6*, 344-0007) Amer Bar Assn.

Ten-Year Index (1976-1985) to Ancestral News. Judy Nacke & Thelma D. Cote. 96p. 1987. pap. 12.00 (*1-889221-35-X*) Ancestral Trails.

***10-Year Spending & Savings Record Book.** Michael Greene, Jr. (Illus.). 148p. 1997. vinyl bd. 20.50 (*1-886197-12-1*) Joy Books.

Ten Years. Grandin Conover. LC 72-77578. 76p. 1972. 15.00 (*0-87023-116-2*); pap. 9.95 (*0-87023-117-0*) U of Mass Pr.

Ten Years Behind the Sacred Desk. Floyd N. Bradley. 1988. pap. 8.99 (*0-88019-232-1*) Schmul Pub Co.

Ten Years' Captivity in the Mahoi's Camp. F. R. Winghate. 482p. 1990. 140.00 (*1-85077-120-0*, Pub. by Darf Pubs Ltd UK) St Mut.

Ten Years' Collected Haiku. William J. Higginson. 32p. 1987. pap. 3.00 (*0-89120-030-4*) From Here.

Ten Years' Digging in Egypt. William F. Petrie. (Illus.). 201p. 1989. pap. 20.00 (*0-89005-107-0*) Ares.

Ten Years Exile. Madam De Stael. 434p. 1969. 35.00 (*0-87556-075-X*) Saifer.

Ten Years' Gatherings, Montana Poems & Stories. Ed. by Gwen Petersen et al. (Illus.). 192p. (Orig.). 1995. 22.95 (*1-887477-01-2*); pap. 14.95 (*1-887477-02-0*) Ranch Cntry.

Ten Years in Japan: A Contemporary Record. Joseph C. Grew. LC 72-4275. (World Affairs Ser.: National & International Viewpoints). (Illus.). 578p. 1972. reprint ed. 40.95 (*0-405-04600-6*) Ayer.

Ten Years in Nevada; or, Life on the Pacific Coast. Mary L. Spence. LC 84-20813. (Illus.). vi, 343p. 1985. reprint ed. pap. 7.50 (*0-8032-8124-2*, Bison Books) U of Nebr Pr.

Ten Years in Oregon. Daniel Lee & Joseph H. Frost. LC 72-9457. (Far Western Frontier Ser.). (Illus.). 348p. 1973. reprint ed. 26.95 (*0-405-04985-4*) Ayer.

Ten Years in the Ranks U. S. Army. Augustus Meyers. Ed. by Richard H. Kohn. LC 78-22387. (American Military Experience Ser.). 1980. reprint ed. lib. bdg. 26.95 (*0-405-11864-3*) Ayer.

Ten Years Later. Alexandre Dumas. 1996. pap. 19.95 (*0-7871-0501-5*, Dove Bks) Dove Audio.

Ten Years Later: Personal Lessons from a Decade of Research & Ministry. George Barna. 150p. 1992. pap. 10.00 (*1-882297-01-6*) Barna Res Grp.

Ten Years of Activities, 1971-1981. Inter-American Commission on Human Rights. LC 83-122693. xix, 403p. 1982. 50.00 (*0-8270-1456-2*) OAS.

Ten Years of Apparitions: New Growth & Recognition of the Pilgrimages. Rene Laurentin. Ed. by Faith Publishing Company Staff. Tr. by Juan Gonzalez, Jr. from FRE. LC 91-77083. 168p. (Orig.). 1991. pap. 6.00 (*1-880033-01-1*) Faith Pub OH.

Ten Years of Concurrency Semantics: Selected Papers of the Amsterdam Concurrency Group. J. W. De Bakker & J. Rutten. LC 92-19669. 420p. 1992. text ed. 109.00 (*981-02-1041-8*) World Scientific Pub.

10 Years of Dolce & Gabbana. Intro. by Isabella Rossellini. (Illus.). 217p. 1996. 67.50 (*0-7892-0277-8*) Abbeville Pr.

Ten Years of Experience in Precast Segmental Construction. (PCI Journal Reprints Ser.). 36p. 1985. pap. 14.00 (*0-318-19747-2*, JR152) P-PCI.

Ten Years of Heat: The Paula Duncan Story "It Can Happen to You" large type ed. Holly Broach-Sowels. Ed. by Jean Daniel. (Illus.). 192p. (Orig.). 1995. pap. 19.95 (*0-9637441-4-3*) Kehori.

***Ten Years of Madness: Oral Histories of China's Cultural Revolution.** Feng Jicai. 272p. 1996. 16.95 (*0-8351-2584-X*) China Bks.

Ten Years of Peter Glen: One Hundred Essays on the Improvement of Work, Life & Other Matters of Consequence. Peter Glen. 330p. 1994. 19.95 (*0-944094-03-1*) ST Pubns.

***Ten Years of Radiofrequency Catheter Ablation.** Ed. by Jeronimo Farre & Concepcion Moro. 1997. write for info. (*0-87993-684-3*) Futura Pub.

10 Years of Research on Porcine Derived Lung Surfactant. H. Walti. (Journal: Biology of the Neonate Ser.: Vol. 67, Suppl. 1, 1995). (Illus.). iv, 92p. 1995. pap. 29.75 (*3-8055-6196-2*) S Karger.

***Ten Years of Superbike.** Julian Ryder. (Illus.). 160p. 1997. pap. 24.95 (*1-85960-404-8*, Pub. by J H Haynes & Co UK) Motorbooks Intl.

Ten Years of Superconductivity, 1980-1990. Ed. by H. R. Ott. LC 92-38477. (Perspectives in Condensed Matter Physics Ser.: Vol. 7). 328p. (C). 1993. lib. bdg. 155.50 (*0-7923-2067-0*) Kluwer Ac.

Ten Years of Training: Developments in France, Federal Republic of Germany & United Kingdom, 1968-1978. ii, 230p. (Orig.). 1980. pap. 15.75 (*92-2-102254-4*) Intl Labour Office.

Ten Years of Turbulence: The Chinese Cultural Revolution. Barbara Barnouin & Yu Changgen. LC 92-2352. (Publication of the Graduate Institute of International Studies, Geneva). 1993. 94.50 (*0-7103-0458-7*, B2340) Routledge Chapman & Hall.

Ten Years of Wall Street. Barnie F. Winkelman. LC 87-80055. 381p. 1987. reprint ed. pap. 21.00 (*0-87034-082-4*) Fraser Pub Co.

Ten Years of Wanderings among the Ethiopians. Thomas J. Hutchinson. 329p. 1967. reprint ed. 39.50 (*0-7146-1817-9*, BHA-01817, Pub. by F Cass Pubs UK) Intl Spec Bk.

Ten Years on a Georgia Plantation since the War (1866-1876) Frances B. Leigh. 141p. 1992. 30.00 (*0-88322-010-5*) Beehive GA.

Ten Years on a Georgian Plantation. Frances B. Leigh. 1973. reprint ed. lib. bdg. 250.00 (*0-8490-1185-X*) Gordon Pr.

Ten Years on in Northern Ireland. Kevin Boyle et al. 1980. 40.00 (*0-900137-16-9*, Pub. by NCCL UK) St Mut.

Ten Years on the Pacific Coast. Francis X. Blanchet. 96p. 1982. 14.95 (*0-87770-281-0*) Ye Galleon.

Ten Years Plant Molecular Biology. Ed. by Robert A. Schilperoort & Leon Dure. LC 92-17645. 200p. (C). 1992. lib. bdg. 86.50 (*0-7923-1480-8*) Kluwer Ac.

Ten Years to Live. Henry J. Schut. (Illus.). 162p. (Orig.). 1990. pap. 6.95 (*0-9627163-1-6*) Arts & Images.

Ten Years under the Earth. Norbert Casteret. Tr. by Burrows Massey. LC 75-26892. (Illus.). 255p. 1975. reprint ed. 10.95 (*0-914264-06-0*); reprint ed. pap. 6.95 (*0-914264-07-9*) Cave Bks MO.

Ten Years Underwater. Ned Middleton. (Illus.). 136p. (C). 1995. 36.00 (*0-907151-43-4*, Pub. by IMMEL Pubng UK) St Mut.

Ten Years' War: An Account of the Battle with the Slum in New York. Jacob A. Riis. LC 70-103655. (Select Bibliographies Reprint Ser.). 1977. 29.95 (*0-8369-5155-7*) Ayer.

Ten Years Women in Design - Chicago: Anniversary Exhibit. Ed. by Mary J. Krysinski. (Illus.). 75p. (Orig.). 1988. pap. write for info. (*0-9620348-0-0*) Women Design.

Ten'a Texts & Tales from Anvik, Alaska...with Vocabulary by Pliny Earle Goddard. John W. Chapman. LC 73-3541. (American Ethnological Society Publications: No. 6). reprint ed. 37.50 (*0-404-58156-0*) AMS Pr.

Tenacious Miss Tamerlane. Kasey Michaels. 192p. 1982. pap. 2.95 (*0-380-79889-1*) Avon.

Tenacity of Prejudice: Anti-Semitism in Contemporary America. Gertude J. Selznick & Stephen Steinberg. LC 78-31365. (Univ of California Five-Year Study of Anti-Semitism). (Illus.). 248p. 1979. reprint ed. text ed. 59.75 (*0-313-20965-0*, SETP) Greenwood.

Tenacity of the Spirit: Biography of Dionisio Q. Quimosing. Thomas A. Bastian. (Illus.). 169p. (Orig.). (C). 1991. pap. 10.75 (*971-10-0450-X*, Pub. by New Day Pub PH) Cellar.

Tenancy & Resource Use Efficiency in Agriculture. M. M. Islam & B. N. Banerjee. 1987. 21.00 (*81-7099-020-3*, Pub. by Mittal II) S Asia.

Tenancy Relations & Agrarian Development: A Study of West Bengal. Sankar K. Bhaumik. LC 93-7495. (Illus.). 208p. (C). 1993. 32.00 (*0-8039-9118-5*) Sage.

Tenant. John Gill. 160p. 1985. pap. 4.95 (*0-89733-141-9*) Academy Chi Pubs.

Tenant: A Novel of Medical Science Fiction. Charles West. 300p. 1996. 21.95 (*1-885173-12-1*) Write Way.

Tenant Advocate's Guide to the South Carolina Residential Landlord & Tenant Act. Stuart M. Andrews. 298p. 1986. 21.00 (*0-685-23182-8*, 41,235) NCLS Inc.

Tenant at Will. Louise Wheeler. 88p. 1994. pap. 12.95 (*0-9640053-0-1*) L Wheeler.

Tenant Improvement Cost Book for Offices 1994. Marshall & Swift. 336p. 1993. per. 89.95 (*1-56842-012-9*) Marshall & Swift.

Tenant Improvement Cost Book...for Offices 1995. 2nd ed. Marshall & Swift Staff. (Illus.). 258p. 1995. pap. 95.95 (*1-56842-025-0*) Marshall & Swift.

Tenant Information Handbook: Apartment Renting in Washington, D.C. Ruth E. Evans. LC 87-288836. (Illus.). pap. write for info. (*0-9620084-5-1*) Essence Creations.

Tenant-Landlord. Kenneth Meiser. (Illus.). 90p. 1989. pap. 35.00 (*0-685-14672-3*) NJ Inst CLE.

Tenant League of Prince Edward Island, 1864-1867: Leasehold Tenure in the New World. Ian R. Robertson. (Illus.). 480p. 1996. 60.00 (*0-8020-0769-4*); pap. 24.95 (*0-8020-7138-4*) U of Toronto Pr.

Tenant of Wildfell Hall. Anne Bronte. Ed. by Herbert Rosengarten. LC 92-29052. (World's Classics Ser.). 512p. 1993. 6.95 (*0-19-282989-0*) OUP.

***Tenant of Wildfell Hall.** Anne Bronte. LC 97-14200. 1997. 19.00 (*0-679-60279-8*, Modern Lib) Random.

Tenant of Wildfell Hall. Anne Bronte. Ed. by G. D. Hargreaves. (English Library). 512p. 1980. pap. 6.95 (*0-14-043137-3*, Penguin Classics) Viking Penguin.

Tenant of Wildfell Hall. Anne Bronte. Ed. & Intro. by Steve Davies. 1996. pap. 7.95 (*0-14-043474-7*) Viking Penguin.

Tenant of Wildfell Hall. large type ed. Anne Bronte. 512p. 1990. 22.95 (*1-85089-363-2*, Pub. by ISIS UK) Transaction Pubs.

***Tenant of Wildfell Hall.** large type ed. Anne Bronte. 799p. 1997. 23.95 (*0-7089-8951-9*) Ulverscroft.

Tenant of Wildfell Hall. Anne Bronte. LC 79-4122. (Banquo Bks.). 389p. 1979. reprint ed. pap. 4.95 (*0-912800-70-4*) Woodbridge Pr.

Tenant Relations Assistant. (Career Examination Ser.: C-3756). pap. 23.95 (*0-8373-3756-9*) Nat Learn.

Tenant Resource & Advocacy Center. Maier Spielberg & Danielson Spielberg. 57p. pap. 5.00 (*0-686-36543-7*) Ctr Responsive Law.

Tenant Retention - Commercial. reprint ed. 9.95 (*0-685-71711-9*, 825) Inst Real Estate.

Tenant Retention Solution: A Revolutionary Approach to Commercial Real Estate Management. Howard K. Lundeen et al. LC 95-11791. (Illus.). 238p. 1995. text ed. 41.95 (*1-57203-008-9*, 742) Inst Real Estate.

***Tenant Retention Solution: A Revolutionary Approach to Commercial Real Estate Management.** Ed. by Howard K. Lundeen et al. 238p. 1995. 120.00 (*0-614-25330-6*, Pub. by R-I-C-S Bks UK) St Mut.

Tenant Right & Agrarian Society in Ulster 1600-1850. Martin W. Dowling. 240p. 1997. 45.00 (*0-7165-2592-5*, Pub. by Irish Acad Pr IE) Intl Spec Bk.

Tenant Smart: How to Win Your Legal Tenancy Rights Without a Lawyer (New York Edition) rev. ed. Benji O. Anosike. (Illus.). 214p. 1994. pap. text ed. 24.95 (*0-932704-28-X*) Do It Yourself Legal Pubs.

Tenant Supervisor. Jack Rudman. (Career Examination Ser.: C-543). 1994. pap. 29.95 (*0-8373-0543-8*) Nat Learn.

Tenants. Bernard Malamud. 230p. 1988. pap. 8.95 (*0-374-52102-6*) FS&G.

Tenants. Bernard Malamud. 176p. 1994. pap. 11.95 (*0-14-018516-X*, Penguin Classics) Viking Penguin.

Tenants & Nomads in Eastern Sudan: A Study of Economic Adaptations in the New Halfa Scheme. Gunnar M. Sorbo. (Illus.). 160p. (Orig.). 1985. pap. text ed. 33.00 (*91-7106-242-4*) Coronet Bks.

Tenants & the American Dream: Ideology & the Tenant Movement. Alan D. Heskin. LC 82-16688. 320p. 1983. text ed. 49.95 (*0-275-91004-0*, C1004, Praeger Pubs) Greenwood.

***Tenants' Complaints & the Reform of Housing Management.** Valerie Karn et al. LC 96-44097. (Illus.). 272p. 1997. text ed. 63.95 (*1-85521-756-2*, Pub. by Dartmth Pub UK) Ashgate Pub Co.

Tenant's Leasing Handbook. Jeanne D. Newman. 216p. 1991. pap. 19.95 (*0-7931-0317-7*, 4105-1101) Dearborn Finan.

Tenants Legal Rights' Kit: How to Win Disputes with Your Landlord. John C. Howell. 1992. 14.95 (*1-880398-06-0*) SJT Enterprises.

Tenants of Malory: A Novel, 3 vols, 1. Joseph S. Le Fanu. Ed. by Devendra P. Varma. LC 76-5276. (Collected Works). 1977. reprint ed. 25.95 (*0-405-09234-2*) Ayer.

Tenants of Malory: A Novel, 3 vols, Set. Joseph S. Le Fanu. Ed. by Devendra P. Varma. LC 76-5276. (Collected Works). 1977. reprint ed. 76.95 (*0-405-09233-4*) Ayer.

Tenants of Malory: A Novel, 3 vols, Vol. 2. Joseph S. Le Fanu. Ed. by Devendra P. Varma. LC 76-5276. (Collected Works). 1977. reprint ed. 25.95 (*0-405-09235-0*) Ayer.

Tenants of Malory: A Novel, 3 vols, Vol. 3. Joseph S. Le Fanu. Ed. by Devendra P. Varma. LC 76-5276. (Collected Works). 1977. reprint ed. 25.95 (*0-405-09236-9*) Ayer.

Tenants of Moonbloom. Edward L. Wallant. LC 63-13501. 245p. 1973. reprint ed. pap. 9.95 (*0-15-688535-2*, Harvest Bks) HarBrace.

Tenants of the Almighty. Arthur F. Raper. LC 76-137184. (Poverty U. S. A. Historical Record Ser.). 1971. reprint ed. 30.95 (*0-405-03122-X*) Ayer.

Tenants of Time. Thomas Flanagan. 864p. 1989. mass mkt. 6.99 (*0-446-35342-6*) Warner Bks.

Tenant's Revenge: How to Tame Your Landlord. Andy Kane. (Illus.). 108p. 1982. pap. 9.95 (*0-87364-258-9*) Paladin Pr.

***Tenants' Rights.** 13th rev. ed. Myron Moskovitz & Ralph Warner. LC 95-39119. (Illus.). 272p. (Orig.). 1997. pap. 19.95 (*0-87337-377-4*) Nolo Pr.

Tenants' Rights: A Guide for Washington State 1991. rev. ed. Barbara A. Isenhour et al. LC 91-12310. 174p. 1991. pap. 10.95 (*0-295-96852-4*) U of Wash Pr.

Tenants' Rights: California Edition. 12th ed. Myron Moskovitz & Ralph Warner. Ed. by Stephen Elias. LC 94-27465. (Illus.). 1996. pap. 18.95 (*0-87337-270-0*) Nolo Pr.

Tenants' Rights to Utility Service: 1993. National Consumer Law Center, Inc. Staff. LC 93-86927. (Utility Law Practice Ser.). 180p. 1994. pap. 60.00 (*1-881793-19-2*) Nat Consumer Law.

***Tenant's Survival Guide.** 2nd rev. ed. Carlton C. Casler. 208p. 1997. pap. 9.95 (*1-881436-03-9*) Consumer Law Bks.

Tenant's Survival Guide for Arizona Renters. Carlton C. Casler. 1994. pap. 9.95 (*1-881436-01-2*) Consumer Law Bks.

Tenascin & Counteradhesive Molecules of the Extracellular Matrix. Kathryn L. Crossin. (Cell Adhesion & Communication Ser.). 1996. text ed. 95.00 (*3-7186-5841-0*) Gordon & Breach.

Tenbow. large type ed. Matt Braun. (Nightingale Ser.). 271p. (Orig.). 1992. pap. 14.95 (*0-8161-5407-4*, GK Hall) Thorndike Pr.

Tench Coxe: A Study in American Economic Development. Harold H. Hutcheson. LC 78-64295. (Johns Hopkins University. Studies in the Social Sciences. Thirtieth Ser. 1912: 26). 248p. 1982. reprint ed. 37.50 (*0-404-61395-0*) AMS Pr.

Tench Coxe: A Study in American Economic Development. Harold H. Hutcheson. LC 77-98690. (American Scene Ser.). 1969. reprint ed. lib. bdg. 32.50 (*0-306-71511-2*) Da Capo.

Tench Coxe & the Early Republic. Jacob E. Cooke. LC 77-28832. (Institute of Early American History & Culture Ser.). (Illus.). xiv, 573p. 1978. 49.95 (*0-8078-1308-7*) U of NC Pr.

Tench Tilghman, the Life & Times of Washington's Aide-de-Camp. L. G. Shreve. LC 82-60330. (Illus.). 286p. 1982. reprint ed. pap. 81.60 (*0-7837-9090-2*, 2049840) Bks Demand.

Tend Your Own Garden First. Nancy Eichman. 1992. pap. 6.50 (*0-89137-457-4*) Quality Pubns.

Tendances Nouvelles: The Complete Run (1904-1914) of the Parisian Revue, 4 vols., Set. (Graphic Arts, Painting & Sculpture Ser.). 1980. reprint ed. 495.00 (*0-306-77581-6*) Da Capo.

Tendances Recentes En Linguistique Francaise et Generale: Volume Dedie A David Gaatone. Ed. by Hava B. Shyldkrot & Lucien Kupferman. LC 95-35085. (Lingvisticae Investigationes Supplementa Ser.: No. 20). xvi, 409p. 1995. 54.00 (*1-55619-750-0*) Benjamins North Am.

Tendencias A Largo Plazo En el Desarrollo Economico De America Latina. Ed. by Miguel Urrutia. 181p. 1993. 18.00 (*0-940602-60-1*) IADB.

Tendencies. Eve K. Sedgwick. LC 93-8369. (Series Q). 304p. 1993. text ed. 49.95 (*0-8223-1408-8*); pap. text ed. 16.95 (*0-8223-1421-5*) Duke.

Tendencies & Tensions of the Information Age: The Production & Distribution of Information in the United States. Jorge R. Schement & Terry Curtis. 381p. (C). 1994. 39.95 (*1-56000-166-6*) Transaction Pubs.

Tendencies & Tensions of the Information Age: The Production & Distribution of Information in the United States. Jorge R. Schement. 285p. 1997. pap. text ed. 21.95 (*1-56000-928-4*) Transaction Pubs.

Tendencies in American Poetry. Amy Lowell. LC 68-54171. (Studies in Poetry: No. 38). 1969. reprint ed. lib. bdg. 75.00 (*0-8383-0588-1*) M S G Haskell Hse.

Tendencies in Modern American Poetry. Amy Lowell. (BCL1-PS American Literature Ser.). 349p. 1992. reprint ed. lib. bdg. 89.00 (*0-7812-6629-7*) Rprt Serv.

Tendencies of Modern English Drama. Arthur E. Morgan. LC 68-29233. (Essay Index Reprint Ser.). 1977. 21.95 (*0-8369-1061-3*) Ayer.

Tendencies of the Modern Novel. Hugh Walpole et al. LC 67-23272. (Essay Index Reprint Ser.). 1977. 19.95 (*0-8369-0929-1*) Ayer.

Tender. Mark Childress. 544p. 1991. mass mkt. 5.99 (*0-345-36526-7*) Ballantine.

***Tender.** Mark Childress. 1997. pap. 12.00 (*0-345-41903-0*) Ballantine.

***Tender.** Toi Derricotte. LC 97-4602. (Poetry Ser.). 80p. 1997. 25.00 (*0-8229-3993-2*) U of Pittsburgh Pr.

***Tender.** Toi Derricotte. LC 97-4602. (Poetry Ser.). 80p. 1997. pap. 12.95 (*0-8229-5640-3*) U of Pittsburgh Pr.

Tender Accents of Sound: Spanish in the Chicano Novel in English. Ernst Rudin. 262p. (Orig.). 1996. pap. 22.00 (*0-927534-52-5*) Biling Rev-Pr.

Tender Agencies. Dennis Denisoff. 1995. per. 12.95 (*1-55152-012-5*, Pub. by Arsenal Pulp CN) LPC InBook.

Tender Assault. Anne Mather. 1994. 2.99 (*0-373-11649-7*) Harlequin Bks.

Tender Assault. large type ed. Anne Mather. (Harlequin Ser.). 1994. lib. bdg. 18.95 (*0-263-13716-3*) Thorndike Pr.

Tender at the Bone: Growing up at the Table. Ruth Reichl. LC 97-14720. 1998. 23.00 (*0-679-44987-6*) Random.

Tender Bargaining: Negotiating an Equal Partnership with the Man You Love. Carol Cassell. 224p. 1993. 22.95 (*1-56565-033-6*, Woman-Woman) Lowell Hse.

Tender Beguilement. Carol A. Osley. (Orig.). 1985. write for info. (*0-910119-12-0*) SOCO Pubns.

Tender Betrayal. F. Rosanne Bittner. 512p. 1993. mass mkt. 5.99 (*0-553-29808-9*) Bantam.

Tender Betrayal. Jennifer Blake. 1993. mass mkt. 4.99 (*0-449-14877-7*, GM) Fawcett.

Tender Betrayal. large type ed. F. Rosanne Bittner. LC 93-33651. 1994. lib. bdg. 22.95 (*0-7862-0069-3*) Thorndike Pr.

Tender Bondage. large type ed. Anne Durham. 1990. 25.99 (*0-7089-2216-3*) Ulverscroft.

Tender Bud: A Physician's Journey Through Breast Cancer. Madeleine Meldin. LC 92-49967. 232p. 1993. 29.95 (*0-88163-157-4*) Analytic Pr.

***Tender Buns.** P. N. Dedeaux. 1996. pap. 5.95 (*1-56333-396-1*) Masquerade.

Tender Buttons. Gertrude Stein. LC 75-188094. 1972. lib. bdg. 250.00 (*0-87968-003-2*) Gordon Pr.

Tender Buttons. Gertrude Stein. (Sun & Moon Classics Ser.: No. 8). 80p. 1990. pap. 9.95 (*1-55713-093-0*) Sun & Moon CA.

Tender Buttons. Gertrude Stein. LC 74-100787. (American Literature Ser.: No. 49). (C). 1970. reprint ed. lib. bdg. 49.95 (*0-8383-0333-1*) M S G Haskell Hse.

***Tender Comrades.** McGilligan. LC 97-16178. 1997. 26.95 (*0-312-17046-7*) St Martin.

Tender Conquest. Lisa Bingham. 352p. (Orig.). 1989. pap. 3.95 (*0-380-75734-6*) Avon.

Tender Courage: Reflections on the Life & Spirit of Catherine Mcauley. M. Joanna Regan & Isabelle Keiss. 158p. (Orig.). 1988. pap. 7.95 (*0-8199-0917-3*, Frncscn Herld) Franciscan Pr.

***Tender Crusader.** Linda L. Bartell. 384p. 1997. mass mkt. 4.99 (*0-8217-5751-2*, Zebra Kensgtn) Kensgtn Pub Corp.

Tender Darkness: A Mary MacLane Anthology. Mary MacLane. Ed. by Elisabeth A. Pruitt. (Illus.). 208p. 1993. reprint ed. pap. 14.95 (*1-883304-01-6*) Abernathy & Brown.

Tender Deceit. Patricia Wilson. (Romance Ser.). 1995. mass mkt. 2.99 (*0-373-03364-8*, 1-03364-6) Harlequin Bks.

Tender Deception. Judith Steel. 448p. 1993. mass mkt. 4.50 (*0-8217-4397-X*, Zebra Kensgtn) Kensgtn Pub Corp.

Tender Deception. large type ed. Lisa Charles. (Linford Romance Library). 272p. 1992. pap. 15.99 (*0-7089-7203-9*, Linford) Ulverscroft.

Tender Ecstasy. Janelle Taylor. (Orig.). 1991. mass mkt. 4.99 (*0-8217-3500-4*, Zebra Kensgtn) Kensgtn Pub Corp.

Tender Ecstasy. Janelle Taylor. 1995. pap. 5.99 (*0-8217-5242-1*) NAL-Dutton.

Tender Farewell of Jesus: Meditations on Chapter 17 of John's Gospel. Adrian Van Kaam. (Christian Living Ser.). 128p. (Orig.). 1996. pap. 8.95 (*1-56548-080-5*) New City.

***Tender Fury.** Connie Mason. 400p. 1996. mass mkt. 5.99 (*0-8439-4196-0*) Dorchester Pub Co.

Tender Geographies: Women & the Origins of the Novel in France. Joan DeJean. 352p. 1991. text ed. 39.50 (*0-231-06230-3*) Col U Pr.

Tender Geographies: Women & the Origins of the Novel in France. Joan Dejean. 1993. pap. 17.50 (*0-231-06231-1*) Col U Pr.

***Tender Guardian.** large type ed. Cathie Linz. LC 96-31686. (Romance-Hall Ser.). 217p. 1996. 22.95 (*0-7838-1909-9*, Thorndike Lrg Prnt) Thorndike Pr.

Tender Hand. Pip Atkin. (C). 1989. pap. 21.00 (*1-85072-114-9*, Pub. by W Sessions UK) St Mut.

***Tender Hearts Book of Days.** Virginia Dixon. 1997. 12.99 (*1-881830-55-1*) Garborgs.

Tender Hours. Paige Phillips. (Intrigue Ser.). 1996. mass mkt. 3.75 (*0-373-22372-2*, 1-22372-6) Harlequin Bks.

Tender Husband. Richard Steele. Ed. by Calhoun Winton. LC 66-25598. (Regents Restoration Drama Ser.). 112p. 1967. reprint ed. pap. 32.00 (*0-608-01704-3*, 2062359) Bks Demand.

Tender Ironies: A Tribute to Lothar Lutze. Ed. by Dilip Chitre et al. 1994. 32.00 (*81-7304-088-5*) S Asia.

***Tender Is the Night.** Fitzgerald. (York Notes Ser.). 1992. pap. text ed. write for info. (*0-582-78275-9*, Pub. by Longman UK) Longman.

***Tender Is the Night.** Fitzgerald. (Longman Literature Ser.). 1993. pap. text ed. write for info. (*0-582-09716-9*, Pub. by Longman UK) Longman.

Tender Is the Night. F. Scott Fitzgerald. (Hudson River Editions Ver.). 315p. 1977. 40.00 (*0-684-15151-0*) S&S Trade.

Tender Is the Night. F. Scott Fitzgerald. 1995. pap. 10.00 (*0-684-80154-X*) S&S Trade.

Tender Is the Night. F. Scott Fitzgerald. 1996. 25.00 (*0-684-83050-7*) S&S Trade.

Tender Is the Night. large type ed. F. Scott Fitzgerald. LC 94-2948. 543p. 1994. lib. bdg. 22.95 (*0-8161-5960-2*, GK Hall) Thorndike Pr.

Tender Is the Night, Pt. I, Vols. 1-2. Ed. by Matthew J. Bruccoli. (F. Scott Fitzgerald Manuscripts: Vol. 4A). 654p. 1990. text ed. 155.00 (*0-8240-5958-1*) Garland.

Tender Is the Night: Essays in Criticism. Ed. by Marvin J. LaHood. LC 77-85091. 222p. reprint ed. pap. 63.30 (*0-8357-9246-3*, 2017625) Bks Demand.

Tender Is the Night: The Broken Universe. Milton R. Stern. (Twayne's Masterwork Studies: 137). 160p. 1994. 23.95 (*0-8057-8380-6*, Twayne); pap. 13.95 (*0-8057-8381-4*, Twayne) Scribnrs Ref.

Tender is the Night see Three Novels of F. Scott Fitzgerald

Tender Is the Night Notes. Carol Poston. (Orig.). 1974. pap. 4.25 (*0-8220-1241-3*) Cliffs.

Tender Is the Night, 1934. Intro. by Matthew J. Bruccoli. (F. Scott Fitzgerald Manuscripts: Vol. 4B). 3214p. 1991. Set. text ed. 675.00 (*0-8240-5960-3*) Garland.

Tender Is the Search. large type ed. Helga Moray. 288p. 1989. 25.99 (*0-7089-2030-6*) Ulverscroft.

Tender Is the Storm. Johanna Lindsey. 336p. 1985. mass mkt. 6.50 (*0-380-89693-1*) Avon.

Tender Is the Touch. Ana Leigh. 384p. (Orig.). 1994. mass mkt. 4.50 (*0-380-77350-3*) Avon.

Tender Lies. Nancy P. Gilsenan. 1984. pap. 5.00 (*0-87129-234-3*, T63) Dramatic Pub.

***Tender Love.** Hybels. pap. 16.50 (*0-8024-6348-7*) Moody.

Tender Loving Rage. Alfred Bester. LC 91-65201. 261p. 1991. 19.95 (*0-9623712-4-6*) Tafford Pub.

***Tender Masquerade.** Linda Cajio. 1997. mass mkt. 4.99 (*0-8217-5752-0*) Kensgtn Pub Corp.

Tender Mercies. Rosellen Brown. 368p. 1994. mass mkt. 5.99 (*0-440-21696-6*) Dell.

Tender Mercies: Applying God's Mercy to Your Life. Ray Bentley. Ed. by Jennie Gillespie. (Illus.). 96p. (Orig.). 1993. pap. 4.95 (*0-9638878-0-7*) In The Word.

Tender Mercies: Inside the World of a Child Abuse Investigator. Keith Richards. LC 91-50624. 280p. (Orig.). 1991. pap. 12.95 (*1-879360-07-1*) Noble Pr.

Tender Moments: Diary of a First-Time Mother. Vivianne Winters. Ed. by Sharon Goldinger. (Illus.). 328p. 1990. 14.95 (*1-878374-36-2*); pap. text ed. 12.95 (*1-878374-35-4*); lib. bdg. 13.95 (*1-878374-37-0*) Pac Coast Pubs.

Tender Obscenity. Jim Teague & Ann Teague. Ed. by Billie Young. LC 73-76537. 1973. 19.95 (*0-87949-012-8*) Ashley Bks.

Tender Offer: A Sneak Attack in Corporate Warfare. Dorman L. Commons. LC 85-1182. 148p. 1985. 30.00 (*0-520-05583-7*) U CA Pr.

Tender Offerings. Meredith Rich. LC 93-42074. 1994. 22.00 (*0-671-78883-3*) S&S Trade.

***Tender Offerings.** large type ed. Meredith Rich. (Black Satin Romance Ser.). 496p. 1996. 25.99 (*1-86110-012-4*) Ulverscroft.

Tender Offers: Defenses, Responses & Planning, 4 vols. Arthur Fleischer, Jr. 280.00 (*0-318-36199-X*) P-H.

Tender Offers: Developments & Commentaries. Ed. by Marc I. Steinberg. LC 84-24947. (Illus.). viii, 363p. 1985. text ed. 65.00 (*0-89930-088-X*, STT/, Quorum Bks) Greenwood.

Tender Offers for Corporate Control. Edward R. Aranow & Herbert A. Einhorn. LC 72-10557. 352p. 1973. text ed. 95.00 (*0-231-03671-X*) Col U Pr.

***Tender Rebel.** Virginia Gaffney. LC 97-12381. (Richmond Chronicles: Bk. 3). 400p. 1997. pap. 9.99 (*1-56507-669-9*) Harvest Hse.

Tender Rebel. Johanna Lindsey. 384p. (Orig.). 1988. mass mkt. 6.99 (*0-380-75086-4*) Avon.

***Tender Redemption.** George F. Hambidge. LC 97-90185. 1997. 16.95 (*0-533-12318-6*) Vantage.

Tender Road Home: The Story of How God Healed a Marriage Crippled by Anger & Abuse. Paul Luchsinger & Susie Luchsinger. LC 97-13819. (Illus.). 224p. 1997. 18.99 (*0-8054-6082-9*, 4260-82) Broadman.

***Tender Roses for Tough Climates.** Douglas Green. LC 96-51616. 1997. 34.95 (*1-57630-031-5*); pap. 19.95 (*1-57630-032-3*) Chapters Pub.

Tender Savage. Phoebe Conn. 480p. 1989. mass mkt. 3.95 (*0-8217-2572-6*, Zebra Kensgtn) Kensgtn Pub Corp.

Tender Scoundrel. Linda L. Bartell. 384p. 1996. mass mkt. 4.99 (*0-8217-5192-1*, Zebra Kensgtn) Kensgtn Pub Corp.

Tender Ship: Governmental Management of Technological Change. Arthur M. Squires. (Illus.). 267p. 1986. 36.50 (*0-8176-3312-X*) Birkhauser.

Tender Taming: When Next We Love, 2 bks. in 1. Heather X. Graham. 368p. 1994. mass mkt., pap. text ed. 4.99 (*0-505-51939-9*, Love Spell) Dorchester Pub Co.

***Tender Thoughts.** (Tender Hearts Collection). 32p. 1997. 9.99 (*1-881830-30-6*, DS18412) Garborgs.

Tender to the Queen of Spain: Poetry Book Society Recommendation. Ken Smith. 64p. 9400. pap. 14.95 (*1-85224-261-2*, Pub. by Bloodaxe Bks UK) Dufour.

***Tender Touch.** Lynn Emery. 1997. pap. 4.99 (*0-7860-0464-9*) Kensgtn Pub Corp.

***Tender Touch.** Lynn Emery. 352p. 1997. mass mkt. 4.99 (*0-7860-0465-7*, Pinncle Kensgtn) Kensgtn Pub Corp.

Tender Touch. Rexella Van Impe. 143p. 1980. pap. 5.00 (*0-934803-16-1*) J Van Impe.

***Tender Touch.** large type ed. Caroline Anderson. (Mills & Boon Large Print Ser.). 288p. 1996. 21.50 (*0-263-14770-3*, Pub. by M & B UK) Ulverscroft.

Tender Touch: Biogenic Fulfillment. Edmond B. Szekely. (Illus.). 120p. 1977. text ed. 5.50 (*0-89564-020-1*) IBS Intl.

Tender Touch, A Guide to Infant Massage. Healthy Alternatives, Inc. Staff. 1986. 29.95 (*0-9618800-0-7*) Healthy Alterntvs.

Tender Touch of God: Turning Your Hurts into Hope. Mike MacIntosh. LC 95-42617. 192p. 1996. pap. 8.99 (*1-56507-408-4*) Harvest Hse.

Tender Trap. Beverly Barton. 1997. mass mkt. 3.50 (*0-373-76047-7*, 1-76047-9) Silhouette.

Tender Trap. Max Shulman. 1956. pap. 5.25 (*0-8222-1118-1*) Dramatists Play.

Tender Triumph. Judith McNaught. Ed. by Linda Marrow. 1991. pap. 6.99 (*0-671-74256-6*) PB.

Tender Tyrant. large type ed. Quenna Tilbury. (Linford Romance Library). 334p. 1984. pap. 15.99 (*0-7089-6028-6*) Ulverscroft.

Tender Warrior. Ed. by Larry R. Libby. 256p. 1993. 18.99 (*0-88070-579-5*, Multnomah Bks) Multnomah Pubs.

Tender Warrior. Fern Michaels. 384p. (Orig.). 1983. mass mkt. 5.99 (*0-345-30358-X*) Ballantine.

Tender Warrior. large type ed. Fern Michaels. LC 95-17739. 587p. 1995. reprint ed. 23.95 (*0-7862-0497-4*) Thorndike Pr.

Tender Warriors: A Novel. Rachel G. DeVries. LC 86-4690. 192p. (Orig.). 1986. pap. 8.95 (*0-932379-14-1*); lib. bdg. 18.95 (*0-932379-15-X*) Firebrand Bks.

Tender Wishes. Jo A. Cassity. 336p. (Orig.). 1993. mass mkt. 4.99 (*1-55773-922-6*) Diamond.

***Tender Years.** Janette Oke. LC 97-21037. (Prairie Legacy Ser.: No. 1). 1997. 15.99 (*1-55661-952-9*); 15.99 (*1-55661-953-7*) Bethany Hse.

***Tender Years.** Janette Oke. LC 97-21037. (Prairie Legacy Ser.). 1997. write for info. (*0-7642-2008-X*) Bethany Hse.

***Tender Years: Toward Developmentally-Sensitive Child Welfare Services for Very Young Children.** Jill D. Berrick & Barbara Needell. (Child Welfare Practice, Policy & Research Ser.). (Illus.). 240p. 1998. pap. text ed. 19.95 (*0-19-511453-1*) OUP.

Tenderfoot. Will James. (Illus.). 32p. 1995. 195.00 (*0-9620327-3-5*) Nygard Pub.

Tenderfoot: Back to the Ranch. Knoll. 1994. pap. 2.99 (*0-373-15542-5*) Harlequin Bks.

Tenderfoot Back to the Ranch. Patricia Knoll. (Romance Ser.). 1994. mass mkt. 2.99 (*0-373-03296-X*, 1-03296-0) Harlequin Bks.

Tenderfoot Bandits: Sam Bass & Joel Collins, Their Lives & Hard Times. Paula Reed & Grover T. Tate. (Great West & Indian Ser.: Vol. 51). (Illus.). 1987. 26.95 (*0-87026-066-9*) Westernlore.

Tenderfoot Bride: Tales from an Old Ranch. Clarice E. Richards. LC 88-14347. (Illus.). viii, 240p. 1988. pap. 7.95 (*0-8032-8930-8*, Bison Books) U of Nebr Pr.

Tenderfoot in Tombstone, the Private Journal of George Whitwell Parksons: The Turbulent Years, 1880-82. Lynn R. Bailey. (Great West & Indian Ser.: Vol. 65). (Illus.). 1996. 36.95 (*0-87026-095-2*) Westernlore.

Tenderfoot Kid on Gyp Water. Carl P. Benedict. LC 86-6911. (Illus.). xiv, 115p. 1986. reprint ed. pap. 4.95 (*0-8032-6079-2*, Bison Books) U of Nebr Pr.

Tenderloin. Bill Kamin. LC 88-92770. (Illus.). 64p. (Orig.). 1989. pap. 14.95 (*0-9621644-0-2*) Black Cat Pr.

Tenderloin Rose. Kathleen Wood. 24p. (Orig.). 1990. pap. 3.00 (*0-929730-24-0*) Zeitgeist Pr.

Tenderly I Care. Albert J. Nimeth. 123p. 1977. pap. 5.00 (*0-8199-0952-1*, Frncscn Herld) Franciscan Pr.

Tenderness. Dorothy Garlock. 384p. (Orig.). 1993. mass mkt. 5.99 (*0-446-36370-7*) Warner Bks.

Tenderness. Joyce Carol Oates. LC 96-1726. 91p. 1996. 18.95 (*0-86538-085-6*) Ontario Rev NJ.

Tenderness. large type ed. Dorothy Garlock. LC 93-26834. (Orig.). 1993. lib. bdg. 20.95 (*0-8161-5851-7*, GK Hall) Thorndike Pr.

Tenderness: A Novel. Robert Cormier. 240p. (YA). 1997. 16.95 (*0-385-32286-0*, Delacorte Pr Bks) BDD Bks Young Read.

***Tenderness & Fire, Vol. 5.** Robert Funderburk. LC 97-4644. (Innocent Years Ser.). 1997. pap. text ed. 8.99 (*1-55661-464-0*) Bethany Hse.

Tenderness of Memory. Christin Swanberg. 89p. (Orig.). 1994. pap. 13.95 (*0-911051-78-3*) Plain View.

Tending & Teaching Babies. Lynda T. Boardman. 84p. (Orig.). 1985. pap. 5.99 (*0-8341-1063-6*) Beacon Hill.

Tending Inner Gardens: The Healing Art of Feminist Psychotherapy. Lesley I. Shore. LC 93-36036. 201p. (C). 1994. 39.95 (*1-56024-885-8*); pap. 14.95 (*1-56023-856-9*) Haworth Pr.

***Tending the Fire.** Juddi Morris. LC 97-12009. 112p. (J). (gr. 3 up). 1997. 12.95 (*0-87358-665-4*, Rising Moon Bks); pap. 6.95 (*0-87358-654-9*, Rising Moon Bks) Northland AZ.

Tending the Fire: The Ritual Men's Group. Wayne Liebman. 64p. 1991. pap. 7.00 (*0-915408-45-7*) Ally Pr.

Tending the Fire Within: How to Protect Male Potency. Larry Brynjuifson. (Illus.). 128p. (Orig.). 1994. pap. text ed. 17.95 (*0-9640877-0-7*) Hid Treas Pub.

Tending the Garden: Essays on Mormon Literature. Ed. by Eugene England & Lavina F. Anderson. LC 94-48077. (Essays on Mormonism Ser.: No. 8). 253p. (Orig.). 1996. pap. 18.95 (*1-56085-019-1*) Signature Bks.

Tending the Light. Mary E. Feagins. LC 84-60120. 1984. pap. 3.00 (*0-87574-255-6*) Pendle Hill.

Tending the Master's Garden: Joyful Thanksgiving for the Beauty of God's Handiwork, Vol. 1. May G. Harris. (Illus.). 72p. 1996. 14.95 (*0-89221-315-9*) New Leaf.

***Tending the Spiritual Land, 9 vols.** Jen Chen Buddhists Staff. Ed. by Ta L. Shih. 190p. (Orig.). (CHI.). Date not set. pap. write for info. (*0-9647369-9-3*) Jen Chen Budd-Houston.

***Tending the Spiritual Land, Vol. 1.** unabridged ed. Jen Chen Buddhists Staff. Ed. by Ta L. Shih. LC 95-79833. 186p. (Orig.). (CHI.). 1995. pap. 6.00 (*0-9647369-0-X*) Jen Chen Budd-Houston.

***Tending the Spiritual Land, Vol. 2.** unabridged ed. Jen Chen Buddhists Staff. Ed. by Ta L. Shih. LC 96-94056. 190p. (Orig.). (CHI.). 1996. pap. 6.00 (*0-9647369-1-8*) Jen Chen Budd-Houston.

***Tending the Spiritual Land, Vol. 3.** unabridged ed. Jen Chen Buddhists Staff. Ed. by Ta L. Shih. 190p. (Orig.). (CHI.). 1998. pap. write for info. (*0-9647369-2-6*) Jen Chen Budd-Houston.

***Tending the Spiritual Land, Vol. 4.** unabridged ed. Jen Chen Buddhists Staff. Ed. by Ta L. Shih. 190p. (Orig.). (CHI.). Date not set. pap. write for info. (*0-9647369-3-4*) Jen Chen Budd-Houston.

Tending to Virginia. Jill McCorkle. 328p. 1987. 15.95 (*0-912697-65-2*) Algonquin Bks.

Tending to Virginia. Jill McCorkle. 1988. mass mkt. 5.99 (*0-449-21624-1*, Crest) Fawcett.

***Tending to Virginia.** Jill McCorkle. 1997. pap. 12.00 (*0-449-91253-1*) Fawcett.

Tendon & Nerve Injuries of the Hand: Surgery & Rehabilitation. Hunter & Schneider. 700p. (C). (gr. 13). 1997. text ed. 165.00 (*0-8151-4740-6*) Mosby Yr Bk.

Tendon Transfers of the Hand & Forearm. Richard J. Smith. (Illus.). 320p. 1987. 102.00 (*0-316-80174-7*) Little.

Tendoy, Chief of the Lemhis. David L. Crowder. LC 75-76336. (Illus.). 139p. (Orig.). reprint ed. pap. 39.70 (*0-8357-7938-6*, 2057011) Bks Demand.

Tendre Secret. Charlotte Lamb. (FRE.). 1994. pap. 3.50 (*0-373-34438-4*, 1-34438-1) Harlequin Bks.

Tendres Stocks. Paul Morand. (FRE.). 1981. pap. 8.95 (*0-7859-4159-2*) Fr & Eur.

Tendril. Vel Gerth. (Illus.). 1983. pap. 2.00 (*0-685-42585-1*) Vardaman Pr.

Tendril, No. 14-15. Ed. by George E. Murphy. 256p. 1983. pap. 5.95 (*0-937504-03-3*) Tendril.

Tendril, No. 16. Ed. by George E. Murphy. 182p. 1983. pap. 5.95 (*0-937504-04-1*) Tendril.

Tendril, No. 17. Ed. by George E. Murphy. 212p. 1984. pap. 5.95 (*0-937504-05-X*) Tendril.

Tendril, Nos. 19-20. Ed. by George E. Murphy. 440p. 1985. pap. 10.95 (*0-937504-07-6*) Tendril.

Tendril in the Mesh. William Everson. (Western Bks.). 1974. pap. 150.00 (*0-9600372-3-3*) Cayucos.

Tendrils of the Eye. Illus. by Edward R. Peres. 58p. (Orig.). 1993. pap. text ed. write for info. (*0-9639765-0-8*) Haiku Moments.

Tendring Peninsula. Peter Ford. 1993. pap. 15.00 (*0-86025-420-8*, Pub. by Ian Henry Pubns UK) Empire Pub Srvs.

Tendryakov: The Trial (Sud) Ed. by Peter Doyle. (Bristol Russian Texts Ser.). 102p. (RUS.). (C). 1990. reprint ed. pap. 19.95 (*0-631-15771-9*, Pub. by Blckwell Pubs UK) Focus Pub-R Pullins.

Tenebreuse Affaire. Honore De Balzac. 1973. 11.95 (*0-685-58347-3*, 2070364682); pap. 11.95 (*0-7859-1760-8*, 2070364682) Fr & Eur.

Tenebreuse Affaire. Honore De Balzac. (Folio Ser.: No. 468). (FRE.). 1973. 9.95 (*2-07-036468-2*) Schoenhof.

***Tenebrionidae (Insecta: Coleoptera)** J. C. Watt. (Fauna of New Zealand Ser.: Vol. 26). (Illus.). 70p. 1992. pap. 27.95 (*0-477-02639-7*, Pub. by Manaaki Whenua NZ) Balogh.

Tenement Conditions in Chicago: Report by the Investigating Committee of the City Homes Association. Robert Hunter. 1972. reprint ed. lib. bdg. 29.00 (*0-8422-8182-7*) Irvington.

Tenement Handbook: An Illustrated Architectural Guide. John Gilbert & Ann Flint. (Illus.). 128p. (C). 1993. pap. 35.00 (*1-873190-14-X*, Pub. by Rutland Pr UK) St Mut.

Tenement House Problem: Including the Report of the New York State Tenement House Commission of 1900, 2 Vols. Ed. by Robert W. DeForest & Lawrence Veiller. LC 75-112537. (Rise of Urban America Ser.). (Illus.). 1974. reprint ed. 65.95 (*0-405-02446-0*) Ayer.

Tenement Landlord. George Sternlieb. LC 75-90260. 290p. reprint ed. pap. 82.70 (*0-7837-5685-2*, 2059113) Bks Demand.

Tenement Landscapes. Paul Mena. 20p. 1995. pap. 3.00 (*1-888431-02-4*) Small Garlic.

Tenement of Clay. Paul West. LC 92-16449. 232p. 1993. 20.00 (*0-929701-27-5*); pap. 12.00 (*0-929701-28-3*) McPherson & Co.

Tenement on the Brome Plantation: Analysis of Surface Finds from an Early 20th- Century Site (18ST1-48) in St. Mary's City, Maryland. Gordon Fine. (Research Papers: No. 5). 60p. 1987. ring bd. 7.00 (*1-878399-37-3*) Div Hist Cult Progs.

Tenement Songs: The Popular Music of Jewish Immigrants. Mark Slobin. LC 81-4932. (Music in American Life Ser.). (Illus.). 232p. 1982. digital audio 24.95 (*0-252-00962-2*) U of Ill Pr.

Tenement Songs: The Popular Music of the Jewish Immigrants. Mark Slobin. 256p. 1995. pap. text ed. 15.95 (*0-252-06562-X*) U of Ill Pr.

***Tenement Songs: The Popular Music of the Jewish Immigrants.** Mark Slobin. (Illus.). 256p. 1996. pap. 24.95 incl. audio (*0-252-06563-8*) U of Ill Pr.

Tenement Writer: An Immigrant's Story. Ben Sonder. LC 92-14400. (Stories of America Ser.). (Illus.). 72p. (J). (gr. 2-5). 1992. lib. bdg. 25.68 (*0-8114-7235-3*) Raintree Steck-V.

Tenements of Chicago, 1908-1935. Edith Abbott. LC 78-112535. (Rise of Urban America Ser.). (Illus.). 1976. reprint ed. lib. bdg. 41.95 (*0-405-02431-2*) Ayer.

***Tenemos Hombre de Jesus.** D. Wilkerson. (SPA.). 9.95 (*0-8297-1967-9*) Life Pubs Intl.

Tener Hijos No es para Cobardes. James Dobson. 168p. (SPA.). 1991. pap. 8.95 (*0-8297-0395-0*) Life Pubs Intl.

Tener Plus Past Participle: A Case Study in Linguistic Description. Catherine E. Harre. (Romance Linguistics Ser.). 256p. (C). (gr. 13). 1992. text ed. 69.95 (*0-415-05647-0*, A6315) Routledge.

Tenerife. (Insight Guides Ser.). (Orig.). 1993. pap. 21.95 (*0-395-66315-6*) HM.

Tenerife! Henk Elsink, pseud. Tr. by H. G. Smittenaar from DUT. 212p. (Orig.). 1992. pap. 7.95 (*1-881164-51-9*) Intercont VA.

***Tenerife.** Paul Murphy. (Essential Travel Guides Ser.). 128p. 1997. pap. 7.95 (*0-8442-4813-4*) NTC Pub Grp.

Teneriffe & Its Six Satellites, or the Canary Islands Past & Present, 2 vols. Olivia M. Stone. 1976. lib. bdg. 250.00 (*0-8490-2734-9*) Gordon Pr.

Teneriffe Lace. Ed. by Jules Kliot & Kaethe Kliot. (Illus.). 96p. 1993. pap. 12.00 (*0-916896-22-6*) Lacis Pubns.

Tenetehara Indians of Brazil. Charles Wagley & Eduardo Galvao. LC 79-82359. (Columbia Univ. Contributions to Anthropology Ser.: Vol. 35). 1969. reprint ed. 31.50 (*0-404-50585-6*) AMS Pr.

Tenets of Islam. 14.50 (*0-933511-75-2*) Kazi Pubns.

Tenets of Stoicism Assembled & Systematized from the Works of L. A. Seneca. H. B. Timothy. 118p. (Orig.). 1973. pap. text ed. 28.50 (*0-317-57965-7*, Pub. by AM Hakkert NE) Coronet Bks.

Tenga una Actitud Mental Positiva. Ed. by Paloma Peers. 130p. (Orig.). (SPA.). 1995. pap. 6.95 (*1-884864-04-X*) Am Success Inst.

Tengo. Nicholas Guillen. Tr. by Richard Carr. (YA). (gr. 12 up). 1974. 7.25 (*0-910296-28-6*) Broadside Pr.

Tengo Prisa. Olga Rosado. (Coleccion Espejo de Paciencia). 1978. pap. 5.00 (*0-89729-197-2*) Ediciones.

Tengo Seis Anos. Ann Morris. (Illus.). 32p. (J). (gr. 1-3). 1996. pap. 5.95 (*0-382-39317-1*); lib. bdg. 15.95 (*0-382-39316-3*) Silver Burdett Pr.

Tengo Todo...Casi Todo. Luis Palau. (Cruzado Ser.). (SPA.). 1991. 1.79 (*1-56063-118-X*, 498013) Editorial Unilit.

***Tengo Todo...Casi Todo.** Luis Palau. (Serie Cruzada - Crusade Ser.). 26p. (SPA.). 1991. pap. write for info. (*0-614-27143-6*) Editorial Unilit.

Tengu Child: Stories by Kikuo Itaya. Kikuo Itaya. Tr. by John Gardner. LC 82-5876. (Illus.). 243p. 1983. 15.95 (*0-8093-1081-3*) S Ill U Pr.

Tenmile! Nearby Canyon of Mystery. Jack Bickers. Ed. by Pat Bickers. (Illus.). 80p. (Orig.). (C). 1991. pap. 6.00 (*0-9621507-8-9*) Four WD Trailguide.

Tenn-Tom Country: The Upper Tombigbee Valley. James Doster & David C. Weaver. LC 85-13974. (Illus.). 256p. 1987. 49.95 (*0-8173-0279-4*) U of Ala Pr.

Tenn-Tom Nitty-Gritty Cruise Guide. 2nd rev. ed. Fred Myers. (Illus.). 95p. (Orig.). 1996. pap. 16.95 (*0-9632005-5-0*) F Myers.

Tennant. A. M. Tennant et al. 356p. 1991. reprint ed. pap. 46.50 (*0-8328-2184-5*); reprint ed. lib. bdg. 56.50 (*0-8328-2183-7*) Higginson Bk Co.

Tenneco Gas Fifty Years. Tenneco Gas Company Staff. 55p. 1993. write for info. (*1-882771-01-X*) Hist Factory.

Tennesse John Stoltzfus: Amish Church-Related Documents & Family Letters. Ed. & Tr. by Paton Yoder from GRE. Tr. by Noah G. Good et al. from GRE. LC 86-80085. (Mennonite Sources & Documents Ser.: No. 1). (Illus.). 296p. 1987. 24.95 (*0-9614479-5-8*) Lancaster Mennonite.

***Tennesse Outdoorsman.** Jimmy Holt & Glen Smith. Date not set. write for info. (*0-688-07280-1*) Morrow.

Tennessean. Anne Royall. LC 78-64092. reprint ed. 37.50 (*0-404-17166-4*) AMS Pr.

T

An Asterisk (*) at the beginning of an entry indicates that the title is appearing in BIP for the first time.

***Tennesseans Before 1800: Washington County.** Marjorie H. Fischer. 1996. lib. bdg. 49.50 (*0-932231-11-X*, TN78) Frontier Pr.

Tennesseans in Texas: As Found in the 1850 Census of Texas. Helen C. Marsh & Timothy R. Marsh. 416p. 1986. 37.50 (*0-89308-561-8*, TN 94) Southern Hist Pr.

Tennesseans in the Civil War: A Military History of Confederate & Union Units with Available Rosters of Personnel, Pt. 1, Military History. Tennessee Historical Commission Staff. 482p. 1964. 38.00 (*0-87402-017-4*) U of Tenn Pr.

Tennesseans in the Civil War: A Military History of Confederate & Union Units with Available Rosters of Personnel, Pt. 2, Rosters. Tennessee Historical Commission Staff. 612p. 1981. reprint ed. 48.00 (*0-87402-018-2*) U of Tenn Pr.

***Tennessee.** Tracy Barrett. LC 96-44983. (Celebrate the States Ser.). (Illus.). 144p. (YA). (gr. 4 up). 1997. lib. bdg. 22.95 (*0-7614-0208-X*, Benchmark NY) Marshall Cavendish.

***Tennessee.** Paul Joseph. LC 97-20636. (The United States Ser.). 1998. write for info. (*1-56239-875-X*) Abdo & Dghtrs.

Tennessee. Romulus Linney. 1980. pap. 3.25 (*0-8222-1119-X*) Dramatists Play.

Tennessee. Sylvia McNair. LC 89-25285. (America the Beautiful Ser.). (Illus.). 144p. (J). (gr. 5-8). 1990. lib. bdg. 28.30 (*0-516-00488-3*) Childrens.

Tennessee. Karen Sirvaitis. (Hello U. S. A. Ser.). 72p. (J). (gr. 3-6). 1991. lib. bdg. 18.95 (*0-8225-2711-1*, Lerner Publctns) Lerner Group.

Tennessee. Karen Sirvaitis. (Hello U. S. A. Ser.). (J). (gr. 3-6). pap. 5.95 (*0-614-15669-6*, First Ave Edns) Lerner Group.

Tennessee. Kathleen Thompson. (Portrait of America Library). 48p. (YA). (gr. 3 up). 1996. lib. bdg. 22.83 (*0-8114-7388-0*) Raintree Steck-V.

Tennessee. Kathleen Thompson. (Portrait of America Library). 48p. (J). (gr. 3 up). 1996. 5.95 (*0-8114-7469-0*) Raintree Steck-V.

Tennessee. James D. Porter. Ed. by Clement A. Evans. (Confederate Military History Extended Edition Ser.: Vol. X). (Illus.). 806p. 1988. reprint ed. 50.00 (*1-56837-029-6*) Broadfoot.

Tennessee. Illus. by Edward Schell. 128p. 1986. reprint ed. 35.00 (*0-9613859-3-6*) Wakestone Bks.

Tennessee: A Bicentennial Celebration. John Netherton. (Illus.). 128p. 1995. 39.95 (*1-56579-126-6*) Westcliffe Pubs.

Tennessee: A Celebration of 200 Years of the University. Betsey B. Creekmore. Ed. by J. Bruce Baumann. LC 94-65024. (Illus.). 128p. 1994. 19.94 (*1-884850-00-6*) Scripps Howard.

Tennessee: A Guide to the State. Federal Writers' Project Staff & Writers Program-WPA Staff. (American Guide Ser.). 1989. reprint ed. lib. bdg. 69.00 (*0-7812-1041-0*, 1041) Rprt Serv.

Tennessee: A Guide to the State. Federal Writers' Project Staff. 558p. 1939. reprint ed. 89.00 (*0-403-02191-X*) Somerset Pub.

Tennessee: A History. rev. ed. Wilma Dykeman. 224p. 1993. reprint ed. pap. 10.95 (*0-9613859-9-5*) Wakestone Bks.

Tennessee: A Photographic Journey. Laura Stephens. (Illus.). 1991. 15.99 (*0-517-05304-7*) Random Hse Value.

Tennessee: A Short History. Robert E. Corlew. LC 80-13553. (Illus.). 652p. 1990. pap. text ed. 18.95 (*0-87049-647-6*) U of Tenn Pr.

Tennessee: A Short History. 2nd ed. Robert E. Corlew. LC 80-13553. (Illus.). 652p. 1990. 36.00 (*0-87049-646-8*) U of Tenn Pr.

Tennessee: Family Adventure Guide. Tim O'Brien. LC 95-17550. (Family Adventure Guide Ser.). (Illus.). 160p. 1995. pap. 9.95 (*1-56440-745-4*) Globe Pequot.

Tennessee: Hello U. S. A. Karen Sirvaitis. (J). 1996. pap. text ed. 5.95 (*0-8225-9726-8*) Lerner Group.

Tennessee: Off the Beaten Path: A Guide to Unique Places. 3rd ed. Tim O'Brien. LC 96-5073. (Off the Beaten Path Ser.). (Illus.). 144p. 1996. pap. 10.95 (*1-56440-897-3*) Globe Pequot.

Tennessee Vol. 1: The Old River, Frontier to Secession. Donald Davidson. LC 91-62454. (Southern Classics Ser.). (Illus.). 342p. (C). 1991. reprint ed. pap. 10.95 (*1-879941-01-5*) J S Sanders.

Tennessee Vol. 2: The New River: Civil War to TVA. Donald Davidson. LC 91-62454. (Southern Classics Ser.). (Illus.). 395p. 1992. reprint ed. pap. 10.95 (*1-879941-08-2*) J S Sanders.

Tennessee see Atlas of Historical County Boundaries

Tennessee - from Sea to Shining Sea. Dennis B. Fradin. LC 92-6385. (From Sea to Shining Sea Ser.). (Illus.). 64p. (J). (gr. 3-5). 1992. pap. 5.95 (*0-516-43842-5*); lib. bdg. 24.00 (*0-516-03842-7*) Childrens.

Tennessee: A Guide to the State see WPA Guide to Tennessee

Tennessee & Other State Greats (Biographies) Carole Marsh. (Carole Marsh Tennessee Bks.). (Illus.). (J). 1994. pap. 19.95 (*0-7933-1054-7*); lib. bdg. 29.95 (*0-7933-1055-5*); disk 29.95 (*0-7933-1056-3*) Gallopade Pub Group.

Tennessee Angler. 32p. 1993. write for info. (*0-9638090-0-8*) Anglers Pr.

Tennessee Antebellum Trail Guidebook. David R. Logsdon. (Illus.). 128p. (Orig.). 1995. pap. text ed. 8.95 (*0-9626018-8-8*) Kettle Mills Pr.

Tennessee Atlas & Gazetteer. 3rd ed. DeLorme Staff. (Illus.). 72p. (Orig.). 1995. pap. 16.95 (*0-89933-240-4*, 5053) DeLorme Map.

Tennessee Attorneys Directory. Joseph L. White & Mary K. Weber. 494p. 1992. 57.00 (*0-614-09393-7*) M Lee Smith.

Tennessee Attorneys Memo: Permanent Edition. Ed. by Bradford Forrister. 680.00 (*0-925773-10-7*) M Lee Smith.

Tennessee Attorneys Memo Vol. 19: Permanent Edition, Set. Ed. by Brad Forrister et al. 1993. 127.00 (*0-925773-15-8*) M Lee Smith.

Tennessee Automotive Directory. Ed. by T. L. Spelman. 1985. 24.95 (*1-55527-030-1*) Auto Contact Inc.

Tennessee Bandits, Bushwackers, Outlaws, Crooks, Devils, Ghosts, Desperadoes & Other Assorted & Sundry Characters! Carole Marsh. (Carole Marsh Tennessee Bks.). (Illus.). (J). 1994. pap. 19.95 (*0-7933-1057-1*); lib. bdg. 29.95 (*0-7933-1058-X*); disk 29.95 (*0-7933-1059-8*) Gallopade Pub Group.

Tennessee Beginnings. Intro. by John Dobson. Bd. with A Short Description of the Tennassee Government (1793). Daniel Smith. LC 74-583.; Constitution of the State of Tennessee, (1796). Intro. by John Dobson. LC 74-583.; Catechetical Exposition of the Constitution of the State of Tennessee, 1803. Willie Blount. LC 74-583. LC 74-583. (Illus.). 144p. 1974. 17.50 (*0-87152-152-0*) Reprint.

Tennessee Biographical Dictionary: People of All Times & All Places Who Have Been Important to the History & Life of the State. LC 93-32358. 1993. 79.00 (*0-403-09941-2*) Somerset Pub.

Tennessee Bookstore Book: A Surprising Guide to Our State's Bookstores & Their Specialties for Students, Teachers, Writers & Publishers. Carole Marsh. (Tennessee Bks.). (Illus.). 1994. pap. 19.95 (*0-7933-2982-5*); lib. bdg. 29.95 (*0-7933-2981-7*); disk 29.95 (*0-7933-2983-3*) Gallopade Pub Group.

***Tennessee Business Directory 1996-1997.** American Business Directories Staff. 1968p. 1996. boxed 445.00 (*1-56105-855-6*) Am Busn Direct.

Tennessee Business Directory 1996-97. rev. ed. American Business Directories Staff. 1696p. 1996. boxed 445.00 (*1-56105-773-8*) Am Busn Direct.

***Tennessee Business Directory 1997-1998.** rev. ed. American Business Directories Staff. 1968p. 1997. boxed 445.00 (*1-56105-942-0*) Am Busn Direct.

Tennessee Census Index 1810, Rutherford Co. & Grainger Co., Vol. 1. Ronald V. Jackson. (Illus.). lib. bdg. 40.00 (*0-89593-778-6*) Accelerated Index.

Tennessee Census Index 1850 Mortality Schedule. (Illus.). 1979. lib. bdg. 59.00 (*0-89593-490-6*) Accelerated Index.

Tennessee Census Index 1860 Anderson-Knox Counties Federal (Every Name), 4 vols., Set. Ronald V. Jackson. (Illus.). lib. bdg. 460.00 (*0-89593-779-4*) Accelerated Index.

Tennessee Census Index 1860 Lake Wilson Counties Federal. Ronald V. Jackson. (Illus.). lib. bdg. write for info. (*0-89593-780-8*) Accelerated Index.

Tennessee Census Index 1860 Mortality Schedule. (Illus.). 1983. lib. bdg. 62.00 (*0-89593-491-4*) Accelerated Index.

Tennessee Census Index 1890 Union Vets. (Illus.). lib. bdg. 69.00 (*0-89593-492-2*) Accelerated Index.

Tennessee Civil War Questionnaires, 5 vols., 1. Ed. by John T. Moore et al. 1985. 30.00 (*0-89308-216-3*) Southern Hist Pr.

Tennessee Civil War Questionnaires, 5 vols., 2. Ed. by John T. Moore et al. 1985. 30.00 (*0-89308-217-1*) Southern Hist Pr.

Tennessee Civil War Questionnaires, 5 vols., 3. Ed. by John T. Moore et al. 1985. 30.00 (*0-89308-218-X*) Southern Hist Pr.

Tennessee Civil War Questionnaires, 5 vols., 4. Ed. by John T. Moore et al. 1985. 30.00 (*0-89308-219-8*) Southern Hist Pr.

Tennessee Civil War Questionnaires, 5 vols., 5. Ed. by John T. Moore et al. 1985. 30.00 (*0-89308-220-1*) Southern Hist Pr.

Tennessee Civil War Questionnaires, 5 vols., Set. Ed. by John T. Moore et al. 1985. 150.00 (*0-89308-221-X*) Southern Hist Pr.

Tennessee Classic Christmas Trivia: Stories, Recipes, Activities, Legends, Lore & More! Carole Marsh. (Carole Marsh Tennessee Bks.). (Illus.). (J). 1994. pap. 19.95 (*0-7933-1060-1*); lib. bdg. 29.95 (*0-7933-1061-X*); disk 29.95 (*0-7933-1062-8*) Gallopade Pub Group.

Tennessee Coastales. Carole Marsh. (Carole Marsh Tennessee Bks.). (Illus.). (J). 1994. pap. 19.95 (*0-7933-2063-1*); lib. bdg. 29.95 (*0-7933-2062-3*); disk 29.95 (*0-7933-2064-X*) Gallopade Pub Group.

Tennessee Coastales! Carole Marsh. (Tennessee Bks.). (J). 1994. lib. bdg. 29.95 (*0-7933-7307-7*) Gallopade Pub Group.

Tennessee Code Annotated, 32 vols. 1955. write for info. (*0-672-84085-5*) MICHIE.

Tennessee Code Annotated. write for info. (*0-614-05972-0*) MICHIE.

Tennessee Corporations. Ronald L. Gilman. LC 79-91162. (Practice Systems Library Manual). ring bd. 120.00 (*0-317-00399-2*) Lawyers Cooperative.

Tennessee Corporations. Ronald L. Gilman. LC 79-91162. (Practice Systems Library Manual). 1993. Suppl. 1993. suppl. ed. 55.00 (*0-317-03165-1*) Lawyers Cooperative.

Tennessee Corporations, Partnerships & Associations Law Annotated, 1993 Edition. 35.00 (*0-614-05973-9*) MICHIE.

Tennessee Country: A Heritage of Natural Places. Kenneth Murray. 1995. pap. text ed. 14.95 (*1-57072-034-7*) Overmountain Pr.

***Tennessee Country: A Heritage of Natural Places.** Kenneth Murray. (Illus.). 120p. (YA). 1995. 22.95 (*1-57072-032-0*) Overmountain Pr.

Tennessee County Maps. rev. ed. Ed. by C. J. Puetz. (Illus.). 144p. 1992. pap. 14.85 (*0-916514-15-3*) Cnty Maps.

Tennessee Court Rules Annotated. Michie Butterworth Editorial Staff. 1993. pap. 42.00 (*0-87473-881-4*) MICHIE.

Tennessee Cousins: A History of Tennessee People. Worth S. Ray. LC 68-24685. (Illus.). 819p. 1994. reprint ed. 40.00 (*0-8063-0289-5*, 4800) Genealog Pub.

Tennessee Crime Perspective 1996. Ed. by Kathleen O. Morgan et al. 24p. 1996. pap. 19.00 (*1-56692-541-X*) Morgan Quitno Corp.

***Tennessee Crime Perspective 1997.** Ed. by Kathleen O. Morgan & Scott E. Morgan. 24p. 1997. pap. 19.00 (*1-56692-791-9*) Morgan Quitno Corp.

Tennessee Criminal Law Case Finder. Sally S. Schneider. 1038p. 1992. 85.00 (*0-87473-954-3*) MICHIE.

Tennessee Criminal Laws Annotated, 1993 Edition. 27.50 (*0-614-05974-7*) MICHIE.

Tennessee "Crinkum-Crankum" A Funny Word Book about Our State. Carole Marsh. (Tennessee Bks.). (Illus.). (J). (gr. 3-12). 1994. 29.95 (*0-7933-4934-6*); pap. 19.95 (*0-7933-4935-4*); disk 29.95 (*0-7933-4936-2*) Gallopade Pub Group.

Tennessee Digest. 2nd ed. 1986. write for info. (*0-318-61350-6*) West Pub.

Tennessee Dingbats! Bk. 1: A Fun Book of Games, Stories, Activities & More about Our State That's All in Code! for You to Decipher. Carole Marsh. (Tennessee Bks.). (Illus.). (J). (gr. 3-12). 1994. pap. 19.95 (*0-7933-3900-6*); lib. bdg. 29.95 (*0-7933-3899-9*); disk 29.95 (*0-7933-3901-4*) Gallopade Pub Group.

Tennessee Early Census, Vol. 1. Ronald V. Jackson. (Illus.). 1981. lib. bdg. 50.00 (*0-89593-746-8*) Accelerated Index.

Tennessee Employer's Guide. Ed. by Charles Lewis. LC 92-18906. 558p. 1996. ring bd. 92.50 (*0-9625969-8-1*) Summers Pr.

Tennessee Employment Law. John B. Phillips, Jr. 89.00 (*0-925773-13-1*) M Lee Smith.

Tennessee Employment Law. John B. Phillips, Jr. 176p. 1989. ring bd. 89.00 (*0-925773-00-X*) M Lee Smith.

Tennessee Facts & Factivities. Carole Marsh. (Carole Marsh State Bks.). (Illus.). 1996. 29.95 (*0-614-11552-3*, C Marsh); teacher ed., pap. 19.95 (*0-7933-7931-8*, C Marsh) Gallopade Pub Group.

***Tennessee Family Histories & Genealogies: A Bibliography.** Donald M. Hehir. xvi, 204p. (Orig.). 1996. pap. 21.00 (*0-7884-0517-9*, H138) Heritage Bk.

Tennessee Farming, Tennessee Farmers: Antebellum Agriculture in the Upper South. Donald L. Winters. LC 94-20835. (Illus.). 254p. (C). 1995. text ed. 34.00 (*0-87049-860-6*) U of Tenn Pr.

Tennessee Federal Census Index, 1820. Ronald V. Jackson. LC 77-86083. (Illus.). lib. bdg. 58.00 (*0-89593-135-4*) Accelerated Index.

Tennessee Federal Census Index, 1830. Ronald V. Jackson. LC 77-86073. (Illus.). 1976. lib. bdg. 79.00 (*0-89593-136-2*) Accelerated Index.

Tennessee Federal Census Index, 1840. Ronald V. Jackson. LC 77-86074. (Illus.). 1976. lib. bdg. 101.00 (*0-89593-137-0*) Accelerated Index.

Tennessee Federal Census Index, 1850. Ronald V. Jackson. LC 77-86075. (Illus.). 1977. lib. bdg. 132.00 (*0-89593-138-9*) Accelerated Index.

Tennessee Festival Fun for Kids! Carole Marsh. (Tennessee Bks.). (Illus.). (YA). (gr. 3-12). 1994. pap. 19.95 (*0-7933-4053-5*); lib. bdg. 29.95 (*0-7933-4052-7*); disk 29.95 (*0-7933-4054-3*) Gallopade Pub Group.

Tennessee Folk Culture: An Annotated Bibliography. Eleanor Goehring. LC 81-16036. 152p. reprint ed. pap. 43.40 (*0-8357-6914-3*, 2037973) Bks Demand.

Tennessee Forms, 3 vols., Set. Jack W. Robinson, Jr. et al. 1991. 300.00 (*0-87473-714-1*) MICHIE.

***Tennessee Gardener's Guide: The What, Where, When, How & Why of Gardening in Tennessee.** Lark Foster & Walter Glenn. (Illus.). 400p. 1997. pap. 18.95 (*1-888608-38-2*) Cool Springs Pr.

Tennessee Genealogical Research. 120p. 1993. pap. 15.00 (*0-913857-05-X*) Genealog Sources.

Tennessee Getaways: A Guide to Bed & Breakfasts & Inns. Don Vandeventer. (Getaways Ser.). (Illus.). 144p. (Orig.). 1996. pap. 12.95 (*1-886443-02-5*) Down Home Pubns.

***Tennessee Government! The Cornerstone of Everyday Life in Our State!** Carole Marsh. (Carole Marsh Tennessee Bks.). (Illus.). (J). (gr. 3-12). 1996. pap. 19.95 (*0-7933-6308-X*); lib. bdg. 29.95 (*0-7933-6307-1*); disk 29.95 (*0-7933-6309-8*) Gallopade Pub Group.

Tennessee Government Officials Directory. Joseph L. White & Mary K. Weber. (1992 Ser.). 49.00 (*0-614-09390-2*) M Lee Smith.

Tennessee Governments Performance Standards, 1990. Ed. by Greg Michels. (Governments Performance Standards Ser.). (Illus.). 150p. 1990. text ed. 125.00 (*1-55507-501-0*) Municipal Analysis.

Tennessee Grassroots Writer. James A. Crutchfield & Peter S. LaPaglia. 96p. 1996. pap. 9.95 (*1-881576-51-5*) Providence Hse.

***Tennessee Handbook.** Jeff Bradley. (Illus.). 450p. (Orig.). 1997. pap. 17.95 (*1-56691-043-9*) Moon Trvl Hdbks.

Tennessee Health Care Perspective 1996. Ed. by Kathleen O. Morgan et al. 24p. 1996. pap. 19.00 (*1-56692-641-6*) Morgan Quitno Corp.

***Tennessee Health Care Perspective 1997.** Ed. by Kathleen O. Morgan & Scott E. Morgan. 24p. 1997. pap. 19.00 (*1-56692-741-2*) Morgan Quitno Corp.

Tennessee Hiking Guide. rev. ed. Ed. by Sierra Club, Tennessee Chapter Staff & Robert S. Brandt. LC 87-30246. (Illus.). 32p. 1988. pap. 4.95 (*0-87049-573-9*) U of Tenn Pr.

Tennessee Hill Folk. Joe Clark. LC 72-2880. (Illus.). 96p. 1972. 14.95 (*0-8265-1183-X*) Vanderbilt U Pr.

Tennessee Historical & Biographical Index, Vol. 1. Ronald V. Jackson. LC 78-53717. (Illus.). 1984. lib. bdg. 30.00 (*0-89593-200-8*) Accelerated Index.

Tennessee History: A Bibliography. Ed. by Sam B. Smith. LC 74-8504. 540p. reprint ed. pap. 153.90 (*0-317-10296-6*, 2019703) Bks Demand.

***Tennessee History! Surprising Secrets about Our State's Founding Mothers, Fathers & Kids!** Carole Marsh. (Carole Marsh Tennessee Bks.). (J). (gr. 3-12). 1996. pap. 19.95 (*0-7933-6155-9*); lib. bdg. 29.95 (*0-7933-6154-0*); disk 29.95 (*0-7933-6156-7*) Gallopade Pub Group.

Tennessee Homecoming Cookbook: Famous Parties, People, Places. Phila Hach. 1986. 9.95 (*0-9606192-6-7*) Hach.

Tennessee Hot Air Balloon Mystery. Carole Marsh. (Carole Marsh Tennessee Bks.). (Illus.). (J). (gr. 2-9). 1994. 29.95 (*0-7933-2696-6*); pap. 19.95 (*0-7933-2697-4*); disk 29.95 (*0-7933-2698-2*) Gallopade Pub Group.

Tennessee in American Histroy. Dickinson & Whiteaker. 1991. 19.60 (*0-536-58007-3*) Ginn Pr.

Tennessee in Perspective 1996. Ed. by Kathleen O. Morgan et al. 26p. 1996. pap. 19.00 (*1-56692-591-6*) Morgan Quitno Corp.

***Tennessee in Perspective 1997.** Ed. by Kathleen O. Morgan & Scott E. Morgan. 26p. 1997. pap. 19.00 (*1-56692-691-2*) Morgan Quitno Corp.

Tennessee Indian Dictionary for Kids! Carole Marsh. (Carole Marsh State Bks.). (J). (gr. 2-9). 1996. 29.95 (*0-7933-7770-6*, C Marsh); pap. 19.95 (*0-7933-7771-4*, C Marsh) Gallopade Pub Group.

Tennessee Jeopardy! Answers & Questions about Our State! Carole Marsh. (Tennessee Bks.). (Illus.). (J). (gr. 3-12). 1994. pap. 19.95 (*0-7933-4206-6*); lib. bdg. 29.95 (*0-7933-4205-8*); disk 29.95 (*0-7933-4207-4*) Gallopade Pub Group.

Tennessee Jobbank. 2nd ed. Ed. by Adams Publishing Staff. (Jobbank Ser.). 420p. 1995. pap. 15.95 (*1-55850-501-6*) Adams Media.

Tennessee JobBank. 3rd ed. Ed. by Adams Publishing Staff. (JobBank Ser.). 416p. 1996. pap. 15.95 (*1-55850-607-1*) Adams Media.

Tennessee "Jography" A Fun Run Thru Our State! Carole Marsh. (Carole Marsh Tennessee Bks.). (Illus.). (J). 1994. pap. 19.95 (*1-55609-089-7*); lib. bdg. 29.95 (*0-7933-2046-1*); disk 29.95 (*0-7933-2047-X*) Gallopade Pub Group.

Tennessee Jurisprudence, 29 vols. Michie Company Editorial Staff. suppl. ed. 185.00 (*0-87473-901-2*) MICHIE.

Tennessee Jurisprudence, 29 vols., Set. Michie Butterworth Editorial Staff. 1991. 1,800.00 (*0-87215-503-X*) MICHIE.

Tennessee Kid's Cookbook: Recipes, How-to, History, Lore & More! Carole Marsh. (Carole Marsh Tennessee Bks.). (Illus.). (J). 1994. pap. 19.95 (*0-7933-1069-5*); lib. bdg. 29.95 (*0-7933-1070-9*); disk 29.95 (*0-7933-1071-7*) Gallopade Pub Group.

Tennessee Land Entries of the First Surveyor's District, 6 vols., Set. Norman T. McGee. (Illus.). 1685p. (Orig.). 1998. write for info. (*0-9622403-8-9*) Lilac Hill Pubns.

Tennessee Land Entries of the First Surveyor's District: Entry Book G, 1813-1815. Norman T. McGee. (Illus.). 270p. (Orig.). 1997. write for info. (*0-9622403-5-4*) Lilac Hill Pubns.

Tennessee Land Entries of the First Surveyor's District: Entry Book H, 1815-1817. Norman T. McGee. (Illus.). 330p. (Orig.). 1998. write for info. (*0-9622403-6-2*) Lilac Hill Pubns.

Tennessee Land Entries of the First Surveyor's District: Entry Book I, 1817-1823. Norman T. McGee. (Illus.). 400p. (Orig.). 1998. write for info. (*0-9622403-7-0*) Lilac Hill Pubns.

Tennessee Land Entries of the First Surveyor's District: Entry Books C & D, 1809-1811. Norman T. McGee. (Illus.). 275p. (Orig.). 1996. write for info. (*0-9622403-3-8*) Lilac Hill Pubns.

Tennessee Land Entries of the First Surveyor's District: Entry Books E & F, 1811-1913. Norman T. McGee. (Illus.). 360p. (Orig.). 1997. write for info. (*0-9622403-4-6*) Lilac Hill Pubns.

Tennessee Land Surveying Law: Questions & Answers. John E. Keen. 48p. (C). 1995. pap. text ed. 20.00 (*1-56569-040-0*) Land Survey.

***Tennessee Landscape, People & Places: 1996 Anthology from the Tennessee Writer's Alliance.** Cool Springs Press Staff. 225p. 1996. pap. 14.95 (*1-888608-32-3*) Cool Springs Pr.

Tennessee Law of Damages with 1992 Cumulative Supplement. Mayo L. Coiner. 405p. 1988. 70.00 (*0-87473-356-1*); suppl. ed. 30.00 (*0-87473-900-4*) MICHIE.

Tennessee Law of Evidence. 2nd ed. Sarah Y. Sheppeard et al. 626p. 1990. suppl. ed. 85.00 (*0-87473-643-9*) MICHIE.

***Tennessee Law of Evidence.** 3rd ed. Sarah Y. Sheppeard et al. 766p. 1995. 95.00 (*1-55834-288-5*, 65803-11) MICHIE.

Tennessee Legal & Business Forms. Ed. by Thomas M. Leveille. LC 94-40878. 1994. 330.00 (*0-615-00380-X*) Lawyers Cooperative.

Tennessee Legal Research Handbook. Lewis L. Laska. LC 77-71305. x, 203p. 1977. lib. bdg. 36.00 (*0-930342-04-6*, 300860) W S Hein.

Tennessee Letters: From Carson Valley, 1857-1860. David Thompson. LC 82-61696. (Illus.). 189p. 1983. 7.50 (*0-913205-02-8*) Grace Dangberg.

Tennessee Library Book: A Surprising Guide to the Unusual Special Collections in Libraries Across Our State for Students, Teachers, Writers & Publishers - Includes Reproducible Mailing Labels Plus Activities for Young People! Carole Marsh. (Tennessee Bks.). (Illus.). 1994. pap. 19.95 (*0-7933-3132-3*); lib. bdg. 29.95 (*0-7933-3131-5*); disk 29.95 (*0-7933-3133-1*) Gallopade Pub Group.

Tennessee Limited Liability Company Forms & Practice Manual. Richard F. Warren & Steven K. Wood. 512p. 1997. ring bd. 149.95 (*1-57400-021-7*) Data Trace Pubng.

***Tennessee Litigation Forms & Analysis.** Thomas M. Leveille & Lori F. Fleishman. LC 95-82074. (Practitioner's Ser.). 1800p. 1995. text ed. write for info. (*0-7620-0031-7*) Lawyers Cooperative.

Tennessee Locator. Harold Rohen. 387p. (Orig.). 1992. pap. 19.95 (*0-9634593-0-9*) Budro.

Tennessee Male Voter Census Index, 1891. Ronald V. Jackson. 1992. 275.00 (*0-89593-859-6*) Accelerated Index.

Tennessee Marriages, Early to 1800. Liahona Research, Inc. Staff. Ed. by Jordan Dodd. 1990. lib. bdg. 25.00 (*1-877677-29-9*) Precision Indexing.

Tennessee Media Book: A Surprising Guide to the Amazing Print, Broadcast & Online Media of Our State for Students, Teachers, Writers & Publishers - Includes Reproducible Mailing Labels Plus Activities for Young People! Carole Marsh. (Tennessee Bks.). (Illus.). 1994. pap. 19.95 (*0-7933-3288-5*); lib. bdg. 29.95 (*0-7933-3287-7*); disk 29.95 (*0-7933-3289-3*) Gallopade Pub Group.

***Tennessee Moon.** Norah Hess. 400p. (Orig.). 1996. mass mkt. 5.99 (*0-8439-4106-5*) Dorchester Pub Co.

Tennessee Motor Vehicle Laws Annotated, 1993 Edition. 25.00 (*0-614-05975-5*) MICHIE.

Tennessee Mountain Bike Adventures. 126p. 1997. reprint ed. 10.95 (*0-9643399-0-0*) TN Mtn Bike.

Tennessee Municipal Handbook. 4th ed. Victor C. Hobday. 1991. reprint ed. write for info. (*0-318-60809-X*) Tenn Muni League.

Tennessee Mystery Van Takes Off! Book 1: Handicapped Tennessee Kids Sneak Off on a Big Adventure. Carole Marsh. (Tennessee Bks.). (Illus.). (J). (gr. 3-12). 1994. 29.95 (*0-7933-5087-5*); pap. 19.95 (*0-7933-5088-3*); disk 29.95 (*0-7933-5089-1*) Gallopade Pub Group.

Tennessee Post Office Murals. Howard Hull. (Illus.). 160p. (Orig.). 1996. pap. 12.95 (*1-57072-030-4*) Overmountain Pr.

Tennessee Private Acts Index. Michie Butterworth Editorial Staff. 652p. 1984. 75.00 (*0-614-05976-3*) MICHIE.

Tennessee Private Acts Index. Michie Company Editorial Staff. 652p. 1991. Suppl. 1991. suppl. ed. 17.50 (*0-87215-870-5*) MICHIE.

Tennessee Private Acts Index, Incl. 1991 Suppl. Michie Company Editorial Staff. 652p. 1984. 75.00 (*0-87215-812-8*) MICHIE.

Tennessee Probate, 2 vols. Albert W. Secor. LC 79-91164. (Practice Systems Library Manual). ring bd. 220.00 (*0-317-00403-4*) Lawyers Cooperative.

Tennessee Probate, 2 vols. Albert W. Secor. LC 79-91164. (Practice Systems Library Manual). 1993. Suppl. 1993. suppl. ed. 87.50 (*0-317-03166-X*) Lawyers Cooperative.

Tennessee Quiz Bowl Crash Course! Carole Marsh. (Carole Marsh Tennessee Bks.). (Illus.). (J). 1994. pap. 19.95 (*0-7933-2060-7*); lib. bdg. 29.95 (*0-7933-2059-3*); disk 29.95 (*0-7933-2061-5*) Gallopade Pub Group.

Tennessee Red Berry Tales. Bob Galbreath. Ed. by Deborah G. Garrett. 97p. (Orig.). (J). (gr. 3 up). 1986. pap. 7.95 (*0-9616918-0-8*) Whites Creek Pr.

Tennessee Research. Afton E. Reintjes. 50p. 1986. pap. 19.50 (*0-940764-45-8*) Genealog Inst.

Tennessee River Cruise Guide. 2nd ed. Fred Myers. (Illus.). 1995. pap. 18.95 (*0-9632005-3-4*) F Myers.

Tennessee Rollercoasters! Carole Marsh. (Tennessee Bks.). (Illus.). (YA). (gr. 3-12). 1994. pap. 19.95 (*0-7933-5351-3*); lib. bdg. 29.95 (*0-7933-5350-5*); disk 29.95 (*0-7933-5352-1*) Gallopade Pub Group.

Tennessee School Trivia: An Amazing & Fascinating Look at Our State's Teachers, Schools & Students! Carole Marsh. (Carole Marsh Tennessee Bks.). (Illus.). (J). 1994. pap. 19.95 (*0-7933-1066-0*); lib. bdg. 29.95 (*0-7933-1067-9*); disk 29.95 (*0-7933-1068-7*) Gallopade Pub Group.

Tennessee Silly Basketball Sportsmysteries, Vol. 1. Carole Marsh. (Carole Marsh Tennessee Bks.). (Illus.). (J). 1994. pap. 19.95 (*0-7933-1063-6*); lib. bdg. 29.95 (*0-7933-1064-4*); disk 29.95 (*0-7933-1065-2*) Gallopade Pub Group.

Tennessee Silly Basketball Sportsmysteries, Vol. 2. Carole Marsh. (Carole Marsh Tennessee Bks.). (Illus.). (J). 1994. pap. 19.95 (*0-7933-2072-0*); lib. bdg. 29.95 (*0-7933-2071-2*); disk 29.95 (*0-7933-2073-9*) Gallopade Pub Group.

Tennessee Silly Football Sportsmysteries, Vol. 1. Carole Marsh. (Carole Marsh Tennessee Bks.). (Illus.). (J). 1994. pap. 19.95 (*0-7933-2051-8*); lib. bdg. 29.95 (*0-7933-2050-X*); disk 29.95 (*0-7933-2052-6*) Gallopade Pub Group.

Tennessee Silly Football Sportsmysteries, Vol. 2. Carole Marsh. (Carole Marsh Tennessee Bks.). (Illus.). (J). 1994. pap. 19.95 (*0-7933-2054-2*); lib. bdg. 29.95 (*0-7933-2053-4*); disk 29.95 (*0-7933-2055-0*) Gallopade Pub Group.

Tennessee Silly Trivia! Carole Marsh. (Carole Marsh Tennessee Bks.). (Illus.). (J). 1994. pap. 19.95 (*1-55609-036-6*); lib. bdg. 29.95 (*0-7933-2044-5*); disk 29.95 (*0-7933-2045-3*) Gallopade Pub Group.

Tennessee Silversmiths. Benjamin H. Caldwell, Jr. LC 88-63431. (Frank L. Horton Ser.). (Illus.). 228p. 1989. 35.00 (*0-945578-01-6*, U of NC Pr) Mus South Deco.

Tennessee Sketches. Louisa P. Looney. (Short Story Index Reprint Ser.). 1977. reprint ed. 23.95 (*0-8369-4020-2*) Ayer.

Tennessee Slave Schedule Index, 1850. Ronald V. Jackson. 1989. 117.00 (*0-89593-857-X*) Accelerated Index.

Tennessee Slave Schedule, 1860. Ronald V. Jackson. 1990. 122.00 (*0-89593-858-8*) Accelerated Index.

Tennessee Soldiers in the Revolution: A Roster of Soldiers Living During the Revolutionary War in the Counties of Washington & Sullivan. Penelope J. Allen. LC 75-970. 71p. 1996. reprint ed. pap. 7.50 (*0-8063-0666-1*) Genealog Pub.

Tennessee State Constitution: A Reference Guide. Lewis L. Laska. LC 90-32454. (Reference Guides to the State Constitutions of the United States Ser.: No. 2). 216p. 1990. text ed. 59.95 (*0-313-26653-0*, LTO/, Greenwood Pr) Greenwood.

Tennessee State Symbols: The Fascinating Stories Behind Our Flag & Capitol, the Mockingbird, Iris & Other Official Emblems. Rob Simbeck. LC 94-79271. (Illus.). 176p. 1995. pap. 10.95 (*0-9642991-8-6*) Altheus Pr.

Tennessee Statistical Abstract, 1969. Ed. by Mary G. Currence. (Illus.). 707p. (C). 1968. pap. text ed. 5.95 (*0-940191-00-8*) Univ TN Ctr Bus Econ.

Tennessee Statistical Abstract, 1971. Ed. by Mary G. Currence. (Illus.). 712p. (C). 1971. pap. text ed. 5.75 (*0-940191-01-6*) Univ TN Ctr Bus Econ.

Tennessee Statistical Abstract, 1974. Ed. by Mary G. Currence. (Illus.). 705p. (C). 1974. pap. text ed. 7.50 (*0-940191-02-4*) Univ TN Ctr Bus Econ.

Tennessee Statistical Abstract, 1977. Ed. by Mickey Lee & Maryann Williams. (Illus.). 737p. (C). 1977. pap. text ed. 15.00 (*0-940191-03-2*) Univ TN Ctr Bus Econ.

Tennessee Statistical Abstract, 1980. Ed. by Patricia D. Postma & Susannah S. Prescott. (Illus.). 720p. (C). 1980. pap. text ed. 18.00 (*0-940191-04-0*) Univ TN Ctr Bus Econ.

Tennessee Statistical Abstract, 1983-1984. Ed. by Betty B. Vickers. (Illus.). 751p. (C). 1983. pap. text ed. 20.95 (*0-940191-05-9*) Univ TN Ctr Bus Econ.

Tennessee Statistical Abstract, 1984-1985. Ed. by Betty B. Vickers. (Illus.). 761p. (C). 1984. pap. text ed. 20.95 (*0-940191-06-7*) Univ TN Ctr Bus Econ.

Tennessee Statistical Abstract, 1985-1986. Ed. by Betty B. Vickers. (Illus.). 759p. (C). 1985. pap. text ed. 22.95 (*0-940191-07-5*) Univ TN Ctr Bus Econ.

Tennessee Statistical Abstract, 1987. Ed. by Melissa A. Wood. (Illus.). 736p. (C). 1990. pap. text ed. 22.95 (*0-940191-08-3*) Univ TN Ctr Bus Econ.

Tennessee Statistical Abstract, 1988. Ed. by Betty B. Vickers. (Illus.). 740p. (C). 1988. pap. text ed. 27.95 (*0-940191-11-3*) Univ TN Ctr Bus Econ.

Tennessee Statistical Abstract, 1989. Ed. by Melissa A. Wood. (Illus.). 779p. (C). 1989. pap. text ed. 27.95 (*0-940191-12-1*) Univ TN Ctr Bus Econ.

Tennessee Statistical Abstract, 1990. Ed. by Melissa A. Kirby. (Illus.). (C). 1990. pap. text ed. write for info. (*0-940191-13-X*) Univ TN Ctr Bus Econ.

Tennessee Statistical Abstract, 1991. Ed. by Betty B. Vickers & Melissa A. Kirby. (Illus.). 760p. 1991. pap. text ed. 32.00 (*0-940191-15-6*) Univ TN Ctr Bus Econ.

Tennessee Statistical Abstract, 1992-1993. Ed. by Betty B. Vickers & Vickie C. Cunningham. (Illus.). 832p. (C). 1993. pap. text ed. 36.00 (*0-940191-17-2*) Univ TN Ctr Bus Econ.

Tennessee Strings: The Story of Country Music in Tennessee. Charles K. Wolfe. LC 77-8052. (Tennessee Three Star Ser.). (Illus.). 128p. 1977. pap. 5.50 (*0-87049-224-1*) U of Tenn Pr.

Tennessee Studies in Literature, Vol. 22. Tennessee Studies in Literature Staff. LC 58-63252. 190p. reprint ed. pap. 49.40 (*0-8357-6291-2*, 2021788) Bks Demand.

Tennessee Studies in Literature, Vol. 23. Tennessee Studies in Literature Staff. LC 58-63252. 139p. reprint ed. pap. 39.70 (*0-8357-6292-0*) Bks Demand.

Tennessee Studies in Literature, Vol. 24. Tennessee Studies in Literature Staff. LC 58-63252. 159p. reprint ed. pap. 45.40 (*0-8357-6293-9*) Bks Demand.

Tennessee Studies in Literature, Vol. 25. Tennessee Studies in Literature Staff. LC 58-63252. 155p. reprint ed. pap. 44.20 (*0-8357-6294-7*) Bks Demand.

Tennessee Studies in Literature, Vol. 26. Tennessee Studies in Literature Staff. LC 58-63252. 191p. reprint ed. pap. 54.50 (*0-8357-6295-5*) Bks Demand.

Tennessee Survival. Betty L. Hall & Ronald E. Galbraith. 160p. (Orig.). (gr. 10-12). 1979. pap. text ed. 5.84 (*0-03-055531-0*) Westwood Pr.

Tennessee Taproots: Courthouses of Tennessee. rev. ed. Sophie Crane & Paul Crane. LC 96-75691. (Illus.). 144p. 1996. 19.95 (*1-881576-26-4*, Hillsboro Pr) Providence Hse.

Tennessee Tax Guide. Ed. by Bradford Forrister. 12.75 (*0-614-09363-5*) M Lee Smith.

Tennessee Tax List Index, 1790. Ronald V. Jackson. 1991. write for info. (*0-89593-827-8*) Accelerated Index.

Tennessee Tax List Index, 1800. Ronald V. Jackson. 1991. write for info. (*0-89593-828-6*) Accelerated Index.

Tennessee Tax List Index, 1810. Ronald V. Jackson. 1991. write for info. (*0-89593-829-4*) Accelerated Index.

Tennessee Tiger. J. L. Kuntz. LC 93-60259. (Illus.). 57p. (J). (ps-3). 1994. 9.95 (*1-55523-611-1*) Winston-Derek.

Tennessee Timeline: A Chronology of Tennessee History, Mystery, Trivia, Legend, Lore & More. Carole Marsh. (Tennessee Bks.). (Illus.). (J). (gr. 3-12). 1994. pap. 19.95 (*0-7933-6002-1*); lib. bdg. 29.95 (*0-7933-6001-3*); disk 29.95 (*0-7933-6003-X*) Gallopade Pub Group.

Tennessee Torts Case Finder. Mayo L. Coiner & Alayne B. Adams. 458p. 1989. 70.00 (*0-87473-522-X*) MICHIE.

Tennessee Towns: From Adams to Yorkville. Tom Siler. (Illus.). 108p. 1985. pap. 5.00 (*0-941199-03-7*) ETHS.

Tennessee Trivia. rev. ed. Ernie Couch & Jill Couch. LC 91-8994. 192p. (Orig.). 1991. pap. 5.95 (*1-55853-109-2*) Rutledge Hill Pr.

Tennessee Valley Authority: Financial Problems Raise Questions about Long-Term Viability. 157p. (Orig.). (C). 1996. pap. text ed. 30.00 (*0-7881-2937-6*) DIANE Pub.

Tennessee Votes, 1799-1976: Studies in Tennessee Politics. Anne H. Hopkins & William Lyons. 393p. (Orig.). 1978. pap. 8.50 (*0-914079-02-6*) U TN Poli Sci.

***Tennessee Walking Horse.** (Learning about Horses Ser.). (Illus.). 48p. (J). (gr. 3-7). 1996. 18.40 (*0-516-20084-4*) Childrens.

Tennessee Walking Horse. Charlotte Wilcox. LC 95-47770. (Learning about Horses Ser.). 48p. (J). (gr. 3-9). 1996. lib. bdg. 17.80 (*1-56065-365-5*) Capstone Pr.

Tennessee Walking Horse National Celebration: World's Greatest Horse Show. Turner Publishing Company Staff. LC 91-75251. 176p. 1991. 29.95 (*1-56311-038-5*) Turner Pub KY.

***Tennessee Waltz.** Elizabeth Leigh. 352p. 1998. mass mkt. 4.99 (*0-8217-5849-7*, Zebra Kensgtn) Kensgtn Pub Corp.

Tennessee Waltz. Jackie Merritt. (Desire Ser.). 1993. pap. 2.89 (*0-373-05774-1*, 5-05774-0) Silhouette.

***Tennessee Waltz.** Trana M. Simmons. (Homespun Ser.). 304p. 1997. mass mkt. 5.99 (*0-515-12135-5*) Jove Pubns.

Tennessee Waltz & Other Stories. Alan Cheuse. LC 92-53615. 160p. 1992. reprint ed. pap. 10.95 (*0-87074-340-6*) SMU Press.

Tennessee Wildlife Viewing Guide. Paul Hamel. LC 93-17495. (Watchable Wildlife Ser.). (Illus.). 96p. (Orig.). 1993. pap. 6.95 (*1-56044-186-0*) Falcon Pr MT.

Tennessee Williams. Benjamin Nelson. 1961. 20.00 (*0-8392-1111-2*) Astor-Honor.

Tennessee Williams: A Bibliography. 2nd ed. Drewey W. Gunn. LC 91-34939. (Author Bibliographies Ser.: No. 89). 471p. 1991. 56.00 (*0-8108-2495-7*) Scarecrow.

Tennessee Williams: A Descsriptive Bibliography. George W. Crandall. (Series in Bibliography). (Illus.). 704p. (C). 1993. text ed. 195.00 (*0-8229-3769-7*) U of Pittsburgh Pr.

Tennessee Williams: Everyone Else Is an Audience. Ronald Hayman. LC 93-24544. (Illus.). 268p. 1994. 30.00 (*0-300-05414-9*) Yale U Pr.

Tennessee Williams: Four Plays. Tennessee Williams. 496p. 1976. 6.95 (*0-451-52512-4*, Sig Classics) NAL-Dutton.

Tennessee Williams see Modern Critical Views Series

Tennessee Williams' A Streetcar Named Desire see Modern Critical Interpretations

Tennessee Williams & Elia Kazan: A Collaboration in the Theatre. Brenda Murphy. (Illus.). 224p. (C). 1992. text ed. 44.95 (*0-521-40095-3*) Cambridge U Pr.

Tennessee Williams in Key West & Miami: A Guide. Marsha Bellavance-Johnson. (Famous Footsteps Ser.). (Illus.). (Orig.). 1989. pap. 4.95 (*0-929709-03-9*) Computer Lab.

Tennessee William's Letters to Donald Windham, 1940-1965. Ed. & Comment by Donald Windham. LC 95-26347. 352p. (C). 1996. pap. 19.95 (*0-8203-1840-X*) U of Ga Pr.

Tennessee Williams' The Glass Menagerie see Modern Critical Interpretations

Tennessee Woman: An Infinite Variety. Wilma Dykeman. (Illus.). 128p. 1993. 14.95 (*1-884450-00-8*) Wakestone Bks.

Tennessee Wonders: A Pictorial Guide to the Parks. Mike Carlton. LC 94-5228. 1994. pap. 18.95 (*1-55853-289-7*) Rutledge Hill Pr.

Tennessee Writers. Thomas D. Young. LC 81-2206. (Tennessee Three Star Ser.). (Illus.). 132p. 1981. pap. 5.50 (*0-87049-320-5*) U of Tenn Pr.

Tennessee's Coal Creek War: Another Fight for Freedom. Chris Cawood. Ed. by Gaynell Seale. LC 95-76607. (Illus.). 272p. (Orig.). 1995. pap. 9.95 (*0-9642231-0-4*) Magnolia Hill.

Tennessee's Forgotten Warriors: Frank Cheatham & His Confederate Division. Christopher Losson. LC 89-33944. (Illus.). 368p. 1990. 28.95 (*0-87049-615-8*) U of Tenn Pr.

Tennessee's Historic Landscapes: A Traveler's Guide. Carroll Van West. LC 94-18717. (Illus.). 528p. 1995. pap. 25.00 (*0-87049-881-9*); text ed. 50.00 (*0-87049-880-0*) U of Tenn Pr.

Tennessee's Indian Peoples: From White Contact to Removal, 1540-1840. Ronald N. Satz. LC 77-21634. (Tennessee Three Star Ser.). (Illus.). 110p. 1979. pap. 5.50 (*0-87049-231-4*); lib. bdg. 11.00 (*0-87049-285-3*) U of Tenn Pr.

Tennessee's (Most Devastating!) Disasters & (Most Calamitous!) Catastrophies! Carole Marsh. (Carole Marsh Tennessee Bks.). (Illus.). (J). 1994. pap. 19.95 (*0-7933-2069-0*); lib. bdg. 29.95 (*0-7933-2068-2*); disk 29.95 (*0-7933-2070-4*) Gallopade Pub Group.

Tennessee's Presidents. Frank B. Williams, Jr. LC 81-3391. (Tennessee Three Star Ser.). (Illus.). 124p. 1981. pap. 5.50 (*0-87049-322-1*) U of Tenn Pr.

Tennessee's South Cumberland: A Hiker's Guide to Trails & Attractions. 2nd ed. Russ Manning & Sondra Jamieson. (Tag-along Bks.). Orig. Title: The South Cumberland & Fall Creek Falls. (Illus.). 144p. 1994. pap. 8.95 (*0-9625122-7-3*) Mtn Laurel Pl.

Tennessee's Unsolved Mysteries (& Their "Solutions") Includes Scientific Information & Other Activities for Students. Carole Marsh. (Tennessee Bks.). (Illus.). (J). (gr. 3-12). 1994. pap. 19.95 (*0-7933-5849-3*); lib. bdg. 29.95 (*0-7933-5848-5*); disk 29.95 (*0-7933-5850-7*) Gallopade Pub Group.

Tennessee's War, 1861-1865: Described by Participants. Stanley F. Horn. LC 65-64988. 364p. 1965. 36.00 (*0-87402-019-0*) U of Tenn Pr.

Tennesses Land Entries of the First Surveyor's District: Entry Books A1, A2, & B, 1807-1809. Norman T. McGee. (Illus.). 380p. (Orig.). 1996. write for info. (*0-9622403-2-X*) Lilac Hill Pubns.

Tenney Family: Or, The Descendants of Thomas Tenney of Rowley, Massachusetts, 1638-1984. M. J. Tenney. (Illus.). 691p. 1989. reprint ed. pap. 99.50 (*0-8328-1159-9*); reprint ed. lib. bdg. 107.50 (*0-8328-1158-0*) Higginson Bk Co.

Tenniel Illustrations to the "Alice" Books. Michael Hancher. LC 84-11842. (Illus.). 176p. 1985. pap. 39.50 (*0-8142-0408-2*) Ohio St U Pr.

Tennis! (J). (ps). 1995. 5.95 (*1-885751-04-4*) Wee Venture.

Tennis. (Take up Sports! Ser.). (Illus.). 64p. pap. 4.95 (*1-56757-057-7*) Appleton Comms.

***Tennis.** LC 96-52604. (Successful Sports Ser.). (J). 1997. lib. bdg. write for info. (*1-57572-200-3*) Rigby Interact Libr.

***Tennis.** (Composite Guide to...Ser.). 64p. (YA). (gr. 3 up). 1997. lib. bdg. 15.95 (*0-7910-4728-8*) Chelsea Hse.

Tennis. Charles Applewhaite & Bill Moss. (Skills of the Game Ser.). (Illus.). 128p. 1996. pap. 19.95 (*1-85223-899-2*, Pub. by Crowood Pr UK) Trafalgar.

***Tennis.** Charles Applewhaite. LC 96-37858. (Know the Sport Ser.). (Illus.). 48p. 1997. pap. 5.95 (*0-8117-2836-6*) Stackpole.

Tennis. Donna Bailey. LC 90-23056. (Sports World Ser.). (Illus.). 32p. (J). (gr. 1-4). 1991. pap. 3.95 (*0-8114-4711-1*); lib. bdg. 21.40 (*0-8114-2904-0*) Raintree Steck-V.

***Tennis.** Brown & Benchmark Staff. (Elements of Learning Ser.). 120p. (C). 1997. per. write for info. (*0-697-29449-8*) Brown & Benchmark.

Tennis. Linda Dawson. (Butterfly Bks.). (J). 1990. 8.95 (*0-86685-476-2*) Intl Bk Ctr.

Tennis. Steve Dimeglio. (The Summer Olympics Ser.). 32p. (J). (gr. 4-8). 1995. 14.79 (*1-887068-07-4*) Smart Apple.

Tennis. Herbert I. Kavet. 64p. 1993. 8.95 (*0-88032-353-1*) Ivory Tower Pub.

Tennis. Anne Pittman. (Sport for Life Ser.). (C). 1988. pap. text ed. 10.50 (*0-673-18346-7*) Addson-Wesley Educ.

Tennis. Keith Reynolds. (Successful Sports Ser.). (J). 1996. write for info. (*1-57572-070-1*) Rigby Interact Libr.

Tennis. Elizabeth Sirimarko. LC 93-27152. (J). 1993. write for info. (*0-86593-343-X*) Rourke Corp.

Tennis. 2nd ed. David Claxton & John Faribault. 112p. (Orig.). (C). 1992. pap. text ed. 14.95 (*0-89787-617-2*) Gorsuch Scarisbrick.

Tennis. 2nd ed. Dewayne J. Johnson et al. (Illus.). 96p. (Orig.). 1996. pap. text ed. 9.95 (*0-89641-283-0*) American Pr.

Tennis. 5th ed. Joel R. Barton, III & William A. Grice. (Illus.). 176p. 1994. pap. text ed. 11.95 (*0-89641-270-9*) American Pr.

Tennis. 6th ed. Joan D. Johnson & Paul Xanthos. 176p. (Orig.). (C). 1992. per. write for info. (*0-697-10117-7*) American Pr.

Tennis. 7th ed. Joan D. Johnson & Paul Xanthos. 176p. (Orig.). (C). 1996. per. write for info. (*0-697-27982-0*) Brown & Benchmark.

Tennis, No. 1. pap. 100.00 (*0-590-06898-9*) Scholastic Inc.

Tennis, No. 2. pap. 100.00 (*0-590-06899-7*) Scholastic Inc.

Tennis, No. 3. rev. ed. pap. 6.00 (*0-590-04942-9*) Scholastic Inc.

Tennis, Set, Nos. 1 & 2. pap. 360.00 (*0-590-06900-4*) Scholastic Inc.

***Tennis: A Cultural History.** Heiner Gillmeister. LC 97-11809. (Illus.). 416p. 1997. 120.00 (*0-7185-0147-0*, Pub. by Leicester Univ Pr) Bks Intl VA.

Tennis: Back to the Basics. 2nd ed. Carole J. Zebas & H. Mardi Johnson. 126p. 1991. pap. text ed. 13.95 (*0-945483-12-0*) E Bowers Pub.

Tennis: Easy on-Easy Off. Eleanor Owens et al. 70p. 1975. 3.95 (*0-938822-10-1*) USTA.

Tennis: Easy Sports Reader. Burt & Hog. (Illus.). 16p. (J). (ps-1). 1996. pap. 2.49 (*1-55734-895-2*) Tchr Create Mat.

Tennis! Great Moments & Dubious Achievements in Tennis History. John S. Snyder. LC 92-29517. 208p. 1993. pap. 6.95 (*0-8118-0312-0*) Chronicle Bks.

Tennis: Keep It Simple. Donald D. Klotz. 64p. (C). 1989. text ed. write for info. (*0-697-08483-3*) Brown & Benchmark.

Tennis: Let's Analyze Your Game. Fred Stolle & Bob G. Knight. (Illus.). 128p. (C). 1992. pap. text ed. 15.95 (*0-89582-236-9*) Morton Pub.

Tennis: Play Like a Pro. Charles Bracken. LC 89-27341. (Be the Best! Ser.). (Illus.). 64p. (J). (gr. 4-8). 1990. lib. bdg. 11.89 (*0-8167-1931-4*) Troll Communs.

Tennis: Play Like a Pro. Charles Bracken. LC 89-27341. (Be the Best! Ser.). (Illus.). 64p. (J). (gr. 4-8). 1997. pap. 3.95 (*0-8167-1932-2*) Troll Communs.

***Tennis: Play Smarter, Not Harder: Tennis Tips, Quips, & Tricks from Curly Davis.** (Illus.). 128p. (Orig.). 1996. pap. 12.95 (*1-889937-02-9*) Crescent Hill Bks.

Tennis: Steps to Success. 2nd ed. Jim Brown. LC 94-43319. (Steps to Success Activity Ser.). (Illus.). (Orig.). 1995. pap. 14.95 (*0-87322-555-4*, PBRO0555) Human Kinetics.

Tennis: Techniques, Tactics, Training. Jeremy Woods. (Illus.). 124p. 1992. pap. 22.95 (*1-85223-467-9*, Pub. by Crowood Pr UK) Trafalgar.

Tennis: The Lifetime Sport. Shimon-Craig Van Collie. (Mature Reader Ser.). 176p. (Orig.). 1993. pap. 8.95 (*1-55867-082-3*) Bristol Pub Ent CA.

Tennis & the Meaning of Life: A Literary Anthology of the Game. Ed. by Jay Jennings. 320p. 1995. 24.00 (*1-55821-378-3*) Lyons & Burford.

An Asterisk (*) at the beginning of an entry indicates that the title is appearing in BIP for the first time.

Tennis & the Meaning of Life: A Literary Anthology of the Game. Jay Jennings. 352p. 1996. pap. 15.00 (*0-15-600407-0*, Harvest Bks) HarBrace.

Tennis Antiques & Collectibles. Jeanne Cherry. (Illus.). 208p. (Orig.). 1995. pap. 39.95 (*0-9646571-0-4*) Amaryllis CA.

Tennis, Anyone? Albert Green. (Illus.). 19p. (Orig.). 1996. pap. 3.25 (*0-88680-421-3*) I E Clark.

Tennis, Anyone? 5th ed. Dick Gould. LC 92-16130. 128p. (C). 1992. pap. 13.95 (*1-55934-168-8*, 1168) Mayfield Pub.

Tennis Charting: The Graphic Way. Peg Greeley. Ed. by Jackie Tucker. (Illus.). (Orig.). 1981. pap. 4.95 (*0-932904-02-5*) Magoos Umbrella.

Tennis Court Oath: A Book of Poems. rev. ed. John Ashbery. LC 62-10596. (Wesleyan Poetry Classics Ser.). 94p. 1997. reprint ed. pap. 11.95 (*0-8195-1013-0*, Wesleyan Univ Pr) U Pr of New Eng.

Tennis Courts Nineteen Ninety - Nineteen Ninety-One. rev. ed. USTA Technical Committee & U. S. Tennis Court & Track Builders Assn. Staff. (Illus.). 192p. 1990. 13.75 (*0-938822-85-3*) USTA.

Tennis Dictionary: Dictionnaire de Tennis. Ed. by P. Rebourgeon. 160p. (FRE.). 1981. 89.95 (*0-8288-4442-9*, M9769) Fr & Eur.

Tennis Doubles, No. 1: Winning Strategies for All Levels. Greg Lappin et al. (Illus.). 144p. (Orig.). 1985. pap. 9.95 (*0-930425-00-6*) KG Bks Co.

Tennis Down Under. Fred Stolle & Kenneth Wydro. LC 85-10685. (Illus.). 135p. 1985. 12.95 (*0-915765-18-7*, Full Court Pr Bks.); pap. 5.95 (*0-915765-07-1*, Full Court Pr Bks.) Natl Pr Bks.

Tennis Drill Book. Sharon Petro. LC 84-47518. (Illus.). 128p. (Orig.). 1986. pap. 13.95 (*0-88011-224-7*, PPET0224) Human Kinetics.

***Tennis Everyone.** 5th ed. Moore & Chafin. 238p. 1994. pap. text ed. 15.95 (*0-88725-205-2*) Hunter Textbks.

Tennis for Beginners. H. A. Murray. 1980. pap. 2.00 (*0-87980-263-4*) Wilshire.

Tennis for Everyone: Uncommon Solutions to Common Problems. Charles Cunningham. 160p. (C). 1994. per., pap. text ed. 15.91 (*0-8403-9751-8*) Kendall-Hunt.

Tennis for Experienced Players. 2nd ed. Robert Gensemer. (Illus.). 170p. (C). 1995. pap. text ed. 15.95 (*0-89582-273-3*) Morton Pub.

***Tennis for Humans: A Simple Blueprint for Winning.** Richard B. Myers. LC 96-54275. 128p. (Orig.). 1997. pap. 13.95 (*0-9639905-8-6*) Two Thous-Three Assocs.

Tennis for Winners!! All about Becoming a Much Better Player: What It Takes & How to Do It. Robert H. Jordan. (Illus.). 144p. (Orig.). 1991. pap. 14.95 (*0-9630897-0-6*) R H Jordan.

Tennis Game. George W. Trow. 1979. pap. 5.25 (*0-8222-1120-3*) Dramatists Play.

Tennis Handbook. Gesele Lajoie & Bob Lajoie. (Illus.). 46p. pap. 5.95 (*0-318-32568-3*) Hancock House.

Tennis Handsome. Barry Hannah. LC 82-48725. (Voices of the South Ser.). 166p. 1995. pap. 9.95 (*0-8071-2008-1*) La State U Pr.

Tennis Party. Madeleine Wickham. 256p. 1996. 22.95 (*0-312-14053-3*) St Martin.

Tennis Party. Madeline Wickham. 256p. 1996. pap. 10.95 (*0-552-99639-4*) Bantam.

Tennis Philately. Lester M. Yerkes. (Illus.). 56p. 1994. pap. text ed. 8.00 (*0-935991-21-2*) Am Topical Assn.

Tennis Players. Lars Gustafsson. Tr. by Yvonne L. Sandstroem from SWE. LC 82-22559. 92p. 1983. 13.00 (*0-8112-0861-3*); pap. 6.25 (*0-8112-0862-1*, NDP551) New Directions.

Tennis Psychology. Harold Geist & Cecelia Martinez. LC 75-17651. (Illus.). 136p. 1976. 24.95 (*0-88229-120-3*) Nelson-Hall.

***Tennis Quotations.** Ed. by Helen Exley. (Quotations Bks.). (Illus.). 60p. 1996. 8.00 (*1-85015-775-8*) Exley Giftbooks.

***Tennis Rules: A Player's Guide.** Barry Newcombe. (Illus.). 80p. 1997. pap. 9.95 (*0-7063-7538-6*, Pub. by Ward Lock UK) Sterling.

Tennis Science for Tennis Players. Howard Brody. LC 86-30735. (Illus.). 168p. (Orig.). 1987. pap. 19.95 (*0-8122-1238-X*) U of Pa Pr.

Tennis Shoes: A Story Rhyme. Story Time Collection Staff. (Illus.). 20p. (Orig.). (J). (ps-6). 1992. pap. text ed. 9.95 (*0-939476-75-4*, Biblio Pr) Prosperity & Profits.

Tennis Shoes: A Story Rhyme. Story Time Stories That Rhyme Staff. (Story Samphlet Edition Ser.). (Illus.). 21p. (J). (gr. 4-7). 1994. pap. 9.95 (*1-56820-012-9*) Story Time.

Tennis Shoes among the Nephites. Chris Heimerdinger. pap. 9.95 (*1-55503-131-5*, 0111732) Covenant Comms.

Tennis Shoes & the Feathered Serpent. Chris Heimerdinger. 1995. pap. 10.95 (*1-55503-805-0*, 01111892) Covenant Comms.

***Tennis Shorts.** Liebman. LC 97-7162. 1997. write for info. (*0-8092-3075-5*) Contemp Bks.

Tennis Skills Test Manual. 1989. 14.00 (*0-88314-442-5*) AAHPERD.

Tennis Sourcebook. Dennis J. Phillips. LC 95-3842. 548p. 1995. 80.00 (*0-8108-3001-9*) Scarecrow.

Tennis Squash & Badminton Bygones. Gerald Gurney. 1989. pap. 25.00 (*0-85263-676-8*, Pub. by Shire UK) St Mut.

Tennis Strokes That Win: Breakthrough Techniques for Mastering the Game. Frank Early. 144p. 1995. pap. 9.95 (*0-8092-3447-5*) Contemp Bks.

Tennis Tactics: Winning Patterns of Play. United States Tennis Association Staff. LC 96-21957. (Illus.). 248p. (Orig.). 1996. pap. 14.95 (*0-88011-499-1*, PUST0499) Human Kinetics.

Tennis Teacher's Guide to Group Instruction. rev. ed. Eve F. Kraft. (Illus.). 96p. 1990. reprint ed. 4.95 (*0-938822-86-1*) USTA.

Tennis Teens. Mary G. Silsby. LC 91-67749. 71p. (Orig.). 1992. pap. 7.00 (*1-56002-155-1*, Univ Edtns) Aegina Pr.

Tennis Ticklers: Tennis Poems to Make You Laugh. Louisa T. Arnold. (Illus.). 80p. 1994. 16.95 (*0-9641835-0-1*) Tengo Pubng.

Tennis Tips from Many Pro's Assembled in One Book. Bill E. Forney. 345p. 1995. pap. 19.95 (*0-614-14351-9*) BEF Pubng.

Tennis Today. Bassett. Date not set. pap. text ed. 21.75 (*0-314-68952-4*) West Pub.

***Tennis Trek.** 3rd ed. LaLance & Short. 162p. (C). 1997. per. 24.95 (*0-7872-3764-7*) Kendall-Hunt.

Tennis Twins. Shaun Gayle & Pat Owsley. 24p. (J). (gr. 5-9). 1995. pap. 8.99 incl. audio (*7-900881-14-X*, 3-1233, Victor Bks) Chariot Victor.

Tennis Twins. Shaun Gayle. (Shaun Gayle's Sports Tales). (Illus.). 24p. (J). (gr. 5-9). 1995. pap. 5.99 (*1-56476-464-8*, 6-3464, Victor Bks) Chariot Victor.

***Tennis Unlimited.** O'Meara & Murray. LC 96-51750. (Winning Edge of Sports Ser.). 144p. (Orig.). 1997. pap. 14.95 (*1-57034-059-5*) ICS Bks.

Tennis-up to Tournament Standard. Ellwanger. (EP Sports Ser.). (Illus.). 1973. 6.95 (*0-7158-0579-7*) Charles River Bks.

Tennis with Baseball Bats: A CoDependent Dance. Jack Veasey. (Illus.). 38p. 1995. pap. 8.00 (*1-879294-09-5*) Warm Spring Pr.

Tennis Workbook, Unit I. rev. ed. Eve F. Kraft. (Illus.). 64p. 1990. reprint ed. 2.95 (*0-938822-87-X*) USTA.

Tennis Workbook, Unit II. rev. ed. Eve F. Kraft. (Illus.). 72p. 1989. reprint ed. 4.95 (*0-938822-88-8*) USTA.

Tennis Workshop: A Complete Game Guide. Alan Jones & Barry Wood. (Illus.). 224p. 1993. pap. 29.95 (*1-85223-729-5*, Pub. by Crowood Pr UK) Trafalgar.

Tennison Gambit. W. John Lutes. (Orig.). 1995. pap. 12.95 (*0-945470-55-X*) Chess Ent.

Tenno Seiji: Direct Imperial Rule. Shinichi Fujii. LC 79-65470. (Studies in Japanese History & Civilization). 415p. 1979. reprint ed. text ed. 79.50 (*0-313-26981-5*, U6981, Greenwood Pr) Greenwood.

Tennozan: The Battle of Okinawa & the Atomic Bomb. George Feifer. (Illus.). 512p. 1994. pap. 14.95 (*0-395-70066-3*) Ticknor & Fields.

Tennyson. Stephen Gwynn. 1972. 59.95 (*0-8490-1186-8*) Gordon Pr.

Tennyson. Stephen Gwynn. LC 74-16313. (Studies in Tennyson: No. 27). 1974. lib. bdg. 59.95 (*0-8383-1796-0*) M S G Haskell Hse.

Tennyson. John D. Jump. (Critical Heritage Ser.). 1967. 67.50 (*0-7100-2941-1*, RKP) Routledge.

Tennyson. A. Lyall. LC 76-53034. (Studies in Tennyson: No. 27). 1977. lib. bdg. 42.95 (*0-8383-2164-X*) M S G Haskell Hse.

Tennyson. Christopher Ricks. (C). 1989. pap. text ed. 40.50 (*0-582-01725-4*) Addison-Wesley.

Tennyson. Ed. by Rebecca Stott. LC 96-1911. (Critical Readers Ser.). 232p. (C). 1996. pap. text ed. 19.50 (*0-582-23712-2*, Pub. by Longman UK) Longman.

Tennyson. Ed. by Rebecca Stott. LC 96-1911. (Critical Readers Ser.). 232p. (C). 1996. text ed. 51.95 (*0-582-23713-0*, Pub. by Longman UK) Longman.

Tennyson. Humbert Wolfe. LC 78-99674. (Select Bibliographies Reprint Ser.). 1977. 17.95 (*0-8369-5103-4*) Ayer.

Tennyson. 4th ed. Arthur C. Benson. LC 76-137369. (Select Bibliographies Reprint Ser.). 1977. reprint ed. 18.95 (*0-8369-5570-6*) Ayer.

Tennyson. Gilbert K. Chesterton. 1977. reprint ed. 17.00 (*0-403-07393-6*) Scholarly.

Tennyson. Garold G. Nicolson. LC 72-2100. (English Literature Ser.: No. 33). 1972. reprint ed. lib. bdg. 75.00 (*0-8383-1458-9*) M S G Haskell Hse.

Tennyson. Humbert Wolfe. (BCL1-PR English Literature Ser.). 60p. 1992. reprint ed. lib. bdg. 59.00 (*0-7812-7700-0*) Rprt Serv.

Tennyson, No. XVI. Ed. by Christopher Ricks & Aidan Day. LC 88-31103. (Tennyson Archive Ser.). 316p. 1989. reprint ed. text ed. 81.50 (*0-8240-4215-8*) Garland.

Tennyson, No. XVII. Ed. by Christopher Ricks & Aidan Day. LC 88-31103. (Tennyson Archive Ser.). 318p. 1989. reprint ed. text ed. 81.50 (*0-8240-4216-6*) Garland.

Tennyson, No. XVIII. Ed. by Christopher Ricks & Aidan Day. LC 88-31103. (Tennyson Archive Ser.). 336p. 1989. reprint ed. text ed. 81.50 (*0-8240-4217-4*) Garland.

Tennyson, No. XIX. Ed. by Christopher Ricks & Aidan Day. LC 88-31103. (Tennyson Archive Ser.). 324p. 1989. reprint ed. text ed. 81.50 (*0-8240-4218-2*) Garland.

Tennyson, No. XX. Ed. by Christopher Ricks & Aidan Day. LC 88-31103. (Tennyson Archive Ser.). 306p. 1989. reprint ed. text ed. 81.50 (*0-8240-4219-0*) Garland.

Tennyson, No. XXI. Ed. by Christopher Ricks & Aidan Day. LC 88-31103. (Tennyson Archive Ser.). 316p. 1989. reprint ed. text ed. 81.50 (*0-8240-4220-4*) Garland.

Tennyson, No. XXII. Ed. by Christopher Ricks & Aidan Day. LC 88-31103. (Tennyson Archive Ser.). 336p. 1989. reprint ed. text ed. 81.50 (*0-8240-4221-2*) Garland.

Tennyson, No. XXIII. Ed. by Christopher Ricks & Aidan Day. LC 88-31103. (Tennyson Archive Ser.). 302p. 1989. reprint ed. text ed. 81.50 (*0-8240-4222-0*) Garland.

Tennyson: A Selected Edition. Alfred Tennyson. Ed. by Christopher Ricks. 1989. 52.00 (*0-520-06588-3*); pap. 17.00 (*0-520-06666-9*) U CA Pr.

Tennyson: An Illustrated Life. Norman Page. (Illus.). 192p. 1993. 30.00 (*1-56131-060-3*) New Amsterdam Bks.

Tennyson: Aspects of His Life. Harold G. Nicolson. LC 74-145209. 308p. 1925. reprint ed. 15.00 (*0-403-00806-9*) Scholarly.

Tennyson: Aspects of His Life, Character & Poetry. Harold G. Nicolson. LC 72-12. (Select Bibliographies Reprint Ser.). 1977. reprint ed. 19.95 (*0-8369-9967-3*) Ayer.

Tennyson: His Art & Relation to Modern Life. Stopford A. Brooke. LC 74-123761. reprint ed. 29.50 (*0-404-01115-2*) AMS Pr.

Tennyson: Interviews & Recollections. Ed. by Norman Page. (Interviews & Recollections Ser.). 218p. 1983. 44.00 (*0-389-20066-2*, N6836) B&N Imports.

Tennyson: Poems. Alfred Tennyson. (Poetry Library). 240p. 1985. pap. 9.95 (*0-14-058502-8*, Penguin Bks) Viking Penguin.

Tennyson: Poet, Philosopher, Idealist. John C. Walters. LC 70-153481. (Studies in Tennyson: No. 27). 1971. reprint ed. lib. bdg. 63.95 (*0-8383-1238-1*) M S G Haskell Hse.

Tennyson: The Growth of a Poet. Jerome H. Buckley. LC 60-13298. 312p. reprint ed. pap. 89.00 (*0-7837-4453-6*, 2057983) Bks Demand.

Tennyson: The Muses' Tug-of-War. Daniel Albright. LC 86-1546. (Virginia Victorian Studies). 267p. reprint ed. pap. 76.10 (*0-7837-4360-2*, 2044070) Bks Demand.

Tennyson, a Modern Portrait. Hugh I. Fausset. (BCL1-PR English Literature Ser.). 309p. 1992. reprint ed. lib. bdg. 89.00 (*0-7812-7696-9*) Rprt Serv.

Tennyson an Occultist. A. P. Sinnett. LC 72-2102. (Studies in Tennyson: No. 27). 1972. reprint ed. lib. bdg. 56.95 (*0-8383-1485-6*) M S G Haskell Hse.

Tennyson & Clio: History in the Major Poems. Henry Kozicki. LC 79-10979. 208p. reprint ed. pap. 59.30 (*0-8357-6619-5*, 2035264) Bks Demand.

Tennyson & His Poetry. Reginald B. Johnson. LC 73-120976. (Poetry & Life Ser.). reprint ed. 27.50 (*0-404-52524-5*) AMS Pr.

Tennyson & Madness. Ann C. Colley. LC 82-13689. 192p. (C). 1983. 25.00 (*0-8203-0648-7*) U of Ga Pr.

Tennyson & Matthew Arnold. Oliver Elton. LC 75-163127. (Studies in Comparative Literature: No. 35). 1971. reprint ed. lib. bdg. 58.95 (*0-8383-1305-1*) M S G Haskell Hse.

Tennyson & Personification: The Rhetoric of "Tithonus" Daniel A. Harris. LC 85-28844. (Nineteenth-Century Studies). 158p. reprint ed. pap. 45.10 (*0-8357-1736-4*, 2070552) Bks Demand.

Tennyson & Scientific Theology. J. W. Hayes. LC 77-434. (Studies in Tennyson: No. 27). 1977. lib. bdg. 22.95 (*0-8383-2163-1*) M S G Haskell Hse.

Tennyson & Swinburne As Romantic Naturalists. Kerry McSweeney. 240p. 1981. 30.00 (*0-8020-2381-9*) U of Toronto Pr.

Tennyson & the Doom of Romanticism. Herbert F. Tucker. LC 87-12978. 495p. 1988. 47.50 (*0-674-87430-7*) HUP.

Tennyson & the Text: The Weaver's Shuttle. Gerhard Joseph. (Illus.). 256p. (C). 1992. text ed. 69.95 (*0-521-41390-7*) Cambridge U Pr.

Tennyson & Tradition. Robert Pattison. LC 79-13247. 178p. 1980. 25.95 (*0-674-87415-3*) HUP.

Tennyson Archive: The Manuscripts at the University Library, Cambridge. LC 91-28998. (Tennyson Archive Ser.: Vol. 26). 264p. 1991. text ed. 81.50 (*0-8240-4225-5*) Garland.

Tennyson Archive: The Manuscripts at the Victoria & Albert Museum, the Robert H. Taylor Collection of Princeton University, & the Alderman Library of the University of Virginia. Ed. by Christopher Ricks & Aidan Day. LC 92-16236. (Tennyson Archive Ser.: Vol. 30). 316p. 1992. text ed. 81.50 (*0-8240-4229-8*) Garland.

Tennyson Archive, Vol. 11: The Manuscripts at Trinity College, Cambridge: Miscellaneous Manuscripts & Notebooks 13-17. Ed. by Day Ricks. LC 88-16352. 318p. 1988. text ed. 81.50 (*0-8240-4210-7*) Garland.

Tennyson Archive, Vol. 12: The Manuscripts at Trinity College, Cambridge: Notebooks 18-25. Ed. by Day Ricks. LC 88-16352. 360p. 1988. text ed. 81.50 (*0-8240-4211-5*) Garland.

Tennyson Archive, Vol. 13: The Manuscripts at Trinity College, Cambridge: Notebooks 26-29. Ed. by Day Ricks. LC 88-16352. 334p. 1988. text ed. 81.50 (*0-8240-4212-3*) Garland.

Tennyson Archive, Vol. 14: The Manuscripts at Trinity College, Cambridge: Notebooks 30-36. Ed. by Day Ricks. LC 88-16352. 424p. 1988. text ed. 81.50 (*0-8240-4213-1*) Garland.

Tennyson Archive, Vol. 15: The Manuscripts at Trinity College, Cambridge: Notebooks 37-40 & Miscellaneous Manuscripts. Ed. by Day Ricks. LC 88-16352. 356p. 1988. text ed. 81.50 (*0-8240-4214-X*) Garland.

Tennyson Archive Volume II. Tennyson. The Harvard Manuscripts: Notebooks 5-15 (MS Eng 952) Alfred Tennyson. Ed. by Christopher Ricks & Aidan Day. LC 86-19585. (Tennyson Archive Ser.). 308p. 1987. text ed. 81.50 (*0-8240-4201-8*) Garland.

Tennyson Archive Volume III. (The Harvard Manuscripts) Notebooks 16-27 (MS Eng 952) Alfred Tennyson. Ed. by Christopher Ricks & Aidan Day. LC 86-19585. (Tennyson Archive Ser.). 306p. 1987. text ed. 81.50 (*0-8240-4202-6*) Garland.

Tennyson Archive Volume I.Tennyson. The Harvard Manuscripts: Notebooks 1-4 (MS Eng 952) Alfred Tennyson. Ed. by Christopher Ricks & Aidan Day. LC 86-19585. (Tennyson Archive Ser.). 1987. text ed. 81.50 (*0-8240-4200-X*) Garland.

Tennyson Archive Volume IV. Tennyson. The Harvard Manuscripts: Notebooks 28-39 (MS Eng 952) Alfred Tennyson. Ed. by Christopher Ricks & Aidan Day. LC 86-19585. (Tennyson Archive Ser.). 322p. 1987. text ed. 81.50 (*0-8240-4203-4*) Garland.

Tennyson Archive Volume IX Tennyson. The Harvard Manuscripts: Loose Papers 114-183 (BMS Eng 952. 1) Alfred Tennyson. Ed. by Christopher Ricks & Aidan Day. LC 86-21711. (Tennyson Archive Ser.: Vol. 9). 322p. 1987. text ed. 81.50 (*0-8240-4208-5*) Garland.

Tennyson Archive Volume V. Tennyson. The Harvard Manuscripts: Notebooks 40-50 (MS Eng 952) Alfred Tennyson. Ed. by Christopher Ricks & Aidan Day. LC 86-19585. (Tennyson Archive Ser.: Vol. 5). 326p. 1987. text ed. 81.50 (*0-8240-4204-2*) Garland.

Tennyson Archive Volume VI. (The Harvard Manuscripts) Notebooks 51-54 (MS Eng 952) Alfred Tennyson. Ed. by Christopher Ricks & Aidan Day. LC 86-19585. (Tennyson Archive Ser.: Vol. 6). 328p. 1987. text ed. 81.50 (*0-8240-4205-0*) Garland.

Tennyson Archive Volume VII. Tennyson. The Harvard Manuscripts: Notebooks 55-70 (MS Eng 952. Alfred Tennyson. Ed. by Christopher Ricks & Aidan Day. LC 86-19585. (Tennyson Archive Ser.: Vol. 7). 294p. 1987. text ed. 81.50 (*0-8240-4206-9*) Garland.

Tennyson Archive Volume VIII. (The Harvard Manuscripts) Loose Papers 1-113 (BMS Eng 952. 1) Alfred Tennyson. Ed. by Christopher Ricks & Aidan Day. LC 86-21711. (Tennyson Archive Ser.: Vol. 8). 312p. 1987. text ed. 81.50 (*0-8240-4207-7*) Garland.

Tennyson Archive Volume X Tennyson the Harvard Manuscripts: Loose Papers 184-275 (BMS Eng 952. 1) & Miscellanea. Alfred Tennyson. Ed. by Christopher Ricks & Aidan Day. LC 86-21711. (Tennyson Archive Ser.: Vol. 10). 320p. 1987. text ed. 81.50 (*0-8240-4209-3*) Garland.

Tennyson As Seen by His Parodists. J. Postma. LC 68-748. (Studies in Tennyson: No. 27). 1969. reprint ed. lib. bdg. 75.00 (*0-8383-0674-8*) M S G Haskell Hse.

Tennyson, Aspects of His Life, Character & Poetry. Harold G. Nicolson. (BCL1-PR English Literature Ser.). 308p. 1992. reprint ed. lib. bdg. 89.00 (*0-7812-7697-7*) Rprt Serv.

Tennyson Dictionary. Arthur E. Baker. LC 67-30807. (Studies in Tennyson: No. 27). 1916. reprint ed. lib. bdg. 75.00 (*0-8383-0706-X*) M S G Haskell Hse.

Tennyson Dictionary. Arthur E. Baker. (BCL1-PR English Literature Ser.). 296p. 1992. reprint ed. lib. bdg. 79.00 (*0-7812-7692-6*) Rprt Serv.

Tennyson Laureate. Valerie Pitt. 304p. reprint ed. pap. 86.70 (*0-8357-4166-4*, 2036940) Bks Demand.

Tennyson MSS from the British Library. Alfred Tennyson. LC 90-3258. (Tennyson Archive Ser.: Vol. 25). 290p. 1990. reprint ed. text ed. 81.50 (*0-8240-4224-7*) Garland.

Tennyson, Ruskin, Mill & Other Literary Estimates. Frederic Harrison. LC 71-111835. (Essay Index Reprint Ser.). 1977. 23.95 (*0-8369-1612-3*) Ayer.

Tennyson, the Manuscripts at the Berg Collection of the New York Public Library & the Harry Ransom Humanities Research Center of the University of Texas at Austin. Alfred Tennyson. Ed. by Christopher Ricks & Aidan Day. LC 91-37461. (Tennyson Archive Ser.: Vol. 28). 258p. 1992. text ed. 81.50 (*0-8240-4227-1*) Garland.

Tennyson, the Manuscripts at the Fitzwilliam Museum, the Bodleian Library of Oxford University & the Sterling Library of the University of London. Alfred Tennyson. Ed. by Christopher Ricks & Aidan Day. LC 91-43681. (Tennyson Archive Ser.: Vol. 29). 214p. 1992. text ed. 81.50 (*0-8240-4228-X*) Garland.

Tennyson, the Manuscripts at the Huntington Library & the Free Library of Philadelphia. Alfred Tennyson. Ed. by Christopher Ricks & Aidan Day. LC 91-38473. (Tennyson Archive Ser.: Vol. 27). 288p. 1991. text ed. 81.50 (*0-8240-4226-3*) Garland.

Tennyson, the Manuscripts in the Minor Collections & the Indexes for the Tennyson Archive. Ed. by Christopher Ricks & Aidan Day. LC 92-36298. 192p. 1993. text ed. 55.00 (*0-8240-4230-1*) Garland.

Tennyson XXIV. Alfred Tennyson. Ed. by Christopher Ricks & Aidan Day. LC 90-3259. (Tennyson Archive Ser.: Vol. 24). 132p. 1990. reprint ed. text ed. 81.50 (*0-8240-4223-9*) Garland.

Tennysonian Love: The Strange Diagonal. Joseph Gerhard. LC 68-57204. 216p. reprint ed. pap. 61.60 (*0-318-39678-5*, 2033261) Bks Demand.

Tennysoniana. 2nd rev. ed. Richard H. Shepherd. LC 70-148302. reprint ed. 31.50 (*0-404-08899-6*) AMS Pr.

Tennyson's Characters: "Strange Faces, Other Minds" David Goslee. LC 89-33468. 333p. 1989. text ed. 42.95 (*0-87745-246-6*) U of Iowa Pr.

Tennyson's Dramas: A Critical Study. Dennis M. Organ. (Graduate Studies: No. 17). 125p. 1979. pap. 7.00 (*0-89672-066-7*) Tex Tech Univ Pr.

Tennyson's Fixations: Psychoanalysis & the Topics of the Early Poetry. Matthew Rowlinson. (Victorian Literature & Culture Ser.). 224p. (C). 1994. text ed. 37.50 (*0-8139-1478-7*) U Pr of Va.

Tennyson's Idylls of the King & Arthurian Story from the Sixteenth Century. Mungo W. Maccallum. LC 73-154159. (Select Bibliographies Reprint Ser.). 1977. reprint ed. 26.95 (*0-8369-5775-X*) Ayer.

Tennyson's in Memoriam. J. F. Genung. LC 76-129342. (Studies in Tennyson: No. 27). 1970. reprint ed. lib. bdg. 55.95 (*0-8383-1146-6*) M S G Haskell Hse.

Tennyson's Language. Donald S. Hair. 212p. 1991. 50.00 (*0-8020-5905-8*) U of Toronto Pr.

Tennyson's Major Poems: The Comic & Ironic Patterns. James R. Kincaid. LC 74-29723. 266p. reprint ed. pap. 75.90 (*0-8357-8344-8*, 2033780) Bks Demand.

Tennyson's Maud: A Definitive Edition. Ed. by Susan Shatto. LC 85-26431. (Illus.). 320p. 1986. 50.00 (*0-8061-1986-1*) U of Okla Pr.

Tennyson's Mystical Poems: The Coming of King Arthur; The Holy Grail; Pellas & Ettarre; The Passing of Arthur; The Higher Pantheism. Alfred Tennyson. 163p. 1996. pap. 16.95 (*1-56459-589-7*) Kessinger Pub.

Tennyson's Poetry. Alfred Tennyson. Ed. by Robert W. Hill, Jr. (Critical Editions Ser.). (C). 1972. pap. text ed. 17.95 (*0-393-09953-9*) Norton.

Tennyson's Use of the Bible. Edna M. Robinson. 119p. (C). 1968. reprint ed. 40.00 (*0-87752-093-3*) Gordian.

Tenoclock Scholar: A Johnnie Baker Mystery. John Miles. 252p. 1996. 22.95 (*0-8027-3273-9*) Walker & Co.

Tenor: Every Woman's Dream. Lisa H. Russell. LC 93-91096. 138p. 1994. pap. 10.00 (*0-9643892-0-7*) Banner Pubng.

Tenor Banjo Chord Chart. Ron Middlebrook. 4p. 1995. pap. text ed. 2.00 (*1-57424-008-0*) Centerstream Pub.

Tenor Banjo Chords. Bay, Mel, Publications, Inc. Staff. 1993. 4.95 (*0-87166-013-X*, 93259) Mel Bay.

Tenor Banjo Melody Chord Playing System. Bay, Mel, Publications, Inc. Staff. 1993. 9.95 (*1-56222-076-4*, 93629) Mel Bay.

Tenor Banjo Pocketbook. William Bay. pap. 0.95 (*0-87166-557-3*, 93756) Mel Bay.

Tenor Saxophone. Bruce Pearson. (Standard of Excellence Ser.: Bk. 1). 1993. 6.45 (*0-8497-5933-1*, W21XB) Kjos.

Tenor Saxophone. Bruce Pearson. (Standard of Excellence Ser.: Bk. 2). 1993. 6.45 (*0-8497-5958-7*, W22XB) Kjos.

Tenor Saxophone. Bruce Pearson. (Standard of Excellence Ser.: Bk. 3). 1996. 6.45 (*0-8497-5982-X*, W23XB) Kjos.

Tenor Saxophonist's Story. Josef Skvorecky. 192p. 1997. 23.00 (*0-88001-461-X*) Ecco Pr.

***Tenor Saxophonist's Story.** Josef Skvorecky. Tr. by Caleb Crain et al. from CZE. 176p. 1997. pap. 13.00 (*0-88001-563-2*) Ecco Pr.

Tenor Voice. Anthony Frissell. 1971. 19.95 (*0-8283-1387-3*) Branden Pub Co.

Tenorman: A Novella. David Huddle. LC 95-12601. 96p. 1995. 12.95 (*0-8118-1027-5*) Chronicle Bks.

Tenors, Tantrums & Trills: An Opera Dictionary from Aida to Zzzz. David Barber. (Illus.). 96p. (Orig.). 1996. pap. 11.95 (*0-920151-19-1*, Pub. by Sound & Vision CN) Firefly Bks Ltd.

***Tens: Clinical Applications & Related Theory.** Deirdre M. Walsh & Eric T. McAdams. LC 96-40892. 1997. write for info. (*0-443-05323-5*) Churchill.

Ten's a Crowd. Judy Delton. (Lottery Luck Ser.: Bk. 3). (Illus.). 96p. (J). (gr. 2-5). 1995. pap. 3.95 (*0-7868-1020-3*) Hyprn Child.

TENS & Electrotherapeutic Devices. (Market Research Reports: No. 321). 148p. 1992. 795.00 (*0-317-05025-7*) Theta Corp.

Tensaurus Italograecus. Gunther A. Saalfeld. 592p. 1964. reprint ed. write for info. (*0-318-70822-1*); reprint ed. write for info. (*0-318-72073-6*) G Olms Pubs.

Tense. Bernard Comrie. (Cambridge Textbooks in Linguistics Ser.). 175p. 1985. pap. text ed. 17.95 (*0-521-28138-5*) Cambridge U Pr.

Tense: New Work by Leslie Bellavance. John Nagus. (Illus.). 15p. (Orig.). 1994. pap. 5.00 (*0-944110-41-X*) Milwauk Art Mus.

***Tense & Aspect: From Semantics to Morphosyntax.** Alessandra Giorgi & Fabio Pianesi. (Oxford Studies in Comparative Syntax). 336p. 1997. 85.00 (*0-19-509192-2*); pap. 35.00 (*0-19-509193-0*) OUP.

Tense & Aspect in Discourse. Ed. by C. Vet & Carl Vetters. LC 94-12275. (Trends in Linguistics, Studies & Monographs: No. 75). 301p. (C). 1994. lib. bdg. 129.25 (*3-11-013813-1*) Mouton.

Tense & Aspect in Eight Languages of Cameroon. Ed. by Stephen C. Anderson & Bernard Comrie. LC 91-65415. (Publications in Linguistics: No. 99). xiv, 255p. (Orig.). 1991. fiche 20.00 (*0-88312-268-5*) Summer Instit Ling.

***Tense & Aspect in Indo-European Languages: Theory, Typology & Diachrony.** John Hewson & Vit Bubenik. LC 97-4482. (Current Issues in Linguistic Theory Ser.: Vol. 145). xii, 403p. 1997. lib. bdg. 89.00 (*1-55619-860-4*) Benjamins North Am.

Tense & Aspect in Korean. Sung-Ock S. Sohn. LC 94-37498. (Center for Korean Studies Monographs: No. 18). 224p. 1995. pap. text ed. 18.00 (*0-8248-1691-9*) UH Pr.

Tense & Mood in English: A Comparison with Danish. Niels Davidsen-Nielsen. (Topics in English Linguistics Ser.: No. 1). x, 224p. (C). 1990. lib. bdg. 65.40 (*3-11-012581-1*) Mouton.

Tense & Narrativity: From Medieval Performance to Modern Fiction. Suzanne Fleischman. LC 89-35579. (Texas Linguistics Ser.). 459p. 1990. text ed. 57.50 (*0-292-78090-7*) U of Tex Pr.

Tense & Tense Logic. John E. Clifford. (Janua Linguarum, Ser. Minor: No. 215). 173p. (Orig.). 1975. pap. text ed. 35.40 (*90-279-3453-3*) Mouton.

Tense-Aspect: Between Semantics & Pragmatics. Ed. by Paul J. Hopper. (Typological Studies in Language: No. 1). x, 350p. 1982. 78.00 (*90-272-2865-5*) Benjamins North Am.

Tense, Aspect, & Action: Empirical & Theoretical Contributions to Language Typology. Ed. by Carl Bache et al. LC 94-25766. (Empirical Approaches to Language Typology Ser.: No. 12). viii, 428p. (C). 1994. lib. bdg. 175.40 (*3-11-012713-X*) Mouton.

Tense-Aspect & the Development of Auxiliaries in Kru Languages. Lynell Marchese. LC 86-60586. (Publications in Linguistics: No. 78). (Illus.). 200p. (Orig.). (C). 1986. fiche 24.00 (*0-88312-407-6*) Summer Instit Ling.

Tense, Attitudes & Scope. Toshiyuki Ogihara. (Studies in Linguistics & Philosophy: Vol. 58). 287p. (C). 1995. lib. bdg. 98.00 (*0-7923-3801-4*) Kluwer Ac.

Tense Marking in Black English: A Linguistic & Social Analysis, with a Chapter on Noun Plural Absence. Ralph W. Fasold & Carolyn Kessler. LC 72-93660. (Urban Language Ser.: No. 8). 272p. reprint ed. pap. 77.60 (*0-8357-3354-8*, 2039589) Bks Demand.

Tense Past: Cultural Essays in Trauma & Memory. Ed. by Paul Antze & Michael Lambek. LC 95-26249. 272p. (C). 1996. pap. 18.95 (*0-415-91563-5*); text ed. 65.00 (*0-415-91562-7*) Routledge.

***Tense Present.** Pasquale Verdicchio. 1997. pap. text ed. 14.00 (*1-888277-03-3*) Incommcdo San Diego.

Tense, Reference, & Worldmaking. James A. McGilvray. 1991. 55.00 (*0-7735-0871-6*, Pub. by McGill CN) U of Toronto Pr.

Tense Significance As the Time of the Action. Oscar E. Johnson. (LD Ser.: No. 21). 1936. pap. 25.00 (*0-527-00767-6*) Periodicals Srv.

Tense Situations. Pamela Hartmann et al. 192p. (C). 1985. pap. text ed. 16.00 (*0-03-069902-9*) HB Coll Pubs.

Tense System in English Relative Clauses: A Corpus-Based Analysis. Ilse Depraetere. (Topics in English Linguistics Ser.: No. 16). xvi, 434p. (C). 1995. lib. bdg. 144.65 (*3-11-014685-1*) Mouton.

Tenshin-en: The Garden of the Heart of Heaven. (Illus.). 48p. 1992. pap. 12.95 (*0-87846-371-2*) Mus Fine Arts Boston.

Tensile Architecture in the Urban Context. Rudi Scheuermann & Keith Boxer. (Illus.). 160p. 1996. 69.95 (*0-7506-0438-7*) Buttrwrth-Heinemann.

Tensile Structures. (Architectural Design Ser.). Date not set. pap. 26.95 (*1-85490-251-2*) Academy Ed UK.

Tensile Testing. Ed. by Patricia Han. (Illus.). 207p. 1992. text ed. 98.00 (*0-87170-440-4*, 6373) ASM.

Tension Between Divine Will & Human Free Will in Milton & the Classical Epic Tradition. Ron Featheringhill. LC 89-13293. (American University Studies: English Language & Literature: Ser. IV, Vol. 113). 347p. (C). 1990. text ed. 69.95 (*0-8204-1165-5*) P Lang Pubng.

Tension Between East & West. Rudolf Steiner. Tr. by B. A. Rowley from GER. 188p. 1983. reprint ed. pap. 10.95 (*0-88010-071-0*) Anthroposophic.

Tension-Free Golf: Unleashing Your Greatest Shots More Often. Dean Reinmuth. (Illus.). 240p. 1995. pap. 19.95 (*1-57243-039-7*) Triumph Bks.

Tension in Boccaccio: Boccaccio & the Fine Arts. Patricia M. Gathercole. LC 74-28151. (Romance Monographs: No. 14). 1975. 22.00 (*84-399-3503-X*) Romance.

Tension-in-Repose: A Basic Home Series Course. Millicent Linden. (Illus.). 100p. 1971. 4.95 (*0-912628-08-1*) M Linden NY.

Tension-in-Repose: An Introduction to Living in a State of Orgasm, Vol. 1. Millicent Linden. LC 62-22285. (Illus.). 1975. 5.00 (*0-912628-09-X*) M Linden NY.

Tension in the Chess Position. rev. ed. Riley Sheffield. 68p. (Orig.). 1981. pap. 6.50 (*0-931462-10-X*) Chess Ent.

Tension in the North: Sweden & Nordic Security. Rodney Kennedy-Minott. (CISA Working Papers: No. 70). 68p. (Orig.). 1989. pap. 15.00 (*0-86682-087-6*) Ctr Intl Relations.

Tension Leg Platform: A State of the Art Review. Ed. by Zeki Demirbilek. 352p. 1989. 33.00 (*0-87262-683-0*) Am Soc Civil Eng.

Tension of Paradox: Donoso's the Obscene Bird of Night as Spriritual Exercises. Pamela Finnegan. (Monographs in International Studies, Latin America Ser.: No. 18). 150p. (Orig.). (C). 1992. pap. text ed. 15.00 (*0-89680-169-1*) Ohio U Pr.

Tension of the Lyre: Poetry in Shakespeare's Sonnets. Hallett C. Smith. LC 80-39610. 184p. reprint ed. pap. 52.50 (*0-7837-5288-1*, 2045042) Bks Demand.

Tension over the Farakka Barrage: A Techno-Political Tangle in South Asia. Khurshida Begum. 1988. 34.00 (*0-8364-2271-6*, Pub. by KP Bagchi IA) S Asia.

Tension Structures: Behavior & Analysis. John W. Leonard. LC 87-3950. 416p. 1988. text ed. 63.00 (*0-07-037226-8*) McGraw.

Tension-Type Headache: Classification, Mechanisms, & Treatment. Ed. by Jes Olesen & Jean Schoenen. LC 93-19572. (Frontiers in Headache Research Ser.: Vol. 3). 320p. 1993. text ed. 100.00 (*0-7817-0070-1*) Lppncott-Raven.

Tension Zone. Sarah Gorham. LC 95-61376. (Award Ser.). 80p. 1996. pap. 11.95 (*1-884800-06-8*) Four Way Bks.

Tensioned Fabric Structures: A Practical Introduction. American Society of Civil Engineers Task Committee Staff. Ed. by R. E. Shaeffer. LC 96-11376. 120p. 1996. 23.00 (*0-7844-0156-X*) Am Soc Civil Eng.

Tensioning of Tendons: Force-Elongation Relationship. (FIP State of the Art Reports). 18p. 1986. 30.00 (*0-7277-0260-2*, Pub. by T Telford UK) Am Soc Civil Eng.

Tensions: Necessary Conflicts in Life & Love. H. A. Williams. 120p. 1992. pap. 10.95 (*0-87243-196-7*) Templegate.

Tensions at the Border: Energy & Environmental Concerns in Canada & the United States. Ed. by Jonathan Lemco. LC 91-34775. 216p. 1992. text ed. 49.95 (*0-275-94001-2*, C4001, Praeger Pubs) Greenwood.

Tensions in American Puritanism. R. Reinitz. LC 70-100325. (Problems in American History Ser.). 208p. reprint ed. pap. 59.30 (*0-8357-9991-3*, 2019292) Bks Demand.

Tensions in Moral Theology. Charles E. Curran. LC 87-40622. 256p. 1988. text ed. 31.00 (*0-268-01866-9*) U of Notre Dame Pr.

Tensions in Social Theory: Groundwork for a Future Moral Sociology. Braulio Munoz. LC 92-26436. (Values & Ethics Ser.). 384p. 1993. 39.95 (*0-8294-0739-1*) Loyola Pr.

Tensions in the Church: Facing the Challenges, Seizing the Opportunities. James J. Bacik. 192p. (Orig.). 1993. pap. 9.95 (*1-55612-624-7*) Sheed & Ward MO.

Tensions in the Performance of Music: Symposium. rev. ed. Ed. by Carola Grindea. (Illus.). 192p. 1987. pap. 12.95 (*0-912483-10-5*) Pro-Am Music.

Tensions in the Territorial Politics of Western Europe. Ed. by R. A. Rhodes & V. Wright. (Illus.). 176p. 1988. text ed. 37.50 (*0-7146-3329-1*, Pub. by F Cass Pubs UK) Intl Spec Bk.

Tensions of Economic Development in Southeast Asia. Ed. by J. C. Daruvala. LC 73-19306. (Illus.). 163p. (C). 1974. reprint ed. text ed. 52.50 (*0-8371-7321-3*, DAED, Greenwood Pr) Greenwood.

***Tensions of Empire: Colonial Cultures in a Bourgeois World.** Ed. by Frederick Cooper & Ann L. Stoler. LC 96-32968. (Illus.). 1997. 55.00 (*0-520-20540-5*); pap. 19.95 (*0-520-20605-3*) U CA Pr.

Tensions of Order & Freedom: Catholic Political Thought, 1789-1848. Bela Menczer. 210p. (C). 1993. text ed. 34.95 (*1-56000-133-X*) Transaction Pubs.

Tensleep: An Em Hansen Mystery. Sarah Andrews. 288p. 1995. mass mkt. 4.99 (*0-451-18606-0*, Sig) NAL-Dutton.

Tensleep: An Em Hansen Mystery. Sarah Andrews. 288p. 1994. 20.00 (*1-883402-33-6*) S&S Trade.

Tensor Analysis: Theory & Applications to Geometry & Mechanics of Continua. 2nd ed. Ivan S. Sokolnikoff. LC 64-13223. (Applied Mathematics Ser.). 373p. reprint ed. pap. 106.40 (*0-317-08559-X*, 2055264) Bks Demand.

Tensor Analysis for Physicists. J. A. Schouten. 289p. 1988. reprint ed. pap. text ed. 8.95 (*0-486-65582-2*) Dover.

Tensor Analysis on Manifolds. Richard Bishop & Samuel Goldberg. (Illus.). 1980. reprint ed. pap. 6.95 (*0-486-64039-6*) Dover.

Tensor Calculus. J. L. Synge & Schild. 1978. pap. text ed. 8.95 (*0-486-63612-7*) Dover.

Tensor Calculus. John L. Synge & A. Schild. LC 75-323720. (Mathematical Expositions Ser.: No. 5). 334p. reprint ed. pap. 95.20 (*0-317-09117-4*, 2014430) Bks Demand.

Tensor Calculus: Theory & Problems. A. N. Srinvastava. 1993. pap. 5.95 (*0-86311-371-0*, Pub. by Universities Pr II) Apt Bks.

Tensor Geometry: The Geometric Viewpoint & Its Uses. 2nd rev. ed. C. T. Dodson & T. Poston. Ed. by J. H. Ewing et al. (Graduate Texts in Mathematics Ser.: Vol. 130). (Illus.). xiv, 432p. 1991. reprint ed. 63.95 (*0-387-52018-X*) Spr-Verlag.

Tensor Norms & Operator Ideals. Andreas Defant & Klaus Floret. LC 92-36408. (Mathematics Studies: Vol. 176). 566p. 1992. 181.00 (*0-444-89091-2*, North Holland) Elsevier.

Tensor Properties of Crystals. David Lovett. 160p. 1989. pap. 32.00 (*0-85274-031-X*) IOP Pub.

Tensor Properties of Crystals. D. R. Lovett. LC 88-34757. (Illus.). 152p. reprint ed. pap. 43.40 (*0-7837-3927-3*, 2057917) Bks Demand.

Tensor Spaces & Exterior Algebra. Takeo Yokonuma. LC 92-16721. (Translation of Mathematical Monographs: No. 108). 131p. 1992. 49.00 (*0-8218-4564-0*, MMONO/108) Am Math.

Tensors & Manifolds: With Applications to Mechanics & Relativity. Robert Wasserman. 432p. (C). 1992. text ed. 48.00 (*0-19-506561-1*) OUP.

Tensors & the Clifford Algebra: Applications to the Physics of Bosons & Fermions. Ed. by Jean-Michel Charlier et al. (Pure & Applied Mathematics Ser.: Vol. 163). 344p. 1992. 160.00 (*0-8247-8666-1*) Dekker.

Tensors Differential Forms. David Lovelock. 1989. pap. 9.95 (*0-486-65840-6*) Dover.

Tensors of Geophysics for Mavericks & Mongrels. Frank Hadsell. Ed. by Eugene Scherrer. LC 95-22789. (Geophysical References Ser.: No. 6). (Illus.). 240p. 1995. text ed. 67.00 (*1-56080-029-1*, 437) Soc Expl Geophys.

Tent: A Parable in One Sitting. Gary Paulsen. 96p. (J). 1996. mass mkt. 4.99 (*0-440-21919-1*) Dell.

Tent: A Parable in One Sitting. Gary Paulsen. 96p. (YA). (gr. 7 up). 1995. 14.00 (*0-15-292879-0*) HarBrace.

Tent & Testament: Camping Tour in Palestine with Some Notes on Scriptural Sites. Herbert Rix. Ed. by Moshe Davis. LC 77-70737. (America & the Holy Land Ser.). (Illus.). 1977. reprint ed. lib. bdg. 33.95 (*0-405-10280-1*) Ayer.

Tent & Town: Rugs & Embroideries from Central Asia. Cathryn Cootner. LC 82-49068. (H. McCoy Jones Collection). (Illus.). 16p. 1982. pap. 2.95 (*0-88401-043-0*) Fine Arts Mus.

Tent & Trail Songs. 72p. 1985. pap. 3.95 (*0-685-25325-2*) Am Camping.

Tent Caterpillars. Terrence D. Fitzgerald. (Comstock Bk.). (Illus.). 338p. 1995. 37.95 (*0-8014-2456-9*) Cornell U Pr.

***Tent for Two.** Janice Maynard. 1997. mass mkt. 1.78 (*0-8217-5774-1*) Kensgtn Pub Corp.

Tent in the Notch. Edward A. Rand. LC 72-2040. (Black Heritage Library Collection). 1977. reprint ed. 24.95 (*0-8369-9054-4*) Ayer.

Tent Life in Siberia: A New Account of an Old Undertaking Adventures among the Koraks & Other Tribes in Kamchatka & Northern Asia. George F. Kennan. LC 79-115572. (Russia Observed, Series I). 1970. reprint ed. 42.95 (*0-405-03037-1*) Ayer.

Tent Life in the Holy Land. William C. Prime. Ed. by Moshe Davis. LC 77-70734. (America & the Holy Land Ser.). (Illus.). 1977. reprint ed. lib. bdg. 42.95 (*0-405-10278-X*) Ayer.

Tent Life with English Gypsies in Norway. 2nd ed. Hubert F. Smith. LC 75-3464. (Illus.). reprint ed. 39.00 (*0-404-16894-9*) AMS Pr.

Tent Man. 2nd rev. ed. Jeff Jackard. Ed. by Douglas M. Eason. (Illus.). 170p. (Orig.). 1996. reprint ed. pap. 16.95 (*0-9647368-0-2*) VC Pr.

Tent Meeting. Levi Lee et al. 1987. pap. 5.25 (*0-8222-1121-1*) Dramatists Play.

Tent of Miracles. Jorge Amado. 1988. pap. 10.00 (*0-380-75472-X*) Avon.

***Tent of Orange Mist.** Paul West. LC 97-9910. 272p. 1997. pap. 13.95 (*0-87951-792-1*) Overlook Pr.

Tent of Orange Mist. large type ed. Paul West. LC 95-47630. 1996. 22.95 (*1-56895-279-1*) Wheeler Pub.

Tent of Orange Mist: A Novel. Paul West. LC 95-9077. 263p. 1995. 22.00 (*0-684-80031-4*) S&S Trade.

***Tent Posts, Vol. 4.** Henri Michaux. (Green Integer Bks.). 1997. pap. text ed. 10.95 (*1-55713-328-X*) Sun & Moon CA.

Tent Too Full. Stephen White. Ed. by Margie Larsen. LC 93-77870. (Barney Book & Tape Ser.). (Illus.). 24p. (J). (ps-3). 1996. pap. 6.95 incl. audio (*1-57064-070-X*) Lyrick Pub.

Tentacles of Progress: Technology Transfer in the Age of Imperialism, 1850-1940. Daniel R. Headrick. (Illus.). 416p. 1988. pap. text ed. 18.95 (*0-19-505116-5*) OUP.

Tentacles of Unreason. Stories. Joan Givner. LC 84-24154. (Illinois Short Fiction Ser.). 144p. 1985. 14.95 (*0-252-01203-8*) U of Ill Pr.

Tentaman Flora Nepalensis, Vol. 1. N. Wallich. (C). 1988. text ed. 60.00 (*0-685-22088-5*, Pub. by Scientific UK) St Mut.

Tentamen Novae Theoriae Musicae see Monuments of Music & Music Literature in Facsimile

Tentamina Semiologica, Sive Quaedam Generalem Theoriam Spectantia: Semiologische Versuche mit dem Ziel der Begrundung einer allgemeinen Zeichentheorie (1789) Johannes C. Hoffbauer. Tr. by R. Innis from LAT. LC 91-16111. (Foundations of Semiotics Ser.: No. 4). xxxii, 118p. 1991. 41.00 (*90-272-3274-1*) Benjamins North Am.

Tentatio et Consolatio: Studien zu Bugenhagens Interpretatio in Librum Psalmorum. Hans H. Holfelder. LC 73-80563. (Arbeiten zur Kirchengeschichte Ser.: Vol. 46). 132p. (GER.). (C). 1974. 98.50 (*3-11-004327-0*) De Gruyter.

Tentation de l'Occident. Andre Malraux. pap. 6.95 (*0-685-34271-9*) Fr & Eur.

Tentation de l'Occident. Andre Malraux. (FRE.). 1972. pap. 10.95 (*0-7859-3096-5*) Fr & Eur.

Tentation de Saint Antoine. Gustave Flaubert. Ed. by Maynial. (Class. Garnier Ser.). pap. 29.95 (*0-685-34903-9*) Fr & Eur.

Tentation de Saint Antoine. Gustave Flaubert. 352p. (FRE.). 1983. pap. 12.95 (*0-7859-2480-9*, 2070374920) Fr & Eur.

Tentation de Saint Antoine. Gustave Flaubert. (Folio Ser.: No. 1492). 346p. (FRE.). 1983. pap. 12.95 (*2-07-037492-0*) Schoenhof.

Tentation d'Exister. E. M. Cioran. (FRE.). 1986. pap. 15.95 (*0-7859-2934-7*) Fr & Eur.

Tentative Inventory of the Habits of Children from Two to Four Years of Age. Ruth Andrus. LC 77-176520. (Columbia University. Teachers College. Contributions to Education Ser.: No. 160). reprint ed. 37.50 (*0-404-55160-2*) AMS Pr.

***Tentative Jewish Pearls.** Jessica Gribetz. LC 97-21243. 1997. pap. write for info. (*0-688-15108-6*) Morrow.

Tentative Pregnancy: How Amniocentesis Changes the Experience of Motherhood. Barbara K. Rothman. 288p. 1993. pap. 9.95 (*0-393-30998-3*) Norton.

Tentative Standard for Proctective Clothing for Fire Fighters. pap. 20.25 (*0-685-58201-9*, 1971-91) Natl Fire Prot.

Tentative Standard for the Safe Use of Electricity in Patient Care Areas of Health Care Facilities. 229p. 1993. pap. 32.25 (*0-685-44142-3*, 99-93) Natl Fire Prot.

Tentative Standard for the Use of Inhalation Anesthetics in Ambulatory Care Facilities. 1993. pap. 32.25 (*0-685-58205-1*, 99-93) Natl Fire Prot.

Tentative Standard on Fire Protection for Limited Access Highways, Tunnels, Bridges & Elevated Structures. 1992. pap. 16.75 (*0-685-58191-8*, 502-92) Natl Fire Prot.

Tentatives de Description d'un Diner de Tetes a Paris-France. Jacques Prevert. 9.65 (*0-685-37053-4*) Fr & Eur.

10th Aerospace Testing Seminar Proceedings, March 1987. LC 62-38584. 247p. (Orig.). 1987. pap. text ed. 100.00 (*0-915414-93-7*) Inst Environ Sci.

Tenth Air Force, 1942. Herbert Weaver & Marrin Rapp. (USAF Historical Studies: No. 12). 191p. 1977. reprint ed. pap. text ed. 32.95 (*0-89126-032-3*) MA-AH Pub.

***10th Anniversary Edition Blessings, Vol. 16.** Chris Thornton. (Illus.). 72p. (Orig.). 1997. pap. 9.50 (*1-56770-394-1*) S Scheewe Pubns.

***Tenth Anniversary Edition of Economic Justice for All.** United States Catholic Conference Staff. 160p. 1997. pap. text ed. 7.95 (*1-57455-135-3*) US Catholic.

Tenth Anniversary of the Regional Advisory Committee on Medical Research for South-East Asia: Proceedings of the Special Session. (WHO Regional Publications South-East Ser.: No. 15). 76p. 1986. pap. text ed. 20.00 (*92-9022-115-1*, 1560015) World Health.

Tenth Anniversary Wishes. Ed. by Catherine Kouts & Laura Cavaluzzo. LC 96-16569. (Illus.). 64p. (J). 1996. 12.95 (*0-87905-651-7*) Gibbs Smith Pub.

Tenth Annual Insurance, Excess, & Reinsurance Coverage Disputes. (Litigation & Administrative Practice Course Handbook, 1983-84 Ser.: Vol. 454). 830p. 1993. 70.00 (*0-685-65531-8*, H4-5148) PLI.

T

An Asterisk (*) at the beginning of an entry indicates that the title is appearing in BIP for the first time.

Tenth Annual Larval Fish Conference. Ed. by R. D. Hoyt. LC 87-72976. (Symposium Ser.: No. 2). 190p. 1987. pap. 21.00 (*0-913235-45-8*) Am Fisheries Soc.

Tenth Annual Outstanding Resumes of College, Business & Law Graduates. 1995. 27.50 (*0-685-67192-5*) Graduate Group.

Tenth Annual Outstanding Resumes of of College, Business, & Law Graduates. 1995. 27.50 (*0-685-71244-3*) Graduate Group.

Tenth Annual Report of the Illinois Animal Poison Information Center, Vols. I & II. Illinois Animal Poison Information Center Staff. 580p. (C). 1990. per. 125.00 (*0-8403-6356-7*) Kendall-Hunt.

Tenth Armored "Tiger" Division. Turner Publishing Company Staff. LC 88-51192. 240p. 1989. 48.00 (*0-938021-27-3*) Turner Pub KY.

Tenth Assembling. Ed. by Richard Kostelanetz et al. LC 80-68188. (Assembling Ser.). (Illus.). 200p. 1981. pap. 10.00 (*0-915066-50-5*) Assembling Pr.

Tenth-Century Latinity: Rather of Verona. Peter L. Reid. LC 80-54672. (Humana Civilitas Ser.: Vol. 6). xiii, 52p. 1981. pap. 22.25 (*0-89003-070-7*) Undena Pubns.

Tenth Circle of Hell: A Memoir of Life in the Death Camps of Bosnia. Rezak Hukanovic. Ed. by Ammiel Alcalay. Tr. by Colleen London et al. LC 96-16631. 192p. 1996. 20.00 (*0-465-08408-7*) Basic.

Tenth Commandment. Lawrence Sanders. 400p. 1987. mass mkt. 6.99 (*0-425-10431-1*) Berkley Pub.

Tenth Commandment. large type ed. Lawrence Sanders. 592p. 1983. 27.99 (*0-7089-8159-3*) Ulverscroft.

Tenth Day of Victory: An Initiation & Beyond. Patrizia Norelli-Bachelet. 300p. (Orig.). 1995. pap. 18.00 (*0-945747-33-0*) Aeon Bks.

Tenth E. C. Photovoltaic Solar Energy Conference. Ed. by Antonio Luque et al. 1490p. (C). 1991. lib. bdg. 387.50 (*0-7923-1389-5*) Kluwer Ac.

Tenth European Anatomical Congress Firenze, September 17-21, 1995, Abstracts: With the Participation of the American Association of Anatomists. Ed. by G. E. Orlandini & S. Zeechi Orlandini. (Journal: Acta Anatomica Ser.: Vol. 152, No. 4, 1995). iv, 130p. 1995. pap. 100.00 (*3-8055-6233-0*) S Karger.

Tenth Fleet. Ladislas Farago. 1962. 27.95 (*0-8392-1112-0*) Astor-Honor.

Tenth Generation: The Origins of the Biblical Tradition. George E. Mendenhall. 266p. 1974. pap. 14.95 (*0-8018-1654-8*) Johns Hopkins.

Tenth Generation of One Hundred & One Aggie Jokes. Illus. by Bob Taylor. (One Hundred & One Aggie Jokes Ser.). 50p. (Orig.). 1983. write for info. (*0-945430-10-8*) Gigem Pr.

Tenth Good Thing about Barney. Judith Viorst. LC 71-154764. (Illus.). 32p. (J). (gr. k-4). 1971. lib. bdg. 14.00 (*0-689-20688-7*, Atheneum Bks Young) S&S Childrens.

Tenth Good Thing about Barney. Judith Viorst. LC 86-25948. (Illus.). 32p. (J). (gr. k-4). 1987. reprint ed. pap. 4.99 (*0-689-71203-0*, Aladdin Paperbacks) S&S Childrens.

Tenth-Grade Abilities & Achievements. Elden A. Bond. LC 79-176577. (Columbia University. Teachers College. Contributions to Education Ser.: No. 813). reprint ed. 37.50 (*0-404-55813-5*) AMS Pr.

***Tenth Insight.** James Redfield. 1996. 8.99 (*0-446-67330-7*) Warner Bks.

Tenth Insight. large type ed. James Redfield. 1996. 20.00 (*0-7862-0817-1*, GK Hall) Thorndike Pr.

Tenth Insight: Holding the Vision. James Redfield. 256p. 1996. 19.95 (*0-446-51908-1*) Warner Bks.

***Tenth Insight: Holding the Vision: An Experiential Guide.** James Redfield. LC 96-3245. 384p. (Orig.). 1996. pap. 11.99 (*0-446-67299-8*) Warner Bks.

***Tenth Insight: Holding the Vision: A Pocket Guide.** James Redfield. 64p. 1997. 6.95 (*0-446-91213-1*) Warner Bks.

Tenth International Conference on Automated Deduction: Proceedings Kaiserslautern, FRG, July 24-27, 1990. Ed. by M. E. Stickel & Joerg H. Siekmann. (Lecture Notes in Artificial Intelligence Ser.: Vol. 449). xvi, 688p. 1990. 79.00 (*0-387-52885-7*) Spr-Verlag.

Tenth International Conference on Numerical Methods in Fluid Dynamics. Ed. by F. G. Zhuang & Y. L. Zhu. (Lecture Notes in Physics Ser.: Vol. 264). xii, 724p. 1986. 90.95 (*0-387-17172-X*) Spr-Verlag.

Tenth International Conference on Sarcoidosis & Other Granulomatous Disorders, Vol. 465. Ed. by Carol J. Johns. 187.00 (*0-89766-325-X*); pap. 187.00 (*0-89766-326-8*) NY Acad Sci.

10th International Congress of Endocrinology Program & Abstracts. 1290p. (Orig.). (C). 1996. pap. text ed. 95.00 (*1-879225-23-9*) Endocrine Soc.

***Tenth International Congress of Logic, Methodology & Philosophy of Science, Florence, August 1995, 2 vols.** Ed. by Maria L. Dalla Chiara. Incl. Vol. 2. Structures & Norms in Science. 512p. (C). 1997. lib. bdg. 257.00 (*0-7923-4384-0*); Vol. 1. Logic & Scientific Methods. 552p. (C). 1997. lib. bdg. 275.00 (*0-7923-4383-2*); LC 96-52731. (Synthese Library). 1996. Set lib. bdg. 470.00 (*0-7923-4385-9*) Kluwer Ac.

Tenth International Congress of Phonetic Sciences: Proceedings. Ed. by A. Cohen & M. P. Van den Broecke. (Netherlands Phonetic Archives Ser.). xviii, 819p. 1984. 229.25 (*90-70176-91-2*) Mouton.

Tenth International Seaweed Symposium. Ed. by Tore Levring. (Illus.). 780p. 1981. 150.00 (*3-11-008389-2*) De Gruyter.

Tenth International Symposium on Endocrinology & Development, Venice, Italy, October 1992: Growth & Metabolism: Obesity, Insulin Action & Use of Anthropometry. Ed. by A. Attanasio. (Journal: Hormone Research: Vol. 39, Suppl. 3, 1993). (Illus.). vi, 118p. 1993. pap. 54.00 (*3-8055-5884-8*) S Karger.

Tenth Irish Division in Gallipoli. Bryan Cooper. 172p. 1993. pap. 15.00 (*0-7165-2517-8*, Pub. by Irish Acad Pr IE) Intl Spec Bk.

***Tenth Justice.** Brad Meltzer. LC 96-44815. 400p. 1997. 23.00 (*0-688-15089-6*, R Weisbach Bks) Morrow.

Tenth Legion. 7th ed. Tom Kelly. LC 73-80205. 119p. 1994. 17.95 (*0-318-39971-7*) Wing Feather Pr.

***Tenth Legion.** Tom Kelly. LC 97-19704. 128p. 1998. reprint ed. 18.95 (*1-55821-539-5*) Lyons & Burford.

Tenth Man. Graham Greene. pap. 3.95 (*0-317-56802-7*, WSP) PB.

Tenth Man. Graham Greene. 1986. mass mkt. 4.99 (*0-671-61171-2*) PB.

Tenth Man. Edward F. Murphy. LC 72-4647. (Black Heritage Library Collection). 1977. reprint ed. 29.95 (*0-8369-9114-1*) Ayer.

Tenth Man: How a Major League Baseball Team Can Gain a 2 to 3 Run Advantage Every Game. Bill Welch & Jeff Moses. (Illus.). 492p. (Orig.). 1989. pap. 14.95 (*0-929633-00-8*) Baseball Analysis.

Tenth Man: The Great Joke (Which Made Lazarus Laugh) Wei Wu-wei. 246p. (C). 1971. pap. text ed. 30.00 (*0-85656-013-8*, Pub. by Hong Kong U Pr HK) St Mut.

Tenth Man see Four Contemporary American Plays

Tenth Men. Allen G. Eastby. LC 85-23138. 384p. 1990. 17.95 (*0-912526-41-6*) Lib Res.

Tenth Mental Measurements Yearbook. Ed. by Jane C. Conoley & Jack J. Kramer. 1000p. 1989. 125.00 (*0-910674-31-0*) Buros Inst Mental.

Tenth Muse. Herbert E. Read. LC 73-99646. (Essay Index Reprint Ser.). 1977. 29.95 (*0-8369-1427-9*) Ayer.

Tenth Muse. Anne Bradstreet. LC 65-10345. 1978. reprint ed. 50.00 (*0-8201-1006-X*) Schol Facsimiles.

Tenth Muse: Classical Drama in Translation. Ed. by Charles Doria. LC 77-88695. vi, 587p. 1980. 30.00 (*0-8040-0781-0*) Swallow.

Tenth Muse: The Psyche of the American Poet. 2nd ed. Albert Gelpi. 327p. (C). 1991. pap. text ed. 21.95 (*0-521-42401-1*) Cambridge U Pr.

Tenth Muse: The Psyche of the American Poet. 2nd ed. Albert Gelpi. 327p. (C). 1991. text ed. 74.95 (*0-521-41339-7*) Cambridge U Pr.

Tenth Muse: The Psyche of the American Poet. Albert Gelpi. LC 74-25038. 349p. 1975. reprint ed. pap. 99.50 (*0-7837-4150-2*, 2057998) Bks Demand.

Tenth Muse: Victorian Philology & the Genesis of the Poetic Language of Gerard Manley Hopkins. Cary H. Plotkin. LC 88-39600. 214p. (C). 1989. 24.95 (*0-8093-1488-6*) S Ill U Pr.

Tenth Muse, Lately Sprung up in America. Anne Bradstreet. 1989. reprint ed. lib. bdg. 79.00 (*0-7812-2041-6*) Rprt Serv.

Tenth National ACCP Pulmonary Board Review Course Syllabus, 2 vols. Prakash et al. Ed. by American College of Chest Physicians Staff. (Illus.). 350p. 1994. pap. text ed. 65.00 (*0-916609-04-9*) Am Chest Phys.

Tenth National Space Symposium Proceedings Report. Ed. by Beth A. Lipskin et al. 244p. 1994. pap. 50.00 (*0-9616962-8-1*) US Space Found.

Tenth of Av. Kenneth D. Roseman. (Do-It-Yourself Jewish Adventure Ser.). 96p. (Orig.). (J). (gr. 4-6). 1988. pap. text ed. 7.95 (*0-8074-0359-8*, 123928) UAHC.

***X Olympiad, Los Angeles 1932 & Garmisch-Partenkirchen 1936.** (Olympic Century Ser.). (Illus.). 1996. 21.95 (*1-888383-10-0*, Wrld Spt) Wld Sport Resch.

Tenth Planet. Edmund Cooper. 1973. 25.00 (*0-399-11187-5*) Ultramarine Pub.

Tenth Process Technology Conference: Modeling in the Iron & Steel Industry, Vol. X. 472p. 1992. 80.00 (*0-932897-74-6*) Iron & Steel.

Tenth Rifle & the Jesse James Gang. Isabel R. Marvin. (J). 1994. pap. 5.00 (*0-932433-12-X*) Windswept Hse.

Tenth Stay at Midnight. Lloyd E. Miller, Jr. (Prestige Classic Ser.). 104p. 1994. reprint ed. pap. 4.95 (*0-9639322-0-9*) Literary Prods.

***Tenth Street Studio Building: Artist-Entrepreneurs from the Hudson River School to the American Impressionists.** Annette Blaugrund. (Illus.). 145p. 1997. pap. 24.95 (*0-295-97635-7*) U of Wash Pr.

Tenth Symposium on Latin-American Geosciences, Berlin 1986. Ed. by H. Miller & U. Rosenfeld. (Zentralblatt Fuer Geologie Ser.). (Illus.). 368p. 1987. pap. 92.40 (*0-945345-26-7*, Pub. by Schweitzerbartsche GW) Lubrecht & Cramer.

Tenth Symposium on Nucleic Acids Chemistry. Compiled by Angela E. Pritchard. (Nucleic Acids Symposium Ser.: No. 11). 296p. 1982. pap. 45.00 (*0-904147-48-7*, IRL Pr) OUP.

***Tenth Systems Administration Conference (LISA '96), September 29-October 4, 1996.** Ed. by Helen E. Harrison & Amy K. Kreiling. 260p. (Orig.). 1996. pap. 38.00 (*1-880446-81-2*) USENIX Assn.

10th Topical Workshop on Proton-Antiproton Collider Physics: Fermi National Accelerator Laboratory, Batavia, IL, May 9-13, 1995. Rajendran Raja & John Yoh. (AIP Conference Proceedings Ser.: No. 357). (Illus.). 734p. 1996. 190.00 (*1-56396-543-7*) Am Inst Physics.

Tenth Trumpeter Swan Society Conference: Proceedings & Papers. Trumpeter Swan Society Staff. Ed. by Donna Compton. (Illus.). 158p. (Orig.). 1988. pap. text ed. 8.00 (*0-9619936-0-X*) Trumpeter Swan Soc.

Tenth Virginia Cavalry. Robert J. Driver, Jr. (Virginia Regimental Histories Ser.). (Illus.). 186p. 1993. 19.95 (*1-56190-039-7*) H E Howard.

Tenth Virginia Infantry. Terrence V. Murphy. (Virginia Regimental Histories Ser.). (Illus.). 186p. 1989. 19.95 (*0-930919-74-2*) H E Howard.

Tenth World Media Conference. 1989. 18.00 (*0-934197-05-9*) World Media Assn.

Tenting on the Plains: Or General Custer in Kansas & Texas. abr. ed. Elizabeth B. Custer. LC 94-11743. (Illus.). 403p. 1994. pap. 12.95 (*0-8061-2668-X*) U of Okla Pr.

Tenting on the Plains: Or General Custer in Kansas & Texas. Elizabeth B. Custer. LC 94-11743. 403p. 1973. reprint ed. 28.95 (*0-87928-042-5*) Corner Hse.

Tenting Tonight. (Civil War Ser.). (Illus.). 176p. 1984. 18.95 (*0-8094-4736-3*); lib. bdg. 25.93 (*0-8094-4737-1*) Time-Life.

Tents & Pyramids: Games & Ideology in Arab Culture from Backgammon to Autocratic Rule. Fuad I. Khuri. 168p. 1990. 39.95 (*0-86356-334-1*, Pub. by Saqi Bks UK) Interlink Pub.

Tents, Clouds & Angels. Lisa Flinn & Barbara Younger. 1992. pap. 3.75 (*1-55673-467-0*, 9249) CSS OH.

Tents, Grandstands & Air Supported Structures. (One Hundred Ser.). 1992. pap. 20.25 (*0-685-58179-9*, 102-92) Natl Fire Prot.

Tents of Kedar: Christian-Jewish Relationships Following the Inquisition. Frieda C. Hyman. 328p. 1995. 16.95 (*965-229-149-8*, Pub. by Gefen Pub Hse IS) Gefen Bks.

Tents of Michael: The Life & Times of Colonel Albert Williamson Goldsmid. Emil Lehman. LC 96-23696. 286p. 1996. lib. bdg. 39.50 (*0-7618-0426-9*) U Pr of Amer.

Tents of Trouble: Verse of D. Runyon. Damon Runyon. 17.95 (*0-8488-0841-X*) Amereon Ltd.

Tenu' ot ha-no' ar ha-Tsiyoniyot ba-Sho ah (eng.) Zionist Youth Movements During the Shoah, 4. Ed. by Asher Cohen & Yehoyakim Cochavi. Tr. by Ted Gorelick from HEB. LC 94-27841. (Studies on the Shoah: Vol. 4). 352p. (C). 1995. pap. text ed. 40.95 (*0-8204-2586-9*) P Lang Pubng.

Tenure & Promotion for Academic Librarians: A Guidebook with Advice & Vignettes. Carol W. Cubberley. LC 96-23959. 135p. 1996. lib. bdg. 32.50 (*0-7864-0238-5*) McFarland & Co.

Tenure Debate. Bardwell L. Smith et al. LC 72-6058. (Jossey-Bass Higher Education Ser.). 272p. reprint ed. pap. 77.60 (*0-8357-9351-6*, 2013962) Bks Demand.

Tenure, Discrimination, & the Courts. 2nd ed. Terry L. Leap. LC 95-8943. 1995. pap. 16.95 (*0-87546-348-7*, ILR Press) Cornell U Pr.

Tenure Dismissal. Susan Galante. write for info. (*0-318-59187-1*) NJ Schl Bds.

Tenure for Socrates: A Study in the Betrayal of the American Professor. Jon H. Huer. LC 90-38827. 232p. 1990. text ed. 49.95 (*0-89789-244-5*, H244, Bergin & Garvey) Greenwood.

Tenure in the Courthouse. Alan L. Clem. 1973. 1.00 (*1-55614-010-X*) U of SD Gov Res Bur.

Tenure of Phil Wisdom: Dialogues. Craig Clifford. 234p. (Orig.). (C). 1995. pap. text ed. 34.00 (*0-7618-0041-7*) U Pr of Amer.

Tenure (Playscript) Bill Wine. LC 93-6131. 1993. pap. 6.00 (*0-88734-263-9*) Players Pr.

***Tenure, Promotion, & Reappointment: Legal & Administrative Implications.** Benjamin Baez & John A. Centra. Ed. by Jonathan D. Fife. LC 96-76556. (ASHE-ERIC Higher Education Reports). (Illus.). 203p. (Orig.). 1996. pap. 21.75 (*1-878380-65-6*) GWU Grad Schl E&HD.

Tenure Track. Joanna H. Kraus & Greer Woodward. LC 92-39691. 1993. pap. 6.00 (*0-88734-256-6*) Players Pr.

Tenure-Track: Historia de Profesores. Silverio Munoz. 427p. (Orig.). (SPA.). 1993. pap. 21.50 (*0-937985-07-4*) Ediciones Arauco.

Tenured Professor. John Kenneth Galbraith. 208p. 1991. pap. 12.95 (*0-395-57424-2*) HM.

Tenured Professor. large type ed. John Kenneth Galbraith. LC 90-45202. 251p. 1990. reprint ed. lib. bdg. 17.95 (*1-56054-060-5*) Thorndike Pr.

Teodoro Luna's Two Kisses. Alberto A. Rios. 96p. 1992. pap. 9.95 (*0-393-30809-X*) Norton.

***Teodoro Moscoso & Puerto Rico's Operation Bootstrap.** A. W. Maldonado. LC 96-49822. (Illus.). 280p. 1997. lib. bdg. 49.95 (*0-8130-1501-4*) U Press Fla.

Teologia Basica. Charles C. Byrie. (SPA.). 1993. 21.99 (*1-56063-194-5*, 498473) Editorial Unilit.

***Teologia Biblica.** Charles C. Ryrie. 625p. (SPA.). 1993. pap. write for info. (*0-614-27144-4*) Editorial Unilit.

Teologia Biblica del Nuevo Testamento. Charles C. Ryrie. 364p. (SPA.). 1979. pap. 10.99 (*0-8254-1637-X*, Edit Portavoz) Kregel.

***Teologia Carismatic de Luces.** Roger Stronstad. (SPA.). 6.95 (*0-8297-1981-4*) Life Pubs Intl.

***Teologia de Conjunto: A Collaborative Hispanic-Protestant Theology.** Jose D. Rodriguez. LC 97-16944. 1997. pap. text ed. 18.00 (*0-664-25665-1*) Westminster John Knox.

***Teologia de la Adoracion.** R. Martin. (SPA.). 1.50 (*0-8297-1834-6*) Life Pubs Intl.

Teologia de la Liberacion. Alberto Barrientos. (SPA.). 1991. 4.99 (*1-56063-093-0*, 497709) Editorial Unilit.

Teologia de la Solidaridad Chrisiana see Theology of Christian Solidarity

Teologia del Antiguo Testamento, Raices para la Fe Neotestamentaria - Old Testament Roots for New Testament Faith. Robert L. Cate. Tr. by Roberto Fricke from ENG. 264p. (Orig.). (SPA.). 1989. pap. 15.99 (*0-311-09110-5*) Casa Bautista.

Teologia del Ministerio Educativo: Perspectivas Latinoamericanas. Daniel S. Schipani. (Nueva Creacion Ser.). 304p. (Orig.). (SPA.). 1993. pap. 15.00 (*0-8028-0919-7*) Eerdmans.

Teologia del Nuevo Testamento. Frank Stagg. Tr. by Arnoldo Canclini. 346p. 1985. reprint ed. pap. 10.99 (*0-311-09077-X*) Casa Bautista.

Teologia Dispensacional. Charles F. Baker. 709p. 1995. 14.95 (*0-89814-025-0*) Grace Publns.

Teologia Reformacional: Un Nuevo Paradigma Para Hacer la Dogmatica. Gordon J. Spykman. 662p. (SPA.). 1994. 22.50 (*0-939125-62-5*) Evangelical Lit.

Teologia Sistematica. 8th ed. Louis Berkhof. 935p. (SPA.). 1993. 28.50 (*0-939125-06-4*) Evangelical Lit.

***Teologia Sistematira Pentecostal.** S. Horton. (SPA.). 24.95 (*0-8297-1854-0*) Life Pubs Intl.

***Teologica Biblica y Sistematica.** M. Pearlman. (SPA.). 9.95 (*0-8297-1372-7*) Life Pubs Intl.

Teoria Cuantica del Momento Angular. 3.50 (*0-685-07487-0*) OAS.

Teoria Cuentistica del Siglo XX: Aproximaciones Hispanicas. Catharina V. De Vallejo. LC 88-80976. (Coleccion Textos). 278p. (Orig.). (SPA.). (C). 1989. pap. 15.00 (*0-89729-485-8*) Ediciones.

Teoria de la Frontera. Jorge Manach. 171p. 1970. 3.00 (*0-8477-2412-3*) U of PR Pr.

Teoria de la Historia: Actualidad e Historia. Carlos A. Trujillo. 213p. (SPA.). (C). 1993. pap. text ed. 10.00 (*1-883341-00-0*) Edit San Diego.

***Teoria de la Musica.** Barbara A. Lewis. (TEE Ser.). 137p. (SPA.). 1983. 5.95 (*1-879892-20-0*) Editorial Bautista.

Teoria de la Musica Spanish: Nueva Edicion. A. Dannhauser. 128p. (SPA.). 1986. per. 12.95 (*0-7935-5537-X*, 50326630) H Leonard.

Teoria de las Incompatibilidades. Jose A. Cardenas & Blandina C. Ramirez. Tr. by Fausto Vergara from ENG. 19p. (SPA.). 1981. pap. text ed. 4.00 (*1-878550-39-X*) Inter Dev Res Assn.

Teoria de Organizacion de la Clase Trabajadora. Victor M. Duran. 126p. (Orig.). (SPA.). 1987. pap. 8.00 (*0-917049-12-8*) Saeta.

Teoria del Conocimiento. Johannes Hessen. Ed. by Victoria Crespo. Tr. by Jose Gaos. (Nueva Austral Ser.: Vol. 207). (SPA.). 1991. pap. text ed. 24.95 (*84-239-7207-0*) Elliots Bks.

Teoria General del Desarrollo Economico. Vernon R. Esteves. 111p. 1985. pap. 7.00 (*0-8477-2642-8*) U of PR Pr.

Teoria Literaria Griega. Jose Alsina. 618p. (SPA.). 1993. 150.00 (*84-249-1457-0*) Elliots Bks.

Teoria Sociologica: Exegesis de los Grandes Sistemas. Roberto D. Agramonte. LC 78-9810. 1024p. (SPA.). (C). 1981. pap. text ed. 12.00 (*0-8477-2487-5*) U of PR Pr.

Teoria y Critica Del Romanticismo Espanol - Spanish Romantic Literary Theory & Criticism. Derek Flitter. Tr. by Benigno F. Salgado. 320p. (SPA.). (C). 1995. pap. text ed. 15.95 (*0-521-47835-9*) Cambridge U Pr.

Teoria y Tecnica del Analisis y Diagnostico de la Empresa en el Sistema Capitalista. Victor M. Duran. 128p. (Orig.). (SPA.). 1987. pap. 8.00 (*0-917049-11-X*) Saeta.

Teorias de la Historia Literaria. Claudio Guillen. (Nueva Austral Ser.: Vol. 106). (SPA.). 1991. pap. text ed. 24.95 (*84-239-1906-4*) Elliots Bks.

Teosofia Universal. Robert Crosbie. (Illus.). 210p. (Orig.). (SPA.). (YA). 1995. pap. 6.50 (*0-938998-36-6*) Theosophy.

Teotihuacan. Eduardo M. Moctezuma. LC 89-43584. 240p. 1990. 75.00 (*0-8478-1198-0*) Rizzoli Intl.

***Teotihuacan: An Experiment in Living.** Esther Pasztory. LC 96-32775. 304p. 1997. 49.95 (*0-8061-2847-X*) U of Okla Pr.

Teotihuacan: Art from the City of the Gods. Ed. by Kathleen Berrin & Esther Pasztory. LC 92-62139. (Illus.). 288p. 1994. pap. 24.95 (*0-500-27767-2*) Thames Hudson.

Teotihuacan: Nuevos Datos, Nuevas Sintesis, Nuevos Problemas. Emily McClung & Evelyn C. Rattray. 526p. 1987. pap. 7.00 (*968-837-968-9*, UN016) UPLAAP.

Teotihuacan Burials & Offerings: A Commentary & Inventory. Ronald M. Spores. (Publications in Anthropology: No. 42). 254p. (Orig.). 1992. pap. 23.00 (*0-935462-33-3*) VUPA.

Teotihuacan Mazapan Figurines & the Xipe Toltec Statue: A Link Between the Basin of Mexico & the Oaxaca Valley. Ronald M. Spores. (Vanderbilt University Publications in Anthropology: No. 44). 125p. (Orig.). 1993. pap. 14.00 (*0-935462-35-X*) VUPA.

Teotihuacan 1980-1982: Nuevas Interpretaciones. Ed. by Ruben Cabrera et al. 400p. 1991. pap. 18.00 (*968-6487-48-4*, IN039) UPLAAP.

Tepee Cookery, or Lets Chew the Fat Indian Style: A Cookbook. Gwen Fisher. LC 86-81885. (Illus.). 74p. 1986. pap. 12.00 (*0-934188-22-X*) Evans Pubns.

Tepee Tales of the American Indian see Dee Brown's Folktales of the Native American Indian: Retold for Our Times

Tepehuan of Chihuahua: Their Material Culture. Campbell W. Pennington. LC 73-99792. (Illus.). 427p. reprint ed. pap. 121.70 (*0-8357-7051-6*, 2033364) Bks Demand.

Tepetotutla Chinantec Syntax. David O. Westley. (Publications in Linguistics: No. 106). xiii, 134p. (Orig.). 1992. fiche 12.00 (*0-88312-628-1*) Summer Instit Ling.

Tepoztlan: Village in Mexico, 1960. Lewis. 104p. (C). 1960. pap. text ed. 13.50 (*0-03-006050-8*) HB Coll Pubs.

Tepoztlan, a Mexican Village: A Study of Folk Life. Robert Redfield. LC 30-15556. (Midway Reprint Ser.). 271p. reprint ed. pap. 77.30 (*0-685-15784-9*, 2026783) Bks Demand.

Teppiche aus Ost Turkestan Bekannt als Khotan, Samarkand, und KansuTeppiche see Carpets from Eastern Turkestan Known As Khotan, Samarkand & Kansu Carpets

Tequila: The Book. Ann Walker & Larry Walker. LC 93-31282. (Illus.). 120p. 1994. pap. 10.95 (*0-8118-0288-4*) Chronicle Bks.

Tequila! The Spirit of Mexico. Lucinda Hutson. LC 94-29104. (Illus.). 160p. 1994. 24.95 (*0-89815-564-9*); pap. 16.95 (*0-89815-663-7*) Ten Speed Pr.

Tequila Cook Book. Lynn Nusom. LC 93-21428. 128p. 1993. pap. 7.95 (*0-914846-89-2*) Golden West Pub.

T

*Tequila Lover's Guide to Mexico. Lance Cutler. 220p. 1998. write for info. (0-614-29909-8) Wine Patrol Pr.

*Tequila Mockingbird: A Fey Croaker Novel. Paul Bishop. 1997. 22.00 (0-684-83009-4) S&S Trade.

TERA Documentation: Onshore Gas & Oil Supply Model, Vol. II. TERA Advisory Committee. 200p. 1979. 15.00 (0-318-12719-9, F20178) Am Gas Assn.

TERA Documentation: The Offshore Gas & Oil Supply Model, Vol. I. TERA Advisory Committee. 195p. 1977. 15.00 (0-318-12720-2, F30078) Am Gas Assn.

Tera, My Journey Home: Alternative Healing for the Body & Spirit. Kathleen A. Milner. (Illus.). 152p. 1997. pap. text ed. 21.95 (1-886903-89-1) K Milner.

Teraphim. Harry Polkinhorn. 60p. (Orig.). 1995. pap. 7.00 (0-926935-98-4) Runaway Spoon.

Terapia Celular, una Nueva Dimension, en la Medicina. Frank Calderon. 192p. (Orig.). (SPA.). 1987. pap. text ed. 4.95 (0-939193-14-0) Edit Concepts.

Terapias de Oxigeno. Nathaniel Altman. (Illus.). (ENG & SPA.). 1995. pap. 12.95 (0-89281-472-1) Inner Tradit.

Teratocarcinoma Stem Cells. Lee M. Silver. (Cold Spring Harbor Conferences on Cell Proliferation Ser.: Vol. 10). 743p. 1983. 105.00 (0-87969-160-3) Cold Spring Harbor.

Teratogenic Effects of Drugs: A Resource for Clinicians: TERIS. Jan M. Friedman & Janine E. Polifka. LC 93-33818. 1994. text ed. 125.00 (0-8018-4800-8) Johns Hopkins.

Teratogens: Chemicals Which Cause Birth Defects. 2nd rev. ed. Ed. by Vera M. Kolb. LC 93-25703. 1993. 243.75 (0-444-81482-5) Elsevier.

Teratogens: Directory of New Medical & Scientific Reviews with Subject Index. Science & Life Consultants Association Staff. 160p. 1995. 47.50 (0-7883-0568-9); pap. 44.50 (0-7883-0569-7) ABBE Pubs Assn.

Teratological Modifications & the Meaning of Flower Parts. M. Guedes. (International Bioscience Monographs: No. 7). 62p. 1979. 8.00 (0-88065-093-1, Messers Today & Tomorrow) Scholarly Pubns.

*Teratologies: A Cultural Study of Cancer. Jackie Stacey. LC 96-37055. 304p. 1997. pap. write for info. (0-415-14960-6) Routledge.

*Teratologies: A Cultural Study of Cancer. Jackie Stacey. LC 96-37055. 304p. (C). 1997. text ed. write for info. (0-415-14959-2) Routledge.

T

Tercentenary Essays in Honor of Andrew Marvell. Ed. by Kenneth Friedenreich. (Illus.). 314p. (C). 1977. lib. bdg. 37.50 (0-208-01567-1, Archon Bks) Shoe String.

Tercentenary History of the Boston Public Latin School, 1635-1935. Pauline Holmes. LC 73-104278. 541p. 1970. reprint ed. text ed. 75.00 (0-8371-3950-3, HOBP, Greenwood Pr) Greenwood.

Tercer Curso de Derecho Internacional Organizado por el Comite Juridico Interamericano: (Julio-Agosto de 1976) 1977. 10.00 (0-8270-5250-2) OAS.

Tercer Ejercito de la U. R. S. S. Francisco-Felix Montiel. LC 88-81600. 116p. (Orig.). (SPA.). 1989. pap. 12.00 (0-89729-497-1) Ediciones.

Tercer Estado y Otros Escritos de 1789. Enmanuel J. Sieyes. Ed. & Tr. by Ramon Maiz. (Nueva Austral Ser.: Vol. 187). (SPA.). 1991. pap. text ed. 29.95 (84-239-1987-0) Elliots Bks.

Tercera Cronica de Alfonso X: La Gran Conquista de Ultramar. Ed. by Cristina Gonzalez. (Monografias A Ser.: No. 146). 166p. (SPA.). (C). 1992. 63.00 (1-85566-011-3) Boydell & Brewer.

Tercera Edad. Editorial America, S. A. Staff. Ed. by Maria E. Del Real. (Illus.). 296p. (Orig.). (SPA.). 1990. pap. write for info. (0-944499-92-9) Editorial Amer.

Tercera Residencia. 4th ed. Pablo Neruda. 112p. (SPA.). 1990. pap. 14.95 (0-7859-4997-6) Fr & Eur.

Tere, Eestimaa! Conversational Estonian. Virgi Jalakas et al. 144p. (Orig.). 1993. pap. text ed. 15.00 (0-9629724-2-8); audio 10.00 (0-9629724-3-6); vhs 20.00 (0-9629724-4-4) Nordic NY.

*Terebrantia (Insecta: Thysanoptera) L. A. Mound & A. K. Walker. (Fauna of New Zealand Ser.: Vol. 1). (Illus.). 113p. 1982. pap. 29.95 (0-477-06687-9, Pub. by Manaaki Whenua NZ) Balogh.

Terena & the Caduveo of Southern Mato Grosso, Brazil. Kalervo Oberg. LC 76-44771. (Smithsonian Institution. Institute of Social Anthropology. Publication Ser.: No. 9). reprint ed. 42.50 (0-404-15959-1) AMS Pr.

Terence: Phormio. Ed. by R. Martin. (Bristol Latin Texts Ser.). (LAT.). 1996. pap. 21.95 (1-85399-258-5, Pub. by Brstl Class Pr UK) Focus Pub-R Pullins.

Terence: The Comedies. Terence. Tr. by Betty Radice. (Classics Ser.). 400p. 1976. pap. 12.95 (0-14-044324-X, Penguin Classics) Viking Penguin.

Terence: The Comedies. Terence. Tr. by Palmer Bovie from LAT. (Roman Drama in Translation Ser.). 424p. 1992. reprint ed. pap. 15.95 (0-8018-4354-5); reprint ed. text ed. 45.00 (0-8018-4353-7) Johns Hopkins.

Terence: The Eunuch, Phormio, the Brothers: A Companion to the Penguin Translation of Betty Radice. J. Barsby. (Classics Companions Ser.). 156p. 1991. pap. 15.95 (1-85399-125-2, Pub. by Brstl Class Pr UK) Focus Pub-R Pullins.

Terence Andria. Richard C. Monti. (Latin Commentaries Ser.). 153p. (Orig.). (C). 1986. pap. text ed. 8.00 (0-929524-58-6) Bryn Mawr Commentaries.

Terence Conrad on Design. Terence Conrad. LC 96-18134. 288p. 1996. 55.00 (0-87951-686-0) Overlook Pr.

Terence Conrans Home Furnishings. Terence Conran. 1989. 29.95 (0-685-33239-X) Random Hse Value.

Terence Conran's Kitchen Book. Terence Conran et al. (Illus.). 224p. 1993. 45.00 (0-87951-513-9) Overlook Pr.

Terence Conran's Kitchen Book. Terence Conran et al. 224p. 1995. pap. 28.95 (0-87951-623-2) Overlook Pr.

Terence Cuneo: Railway Painter of the Century. Narisa Chakra. 1992. 55.00 (0-904568-74-1) Schiffer.

Terence Gray & the Cambridge Festival Theatre. Richard Cave. (Theatre in Focus Ser.). (Illus.). 90p. (Orig.). 1980. pap. text ed. 105.00 incl. sl. (0-85964-069-8) Chadwyck-Healey.

Terence La Noue. Dore Ashton. LC 91-58632. (Illus.). 168p. 1992. 75.00 (1-55595-052-3) Hudson Hills.

Terence Main: Terrestrial Tale. John Ash et al. LC 96-83582. (Illus.). 80p. (Orig.). 1996. pap. write for info. (0-9651328-0-3) Art Et Industrie.

*Terence Rattigan. Wansell. 1997. 29.95 (0-312-16521-8) St Martin.

Terence Rattigan: The Man & His Work. Michael Darlow & Gillian Hodson. 25.00 (0-7043-2160-2, Pub. by Quartet UK) Charles River Bks.

Terence's Bembine Phormio: A Palaeographic Examination. Elaine Coury. LC 81-71636. (Illus.). 150p. 59.00 (0-86516-011-2) Bolchazy-Carducci.

Teresa see Hola, Amigos!

Teresa: A Woman: A Biography of Teresa of Avila. Victoria Lincoln. LC 84-8561. (SUNY Series in Cultural Perspectives). 440p. 1985. text ed. 64.50 (0-87395-936-1); pap. text ed. 19.95 (0-87395-937-X) State U NY Pr.

Teresa Carreno "By the Grace of God" Marta Milinowski. LC 76-58931. (Music Reprint Ser.). 1977. reprint ed. lib. bdg. 45.00 (0-306-70870-1) Da Capo.

Teresa Come Por Dos Brochure. (SPA.). 1994. 0.50 (0-8151-3865-2) Mosby Yr Bk.

Teresa Neumann: The Stigmatist of Konnesreuth. Paola Giovetti. 136p. (C). 1990. text ed. 49.00 (0-85439-346-3, Pub. by St Paul Pubns UK) St Mut.

Teresa of Avila. Rowan Williams. LC 90-25030. (Outstanding Christian Thinkers Ser.). 177p. (Orig.). 1991. pap. 12.95 (0-8192-1496-5) Morehouse Pub.

Teresa of Avila: An Introduction to Her Life & Writings. Tessa Bielecki. 208p. 1994. pap. 27.00 (0-86012-233-6, Pub. by Srch Pr UK) St Mut.

Teresa of Avila: Ecstasy & Common Sense. Teresa of Avila. Ed. by Tessa Bielecki. LC 96-13513. 168p. (Orig.). 1996. pap. 10.00 (1-57062-167-5) Shambhala Pubns.

Teresa of Avila: Her Story: A Compelling Biography of One of the Most Remarkable Women of All Time. Shirley Du Boulay. 260p. 1995. pap. 10.99 (0-89283-893-0, Charis) Servant.

Teresa of Avila: Mystical Writings. Tessa Bielecki. (Spiritual Legacy Ser.). 176p. (Orig.). 1994. pap. 12.95 (0-8245-2504-3) Crossroad NY.

Teresa of Avila: The Interior Castle. Tr. by Kieran Kavanaugh & Otilio Rodrigues from SPA. LC 79-66484. (Classics of Western Spirituality Ser.). 256p. 1979. pap. 14.95 (0-8091-2254-5) Paulist Pr.

Teresa of Avila & the Politics of Sanctity. Gillian T. Ahlgren. 240p. 1996. 29.95 (0-8014-3232-4) Cornell U Pr.

Teresa of Avila & the Rhetoric of Femininity. Alison Weber. 194p. 1990. pap. text ed. 14.95 (0-691-02744-7) Princeton U Pr.

Teresa of Avila's Way. J. Mary Luti. (Way of the Christian Mystics Ser.: No. 13). 208p. (Orig.). 1991. pap. text ed. 14.95 (0-8146-5548-3) Liturgical Pr.

Teresa of Calcutta. D. Jeanene Watson. LC 84-60313. (Sower Ser.). (J). (gr. 3-6). 1984. pap. 7.99 (0-88062-012-9) Mott Media.

Teresa of Calcutta: A Pencil in God's Hand. Franca Zambonini. Tr. by Jordan Aumann. LC 93-1046. 207p. 1993. pap. 9.95 (0-8189-0670-7) Alba.

Teresa of the Poor: The Story of Her Life. Renzo Allegri. 140p. 1996. 14.99 (0-89283-937-6, Charis) Servant.

Teresa of Watling Street. Arnold Bennett. LC 74-17051. (Collected Works of Arnold Bennett: Vol. 78). 1977. reprint ed. 21.95 (0-518-19159-1) Ayer.

Teresa y Los Otros: Voces Narrativas En la Novelistica De Hilda Perera. Wilma Detjens. LC 92-74698. (Coleccion Polymita). 83p. (Orig.). (SPA.). 1993. pap. 9.95 (0-89729-661-3) Ediciones.

Terese & Alvin S. Lane Collection: Twentieth-Century Sculpture & Sculptors' Works on Paper. Alvin S. Lane & Doug Dreishpoon. (Illus.). 1995. pap. 34.95 (0-932900-40-2) Elvejhem Mus.

Teresina in America, 2 Vols. Maria T. Longworth. LC 73-13158. (Foreign Travelers in America, 1810-1935 Ser.). 734p. 1974. reprint ed. 57.95 (0-405-05478-5) Ayer.

Teresita. William C. Holden. LC 78-2321. (Illus.). 256p. 1978. pap. 10.95 (0-916144-25-9) Stemmer Hse.

Tereza Batista: Home from the Wars. Jorge Amado. Tr. by Barbara S. Merello. 576p. 1988. pap. 9.95 (0-380-75468-1) Avon.

*Terezienstadt Diary. Roubicek. LC 97-18576. 1997. 16.95 (0-8050-5352-2) H Holt & Co.

Terezin Diary of Gonda Redlich. Ed. by Saul S. Friedman. Tr. by Laurence Kutler from CZE. LC 92-11357. 192p. (C). 1993. 24.00 (0-8131-1804-2) U Pr of Ky.

*Teri King's: Aquarius '98. Teri King. 192p. 1997. pap. 4.95 (1-85230-975-X) Element MA.

*Teri King's: Aries '98. Teri King. 192p. 1997. pap. 4.95 (1-85230-977-6) Element MA.

*Teri King's: Cancer '98. Teri King. 192p. 1997. pap. 4.95 (1-85230-984-9) Element MA.

*Teri King's: Capricorn '98. Teri King. 192p. 1997. pap. 4.95 (1-85230-974-1) Element MA.

*Teri King's: Gemini '98. Teri King. 192p. 1997. pap. 4.95 (1-85230-979-2) Element MA.

*Teri King's: Leo '98. Teri King. 192p. 1997. pap. 4.95 (1-85230-976-8) Element MA.

*Teri King's: Libra '98. Teri King. 192p. 1997. pap. 4.95 (1-85230-981-4) Element MA.

*Teri King's: Pisces '98. Teri King. 192p. 1997. pap. 4.95 (1-85230-980-6) Element MA.

*Teri King's: Sagittarius '98. Teri King. 192p. 1997. pap. 4.95 (1-85230-978-4) Element MA.

*Teri King's: Scorpio '98. Teri King. 192p. 1997. pap. 4.95 (1-85230-983-0) Element MA.

*Teri King's: Taurus '98. Teri King. 192p. 1997. pap. 4.95 (1-85230-985-7) Element MA.

*Teri King's: Virgo '98. Teri King. 192p. 1997. pap. 4.95 (1-85230-982-2) Element MA.

Teri King's Astrological Horoscopes for 1997: Aquarius. Teri King. 1996. pap. 4.95 (1-85230-830-3) Element MA.

Teri King's Astrological Horoscopes for 1997: Aries. Teri King. 1996. pap. 4.95 (1-85230-820-6) Element MA.

Teri King's Astrological Horoscopes for 1997: Capricorn. Teri King. 1996. pap. 4.95 (1-85230-829-X) Element MA.

Teri King's Astrological Horoscopes for 1997: Gemini. Teri King. 1996. pap. 4.95 (1-85230-822-2) Element MA.

Teri King's Astrological Horoscopes for 1997: Leo. Teri King. 1996. pap. 4.95 (1-85230-824-9) Element MA.

Teri King's Astrological Horoscopes for 1997: Pisces. Teri King. 1996. pap. 4.95 (1-85230-831-1) Element MA.

Teri King's Astrological Horoscopes for 1997: Sagittarius. Teri King. 1996. pap. 4.95 (1-85230-828-1) Element MA.

Teri King's Astrological Horoscopes for 1997: Taurus. Teri King. 1996. pap. 4.95 (1-85230-821-4) Element MA.

Teri King's Astrological Horoscopes for 1997: Virgo. Teri King. 1996. pap. 4.95 (1-85230-825-7) Element MA.

Teri King's Complete Guide to Your Stars. Teri King. 1995. pap. 7.95 (1-85230-638-6) Element MA.

Terioki Crossing. large type ed. Alan Fisher. 544p. 1985. 27.99 (0-7089-8283-2) Ulverscroft.

Term Bank Notes. (How to Borrow Workbooks Ser.). Date not set. 83.00 (0-614-17082-6, Pub. by IFR Pub UK) Am Educ Systs.

*Term Graph Rewriting: Theory & Practice. Ed. by M. R. Sleep et al. LC 93-3426. (Illus.). 399p. reprint ed. pap. 113.80 (0-608-05313-9, 2065851) Bks Demand.

Term Indexing. Peter Graf. LC 96-4089. (Lecture Notes in Artificial Intelligence: Vol. 1053). 284p. 1996. pap. 49.00 (3-540-61040-5) Spr-Verlag.

Term Lending to Business. Neil H. Jacoby & Raymond J. Saulnier. (Financial Research Program III: Studies in Business Financing: No. 1). 183p. 1942. reprint ed. 47.60 (0-87014-129-5); reprint ed. mic. film 23.80 (0-685-61228-7) Natl Bur Econ Res.

Term Limits & Legislative Representation. John M. Carey. (Illus.). 192p. (C). 1996. text ed. 59.95 (0-521-55233-8) Cambridge U Pr.

Term Limits for Congress? . Barbara S. Feinberg. LC 95-34220. (Inside Government Ser.). (Illus.). 64p. (J). (gr. 5-8). 1996. lib. bdg. 15.98 (0-8050-4099-4) TFC Bks NY.

Term Loan Handbook. 3rd ed. American Bar Association Staff. 268p. 1983. write for info. (0-318-65471-7, H4285X) P-H.

Term Paper. 4th ed. Cooper. iv, 33p. (C). 1986. pap. 1.95 (0-8047-0348-5) Stanford U Pr.

Term Paper Study Aids. John Moran et al. (J). 1986. pap. 2.25 (0-87738-025-2) Youth Ed.

Term Paper Writing: The Fastest Easiest Legitimate Method Known to Man. rev. ed. L. Michael Tompkins. 1980. pap. 6.00 (0-931324-01-7) La Grange.

Term Papers & Reports: The Wilmington College Style Guide. Ed. by John J. Malarkey, 3rd. 120p. (Orig.). (C). 1993. pap. text ed. 4.95 (0-9636944-0-5) Wilmington Coll.

Term Rewriting: Advanced Course Held at the French Spring School of Theoretical Computer Science, Font Romeux, France, May 17-21, 1993. French Spring School of Theoretical Computer Science Staff. Ed. by Hubert Common & Jean-Pierre Jouannaud. LC 95-15960. (Lecture Notes in Computer Science Ser.: Vol. 909). 1995. write for info. (0-387-59340-3) Spr-Verlag.

Term Rewriting: Advanced Course Held at the French Spring School of Theoretical Computer Science, Font Romeux, France, May 17-21, 1993. French Spring School of Theoretical Computer Science Staff. Ed. by Hubert Common & Jean-Pierre Jouannaud. LC 95-15960. (Lecture Notes in Computer Science Ser.: Vol. 909). 221p. 1995. 43.00 (3-540-59340-3) Spr-Verlag.

*Term Rewriting & All That. Franz Baader & Tobias Nipkow. (Illus.). 250p. (C). 1997. write for info. (0-521-45520-0) Cambridge U Pr.

Term Rewriting Systems. Ed. by C. Kirchner & H. Kirchner. Date not set. text ed. write for info. (0-444-88754-7, North Holland) Elsevier.

Term Rewriting Systems. J. W. Klop & R. C. De Vrijer. (Tracts in Theoretical Computer Science Ser.: No. 25). (Illus.). 400p. (C). Date not set. text ed. 39.50 (0-521-39115-6) Cambridge U Pr.

Term Structure of Interest Rates. J. C. Dods & J. L. Fori. (Modern Revivals in Economics Ser.). 325p. 1992. 61.95 (0-7512-0097-2, Pub. by Gregg Pub UK) Ashgate Pub Co.

Term Structure of Interest Rates: Expectations & Behavior Patterns. Burton G. Malkiel. LC 66-21836. (Illus.). 293p. reprint ed. pap. 83.60 (0-317-08743-6, 2051944) Bks Demand.

Term Structure of Interest Rates in the United States, 1884-1914. Jean M. Gray. LC 77-14785. (Dissertations in American Economic History Ser.). 1978. 25.95 (0-405-11037-5) Ayer.

Terman's Kids: The Groundbreaking Study of How the Gifted Grow Up. Joel N. Shurkin. 288p. 1992. 22.95 (0-316-78890-2) Little.

Termcap & Terminfo. 3rd ed. John Strang et al. (Nutshell Handbook Ser.). Orig. Title: Reading & Writing Termcap Entries. 270p. 1988. pap. 21.95 (0-937175-22-6) OReilly & Assocs.

Termcap Manual. 3rd ed. Richard M. Stallman. (Illus.). 68p. 1996. spiral bd. 15.00 (1-882114-87-6) Free Software.

Termes de la Ley: or Certain Difficult & Obscure Words & Terms of the Common & Statute Laws of England. John Rastell. iv, 392p. 1993. reprint ed. lib. bdg. 85.00 (0-8377-2575-5) Rothman.

Termes Techniques Nouveaux: Termes Officielement Recommendes par le Gouvernement Francais: French-English, English-French. B. De Besse. 366p. (ENG & FRE.). 1982. pap. 95.00 (0-7859-7143-2) Fr & Eur.

Terminal. Robin Cook. pap. 6.98 (0-8317-4385-9) Smithmark.

Terminal. Robin Cook. 1996. mass mkt. 6.99 (0-425-15506-4) Berkley Pub.

Terminal. Colin Forbes. 317p. (Orig.). 1995. pap. 14.95 (0-330-28813-X, Pub. by Pan Books UK) Trans-Atl Phila.

Terminal. large type ed. Robin Cook. LC 93-18332. 1993. Alk. paper. 23.95 (1-56054-689-1) Thorndike Pr.

Terminal. large type ed. Robin Cook. LC 93-18332. 1994. Alk. paper. pap. 15.95 (1-56054-880-0) Thorndike Pr.

Terminal Aleph. Pamela Edwards. (Illus.). 80p. 1986. pap. 6.00 (0-915572-40-0) Panjandrum.

Terminal & Life-Threatening Illness: An Occupational Behavioral Perspective. Kent N. Tigges & William M. Marcil. LC 87-43327. 300p. 1988. pap. 20.00 (1-55642-022-6) SLACK Inc.

Terminal Arrrangements. large type ed. Joan Pennycook. (Dales Mystery Ser.). 255p. 1993. pap. 17.99 (1-85389-395-1) Ulverscroft.

*Terminal Bar. Bill Shively. 26p. 1995. 5.00 (0-614-30118-1) Skydog OR.

Terminal Beach. J. G. Ballard. 1987. reprint ed. pap. 3.50 (0-88184-370-9) Carroll & Graf.

Terminal Cafe. Jon Tuttle. 1996. pap. 5.25 (0-8222-1497-0) Dramatists Play.

Terminal Cancer & AIDS Patients: How They are Getting Well with Alternative Therapies: Vital Consumer Information Handbook. Douglas Gray, pseud. 132p. (Orig.). 1994. pap. 12.00 (0-9642592-0-6) D Gray.

Terminal Care: A Source Guide. 1991. lib. bdg. 76.00 (0-8490-4840-0) Gordon Pr.

Terminal Care for People with AIDS. Sims. 128p. 1992. pap. 45.00 (1-56593-547-0, 0517) Singular Publishing.

Terminal Care Support Teams: The Hospital-Hospice Interface. R. J. Dunlop & J. M. Hockley. 112p. 1990. pap. 19.95 (0-19-261915-2) OUP.

*Terminal Case of the Uglies, Vol. 14. Betsy Haynes. (Bone Chillers Ser.). 1997. pap. text ed. 3.99 (0-06-106429-7, HarpT) HarpC.

Terminal Command. Phillip Sanni. 1995. 18.95 (0-533-11297-4) Vantage.

Terminal Compromise: Computer Terrorism in a Networked Society. Winn Schwartau. 501p. 1991. pap. 19.95 (0-9628700-0-5) Inter Pact Pr.

Terminal Degrees: The Job Crisis in Higher Education. Emily K. Abel. LC 83-26876. 240p. 1984. text ed. 45.00 (0-275-91108-X, C1108, Praeger Pubs) Greenwood.

Terminal Disasters: Computer Applications in Emergency Management. Ed. by Sallie A. Marston. (Program on Environment & Behavior Monograph Ser.: No. 39). 218p. (Orig.). (C). 1986. pap. 10.00 (0-685-28113-2) Natural Hazards.

Terminal Identity: The Virtual Subject in Postmodern Science Fiction. Scott Bukatman. LC 92-39981. (Illus.). 420p. (C). 1993. text ed. 59.95 (0-8223-1332-4); pap. text ed. 18.95 (0-8223-1340-5) Duke.

Terminal Illness: A Guide to Nursing. Charles Kemp. LC 94-16166. 352p. 1994. pap. text ed. 35.95 (0-397-55123-1) Lppncott-Raven.

Terminal Justice. Steve Canton. 135p. 1994. 15.95 (1-883114-04-7) C B McFadden.

*Terminal Logic: What Rules Apply When the Killer Isn't Human? Jefferson Scott. LC 97-17235. 320p. (Orig.). 1997. pap. 9.99 (1-57673-038-7, Multnomah Bks) Multnomah Pubs.

Terminal Man. Michael Crichton. 1972. 23.00 (0-394-44768-9) Knopf.

Terminal Man. Michael Crichton. 1988. mass mkt. 6.99 (0-345-35462-1, Del Rey) Ballantine.

*Terminal Man. Michael Crichton. 1997. pap. 12.00 (0-345-41901-4) Ballantine.

Terminal Nerve (Nervus Terminalis) Structure, Function & Evolution. Ed. by Leo S. Demski & Marlene Schwanzel-Fukuda. (Annals Ser.: Vol. 519). 469p. 1987. 117.00 (0-89766-433-7) NY Acad Sci.

Terminal Operations, Vol. II. Cargo Systems Staff. 1980. 195.00 (0-907499-12-0, Pub. by Cargo Systs UK) St Mut.

Terminal Operations, Vol. III. Ed. by Cargo Systems Staff. 1983. 195.00 (0-907499-39-2, Pub. by Cargo Systs UK) St Mut.

Terminal Operations Conference, 5th. Ed. by Cargo Systems International Staff. (C). 1988. 200.00 (0-907499-59-7, Pub. by Cargo Systs UK) St Mut.

Terminal Operations Conference, 6th. Ed. by Cargo Systems International Staff. (C). 1990. 200.00 (0-907499-69-4, Pub. by Cargo Systs UK) St Mut.

*Terminal Option. Pendleton. (Executioner Ser.: No. 228). 1997. mass mkt. 3.75 (0-373-64228-8) Harlequin Bks.

Terminal Option. John Rogers. 168p. (Orig.). 1992. pap. 8.99 (1-56043-656-5) Destiny Image.

Terminal Paradox: The Novels of Milan Kundera. Maria N. Banerjee. 304p. 1991. pap. 12.95 (0-8021-3233-2, Grove) Grove-Atltic.

Terminal Renal Failure: Therapeutic Problems, Possibilities & Potentials. Ed. by H. Klinkmann. (Contributions to Nephrology Ser.: Vol. 78). (Illus.). x, 252p. 1990. 189.75 (3-8055-5086-3) S Karger.

An Asterisk (*) at the beginning of an entry indicates that the title is appearing in BIP for the first time.

Terminal Shock. Franklin W. Dixon. Ed. by Ann Greenberg. (Hardy Boys Ser.: No. 102). 160p. (YA). (gr. 3-6). pap. 3.99 (*0-671-69288-7*, Minstrel Bks) PB.

Terminal Signs: Computers & Social Change in Africa. Bennetta Jules-Rosette. (Approaches to Semiotics Ser.: No. 90). xvi, 424p. (C). 1990. lib. bdg. 136.95 (*3-11-012221-9*) Mouton.

Terminal Velocities. Ed. by Andrew Joron. LC 92-44108. 144p. (Orig.). 1993. pap. 19.95 (*0-938075-26-8*) Ocean View Bks.

Terminal Velocities. Ed. by Andrew Joron. 142p. (Orig.). 1992. pap. 10.00 (*0-685-60857-3*) Pantograph Pr.

Terminal Velocities. Ed. by Andrew Joron. LC 92-44108. (Orig.). 1993. write for info. (*1-880766-03-5*) Pantograph Pr.

***Terminal Velocity.** Blanche Boyd. LC 97-5825. 1997. 23.00 (*0-679-43008-3*) Knopf.

Terminal Velocity. Bob Shaw. 192p. 1992. 23.95 (*0-575-04917-0*, Pub. by V Gollancz UK) Trafalgar.

Terminal Velocity Official Strategy Guide. Robert Waring. (Illus.). 324p. (Orig.). 1995. pap. 19.99 (*1-56686-343-0*) Brady Pub.

Terminal Visions: The Literature of Last Things. W. Warren Wagar. LC 81-48625. 256p. 1982. 31.50 (*0-253-35847-7*) Ind U Pr.

Terminal Weird. Jack Remick. 160p. (Orig.). 1994. pap. 10.95 (*0-930773-34-9*); lib. bdg. 20.95 (*0-930773-33-0*) Black Heron Pr.

***Terminating Public Programs: An American Political Paradox.** Mark R. Daniels. LC 97-10553. 128p. (C). (gr. 13). 1997. text ed. 35.00 (*0-7656-0124-9*); pap. text ed. 14.95 (*0-7656-0125-7*) M E Sharpe.

Terminating the "Socially Inadequate" A History of the American Eugenicists & the German Race Hygienists, California to Cold Spring Harbor, Long Island to Germany. Marvin D. Miller. LC 95-76356. (Illus.). 365p. (Orig.). 1996. pap. 15.95 (*0-9610466-1-9*) Malamud-Rose.

Termination. Sean Dalton. 224p. (Orig.). 1995. mass mkt. 4.99 (*0-441-00201-3*) Ace Bks.

Termination: The Closing at Baker Plant. Alfred Slote. LC 69-13100. 360p. 1977. reprint ed. 12.00 (*0-87944-219-0*) Inst Soc Res.

Termination & Renewal of Property/Casualty Insurance Policies - 1996. annuals 246p. 1996. ring bd. 129.00 (*0-614-13250-9*) Am Ins NY.

Termination & Revision of Treaties in the Light of New Customary International Law. A. Kontou. (Monographs in International Law). 280p. 1995. 59.00 (*0-19-825842-9*) OUP.

Termination Dust. Sue Henry. (Alex Jensen Ser.). 320p. 1996. mass mkt. 5.99 (*0-380-72406-5*) Avon.

Termination in Psychoanalysis. Stephen K. Firestein. LC 76-46811. 261p. 1978. 40.00 (*0-8236-6450-3*) Intl Univs Pr.

Termination of Employment. 3rd ed. John Bowers. (Practice Notes Ser.). 99p. 1995. pap. 32.00 (*0-7520-0080-2*, Pub. by Cavendish UK) Gaunt.

***Termination of Employment in Germany.** Michael Tepass. Date not set. 60.00 (*0-86640-057-5*) German Am Chamber.

Termination of Employment Statutes. Tony Kerr. 1994. pap. 56.00 (*0-421-53080-4*, Pub. by Sweet & Maxwll UK) Gaunt.

Termination of Multipartite Treaties. Harold J. Tobin. LC 33-34572. (Columbia University. Studies in the Social Sciences: No. 388). reprint ed. 31.50 (*0-404-51388-3*) AMS Pr.

***Termination of School Employees: Legal Issues & Techniques.** NSBA Council of School Attorneys Staff. 316p. 1997. pap. text ed. 35.00 (*0-88364-210-7*, 06-163) Natl Sch Boards.

Termination Proofs for Logic Programs. Lutz Plumer. Ed. by Joerg H. Siekmann. (Lecture Notes in Artificial Intelligence Ser.: Vol. 446). viii, 142p. 1990. 25.00 (*0-387-52837-7*) Spr-Verlag.

Terminations. Henry James. LC 71-134966. (Short Story Index Reprint Ser.). 1977. 18.95 (*0-8369-3696-5*) Ayer.

Terminations for Convenience: A Contractor's Guide. Robert B. Holland. 205p. Date not set. ring bd. 99.00 (*1-56726-029-2*, B583) Holbrook & Kellogg.

***Terminator.** Sean French. (BFI Modern Classics Ser.). (Illus.). 72p. 1996. pap. 9.95 (*0-85170-553-7*, Pub. by British Film Inst UK) Ind U Pr.

Terminator II. Marvel Comics Staff et al. 64p. 1991. 4.95 (*0-87135-756-9*) Marvel Entmnt.

Terminator 2: Judgment Day: The Book of the Film. James Cameron & William Wisher. (Screenplay Ser.). (Illus.). 336p. (Orig.). 1991. pap. 17.95 (*1-55783-097-5*) Applause Theatre Bk Pubs.

Terminators. Donald Hamilton. (Matt Helm Ser.). 224p. 1980. pap. 1.95 (*0-449-14035-0*, GM) Fawcett.

***Terminatrix Progeny.** Stanya Kahn et al. (Orig.). Date not set. pap. 8.00 (*1-881430-52-9*) AFP.

Terminological Dictionary of Automatic Control. deluxe ed. 641p. 1977. 39.95 (*0-8288-5523-4*, M9059) Fr & Eur.

Terminological Dictionary of Ecology, Geobotany & Pedology. T. Goryshkina. 248p. (C). 1988. 75.00 (*0-685-46865-8*, Pub. by Collets) St Mut.

Terminological Dictionary of the European Community: Diccionario Terminologico de las Comunidades Europeas. Daniel Busturia et al. 680p. (SPA.). 1982. 85.00 (*0-7859-4969-0*) Fr & Eur.

Terminologie Bancaire, Financier et Economique Francais-Anglais. J. Cicile. 192p. (FRE.). 1995. 110.00 (*0-7859-9880-2*) Fr & Eur.

Terminologie de la Documentation. Ulrich Neveling. Ed. by Gernot Wersig. 274p. (ENG, FRE, GER, RUS & SPA.). 1976. pap. 85.00 (*0-8288-5756-3*, M6529) Fr & Eur.

Terminologie de la Gestion: Le Organigrammes: Management Terminology. L. Larouche & J. Pilon. Ed. by M. Cote. 223p. 1974. pap. 24.95 (*0-8288-6215-X*, M-9220) Fr & Eur.

Terminologie de la Geston des Imprimes Administratifs. M. Viller & A. Drollet. Ed. by Jean-Claude Corbeil. 92p. 1981. pap. 7.95 (*0-8288-5948-5*, M9221) Fr & Eur.

Terminologie de l'Etiquetage: Anglais-Francais: English - French Labelling Technology. M. Villers. 42p. 1974. pap. 7.95 (*0-8288-6214-1*, M-9233) Fr & Eur.

Terminologie et Lexicographie Medicales. 60p. (FRE.). 1967. pap. 29.95 (*0-8288-6693-7*, M-6530) Fr & Eur.

Terminologie Fondamentale en Odonto-Stomatologie et Lexique: Francais-Anglais, Anglais-Francais. Roucoules. 259p. (ENG & FRE.). 1977. 35.95 (*0-8288-5524-2*, M6492) Fr & Eur.

Terminology: Applications in Interdisciplinary Communication. Ed. by Helmi B. Sonneveld & Kurt L. Loening. LC 93-13089. viii, 228p. 1993. 59.00 (*1-55619-487-0*) Benjamins North Am.

Terminology & Concepts in Mental Retardation. Joel R. Davitz et al. LC 61-62621. (TC Series in Special Education). 135p. reprint ed. pap. 38.50 (*0-685-44070-2*, 2030145) Bks Demand.

Terminology Bulletin: Country Names, No. 342. 1991. 10.00 (*92-1-002055-3*, 91.I.9) UN.

Terminology, Definitions & Diagnostic Criteria in Digestive Endoscopy. 3rd rev. ed. Ed. by Zdenek Maratka. (Illus.). 130p. (C). 1994. 35.00 (*0-926592-01-7*) Normed Verlag.

Terminology, Dimensions & Safety Practices for Indicating Variable Area Meters: Rotameters, Glass Tube, Metal Tube, Extension Type Glass Tube. 1959. pap. 20.00 (*0-87664-342-X*, RP16.1,2,3) ISA.

Terminology for Allied Health Professionals. 3rd ed. Carolee Sormunen. 1995. pap. 44.95 (*0-538-71151-5*) S-W Pub.

Terminology for Grazing Lands & Grazing Animals. Forage & Grazing Lands Terminology Committee Staff. LC 91-22278. 46p. 1992. pap. 5.00 (*0-936015-31-4*) Pocahontas Pr.

Terminology for the Devil & Evil Spirits in the Apostolic Fathers. Francis X. Gokey. LC 79-8100. 224p. reprint ed. 36.00 (*0-404-18412-X*) AMS Pr.

Terminology for the Theory of Machines & Mechanisms. Ed. by G. Bogelsack et al. 30p. 1984. pap. 11.00 (*0-08-031140-7*, Pergamon Pr) Elsevier.

***Terminology, LSP & Translation: Studies in Language Engineering in Honour of Juan C. Sager.** Juan C. Sager. Ed. by Harold L. Somers. LC 96-49436. (Translation Library: Vol. 18). xii, 250p. 1997. lib. bdg. 69.00 (*1-55619-700-4*) Benjamins North Am.

Terminology of Communication Disorders: Speech - Language - Hearing. 3rd ed. Lucille Nicolosi. 375p. 1988. pap. text ed. 29.95 (*0-683-06500-9*) Williams & Wilkins.

Terminology of Communication Disorders: Speech-Language-Hearing. 4th ed. Lucille Nicolosi et al. 373p. 1996. 33.00 (*0-683-06505-X*) Williams & Wilkins.

Terminology of Environmental Pollutants. European Parliament Staff. 108p. (DAN, DUT, ENG, FRE, GER, GRE & ITA.). 1984. pap. 49.95 (*0-8288-0944-5*, M8742) Fr & Eur.

Terminology of Human Rights. European Parliament Staff. 342p. (DAN, DUT, ENG, FRE, GER, GRE & ITA.). 1982. pap. 49.95 (*0-8288-0409-5*, M6429) Fr & Eur.

Terminology of Swiss Civil Rights. 6th ed. A. Schreiber. 46p. (ENG, FRE, GER & ITA.). 1983. pap. 24.95 (*0-8288-0414-1*, M15826) Fr & Eur.

Terminology of Technical & Vocational Education: With English-Arabic Supplement. UNESCO Staff. 144p. (ENG, FRE, RUS & SPA.). 1984. pap. 29.95 (*0-8288-8018-2*) Fr & Eur.

Terminology of the European Company. 3rd ed. European Parliament Staff. 319p. (DAN, DUT, ENG, FRE, GER & ITA.). 1981. pap. 19.95 (*0-8288-0143-6*, M8201) Fr & Eur.

Terminology of the European Patent. European Parliament Staff. 527p. (DAN, DUT, ENG, FRE, GER & ITA.). 1981. pap. 29.95 (*0-8288-0410-9*, M6344) Fr & Eur.

Terminology of Waste Management. European Parliament Staff. 284p. (DAN, DUT, ENG, FRE, GER, GRE & ITA.). 1984. pap. 24.95 (*0-8288-0945-3*, M15891) Fr & Eur.

Terminology of Water Supply & Environmental Sanitation: A World Bank-UNICEF Glossary. Paul J. Biron. 176p. 1987. 23.95 (*0-8213-0585-9*, 10585) World Bank.

Terminorum Musicae Diffinitorium see Monuments of Music & Music Literature in Facsimile

Terminus. Boileau-Narcejac. (FRE.). 1982. pap. 10.95 (*0-7859-2222-9*, 207037386X) Fr & Eur.

Terminus. Pierre Boileau & Thomas Narcejac. (Folio Ser.: No. 1386). (Orig.). (FRE.). pap. 8.95 (*2-07-037386-X*) Schoenhof.

Terminus. large type ed. Andrew A. Puckett. 368p. 1992. 25.99 (*0-7089-2751-3*) Ulverscroft.

***Terminus Brain: The Environmental Threats to Human Intelligence.** Christopher Williams. LC 96-29928. (Global Issues Ser.). 288p. 1997. 90.00 (*0-304-33856-7*) Cassell.

***Terminus Brain: The Environmental Threats to Human Intelligence.** Christopher Williams. LC 96-29928. (Global Issues Ser.). 288p. 1997. pap. 27.95 (*0-304-33857-5*) Cassell.

***Terminus Cauchemar.** Denis Cote. (Novels in the Roman Plus Ser.). 160p. (FRE.). (YA). (gr. 8 up). 1996. pap. 7.95 (*2-89021-149-5*, Pub. by Les Editions CN) Firefly Bks Ltd.

Terminus English & German Pocket Dictionary Civil Engineering & Architecture. Hans-Dieter Junge. 216p. (ENG & GER.). 1986. pap. 85.00 (*0-8288-0208-4*, M15514) Fr & Eur.

Terminus English & German Pocket Dictionary Steam Generators. Hans-Dieter Junge. 88p. (ENG & GER.). 1986. pap. 59.95 (*0-8288-0699-3*, M15517) Fr & Eur.

Terminus German & English Pocket Dictionary of Robotics. Hans-Dieter Junge. 112p. (ENG & GER.). 1986. pap. 59.95 (*0-8288-0628-4*, M15515) Fr & Eur.

Termite Genus Amitermes in Africa & the Middle East. W. A. Sands. 1992. pap. 45.00 (*0-85954-319-6*, Pub. by Nat Res Inst UK) St Mut.

Termite Life & Termite Control in Tropical South Asia. M. L. Roonwal. 117p. (C). 1979. 80.00 (*81-85046-02-6*, Pub. by Scientific UK) St Mut.

Termite Repair: How to: Make Repairs, Use Chemicals, Save Money. 2nd rev. ed. George T. Demaree. (Illus.). 128p. (Orig.). 1987. pap. 18.95 (*0-935831-00-2*) Tradesman Pub.

Termite Report: The Homeowner & Buyer's Guide to Structural Pest Control. Donald V. Pearman. (Illus.). 140p. (Orig.). 1988. pap. 16.95 (*0-943743-00-1*) Pear Pub.

Termite Slide Kit: Termite Pests of Crops, Trees, Rangeland & Foodstores. M. J. Pearce. 1995. pap. 45.00 (*0-85954-390-0*, Pub. by Nat Res Inst UK) St Mut.

***Termites: Biology & Pest Management.** M. J. Pearce. 192p. 1997. 60.00 (*0-85199-130-0*) OUP.

Termites et Champignons: Les Champignons termitophiles d'Afrique Noire et d'Asie Meridionale. Roger Heim. (Collection "Flores et Faunes Acruelles"). (Illus.). 207p. (FRE.). 1977. lib. bdg. 110.00 (*2-85004-004-5*) Lubrecht & Cramer.

***Termo to Madeline: Northern California's Last Frontier.** Donald T. Garate. (Illus.). 436p. Date not set. 14.95 (*0-938373-18-8*) Lahontan Images.

Termodinamika Kriticheskogo Sostoianiia Individualnykh Veshchestv see Thermodynamics of the Critical State of Individual Substances: Termodinamika Kriticheskogo Sostoianiia Individual Nykh Veshchestv

Termoluminiscencia en el Fechamiento de Sitios Arqueologicos. Maria M. De los Rios. 191p. 1989. pap. 6.50 (*968-6068-07-4*, IN004) UPLAAP.

***Terms & Conditions of Contract.** R. W. Oliver & A. D. Allwright. 125p. 1989. 65.00 (*0-317-43795-X*, Pub. by Inst Pur & Supply UK) St Mut.

Terms & Conditions of Contract for Land Surveying Services. RICS Staff. (C). 1989. text ed. 59.00 (*0-85406-418-4*, Pub. by Surveyors Pubns) St Mut.

Terms & Conditions of Employment. Ed. by IPM Personnel Management Services Ltd. Staff. 160p. (C). 1991. pap. text ed. 120.00 (*0-85292-452-6*, Pub. by IPM Hse UK) St Mut.

Terms & Methods for Technical Archiving of Audiovisual Material. Compiled by Gunter & Schultz. (Film-Television-Sound Archive Ser.: Vol. 4). 88p. (ENG, FRE, GER, RUS & SPA.). 1993. lib. bdg. 60.00 (*3-598-22592-X*) K G Saur.

Terms & Renewals. Peter Wild. (Orig.). 1970. pap. 8.00 (*0-912136-20-0*) Twowindows Pr.

Terms for Geotechnical Engineering Services. 10.00 (*0-614-05200-9*, BPCMA06895M) ASFE.

Terms for Order. Kenneth Burke. Ed. by Stanley E. Hyman. 206p. reprint ed. pap. 58.80 (*0-685-43702-7*, 2056218) Bks Demand.

Terms of Abuse for Some Chicago Social Groups see Lexicon of the Sports & Racing Car Enthusiast

Terms of Address: Problems of Patterns & Usage in Various Languages & Cultures. Friederike Braun. (Contributions to the Sociology of Language Ser.: No. 50). xiv, 374p. (C). 1988. lib. bdg. 111.55 (*0-89925-432-2*) Mouton.

Terms of Astrology (English-Chinese, Chinese-English) China National Committee for Natural Scientific Terms. 120p. (CHI & ENG.). 1989. 49.95 (*0-8288-7331-3*, 7030012976) Fr & Eur.

Terms of Atmosphere Science (English-Chinese, Chinese-English) China National Committee for Natural Scientific Terms. 70p. (CHI & ENG.). 1989. 29.95 (*0-8288-7332-1*, 703001510X) Fr & Eur.

Terms of Conflict: Ideology in Latin American Politics. Ed. by Morris J. Blachman & Ronald G. Hellman. LC 76-54814. (Inter-American Politics Ser.: Vol. 1). 288p. reprint ed. pap. 82.10 (*0-317-42085-2*, 2025709) Bks Demand.

Terms of Cultural Criticism: The Frankfurt School, Existentialism, Poststructuralism. Richard Wolin. 256p. 1992. text ed. 39.50 (*0-231-07664-9*) Col U Pr.

Terms of Cultural Criticism: The Frankfurt School, Existentialism, Poststructuralism. Richard Wolin. 256p. 1995. pap. 16.00 (*0-231-07665-7*) Col U Pr.

Terms of Endearment. Larry McMurtry. Ed. by Bill Grose. 1992. mass mkt. 6.99 (*0-671-75872-1*) PB.

Terms of Endearment. Larry McMurtry. 416p. 1989. pap. 8.95 (*0-671-68208-3*, Touchstone Bks) S&S Trade.

Terms of Forestry (English-Chinese, Chinese-English) China National Committee for Natural Scientific Terms. 134p. (CHI & ENG.). 1989. 39.95 (*0-8288-7336-4*, 7030014952) Fr & Eur.

Terms of Geography (English-Chinese, Chinese-English) China National Committee for Natural Scientific Terms. 85p. (CHI & ENG.). 1989. 29.95 (*0-8288-7333-X*, 703001152X) Fr & Eur.

***Terms of Love.** Shirl Henke. 448p. (Orig.). 1997. mass mkt. 5.99 (*0-8439-4201-0*) Dorchester Pub Co.

Terms of Microbiology (English-Chinese, Chinese-English) China National Committee for Natural Scientific Terms. 98p. (CHI & ENG.). 1989. 29.95 (*0-8288-7334-8*, 7030014060) Fr & Eur.

Terms of Pedology (English-Chinese, Chinese-English) China National Committee for Natural Scientific Terms. 103p. (CHI & ENG.). 1988. 39.95 (*0-8288-7335-6*, 7030007751) Fr & Eur.

Terms of Physics (English-Chinese, Chinese-English) China National Committee for Natural Scientific Terms. 145p. (CHI & ENG.). 1989. 49.95 (*0-8288-7330-5*, 7030012488) Fr & Eur.

Terms of Possession. Elizabeth Power. (Presents Ser.). 1996. mass mkt. 3.50 (*0-373-11838-4*, 1-11838-9) Harlequin Bks.

Terms of Reference of an International Copper Study Group. 15p. 1989. mass mkt. 6.00 (*92-1-112278-3*, 89. II.D.12) UN.

Terms of Reference of the International Tin Study Group. 15p. 1989. 6.00 (*92-1-112277-5*, 89.II.D.11) UN.

Terms of Response: Language & the Audience in Seventeenth- & Eighteenth-Century Theory. Robert L. Montgomery. 208p. 1991. 30.00 (*0-271-00764-8*) Pa St U Pr.

Terms of Surrender. Janet Dailey. 1993. mass mkt. 5.99 (*0-671-87519-1*) PB.

Terms of Surrender. Shirl Henke. 448p. (Orig.). 1993. mass mkt., pap. text ed. 4.99 (*0-8439-3424-7*) Dorchester Pub Co.

Terms of Surrender. Kate Hoffmann. (Weddings by DeWilde Ser.). 1996. mass mkt. 4.50 (*0-373-82544-7*, 1-82544-7) Harlequin Bks.

Terms of Survival. (Stony Man Ser.). 1996. mass mkt. 4.99 (*0-373-61904-9*, 1-61904-8, Wrldwide Lib) Harlequin Bks.

Terms of Survival. 2nd ed. Judith O. Cofer. LC 87-70270. 1995. pap. 7.00 (*1-55885-079-1*) Arte Publico.

Terms of Survival: The Jewish World since 1945. Robert S. Wistrich. LC 94-22069. (Illus.). 432p. (C). 1995. text ed. 99.95 (*0-415-10056-9*, C0148) Routledge.

Terms of the Trade: A Reference for the Forest Products Industry. 2nd ed. Ed. by William Dean. LC 77-95459. (Illus.). 1984. 21.95 (*0-9614042-0-5*) Random Lgths Pubns.

Terms of the Trade: A Reference for the Forest Products Industry. 3rd rev. ed. Ed. by David Evans. (Illus.). 360p. 1993. 39.95 (*0-9614042-8-0*) Random Lgths Pubns.

Terms of Trade: The Language of International Trade Law, Policy & Diplomacy. Ed. by Thomas F. O'Herron. 110p. (C). 1989. pap. 12.00 (*0-9624861-1-6*) Intl Advisory Serv.

Terms of Trade & the Real Exchange Rate in the CFA Zone: Implications for Income Distribution in Niger. Paul A. Dorosh et al. (Working Papers: No. 57). 38p. (C). 1994. pap. 7.00 (*1-56401-157-7*) Cornell Food.

***Terms on Environment Related to Agriculture.** 178p. (ENG, FRE & SPA.). 1985. 25.00 (*92-5-000819-8*, F8198, Pub. by FAO IT) Bernan Associates.

Terms to Be Met. George Bradley. LC 85-22584. (Younger Poets Ser.: No. 18). 96p. 1986. 10.00 (*0-300-03598-5*) Yale U Pr.

***Ternary Alloys: A Comprehensive Compendium of Evaluated Constitutional Data & Phase Diagrams, 40 vols.** Incl. Vol. 13 Au Systems. Ed. by G. Petzow & G. Effenberg. (Illus.). xxv, 600p. 1995. lib. bdg. (*3-527-29234-9*, VCH); Vol. 12 Au Systems. Ed. by G. Petzow & G. Effenberg. (Illus.). xxv, 600p. 1995. lib. bdg. (*3-527-29233-0*, VCH); Vol. 11 As-In-Ir to AsYb-Zn. Ed. by G. Petzow & G. Effenberg. (Illus.). xxv, 586p. 1994. lib. bdg. (*3-527-29232-2*, VCH); Vol. 10 As-Cr-Fe to As-Xy. Ed. by G. Petzow & G. Effenberg. (Illus.). xxv, 582p. 1994. lib. bdg. (*3-527-29037-0*, VCH); Vol. 9 As-Au-Ca to As-Co-V. Ed. by G. Petzow & G. Effenberg. (Illus.). xx, 600p. 1994. lib. bdg. (*3-527-29038-9*, VCH); Vol. 8 Al-Ni-Tb to Al-Zn-Zr. Ed. by G. Petzow & G. Effenberg. (Illus.). xix, 489p. 1993. lib. bdg. (*3-527-29046-X*, VCH); Vol. 7 Al-Mg-Se to Al-Ni-Ta. Ed. by G. Petzow & G. Effenberg. (Illus.). xvii, 497p. 1993. lib. bdg. (*3-527-28370-6*, VCH); Vol. 6 Al-Gd-Tb to Al-Mg-Sc. Ed. by G. Petzow & G. Effenberg. (Illus.). xix, 492p. 1993. lib. bdg. (*3-527-28369-2*, VCH); Vol. 5 Al-Cu-S to Al-Gd-Sn. Ed. by G. Petzow et al. (Illus.). xix, 695p. 1992. lib. bdg. 800.00 (*3-527-27890-7*, VCH); Vol. 4 Al-Cd-Ce to Al-Cu-Ru. Ed. by G. Petzow & G. Effenberg. (Illus.). xix, 652p. 1991. lib. bdg. 800.00 (*3-527-27889-3*, VCH); Vol. 3 Al-Ar-O to Al-Ca-Zn. Ed. by G. Petzow & G. Effenberg. (Illus.). xx, 611p. 1990. lib. bdg. 800.00 (*3-527-27888-5*, VCH); Vol. 2 Ag-Cu-Pb to Ag-Zn-Zr. Ed. by G. Petzow & G. Effenberg. (Illus.). xviii, 624p. 1989. lib. bdg. 800.00 (*3-527-26942-8*, VCH); Vol. 1 Ag-Al-Au to Ag-Cu-P. Ed. by G. Petzow & G. Effenberg. (Illus.). xvii, 646p. 1989. lib. bdg. 800.00 (*3-527-26941-X*, VCH); Vol. 14 Ag-Al-Li to H-Li-Zr. Ed. by G. Petzow et al. (Illus.). 458p. 1995. lib. bdg. 800.00 (*3-527-29367-1*, VCH); Vol. 15 Hf-Li-N to Li-Y-Zr. Ed. by G. Petzow et al. (Illus.). xxv, 458p. 1995. lib. bdg. 800.00 (*3-527-29368-X*, VCH); write for info. (*0-614-20834-3*, VCH) Wiley.

Ternary & Multicomponent Systems. H. Stephen & T. Stephen. LC 79-40319. (Solubilities of Inorganic & Organic Compounds Ser.: Vol. 2, Pt. 2). 1964. 489.00 (*0-08-009926-2*, Pub. by Pergamon Repr UK) Franklin.

Ternary & Multinary Compounds, Vol. TMC. Ed. by Satyen Deb & Alex Zunger. 1987. text ed. 17.50 (*0-931837-57-X*) Materials Res.

Ternary Chalcopyrite Semiconductors: Growth, Electronic Properties & Applications. J. L. Shay & J. H. Wernick. LC 74-5763. 1975. 118.00 (*0-08-017883-9*, Pub. by Pergamon Repr UK) Franklin.

Ternary Quadratic Forms & Norms. Taussky. (Lecture Notes in Pure & Applied Mathematics Ser.: Vol. 79). 152p. 1982. 99.75 (*0-8247-1651-5*) Dekker.

T

Terns of Europe & North America. Klaus M. Olsen & Hans Larsson. LC 94-39312. 176p. 1995. text ed. 39.50 (0-691-04387-6) Princeton U Pr.

Terpenes, Vol. 3. 2nd ed. John Simonsen. Ed. by D. H. Barton. 591p. reprint ed. pap. 168.50 (0-317-20816-0, 2024537) Bks Demand.

Terpenoids & Steroids, Vol. 12. Royal Society of Chemistry Staff. 1989. 166.00 (0-85186-356-6) CRC Pr.

Terpenoids & Steroids, Vols. 1-9. Incl. Vol. 1. 1969-70 Literature. LC 74-615720. 1971. 47.00 (0-85186-256-X); Vol. 2. 1970-71 Literature. LC 72-78528. 1972. 41.00 (0-85186-266-7); Vol. 3. 1971-72 Literature. LC 74-615720. 1973. 47.00 (0-85186-276-4); Vol. 4. 1972-73 Literature. LC 74-615720. 1974. 54.00 (0-85186-286-1); Vol. 5. 1973-74 Literature. LC 74-615720. 1975. 54.00 (0-85186-296-9); Vol. 6. 1974-75 Literature. LC 74-615720. 1976. 54.00 (0-85186-306-X); Vol. 7. 1975-76 Literature. LC 74-615720. 1977. 65.00 (0-85186-316-7); Vol. 8. 1976-77 Literature. LC 79-67610. 1978. 59.00 (0-85186-326-4); Vol. 9. . Ed. by J. R. Hanson. LC 74-615720. 1979. 72.00 (0-85186-650-6); LC 74-615720. write for info. (0-318-50488-X) Am Chemical.

Terpin. Tor Seidler. LC 82-11734. 96p. (J). (gr. 7 up). 1982. 12.00 (0-374-37413-9) FS&G.

***Terpsichore at Louis-le-Grand: Baroque Dance on the Jesuit Stage in Paris.** unabridged ed. Judith Rock. LC 96-79049. (Original Studies Composed in English: No. 15). viii, 212p. (Orig.). 1996. pap. 22.95 (1-880810-22-0) Inst Jesuit.

Terpsichore in Sneakers: Post-Modern Dance. Sally Banes. LC 86-7829. (Illus.). 311p. 1987. pap. 18.95 (0-8195-6160-6, Wesleyan Univ Pr) U Pr of New Eng.

Terqa Final Reports, No. 1: L'Archive de Puzurum. Olivier Rouault. LC 81-71741. (Bibliotheca Mesopotamica Ser.: Vol. 16). (Illus.). 130p. (AKK, ENG & FRE.). 1984. pap. 24.25 (0-89003-102-9) Undena Pubns.

Terqa Preliminary Report, No. 12: Digital Plotting of Archaeological Floor Plans. Oliver Rouault & G. Buccellati. (Computer Aided Research in Near Eastern Studies: Vol. 1, Pt. 1). 40p. 1983. pap. text ed. 8.00 (0-89003-146-0) Undena Pubns.

Terqa Preliminary Reports, No. 10: The Fourth Season, Introduction & the Stratigraphic Record. Giorgio Buccellati & J. Knudstad. (Bibliotheca Mesopotamica Ser.: Vol. 10). (Illus.). 150p. 1979. 43.00 (0-89003-042-1); pap. 30.50 (0-89003-043-X) Undena Pubns.

Terra. Ken A. Smith. 94p. 8600. pap. 11.95 (0-906427-94-0, Pub. by Bloodaxe Bks UK) Dufour.

***Terra: Struggle of the Landless.** (Illus.). 144p. 1997. 55.00 (0-7148-3636-2, Pub. by Phaidon Press UK) Chronicle Bks.

Terra Amata. Kathryn B. Gurkin. Ed. by Ronald H. Bayes. (Illus.). 1979. pap. 10.00 (0-932662-31-5) St Andrews NC.

Terra Amata & the Middle Pleistocene Archaeological Record of Southern France. Paola Villa. LC 83-1392. (University of California Publications in Anthropology: No. 13). 339p. 1983. pap. 96.70 (0-7837-8432-5, 2049234) Bks Demand.

***Terra Cognita.** Kai Brodersen. (Spudasmata Ser.: Vol. 59). 354p. (GER.). 1995. write for info. (3-487-10008-8) G Olms Pubs.

Terra Cognita: The Mental Discovery of America. Eviatar Zerubavel. LC 92-5563. (Illus.). 180p. 1992. 35.00 (0-8135-1897-0); pap. 15.95 (0-8135-1898-9) Rutgers U Pr.

Terra Cotta Army of Emperor Qin. Caroline Lazo. LC 92-26189. (Illus.). 80p. (YA). (gr. 6 up). 1993. lib. bdg. 14.95 (0-02-754631-4, Mac Bks Young Read) S&S Childrens.

Terra Cotta ...Don't Take It for Granite: 3 Walks in New York City Neighborhoods. Susan Tunick. (Illus.). 64p. (Orig.). 1995. spiral bd. 10.00 (0-9636061-2-3) Frnds of TC.

***Terra Cotta Skyline: New York's Architectural Ornament.** Susan Tunick. LC 96-52343. (Illus.). 176p. 1997. 45.00 (1-56898-105-8) Princeton Arch.

Terra-Cottas from Nippur. L. Legrain. (Publications of the Babylonian Section). (Illus.). 52p. 1930. 60.00 (0-686-11926-6) U PA Mus Pubns.

Terra Firma. Thomas Centolella. LC 89-81835. (National Poetry Ser.). 96p. (Orig.). 1990. pap. 10.00 (1-55659-030-X) Copper Canyon.

***Terra Firma.** Intro. by Terry Gips. (Illus.). 20p. (Orig.). 1997. pap. 4.00 (0-937123-34-X) Am Gal U MD.

***Terra Firma, U. S. A.** Jordan Green. 64p. 1995. pap. write for info. (1-887128-10-7) Soft Skull Pr.

Terra in Piazza: An Interpretation of the Palio of Siena. Alan Dundes & Alessandro Falassi. (Illus.). 325p. 1975. pap. 15.00 (0-520-04771-0) U CA Pr.

Terra Incognita. Ed. by Polly Schaafsma. LC 88-81876. (Illus.). 31p. 1988. pap. 5.00 (0-912089-06-7) Haffenreffer Mus Anthro.

Terra Incognita: The Recent Sculpture of Charles Fahlen. John B. Jackson & Stephen Westfall. (Illus.). 48p. 1991. pap. 15.00 (0-88454-062-6) U of Pa Contemp Art.

***Terra Maria: or Threads of Maryland Colonial History.** Edward D. Neill. (Illus.). 260p. 1997. reprint ed. lib. bdg. 32.50 (0-8328-5940-0) Higginson Bk Co.

Terra Non Firma: Understanding & Preparing for Earthquakes. James M. Gere & Haresh C. Shah. (Portable Stanford Bks.). 191p. 1984. pap. 12.95 (0-916318-13-3) Stanford Alumni Assn.

Terra Nostra. Carlos Fuentes. Tr. by Margaret S. Peden from SPA. 786p. 1987. pap. 25.00 (0-374-51750-9) FS&G.

Terra Nostra, Tome II. Carlos Fuentes. 470p. (FRE.). 1989. pap. 15.95 (0-7859-2659-3, 207038196X) Fr & Eur.

Terra Nostra, I. Carlos Fuentes. Ed. by Javier Ordiz. (Nueva Austral Ser.: Vol. 264). (SPA.). 1993. pap. text ed. 19.95 (84-239-7264-X) Elliots Bks.

Terra Nostra, II. Carlos Fuentes. Ed. by Javier Ordiz. (Nueva Austral Ser.: Vol. 265). (SPA.). 1993. pap. text ed. 19.95 (84-239-7265-8) Elliots Bks.

Terra Nostra Tome I. Carlos Fuentes. 756p. (FRE.). 1989. pap. 17.95 (0-7859-2571-6, 2070381412) Fr & Eur.

Terra Nova. Wallace B. Shute. 1988. 14.00 (0-8309-0513-8) Herald Hse.

Terra Nova. Ted Tally. 1981. pap. 5.25 (0-8222-1122-X) Dramatists Play.

Terra Nova Official Strategy Guide. BradyGAMES Staff. (Illus.). 238p. (Orig.). 1996. 19.99 (1-56686-349-X) Brady Pub.

Terra-Phaza. Lenora Boneck. (Illus.). 182p. 1988. pap. 8.95 (0-940415-07-0) B & K Pub Hse.

***Terra Sourcebook.** (Torg Ser.). 18.00 (0-87431-353-8, 20515) West End Games.

TERRA-1: Understanding the Terrestrial Environment - The Role of Earth Observations from Space. Ed. by Paul M. Mather. LC 92-18705. 1992. 99.00 (0-7484-0044-3, Pub. by Tay Francis Ltd UK) Taylor & Francis.

Terra 2: Understanding the Terrestrial Environment: Remote Sensing Data Systems & Networks. Ed. by Paul M. Mather. LC 94-23083. 237p. 1995. text ed. 110.00 (0-471-95405-5) Wiley.

Terrace Gardener's Handbook: Raising Plants on a Balcony, Terrace, Rooftop, Penthouse or Patio. Linda Yang. LC 81-23249. 283p. 1982. pap. 13.95 (0-917304-17-9) Timber.

Terrace Hill: The Home of Iowa's Governor. Bill Witt. Ed. by Charles Roberts & Mary H. Tone. (Illus.). 24p. (Orig.). 1983. pap. 3.50 (0-685-08480-9) Mid Am Pub.

Terrace of the Great God at Abydos: The Offering Chapels of Dynasties 12 & 13, Vol. 5. William K. Simpson. LC 73-88231. 1974. 25.00 (0-686-05519-5) Penn-Yale Expedit.

Terracotta: The Technique of Fired Clay Sculpture. Bruno Lucchesi. (Illus.). 160p. 1977. 24.95 (0-8230-5320-2, Watsn-Guptill) Watsn-Guptill.

Terracotta Figurines from Kourion in Cyprus. J. H. Young & S. H. Young. (University Museum Monographs: No. 11). (Illus.). x, 260p. 1955. pap. 25.00 (0-934718-03-2) U PA Mus Pubns.

Terracotta Lamps. Oscar Broneer. LC 76-362971. (Isthmia Ser.: Vol. 3). (Illus.). xii, 122p. 1977. 30.00 (0-87661-933-2) Am Sch Athens.

Terracotta Revival: Building Innovation & the Image of the Industrial City in Britain & North America. Michael Stratton. (Illus.). 256p. 1994. 55.00 (0-575-05433-6, Pub. by V Gollancz UK) Trafalgar.

Terraformers. Stone Waters. 155p. (Orig.). 1996. mass mkt. 4.99 (1-55197-122-4, 1551971224, Pub. by Comnwlth Pub CN) Partners Pubs Grp.

Terraforming: Engineering Planetary Environments. Martyn J. Fogg. LC 95-10546. 560p. 1995. 49.00 (1-56091-609-5, R-153) Soc Auto Engineers.

Terrain Analysis. (Military Operations Ser.). 1991. lib. bdg. 75.00 (0-8490-4067-1) Gordon Pr.

Terrain Analysis & Distributed Modelling in Hydrology. Ed. by Keith J. Bevin & I. D. Moore. (Advances in Hydrological Processes Ser.). 249p. (Orig.). 1993. pap. text ed. 90.00 (0-471-93886-6) Wiley.

Terrain & Tactics. Patrick O'Sullivan. LC 91-12223. (Contributions in Military Studies: No. 115). 192p. 1991. text ed. 49.95 (0-313-27923-3, OTT, Greenwood Pr) Greenwood.

Terrain Factors in the Russian Campaign. 1995. lib. bdg. 250.95 (0-8490-6660-3) Gordon Pr.

Terrain of Comedy. Ed. by Louise Cowan. LC 84-22667. 259p. (Orig.). 1984. pap. 16.00 (0-911005-05-6) Dallas Inst Pubns.

Terrain Skiing: How to Master Tough Skiing Like the Experts. Seth Masia. (Illus.). 144p. 1996. pap. 12.95 (0-8092-3202-2) Contemp Bks.

Terrains & Pathology in Acupuncture, Vol. 1. Yves Requena. Ed. by Robert L. Felt. Tr. by Allan Ducharne from FRE. (Illus.). 443p. (FRE.). 1985. pap. 30.00 (0-912111-09-7) Paradigm Publns.

Terrains & Pathology in Acupuncture, Vol. 2. Yves Requena. Ed. by Robert L. Felt. Tr. by Allan Ducharne. (Illus.). 448p. (FRE.). Date not set. pap. 30.00 (0-912111-49-6) Paradigm Publns.

Terrains of Resistance: Nonviolent Social Movements & the Contestation of Place in India. Paul Routledge. 200p. 1993. text ed. 49.95 (0-275-94517-0, C4517, Praeger Pubs) Greenwood.

Terrakotta-Arulae Aus Sizilien und Unteritalien. Hellebora Van Der Meijden. (Illus.). xii, 394p. 1993. pap. 180.00 (90-256-1022-6, Pub. by A M Hakkert NE) Benjamins North Am.

***Terrakottafiguren von Myrina: Eine Untersuchung ihrer Moglichen Bedeutung und Funktion im Grabzusammenhang.** Ute Mrogenda. (Europaische Hochschulschriften, Reihe 38: Bd. 63). 200p. (GER.). 1996. 42.95 (3-631-30962-7) P Lang Pubng.

Terrakotten aus dem Kabirion bei Theben: Teil 1, Menschenaehnliche Figuren, Menschliche Figuren und Geraete. Bernhard Schmaltz. LC 74-77212. (Kabirenheiligtum bei Theben Ser.: Vol. 5). (C). 1974. 129.25 (3-11-004473-0) De Gruyter.

Terrakotten Von Pergamon. Eva Toepperwein. (Pergamenische Forschungen Ser.: Vol. 3). (C). 1976. 176.95 (3-11-005970-3) De Gruyter.

Terramechanics & off Road Vehicles. J. Y. Wong. 252p. 1989. 158.25 (0-444-88301-0) Elsevier.

Terrane Accretion & Orogenic Belts. Ed. by E. C. Leitch & E. Scheibner. (Geodynamics Ser.: Vol. 19). (Illus.). 343p. 1987. 38.00 (0-87590-516-1) Am Geophysical.

Terranes in the Circum-Atlantic Paleozoic Orogens. Ed. by R. David Dallmeyer. (Special Papers: No. 230). (Illus.). 281p. 1989. pap. 14.00 (0-8137-2230-6) Geol Soc.

Terranglia: The Case for English As World Literature. Joseph Jones. LC 65-24395. 110p. 1965. 22.50 (0-8290-0211-1) Irvington.

Terrapin, Bk. A. Mandell. Date not set. teacher ed., pap. text ed. 37.95 (0-314-87128-4) West Pub.

Terrapin Logo. Mandell. Date not set. teacher ed., pap. text ed. 25.95 (0-314-90685-1) West Pub.

Terrapin Logo Time. Mandell. Date not set. pap. text ed. 27.25 (0-314-90684-3) West Pub.

Terrarium. Scott Russell & Scott R. Sanders. 288p. (Orig.). 1996. pap. 12.95 (0-253-21021-6) Ind U Pr.

Terrarium. Scott R. Sanders. 288p. (Orig.). 1996. 22.95 (0-253-32956-6) Ind U Pr.

Terrarium Habitats. Kimi Hosoume & Jacqueline Barber. Ed. by Kay Fairwell et al. (Great Explorations in Math & Science (GEMS) Ser.). (Illus.). 92p. (Orig.). (J). (gr. k-6). 1994. teacher ed., pap. 13.50 (0-912511-85-0) Lawrence Science.

Terrariums. Lyn Stratmann. 1993. 12.98 (1-55521-845-8) Bk Sales Inc.

Terrariums - Animal & Plant Interactions: Hands on Elementary School Science. Linda Poore. 38p. 1994. teacher ed. 35.00 (1-883410-04-5) L Poore.

Terrariums for Your New Pet. Mervin F. Roberts. (Illus.). 64p. (Orig.). 1990. pap. 6.95 (0-86622-525-0, TU-017) TFH Pubns.

Terrasses de l'Ille d'Elbe. Jean Giono. 192p. (FRE.). 1976. 19.95 (0-7859-0099-3, M3504) Fr & Eur.

Terratopia - The Graphic Adventure: The First Four Tales. Steve Beck et al. Ed. by Vicki Dobbs. (Tales of Terratopia Ser.). (Illus.). 118p. (J). (gr. k-5). 1994. 19.95 (1-883871-02-6) Nature Co.

Terre. Emile Zola. (Coll. Diamant). (FRE.). 1989. pap. 13.95 (0-7859-1600-8, 208070267X) Fr & Eur.

Terre. Emile Zola. Ed. by Marcel Girard. (Folio Ser.: No. 1177). (FRE.). 1973. 12.95 (2-07-037177-8) Schoenhof.

Terre. Emile Zola. Ed. by Marcel Girard. 1973. write for info. (0-318-63602-6) Fr & Eur.

Terre de fer, Ciel de Cuivre. Yachar Kemal. (Au-Dela de la Montagne Ser.: No. II). 544p. (FRE.). 1988. pap. 16.95 (0-7859-2469-8, 2070374319) Fr & Eur.

Terre des Hommes. Antoine de Saint-Exupery. 1972. write for info. (0-318-63063-4); pap. 10.95 (0-8288-3733-3, F123555) Fr & Eur.

Terre des Hommes. Antoine de Saint-Exupery. (Folio Ser.: No. 21). (FRE.). 1972. 6.95 (2-07-036021-0) Schoenhof.

Terre Est Ronde. Armand Salacrou. 192p. (FRE.). 1973. pap. 10.95 (0-7859-1369-6, 2070364976) Fr & Eur.

Terre et la Monde Souterrain. Paul Sebillot. (FRE.). 1983. pap. 39.95 (0-7859-1567-2, 2902702116) Fr & Eur.

Terre Haute: A Pictorial History. Judity Calvert & Dorothy W. Jerse. (Indiana Pictorial History Ser.). (Illus.). 1993. write for info. (0-943963-33-8) G Bradley.

Terre Natale. Marcel Arland. 256p. (FRE.). 1972. pap. 10.95 (0-7859-1715-2, 2070362507) Fr & Eur.

Terre Promise. Andre Maurois. 340p. 9.95 (0-686-55499-X); pap. 16.50 (0-685-36962-5) Fr & Eur.

Terre Qui Meurt. Herve Bazin. (FRE.). 1988. pap. 10.95 (0-7859-3217-8, 2266022679) Fr & Eur.

Terre Tragique. Erskine Caldwell. 224p. (FRE.). 1986. pap. 10.95 (0-7859-2049-8, 2070377733) Fr & Eur.

Terrell on the Law of Patents Vol. 1. 14th ed. David Young et al. 1994. 240.00 (0-421-40890-1, Pub. by Sweet & Maxwll UK) Gaunt.

Terrence McNally, Vol. II. Terrence McNally. (Contemporary American Playwrights Ser.). 176p. (Orig.). 1996. pap. 14.95 (1-57525-061-6) Smith & Kraus.

***Terrence McNally: A Casebook.** Ed. by Toby S. Zinman. LC 96-45085. (Casebooks on Modern Dramatists Ser.: Vol. 22). 216p. 1997. text ed. 35.00 (0-8153-2100-7, H1933) Garland.

Terrence McNally Vol. I: 15 Short Plays. Terrence McNally. (Contemporary Playwrights Ser.). 348p. 1994. pap. 16.95 (1-880399-34-2) Smith & Kraus.

Terrence the Turtle. Judith Jango-Cohen. (Head & Tale Bks.). (Illus.). 20p. (J). (ps-k). 1997. 7.99 (0-88705-974-0) Joshua Morris.

Terres Au Bout du Monde. Jorge Amado. 379p. (FRE.). 1991. pap. 18.95 (0-7859-2241-5, 207038425X) Fr & Eur.

***Terrestrial Algae of Signy Island, South Orkney Islands.** P. A. Broady. (British Antarctic Survey Report Ser.: No. 98). 120p. 1979. 30.00 (0-85665-056-0, Pub. by Brit Antarctic Surv UK) Balogh.

Terrestrial & Freshwater Fauna of the Wadden Sea Area: Final Report of the Section "Terrestrial Fauna" of the Wadden Sea Working Group. Ed. by C. Smit et al. 276p. (C). 1982. text ed. 70.00 (90-6191-060-9, Pub. by A A Balkema NE) Ashgate Pub Co.

Terrestrial & Shallow Marine Geology of the Bahamas & Bermuda. Ed. by H. Allen Curran & Brian White. (Special Papers: No. 300). (Illus.). 1995. pap. 93.00 (0-8137-2300-0) Geol Soc.

Terrestrial & Space Techniques in Earthquake Prediction Research. Ed. by Andreas Vogel. (Progress in Earthquake Prediction Research Ser.: Vol. 1). (Illus.). viii, 712p. (C). 1979. 98.00 (3-528-08406-5, Pub. by Vieweg & Sohn GW) Informatica.

Terrestrial Behavior of Pesticides. I. Scheunert & H. Parlar. (Chemistry of Plant Protection Ser.: No. 8). 141p. 1992. 121.95 (0-387-54238-8) Spr-Verlag.

Terrestrial Biology II. Ed. by B. Parker. (Antarctic Research Ser.: Vol. 37). 170p. 37.00 (0-87590-185-9) Am Geophysical.

Terrestrial Biology Three, 9 papers, Paper 5. Ed. by B. Parker. (Antarctic Research Ser.: Vol. 30). (Illus.). 155p. 1979. write for info. (0-87590-148-4) Am Geophysical.

Terrestrial Biology Three, 9 papers, Set 30-9. Ed. by B. Parker. (Antarctic Research Ser.: Vol. 30). (Illus.). 155p. 1979. Papers 2 & 3: Ecological Investigations of Yeasts in Antarctic Soils & Taxonomy of Antarctic Bacteri. write for info. (0-87590-146-8); Paper 4: Crustacean Branchiopid Distribution & Speciation in Mesozoic Lakes of the Southern Continen. write for info. (0-87590-147-6); Paper 1: Identification of Some Fungi from Soil & Air of Antarctica, 26p. write for info. (0-87590-145-X) Am Geophysical.

Terrestrial Biology Three: Feeding Chases in the Adelie Penguin; the Mummified Seals of Southern Victoria Land, 9 papers, Set 30-9. Ed. by B. Parker. (Antarctic Research Ser.: Vol. 30). (Illus.). 155p. 1979. Papers 6-9: Feeding Chases in the Adelie Penguin; The Mummified Seals of Southern Victoria Land, Ant. write for info. (0-87590-175-1) Am Geophysical.

Terrestrial Biospheric Carbon Fluxes: Quantification of Sinks & Sources of CO2. Ed. by Joe Wisniewski & R. Neil Sampson. LC 93-31134. 1993. lib. bdg. 292.50 (0-7923-2502-8) Kluwer Ac.

Terrestrial Digital Microwave Communications. Intro. by Ferdo Ivanek. (Artech House Microwave Library). (Illus.). 320p. (C). 1989. write for info. (0-89006-302-8) Artech Hse.

Terrestrial Digital Microwave Communications. Ed. by Ferdo Ivanek. LC 89-6773. (Artech House Microwave Library). (Illus.). 367p. 1989. reprint ed. pap. 104.60 (0-7837-9695-1, 2060425) Bks Demand.

Terrestrial Ecosystems. Aber. 368p. (C). 1991. pap. write for info. (0-03-047443-4) HB Coll Pubs.

***Terrestrial Ecosystems in Changing Environments.** Herman H. Shugart. (Studies in Ecology). (Illus.). 524p. (C). 1997. write for info. (0-521-56342-9) Cambridge U Pr.

***Terrestrial Ecosystems in Changing Environments.** Herman H. Shugart. (Studies in Ecology). (Illus.). 524p. (C). 1997. pap. text ed. 34.95 (0-521-56523-5) Cambridge U Pr.

Terrestrial Ecosystems Through Time: Evolutionary Paleoecology of Terrestrial Plants & Animals. Anna K. Behrensmeyer et al. LC 91-44166. (Illus.). 588p. 1992. pap. text ed. 32.50 (0-226-04155-7) U Ch Pr.

Terrestrial Ecosystems Through Time: Evolutionary Paleoecology of Terrestrial Plants & Animals. Anna K. Behrensmeyer et al. LC 91-44166. (Illus.). 588p. 1992. lib. bdg. 86.50 (0-226-04154-9) U Ch Pr.

Terrestrial Eocene-Oligocene Transition in North America. Ed. by Donald R. Prothero & Robert J. Emry. (Illus.). 550p. (C). 1996. text ed. 95.00 (0-521-43387-8) Cambridge U Pr.

Terrestrial Fishing: The History & Development of the Jassid, Beetle, Cricket, Hopper, Ant, & Inchworm on Pennsylvania's Legendary Letort. Ed Koch. LC 89-36114. (Illus.). 176p. 1990. 24.95 (0-8117-0928-0) Stackpole.

Terrestrial Heat Flow & the Litosphere Structure. Ed. by V. Cermak & L. Rybach. (Exploration of the Deep Continental Crust Ser.). (Illus.). xi, 507p. 1991. 199.95 (0-387-52404-5) Spr-Verlag.

Terrestrial Invasion: An Ecophysiological Approach to the Origins of Land Animals. Colin Little. (Cambridge Studies in Ecology). (Illus.). 320p. (C). 1990. text ed. 110.00 (0-521-33447-0); pap. text ed. 38.95 (0-521-33669-4) Cambridge U Pr.

Terrestrial Isopod Biology. A. M. Alikhan. (Crustacean Issues Ser.: Vol. 9). (Illus.). 220p. (C). 1995. text ed. 110.00 (90-5410-193-8, Pub. by A A Balkema NE) Ashgate Pub Co.

Terrestrial Orchids: From Seed to Mycotrophic Plant. Hanne N. Rasmussen. (Illus.). 332p. (C). 1995. text ed. 69.95 (0-521-45165-5) Cambridge U Pr.

***Terrestrial Planisphere: Map of the Complete World.** Paperblanks Books Staff. 1994. 10.95 (1-55156-001-1, Pub. by Paperblank Bk CN) Consort Bk Sales.

Terrestrial Plant Ecology. 2nd rev. ed. Michael G. Barbour et al. (C). 1987. text ed. 49.50 (0-8053-0541-6) Benjamin-Cummings.

Terrestrial Slugs: Biology, Ecology & Control. A. South. (Illus.). 448p. (C). (gr. 13). 1992. text ed. 114.95 (0-412-36810-2, A6601) Chapman & Hall.

Terrestrial Space Radiation & Its Biological Effects. Ed. by P. D. McCormack et al. (NATO ASI Series A, Life Sciences: Vol. 154). (Illus.). 850p. 1988. 175.00 (0-306-43020-7, Plenum Pr) Plenum.

***Terrestrial Talitridae (Crustacea: Amphipoda)** K. W. Duncan. (Fauna of New Zealand Ser.: Vol. 31). 128p. 1994. pap. 36.00 (0-478-04533-6, Pub. by Manaaki Whenua NZ) Balogh.

Terrestrial Vegetation of California. 2nd ed. Ed. by Michael G. Barbour & Jack Major. (Special Publication Ser.: No. 9). 1040p. (Orig.). 1988. 50.00 (0-943460-13-1) Calif Native.

Terrestrials: A Modern Approach to Fishing & Tying with Synthetic & Natural Materials. Harrison R. Steeves, III & Ed Koch. (Illus.). 272p. 1994. 29.95 (0-8117-0629-X) Stackpole.

Terri. John Benton. 192p. (J). (gr. 7-12). 1981. pap. 3.50 (0-8007-8408-1) J Benton Bks.

Terri Murphy's Listing & Selling Secrets: How to Become a Million Dollar Producer. Terri Murphy. 168p. 1995. 24.95 (0-7931-1545-0, 1907-1601, Real Estate Ed) Dearborn Finan.

Terrible Angel: Surviving the First Five Years of Motherhood. Patricia H. Clifford. 1991. pap. 5.95 (0-8091-3192-7) Paulist Pr.

Terrible Anger: The 1934 Waterfront & General Strikes in San Francisco. David F. Selvin. LC 96-11397. (Illus.). 272p. (Orig.). 1996. pap. 26.95 (0-8143-2610-2) Wayne St U Pr.

Terrible Beauty. Diana Norman. 320p. 1988. pap. 12.95 (*1-85371-007-5*) Dufour.

Terrible Beauty: The Easter Rebellion & Yeats's "Great Tapestry" Carmel Jordan. LC 86-47550. 136p. 1987. 32.50 (*0-8387-5107-5*) Bucknell U Pr.

Terrible Beauty: Yeats, Joyce, Ireland, & the Myth of the Devouring Female. Patrick J. Keane. LC 88-4792. 168p. 1988. text ed. 27.50 (*0-8262-0686-7*) U of Mo Pr.

Terrible Beyond Endurance? The Foreign Policy of State Terrorism. Ed. by Michael Stohl & George A. Lopez. LC 87-251. (Contributions in Political Science Ser.: No. 180). 368p. 1988. text ed. 65.00 (*0-313-25297-1*, SFN/, Greenwood Pr) Greenwood.

Terrible but Unfinished Story of Norodom Sihanouk, King of Cambodia. Helene Cixous. Tr. by Juliet F. MacCannell et al. LC 93-1916. (European Women Writers Ser.). xxvii, 233p. (ENG & FRE.). 1994. pap. 13.95 (*0-8032-6361-9*, Bison Books) U of Nebr Pr.

Terrible Fitzball: The Melodramatist of the Macabre. Larry Clifton. LC 92-74879. 192p. (C). 1993. 39.95 (*0-87972-608-3*); pap. 15.95 (*0-87972-609-1*) Bowling Green Univ Popular Press.

Terrible Girls. Rebecca Brown. 144p. (Orig.). 1992. pap. 8.95 (*0-87286-266-6*) City Lights.

***Terrible Hard Biscuits: A Reader in Aboriginal History.** Ed. by Valerie Chapman & Peter Read. 304p. 1997. pap. 29.95 (*1-86373-964-5*, Pub. by Allen Unwin AT) Paul & Co Pubs.

Terrible Honesty: Mongrel Manhattan in the 1920s. Ann Douglas. LC 94-10892. 606p. 1995. 27.50 (*0-374-11620-2*) FS&G.

Terrible Honesty: Mongrel Manhattan in the 1920's. Ann Douglas. 608p. 1996. pap. 15.00 (*0-374-52462-9*) FS&G.

Terrible Itch. Shen Roddie. (Illus.). 24p. (J). (ps-1). 1993. boxed 13.00 (*0-671-79169-9*, S&S Bks Young Read) S&S Childrens.

Terrible Leak. Yoshiko Uchida. (Creative Short Stories Ser.). (YA). (gr. 4-12). 1989. 13.95 (*0-88682-357-9*, 97223-098) Creative Ed.

Terrible Meek: Essays on Religion & Revolution. Ed. by Lonnie D. Kliever. LC 86-25317. 220p. 1987. pap. 12.95 (*0-88702-215-4*) Washington Inst Pr.

Terrible Perfection: Women & Russian Literature. Barbara Heldt. LC 86-45893. 192p. 1987. text ed. 27.50 (*0-253-35838-8*) Ind U Pr.

Terrible Perfection: Women & Russian Literature. Barbara Heldt. LC 86-45893. 192p. 1992. reprint ed. pap. text ed. 5.95 (*0-253-20647-2*, MB-647) Ind U Pr.

***Terrible Secret.** Ginette Anfousse. (Novels in the Roman Plus Ser.). 160p. (FRE.). (YA). (gr. 8 up). 1996. pap. 7.95 (*2-89021-107-X*, Pub. by Les Editions CN) Firefly Bks Ltd.

Terrible Shears: Scenes from a Twenties Childhood. D. J. Enright. LC 74-5966. (Wesleyan Poetry Program Ser.: Vol. 73). 71p. 1974. pap. 11.95 (*0-8195-1073-4*, Wesleyan Univ Pr) U Pr of New Eng.

Terrible Siren: Victoria Woodhull (1838-1927) Emanie S. Arling. LC 72-2587. (American Women Ser.: Images & Realities). (Illus.). 478p. 1978. reprint ed. 29.95 (*0-405-04474-7*) Ayer.

Terrible Sociability: The Text of Manners in Laclos, Goethe, & James. Susan Winnett. LC 92-24579. 264p. 1993. 37.50 (*0-8047-2140-8*) Stanford U Pr.

Terrible Speller: A Quick-&-Easy Guide to Enhancing Your Spelling Ability. William Proctor. 192p. 1995. pap. 7.95 (*0-688-14229-X*) Morrow.

Terrible Stories. Lucille Clifton. (American Poets Continuum Ser.: Vol. 38). 72p. 1996. 20.00 (*1-880238-36-5*); pap. 12.50 (*1-880238-37-3*) BOA Edns.

Terrible Swift Sword. William R. Forstchen. (Lost Regiment Ser.: No. 3). 464p. 1992. pap. 5.99 (*0-451-45137-6*, ROC) NAL-Dutton.

Terrible Tattoo Parlor. Mary Chase. 1981. pap. 3.25 (*0-8222-1123-8*) Dramatists Play.

***Terrible Teresa & Other Very Short Stories.** Mittie Cuetara. LC 96-29727. (Illus.). (J). 1997. pap. 14.99 (*0-525-45768-2*) NAL-Dutton.

Terrible, Terrible Tiger. Colin Hawkins & Jacqui Hawkins. LC 87-40675. (Early Reader Ser.). (Illus.). 32p. (J). (ps-3). 1988. bds. 5.95 (*1-55782-043-0*, Warner Juvenile Bks) Little.

Terrible Thing. June M. Milam. Ed. by Laura L. Nelson & Chris Gilmer. (Drugless Douglass Tales Ser.). (Illus.). 20p. (J). (ps-k). 1994. pap. text ed. 42.95 (*1-884307-13-2*) Dev Res Educ.

***Terrible Thing.** June M. Milam. Ed. by Charlotte C. Daley. Tr. by Carmen Miranda. (Drugless Douglass Tales Ser.). (Illus.). 24p. (Orig.). (SPA.). (J). (ps). 1997. pap. 32.95 (*1-884307-32-9*) Dev Res Educ.

***Terrible Thing.** June M. Milam. Ed. by Charlotte C. Daley. Tr. by Carmen Miranda. (Drugless Douglass Tales Ser.). (Illus.). 24p. (Orig.). (SPA.). (J). (ps). 1997. pap. 6.95 (*1-884307-33-7*) Dev Res Educ.

Terrible Thing. Ed. by Laura L. Nelson et al. (Drugless Douglass Tales Ser.). (Illus.). 20p. (J). (ps-k). 1994. 4.95 (*1-884307-14-0*) Dev Res Educ.

Terrible Thing That Happened at Our House. Marge Blaine. (Illus.). 32p. (J). (gr. 1-4). 1991. pap. 3.95 (*0-590-42371-1*) Scholastic Inc.

Terrible Things: An Allegory of the Holocaust. rev. ed. Eve Bunting. (Illus.). 32p. (J). (gr. 1-4). reprint ed. 11.95 (*0-8276-0325-8*) JPS Phila.

Terrible Things: An Allegory of the Holocaust. rev. ed. Eve Bunting. (Illus.). 24p. (J). (gr. 1-4). 1989. reprint ed. pap. 7.95 (*0-8276-0507-2*) JPS Phila.

Terrible Tide. Alisa Craig, pseud. 192p. 1987. mass mkt. 3.99 (*0-380-70336-X*) Avon.

Terrible Tiger. Jack Prelutsky. LC 88-7901. (Illus.). 32p. (J). (ps-2). 1989. reprint ed. pap. 3.95 (*0-689-71300-2*, Aladdin Paperbacks) S&S Childrens.

Terrible Tilly (Tillamook Rock Light House) An Oregon Documentary, the Biography of a Light House. Bert Webber & Margie Webber. LC 91-374. (Illus.). 128p. (Orig.). 1992. pap. 10.95 (*0-936738-13-8*) Webb Research.

Terrible Tooths: Survival Cookbook. Susan G. Clark. 150p. (J). 1991. 12.95 (*0-9631133-0-5*) La Petite.

Terrible Tragadabas: El Terrible Tragadabas. Joe Hayes. (Illus.). 32p. (Orig.). (J). (ps-4). 1987. pap. 4.95 (*0-939729-02-4*); audio 8.95 (*0-939729-03-2*) Trails West Pub.

Terrible Trail: The Meek Cutoff, 1845. rev. ed. Keith Clark & Lowell Tiller. LC 93-16761. (Illus.). 250p. 1993. reprint ed. pap. 14.95 (*0-89288-233-6*) Maverick.

Terrible Trio. Brian Scott. 120p. (C). 1996. pap. 23.00 (*0-85976-306-4*, Pub. by J Donald UK) St Mut.

Terrible Truth about Lawyers: What I Should Have Learned at Yale Law School. Mark H. McCormack. 1988. mass mkt. 4.95 (*0-380-70652-0*) Avon.

Terrible Truth about Third Grade. Leslie McGuire. LC 90-26788. (Making the Grade Ser.). (Illus.). 96p. (J). (gr. 2-4). 1997. pap. 3.95 (*0-8167-2383-4*) Troll Communs.

Terrible Tuesday see Black History Series I

Terrible Turnoff & Me. Joan Thompson. Ed. by Patricia MacDonald. 160p. (Orig.). (J). (gr. 3-6). 1994. pap. 2.99 (*0-671-86845-4*, Minstrel Bks) PB.

Terrible Twos. Ishmael Reed. 192p. 1988. pap. 9.95 (*0-689-70727-4*, Pub. by Ctrl Bur voor Schimmel NE) Macmillan.

***Terrible Tyrannosaurus.** Jinny Johnson. (J). 1996. pap. 8.95 (*0-590-86403-3*) Scholastic Inc.

***Terrible Tyrannosaurus & Other Prehistoric Creatures.** Jinny Johnson. (J). (gr. 1-5). Date not set. 8.95 (*0-614-19202-1*, Blue Ribbon Bks) Scholastic Inc.

Terrible Wave: Memorial Edition. Marden A. Dahlstedt. LC 72-76687. (Illus.). 125p. (YA). (gr. 7 up). 1988. reprint ed. pap. 5.00 (*0-9621827-0-2*) R R Dahlstedt.

Terrible Wonderful Day. Yaffa Ganz. (Illus.). 1986. 10.95 (*0-87306-423-2*) Feldheim.

Terrible, Wonderful Tellin' at Hog Hammock. Kim L. Siegelson. LC 95-30005. (Illus.). 96p. (J). (gr. 2-5). 1996. 13.95 (*0-06-024877-5*) HarpC Child Bks.

Terrible, Wonderful Tellin' at Hog Hammock. Kim L. Siegelson. LC 95-30005. (Illus.). 96p. (J). (gr. 2-5). 1996. lib. bdg. 13.89 (*0-06-024878-3*) HarpC Child Bks.

Terribly Gross Jokes, Vol. XIX. Julius Alvin. 160p. 1995. mass mkt. 3.50 (*0-8217-4873-4*, Zebra Kensgtn) Kensgtn Pub Corp.

Terribly Tasteless. Davis. Date not set. pap. 4.95 (*0-312-79202-6*) St Martin.

Terricolas. Fausto Avendano. 120p. 1992. pap. 7.25 (*1-881781-01-1*) Spanish Press.

Terrier Breeds. Barbara J. Patten. LC 96-23074. (Read All about Dogs Ser.). (J). 1996. write for info. (*0-86593-458-4*) Rourke Corp.

Terrier of Fleete, Lincolnshire. Ed. by N. Neilson. Bd. with Eleventh Century Inquisition of St. Augustine's Canterbury. (British Academy, London, Records of the Social & Economic History of Wngland & Wales. Series: Vol. 4). 1974. reprint ed. Set pap. 50.00 (*0-8115-1244-4*) Periodicals Srv.

Terriers in the Trenches: The Post Office Rifles at War, 1914-1918. Ed. by Charles Messenger. 170p. (C). 1987. 100.00 (*0-317-90379-9*, Pub. by Picton UK) St Mut.

Terriers in the Trenches: The Post Office Rifles at War, 1914-1918. Picton Publishing (Chippenham) Ltd. Staff. (C). 1987. 65.00 (*0-685-39338-0*, Pub. by Picton UK) St Mut.

Terriers Vocation. Geoffrey Sparrow. (Illus.). 120p. 1990. pap. 21.00 (*0-85131-111-3*, Pub. by J A Allen & Co UK) St Mut.

Terrific Bee on Terrific Me. Nancy E. Conkle. (Illus.). 32p. (Orig.). (J). (ps-1). 1993. pap. 9.50 (*0-9639061-0-0*) N Conkle.

***Terrific, No Tears Bedtime Book: A Child's Delightful Bedtime Routine with a Definite Beginning & a Definite, No Tears Ending - Ages 2-6 Years.** Marjorie R. Nelsen. (Illus.). 8p. (Orig.). 1996. pap. 8.95 (*0-9630495-2-6*) Partners in Learn.

***Terrific Number 2: Amazing Facts about the Number Two.** Kitty Higgins. (Birthday Book Ser.). 1998. 6.95 (*0-8362-3218-6*) Andrews & McMeel.

Terrific Pacific Cookbook: The Vibrant Foods of Thailand, Bali, Vietnam, Penang, Singapore, and Australia. Anya Von Bremzen & John Welchman. LC 95-2381. (Illus.). 480p. 1995. 24.95 (*1-56305-868-5*, 3868); pap. 15.95 (*1-56305-172-9*, 3172) Workman Pub.

Terrific Parties for Kids. Janice Hubbard-Holmes. 96p. 1991. pap. 10.98 (*0-88290-419-1*) Horizon Utah.

Terrific Stencils & Stamps. Jo'Anne Kelly. LC 95-26033. 80p. 1996. 19.95 (*1-895569-38-9*, Pub. by S Milner AT) Sterling.

***Terrific Stencils & Stamps.** Jo'Anne Kelly. (Illus.). 96p. 1997. pap. 10.95 (*1-895569-15-X*, Pub. by Tamos Bks CN) Sterling.

***Terrific Tales to Tell: From the Storyknifing Tradition.** Valerie Marsh. LC 96-43080. 1997. pap. 12.95 (*0-917846-60-5*) Highsmith Pr.

Terrific Tappers. Bonnie Nemeth. Ed. by Wolf Nemeth & Debby Bouldin. (Timeless Tap Ser.: Level 4, Bk. 4, Vol. 4). (Illus.). 72p. (Orig.). (J). (gr. 4-7). 1996. pap. 12.00 (*1-888199-54-7*) Dance Innovators.

***Terrific Tennessee.** Kenneth Beck. LC 96-71358. 128p. (Orig.). 1996. pap. 6.95 (*1-887654-23-2*) Premium Pr TN.

Terrific Tomatoes: Simple Secrets for Glorious Gardens, Indoors & Out. Mimi Luebbermann. LC 93-6088. (Illus.). 96p. 1994. pap. 12.95 (*0-8118-0551-4*) Chronicle Bks.

Terrifying Love: Why Battered Women Kill & How Society Responds. Lenore E. Walker. LC 89-11228. 352p. 1990. reprint ed. pap. 13.50 (*0-06-092006-8*, PL) HarpC.

Terrifying News, Vol. 7. Hilda Stahl. (Elizabeth Gail Ser.: Vol. 7). 128p. (J). 1989. pap. 5.99 (*0-8423-0812-1*) Tyndale.

***Terrifying Steamboat Stories.** 2nd rev. ed. James Donahue. 209p. 1997. reprint ed. pap. 14.95 (*1-882376-36-6*) Thunder Bay Pr.

Terrifying Steamboat Stories: Seventy-Five True Tales of Shipwreck, Death & Disaster on the Great Lakes. James Donahue. 264p. 1991. pap. 15.95 (*1-878005-10-3*) Northmont Pub.

Terrifying Three: Uzi, Ingram, & Intratec Weapons Families. Duncan Long. (Illus.). 136p. 1989. pap. 20.00 (*0-87364-523-5*) Paladin Pr.

Terrigenous Clastic Depositional Systems: Applications to Fossil Fuel & Groundwater Resources. 2nd enl. rev. ed. William E. Galloway & David K. Hobday. LC 95-47132. (Illus.). 480p. 1996. 89.00 (*3-540-60232-1*) Spr-Verlag.

Terrigenous Clastic Depositional Systems: Applications to Fossil Fuel & Groundwater Resources. 2nd enl. rev. ed. William E. Galloway & David K. Hobday. LC 95-47132. 1996. 89.00 (*0-387-60232-1*) Spr-Verlag.

Terrigenous Elastic Depositional Systems. W. E. Galloway. (Illus.). 420p. 1989. 86.95 (*0-387-90827-7*) Spr-Verlag.

Terri's Winter. John F. Cullicott. (Orig.). (J). (gr. 1-3). 1995. pap. 3.00 (*0-89824-219-3*) Royal Fireworks.

***Territorial Acquisition, Disputes, And International Law.** Surya P. Sharma. LC 96-53036. (Developments in International Law Ser.). 1997. lib. bdg. 129.00 (*90-411-0362-7*, Pub. by M Nijhoff NE) Kluwer Ac.

Territorial Allocation by Imperial Rivalry: The Human Legacy in the Near East. LC 86-25013. (University of Chicago Department of Geography Research Paper Ser.: Vol. 221). 149p. 1987. reprint ed. pap. 42.50 (*0-608-02430-9*, 2063073) Bks Demand.

***Territorial Ambitions & the Gardens of Versailles.** Chandra Mukerji. (Cultural Social Studies). (Illus.). 300p. (C). 1997. text ed. 79.95 (*0-521-49675-6*) Cambridge U Pr.

***Territorial Ambitions & the Gardens of Versailles.** Chandra Mukerji. (Cultural Social Studies). (Illus.). 300p. (C). 1997. pap. write for info. (*0-521-59959-8*) Cambridge U Pr.

Territorial Army 1906-1940. Peter Dennis. (Royal Historical Society: Studies in History: No. 51). 282p. 1987. 63.00 (*0-86193-208-0*) Boydell & Brewer.

Territorial Basis of Government under the State Constitutions. Alfred Z. Reed. LC 68-56685. (Columbia University. Studies in the Social Sciences: No. 106). reprint ed. 39.50 (*0-404-51106-6*) AMS Pr.

Territorial Battalions 1859-1985. Ray Westlake & James D. Goldsmid. 256p. (C). 1991. 130.00 (*0-946771-68-5*, Pub. by Spellmount UK) St Mut.

Territorial Changes & International Conflict. Gary Goertz & Paul Diehl. 224p. (C). 1992. text ed. 59.95 (*0-415-07597-1*, A8257) Routledge.

Territorial Competition in an Integrating Europe. Ed. by Paul C. Cheshire & Ian R. Gordon. 336p. 1995. 68.95 (*1-85972-112-5*, Pub. by Avebury Pub UK) Ashgate Pub Co.

Territorial Dimension in Government: Understanding the United Kingdom. Richard Rose. LC 82-9680. 240p. reprint ed. pap. 68.40 (*0-8357-4827-8*, 2037764) Bks Demand.

Territorial Dimension of Judaism. W. D. Davies. LC 81-53. (Quantum Bks.: No. 23). 160p. 1982. 35.00 (*0-520-04331-6*) U CA Pr.

Territorial Disputes: Maps & Mapping Strategies in Contemporary Canadian Australian Fiction. Graham Huggan. LC 94-204015. (Theory - Culture Ser.). 198p. 1995. 40.00 (*0-8020-2923-X*) U of Toronto Pr.

Territorial Experience: Human Ecology As Symbolic Interaction. Ephraim G. Ericksen. LC 80-14861. (Illus.). 224p. 1980. pap. 63.90 (*0-7837-8954-8*, 2049667) Bks Demand.

Territorial Forces. Ngo Q. Truong. 154p. 1994. pap. text ed. 17.50 (*0-923135-28-6*) Dalley Bk Service.

Territorial Foundations of the Gulf States. Ed. by Richard Schofield. LC 93-44300. (SOAS-GRC Geopolitics Ser.). 1994. text ed. 55.00 (*0-312-12061-3*) St Martin.

***Territorial Games: Understanding & Ending Turf Wars at Work.** Annette Simmons. LC 97-25819. 208p. 1997. 22.95 (*0-8144-0383-2*) AMACOM.

Territorial Giants: Florida's Founding Fathers. Louise M. Porter & Charles B. Smith. 136p. 1990. 12.00 (*0-9636228-1-1*) St Joseph Hist.

Territorial History of Socorro, New Mexico. Bruce Ashcroft. (Southwestern Studies: No. 85). (Orig.). 1988. pap. 10.00 (*0-87404-169-4*) Tex Western.

Territorial Imperative: A Personal Inquiry into the Animal Origins of Property & Nations. Robert Ardrey. Ed. by Philip Turner. LC 96-45037. 400p. 1997. reprint ed. pap. 15.00 (*1-56836-144-0*, Kodansha Globe) Kodansha.

Territorial Imperative: Pluralism, Corporatism & Economic Crisis. Jeffrey J. Anderson. (Illus.). 262p. (C). 1992. text ed. 69.95 (*0-521-41378-8*) Cambridge U Pr.

***Territorial Indicators of Employment: Focusing on Rural Development.** OECD Staff. 169p. (Orig.). 1996. pap. 30.00 (*92-64-15276-8*, 04-96-08-1) OECD.

Territorial Management of Ethnic Conflict. John Coakley. LC 93-10948. (Regions & Regionalism Ser.: No. 2). 230p. 1993. text ed. 39.50 (*0-7146-3465-4*, Pub. by F Cass Pubs UK) Intl Spec Bk.

Territorial Masonry: The Story of Freemasonry & the Louisiana Purchase, 1804-1821. Ray V. Denslow. 300p. 1996. pap. 19.95 (*1-56459-551-X*) Kessinger Pub.

Territorial Papers of the United States, 26 vols. in 25. Ed. by Clarence E. Carter. LC 76-38840. reprint ed. Set. lib. bdg. 3,465.00 (*0-404-01450-X*) AMS Pr.

Territorial Papers of the United States. General Introduction to the Series., Vols. 1 & 2. Ed. by Clarence E. Carter. Bd. with Territory Northwest of the River Ohio, 1787-1803. reprint ed. 138.60 (*0-404-01451-8*) AMS Pr.

Territorial Rights of Peoples. Ed. by John R. Jacobson. LC 89-12457. (Studies in World Peace: Vol. 2). 352p. 1990. lib. bdg. 99.95 (*0-88946-588-6*) E Mellen.

Territorial Subdivisions & Boundaries of the Wampanoag, Massachusett, & Nauset Indians. Frank G. Speck. LC 76-43847. (MAI. Indian Notes & Monographs. Miscellaneous: No. 44). reprint ed. 39.50 (*0-404-15701-7*) AMS Pr.

Territorial Trademark Rights & the Antitrust Laws. Richard F. Dole, Jr. LC 66-63307. (Michigan Legal Publications). vi, 150p. 1985. reprint ed. lib. bdg. 39.50 (*0-89941-381-1*, 303510) W S Hein.

Territories & Possessions: Puerto Rico, U. S. Virgin Islands, Guam, American Samoa, Wake, Midway, & Other Islands, Micronesia. Thomas G. Aylesworth & Virginia L. Aylesworth. LC 94-45827. (J). 1995. pap. 8.95 (*0-7910-3431-3*); lib. bdg. 18.95 (*0-7910-3413-5*) Chelsea Hse.

Territories, Boundaries & Consciousness: The Changing Geographies of the Finnish-Russian Boundary. Anssi Paasi. (Studies in Political Geography). 300p. 1996. text ed. 85.00 (*0-471-96119-1*, Belhaven) Halsted Pr.

***Territories, Here & Elsewhere.** Judith McCombs. pap. 6.00 (*0-932412-10-6*) Mayapple Pr.

Territories of Grace: Cultural Change in the Seventeenth-Century Diocese of Grenoble. Keith P. Luria. LC 90-38259. (Studies on the History of Society & Culture: No. 11). (Illus.). 275p. 1991. 42.50 (*0-520-06810-6*) U CA Pr.

Territories of the Voice: Contemporary Stories by Irish Women Writers. Ed. by Louise Desalvo et al. LC 89-42597. 270p. 1991. pap. 15.00 (*0-8070-8325-9*) Beacon Pr.

Territorium Artis. Jasper Johns et al. (Illus.). 394p. 75.00 (*3-7757-0400-0*) Dist Art Pubs.

Territory & Function: The Evolution of Regional Planning. John Friedmann & Clyde Weaver. LC 79-64482. 240p. reprint ed. pap. 68.40 (*0-7837-4815-9*, 2044462) Bks Demand.

Territory & State Power in Latin America: The Peruvian Case. David Slater. LC 89-30608. (Illus.). 280p. 1989. text ed. 45.00 (*0-312-03073-8*) St Martin.

Territory in Bird Life. Henry E. Howard. Ed. by Keir B. Sterling. LC 77-84443. (Biologists & Their World Ser.). (Illus.). 1978. reprint ed. lib. bdg. 28.95 (*0-405-10696-3*) Ayer.

Territory Northwest of the River Ohio, 1787-1803. Ed. by Clarence E. Carter. (Territorial Papers of the United States: Vol. 3). reprint ed. 138.60 (*0-404-01453-4*) AMS Pr.

Territory Northwest of the River Ohio, 1787-1803 see Territorial Papers of the United States. General Introduction to the Series.

Territory of Alabama, 1817-1819. Ed. by Clarence E. Carter. (Territorial Papers of the United States: Vol. 18). reprint ed. 138.60 (*0-404-01468-2*) AMS Pr.

Territory of Arkansas, 1819-1825. Ed. by Clarence E. Carter. (Territorial Papers of the United States: Vol. 19). reprint ed. 138.60 (*0-404-01469-0*) AMS Pr.

Territory of Arkansas, 1825-1829. Ed. by Clarence E. Carter. (Territorial Papers of the United States: Vol. 20). reprint ed. 138.60 (*0-404-01470-4*) AMS Pr.

Territory of Arkansas, 1829-1836. Ed. by Clarence E. Carter. (Territorial Papers of the United States: Vol. 21). reprint ed. 138.60 (*0-404-01471-2*) AMS Pr.

Territory of Florida, 1821-1825. Ed. by Clarence E. Carter. (Territorial Papers of the United States: Vol. 22). reprint ed. 138.60 (*0-404-01472-0*) AMS Pr.

Territory of Florida, 1824-1828. Ed. by Clarence E. Carter. (Territorial Papers of the United States: Vol. 23). reprint ed. 138.60 (*0-404-01473-9*) AMS Pr.

Territory of Florida, 1828-1834. Ed. by Clarence E. Carter. (Territorial Papers of the United States: Vol. 24). reprint ed. 138.60 (*0-404-01474-7*) AMS Pr.

Territory of Florida, 1834-1839. Ed. by Clarence E. Carter. (Territorial Papers of the United States: Vol. 25). reprint ed. 138.60 (*0-404-01475-5*) AMS Pr.

Territory of Florida, 1839-1845. Ed. by Clarence E. Carter. (Territorial Papers of the United States: Vol. 26). reprint ed. 138.60 (*0-404-01476-3*) AMS Pr.

Territory of Illinois, 1809-1814. Ed. by Clarence E. Carter. (Territorial Papers of the United States: Vol. 16). reprint ed. 138.60 (*0-404-01466-6*) AMS Pr.

Territory of Illinois, 1814-1818. Ed. by Clarence E. Carter. (Territorial Papers of the United States: Vol. 17). reprint ed. 138.60 (*0-404-01467-4*) AMS Pr.

Territory of Indiana, 1800-1810. Ed. by Clarence E. Carter. (Territorial Papers of the United States: Vol. 7). reprint ed. 138.60 (*0-404-01457-7*) AMS Pr.

Territory of Indiana, 1810-1816. Ed. by Clarence E. Carter. (Territorial Papers of the United States: Vol. 8). reprint ed. 138.60 (*0-404-01458-5*) AMS Pr.

***Territory of Information.** Akio Kamio. LC 97-15576. (Pragmatics & Beyond NS Ser.: No. 48). 227p. 1997. lib. bdg. 68.00 (*1-55619-810-8*) Benjamins North Am.

Territory of Iowa (1838-1846) Donald L. Kimball & Jo A. Zimmerman. LC 90-85024. (Sesquicentennial History of Iowa Ser.). Orig. Title: A History of Iowa. (Illus.). 400p. 1990. 49.00 (*0-685-47411-9*); lib. bdg. 49.00 (*0-685-47412-7*) Trends & Events.

Territory of Language: Linguistics, Stylistics, & the Teaching of Composition. Ed. by Donald A. McQuade. LC 85-2080. 376p. (Orig.). (C). 1986. text ed. 29.95 (*0-8093-1217-4*); pap. text ed. 19.95 (*0-8093-1215-8*) S Ill U Pr.

Territory of Lies. Wolf Blitzer. 368p. 1990. mass mkt. 4.95 (0-06-100024-8, Harp PBks) HarpC.

Territory of Louisiana-Missouri, 1803-1806. Ed. by Clarence E. Carter. (Territorial Papers of the United States: Vol. 13). reprint ed. 138.60 (0-404-01463-1) AMS Pr.

Territory of Louisiana-Missouri, 1806-1814. Ed. by Clarence E. Carter. (Territorial Papers of the United States: Vol. 14). reprint ed. 138.60 (0-404-01464-X) AMS Pr.

Territory of Louisiana-Missouri, 1815-1821. Ed. by Clarence E. Carter. (Territorial Papers of the United States: Vol. 15). reprint ed. 138.60 (0-404-01465-8) AMS Pr.

Territory of Michigan, 1805-1820. Ed. by Clarence E. Carter. (Territorial Papers of the United States: Vol. 10). reprint ed. 138.60 (0-404-01460-7) AMS Pr.

Territory of Michigan, 1820-1829. Ed. by Clarence E. Carter. (Territorial Papers of the United States: Vol. 11). reprint ed. 138.60 (0-404-01461-5) AMS Pr.

Territory of Michigan, 1829-1837. Ed. by Clarence E. Carter. (Territorial Papers of the United States: Vol. 12). reprint ed. 138.60 (0-404-01462-3) AMS Pr.

Territory of Mississippi, 1798-1817. Ed. by Clarence E. Carter. (Territorial Papers of the United States: Vol. 5). reprint ed. 138.60 (0-404-01455-0) AMS Pr.

Territory of Mississippi, 1809-1817. Ed. by Clarence E. Carter. (Territorial Papers of the United States: Vol. 6). reprint ed. 138.60 (0-404-01456-9) AMS Pr.

Territory of Orleans, 1803-1812. Ed. by Clarence E. Carter. (Territorial Papers of the United States: Vol. 9). reprint ed. 138.60 (0-404-01459-3) AMS Pr.

Territory South of the River Ohio, 1790-1796. Ed. by Clarence E. Carter. (Territorial Papers of the United States: Vol. 4). reprint ed. 138.60 (0-404-01454-2) AMS Pr.

Territory, Time & State: The Archaeological Development of the Gubbio Basin. Ed. by Simon Stoddart & Caroline Malone. (Illus.). 208p. (C). 1994. text ed. 105.00 (0-521-35568-0) Cambridge U Pr.

Terrocotta. Margit Malmstrom. 1996. pap. text ed. 19.95 (0-8230-5321-0) Watsn-Guptill.

Terror. J. Ahern. 1989. pap. 2.95 (0-8217-2775-3) NAL-Dutton.

Terror. Jerry Ahern. (Survivalist Ser.: No. 14). 224p. 1987. mass mkt. 2.50 (0-8217-1972-6, Zebra Kensgtn) Kensgtn Pub Corp.

Terror. Marcus Van Heller. (Orig.). 1995. mass mkt. 5.95 (1-56333-247-7) Masquerade.

Terror: The Inside Story of the Terrorist Conspiracy in America. Yossef Bodansky. 1993. pap. 5.99 (1-56171-301-5, S P I Bks) Sure Seller.

***Terror Academy, Box set.** Nicholas Pine. 1994. pap. 14.00 (0-425-14597-2) Berkley Pub.

Terror Academy: Boy Crazy, No. 15. Nicholas Pine. 192p. (Orig.). (YA). 1995. mass mkt. 3.99 (0-425-14727-4) Berkley Pub.

Terror Academy No. 11: Summer School. Nicholas Pine. 192p. (Orig.). (J). (gr. 4 up). 1994. mass mkt. 3.50 (0-425-14338-4) Berkley Pub.

Terror Academy No. 12: Breaking Up. Nicholas Pine. 192p. 1994. mass mkt. 3.50 (0-425-14398-8) Berkley Pub.

Terror Academy No. 14: School Spirit. Nicholas Pine. 192p. (Orig.). 1995. mass mkt. 3.99 (0-425-14644-8) Berkley Pub.

Terror Academy Four: Spring Break. Nicholas Pine. 208p. (Orig.). 1993. mass mkt. 3.50 (0-425-13969-7) Berkley Pub.

Terror Academy Three: Sixteen Candles. Nicholas Pine. 192p. (Orig.). 1993. mass mkt. 3.50 (0-425-13841-0) Berkley Pub.

Terror Academy Two: Stalker. Nicholas Pine. 192p. (Orig.). 1993. mass mkt. 3.50 (0-425-13814-3) Berkley Pub.

Terror & Decorum: Poems, Nineteen Forty to Nineteen Forty-Eight. Peter R. Viereck. LC 78-178796. 110p. 1973. reprint ed. text ed. 45.00 (0-8371-6296-3, VTDE, Greenwood Pr) Greenwood.

Terror & Everyday Life: Singular Moments in the History of the Horror Film. Jonathan L. Crane. 235p. 1994. 39.95 (0-8039-5848-X) Sage.

Terror & Everyday Life: Singular Moments in the History of the Horror Film. Jonathan L. Crane. 1994. pap. 19.50 (0-8039-5849-8) Sage.

Terror & Progress U. S. S. R. Barrington Moore, Jr. LC 54-5995. (Russian Research Center Studies: No. 12). 278p. 1954. 29.00 (0-674-87450-1) HUP.

Terror & Taboo: The Follies, Fables & Faces of Terrorism. Joseba Zulaika & William A. Douglass. LC 95-46989. 304p. (C). 1996. pap. 18.95 (0-415-91759-X); text ed. 65.00 (0-415-91758-1) Routledge.

Terror & Tombstones Dingbats Book. Carole Marsh. (Carole Marsh Dingbats Bks.). (Illus.). (J). (gr. 3-12). 1994. pap. 19.95 (0-7933-5402-1); lib. bdg. 29.95 (0-7933-5401-3); disk 29.95 (0-7933-5403-X) Gallopade Pub Group.

Terror & Triumph: The Saga of Frank Carden. John Harllee. LC 90-50350. 328p. (Orig.). 1990. pap. 9.95 (0-923568-11-5) Wilderness Adventure Bks.

Terror & Urban Guerillas: A Study of Tactics & Documents. Ed. by Jay Mallin. LC 79-163842. 1983. 13.95 (0-87024-223-7) U of Miami Pr.

Terror at Forbidden Falls. Lee Roddy. LC 93-3379. (Ladd Family Adventure Ser.: Vol. 8). (J). 1993. pap. 5.99 (1-56179-137-7) Focus Family.

***Terror at High Tide Hardy Boys: Digest 145.** Dixon. (J). 1997. pap. 3.99 (0-671-00057-8) S&S Trade.

Terror at Sea: True Tales of Shipwrecks, Cannibalism, Pirates, Fire at Sea, & Other Dire Disasters in the 18th & 19th Centuries. Barbara D. Smith. 1995. write for info. (0-931675-04-9) Prov Pr Maine.

***Terror at the Atlanta Olympics.** 220p. 1996. pap. write for info. (1-57745-005-1) Artex Pub.

***Terror at the Atlanta Olympics.** Kenneth Alonso. 143p. 1996. 12.00 (1-890731-00-5) Allegro Pr.

Terror at the Hargrove Mansion. Johnny K. Gonzales. 1994. 11.95 (0-533-10986-8) Vantage.

***Terror at the Soo Locks: A Novel.** Ronald J. Lewis. LC 96-85424. 250p. (Orig.). Date not set. 12.95 (0-9642436-1-X) Agawa Pr.

Terror at the Zoo. Peg Kehret. 160p. (YA). (gr. 5 up). 1992. pap. 14.99 (0-525-65083-0, Cobblehill Bks) Dutton Child Bks.

Terror at the Zoo. Peg Kehret. 144p. (J). (gr. 4-7). 1993. pap. 3.99 incl. 5.25 hd (0-671-79394-2, Minstrel Bks) PB.

Terror at Twilight. Teddy Keller. 1984. pap. 1.75 (0-912963-02-6) Eldridge Pub.

***Terror Below! True Shark Stories.** Dana Del Prado. (All Aboard Reading Ser.). (Illus.). 48p. (Orig.). (J). (gr. 1-4). 1997. pap. 3.95 (0-448-41124-5, G&D) Putnam Pub Group.

***Terror Below! True Shark Stories.** Dana Del Prado. (Illus.). (J). 13.99 (0-614-28811-8, G&D) Putnam Pub Group.

Terror by Gaslight. Tim Kelly. 1980. pap. 5.25 (0-8222-1124-6) Dramatists Play.

Terror Cruise. Roger Elwood. 1991. pap. 5.99 (0-8499-3302-1) Word Pub.

Terror for Sale: Larry & Stretch. large type ed. Marshall Grover. (Western Library). 288p. 1995. pap. 15.99 (0-7089-7684-0, Linford) Ulverscroft.

Terror, Force, & States: The Path from Modernity. Rosemary H. O'Kane. LC 95-34568. 224p. 1996. 80.00 (1-85278-694-9) E Elgar.

Terror from the Extreme Right. Ed. by Tore Bjorgo. LC 95-21435. (Cass Series on Political Violence: Vol. 1). 200p. 1995. 39.50 (0-7146-4663-6, Pub. by F Cass Pubs UK); pap. 19.50 (0-7146-4196-0, Pub. by F Cass Pubs UK) Intl Spec Bk.

Terror from the Skies! Peter R. Chaston. (Illus.). 136p. (Orig.). (C). 1995. pap. 29.00 (0-9645172-1-3) Chaston Scient.

Terror in Branco Grande. Jerry B. Jenkins. LC 96-30714. (Global Air Troubleshooters Ser.: Bk. 2). 128p. 1996. pap. text ed. 4.99 (0-88070-971-5, Multnomah Bks) Multnomah Pubs.

Terror in St. Augustine. Lillian M. Wirth. LC 94-90166. (Illus.). 64p. (Orig.). (J). 1995. pap. 6.00 (1-56002-451-8, Univ Edtns) Aegina Pr.

***Terror in the French Revolution.** Hugh Gough. LC 97-19539. 1997. pap. 10.95 (0-312-17673-2) St Martin.

Terror in the Heartland: The Oklahoma City Bombing. John Hamilton. LC 95-23252. (Day of the Disaster Ser.). (J). 1995. lib. bdg. 12.98 (1-56239-524-6) Abdo & Dghtrs.

Terror in the Mirror. Jim Razzi. LC 89-5230. (Horror Show Ser.). 96p. (YA). (gr. 7 up). 1990. lib. bdg. 10.50 (0-8167-1684-6) Troll Communs.

Terror in the Mirror. Jim Razzi. LC 89-5230. (Horror Show Ser.). 96p. (YA). (gr. 7 up). 1996. pap. 2.95 (0-8167-1685-4) Troll Communs.

Terror in the Night: The Klan's Campaign Against Jews. Jack Nelson. (Illus.). 288p. 1996. reprint ed. pap. 16.00 (0-87805-907-5) U Pr of Miss.

Terror in the Night: The Klan's Campaign Against the Jews. Jack Nelson. LC 92-29539. (Illus.). 304p. 1993. 22.00 (0-671-69223-2) S&S Trade.

Terror in the Prisons. David J. Friar & Carl Weiss. LC 73-22667. 1974. 8.95 (0-672-51996-8, Bobbs) Macmillan.

Terror in the Skies: The Inside Story of the World's Worst Air Crashes. (Illus.). 256p. (YA). 1988. 16.95 (0-8065-1091-9, Citadel Pr) Carol Pub Group.

Terror in the Sky. Lee Roddy. (American Adventure Ser.: Vol. 6). 176p. (Orig.). (J). (gr. 3-8). 1991. pap. 5.99 (1-55661-096-3) Bethany Hse.

Terror in the Towers: Amazing Stories from the World Trade Center Disaster. Adrian Kerson. (Read It to Believe It! Ser.). 80p. (Orig.). (J). (gr. 2-7). 1993. lib. bdg. 9.99 (0-679-95332-9, Bullseye Bks) Random Bks Yng Read.

Terror in the Town. large type ed. Edward S. Aarons. (Linford Mystery Library). 400p. 1995. pap. 15.99 (0-7089-7712-X, Linford) Ulverscroft.

Terror in Tiny Town. A. G. Cascone. (Deadtime Stories Ser.). 128p. (J). (gr. 3-7). 1996. pap. 3.50 (0-8167-4135-2) Troll Communs.

***Terror in Tiny Town.** A. G. Cascone. (Deadtime Stories Ser.: Vol. 1). 1996. pap. 1.75 (0-8167-4258-8) Troll Communs.

Terror in Winnipeg. Eric Wilson. 112p. (J). (gr. 3-6). 1992. pap. text ed. 3.95 (0-7736-7369-5, Pub. by Stoddart Pubng CN) Genl Dist Srvs.

***Terror Intent.** (Executioner Ser.). 1997. mass mkt. 3.75 (0-373-64219-9, 1-64219-8, Wrldwide Lib) Harlequin Bks.

Terror of Earth. Tom La Farge. LC 96-24616. (Sun & Moon Classics Ser.: No. 136). 136p. (Orig.). 1996. pap. 11.95 (1-55713-261-5) Sun & Moon CA.

Terror of Tellico Plains: The Memoirs of Ray H. Jenkins. Ray H. Jenkins. LC 78-11623. (Illus.). 199p. 1978. 11.00 (0-941199-05-3) ETHS.

***Terror of the Coast: The 1863 Colonial War on the East Coast of Vancouver Island & the Gulf Islands.** Chris Arnett. 256p. 1997. pap. 14.95 (0-88922-318-1, Pub. by Talonbooks CN) Genl Dist Srvs.

Terror of the Machine: Technology, Work, Gender, & Ecology on the U. S.-Mexico Border. Devon S. Pena. LC 96-2352. (Border & Migration Studies). (Illus.). 412p. (Orig.). 1995. pap. 19.95 (0-292-76562-2); text ed. 45.00 (0-292-76561-4) U of Tex Pr.

***Terror of the Situation: Synchronicity's Scream: An Attempt to Be Human - the Story of a Seeker.** Robert M. Hoffstein. 124p. (Orig.). 1996. pap. write for info. (0-913002-04-6) Tsimtsum Hse.

Terror on Cemetery Hill: A Sarah Capshaw Mystery. Drew Stevenson. (Illus.). 112p. (J). (gr. 4-6). 1996. pap. 14.99 (0-525-65217-5) NAL-Dutton.

Terror on Kamikaze Run. Sigmund Brouwer. (Accidental Detective Ser.: Vol. 12). 132p. (Orig.). (J). (gr. 3-7). 1994. pap. 5.99 (1-56476-381-1, 6-3381, Victor Bks) Chariot Victor.

Terror on Tape: A Complete Guide to Over 2,000 Horror Movies on Video. James O'Neill. LC 94-25496. (Illus.). 400p. 1994. pap. 16.95 (0-8230-7612-1, Billboard Bks) Watsn-Guptill.

Terror on the Titanic. Raymond A. Montgomery. (Choose Your Own Adventure Ser.: No. 169). 128p. (J). 1996. pap. 3.50 (0-553-56622-9) Bantam.

Terror on Track. Franklin W. Dixon & Anne Greenberg. (Hardy Boys Casefiles Ser.: No. 57). 160p. (Orig.). (J). (gr. 6 up). pap. 3.99 (0-671-73093-2, Archway) PB.

Terror on Tulip Lane. Anne Schraff. Ed. by Carol Newell. (Standing Tall Mystery Ser.). 52p. (Orig.). (J). (gr. 5-9). 1995. pap. 4.95 (1-56254-157-9, SP1579) Saddleback Pubns.

Terror Out of Zion: The Fight for Israeli Independence. J. Bowyer Bell. LC 95-49992. 400p. 1996. pap. text ed. 24.95 (1-56000-870-9) Transaction Pubs.

Terror Runs Deep. Richard Posner. Ed. by Patricia MacDonald. 240p. (Orig.). (YA). (gr. 7 up). 1995. pap. 3.50 (0-671-88745-9, Archway) PB.

***Terror Spin.** 1997. mass mkt. 5.50 (0-373-61456-X, 1-61456-9, Wrldwide Lib) Harlequin Bks.

Terror That Comes in the Night: An Experience-Centered Study of Supernatural Assault Traditions. David J. Hufford. LC 82-40350. (Publications of the American Folklore Society, Bibliographical & Special Ser.). 352p. 1982. pap. 19.95 (0-8122-1305-X) U of Pa Pr.

Terror Tournament. large type ed. J. M. Flynn. 1990. pap. 15.99 (0-7089-6906-2, Trailtree Bookshop) Ulverscroft.

Terror Within. Ken Michael. 414p. 1996. pap. 12.95 (1-85756-178-3, Pub. by Janus Pubng UK) Paul & Co Pubs.

Terror/Counterterror. Lisa Smedman et al. Ed. & Illus. by Charles Ryan. 143p. (Orig.). 1996. pap. 15.00 (1-887990-04-6, 012-007) Chameleon Eclectic.

***Terrorism.** Ann Gaines. (Crime, Justice, & Punishment Ser.). (Illus.). (J). (gr. 3 up). 1997. lib. bdg. 19.95 (0-7910-4596-X) Chelsea Hse.

Terrorism. Connor Gearty. (International Library of Criminology, Criminal Justice & Penology). (Illus.). 608p. 1996. text ed. 145.95 (1-85521-548-9, Pub. by Dartmth Pub UK) Ashgate Pub Co.

Terrorism. John P. Holms & Tom J. Burke. 288p. 1994. mass mkt. 4.99 (0-7860-0057-0, Pinncle Kensgtn) Kensgtn Pub Corp.

Terrorism. Albert W. Parry. 1980. 24.50 (0-8149-0746-6) Random.

Terrorism. Philip Steele. LC 91-39803. (Past & Present Ser.). (Illus.). 48p. (YA). (gr. 6 up). 1992. lib. bdg. 12.95 (0-02-735401-6, Mac Bks Young Read) S&S Childrens.

Terrorism. Ed. by Michael Wallace. LC 78-19595. (Great Contemporary Issues Ser.). 1979. lib. bdg. 27.95 (0-405-11525-3) Ayer.

Terrorism, Vol. 11. J. L. Scherer. 1996. 45.00 (0-685-67189-5) J L Scherer.

Terrorism: A Bibliography. 52p. (Orig.). (C). 1993. pap. text ed. 30.00 (1-56806-865-4) DIANE Pub.

Terrorism: A Reference Handbook. Stephen E. Atkins. LC 92-28530. (Contemporary World Issues Ser.). 199p. 1992. lib. bdg. 39.50 (0-87436-670-4) ABC-CLIO.

Terrorism: An Annotated Bibliography. Susheela Bhan. (C). 1989. 44.00 (81-7022-256-7, Pub. by Concept II) S Asia.

Terrorism: An International Resource File: 1970-1979 Index. Ed. by Yonah Alexander. 389p. 1990. write for info. (0-8357-2117-5) Univ Microfilms.

Terrorism: An International Resource File: 1970-1989 Bibliography. Ed. by Yonah Alexander. 241p. 1991. write for info. (0-8357-2118-3) Univ Microfilms.

Terrorism: An International Resource File: 1980-1985 Index. Ed. by Yonah Alexander. 335p. 1989. 350.00 (0-685-46002-9) Univ Microfilms.

Terrorism: An International Resource File: 1986 Index. Ed. by Yonah Alexander. 332p. 1987. 195.00 (0-8357-0756-3) Univ Microfilms.

Terrorism: An International Resource File: 1987 Index. Ed. by Yonah Alexander. 177p. 1988. 195.00 (0-8357-0800-4) Univ Microfilms.

Terrorism: An International Resource File: 1988 Index. Ed. by Yonah Alexander. 316p. 1989. 195.00 (0-8357-0883-7) Univ Microfilms.

Terrorism: An International Resource File: 1989 Index. Ed. by Yonah Alexander. 158p. 1990. write for info. (0-8357-0948-5) Univ Microfilms.

Terrorism: An International Resource File: 1990 Index. Ed. by Yonah Alexander. 185p. 1991. write for info. (0-8357-2119-1) Univ Microfilms.

Terrorism: An Introduction. Jonathan R. White. LC 90-37132. 400p. (C). 1991. pap. 34.95 (0-534-13920-5) Wadsworth Pub.

***Terrorism: An Introduction.** 2nd ed. Jonathan R. White. (Criminal Justice Ser.). (C). 1997. pap. text ed. 31.95 (0-534-52699-3) Wadsworth Pub.

Terrorism: Avoidance & Survival. Chester L. Quarles. 224p. 1991. 44.95 (0-7506-9176-X) Buttrwrth-Heinemann.

Terrorism: British Perspective. Paul Wilkinson. (International Library of Terrorism: No. 1). 431p. 1994. 50.00 (0-8161-1999-6) G K Hall.

Terrorism: Documents of International & Local Control, 12 vols. Robert A. Friedlander. LC 78-26126. 1979. Set. lib. bdg. 830.00 (0-379-00690-1) Oceana.

***Terrorism: First Response, Leaders Guide.** John Ronan & Shirley Ayers. Ed. by Gordon Massingham. (Orig.). 1997. pap. write for info. (0-945790-12-0) Detrick Lawrence.

Terrorism: From Popular Struggle to Media Spectacle. Gerard Chaliand. 39.95 (0-86356-168-3, Pub. by Saqi Books UK); pap. 9.95 (0-86356-083-0, Pub. by Saqi Bks UK) Interlink Pub.

Terrorism: How the West Can Win. Ed. by Benjamin Netanyahu. 272p. 1987. mass mkt. 4.50 (0-380-70321-1) Avon.

Terrorism: Is It Revolutionary? Gil Green. 1970. pap. 0.50 (0-87898-054-7) New Outlook.

Terrorism: Its Goals, Its Targets, Its Methods - The Solutions. Michael Connor. 272p. 1987. text ed. 22.95 (0-87364-404-2) Paladin Pr.

Terrorism: Political Violence & Security of Nations. Attar Chand. 1988. 67.50 (81-212-0199-3, Pub. by Gian Publng Hse II) S Asia.

Terrorism: Pragmatic International Deterrence & Cooperation. Richard Allan. (East-West Occasional Papers). 710p. 1991. pap. text ed. 14.85 (0-8133-8132-0) Westview.

Terrorism: Report of the Senate Special Committee on Terrorism & the Public Safety (Canada) 151p. (Orig.). (C). 1995. pap. text ed. 40.00 (0-7881-2572-9) DIANE Pub.

Terrorism: Roots, Impact, Responses. Ed. by Lawrence C. Howard. LC 91-37252. 208p. 1992. text ed. 47.95 (0-275-94020-9, C4020, Praeger Pubs) Greenwood.

***Terrorism: Special Studies, 1992-1995: Third Supplement.** Blair D. Hydrick. LC 96-41846. (Special Studies). 1996. write for info. (1-55655-540-7) U Pubns Amer.

Terrorism: The Cuban Connection. Roger W. Fontaine. Ed. by Ray S. Cline. (International Book Series on Terrorism). (Illus.). 200p. (C). 1988. text ed. 42.00 (0-8448-1521-7, Crane Russak); pap. text ed. 21.00 (0-8448-1522-5, Crane Russak) Taylor & Francis.

Terrorism: The New Menace. Keith Greenberg. LC 93-23565. (Headliners Ser.). (Illus.). 64p. (J). (gr. 5-8). 1994. lib. bdg. 17.40 (1-56294-488-6) Millbrook Pr.

Terrorism: The Newest Face of Warfare. D. J. Hanle. (Terrorism Library Book Ser.). 272p. 1989. 27.00 (0-08-036742-9) Brasseys Inc.

Terrorism: The North Korean Connection. Joseph S. Bermundez, Jr. 240p. (C). 1990. text ed. 52.00 (0-8448-1609-4, Crane Russak); pap. text ed. 29.00 (0-8448-1610-8, Crane Russak) Taylor & Francis.

Terrorism: The PLO Connection. Yonah Alexander & Joshua Sinai. Ed. by Ray S. Cline. (Terrorism Ser.). (Illus.). 150p. (C). 1989. text ed. 62.00 (0-8448-1604-3, Crane Russak); pap. text ed. 31.00 (0-8448-1605-1, Crane Russak) Taylor & Francis.

Terrorism: The Solutions. 1991. lib. bdg. 64.75 (0-8490-4717-X) Gordon Pr.

Terrorism: The Soviet Connection. Ray S. Cline & Yonah Alexander. LC 83-23162. 165p. 1984. pap. 26.00 (0-8448-1471-7, Crane Russak) Taylor & Francis.

Terrorism: Threat & Response. Jill W. Brennan. 73p. (YA). (gr. 7-12). 1992. pap. 6.95 (1-57515-010-7) PPI Pubng.

Terrorism: Threat & Response. Eric Morris & Alan Hoe. LC 87-30696. 180p. 1988. text ed. 55.00 (0-312-01594-1) St Martin.

Terrorism: Why America Is the Target! Mohammad T. Mehdi. LC 87-62974. 128p. 1988. pap. 10.00 (0-911119-10-8) New World Press NY.

Terrorism: World under Siege. S. K. Ghosh. xxi, 678p. 1995. 59.00 (81-7024-665-2, Pub. by Ashish Pub Hse II) Nataraj Bks.

Terrorism & Collective Responsibility. Burleigh T. Wilkins. (Points of Conflict Ser.). 160p. (Orig.). (C). 1992. pap. 14.95 (0-415-04152-X, A6677) Routledge.

Terrorism & Collective Responsibility. Burleigh T. Wilkins. (Points of Conflict Ser.). 160p. (Orig.). (C). (gr. 13). 1992. text ed. 45.00 (0-415-07186-0, A6673) Routledge.

Terrorism & Communism: A Reply to Karl Kautsky. Leon Trotsky. LC 86-356. 238p. 1986. reprint ed. text ed. 59.75 (0-313-25212-2, TRTE, Greenwood Pr) Greenwood.

Terrorism & Democracy: Some Contemporary Cases. Ed. by Peter Janke. LC 91-31619. 256p. 1992. text ed. 69.95 (0-312-06822-0) St Martin.

***Terrorism & Drug Trafficking: Technologies for Detecting Explosives & Narcotics.** (Illus.). 28p. (Orig.). (C). 1996. pap. 25.00 (0-7881-3569-4) DIANE Pub.

Terrorism & Drug Trafficking in Europe in the 1990s. Ed. by Alison Jamieson. (Research Institute for the Study of Conflict & Terrorism Ser.). 300p. 1994. 59.95 (1-85521-532-2, Pub. by Dartmth Pub UK) Ashgate Pub Co.

Terrorism & Fear: Enter the Third Level. Gerald McNerney. LC 93-86071. 210p. (Orig.). 1994. pap. 10.95 (0-9637293-5-7) Storm Pub.

***Terrorism & Hostages in International Law: A Commentary on the Hostages Convention 1979.** 454p. 1993. text ed. 99.95 (0-521-46329-7) Cambridge U Pr.

Terrorism & Hostages in International Law: A Commentary on the Hostages Convention 1979. Ed. by Joseph J. Lambert. 454p. (C). 1990. 220.00 (0-949009-46-6, Pub. by Grotius Pubns UK) St Mut.

Terrorism & Insurgency in India: Study of the Human Element. Ashish Sonal. (C). 1994. 17.50 (1-897829-80-9, Pub. by Lancer India II) S Asia.

Terrorism & International Cooperation. Martha Crenshaw. 91p. 1989. pap. text ed. 14.85 (0-8133-7797-8) Westview.

***Terrorism & International Law.** Ed. by Rosalyn Higgins & Maurice Flory. 368p. (C). 1997. text ed. 99.95 (0-415-11606-6) Routledge.

An Asterisk (*) at the beginning of an entry indicates that the title is appearing in BIP for the first time.

***Terrorism & Local Law Enforcement: A Multidimensional Challenge for the Twenty-First Century.** Philip M. McVey. LC 97-7427. 1997. write for info. (0-398-06774-0); pap. write for info. (0-398-06775-9) C C Thomas.

Terrorism & Modern Drama. Ed. by John Orr & Dragan Klaic. 1991. text ed. 49.00 (0-7486-0173-2, Pub. by Edinburgh U Pr UK) Col U Pr.

Terrorism & Modern Drama. Ed. by John Orr & Dragan Klaic. 288p. 1992. pap. 24.95 (0-7486-0195-3, Pub. by Edinburgh U Pr UK) Col U Pr.

Terrorism & Political Destabilization, Vol. I. Veenaskay & Sahar Muakasa. LC 85-901540. 160p. 1986. 40.00 (0-944025-04-8) Advance Research.

Terrorism & Political Destabilization, Vol. II. Veenaskay & Sahar Muakasa. 200p. 1988. write for info. (0-944025-06-4) Advance Research.

Terrorism & Political Violence: An Egyptian Perspective. Ahmed G. Ezeldin. Tr. by Sanaa Ragheb from ARA. (Studies in Terrorism). 144p. 1987. text ed. 19.00 (0-942511-03-4); pap. text ed. 14.00 (0-942511-02-6) OICJ.

Terrorism & Political Violence: Limits & Possibilities of Legal Control. Henry H. Han. LC 92-11462. (Terrorism, Documents of International & Local Control, Second Ser.: Vol. 2). 452p. 1993. lib. bdg. 60.00 (0-379-00906-4) Oceana.

Terrorism & Politics. Ed. by Barry Rubin. 174p. 1991. text ed. 39.95 (0-312-06068-8) St Martin.

Terrorism & the American Response. Alvin H. Buckelew. LC 84-61050. 161p. (Orig.). (C). 1984. 12.95 (0-917919-00-9) MIRA.

Terrorism & the Liberal State. enl. rev. ed. Paul Wilkinson. LC 85-15303. 336p. (C). 1986. pap. 18.50 (0-8147-9207-3) NYU Pr.

Terrorism & the Liberal State. 2nd enl. rev. ed. Paul Wilkinson. LC 85-15303. 336p. (C). 1986. text ed. 36.00 (0-8147-9206-5) NYU Pr.

Terrorism & the Media. Ed. by David L. Paletz & Alex P. Schmid. (Illus.). 320p. (C). 1992. 44.00 (0-8039-4482-9); pap. 19.50 (0-8039-4483-7) Sage.

Terrorism & the Media: From the Iran Hostage Crisis to the Oklahoma City Bombing. Brigitte L. Nacos. 214p. 1996. pap. 16.50 (0-231-10015-9) Col U Pr.

Terrorism & the Media: From the Iran Hostage Crisis to the World Trade Center Bombing. Brigitte L. Nacos. LC 94-4602. 224p. 1994. 32.50 (0-231-10014-0) Col U Pr.

Terrorism & the News Media: A Selected, Annotated Bibiliography. A. Odasuo Alali & Gary W. Byrd. LC 94-2923. 214p. 1994. pap. 42.50 (0-89950-904-5) McFarland & Co.

Terrorism & the Red Brigades in Italy. Ed. by Raimondo Cantanzaro. 256p. 1991. text ed. 49.95 (0-312-05745-8) St Martin.

Terrorism & the State. William D. Perdue. LC 88-34029. 240p. 1989. text ed. 55.00 (0-275-93140-4, Greenwood Pr) Greenwood.

Terrorism, Drugs & Crime in Europe After 1992. Richard Clutterbuck. 256p. (C). (gr. 13). 1990. text ed. 59.95 (0-415-05443-5, A4724) Routledge.

Terrorism, Drugs, International Law & the Protection of Human Liberty. Christopher L. Blakesley. 349p. (C). 1992. lib. bdg. 75.00 (0-941320-62-6) Transnatl Pubs.

Terrorism, Guerrilla Warfare & Insurrections, Vol. 3, No. 4. Keith Hartley. (Studies in Defence Economics). 99p. 1992. pap. text ed. 87.00 (3-7186-5372-9, Harwood Acad Pubs) Gordon & Breach.

Terrorism, History & Facets in the World & India. N. S. Saksena. 1985. 18.50 (81-7017-201-2, Pub. by Abhinav II) S Asia.

Terrorism in Africa. Ed. by Martha Crenshaw. LC 93-38368. (International Library of Terrorism: No. 4). 535p. 1994. 50.00 (0-8161-7336-2) G K Hall.

Terrorism in America: Pipebombs & Pipedreams. Brent L. Smith. LC 93-6941. (SUNY Series in New Directions in Crime & Justice Studies). 256p. (C). 1994. text ed. 74.50 (0-7914-1759-X); pap. text ed. 24.95 (0-7914-1760-3) State U NY Pr.

Terrorism in an Unstable World. Richard Clutterbuck. LC 93-36839. 240p. (C). (gr. 13). 1994. 35.00 (0-415-10340-1, Routledge NY) Routledge.

Terrorism in Context. Ed. by Martha Crenshaw. LC 93-13785. 656p. 1995. 75.00 (0-271-01014-2); pap. 25.00 (0-271-01015-0) Pa St U Pr.

Terrorism in Europe: An International Comparative Legal Analysis. Antonio Vercher. 450p. 1992. 95.00 (0-19-825437-7) OUP.

Terrorism in India. Shaileshwar Nath. 350p. 1980. 25.95 (0-940500-27-2) Asia Bk Corp.

Terrorism in Ireland. Ed. by Yonah Alexander & Alan O'Day. LC 83-3106. 277p. 1984. text ed. 39.95 (0-312-79260-3) St Martin.

Terrorism in Northern Ireland. Alfred M. Lee. LC 83-80158. 253p. 1983. lib. bdg. 38.95 (0-930390-51-2) Gen Hall.

Terrorism in Punjab: Selected Articles & Speeches. Darshan S. Canandian. Ed. by Satyapal Dang. 1987. 12.50 (81-7050-040-0, Pub. by Patriot II) S Asia.

Terrorism in the U. S. (1993) (Illus.). 30p. (Orig.). (C). 1995. pap. text ed. 20.00 (0-7881-2381-5) DIANE Pub.

***Terrorism in the United States.** Frank McGuckin. LC 97-3423. (Reference Shelf Ser.). 1997. 15.00 (0-8242-0914-1) Wilson.

Terrorism in the United States & Europe, 1800-1959: An Annotated Bibliography. Michael Newton & Judy A. Newton. LC 88-21848. 522p. 1988. text ed. 85.00 (0-8240-5747-3) Garland.

Terrorism in the United States & the Potential Threat to Nuclear Facilities. Bruce R. Hoffman. LC 86-492. 1986. pap. 7.50 (0-8330-0694-0, R-3351-DOE) Rand Corp.

Terrorism in the 21st Century. Combs. LC 96-28270. 304p. (C). 1996. pap. text ed. 22.67 (0-13-490731-0) P-H.

***Terrorism in Vegas.** Wilson Whitenton. 176p. (Orig.). 1997. mass mkt. 4.99 (1-55197-611-0, Pub. by Comnwlth Pub CN) Partners Pubs Grp.

Terrorism in War: The Law of War Crimes. Howard S. Levie. LC 93-25148. (Terrorism Documents of International & Local Control Second Ser.). 721p. 1993. lib. bdg. 105.00 (0-379-20148-8) Oceana.

Terrorism, Interdisciplinary Perspectives. David A. Soskis. LC 82-24393. 200p. reprint ed. pap. 57.00 (0-8357-2804-8, 2036161) Bks Demand.

Terrorism, Justice & Social Values. Ed. by Creighton Peden & Yeager Hudson. LC 90-24911. (Studies in Social & Political Theory: Vol. 11). 456p. 1991. lib. bdg. 109.95 (0-88946-739-0) E Mellen.

Terrorism, Legitimacy, & Power: The Consequences of Political Violence: Essays. Ed. by Martha Crenshaw. LC 82-23756. 1983. reprint ed. pap. 49.60 (0-608-02317-5, 2062958) Bks Demand.

Terrorism Nineteen Eighty to Nineteen Eighty-Seven: A Selectively Annotated Bibliography. Ed. by Edward F. Mickolus & Peter A. Flemming. LC 87-32275. (Bibliographies & Indexes in Law & Political Science Ser.: No. 8). 328p. 1988. text ed. 95.00 (0-313-26248-9, MKT/) Greenwood.

Terrorism, Politics, & Law: The Achille Lauro Affair. Antonio Cassese. LC 89-3971. 174p. 1989. reprint ed. pap. 49.60 (0-7837-9494-0, 2060238) Bks Demand.

Terrorism, Protest & Power. Martin Warner & Roger Crisp. 208p. 1990. text ed. 75.00 (1-85278-202-1) E Elgar.

Terrorism Research & Public Policy. Ed. by Clark McCauley. 168p. 1991. 35.00 (0-7146-3429-8, Pub. by F Cass Pubs UK) Intl Spec Bk.

Terrorism, Security, & Nationality: An Introductory Study in Applied Political Philosophy. Paul Gilbert. LC 93-48161. 224p. (C). (gr. 13). 1994. text ed. 59.95 (0-415-09175-6, B4402, Routledge NY) Routledge.

Terrorism, Security, & Nationality: An Introductory Study in Applied Political Philosophy. Paul Gilbert. LC 93-48161. 224p. (C). 1995. pap. 17.95 (0-415-09176-4, B4406, Routledge NY) Routledge.

Terrorism, the Media, & the Law. Ed. by Abraham H. Miller. LC 82-11020. 232p. 1982. lib. bdg. 30.00 (0-941320-04-9) Transnatl Pubs.

Terrorism, the Middle East & You. Joe E. Pierce. 132p. 1986. pap. 5.50 (0-913244-65-1) Hapi Pr.

Terrorism, U. S. Strategy & Reagan Policies. Marc A. Celmer. LC 86-33647. (Symposium Papers IX: Vol. 22). 142p. 1987. text ed. 47.95 (0-313-25632-2, Greenwood Pr) Greenwood.

Terrorism, Violence & Human Destruction: Causes, Effects, & Control Measures. N. P. Rao. (C). 1992. 15.00 (81-7041-568-3, Pub. by Anmol II) S Asia.

***Terrorism with Chemical & Biological Weapons: Calibrating the Risks & Responses.** Ed. by Brad Roberts. 140p. (Orig.). 1997. pap. 12.95 (0-9656168-0-0) Chemical & Biological.

Terrorism, 1988-1991: A Chronology of Events & a Selectively Annotated Bibliography. Edward F. Mickolus. LC 92-46525. (Bibliographies & Indexes in Military Studies: No. 6). 928p. 1993. text ed. 135.00 (0-313-28970-0, GR8970, Greenwood Pr) Greenwood.

***Terrorism, 1992-1995: A Chronology of Events & a Selectively Annotated Bibliography.** Edward F. Mickolus & Susan L. Simmons. LC 97-9149. (Bibliographies & Indexes in Military Studies: vOL. 9). 980p. 1997. text ed. 145.00 (0-313-30468-8, Greenwood Pr) Greenwood.

Terrorism's Laboratory: The Case of Northern Ireland. Ed. by Alan O'Day. LC 95-3902. 1995. 59.95 (1-85521-457-1, Pub. by Dartmth Pub UK) Ashgate Pub Co.

***Terrorist.** Caroline B. Cooney. LC 96-42352. (J). 1997. 15.95 (0-590-22853-6) Scholastic Inc.

Terrorist Attacks: A Protective Service Guide for Executives, Bodyguards & Policemen. R. P. Siljander. (Illus.). 342p. 1980. 52.95 (0-398-04028-1); pap. 36.95 (0-398-06428-8) C C Thomas.

Terrorist Group Profiles. (Illus.). 55p. (C). 1993. pap. text ed. 25.00 (1-56806-864-6) DIANE Pub.

Terrorist Group Profiles. 1993. lib. bdg. 256.75 (0-8490-8929-8) Gordon Pr.

Terrorist Handbook & Manual. 1991. lib. bdg. 79.95 (0-8490-4142-2) Gordon Pr.

Terrorist Killers. Geoffrey Metcalf. (Critic's Choice Paperbacks Ser.). 1988. pap. 3.95 (1-55547-269-9, Univ Books) Carol Pub Group.

Terrorist Lives. Maxwell Taylor. 256p. 1994. 30.00 (0-08-041327-7, Pub. by Brasseys UK) Brasseys Inc.

Terrorist or Freedom Fighter? The Cost of Confusion. Ed. by William McGurn. (C). 1990. 35.00 (0-907967-83-3, Pub. by Inst Euro Def & Strat UK) St Mut.

***Terrorist Prince.** Raja Anwar. Date not set. 25.00 (1-85984-886-9) Routledge Chapman & Hall.

Terrorist Propaganda. Joanne Wright. 272p. 1991. text ed. 49.95 (0-312-04761-4) St Martin.

Terrorist Spectaculars: Should TV Coverage Be Curbed? - A Twentieth Century Fund Paper. Michael J. O'Neill. 109p. (Orig.). (C). 1986. pap. text ed. 7.50 (0-87078-202-9) TCFP-PPP.

Terrorist Trap: America's Experience with Terrorism. Jeffrey D. Simon. LC 94-5161. 484p. 1994. 29.95 (0-253-35249-5) Ind U Pr.

Terrorists. Randolph Harris. 176p. (Orig.). (J). 1987. mass mkt. 2.50 (0-87067-283-5) Holloway.

Terrorists: Their Weapons, Leaders & Tactics. Christopher Dobson & Ronald Payne. LC 82-1438. (Illus.). 284p. reprint ed. pap. 81.00 (0-7837-5347-0, 2045090) Bks Demand.

Terrorists & Social Democrats: The Russian Revolutionary Movement under Alexander III. Norman M. Naimark. (Russian Research Center Studies: No. 82). 328p. 1983. 37.00 (0-674-87464-1) HUP.

Terrorists' Madonna. Elyssa Jordan. 400p. (Orig.). 1993. pap. 5.50 (1-56171-155-1, S P I Bks) Sure Seller.

Terrormazia. Anna Nilsen. LC 95-67535. (Candlewick Gamebooks Ser.). (Illus.). 32p. (J). (gr. 1-4). 1996. reprint ed. pap. 7.99 (1-56402-865-8) Candlewick Pr.

Terrormazia: A Hole New Kind of Maze Game. Anna Nilsen. LC 95-67535. (Illus.). (J). (gr. k up). 1995. 12.95 (1-56402-461-X) Candlewick Pr.

Terrors & Experts. Adam Phillips. LC 95-38506. 110p. 1996. 19.95 (0-674-87479-X) HUP.

***Terrors & Experts.** Adam Phillips. 1997. pap. text ed. 12.00 (0-674-87480-3) HUP.

Terrors of Ice & Darkness. Christopher Ransmayr. Tr. by John E. Woods from GER. 240p. 1996. reprint ed. pap. 12.00 (0-8021-3459-9, Grove) Grove-Atltic.

Terrors of Paradise. Paul Quenon. 54p. 1996. pap. text ed. 14.95 (0-88753-278-0, Pub. by Black Moss Pr CN) Firefly Bks Ltd.

Terrors of the Law: Being the Portraits of Three Lawyers "Bloody Jeffreys", "The Bluidy Advocate MacKenzie" & the Original Weir of Hermiston. Francis Watt. 129p. 1985. reprint ed. 20.00 (0-8377-1338-2) Rothman.

Terrors of Uncertainty: The Cultural Contexts of Horror Fiction. Joseph Grixti. 224p. 1989. 45.00 (0-415-02597-4, A3452); pap. text ed. 14.95 (0-415-02598-2, A3782) Routledge.

***Terry.** Date not set. pap. 12.95 (0-452-27833-3, Plume) NAL-Dutton.

***Terry.** George McGovern. LC 97-11886. 1997. pap. 11.95 (0-452-27823-6, Plume) NAL-Dutton.

Terry: My Daughter's Life & Death Struggle with Alcoholism. George McGovern. (Illus.). 208p. 1996. 21.00 (0-679-44797-0, Villard Bks) Random.

Terry Adkins. Steven High & Anne Morgan. 1991. 5.00 (0-935519-12-2) Anderson Gal.

Terry Allen: A Simple Story (Juarez) Terry Allen. LC 92-85535. (Illus.). 80p. (Orig.). 1991. pap. 20.00 (1-881390-02-0) OSU Wexner Ctr.

Terry Allen: Youth in Asia. Craig Adcock et al. Ed. by Nancy H. Margolis. (Illus.). 112p. (Orig.). (C). 1992. pap. 22.00 (0-9611560-0-7) SEC Contemp Art.

Terry & the Bully. Mike Rucker. LC 94-90111. (Illus.). 64p. (Orig.). (J). 1995. pap. 3.95 (1-56002-449-6, Univ Edtns) Aegina Pr.

Terry Black: Fiery Vision Bright. Terry Black. Ed. by Laurel Gasque & Dal Schindell. 36p. (Orig.). (C). 1995. reprint ed. pap. write for info. (1-57383-044-5) Regent College.

Terry Bradshaw. G. S. Prentzas. LC 94-5780. (Football Legends Ser.). (Illus.). 64p. (J). (gr. 3 up). 1994. lib. bdg. 15.95 (0-7910-2451-2) Chelsea Hse.

Terry Bradshaw Fantasy Football Journal, 1996 Edition. Terry Bradshaw. 250p. (Orig.). 1996. pap. 9.95 (0-9636895-5-X) Fantasy Spts.

***Terry Bradshaw Fantasy Football Journal '97.** Larry Weisman & Terry Bradshaw. 350p. (Orig.). 1997. pap. 11.95 (0-9636895-7-6) Fantasy Spts.

Terry Clock Company, 1875. 1981. pap. 5.00 (0-930476-10-7) Am Clock & Watch.

Terry, Come Home: The Story of a Pastor & the Family of Terry Anderson. Thomas W. Vickers. LC 87-38064. 158p. 1988. reprint ed. pap. 45.10 (0-608-00223-2, 2061018) Bks Demand.

Terry Farrell. Images Publ. Group Staff. (Master Architect Staff). (Illus.). 256p. 1994. 69.95 (1-875498-16-8, Pub. by Images Publ AT) Bks Nippan.

Terry Farrell. Ed. by Andreas Papadakis. (Architectural Monographs: No. 9). (Illus.). 128p. 1984. pap. 30.00 (0-85670-842-9) Academy Ed UK.

Terry Farrell: An Academy Architectural Monograph. Ed. by Frank Russell. (Illus.). 120p. 1985. pap. 24.95 (0-312-79286-7) St Martin.

Terry Farrell: Urban Design. Terry Farrell. (Illus.). 312p. 1993. 80.00 (1-85490-125-7) Academy Ed UK.

Terry Fox: Articulations. Moore College of Arts & Design Staff. (Labyrinth - Text Works). (Illus.). 46p. 1992. pap. 15.00 (0-685-67186-0) Feldman Fine Arts.

Terry Frost. David Lewis. Ed. by Elizabeth Knowles. (Illus.). 252p. 1994. 75.00 (1-85928-041-2, Pub. by Scolar Pr UK) Ashgate Pub Co.

Terry Johnston Boxed Set #1. Johnston. 1993. pap. 17.97 (0-312-95110-8) Tor Bks.

Terry Johnston Boxed Set #2. Johnston. 1993. pap. write for info. (0-312-95174-4) St Martin.

Terry Jones' Fairy Tales. Terry Jones. (Storybooks Ser.). (Illus.). 128p. (J). (ps up). 1986. pap. 8.95 (0-14-031642-6, Puffin) Puffin Bks.

Terry Jones' Fantastic Stories. Terry Jones. (Illus.). 128p. (J). 1993. pap. 16.99 (0-670-84899-9) Viking Child Bks.

Terry LaGerould's Pasteboard Presentations. Wayne Whiting & Terry LaGerould. (Illus.). 122p. 1992. 22.00 (0-945296-06-1) Hermetic Pr.

Terry Lee. Sally Jaster. LC 86-70629. 320p. (Orig.). 1987. pap. 11.95 (0-916383-09-1) Aegina Pr.

Terry Letters: The Letters of General Alfred Howe Terry to His Sisters During the Indian War of 1876. James Willert. (Illus.). 78p. 1980. 25.00 (0-930798-03-1) J Willert.

Terry Madewell's Catfishing from A to Z: A Manual of Modern Catfishing Techniques. Terry Madewell. Ed. by Jacki Reeser. 52p. 1993. 8.00 (0-9615455-4-2) J T Pub Co.

Terry on the Fence. Bernard Ashley. LC 76-39898. (Illus.). (J). (gr. 5-9). 1977. 24.95 (0-87599-222-6) S G Phillips.

Terry Pratchett's Discworld: The Official Strategy Guide. PCS Staff. 1995. pap. text ed. 19.95 (0-7615-0218-1) Prima Pub.

Terry Rosenberg: Drawings, Inside the Dance. Jeffrey Hogrefe. (Illus.). 64p. (Orig.). (C). 1995. pap. 18.00 (0-9643821-0-5) T Rosenberg.

Terry Savage Talks Money: The Common-Sence Guide to Money Matters. Terry Savage. LC 91-55109. 416p. 1993. pap. 13.00 (0-88730-623-3) HarpC.

Terry Savage Talks Money: The Common-Sense Guide to Money Matters. Terry Savage. 400p. 1990. 22.95 (0-7931-0010-0, 5608-2601) Dearborn Finan.

Terry Savage's New Money Strategies for the '90s: Simple Steps to Creating Wealth & Building Financial Security. Terry Savage. LC 92-53340. (Illus.). 576p. 1994. pap. 14.00 (0-88730-668-3) Harper Busn.

Terry Texas Ranger Trilogy: Reminiscences of the Terry Rangers, Terry's Texas Rangers, & the Diary of Ephraim Shelby Dodd. J. K. Blackburn et al. LC 96-22469. (Illus.). 256p. 1996. 24.95 (1-880510-45-6); pap. 17.95 (1-880510-46-4) State House Pr.

Terry Texas Ranger Trilogy: Reminiscences of the Terry Rangers, Terry's Texas Rangers, & the Diary of Ephraim Shelby Dodd. limited ed. J. K. Blackburn et al. LC 96-22469. (Illus.). 256p. 1996. 60.00 (1-880510-47-2) State House Pr.

Terry the Athlete. Mike Rucker. LC 95-90136. (Terry the Tractor Ser.: No. 3). (Illus.). 64p. (Orig.). (J). (gr. 3-4). 1996. pap. 3.95 (1-56002-560-3, Univ Edtns) Aegina Pr.

Terry the Tractor. Mike Rucker. LC 93-94079. (Illus.). 64p. (J). (gr. k up). 1994. pap. 3.95 (1-56002-382-1, AndeLear Pub) Aegina Pr.

Terry-Thomas: Tells Tales. Terry Thomas & Terry Daum. (Illus.). 213p. 1992. 29.95 (0-86051-662-8, Robson-Parkwest) Parkwest Pubns.

Terry-Thomas: Tells Tales, an Autobiography. Terry Daum. 1993. pap. 11.95 (0-86051-795-0, Pub. by Robson UK) Parkwest Pubns.

Terry-Thomas Tells Tales: An Autobiography. large type ed. Terry Thomas & Terry Daum. 279p. 1991. 23.95 (1-85089-501-5, Pub. by ISIS UK) Transaction Pubs.

***Terry Toots.** Bernadette Gervais & Francisco Pittau. LC 96-27141. (Illus.). (J). (ps-1). 1997. 7.95 (0-8118-1637-0) Chronicle Bks.

Terry Trucco's Where to Find It: Essential Guide Hard to Locate Goods A to Z. Terry Trucco. 288p. 1996. pap. 14.00 (0-684-80165-5, Touchstone Bks) S&S Trade.

Terry Waite. Trevor Barnes. (Men of Faith Ser.). 160p. (Orig.). 1992. mass mkt. 4.99 (1-55661-303-2) Bethany Hse.

Terry Winters. Lisa Phillips. (Illus.). 204p. 1992. 75.00 (0-8109-3963-0) Abrams.

Terry's Temper: A Program about Anger for Students in Grades One Through Four. Timothy G. Ludwig. LC 94-77205. 316p. (J). (gr. 1-4). 1991. 4.95 (1-988406-32-3) Mar Co Prods.

Terry's Universe. Ed. by Beth Meacham. 288p. 1989. pap. 3.95 (0-8125-4592-3) Tor Bks.

Terse Verse - Jest for Fun. Al Joneson. (Illus.). 90p. (Orig.). 1984. pap. 3.75 (0-9613668-0-X) OAvel Pr.

Tersery Versery: World's First Individual Collection of Double Dactyls. Anthony Harrington. (Illus.). 120p. (Orig.). 1982. pap. 5.95 (0-943764-00-9) HAPCO.

***Tert-Butanol Health & Safety Guide.** WHO Staff. (Health & Safety Guides: No. 7). 38p. 1987. 5.00 (92-4-154565-8) World Health.

Tertiary & Cretaceous Coals in the Rocky Mountains Region. Ed. by Romeo M. Flores. (IGC Field Trip Guidebooks Ser.). 64p. 1989. 21.00 (0-87590-584-6, T132) Am Geophysical.

Tertiary & Pleistocene Coralline Algae from Lau, Fiji. H. H. Johnson & B. J. Ferris. (BMB Ser.). 1950. pap. 25.00 (0-527-02309-4) Periodicals Srv.

Tertiary Basins of Spain: The Stratigraphic Record of Crustal Kinematics. Ed. by Peter F. Friend & Cristino J. Dabrio. (World & Regional Geology Ser.: No. 6). (Illus.). 450p. (C). 1996. text ed. 200.00 (0-521-46171-5) Cambridge U Pr.

Tertiary Bauxite Belt on Tectonic Uolift Areas in the Serra da Mantiqueira, South-East Brazil. I. Veleton et al. (Contributions to Sedimentology Ser.: No. 17). (Illus.). 101p. 1991. pap. text ed. 47.00 (3-510-57017-0, Pub. by E Schweizerbartsche GW) Lubrecht & Cramer.

Tertiary College: Assuring Our Future. David Terry. 172p. 1987. 85.00 (0-335-10286-7, Open Univ Pr); pap. 32.00 (0-335-10285-9, Open Univ Pr) Taylor & Francis.

Tertiary Record of Rodents in North America. W. Korth. (Topics in Geobiology Ser.: Vol. 12). (Illus.). 230p. (C). 1994. 85.00 (0-306-44696-0) Plenum.

Tertiary Spiders & Opilionids of North America. Alexander Petrunkevitch. (Connecticut Academy of Arts & Sciences Ser., Trans.: Vol. 25). 1922. pap. 75.00 (0-685-22826-6) Elliots Bks.

Tertiary Stratigraphy & Paleontology, Chesapeake Bay Region, Virginia & Maryland, No. T216. Ed. by Ward. (IGC Field Trip Guidebooks Ser.). 72p. 1989. write for info. (0-87590-660-5) Am Geophysical.

Tertiary Tectonics & Sedimentation in the Cuyama Basin, San Luis Obispo, Santa Barbara & Ventura Counties, California. Ed. by W. J. Bazeley. (Illus.). 173p. (Orig.). 1988. pap. 14.00 (1-878861-10-7) Pac Section SEPM.

***Tertio Millennio Adveniente.** Pope John Paul, II. 62p. pap. 2.50 (0-8198-7381-0) Pauline Bks.

Tertius & Pliny. B. Frankel. Ed. by E. Clark. (J). 1992. 13.95 (0-15-200604-4, Gulliver Bks) HarBrace.

Tertulia. Davis. (C). 1994. teacher ed., pap. text ed. 33.75 (0-03-012968-0) HB Coll Pubs.

Tertulia: Conversational Skills. Davis. (C). 1995. pap. 37.00 (0-03-098568-4) HB Coll Pubs.

T

Tertullian: Apologetical Works, & Minucius Felix: Octavius. Tertullian. Tr. by Rudolph Arbesmann et al. (Fathers of the Church Ser.: Vol. 10). 450p. 1985. reprint ed. pap. 128.30 (*0-7837-9141-0*, 2049941) Bks Demand.
Tertullian & the Church. David Rankin. 270p. (C). 1995. text ed. 54.95 (*0-521-48067-1*) Cambridge U Pr.
***Tertullian, First Theologian of the West.** Eric Osborn. 304p. (C). 1997. text ed. 59.95 (*0-521-59035-3*) Cambridge U Pr.
Tertullian the Puritan & His Influences. Cahal B. Daly. 240p. 1993. text ed. 45.00 (*1-85182-110-4*, Pub. by Irish Acad Pr IE) Intl Spec Bk.
Tertullian, the Treatise Against Hermogenes. Ed. by W. J. Burghardt et al. LC 56-13257. (Ancient Christian Writers Ser.: No. 24). 179p. 1956. 14.95 (*0-8091-0148-3*) Paulist Pr.
Tertullian, Treatise on Marriage & Remarriage: To His Wife, an Exhortation to Chastity Monogamy. Ed. by W. J. Burghardt et al. LC 78-62462. (Ancient Christian Writers Ser.: No. 13). 103p. 1951. 14.95 (*0-8091-0149-1*) Paulist Pr.
Tertullian, Treatise on Penance: On Penitence & on Purity. Ed. by W. J. Burghardt et al. LC 58-10746. (Ancient Christian Writers Ser.: No. 28). 138p. 1959. 21.95 (*0-8091-0150-5*) Paulist Pr.
Tertullianus - Concordance Verbale du "De Corona" de Tertullien. Ed. by Henri Quellet. (Alpha-Omega, Reihe A Ser.: Vol. XXIII). 434p. (GER.). 1975. write for info. (*3-487-05763-8*) G Olms Pubs.
Tertullianus - Concordance Verbale du de Cultu Feminarum de Tertullien. Henri Quellet. (Alpha-Omega, Reihe A Ser.: Vol. LX). iv, 382p. (GER.). 1986. write for info. (*3-487-07769-8*) G Olms Pubs.
Tertullianus - Concordance Verbale du "De Exhortatione Castitatis" de Tertullien. Henri Quelle. (Alpha-Omega, Reihe A Ser.: Bd. CXXXI). iv, 226p. (GER.). 1993. write for info. (*3-487-09501-7*) G Olms Pubs.
Tertullianus - Concordance Verbale du "De Patientia" de Tertullien. Ed. by Henri Quellet. (Alpha-Omega, Reihe A Ser.: Vol. XCVII). iv, 346p. (GER.). 1988. write for info. (*3-487-07994-1*) G Olms Pubs.
Tertullianus, De Idololatria: Critical Text, Translation & Commentary. J. Van Winden & Jan H. Waszink. (Supplements to Vigiliae Christianae Ser.: Suppl. 1). xii, 317p. 1987. 105.50 (*90-04-08105-4*) E J Brill.
Tertullien: Etude sur les sentiments a l'egard de l'empire et de la societe civile. Charles A. Guinebert. LC 82-45819. reprint ed. 57.50 (*0-404-62386-7*) AMS Pr.
Terzaghi Lectures: 1963-1972. Karl Terzaghi. (Terzaghi Lecture Ser.: Nos. 1-9). (Illus.). 429p. reprint ed. pap. 122.30 (*0-317-09410-6*, 2017761) Bks Demand.
Terzaghi Lectures, Nineteen Seventy-Four to Nineteen Eighty-Two. (Geotechnical Special Publications: No. 1). 435p. 1986. 42.00 (*0-87262-532-X*) Am Soc Civil Eng.
T'Es le Meilleur, Charlie Brown. Charles M. Schulz. (Peanuts Ser.). (FRE.). (J). 1985. 4.95 (*0-8288-4521-2*) Fr & Eur.
Tesalonicenses: El Senor Viene. Juan C. Cevallos. 160p. (SPA.). 1991. pap. 7.50 (*0-311-04361-5*) Casa Bautista.
***Tesauro de Datos Historicos, Vol. II.** Adolfo De Hostos. 978p. (SPA.). Date not set. 30.00 (*0-8477-0896-9*) U of PR Pr.
Tesauro de Datos Historicos, Vol. 4. Adolfo De Hostos. 976p. (SPA.). 1994. 30.00 (*0-8477-0199-9*) U of PR Pr.
Tesauro de Datos Historicos, Vol. 5. Adolfo De Hostos. 832p. (SPA.). 1995. 30.00 (*0-8477-0890-X*) U of PR Pr.
Tesauro de Datos Historicos de Puerto Rico, Vol. I. Adolfo De Hostos. 932p. (SPA.). 1990. 30.00 (*0-8477-0889-6*) U of PR Pr.
Tesauro de Datos Historicos-Oficina del Indice Historico de PR, Vol. II. Adolfo De Hostos. 1992. 30.00 (*0-8477-0897-7*) U of PR Pr.
***Tesauro de Terminos para Ciencias Acuaticas y Pesqueras.** 209p. (SPA.). 1985. 30.00 (*92-5-302233-7*, Pub. by FAO IT) Bernan Associates.
Tesaurus: Manufacturing Engineering Terms. Society of Manufacturing Engineers Staff. 70p. 1984. reprint ed. pap. 25.00 (*0-7837-9727-3*, 2060458) Bks Demand.
Teshuvah: A Guide for the Newly Observant Jew. Adin Steinsaltz. LC 96-24952. 192p. 1996. 25.00 (*0-7657-5950-0*) Aronson.
Tesio Myth. Franco Varola. 310p. 1990. 60.00 (*0-85131-388-4*, Pub. by J A Allen & Co UK) St Mut.
Tesios As I Knew Them. Mario Incisa della Rochetta. 113p. 1990. 32.00 (*0-85131-313-2*, Pub. by J A Allen & Co UK) St Mut.
Tesla. Tad Wise. LC 94-4024. 1994. 21.95 (*1-878685-36-8*) Turner Pub GA.
Tesla. Tad Wise. 1995. pap. 9.95 (*1-57036-163-0*) Turner Pub GA.
Tesla: Complete Patents. Ed. by John T. Ratzlaff. (Nikola Tesla Ser.). 1986. lib. bdg. 125.00 (*0-8490-3838-3*) Gordon Pr.
Tesla: Man Out of Time. Margaret Cheney. (Illus.). 336p. 1983. mass mkt. 6.50 (*0-440-39077-X*, LE) Dell.
Tesla: Time's Makin' Changes. 64p. 1995. pap. 19.95 (*0-89524-970-7*) Cherry Lane.
Tesla - Bust a Nut. 131p. (Orig.). (YA). 1994. pap. text ed. 19.95 (*0-89524-872-7*, 02501245) Cherry Lane.
Tesla - Five Man Acoustical Jam: Play-It-Like-It-Is-Guitar. 1994. pap. 19.95 (*0-89524-823-9*) Cherry Lane.
Tesla - Five of the Best: Play-It-Like-It-Is-Guitar. pap. 8.95 (*0-89524-528-0*) Cherry Lane.
Tesla - Mechanical Resonance: Bass Guitar. Ed. by Mark Phillips. (Illus.). 71p. (Orig.). 1990. pap. text ed. 14.95 (*0-89524-429-2*) Cherry Lane.
Tesla - Mechanical Resonance: Guitar - Vocal. Ed. by Mark Phillips. (Illus.). 70p. (Orig.). 1990. pap. text ed. 19.95 (*0-89524-393-8*) Cherry Lane.
Tesla - Psychotic Supper: Play-It-Like-It-Is-Bass. pap. 17.95 (*0-89524-759-3*) Cherry Lane.
Tesla - Psychotic Supper: Play-It-Like-It-Is-Guitar. pap. 19.95 (*0-685-75229-1*) Cherry Lane.
Tesla - The Great Radio Controversy: Play-It-Like-It-Is-Bass. pap. 14.95 (*0-89524-483-7*) Cherry Lane.
Tesla - The Great Radio Controversy: Play-It-Like-It-Is-Guitar. pap. 19.95 (*0-89524-459-4*) Cherry Lane.
Tesla Coil. Nikola Tesla. 1991. lib. bdg. 250.00 (*0-87700-944-9*) Revisionist Pr.
Tesla Coil Builder's Guide to the Colorado Springs Notes of Nikola Tesla. Richard L. Hull. (Illus.). 142p. (Orig.). 1994. pap. 27.50 (*0-9636012-2-9*) Twty Frst Cent.
Tesla Experiment-Lightning & Earth Resonance. 1987. 10.95 (*0-914119-21-4*) Tesla Bk Co.
Tesla Experiments with Alternate Currents. 1986. reprint ed. pap. 9.95 (*0-917914-39-2*) Lindsay Pubns.
Tesla High Frequency Coil: Its Construction & Uses. G. F. Haller & E. T. Cunningham. (Nikola Tesla Ser.). 1991. lib. bdg. 75.00 (*0-8490-4379-4*) Gordon Pr.
Tesla Man of Mystery. 1992. lib. bdg. 75.00 (*0-8490-8709-0*) Gordon Pr.
Tesla Psychotic Supper: With Tablature. 1992. 19.95 (*0-89524-694-5*, 02501197) Cherry Lane.
Tesla Said. John T. Ratzlaff. LC 83-72252. (Illus.). 292p. (Orig.). 1984. pap. text ed. 28.00 (*0-914119-00-1*) Tesla Bk Co.
Tesla Speaks: Philosophers. Ruth E. Norman. (Tesla Speaks Ser.: Vol. 2). 478p. 1973. 18.00 (*0-932642-21-7*) Unarius Acad Sci.
Tesla's Engine: A New Dimension for Power. Ed. by Jeffery A. Hayes. LC 94-60502. (Illus.). 220p. (Orig.). 1994. pap. text ed. 19.95 (*1-884917-33-X*) Tesla Engine.
Tesla's Fuelless Generator & Wireless Method. Oliver Nichelson. v, 48p. (Orig.). 1993. pap. 9.00 (*0-9636012-0-2*) Twty Frst Cent.
Tesnic. Peter Mann. 216p. 1994. pap. 16.00 (*0-8059-3556-8*) Dorrance.
TESOL Membership Directory 1992. LC 82-640189. 308p. 1992. pap. 158.00 (*0-939791-38-2*) Tchrs Eng Spkrs.
TESOL Techniques & Procedures. J. Donald Bowen et al. 1985. pap. 27.95 (*0-8384-2680-8*, Newbury) Heinle & Heinle.
Tesoro: The Treasure. Uri Shulevitz. Tr. by Maria Negroni. (Illus.). 32p. (SPA.). (J). (ps-3). 1992. 16.00 (*0-374-37422-8*, Mirasol) FS&G.
Tesoro de la Lengua Castellana, O Espanola. Sebastian De Covarrubias Horozco. (SPA.). 1927. 25.00 (*0-87535-020-8*) Hispanic Soc.
***Tesoro de Novenas.** Lawrence G. Lovasik. (SPA.). 1988. vinyl bd. 7.95 (*0-89942-346-9*, 346/22S) Catholic Bk Pub.
Tesoro de Rackham. Herge. (Illus.). 62p. (SPA.). (J). 19.95 (*0-8288-5081-X*) Fr & Eur.
Tesoro del Amor. Suzanne Simms. (Deseo Ser.). 1996. mass mkt. 3.50 (*0-373-35146-1*, 1-35146-9) Harlequin Bks.
Tesoro di Rakam. Herge. (Illus.). 62p. (ITA.). (J). pap. 19.95 (*0-8288-5082-8*) Fr & Eur.
Tesoros Biblicos: Temas Dificiles de la Biblia. Domingo Fernandez. (Libros Nueva Vida). (SPA.). 1991. 5.99 (*1-56063-078-7*, 498485) Editorial Unilit.
***Tesoros Biblicos: Temas Dificiles de la Biblia.** Domingo Fernandez. 160p. (SPA.). 1991. pap. write for info. (*0-614-27145-2*) Editorial Unilit.
Tesoros De Espana, Ten Centuries of Spanish Books. Ed. by Luis Revenga & M. L. Lopez-Vidriero. (Illus.). 440p. (ENG & SPA.). 1985. pap. 19.95 (*84-398-4960-5*) NY Pub Lib.
Tesoros del Espiritu - Treasures of the Spirit: A Portrait in Sound of Hispanic New Mexico. Enrique E. Lamadrid. LC 94-20165. 192p. 1995. pap. 24.95 (*0-929820-05-3*) U of NM Pr.
***Tesoros Lexicos de Palabra de Dios.** A. Palma. (SPA.). 1.50 (*0-8297-2036-7*) Life Pubs Intl.
Tesoros Para el Corazon (Treasures for Heart) (SPA.). 1.00 (*0-685-74984-3*, 490262) Editorial Unilit.
Tess. Katherine Burton. (Calloway Corners Ser.). 1993. mass mkt. 3.50 (*0-373-83280-X*, 1-83280-7) Harlequin Bks.
Tess. Hazel Hutchins. (Illus.). 32p. (J). (gr. 1-5). 1995. per., pap. 5.95 (*1-55037-394-3*, Pub. by Annick CN) Firefly Bks Ltd.
Tess. Hazel Hutchins. (Illus.). 32p. (J). (gr. 1-5). 1995. lib. bdg. 16.95 (*1-55037-395-1*, Pub. by Annick CN) Firefly Bks Ltd.
Tess & Tim. Marc Gave. LC 88-12418. (Illus.). 48p. (J). (ps-3). 1988. 5.95 (*0-8193-1185-5*) Parents.
Tess Gallagher. Ron McFarland. LC 95-75727. (Western Writers Ser.: No. 120). (Illus.). 55p. (C). 1995. pap. 4.95 (*0-88430-119-2*) Boise St U W Writ Ser.
Tess Jaray: Prints & Drawings, 1964-1984. Intro. by Deana Patherbridge. (Illus.). 32p. 1984. pap. 9.95 (*0-907849-06-7*, 067, Pub. by Ashmolean Mus UK) A Schwartz & Co.
Tess Mallos Fillo Pastry Cookbook. Tess Mallos. (Illus.). 96p. (Orig.). 1995. pap. 12.95 (*0-85091-695-X*, Pub. by Lothian Pub AT) Seven Hills Bk.
***Tess of D'Urbervilles.** McDougal. (J). Date not set. pap. 14.24 (*0-395-78404-2*) HM.
Tess of the D'Urbervilles. Thomas Hardy. (Airmont Classics Ser.). (YA). (gr. 11 up). 1963. mass mkt. 3.50 (*0-8049-0082-5*, CL-82) Airmont.
Tess of the D'Urbervilles. Thomas Hardy. 1976. 29.95 (*0-8488-0516-X*) Amereon Ltd.
Tess of the D'Urbervilles. Thomas Hardy. Ed. by William E. Buckler. LC 60-707. (YA). (gr. 9 up). 1960. pap. 11.56 (*0-395-05144-4*, RivEd) HM.
Tess of the D'Urbervilles. Thomas Hardy. (Study Texts Ser.). 1900. pap. text ed. 5.95 (*0-582-01978-8*) Longman.
***Tess of the D'Urbervilles.** Thomas Hardy. (Longman Literature Ser.). 1993. pap. text ed. write for info. (*0-582-09715-0*, Pub. by Longman UK) Longman.
Tess of the D'Urbervilles. Thomas Hardy. 432p. 1964. pap. 4.95 (*0-451-52546-9*, Sig Classics) NAL-Dutton.
Tess of the D'Urbervilles. Thomas Hardy. LC 51-2271. 1979. 8.95 (*0-394-60484-9*, Modern Lib) Random.
Tess of the D'Urbervilles. Thomas Hardy. Date not set. text ed. 35.00 (*0-312-16375-4*) St Martin.
***Tess of the D'Urbervilles.** Thomas Hardy. Date not set. pap. text ed. write for info. (*0-312-10688-2*) St Martin.
Tess of the D'Urbervilles. Thomas Hardy. 560p. 1991. 20.00 (*0-679-40586-0*, Everymans Lib) Knopf.
Tess of the d'Urbervilles. Thomas Hardy. (Classics Ser.). 448p. (YA). (gr. 9-12). 1984. mass mkt. 3.95 (*0-553-21168-4*, Bantam Classics) Bantam.
***Tess of the d'Urbervilles.** Thomas Hardy. Ed. by Rex Gibson. (Cambridge Literature Ser.). 448p. (C). 1996. pap. text ed. 10.95 (*0-521-56714-9*) Cambridge U Pr.
Tess of the d'Urbervilles. Thomas Hardy. Ed. by James Gibson. LC 92-29776. 447p. 1993. pap. 4.95 (*0-460-87344-X*, Sig Classics) NAL-Dutton.
Tess of the d'Urbervilles. Thomas Hardy et al. Ed. by Simon Gatrell & Nancy Barrineau. (World's Classics Ser.). 456p. 1988. pap. 5.95 (*0-19-281826-0*) OUP.
Tess of the d'Urbervilles. Thomas Hardy. Ed. by Peter Widdowson. LC 92-29776. (New Casebooks Ser.). 224p. 1993. text ed. 39.95 (*0-312-09092-7*) St Martin.
Tess of the d'Urbervilles. Thomas Hardy. Ed. by David Skilton. (English Library). 536p. 1978. pap. 6.95 (*0-14-043135-7*, Penguin Classics) Viking Penguin.
Tess of the D'urbervilles. Thomas Hardy. Ed. by Sarah Maier. 280p. 1996. pap. 9.95 (*1-55111-066-0*) Broadview Pr.
Tess of the d'Urbervilles. Thomas Hardy. (Literary Classics Giant Ser.). 528p. 1995. 7.98 (*1-56138-653-7*) Courage Bks.
Tess of the d'Urbervilles. 3rd ed. Thomas Hardy. Ed. by Scott Elledge. (Critical Editions Ser.). (C). 1990. pap. text ed. 11.95 (*0-393-95903-1*) Norton.
Tess of the D'Urbervilles. Thomas Hardy. 432p. 1987. reprint ed. lib. bdg. 35.95 (*0-89966-624-8*) Buccaneer Bks.
Tess of the D'Urbervilles: Movie Tie-in Edition. Thomas Hardy. 1964. pap. 2.95 (*0-451-51924-8*, CE1686, Sig Classics) NAL-Dutton.
Tess of the D'Urbervilles (Hardy) Berc. (Book Notes Ser.). (C). 1984. pap. 2.50 (*0-8120-3445-7*) Barron.
Tess of the D'Urbervilles Notes. Lorraine M. Force. 1966. pap. 3.95 (*0-8220-1273-1*) Cliffs.
Tessa. Jean Giraudoux. pap. 9.95 (*0-685-33931-9*) Fr & Eur.
Tessa: The Beckoning Breeze. Lyn Davenport. (Orig.). 1994. mass mkt. 5.95 incl. mac hd (*1-56201-069-7*) Blue Moon Bks.
Tessa see Theatre
Tessa Becomes a Ballerina. Rocco Rotunno & Betsy Rotunno. (Stamptime Stories Ser.). (Illus.). 12p. (J). (gr. 2-6). 1992. Mixed Media Pkg. incls. stamp pad, stamps, box of 4 crayons. 7.00 (*1-881980-01-4*) Noteworthy.
Tessa on Her Own. Alyssa Chase. (Key Concepts in Personal Development Ser.). (Illus.). 32p. (J). (gr. 1-4). 1994. 16.95 (*1-55942-064-2*, 7659) Marsh Media.
Tessa Snaps Snakes. Alison Lester. LC 91-2665. (Illus.). 32p. (J). (ps). 1991. pap. 13.95 (*0-685-52551-1*, Sandpiper) HM.
***Tessa's Child.** Dallas Schulze. 1997. mass mkt. 5.99 (*0-373-48339-2*, 1-48339-5) Harlequin Bks.
Tessa's Holidays. Lyn Davenport. (Orig.). 1996. mass mkt. 5.95 (*1-56333-377-5*) Masquerade.
Tesse, Are You Really a Cat? D. C. Harrold. (Illus.). 102p. 1986. 19.95 (*0-317-64554-4*) Tesse Enter.
Tessellations. Jackie Robinson. 46p. 1992. pap. text ed. 12.00 (*1-885156-03-0*) Animas Quilts.
Tessellations & Variations: Creating One & Two Patch Quilt Designs. Barbara A. Caron. 1995. pap. 14.95 (*0-89145-844-1*) Collector Bks.
Tessellations File. Chris De Cordova. 32p. (Orig.). 1986. pap. 5.50 (*0-906212-35-9*, Pub. by Tarquin UK) Parkwest Pubns.
***Tessellations File.** Chris De Cordova. teacher ed., pap. 9.95 (*0-906212-80-4*, Pub. by Tarquin UK) Parkwest Pubns.
TesselMania Math Connection: Activity Book. Lois Edwards & Kevin Lee. 1994. pap. 12.95 (*1-55953-076-6*) Key Curr Pr.
Tesserae. Denise Levertov. LC 95-2954. 160p. 1995. 18.95 (*0-8112-1292-0*) New Directions.
Tesserae: And Other Poems. John Hollander. LC 92-54792. 1993. 20.00 (*0-679-42222-6*) Knopf.
Tesserae: And Other Poems. John Hollander. 1995. pap. 12.00 (*0-679-76200-0*) Knopf.
Tesserae: Memories & Suppositions. Denise Levertov. LC 95-2954. 160p. 1996. pap. 9.95 (*0-8112-1337-4*, NDP832) New Directions.
***Tessie & Pearlie.** Horowitz. 1997. pap. 12.00 (*0-684-83347-6*, Touchstone Bks) S&S Trade.
Tessie & Pearlie: A Grandaughter's Report. Joy Horowitz. 240p. 1996. 20.00 (*0-684-00312-0*) S&S Trade.
Tessie & Pearlie: A Granddaughter's Story. Joy Horowitz. 288p. 1996. 21.00 (*0-684-81395-5*, S&S) S&S Trade.
Tessie & Pearlie: A Granddaugter's Story. large type ed. Joy Horowitz. 480p. 1996. lib. bdg. 23.95 (*0-7862-0809-0*, Thorndike Lrg Prnt) Thorndike Pr.
Test. Dorothy Bryant. LC 91-72556. 146p. 1991. 16.95 (*0-931688-15-9*); pap. 8.95 (*0-931688-16-7*) Ata Bks.
***Test.** Casey Czichas. (Orig.). 1997. mass mkt. 4.99 (*1-55197-873-3*, Pub. by Comnwlth Pub CN) Partners Pubs Grp.
Test. Shahar Yonay & Rina Yonay. (J). (gr. 7-12). 1988. 14.95 (*0-9616783-4-8*) S Yonay.
***Test: A Single Man's Guide to Quality Women.** Branyon Davis. 1997. pap. text ed. 10.95 (*0-8065-1895-2*, Citadel Pr) Carol Pub Group.
Test: Numbers 1-35. Nov. 6, 1756-July 9, 1757, 2 vols. in 1. Bd. with Con-Test: Numbers 1-38. Nov. 23, 1756-Aug. 6, 1757. LC 73-176144. LC 73-176144. reprint ed. 70.00 (*0-686-76933-3*) AMS Pr.
Test & Drill English Grammar, Book 2. Dixson. 1987. pap. text ed. 9.50 (*0-13-903741-1*) P-H.
***Test & Evaluation: DOD Has Been Slow in Improving Testing of Software Intensive Systems.** Michael E. Motley & Lester C. Farrington. (Illus.). 56p. (C). 1997. reprint ed. pap. text ed. 30.00 (*0-7881-4132-5*) DIANE Pub.
Test & Evaluation of Complex Systems. Matthew T. Reynolds. LC 96-28134. 168p. 1996. text ed. 69.95 (*0-471-96719-X*) Wiley.
Test & Improve Your Chess. Lev Alburt. 127p. 1994. pap. 12.95 (*1-85744-061-7*) S&S Trade.
Test & Improve Your Chess: A Grandmaster Method of Chess Evaluation. L. Alburt. (Chess Ser.). 100p. 1989. 27.90 (*0-08-032041-4*, Pergamon Pr); pap. 15.90 (*0-08-032042-2*, Pergamon Pr) Elsevier.
Test & Measurement Equipment '94. Market Intelligence Staff. 298p. 1994. 545.00 (*1-56753-960-2*) Frost & Sullivan.
***Test & Practise Your English 2: Intermediate to Advanced.** Coe Fowler. 1992. pap. text ed. write for info. (*0-17-555750-0*) Addison-Wesley.
Test Anxiety: Applied Research, Assessment, & Treatment Intervention. Marty Sapp. LC 92-42456. (C). 1993. 69.50 (*0-8191-9039-X*); pap. 38.50 (*0-8191-9040-3*) U Pr of Amer.
Test Anxiety Prevention. Howard Rosenthal. 1994. audio 9.95 (*1-55959-067-X*) Accel Devel.
Test Assessment & Impressions: Grade 1. Booth. 1991. teacher ed., pap. text ed. 12.50 (*0-03-927238-9*) HB Schl Dept.
Test Assessment & Impressions: Grade 2. Booth. 1991. teacher ed., pap. text ed. 12.50 (*0-03-927239-7*) HB Schl Dept.
Test Assessment & Impressions: Grade 3. Booth. 1991. teacher ed., pap. text ed. 12.50 (*0-03-927240-0*) HB Schl Dept.
Test Assessment & Impressions: Grade 4. Booth. 1991. teacher ed., pap. text ed. 12.50 (*0-03-927241-9*) HB Schl Dept.
Test Assessment & Impressions: Grade 5. Booth. 1991. teacher ed., pap. text ed. 12.50 (*0-03-927242-7*) HB Schl Dept.
Test Assessment & Impressions: Grade 6. Booth. 1991. teacher ed., pap. text ed. 12.50 (*0-03-927243-5*) HB Schl Dept.
Test Ban Treaty. David W. Felder. 44p. 1996. pap. text ed. 8.95 (*0-910959-58-7*, B&G 11D) Wellington Pr.
Test Bank. Bruce M. Russett. (C). 1995. pap. text ed. write for info. (*0-7167-2375-1*) W H Freeman.
Test Bank - Sociology In A Changing World. 4th ed. William Kornblum. (C). 1996. pap. text ed. 28.00 (*0-15-503293-3*) HarBrace.
Test Bank Biology. 2nd ed. Villee. (C). 1989. student ed., suppl. ed., pap. text ed. 34.00 (*0-03-025388-8*) HB Coll Pubs.
Test Bank for Our Land Our Time. Conlin. 1987. suppl. ed., pap. text ed. 10.00 (*0-15-772002-0*) HR&W Schl Div.
Test Bank Macroeconomics. Eaton. 1995. write for info. (*0-7167-2184-8*) W H Freeman.
Test Bank to Accompany Bank Management. 3rd ed. Timothy W. Koch. 224p. (C). 1995. pap. text ed. 36.75 (*0-03-016322-6*) Dryden Pr.
Test Bank to Accompany Governmental & Nonprofit Accounting. 2nd ed. Patricia Douglas & Darlene Bay. 132p. (C). 1995. pap. text ed. 33.75 (*0-03-007438-X*) Dryden Pr.
Test Bank to Accompany Intermediate Microeconomics & Its Application. 6th ed. Walter Nicholson. 97p. (C). 1994. pap. text ed. 33.75 (*0-03-006457-0*) Dryden Pr.
Test Book Chemistry. Donald A. McQuarrie. 1995. write for info. (*0-7167-2222-4*) W H Freeman.
Test Book of Statistics. N. M. Kapoor. 684p. 1990. pap. 65.00 (*81-209-0006-5*, Pub. by Pitambar Pub II) St Mut.
Test Book to Accompany Living with Computers Version 5.0. 5th ed. Margaret Anderson et al. 903p. (C). 1995. teacher ed., pap. text ed. 36.75 (*0-03-015357-3*) Dryden Pr.
Test Booklet for HBJ General Mathematics 1987. Gerardi. 1987. suppl. ed., pap. 9.00 (*0-15-353594-6*) HB Schl Dept.
Test Booklet for Reading & Language. 2nd ed. Bader. 1994. pap. text ed. 5.00 (*0-02-305112-4*, Macmillan Coll) P-H.
Test Buster Pep Rally. Robert P. Bowman. Ed. by Don L. Sorenson. Tr. by Merle. 180p. ring bd. 79.95 (*0-932796-21-4*) Ed Media Corp.
Test Conference, 25th Anniversary Compendium International (ITC 1970-1994) T. W. Williams. LC 94-77462. 816p. 1994. 50.00 (*0-8186-6617-X*, BP06617) IEEE Comp Soc.
Test Construction: A Bibliography of Selected Resources. Nancy P. O'Brien. LC 87-25119. 320p. 1988. text ed. 59.95 (*0-313-23435-3*, CTC/, Greenwood Pr) Greenwood.
Test Critiques, Vol. I. Ed. by Daniel J. Keyser & Richard C. Sweetland. LC 84-26895. (Illus.). 800p. 1984. 89.00 (*0-9611286-6-6*, 1901) PRO-ED.
Test Critiques, Vol. II. Ed. by Daniel J. Keyser & Richard C. Sweetland. LC 84-26895. (Illus.). 872p. 1985. text ed. 89.00 (*0-9611286-7-4*, 1902) PRO-ED.
Test Critiques, Vol. III. Ed. by Daniel J. Keyser & Richard C. Sweetland. LC 84-26895. (Illus.). 784p. 1985. text ed. 89.00 (*0-9611286-8-2*, 1903) PRO-ED.
Test Critiques, Vol. III. Ed. by Daniel J. Keyser & Richard C. Sweetland. LC 84-26895. (Illus.). 810p. (C). 1991. text ed. 89.00 (*0-89079-254-2*, 1908) PRO-ED.

An Asterisk (*) at the beginning of an entry indicates that the title is appearing in BIP for the first time.

Test Critiques, Vol. IV. Ed. by Daniel J. Keyser & Richard C. Sweetland. LC 84-26895. (Illus.). 768p. 1986. text ed. 89.00 (0-933701-02-0, 1904) PRO-ED.

Test Critiques, Vol. V. Ed. by Daniel J. Keyser & Richard C. Sweetland. LC 84-26895. (Illus.). 624p. (C). 1987. text ed. 89.00 (0-933701-04-7, 1905) PRO-ED.

Test Critiques, Vol. VI. Ed. by Daniel J. Keyser & Richard C. Sweetland. LC 84-26895. (Illus.). 800p. 1987. 89.00 (0-933701-10-1, 1906) PRO-ED.

Test Critiques, Vol. VII. Ed. by Daniel J. Keyser & Richard C. Sweetland. LC 84-26895. (Illus.). 720p. 1988. 89.00 (0-933701-20-9) PRO-ED.

Test Critiques, Vol. IX. Ed. by Daniel J. Keyser & Richard C. Sweetland. LC 84-26895. (Illus.). 1992. text ed. 89.00 (0-89079-521-5, 1909) PRO-ED.

Test Critiques, Vol. 10. 1993. 89.00 (0-685-59036-4, 072404) Gale.

Test Critiques, Vol. X. 700p. 1994. 92.00 (0-89079-596-7) Gale.

***Test Critiques, Vol. 11.** 1998. 92.00 (0-7876-0941-2, 00109046, Gale Res Intl) Gale.

***Test-Driving Marriage.** Beliza A. Furman. 1998. 22.00 (1-56980-122-3) Barricade Bks.

Test Economics & Design for Testability for Electronic Circuits & Systems. Ed. by C. Dislis et al. LC 94-30448. (Ellis Horwood Electrical & Electronic Engineering Ser.). 206p. 1995. text ed. 53.00 (0-13-108994-3, Pub. by E Horwood UK) P-H.

Test Eleven: Great Ashes Battles. Barnard Whimpress & Nigel Hart. (Illus.). 304p. 1996. pap. 19.95 (0-233-98947-1, Pub. by A Deutsch UK) Trafalgar.

Test Equating: Methods & Practices. N. Wermuth & K. Krickebert. LC 95-5883. (Springer Series in Statistics). (Illus.). 328p. 1995. 49.95 (0-387-94486-9) Spr-Verlag.

Test Equipment. Multi - AMP Institute Staff. LC 93-20199. 241p. 1992. pap. 33.00 (0-8273-4923-8) Delmar.

Test Equipment - Instructor's Guide. AVO Multi-Amp Institute Staff. 86p. 1992. 15.50 (0-8273-4924-6) Delmar.

***Test Equipment Blue Book - 1998.** rev. ed. 1997. lib. bdg. 89.00 (0-932089-81-X) Orion Res.

***Test Equipment Guide.** Electronic Servicing & Technology Staff. 1997. pap. text ed. 18.95 (0-7906-1089-2) Prompt Publns.

Test Everything: Hold Fast to What Is Good. Hans U. Von Balthasar & Angelo Scola. Tr. by Maria Shrady from GER. LC 87-80660. 93p. (Orig.). 1989. pap. 8.95 (0-89870-196-1) Ignatius Pr.

Test Excavation & Data Recovery at the Awl Site, 4-SBr-4562, a Pinto Site at Fort Irwin, San Bernardino County, California. fac. ed. D. L. Jenkins & C. N. Warren. (Fort Irwin Archaeology Project, Research Reports: No. 22). (Illus.). 284p. 1986. reprint ed. pap. text ed. 25.00 (1-55567-548-4) Coyote Press.

Test Excavation & Significance Assessment of Archaeological Site SBr-4448, a Rockshelter in the Drinkwater Basin, Fort Irwin, San Bernardino County, California. fac. ed. D. L. Jenkins. (Fort Irwin Archaeology Project, Research Reports: No. 2). (Illus.). 85p. (C). 1982. reprint ed. pap. text ed. 7.75 (1-55567-524-7) Coyote Press.

Test Excavations at CA-FRE-61, Fresno County, California. Kelly R. McGuire. (Anthropology Occasional Papers in Anthropology: No. 5). (Illus.). 138p. (Orig.). (C). 1995. pap. 10.00 (0-9632633-4-X) CSU Bakerfld Mus.

***Test Excavations at Painted Rock Reservoir: Sites AZ Z:1:7, AZ Z:1.8, & AZ S:16:36.** Lynn S. Teague. (Archaeological Ser.: Vol. 143). (Illus.). 98p. 1981. 6.95 (1-889747-13-0) Ariz St Mus.

Test Excavations at the May Site (CA-SIS-57) in Seiad Valley, Northwestern, California, Vol. 17. Joseph L. Chartkoff. (Archives of California Prehistory Ser.: Vol. 17). (Illus.). 86p. (Orig.). (C). 1988. pap. text ed. 7.75 (1-55567-051-2) Coyote Press.

Test Excavations in the Mangum Reservoir Area of Southwestern Oklahoma. Frank C. Leonhardy. (Contributions of the Museum of the Great Plains Ser.: No. 2). (Illus.). 1966. 4.00 (0-685-85507-4) Mus Great Plains.

Test File. Suzuki. 1995. write for info. (0-7167-2047-7) W H Freeman.

Test Firing & Emissions Analysis of Densified RDF Combustion in a Small Power Boiler. (Illus.). 58p. (Orig.). (C). 1994. pap. text ed. 25.00 (0-7881-0614-7) DIANE Pub.

Test Flights. Kerry P. May. 71p. (Orig.). 1995. pap. 8.95 (0-931122-79-1) West End.

Test Flying at Old Wright Field. Wright Stuff Pilots & Engineers Staff. Ed. & Frwd. by Ken Chilstrom. (Illus.). 276p. (Orig.). 1991. pap. 24.00 (0-9617917-2-1) Westchester Hse.

Test for Differences. Mary L. LaBrake. LC 92-16719. 1992. write for info. (0-201-63411-2) Addison-Wesley.

Test for Homoscedasticity: The B-H Critical Values. V. Shvyrkov & A. C. Davis, III. LC 84-50865. (Illus.). 83p. (Orig.). 1984. text ed. 21.19 (0-942004-10-8) Throwkoff Pr.

Test for Pack Set. 1991. 50.00 (0-06-009976-3, HarpT) HarpC.

Test for "The Learnables", American English. Harris Winitz. 160p. (Orig.). (YA). (gr. 7 up). 1995. pap. 50.00 (0-939990-99-7) Intl Linguistics.

Test Gear & Measurement Projects. Danny Stewart. (Illus.). 208p. 1996. pap. 19.95 (0-7506-2601-1) Buttrwrth-Heinemann.

***Test Generation Technology for Digital Integrated Circuits: Foundations, Technology, Tools.** Ed. by H. T. Vierhaus & U. Glaeser. (Monographs in Computer Science). 250p. 1997. 49.95 (0-387-98208-6) Spr-Verlag.

Test Item Bias. Steven J. Osterlind. (Quantitative Applications in the Social Sciences Ser.: Vol. 30). 88p. 1983. pap. 9.95 (0-8039-1989-1) Sage.

Test Lessons in Primary Reading. 2nd ed. William A. McCall & Mary L. Harby. (J). (gr. 2-3). 1980. teacher ed. 2.95 (0-8077-5966-X) Tchrs Coll.

Test Lessons in Primary Reading. 2nd ed. William A. McCall & Mary L. Harby. (J). (gr. 2-3). 1980. pap. text ed. 3.95 (0-8077-5965-1) Tchrs Coll.

Test Lessons in Reading Figurative Language. William A. McCall et al. (gr. 9-12). 1980. teacher ed. 1.95 (0-8077-5971-6) Tchrs Coll.

Test Lessons in Reading Figurative Language. William A. McCall et al. (YA). (gr. 9-12). 1980. pap. text ed. 7.95 (0-8077-5970-8) Tchrs Coll.

***Test Method for Measurement of Hot Creep of Polymeric Insulations.** 15.00 (0-614-18686-2, T-28-562-1995) Insulated Cable.

Test Methods & Design Allowables for Fibrous Composites, Vol. 2. Ed. by C. C. Chamis. LC 88-38493. (Special Technical Publication Ser.: No. STP 1003). (Illus.). 300p. 1989. text ed. 54.00 (0-8031-1196-7, 04-010030-33) ASTM.

Test Methods & Design Allowables for Fibrous Composites - STP 734. Ed. by C. C. Chamis. 429p. 1981. 44.00 (0-8031-0700-5, 04-734000-33) ASTM.

***Test Methods, Ext. Dielectrics.** 28.00 (0-614-18704-4, T-27-581) Insulated Cable.

Test Methods for Composite Materials (Seminar Notes) 162p. 1993. 149.95 (0-87762-985-4) Technomic.

Test Methods for Explosives. Muhamed Suceska. LC 95-19429. (High Pressure Shock Compression of Condensed Matter Ser.). (Illus.). 240p. 1995. 69.95 (0-387-94555-5) Spr-Verlag.

Test Methods for Rating Motor, Diesel, & Aviation Fuels see 1997 Annual Book of ASTM Standards: Petroleum Products, Lubricants, & Fossil Fuels, Section 5

Test Methods for UV & EB Curable Systems. C. Lowe & Peter K. Oldring. (Illus.). 214p. 1994. text ed. 100.00 (0-947798-47-1) Scholium Intl.

Test Methods for Vertebrate Pest Control & Management Materials - STP 625. Ed. by W. B. Jackson & R. E. Marsh. 256p. 1977. 26.00 (0-8031-0199-6, 04-625000-48) ASTM.

Test Methods in Filtration. Al Johnston. 140p. 1995. 79.00 (0-88415-816-0) Gulf Pub.

Test Most People Never Take. Mark Hitchcock. 40p. (Orig.). 1994. pap. 2.50 (1-879366-84-3) Hearthstone OK.

Test of Academic Achievement Skills: Reading, Arithmetic, & Spelling. Morrison F. Gardner. 1989. teacher ed., pap. 16.95 (0-931421-60-8); teacher ed. 23.95 (0-931421-44-6); 8.95 (0-685-45311-1) Psychol Educ Pubns.

Test of Auditory Analysis Skills (TAAS) Jerome Rosner. 1988. teacher ed. 14.00 (0-87879-630-4) Acad Therapy.

Test of Auditory-Perceptual Skills: Upper Level. Morrison F. Gardner. 1994. pap. 16.95 (0-931421-84-5); pap. 54.50 (0-931421-90-X) Psychol Educ Pubns.

Test of Auditory Reasoning & Processing Skills. Morrison F. Gardner. 1992. teacher ed., pap. 14.95 (0-931421-79-9) Psychol Educ Pubns.

Test of Battle: The American Expeditionary Forces in the Meuse-Argonne Campaign. Paul Braim. LC 85-40991. (Illus.). 240p. 1988. 40.00 (0-87413-301-7) U Delaware Pr.

Test of English As a Foreign Language (TOEFL) Jack Rudman. (Admission Test Ser.: ATS-30). 1994. pap. 29.95 (0-8373-5030-1) Nat Learn.

***Test of Faith.** Eric I. Soyland. 156p. (Orig.). 1997. pap. 12.95 (0-9656278-0-2, 101) dnalyos Pub.

Test of Fire. Ben Bova. 320p. 1985. pap. 2.95 (0-8125-3208-2) Tor Bks.

Test of General Educational Development (GED) Jack Rudman. (Admission Test Ser.: ATS-61). 1994. pap. 23.95 (0-8373-5061-1) Nat Learn.

Test of Greatness: Britain's Struggle for the Atom Bomb. Brian Cathcart. (Illus.). 301p. 1995. 45.00 (0-7195-5225-7, Pub. by John Murray UK) Trafalgar.

Test of Love: A Revaluation of the New Testament. Norman Weeks. 322p. (C). 1992. 29.95 (0-87975-741-8) Prometheus Bks.

Test of Love: Can Love Survive Murder & Betrayal? Edward L. Tottle. LC 92-70456. (Illus.). 224p. (Orig.). 1993. pap. 15.00 (0-937117-07-2) Educ Materials.

Test of Loyalty. James M. Hiatt. LC 73-39089. (Black Heritage Library Collection). 1977. reprint ed. 21.95 (0-8369-9027-7) Ayer.

Test of Pictures - Forms - Letters - Numbers - Spatial Orientation & Sequencing Skills. Morrison F. Gardner. 1991. pap. 16.95 (0-931421-64-0); teacher ed. 34.95 (0-931421-70-5) Psychol Educ Pubns.

Test of Poetry. Louis Zukofsky. 1981. 6.95 (0-393-01446-0) Norton.

Test of Purchasing Power Parity on the Texas-Mexico Border. V. Howard Savage & Eric Blankmeyer. 9p. (Orig.). (C). 1985. pap. text ed. 10.00 (0-937795-06-2) Border Res Inst.

Test of the Tenderfoot. Vera Saban. LC 89-9729. (Illus.). 147p. (YA). (gr. 5-8). 1989. 6.95 (0-914565-35-4, Timbertrails) Capstan Pubns.

Test of the Tribal Challenge. Shel Arensen. (Rhino Tales Ser.: No. 6). 128p. 1996. pap. 4.99 (0-88070-901-4, Multnomah Bks) Multnomah Pubs.

Test of the Twins, Vol. III. Margaret Weis & Tracy Hickman. (Dragon Lance Legends Ser.: Vol. III). 1995. pap. 5.99 (0-7869-0264-7) TSR Inc.

Test of Time. Gary Kasparov. (Russian Chess Ser.). 300p. 1986. 35.90 (0-08-034043-1, Pub. by PPL UK) Elsevier.

Test of Time. Jayne Ann Krentz. 1995. mass mkt. 4.99 (1-55166-013-X, Mira Bks) Harlequin Bks.

Test of Time. Jayne Ann Krentz. 1994. mass mkt. 4.50 (0-373-83292-3, 1-83292-2) Harlequin Bks.

Test of Time: A One Hundred Year History of St. Mary's Home for Boys. Wilfred P. Schoenberg. Ed. by Emma Dennis & Adam Heineman. 210p. 1990. pap. write for info. (0-9625179-1-7) St Marys Home.

Test of Time: A One Hundred Year History of St. Mary's Home for Boys. Wilfred P. Schoenberg. Ed. by Emma Dennis & Adam Heineman. 210p. 1990. write for info. (0-9625179-0-9) St Marys Home.

Test of Visual - Motor Skills - Upper Level (Adolescent & Adult) Morrison F. Gardner. 1992. teacher ed., pap. 16.95 (0-931421-72-1); teacher ed. 43.95 (0-931421-73-X) Psychol Educ Pubns.

Test of Visual Analysis Skills (TVAS) Jerome Rosner. teacher ed. 4.00 (0-87879-678-9) Acad Therapy.

Test of Visual Analysis Skills (TVAS) Jerome Rosner. 1988. teacher ed. 15.00 (0-685-53819-2) Acad Therapy.

Test of Visual-Motor Skills. Morrison F. Gardner. 60p. (Orig.). 1986. teacher ed., pap. 14.95 (0-931421-09-8); pap. 23.50 (0-931421-08-X) Psychol Educ Pubns.

Test of Visual-Perceptual Skills (Non-Motor) Morrison F. Gardner. 1988. student ed., teacher ed., pap. 18.50 (0-931421-40-3); teacher ed. 55.95 (0-931421-41-1); lp 9.95 (0-931421-42-X) Psychol Educ Pubns.

Test of Visual-Perceptual Skills (Non-Motor) Upper Level. Morrison F. Gardner. 1992. teacher ed., pap. 17.50 (0-931421-78-0); teacher ed. 46.95 (0-931421-77-2) Psychol Educ Pubns.

Test of Wills. Charles Todd. 320p. 1996. 22.95 (0-312-14431-8) St Martin.

***Test of Wills.** Charles Todd. 1994. 165.00 (0-7838-2232-4) Thorndike Pr.

***Test of Wills.** large type ed. Charles Todd. LC 96-44453. (Mystery-Hall Ser.). 416p. 1997. lib. bdg. 25.95 (0-7838-2023-2, GK Hall) Thorndike Pr.

Test of Written English (TWE) Velma R. Andersen & Sheryl K. Thompson. 1979. student ed. 36.00 (0-685-44977-7); teacher ed., pap. 19.00 (0-87879-234-1); teacher ed. 18.00 (0-685-31200-3) Acad Therapy.

Test Pilot. Keith E. Greenberg. Ed. by Bruce Glassman. LC 95-38806. (Risky Business Ser.). (Illus.). 32p. (J). (gr. 2-5). 1996. lib. bdg. 14.95 (1-56711-158-0) Blackbirch.

Test Pilot. Neville Duke. (Grub Street Aviation Classics Ser.). (Illus.). 224p. 1993. reprint ed. 29.95 (0-948817-63-1, Pub. by Grub St Pubns UK) Seven Hills Bk.

Test Pilots. Ed. by Gene Gurney & James B. Gilbert. LC 79-7265. (Flight: Its First Seventy-Five Years Ser.). (Illus.). 1980. reprint ed. lib. bdg. 28.95 (0-405-12175-X) Ayer.

Test Pilots: The Frontiersmen of Flight. Richard P. Hallion. LC 87-28846. (Illus.). 432p. 1988. pap. 19.95 (0-87474-549-7) Smithsonian.

Test Policy & Test Performance: Education, Language, & Culture. Ed. by Bernard R. Gifford. 320p. 1989. lib. bdg. 71.00 (0-7923-9014-8) Kluwer Ac.

Test Policy & the Politics of Opportunity Allocation: The Workplace & the Law. Ed. by Bernard R. Gifford. 326p. 1989. lib. bdg. 71.00 (0-7923-9015-6) Kluwer Ac.

Test Policy in Defense: Lessons from the Military for Education, Training, & Employment. Ed. by Bernard R. Gifford & Linda C. Wing. (Evaluation in Education & Human Services Ser.: No. 29). 288p. (C). 1991. lib. bdg. 81.00 (0-7923-9176-4) Kluwer Ac.

***Test-Prep Mathematics.** rev. ed. Pamela Cohen & Walter Antoniotti. (Quick Notes Learning System Ser.). (Illus.). 252p. (YA). (gr. 4-12). 1995. pap. text ed. write for info. (0-9632772-6-X) Twen Frst Cent Lrn.

***Test Preparation for the Computer-Adaptive GMAT.** 1997. pap. 59.95 (0-446-39636-2) Warner Bks.

Test Preparation Guide for Agency Administration. Ed. by Martha Parker. 104p. 1995. pap. text ed. 12.00 (0-939921-82-0) Life Office.

Test Preparation Guide for Course 2. Ed. by Martha Humbard. 88p. (C). 1992. pap. text ed. 10.00 (0-939921-43-X) Life Office.

Test Preparation Guide for Course 3 (Canada) Iris F. Hartley. 1992. pap. text ed. 12.00 (0-939921-33-2) Life Office.

Test Preparation Guide for Course 4. Ed. by David A. Lewis. (Orig.). 1990. pap. text ed. 10.00 (0-939921-23-5) Life Office.

Test Preparation Guide for Course 6/Course 340. Joseph Scott. 1995. pap. text ed. 10.00 (0-939921-72-3) Life Office.

Test Preparation Guide for Economics & Investments. Ed. by Robert Hartley. 1995. pap. text ed. 10.00 (0-939921-62-6) Life Office.

***Test Preparation Guide for Foundations of Customer Service.** (Associate, Customer Service Program Ser.). 100p. 1997. pap. text ed. 18.00 (1-57974-003-0) Life Office.

Test Preparation Guide for Legal Aspects of Life & Health Insurance (U. S.) Ed. by Patsy L. Heil. 84p. (C). 1994. pap. text ed. 10.00 (0-939921-59-6) Life Office.

Test Preparation Guide for Microsoft Windows NT Workstation 3.5 Microsoft Certified Professional. Michael A. Pastore. Ed. by James C. Baker. (Illus.). 208p. 1995. pap. 69.95 (0-89716-566-7) P B Pubng.

Test Procedures for Basic Electronics. Irving M. Gottlieb. 356p. 1994. pap. 16.95 (0-7906-1063-9) Prompt Publns.

Test Procedures for Characterizing Dynamic Stress-Strain Properties of Pavement Materials. (Special Reports: No. 162). 40p. 1976. 4.00 (0-309-02468-4) Transport Res Bd.

***Test Procedures for Extended Time-Testing of Wire & Cable Insulations for Service in Wet Locations.** rev. ed. 1983. 15.00 (0-614-18688-9, T-22-294) Insulated Cable.

Test Procedures for Short Term Thermal Stores. Ed. by H. Visser & H. A. Van Dijk. (C). 1991. lib. bdg. 97.00 (0-7923-1131-0) Kluwer Ac.

Test Procedures for the Blood Compatibility of Biomaterials. Ed. by Steen Dawids. LC 92-41726. 1993. lib. bdg. 211.50 (0-7923-2107-3) Kluwer Ac.

Test Quality for Construction, Materials & Structures: Proceedings of the International RILEM-ILAC Symposium. Ed. by M. Fickelson. (Illus.). 352p. 1991. 88.95 (0-442-31360-8) Chapman & Hall.

Test Questions Social Animal. 7th ed. Gary A. Thibodeau et al. 1995. write for info. (0-7167-2704-8) W H Freeman.

Test Questions the Brain. 2nd ed. Martha Berg. 1995. write for info. (0-7167-2514-2) W H Freeman.

***Test Review Guide for Bilingual Children: Cognitive Assessment.** Sharon-Ann Gopaul-McNicol & National League for Nursing Staff. LC 97-20784. 1997. write for info. (0-88737-748-3) Natl League Nurse.

Test Score Decline: Meaning & Issues. Ed. by Lawrence Lipsitz. LC 76-13169. (Illus.). 240p. 1977. 34.95 (0-87778-095-1) Educ Tech Pubns.

Test Scores & What They Mean. 4th ed. Howard B. Lyman. (Illus.). 204p. (C). 1986. pap. text ed. write for info. (0-13-903832-9) P-H.

Test Scores & What They Mean. 5th ed. Howard B. Lyman. 1990. pap. text ed. 38.00 (0-13-904178-8) P-H.

***Test Smart! Ready-to-Use Test-Taking Strategies & Activities.** Gary W. Abbamont & Antoinette Brescher. LC 96-39568. 1997. pap. 29.95 (0-87628-916-2) Ctr Appl Res.

***Test Smart Math.** Mark A. Stewart. 1998. pap. 12.95 (0-02-862181-6) Macmillan.

***Test Smart Words.** Mark A. Stewart. 1998. pap. 12.95 (0-02-862188-3) Macmillan.

***Test Smarter! Train Your Brain to Perform Better on Test of All Kinds.** Gary W. Abbamont. LC 97-25947. 1997. pap. text ed. 11.95 (0-13-647397-0) P-H.

Test Success: Test-Taking Techniques for Beginning Nursing Students. 2nd ed. Patricia M. Nugent & Barbara A. Vitale. (Illus.). 288p. (C). 1996. pap. text ed. 21.95 (0-8036-0109-3) Davis Co.

Test Success: Test Taking Techniques for the Healthcare Student. Barbara A. Vitale & Patricia M. Nugent. LC 95-31144. (Illus.). 244p. (C). 1995. pap. text ed. 21.95 (0-8036-0089-5) Davis Co.

Test Taking. rev. ed. Herman Ohme. Ed. by Jean Ohme. (Illus.). 54p. 1989. pap. 5.00 (0-936047-05-4) CA Educ Plan.

Test Taking: Grades 1-3. unabridged ed. Karla Dencker-Koenig. Ed. by Mary L. Muffoletto. (Illus.). 64p. 1996. teacher ed., pap. 6.95 (1-889369-09-8, TI0020) Teaching Ink.

Test Taking Advantage Strategy Manual. Richard T. Abresch & Roger G. Kern. (Illus.). 181p. (YA). (gr. 10-12). 1990. pap. text ed. 35.50 (0-9627360-0-7) Test Taking Advan.

Test Taking Strategies. Judi Kesselman-Turkel & Franklynn Peterson. 132p. (Orig.). 1981. pap. 8.86 (0-8092-5850-1) Contemp Bks.

Test Target & Test Method for Determining Output of 35 mm Microfilm Duplicators: ANSI-AIIM MS46-1990. Association for Information & Image Management Staff. 1996. pap. 33.00 (0-89258-200-6, MS46) Assn Inform & Image Mgmt.

Test Target for Use in Microrecording Engineering Graphics on 35mm Microfilm: (ANSI-AIIM MS24-1980 (R1987) Association for Information & Image Management Staff. (Standards Ser.). 1980. pap. 33.00 (0-89258-109-3, MS24) Assn Inform & Image Mgmt.

Test Theory for a New Generation of Tests. Ed. by Norman Frederikson et al. 416p. 1993. text ed. 79.95 (0-8058-0593-1) L Erlbaum Assocs.

Test Tube Conception. Carl Wood & Ann Westmore. (Illus.). 144p. 1984. pap. 6.95 (0-685-07921-X) P-H.

Test-Tube Conception: A Blend of Love & Science. E. Peter Volpe. LC 87-22061. 160p. (C). 1987. 24.95 (0-86554-287-2, H257); pap. 14.95 (0-86554-291-0, MUP/P050) Mercer Univ Pr.

Test Tube Women. 2nd ed. Ed. by Rita Arditti et al. 460p. 1989. pap. 11.95 (0-04-440429-8) Routledge Chapman & Hall.

Test Validity. Howard Wainer & Henry Braun. 272p. (C). 1988. text ed. 55.00 (0-89859-997-0) L Erlbaum Assocs.

Test Way & the Clarendon Way. Barry Shurlock. 128p. 1987. 30.00 (0-948176-03-2) St Mut.

Test Wise. Rona F. Flippo. (YA). (gr. 7-12). 1988. pap. 14.99 (0-8224-6939-1) Fearon Teach Aids.

Test Wiseness: Cultural Orientation & Job Related Factors in the Design of Multiple Choice Test Questions see IPMA Assessment Council Monograph Series, Vol. II

Test Your Baseball IQ. Dom Forker. LC 92-44925. (Illus.). 128p. 1993. pap. 5.95 (0-8069-8802-9) Sterling.

Test Your Baseball Literacy. R. Wayne Schmittberger. LC 00-90. 234p. 1991. pap. text ed. 14.95 (0-471-53622-9) Wiley.

Test Your Bible Knowledge. Carl S. Shoup. 144p. 1994. mass mkt. 1.99 (1-55748-541-0) Barbour & Co.

***Test Your Bible Power.** 2nd ed. Jerry Agel. 1997. pap. 12.95 (0-8038-9397-3) Hastings.

Test Your Bridge Play, Vol. 1. Edwin B. Kantar. 1974. pap. 10.00 (0-87980-286-3) Wilshire.

Test Your Bridge Play, Vol. 2. Edwin B. Kantar. 1981. pap. 10.00 (0-87980-390-8) Wilshire.

Test Your Card Play, No. 3. Hugh Kelsey. 80p. 1992. pap. 11.95 (0-575-05117-5, Pub. by V Gollancz UK) Trafalgar.

Test Your Card Play, No. 4. Hugh Kelsey. 80p. 1992. pap. 11.95 (0-575-05119-1, Pub. by V Gollancz UK) Trafalgar.

An Asterisk (*) at the beginning of an entry indicates that the title is appearing in BIP for the first time.

Test Your Card Play Vols. 1 & 2. Hugh Kelsey. LC 92-35311. 160p. 1993. pap. 8.95 (0-395-65665-6) HM.

Test Your Card Play Five. Hugh Kelsey. 80p. 1993. pap. 11.95 (0-575-05312-7, Pub. by V Gollancz UK) Trafalgar.

Test Your Card Play Six. Hugh Kelsey. 80p. 1993. pap. 11.95 (0-575-05313-5, Pub. by V Gollancz UK) Trafalgar.

Test Your Card Play 1. Hugh Kelsey. (Illus.). 80p. 1991. pap. 11.95 (0-575-04795-X, Pub. by V Gollancz UK) Trafalgar.

Test Your Card Play 2. Hugh Kelsey. (Illus.). 80p. 1991. pap. 11.95 (0-575-04796-8, Pub. by V Gollancz UK) Trafalgar.

Test Your Cat's Intelligence. Burton Silver & Heather Busch. 48p. 1996. pap. 12.95 (0-89815-879-6) Ten Speed Pr.

***Test Your Cat's Mental Health.** Missy Dizick. LC 96-54733. 1997. pap. text ed. 6.95 (1-55850-712-4) Adams Media.

Test Your Chess: Piece Power. John Walker. 1995. pap. 14.95 (1-85744-185-0) Macmillan.

Test Your Chess I. Q., 2 bks. Ed. by August Livshitz & Kenneth P. Neat. Incl. Bk. 1. . LC 80-41072. 128p. 1981. 20.00 (0-08-023120-9); Bk. 1. . LC 80-41072. 128p. 1981. pap. 11.50 (0-08-024118-2); Bk. 2. . LC 80-41072. 233p. 1981. 26.00 (0-08-026881-1); Bk. 2. . LC 80-41072. 233p. 1981. pap. 17.25 (0-08-026880-3); LC 80-41072. (Russian Chess Ser.). (Illus.). 1981. Set pap. write for info. (0-318-55234-5) Elsevier.

Test Your Chess I. Q., Bk. 2. 2nd ed. August Livshitz. Tr. by Kenneth P. Neat. (Russian Chess Ser.). (Illus.). 125p. 1988. 33.90 (0-08-032072-4, Pergamon Pr) Elsevier.

Test Your Chess IQ, Bk. 1. 2nd ed. August Livshitz. LC 87-21595. 1988. 31.95 (0-08-032065-1, Pergamon Pr) Elsevier.

Test Your Chess IQ: Grandmaster Challenge, Bk. 3. 3rd ed. August Livshitz. 1993. pap. 19.95 (1-85744-002-1, Maxwell Macmillan) Macmillan.

Test Your Child: Birth to 6. Judy K. Sargent & Janmarie P. Scarr. LC 94-14755. (Illus.). 200p. (Orig.). 1995. pap. 14.95 (0-940159-28-7) Camino Bks.

Test Your Child's IQ. Martin Lubin. 1996. pap. text ed. 4.98 (1-884822-71-1) Blck Dog & Leventhal.

Test Your Communications. Hugh Kelsey. (Master Bridge Ser.). (Illus.). 80p. 1982. pap. 8.95 (0-575-03171-9, Pub. by V Gollancz UK) Trafalgar.

Test Your Consciousness. Gabriel. (Orig.). 1994. pap. 9.99 (0-9641745-0-2) Bell Rock.

Test Your Countercultural Literacy. Diane Zahler & Kathy A. Zahler. 1989. pap. 8.95 (0-685-29712-8) P-H.

Test Your Cultural Literacy. 2nd ed. Diane Zahler & Kathy A. Zahler. (Illus.). 320p. 1993. pap. 10.00 (0-671-84716-3, Arco) Macmillan Gen Ref.

Test Your Defensive Play. Hugh Kelsey. (Master Bridge Ser.). 80p. 1985. pap. 8.95 (0-575-03672-9, Pub. by V Gollancz UK) Trafalgar.

Test Your Elimination Play. Hugh Kelsey. (Master Bridge Ser.). 80p. 1984. pap. 8.95 (0-575-03466-1, Pub. by V Gollancz UK) Trafalgar.

***Test Your English Bk. 1.** Coe Fowler. 1992. pap. text ed. write for info. (0-17-555247-9) Addison-Wesley.

***Test Your English Bk. 2.** Coe Fowler. 1992. pap. text ed. write for info. (0-17-555248-7) Addison-Wesley.

***Test Your English Bk. 3.** Coe Fowler. 1992. pap. text ed. write for info. (0-17-555241-X) Addison-Wesley.

Test Your Fitness I. Q. Marcia Rosen & Eunice A. Lisk. (Illus.). 96p. 1986. pap. 6.95 (0-13-906868-6) P-H.

Test Your Go Strength: Fifty Whole Board Problems. Naoki Miyamoto. Tr. by Richard Bozulich from JPN. (Illus.). 216p. 1991. reprint ed. pap. 12.95 (4-87187-018-9, G18) Ishi Pr Intl.

Test Your Grammar. Rachel Bladon. (Test Yourself Ser.). (Illus.). 32p. (J). (gr. 4 up). 1995. pap. 5.95 (0-7460-1723-5, Usborne); lib. bdg. 13.95 (0-88110-740-9, Usborne) EDC.

Test Your I. Q. 3rd ed. Alfred W. Munzert. 1994. pap. 7.00 (0-671-87459-4) P-H Gen Ref & Trav.

***Test Your I. Q.** 4th ed. 1997. 6.95 (0-02-861936-6) Macmillan.

Test Your IQ. Hans Eysenck & Darrin Evans. 224p. 1995. pap. 9.95 (0-14-024962-1, Penguin Bks) Viking Penguin.

Test Your I.Q. Alfred W. Munzert. LC 96-31149. 1996. 5.99 (0-517-18287-4) Random Hse Value.

Test Your IQ. Ken A. Russell & Philip J. Carter. (Illus.). 128p. 1992. pap. 5.95 (0-7063-7059-7, Pub. by Ward Lock UK) Sterling.

Test Your IQ Skills: Exercise Your Brain with 100 Intellectual Work-Outs. Sullivan. 64p. 1996. spiral bd. 4.98 (1-884822-32-0, 80032) Blck Dog & Leventhal.

Test Your Knowledge Series. Jack Rudman. 1994. write for info. (0-8373-7200-3); pap. write for info. (0-8373-7000-0) Nat Learn.

Test Your Lateral Thinking IQ. Paul Sloane. LC 84-12348. (Illus.). 96p. 1994. pap. 4.95 (0-8069-0684-7) Sterling.

Test Your Logic: Fifty Puzzles in Deductive Reasoning. George J. Summers. LC 68-19447. 1972. pap. 2.95 (0-486-22877-0) Dover.

Test Your Math IQ. Steve Ryan. (Illus.). 96p. 1994. pap. 5.95 (0-8069-0724-X) Sterling.

Test Your Nineteen Eighties Literacy. Carol O. Madigan & Ann Elwood. 288p. 1990. pap. 8.95 (0-685-32623-3) P-H.

Test Your Own Job Aptitude: Exploring Your Career Potential. rev. ed. Jim Barrett & Geoff Williams. 224p. 1992. pap. 11.95 (0-14-016834-6, Penguin Bks) Viking Penguin.

Test Your Pairs Play. Hugh Kelsey. (Master Bridge Ser.). 80p. 1985. pap. 9.95 (0-575-03673-7, Pub. by V Gollancz UK) Trafalgar.

Test Your Positional Play. Robert Bellin & Pietro Ponzetto. (Illus.). 192p. 1985. pap. 13.95 (0-02-028090-4) Macmillan.

***Test Your Psychic Powers.** Susan J. Blackmore & Adam Hart-Davis. LC 96-52315. 168p. 1997. pap. 9.95 (0-8069-9669-2) Sterling.

Test Your Punctuation. Victoria Parker. (Test Yourself Ser.). (Illus.). 32p. (J). (gr. 4 up). 1995. pap. 5.95 (0-7460-1749-9, Usborne); lib. bdg. 13.95 (0-88110-766-2, Usborne) EDC.

Test Your Puzzle IQ. Steve Ryan. (Illus.). 96p. (YA). (gr. 10-12). 1993. pap. 5.95 (0-8069-0344-9) Sterling.

Test Your Salvation. Kent A. Field. 1987. reprint ed. pap. text ed. 1.00 (0-9623100-0-X) KAF Minsts.

Test Your Spelling. Victoria Parker. (Test Your self Ser.). (Illus.). 32p. (J). (gr. 4 up). 1995. pap. 5.95 (0-7460-1735-9, Usborne); lib. bdg. 13.95 (0-88110-754-9, Usborne) EDC.

Test Your Tactical Ability. Neishtadt. 1992. pap. 27.50 (0-7134-4013-9, Pub. by Batsford UK) Trafalgar.

Test Your Timing. Hugh Kelsey. (Master Bridge Ser.). 80p. 1983. pap. 8.95 (0-575-03309-6, Pub. by V Gollancz UK) Trafalgar.

Test Your Vocabulary for Computing. 48p. 1995. student ed., pap. 6.95 (0-948549-58-0) IBD Ltd.

Test Your Vocabulary for Medicine. 48p. 1995. student ed., pap. 6.95 (0-948549-59-9) IBD Ltd.

Test Your Word Play IQ. Steve Ryan. (Illus.). 96p. 1993. pap. 5.95 (0-8069-0412-7) Sterling.

Test Yourself: American Government. Larry Elowitz. 192p. 1996. pap. text ed. 11.95 (0-8442-2350-6) NTC Pub Grp.

Test Yourself: Find Your Hidden Talent. Jack Shafer. 1979. pap. 3.00 (0-87980-259-6) Wilshire.

Test Yourself American Government. Larry Elowitz. (Test Yourself Ser.). 192p. (Orig.). 1996. pap. 11.95 (0-614-11790-9, NTC LrningWrks) NTC Pub Grp.

Test Yourself Basic Math. Patricia J. Newell. LC 96-47152. (Test Yourself Ser.). 192p. (Orig.). 1996. pap. 11.95 (0-8442-2351-4, NTC LrningWrks) NTC Pub Grp.

Test Yourself Business Calculus. Lawrence A. Trivieri. (Test Yourself Ser.). 192p. (Orig.). 1996. pap. 14.95 (0-8442-2352-2, NTC LrningWrks) NTC Pub Grp.

Test Yourself College Chemistry. Drew H. Wolfe. (Test Yourself Ser.). 192p. (Orig.). 1996. pap. 12.95 (0-8442-2353-0, NTC LrningWrks) NTC Pub Grp.

Test Yourself Elementary Algebra. Lawrence A. Trivieri. (Test Yourself Ser.). 192p. (Orig.). 1996. pap. 12.95 (0-8442-2356-5, NTC LrningWrks) NTC Pub Grp.

Test Yourself English Grammar. Elaine Bender. (Test Yourself Ser.). 192p. (Orig.). 1996. pap. 9.95 (0-8442-2357-3, NTC LrningWrks) NTC Pub Grp.

Test Yourself Finite Math. Karen Benbury. (Test Yourself Ser.). 192p. (Orig.). 1996. pap. 14.95 (0-8442-2358-1, NTC LrningWrks) NTC Pub Grp.

Test Yourself for Maximum Health. Charles B. Inlander. 1994. pap. 14.95 (1-882606-11-6) Peoples Med Soc.

Test Yourself French Grammar. Didier Bertrand. LC 96-47422. (Test Yourself Ser.). 192p. (Orig.). (ENG & FRE.). 1996. pap. 11.95 (0-8442-2360-3, NTC LrningWrks) NTC Pub Grp.

Test Yourself in (A) Evidence, (B) Civil Procedure, (C) Criminal Procedure, (D) Sentencing, Vol. 1. 160p. 1994. pap. text ed. 30.00 (1-85431-389-4, Blckstone AT) Gaunt.

***Test Yourself in (A) Evidence (B) Civil Procedure (C) Criminal Procedure (D) Sentencing.** 3rd ed. 174p. 1996. pap. 30.00 (1-85431-605-2, Pub. by Blackstone Pr UK) Gaunt.

***Test Yourself in Clinical Pharmacology for Nurses.** John R. Trounce & Dinah Gould. LC 96-54720. 1997. write for info. (0-443-05783-4) Churchill.

Test Yourself in A< Evidence B< Civil Procedure C< Criminal Procedure D< Sentencing. 2nd ed. 164p. 1995. pap. 26.00 (1-85431-497-1, Pub. by Blackstone Pr UK) Gaunt.

Test Yourself Intermediate Algebra. Joan Van Glabak. (Test Yourself Ser.). 192p. (Orig.). 1996. pap. 12.95 (0-8442-2361-1, NTC LrningWrks) NTC Pub Grp.

Test Yourself Introduction to Calculus. (Test Yourself Ser.). 128p. (Orig.). 1996. pap. 12.95 (0-8442-2365-4, NTC LrningWrks) NTC Pub Grp.

Test Yourself Introduction to Psychology. Deborah Winter. LC 96-41278. (Test Yourself Ser.). 192p. (Orig.). 1996. pap. 11.95 (0-8442-2366-2, NTC LrningWrks) NTC Pub Grp.

Test Yourself Introduction to Sociology. Norman Goodman. (Test Yourself Ser.). 192p. (Orig.). 1996. pap. 11.95 (0-8442-2367-0, NTC LrningWrks) NTC Pub Grp.

Test Yourself Organic Chemistry: Second Semester. Drew H. Wolfe. (Test Yourself Ser.). 192p. (Orig.). 1996. pap. 14.95 (0-8442-2368-9, NTC LrningWrks) NTC Pub Grp.

Test Yourself Principles of Macroeconomics. Kenneth Parzych. (Test Yourself Ser.). 192p. (Orig.). 1996. pap. 9.95 (0-8442-2371-9, NTC LrningWrks) NTC Pub Grp.

Test Yourself Principles of Marketing. Majorie Cooper. (Test Yourself Ser.). 164p. (Orig.). 1996. pap. 11.95 (0-8442-2373-5, NTC LrningWrks) NTC Pub Grp.

Test Yourself Principles of Microeconomics. Kenneth Parzych. (Test Yourself Ser.). 128p. (Orig.). 1996. pap. 9.95 (0-8442-2372-7, NTC LrningWrks) NTC Pub Grp.

Test Yourself Spanish Grammer. Gladys Verona-Lacey. (Test Yourself Ser.). 192p. (Orig.). (ENG & SPA.). 1996. pap. 11.95 (0-8442-2374-3, NTC LrningWrks) NTC Pub Grp.

Test Yourself Trigonometry. (Test Yourself Ser.). 192p. (Orig.). 1996. pap. 12.95 (0-8442-2375-1, NTC LrningWrks) NTC Pub Grp.

Testability Concepts for Digital ICs: The Macro Test Approach. F. P. Beenker et al. (Frontiers in Electronic Testing Ser.). 224p. (C). 1995. lib. bdg. 97.50 (0-7923-9658-8) Kluwer Ac.

Testability of Distributed Real-Time Systems. Werner Schutz. LC 93-26518. (International Series in Engineering & Computer Science, VLSI, Computer Architecture, & Digital Screen Processing). 160p. 1993. lib. bdg. 86.50 (0-7923-9386-4) Kluwer Ac.

Testament. Valerie J. Freireich. 304p. (Orig.). 1995. mass mkt. 5.99 (0-451-45459-6, ROC) NAL-Dutton.

Testament. David Morrell. 352p. 1993. mass mkt. 5.99 (0-446-36448-7) Warner Bks.

Testament, 3 vols. in 1. Jean Meslier. lxv, 1162p. 1974. reprint ed. write for info. (3-487-05278-4) G Olms Pubs.

Testament: Commentaire, Vol. 2. Francois Villon. 304p. (FRE.). 1974. pap. 59.95 (0-7859-5505-4) Fr & Eur.

Testament: Life & Work of M. G. Smith 1921-1993. Research Institute for the Study of Man Staff. (InterAmericas Ser.: No. 3). 47p. (Orig.). 1994. 7.00 (0-9633741-3-3) RI Study of Man.

Testament: Low. Ed. by Jeannette DeLisa & Aaron Stang. 156p. (Orig.). (YA). 1995. pap. text ed. 24.95 (0-89724-461-3, P1090GTX) Warner Brothers.

Testament: Texte, Vol. 1. Francois Villon. Ed. by Jean Rychner & Albert Henry. 151p. (FRE.). 1974. pap. 16.95 (0-7859-5504-6) Fr & Eur.

Testament: The Ritual with Notes & Tablature. 128p. 1992. otabind 19.95 (0-7935-1746-X, 00694846) H Leonard.

***Testament: Transcribed by Mark Russell Bell.** Ed. by Mark R. Bell. LC 96-71184. (Illus.). 1100p. (Orig.). 1997. pap. 21.95 (0-9654916-0-9) Oracle Pr CA.

Testament & Poesies Diverses. Francois Villon. Ed. by Barbara N. Sargent. LC 67-22704. (Medieval French Literature Ser.). (Illus.). (Orig.). (FRE.). 1967. pap. text ed. 5.95 (0-89197-447-4) Irvington.

Testament Donadieu, l'Assassin, le Blanc a Lunettes. Georges Simenon. 1000p. (FRE.). 1992. 49.95 (0-7859-0492-1, 2258035252) Fr & Eur.

Testament d'un Excentrique. abr. ed. Jules Verne. (Illus.). 472p. (FRE.). 1979. reprint ed. pap. 18.95 (0-7859-1223-1, 2010055934) Fr & Eur.

Testament d'un Poete Juif Assassine. Elie Wiesel. (FRE.). 1981. pap. 16.95 (0-7859-2684-4) Fr & Eur.

Testament Francais. A. Makine. (FRE.). 1995. pap. 34.95 (2-7152-1936-9) Schoenhof.

Testament Francais. large type ed. Andrei Makine. 1996. pap. 25.99 (2-84011-144-6) Ulverscroft.

Testament from a Prison Cell. Benigno S. Aguino, Jr. Ed. by Consuelo Fernandez et al. (Illus.). 190p. (Orig.). (C). 1989. 18.75 (0-9621695-0-1); pap. 7.95 (0-9621695-1-X) Philippine Jrnl.

Testament Grec d'Abraham. Francis Schmidt. 200p. 1986. lib. bdg. 72.50 (3-16-144949-5, Pub. by J C B Mohr GW) Coronet Bks.

Testament of Abraham: The Greek Recensions. Bible, O T, Apocryphal Books, Testament of Abraham, English, 1972, Stone Staff. Tr. by Michael E. Stone. LC 72-88770. (Texts & Translations Ser.: No. 2). 97p. reprint ed. pap. 27.70 (0-7837-5401-9, 2045165) Bks Demand.

Testament of Adam: An Examination of the Syriac & Greek Traditions. Stephen E. Robinson. LC 80-12209. (Society of Biblical Literature. Dissertation Ser.: No. 52). 208p. reprint ed. pap. 59.30 (0-7837-5440-X, 2045205) Bks Demand.

Testament of Adolf Hitler. Adolf Hitler. (Illus.). 1978. pap. 5.00 (0-911038-44-2, Noontide Pr) Legion Survival.

Testament of Beauty: A Poem in Four Books. Robert S. Bridges. (BCL1-PR English Literature Ser.). 175p. 1992. reprint ed. lib. bdg. 69.00 (0-7812-7450-8) Rprt Serv.

Testament of Caspar Schultz. Jack Higgins. 1978. pap. 1.75 (0-449-13963-8, GM) Fawcett.

Testament of Cremer, the English Alchemist. John Cremer. 1984. pap. 3.95 (0-916411-96-6) Holmes Pub.

***Testament of Devotion.** (Great Devotional Classics Ser.). pap. 1.85 (0-687-61157-1) Abingdon.

***Testament of Devotion.** Kelly. pap. 2.00 (0-8358-0086-5) Upper Room Bks.

Testament of Devotion. large type ed. Thomas R. Kelly. 1987. 9.95 (0-8027-2571-6) Walker & Co.

Testament of Devotion. Thomas R. Kelly. LC 96-6845. 1996. reprint ed. pap. 11.00 (0-06-064361-7) Harper SF.

Testament of Hope: The Essential Speeches & Writings of Martin Luther King, Jr. Martin Luther King, Jr. Ed. by James M. Washington. LC 85-45370. 704p. 1990. pap. 22.50 (0-06-064691-8) Harper SF.

Testament of Job. Robert A. Kraft. LC 74-15201. (Society of Biblical Literature. Texts & Translations Ser.: No. 5). 93p. reprint ed. pap. 26.60 (0-8357-9580-2, 2017530) Bks Demand.

Testament of Joy: Studies in Philippians. David Ewert. (Luminaire Studies: Vol. 5). 155p. (Orig.). 1995. pap. 8.95 (0-921788-21-5) Kindred Prods.

Testament of Nizamulmulk. K. Mahadev. (Writers Workshop Redbird Ser.). 1975. 8.00 (0-88253-654-0); pap. text ed. 4.00 (0-88253-653-2) Ind-US Inc.

Testament of Our Times. C. Kent Dunford. 1993. 8.95 (0-88494-878-1) Bookcraft Inc.

Testament of St. Colette. St. Colette. Tr. by Mother Mary Francis. 13p. 1987. pap. 0.60 (0-8199-0908-4, Frncscn Herld) Franciscan Pr.

Testament of Stone: Themes of Idealism & Indignation from the Writings of Louis Sullivan. Louis H. Sullivan. LC 63-15297. 256p. reprint ed. pap. 73.00 (0-685-09005-1, 2006895) Bks Demand.

***Testament of the Dragon: An Illustrated Novel.** Margaret Weis. 1997. 22.00 (0-06-105543-3, HarperPrism) HarpC.

***Testament of the Weekend Warrior.** Dale Grubba. (Illus.). 96p. (YA). (gr. 6 up). 1997. 14.95 (0-614-21801-2) Aztex.

Testament of Vision. Henry Zylstra. LC 58-7572. 144p. reprint ed. pap. 41.10 (0-317-09777-6, 2012746) Bks Demand.

Testament of Xanthippus. Stewart Easton. 215p. 1990. pap. 9.95 (0-9510886-0-2, 1066) Anthroposophic.

Testament of Youth. Vera Brittain. 672p. 1989. pap. 10.95 (0-14-012251-6, Penguin Bks) Viking Penguin.

Testament of Youth. Vera Brittain. 672p. 1994. pap. 14.95 (0-14-018844-4, Penguin Classics) Viking Penguin.

Testament to Freedom: The Essential Writings of Dietrich Bonhoeffer. Dietrich Bonhoeffer. 1995. pap. 18.00 (0-06-064214-9) Harper SF.

Testament to Ruthenian: A Linguistic Analysis of the Smotryc'kyj Variant. Stefan M. Pugh. (Series in Ukrainian Studies). (Illus.). 314p. 1996. 39.95 (0-916458-75-X) Harvard Ukrainian.

Testament to Ruthenian: A Morphological Analysis of the Smotryc'kyj Variant. (Harvard Series in Ukrainian Studies). 300p. (C). 1994. pap. 17.00 (0-685-71133-1); text ed. 29.95 (0-916458-46-6) Harvard Ukrainian.

Testament to the Earth. Robert Muller. (Chrysalis Bks.). 176p. 1988. pap. 9.95 (0-317-65997-9) Amity Hse Inc.

Testament to the Wilderness: Essays on an Address by C. A. Meir. Jane H. Wheelwright. LC 85-50886. 142p. 1985. 25.00 (0-932499-12-0); pap. 12.50 (0-932499-13-9) Lapis Pr.

Testament to the Wilderness: Ten Essays on an Address by C. A. Meier. 142p. 1995. pap. 15.00 (3-85630-503-3, Pub. by Daimon Pubs SZ) Continuum.

***Testament to Truth.** Gandhi. 30.00 (0-06-063065-5) HarpC.

Testamentary Acts: Browning, Tennyson, James, Hardy. Michael Millgate. 224p. 1992. 65.00 (0-19-811276-9) OUP.

Testamentary Acts: Browning, Tennyson, James, Hardy. Michael Millgate. 284p. 1995. reprint ed. pap. 19.95 (0-19-818366-6) OUP.

Testamentary Executor in England & Elsewhere. R. J. Goffin. Ed. by R. H. Helmholz & Bernard D. Reams, Jr. LC 80-84960. (Historical Writings in Law & Jurisprudence Ser.: No. 26, Bk. 40). 154p. 1981. reprint ed. lib. bdg. 38.50 (0-89941-092-8, 302190) W S Hein.

Testaments Betrayed. Milan Kundera. Tr. by Linda Asher from ENG. LC 95-32148. 280p. 1995. 24.00 (0-06-017145-6, HarpT) HarpC.

Testaments Betrayed: An Essay in 9 Parts. Milan Kundera. 288p. 1996. pap. 13.00 (0-06-092751-8) HarpC.

Testaments in Wood: Finnish Log Structures at Embarrass, Minnesota. Photos by Wayne Gudmundson. LC 91-16556. (Illus.). x, 83p. 1991. pap. 16.95 (0-87351-268-5) Minn Hist.

Testaments of Courage: Selections from Men's Slave Narratives. Mary Young & Gerald Horne. (African-American Experience Ser.). (Illus.). 144p. (YA). (gr. 7 up). 1995. lib. bdg. 22.70 (0-531-11205-5) Watts.

Testaments of the Twelve Patriarchs: A Critical History of Research. H. Dixon Slingerland. LC 75-34233. (Society of Biblical Literature. Monograph Ser.: No. 21). 132p. reprint ed. pap. 37.70 (0-7837-5454-X, 2045219) Bks Demand.

Testbank to Accompany Automotive Technology: A Systems Approach. Jack Erjavec & Robert Scharff. 1992. pap. 26.95 (0-8273-5126-7) Delmar.

Testbank to Accompany Nursing Care of the Childbearing Family. 2nd ed. Morin. (C). 1995. teacher ed. write for info. (0-8385-7089-5, A7089-4) Appleton & Lange.

Testbank to Accompany Systems Analysis & Design: An Organizational Approach, by R. McLeod. Nilakantan Nagarajan. 176p. (C). 1994. pap. text ed. 36.75 (0-03-076683-4) Dryden Pr.

Testbank/Continuing Physical Geology. 3rd ed. Levin. (C). 1990. student ed., suppl. ed., pap. text ed. 34.00 (0-03-032659-1) HB Coll Pubs.

Testbook English Writing & Skills 1988. Henry Holt Company Staff. 1988. 14.25 (0-03-014647-X) HR&W Schl Div.

Testbook English Writing & Skills 1988: Grades 7. Holt. 1988. 14.25 (0-03-014634-8) HR&W Schl Div.

Testbook to Accompany Lawlor, Computer Information Systems. 3rd ed. Ronald L. Weir. 351p. (C). 1994. pap. text ed. 36.75 (0-03-098194-8) Dryden Pr.

Testbusters Study Smarter, Not Harder: A Guide for Parents. Deborah C. Beidel & Jill C. Taylor. 130p. 1994. pap. write for info. (1-886344-03-5) Turndel.

Testbusters Study Smarter, Not Harder: A Guide for Teachers. Deborah C. Beidel & Jill C. Taylor. 130p. 1994. teacher ed., pap. write for info. (1-886344-02-7) Turndel.

Testbusters Study Smarter, Not Harder: Student Workbook. Deborah C. Beidel & Jill C. Taylor. 100p. 1994. pap. write for info. (1-886344-04-3) Turndel.

Testcard F: Television, Mythinformation & Social Control. (Illus.). 80p. (Orig.). 1994. pap. 6.00 (1-873176-91-0, AK Pr San Fran) AK Pr Dist.

Teste Dein Deutsch! Stufe 1. Marianne Zingel. 175p. 1980. pap. 11.25 (3-468-38525-0) Langenscheidt.

Teste Dein Deutsch! Stufe 2. Marianne Zingel. 191p. 1981. pap. 11.25 (3-468-38526-9) Langenscheidt.

Teste Dein Wirtschaftsdeutsch. Charlotte Lissok. 112p. (GER.). 1983. pap. 11.25 (3-468-38527-7) Langenscheidt.

Tested Advertising Methods. 4th ed. John Caples. 318p. 1986. 14.95 (0-13-906909-7, Busn); 9.95 (0-13-906891-0, Busn) P-H.

Tested Advertising Methods. 5th ed. John Caples. LC 96-47752. 320p. 1996. 29.95 (0-13-244609-X) P-H.

Tested by Fire: A Study of the Christian's Heavenly Rewards. 2nd ed. Woodrow M. Kroll. LC 90-24666. Orig. Title: It Will Be Worth It All: A Study in the Believer's Rewards. 123p. 1991. reprint ed. pap. 8.99 (0-87213-475-X) Loizeaux.

T

An Asterisk (*) at the beginning of an entry indicates that the title is appearing in BIP for the first time.

Tested by the Cross. Anne E. Carr. 1993. pap. 10.00 (*0-00-627626-1*) Harper SF.

Tested Demonstrations in Chemistry & Selected Demonstrations from the Journal of Chemical Education, 2 vols., Set, Vol. I & II. George L. Gilbert et al. 804p. (C). 1994. pap. text ed. 45.00 (*0-9645053-2-0*) G L Gilbert.

Tested Demonstrations in Chemistry & Selected Demonstrations from the Journal of Chemical Education, Vol. I. George L. Gilbert et al. 804p. (C). 1994. pap. text ed. 45.00 (*0-9645053-0-4*) G L Gilbert.

Tested Demonstrations in Chemistry & Selected Demonstrations from the Journal of Chemical Education, Vol. II. George L. Alyea et al. 804p. (C). 1994. pap. text ed. 45.00 (*0-9645053-1-2*) G L Gilbert.

Tested Electronic Troubleshooting Methods. 2nd ed. Walter H. Buchsbaum. LC 82-13167. 272p. 1982. 24.95 (*0-13-906966-6*) P-H.

Tested Electronic Troubleshooting Methods. 2nd ed. Walter H. Buchsbaum. (Illus.). 272p. 1987. 12.95 (*0-13-906942-9*, Busn) P-H.

Tested Humor: And How to Use It. A. L. Kirkpatrick. 288p. 1995. 19.95 (*0-9639099-0-8*); pap. 9.95 (*0-9639099-1-6*) Impetus Pr.

Tested Man. John C. Fine. Ed. by Kate Whitaker. LC 93-61534. 130p. (Orig.). (YA). 1994. pap. 10.00 (*1-883650-00-3*) Windswept Hse.

Tested Positive. John D. Collins. 116p. 1994. pap. 15.00 (*0-938245-13-9*) Inverted-A.

***Tested Studies for Laboratory Teaching Vol. 16: Proceedings of the 16th Workshop-Conference of the Association for Biology Laboratory Education.** Ed. by Corey Goldman. LC 95-79492. (Illus.). (Orig.). (C). 1995. pap. text ed. 15.00 (*0-9626182-8-4*) ABLE GA.

***Tested Studies for Laboratory Teaching Vol. 17: Proceedings of the 17th Workshop-Conference of the Association for Biology Laboratory Education.** Ed. by Jon C. Glase. (Illus.). (Orig.). (C). 1996. pap. text ed. 15.00 (*0-614-27175-4*) ABLE GA.

Tested Studies for Laboratory Teaching Vol. 17: Proceedings of the 17th Workshop-Conference of the Association for Biology Laboratory Education (ABLE) Ed. by Jon C. Glass. (Illus.). 354p. (Orig.). 1996. pap. 15.00 (*0-9626182-9-2*) ABLE GA.

***Tested Studies for Laboratory Teaching Vol. 18: Proceedings of the 18th Workshop-Conference of the Association for Biology Laboratory Education.** Ed. by Corey Goldman. (Illus.). (Orig.). (C). 1996. pap. text ed. 15.00 (*0-614-27176-2*) ABLE GA.

Tested Studies for Laboratory Teaching, Vol. 11: Proceedings of the 11th Workshop-Conference of the Association for Biology Laboratory Education (ABLE) Ed. by Corey A. Goldman. LC 90-81536. (Illus.). (Orig.). (C). 1990. pap. text ed. 15.00 (*0-9626182-0-9*) ABLE GA.

Tested Studies for Laboratory Teaching, Vol. 12: Proceedings of the 12th Workshop-Conference of the Association for Biology Laboratory Education (ABLE) Ed. by Corey A. Goldman. LC 91-70799. (Illus.). (C). 1991. pap. text ed. 15.00 (*0-9626182-1-7*) ABLE GA.

Tested Studies for Laboratory Teaching, Vol. 14: Proceedings of the 14th Workshop-Conference of the Association for Biology Laboratory Education (ABLE) Ed. by Corey A. Goldman. LC 93-71236. (Illus.). (Orig.). (C). 1993. pap. text ed. 15.00 (*0-9626182-6-8*) ABLE GA.

Tested Studies for Laboratory Teaching, Vol. 15: Proceedings of the 15th Workshop-Conference of the Association for Biology Laboratory Education (ABLE) Ed. by Corey A. Goldman. LC 94-70908. (Illus.). (Orig.). (C). 1994. pap. text ed. 15.00 (*0-9626182-7-6*) ABLE GA.

Tested Studies for Laboratory Teaching, Vol. 5: Proceedings of the 5th Workshop-Conference of the Association for Biology Laboratory Education (ABLE) Ed. by Corey A. Goldman et al. LC 93-71234. (Illus.). (Orig.). (C). 1993. pap. text ed. 15.00 (*0-9626182-4-1*) ABLE GA.

Tested Studies for Laboratory Teaching, Vol. 6: Proceedings of the 6th Workshop-Conference of the Association for Biology Laboratory Education (ABLE) Ed. by Corey A. Goldman et al. LC 92-71632. (Illus.). (Orig.). (C). 1992. pap. text ed. 15.00 (*0-9626182-3-3*) ABLE GA.

Tested Studies for Laboratory Teaching, Vols. 7-8: Proceedings of the 7th & 8th Workshop-Conference of the Association for Biology Laboratory Education (ABLE) Ed. by Corey A. Goldman & P. Lynn Hauta. LC 93-71235. (Illus.). (Orig.). (C). 1993. pap. text ed. 15.00 (*0-9626182-5-X*) ABLE GA.

Tested Studies for Laboratory Testing, Vol. 13: Proceedings of the 13th Workshop-Conference of the Association for Biology Laboratory Education (ABLE) Ed. by Corey A. Goldman. LC 92-71490. (Illus.). (Orig.). (C). 1992. pap. text ed. 15.00 (*0-9626182-2-5*) ABLE GA.

Tested Ways to Successful Fund Raising. George A. Brakeley. LC 79-54828. 185p. reprint ed. pap. 52.80 (*0-317-27059-1*, 2023544) Bks Demand.

Testen und Prufen in der Grundstufe. H. G. Albers & S. Bolton. Ed. by Gerd Neuner. (Fernstudienangebot Ser.). 176p. (GER.). 1996. 11.25 (*3-468-49673-7*) Langenscheidt.

Testers & Testing: The Sociology of School Psychology. Carl Milofsky. LC 88-28293. 304p. (C). 1989. text ed. 40.00 (*0-8135-1407-X*); pap. text ed. 17.00 (*0-8135-1408-8*) Rutgers U Pr.

Testfact: Test Scoring, Item Statistics, & Item Factor Analysis. 2nd ed. Douglas T. Wilson et al. 1991. ring bd. 30.00 (*0-89498-027-0*) Sci Ware.

Testfragen Wirtschaftsdeutsch: Testbuch. W. Brueggemann & K. Hemberger. 104p. (GER.). (C). 1993. pap. text ed. 11.00 (*3-12-675230-6*, Pub. by Klett Edition GW) Intl Bk Import.

Testicles: The Ball Book. 4th rev. ed. Gary Griffin. 96p. 1993. pap. 9.95 (*1-879967-09-X*) Added Dimensns.

***Testicular Cancer.** 2nd ed. A. Horwich. (Illus.). 344p. 1996. 155.95 (*0-412-61210-0*, Chap & Hall NY) Chapman & Hall.

Testicular Cancer: Diagnosis, Surgical & Medical Therapy, Heinrich Warner Stiftung, 4th Symposium, Hamburg, November 1992. Ed. by H. Huland & U. Helmchen. (Journal: European Urology: Vol. 23, Suppl. 2, 1993). (Illus.). vi, 78p. 1993. pap. 44.50 (*3-8055-5789-2*) S Karger.

Testicular Development, Structure, & Function. fac. ed. NICHHD Workshop on the Testis Staff. Ed. by Anna Steinberger & Emil Steinberger. LC 78-68530. (Illus.). 556p. pap. 158.50 (*0-7837-7249-1*, 2047056) Bks Demand.

Testicular Tumors. Robert H. Young & Robert E. Scully. (Illus.). 240p. 1990. 125.00 (*0-89189-295-8*) Am Soc Clinical.

Testifica! Como Superar Obstaculos que Impiden la Evangelizacion Personal (Overcoming Barriers to Witnessing) Delos Miles. Tr. by Jorge A. Gonzalez. 128p. (Orig.). (SPA.). 1991. pap. 5.99 (*0-311-13850-0*) Casa Bautista.

Testifying in Court. Richard A. Gardner. LC 95-11203. xxiv, 273p. 1995. pap. 30.00 (*0-933812-39-6*) Creative Therapeutics.

Testifying in Court. 4th ed. Jack E. Horsley & John Carlova. Ed. by Melanie C. Karaffa & Jill Brittenham. 150p. 1992. 49.95 (*1-878487-47-7*) Practice Mgmt Info.

Testifying in Court: A Guide for Physicians. 3rd ed. Jack E. Horsley & John Carlova. 200p. 1988. 44.95 (*0-87489-465-4*) Med Econ.

Testifying in Court: Guidelines & Maxims for the Expert Witness. Stanley L. Brodsky. LC 91-16296. (Illus.). 208p. (Orig.). 1991. pap. 19.95 (*1-55798-128-0*) Am Psychol.

Testifying in Criminal Court: Emotional Effects of Criminal Court Testimony on Child Sexual Assault Victims. Gail S. Goodman et al. (Monographs of the Society for Research in Child Development: No. 229, Vol. 57, No. 5). 169p. (C). 1992. pap. text ed. 15.00 (*0-226-30323-3*) U Ch Pr.

Testigo de la Esperanza. Francisco Matos-Paoli. (UPREX, Poesia Ser.: No. 29). 132p. (C). 1975. pap. 1.50 (*0-8477-0029-1*) U of PR Pr.

Testigos de Jehova. Walter Martin. 144p. 1988. 3.95 (*0-88113-285-3*) Edit Betania.

***Testigos de Jehova? Una Respuesta Esclarecedora.** Fernandez. 88p. (SPA.). pap. write for info. (*0-7899-0244-3*) Editorial Unilit.

Testigos de Jehova a la Luz de la Biblia. Jose Garcia. 1996. pap. 8.99 (*0-8254-1253-6*, Edit Portavoz) Kregel.

Testimonial to Grace see Testimonial to Grace & Reflections on a Theological Journey

***Testimonial to Grace & Reflections on a Theological Journey.** 50th anniversary rev. ed. Avery Dulles. Orig. Title: A Testimonial to Grace. 160p. 1996. 24.95 (*1-55612-904-1*, LL1904) Sheed & Ward MO.

***Testimonials by Unarius Students.** 2nd unabridged ed. Ruth E. Norman. (Illus.). 145p. (Orig.). 1987. pap. 8.00 (*0-932642-99-3*) Unarius Acad Sci.

Testimonie of Antique. Abbot Aelfric. LC 73-36208. (English Experience Ser.: No. 214). 1970. reprint ed. 35.00 (*90-221-0214-9*) Walter J Johnson.

Testimonies. Michael Hamburger. 320p. 1989. text ed. 39.95 (*0-312-02701-X*) St Martin.

Testimonies: A Novel. Patrick O'Brian. 224p. 1995. pap. 11.95 (*0-393-31316-6*, Norton Paperbks) Norton.

Testimonies: Four Plays. Emily Mann. LC 96-7092. 1996. pap. text ed. 15.95 (*1-55936-117-4*) Theatre Comm.

Testimonies: Lesbian Coming Out Stories. Ed. by Karen Barber & Sarah Holmes. 170p. (Orig.). 1994. pap. 7.95 (*1-55583-245-8*) Alyson Pubns.

Testimonies & Reflections: Essays of Louis Massignon. Ed. & Tr. by Herbert Mason from FRE. LC 88-40327. (C). 1989. text ed. 29.00 (*0-268-01733-6*) U of Notre Dame Pr.

***Testimonies & Reflections: Essays of Louis Massignon.** Herbert Mason. 182p. 1996. 24.95 (*0-614-21244-8*, 1225) Kazi Pubns.

Testimonies Concerning Slavery. Moncure D. Conway. LC 77-82187. (Anti-Slavery Crusade in America Ser.). 1977. reprint ed. 20.95 (*0-405-00625-X*) Ayer.

Testimonies for the Church, 9 vols. Ellen G. White. 1948. 11.99 (*0-8163-0152-2*); Set. 99.99 (*0-8163-0153-0*, 20140-0) Pacific Pr Pub Assn.

Testimonies in the Life, Character, Revelations, & Doctrines of Mother Ann Lee. 2nd ed. Shakers Staff. LC 72-2994. reprint ed. 47.50 (*0-404-10756-7*) AMS Pr.

Testimonies of Exile. Abena P. Busia. LC 90-81310. (Illus.). 100p. (C). 1990. 19.95 (*0-86543-160-4*); pap. 7.95 (*0-86543-161-2*) Africa World.

Testimonies of Jews Who Believe in Jesus: If Jesus Is the Messiah at All, Then He Is the Messiah for All. rev. ed. Ruth C. Rosen. LC 92-3656. Orig. Title: Jesus for Jews. 349p. 1992. pap. 5.95 (*1-881022-00-5*) Purple Pomegranate.

Testimonies of the Life, Character, Revelations & Doctrines of Mother Ann Lee (Rufus Bishop) fac. ed. vi, 302p. 1991. Facsimile ed. (1888). 13.95 (*0-915836-21-1*) United Soc Shakers.

Testimonies to Ministers. Ellen G. White. 1923. 12.99 (*0-8163-0986-8*) Pacific Pr Pub Assn.

Testimonio Hispanamericano: Historia, Teoria, Poetica. Elzbieta Sklodowska. LC 91-31781. 219p. (SPA.). (C). 1993. text ed. 52.95 (*0-8204-1705-X*) P Lang Pubng.

Testimonios de una Gestion Universitaria. Arturo Morales-Carrion. LC 77-11056. (Illus.). 329p. 1978. pap. 3.00 (*0-8477-2740-8*) U of PR Pr.

Testimony. C. A. Coady. 376p. 1992. 59.00 (*0-19-824786-9*) OUP.

Testimony. large type ed. Frank Palmer. (Dales Large Print Ser.). 1996. pap. 17.99 (*1-85389-611-X*, Dales) Ulverscroft.

Testimony: A Philosophical Study. C. A. Coady. 336p. 1995. pap. 24.00 (*0-19-823551-8*) OUP.

Testimony: An Introduction to Christian Doctrine. Morton H. Smith. (Orig.). 1986. teacher ed. 3.95 (*0-934688-26-5*); pap. text ed. 5.95 (*0-934688-25-7*) Great Comm Pubns.

Testimony: Contemporary Writers Make the Holocaust Personal. Ed. by David Rosenberg. LC 89-40185. 1989. 24.95 (*0-8129-1817-7*, Times Bks) Random.

Testimony: Crises of Witnessing in Literature, Psychoanalysis & History. Shoshana Felman & Dori Laub. (Illus.). 288p. (C). (gr. 13). 1991. pap. 17.95 (*0-415-90392-0*, A5241, Routledge NY); text ed. 62.95 (*0-415-90391-2*, A5237, Routledge NY) Routledge.

Testimony: Death of a Guatemalan Village. Victor Montejo. Tr. by Victor Perera. LC 86-71063. 124p. 1987. pap. 9.95 (*0-915306-65-4*) Curbstone.

Testimony: Memoirs of Dmitri Shostakovich. Ed. by Solomon Volkov. Tr. by Antonina W. Bouis from RUS. LC 84-4399. (Illus.). 336p. (C). 1984. reprint ed. pap. 17.95 (*0-87910-021-4*) Limelight Edns.

Testimony: Selected Poems, 1954-1986. Hans Juergensen. 112p. 1989. pap. 11.95 (*0-8130-0916-2*) U Press Fla.

***Testimony: Selected Poems, 1954-1986.** Hans Juergensen. LC 88-33789. 117p. reprint ed. pap. 33.40 (*0-608-04489-X*, 2065234) Bks Demand.

Testimony: Stories. Jean R. Matthew. LC 86-16126. 80p. 1987. pap. 12.95 (*0-8262-0623-9*, 83-36315) U of Mo Pr.

Testimony: The United States, 1885-1915, Vol. 1. Charles Reznikoff. Ed. by Seamus Cooney. LC 78-7618. 280p. (Orig.). 1978. 25.00 (*0-87685-322-X*); pap. 13.00 (*0-87685-321-1*) Black Sparrow.

Testimony: The United States, 1885-1915, Vol. 2. Charles Reznikoff. Ed. by Seamus Cooney. LC 78-7618. 250p. (Orig.). 1979. 25.00 (*0-87685-333-5*); pap. 13.00 (*0-87685-332-7*) Black Sparrow.

Testimony: Writers of the West Speak on Behalf of Utah Wilderness. Ed. by Terry T. Williams & Stephen A. Trimble. 1996. pap. 6.95 (*1-57131-212-9*) Milkweed Ed.

Testimony: Young African-Americans on Self-Discovery & Black Identity. Ed. by Natasha Tarpley. LC 94-14362. 304p. 1994. 40.00 (*0-8070-0928-8*); pap. 14.00 (*0-8070-0929-6*) Beacon Pr.

Testimony & Demeanor. John Casey. 224p. 1990. reprint ed. pap. 8.95 (*0-380-71239-3*) Avon.

Testimony Before the Joint Commission to Consider the Present Organizations of the Signal Service, Geological Survey, Coast & Geodetic Survey, & the Hydrographic Office of the Navy Department: With a View to Secure Greater Efficiency, Vol. 1. United States Commission to Consider the Present Organizations of the Signal Service, Geological Survey, Coast & Geodetic Survey, & Hydrographic Offic. 1980. 53.95 (*0-405-12518-6*) Ayer.

Testimony Before the Joint Commission to Consider the Present Organizations of the Signal Service, Geological Survey, Coast & Geodetic Survey, & the Hydrographic Office of the Navy Department: With a View to Secure Greater Efficiency & Economy of Administration of the Public in Said Bureaus, 2 Vols. U. S. Senate Joint Commission, 49th Congress, 1st Session, Mis. Doc. No. 82. Ed. by I. Bernard Cohen. LC 79-7946. (Three Centuries of Science in America Ser.). 1980. reprint ed. Set. lib. bdg. 107.95 (*0-405-12527-5*) Ayer.

Testimony in Stone. J. Bernard Nicklin. 1961. 6.00 (*0-685-08818-9*) Destiny.

Testimony of a Confucian Woman: The Autobiography of Mrs. Nie Zeng Jifen, 1852-1942. Nie Zeng Jifen. Ed. by Micki Kennedy & Thomas L. Kennedy. LC 92-22989. (Illus.). 240p. 1993. 35.00 (*0-8203-1509-5*) U of Ga Pr.

Testimony of Existence. Narciso V. Vasquez. 56p. 1995. pap. 7.00 (*0-8059-3735-8*) Dorrance.

Testimony of God. Watchman Nee. Tr. by Stephen Kaung. 123p. 1979. pap. 4.00 (*0-935008-44-6*) Christian Fellow Pubs.

Testimony of God Against Slavery, or a Collection of Passages from the Bible, Which Show the Sin Holding Property in Man. La Roy Sunderland. LC 73-92444. 1970. reprint ed. 17.00 (*0-403-03707-7*, 403-00183-8) Scholarly.

Testimony of Images: Pre-Columbian Art. Donald McVicker et al. LC 92-85435. (Illus.). 200p. (Orig.). (C). 1992. pap. 25.00 (*0-940784-15-7*) Miami Univ Art.

Testimony of Justin Martyr to Early Christianity. George T. Purves. 1977. lib. bdg. 59.95 (*0-8490-2735-7*) Gordon Pr.

Testimony of Leon Fraser on the Bretton Woods Agreement Act. Leon Fraser. LC 84-80692. 84p. 1984. reprint ed. pap. 11.00 (*0-87034-073-5*) Fraser Pub Co.

Testimony of Light. Helen Greaves. 190p. 1969. pap. 11.95 (*0-85435-164-7*, Pub. by C W Daniel UK) Natl Bk Netwk.

Testimony of Light. 10th ed. Helen Greaves. 146p. 1993. pap. 17.95 (*0-8464-4300-7*) Beekman Pubs.

***Testimony of Lives: Narrative & Memory in Post-Soviet Latvia.** Vieda Skultans. LC 97-12949. 256p. (C). 1997. pap. write for info. (*0-415-16290-4*); text ed. write for info. (*0-415-16289-0*) Routledge.

Testimony of St. Paul. Ed. by Carlo M. Martini. (C). 1988. 6.95 (*0-8245-0958-7*) Crossroad NY.

Testimony of St. Paul. Carlo M. Martini. 104p. (C). 1990. 39.00 (*0-85439-221-1*, Pub. by St Paul Pubns UK) St Mut.

Testimony of Teeth: Forensic Aspects of Human Dentition. Spencer L. Rogers. (Illus.). 126p. (C). 1988. text ed. 35.95 (*0-398-05450-9*) C C Thomas.

Testimony of the Evangelists: The Gospels Examined by the Rules of Evidence. Simon Greenleaf. LC 94-38149. 144p. 1995. pap. 7.99 (*0-8254-2747-9*, Kregel Class) Kregel.

Testimony of the Holy Quran. Hazrat M. Sahib. Tr. & Intro. by Zahid Aziz. 100p. 1989. pap. 4.95 (*0-913321-43-5*) Ahmadiyya Anjuman.

Testimony of the Rocks: Or, Geology in Its Bearings on Two Theologies, Natural & Revealed. Hugh G. Miller. Ed. by Stephen J. Gould. LC 79-8336. (History of Paleontology Ser.). (Illus.). 1980. reprint ed. lib. bdg. 46.95 (*0-405-12720-0*) Ayer.

Testimony of the Twentieth Century: Before & After the Berlin Wall. Marie Ueda. Ed. by Sofia Marchant & Michele Navarrete. (Illus.). 488p. 1996. 70.00 (*0-9650299-0-5*) M I Prods.

Testimony of Two. Mary Youmans & Roger Youmans. pap. 5.95 (*0-910924-91-0*) Macalester.

Testimony of Two Men. Taylor Caldwell. 704p. 1984. mass mkt. 5.95 (*0-449-20572-X*, Crest) Fawcett.

Testimony Studies on Diet & Food. E. G. White. (Seventh Day Adventist Health & Nutrition Ser.). 1991. lib. bdg. 75.00 (*0-87700-954-6*) Revisionist Pr.

Testimony, the United States 1885-1890, Recitative. Charles Reznikoff. LC 65-15675. 1965. 10.00 (*0-685-79043-6*); 5.00 (*0-685-79044-4*) SPD-Small Pr Dist.

Testimony to the Invisible & Other Essays on Swedenborg: Essays on Swedenborg. Kathleen Raine et al. Ed. by James F. Lawrence. 176p. (Orig.). 1995. pap. 11.95 (*0-87785-149-2*) Swedenborg.

Testing: Concepts, Policy, Practice, & Research. Ed. by Robert Glaser & Lloyd Bond. (Special Issue, American Psychologist Ser.: Vol. 36, No. 10). 211p. 1981. pap. 16.00 (*1-55798-001-2*) Am Psychol.

Testing: Theoretical & Applied Perspectives. Ed. by Ronna R. Dillon & James W. Pelligrino. LC 88-316. 274p. 1989. text ed. 65.00 (*0-275-92759-8*, C2759, Praeger Pubs) Greenwood.

***Testing a Nuclear Test Ban: What Should Be Prohibited by a 'Comprehensive' Treaty?** David A. Koplow. LC 96-43127. (Illus.). 192p. 1996. text ed. 62.95 (*1-85521-806-2*, Pub. by Dartmth Pub UK) Ashgate Pub Co.

T

Testing Active & Passive Electronic Components. Powell. (Electrical Engineering & Electronics Ser.: Vol. 38). 232p. 1987. 125.00 (*0-8247-7705-0*) Dekker.

***Testing African American Students.** Asa G. Hilliard. 1996. pap. text ed. 14.95 (*0-88378-152-2*) Third World.

Testing African American Students, Vol. XXXVIII, Nos. 2, 3: Special Issue of the Negro Educational Review. Intro. by Asa G. Hilliard. 217p. (C). 1990. reprint ed. text ed. 22.95 (*0-685-45607-2*); reprint ed. pap. text ed. 14.95 (*0-685-45608-0*) J Richardson.

***Testing & Acceptance Criteria for Geosynthetic Clay Liners, Vol. STP 1308.** Ed. by Larry W. Well. LC 96-45669. (Illus.). 275p. 1997. text ed. 46.00 (*0-8031-2471-6*, 04-01308-38) ASTM.

Testing & Assessment. Charles Desforges. Ed. by C. E. Wragg. (Education Matters Ser.). 128p. 1989. text ed. 45.00 (*0-304-31713-6*); pap. text ed. 18.95 (*0-304-31711-X*) Cassell.

Testing & Assessment in Occupational & Technical Education. Paul A. Bott. LC 95-1709. 1995. pap. text ed. 36.00 (*0-205-16878-7*) Allyn.

Testing & Assessment in Vocational Education. (Illus.). 128p. (Orig.). (C). 1994. pap. text ed. 30.00 (*0-7881-1039-X*) DIANE Pub.

Testing & Balancing HVAC Air & Water Systems. Samuel C. Monger. LC 88-45792. 300p. 1989. text ed. 67.00 (*0-88173-075-0*) Fairmont Pr.

Testing & Balancing HVAC Air & Water Systems. 2nd ed. Sam Monger. LC 95-17282. 1995. write for info. (*0-88173-210-9*) Fairmont Pr.

Testing & Balancing HVAC Air & Water Systems. 2nd ed. Samuel C. Monger. LC 88-45792. 290p. (C). 1995. text ed. 69.00 (*0-13-462276-6*) P-H.

Testing & Cognition. Merlin C. Wittrock & Eva L. Baker. 192p. (C). 1990. pap. text ed. 32.00 (*0-13-906991-7*) P-H.

Testing & Completing. 2nd ed. Ed. by Mark Longley. (Rotary Drilling Ser.: Unit II, Lesson 5). (Illus.). 72p. (C). 1983. pap. text ed. 14.00 (*0-88698-120-4*, 2.20520) PETEX.

Testing & Control in the Wool Industry. Ed. by Wira Staff. 1955. 75.00 (*0-317-43609-0*) St Mut.

Testing & Control in the Wool Industry. Wira Staff. (C). 1955. 125.00 (*0-900820-04-7*, Pub. by British Textile Tech UK) St Mut.

Testing & Diagnosis of Analog Circuits & Systems. Ed. by Ruey-Wen Liu. LC 90-45217. (Illus.). 240p. 1991. text ed. 64.95 (*0-442-25932-8*) Van Nos Reinhold.

Testing & Diagnosis of VLSI & ULSI. Ed. by Fabrizio Lombardi & Mariagiovanna Sami. (C). 1988. lib. bdg. 167.00 (*90-247-3794-X*) Kluwer Ac.

Testing & Evaluation of Agricultural Machinery & Equipment: Principles & Practices. D. W. Smith et al. (Agricultural Services Bulletin Ser.: 110). 277p. 1994. pap. 30.00 (*92-5-103458-3*, F34583) Bernan Associates.

Testing & Evaluation of Drugs of Abuse. Martin W. Adler & Alan Cowan. LC 90-12025. (Modern Methods in Pharmacology Ser.). 306p. 1990. text ed. 144.95 (*0-471-56743-4*) Wiley.

Testing & Evaluation of Infrared Imaging Systems. Gerald C. Holst. (Illus.). xiv, 348p. (C). 1993. text ed. 75.00 (*0-9640000-0-8*) JCD Pubng.

An Asterisk (*) at the beginning of an entry indicates that the title is appearing in BIP for the first time.

Testing & Evaluation of Life Saving Appliances. IMO Staff. (C). 1985. English ed. 59.00 (0-7855-0028-6, IMO 982E, Pub. by Intl Maritime Org UK); French ed. 55.00 (0-685-74535-X, IMO 983F, Pub. by Intl Maritime Org UK); Spanish ed. 55.00 (0-685-74536-8, IMO 984S, Pub. by Intl Maritime Org UK) St Mut.

Testing & Evaluation of Solidified High-Level Radioactive Waste. Ed. by A. R. Hall. (C). 1987. pap. text ed. 168.50 (0-86010-893-7, Pub. by Graham & Trotman UK) Kluwer Ac.

Testing & Grading: Tips for Classroom Practice. John C. Ory & Katherine E. Ryan. (Survival Skills for Scholars Ser.: Vol. 4). (Illus.). 128p. (C). 1993. text ed. 35.00 (0-8039-4973-1); pap. text ed. 15.95 (0-8039-4974-X) Sage.

Testing & Instrumentation: SAE International Congress & Exposition 1994, 10 papers. (Special Publications). 133p. 1994. pap. 31.00 (1-56091-491-2, SP-1039) Soc Auto Engineers.

Testing & Reclaiming Your Call to Ministry. Robert Schnase. LC 90-48632. 1991. pap. 5.18 (0-687-41274-9) Abingdon.

Testing & Reliable Design of CMOS Circuits. Niraj K. Jha & Sandip Kundu. (C). 1989. lib. bdg. 91.00 (0-7923-9056-3) Kluwer Ac.

Testing & Reporting Performance Results of Ventricular Arrhythmia Detection Algorithms. 16p. 1987. pap. 70.00 (0-910275-72-6, ECAR-238) Assn Adv Med Instrn.

Testing & Retention of Young Children. 8p. 1990. 4.00 (0-317-05351-5) NASBE.

Testing & Screening for Drugs of Abuse: Techniques, Issues, & Clinical Implications. Gerald G. DeAngelis. LC 75-40843. (Illus.). 152p. reprint ed. pap. 43.40 (0-7837-0839-4, 2041153) Bks Demand.

Testing & Servicing of Steam Boilers. Parilov & Ushakov. 1990. 154.00 (1-56032-094-X) Hemisp Pub.

Testing & Teaching for Oral Proficiency. Lisken-Gasparro. 171p. 1987. pap. 25.95 (0-8384-1505-9) Heinle & Heinle.

Testing & Teaching for Oral Proficiency: ETS Familiarization Kits. Judith Liskin-Gasparro. 1987. French Kit. pap. 55.95 (0-8384-1896-1); German Kit. pap. 55.95 incl. audio (0-8384-1897-X) Heinle & Heinle.

Testing & Test Methods of Fibre Cement Composites: RILEM Symposium held April 5-7, 1978. RILEM International Symposium Staff. Ed. by R. N. Swamy. (Illus.). 555p. reprint ed. pap. 158.20 (0-317-08289-2, 2019629) Bks Demand.

Testing & Testability for Integrated Circuits. A. P. Ambler. 352p. 1992. boxed 41.00 (0-13-911793-8) P-H.

***Testing & Testable Design of High-Density Random-Access Memories.** Pinaki Mazumder & Kanad Chakraborty. LC 96-2750. (Frontiers in Electronic Testing Ser.). 424p. (C). 1996. lib. bdg. 127.00 (0-7923-9782-7) Kluwer Ac.

Testing Automotive Materials & Components. Don H. Wright. 250p. 1993. 29.00 (1-56091-377-0, R-124) Soc Auto Engineers.

***Testing Carbide Hobs & Modified 1600 Gould & Eberhardt Hobbing Machine.** A. J. Krogg & R. W. Righter. (Technical Papers). 1945. pap. text ed. 30.00 (1-55589-170-5) AGMA.

Testing Christianity's Truth Claims: Approaches to Christian Apologetics. Gordon R. Lewis. 363p. (C). 1990. reprint ed. pap. text ed. 29.50 (0-8191-7838-1) U Pr of Amer.

Testing Cleanrooms, IES-RP-CC006.2. Institute of Environmental Sciences Staff. Ed. by Vinette Kopetz. (Recommended Practice for Contamination Control Ser.). 36p. 1993. 125.00 (1-877862-26-6, IES-RP-CC024.1) Inst Environ Sci.

Testing Client - Server Applications. Patricia A. Goglia. 320p. 1993. text ed. 49.95 (0-471-56527-X) Wiley.

Testing Client Server Software. Mosley. 1996. text ed. 40.00 (0-13-183880-6) P-H.

***Testing Client Server Systems.** Kelly C. Bourne. LC 97-22888. 1997. pap. text ed. 49.95 (0-07-006688-4) McGraw.

Testing Computer Software. 2nd ed. Cem Kaner. (C). 1993. pap. text ed. 32.95 (1-85032-847-1) ITCP.

Testing Computer Software. 2nd ed. Cem Kaner et al. 1993. pap. 30.95 (0-442-01361-2) Van Nos Reinhold.

***Testing Computer Software.** 3rd ed. Cem Kaner. (ITCP-US Computer Science Ser.). 1998. pap. 44.99 (1-85032-908-7) ITCP.

Testing Computer Telephony Systems & Networks. Steve Gladstone. 24.95 (0-936648-57-0) Flatiron Pubng.

Testing, Counseling & Supportive Services for Disadvantaged Youth. Jesse E. Gordon. (Orig.). 1969. pap. 5.00 (0-87736-309-9) U of Mich Inst Labor.

Testing Democracy: Electoral Behavior & Progressive Reform in New Jersey, 1880-1920. John F. Reynolds. LC 87-31947. (Illus.). xvii, 245p. (C). 1988. 55.00 (0-8078-1789-9) U of NC Pr.

***Testing Democracy: Electoral Behavior & Progressive Reform in New Jersey, 1880-1920.** John F. Reynolds. LC 87-31947. (Illus.). 263p. pap. 75.00 (0-608-05222-1, 2065759) Bks Demand.

Testing Digital Circuits. A. Wilkins. (C). 1986. pap. text ed. 43.95 (0-412-38360-8) Chapman & Hall.

Testing Drugs for the Aging Brain. (Journal: Gerontology: Vol. 28, Suppl. 2). (Illus.). xiv, 58p. 1983. pap. 44.00 (3-8055-3659-3) S Karger.

Testing During Concrete Construction: Proceedings of RILEM Colloquium, Darmstadt, 1990. Ed. by H. W. Reinhardt. (Illus.). 420p. 1991. 85.95 (0-442-31389-6) Chapman & Hall.

Testing Early Jets: Compressibility & the Supersonic Era. Roland P. Beamont. (Illus.). 160p. (C). 1991. text ed. 46.00 (1-56098-109-1) Smithsonian.

Testing, Evaluation & Measurements in Metal Casting. Sarat C. Panigrahi. 304p. (C). 1987. 15.00 (81-204-0171-9, Pub. by Oxford IBH II) S Asia.

Testing, Evaluation & Shallow Land Burial of Low & Medium Radioactive Waste Forms. Ed. by W. Krischer & R. A. Simon. (Radioactive Waste Management Ser.: Vol. 13). 228p. 1984. text ed. 145.00 (3-7186-0206-7) Gordon & Breach.

Testing Exogeneity. Ed. by Neil Ericsson. (Advanced Texts in Econometrics Ser.). 384p. 1995. 72.00 (0-19-877401-X); pap. 32.00 (0-19-877404-4) OUP.

Testing Fluid Power Components. Robert A. Nasca. (Illus.). 352p. 1990. 49.95 (0-8311-3002-4) Indus Pr.

Testing for Abuse Liability of Drugs in Humans. 1990. lib. bdg. 75.00 (0-8490-4024-8) Gordon Pr.

Testing for Electrical Safety in Hospitals. Noel L. Mhyre. (Illus.). 27p. 1975. 2.00 (0-917054-03-2) Med Communications.

Testing for HIV: What Your Lab Results Mean. Ed. by N. L. Gifford. 22p. (Orig.). (C). 1995. pap. 5.00 (1-881818-07-1) TBL.

Testing for Language Teachers. Arthur Hughes. (Cambridge Handbooks for Language Teachers Ser.). (Illus.). 256p. (C). 1989. pap. text ed. 17.95 (0-521-27260-2) Cambridge U Pr.

Testing for Learning: How New Approaches to Evaluation Can Improve American Schools. Ruth Mitchell. 222p. 1992. 27.95 (0-02-921465-3, Free Press) Free Pr.

Testing for Prediction of Material Performance in Structures & Components: A Symposium. Presented at the Annual Meeting, American Society & Materials. American Society for Testing & Materials Staff. LC 72-79572. (American Society for Testing & Materials: No. 515). 319p. reprint ed. pap. 91.00 (0-317-08194-2, 2015505) Bks Demand.

Testing for Short-Termism in the U.K. Stock Market. fac. ed. David H. Miles. (Bank of England, Economics Division, Working Paper Ser.). 42p. 1992. reprint ed. pap. 25.00 (0-7837-8335-3, 2049122) Bks Demand.

Testing for Substance Use & Abuse in the Transportation Industry (1987) 121p. 1987. pap. text ed. 5.00 (1-56986-062-9) Federal Bar.

Testing for Teacher Certification. Ed. by Gorth & Chernoff. 288p. (C). 1985. text ed. 49.95 (0-89859-758-7) L Erlbaum Assocs.

Testing For Teachers. 2nd ed. Bruce W. Tuckman. 248p. (C). 1988. pap. text ed. 18.75 (0-15-591435-9) HB Coll Pubs.

***Testing Forms: Reproducible.** Katherine E. Anderson. (Illus.). 50p. (Orig.). 1997. spiral bd., pap. 12.95 (1-57876-950-7) Triple U Prods.

Testing Guidebook. L. D. Hahn. 40p. (Orig.). 1992. pap. 24.00 (0-89852-474-1, 0101R174) TAPPI.

Testing Handicapped People. Willingham. 256p. (C). 1988. text ed. 42.00 (0-205-11388-5, H13881) Allyn.

Testing HEPA & ULPA Filters Media. (Recommended Practice Ser.). 34p. 1994. pap. text ed. 125.00 (1-877862-21-5, IES-RP-CC021.1) Inst Environ Sci.

Testing in American Schools: Asking the Right Questions. (Illus.). 96p. (Orig.). (C). 1992. pap. text ed. 20.00 (0-941375-75-7) DIANE Pub.

Testing in Counseling Practice. Campbell & Watkins, Jr. Ed. by W. Bruce Walsh & Samuel H. Osipow. (Contemporary Topics in Vocational Psychology Ser.). 512p. 1993. reprint ed. pap. 39.95 (0-8058-1439-6) L Erlbaum Assocs.

Testing in Counseling, Uses & Misuses. Harley D. Christiansen. LC 81-3715. (Illus.). 96p. (Orig.). (C). 1981. pap. text ed. 15.95 (0-915456-03-6) P Juul Pr.

Testing in Language Programs. 2nd ed. Brown. (Illus.). 544p. 1995. pap. 24.95 (0-13-124157-5) P-H.

Testing in Software Development. Ed. by Martyn A. Ould & Charles Unwin. (British Computer Society Monographs in Informatics). 130p. 1987. pap. text ed. 28.95 (0-521-33786-0) Cambridge U Pr.

Testing in the Workplace, 4th Circuit Conference (1988) 68p. 1988. pap. text ed. 10.00 (1-56986-063-7) Federal Bar.

Testing Language Proficiency. Bernard J. Spolsky. LC 75-13740. 152p. reprint ed. pap. 43.40 (0-8357-3352-1, 2039586) Bks Demand.

Testing Machine Tools: For the Use of Machine Tool Makers, Users, Inspectors & Plant Engineers. 8th rev. ed. G. Schlesinger & F. Koenigsberger. LC 77-30267. (Materials Engineering Practice Ser.). 1978. 60.00 (0-08-021685-4, Pub. by Pergamon Repr UK) Franklin.

Testing Macroeconometric Models. Ray C. Fair. LC 94-13914. (Illus.). 445p. 1994. text ed. 45.00 (0-674-87503-6, FAITES) HUP.

Testing Methods in Food Microbiology. Ed. by Istvan Kiss. (Developments in Food Science Ser.: Vol. 6). 448p. 1984. 190.75 (0-444-99648-6, I-045-84) Elsevier.

Testing Object-Oriented Software. Robert Binder. (C). 1998. text ed. write for info. (0-201-80938-9) Addison-Wesley.

Testing of Adhesives: A Project of the Adhesives Testing Committee. Technical Association of the Pulp & Paper Industry Staff. Ed. by R. Gregory Meese. LC 73-88201. (TAPPI Monographs: No. 35). 224p. reprint ed. pap. 63.90 (0-317-28875-X, 2020303) Bks Demand.

Testing of Agricultural Technological Processes: A Systems Approach. Ed. by S. V. Kradashevskii et al. Tr. by J. P. Saxena from RUS. 311p. (C). 1986. text ed. 155.00 (90-6191-460-4, Pub. by A A Balkema NE) Ashgate Pub Co.

***Testing of Communicating Systems.** Ed. by Alan Baumgarten et al. 432p. 1996. text ed. write for info. (0-412-78790-3, Chap & Hall NY) Chapman & Hall.

***Testing of Concrete in Structures.** 3rd ed. Bungey & Millard. (Illus.). 296p. 1996. text ed. 101.95 (0-7514-0241-9, Pub. by Blackie Acad & Prof UK) Routledge Chapman & Hall.

Testing of Engineering Materials. 4th ed. Harmer E. Davis et al. 480p. 1982. text ed. write for info. (0-07-015656-5) McGraw.

Testing of Fiber Reinforced Concrete. 254p. 1995. pap. 36.95 (0-614-11138-2, OSP155.BOW6) ACI.

Testing of Hanna Senesh. Ruth Whitman. LC 86-23392. 116p. 1986. 17.95 (0-8143-1853-3); pap. 11.95 (0-8143-1854-1) Wayne St U Pr.

Testing of M. Falk Gjertsen. Nina Draxten. (Topical Studies: Vol. 4). (Illus.). 140p. 1988. 15.00 (0-87732-074-8) Norwegian-Am Hist Assn.

Testing of Metallic & Inorganic Coatings. Ed. by W. B. Harding & G. A. Di Bari. LC 87-11505. (Special Technical Publication Ser.: No.947). (Illus.). 380p. 1987. text ed. 59.00 (0-8031-0947-4, 04-947000-04) ASTM.

Testing of Metals for Structures: Proceedings of the International Workshop. Ed. by Federico M. Mazzolani. (RILEM Proceedings Ser.: No. 12). (Illus.). 500p. 1991. write for info. (0-412-42650-1, E & FN Spon) Routledge Chapman & Hall.

Testing of Peats & Organic Soils: A Symposium - Sponsored by ASTM Committee D-18 on Soil & Rock, Toronto, Canada, 23 June 1982. American Society for Testing & Materials Staff. Ed. by P. M. Jarrett. LC 83-70259. (ASTM Special Technical Publication Ser.: No. 820). (Illus.). 249p. reprint ed. pap. 71.00 (0-8357-3565-6, 2034269) Bks Demand.

Testing of Tertius. Robert Newman. (Illus.). (J). (gr. 5-9). 1990. 20.25 (0-8446-6188-0) Peter Smith.

Testing of the Standard Model: Proceedings of the Eleventh International School of Theoretical Physics. M. Zralek & R. Manka. 496p. 1988. text ed. 109.00 (9971-5-0634-3) World Scientific Pub.

Testing Peripheries: U.S.-Yugoslav Economic Relations in the Interwar Years. Linda Killen. LC 93-72245. (East European Monographs: No. CCCLXXXII). 234p. 1994. 50.50 (0-88033-279-4) East Eur Monographs.

Testing Positive: Sexually Transmitted Disease & the Public Health Response. Patricia A. Donovan. 47p. 1993. pap. 10.00 (0-939253-28-3) Guttmacher Inst.

Testing Principles in Clinical & Preclinical Trials. Ed. by Joachim Vollmar. (Biometrics in the Chemical/Pharmaceutical Industry Ser.: Vol. 6). (Illus.). x, 133p. 1995. pap. 35.00 (3-437-20513-7, Pub. by G Fischer Verlag GW) Lubrecht & Cramer.

Testing Problems with Linear or Angular Inequality Constraints. J. C. Akkerboom. (Lecture Notes in Statistics Ser.: Vol. 62). xii, 291p. 1990. 57.95 (0-387-97232-3) Spr-Verlag.

Testing Program for Ciao! 3rd ed. Carla Federici. (C). 1994. pap. text ed. 33.75 (0-15-500673-8) HB Coll Pubs.

Testing Program for Habla Espanol ESS. 5th ed. Mendez. (SPA.). (C). 1994. pap. text ed. 33.75 (0-15-500679-7) HB Coll Pubs.

Testing Program for Up with Math. 2nd ed. Roland C. McCully. Ed. by Erika Jacobs. 139p. 1995. teacher ed., pap. 15.95 (0-918272-25-4, 117) Jacobs.

Testing Programs for Behavior Toxicology Test Guides: Methodology & Interpretation of Data. Phyllis Mullinex. 1989. 58.00 (0-911131-21-3) Princeton Sci Pubs.

Testing, Rationality, & Progress: Essays on the Popperian Tradition in Economic Methodology. D. Wade Hands. 256p. (C). 1992. text ed. 46.50 (0-8476-7724-9) Rowman.

Testing Real Interest Parity in the European Monetary System. fac. ed. Andrew G. Haldane & Mahmood Pradhan. LC 93-4996. (Bank of England, Economics Division, Working Paper Ser.: No. 2). 36p. 1992. reprint ed. pap. 25.00 (0-7837-8294-2, 2049076) Bks Demand.

Testing, Reform & Rebellion. H. Dickson Corbett & Bruce L. Wilson. Ed. by George Nobilt & William Pink. (Interpretive Perspectives on Education & Policy Ser.). 192p. 1991. pap. 39.50 (1-56750-083-8); text ed. 73.25 (0-89391-719-2) Ablex Pub.

Testing Regression Models Based on Sample Survey Data. M. Ishaq Bhatti. 216p. (C). 1995. 59.95 (1-85628-642-8, Pub. by Avebury Pub UK) Ashgate Pub Co.

Testing Research Hypotheses Using Multiple Linear Regression. Keith McNeil et al. LC 75-6639. 600p. 1975. pap. text ed. 7.95 (0-8093-0755-3) S Ill U Pr.

Testing Research Hypotheses with the General Linear Model. Keith McNeil et al. 416p. 1996. 49.95 (0-8093-2019-3); pap. 24.95 (0-8093-2020-7) S Ill U Pr.

Testing Semiconductor Memories: Theory & Practice. A. J. Van de Goor. LC 91-20658. 512p. 1991. text ed. 98.00 (0-471-92586-1) Wiley.

Testing Sex Offenders for HIV. Lucind L. Bryant & Tracey A. Hooker. (State Legislative Reports: Vol. 16, No. 7). 12p. 1991. pap. text ed. 5.00 (1-55516-306-8, 7302-1607) Natl Conf State Legis.

Testing Spoken Language: A Handbook of Oral Testing Techniques. Nicholas Underhill. (Cambridge Handbooks for Language Teachers Ser.). 112p. 1987. pap. text ed. 15.95 (0-521-31276-0) Cambridge U Pr.

***Testing Statistical Hypotheses.** 2nd ed. E. Lehmann. (C). (gr. 13 up). 1991. text ed. 63.95 (0-412-05321-7) Chapman & Hall.

***Testing Statistical Hypotheses.** 2nd ed. E. L. Lehmann. LC 96-48846. (Springer Texts in Statistics Ser.). 600p. 1997. 64.95 (0-387-94919-4) Spr-Verlag.

Testing Structural Equation Models. Ed. by Kenneth A. Bollen & J. Scott Long. (Focus Editions Ser.: Vol. 154). (Illus.). 280p. (C). 1993. text ed. 54.00 (0-8039-4506-X); pap. text ed. 24.95 (0-8039-4507-8) Sage.

***Testing Students with Disabilities: Practical Strategies for Complying with District & State Requirements.** Martha L. Thurlow et al. LC 97-21048. 1997. write for info. (0-8039-6551-6); pap. write for info. (0-8039-6552-4) Corwin Pr.

Testing Techniques for Rock Mechanics. American Society for Testing & Materials Staff. LC 66-24783. (American Society for Testing & Materials Special Technical Publication Ser.: Special Technical Publication, No. 402). 304p. reprint ed. pap. 86.70 (0-317-11253-8, 2001129) Bks Demand.

Testing Technology of Metal Matrix Composites STP 964. Ed. by P. R. DiGiovanni & N. R. Adsit. LC 88-15451. (Special Technical Publication (STP) Ser.). (Illus.). 472p. 1988. text ed. 64.00 (0-8031-0967-9, 04-964000-33) ASTM.

Testing Testing: Social Consequences of the Examined Life. F. Allan Hanson. LC 92-32639. 1994. pap. 14.00 (0-520-08648-1) U CA Pr.

Testing Testing: The Social Consequences of the Examined Life. F. Allan Hanson. LC 92-32639. 390p. 1993. 35.00 (0-520-08060-2) U CA Pr.

Testing the AGN Paradigm. Ed. by Stephen S. Holt et al. LC 92-52780. (Conference Proceeding Ser.: No. 254). (Illus.). 720p. 1992. lib. bdg. 99.00 (1-56396-009-5) Am Inst Physics.

Testing the Boundaries: Windows to Lutheran Identity. Charles P. Arand. LC 95-36697. (Concordia Scholarship Today Ser.). 1995. 12.99 (0-570-04839-7, 12-3276) Concordia.

Testing the Efficiency of Wood-Burning Cookstoves: International Provisional Standards. Volunteers in Technical Assistance Staff. 76p. 1985. English, 76p. 9.75 (0-86619-229-8, E-11082); French, 76p. 9.75 (0-86619-235-2, F-19082); Spanish, 90p. 9.75 (0-86619-236-0, S-18082) Vols Tech Asst.

Testing the Faith: The New Catholic Fiction in America. Anita Gandolfo. LC 91-24836. (Contributions in American Studies: No. 100). 264p. 1992. text ed. 49.95 (0-313-27843-1, GCY, Greenwood Pr) Greenwood.

Testing the Link Between Devaluation & Inflation: Time Series Evidence from Ghana. CFNPP Staff & Stephen D. Younger. (Working Papers). (C). 1992. pap. 7.00 (1-56401-124-0) Cornell Food.

Testing the Medical Covenant: Active Euthanasia & Health Care Reform. William F. May. LC 96-26076. 146p. 1996. pap. 14.00 (0-8028-4204-6) Eerdmans.

Testing the Roosevelt Coalition: Connecticut Society & Politics in the Era of World War II. John W. Jeffries. LC 78-14550. (Twentieth-Century America Ser.). 327p. reprint ed. pap. 93.20 (0-7837-1318-5, 2041466) Bks Demand.

Testing the Social Safety Net: The Impact of Changes in Support Programs During the Reagan Administration. Martha R. Burt & Karen J. Pittman. 183p. (Orig.). 1985. pap. text ed. 19.50 (0-87766-392-0) Urban Inst.

Testing the Spirits. Elizabeth L. Hillstrom. LC 94-41678. 240p. (Orig.). 1995. pap. 12.99 (0-8308-1604-6, 1604) InterVarsity.

Testing the Standard Model: TASI Workshop 1990. Ed. by Mirjam Cvetic & Paul Langacker. 936p. (C). 1991. text ed. 124.00 (981-02-0314-4); pap. text ed. 61.00 (981-02-0315-2) World Scientific Pub.

Testing the Theories of Aging. Ed. by Richard C. Adelman & George S. Roth. 304p. 1982. 304.00 (0-8493-5829-9, QP86, CRC Reprint) Franklin.

***Testing the Waters: Basic Tenets of Faith.** Jeff Wright & Lani Wright. (Generation Why: Vol. 2:8). 44p. (YA). (gr. 9-12). 1997. pap. 14.95 (0-87303-271-3) Faith & Life.

***Testing the Waters: Chemical & Physical Vital Signs of a River.** River Watch Staff. 240p. 1997. per. 24.95 (0-7872-3492-3) Kendall-Hunt.

***Testing the Wind.** Terry Deffenbaugh. 75p. 1993. pap. 12.95 (1-877871-49-4, 8421) Ed Ministries.

***Testing To Learn--Learning To Test.** Joanne Capper. LC 96-32876. 1996. pap. 28.95 (0-87207-145-6) Intl Reading.

Testing, Troubleshooting, & Tuning Local Area Networks: Techniques & Tools to Isolate Problems & Boost Performance. Gilbert Held. LC 95-53982. 250p. 1996. text ed. 59.95 (0-471-95880-8) Wiley.

Testing Ulpa Filters: IES-RP-CC007.1. Working Group Staff. (Recommended Practice Ser.). 32p. 1992. pap. text ed. 125.00 (1-877862-37-1) Inst Environ Sci.

Testing Very Big Systems. David M. Marks. 240p. 1991. 39.95 (0-8306-2555-0) McGraw-Hill Prof.

***Testing Yeast & Bacteria.** Katherine E. Anderson. (Illus.). 60p. (Orig.). 1996. spiral bd., pap. 9.95 (1-57876-904-3) Triple U Prods.

Testing Young Children: A Reference Guide for Developmental, Psychoeducational, & Psychosocial Assessments. Ed. by Jan L. Culbertson & Diane J. Willis. LC 92-11515. 600p. 1992. text ed. 41.00 (0-89079-550-9, 1924) PRO-ED.

Testing Your Grammar. Susan M. Reinhart. 1985. pap. text ed. 12.95 (0-472-08054-7) U of Mich Pr.

Testis. 2nd ed. Ed. by Henry Burger & David De Kretser. (Comprehensive Endocrinology Ser.). 605p. 1989. text ed. 121.50 (0-88167-543-1, 2013) Lppncott-Raven.

TestMaster ACT. Jill Horner. 175p. 1993. teacher ed. 99.00 (1-883859-08-5); 79.00 incl. vhs (1-883859-07-7) Resource Netwrk.

TestMaster ACT Review. Margaret Whyte & Jill Horner. 175p. 1993. teacher ed. 49.00 (1-883859-02-6); pap. 12.00 (1-883859-01-8) Resource Netwrk.

TestMaster SAT Review. Margaret Whyte. Ed. by Jill Horner. 110p. 1996. teacher ed. 49.00 (1-883859-05-0); student ed. 12.00 (1-883859-04-2) Resource Netwrk.

An Asterisk (*) at the beginning of an entry indicates that the title is appearing in BIP for the first time.

Testment of Cresseid & Other Poems. Robert Henryson. 96p. 1989. pap. 8.95 (*0-14-044507-2*, Penguin Classics) Viking Penguin.

Testology: Secrets on How to Take Examinations. Larry A. Zadnikar, Jr. (Winning at the Educational Game Ser.: Vol. 1). (Illus.). vi, 26p. (Orig.). 1996. pap. 5.95 (*1-888794-00-3*) I Can Learn.

Testosterone - Action, Deficiency, Substitution. Ed. by E. Nieschlag & H. M. Behre. (Illus.). 352p. 1990. 70.00 (*0-387-52763-X*) Spr-Verlag.

***Testosterone Replacement Therapy.** Fred C. Wu. (Illus.). 55p. (Orig.). 1996. pap. text ed. 14.95 (*1-898099-12-X*) Blackwell Sci.

***Testosterone Solution.** Aubrey Hill. LC 97-13864. 240p. 1997. per. 14.00 (*0-7615-1022-2*) Prima Pub.

Tests. 4th ed. 1994. 89.00 (*0-685-58990-0*) Gale.

Tests. 5th ed. 1996. 89.00 (*0-685-58995-1*) Gale.

Tests: A Comprehensive Reference for Assessments in Psychology, Education, & Business. 3rd ed. Ed. by Daniel J. Keyser & Richard C. Sweetland. LC 89-78495. 1251p. (C). 1991. text ed. 89.00 (*0-89079-255-0*, 1939); pap. text ed. 69.00 (*0-89079-256-9*, 1940) PRO-ED.

***Tests: A Comprehensive Reference for Assessments in Psychology, Education & Business.** 4th ed. Taddy Maddox. LC 96-38299. 1997. 89.00 (*0-89079-707-2*) PRO-ED.

***Tests: A Comprehensive Reference for Assessments in Psychology, Education & Business.** 4th ed. Taddy Maddox. LC 96-38299. 1997. 69.00 (*0-89079-709-9*) PRO-ED.

Tests see Deutsch Konkret, Level 2

Tests see Deutsch Konkret, Level 3

Tests - Harcourt Brace Language. 90th ed. Strickland. 1990. teacher ed., pap. 11.00 (*0-15-316480-8*); teacher ed., pap. 11.00 (*0-15-316481-6*); teacher ed., pap. 11.75 (*0-15-316482-4*); teacher ed., pap. 11.75 (*0-15-316483-2*); teacher ed., pap. 11.75 (*0-15-316484-0*); teacher ed., pap. 11.75 (*0-15-316485-9*); teacher ed., pap. 11.75 (*0-15-316486-7*); teacher ed., pap. 11.75 (*0-15-316487-5*) HB Schl Dept.

Tests & Assessment. 3rd ed. Bruce Walsh & Nancy E. Betz. LC 94-35182. 512p. 1994. text ed. 68.33 (*0-13-173171-8*) P-H.

Tests & Checkpoints for the Reading Program. Amy Awtrey & Carol Markos. (Reading Program Ser.). 100p. (gr. 10-12). 1982. ring bd. 15.00 (*0-88069-013-5*) L A Meyer.

Tests & Criteria for the Recommendations on the Transport of Dangerous Goods. 6th ed. United Nations Economic & Social Council Staff. (Illus.). 1990. ring bd. 65.00 (*0-685-33036-2*, UN-TEST) Labelmaster.

Tests & Measurement Specialist. Jack Rudman. (Career Examination Ser.: C-3484). 1994. pap. 39.95 (*0-8373-3484-5*) Nat Learn.

Tests & Measurements. Jack Rudman. (College Level Examination Ser.: CLEP-27). 1994. pap. 23.95 (*0-8373-5327-0*) Nat Learn.

Tests & Measurements. 4th ed. W. Bruce Walsh. 160p. (C). 1989. pap. text ed. 19.00 (*0-13-906918-6*) P-H.

Tests & Measurements for Behavioral Optometrists. Harold A. Solan & Irwin B. Suchoff. Ed. by Sally M. Corngold. LC 91-32164. (Illus.). 70p. (C). 1991. lib. bdg. 15.00 (*0-943599-21-0*) OEPF.

Tests & Measurements in Child Development: Handbook II, 2 vols., Vol. 1. Orval G. Johnson. LC 76-11890. (Jossey-Bass Behavioral Science Ser.). 688p. reprint ed. pap. 180.00 (*0-8357-4894-4*, 2037825) Bks Demand.

Tests & Measurements in Child Development: Handbook II, 2 vols., Vol. 2. Orval G. Johnson. LC 76-11890. (Jossey-Bass Behavioral Science Ser.). 666p. reprint ed. pap. 180.00 (*0-8357-4895-2*, 2037825) Bks Demand.

Tests & Measurements in Child Development: Handbook One. Orval G. Johnson & James W. Bommarito. LC 76-110636. (Jossey-Bass Behavioral Science Ser.). 540p. reprint ed. pap. 153.90 (*0-8357-4989-4*, 2037922) Bks Demand.

Tests & Measurements in Health & Physical Education. 3rd ed. Charles H. McCloy & Norma D. Young. (Illus.). 1979. reprint ed. text ed. 29.50 (*0-89197-448-2*) Irvington.

Tests for American Civics 1987. Hartley. 1987. suppl. ed., teacher ed., pap. text ed. 8.75 (*0-15-371449-2*) HR&W Schl Div.

Tests for HBJ Health 1987 Grade 5. rev. ed. HBJ Staff. 1987. suppl. ed., pap. 4.25 (*0-15-369028-3*) HB Schl Dept.

Tests for HBJ Health 1987 Grade 6. rev. ed. HBJ Staff. 1987. suppl. ed., pap. 4.25 (*0-15-369029-1*) HB Schl Dept.

Tests for HBJ Health 1987 Grade 7. rev. ed. HBJ Staff. 1987. suppl. ed., pap. 4.25 (*0-15-369030-5*) HB Schl Dept.

Tests for HBJ Health 1987 Grade 8. rev. ed. HBJ Staff. 1987. suppl. ed., pap. 4.25 (*0-15-369031-3*) HB Schl Dept.

Tests for HBJ Introduction to Algebra 1 '88. Jacobs. 1988. teacher ed., pap. text ed. 10.00 (*0-15-357860-2*) HR&W Schl Div.

Tests for People & Nations: World History 1987. Mazour. 1987. suppl. ed., pap. text ed. 11.00 (*0-15-373469-8*) HR&W Schl Div.

Tests for United States History. Reich. 1988. teacher ed., pap. text ed. 10.00 (*0-03-014812-X*) HR&W Schl Div.

Tests for 250 Young Adult Novels see Teaching Guides for 50 Young Adult Novels & Tests for 250 Young Adult Novels

***Tests-Horizontes.** 3rd ed. Gilman. (College Spanish Ser.). 1997. pap. 17.95 (*0-8384-6090-9*) Heinle & Heinle.

Tests-Horizontes 3E. 3rd ed. Gilman. (Miscellaneous/Catalogs Ser.). 1997. pap. 12.75 (*0-8384-7112-9*) Wadsworth Pub.

Tests in Print: A Comprehensive Bibliography of Tests for Use in Education, Psychology & Industry. Ed. by Oscar K. Buros et al. LC 61-16302. 511p. reprint ed. pap. 145.70 (*0-317-41871-8*, 2026110) Bks Demand.

Tests in Print No. IV, 2 vols., Set. Ed. by Linda U. Murphy et al. 1473p. (C). 1994. text ed. 325.00 (*0-910674-53-1*) Buros Inst Mental.

Tests in Print III. Ed. by James V. Mitchell, Jr. LC 83-18866. xxxii, 714p. 1983. 150.00 (*0-910674-52-3*) U of Nebr Pr.

Tests in Voice & Speech-Language Pathology. Kersner. 320p. 1992. 59.50 (*1-56593-569-1*, 0424) Singular Publishing.

Tests: Listening Comprehension, Other Skills see Foreign Language Teachers & Tests

Tests Math Plus 1992: Grade 1. 1992. teacher ed., pap. text ed. 35.00 (*0-15-301015-0*) HB Schl Dept.

Tests Math Plus 1992: Grade 2. 1992. teacher ed., pap. text ed. 35.00 (*0-15-301016-9*) HB Schl Dept.

Tests Math Plus 1992: Grade 3. 1992. teacher ed., pap. text ed. 35.00 (*0-15-301017-7*) HB Schl Dept.

Tests Math Plus 1992: Grade 4. 1992. teacher ed., pap. text ed. 35.00 (*0-15-301018-5*) HB Schl Dept.

Tests Math Plus 1992: Grade 5. 1992. teacher ed., pap. text ed. 35.00 (*0-15-301019-3*) HB Schl Dept.

Tests Math Plus 1992: Grade 6. 1992. teacher ed., pap. text ed. 35.00 (*0-15-301020-7*) HB Schl Dept.

Tests Math Plus 1992: Grade 7. 1992. teacher ed., pap. text ed. 35.00 (*0-15-301021-5*) HB Schl Dept.

Tests Math Plus 1992: Grade 8. 1992. teacher ed., pap. text ed. 35.00 (*0-15-301022-3*) HB Schl Dept.

Tests of Being. Nur Cheyenne. (Illus.). 159p. (Orig.). 1996. pap. 12.95 (*1-56072-329-7*) Nova Sci Pubs.

***Tests of Character: Epic Flights by Legendary Test Pilots.** Donald Middleton. 224p. 1995. 35.00 (*1-56091-671-0*) Soc Auto Engineers.

Tests of Electroweak Theories, Polarized Processes & Other Phenomena: Proceedings of the 2nd ICTP Conference on Tests of Electroweak Physics, Trieste, Italy, June 1985. Ed. by B. W. Lynn & C. Verzegnassi. 476p. 1987. pap. 51.00 (*9971-5-0305-0*); text ed. 124.00 (*9971-5-0300-X*) World Scientific Pub.

Tests of Eternal Life: Studies in First John. Herbert W. Butt. pap. 0.99 (*0-87377-034-X*) GAM Pubns.

Tests of Literary Vocabulary for Teachers of English. L. H. Kennon. LC 70-176966. (Columbia University. Teachers College. Contributions to Education Ser.: No. 223). reprint ed. 37.50 (*0-404-55223-4*) AMS Pr.

Tests of Practical Mental Classification see Report

Tests of Significance. Ramon E. Henkel. (Quantitative Applications in the Social Sciences Ser.: Vol. 4). 92p. 1976. 9.95 (*0-8039-0652-8*) Sage.

Tests of Subsurface Storage of Freshwater at Hialeah, Dade County, Florida & Digital Simulation of the Salinity of Recovered Water. Michael L. Merritt. 1995. write for info. (*0-615-00059-2*) US Geol Survey.

Tests of the Standard Theory of Electroweak Interactions. C. Kiesling. (Tracts in Modern Physics Ser.: Vol. 112). (Illus.). 225p. 1989. 86.95 (*0-387-17513-X*) Spr-Verlag.

Tests of Time Reversal Invariance in Neutron Physics: Proceedings of the Aqueduct Conference Center, N. C. Ed. by N. Roberson et al. 216p. (C). 1987. text ed. 97.00 (*9971-5-0463-4*) World Scientific Pub.

***Tests of Wormgear Speed Reducers for Power Capacity & Lubrication Data.** C. B. Hamilton. (Technical Papers). 1933. pap. text ed. 30.00 (*1-55589-421-6*) AGMA.

Tests on Two Thirty-Year-Old Prestressed Concrete Beams. (PCI Journal Reprints Ser.). 4p. 1980. pap. 6.00 (*0-686-40138-7*, JR234) P-PCI.

Tests That Help Teaching. W. James Popham. 43p. (Orig.). 1995. pap. 25.00 (*0-614-14879-0*) IOX Amnt Assocs.

Tests to Determine the Lateral Distribution of Vertical Loads in a Long-Span Hollow-Core Floor Assembly. (PCI Journal Reprints Ser.). 18p. 1983. pap. 14.00 (*0-318-19801-0*, JR290) P-PCI.

Testudines. M. Minarski. (Encyclopedia of Paleoherpetology Ser.: Pt. 7). (Illus.). 130p. 1976. text ed. 70.00 (*3-437-30236-1*) Lubrecht & Cramer.

Testwell College Inventory. National Wellness Staff. 16p. (C). 1993. write for info. (*0-697-21131-2*) Brown & Benchmark.

Tesuji & Anti-Suji of Go: Playing in Good Form & Making Correct Shape. Sakata Eio. Tr. by Robert J. Terry from JPN. (Illus.). 224p. (Orig.). 1995. pap. text ed. write for info. (*0-9641847-5-3*) Yutopian Ent.

Tesuque Poems. Victor Di Suvero. (Blue Ser.). 6.00 (*0-938631-17-9*) Pennywhistle Pr.

Tesy. 1976. pap. 111.00 (*0-380-88888-2*) Avon.

T.E.T. Teacher Effectiveness Training. Thomas Gordon. 14.95 (*0-317-62732-5*) McKay.

TET: The Crucial Year of Nineteen Sixty-Eight. Clark Dougan. Ed. by Boston Publishing Company Editors. (Vietnam Experience Ser.). (Illus.). 192p. 1983. 16.30 (*0-201-11326-0*) Addison-Wesley.

Tet: Vietnamese New Year. Dianne M. MacMillan. LC 93-46184. (Best Holiday Bks.). (Illus.). 48p. (J). (gr. 1-4). 1994. lib. bdg. 17.95 (*0-89490-501-5*) Enslow Pubs.

Tet Marine: An Autobiography. W. J. Davis. 185p. 1987. pap. 11.00 (*1-885541-02-3*) Marine Bks.

Tet Offensive. Ed. by Marc J. Gilbert & William Head. LC 95-49604. 312p. 1996. text ed. 69.50 (*0-275-95480-3*, Praeger Pubs) Greenwood.

Tet Offensive. Ed. by Marc J. Gilbert & William Head. LC 95-49604. 312p. 1996. pap. text ed. 24.95 (*0-275-95481-1*, Praeger Pubs) Greenwood.

Tet Offensive. Earle Rice, Jr. LC 96-14227. (Great Battles Ser.). (Illus.). 112p. (J). (gr. 5-12). 1996. lib. bdg. 20.96 (*1-56006-422-6*) Lucent Bks.

Tet Offensive. Charles Wills. (Turning Points in American History Ser.). (Illus.). 64p. (J). (gr. 5 up). 1989. lib. bdg. 14.95 (*0-382-09849-8*) Silver Burdett Pr.

Tet Offensive. Charles Wills. (Turning Points in American History Ser.). (Illus.). 64p. (YA). (gr. 5 up). 1989. pap. 7.95 (*0-382-09855-2*) Silver Burdett Pr.

Tet Offensive: Intelligence Failure in War. James J. Wirtz. (Cornell Studies in Security Affairs). 304p. 1994. pap. 16.95 (*0-8014-8209-7*) Cornell U Pr.

Tet-Offensive, 1968. James R. Arnold. (Campaign Ser.: No. 4). (Illus.). 96p. 1990. pap. 14.95 (*0-85045-960-5*, 9503, Pub. by Osprey Pubng Ltd UK) Stackpole.

TET! The Turning Point in the Vietnam War. Don Oberdorfer. (Quality Paperbacks Ser.). (Illus.). 400p. 1984. pap. 11.95 (*0-306-80210-4*) Da Capo.

***Tet-Vietnam War Games.** 1991. 40.00 (*1-55878-075-0*) Game Designers.

Tet 1968: Understanding the Surprise. Ronnie E. Ford. 240p. 1995. pap. 19.50 (*0-7146-4166-9*) Intl Spec Bk.

Tet 1968: Understanding the Surprise. W. C. Westmoreland. LC 94-39310. (Studies in Intelligence). 240p. 1995. 39.50 (*0-7146-4587-7*, Pub. by F Cass Pubs UK) Intl Spec Bk.

Tetanus. Farokh E. Udwadia. (Illus.). 176p. 1994. 57.50 (*0-19-563578-7*) OUP.

Tetbury. John Hudson. (Towns & Villages of England Ser.). (Illus.). 1994. pap. 10.00 (*0-7509-0538-7*, Pub. by Sutton Pubng UK) Bks Intl VA.

Tete: Cornrows Say the African Healer's Life. Julianna Free. Tr. by Howell Wechsler. (Illus.). 128p. 1996. pap. 17.95 (*0-9605700-8-X*) Lifeline Res.

Tete a Tete. Gorrell. 1992. pap. 36.95 (*0-8384-3682-X*) Heinle & Heinle.

Tete Contre les Murs. Herve Bazin. (FRE.). 1956. pap. 12.95 (*0-7859-3069-8*) Fr & Eur.

Tete Coupable. Romain Gary. 304p. (FRE.). 1968. 19.95 (*0-8288-9771-9*, F101642) Fr & Eur.

Tete Coupable see Frere Ocean

Tete De Chien. Jean Dutourd. 154p. (FRE.). 1988. pap. 10.95 (*0-7859-2103-6*, 2070380866) Fr & Eur.

Tete des Autres. Marcel Ayme. 192p. (FRE.). 1956. pap. 10.95 (*0-7859-0371-2*, F84050) Fr & Eur.

Tete d'Or. Paul Claudel. (FRE.). 1987. pap. 10.95 (*0-8288-3633-7*, M3266) Fr & Eur.

Tete d'Or. Paul Claudel. (Folio Ser.: No. 308). 326p. (FRE.). 1959. pap. 8.95 (*2-07-036308-2*) Schoenhof.

Tetes Mortes. Samuel Beckett. pap. 8.95 (*0-685-37201-4*, F86110) Fr & Eur.

Teth. Sheila Murphy. 88p. (Orig.). 1990. pap. 9.00 (*0-925904-05-8*) Chax Pr.

Tether. Lorrie Goldensohn. LC 82-21685. 65p. pap. 4.95 (*0-934332-39-8*) LEpervier Pr.

***Tetherballs of Bougainville.** Mark Leyner. LC 97-10699. 1997. 21.00 (*0-517-70101-4*, Harmony) Crown Pub Group.

Tethered Cord Syndrome. Ed. by Shokei Yamada. (Special Topics Ser.). (Illus.). 200p. 1995. 95.00 (*1-879284-37-5*) Am Assn Neuro.

Tethered Deer: Government & Economy in a Chinese County. Marc J. Blecher. LC 95-19174. 322p. 1996. 39.50 (*0-8047-2565-9*) Stanford U Pr.

Tether's End. Margery Allingham. 176p. reprint ed. lib. bdg. 16.95 (*0-89190-197-3*, Rivercity Pr) Amereon Ltd.

Tether's End: An Albert Campion Mystery. Margery Allingham. 208p. 1996. mass mkt. 4.95 (*0-7867-0383-0*) Carroll & Graf.

Tethers in Space. Ed. by Peter M. Bainum et al. (Advances in the Astronautical Sciences Ser.: Vol. 62). (Illus.). 784p. 1987. pap. 70.00 (*0-87703-265-3*); lib. bdg. 80.00 (*0-87703-264-5*) Univelt Inc.

Teton Classics: Fifty Selected Climbs in Grand Teton National Park. 2nd ed. Richard Rossiter. (Illus.). 126p. (Orig.). 1994. pap. 15.00 (*0-934641-71-4*) Chockstone Pr.

Teton Country Anthology. Ed. by Robert W. Righter. (Illus.). 210p. 1990. pap. 12.50 (*0-911797-73-4*) R Rinehart.

Teton Sioux see Indians of North America

Teton Sioux Indians see Junior Library of American Indians

Teton Sioux Music. Frances Densmore. (Bureau of American Ethnology Buletins Ser.). 561p. 1995. lib. bdg. 119.00 (*0-7812-4061-1*) Rprt Serv.

Teton Sioux Music. Frances Densmore. 1988. reprint ed. lib. bdg. 75.00 (*0-7812-0222-1*) Rprt Serv.

Teton Sioux Music & Culture. Frances Densmore. LC 92-16223. (Illus.). xviii, 644p. 1992. pap. 19.95 (*0-8032-6593-X*, Bison Books) U of Nebr Pr.

Teton Skiing: A Guide to Skiing the Teton Range. Thomas Turiano. (Illus.). (Orig.). 1995. pap. 16.95 (*0-943972-43-4*) Homestead WY.

Teton Tale Embracing Life with No Regrets. Paul K. Petzoldt. LC 95-24428. 1995. 14.95 (*1-57034-015-3*) ICS Bks.

Teton Trails: A Guide to the Trails of Grand Teton National Park. Darwin Wile & Katy Duffy. Ed. by Sharlene Milligan. (Illus.). 175p. (Orig.). 1995. pap. 7.95 (*0-931895-35-9*) Grand Teton NHA.

Tetons: Interpretation of a Mountain Landscape. Fritiof Fryxell. (Illus.). 77p. 1938. reprint ed. 24.95 (*0-931895-06-5*); reprint ed. pap. 9.95 (*0-931895-05-7*) Grand Teton NHA.

Tetra Encyclopedia of Freshwater Tropical Aquarium Fishes. rev. ed. Gwynne Vevers & D. L. Mills. (Illus.). 211p. 1995. 31.95 (*1-56465-131-2*, 16060) Tetra Pr.

Tetra Encyclopedia of Koi. Tetra Press Staff et al. 211p. 1994. 31.95 (*1-56465-145-2*, 16097) Tetra Pr.

Tetra Encyclopedia of the Marine Aquarium. Dick Mills. (Illus.). 208p. 31.95 (*1-56465-141-X*, 16059) Tetra Pr.

Tetraalkyl Halides. Abraham. (IUPAC Solubility Data Ser.). Date not set. 130.01 (*0-08-026189-2*, Pergamon Pr) Elsevier.

Tetraalkyl Halides. S. Abraham. 1993. 105.31 (*0-08-026188-4*, Pergamon Pr) Elsevier.

Tetrabiblos. Claudius Ptolemy. (Loeb Classical Library: No. 435). 502p. (C). 1980. text ed. 18.95 (*0-674-99479-5*) HUP.

Tetrabiblos. Claudius Ptolemy. LC 76-41123. 1974. 10.50 (*0-912504-31-5*); pap. 7.50 (*0-912504-24-2*) Sym & Sign.

Tetrabromobisphenol A & Derivatives. (Environmental Health Criteria Ser.: Vol. 172). 139p. (C). 1995. pap. 29.00 (*92-4-157172-1*, 1160172) World Health.

***Tetrachloroethylene.** (Environmental Health Criteria Ser.: No. 31). 48p. 1984. pap. text ed. 12.00 (*92-4-154091-5*, 1160031) World Health.

***Tetrachloroethylene Health & Safety Guide.** WHO Staff. (Health & Safety Guides). 42p. 1987. 5.00 (*92-4-154331-0*) World Health.

Tetradifon. (Environmental Health Criteria Ser.: No. 67). 47p. 1986. pap. text ed. 11.00 (*92-4-154267-5*, 1160067) World Health.

***Tetradifon Health & Safety Guide.** WHO Staff. (Health & Safety Guides: No. 11). 38p. 1987. 5.00 (*92-4-154367-1*) World Health.

Tetradrachmenpragung Von Syrakus, in der Periode der Signierenden Kunstler. L. O. Tudeer. (Illus.). 1979. 40.00 (*0-916710-53-X*) Obol Intl.

Tetradrachms of Roman Egypt. 2nd ed. James Curtis. Ed. by S. Durst. LC 88-72315. (Illus.). 420p. 1990. text ed. 45.00 (*0-942666-61-5*) S J Durst.

Tetragrammaton. Steven Jacobsen. 321p. 1993. pap. 20.00 (*1-883657-02-4*) Earth Rose Pr.

Tetragrammaton: The Secret to Evoking Angelic Powers & the Key to the Apocalypse. Donald Tyson. LC 95-31174. (Llewellyn's High Magick Ser.). 304p. 1995. pap. 19.95 (*1-56718-744-7*) Llewellyn Pubns.

Tetrahedrally-Bonded Amorphous Semiconductors. Ed. by David A Adler & Hellmut Fritzsche. (Institute for Amorphous Studies). 580p. 1985. 145.00 (*0-306-42076-7*, Plenum Pr) Plenum.

Tetrahedrally Bonded Amorphous Semiconductors: Carefree, AZ, 1981. Ed. by R. A. Street et al. (AIP Conference Proceedings Ser.: No. 73). 338p. 1981. lib. bdg. 31.75 (*0-88318-172-X*) Am Inst Physics.

Tetrahedrally Bonded Amorphous Semiconductors: Proceedings of the Conference, No. 20, Yorktown Heights. D. L. Weaire. LC 74-80145. 369p. 1974. 16.00 (*0-88318-119-3*) Am Inst Physics.

***Tetrahydrobiopterin: Basic Biochemistry & Role in Human Disease.** Seymour Kaufman. LC 96-39275. (Illus.). 448p. 1997. text ed. 90.00 (*0-8018-5344-3*) Johns Hopkins.

Tetramethrin. (Environmental Health Criteria Ser.: No. 98). 69p. 1990. pap. text ed. 19.00 (*92-4-154298-5*, 1160098) World Health.

***Tetramethrin Health & Safety Guide.** WHO Staff. (Health & Safety Guides: No. 31). 28p. 1989. 5.00 (*92-4-154352-3*) World Health.

Tetraphenylborates. Popovych. (Solubility Data Ser.). 1981. 130.00 (*0-08-023965-X*, Pergamon Pr) Elsevier.

Tetraphenylborates see Solubility Data Series

Tetraplegia & Paraplegia: A Guide for Physiotherapists. 4th ed. Ida Bromley. (Illus.). 219p. 1991. pap. text ed. 39.95 (*0-443-04215-2*) Churchill.

Tetra's Popular Guide to Tropical Cichlids. Paul V. Loiselle et al. LC 94-23254. 1994. 21.95 (*1-56465-147-9*, 16004) Tetra Pr.

Tetrathiooxalate Darstellung Eigenschaften & Reaktionen, Vol. 7. P. Jeroschewski. (Sulfur Reports). 44p. 1986. pap. text ed. 41.00 (*3-7186-0373-X*, Harwood Acad Pubs) Gordon & Breach.

Tetrato Literario en Sor Juana Ines de la Cruz. Sylvia G. Carullo. LC 91-23. (American University Studies: Romance Languages & Literature: Ser. II, Vol. 164). 232p. (SPA.). (C). 1991. text ed. 38.95 (*0-8204-1468-9*) P Lang Pubng.

Tetrazolium-Formazan System: Design & Histochemistry. Eberhard Seidler. (Progress in Histochemistry & Cytochemistry Ser.: Vol. 24, No. 1). (Illus.). 70p. (Orig.). 1991. 60.00 (*0-685-54389-7*, Pub. by G Fischer Verlag GW) Lubrecht & Cramer.

Tetrazolium-Formazan System: Design & Histochemistry. Eberhard Seidler. (Progress in Histochemistry & Cytochemistry Ser.: Vol. 24/1). (Illus.). 70p. (Orig.). 1991. pap. 70.00 (*1-56081-315-6*, Pub. by G Fischer Verlag GW) Lubrecht & Cramer.

Tetsubin. P. L. Arts. (Illus.). 582p. 1987. 39.50 (*90-72370-01-5*, Pub. by Bamboo Pub UK) Antique Collect.

Tettigoniidae, Vol. 1. D. C. Rentz. 384p. 1985. text ed. 80.00 (*0-643-03839-6*, Pub. by CSIRO AT) Aubrey Bks.

Tettigoniidae of Australia Vol. 2: The Austrosaginae, Zaprochilinae & Phasmodinae. D. C. Rentz. (Illus.). 386p. 1993. text ed. 80.00 (*0-643-05424-3*, Pub. by CSIRO AT) Aubrey Bks.

Tetum Ghosts & Kin: Fieldwork in an Indonesian Community. David Hicks. LC 76-28114. (Illus.). 143p. (C). 1988. reprint ed. pap. text ed. 9.95 (*0-88133-320-4*) Waveland Pr.

Teudar: A King of Cornwall. W. H. Pascoe. (C). 1989. 40.00 (*1-85022-001-8*, Pub. by Dyllansow Truran UK) St Mut.

Teufelbuecher in Auswahl, 3 vols., Vol. 1. Ed. by Ria Stambaugh. (Ausgaben Deutscher Literatur des XV bis XVIII Jahrhunderts Ser.). (C). 1970. 334.60 (*3-11-006388-3*) De Gruyter.

Teufelbuecher in Auswahl, 3 vols., Vol. 2. Ed. by Ria Stambaugh. (Ausgaben Deutscher Literatur des XV bis XVIII Jahrhunderts Ser.). (C). 1972. 311.55 (*3-11-003924-9*) De Gruyter.

T

Teufelbuecher in Auswahl, 3 vols., Vol. 3. Ed. by Ria Stambaugh. (Ausgaben Deutscher Literatur des XV bis XVIII Jahrhunderts Ser.). (C). 1972. 303.85 (*3-11-004127-8*) De Gruyter.
Teufelbuecher in Auswahl, Vol. 4. Ed. by Ria Stambaugh. (Ausgaben Detuscher Literatur des XV bis XVIII Jahrhunderts Ser.). (C). 1978. 280.75 (*3-11-007331-5*) De Gruyter.
Teufelliteratur des 16 Jahrhunderts. Max Osborn. vi, 236p. 1972. reprint ed. write for info. (*0-318-71850-2*) G Olms Pubs.
Teufels General. Carl Zuckmayer. 156p. (GER.). 1996. pap. 11.75 (*3-596-27019-7*, Pub. by Fischer Taschbch Verlag GW) Intl Bk Import.
***Teufelskreis.** L. Tilkovszky. 1989. pap. 145.00 (*963-05-4980-8*, Pub. by Akad Kiado HU) St Mut.
Teuton & the Roman: Abridged from the Work of Charles Kingsley. Charles Kingsley. Ed. by R. Peterson. (Illus.). 122p. (Orig.). 1995. pap. 16.00 (*1-878465-12-0*) Scott-Townsend Pubs.
Teutonic Knights. Henryk Sienkiewicz. (Illus.). 400p. 1996. 30.00 (*0-7818-0433-7*) Hippocrene Bks.
Teutonic Legends in the Nibelungen Lied & the Nibelungen Ring. W. C. Sawyer. 1976. lib. bdg. 59.95 (*0-8490-2736-5*) Gordon Pr.
Teutonic Magic: The Magical & Spiritual Practices of the Germanic Peoples. Kveldulf Gundarsson. LC 90-39289. (Teutonic Magick Ser.). (Illus.). 336p. (Orig.). 1990. pap. 12.95 (*0-87542-291-8*) Llewellyn Pubns.
Teutonic Mythology of Richard Wagner's "The Ring of The Nibelung", Vol. 1: Nine Properties. William O. Cord. LC 89-12612. (Studies in the History & Interpretation of Music: Vol. 16). 160p. 1989. 69.95 (*0-88946-441-3*) E Mellen.
Teutonic Mythology of Richard Wagner's "The Ring of the Nibelung", Vol. 2: The Family of Gods. William O. Cord. LC 89-12612. (Studies in the History & Interpretation of Music: Vol. 17). 1990. 89.95 (*0-88946-442-1*) E Mellen.
Teutonic Mythology of Richard Wagner's "The Ring of the Nibelung", Vol. 3: The Natural & Supernatural Worlds, 2 pts. William O. Cord. LC 89-12612. (Studies in the History & Interpretation of Music: Vol. 18). 604p. 1990. 129.95 (*0-88946-443-X*) E Mellen.
Teutonic Religion: Folk Beliefs & Practices of the Northern Tradition. Kveldulf Gundarsson. LC 92-40589. (Llewllyn's Teutonic Magic Ser.). (Illus.). 412p. 1993. pap. 13.00 (*0-87542-260-8*) Llewellyn Pubns.
Teutonic Visions of Social Perfection for Emerson. Ed. by Karl J. Arndt. (Illus.). 263p. (Orig.). 1988. pap. 35.00 (*0-937640-04-2*) Harmony Soc.
Teutsch Spraach. Josua Maaler. xvi, 1072p. (GER.). 1971. reprint ed. write for info. (*0-318-70473-0*) G Olms Pubs.
Teutsches Kunstlerlexikon, 3 vols. Johann G. Meusel. reprint ed. write for info. (*0-318-71930-4*) G Olms Pubs.
TeV Physics, Vol. 8. Ed. by T. C. Huang et al. (China Center of Advanced Science & Technology (World Laboratory) Symposium - Workshop Proceedings Ser.). ix, 461p. 1991. pap. text ed. 132.00 (*2-88124-830-6*) Gordon & Breach.
TeV Physics: Proceedings of the Johns Hopkins Workshop on Current Problems in Particle Theory 12. G. Domokos & S. Kovsei-Domokos. 336p. 1989. text ed. 89.00 (*9971-5-0822-2*) World Scientific Pub.
TeV Physics & Beyond: Proceedings of the 8th & Nuclear Particle Physics Summer School. Ed. by R. Delbourgo & J. Fox. 324p. (C). 1987. pap. 79.00 (*9971-5-0304-2*); text ed. 144.00 (*9971-5-0301-8*) World Scientific Pub.
Tevilas Kelim: A Comprehensive Guide. Zvi Cohen. 160p. 1988. 12.95 (*0-944070-06-X*) Targum Pr.
Teville Obsession. Caroline Stafford. 1979. pap. 1.75 (*0-449-24077-0*, Crest) Fawcett.
Tevya & His Daughters. Arnold Perl. 1957. pap. 5.25 (*0-8222-1125-4*) Dramatists Play.
Tevye the Dairyman. Sholem Aleichem. 1996. pap. 15.00 (*0-8052-1069-5*) Random Hse Value.
Tevye the Dairyman: Complete, Illustrated. Sholem-Aleykhem. Ed. by Joseph Simons. Tr. by Miriam Katz. (Illus.). 160p. (YID.). (YA). (gr. 10-12). 1994. pap. 12.95 (*0-934710-31-7*) J Simon.
Tewa Tales. Elsie C. Parsons. 304p. 1994. reprint ed. pap. 17.95 (*0-8165-1452-6*) U of Ariz Pr.
Tewa World: Space, Time, Being, & Becoming in a Pueblo Society. Alfonso Ortiz. LC 72-94079. 216p. 1972. pap. text ed. 10.95 (*0-226-63307-1*, P447) U Ch Pr.
Tex. S. E. Hinton. 192p. (J). (gr. k up). 1989. mass mkt. 3.99 (*0-440-97850-5*, LLL BDD) BDD Bks Young Read.
Tex. S. E. Hinton. 1995. pap. text ed. 8.95 (*84-204-3924-X*) Santillana.
Tex. Donald E. Knuth. LC 86-1232. (Computers & Typesetting Ser.: Vol. B). 608p. (C). 1986. text ed. 46.25 (*0-201-13437-3*) Addison-Wesley.
Tex & Molly in the Afterlife. Richard Grant. 496p. 1996. 24.00 (*0-380-97304-9*) Avon.
***Tex & Molly in the Afterlife.** Richard Grant. 1997. mass mkt. 6.99 (*0-380-78676-1*) Avon.
Tex Avery: Artist, Animator, & Director from the Golden Age of Animated Cartoons. John Canemaker. LC 96-18813. 1996. 34.95 (*1-57036-291-2*) Turner Pub GA.
Tex Avery: King of Cartoons. Joe Adamson. (Quality Paperbacks Ser.). (Illus.). 238p. 1985. reprint ed. pap. 15.95 (*0-306-80248-1*) Da Capo.
TEX by Example: A Beginner's Guide. Arvind Borde. (Illus.). 169p. 1993. pap. text ed. 25.00 (*0-12-117651-7*, AP Prof) Acad Pr.
TEX by Topic: A Texnicians Reference. Victor Eijkhout. (C). 1992. pap. text ed. 29.25 (*0-201-56882-9*) Addison-Wesley.
TEX for Scientific Documentation. Ed. by J. Desarmenien. (Lecture Notes in Computer Science Ser.: Vol. 236). vi, 204p. 1988. 33.00 (*0-387-16807-9*) Spr-Verlag.
TEX for the Beginner. Wynter Snow. (Illus.). 320p. (C). 1992. pap. text ed. 29.25 (*0-201-54799-6*) Addison-Wesley.
TEX for the Impatient. Paul W. Abrahams et al. (Computer Science Ser.). (Illus.). 352p. (C). 1990. pap. text ed. 29.25 (*0-201-51375-7*) Addison-Wesley.
TEX from Square One. Michael Doob. LC 93-26025. 114p. 1994. 29.95 (*0-387-56441-1*) Spr-Verlag.
TEX from Square 1. Michael Doob. viii, 122p. 1993. pap. write for info. (*3-540-56441-1*) Spr-Verlag.
TEX in Practice, 4 vols., Set. Stephen V. Bechtolsheim. Ed. by David F. Rogers. (Monographs in Visual Communication). (Illus.). 1872p. 1994. 204.95 (*0-387-97296-X*) Spr-Verlag.
TEX in Practice, 4 vols., Vol. I: Basics. Stephen V. Bechtolsheim. Ed. by David F. Rogers. (Monographs in Visual Communication). (Illus.). 384p. 1994. 59.95 (*0-387-97595-0*) Spr-Verlag.
TEX in Practice, 4 vols., Vol. II: Paragraphs, Math & Fonts. Stephen V. Bechtolsheim. Ed. by David F. Rogers. (Monographs in Visual Communication). (Illus.). 368p. 1994. 59.95 (*0-387-97596-9*) Spr-Verlag.
TEX in Practice, 4 vols., Vol. III: Tokens, Macros. Stephen V. Bechtolsheim. Ed. by David F. Rogers. (Monographs in Visual Communication). (Illus.). 544p. 1994. 59.95 (*0-387-97597-7*) Spr-Verlag.
TEX in Practice, 4 vols., Vol. IV: Output Routines, Tables. Richard L. Scheaffer et al. Ed. by David F. Rogers. LC 95-37626. (Textbooks in Mathematical Sciences Ser.). (Illus.). 576p. 1993. 65.95 (*0-387-97598-5*) Spr-Verlag.
Tex Johnston: Jet-Age Test Pilot. A. M. Johnston & Charles Barton. LC 90-9962. (Illus.). 320p. (C). 1991. 33.00 (*1-56098-013-3*) Smithsonian.
***Tex-Mex Cookbook.** (Orig.). Date not set. pap. text ed. write for info. (*1-56944-137-5*) Terrell Missouri.
Tex-Mex Cooking. Ed. by Jillian Stewart. (Illus.). 96p. 1994. 12.98 (*1-56138-447-X*) Courage Bks.
Tex-Mex Rex & Other Dancing Dinosaurs. 24p. 1994. pap. 5.95 (*0-7935-2799-6*, 00290440) H Leonard.
Tex R Masaur: Down in the Dump. Sue A. Holcomb & J. Paul Holcomb. (Tex R Masaur, Dinodillo Bks.). (Illus.). 32p. (Orig.). (J). (gr. k-3). pap. 3.95 (*0-9636122-2-0*) Post Oak Hill.
Tex R Masaur: The Beginning. J. Paul Holcomb & Sue A. Holcomb. (Tex R Masaur, Dinodillo Bks.). (Illus.). 32p. (Orig.). (J). (gr. k-3). 1993. pap. 3.95 (*0-9636122-1-2*) Post Oak Hill.
Tex the Cowboy. Sarah Garland. LC 94-36987. 1995. pap. 12.99 (*0-525-45418-7*) Dutton Child Bks.
Tex Thorne Comes out of the West. Zane Grey. 300p. reprint ed. lib. bdg. 23.95 (*0-89190-761-0*, Rivercity Pr) Amereon Ltd.
***TeX Unbound: LaTex & TeX Strategies for Fonts, Graphics, & More.** Alan Hoenig. 640p. 1998. 60.00 (*0-19-509685-1*); pap. 35.00 (*0-19-509686-X*) OUP.
Texaco: A Novel. Patrick Chamoiseau et al. LC 96-26976. 416p. 1997. 27.00 (*0-679-43235-3*, Vin) Random.
Texaco Collectibles with Price Guide. Robert Ball. LC 94-65616. (Illus.). 127p. (Orig.). 1994. pap. 24.95 (*0-88740-656-4*) Schiffer.
***Texaco Collector's Guide.** Scott Benjamin. (Illus.). 128p. 1997. pap. 19.95 (*0-7603-0291-X*) Motorbooks Intl.
Texaco Environment, Health & Safety Audit Working Copy. Date not set. spiral bd. write for info. (*0-88061-190-1*) Intl Loss Cntrl.
Texaco Environment, Health & Safety Audit Working Copy. (SPA.). Date not set. spiral bd. write for info. (*0-88061-191-X*) Intl Loss Cntrl.
Texaco Environment, Health & Safety Guidelines. Date not set. ring bd. write for info. (*0-88061-189-8*) Intl Loss Cntrl.
Texaco, Inc. A Report on the Company's Environmental Policies & Practices. (Illus.). 35p. (C). 1994. reprint ed. pap. text ed. 250.00 (*0-7881-0985-5*, Coun on Econ) DIANE Pub.
Texan & the Lady. Jodi Thomas. 352p. (Orig.). 1994. mass mkt. 4.99 (*1-55773-970-6*) Diamond.
Texan in Search of a Fight. John C. West. 189p. (C). 1994. 20.00 (*0-935523-44-8*) Butternut & Blue.
Texan Jazz. Dave Oliphant. (Illus.). 480p. (C). 1996. pap. 24.95 (*0-292-76045-0*); text ed. 50.00 (*0-292-76044-2*) U of Tex Pr.
Texan Looks at Lyndon. J. Evetts Haley. 1993. reprint ed. lib. bdg. 16.95 (*1-56849-009-7*) Buccaneer Bks.
Texan Ranch Life. Mary J. Jaques. LC 88-32637. (Southwest Landmark Ser.: No. 7). (Illus.). 378p. 1989. reprint ed. 19.95 (*0-89096-394-0*) Tex A&M Univ Pr.
Texan (Rebels & Rogues) Janice Kaiser. 1995. mass mkt. 3.25 (*0-373-25656-6*) Harlequin Bks.
Texan Revolution of Eighteen Thirty-Six: A Concise Historical Perspective, Based on Original Sources. Roger Borroel. LC 89-90463. (Illus.). 160p. (J). (ps-12). 1990. pap. 14.99 (*0-9624727-6-X*) LaVillita Pubns.
Texan Scouts. Joseph A. Altsheler. (Texan Ser.). 1985. 21.95 (*0-8488-0202-0*, American Hse) Amereon Ltd.
Texan Scouts. Joseph A. Altsheler. 26.95 (*0-8488-0730-8*) Amereon Ltd.
Texan Scouts. Joseph A. Altsheler. 1993. reprint ed. lib. bdg. 21.95 (*0-89968-569-2*) Buccaneer Bks.
Texan Star. Joseph A. Altsheler. (Texan Ser.). 1985. 21.95 (*0-8488-0201-2*, American Hse) Amereon Ltd.
Texan Star. Joseph A. Altsheler. 26.95 (*0-8488-0729-4*) Amereon Ltd.
Texan Star. Joseph A. Altsheler. 1993. reprint ed. lib. bdg. 21.95 (*0-89968-570-6*) Buccaneer Bks.
Texan Takes a Wife. Kristine Rolofson. (Temptation Ser.). 1996. mass mkt. 3.50 (*0-373-25704-X*, 1-25704-7) Harlequin Bks.
Texan Triumph. Joseph A. Altsheler. (Texan Ser.). 1985. 21.95 (*0-8488-0203-9*, American Hse) Amereon Ltd.
Texan Triumph. Joseph A. Altsheler. 24.95 (*0-8488-0731-6*) Amereon Ltd.
Texan Triumph. Joseph A. Altsheler. 1993. reprint ed. lib. bdg. 21.95 (*0-89968-571-4*) Buccaneer Bks.
Texana at the University of Texas. Illus. by Kim Taylor. LC 62-63428. 1962. pap. 8.00 (*0-87959-025-4*) U of Tex H Ransom Ctr.
Texana Catalogue Prices, 1995 Vol. 13: 11,000 Price Entries on Texas Material Offered for Sale in 1995. Shelly O. Morrison. 136p. (Orig.). 1996. pap. 38.50 (*0-926158-25-2*) W M Morrison.
Texans. Gail Stewart. (Wild West in American History Ser.). (Illus.). 32p. (J). (gr. 3-8). 1990. lib. bdg. 18.00 (*0-86625-408-0*); lib. bdg. 13.50 (*0-685-58650-2*) Rourke Corp.
Texans: A Story of Texan Cultures for Young People. 2nd ed. Barbara E. Stanush. LC 88-50983. (Illus.). 67p. 1994. teacher ed., pap. 4.95 (*0-86701-068-1*) U of Tex Inst Tex Culture.
Texans: A Story of Texan Cultures for Young People. 2nd ed. Barbara E. Stanush. LC 88-50983. (Illus.). 122p. (J). (gr. 4-7). 1994. ring bd. 21.95 (*0-86701-067-3*) U of Tex Inst Tex Culture.
Texans & Government: What Citizens Want. Susan Hadden et al. 30p. 1987. pap. 5.00 (*0-89940-506-1*) LBJ Sch Pub Aff.
Texan's Garden of Trivia. June R. Welch. 200p. 1984. pap. 7.95 (*0-912854-15-4*) Yellow Rose Pr.
Texans in Gray: The Eighteenth Texas Infantry Walker's Texas Division in the Civil War. James H. Davis. LC 93-79082. 200p. 1994. lib. bdg. 19.95 (*0-9630768-8-4*) Heritage Oak.
Texans in Revolt: The Battle for San Antonio, 1835. Alwyn Barr. (Illus.). 112p. 1991. reprint ed. 18.95 (*0-292-77042-1*); reprint ed. pap. 7.95 (*0-292-78120-2*) U of Tex Pr.
Texans in the Confederate Cavalry. Anne J. Bailey. LC 95-11704. (Civil War Campaigns & Commanders Ser.). (Illus.). 95p. (Orig.). 1995. pap. 11.95 (*1-886661-02-2*, 61022) Ryan Place Pub.
Texan's Lady. Lauren Wilde. 480p. 1984. mass mkt. 3.50 (*0-8217-1420-1*, Zebra Kensgtn) Kensgtn Pub Corp.
***Texans of Valor: Military Heroes of the Twentieth Century.** Dede Casad. (YA). (gr. 8-12). 1997. 16.95 (*0-614-28730-8*, Eakin Pr) Sunbelt Media.
***Texar the Southerner.** Jules Verne. lib. bdg. 22.95 (*0-8488-2060-6*) Amereon Ltd.
Texas. (Insight Guides Ser.). 1993. pap. 22.95 (*0-395-66292-3*) HM.
***Texas.** Mary L. Abbott. (Travel Smart Trip Planner Ser.). (Illus.). 272p. (Orig.). 1998. pap. 15.95 (*1-56261-378-2*) John Muir.
Texas. Capstone Press Geography Department Staff. (One Nation Ser.). 48p. (J). (gr. 3-9). 1996. lib. bdg. 17.80 (*1-56065-355-8*) Capstone Pr.
***Texas.** Capstone Press Geography Department Staff. (One Nation Ser.). (Illus.). 48p. (J). (gr. 3-7). 1996. 18.40 (*0-516-20110-7*) Childrens.
Texas. Dennis B. Fradin. LC 92-9189. (From Sea to Shining Sea Ser.). (Illus.). 64p. (J). (gr. 3-5). 1992. pap. 5.95 (*0-516-43843-3*); lib. bdg. 24.00 (*0-516-03843-5*) Childrens.
Texas. Jennifer Grambs. (American Traveler Ser.). 1990. 7.98 (*0-8317-8839-9*) Smithmark.
Texas. James Marten. LC 93-215090. (World Bibliographical Ser.). 229p. 1992. lib. bdg. 79.25 (*1-85109-184-X*) ABC-CLIO.
Texas. James A. Michener. 1344p. 1987. mass mkt. 6.99 (*0-449-21092-8*, Crest) Fawcett.
Texas. Kathy Pelta. LC 93-33390. (Hello U. S. A. Ser.). (Illus.). 72p. (J). (gr. 3-6). 1994. lib. bdg. 18.95 (*0-8225-2749-9*, Lerner Publctns) Lerner Group.
Texas. Kathy Pelta. (J). (gr. 3-6). 1995. pap. text ed. 5.95 (*0-8225-9667-9*) Lerner Group.
Texas. Dick J. Reavis. LC 94-27287. (Compass American Guides Ser.). (Illus.). 1995. pap. 17.95 (*1-878867-64-4*) Fodors Travel.
Texas. R. Conrad Stein. LC 88-38400. (America the Beautiful Ser.). (Illus.). 144p. (J). (gr. 4 up). 1989. lib. bdg. 28.30 (*0-516-00489-1*) Childrens.
Texas. Kathleen Thompson. LC 95-30264. (Portrait of America Library). (J). 1996. lib. bdg. 22.83 (*0-8114-7389-9*) Raintree Steck-V.
Texas. Kathleen Thompson. LC 85-9980. (Portrait of America Library). 48p. (J). (gr. 3 up). 1996. pap. text ed. 5.95 (*0-8114-7474-1*) Raintree Steck-V.
Texas. 2nd ed. Gousha, H. M., Editors. 1992. pap. 2.95 (*0-671-52920-X*, H M Gousha) P-H Gen Ref & Trav.
***Texas.** 2nd ed. Dick J. Reavis. LC 96-49826. (Compass American Guides Ser.). 1997. pap. 18.95 (*1-878867-98-9*, Compass Amrcn) Fodors Travel.
***Texas.** 4th ed. Robert R. Rafferty. (Texas Monthly Guidebooks Ser.). 800p. 1998. pap. 18.95 (*0-87719-317-7*, 9317) Gulf Pub.
Texas. 7th ed. Richardson & Anderson. 464p. (C). 1996. pap. text ed. 34.40 (*0-13-487000-X*) P-H.
Texas. Mary A. Holley. LC 85-51947. (Illus.). 434p. 1991. reprint ed. 24.95 (*0-87611-075-8*); reprint ed. pap. 14.95 (*0-87611-074-X*) Tex St Hist Assn.
Texas. O. M. Roberts. Ed. by Clement A. Evans. (Confederate Military History Extended Edition Ser.: Vol. XV). (Illus.). 713p. 1989. reprint ed. 50.00 (*1-56837-034-2*) Broadfoot.
Texas: A Conquest of Civilizations. George Pierce Garrison. LC 72-3753. (American Commonwealths Ser.: No. 15). reprint ed. 37.50 (*0-404-57215-4*) AMS Pr.
Texas: A Geography. Terry G. Jordan & William M. Holmes. LC 83-6642. (Geographies of the United States Ser.). 288p. (C). 1984. pap. text ed. 35.95 (*0-86531-481-0*) Westview.
Texas: A Geography. Terry G. Jordan & William M. Holmes. LC 83-6642. (Geographies of the United States Ser.). 288p. (C). 1984. text ed. 47.00 (*0-86531-088-2*) Westview.
Texas: A Guide to the Lone Star State. Federal Writers' Project Staff. LC 40-10658. 717p. 95.00 (*0-403-02192-8*) Somerset Pub.
Texas: A Guide to the Lone Star State. Federal Writers' Project Staff & Writers Program-WPA Staff. (American Guide Ser.). 1989. reprint ed. lib. bdg. 99.00 (*0-7812-1042-9*, 1042) Rprt Serv.
Texas: A Literary Portrait. Don Graham. LC 85-71202. (Illus.). 250p. 1985. 37.50 (*0-931722-40-3*); pap. 16.95 (*0-931722-41-1*) Corona Pub.
Texas: A Modern History. David G. McComb. LC 89-31666. (Illus.). 208p. 1989. 24.95 (*0-292-73048-9*); pap. 12.95 (*0-292-74665-2*) U of Tex Pr.
Texas: A Photographic Celebration. American Geographic Publishing Staff. (Illus.). 96p. (Orig.). 1989. pap. 6.95 (*0-938314-73-4*) Am Wrld Geog.
Texas: A Photographic Journey. 1990. 15.99 (*0-517-01492-0*) Random Hse Value.
Texas: A Picture Memory. (Illus.). 1990. 8.99 (*0-517-02539-6*) Random Hse Value.
Texas: A Salute from Above. T. R. Fehrenbach. 1988. 17.99 (*0-517-66469-0*) Random Hse Value.
Texas: A Sesquicentennial Celebration. Ed. by Donald W. Whisenhunt. 440p. 1984. pap. 12.95 (*0-89015-488-0*) Sunbelt Media.
Texas: A World in Itself. George S. Perry & Arthur Fuller. (Illus.). 293p. 1975. reprint ed. 9.95 (*0-88289-094-8*) Pelican.
Texas: All Hail the Mighty State. Archie P. McDonald. 288p. 1983. pap. 14.95 (*0-89015-389-2*) Sunbelt Media.
Texas: Amazing but True. Jack Maguire. (Illus.). 200p. 1984. pap. 14.95 (*0-89015-487-2*) Sunbelt Media.
Texas: An Educational Coloring Book. Spizzirri Publishing Co. Staff. Ed. by Linda Spizzirri. (Illus.). 32p. (J). (gr. 1-8). 1985. pap. 1.99 (*0-86545-070-6*) Spizzirri.
Texas: An Illustrated History. David G. McComb. (Oxford Illustrated Histories Ser.). (Illus.). 144p. (J). 1995. pap. 22.95 (*0-19-509246-5*); lib. bdg. 25.00 (*0-19-509247-3*) OUP.
Texas: Between Two Worlds. Text by Peter Doroshenko. LC 93-72062. (Illus.). 82p. 1993. pap. 24.95 (*0-936080-33-7*) Cont Arts Museum.
Texas: Family Adventure Guide: Great Things to See & Do for the Entire Family. Allan C. Kimball. LC 96-47418. (Family Adventure Guide Ser.). (Illus.). 224p. 1997. pap. 11.95 (*1-56440-965-1*) Globe Pequot.
Texas: From the Frontier to Spindletop. James L. Haley. (Illus.). 304p. 1991. pap. 15.95 (*0-312-06479-9*) St Martin.
Texas: Generations of Harvest. Ed. by Caleb Pirtle, III et al. 96p. write for info. (*1-879234-11-4*) Herit Pub TX.
Texas: Its Geography, Natural History & Topography. William P. Kennedy. 1993. reprint ed. lib. bdg. 75.00 (*0-7812-5888-X*) Rprt Serv.
***Texas: Its Land & Its People.** James Killoran et al. (Illus.). 368p. (YA). (gr. 4 up). 1997. pap. text ed. 24.95 (*1-882422-20-1*) Jarrett Pub.
Texas: Observations, Historical, Geographical & Descriptive. Mary A. Holley. LC 72-9451. (Far Western Frontier Ser.). (Illus.). 172p. 1973. reprint ed. 17.95 (*0-405-04979-X*) Ayer.
Texas: Off the Beaten Path: A Guide to Unique Places. June N. Rodriguez. LC 94-12357. (Off the Beaten Path Ser.). (Illus.). 160p. 1994. pap. 12.95 (*1-56440-483-8*) Globe Pequot.
Texas: One Hundred Years Ago. Compiled by Skip Whitson. (Historical Ser.). (Illus.). (Orig.). 1976. pap. 3.50 (*0-89540-030-8*, SB-030) Sun Pub.
Texas: Photos of Laurence Parent. Photos by Laurence E. Parent. 1995. 39.95 (*1-55868-202-3*) Gr Arts Ctr Pub.
Texas: Politics & Public Policy. Richard L. Cole & Delbert A. Taebel. 411p. (C). 1987. teacher ed. write for info. (*0-318-61980-6*); pap. text ed. 21.50 (*0-15-591460-X*) HB Coll Pubs.
Texas: Rise, Progress & Prospects of the Republic of Texas, 2 vols., Set. William P. Kennedy. 1993. reprint ed. lib. bdg. 150.00 (*0-7812-5887-1*) Rprt Serv.
Texas! Sage. Sandra Brown. 352p. 1992. mass mkt. 6.50 (*0-553-29500-4*) Bantam.
Texas: The Lone Star State. 4th ed. Rupert N. Richardson et al. (Illus.). 464p. 1981. text ed. write for info. (*0-13-912444-6*) P-H.
Texas: The Newest, the Biggest, the Most Complete Guide to All of Texas! 3rd ed. Robert R. Rafferty. (Texas Monthly Guidebooks Ser.). 1993. 29.95 (*0-87719-240-5*) Gulf Pub.
Texas: The Newest, the Biggest, the Most Complete Guide to All of Texas! 3rd rev. ed. Ed. by Robert R. Rafferty et al. LC 92-45102. (Texas Monthly Guidebooks Ser.). 1993. pap. 18.95 (*0-87719-209-X*) Gulf Pub.
Texas: The State & Its Educational System. Harold L. Hodgkinson. (Orig.). 1986. pap. 2.00 (*0-937846-88-0*) Inst Educ Lead.
Texas: The Way It Was. Willie E. Leighton. (Illus.). 272p. 1990. 19.95 (*0-9626069-0-1*) Insite Pub.
Texas? What Do You Know about the Lone Star State? Archie P. McDonald. LC 93-14665. (Illus.). 190p. (C). 1993. pap. 12.95 (*0-87565-120-8*) Tex Christian.
Texas: With Particular Reference to German Immigration & the Physical Appearance of the Country. Ferdinand Roemer. 1993. reprint ed. lib. bdg. 75.00 (*0-7812-5973-8*) Rprt Serv.
Texas see Crossword Treasury
Texas see Celebrate the States - Group 1
Texas - Collected Works of Federal Writers Project, 2 vols. Federal Writers' Project Staff. 1991. reprint ed. Set. lib. bdg. 148.00 (*0-7812-5782-4*) Rprt Serv.

An Asterisk (*) at the beginning of an entry indicates that the title is appearing in BIP for the first time.

Texas - de Mar a Mar. Dennis B. Fradin. LC 92-9189. (From Sea to Shining Sea - Spanish Ser.). (Illus.). 64p. (SPA.). (J). (gr. 3-5). 1993. pap. 5.95 (*0-516-53843-8*); lib. bdg. 23.50 (*0-516-33843-9*) Childrens.

Texas - ESO-CERN Symposium on Relativistic Astrophysics, Cosmology, & Fundamental Physics: 1990, Brighton, England. LC 92-6391. (Annals Ser.: Vol. 647). 840p. 1992. pap. 190.00 (*0-89766-708-5*, QB462) NY Acad Sci.

Texas A & M: Traditions & Spirit. Carolyn Bible. (Illus.). 80p. (Orig.). 1990. pap. 5.95 (*0-9627306-0-2*) C Bible.

Texas A & M University: A Pictorial History, 1876-1996. 2nd ed. Henry C. Dethloff. LC 96-17320. (Centennial Series of the Association of Former Students: No. 63). (Illus.). 248p. 1996. 29.95 (*0-89096-704-0*) Tex A&M Univ Pr.

Texas A&M University Campus Map. W. Chris Smith. (Illus.). 1994. 3.95 (*0-89096-660-5*) Tex A&M Univ Pr.

Texas Academic Skill. Patricia Juelg. 1990. pap. text ed. 69.00 (*0-02-361475-7*, Macmillan Coll) P-H.

Texas Academic Skills Program (TASP) (Admission Test Ser.: ATS-110). pap. 29.95 (*0-8373-5810-8*) Nat Learn.

Texas' Action History. Patrick M. Reynolds. (Texas Lore Ser.: Vol. 7). (Illus.). 56p. (Orig.). 1990. pap. 3.75 (*0-932514-21-9*) Red Rose Studio.

Texas Air Museums. Ron Swartley. (Illus.). 80p. (Orig.). 1995. pap. 10.95 (*0-9634309-6-3*) Frontier Image.

Texas Alcoholic Beverage Code: With Tables & Index: As Amended Through the 1983 Regular & First Called Sessions of the 68th Legislature. Texas Legislature Staff. 147p. write for info. (*0-318-59332-7*) West Pub.

Texas Almanac 1998-99: State Industrial Guide. Ed. by Mary G. Ramos. (Illus.). 672p. 1997. pap. 12.95 (*0-914511-25-4*) Dallas Morning.

***Texas Almanac 1998-99: State Industrial Guide.** Ed. by Mary G. Ramos. (Illus.). 672p. 1997. 19.95 (*0-914511-26-2*) Dallas Morning.

***Texas Almanac 1998-99: State Industrial Guide.** Ed. by Mary G. Ramos. 100p. 1997. pap. 9.95 (*0-914511-27-0*) Dallas Morning.

Texas Almanac's Political History of Texas. Mike Kingston et al. (Illus.). 339p. (Orig.). (C). 1992. pap. 16.95 (*0-89015-855-X*) Dallas Morning.

Texas Alphabet. James Rice. LC 87-31159. (Illus.). 132p. (J). (gr. k-5). 1988. 13.95 (*0-88289-692-X*) Pelican.

Texas Alternative Dispute Resolution. James L. Branton & Jim D. Lovett. (Trial Lawyer's Ser.: Vol. 10). 1992. ring bd. 135.00 (*1-878337-33-5*) Knowles Law.

***Texas Alternative Dispute Resolution Practice Guide.** Jerome S. Levy & Robert C. Prather. Ed. by Susan Thomas & Edward K. Esping. LC 95-80676. 600p. 1995. text ed. write for info. (*0-7620-0013-9*) Lawyers Cooperative.

Texas & Christmas: A Collection of Traditions, Memories & Folklore. Ed. by Judy Alter & Joyce G. Roach. LC 83-4717. (Illus.). 86p. 1983. pap. 6.50 (*0-912646-81-0*) Tex Christian.

Texas & Northeastern Mexico, 1630-1690. Juan B. Chapa. LC 96-25202. (Illus.). 248p. 1996. 24.95 (*0-292-71188-3*) U of Tex Pr.

Texas & Other State Greats (Biographies) Carole Marsh. (Carole Marsh Texas Bks.). (Illus.). (J). 1994. pap. 19.95 (*0-7933-2098-4*); lib. bdg. 29.95 (*0-7933-2097-6*); disk 29.95 (*0-7933-2099-2*) Gallopade Pub Group.

Texas & Southwestern Lore. Ed. by J. Frank Dobie. LC 33-1131. (Texas Folklore Society Publications: No. 6). 259p. 1982. reprint ed. 13.95 (*0-87074-044-X*) UNTX Pr.

Texas & Texans. Glencoe Staff. Date not set. 38.49 (*0-02-800459-0*) Glencoe.

Texas & Texans in the Civil War. Ralph A. Wooster. LC 95-35743. (Illus.). 20p. 1996. 27.95 (*1-57168-042-X*, Eakin Pr) Sunbelt Media.

Texas & the American Revolution. (Illus.). 72p. 1975. pap. text ed. 1.95 (*0-933164-23-8*) U of Tex Inst Tex Culture.

***Texas & the Arkansas River Valley.** Alice Gordon et al. LC 96-40548. (Smithsonian Guide to Historic America Ser.). 1998. write for info. (*1-55670-642-1*) Stewart Tabori & Chang.

Texas & the Arkansas River Valley: Texas, Oklahoma, Arkansas. Alice Gordon et al. Ed. by Roger G. Kennedy. LC 89-4605. (Smithsonian Guide to Historic America Ser.). (Illus.). 496p. 1990. 24.95 (*1-55670-122-5*); pap. 18.95 (*1-55670-124-1*) Stewart Tabori & Chang.

Texas & the Gulf of Mexico; or Yachting in the New World. Matilda C. Houstoun. (Library of Texas). (Illus.). xviii, 274p. 1991. reprint ed. 55.00 (*0-935072-21-7*) W T Taylor.

Texas & the Mexican War: A Chronicle of the Winning of the Southwest. Nathaniel W. Stephenson. (BCL1 - United States Local History Ser.). 273p. 1991. reprint ed. text ed. 79.00 (*0-7812-6312-3*) Rprt Serv.

Texas & the Southwest, 1985. Connie Sherley. Ed. by Robert C. Fisher. (Fisher Annotated Travel Guides Ser.). (Illus.). 1984. pap. 12.95 (*0-8116-0016-5*) NAL-Dutton.

Texas & the Texans, 2 vols., Set. Henry S. Foote. 1993. reprint ed. lib. bdg. 150.00 (*0-7812-5879-0*) Rprt Serv.

Texas & Western American Maps, Catalogue Prices, 1987-1990: Chronological Listing of over 3,000 Price Entries on Maps Featuring the U. S. West of the Mississippi. Richard Morrison & Shelly O. Morrison. 75p. (Orig.). 1991. pap. 22.50 (*0-926158-12-0*) W M Morrison.

Texas Angler's Guide: Your Personal Guide to Fishing Texas' Top Lakes. Charles R. Dickinson & David Vance. Ed. by T. Dickinson. 200p. (Orig.). 1994. pap. 14.00 (*0-9639724-0-5*) Print Comm.

Texas Annotated Penal Statutes with Forms Branch's, 5 vols. 3rd ed. LC 74-81698. 1993. Suppl. 1993. suppl. ed. 60.00 (*0-317-00408-5*) Lawyers Cooperative.

Texas Annotated Penal Statutes with Forms Branch's, 5 vols., Incl. 1992 Suppl. 3rd ed. LC 74-81698. 280.00 (*0-317-00407-7*) Lawyers Cooperative.

Texas Appellate Practice Manual, 2 vols. 2nd ed. Ed. by Roger D. Townsend. LC 92-63334. 926p. 1993. ring bd. 195.00 (*0-938160-65-6*, 6210) State Bar TX.

Texas Army: A History of the Thirty-Sixth Division in the Italian Campaign. limited ed. Robert L. Wagner. LC 91-21289. (Illus.). 307p. 1991. reprint ed. 60.00 (*0-938349-77-5*) State House Pr.

Texas Army: A History of the Thirty-Sixth Division in the Italian Campaign. Robert L. Wagner. LC 91-21289. (Illus.). 307p. 1991. reprint ed. 24.95 (*0-938349-76-7*) State House Pr.

Texas Art. Marilyn A. Zeitlin et al. LC 88-60136. 25p. 1988. pap. 5.00 (*0-939594-09-9*) Menil Collect.

Texas Arts Journal. pap. 10.00 (*0-686-78140-6*) New London Pr.

Texas Atlas & Gazetteer. (Illus.). 168p. 1995. 24.95 (*0-89933-241-2*, 5103) DeLorme Map.

Texas Auto Trails: The Northeast. Myra H. McIlvain. (Illus.). 277p. 1984. pap. 9.95 (*0-292-78055-9*) U of Tex Pr.

Texas Auto Trails: The South & the Rio Grande Valley. Myra H. McIlvain. (Illus.). 256p. 1985. pap. 9.95 (*0-292-78064-8*) U of Tex Pr.

Texas Auto Trails: The Southeast. Myra H. McIlvain. (Illus.). 293p. 1982. pap. 8.95 (*0-292-78050-8*) U of Tex Pr.

Texas Automobiles. James L. Branton & Jim D. Lovett. (Trial Lawyer's Ser.: Vol. 2). (Illus.). 385p. 1984. ring bd. 135.00 (*1-878337-02-5*) Knowles Law.

Texas Automotive Directory. Ed. by T. L. Spelman. 1985. 24.95 (*1-55527-031-X*) Auto Contact Inc.

***Texas Baby.** Pickart. 1997. mass mkt. 3.99 (*0-373-24141-0*) Harlequin Bks.

Texas Bandits, Bushwackers, Outlaws, Crooks, Devils, Ghosts, Desperadoes & Other Assorted & Sundry Characters! Carole Marsh. (Carole Marsh Texas Bks.). (Illus.). (J). 1994. pap. 19.95 (*0-7933-1081-4*); lib. bdg. 29.95 (*0-7933-1082-2*); disk 29.95 (*0-7933-1083-0*) Gallopade Pub Group.

Texas Bank Robbing Company. Giles Tippette. 240p. 1994. mass mkt. 4.50 (*0-515-11475-8*) Jove Pubns.

Texas Baptist Leadership & Social Christianity, 1900-1980. John W. Storey. LC 85-40747. (Southwestern Studies: No. 5). (Illus.). 252p. 1986. 24.95 (*0-89096-251-0*) Tex A&M Univ Pr.

Texas Baptist Orphanage: My Heritage of Dreams & Happiness. Georgia D. Edwards. (Illus.). 120p. 1987. 17.95 (*0-943639-00-X*) Anchor Pub Co.

Texas Barbeque. Paris Permenter & John Bigley. 160p. (Orig.). 1994. pap. 14.95 (*0-925175-20-X*) Pig Out Pubns.

Texas Bed & Breakfast. 3rd ed. Ann Ruff et al. LC 93-10528. (Texas Monthly Guidebooks Ser.). 208p. 1993. 14.95 (*0-87719-239-1*) Gulf Pub.

***Texas Bed & Breakfast.** 4th ed. Marjie M. Acheson et al. LC 97-3974. (Texas Monthly Guidebook Ser.). 1997. pap. 16.95 (*0-88415-868-3*, 5868) Gulf Pub.

Texas Bed & Breakfast Directory: Over 500 Alternatives. Sandra Rinaldo-Watson. 1995. pap. 19.95 (*0-9646258-1-4*) Golden Pen Pub.

Texas' Big Bend Country. George Wuerthner. 104p. (Orig.). 1989. pap. 6.95 (*0-938314-64-5*) Am Wrld Geog.

Texas Big Debt Survival Guide, 1988. McKinney & McKinney Staff. 1988. pap. 19.95 (*0-9620366-0-9*) Marshall TX.

Texas Big Rich. Sandy Sheehy. 1992. mass mkt. 5.99 (*0-312-92712-6*) St Martin.

Texas Bill of Rights: A Commentary & Litigation Manual. James C. Harrington. 500p. 1994. ring bd. 95.00 (*0-409-25636-6*) MICHIE.

Texas Bill of Rights, 1987-1991: A Commentary & Litigation Manual. James C. Harrington. 330p. 1992. suppl. ed. 45.00 (*0-685-73970-8*) MICHIE.

Texas Birds: Where They Are & How to Find Them. Edward A. Kutac. 1985. pap. text ed. 9.95 (*0-88415-063-1*) Gulf Pub.

Texas Blood. Hascal Giles. 1992. mass mkt. 3.50 (*0-8217-3725-2*, Zebra Kensgtn) Kensgtn Pub Corp.

Texas Blood Kill. Jason Manning. 1991. mass mkt. 3.50 (*0-8217-3577-2*, Zebra Kensgtn) Kensgtn Pub Corp.

Texas Blue Norther. Lass Small. (Desire Ser.). 1996. mass mkt. 3.50 (*0-373-76027-2*, 1-76027-1) Silhouette.

Texas Bluebonnet Trails. Jay Woodard. 24p. (Orig.). 1988. pap. 9.95 (*0-9618888-0-6*) Anglo-Am TX.

Texas Bookstore Book: A Surprising Guide to Our State's Bookstores & Their Specialties for Students, Teachers, Writers & Publishers. Carole Marsh. (Texas Bks.). (Illus.). 1994. pap. 19.95 (*0-7933-2985-X*); lib. bdg. 29.95 (*0-7933-2984-1*); disk 29.95 (*0-7933-2986-8*) Gallopade Pub Group.

Texas Born. Judith Gould. 480p. (Orig.). 1992. pap. 5.99 (*0-451-17421-6*, Onyx) NAL-Dutton.

***Texas Bound.** Jason Manning. 1997. mass mkt. 5.99 (*0-451-19142-0*) Viking Penguin.

Texas Bound: Nineteen Texas Stories. Ed. by Kay Cattarulla. LC 93-45385. (Southwest Life & Letters Ser.). 262p. 1994. 22.50 (*0-87074-367-8*); pap. 10.95 (*0-87074-368-6*) SMU Press.

Texas Boundaries: Evolution of the State's Counties. Luke Gournay. LC 95-13850. (Centennial Series of the Association of Former Students: No. 59). (Illus.). 176p. (C). 1995. 29.50 (*0-89096-653-2*) Tex A&M Univ Pr.

Texas Brazos. G. Clifton Wisler. 448p. (gr. k). 1987. mass mkt. 3.95 (*0-8217-1969-6*, Zebra Kensgtn) Kensgtn Pub Corp.

Texas Brazos. G. Clifton Wisler. 1987. pap. 3.95 (*0-8217-2164-X*) NAL-Dutton.

Texas Brazos: Caddo Creek. G. Clifton Wisler. 432p. 1988. mass mkt. 3.95 (*0-8217-2257-3*, Zebra Kensgtn) Kensgtn Pub Corp.

Texas Brazos: Fortune Bend. G. Clifton Wisler. 432p. 1987. mass mkt. 3.95 (*0-8217-2069-4*, Zebra Kensgtn) Kensgtn Pub Corp.

***Texas Budget: Facing Changes in State-Federal Relations.** Thomas M. Keel. (Policy Research Project Report: Vol. 118). 136p. 1997. pap. 13.50 (*0-89940-726-9*) LBJ Sch Pub Aff.

Texas Business & Commerce Code: With Tables & Index, As Amended Through the 1983 Regular & First Called Sessions of the 68th Legislature. West Publishing Company Editorial Staff. 222p. write for info. (*0-318-59333-5*) West Pub.

***Texas Business Directory 1996-1997.** rev. ed. American Business Directories Staff. 6160p. 1996. boxed 795.00 (*1-56105-860-2*) Am Busn Direct.

Texas Business Directory 1996-97. rev. ed. American Business Directories Staff. 5552p. 1996. boxed 795.00 (*1-56105-778-9*) Am Busn Direct.

***Texas Business Directory 1997-1998.** rev. ed. American Business Directories Staff. 6160p. 1997. boxed 795.00 (*1-56105-948-X*) Am Busn Direct.

Texas Business Law. 3rd ed. Don A. Evans. 864p. (Orig.). (C). 1995. pap. 35.00 (*1-56554-116-2*) Pelican.

Texas Business Law Workbook. Don A. Evans. 336p. (C). 1982. pap. text ed. 12.95 (*0-88289-305-X*) Pelican.

Texas Business Statutes & Securities Rules. Ed. by Butterworth Staff. 500p. 1994. pap. 35.00 (*0-250-44807-6*) MICHIE.

Texas by the Tail. Jim Thompson. 1994. pap. 10.00 (*0-679-74011-2*, Vin) Random.

Texas Camel Tales. Chris Emmett. 1993. reprint ed. lib. bdg. 75.00 (*0-7812-5929-0*) Rprt Serv.

Texas Cannibals, or, Why Father Serra Came to California. Sibley S. Morrill. 28p. 1964. 5.00 (*0-910740-04-6*) Holmes.

Texas Capitol Collection Vol. I: Cookery, Commentary, Portraiture. Saxon Fox. (Illus.). 210p. (Orig.). 1991. pap. 15.95 (*0-9629382-1-1*) Fox Pr.

Texas Celebrity Cookbook. Ed. by Russell M. Gardener & F. Chris Farkas. LC 84-82018. (Illus.). 256p. 1984. 15.95 (*0-9613874-0-8*) Gardner Farkas Pr.

Texas Census Index 1820-1829. Ronald V. Jackson. (Illus.). 1981. lib. bdg. 49.00 (*0-89593-782-4*) Accelerated Index.

Texas Census Index 1830-1839. Ronald V. Jackson. (Illus.). 1982. lib. bdg. 53.00 (*0-89593-783-2*) Accelerated Index.

Texas Census Index 1840-1849, Vol. 1. Ronald V. Jackson. (Illus.). lib. bdg. 65.00 (*0-89593-784-0*) Accelerated Index.

Texas Census Index 1850 Mortality Schedule. (Illus.). 1979. lib. bdg. 53.00 (*0-89593-493-0*) Accelerated Index.

Texas Census Index 1850 Slave Schedule. (Illus.). 1988. lib. bdg. 95.00 (*0-89593-494-9*) Accelerated Index.

Texas Census Index 1860 Mortality Schedule. (Illus.). 1979. lib. bdg. 57.00 (*0-89593-495-7*) Accelerated Index.

Texas Census Index 1870 Mortality Schedule. (Illus.). 1983. lib. bdg. 64.00 (*0-89593-497-3*) Accelerated Index.

Texas Census Index, 1880, 2 vols., Set. (Illus.). 1989. lib. bdg. 460.00 (*0-89593-498-1*) Accelerated Index.

Texas Census Index 1880 Mortality Schedule. (Illus.). lib. bdg. write for info. (*0-89593-499-X*) Accelerated Index.

Texas Census Index 1890 Union Veterans. (Illus.). lib. bdg. 65.00 (*0-89593-500-7*) Accelerated Index.

Texas Challenge: Population Change & the Future of Texas. Steve H. Murdock et al. LC 96-23954. 256p. (Orig.). 1996. 19.95 (*0-89096-724-5*) Tex A&M Univ Pr.

Texas! Chase. Sandra Brown. 352p. 1991. 6.50 (*0-553-28990-X*) Bantam.

Texas! Chase. large type ed. Sandra Brown. LC 91-35829. 382p. 1992. reprint ed. lib. bdg. 20.95 (*1-56054-296-9*) Thorndike Pr.

Texas! Chase. large type ed. Sandra Brown. LC 91-35829. 382p. 1992. pap. 14.95 (*1-56054-941-6*) Thorndike Pr.

Texas Cheerleaders: The Spirit of America. John Hawkins. (Illus.). 176p. 1992. pap. 13.95 (*0-312-08315-7*) St Martin.

Texas Cherokees: A People Between Two Fires, 1819-1840. Dianna Everett. LC 90-50233. (Civilization of the American Indian Ser.: Vol. 203). (Illus.). 192p. 1995. pap. 12.95 (*0-8061-2720-1*) U of Okla Pr.

Texas Child's Harvest: For Anyone Who Has Ever Been a Child. Pearl E. Bethune. LC 88-70480. (Illus.). 64p. 1988. 29.95 (*0-9620124-0-8*) Bethune Pubns.

Texas Christmas: As Celebrated under 6 Flags. Elizabeth D. Morgan. LC 95-35770. (Illus.). 57p. (J). (gr. 3-7). 1995. 12.95 (*1-57168-067-5*, Eakin Pr) Sunbelt Media.

Texas Chronicles. Leon Hale. 256p. 1989. 16.95 (*0-940672-50-2*) Shearer Pub.

Texas Chronicles: The Heritage & Enterprise of the Lone Star State. Darwin Payne. (Illus.). 176p. 1994. 39.95 (*1-882933-04-4*) Cherbo Pub Grp.

Texas Cities in the Microcomputer Age. David W. Tees & Andrew D. Seidel. 120p. (Orig.). 1985. pap. text ed. 20.00 (*0-936440-65-1*) U TX SUPA.

Texas City - La Marque - Hitchcock. San Antonio Cartographers Staff. 1996. 2.95 (*0-671-56291-6*) Macmillan.

***Texas City Disaster, 1947.** Hugh W. Stephens. LC 96-35657. (Illus.). 160p. 1997. 30.00 (*0-292-77722-1*); pap. 16.95 (*0-292-77723-X*) U of Tex Pr.

Texas City, Nineteen Forty-Seven. deluxe ed. James Lee Burke. 30p. 1992. 75.00 (*0-935716-61-0*) Lord John.

Texas Civil Appeals Forms. Richard C. Robins. 420p. 1991. ring bd. 115.00 (*0-409-25502-5*) MICHIE.

Texas Civil Procedure: Pre-Trial Litigation. 3rd ed. Dorsaneo & Crump. 1989. write for info. (*0-8205-0471-8*, 709) Bender.

Texas Civil Procedure 1993: Trial & Appellate Practices. 2nd ed. William Dorsaneo, III & Despo Dorsaneo. (C). 1993. suppl. ed. 9.95 (*0-8205-0463-7*) Irwin.

Texas Civil Trial Guide, 5 vols. Johnson & Dorsaneo. 1989. Updates. ring bd. write for info. (*0-8205-1741-0*) Bender.

Texas Classic Christmas Trivia: Stories, Recipes, Activities, Legends, Lore & More! Carole Marsh. (Carole Marsh Texas Bks.). (Illus.). (J). 1994. pap. 19.95 (*0-7933-1084-9*); lib. bdg. 29.95 (*0-7933-1085-7*); disk 29.95 (*0-7933-1086-5*) Gallopade Pub Group.

Texas Coastal Bend: A Visitor's Guide. Marilyn Bennett. (Illus.). 192p. (Orig.). 1992. pap. 12.95 (*0-89015-834-7*) Sunbelt Media.

Texas Coastal Bend Trilogy. Hobart Huson. 176p. 1994. 24.95 (*0-89015-915-7*) Sunbelt Media.

Texas Coastal Zone Issues. Contrib. by Stephen H. Spurr. (Policy Research Project Report: No. 39). 77p. 1980. pap. 4.95 (*0-89940-639-4*) LBJ Sch Pub Aff.

Texas Coastales. Carole Marsh. (Carole Marsh Texas Bks.). (Illus.). (J). 1994. pap. 19.95 (*1-55609-121-4*); lib. bdg. 29.95 (*0-7933-2092-5*); disk 29.95 (*0-7933-2093-3*) Gallopade Pub Group.

Texas Coastales! Carole Marsh. (Texas Bks.). (J). 1994. lib. bdg. 29.95 (*0-7933-7308-5*) Gallopade Pub Group.

Texas Codes & Rules of Litigation. 1991. write for info. (*0-8205-1892-1*) Bender.

Texas Collections Manual, 2 vols. 2nd ed. Ed. by Daniel J. Goldberg & Roger A. Bartlett. LC 87-60410. 1472p. 1987. Set. suppl. ed., ring bd. 230.00 (*0-938160-45-1*, 6302) State Bar TX.

Texas Collections Manual: 1990 Supplement. Ed. by Daniel J. Goldberg & Roger A. Bartlett. LC 87-60410. 832p. 1990. ring bd. 85.00 (*0-938160-62-1*, 6304) State Bar TX.

Texas Collections Manual, 1988 Supplement. 2nd ed. Ed. by Daniel J. Goldberg & Roger A. Bartlett. LC 87-60410. 372p. 1988. ring bd. 55.00 (*0-938160-52-4*, 6303) State Bar TX.

***Texas Collections Manual, 1996 Supplement.** 52p. ring bd. 23.00 (*0-938160-86-9*) State Bar TX.

Texas Collector. Gaines De Graffenried. 1988. 21.95 (*0-87244-080-X*) Texian.

Texas College & University Handbook. Lane B. Stephenson. LC 95-18737. (Centennial Series of the Association of Former Students: No. 60). (Illus.). 128p. (Orig.). (C). 1995. pap. 14.95 (*0-89096-685-0*) Tex A&M Univ Pr.

Texas Colonists & Religion, 1821-1836. William S. Red. 1993. reprint ed. lib. bdg. 75.00 (*0-7812-5947-9*) Rprt Serv.

Texas Commercial Real Estate Forms, 1990-1993. David A. Bankus. 300p. 1993. ring bd. 115.00 (*0-409-25467-3*); suppl. ed. 45.00 (*1-56257-969-X*) MICHIE.

Texas Confederate Scrip Grantees. Thomas L. Miller. LC 85-71227. 165p. (Orig.). 1985. pap. 15.00 (*0-911317-38-4*) Ericson Bks.

Texas Connection. Theodore A. Schendel. LC 92-91194. 104p. 1993. pap. 9.00 (*1-56002-285-X*, Univ Edtns) Aegina Pr.

Texas Connection: The Assassination of John F. Kennedy. Craig I. Zirbel. 304p. 1992. mass mkt. 4.99 (*0-446-36433-9*) Warner Bks.

Texas Connection: The Assassination of John F. Kennedy. Craig I. Zirbel. 323p. 1992. reprint ed. 21.95 (*0-9631449-0-1*) TX Connect Co.

Texas Connection with the American Revolution. Robert H. Thonhoff. (Illus.). 128p. 1981. 15.95 (*0-89015-277-2*) Sunbelt Media.

Texas Conservation Guide for Municipal Services: A Report to Texas Cities. Jacilyn G. Walker & Martha L. DeHaven. 33p. 1977. 6.00 (*0-936440-18-X*) U TX SUPA.

Texas Construction Law Manual. Shepard's Citation, Inc. Staff & Rudolph W. Fisher. LC 78-23511. 600p. 1981. text ed. 110.00 (*0-07-056702-6*) Shepards.

Texas Consumer Law Vol. 3: Buying, Renting & Borrowing in Texas. 3rd rev. ed. Clyde Farrell & Joe Fiore. Orig. Title: Buying, Renting & Borrowing in Texas. Date not set. pap. write for info. (*0-614-13840-X*) Tex Consumer.

Texas Cookbook. 1993. pap. 5.95 (*0-914846-78-7*) Golden West Pub.

Texas Cookbook. Mary F. Koock. 1982. 22.00 (*0-316-50182-4*) Little.

Texas Cooking: Lone Star Style. Telephone Pioneers of America Staff. LC 91-6958. 1994. spiral bd., pap. 14.95 (*0-87197-295-6*) Favorite Recipes.

Texas Cool Cat Coloring Book. Maxine S. Sommers. (Texas Cool Cat Children's Bks.). (Illus.). 10p. (Orig.). (J). (gr. k-1). 1991. pap. 1.50 (*0-943991-20-X*) Pound Sterling Pub.

Texas Corporation Law. Lawrence G. Newman. 850p. 1994. ring bd. 115.00 (*1-55943-158-X*) MICHIE.

Texas Corporation Law, No. 1. Lawrence G. Newman. 850p. 1988. Suppl. 1, 10/88. suppl. ed. 40.00 (*0-685-66113-X*) MICHIE.

Texas Corporation Law, No. 2. Lawrence G. Newman. 850p. 1990. Suppl. 2, 11/90. suppl. ed. 32.50 (*0-685-66114-8*) MICHIE.

Texas Corporation Law, No. 3. Lawrence G. Newman. 850p. 1992. Suppl. 3, 8/92. suppl. ed. 35.00 (*0-685-70055-0*) MICHIE.

Texas Corporation Laws: Civil Statutes, Title 32, Corporations & Business Corporation Act with Index: As Amended Through the 1983 Regular & First Called Sessions of the 68th Legislature. Texas Legislature Staff. 294p. write for info. (*0-318-59334-3*) West Pub.

Texas Corporations: Law & Practice. Barbara B. Aldave & Michael M. Boone. LC 84-71521. 1984. Updates. ring bd. write for info. (*0-8205-1707-0*) Bender.

T

***Texas Correllations to Essent Elements.** McCloskey. (Secondary ESL Ser.). 1997. text ed. write for info. (*0-8384-7583-3*) Heinle & Heinle.

Texas Country: The Changing Rural Scene. Ed. by Glen E. Lich & Dona B. Reeves-Marquardt. LC 86-40216. (Illus.). 280p. 1986. 21.95 (*0-89096-247-2*) Tex A&M Univ Pr.

Texas Country Reporter Cookbook. Phillips Production, Inc., Staff. 256p. 1990. pap. 13.95 (*0-940672-54-5*) Shearer Pub.

Texas County Missouri Heritage, Vol. III. 487p. 1992. 45.00 (*0-9622893-3-7*) TCMG&HS.

Texas Courthouse Revisited. June R. Welch. (Illus.). 280p. 1984. 29.95 (*0-912854-14-6*) Yellow Rose Pr.

Texas Courtroom Evidence. 4th ed. Phillip D. Hardberger. 590p. 1990. suppl. ed. 31.50 (*0-685-66085-0*) MICHIE.

Texas Courtroom Evidence. 4th ed. Phillip D. Hardberger. 590p. 1991. suppl. ed. 31.50 (*0-685-66086-9*) MICHIE.

Texas Courtroom Evidence. 4th ed. Phillip D. Hardberger. 590p. 1993. suppl. ed. 35.00 (*0-250-42751-6*) MICHIE.

Texas Courtroom Evidence. 4th ed. Phillip D. Hardberger. 1993. suppl. ed., ring bd. 42.50 (*0-318-68972-3*) MICHIE.

Texas Courtroom Evidence. 4th ed. Phillip D. Hardberger. 590p. 1994. spiral bd. 115.00 (*1-55943-133-4*) MICHIE.

***Texas Courts.** 5th ed. R. P. Adams et al. 68p. 1997. pap. text ed. 13.95 (*0-929563-37-9*) Pearson Pubns.

Texas Court's Charge Series, 8 vols., Set. Ed. by Will G. Barber. 1992. spiral bd. 544.00 (*0-409-25689-7*) MICHIE.

Texas Cowboy. Rita Kerr. LC 96-24037. (Illus.). 96p. (J). (gr. 2-4). 1996. 12.95 (*1-57168-105-1*, Eakin Pr) Sunbelt Media.

Texas Cowboy. Texas Cowboy Artists Association Staff & Donald Worcester. LC 85-50540. 138p. 1986. 29.95 (*0-87565-022-8*) Tex Christian.

Texas Cowboy: The Oral Memoirs of Roland A. Warnock & His Life on the Texas Frontier. Kirby F. Warnock. LC 92-63082. 1992. pap. text ed. 10.75 (*0-9635326-0-X*) Trans Pecos Prods.

Texas Cowboy or Fifteen Years on the Hurricane Deck of a Spanish Pony, Including 1886 Addenda. Charles A. Siringo. LC 79-63094. (Illus.). xl, 216p. 1979. pap. 10.00 (*0-8032-9111-6*, Bison Books) U of Nebr Pr.

Texas Cowboy: or Fifteen Years on the Hurricane Deck of a Spanish Pony, Taken from Real Life. Charles A. Siringo. (American Biography Ser.). 216p. 1991. reprint ed. lib. bdg. 69.00 (*0-7812-8355-8*) Rprt Serv.

Texas Cowboys. Dane Coolidge. LC 85-16333. (Illus.). 162p. 1985. reprint ed. pap. 10.95 (*0-8165-0947-6*) U of Ariz Pr.

***Texas Cowboys: Cowboys of the Lone Star State, a Photographic Portrayal.** Ed. by Dan Streeter. LC 97-65948. (Illus.). 252p. 1997. 60.00 (*0-922029-60-1*) Stoecklein Pub.

Texas Cowboys: Memories of the Early Days. Ed. by Jim Lanning & Judy Lanning. LC 83-40494. (Illus.). 256p. (Orig.). 1995. pap. 14.95 (*0-89096-658-3*) Tex A&M Univ Pr.

Texas Creative Sourcebook, 1996/1997. Ed. by Joey D. Petelle. (Illus.). 350p. 1996. 50.00 (*1-886295-07-7*) Everest Pubng.

Texas Crime Perspective 1996. Ed. by Kathleen O. Morgan et al. 24p. 1996. pap. 19.00 (*1-56692-542-8*) Morgan Quitno Corp.

***Texas Crime Perspective 1997.** Ed. by Kathleen O. Morgan & Scott E. Morgan. 24p. 1997. pap. 19.00 (*1-56692-792-7*) Morgan Quitno Corp.

Texas Crime Poll: Special Survey on Legislative Issues. Raymond H. Teske & Robert H. Meyer. 20p. 1983. 2.00 (*0-318-02513-2*) S Houston Employ.

Texas Crime Victims Handbook. Ken Anderson. 132p. (Orig.). 1995. pap. 22.50 (*0-9644421-0-8*) Georgetwn Pr.

Texas Criminal Defense Forms Annotated. W. V. Dunham, Jr. 410p. 1984. ring bd. 135.00 (*1-878337-19-X*) Knowles Law.

Texas Criminal Law. Cliff Roberson. 1995. 59.95 (*0-8039-7364-0*); pap. 24.95 (*0-8039-7365-9*) Sage.

Texas Criminal Law & Motor Vehicle Handbook: 1995-1996 Edition. rev. ed. Gould Publications Editorial Staff. 1500p. 1995. ring bd. 24.95 (*0-9629210-1-7*) Gould.

Texas Criminal Practice Guide, 6 vols. Bender's Editorial Staff & Marvin O. Teague. 1979. Set. Updates available. ring bd. write for info. (*0-8205-1712-7*) Bender.

Texas Criminal Procedure. Dix & Dawson. 1988. Supplement 1988. suppl. ed. write for info. (*0-8205-0482-3*) Bender.

Texas Criminal Procedure Code Rules, 1992. West Publishing Company Editorial Staff. 1991. pap. 27.50 (*0-314-00044-5*) West Pub.

Texas "Crinkum-Crankum" A Funny Word Book about Our State. Carole Marsh. (Texas Bks.). (Illus.). (J). (gr. 3-12). 1994. 29.95 (*0-7933-4937-0*); pap. 19.95 (*0-7933-4938-9*); disk 29.95 (*0-7933-4939-7*) Gallopade Pub Group.

Texas Currents. Howard J. Smagula. LC 85-61314. (Illus.). 64p. (Orig.). 1985. pap. 12.50 (*0-9614862-0-1*) San Antonio Art.

Texas Damages. James L. Branton & Jim D. Lovett. (Trial Lawyer's Ser.: Vol. 4). (Illus.). 520p. 1987. ring bd. 135.00 (*1-878337-04-1*) Knowles Law.

***Texas Damages Awards: 1996 Edition.** rev. ed. Ed. by Timothy M. Hall. LC 94-76225. 600p. 1996. pap. text ed. write for info. (*0-7620-0084-8*) Lawyers Cooperative.

***Texas Dawn.** Joan E. Pickart. (Family Men Ser.). 1997. mass mkt. 3.99 (*0-373-24100-3*, 1-24100-9) Silhouette.

***Texas Death Row.** Ken Light & Suzanne Donovan. LC 96-41256. (Illus.). 1997. write for info. (*0-87805-950-4*); pap. write for info. (*0-87805-951-2*) U Pr of Miss.

Texas Deceptive Trade Practices. 3rd ed. Richard Alderman. LC 94-72967. 576p. 1994. pap. 48.75 (*0-916081-37-0*) J Marshall Pub Co.

***Texas Democracy.** Gambitta. (C). 1996. text ed. write for info. (*0-15-500957-5*) HB Coll Pubs.

Texas Democrats vs. Party Reform, 1950-1973. Daniel M. Siewert. LC 94-13972. (Illus.). viii, 112p. 1994. pap. 12.00 (*0-86663-207-7*) Ide Hse.

Texas Department of Human Services Directory of Licensed Administrators & Child Care Institutions, 1989. Ed. by Silent Partners, Inc. Staff. 72p. 1989. pap. write for info. (*1-878353-03-9*) Silent Partners.

Texas Department of Human Services Directory of Licensed Administrators & Child Care Institutions 1990. Ed. by Silent Partners, Inc. Staff. 72p. (Orig.). 1990. pap. write for info. (*1-878353-18-7*) Silent Partners.

Texas Department of Human Services Directory of Licensed Administrators & Child Care Institutions 1991. Ed. by Silent Partners, Inc. Staff. 72p. (Orig.). 1991. pap. write for info. (*1-878353-19-5*) Silent Partners.

Texas Department of Human Services Directory of Licensed Administrators & Child Care Institutions, 1992. 75p. (Orig.). 1992. pap. write for info. (*1-878353-27-6*) Silent Partners.

Texas Department of Human Services Directory of Social Workers, 1989. Ed. by Silent Partners, Inc. Staff. 201p. (Orig.). 1989. pap. write for info. (*1-878353-04-7*) Silent Partners.

Texas Department of Human Services Directory of Social Workers 1990. Ed. by Silent Partners, Inc. Staff. 200p. (Orig.). 1990. pap. write for info. (*1-878353-17-9*) Silent Partners.

Texas Department of Human Services Directory of Social Workers 1991. Ed. by Silent Partners, Inc. Staff. 328p. (Orig.). 1991. pap. write for info. (*1-878353-16-0*) Silent Partners.

Texas Department of Human Services Directory of Social Workers, 1992. 356p. (Orig.). 1992. pap. write for info. (*1-878353-26-8*) Silent Partners.

Texas Department of Human Services Directory of Social Workers, 1993. 326p. 1993. pap. write for info. (*1-878353-28-4*) Silent Partners.

Texas Department of Protective & Regulatory Services Directory of Licensed Administrators & Child Care Institutions 1993. 77p. 1993. pap. write for info. (*1-878353-31-4*) Silent Partners.

Texas Depositions, Vols. 1 & 1A. James L. Branton & Jim D. Lovett. (Trial Lawyer's Ser.: Vols. 1 & 1A). (Illus.). 1982. Vol. 1, 334 pp., Vol. 1A, 410 pp. ring bd. 185.00 (*1-878337-08-4*) Knowles Law.

***Texas Destiny.** Lorain Heath. 1997. pap. 5.99 (*0-451-40752-0*, Onyx) NAL-Dutton.

Texas Diary, 1835-1838. Mary A. Holley. (American Biography Ser.). 120p. 1991. reprint ed. lib. bdg. 59.00 (*0-7812-8188-1*) Rprt Serv.

Texas Dingbats! Bk. 1: A Fun Book of Games, Stories, Activities & More about Our State That's All in Code! for You to Decipher. Carole Marsh. (Texas Bks.). (Illus.). (J). (gr. 3-12). 1994. pap. 19.95 (*0-7933-3903-0*); lib. bdg. 29.95 (*0-7933-3902-2*); disk 29.95 (*0-7933-3904-9*) Gallopade Pub Group.

Texas Directory of Economic Development Officials 1988. Ed. by Charles W. Graham & Thomas M. Walusek. 70p. (Orig.). 1987. pap. 31.25 (*0-945331-00-2*) Environetics Commns.

Texas Discovery. James L. Branton & Jim D. Lovett. (Trial Lawyer's Ser.: Vol. 6). (Illus.). 319p. 1988. ring bd. 135.00 (*1-878337-10-6*) Knowles Law.

Texas Discovery Forms, 1991-1992. Richard C. Robins. 360p. 1994. spiral bd. 115.00 (*0-409-25534-3*) MICHIE.

Texas Divided: Loyalty & Dissent in the Lone Star State, 1856-1874. James Marten. LC 89-48256. 256p. 1990. 28.00 (*0-8131-1700-3*) U Pr of Ky.

Texas Drawdown. Patrick E. Andrews. 224p. 1991. mass mkt. 3.50 (*0-8217-3399-0*, Zebra Kensgtn) Kensgtn Pub Corp.

Texas Drive. Bill Dugan. 192p. 1996. mass mkt. 2.50 (*0-06-101121-5*, Harp PBks) HarpC.

Texas Drunk Driving Law, 1991-92, 2 vols., Set. 2nd ed. J. Gary Trichter & W. Troy McKinney. 600p. 1994. spiral bd. 195.00 (*0-409-26192-0*) MICHIE.

Texas Earth Surfaces: A Photographic Essay. Jim Bones. (Illus.). 1970. 20.00 (*0-88426-016-X*) Encino Pr.

Texas Economic Development in Transition: Opportunities for Public-Private Collaboration. Ed. by Sherman M. Wyman & Robert R. Weaver. 163p. (Orig.). 1989. pap. text ed. 12.50 (*0-936440-78-3*) U TX SUPA.

Texas Economic Growth, 1890 to World War II: From Frontier to Industrial Giant. Robert S. Maxwell. (Texas History Ser.). (Illus.). 42p. 1982. pap. text ed. 8.95 (*0-89641-099-4*) American Pr.

Texas Economics: Free Enterprise 1988. O'Connor. 1988. text ed. 71.25 (*0-15-374216-X*); text ed. 61.25 (*0-15-374215-1*) HR&W Schl Div.

Texas Economy: 21st Century Economic Challenges. Ed. by Louis J. Rodriguez & Yoshi Fukasawa. LC 96-9266. 278p. 1996. 47.50 (*0-915323-09-5*) Midwestern St U Pr.

Texas Economy since World War II. Mary A. Norman. (Texas History Ser.). (Illus.). 38p. (Orig.). 1983. pap. text ed. 8.95 (*0-89641-126-5*) American Pr.

Texas Education Code. 579p. write for info. (*0-318-59782-9*) West Pub.

Texas Electric Railway: Bulletin No. 121. Johnnie J. Myers. Ed. by LeRoy O. King, Jr. LC 82-71474. (Illus.). 256p. 1982. 36.00 (*0-915348-21-7*) Central Electric.

***Texas Embrace.** F. Rosanne Bittner. 320p. 1997. mass mkt. 5.99 (*0-8217-5625-7*, Zebra Kensgtn) Kensgtn Pub Corp.

***Texas Empire.** Matt Bruan. 1996. mass mkt. 5.99 (*0-312-96036-0*) St Martin.

Texas Employers' Guide. Michael P. Maslanka. 1992. write for info. (*0-8205-1005-X*) Bender.

Texas Employer's Guide to Employee Policy Handbooks. Michael P. Maslanka. 390p. 1995. ring bd. 187.00 (*0-925773-22-0*) M Lee Smith.

Texas Employment Law, Pt. I. Richard R. Carlson. Ed. by Charles Neighbors. 640p. (Orig.). Part I. 55.00 (*0-945701-05-5*) Sterling TX.

Texas Employment Law, Pt. II. Richard R. Carlson. Ed. by Charles Neighbors. 640p. (Orig.). Part II. 55.00 (*0-685-35545-4*) Sterling TX.

Texas Employment Laws & Regulations: How to Comply. Ed. by McGinnis et al. 148p. 1995. pap. 75.00 (*0-685-67824-5*) Amer CC Pubs.

Texas Energy Issues: 1978, No. 25. Contrib. by Stephen H. Spurr. (Policy Research Project Report). 123p. 1978. pap. 4.00 (*0-89940-618-1*) LBJ Sch Pub Aff.

Texas Energy Issues: 1979, No. 36. Contrib. by Stephen H. Spurr. (Policy Research Project Report). 135p. 1979. pap. 4.00 (*0-89940-636-X*) LBJ Sch Pub Aff.

Texas Energy Issues: 1980. Contrib. by Stephen H. Spurr. (Policy Research Project Report: No. 40). 95p. 1980. pap. 4.95 (*0-89940-640-8*) LBJ Sch Pub Aff.

***Texas Environmental Law Handbook.** Fulbright & Jaworsky. (State Environmental Law Ser.). 524p. (Orig.). 1996. pap. text ed. 99.00 (*0-86587-544-8*) Gov Insts.

Texas Estate Planning, 3 vols. Kenneth McLaughlin, Jr. & Lisa S. Robinson. 1992. Set. write for info. (*0-8205-1238-9*) Bender.

Texas Ethics Commission: Study & Recommendations. 73p. (Orig.). (C). 1994. pap. text ed. 20.00 (*0-7881-0632-5*) DIANE Pub.

Texas Evidence: A User's Guide to Texas Civil Evidence. annuals James L. Branton & Jim D. Lovett. (Trial Lawyer's Ser.: Vol. 8). 375p. 1991. suppl. ed., ring bd. 135.00 (*1-878337-28-9*) Knowles Law.

Texas Evidentiary Foundations. David A. Schlueter et al. 503p. 1992. 75.00 (*0-87473-997-7*) MICHIE.

Texas Experience: Published for Texas Committee for the Humanities. Compiled by Archie P. McDonald. LC 85-40755. (Illus.). 192p. 1986. 19.95 (*0-89096-281-2*) Tex A&M Univ Pr.

Texas Fact Book, 1989. LC 78-67923. (Illus.). 150p. 1989. pap. text ed. 15.00 (*0-87755-299-1*) Bureau Busn TX.

Texas Facts & Factivities. Carole Marsh. (Carole Marsh State Bks.). 1996. 29.95 (*0-614-11553-1*, C Marsh); teacher ed., pap. 19.95 (*0-7933-7933-4*, C Marsh) Gallopade Pub Group.

Texas Family Code. 132p. write for info. (*0-318-59783-7*) West Pub.

Texas Family Code, 1992. West Publishing Company Editorial Staff. 1991. pap. 20.95 (*0-314-00049-6*) West Pub.

Texas Family Law. James L. Branton & Jim D. Lovett. Ed. by Brian L. Webb. (Trial Lawyer's Ser.: Vol. 7). (Illus.). 350p. 1990. ring bd. 135.00 (*1-878337-23-8*) Knowles Law.

Texas Family Law. 7th rev. ed. Gaylord A. Jentz. LC 86-71681. 166p. (Orig.). 1992. pap. 15.00 (*0-87755-323-8*) Bureau Busn TX.

***Texas Family Law Practice Manual, 5 vols.** 2nd ed. State Bar of Texas Council of Family Law Section Staff. 2752p. 1997. ring bd. 495.00 (*0-938160-90-7*) State Bar TX.

Texas Family Law Service, 8 vols. LC 88-72209. 1988. 858.00 (*0-318-57141-2*) Lawyers Cooperative.

Texas Family Law Trial Guide, 1 vol. Jo L. Merrill. 750p. Updates available. 115.00 (*0-8205-1767-4*) Juris Pubng.

Texas Favorites. 1986. write for info. (*0-936769-05-X*) Gateway Prod.

Texas Federal Census Index, 1850. Ronald V. Jackson. LC 77-86076. (Illus.). 1976. lib. bdg. 68.00 (*0-89593-139-7*) Accelerated Index.

Texas Federal Census Index, 1860. Ronald V. Jackson. (Illus.). 1985. lib. bdg. 129.00 (*0-89593-550-3*) Accelerated Index.

Texas Federal Census Index, 1870. (Illus.). 1987. lib. bdg. 290.00 (*0-89593-496-5*) Accelerated Index.

***Texas Federal Court Rules.** annot. ed. LC 96-76323. 1000p. 1996. pap. text ed. write for info. (*0-7620-0065-1*) Lawyers Cooperative.

Texas Festival Fun for Kids! Carole Marsh. (Texas Bks.). (Illus.). (YA). (gr. 3-12). 1994. pap. 19.95 (*0-7933-4056-X*); lib. bdg. 29.95 (*0-7933-4055-1*); disk 29.95 (*0-7933-4057-8*) Gallopade Pub Group.

Texas Financial Institutions Directory & Fact Book: Spring - Summer 1993 Edition. 600p. 1993. text ed. 22.95 (*1-883566-08-8*) R L Polk.

Texas Five Hundred: Hoover's Guide to the Top Texas Companies, 1994-1995. Ed. by Reference Press Staff. 300p. (Orig.). 1993. lib. bdg. 24.95 (*1-878753-46-0*) Hoovers TX.

Texas Five Hundred: Hoover's Guide to the Top Texas Companies, 1994-1995. Ed. by Reference Press Staff. 300p. (Orig.). 1994. pap. 14.95 (*1-878753-39-8*) Hoovers TX.

Texas Flame. Catherine Creel. 1981. mass mkt. 2.75 (*0-89083-797-X*, Zebra Kensgtn) Kensgtn Pub Corp.

Texas Flowerscaper: A Seasonal Guide to Bloom, Height, Color & Texture. Kathy Huber. (Illus.). 144p. 1996. 21.95 (*0-87905-706-8*) Gibbs Smith Pub.

Texas Folk Medicine, Vol. 5. Ed. by John Q. Anderson. (Texas Folklore Society Paisano Books Ser.). 1970. 15.00 (*0-88426-013-5*) Encino Pr.

Texas Folk Songs. rev. ed. Compiled & Rev. by William A. Owens. LC 76-43005. (Texas Folklore Society Publications: No. 23). (Illus.). 210p. 1976. reprint ed. 15.00 (*0-87074-157-8*) UNTX Pr.

Texas Folklife Festival: A Children's Guide. Kathy Wicks. (Illus.). 30p. (J). 2.25 (*0-86701-035-5*) U of Tex Inst Tex Culture.

Texas Folklore Society, 1909-1943, Vol. I. Francis E. Abernethy. LC 92-12273. (Texas Folklore Society Publications: No. 51). (Illus.). 326p. 1992. 29.95 (*0-929398-42-4*) UNTX Pr.

Texas Folklore Society, 1943-1971 Vol. 2, Vol. II. Francis E. Abernethy. LC 92-12273. (Texas Folklore Society Publications: No. 53). (Illus.). 320p. 1994. 29.95 (*0-929398-78-5*) UNTX Pr.

Texas Footprints. Rita Kerr. (J). (gr. 3-7). 1988. 12.95 (*0-89015-676-X*) Sunbelt Media.

Texas Foreclosure: Law & Practice. W. Michael Baggett. LC 84-5376. 562p. 1984. text ed. 120.00 (*0-07-003027-8*) Shepards.

Texas Foreclosure Manual. William H. Locke, Jr. & Ralph M. Novak, Jr. LC 91-65392. 484p. 1991. ring bd. 150.00 (*0-938160-63-X*, 6207) State Bar TX.

Texas Forever. Rita Kerr. LC 93-11134. 1993. 12.95 (*0-89015-921-1*) Sunbelt Media.

Texas Forever!! The Paintings. J. C. Martin et al. (Illus.). 100p. (YA). (gr. 9 up). 1991. 39.95 (*0-9627589-0-6*) Oak Creek Pr.

Texas' Forgotten Ports. Keith Guthrie. (Illus.). 224p. 1988. 18.95 (*0-89015-661-1*) Sunbelt Media.

Texas Forgotten Ports, Vol. 2. Keith Guthrie. 1994. 22.95 (*0-89015-898-3*) Sunbelt Media.

Texas Forms: Legal & Business, 15 vols., Set Incl. Suppl. 1994. LC 78-6994. 1992. Set; Suppl. 1994. 1,070.00 (*0-318-57139-0*) Lawyers Cooperative.

Texas Fossils: An Amateur Collector's Handbook. W. H. Matthews, III. (Guidebook Ser.: GB 2). (Illus.). 123p. 1960. reprint ed. pap. 3.50 (*0-686-29311-8*) Bur Econ Geology.

Texas Frontier: The Clear Fork Country & Fort Griffin, 1849-1887. Ty Cashion. LC 95-41192. (Illus.). 384p. (C). 1996. 24.95 (*0-8061-2791-0*) U of Okla Pr.

***Texas Frontier: The Clear Fork Country & Fort Griffin, 1849-1887.** Ty Cashion. LC 95-41192. (Illus.). 384p. 1997. pap. 17.95 (*0-8061-2855-0*) U of Okla Pr.

Texas Fury. Fern Michaels. 1989. mass mkt. 5.99 (*0-345-31375-5*) Ballantine.

Texas Fury. Fern Michaels. 1996. pap. 8.95 (*0-345-40569-2*) Ballantine.

***Texas Fury.** large type ed. Jackson Cole. LC 97-13073. 1997. write for info. (*0-7838-8203-3*) G K Hall.

Texas Fury. large type ed. Fern Michaels. LC 93-13197. 1993. lib. bdg. 22.95 (*1-56054-754-5*) Thorndike Pr.

Texas Gambler in My Kitchen. 4.00 (*0-943768-09-8*) C Coleman.

***Texas Garden Almanac, 1997.** Mike Peters & Texas Gulf Coast Gardener Staff. 264p. 1996. pap. 10.95 (*0-9654378-0-9*, 37809, TX Grdn Almanac) McMillen Pubng.

***Texas Gardener's Guide: The What, Where, When, How & Why of Gardening in Texas.** Dale Groom. (Illus.). 400p. (Orig.). 1997. pap. 19.95 (*1-888608-30-7*) Cool Springs Pr.

Texas Gardener's Guide to Growing & Using Herbs. Diane M. Sitton. (Illus.). 144p. 1987. 12.95 (*0-914641-08-5*) TX Gardener Pr.

Texas Garderner's Guide to Growing Tomatoes. Mary G. Rundell. 128p. (Orig.). 1984. pap. text ed. 6.95 (*0-914641-00-X*) TX Gardener Pr.

Texas Gateways for Two. Paris Permenter & John Bigley. (Illus.). 200p. (Orig.). 1996. pap. 14.95 (*1-878686-24-0*) Two Lane Pr.

***Texas Glory.** Lorraine Heath. 1998. mass mkt. 5.99 (*0-451-40753-9*, Onyx) NAL-Dutton.

***Texas Glory.** Joan E. Pickart. 1997. pap. 3.50 (*0-373-76088-4*, 1-76088-3) Silhouette.

Texas Glory Vol. 1: An Epic of the Alamo. Robert Vaughan. 1996. mass mkt. 5.99 (*0-312-95938-9*) St Martin.

Texas Gold. Joan Hohl. 1993. mass mkt. 4.50 (*0-373-48282-5*) Harlequin Bks.

***Texas Gold: Growing up in a Texas Oil Camp.** Joyce Shaughnessy. Ed. by Pete Billac. Tr. by Sharon Davis. (Illus.). 128p. 1996. pap. 9.95 (*0-943629-24-1*) Swan Pub.

Texas Golf Legends. Curt Sampson. LC 92-38712. (Illus.). 144p. (C). 1993. 350.00 (*0-89672-314-3*) Tex Tech Univ Pr.

***Texas Goverment.** 5th ed. Hill. (C). 1998. pap. text ed. 27.50 (*0-15-505615-8*) HB Coll Pubs.

Texas Government. Coleman & Calvi. 1995. pap. text ed. 34.00 (*0-13-912932-4*) P-H.

Texas Government. Susan Coleman et al. LC 95-14145. 1995. pap. write for info. (*0-614-07804-0*) P-H.

Texas Government: Policy & Politics. abr. ed. Neal R. Tannahill. (C). 1995. teacher ed. write for info. (*0-673-54323-4*) Addson-Wesley Educ.

Texas Government: Policy & Politics. abr. ed. Neal R. Tannahill. 272p. (C). 1996. text ed. 33.50 (*0-673-52470-1*) Addson-Wesley Educ.

Texas Government: Policy & Politics. 4th ed. Neal R. Tannahill. LC 92-28688. (C). 1992. 26.00 (*0-673-52178-8*) Addson-Wesley Educ.

***Texas Government: Policy & Politics.** 5th ed. Ed. by Tannahill. (C). 1997. student ed., pap. text ed. 18.95 (*0-673-52557-0*) Addison-Wesley.

Texas Government: Policy & Politics. 5th ed. Neal R. Tannahill. LC 96-16347. (C). 1997. text ed. 35.95 (*0-673-52469-8*) Addson-Wesley Educ.

Texas Government: Politics & Economics. 4th ed. Kim Q. Hill & Kenneth R. Mladenka. (C). 1995. pap. text ed. 39.25 (*0-534-25440-3*) HarBrace.

An Asterisk (*) at the beginning of an entry indicates that the title is appearing in BIP for the first time.

***Texas Government! The Cornerstone of Everyday Life in Our State!** Carole Marsh. (Carole Marsh Texas Bks.). (Illus.). (J). (gr. 3-12). 1996. pap. 19.95 (*0-7933-6311-X*); lib. bdg. 29.95 (*0-7933-6310-1*); disk 29.95 (*0-7933-6312-8*) Gallopade Pub Group.

Texas Government Handbook. 2nd ed. Jeffrey M. Gamso. Ed. by Louise Cummins et al. (Illus.). 44p. 1989. pap. 5.00 (*0-915757-12-5*) League Women Voters TX.

Texas Government National Perspective. 3rd ed. Leon Blevins. 1994. pap. text ed. write for info. (*0-07-005929-2*) McGraw.

Texas Government Today. 5th ed. Bland. (C). 1991. pap. text ed. 28.00 (*0-534-15199-X*) HarBrace.

Texas Government Today. 5th ed. Randall W. Bland et al. 528p. (C). 1991. pap. text ed. 35.00 (*0-534-15198-1*) HarBrace.

Texas Governments Performance Standards, 1990. Ed. by Greg Michels. (Governments Performance Standards Ser.). (Illus.). 150p. 1990. text ed. 125.00 (*1-55507-502-9*) Municipal Analysis.

Texas Governor. June R. Welch. (Illus.). 1977. 17.95 (*0-912854-09-X*) Yellow Rose Pr.

Texas Granite: The Story of First Lieutenant Jack Lummus, World War II Hero. Mary Hartman. LC 96-39051. (Illus.). (Orig.). 1997. pap. 17.95 (*1-885777-07-8*) Hendrick-Long.

Texas Graveyards: A Cultural Legacy. Terry G. Jordan. (Elma Dill Russell Spencer Foundation Ser.: No. 13). (Illus.). 160p. 1982. pap. 24.95 (*0-292-78044-3*); pap. 13.95 (*0-292-78070-2*) U of Tex Pr.

***Texas Guide.** Judy Moore. 1997. pap. 14.95 (*1-883323-59-2*) Open Rd Pub.

Texas Guinan, Queen of the Night Clubs. Louise Berliner. LC 92-1720. (Illus.). 253p. 1993. 24.95 (*0-292-78111-3*) U of Tex Pr.

Texas Gulf Coast: Interpretations by Nine Artists. Intro. by Leon Hale. LC 79-7416. (Joe & Betty Moore Texas Art Ser.: No. 4). (Illus.). 114p. 1979. 29.95 (*0-89096-082-8*) Tex A&M Univ Pr.

Texas Gulf Historical & Biographical Record: General Index, Volumes I-XXX, 1965-1994. Compiled by Howell H. Gwin, Jr. LC 95-34778. 1995. write for info. (*1-57168-059-4*) Sunbelt Media.

Texas Gun - Gringo. Nelson Nye. 320p. 1995. mass mkt., pap. text ed. 4.99 (*0-8439-3822-6*) Dorchester Pub Co.

Texas Gun Owner's Guide: Who Can Bear Arms? Where Are Guns Forbidden? When Can You Shoot to Kill? Alan Korwin & Georgene Lockwood. LC 95-77340. (Illus.). 256p. (Orig.). 1995. pap. 14.95 (*0-9621958-5-5*) Bloomfield Pr.

Texas Gundown. Jason Manning. 1990. mass mkt. 2.95 (*0-8217-2970-5*, Zebra Kensgtn) Kensgtn Pub Corp.

Texas Gunsmoke. Frank Cannon. 192p. 1988. mass mkt. 2.50 (*0-8217-2488-6*, Zebra Kensgtn) Kensgtn Pub Corp.

Texas Handbook. 3rd ed. Joe Cummings. (Moon Travel Handbooks Ser.). (Illus.). 598p. (Orig.). 1996. pap. 17.95 (*1-56691-063-3*) Moon Trvl Hdbks.

Texas Health Care Perspective 1996. Ed. by Kathleen O. Morgan et al. 24p. 1996. pap. 19.00 (*1-56692-642-4*) Morgan Quitno Corp.

***Texas Health Care Perspective 1997.** Ed. by Kathleen O. Morgan & Scott E. Morgan. 24p. 1997. pap. 19.00 (*1-56692-742-0*) Morgan Quitno Corp.

Texas Health Care Reform: The Best & Worst Ideas. John C. Goodman & Merrill Matthews, Jr. (Illus.). 61p. (Orig.). 1993. pap. text ed. 10.00 (*1-56808-012-3*) Natl Ctr Pol.

Texas Heartland: A Hill Country Year. Jim Bones, Jr. & John Graves. LC 75-16352. (Illus.). 104p. 1982. 29.95 (*0-89096-002-X*) Tex A&M Univ Pr.

***Texas Heat.** Barbara McCauley. (Silhouette Romance Ser.). 1996. 19.95 (*0-373-59747-9*) Thorndike Pr.

Texas Heat. Fern Michaels. 640p. 1986. mass mkt. 5.99 (*0-345-33100-1*) Ballantine.

Texas Heat. large type ed. Fern Michaels. LC 92-42500. 1993. lib. bdg. 20.95 (*1-56054-660-3*) Thorndike Pr.

Texas Heat. Fern Michaels. 1989. reprint ed. 20.00 (*0-7278-4007-X*) Severn Hse.

Texas Heat: (Hearts of Stone) Barbara McCauley. (Desire Ser.). 1995. mass mkt. 3.25 (*0-373-05917-5*, 1-05917-9) Silhouette.

Texas Helltown. Jason Manning. 1990. mass mkt. 2.95 (*0-8217-3218-8*, Zebra Kensgtn) Kensgtn Pub Corp.

***Texas, Her Texas: The Life & Times of Frances Goff.** Nancy B. Young et al. LC 96-52778. (Barker Texas History Center Ser.). 1997. write for info. (*0-87611-159-2*) Tex St Hist Assn.

Texas Heritage. 2nd ed. Ed. by Ben Procter & Archie P. McDonald. 366p. 1992. pap. text ed. write for info. (*0-88295-880-1*) Harlan Davidson.

***Texas Heritage.** 3rd ed. Ben Procter & Archie P. McDonald. LC 97-6788. (Illus.). 288p. (C). Date not set. pap. text ed. 17.95 (*0-88295-976-X*) Harlan Davidson.

Texas Heritage Songbook Grade 7-8. Boardman. (J). (gr. 7-8). 1988. pap. 23.25 (*0-03-014058-7*) HB Schl Dept.

Texas Hero. Ruth R. Langan. (Historical Ser.). 1993. mass mkt. 3.99 (*0-373-28780-1*, 1-28780-4) Harlequin Bks.

Texas Highschool Basketball Scrapbook. Ivy McLemore. Ed. by Edwin M. Eakin. (Illus.). 128p. (Orig.). 1989. pap. 12.95 (*0-89015-723-5*) Sunbelt Media.

Texas Highway Cost Index: An Assessment. Michael C. Walton et al. LC 84-81399. (Policy Research Institute Ser.: No. 1). 216p. 1984. pap. 3.00 (*0-89940-150-3*) LBJ Sch Pub Aff.

Texas Highway Humor. Wallace O. Chariton. (Regional Bks.). (Illus.). 144p. (Orig.). 1991. pap. 10.95 (*1-55622-176-2*, Rep of TX Pr) Wordware Pub.

Texas Highways Cookbook. Joanne Smith. LC 86-4949. (Illus.). 128p. 1991. reprint ed. pap. 19.95 (*0-292-78088-5*) U of Tex Pr.

Texas Hill Country. George O. Miller. LC 91-13082. (Illus.). 96p. 1991. 21.95 (*0-89658-164-0*) Voyageur Pr.

Texas Hill Country: A Complete Guide. Eleanor Morris. LC 96-18635. (Great Destinations Ser.). 1997. 17.95 (*0-936399-84-8*) Berkshire Hse.

Texas Hill Country: A Postcard Book. Laurence E. Parent. (Illus.). 48p. (Orig.). 1992. pap. 8.95 (*0-9634758-0-0*) L Parent Photo.

Texas Hill Country: Interpretations by Thirteen Artists. Intro. by A. C. Greene. LC 81-40400. (Joe & Betty Moore Texas Art Ser.: No. 5). (Illus.). 122p. (Orig.). 1981. 29.95 (*0-89096-116-6*) Tex A&M Univ Pr.

Texas Hill Country: Interpretations by Thirteen Artists. Intro. by A. C. Greene. LC 81-40400. (Joe & Betty Moore Texas Art Ser.: No. 5). (Illus.). 122p. (Orig.). 1986. pap. 18.95 (*0-89096-359-2*) Tex A&M Univ Pr.

Texas Hill Country: Littlebook. Photos by Richard Reynolds. (Illus.). 1996. 14.95 (*1-56579-145-2*) Westcliffe Pubs.

Texas Hill Country Cookbook. Blue Lake-Deerhaven Cookbook Staff. (Illus.). 406p. 1983. reprint ed. pap. 12.95 (*0-9609210-0-1*) RAR Enterprises.

Texas Historic Inns Cookbook. Ann Ruff & Gail Drago. Ed. by Scott Lubeck. (Illus.). 224p. 1984. pap. 11.95 (*0-932012-45-0*, 0245) Gulf Pub.

Texas Historical & Biographical Index, Vol. 1. Ronald V. Jackson. LC 78-53718. (Illus.). 1984. lib. bdg. 30.00 (*0-89593-201-6*) Accelerated Index.

Texas History. 2nd ed. Ed. by Walter L. Buenger. (Texas History Ser.). (Illus.). 546p. 1983. pap. text ed. 24.95 (*0-89641-138-9*) American Pr.

Texas History. 2nd ed. Ed. by Frank H. Smyrl. (Texas History Ser.). (Illus.). 474p. 1985. pap. text ed. 21.95 (*0-89641-159-1*) American Pr.

***Texas History! Surprising Secrets about Our State's Founding Mothers, Fathers & Kids!** Carole Marsh. (Carole Marsh Texas Bks.). (Illus.). (J). (gr. 3-12). 1996. pap. 19.95 (*0-7933-6158-3*); lib. bdg. 29.95 (*0-7933-6157-5*); disk 29.95 (*0-7933-6159-1*) Gallopade Pub Group.

Texas History According to Us. Intro. by Michael C. Hennech. (Illus.). 116p. (Orig.). (YA). (gr. 7). 1991. pap. 7.95 (*1-881301-01-X*) Ale Pub.

Texas History Movies. 65p. 1986. pap. 4.50 (*0-87611-080-4*) Tex St Hist Assn.

Texas History Stories. E. G. Littlejohn. LC 86-62880. (Illus.). 188p. (J). (gr. 3-7). 1986. reprint ed. pap. 11.95 (*0-938349-07-4*) State House Pr.

Texas History Stories Activity Book. Deborah E. Brothers & Thomas A. Munnerlyn. LC 86-62880. (Illus.). 32p. (J). (gr. 3-7). 1986. reprint ed. student ed., pap. 6.95 (*0-938349-10-4*) State House Pr.

Texas History Time Line: From Indians to Astronauts. Betsy Warren. (Illus.). 64p. (Orig.). (YA). (gr. 4 up). 1996. pap. 12.95 (*1-885777-13-2*) Hendrick-Long.

Texas HIV-AIDS Community Resource Directory. 9th ed. 141p. 1996. pap. text ed. 25.00 (*0-7881-2841-8*) DIANE Pub.

***Texas Hold'Em Poker for Low-Limit Players.** Ken Warren. 1997. pap. text ed. 14.95 (*0-940685-70-1*) Cardoza Pub.

***Texas Holiday Cookbook.** Dotty Griffith. LC 97-24683. 1997. 24.95 (*0-88415-869-1*, 5869) Gulf Pub.

Texas Home Cooking. Cheryl A. Jamison & Bill Jamison. Ed. by Linda Ziedrich. LC 93-29035. (Illus.). 592p. 1993. 29.95 (*1-55832-058-X*); pap. 17.95 (*1-55832-059-8*) Harvard Common Pr.

Texas Homebuyer's Manual. State Bar of Texas, Real Estate, Probate & Trust Law Section Staff. Ed. by Michael Graham. LC 86-3084. 92p. (Orig.). 1986. pap. 6.95 (*0-87201-836-9*) Gulf Pub.

Texas Horse Trading Co. No. 4: Devil's Deathbed. Gene Shelton. 192p. (Orig.). 1995. mass mkt. 4.50 (*0-515-11567-3*) Jove Pubns.

Texas Hospital Law, 2 vols. 2nd ed. Richard L. Griffith & Dewey M. Johnston. 690p. 1993. suppl. ed. 65.00 (*0-685-74473-6*) MICHIE.

Texas Hospital Law, 2 vols., Set. 2nd ed. Richard L. Griffith & Dewey W. Johnston. 654p. 1995. spiral bd. 160.00 (*0-409-25657-9*) MICHIE.

Texas Hot Air Balloon Mystery. Carole Marsh. (Carole Marsh Texas Bks.). (Illus.). (J). (gr. 2-9). 1994. 29.95 (*0-7933-2705-9*); pap. 19.95 (*0-7933-2706-7*); disk 29.95 (*0-7933-2707-5*) Gallopade Pub Group.

Texas Humoresque: Lone Star Humorists from Then Till Now. Charles L. Sonnichsen. LC 89-37113. (Illus.). 322p. (Orig.). 1990. pap. 14.95 (*0-87565-046-5*) Tex Christian.

***Texas Hunting & Fishing.** Luke Clayton. (Illus.). 176p. (Orig.). 1997. pap. 14.95 (*0-87833-967-1*) Taylor Pub.

Texas Hunting & Fishing Leases. Keith Phillips. 1996. pap. text ed. 9.95 (*1-888103-00-0*) Trophy Pubng.

***Texas Iconoclast: Maury Maverick, Jr.** Maury Maverick, Jr. Ed. by Allan O. Kownslar. LC 96-31443. (Illus.). 300p. (Orig.). 1997. pap. 16.95 (*0-87565-172-0*) Tex Christian.

Texas in Bloom: Photographs from Texas Highways Magazine. Intro. by Glen Evans. LC 83-40500. (Louise Lindsey Merrick Texas Environment Ser.: No. 7). (Illus.). 148p. 1991. reprint ed. 24.95 (*0-89096-180-8*) Tex A&M Univ Pr.

Texas in Eighteen Forty-Eight. Viktor Bracht. 1993. reprint ed. lib. bdg. 75.00 (*0-7812-5919-3*) Rprt Serv.

Texas in Eighteen Forty: or The Emigrant's Guide to the New Republic. 1973. 23.95 (*0-405-04997-8*) Ayer.

Texas in Gray: The Civil War Years, 1861-1865. Frank H. Smyrl. (Texas History Ser.). 55p. (Orig.). (C). 1983. pap. text ed. 8.95 (*0-89641-130-3*) American Pr.

Texas in Historic Sites & Symbols. Betsy Warren. (Illus.). 32p. (J). (gr. k-3). 1982. pap. 6.95 (*0-937460-05-2*) Hendrick-Long.

Texas in Maps. James P. Bryan & Walter K. Hanak. (Illus.). 40p. 1961. pap. 10.00 (*0-87959-126-9*) U of Tex H Ransom Ctr.

Texas in My Heart. Claudia L. Boysen & Christine L. Brownlie. (Illus.). 120p. 1992. spiral bd. write for info. (*1-879127-15-6*) Lighten Up Enter.

Texas in Perspective 1996. Ed. by Kathleen O. Morgan et al. 26p. 1996. pap. 19.00 (*1-56692-592-4*) Morgan Quitno Corp.

***Texas in Perspective 1997.** Ed. by Kathleen O. Morgan & Scott E. Morgan. 26p. 1997. pap. 19.00 (*1-56692-692-0*) Morgan Quitno Corp.

Texas in Poetry: A 150-Year Anthology. Billy B. Hill. 358p. (C). 1994. 29.95 (*1-885196-01-6*) Ctr Tex Studies.

Texas in Seventeen Seventy-Six: A Historical Description. Seymour V. Connor. LC 75-37049. 112p. 1975. 20.00 (*0-8363-0136-6*, V24-10-7228) Jenkins.

Texas in the Middle Eighteenth Century. Herbert E. Bolton. 1993. reprint ed. lib. bdg. 75.00 (*0-7812-5868-5*) Rprt Serv.

***Texas in the Morning: The Love Story of Madeleine Duncan Brown & President Lyndon Baines-Johnson.** Madeleine D. Brown. LC 97-66180. (Harrison Edward Livingstone Bks.). (Illus.). 255p. 1997. 25.00 (*0-941401-06-5*) Conservatory.

Texas in Transition. Bill Broyles et al. Ed. by Michael L. Gillette. (Symposia Ser.). (Illus.). 254p. 1986. pap. 7.00 (*0-89940-419-7*) LBJ Sch Pub Aff.

Texas Indian Dictionary for Kids! Carole Marsh. (Carole Marsh State Bks.). (J). (gr. 2-9). 1996. 29.95 (*0-7933-7773-0*, C Marsh); pap. 19.95 (*0-7933-7774-9*, C Marsh) Gallopade Pub Group.

Texas Instruments Computer Program Writing Workbook. Len Turner. 96p. 1983. 4.95 (*0-86668-812-9*) ARCsoft.

Texas Instruments Graphing Calculator. Moore. suppl. ed., pap. text ed. write for info. (*0-7167-2923-7*) W H Freeman.

Texas Instruments Home Computer Games Programs. Len Turner. 96p. 1983. 8.95 (*0-86668-032-2*) ARCsoft.

Texas Instruments Home Computer Graphics Programs. Len Turner. 112p. 1983. 9.95 (*0-86668-031-4*) ARCsoft.

Texas Insurance Code: With Tables & Index, As Amended Through the 1983 Regular & First Called Sessions of the 68th Legislature. Texas Legislature Staff. 600p. write for info. (*0-318-59335-1*) West Pub.

Texas Insurance Law Reporter. Ed. by Richard S. Geiger & Leo J. Jordan. 20p. 1980. ring bd. 96.00 (*0-614-05977-1*) MICHIE.

Texas Is ...(the Sesquicentennial Remembered) Mark Holbrook. (Illus.). 200p. 1986. 50.00 (*0-9617487-0-2*) Ringtail Prod.

Texas Jack at the Alamo. James Rice. LC 88-31691. (Illus.). 40p. (J). 1989. 13.95 (*0-88289-725-X*) Pelican.

Texas Jeopardy! Answers & Questions about Our State! Carole Marsh. (Texas Bks.). (Illus.). (J). (gr. 3-12). 1994. pap. 19.95 (*0-7933-4209-0*); lib. bdg. 29.95 (*0-7933-4208-2*); disk 29.95 (*0-7933-4210-4*) Gallopade Pub Group.

***Texas Jingo.** Gary Grimm. (Illus.). 32p. (J). (gr. 1-6). 1997. 12.00 (*1-56490-048-7*) G Grimm Assocs.

Texas "Jography" A Fun Run Thru Our State! Carole Marsh. (Carole Marsh Texas Bks.). (Illus.). (J). 1994. pap. 19.95 (*1-55609-087-0*); lib. bdg. 29.95 (*0-7933-2076-3*); disk 29.95 (*0-7933-2077-1*) Gallopade Pub Group.

Texas Jurisprudence, 77 vols., Set Incl. Suppl. 1993. 3rd ed. LC 79-51183. 1991. Set; Suppl. 1993. 5,000.00 (*0-318-57138-2*) Lawyers Cooperative.

Texas Jurisprudence Pleading & Practice Forms 2d, 13 vols. LC 72-88069. suppl. ed. 1,080.00 (*0-318-57140-4*) Lawyers Cooperative.

***Texas Juvenile Justice Systems.** Cuvelier. 1997. pap. text ed. 10.60 (*0-13-675570-4*) P-H.

Texas Kickapoo: Keepers of Tradition. Bill Wright & John Gesick. 1996. 45.00 (*0-87404-239-9*) Tex Western.

Texas Kidnappers. T. Edson. 192p. 1996. mass mkt. 4.99 (*0-440-22213-3*) Dell.

Texas Kid's Cookbook: Recipes, How-To, History, Lore & More! Carole Marsh. (Carole Marsh Texas Bks.). (Illus.). (J). 1994. pap. 19.95 (*0-7933-1093-8*); lib. bdg. 29.95 (*0-7933-1094-6*); disk 29.95 (*0-7933-1095-4*) Gallopade Pub Group.

Texas Kiss. Alexandra Blackstone. (Wildflower Ser.). 320p. (Orig.). 1995. mass mkt. 5.50 (*0-515-11638-6*) Jove Pubns.

***Texas Land Ethics.** Pete A. Gunter & Max Oelschlaeger. LC 96-51314. (Illus.). 176p. 1998. pap. 18.95 (*0-292-72802-6*) U of Tex Pr.

Texas Land Surveying Law: Questions & Answers. John E. Keen. 66p. (C). 1995. pap. text ed. 20.00 (*1-56569-041-9*) Land Survey.

Texas Land Use Law. Arthur J. Anderson. LC 91-22845. (Real Estate Practice Library Ser.). 418p. 1991. ring bd. 140.00 (*0-471-55339-5*) Wiley.

Texas Law Finder: A New Topical Reference Guide for Coordinated Research Providing Comprehensive References to the Following West Publications, Vernon's Texas Statutes & Codes Annotated, Vernon's Texas Rules Annotated, Texas Practice Series, West's Texas Forms, Texas Digest, United States Code Annotated, Corpus Juris Secundum, Federal Publications, Key Number Publications, Texts & Treatises, 1982. West Publishing Company Editorial Staff. LC 82-830775. vi, 1201p. 1985. 26.00 (*0-685-06764-5*) West Pub.

Texas Law in Layman's Language. 5th rev. ed. Charles Turner & Ralph Walton. LC 95-2226. (Illus.). 254p. 1990. pap. 14.95 (*0-88415-854-3*, 5854) Gulf Pub.

Texas Law Locator, 15 vols., Set. Shepard's Citation, Inc. Staff. (Law Locators Ser.). 1,150.00 (*0-317-38905-X*) Shepards.

Texas Law of Oil & Gas, 1989-1991, 3 vols. Jacqueline L. Weaver. 1994. suppl. ed., ring bd. 125.00 (*0-685-44584-4*) MICHIE.

Texas Law of Oil & Gas, 1989-1991, 3 vols., Set. Ernest E. Smith & Jacqueline L. Weaver. 1400p. 1994. spiral bd. 350.00 (*0-409-25189-5*) MICHIE.

Texas Law Office Handbook. 3rd ed. Texas Assn. of Legal Secretaries Staff. 440p. 1993. suppl. ed. 35.00 (*0-250-42758-3*) MICHIE.

Texas Law Office Handbook. 3rd ed. Ed. by Texas Association of Legal Secretaries Staff. 440p. 1994. ring bd. 85.00 (*1-55943-163-6*) MICHIE.

Texas Law Office Handbook, No. 1. 3rd ed. Texas Assn. of Legal Secretaries Staff. 440p. 1991. Suppl. 1, 6/91. suppl. ed. 31.00 (*0-685-66116-4*) MICHIE.

Texas Law Office Handbook, No. 2. 3rd ed. Texas Assn. of Legal Secretaries Staff. 440p. 1992. Suppl. 2, 7/92. suppl. ed. 33.00 (*0-685-70056-9*) MICHIE.

Texas Law Review: 1922-1995/96, 74 vols., Set. Bound set, with index. 4,125.00 (*0-8377-9163-4*) Rothman.

Texas League: A Century of Baseball. Bill O'Neal. Ed. by Melissa Roberts. (Illus.). 389p. 1987. pap. 17.95 (*0-89015-609-3*) Sunbelt Media.

Texas Legacy of Katherine Anne Porter. James T. Tanner. LC 90-23052. (Texas Writers Ser.: Vol. 3). 237p. 1991. 19.95 (*0-929398-22-X*) UNTX Pr.

Texas Legal Assistant: Personal Injury, Set. T. Hartley et al. 1992. write for info. (*0-8205-0648-6*) Bender.

Texas Legal Practice Forms, 4 vols. Dennis Taylor & S. Stevenson. LC 82-20673. 1020p. 1990. 295.00 (*0-8321-0053-6*) Bancroft Whitney Co.

Texas Legal Research. 2nd ed. Pamela R. Tepper. (Paralegal Ser.). 496p. 1996. text ed. 37.95 (*0-8273-7682-0*) Delmar.

Texas Legal Research. 2nd ed. Pamela R. Tepper. (Paralegal Ser.). 1997. teacher ed. 16.00 (*0-8273-7683-9*) Delmar.

***Texas Legends.** Retold by J. Havenhill. (YA). (gr. 5 up). 1997. pap. 9.99 (*0-88092-354-7*) Royal Fireworks.

Texas Legends, No. 2: Captain Jack. Gene Shelton. 208p. (Orig.). 1993. mass mkt. 4.50 (*0-515-11192-9*) Jove Pubns.

***Texas Legislative Almanac.** Harvey Tucker & Gary Halter. (Illus.). 400p. (C). 1997. pap. 39.95 (*0-89096-766-0*) Tex A&M Univ Pr.

***Texas Legislative Handbook.** 1995. pap. 4.95 (*0-934367-33-7*) TX St Direct.

***Texas Legislative Manual.** Scott Sayers & Julie Sayers. (Illus.). 104p. 1997. pap. 8.95 (*0-934367-34-5*) TX St Direct.

Texas Library Book: A Surprising Guide to the Unusual Special Collections in Libraries Across Our State for Students, Teachers, Writers & Publishers - Includes Reproducible Mailing Labels Plus Activities for Young People! Carole Marsh. (Texas Bks.). (Illus.). 1994. pap. 19.95 (*0-7933-3135-8*); lib. bdg. 29.95 (*0-7933-3134-X*); disk 29.95 (*0-7933-3136-6*) Gallopade Pub Group.

Texas Lignite: Near-Surface & Deep-Basin Resources. W. R. Kaiser. (Report of Investigations Ser.: RI 79). (Illus.). 70p. 1974. reprint ed. pap. 3.00 (*0-318-03203-1*) Bur Econ Geology.

***Texas Lily.** Fackler. LC 96-54233. 1997. 25.95 (*0-312-85912-0*) St Martin.

Texas Lily. Patricia Rice. 384p. (Orig.). 1994. pap. 4.99 (*0-451-40468-8*, Topaz) NAL-Dutton.

Texas Limitations Manual, 1987-1993. Jennifer N. Mellett. 650p. 1993. pap. 95.00 (*0-409-25254-9*); suppl. ed. 85.00 (*0-685-17764-5*) MICHIE.

Texas Limited Liability Company Forms & Practice Manual. William P. Bowers & Philip M. Kinkaid. 632p. 1995. ring bd. 149.95 (*0-9637468-3-9*) Data Trace Pubng.

Texas Limited Liability Company Forms & Practice Manual. 2nd rev. ed. William P. Bowers & Philip M. Kinkaid. LC 94-46843. 660p. 1996. suppl. ed., ring bd. 79.95 (*1-57400-008-X*) Data Trace Pubng.

Texas Litigation Guide, 21 vols. W. Dorsaneo et al. 1977. write for info. (*0-8205-1719-4*) Bender.

Texas Livestock Auctions: A Folklife Ethnography. George A. Boeck, Jr. LC 89-45369. (Studies in Anthropology: No. 8). 1990. 49.50 (*0-404-62608-4*, HD 9433) AMS Pr.

Texas Log Buildings: A Folk Architecture. Terry G. Jordan. LC 77-24559. (Illus.). 240p. (C). 1994. reprint ed. pap. 19.95 (*0-292-78051-6*) U of Tex Pr.

Texas Lonesome. Alice Duncan. 352p. 1996. mass mkt. 4.99 (*0-06-108414-X*) HarpC.

Texas Long Grain: Photographs by the Kearney Street Workshop. Kearny Street Workshop Staff. (Illus.). 1982. pap. 5.00 (*0-9609630-1-4*) Kearny St Wkshop.

Texas Longhorn: Relic of the Past, Asset for the Future. Don Worcester. LC 86-6025. (Elma Dill Russell Spencer Series in the West & Southwest: No. 8). (Illus.). 112p. 1994. pap. 9.95 (*0-89096-625-7*) Tex A&M Univ Pr.

Texas Looks Ahead, Vol. 1. The Resources Of Texas. Texas University Staff. Ed. by Lorena Drummond. LC 68-58814. (Essay Index Reprint Ser.). 1977. 26.95 (*0-8369-0093-6*) Ayer.

Texas Lore, Vol. 5. Patrick M. Reynolds. (Illus.). 56p. (Orig.). 1987. pap. 3.75 (*0-932514-15-4*) Red Rose Studio.

Texas Lore, Vol. 9. Patrick M. Reynolds. (Illus.). 56p. (Orig.). 1991. pap. 3.75 (*0-932514-26-X*) Red Rose Studio.

Texas Lore, Vols. 1, 2, 3, & 4. Patrick M. Reynolds. (Illus.). 228p. (Orig.). (YA). (gr. 8-12). 1992. pap. 12.95 (*0-932514-27-8*) Red Rose Studio.

Texas Lore: The Era of the Missions, Vols. 11 & 12. Patrick M. Reynolds. (Texas Lore Ser.). (Illus.). 104p. (Orig.). 1995. pap. 6.95 (*0-932514-30-8*) Red Rose Studio.

Texas Lore Ten. Patrick M. Reynolds. (Texas Lore Ser.). (Illus.). 56p. (Orig.). 1992. pap. 3.75 (*0-932514-28-6*) Red Rose Studio.

Texas Lost: Vanishing Heritage. Andrew Sansom. Ed. by Jan Reid. (Illus.). 160p. 1995. 39.95 (*0-9647023-0-4*, 02304) Parks & Wildlife.

***Texas Love Song.** Jodi Thomas. 336p. 1996. mass mkt. 5.99 (*0-515-11953-9*) Jove Pubns.

Texas Lover. Sobolak. 400p. 1996. mass mkt. 5.50 (*0-553-57481-7*, Fanfare) Bantam.

Texas! Lucky. Sandra Brown. 288p. 1991. 6.50 (*0-553-28951-9*) Bantam.

Texas! Lucky. large type ed. Sandra Brown. 382p. 1992. reprint ed. lib. bdg. 19.95 (*1-56054-295-0*) Thorndike Pr.

Texas! Lucky. large type ed. Sandra Brown. 382p. 1992. lib. bdg. 14.95 (*1-56054-942-4*) Thorndike Pr.

Texas Mammals East of the Balcones Fault Zone. David J. Schmidly. LC 83-45098. (W. L. Moody, Jr. Natural History Ser.: No. 6). (Illus.). 418p. 1983. 24.95 (*0-89096-158-1*); pap. 16.95 (*0-89096-171-9*) Tex A&M Univ Pr.

Texas Marital Property Rights. 2nd ed. J. Thomas Oldham. 588p. (Orig.). 1992. pap. 55.00 (*0-916081-30-3*) J Marshall Pub Co.

Texas Marriages, Early to 1850. Liahona Research, Inc. Staff. Ed. by Jordan Dodd. 1990. lib. bdg. 60.00 (*1-877677-26-4*) Precision Indexing.

Texas Marvel. Rita Kerr. Ed. by Melissa Roberts. 120p. (J). (gr. 4-7). 1987. 12.95 (*0-89015-597-6*) Sunbelt Media.

Texas Maverick. Hascal Giles. 1990. mass mkt. 2.95 (*0-8217-3103-3*, Zebra Kensgtn) Kensgtn Pub Corp.

Texas Media Book: A Surprising Guide to the Amazing Print, Broadcast & Online Media of Our State for Students, Teachers, Writers & Publishers - Includes Reproducible Mailing Labels Plus Activities for Young People! Carole Marsh. (Texas Bks.). (Illus.). 1994. pap. 19.95 (*0-7933-3291-5*); lib. bdg. 29.95 (*0-7933-3290-7*); disk 29.95 (*0-7933-3292-3*) Gallopade Pub Group.

Texas Medicaid in Perspective. Anne Dunkelberg. (Illus.). 159p. (Orig.). (C). 1995. pap. text ed. 35.00 (*0-7881-1535-9*) DIANE Pub.

Texas Medicaid Program. Dawn Jahn & Thomas Ortiz. (Working Paper Ser.: No. 65). 63p. 1992. pap. 5.50 (*0-89940-547-9*) LBJ Sch Pub Aff.

Texas Medico. large type ed. Len Turner. (Linford Western Library). 272p. 1994. pap. 15.99 (*0-7089-7575-5*, Linford) Ulverscroft.

Texas-Mexican Cancionero: Folksongs of the Lower Border. Americo Paredes. (Illus.). 218p. (SPA.). 1995. pap. 10.95 (*0-292-76558-4*) U of Tex Pr.

Texas-Mexican Conjunto: History of a Working-Class Music. Manuel Pena. (Mexican American Monographs: No. 9). (Illus.). 238p. 1985. pap. 14.95 (*0-292-78080-X*); text ed. 22.95 (*0-292-78068-0*) U of Tex Pr.

Texas-Mexico Multimodal Transportation. (Policy Research Project Report: No. 104). 168p. 1993. pap. 12.50 (*0-89940-712-9*) LBJ Sch Pub Aff.

Texas-Mexico Transborder Transportation System: Regulatory & Infrastructure Obstacles to Free Trade. Leigh B. Boske & Sidney Weintraub. (Policy Research Project Report: No. 98). 180p. 1991. pap. 12.50 (*0-89940-706-4*) LBJ Sch Pub Aff.

Texas Military Experience: From the Revolution Through World War II. Ed. by Joseph G. Dawson, 3rd. LC 95-3321. (Military History Ser.: No. 43). (Illus.). 264p. (C). 1995. 29.50 (*0-89096-655-9*) Tex A&M Univ Pr.

Texas Missions. Nancy H. Foster. (Texas Monthly Guidebooks Ser.). (Illus.). 192p. 1995. pap. 14.95 (*0-87719-276-6*, 9276) Gulf Pub.

***Texas Moon.** Joan E. Pickart. (Desire Ser.). 1997. 3.50 (*0-373-76051-5*, 1-76051-1) Silhouette.

***Texas Motor Speedway Week.** Ed. by Wallace D. Sears. (Illus.). 208p. 1997. 39.95 (*0-614-29788-5*) Pachyderm AL.

***Texas Motor Speedway Week.** Ed. by Wallace D. Sears. (Illus.). 208p. 1997. lthr. 89.95 (*0-614-29789-3*) Pachyderm AL.

Texas Municipal Zoning Law. 2nd ed. John Mixon. 500p. 1993. suppl. ed. 55.00 (*0-685-74604-6*) MICHIE.

Texas Municipal Zoning Law. 2nd ed. John Mixon. 500p. 1994. spiral bd. 115.00 (*0-409-25656-0*) MICHIE.

Texas Museums: A Guidebook. Paula E. Tyler & Ron Tyler. (Illus.). 327p. 1983. 16.95 (*0-292-78062-1*); pap. 8.95 (*0-292-78063-X*) U of Tex Pr.

Texas Mushrooms: A Field Guide. Susan Metzler & Van Metzler. LC 91-2239. (Corrie Herring Hooks Ser.: No. 18). (Illus.). 358p. 1992. 39.95 (*0-292-75125-7*); pap. 19.95 (*0-292-75126-5*) U of Tex Pr.

***Texas Music Encyclopedia.** Koster. Date not set. write for info. (*0-312-18193-0*) St Martin.

Texas, My Texas. James W. Lee. LC 92-38219. 102p. 1993. pap. 9.95 (*0-929398-54-8*) UNTX Pr.

Texas Mystery Van Takes Off! Book 1: Handicapped Texas Kids Sneak Off on a Big Adventure. Carole Marsh. (Texas Bks.). (Illus.). (J). (gr. 3-12). 1994. 29.95 (*0-7933-5090-5*); pap. 19.95 (*0-7933-5091-3*); disk 29.95 (*0-7933-5092-1*) Gallopade Pub Group.

Texas Myths: Published for the Texas Committee for the Humanities. Ed. by Robert F. O'Connor. LC 85-40743. 264p. 1986. 18.95 (*0-89096-264-2*) Tex A&M Univ Pr.

Texas Natural Resources Code: With Tables & Index, As Amended Through the 1983 Regular & First Called Sessions of the 68th Legislature. Texas Legislature Staff. 315p. 1985. write for info. (*0-318-59336-X*) West Pub.

Texas Navy: Freedom Fighters for the Republic of Texas. Linda E. Devereaux. Ed. by Joe Ericson. LC 83-81716. (Illus.). 1983. pap. 14.50 (*0-911317-21-X*) Ericson Bks.

Texas, New Mexico, & the Compromise of 1850: Boundary Dispute & Sectional Crisis. Mark J. Stegmaier. LC 95-37378. (Illus.). 575p. 1996. 39.00 (*0-87338-529-2*) Kent St U Pr.

Texas Night Before Christmas. James Rice. LC 86-9445. (Illus.). 32p. (J). (gr. 1-6). 1986. reprint ed. 14.95 (*0-88289-603-2*) Pelican.

Texas Night Before Christmas Coloring Book. James Rice. (Illus.). 32p. (J). 1989. pap. 2.95 (*0-88289-727-6*) Pelican.

***Texas Night Riders.** Ray Slater, pseud. 160p. 1997. 35.00 (*0-9649890-1-8*) Subtrrnean Pr.

Texas Nighthawks. large type ed. Wes Calhoun. (Linford Western Library). 256p. 1992. pap. 15.99 (*0-7089-7174-1*, Linford) Ulverscroft.

Texas Notary Law Primer. 5th ed. National Notary Association Editors. LC 0980058X. 124p. 1995. pap. 12.95 (*0-933134-47-9*) Natl Notary.

Texas Notary Manual. Eugene E. Hines. Ed. by Lisa K. Fisher. LC 94-72335. 93p. Date not set. pap. 9.45 (*0-614-12966-4*) Am Soc Notaries.

Texas Objections at Trial. Susan Crump et al. LC 92-20557. 192p. (Orig.). 1992. pap. 39.50 (*0-88063-827-3*) MICHIE.

***Texas: Off the Beaten Path: A Guide to Unique Places.** 2nd rev. ed. June N. Rodriguez. LC 97-22102. (Off the Beaten Path Ser.). (Illus.). 256p. 1997. pap. 12.95 (*0-7627-0102-1*) Globe Pequot.

Texas Oil, American Dreams: A Study of the Texas Independent Producers & Royalty Owners Association. Lawrence R. Goodwyn. LC 96-17467. (Barker Texas History Center Ser.: No. 5). 1996. write for info. (*0-87611-158-4*) Tex St Hist Assn.

Texas Oil & Gas Law Journal. Ed. by Owen Anderson & Jane F. Romanov. 20p. 1986. ring bd. 125.00 (*0-409-25264-6*) MICHIE.

Texas Oil Directory. Ed. by Lalla Howell. (Illus.). 1985. pap. 90.00 (*0-317-40908-5*) Tradex Pubns.

Texas on My Mind. Intro. by A. C. Greene. LC 89-80766. (America on My Mind Ser.). (Illus.). 120p. 1989. 29.95 (*0-937959-69-3*) Falcon Pr MT.

Texas on Stamps. Jon L. Allen. LC 96-14898. (Illus.). 128p. (Orig.). 1996. pap. 14.95 (*0-87565-164-X*) Tex Christian.

Texas One Day Adventures & Weekend Getaways. Gerald E. McLeod. 1994. pap. 8.95 (*1-56943-033-0*, Tribune) Contemp Bks.

Texas Open Meetings Act. Warren Weir & Charles H. Weir. (Texas Open Meetings & Open Records Handbook Ser.). 356p. (Orig.). pap. 89.00 (*0-945701-09-8*) Sterling TX.

Texas Orphans: A Story of the Orphan Trail Children. Rita Kerr. LC 94-1995. (Illus.). (J). 1994. 12.95 (*0-89015-962-9*) Sunbelt Media.

***Texas, Our Texas.** Willoughby. 1993. text ed. 52.00 (*0-03-075431-3*) HR&W Schl Div.

Texas, Our Texas. Willoughby. (J). 1993. teacher ed., pap. text ed. 78.00 (*0-03-075432-1*) HR&W Schl Div.

Texas Outdoors: Read 'n Color Book. Tony Elliott. (This Is America Ser.). (Illus.). (J). (gr. 1-8). 1986. pap. 4.50 (*0-914565-24-9*, 24-9, Timbertrails) Capstan Pubns.

Texas Outlaw. Adrienne Dewolfe. 368p. 1995. mass mkt. 4.99 (*0-553-57395-0*, Fanfare) Bantam.

Texas Overland Expedition of 1863. Richard Lowe. LC 95-51437. (Civil War Campaigns & Commanders Ser.). (Illus.). 122p. (Orig.). 1996. pap. 11.95 (*1-886661-12-X*, 6112X) Ryan Place Pub.

Texas Parks: A History & Guide. Ray Miller. (Eyes of Texas Travel Guides Ser.). (Illus.). 232p. 1987. pap. 10.95 (*0-88415-217-0*) Gulf Pub.

Texas Parks & Campgrounds: A Vacation Guide. 3rd ed. George O. Miller. (Texas Monthly Guidebook Ser.). 224p. 1995. pap. 14.95 (*0-87719-265-0*, 9265) Gulf Pub.

Texas Parks Guide. Barbara McCaig. Ed. by Chris Boyce. 100p. (Orig.). 1988. pap. text ed. 5.95 (*0-935201-40-8*) Affordable Adven.

Texas Party Food...with Love from Corpus Christi! large type ed. Maxine S. Sommers. (Illus.). 24p. (Orig.). 1996. spiral bd. 4.00 (*0-943991-41-2*) Pound Sterling Pub.

Texas Passion. Sara Orwig. 432p. 1994. mass mkt. 4.50 (*0-8217-4746-0*, Zebra Kensgtn) Kensgtn Pub Corp.

***Texas Past.** Andrew Sansom. (Illus.). 150p. (Orig.). 1997. 39.95 (*1-885696-19-1*) U of Tex Pr.

***Texas Pattern Jury Charges: Business, Consumer, Employment.** State Bar of Texas, Committee on Pattern Jury Charges. 326p. 1997. suppl. ed., pap. write for info. (*0-938160-92-3*, 6284) State Bar TX.

***Texas Pattern Jury Charges: Family.** State Bar of Texas, Committee on Pattern Jury Charges. 219p. 1996. suppl. ed., pap. 85.00 (*0-938160-88-5*, 6285) State Bar TX.

***Texas Pattern Jury Charges: General Negligence & Motor Vehicles.** 2nd ed. State Bar of Texas, Committee on Pattern Jury Charges. 189p. 1997. suppl. ed., pap. 70.00 (*0-938160-89-3*, 6281) State Bar TX.

Texas Pattern Jury Charges, Malpractice, Premises, Products. 2nd ed. State Bar of Texas, Committee on Pattern Jury Charges. LC 87-62226. 313p. 1997. pap. 90.00 (*0-938160-59-1*, 6283) State Bar TX.

Texas Peace Officer, 2 vols. 5th ed. Ray K. Robbins et al. LC 95-767555. 707p. 1995. 60.00 (*0-8211-1759-9*) McCutchan.

***Texas Penal Code.** 10th ed. West Publishing Company Editorial Staff. 1994. pap. 19.00 (*0-314-03231-2*) West Pub.

***Texas Penal Code.** 12th ed. West Publishing Staff. 1995. pap. text ed. 20.75 (*0-314-07700-6*) West Pub.

Texas Penal Code Flip Code. 1995. 8.95 (*0-9629210-3-3*) Gould.

Texas Penal Code, 1992. West Publishing Company Editorial Staff. 1991. pap. 21.50 (*0-314-00042-9*) West Pub.

Texas Personal Injury Forms. 2nd ed. Ruth Tone. 420p. 1993. suppl. ed. 52.50 (*0-685-74474-4*); ring bd. 115.00 (*0-409-25692-7*) MICHIE.

Texas Personal Injury Law. Jennifer N. Mellett. 1020p. 1994. ring bd. 170.00 (*0-409-25659-5*) MICHIE.

Texas Personal Injury Law Reporter. Frank R. Southers. 16p. 1994. ring bd. 145.00 (*0-409-25002-3*) MICHIE.

Texas Personal Injury Law, 1981-1992, 2 vols. 2nd ed. Suppl. by Jennifer N. Mellett. 1994. suppl. ed., ring bd. 65.00 (*0-685-74466-3*) MICHIE.

Texas Personal Injury Law, 1981-1992, 2 vols., Set. 2nd ed. Suppl. by Jennifer N. Mellett. 1024p. ring bd. 170.00 (*0-409-25621-8*) MICHIE.

Texas Pilgrim. large type ed. Bret Rey. (Linford Western Library). 1995. pap. 15.99 (*0-7089-7767-7*, Linford) Ulverscroft.

Texas Pioneer: Early Staging & Overland Freighting. August Santleben. 1993. reprint ed. lib. bdg. 75.00 (*0-7812-5899-5*) Rprt Serv.

Texas Playparty: A LaVaca County Life 1906 to Today. Kenneth Munson. 175p. 1992. 15.95 (*1-878208-15-2*) Guild Pr IN.

Texas Plays. Ed. by William B. Martin. LC 89-42893. (Southwest Life & Letters Ser.). (Illus.). 480p. 1990. pap. 16.95 (*0-87074-301-5*); text ed. 35.00 (*0-87074-300-7*) SMU Press.

Texas Policies & Procedures Manual. 6th ed. Mattie Locke. 383p. (C). 1993. ring bd. 75.00 (*1-877735-01-9*, 102) M&H Pub Co TX.

Texas Politics, 9 Vols. (C). 1994. pap. 38.76 (*0-395-70839-7*) HM.

Texas Politics. Benson. (C). 1996. teacher ed., pap. text ed. 42.00 (*0-15-503540-1*) HB Coll Pubs.

Texas Politics. Anthony Champagne. LC 96-30351. (C). 1996. pap. text ed. 14.95 (*0-393-96867-7*) Norton.

***Texas Politics.** Edwin L. Dickens. 160p. (C). 1996. pap. text ed. 11.56 (*0-669-41706-8*) HM College Div.

Texas Politics, 9 Vols. Jones. (C). Date not set. suppl. ed., teacher ed., pap. write for info. (*0-395-71716-7*) HM.

Texas Politics, 9 Vols. Jones. (C). 1995. teacher ed., pap. 11.96 (*0-395-72557-7*) HM.

Texas Politics, 9 Vols. Jones. (C). 1994. student ed., pap. 18.76 (*0-395-72558-5*) HM.

Texas Politics. Todd. (C). Date not set. pap. 37.96 (*0-395-71736-1*) HM.

Texas Politics. Todd. (C). 1995. pap. 37.96 (*0-395-48967-9*) HM.

Texas Politics. Todd. (C). 1996. student ed., pap. text ed. 16.76 (*0-395-48968-7*) HM.

Texas Politics. 5th ed. Richard H. Kraemer & Charldean Newell. Ed. by Clyde Perlee. LC 92-35571. 450p. (C). 1993. pap. text ed. 37.00 (*0-314-01066-1*) West Pub.

Texas Politics. 6th ed. Anderson et al. (C). 1991. text ed. 33.50 (*0-06-500511-2*) Addson-Wesley Educ.

Texas Politics. 6th ed. Richard H. Kraemer et al. LC 95-34832. 500p. (C). 1996. pap. text ed. 37.00 (*0-314-06700-0*) West Pub.

***Texas Politics.** 7th ed. Maxwell. (Political Science Ser.). (C). 1995. student ed., pap. 13.50 (*0-314-05992-X*) West Pub.

Texas Politics: Economics, Power, & Policy. 5th ed. James W. Lamare. Ed. by Clyde Perlee. LC 94-4546. 250p. (C). 1994. pap. text ed. 37.00 (*0-314-02849-8*) West Pub.

***Texas Politics: Economics, Power, & Policy.** 6th ed. James W. Lamare. LC 97-23747. (C). 1997. pap. text ed. 37.95 (*0-314-20481-4*) Wadsworth Pub.

Texas Politics: Roots, Culture, & Reform. Ginny Stowitts & Sandra Giesler. 576p. (C). 1996. per. 47.95 (*0-7872-0609-1*) Kendall-Hunt.

***Texas Politics: The Challenge of Change.** John R. Todd. (C). 1995. teacher ed., text ed. 11.96 (*0-395-77693-7*) HM.

Texas Politics & Government: A Concise Survey. 2nd ed. Kim Q. Hill & Kenneth R. Mladenka. 176p. (C). 1996. pap. 27.00 (*0-205-19891-0*) Allyn.

***Texas Politics & Government: Ideas, Institutions & Policies.** Stefan Haag. (C). 1997. student ed., pap. text ed. 16.88 (*0-673-99954-8*) Addison-Wesley.

***Texas Politics & Government: Ideas, Institutions, & Policies.** Stefan D. Haag et al. LC 96-17947. (C). 1997. text ed. 35.95 (*0-673-99768-5*) Longman.

Texas Politics in My Rearview Mirror. Waggoner Carr & Byron D. Varner. LC 92-30785. (Illus.). 168p. 1992. pap. 12.95 (*1-55622-314-5*, Rep of TX Pr) Wordware Pub.

Texas Politics in the Gilded Age, 1873-1890. Cary D. Wintz. (Texas History Ser.). (Illus.). 64p. (Orig.). 1983. pap. text ed. 8.95 (*0-89641-129-X*) American Pr.

Texas Politics Today. 6th ed. William E. Maxwell & Ernest Crain. Ed. by Simon. 416p. (C). 1992. text ed. 36.50 (*0-314-89956-1*) West Pub.

Texas Politics Today. 7th ed. William E. Maxwell & Ernest Crain. LC 94-3694. 396p. (C). 1995. pap. text ed. 37.00 (*0-314-04324-1*) West Pub.

***Texas Politics Today.** 8th ed. Maxwell. (Political Science Ser.). (C). 1998. pap. 17.95 (*0-534-54062-7*) Wadsworth Pub.

***Texas Politics Today.** 8th ed. William E. Maxwell et al. (Political Science Ser.). (C). 1997. pap. text ed. 37.95 (*0-314-12781-X*) Wadsworth Pub.

Texas Practice Guide: Personal Injury, 2 vols. Thomas G. Gee et al. 1990. 160.00 (*0-8321-0054-4*) Bancroft Whitney Co.

Texas Premises Liability. James L. Branton & Jim D. Lovett. (Trial Lawyer's Ser.: Vols. 3 & 3A). (Illus.). 1986. ring bd. 185.00 (*1-878337-12-2*) Knowles Law.

Texas Pride. Barbara McCauley. 1995. mass mkt. 3.25 (*0-373-05971-X*, 1-05971-6) Silhouette.

Texas Probate, 3 vols. Kenneth McLaughlin, Jr. 1992. Set. write for info. (*0-8205-1708-9*) Bender.

Texas Probate. 7th rev. ed. Charles A. Saunders. 190p. 1995. pap. 12.95 (*0-88415-399-1*, 5399) Gulf Pub.

Texas Probate Code Manual. Jennifer N. Mellett. 1200p. 1994. ring bd. 175.00 (*0-614-05979-8*) MICHIE.

Texas Probate Code Manual, 1984-1993, 2 vols. Jennifer N. Mellett. 1040p. 1993. suppl. ed. 49.00 (*0-685-46136-X*) MICHIE.

Texas Probate, Estate, & Trust Administration. Ed. by Kenneth McLaughlin. 1994. cd-rom write for info. (*0-614-16737-X*) Bender.

Texas Probate, Estate, & Trust Administration, 4 vols., Set. Ed. by Kenneth McLaughlin. 1994. ring bd. write for info. (*0-614-16736-1*) Bender.

Texas Probate System. 2nd rev. ed. James E. Brill. LC 93-84172. 852p. 1993. 160.00 (*0-938160-76-1*, 6224) State Bar TX.

Texas Probation Officers' Attitudes & Alternatives to Incarceration. Contrib. by Laura Lein & Robert C. Richards. (Policy Research Project Report: No. 95). 90p. 1992. pap. 9.50 (*0-89940-703-X*) LBJ Sch Pub Aff.

Texas Production Manual: A Source Book for the Motion Picture, Television & Video Industries, Vol. XV. (Illus.). 275p. (Orig.). (C). 1995. pap. text ed. 45.00 (*0-7881-1409-3*) DIANE Pub.

Texas Products Liability. James L. Branton et al. (Trial Lawyer's Ser.: Vol. 9). 560p. 1992. ring bd. 135.00 (*1-878337-30-0*) Knowles Law.

Texas Products Liability Law. William C. Powers, Jr. 380p. 1993. suppl. ed. 55.00 (*0-685-46138-6*) MICHIE.

Texas Products Liability Law. 2nd ed. William C. Powers, Jr. 380p. 1994. spiral bd. 115.00 (*1-56257-955-X*) MICHIE.

Texas Professional Liability. James L. Branton & Jim D. Lovett. (Trial Lawyer's Ser.: Vol. 5). (Illus.). 349p. 1988. ring bd. 135.00 (*1-878337-14-9*) Knowles Law.

***Texas Provider Utilization & Financial Data.** Nicole Abend. (Working Paper Ser.: Vol. 63). 61p. 1992. pap. 5.50 (*0-89940-545-2*) LBJ Sch Pub Aff.

***Texas Provincial Kitchen.** Melissa M. Guerra. (Illus.). (Orig.). 1997. pap. 24.95 (*0-9657658-0-6*) TX Provincial.

Texas Public School Organization & Administration: 1996. James A. Vornberg. 576p. (C). 1996. per., pap. text ed. 38.79 (*0-7872-1819-7*) Kendall-Hunt.

Texas Quest for New Mexico, 1836-1850. Gene Brack. (Texas History Ser.). (Illus.). 37p. (Orig.). 1984. pap. text ed. 8.95 (*0-89641-144-3*) American Pr.

Texas Quiz Bowl Crash Course! Carole Marsh. (Carole Marsh Texas Bks.). (Illus.). (J). 1994. pap. 19.95 (*0-7933-2090-9*); lib. bdg. 29.95 (*0-7933-2089-5*); disk 29.95 (*0-7933-2091-7*) Gallopade Pub Group.

Texas Radio Directory. David Stall. 64p. (Orig.). 1939. pap. 14.95 (*1-878884-12-3*) Luna Lumen Pr.

Texas Range Plants. Stephan L. Hatch & Jennifer Pluhar. LC 92-5073. (W. L. Moody, Jr. Natural History Ser.: No. 13). (Illus.). 344p. 1992. 35.00 (*0-89096-538-2*) Tex A&M Univ Pr.

Texas Range Plants. Stephan L. Hatch & Jennifer Pluhar. LC 92-5073. (W. L. Moody, Jr. Natural History Ser.: No. 13). (Illus.). 344p. 1995. pap. 16.95 (*0-89096-521-8*) Tex A&M Univ Pr.

***Texas Ranger.** N. A. Jennings. LC 96-44442. 176p. 1997. pap. 9.95 (*0-8061-2903-4*) U of Okla Pr.

Texas Ranger. Herman Toepperwein. pap. 1.75 (*0-910722-10-2*) Highland Pr.

Texas Ranger: Jack Hays in the Frontier Southwest. James K. Greer. LC 93-4302. (Centennial Series of the Association of Former Students: No. 50). (Illus.). 240p. (Orig.). 1993. 24.50 (*0-89096-567-6*); pap. 13.95 (*0-89096-572-2*) Tex A&M Univ Pr.

Texas Ranger in the Oil Patch. John M. Wood. Ed. by Betty W. Cox. LC 94-61220. (Illus.). 123p. (Orig.). 1994. pap. 12.50 (*0-9643126-0-3*) Woodburner Pr.

***Texas Ranger Tales.** Mike Cox. 248p. 1997. pap. 16.95 (*1-55622-537-7*, Rep of TX Pr) Wordware Pub.

Texas Rangers. Mike Cox. (Illus.). 144p. (J). (gr. 6-9). 1994. 15.95 (*0-89015-818-5*) Sunbelt Media.

Texas Rangers. S. Hardin. (Elite Ser.: No. 36). (Illus.). 64p. pap. 12.95 (*1-85532-155-6*, 9451, Pub. by Osprey UK) Stackpole.

Texas Rangers. Bob Italia. LC 96-23795. (America's Game Ser.). (J). 1997. lib. bdg. 15.95 (*1-56239-678-1*) Abdo & Dghtrs.

Texas Rangers. Richard Rambeck. (Baseball: The Great American Game Ser.). 48p. (J). (gr. 4-10). 1992. lib. bdg. 14.95 (*0-88682-443-5*) Creative Ed.

***Texas Rangers.** Richard Rambeck. LC 97-9230. (Baseball Ser.). (Illus.). 32p. (YA). (gr. 4 up). 1998. lib. bdg. 15.95 (*0-88682-927-5*) Creative Ed.

Texas Rangers. Walter P. Webb. 1993. reprint ed. lib. bdg. 75.00 (*0-7812-5981-9*) Rprt Serv.

Texas Rangers: A Century of Frontier Defense. Walter P. Webb. 606p. 1965. 29.95 (*0-292-73400-X*); pap. 16.95 (*0-292-78110-5*) U of Tex Pr.

Texas Rangers: Images & Incidents. John L. Davis. (Illus.). 1992. 29.95 (*0-86701-052-5*) U of Tex Inst Tex Culture.

Texas Rangers: Notes from the Architectural Underground. Alexander Caragonne. (Illus.). 400p. 1995. 50.00 (*0-262-03218-X*) MIT Pr.

***Texas Rangers: The Authorized History.** Eric Nadel. LC 97-9629. (Illus.). 256p. 1997. 36.95 (*0-87833-139-5*) Taylor Pub.

***Texas Rangers: The Authorized History.** Eric Nadel. LC 97-9629. (Illus.). 256p. 1997. 75.00 (*0-87833-140-9*) Taylor Pub.

***Texas Rangers Facts & Trivia.** Gary Stratton. (Illus.). 192p. (Orig.). 1997. pap. 9.99 (*0-938313-27-4*) E B Houchin.

Texas RE Agency. John W. Reilly & Thomas Terrell. 260p. 1994. pap. 26.95 (*0-7931-0985-X*, 156005-01, Real Estate Ed) Dearborn Finan.

T

An Asterisk (*) at the beginning of an entry indicates that the title is appearing in BIP for the first time.

***Texas Real Estate.** 2nd ed. Deroberti & Irwin. 1995. pap. 30.50 (*0-13-777756-6*) P-H.

Texas Real Estate. 6th ed. Charles J. Jacobus & Bruce M. Harwood. LC 94-19179. 800p. 1994. text ed. 51.00 (*0-13-165010-6*) P-H Gen Ref & Trav.

Texas Real Estate: Principles & Practices. 2nd ed. Samuel P. DeRobertis & Joseph N. Irwin. LC 96-9333. (Illus.). 468p. (C). 1995. pap. text ed. 30.95 (*0-89787-947-3*) Gorsuch Scarisbrick.

Texas Real Estate Agency. 2nd ed. John W. Reilly & Thomas Terrell. 256p. 1996. pap. 26.95 (*0-7931-1639-2*, 15600502, Real Estate Ed) Dearborn Trade.

Texas Real Estate Appraisal. J. B. Featherston et al. LC 85-26479. 418p. 1986. pap. text ed. 38.95 (*0-471-82299-X*) P-H.

Texas Real Estate Contracts. Ralph Tamper. 1997. pap. 29.95 (*0-7931-1763-1*, 15601801, Real Estate Ed) Dearborn Finan.

Texas Real Estate Finance. Richard L. Chumbley et al. 365p. 1987. pap. text ed. 34.50 (*0-471-82300-7*) P-H.

Texas Real Estate Finance. 5th ed. Tom J. Morton. LC 94-6528. 379p. 1994. 39.95 (*0-7931-1020-3*, 1557-1705) Dearborn Finan.

Texas Real Estate Law. 2nd ed. Madeline Johnson. 714p. 1996. pap. 39.95 (*0-7931-1441-1*, 1560-0602, Real Estate Ed) Dearborn Finan.

Texas Real Estate Law. 4th ed. Charles J. Jacobus. (C). 1985. teacher ed. write for info. (*0-8359-7577-0*, Reston) P-H.

Texas Real Estate Law. 7th ed. Charles J. Jacobus. 1995. text ed. 47.00 (*0-13-763582-6*) P-H.

Texas Real Estate Law Reporter. Ed. by Charles J. Jacobus. 1220p. 1985. ring bd. 125.00 (*0-614-05980-1*) MICHIE.

Texas Real Estate License Examinations Guide. Jack P. Friedman & John S. Baen. write for info. (*0-318-59700-4*) S&S Trade.

Texas Rebel. Rita Kerr. Ed. by Edwin M. Eakin. (Illus.). 80p. (J). (gr. 4-6). 1989. 12.95 (*0-89015-695-6*) Sunbelt Media.

Texas Reflections: Littlebook. Photos by Richard Reynolds. (Illus.). 64p. 1996. 14.95 (*1-56579-144-4*) Westcliffe Pubs.

Texas Renegade. Dana Ransom. 384p. 1996. mass mkt. 4.99 (*0-8217-5267-7*, Zebra Kensgtn) Kensgtn Pub Corp.

Texas Renegade. Jack Slade. 176p. (Orig.). 1993. mass mkt., pap. text ed. 3.99 (*0-8439-3495-6*) Dorchester Pub Co.

Texas Republic: A Social & Economic History. rev. ed. William R. Hogan. LC 68-59357. (Texas History Paperbacks Ser.: No. 3). 352p. 1969. pap. 14.95 (*0-292-78423-6*) U of Tex Pr.

Texas Residential Landlord-Tenant Law, 1986-1992, 2 vols., Set. James C. Hauser et al. 1360p. 1995. spiral bd. 125.00 (*0-409-25079-1*) MICHIE.

Texas Revenue Alternatives: A National Survey on Alternatives & Comparisons. 226p. (Orig.). (C). 1993. pap. text ed. 45.00 (*1-56806-999-5*) DIANE Pub.

Texas Revolution. William C. Binkley. LC 79-63065. 1979. reprint ed. 12.95 (*0-87611-041-3*) Tex St Hist Assn.

Texas Revolution & Republic: Materials Relating to the Period from the Beginning of Anglo-American Settlement to Annexation. John H. Jenkins. (Illus.). 224p. 1986. 10.00 (*0-318-37955-4*, PA-97-26741) Jenkins.

Texas Revolutionary Experience: A Political & Social History, 1835-1836. Paul D. Lack. LC 91-23368. (Texas A&M Southwestern Studies: No. 10). 360p. 1996. 41.95 (*0-89096-497-1*); pap. 19.95 (*0-89096-721-0*) Tex A&M Univ Pr.

Texas Rhythm, Texas Rhyme. rev. ed. Larry Willoughby. (Illus.). 160p. 1991. reprint ed. pap. 14.95 (*0-89015-802-9*) Sunbelt Media.

Texas Rib-Ticklers! Ed. by Claire Ottenstein. (Illus.). 84p. 1990. lib. bdg. 7.95 (*1-878149-00-8*) Counterpoint Pub.

Texas Rich. Fern Michaels. 640p. 1987. mass mkt. 5.95 (*0-345-33540-6*) Ballantine.

Texas Rich. large type ed. Fern Michaels. LC 92-42501. (Americana Ser.). 921p. 1993. reprint ed. lib. bdg. 23.95 (*1-56054-662-X*) Thorndike Pr.

Texas Rich: The Hunt Dynasty from the Early Oil Days Through the Silver Crash. Harry Hurt, III. (Illus.). 448p. 1982. pap. 10.95 (*0-393-30037-4*) Norton.

Texas Riviera Is Cooking: The Official Sesquincentennial Cookbook of Corpus Christi, Texas. 2nd ed. LC 86-70198. (Illus.). 300p. 1986. pap. write for info. (*0-9615283-0-3*) Am Assn U Women.

Texas Road Atlas. H. M. Gousha Staff. 1994. pap. 6.95 (*0-671-88836-6*, H M Gousha) P-H Gen Ref & Trav.

Texas Rocks & Minerals: An Amateur's Guide. R. M. Girard. (Guidebook Ser.: GB 6). (Illus.). 109p. 1964. reprint ed. pap. 2.50 (*0-686-29314-2*) Bur Econ Geology.

***Texas Rodeo Showdown.** Eric Wiggin. (Hannah's Island Ser.: Bk. 6). (Orig.). (J). (gr. 3-7). 1997. pap. 5.99 (*1-883002-29-X*) Emerald WA.

Texas Rollercoasters! Carole Marsh. (Texas Bks.). (Illus.). (YA). (gr. 3-12). 1994. pap. 19.95 (*0-7933-5354-8*); lib. bdg. 29.95 (*0-7933-5353-X*); disk 29.95 (*0-7933-5355-6*) Gallopade Pub Group.

Texas Rose: Dilue Rose Harris. Rita Kerr. 64p. 1986. 12.95 (*0-89015-578-X*) Sunbelt Media.

Texas Roundup: Life on the Range. Catherine E. Chambers. LC 83-18281. (Adventures in Frontier America Ser.). (Illus.). 32p. (J). (gr. 5-9). 1984. pap. text ed. 3.50 (*0-8167-0048-6*) Troll Communs.

Texas Routine Case Manual: Access to Attorneys. Norma Martinez & H. Clyde Farrell. 66p. pap. 6.50 (*0-685-23157-7*, 41,575A) NCLS Inc.

Texas Rules of Appellate Procedure, 1986-1992. Butterworth Staff. 130p. 1992. ring bd. 39.50 (*0-409-25255-7*) MICHIE.

Texas Rules of Civil Evidence. Warren Weir. 89.00 (*0-685-52374-8*, B4) Sterling TX.

Texas Rules of Civil Procedure, 1984-1990. Butterworth Staff. 400p. 1993. spiral bd. 39.50 (*0-409-25020-1*) MICHIE.

Texas Rules of Civil Procedure, 1984-1990. Butterworths Staff. 430p. 1993. suppl. ed. 25.00 (*1-56257-970-3*) MICHIE.

Texas Rules of Evidence Handbook & Supplement. Newell H. Blakely et al. 878p. 1987. 61.40 (*0-317-61183-6*) Houston Law Review.

Texas Rules of Evidence Manual. 3rd rev. ed. Robert Barton et al. (C). 1994. student ed. 35.50 (*0-256-18119-5*) Irwin.

Texas Safari: World Class Big Game Hunting in the State of Texas. A. M. Micallef. (Illus.). 256p. 1986. 25.00 (*0-9616868-0-4*) Clear Fork Ranch.

Texas! Sage. large type ed. Sandra Brown. 380p. 1992. reprint ed. lib. bdg. 19.95 (*1-56054-297-7*) Thorndike Pr.

Texas! Sage. large type ed. Sandra Brown. 380p. 1992. pap. 14.95 (*1-56054-940-8*) Thorndike Pr.

Texas Sampler. Junior League of Richardson. 1995. 16.95 (*0-9612810-5-7*) Jr Leag Richardson.

Texas Sayings. Anne Dingus. LC 96-16538. (Illus.). 128p. 1996. pap. 9.95 (*0-87719-292-8*, 9292) Gulf Pub.

Texas School Dropout Project: A Summary of Findings. Josie D. Supik et al. (Illus.). 58p. (Orig.). 1986. pap. text ed. 6.50 (*1-878550-37-3*) Inter Dev Res Assn.

Texas School Dropout Project, Vol. 6: Program Responses - Their Nature & Effectiveness. Josie D. Supik et al. 103p. (Orig.). 1986. pap. text ed. 8.50 (*1-878550-34-9*) Inter Dev Res Assn.

Texas School Dropout Survey Project, 7 vols., Set. (Orig.). 1986. pap. text ed. 58.50 (*1-878550-36-5*) Inter Dev Res Assn.

Texas School Dropout Survey Project: Benefit-Cost Impact of the Dropout Problem, Vol. 5. Josie D. Supik et al. 44p. (Orig.). 1986. pap. text ed. 8.50 (*1-878550-33-0*) Inter Dev Res Assn.

Texas School Dropout Survey Project, Vol. 1: Magnitude of the Problem-Census Analysis. David J. Halton. 103p. (Orig.). 1986. pap. text ed. 39.00 (*1-878550-29-2*) Inter Dev Res Assn.

Texas School Dropout Survey Project, Vol. 3: Magnitude of the Problem - School District Research & Procedures. Josie D. Supik et al. 192p. (Orig.). 1986. pap. text ed. 8.50 (*1-878550-31-4*) Inter Dev Res Assn.

Texas School Dropout Survey Project, Vol. 4: Magnitude of the Problem - School District Research & Procedures. Josie D. Supik et al. 192p. (Orig.). 1986. pap. text ed. 8.50 (*1-878550-32-2*) Inter Dev Res Assn.

Texas School Dropout Survey Project, Vol. 7: Study Methods & Procedures. Josie D. Supik et al. 119p. (Orig.). 1986. pap. text ed. 8.50 (*1-878550-35-7*) Inter Dev Res Assn.

Texas School Dropout Survey, Vol. 2: Magnitude of the Problem - Attrition Analyses. Josie D. Supik et al. 103p. (Orig.). 1986. pap. text ed. 8.50 (*1-878550-30-6*) Inter Dev Res Assn.

Texas School Finance Reform: An IDRA Perspective. Jose A. Cardenas. 387p. 1997. 30.00 (*1-878550-63-2*) Inter Dev Res Assn. A master story-teller, Dr. Jose A. Cardenas, offers us an insider's view of the 28-year history of school finance in Texas. Dr. Cardenas is the founder & director emeritus of IDRA & is the only person who has been actively involved in the entire school finance reform effort since the early days of the RODRIGUEZ VS. SAN ANTONIO ISD litigation when he was superintendent of the Edgewood Independent School District. More than a history, this book provides a blueprint for persons interested in bringing about future reform in schools & other social institutions. Beginning with a description of the Texas system in 1950, the account covers court cases, legislation, & advocacy efforts & concludes with the status & future of school finance reform. Personal vignettes sprinkled throughout offer glimpses of those special untold moments that impacted history. Much of this volume - including the myths of school finance & lessons learned - relate to reform efforts in other states as well. Dr. James A. Kelly, president of the National Board of Professional Teaching Standards, provides a foreword, "Fighting the Good Fight," describing Dr. Cardenas as a trailblazer & pioneer. (ISBN 1-878550-63-2; 1997; 387 pages; hardback) Distributed exclusively by the Intercultural Development Research Association (IDRA); 210-684-8180; FAX: 210-684-5389; E-mail: idra@idra.org; URL: www.idra.org.** ***Publisher Provided Annotation.

***Texas School Law: A Practical Guide.** Ed. by Kelly Frels et al. 349p. 1996. text ed. 35.00 (*1-56534-070-1*) Ed Law Assn.

Texas School Trivia: An Amazing & Fascinating Look at Our State's Teachers, Schools & Students! Carole Marsh. (Carole Marsh Texas Bks.). (Illus.). (J). 1994. pap. 19.95 (*0-7933-1090-3*); lib. bdg. 29.95 (*0-7933-1091-1*); disk 29.95 (*0-7933-1092-X*) Gallopade Pub Group.

Texas Scrap-Book: Made up of the History, Biography, & Miscellany of Texas & Its People. D. W. Baker. 1991. 34.95 (*0-87611-108-8*) Tex St Hist Assn.

Texas Scrap-Book: Made up of the History, Biography, & Miscellany of Texas & Its People. limited ed. D. W. Baker. 1991. boxed 85.00 (*0-87611-113-4*) Tex St Hist Assn.

Texas Seaport & Inland Waterway System. Contrib. by Leigh B. Boske & Robert Harrison. (Policy Research Project Report: No. 114). 309p. 1995. pap. 18.00 (*0-89940-722-6*) LBJ Sch Pub Aff.

Texas Search & Seizure. R. Barton. 500p. 95.00 (*0-07-172489-3*) Juris Pubng.

Texas Senate: Vol. I, Republic to Civil War 1836-1861. Ed. by Patsy M. Spaw. LC 90-10988. 408p. 1991. 50.00 (*0-89096-442-4*) Tex A&M Univ Pr.

***Texas Sheep & Goat Raisers Association History.** Ross McSwain. (Illus.). 288p. 1996. 42.75 (*0-943639-27-1*) Anchor Pub Co.

Texas Sheepman. Robert Maudslay. Ed. by Winifred Kupper. LC 78-157347. (Select Bibliographies Reprint Ser.). (Illus.). 1977. reprint ed. 20.95 (*0-8369-5808-X*) Ayer.

Texas Sheriff. large type ed. Eugene Cunningham. LC 93-26430. 1993. lib. bdg. 16.95 (*1-56054-777-4*) Thorndike Pr.

Texas Short Fiction: A World in Itself II. Ed. by Billy B. Hill & Michael C. Hennech. LC 94-73039. 304p. (Orig.). 1995. pap. 15.95 (*1-881301-05-2*) Ale Pub.

Texas Short Fiction: A World in Itself: Texas Short Story Anthology by 21 Authors. Ed. by Michael C. Hennech. LC 93-70393. 256p. (Orig.). 1993. pap. 12.95 (*1-881301-04-4*) Ale Pub.

Texas Short Stories. Ed. by Billy B. Hill. 325p. (Orig.). 1997. pap. 16.99 (*0-9651359-1-8*) Browder Springs. These fifty-five previously unpublished short stories have their settings in diverse Texas places & times, from the Old West to Winn-Dixie. Author Annette Sanford describes the collection as "a generous outpouring of Texas voices." Novelist Sarah Bird further comments: "At a time when lots of Lone Star writers are banking on crime novels & film scripts, Texas short story writers continue to patrol the smaller venues, sending back microcosmic reports from off-ramp towns, core samplings from burgeoning metroplexes, keeping the faith. Billy Bob Hill's new anthology contains a wealth of Texas tales." TEXAS SHORT STORIES, which contains selections by some of the state's best writers, is certainly a good read, & perhaps, it says something new about a place & a people. To order contact: Browder Springs Publishing Co., P.O. Box 823521, Dallas, TX 75382, phone: (214) 368-4360.** ***Publisher Provided Annotation.

***Texas Shout: How Dixieland Jazz Works.** Tex Wyndham. (Illus.). 300p. (Orig.). 1997. pap. 19.95 (*0-9645795-1-0*) Light Words & Music.

Texas Shrimpers: Community, Capitalism, & the Sea. Robert L. Maril. LC 82-45897. (Illus.). 256p. 1983. 21.95 (*0-89096-147-6*) Tex A&M Univ Pr.

Texas Silly Basketball Sportsmysteries, Vol. 1. Carole Marsh. (Carole Marsh Texas Bks.). (Illus.). (J). 1994. pap. 19.95 (*0-7933-1087-3*); lib. bdg. 29.95 (*0-7933-1088-1*); disk 29.95 (*0-7933-1089-X*) Gallopade Pub Group.

Texas Silly Basketball Sportsmysteries, Vol. 2. Carole Marsh. (Carole Marsh Texas Bks.). (Illus.). (J). 1994. pap. 19.95 (*0-7933-2101-8*); lib. bdg. 29.95 (*0-7933-2100-X*); disk 29.95 (*0-7933-2102-6*) Gallopade Pub Group.

Texas Silly Football Sportsmysteries, Vol. 1. Carole Marsh. (Carole Marsh Texas Bks.). (Illus.). (J). 1994. pap. 19.95 (*0-7933-2081-X*); lib. bdg. 29.95 (*0-7933-2080-1*); disk 29.95 (*0-7933-2082-8*) Gallopade Pub Group.

Texas Silly Football Sportsmysteries, Vol. 2. Carole Marsh. (Carole Marsh Texas Bks.). (Illus.). (J). 1994. pap. 19.95 (*0-7933-2084-4*); lib. bdg. 29.95 (*0-7933-2083-6*); disk 29.95 (*0-7933-2085-2*) Gallopade Pub Group.

Texas Silly Trivia! Carole Marsh. (Carole Marsh Texas Bks.). (Illus.). (J). 1994. pap. 19.95 (*1-55609-081-1*); lib. bdg. 29.95 (*0-7933-2074-7*); disk 29.95 (*0-7933-2075-5*) Gallopade Pub Group.

***Texas Silver.** Holly Harte. 320p. 1997. mass mkt. 4.99 (*0-8217-5707-5*, Zebra Kensgtn) Kensgtn Pub Corp.

Texas Society of Certified Public Accountants: A History 1915-1981. James A. Tinsley. LC 82-45890. (Illus.). 216p. 1983. reprint ed. 29.95 (*0-89096-152-2*) Tex A&M Univ Pr.

***Texas Source Book.** 3rd ed. Macmillan Services Group Staff. Date not set. write for info. (*0-688-11005-3*) Morrow.

***Texas Sourcebook.** Macmillan Services Group Staff. 1991. 22.50 (*0-688-09818-5*) Morrow.

Texas Special Issues Forms, 1988-1993. Richard C. Robins. LC 88-2589. 640p. 1994. suppl. ed., ring bd. 65.00 (*0-685-44084-2*) MICHIE.

Texas Special Issues Forms, 1988-1993. Richard C. Robins. LC 88-2589. 640p. 1995. spiral bd. 115.00 (*0-409-25339-1*) MICHIE.

Texas Standoff. Ruth A. Smith. (Superromance Ser.). 1996. mass mkt. 3.99 (*0-373-70707-X*, 1-70707-4) Harlequin Bks.

***Texas State & Federal Local Court Rules.** LC 96-76559. 800p. 1996. pap. text ed. write for info. (*0-7620-0069-4*) Lawyers Cooperative.

Texas State Capitol: Selected Essays from the Southwestern Historical Quaterly. LC 95-16736. (Fred H. & Ella Mae Moore Texas History Reprint Ser.: vol. 14). 1995. pap. 13.95 (*0-87611-150-9*) Tex St Hist Assn.

Texas State Constitution: A Reference Guide. Janice May. LC 96-539. (Reference Guides to the State Constitutions of the United States: No. 26). 512p. 1996. text ed. 99.50 (*0-313-26637-9*, Greenwood Pr) Greenwood.

Texas State Debt Management. Thomas M. Keel & Beverly S. Bunch. (Policy Research Project Report: No. 115). 165p. 1995. 15.00 (*0-89940-723-4*) LBJ Sch Pub Aff.

***Texas State Directory.** 40th rev. ed. Julie Sayers. 640p. 1997. pap. 27.50 (*0-934367-32-9*) TX St Direct.

Texas Stories. Ed. by John Miller & Kirsten Miller. LC 94-37904. 256p. 1995. pap. 11.95 (*0-8118-0845-9*) Chronicle Bks.

Texas Stories of Nelson Algren. Nelson Algren. Ed. & Intro. by Bettina Drew. LC 95-12195. 208p. 1995. pap. 12.95 (*0-292-70468-2*); text ed. 27.50 (*0-292-71577-3*) U of Tex Pr.

Texas Storm. Deana James. mass mkt. 3.95 (*0-317-43143-9*, Zebra Kensgtn) Kensgtn Pub Corp.

Texas Studies in Bilingualism. Ed. by Glenn G. Gilbert. (Studia Linguistica Germanica: Vol. 3). 1970. 130.80 (*3-11-002691-0*) De Gruyter.

Texas Suffragist: Diaries & Writings of Jane Y. McCallum. Janet G. Humphrey. (Illus.). 176p. (Orig.). 1988. pap. 14.95 (*0-936650-06-0*) E C Temple.

***Texas Summer.** Terry Southern. 174p. 3.98 (*0-8317-7062-7*) Smithmark.

Texas Summer. Terry Southern. 184p. 1993. reprint ed. pap. 9.95 (*1-55970-215-X*) Arcade Pub Inc.

Texas Sunrise. Fern Michaels. 1994. mass mkt. 6.99 (*0-345-36593-3*) Ballantine.

Texas Sunrise. large type ed. Fern Michaels. LC 93-13194. 1994. lib. bdg. 22.95 (*1-56054-755-3*) Thorndike Pr.

Texas Supreme Court: An Index of Selected Sources on the Court & Its Members, 1836 to 1981. Linda Gardner. (Legal Bibliography Ser.: No. 25). 142p. 1983. pap. 15.00 (*0-935630-08-2*) U of Tex Tarlton Law Lib.

Texas Survival. Betty L. Hall. 158p. (Orig.). (gr. 10-12). 1979. pap. text ed. 5.84 (*0-03-046971-6*) Westwood Pr.

Texas Sweets from Grandma's Kitchen. Donna D. Jomaa. LC 87-90679. 158p. (Orig.). 1988. pap. 9.95 (*0-9619202-0-3*) Straw Hat Prodns.

Texas Symposium on Relativistic Astrophysics , 9th. Ed. by Jurgen Ehlers et al. LC 80-11614. (Annals Ser.: Vol. 336). 599p. 1980. 107.00 (*0-89766-045-5*) NY Acad Sci.

Texas Symposium on Relativistic Astrophysics, Tenth: Proceedings, Vol. 375. 467p. 1981. 102.00 (*0-89766-139-7*); pap. 102.00 (*0-89766-140-0*) NY Acad Sci.

Texas Tacky. Martha Ebersole. (Illus.). 60p. (Orig.). 1985. pap. 4.50 (*0-88680-232-6*) I E Clark.

Texas Tae Ven Conmigo! 97th ed. (SPA.). 1997. text ed. 65.25 (*0-03-095781-8*); text ed. 66.50 (*0-03-095783-4*); text ed. 66.50 (*0-03-095785-0*) HR&W Schl Div.

Texas Tales Your Teacher Never Told You. Charlie Eckhardt. LC 91-17179. (Illus.). 224p. (Orig.). 1991. pap. 12.95 (*1-55622-141-X*, Rep of TX Pr) Wordware Pub.

***Texas Tapestry.** Houston Junior Woman's Club Staff. 1995. 17.95 (*0-9644109-0-7*) Houston Jr Womans.

Texas Teacher Edition for Music Grade 7. Boardman. 1988. teacher ed., pap. 99.00 (*0-03-014054-4*) HB Schl Dept.

Texas Teacher Edition for Music Grade 8. Boardman. 1988. teacher ed., pap. 99.00 (*0-03-014057-9*) HB Schl Dept.

Texas Teacher's Guide. Ndir. 1985. pap. 7.32 (*0-395-39027-3*) HM.

***Texas Teamwork.** J. T. Edson. 1997. mass mkt. 5.50 (*0-440-22416-0*) Dell.

Texas Tears & Texas Sunshine: Voices of Frontier Women. Ed. by Jo E. Exley. LC 84-40140. (Centennial Series of the Association of Former Students: No. 17). (Illus.). 296p. 1996. reprint ed. 29.95 (*0-89096-215-4*); reprint ed. pap. 15.95 (*0-89096-453-X*) Tex A&M Univ Pr.

Texas Temptation. Barbara McCauley. (Desire Ser.). 1995. mass mkt. 3.25 (*0-373-05948-5*, 1-05948-4) Silhouette.

Texas Temptations. Members of TFCE Staff. 350p. 1993. 12.00 (*0-9637300-0-2*) TX Assn Fmly.

***Texas Tender.** Sharon Gillenwater. LC 97-14402. 286p. 1997. pap. 8.99 (*1-57673-111-1*, Palisades OR) Multnomah Pubs.

Texas the Beautiful Cookbook. Elizabeth Germaine. (Illus.). 208p. 1989. 29.99 (*0-517-69220-1*) Random Hse Value.

Texas the Beautiful Cookbook: Authentic Recipes from the Regions of Texas. Patsy Swendson. LC 94-45573. (Illus.). 1995. 50.00 (*0-00-225035-7*) HarpC West.

Texas, the Dark Corner of the Confederacy: Contemporary Accounts of the Lone Star State in the Civil War. 3rd ed. Ed. by B. P. Gallaway. LC 93-37186. (Illus.). xii, 286p. 1994. text ed. 45.00 (*0-8032-2148-7*) U of Nebr Pr.

Texas, the Dark Corner of the Confederacy: Contemporary Accounts of the Lone Star State in the Civil War. 3rd ed. Ed. by B. P. Gallaway. LC 93-37186. (Illus.). xii, 286p. 1994. pap. 16.95 (*0-8032-7036-4*, Bison Books) U of Nebr Pr.

Texas Through Time: Evolving Interpretations. Ed. by Walter L. Buenger & Robert A. Calvert. LC 90-43716. 408p. 1991. 35.00 (*0-89096-490-4*); pap. 17.95 (*0-89096-468-8*) Tex A&M Univ Pr.

***Texas Ties: Recipes & Remembrances from the Junior League of North Harris County.** Junior League of North Harris. 1997. 19.95 (*0-9657063-0-3*) Jr League N Harris.

Texas Timeline: A Chronology of Texas History, Mystery, Trivia, Legend, Lore & More. Carole Marsh. (Texas Bks.). (Illus.). (J). (gr. 3-12). 1994. pap. 19.95 (*0-7933-6005-6*); lib. bdg. 29.95 (*0-7933-6004-8*); disk 29.95 (*0-7933-6006-4*) Gallopade Pub Group.

Texas Title Insurance. rev. ed. Billie J. Ellis & Charles J. Jacobus. LC 95-47014. (Texas Law Ser.). 1995. write for info. (*0-07-172791-4*) Shepards.

Texas Torment. Catherine Creel. 1985. mass mkt. 3.95 (*0-8217-1622-0*, Zebra Kensgtn) Kensgtn Pub Corp.

Texas Tortes: A Collection of Recipes from the Heart ... of Texas. Arthur L. Meyer. LC 96-9422. 1997. write for info. (*0-292-75202-4*) U of Tex Pr.

Texas Tortes: A Collection of Recipes from the Heart ... of Texas. Arthur L. Meyer. LC 96-9422. (Illus.). 120p. 1997. 17.95 (*0-292-75201-6*) U of Tex Pr.

Texas Torts & Remedies, 5 Vols. J. Hadley Edgar & James B. Sales. 1987. Updates. ring bd. write for info. (*0-8205-1706-2*) Bender.

Texas Touch. Kate Thomas. (Romance Ser.). 1994. pap. 2.75 (*0-373-19023-9*, 1-19023-0) Harlequin Bks.

Texas Tough. Hascal Giles. 320p. 1992. mass mkt. 3.50 (*0-8217-3855-0*, Zebra Kensgtn) Kensgtn Pub Corp.

Texas Tough: Dangerous Men in Dangerous Times. Gra'Delle Duncan. Ed. by Edwin M. Eakin. (Illus.). 128p. 1990. 12.95 (*0-89015-697-2*) Sunbelt Media.

***Texas Towns from A to Z: Pronunciation Guide.** Ed. by Bill Bradfield & Clare Bradfield. 118p. 1996. text ed. 14.00 (*0-9637629-5-8*) Three Forks.

Texas Toys & Games. Ed. by Francis E. Abernethy. LC 89-42896. (Texas Folklore Society Publications: No. 48). (Illus.). 256p. 1989. 24.95 (*0-87074-293-0*) UNTX Pr.

***Texas Toys & Games.** Ed. by Francis E. Abernethy. LC 97-10584. (Texas Folklore Society Publications: Vol. 48). (Illus.). 256p. 1997. reprint ed. pap. 16.95 (*1-57441-037-7*) UNTX Pr.

Texas Trackers. Doyle Trent. 256p. 1992. mass mkt. 3.50 (*0-8217-3850-X*, Zebra Kensgtn) Kensgtn Pub Corp.

Texas Trade & Professional Associations/1996. Ed. by Rita J. Wright. 100p. (Orig.). 1996. pap. 15.00 (*0-87755-339-4*) Bureau Busn TX.

Texas Traditions: The Culture of the Lone Star State. Robyn M Turner. LC 95-34360. (Illus.). 96p. (J). (gr. 4 up). 1996. 19.95 (*0-316-85675-4*) Little.

Texas Traditions: The Culture of the Lone Star State. Robyn M. Turner. LC 95-34360. (Illus.). 96p. (J). (gr. 4 up). 1996. pap. 12.95 (*0-316-85639-8*) Little.

Texas Trails of Our Tollett Family. Mary L. Donnelly. (Illus.). 288p. 1994. 33.00 (*0-939142-13-9*) M L Donnelly.

Texas Transaction Guide: Legal Forms, 15 vols. John J. Kendrick & Bender's Editorial Staff. 1985. Set. Updates available. ring bd. write for info. (*0-8205-1727-5*) Bender.

Texas Trash: And Other Great Recipes from Good Friends in the Lone Star State. Barbara L. Lacy. (Illus.). 123p. (Orig.). 1991. spiral bd. 6.95 (*0-9617721-3-1*) Golightly Pubns.

Texas Treasure Coast. 2nd rev. ed. Tom Townsend. (Illus.). 178p. 1996. pap. 16.95 (*1-57168-043-8*, Eakin Pr) Sunbelt Media.

Texas Trees: A Friendly Guide. Paul W. Cox & Patty Leslie. LC 87-72604. (Illus.). 260p. 1988. pap. 14.95 (*0-931722-67-5*) Corona Pub.

Texas Trends in Biotechnology. Center for Occupational Research & Development Staff. 111p. 1988. pap. text ed. 16.00 (*1-55502-359-2*) CORD Commns.

Texas Trial Handbook. 2nd ed. Walter E. Jordan. LC 81-65548. 760p. 200.00 (*0-317-00416-6*) Lawyers Cooperative.

Texas Trial Handbook. 2nd ed. Walter E. Jordan. LC 81-65548. 760p. 1992. Suppl. 1992. suppl. ed. 25.50 (*0-317-03168-6*) Lawyers Cooperative.

Texas Trigger. large type ed. Jackson A. Cole. (Linford Western Library). 272p. 1992. pap. 15.99 (*0-7089-7250-0*, Linford) Ulverscroft.

Texas Triggers. Jon Sharpe. (Trailsman Ser.: No. 136). 176p. (Orig.). 1993. pap. 3.50 (*0-451-17565-4*, Sig) NAL-Dutton.

***Texas Triggers: A Western Novel.** large type ed. Eugene Cunningham. LC 97-13094. 1997. write for info. (*0-7838-8204-1*) G K Hall.

Texas Trivia. rev. ed. Jill Couch & Ernie Couch. LC 91-9502. 192p. (Orig.). 1991. pap. 6.95 (*1-55853-114-9*) Rutledge Hill Pr.

Texas Twostep. (Ballroom Dance Ser.). 1985. lib. bdg. 70.00 (*0-87700-793-4*) Revisionist Pr.

Texas Uniform Commercial Code. Ed. by Butterworth Staff. 150p. 1994. pap. 25.00 (*0-250-44763-0*) MICHIE.

Texas Vehicle Laws Flip Code. 1995. 8.95 (*0-9629210-2-5*) Gould.

Texas Venue. J. Patrick Hazel. 304p. (Orig.). 1996. pap. text ed. 30.00 (*0-9648201-1-0*) Grail & Tucker.

Texas Veterans in the Mexican War: Muster Rolls of Texas Military Units. Charles D. Spurlin. LC 84-80189. 275p. 1984. pap. 20.00 (*0-911317-29-5*) Ericson Bks.

Texas Vistas: Selections from the Southwestern Historical Quarterly. Ed. by Ralph A. Wooster & Robert A. Calvert. LC 80-52706. 1990. reprint ed. pap. 9.95 (*0-87611-048-0*) Tex St Hist Assn.

***Texas vs. Johnson: The Flag-Burning Case.** J. Anthony Miller. LC 96-34850. (Landmark Supreme Court Cases Ser.). (Illus.). 112p. (YA). (gr. 6 up). 1997. lib. bdg. 18.95 (*0-89490-858-8*) Enslow Pubs.

Texas Wanderlust: The Adventures of Dutch Wurzbach. Douglas V. Meed. LC 96-27122. (Centennial Series of the Association of Former Students: No. 65). (Illus.). 192p. 1996. 29.95 (*0-89096-726-1*); pap. 12.95 (*0-89096-734-2*) Tex A&M Univ Pr.

***Texas Warrior.** J. T. Edson. 1997. mass mkt. 5.50 (*0-440-22396-2*) Dell.

***Texas Warrior.** J. T. Edson. 1997. pap. 5.50 (*0-440-22399-7*, Island Bks) Dell.

Texas Water Law, Pt. I. Frank F. Skillern. (Texas Water Law Ser.). 348p. (Orig.). Part I. pap. 125.00 (*0-945701-07-1*) Sterling TX.

Texas Water Law, Pt. II. Frank F. Skillern. (Texas Water Law Ser.). 348p. (Orig.). Part II. pap. 125.00 (*0-685-45919-5*) Sterling TX.

Texas Water Management Issues. Contrib. by J. Gronouski & E. Smerdon. (Policy Research Project Report: No. 77). 234p. 1987. pap. 10.00 (*0-89940-681-5*) LBJ Sch Pub Aff.

Texas Way. Jan Freed. (Superromance Ser.). 1996. mass mkt. 3.75 (*0-373-70676-6*, 1-70676-1) Harlequin Bks.

Texas Weather. 2nd rev. ed. Rev. by George W. Bomar. LC 93-48572. (Illus.). 288p. (C). 1994. pap. 17.95 (*0-292-70811-4*); text ed. 37.50 (*0-292-70810-6*) U of Tex Pr.

Texas West of the Pecos. Jim Bones, Jr. LC 81-40397. (Louise Lindsey Merrick Texas Environment Ser.: No. 4). (Illus.). 138p. 1981. 35.00 (*0-89096-117-4*) Tex A&M Univ Pr.

Texas Whitetails - Class of '92. Ray Sasser. 288p. 1993. 25.00 (*0-9632969-1-4*) Collect Covey.

Texas Whitetails, 1993-94. Ray Sasser. 288p. 1994. 25.00 (*0-9632969-2-2*) Collect Covey.

Texas Whitetails 1994-95. Ray Sasser. 300p. 1995. 29.95 (*0-9632969-5-7*) Collect Covey.

Texas: Why Stop? A Guide to Texas Historical Roadside Markers. 3rd rev. ed. Texas Historical Commission Staff et al. LC 92-12161. 1992. 16.95 (*0-88415-059-3*) Gulf Pub.

***Texas Wildcat.** Adrienne Dewolfe. 1997. mass mkt. 5.50 (*0-553-57482-5*, Fanfare) Bantam.

Texas Wildflower Postcard Collection Reprinted. Susan Gibler. (Illus.). 30p. (Orig.). 1997. pap. 8.95 (*0-89658-145-4*) Voyageur Pr.

Texas Wildflowers. Beverly Magley. LC 92-55083. 32p. 1993. pap. text ed. 6.95 (*1-56044-386-3*) Falcon Pr MT.

Texas Wildflowers. Leo Meier. 1990. 29.99 (*0-517-05059-5*) Random Hse Value.

Texas Wildflowers: A Field Guide. Campbell Loughmiller & Lynn Loughmiller. (Illus.). 287p. 1984. 27.95 (*0-292-78059-1*); pap. 12.95 (*0-292-78060-5*) U of Tex Pr.

Texas Wildflowers: Littlebook. Photos by Richard Reynolds. (Illus.). 64p. 1996. 14.95 (*1-56579-143-6*) Westcliffe Pubs.

Texas Wildlife: Photographs from Texas Parks & Wildlife Magazine. Intro. by David Baxter et al. LC 77-99281. (Louise Lindsey Merrick Natural Environment Ser.: No. 1). (Illus.). 192p. 1993. reprint ed. 24.95 (*0-89096-047-X*) Tex A&M Univ Pr.

Texas Wildlife Coloring Book. Illus. by John Carter & Chris Dodge. 40p. 1984. 2.95 (*0-89015-483-X*) Sunbelt Media.

Texas Wildlife Viewing Guide. Gary Graham. Ed. by Chris Cauble. LC 91-5880. (Watchable Wildlife Ser.). (Illus.). 160p. (Orig.). 1992. pap. 10.95 (*1-56044-092-9*) Falcon Pr MT.

Texas Wit & Wisdom. Wallace O. Chariton. (Regional Bks.). (Illus.). 252p. 1989. pap. 9.95 (*1-55622-257-2*, Rep of TX Pr) Wordware Pub.

Texas Woman. Connie Harwell. 400p. (Orig.). 1991. mass mkt., pap. text ed. 4.50 (*0-8439-3072-1*) Dorchester Pub Co.

Texas Women: Legends in Their Own Time. C. Dee Seligman. LC 89-1731. (Illus.). 112p. (J). (gr. 4 up). 1989. pap. 14.95 (*0-937460-59-1*) Hendrick-Long.

***Texas Women Writers: A Tradition of Their Own.** Ed. by Sylvia A. Grider & Lou H. Rodenberger. LC 97-7048. (Tarleton State University Southwestern Studies in the Humanities: Vol. 8). 448p. (C). 1997. pap. 17.95 (*0-89096-765-2*); text ed. 39.95 (*0-89096-752-0*) Tex A&M Univ Pr.

Texas Woollybacks: The Range Sheep & Goat Industry. Paul H. Carlson. LC 82-40311. (Illus.). 256p. 1982. 29.95 (*0-89096-133-6*) Tex A&M Univ Pr.

Texas Workers' Compensation Law. Howard Nations & John Kilpatrick. 1990. write for info. (*0-8205-1735-6*, 735) Bender.

Texas Workers' Compensation Trial Manual. 2nd ed. Phillip D. Hardberger. 1280p. 1991. ring bd. 115.00 (*1-55943-522-4*) MICHIE.

***Texas Writers of Today.** 1980. 53.00 (*0-8103-3734-7*, 00006303, Gale Res Intl) Gale.

Texas Yankee - Bullets for the Doctor, 2 vols. in 1. Will Cook. 320p. 1994. mass mkt., pap. text ed. 4.99 (*0-8439-3682-7*) Dorchester Pub Co.

Texas Yesterday, Today & Tomorrow. Ed. by S. Charles Maurice & Svetozar Pejovich. (Series on Public Issues: No. 22). 1986. pap. 2.00 (*0-86599-026-3*) PERC.

Texas' Youth, Texas' Future. National Health - Education Consortium Staff. 20p. 1993. 12.00 (*0-937846-50-3*) Inst Educ Lead.

Texas Zoning & Land Use Forms. Arthur J. Anderson & William S. Dahlstrom. LC 92-40671. 400p. 1992. spiral bd. 115.00 (*1-56257-953-3*) MICHIE.

Texas, 1844-45. Carl E. Prince. 1993. reprint ed. lib. bdg. 75.00 (*0-7812-5962-2*) Rprt Serv.

Texas 2077. Carlos Miralejos. Ed. by Orlando N. Acosta. 300p. Date not set. 19.95 (*0-9625266-4-9*, 97F002) Outer Space Pr.

Texas's (Most Devastating!) Disasters & (Most Calamitous!) Catastrophies! Carole Marsh. (Carole Marsh Texas Bks.). (Illus.). (J). 1994. pap. 19.95 (*0-7933-1078-4*); lib. bdg. 29.95 (*0-7933-1079-2*); disk 29.95 (*0-7933-1080-6*) Gallopade Pub Group.

Texas's Unsolved Mysteries (& Their "Solutions") Includes Scientific Information & Other Activities for Students. Carole Marsh. (Texas Bks.). (Illus.). (J). (gr. 3-12). 1994. pap. 19.95 (*0-7933-5852-3*); lib. bdg. 29.95 (*0-7933-5851-5*); disk 29.95 (*0-7933-5853-1*) Gallopade Pub Group.

Texasville. Larry McMurtry. Ed. by Bill Grose. 576p. 1990. pap. 6.99 (*0-671-73517-9*) PB.

Texe Marrs Book of New Age Cults & Religions. Texe Marrs. (Illus.). 336p. 1990. 17.95 (*0-9620086-4-8*) Living Truth Pubs.

Texfake: An Account of Theft & Forgery of Early TX Printed Documents. W. Thomas Taylor. (Illus.). 178p. 1991. 39.95 (*0-935072-20-9*, 33467) W T Taylor.

Texian Iliad: A Military History of the Texas Revolution. Stephen L. Hardin. LC 94-1564. (Illus.). 272p. (Orig.). 1994. 24.95 (*0-292-73086-1*) U of Tex Pr.

Texian Iliad: A Military History of the Texas Revolution. Stephen L. Hardin. (Orig.). (C). 1996. pap. 15.95 (*0-292-73102-7*) U of Tex Pr.

Texians. Dan Parkinson & David Hicks. 1990. mass mkt. 3.95 (*0-8217-3097-5*, Zebra Kensgtn) Kensgtn Pub Corp.

Texican. Dane Coolidge. 1975. lib. bdg. 16.30 (*0-89966-065-7*) Buccaneer Bks.

Texican Blood Fight. Patrick E. Andrews. 1992. mass mkt. 3.50 (*0-8217-3699-X*, Zebra Kensgtn) Kensgtn Pub Corp.

Texinfo: The GNU Documentation Format 2.20. Robert J. Chassell & Richard M. Stallman. 244p. (Orig.). (C). 1995. per., pap. 20.00 (*1-882114-63-9*) Free Software.

Tex's Tales. Rita Kerr. 1990. 12.95 (*0-89015-746-4*) Sunbelt Media.

Text: The Genealogy of an Antidisciplinary Object. John Mowitt. LC 92-11618. (Post-Contemporary Interventions Ser.). (Illus.). 256p. 1992. text ed. 43.95 (*0-8223-1251-4*); pap. text ed. 16.95 (*0-8223-1273-5*) Duke.

Text: Transactions of the Society for Textual Scholarship, 6 vols. Ed. by D. C. Greetham & W. Speed Hill. LC 83-45281. (Illus.). 1988. write for info. (*0-404-62550-9*) AMS Pr.

***Text: Transactions of the Society for Textual Scholarship, Vol. 8.** Ed. by D. C. Greetham et al. 500p. 59.50 (*0-472-10716-X*) U of Mich Pr.

TEXT: Transactions of the Society for Textual Scholarship, Vol. 9. Ed. by D. C. Greetham & W. Speed Hill. (C). 1996. 59.50 (*0-472-10774-7*) U of Mich Pr.

TEXT Vol. 8: Transactions of the Society for Textual Scholarship. Ed. by D. C. Greetham & W. Speed Hill. (C). 1995. 59.50 (*0-472-10615-5*) U of Mich Pr.

Text see Iwein: Eine Erzaehlung

Text see Philosophical Notebook

Text see Style & Evolution of the Earliest Motets

Text - Clinical Manual Package. 2nd ed. Ruth P. Rawlins. 1992. 67.95 (*0-8016-7360-7*) Mosby Yr Bk.

Text - Enlaces. Glisan. (College Spanish Ser.). 1991. pap. 40.95 (*0-8384-1988-7*) Wadsworth Pub.

Text - Politics in Island Southeast Asia: Essays in Interpretation. Ed. by D. M. Roskies. (Monographs in International Studies, Southeast Asia Ser.: No. 91). x, 360p. (C). 1993. pap. text ed. 25.00 (*0-89680-175-6*, Ohio U Ctr Intl) Ohio U Pr.

Text - Workbook Nursing Assistant Package. 3rd ed. Sheila A. Sorrentino. (gr. 13). 1991. 34.95 (*0-8016-6436-5*) Mosby Yr Bk.

Text-Aided Archaeology. Barbara J. Little. 240p. 1991. 76.95 (*0-8493-8853-8*, E159) CRC Pr.

Text Algorithms. Maxime Crochemore & Wojciech Rytter. (Illus.). 432p. 1994. text ed. 115.00 (*0-19-508609-0*) OUP.

Text Analyses of Three Yana Dialects. fac. ed. Edward Sapir. (University of California Publications in American Archaeology & Ethnology: Vol. 20: 15). 32p. (C). 1923. reprint ed. pap. text ed. 3.10 (*1-55567-251-5*) Coyote Press.

Text Analysis for the Social Sciences: Methods for Drawing Statistical Inferences from Texts & Transcripts. Ed. by Carl W. Roberts. LC 96-40299. (Communication Ser.). 320p. (C). 1997. text ed. 74.50 (*0-8058-1734-4*); pap. text ed. 39.95 (*0-8058-1735-2*) L Erlbaum Assocs.

Text & Act: Essays on Music & Performance. Richard F. Taruskin. (Illus.). 336p. 1995. pap. 19.95 (*0-19-509458-1*) OUP.

Text & Atlas of Arterial Imaging: Modern & Developing Technology. Ed. by Douglas M. Cavaye & Rodney A. White. LC 92-49001. (Medical Atlas Ser.: Vol. 11). 160p. (gr. 13). 1993. text ed. 143.95 (*0-412-46150-1*) Chapman & Hall.

Text & Atlas of Clinical Retinopathies. J. Gibxon et al. (Medical Atlas Ser.). (Illus.). 250p. (gr. 13). 1994. text ed. 99.95 (*0-412-35930-8*) Chapman & Hall.

Text & Atlas of Diagnostic Imaging of the Head & Neck. J. E. Gillespie & A. Gholkar. (Illus.). 300p. (gr. 13). 1994. text ed. 94.95 (*0-412-45200-6*) Chapman & Hall.

Text & Atlas of Endoscopic Retrograde Cholangiopancreatography. Ed. by Stephen E. Silvis et al. LC 94-11089. (Illus.). 496p. 1994. 155.00 (*0-89640-265-7*) Igaku-Shoin.

Text & Atlas of Liver Ultrasound. H. Bismuth et al. (Medical Atlas Ser.: No. 6). (Illus.). 249p. (gr. 13). 1991. text ed. 147.95 (*0-412-36790-4*) Chapman & Hall.

Text & Atlas of Paediatric Orofacial Medicine & Pathology. R. K. Hall. LC 92-49028. (Medical Atlas Ser.: Vol. 13). (Illus.). 432p. (gr. 13). 1993. text ed. 220.95 (*0-412-34860-8*) Chapman & Hall.

Text & Audiotape Package for Exploring Medical. 3rd ed. Lafleur & Brooks. 612p. (C). (gr. 13). 1993. 40.00 (*0-8016-7679-7*) Mosby Yr Bk.

Text & Beyond: Essays in Literary Linguistics. Ed. by Cynthia G. Bernstein. LC 93-29447. 328p. (C). 1994. pap. text ed. 29.95 (*0-8173-0699-4*) U of Ala Pr.

Text & Checklists Package to Accompany Clinical Nursing Skills. Perry. 304p. 1993. 46.95 (*0-8016-7746-7*) Mosby Yr Bk.

Text & Concept in Leviticus 1. Rolf P. Knierim. (Forschungen zum Alten Testament Ser.: No. 2). 125p. 1992. 74.50 (*3-16-145859-1*, Pub. by J C B Mohr GW) Coronet Bks.

Text & Concordance of Biblioteca Nacional, Madrid, MS10289: Moses Maimonides, Mostrador e Ensennador de los Turbados. Ed. by Moshe Lazar. Tr. by Pedro Toledo. (Spanish-Jewish Ser.: No. 1). 12p. (SPA.). 1987. 10.00 incl. fiche (*0-942260-84-8*) Hispanic Seminary.

Text & Concordance of Biblioteca Nacional, Madrid, MS171812: The Book of the Kuzari, a 15th Century Ladino Translation. Yehuda Halevi. Ed. by Moshe Lazar. (Spanish-Jewish Ser.: No. 2). 12p. (SPA.). 1989. 10.00 incl. fiche (*0-942260-97-X*) Hispanic Seminary.

Text & Concordance of Biblioteca Nacional Manuscript Res. 270-217: Libro Que Es Hecho de las Animalias Que Cazan: The Book of Moamin. Anthony J. Cardenas. (Spanish Ser.: No. 38). 24p. 1987. 10.00 incl. fiche (*0-942260-99-6*) Hispanic Seminary.

Text & Concordance of Biblioteca Nacional Manuscript 18052, Visita y consejo de medicos. Ed. by Enrica J. Ardemagni et al. (Medieval Spanish Medical Texts Ser.: No. 3). 8p. 1988. 10.00 incl. fiche (*0-942260-54-6*) Hispanic Seminary.

Text & Concordance of Biblioteca Nacional Manuscript 2153 Cirugia Rimada. Ed. by Victoria G. Serrano & Michael R. Solomon. (Medieval Spanish Medical Texts Ser.: No. 6). 1986. 10.00 incl. fiche (*0-942260-72-4*) Hispanic Seminary.

Text & Concordance of Biblioteca Nacional Manuscript 3356: Speculum al Foderi. Michael R. Solomon. (Medieval Spanish Medical Texts Ser.: No. 4). 22p. 1986. 10.00 incl. fiche (*0-942260-60-0*) Hispanic Seminary.

Text & Concordance of Biblioteca Nacional Manuscript 4987: Tratado Juridico. Ed. by Michelle A. Fuerch. (Spanish Aljamiado Texts Ser.: No. 1). 10p. (SPA.). 1986. 10.00 incl. fiche (*0-942260-82-1*) Hispanic Seminary.

Text & Concordance of Biblioteca Nacional Manuscript 9218 Historia del gran Tamerlan. Ed. by Juan L. Rodriguez et al. (Spanish Ser.: No. 20). 8p. 1986. 10.00 incl. fiche (*0-942260-62-7*) Hispanic Seminary.

Text & Concordance of Biblioteca Nacional, MS2147: Compendio de Cirugia. Ed. by Enrica J. Ardemagni. (Medieval Spanish Medical Texts Ser.: No. 24). 10p. (SPA.). 1988. 10.00 incl. fiche (*0-940639-23-8*) Hispanic Seminary.

Text & Concordance of Biblioteca Nacional, MS2165: Arte Complida de Cirugia. Guido Lanfranc De Milan. Ed. by Cynthia M. Wasick & Enrica Ardemagni. (Medieval Spanish Medical Texts Ser.: No. 26). 10p. (SPA.). 1988. 10.00 incl. fiche (*0-940639-25-4*) Hispanic Seminary.

Text & Concordance of Biblioteca Universitaria, Salamanca, MS2262: Doctor Gomez de Salamanca, Propiedades del Romero. Ed. by Marcela Lopez. (Medieval Spanish Medical Texts Ser.: No. 21). 6p. (SPA.). 1987. 10.00 incl. fiche (*0-940639-17-3*) Hispanic Seminary.

Text & Concordance of Escorial Manuscript f. iv. 1. Arte Cisoria. Enrique De Villena. Ed. by John O'Neill. (Spanish Ser.: No. 37). 8p. 1987. 10.00 incl. fiche (*0-942260-98-8*) Hispanic Seminary.

Text & Concordance of Escorial Manuscript M.III 7: Viajes de John of Mandeville. Ed. by Maria Del Mar Martinez Rodriquez & Juan L. Rodriguez Bravo. (Dialect Ser.: No. 7). 8p. 1984. text ed. 10.00 incl. fiche (*0-942260-46-5*) Hispanic Seminary.

Text & Concordance of Especulo, Alfonso el Sabio, MS10. 123: Biblioteca Nacional de Madrid. Ed. by Robert A. MacDonald. (Spanish Legal Texts Ser.: No. 4). 12p. (SPA.). 1989. 10.00 incl. fiche (*0-940639-37-8*) Hispanic Seminary.

Text & Concordance of Invencionario by Alfonso de Toledo, MS. 9219 of the Biblioteca Nacional, Madison. Ed. by Philip O. Gericke. (Spanish Ser.: No. 73). 8p. 1992. 10.00 incl. fiche (*0-940639-74-2*) Hispanic Seminary.

Text & Concordance of Kungliga Biblioteket, Stockholm, MSD1272a: Obra Sacada de las Cronicas de San Isidoro, Arcebispo de Sevilla. Ed. by Regina A. Geijerstam & Cynthia M. Wasick. (Dialect Ser.: No. 9). 14p. (SPA.). 1988. 10.00 incl. fiche (*0-940639-24-6*) Hispanic Seminary.

Text & Concordance of MS1-17: Biblioteca Colombina, Tesoro de los Remedios. Ed. by Maria Purificacion Zabia. (Medieval Spanish Medical Texts Ser.: No. 22). 6p. (SPA.). 1987. 10.00 incl. fiche (*0-940639-20-3*) Hispanic Seminary.

Text & Concordance of the Aragonese Translation of Brunetto Latini's Li Livres dou Tresor, Garona Cathedral, MS20-2-5. Ed. by Dawn E. Prince. (Dialect Ser.: No. 11). 16p. (SPA.). 1990. 10.00 incl. fiche (*0-940639-46-7*) Hispanic Seminary.

Text & Concordance of the Biblioteca del Palacio Real, MS3063: El Libro de Recetas de Gilberto. Ed. by Isabel Zurron. (Medieval Spanish Medical Texts Ser.: No. 23). 6p. (SPA.). 1988. 10.00 incl. fiche (*0-940639-22-X*) Hispanic Seminary.

Text & Concordance of the Leyes de Estilo, MS5764: Biblioteca Nacional, Madrid. Ed. by Terrence A. Mannetter. (Spanish Legal Texts Ser.: No. 6). 8p. (SPA.). 1989. 10.00 incl. fiche (*0-940639-43-2*) Hispanic Seminary.

Text & Concordance of the Leyes del Estilo, MS. Z.III.11, Escorial. Ed. by Terrence A. Mannetter et al. (Spanish Legal Texts Ser.: No. 8). 6p. 1990. 10.00 incl. fiche (*0-940639-47-5*) Hispanic Seminary.

Text & Concordance of the Libro de los Fueros de Castiella, MS431: Biblioteca Nacional, Madrid. Ed. by Kathryn Bares & Jerry R. Craddock. (Spanish Legal Texts Ser.: No. 5). 8p. (SPA.). 1989. 10.00 incl. fiche (*0-940639-41-6*) Hispanic Seminary.

Text & Concordance of the Ordenanzas Reales, I-1338: Biblioteca Nacional, Madrid. Ed. by Ivy A. Corfis & Carlos Petit. (Spanish Legal Texts Ser.: No. 7). 24p. (SPA.). 1990. 10.00 incl. fiche (*0-940639-42-4*) Hispanic Seminary.

Text & Concordance of the Suma de la Flor de Cirugia: Biblioteca Nacional Madrid 3383. Maria C. Villar. (Spanish Medical Texts Ser.: No. 10). 4p. 1987. 10.00 incl. fiche (*0-940639-06-8*) Hispanic Seminary.

Text & Concordance of the Tratado de la Generacion de la Criatura: I-51 Biblioteca Nacional, Madrid. Maria J. Mancho. (Spanish Medical Texts Ser.: No. 11). 12p. 1987. 10.00 incl. fiche (*0-940639-07-6*) Hispanic Seminary.

Text & Concordance of the Tratado de Patologia General: Biblioteca Nacional Madrid, 10.051. Maria T. Herrera. (Spanish Medical Texts Ser.: No. 15). 4p. 1987. 10.00 incl. fiche (*0-940639-11-4*) Hispanic Seminary.

***Text & Concordance of the Vatican Manuscript 6428 Cuento de Tristan de Leonis.** Ed. by Ivy A. Corfis. (Spanish Ser.: No. 26). 8p. 1985. 10.00 incl. fiche (*0-942260-68-6*) Hispanic Seminary.

Text & Concordances of Biblioteca Nacional Manuscript 3384 Espejo de Medicina. Alfonso Chirino. Ed. by Cynthia M. Wasick & Enrica J. Ardemagni. (Medieval Spanish Medical Texts Ser.: No. 5). 9p. 1988. 10.00 incl. fiche (*0-942260-56-2*) Hispanic Seminary.

Text & Concordances of Escorial Manuscript M.I.28: Tratado de las Fiebres. 2nd ed. Isaac Israeli & Ruth M. Richards. (Medieval Spanish Medical Texts Ser.: No. 1). 13p. 1984. 10.00 incl. fiche (*0-942260-44-9*) Hispanic Seminary.

Text & Concordances of Fernando del Pulgar - Claros Varones de Castilla & Letras, Seville, 1500. Ed. by Michael L. Dangerfield. (Spanish Ser.: No. 29). 6p. 1986. 10.00 incl. fiche (*0-942260-71-6*) Hispanic Seminary.

Text & Concordances of Macer Herbolario Seville Colombina Manuscript 7-6-27. Ed. by Porter Conerly et al. (Medieval Spanish Medical Texts Ser.: No. 7). 10p. 1986. 10.00 incl. fiche (*0-942260-78-3*) Hispanic Seminary.

***Text & Concordances of Sermones Contra Iudios e Moros, MS 25H: Biblioteca Publica y Provincial de Soria.** Alfonso De Valladolid. Ed. by John Dagenais et al. (Spanish Ser.: No. 65). 12p. (SPA.). 1991. 40.00 incl. fiche (*0-940639-59-9*) Hispanic Seminary.

Text & Concordances of the Escorial Manuscript of the Arcipreste de Talavera of Alfonso Martinez de Toledo. Ed. by Eric W. Naylor. (Spanish Ser.: No. 12). 6p. 1983. 10.00 incl. fiche (*0-942260-38-4*) Hispanic Seminary.

Text & Context: Cross-Disciplinary Perspectives on Language Study. Ed. by Claire Kramsch & Sally McConnell-Ginet. (Series on Foreign Language Acquisition Research & Instruction: Vol. 2). 286p. (C). 1992. pap. text ed. 34.76 (*0-669-27024-5*) HM College Div.

Text & Context: Document Storage & Processing. S. Jones. (Illus.). xiii, 298p. 1991. pap. text ed. 39.00 (*0-387-19604-8*) Spr-Verlag.

Text & Context: Studies in the Armenian New Testament: Papers Presented to the Conference on the Armenian New Testament, May 22-28 1992. M. E. Stone. LC 94-31345. (Armenian Texts & Studies: Vol. 13). 136p. 1994. 39.95 (*0-7885-0033-3*, 210213) Scholars Pr GA.

Text & Context Folksong in a Bosnian Muslim Village. Yvonne R. Lockwood. (Illus.). 220p. (Orig.). 1983. pap. 21.95 (*0-89357-120-2*) Slavica.

Text & Corpus Analysis: Computer-Assisted Studies of Language & Culture. Michael Stubbs. (Language in Society Ser.). (Illus.). 272p. (C). 1996. 59.95 (*0-631-19511-4*); pap. 24.95 (*0-631-19512-2*) Blackwell Pubs.

Text & Culture: The Politics of Interpretation. Daniel Cottom. LC 88-17341. (Theory & History of Literature Ser.: Vol. 62). 177p. (Orig.). 1989. pap. text ed. 14.95 (*0-8166-1763-5*) U of Minn Pr.

Text & Discourse Analysis. Raphael Salkie. LC 94-44507. (Language Workbook Ser.). 128p. (C). 1995. pap. 12.95 (*0-415-09278-7*, C0229) Routledge.

Text & Discourse Connectedness: Proceedings of the Conference on Connexity & Coherence, Urbino, July 16-21, 1984. Ed. by Marie-Elizabeth Conte et al. LC 88-7543. (Studies in Language Companion: Vol. 16). xi, 570p. (C). 1989. 156.00 (*90-272-3017-X*) Benjamins North Am.

Text & Discourse Constitution: Empirical Aspects, Theoretical Approaches. Ed. by Janos S. Petofi. (Research in Text Theory Ser.: Vol. 4). 516p. (C). 1987. lib. bdg. 215.40 (*3-11-007566-0*) De Gruyter.

Text & Epistemology. William Frawley. Ed. by Roy O. Freedle. LC 87-1847. (Advances in Discourse Processes Ser.: Vol. 24). 224p. 1987. text ed. 78.50 (*0-89391-397-9*) Ablex Pub.

Text & Experience: Toward a Cultural Exegesis of the Bible. Ed. by Daniel S. Christopher. (Biblical Seminar Ser.: No. 35). 350p. 1995. pap. text ed. 24.50 (*1-85075-740-2*, Pub. by Sheffield Acad UK) CUP Services.

Text & Graphics in the Electronic Age: Desktop Publishing for Scientists. William E. Russey et al. 359p. 1995. 50.00 (*3-527-28519-9*, VCH) Wiley.

Text & Iconography of Joinville's Credo. Lionel J. Friedman. LC 58-7918. (Medieval Academy Bks.: No. 68). 1958. 20.00 (*0-910956-42-1*) Medieval Acad.

Text & Interpretation: New Approaches in the Criticism of the New Testament. P. J. Hartin & J. H. Petzer. LC 91-11887. (New Testament Tools & Studies: No. 15). viii, 326p. 1991. 99.75 (*90-04-09401-6*) E J Brill.

Text & Interpretation: Studies in the New Testament. Ed. by Ernest Best & R. McL. Wilson. LC 78-2962. 286p. reprint ed. pap. 81.60 (*0-317-26088-X*, 2024416) Bks Demand.

Text & Intertext in Medieval Arthurian Literature. Keith Busby. Ed. by Norris J. Lacy. LC 96-2392. 256p. 1996. text ed. 38.00 (*0-8153-2385-9*, H1997) Garland.

Text & Its Margins. M. Alexiou & V. Lambropoulos. LC 85-62596. 288p. 1985. 25.00 (*0-918618-30-4*); pap. 12.00 (*0-918618-29-0*) Pella Pub.

Text & Logos: The Humanistic Interpretation of the New Testament. Ed. by Theodore W. Jennings. (Homage Ser.). 324p. 1990. 69.95 (*1-55540-508-8*, 001616) Scholars Pr GA.

Text & Materials for Bar Management Certification: Managing a Bar for Maximum Profit. Bob Johnson. 246p. 1995. wbk. ed. 115.00 (*0-9648379-3-5*) Hughes Co.

Text & Matter: New Critical Perspectives of the Pearl Poet. Ed. by Robert J. Blanch et al. 254p. 1990. 30.00 (*0-87875-402-4*) Whitston Pub.

Text & Meaning. Gert Jager et al. (Kent Forum on Translation Studies: Vol. 1). 176p. 1993. pap. text ed. 19.00 (*0-9637204-0-6*) KSU Appl Ling.

Text & Nation: Cross-Disciplinary Essays on National & Cultural Identities. Ed. by Peter C. Pfeiffer & Laura Garcia-Moreno. LC 96-18398. (GERM Ser.). xii, 212p. 1996. 58.00 (*1-57113-105-1*) Camden Hse.

Text & Presentation. Ed. by Karelisa V. Hartigan. LC 88-3536. (Comparative Drama Conference Papers: Vol. VIII). (Illus.). 232p. (C). 1988. lib. bdg. 41.50 (*0-8191-6907-2*) U Pr of Amer.

Text & Presentation. Ed. by Karelisa V. Hartigan. LC 89-5614. (Comparative Drama Conference Papers: Vol. IX). (Illus.). 178p. (C). 1989. lib. bdg. 31.50 (*0-8191-7420-3*) U Pr of Amer.

Text & Presentation: The University of Florida Dept. of Classics Comparative Drama Conference, Vol. X. Ed. by Karelisa V. Hartigan. 122p. (Orig.). 1990. lib. bdg. 38.50 (*0-8191-7784-9*) U Pr of Amer.

Text & Quality: Studies of Educational Texts. Ed. by Peder Skyum-Nielsen. 187p. 1995. 40.00 (*82-00-22453-8*) Scandnvan Univ Pr.

Text & Readings on Jurisprudence: The Philosophy of Law. George C. Christie. 1056p. 1989. reprint ed. text ed. 48.50 (*0-314-28171-1*) West Pub.

Text & Reality: Aspects of Reference in Biblical Texts. Bernard C. Lategan & Willem S. Vorster. 123p. 1975. 22.95 (*0-89130-822-9*, 06 06 14); pap. 16.95 (*0-89130-823-7*) Scholars Pr GA.

***Text & Review Package.** 7th ed. Scott et al. 1994. text ed. 145.00 (*0-397-51486-7*) Lppncott-Raven.

Text & Special Fonts, Menus, & Printing. Richard P. Braden. (Hands-on-Windows Programming Ser.: Bk. 6). 168p. (Orig.). 1995. pap. 15.95 incl. disk (*1-55622-453-2*) Wordware Pub.

Text & Supertext in Ibsen's Drama. Brian Johnston. LC 88-12488. 306p. 1989. lib. bdg. 35.00 (*0-271-00644-7*) Pa St U Pr.

Text & Tagmeme. Kenneth Pike & Evelyn Pike. 144p. 1983. text ed. 73.25 (*0-89391-210-7*) Ablex Pub.

Text & Teaching: The Search for Human Excellence. William J. Brennan, Jr. et al. Ed. by Michael Collins & Francis J. Ambrosio. LC 91-43554. 175p. (C). 1991. pap. 20.00 (*0-87840-529-1*) Georgetown U Pr.

Text & Technology: In Honour of John Sinclair. Ed. by Mona Baker et al. LC 93-17441. xii, 361p. 1993. 74.00 (*1-55619-494-3*) Benjamins North Am.

***Text & Testimony: Essays on New Testament & Apocryphal Literature in Honour of A.F.J. Klijn.** Ed. by Tjitze Baarda et al. 286p. 1988. 49.90 (*90-242-3404-2*, Pub. by KOK Pharos NE) Eisenbrauns.

***Text & Text Processing.** G. Denhiere & J. P. Rossi. (Advances in Psychology Ser.: Vol. 79). 414p. 1991. 173.50 (*0-444-88484-X*, North Holland) Elsevier.

Text & Texture: Patterns of Cohesion. Sally Stoddard. Ed. by Roy Freedle. (Advances in Discourse Processes Ser.: Vol. 40). 152p. (C). 1991. text ed. 78.50 (*0-89391-695-1*) Ablex Pub.

Text & the Voice: Writing, Speaking, & Democracy in American Literature. Alessandra Portelli. 1994. 29.50 (*0-231-08498-6*) Col U Pr.

Text & Thinking: On Some Role of Thinking in Text Interpretation. Roger G. Van De Velde. LC 92-23305. (Research in Text Theory Ser.: No. 18). xvi, 328p. (C). 1992. lib. bdg. 138.50 (*3-11-013250-8*) De Gruyter.

Text & Tradition: The Hebrew Bible & Folklore. Ed. by Susan Niditch. (Society of Biblical Literature Semeia Studies). 247p. 1990. 29.95 (*1-55540-440-5*, 06 06 20); pap. 19.95 (*1-55540-441-3*, 06 06 20) Scholars Pr GA.

Text & Tradition of Layamon's Brut. Ed. by Francoise LeSaux. LC 94-10443. (Arthurian Studies: No. XXXIII). (Illus.). 284p. (C). 1994. 53.00 (*0-85991-412-7*, DS Brewer) Boydell & Brewer.

Text & Transmission: An Empirical Model for the Literacy Development of Old Testament Narratives. Hans J. Tertel. LC 94-12755. (Beihefte zur Zeitschrift fuer die Alttestamentliche Wissenschaft Ser.: Vol. 221). x, 311p. (C). 1994. lib. bdg. 116.95 (*3-11-013921-9*) De Gruyter.

Text & Trauma: An East-West Primer. Ian R. Netton. 176p. (C). 1995. 65.00 (*0-7007-0325-X*, Pub. by Curzon Pr UK); pap. 25.00 (*0-7007-0326-8*, Pub. by Curzon Pr UK) Paul & Co Pubs.

Text As Picture: Studies in the Literary Transformation of Pictures. Hans Lund. (Illus.). 228p. 1992. lib. bdg. 89.95 (*0-7734-9449-9*) E Mellen.

Text As Pretext: Essays in Honour of Robert Davidson. R. P. Carroll. (JSNT Supplement Ser.: No. 138). 300p. (C). 1992. 60.00 (*1-85075-295-8*, Pub. by Sheffield Acad UK) CUP Services.

Text As Thou: Martin Buber's Dialogical Hermeneutics & Narrative Theology. Steven Kepnes. LC 92-7725. 244p. 1992. 35.00 (*0-253-33127-7*) Ind U Pr.

Text As Topos in the Religious Literature of the Spanish Golden Age. M. Louise Salstad. (North Carolina Studies in the Romance Languages & Literatures Ser.). 500p. 1995. pap. text ed. 30.00 (*0-8078-9252-1*) U of NC Pr.

Text-Atlas of Cat Anatomy. James E. Crouch. LC 68-25206. 415p. reprint ed. pap. 118.30 (*0-317-27963-7*, 2056016) Bks Demand.

Text-Atlas of Histology. C. Roland Leeson et al. (Illus.). 768p. 1988. text ed. 75.00 (*0-7216-2386-7*) Saunders.

Text-Atlas of Histology Slide Set. C. Roland Leeson et al. 1989. 389.00 (*0-7216-2824-9*) Saunders.

Text Atlas of Urogenital Ultrasound. Dennis Cochlin et al. (Illus.). 448p. 1994. text ed. 139.00 (*0-397-51424-7*) Lppncott-Raven.

Text-Based Intelligent Systems: Current Research & Practice in Information Extraction & Retrieval. Ed. by Paul S. Jacobs. 296p. 1992. text ed. 59.95 (*0-8058-1188-5*) L Erlbaum Assocs.

Text-Based Learning & Reasoning: Studies in History. Charles A. Perfetti et al. 232p. 1995. text ed. 49.95 (*0-8058-1643-7*) L Erlbaum Assocs.

Text Blocks. John Byrum. 18p. (Orig.). 1995. pap. 5.00 (*1-57141-004-X*) Runaway Spoon.

Text Blocks, Drawn. John Byrum. (Illus.). 24p. (Orig.). 1995. pap. 5.00 (*1-57141-010-4*) Runaway Spoon.

Text Book. 2nd ed. Scholes. 1994. teacher ed., pap. text ed. 0.52 (*0-312-10123-6*) St Martin.

Text Book. 2nd ed. Scholes. 1994. teacher ed., pap. text ed. 18.50 (*0-312-10124-4*) St Martin.

Text Book: An Introduction to Literary Language. 2nd ed. Robert Scoles et al. 352p. 1994. pap. text ed. 17.50 (*0-312-04837-8*) St Martin.

Text Book of Advanced Freemasonry: Containing for the Instruction of the Candidates, the Complete Rituals of the Higher Degrees, viz., Royal Ark Mariners, Mark Master, Royal Arch, Red Cross of Rome & Constantine, & Perfect Prince Mason, Knights Templar & Rose Croix, & Also Monitorial Instructions in the 30th to 33rd & Last Degree of Freemasonry. 280p. 1993. pap. 18.95 (*1-56459-334-7*) Kessinger Pub.

Text Book of Calculus. S. C. Arora & Ramesh Kumar. 550p. 1992. 65.00 (*81-209-0170-3*, Pub. by Pitambar Pub II) St Mut.

Text Book of Coordinate Geometry. P. N. Arora & P. C. Bagga. 260p. 1989. pap. 25.00 (*81-209-0206-8*, Pub. by Pitambar Pub II) St Mut.

Text Book of Differential Equations. N. M. Kapoor. 732p. 1992. pap. 80.00 (*81-209-0012-X*, Pub. by Pitambar Pub II) St Mut.

Text Book of English Legal History. V. D. Kulshreshtha. 296p. 1983. pap. text ed. 36.00 (*0-317-54606-6*) St Mut.

Text Book of English Legal History. 2nd ed. V. D. Kulshrestha. (C). 1990. 50.00 (*0-685-39635-5*) St Mut.

Text Book of Gynaecology. D. C. Dutta. (C). 1989. 135.00 (*0-89771-375-3*, Pub. by Current Dist II) St Mut.

Text Book of Irish Literature, 2 Vols, Set. Eleanor Hull. LC 70-153595. reprint ed. 105.00 (*0-404-09244-6*) AMS Pr.

Text Book of Mathematics, Vol. 1. M. K. Singhal & A. R. Singhal. 768p. 1992. 85.00 (*81-209-0178-9*, Pub. by Pitambar Pub II) St Mut.

Text Book of Mathematics, Vol. 2. M. K. Singhal & A. R. Singhal. 1008p. 1991. 95.00 (*81-209-0179-7*, Pub. by Pitambar Pub II) St Mut.

Text Book of Medical Entomology. W. S. Patton & F. W. Cragg. 764p. 1984. pap. 175.00 (*0-7855-0400-1*, Pub. by Intl Bks & Periodicals II) St Mut.

Text Book of Medicine. G. C. Mookherjee. (C). 1989. 150.00 (*0-89771-371-0*, Pub. by Current Dist II) St Mut.

Text Book of Medicine. 3rd ed. N. Das. (C). 1989. 110.00 (*0-685-36184-5*, Pub. by Current Dist II) St Mut.

Text Book of Obstetrics. D. C. Dutta. (C). 1989. 265.00 (*0-89771-374-5*, Pub. by Current Dist II) St Mut.

Text-Book of Palaeontology, 3 vols., Set. Incl. Vol. 2. Vertebrates I: Pisces, Amphibia, Reptile, Aves. Ed. by K. A. Von Zittel et al. 1964. 35.00 (*3-7682-7101-3*); Vol. 3. Mammalia. K. A. Von Zittel. Ed. by C. R. Eastmann & A. Smith Woodward. LC 67-23158. 35.00 (*3-7682-7103-X*); 1964. 150.00 (*3-7682-7100-5*) Lubrecht & Cramer.

Text-Book of Roman Law from Augustus to Justinian. W. W. Buckland. LC 90-55180. xiv, 756p. 1990. reprint ed. lib. bdg. 99.00 (*0-912004-82-7*) Gaunt.

Text Book of Waves & Acoustics. P. K. Chakrabarti. (C). 1989. 75.00 (*0-89771-402-4*, Pub. by Current Dist II) St Mut.

Text-Book on Campbellism. D. B. Ray. 1991. reprint ed. 19.50 (*0-685-40811-6*) Church History.

Text, Cases & Materials on Sex-Based Discrimination. 3rd ed. Herma H. Kay. (American Casebook Ser.). 1001p. 1993. reprint ed. text ed. 49.00 (*0-314-39751-5*) West Pub.

Text Coherence in Translation. Klaus Schubert. (Distributed Language Translation Ser.). 180p. (Orig.). (C). 1988. pap. 52.35 (*3-11-013107-2*) Mouton.

Text Comprehension & Learning from Text. Wolfgang Schnotz. Ed. by Bernadette H. Van Hout-Wolters. LC 92-34188. 212p. 1992. pap. 33.75 (*90-265-1283-X*) Swets.

Text, Context, & Hypertext: Writing with & for the Computer. Ed. by Edward Barrett. (Information Systems Ser.). 250p. 1988. 50.00 (*0-262-02275-3*) MIT Pr.

Text Counter Text: Rereading in Russian Literary History. Alexander Zholkovsky. LC 93-36232. 382p. (Orig.). 1996. pap. 17.95 (*0-8047-2703-1*) Stanford U Pr.

Text Counter Text: Rereadings in Russian Literary History. Alexander Zholkovsky. LC 93-36232. 392p. (C). 1994. 49.50 (*0-8047-2316-8*) Stanford U Pr.

Text-Critical Study of the Epistle of Jude. Charles Landon. (JSNTS Ser.: No. 135). 197p. 1996. 45.00 (*1-85075-636-8*, Pub. by Sheffield Acad UK) CUP Services.

Text-Critical Use of the Septuagint in Biblical Research. Emmanuel Tov. (Jerusalem Biblical Studies: Vol. 3). 343p. (C). 1981. pap. text ed. 25.00 (*965-242-003-4*, Pub. by Simor Ltd IS) Eisenbrauns.

Text der Aristotelischen Rhetorik: Prolegomena zu einer kritischen Ausgabe. Rudolfo Kassel. (Peripatoi Ser.: Vol. 3). 151p. (C). 1971. 102.35 (*3-11-003740-8*) De Gruyter.

Text, Discourse & Context: Representations of Poverty in Britain. Ed. by Ulrike Meinho & Kay Richardson. LC 93-50744. (Real Language Ser.). 1994. write for info. (*0-582-10214-6*, Pub. by Longman Grp UK); pap. write for info. (*0-582-10213-8*, Pub. by Longman Grp UK) Longman.

Text, Discourse & Process - Toward a Multidisciplinary Science of Texts. Robert De Beaugrande. (Advances in Discourse Processes Ser.: Vol. 4). 368p. 1980. text ed. 78.50 (*0-89391-033-3*) Ablex Pub.

Text Displays: Analysis & Systematic Design. George L. Gropper. LC 90-13993. (Illus.). 395p. 1991. pap. 44.95 (*0-87778-231-8*) Educ Tech Pubns.

Text Editing: Keyboarding, Applications & Exercises. Arnold Rosen & William H. Hubbard. LC 84-27090. 231p. 1985. pap. text ed. 30.95 (*0-471-81068-1*) P-H.

Text Encoding Initiative: Background & Contexts. Ed. by Nancy Ide & Jean Veronis. LC 95-31289. 1995. lib. bdg. 99.00 (*0-7923-3689-5*) Kluwer Ac.

Text for Scientific Documentation of the First European Conference Como, Italy. Ed. by Dario Lucarella. 224p. 1986. pap. write for info. (*0-201-13399-7*) Addison-Wesley.

Text for the Learnables, American English, Bk. 1. Harris Winitz. 36p. (YA). (gr. 3 up). 1990. pap. text ed. 6.50 (*0-939990-69-5*) Intl Linguistics.

Text for the Learnables, French, Bk. 1. Carmen Waggoner. 36p. (FRE.). 1991. pap. text ed. 6.50 (*0-939990-79-2*) Intl Linguistics.

T

Text for the Learnables, Spanish, Bk. 1. Harris Winitz. Tr. by Blanca Sagarna. 36p. (SPA.). (J). (gr. 3 up). 1990. pap. text ed. 6.50 (*0-939990-68-7*) Intl Linguistics.

Text Generation: Using Discourse Strategies & Focus Constraints to Generate Natural Language Text. Kathleen R. McKeown. (Studies in Natural Language Processing). (Illus.). 256p. (C). 1992. pap. text ed. 19.95 (*0-521-43802-0*) Cambridge U Pr.

Text Generation & Systemic-Functional Linguistics. M. I. Christian et al. 384p. 1992. text ed. 69.00 (*0-86187-711-X*) St Martin.

Text, Image, Message: Saints in Medieval Manuscript Illustrations. Leslie Ross. LC 93-35869. (Contributions to the Study of Art & Architecture Ser.: No. 3). 280p. 1994. text ed. 59.95 (*0-313-29046-6*, Greenwood Pr) Greenwood.

Text in Context: Contributions to Ethnomethodology. Graham Watson & Robert M. Seiler. (Focus Editions Ser.: Vol. 132). (Illus.). 320p. (C). 1992. text ed. 54.00 (*0-8039-4253-2*); pap. text ed. 24.95 (*0-8039-4254-0*) Sage.

Text in Context: Contributions to Ethnomethodology. Ed. by Graham Watson & Robert M. Seiler. LC 91-2619. (Sage Focus Editions Ser.: No. 132). 251p. 1992. reprint ed. pap. 71.60 (*0-608-01536-9*, 2059580) Bks Demand.

***Text in the Book Format.** Keith A. Smith. (Illus.). 128p. (Orig.). pap. 17.50 (*0-614-18198-4*) Visual Studies.

Text in the Book Format Bk. 120. 2nd ed. Keith A. Smith. LC 95-92070. 1995. pap. 17.50 (*0-9637682-3-9*) K A Smith Bks.

Text Information Retrieval Systems. Charles T. Meadow. (Library & Information Science Ser.). (Illus.). 302p. 1992. text ed. 52.00 (*0-12-487410-X*) Acad Pr.

Text, Interpretation, Theory. Michael Payne & James M. Heath. LC 85-5893. (Bucknell Review Ser.: Vol. 29. No. 2). 176p. 1985. 22.00 (*0-8387-5097-4*) Bucknell U Pr.

Text Knowledge & Object Knowledge. Annely Rothkegel. LC 92-44023. (Communication in Artificial Intelligence Ser.). 220p. 1993. 59.00 (*1-86187-136-8*) St Martin.

Text, Lies & Videotape: Stories About Life, Literacy, & Learning. Patrick Shannon. LC 95-1840. 144p. 1995. pap. 14.95 (*0-435-08120-9*, 08120) Heinemann.

Text-Netscape Navigator 2.0 Windows 3.1. Gary B. Shelly. 1996. pap. 21.35 (*0-7895-1279-3*) S-W Pub.

Text-Netscape Navigator 2.0 Windows 95. Gary B. Shelly. 1997. pap. 21.35 (*0-7895-1280-7*) S-W Pub.

Text of Chaucer's Legend of Good Women. Ernest F. Amy. LC 65-21088. (Studies in Chaucer: No. 6). 1969. reprint ed. lib. bdg. 39.95 (*0-8383-0502-4*) M S G Haskell Hse.

Text of Chinese Military Terms. Ed. by P. K. Li. 390p. (CHI & ENG.). 1972. pap. 12.95 (*0-7859-0792-0*, M-9577) Fr & Eur.

***Text of Great Britain: Theme & Design in Defoe's Tour.** Pat Rogers. LC 97-727. 1997. write for info. (*0-87413-617-2*) U Delaware Pr.

Text of Othello & Shakespearian Revision. E. A. Honigmann. LC 95-35947. 208p. (C). 1996. 49.95 (*0-415-09271-X*, Routledge NY) Routledge.

Text of Paradise Lost: A Study in Editorial Procedure. R. G. Moyles. 198p. 1985. 30.00 (*0-8020-5634-2*) U of Toronto Pr.

Text of Shakespeare. Thomas R. Lounsbury. LC 74-130240. reprint ed. 62.50 (*0-404-04035-7*) AMS Pr.

Text of Sidney's Arcadian World. Michael McCanles. LC 88-26742. 224p. (C). 1989. text ed. 41.95 (0-8223-0797-9) Duke.

Text of the Book of Llan Dav. Ed. by John G. Evans & John Rhys. LC 78-72667. (Series of Old Welsh Texts: Vol. 4). reprint ed. 62.50 (0-404-60584-2) AMS Pr.

Text of the Bruts from the Red Book of Hergest. Ed. by John Rhys & John G. Evans. LC 78-72662. (Series of Old Welsh Texts: Vol. 2). reprint ed. 62.50 (0-404-60582-6) AMS Pr.

Text of the Fourth Gospel in the Writings of Origen. Bart D. Ehrman et al. LC 92-33409. (Society of Biblical Literature New Testament in the Greek Fathers Ser.: No. 3). 499p. 1992. 44.95 (1-55540-788-9, 063003); pap. 29.95 (1-55540-789-7) Scholars Pr GA.

Text of the Holocaust: A Documentation of the Nazis' Extermination Propaganda from 1919-45. C. C. Aronsfeld. LC 85-351. 1985. 20.00 (0-916288-17-X); pap. 12.00 (0-916288-18-8) Micah Pubns.

Text of the Mabinogion from the Red Book of Hergest. Ed. by John Rhys & John G. Evans. LC 78-72663. (Series of Old Welsh Texts: Vol. 1). reprint ed. 52.50 (0-404-60581-8) AMS Pr.

Text of the New Testament. rev. ed. Kurt Aland & Barbara Aland. 1995. pap. 25.00 (0-8028-4098-1) Eerdmans.

Text of the New Testament. 3rd ed. Bruce M. Metzger. (Illus.). 320p. (C). 1992. pap. text ed. 19.95 (0-19-507297-9) OUP.

Text of the New Testament in Contemporary Research: Essays on the Status Quaestionis. Ed. by Bart D. Ehrman & Michael W. Holmes. LC 94-40616. (Studies & Documents: Vol. 46). 379p. 1995. text ed. 40.00 (0-8028-2440-4) Eerdmans.

Text of the Old Testament. E. Naville. (British Academy, London, Schweich Lectures on Biblical Archaeology Series, 1930). 1974. reprint ed. pap. 25.00 (0-8115-1257-6) Periodicals Srv.

Text of the Old Testament: An Introduction to the Biblia Hebraica. 2nd rev. ed. Ernst Wurthwein. LC 94-23307. 1994. pap. 20.00 (0-8028-0788-7) Eerdmans.

Text of the Old Testament in Anglo-Saxon England. Richard Marsden. (Studies in Anglo-Saxon England: No. 15). (Illus.). 400p. (C). 1995. text ed. 85.00 (0-521-46477-3) Cambridge U Pr.

Text of the Septuagint: Its Corruptions & Their Emendation. Peter Katz. Ed. by D. W. Gooding. LC 74-161292. 440p. reprint ed. pap. 125.40 (0-317-28405-3, 2022451) Bks Demand.

Text of the Talmud: Misnah, 3 vols., Set. Hyman E. Goldin. 1933. 10.00 (0-88482-838-7) Hebrew Pub.

Text of the Targum of Job: An Introduction & Critical Edition. David M. Stec. LC 94-950. (Arbeiten zur Geschichte des Antiken Judentums & des Urchristentums Ser.: Vol. 0169-734x). 1994. 122.50 (90-04-09874-7) E J Brill.

Text of Yi King: (And Its Appendixes) Z. D. Sung. 374p. 1997. pap. 32.00 (0-89540-318-8) Sun Pub.

***Text of 1 Corinthians in the Writings of Origen.** Darrell D. Hannah. LC 97-2100. (New Testament in the Greek Fathers Ser.). 308p. 1997. 44.95 (0-7885-0338-3, 063004) Scholars Pr GA.

Text, Play, & Story: The Construction & Reconstruction of Self & Society. Edward M. Bruner. (Illus.). 364p. (C). 1988. reprint ed. pap. text ed. 16.95 (0-88133-365-4) Waveland Pr.

Text Primer for Scientists. Steven G. Krantz. 416p. 1994. 31.95 (0-8493-7159-7) CRC Pr.

Text Processing. Ed. by Wolfgang Burghardt & Klaus Hoelker. (Research in Text Theory Ser.). 466p. (C). 1979. text ed. 142.35 (3-11-007565-2) De Gruyter.

Text Processing. Joyce Stananought & Derek Stananought. 256p. (Orig.). 1990. teacher ed. 28.50 (0-273-03056-6, Pub. by Pitman Pub Ltd UK); pap. 32.50 (0-273-03055-8, Pub. by Pitman Pub Ltd UK) Trans-Atl Phila.

Text Processing: Text Analysis & Generation. Sture Allen. (Data Linguistica Ser.). 653p. (Orig.). 1982. pap. text ed. 85.00 (91-22-00594-3) Coronet Bks.

Text Processing & Document Manipulation: Proceedings of the International Conference Nottingham, April 1986. Ed. by J. C. Van Vliet. (British Computer Society Workshop Ser.). 250p. 1986. text ed. 74.95 (0-521-32592-7) Cambridge U Pr.

Text Processing with UNIX. David W. Barron & Michael J. Rees. 240p. (C). 1987. pap. text ed. 26.95 (0-201-14219-8) Addison-Wesley.

Text Production. Michael Riffaterre. Tr. by Therese Lyons. LC 82-25509. 336p. 1983. text ed. 49.50 (0-231-05334-7) Col U Pr.

Text Production: Forward a Science of Composition. Robert de Beaugrande. Ed. by Roy O. Freedle. LC 83-25756. (Advances in Discourse Processes Ser.: Vol. 11). 416p. (C). 1984. pap. 42.50 (0-89391-159-3); text ed. 78.50 (0-89391-158-5) Ablex Pub.

***Text, Role, & Context: Developing Academic Literacies.** Ann M. Johns. (Applied Linguistics Ser.). (Illus.). 192p. (C). 1997. text ed. 47.95 (0-521-56138-8) Cambridge U Pr.

***Text, Role, & Context: Developing Academic Literacies.** Ann M. Johns. (Applied Linguistics Ser.). (Illus.). 192p. (C). 1997. pap. text ed. 18.95 (0-521-56761-0) Cambridge U Pr.

Text Searching Algorithms. Ricardo A. Baeza-Yates. (Computers & Their Applications Ser.). 200p. 1991. text ed. 49.95 (0-13-912338-5, 540701) P-H.

Text-Sound Texts. Ed. by Richard Kostelanetz. LC 78-72281. 10.00 (0-932360-60-2) Archae Edns.

***Text, Theory, Space: Postcolonial Representations & Identity.** Ed. by Sarah Nuttall & Liz Gunner. 280p. (C). 1996. pap. 18.95 (0-415-12408-5); text ed. 69.95 (0-415-12407-7) Routledge.

Text to Reader: A Communicative Approach to Fowles, Barth, Cortazar & Boon. Theo D'Haen. (Utrecht Publications in Comparative Literature: 16). x, 162p. 1983. 59.00 (90-272-2191-X); pap. 32.95 (90-272-2201-0) Benjamins North Am.

Text to Text Pours Forth Speech: Voices of Scripture in Luke-Acts. Robert L. Brawley. LC 95-2379. (Indiana Studies in Biblical Literature). 208p. 1995. 27.95 (0-253-32939-6) Ind U Pr.

Text, Tone & Music: Parameters of Music in Multicultural Perspective. Ed. by Bonnie C. Wade. (C). 1993. 36.00 incl. audio (81-204-0689-3, Pub. by Oxford IBH II) S Asia.

Text und Textwert der Griechischen Handschriften des Neuen Testaments II: Die Paulinischen Briefe, 1. Ed. by Kurt Aland. (Arbeiten zur Neutestamentlichen Testforschung Ser.). xxii, 806p. (GER.). (C). 1991. lib. bdg. 215.40 (3-11-013442-X) De Gruyter.

Text und Textwert der Griechischen Handschriften des Neuen Testaments II: Die Paulinischen Briefe, 2. Ed. by Kurt Aland. (Arbeiten zur Neutestamentlichen Testforschung Ser.). vi, 819p. (GER.). (C). 1991. lib. bdg. 215.40 (3-11-013443-8) De Gruyter.

Text und Textwert der Griechischen Handschriften des Neuen Testaments II: Die Paulinischen Briefe, 3. Ed. by Kurt Aland. (Arbeiten zur Neutestamentlichen Testforschung Ser.). vi, 658p. (GER.). (C). 1991. lib. bdg. 175.40 (3-11-013444-6) De Gruyter.

Text und Textwert der Griechischen Handschriften des Neuen Testaments II: Die Paulinischen Briefe, 4. Ed. by Kurt Aland. (Arbeiten zur Neutestamentlichen Testforschung Ser.). vi, 941p. (GER.). (C). 1991. lib. bdg. 244.65 (3-11-013445-4) De Gruyter.

Text und Textwert der Griechischen Handschriften Des Neuen Testaments Drei, Die Apostelgeschichte, 2 vols., No. 1, Untersuchungen und Ergaenzungsliste. Ed. by Kurt Aland. (Arbeiten zur Neutestamentlichen Testforschung Ser.: Nos. 20-21). xii, 719p. (GER.). (C). 1993. lib. bdg. 215.40 (3-11-014055-1) De Gruyter.

Text und Textwert der Griechischen Handschriften Des Neuen Testaments Drei, Die Apostelgeschichte, 2 vols., No. 2, Hauptliste. Ed. by Kurt Aland. (Arbeiten zur Neutestamentlichen Testforschung Ser.: Nos. 20-21). ix, 806p. (GER.). (C). 1993. lib. bdg. 221.55 (3-11-014056-X) De Gruyter.

Text und Variantenkonkordanz zu Schillers "Kabale und Liebe" Peter M. Daly & Claus O. Lappe. (C). 1976. 484.65 (3-11-002225-7) De Gruyter.

Text Understanding in LILOG: Integrating Computational Linguistics & Artificial Intelligence - Final Report on the LILOG-Project. Ed. by O. Herzog et al. (Lecture Notes in Artificial Intelligence: Vol. 546). xii, 738p. 1991. 74.95 (0-387-54594-8) Spr-Verlag.

Text-World Wide Web. Gary B. Shelly. 1998. pap. 33.95 (0-7895-1277-7) S-W Pub.

Text 1 see Hablemos en Espanol

Text 1 see Orientation in American English

Text 1 see Orientation in Business English

Text 1 see SR French: Parlons Francais

Text 1 see SR Italian: Lo Dica in Italiano

Text 2 see Hablemos en Espanol

Text 2 see Orientation in American English

Text 2 see Orientation in Business English

Text 2 see SR French: Parlons Francais

Text 4 see Orientation in American English

Text 5 see Orientation in American English

Text 6 see Orientation in American English

Textaufbau in den Erzahlungen Dostoevskijs. Wolf Schmid. (Beihefte zu Poetica Ser.: No. 10). 318p. 1986. 50.00 (90-6032-253-3, Pub. by B R Gruener NE) Benjamins North Am.

Textband see Opicinus de Canistris: Weltbild & Bekenntnisse Eines Avignonesischen Klerikers des 14 Jahrhunderts

Textbook. Donald E. Knuth. Vol. A. 496p. 1986. text ed. write for info. (0-318-60950-9) Addison-Wesley.

TEXtbook. Donald E. Knuth. LC 83-830. 483p. 1988. pap. 35.00 (0-201-13448-9, TEXBK) Am Math.

Textbook see Deutsch Konkret, Level 2

Textbook see Hazardous Materials: Managing the Incident

Textbook & Atlas of Diagnostic Microbiology. 5th ed. Elmer W. Koneman. LC 96-37818. 1088p. 1997. text ed. 66.95 (0-397-51529-4) Lppncott-Raven.

Textbook & Color Atlas of the Temporomandibular Joint: Diseases, Disorders, Surgery. Ed. by John E. De Burgh Norman & Paul Bramley. (Illus.). 272p. (C). (gr. 13). 1990. 179.00 (0-8151-6429-7, Yr Bk Med Pubs) Mosby Yr Bk.

Textbook & Color Atlas of Traumatic Injuries to the Teeth. 3rd ed. Andreasen. (Illus.). 762p. (C). (gr. 13 up). 1994. 255.00 (0-8151-0127-9, 24309) Mosby Yr Bk.

Textbook & Colour Atlas of the Cardiovascular System. C. Thomas et al. (Illus.). 160p. (gr. 13). 1992. pap. text ed. 30.50 (0-412-43520-9) Chapman & Hall.

Textbook Controversy: Issues, Aspects & Perspectives. Ed. by John G. Herlihy. 176p. (C). 1992. text ed. 73.25 (0-89391-748-6) Ablex Pub.

Textbook Development As an Art & a Science. 1994. pap. 5.50 (1-880407-12-4) Edit Freelancers.

Textbook for an Introductory Course in the Microbiology & Engineering of Sterilization Processes. 7th ed. I. J. Pflug. 454p. (C). 1990. pap. write for info. (0-929340-01-9) Environ Sterilization Lab.

***Textbook for Beginning Arabic.** Kristen Brustad. 224p. 1996. pap. 35.00 (0-614-21657-5, 1386) Kazi Pubns.

Textbook for Beginning Arabic see Al-Kitaab: A Textbook for Beginning Arabic

Textbook for Dental Nurses. 7th ed. H. Levison. (Illus.). 384p. 1991. pap. 29.95 (0-632-02956-0) Blackwell Sci.

***Textbook for Dental Nurses.** 8th ed. H. Levison. LC 97-1020. 1997. pap. write for info. (0-632-04031-9) Blackwell Sci.

Textbook for Nursing Assistants. 2nd ed. Sorretino. 512p. (C). (gr. 13). 1988. text ed. 25.95 (0-8016-5257-X) Mosby Yr Bk.

Textbook for Pressman Training. 2nd ed. Frank Drazan. (Illus.). 106p. 1986. pap. 20.00 (0-318-21789-9) F Drazan.

Textbook for the Clinical Application of Therapeutic Drug Monitoring. Ed. by William J. Taylor & Mary H. Diers-Caviness. LC 85-71233. (Illus.). 500p. (C). text ed. 85.00 (0-9614903-0-6, 9520-55) Abbott Laboratories.

Textbook for World Peace. Sun Myung Moon & Hak Ja Han Moon. 64p. 1992. pap. text ed. 4.95 (0-910621-64-0) HSA Pubns.

***Textbook, Force.** 1990. pap. text ed. 4.24 (1-55502-372-X) CORD Commns.

Textbook in American Education. Ed. by Ramsey W. Selden et al. 300p. (C). 1996. text ed. 52.50 (0-89391-530-0); pap. text ed. 24.50 (0-89391-689-7) Ablex Pub.

Textbook in American Society: A Volume Based on a Conference at the Library of Congress on May 2-3, 1979. LC 80-27657. 68p. 1981. 5.95 (0-8444-0355-5) Lib Congress.

Textbook in Analytic Group Psychotherapy. S. R. Slavson. LC 64-15375. 563p. 1964. 65.00 (0-8236-6460-0) Intl Univs Pr.

Textbook in Applied Mechanics. M. M. Malhotra & R. Subramaninian. 1994. write for info. (81-224-0645-9, Pub. by Wiley Estrn II) Franklin.

Textbook in Methods of Instruction see Methods of Instruction

Textbook in Psychiatric Epidemiology. Ed. by Ming T. Tsuang et al. LC 94-47953. 483p. 1995. text ed. 64.95 (0-471-59375-3) Wiley.

Textbook in the History of Education. Paul Monroe. LC 77-109914. reprint ed. 49.50 (0-404-04357-7) AMS Pr.

Textbook in the Kaleidoscope: A Critical Survey of Literature & Research of Education Texts. Egil B. Johnsen. (Scandinavian University Press Publication). 455p. (C). 1993. 39.50 (82-00-21506-7, 14457) Scandnvan Univ Pr.

Textbook National Medicine. 600p. 1986. 150.00 (0-318-23858-6) John Bastyr.

Textbook of Abdominal Ultrasound. Ed. by Barry B. Goldberg. LC 92-49049. (Illus.). 552p. 1993. 135.00 (0-683-03624-6) Williams & Wilkins.

***Textbook of Accident & Emergency Medicine.** Yates. 200p. (C). (gr. 13 up). 1997. text ed. 187.00 (0-412-45760-1) Chapman & Hall.

Textbook of Acupuncture. Felix Mann. (Illus.). 640p. 1987. text ed. 95.00 (0-7506-1895-7) Buttrwrth-Heinemann.

Textbook of Acute Pain Management. Paris. 1998. pap. text ed. write for info. (0-7216-6644-2) Saunders.

Textbook of Administrative Psychiatry. Ed. by John A. Talbott et al. LC 92-2579. 610p. 1992. boxed 59.95 (0-88048-400-4, 8400) Am Psychiatric.

Textbook of Adolescent Medicine. Elizabeth R. McAnarney et al. (Illus.). 1269p. 1992. text ed. 145.00 (0-7216-3077-4) Saunders.

Textbook of Advanced Cardiac Life Support. American Heart Association Staff. Ed. by Richard O. Cummins. (Illus.). 348p. 1994. pap. text ed. write for info. (0-87493-626-8) Am Heart.

Textbook of Advanced Phacoemulsification Techniques. Ed. by Paul S. Koch & James Davison. LC 89-43329. 414p. 1990. 100.00 (1-55642-158-3) SLACK Inc.

Textbook of Adverse Drug Reactions. 4th ed. D. M. Davies. 896p. 1991. 179.50 (0-19-262045-2) OUP.

Textbook of Agricultural Statistics. R. Rangaswamy. 1995. write for info. (81-224-0758-7, Pub. by Wiley Estrn II) Franklin.

Textbook of Agriculture, 2 vols. Ed. by W. Fream. 720p. 1989. 480.00 (81-7158-089-0, Pub. by Scientific Pubs II) St Mut.

Textbook of AIDS Medicine. Ed. by Samuel Broder et al. LC 93-8436. (Illus.). 1200p. 1993. 155.00 (0-683-01072-7) Williams & Wilkins.

Textbook of Algebra. Ravinder Kumar & S. K. Wasan. 336p. 1989. pap. 38.50 (81-209-0009-X, Pub. by Pitambar Pub II) St Mut.

Textbook of Algebra, Set, Vols. I & II. 7th ed. George Chrystal. LC 64-21987. (YA). (gr. 9-12). text ed. 39.90 (0-8284-0084-9) Chelsea Pub.

Textbook of Algebra, Vol. I. 7th ed. George Chrystal. LC 64-21987. (YA). (gr. 9-12). text ed. 19.95 (0-614-14593-7) Chelsea Pub.

Textbook of Algebra, Vol. II. 7th ed. George Chrystal. LC 64-21987. (YA). (gr. 9-12). text ed. 19.95 (0-614-14592-9) Chelsea Pub.

Textbook of Anaesthesia. 2nd ed. G. Smith & A. R. Aitkenhead. (Illus.). 640p. (Orig.). 1990. pap. text ed. 65.00 (0-443-03957-7) Churchill.

***Textbook of Anaesthesia.** 3rd ed. Alan R. Aitkenhead. 1996. pap. text ed. 85.95 (0-443-05056-2) Churchill.

***Textbook of Anal Diseases.** Ed. by Steen L. Jensen & Ole V. Nielsen. 1996. text ed. 89.00 (3-7186-5498-9, Harwood Acad Pubs) Gordon & Breach.

Textbook of Analytical Chemistry. S. P. Banerjee. 1985. text ed. 79.00 (0-317-38800-2, Pub. by Current Dist II) St Mut.

Textbook of Anatomy. A. W. Rogers. (Illus.). 779p. (Orig.). 1992. pap. text ed. 45.95 (0-443-02672-6) Churchill.

Textbook of Anatomy & Physiology. W. E. Arnould-Taylor. 112p. (C). 1988. pap. 35.00 (0-85950-937-0, Pub. by S Thornes Pubs UK) St Mut.

Textbook of Anatomy & Physiology: High School Edition. 13th ed. Gary A. Thibodeau & Catherine P. Anthony. (Illus.). 840p. (C). (gr. 13). 1989. text ed. 42.95 (0-8016-6079-3) Mosby Yr Bk.

Textbook of Animal Husbandry. 7th rev. ed. G. C. Banerjee. (C). 1991. 27.00 (81-204-0066-6, Pub. by Oxford IBH II) S Asia.

Textbook of Aramaic Documents from Ancient Egypt Vol. 1: Letters, Vol. 1: Letters. Ed. by Bezalel Porten & Ada Yardeni. Tr. by Ada Yardeni. ix, 143p. (ENG & HEB.). 1986. pap. 49.00 (965-222-075-2) Eisenbrauns.

Textbook of Aramaic Documents from Ancient Egypt Vol. 2: Contracts, Vol. 2: Contracts, incl. 37 plates. Ed. by Bezalel Porten & Ada Yardeni. Tr. by Ada Yardeni. liv, 191p. (ENG & HEB.). 1989. pap. 78.00 (965-350-003-1) Eisenbrauns.

Textbook of Aramaic Documents from Ancient Egypt Vol. 3: Literature, Accounts, Lists, Vol. 3: Literature, Accounts, Lists, incl. 36 plt. Ed. by Bezalel Porten & Ada Yardeni. Tr. by Ada Yardeni. ixvi, 295p. (ENG & HEB.). 1993. pap. 84.00 (965-350-014-7) Eisenbrauns.

Textbook of Automatic Pistols. Wilson. (Library Classics Ser.). 1990. 54.00 (0-935632-89-1) Wolfe Pub Co.

Textbook of Aviation Physiology. J. Gillies. LC 65-15380. 1965. 532.00 (0-08-018999-7, Pub. by Pergamon Repr UK) Franklin.

Textbook of Basic Life Support for Healthcare Providers. (Illus.). 116p. pap. text ed. write for info. (0-87493-615-2) Am Heart.

Textbook of Basic Nursing. 6th ed. Caroline B. Rosdahl. LC 94-30640. 1,616p. 1995. text ed. 48.95 (0-397-55109-6) Lppncott-Raven.

***Textbook of Biochemistry: With Clinical Correlations.** 4th ed. Ed. by Thomas M. Devlin. pap. text ed. write for info. (0-471-17162-X) Wiley.

***Textbook of Biochemistry: With Clinical Correlations.** 4th ed. Ed. by Thomas M. Devlin. LC 97-1078. 1997. text ed. write for info. (0-471-15451-2) Wiley.

Textbook of Biological Feedback. Mariella Fischer-Williams et al. LC 80-15235. 511p. 1981. 54.95 (0-89885-014-2); pap. 29.95 (0-89885-261-7) Human Sci Pr.

Textbook of Blood Banking & Transfusion Medicine. Ed. by Sally V. Rudmann. LC 93-49788. 1994. text ed. 47.00 (0-7216-3453-2) Saunders.

Textbook of Breast Disease. Ed. by John H. Issacs. LC 92-8464. 370p. (gr. 13). 1992. text ed. 102.00 (1-55664-283-0) Mosby Yr Bk.

Textbook of Bronchoscopy. Steven H. Feinsilver & Alan Fein. 600p. 1995. 125.00 (0-683-03107-4) Williams & Wilkins.

Textbook of Bunion Surgery. 2nd ed. Joshua Gerbert. (Illus.). 592p. 1991. 80.00 (0-87993-388-7) Futura Pub.

***Textbook of Cardiovascular Medicine.** Topol. 3008p. 1997. text ed. write for info. (0-397-51592-8) Lppncott-Raven.

Textbook of Cardiovascular Technology. Lunn Bronson. LC 65-8907. (Illus.). 388p. 1988. text ed. 39.95 (0-397-50726-7, Lippncott) Lppncott-Raven.

Textbook of Cell Biology. P. K. Nair & K. Prabhakar Achar. 224p. 1990. text ed. 25.00 (81-220-0123-8, Pub. by Konark Pubs Pvt Ltd II) Advent Bks Div.

Textbook of Child & Adolescent Psychiatry. 2nd ed. Ed. by Jerry M. Wiener. 960p. 1997. boxed 140.00 (1-882103-03-3, 0303) Am Psychiatric.

Textbook of Child Behavior & Development. 3rd rev. ed. B. Kuppuswamy. 300p. 1990. text ed. 30.00 (81-220-0163-7, Pub. by Konark Pubs Pvt Ltd II) Advent Bks Div.

Textbook of Child Behaviour & Development. 3rd rev. ed. B. Kuppuswamy. 1992. pap. 12.95 (81-220-0162-9, Pub. by Konark Pubs Pvt Ltd II) Advent Bks Div.

Textbook of Child Neurology. 5th ed. John H. Menkes. LC 94-13052. 1995. 99.50 (0-683-05920-3) Williams & Wilkins.

Textbook of Chiropractic. 1991. lib. bdg. 75.00 (0-8490-5039-1) Gordon Pr.

Textbook of Chiropractic. American College of Mechano-Therapy Staff. 96p. 1962. reprint ed. spiral bd. 8.00 (0-7873-0032-2) Hlth Research.

Textbook of Christian Ethics. Robin Gill. 586p. 1986. pap. 24.95 (0-567-29280-0, Pub. by T & T Clark UK) Bks Intl VA.

Textbook of Clinical Chiropractic. Ed. by Gregory Plaugher. LC 92-5613. (Illus.). 550p. 1992. 89.00 (0-683-06897-0) Williams & Wilkins.

Textbook of Clinical Echocardiography. Catherine M. Otto & Alan S. Pearlman. LC 94-6846. (Illus.). 416p. 1994. text ed. 105.00 (0-7216-6634-5) Saunders.

Textbook of Clinical Electrocardiography. A. Bayes De Luna. 1987. pap. text ed. 129.50 (0-89838-835-X); lib. bdg. 253.50 (0-89838-826-0) Kluwer Ac.

Textbook of Clinical Neurology. Goetz. 1998. text ed. write for info. (0-7216-6423-7) HarBrace.

Textbook of Clinical Neuropharmacology. fac. ed. Harold L. Klawans & William J. Weiner. LC 81-12156. 381p. pap. 108.60 (0-7837-7251-3, 2047054) Bks Demand.

Textbook of Clinical Neuropharmacology & Therapeutics. 2nd ed. Harold L. Klawans et al. 672p. 1991. text ed. 110.50 (0-88167-797-3) Lppncott-Raven.

Textbook of Clinical Neurophysiology. Ed. by A. M. Halliday et al. LC 86-18909. (Illus.). 742p. reprint ed. pap. 180.00 (0-8357-8626-9, 2035049) Bks Demand.

Textbook of Clinical Occupational & Environmental Medicine. Linda Rosenstock & Mark R. Cullen. LC 93-8640. (Illus.). 944p. 1994. text ed. 139.00 (0-7216-3482-6) Saunders.

Textbook of Clinical Ophthalmology. 2nd ed. Ronald P. Crick & Peng Khaw. 500p. 1997. text ed. 99.00 (981-02-2262-9); pap. text ed. 48.00 (981-02-2373-0) World Scientific Pub.

T

An Asterisk (*) at the beginning of an entry indicates that the title is appearing in BIP for the first time.

Textbook of Clinical Pharmacology. 3rd ed. James M. Ritter et al. 736p. 1995. 35.00 (*0-340-55864-4*, Pub. by Ed Arnold UK) OUP.

Textbook of Coal Petrology. 3rd enl. rev. ed. E. Stach et al. Ed. by D. G. Murchison et al. (Illus.). 536p. 1982. lib. bdg. 93.80 (*3-443-01018-0*) Lubrecht & Cramer.

Textbook of Community Medicine in South-East Asia. Wai-On Phoon & P. C. Chen. LC 84-5073. (Wiley-Medical Publication Ser.). (Illus.). 629p. reprint ed. pap. 179.30 (*0-7837-1878-0*, 2042079) Bks Demand.

Textbook of Complete Dentures. 5th ed. Arthur Rahn & Charles M. Heartwell, Jr. (Illus.). 600p. 1993. text ed. 65.95 (*0-8121-1523-6*) Williams & Wilkins.

Textbook of Contact Dermatitis. Ed. by P. J. Frosch et al. LC 92-2195. (Illus.). xxiv, 839p. 1992. 243.00 (*0-387-54562-X*) Spr-Verlag.

Textbook of Contact Dermatitis. 2nd enl. rev. ed. Torkil Menne et al. LC 94-34409. (Illus.). 840p. 1994. 165.00 (*3-540-57943-5*) Spr-Verlag.

Textbook of Contact Dermatitis. 2nd enl. rev. ed. Ed. by Torkil Menne et al. LC 94-34409. 900p. 1994. 236.00 (*0-387-57943-5*) Spr-Verlag.

Textbook of Cooperative Management. P. C. Dhal. 120p. 1990. text ed. 7.95 (*81-220-0158-0*, Pub. by Konark Pubs Pvt Ltd II) Advent Bks Div.

Textbook of Critical Care. 3rd ed. William C. Shoemaker et al. LC 94-27360. (Illus.). 1584p. 1995. text ed. 119.00 (*0-7216-5422-3*) Saunders.

***Textbook of Critical Care.** 4th ed. William C. Shoemaker. Date not set. text ed. write for info. (*0-7216-7246-9*) Saunders.

Textbook of Dendrology. 7th ed. William M. Harlow et al. 512p. 1991. text ed. write for info. (*0-07-026571-2*) McGraw.

Textbook of Dendrology. 8th ed. William M. Harlow et al. (Series in Forest Resources). 1996. pap. text ed. write for info. (*0-07-026572-0*) McGraw.

Textbook of Dental Assisting. Humphrey. text ed. write for info. (*0-7216-6136-X*); student ed., pap. text ed. write for info. (*0-7216-6138-6*) Saunders.

Textbook of Dental Homeopathy: For Dental Surgeons, Homeopathists & General Medicine Practitioners. Colin Lessell. 111p. 1995. pap. 25.95 (*0-85207-281-3*, Pub. by C W Daniel UK) Natl Bk Netwk.

Textbook of Dental Pharmacology & Therapeutics. John G. Walton et al. (Illus.). 304p. 1994. pap. 54.00 (*0-19-262506-3*) OUP.

Textbook of Dental Pharmacology & Therapeutics. 2nd ed. John G. Walton et al. (Illus.). 304p. 1994. 120.00 (*0-19-262507-1*) OUP.

Textbook of Dental Radiology. 2nd ed. Olaf E. Langland et al. (Illus.). 684p. (C). 1984. 67.95 (*0-398-04910-6*) C C Thomas.

***Textbook of Dermatologic Surgery.** Ed. by John L. Ratz et al. (Illus.). 1000p. 1997. text ed. 185.00 (*0-397-51495-6*) Lppncott-Raven.

Textbook of Dermatology, 4 vols. 5th ed. Ed. by Robert H. Champion et al. (Illus.). 3160p. 1992. CD-ROM version, 07/1992. cd-rom 295.00 (*0-86542-234-6*) Blackwell Sci.

Textbook of Dermatology, 4 vols., Set. 5th ed. Robert H. Champion et al. (Illus.). 3452p. 1991. 595.00 (*0-632-02396-1*) Blackwell Sci.

Textbook of Dermatopathology. Ed. by Raymond Barnhill. (Illus.). 912p. 1997. 150.00 (*0-07-005726-5*) McGraw-Hill HPD.

Textbook of Developmental Paediatrics. Margaret Pollak. LC 92-22842. (Illus.). 512p. 1993. text ed. 65.00 (*0-443-04169-5*) Churchill.

Textbook of Developmental Pediatrics. Ed. by Marvin I. Gottlieb & John E. Williams. LC 83-30411. 568p. 1987. 79.50 (*0-306-42334-0*, Plenum Med Bk) Plenum.

Textbook of Diabetes. 2nd ed. John C. Pickup & Gareth Williams. LC 96-25940. 1996. write for info. (*0-86542-730-5*) Blackwell Sci.

Textbook of Diabetes. 2nd ed. John C. Pickup & Gareth Williams. LC 96-25940. (Illus.). 1600p. 1997. 275.00 (*0-632-03802-0*) Blackwell Sci.

Textbook of Diabetes. 2nd ed. John C. Pickup & Gareth Williams. LC 96-25940. 1996. write for info. (*0-86542-747-X*) Blackwell Sci.

Textbook of Diabetes, 2 vols., Set. J. Pickup & G. Williams. (Illus.). 1104p. 1991. 295.00 (*0-632-02594-8*) Blackwell Sci.

Textbook of Diabetes Slide Atlas. J. C. Pickup & G. Williams. (Illus.). 20p. 1993. 99.95 (*0-632-03569-2*) Blackwell Sci.

Textbook of Diagnostic Imaging, 2 vols. 2nd ed. Charles E. Putman & Carl E. Ravin. LC 94-4061. (Illus.). 2368p. 1994. text ed. 299.00 (*0-7216-3697-7*) Saunders.

Textbook of Diagnostic Medicine. Ed. by A. H. Samiy et al. LC 85-23966. 924p. reprint ed. pap. 180.00 (*0-7837-2744-5*, 2043124) Bks Demand.

Textbook of Diagnostic Microbiology. Ed. by Connie Mahon et al. LC 94-21550. (Illus.). 1152p. 1995. text ed. 65.00 (*0-7216-4028-1*) Saunders.

Textbook of Diagnostic Ultrasonography. 4th ed. Sandra L. Hagen-Ansert. LC 94-22472. (Illus.). (gr. 13). 1994. 175.00 (*0-8016-7948-6*) Mosby Yr Bk.

Textbook of Diseases of Nose, Throat & Ear. Ed. by P. B. Rao. 340p. (C). 1990. 90.00 (*0-685-57271-4*, Pub. by Interprint II) St Mut.

Textbook of Disorders & Injuries of Musculoskeletal Structure. 2nd ed. Robert B. Salter. (Illus.). 578p. 1983. text ed. 56.00 (*0-683-07500-4*) Williams & Wilkins.

Textbook of Disturbances of Mental Life: Disturbances of the Soul & Their Treatment, Vol. 1 Theory. Johann C. Heinroth. reprint ed. pap. 76.80 (*0-317-19872-6*, 2023102) Bks Demand.

Textbook of Disturbances of Mental Life: Disturbances of the Soul & Their Treatment, Vol. 2 Practice. Johann C. Heinroth. reprint ed. pap. 61.00 (*0-317-19873-4*) Bks Demand.

Textbook of Dr. Vodder's Manual Lymph Drainage, Vol. 2, Therapy I. 3rd ed. Ingrid Kurz. Tr. by Robert H. Harris. (Ingrid Kurz Ser.). (Illus.). 100p. (Orig.). (GER.). 1993. pap. text ed. 19.00 (*2-8043-4006-6*, Pub. by K F Haug Pubs) Medicina Bio.

Textbook of Dr. Vodder's Manual Lymph Drainage, Vol. 3, Therapy II. 3rd rev. ed. Ingrid Kurz. Tr. by Robert H. Harris. (Ingrid Kurz Ser.). (Illus.). 139p. (Orig.). (GER.). 1996. pap. text ed. 21.00 (*2-8043-4017-1*, Pub. by K F Haug Pubs) Medicina Bio.

Textbook of Dr. Vodder's Manual Lymph Drainage Vol. 1: Basic Course. 5th ed. Hildegard Wittlinger & Gunther Wittlinger. (Illus.). 126p. 1995. 19.00 (*2-8043-4016-3*, Pub. by Edits Haug Intl) Medicina Bio.

Textbook of Drug Design & Development. Ed. by Povl Krogsgaard-Larsen & H. Bundgaard. 643p. 1991. text ed. 227.00 (*3-7186-5099-1*, Harwood Acad Pubs); pap. text ed. 64.00 (*3-7186-5100-9*, Harwood Acad Pubs) Gordon & Breach.

Textbook of Drug Design & Development. 2nd ed. Ed. by Povl Krogsgaard-Larsen et al. 1996. pap. text ed. 45.00 (*3-7186-5867-4*, Harwood Acad Pubs) Gordon & Breach.

Textbook of Drug Design & Development. 2nd ed. Ed. by Povl Krogsgaard-Larsen et al. 1996. text ed. 165.00 (*3-7186-5866-6*, Harwood Acad Pubs) Gordon & Breach.

Textbook of Dynamics. 2nd ed. Frank Chorlton. LC 82-25484. (Mathematics & Its Applications Ser.). 271p. 1983. text ed. 65.95 (*0-470-27407-7*) P-H.

Textbook of Echocardiography. Natasa Pandian & Stephen P. Sanders. 750p. 1994. write for info. (*0-683-06744-3*) Williams & Wilkins.

Textbook of Echocardiography. Ed. by Martin S. Sutton & Paul J. Oldershaw. (Illus.). 912p. 1989. 135.00 (*0-86542-032-7*) Blackwell Sci.

Textbook of Echocardiography & Doppler in Adults & Children. 2nd ed. Ed. by Martin G. St. John Sutton et al. 1008p. 1996. 195.00 (*0-86542-287-7*) Blackwell Sci.

Textbook of Economic Geography. 2nd ed. S. P. Chatterjee. 142p. 1988. pap. 7.95 (*0-86131-842-0*, Pub. by Orient Longman Ltd II) Apt Bks.

Textbook of Economics. 4th ed. Frank Livesey. LC 94-30854. 1995. write for info. (*0-582-23867-6*) Longman.

Textbook of Endocrine Physiology. 3rd ed. Ed. by James Griffin & Sergio R. Ojeda. (Illus.). 408p. 1996. 55.00 (*0-19-510754-3*); pap. 27.95 (*0-19-510755-1*) OUP.

Textbook of Endocrine Surgery. Orlo H. Clark & Quan-Yang Duh. Ed. by Larry McGrew. (Illus.). 560p. 1997. text ed. 145.00 (*0-7216-5882-2*) Saunders.

Textbook of Endourology. R. Ernest Sosa et al. Ed. by Sandra Valhoff. LC 95-41654. (Illus.). 784p. 1996. text ed. 195.00 (*0-7216-5316-2*) Saunders.

Textbook of Entomology. Mohammed Sulaiman. (Illus.). 1992. 27.50 (*81-7040-499-1*, Pub. by Himalaya II) Apt Bks.

Textbook of Entomology. Herbert H. Ross et al. 704p. (C). 1991. reprint ed. lib. bdg. 77.50 (*0-89464-497-1*) Krieger.

Textbook of Environmental Physiology. 2nd ed. George E. Folk. LC 73-8683. 482p. reprint ed. pap. 137.40 (*0-317-28604-8*, 2055425) Bks Demand.

Textbook of Epilepsy. 4th ed. Ed. by David Chadwick et al. LC 92-12309. 768p. 1993. 185.00 (*0-443-04473-2*) Churchill.

Textbook of Ethics in Pediatric Research. Ed. by Gideon Koren. 346p. (C). 1993. 39.50 (*0-89464-559-5*) Krieger.

Textbook of European Musical Instruments. Francis W. Galpin. 1977. lib. bdg. 59.95 (*0-8490-2737-3*) Gordon Pr.

Textbook of European Musical Instruments. Francis W. Galpin. LC 75-36509. (Illus.). 256p. 1976. reprint ed. text ed. 35.00 (*0-8371-8648-X*, GAEM, Greenwood Pr) Greenwood.

Textbook of Family Medicine. Ian R. McWhinney. (Illus.). 400p. 1989. pap. 33.50 (*0-19-505037-1*) OUP.

***Textbook of Family Medicine.** 2nd ed. Ian R. McWhinney. (Illus.). 496p. 1997. 60.00 (*0-19-511517-1*); pap. 34.95 (*0-19-511518-X*) OUP.

Textbook of Family Practice. Robertson & Estes. 1991. write for info. (*0-8151-7407-1*, Yr Bk Med Pubs) Mosby Yr Bk.

Textbook of Family Practice. 5th ed. Robert E. Rakel. (Illus.). 1760p. 1995. text ed. 119.00 (*0-7216-4053-2*) Saunders.

Textbook of Fetal & Perinatal Pathology. 2nd ed. Wigglesworth. 1380p. 1990. 295.00 (*0-86542-118-8*) Blackwell Sci.

***Textbook of Fetal & Perinatal Pathology.** 2nd ed. Jonathan S. Wigglesworth & Don B. Singer. LC 97-21930. 1997. write for info. (*0-86542-396-2*) Blackwell Sci.

***Textbook of Fetal Cardiology.** Erik J. Meijboom. 300p. 1997. text ed. write for info. (*0-7817-0295-X*) Lppncott-Raven.

Textbook of Fetal Physiology. Ed. by Geoffrey D. Thorburn & Richard Harding. (Illus.). 480p. 1994. 95.00 (*0-19-857748-6*) OUP.

Textbook of Fire Assaying. 3rd ed. Edward E. Bugbee. Ed. by Jon W. Raese. LC 81-17021. (Illus.). 314p. (C). 1981. reprint ed. text ed. 21.00 (*0-918062-47-0*) Colo Sch Mines.

***Textbook of Fire Assaying.** 4th rev. ed. Edward E. Bugbee. LC 81-17021. (Illus.). 235p. 1991. pap. 17.95 (*0-9653923-2-5*) Western Tales.

Textbook of Fish Culture: Breeding & Cultivation of Fish. 1978. 80.00 (*0-685-63460-4*) St Mut.

Textbook of Fish Culture: Breeding & Cultivation of Fish. 2nd ed. Marcel Huet. (Fishing News Bks.). Orig. Title: Traite de Pisicultur. (Illus.). 456p. 1994. pap. 55.00 (*0-85238-219-7*) Blackwell Sci.

Textbook of Fish Health. George Post. (Illus.). 256p. 1987. 35.95 (*0-86622-491-2*, H-1043) TFH Pubns.

Textbook of Foods, Nutrition & Dietetics. 2nd enl. rev. ed. M. Raheena Begum. x, 357p. 1991. text ed. 40.00 (*81-207-0965-9*, Pub. by Sterling Pubs II) Apt Bks.

Textbook of Forensic Pharmacy. 8th ed. M. Mithal. (C). 1988. 80.00 (*0-685-36221-3*, Pub. by Current Dist II) St Mut.

Textbook of Gastroenterology, 2. 2nd ed. Ed. by Tadataka Yamada et al. Incl. Vol. 1. Textbook of Gastroenterology. , 2 vols. 2nd ed. LC 94-23213. (Illus.). 1995. (*0-397-51491-3*); LC 94-23213. 3,456p. 1995. text ed. 235.00 (*0-397-51314-3*) Lppncott-Raven.

***Textbook of Gastroenterology.** 3rd ed. Tadataka Yamada. 1998. text ed. write for info. (*0-397-58735-X*) Lppncott-Raven.

Textbook of Gastroenterology, 2 vols., Vol. 2. Ed. by Tadataka Yamada et al. LC 94-23213. (Illus.). 1995. write for info. (*0-397-51492-1*) Lppncott-Raven.

Textbook of Gastroenterology: Self-Assessment Review. 2nd ed. Ed. by Tadataka Yamada et al. LC 95-9616. 344p. 1995. pap. text ed. 39.95 (*0-397-51541-3*) Lppncott-Raven.

Textbook of Gastroenterology see Textbook of Gastroenterology

Textbook of Gastroenterology & Nutrition in Infancy. 2nd ed. Emanuel Lebenthal. 1406p. 1989. text ed. 199.00 (*0-88167-522-9*) Lppncott-Raven.

Textbook of Gastrointestinal Radiology, 2 vols., 1. Ed. by Richard M. Gore et al. LC 93-24075. (Illus.). 2240p. 1993. write for info. (*0-7216-3978-X*) Saunders.

Textbook of Gastrointestinal Radiology, 2 vols., 2. Ed. by Richard M. Gore et al. LC 93-24075. (Illus.). 2240p. 1993. write for info. (*0-7216-3979-8*) Saunders.

Textbook of Gastrointestinal Radiology, 2 vols., Set. Ed. by Richard M. Gore et al. LC 93-24075. (Illus.). 2240p. 1993. text ed. 325.00 (*0-7216-3977-1*) Saunders.

Textbook of General Hospital Psychiatry. Geoffrey Lloyd. 256p. 1991. pap. text ed. 36.00 (*0-443-02469-3*) Churchill.

Textbook of General Medicine & Primary Care. Ed. by John Noble. 2320p. 1987. text ed. 85.00 (*0-317-53603-6*, Little Med Div) Little.

Textbook of Genetics & Evolution. P. K. Nair & K. Prabhakar Achar. (Illus.). 356p. 1990. text ed. 30.00 (*81-220-0127-0*, Pub. by Konark Pubs Pvt Ltd II) Advent Bks Div.

Textbook of Genitourinary Surgery. 2nd ed. Hugh Whitfield et al. LC 96-27776. 1664p. 1997. text ed. 595.00 (*0-632-03774-1*) Blackwell Sci.

Textbook of Geriatric Medicine. Ed. by P. De V. Meiring. (Illus.). 433p. (C). 1990. pap. text ed. 65.25 (*0-7021-2387-0*, Pub. by Juta & Co SA) Intl Spec Bk.

Textbook of Geriatric Medicine & Gerontology. 4th ed. Ed. by John C. Brocklehurst et al. (Illus.). 1096p. 1992. 198.00 (*0-443-04276-4*) Churchill.

Textbook of Gerontologic Nursing. Annette Lueckenotte. 864p. (C). (gr. 13). 1995. text ed. 55.00 (*0-8016-7414-X*) Mosby Yr Bk.

Textbook of Glaucoma. 3rd ed. M. Bruce Shields. (Illus.). 696p. 1991. 105.00 (*0-683-07695-7*) Williams & Wilkins.

***Textbook of Glaucoma.** 4th ed. Bruce M. Shields. LC 97-983. 1997. write for info. (*0-683-07693-0*) Williams & Wilkins.

Textbook of Gynaecology. D. Datta. (C). 1989. 160.00 (*0-685-36215-9*, Pub. by Current Dist II) St Mut.

Textbook of Gynaecology. A. K. Ghosh. (C). 1982. 45.00 (*0-89771-349-4*, Pub. by Current Dist II) St Mut.

Textbook of Gynaecology. Ajoy K. Ghosh. 552p. 1983. text ed. 69.00 (*0-317-38799-5*, Pub. by Current Dist II) St Mut.

***Textbook of Gynecologic Oncology.** Ed. by G. R. Blackledge et al. (Illus.). 512p. 1991. write for info. (*0-7020-1410-9*, Pub. by W B Saunders UK) Saunders.

Textbook of Gynecology. Ed. by Larry J. Copeland. (Illus.). 1216p. 1993. text ed. 115.00 (*0-7216-3401-X*) Saunders.

Textbook of Gynecology. 2nd ed. Copeland. text ed. write for info. (*0-7216-5526-2*) Saunders.

Textbook of Gynecology. Ed. by Russell R. De Alvarez. LC 76-10816. 562p. reprint ed. pap. 160.20 (*0-317-28609-9*, 2055418) Bks Demand.

Textbook of Head & Neck Anatomy. 2nd ed. James L. Hiatt. (Illus.). 384p. 1987. text ed. 40.00 (*0-683-03975-X*) Williams & Wilkins.

Textbook of Head Injury. Donald P. Becker et al. (Illus.). 576p. 1989. text ed. 210.00 (*0-7216-1614-3*) Saunders.

Textbook of Healthcare Ethics. E. H. Loewy. LC 96-20314. (Illus.). 299p. (C). 1996. 49.50 (*0-306-45240-5*, Plenum Pr) Plenum.

Textbook of Hematology. Shirlyn B. McKenzie. LC 87-3834. (Illus.). 507p. 1988. text ed. 48.50 (*0-8121-1096-X*) Williams & Wilkins.

Textbook of Hematology. 2nd ed. Shirlyn B. McKenzie. 733p. 1996. 56.95 (*0-683-18016-9*) Williams & Wilkins.

Textbook of Hemodialysis for Patient Care Personnel. Mark A. Newberry. (Illus.). 606p. 1989. pap. 54.95 (*0-398-06305-2*) C C Thomas.

Textbook of Hemodialysis for Patient Care Personnel. Mark A. Newberry. (Illus.). 606p. (C). 1989. text ed. 99.95 (*0-398-05516-5*) C C Thomas.

Textbook of Holistic Aromatherapy: The Use of Essential Oils Treatments. 2nd ed. W. E. Arnould-Taylor. 104p. 1992. pap. 39.00 (*0-7487-1551-7*, Pub. by Stanley Thornes UK) Trans-Atl Phila.

Textbook of Homosexuality & Mental Health. Ed. by Robert P. Cabaj & Terry S. Stein. 1022p. 1996. text ed. 89.95 (*0-88048-716-X*, 8716) Am Psychiatric.

Textbook of Horseshoeing for Horseshoers & Veterinarians. Anton Lungwitz. Tr. by John W. Adams. LC 66-28443. (Illus.). 216p. 1995. reprint ed. pap. 19.95 (*0-87071-026-5*) Oreg St U Pr.

Textbook of Human Biology. 3rd ed. J. K. Inglis. (Illus.). 437p. 1986. pap. text ed. 36.95 (*0-08-029806-0*, Prgamon Press) Buttrwrth-Heinemann.

Textbook of Human Genetics. 3rd ed. Max Levitan. (Illus.). 456p. 1988. 49.95 (*0-19-504935-7*) OUP.

Textbook of Human Resource Management. Ed. by George Thomason. 640p. (C). 1988. 90.00 (*0-85292-403-8*) St Mut.

Textbook of Hyperbaric Medicine. 2nd expanded rev. ed. K. K. Jain. (Illus.). 600p. 1996. 128.00 (*0-88937-127-X*) Hogrefe & Huber Pubs.

Textbook of Immunology. 2nd ed. Constantin A. Bona. 300p. 1996. text ed. 80.00 (*3-7186-0596-1*, Harwood Acad Pubs) Gordon & Breach.

Textbook of Immunology. 2nd ed. Constantin A. Bona. 300p. 1996. pap. text ed. 29.50 (*3-7186-0597-X*, Harwood Acad Pubs) Gordon & Breach.

Textbook of Immunology: International Edition. 5th ed. James T. Barrett. (Illus.). 496p. (C). (gr. 13). 1987. International Edition. 23.00 (*0-8016-0406-0*) Mosby Yr Bk.

Textbook of Immunopharmacology. 3rd ed. Ed. by M. Maureen Dale et al. LC 93-19411. (Illus.). 384p. 1994. pap. 20.00 (*0-632-03025-9*, Pub. by Blckwell Sci Pubns UK) Blackwell Sci.

Textbook of Indian Epigraphy. K. Satya Murty. (C). 1992. text ed. 14.00 (*81-85418-88-8*, Pub. by Low Price II) S Asia.

Textbook of Industrial Relations Management. George Thomason. 656p. (C). 1984. 105.00 (*0-85292-302-3*) St Mut.

Textbook of Insurance Broking. R. Clews. (C). 1987. 250.00 (*0-685-32686-1*, Pub. by Witherby & Co UK) St Mut.

***Textbook of Intensive Care.** Ed. by David R. Goldhill & P. Stuart Withington. (Illus.). 672p. 1997. text ed. 82.95 (*0-412-60130-3*, Chap & Hall NY) Chapman & Hall.

Textbook Of Internal Medicine. 3rd ed. 2496p. 1996. text ed. 125.00 (*0-397-51540-5*) Lppncott-Raven.

Textbook of Internal Medicine. 3rd ed. Ed. by William N. Kelley et al. LC 96-14758. 2,496p. 1996. text ed. 99.00 (*0-397-51283-X*) Lppncott-Raven.

Textbook of International Health. Paul F. Basch. (Illus.). 448p. 1989. 45.00 (*0-19-504897-0*) OUP.

Textbook of Interventional Cardiology. 2nd ed. Ed. by Eric J. Topol. (Illus.). 1384p. 1993. text ed. 210.00 (*0-7216-6722-8*) Saunders.

Textbook of Intravenous Anesthesia. Paul F. White. LC 96-15025. 1996. write for info. (*0-683-02125-7*) Williams & Wilkins.

***Textbook of Intravenous Anesthesia.** Paul F. White. LC 96-15025. 1996. write for info. (*0-683-09000-3*) Williams & Wilkins.

Textbook of Israeli Hebrew: With an Introduction to the Classical Language. 2nd ed. Haiim B. Rosen. LC 62-9116. 424p. 1976. pap. text ed. 27.50 (*0-226-72603-7*, P689) U Ch Pr.

Textbook of Labour & Industrial Laws. V. N. Pandey. 416p. 1980. 90.00 (*0-317-54680-5*) St Mut.

Textbook of Laparoscopy. 2nd ed. Jaroslav F. Hulka & Harry Reich. LC 92-48883. (Illus.). 432p. 1993. text ed. 169.00 (*0-7216-3643-8*) Saunders.

Textbook of Laparoscopy. 3rd ed. Jaroslav F. Hulka & Harry Reich. Ed. by William Schmitt. (Illus.). 624p. 1997. text ed. 150.00 (*0-7216-6805-4*) Saunders.

Textbook of Limnology. 4th rev. ed. Gerald A. Cole. (Illus.). 412p. (C). 1994. text ed. 37.95 (*0-88133-800-1*) Waveland Pr.

Textbook of Mammography. Ed. by Audrey K. Tucker. LC 92-49320. 288p. 1993. text ed. 150.00 (*0-443-04208-X*) Churchill.

Textbook of Materia Medica & Therapeutics of Rare Homeopathic Remedies. Oscar Hansen. 1991. lib. bdg. 75.00 (*0-87700-938-4*) Revisionist Pr.

Textbook of Materia Medica & Therapeutics of Rare Homeopathic Remedies. Oscar Hansen. 121p. 1993. reprint ed. spiral bd. 9.00 (*0-7873-0370-4*) Hlth Research.

Textbook of Materials Technology. Lawrence H. Van Vlack. LC 70-190614. (C). 1973. teacher ed. write for info. (*0-201-08067-2*) Addison-Wesley.

Textbook of Medical Ethics. E. H. Loewy. (Illus.). 270p. 1989. 39.50 (*0-306-43280-3*, Plenum Med Bk) Plenum.

Textbook of Medical Pathology. Paglia et al. 692p. 1979. 60.00 (*1-55664-193-1*) Mosby Yr Bk.

Textbook of Medical Physiology. 9th ed. Arthur C. Guyton & John E. Hall. LC 94-40510. (Illus.). 1072p. 1995. text ed. 59.95 (*0-7216-5944-6*) Saunders.

Textbook of Medical Record Linkage. Ed. by J. A. Baldwin et al. (Illus.). 364p. 1987. 79.00 (*0-19-261319-7*) OUP.

Textbook of Medical Treatment. 15th ed. Ed. by Ronald H. Girdwood & J. C. Petrie. LC 87-10282. (Illus.). 605p. (C). 1987. pap. text ed. 72.00 (*0-443-03211-4*) Churchill.

Textbook of Medicine. P. C. Das. (C). 1989. 150.00 (*0-89771-343-5*, Pub. by Current Dist II) St Mut.

Textbook of Medicine. Robert L. Souhami. (Illus.). 1198p. 1990. pap. text ed. 48.00 (*0-443-03434-6*) Churchill.

Textbook of Medicine. 2nd ed. Robert L. Souhami. LC 93-21174. 1994. pap. 48.00 (*0-443-04664-6*) Churchill.

Textbook of Medicine MCQs. Robert L. Souhami. LC 92-12584. 216p. 1992. pap. 19.95 (*0-443-04663-8*) Churchill.

Textbook of Microbiology. S. K. Sarkar. 1985. 50.00 (*0-317-39562-9*, Pub. by Current Dist II) St Mut.

Textbook of Microbiology. 2nd ed. R. Ananthanarayan & Jayaram Paniker. (Illus.). 618p. 1982. text ed. 25.00 (*0-86131-293-7*, Pub. by Orient Longman Ltd II) Apt Bks.

T

An Asterisk (*) at the beginning of an entry indicates that the title is appearing in BIP for the first time.

Textbook of Microscopic Anatomy. Kurt E. Johnson. 1988. write for info. (0-471-88247-X) Churchill.

Textbook of Microsurgery. Ed. by Giorgio Brunelli. 1054p. 1988. text ed. 146.00 (88-214-1825-1) Lppncott-Raven.

***Textbook of Modern Karate.** Teruyuki Okazaki. 1997. pap. text ed. 32.95 (4-7700-2141-0, Pub. by Kodansha Int JA) OUP.

Textbook of Modern Toxicology. Ernest Hodgson & Patricia E. Levi. 500p. 1987. text ed. 65.00 (0-8385-8915-4, A8915-9) Appleton & Lange.

Textbook of Modern Western Armenian. Kevork B. Bardakjian & Robert W. Thomson. LC 77-1774. 1985. pap. 15.00 (0-88206-504-1) Caravan Bks.

***Textbook of Molecular Medicine.** Larry J. Jameson & D. A. Ausiello. LC 97-14315. 1997. write for info. (0-86542-414-4) Blackwell Sci.

Textbook of Natural Medicine, 2 vols., Set, Vols. 1-2. rev. ed. Joseph E. Pizzorno et al. (Illus.). 1230p. (C). 1993. Set. ring bd. 295.00 (0-9618764-0-9, K03V2) John Bastyr.

Textbook of Natural Medicine, 2 vols., Vol. 1. rev. ed. Joseph E. Pizzorno et al. (Illus.). 750p. (C). 1993. write for info. (0-9618764-1-7) John Bastyr.

Textbook of Natural Medicine, 2 vols., Vol. 2. rev. ed. Joseph E. Pizzorno et al. (Illus.). 400p. (C). 1993. write for info. (0-9618764-2-5) John Bastyr.

***Textbook of Neonatal Medicine: A Chinese Perspective.** Ed. by Victor Y. Yu et al. (Illus.). 912p. (Orig.). 1996. pap. 115.00 (962-209-417-1, Pub. by Hong Kong Univ Pr HK) Coronet Bks.

Textbook of Neonatal Resuscitation. American Academy of Pediatrics Staff & American Heart Association Staff. 376p. 1994. spiral bd. 25.00 (0-910761-61-2) Am Acad Pediat.

Textbook of Neonatology. Dharmapuri Vidyasagar. 462p. (C). 1990. 185.00 (81-85017-38-7, Pub. by Interprint II) St Mut.

Textbook of Neonatology. 2nd ed. Ed. by N. R. Roberton. (Illus.). 1329p. 1992. text ed. 275.00 (0-443-04088-5) Churchill.

***Textbook of Nephrology.** Ed. by Jamison & Wilkinson. (Illus.). 896p. 1997. text ed. write for info. (0-412-60930-4, Chap & Hall NY) Chapman & Hall.

Textbook of Nephrology. 3rd ed. Ed. by Shaul G. Massry & Richard J. Glassock. LC 94-904. 2104p. 1994. 295.00 (0-683-05621-2) Williams & Wilkins.

Textbook of Neuroanatomy. Burt. 1993. pap. text ed. 41.00 (0-7216-2199-6) Saunders.

Textbook of Neuroanatomy: With an Atlas & Dissection Guide. William T. Mosenthal. (Illus.). 525p. (C). 1994. pap. text ed. 32.95 (1-85070-587-9) Prthnon Pub.

Textbook of Neuroanesthesia: With Neurosurgical & Neuroscience Perspectives. Maurice S. Albin. LC 96-24790. (Illus.). 1500p. 1996. text ed. 165.00 (0-07-000966-X) McGraw-Hill HPD.

Textbook of Neurology. Ed. by Robert K. Jackler & Derald E. Brackmann. LC 93-34012. (Illus.). 992p. (C). (gr. 13). 1994. text ed. 195.00 (0-8016-6383-0) Mosby Yr Bk.

Textbook of Neuropathology. 2nd ed. Richard Davis & David Robertson. (Illus.). 1176p. 1990. 180.00 (0-683-02344-6) Williams & Wilkins.

Textbook of Neuropathology. 3rd ed. Ed. by Richard L. Davis & David M. Robertson. LC 96-15265. 1409p. 1996. 195.00 (0-683-02355-1) Williams & Wilkins.

***Textbook of Nuclear Medicine.** Ed. by Michael A. Wilson. (Illus.). 380p. 1997. text ed. 70.00 (0-7817-0303-4) Lppncott-Raven.

Textbook of Nuclear Medicine, Vol. 1: Basic Science. 2nd ed. John Harbert & Antonio F. Goncalves Da Rocha. LC 83-25594. 540p. reprint ed. pap. 153.90 (0-7837-2714-3, 2043094) Bks Demand.

Textbook of Nuclear Medicine, Vol. 2: Clinical Applications. 2nd ed. Ed. by John Harbert & Antonio F. Goncalves Da Rocha. LC 83-25594. 740p. reprint ed. pap. 180.00 (0-7837-2984-7, 2057469) Bks Demand.

Textbook of Obstetrics. D. Datta. (C). 1987. 150.00 (0-685-36214-0, Pub. by Current Dist II) St Mut.

Textbook of Occlusion. George A. Zarb. (Illus.). 413p. 1988. text ed. 56.00 (0-86715-167-6, 1676) Quint Pub Co.

Textbook of Occupational Medicine Practice. J. Jeyaratnam & D. Koh. 500p. 1996. text ed. 84.00 (981-02-2322-6); pap. text ed. 42.00 (981-02-2415-X) World Scientific Pub.

***Textbook of Ocular Pharmacology.** Ed. by Thom J. Zimmerman et al. LC 97-1434. (Illus.). 600p. 1997. text ed. 175.00 (0-7817-0306-9) Lppncott-Raven.

Textbook of Operative Dentistry. 3rd ed. Lloyd Baum et al. LC 94-8371. (Illus.). 688p. 1994. text ed. 69.95 (0-7216-3484-2) Saunders.

Textbook of Operative Urology. Fray F. Marshall. Ed. by Sandra Valkhoff et al. LC 95-17717. 992p. 1996. text ed. 185.00 (0-7216-5510-6) Saunders.

Textbook of Ophthalmic Plastic & Reconstructive Surgery. Roger Kohn. LC 87-26042. 360p. reprint ed. pap. 102.60 (0-7837-2722-4, 2043102) Bks Demand.

***Textbook of Ophthalmology.** Ed. by Kenneth W. Wright. LC 96-24216. 932p. 1996. 169.00 (0-683-09292-8, RE46) Williams & Wilkins.

Textbook of Ophthalmology. 2nd ed. G. N. Seal. 512p. 1982. 80.00 (0-317-39563-7, Pub. by Current Dist II) St Mut.

Textbook of Oral Pathology. 4th ed. William G. Shafer et al. (Illus.). 944p. 1983. text ed. 69.00 (0-7216-8128-X) Saunders.

Textbook of Oral Surgery. Gordon W. Pedersen. (Illus.). 528p. 1988. pap. text ed. 55.00 (0-7216-2426-X) Saunders.

Textbook of Ore Dressing. 3rd rev. ed. Robert H. Richards et al. LC 40-10540. 624p. reprint ed. pap. 177.90 (0-317-29998-0, 2051848) Bks Demand.

Textbook of Orthodontics. 2nd ed. W. J. B. Houston et al. (Illus.). 325p. 1992. pap. text ed. 65.00 (0-7236-0986-1) Buttrwrth-Heinemann.

Textbook of Orthopaedic Medicine. 8th ed. James Cyriax. 1983. text ed. 85.00 (0-7216-0777-2) Saunders.

Textbook of Orthopaedic Medicine, Vol. 2. 11th ed. Cyriax. 1984. text ed. 60.00 (0-7216-0960-0) Saunders.

Textbook of Orthopaedic Medicine: Diagnosis of Soft Tissue Lesions, Vol. 1. 8th ed. James Cyriax. (Illus.). 1982. text ed. 85.00 (0-7020-0935-0, Bailliere-Tindall) Saunders.

Textbook of Orthopaedic Medicine: Treatment by Manipulation, Massage & Injection, Vol. 2. 11th ed. James Cyriax & Margaret Coldham. (Illus.). 288p. 1984. text ed. 60.00 (0-7020-1037-5, Bailliere-Tindall) Saunders.

***Textbook of Orthopaedics & Fractures.** Sean P. Hughes & Richard W. Porter. LC 97-639. 256p. 1997. pap. text ed. 24.50 (0-340-61381-5, Pub. by Ed Arnold UK) OUP.

Textbook of Osteopathy. American College of Mechano Therapy Staff. 96p. 1994. reprint ed. spiral bd. 9.00 (0-7873-1155-3) Hlth Research.

Textbook of Osteoporosis. John A. Kanis. LC 93-43053. (Illus.). 432p. 1996. 175.00 (0-632-03426-2, Pub. by Blckwell Sci Pubns UK) Blackwell Sci.

Textbook of Otolaryngology. Collin S. Karmody. LC 83-14868. 281p. 1983. reprint ed. pap. 80.10 (0-7837-2983-9, 2057471) Bks Demand.

***Textbook of Paediatric Anaesthetic Practice.** Edward Sumner & David Hatch. (Illus.). 616p. 1989. write for info. (0-7020-1336-6, Pub. by W B Saunders UK) Saunders.

Textbook of Paediatric Nutrition. 3rd ed. Ed. by Donald S. McLaren et al. (Illus.). 616p. 1991. text ed. 149.95 (0-443-04090-7) Churchill.

Textbook of Pain. 2nd fac. ed. Ed. by Patrick D. Wall & Ronald Melzack. LC 88-16154. (Illus.). 1077p. 1989. pap. 180.00 (0-7837-7556-3, 2047309) Bks Demand.

Textbook of Pain. 3rd ed. Ed. by Patrick D. Wall & Ronald Melzack. (Illus.). 1994. 225.00 (0-443-04757-X) Churchill.

Textbook of Pathology. N. C. Dey. (C). 1988. 200.00 (0-685-36195-0, Pub. by Current Dist II) St Mut.

Textbook of Pediatric Advanced Life Support. (Illus.). 148p. pap. text ed. write for info. (0-87493-635-7) Am Heart.

Textbook of Pediatric Basic Life Support. (Illus.). 120p. pap. text ed. write for info. (0-87493-620-9) Am Heart.

Textbook of Pediatric Critical Care. Peter R. Holbrook. (Illus.). 1256p. 1992. text ed. 169.00 (0-7216-2352-2) Saunders.

Textbook of Pediatric Dermatology. Ed. by Lawrence C. Parish et al. (Illus.). 880p. 1989. text ed. 243.00 (0-8089-1863-X, 793249, Grune) Saunders.

Textbook of Pediatric Emergency & Critical Care Procedures. Steven M. Selbst. LC 96-46924. 890p. (C). (gr. 13). 1996. text ed. 150.00 (0-8016-8102-2) Mosby Yr Bk.

Textbook of Pediatric Emergency Medicine. 3rd ed. Ed. by Gary R. Fleisher et al. LC 92-21068. (Illus.). 1844p. 1993. 169.00 (0-683-03255-0) Williams & Wilkins.

Textbook of Pediatric Infectious Diseases. 4th ed. Ralph D. Feigin & James D. Cherry. Ed. by Judy Fletcher. (Illus.). 3136p. 1997. text ed. write for info. (0-7216-6448-2) Saunders.

Textbook of Pediatric Infectious Diseases, 2 vols., Set. 3rd ed. Ralph D. Feigin & James D. Cherry. (Illus.). 2630p. 1992. text ed. 285.00 (0-7216-3656-X) Saunders.

Textbook of Pediatric Intensive Care. 2nd ed. Mark C. Rogers. (Illus.). 1792p. 1992. text ed. 195.00 (0-683-07319-2) Williams & Wilkins.

Textbook of Pediatric Intensive Care. 3rd ed. Ed. by Mark C. Rogers & David G. Nichols. LC 96-14624. 1710p. 1996. 179.00 (0-683-18034-7) Williams & Wilkins.

Textbook of Pediatric Neurology. Gerald S. Golden. LC 86-30432. (Topics in Pediatrics Ser.). 346p. 1987. 69.50 (0-306-42359-6, Plenum Med Bk) Plenum.

***Textbook of Pediatric Neuropsychiatry.** C. Edward Coffey & Roger A. Brumback. LC 97-15724. 1998. write for info. (0-88048-766-6) Am Psychiatric.

Textbook of Pediatric Nursing. 6th ed. Dorothy R. Marlow. (Illus.). 1358p. 1988. text ed. 71.95 (0-7216-6100-9) Saunders.

Textbook of Pediatric Nutrition. fac. ed. Ed. by Robert M. Suskind. LC 78-24628. (Illus.). 680p. pap. 180.00 (0-7837-7156-8, 2047141) Bks Demand.

Textbook of Pediatric Nutrition. 2nd ed. Robert M. Suskind & Leslie Lewinter-Suskind. 592p. 1992. text ed. 126.00 (0-88167-897-1) Lppncott-Raven.

Textbook of Pediatric Respiratory Medicine. Taussig & L. Landau. 1500p. (C). (gr. 13). 1998. text ed. 175.00 (0-8016-7406-9) Mosby Yr Bk.

Textbook of Pediatric Rheumatology. 2nd ed. James T. Cassidy & Ross E. Petty. LC 89-22236. (Illus.). 619p. reprint ed. pap. 176.50 (0-7837-6713-7, 2046340) Bks Demand.

Textbook of Pediatric Rheumatology. 3rd ed. James T. Cassidy & Ross E. Petty. LC 94-33337. (Illus.). 622p. 1994. text ed. 137.00 (0-7216-5244-1) Saunders.

Textbook of Pediatric Rheumatology. James T. Cassidy. LC 82-4951. (Illus.). 700p. reprint ed. pap. 180.00 (0-8357-6572-5, 2035953) Bks Demand.

Textbook of Pediatric Transport Medicine. McCloskey & Orr. 900p. (C). (gr. 13). 1995. text ed. 125.00 (0-8016-7817-X) Mosby Yr Bk.

Textbook of Pediatrics. Tom Lissauer & Graham Clayden. (Illus.). 330p. 1996. pap. 39.95 (0-7234-1657-5) Mosby Yr Bk.

Textbook of Penetrating Trauma. Ed. by Rao R. Ivatury & Gene C. Cayten. LC 94-29198. 1995. 185.00 (0-683-04338-2) Williams & Wilkins.

***Textbook of Performing Arts Medicine.** Ed. by Robert T. Sataloff. 448p. 1991. 92.50 (1-56593-743-0, 0638) Singular Publishing.

Textbook of Performing Arts Medicine. Robert T. Sataloff et al. 448p. 1990. text ed. 97.50 (0-88167-698-5, 2168) Lppncott-Raven.

Textbook of Peritoneal Dialysis. Ed. by Ram Gokal & Karl D. Nolph. LC 93-40474. 800p. (C). 1994. lib. bdg. 247.00 (0-7923-2661-X) Kluwer Ac.

Textbook of Phacoemulsification. Maloney & Grindle. LC 87-28607. (Illus.). 1988. 68.00 (0-918916-06-2) Lasenda.

Textbook of Pharmaceutical Analysis. 3rd ed. Kenneth A. Connors. LC 81-19742. 664p. 1982. text ed. 99.95 (0-471-09034-4) Wiley.

Textbook of Pharmaceutical Medicine. Ed. by R. E. Mann et al. (Illus.). 500p. 1993. text ed. 135.00 (1-85070-341-8) Prthnon Pub.

Textbook of Pharmacology. Smith. 1991. text ed. 58.50 (0-7216-2442-1) Saunders.

Textbook of Pharmacology & Nursing Care: Using the Nursing Process. Roger T. Malseed & Harrigan. LC 64-3737. (Illus.). 1749p. 1989. text ed. 52.50 (0-397-54432-4) Lppncott-Raven.

Textbook of Pharmacotherapy for Child & Adolescent Psychiatric Disorders. Ed. by David Rosenberg et al. LC 94-6401. 576p. 1994. text ed. 67.95 (0-87630-740-3) Brunner-Mazel.

Textbook of Physical Diagnosis: History & Examination. 2nd ed. Mark H. Swartz. LC 93-31155. 1994. text ed. 53.95 (0-7216-5530-0) Saunders.

***Textbook of Physical Diagnosis: History & Examination.** 3rd ed. Mark H. Swartz. Ed. by William Schmitt. (Illus.). 848p. 1997. text ed. write for info. (0-7216-7514-X) Saunders.

Textbook of Physics, 2 vols. Alok Chakrabarty. 1985. text ed. 82.00 (0-317-38802-9, Pub. by Current Dist II) St Mut.

Textbook of Physiology. 2nd ed. Ed. by Sarada Subrahmanyam & K. Madhaven Kutty. 818p. 1979. 30.00 (0-86125-415-5, Pub. by Orient Longman Ltd II) Apt Bks.

Textbook of Physiology, 2 vols., Set. 21th ed. Patton et al. 1989. text ed. 139.00 (0-7216-1990-8) Saunders.

Textbook of Plastic, Mexillofacial, & Reconstructive Surgery, 2 vols., Set. 2nd ed. Gregory S. Georgiade et al. (Illus.). 1520p. 1992. 250.00 (0-683-03454-5) Williams & Wilkins.

Textbook of Polymer Science. 3rd ed. Fred W. Billmeyer, Jr. LC 83-19870. 608p. 1984. text ed. 69.95 (0-471-03196-8) Wiley.

Textbook of Prematurity: Antecedents, Treatment, & Outcome. Ed. by Frank R. Witter & Louis G. Keith. LC 92-48895. (Illus.). 335p. 1993. 95.00 (0-316-94917-5) Little.

Textbook of Pressman Training Classroom Guide. 100p. spiral bd. 25.00 (0-318-23318-5) F Drazan.

Textbook of Psoriasis. Ed. by Paul D. Mier & Peter C. Van de Kerkhof. LC 85-16669. (Illus.). 292p. 1986. text ed. 156.00 (0-443-03210-6) Churchill.

***Textbook of Psychiatry.** Ed. by Linford Rees et al. (Illus.). 250p. 1996. pap. 27.50 (0-340-57195-0, Pub. by Ed Arnold UK) OUP.

Textbook of Psychiatry. Eugen Bleuler. LC 75-16685. (Classics in Psychiatry Ser.). (Illus.). 1977. reprint ed. 54.95 (0-405-07417-4) Ayer.

Textbook of Psychoanalysis. Ed. by Edward Nersessian & Richard G. Kopff, Jr. 768p. 1995. text ed. 110.00 (0-88048-507-8, 8507) Am Psychiatric.

Textbook of Psychology. 4th ed. Donald O. Hebb & D. C. Donderi. LC 86-23931. 396p. reprint ed. pap. 112.90 (0-7837-3163-9, 2042818) Bks Demand.

Textbook of Psychology. Edward B. Titchener. LC 80-14831. (History of Psychology Ser.). 1981. reprint ed. 75.00 (0-8201-1354-9) Schol Facsimiles.

Textbook of Psychology & the Study of Psychology see Outlines of Psychology

Textbook of Psychotherapy. Vimala Veeraraghavan. 1986. text ed. 25.00 (81-207-0030-9, Pub. by Sterling Pubs II) Apt Bks.

Textbook of Psychotherapy in Psychiatric Practice. Ed. by Jeremy Holmes. (Illus.). 580p. 1991. text ed. 72.00 (0-443-04197-0) Churchill.

Textbook of Pulmonary Diseases. 3rd ed. Ed. by Gerald L. Baum. 1983. 99.00 (0-316-08386-0) Little.

***Textbook of Pulmonary Diseases, 2 vols.** 6th ed. Ed. by Gerald L. Baum & Emanuel Wolinsky. (Illus.). 2040p. 1997. text ed. write for info. (0-316-08434-4) Lppncott-Raven.

Textbook of Pulmonary Diseases, 2 vols., Set. 5th ed. Ed. by Gerald L. Baum & Emanuel Wolinsky. (Illus.). 1760p. 1993. text ed. 250.00 (0-316-08410-7) Lppncott-Raven.

Textbook of Radiographic Positioning & Related Anatomy. Bontrager. 768p. (gr. 13). 1996. text ed. 110.00 (0-8151-0947-4) Mosby Yr Bk.

Textbook of Radiology & Imaging, 2 vols. 5th ed. Ed. by David Sutton. (Illus.). 1768p. 1993. text ed. 325.00 (0-443-04352-3) Churchill.

Textbook of Radiopharmacy: Theory & Practice. 2nd ed. Ed. by Charles B. Sampson. LC 94-7006. (Nuclear Medicine Ser.: Vol. 3). 1994. 150.00 (2-88124-951-5); pap. text ed. 75.00 (2-88124-973-6) Gordon & Breach.

Textbook of Receptor Pharmacology. Ed. by John C. Foreman & Torben Johansen. LC 96-14485. 320p. 1996. 69.95 (0-8493-9227-6) CRC Pr.

Textbook of Relaxation Skills: Training for Stress Relief & Pain Control. Carol Horrigan. 256p. 1996. pap. write for info. (0-7506-2439-6) Buttrwrth-Heinemann.

Textbook of Renal Disease. 2nd ed. Ed. by Judith A. Whitworth & J. R. Lawrence. (Illus.). 505p. 1994. 85.00 (0-443-04786-3) Churchill.

Textbook of Reproductive Medicine. Bruce R. Carr & Richard E. Blackwell. 645p. 1993. text ed. 90.00 (0-8385-8914-6, A8914-2) Appleton & Lange.

Textbook of Respiratory Medicine, 2 vols., Set. 2nd ed. Ed. by John F. Murray & Jay A. Nadel. LC 92-48497. (Illus.). 2816p. 1994. text ed. 289.00 (0-7216-3890-2) Saunders.

Textbook of Rheumatology. 5th ed. William N. Kelley et al. Ed. by Richard Zorab. (Illus.). 1792p. 1996. text ed. 235.00 (0-7216-5692-7) Saunders.

Textbook of Roman Law. J. A. Thomas. 562p. 1982. 111.75 (0-7204-0513-0, North Holland) Elsevier.

Textbook of Roman Law. J. A. Thomas. 562p. 1976. pap. 32.00 (0-7021-0517-1, Pub. by Juta SA) Gaunt.

Textbook of Science for the Health Professions. Barry Hinwood. LC 92-49020. 512p. 1993. pap. 57.50 (1-56593-027-4, 0271) Singular Publishing.

***Textbook of Secretory Diarrhea.** Ed. by Emanuel Lebenthal & Michael E. Duffey. LC 90-8463. 456p. 1990. reprint ed. pap. 130.00 (0-608-03426-6, 2064125) Bks Demand.

Textbook of Sedimentry Petrology. V. K. Verma. 134p. (C). 1981. text ed. 75.00 (0-89771-673-6, Pub. by Intl Bk Distr II) St Mut.

***Textbook of Silviculture.** A. P. Dwivedi. 523p. 1993. pap. 150.00 (81-7089-198-1, Pub. by Intl Bk Distr II) St Mut.

***Textbook of Small Animal Medicine.** Ed. by John Dunn. (Illus.). 1100p. 1997. write for info. (0-7020-1582-2, Pub. by W B Saunders UK) Saunders.

Textbook of Small Animal Surgery, 2 vols., Set. 2nd ed. Ed. by Douglas H. Slatter. LC 92-21883. (Illus.). 2496p. 1993. text ed. 195.00 (0-7216-8330-4) Saunders.

Textbook of Social Dancing. Agnes Marsh. (Ballroom Dance Ser.). 1986. lib. bdg. 79.95 (0-8490-3314-4) Gordon Pr.

Textbook of Social Dancing. Agnes Marsh. (Ballroom Dance Ser.). 1985. lib. bdg. 75.95 (0-87700-817-5) Revisionist Pr.

Textbook of Soil Chemical Analysis. P. R. Hesse. (C). 1972. 85.00 (0-8206-0242-6) Chem Pub.

Textbook of Spinal Disorders. Stephen I. Esses. (Illus.). 480p. 1994. text ed. 82.50 (0-397-51346-1) Lppncott-Raven.

Textbook of Spinal Surgery, 2 vols., Set. 2nd ed. Ed. by Keith H. Bridwell et al. LC 96-7784. 2,632p. 1996. text ed. 375.00 (0-397-51384-4) Lppncott-Raven.

Textbook of Spinal Surgery, Vol. 1. 2nd ed. Ed. by Keith H. Bridwell et al. LC 96-7784. 8p. 1996. write for info. (0-395-75179-9) Lppncott-Raven.

Textbook of Spinal Surgery, Vol. 2. 2nd ed. Ed. by Keith H. Bridwell et al. LC 96-7784. 1996. write for info. (0-397-51800-5) Lppncott-Raven.

Textbook of Stagecraft. Susan Richmond. 140p. (Orig.). 1994. pap. 6.00 (0-88734-908-0) Empire Pub Srvs.

Textbook of Surgery: The Biological Basis of Modern Surgical Practice. 14th ed. Sabeston. (Illus.). 2272p. 1991. write for info. (0-7216-3490-7) Saunders.

Textbook of Surgery: The Biological Basis of Modern Surgical Practice. 15th ed. David C. Sabiston. Ed. by Lisette Bralow. (Illus.). 2304p. 1996. text ed. 110.00 (0-7216-5887-3) Saunders.

Textbook of Surgery Pocket Companion. 2nd ed. David C. Sabiston & H. Kim Lyerly. Ed. by Lisette Bralow. 768p. 1996. pap. text ed. 29.95 (0-7216-8670-2) Saunders.

Textbook of Surgical Technology. Keegan. Date not set. text ed. write for info. (0-7216-8657-5) HarBrace.

Textbook of Techniques & Strategies in Personnel Management. Ed. by David Guest & Terence Kenny. 352p. (C). 1983. 90.00 (0-85292-269-8) St Mut.

Textbook of Temporomandibular Disorders. Joel A. Kaplan. (Illus.). 848p. 1991. text ed. 205.00 (0-7216-5286-7) Saunders.

Textbook of the English Language, 2. 2nd ed. N. A. Bonk. 639p. 1993. 95.00 (0-7859-9100-X) Fr & Eur.

Textbook of the Origin & History of the Colored People. James Pennington. LC 77-92437. 1841. 29.00 (0-403-00169-2) Scholarly.

***Textbook of Theosophy.** Charles W. Leadbeater. 1912. 12.95 (81-7059-246-1) Theos Pub Hse.

Textbook of Therapeutics: Drug & Disease Management. 6th ed. Eric T. Herfindal & Dick R. Gourley. LC 96-5665. 1958p. 1996. 105.00 (0-683-03969-5) Williams & Wilkins.

Textbook of Thoracic Surgery. Peter Goldstraw. (Illus.). 936p. 1995. text ed. 250.00 (0-7506-1384-X) Buttrwrth-Heinemann.

Textbook of Total Quality in Healthcare. A. F. Al-Assaf & June Schmele. LC 93-31083. (Illus.). 310p. 1993. 47.95 (0-9634030-4-4) St Lucie Pr.

Textbook of Toxicology: Principles & Applications. Ed. by John De Vries et al. 1328p. 1996. 125.00 (0-8493-9232-2, 9232) CRC Pr.

Textbook of Transpersonal Psychiatry & Psychology. Ed. by Bruce Scotton et al. 443p. 1996. text ed. 55.00 (0-465-09530-5) Basic.

Textbook of Trauma Anesthesia & Critical Care. Christopher M. Grande et al. LC 92-49406. 1992. write for info. (0-8016-2153-4) Mosby Yr Bk.

Textbook of Traumatic Injuries of the Teeth. 3rd ed. Andreasen. 500p. 1993. 135.00 (87-16-10637-7) Mosby Yr Bk.

***Textbook of Travel Medicine & Health.** Herbert L. Dupont. 1996. 125.00 (1-55009-037-2, Pub. by B C Decker CN) Blackwell Sci.

Textbook of Tuberculosis. Ed. by K. N. Rao. 607p. 1981. 24.95 (0-318-36372-0) Asia Bk Corp.

Textbook of Uncommon Cancer. Raghav et al. Ed. by C. J. Williams et al. LC 87-23141. 900p. 1988. text ed. 315.00 (0-471-90968-8) Wiley.

Textbook of Urdu. J. Willatt. 188p. (ENG & URD.). 1994. 17.95 (0-7859-9824-1) Fr & Eur.

An Asterisk (*) at the beginning of an entry indicates that the title is appearing in BIP for the first time.

Textbook of Urdu: In the Roman Script. J. Willatt. (C). 1994. text ed. 18.00 (*81-206-0956-5*, Pub. by Asian Educ Servs II) S Asia.

Textbook of Uroradiology. N. Reed Dunnick et al. (Illus.). 505p. 1990. 125.00 (*0-683-02696-8*) Williams & Wilkins.

Textbook of Uroradiology. 2nd ed. N. Reed Dunnick et al. LC 96-14722. 520p. 1996. 125.00 (*0-683-02697-6*) Williams & Wilkins.

Textbook of Vascular Medicine. John Tooke & Gordon D. Lowe. 674p. 1996. 150.00 (*0-340-55791-5*, Pub. by Ed Arnold UK) OUP.

Textbook of Vertebrate Zoology. 14th ed. S. N. Prasad & Vasantika Kashyap. (C). 1989. pap. 17.50 (*0-85226-928-5*) S Asia.

Textbook of Veterinary Anatomy. 2nd ed. K. M. Dyce et al. (Illus.). 992p. 1995. text ed. 86.00 (*0-7216-4961-0*) Saunders.

Textbook of Veterinary Diagnostic Radiology. 2nd ed. Ed. by Donald E. Thrall. LC 93-10675. (Illus.). 608p. 1993. text ed. 75.00 (*0-7216-3143-6*) Saunders.

Textbook of Veterinary Diagnostic Radiology. 3rd ed. Charles A. Thrall. Ed. by Ray Kersey. LC 97-6593. (Illus.). 656p. 1997. text ed. write for info. (*0-7216-5092-9*) Saunders.

Textbook of Veterinary Histology. 4th ed. Horst-Dieter Dellmann. (Illus.). 420p. 1992. text ed. 55.00 (*0-8121-1553-8*) Williams & Wilkins.

Textbook of Veterinary Internal Medicine, 2 vols. 4th ed. Stephen J. Ettinger & Edward C. Feldman. LC 93-31785. (Illus.). 2656p. 1994. text ed. 194.00 (*0-7216-6795-3*) Saunders.

Textbook of Veterinary Internal Medicine, 2 vols., Vol. 1. 4th ed. Stephen J. Ettinger & Edward C. Feldman. LC 93-31785. (Illus.). 2656p. 1994. text ed. write for info. (*0-7216-6796-1*) Saunders.

Textbook of Veterinary Internal Medicine, 2 vols., Vol. 2. 4th ed. Stephen J. Ettinger & Edward C. Feldman. LC 93-31785. (Illus.). 2656p. 1994. text ed. write for info. (*0-7216-6797-X*) Saunders.

Textbook of Veterinary Internal Medicine: Diseases of the Dog & Cat, 2 vols., 1. 3rd ed. Ettinger. 2464p. 1989. text ed. write for info. (*0-7216-1942-8*) Saunders.

Textbook of Veterinary Internal Medicine: Diseases of the Dog & Cat, 2 vols., 2. 3rd ed. Ettinger. 2464p. 1989. text ed. write for info. (*0-7216-1943-6*) Saunders.

Textbook of Veterinary Ophthalmology. 3rd ed. Kirk N. Gelatt. (Illus.). 765p. 1991. text ed. 129.00 (*0-8121-1365-9*) Williams & Wilkins.

Textbook of Veterinary Physiology. Cunninghan. (Illus.). 656p. 1991. text ed. 84.00 (*0-7216-2306-9*) Saunders.

Textbook of Veterinary Physiology. 2nd ed. James G. Cunningham. Ed. by Ray Kersey. LC 96-29043. 688p. 1997. text ed. 82.50 (*0-7216-6424-5*) Saunders.

Textbook of Veterinary Physiology. Ed. by James E. Breazile. LC 71-135683. (Illus.). 584p. reprint ed. pap. 166.50 (*0-685-44437-6*, 2056677) Bks Demand.

***Textbook of Videoscopic Surgery.** Ed. by Douglas Olsen et al. 1996. text ed. 220.00 (*3-7186-5495-4*, Harwood Acad Pubs) Gordon & Breach.

***Textbook of Women's Health.** Lila Wallis et al. (Illus.). 1000p. 1997. text ed. write for info. (*0-316-91991-8*) Lppncott-Raven.

Textbook of Wood Technology, Vol. 1. 4th ed. A. J. Panshin & Carl De Zeeuw. 1980. text ed. write for info. (*0-07-048441-4*) McGraw.

Textbook of Work Physiology. 3rd ed. Per-Olof Astrand & Kaare Rodahl. 768p. (C). 1986. text ed. write for info. (*0-07-002416-2*) McGraw.

Textbook of World Health: A Practical Guide to Global Healthcare. Russell F. Whaley. 256p. 1995. 39.00 (*1-85070-473-2*) Prthnon Pub.

Textbook of Yoga. Yogeswar. (Illus.). 574p. 1982. 34.95 (*0-940500-37-X*) Asia Bk Corp.

Textbook of Yoga Psychology. Rammurti S. Mishra. 464p. 1987. pap. 10.95 (*0-517-56434-3*, Harmony) Crown Pub Group.

Textbook of Zoology, 2 vols. D. Mukerji. 1985. text ed. 95.00 (*0-317-38806-1*, Pub. by Current Dist II) St Mut.

Textbook on "A" Level Law. Patricia Hirst. 476p. 1996. pap. 34.00 (*1-85431-506-4*, Pub. by Blackstone Pr UK) Gaunt.

Textbook on Administrative Law. Peter Leyland et al. 398p. 1994. pap. 38.00 (*1-85431-318-5*, Pub. by Blackstone Pr UK) Gaunt.

Textbook on Alcoholism & Drug Abuse in the Soviet Union. Edward A. Babayan & M. W. Gonopolsky. Tr. by V. Bobrov from RUS. LC 85-18086. (Illus.). vii, 353p. 1985. 40.00 (*0-8236-6470-8*) Intl Univs Pr.

Textbook on Chiropractic & Pregnancy. Joan M. Fallon. Ed. by Molly Rangnath. 222p. (C). 1994. text ed. 56.00 (*1-886190-00-3*) Intl Chiropractors Assn.

Textbook on Civil Liberties. Richard Stone. 398p. 1994. pap. 40.00 (*1-85431-278-2*, Pub. by Blackstone Pr UK) Gaunt.

Textbook on Commercial Law. Iwan Davies. xli, 541p. 1992. pap. 48.00 (*1-85431-195-6*, Pub. by Blackstone Pr UK) Gaunt.

Textbook on Constitutional & Administrative Law. Brian Thompson. 442p. 1993. pap. 38.00 (*1-85431-196-4*, Pub. by Blackstone Pr UK) Gaunt.

Textbook on Constitutional & Administrative Law. 2nd ed. Brian Thompson. 516p. 1995. pap. 34.00 (*1-85431-445-9*, Pub. by Blackstone Pr UK) Gaunt.

Textbook on Consumer Law. David W. Oughton & John Lowry. 1996. 18.00 (*1-85431-538-2*, Pub. by Blackstone Pr UK) Gaunt.

Textbook on Contract. T. A. Downes. 360p. (C). 1991. 40.00 (*1-85431-150-6*, Pub. by Blackstone Pr UK) Gaunt.

Textbook on Contract. T. A. Downes. 360p. (C). 1987. 160.00 (*1-85185-076-7*, Pub. by Blackstone Pr UK) St Mut.

Textbook on Contract. 4th ed. T. Antony Downes. 464p. 1995. pap. 32.00 (*1-85431-453-X*, Pub. by Blackstone Pr UK) Gaunt.

Textbook on Contracts. 3rd ed. T. Antony Downs. 405p. 1993. pap. 36.00 (*1-85431-285-5*, Pub. by Blackstone Pr UK) Gaunt.

Textbook on Criminal Law. 2nd ed. Michael J. Allen. 396p. 1993. pap. 38.00 (*0-685-73074-3*, Pub. by Blackstone Pr UK) Gaunt.

Textbook on Criminal Law. 3rd ed. Michael J. Allen. 468p. 1993. 48.00 (*1-85431-447-5*, Pub. by Blackstone Pr UK) Gaunt.

Textbook on Criminology. K. Williams. (C). 1991. 125.00 (*1-85431-012-7*) St Mut.

Textbook on Criminology. 2nd ed. Katherine S. Williams. 500p. 1994. 17.95 (*1-85431-336-3*, Pub. by Blackstone Pr UK) Gaunt.

Textbook on EC Law. 4th ed. Josephine Steiner. 486p. 1994. pap. 40.00 (*1-85431-335-5*, Pub. by Blackstone Pr UK) Gaunt.

***Textbook on EC Law.** 5th ed. Josephine Steiner & Lorna Woods. 492p. 1996. pap. 40.00 (*1-85431-553-6*, Pub. by Blackstone Pr UK) Gaunt.

Textbook on Foreign Exchange. 2nd ed. Einzig. 1969. 25.95 (*0-333-07649-4*, Pub. by Macm UK) St Martin.

Textbook on Forest Management. M. R. Jerram. 156p. 1980. 75.00 (*0-685-54020-0*, Pub. by Intl Bk Distr II) St Mut.

Textbook on Forest Management. M. R. Jerram. (C). 1980. text ed. 75.00 (*0-89771-551-9*, Pub. by Intl Bk Distr II) St Mut.

Textbook on Gerontological Nursing. Wade. 1996. pap. text ed. 32.50 (*0-7020-1603-9*) HarBrace.

Textbook on Heat Transfer. 3rd rev. ed. S. O. Sukhatme. (Illus.). x, 265p. (C). 1988. pap. text ed. 15.95 (*0-86131-073-X*, Pub. by Orient Longman Ltd II) Apt Bks.

Textbook on International Law. 2nd ed. Martin Dixon. 332p. 1993. pap. 36.00 (*1-85431-257-X*, Pub. by Blackstone Pr UK) Gaunt.

Textbook on International Law. 3rd ed. Martin Dixon. 340p. 1996. pap. 38.00 (*1-85431-444-0*, Pub. by Blackstone Pr UK) Gaunt.

Textbook on Jurisprudence. Hilaire McCoubrey & Nigel D. White. 270p. 1993. pap. 36.00 (*1-85431-265-0*, Pub. by Blackstone Pr UK) Gaunt.

Textbook on Jurisprudence. 2nd ed. Hilaire McCoubrey & Nigel D. White. 299p. 1996. pap. 36.00 (*1-85431-582-X*, Pub. by Blackstone Pr UK) Gaunt.

Textbook on Labour Law. 3rd ed. John Bowers & Simon Honeyball. 476p. 1993. pap. 40.00 (*1-85431-302-9*, Pub. by Blackstone Pr UK) Gaunt.

Textbook on Muslim Personal Law. David Pearl. 304p. 1987. pap. 39.95 (*0-7099-4089-0*, Pub. by Croom Helm UK) Routledge Chapman & Hall.

Textbook on Rhetoric. Brainerd Kellogg. LC 90-33879. 1990. 50.00 (*0-8201-1442-1*) Schol Facsimiles.

Textbook on Roman Law. Andrew Borkowski. 382p. 1994. pap. text ed. 40.00 (*1-85431-313-4*) Gaunt.

Textbook on Sedimentary Petrology. V. K. Verma. 134p. (C). 1981. 75.00 (*0-685-21833-3*, Pub. by Intl Bk Distr II) St Mut.

Textbook on Spherical Astronomy. 6th ed. W. M. Smart. LC 76-50643. (Illus.). 446p. 1977. pap. text ed. 30.95 (*0-521-29180-1*) Cambridge U Pr.

Textbook on Torts. Michael A. Jones. 442p. (C). 1989. 160.00 (*1-85431-047-X*, Pub. by Blackstone Pr UK) St Mut.

Textbook on Torts. 4th ed. Michael A. Jones. 520p. 1993. 46.00 (*1-85431-268-5*, Pub. by Blackstone Pr UK) Gaunt.

Textbook on Torts. 5th ed. Michael A. Jones. 567p. 1996. pap. 38.00 (*1-85431-551-X*, Pub. by Blackstone Pr UK) Gaunt.

Textbook on Trusts. 3rd ed. Paul Todd. 406p. 1996. pap. 40.00 (*1-85431-552-8*, Pub. by Blackstone Pr UK) Gaunt.

***Textbook on Veterinary Internal Medicine.** 5th ed. Ettinger. Date not set. text ed. write for info. (*0-7216-7256-6*) Saunders.

Textbook Physiology, Vol. 1. 21th ed. Patton. 1989. text ed. 87.00 (*0-7216-2523-1*) HarBrace.

Textbook Physiology, Vol. 2. 21th ed. Patton. 1989. text ed. 75.00 (*0-7216-2524-X*) HarBrace.

Textbooks & the Students Who Can't Read Them: A Guide for the Teaching of Content. Jean Ciborowski. 1993. pap. text ed. 21.95 (*0-914797-57-3*) Brookline Bks.

Textbooks in American Society: Politics, Policy, & Pedagogy. Ed. by Philip G. Altbach et al. LC 90-43397. (SUNY Series, Frontiers in Education). 261p. (C). 1991. pap. text ed. 24.95 (*0-7914-0670-9*) State U NY Pr.

Textbooks in American Society: Politics, Policy, & Pedagogy. Ed. by Philip G. Altbach et al. LC 90-43397. (SUNY Series, Frontiers in Education). 261p. (C). 1991. text ed. 74.50 (*0-7914-0669-5*) State U NY Pr.

Textbooks in School & Society: An Annotated Bibliography & Guide to Research. Ed. by Arthur Woodward et al. LC 87-35302. (Bibliographies in Contemporary Education Ser.). 182p. 1988. text ed. 36.00 (*0-8240-8390-3*) Garland.

Textbooks in the Third World: Policy, Content & Context. Philip G. Altbach & Gail P. Kelly. LC 88-21825. 284p. 1988. text ed. 49.00 (*0-8240-4294-8*) Garland.

***Text/Countertext: Postmodern Paranoia in Samuel Beckett, Doris Lessing & Philip Roth.** Marie F. Danziger. (Studies in Literary Criticism & Theory). 128p. (C). 1996. text ed. 34.95 (*0-8204-2871-X*) P Lang Pubng.

Texte du Roman. Julia Kristeva. (Approaches to Semiotics Ser.: No. 6). 1976. text ed. 45.40 (*90-279-3304-9*) Mouton.

Texte et Ideologie: Images de la Noblesse et de la Bourgeoisies dans le Roman Francais, dex annees 1750 a 1830. Norbert Sclippa. (Reading Plus Ser.: Vol. 4). 299p. (C). 1988. text ed. 52.90 (*0-8204-0468-3*) P Lang Pubng.

Texte Horen, Lesen und Verstehen. Gerd Solmecke. 112p. (GER.). 1993. 20.00 (*3-468-49447-5*) Langenscheidt.

Texte und Kontexte: Intermediate German. Monica D. Clyde et al. (GER.). 1989. write for info. (*0-07-557397-0*) McGraw.

Texte und Kontexte: Intermediate German. Monica D. Clyde et al. (GER.). 1989. text ed. write for info. (*0-07-557842-5*) McGraw.

Texte und Kontexte: Intermediate German. Monica D. Clyde et al. (GER.). 1989. lab manual ed., wbk. ed., pap. text ed. write for info. (*0-07-557723-2*) McGraw.

Texte Visualise: Le Calligramme de l'Epoque Alexandrine a l'Epoque Cubiste. Nicole M. Mosher. (American University Studies: Romance Languages & Literature: Ser. II, Vol. 119). 188p. (C). 1989. text ed. 42.95 (*0-8204-0924-3*) P Lang Pubng.

TexTerm Cooling Towers. A. Junker & P. Schmitt. (Illus.). 290p. (Orig.). (ENG & GER.). 1991. pap. 45.00 (*3-527-28215-7*, VCH) Wiley.

***TexTerm Four Wheel Drive: English/German-German/English.** M. Donnevert. (TexTerm Ser.). (Illus.). xii, 131p. (ENG & GER.). 1989. pap. 30.00 (*3-527-27869-9*, VCH) Wiley.

TexTerm Polarography & Voltammetry. Ed. by I. Eisenhardt & P. A. Schmitt. (Illus.). 130p. (ENG & GER.). 1990. pap. 45.00 (*3-527-28214-9*, VCH) Wiley.

Textermination. Christine Brooke-Rose. LC 92-17328. 192p. 1992. 21.95 (*0-8112-1230-0*); pap. 10.95 (*0-8112-1216-5*, NDP756) New Directions.

Textes. Aime Cesaire. Ed. by R. Mercier et al. (Classiques du Monde, Litterature Africaine Ser.). pap. 8.95 (*0-685-35627-2*) Fr & Eur.

Textes. Bernard B. Dadie. Ed. by R. Mercier et al. (Classiques du Monde, Litterature Africaine Ser.). pap. 8.95 (*0-685-35632-9*) Fr & Eur.

Textes & Chansons. Boris Vian. 6.95 (*0-686-55705-0*) Fr & Eur.

Textes & Litterature. Incl. Moyen Age. 7.95 (*0-685-35942-5*); XVIe Siecle. L. Michard. 8.95 (*0-685-35943-3*); XVIIe Siecle. L. Michard. 9.50 (*0-685-35944-1*); XVIIIe Siecle. L. Michard. 9.50 (*0-685-35945-X*); XIXe Siecle. L. Michard. 11.50 (*0-685-35946-8*); XXe Siecle. L. Michard. 15.50 (*0-685-35947-6*); write for info. (*0-318-52270-5*) Fr & Eur.

Textes Choisis, 3 vols., Set. Pierre De Coubertin. xxxviii, 2252p. write for info. (*3-296-18000-1*) G Olms Pubs.

Textes Culinaires Mesopotamien: Mesopotamian Culinary Texts. Jean Bottero. LC 94-23705. (Mesopotamian Civilizations Ser.: Vol. 6). (Illus.). x, 252p. 1995. text ed. 45.00 (*0-931464-92-7*) Eisenbrauns.

Textes d'Auteurs Grecs & Latines Relatifs a l'Extreme Orient. Georges Coedes. xxxii, 184p. 1979. reprint ed. 30.00 (*0-89005-289-1*) Ares.

Textes d'Auteurs Grecs et Latins Relatifs a l'Extreme Orient. George Coedes. xxxi, 187p. 1977. reprint ed. 50.00 (*3-487-06322-0*) G Olms Pubs.

Textes d'Auteurs Grecs et Romains Relatifs au Judaisme. Theodore Reinach. xx, 376p. 1983. reprint ed. write for info. (*3-487-00346-5*) G Olms Pubs.

Textes Dramatiques Inedits par J. Richer. Alfred De Musset. 213p. (FRE.). 1953. pap. 18.95 (*0-7859-5490-2*) Fr & Eur.

Textes Grecs & Latines Relatifs a l'Histoire de la Peinture Ancienne. A. Reinach. 429p. 1921. 40.00 (*0-89005-390-1*) Ares.

Textes Oublies. Jules Verne. 8.95 (*0-686-55954-1*) Fr & Eur.

Textes Politiques. Denis Diderot. 214p. (FRE.). 1971. 29.95 (*0-8288-7428-X*) Fr & Eur.

Textes Politiques, Sociaux & Philosophiques Choisis. Romain Rolland. Ed. by Jean Albertini. (FRE.). 1973. pap. 13.95 (*0-7859-5466-X*) Fr & Eur.

Textes pour une Psycholinguistique. Jacques A. Mehler. (Textes de Sciences Sociales Ser.: No. 10). 1974. pap. 41.55 (*90-279-7285-0*) Mouton.

Textes sous une Occupation (1940-1944) Henry De Montherlant. pap. 9.95 (*0-685-36989-7*) Fr & Eur.

Textgrammatik der Deutsch Sprache. Harald Weinrich. 1111p. (GER.). 1992. 82.95 (*3-411-05261-9*) Langenscheidt.

Textil-Fachwoerterbuch. 2nd ed. R. Huenlich. 144p. (GER.). 1970. pap. 24.95 (*0-8288-6556-6*, M-7665) Fr & Eur.

Textile. Boy Scouts of America. 64p. (J). (gr. 6-12). 1972. pap. 2.40 (*0-8395-3344-6*, 33344) BSA.

Textile & Paper Chemistry & Technology, No. 49. Ed. by Jett C. Arthur, Jr. LC 77-7938. 1977. 30.95 (*0-8412-0377-6*) Am Chemical.

Textile Art of Japan. Sunny Yang & Rochelle M. Narasin. 160p. 1990. 34.00 (*0-87040-773-2*) Japan Pubns USA.

Textile Art of Okinawa: Collection of Okinawa Prefectural Museum. Reiko M. Brandon & Barbara B. Stephan. (Illus.). 60p. (C). 1990. pap. 14.50 (*0-937426-12-1*) Honolu Arts.

Textile Art of Peru. James Reid & Raul Apesteguia. Ed. by Jose A. De Lavalle & Jose A. Gonzalez. Tr. by Isabel Hare. (Illus.). 373p. (Orig.). 1993. 65.00 (*0-9647468-0-8*) Industrial Textil.

Textile Artistry. Ed. by Valerie Campbell-Harding. 1996. pap. 17.95 (*0-8019-8780-6*) Chilton.

Textile Arts Index, 1950-1987. Sadye T. Wilson & Ruth D. Jackson. LC 88-72005. 1006p. 1988. 28.00 (*0-9616526-2-4*) Tunstede.

Textile Arts of India. Kokyo Hatanaka. LC 96-14931. (Illus.). 344p. 1996. 60.00 (*0-8118-1084-4*) Chronicle Bks.

Textile Chemistry, Vols. 2 & 3. Raymond H. Peters. Incl. Impurities in Fibres. 374p. 1967. 100.00 (*0-444-40452-X*); Physical Chemistry of Dyeing Vol. 3. 890p. 1975. 205.25 (*0-444-41120-8*); write for info. (*0-318-51826-0*) Elsevier.

***Textile Chemistry: Theory, Technology & Equipment.** Ed. by A. P. Moryganov. 305p. (C). 1997. lib. bdg. 79.00 (*1-56072-439-0*) Nova Sci Pubs.

***Textile Coating & Laminating, Fifth International Conference: November 13-14, 1995, Williamsburg, VA, Vol. 5.** 157p. 1995. ring bd. 89.95 (*1-56676-402-5*, 764025) Technomic.

Textile Coating & Laminating, First International Conference: November 6-7, 1991, Charlotte NC, Vol. 1. 204p. 1991. ring bd. 29.95 (*0-87762-916-1*, 629161) Technomic.

Textile Coating & Laminating, Fourth International Conference: November 8-9, 1994, Zurich, Vol. 4. 226p. 1994. ring bd. 89.95 (*1-56676-248-0*, 762480) Technomic.

Textile Coating & Laminating, Second International Conference: November 9-10, 1992, Zurich, Vol. 2. 251p. 1992. ring bd. 49.95 (*1-56676-022-4*, 760224) Technomic.

Textile Coating & Laminating, Third International Conference: November 3-4, 1993, Atlanta, Vol. 3. 305p. 1993. ring bd. 89.95 (*1-56676-130-1*, 761301) Technomic.

Textile Coloration & Finishing. Warren S. Perkins. LC 96-2516. (Illus.). 248p. 1996. boxed 75.00 (*0-89089-885-5*) Carolina Acad Pr.

Textile Conservation. Ed. by Jentina E. Leene. LC 74-179287. (Illus.). 285p. reprint ed. pap. 81.30 (*0-317-10509-4*, 2004628) Bks Demand.

Textile Conservator's Manual. 2nd ed. Sheila Landi. 368p. 1992. 160.00 (*0-7506-0352-6*) Buttrwrth-Heinemann.

Textile Design. Carol Joyce. LC 92-38380. (Illus.). 160p. 1993. 39.95 (*0-8230-5325-3*, Watsn-Guptill) Watsn-Guptill.

***Textile Design.** PBC International Staff. 1992. 59.95 (*0-688-10918-7*) Morrow.

***Textile Design - Journal of the Textile Institute: Special Edition.** John W. Hearle. 1989. pap. 54.00 (*0-614-20867-X*, Pub. by Textile Inst UK) St Mut.

***Textile Designs.** Susan Meller. 1991. 90.00 (*0-500-23628-3*) Thames Hudson.

Textile Designs: Two Hundred Years of European & American Patterns for Printed Fabrics. Susan Meller & Joost Elffers. (Illus.). 464p. 1991. 85.00 (*0-8109-3853-7*) Abrams.

***Textile Dictionary.** 2nd ed. 1991. 335.00 (*0-614-20931-5*, Pub. by Textile Inst UK) St Mut.

Textile Dictionary: English, French, German, Italian, Spanish. 2nd ed. Verein Deutsch Ingenieure Staff. 885p. (ENG, FRE, GER, ITA & SPA.). 1991. 350.00 (*0-7859-9958-2*) Fr & Eur.

Textile Dictionary: English, French, German, Spanish, Italian. 2nd ed. 800p. (FRE & GER.). 1995. 365.00 (*3-18-400876-2*, Pub. by Woodhead Pubng UK) Am Educ Systs.

Textile Dictionary: Fachwoerterbuch Textil. 4th ed. Derrick O. Michelson & G. Wagner. 120p. (FRE & GER.). 1987. 49.95 (*0-8288-0744-2*, M 7404) Fr & Eur.

Textile Dictionary, German-English/English-German. 6th ed. Joachim Schubert. 448p. (ENG & GER.). 1994. 195.00 (*0-7859-9253-7*) Fr & Eur.

Textile Dictionary in Four Languages. Nuri Ozbalkan. 1053p. (ENG, FRE, GER & TUR.). 98.75 (*0-88431-308-5*) IBD Ltd.

Textile Dyeing: The Step-by-Step Guide & Showcase. Kate Broughton. 144p. 1996. 29.99 (*1-56496-213-X*) Rockport Pubs.

***Textile Dyeing & Coloration.** J. R. Aspland. (Illus.). 416p. 1997. 65.00 (*0-9613350-1-7*, 9615) AATCC.

Textile Equipment & Its Working Environment. Ingvild Oye. (The Bryggen Papers Main Ser.: Vol. 2). 152p. 1988. pap. 37.00 (*82-00-02537-3*) Scandnvan Univ Pr.

Textile Evaluation. Judith Forney. 93p. (C). 1994. 14.56 (*1-56870-134-9*) RonJon Pub.

Textile Fabrics of Ancient Peru. William H. Holmes. (Bureau of American Ethnology Bulletins Ser.). 99p. 1995. lib. bdg. 89.00 (*0-7812-4007-7*) Rprt Serv.

Textile Fibres under the Microscope. Shirley Inst. Staff. (C). 1987. 120.00 (*0-685-46365-6*, Pub. by British Textile Tech UK) St Mut.

Textile Finishing. P. W. Harrison. 326p. 1978. 75.00 (*0-686-63799-2*) St Mut.

Textile Finishing Chemicals: An Industrial Guide. Ernest W. Flick. LC 90-6737. (Illus.). 682p. 1990. 76.00 (*0-8155-1234-1*) Noyes.

Textile Floorcoverings. G. H. Crawshaw & J. Ince. 84p. 1977. 110.00 (*0-686-63800-X*) St Mut.

Textile Handbook. 5th ed. American Home Economics Association Staff. LC 74-31289. 127p. reprint ed. pap. 36.20 (*0-7837-4785-3*, 2044541) Bks Demand.

Textile Industries of the United States: Vol. 1, 1639-1810. William R. Bagnall. LC 68-22370. (Library of Early American Business & Industry: No. 15). xxii, 660p. 1971. reprint ed. 65.00 (*0-678-00735-7*) Kelley.

***Textile Industry, 4 vols.** Ed. by S. D. Chapman. 1996. boxed 750.00 (*1-86064-057-5*, Pub. by Textile Inst UK) St Mut.

Textile Industry: A Case Study of Industrial Development in the Philippines. Laurence D. Stifel. LC 64-2724. (Cornell University, Southeast Asia Program, Data Paper Ser.: No. 49). 218p. reprint ed. pap. 62.20 (*0-8357-3566-4*, 2034596) Bks Demand.

Textile Industry & Its Business Climate, No. 8. Ed. by Akio Okochi & Shin-ichi Yonekawa. 299p. 1982. 42.50 (*0-86008-298-9*, Pub. by U of Tokyo JA) Col U Pr.

Textile Industry & the Environment. (Technical Reports: No. 16). 120p. 1993. 25.00 (*92-807-1367-1*) UN.

Textile Industry Dictionary. Ed. by A. M. Sabriel et al. 394p. (ARA, ENG, FRE & GER.). 1975. 75.00 (*0-8288-5949-3*, M9763) Fr & Eur.

***Textile Industry Division Symposium Vol. 1: 1996: Presented at North Carolina State University, Raleigh, NC, May 22-23, 1996.** Instrument Society of America Staff. LC 96-647624. (Illus.). 74p. 1996. reprint ed. pap. 25.00 (*0-608-04249-8*, 2065005) Bks Demand.

Textile Industry Effluents. Ed. by Wira Staff. 1988. 50.00 (*0-317-43605-8*) St Mut.

Textile Industry in Antebellum South Carolina. Ernest M. Lander. LC 69-12590. 140p. 1969. pap. 39.90 (*0-7837-8522-4*, 2049331) Bks Demand.

Textile Industry in North Carolina: A History. Brent D. Glass. (Illus.). xiv, 119p. (Orig.). 1992. pap. 6.00 (*0-86526-256-X*) NC Archives.

Textile Industry Information Sources. Ed. by Joseph V. Kopycinski. LC 64-25644. (Management Information Guide Ser.: No. 4). 194p. 1974. 68.00 (*0-8103-0804-5*) Gale.

***Textile Institute Membership Directory '96.** 1995. pap. 950.00 (*0-614-20932-3*, Pub. by Textile Inst UK) St Mut.

Textile League Baseball: South Carolina's Mill Teams, 1880-1955. Thomas K. Perry. LC 92-56680. (Illus.). 327p. 1993. lib. bdg. 28.50 (*0-89950-875-8*) McFarland & Co.

Textile Lexicon: Lexique Textile: Francais-Allemand. Pierre Hirsch. 235p. (FRE & GER.). 1983. pap. 69.95 (*0-7859-4986-0*) Fr & Eur.

Textile Machinery. J. Shaw & A. A. Chisholm. 69p. 1969. 70.00 (*0-686-63801-8*) St Mut.

Textile Machines. Anna P. Benson. 1989. pap. 25.00 (*0-85263-647-4*, Pub. by Shire UK) St Mut.

Textile Manufacturers' Bookkeeping for the Counting House, Mill & Warehouse. 3rd ed. George P. Norton. LC 75-18478. (History of Accounting Ser.). 1979. reprint ed. 25.95 (*0-405-07560-X*) Ayer.

Textile Markets: Their Structure in Relation to Price Research. (Conference on Price Research Ser.: No. 2). 288p. 1939. reprint ed. 74.90 (*0-87014-188-0*); reprint ed. mic. film 37.50 (*0-685-61196-5*) Natl Bur Econ Res.

Textile Masterpieces of Ancient Peru. James W. Reid. (Illus.). 80p. 1987. pap. 10.95 (*0-486-25246-9*) Dover.

Textile Mathematics, Vol. 1. J. E. Booth. 162p. 1975. 70.00 (*0-686-63802-6*) St Mut.

Textile Mathematics, Vol. 3. J. E. Booth. 144p. 1977. 40.00 (*0-686-63804-2*) St Mut.

***Textile Opportunities: Making It Happen in the New Europe.** 1993. spiral bd. 90.00 (*0-614-20913-7*, Pub. by Textile Inst UK) St Mut.

Textile Pattern Book. Ed. by Wolfgang Hageney. (Illus.). 312p. (ENG, FRE, GER, ITA & SPA.). 1988. 59.95 (*88-7070-076-3*) Belvedere USA.

Textile Patternbook, Vol. 1: Floral. Ed. by Wolfgang Hageney. (Illus.). 112p. 1990. pap. 26.95 (*88-7070-142-5*) Belvedere USA.

Textile Patternbook, Vol. 2: Graphic. Ed. by Wolfgang Hageney. (Illus.). 112p. 1990. pap. 26.95 (*88-7070-143-3*) Belvedere USA.

Textile Patternbook, Vol. 3: Geometric. Ed. by Wolfgang Hageney. (Illus.). 112p. 1990. pap. 26.95 (*88-7070-144-1*) Belvedere USA.

Textile Print Design. Richard Fisher & Dorothy Wolfthal. (Illus.). 224p. 1986. 39.00 (*0-87005-513-5*) Fairchild.

***Textile Printing.** 2nd ed. Ed. by L. W. Miles. 1994. pap. 55.00 (*0-901956-57-0*, Pub. by Textile Inst UK) St Mut.

Textile Processing & Properties: Preparation, Dyeing, Finishing, & Performance. Tyrone L. Vigo. LC 94-1623. (Textile Science & Technology Ser.: Vol. 11). 498p. 1994. 304.50 (*0-444-88224-3*) Elsevier.

***Textile Processing & Properties: Preparation, Dyeing, Finishing & Performance.** T. L. Vigo. (Textile Science & Technology Ser.: Vol. 11). 498p. 1994. reprint ed. pap. 62.50 (*0-444-82623-8*) Elsevier.

Textile Product Serviceability: By Specification. Robert S. Merkel. 400p. (C). 1991. text ed. 55.51 (*0-02-380565-X*, Macmillan Coll) P-H.

***Textile Project Management.** A. Omerod. 1992. 360.00 (*1-870812-38-7*, Pub. by Textile Inst UK) St Mut.

***Textile Quality.** M. Bona. 1994. pap. 99.00 (*1-870812-60-3*, Pub. by Textile Inst UK) St Mut.

Textile Rental & Maintenance Services. 180p. 1987. 695.00 (*0-318-01948-5*) Busn Trend.

Textile Science. Kathryn L. Hatch. Ed. by LaMarre. (Illus.). 500p. (C). 1993. text ed. 63.00 (*0-314-90471-9*) West Pub.

***Textile Science: An Outline.** Charles Kim. 180p. 1996. per., pap. text ed. 31.44 (*0-7872-2785-4*) Kendall-Hunt.

***Textile Science: An Outline.** Charles Kim. 178p. (C). 1996. per., pap. text ed. 29.95 (*0-7872-3037-5*) Kendall-Hunt.

***Textile Sizing.** B. C. Goswami et al. 1996. write for info. (*0-8247-8976-8*) Dekker.

Textile Structural Composite. Ed. by T. W. Chou & F. Ko. (Composite Materials Ser.: No. 3). 388p. 1989. 244.50 (*0-444-42992-1*) Elsevier.

Textile Structure, Draft & Analysis. Harriet Tidball. LC 76-24008. (Guild Monographs: No. 18). (Illus.). 31p. 1966. pap. 9.95 (*0-916658-18-X*) Shuttle Craft.

Textile Systems for Endomorphisms & Automorphisms of the Shift. Masakazu Nasu. LC 94-43210. (Memoirs Ser.: Vol. 546). 1995. pap. 43.00 (*0-8218-2606-9*, MEMO/114/546) Am Math.

Textile Techniques in Metal: For Jewelers, Sculptors, & Textile Artists. rev. ed. Arline M. Fisch. LC 95-40789. (Illus.). 160p. 1995. 26.95 (*0-937274-93-3*) Lark Books.

Textile Terms & Definitions. Wira Staff. 1986. 130.00 (*0-317-56738-1*) St Mut.

***Textile Terms & Definitions.** 10th ed. Ed. by J. E. McIntyre & P. N. Daniels. 1995. 90.00 (*1-870812-77-8*, Pub. by Textile Inst UK) St Mut.

***Textile Trade: Operations of the Committee for the Implementation of Textile Agreements (CITA)** (Illus.). 111p. (Orig.). (C). 1996. pap. 35.00 (*0-7881-3574-0*) DIANE Pub.

Textile Traditions of Mesoamerica & the Andes: An Anthology. Ed. by Margot B. Schevill et al. LC 96-10252. (Illus.). 523p. (Orig.). 1996. reprint ed. pap. 19.95 (*0-292-77714-0*) U of Tex Pr.

Textile Treasures: A Sampling of the Museum's Collections Sigrun Marrocco & Carolyn Samonds. (Illus.). 32p. 1987. 8.25 (*0-916746-53-4*) Springfield Lib & Mus.

Textile Washing Products: The International Market. Euromonitor Staff. 112p. (C). 1988. 2,925.00 (*0-685-30316-0*, Pub. by Euromonitor Pubns UK) Gale.

Textile Wet Processing & Pollution Abatement Technology: A Survey. Ed. by Scientific Publishers Staff. (C). 1989. 100.00 (*0-685-54211-4*, Pub. by Scientific UK) St Mut.

Textile Wet Processing & Pollution Abatement Technology Environment, Canada. Ed. by Scientific Publishers Staff. (C). 1989. text ed. 50.00 (*81-85312-07-9*, Pub. by Scientific Pubs II) St Mut.

Textile Workers in Brazil & Argentina: A Study of the Interrelationships Between Work & Household. 305p. 1991. 35.00 (*92-808-0753-6*, E.91.III.A.1) UN.

***Textile World at a Crossroads.** 1991. pap. 72.00 (*1-870812-34-4*, Pub. by Textile Inst UK) St Mut.

Textiles. LC 96-13080. (World Crafts Ser.). (J). 1997. lib. bdg. 18.00 (*0-531-14432-1*) Watts.

Textiles. Elsasser. (Fashion Merchandising Ser.). 1997. teacher ed. 15.95 (*0-8273-7687-1*) Delmar.

Textiles. Amrita Kumar. (C). 1994. 7.50 (*81-7167-212-4*, Pub. by Rupa II) S Asia.

Textiles. 7th ed. Sara J. Kadolph et al. LC 92-20613. 416p. (C). 1992. text ed. 63.00 (*0-02-361601-6*, Macmillan Coll) P-H.

***Textiles.** 8th ed. Kadolph & Langford. 1997. text ed. 60.00 (*0-13-494592-1*) P-H.

Textiles: A Classification of Techniques. Annemarie Seiler-Baldinger. (Illus.). 272p. 1992. text ed. 49.00 (*1-56098-509-7*) Smithsonian.

***Textiles: A Classification of Techniques.** 2nd ed. Annemarie Seiler-Baldinger. 1994. pap. 54.00 (*1-86333-110-7*, Pub. by Textile Inst UK) St Mut.

Textiles: A Handbook for Designers. Marypaul Yates. 192p. 1991. pap. 19.95 (*0-8306-1843-0*, Design Pr) TAB Bks.

Textiles: A Handbook for Designers. rev. ed. Marypaul Yates. (Illus.). 208p. 1995. pap. 25.00 (*0-393-73003-4*) Norton.

Textiles: Concepts & Principles. Elsasser. LC 96-35771. (Fashion Merchandising Ser.). 1997. 44.95 (*0-8273-7686-3*) Delmar.

***Textiles: Fashioning the Future.** 1990. pap. 45.00 (*1-870812-23-9*, Pub. by Textile Inst UK) St Mut.

***Textiles: Fiber to Fabric.** 6th ed. B. P. Corbman. 1983. pap. 35.00 (*0-07-066236-3*) McGraw.

Textiles: Fiber to Fabric. 6th ed. Bernard P. Corbman. 608p. 1983. text ed. 38.95 (*0-07-013137-6*) McGraw.

Textiles: Product Design & Marketing. Textile Institute Staff. 316p. (C). 1987. pap. text ed. 45.00 (*0-900739-98-3*, Pub. by Textile Inst UK) St Mut.

***Textiles: Production, Trade & Demand.** Maureen F. Mazzaoui. LC 96-52046. (Expanding World Ser.: No. 12). 350p. 1997. text ed. 98.95 (*0-86078-509-2*, Pub. by Variorum UK) Ashgate Pub Co.

Textiles: Properties & Behavior. Edward Miller. (Illus.). 192p. 1984. pap. 34.95 (*0-7134-7235-9*, Pub. by Batsford UK) Trafalgar.

Textiles Vol. 1: Dictionnaire des Termes Normalises. 5th ed. Afnor Staff. 298p. (FRE.). 1988. pap. 145.00 (*0-7859-7737-6*, 2120707006) Fr & Eur.

Textiles - Isabella Stewart Gardner Museum. Adolph S. Cavallo. LC 85-51863. (Illus.). 223p. 1986. 49.50 (*0-914660-09-8*); pap. 32.50 (*0-914660-10-1*) I S Gardner Mus.

***Textiles - the Technology for a Better Future.** 1995. spiral bd. 90.00 (*1-870812-82-4*, Pub. by Textile Inst UK) St Mut.

Textiles & Apparel in the Global Economy. 2nd ed. Kitty G. Dickerson. LC 94-19854. Orig. Title: Textiles & Apparel in the International Economy. 608p. (C). 1994. text ed. 66.00 (*0-02-329502-3*, Macmillan Coll) P-H.

Textiles & Apparel in the International Economy see Textiles & Apparel in the Global Economy

***Textiles & Capitalism in Mexico: An Economic History of the Obrajes, 1539-1840.** Richard J. Salvucci. LC 87-45535. 265p. 1987. reprint ed. pap. 75.60 (*0-608-03307-3*, 2064019) Bks Demand.

Textiles & Industrial Transition in Japan. Dennis L. McNamara. LC 94-43122. 288p. 1995. 37.50 (*0-8014-3100-X*) Cornell U Pr.

Textiles & Ornaments of India. Pupul Jayakar & John Irwin. Ed. by Monroe Wheeler. LC 75-169305. (Museum of Modern Art Publications in Reprint). (Illus.). 96p. 1972. reprint ed. 23.95 (*0-405-01564-X*) Ayer.

Textiles & Politics: The Life of B. Everett Jordan - From Saxapahaw to the United States Senate. Ben F. Bulla. LC 91-76747. (Illus.). 402p. 1992. 24.95 (*0-89089-486-8*) Carolina Acad Pr.

***Textiles & Technology.** K. Baulch & K. Opperman. 1994. pap. 18.00 (*0-521-43784-9*) Cambridge U Pr.

Textiles & the Tai Experience in Southeast Asia. Mattiebelle Gittinger & H. Leedon Lefferts, Jr. Ed. by Henrietta Consentino. (Illus.). 288p. (Orig.). 1992. pap. 45.00 (*0-87405-030-8*) Textile Mus.

Textiles As Art: Selecting, Framing & Maintaining Textile Art. Laurence Korwin. (Illus.). 112p. 1990. pap. 29.95 (*0-9624118-0-9*) Korwin Design.

Textiles by William Morris & Co. Oliver Fairclough & Emmeline Leary. (Illus.). (Orig.). 1981. pap. 20.00 (*0-686-79147-9*) Eastview.

***Textiles for Modern Living.** 5th ed. Gohl & Vilensky. 1993. pap. text ed. write for info. (*0-582-80113-3*, Pub. by Longman UK) Longman.

***Textiles for People.** Wilkinson. Date not set. pap. text ed. write for info. (*0-582-22476-4*, Pub. by Longman UK) Longman.

Textiles for the Consumer. rev. ed. Nancy Belck. 380p. (C). 1990. pap. text ed. 40.00 (*0-87013-237-7*) Mich St U Pr.

Textiles for Today's Interiors. K. Nielson. 1991. text ed. write for info. (*0-442-01202-0*) Van Nos Reinhold.

Textiles for You. E. Pomeroy & J. Pomeroy. (C). 1988. 65.00 (*0-685-47486-0*, Pub. by S Thornes Pubs UK) St Mut.

Textiles from Beneath the Temple of Pachacamac, Peru. Ina Van Stan. (University Museum Monographs: No. 30). (Illus.). vii, 91p. 1967. pap. 15.00 (*0-934718-22-9*) U PA Mus Pubns.

Textiles from Medieval Egypt, A.D. 300-1300. Thelma K. Thomas. LC 89-85825. (Illus.). 72p. (Orig.). (C). 1990. pap. text ed. 8.95 (*0-911239-20-0*) Carnegie Mus.

Textiles Handbook. Rebecca Davis & Carol Tuntland. (Illus.). (Orig.). (C). 1996. pap. 15.95 (*0-916434-11-7*) Plycon Pr.

Textiles (I): D 76-D 3218 see 1997 Annual Book of ASTM Standards: Textiles, Section 7

Textiles (II): D 3333-Latest see 1997 Annual Book of ASTM Standards: Textiles, Section 7

Textiles in Ancient India. Kiran Singh. (C). 1994. 21.00 (*81-7124-121-2*, Pub. by Manohar II) S Asia.

Textiles in Archaeology. John P. Wild. (Archaeology Ser.). (Illus.). 68p. 1988. pap. text ed. 10.50 (*0-85263-931-7*, Pub. by Shire Pubns UK) Lubrecht & Cramer.

Textiles in Bali. Brigitta Hauser-Schaublin et al. Tr. by Dennis Q. Stephenson from GER. 160p. 1991. 45.00 (*0-945971-29-X*) Periplus.

Textiles in Perspective. Betty Smith & Ira Block. (Illus.). 512p. (C). 1982. text ed. 50.27 (*0-13-912808-5*) P-H.

Textiles in the Art Institute of Chicago. Christa C. Thurman. LC 92-12418. (Illus.). 152p. 1992. 35.00 (*0-8109-3856-1*) Abrams.

Textiles in Transition: Technology, Wages, & Industry Relocation in the U. S. Textile Industry, Eighteen Eighty to Nineteen Thirty. Nancy F. Kane. LC 87-24950. 208p. 1988. text ed. 49.95 (*0-313-25529-6*, KIW/, Greenwood Pr) Greenwood.

Textiles of Ancient Mesopotamia, Persia, & Egypt. Florence E. Petzel. LC 87-90471. 226p. 1987. pap. text ed. 11.00 (*0-9618476-0-3*) F E Petzel.

Textiles of Ancient Peru & Their Techniques. Raoul D'Harcourt. Ed. by Grace G. Denny & Carolyn M. Osborne. Tr. by Sadie Brown from FRE. LC 62-17150. (Illus.). 320p. 1987. reprint ed. pap. 19.95 (*0-295-95331-4*) U of Wash Pr.

Textiles of India - A Living History: A Study of Regional Surface Design Traditions in India. Elsa Screenivasam. (Illus.). 46p. (Orig.). 1989. pap. 15.00 (*0-317-94018-X*) Octagon Ctr Arts.

Textiles of Late Antiquity. Annemarie Stauffer. 1995. pap. 8.95 (*0-87099-768-8*) Metro Mus Art.

Textiles of Southeast Asia: Tradition, Trade, & Transformation. Robyn Maxwell. (Illus.). 440p. 1990. reprint ed. 145.00 (*0-19-553186-8*) OUP.

Textiles of the Arts & Crafts Movement. Linda Parry. LC 87-51290. (Illus.). 200p. 1988. pap. 22.50 (*0-500-27497-5*) Thames Hudson.

Textiles of the Kuna Indians of Panama. Herta Puls. 1989. pap. 30.00 (*0-85263-942-2*, Pub. by Shire UK) St Mut.

Textiles of the Southern Philippines. Lynda A. Reyes. 170p. (C). 1992. text ed. 28.00 (*971-542-005-2*, Pub. by U of Philippines Pr PH); pap. text ed. 17.95 (*971-542-006-0*, Pub. by U of Philippines Pr PH) UH Pr.

***Textiles Towards World Class.** 1989. spiral bd. 63.00 (*0-614-20914-5*, Pub. by Textile Inst UK) St Mut.

Textiles, Towns & Trades: Essays in the Economic History of Late-Medieval England & the Low Countries. John H. Munro. LC 94-4405. (Collected Studies: No. 442). 350p. 1994. 92.95 (*0-86078-404-5*, Pub. by Variorum UK) Ashgate Pub Co.

Textiles, 5000 Years: An International History & Illustrated Survey. Ed. by Jennifer Harris. LC 93-16980. (Illus.). 1993. 75.00 (*0-8109-3875-8*) Abrams.

Textilien in Bali. Brigitta Hauser-Schaublin et al. 142p. (GER.). 1991. 45.00 (*0-945971-50-8*) Periplus.

Textiltechnisches Woerterbuch: English-American-French-German-Spanish. Jean-Marie Ducrot. 535p. (ENG, FRE & GER.). 1979. 350.00 (*0-7859-6868-7*) Fr & Eur.

Textmaps: A Chapter - By - Chapter Guide For Exploring. 4th ed. Ruth Taylor & Eric Berkowitz. (C). 1994. pap. 14.50 (*0-256-18435-6*) Irwin.

Texto e Ideologia en la Narrativa Chilena. Lucia G. Cunningham. LC 87-20006. (Towards a Social History of Hispanic & Luso-Brazilian Literature Ser.). 256p. (Orig.). (SPA.). 1988. pap. 9.95 (*0-910235-28-7*) Prisma Bks.

Texto en llamas: El arte narrative de Juan Rulfo. Terry J. Peavler. (University of Texas Studies in Contemporary Spanish-American Fiction: Vol. 1). 198p. (C). 1989. text ed. 35.50 (*0-8204-0673-2*) P Lang Pubng.

Texto General de Cosmetologia. Milady Editors. (SPA.). 1989. student ed., pap. 6.50 (*0-87350-879-3*) Milady Pub.

Texto General de Cosmetologia. 2nd ed. Milady Publishing Company Staff. LC 95-2982. 656p. (ENG & SPA.). 1995. pap. 40.95 (*1-56253-254-5*) Milady Pub.

Texto General De Cosmetologia, Respuestas a las Preguntas de Repaso. Milady Publishing Company Staff. 19p. (SPA.). 1993. teacher ed., pap. write for info. (*1-56253-143-3*) Milady Pub.

Texto General de Cosmetologia: Answers Practical. Milady Publishing Company Staff. 288p. (SPA.). 1996. teacher ed. 29.95 (*1-56253-258-8*) Milady Pub.

Texto General de Cosmetologia: Answers to Theory Workbook. Milady Publishing Company Staff. 144p. (SPA.). 1996. 29.95 (*1-56253-260-X*) Milady Pub.

Texto General de Cosmetologia: Workbook Cuaderno Practico. Milady Publishing Company Staff. 288p. (SPA.). 1996. 21.00 (*1-56253-257-X*) Milady Pub.

Texto General de Cosmetology: Revision del Examen. Milady Publishing Company Staff. (Cosmetology Ser.). 144p. (SPA.). 1996. student ed., pap. 14.50 (*1-56253-256-1*) Milady Pub.

Texto Libre de Prejuicios Sexuales y Raciales: Guia para la Preparacion de Materiales de Ensenanza. Isabel Pico & Idsa Alegria. 56p. (SPA.). 1989. pap. 6.50 (*0-8477-2470-0*) U of PR Pr.

***Texto Of Oro de las Sagradas Escrituras.** Ed Morrell. Ed. by Gary Hilliker. 24p. (SPA.). 1994. 0.50 (*1-879892-46-4*) Editorial Bautista.

Texto Theory Workbook. 2nd rev. ed. Milady Publishing Company Staff. 144p. (SPA.). 1996. 21.00 (*1-56253-259-6*) Milady Pub.

Texto y Concordancia del Compendio de los Boticarios, Saladino de Ascoli, Valladolid, 1515. Ed. by Thomas M. Capuano. (Medieval Spanish Medical Texts Ser.: No. 30). 36p. (SPA.). 1990. 10.00 incl. fiche (*0-940639-60-2*) Hispanic Seminary.

Texto y Concordancias de De las Melecinas, MS1743: Salamanca, Universitaria. Ed. by Sylvia Fernandez. (Medieval Spanish Medical Texts Ser.: No. 27). 8p. (SPA.). 1989. 10.00 incl. fiche (*0-940639-29-7*) Hispanic Seminary.

Texto y Concordancias de la Defenssa de Virtuossas Mugeres de Mosen Diego de Valera, MS. 1341 de la Biblioteca Nacional. Ed. by Maria I. Montoya-Ramirez. (Spanish Ser.: No. 72). 8p. 1992. 10.00 incl. fiche (*0-940639-73-4*) Hispanic Seminary.

Texto y Concordancias de Libro de las Donas, Escorial MS. h.III.20. Ed. by Gracia Lozano-Lopez. (Spanish Ser.: No. 67). 20p. 1992. 10.00 incl. fiche (*0-940639-63-7*) Hispanic Seminary.

Texto y Concordancias de los Doze Trabajos de Hercules, Enrique de Villena, Biblioteca Nacional MS. 27. Ed. by Francisco G. Jover. (Spanish Ser.: No. 68). 10p. 1991. 10.00 incl. fiche (*0-940639-68-8*) Hispanic Seminary.

Texto y Espectaculo: Proceedings of the Fourteenth International Golden Age Spanish Theatre Symposium (March 9-12, 1994) at the University of Texas, El Paso. Ed. by Jose L. Garcia. LC 94-67247. 140p. (Orig.). (ENG & SPA.). (C). 1995. 12.00 (*0-614-10353-3*) Spanish Lit Pubns.

Texto y Espectaculo: Proceedings of the Thirteenth International Golden Age Spanish Theatre Symposium (March 17-20, 1993) at the University of Texas, El Paso. Ed. by Jose L. Garcia. LC 94-67247. 133p. (Orig.). (ENG & SPA.). (C). 1995. pap. 12.00 (*0-938972-25-1*) Spanish Lit Pubns.

Texto y Espectaculo: Selected Proceedings of the Symposium on Spanish Golden Age Theatre, March 11, 12, 13, 1987 the University of Texas at El Paso. Ed. by Barbara Mujica. LC 88-37834. 172p. (C). 1989. lib. bdg. 34.50 (*0-8191-7312-6*) U Pr of Amer.

Texto y Vida: Introduccion a la Literatura Espanola. Barbara Mujica. Ed. by Katherine L. Vardy. 608p. (C). 1990. pap. text ed. 40.00 (*0-03-013164-2*) HB Coll Pubs.

Texto y Vida: Introduccion a la Litteratura Hispano Americana. Barbara Mujica. (Illus.). 608p. (SPA.). (C). 1992. pap. text ed. 41.75 (*0-03-026237-2*) HB Coll Pubs.

Textos y Concordancia de la obra completa de Juan Manuel. Ed. by Reinaldo Ayerbe-Chaux. (Spanish Ser.: No. 28). 12p. 1986. 15.00 incl. fiche (*0-942260-70-8*) Hispanic Seminary.

Textos y Concordancias: Fabula de Polyfemo y Galathea, y las Soledades. Ed. by Alfonso Callejo & Maria T. Pajares. (Spanish Ser.: No. 25). iv, 128p. 1985. 15.00 (*0-942260-67-8*) Hispanic Seminary.

Textos y Concordancias del Libro de los Olios, MS2262: Salamanca, Universitaria. Ed. by M. Lopez Hernandez. (Medieval Spanish Medical Texts Ser.: No. 28). 8p. (SPA.). 1989. 10.00 incl. fiche (*0-940639-38-6*) Hispanic Seminary.

Textos y Concordancias del Libro de Medecina Llamado Macer: Andres de Burgos, Granada 1518 y 1519. Ed. by Thomas M. Capuano. (Medieval Spanish Medical Texts Ser.: No. 32). 20p. (SPA.). 1991. 10.00 incl. fiche (*0-940639-66-1*) Hispanic Seminary.

Textos y Contextos en Torno al Tema de la Espada y la Cruz en Tres Cronicas Novelescas Vol. 12: Cautiverio Feliz; El Carnero; Infortunios de Alonso Ramirez. Norma Hernandez De Ross. (Iberica Ser.). 168p. (SPA.). (C). 1996. text ed. 40.95 (*0-8204-2574-5*) P Lang Pubng.

Textos y Pretextos. Rafael C. Pereda. LC 85-14137. 114p. (SPA.). 1986. pap. 6.00 (*0-8477-3516-8*) U of PR Pr.

Texts: Ontological Status, Identity, Author, Audience. Jorge J. Gracia. LC 95-9554. (SUNY Series in Philosophy). 225p. 1996. text ed. 73.50 (*0-7914-2901-6*); pap. text ed. 24.95 (*0-7914-2902-4*) State U NY Pr.

Texts & Calendars: An Analytical Guide to Serial Publications, 1957-1982, Vol. 2. E. L. Mullins. (Royal Historical Society Guides & Handbooks Ser.: No.12). 335p. 27.00 (*0-86193-100-9*) David Brown.

An Asterisk (*) at the beginning of an entry indicates that the title is appearing in BIP for the first time.

Texts & Concordances of Escorial Manuscript b.IV.34: Menor dano de medicina. Alfonso Chirino et al. Ed. by Enrica J. Ardemagni. (Medieval Spanish Medical Texts Ser.: No. 2). 11p. 1984. 10.00 incl. fiche (*0-942260-41-4*) Hispanic Seminary.

Texts & Concordances of Manuscript Esp. 226 of the Bibliotheque Nationale, Paris: Cancionero Castellano Y Catalan de Paris. Ed. by Robert G. Black. (Spanish Ser.: No. 23). 16p. 1985. text ed. 10.00 incl. fiche (*0-942260-65-1*) Hispanic Seminary.

Texts & Concordances of the Armenian Adam Literature Vol. 1: Genesis 1-4, Penitence of Adam, Book of Adam. Michael E. Stone. LC 96-21615. (SBL Early Judaism & Its Literature Ser.). 334p. (ARM.). 1996. 49.95 (*0-7885-0278-6*, 063512) Scholars Pr GA.

Texts & Contexts: A Contemporary Approach to College Writing. William S. Robinson & Stephanie Tucker. 412p. (C). 1991. pap. 24.95 (*0-534-13044-5*) Wadsworth Pub.

Texts & Contexts: A Contemporary Approach to College Writing. 2nd ed. William S. Robinson & Stephanie Tucker. 526p. 1994. pap. 27.25 (*0-534-21474-6*) Wadsworth Pub.

Texts & Contexts: A Contemporary Approach to College Writing. 3rd ed. Robinson. (Developmental Study/Study Skill Ser.). 1997. pap. 35.95 (*0-534-52335-8*) Wadsworth Pub.

Texts & Contexts: A Guide to Careful Thinking & Writing about the Bible. Michael J. Gorman. 51p. (YA). (gr. 9-12). 1989. pap. 15.75 (*1-881678-04-0*) CRIS.

Texts & Contexts: Biblical Texts in Their Textual & Situational Contexts. Ed. by Tord Fornberg & David Hellholm. 1099p. 1995. 98.00 (*82-00-22446-5*) Scandnvan Univ Pr.

Texts & Contexts: Writing about Literature. Lynn. (C). 1994. pap. text ed. 20.50 (*0-06-500099-4*) Addison-Wesley Educ.

***Texts & Contexts in Ancient & Medieval Science: Studies on the Occasion of John E. Murdoch's Seventieth Birthday.** Ed. by Edith Sylla & Michael McVaugh. LC 97-18497. (Studies in Intellectual History: No. 78). (Illus.). 224p. 1997. 78.25 (*90-04-10823-8*) E J Brill.

Texts & Contexts in Idea Vilarino's Poetry. Judy Berry-Bravo. LC 93-86774. (Illus.). 270p. (C). 1994. 32.00 (*0-938972-21-9*) Spanish Lit Pubns.

***Texts & Contexts, Writing about Literature with Critical Theory.** 2nd ed. Lynn. (C). 1998. pap. text ed. write for info. (*0-321-01979-2*) Addison-Wesley.

***Texts & Cultural Change in Early Modern England.** Cedric C. Brown & Arthur F. Marotti. LC 97-24801. (Early Modern Literature in History Ser.). 1997. write for info. (*0-312-17728-3*) St Martin.

Texts & Dialogues. Maurice Merleau-Ponty. Ed. by Hugh J. Silverman & James Barry, Jr. Tr. by Michael B. Smith et al. LC 90-46082. 232p. (C). 1996. pap. 17.50 (*0-391-03962-8*) Humanities.

Texts & Practices: Readings in Critical Discourse Analysis. Compiled by Carmen R. Caldas-Coulthard & Malcolm Coulthard. LC 95-10857. 294p. (C). 1995. pap. 18.95 (*0-415-12143-4*) Routledge.

Texts & Practices: Readings in Critical Discourse Analysis. Compiled by Carmen R. Caldas-Coulthard & Malcolm Coulthard. LC 95-10857. 232p. (C). (gr. 13). 1995. text ed. 74.95 (*0-415-12142-6*) Routledge.

Texts & Textuality: Textual Instability, Theory & Interpretation. Philip G. Cohen. LC 96-23047. (Wellesley Studies in Critical Theory, Literary History & Culture). 355p. 1997. text ed. 65.00 (*0-8153-1956-8*) Garland.

***Texts & the Self in the Twelfth Century.** Sarah Spence. (Studies in Medieval Literature: No. 30). 181p. (C). 1997. text ed. 49.95 (*0-521-57279-7*) Cambridge U Pr.

Texts & Their Contexts: Papers from the Early Book Society. Ed. by Julia Boffey & John Scattergood. (Illus.). 240p. 1997. boxed 55.00 (*1-85182-209-7*, Pub. by Four Cts Pr IE) Intl Spec Bk.

Texts & Their Traditions in the Medieval Library of Rochester Cathedral Priory. Mary P. Richards. LC 87-72869. (Transactions Ser.: Vol. 78, Pt. 3). (Illus.). 212p. (C). 1988. pap. 20.00 (*0-87169-783-1*, T783-RIM) Am Philos.

Texts & Their Transformations: Continuity & Change in the Classical Tradition. Mark D. Usher. LC 94-39078. 1994. pap. 8.00 (*0-943056-22-5*) Univ Chi Lib.

Text's Boyfriend. deluxe ed. Harrison Fisher. (Burning Deck Poetry Chapbooks Ser.). 24p. (Orig.). 1980. pap. 15.00 (*0-930900-85-5*) Burning Deck.

Texts, Facts & Feminity: Exploring the Relations of Ruling. Dorothy E. Smith. 256p. (C). 1993. pap. 17.95 (*0-415-10244-8*) Routledge.

Texts for Preaching: A Lectionary Commentary Based on the NRSV - Year C. Charles B. Cousar et al. 624p. 1994. 32.00 (*0-664-22000-2*) Westminster John Knox.

Texts for Preaching: A Lectionary Commentary Based on the NRSV Year A. Walter Brueggemann et al. 608p. 1995. 32.00 (*0-664-21927-6*) Westminster John Knox.

Texts for Preaching: A Lectionary Commentary Based on the NRSV, Year B. James D. Newsome et al. LC 93-8023. 704p. 1993. text ed. 32.00 (*0-664-21970-5*) Westminster John Knox.

Texts from Tall-i Malyan: Elamite Administrative Texts. Matthew W. Stolper. (Occasional Publications of the Babylonian Fund: No. 6). xix, 159p. 1984. text ed. 30.00 (*0-934718-61-X*) U PA Mus Pubns.

Texts from the Amarna Period in Egypt. William J. Murnane. Ed. by Edmund S. Meltzer. LC 94-5147. (Writings from the Ancient World Ser.: Vol. 5). 310p. 1994. 49.95 (*1-55540-965-2*, 06 15 05); pap. 34.95 (*1-55540-966-0*, 06 15 05) Scholars Pr GA.

Texts from the British Museum. Marcel Sigrist. LC 93-21403. (Sumerian Archival Texts Ser.: Vol. 1). 167p. (C). 1994. 48.00 (*1-883053-03-X*) CDL Pr.

Texts from the Buddhist Canon. Dhammapada. Tr. by Samuel Beal from CHI. LC 78-72420. reprint ed. 22.50 (*0-404-17284-9*) AMS Pr.

Texts from the Time of Nebuchadnezzar. David B. Weisberg. LC 79-16038. (Yale Oriental Series, Babylonion Texts: Vol. XVII). 256p. 1980. text ed. 60.00 (*0-300-02338-3*) Yale U Pr.

Texts in Context: Critical Dialogues on Significant Episodes in American Political Rhetoric. Ed. by Michael C. Leff & Fred J. Kauffeld. 225p. (Orig.). (C). 1989. 15.50 (*0-9611800-5-6*, Hermagoras); pap. 9.95 (*0-9611800-4-8*, Hermagoras) L Erlbaum Assocs.

Texts in Context: Revisionist Methods for Studying the History of Ideas. David Boucher. (Martinus Nijhoff Philosophy Library: No. 12). 290p. 1985. lib. bdg. 107.50 (*90-247-3121-6*, Pub. by M Nijhoff NE) Kluwer Ac.

Texts in Context: Traditional Hermeneutics in South Asia. Ed. by Jeffrey R. Timm. LC 90-49428. 320p. (C). 1991. text ed. 59.50 (*0-7914-0795-0*); pap. text ed. 19.95 (*0-7914-0796-9*) State U NY Pr.

Texts in the Mastabeh of Se'n-Wosret-Ankh at Lisht: Metropolitan Museum of Art Egyptian Expedition Publications, Vol. 12. William C. Hayes. LC 70-168407. (Metropolitan Museum of Art Publications in Reprint). (Illus.). 64p. 1973. reprint ed. 19.95 (*0-405-02240-9*) Ayer.

Texts in Transit: A Study of New Testament Passages That Shaped the Brethren. fac. ed. Graydon F. Snyder & Kenneth M. Shaffer. (Church of the Brethren, Heritage Learning Program Ser.). 57p. 1976. pap. 25.00 (*0-7837-7550-4*, 2047303) Bks Demand.

Texts in Transit II. Kenneth M. Shaffer, Jr. & Graydon F. Snyder. 256p. 1991. pap. 9.95 (*0-87178-837-3*, 8373) Brethren.

Texts in Translation - Kielikannas: FATA Annual III. Ed. by Steve Stone. 96p. (Orig.). 1992. pap. write for info. (*1-880474-04-2*) FATA.

Texts of Desire: Essays on Fiction, Femininity & Schooling. Ed. by Linda K. Christian-Smith. (Critical Perspectives on Literacy & Education Ser.). 224p. 1993. 80.00 (*0-7507-0003-3*, Falmer Pr); pap. 29.00 (*0-7507-0004-1*, Falmer Pr) Taylor & Francis.

Texts of Keat's Poems. Jack Stillinger. LC 73-86940. 317p. reprint ed. pap. 90.40 (*0-7837-5944-4*, 2045743) Bks Demand.

Texts of Paulo Freire. Paul V. Taylor. LC 92-27643. 1993. 90.00 (*0-335-19020-0*, Open Univ Pr); pap. 27.50 (*0-335-19019-7*, Open Univ Pr) Taylor & Francis.

Texts of Power: Emerging Disciplines in Colonial Bengal. Ed. by Partha Chatterjee. 232p. 1995. text ed. 57.95 (*0-8166-2686-3*); pap. text ed. 22.95 (*0-8166-2687-1*) U of Minn Pr.

Texts of Taoism, Vol. 1. Ed. by F. Max Muller. Tr. by James Legge. 396p. 1891. pap. 9.95 (*0-486-20990-3*) Dover.

Texts of Taoism, Vol. 2. Ed. by F. Max Muller. Tr. by James Legge. 396p. 1891. pap. 9.95 (*0-486-20991-1*) Dover.

Texts of Terror: Literary-Feminist Readings of Biblical Narratives. Phyllis Trible. LC 83-48906. (Overtures to Biblical Theology Ser.). 144p. 1984. pap. 14.00 (*0-8006-1537-9*, 1-1537, Fortress Pr) Augsburg Fortress.

Texts of the Kaibab Paiutes & Uintah Utes see Southern Paiute

Texts of the Passion: Latin Devotional Literature & Medieval Society. Thomas H. Bestul. LC 96-26705. (Middle Ages Ser.). 288p. 1996. text ed. 39.95 (*0-8122-3376-X*) U of Pa Pr.

Texts of the Peace Conference at the Hague, 1899 & 1907 with English Translation & Appendix of Related Documents. Ed. by James B. Scott. 1977. 26.95 (*0-8369-7168-X*, 8000) Ayer.

Texts of the Songs. Ed. by Elise B. Jorgens. LC 86-751946. (English Song 1600-1675 Ser.: Vol. 12). 608p. 1989. text ed. 75.00 (*0-8240-8242-7*) Garland.

Texts of the Ukraine "Peace" with Maps. Ed. by Paul R. Magocsi. (Revolution & Nationalism in the Modern World Ser.: No. 3). 184p. 1981. reprint ed. pap. 12.00 (*0-939738-02-3*) Zubal Inc.

Texts of the White Yajurveda. Tr. by Ralph T. Griffith. xi, 388p. (C). 1987. 31.00 (*81-215-0047-8*, Pub. by Munshiram Manoharial II) S Asia.

Texts on Zulu Religion: Traditional Zulu Ideas about God. Ed. by Irving Hexham. LC 87-10992. (African Studies: Vol. 6). 496p. 1987. lib. bdg. 109.95 (*0-88946-181-3*) E Mellen.

Texts Pertaining to the Invention of the Balloon in 1782. Ed. & Tr. by Paul Maravelas from FRE. Tr. by Scott Carpenter from FRE. (Illus.). 28p. 1985. text ed. 95.00 (*0-318-19997-1*) P Maravelas.

Texts, Temples, & Traditions: A Tribute to Menahem Haran. Ed. by Michael Klein et al. LC 96-5780. 630p. (ENG & HEB.). 1996. 55.00 (*1-57506-003-5*) Eisenbrauns.

Texts under Negotiation: The Bible & Postmodern Imagination. Walter Brueggemann. LC 93-18154. 128p. 1993. pap. 12.00 (*0-8006-2736-9*, 1-2736, Fortress Pr) Augsburg Fortress.

***Textstrukturen Im Medienwandel.** Ernest W. Hess-Luttich et al. (Forum Angewandte Linguistik Ser.: Bd. 29). (Illus.). 209p. 1996. 42.95 (*3-631-50014-9*) P Lang Pubng.

***TextTanzTheater: Eine Untersuchung des Dramatischen Motivs und Theatralen Ereignisses Tanz am Beispiel von Frank Wedekinds "Buchse der Pandora" und Hugo von Hofmannsthals "Elektra"** Susanne Marschall. Ed. by Dieter Kafitz et al. (Studien zur Deutschen und Europaischen Literatur des 19. und 20. Jahrhunderts: Bd. 36). 298p. (GER.). 1996. 57.95 (*3-631-30476-5*) P Lang Pubng.

Textual Analysis: Some Readers Reading. Ed. by Mary A. Caws. LC 85-18808. viii, 327p. 1986. pap. text ed. 8.00 (*0-87352-141-2*, T121P); lib. bdg. 12.00 (*0-87352-140-4*, T121C) Modern Lang.

Textual Analysis Vol. 1 & 2: A Scientific Approach for Assessing Cases of Sexual Abuse: The Theoretical Framework; the Psychology of Lying; & Cases of Older Children: Cases of Younger Children; & the Shortcomings of Judicial Logic, 2 vols., Set. Max Scharnberg. (Uppsala Studies in Education: Vol. 64). 650p. (Orig.). 1996. pap. 97.50 (*91-554-3679-X*) Coronet Bks.

Textual Analysis of Marlowe's Doctor Faustus with Director's Book: Stage Action As Metaphor. Louise C. Jones. LC 95-46717. (Studies in Renaissance Literature: Vol. 12). 180p. 1996. text ed. 79.95 (*0-7734-8802-2*) E Mellen.

Textual & Literary Criticism. Fredson T. Bowers. (Sanders Lectures in Bibliography: 1957-58). 196p. reprint ed. pap. 55.90 (*0-317-26059-6*, 2024423) Bks Demand.

Textual & Stylistic Commentary on Theocritus' Idyll XXV. G. Chryssafis. (London Studies in Classical Philology: Vol. I). 289p. (Orig.). (C). 1981. pap. 80.00 (*90-70265-21-4*, Pub. by Gieben NE) Benjamins North Am.

Textual & Subject Indexes of C. H. Spurgeon's Sermons. Charles H. Spurgeon. 1971. 6.00 (*1-56186-108-1*) Pilgrim Pubns.

Textual & Theatrical Shakespeare: Questions of Evidence. Ed. by Edward Pechter. LC 95-50872. (Studies in Theatre History & Culture). (Illus.). 256p. 1996. text ed. 35.00 (*0-87745-545-7*) U of Iowa Pr.

Textual Bodies: Changing Boundaries of Literary Representation. Ed. by Lori H. Lefkovitz. LC 96-21758. (SUNY Series, The Body in Culture, History, & Religion). 292p. 1997. text ed. 65.50 (*0-7914-3161-4*); pap. text ed. 21.95 (*0-7914-3162-2*) State U NY Pr.

Textual Bodies: Modernism, Postmodernism, & Print. Michael Kaufmann. LC 92-56603. (C). 1994. 29.50 (*0-8387-5260-8*) Bucknell U Pr.

Textual Carnivals: The Politics of Composition. Susan Miller. LC 90-34244. 288p. (C). 1993. pap. 14.95 (*0-8093-1922-5*) S Ill U Pr.

Textual Communication: A Print-Based Theory of the Novel. Maurice Couturier. 208p. (C). (gr. 13). 1990. text ed. 89.95 (*0-415-03920-7*, A4846) Routledge.

Textual Companion to Doctor Faustus. Eric Rasmussen. LC 93-18696. (Revels Plays Companion Library). 1994. text ed. 74.95 (*0-7190-1562-6*, Pub. by Manchester Univ Pr UK) St Martin.

Textual Concordance of the Holy Scriptures: (Bible Passages Taken from the Douay-Rheims Bible) Ed. by Thomas D. Williams. LC 85-52025. 848p. (Orig.). 1994. reprint ed. pap. 35.00 (*0-89555-286-8*) TAN Bks Pubs.

Textual Condition. Jerome J. McGann. (Illus.). 210p. 1991. text ed. 35.00 (*0-691-06931-X*); pap. text ed. 13.95 (*0-691-01518-X*) Princeton U Pr.

Textual Confrontations: Comparative Readings in Latin American Literature. Alfred J. MacAdam. LC 86-24913. 288p. 1987. 23.95 (*0-226-49990-1*) U Ch Pr.

Textual Connections in Acts. Stephen H. Levinsohn. LC 86-20238. (Society of Biblical Literature Monographs). 197p. 1987. 30.95 (*1-55540-060-4*, 06-00-31); pap. 19.95 (*1-55540-061-2*) Scholars Pr GA.

Textual Criticism & Editorial Technique. M. L. West. 150p. 1973. 59.95 (*3-519-07402-8*); pap. 45.95 (*3-519-07401-X*) Adlers Foreign Bks.

Textual Criticism & Literary Interpretation. Jerome J. McGann. LC 84-16174. (Illus.). 250p. 1985. lib. bdg. 26.50 (*0-226-55842-8*) U Ch Pr.

Textual Criticism & Middle English Texts. Tim W. Machan. LC 94-5441. 1994. text ed. 40.00 (*0-8139-1508-2*) U Pr of Va.

Textual Criticism & Scholarly Editing. G. Thomas Tanselle. 367p. 1991. text ed. 40.00 (*0-8139-1303-9*) U Pr of Va.

Textual Criticism of Inscriptions. Roland G. Kent. (LM Ser.: No. 2). 1926. pap. 25.00 (*0-527-00806-0*) Periodicals Srv.

Textual Criticism of the Hebrew Bible. Emanuel Tov. LC 92-22889. 496p. 1992. 42.00 (*0-8006-2687-7*, 1-2687, Fortress Pr) Augsburg Fortress.

Textual Criticism since Greg: A Chronicle, 1950-1985. Intro. by G. Thomas Tanselle. LC 87-23758. 150p. 1988. pap. text ed. 12.95 (*0-8139-1166-4*) U Pr of Va.

Textual Decorum: A Rhetoric of Attitudes in Medieval Literature. Scott D. Troyan. LC 94-25358. (Garland Studies in Medieval Literature: No. 12). 304p. 1994. text ed. 20.00 (*0-8153-1555-4*) Garland.

***Textual Development of the Qumran Community Rule.** Sarianna Metso. LC 96-17974. (Studies on the Texts of the Desert of Judah). (Illus.). 200p. 1996. 77.50 (*90-04-10683-9*) E J Brill.

***Textual Diaries of James Joyce.** Danis Rose. 198p. 9500. 39.95 (*1-874675-58-9*) Dufour.

Textual Dynamics of the Professions: Historical & Contemporary Studies of Writing in Professional Communities. Ed. by Charles Bazerman & James Paradis. LC 90-50079. (Rhetoric of the Human Sciences Ser.). 416p. (Orig.). (C). 1991. text ed. 42.50 (*0-299-12590-4*); pap. text ed. 17.50 (*0-299-12594-7*) U of Wis Pr.

***Textual Encounters.** Allison. (C). Date not set. text ed. 51.25 (*0-15-502857-X*); teacher ed., pap. text ed. 15.00 (*0-15-502858-8*) HB Coll Pubs.

Textual Escap-e-ades: Mobility, Maternity & Textuality in Contemporary Fiction by Women. Lindsey Tucker. LC 94-16130. (Contributions in Women's Studies: No. 146). 160p. 1994. text ed. 49.95 (*0-313-29156-X*, Greenwood Pr) Greenwood.

Textual Exile: The Reader in Sterne & Foscolo. Sante Matteo. (American University Studies: Comparative Literature: Ser. III, Vol. 15). 283p. 1985. text ed. 35.00 (*0-8204-0168-4*) P Lang Pubng.

Textual Fidelity & Textual Disregard. Ed. by Bernard Dauenhauer. LC 89-27808. (American University Studies: Comparative Literature: Ser. III, Vol. 33). 182p. 1990. text ed. 40.95 (*0-8204-1221-X*) P Lang Pubng.

Textual History & the Divine Comedy. John Guzzardo. 150p. 1990. 40.50 (*0-916379-58-2*) Scripta.

Textual History of the Huai-nan Tzu. Harold D. Roth. LC 90-85256. (Monographs: No. 46). (Illus.). xvi, 470p. (Orig.). (CHI.). (C). 1992. 36.00 (*0-924304-05-7*); pap. 20.00 (*0-924304-06-5*) Assn Asian Studies.

Textual Intercourse: Collaboration, Authorship, & Sexualities in Renaissance Drama. Jeffrey Mastern. LC 96-2949. (Studies in Renaissance Literature & Culture: No. 14). (Illus.). 237p. (C). 1997. text ed. 54.95 (*0-521-57260-6*) Cambridge U Pr.

Textual Intercourse: Collaboration, Authorship, & Sexualities in Renaissance Drama. Jeffrey Mastern. LC 96-2949. (Studies in Renaissance Literature & Culture: No. 14). (Illus.). 237p. (C). 1997. pap. text ed. 18.95 (*0-521-58920-7*) Cambridge U Pr.

Textual Intervention: Critical & Creative Strategies for Literary Studies. Rob Pope. LC 94-4022. (Interface Ser.). 350p. (C). (gr. 13). 1994. pap. 18.95 (*0-415-05437-0*); text ed. 69.95 (*0-415-05436-2*) Routledge.

Textual Introduction to Social & Political Theory. Ed. by Richard Bellamy & Angus Ross. LC 95-36976. 350p. (C). 1996. text ed. 24.95 (*0-7190-4639-4*) St Martin.

Textual Life of the Savants. Gisli Palsson. (Studies in Anthropology & History). 1995. pap. text ed. 24.00 (*3-7186-5722-8*, Harwood Acad Pubs) Gordon & Breach.

Textual Life of the Savants, Vol. 18. Gisli Palsson. (Studies in Anthropology & History). 240p. 1995. text ed. 54.00 (*3-7186-5721-X*, Harwood Acad Pubs) Gordon & Breach.

Textual Notes on the New American Bible. Ed. by Patrick W. Skehan. 124p. 1.30 (*0-318-13671-6*) Catholic Bibl Assn.

***Textual Optimism: A Critique of the United Bible Societies Greek New Testament.** Kent D. Clarke. (JSNTS Ser.: Vol. 138). 360p. 1997. 70.00 (*1-85075-649-X*, Pub. by Sheffield Acad UK) CUP Services.

Textual Orientations: Lesbian & Gay Students & the Making of Discourse Communities. Harriet Malinowitz. LC 94-36734. 294p. 1995. pap. text ed. 25.00 (*0-86709-353-6*, 0353) Boynton Cook Pubs.

Textual Poachers: Television Fans & Participatory Culture. Henry Jenkins. 256p. (C). (gr. 13). 1992. pap. 16.95 (*0-415-90572-9*, Routledge NY); text ed. 59.95 (*0-415-90571-0*, A7147, Routledge NY) Routledge.

Textual Poetics of German Manuscripts, 1300-1500. Sarah Westphal. LC 92-30499. (GERM Ser.). 244p. 1993. 59.95 (*1-879751-36-4*) Camden Hse.

Textual Politics: Discourse & Social Dynamics. J. Lemke. (Critical Perspectives on Literacy & Education Ser.). 240p. 1995. 80.00 (*0-7484-0215-2*); pap. 26.00 (*0-7484-0216-0*) Taylor & Francis.

Textual Politics & the Language Poets. George Hartley. LC 88-46024. (Illus.). 128p. 1989. 22.50 (*0-253-32716-4*) Ind U Pr.

***Textual Politics & the Language Poets.** George Hartley. LC 88-46024. 123p. pap. 35.10 (*0-608-05026-1*, 2059687) Bks Demand.

Textual Power: Literary Theory & the Teaching of English. Robert Scholes. LC 84-19628. (Illus.). 192p. 1986. pap. 12.00 (*0-300-03726-0*) Yale U Pr.

***Textual Practice, Vol. 9.** 148p. (C). 1995. pap. 13.95 (*0-415-12383-6*, Routledge NY) Routledge.

Textual Practice: Journal, Vol. 8, Issue 2. Ed. by Terence Hawkes & Jean Howard. 144p. (C). 1995. pap. 12.95 (*0-415-11098-X*, B3753) Routledge.

Textual Practice: Journal, Vol. 8, Issue 3. Ed. by Terence Hawkes & Jean Howard. 144p. (C). 1995. pap. 12.95 (*0-415-11099-8*, B3757) Routledge.

***Textual Practice No. 101: Photography & Cultural Representation.** Ed. by Alan Sinfeld. 243p. (C). 1997. pap. 12.95 (*0-415-14564-3*) Routledge.

Textual Practice Journal Vol. 8. Ed. by Terence Hawks & Jean Howard. 144p. 1995. pap. 12.95 (*0-415-11097-1*, Routledge NY) Routledge.

***Textual Practice 112.** Ed. by Alan Sinfield & Lindsay Smith. 171p. (C). 1997. pap. 12.95 (*0-415-16176-2*, Routledge NY) Routledge.

***Textual Practice 113: Luxurious Sexualities.** Ed. by Alan Sinfield & Jean E. Howard. 248p. (C). 1997. pap. 12.95 (*0-415-16177-0*, Routledge NY) Routledge.

Textual Scholarship: An Introduction. David C. Greetham. LC 91-24657. (Medieval Texts Ser.). (Illus.). 564p. 1992. text ed. 60.00 (*0-8153-0058-1*, H1417) Garland.

Textual Scholarship: An Introduction. David C. Greetham. LC 94-9786. (Reference Library of the Humanities: Vol. 1417). 564p. 1994. pap. text ed. 21.95 (*0-8153-1791-3*) Garland.

***Textual Society.** Edwina Taborsky. (Toronto Studies in Semiotics). 256p. 1996. 50.00 (*0-8020-0812-7*); pap. 17.95 (*0-8020-7180-5*) U of Toronto Pr.

T

An Asterisk (*) at the beginning of an entry indicates that the title is appearing in BIP for the first time.

Textual Sources for the Study of Hinduism. Ed. & Tr. by Wendy D. O'Flaherty. Tr. by Daniel H. Gold et al. (Sources for the Textual Study of Religion Ser.). xii, 224p. 1990. pap. text ed. 17.95 (*0-226-61847-1*) U Ch Pr.

Textual Sources for the Study of Islam. Ed. by Andrew Rippen & Jan Knappert. Tr. by Jan Knappert. (Textual Sources for the Study of Religion Ser.). (Illus.). xii, 222p. 1990. pap. text ed. 17.95 (*0-226-72063-2*) U Ch Pr.

Textual Sources for the Study of Judaism. Ed. & Tr. by Philip S. Alexander. (Textual Sources for the Study of Religion Ser.). 208p. 1990. pap. text ed. 17.95 (*0-226-01297-2*) U Ch Pr.

Textual Sources for the Study of Sikhism. Ed. & Tr. by W. H. McLeod. (Textual Sources for the Study of Religion Ser.). (Illus.). x, 176p. 1990. pap. text ed. 15.95 (*0-226-56085-6*) U Ch Pr.

Textual Sources for the Study of Zoroastrianism. Ed. & Tr. by Mary Boyce. (Textual Sources for the Study of Religion Ser.). (Illus.). x, 176p. 1990. pap. text ed. 15.95 (*0-226-06930-3*) U Ch Pr.

Textual Strategies: Perspectives in Post-Structuralist Criticism. Intro. by Josue V. Harari. LC 79-7617. 464p. 1979. 55.00 (*0-8014-1218-8*); pap. 17.95 (*0-8014-9180-0*) Cornell U Pr.

Textual Studies in Ancient & Medieval Geometry. Wilbur R. Knorr. 864p. 1989. 149.50 (*0-8176-3387-1*) Birkhauser.

Textual Studies in Hinduism. Arvind Sharma. 183p. 1980. 14.95 (*0-318-37166-9*) Asia Bk Corp.

Textual Studies in Hinduism. Arvind Sharma. 1980. lib. bdg. 14.95 (*0-914914-15-4*) New Horizons.

Textual Studies in Hinduism. Arvind Sharma. 1985. 12.50 (*0-8364-1291-5*, Pub. by Manohar II) S Asia.

Textual Studies in the Book of Joshua. Leonard Greenspoon. LC 83-3434. (Harvard Semitic Monographs). 412p. (C). 1983. 24.95 (*0-89130-622-6*, 04 00 28) Scholars Pr GA.

Textual Studies of Goethe's Faust. H. G. Fiedler. LC 73-20371. (Studies in Goethe: No. 61). 1974. lib. bdg. 75.00 (*0-8383-1809-6*) M S G Haskell Hse.

Textual Sublime: Deconstruction & Its Differences. Ed. by Hugh J. Silverman & Gary E. Aylesworth. LC 88-37124. (International Association of Philosophy & Literature (IAPL) Ser.). 274p. (Orig.). 1990. text ed. 64.50 (*0-7914-0074-3*); pap. text ed. 21.95 (*0-7914-0075-1*) State U NY Pr.

Textual Tradition of Strabo's Geography. A. Diller. iv, 222p. (Orig.). 1975. pap. text ed. 64.50 (*0-317-57966-5*, Pub. by AM Hakkert NE) Coronet Bks.

Textual Transgressions: Essays Toward the Construction of a Biobibliography. David Greetham. LC 95-43554. (Reference Library of the Humanities: Vol. 1739). 1996. text ed. 70.00 (*0-8153-1340-3*) Garland.

Textualities: Between Hermeneutics & Deconstruction. Hugh J. Silverman. 288p. (C). 1994. pap. 17.95 (*0-415-90819-1*, B0760, Routledge NY) Routledge.

Textuality & Legitimacy in the Printed Constitution. Michael Warner. (Illus.). 30p. 1987. reprint ed. pap. 4.50 (*0-912296-96-8*) Am Antiquarian.

Textuality & Sexuality: Reading Theories & Practices. Ed. by Judith Still & Michael Worton. LC 92-21096. (Illus.). 304p. (C). 1993. text ed. 75.00 (*0-7190-3604-6*, Pub. by Manchester Univ Pr UK) St Martin.

Textuality & Subjectivity: Essays on Language & Being. Ed. by Eitel Timm et al. (ENGL Ser.: Vol. 9). viii, 108p. 1992. 29.50 (*1-879751-07-0*) Camden Hse.

Textuality & Tectonics: Troubling Social & Psychological Science. Beryl Curt. 192p. 1994. 79.00 (*0-335-19064-2*, Open Univ Pr); pap. 27.50 (*0-335-19063-4*, Open Univ Pr) Taylor & Francis.

Textuality of Old English Poetry. Carol B. Pasternack. (Studies in Anglo-Saxon England: No. 13). (Illus.). 243p. (C). 1995. text ed. 59.95 (*0-521-46549-4*) Cambridge U Pr.

Textualizing the Feminine: On the Limits of Genre. Shari Benstock. LC 91-2516. (Project for Discourse & Theory Ser.: Vol. 7). (Illus.). 288p. 1991. 29.95 (*0-8061-2358-3*); pap. 14.95 (*0-8061-2383-4*) U of Okla Pr.

Textualterity: Art, Theory & Textual Criticism. Joseph Grigely. LC 95-16051. (Editorial Theory & Literary Criticism Ser.). (Illus.). 1995. text ed. 44.50 (*0-472-10579-5*) U of Mich Pr.

Textura: Russian Essays on Visual Culture. Ed. by Alla Efimova & Lev Manovich. Tr. by Lev Manovich. LC 93-7803. (Illus.). 264p. 1993. pap. text ed. 13.95 (*0-226-95124-3*); lib. bdg. 34.95 (*0-226-95123-5*) U Ch Pr.

Textural Tradition of Euripides' "Phoinissai" Donald J. Mastronarde & Jan M. Bremer. LC 82-13492. (UC Publications in Classical Studies: Vol. 27). 464p. (C). 1983. pap. 42.00 (*0-520-09664-9*) U CA Pr.

Texture. Karen Bryant-Mole. LC 95-48063. (J). 1996. pap. 4.95 (*0-382-39621-9*, Silver Pr NJ); lib. bdg. 10.95 (*0-382-39585-9*) Silver Burdett Pr.

Texture: How to Draw It, How to Paint It. Martin Davidson. 1992. 17.98 (*1-55521-790-7*) Bk Sales Inc.

Texture: Journal of Writing & Art, No. 6. Ed. by Susan S. Nash. 200p. (Orig.). 1995. pap. 10.00 (*0-9641837-2-2*) Texture Pr.

*****Texture: Web Site Construction with Future.** Taylor. LC 97-21893. (U. S. Computer Science Ser.). 1977. pap. 34.99 (*1-85032-893-5*) ITCP.

Texture & Detail in Watercolour. Richard Bolton. (Illus.). 128p. 1996. 35.00 (*0-7134-7222-7*, Pub. by Batsford UK) Trafalgar.

*****Texture & Detail in Watercolour.** Richard Bolton. LC 96-41746. (Illus.). 128p. 1997. reprint ed. pap. text ed. 14.95 (*0-486-29509-5*) Dover.

Texture Measurement of Foods: Psychophysical Fundamentals-Sensory, Mechanical & Chemical Procedures & Their Interrelationships. Ed. by A. Kramer et al. LC 72-93271. 175p. 1973. lib. bdg. 88.00 (*90-277-0307-8*) Kluwer Ac.

Texture of Identity: Ceramic Works by Aora Ellis, Fabric Works by Sue Klebanoff, Fabric & Found Object Constructions by Carol Hamoy. Ori Z. Soltes. (Illus.). (Orig.). pap. text ed. write for info. (*1-881456-20-X*) B B K Natl Jew Mus.

*****Texture of Industry: An Archaeological View of the Industrialization of North America.** Gordon & Malone. 464p. Date not set. pap. 24.95 (*0-340-51114-1*) OUP.

Texture of Industry: An Archaeological View of the Industrialization of North America. Robert B. Gordon & Patrick M. Malone. LC 92-17396. 464p. 1994. 55.00 (*0-19-505885-2*) OUP.

Texture of Industry: An Archaeological View of the Industrialization of North America. Robert B. Gordon & Patrick M. Malone. (Illus.). 464p. 1997. reprint ed. pap. 24.95 (*0-19-511141-9*) OUP.

Texture of Knowledge: An Essay on Religion & Science. James W. Jones. LC 80-69036. 112p. 1981. pap. text ed. 16.50 (*0-8191-1361-1*) U Pr of Amer.

*****Texture of Memory: Holocaust Memorials & Meaning.** James E. Young. 398p. 40.00 (*0-8276-0600-1*) JPS Phila.

Texture of Memory: Holocaust Memorials & Meaning in Europe, Israel, & America. James E. Young. LC 92-40888. 398p. (C). 1993. pap. 22.50 (*0-300-05991-4*); text ed. 45.00 (*0-300-05383-5*) Yale U Pr.

Textured Embroidery. Jenny Bradford. (Illus.). 112p. 1994. pap. 12.95 (*1-86351-076-1*, Pub. by S Milner AT) Sterling.

Textured Lives: Women, Art, & Representation in Modern Mexico. Claudia Schaefer. LC 91-30584. 163p. 1992. 36.00 (*0-8165-1250-7*) U of Ariz Pr.

Textured Lives: Women, Art & Representation in Modern Mexico. Claudia Schaefer. LC 91-30584. 163p. 1994. reprint ed. pap. 13.95 (*0-8165-1474-7*) U of Ariz Pr.

Texturen: Essays und Anderes zu Hans Magnus Enzenberger. Reinhold Grimm. LC 83-48820. (New York University Ottendorfer Ser.: Vol. 19). 224p. (C). 1985. text ed. 19.50 (*0-8204-0059-9*) P Lang Pubng.

*****Textures.** Joanne Barkan. (J). 1998. write for info. (*0-679-89024-6*) Random Bks Yng Read.

*****Textures.** Barrons. 1997. 9.95 (*0-7641-5061-8*) Barron.

*****Textures.** Barron's Publishing Staff. (Barron's Art Handbook Ser.). 1997. 9.95 (*0-7641-5013-8*) Barron.

Textures. Ed. by Wolfgang Hageney. (Illus.). 112p. 1986. pap. 26.95 (*88-7070-065-8*) Belvedere USA.

Textures. Rhett S. James. (Illus.). 100p. (Orig.). 1995. pap. 14.00 (*0-9643538-1-4*) Wstrn Profiles.

Textures: A Photographic Album for Artists & Designers. Phil Brodatz. (Illus.). (Orig.). 1966. pap. 8.95 (*0-486-21669-1*) Dover.

Textures: Photographs. Truitt. (Illus.). 1995. per. 27.50 (*0-85449-128-7*, Pub. by Gay Mens Pr UK) LPC InBook.

Textures: Strategies for Reading & Writing. Grace W. Ellis. LC 92-53794. 800p. (Orig.). (C). 1993. text ed. 21.50 (*0-03-020588-3*) HB Coll Pubs.

Textures in Non-Ferrous Metals & Alloys: Proceedings of a Symposium - Sponsored by the Non-Ferrous Metals Committee of the Metallurgical Society of AIME, Detroit, MI, September 19-20, 1984. Harish D. Merchant. LC 85-11569. 239p. reprint ed. pap. 68.20 (*0-8357-2521-9*, 2052401) Bks Demand.

Textures of Irish America. Lawrence J. McCaffrey. (Irish Studies). (Illus.). 300p. 1992. 34.95 (*0-8156-0267-7*) Syracuse U Pr.

*****Textures of Light: Vision & Touch in Irigaray, Levinas, & Merleau-Ponty.** Cathryn Vasseleu. LC 97-17425. (Warwick Studies in European Philosophy). 1998. write for info. (*0-415-14273-3*); pap. write for info. (*0-415-14274-1*) Routledge.

Textures, Spaces, Wonders. Frederic Will. LC 93-7832. 88p. 1993. text ed. 49.95 (*0-7734-3036-9*) E Mellen.

Texturing & Modeling: A Procedural Approach. David S. Ebert et al. (Illus.). 332p. 1994. text ed. 39.95 incl. disk (*0-12-228760-6*, AP Prof) Acad Pr.

Texturing Today. Shirley Inst. Staff. (C). 1983. 125.00 (*0-685-36029-6*, Pub. by British Textile Tech UK) St Mut.

Teyku: The Unsolved Problem in the Babylonian Talmus. Louis Jacobs. LC 80-70887. 312p. 1981. 20.00 (*0-8453-4501-X*, Cornwall Bks) Assoc Univ Prs.

Teyr-al Nader dar Sharhe Seyr-al Saer va Teyr-al Nader. Ali N. Salaheddin. LC 85-80048. 81p. (PER.). 1985. 55.00 (*0-910735-39-5*); pap. 25.00 (*0-910735-37-9*) MTO Printing & Pubn Ctr.

Tezen. Serge Madhere. 72p. 1989. pap. text ed. write for info. (*1-881686-01-9*) Madhere.

TFB: Typewriting for Business. Leger Morrison. 208p. 1985. reprint ed. student ed. 5.00 (*0-935920-35-8*, Ntl Pubs Blck); reprint ed. pap. text ed. 11.50 (*0-935920-34-X*, Ntl Pubs Blck) P-H.

TFP's Defense Against Fidelity's Onslaught. Study Commission of the American TFP Staff. Ed. by American TFP Staff. LC 89-85246. 170p. (Orig.). 1989. pap. text ed. 10.00 (*1-877905-20-8*) Am Soc Defense TFP.

*****TFT-LCD: Liquid-Crystal Displays Addressed by Thin-Film Transistors.** Toshihisa Tsukuda. (Japanese Tecnology Reviews Ser., Section A). 1996. pap. text ed. 70.00 (*2-919875-01-9*) Gordon & Breach.

TGIF: But What Will I Do on Monday? Susan L. Fister & Karen A. Kemp. (Illus.). 178p. 1995. teacher ed., pap. text ed. 19.50 (*1-57035-039-6*, 61TG) Sopris.

TGIF: Making It Work on Monday. Susan L. Fister & Karen A. Kemp. (Illus.). 204p. 1995. teacher ed., pap. text ed. 16.95 (*1-57035-040-X*, 61CP) Sopris.

TH Influenza UV Logik. Bill Bissett. 1996. pap. text ed. 11.95 (*0-88922-357-2*) Genl Dist Srvs.

Th Thorium: Compound with F, CI, Br, I, Vol. C4. 175p. 1993. 785.00 (*0-387-93666-1*) Spr-Verlag.

Th Thorium: Compounds with Si, P, As, Sb, Bi, & Ge. Planck, Max Society for the Advancement of Science, the Gmelin Institute for Inorganic Chemistry Staff. (Gmelin Handbuch der Anorganischen Chemie Ser.). (Illus.). xxiii, 301p. 1993. 1,310.00 (*0-387-93675-0*) Spr-Verlag.

Thackeray. M. Elqin. 1972. 59.95 (*0-8490-1187-6*) Gordon Pr.

Thackeray. Geoffrey U. Ellis. LC 79-160465. (English Literature Ser.: No. 33). 1971. reprint ed. lib. bdg. 43.95 (*0-8383-1300-0*) M S G Haskell Hse.

Thackeray. Anthony Trollope. Ed. by John Morley. LC 68-58404. (English Men of Letters Ser.). reprint ed. lib. bdg. 34.50 (*0-404-51736-6*) AMS Pr.

Thackeray. Anthony Trollope. (BCL1-PR English Literature Ser.). 206p. 1992. reprint ed. lib. bdg. 79.00 (*0-7812-7703-5*) Rprt Serv.

Thackeray: The Major Novels. Juliet McMaster. LC 76-151380. (Illus.). 246p. reprint ed. pap. 70.20 (*0-8357-8345-6*, 2034019) Bks Demand.

Thackeray: The Sentimental Cynic. Lambert Ennis. (Northwestern University. Humanities Ser.: No. 25). reprint ed. 28.00 (*0-404-50725-5*) AMS Pr.

Thackeray & Form of Fiction. John Loofbourow. LC 75-42172. 224p. 1976. reprint ed. 45.00 (*0-87752-177-8*) Gordian.

Thackeray & Slavery. Deborah A. Thomas. (Illus.). 275p. (C). 1993. text ed. 45.00 (*0-8214-1038-5*) Ohio U Pr.

Thackeray & Women. Micael M. Clarke. LC 94-36979. (Illus.). 250p. 1995. lib. bdg. 30.00 (*0-87580-197-8*) N Ill U Pr.

Thackeray in the United States. James Wilson. LC 70-119439. (Studies in Comparative Literature: No. 35). 1970. reprint ed. lib. bdg. 150.00 (*0-8383-1067-2*) M S G Haskell Hse.

Thackeray the Humourist & the Man of Letters. Theodore Taylor. LC 72-174687. (English Literature Ser.: No. 33). 1971. reprint ed. lib. bdg. 59.95 (*0-8383-1339-6*) M S G Haskell Hse.

Thackerayana (1901) William Makepeace Thackeray. LC 71-137436. (English Literature Ser.: No. 33). 1970. reprint ed. lib. bdg. 75.00 (*0-8383-1191-1*) M S G Haskell Hse.

Thackeray's Canvass of Humanity: An Author & His Public. Robert A. Colby. LC 78-27465. (Illus.). 1979. 55.00 (*0-8142-0282-9*) Ohio St U Pr.

Thackeray's Cultural Frame of Reference: Allusion in The Newcomes. R. D. McMaster. 234p. (C). 1991. text ed. 57.95 (*0-7735-0838-4*, Pub. by McGill CN) U of Toronto Pr.

Thackeray's "English Humourists" Edgar F. Harden. LC 84-40411. 280p. 1985. 40.00 (*0-87413-274-6*) U Delaware Pr.

Thackery Jewels: Amethyst; Emerald; Topaz. Phyllis T. Pianka. (Regency Romance Ser.). 1994. mass mkt. 5.99 (*0-373-31216-4*, 1-31216-4) Harlequin Bks.

Thaddeus. Illus. by Joyce Alexander. 1972. pap. 9.00 (*0-912020-20-2*) Turtles Quill.

Thaddeus Jones & the Dragon. J. Hjelm. LC 68-56830. (Illus.). 64p. (J). (gr. 2-5). 1968. lib. bdg. 10.95 (*0-87783-039-8*) Oddo.

Thaddeus Jones & the Dragon. deluxe ed. J. Hjelm. LC 68-56830. (Illus.). 64p. (J). (gr. 2-5). 1968. pap. 3.94 (*0-87783-110-6*) Oddo.

*****Thaddeus Kosciuszko: Purest Son of Liberty.** James S. Pula. 350p. 1997. 29.95 (*0-7818-0576-7*) Hippocrene Bks.

*****Thaddeus Mosley: African-American Sculptor.** David Lewis. (Illus.). 128p. 1997. 45.00 (*0-8229-3985-1*); pap. 24.95 (*0-8229-5634-9*) U of Pittsburgh Pr.

Thaddeus of Warsaw. rev. ed. Jane Porter. LC 70-162883. (Bentley's Standard Novels Ser.: No. 4). (Illus.). reprint ed. 37.50 (*0-404-54404-5*) AMS Pr.

Thaddeus Stevens. Ralph Korngold. LC 74-12629. 460p. 1974. reprint ed. text ed. 75.00 (*0-8371-7733-2*, KOTS, Greenwood Pr) Greenwood.

Thaddeus Stevens. Samuel W. McCall. Ed. by John T. Morse, Jr. LC 78-128951. (American Statesmen Ser.: No. 31). reprint ed. 45.00 (*0-404-50881-2*) AMS Pr.

*****Thaddeus Stevens: Nineteenth-Century Egalitarian.** Hans L. Trefousse. LC 96-35004. (Civil War America Ser.). 352p. (C). (gr. 13). 1997. 39.95 (*0-8078-2335-X*) U of NC Pr.

Thaddeus Stevens, Commoner. Edward B. Callender. LC 70-39881. reprint ed. 34.00 (*0-404-00011-8*) AMS Pr.

Thaddeus Stevens Papers: Guide & Index to the Microfilm Edition. Ed. by Beverly W. Palmer & Holly B. Ochoa. LC 94-2585. 184p. 1994. pap. 40.00 (*0-8420-4146-X*) Scholarly Res Inc.

Thai, Vol. 1. Foreign Service Institute Staff. 427p. 1980. pap. text ed. 195.00 incl. audio (*0-88432-050-2*, AFD300) Audio-Forum.

Thai, Vol. 2. Foreign Service Institute Staff. 410p. (C). 1970. pap. text ed. 215.00 incl. audio (*0-88432-104-5*, AFD350) Audio-Forum.

Thai & Cambodian Sculpture: From the 6th to the 17th Centuries. Wolfgang Felten & Martin Lerner. (Illus.). 256p. 1989. 150.00 (*0-85667-361-7*, Pub. by P Wilson Pubs) Sothebys Pubns.

Thai Boxing Dynamite: The Explosive Art of Muay Thai. Zoran Rebac. (Illus.). 120p. 1987. reprint ed. pap. 14.00 (*0-87364-426-3*) Paladin Pr.

Thai Cassette Pack. Berlitz Editors. (Cassette Pack Ser.). (Illus.). 192p. 1994. 15.95 incl. audio (*2-8315-1109-7*) Berlitz.

Thai Ceramics: The James & Elaine Connell Collection. Asian Art Museum of San Francisco Staff. (Illus.). 188p. 1994. pap. 85.00 (*967-65-3043-3*) OUP.

Thai Ceramics from the Sosai Collection. Kenji Itoi. (Asia Collection). (Illus.). 136p. 1989. 35.00 (*0-19-588918-5*) OUP.

*****Thai Cooking.** Carol Bowen. (Cooking for Today Ser.). 1996. 4.98 (*0-7651-9660-3*) Smithmark.

Thai Cooking. Kelly Simon. (Foods of the World Ser.). (Illus.). 120p. 1993. 12.95 (*0-8048-1979-3*) C E Tuttle.

*****Thai Cooking.** Akiko Ujlle. (Illus.). 84p. (Orig.). 1997. pap. 12.95 (*0-89346-841-X*) Heian Intl.

Thai Cooking Class. Somi A. Miller & Patricia Lake. (Illus.). 96p. (Orig.). 1993. pap. 7.00 (*0-685-66882-7*, Pub. by Angus & Robertson AT) HarpC.

Thai Cooking from the Siam Cuisine Restaurant. Diana Hiranaga & Somchai Aksomboom. (Illus.). 191p. (Orig.). 1989. 25.00 (*1-55643-075-2*); pap. 16.95 (*1-55643-074-4*) North Atlantic.

Thai Cooking Made Easy. Wei Chaun. 96p. (CHI & ENG.). 1992. pap. 15.95 (*0-941676-28-5*) Wei-Chuan Pub.

Thai Cultural Reader, Bk. 1. rev. ed. Robert B. Jones et al. 517p. (THA.). (C). 1994. pap. text ed. 18.00 (*0-87727-503-3*) Cornell SE Asia.

Thai Cultural Reader, Bk. 1. 2nd rev. ed. Robert Jones. 525p. (ENG & THA.). reprint ed. pap. 149.70 (*0-7837-1664-8*, 2041963) Bks Demand.

Thai Dictionary. (Handy Dictionaries Ser.). 120p. (Orig.). 1991. pap. 8.95 (*0-87052-963-3*) Hippocrene Bks.

Thai Economy in Transition. Ed. by Peter G. Warr. (Trade & Development Ser.: No. 5). (Illus.). 488p. (C). 1994. text ed. 65.00 (*0-521-38186-X*) Cambridge U Pr.

Thai-English & English-Thai Dictionary. 1974. 29.50 (*0-87557-087-9*) Saphrograph.

Thai-English Dictionary. George B. McFarland. xxi, 1060p. 1944. 45.00 (*0-8047-0383-3*) Stanford U Pr.

Thai-English Student's Dictionary. Ed. by Mary R. Haas. xxix, 638p. 1964. 35.00 (*0-8047-0567-4*) Stanford U Pr.

Thai Forms. Jean-Michel Beurdeley. (Illus.). 128p. 1980. 47.50 (*0-8348-0150-7*, 28518) Weatherhill.

*****Thai Garden Style.** Photos by Luca Invernizzi. (Illus.). 1997. 39.95 (*0-614-27255-6*) C E Tuttle.

Thai-German Dictionary: Thai-Deutsches Woerterbuch. Ampha Otrakul. 779p. (GER & THA.). 1986. write for info. (*0-8288-1722-7*, F65790) Fr & Eur.

Thai Hill Tribes Phrasebook. David Bradley. 184p. (Orig.). 1991. pap. 4.95 (*0-86442-131-1*) Lonely Planet.

Thai Home Cooking. Kamolmal Pootaraksa & William Crawford. 1986. pap. 12.95 (*0-452-26133-3*, Plume) NAL-Dutton.

Thai Home-Cooking from Kamolmal's Kitchen. William Crawford & Kamolmal Pootaraksa. 1986. pap. 9.95 (*0-452-25834-0*, Plume) NAL-Dutton.

Thai Horse. William Diehl. 1989. mass mkt. 6.99 (*0-345-32745-4*) Ballantine.

Thai Horse. William Diehl. 1996. mass mkt. 5.99 (*0-345-90985-2*) Ballantine.

Thai in 7 Days. Somsong Buasai et al. (Language in 7 Days Ser.). 96p. (THA.). 1995. pap. 12.95 incl. audio (*0-8442-9142-0*, Natl Textbk) NTC Pub Grp.

Thai Manuscript Painting. Henry Ginsburg. LC 89-20259. (Illus.). 112p. 1989. text ed. 34.00 (*0-8248-1295-6*) UH Pr.

Thai Music & Musicians in Contemporary Bangkok. Pamela Myers-Moro. LC 93-32327. (Center for Southeast Asia Studies: No. 34). 271p. 1993. pap. text ed. 22.50 (*0-944613-20-9*) UC Berkeley Ctrs SE Asia.

Thai Phrase Book. (Hugo Ser.). (Illus.). 128p. (Orig.). 1991. pap. 4.95 (*0-85285-154-5*) Hunter NJ.

Thai Phrase Book. Berlitz Editors. (Phrase Bk.). 192p. 1994. pap. 6.95 (*2-8315-0931-9*) Berlitz.

Thai Phrase Handbook: What You See Is What You Say. E. G. Allyn. Ed. by Somboon Inpradith & Nukul Benchamat. LC 91-76316. (Illus.). 304p. (Orig.). (C). 1993. pap. 14.95 (*0-942777-04-2*) Floating Lotus.

Thai Phrasebook: A Language Survival Kit. 3rd ed. Joe Cummings. (Illus.). 208p. 1995. pap. 5.95 (*0-86442-275-X*) Lonely Planet.

*****Thai Puppets & Khon Masks.** Natthapatra Chandavij. (Illus.). 160p. 1997. 39.95 (*974-8225-23-2*, Pub. by River Books TH) Weatherhill.

Thai Radical Discourse: The Real Face of Thai Feudalism Today. Craig J. Reynolds. (Studies on Southeast Asia: No. 3). (Illus.). 186p. (Orig.). (C). 1994. pap. text ed. 16.00 (*0-87727-702-8*) Cornell SE Asia.

Thai Radical Discourse: The Real Face of Thai Feudalism Today. Craig J. Reynolds. (Studies on Southeast Asia). (Illus.). 192p. (Orig.). reprint ed. pap. 54.80 (*0-8357-3117-0*, 2039375) Bks Demand.

Thai Reader. Mary Haas. LC 79-92824. 216p. (THA.). (C). 1978. reprint ed. pap. 15.00 (*0-87950-264-9*) Spoken Lang Serv.

Thai Reading. 164p. 1979. pap. 9.00 (*0-87727-511-4*) Cornell SE Asia.

Thai Scene. Michael Notcutt. 1995. pap. 12.95 (*0-85449-224-0*) LPC InBook.

*****Thai Sound System & Reading Rules.** Prawet Jantharat. 215p. (Orig.). (C). Date not set. pap. text ed. 15.00 (*1-877979-31-7*) SE Asia.

Thai Style. William Warren. LC 88-43422. (Illus.). 224p. 1990. 45.00 (*0-8478-1043-7*) Rizzoli Intl.

Thai Syntax: An Outline. Udom Warotamasikkhadit. LC 71-159472. (Janua Linguarum, Ser. Practica: No. 68). 77p. (Orig.). 1972. pap. text ed. 26.15 (*90-279-2095-8*) Mouton.

Thai System of Writing. Mary R. Haas. LC 79-92825. 130p. 1979. reprint ed. pap. 5.00 (*0-87950-266-5*) Spoken Lang Serv.

An Asterisk (*) at the beginning of an entry indicates that the title is appearing in BIP for the first time.

Thai Tales: Folktales of Thailand. Supaporn Vathanaprida. Ed. by Margaret R. MacDonald. (World Folklore Ser.). (Illus.). xviii, 152p. 1994. lib. bdg. 23.50 (*1-56308-096-6*) Libs Unl.

Thai Tellings of Phra Malai: Texts & Rituals Concerning a Popular Buddhist Saint. Bonnie P. Brereton. (Illus.). xiii, 252p. (Orig.). 1995. pap. 24.95 (*1-881044-07-6*) ASU Prog SE Asian.

Thai Temples & Temple Murals. Rita Ringis. (Illus.). 196p. 1990. 60.00 (*0-19-588933-9*) OUP.

Thai Textiles. Susan Conway. (Illus.). 192p. 1992. pap. 35.00 (*0-7141-2506-7*) U of Wash Pr.

Thai Titles & Ranks: Including a Translation of Traditions of Royal Lineage in Siam by King Chulalongkorn. Robert B. Jones. LC 79-30150. (Cornell University, Southeast Asia Program, Data Paper Ser.: Data Paper No. 81). 174p. reprint ed. pap. 49.60 (*0-317-08926-9*, 2010482) Bks Demand.

Thai Travel Pack. (Hugo Ser.). (Illus.). 128p. (Orig.). 1991. pap. 14.95 incl. audio (*0-85285-157-X*) Hunter NJ.

Thai Vegetarian Cooking. Vatcharin Bhumichitr. (Illus.). 192p. 1991. 32.50 (*0-517-58167-1*, C P Pubs) Crown Pub Group.

***Thai Vegetarian Cooking.** Vatcharin Bhumichitr. (Illus.). 160p. 1997. pap. 19.95 (*1-86205-092-9*, Pub. by Pavilion UK) Trafalgar.

Thai Vocabulary. Mary R. Haas. LC 79-92827. 373p. (THA.). (C). 1980. reprint ed. pap. 15.00 (*0-87950-265-7*) Spoken Lang Serv.

Thai Women in Buddhism. Chatsumarn Kabilsingh. LC 91-42293. 113p. 1991. pap. 12.00 (*0-938077-84-8*) Parallax Pr.

Thai Writing. 99p. 1979. pap. 9.00 (*0-87727-512-2*) Cornell SE Asia.

Thaianic Oscillations & Signaling. Mircea Steriade et al. 431p. 1990. text ed. 188.00 (*0-471-51508-6*) Wiley.

THAID: A Sequential Analysis Program for the Analysis of Nominal Scale Dependent Variables. James N. Morgan & Robert C. Messenger. LC 72-619720. 98p. 1973. 12.00 (*0-87944-137-2*) Inst Soc Res.

Thailand. (RAC Travel Guides Ser.). (Illus.). 96p. 1990. pap. 6.95 (*0-7117-0485-6*) Hunter NJ.

Thailand. (Insider's Guides Ser.). (Illus.). 224p. 1991. pap. 16.95 (*1-55650-054-8*) Hunter NJ.

Thailand. (Nelles Guides Ser.). (Illus.). 256p. 1992. pap. 14.95 (*3-88618-364-5*, Pub. by Nelles Verlag GW) Seven Hills Bk.

Thailand. 200p. 1995. spiral bd. 19.95 (*1-870049-05-5*) Oliver Bks.

***Thailand.** LC 97-5191. (Eyewitness Travel Guides Ser.). 504p. 1997. 24.95 (*0-7894-1949-1*) DK Pub Inc.

Thailand. Donna Bailey. LC 91-22044. (Where We Live Ser.). (Illus.). 32p. (J). (gr. 1-4). 1992. lib. bdg. 21.40 (*0-8114-2570-3*) Raintree Steck-V.

Thailand. Ben Davies. (Passport's Illustrated Travel Guides from Thomas Cook Ser.). (Illus.). 192p. 1994. pap. 12.95 (*0-8442-9049-1*, Passport Bks) NTC Pub Grp.

Thailand. Francis Hill. (Illus.). (C). 1989. 40.00 (*1-85368-048-6*, Pub. by New Holland Pubs UK) St Mut.

***Thailand.** John Hoskin. (Globetrotter Travel Guide Ser.). 1995. pap. 9.95 (*1-85368-360-4*) St Mut.

Thailand. Karen Jacobsen. LC 89-34413. (New True Bks.). (Illus.). 48p. (J). (gr. k-4). 1989. pap. 5.50 (*0-516-41179-9*); lib. bdg. 19.00 (*0-516-01179-0*) Childrens.

Thailand. Sylvia McNair. LC 86-29933. (Enchantment of the World Ser.). (Illus.). 128p. (J). (gr. 5-9). 1987. lib. bdg. 30.00 (*0-516-02792-1*) Childrens.

Thailand. Nicholas T. Parsons. write for info. (*0-614-17425-2*, Pub. by Euromoney UK) Am Educ Systs.

***Thailand.** John Villiers & Gavin Pattison. (Blue Guides Ser.). (Illus.). 416p. (Orig.). 1997. pap. 23.00 (*0-393-31583-5*) Norton.

Thailand. 2nd ed. Frank Kusy & Frances Capel. (Cadogan Country Guides Ser.). (Illus.). 408p. 1991. pap. 14.95 (*0-87106-154-6*) Globe Pequot.

***Thailand.** 5th ed. Insight Guides Staff. (Insight Guides Ser.). 1996. pap. 22.95 (*0-395-81932-6*) HM.

***Thailand.** 7th ed. Joe Cummings. (Illus.). 800p. 1997. pap. 19.95 (*0-86442-411-6*) Lonely Planet.

***Thailand, Vol. 65.** rev. ed. David Smyth. (World Bibliographical Ser.). 330p. 1997. 91.00 (*1-85109-254-4*) ABC-CLIO.

Thailand: A Country Study. 6th ed. Ed. by Barbara L. LePoer. LC 88-600485. (Area Handbook Ser.). (Illus.). 396p. 1989. text ed. 23.00 (*0-16-001732-7*, S/N 008-020-01184-3) USGPO.

Thailand: A Short History. David K. Wyatt. LC 83-25953. (Illus.). 354p. 1986. pap. 18.00 (*0-300-03582-9*, Y-565) Yale U Pr.

Thailand: A Socio-Economic Profile. Suchart Prasith-Rathsint. (Asian Social Science Research Council UNESCO Ser.). 1993. text ed. 30.00 (*81-207-0988-8*, Pub. by Sterling Pubs II) Apt Bks.

Thailand: Adjusting to Success: Current Policy Issues. David Robinson et al. (Occasional Paper Ser.: No. 85). viii, 50p. (Orig.). 1991. pap. 10.00 (*1-55775-221-4*) Intl Monetary.

Thailand: Economy & Politics. Pasuk Phongpaichit & Chris Baker. (Illus.). 450p. 1996. 59.00 (*967-65-3097-2*) OUP.

Thailand: Its People, Its Society, Its Culture. Frank J. Moore et al. LC 74-79218. (Survey of World Cultures Ser.: No. 15). 629p. reprint ed. pap. 179.30 (*0-317-11189-2*, 2010454) Bks Demand.

Thailand: Land of Smiles. Karen Schwabach. LC 90-40848. (Discovering Our Heritage Ser.). (Illus.). 128p. (YA). (gr. 5 up). 1991. lib. bdg. 14.95 (*0-87518-454-5*, Dillon Silver Burdett) Silver Burdett Pr.

***Thailand: Land of the White Elephant.** 96p. 1997. 6.50 (*0-8341-1642-1*) Nazarene.

Thailand: Nelles Guide. rev. ed. Nelles Verlag Staff. (Nelles Guides Ser.). (Illus.). 256p. (Orig.). 1996. pap. 14.95 (*3-88618-047-6*, Pub. by Nelles Verlag GW) Seven Hills Bk.

Thailand: Politics, Economy, & Socio-Cultural Setting. Woodworth G. Thrombley & William J. Siffin. LC 76-6602. reprint ed. pap. 47.50 (*0-404-15297-X*) AMS Pr.

Thailand: Society & Politics. John L. Girling. LC 80-69822. (Politics & International Relations of Southeast Asia Ser.). 306p. (C). 1985. pap. 14.95 (*0-8014-9328-5*) Cornell U Pr.

Thailand: The Complete Guide to the Exotic Land: Bangkok, the Temples, Beaches & Resorts. 4th ed. Fodor's Travel Staff. 1997. pap. 15.00 (*0-679-03290-8*) Fodors Travel.

Thailand: The Institutional & Political Underpinnings of Growth. Scott Christensen et al. LC 93-23260. (Lessons of East Asia Ser.). 46p. 1993. 6.95 (*0-8213-2608-2*, 12608) World Bank.

***Thailand: The Road to Sustained Growth.** LC 96-48790. (Occasional Papers: No. 146). 1996. 15.00 (*1-55775-603-1*) Intl Monetary.

Thailand see Cultures of the World - Group 3

Thailand - Bloody May: Excessive Use of Lethal Force in Bangkok. Physicians for Human Rights - Asia Watch Staff. 50p. 1992. pap. 7.00 (*1-879707-11-X*) Phy Human Rights.

Thailand - U. S. Relations: Changing Political, Strategic, & Economic Factors. Ed. by Ansil Ramsay & Wiwat Mungkandi. LC 88-8027. (Research Papers & Policy Studies: No. 23). 330p. (Orig.). 1988. pap. 10.00 (*1-55729-001-6*) IEAS.

Thailand & Burma. 3rd ed. (Handbooks of the World Ser.). 1994. 19.95 (*0-8442-8981-7*, Passport Bks) NTC Pub Grp.

Thailand & Burman Handbook. 4th ed. Ed. by Joshua Eliot et al. 736p. 1995. 21.95 (*0-8442-8885-3*, Passport Bks) NTC Pub Grp.

Thailand & Japan's Southern Advance, 1940-1945. E. Bruce Reynolds. LC 93-26125. 1994. text ed. 55.00 (*0-312-10402-2*) St Martin.

Thailand & the Philippines: Case Studies in U. S. IMET Training & Its Role in Internal Defense & Development. Jennifer M. Taw. LC 93-7185. 1994. pap. 13.00 (*0-8330-1347-5*, MR-159-USDP) Rand Corp.

Thailand & the United States: Development, Security, & Foreign Aid. Robert J. Muscat. (Studies of the East Asian Institute). 352p. 1990. text ed. 49.50 (*0-231-07144-2*) Col U Pr.

Thailand Atlas. Globe Pequot Press Staff. 1996. pap. text ed. 12.95 (*1-85368-447-3*) Globe Pequot.

***Thailand Green Guide.** Michelin Staff. 1997. per. 20.00 (*2-06-159601-0*, 1596) Michelin.

***Thailand Guide.** Lou Bechtel. 1997. pap. text ed. 16.95 (*1-883323-53-3*) Open Rd Pub.

***Thailand Handbook.** 1997. 19.95 (*0-8442-4918-1*) NTC Pub Grp.

Thailand Handbook. 2nd rev. ed. Carl Parkes. (Moon Travel Handbooks Ser.). (Illus.). 800p. (Orig.). 1997. pap. 19.95 (*1-56691-042-0*) Moon Trvl Hdbks.

Thailand in Pictures. Ed. by Lerner Publications, Department of Geography Staff. (Visual Geography Ser.). (Illus.). 64p. (YA). (gr. 5 up). 1994. lib. bdg. 19.95 (*0-8225-1866-X*, Lerner Publctns) Lerner Group.

***Thailand in Your Pocket Guide.** (In Your Pocket Guides Ser.). 1997. per. 9.95 (*2-06-651301-6*, 6513) Michelin.

Thailand, Indochina & Burma Handbook, 1994. Joshua Eliot. 864p. 1994. pap. 24.95 (*0-8442-9981-2*, Passport Bks) NTC Pub Grp.

Thailand Law Yearbook 1995. 120p. 1995. 70.00 (*962-7708-67-4*, Pub. by Euromoney UK) Am Educ Systs.

Thailand, Malaysia, & Singapore by Rail. Brian McPhee. (Bradt Rail Guides Ser.). (Illus.). 214p. 1993. pap. 14.95 (*1-56440-560-5*, Pub. by Bradt Pubns UK) Globe Pequot.

Thailand Pocket Guide. rev. ed. Berlitz Editors. (Pocket Guides Ser.). (Illus.). 160p. 1994. pap. 7.95 (*2-8315-2568-3*) Berlitz.

Thailand Product Guide. Ed. by C. DePaula. 350p. 1992. pap. 75.00 (*0-915344-47-5*) Todd Pubns.

Thailand Strategy for Fertilizer Development a Prefeasibility Study. Edwin C. Kapusta et al. (Technical Bulletin Ser.: No. T-17). (Illus.). 36p. (Orig.). 1980. pap. 4.00 (*0-88090-016-4*) Intl Fertilizer.

Thailand the Beautiful Cookbook. Panurat Poladitmontri & Judy Lew. (Beautiful Cookbook Ser.). 256p. 1992. 45.00 (*0-00-255029-6*) Collins SF.

Thailand, the Kingdom of Siam. (Asian Guides Ser.). 222p. 1992. pap. 12.95 (*0-8442-9717-8*, Passport Bks) NTC Pub Grp.

Thailand Travel Atlas. Joe Cummings. (Illus.). 44p. 1995. pap. 8.95 (*0-86442-269-5*) Lonely Planet.

Thailand, 1995: The MFC Investment Handbook. 404p. 1995. pap. 46.95 (*974-89251-8-8*) Hoovers TX.

***Thailande Green Guide.** (FRE.). 1997. per. 20.00 (*2-06-059601-7*, 596) Michelin.

Thailand's Agriculture. F. D. O'Reilly & P. I. McDonald. 98p. 1983. write for info. (*963-05-3360-X*, Pub. by Akad Kiado HU) St Mut.

Thailand's Durable Premier: Phibun Through Three Decades, 1932-1957. Kobkua Suwannathat-Pian. (Illus.). 320p. 1995. 38.00 (*967-65-3053-0*) OUP.

Thailand's Industrialization & Its Consequences. Medhi Krongkaew. LC 94-33766. (Series Studies in the Economies of East & Southeast Asia). 390p. 1995. text ed. 69.95 (*0-312-12458-9*) St Martin.

***Thailand's Islands & Beaches.** Joe Cummings & Nicko Goncharoff. (Illus.). 400p. (Orig.). 1998. pap. 15.95 (*0-86442-540-6*) Lonely Planet.

Thailand's Macroeconomic Miracle: Stable Adjustment & Sustained Growth. Peter G. Warr & Bhanupong Nidhiprabha. LC 95-13672. (Comparative Macroeconomic Study Ser.). 266p. 1996. 19.95 (*0-8213-2654-6*, 12654) World Bank.

Thailand's Reproductive Revolution: Rapid Fertility Decline in a Third World Setting. John Knodel et al. LC 87-8172. (Social Demography Ser.). (Illus.). 272p. 1987. text ed. 45.00 (*0-299-11050-8*); pap. text ed. 19.95 (*0-299-11054-0*) U of Wis Pr.

Thailand's Struggle for Democracy: The Life & Times of M. R. Seni Pramoi. David Van Praagh. (Illus.). 300p. (C). 1996. 34.95 (*0-8419-1321-8*) Holmes & Meier.

Thais: Rotisserie de la Reine Pedauque. Anatole France. 1976. 19.95 (*0-8488-0492-9*) Amereon Ltd.

Thais: Rotisserie de la Reine Pedauque. Anatole France. (Coll. Bleue). 224p. 1966. 17.95 (*0-7859-5259-4*) Fr & Eur.

Thakalis of North Western Nepal. Susanne Van Der Heide. 1988. 100.00 (*0-7855-0236-X*, Pub. by Ratna Pustak Bhandar) St Mut.

Thakalis of North Western Nepal. Susanne Von der Heide. 97p. (C). 1988. 200.00 (*0-89771-045-2*, Pub. by Ratna Pustak Bhandar) St Mut.

Thalaba the Destroyer. Robert Southey. LC 91-30166. 670p. 1991. reprint ed. 75.00 (*1-85477-080-2*, Pub. by Woodstock Bks UK) Cassell.

Thalamic Networks for Relay & Modulation. Ed. by Diego Minciacchi et al. LC 93-21166. (Studies in Neuroscience). 462p. 1993. 185.25 (*0-08-042274-8*, Pergamon Pr) Elsevier.

Thalamus. Ed. by E. G. Jones et al. 1400p. 1996. text ed. write for info. (*0-08-042507-0*, Pergamon Pr) Elsevier.

Thalamus. Edward G. Jones. 918p. 1985. 165.00 (*0-306-41856-8*, Plenum Pr) Plenum.

Thalassa. Andrea F. Litkei. (Illus.). 61p. 1967. pap. 6.95 (*1-880165-05-8*) Hanlit Pubns.

Thalassa: A Theory of Genitality. Sandor Ferenczi. 128p. 1990. reprint ed. pap. 25.95 (*0-946439-61-3*, Pub. by Karnac Bks UK) Brunner-Mazel.

Thalassemia: An Interdisciplinary Approach. Ed. by John T. Chirban. (Illus.). 106p. (C). 1987. lib. bdg. 35.50 (*0-8191-5675-2*) U Pr of Amer.

Thalatta: Der Weg der Griechen Zum Meer. Albin Lesky. LC 72-7899. (Greek History Ser.). (GER.). 1980. reprint ed. 31.95 (*0-405-04798-3*) Ayer.

Thales to Dewey: A History of Philosophy. 2nd ed. Gordon H. Clark. Ed. & Intro. by John W. Robbins. 548p. 1989. 21.95 (*0-940931-96-6*) Trinity Found.

Thales to Zeno see Jean Piaget

Thallium--201 Myocardial Imaging. fac. ed. Ed. by James L. Ritchie. LC 78-3004. (Illus.). 166p. pap. 47.40 (*0-7837-7357-9*, 2047166) Bks Demand.

Thallium-Based High-Temperature Superconductors. Ed. by Hermann & Yakhmi. (Applied Physics Ser.: Vol. 2). 640p. 1993. 195.00 (*0-8247-9114-2*) Dekker.

***Thallium in the Environment.** Ed. by Jerome O. Nriagu. LC 97-14871. (Advances in Environmental Science & Technology Ser.). 278p. 1998. text ed. 89.95 (*0-471-17755-5*) Wiley.

Thallium Myocardial Perfusion Tomography in Clinical Cardiology. D. C. Costa et al. (Illus.). 240p. 1994. 242.00 (*0-387-19675-7*) Spr-Verlag.

Thallium-201 & Technettium-99m-Pyrophosphate Nyocardial Imaging in the Coronary Care Unit. Ed. by Frans J. Wackers. (Developments in Cardiovascular Medicine Ser.: No. 9). (Illus.). 255p. 1980. lib. bdg. 104.50 (*90-247-2396-5*) Kluwer Ac.

Tham Khwan: How to Contain the Essence of Life: A Socio-Psychological Comparison of a Thai Custom. Ruth-Inge Heinze. 192p. 1982. 39.50 (*9971-69-047-0*, Pub. by Sgapore Univ SI) Coronet Bks.

Thames. Daniel Rogers. LC 92-44702. (Rivers of the World Ser.). (Illus.). 48p. (J). (gr. 5-6). 1993. lib. bdg. 24.26 (*0-8114-3104-5*) Raintree Steck-V.

Thames & Hudson Dictionary Art Terms. Edward Lucie-Smith. LC 83-51331. (World of Art Ser.). (Illus.). 208p. 1988. pap. 14.95 (*0-500-20222-2*) Thames Hudson.

Thames & Hudson Dictionary of Art & Artists. rev. ed. Herbert Read & Nikos Stangos. LC 93-61272. (World of Art Ser.). (Illus.). 352p. 1994. pap. 14.95 (*0-500-20274-5*) Thames Hudson.

Thames & Hudson Dictionary of Art & Artists. rev. ed. Ed. by Herbert E. Read & Nikos Stangos. LC 87-50342. (World of Art Ser.). (Illus.). 1988. 19.95 (*0-500-52340-1*) Thames Hudson.

Thames & Hudson Encyclopaedia of British Art. Ed. by David Bindman. LC 84-51499. (World of Art Ser.). (Illus.). 320p. 1988. pap. 14.95 (*0-500-20229-X*) Thames Hudson.

Thames & Hudson Encyclopaedia of Graphic Design & Designers. Alan Livingston & Isabella Livingston. LC 92-70862. (World of Art Ser.). (Illus.). 216p. 1992. pap. 14.95 (*0-500-20259-1*) Thames Hudson.

Thames & Hudson Encyclopaedia of the Italian Renaissance. Ed. by J. R. Hale. (World of Art Ser.). (Illus.). 360p. 1985. pap. 14.95 (*0-500-20191-9*) Thames Hudson.

Thames & Hudson Encyclopaedia of the Italian Renaissance. Ed. by J. R. Hale. (World of Art Ser.). (Illus.). 360p. 1985. 19.95 (*0-500-23333-0*) Thames Hudson.

Thames & Hudson Encyclopaedia of 20th-Century Music. Paul Griffiths. LC 85-51468. (World of Art Ser.). (Illus.). 208p. 1989. reprint ed. pap. 14.95 (*0-500-20235-4*) Thames Hudson.

Thames & Hudson Encyclopedia of Impressionism. Bernard Denvir. (World of Art Ser.). (Illus.). 1990. pap. 14.95 (*0-500-20239-7*) Thames Hudson.

Thames & Hudson Encyclopaedia of Twentieth Century Design & Designers. Guy Julier. LC 93-60123. (World of Art Ser.). (Illus.). 216p. 1993. pap. 14.95 (*0-500-20269-9*) Thames Hudson.

Thames & Hudson Manual of Bookbinding. Arthur W. Johnson. (Illus.). 224p. 1992. reprint ed. pap. 15.95 (*0-500-68011-6*) Thames Hudson.

Thames & Hudson Manual of Dyes & Fabrics. Joyce Storey. (Manuals Ser.). (Illus.). 192p. 1992. pap. 14.95 (*0-500-68016-7*) Thames Hudson.

Thames & Hudson Manual of Etching & Engraving. Walter Chamberlain. (Illus.). 200p. 1992. pap. 14.95 (*0-500-68001-9*) Thames Hudson.

Thames & Hudson Manual of Rendering with Pen & Ink. Robert W. Gill. LC 89-51867. (Illus.). 400p. 1990. reprint ed. pap. 15.95 (*0-500-68026-4*) Thames Hudson.

Thames & Hudson Manual of Screen Printing. Tim Mara. (Illus.). 1979. 18.95 (*0-500-67019-6*) Thames Hudson.

Thames & Hudson Manual of Typography. Ruari McLean. LC 80-50803. (Illus.). 216p. 1992. pap. 15.95 (*0-500-68022-1*) Thames Hudson.

Thames Barrier. Stuart Gilbert & Ray Horner. 216p. 1984. 31.00 (*0-7277-0182-7*, Pub. by T Telford UK) Am Soc Civil Eng.

Thames Barrier Design: Conference Proceedings. 208p. 1978. 50.00 (*0-7277-0057-X*, Pub. by T Telford UK) Am Soc Civil Eng.

Thames Cavalcade. L. M. Bates. 208p. 1994. 65.00 (*0-86138-090-8*, Pub. by T Dalton UK) St Mut.

Thames Doesn't Rhyme with James. Paula Danziger. 192p. (Orig.). (J). 1995. pap. 3.99 (*0-425-15015-1*) Berkley Pub.

Thames Doesn't Rhyme with James. Paula Danziger. 176p. (Orig.). (YA). 1994. 15.95 (*0-399-22526-9*, Putnam) Putnam Pub Group.

Thames Gateway - The Thames Gateway Planning Framework. (Regional Planning Guidance Notes Ser.: Ser. 9A). 70p. 1995. pap. 45.00 (*0-11-753109-X*, HM3109X, Pub. by Stationery Ofc UK) Bernan Associates.

Thames Groundwater Scheme: Conference Proceedings. 245p. 1978. 49.00 (*0-7277-0060-X*, Pub. by T Telford UK) Am Soc Civil Eng.

Thames of Henry Taunt. Henry Taunt. Ed. by Susan Read. (Illus.). 256p. 1990. 28.00 (*0-86299-616-3*, Pub. by Sutton Pubng UK) Bks Intl VA.

Thames on Fire: The Battle of London River, 1939-1945. L. M. Bates. 200p. 1990. 39.00 (*0-86138-037-1*, Pub. by T Dalton UK) St Mut.

Thames Ship Towage 1933-1992. John E. Reynolds. (C). 1989. text ed. 75.00 (*1-85821-028-3*, Pub. by Pentland Pr UK) St Mut.

Thames Strategy - A Study of Thames. 96p. 1995. pap. 55.00 (*0-11-753065-4*, HM30654, Pub. by Stationery Ofc UK) Bernan Associates.

Thames Valley Papists-from Reformation to Emancipation, 1534-1829. Tony Hadland. (C). 1993. 65.00 (*0-9507431-4-3*, Pub. by Chartered Pub Survey UK) St Mut.

Thamesway Soft Commission Handbook, Set. Ed. by Richard Waters. 295p. 1993. 245.00 (*1-85564-290-5*, Pub. by Euromoney UK) Am Educ Systs.

***Thanatochemistry.** 2nd ed. Dorn & Hopkins. 1997. text ed. 64.00 (*0-13-654195-X*) P-H.

Thanatologic Aspects of Aging. Ed. by Margot Tallmer et al. LC 78-70537. (Thanatology Service Ser.). 190p. 1980. pap. 9.95 (*0-930194-25-X*) Ctr Thanatology.

Thanatology: Through The Veil. Bruce. 1993. pap. text ed. write for info. (*0-07-008574-9*) McGraw.

Thanatology Abstracts, 1977. Otto S. Margolis & Daniel J. Cherico. 1980. 19.95 (*0-405-12503-8*) Ayer.

Thanatology Abstracts 1979. Otto S. Margolis & Daniel J. Cherico. 1981. 18.95 (*0-405-14222-6*, 19702) Ayer.

Thanatology Community & the Needs of the Movement. Ed. by Elizabeth J. Clark & Austin H. Kutscher. LC 92-10750. (Loss, Grief & Care Ser.: Vol. 6, No. 1). 125p. 1992. text ed. 29.95 (*1-56024-218-3*) Haworth Pr.

Thanatology Course Outlines, Vol. 2. Daniel J. Cherico & Otto S. Margolis. 1979. 18.95 (*0-405-12514-3*) Ayer.

Thanatology Curriculum-Medicine. Ed. by Robert De Bellis et al. LC 88-2934. (Loss, Grief & Care Ser.: Vol. 2, Nos. 1 & 2). (Illus.). 132p. 1988. text ed. 39.95 (*0-86656-738-0*) Haworth Pr.

Thanatology Thesaurus. Ed. by Roberta Halporn. (Thanatology Service Ser.). 50p. 1997. ring bd. 15.95 (*0-930194-17-9*) Ctr Thanatology.

Thanatopics: Activities & Exercises for Confronting Death. 2nd ed. J. Eugene Knott et al. 125p. pap. 22.95 (*0-669-20871-X*, Lexington) Jossey-Bass.

Thanatopsis Wings, No. 48. Ed. by Jackson Wilcox. (Wings Ser.). (Illus.). 36p. (Orig.). 1988. pap. 3.50 (*0-944231-02-0*) Slvr Wings CA.

Thanatos: Earth Poems. Thomas Parkinson. 1976. pap. 2.00 (*0-685-79271-4*) Oyez.

Thanatos Syndrome. Walker Percy. 1987. 17.95 (*0-374-27354-5*) FS&G.

***Thanatos Syndrome.** Walker Percy. 1996. pap. 12.00 (*0-449-91196-9*) Fawcett.

Thanatos Syndrome. Walker Percy. 416p. 1988. reprint ed. mass mkt. 6.99 (*0-8041-0220-1*) Ivy Books.

Thanatos to Eros: Thirty-Five Years of Psychedelic Exploration Ethnomedicine & the Study of Consciousness. Myron J. Stolaroff. 192p. 1994. 22.95 (*3-86135-453-5*, Pub. by VWB GW) Thaneros Pr.

Thanet at War, 1939-45. Roy Humphreys. LC 92-38201. 1993. pap. 20.00 (*0-7509-0297-3*, Pub. by Sutton Pubng UK) Bks Intl VA.

***Thang That Ate My Grandaddy's Dog.** John C. Rainey. LC 97-4447. 368p. 1997. 18.95 (*1-56164-130-8*); pap. 12.95 (*1-56164-133-2*) Pineapple Pr.

Thangam Philip Book of Cooking. Thangam E. Philip. 122p. 1982. pap. 3.50 (*0-86131-285-6*) Apt Bks.

Thangliena: The Life of T. H. Lewin. John Whitehead. (Illus.). 438p. (C). 1995. 40.00 (*1-870838-06-8*, Pub. by Kiscadale UK) Weatherhill.

Thangs Yankee Don't Know. 2.95 (*0-936672-31-5*) Aerial Photo.

Thanh Kinh Tan-Uoc. Tran N. Thao et al. 1300p. text ed. 20.50 (*1-885550-01-4*) Du-Sinh St Joseph.

***Thanhouser Films, 1909-1917: An Illustrated History.** Q. David Bowers. (Illus.). 200p. 1998. 45.00 (*1-879511-33-9*) Emprise NY.

Thank a Bored Angel: Selected Poems. Samuel Hazo. LC 83-4129. 128p. 1983. 14.00 (*0-8112-0869-9*); pap. 6.25 (*0-8112-0868-0*, NDP555) New Directions.

Thank God: Prayers for Jews & Christians Together. Carol F. Jegen & Byron Sherwin. 58p. (Orig.). 1989. pap. 6.50 (*0-929650-05-0*, JCPRAY) Liturgy Tr Pubns.

Thank God Ahead of Time: The Life & Spirituality of Solanus Casey. Michael H. Crosby. 334p. 1985. pap. 9.50 (*0-8199-0879-7*, Frncscn Herld) Franciscan Pr.

Thank God for Black Power. 2nd ed. James H. Boykin. LC 83-90000. 172p. 1983. pap. 16.99 (*0-9603342-2-X*) Boykin.

Thank God for Everything, Mini bk. Frederick K. Price. 32p. 1977. pap. 0.99 (*0-89274-056-6*, HH-056) Harrison Hse.

Thank God for His Grace. H. B. Sharp, Jr. 88p. (Orig.). 1996. pap. text ed. 7.00 (*1-57502-212-5*) Morris Pubng.

Thank God for Prayer. Russell W. Lake. LC 83-50397. 293p. 1983. 6.95 (*0-87159-159-6*) Unity Bks.

Thank God, I Am Alive. Frank Jakubowsky. 50p. (Orig.). 1989. pap. 5.00 (*0-932588-13-1*) Jesus Bks.

Thank God I'm Humble. Warren Schrader. 1992. pap. 6.50 (*0-85819-733-2*, Pub. by JBCE AT) Morehouse Pub.

Thank God I'm Manic. Rosemary Wren. (Illus.). 128p. (Orig.). 1993. pap. 10.00 (*0-9635408-0-7*) R Wren Prods.

Thank God, It's Monday! William E. Diehl. LC 81-71390. 108p. 1982. pap. 11.99 (*0-8006-1656-1*, 1-1656, Fortress Pr) Augsburg Fortress.

Thank God It's Monday: Discover Your Ministry Where You Work. Pat Klingaman. 180p. 1996. pap. 9.99 (*1-56476-538-5*, 6-3538, Victor Bks) Chariot Victor.

***Thank God It's Only Cancer.** Steve Gould. (Illus.). 56p. (Orig.). 1996. pap. write for info. (*0-9655160-1-6*) Mondays.

Thank Goodness for People. Charles M. Schulz. LC 76-8678. 192p. 1976. pap. 3.95 (*0-03-018121-6*) H Holt & Co.

Thank Goodness for People. Charles M. Schulz. 128p. 1991. pap. 7.95 (*0-8050-1693-7*, Owl) H Holt & Co.

Thank Goodness It Isn't a Hate Crime! Cartoons by Wayne Stayskal. Wayne Stayskal. (Illus.). 96p. (Orig.). (YA). (gr. 10). 1995. pap. 5.99 (*0-8010-5060-X*) Baker Bks.

Thank Gutenberg for Shakespeare & Ben Franklin. John M. Fontana. 24p. 1964. pap. 1.25 (*0-685-26780-6*) J M Fontana.

Thank Heaven for Little Girls. Tracy Sinclair. 1996. mass mkt. 3.99 (*0-373-24058-9*, 1-24058-9) Silhouette.

Thank Heavens for Friends. Helen Exley. (Suedel Giftbooks Ser.). (Illus.). 60p. 1993. 9.99 (*1-85015-451-1*) Exley Giftbooks.

***Thank Heavens for Pegasus! A Squeeze Me Book.** Walt Disney. (Hercules Ser.). (J). 1997. pap. 6.98 (*1-57082-536-X*) Mouse Works.

Thank You! (Miniature Pop-up Bks.). (Illus.). 14p. 1995. 4.95 (*1-56138-605-7*, Running Pr Mini Edtns) Running Pr.

Thank You. Adventure Staff. (Small Wonders Ser.). 120p. 1995. spiral bd. 4.99 (*1-879127-52-0*) Lighten Up Enter.

***Thank You.** Andrews & McMeel Staff. (Tiny Tomes Ser.). (J). 1997. 3.95 (*0-8362-3647-5*) Andrews & McMeel.

***Thank You.** Ariel Books Staff. 1996. 3.95 (*0-8362-0978-8*, Arie Bks) Andrews & McMeel.

Thank You. Chariot Books Staff. LC 50-6525. (Talking with God Ser.). 22p. (J). (ps). 1993. bds. 3.29 (*0-7814-0106-2*, Chariot Bks) Chariot Victor.

Thank You. Mary Engelbreit. (Illus.). 32p. 1993. 6.95 (*0-8362-4610-1*) Andrews & McMeel.

***Thank You.** Photos by Robert Frank. (Illus.). 80p. 1996. pap. 19.95 (*3-931141-27-6*, 620181, Pub. by Scalo Pubs) Dist Art Pubs.

Thank-You. Janet Riehecky. LC 88-16840. (Manners Matter Ser.). (Illus.). 32p. (J). (ps-2). 1989. lib. bdg. 18.50 (*0-89565-387-7*) Childs World.

Thank You. St. Paul Publications Staff. (C). 1990. text ed. 35.00 (*0-85439-356-0*, Pub. by St Paul Pubns UK) St Mut.

Thank You! Liesl Vazquez. (Charming Petites Ser.). (Illus.). 80p. 1995. 4.95 (*0-88088-789-3*) Peter Pauper.

***Thank You: A Changing Picture Book.** Ed. by Intervisual Books Staff. (Changing Picture Ser.). (Illus.). 80p. 1997. 4.95 (*0-8362-2682-8*) Andrews & McMeel.

***Thank You: Thoughts on Gratitude & Friendship.** Ariel Books Staff. 1997. pap. text ed. 5.95 (*0-8362-3625-4*, Arie Bks) Andrews & McMeel.

Thank You Amelia Bedelia. (J). pap. 1.95 (*0-590-38075-3*) Scholastic Inc.

Thank You, Amelia Bedelia. Peggy Parish. LC 92-5746. (I Can Read Bk.). (Illus.). 64p. (J). (gr. k-3). 1993. 14.95 (*0-06-022979-9*); lib. bdg. 14.89 (*0-06-022980-2*) HarpC Child Bks.

Thank You, Amelia Bedelia. Peggy Parish. (Illus.). (J). (ps-3). 1995. pap. 6.95 incl. audio (*0-694-70002-9*) HarperAudio.

Thank You, Amelia Bedelia: Newly Illustrated Edition. Peggy Parish. LC 92-5746. (Trophy I Can Read Bk.). (Illus.). 64p. (J). (ps-3). 1993. pap. 3.75 (*0-06-444171-7*, Trophy) HarpC Child Bks.

Thank You & OK! An American Zen Failure in Japan. David Chadwick. 464p. (Orig.). 1994. pap. 13.95 (*0-14-019457-6*, Arkana) Viking Penguin.

Thank-You Book. LC 96-30242. 1996. 5.99 (*0-87788-804-3*) Shaw Pubs.

Thank-You Book. abr. ed. Robyn F. Spizman. LC 93-81143. 96p. 1994. pap. 7.95 (*1-56352-141-5*) Longstreet Pr Inc.

Thank You, Brother Bear. Hans Bauman. (J). 1995. pap. 4.95 (*0-590-25487-1*) Scholastic Inc.

Thank You, Dr. Martin Luther King, Jr. Eleanora E. Tate. 240p. (J). (gr. 4-7). 1992. pap. 4.50 (*0-553-15886-4*) Bantam.

***Thank You, Dr. Martin Luther King, Jr.** Eleanora E. Tate. 240p. (J). 1992. pap. 4.50 (*0-440-41407-5*) BDD Bks Young Read.

Thank You for Asking. rev. ed. Christopher F. Givan. 24p. 1995. 5.00 (*0-936908-02-5*) Broncho Pr.

Thank You for Being. Clinton Weyand. (Illus.). 104p. (Orig.). 1978. 8.95 (*0-938292-07-2*) Being Bks.

***Thank You for Being Concerned & Sensitive.** Jim Henry. (Iowa Short Fiction Award Ser.). 152p. 1997. 24.95 (*0-87745-610-0*) U of Iowa Pr.

***Thank You for Being Such a Pain.** Mark Rosen. LC 97-23784. 1998. write for info. (*0-609-60099-0*, Harmony) Crown Pub Group.

Thank You for Calling. large type ed. Jeanette Nagai & Becky G. Olsen. Ed. by Cindy Drolet. 96p. (C). 1995. wbk. ed., spiral bd. 56.00 incl. audio (*1-883315-12-3*, 4032) Imaginart Pr.

Thank You for Coming: A Book to Help Children Be a Part of the Funeral Rituals. Janice Roberts & Joy Johnson. (Illus.). 48p. 1994. pap. 5.75 (*1-56123-071-5*) Centering Corp.

Thank You for Listening, But I Wasn't Quite Through. Perry A, pseud. 80p. (Orig.). 1995. pap. 11.95 (*1-887879-03-X*) Perry Prods.

***Thank You for Loving Me! The Psychology of Loving & Healing.** rev. ed. John R. Rice. Ed. by Thomas J. Botheroyd & Zachary A. Knaack. LC 84-60233. 116p. (Orig.). 1997. pap. 16.99 (*0-9655602-0-1*) Profssnl Dev Commn.

Thank You for Sharing. Philip Berk. LC 94-7451. 254p. 1996. pap. 12.95 (*1-885487-11-8*) Brownell & Carroll.

Thank You for Smoking: A Novel. Christopher Buckley. LC 95-10356. 288p. 1995. pap. 12.00 (*0-06-097662-4*, PL) HarpC.

Thank You for This Food: Action Prayers, Songs, & Blessings for Mealtime. Debbie T. O'Neal. LC 94-78747. (Illus.). 32p. (J). (ps). 1994. pap. 5.99 (*0-8066-2603-8*, Augsburg) Augsburg Fortress.

Thank You, Friend. Melanie Jongsma. (Friendship Ser.). (Illus.). 48p. (Orig.). 1996. pap. 0.55 (*1-882536-30-4*, A100-0065) Bible League.

Thank You God. 16p. Date not set. pap. 1.25 (*1-85792-094-5*, Pub. by Christian Focus UK) Spring Arbor Dist.

***Thank You, God.** Sally A. Conan. LC 97-7497. (Illus.). (J). 1997. write for info. (*0-8091-6643-7*) Paulist Pr.

Thank You God. George Donigian. (Storytelling Bks.). (Illus.). 8p. (J). (ps-3). 1995. pap. text ed. 1.95 (*0-687-00658-9*) Abingdon.

Thank You God. M. Rogers. (My First Prayers Ser.). 12p. (J). (ps). 1995. bds. 2.98 (*0-86112-196-1*) Brimax Bks.

Thank You, God: A Jewish Child's Book of Prayers. Judyth Groner & Madeline Wikler. LC 93-7550. (Illus.). 32p. (ENG & HEB.). (J). (ps-2). 1993. 14.95 (*0-929371-65-8*) Kar-Ben.

***Thank You, God: The Prayers of Children.** LC 96-49895. (Illus.). 64p. (J). (gr. k-2). 1997. 10.95 (*1-885223-53-6*) Beyond Words Pub.

***Thank You God: The Prayers of Children.** Compiled by Fiona Corbridge. (J). 1997. pap. 10.95 (*0-614-28639-5*) Beyond Words Pub.

Thank You God Book. Rachel N. Luna. 10p. (J). (ps). 1994. pap. 7.95 (*1-886551-00-6*) R N Luna.

***Thank You God for All My Friends.** Kath Mellentin & Tim Wood. (Thank You God Ser.). (Illus.). 24p. (J). (ps). 1997. 6.99 (*1-884628-07-9*) Flying Frog.

Thank You God for Baby Jesus. George Donigian. (Storytelling Bks.). (Illus.). 8p. (J). (ps-3). 1995. pap. 1.95 (*0-687-01701-7*) Abingdon.

Thank You, God, for Christmas. (Happy Day Coloring Bks.). (Illus.). 16p. (J). 1988. pap. 1.49 (*0-87403-467-1*, 02027) Standard Pub.

Thank You God for Jesus. George Donigian. (Storytelling Bks.). (Illus.). 8p. (J). (ps-3). 1995. pap. 1.95 (*0-687-00447-0*) Abingdon.

Thank You God for Me. George Donigian. (Storytelling Bks.). (Illus.). 8p. (J). (ps-3). 1995. pap. 1.95 (*0-687-00445-4*) Abingdon.

Thank You, God, for Me. Marybeth Hageman. (Christian Self-Discovery Ser.). (Illus.). 24p. (J). (ps). 1987. pap. 2.99 (*0-570-09114-4*, 56-1589) Concordia.

Thank You God for My Two Ears. Christine H. Tangvald. 12p. (J). 1993. 5.99 (*0-7814-0507-6*) Chariot Victor.

Thank You God for My Two Eyes. Christine H. Tangvald. 12p. (J). (gr. 1 up). 1993. 5.99 (*0-7814-0497-5*) Chariot Victor.

Thank You, God, for My Two Feet. Christine H. Tangvald. Date not set. 5.99 (*1-55513-931-0*) Cook.

Thank You, God, for My Two Hands. Christine H. Tangvald. (J). Date not set. bds. 5.99 (*1-55513-930-2*) Cook.

***Thank You God for the Wonderful World.** Kath Mellentin & Tim Wood. (Thank You God Ser.). (Illus.). 24p. (J). (ps). 1997. 6.99 (*1-884628-32-X*) Flying Frog.

Thank You Hashem. Yaffa Rosenthal. (ArtScroll Youth Ser.). (Illus.). 32p. (J). (gr. 1-8). 1983. 13.99 (*0-89906-777-8*); pap. 9.99 (*0-89906-778-6*) Mesorah Pubns.

Thank You, Jackie Robinson. Barbara Cohen. 128p. (J). 1989. pap. 3.99 (*0-590-42378-9*) Scholastic Inc.

***Thank You, Jackie Robinson.** Barbara Cohen. 1997. pap. 4.95 (*0-688-15293-7*, Mulberry) Morrow.

Thank You, Jeeves. P. G. Wodehouse. reprint ed. lib. bdg. 23.95 (*0-89190-294-5*, Rivercity Pr) Amereon Ltd.

Thank You, Jeeves. P. G. Wodehouse. LC 82-48821. 92p. 1989. reprint ed. pap. 10.00 (*0-06-097249-1*, PL) HarpC.

Thank You, Jesus. pap. 3.50 (*0-89066-194-4*) World Wide Pubs.

Thank you, Jesus: Luke 17: 11-19; Jesus Heals Ten Men with Leprosy. Mary M. Simon. LC 93-36192. (Hear Me Read Ser.: Level 2). (Illus.). 32p. (J). (gr. 1-3). 1994. pap. 3.99 (*0-570-04762-5*, 56-1781) Concordia.

Thank You, Jesus, for Puppy Dogs & Everything Else I Love. Barbara Lockwood. 10p. (J). 1992. bds. 4.29 (*1-55513-742-3*) Cook.

Thank You Lord. Louise Reece. (Illus.). 164p. (Orig.). 1983. pap. 3.95 (*0-9614264-0-3*) Lovejoy Pr.

Thank You, Lord, for Life! A Journal with Illustrations & a Reflection for Each Month of the Year. Joan Hutson. (Illus.). 154p. (J). (gr. 5-12). 1996. 9.95 (*0-8198-7383-7*) Pauline Bks.

Thank You M'am. Langston Hughes. (Classic Short Stories Ser.). (J). 1991. lib. bdg. 13.95 (*0-88682-478-8*) Creative Ed.

Thank You, Mom. Richard Haffey. (Greeting Book Line Ser.). 32p. (Orig.). 1986. pap. 1.95 (*0-89622-306-X*) Twenty-Third.

***Thank You, Mr. Falkner.** Patricia Polacco. LC 97-18685. (Illus.). 40p. (J). (ps-3). 1998. 15.95 (*0-399-23166-8*, Philomel Bks) Putnam Pub Group.

Thank You Mr. President. Merriman Smith. LC 75-31769. (FDR & the Era of the New Deal Ser.). 1975. reprint ed. lib. bdg. 39.50 (*0-306-70740-3*) Da Capo.

Thank You Music Lovers: A Bio-Discography of Spike Jones & His City Slickers, 1941-1965. Compiled by Jack Mirtle. LC 85-27128. (Discographies Ser.: No. 20). 448p. 1986. text ed. 69.50 (*0-313-24814-1*, MSN/, Greenwood Pr) Greenwood.

Thank You, Santa. Margaret Wild. (Illus.). 32p. (J). 1992. 12.95 (*0-590-45805-1*, Scholastic Hardcover) Scholastic Inc.

Thank You, Santa. Margaret Wild. (J). (ps-3). 1994. pap. 4.95 (*0-590-48100-2*) Scholastic Inc.

Thank You, St. Jude: Women's Devotion to the Patron Saint of Hopeless Causes. Robert A. Orsi. (Illus.). 336p. 1996. 30.00 (*0-300-06476-4*) Yale U Pr.

Thank You Stickers. Nina Barbaresi. (Illus.). (J). (gr. k-3). 1991. pap. 1.00 (*0-486-27197-8*) Dover.

***Thank You, Thank You, Thank You, God.** 24p. (J). 1993. write for info. (*0-7814-0006-6*) Chariot Victor.

Thank You, Toronto & Happy Birthday. Ansara Ali. LC 93-60619. (Illus.). 96p. (Orig.). 1993. pap. 13.95 (*0-9636170-3-6*) Royal Rags.

Thank You Very Much. Holly Stiel. 144p. (Orig.). 1995. pap. 6.95 (*0-89815-673-4*) Ten Speed Pr.

***Thank Your Mother for the Rabbits.** John Mills. 272p. 1993. pap. 14.95 (*0-88984-160-8*, Pub. by Porcupines Quill CN) Genl Dist Srvs.

***Thankful.** Furman Bisher. 1997. 9.95 (*1-56352-384-1*) Longstreet Pr Inc.

Thankful Blossom, & Other Eastern Tales & Sketches. Bret Harte. LC 72-37546. (Short Story Index Reprint Ser.). 1977. reprint ed. 27.95 (*0-8369-4105-5*) Ayer.

Thankful Days: Verses for Children. Merna B. Shank. (J). 1982. pap. 1.95 (*0-87813-212-0*) Christian Light.

Thankful Praise. Keith Watkins. LC 86-24514. 192p. (Orig.). 1987. pap. 10.99 (*0-8272-3650-6*) Chalice Pr.

Thankful Praise: A Studyguide. Cy Rowell. 24p. (Orig.). 1987. pap. 2.50 (*0-8272-3651-4*) Chalice Pr.

Thankless Gift. Slightly Off-Center Writers Group Staff. (Life's Roadmap Ser.). (Illus.). 60p. (J). (gr. 3-5). 1994. pap. 6.95 (*1-56721-025-2*) Twnty-Fifth Cent Pr.

***Thanks.** 1995. pap. 1.20 (*0-8341-9382-5*) Lillenas.

Thanks. Harriet Bacso. 224p. 1996. pap. 11.95 (*0-9649008-0-7*) TreeTop Books.

Thanks: Lovable, Livable, Laughable Lines. Marcia Kaplan & David Kaplan. (Illus.). 96p. (Orig.). 1989. pap. text ed. 6.95 (*0-9617744-4-4*) Cheers.

Thanks: What Does It Mean? Ruth S. Odor. LC 79-23926. (What Does It Mean? Ser.). (Illus.). 32p. (J). (ps-2). 1980. lib. bdg. 18.50 (*0-89565-113-0*) Childs World.

Thanks a Lot! Lucille Kraiman. 96p. (Orig.). (J). 1995. pap. 9.95 (*1-884362-05-2*) Butte Pubns.

Thanks Again, God. Eleanor S. Antrim. 1980. pap. 3.50 (*0-913342-29-7*) Barclay Pr.

Thanks & Hurrah. Peggy Day. 1991. pap. 5.98 (*1-879997-06-1*) Mystic Child Stu.

***Thanks & Praise.** (St. Joseph's Coloring Bks.). (Illus.). 32p. (Orig.). (J). (ps-3). 1988. pap. 0.99 (*0-89942-684-0*, 684/00) Catholic Bk Pub.

Thanks, Awfully! Jean L. Latham. 30p. (YA). 1929. pap. 3.00 (*0-87129-654-3*, T18) Dramatic Pub.

Thanks Be to God: Prayers from Around the World. Illus. & Compiled by Pauline Baynes. LC 89-28622. 32p. (J). (ps up). 1990. text ed. 13.95 (*0-02-708541-4*, Mac Bks Young Read) S&S Childrens.

Thanks, But No Banks! Great Ways to Finance Your Business. Patricia Ayres. 100p. (Orig.). 1994. pap. text ed. 14.95 (*0-9643237-0-2*) Am Womans Econ.

Thanks, Dad. Allen Appel. 80p. 1994. 8.95 (*0-312-10556-8*) St Martin.

Thanks, Dad - You Really Were a "Wise" Guy Afterall. Bill Bailey & Patrick Murphy. (Heartlines Ser.). 128p. 1994. pap. 6.95 (*1-881139-09-3*) Glovebox Guidebks.

***Thanks for Being My Friend.** Grampa Gray. (Tree of Life Mini-Books Ser.: Vol. 6). (Illus.). 12p. (Orig.). 1996. pap. 2.50 (*1-885631-33-2*, 33-2) G F Hutchison.

***Thanks for Coming By.** Chester F. Powell. LC 97-66268. 72p. (Orig.). 1997. 10.95 (*0-9632886-5-2*, 0-9766268) Plum Lick Pub.

Thanks for Giving & Other Poems. Marian Bitker. LC 90-93454. 63p. (Orig.). (YA). 1991. 15.00 (*0-9628150-0-4*); pap. 10.00 (*0-9628150-1-2*) M Bitker.

Thanks for Listening. Jack Brickhouse et al. LC 86-2103. (Illus.). 264p. 1995. pap. 12.95 (*0-912083-92-1*) Diamond Communications.

Thanks for Thanksgiving. Dottie Poole. (Illus.). 55p. (Orig.). (J). (gr. 3-8). 1995. pap. text ed. 8.95 (*1-887172-09-2*) G Bowden.

***Thanks for the Mammaries: The Untold Truth about Pregnancy.** Tina Hooper. (Illus.). 128p. (Orig.). 1997. pap. text ed. 6.95 (*0-9646452-7-0*) Dowling Pr.

Thanks for the Memories. Perry Tanksley. 4.50 (*0-686-15451-7*) Allgood Bks.

Thanks for the Memos. Michael Feldman. LC 95-3269. 141p. 1995. pap. 8.95 (*1-56079-523-9*, Petersons Pacesetter) Petersons.

Thanks from the Heart. Mark Ortman. Ed. by Patrick Caton. 168p. (Orig.). 1996. pap. 5.95 (*1-56245-237-1*) Great Quotations.

Thanks Lord, I Needed That! Charlene Potterbaum. LC 77-86470. 155p. 1979. pap. 4.95 (*0-88270-411-7*) Bridge-Logos.

Thanks, Mom. Allen Appel. 80p. 1994. 8.95 (*0-312-10557-6*) St Martin.

***Thanks, Mom.** Sherry C. Appel. LC 96-48917. 1997. 9.95 (*0-312-15222-1*) St Martin.

***Thanks, Mom, for Everything.** Susan A. Yates & Allison Y. Gaskins. LC 96-53836. 120p. 1997. 12.99 (*1-56955-017-4*, Vine Bks) Servant.

Thanks, Mr. President: The Trail-Blazing Second Term of George Washington. North Callahan. LC 90-84706. (Illus.). 256p. 1992. 19.95 (*0-8453-4835-3*, Cornwall Bks) Assoc Univ Prs.

Thanks of the Fatherland: German Veterans after the Second World War. James M. Diehl. LC 92-50811. xiv, 346p. (C). 1993. 49.95 (*0-8078-2077-6*) U of NC Pr.

Thanks, Santa, but Who's Gonna Put It Together? Owen Canfield. 177p. 1996. 17.95 (*1-56698-192-1*) Actex Pubns.

Unruly Christmas trees that refuse to remain standing, holiday gifts marked with the dreaded label "some assembly required," indoor football games & Christmas lasagnas. These are the things that create the laughter & the tears of Christmas. These are the things that Owen Canfield serves up for us in THANKS, SANTA, BUT WHO'S GONNA PUT IT TOGETHER? This beautiful book is a collection of Christmas Day columns written by Owen Canfield that originally appeared in THE HARTFORD COURANT from 1965 to 1994. In these columns, Mr. Canfield shared his Christmas memories that took place in a house on Woodbine Street in Torrington with ten children & a wife who, year after year, managed to turn a sportswriter's salary into Christmas magic. Interwoven with the Christmas tales are "love poems" written by Mr. Canfield to his wife, Ethel. The reader is treated to the memories of a man who is unashamedly in love with his wife & shares this love on nearly every page. There are columns of tribute to Ethel written after her death & columns of thanks for all she did as the family's Christmas Star. The author was a sportswriter & columnist for the Hartford Courant for thirty years. He has been selected six times as "Connecticut Sportswriter of the Year" by the National Sportscasters & Sportswriters Association. Through his annual accounts of the holiday antics of "the gallant ten," as well as photographs of the family & commentary on each column by the author, we are able to recall & relive our own Christmas magic. An excellent Christmas gift. For information or orders please contact the publisher: ACTEX Publications, 140 Willow Street, P.O. Box 974, Winsted, CT 06098. Phone (800) 282-2839, FAX (860) 738-3152, e-mail retail@actexmadriver.com. ***Publisher Provided Annotation.***

Thanks to Cows. Allan Fowler. LC 91-35062. (Rookie Read-about Science Ser.). (Illus.). 32p. (J). (ps-2). 1992. pap. 3.95 (*0-516-44924-9*); lib. bdg. 17.30 (*0-516-04924-0*) Childrens.

Thanks to Cows, Big bk. Allan Fowler. LC 91-35062. (Rookie Read-about Science Big Bks.). (Illus.). 32p. (J). (ps-2). 1992. pap. 32.40 (*0-516-49625-5*) Childrens.

Thanks to God & the Revolution: Popular Religion & Class Consciousness in the New Nicaragua. Roger N. Lancaster. 280p. 1988. pap. text ed. 16.50 (*0-231-06731-3*) Col U Pr.

Thanks to God & the Revolution: The Oral History of a Nicaraguan Family. Dianne W. Hart. LC 90-50090. (Illus.). 328p. (C). 1990. 15.95 (*0-299-12610-2*) U of Wis Pr.

An Asterisk (*) at the beginning of an entry indicates that the title is appearing in BIP for the first time.

***Thanks to My Mother.** Schoschana Rabinovici et al. LC 97-14407. (J). 1998. write for info. (*0-8037-2235-4*) Dial Bks Young.

Thanks to You! Miriam L. Elias. LC 94-44850. (J). 1994. 12.95 (*0-87306-663-4*); pap. 9.95 (*0-87306-664-2*) Feldheim.

Thanksgiving. Laura Alden. LC 93-13019. (Circle the Year with Holidays Ser.). (Illus.). 32p. (J). (ps-2). 1993. pap. 3.95 (*0-516-40688-4*); lib. bdg. 17.50 (*0-516-00688-6*) Childrens.

Thanksgiving. Judy Beach & Kathleen Spencer. (Teachers' Holiday Helpers Ser.). (J). (gr. 1-3). 1987. pap. 6.99 (*0-8224-6772-0*) Fearon Teach Aids.

***Thanksgiving.** Martin Hintz & Kate Hintz. (Celebrate! Ser.). (Illus.). 48p. (J). (gr. 3-7). 1996. 18.40 (*0-516-20087-9*) Childrens.

***Thanksgiving.** Kristine Kidd & Chuck Williams. LC 96-29831. (Williams-Sonoma Kitchen Library). (Illus.). 108p. 1997. write for info. (*0-7835-0324-5*) Time-Life.

Thanksgiving. Miriam Nerlove. Ed. by Judith Mathews. LC 89-49363. (Illus.). 24p. (J). (ps-1). 1990. lib. bdg. 12.95 (*0-8075-7818-5*) A Whitman.

Thanksgiving. Miriam Nerlove. (J). (ps-3). 1993. pap. 4.95 (*0-8075-7817-7*) A Whitman.

Thanksgiving. Shelly Nielsen. Ed. by Rosemary Wallner. LC 91-73033. (Holiday Celebrations Ser.). (J). 1992. lib. bdg. 13.98 (*1-56239-068-6*) Abdo & Dghtrs.

Thanksgiving. Lynda Sorensen. LC 94-17723. (Holidays Ser.). (J). (gr. k up). 1994. write for info. (*1-57103-072-7*) Rourke Pr.

***Thanksgiving.** Wendy Watson. (J). Date not set. write for info. (*0-688-09564-X*); lib. bdg. write for info. (*0-688-09565-8*) Lothrop.

Thanksgiving. Alana Willoughby. Ed. by Alton Jordan. (Holiday Set). (Illus.). (J). (gr. k-3). 1984. 7.95 (*0-89868-024-7*, Read Res); pap. 3.95 (*0-89868-057-3*, Read Res) ARO Pub.

Thanksgiving: A Thematic Unit. Ireta S. Graube. (Thematic Units Ser.). (Illus.). 80p. (Orig.). (gr. 1-3). 1992. student ed. 9.95 (*1-55734-258-X*) Tchr Create Mat.

***Thanksgiving: Prayer, Pilgrims, Native Americans.** Amanda Bennett. (Unit Study Adventures Ser.). 108p. Date not set. pap. 13.99 (*1-888306-12-2*, Home School Pr) GCB.

Thanksgiving: Stories & Poems. Caroline Feller Bauer. LC 93-18631. (Illus.). 96p. (J). (gr. 2-5). 1994. lib. bdg. 14.89 (*0-06-023327-3*) HarpC Child Bks.

Thanksgiving: Stories & Poems. Caroline Feller Bauer. LC 93-18631. (Illus.). 96p. (J). (gr. 2-5). 1994. 14.00 (*0-06-023326-5*) HarpC Child Bks.

Thanksgiving: Why We Celebrate It the Way We Do. Martin Hintz & Kate Hintz. LC 95-25928. 48p. (J). (gr. 3-9). 1996. lib. bdg. 17.80 (*1-56065-328-0*) Capstone Pr.

Thanksgiving see Set 6

Thanksgiving Activities. 16p. 1996. wbk. ed., pap. 2.95 (*1-55734-796-4*) Tchr Create Mat.

Thanksgiving Activity Book. Illus. by Dan Hayes. 24p. (J). (ps-3). 1992. pap. 4.95 (*0-8249-8550-8*, Ideals Child) Hambleton-Hill.

Thanksgiving Address: Greetings to the Natural World. 3rd ed. John Stokes. Tr. by Dan Thompson. (Illus.). 40p. (Orig.). (YA). (gr. 7-12). 1996. pap. 5.00 (*0-9643214-0-8*) Six Nations.

Thanksgiving Address: Greetings to the Natural World see Worte des Dankes: Ein Gruss an Die Naturwelt

***Thanksgiving Alphabet.** Ed. by Phyllis Wezeman. 66p. 1993. pap. 9.50 (*1-877871-57-5*, 2690) Ed Ministries.

Thanksgiving & Praise. deluxe ed. M. Countryman. 336p. 1989. ring bd. 14.95 (*0-937347-22-1*) C & D Intl.

Thanksgiving at Obaachan's. Janet M. Brown. LC 93-43933. (Illus.). (J). 1994. 12.95 (*1-879965-07-0*) Polychrome Pub.

Thanksgiving at Our House. Wendy Watson. (J). (ps-2). 1994. pap. 5.95 (*0-395-69944-4*, Clarion Bks) HM.

Thanksgiving at the Tappletons' Eileen Spinelli. LC 84-40793. (Illus.). 32p. (J). (gr. k-3). 1984. 11.95 (*0-201-15892-2*, Lipp Jr Bks) HarpC Child Bks.

Thanksgiving at the Tappletons' Eileen Spinelli. LC 91-33250. (Trophy Picture Bk.). (Illus.). 32p. (J). (gr. k-3). 1992. pap. 4.95 (*0-06-443204-1*, Trophy) HarpC Child Bks.

Thanksgiving at the Tappletons' Eileen Spinelli. LC 91-33250. (Illus.). 32p. (J). (ps-3). 1992. 15.00 (*0-06-020871-6*); lib. bdg. 14.89 (*0-06-020872-4*) HarpC Child Bks.

Thanksgiving Book. 3rd ed. Susan O. Higgins. Ed. by V. I. Wexner. (Holiday Ser.). 74p. (J). (ps-3). 1984. reprint ed. pap. 3.95 (*0-939973-01-4*) Pumpkin Pr Pub Hse.

Thanksgiving Book: An Illustrated Treasury of Lore, Tales, Poems, Prayers. Jerome Agel. 1995. 5.98 (*0-8317-8020-7*) Smithmark.

***Thanksgiving by the (Cook) Book.** James W. Baker et al. (Illus.). 52p. (Orig.). 1996. pap. 9.95 (*0-940628-53-8*) Pilgrim Soc.

Thanksgiving Cookbook. Holly Garrison. 1995. 12.00 (*0-02-860377-X*) Macmillan.

Thanksgiving Cookery. James W. Baker & E. Brabb. LC 93-70949. (Traditional Country Life Recipe Ser.). (Illus.). 96p. (Orig.). 1994. pap. 9.95 (*1-883283-03-5*) Brick Tower.

Thanksgiving Crafts. Judith H. Corwin. LC 93-6369. (Holiday Craft Bks.). (Illus.). 48p. (J). (gr. 3-5). 1996. pap. 5.95 (*0-531-15736-9*) Watts.

Thanksgiving Crafts. Judith H. Corwin. (Holiday Craft Bks.). (Illus.). 48p. (J). (gr. 3-5). 1995. lib. bdg. 19.80 (*0-531-11147-4*) Watts.

Thanksgiving Day. Gail Gibbons. LC 83-175. (Illus.). 32p. (J). (ps-3). 1983. lib. bdg. 15.95 (*0-8234-0489-7*) Holiday.

Thanksgiving Day. Gail Gibbons. LC 83-175. (Illus.). 32p. (J). (ps-3). 1985. pap. 6.95 (*0-8234-0576-1*) Holiday.

Thanksgiving Day. Gail Gibbons. (Illus.). (J). (gr. k-3). 1984. flmstrp 32.95 (*0-941078-60-4*) Live Oak Media.

Thanksgiving Day. Gail Gibbons. (Illus.). (J). (gr. k-3). 1985. 22.95 incl. audio (*0-941078-63-9*); pap. 15.95 incl. audio (*0-941078-61-2*) Live Oak Media.

***Thanksgiving Day.** Dianne M. MacMillan. LC 96-31395. (Best Holiday Bks.). 48p. (J). (gr. 1-4). 1997. lib. bdg. 17.95 (*0-89490-822-7*) Enslow Pubs.

Thanksgiving Day, 4 bks., Set. Gail Gibbons. (Illus.). (J). (gr. k-3). 1985. pap. 36.95 incl. audio (*0-941078-62-0*) Live Oak Media.

Thanksgiving Day: Let's Meet the Wampanoags & the Pilgrims. Barbara DeRubertis. (Holidays & Heroes Ser.). (Orig.). (J). (gr. 1-5). 1991. pap. 4.95 (*0-7915-1911-2*) Kane Pr.

Thanksgiving Day: Let's Meet the Wampanoags & the Pilgrims. Barbara DeRubertis. (Holidays & Heroes Ser.). 32p. (Orig.). (ENG & SPA.). (J). (gr. 1-5). 1996. pap. 7.95 incl. audio (*1-57565-012-6*) Kane Pr.

Thanksgiving Day Murder. Lee Harris. (Holiday Mysteries Ser.). 1995. mass mkt. 5.99 (*0-449-14923-4*, GM) Fawcett.

Thanksgiving Day Parade Mystery. Marion M. Markham. (Illus.). 64p. (J). 1990. pap. 2.95 (*0-380-70967-8*, Camelot) Avon.

Thanksgiving Feast: The First American Holiday. June Behrens. Ed. by Pauline Brower. LC 96-60569. (Holiday Play Series). (Illus.). 32p. (Orig.). (J). (gr. 2-5). 1996. pap. text ed. 5.95 (*1-889121-01-0*) York Hse Pubs.

***Thanksgiving Fiesta.** Laura E. Williams. (Let's Have a Party Ser.: No. 6). (Illus.). (J). 1997. pap. 3.99 (*0-380-79257-5*) Avon.

Thanksgiving Fun. Judith H. Corwin. (Holiday Fun Ser.). (Illus.). 64p. (J). (gr. 3 up). 1984. pap. 5.95 (*0-671-50849-0*, Julian Messner) Silver Burdett Pr.

Thanksgiving Fun: A Bountiful Harvest of Crafts, Recipes, & Games. Beth Murray. LC 92-75841. (Illus.). 32p. (Orig.). (J). (gr. 2-7). 1993. pap. 3.95 (*1-56397-280-8*) Boyds Mills Pr.

Thanksgiving Fun: Great Things to Make & Do. Ronne Randall. LC 93-48615. (Illus.). 32p. (J). (gr. 3-7). 1994. pap. 4.95 (*1-85697-500-2*, Kingfisher LKC) LKC.

Thanksgiving Holiday Grab Bag. Judith B. Stamper. LC 92-13420. (Illus.). 48p. (J). (gr. 2-5). 1992. lib. bdg. 13.95 (*0-8167-2906-9*) Troll Communs.

Thanksgiving Ideals 1995. Ideals Editorial Staff. (Illus.). 80p. 1995. pap. 5.95 (*0-8249-1131-8*) Ideals.

***Thanksgiving Ideals 1997.** Ideals Editors. (Illus.). 88p. 1997. pap. 5.95 (*0-8249-1145-8*, Ideals TN) Ideals.

Thanksgiving in Vegas. Curt Johnson. 112p. 1995. pap. 12.50 (*0-913204-33-1*) December Pr.

***Thanksgiving Is...** Louise Borden. LC 97-8767. (Hello Reader Ser.!). (Illus.). (J). 1997. 1.95 (*0-590-33128-0*) Scholastic Inc.

***Thanksgiving Monster: A Lift-the-Flap Book.** Alison Inches. (Illus.). 1997. pap. 5.99 (*0-14-056239-7*) Viking Penguin.

Thanksgiving over Water. Stephen Sandy. 1994. pap. 11.00 (*0-679-75278-1*) Random.

Thanksgiving Parade: The Good News Kids Learn about Faithfulness. Dorothy K. Mock. LC 93-2988. (Good News Kids Ser.). (Illus.). 32p. (Orig.). (J). (ps-2). 1993. pap. 4.99 (*0-570-04743-9*, 56-1762) Concordia.

Thanksgiving Poems. Ed. by Myra C. Livingston. LC 85-762. (Illus.). 32p. (J). (ps-4). 1985. lib. bdg. 14.95 (*0-8234-0570-2*) Holiday.

Thanksgiving Program Builder, No. 2. Compiled by Evelyn Stenbock. 1981. 4.50 (*0-8341-9280-2*, MP-404) Lillenas.

Thanksgiving Program Builder, No. 3. Compiled by Diane K. Cunningham. 1989. 4.50 (*0-685-68755-4*, MP-405) Lillenas.

Thanksgiving Story. Alice Dalgliesh. LC 87-11471. (Illus.). 32p. (J). (gr. k-3). 1985. pap. 5.99 (*0-689-71053-4*, Aladdin Paperbacks) S&S Childrens.

Thanksgiving Story. Alice Dalgliesh. LC 88-4448. (Illus.). 32p. (J). (gr. k-3). 1988. reprint ed. lib. bdg. 15.00 (*0-684-18999-2*, C Scribner Sons Young) S&S Childrens.

Thanksgiving Story Continues. Grace Reynolds. Ed. by Betse Grace. (Illus.). 80p. (Orig.). 1989. pap. 3.95 (*1-878374-27-3*) Pac Coast Pubs.

Thanksgiving Story in Vermont - 1852. Jeff Barth. (Illus.). 60p. (Orig.). (J). (gr. 3-8). 1989. pap. write for info. (*0-9624067-0-8*) Parable Pub.

Thanksgiving Surprise. Carolyn Keene. (Nancy Drew Notebooks Ser.: No. 9). (J). (gr. 2-4). 1995. pap. 3.50 (*0-671-52707-X*) PB.

Thanksgiving Tea Man. A. H. Brennan. 1986. 4.00 (*0-02-657930-8*) Macmillan.

Thanksgiving Treat. Catherine Stock. LC 89-49528. (Festive Year Ser.). (Illus.). 32p. (J). (ps-1). 1990. lib. bdg. 13.00 (*0-02-788402-3*, Bradbury S&S) S&S Childrens.

Thanksgiving Treat. Catherine Stock. LC 92-43690. (Illus.). 32p. (J). (ps-1). 1993. reprint ed. pap. 4.99 (*0-689-71726-1*, Aladdin Paperbacks) S&S Childrens.

Thanksgiving Uncles. Willey. (J). 15.00 (*0-06-026469-1*); lib. bdg. 14.89 (*0-06-026474-8*) HarpC Child Bks.

Thanksgiving Uncles. Margaret Willey. LC 95-43627. (Illus.). (J). 1997. write for info. (*0-06-027113-2*); lib. bdg. write for info. (*0-06-027114-0*) HarpC.

Thanksgiving Visitor. Truman Capote. 1968. 19.95 (*0-394-44824-3*) Random.

Thanksgiving Visitor. Truman Capote. LC 95-1503. (Illus.). 40p. (J). 1996. 19.00 (*0-679-83898-8*) Knopf.

Thannhauser Collection. Vivian E. Barnett et al. Orig. Title: Justin K. Thannhauser Collection. (Illus.). 192p. 1991. 45.00 (*0-89207-074-9*) S R Guggenheim.

Thanos Quest, Bk. I. Jim Starlin et al. 48p. 1990. 4.95 (*0-87135-681-3*) Marvel Entmnt.

Thanos Quest, Bk. II. Jim Starlin et al. 48p. 1990. 4.95 (*0-87135-682-1*) Marvel Entmnt.

***Thanzaloria Sticks Her Neck Out.** Donna H. Turner. (Illus.). 64p. (Orig.). (J). 1997. pap. 8.00 (*1-56002-654-5*, Univ Edtns) Aegina Pr.

Thape: In Search of the Bigfoot Myth. Ron T. Shaw et al. 144p. 1995. 20.00 (*0-8059-3706-4*); pap. 11.00 (*0-8059-3700-5*) Dorrance.

Thaqafat al-Tifl . . . Waqi wa-Afaq. Abd-al-Wahid Ulwani. 184p. (Orig.). (ARA.). 1995. pap. 4.95 (*1-57547-221-X*) Dar Al-Fikr.

***Thar She Blows.** Sue Kassirer. (Illus.). 32p. (J). (gr. 1-4). 1997. 14.95 (*1-56899-507-5*) Soundprints.

***Thar She Blows.** Sue Kassirer. (Illus.). 32p. (J). (gr. 1-4). 1997. pap. 5.95 (*1-56899-508-3*) Soundprints.

***Thar She Blows.** Sue Kassirer. (Illus.). 32p. (J). (gr. 1-4). 1997. 19.95 incl. audio (*1-56899-512-1*) Soundprints.

***Thar She Blows.** Sue Kassirer. (Illus.). (J). (gr. 1-4). 1997. audio 5.00 (*1-56899-515-6*) Soundprints.

***Thar She Blows, Incl. toy.** Sue Kassirer. (Illus.). 32p. (J). (gr. 1-4). 1997. 29.95 (*1-56899-509-1*) Soundprints.

***Thar She Blows, Incl. toy.** Sue Kassirer. (Illus.). 32p. (J). (gr. 1-4). 1997. pap. 17.95 (*1-56899-510-5*) Soundprints.

***Thar She Blows, Incl. toy.** Sue Kassirer. (Illus.). 32p. (J). (gr. 1-4). 1997. pap. write for info. incl. audio (*1-56899-511-3*) Soundprints.

***Thar She Blows, Incl. toy.** Sue Kassirer. (Illus.). 32p. (J). (gr. 1-4). 1997. write for info. incl. audio (*1-56899-513-X*) Soundprints.

***Thar She Blows, Incl. toy.** Sue Kassirer. (Illus.). (J). (gr. 1-4). 1997. audio write for info. (*1-56899-514-8*) Soundprints.

Tharkold Sourcebook: Torg. (Torg Ser.). 18.00 (*0-87431-329-5*, 20512) West End Games.

That All May Be Edified. Boyd K. Packer. 1982. 10.95 (*0-88494-473-5*) Bookcraft Inc.

***That All May Be One: Hierarchy & Participation in the Church.** Terence Nichols. LC 97-21588. 1997. pap. 29.95 (*0-8146-5857-1*, M Glazier) Liturgical Pr.

That All People May Be One People, Send Rain to Wash the Face of the Earth. Chief Joseph. LC 94-77351. (Illus.). 60p. (Orig.). 1995. pap. 12.95 (*0-945519-15-X*) Mountn Meadw Pr.

That Alluring Land: Slovak Stories by Timrava. N. Rudinsky. LC 91-38744. (Russian & East European Studies). 288p. (C). 1992. 49.95 (*0-8229-3709-3*); pap. 15.95 (*0-8229-5473-7*) U of Pittsburgh Pr.

***That Amazing Grace: The Role of Clarence & Grace S. in Alcoholics Anonymous.** Dick B. LC 95-92858. 160p. (Orig.). 1996. pap. 16.95 (*0-614-28307-8*) Paradise Res Inc.

***That & This.** Phillip D. Neugebauer. (Illus.). 228p. (Orig.). 1997. pap. 15.00 (*1-57502-494-2*, P01466) Morris Pubng.

That Art of Difference: Documentary-Collage & English-Canadian Writing. Manina Jones. 198p. 1993. 40.00 (*0-8020-2871-3*) U of Toronto Pr.

That Art Thou. Rajneesh Osho Staff. Ed. by Ma D. Sagar. (Early Talks Ser.). (Illus.). (Orig.). 1987. pap. 17.95 (*3-89338-011-6*, Pub. by Rebel Hse GW) Osho America.

That Awful Mess on Via Merulana. Carlo E. Gadda. LC 65-19320. 388p. 1984. pap. 8.95 (*0-8076-1093-3*) Braziller.

That Balance So Rare: The Story of Oregon. Terence O'Donnell. (Illus.). 152p. (Orig.). 1988. pap. 11.95 (*0-87595-202-X*) Oregon Hist.

That Black Day: Manuscripts of Crazy Jane on the Day of Judgement. David R. Clark. (Illus.). 55p. 1980. pap. 10.95 (*0-318-39998-9*, Pub. by Colin Smythe Ltd UK) Dufour.

That Bloody Bozeman Trail & Stagecoach West. Frank Bonham. 1990. pap. 3.50 (*0-8125-0534-4*) Tor Bks.

That Book about Drugs. Peter McWilliams. 384p. pap. 5.95 (*0-931580-60-9*) Prelude Press.

That Bothered Kate. Sally Noll. LC 92-40167. (Illus.). 32p. (J). (ps-3). 1993. pap. 4.99 (*0-14-054885-8*, Puffin) Puffin Bks.

That Boy, That Girl. Beverly Amstutz. LC 80-80372. (Illus.). 24p. (J). (gr. k-7). 1979. pap. 2.50 (*0-937836-01-X*) Precious Res.

***That Bringas Woman.** Benito Perez Galdos. Tr. by Catherine Jagoe. 256p. 1996. pap. 7.95 (*0-460-87636-8*, Everyman's Classic Lib) C E Tuttle.

That Buck Rogers Stuff. Jerry Pournelle. Ed. by Gavin Claypool. (Illus.). 101p. 1977. 9.00 (*0-935892-01-X*) Extequer.

That Burke Man: (Man of the Month) Diana Palmer. (Desire Ser.). 1995. pap. 3.25 (*0-373-05913-2*, 1-05913-8) Silhouette.

That Burning Question of Final Perseverance. unabridged ed. Harry E. Jessop. 48p. 1995. reprint ed. pap. 3.99 (*0-88019-340-9*) Schmul Pub Co.

That Camden Summer. LaVyrle Spencer. 1996. pap. 49.95 (*0-7871-0614-3*, Dove Bks) Dove Audio.

That Camden Summer. LaVyrle Spencer. 384p. 1996. 23.95 (*0-399-14120-0*, Putnam) Putnam Pub Group.

***That Camden Summer.** LaVyrle Spencer. 1997. mass mkt. 6.99 (*0-614-27757-4*) Jove Pubns.

That Camden Summer. large type ed. LaVyrle Spencer. 1997. pap. 24.95 (*0-7838-1606-5*, GK Hall) Thorndike Pr.

***That Camden Summer.** LaVyrle Spencer. 400p. 1997. reprint ed. mass mkt. 6.99 (*0-515-11992-X*) Jove Pubns.

That Carolina Summer. Janet Dailey. (Janet Dailey Americana Ser.: No. 883). 1992. mass mkt. 3.59 (*0-373-89883-5*, 1-89883-2) Harlequin Bks.

That Cat! Eve B. Feldman. LC 94-280. (Illus.). (J). 1994. 14.00 (*0-688-13310-X*, Tambourine Bks) Morrow.

That Cat Won't Flush. Wallace O. Chariton. LC 90-23139. (Illus.). 288p. (Orig.). 1990. pap. 12.95 (*1-55622-175-4*, Rep of TX Pr) Wordware Pub.

That Certain Style. Eleanora Brownleigh. (Lucky in Love Ser.: No. 23). 320p. 1993. mass mkt. 3.50 (*0-8217-4082-2*, Zebra Kensgtn) Kensgtn Pub Corp.

That Championship Season. Jason Miller. 1972. pap. 5.25 (*0-8222-1126-2*) Dramatists Play.

That Championship Season: The 1995 Northwestern Wildcats' Road to the Rose Bowl. Ed. by Francis J. Fitzgerald. LC 95-83850. (Illus.). 160p. (Orig.). 1996. pap. 19.95 (*1-887761-02-0*) AdCraft.

That Childhood Country. Deirdre Purcell. 528p. 1994. pap. 5.99 (*0-451-17871-8*, Sig) NAL-Dutton.

That Christ May Dwell in Your Hearts: Sermons on the Heidelberg Catechism Lord's Day I-XX. Ed. by N. D. Kloosterman. (Illus.). 190p. (Orig.). (C). 1988. pap. 4.95 (*0-9621146-0-X*) Mid-Am Refrm Seminary.

That Christmas Feeling, Vol. 134. 48p. 1980. pap. 6.95 (*0-7935-0983-1*, 00100586) H Leonard.

That Compassionate Touch of Ma Anadamayee. Narayan Chaudhuri. vii, 171p. 1986. reprint ed. 12.50 (*81-208-0204-7*, Pub. by Motilal Banarsidass II) S Asia.

That Constant Coyote: California Stories. Gerald W. Haslam. LC 89-70764. 192p. (Orig.). 1990. 22.00 (*0-87417-160-1*); pap. 14.00 (*0-87417-161-X*) U of Nev Pr.

That Crazy Vacuum. Carol Beich. (Illus.). 25p. (Orig.). (J). (gr. k-4). 1996. pap. 4.95 (*0-9631098-1-2*) Beich Pubng.

***That Crimson Flame.** Alison Bielski. 157p. 1996. pap. 14.95 (*3-7052-0784-9*, Pub. by Univ of Salzburg AT) Intl Spec Bk.

That Crow That Visited Was Flying Backwards. John Brandi. (Illus.). 56p. 1982. pap. 6.00 (*0-940510-05-7*) Tooth of Time.

That D--D Brownlow. Steve Humphrey. LC 77-18345. 1978. 12.95 (*0-913239-28-3*); pap. 6.95 (*0-913239-29-1*) Appalach Consortium.

That Dada Strain. Jerome Rothenberg. LC 82-18827. 96p. 1983. pap. 7.25 (*0-8112-0860-5*, NDP550) New Directions.

That Damn Romantic Fool. Michael Daniels. 14.00 (*0-89253-624-1*); 6.75 (*0-89253-625-X*) Ind-US Inc.

That Damn Single Shot. large type ed. Jim Miller. 1990. pap. 15.99 (*0-7089-6864-3*, Trailtree Bookshop) Ulverscroft.

That Damned Cowboy: Theodore Roosevelt & the American West, 1883-1898. Michael L. Collins. (Recent American History Ser.: Vol. 2). 229p. (C). 1989. text ed. 58.95 (*0-8204-1004-7*) P Lang Pubng.

That Dangerous & Persuasive Woman: Vida Goldstein. Janette Bomford. 208p. 1994. pap. 29.95 (*0-522-84542-8*, Pub. by Melbourne Univ Pr AT) Paul & Co Pubs.

That Dark & Bloody River: Chronicles of the Ohio River Valley. Allan W. Eckert. LC 95-17112. (Illus.). 864p. 1995. 27.95 (*0-553-09448-3*) Bantam.

That Dark & Bloody River: Chronicles of the Ohio River Valley. Allan W. Eckert. 832p. 1996. pap. 12.95 (*0-553-37865-1*) Bantam.

***That Dark & Bloody River: Chronicles of the Ohio River Valley.** Allan W. Eckert. 1996. pap. 12.95 (*0-614-20745-2*) Bantam.

That Darn Cat. Shannon O'Connell. (Romance Ser.: No. 859). 1992. pap. 2.69 (*0-373-08859-0*, 5-08859-6) Silhouette.

***That Day: Searching the Past to Unveil the Future Day of the Lord.** Norma C. Peters. 264p. (Orig.). 1997. pap. 12.99 (*0-9656749-0-8*) ACW Press.

That Day at the Quarry: An Autobiographical Novel. Tom Shaw. 156p. (Orig.). 1994. pap. 8.95 (*0-9640291-5-4*) Outbound Pr.

***That Day the Rabbi Left Town.** Harry Kemelman. 1997. mass mkt. 5.99 (*0-614-27741-8*, Crest) Fawcett.

***That Dear Land.** Charles S. Fox. 98p. (Orig.). 1997. pap. 12.95 (*1-57502-422-5*, PO1296) Morris Pubng.

That Devil Forrest: Life of General Nathan Bedford Forrest. John A. Wyeth. LC 89-8174. (Illus.). 672p. 1989. pap. 19.95 (*0-8071-1578-9*) La State U Pr.

That Dirty Fat. Michael Hobson. 1994. pap. 7.95 (*0-913923-95-8*) Woodland UT.

That Does Not Compute: A Handbook for the Baffled Computer Owner. Timothy J. Connor. (Illus.). 204p. (Orig.). 1992. pap. 19.95 (*0-9632910-1-7*) Disk Org Srvs.

That Elusive Extra Trick. Terence Reese & David Bird. 128p. 1995. pap. 13.95 (*0-575-05816-1*, Pub. by V Gollancz UK) Trafalgar.

That Enchantress. large type ed. Doris Leslie. (Shadows of the Crown Ser.). 1974. 25.99 (*0-85456-593-0*) Ulverscroft.

That Every Man Be Armed: The Evolution of a Constitutional Right. Stephen P. Halbrook. 1994. pap. 16.95 (*0-945999-38-0*) Independent Inst.

That Family Circus Feeling. Bill Keane. LC 81-72010. (Illus.). 104p. 1982. pap. text ed. 5.95 (*0-8362-1125-1*) Andrews & McMeel.

That Far-Off Self: The Collected Poetry of Maruyama (Family) Kaoru (Given) 2nd rev. ed. Maruyama Kaoru. Tr. & Intro. by Robert Epp. 360p. (C). 1994. text ed. 35.00 (*1-880276-49-6*) Yakusha.

That Fat Hat. Joanne Barkan. LC 92-7414. (Hello Reader! Ser.). (Illus.). (J). (gr. 1-2). 1992. 2.95 (*0-590-45643-1*) Scholastic Inc.

That Fierce Virgin. Date not set. pap. 6.95 (*0-14-010931-5*, Viking) Viking Penguin.

That Final Summer. M. Smith. 1995. 4.99 (*1-871676-91-6*, Pub. by Christian Focus UK) Spring Arbor Dist.

That Fine Italian Hand: A Wry Close-up of a Resourceful People. Paul Hofmann. 256p. 1991. pap. 12.95 (*0-8050-1729-1*, Owl) H Holt & Co.

That First Affair: Other Sketches. John A. Mitchell. LC 77-98587. (Short Story Index Reprint Ser.). 1977. 19.95 (*0-8369-3161-0*) Ayer.

T

That First Bite: Journal of a Compulsive Overeater. Karen Rose. 1990. 8.95 (*0-88282-070-2*) New Horizon NJ.

That First Bite - Chance or Choice? A Working Guide Empowering Choice for Those with Eating Disorders. Rosemarie Durphy & Mary Sullivan. 128p. (Orig.). 1992. pap. 7.95 (*0-9631517-6-2*) Jeremiah Pr.

That First Time. Hiroaki Sato. 82p. Date not set. 14.00 (*0-932662-68-4*) St Andrews NC.

That First Time: Renga on Love & Other Poems. Hiroaki Sato. 84p. 1988. 14.00 (*0-932662-74-9*) St Andrews NC.

That Fortune. Charles D. Warner. (BCL1-PS American Literature Ser.). 393p. 1992. reprint ed. lib. bdg. 89.00 (*0-7812-6894-X*) Rprt Serv.

That Frenchman, John Calvin. Robert W. Miles. LC 83-45625. reprint ed. 29.00 (*0-404-19843-0*) AMS Pr.

That Further Hill. MacDonald Carey. 1987. pap. 5.95 (*0-941017-12-5*) Bombshelter Pr.

That Gallant Ship USS Yorktown (CV-5) Robert J. Cressman. LC 84-62874. (Illus.). 196p. 1985. pap. 10.95 (*0-933126-57-3*) Pictorial Hist.

That Gentle Strength: Historical Perspectives on Women in Christianity. Ed. by Katherine J. Haldane & Elisabeth W. Sommer. 352p. 1990. text ed. 35.00 (*0-8139-1286-5*); pap. text ed. 17.50 (*0-8139-1293-8*) U Pr of Va.

That Girl from Texas. Albert Green. 72p. 1976. pap. 4.00 (*0-88680-190-7*) I E Clark.

That Goddess. Ivan Arguelles. 104p. 1991. pap. 8.95 (*1-880766-00-0*) Pantograph Pr.

That Godless Court? Supreme Court Decisions on Church-State Relationships. Ronald B. Flowers. LC 94-11019. 208p. (Orig.). 1994. pap. 16.00 (*0-664-25562-0*) Westminster John Knox.

That Good Between Us. Howard Barker. (Orig.). 1981. pap. 10.95 (*0-7145-3765-9*) Riverrun NY.

That Good Old Baylor Line. Denne Freeman. LC 75-260701. (College Sports Bks.). 1975. 10.95 (*0-87397-063-2*, Strode Pubs) Circle Bk Service.

That Grand Whig Milton. George F. Sensabaugh. LC 67-29815. 213p. 1972. reprint ed. 21.95 (*0-405-08948-1*, Pub. by Blom Pubns UK) Ayer.

That Great Sanity: Critical Essays on May Sarton. Ed. by Susan Swartzlander & Marilyn R. Mumford. (Illus.). 224p. (C). 1992. text ed. 42.50 (*0-472-10259-1*) U of Mich Pr.

That Great Sanity: Critical Essays on May Sarton. Susan Swartzlander. 1995. pap. 16.95 (*0-472-08323-6*) U of Mich Pr.

That Greater Freedom. Margaret Kirk. 1986. pap. 4.95 (*9971-972-34-4*) OMF Bks.

***That Gunk on Your Car.** Mark Hostetler. LC 97-18864. (Illus.). 104p. 1997. pap. 9.95 (*0-89815-961-X*) Ten Speed Pr.

***That Gunk on Your Car: A Unique Guide to Insects of the United States.** Mark Hostetler. (Illus.). 104p. (Orig.). 1996. pap. 10.00 (*0-9653788-0-2*) Brazen Cockrches.

***That Hair Thing: And the Sisterlocks Approach.** JoAnne Cornwell. (Illus.). 192p. (Orig.). 1997. pap. 19.95 (*0-9657426-5-2*) Sisterlocks.

That Half-Barbaric Twang: The Banjo in American Popular Culture. Karen Linn. (Music in American Life Ser.). (Illus.). 208p. 1991. 29.95 (*0-252-01780-3*) U of Ill Pr.

That Half-Barbaric Twang: The Banjo in American Popular Culture. Karen Linn. 208p. 1994. 12.95 (*0-252-06433-X*) U of Ill Pr.

That Hardhead Cinnamon. Jo Jones. LC 89-92753. (Illus.). 36p. (Orig.). (J). (gr. 2-5). 1989. pap. 6.95 (*0-9602266-1-3*) Jo-Jo Pubns.

That Hideous Strength. C. S. Lewis. 384p. 1996. pap. 6.95 (*0-684-82385-3*) S&S Trade.

That Hideous Strength. C. S. Lewis. LC 96-20722. 1997. 22.00 (*0-684-83367-0*) S&S Trade.

That Hideous Strength. C. S. Lewis. 382p. 1990. reprint ed. 60.00 (*0-02-571255-1*, Hudson Rvr Edtn) S&S Trade.

That Horse Whiskey! C. S. Adler. 160p. (J). 1996. pap. 3.99 (*0-380-72601-7*, Camelot) Avon.

That House in Manawaka: Margaret Laurence's A Bird in the House. Jon Kertzer. (Canadian Fiction Studies: No. 11). 95p. (C). 1992. pap. text ed. 14.95 (*1-55022-124-8*, Pub. by ECW Press CN) Genl Dist Srvs.

***That Hungarian's in My Kitchen: 125 Hungarian/American/Kosher Recipes.** Linda F. Radke. Ed. by Mary E. Hawkins. 179p. 1997. reprint ed. pap. 14.95 (*1-877749-28-1*) Five Star AZ.

That Hungarian's in My Kitchen, One Hundred Twenty-Five Hungarian - American Recipes. 3rd ed. Linda F. Radke. Ed. by Mary E. Hawkins. 179p. 1995. spiral bd. 14.95 (*1-877749-02-8*) Five Star AZ.

That I May Know Him. Joyce Fowler. 200p. (Orig.). 1989. pap. text ed. write for info. (*0-932281-00-1*) Quill Pubns GA.

That I May See: A Prayerful Discovery Through Imagination. Salvino Briffa. 140p. 1986. pap. 8.95 (*0-87193-251-2*) Dimension Bks.

That Incredible Christian. Aiden W. Tozer. 137p. 1986. pap. 8.99 (*0-87509-197-0*) Chr Pubns.

That Italian Summer. large type ed. Jean Davidson. (Linford Romance Library). 1991. pap. 15.99 (*0-7089-7048-6*) Ulverscroft.

That Jesus Christ Was Born a Jew: Karl Barth's "Doctrine of Israel" Katherine Sonderegger. 224p. 1992. 32.50 (*0-271-00818-0*) Pa St U Pr.

***That Kennedy Girl: A Biographical Novel.** Robert Demaria. 1997. 22.95 (*1-57036-395-1*) Turner Pub GA.

That Kind of Danger. Donna Masini. LC 93-36956. 128p. 1994. 22.00 (*0-8070-6822-5*); pap. 12.00 (*0-8070-6823-3*) Beacon Pr.

***That Kind of Woman.** Ed. by Bronte Adams & Trudi Tate. 10.95 (*0-7867-0963-4*) Carroll & Graf.

That Kind of Woman. Ed. by Bronte Adams & Trudi Tate. 304p. 1993. pap. 10.95 (*0-88184-963-4*) Carroll & Graf.

That Kookoory! Margaret W. Froehlich. LC 93-41833. (Illus.). 40p. (J). (gr. k-3). 1995. 15.00 (*0-15-277650-8*, Browndeer Pr) HarBrace.

***That Land Beyond.** Jenni Doherty & Liz Doherty. (Illus.). 47p. 1996. pap. 5.95 (*0-946451-24-9*, Pub. by Guildhall Pr IE) Irish Bks Media.

That Lass O'Lowries, 2 vols. in 1. Frances Hodgson Burnett. LC 79-3329. reprint ed. 44.50 (*0-404-61798-0*) AMS Pr.

***That Lass O'Lowrie's (1878)** Frances H. Burnett. (Pocket Classics Ser.). 160p. 1997. pap. 10.95 (*0-7509-1410-6*, Pub. by Sutton Pubng UK) Bks Intl VA.

That Looks Like a Nice House. Carrie E. Wynne. LC 94-898. (Illus.). 42p. (Orig.). (YA). (gr. 8). 1987. pap. 6.95 (*0-9613205-3-2*) Launch Pr.

That Magnetic Dog. Bruce Whatley. (J). (ps-3). 1996. pap. 7.00 (*0-207-18420-8*) HarperColl Wrld.

That Magnificent Cestrian-William Darlington: Being a Short Biography, 1782-1863. Dorothy I. Lansing. 87p. (Orig.). 1985. pap. 14.95 (*0-9619411-0-3*) Serpentine Pr.

That Man: Reading Level 3. (Sundown Fiction Collection). 1993. 3.95 (*0-88336-766-1*); audio 17.95 (*0-88336-263-5*) New Readers.

That Man Callahan! Catherine Spencer. 1996. mass mkt. 3.50 (*0-373-11812-0*, 1-11812-4) Harlequin Bks.

That Man Tate & Other Kindred Spirits: With Stories from the Allagash. Norman E. Marshall. LC 93-60020. (Orig.). 1993. pap. 12.95 (*0-9636231-0-9*) TreeTop MA.

That Marvel the Movie. E. S. Van Zile. 1976. lib. bdg. 59.95 (*0-8490-2738-1*) Gordon Pr.

That Mighty Sculptor, Time. Marguerite Yourcenar. Tr. by Walter Kaiser from FRE. 240p. 1992. 22.00 (*0-374-27358-8*) FS&G.

That Mighty Sculptor, Time. Marguerite Yourcenar. 240p. 1993. pap. 12.00 (*0-374-52375-4*, Noonday) FS&G.

That Most Subtle Question (Quaestio Subtilissima) The Metaphysical Bearing of Medieval & Contemporary Linguistic Disciplines. Desmond P. Henry. (Modern Revivals in Philosophy Ser.). 368p. 1993. 69.95 (*0-7512-0128-6*, Pub. by Gregg Pub UK) Ashgate Pub Co.

That Mushy Stuff. Judy Delton. (Pee Wee Scouts Ser.: No. 8). 80p. (Orig.). (J). (gr. k-6). 1989. pap. 3.50 (*0-440-40176-3*, YB BDD) BDD Bks Young Read.

That Must Have Been ESP! An Examination of Psychic Experiences. Leea Virtanen. Tr. by John Atkinson & Thomas DuBois from FIN. LC 89-45411. (Folklore Today Ser.). 192p. 1990. 31.50 (*0-253-36264-4*); pap. 5.95 (*0-253-20556-5*, MB-556) Ind U Pr.

That Myriad-Minded Man: A Biography of G. W. Russell, A. E. 1867-1935. Henry Summerfield. 354p. 7500. 49.95 (*0-900675-69-1*, Pub. by Colin Smythe Ltd UK) Dufour.

That Mystery Called Life. 84p. 1990. pap. 3.00 (*0-934803-74-9*) J Van Impe.

That Nakedness. Phyllis Koestenbaum. 1982. 6.50 (*0-941220-06-0*) Jungle Garden.

That Nelson! Tom Sullivan. (Illus.). 32p. (J). 1995. pap. 6.95 (*1-56189-392-7*, 85210) Amer Educ Pub.

That New Baby. Sara B. Stein. LC 73-15271. (Open Family Ser.). (Illus.). 48p. (J). (gr. 1 up). 1974. 12.95 (*0-8027-6175-5*) Walker & Co.

That New Baby. Sara B. Stein. LC 73-15271. (Open Family Ser.). (Illus.). 48p. (J). 1984. pap. 8.95 (*0-8027-7227-7*) Walker & Co.

That Nice Miss Smith. large type ed. Nigel Morland. 1990. 25.99 (*0-7089-2337-2*) Ulverscroft.

That Noble Dream: The Objectivity Question & the American Historical Profession. Peter Novick. (Ideas in Context Ser.). 500p. 1988. text ed. 80.00 (*0-521-34328-3*); pap. text ed. 19.95 (*0-521-35745-4*) Cambridge U Pr.

That None Should Die. Frank Slaughter. 28.95 (*0-89190-286-4*) Amereon Ltd.

That None Should Die. large type ed. Frank G. Slaughter. 656p. 1984. 25.99 (*0-7089-1120-X*) Ulverscroft.

That None Should Perish. Janet Graybill. 62p. (Orig.). 1994. pap. write for info. (*0-9619928-5-9*) Messg Love Victry.

That None Should Perish: How to Reach Entire Cities for Christ Through Prayer Evangelism. Ed Silvoso. Ed. by Virginia Woodard. LC 94-17579. (Illus.). 300p. 1994. 16.99 (*0-8307-1688-2*, 5112481) Regal.

That Noodlehead Epaminondas. Retold by Eve Merriam. (Illus.). (J). 1992. reprint ed. pap. 8.95 (*0-89966-962-X*) Buccaneer Bks.

That Nothing Be Wasted: My Experience with the Suicide of My Son. Mary Langford. 64p. (Orig.). 1989. pap. text ed. 2.95 (*0-936625-61-9*, New Hope AL) Womans Mission Union.

That Nun from Saint Luis: To Catch a Snake. Leona Ruby. (Illus.). 300p. 1996. pap. 10.00 (*0-8059-3726-9*) Dorrance.

That Old Black Magic. large type ed. Pepper Adams. 226p. 1992. reprint ed. lib. bdg. 13.95 (*1-56054-410-4*) Thorndike Pr.

***That Old Black Magic: Essays, Images & Verse on the Joys of Loving Black Men.** D. Anne Browne. 250p. (Orig.). 1997. pap. 13.95 (*1-878647-35-0*) Duncan & Duncan.

That Old Devil Moon (Women Who Dare) Anne Logan. (Superromance Ser.). 1996. mass mkt. 3.99 (*0-373-70688-X*, 1-70688-6) Harlequin Bks.

That Old Overland Stagecoaching. Eva J. Boyd. (Illus.). 224p. (Orig.). 1992. pap. 12.95 (*1-55622-250-5*, Rep of TX Pr) Wordware Pub.

That Old Serpent, the Devil. F. J. Huegel. pap. 4.99 (*0-88019-113-9*) Schmul Pub Co.

That Old Studebaker. Lee Lynch. 272p. (Orig.). 1991. pap. 9.95 (*0-941483-82-7*) Naiad Pr.

That Old-Time Religion. Archibald T. Robertson. LC 78-24159. 282p. 1979. reprint ed. text ed. 59.75 (*0-313-20823-9*, ROOT, Greenwood Pr) Greenwood.

That Old-Time Religion: Poetry Book Society Recommendation. Peter Didsbury. 64p. 9400. pap. 14.95 (*1-85224-255-8*, Pub. by Bloodaxe Bks UK) Dufour.

That Old Time Rock & Roll: A Chronicle of an Era, 1954-1963. Richard Aquila. 375p. 1989. 25.00 (*0-02-870082-1*) Schirmer Bks.

***That Old Tin Can.** Bird & Falk. (New Trend Fiction A Ser.). (J). 1993. pap. text ed. write for info. (*0-582-91192-3*, Pub. by Longman UK) Longman.

That Other Brightness. Virginia Gilbert. 109p. 1995. pap. 9.95 (*1-887810-40-4*) Blck Star Pr.

That Other God. David Beasley. 340p. 1993. pap. 18.95 (*0-915317-02-8*) Davus Pub.

That Others Might Live: The U. S. Life-Saving Service, 1878-1915. Dennis L. Noble. LC 93-37539. (Illus.). 198p. 1994. 28.95 (*1-55750-627-2*) Naval Inst Pr.

That Outlaw Attitude. Noreen Brownlie. 1994. 3.50 (*0-373-09888-X*) Silhouette.

That Pale Mother Rising: Sentimental Discourses & the Imitation of Motherhood in Nineteenth-Century America. Eva Cherniavsky. LC 94-13186. 176p. 1995. 25.00 (*0-253-31343-0*); pap. 10.95 (*0-253-20934-X*) Ind U Pr.

That Paralysing Apparition, Beauty. Untersuchunen zu Christopher Caudwells Ideologie und Widerspiegelungatheorie. Juergen Schmidt. (Bochum Studies in English: No. 14). 622p. (Orig.). 1982. 49.00 (*90-6032-235-5*, Pub. by B R Gruener NE) Benjamins North Am.

That Pesky Toaster. large type ed. Ben Hillman. LC 94-9831. (Illus.). 32p. (J). 1995. 13.95 (*0-7868-0033-X*); lib. bdg. 13.89 (*0-7868-2028-4*) Hyprn Child.

That Printer of Udell's. Harold B. Wright. LC 95-26339. 352p. 1996. reprint ed. pap. 5.95 (*1-56554-121-9*) Pelican.

That Pup Blueberry. (J). (gr. 4 up). 1994. 3.50 (*0-9614746-0-2*) Berry Bks.

That Quail, Robert. Margaret Stanger. LC 92-52614. 128p. 1992. pap. 5.00 (*0-06-081246-X*, PL) HarpC.

That Quail, Robert. Margaret A. Stanger. 18.95 (*0-8488-1468-1*) Amereon Ltd.

That Quail, Robert. Margaret A. Stanger. 128p. 1986. reprint ed. lib. bdg. 25.95 (*0-89966-565-9*) Buccaneer Bks.

That Red Wheelbarrow: Selected Literary Essays. Robert Coles. LC 88-14281. 368p. 1988. 28.95 (*0-87745-208-3*) U of Iowa Pr.

That Reminds Me. Girault M. Jones. (Illus.). xiv, 211p. (Orig.). 1984. pap. 10.00 (*0-918769-08-6*) Univ South Pr.

That Reminds Me: Canada's Authors Relive Their Most Embarrassing Moments. Ed. by Marta Kurc. 172p. 1990. 19.95 (*0-7737-2418-4*) Genl Dist Srvs.

That Reminds Me of a Story: The Life of Abraham Lincoln. Richard E. Swanson. (Illus.). 130p. (Orig.). 1995. pap. 19.95 (*0-9640857-1-2*) Busn Connect.

That Reminds Me of a Story About... Bearl S. King. 1992. pap. text ed. 7.95 (*1-879243-06-7*) Writers Helpers.

That Reminds Me of the One. Ed. by Tom Petrie & Chuck Petrie. 256p. 1995. 22.50 (*1-57223-024-X*) Idyll Arbor.

That Ribbon of Highway: Highway 99 from the Oregon Border to the State Capital. Jill Livingston. (Illus.). 176p. (Orig.). 1996. pap. 14.99 (*0-9651377-0-8*) Liv Gold Pr.

***That Ribbon of Highway II: Highway 99 from Sacramento to Mexico.** Jill Livingston. (Illus.). (Orig.). 1997. pap. write for info. (*0-9651377-2-4*) Liv Gold Pr.

***That Same Flower: Floria Aemilia's Letter to St. Augustine.** Jostein Gaarder. 1998. 21.00 (*0-374-25384-6*) FS&G.

That Same Old Feeling. Judith Duncan. (Intimate Moments Ser.). 1994. mass mkt. 3.50 (*0-373-07577-4*, 1-07577-9) Harlequin Bks.

That Saved a Wretch Like Me: The True Story of a Life God Turned Around. Marvin N. Dixon. LC 93-20016. 152p. (Orig.). 1993. pap. 10.99 (*0-8272-3631-X*) Chalice Pr.

That Scoundrel Scapin see Miser & Other Plays

That Seeing, They May Believe: Children's Object Lessons. Kenneth A. Mortonson. LC 93-18007. 1993. pap. 9.50 (*1-55673-652-5*, 9352) CSS OH.

That Serious He-Man Ball. Alonzo D. Lamont, Jr. 1992. pap. 5.25 (*0-8222-1127-0*) Dramatists Play.

That Shakespeherian Rag: Essays on a Critical Process. Terence Hawkes. 200p. 1986. 25.00 (*0-416-38530-3*, 9736) Routledge Chapman & Hall.

That Shining Place. Simone Poirier-Bures. 96p. 1995. 23.95 (*0-7780-1017-1*, Pub. by Oberon Pr CN); pap. 11.95 (*0-7780-1019-8*, Pub. by Oberon Pr CN) Pocahontas Pr.

That Special Friend: A Token of Love. Suzanne S. Zenkel. (Keepsakes with CDs Ser.). (Illus.). 56p. 1996. 13.99 (*0-88088-866-0*) Peter Pauper.

That Special Magic. Elizabeth S. Montfort. LC 87-71719. (Illus.). 53p. (Orig.). (J). (gr. 2-3). 1988. pap. 5.00 (*0-916383-37-7*) Aegina Pr.

That Special Mother: Loving Reflections. Ed. & Compiled by Phyllis D. Alston. (Keepsakes with CDs Ser.). (Illus.). 56p. 1995. 13.99 incl. audio compact disk (*0-88088-870-9*) Peter Pauper.

That Special Summer. Linda Swift. 544p. 1994. mass mkt. 4.99 (*0-8217-4431-3*, Zebra Kensgtn) Kensgtn Pub Corp.

That Special Touch. Sandra P. Davis. LC 89-92544. (Illus.). 140p. 1990. 39.95 (*0-9625232-0-8*) Special Touch.

That Special Woman: Getting Older, Getting Better. Ed. by Lois L. Kaufman. (Keepsakes Ser.). (Illus.). 56p. 1994. 13.99 incl. audio compact disk (*0-88088-869-5*) Peter Pauper.

That Special You: Feeling Good about Yourself. Rita Freedman. (Keepsakes Ser.). (Illus.). 56p. 1994. 13.99 incl. audio compact disk (*0-88088-867-9*) Peter Pauper.

That Sterling Soldier: The Life of David A. Russell. A. D. Slade. 216p. 1995. 30.00 (*0-89029-324-4*) Morningside Bkshop.

That Strange Divine Sea: Reflections on Being a Catholic. Christopher Derrick. LC 83-80190. 189p. (Orig.). 1983. pap. 8.95 (*0-89870-029-9*) Ignatius Pr.

That Stuff Will Never Work Here. Robin E. McDermott et al. (Illus.). 17p. (C). 1995. teacher ed. 5.00 (*1-882307-05-4*) Res Engineering.

That Summer. Sarah Dessen. LC 96-7643. 208p. (YA). (gr. 7 up). 1996. lib. bdg. 17.99 (*0-531-08888-X*) Orchard Bks Watts.

That Summer. Sarah Dessen. LC 96-7643. 208p. (YA). (gr. 7 up). 1996. 16.95 (*0-531-09538-X*) Orchard Bks Watts.

That Summer. David Edgar. 80p. (C). 1988. pap. 9.95 (*0-413-17450-6*, A0283, Pub. by Methuen UK) Heinemann.

That Summer. large type ed. Mary Raymond. (Romance Ser.). 288p. 1986. 25.99 (*0-7089-1507-8*) Ulverscroft.

***That Summer in Eagle Street.** large type ed. Harry Bowling. (Magna Large Print Ser.). 616p. 1997. 27.50 (*0-7505-1063-3*) Ulverscroft.

That Sweet Diamond: Baseball Poems. Paul B. Janeczko. LC 97-5044. (J). 1998. 16.00 (*0-689-80735-X*) S&S Childrens.

That Tantalus. William Bronk. 1971. pap. 8.00 (*0-685-00987-4*) Elizabeth Pr.

That Terrible Baby. Jennifer Armstrong. LC 93-14727. (Illus.). 32p. (J). 1994. 14.00 (*0-688-11832-1*, Tambourine Bks); lib. bdg. 13.93 (*0-688-11833-X*, Tambourine Bks) Morrow.

That Terrible Halloween Night. James Stevenson. LC 79-27775. (Illus.). 32p. (J). (ps). 1980. lib. bdg. 15.93 (*0-688-84281-X*) Greenwillow.

That Terrible Halloween Night. James Stevenson. LC 79-27775. (Illus.). 32p. (J). (ps up). 1990. pap. 3.95 (*0-688-09932-7*, Mulberry) Morrow.

That Terrible Night Santa Got Lost in the Woods. Larry L. King. (Illus.). 29p. 1981. 20.00 (*0-88426-060-7*) Encino Pr.

***That the People Might Live: Native American Literature & Native American Community.** Jace Weaver. LC 97-3273. 256p. 1997. pap. 17.95 (*0-19-512037-X*) OUP.

***That the People Might Live: Native American Literatures & Native American Community.** Jace Weaver. LC 97-3273. 256p. 1997. 45.00 (*0-19-511852-9*) OUP.

That the World May Believe. Tony Higton. 1992. pap. 4.99 (*0-551-01261-7*) Zondervan.

That the World May Know. Earl Paulk. 189p. (Orig.). 1987. pap. 7.95 (*0-917595-15-7*) Kingdom Pubs.

***That the World May Know.** Laan R. Vander. 1997. pap. 18.00 (*1-56179-420-1*) Focus Family.

That the World May Know. Ray Vander Laan. 1996. 29.95 (*1-56179-413-9*) Focus Family.

***That the World May Know, No. 3.** Raymond Vander Laan. 1996. teacher ed., pap. 53.00 incl. bmax (*1-56179-506-2*) Focus Family.

***That the World May Know, No. 3.** Raymond Vander Laan. 1996. pap. 18.00 (*1-56179-419-8*) Focus Family.

***That the World May Know, No. 3.** Raymond Vander Laan. 1996. teacher ed., pap. write for info. incl. bmax, trans. (*1-56179-507-0*) Focus Family.

***That the World May Know, No. 4.** Ray Vander Laan. 1997. teacher ed. 76.00 incl. vhs (*1-56179-523-2*) Focus Family.

***That the World May Know, Set No. 4.** Ray Vander Laan. 1997. teacher ed. 170.00 incl. trans., vhs (*1-56179-524-0*) Focus Family.

***That the World May Know, Set No. 4.** Ray Vander Laan. 1997. 50.00 incl. vhs (*1-56179-525-9*) Focus Family.

***That the World May Know: With Personal Devotion Guide, No. 3.** Raymond Vander Laan. 1996. pap. 35.00 incl. bmax (*1-56179-505-4*) Focus Family.

That There Be No Stain upon My Stones: Lieutenant Colonel William L. McLeod, 38th Georgia Regiment, 1842-1863. Michael W. Hofe. (Illus.). 48p. (C). 1995. pap. text ed. 5.95 (*0-939631-84-9*) Thomas Publications.

***That They All May Be One: Relating to Different Backgrounds in the Church.** Philip Cohen. 80p. 1997. pap. text ed. 6.00 (*0-9656046-1-6*) Lghthse Pub TN.

That They Be One: The Social Teaching of the Papal Encyclicals 1740-1989. Michael Schuck. LC 90-44235. 240p. (Orig.). (C). 1991. pap. 14.95 (*0-87840-489-9*) Georgetown U Pr.

That They May All Be One. Elbridge B. Linn. 1969. 4.50 (*0-88027-020-9*) Firm Foun Pub.

That They May Be Many: Voices of Women, Echoes of God. Ann K. Wetherilt. 176p. (C). 1994. 19.95 (*0-8264-0691-2*) Continuum.

That They May Be One. Loretta Ross-Gotta. 12p. 1995. pap. text ed. 7.00 (*1-888821-05-1*) Sanctuary.

That They May Be One: On Commitment to Ecumenism. Pope John Paul, II. 115p. (Orig.). 1995. pap. 6.95 (*1-57455-050-0*) US Catholic.

That They May Have Life: The Story of the American University of Beirut, 1866-1941. Stephen B. Penrose, Jr. 1970. 17.95 (*0-8156-6000-6*, Am U Beirut) Syracuse U Pr.

That They Might Know: Remembrances of a Christian Southwest Missionary. Richard Kruis. (Illus.). 136p. 1995. pap. 9.95 (*1-880047-32-2*) Creative Des.

That They Might Live: Power, Empowerment, & Leadership in the Church. Ed. by Michael Downey. 272p. 1991. 19.95 (*0-8245-1072-0*) Crossroad NY.

That They Were At the Beach. Leslie Scalapino. LC 85-60854. 128p. (Orig.). 1985. 9.50 (*0-86547-211-4*) O Bks.

An Asterisk (*) at the beginning of an entry indicates that the title is appearing in BIP for the first time.

That Tickles! The Disney Book of Senses. Cindy West. LC 92-53444. (Illus.). 32p. (J). (ps). 1993. 9.95 (*1-56282-383-3*) Disney Pr.

That Time & Place: A Greenwich Village Memoir. Anatole Broyard. LC 93-7830. 1993. 18.00 (*0-685-65374-9*, Crown) Crown Pub Group.

That Time in Malomba. James Hamilton-Paterson. LC 90-9976. 180p. 1992. 9.95 (*0-939149-68-0*) Soho Press.

That Time o' Day. John Booth. 1993. pap. 12.00 (*0-86025-404-6*, Pub. by Ian Henry Pubns UK) Empire Pub Srvs.

That Tricky Coyote! Gretchen W. Mayo. LC 92-12440. (Native American Trickster Tales Ser.). (Illus.). 32p. (J). (gr. 1-5). 1993. 12.95 (*0-8027-8200-0*); lib. bdg. 13.85 (*0-8027-8201-9*) Walker & Co.

That Unknown Day. Carlos E. Portillo. LC 85-52117. (Illus.). 400p. (Orig.). 1986. 14.95 (*0-937365-00-9*); pap. 9.95 (*0-937365-01-7*) WCP Pubns.

That VanDam Book - New York City: Unique Pocket Guide & Pop-up Map. Stephan C. Van Dam. (That Vandam Bk.). (Illus.). 155p. 1993. pap. text ed. 9.95 (*0-931141-56-7*) VanDam Inc.

That Various Field for James Schuyler. Ed. by Corbett & Young. (Illus.). 56p. 1991. pap. 7.50 (*0-935724-51-6*) Figures.

That Very Special Person - Me: Self Esteem for Teens. Margaret Houk. LC 89-29003. 136p. (Orig.). (YA). 1990. pap. 6.99 (*0-8361-3514-8*) Herald Pr.

That Voice. Robert Pinget. Tr. by Barbara Wright. LC 82-60910. 114p. 1983. 10.95 (*0-87376-041-7*) Red Dust.

That Voice Behind You: God's Guidance in Daily Decisions. Charles G. Coleman. LC 77-6796. 175p. 1991. student ed., pap. 8.99 (*0-87213-087-8*) Loizeaux.

***That Was the Best Party Ever! How to Give Birthday Parties Kids Will Never Forget.** Sharron W. Krull. Ed. by Mary Humphrey. LC 95-92669. (Illus.). 259p. (Orig.). 1996. pap. 16.95 (*1-885650-03-5*) Play Power.

That Was Then, This Is Now. Fred L. Fifer & Cynthia E. Ledbetter. (Do It Now Ser.). 180p. (J). 1990. student ed. 15.95 (*1-885568-08-8*) SCE Assocs.

That Was Then This Is Now. Thomas Gahn, Jr. 156p. 1991. pap. 10.95 (*0-9630966-0-5*) T Gahn.

That Was Then, This Is Now. S. E. Hinton. 224p. (J). (gr. k up). 1989. mass mkt. 4.50 (*0-440-98652-4*, LLL BDD) BDD Bks Young Read.

That Was Then, This Is Now. S. E. Hinton. (YA). (gr. 7 up). 1971. 18.50 (*0-8446-6371-9*) Peter Smith.

That Was Then, This Is Now. S. E. Hinton. (Illus.). (YA). (gr. 7 up). 1971. pap. 15.99 (*0-670-69798-2*) Viking Child Bks.

That Was Then This Is Now - Esto Ya Es Otra Historia. S. E. Hinton. (SPA.). (J). 6.95 (*84-204-4121-X*) Santillana.

***That Way Lies Camelot.** Janny Wurts. 320p. 1997. mass mkt. 5.50 (*0-06-105778-9*, HarperPrism) HarpC.

That We May Be One: Let's Quit Fighting about the Holy Spirit. James G. Sigountos. 176p. 1994. pap. 10.99 (*0-310-48011-6*) Zondervan.

That We May Be One: The Autobiography of Ambassador Jolly Tanko Yusuf, C.O.N. Jolly T. Yusuf. LC 95-38879. 139p. 1995. pap. 15.00 (*0-8028-4139-2*) Eerdmans.

That We May Be Willing to Receive. Elise N. Morgan. (Meditation Ser.). 1938. 6.95 (*0-87516-331-9*) DeVorss.

That We May Join Earth & Heaven: Lay Religious Community for the 21st Century. Pia Gyger. LC 95-44314. 126p. (Orig.). 1996. pap. 12.95 (*1-55612-816-9*, LL1816) Sheed & Ward MO.

That We Might Have Joy. Howard W. Hunter. LC 94-68367. vi, 197p. 1994. 14.95 (*0-87579-876-4*) Deseret Bk.

That Which Concerneth Me. J. Baxter & L. Harvey. LC 79-178468. (Black Heritage Library Collection). 1977. reprint ed. 19.95 (*0-8369-8911-2*) Ayer.

That Which Is Crooked. Doris M. Disney. 1989. mass mkt. 3.50 (*0-8217-2848-2*, Zebra Kensgtn) Kensgtn Pub Corp.

That Which Transpires Behind That Which Appears: The Experience of Sufism. Vilayat I. Khan. (Illus.). 211p. 1994. 21.00 (*0-930872-50-9*); pap. 13.00 (*0-930872-49-5*) Omega Pubns NY.

That Which Was Once a War: A Winter Soldier's Poems. Sydney Kessler. LC 95-67037. 63p. 1995. per., pap. 8.95 (*1-884768-03-2*) Charming Forge.

That Which You Are Seeking Is Causing You to Seek. Cheri Huber. (Illus.). 123p. 1991. pap. text ed. 10.00 (*0-9614754-2-0*) Zen Med Ctr.

That Whiff of Sulphur. Angeline Bennett. 64p. (Orig.). 1995. pap. 9.75 (*1-880222-22-1*) Red Apple Pub.

That Why Child: Problems in Psychotherapy & Counselling. Carol Jeffrey. 180p. (C). 1996. 45.00 (*1-85343-338-1*); pap. 20.00 (*1-85343-339-X*) NYU Pr.

That Wild Berries Should Grow. Gloria Whelan. LC 93-41106. 122p. (J). (gr. 4-6). 1994. pap. 6.00 (*0-8028-5091-X*) Eerdmans.

That Wild Fellow John Neal & the American Literary Revolution. Benjamin Lease. LC 72-81630. 255p. reprint ed. pap. 72.70 (*0-317-26518-0*, 2024054) Bks Demand.

***That Wild Stallion.** Shirley Larson. 1997. mass mkt. 3.99 (*0-373-24109-7*, 1-24109-0) Silhouette.

***That Wilder Man.** Susan Liepitz. 1997. mass mkt. 3.50 (*0-373-25752-X*, 1-25752-6) Harlequin Bks.

That Winning Feeling! Jane Savoie. 150p. (C). 1990. 60.00 (*0-85131-565-8*, Pub. by J A Allen & Co UK) St Mut.

***That Winning Feeling: Program Your Mind for Peak Performance.** Jane Savoie. LC 97-121. (Illus.). 160p. 1997. pap. 14.95 (*1-57076-049-7*, Trafalgar Sq Pub) Trafalgar.

That Winter. Pamela Gillilan. 8600. pap. 11.95 (*1-85224-005-9*, Pub. by Bloodaxe Bks UK) Dufour.

That Woman. large type ed. Helga Moray. 384p. 1986. 25.99 (*0-7089-1449-7*) Ulverscroft.

That Woman I Married. Melvin R. Miller. 104p. 1986. pap. 3.95 (*0-88144-061-2*) Christian Pub.

That Woman in Proverbs. Vernelle B. Allen. 95p. 1994. pap. write for info. (*1-885984-11-1*) Wings of Healing.

That Would Explain the Violinist. Sunil Freeman. LC 92-72280. 64p. (Orig.). 1993. pap. 7.95 (*0-945144-03-2*) Gut Punch Pr.

That Yankee Cat: The Maine Coon. rev. ed. Marilis Hornidge. (Illus.). 112p. (Orig.). 1992. pap. 14.95 (*0-88448-088-7*) Tilbury Hse.

That Ye May Believe. Neal A. Maxwell. 1992. 11.95 (*0-88494-843-9*) Bookcraft Inc.

That Year of Our War. large type ed. Gloria Goldreich. LC 94-29779. 1994. pap. 20.95 (*1-56895-081-0*) Wheeler Pub.

That You May Believe. Dan R. Owen. 1993. pap. 7.50 (*0-89137-337-3*) Quality Pubns.

That You May Believe: Studies in the Gospel of John. Homer Hailey. (Illus.). 1982. pap. 9.95 (*0-913814-51-2*) Nevada Pubns.

That You May Know Christ: Studies from Philippians. Leon Barnes. 182p. 1993. pap. write for info. (*0-945441-14-2*) Res Pubns AR.

That You May Prosper: Dominion by Covenant. 2nd ed. Ray R. Sutton. LC 91-22625. 347p. 1992. reprint ed. 15.95 (*0-930464-11-7*) Inst Christian.

***That Your Days May Be Long: A Collection of Plays for the Church.** Kenneth L. Gibble. LC 90-40775. 128p. 1990. reprint ed. pap. 36.50 (*0-608-04174-2*, 2064908) Bks Demand.

That Your Joy May Be Complete: The Secret of Becoming a Joyful Person. 3rd ed. George A. Maloney. LC 93-47943. 144p. 1994. 8.95 (*1-56548-062-7*) New City.

That Your Joy May Be Full. 3.50 (*0-318-02211-7*) Chrstphrs NY.

That Your Joy Might Be Full. Joseph L. Palotta. 247p. 1981. pap. 6.95 (*0-9604852-1-X*) Revelation Hse.

Thatch & Thatching. Jacqueline Fearn. 1989. pap. 25.00 (*0-85263-337-8*, Pub. by Shire UK) St Mut.

Thatched Kitchen: Harvest & Holiday Cookbook. Patricia Collier. LC 72-87655. 1972. 5.95 (*0-88351-008-1*) Test Recipe.

***Thatcher & Thatcherism.** Eric J. Evans. LC 97-4317. (Making of the Contemporary World Ser.). 192p. (C). 1997. pap. write for info. (*0-415-13694-6*) Routledge.

Thatcher Effect: A Decade of Change. Ed. by Dennis A. Kavanagh & Anthony Seldon. (Illus.). 376p. 1989. pap. text ed. 14.95 (*0-19-827746-6*) OUP.

Thatcher Magoun. An American Clipper Ship. Her Owners, Captains, & Model. Hollis French. (Illus.). 70p. 1934. write for info. (*1-879886-01-4*) Addison Gallery.

Thatcher, Reagan, & Mulroney: In Search of a New Bureaucracy. Donald J. Savoie. (Policy & Institutional Studies). 416p. (C). 1994. text ed. 49.95 (*0-8229-3775-1*); pap. text ed. 22.95 (*0-8229-5519-9*) U of Pittsburgh Pr.

Thatcher, Reagan, & Mulroney: In Search of a New Bureaucracy. Donald J. Savoie. 1994. pap. 22.95 (*0-8020-6993-2*) U of Toronto Pr.

Thatcherism & British Politics: The End of Consensus? 2nd ed. Dennis A. Kavanagh. (Illus.). 352p. 1990. pap. text ed. 17.95 (*0-19-827755-5*) OUP.

***Thatcherism & Planning: The Case of Simplified Planning Zones.** Philip Allmendinger. (Illus.). 206p. 1997. text ed. 59.95 (*1-85972-671-2*, Pub. by Ashgate UK) Ashgate Pub Co.

Thatcherism & Territorial Politics: A Welsh Case Study. Dylan Griffiths. 192p. 1996. 55.95 (*1-85972-296-2*, Pub. by Avebury Pub UK) Ashgate Pub Co.

Thatcherism at Work: Industrial Relations & Economic Change. John MacInnnes. 192p. 1987. 85.00 (*0-335-15517-0*, Open Univ Pr); pap. 29.00 (*0-335-15516-2*, Open Univ Pr) Taylor & Francis.

Thatcher's Children? Politics, Childhood, & Society in the 1980s & 1990s. Jane Pilcher & Stephen Wagg. (World of Childhood & Adolescence Ser.). 240p. 1996. 75.00 (*0-7507-0461-6*, Falmer Pr); pap. 24.95 (*0-7507-0462-4*, Falmer Pr) Taylor & Francis.

Thatcher's Diplomacy: The Revival of British Foreign Policy. Paul Sharp. LC 96-28748. (Contemporary History in Context Ser.). 1996. text ed. 65.00 (*0-312-16440-8*) St Martin.

Thatching: A Handbook. Nicholas Hall. 40p. (Orig.). 1988. pap. 13.50 (*1-85339-060-7*, Pub. by Intermed Tech UK) Women Ink.

That's a Fact Picture. Lucille R. Penner. write for info. (*0-679-96212-3*) Random.

***That's a Good Question.** William MacDonald. 30p. (Orig.). 1995. pap. 1.50 (*1-884838-02-2*) Walterick Pubs.

That's a Good Question. 2nd ed. Roger Forster & Paul Marston. Tr. by Hugo S. Sun & Silas Chan. 204p. (CHI.). 1982. pap. write for info. (*0-941598-01-2*) Living Spring Pubns.

That's a Lot of Bulletin: The Lehigh World According to Ray Armstrong. Ray Armstrong. Ed. by Jack DeBellis. (Illus.). (C). 1989. text ed. 19.95 (*0-9624866-0-4*) Lehigh U PA.

That's All: Bobby Darin on Record, Stage & Screen. Jeffrey Bleiel. LC 93-83934. (Rock & Roll Reference Ser.: No. 38). (Illus.). 304p. 1993. lib. bdg. 40.00 (*1-56075-031-6*) Popular Culture.

***That's All Folks: Black Images in Animated Cartoons, 1900-1960.** LC 96-49987. 1997. write for info. (*0-8108-3250-X*) Scarecrow.

That's All Folks! The Art of the Warner Brothers Animation. Stephen Schneider. LC 88-81823. 256p. 1990. pap. 19.95 (*0-8050-1485-3*, Owl) H Holt & Co.

That's All Right, Mama. Gerald Duff. 278p. 1995. 21.00 (*1-880909-33-2*) Baskerville.

That's All They're Good For. Tim Jackson. (What Are Friends For? Ser.: No. 3). (Illus.). 20p. (J). (gr. 5-9). 1986. pap. 1.95 (*0-942675-02-9*) Creative License.

That's Alright: My Life with Elvis. Moore & Dickerson. LC 96-6614. 1997. 25.00 (*0-02-864599-5*) Mac Lib Ref.

***That's Alright, Elvis: The Untold Story of Elvis' First Guitarist & Manager, Scotty Moore.** Scotty Moore & James Dickerson. 1997. 25.00 (*0-614-28026-5*) Schirmer Bks.

That's Blaxploitation! Roots of the Baadasssss 'Tude. Darius James. LC 95-17149. 224p. (Orig.). 1995. pap. 14.95 (*0-312-13192-5*, Griffin) St Martin.

That's Dangerous. Isabel Bissett. LC 92-31947. (Voyages Ser.). (Illus.). (J). 1993. 3.75 (*0-383-03596-1*) SRA McGraw.

That's Easy! Classics for Alto Saxophone. Peter Evans. (Illus.). 32p. 1993. pap. 8.95 (*0-7119-3421-5*, AM91090) Music Sales.

That's Easy! Classics for Clarinet - Tenor Sax. Peter Evans. (Illus.). 32p. 1993. pap. 8.95 (*0-7119-3422-3*, AM91091) Music Sales.

That's Easy! Classics for Flute. Peter Evans. (Illus.). 32p. 1993. pap. 8.95 (*0-7119-3423-1*, AM91092) Music Sales.

That's Easy! Classics for Trumpet. Peter Evans. (Illus.). 32p. 1993. pap. 8.95 (*0-7119-3424-X*, AM91093) Music Sales.

***That's Easy for You to Say: A Guide to Pronouncing Bible Names.** W. Murray Severance. LC 97-25039. 1997. pap. write for info. (*1-55819-695-1*) Broadman.

That's Edutainment! A Parents Guide to Educational Software. Eric Brown. 400p. 1995. pap. text ed. 29.95 (*0-07-882083-9*) Osborne-McGraw.

That's Enough, Maddie! Louise Leblanc. (First Novels Ser.). (Illus.). 64p. (J). (gr. 1-4). 1995. pap. 4.95 (*0-88780-090-4*); bds. 14.95 (*0-88780-091-2*) Formac Dist Ltd.

That's Entertainment. CPP Belwin Staff. 1994. pap. 22.50 (*0-89898-979-5*) Warner Brothers.

***That's Entertainment.** Graphic Showbiz Staff. 1997. pap. 39.95 (*0-86636-480-3*) St Martin.

That's Entertainment. Steven Heller & Anne Fink. LC 95-13985. 184p. 1996. 42.50 (*0-86636-344-0*) PBC Intl Inc.

***That's Entertainment.** PBC International Staff. 1996. 45.00 (*0-688-14429-2*) Morrow.

***That's Entertainment: The Graphics of Showbiz.** Steven Heller & Anne Fink. (Illus.). 1997. pap. 39.95 (*0-614-28155-5*) PBC Intl Inc.

That's Entertainment! Hollywood's Greatest Musicals see MGM's Greatest Musicals: The Arthur Freed Unit

That's EZ: Mozart for Clarinet. 1994. 8.95 (*0-7119-3987-X*, AM91875) Omnibus NY.

That's EZ: Mozart for Tenor Sax. 1994. 8.95 (*0-7119-4238-2*, AM92112) Omnibus NY.

That's EZ Beethoven for Alto Sax. 1994. 8.95 (*0-7119-4000-2*, AM91884) Omnibus NY.

That's EZ Beethoven for Clarinet. 1994. 8.95 (*0-7119-3998-5*, AM91882) Omnibus NY.

That's EZ Beethoven for Flute. 1994. 8.95 (*0-7119-3999-3*, AM91883) Omnibus NY.

That's EZ Beethoven for Tenor Sax. 1994. 8.95 (*0-7119-4227-7*, AM92101) Omnibus NY.

That's EZ Beethoven for Trumpet. 1994. 8.95 (*0-7119-4001-0*, AM91885) Omnibus NY.

That's EZ Hymns & Spirituals Alto Sax. 1994. 8.95 (*0-7119-4288-9*, AM92155) Omnibus NY.

That's EZ Hymns & Spirituals Clarinet. 1994. 8.95 (*0-7119-4286-2*, AM92153) Omnibus NY.

That's EZ Hymns & Spirituals for Flute. 1994. 8.95 (*0-7119-4287-0*, AM92154) Omnibus NY.

That's EZ Hymns & Spirituals Tenor Sax. 1994. 8.95 (*0-7119-4289-7*, AM92156) Omnibus NY.

That's EZ Hymns & Spirituals Trumpet. 1994. 8.95 (*0-7119-4290-0*, AM92157) Omnibus NY.

That's EZ Mozart for Alto Sax. 1994. 8.95 (*0-7119-3989-6*, AM91877) Omnibus NY.

That's EZ Mozart for Flute. 1994. 8.95 (*0-7119-3988-8*, AM91876) Omnibus NY.

That's EZ Mozart for Trumpet. 1994. 8.95 (*0-7119-3990-X*, AM91878) Omnibus NY.

That's for Shore: Riddles from the Beach. June Swanson. (You Must Be Joking! Ser.). (Illus.). 32p. (J). (gr. 1-4). 1991. lib. bdg. 9.50 (*0-8225-2332-9*, Lerner Publctns) Lerner Group.

That's for Shore: Riddles from the Beach. June Swanson. (J). (gr. 1-4). 1991. pap. 3.95 (*0-8225-9592-3*, Lerner Publctns) Lerner Group.

That's Fresh! Seasonal Recipes for Young Cooks. Braiden Rex-Johnson & David Wasson. (Illus.). 96p. (Orig.). (J). (gr. 2 up). 1995. pap. 14.95 (*1-57061-017-7*) Sasquatch Bks.

That's Funny. 128p. 1996. pap. text ed. 8.95 (*0-8362-1502-8*, Cader Bks) Andrews & McMeel.

That's Funny, You Don't Look Buddhist: Why Jews Are Attracted to Buddhism & How Both Traditions Can Enrich Our Lives. Sylvia Boorstein & Sharon Lebell. LC 96-16447. 1996. 23.00 (*0-06-060957-5*); pap. write for info. (*0-06-060958-3*) Harper SF.

That's Funny You Don't Look Like a Teacher: Interrogating Images, Identity, & Popular Culture. Sandra J. Weber & Claudia Mitchell. (World of Childhood & Adolescence Ser.: No. 3). 192p. 1995. 75.00 (*0-7507-0412-8*, Falmer Pr); pap. 23.00 (*0-7507-0413-6*, Falmer Pr) Taylor & Francis.

That's Good! That's Bad! Margery Cuyler. LC 90-49353. (Illus.). 32p. (J). (ps-2). 1993. pap. 5.95 (*0-8050-2954-0*, Bks Young Read) H Holt & Co.

That's Good! That's Bad! Margery Cuyler. (Illus.). (J). (ps-3). 1996. 22.95 incl. audio (*0-87499-377-6*); pap. 15.95 incl. audio (*0-87499-376-8*) Live Oak Media.

That's Good! That's Bad!, 4 bks., Set. Margery Cuyler. (Illus.). (J). (ps-3). 1996. pap. 33.95 incl. audio (*0-87499-378-4*) Live Oak Media.

***That's How It Is When We Draw.** Ruth Bornstein. LC 96-49646. (J). 1997. 14.00 (*0-395-82509-1*) HM.

That's How It Was. Eruch Jessawala. Ed. & Intro. by Steve Klein. LC 95-69857. 406p. (Orig.). 1995. pap. 15.00 (*1-880619-14-8*) Sheriar Found.

That's How Love Is. Joan Howes. LC 91-316. (Illus.). 32p. (J). (gr. k-4). 1991. 12.95 (*0-938349-62-7*); pap. 6.95 (*0-938349-63-5*) State House Pr.

That's How the Light Gets In: A Credo of Friendship. Donald B. Harris. LC 94-92445. 350p. (Orig.). 1994. pap. 18.95 (*0-9643691-0-9*) Credo Inst.

That's in the Bible? The Ultimate Learn as You Play Bible Quizbook. Wick Allison & Christine Allison. LC 94-6690. 1994. 16.95 (*0-385-31097-8*) Delacorte.

That's It, Folks! Mark O'Donnell. 1983. pap. 5.25 (*0-8222-1128-9*) Dramatists Play.

That's Life. (J). (gr. 1). 1990. student ed. 3.50 (*1-56117-054-2*) Telesis CA.

That's Life. (YA). (gr. 10). 1990. student ed. 3.50 (*1-56117-076-3*) Telesis CA.

That's Life. (J). (gr. 2). 1990. student ed. 3.50 (*1-56117-056-9*) Telesis CA.

That's Life. (J). (gr. 3). 1990. student ed. 3.50 (*1-56117-057-7*) Telesis CA.

That's Life. (J). (gr. 4). 1990. student ed. 3.50 (*1-56117-058-5*) Telesis CA.

That's Life. (J). (gr. 5). 1990. student ed. 3.50 (*1-56117-059-3*) Telesis CA.

That's Life. (J). (gr. 6). 1990. student ed. 3.50 (*1-56117-060-7*) Telesis CA.

That's Life. (J). (gr. 7). 1990. student ed. 3.50 (*1-56117-061-5*) Telesis CA.

That's Life. (J). (gr. 8). 1990. student ed. 3.50 (*1-56117-062-3*) Telesis CA.

That's Life. (YA). (gr. 9). 1990. student ed. 3.50 (*1-56117-075-5*) Telesis CA.

That's Life. (J). (gr. 1). 1994. 65.00 (*1-56117-019-4*) Telesis CA.

That's Life. (J). (gr. 2). 1994. 65.00 (*1-56117-020-8*) Telesis CA.

That's Life. (J). (gr. 3). 1994. 65.00 (*1-56117-021-6*) Telesis CA.

That's Life. (J). (gr. 4). 1994. 65.00 (*1-56117-022-4*) Telesis CA.

That's Life. (J). (gr. 5). 1994. 65.00 (*1-56117-023-2*) Telesis CA.

That's Life. (J). (gr. 6). 1994. 65.00 (*1-56117-045-3*) Telesis CA.

That's Life. (J). (gr. 7). 1994. 65.00 (*1-56117-046-1*) Telesis CA.

That's Life. (J). (gr. 8). 1994. 65.00 (*1-56117-048-8*) Telesis CA.

That's Life. (SPA.). (J). (gr. k). 1990. student ed. 3.95 (*1-56117-077-1*) Telesis CA.

That's Life. (SPA.). (J). (gr. 1). 1990. student ed. 3.95 (*1-56117-079-8*) Telesis CA.

That's Life. (SPA.). (YA). (gr. 10). 1990. student ed. 3.95 (*1-56117-090-9*) Telesis CA.

That's Life. (SPA.). (J). (gr. 2). 1990. student ed. 3.95 (*1-56117-080-1*) Telesis CA.

That's Life. (SPA.). (J). (gr. 3). 1990. student ed. 3.95 (*1-56117-082-8*) Telesis CA.

That's Life. (SPA.). (J). (gr. 4). 1990. student ed. 3.95 (*1-56117-083-6*) Telesis CA.

That's Life. (SPA.). (J). (gr. 5). 1990. student ed. 3.95 (*1-56117-084-4*) Telesis CA.

That's Life. (SPA.). (J). (gr. 6). 1990. student ed. 3.95 (*1-56117-085-2*) Telesis CA.

That's Life. (SPA.). (J). (gr. 7). 1990. student ed. 3.95 (*1-56117-087-9*) Telesis CA.

That's Life. (SPA.). (J). (gr. 8). 1990. student ed. 3.95 (*1-56117-088-7*) Telesis CA.

That's Life. (SPA.). (YA). (gr. 9). 1990. student ed. 3.95 (*1-56117-089-5*) Telesis CA.

That's Life. (YA). (gr. 10). 1994. 65.00 (*1-56117-051-8*) Telesis CA.

That's Life. (YA). (gr. 9). 1994. 65.00 (*1-56117-049-6*) Telesis CA.

That's Life, 13 vols. David Cleveland. (Telesis Drug Education Ser.). (Illus.). (J). (gr. k). 1990. student ed. 3.50 (*1-56117-043-7*) Telesis CA.

That's Life, 13 vols. David Cleveland. (Telesis Drug Education Ser.). (Illus.). (J). (ps). 1990. 35.00 (*1-56117-042-9*) Telesis CA.

That's Life, 13 vols. David Cleveland. (Telesis Drug Education Ser.). (Illus.). (J). 1994. student ed. 65.00 (*1-56117-044-5*) Telesis CA.

That's Life. William Herrick. LC 84-27378. 256p. 1985. 17.50 (*0-8112-0946-6*); pap. 9.95 (*0-8112-0947-4*, NDP596) New Directions.

That's Life. Joaquin. 1995. write for info. (*0-8477-0247-2*) U of PR Pr.

That's Life. Arlene Maass. LC 93-8592. 87p. 1993. pap. 6.00 (*0-940895-14-5*) Cornerstone IL.

That's Life: Featuring the Wit & Wisdom of Bernadette McCarver Snyder. Bernadette M. Snyder. LC 91-62108. (Illus.). 96p. (Orig.). 1991. pap. 3.95 (*0-89243-408-2*) Liguori Pubns.

***That's Life Basic Set, 8 bks.** Tana Reiff. 1994. pap. 49.95 (*0-7854-1084-8*, 40700) Am Guidance.

***That's Life Classroom Library, 24 bks.** Tana Reiff. 1994. teacher ed., pap. 99.95 (*0-7854-1083-X*, 40710) Am Guidance.

***That's Life Curriculum Guide.** Tana Reiff. 272p. 1994. pap. 29.95 (*0-7854-1094-5*, 40709) Am Guidance.

***That's Life DramaTapes Cassette Program, 8 bks.** Tana Reiff & Vince Clews. 1994. teacher ed., pap. 99.95 incl. audio (*0-7854-1085-6*, 40720) Am Guidance.

T

An Asterisk (*) at the beginning of an entry indicates that the title is appearing in BIP for the first time.

That's Me in Here. Jean Darby. (Illus.). 43p. (Orig.). (J). (gr. 1-2). 1989. pap. 4.95 (*0-8198-7345-4*) Pauline Bks.

That's Ms. Bulldyke to You, Charlie! Jane Caminos. LC 92-60819. (Illus.). 1992. pap. 8.95 (*0-9630822-1-3*) Madwoman Pr.

That's Muscle Control. Ed. by Jubinville Staff. 150p. 1986. 19.95 (*0-935783-08-3*) Fitness Ctr Info.

That's My Baby. Norma Klein. 208p. 1990. mass mkt. 3.95 (*0-449-70356-8*, Juniper) Fawcett.

That's My Baby. A. Wayne Von Konigslow. (Illus.). 24p. (J). (ps-8). 1986. 12.95 (*0-920303-56-0*, Pub. by Annick CN); pap. 4.95 (*0-920303-57-9*, Pub. by Annick CN) Firefly Bks Ltd.

That's My Buddy! Friendship & Learning Across the Grades: Ideas from the Child Development Project. Developmental Studies Center Staff. 128p. (Orig.). 1996. pap. 14.95 (*1-885603-81-9*) Develop Studies.

***That's My Buddy! Collegial Study Guide.** Developmental Studies Center Staff. (Building Schoolwide Community Ser.). (Illus.). 48p. 1997. pap. 9.95 (*1-57621-136-3*) Develop Studies.

That's My Buddy! (Overview Video) Friendship & Learning Across the Grades. Developmental Studies Center Staff. (Orig.). 1996. vhs 29.95 (*1-885603-82-7*) Develop Studies.

That's My Child: Strategies for Parents of Children with Disabilities. Lizanne Capper. 200p. (Orig.). 1996. pap. text ed. 12.95 (*0-87868-595-2*, Child-Family Pr) Child Welfare.

That's My Cousin: Manuscript Edition. Kurtz Gordon. 1957. pap. 13.00 (*0-8222-1129-7*) Dramatists Play.

That's Not All! Rex Schneider. Ed. by Barbara Gregorich. (Start to Read! Ser.). (Illus.). 16p. (Orig.). (J). (gr. k-2). 1985. pap. 2.25 (*0-88743-019-8*, 06019) Sch Zone Pub Co.

That's Not All! Rex Schneider. Ed. by Barbara Gregorich. (Start to Read! Ser.). (Illus.). 32p. (Orig.). (J). (gr. k-2). 1992. pap. 3.95 (*0-88743-417-7*, 06069) Sch Zone Pub Co.

That's Not Fair! Earth Friendly Tales. Joe Hayes. (Illus.). 32p. (Orig.). (J). (gr. k-6). 1991. pap. 5.95 (*0-939729-21-0*) Trails West Pub.

That's Not Santa! Leonard Kessler. LC 93-39653. (Hello Reader! Ser.: Level 1). (J). (ps-1). 1994. 3.50 (*0-590-48140-1*) Scholastic Inc.

***That's Not Santa.** Leonard Kessler. (Hello Reader! (Je Peux Lire!) Ser.). (FRE.). (J). pap. 5.99 (*0-590-24360-8*) Scholastic Inc.

That's Not the Way It Was: (Almost) Everything They've Told You about Sports Is Wrong. Allen Barra. LC 94-13273. 256p. 1995. pap. 10.95 (*0-7868-8053-8*) Hyperion.

That's Not What I Meant. Deborah Tannen. 214p. 1992. pap. 12.00 (*0-345-37972-1*) Ballantine.

That's Not What I Meant: How Conversational Style Makes or Breaks Relationships. Deborah Tannen. 1987. mass mkt. 5.99 (*0-345-34090-6*) Ballantine.

That's Only the Down Payment: A Survival Manual for the Father of the Bride. Michael M. Warren. LC 92-73432. (Illus.). 109p. (Orig.). 1995. pap. 11.95 (*0-9627775-2-8*) Ledero Pr.

That's Our New Ad Campaign...? Dick Wasserman. 188p. pap. 18.95 (*0-669-27668-5*, Lexington) Jossey-Bass.

That's Outrageous, Boliver Boggs! Jo Harper. LC 95-6029. (Illus.). (J). 1995. write for info. (*0-02-742755-2*, S&S Bks Young Read) S&S Childrens.

That's Philomena! Catherine Bancroft & Hannah C. Gruenberg. (J). 1995. text ed. 15.00 (*0-02-708326-8*, S&S Bks Young Read) S&S Childrens.

That's Racing. Sean Magee. Ed. by Peter O'Sullevan. (Illus.). 208p. 1996. pap. 22.95 (*1-85158-828-0*, Pub. by Mnstream UK) Trafalgar.

That's Sick! A Collection of the Rudest & Crudest Cartoons from National Lampoon. National Lampoon Editors. 128p. 1994. pap. 8.95 (*0-8092-3695-8*) Contemp Bks.

That's That. Dwight Bolinger. (Janua Linguarum, Ser. Minor: No. 155). 79p. (Orig.). 1972. pap. text ed. 23.10 (*90-279-2319-1*) Mouton.

That's the Spirit, Claude. Joan L. Nixon. (Illus.). 32p. (J). (gr. k-3). 1994. pap. 4.99 (*0-14-054290-6*) Puffin Bks.

That's the Spirit, Claude. Joan L. Nixon. (Illus.). 32p. (J). (ps-3). 1992. pap. 13.00 (*0-670-83434-3*) Viking Child Bks.

That's the Way I See It. David Hockney. 240p. 1993. 40.00 (*0-8118-0506-9*) Chronicle Bks.

That's the Way I See It. David Hockney. (Illus.). 240p. 1996. reprint ed. pap. 24.95 (*0-8118-1487-4*) Chronicle Bks.

***That's the Way It Once Was.** Arnold H. Marzolf. 1995. pap. 10.50 (*0-614-23869-2*) Am Hist Soc Ger.

That's What a Friend Is. P. K. Hallinan. 24p. (J). (ps-3). 1990. per., pap. 4.95 (*0-8249-8492-7*, Ideals Child) Hambleton-Hill.

That's What Counts: A Tapley P. Bear Book. Jane D. Weinberger. LC 87-50549. (Illus.). 40p. (J). (ps-4). 1987. reprint ed. pap. 3.95 (*0-932433-33-2*) Windswept Hse.

That's What Friends Are For: A Changing Picture Book. Mary Engelbreit. (Illus.). 10p. 1995. 6.95 (*0-8362-4631-4*) Andrews & McMeel.

***That's What Friends Are For: A Novel.** Joni Hilton. LC 97-8703. 300p. 1997. pap. 9.95 (*1-57734-111-2*) Covenant Comms.

That's What God Is Like, No. 3. Ed. by Henrietta Gambill. (Acetate Window Bks.). (Illus.). 16p. (J). (ps). 1994. 6.99 (*0-7847-0153-9*, 03703) Standard Pub.

That's What Grandfathers Are For. Arlene Uslander. 24p. (Orig.). 1996. pap. 5.95 (*1-886094-39-X*) Chicago Spectrum.

That's What Grandmothers are For. Arlene Uslander. 32p. (Orig.). 1995. pap. 5.95 (*1-886094-13-6*) Chicago Spectrum.

That's What Happens When It's Spring. Elaine W. Good. LC 87-14964. (Illus.). 32p. (J). (ps-1). 1987. 12.95 (*0-934672-53-9*) Good Bks PA.

That's What Happens When It's Spring. Elaine W. Good. LC 87-14964. (Seasonal Ser.). (Illus.). 32p. (J). (ps-3). 1995. pap. 6.95 (*1-56148-145-9*) Good Bks PA.

That's What I Like (about the South) Other New Southern Stories for the Nineties. Ed. by George Garrett & Paul Ruffin. LC 92-43168. 418p. (C). 1993. pap. 14.95 (*0-87249-864-6*); text ed. 34.95 (*0-87249-863-8*) U of SC Pr.

That's What She Said: Contemporary Poetry & Fiction by Native American Women. Ed. by Rayna Green. LC 83-49002. (Illus.). 352p. 1984. 31.50 (*0-253-35855-8*); pap. 15.95 (*0-253-20338-4*, MB-338) Ind U Pr.

***That's What the Main Said.** Dunnam. 11.85 (*0-687-61161-X*) Abingdon.

That's What the Man Said: The Sayings of Jesus. Maxie Dunnam. 128p. (Orig.). 1989. pap. 8.95 (*0-8358-0599-9*) Upper Room Bks.

That's Where the Town's Going. Tad Mosel. 1963. pap. 5.25 (*0-8222-1130-0*) Dramatists Play.

Thauma Idesthai: The Phenomenology of Sight & Appearance in Archaic Greek. Raymond A. Prier. 312p. 1989. lib. bdg. 49.95 (*0-8130-0919-7*) U Press Fla.

Thaurmatin. Witty. 216p. 1994. 167.95 (*0-8493-5196-0*) CRC Pr.

Thaw Collection: Master Drawings & New Acquisitions. Cara D. Denison et al. (Pierpont Morgan Library). (Illus.). 284p. 1994. 37.50 (*0-87598-106-2*) Pierpont Morgan.

Thaw Generation: Coming of Age in the Post-Stalin Era. Ludmilla Alexeyeva & Paul Goldberg. LC 92-50913. (Russian & East European Studies: Vol. 19). (Illus.). 368p. 1993. reprint ed. 16.95 (*0-8229-5911-9*) U of Pittsburgh Pr.

Thaw in Bulgarian Literature. Atanas Slavov. (East European Monographs: No. 84). 190p. 1981. text ed. 52.50 (*0-914710-78-8*) East Eur Monographs.

Thawing of Mara. Janet Dailey. (Americana Ser.: No. 888). 1992. mass mkt. 3.59 (*0-373-89888-6*) Harlequin Bks.

Thawing Out. Philip K. Jason. LC 79-15901. pap. 7.95 (*0-931848-27-X*) Dryad Pr.

Thayer: Genealogy of Ephraim & Sarah Thayer with Their 14 Children, from the Time of Their Marriage to 1835. E. Thayer. 97p. 1993. reprint ed. pap. 18.00 (*0-8328-3418-1*) Higginson Bk Co.

Thayer's Greek-English Lexicon of the New Testament: Coded to Strong's Numbering System. Joseph H. Thayer. 784p. 1995. reprint ed. 24.95 (*1-56563-209-5*) Hendrickson MA.

Thayer's Life of Beethoven, Pt. 1. Elliot Forber. 632p. 1967. pap. text ed. 19.95 (*0-691-02717-X*) Princeton U Pr.

Thayer's Life of Beethoven, Pt. 2. Elliot Forber. 542p. 1967. pap. text ed. 19.95 (*0-691-02718-8*) Princeton U Pr.

Thayer's Life of Beethoven, Set. Elliot Forber. 117p. 1967. pap. text ed. 34.00 (*0-691-02719-6*) Princeton U Pr.

Thayer's Life of Beethoven, Vol. 1. Alexander W. Thayer. LC 66-29831. 633p. 1967. reprint ed. pap. 180.00 (*0-7837-9337-5*, 2060078) Bks Demand.

Thbo Tsrm Adrnm Wod Tsornm. Mark McMenamin. (Illus.). 23p. (Orig.). 1996. pap. text ed. 9.95 (*0-9651136-0-4*, 100) Meanma Pr.

The Abuse of Elderly People see Abuse of Older People: A Training Manual for Detection & Prevention

The Adventures of Haji Baba of Isphahan see Sargozasht-e Haji Baba-Ye Isfahani Haji Baba-Ye Isfahani

The Afternoon Tea Guide by Ellen Easton see Tea Travels

The AIVF Guide to International Film & Video Festivals see AIVF Guide to International Film & Video Festivals

The American School, 1642 - 1985 see American School, 1642-1994

The American Who Couldn't Say Noh see Japan for Starters: Almost Everything You Need to Know

The Ancient Aramaic Prayer of Jesus: The Lords Prayer see Setting a Trap for God: The Aramaic Prayer of Jesus

The Ancient Schools of Wisdom - A Selection of Teachings from Ramtha see Ramtha - Die Alten Schulen der Weisheit

The Animal World see Amazing Creatures

The Art of Information Gathering see Uncover the Truth

The Bantam New College French & English Dictionary see New International Webster's French & English Dictionary

The Bantam New College German & English Dictionary see New International Webster's German & English Dictionary

The Bantam New College Italian & English Dictionary see New International Webster's Italian & English Dictionary

The Bantam New College Spanish & English Dictionary see New International Webster's Spanish & English Dictionary

The Bassoonist's Scrapbook see Bassoonist's Memo Pad: A Gathering Place for Reed Tips

The Biography of Chet Bitterman see Hora de Morir: Biografia de Chet Bitterman

Bologna Annual '96. 176p. (J). Date not set. 45.00 (*1-55858-594-X*) North-South Bks NYC.

Bologna Annual '96. 150p. (J). Date not set. 45.00 (*1-55858-595-8*) North-South Bks NYC.

Bologna Annual '93: 1993 Bologna Illustrator's Exhibition Annual. (Illus.). 176p. (J). Date not set. 39.95 (*1-55858-236-3*) North-South Bks NYC.

***Bologna Annuals '97.** North-South Books Staff. 176p. (J). 1997. 45.00 (*1-55858-743-8*) North-South Bks NYC.

***Bologna Annuals '97.** North-South Books Staff. 150p. (J). 1997. 45.00 (*1-55858-744-6*) North-South Bks NYC.

The Bomb see H: A Hiroshima Novel

The Briar Patch: The People of the State of New York V. Lusmumba Shakur Et Al see Briar Patch: The Trial of the Panther 21

The Cardiologist's Painless Prescription for a Healthy Heart & a Longer Life see Healthy Heart Longer Life

The Chemotherapy Survival Guide see Chemotherapy & Radiation Therapy Survival Guide: Information, Suggestions, & Support to Help You Get Through Treatment

The Child with a Handicap see Child with a Disability

The Clarinetist's Scrapbook see Single-Reed Player's Memo Pad: A Gathering Place for Reed Tips

The Compelling Christ see Evidence You Never Knew Existed: Reasons to Trust Jesus & the Bible

The Complaint, & The Consolation see Night Thoughts: Or, The Complaint & the Consolation

The Complete Arizona Construction Study Guide see Complete Contractors' Study Guide: Business Management & Law

The Complete Book of Macra-Tack see Art of Braiding Quality Custom Tack: An Illustrated Guide with Step-by-Step Instructions Featuring 17 Braiding Techniques & Styles

The Complete Book of Water Therapy see Complete Book of Water Healing

The de Nemethy Method see Classic Show Jumping

The Demjanjuk Affair see Defending Ivan the Terrible: The Conspiracy to Convict John Demjanjuk

The Direct System of Ladies' Tailoring see Late Victorian Women's Tailoring: The Direct System of Ladies' Cutting (1897)

The Divine Pity: A Study in the Social Implications of the Beatitudes see Seven Sweet Blessings of Christ: And How to Make Them Yours

The Dream Lives On see New Life for Dying Churches: It Can Happen Anywhere!

***18th Century: Artists, Writers & Composers.** Sarah Halliwell. LC 97-11620. (Who & When Ser.). (J). 1998. write for info. (*0-8172-4727-0*) Raintree Steck-V.

The End of Bureaucracy & the Risk of the Intelligent Organization see Intelligent Organization: Engaging the Talent & Initiative of Everyone in the Workplace

The Fascinating Girl see Secrets of Winning Men

The Faux Gourmet see Dish!: A Single Woman's Confessions on Food & Sex

The Fitness Option see Five Weeks to Healing Stress: The Wellness Option

***5 Minute Child Health Advisor.** William M. Schwartz & Bruce Goldfarb. LC 97-24983. 1997. write for info. (*0-683-30433-X*) Williams & Wilkins.

***5 Minute Family Health Advisor.** Mark R. Dambro & Bruce Goldfarb. LC 97-24984. 1997. write for info. (*0-683-30435-6*) Williams & Wilkins.

The Gambler's Tale see Confessions of a Yakuza

The Gold-Mines of Midian & the Ruined Midianite Cities see Gold-Mines of Midian

The Good Ship Venus see Venus Bound: The Erotic Voyage of the Olympia Press & Its Writers

The Great Inventions see Great Inventions

The Hamlyn Book of Knots see Complete Book of Knots

The Handbook of Surgical Knot Tying see Medical Knots & Suture Technique: A Handbook for Students of Surgery

The Heart see Hurst's the Heart: Update 1

The Hidden Charles see Exploring the Hidden Charles: A Guide to Outdoor Activities on Boston's Celebrated River

100 Best Stocks You Can Buy. John Slatter. LC 96-20253. 304p. 1996. pap. 12.95 (*1-55850-650-0*) Adams Media.

The Illustrated Contemporary Dictionary-Encyclopedic see New International Webster's Concise Dictionary of the English Language: Deluxe Padded Edition

The Illustrated Contemporary Dictionary-Encyclopedia see New International Webster's Concise Dictionary of the English Language: Standard Edition

The Immunization Decision see Vaccine Guide: Making an Informed Choice

The Joy of Primary Music see Joy of Children's Music

The Last Victory see Lane Victory: The Last Victory Ship in War & in Peace

The Laugh & Cry Movie Guide: How to Use Movies to Feel Better About Life's Changes see Laugh & Cry Movie Guide: A Little Escape from Every Day Stress

The Learning-Disabled Child see LD Child & the ADHD Child: Ways Parents & Professionals Can Help

The Life of Lee Wulff see Lee Wulff

The Linton Register see Linton Trainer's Resource Directory

The Literature of the Ancient Egyptians see Ancient Egyptian Poetry & Prose

The Making of Urban Europe, 1000-1950 see Making of Urban Europe, 1000-1994

The Man on Fire see Saint Paul the Apostle: The Story of the Apostle to the Gentiles

The Mastery of Grief (1913) see Halo of Grief: A Companion on Your Journey Through Loss

The Missile Crisis of October 1962 see Cuba-Caribbean Missile Crisis of October 1962

The Mother's Almanac II see Mother's Almanac Goes To School: Your Child From Six To Twelve

The Nature of Foxes see World of the Fox

The NBA Finals: The Official Illustrated History see NBA Finals: 50th Anniversary Celebration

The Negro in American Life & Thought see Betrayal of the Negro from Rutherford B. Hayes to Woodrow Wilson: From Rutherford B. Hayes to Woodrow Wilson

The New Sobriety see Art & Politics in the Weimar Period: The New Sobriety 1917-1933

The New Three Minute Meditator see Three Minute Meditator: 30 Simple Ways to Unwind Your Mind While Enhancing Your Emotional Intelligence

The New York Book of Beauty see Beauty: The Little Black Book for New York Glamour Girls

The New York Book of Coffee & Cake see Big Cup: A Guide to New York's Coffee Culture

1995 Accessible Building Product Guide. John P. Salmen & Julee Quarve-Peterson. 192p. 1995. pap. text ed. 69.95 (*0-471-10947-9*) Wiley.

***1996 Presidential Election in the South: Southern Party Systems in the 1990s.** Ed. by Laurence W. Moreland & Robert P. Steed. LC 97-19236. 1998. text ed. write for info. (*0-275-95951-1*, Praeger Pubs) Greenwood.

The Oboist's Scrapbook see Oboist's Memo Pad: A Gathering Place for Reed Tips

100 Best Annuities You Can Buy. Gordon K. Williamson. LC 94-38102. 224p. 1995. pap. text ed. 19.95 (*0-471-01025-1*) Wiley.

101st Airborne Division, No. EM 13. Barry Smith. (Windrow & Greene Ser.). (Illus.). 66p. 1993. pap. 15.95 (*1-872004-53-9*) Motorbooks Intl.

The Other Side of History see Takeover: How Euroman Changed the World

The Papal Sin see Buddhist Manifesto: The Papal Sin

***...The Path of the Bird.** Vincent Tripi. 72p. 1996. pap. 10.00 (*0-9629902-3-X*) Hummngbrd WI.

The Penguin Book of Interviews: An Anthology from 1859 to the Present Day see Norton Book of Interviews

The Penguin Complete Children's Classics see Penguin Book of Classic Children's Characters

The Philosophical Foundations of Education see Classic & Contemporary Readings in the Philosophy of Education

The Pirate Princess see Princesa Pirata

The Ponca Chief see Standing Bear & the Ponca Chiefs

The Portable Edmund Wilson see Edmund Wilson Reader

The Poverty Pentagon see Triumphs of Joseph

The Question of Autonomy for the United States Air Arm, 1907-1945 see Autonomy of the Air Arm

The Sampler Quilt see New Sampler Quilt

The Second World War see Great Battles & Leaders of the Second World War: An Illustrated History

***17th Century: Artists, Writers & Composers.** Sarah Halliwell. LC 97-11621. (Who & When Ser.). (J). 1998. write for info. (*0-8172-4726-2*) Raintree Steck-V.

The South Cumberland & Fall Creek Falls see Tennessee's South Cumberland: A Hiker's Guide to Trails & Attractions

The Spiritual Conferences see Art of Loving God: Simple Virtues for the Christian Life

The Story About Ping see Historia De Ping

The Story of Hillside Cemetery Burials 1872-1988 see Over My Dead Body!: The Story of Hillside Cemetery, Silverton, Colorado

The Story of Opal: The Journal of an Understanding Heart see Diary of Opal Whiteley

The Super Forcing System see Yang's Jump Shifts - A Powerful Bidding Approach for Slams

The Survivor's Nutritional Pharmacy see How to Survive Disasters with Natural Medicines

10 Hottest Consulting Practices: What They Are, How to Get into Them. Ronald Tepper. LC 95-4261. 210p. 1995. text ed. 27.95 (*0-471-11000-0*) Wiley.

The Tenth Moon see Come Back to Sorrento

13 Nights of Halloween. Rebecca Dickinson. LC 95-30065. (J). 1996. 4.99 (*0-590-47586-X*) Scholastic Inc.

36-Hour Day. large type ed. Nancy L. Mace & Peter V. Rabins. 1995. 27.99 (*0-7089-5801-X*) Ulverscroft.

Top 500 Poems. Ed. by William Harmon. 1,132p. (C). 1992. 29.95 (*0-231-08028-X*) Col U Pr.

***Top 10 Career Strategies for the Year 2000 & Beyond: For the Year 2000 & Beyond.** Gary J. Grappo. 160p. 1997. pap. 12.00 (*0-425-15792-X*, Berkley Trade) Berkley Pub.

The Trail Guide to Olympic National Park see Hiking Olympic National Park

The Truth about the Titanic see Titanic: A Survivor's Story

The Wall Between see Women Behind Bars in Romania

***Watershed Trilogy 3: War of Three Waters, Vol. 3.** Douglas Niles. (Watershed Ser.). 384p. 1997. pap. 14.00 (*0-441-00442-3*) Ace Bks.

The Way Back see Qabalah, Tarot & the Wistern Mystery Tradition: The 22 Connecting Paths on the Tree of Life

The Way to Write see Classic Guide to Better Writing: Step-by-Step Techniques & Exercises to Write Simply, Clearly & Correctly

Wealthy 100: From Benjamin Franklin to Bill Gates - a Ranking of the Richest Americans, Past & Present. Michael M. Klepper & Robert Gunther. LC 95-50109. (Illus.). 400p. Date not set. 25.95 (*0-8065-1800-6*, Citadel Pr) Carol Pub Group.

The Westminster Shorter Catechism see Shorter Catechism: A Modest Revision for Baptists Today

The Winning Attitude see Actitud Triunfadora: Minibook

The Writer's Book of Checklists see 1,818 Ways to Write Better & Get Published

The Written Word Endures see Milestone Documents of American History

The Yearbook of School Law see Yearbook of Education Law 1996

Thea Bowman: Handing on Her Legacy. Ed. by Christian Koontz. LC 91-61104. 120p. (Orig.). 1991. pap. 8.95 (*1-55612-458-9*, LL1458) Sheed & Ward MO.

Thea Musgrave: A Bio-Bibliography. Donald L. Hixon. LC 83-22705. (Bio-Bibliographies in Music Ser.: No. 1). iv, 187p. 1984. text ed. 49.95 (*0-313-23708-5*, HTM/, Greenwood Pr) Greenwood.

***Thea Von Harbou und der Deutsche Film Bis 1933.** Reinhold Keiner. (Studien Zur Filmgeschichte Ser.: Vol. 2). x, 311p. (GER.). 1991. write for info. (*3-487-07467-2*) G Olms Pubs.

Theaetetus. Plato. Tr. by M. J. Levett from GRE. LC 92-28261. 128p. (C). 1992. 27.95 (*0-87220-159-7*); pap. 6.95 (*0-87220-158-9*) Hackett Pub.

T

An Asterisk (*) at the beginning of an entry indicates that the title is appearing in BIP for the first time.

Theaetetus. Plato. Tr. by John McDowell. (Clarendon Plato Ser.). 272p. 1977. pap. 24.95 (*0-19-872083-1*) OUP.

Theaetetus. Plato. Tr. by Robin A. Waterfield. 256p. 1987. pap. 8.95 (*0-14-044450-5*, Penguin Classics) Viking Penguin.

Theaetetus, & Sophist, Vol. VII. Plato. (Loeb Classical Library: No. 123). 474p. 1923. text ed. 18.95 (*0-674-99137-0*) HUP.

Theaetetus of Plato. Myles Burnyeat. LC 89-26936. 372p. (C). 1990. reprint ed. pap. text ed. 14.95 (*0-915144-81-6*); reprint ed. lib. bdg. 34.95 (*0-915144-82-4*) Hackett Pub.

Theaetetus of Plato. Plato. LC 72-9287. (Philosophy of Plato & Aristotle Ser.). 1977. reprint ed. 21.95 (*0-405-04837-8*) Ayer.

Theagenes Oder Wissenscshaftliche Darstellung der Gymnastik, Agonistik und Festspiele der Hellenen. Johann Krause. xxx, 256p. 1975. reprint ed. write for info. (*3-487-05498-1*) G Olms Pubs.

Theages, Charmides, Laches, Lysis, Euthydemus, Protagoras, Gorgias, Meno, Hippias Maior, Hippas Minor, Io, Menexenus see Opera

Theandric: Julian Beck's Last Notebooks, Vol. 2. Ed. by Erica Bilder. (Contemporary Theatre Studies). 195p. 1992. text ed. 46.00 (*3-7186-5192-0*, Harwood Acad Pubs); pap. text ed. 23.00 (*3-7186-5193-9*, Harwood Acad Pubs) Gordon & Breach.

Theater. Boy Scouts of America. 64p. (J). (gr. 6-12). 1968. pap. 2.40 (*0-8395-3328-4*, 33328) BSA.

Theater. Andrea Gironemeyer. (Crash Course Ser.). 192p. 1996. 12.95 (*0-8120-9774-2*) Barron.

Theater. Jane Mason. LC 93-5744. (Now Hiring Ser.). (J). 1994. pap. 5.95 (*0-382-24750-7*, Crstwood Hse) Silver Burdett Pr.

***Theater: The Lively Art.** 2nd ed. Edwin Wilson & Alvin Goldfarb. 1995. pap. text ed. write for info. (*0-07-070687-5*) McGraw.

Theater: The Lively Art. 2nd ed. Edwin Wilson & Alvin Goldfarb. LC 95-35794. 1995. pap. text ed. write for info. (*0-07-070764-2*) McGraw.

Theater Air & Missile Defense (TAMD) A Context for the Roles & Missions Debate. Richard F. Mesic. LC 95-48458. Date not set. pap. 15.00 (*0-8330-2346-2*) Rand Corp.

Theater Analysis & Modeling in an Era of Uncertainty: The Present & Future of Warfare. Bruce W. Bennett et al. LC 94-4161. 1994. pap. text ed. 13.00 (*0-8330-1511-7*, MR-380-NA) Rand Corp.

Theater & Its Double. Antonin Artaud. Tr. by Mary C. Richards from FRE. 159p. 1988. pap. 11.00 (*0-8021-5030-6*, Grove) Grove-Atltic.

Theater & Politics. Zygmunt Hubner. Ed. & Tr. by Jadwiga Kosicka from POL. (Illus.). 350p. (Orig.). 1992. 35.00 (*0-8101-1022-9*) Northwestern U Pr.

***Theater & Politics: An International Anthology: Includes: Black Wedding Candles for Blessed Antigone, A Season in the Congo, Burn River Burn, Olympe & the Executioner, Mephisto, 5 plays.** Sylvain Bemba et al. Ed. by Francoise Kourilsky & Catherine Temerson. Tr. by Townsend Brewster et al. 470p. (Orig.). 1990. pap. 15.95 (*0-913745-32-4*) Ubu Repertory.

Theater & Revolution in France since 1968. Judith G. Miller. LC 76-47500. (French Forum Monographs: No. 4). 169p. (Orig.). 1977. pap. 10.95 (*0-917058-03-8*) French Forum.

Theater & Society in the Classical World. Ed. by Ruth Scodel. 300p. (C). 1992. text ed. 47.50 (*0-472-10281-8*) U of Mich Pr.

Theater & the Adolescent Actor: Building a Successful School Program. Camille L. Poisson. LC 93-36406. (Illus.). x, 228p. (C). 1994. lib. bdg. 29.50 (*0-208-02380-1*, Archon Bks) Shoe String.

Theater & World: The Problematics of Shakespeare's History. Jonathan Hart. 224p. 1991. text ed. 47.50 (*1-55553-110-5*) NE U Pr.

Theater As Music: The Bunraku Play "Mt. Imo & Mt. Se: An Exemplary Tale of Womanly Virtue" C. Andrew Gerstle et al. LC 89-25139. (Michigan Monographs in Japanese Studies: No. 4). (Illus.). xii, 289p. 1990. 46.95 incl. audio (*0-939512-38-6*) U MI Japan.

Theater As Problem: Modern Drama & Its Place in Literature. Benjamin Bennett. LC 90-55115. 296p. 1990. 45.00 (*0-8014-2443-7*); pap. 16.95 (*0-8014-9730-2*) Cornell U Pr.

Theater at the Margins: Texts for a Post-Structured Stage. Erik MacDonald. (Theater: Theory - Text - Performance Ser.). 184p. (C). 1993. text ed. 39.50 (*0-472-10311-3*) U of Mich Pr.

Theater Book of the Year 1947-1948. George J. Nathan. 350p. 29.50 (*0-8386-1176-1*) Fairleigh Dickinson.

Theater Criticisms. Stanley Kauffmann. 1984. 19.95 (*0-933826-57-5*); pap. 14.95 (*0-933826-58-3*) PAJ Pubns.

***Theater Design.** 2nd ed. George C. Izenour. (Illus.). 666p. 1996. 150.00 (*0-300-06775-5*) Yale U Pr.

Theater Dictionary: British & American Terms in the Drama, Opera & Ballet. Wilfred Granville. LC 76-110046. 227p. 1970. reprint ed. text ed. 67.50 (*0-8371-4428-0*, GRTD, Greenwood Pr) Greenwood.

Theater Duke: Georg II of Saxe-Meiningen & the German Stage. Ann M. Koller. LC 82-42911. (Illus.). xiv, 257p. 1984. 39.50 (*0-8047-1196-8*) Stanford U Pr.

Theater Enough: American Culture & the Metaphor of the World Stage, 1607-1789. Jeffrey H. Richards. LC 90-47943. 359p. 1991. text ed. 34.95 (*0-8223-1107-0*) Duke.

Theater Essays of Arthur Miller. 2nd expanded rev. ed. Arthur Miller. Ed. by Robert A. Martin & Steven R. Centola. LC 96-16452. 686p. 1996. pap. 17.95 (*0-306-80732-7*) Da Capo.

Theater Experience. 6th ed. Edwin Wilson. 1994. pap. text ed. write for info. (*0-07-070685-9*) McGraw.

Theater Experience. 6th ed. Edwin Wilson. 1995. pap. text ed. write for info. (*0-07-912056-3*) McGraw.

***Theater Experience.** 7th ed. Edwin Wilson. LC 96-37201. 1997. pap. text ed. write for info. (*0-07-070691-3*) McGraw.

Theater Experience, Third Edition. 3rd ed. Edwin Wilson. 1985. text ed. write for info. (*0-07-070673-5*) McGraw.

Theater Facility Impact Study: Theater Facilities: Guidelines & Strategies, Vol. 1. Robert M. Beckley & Sherrill M. Myers. (Publications in Architecture & Urban Planning: No. R81-9). (Illus.). vi, 139p. 1981. 12.50 (*0-938744-21-6*) U of Wis Ctr Arch-Urban.

Theater for Development: A Guide to Training. Martin L. Byram. (Illus.). 65p. (Orig.). (C). 1985. pap. text ed. 4.00 (*0-932288-76-6*) Ctr Intl Ed U of MA.

Theater Game File. Viola Spolin. 1989. Handbook plus 210 index cards. 49.95 (*0-8101-4007-1*) Northwestern U Pr.

Theater Games for Rehearsal: A Director's Handbook. Viola Spolin. 117p. 1985. pap. 26.95 (*0-8101-4002-0*); text ed. 26.95 (*0-8101-4001-2*) Northwestern U Pr.

Theater Games for the Classroom: A Teacher's Handbook. Viola Spolin. 233p. 1986. 29.95 (*0-8101-4003-9*); pap. 13.95 (*0-8101-4004-7*) Northwestern U Pr.

Theater in America: 250 Years of Plays, Players, & Productions. Mary C. Henderson. (Illus.). 352p. 1996. 60.00 (*0-8109-3884-7*) Abrams.

Theater in Israel. Linda Ben-Zvi. LC 95-46189. (C). 1996. 52.50 (*0-472-10607-4*) U of Mich Pr.

Theater in Southeast Asia. James R. Brandon. LC 67-14338. (Illus.). 383p. 1974. pap. 15.95 (*0-674-87587-7*) HUP.

Theater in Soviet Russia. Nikolai A. Gorchakov. Tr. by Edgar Lehrman. LC 72-2996. (Select Bibliographies Reprint Ser.). 1977. reprint ed. 47.95 (*0-8369-6869-7*) Ayer.

Theater in the South. Ed. by Rebecca Ranson. (Southern Exposure Ser.). (Illus.). 120p. (Orig.). 1986. pap. 4.00 (*0-943810-21-3*) Inst Southern Studies.

***Theater-Level Campaign Model: A Research Prototype for a New Generation of Combat Model.** Richard J. Hillestad & Louis Moore. LC 96-39447. (Illus.). 201p. 1996. pap. text ed. 13.00 (*0-8330-2465-5*, MR-388-A/AF) Rand Corp.

Theater Magic. Houghton Mifflin Company Staff. (Literature Experience 1993 Ser.). (J). (gr. 3). 1992. pap. 8.48 (*0-395-61786-3*) HM.

Theater Magic: Behind the Scenes at a Children's Theater. Cheryl W. Bellville. LC 86-9757. (Carolrhoda Photo Bks.). (Illus.). 48p. (J). (ps-5). 1986. lib. bdg. 19.95 (*0-87614-278-1*, Carolrhoda) Lerner Group.

Theater of Andrzej Wajda. Maciej Karpinski. (Directors in Perspective Ser.). (Illus.). 200p. (C). 1989. text ed. 69.95 (*0-521-32246-4*) Cambridge U Pr.

Theater of Animals: Poems. Samn Stockwell. LC 94-46117. (National Poetry Ser.). 72p. 1995. 10.95 (*0-252-06476-3*) U of Ill Pr.

Theater of Claude Billard: A Study in Post-Renaissance Dramatic Esthetics, Vol. 9. Thomas L. Zamparelli. 188p. 1978. pap. 7.00 (*0-912788-08-9*) Tulane Romance Lang.

Theater of Confinement: Language & Survival in the Milieu Plays of Marieluise Fleisser & Franz Xaver Kroetz. Donna L. Hoffmeister. LC 82-72261. (GERM Ser.: Vol. 11). (Illus.). xiv, 176p. 1983. 34.00 (*0-938100-12-2*) Camden Hse.

Theater of Devotion: East Anglican Drama & Society in the Late Middle Ages. Gail M. Gibson. (Illus.). xvi, 268p. 1994. pap. text ed. 14.95 (*0-226-29102-2*) U Ch Pr.

Theater of Diaspora: Two Plays, the Ass & Rex Cinema Trial. Parviz Sayyad. Ed. by Hamid Dabashi. 224p. (Orig.). 1992. pap. 15.00 (*0-939214-94-6*) Mazda Pubs.

Theater of Essence. Jan Kott. LC 84-61440. 218p. 1984. pap. 14.95 (*0-8101-0665-5*) Northwestern U Pr.

Theater of Fine Devices. Thomas Combe. (Illus.). 240p. 1990. text ed. 56.95 (*0-85967-769-9*, Pub. by Scolar Pr UK) Ashgate Pub Co.

Theater of Franz Xaver Kroetz. Ingeborg C. Walther. Ed. by Peter D. Brown. LC 90-6203. (Studies in Modern German Literature: Vol. 40). xi, 276p. (C). 1990. 47.95 (*0-8204-1397-6*) P Lang Pubng.

Theater of Healing. E. D. Karampetsos. (American University Studies: Ser. XXVI, Vol. 24). 152p. (C). 1995. text ed. 32.95 (*0-8204-2651-2*) P Lang Pubng.

Theater of His Glory: Nature & the Natural Order in the Thought of John Calvin. Susan E. Schreiner. (Studies in Historical Theology: Vol. 3). 196p. 1991. lib. bdg. 30.00 (*0-939464-51-9*, Labyrinth) Baker Bks.

Theater of Isthmia. Elizabeth R. Gebhard. LC 72-80813. (Illus.). 174p. reprint ed. pap. 49.60 (*0-317-10659-7*, 2015756) Bks Demand.

Theater of Maxim Gorky see Lower Depths & Other Plays

Theater of Memory: Three Plays of Kalidasa. Ed. by Barbara S. Miller et al. LC 83-26362. (Translations from the Oriental Classics Ser.). 384p. (Orig.). 1984. text ed. 59.00 (*0-231-05838-1*); pap. text ed. 21.50 (*0-231-05839-X*) Col U Pr.

Theater of Michel Vinaver. David Bradby. (Theater: Theory - Text - Performance Ser.). 140p. 1993. text ed. 37.50 (*0-472-10326-1*) U of Mich Pr.

***Theater of Nature: Jean Bodin & Renaissance Science.** LC 96-40164. 1997. write for info. (*0-691-05675-7*) Princeton U Pr.

***Theater of Recollection: Paintings & Prints by John Walker.** John R. Stomberg. (Illus.). 32p. (Orig.). 1997. pap. 10.00 (*1-881450-08-2*) Boston U Art.

Theater of Refusal: Black Art & Mainstream Criticism. Maurice Berger et al. (Illus.). 88p. (Orig.). 1993. pap. 16.50 (*1-884355-00-5*) U CA Fine Arts.

Theater of Solitudes: The Drama of Alfred de Musset. David Sices. LC 73-89286. (Illus.). 284p. reprint ed. pap. 81.00 (*0-685-44069-9*, 2030032) Bks Demand.

Theater of Spontaneity. 3rd ed. Ed. by J. L. Moreno. 1983. pap. 15.00 (*0-685-42742-0*) Beacon Hse.

Theater of Sport. Ed. by Karl B. Raitz. (Illus.). 384p. 1995. pap. 19.95 (*0-8018-4909-8*); text ed. 45.00 (*0-8018-4908-X*) Johns Hopkins.

Theater of the Absurd. rev. ed. Martin Esslin. LC 72-94410. 424p. 1973. reprint ed. 35.00 (*0-87951-005-6*) Overlook Pr.

Theater of the Bauhaus. Ed. by Walter Gropius & Arthur S. Wensinger. Tr. by Arthur S. Wensinger from GER. LC 96-33458. (PAJ Bks.). 109p. 1996. reprint ed. pap. text ed. 14.95 (*0-8018-5528-4*) Johns Hopkins.

Theater of the Ears. Valere Novarina. Tr. by Allen S. Weiss from FRE. (Sun & Moon Classics Ser.: No. 85). 220p. 1996. pap. 13.95 (*1-55713-251-8*) Sun & Moon CA.

Theater of the Object, 1958-1972: Reconstruction, Re-Creation, Reconsideration. Alternative Museum Staff. LC 89-84275. (Illus.). 1989. pap. 7.00 (*0-932075-26-6*) Alternative Mus.

***Theater of the Soul: The Higher Self & Multi-Incarnational Exploration. Susan Harris. x, 150p. (Orig.). 1996. pap. 12.95 (*0-9653413-0-5*) Wndhorse Pubs.**

Susan Harris, a psychotherapist & former Director of the European Light Institute, reveals the use of multi-incarnational exploration as a profound tool for inner clarity & healing. She has discovered that truth is always with us as the Inner Self, that it is only our misperceptions about ourselves & reality that draw our attention away. When these patterns become conscious, they can be seen for what they are & released. Viewing the many dramas that live inside us is a natural way to accomplish this. By entering the perspective of our lives being "theater" we gain wisdom & freedom from suffering, allowing us to remember the deep abiding peace that lives inside all of us. THEATER OF THE SOUL covers: * COMING HOME TO THE SELF. Self-inquiry. Living in constant communion with our Inner Self is easy. What has made it so difficult? * USING OUR EMOTIONAL BODY as an instrument of ecstasy, not pain. Bridging the psychological with the spiritual. * MULTI-INCARNATIONAL EXPLORATION is a powerful tool for clearing repetitive patterns & blocks. Stories can also be seen as metaphors. * LIVING IT - "walking our talk." Not as fancy ideas, but as real life. Order from: Windhorse Publications, P.O. Box 9939, Santa Fe, NM 87504-9939, or call 505-984-1274; FAX 505-984-8410. *Publisher Provided Annotation.*

Theater Props Handbook: The Property Builders Encyclopedia. Thurston James. (Illus.). 288p. (Orig.). 1987. pap. 19.99 (*0-932620-86-8*, Betrwy Bks) F & W Pubns Inc.

Theater Subject Headings. 2nd enl. large type ed. New York Public Library Staff. 1994. 165.00 (*0-7838-2319-3*, GK Hall) Thorndike Pr.

***Theater Technology.** 2nd ed. George C. Izenour. (Illus.). 594p. 1996. 150.00 (*0-300-06766-6*) Yale U Pr.

Theater, Theory, Speculation: Walter Benjamin & the Scenes of Modernity. Rainer Nagele. LC 90-45358. 208p. 1991. text ed. 40.00 (*0-8018-4123-2*) Johns Hopkins.

Theater Tips & Strategies for Jury Trials. David Ball. 166p. 1994. pap. 22.95 (*1-55681-410-0*) Natl Inst Trial Ad.

Theater von Milet I: Das hellenistische Theater. Friedrich Krauss. LC 72-75866. (Milet Ser.: Vol. 4, 1). (C). 1973. 246.15 (*3-11-004211-8*) De Gruyter.

Theaterperiodika des 18 Jahrhunderts: Teil 2: 1781-1790. 1996. write for info. (*3-598-23183-0*) K G Saur.

Theaterperiodika des 18 Jahrhunderts: Teil 3: 1791-1799. 1998. write for info. (*3-598-23184-9*) K G Saur.

Theaters & Halls. (Illus.). 224p. 1995. 85.00 (*4-938812-19-3*, Pub. by Meisei Co Ltd JA) Bks Nippan.

***Theaters & Halls.** Meisei Publications Editorial Staff. 1996. 89.95 (*4-938812-09-6*, Nippan Pubns) Bks Nippan.

Theaters of the Body: A Psychoanalytic View of Psychosomatic Illness. Joyce McDougall. (C). 1989. 22.95 (*0-393-70082-8*) Norton.

***Theaters of the Heart & Mind.** Alice Barter. LC 97-65993. 128p. 1997. pap. 13.50 (*0-88739-124-9*) Creat Arts Bk.

Theaters of the Mind: Illusion & Truth on the Psychoanalytic Stage. Joyce McDougall. LC 91-20628. 320p. 1991. pap. text ed. 28.95 (*0-87630-648-2*) Brunner-Mazel.

Theatine Spirituality: Selected Writings. Ed. & Tr. by William V. Hudon. (Classics of Western Spirituality Ser.: CWS 87). 416p. 1996. 29.95 (*0-8091-0479-2*, 0479-2) Paulist Pr.

Theatine Spirituality: Selected Writings. Tr. by William V. Hudon. (Classics of Western Spirituality Ser.: No. 87). 416p. 1996. pap. 22.95 (*0-8091-3637-6*, 3637-6) Paulist Pr.

Theatralite dans l'Oeuvre d'Alfred Jarry. Linda K. Stillman. LC 78-74000. 179p. (FRE.). 1981. 14.95 (*0-917786-12-2*) Summa Pubns.

Theatre. Henri De Montherlant. Ed. by Armand Laprade. 1472p. (FRE.). 1955. lib. bdg. 115.00 (*0-7859-3768-4*, 2070103749) Fr & Eur.

Theatre, 5 vols. Henry De Montherlant. (Illus.). 380p. (FRE.). 1966. Set. 525.00 (*0-8288-9885-5*, F115190) Fr & Eur.

Theatre. Carlo Goldino. (FRE.). 1972. 110.00 (*0-8288-3493-8*, F10161) Fr & Eur.

Theatre. Incl. Impromptu de l'Alma. (*0-318-52297-7*); Tuers sans Gages. (*0-318-52298-5*); Nouveau Locataire. (*0-318-52299-3*); Avenir Est dans les Oeufs. (*0-318-52300-0*); Maitre. (*0-318-52301-9*); Jeune Fille a Marier. (*0-318-52302-7*); Cantatrice Chauve. (*0-318-63605-0*); Lecon. (*0-318-63606-9*); Jacques ou la Soumission. (*0-318-63607-7*); Chaises. (*0-318-63608-5*); Victimes du Devoir. (*0-318-63609-3*); Amedee. (*0-318-63610-7*); Ou Comment s'en Debarrasser. (*0-318-63611-5*); write for info. (*0-318-63604-2*) Fr & Eur.

Theatre. Gabriela Kohen. (This Is Entertainment Ser.). (Illus.). 24p. (Orig.). (J). (gr. 2-6). 1992. lib. bdg. 9.95 (*1-56492-012-7*) Laredo.

Theatre. 3rd ed. Robert Cohen. LC 92-46052. 512p. 1993. pap. text ed. 39.95 (*1-55934-142-4*, 1142) Mayfield Pub.

Theatre. 3rd ed. Robert Cohen. (Illus.). (C). 1993. disk 36.95 (*0-685-70423-8*) Mayfield Pub.

Theatre. 4th rev. ed. Robert Cohen. LC 96-13608. (Illus.). 535p. (C). 1996. pap. text ed. 39.95 (*1-55934-666-3*, 1666) Mayfield Pub.

Theatre. W. Somerset Maugham. LC 75-25365. (Works of W. Somerset Maugham). 1977. reprint ed. 23.95 (*0-405-07823-4*) Ayer.

Theatre, 5 tomes, 1. Eugene Ionesco. (Gallimard Ser.: Tome I). (FRE.). pap. 31.95 (*2-07-023301-4*) Schoenhof.

Theatre, 2 vols., 2. Paul Claudel. Ed. by Madaule. (Bibliotheque de la Pleiade Ser.). (FRE.). 1966. 110.00 (*0-685-73336-X*, F93762) Fr & Eur.

Theatre, 5 tomes, 2. Eugene Ionesco. (Gallimard Ser.: Tome I). (FRE.). pap. 19.95 (*2-07-023302-2*) Schoenhof.

Theatre, 5 tomes, 3. Eugene Ionesco. (Gallimard Ser.: Tome I). (FRE.). pap. 29.95 (*2-07-023306-5*) Schoenhof.

Theatre, 5 tomes, 4. Eugene Ionesco. (Gallimard Ser.: Tome I). (FRE.). pap. 31.95 (*2-07-023308-1*) Schoenhof.

Theatre, 5 tomes, 5. Eugene Ionesco. (Gallimard Ser.: Tome I). (FRE.). pap. 20.95 (*2-07-028969-9*) Schoenhof.

Theatre, Set. Incl. Electre. Jean Giraudoux. 1959. (*0-318-52285-3*); Supplement au Voyage de Cook. Jean Giraudoux. 1959. (*0-318-52286-1*); Impromptu de Paris. Jean Giraudoux. 1959. (*0-318-52287-X*); Cantique des Cantiques. Jean Giraudoux. 1959. (*0-318-52288-8*); Ondine. (*0-318-52289-6*); Siegfried. (*0-318-52290-X*); Fin de Siegfried. (*0-318-52291-8*); Amphitryon 38. (*0-318-52292-6*); Judith. (*0-318-52293-4*); Intermezzo. (*0-318-52294-2*); Tessa. (*0-318-52295-0*); Guerre de Troie n'Aura pas Lieu. (*0-318-52296-9*); 1959. 37.95 (*0-8288-9792-1*, F103905); 110.00 (*0-8288-9793-X*) Fr & Eur.

Theatre, 5 tomes, Set. Henri De Montherlant. 525.00 (*0-685-11587-9*) Fr & Eur.

Theatre, Tome II. Incl. Impromptu de l'Alma. (*0-318-52297-7*); Tuers sans Gages. (*0-318-52298-5*); Nouveau Locataire. (*0-318-52299-3*); Avenir Est dans les Oeufs. (*0-318-52300-0*); Maitre. (*0-318-52301-9*); Jeune Fille a Marier. (*0-318-52302-7*); Cantatrice Chauve. (*0-318-63605-0*); Lecon. (*0-318-63606-9*); Jacques ou la Soumission. (*0-318-63607-7*); Chaises. (*0-318-63608-5*); Victimes du Devoir. (*0-318-63609-3*); Amedee. (*0-318-63610-7*); Ou Comment s'en Debarrasser. (*0-318-63611-5*); (Blanche Ser.). 13.50 (*0-685-34247-6*) Fr & Eur.

Theatre, Tome III. Incl. Electre. Jean Giraudoux. 1959. (*0-318-52285-3*); Supplement au Voyage de Cook. Jean Giraudoux. 1959. (*0-318-52286-1*); Impromptu de Paris. Jean Giraudoux. 1959. (*0-318-52287-X*); Cantique des Cantiques. Jean Giraudoux. 1959. (*0-318-52288-8*); Ondine. (*0-318-52289-6*); Siegfried. (*0-318-52290-X*); Fin de Siegfried. (*0-318-52291-8*); Amphitryon 38. (*0-318-52292-6*); Judith. (*0-318-52293-4*); Intermezzo. (*0-318-52294-2*); Tessa. (*0-318-52295-0*); Guerre de Troie n'Aura pas Lieu. (*0-318-52296-9*); 1959. 37.95 (*0-685-35877-1*) Fr & Eur.

Theatre, Vol. 1. Paul Claudel. (FRE.). 1966. 99.50 (*0-8288-3460-1*, F93761) Fr & Eur.

Theatre, Vol. 1. Eugene Labiche. (FRE.). 1990. pap. 16.95 (*0-7859-3002-7*) Fr & Eur.

Theatre, Vol. 1. Charles Vildrac. 288p. (FRE.). 1943. pap. 14.95 (*0-7859-1333-5*, 2070265331) Fr & Eur.

Theatre, Vol. 2. Paul Claudel. (FRE.). 1966. 110.00 (*0-8288-3461-X*, F93762) Fr & Eur.

Theatre, Vol. 2. Eugene Labiche. (FRE.). 1991. pap. 14.95 (*0-7859-3003-5*) Fr & Eur.

Theatre, Vol. 3. Eugene Labiche. 509p. (FRE.). 1964. 10.95 (*0-8288-9835-9*, F108552) Fr & Eur.

Theatre, Vol. 3. Alfred Musset. 512p. (FRE.). 1964. 10.95 (*0-8288-9650-X*, FC1473) Fr & Eur.

Theatre, Vol. 4. Jacques Audiberti. (FRE.). 1970. pap. 39.95 (*0-7859-3957-1*, 2070203492) Fr & Eur.

Theatre, Vol. 4. Jacques Audiberti. 1970. pap. 29.95 (*0-686-54507-9*) Fr & Eur.

Theatre: A Concise History. rev. ed. Phyllis Hartnoll. (World of Art Ser.). (Illus.). 262p. 1985. pap. 14.95 (*0-500-20073-4*) Thames Hudson.

Theatre: A Contemporary Introduction. 3rd ed. Jerry V. Pickering. (Illus.). 389p. (C). 1981. pap. text ed. 43.75 (*0-8299-0403-4*) West Pub.

Theatre: A Model of the World. Alvin J. Schnupp. 368p. (C). 1994. per. 41.94 (*0-8403-8434-3*) Kendall-Hunt.

Theatre: A Way of Seeing. 3rd ed. Milly S. Barranger. 393p. (C). 1991. pap. 35.95 (*0-534-14418-7*) Wadsworth Pub.

Theatre: A Way of Seeing. 4th ed. Milly S. Barranger. 416p. 1995. pap. 44.95 (*0-534-24024-0*) Wadsworth Pub.

Theatre: Art & Craft. 3rd ed. Stephen M. Archer. (Illus.). 318p. pap. text ed. 21.90 (*0-685-69334-1*) Collegiate Pr.

Theatre: Avec: Atlas-Hôtel, Vol. 2. Armand Salacrou. 346p. (FRE.). 1978. pap. 24.95 (0-7859-1592-3, 207028574X) Fr & Eur.

Theatre: Avec: Boubouroche, La Peur des Coups. Georges Courteline. 253p. (FRE.). 1965. 10.95 (0-7859-1168-5, 2080700650) Fr & Eur.

Theatre: Avec: Guernica, Le Labyrinthe, Le Tricycle,Pique-Nique en Campagne, La Bicyclette du Condamne, Vol. 2. 221p. 1968. 9.95 (0-686-54464-1) Fr & Eur.

Theatre: Avec: La Querre de Mil Ans, Bella Ciao, Vol. 10. 5.95 (0-686-54469-2) Fr & Eur.

Theatre: Avec: La Terre est Ronde, Vol. 4. Armand Salacrou. 284p. (FRE.). 1945. pap. 14.95 (0-7859-1316-5, 2070257029) Fr & Eur.

Theatre: Avec: Le Barbier de Seville, Le Marriage de Figaro, La Mere Coupable. Pierre de Beaumarchais & Rene Pomeau. 320p. (FRE.). 1965. pap. 10.95 (0-7859-0671-1) Fr & Eur.

Theatre: Avec: Le Ciel et la Mer, La Grande Revue du 20e Siecle, Vol. 9. Fernando Arrabal. 261p. 1969. 15.95 (0-686-54468-4) Fr & Eur.

Theatre: Avec: Le Jardin des Delices, Bestialite Erotique, Une Torture Nommee Dostoievsky, Vol. 6. Fernando Arrabal. 192p. 1969. 9.95 (0-686-54466-8) Fr & Eur.

Theatre: Avec: Les Fiances du Havre, Vol. 5. Armand Salacrou. 366p. (FRE.). 1947. pap. 15.95 (0-7859-1317-3, 2070257037) Fr & Eur.

Theatre: Avec: Operas Paniques, Ars Amandi, Dieu Tente par le Mathematiques, Vol. 8. Fernando Arrabal. 192p. 1970. 9.95 (0-686-54467-6) Fr & Eur.

Theatre: Avec: Pomme, Pomme, Pomme, Baton et Ruban, Boutique Fermee, La Brigitta, Vol. 5. 264p. 1962. 5.95 (0-686-54508-7) Fr & Eur.

Theatre: Avec: Pourquoi pas moi?, Vol. 7. Armand Salacrou. 288p. (FRE.). 1957. pap. 13.95 (0-7859-1319-X, 2070257088) Fr & Eur.

Theatre: Avec: Une Femme Libre, Vol. 3. Armand Salacrou. 336p. (FRE.). 1942. pap. 16.95 (0-7859-1393-9, 2080256995) Fr & Eur.

Theatre: Big Book. Gabriela Kohen. (This Is Entertainment Ser.). (Illus.). 24p. (Orig.). (J). (gr. 2-6). 1992. pap. 19.95 (1-56492-013-5) Laredo.

Theatre: Choice in Action. Arden Fingerhut. 416p. 1994. 32.50 (0-8230-4957-4, Back Stage Bks) Watsn-Guptill.

Theatre: Choice of Action. Arden Fingerhut. (C). 1995. text ed. 43.50 (0-673-46489-X) Addson-Wesley Educ.

Theatre: Edition Definitive, Vol. 1. Armand Salacrou. 279p. (FRE.). 1977. pap. 18.95 (0-7859-1350-5, 2070297470) Fr & Eur.

Theatre: Essays on the Arts of the Theatre. Ed. by Edith J. Isaacs. LC 68-22919. (Essay Index Reprint Ser.). 1977. 23.95 (0-8369-0561-X) Ayer.

Theatre: La Locandiera, Le Valet de deux Maitres, La Trilogie de la Villegiature. Goldini. 1584p. 41.50 (0-686-56517-7) Fr & Eur.

Theatre: Romans et Nouvelles. Prosper Merimee. (FRE.). 1979. lib. bdg. 110.00 (0-8288-3566-7, F68014) Fr & Eur.

Theatre: Romans et Nouvelles. rev. ed. Prosper Merimee. 54.95 (0-686-56540-1) Fr & Eur.

Theatre: Stage to Screen to Television, 2 vols. William T. Leonard. LC 80-22987. 1812p. 1981. Set. 92.50 (0-8108-1374-2) Scarecrow.

Theatre: The Dynamics of the Art. 2nd ed. Brian Hansen. 320p. (C). 1990. pap. text ed. 50.00 (0-13-913047-0) P-H.

Theatre: The Rediscovery of Style. Michel Saint-Denis. LC 60-10492. 1968. reprint ed. pap. 9.95 (0-87830-523-8, Thtre Arts Bks) Routledge.

Theatre Vol. 1: Quoat-Quoat, l'Ampelour, les Femmes de Boeuf, la Mal Court. Jacques Audiberti. 200p. (FRE.). 1970. pap. 39.95 (0-7859-0355-0, F83650) Fr & Eur.

Theatre see Oeuvres

Theatre see Oeuvres Completes

Theatre - Poesies see Oeuvres Completes

Theatre According to the Natyasastra of Bharata. R. P. Kulkarni. (C). 1994. 20.00 (81-85475-81-4, Pub. by Kanishka) S Asia.

Theatre Advancing. Edward G. Craig. 1980. 34.95 (0-405-09144-3, 1708) Ayer.

Theatre Alive! An Introductory Anthology of World Drama. rev. ed. Ed. by Norman Bert et al. LC 94-41533. 848p. 1994. pap. text ed. 24.95 (1-56608-008-8, B178) Meriwether Pub.

Theatre & Allied Arts. Blanch M. Baker. LC 66-12284. 1972. reprint ed. 47.95 (0-405-08230-4, Pub. by Blom Pubns UK) Ayer.

Theatre & Change in South Africa. Ed. by Geoffrey V. Davis & Anne Fuchs. (Contemporary Theatre Studies: Vol. 12). 352p. 1996. text ed. 99.00 (3-7186-5650-7, ECU76, Harwood Acad Pubs); pap. text ed. 33.00 (3-7186-5651-5, ECU25, Harwood Acad Pubs) Gordon & Breach.

Theatre & Cinema Architecture: A Guide to Information Sources. Ed. by Richard Stoddard. LC 78-14820. (Performing Arts Information Guide Ser.: Vol. 5). 384p. 1978. 68.00 (0-8103-1426-6) Gale.

Theatre & Drama for the Gifted: An Advanced Course of Study for the Secondary & Post-Secondary Levels. Phyllis Girard. 1987. pap. text ed. 15.00 (0-910609-15-2) Gifted Educ Pr.

Theatre & Drama in Francophone Africa: A Critical Introduction. John Conteh-Morgan. 240p. (C). 1995. text ed. 69.95 (0-521-43453-X) Cambridge U Pr.

Theatre & Drama in the Making: The Greeks to the Elizabethans. rev. ed. John Gassner & Ralph G. Allen. 534p. 1992. pap. 18.95 (1-55783-073-8) Applause Theatre Bk Pubs.

Theatre & Dramatic Theory. Allardyce Nicoll. LC 78-5609. 221p. 1978. reprint ed. text ed. 55.00 (0-313-20433-0, NITD, Greenwood Pr) Greenwood.

Theatre & Everyday Life. Alan Read. 304p. (C). 1995. pap. 18.95 (0-415-06941-6, A7978) Routledge.

Theatre & Everyday Life: A Theoretical Introduction. Alan Read. LC 92-11913. (Illus.). 244p. (C). (gr. 13). 1993. text ed. 59.95 (0-415-06940-8, A7974) Routledge.

Theatre & Fashion: Oscar Wilde to the Suffragettes. Joel H. Kaplan & Sheila Stowell. (Illus.). 240p. (C). 1994. text ed. 59.95 (0-521-41510-1) Cambridge U Pr.

Theatre & Fashion: Oscar Wilde to the Suffragettes. Joel H. Kaplan & Sheila Stowell. 234p. 1995. pap. text ed. 18.95 (0-521-49950-X) Cambridge U Pr.

Theatre & Feminist Aesthetics. Ed. by Karen Laughlin & Catherine Schuler. LC 94-20057. 1995. 45.00 (0-8386-3549-0) Fairleigh Dickinson.

Theatre & Film in Exile: German Artists in Great Britain, 1933-1945. Ed. by Gunter Berghaus. LC 89-116. (Illus.). 304p. 1990. 19.95 (0-85496-025-2) Berg Pubs.

Theatre & Friendship. Henry James. (Select Bibliographies Reprint Ser.). 1977. 29.95 (0-8369-5156-5) Ayer.

Theatre & Government under the Early Stuarts. Ed. by J. R. Mulryne & Margaret Shewring. LC 92-33796. 264p. (C). 1993. text ed. 69.95 (0-521-40159-3) Cambridge U Pr.

***Theatre & Holy Script.** Ed. by Shimon Levy. 272p. 1997. 59.50 (1-898723-53-2, Pub. by Sussex Acad Pr UK) Intl Spec Bk.

Theatre & Ideology. Ben B. Halm. LC 94-10125. 1995. 38.50 (0-945636-62-8) Susquehanna U Pr.

Theatre & Incarnation. Max Harris. 240p. 1990. text ed. 45.00 (0-312-03699-X) St Martin.

Theatre & Its Players in Shakespeare's Time: A Guide to the Microfiche Collection. (Shakespeariana Ser.). 33p. (Orig.). 1991. pap. 20.00 (0-8357-2156-6) Univ Microfilms.

Theatre & Nationalism in Twentieth-Century Ireland. Seminar in Irish Studies (2nd: 1968: University of Toronto) Staff. Ed. by Robert O'Driscoll. LC 77-151383. 222p. reprint ed. pap. 63.30 (0-8357-3769-1, 2036498) Bks Demand.

Theatre & Performance in Austria: From Mozart to Jelinek. Ed. by Ritchie Robertson & Edward Timms. LC 93-239291. (Austrian Studies: No. 4). 218p. 1994. 55.00 (0-7486-0436-7, Pub. by Edinburgh U Pr UK) Col U Pr.

Theatre & Performing Arts Collections. Ed. by Louis A. Rachow. LC 81-6567. (Special Collections: Vol. 1, No. 1). 166p. 1981. text ed. 49.95 (0-917724-47-X) Haworth Pr.

Theatre & Politics in Nineteenth-Century Spain: Juan de Grimaldi As Impresario & Government Agent. David T. Gies. (Cambridge Iberian & Latin American Studies). 272p. 1988. text ed. 59.95 (0-521-34293-7) Cambridge U Pr.

Theatre & Reformation: Protestantism, Patronage, & Playing in Tudor England. Paul W. White. (Illus.). 240p. (C). 1993. text ed. 69.95 (0-521-41817-8) Cambridge U Pr.

***Theatre & Social Change in Zambia: The Chikwakwa Theatre.** Patrick E. Idoye. LC 96-31142. (African Studies: Vol. 43). 212p. 1997. text ed. 89.95 (0-7734-8959-2) E Mellen.

Theatre & Song. Ed. by Peter Davison et al. LC 77-90616. (Literary Taste, Culture & Mass Communication Ser.: Vol. 8). 279p. 1978. lib. bdg. 90.00 (0-85964-043-4) Chadwyck-Healey.

***Theatre & Sport: Mime Journal - 1996.** Ed. by Thomas Leabhart et al. (Illus.). 112p. (Orig.). 1996. pap. 20.00 (1-887482-01-6) Mime Jour.

Theatre & State in France, 1760-1905. F. W. Hemmings. 308p. (C). 1994. text ed. 69.95 (0-521-45088-8) Cambridge U Pr.

Theatre & the World: Essays on Performance & Politics of Culture. Rustom Bharucha. 1990. 24.00 (0-945921-13-6, Pub. by S Asia Pubs II) S Asia.

Theatre & the World: Performance & the Politics of Culture. Rustom Bharucha. LC 93-18374. 272p. (C). 1993. pap. 17.95 (0-415-09216-7) Routledge.

Theatre & the World: Performance & the Politics of Culture. Rustom Bharucha. LC 93-18374. 272p. (C). (gr. 13). 1993. text ed. 65.00 (0-415-09215-9) Routledge.

***Theatre & Theatre, Brief Version Test Bank.** 4th rev. ed. Robert Cohen & Marilyn F. Moriarty. 157p. (C). 1996. pap. text ed. write for info. (1-55934-742-2, 1743) Mayfield Pub.

Theatre & You: A Beginning. Marsh Cassady. Ed. by Arthur L. Zapel. LC 92-14993. (Illus.). 256p. (Orig.). 1992. pap. text ed. 15.95 (0-916260-83-6, B115) Meriwether Pub.

Theatre Anthology: Plays & Documents. Ed. by David Willinger & Charles Gattnig. 376p. (Orig.). (C). 1990. pap. text ed. 32.00 (0-8191-7731-8) U Pr of Amer.

***Theatre Antique et Sa Reception: Hommage a Walter Sporri.** Ed. by Jurgen Soring et al. 221p. 1994. 39.95 (3-631-47280-3) P Lang Pubng.

Theatre Architecture & Stage Machines: Engravings from the Encyclopedie, ou Dictionnaire Raisonne des Sciences, des Arts, et des Metiers. Denis Diderot & Jean L. Alembert. 1972. 27.95 (0-405-09139-7, 1713) Ayer.

Theatre, Aristocracy & Pornocracy: The Orgy Calculus. Karl Toepfer. 1990. 35.00 (1-55554-055-4); pap. 14.95 (1-55554-056-2) PAJ Pubns.

Theatre Arts: The Dynamics of Acting. 4th rev. ed. Dennis Caltagirone. (J). 1995. write for info. (0-8442-5165-8) NTC Pub Grp.

Theatre Arts: 1916-17, I. 1971. pap. 60.95 (0-405-03473-3, 604) Ayer.

Theatre Arts: 1916-19, I-III. 1971. 84.95 (0-405-03451-2, 582) Ayer.

Theatre Arts: 1916-1941, 21 Vols., Set. LC 71-155055. (Illus.). 21000p. 1,617.00 (0-405-03450-4) Ayer.

Theatre Arts: 1917-18, II. 1971. pap. 60.95 (0-405-03474-1, 605) Ayer.

Theatre Arts: 1919, III. 1971. pap. 60.95 (0-405-03475-X, 606) Ayer.

Theatre Arts: 1920, IV. 1971. pap. 60.95 (0-405-03476-8, 607) Ayer.

Theatre Arts: 1920-21, IV-V. 1971. 84.95 (0-405-03452-0, 583) Ayer.

Theatre Arts: 1921, V. 1971. pap. 60.95 (0-405-03477-6, 608) Ayer.

Theatre Arts: 1922, VI. 1971. pap. 60.95 (0-405-03478-4, 609) Ayer.

Theatre Arts: 1922, VI-VII. 1971. 84.95 (0-405-03453-9, 584) Ayer.

Theatre Arts: 1923, VII. 1971. pap. 60.95 (0-405-03479-2, 610) Ayer.

Theatre Arts: 1924, VIII. 1971. pap. 60.95 (0-405-03480-6, 585) Ayer.

Theatre Arts: 1925, IX. 1971. 84.95 (0-405-03455-5, 586); 55.00 (0-685-11356-6, 612) Ayer.

Theatre Arts: 1926, X. 1971. 77.00 (0-685-43156-8, 587); pap. 60.95 (0-405-03482-2, 613) Ayer.

Theatre Arts: 1927, XI. 1971. 84.95 (0-405-03457-1, 588) Ayer.

Theatre Arts: 1928, XII. 1971. pap. 60.95 (0-405-03484-9, 615) Ayer.

Theatre Arts: 1929, XIII. 1971. 84.95 (0-405-03459-8, 590); pap. 60.95 (0-405-03485-7, 616) Ayer.

Theatre Arts: 1930, XIV. 1971. 84.95 (0-405-03460-1, 591); pap. 60.95 (0-405-03486-5, 617) Ayer.

Theatre Arts: 1931, XV. 1971. 84.95 (0-405-03461-X, 599); pap. 60.95 (0-405-03487-3, 618) Ayer.

Theatre Arts: 1932, XVI. 1971. 84.95 (0-405-03462-8, 593) Ayer.

Theatre Arts: 1934, XVII. 1971. pap. 60.95 (0-405-03490-3, 621) Ayer.

Theatre Arts: 1934, XVIII. 1971. 84.95 (0-405-03464-4, 595) Ayer.

Theatre Arts: 1935, XIX. 1971. 84.95 (0-405-03465-2, 596); pap. 60.95 (0-405-03491-1, 622) Ayer.

Theatre Arts: 1936, XX. 1971. 84.95 (0-405-03466-0, 597); pap. 60.95 (0-405-03492-X, 623) Ayer.

Theatre Arts: 1937, XXI. 1971. 84.95 (0-405-03467-9, 598); pap. 60.95 (0-405-03493-8, 624) Ayer.

Theatre Arts: 1938, XXII. 1971. 84.95 (0-405-03468-7, 599); pap. 60.95 (0-405-03494-6, 625) Ayer.

Theatre Arts: 1939, XXIII. 1971. 84.95 (0-405-03469-5, 600); pap. 55.00 (0-685-43154-1, 626) Ayer.

Theatre Arts: 1940, XXIV. 1971. 84.95 (0-405-03470-9, 601); pap. 60.95 (0-405-03496-2, 627) Ayer.

Theatre Arts: 1941, XXV. 1971. 84.95 (0-405-03471-7, 602); pap. 55.00 (0-685-43153-3, 628) Ayer.

***Theatre Arts I Student Handbook.** Penny Englesman & Alan Englesman. Ed. by Rebecca Wendling. LC 97-3803. 1997. pap. 19.95 (1-56608-031-2, B208) Meriwether Pub.

***Theatre Arts I Teacher's Course Guide.** Penny Englesman & Alan Englesman. Ed. by Rebecca Wendling. 1997. pap. 24.95 (1-56608-032-0, B210) Meriwether Pub.

Theatre Arts in the Elementary Classroom, Vol. 1. Barbara Salisbury-Willis. 272p. (J). (gr. k-3). 1986. 32.00 (0-87602-024-4) Anchorage.

Theatre Arts in the Elementary Classroom Vol. 1: Kindergarten Through Third Graade. 2nd ed. Barbara S. Wills. 330p. 1996. teacher ed. 36.00 (0-87602-033-3) Anchorage.

Theatre Arts in the Elementray Classroom Vol. 2: Fourth Grade Through Grade Six. 2nd ed. Barbara S. Wills. 396p. 1996. teacher ed. 36.00 (0-87602-034-1) Anchorage.

Theatre Arts Two - Student Handbook: On Stage & Off Stage Roles. Alan Engelsman & Penny Engelsman. 170p. (YA). (gr. 6-12). 1991. pap. text ed. 18.50 (1-879692-00-7) Alpen & Jeffries.

Theatre Arts Two - Teacher's Manual: On Stage & Off Stage Roles: Fitting the Pieces Together. Alan Engelsman & Penny Engelsman. 126p. 1991. ring bd. 28.75 (1-879692-01-5) Alpen & Jeffries.

Theatre As a Weapon: Workers' Theatre in the Soviet Union, Germany & Britain, 1917-1934. Richard Stourac & Kathleen McCreery. (Illus.). 384p. 1986. lib. bdg. 60.00 (0-7100-9770-0, RKP) Routledge.

Theatre As Action: Soviet Russian Avant-Garde Aesthetics. Lars Kleberg. 168p. (C). 1993. 40.00 (0-333-56694-7); pap. 16.00 (0-333-56817-6) NYU Pr.

Theatre As Sign System. Elaine Aston. 224p. (C). 1992. pap. 16.95 (0-415-04932-6, Pub. by Tavistock UK) Routledge Chapman & Hall.

Theatre. Asmodee: Avec: Les Mal Aimes. Francois Mauriac. (Illus.). 12.50 (0-686-55478-7) Fr & Eur.

Theatre at Stratford-Upon-Avon: A Catalogue-Index to Productions of the Shakespeare Memorial-Royal Shakespeare Theatre, 1879 to 1978, 2 vols. Compiled by Michael Mullin. LC 79-8578. 1980. Set. text ed. 150.00 (0-313-22126-X, MSH/) Greenwood.

Theatre at Stratford-Upon-Avon: A Catalogue-Index to Productions of the Shakespeare Memorial-Royal Shakespeare Theatre, 1879 to 1978, 2 vols., 1. Compiled by Michael Mullin. LC 79-8578. 1980. text ed. 85.00 (0-313-22169-3, MSH/1) Greenwood.

Theatre at Stratford-Upon-Avon: A Catalogue-Index to Productions of the Shakespeare Memorial-Royal Shakespeare Theatre, 1879 to 1978, 2 vols., Vol. 2. Compiled by Michael Mullin. LC 79-8578. 1980. text ed. 85.00 (0-313-22170-7, MSH/2) Greenwood.

Theatre at Stratford-Upon-Avon: First Supplement, A Catalogue-Index to Productions of the Royal Shakespeare Company, 1979-1993. Michael Mullin. LC 94-22456. (Bibliographies & Indexes in the Performing Arts Ser.: Vol. 17). 352p. 1994. text ed. 95.00 (0-313-25028-6, Greenwood Pr) Greenwood.

Theatre at the Crossroads of Culture. Patrice Pavis. Tr. by Loren Kruger from FRE. 256p. (C). 1991. pap. text ed. 17.95 (0-415-06038-9, A6320) Routledge.

Theatre at the Crossroads of Culture. Patrice Pavis. Tr. by Loren Kruger from FRE. 256p. (C). (gr. 13). 1992. text ed. 79.95 (0-415-06037-0, A6316) Routledge.

***Theatre at War 1914-18.** Collins. LC 97-10633. 1997. text ed. 55.00 (0-312-17598-1) St Martin.

Theatre Audiences: A Theory of Production & Reception. Susan Bennett. LC 89-10955. (Illus.). 224p. (C). (gr. 13). 1990. text ed. 74.95 (0-415-04495-2, A4245) Routledge.

***Theatre Audiences: A Theory of Production & Reception.** 2nd ed. Susan Bennett. LC 97-11461. 1998. write for info. (0-415-15722-6); pap. write for info. (0-415-15723-4) Routledge.

Theatre Backstage from A to Z. rev. ed. Warren C. Lounsbury. LC 89-14715. (Illus.). 242p. 1989. pap. 22.50 (0-295-96828-1) U of Wash Pr.

Theatre Book of the Year, 1942-1943. George J. Nathan. LC 75-120099. (Illus.). 350p. 1975. 29.50 (0-8386-7946-3) Fairleigh Dickinson.

Theatre Book of the Year, 1943-1944. George J. Nathan. LC 75-120099. 350p. 1975. 29.50 (0-8386-7962-5) Fairleigh Dickinson.

Theatre Book of the Year, 1944-1945. George J. Nathan. LC 75-120099. 350p. 1975. 29.50 (0-8386-7961-7) Fairleigh Dickinson.

Theatre Book of the Year 1945-1946. George J. Nathan. LC 75-120099. (Theatre World of George Jean Nathan Ser.). 350p. 1974. 29.50 (0-8386-1174-5) Fairleigh Dickinson.

Theatre Book of the Year 1946-1947. George J. Nathan. LC 75-120099. (Theatre World of George Jean Nathan Ser.). 350p. 1975. 29.50 (0-8386-1175-3) Fairleigh Dickinson.

Theatre Bouffe, Vol. 12. Fernando Arrabal. 240p. 1978. 19.95 (0-686-54470-6) Fr & Eur.

Theatre, Brief Version. 3rd ed. Robert Cohen. LC 92-46051. 329p. (C). 1993. pap. text ed. 31.95 (1-55934-143-2, 1143) Mayfield Pub.

Theatre, Brief Version. 4th rev. ed. Robert Cohen. (Illus.). 348p. (C). 1996. pap. text ed. 31.95 (1-55934-669-8, 1669) Mayfield Pub.

Theatre, Brief Version, Instructor's Manual. 3rd ed. Robert Cohen. (C). 1993. teacher ed., pap. text ed. write for info. (1-55934-344-3, 1344) Mayfield Pub.

Theatre Builders: A Collaborative Art. James Steele. (Builders Ser.). (Illus.). 264p. 1996. 70.00 (1-85490-450-7) Academy Ed UK.

Theatre Career of Charles Dibdin the Elder (1745-1814) Robert Fahrner. (American University Studies: Fine Arts: Ser. XX, Vol. 8). 250p. (C). 1989. text ed. 38.95 (0-8204-0798-4) P Lang Pubng.

Theatre, Children & Youth. rev. ed. Jed H. Davis & Mary J. Evans. (Illus.). 360p. 1987. pap. text ed. 32.00 (0-87602-026-0) Anchorage.

Theatre Companies of the World, 2 vols., 1. Ed. by Colby H. Kullman & William C. Young. LC 84-539. 1024p. 1986. text ed. 85.00 (0-313-25667-5, YTC/01) Greenwood.

Theatre Companies of the World, 2 vols., Set. Ed. by Colby H. Kullman & William C. Young. LC 84-539. 996p. 1986. text ed. 150.00 (0-313-21456-5, YTC/) Greenwood.

Theatre Companies of the World, 2 vols., Vol. 2. Ed. by Colby H. Kullman & William C. Young. LC 84-539. 1024p. 1986. text ed. 85.00 (0-313-25668-3, YTC/02) Greenwood.

Theatre Complet, 9 tomes. Jean Anouilh. Set. 126.95 (0-685-11593-3, F81760) Fr & Eur.

Theatre Complet. Pierre de Beaumarchais. 45.00 (0-686-54088-3) Fr & Eur.

Theatre Complet. Alfred De Musset. Ed. by Andre Jeune. (FRE.). 1990. lib. bdg. 160.00 (0-7859-3890-7) Fr & Eur.

Theatre Complet. Jean Giraudoux. Ed. by Jacques Body. 1904p. (FRE.). 1982. lib. bdg. 140.00 (0-7859-3852-4) Fr & Eur.

Theatre Complet. Jean Giraudoux. (FRE.). 1991. pap. 56.95 (0-7859-3159-7, 2253055093) Fr & Eur.

Theatre Complet. Johann Wolfgang Von Goethe. 1376p. write for info. (0-318-52303-5) Fr & Eur.

Theatre Complet. Johann Wolfgang Von Goethe. (FRE.). 1988. 150.00 (0-8288-3491-1, M5856) Fr & Eur.

Theatre Complet. Eugene Ionesco. (FRE.). 1990. 125.00 (0-8288-3507-1, F120230) Fr & Eur.

Theatre Complet. A. Marivaux. (FRE.). 1950. lib. bdg. 110.00 (0-8288-3554-3, F48010) Fr & Eur.

Theatre Complet, 3 vols. Jean-Baptiste Racine. (Illus.). Set. 200.00 (0-686-54715-2) Fr & Eur.

Theatre Complet. deluxe ed. Eugene Ionesco. (Pleiade Ser.). (FRE.). 119.95 (2-07-011198-9) Schoenhof.

Theatre Complet. rev. ed. Pierre C. Marivaux. Ed. by Marcel Arland. (Bibliotheque de la Pleiade Ser.). 1125p. (FRE.). 1989. pap. 49.95 (0-685-11591-7, 2040173455) Fr & Eur.

Theatre Complet, Tome 1. Jean-Baptiste Racine. (Folio Ser.: No. 1412). (FRE.). pap. 15.95 (2-07-037412-2) Schoenhof.

Theatre Complet, Tome 1. deluxe ed. Victor Hugo. (Pleiade Ser.). 1836p. (FRE.). 1963. 82.95 (2-07-010265-3) Schoenhof.

Theatre Complet, Tome 2. Jean-Baptiste Racine. (Folio Ser.: No. 1495). (FRE.). pap. 15.95 (2-07-037495-5) Schoenhof.

Theatre Complet, Tome 2. deluxe ed. Victor Hugo. (Pleiade Ser.). 1936p. (FRE.). 1979. 82.95 (2-07-010266-1) Schoenhof.

Theatre Complet, Vol. 1. Alexandre Dumas. (Illus.). 588p. (FRE.). 1974. 33.95 (0-7859-0067-5, M2279) Fr & Eur.

An Asterisk (*) at the beginning of an entry indicates that the title is appearing in BIP for the first time.

Theatre Complet, Vol. 1. Luigi Pirandello. 1536p. 45.00 (*0-686-56547-9*) Fr & Eur.
Theatre Complet, Vol. 1. Jean-Baptiste Racine. (FRE.). 1982. pap. 19.95 (*0-7859-2901-0*) Fr & Eur.
Theatre Complet, Vol. 1. deluxe ed. Luigi Pirandello. Ed. by Andre Bouissy. 1536p. (FRE.). 1977. 120.00 (*0-7859-3832-X*, 2070108791) Fr & Eur.
Theatre Complet, Vol. 2. Luigi Pirandello. Ed. by Andre Bouissy. (FRE.). 1985. lib. bdg. 150.00 (*0-7859-3869-9*) Fr & Eur.
Theatre Complet: Avec Bajazet, Mithridate, Iphigenie, Phedre, Esther, Athalie, Vol. 2. Jean-Baptiste Racine. Ed. by Andre Stegmann. 378p. 1983. pap. 19.95 (*0-7859-2905-3*) Fr & Eur.
Theatre Complet: Avec: La Thebaide, Alexandre le Grand, Andromaque, Les Plaideurs, Britannicus, Berenice, Vol. 1. Jean-Baptiste Racine. Ed. by Andre Stegmann. 436p. 5.95 (*0-686-54713-6*) Fr & Eur.
Theatre Complet: Christine ou Stockholm, Fontainebleau et Rome, Vol. 1, Pt. 6. Alexandre Dumas. 186p. (FRE.). 1976. pap. 27.95 (*0-7859-5434-1*) Fr & Eur.
Theatre Complet: Comment je devins Auteur Dramatique. Ivanhoe, Vol. 1, Pt. 1. Alexandre Dumas & Fernande Bassan. 144p. (FRE.). 1976. pap. 22.95 (*0-7859-5430-9*) Fr & Eur.
Theatre Complet: Flesque de Lavagna, Vol. 1, Pt. 4. Alexandre Dumas. 166p. (FRE.). 1976. pap. 22.95 (*0-686-55208-3*) Fr & Eur.
Theatre Complet: Henry III et sa Cour, Vol. 1, Pt. 5. Alexandre Dumas. 152p. (FRE.). 1976. pap. 22.95 (*0-7859-5433-3*) Fr & Eur.
Theatre Complet: La Chasse et l'Amour, La Noce et l'Enterrement, Vol. 1, Pt. 2. Alexandre Dumas. 126p. (FRE.). 1976. pap. 22.95 (*0-7859-5431-7*) Fr & Eur.
Theatre Complet, Parades, Lettres Relatives a son Theatre. Pierre-Augustin C. De Beaumarchais. Ed. by Maurice Allem & Paul N. Courant. (Bibliotheque de la Pleiade Ser.). 876p. (FRE.). 1934. 85.00 (*0-7859-1074-3*, 2070100529) Fr & Eur.
Theatre Complet Tome I, Tome I. Aristophane. 509p. (FRE.). 1987. pap. 15.95 (*0-7859-2233-4*, 207037789X) Fr & Eur.
Theatre Complet Tome I, Tome II. Aristophane. 511p. (FRE.). 1987. pap. 15.95 (*0-7859-2056-0*, 2070377903) Fr & Eur.
Theatre Complet, Vol. 1: Avec: Cromwell. deluxe ed. Victor Hugo. 1836p. (FRE.). 1836. 110.00 (*0-8288-9995-9*, F63681) Fr & Eur.
Theatre Complet, Vol. 2: Avec: Les Burgraves. deluxe ed. Victor Hugo. 1936p. (FRE.). 1979. 120.00 (*0-7859-4678-0*) Fr & Eur.
Theatre Complete. deluxe ed. A. Marivaux. Ed. by Henri Coulet & Michel Gilot. 11376p. (FRE.). 1993. 150.00 (*0-7859-0967-2*, 2070112594) Fr & Eur.
Theatre Complete see Oeuvres Completes
Theatre Criticism. Irving Wardle. LC 91-39222. (Theatre Concepts Ser.). 128p. (C). 1992. pap. 13.95 (*0-415-03181-8*, A7122) Routledge.
Theatre Criticism. Irving Wardle. LC 91-39222. (Theatre Concepts Ser.). 128p. (C). (gr. 13). 1992. text ed. 49.95 (*0-415-03180-X*, A7118) Routledge.
***Theatre Culture in America, 1825-1860.** Rosemari K. Bank. (Studies in American Theatre & Drama: No. 7). (Illus.). 272p. (C). 1997. text ed. 59.95 (*0-521-56387-9*) Cambridge U Pr.
Theatre de Clara Gazul. Prosper Merimee. (FRE.). 1968. 7.95 (*0-7859-0028-4*, F68310) Fr & Eur.
Theatre de la Gaite. Victor Hugo. (FRE.). 1961. pap. 24.95 (*0-7859-5555-0*) Fr & Eur.
Theatre de Pagnol: Personnages et Themes Dans les Oeuvres de Jeunesse. P. Gounelle Kline. (American University Studies: Romance Languages & Literature: Ser. II, Vol. 46). 161p. 1987. text ed. 26.50 (*0-8204-0320-2*) P Lang Pubng.
Theatre de Situations. Jean-Paul Sartre. (FRE.). 1992. pap. 24.95 (*0-7859-2827-8*) Fr & Eur.
Theatre de Situations. Jean-Paul Sartre. Ed. by Michel Contat & Michel Rybalka. (Folio Essais Ser.). 384p. 1973. 9.95 (*2-07-032691-8*) Schoenhof.
Theatre Des Bons Engins. Guillaume D. La Perriere. LC 63-7783. 1963. reprint ed. 50.00 (*0-8201-1036-1*) Schol Facsimiles.
Theatre des Bons Engins with la Morosophie. Guillaume De La Perriere. Ed. by Alison Saunders. (Emblem Ser.). 468p. 1993. 65.95 (*0-85967-979-9*, Pub. by Scolar Pr UK) Ashgate Pub Co.
Theatre des Varietes. Joseph Long. (Theatre in Focus Ser.). (Illus.). 120p. (Orig.). 1980. pap. text ed. 105.00 incl. sl. (*0-85964-063-9*) Chadwyck-Healey.
Theatre Directory 1996-97. Compiled by Theatre Communications Group Staff. 96p. (Orig.). 1996. pap. 5.95 (*1-55936-121-2*) Theatre Comm.
***Theatre Directory, 1997-1998.** Theatre Communications Group Staff. 1997. pap. text ed. 5.95 (*1-55936-145-X*) Theatre Comm.
Theatre, Drama, & Audience in Goethe's Germany. Walter H. Bruford. LC 73-10579. 388p. 1974. reprint ed. text ed. 65.00 (*0-8371-7016-8*, BRTD, Greenwood Pr) Greenwood.
Theatre Du XVII Siecle, 3 tomes, 1. deluxe ed. (Pleiade Ser.). (FRE.). 83.95 (*2-07-010794-9*) Schoenhof.
Theatre Du XVII Siecle, 3 tomes, 2. deluxe ed. (Pleiade Ser.). (FRE.). 89.95 (*2-07-011107-5*) Schoenhof.
Theatre du XVII Siecle, Vol. 2. Jacques Scherer & Truchet Scherer. (FRE.). 1986. lib. bdg. 140.00 (*0-7859-3873-7*) Fr & Eur.
Theatre Du XVII Siecle, 3 tomes, Vol. 3. deluxe ed. (Pleiade Ser.). (FRE.). 109.95 (*2-07-011232-2*) Schoenhof.
Theatre du XVIII Siecle, Vol. 1. Jacques Truchet. Ed. by Albert Truchet. (FRE.). 1973. lib. bdg. 110.00 (*0-7859-3822-2*) Fr & Eur.
Theatre du XVIII Siecle, Vol. 2. Jacques Truchet. (FRE.). 1974. lib. bdg. 120.00 (*0-7859-3823-0*) Fr & Eur.
Theatre Du XVIII Siecle: Crebillon, Le Sage, Voltaire, Piron, Destouches, Fagan, Gresset, Theatre des Boulevards, etc., Vol. 1. deluxe ed. (Pleiade Ser.). 1568p. (FRE.). 61.95 (*2-07-010778-7*) Schoenhof.
Theatre Du XVIII Siecle: Diderot, Palissot, Favart, Sedaine, Colle, Carmontelle, La Harpe, M. J. Chenier, Sade, etc., Vol. 2. deluxe ed. (Pleiade Ser.). 1584p. (FRE.). 75.95 (*2-07-010779-5*) Schoenhof.
Theatre Education: Mandate for Tomorrow. Ed. by Jed H. Davis. 60p. 1985. pap. 7.50 (*0-87602-023-6*) Anchorage.
Theatre en France Depuis Nineteen Hundred. Rene Lalou. 127p. 1951. 9.95 (*0-8288-7412-3*) Fr & Eur.
Theatre Espagnol du XVI Siecle. Robert Marrast & Sylvie Marrast. (FRE.). 1983. lib. bdg. 100.00 (*0-7859-3862-1*) Fr & Eur.
Theatre et Nouvelles see Oeuvres Choisies
Theatre et Poesie Surrealistes: Vitrac et la Scene Virtuelle. Martine Antle. LC 88-60341. (Illus.). 136p. (FRE.). 1988. lib. bdg. 22.95 (*0-917786-61-0*) Summa Pubns.
Theatre et Son Double. Antonin Artaud. (Folio Essais Ser.: No. 14). 256p. (FRE.). 1971. 9.95 (*2-07-032301-3*) Schoenhof.
Theatre et Son Double: Le Theatre de Seraphin. Antonin Artaud. 251p. (FRE.). 1985. pap. 12.95 (*0-7859-2795-6*, 2070323013) Fr & Eur.
Theatre Experience. Carl M. Hinrichs. 128p. (C). 1995. spiral bd. 21.99 (*0-8403-9130-7*) Kendall-Hunt.
Theatre Festivals of the Medici, 1539-1637. A. M. Nagler. LC 76-8447. (Music Reprint Ser.). 190p. 1976. reprint ed. lib. bdg. 32.50 (*0-306-70779-9*) Da Capo.
Theatre for Cannibals: Rodolfo Usigli & the Mexican State. Peter Beardsell. LC 90-56174. 248p. 1992. 39.50 (*0-8386-3436-2*) Fairleigh Dickinson.
***Theatre for Children in the United States: A History.** Nellie McCaslin. Ed. by William-Alan Landes. LC 96-47570. (Illus.). 425p. (Orig.). 1997. pap. 40.00 (*0-88734-677-4*) Players Pr.
Theatre for Shakespeare. Alfred Harbage. LC 56-1874. (Alexander Lectures, 1954-55). 130p. reprint ed. pap. 37.10 (*0-8357-4728-X*, 2037644) Bks Demand.
Theatre for the Ninety-Eight Percent. Maxine Klein. LC 77-86334. (Illus.). 175p. 1978. 30.00 (*0-89608-001-3*); pap. 10.00 (*0-89608-000-5*) South End Pr.
Theatre for the Young. Alan England. LC 89-6391. (Modern Dramatists Ser.). 200p. 1990. text ed. 29.95 (*0-312-03459-8*) St Martin.
Theatre for Voluptuous Worldlings. Jan Van Der Noot. LC 43-1514. 1977. reprint ed. 50.00 (*0-8201-1179-1*) Schol Facsimiles.
Theatre for Working-Class Audiences in the United States, 1830-1980. Ed. by Bruce A. McConachie & Daniel P. Friedman. LC 84-19773. (Contributions in Drama & Theatre Studies: No. 14). (Illus.). viii, 264p. 1985. text ed. 59.95 (*0-313-24629-7*, MTU/) Greenwood.
***Theatre for Young Audiences.** Jennings. Date not set. write for info. (*0-312-18194-9*) St Martin.
Theatre for Young Audiences: Around the World in Twenty-One Plays. Ed. by Lowell Swortzell. 644p. 1996. 29.95 (*1-55783-263-3*) Applause Theatre Bk Pubs.
Theatre for Young People: A Creative Workbook. Pam B. Dunne. (Illus.). 52p. (Orig.). 1993. pap. 18.00 (*1-888657-00-6*) Drama Thrpy Inst.
Theatre for Young People: A Sense of Occasion. Helane S. Rosenberg & Christine Prendergast. 366p. (C). 1983. pap. text ed. 33.25 (*0-03-039911-4*) HB Coll Pubs.
Theatre for Youth: Twelve Plays with Mature Themes. Ed. by Coleman A. Jennings & Gretta Berghammer. LC 85-26515. 524p. (J). (gr. 8 up). 1986. 30.00 (*0-292-78081-8*); pap. 17.95 (*0-292-78085-0*) U of Tex Pr.
Theatre Francois. Samuel Chapuzeau. 248p. reprint ed. write for info. (*0-318-71327-6*) G Olms Pubs.
Theatre from Nigeria, 5 vols. in 1, Set. Sebastian S. Bondy et al. (B. E. Ser.: No. 109). 1967. Five works in one unit. 25.00 (*0-8115-3040-X*) Periodicals Srv.
Theatre Games. Clive Barker. 226p. (C). 1988. pap. 13.95 (*0-413-45380-4*, A0285) Heinemann.
***Theatre Games.** David Trembley & Lo-Ann Trembley. 15p. 1994. pap. 5.50 (*1-877871-79-6*, 3703) Ed Ministries.
***Theatre Games for Playwrights: Working Through Craft.** Michael Wright. 1997. pap. 17.95 (*0-614-27391-9*) Heinemann.
Theatre Games for Young Performers: Improvisations & Exercises for Developing Acting Skills. Maria C. Novelly. Ed. by Kathy Pijanowski & Arthur L. Zapel. LC 85-60572. (Illus.). 160p. (Orig.). (J). (gr. 6-10). 1985. pap. text ed. 12.95 (*0-916260-31-3*, B188) Meriwether Pub.
Theatre Guild. Walter P. Eaton. 1988. reprint ed. lib. bdg. 75.00 (*0-7812-0046-6*) Rprt Serv.
Theatre Guild, the First Ten Years. Walter P. Eaton. 1971. reprint ed. 49.00 (*0-403-00922-7*) Scholarly.
Theatre Guild, the First Ten Years, with Articles by the Directors. Walter P. Eaton. LC 75-107799. (Select Bibliographies Reprint Ser.). 1977. 29.95 (*0-8369-5180-8*) Ayer.
Theatre in a Tent: The Development of a Provincial Entertainment. William L. Slout. LC 72-188635. 153p. 1972. 15.00 (*0-87972-028-X*) Bowling Green Univ Popular Press.
Theatre in Action. Geoffrey Whitworth. LC 77-173186. (Illus.). 1972. reprint ed. 31.95 (*0-405-09074-9*) Ayer.
Theatre in America During the Revolution. Jared Brown. (Studies in American Theatre & Drama: No. 4). 272p. (C). 1995. text ed. 59.95 (*0-521-49537-7*) Cambridge U Pr.
Theatre in Ancient Greek Society. Green. Date not set. pap. 18.95 (*0-415-13819-1*) Routledge.
***Theatre in Ancient Greek Society.** Green. 1996. pap. 18.95 (*0-415-14395-0*) Routledge.
***Theatre in Ancient Greek Society.** J. R. Green. 256p. (C). 1996. pap. 18.95 (*0-415-14359-4*) Routledge.
Theatre in Ancient India. Siddheswar Chattopadhyay. (C). 1993. 16.00 (*81-7304-016-8*, Pub. by Manohar II) S Asia.
Theatre in Crisis: Sophocles' Reconstruction of Genre & Politics in "Philoctetes" Carola Greengard. 106p. 1987. pap. 34.00 (*90-256-0836-1*, Pub. by A M Hakkert NE) Benjamins North Am.
Theatre in Dada & Surrealism. J. H. Matthews. LC 73-16286. 300p. reprint ed. pap. 85.50 (*0-8357-7052-4*, 2033443) Bks Demand.
Theatre in Greek Society. J. R. Green. LC 93-35468. 240p. (C). (gr. 13). 1994. 62.95 (*0-415-04751-X*, Routledge NY) Routledge.
Theatre in Latin America: Religion, Politics, & Culture from Cortes to the 1980s. Adam Versenyi. LC 92-33869. 229p. (C). 1993. 49.95 (*0-521-41938-7*) Cambridge U Pr.
Theatre in Life. Nikolai Evreino. LC 76-149211. 1972. 26.95 (*0-405-08492-7*, Pub. by Blom Pubns UK) Ayer.
Theatre in Nineteenth-Century Spain. David T. Gies. LC 93-31543. 376p. (C). 1994. text ed. 47.95 (*0-521-38046-4*) Cambridge U Pr.
Theatre in Spain, 1490-1700. Melveena McKendrick. (Illus.). 312p. (C). 1992. pap. text ed. 23.95 (*0-521-42901-3*) Cambridge U Pr.
Theatre in the East. Faubion Bowers. LC 79-7753. (Dance Ser.). (Illus.). 1980. reprint ed. lib. bdg. 67.95 (*0-8369-9278-4*) Ayer.
Theatre in the Middle Ages. Ed. by H. Braet et al. No. 13. 388p. (Orig.). 1985. pap. 67.50 (*90-6186-175-6*, Pub. by Leuven Univ BE) Coronet Bks.
Theatre in the Solovki Prison Camp. Natalia Kuziakina. 225p. 1995. pap. text ed. 33.00 (*3-7186-5440-7*, ECU15, Harwood Acad Pubs) Gordon & Breach.
Theatre in the Solovki Prison Camp. Natalia Kuziakina. 225p. 1995. text ed. 67.00 (*3-7186-5439-3*, ECU30, Harwood Acad Pubs) Gordon & Breach.
Theatre in the Third Reich, the Pre-War Years: Essays on Theatre in Nazi Germany. Glen W. Gadberry. LC 94-36642. (Contributions to the Study of World History Ser.: Vol. 49). 200p. 1995. text ed. 55.00 (*0-313-29516-6*, Greenwood Pr) Greenwood.
Theatre in the Twentieth Century. Tulane Drama Review Staff. Ed. by Robert W. Corrigan. LC 70-111867. (Essay Index Reprint Ser.). 1977. 30.95 (*0-8369-1631-X*) Ayer.
Theatre in the United States Vol. 1: A Documentary History: 1750-1915: Theatre in the Colonies & United States. Ed. by Barry B. Witham. (Illus.). 450p. (C). 1996. text ed. 89.95 (*0-521-30858-5*) Cambridge U Pr.
Theatre in the Victorian Age. Michael R. Booth. (Illus.). 200p. (C). 1991. pap. text ed. 21.95 (*0-521-34837-4*) Cambridge U Pr.
Theatre in Vienna: A Critical History, 1776-1995. W. E. Yates. (Studies in German). (Illus.). 352p. (C). 1996. text ed. 59.95 (*0-521-42100-4*) Cambridge U Pr.
Theatre Industry in Nineteenth-Century France. F. W. Hemmings. LC 92-35031. 296p. (C). 1993. text ed. 69.95 (*0-521-44142-0*) Cambridge U Pr.
Theatre Inedit. Maurice Maeterlinck. (FRE.). 1967. reprint ed. pap. 11.95 (*0-7859-4703-5*) Fr & Eur.
Theatre, Instructor's Manual. 3rd ed. Robert Cohen. 1993. teacher ed., pap. text ed. write for info. (*1-55934-343-5*, 1343) Mayfield Pub.
Theatre Language, a Dictionary. Walter P. Bowman & Robert H. Ball. LC 60-10495. 1976. pap. 8.95 (*0-87830-551-3*, Thtre Arts Bks) Routledge.
Theatre Lethbridge: A History of Theatrical Production in Lethbridge, Alberta (1885-1988) George Mann. (Illus.). 440p. (Orig.). 1993. pap. 29.95 (*1-55059-055-3*) Temeron Bks.
Theatre Lighting from A to Z. Norman C. Boulanger & Warren C. Lounsbury. LC 92-14620. (Illus.). 206p. 1992. pap. 24.95 (*0-295-97214-9*) U of Wash Pr.
Theatre Lover's Cookbook. Mollie A. Meserve & Walter J. Meserve. 208p. 1992. pap. 9.95 (*0-937657-11-5*) Feedbk Theabks & Prospero.
Theatre Management & Production in America: Commercial, Stock, Resident, College, Community, Theatre, & Presenting Organizations. Stephen Langley. (Illus.). 702p. (C). 1990. pap. 37.50 (*0-89676-143-6*, Drama Pubs) QSMG Ltd.
Theatre Museum, London. Alexander Schouvaloff. (Illus.). 144p. 1987. 25.00 (*0-935748-76-8*) Scala Books.
Theatre Nineteen Seventy, Bob Wilson. 2nd ed. Jose L. Arriaga. 336p. (SPA.). 1980. pap. 19.95 (*0-8288-2192-5*, S25771) Fr & Eur.
Theatre Noir: Encyclopedie des Pieces Ecrites en Francais par des Auteurs Noirs. Harold A. Waters. 296p. (FRE.). 1988. 30.00 (*0-89410-627-9*, Three Contnts) Lynne Rienner.
***Theatre Noir: Encyclopedie des Pieces Ecrites en Francais par des Auteurs Noirs.** Harold A. Waters. 296p. (FRE.). 1988. pap. 8.00 (*1-57889-066-7*) Passeggiata.
Theatre Nursing. 6th ed. West. 1992. pap. text ed. 16.95 (*0-7020-1605-5*) HarBrace.
***Theatre of Apollo: Divine Justice & Sophocles' Oedipus the King.** R. Drew Griffith. 147p. 1996. 44.95 (*0-7735-1500-3*, PA4413, Pub. by McGill CN) U of Toronto Pr.
Theatre of Aurand Harris. Aurand Harris. Ed. by Lowell Swortzell. (Illus.). 1000p. (J). 1996. 40.00 (*0-87602-035-X*) Anchorage.
Theatre of Black Americans. Ed. by Errol Hill. 432p. (Orig.). 1986. pap. 16.95 (*0-936839-27-9*) Applause Theatre Bk Pubs.
***Theatre of Chaos: Beyond Absurdism, into Orderly Disorder.** William W. Demastes. (Illus.). 192p. (C). 1997. text ed. 49.95 (*0-521-58245-8*) Cambridge U Pr.
***Theatre of Death: The Ritual Management of Royal Funerals in Renaissance England 1570-1625.** Jennifer Woodward. LC 97-15603. (Illus.). 352p. 1997. 81.00 (*0-85115-704-1*) Boydell & Brewer.
Theatre of Discord: Dissonance in Beckett, Albee, & Pinter. Bob Mayberry. LC 88-45786. 96p. 1989. 22.50 (*0-8386-3353-6*) Fairleigh Dickinson.
Theatre of Don Juan: A Collection of Plays & Views, 1630-1963. Ed. by Oscar Mandel. LC 86-1491. (Illus.). x, 731p. 1986. pap. text ed. 30.00 (*0-8032-8137-4*, Bison Books) U of Nebr Pr.
Theatre of Donald Oenslager. Donald Oenslager. LC 77-16026. (Illus.). 194p. reprint ed. pap. 55.30 (*0-685-23378-2*, 2032491) Bks Demand.
Theatre of Eduardo De Filippo: An Introductory Study. Marco Ciolli. 1993. pap. 17.95 (*0-533-08341-9*) Vantage.
Theatre of Edward Gordon Craig. Denis Bablet. Tr. by D. Woodward. LC 66-23134. Orig. Title: Edward Gordon Craig. (Illus.). 1966. pap. 8.95 (*0-87830-581-5*, Thtre Arts Bks) Routledge.
Theatre of Edward Gordon Craig. Denis Bablet. Tr. by D. Woodward. LC 66-23134. Orig. Title: Edward Gordon Craig. (Illus.). 160p. (gr. 13). 1993. pap. 16.95 (*0-87830-042-2*, Thtre Arts Bks) Routledge.
Theatre of Erwin Piscator: Half a Century of Politics in the Theatre. John Willett. LC 79-11941. (Illus.). 224p. 1979. 42.95 (*0-8419-0501-0*) Holmes & Meier.
Theatre of Fine Devices. Thomas Combe. (Illus.). 120p. 1982. pap. 3.00 (*0-87328-075-X*) Huntington Lib.
Theatre of Frustration: Super Realism in the Dramatic Work of F. X. Kroete & Michel Tremblay. Renate Usmiani. LC 90-22234. (Studies in Comparative Literature). 240p. 1991. reprint ed. 20.00 (*0-8240-5469-5*) Garland.
Theatre of Galdos: Realidad (Eighteen Ninety-Two) annot. ed. Benito Perez Galdos. Ed. by Lisa P. Conde. LC 92-45901. (Hispanic Literature Ser.: Vol. 16). 232p. 1993. text ed. 89.95 (*0-7734-9254-2*) E Mellen.
Theatre of Grotowski. Jennifer Kumiega. 256p. (C). 1988. pap. 21.95 (*0-413-58040-7*, A0286, Pub. by Methuen UK) Heinemann.
Theatre of Her Mind. 1990. pap. 4.50 (*0-8216-5085-8*, Univ Books) Carol Pub Group.
Theatre of Her Mind, Bk. 2. 1991. pap. 4.50 (*0-8216-5090-4*, Univ Books) Carol Pub Group.
Theatre of Horror: Crime & Punishment in Early Modern Germany. Richard Van Dulmen. Tr. by Elisabeth Neu. 200p. (C). 1991. 40.95 (*0-7456-0616-4*) Blackwell Pubs.
Theatre of Images. Ed. by Bonnie Marranca. (PAJ Publications). (Illus.). 176p. 1996. reprint ed. pap. text ed. 14.95 (*0-8018-5243-9*) Johns Hopkins.
Theatre of Jean Paul Sartre. Dorothy McCall. 1969. text ed. 49.50 (*0-231-03180-7*) Col U Pr.
Theatre of Jose Martin Recuerda, Spanish Dramatist: Dramas of Franco & Post-Franco Spain. Jose M. Recuerda. Ed. by Sixto E. Torres. LC 93-30131. (Hispanic Literature Ser.: Vol. 22). 408p. 1993. 109.95 (*0-7734-9356-5*) E Mellen.
Theatre of Kanhailal: Pebet & Memoirs of Africa. Rustom Bharucha. (C). 1992. pap. text ed. 14.00 (*81-7046-094-8*, Pub. by Seagull Bks II) S Asia.
Theatre of Love. large type ed. Lydia Balmain. 328p. 1993. 25.99 (*0-7505-0471-4*) Ulverscroft.
Theatre of Marco Antonio de la Parra: Translations & Commentary. Marco A. De la Parra. Tr. by Charles P. Thomas. LC 93-8865. (Taft Memorial Fund & University of Cincinnati Studies in Latin American, Chicano & U. S. Latino Theatre: Vol. 2). 384p. (SPA.). (C). 1995. text ed. 62.95 (*0-8204-2141-3*) P Lang Pubng.
Theatre of Max Reinhardt. Huntly Carter. LC 64-14700. (Illus.). 1972. 24.95 (*0-405-08344-0*, Pub. by Blom Pubns UK) Ayer.
Theatre of Medieval Europe: New Research in Early Drama. Ed. by Eckehard Simon. (Studies in Medieval Literature: No. 9). 336p. (C). 1991. text ed. 74.95 (*0-521-38514-8*) Cambridge U Pr.
Theatre of Meyerhold & Brecht. Katherine Eaton. LC 85-9910. (Contributions in Drama & Theatre Studies: No. 19). (Illus.). xi, 142p. 1985. text ed. 47.95 (*0-313-24590-8*, EMB, Greenwood Pr) Greenwood.
Theatre of Mixed Means. Richard Kostelanetz. LC 68-10828. 336p. 1981. reprint ed. pap. 15.00 (*0-932360-28-9*) Archae Edns.
Theatre of Power: The Art of Diplomatic Signalling. Raymond Cohen. LC 86-15300. 239p. (Orig.). reprint ed. pap. 68.20 (*0-7837-1586-2*, 2041878) Bks Demand.
Theatre of Praise: The Panegyric Tradition in Seventeenth-Century English Drama. Joanne Altieri. LC 84-40479. 240p. 1986. 40.00 (*0-87413-275-4*) U Delaware Pr.
Theatre of Rafael Alberti. Louise B. Popkin. (Monografias A Ser.: No. 47). 183p. (C). 1975. 45.00 (*0-7293-0004-8*, Pub. by Tamesis Bks Ltd UK) Boydell & Brewer.
Theatre of Recollection: A Cultural Study of Modern Dramatic Tradition in Ireland & Poland. Nina Witoszek. (Illus.). 235p. (Orig.). 1988. pap. 37.50 (*91-7146-384-4*, Pub. by Stockholms Universitet SW) Coronet Bks.
Theatre of Revolt: Studies in Modern Drama from Ibsen to Genet. Robert Brustein. 456p. 1991. reprint ed. pap. 13.95 (*0-929587-53-7*, Elephant Paperbacks) I R Dee.

*Theatre of Robert Wilson. Arthur Holmberg. (Directors in Perspective Ser.). (Illus.). 256p. (C). 1997. text ed. 54.95 (0-521-36492-2) Cambridge U Pr.

Theatre of Roger Planchon. David Bradby. (Theatre in Focus Ser.). (Illus.). 120p. 1984. pap. 105.00 incl. sl. (0-85964-153-8) Chadwyck-Healey.

*Theatre of Sam Shepard: States of Crisis. Stephen J. Bottoms. (Studies in American Theatre & Drama: Vol. 9). (Illus.). 272p. (C). 1997. text ed. 54.95 (0-521-58242-3) Cambridge U Pr.

*Theatre of Sam Shepard: States of Crisis. Stephen J. Bottoms. (Studies in American Theatre & Drama: Vol. 9). (Illus.). 272p. (C). 1997. pap. text ed. 17.95 (0-521-58791-3) Cambridge U Pr.

Theatre of Science. Robert Grau. LC 68-56483. (Illus.). 1972. 30.95 (0-405-08573-7, Pub. by Blom Pubns UK) Ayer.

Theatre of Self-Expression: Dramatherapy & Its Application in the Clinical Setting. Ed. by Steve Mitchell. 180p. 1996. pap. 27.00 (1-85302-283-7) Taylor & Francis.

Theatre of Shadows: From All That Fall to Footfalls, Samuel Beckett's D. Rosemary Pountney. (Irish Literary Studies: Vol. # 28). 310p. 8800. 45.00 (0-86140-256-1, Pub. by Colin Smythe Ltd UK) Dufour.

Theatre of Steven Berkoff. Steven Berkoff. 1992. 39.95 (0-413-66150-4, A0626, Pub. by Methuen UK) Heinemann.

Theatre of Steven Berkoff. Steven Berkoff. 176p. (C). 1992. pap. 25.00 (0-413-67340-5, A0691) Heinemann.

*Theatre of Struggle: Vietnam. George Carver. Date not set. write for info. (0-688-06599-6) Morrow.

Theatre of Tennessee Williams Vol. I: Battle of Angels, A Streetcar Named Desire, The Glass Menagerie. Tennessee Williams. LC 90-5998. 432p. 1971. 35.00 (0-8112-0417-0) New Directions.

Theatre of Tennessee Williams Vol. I: Battle of Angels, A Streetcar Named Desire, The Glass Menagerie. Tennessee Williams. LC 90-5998. 432p. 1990. pap. 19.95 (0-8112-1135-5, NDP694) New Directions.

Theatre of Tennessee Williams Vol. II: The Eccentricities of a Nightingale, Summer & Smoke, The Rose Tattoo, Camino Real. Tennessee Williams. LC 90-5998. 600p. 1971. 35.00 (0-8112-0418-9) New Directions.

Theatre of Tennessee Williams Vol. II: The Eccentricities of a Nightingale, Summer & Smoke, The Rose Tattoo, Camino Real. Tennessee Williams. LC 90-5998. 600p. 1990. pap. 21.95 (0-8112-1136-3, NDP695) New Directions.

Theatre of Tennessee Williams Vol. III: Cat on a Hot Tin Roof, Orpheus Descending, Suddenly Last Summer. Tennessee Williams. LC 90-5998. 432p. 1971. 35.00 (0-8112-0419-7) New Directions.

Theatre of Tennessee Williams Vol. III: Cat on a Hot Tin Roof, Orpheus Descending, Suddenly Last Summer. Tennessee Williams. LC 90-5998. 432p. 1991. pap. 19.95 (0-8112-1196-7, NDP736) New Directions.

*Theatre of Tennessee Williams Vol. IV: Sweet Bird of Youth, Period of Adjustment & The Night of the Iguana. Tennessee Williams. LC 90-65998. 384p. 1972. 35.00 (0-8112-0422-7, NDP773) New Directions.

Theatre of Tennessee Williams Vol. IV: Sweet Bird of Youth, Period of Adjustment & The Night of the Iguana. Tennessee Williams. LC 90-5998. 384p. 1993. reprint ed. pap. 19.95 (0-8112-1257-2, NDP773) New Directions.

Theatre of Tennessee Williams Vol. V: The Milk Train Doesn't Stop Here Anymore, Kingdom of Earth, Small Craft Warnings, The Two Character Play. Tennessee Williams. LC 90-5998. 1976. 35.00 (0-8112-0593-2) New Directions.

Theatre of Tennessee Williams Vol. V: The Milk Train Doesn't Stop Here Anymore, Kingdom of Earth, Small Craft Warnings, The Two Character Play. Tennessee Williams. LC 90-5998. 1990. pap. 19.95 (0-8112-1137-1, NDP696) New Directions.

Theatre of Tennessee Williams Vol. VI: Twenty-Seven Wagons Full of Cotton & Other Short Plays. Tennessee Williams. LC 90-5998. 368p. 1981. pap. 19.95 (0-8112-1215-7, NDP748) New Directions.

Theatre of Tennessee Williams Vol. VII: In the Bar of a Tokyo Hotel & Other Plays. Tennessee Williams. LC 90-5998. 384p. (C). 1981. 35.00 (0-8112-0795-1) New Directions.

Theatre of Tennessee Williams Vol. VII: In the Bar of a Tokyo Hotel & Other Plays. Tennessee Williams. LC 90-5998. 384p. (C). 1994. pap. 19.95 (0-8112-1286-6, NDP797) New Directions.

Theatre of Tennessee Williams Vol. VIII: Vieux Carre, A Lovely Sunday for Creve Coeur, Clothes for a Summer Hotel, The Red Devil Battery Sign. Tennessee Williams. LC 90-5998. 400p. 1992. 35.00 (0-8112-1201-7) New Directions.

Theatre of Terrestrial Astronomy. Edward Kelly. Ed. by A. E. Waite. 1984. reprint ed. pap. 7.95 (0-916411-46-X) Holmes Pub.

Theatre of Terror: The Mass Media & International Terrorism. Gabriel Weimann & Conrad Winn. LC 92-46571. 295p. (C). 1994. pap. text ed. 26.50 (0-8013-1101-2, 79559) Longman.

Theatre of the Absurd. 4th ed. Martin Esslin. 480p. 1987. pap. 13.95 (0-14-013728-9, Penguin Bks) Viking Penguin.

Theatre of the Dream. Salomon Resnik. LC 87-6538. 260p. (C). 1987. lib. bdg. 45.00 (0-422-61040-2, Pub. by Tavistock UK) Routledge Chapman & Hall.

Theatre of the Dream. Salomon Resnik. LC 87-6538. 260p. (C). 1995. pap. text ed. 13.95 (0-422-61830-6, Pub. by Tavistock UK) Routledge Chapman & Hall.

Theatre of the English & Italian Renaissance. Ed. by J. R. Mulryne & Margaret Shewring. LC 91-21021. 268p. 1991. text ed. 49.95 (0-312-06771-2) St Martin.

Theatre of the Fraternity: Staging the Ritual Space of the Scottish Rite of Freemasonry. Ed. by C. Lance Brockman. (Illus.). 160p. 1996. pap. 35.00 (0-87805-947-4) U Pr of Miss.

Theatre of the Greeks. John W. Donaldson. LC 72-2095. (Studies in Drama: No. 39). 1972. reprint ed. lib. bdg. 75.00 (0-8383-1495-3) M S G Haskell Hse.

Theatre of the Holocaust: Four Plays. Ed. & Intro. by Robert Skloot. LC 81-69829. 344p. 1982. reprint ed. pap. 98.10 (0-608-01863-5, 2062515) Bks Demand.

Theatre of the Imagination. Jonathan Levy. 56p. pap. 7.95 (0-932720-75-7) New Plays Inc.

Theatre of the Impossible: Puppet Theatre in Australia. Maeve Vella. 168p. 1989. text ed. 60.00 (0-947131-21-3) Gordon & Breach.

Theatre of the Mind. Henryk Skolimowski. LC 84-40165. (Illus.). 182p. (Orig.). 1984. pap. 6.75 (0-8356-0588-4, Quest) Theos Pub Hse.

Theatre of the Mind: A Study of Unacted Drama in Nineteenth-Century England. Shou-ren Wang. LC 89-34365. 256p. 1989. text ed. 49.95 (0-312-03525-X) St Martin.

Theatre of the Moment. George J. Nathan. LC 75-120099. (Theatre World of George Jean Nathan Ser.). 310p. 1975. 25.00 (0-8386-7775-4) Fairleigh Dickinson.

Theatre of the Oppressed. Augusto Boal. 208p. 1985. pap. 10.95 (0-930452-49-6) Theatre Comm.

Theatre of the Planetary Houres for All the Days of the Yeare. George Simotta. Tr. by G. Baker from GRE. LC 73-171791. (English Experience Ser.: No. 414). 40p. 1971. reprint ed. 15.00 (90-221-0414-1) Walter J Johnson.

*Theatre of the Ridiculous. Bonnie Marranca et al. LC 97-15815. 1998. write for info. (0-8018-5697-3); pap. write for info. (0-8018-5698-1) Johns Hopkins.

Theatre of the Weimar Republic. John Willett. (Illus.). 360p. Date not set. pap. 24.00 (0-8419-1357-9) Holmes & Meier.

Theatre of the Weimar Republic. John Willett. LC 87-19773. 224p. (C). 1988. 79.50 (0-8419-0759-5) Holmes & Meier.

Theatre of To-Day. Hiram K. Moderwell. LC 72-7078. (Select Bibliographies Reprint Ser.). 1977. reprint ed. 40.95 (0-8369-6950-2) Ayer.

*Theatre of Tom Stoppard. 216p. 1989. pap. text ed. 19.95 (0-521-37974-1) Cambridge U Pr.

Theatre of Valle-Inclan. John Lyon. LC 83-7368. (Cambridge Iberian & Latin American Studies). 241p. reprint ed. pap. 68.70 (0-317-55473-5, 2029222) Bks Demand.

Theatre of Visions: Robert Wilson. Stefan Brecht. 440p. (Orig.). 1984. pap. 14.95 (3-518-02488-4, 9413) Routledge Chapman & Hall.

Theatre of Wonders: Six Contemporary American Plays. Len Jenkin et al. Ed. by Mac Wellman. 326p. 1986. 16.95 (0-940650-38-X) Sun & Moon CA.

Theatre of Wonders: Six Contemporary American Plays. Len Jenkin et al. Ed. by Mac Wellman. (American Theatre & Performance Ser.: No. 1). 326p. 1986. pap. 10.95 (0-940650-39-8) Sun & Moon CA.

Theatre of Yesterday & Tomorrow: Commedia Dell'Arte on the Modern Stage. James Fisher. LC 92-14529. (Illus.). 424p. 1992. lib. bdg. 109.95 (0-7734-9529-0) E Mellen.

Theatre on Paper. Alexander Schouvaloff. (Illus.). 248p. 1989. 60.00 (0-85667-373-0, Pub. by P Wilson Pubs) Sothebys Pubns.

Theatre on the Frontier: The Early Years of the St. Louis Stage. 2nd rev. ed. William G. Carson. LC 65-16229. (Illus.). 1972. reprint ed. 35.95 (0-405-08342-4, Pub. by Blom Pubns UK) Ayer.

Theatre on Trial: Samuel Beckett's Later Drama. Audrey McMullan. LC 92-30605. 176p. (C). (gr. 13). 1993. text ed. 59.95 (0-415-05202-5, B0359) Routledge.

Theatre One. Samuel Beckett. Incl. En Attendant Godot. (0-318-52304-3); Fin de Partie. (0-318-52305-1); Acte sans paroles I et II. (0-318-52306-X); 29.95 (0-685-37195-6) Fr & Eur.

Theatre, Opera, & Audiences in Revolutionary Paris: Analysis & Repertory. Emmet Kennedy et al. LC 95-5677. (Contributions in Drama & Theatre Studies: Vol. 62). 424p. 1996. text ed. 79.50 (0-313-28960-3, Greenwood Pr) Greenwood.

Theatre Organ World. Jack Courtnay. (Illus.). 230p. 1946. pap. 38.00 (0-913746-33-9) Organ Lit.

Theatre Philatelic. Harrold C. Shiffler. 264p. 1994. pap. text ed. 20.00 (0-935991-22-0) Am Topical Assn.

Theatre Pieces, an Anthology. Liliane Atlan. Ed. by Bettina L. Knapp. Tr. by Marguerite Feitlowitz from FRE. (Modern Literatures Annual Ser.: Vol. I). 225p. 1985. lib. bdg. 15.00 (0-913283-03-7) Penkevill.

Theatre Posters. Aileen A. Reid. 1994. 14.98 (0-8317-8752-X) Smithmark.

Theatre Primer: A Manual for Success in Early College or University Theatre Courses. Briant H. Lee. 192p. (C). 1991. per., pap. text ed. 15.12 (0-8403-6910-7) Kendall-Hunt.

Theatre Profane. Marguerite D'Angouleme. Ed. by V. L. Saulnier. 357p. (FRE.). 1965. 17.95 (0-8288-9920-7, F30310) Fr & Eur.

Theatre Profiles Vol. 12: The Illustrated Guide to America's Nonprofit Professional Theatres. Steven Samuels. (Illus.). 1996. pap. text ed. 22.95 (1-55936-118-2) Theatre Comm.

Theatre Profiles Eight. Ed. by John Istel. (Illus.). 208p. (Orig.). 1988. pap. 18.95 (0-930452-77-1) Theatre Comm.

Theatre Profiles Nine: The Illustrated Guide to America's Nonprofit Professional Theatre. (Illus.). 240p. (Orig.). 1990. pap. 21.95 (1-55936-007-0) Theatre Comm.

Theatre Profiles, No. 11: The Illustrated Guide to America's Nonprofit Professional Theatre. Steven Samuels. (Illus.). 256p. 1994. pap. 21.95 (1-55936-077-1) Theatre Comm.

Theatre Profiles Seven: The Illustrated Guide to America's Nonprofit Professional Theatre. 25th ed. Ed. by Laura Ross. (Illus.). 388p. 1986. pap. 18.95 (0-930452-52-6) Theatre Comm.

Theatre Profiles Ten: The Illustrated Guide to America's Nonprofit Professional Theatre. (Theatre Profiles Ser.). (Illus.). 240p. (Orig.). 1992. pap. 21.95 (1-55936-040-2) Theatre Comm.

Theatre, Recits et Nouvelles. Albert Camus. Ed. by Claude Quilliot. 2128p. (FRE.). 1962. lib. bdg. 125.00 (0-7859-3744-7, 2070101037) Fr & Eur.

Theatre, Recits et Nouvelles. Albert Camus. (Pleiade Ser.). (FRE.). 1962. 87.95 (2-07-010103-7) Schoenhof.

Theatre, Ritual & Transformation: The Senoi Temiar. Sue Jennings. LC 94-21644. (Illus.). 224p. (C). 1995. pap. 17.95 (0-415-11990-1, C0473) Routledge.

Theatre, Ritual & Transformation: The Senoi Temiar. Sue Jennings. LC 94-21644. (Illus.). 240p. (C). (gr. 13). 1995. text ed. 62.95 (0-415-05229-7, C0348) Routledge.

Theatre Royal at Bath. William Lowndes. 1988. 39.00 (0-317-20314-2, Pub. by Redcliffe Pr Ltd) St Mut.

Theatre Scenecraft. rev. ed. Vern Adix. 310p. 1981. pap. 22.50 (0-87602-013-9) Anchorage.

Theatre Semiotics: Signs of Life. Marvin Carlson. LC 89-45193. (Advances in Semiotics Ser.). 144p. 1990. 25.95 (0-253-31315-5) Ind U Pr.

Theatre Semiotics: Text & Staging in Modern Theatre. Fernando De Toro. (Studies in Semiotics). 256p. 1995. 60.00 (0-8020-0634-5); pap. 18.95 (0-8020-7589-4) U of Toronto Pr.

Theatre Street. Tamara Karsavina. LC 79-7771. (Dance Ser.). (Illus.). 1980. reprint ed. lib. bdg. 26.95 (0-8369-9298-9) Ayer.

Theatre Street: The Reminiscences of Tamara Karsavina. 2nd ed. Tamara Karsavina. (Illus.). 362p. 1981. 29.95 (0-903102-47-1, Pub. by Dance Bks UK) Princeton Bk Co.

Theatre Symposium: A Journal of the Southeastern Theatre Conference, Commedia dell'Arte Performance: Contents & Contexts, Vol. 1. Ed. by Philip G. Hill & Paul C. Castagno. 144p. 1993. pap. text ed. 20.00 (0-8173-0810-5) U of Ala Pr.

Theatre Symposium Vol. 4: A Journal of the Southeastern Theatre Conference - Theatrical Spaces & Dramatic Places - The Reemergence of the Theatre Building in the Renaissance. Ed. by Paul C. Castagno. 144p. 1996. pap. text ed. 20.00 (0-8173-0854-7) U of Ala Pr.

*Theatre Team: Playwright, Producer, Director, Designers & Actors. Ed. by Jeane Luere & Sidney Berger. (Contributions in Drama & Theatre Studies: Vol. 80). 1998. text ed. write for info. (0-313-30050-X, Greenwood Pr) Greenwood.

*Theatre Theory: An Introduction. Mark Fortier. LC 96-46380. 208p. (C). 1997. pap. write for info. (0-415-16165-7); text ed. write for info. (0-415-16164-9) Routledge.

Theatre, Theory, Postmodernism. Johannes Birringer. LC 90-24442. (Drama & Performance Studies). (Illus.). 256p. 1991. 39.95 (0-253-31195-0) Ind U Pr.

Theatre, Theory, Postmodernism. Johannes Birringer. LC 90-24442. (Drama & Performance Studies). (Illus.). 256p. 1993. pap. 11.95 (0-253-20845-9) Ind U Pr.

Theatre Through Its Stage Door. David Belasco. Ed. by Louis V. Defoe. LC 69-56534. (Illus.). 1972. reprint ed. 24.95 (0-405-08261-4, Pub. by Blom Pubns UK) Ayer.

Theatre to Change Men's Souls: The Artistry of Adrian Hall. Jeannie M. Woods. LC 91-51140. (Illus.). 288p. 1993. 42.50 (0-87413-451-X) U Delaware Pr.

*Theatre to Cinema: Stage Pictorialism & the Early Feature Film. Benjamin R. Brewster & Lea Jacobs. (Illus.). 300p. 1997. 75.00 (0-19-818267-8); pap. 24.95 (0-19-815950-1) OUP.

Theatre Unbound. Alexander Bakshy. LC 68-56535. 1972. reprint ed. 23.95 (0-405-08232-0, Pub. by Blom Pubns UK) Ayer.

Theatre under Deconstruction? A Question of Approach. Stratos E. Constantinidis. LC 92-24320. (Studies in Modern Drama: Vol. 2). 360p. 1993. text ed. 59.00 (0-8153-0872-8, H1605) Garland.

Theatre, Vol. 1: Avec: Les Batisseurs d'Empire, Le Gouter des Generaux, L'Equarrissage pour Tous, Le Dernier des Metiers. Boris Vian. 361p. (FRE.). 1971. pap. 26.95 (0-7859-5500-3, 2264001461) Fr & Eur.

Theatre, Vol. 1: Avec: Les Eaux et Forets, Le Square, La Musica. Marguerite Duras. (Gallimard Ser.). 176p. (FRE.). 1956. 26.95 (2-07-022103-2) Schoenhof.

Theatre, Vol. 1: Avec: Les Marrons de feu, La Nuit Ventienne, La Coup et les Levres, A quoi revent les Jeunes Filles, Andre del Sorto, Les Caprices de Marianne. Alfred Musset. 448p. (FRE.). 1964. 10.95 (0-8288-9652-6, FC1471) Fr & Eur.

Theatre, Vol. 1: Les Marrons de Feu; La Nuit Venitienne. Alfred De Musset. (FRE.). 1964. pap. 10.95 (0-7859-2956-8) Fr & Eur.

Theatre, Vol. 1: Melite; La Galerie du Palais. Pierre Corneille. (FRE.). 1968. pap. 19.95 (0-7859-2963-0) Fr & Eur.

Theatre, Vol. 1: Rendre a Cesar, la Petite Sirene, le Dialogue Dans le Marecage. Marguerite Yourcenar. (FRE.). 1987. 39.95 (0-7859-0454-9, 2070279391) Fr & Eur.

Theatre, Vol. 2: Avec: Le Quenouille de Barberine, Le Chandelier, Il Ne Faut Jurer de Rein, Un Caprice, Il Faut Qu'Une Port Soit Ouverte ou Fermee. Alfred Musset. Ed. by Maurice Rat. 448p. (FRE.). 1964. 10.95 (0-8288-9651-8, FC1472) Fr & Eur.

Theatre, Vol. 2: Clitandre; Medee; Le Cid. Pierre Corneille. (FRE.). 1980. pap. 17.95 (0-7859-2964-9) Fr & Eur.

Theatre, Vol. 2: Electre Ou la Chute Des Masques, le Mystere d'Alceste, Qui n'as Pas Son Minotaure. Marguerite Yourcenar. 235p. (FRE.). 1971. 39.95 (0-7859-0455-7, 2070280489) Fr & Eur.

Theatre, Vol. 2: Pucelle, La Fete Noire, Les Naturels du Borelais. Jacques Audiberti. 312p. (FRE.). 1970. pap. 39.95 (0-7859-0356-9, F83651) Fr & Eur.

Theatre, Vol. 2: Suzanne Andler, des Journees Entieres Dans les Arbres, Yes Peut-Etre?, le Shape, Etc. Marguerite Duras. (Gallimard Ser.). 298p. (FRE.). 1968. pap. 29.95 (2-07-026964-7) Schoenhof.

Theatre, Vol. 2: Suzanne Andler, des Journees Entieres Dans les Arbres, Yes Peut-Etre?, le Shape, Etc., 3. Marguerite Duras. (Gallimard Ser.). 298p. (FRE.). 1968. 25.95 (2-07-070175-1) Schoenhof.

Theatre, Vol. 3: La Logeuse, Opera Parle, le Oullou, Aetanima. Jacques Audiberti. 264p. (FRE.). 1956. pap. 24.95 (0-7859-0357-7, F83652) Fr & Eur.

Theatre, Vol. 4: Avec: Sodome et Gommorrhe, L'Appollon de Bellac, La Folle de Chaillot, Pour Lucrece. Jean Giraudoux. 340p. (FRE.). 1959. 26.95 (0-8288-9791-3, F103903) Fr & Eur.

Theatre, Vol. 5: Pomme, Pomme, Pomme; Baton et Ruban; Boutique Fermee; La Brigitta. Jacques Audiberti. 264p. (FRE.). 1962. pap. 45.00 (0-7859-3958-X, 2070203506) Fr & Eur.

Theatre We Worked for: The Letters of Eugene O'Neill to Kenneth Macgowan. Eugene O'Neill. Ed. by Jackson R. Bryer. LC 81-299. (Illus.). 292p. (C). 1982. 40.00 (0-300-02583-1) Yale U Pr.

Theatre Workshop Story. Howard Goorney. Ed. by Malcolm Hay & P. Roberts. 226p. (C). 1988. pap. 15.95 (0-413-48760-1, A0290, Pub. by Methuen UK) Heinemann.

Theatre World Drawings of Reginald Marsh, 1972. Walter Kerr. LC 41-50522. (Illus.). 1972. 0.50 (0-614-10419-X) W Benton Mus.

Theatre World, 1990-1991, Vol. 47. John Willis. (Illus.). 1992. pap. 24.95 (1-55783-126-2) Applause Theatre Bk Pubs.

Theatre World 1990-1991, Vol. 47. John Willis. 1992. 45.00 (1-55783-125-4) Applause Theatre Bk Pubs.

Theatre World, 1992-1993, Vol. 49. Ed. by John Willis. (Theatre World Ser.). (Illus.). 254p. (Orig.). 1995. 45.00 (1-55783-203-X); pap. 24.95 (1-55783-204-8) Applause Theatre Bk Pubs.

Theatre World 1993-1994, Vol. 50. Ed. by John Willis. (Theatre World Ser.). (Illus.). 272p. (Orig.). 1996. 45.00 (1-55783-235-8); pap. 25.95 (1-55783-236-6) Applause Theatre Bk Pubs.

Theatre World 1994-95, Vol. 51. Ed. by John Willis. (Theatre World Ser.). (Illus.). 272p. 1996. 49.95 (1-55783-250-1); pap. 25.95 (1-55783-251-X) Applause Theatre Bk Pubs.

Theatre Year 1983. Donald Cooper. (Illus.). 132p. 1988. pap. 11.95 (0-413-75783-8, A0291, Pub. by Methuen UK) Heinemann.

Theatre 1969: La Contestation, Vol. 1. 288p. 1969. 8.95 (0-686-54471-4) Fr & Eur.

Theatre 1969: Le Grand Guignol, Vol. 2. 304p. 1969. 9.95 (0-686-54472-2) Fr & Eur.

Theatre 1970: Bob Wilson. Fernando Arrabal. 208p. (FRE.). 1972. pap. 9.95 (0-7859-5370-1) Fr & Eur.

Theatre 1971: Les Monstres. Fernando Arrabal. 19.95 (0-686-54474-9) Fr & Eur.

Theatre 1972: Bob Wilson. Fernando Arrabal. 19.95 (0-686-54475-7) Fr & Eur.

*Theatregoer's Almanac: A Collection of Lists, People, History & Commentary on the American Theatre. Thomas S. Hischak. LC 96-43782. 296p. 1997. text ed. 45.00 (0-313-30246-4, Greenwood Pr) Greenwood.

Theatres: Planning Guidance for Design & Adaptation. Roderick Ham. 224p. 1988. 87.95 (0-85139-418-3) Buttrwrth-Heinemann.

Theatres: Romans et Nouvelles, Philosophie, Ecrits Divers. Georges Courteline. (FRE.). 1990. pap. 48.95 (0-7859-3030-2) Fr & Eur.

Theatres for Drama Performance: Recent Experiences in Acoustical Design. Ed. by R. E. Boner & Richard H. Talaske. LC 86-72934. 167p. 1987. pap. 26.00 (0-88318-516-4) Acoustical Soc Am.

Theatres in Roman Palestine & Provincia Arabia. Arthur Segal. LC 94-3484. (Mnemosyne, Bibliotheca Classica Batava: Supplementum: Vol 140). 1994. 87.50 (90-04-10145-4) E J Brill.

Theatres of Accumulation: Studies in Asian & Latin America Urbanization. Warwick Armstrong & Terence McGee. 320p. 1985. text ed. 40.00 (0-416-78570-0, 9706); pap. text ed. 14.95 (0-416-39800-6, 9528) Routledge Chapman & Hall.

*Theatres of Bharata & Some Aspects of Sanskrit Play-Production. Goverdhan Panchal. 1996. 32.50 (81-215-0661-1, Pub. by M Manoharial II) Coronet Bks.

Theatres of Inigo Jones & John Webb. John Orrell. (Illus.). 240p. 1985. 59.95 (0-521-25546-5) Cambridge U Pr.

Theatres of London. Raymond Mander & Joe Mitchenson. LC 78-11808. 292p. 1979. reprint ed. text ed. 59.75 (0-313-21227-9, MATL, Greenwood Pr) Greenwood.

Theatres of Memory: Past & Present in Contemporary British Culture. Raphael Samuel. 300p. (C). (gr. 13). 1995. text ed. 65.00 (0-86091-209-4, A2677, Pub. by Vrso UK) Norton.

An Asterisk (*) at the beginning of an entry indicates that the title is appearing in BIP for the first time.

Theatres of Memory Vol. 1: Past & Present in Contemporary Culture. Raphael Samuel. 496p. 1996. pap. 20.00 (*1-85984-077-9*, Pub. by Vrso UK) Norton.
Theatres of the Left, Eighteen Eighty to Nineteen Thirty-Five. Ed. by Raphael Samuel. (History Workshop Ser.). 288p. (Orig.). 1985. pap. 18.95 (*0-7100-0901-1*, RKP) Routledge.
Theatres of War: Performance, Politics, & Society 1793-1815. Gillian Russell. (Illus.). 264p. 1995. 55.00 (*0-19-812263-2*) OUP.
***Theatresports down Under.** 2nd ed. Lyn Pierse. Ed. by Irma Havlicek. (Illus.). 427p. 1997. reprint ed. pap. 60.00 (*0-646-23861-2*) Players Pr.
Theatrewritings. Bonnie Marranca. 1984. 28.50 (*0-933826-67-2*); pap. 14.95 (*0-933826-68-0*) PAJ Pubns.
Theatric Aspects of Sanskrit Drama. G. K. Bhat. 1985. 12.50 (*0-8364-1365-2*, Bhanarkar Oriental Inst) S Asia.
Theatrical City: Culture, Theatre & Politics in London, 1576-1649. Ed. by David L. Smith et al. (Illus.). 288p. (C). 1995. text ed. 54.95 (*0-521-44126-9*) Cambridge U Pr.
Theatrical Costume: A Guide to Information Sources. Ed. by Jackson Kesler. LC 79-22881. (Performing Arts Information Guide Ser.: Vol. 6). 320p. 1979. 68.00 (*0-8103-1455-X*) Gale.
Theatrical Costume, Masks, Make-Up & Wigs: A Bibliography. large type ed. Jowers. 1997. 205.00 (*0-7838-1690-1*, GK Hall) Thorndike Pr.
Theatrical Craftsmanship of Richard Brinsley Sheridan's 'School for Scandal' Thomas H. Jordan. 1974. 250.00 (*0-87700-209-6*) Revisionist Pr.
Theatrical Criticism in London to Seventeen Ninety-Five. Charles H. Gray. LC 64-14708. 1972. 20.95 (*0-405-08574-5*) Ayer.
Theatrical Design & Production: An Introduction to Scene Design & Construction, Light, Sound, Costume, & Makeup. 2nd ed. J. Michael Gillette. LC 91-29991. 557p. (C). 1992. text ed. 44.95 (*1-55934-102-5*, 1102) Mayfield Pub.
Theatrical Design & Production: An Introduction to Scene Design & Construction, Lighting, Sound, Costume, & Makeup. 3rd rev. ed. J. Michael Gillette. LC 96-21642. (Illus.). 573p. (C). 1996. text ed. 44.95 (*1-55934-701-5*, 1701) Mayfield Pub.
Theatrical Design in the Twentieth Century: An Index to Photographic Reproductions of Scenic Designs. Compiled by W. Patrick Atkinson. LC 96-4975. (Bibliographies & Indexes in the Performing Arts Ser.). 488p. 1996. text ed. 95.00 (*0-313-29701-0*, Greenwood Pr) Greenwood.
Theatrical Designers: An International Biographical Dictionary. Ed. by Tom Mikotowicz. LC 91-28086. 360p. 1992. text ed. 69.50 (*0-313-26270-5*, MZT/, Greenwood Pr) Greenwood.
Theatrical Designs from Baroque Through Neoclassicism. Janos Scholz. 1976. reprint ed. lib. bdg. write for info. (*0-87817-179-7*) Hacker.
Theatrical Designs of Charles Ricketts. Eric Binnie. Ed. by Bernard Beckerman. LC 84-23921. (Theater & Dramatic Studies: No. 23). 200p. reprint ed. pap. 56.80 (*0-8357-1584-1*, 2070430) Bks Demand.
Theatrical Directors: A Biographical Dictionary. Ed. by John W. Frick & Stephen Vallillo. LC 93-1138. 584p. 1994. Alk. papers. text ed. 95.00 (*0-313-27478-9*, FTF/, Greenwood Pr) Greenwood.
Theatrical Gamut: Notes for a Post-Beckettian Stage. Ed. by Enoch Brater. LC 95-2385. (Theater: Theory - Text - Performance Ser.). 1995. text ed. 44.50 (*0-472-10583-3*) U of Mich Pr.
Theatrical Image. James H. Clay & Daniel Krempel. LC 85-91268. (Illus.). 314p. 1985. reprint ed. pap. text ed. 27.00 (*0-8191-4978-0*) U Pr of Amer.
Theatrical Imagination. Huberman. (C). 1993. suppl. ed., teacher ed., pap. text ed. 6.00 (*0-03-030833-X*) HB Coll Pubs.
Theatrical Imagination. Jeffrey Huberman & James Ludwig. (Illus.). 500p. (Orig.). (C). 1993. text ed. 40.00 (*0-03-030832-1*) HB Coll Pubs.
Theatrical Imagination. 2nd ed. Jeffrey H. Hoberman et al. 560p. (C). 1996. pap. text ed. write for info. (*0-15-503024-8*) HB Coll Pubs.
Theatrical Imagination. 2nd ed. Huberman. (C). 1996. pap. text ed. 28.00 (*0-15-503025-6*) HarBrace.
Theatrical Instinct: Nikolai Evreinov & the Russian Theatre of the Early Twentieth Century. Sharon M. Carnicke. LC 88-31364. (American University Studies: Theatre Arts: Ser. XXVI, Vol. 2). 247p. (C). 1989. text ed. 45.50 (*0-8204-1073-X*) P Lang Pubng.
Theatrical Legitimation: Allegories of Genius in 17th-Century England & France. Timothy Murray. (Illus.). 304p. 1987. 55.00 (*0-19-504268-9*) OUP.
Theatrical Life of George Henry Boker. Thomas M. Kitts. LC 93-14564. (Artists & Issues in the Theatre Ser.: Vol. 3). 204p. (C). 1994. text ed. 44.95 (*0-8204-2248-7*) P Lang Pubng.
Theatrical Makeup. Bert Broe. (Illus.). 96p. 1985. 13.95 (*0-8253-0295-1*) Beaufort Bks NY.
***Theatrical Makeup: A Practical Approach for Church Drama.** Ginger Shew. Date not set. 8.99 (*0-8341-9304-3*) Lillenas.
Theatrical Management in the West & South for Thirty Years. Sol Smith. LC 67-13343. (Illus.). 1972. reprint ed. 23.95 (*0-405-08983-X*) Ayer.
Theatrical Movement: A Bibliographical Anthology. Ed. by Bob Fleshman. LC 85-1795. 756p. 1986. 69.50 (*0-8108-1789-6*) Scarecrow.
Theatrical Notes. Joseph Knight. LC 70-82835. 309p. 1972. 20.95 (*0-405-08712-8*, Pub. by Blom Pubns UK) Ayer.
Theatrical Performance in the Ancient World: Hellenistic & Early Roman Theatre. Bruno Gentili. (London Studies in Classical Philology: No. 2). 117p. 1979. pap. 30.00 (*90-70265-31-1*, Pub. by Gieben NE) Benjamins North Am.
Theatrical Presentation. Ed. by Gloria B. Beckerman & William Coco. 256p. (C). (gr. 13). 1990. pap. 16.95 (*0-415-90281-9*, A3444, Routledge NY) Routledge.
Theatrical Rambles of Mr. & Mrs. John Greene. Charles Durang. Ed. by William L. Slout. LC 84-11165. (Clipper Studies in the Theater: No. 1). 142p. (Orig.). 1987. pap. 19.00 (*0-89370-460-1*); lib. bdg. 29.00 (*0-89370-360-5*) Borgo Pr.
Theatrical Reflections: Notes on the Form & Practice of Drama. Bert Cardullo. LC 92-22552. (American University Studies: Theatre Arts: Ser. XXVI, Vol. 15). 276p. (C). 1993. text ed. 49.95 (*0-8204-1935-4*) P Lang Pubng.
Theatrical Scene Painting: A Lesson Guide. William H. Pinnell. LC 86-15500. (Illus.). 160p. (Orig.). (C). 1987. pap. 24.95 (*0-8093-1332-4*) S Ill U Pr.
Theatrical Seasonings-Encore! Ed. by Joan M. Good et al. LC 83-50926. (Illus.). 336p. (Orig.). 1983. spiral bd. 11.95 (*0-9612330-0-1*) Stage Guild.
Theatrical Space: A Guide for Directors & Designers. William F. Condee. LC 95-3311. (Illus.). 242p. 1995. 39.50 (*0-8108-3007-8*) Scarecrow.
Theatrical Space & Historical Place in Sophocles' Oedipus at Colonus. Lowell Edmunds. LC 96-23870. 208p. 1996. 57.50 (*0-8476-8319-2*); pap. 22.95 (*0-8476-8320-6*) Rowman.
Theatrical Space in Ibsen, Chekhov & Strindberg: Public Forms of Privacy. Freddie Rokem. Ed. by Oscar G. Brockett. LC 85-16415. (Theater & Dramatic Studies: No. 32). (Illus.). 106p. reprint ed. pap. 34.00 (*0-8357-1707-0*, 2070441) Bks Demand.
Theatrical Tapes of Leo Thynn. Adrian Plass. 1993. pap. 6.99 (*0-551-01875-5*) Zondervan.
Theatrical Touring & Founding in North America. Ed. by L. W. Conolly. LC 81-23766. (Contributions in Drama & Theatre Studies: No. 5). (Illus.). xiv, 245p. 1982. text ed. 55.00 (*0-313-22595-8*, CTH/, Greenwood Pr) Greenwood.
Theatrical Training During the Age of Shakespeare. David P. Edgecombe. LC 95-17480. (Studies in Theatre Arts: Vol. 2). 136p. 1995. 69.95 (*0-7734-8881-2*) E Mellen.
Theatrical Trip for a Wager. Horton Rhys. LC 73-81217. 1972. 24.95 (*0-405-08884-1*, Pub. by Blom Pubns UK) Ayer.
Theatrical "World" William Archer. LC 77-82818. 1972. reprint ed. 24.95 (*0-405-08211-8*, Pub. by Blom Pubns UK); reprint ed. 24.95 (*0-405-08210-X*, Pub. by Blom Pubns UK) Ayer.
Theatrical Writings of Fabrizio Carini Motta. Ed. by Orville K. Larson. LC 87-4296. (Illus.). 145p. (C). 1987. text ed. 19.95 (*0-8093-1337-5*) S Ill U Pr.
Theatrically Speaking: A Guide to Operations for the Nonprofit Arts Organization. Enid Holm. (Illus.). 324p. (C). 1995. 35.00 (*0-9650713-0-8*) TX Non-Profit.
Theatricals: Two Comedies. Henry James. 1971. reprint ed. 39.00 (*0-403-01043-8*) Scholarly.
Theatricals - Two Comedies: Tenants, Disengaged. Henry James. (BCL1-PS American Literature Ser.). 325p. 1992. reprint ed. lib. bdg. 89.00 (*0-7812-6762-5*) Rprt Serv.
Theatro de los Theatros de los Passados Y Presentes Siglos. Francisco B. Candamo. Ed. by Duncan W. Moir. (Textos B Ser.: No. 3). 191p. (SPA.). (C). 1970. pap. 36.00 (*0-900411-09-0*, Pub. by Tamesis Bks Ltd UK) Boydell & Brewer.
Theatrum Anonymorum et Pseudonymorum Ex Symbolis et Collatione Virorum Per Europam Doctissimorum Ac Celeberrimorum Post Syntagma Dudum Editum, 2 vols. Vicentius Placcius. reprint ed. Set. write for info. (*0-318-71941-X*) G Olms Pubs.
Theatrum Arbitri: Theatrical Elements in the Satyrica of Petronius. Costas Panayotakis. LC 94-40910. (Mnemosyne, Bibliotheca Classica Batava). 1995. 71.50 (*90-04-10229-9*) E J Brill.
Theatrum Chemicum Britannicum. Elias Ashmole. 1968. reprint ed. 145.00 (*0-318-71886-3*) G Olms Pubs.
Theatrum Chemicum Britannicum. Elias Ashmole. 494p. 1992. reprint ed. pap. 32.50 (*0-922802-89-0*) Kessinger Pub.
Theatrum Chemicum Praecipuos Selectorum Auctorum Tractatus de Chemia et Lapide Philosophica Antiquitate, Veritate, Jure, Praestantia et Operationibus Continens, 6 vols. Lazarus Zetzner. reprint ed. write for info. (*0-318-71883-9*) G Olms Pubs.
Theatrum Majorum, the Cambridge of 1776: Diary of Dorothy Dudley. Dorothy Dudley. LC 73-140861. (Eyewitness Accounts of the American Revolution Ser., No. 1). (Illus.). 1971. reprint ed. 16.95 (*0-405-01228-4*) Ayer.
Theatrum Poetarum: or a Compleat Collection of the Poets, Especially the Most Eminent, of All Ages. Edward Phillips. (Anglistica & Americana Ser.: No. 61). 453p. 1970. reprint ed. 76.70 (*0-685-66501-1*, 05102475) G Olms Pubs.
Thebaid. Statius. Tr. by A. D. Melville. (Illus.). 288p. 1992. 95.00 (*0-19-814782-1*) OUP.
Thebaid. Statius. Tr. by A. D. Melville. (The World's Classics Ser.). 432p. 1995. pap. 12.95 (*0-19-282453-8*) OUP.
Thebaid the Ninth. Statius. Ed. by M. J. Dewar. (Oxford Classical Monographs). 256p. 1991. 80.00 (*0-19-814480-6*) OUP.
Theban Hegemony, 371-362 B. C. John Buckler. (Historical Studies: No. 98). (Illus.). 355p. 1980. 25.00 (*0-674-87645-8*) HUP.
Theban Mysteries. Amanda Cross. 192p. 1979. mass mkt. 4.99 (*0-380-45021-6*) Avon.
Theban Necropolis, Vol. 01-1: Private Tombs. Malek. (Topographical Bibliography of Ancient Egyptian Hieroglyphic Texts Ser.: Reliefs & Paintings, Vol. 1-1). 1985. 91.50 (*0-900416-10-6*, Pub. by Aris & Phillips UK) David Brown.
Theban Necropolis, Vol. 01-2: Royal Tombs & Smaller Cemeteries. Malek. (Topographical Bibliography of Ancient Egyptian Hieroglyphic Texts Ser.: Reliefs & Paintings, Vol. 1-2). 1973. 99.00 (*0-900416-15-7*, Pub. by Aris & Phillips UK) David Brown.
Theban Plays. Incl. King Oedipus. Sophocles. Tr. by E. F. Watling. 1950. pap. (*0-318-55098-9*); Oedipus at Colonus. (*0-318-55099-7*); Antigone. (*0-318-55100-4*); (Classics Ser.). 168p. (Orig.). (YA). (gr. 9 up). 1950. pap. 9.95 (*0-14-044003-8*, Penguin Classics) Viking Penguin.
Theban Plays. Sophocles. LC 94-5984. (Everyman's Library of Children's Classics). 1994. 17.00 (*0-679-43132-2*) Knopf.
Theban Plays: King Oedipus, Antigone, Oedipus at Kollonos & Omma. Sophocles. 1994. pap. text ed. 15.95 (*0-948230-71-1*, Pub. by N Hern Bks UK) Theatre Comm.
Theban Temples. Malek. (Topographical Bibliography of Ancient Egyptian Hieroglyphic Texts Ser.: Reliefs & Paintings, Vol. 2). 1972. 91.50 (*0-900416-18-1*, Pub. by Aris & Phillips UK) David Brown.
Thebans: Oedipus Tyrannos, Oedipus at Colonus & Antigone. Timberlake Wertenbaker. 256p. (Orig.). 1992. pap. 12.95 (*0-571-16711-X*) Faber & Faber.
Thebes. Dale Jensen. Ed. by Edward Mycue. (Took Modern Poetry in English Ser.: No. 14). (Illus.). 28p. (Orig.). 1991. pap. 3.00 (*1-879457-12-1*) Norton Coker Pr.
Thecla Merlo: Messenger of the Good News. Domenica Agasso. Tr. by John Moore from ITA. (Illus.). 232p. (Orig.). 1994. pap. 8.50 (*0-8198-7376-4*) Pauline Bks.
Theda Bara: A Biography of the Silent Screen Vamp, with a Filmography. Ronald Genini. LC 96-11764. (Illus.). 168p. 1996. lib. bdg. 29.95 (*0-7864-0202-4*) McFarland & Co.
Thedford Two: A Paleo-Indian Site in the Ausable River Watershed of Southwestern Ontario. D. Brian Deller & Christopher J. Ellis. LC 91-25892. (Memoirs Ser.: No. 24). (Illus.). xii, 158p. (Orig.). (C). 1992. pap. 20.00 (*0-915703-25-4*) U Mich Mus Anthro.
***Thee First Garden.** Robert B. Ward. (Illus.). 40p. (Orig.). (J). 1996. pap. 4.95 (*0-7880-0652-5*) CSS OH.
Thee Generation: Reflections on the Coming Revolution. Tom Regan. 176p. 1991. 24.95 (*0-87722-758-6*); pap. 16.95 (*0-87722-772-1*) Temple U Pr.
Theft. Saul Bellow. 1989. pap. 6.95 (*0-318-41472-4*, Penguin Bks) Viking Penguin.
Theft & Drugs in the Workplace: A Management Guide. K. C. Bettencourt. Ed. by D. Parker. LC 90-63054. (Illus.). 140p. (Orig.). 1991. pap. 14.95 (*0-88247-852-4*) R & E Pubs.
Theft by Deception. David Benoit & Charles G. Graff. (Illus.). 12p. (Orig.). (YA). (gr. 7 up). 1987. pap. text ed. 1.50 (*0-923105-08-5*) Glory Ministries.
Theft of a Nation. 3rd rev. ed. William W. Baker. 192p. (Orig.). 1989. pap. 15.00 (*0-910643-00-8*); pap. 10.00 (*0-317-99885-4*) Defenders Pubns.
Theft of an Idol: Text & Context in the Representation of Collective Violence. Paul R. Brass. LC 96-9315. (Princeton Studies In Culture, Power & History). 1997. write for info. (*0-691-02651-3*); pap. text ed. 17.95 (*0-691-02650-5*) Princeton U Pr.
Theft of the City: Readings on Corruption in Urban America. Ed. by John A. Gardiner & David J. Olson. LC 73-16519. 447p. reprint ed. pap. 127.40 (*0-8357-6697-7*, 2056877) Bks Demand.
Theft of the Spirit: A Journey to Spiritual Healing s. Carl A. Hammerschlag. 176p. 1994. pap. 10.00 (*0-671-88553-7*, Fireside) S&S Trade.
Theft of the Spirit: The Journey to Spiritual Healing with Native Americans. Carl A. Hammerschlag. 256p. 1993. 18.00 (*0-671-78023-9*) S&S Trade.
Theft of Thor's Hammer. Illus. by Dave Bowyer. (Myths & Legends Ser.). (J). 1996. lib. bdg. write for info. (*1-57572-014-0*) Rigby Interact Libr.
***Theilheimer's Synthetic Method of Organic Chemistry Series, Vol. 51, 1997.** Ed. by Alan F. Finch. xxiv, 296p. 1997. 391.50 (*3-8055-6529-1*) S Karger.
***Theilheimer's Synthetic Methods of Organic Chemistry, Vol. 52, 1997.** Ed. by Alan F. Finch. xx, 250p. 1997. 391.50 (*3-8055-6530-5*) S Karger.
Theilheimer's Synthetic Methods of Organic Chemistry: Synthetische Methoden der Organischen Chemie, 32 vols. Incl. Vol. 1. Thesaurus. 2nd ed. Tr. by H. Wynberg from GER. 1975. 66.25 (*3-8055-2226-6*); Vol. 2. Thesaurus. 2nd ed. Tr. by A. Ingberman from GER. 1975. 84.50 (*3-8055-2227-4*); Vol. 3. Repertorium. Ed. by W. Theilheimer. 1975. 123.50 (*3-8055-2228-2*); Vol. 6. Annual Survey, 1952. 2nd ed. Ed. by W. Theilheimer. 1952. 104.50 (*3-8055-2229-0*); Vol. 7. Annual Survey, 1952. 2nd ed. Ed. by W. Theilheimer. 1953. 117.50 (*3-8055-2230-4*); Vol. 8. Annual Survey, 1954. 2nd ed. Ed. by W. Theilheimer. 1977. 132.25 (*3-8055-2231-2*); Vol. 9. Annual Survey, 1955. Ed. by W. Theilheimer. 1955. 81.75 (*3-8055-0643-0*); Vol. 10. Yearbook, 1956. 2nd ed. Ed. by W. Theilheimer. 1975. 194.00 (*3-8055-2232-0*); Vol. 11. Yearbooks, 1957. 2nd ed. Ed. by W. Theilheimer. 1975. 128.75 (*3-8055-2233-9*); Vol. 12. Yearbooks, 1957. 2nd ed. Ed. by W. Theilheimer. 1975. 141.75 (*3-8055-2234-7*); Vol. 13. Yearbooks, 1957. 2nd ed. Ed. by W. Theilheimer. 1959. 156.75 (*3-8055-2235-5*); Vol. 14. Yearbooks, 1957. 2nd ed. Ed. by W. Theilheimer. 1960. 142.75 (*3-8055-2236-3*); Vol. 16. Yearbook, 1962. Ed. by W. Theilheimer. 1962. 156.75 (*3-8055-0647-3*); Vol. 17. Yearbook, 1963. Ed. by W. Theilheimer. 1963. 156.75 (*3-8055-0648-1*); Vol. 18. Yearbook, 1964. Ed. by W. Theilheimer. 1964. 177.50 (*3-8055-0650-3*); Vol. 19. Yearbook, 1965. Ed. by W. Theilheimer. 1965. 177.50 (*3-8055-0651-1*); Vol. 20. Yearbook, 1966. Ed. by W. Theilheimer. 1966. 256.75 (*3-8055-0653-8*); Vol. 21. Yearbooks, 1967. Ed. by W. Theilheimer. 1967. 203.50 (*3-8055-0654-6*); Vol. 22. Yearbooks, 1968. Ed. by W. Theilheimer. 1968. 236.75 (*3-8055-0655-4*); Vol. 23. Yearbooks, 1969. Ed. by W. Theilheimer. 1969. 275.75 (*3-8055-0656-2*); Vol. 24. Yearbooks, 1970. Ed. by W. Theilheimer. 1970. 261.00 (*3-8055-0657-0*); Vol. 25. Yearbook, 1971. Ed. by W. Theilheimer. 1971. 257.50 (*3-8055-1198-1*); Vol. 26. Yearbooks, 1972. Ed. by W. Theilheimer. 1972. 248.00 (*3-8055-1390-9*); Vol. 27. Yearbooks, 1973. Ed. by W. Theilheimer. 1973. 277.50 (*3-8055-1565-0*); Vol. 28. Yearbooks, 1974. Ed. by W. Theilheimer. 1974. 426.25 (*3-8055-1680-0*); Vol. 29. Yearbooks, 1975. Ed. by W. Theilheimer. 1975. 400.00 (*3-8055-2095-6*); Vol. 30. Yearbook, 1976. Ed. by W. Theilheimer. 1976. 456.75 (*3-8055-2256-8*); Vol. 31. Yearbooks, 1977. Ed. by W. Theilheimer. 1977. 433.25 (*3-8055-2432-3*); Vol. 32. Yearbooks, 1978. Ed. by W. Theilheimer. 1978. 426.25 (*3-8055-2818-3*); write for info. (*0-318-55594-8*) S Karger.
Theios Aner & the Markan Miracle Traditions: A Critique of the Theios Aner Concept As an Interpretative Background of the Miracle Traditions Used by Mark. Barry Blackburn. (WissUNT Neuen Testament Ser.: No. 2-40). 308p. (Orig.). 1990. pap. 61.00 (*3-16-145503-7*, Pub. by J C B Mohr GW) Coronet Bks.
Their Ancient Glittering Eyes: Remembering Poets & More Poets. Donald Hall. 348p. 1993. pap. 11.95 (*0-89919-980-1*) Ticknor & Fields.
Their Angel Reach. Livi Michael. 1995. pap. 9.99 (*0-7493-2163-6*, Reed Trade) Buttrwrth-Heinemann.
***Their Blood Cries Out.** Paul Marshall. 304p. 1997. pap. 12.99 (*0-8499-4020-6*) Word Pub.
Their Blood Runs Cold: Adventures with Reptiles & Amphibians. Whit Gibbons. LC 82-17395. (Illus.). 184p. (Orig.). 1983. pap. 14.95 (*0-8173-0133-X*) U of Ala Pr.
Their Brothers' Keepers. Philip Friedman. LC 57-8773. 232p. 1978. pap. 12.95 (*0-89604-002-X*, Holocaust Library) US Holocaust.
Their Brothers' Keepers: Moral Stewardship in the United States, 1800 to 1865. Clifford S. Griffin. LC 83-8563. xv, 332p. 1983. reprint ed. text ed. 67.50 (*0-313-24059-0*, GRTB, Greenwood Pr) Greenwood.
Their Brothers' Keepers: The Christian Heroes & Heroines Who Helped the Oppressed Escape the Nazi Terror. Philip Friedman. 232p. reprint ed. 12.95 (*0-686-95090-9*) ADL.
Their Child. Robert Herrick. (Collected Works of Robert Herrick). 1988. reprint ed. lib. bdg. 59.00 (*0-7812-1266-9*) Rprt Serv.
Their Child see Collected Works of Robert Herrick
Their Day in the Sun: Women of the 1932 Olympics. Doris H. Pieroth. (Samuel & Althea Stroum Bks.). (Illus.). 208p. 1996. pap. 16.95 (*0-295-97554-7*); text ed. 30.00 (*0-295-97553-9*) U of Wash Pr.
Their Earthshaking News: When Science & Theology Speak the Same Urgent Language. Helen T. Otto. 437p. 1996. pap. 18.00 (*0-9639553-4-9*) Verenikia Pr.
Their Eyes Were Watching God. Zora Neale Hurston. 286p. 1990. pap. 13.00 (*0-06-091650-8*, PL) HarpC.
Their Eyes Were Watching God. Zora Neale Hurston. (Illus.). 288p. 1991. 24.95 (*0-252-01778-1*) U of Ill Pr.
Their Eyes Were Watching God. Zora Neale Hurston. 1995. pap. write for info. (*0-06-502316-1*) Addson-Wesley Educ.
Their Eyes Were Watching God. large type ed. Zora Neale Hurston. LC 96-22001. 289p. 1996. lib. bdg. 24.95 (*0-7838-1884-X*, GK Hall) Thorndike Pr.
Their Eyes Were Watching God. Zora Neale Hurston. 1995. reprint ed. lib. bdg. 24.95 (*1-56849-625-7*) Buccaneer Bks.
Their Eyes Were Watching God: A Novel. Zora Neale Hurston. 286p. (C). 1990. reprint ed. lib. bdg. 35.00 (*0-8095-9019-0*) Borgo Pr.
Their Eyes Were Watching God: Notes. Mary Ella Randall. (Illus.). 86p. 1995. pap. text ed. 4.25 (*0-8220-1275-8*) Cliffs.
Their Faces Toward Zion. Richard N. Holzapfel. 1996. 34.95 (*1-57008-266-9*) Bookcraft Inc.
Their Fathers' Daughters: Hannah More, Maria Edgeworth, & Patriarchal Complicity. Elizabeth Kowaleski-Wallace. 256p. 1991. 45.00 (*0-19-506853-X*) OUP.

Their Fathers' God. Ole E. Rolvaag. LC 82-17636. x, 338p. 1983. reprint ed. pap. 12.00 (0-8032-8911-1, Bison Books) U of Nebr Pr.

Their Fathers' Voice: Vassily Aksyonov, Venedikt Erofeev, Eduard Limonov, & Sasha Sokolov. Cynthia Simmons. LC 93-623. (Middlebury Studies in Russian Language & Literature: Vol. 4). 218p. 1993. 52.95 (0-8204-2160-X) P Lang Pubng.

Their Fight Continued: America & American POW's. Craig Howes. LC 92-41091. 304p. 1993. pap. 19.95 (0-19-508680-5) OUP.

Their Finest Hour. Winston S. Churchill. 1986. pap. 14.95 (0-395-41056-8) HM.

Their Finest Hour: The Battle of Britain Remembered. Richard Collier & Philip Kaplan. (Illus.). 224p. 1989. 29.98 (1-55859-047-1) Abbeville Pr.

Their Finest Hour: The War in the First Person. Ed. by Allan A. Michie & Walter Graebner. LC 41-2009. 213p. reprint ed. pap. 60.80 (0-317-28769-9, 2051682) Bks Demand.

Their Finest Hour: Thrilling Moments in Ancient History. Herbert Lockyer. 160p. (gr. 10). 1996. pap. 9.99 (0-8007-5589-8) Revell.

Their Finest Hour see Second World War

Their First Noel. Leigh Greenwood et al. 400p. (Orig.). 1995. mass mkt., pap. text ed. 5.99 (0-8439-3865-X) Dorchester Pub Co.

Their Future Is Now: Today Is for Children. Ed. by Laura L. Dittmann & Marjorie E. Ramsey. LC 82-22716. (Illus.). 48p. 1982. pap. 6.25 (0-87173-102-9) ACEI.

Their Highest Potential: An African American School Community in the Segregated South. Vanessa S. Walker. LC 95-39504. (Illus.). 272p. (C). 1996. lib. bdg. 34.95 (0-8078-2276-0) U of NC Pr.

Their Highest Potential: An African American School Community in the Segregated South. Vanessa S. Walker. LC 95-39504. (Illus.). 272p. (C). 1996. pap. 14.95 (0-8078-4581-7) U of NC Pr.

Their Hollow Inheritance: A Comprehensive Refutation of the New Testament & Its Missionaries. Michoel Drazin. 210p. 1992. 18.00 (965-229-070-X, Pub. by Gefen Pub Hse IS) Gefen Bks.

Their Honor Was Loyalty: Knight's Cross Holders of the Waffen-SS. Jost W. Schneider. (Illus.). 520p. 1993. 44.95 (0-912138-51-3) Bender Pub CA.

Their Infinite Variety: Essays on Indiana Politicians. 488p. 1981. pap. 19.95 (1-885323-31-X) IN Hist Bureau.

Their Island of Dreams. large type ed. Ravey Sillars. (Linford Romance Library). 288p. 1994. pap. 15.99 (0-7089-7548-8, Linford) Ulverscroft.

Their Kind of Town. Richard Whittingham. 1996. mass mkt. 5.99 (0-380-72502-9) Avon.

***Their Last Ride Together.** Marion Morrison. 1998. pap. text ed. 9.95 (1-883283-14-0) Brick Tower.

Their Light Still Shines: Inspiring Stories of Faith & Courage. Lewann Sotnak. LC 93-36828. 136p. 1994. pap. 10.99 (0-8066-2605-4) Augsburg Fortress.

Their Lives & Numbers: The Condition of Working People in Massachusetts, 1870-1900. Ed. by Henry F. Bedford. LC 94-23402. (Documents in American Social History Ser.). (Illus.). 264p. 1995. 37.50 (0-8014-3032-1) Cornell U Pr.

Their Lives & Numbers: The Condition of Working People in Massachusetts, 1870-1900. Ed. by Henry F. Bedford. LC 94-23402. (Documents in American Social History Ser.). (Illus.). 264p. 1995. pap. 15.95 (0-8014-8258-5) Cornell U Pr.

Their Majesties' Servants: Or Annals of the English Stage, 3 Vols. John Doran. Ed. by R. W. Lowe. LC 68-58985. reprint ed. Set. 185.00 (0-404-02170-0) AMS Pr.

Their Misty Years: Childhood Entanglement - The Magic Raindrop - Sammy Crow Saves the Day - Smoky's Friend "The Thief" Pearline W. Mitchell. Tr. by Rebecca Brinson. (Illus.). 32p. (J). 1994. text ed. 12.50 (0-930329-85-6) Kabel Pubs.

Their Morals & Ours. Leon Trotsky et al. LC 73-82168. 116p. 1973. reprint ed. pap. 14.95 (0-87348-319-7); reprint ed. lib. bdg. 35.00 (0-87348-318-9) Pathfinder NY.

Their Music Is Mary. Ed. by Clifford J. Laube. 1961. 3.50 (0-910984-11-5) Montfort Pubns.

Their Mysterious Patient. large type ed. Petra Sawley. (Linford Romance Library). 224p. 1993. pap. 15.99 (0-7089-7339-6, Linford) Ulverscroft.

Their Name Is Pius. Lillian Olf. LC 74-107729. (Essay Index Reprint Ser.). 1977. 30.95 (0-8369-1768-5) Ayer.

Their Number Become Thinned: Native American Population Dynamics in Eastern North America. Henry F. Dobyns. LC 83-5952. (Native American Historic Demography Ser.). 396p. 1983. text ed. 40.00 (0-87049-400-7); pap. text ed. 19.00 (0-87049-401-5) U of Tenn Pr.

***Their Only Child.** Cassidy. 1997. mass mkt. 3.75 (0-373-22447-8) Harlequin Bks.

Their Own Worst Enemies: Women As Writers of Popular Fiction. Daphne Watson. 192p. (C). 59.95 (0-7453-0655-1, Pub. by Pluto Pr UK) LPC InBook.

Their Pavel. Marie Von Ebner-Eschenbach. Tr. by Lynne Tatlock. LC 96-82. (Studies in German Literature, Linguistics & Culture). 151p. 1996. 55.95 (1-57113-078-0) Camden Hse.

***Their Pavel.** Marie Von Ebner-Eschenbach. (GERM Ser.). 1996. 55.95 (1-57113-019-5) Camden Hse.

Their Place on the Stage: Black Women Playwrights in America. Elizabeth Brown-Guillory. LC 88-10237. (Contributions in Afro-American & African Studies: No. 117). 177p. 1988. text ed. 55.00 (0-313-25985-2, BGY/, Greenwood Pr) Greenwood.

Their Place on the Stage: Black Women Playwrights in America. Elizabeth Brown-Guillory. LC 89-26672. 184p. 1990. pap. text ed. 12.95 (0-275-93566-3, B3566, Praeger Pubs) Greenwood.

Their Promised Land: Arab & Jew in History's Cauldron - One Valley in the Jerusalem Hills. Marcia Kunstel & Joseph Albright. 1990. 19.95 (0-517-57231-1, Crown) Crown Pub Group.

Their Religion. Arthur J. Russell. LC 78-128308. (Essay Index Reprint Ser.). 1977. 23.95 (0-8369-2131-3) Ayer.

Their Revolution or Ours. Helen Bugbee. 140p. 1990. pap. 8.95 (0-89697-263-1) Intl Univ Pr.

Their Ruling Passions. Percy Colson. LC 70-136645. (Biography Index Reprint Ser.). 1977. 23.95 (0-8369-8040-9) Ayer.

Their Shadows Before: A Story of the Southampton Insurrection. Pauline C. Bouve. LC 72-39078. (Black Heritage Library Collection). 1977. reprint ed. 25.95 (0-8369-9016-1) Ayer.

Their Silence a Language. Jeremy T. Hooker & Lee Grandjean. (Illus.). 79p. 9400. pap. 21.00 (1-870612-23-X, Pub. by Enitha Pr UK) Dufour.

Their Silver Wedding Journey. William Dean Howells. (Notable American Authors Ser.). 1992. reprint ed. lib. bdg. 75.00 (0-7812-3253-8) Rprt Serv.

Their Sisters' Keepers: Prostitution in New York City, 1830-1870. Marilyn W. Hill. (Illus.). 370p. 1994. 35.00 (0-520-07834-9) U CA Pr.

Their Sister's Keepers: Women's Prison Reform in America, 1830-1930. Estelle B. Freedman. LC 80-24918. (Women & Culture Ser.). 272p. 1981. pap. 17.95 (0-472-08052-0) U of Mich Pr.

Their Solitary Way: The Puritan Social Ethic in the First Century of Settlement in New England. Stephen Foster. LC 76-151573. (Yale Historical Publications: Miscellany: No. 94). 238p. reprint ed. pap. 67.90 (0-317-29587-X, 2021997) Bks Demand.

Their Stories, Our Stories: Women of the Bible, Vol. 1. Rose S. Kam. 284p. 1995. pap. text ed. 18.95 (0-8264-0804-4) Continuum.

Their Story: Twentieth Century Pentecostals. Fred J. Foster. LC 86-26718. (Illus.). 192p. 1983. pap. 7.99 (0-912315-05-9) Word Aflame.

Their Tattered Flags: The Epic of the Confederacy. Frank E. Vandiver. LC 87-6520. (Military History Ser.: No. 5). (Illus.). 376p. (Orig.). 1994. reprint ed. pap. 16.95 (0-89096-355-X) Tex A&M Univ Pr.

Their There They're Easy Guide to Better Spelling. Teri Gordon. LC 90-93115. 129p. (Orig.). 1990. pap. 5.95 (0-9619870-3-0) T Gordon Pub.

Their Trotsky & Ours: Communist Continuity Today. Jack Barnes. 156p. 1983. reprint ed. pap. 8.00 (0-87348-636-6) Pathfinder NY.

Their Wedding Day. Emma Darcy. 1996. mass mkt. 3.50 (0-373-11848-1, 1-11848-8) Harlequin Bks.

***Their Wedding Day.** Emma Darcy. (Harlequin Ser.). 1997. 20.95 (0-263-14992-7, Pub. by Mills & Boon UK) Thorndike Pr.

Their Wedding Journey. William Dean Howells. 240p. 1976. reprint ed. lib. bdg. 21.95 (0-89190-457-3, Queens House) Amereon Ltd.

Their Wedding Journey. William Dean Howells. (Notable American Authors Ser.). 1992. reprint ed. lib. bdg. 75.00 (0-685-54682-9) Rprt Serv.

Their Words, My Thoughts. (Illus.). 158p. 1981. Student's ed. student ed., pap. text ed. 10.95 (0-19-917034-7) OUP.

Their World, Our World: Reflections on Childhood. Kaoru Yamamoto. LC 92-42868. 190p. 1993. text ed. 49.95 (0-275-94343-7, C4343, Praeger Pubs) Greenwood.

Their Yesterdays. Harold B. Wright. 1975. lib. bdg. 17.85 (0-89966-207-2) Buccaneer Bks.

Theirs be the Power: The Moguls of Eastern Kentucky. Harry M. Caudill. LC 83-5771. 224p. reprint ed. pap. 63.90 (0-7837-5734-4, 2045395) Bks Demand.

Theirs Is the Kingdom. Mairin Healy. (Short Play Ser.). 1969. pap. 0.50 (0-912262-17-6) Proscenium.

Theirs Is the Kingdom. Robert D. Lupton. 1989. write for info. (0-318-65615-9) Harper SF.

Theirs Is the Kingdom. Robert D. Lupton. LC 89-45252. 1989. pap. 11.00 (0-06-065307-8, PL) HarpC.

Theirs Was the Kingdom: Lila & DeWitt Wallace & the Story of the Reader's Digest. John Heidenry. 704p. 1994. pap. 10.95 (0-393-31227-5) Norton.

Theis Made Easy, New Methods & a Computer Program in Well Hydraulics. Michael Kasenow. 1994. pap. 85.00 (0-918334-85-3) WRP.

Theism. Clement Dore. (Philosophical Studies: 30). 212p. 1984. lib. bdg. 97.00 (90-277-1683-8) Kluwer Ac.

Theism. John Stuart Mill. Ed. by Richard Taylor. 1957. pap. 2.25 (0-672-60238-5, Bobbs) Macmillan.

Theism: The Implication of Experience. William W. Fenn. 1969. 10.00 (0-87233-005-2) Bauhan.

Theism & Cosmology. John Laird. LC 74-84317. (Essay Index Reprint Ser.). 1977. 23.95 (0-8369-1147-4) Ayer.

Theism & Thought: A Study in Familiar Beliefs. Arthur J. Balfour. LC 77-27208. (Gifford Lectures: 1922-23). reprint ed. 45.00 (0-404-60469-2) AMS Pr.

Theism, Atheism, & Big Bang Cosmology. William L. Craig & Quentin Smith. (Illus.). 352p. 1995. pap. 19.95 (0-19-826383-X) OUP.

Theism, Atheism & the Doctrine of the Trinity: Trinitarian Theologies of Karl Barth & Jurgen Moltmann in Response to Protest Atheism. W. Waite Willis, Jr. LC 86-6640. (American Academy of Religion Academy Ser.). 200p. 1987. pap. 15.95 (1-55540-021-3) Scholars Pr GA.

Theism... Comprising the Deems Lectures for 1902. Borden P. Bowne. LC 75-3075. (Philosophy in America Ser.). reprint ed. 37.50 (0-404-59076-4) AMS Pr.

Theism in an Age of Science. Phillip H. Wiebe. 188p. (Orig.). (C). 1988. pap. text ed. 20.00 (0-8191-6820-3) U Pr of Amer.

Theism in Medieval India. J. Estlin Carpenter. 564p. reprint ed. text ed. 37.50 (0-685-13399-0) Coronet Bks.

Theism in Medieval India. Joseph E. Carpenter. LC 77-27152. (Hibbert Lectures: 1919). reprint ed. 62.50 (0-404-60419-6) AMS Pr.

Theism in the Discourse of Jonathan Edwards. R. C. De Prospo. LC 84-40406. 296p. 1986. 42.50 (0-87413-281-9) U Delaware Pr.

Theism of Edgar Sheffied Brightman. James J. McLarney. LC 75-3089. reprint ed. 29.50 (0-404-59087-X) AMS Pr.

Theist & Atheist: A Typology of Non-Belief. Thomas Molnar. 1979. text ed. 60.80 (90-279-7788-7) Mouton.

Thelephoraceae of North America, 15 Pts. Edward A. Burt. (Illus.). 900p. 1966. reprint ed. lib. bdg. 50.00 (0-945345-04-6) Lubrecht & Cramer.

Thelma & Louise - Something to Talk About: Screenplays. Callie Khouri. 288p. 1996. pap. 12.00 (0-8021-3462-9, Grove) Grove-Atltic.

Thelma D. Sullivan's Compendium of Nahuatl Grammar. Thelma D. Sullivan. Ed. by Wick R. Miller & Karen Dakin. Tr. by Neville Stiles from SPA. LC 88-17082. 352p. 1988. 25.00 (0-87480-282-2) U of Utah Pr.

***Thelma's Country Clatter.** Thelma Gibson. 192p. 1996. pap. 9.95 (0-87012-569-9) McClain.

***Thelma's Treasures.** Susanna Thomas. 1997. pap. 9.95 (1-56352-373-6) Longstreet Pr Inc.

Thelma's Treasures: The Secret Recipes of "The Best Cook in Harrodsburg" Susanna Thomas. (Illus.). 112p. 1992. write for info. (0-9638478-8-0) Little Barter.

***Thelonious Monk: His Life & Music.** Thomas Fitterling. Tr. by Robert Dobbin. (Illus.). 240p. (Orig.). (GER.). 1997. pap. 15.95 (0-9653774-1-5) Berkeley Hills.

Thelonious Monk: Originals & Standards. Ed. by Charley Gerard. 109p. (Orig.). 1991. pap. 15.00 (0-9628467-0-8) Gerard Sarzin Pub.

Them. William W. Johnstone. 352p. 1992. mass mkt. 4.50 (0-8217-3992-1, Zebra Kensgtn) Kensgtn Pub Corp.

Them. Joyce Carol Oates. 480p. 1984. mass mkt. 6.99 (0-449-20692-0, Crest) Fawcett.

THEM. Marjorie Spiegel. (Illus.). write for info. (0-9624493-2-6) Mirror Bks.

Them - More Labor Cartoons. Gary Huck & Mike Konopacki. 112p. (Orig.). 1991. pap. 12.00 (0-88286-204-9) C H Kerr.

***Them & Us.** Afterword by Mark McColloch & Peter Gilmore. 1995. pap. 6.00 (0-916180-20-4) United Elec R&M.

Them Children: A Study in Language Learning. George D. Spindler. (Case Studies in Education & Culture). 112p. 1982. reprint ed. pap. text ed. 6.95 (0-8290-0323-1) Irvington.

Them Children: A Study in Language Learning. Martha C. Ward. (Illus.). 99p. (C). 1986. reprint ed. pap. text ed. 8.95 (0-88133-213-5) Waveland Pr.

Them Cow Pokes. 64p. 1962. 5.95 (0-917207-03-3) Cowpoke.

Them Damned Pictures: Explorations in American Political Cartoon Art. Roger A. Fischer. LC 95-8892. (Illus.). xiv, 253p. (C). 1996. lib. bdg. 37.50 (0-208-02298-8, Archon Bks) Shoe String.

Them Dark Days: Slavery in the American Rice Swamps. William Dusinberre. 512p. 1996. 55.00 (0-19-509021-7) OUP.

Them Gospel Songs: Love of the Black Church Experience. Big Mama. (Illus.). 101p. (Orig.). 1990. pap. text ed. 8.95 (0-9620373-1-1) Cultral Alliance Foundation.

***Them Gospel Songs: Love of the Black Church Experience.** Big Mama. LC 90-63230. (Illus.). 70p. 1990. pap. 8.95 (0-88100-071-X) Cultral Alliance Foundation.

Them or Us: Archetypal Interpretations of Fifties Alien Invasion Films. Patrick Lucanio. LC 86-43049. (Illus.). 206p. 1988. 29.95 (0-253-35871-X) Ind U Pr.

Them Ornery Mitchum Boys: The Adventures of Robert & John Mitchum. John Mitchum. Ed. by John Stanley. LC 88-92904. (Illus.). 400p. (Orig.). 1989. pap. 11.95 (0-940064-06-5) Creatures at Large.

Them Was the Days: An American Saga of the 70's. Martha F. McKeown. 298p. reprint ed. pap. 85.00 (0-7837-1641-9, 2041935) Bks Demand.

Thematic Activities for Student Portfolios. Kathy Balsamo. (Illus.). 112p. 1994. 12.95 (1-880505-11-8, CLC0169) Pieces of Lrning.

Thematic Analysis of Francois Mauriac's "Genitrix, le Desert De L'amour, & le Noeud De Viperes" Ruth B. Paine. LC 76-8024. (Romance Monographs: No. 20). 1976. 26.00 (84-399-4950-2) Romance.

Thematic Analysis of Mme. D'Aulnoy's "Contes De Fees" Jane T. Mitchell. LC 78-6947. (Romance Monographs: No. 30). 1978. 24.00 (84-399-8448-0) Romance.

Thematic & Alphabetic Dictionary of Agriculture. 5th ed. G. Haensch & G. Haberkamp De Anton. 1264p. (ENG, FRE, GER, ITA & SPA.). 1987. 395.00 (0-8288-9444-2) Fr & Eur.

Thematic Apperception Test. Henry A. Murray. LC 43-3797. 20p. 1943. Manual with cards. student ed. 25.00 (0-674-87720-9); pap. 3.95 (0-674-87721-7) HUP.

Thematic Apperception Test, the Children's Apperception Test, & the Senior Apperception Technique in Clinical Use. 6th rev. ed. Leopold Bellak & David M. Abrams. 512p. 1996. 66.95 (0-205-18999-7) Allyn.

Thematic Atlases for Public, Academic, and High School Libraries. Diane K. Podell. LC 94-4326. 208p. 1994. 27.50 (0-8108-2866-9) Scarecrow.

Thematic Bibliography. Cheryl Buhler et al. (Illus.). 176p. 1993. student ed. 14.95 (1-55734-373-X) Tchr Create Mat.

Thematic Book Reports for Holidays: Literature Lists & Ready-to-Use Book Reports. Linda Milliken. (Illus.). 64p. 1994. student ed., pap. 6.95 (1-56472-021-7) Edupress.

Thematic Book Reports for Math: Literature Lists & Ready-to-Use Book Reports. Linda Milliken. (Illus.). 64p. 1994. student ed., pap. 6.95 (1-56472-022-5) Edupress.

Thematic Book Reports for Science: Literature Lists & Ready-to-Use Book Reports. Nancy Shaw. (Illus.). 64p. 1994. student ed., pap. 6.95 (1-56472-023-3) Edupress.

Thematic Book Reports for Social Studies: Literature Lists & Ready-to-Use Book Reports. Terry Link. (Illus.). 64p. 1995. student ed., pap. 6.95 (1-56472-024-1) Edupress.

Thematic Cartography & Remote Sensing. Ed. by Prithvish Nag. (C). 1992. 38.00 (81-7022-410-1, Pub. by Concept II) S Asia.

Thematic Catalogue. Ed. by Ernest Warburton. (Johann Christian Bach Ser.: Vol. 48). 400p. 1997. text ed. 161.00 (0-8240-6097-0) Garland.

Thematic Catalogue of the Works of Giovanni Battista Sammartini. Ed. by Newell Jenkins & Bathia Churgin. 291p. 1976. 40.00 (0-674-87735-7) HUP.

Thematic Catalogue of Troubadour & Trouvere Melody. Donna Mayer-Martin. (Thematic Catalogues Ser.: No. 18). (Illus.). 1997. lib. bdg. 76.00 (0-918728-82-7) Pendragon NY.

Thematic Catalogues in Music: An Annotated Bibliography. 2nd ed. Barry S. Brook & Richard J. Viano. LC 97-2411. (Rilm Retro Ser.: No. 5). 602p. 1997. 68.00 (0-918728-86-X) Pendragon NY.

Thematic Concordance of Julien Green's Journal. Kathryn E. Wildgen. LC 94-66520. 236p. 1995. lib. bdg. 35.95 (1-883479-03-7) Summa Pubns.

Thematic Development in Chilean Theatre since 1973: In Search of the Dramatic Conflict. Catherine M. Boyle. 1992. 39.50 (0-8386-3363-3) Fairleigh Dickinson.

Thematic Development in English Texts. Ed. by Mohsen Ghadessy. LC 95-9963. (Open Linguistics Ser.). 1995. 79.95 (1-85567-333-9) St Martin.

Thematic Dictionary of Literary Terms: Diccionario Tematico des Terminos Literarios. L. Madariaga. 572p. (SPA.). 1980. 29.95 (0-8288-1578-X, S39853) Fr & Eur.

Thematic Dictionary of Modern Persian. Colin Turner. 550p. 1996. 98.00 (0-7007-0458-2, Pub. by Curzon Pr UK) Paul & Co Pubs.

Thematic Dictionary of Synonyms & Antonyms: Diccionario Tematico de Sinonimos y Antonimos. 3rd ed. Everest Staff. 638p. (SPA.). 1983. 19.95 (0-8288-2019-8, S8987) Fr & Eur.

Thematic Encyclopedia of Psychology: Enciclopedia Tematica de Psicologia, 2 vols. Leonardo Ancona. 1892p. 1985. 150.00 (0-8288-2213-1, S35828) Fr & Eur.

Thematic French-Argot Dictionary: Dictionnaire Thematique Francais-Argot. H. Leveque. (FRE.). 1991. 49.95 (0-8288-3914-X, F83770) Fr & Eur.

Thematic Guide to Documents on the Human Rights of Women: Global & Regional Standards Adopted by Intergovernmental Organizations, International Non-Governmental Organizations & Professional Associations. Ed. by Gudmundur Alfredsson & Katarina Tomasevski. (Raoul Wallenberg Institute Human Rights Guides Ser.: Vol. 1). 448p. (C). 1995. lib. bdg. 182.50 (90-411-0094-6, Pub. by M Nijhoff NE) Kluwer Ac.

Thematic Index of the Works of Francois Couperin. Maurice Cauchie. LC 74-24057. reprint ed. 37.50 (0-404-12879-3) AMS Pr.

Thematic Journal: A Diary for Self-Observation & Self-Revelation. Alan K. White. 100p. (Orig.). 1984. pap. 7.00 (0-914865-00-5) Mstque Pubns.

Thematic Learning Adventures for Young Children: Weekly Integrated Curriculum Units for the Whole Year. Debbie Duguran & Margot Hopkins. Ed. by Jan Keeling & Leslie Britt. (Illus.). 192p. (Orig.). 1994. pap. text ed. 14.95 (0-86530-283-9) Incentive Pubns.

Thematic Literature Units on U. S. Wars. Phyllis K. Kennemer. 150p. 1991. pap. text ed. 24.95 (0-87436-604-6) ABC-CLIO.

Thematic Locator for the Works of Jean-Baptiste Lully. Bruce Gustafson & Matthew Leshinskie. iii, 56p. (Orig.). 1989. pap. 20.00 (0-943930-52-9) Performers Edit.

Thematic Mapping from Satellite Imagery: A Guidebook. J. Denegre. LC 94-19073. (International Catalog of Sources for History of Physics & Allied Sciences Ser.). 200p. (ENG & FRE.). 1994. 118.75 (0-08-042351-5, Pergamon Pr) Elsevier.

Thematic Mapping from Satellite Imagery: An International Report. Ed. by J. Denegre. 214p. 1988. 115.50 (1-85166-217-0) Elsevier.

Thematic Maps. D. Cuff. (C). pap. text ed. 14.91 (0-7870-0000-0) Digital Print.

Thematic Maps. David J. Cuff & Mark T. Mattson. (Illus.). 176p. 1983. 15.95 (0-415-90158-8, NO. 2893, Routledge NY); teacher ed. 4.95 (0-416-34320-1, NO. 3731, Routledge NY) Routledge.

Thematic Methods & Strategies in Learning Disabilities: A Textbook for Practitioners. M. E. Lewis. LC 92-42082. (Illus.). 210p. (Orig.). (C). 1993. pap. text ed. 29.95 (1-879105-95-0, 0353) Singular Publishing.

Thematic Origins of Scientific Thought: Kepler to Einstein. rev. ed. Gerald J. Holton. LC 87-34163. 504p. 1988. reprint ed. pap. text ed. 16.95 (0-674-87748-9) HUP.

Thematic Patterns in Sonatas of Beethoven. Rudolph Reti. (Music Reprint Ser.). 1992. 27.50 (0-306-79714-3) Da Capo.

Thematic Poems, Songs, & Fingerplays: Forty-Five Irresistible Rhymes & Activities to... Meish Goldish. 96p. (J). 1994. pap. 12.95 (0-590-49638-7) Scholastic Inc.

An Asterisk (*) at the beginning of an entry indicates that the title is appearing in BIP for the first time.

Thematic Process in Music. Rudolph R. Reti. LC 77-13622. 362p. 1978. reprint ed. text ed. 69.75 (0-8371-9875-5, RETH, Greenwood Pr) Greenwood.

*Thematic Reader. Axelrod. 1997. pap. text ed. 10.00 (0-312-15717-7) St Martin.

Thematic Relations & Relational Grammar. Patrick Farrell. LC 93-41177. (Outstanding Dissertations in Linguistics Ser.). 304p. 1994. text ed. 20.00 (0-8153-1686-0) Garland.

Thematic Relations & Transitivity in English, Japanese, & Korean. Nam-Sung Song. LC 93-29693. (Center for Korean Studies Monograph: No. 17). 1994. pap. text ed. 15.00 (0-8248-1580-7) UH Pr.

*Thematic Roles in Production. Anne Whitworth. (Illus.). 1996. 195.00 (1-56593-789-9, 1540) Singular Publishing.

Thematic Sophocles. Richard Minadeo. viii, 200p. 1994. pap. 60.00 (90-256-1056-0, Pub. by A M Hakkert NE) Benjamins North Am.

Thematic Structure in Syntax. Edwin B. Williams. (Linguistic Inquiry Monographs: No. 23). (Illus.). 196p. 1994. 35.95 (0-262-23173-5); pap. 21.00 (0-262-73106-1) MIT Pr.

Thematic Studies in Phenomenology & Pragmatism. Patrick L. Bourgeois & Sandra B. Rosenthal. viii, 147p. (Orig.). 1983. pap. 22.00 (90-6032-238-X) Benjamins North Am.

Thematic Teaching. Linda Holliman & Jo E. Moore. (Teaching Strategies Ser.). (Illus.). 86p. (J). (gr. k-6). 1994. teacher ed., pap. 14.95 (1-55799-197-9, EMC 996) Evan-Moor Corp.

Thematic Units: An Interactive Approach Teaching Science & Social Studies. Anthony D. Fredericks et al. (C). 1993. text ed. 36.50 (0-06-500892-8) Addson-Wesley Educ.

Thematic Units for Kinder-Garten. Kristen Schlosser. 1994. pap. text ed. 12.95 (0-590-49579-8) Scholastic Inc.

Thematics: New Approaches. Ed. by Claude Bremond et al. LC 94-72. (SUNY Series, The Margins of Literature). 229p. 1994. text ed. 49.50 (0-7914-2167-8); pap. text ed. 16.95 (0-7914-2168-6) State U NY Pr.

*Thematics of Commitment: The Tower & the Plain. Peter M. Cryle. LC 84-42590. 470p. 1985. reprint ed. pap. 134.00 (0-608-02890-8, 2063954) Bks Demand.

Thematischer Grund- und Aufbauwortschatz Deutsch. G. Forst & M. Crellin. 450p. (GER.). (C). 1995. pap. text ed. 22.50 (3-12-675260-8, Pub. by Klett Edition GW) Intl Bk Import.

Themba. Margaret Sacks. (Illus.). 48p. (J). (gr. 2-6). 1994. pap. 3.99 (0-14-036445-5) Puffin Bks.

Theme-A-Saurus: The Great Big Book of Mini Teaching Topics. Jean Warren. Ed. by Gayle Bittinger. LC 88-51450. (Theme-A-Saurus Ser.). (Illus.). 280p. (Orig.). (J). (ps-1). 1989. pap. 21.95 (0-911019-20-0, WPH 1001) Warren Pub Hse.

Theme-A-Saurus II: The Great Big Book of More Teaching Units. Jean Warren. Ed. by Gayle Bittinger. LC 89-51179. (Theme-A-Saurus Ser.). (Illus.). 280p. (Orig.). (J). (ps-1). 1990. pap. 21.95 (0-911019-26-X, WPH 1002) Warren Pub Hse.

Theme Adventures. Veronica Terrill. (Illus.). 128p. 1992. 10.99 (0-86653-662-0, GA1394) Good Apple.

*Theme & Amusement Parks. 1997. pap. text ed. 39.95 (0-8230-5350-4) Watsn-Guptill.

*Theme & Amusement Parks. Date not set. 42.50 (0-688-15417-4) Morrow.

Theme & Context in Biblical Lists, Vol. 119. Benjamin E. Scolnic. LC 95-34240. (South Florida Studies in the History of Judaism Ser.). 185p. 1995. 74.95 (0-7885-0145-3, 24 01 19) Scholars Pr GA.

Theme & Entertainment Parks: Planning, Design, Development & Management. Stephen J. Rebori. (CPL Bibliographies Ser.: No. 319). 97p. 1995. 10.00 (0-86602-319-4, Sage Prdcls Pr) Sage.

Theme & Improvisation: Kadinsky & the American Avant-Garde 1912-1950. Dayton Art Institute Staff et al. (Illus.). 272p. 1992. pap. 35.00 (0-8212-1927-8) Bulfinch Pr.

Theme & Strategy. Ronald R. Tobias. (Elements of Fiction Writing Ser.). 176p. 1990. 14.99 (0-89879-392-0, Wrtrs Digest Bks) F & W Pubns Inc.

Theme & Style in African Poetry. Isaac I. Elimimian. LC 91-28877. 272p. 1991. lib. bdg. 89.95 (0-7734-9675-0) E Mellen.

Theme & Variation. Ray Cook. 59p. (Orig.). (C). 1981. pap. text ed. 15.00 (0-9602002-3-1) Ray Cook.

Theme & Variation in the Short Story. Ed. by John D. Ferguson et al. LC 74-37541. (Short Story Index Reprint Ser.). 1972. reprint ed. 27.95 (0-8369-4100-4) Ayer.

Theme & Variations. Samuil Alyoshin. Tr. by Michael Glenny from RUS. 1979. pap. 5.00 (0-87129-128-2, T83) Dramatic Pub.

Theme & Variations on Happy Birthday. Louise Kupelian. 11p. 1995. pap. 3.95 (0-87487-910-8) Summy-Birchard.

Theme Artistry. rev. ed. Eugene A. Furst. (Artistry Series of Chess Encyclopedias: Vol. 1). (Illus.). 320p. 1991. pap. 19.95 (1-879394-01-4, 1-979-448) Caissas Pr.

Theme Centers for Dramatic Play. Judie Bertolino et al. (Illus.). 304p. 1996. wbk. ed., pap. 24.95 (1-56472-106-X) Edupress.

Theme Day Play for Younger Years. Joyce Hamman. Ed. by Linda Milliken. (Illus.). 128p. 1993. pap. 11.95 (1-56472-015-2) Edupress.

*Theme Day Treats. Shirley Stevens. 200p. 1993. pap. 15.95 (1-877871-47-8, 5409) Ed Ministries.

Theme du Regard dans l'Oeuvre d'Andre Langevin, Ecrivain Quebecois: La Fleche dans l'Oeil de Narcisse. Karin M. Egloff. LC 94-39576. 124p. (FRE.). 1995. text ed. 59.95 (0-7734-2916-6) E Mellen.

Theme et Variations: An Introduction to French Language & Culture. 4th ed. Ed. by Peter M. Hagiwara & Francoise De Rocher. Incl. . 4th ed. LC 88-27815. (FRE.). 551p. 1989. pap. text ed. 41.00 (0-471-63133-7); . 1989. (0-471-63131-0); . 1989. 43.50 (0-471-60853-X); . 4th ed. 1989. 25.00 (0-471-51376-8); . 1989. disk (0-318-63973-4); . 1989. (0-471-60854-8); . 1989. (0-318-63974-2); . 4th ed. 1989. audio 0.01 (0-471-51663-5); . 104p. 1989. 10.00 (0-471-60855-6); 551p. 1989. write for info. (0-318-63972-6) Wiley.

Theme Exploration: A Voyage of Discovery. Connie Weaver et al. LC 93-13263. 230p. 1993. pap. text ed. 19.50 (0-435-08780-0, 08780) Heinemann.

*Theme for a Day. Julia Jasmine et al. (J). (gr. 1-2). 1995. pap. text ed. 14.95 (1-55734-507-4) Tchr Create Mat.

Theme for a Day. Lisa Rogulic-Newsome. 128p. (J). (gr. 1-6). 1990. 10.99 (0-86653-545-4, GA1154) Good Apple.

Theme for Diverse Instruments. Jane Rule. 208p. 1990. pap. 8.95 (0-941483-63-0) Naiad Pr.

*Theme for Diverse Instruments. Jane Rule. 192p. pap. 12.95 (0-88922-060-3) LPC InBook.

Theme from Dead Poets Society: For Harp. M. Jarre. 1981. pap. 4.95 (0-7935-0696-4, 00720200) H Leonard.

Theme from Star Trek Generations. Den McCarthy. 4p. 1995. 3.95 (0-7935-4313-4, 00294011) H Leonard.

Theme Gardens. Barbara Damrosch. LC 82-60062. (Illus.). 224p. 1982. pap. 18.95 (0-89480-217-8, 487) Workman Pub.

Theme Immersion: Inquiry-Based Curriculum in Elementary & Middle Schools. Gary L. Manning et al. LC 93-43027. (Illus.). 192p. (YA). 1994. pap. text ed. 23.50 (0-435-08806-8, 08806) Heinemann.

*Theme Immersion Compendium for Social Studies Teaching. Maryann M. Manning et al. LC 97-22906. 1997. write for info. (0-435-07238-2); write for info. (0-435-08884-X) Heinemann.

Theme in English Expository Discourse. 2nd rev. ed. Linda K. Jones. LC 78-100090. (Edward Sapir Monograph Ser. in Language, Culture & Cognition: No. 2). xiv, 241p. (C). 1980. pap. 32.00 (0-933104-10-3) Jupiter Pr.

Theme in Oral Epic & in Beowulf. Francelia M. Clark. LC 94-43067. (Milman Parry Studies in Oral Tradition). 1995. 649.00 (0-8153-1235-0) Garland.

Theme in Oral Epic & in Beowulf. rev. ed. Francelia M. Clark. LC 94-43067. (Milman Parry Studies in Oral Tradition). 288p. 1995. text ed. 75.00 (0-8153-1874-X) Garland.

Theme in Search of a Movie. Date not set. 40.00 (0-7935-4834-9, 00000800) H Leonard.

Theme Is Freedom. John R. Dos Passos. LC 71-99632. (Essay Index Reprint Ser.). 1977. 24.95 (0-8369-1460-0) Ayer.

Theme Is Freedom: Religion, Politics, & the American Tradition. M. Stanton Evans. LC 94-528. 1994. 24.95 (0-89526-497-8) Regnery Pub.

Theme Is Freedom: Religion, Politics, & the American Tradition. M. Stanton Evans. LC 94-528. 366p. 1996. pap. 14.95 (0-89526-718-7) Regnery Pub.

Theme of Acquisitiveness in Bentham's Political Thought. Allison Dube. LC 91-11375. (Political Theory & Political Philosophy Ser.). 384p. 1991. text ed. 25.00 (0-8153-0132-4) Garland.

Theme of Childhood in Elsa Morante. Grace Z. Kalay. (Romance Monographs: No. 50). 122p. (Orig.). 1996. pap. 25.00 (1-889441-00-7) Romance.

Theme of Enclosure in Selected Works of Doris Lessing. Shirley Budhos. LC 86-50290. 128p. 1987. 15.00 (0-87875-314-1) Whitston Pub.

Theme of Government in Piers Plowman. Anna P. Baldwin. (Piers Plowman Studies: No. I). 115p. 1987. 59.00 (0-85991-073-3) Boydell & Brewer.

*Theme of Music in Peter Russell's Work. Helga Denkmayr. 70p. 1996. pap. 12.95 (3-7052-0980-9, Pub. by Univ of Salzburg AT) Intl Spec Bk.

Theme of Recompense in Matthew's Gospel. Charette et al. (JSNT Supplement Ser.: No. 79). 200p. 1992. 50.00 (1-85075-385-7, Pub. by Sheffield Acad UK) CUP Services.

Theme of Spenser's "Foure Hymnes" J. W. Bennett. LC 76-100731. 1970. reprint ed. pap. 39.95 (0-8383-0003-0) M S G Haskell Hse.

Theme of the Month. Dona Rice & Blanca A. La Bounty. (J). (gr. 1-3). 1995. pap. text ed. 14.95 (1-55734-509-0) Tchr Create Mat.

Theme of the Nazi Concentration Camp in French Literature. Cynthia Haft. (New Babylon Studies in the Social Sciences: No. 12). 1973. 27.70 (90-279-7190-0) Mouton.

Theme of the Pentateuch. 2nd rev. ed. David J. Clines. (Journal for the Study of the Old Testament Supplement Ser.: Vol. 10). 152p. 1997. pap. 12.95 (1-85075-792-5, Pub. by Sheffield Acad UK) CUP Services.

Theme of the Week. Lisa Rogulic-Newsome. 208p. 1991. 13.99 (0-86653-602-7, GA1321) Good Apple.

*Theme Parks, Leisure Centres, Zoos, & Aquria. Anthony Wylson & Patricia Wylson. LC 93-28642. (Longman Building Studies). 191p. 1994. reprint ed. pap. 54.50 (0-608-03612-9, 2064435) Bks Demand.

*Theme Restaurant Design. Martin M. Pegler. 1997. 59.95 (0-07-049413-4) McGraw.

*Theme Restaurant Design. Retail Reporting Staff. Date not set. 39.95 (0-688-15552-9) Morrow.

Theme Restaurant Design, No. 9. Ed. by Martin M. Pester. (Illus.). 178p. 1997. 59.95 (0-934590-87-7) Retail Report.

*Theme Restaurants. Michael Kaplan. LC 97-5302. 1997. pap. write for info. (0-86636-579-6) PBC Intl Inc.

*Theme Restaurants. Michael Kaplan. LC 97-5302. 1997. 37.50 (0-86636-542-7) PBC Intl Inc.

*Theme Restaurants. PBC International Staff. Date not set. 39.95 (0-688-15075-6) Morrow.

Theme Song for Recovery: An Intervention Guide for Families. rev. ed. Sandra Inskeep-Fox. 1997. pap. 0.50 (0-89230-198-8) Do It Now.

Theme Songs. write for info. (1-879104-01-6) Overly Pub.

Theme Studies: A Practical Guide. Penny Strube. 1993. pap. text ed. 15.95 (0-590-49272-1) Scholastic Inc.

Theme Teaching with Art Reproductions. Janet Amman. 150p. (Orig.). 1992. pap. 14.95 (0-935493-26-3) Modern Learn Pr.

*Themed Environment, Vol. 1. Gottdeiner. Date not set. pap. text ed. write for info. (0-312-11500-8) St Martin.

Themersons & the Gaberbocchus Press: An Experiment in Publishing, 1948-1979. Jan Kubasiewicz et al. (Illus.). 100p. (Orig.). 1993. pap. 25.00 (0-9639239-0-0) MJS Bks & Graphics.

Themes Across the Curriculum: Ready-to-Use Activities & Projects for the Elementary Classroom. Karl A. Matz. 1994. spiral bd. 27.95 (0-87628-907-3) Ctr Appl Res.

Themes & Conclusions. Igor Stravinsky. 328p. 1983. pap. 10.95 (0-520-04652-8) U CA Pr.

Themes & Conventions of Elizabethan Tragedy. 2nd ed. Muriel C. Bradbrook. (History of Elizabethan Drama Ser.). 270p. 1980. pap. text ed. 24.95 (0-521-29695-1) Cambridge U Pr.

Themes & Foundations of Art. Elizabeth L. Katz et al. LC 93-38676. 1994. text ed. 61.50 (0-314-02945-1) West Pub.

Themes & Images in the Fictional Works of Madame de Lafayette. Ruth Willard. LC 90-3557. (American University Studies: Romance Languages & Literature: Ser. II, Vol. 154). 154p. (C). 1991. text ed. 43.95 (0-8204-1392-5) P Lang Pubng.

*Themes & Issues in Christianity. Douglas J. Davies. Ed. by Clare Drury. LC 96-52966. (World Religions). 224p. 1997. 59.95 (0-304-33848-6); pap. 24.95 (0-304-33849-4) Cassell.

*Themes & Issues in Hinduism. Paul Bowen. LC 97-15235. 1997. write for info. (0-304-33850-8, Pub. by Cassell UK); pap. write for info. (0-304-33851-6, Pub. by Cassell UK) Sterling.

Themes & Perspectives in Indian Sociology. D. N. Dhanagare. (C). 1993. 18.50 (81-7033-198-6, Pub. by Rawat II) S Asia.

Themes & Perspectives in Nursing. 2nd ed. Keith Soothill et al. 352p. (C). 1996. pap. text ed. 42.99 (1-56593-466-0, 1119) Singular Publishing.

Themes & Settings in Fiction: A Bibliography of Bibliographies. Compiled by Donald K. Hartman & Jerome Drost. LC 88-25082. (Bibliographies & Indexes in World Literature Ser.: No. 14). 238p. 1988. text ed. 69.50 (0-313-25866-X, HTH/, Greenwood Pr) Greenwood.

*Themes & Structures: Studies in German Literature from Goethe to the Present. A Festschrift for Theodore Ziolkowski. Alexander Stephan. LC 97-2585. (GERM Ser.). 280p. 1997. 59.95 (1-57113-087-X) Camden Hse.

Themes & Texts: Toward a Poetics of Expressiveness. Alexander Zholkovsky. LC 83-45152. 304p. 1983. 55.00 (0-8014-1505-5) Cornell U Pr.

Themes & Theories in Modern Japanese History: Essays in Memory of Richard Storry. Ed. by Sue Henny & Jean-Pierre Lehmann. LC 86-17259. 320p. (C). 1988. text ed. 65.00 (0-485-11242-6, Pub. by Athlone Pr UK) Humanities.

Themes & Theses of Six Recent Papal Documents: A Commentary. Robert F. Morneau. LC 84-29034. 160p. (Orig.). 1985. pap. 5.95 (0-8189-0482-8) Alba.

Themes & Variations. John Cage. LC 81-13626. (Illus.). 150p. 25.00 (0-930794-22-2); pap. 9.95 (0-930794-23-0) Station Hill Pr.

Themes & Variations. Aldous Huxley. LC 79-128264. (Essay Index Reprint Ser.). 1977. 21.95 (0-8369-1883-5) Ayer.

Themes & Variations: A College Reader. W. Ross Winterowd & Charlotte Preston. 425p. (C). 1985. teacher ed. write for info. (0-15-591471-5); pap. text ed. 18.75 (0-15-591470-7) HB Coll Pubs.

Themes & Variations: A Study of Action in Biblical Narrative. Robert C. Culley. LC 92-26201. (Society of Biblical Literature Semeia Studies). 204p. 1992. 44.95 (1-55540-757-9, 060623); pap. 29.95 (1-55540-758-7) Scholars Pr GA.

Themes & Variations: Classics to Moderns. (Music for Millions Ser.: Vol. 77). 1974. pap. 12.95 (0-8256-4077-6, AM48745) Music Sales.

Themes & Variations: Writings on Music in Honor of Rulan Chao Pian. Ed. by Bell Yung & Joseph S. Lam. LC 94-26322. 1994. text ed. 34.95 (0-674-87749-7) HUP.

Themes & Variations - Temy i Variatsii: In Honor of Lazar Fleishman. V. V. Ivanov et al. Ed. by Konstantin Polivanov et al. (Stanford Slavic Studies: Vol. 8). 550p. (Orig.). (ENG & RUS.). (C). 1995. pap. 60.00 (1-57201-009-6) Berkeley Slavic.

Themes & Variations from the Foot-Hook Rag. Georgette W. Amowitz. (Illus.). (Orig.). 1990. spiral bd. 15.00 (1-878084-02-X) Danscores.

Themes & Variations in Community Policing: Case Studies in Community Policing. Carl W. Hawkins, Jr. et al. LC 96-67352. 92p. (Orig.). (C). 1996. pap. 16.50 (1-878734-42-3) Police Exec Res.

Themes & Variations in European Psychiatry: An Anthology. Ed. by Steven R. Hirsch & Michael Shepard. LC 73-86374. (Illus.). 480p. reprint ed. pap. 136.80 (0-8357-3145-6, 2039408) Bks Demand.

Themes & Variations in Pasternak's Poetics. K. Pomorska. 92p. 1975. pap. 21.00 (0-685-53318-2) Benjamins North Am.

Themes Apple Westest. Katz. Date not set. write for info. (0-314-04886-3) West Pub.

*Themes, Dreams & Schemes: Banquet Menu Ideas, Concepts & Thematic Experiences. G. Eugene Wigger. LC 96-38128. 1997. text ed. 75.00 (0-471-15391-5) Wiley.

Themes et Discussions. Thomas H. Brown. 223p. (FRE.). (C). 1982. pap. text ed. 31.16 (0-669-02844-4) HM College Div.

*Themes for Classical Studies. 64p. 1991. ring bd. 69.95 (0-521-40831-8) Cambridge U Pr.

Themes for Today. Smith. (College ESL Ser.). 1996. pap. 21.95 (0-8384-5252-3) Heinle & Heinle.

Themes for Writers. Alfred F. Rosa. 544p. 1994. pap. text ed. 21.00 (0-312-09204-0) St Martin.

*Themes for Writers. 2nd ed. Eschholz. Date not set. pap. text ed. write for info. (0-312-13746-X) St Martin.

Themes for Writing. Eschholz. 1994. teacher ed., pap. text ed. 23.00 (0-312-09217-2) St Martin.

Themes for Writing. Escholz. 1994. teacher ed., pap. text ed. 5.00 (0-312-09457-4) St Martin.

Themes from a Letter to Rome. Daniel L. Segraves. LC 95-39200. 270p. (Orig.). 1995. pap. 9.99 (1-56722-136-X) Word Aflame.

Themes from Isaiah see Temas de Isaias

Themes from Kaplan. Ed. by Joseph Almog et al. (Illus.). 624p. 1989. 60.00 (0-19-505217-X) OUP.

Themes from Masterworks, 3 bks., Bk. 1. Ed. by Louise Goss. (Frances Clark Library for Piano Students). 16p. (Orig.). (J). (gr. k-12). 1970. pap. text ed. 5.95 (0-87487-191-3) Summy-Birchard.

Themes from Masterworks, 3 bks., Bk. 2. Ed. by Louise Goss. (Frances Clark Library for Piano Students). 16p. (Orig.). (J). (gr. k-12). 1970. pap. text ed. 5.95 (0-87487-192-1) Summy-Birchard.

Themes from Masterworks, 3 bks., Bk. 3. Ed. by Louise Goss. (Frances Clark Library for Piano Students). 16p. (Orig.). (J). (gr. k-12). 1970. pap. text ed. 5.95 (0-87487-193-X) Summy-Birchard.

Themes from the Philokalia, Vol. I. A. Ioannikios. 1989. pap. 9.95 (0-937032-59-X) Light&Life Pub Co MN.

Themes I. A. L. Staveley. 1981. 20.00 (0-89756-005-1) Two Rivers.

Themes II. A. L. Staveley et al. 112p. 1982. 20.00 (0-89756-010-8) Two Rivers.

Themes III. A. L. Staveley et al. 1984. 20.00 (0-89756-013-2) Two Rivers.

Themes in African & World History: A Schema for Integrating Africa into World History; Tropical Africa: The Colonial Heritage; The African Heritage & the Slave Trade. rev. ed. George E. Brooks, Jr. (African Humanities Ser.). 59p. 1983. pap. text ed. 5.00 (0-941934-06-3) Indiana Africa.

Themes in American Painting: A Reference Work to Common Styles & Genres. Robert Henkes. LC 92-53599. (Illus.). 280p. 1993. lib. bdg. 39.95 (0-89950-734-4) McFarland & Co.

Themes in Australian History. Frank Farrell. 240p. 1990. pap. 27.95 (0-86840-212-5, Pub. by New South Wales Univ Pr AT) Intl Spec Bk.

Themes in Contemporary Physics II: Essays in Honor of Julian Schwinger's 70th Birthday. Ed. by S. Deren & R. J. Finkelstein. 104p. (C). 1989. text ed. 54.00 (9971-5-0961-X) World Scientific Pub.

Themes in Cultural Psychiatry: An Annotated Bibliography 1975-1980. Armando R. Favazza & Ahmed D. Faheem. LC 82-2738. 208p. 1982. 32.50 (0-8262-0377-9) U of Mo Pr.

Themes in Development Economics: Essays in Honour of Malcolm Adiseshiah. Ed. by S. Subramanian. 360p. 1993. 39.95 (0-19-563030-0) OUP.

Themes in Development Economics: Essays on Method, Peasants & Governmental. Ed. by Max Lundahl. 400p. 1995. 76.95 (1-85628-689-4, Pub. by Avebury Pub UK) Ashgate Pub Co.

Themes in Geography: An Interactive Study Guide. Craig L. Torbenson. 256p. (C). 1996. spiral bd. 38.79 (0-8403-9394-6) Kendall-Hunt.

Themes in Greek Linguistics: Papers from the First International Conference on Greek Linguistics, Reading, September 1993. Ed. by Irene Philippaki-Warburton et al. LC 94-38050. (Current Issues in Linguistic Theory Ser.: No. 117). xviii, 534p. 1994. 79.00 (1-55619-571-0) Benjamins North Am.

Themes in Immigration History. George E. Pozzetta. LC 90-49051. (Immigration & Ethnicity Ser.: Vol. 1). 368p. 1991. reprint ed. text ed. 60.00 (0-8240-7401-7) Garland.

Themes in Linguistics: The Nineteen Seventies. Ed. by Eric P. Hamp. LC 72-94473. (Janua Linguarum, Ser. Minor: No. 172). (Illus.). 129p. 1973. pap. text ed. 41.55 (90-279-2365-5) Mouton.

Themes in Macroeconomic History: The U. K. Economy 1919-1939. Solomos Solomou. 160p. (C). 1996. pap. text ed. 16.95 (0-521-43621-4) Cambridge U Pr.

Themes in Macroeconomic History: The U. K. Economy 1919-1939. Solomos Solomou. 160p. (C). 1996. text ed. 54.95 (0-521-43033-X) Cambridge U Pr.

Themes in Medical Geography: Environment & Health. Ed. by Rais Akhtar. 1991. 78.50 (81-7024-332-7, Pub. by Ashish II) S Asia.

Themes in Medieval Arabic Literature. Gustave E. Von Grunebaum. Ed. by Dunning S. Wilson. (Collected Studies: No. CS133). 360p. (C). 1981. reprint ed. lib. bdg. 69.95 (0-86078-079-1, Pub. by Variorum UK) Ashgate Pub Co.

Themes in Modern European History: 1830 - 1890. Ed. by Bruce Waller. 288p. (C). 1990. pap. 19.95 (0-04-445453-8) Routledge Chapman & Hall.

Themes in Modern European History, 1780-1830. Pamela M. Philbeam. LC 94-28278. (Themes in Modern European History Ser.). (Illus.). 224p. (C). 1995. pap. 17.95 (0-415-10173-5, C0167) Routledge.

Themes in Modern European History, 1780-1830. Pamela M. Philbeam. LC 94-28278. (Themes in Modern European History Ser.). (Illus.). 224p. (C). (gr. 13). 1995. text ed. 59.95 (*0-415-10172-7*, C0166) Routledge.

***Themes in Modern European History 1830-1890.** Ed. by Bruce Waller. 288p. 1990. pap. 19.95 (*0-415-09075-X*) Routledge.

Themes in Modern European History 1830-1890. Ed. by Bruce Waller. 288p. (C). 1990. text ed. 49.95 (*0-04-445695-6*); pap. text ed. 19.95 (*0-04-445696-4*) Routledge Chapman & Hall.

Themes in Modern European History 1890-1945. Ed. by Paul Hayes. 336p. (C). 1992. pap. 19.95 (*0-415-07905-5*, A7987) Routledge.

Themes in Motor Development. Ed. by H. T. Whiting & M. G. Wade. 1986. lib. bdg. 160.50 (*90-247-3390-1*) Kluwer Ac.

Themes in Old Testament Theology. William A. Dyrness. LC 79-2380. 252p. 1980. pap. 13.99 (*0-87784-726-6*, 726) InterVarsity.

Themes in Rural History of the Western World. Ed. by Richard Herr. LC 93-3515. (Henry A. Wallace Series on Agricultural History & Rural Studies). (Illus.). 292p. (C). 1993. text ed. 44.95 (*0-8138-1492-8*) Iowa St U Pr.

Themes in Southwest Prehistory. Ed. by George J. Gumerman. (Advanced Seminar Ser.). (Illus.). 330p. 1994. pap. 22.50 (*0-933452-84-5*) Schol Am Res.

Themes in Soviet Marxist Philosophy: Selected Articles from the Sovetskaja Enciklopedija. Ed. by Thomas J. Blakeley. (Sovietica Ser.: No. 37). 235p. 1975. lib. bdg. 104.50 (*90-277-0637-9*, D Reidel) Kluwer Ac.

***Themes in the Current Reformation in Religious Thinking: The Covenantal Friendship of God.** John W. Lynes. LC 97-2069. (Studies in Religion & Society: Vol. 36). 220p. 1997. text ed. 89.95 (*0-7734-8674-7*) E Mellen.

Themes of Adulthood Through Literature. Sharan B. Merriam. 1983. pap. text ed. 21.95 (*0-8077-2731-8*) Tchrs Coll.

Themes of Indigenous Acculturation in Northwest Mexico. Ed. by Thomas B. Hinton & Phil C. Weigand. LC 80-39646. (Anthropological Papers: No. 38). 76p. 1981. pap. 9.95 (*0-8165-0324-9*) U of Ariz Pr.

***Themes of Islamic Civilization.** Ed. by John A. Williams. 382p. 1996. pap. 16.95 (*0-614-21632-X*, 1227) Kazi Pubns.

Themes of Magic in Nineteenth Century French Fiction. Emile Caillet. 1972. 59.95 (*0-8490-1188-4*) Gordon Pr.

Themes of Peace in Renaissance Poetry. James Hutton. Ed. by Rita Guerlac. LC 84-7631. (Illus.). 280p. 1984. 49.95 (*0-8014-1613-2*) Cornell U Pr.

Themes of Renewal. Rembert G. Weakland. 226p. (Orig.). 1995. pap. text ed. 12.95 (*1-56929-027-X*) Pastoral Pr.

Themes of Work & Love in Adulthood. Ed. by Neil J. Smelser & Erik H. Erikson. LC 79-26130. (Harvard Paperbacks Ser.). 307p. 1981. pap. 16.50 (*0-674-87751-9*) HUP.

***Themes of 007 - Bond's Greatest Hits.** Ed. by Carol Cuellar. 72p. (Orig.). (C). 1996. pap. text ed. 12.95 (*0-7692-0831-2*, TSF0053A) Warner Brothers.

Themes out of School: Effects & Causes. Stanley Cavell. 282p. 1988. pap. 14.95 (*0-226-09788-9*) U Ch Pr.

Themes, Scenes & Taste in the History of Japanese Garden Art. Wybe Kuitert. (Japonica Neerlandica Ser.: Vol. 3). (Illus.). xiii, 348p. (C). 1988. 54.00 (*90-5063-021-9*, Pub. by Gieben NE) Benjamins North Am.

Themes Teachers Use: Classroom-Tested Units for Young Children. Ed. by Marjorie J. Kostelnik. LC 95-24821. 600p. (Orig.). 1995. pap. 29.95 (*0-673-36076-8*, GoodYrBooks) Addson-Wesley Educ.

***Themes They Try to Tame.** unabridged ed. A. M. Onoapoi. LC 96-94707. 56p. (Orig.). 1996. pap. 12.95 (*0-9654513-0-5*); lib. bdg. 18.95 (*0-614-24606-7*) Think Pen.

Themes Through Time: Readings in Art History. Lou A. Culley. 192p. (C). 1992. pap. text ed. 29.34 (*0-8403-8048-8*) Kendall-Hunt.

***Themes with a Difference: 228 New Activities for Young Children.** Moira D. Green. LC 97-13490. 1997. write for info. (*0-7668-0009-1*) Delmar.

Themestorming. Joni Becker et al. (Illus.). 308p. (Orig.). 1994. pap. text ed. 24.95 (*0-87659-170-5*) Gryphon Hse.

Theming of America: Dreams, Visions, & Commercial Spaces. Mark Gottdiener. LC 96-38569. 1996. text ed. 69.00 (*0-8133-3188-9*) Westview.

Theming of America: Dreams, Visions, & Commercial Spaces. Mark Gottdiener. LC 96-38569. (C). 1996. pap. text ed. 19.95 (*0-8133-3189-7*) Westview.

Themis: A Study of the Social Origins of Greek Religion. Jane E. Harrison. (C). 1977. pap. 19.95 (*0-85036-229-6*, Pub. by Merlin Pr UK) Humanities.

Themis, Dike und Verwandtes. Rudolf Hirzel. vi, 445p. 1966. reprint ed. write for info. (*0-318-70941-4*) G Olms Pubs.

Themistius & the Imperial Court: Oratory, Civic Duty, & Paideia from Constantius to Theodosius. John Vanderspoel. LC 95-12268. 1995. text ed. 44.50 (*0-472-10485-3*) U of Mich Pr.

Them...Within Us. T. D. Gross. 1994. pap. 5.95 (*0-88145-113-4*) Broadway Play.

Then. Carroll Arnett. 1965. pap. 3.00 (*0-685-00981-5*) Elizabeth Pr.

Then: Photographs 1924-1994. Comment by Alexander Liberman. LC 95-34077. 272p. 1995. 65.00 (*0-679-44524-2*) Random.

Then Again, Maybe I Won't. Judy Blume. 128p. (J). (gr. 6 up). 1976. mass mkt. 3.99 (*0-440-98659-1*, LLL BDD) BDD Bks Young Read.

Then Again, Maybe I Won't. Judy Blume. 164p. (J). (gr. 5-8). 1986. mass mkt. 4.50 (*0-440-48659-9*, YB BDD) BDD Bks Young Read.

Then Again, Maybe I Won't. Judy Blume. LC 77-156548. 176p. (J). (gr. 5-7). 1982. lib. bdg. 16.00 (*0-02-711090-7*, Bradbury S&S) S&S Childrens.

Then Again, Maybe I Won't - Quiza No lo Haga. Judy Blume. (SPA.). (J). 8.50 (*84-204-4626-2*) Santillana.

Then Again...Annapolis, 1900-1965. Mame Warren. LC 90-71343. (Illus.). 216p. 1990. 42.00 (*0-9627799-0-3*); pap. 27.50 (*0-9627799-1-1*) Annapol Pubng.

***Then an Angel Came.** Carol Gino. 304p. 1997. 22.00 (*1-57566-231-0*, Knsington) Kensgtn Pub Corp.

Then & Now. Ed. by Anna Brinton. LC 72-128214. (Essay Index Reprint Ser.). 1977. 23.95 (*0-8369-1905-X*) Ayer.

Then & Now. Illus. by Peter Firmin. (Talkabout Bks.). 16p. (J). (ps-1). 1986. pap. 4.50 (*0-7460-0794-9*) EDC.

***Then & Now.** Barbara Hughes. (Livewire Ser.). (YA). (gr. 6-9). pap. 7.95 (*0-7043-4930-2*, Pub. by Womens Press UK) Trafalgar.

Then & Now. Willard Simms. 1989. pap. 5.25 (*0-8222-1131-9*) Dramatists Play.

Then & Now. W. Somerset Maugham. LC 75-25364. (Works of W. Somerset Maugham). 1977. reprint ed. 25.95 (*0-405-07822-6*) Ayer.

Then & Now: A Photographic History of Vegetation Change in the Central Great Basin Desert. Garry F. Rogers. LC 82-4825. (Illus.). 164p. (Orig.). reprint ed. pap. 46.80 (*0-7837-6865-6*, 2046695) Bks Demand.

Then & Now: Cartoons about Airline Pilots. Michael J. Ray. 96p. (Orig.). 1986. pap. 6.95 (*0-936283-00-9*) U Temecula Pr.

Then & Now: On the One Hundreth Anniversary of the First General Strike in the U. S. Terry Moon & Ron Brokmeyer. (Illus.). 50p. 1977. pap. 1.00 (*0-914441-17-5*) News & Letters.

Then & Now: The Personal Past in the Poetry of Robert Penn Warren. Floyd C. Watkins. LC 81-51016. 198p. 1982. reprint ed. pap. 56.50 (*0-608-02124-5*, 2062773) Bks Demand.

Then & Now: The Wonders of the Ancient World Brought to Life in Vivid See-Through Reproductions. Stefania Perring & Dominic Perring. (Illus.). 144p. 1991. 29.95 (*0-02-599461-1*) Macmillan.

***Then & Now Bible Map Book.** (Illus.). 24p. 1997. spiral bd. 24.95 (*0-9655082-0-X*, 306X) Rose Publshg.

***Then & Now Bible Map Transparencies.** (Illus.). (J). (gr. 2-8). 1997. trans. 19.95 (*0-9655082-3-4*) Rose Publshg.

Then & Now in Education, Eighteen Forty-Five to Nineteen Twenty-Three. Otis W. Caldwell & Stuart A. Courtis. LC 77-165711. (American Education Ser. No. 2). 1972. reprint ed. 21.95 (*0-405-03700-7*) Ayer.

Then Badger Said This. Elizabeth Cook-Lynn. (Illus.). 42p. 1983. pap. 5.00 (*0-87770-307-8*) Ye Galleon.

Then Came the French: The History of the French in Tuolumne County, California. Mary G. Paquette. LC 96-60553. (Illus.). ix, 160p. (Orig.). 1996. pap. 17.50 (*0-9652608-0-1*) Tuolumne Cnty.

Then Came the Glory. Nona Freeman. Ed. by Nell Perry. 204p. 1994. pap. 8.00 (*1-878366-08-4*) Nonas Bk Sales.

Then Came Violence. large type ed. John Ball. 352p. 1982. 25.99 (*0-7089-0870-5*) Ulverscroft.

Then Came You. Lisa Kleypas. 416p. (Orig.). 1993. mass mkt. 5.99 (*0-380-77013-X*) Avon.

Then Comes the Baby in the Baby Carriage. Charles S. Mueller. LC 94-25525. 224p. 1994. pap. 10.99 (*0-570-04666-1*, 12-3238) Concordia.

***Then Comes the Morning.** F. J. Bayhi. 1986. pap. 20.00 (*0-614-30819-4*, BTHENC) Claitors.

***Then God Created Woman: How to Find Fulfillment As the Woman God Intended You to Be.** Deborah Newman. LC 97-1429. 1997. pap. 10.99 (*1-56179-533-X*) Focus Family.

***Then God Showed Up.** (Illus.). 100p. Date not set. pap. 22.99 (*0-9633356-0-X*) Harvest Time.

Then Hang All the Liars. Alice Storey. 1989. mass mkt. 3.50 (*0-671-64530-7*) PB.

Then I Got Three Scoops. Getzel. 1992. 9.99 (*0-89906-412-4*) Mesorah Pubns.

Then I Was Guided. Muhammad al-Tijani al-Samawi. LC 91-66698. 232p. 1993. pap. 6.00 (*1-879402-06-8*, OO) Tahrike Tarsile Quran.

Then King Down Came. Richard Johnson. (Orig.). 1970. pap. 2.00 (*0-932264-14-X*) Trask Hse Bks.

Then Ninth Vibration, & Other Stories. Douglas A. Menville. LC 75-46251. (Supernatural & Occult Fiction Ser.). 1976. reprint ed. lib. bdg. 26.95 (*0-405-08111-1*) Ayer.

Then Now & Forever. Carmel J. Rapisardi. 271p. 1992. pap. write for info. (*0-9632702-0-6*) Lightning.

***Then Shall Your Light Rise: Spiritual Formation & Social Witness.** Joyce Hollyday. LC 97-8990. (Orig.). 1997. 9.95 (*0-8358-0816-5*) Upper Room Bks.

***Then Shall Your Light Rise: Spiritual Formation & Social Witness.** Joyce Hollyday. Ed. by Rita Collett. 112p. (Orig.). 1997. pap. 9.95 (*0-8358-0826-2*, UR826) Upper Room Bks.

Then She Found Me. Elinor Lipman. Ed. by Jane Rosenman. 320p. 1991. reprint ed. pap. 12.00 (*0-671-68615-1*, WSP) PB.

Then the Americans Came: Voices from Vietnam. Martha Hess. LC 92-38999. (Illus.). 300p. 1993. 22.95 (*0-941423-92-1*) FWEW.

Then the Americans Came: Voices from Vietnam. Martha Hess. (Illus.). 239p. (C). 1994. reprint ed. pap. 14.95 (*0-8135-2145-9*) Rutgers U Pr.

***Then the End Will Come: Great News about the Great Commission.** Jim Montgomery. LC 96-49863. 216p. (Orig.). 1997. pap. 7.95 (*0-87808-272-7*) William Carey Lib.

Then, the Toaster Said... Bill Harvey. (Illus.). 144p. (Orig.). 1985. pap. 5.95 (*0-930297-18-0*, 84-081379) Ike & Dudatt Pubns.

Then the Wind Changed in Africa: Nigerian Letters of Robert Hepburn Wright. Ed. by Robert Pearce. (Illus.). 256p. (C). 1993. text ed. 39.50 (*1-85043-573-1*, Pub. by I B Tauris UK) St Martin.

***Then There Was Murder.** large type ed. Brian Parvin. (Dales Large Print Ser.). 227p. 1996. pap. 17.99 (*1-85389-671-3*, Dales) Ulverscroft.

***Then There Were Five.** Elizabeth Enright. LC 97-14307. 1997. pap. 4.99 (*0-14-038397-2*) Viking Penguin.

***Then They Leave Home: Parenting after the Kids Grow Up.** Boni Piper & Judith K. Balswick. LC 97-12915. 204p. 1997. pap. 10.99 (*0-8308-1964-9*, 1964) InterVarsity.

Then to the Rock Let Me Fly: Luther Bohanon & Judicial Activism. Jace Weaver. LC 93-2441. 1993. 24.95 (*0-8061-2554-3*) U of Okla Pr.

Then Troll Heard Squeek. Smithmark Staff. pap. 4.98 (*0-8317-1078-0*) Smithmark.

Then Truth Will Out. Leonard E. Read. 177p. 1971. pap. 8.95 (*0-910614-27-X*) Foun Econ Ed.

Then upon the Evil Season. Noel Virtue. 144p. 8900. 24.00 (*0-7206-0717-5*, Pub. by P Owen Ltd UK) Dufour.

Thence Round Cape Horn. Robert E. Johnson. LC 79-6111. (Navies & Men Ser.). (Illus.). 1980. reprint ed. lib. bdg. 31.95 (*0-405-13040-6*) Ayer.

Thendara House. Marion Zimmer Bradley. (Darkover Ser.). 416p. 1983. mass mkt. 5.99 (*0-88677-240-0*) DAW Bks.

Thendara House. Marion Zimmer Bradley. 416p. 1995. reprint ed. 22.00 (*0-7278-4723-6*) Severn Hse.

Thennberg or Seeking to Go Home Again. Gyorgy Sebestyen. Tr. by Lisa Fleisher. (Studies in Austrian Literature, Culture, & Thought. Translation Ser.). 1995. pap. 14.95 (*0-929497-84-8*) Ariadne CA.

Theo. Mark Dunster. 14p. (Orig.). 1988. pap. 4.00 (*0-89642-165-1*) Linden Pubs.

Theo: The Autobiography of Theodore Bikel. Theodore Bikel. LC 94-9280. (Illus.). 416p. 1994. 27.50 (*0-06-019044-2*, A Asher Bks) HarpC.

Theo-Drama: Theological Dramatic Theory, Vol. II: Dramatis Personae. Hans U. Von Balthasar. LC 89-83257. 437p. 1990. 40.00 (*0-89870-287-9*) Ignatius Pr.

Theo-Drama Vol. I: Theological Dramatic Theory: Prolegomena. Hans U. Von Balthasar. Tr. by Graham Harrison from GER. LC 88-80725. (Glory of the Lord Ser.). 663p. 1988. 40.00 (*0-89870-185-6*) Ignatius Pr.

Theo-Drama Vol. III: Dramatis Personae - Persons in Christ. Hans Urs von Balthasar. Tr. by Graham Harrison from GER. LC 86-80725. 546p. 1992. 40.00 (*0-89870-295-X*) Ignatius Pr.

Theo-Economics: The Call to Responsibility. Roland J. Hill. Ed. by Kenneth McFarland. 175p. 1994. 25.00 (*0-9639357-0-4*) Helping Hands.

Theo-Monistic Mysticism: A Hindu-Christian Comparison. Michael Stoeber. LC 93-34044. 1994. text ed. 55.00 (*0-312-10746-3*) St Martin.

Theo or the New Era. Robert Pinget. Tr. by Barbara Wright from FRE. 32p. 1994. pap. 6.95 (*0-87376-079-4*) Red Dust.

Theo R. Schwalm Memories of My Life. Theo R. Schwalm. Ed. by R. Carl Barth. (Illus.). 348p. 1992. text ed. 15.00 (*0-939016-20-6*) Johannes Schwalm Hist.

***Theo Takes Off.** Peter Hartling. (J). Date not set. write for info. (*0-688-09263-2*) Lothrop.

Theo, the Indian Fighter. Wells Teague. Ed. by Edwin M. Eakin. (Illus.). 112p. (J). (gr. 4-7). 1987. 8.95 (*0-89015-614-X*) Sunbelt Media.

Theo Van Doesburg: Propagandist & Practitioner of the Avant-Garde, 1909-1923. Hannah L. Hedrick. LC 79-24699. (Studies in the Fine Arts: The Avant-Garde: No. 5). 173p. reprint ed. pap. 49.40 (*0-685-20851-6*, 2070086) Bks Demand.

Theocracy in Massachusetts: Reformation & Separation in Early Puritan New England. Avihu Zahai. LC 93-37010. 412p. 1993. text ed. 109.95 (*0-7734-9970-9*) E Mellen.

Theocritis' "Idyll XVII" A Stylistic Commentary. Mary A. Rossi. vii, 249p. 1989. pap. 78.00 (*90-256-0967-8*, Pub. by A M Hakkert NE) Benjamins North Am.

***Theocritus.** Ed. by M. A. Harder et al. (Hellenistica Groningana Ser.: Vol. 2). 266p. 1996. pap. 57.00 (*0-614-20978-1*, Pub. by Egbert Forsten NE) Benjamins North Am.

Theocritus. Theocritus. Tr. by Charles S. Calverley. LC 73-39212. (Select Bibliographies Reprint Ser.). 1977. reprint ed. 19.95 (*0-8369-6814-X*) Ayer.

Theocritus: Select Poems. K. Dover. (Bristol Greek Texts Ser.). 400p. 1985. reprint ed. pap. 27.95 (*0-86292-147-3*, Pub. by Brstl Class Pr UK) Focus Pub-R Pullins.

Theocritus: Select Poems. Ed. & Tr. by Kenneth J. Dover from GRE. 323p. (ENG & GRE.). (C). 1987. reprint ed. pap. 20.00 (*0-86516-204-2*) Bolchazy-Carducci.

Theocritus & the Archaeology of Greek Poetry. Richard L. Hunter. 220p. (C). 1996. text ed. 54.95 (*0-521-56040-3*) Cambridge U Pr.

Theocritus' Idyll XXIV: A Commentary. Heather White. 164p. 1979. pap. 50.00 (*90-256-0827-2*, Pub. by A M Hakkert NE) Benjamins North Am.

Theocritus' Pastoral Analogies: The Formation of a Genre. Kathryn J. Gutzwiller. LC 91-7616. (Studies in Classics). 320p. (Orig.). (C). 1991. pap. 21.50 (*0-299-12944-6*); lib. bdg. 47.50 (*0-299-12940-3*) U of Wis Pr.

Theocritus's Urban Mimes: Mobility, Gender, & Patronage. Joan B. Burton. LC 94-28938. (Hellenistic Culture & Society Ser.: Vol. XIX). 307p. 1995. 40.00 (*0-520-08858-1*) U CA Pr.

Theoderic in Italy. John Moorhead. 352p. 1993. 69.00 (*0-19-814781-3*) OUP.

Theodicee Plotinienne, Theodicee Gnostique. Denis O'Brien. LC 92-9638. (Philosophia Antiqua Ser.: Vol. 57). 117p. (FRE.). 1993. 57.00 (*90-04-09618-3*) E J Brill.

Theodicies in Conflict: A Dilemma in Puritan Ethics & Nineteenth-Century American Literature. Richard Forrer. LC 85-27220. (Contributions to the Study of Religion Ser.: No. 17). 302p. 1986. text ed. 55.00 (*0-313-25191-6*, FTS/, Greenwood Pr) Greenwood.

***Theodicy.** Ed. by Dan Cohn-Sherbok. LC 97-3725. (Jewish Studies: Vol. 18). 104p. 1997. text ed. 59.95 (*0-7734-8690-9*) E Mellen.

Theodicy in Islamic Thought. Eric L. Ormsby. LC 84-3396. 320p. 1984. text ed. 49.50 (*0-691-07278-7*) Princeton U Pr.

Theodicy of Alfred North Whitehead: A Logical & Ethical Vindication. R. Maurice Barineau. 212p. (Orig.). (C). 1991. lib. bdg. 46.50 (*0-8191-8167-6*) U Pr of Amer.

Theodicy of Suffering. Albert W. J. Harper. LC 90-36666. (Toronto Studies in Theology: Vol. 52). 116p. 1990. lib. bdg. 59.95 (*0-88946-842-7*) E Mellen.

Theodis Boneright in the Land of Make Believe. Richard H. Moore. (Illus.). 32p. (J). (gr. 2-5). 10.00 (*0-9648170-0-4*) World Crusade.

Theodontia. A. J. Charig et al. (Encyclopedia of Paleoherpetology Ser.: Pt. 13). (Illus.). 137p. 1976. lib. bdg. 120.00 (*3-437-30184-5*) Lubrecht & Cramer.

Theodor Adorno: A Bibliography. Ed. by Joan Nordquist. (Social Theory: A Bibliographic Ser.: No. 10). 60p. (Orig.). 1988. pap. 15.00 (*0-937855-18-9*) Ref Rsch Serv.

Theodor Adorno Vol. 2: A Bibliography. (Social Theory: A Bibliographic Ser.: No. 35). 72p. (C). 1994. pap. 15.00 (*0-937855-69-3*) Ref Rsch Serv.

Theodor Billroth - Ein Leben fuer die Chirurgie. W. A. Kozuschek. (Illus.). x, 92p. 1992. 55.00 (*3-8055-5623-3*) S Karger.

Theodor Billroth Privat: Die Billroth Seegen Briefe. Ed. by Karel B. Absolon & Ernst Kern. (Illus.). 291p. 1987. 39.50 (*0-930329-07-4*) Kabel Pubs.

Theodor Billroth 1829-1894. Karel B. Absolon. Tr. by Ubaldo Brancato. (Illus.). 350p. (ITA.). (C). 1995. text ed. 39.50 (*0-930329-76-7*) Kabel Pubs.

Theodor Boveri: Life & Work of a Great Biologist, 1862-1915. Friedrich Baltzer. LC 67-21996. (Illus.). 187p. reprint ed. pap. 53.30 (*0-685-20495-2*, 2029943) Bks Demand.

Theodor Fahrner Jewelry...Between Avante Garde & Tradition. Ulrike Von Hase-Schmundt et al. LC 91-65661. (Illus.). 288p. 1991. 69.95 (*0-88740-326-3*) Schiffer.

Theodor Fontane: An Introduction to the Man & His Work. A. R. Robinson. LC 76-383573. 219p. (ENG & GER.). reprint ed. pap. 62.50 (*0-7837-5190-7*, 2044924) Bks Demand.

Theodor Fontane und das Schau-Spiel: Die Kunstlergestalten seines Romanwerks. Sylvain Guarda. LC 89-37985. (American University Studies: Germanic Languages & Literature: Ser. I, Vol. 87). 125p. 1990. text ed. 33.50 (*0-8204-1140-X*) P Lang Pubng.

***Theodor Fontane und Friedrich Eggers Briefwechsel: Mit Fontanes Briefen an Karl Eggers und der Korrespodenz von Friedrich Eggers an Emilie Fontane.** Ed. by Roland Berbig. (Schriften der Theodor Fontane-Gesellschaft Ser.). 480p. (GER.). (C). 1997. lib. bdg. 156.00 (*3-11-014987-7*) De Gruyter.

Theodor Fontanes Irrungen, Wirrungen, Die "Erste Seite" als Schlussel zum Werk. G. H. Hertling. (Germanic Studies in America: Band 54). 1985. text ed. 15.00 (*0-8204-0314-8*) P Lang Pubng.

***Theodor Herzl: An Illustrated Biography.** Julius H. Schoeps. LC 96-50317. (Illus.). 224p. 1997. 35.00 (*0-87951-778-6*) Overlook Pr.

Theodor Herzl: Architect of a Nation. (Lerner Biography Ser.). 120p. (YA). (gr. 5 up). 1991. lib. bdg. 22.95 (*0-8225-4913-1*, Lerner Publctns) Lerner Group.

Theodor Herzl: From Assimilation to Zionism. Jacques Kornberg. LC 93-18399. (Jewish Literature & Culture Ser.). (C). 1993. 25.95 (*0-253-33203-6*) Ind U Pr.

Theodor Herzl: The Road to Israel. Miriam Gurko. (Young Biography Ser.). (Illus.). 96p. (J). (gr. 3-7). 1988. 14.95 (*0-8276-0312-6*) JPS Phila.

***Theodor Mommsen und Adolf Harnack: Wissenschaft und Politik im Berlin des Ausgehenden 19. Jahrhunderts, Mit Einem Anhang: Edition und Kommentierung des Briefwechsels.** Stefan Rebenich. xxi, 1018p. (GER.). (C). 1997. lib. bdg. 248.60 (*3-11-015079-4*) De Gruyter.

Theodor Storm. A. Tilo Alt. LC 72-2793. (Twayne's World Authors Ser.). 157p. (C). 1973. text ed. 17.95 (*0-8290-1757-7*) Irvington.

Theodor Storm: Ein Bild Seines Lebens, 2 vols. in 1. Gertrud Storm. 1991. reprint ed. write for info. (*3-487-09411-8*) G Olms Pubs.

Theodor Storm: Studies in Ambivalence. David Artiss. (German Language & Literature Monographs: No. 5). xix, 215p. 1978. 52.00 (*90-272-0965-0*) Benjamins North Am.

Theodor Storm: The Writer As Democratic Humanitarian. David A. Jackson. 287p. 1992. 19.95 (*0-85496-593-9*) Berg Pubs.

Theodor Storm's Craft of Fiction: The Torment of a Narrator. Clifford A. Bernd. LC 67-64644. (North Carolina. University. Studies in the Germanic Languages & Literatures: No. 43). reprint ed. 34.00 (*0-404-50943-6*) AMS Pr.

***Theodor Storm's Immensee from Critical Vantagepoint.** Wiebke Strehl. (GERM Ser.). Date not set. 49.95 (*1-57113-133-7*) Camden Hse.

Theodor Storm's Novellen: Essays on Literary Technique. E. Allen McCormick. LC 64-64253. (North Carolina. University. Studies in the Germanic Languages & Literatures: No. 47). reprint ed. 27.00 (*0-404-50947-9*) AMS Pr.

Theodora: Portrait in a Byzantine Landscape. Antony Bridge. 194p. 1993. reprint ed. pap. 10.00 (*0-89733-394-2*) Academy Chi Pubs.

An Asterisk (*) at the beginning of an entry indicates that the title is appearing in BIP for the first time.

Theodorakis: Myth & Politics in Modern Greek Music. Gail Holst. xvi, 264p. 1980. pap. 38.00 (*90-256-0795-0*, Pub. by A M Hakkert NE) Benjamins North Am.

Theodora's Dreadful Mistake. Carol Proctor. (Regency Romance Ser.). 224p. (Orig.). 1992. pap. 3.99 (*0-451-17351-1*, Sig) NAL-Dutton.

Theodore All Grown Up. Ellen S. Walsh. LC 94-24406. (Illus.). 32p. (J). (ps-3). 1995. pap. 5.00 (*0-15-285053-8*, Voyager Bks) HarBrace.

Theodore & Alice - A Love Story: The Life & Death of Alice Lee Roosevelt. William E. Monk. 80p. 1994. lib. bdg. 20.00 (*1-55787-117-5*, NY71061, Empire State Bks) Hrt of the Lakes.

Theodore Besterman, Bibliographer & Editor: A Selection of Representative Texts. Ed. by Francesco Cordasco. LC 91-45136. (Great Bibliographers Ser.: No. 9). 497p. 1992. 67.50 (*0-8108-2497-3*) Scarecrow.

Theodore Beza's Doctrine of Predestination. John S. Bray. 153p. 1975. 57.50 (*90-6004-334-0*, Pub. by B De Graaf NE) Coronet Bks.

Theodore Blegen. John T. Flanagan. 181p. 1977. 10.00 (*0-87732-060-8*) Norwegian-Am Hist Assn.

Theodore Chasseriau: Illustrations for Othello. Jay M. Fisher. LC 79-67570. 1980. pap. 6.98 (*0-912298-50-2*) Baltimore Mus.

Theodore Clement Steele: An American Master of Light. William H. Gerdts. (Illus.). 80p. 1996. 25.00 (*0-915829-66-5*) Chameleon Bks.

Theodore Clement Steele, an American Master of Light. Text by William H. Gerdts. LC 95-40830. 1995. write for info. (*0-614-09351-1*) Chameleon Bks.

Theodore Dreiser. Wilbur M. Frohock. LC 72-619529. (University of Minnesota Pamphlets on American Writers Ser.: No. 102). 48p. reprint ed. pap. 25.00 (*0-7837-2887-5*, 2057568) Bks Demand.

Theodore Dreiser. Francis O. Matthiessen. LC 72-7876. (American Men of Letters Ser.). (Illus.). 267p. 1973. reprint ed. text ed. 35.00 (*0-8371-6550-4*, MATD, Greenwood Pr) Greenwood.

Theodore Dreiser. B. Rascoe. LC 72-3569. (American Literature Ser.: No. 49). (C). 1972. reprint ed. lib. bdg. 49.95 (*0-8383-1545-3*) M S G Haskell Hse.

Theodore Dreiser: A Primary Bibliography & Reference Guide. Donald Pizer. (Reference Guides to Literature Ser.). 450p. 1991. 80.00 (*0-8161-8976-5*, Hall Reference) Macmillan.

Theodore Dreiser: A Selection of Uncollected Prose. Theodore Dreiser. Ed. by Donald Pizer. LC 77-771. 341p. reprint ed. pap. 97.20 (*0-7837-3658-4*, 2043529) Bks Demand.

Theodore Dreiser: American Editor & Novelist. Alan L. Paley. Ed. by D. Steve Rahmas. (Outstanding Personalities Ser.: No. 55). 32p. 1973. lib. bdg. 7.25 (*0-87157-557-4*) SamHar Pr.

Theodore Dreiser: An American Journey. abr. ed. Richard Lingeman. LC 92-40559. 672p. 1993. pap. text ed. 19.95 (*0-471-57426-0*) Wiley.

Theodore Dreiser: Beyond Naturalism. Ed. by Miriam Gogol. 320p. (C). 1995. 45.00 (*0-8147-3073-6*) NYU Pr.

Theodore Dreiser: Beyond Naturalism. Ed. by Miriam Gogol. 320p. (Orig.). (C). 1995. pap. 18.95 (*0-8147-3074-4*) NYU Pr.

*__Theodore Dreiser: Great American Short Stories III.__ Illus. by James Balkovek. LC 95-76748. (Classic Short Stories Ser.). 80p. (YA). (gr. 6-12). 1995. pap. 5.95 (*0-7854-0598-4*, 40084) Am Guidance.

Theodore Dreiser & the Critics, 1911 - 1982: A Bibliography with Selective Annotations. Jeanetta Boswell. LC 85-14405. (Author Bibliographies Ser.: No. 73). 319p. 1986. 32.50 (*0-8108-1837-X*) Scarecrow.

Theodore Dreiser's Ev'ry Month. Ed. by Nancy W. Barrineau. LC 95-36582. 1996. 50.00 (*0-8203-1816-7*) U of Ga Pr.

Theodore Dreiser's "Heard in the Corridors" Articles & Related Writings. Theodore Dreiser. LC 87-13095. 179p. 1988. reprint ed. pap. 51.10 (*0-608-00013-2*, 2060779) Bks Demand.

Theodore Dwight Woolsey: His Political & Social Ideas. George A. King. LC 56-12108. (Jesuit Studies). 319p. reprint ed. 91.00 (*0-8357-9432-6*, 2015063) Bks Demand.

Theodore DwightWeld - This Was A Man! Mary E. Pitts. 30p. 1987. pap. 5.00 (*0-913553-05-0*) Albert Hse Pub.

Theodore Foster's Minutes of the Convention. Theodore Foster. LC 79-137375. (Select Bibliographies Reprint Ser.). 1977. 15.95 (*0-8369-5576-5*) Ayer.

Theodore Francis Green: The Rhode Island Years, 1906-1936. Erwin L. Levine. LC 63-18096. (Brown University Bicentennial Publications). 234p. reprint ed. 66.70 (*0-685-15697-4*, 2027511) Bks Demand.

Theodore Francis Green: The Washington Years, 1937-1960. Erwin L. Levine. LC 73-127366. 191p. reprint ed. 54.50 (*0-685-15710-5*, 2027512) Bks Demand.

Theodore Gericault: 1791-1824. Lorenz E. Eitner & Steven A. Nash. LC 88-83910. (Illus.). 72p. (Orig.). (C). 1989. pap. 14.95 (*0-88401-064-3*) Fine Arts Mus.

Theodore H. White & Journalism As Illusion. Joyce Hoffman. 208p. 1995. text ed. 27.50 (*0-8262-1010-4*) U of Mo Pr.

Theodore Hamm in Minnesota: His Family & Brewery. John T. Flanagan. LC 89-61426. (Illus.). 128p. 1989. pap. 12.00 (*0-9617767-5-7*) Pogo Pr.

*__Theodore Henry Hittell's the California Academy of Sciences, 1853-1906.__ unabridged ed. Ed. by Alan E. Leviton & Michele L. Aldrich. (Memoirs of the California Academy of Sciences Ser.: Vol. 22). (Illus.). 640p. 1997. lib. bdg. 42.00 (*0-940228-39-4*) Calif Acad Sci.

Theodore Hook & His Novels. Myron F. Brightfield. (BCL1-PR English Literature Ser.). 381p. 1992. reprint ed. lib. bdg. 89.00 (*0-7812-7564-4*) Rprt Serv.

Theodore M. Hesburgh: A Bio-Bibliography. Theodore M. Hesburgh. LC 89-38277. (Bio-Bibliographies in Education Ser.: No. 1). 280p. 1989. text ed. 47.95 (*0-313-26508-9*, ATH/, Greenwood Pr) Greenwood.

Theodore Meliteniote: Tribiblos Astronomique, Livre I. Regine Leurquin. (Corpus des Astronomes Byzantins Ser.: Vol. 4). 436p. (FRE.). 1990. pap. 94.00 (*90-5063-045-6*, Pub. by Gieben NE) Benjamins North Am.

Theodore Metochite: Une Reevaluation. Eva De Vries-van der Velden. x, 276p. (FRE.). (C). 1987. 74.00 (*90-70265-58-3*, Pub. by Gieben NE) Benjamins North Am.

Theodore Parker: A Biography. Octavius B. Frothingham. (Notable American Authors Ser.). 1992. reprint ed. lib. bdg. 75.00 (*0-7812-2905-7*) Rprt Serv.

Theodore Parker: Preacher & Reformer. John W. Chadwick. LC 72-144939. 1971. reprint ed. 39.00 (*0-403-00925-1*) Scholarly.

Theodore Parker: Yankee Crusader. H. S. Commager. 1990. 14.50 (*0-8446-1884-5*) Peter Smith.

Theodore Parker Lukens: Father of Forestry. Shirley Sargent. (Illus.). x, 91p. 1969. 10.00 (*0-87093-080-X*) Dawsons.

Theodore Rex. Jane B. Mason. (J). 1996. pap. 2.99 (*0-590-67784-5*) Scholastic Inc.

Theodore Rex Digest. J. J. Gardner. (J). 1996. pap. 3.50 (*0-590-67786-1*) Scholastic Inc.

Theodore Rex Storybook. Nancy E. Krulik. (J). 1996. pap. 5.95 (*0-590-67785-3*) Scholastic Inc.

Theodore Roethke: A Bioliography. LC 72-158715. (Serif Series: Bibliographies & Checklists: No.27). 285p. reprint ed. pap. 81.30 (*0-317-10828-X*, 2014599) Bks Demand.

Theodore Roethke: A Manuscript Checklist. James R. McLeod. LC 70-121652. (Serif Series: Bibliographies & Checklists: No. 21). 315p. reprint ed. pap. 89.80 (*0-7837-0566-2*, 2040910) Bks Demand.

Theodore Roethke: The Garden Master. Rosemary Sullivan. LC 75-15527. 236p. 1975. 25.00 (*0-295-95429-9*) U of Wash Pr.

Theodore Roethke: The Journey from I to Otherwise. Neal Bowers. LC 81-10410. 240p. 1982. text ed. 29.95 (*0-8262-0347-7*) U of Mo Pr.

Theodore Roethke's Far Fields: The Evolution of His Poetry. Peter Balakian. LC 88-29212. 176p. 1989. text ed. 27.50 (*0-8071-1489-8*) La State U Pr.

Theodore Roethke's Meditative Sequences: Contemplation & the Creative Process. Ann T. Foster. LC 85-3041. (Studies in Art & Religious Interpretation: Vol. 4). 210p. 1985. lib. bdg. 89.95 (*0-88946-555-X*) E Mellen.

Theodore Roosevelt. Kathleen Dalton. Date not set. pap. write for info. (*0-679-44663-X*) Random.

Theodore Roosevelt. Zachary Kent. LC 87-35184. (Encyclopedia of Presidents Ser.). (Illus.). 100p. (J). (gr. 3 up). 1988. lib. bdg. 22.00 (*0-516-01354-8*) Childrens.

Theodore Roosevelt. Lois Markham. (World Leaders - Past & Present Ser.). (Illus.). 112p. (YA). (gr. 5 up). 1985. lib. bdg. 19.95 (*0-87754-553-7*) Chelsea Hse.

*__Theodore Roosevelt.__ Steve Potts. (Read-&-Discover Biographies Ser.). (Illus.). 24p. (J). (gr. k-3). 1996. 13.25 (*0-516-20279-0*) Childrens.

*__Theodore Roosevelt.__ Michael A. Schuman. LC 97-7272. (United States Presidents Ser.). (Illus.). 128p. (YA). (gr. 5 up). 1997. lib. bdg. 18.95 (*0-89490-836-7*) Enslow Pubs.

Theodore Roosevelt: A Biography. Henry F. Pringle. LC 56-13739. 435p. 1956. pap. 15.00 (*0-15-688943-9*, HB15, Harvest Bks) HarBrace.

Theodore Roosevelt: A Life. Nathan Miller. 1994. pap. 15.00 (*0-688-13220-0*, Quill) Morrow.

Theodore Roosevelt: A Photo-Illustrated Biography. Steve Potts. LC 96-25855. (Read & Discover Photo-Illustrated Biographies Ser.). 24p. (J). (gr. 1-2). 1996. 13.25 (*1-56065-452-X*) Capstone Pr.

Theodore Roosevelt: An American Hero in Caricature. J. David Valaik. Ed. by Elizabeth Foy. (Illus.). 99p. 1993. 34.95 (*1-878097-11-3*) Canisius Coll Pr.

Theodore Roosevelt: An American Mind: Selected Writings. Ed. & Intro. by Mario R. DiNunzio. (Illus.). 384p. 1995. pap. 13.95 (*0-14-024520-0*, Penguin Bks) Viking Penguin.

*__Theodore Roosevelt: Conservation, Vol. 1.__ Destefano. 1993. 14.98 (*0-8050-2788-2*) H Holt & Co.

Theodore Roosevelt: Conservation President. Susan DeStefano. (Earth Keepers Ser.). (Illus.). 80p. (J). (gr. 4-7). 1993. lib. bdg. 14.98 (*0-8050-2122-1*) TFC Bks NY.

Theodore Roosevelt: Many-Sided American. Ed. by Natalie A. Naylor et al. (Long Island Studies). (Illus.). 678p. 1992. lib. bdg. 55.00 (*1-55787-085-3*, NY71048) Hrt of the Lakes.

Theodore Roosevelt: Mini-Play. (President's Choice Ser.). (J). (gr. 5 up). 1979. 6.50 (*0-89550-316-6*) Stevens & Shea.

Theodore Roosevelt: The Making of a Conservationist. Paul R. Cutright. LC 84-16205. (Illus.). 306p. 1985. text ed. 29.95 (*0-252-01190-2*) U of Ill Pr.

Theodore Roosevelt: The Story Behind the Scenery. Henry A. Schoch & Bruce M. Kye. Tr. by Sigrid Sommer. (Illus.). 48p. (Orig.). (GER.). 1993. pap. 8.95 (*0-88714-757-7*) KC Pubns.

Theodore Roosevelt: The Story Behind the Scenery. rev. ed. Henry A. Schoch & Bruce M. Kaye. LC 93-77027. (Illus.). 48p. (Orig.). 1993. pap. 7.95 (*0-88714-073-4*) KC Pubns.

Theodore Roosevelt: 26th President of the United States. Rebecca Stefoff. Ed. by Richard G. Young. LC 87-35953. (Presidents of the United States Ser.). (Illus.). (J). (gr. 5-9). 1988. lib. bdg. 17.26 (*0-944483-09-7*) Garrett Ed Corp.

*__Theodore Roosevelt - Typical American.__ Charles E. Banks & Leroy Armstrong. (Roosevelt Anthology Ser.: Vol. 4). (Illus.). 140p. 1997. 7.95 (*1-58057-012-7*, TRTA001B) Digital Antiq.

*__Theodore Roosevelt, American Politician: An Assessment.__ David H. Burton. LC 96-29718. 176p. 1997. 29.50 (*0-8386-3727-2*) Fairleigh Dickinson.

Theodore Roosevelt Among the Humorists: W. D. Howells, Mark Twain & Mr. Dooley. William M. Gibson. LC 79-17592. (Hodges Lectures). 96p. reprint ed. pap. 27.40 (*0-8357-6913-5*, 2037972) Bks Demand.

*__Theodore Roosevelt & Friends of the Indian.__ William T. Hagan. LC 97-4517. (Illus.). 1997. 25.95 (*0-8061-2954-9*) U of Okla Pr.

Theodore Roosevelt & His America. Milton Meltzer. LC 94-17369. (Illus.). 160p. (YA). (gr. 9-12). 1994. lib. bdg. 25.80 (*0-531-11192-X*) Watts.

Theodore Roosevelt & His Times. Harold J. Howland. (History - United States Ser.). 289p. 1992. reprint ed. lib. bdg. 79.00 (*0-7812-6219-4*) Rprt Serv.

Theodore Roosevelt & Labor in New York State, 1880-1900. Howard L. Hurwitz. LC 68-58592. (Columbia University. Studies in the Social Sciences: No. 500). reprint ed. 20.00 (*0-404-51500-2*) AMS Pr.

Theodore Roosevelt & the British Empire. William N. Tilchin. LC 96-48922. 320p. 1996. text ed. 49.95 (*0-312-12091-5*) St Martin.

*__Theodore Roosevelt & the Great White Fleet: American Seapower Comes of Age.__ Kenneth Wimmel. (Illus.). 304p. 1997. 24.95 (*1-57488-153-1*) Brasseys Inc.

Theodore Roosevelt & the Idea of Race. Thomas G. Dyer. LC 79-20151. 182p. (C). 1992. pap. text ed. 11.95 (*0-8071-1808-7*) La State U Pr.

Theodore Roosevelt & the International Rivalries. Raymond A. Esthus. LC 71-102172. (Topics in American Diplomatic History Ser.). 165p. (C). 1982. reprint ed. 19.95 (*0-941690-04-0*); reprint ed. pap. 11.95 (*0-941690-05-9*) Regina Bks.

Theodore Roosevelt & the Politics of Power. G. Wallace Chessman. 214p. (C). 1994. reprint ed. pap. text ed. 10.50 (*0-88133-795-1*) Waveland Pr.

Theodore Roosevelt & the Rhetoric of Militant Decency. Robert V. Friedenberg. LC 90-3648. (Great American Orators: Critical Studies, Speeches & Sources: No. 9). 232p. 1990. text ed. 59.95 (*0-313-26448-1*, FRV/, Greenwood Pr) Greenwood.

Theodore Roosevelt & the Rise of the Modern Navy. Gordon C. O'Gara. LC 69-14016. 138p. 1970. reprint ed. text ed. 38.50 (*0-8371-1480-2*, OGTR, Greenwood Pr) Greenwood.

Theodore Roosevelt & the Rise of the Modern Navy. Gordon C. O'Gara. (History - United States Ser.). 138p. 1993. reprint ed. lib. bdg. 69.00 (*0-7812-4858-2*) Rprt Serv.

Theodore Roosevelt Cyclopedia. 2nd rev. ed. John A. Gable. LC 87-31012. 680p. 1989. text ed. 125.00 (*0-313-28089-4*, GTI/, Greenwood Pr) Greenwood.

Theodore Roosevelt on Race, Riots, Immigration & Crime. J. W. Jamieson. 116p. 1996. pap. 15.00 (*1-878465-19-8*) Scott-Townsend Pubs.

Theodore Roosevelt on Race, Riots, Reds, & Crime. 2nd ed. Theodore Roosevelt. Ed. by Archibald Roosevelt. 101p. 1983. pap. 5.00 (*0-89562-174-6*) Sons Lib.

Theodore Roosevelt Outdoorsman. R. L. Wilson. LC 94-60942. (Illus.). xx, 326p. 1994. 85.00 (*1-882458-03-6*) Trophy Rm Bks.

Theodore Roosevelt Takes Charge. Nancy Whitelaw. Ed. by Abby Levine. LC 90-29181. 192p. (J). (gr. 4-8). 1992. 14.95 (*0-8075-7849-5*) A Whitman.

Theodore Roosevelt, the Citizen. Jacob A. Riis. LC 71-101270. reprint ed. 34.50 (*0-404-05335-1*) AMS Pr.

Theodore Roosevelt, the Citizen. Jacob A. Riis. (History - United States Ser.). 471p. 1992. reprint ed. lib. bdg. 99.00 (*0-7812-6220-8*) Rprt Serv.

Theodore Roosevelt, the Citizen. Jacob A. Riis. LC 77-108531. 1970. reprint ed. 15.00 (*0-403-00224-9*) Scholarly.

Theodore Roosevelt's America: American Naturalists Ser. Farida A. Wiley. (Selections from the Writings of the Oyster Bay Naturalist). (Illus.). 1955. 14.95 (*0-8159-6714-4*) Devin.

Theodore Roosevelt's Caribbean: The Panama Canal, the Monroe Doctrine, & the Latin American Context. Richard H. Collin. LC 89-28161. 520p. 1990. text ed. 62.50 (*0-8071-1507-X*) La State U Pr.

Theodore Roosevelt's Night Ride to the Presidency. Eloise C. Murphy. (Adirondack Museum Monographs). (Illus.). 36p. 1996. reprint ed. pap. 4.95 (*0-910020-33-7*) Adirondack Mus.

Theodore Roszak: The Drawings. Joan M. Marter. (Illus.). 96p. (Orig.). 1992. pap. 29.95 (*0-9633559-0-2*) Drawing Soc.

Theodore Roszak: The Drawings. Joan M. Marter. (Illus.). 96p. 1993. pap. 29.95 (*0-295-97237-8*) U of Wash Pr.

Theodore Roszak: The Early Works, 1929-1943. Howard E. Wooden. LC 86-51185. (Illus.). 64p. 1986. pap. 12.00 (*0-939324-26-1*) Wichita Art Mus.

Theodore Strong Van Dyke. Peter Wild. LC 95-75728. (Western Writers Ser.: No. 121). (Illus.). 54p. (C). 1995. pap. 4.95 (*0-88430-120-6*) Boise St U W Writ Ser.

Theodore Sturgeon. Lahna Diskin. Ed. by Roger C. Schlobin. LC 80-21423. (Starmont Reader's Guide Ser.: Vol. 7). (Illus.). 72p. 1981. pap. 15.00 (*0-916732-18-5*); lib. bdg. 25.00 (*0-89370-026-6*) Borgo Pr.

Theodore Sturgeon: Sculptor of Love & Hate: A Working Bibliography. Phil Stephensen-Payne & Gordon Benson, Jr. (Galactic Central Bibliographies Ser.: No. 32). ix, 75p. (C). 1990. lib. bdg. 25.00 (*0-8095-4730-9*) Borgo Pr.

Theodore Thomas: A Musical Autobiography. 2nd ed. Ed. by George P. Upton. LC 64-18990. (Music Reprint Ser.). 1964. reprint ed. lib. bdg. 45.00 (*0-306-70904-X*) Da Capo.

Theodore Thomas: A Musical Autobiography, 2 vols. Theodore Thomas. 1990. reprint ed. lib. bdg. 140.00 (*0-7812-9006-6*) Rprt Serv.

Theodore Thomas: America's Conductor & Builder of Orchestras, 1835-1905. Ezra Schabas. (Music in American Life Ser.). (Illus.). 352p. 1989. text ed. 29.95 (*0-252-01610-6*) U of Ill Pr.

Theodore Von Karman Memorial Seminar: Proceedings of the Theodore Von Karman Memoirial Seminar, Los Angeles, 1965. Theodore Von Karman Memorial Seminar Staff. Ed. by Shirley Thomas. (Science & Technology Ser.: Vol. 7). 1966. 30.00 (*0-87703-035-9*) Univelt Inc.

Theodore Waddell: Seasons of Change. David G. Turner & Jennifer Complo. Ed. by Mike Leslie. (Illus.). 68p. (Orig.). 1993. pap. 18.00 (*0-9635492-1-9*) Eiteljorg Mus.

Theodore Watts-Dunton: Poet, Novelist, Critic. James Douglas. LC 72-1509. (English Literature Ser.: No. 33). (Illus.). 1972. reprint ed. lib. bdg. 73.95 (*0-8383-1447-3*) M S G Haskell Hse.

Theodore Winthrop. Elbridge Colby. (Twayne's United States Authors Ser.). 1965. pap. 13.95 (*0-8084-0296-X*, T84) NCUP.

Theodore Wores: An American Artist in Meiji Japan. (Illus.). 132p. 1993. pap. 22.00 (*1-877921-10-6*) Pacific Asia.

Theodoret of Cyrus: On Divine Providence. Ed. by Thomas Halton. (Ancient Christian Writers Ser.: No. 49). 1989. 19.95 (*0-8091-0420-2*) Paulist Pr.

Theodoret von Cyrus und der Neunizaenismus: Aspekte der Altkirchlichen Trinitaetslehre. Silke-Petra Bergjan. (Arbeiten zur Kirchengeschichte Ser.: No. 60). x, 246p. (GER.). 1993. lib. bdg. 113.85 (*3-11-013955-3*) De Gruyter.

Theodori Studitae Epistulae: Pars Prior: Prolegomena et Textum epp. 1-70 continens Pars Altera: Textum epp. 71-560 et Indices continens. Ed. by Georgios Fatouros. (Corpus Fontium Historiae Byzantinae Ser.: Vol. XXXXI - 1 et 2). (LAT.). (C). 1991. lib. bdg. 761.55 (*3-11-008808-8*) De Gruyter.

Theodoric the Goth. Thomas Hodgkin. LC 73-14449. (Heroes of the Nations Ser.). reprint ed. 45.00 (*0-404-58267-2*) AMS Pr.

Theodoric the Goth: Barbarian Champion of Civilization. T. Hodgkin. 1977. lib. bdg. 59.95 (*0-8490-2739-X*) Gordon Pr.

Theodorich's Description of the Holy Places see Guide to the Holy Land

Theodoric's Rainbow. Stephen Kramer. LC 95-11469. (Illus.). 32p. (J). 1995. 17.95 (*0-7167-6603-5*, Sci Am Yng Rdrs) W H Freeman.

Theodoros Dukas Laskaris: Der Naturliche Zusammenhang: Ein Zeugnis vom Stand der Byzantinischen Philosophie in der Mitte des 13. Jahrhunderts. Gerhard Richter. viii, 258p. (Orig.). (GER.). 1989. pap. 78.00 (*90-256-0944-9*, Pub. by A M Hakkert NE) Benjamins North Am.

Theodoros Stamos. Barbara Cavaliere. Ed. by Martin Bush. Tr. by Alan Cress. (Illus.). 63p. (Orig.). 1991. pap. 30.00 (*0-925315-98-2*) ACA Galleries.

Theodosia Bk. 1: Celebrating the American Woman. Meredith B. McMath. 350p. 1995. pap. 11.99 (*0-89283-890-6*, Vine Bks) Servant.

Theodosian Code. Ed. by Jill Harries & Ian Wood. LC 93-17596. 264p. 1993. 49.95 (*0-8014-2946-3*) Cornell U Pr.

Theodosian Code & Novels, & the Sirmondian Constitutions. Codex Theodosianus. Tr. by Clyde Pharr. LC 71-91756. xxvi, 643p. 1970. reprint ed. text ed. 85.00 (*0-8371-2494-8*, THC, Greenwood Pr) Greenwood.

Theodosian Empresses: Women & Imperial Dominion in Late Antiquity. Kenneth G. Holum. LC 81-43690. (Transformation of the Classical Heritage Ser.: Vol. III). 325p. 1982. pap. 16.00 (*0-520-06801-7*) U CA Pr.

Theodynamics: NeoChristian Perspectives for the Modern World. John A. Creager. 452p. (Orig.). (C). 1994. lib. bdg. 59.00 (*0-8191-9363-1*) U Pr of Amer.

Theogenesis. Ed. by Temple of the People Publications Staff. (Illus.). 548p. 1981. 24.00 (*0-933797-06-0*) Halcyon Bk.

*__Theognis of Megara: Poetry & the Polis.__ Ed. by Thomas J. Figueira & Gregory Nagy. LC 84-21832. 350p. 1985. reprint ed. pap. 99.80 (*0-608-03696-X*, 2064521) Bks Demand.

Theogonia, Opera et Dies, Scutum, Fragmenta Selecta. 3rd ed. Reinholdo Merkelbach. (Oxford Classical Texts Ser.). 282p. 1990. 26.00 (*0-19-814071-1*) OUP.

Theogony & Works & Days. Hesiod. Ed. by M. L. West. (World's Classics Ser.). 120p. 1988. pap. 7.95 (*0-19-281788-4*) OUP.

Theogony Hesiod. Norman O. Brown. 96p. (C). 1953. pap. text ed. 11.20 (*0-02-315310-5*, Macmillan Coll) P-H.

Theologia Cartesiana. J. R. Armogathe. (International Archives of the History of Ideas Ser.: No. 84). 157p. 1977. lib. bdg. 104.50 (*90-247-1869-4*, Pub. by M Nijhoff NE) Kluwer Ac.

*__Theologia Germanica.__ pap. 2.00 (*0-8358-0159-4*) Upper Room Bks.

Theologia Germanica. Martin Luther. 240p. 1992. reprint ed. pap. 19.95 (*1-56459-012-7*) Kessinger Pub.

Theologia Germanica of Martin Luther. Ed. by Bengt Hoffman. LC 80-50155. (Classics of Western Spirituality Ser.). 224p. 1980. pap. 14.95 (*0-8091-2291-X*) Paulist Pr.

Theologia Mystica. Rajneesh Osho Staff. Ed. by Ma P. Asha. LC 83-11086. (Western Mystics Ser.). 400p. (Orig.). 1983. pap. 4.95 (*0-88050-655-5*) Osho America.

Theologia Platonica. Marsilius Ficinus. 735p. 1975. reprint ed. write for info. (*3-487-05183-4*) G Olms Pubs.

T

Theologia Twenty-One, 3 vols. Ed. by A. S. Otto. 150p. 1991. Set. vinyl bd. 69.95 (0-912132-08-6) Dominion Pr.

Theologia Twenty-One Encyclopedia, 3 vols. Ed. by A. S. Otto. 700p. 1991. Set. vinyl bd. 54.95 (0-912132-16-7) Dominion Pr.

Theologians & Authority Within the Living Church. James J. Mulligan. LC 86-30542. 139p. (Orig.). 1987. pap. 13.95 (0-935372-18-0) Pope John Ctr.

***Theologians of a New World Order: Rheinhold Niebuhr & the Christian Realists, 1920-1948.** Heather A. Warren. (Religion in America Ser.). 224p. 1997. 37.00 (0-19-511438-8) OUP.

Theologians of Methodism. 1992. reprint ed. pap. 7.99 (0-88019-287-9) Schmul Pub Co.

Theologians of Our Time. Ed. by Leonhard Reinisch. LC 64-17067. 1964. pap. 10.50 (0-268-00378-5) U of Notre Dame Pr.

Theological Aesthetics of Hans Urs von Balthasar. Louis Roberts. LC 86-28321. 272p. 1987. reprint ed. pap. 77.60 (0-7837-9118-6, 2049919) Bks Demand.

Theological Analyses of the Clinical Encounter. Jonathan R. Sande. Ed. by Gerald P. Mckenney. LC 93-17958. (Theology & Medicine Ser.: Vol. 3). 256p. 1994. lib. bdg. 127.00 (0-7923-2362-9, Pub. by Klwr Acad Pubs NE) Kluwer Ac.

Theological & Aesthetic Roots in the Stone-Campbell Movement. Dale A. Jorgenson. (Illus.). 360p. (C). 1989. lib. bdg. 47.50 (0-943549-04-3) TJU Pr.

Theological & Miscellaneous Works, 25 vols. in 26. Joseph Priestley. 1974. reprint ed. Set. pap. 1,900.00 (0-527-72751-2) Periodicals Srv.

Theological & Religious Reference Materials: General Resources & Biblical Studies. G. E. Gorman & Lyn Gorman. LC 83-22759. (Bibliographies & Indexes in Religious Studies: No. 1). xvi, 526p. 1984. text ed. 89.50 (0-313-20924-3, GRM/) Greenwood.

Theological & Religious Reference Materials: Practical Theology. Ed. by Lyn Gorman & Donald N. Matthews. LC 86-380. (Bibliographies & Indexes in Religious Studies: No. 7). 402p. 1986. text ed. 79.50 (0-313-25397-8, GPA/, Greenwood Pr) Greenwood.

Theological & Religious Reference Materials: Systematic Theology & Church History. G. E. Gorman & Lyn Gorman. LC 83-22759. (Bibliographies & Indexes in Religious Studies: No. 2). xiv, 401p. 1985. text ed. 95.00 (0-313-24779-X, GOS/) Greenwood.

Theological Anthropology. Ed. & Tr. by J. Patout Burns. LC 81-43080. (Sources of Early Christian Thought Ser.). 136p. (Orig.). 1981. pap. 13.00 (0-8006-1412-7, 1-1412, Fortress Pr) Augsburg Fortress.

Theological Approaches to Christian Education. Ed. by Jack L. Seymour & Donald E. Miller. LC 90-35784. 1990. pap. 20.95 (0-687-41355-9) Abingdon.

Theological Biology: The Case for a New Modernism. Kenneth Cauthen. LC 91-41520. (Toronto Studies in Theology: Vol. 62). 320p. 1991. lib. bdg. 99.95 (0-7734-9655-6) E Mellen.

Theological Cautions. Paul Toinet. Tr. by Michael J. Wrenn. 165p. 1982. 5.00 (0-8199-0835-5, Frncscn Herld) Franciscan Pr.

***Theological Consensus in the Episcopal Church, 1801-73.** Robert W. Prichard. LC 96-25380. 1997. text ed. 29.95 (0-252-02309-9) U of Ill Pr.

Theological Context for Pastoral Caregiving: Word in Deed. Howard W. Stone. LC 96-355. 190p. 1996. 29.95 (0-7890-0072-5, Haworth Pastrl); pap. 19.95 (0-7890-0125-X) Haworth Pr.

***Theological Convictions.** Vern Elefson. 106p. (Orig.). 1997. pap. 6.00 (1-57502-397-0, P01237) Morris Pubng.

***Theological Dicionary of the Old Testament, Vol. III.** Ed. by G. Johannes Botterweck et al. 584p. 1996. 45.00 (0-8028-2332-7) Eerdmans.

Theological Dictionary of the New Testament. abr. ed. Ed. by Gerhard Kittel & Gerhard Friedrich. Tr. by Geoffrey W. Bromiley from GER. 1300p. (C). 1985. 60.00 (0-8028-2404-8) Eerdmans.

Theological Dictionary of the New Testament, 10 vols, Set. Ed. by Gerhard Kittel & Gerhard Friedrich. Incl. Vol. 1. Theological Dictionary of the New Testament. 1964. 60.00 (0-8028-2243-6); Vol. 2. . 1965. 60.00 (0-8028-2244-4); Vol. 3. . 1966. 60.00 (0-8028-2245-2); Vol. 4. . 1967. 60.00 (0-8028-2246-0); Vol. 5. . 1968. 60.00 (0-8028-2247-9); Vol. 6. . 1969. 60.00 (0-8028-2248-7); Vol. 7. . 1971. 60.00 (0-8028-2249-5); Vol. 8. . 1972. 60.00 (0-8028-2250-9); Vol. 9. . 1974. 60.00 (0-8028-2322-X); Vol. 10. . 1976. 60.00 (0-8028-2323-8); 1984. 550.00 (0-8028-2324-6) Eerdmans.

Theological Dictionary of the New Testament, Vol. 1. Ed. by Gerhard Kittel & Gerhard Friedrich. Incl. Vol. 1. Theological Dictionary of the New Testament. 1964. 60.00 (0-8028-2243-6); Vol. 2. . 1965. 60.00 (0-8028-2244-4); Vol. 3. . 1966. 60.00 (0-8028-2245-2); Vol. 4. . 1967. 60.00 (0-8028-2246-0); Vol. 5. . 1968. 60.00 (0-8028-2247-9); Vol. 6. . 1969. 60.00 (0-8028-2248-7); Vol. 7. . 1971. 60.00 (0-8028-2249-5); Vol. 8. . 1972. 60.00 (0-8028-2250-9); Vol. 9. . 1974. 60.00 (0-8028-2322-X); Vol. 10. . 1976. 60.00 (0-8028-2323-8); (Theological Dictionary of the New Testament). 1964. 60.00 (0-8028-2243-6) Eerdmans.

Theological Dictionary of the New Testament see Theological Dictionary of the New Testament

Theological Dictionary of the Old Testament, 8 vols. Ed. by G. Johannes Botterweck & Helmer Ringgren. 560p. 1978. 350.00 (0-8028-2338-6) Eerdmans.

Theological Dictionary of the Old Testament, 7 vols., Vol. 1. Ed. by G. Johannes Botterweck & Helmer Ringgren. 560p. 1974. 45.00 (0-8028-2325-4) Eerdmans.

Theological Dictionary of the Old Testament, 7 vols., Vol. 2. Ed. by G. Johannes Botterweck & Helmer Ringgren. 560p. 1975. 45.00 (0-8028-2326-2) Eerdmans.

Theological Dictionary of the Old Testament, 7 vols., Vol. 3. Ed. by G. Johannes Botterweck & Helmer Ringgren. 560p. 1979. 45.00 (0-8028-2327-0) Eerdmans.

Theological Dictionary of the Old Testament, 7 vols., Vol. 4. Ed. by G. Johannes Botterweck & Helmer Ringgren. 560p. 1981. 45.00 (0-8028-2328-9) Eerdmans.

Theological Dictionary of the Old Testament, 7 vols., Vol. 5. Ed. by G. Johannes Botterweck & Helmer Ringgren. 560p. 1986. 45.00 (0-8028-2329-7) Eerdmans.

Theological Dictionary of the Old Testament, 7 vols., Vol. 6. Ed. by G. Johannes Botterweck & Helmer Ringgren. 560p. 1990. 45.00 (0-8028-2330-0) Eerdmans.

Theological Dictionary of the Old Testament, 7 vols., Vol. 7. Ed. by G. Johannes Botterweck et al. 600p. 1995. text ed. 45.00 (0-8028-2331-9) Eerdmans.

Theological Diversity & the Authority of the Old Testament. John Goldingay. 240p. (Orig.). 1987. pap. 15.00 (0-8028-0229-X) Eerdmans.

Theological Dramatic Theory IV: The Action. Hans U. Von Balthasar. 510p. (Orig.). 1994. pap. 40.00 (0-89870-471-5) Ignatius Pr.

***Theological Education in the Catholic Tradition: Contemporary Challenges.** Ed. by Patrick W. Carey & Earl C. Muller. LC 96-51970. 396p. (Orig.). 1997. pap. 29.95 (0-8245-1672-9, Crossrd Herd) Crossroad NY.

***Theological Education in the Evangelical Tradition.** Ed. by R. Albert Mohler, Jr. & D. G. Hart. LC 96-35212. 320p. (C). 1996. pap. 24.99 (0-8010-2061-1) Baker Bks.

Theological Essays. Eberhard Jungel. Ed. & Tr. by J. B. Webster from GER. Tr. by U. Lohmann from GER. 236p. 1989. 43.95 (0-567-09502-9, Pub. by T & T Clark UK) Bks Intl VA.

Theological Essays, 2 vols. in 1. W. G. Shedd. 692p. 1987. lib. bdg. 27.99 (0-8254-5230-9, Kregel Class) Kregel.

Theological Essays II. Eberhard Jungel. Ed. & Tr. by John Webster from GER. Tr. by Arnold Neufeldt-Fast from GER. 272p. 1995. text ed. 47.95 (0-567-09706-4, Pub. by T & T Clark UK) Bks Intl VA.

Theological Ethics, Vol. 1. Helmut Thielicke. LC 78-31858. 731p. reprint ed. 180.00 (0-685-15957-4, 2027550) Bks Demand.

Theological Ferment: Personal Reflections. Paul Clasper. 226p. (Orig.). 1982. pap. 9.50 (971-10-0042-3, Pub. by New Day Pub PH) Cellar.

Theological Formulations. Richard S. Taylor. (Exploring Christian Holiness Ser.: Vol. 3). 260p. 1985. 19.99 (0-8341-1077-6) Beacon Hill.

Theological Foundations, Vol. 1. Robert M. Doran. LC 95-41772. (Studies in Theology: No. 8). 500p. (C). 1995. pap. 50.00 (0-87462-632-3) Marquette.

Theological Foundations, Vol. 2. Robert M. Doran. LC 95-41772. (Studies in Theology: No. 9). 550p. (C). 1995. pap. 55.00 (0-87462-633-1) Marquette.

***Theological Foundations for Ministry.** Anderson. pap. 24.95 (0-567-22355-8, Pub. by T & T Clark UK) Bks Intl VA.

Theological Hermeneutics: Development & Significance. Werner G. Jeanrond. 192p. 1991. 22.95 (0-8245-1117-4) Crossroad NY.

Theological Interpretation of Scripture: Classic & Contemporary Readings. Stephen Fowl. LC 96-19722. (Blackwell Readings in Modern Theology Ser.). (C). 1997. 64.95 (1-55786-834-4) Blackwell Pubs.

Theological Interpretation of Scripture: Classic & Contemporary Readings. Stephen Fowl. LC 96-19722. 400p. (C). 1997. pap. 24.95 (1-55786-835-2) Blackwell Pubs.

Theological Introduction to the Book of Psalms: The Psalms As Torah. J. Clinton McCann. 224p. (Orig.). 1993. pap. 19.95 (0-687-41468-7) Abingdon.

Theological Introduction to the New Testament. Eduard Schweizer. 1991. pap. 7.58 (0-687-41469-5) Abingdon.

Theological Investigations, Vols. 1-17, 20. Karl Rahner. Incl. Vol. 2. Man & the Church. 1975. 29.50 (0-8245-0378-3); Vol. 5. Later Writings. 1975. 29.50 (0-8245-0381-3); Vol. 7. Further Theology of the Spiritual Life I. 1975. 29.50 (0-8245-0383-X); Vol. 15. Penance in the Early Church. 500p. 1975. 29.50 (0-8245-0025-3); Vol. 17. Jesus, Man & the Church. 1975. 29.50 (0-8245-0026-1); 1975. write for info. (0-318-51489-3) Crossroad NY.

Theological Investigations, Vol. 22: Humane Society & the Church of Tomorrow. Karl Rahner. 288p. 1987. 29.50 (0-8245-0924-2) Crossroad NY.

Theological Investigations, Vol. 23: Final Writings. Karl Rahner. 240p. 1992. 29.50 (0-8245-1165-4) Crossroad NY.

***Theological Issues in the Letters of Paul.** J. Louis Martyn. LC 97-15082. 1997. write for info. (0-687-05622-5) Abingdon.

Theological Lexicon of the Old Testament. Ed. by Ernst Jenni & Claus Westermann. Tr. by Mark Biddle. LC 97-5604. 1600p. 1997. 119.95 (1-56563-133-1) Hendrickson MA.

Theological Lexion of the New Testament, 3 vols. Ceslas Spicq. Tr. by James D. Ernest from FRE. 1888p. (C). 1995. Set. 99.95 (1-56563-035-1) Hendrickson MA.

Theological Method in Jacques Ellul. Daniel B. Clendenin. LC 87-10506. 184p. (Orig.). (C). 1987. pap. text ed. 19.50 (0-8191-6428-3) U Pr of Amer.

Theological Method of Karl Rahner. Anne Carr. LC 76-51639. (American Academy of Religion, Dissertation Ser.: No. 19). 289p. reprint ed. pap. 82.40 (0-317-08410-0, 2017556) Bks Demand.

Theological Methodology of Hans Kung. Catherine M. LaCugna. LC 81-16654. (American Academy of Religion Academy Ser.). 244p. 1982. 19.95 (0-89130-546-7, 01 01 39) Scholars Pr GA.

Theological Models for the Parish. Sabbas Kilian. LC 76-42986. 1977. pap. 5.95 (0-8189-0389-9) Alba.

Theological Music: Introduction to Theomusicology. Jon M. Spencer. LC 91-9254. (Contributions to the Study of Music & Dance Ser.: No. 23). 200p. 1991. text ed. 45.00 (0-313-27953-5, SKW/, Greenwood Pr) Greenwood.

Theological Notebook, Vol. I. Donald G. Bloesch. LC 88-24566. 256p. 1989. pap. 18.95 (0-939443-12-0) Helmers Howard Pub.

Theological Notebook, Vol. 2. Donald G. Bloesch. LC 88-24566. (Spiritual Journals of Donald G. Bloesch). 219p. 1991. pap. 18.95 (0-939443-13-9) Helmers Howard Pub.

Theological Paradox-Das Theologische Paradox: Interdisciplinary Reflections on the Centre of Paul Tillich's Thought/Interdisziplinaere Reflexionen Zur Mitte Von Paul Tillichs Denken. Ed. by Gert Hummel. LC 95-40722. (Theologische Bibliothek Toepelmann Ser.: Vol. 74). xvii, 264p. (ENG & GER.). (C). 1995. lib. bdg. 106.15 (3-11-014995-8) De Gruyter.

Theological Pastoral Resources: A Collection of Articles on Homosexuality from a Pastoral Perspective. rev. ed. Ed. by Kathleen Leopold & Thomas Orians. LC 81-69476. 81p. 1985. pap. 4.00 (0-940680-01-7) Dignity Inc.

***Theological Perspectives on Christian Formation: A Reader on Theology & Christian Education.** Ed. by Jeff Astley et al. 472p. 1997. pap. text ed. 34.00 (0-8028-0777-1) Eerdmans.

Theological Principles of Egyptian Religion. Vincent A. Tobin. (American University Studies: Theology & Religion: Ser. VII, Vol. 59). 221p. (C). 1989. text ed. 36.95 (0-8204-1082-9) P Lang Pubng.

Theological Questions: Analysis & Argument. Owen C. Thomas. LC 83-60658. 134p. (Orig.). 1983. pap. 8.95 (0-8192-1328-4) Morehouse Pub.

Theological Reading of Four Novels by Marie Chauvet: In Search of Christic Voices. Pedro A. Sandin-Fremaint. LC 92-7642. 380p. 1992. lib. bdg. 99.95 (0-7734-9826-5) E Mellen.

Theological Reading of Hegel's Phenomenology of Spirit, with Particular Reference to Its Themes of Identity, Alienation, & Community: Salvation in a Social Context. Esther D. Reed. LC 95-20526. 240p. 1996. write for info. (0-7734-8874-X, Mellen Univ Pr) E Mellen.

Theological Reflections: Essays on Related Themes. Henry Stob. LC 81-1472. 277p. reprint ed. pap. 79.00 (0-317-20015-1, 2023223) Bks Demand.

***Theological Resources for Ministry: A Bibliography of Works in Theological Studies.** Don Thorsen. LC 96-86314. 192p. (Orig.). 1996. pap. 10.00 (0-916035-71-9) Evangel Indiana.

Theological Roots of Pentecostalism. Donald W. Dayton. 204p. 1991. pap. 14.95 (0-943575-79-6) Hendrickson MA.

Theological Science. Thomas F. Torrance. 400p. 1996. pap. 29.95 (0-567-08514-7, Pub. by T & T Clark UK) Bks Intl VA.

***Theological Study Informed by the Theory of Paul Tillich & the Latin American Experience: The Ambivalence of Science.** Eduardo R. Cruz. LC 96-50188. 354p. 1997. text ed. 99.95 (0-7734-2280-3, Mellen Univ Pr) E Mellen.

Theological Themes in the American Protestant World see Modern American Protestantism & Its World

Theological Themes on the Holy Spirit. David Mendez & Ken Chant. 100p. (Orig.). 1990. pap. 7.00 (1-56428-002-0) Logos Intl Pub.

Theological Thinking: An Inquiry. Carl Raschke. LC 87-26604. (Studies in Religion). 169p. 1988. 20.95 (1-55540-187-2, 01-00-53); pap. 13.95 (1-55540-188-0) Scholars Pr GA.

Theological Tractates. Boethius. Bd. with Consolation of Philosophy. (Loeb Classical Library: No. 74). 15.50 (0-674-99083-8) HUP.

Theological Transition in American Methodism, 1790-1935. Robert E. Chiles. LC 83-16666. 238p. 1983. reprint ed. pap. text ed. 22.00 (0-8191-3551-8) U Pr of Amer.

Theological Treatises on the Trinity. Marius Victorinus. LC 79-15587. (Fathers of the Church Ser.: Vol. 69). 371p. 1981. 26.95 (0-8132-0069-5) Cath U Pr.

Theological Turning Points: Major Issues in Christian Thought. Donald K. McKim. LC 88-45432. 240p. 1988. pap. 18.00 (0-8042-0702-X) Westminster John Knox.

Theological Voices in Medical Ethics. Ed. by Allen Verhey & Stephen E. Lammers. LC 92-42800. 266p. (Orig.). 1993. pap. 13.00 (0-8028-0664-3) Eerdmans.

Theological Wordbook of the Old Testament, 2 vols. R. Laird Harris et al. Ed. by Bruce K. Waltke. LC 80-28047. 1800p. (C). 1980. text ed. 69.99 (0-8024-8631-2) Moody.

Theological Works of Isaac Barrow, 9 Vols. Isaac Barrow. Ed. by Alexander Napier. LC 72-161751. reprint ed. Set. lib. bdg. 215.00 (0-404-00670-1) AMS Pr.

Theological Worlds: Understanding the Alternative Rhythms of Christian Belief. W. Paul Jones. LC 89-35389. 240p. 1989. pap. 18.95 (0-687-41470-9) Abingdon.

Theologico-Political Treatise: Political Treatise. Benedict Spinoza. Tr. by R. H. Elwes. pap. text ed. 6.95 (0-486-20249-6) Dover.

Theologie als Gestaltmetaphysik: Die Vermittlung von Gott & Welt im Fruehwerk Paul Tillichs. Hannelore Jahr. (Theologische Bibliothek Toepelmann Ser.: Vol. 46). xiv, 482p. (GER.). (C). 1989. lib. bdg. 106.95 (3-11-011906-4) De Gruyter.

***Theologie der Bekenntnisschriften der Evangelisch-Lutherischen Kirche Vol. 1: Eine Historische und Systematische Einfuehrung in das Konkordienbuch.** Gunther Wenz. 719p. (GER.). (C). 1996. pap. text ed. 50.40 (3-11-015239-8, 108/96); lib. bdg. 80.00 (3-11-015238-X, 108/96) De Gruyter.

Theologie des Markell Von Ankyra. Klaus Seibt. (Arbeiten zur Kirchengeschichte Ser.: Vol. 59). xiv, 558p. 1994. lib. bdg. 198.50 (3-11-014027-6) De Gruyter.

Theologie des Neuen Testaments. Georg Strecker. Ed. by Friedrich W. Horn. xvi, 744p. (C). 1995. pap. text ed. 60.00 (3-11-014896-X); lib. bdg. 90.75 (3-11-012674-5) De Gruyter.

***Theologie Im Pianissimo & Zwischen Rationalitat und Dekonstruktion: Die Aktualitat der Denkfiguren Adornos und Levinas'** Hent De Vries. (Studies in Philosophical Theology: Vol. 1). 355p. 1989. pap. 46.00 (90-242-5179-6, Pub. by KOK Pharos NE) Eisenbrauns.

Theologie Portative ou Dictionnaire Abrege de la Religion Chretienne. rev. ed. Paul H. D'Holbach. 229p. 1977. 55.00 (3-487-06411-1) G Olms Pubs.

***Theologie und Anthropologie: Die Erziehung des Menschengeschlechts Bei Johann Gottfried Herder.** Claudia Leuser. (Wurzburger Studien Zur Fundamentaltheologie Ser.: Bd. 19). 472p. (GER.). 1996. 76.95 (3-631-30388-2) P Lang Pubng.

Theologie und Gesellschaft Im 2 Lund 3 Jahrundert Hidschra, Vol. 5: Eine Geschichte Des Religioesen Denkens im Fruehen Islam. Josef Van Ess. x, 457p. (GER.). 1993. lib. bdg. 238.50 (3-11-013726-7) De Gruyter.

Theologie und Gesellschaft im 2. und 3. Jahrhundert Hidschra, Vol. 3: Eine Geschichte des Religioesen Denkens im Fruehen Islam. Josef Van Ess. xii, 508p. (GER.). (C). 1992. lib. bdg. 264.65 (3-11-013161-7) De Gruyter.

Theologie und Gesellschaft im 2. und 3. Jahrhundert Hidschra, Bd. II: Eine Geschichte des Religosen im Fruhen Islam. Josef Van Ess. xi, 742p. (GER.). (C). 1991. lib. bdg. 307.70 (3-11-012212-X, 243-91) De Gruyter.

Theologies & Liberation in Peru: The Role of Ideas in Social Movements. Milagros Pena. 240p. (Orig.). (C). 1995. text ed. 49.95 (1-56639-294-2) Temple U Pr.

Theologies of Religious Education. Ed. by Randolph C. Miller. LC 95-11226. 378p. (Orig.). 1995. pap. 19.95 (0-89135-096-9) Religious Educ.

Theologies of the Body: Humanist & Christian. Benedict Ashley. LC 84-15031. (Illus.). 770p. (Orig.). 1995. reprint ed. pap. 25.95 (0-935372-15-6) Pope John Ctr.

Theologische Enzyklopadie (1831-32) Kurt-Victor Selge et al. Ed. by Friedrich Schleiermacher. (Schleiermacher-Archiv Ser.: Band 4). 256p. (C). 1987. lib. bdg. 97.70 (3-11-010894-1) De Gruyter.

Theologische Grundstrukturen des Alten Testaments. Georg Fohrer. (Theologische Bibliothek Toepelmann Ser.: Vol. 24). (C). 1972. pap. 52.35 (3-11-003874-9) De Gruyter.

Theologische Realenzyklopaedie: Agende-Anselm Von Cantebury, Vol. 2. Ed. by Michael Wolter. (Illus.). (C). 1978. 344.65 (3-11-007379-X) De Gruyter.

Theologische Realenzyklopaedie: Teil I, Band 1-17 und Registerband. Ed. by Gerhard Mueller. (TRE Ser.). (Orig.). (GER.). (C). 1993. Set. pap. text ed. 795.00 (3-11-013898-0) De Gruyter.

Theologischen Fakultaeten Im Dritten Reich. Kurt Meier. vi, 500p. (GER.). (C). 1996. text ed. 80.00 (3-11-015226-6); pap. text ed. 50.40 (3-11-013761-5) De Gruyter.

Theologizing Gay. J. Michael Clark. LC 91-13732. 80p. 1991. pap. 6.00 (0-926899-03-1) Minuteman Pr.

Theology. Christ. 19.00 (0-06-061328-9, HarpT) HarpC.

Theology, 5 vols., Set. Timothy Dwight. LC 75-3132. reprint ed. 200.00 (0-404-59136-1) AMS Pr.

Theology: An Assessment of Current Trends Report. Lutheran Church in America Task Group for Long-Range Planning. LC 68-55757. 174p. reprint ed. pap. 49.60 (0-685-15423-8, 2026880) Bks Demand.

Theology: An Orthodox Standpoint. Apostolos Makrakis. Ed. by Orthodox Christian Educational Society Staff. Tr. by Denver Cummings. (Logos & Holy Spirit in the Unity of Christian Thought Ser.: Vol. 4). 216p. 1977. reprint ed. pap. 5.00 (0-938366-03-3) Orthodox Chr.

Theology: Love's Question. Terry J. Tekippe. 160p. (C). 1992. pap. text ed. 22.50 (0-8191-8433-0); lib. bdg. 45.00 (0-8191-8432-2) U Pr of Amer.

Theology Vol. 3: Revisioning the Church. Ed. by Richard Brown. (Theology Colloquy Papers). 164p. (Orig.). 1995. pap. text ed. 12.00 (0-8309-0722-X) Herald Hse.

***Theology Vol. 4: Justice or Just Us?** Ed. by Richard A. Brown. 206p. (Orig.). 1997. pap. text ed. 13.00 (0-8309-0754-8) Herald Hse.

Theology after Freud: An Interpretive Inquiry. Peter Homans. LC 76-84162. 1970. 29.50 (0-672-51245-9); pap. text ed. 16.95 (0-8290-1399-7) Irvington.

***Theology after the Storm: Reflections on the Upheavals in Modern Theology & Culture.** John McIntyre. Ed. & Intro. by Gary Badcock. 296p. 1996. pap. 25.00 (0-8028-4110-4) Eerdmans.

Theology after Vedanta: An Experiment in Comparative Theology. Francis X. Clooney. LC 92-14007. (SUNY Series, Toward a Comparative Philosophy of Religions). 265p. 1993. text ed. 24.50 (0-7914-1365-9) State U NY Pr.

Theology & Canon Law: New Horizons for Legislation & Interpretation. Ladislas M. Orsy. 200p. (Orig.). 1992. pap. text ed. 19.95 (0-8146-5011-2) Liturgical Pr.

Theology & Canon Law: The Theories of Klaus Morsdorf & Eugenio Corecco. Myriam Wijlens. 250p. (Orig.). (C). 1992. lib. bdg. 48.00 (0-8191-8498-5) U Pr of Amer.

Theology & Contemporary Critical Theory. Graham Ward. LC 96-17547. (Studies in Literature & Religion). 175p. 1996. text ed. 49.95 (0-312-15942-0) St Martin.

Theology & Dialogue: Essays in Conversation with George Lindbeck. Ed. by Bruce D. Marshall. LC 90-70847. 288p. (C). 1990. text ed. 34.50 (0-268-01873-1) U of Notre Dame Pr.

Theology & Dialogue: Essays in Conversation with George Lindbeck. Ed. by Bruce D. Marshall. LC 90-70847. (C). 1992. pap. text ed. 17.50 (*0-268-01874-X*) U of Notre Dame Pr.

Theology & Difference: The Wound of Reason. Walter Lowe. LC 92-26531. (Indiana Series in the Philosophy of Religion). 204p. 1993. 31.50 (*0-253-33611-2*) Ind U Pr.

Theology & Embodiment: The Post-Patriarchal Reconstruction of Female Sacrality. Melissa Raphael. (Feminist Theology Ser.). 320p. 1996. pap. 19.95 (*1-85075-757-7*, Pub. by Sheffield Acad UK) CUP Services.

***Theology & Ethics in Paul & His Interpreters: Essays in Honor of Victor Paul Furnish.** Ed. by Eugene H. Lovering, Jr. & Jerry L. Sumney. 288p. 1996. pap. 19.95 (*0-687-00767-4*) Abingdon.

Theology & Evangelism in the Wesleyan Heritage: Essays in the Theology of Evangelism. Ed. by James C. Logan. LC 93-6428. (Kingswood Ser.). 224p. (Orig.). 1994. pap. 14.95 (*0-687-41395-8*) Abingdon.

Theology & Feminism. Daphne Hampson. (Signposts in Theology Ser.). 192p. 1990. pap. text ed. 21.95 (*0-631-14944-9*) Blackwell Pubs.

Theology & History of the Augustinian Order in the Middle Ages. Adolar Zumkeller & John E. Rotelle. LC 96-24004. (Augustinian Ser.). 1996. pap. 19.95 (*0-941491-93-5*) Augustinian Pr.

Theology & Identity: Traditions, Movements & Polity in the United Church of Christ. Ed. by Charles E. Hambrick-Stowe & Daniel L. Johnson. LC 89-78141. 208p. (Orig.). (C). 1990. pap. 16.95 (*0-8298-0807-8*) Pilgrim OH.

Theology & Integration: Four Essays in Philosophical Theology. Anders Jeffner. (Acta Universitatis Upsaliensis Ser.). 73p. (Orig.). 1987. pap. 31.50 (*91-554-2087-7*, Pub. by Uppsala Univ Acta Univ Uppsaliensis SW) Coronet Bks.

Theology & Meaning: A Critique of Metatheological Scepticism. Raeburne S. Heimbeck. LC 68-13146. 276p. 1969. 35.00 (*0-8047-0704-9*) Stanford U Pr.

Theology & Modern Life. Paul A. Schilpp. LC 70-117852. (Essay Index Reprint Ser.). 1977. 21.95 (*0-8369-1727-8*) Ayer.

Theology & Modern Life: Essays in Honor of Harris Franklin Rall. Ed. by Paul A. Schilpp. (Essay Index Reprint Ser.). 307p. 1982. reprint ed. lib. bdg. 18.00 (*0-686-79705-1*) Irvington.

Theology & Modern Literature. Amos N. Wilder. LC 58-11556. 157p. reprint ed. pap. 44.80 (*0-317-10086-6*, 2003002) Bks Demand.

Theology & Narrative: A Critical Introduction. Michael Goldberg. LC 90-23328. 304p. (Orig.). (C). 1991. reprint ed. pap. 15.95 (*1-56338-010-2*) TPI PA.

Theology & Narrative: Selected Essays. Hans W. Frei. Ed. by George Hunsinger & William C. Placher. LC 92-36161. 288p. 1993. 45.00 (*0-19-507880-2*) OUP.

Theology & Pastoral Counseling: A New Interdisciplinary Approach. Deborah V. Hunsinger. LC 95-12857. 256p. 1995. pap. 19.00 (*0-8028-0842-5*) Eerdmans.

Theology & Poetry: Studies in the Medieval Piyyut. Ed. by Jakob J. Petuchowski. Tr. by Jacob J. Petuchowski. (Littman Library of Jewish Civilization). 250p. 1978. 21.00 (*0-19-710014-7*) Bnai Brith Bk.

Theology & Practice. Ed. by Duncan Forrester. 144p. (Orig.). (C). 1990. pap. 12.95 (*0-7162-0466-5*, Epworth Pr) TPI PA.

Theology & Praxis: Epistemological Foundations. Clodovis Boff. Tr. by Robert R. Barr from POR. LC 86-21671. 416p. (Orig.). 1987. reprint ed. pap. 118.60 (*0-7837-9856-3*, 2060585) Bks Demand.

Theology & Sanity. Francis J. Sheed. LC 93-78529. 468p. 1993. 17.95 (*0-89870-470-7*) Ignatius Pr.

Theology & Science in the Fourteenth Century: Three Questions on the Unity & Subalternation of the Sciences from John of Reading's Commentary on the Sentences. Steven J. Livesey. LC 89-909. (Studien und Texte zur Geistesgeschichte des Mittelalters Ser.: Vol. XXV). viii, 229p. (Orig.). 1989. pap. text ed. 85.75 (*90-04-09023-1*) E J Brill.

Theology & Scientific Knowledge: Changing Models of God's Presence in the World. Christopher F. Mooney. LC 95-16517. 288p. (C). 1996. text ed. 34.95 (*0-268-04200-4*) U of Notre Dame Pr.

***Theology & Scientific Knowledge: Changing Models of God's Presence in the World.** Christopher F. Mooney. 256p. 1996. pap. text ed. 15.00 (*0-614-18897-0*) U of Notre Dame Pr.

Theology & Setting of Discipleship in the Gospel of Mark. John R. Donahue. LC 83-60749. (Pere Marquette Lectures). (C). 1983. 15.00 (*0-87462-538-6*) Marquette.

Theology & Social Theory: Beyond Secular Reason. John Milbank. (Signposts in Theology Ser.). 448p. 1993. pap. text ed. 27.95 (*0-631-18948-3*) Blackwell Pubs.

***Theology & Sociology: A Reader.** Ed. by Robin Gill. 480p. 1996. pap. 27.00 (*0-304-33839-7*) Cassell.

Theology & the Church. Dumitru Staniloae. Tr. by Robert Barringer from RUM. LC 80-19313. 240p. 1980. pap. 10.95 (*0-913836-69-9*) St Vladimirs.

Theology & the Community of God. Stanley J. Grenz. LC 93-26963. 1994. 39.99 (*0-8054-2801-1*, 4228-01) Broadman.

Theology & the Dialectics of History. Robert M. Doran. 752p. 1989. 95.00 (*0-8020-2713-X*); pap. 45.00 (*0-8020-6777-8*) U of Toronto Pr.

Theology & the Dialectics of Otherness: On Reading Bonhoeffer & Adorno. Wayne W. Floyd, Jr. LC 88-5428. 368p. (Orig.). (C). 1988. lib. bdg. 52.00 (*0-8191-6974-9*) U Pr of Amer.

Theology & the Human Spirit: Essays in Honor of Perry D. LeFevre. Ed. by Susan B. Thistlethwaite. LC 92-73228. (Studies in Ministry & Parish Life). 124p. 1994. text ed. 21.95 (*0-913552-48-8*) Exploration Pr.

Theology & the Interhuman: Essays in Honor of Edward Farley. Robert R. Williams. LC 95-23845. 288p. (Orig.). 1995. 40.00 (*1-56338-126-5*); pap. 25.00 (*1-56338-127-3*) TPI PA.

Theology & the Justification of Faith: Constructing Theories in Systematic Theology. Wentzel Van Huyssteen. 1989. pap. 19.00 (*0-8028-0366-0*) Eerdmans.

Theology & the Option for the Poor. John O'Brien. (Theology & Life Ser.: Vol. 22). 167p. (Orig.). 1992. pap. text ed. 14.95 (*0-8146-5787-7*) Liturgical Pr.

Theology & the Practice of Responsibility: Essays on Dietrich Bonhoeffer. Ed. by Wayne W. Floyd & Charles Marsh. LC 94-15801. 320p. (Orig.). (C). 1994. pap. 25.00 (*1-56338-077-3*) TPI PA.

Theology & the Scientific Imagination from the Middle Ages to the Seventeenth Century. Amos Funkenstein. LC 85-43281. (Illus.). 368p. (C). 1986. pap. text ed. 23.50 (*0-691-02425-1*) Princeton U Pr.

Theology & the University, Vol. 33. Ed. by John V. Apczynski. 290p. (Orig.). (C). 1990. pap. text ed. 25.00 (*0-8191-7473-4*); lib. bdg. 46.50 (*0-8191-7472-6*) U Pr of Amer.

Theology & the University: Essays in Honor of John B. Cobb, Jr. Ed. by David R. Griffin & Joseph C. Hough, Jr. LC 90-36908. 276p. 1991. pap. text ed. 19.95 (*0-7914-0593-1*) State U NY Pr.

Theology & the University: Essays in Honor of John B. Cobb, Jr. Ed. by David R. Griffin & Joseph C. Hough, Jr. LC 90-36908. 276p. 1991. text ed. 59.50 (*0-7914-0592-3*) State U NY Pr.

Theology & Violence: The South African Debate. Ed. by Charles Villa-Vicencio. LC 87-37524. 313p. reprint ed. pap. 89.30 (*0-7837-3172-8*, 2042806) Bks Demand.

Theology & Women's Ministry in Seventeenth-Century English Quakerism: Handmaids of the Lord. Catherine M. Wilcox. LC 94-38870. (Studies in Women & Religion: Vol. 35). 300p. 1995. text ed. 89.95 (*0-7734-8982-7*) E Mellen.

Theology As a Way of Thinking. Richard Grigg. (American Academy of Religion, Religion & the Arts & Society of Biblical Literature Ser.). 144p. 1990. 29.95 (*1-55540-275-5*, 09 02 01); pap. 14.95 (*1-55540-535-5*, 09 02 01) Scholars Pr GA.

Theology As an Empirical Science. Douglas C. Macintosh. Ed. by Edwin S. Gaustad. LC 79-52601. (Baptist Tradition Ser.). 1980. reprint ed. lib. bdg. 25.95 (*0-405-12466-X*) Ayer.

***Theology as Big as the City.** Ray Bakke. LC 96-29820. 240p. 1997. pap. 12.99 (*0-8308-1890-1*, 1890) InterVarsity.

Theology as Hermeneutics: Paul Ricoeur's Theory of Text Interpretation & Method in Theology. Joseph Putti. LC 93-39087. 1995. 64.95 (*1-883255-23-6*); pap. 44.95 (*1-883255-22-8*) Intl Scholars.

Theology as Hermeneutics: Rudolf Bultmann's Interpretation of the History of Jesus. John Painter. (Historic Texts & Interpreters Ser.: Vol. 265). 265p. 18.95 (*1-85075-051-3*) CUP Services.

Theology at the End of Modernity. Ed. by Sheila G. Davaney. LC 91-13306. 288p. (C). 1991. pap. 24.95 (*1-56338-017-X*) TPI PA.

Theology at the End of the Century: A Dialogue on the Postmodern with Thomas J. J. Altizer, Mark C. Taylor, Charles E. Winquist & Robert P. Scharlemann. Robert P. Scharlemann. (Studies in Religion & Culture). (Illus.). 176p. 1990. text ed. 28.50 (*0-8139-1246-6*) U Pr of Va.

Theology Beyond Christendom. Essays on the Centenary of the Birth of Karl Barth, May 10, 1886. Ed. by John Thompson. LC 86-2377. (Princeton Theological Monographs: No. 6). (Orig.). 1986. pap. 24.95 (*0-915138-85-9*) Pickwick.

Theology by the People: Reflections on Doing Theology in Community. Ed. by Samuel Amirtham & John S. Pobee. LC 86-211214. 153p. reprint ed. pap. 43.70 (*0-7837-6007-8*, 2045817) Bks Demand.

Theology Conflict & Other Writings on Nonviolence. Dominique Barbe. LC 89-8827. 199p. 1989. reprint ed. pap. 56.80 (*0-7837-9832-6*, 2060561) Bks Demand.

Theology, Ethics, & the Nineteenth-Century American College Ideal: Conserving a Rational World. Thomas E. Frank. LC 92-44659. 292p. 1993. text ed. 89.95 (*0-7734-2208-0*, Mellen Univ Pr) E Mellen.

Theology Explained & Defended. Timothy Dwight. (Notable American Authors Ser.). 1992. reprint ed. lib. bdg. 75.00 (*0-7812-2743-7*) Rprt Serv.

Theology for a Liberating Church: The New Praxis of Freedom. Alfred Hennelly. LC 88-24701. 203p. (Orig.). 1989. pap. 10.95 (*0-87840-474-0*) Georgetown U Pr.

Theology for a Nuclear Age. Gordon D. Kaufman. LC 84-25803. 78p. (C). 1985. pap. 11.00 (*0-664-24628-1*, Westminster) Westminster John Knox.

Theology for a Scientific Age: Being & Becoming - Natural, Divine, & Human. Arthur Peacocke. LC 93-30674. (Theology & the Sciences Ser.). 416p. 1993. pap. 23.00 (*0-8006-2759-8*, 1-2759, Fortress Pr) Augsburg Fortress.

Theology for Beginners. rev. ed. Francis J. Sheed. 196p. 1982. pap. 9.99 (*0-89283-124-3*) Servant.

Theology for Disciples. Gilbert W. Stafford. Ed. by Richard Craghead. 640p. (Orig.). 1996. 24.95 (*0-87162-674-8*) Warner Pr.

Theology for Earth Community: A Field Guide. Ed. by Dieter T. Hessel. LC 95-50663. (Ecology & Justice Ser.). 300p. (Orig.). 1996. pap. 20.00 (*1-57075-052-1*) Orbis Bks.

Theology for Everyman. John H. Gerstner. 127p. 1991. reprint ed. pap. 7.95 (*1-877611-40-9*) Soli Deo Gloria.

Theology for Non-Theologians. James Cantelon. 288p. 1989. pap. 8.95 (*0-02-084280-5*) Macmillan.

Theology for Ordinary People: What You Should Know to Make Sense Out of Life. Bruce L. Shelley. LC 92-34568. (Illus.). 218p. (Orig.). 1993. pap. 10.99 (*0-8308-1342-X*, 1342) InterVarsity.

Theology for Pew & Pulpit: The Everlasting Song. Joseph A. Bassett. LC 95-46836. 184p. (Orig.). (C). 1996. pap. 24.95 (*0-942597-90-7*, Ragged Edge) White Mane Pub.

Theology for Preaching. Mack Stokes. 450p. (Orig.). 1994. pap. 17.95 (*0-917851-97-8*) Bristol Hse.

***Theology for Preaching: Authority, Truth & Knowledge of God in a Postmodern Ethos.** Ronald J. Allen et al. LC 97-7471. 176p. 1997. pap. 14.95 (*0-687-01717-3*) Abingdon.

Theology for Skeptics: Reflections on God. Dorothee Solle. LC 94-2828. 1994. 14.00 (*0-8006-2788-1*, Fortress Pr) Augsburg Fortress.

***Theology for the Church: Writings by Marlin E. Miller.** Marlin E. Miller. Ed. by Richard A. Kauffman & Gayle G. Koontz. (Test Reader Ser.: No. TR7). 264p. (C). 1997. pap. 15.00 (*0-936273-24-0*) Inst Mennonite.

***Theology for the Social Gospel.** Walter Rauschenbusch. 289p. 1996. pap. 16.00 (*1-57910-022-8*) Wipf & Stock.

***Theology for the Social Gospel.** Walter Rauschenbush. LC 97-1589. (Library of Theological Ethics). (Orig.). 1997. pap. 17.00 (*0-664-25730-5*) Westminster John Knox.

Theology for Youth: God 101. Scott M. Montgomery. 128p. (YA). (gr. 9-12). 1994. pap. 7.95 (*0-9641817-0-3*) S M Montgomery.

***Theology from Three Worlds: Liberation & Evangelization for the New Europe.** Michael I. Bochenski. LC 97-14480. (Regent's Study Guides Ser.). 1997. write for info. (*1-57312-168-1*) Smyth & Helwys.

Theology, from Tradition to Task. LC 93-11566. 1993. pap. 12.00 (*0-8309-0641-X*) Herald Hse.

Theology, History, & Culture: Major Unpublished Writings. H. Richard Niebuhr. 1996. write for info. (*0-300-06370-9*) Yale U Pr.

Theology, Ideology & Liberation: Towards a Liberative Theology. Peter Scott. (Cambridge Studies in Ideology & Religion: No. 6). 300p. (C). 1995. text ed. 65.00 (*0-521-46476-5*) Cambridge U Pr.

Theology in a New Key: Responding to Liberation Themes. Robert M. Brown. LC 78-6494. 212p. 1978. pap. 11.00 (*0-664-24204-9*, Westminster) Westminster John Knox.

Theology in a Polanyian Universe Vol. 174: The Theology of Thomas Torrance. Colin Weightman. LC 93-41340. (American University Studies: No. VII). 315p. (C). 1994. text ed. 51.95 (*0-8204-2391-2*) P Lang Pubng.

Theology in Anglicanism. Arthur A. Vogel et al. LC 84-60624. (Anglican Studies Ser.). 160p. (Orig.). 1984. pap. 9.95 (*0-8192-1344-6*) Morehouse Pub.

Theology in Dialogue. John H. Gerstner. 621p. 1996. 29.95 (*1-57358-038-4*) Soli Deo Gloria.

Theology in Exodus: Biblical Theology in the Form of a Commentary. Donald E. Gowan. LC 94-8689. 1994. 28.00 (*0-664-22057-6*) Westminster John Knox.

***Theology in History.** Henri De Lubac. 615p. 1996. pap. text ed. 29.95 (*0-89870-472-3*) Ignatius Pr.

Theology in Hymns: Reflections on the "Collection of Hymns for the Use of the People Called Methodists (1780)" Teresa Berger. (Kingswood Ser.). 224p. (Orig.). 1995. pap. 14.95 (*0-687-00281-8*) Abingdon.

Theology in Postliberal Perspective. Daniel Liechty. LC 90-38708. 128p. (Orig.). (C). 1990. pap. 10.95 (*0-334-02481-1*) TPI PA.

***Theology in Rabbinic Stories.** Chaim Pearl. 176p. (Orig.). 1997. pap. 12.95 (*1-56563-285-0*) Hendrickson MA.

***Theology in Reconciliation.** Thomas F. Torrance. 303p. 1996. pap. 20.00 (*1-57910-023-6*) Wipf & Stock.

***Theology in Reconstruction.** Thomas F. Torrance. 288p. 1996. pap. 20.00 (*1-57910-024-4*) Wipf & Stock.

Theology in the Age of Scientific Reasoning. Nancey C. Murphy. LC 89-39375. (Cornell Studies in the Philosophy of Religion). 232p. 1993. pap. 13.95 (*0-8014-8114-7*) Cornell U Pr.

Theology in the Americas. Ed. by Sergio Torres & John Eagleson. LC 76-22545. 465p. reprint ed. pap. 132.60 (*0-8357-7053-2*, 2033546) Bks Demand.

Theology in the English Poets. Stopford A. Brooke. 1972. 59.95 (*0-8490-1189-2*) Gordon Pr.

Theology in the English Poets: Cowper, Coleridge, Wordsworth & Burns. 6th ed. Stopford A. Brooke. LC 79-129367. reprint ed. 29.50 (*0-404-01116-0*) AMS Pr.

Theology in the Russian Diaspora: Church, Fathers, Eucharist in Nikolai Afanas'ev (1893-1966) Aidan Nichols. 280p. (C). 1990. text ed. 80.00 (*0-521-36543-0*) Cambridge U Pr.

Theology in the Shape of Dance: Using Dance in Worship & Theological Process. Judith Rock. 1977. pap. 3.00 (*0-941500-16-0*) Sharing Co.

Theology Interpreted: A Guide to Christian Doctrine - God, the World & Mankind, Vol. I. Joseph Pungur. LC 87-8250. (Christian Doctrine of God, Revelation, Creation, Providence, Man & Sin Ser.). 246p. (Orig.). (C). 1987. pap. text ed. 24.00 (*0-8191-6355-4*); lib. bdg. 43.50 (*0-8191-6354-6*) U Pr of Amer.

Theology Interpreted, Vol. 2: A Guide to Christian Doctrine. Joseph Pungur. 226p. (Orig.). (C). 1992. pap. text ed. 27.50 (*0-8191-8892-1*); lib. bdg. 54.00 (*0-8191-8891-3*) U Pr of Amer.

Theology Investment SCI CHR, Vol. 21. Karl Rahner. (Theological Investigations Ser.: Vol. 21). 352p. 1988. 29.50 (*0-8245-0888-2*) Crossroad NY.

Theology Is for Proclamation. Gerhard O. Forde. LC 90-33374. 208p. (Orig.). 1990. pap. 15.00 (*0-8006-2425-4*, 1-2425) Augsburg Fortress.

Theology Meets Progress: Human Implications of Development. Ed. by Philip Land. 1971. pap. 6.50 (*0-8294-0326-4*, Pub. by Gregorian Univ Pr IT) Loyola Pr.

Theology of a Protestant Catholic. Adrian Hastings. LC 90-31484. 224p. (Orig.). (C). 1990. pap. text ed. 19.95 (*0-334-02441-2*) TPI PA.

Theology of Albert Schweitzer. E. N. Mozley. LC 73-16630. 108p. 1974. reprint ed. text ed. 35.00 (*0-8371-7204-7*, SCTH, Greenwood Pr) Greenwood.

Theology of Albert Schweitzer for Christian Inquirers. Albert Schweitzer. Ed. by E. N. Mozley. 1977. lib. bdg. 59.95 (*0-8490-2740-3*) Gordon Pr.

Theology of Anabaptism: An Interpretation. Robert Friedmann. LC 73-7886. (Studies in Anabaptist & Mennonite History: No. 15). 184p. reprint ed. pap. 52.50 (*0-7837-5108-7*, 2044807) Bks Demand.

Theology of Ancient Judaism, 2 vols, Set. Abraham J. Heschel. (HEB.). 1973. 27.95 (*0-900689-75-7*) Bloch.

Theology of Arithmetic. Iamblichus. Tr. by Robin Waterfield from GRE. LC 88-23012. (Illus.). 150p. (Orig.). 1988. pap. 17.00 (*0-933999-72-0*) Phanes Pr.

Theology of Atonement & Paul's Vision of Christianity. Anthony J. Tambasco. (Zaachaeus Studies: New Testament). 120p. (Orig.). 1991. pap. text ed. 7.95 (*0-8146-5679-X*) Liturgical Pr.

Theology of Bernard Lonergan. Hugo A. Meynell. (Studies in Religion). 235p. (C). 1986. pap. 15.95 (*1-55540-016-7*, 01 00 42) Scholars Pr GA.

Theology of Canon Law: A Methodological Question. Eugenio Corecco. LC 91-38559. 172p. (C). 1992. text ed. 21.50 (*0-8207-0238-2*) Duquesne.

Theology of Change: A Christian Concept of God in an Eastern Perspective. Jung Y. Lee. LC 78-16745. 160p. reprint ed. pap. 45.60 (*0-8357-7054-0*, 2033547) Bks Demand.

***Theology of Chaplaincy.** Paul Wells. 40p. 1997. pap. 8.00 (*0-8059-4086-3*) Dorrance.

Theology of Christian Counseling: More Than Redemption. Jay E. Adams. (Jay Adams Library). 352p. 1986. pap. 15.99 (*0-310-51101-1*, 12122P) Zondervan.

Theology of Christian Solidarity. Jon Sobrino & Juan H. Pico. Tr. by Phillip Berryman from SPA. LC 84-16533. Orig. Title: Teologia de la Solidaridad Chrisiana. 112p. (Orig.). reprint ed. pap. 32.00 (*0-7837-5529-5*, 2045299) Bks Demand.

Theology of Compromise: A Study of Method in the Ethics of Charles E. Curran. Richard Grecco. LC 91-3823. (American University Studies: Theology & Religion: Ser. VII, Vol. 104). 250p. 1991. 45.95 (*0-8204-1538-3*) P Lang Pubng.

Theology of Congregationalism. Karl Pruter. LC 85-12844. 100p. 1985. reprint ed. pap. 17.00 (*0-912134-09-7*); reprint ed. lib. bdg. 27.00 (*0-89370-597-7*) Borgo Pr.

***Theology of Creation in an Evolutionary World.** Karl Schmitz-Moormann. 192p. (Orig.). 1997. pap. 18.95 (*0-8298-1215-6*) Pilgrim OH.

Theology of Culture. Paul Tillich. Ed. by Robert C. Kimball. 224p. 1964. pap. 10.95 (*0-19-500711-5*) OUP.

Theology of Deuteronomy: Collected Essays of Georg Braulik, O.S.B. Georg Braulik. Tr. by Ulrika Lindblad from GER. (Collected Essays Ser.: No. 2). 320p. 1995. pap. 18.95 (*0-941037-30-4*) BIBAL Pr.

Theology of Discontent: The Ideological Foundations of the Islamic Revolution in Iran. Hamid Dabashi. 600p. (C). 1992. 75.00 (*0-8147-1839-6*); pap. 25.00 (*0-8147-1840-X*) NYU Pr.

Theology of Doubt. Scott Cairns. (CSU Poetry Ser.: No. XVIII). 58p. (Orig.). 1985. pap. 6.00 (*0-914946-52-8*) Cleveland St Univ Poetry Ctr.

Theology of Electricity: On the Encounter & Dialogue Between Theology & the Natural Sciences in the Seventeenth & Eighteenth Centuries. Ernst Benz. Tr. by Wolfgang Taraba. (Princeton Theological Monographs: No. 19). xix, 108p. (Orig.). 1990. pap. 19.95 (*0-915138-92-1*) Pickwick.

Theology of Encounter: The Ontological Ground for a New Christology. Charles B. Ketcham. LC 77-21905. 1978. 30.00 (*0-271-00520-3*) Pa St U Pr.

Theology of Existence. Fritz Buri. Tr. by Harold H. Oliver. 128p. 1965. 6.00 (*0-87921-001-X*) Attic Pr.

Theology of Familycare. James Stone. 116p. (Orig.). 1987. pap. 5.95 (*0-934942-71-4*) White Wing Pub.

Theology of Freedom: The Legacy of Jacque Maritain & Reinhold Niebuhr. John W. Cooper. LC 85-13852. ix, 186p. 1985. text ed. 19.95 (*0-86554-172-8*, MUP-H162) Mercer Univ Pr.

Theology of Fulfillment. Fred G. Zaspel. LC 93-61277. 39p. 1994. pap. 3.95 (*0-944788-90-4*) IBRI.

Theology of Grace & the American Mind: A Representation of Catholic Doctrine. Daniel Liderbach. LC 83-22154. (Toronto Studies in Theology: Vol. 15). 170p. 1983. lib. bdg. 79.95 (*0-88946-761-7*) E Mellen.

Theology of Haham David Nieto. Jakob J. Petuchowski. 1970. 10.00 (*0-87068-015-3*) Ktav.

Theology of Henri de Lubac: An Overview. Hans U. Von Balthasar. Tr. by Joseph Fessio et al. from GER. LC 91-71631. 127p. (Orig.). 1991. pap. 12.95 (*0-89870-350-6*) Ignatius Pr.

Theology of History. Hans U. Von Balthasar. LC 93-7536. 154p. pap. 12.95 (*0-89870-460-X*) Ignatius Pr.

Theology of History According to St. Bonaventure. Joseph C. Ratzinger. Tr. by Zachary Hayes from GER. 268p. 1989. pap. 12.50 (*0-8199-0415-5*, Frncscn Herld) Franciscan Pr.

Theology of History & Apologetic Historiography in Heinrich Bullinger: Truth in History. Aurelio A. Archilla. LC 92-11975. 344p. 1992. lib. bdg. 99.95 (*0-7734-9828-1*) E Mellen.

An Asterisk (*) at the beginning of an entry indicates that the title is appearing in BIP for the first time.

Theology of Holiness. unabridged ed. Dougan Clark. 112p. 1996. reprint ed. pap. 7.99 (*0-88019-347-6*) Schmul Pub Co.

Theology of Holiness & Love. Kenneth E. Jones. LC 95-23280. 334p. (Orig.). (C). 1995. pap. text ed. 37.00 (*0-7618-0035-2*) U Pr of Amer.

Theology of Hope: On the Ground & the Implications of a Christian Eschatology. Jurgen Moltmann. Tr. by James W. Leitch. LC 93-29966. (Works of Jurgen Moltmann). 352p. 1993. pap. 18.00 (*0-8006-2824-1*, 1-2824, Fortress Pr) Augsburg Fortress.

Theology of Inclusion in Jesus & Paul: The God of Outcasts & Sinners. William A. Simmons. LC 95-32214. (Biblical Press Ser.: Vol. 39). 216p. 1996. 89.95 (*0-7734-2436-9*, Mellen Biblical Pr) E Mellen.

***Theology of Jewish Christian Reality Pt. 1: Discerning the Way.** Van Buren. pap. 25.95 (*0-06-068823-8*, Pub. by T & T Clark UK) Bks Intl VA.

***Theology of Jewish Christian Reality Pt. 2: A Christian Theology of the People of Israel.** Van Buren. pap. 25.95 (*0-06-254751-8*, Pub. by T & T Clark UK) Bks Intl VA.

Theology of John Calvin. Karl Barth. Tr. by Geoffrey W. Bromiley. 1995. pap. 25.00 (*0-8028-0696-1*) Eerdmans.

Theology of John Fisher: A Study in the Intellectual Origins of the Counter-Reformation. Richard Rex. 250p. (C). 1991. text ed. 75.00 (*0-521-39177-6*) Cambridge U Pr.

Theology of Jonathan Edwards: A Reappraisal. Conrad Cherry. LC 89-45471. 300p. 1990. 12.95 (*0-253-31342-2*); pap. 7.95 (*0-253-20559-X*, MB 559) Ind U Pr.

Theology of Jurgen Moltmann. Richard J. Bauckham. 1995. pap. 27.95 (*0-567-29277-0*) Bks Intl VA.

Theology of Karl Barth: Exposition & Interpretation. Hans U. Von Balthasar. Tr. by Edward T. Oakes from GER. LC 92-71929. 451p. (Orig.). 1992. pap. 21.95 (*0-89870-398-0*) Ignatius Pr.

Theology of "La Lozana Andaluza" Pamela Brakhage. 27.50 (*0-916379-34-5*) Scripta.

Theology of Law & Authority in the English Reformation. Joan L. O'Donovan. 421p. 1991. 39.95 (*1-55540-628-9*, 70 03 01); pap. 24.95 (*1-55540-629-7*, 70 03 01) Scholars Pr GA.

Theology of Liberation: History, Politics, & Salvation. annuals 15th rev. ed. Gustavo Gutierrez. Tr. by Caridad Inda & John Eagleson from SPA. LC 87-34793. 272p. 1988. pap. 18.50 (*0-88344-542-5*) Orbis Bks.

Theology of Love. Mildred B. Wynkoop. 376p. 1972. 21.99 (*0-8341-0102-5*) Beacon Hill.

Theology of Martin Luther. Paul Althaus. Tr. by Robert C. Schultz from GER. LC 66-17345. 480p. 1966. pap. 21.00 (*0-8006-1855-6*, 1-1855, Fortress Pr) Augsburg Fortress.

Theology of Meaning. Margaret Larkin. (American Oriental Ser.: Vol. 79). ix, 220p. 1995. 35.00 (*0-940490-79-X*) Am Orient Soc.

Theology of Medicine: The Political-Philosophical Foundations of Medical Ethics. 2nd ed. Thomas Szasz. 170p. (C). 1988. reprint ed. pap. 14.95 (*0-8156-0225-1*) Syracuse U Pr.

Theology of Ministry. Michael G. Lawler. LC 89-61929. 152p. (Orig.). 1990. pap. 10.95 (*1-55612-310-8*) Sheed & Ward MO.

Theology of Ministry. Thomas F. O'Meara. LC 82-60588. 1983. pap. 12.95 (*0-8091-2487-4*) Paulist Pr.

Theology of Ministry in the "Lima Document" A Roman Catholic Critique. Conrad T. Gromada. (Catholic Scholars Press Ser.). 525p. (C). 1995. pap. 44.95 (*1-883255-96-1*); text ed. 64.95 (*1-883255-97-X*) Intl Scholars.

Theology of Music for Worship Derived from the Book of Revelation. Thomas A. Seel. LC 94-98093. (Studies in Liturgical Musicology: No. 3). 323p. 1995. 29.50 (*0-8108-2989-4*) Scarecrow.

Theology of Nahmanides Systematically Presented. David Novak. LC 92-35709. (Brown Judaic Studies: No. 271). 149p. 1993. 59.95 (*1-55540-802-8*, 14 02 71) Scholars Pr GA.

Theology of Ordained Ministry in the Letters of Augustine of Hippo. Lee F. Bacchi. (Catholic Scholars Press Ser.). 320p. 1997. 69.95 (*1-57309-047-6*, Cath Scholar Pr); pap. 49.95 (*1-57309-046-8*, Cath Scholar Pr) Intl Scholars.

***Theology of Paul the Apostle.** James D. Dunn. LC 97-23189. 1997. write for info. (*0-8028-3844-8*) Eerdmans.

Theology of Paul's Letter to the Galatians. Ed. by James D. Dunn. LC 93-9. (New Testament Theology Ser.). 170p. (C). 1993. text ed. 49.95 (*0-521-35127-8*); pap. text ed. 16.95 (*0-521-35953-8*) Cambridge U Pr.

Theology of Peace. Victorino R. Rodriguez. LC 88-70763. (Illus.). 62p. (Orig.). (C). 1988. pap. 4.00 (*1-877905-04-6*) Am Soc Defense TFP.

Theology of Peace. Paul Tillich & Ronald H. Stone. 192p. (Orig.). 1990. pap. 14.00 (*0-664-25118-8*) Westminster John Knox.

Theology of Plato: Compared with the Principles of Oriental & Grecian Philosophers. John Ogilvie. xxiii, 205p. 1976. reprint ed. 37.70 (*3-487-05710-7*) G Olms Pubs.

Theology of Politics. Nathaniel Micklem. 1977. 13.95 (*0-8369-7119-1*, 7953) Ayer.

Theology of Power: Domination & Being. Kyle A. Pasewark. LC 92-19343. 400p. 1992. 22.00 (*0-8006-2605-2*, 1-2605) Augsburg Fortress.

***Theology of Preaching.** Lischer. 14.80 (*0-8010-2036-0*) Baker Bks.

Theology of Preaching: The Dynamics of the Gospel. Richard Lischer. 115p. (Orig.). 1993. reprint ed. pap. 9.95 (*0-939464-53-5*, Labyrinth) Baker Bks.

Theology of Presence: The Search for Meaning in the American Catholic Experience. Dick Westley. LC 88-72012. 168p. 1988. pap. text ed. 9.95 (*0-89622-373-6*) Twenty-Third.

Theology of Reconstruction: Nation-Building & Human Rights. Charles Villa-Vicencio. (Studies in Ideology & Religion: No. 1). 328p. (C). 1992. text ed. 69.95 (*0-521-41625-6*); pap. text ed. 21.95 (*0-521-42628-6*) Cambridge U Pr.

Theology of Revelation. Rene Latourelle. LC 65-15734. 1966. pap. 17.95 (*0-8189-0401-1*) Alba.

Theology of Revelation of Avery Dulles, 1980-1994: Symbolic Mediation. Ross A. Shecterle. LC 95-50929. (Roman Catholic Studies: Vol. 8). 268p. 1996. text ed. 89.95 (*0-7734-4248-0*, Mellen Univ Pr) E Mellen.

Theology of Ronald Gregor Smith. K. W. Clements. (Zeitschrift fur Religions- und Geistesgeschichte Ser.: No. 27). xii, 328p. 1986. pap. 85.75 (*90-04-07298-5*) E J Brill.

Theology of Salomon Ludwig Steinheim. Aharon Shear-Yashuv. (Studies in Judaism in Modern Times: Vol. 7). (Illus.). x, 115p. 1986. 46.00 (*90-04-07670-0*) E J Brill.

Theology of Schleiermacher. Karl Barth. 1996. 47.95 (*0-567-09339-5*) Bks Intl VA.

Theology of Schleiermacher: Lectures at Gottingen, Winter Semester of 1923-24. Karl Barth. Ed. by Dietrich Ritschl. Tr. by Geoffrey W. Bromiley. LC 82-2330. 307p. reprint ed. pap. 87.50 (*0-8357-4353-5*, 2037180) Bks Demand.

Theology of Stewardship in Light of Orthodox Tradition. Paul Wesche. 1990. pap. 7.95 (*0-937032-71-9*) Light&Life Pub Co MN.

Theology of the Acts of the Apostles. Jacob Jervell. (New Testament Theology Ser.). 160p. (C). 1996. text ed. 39.95 (*0-521-41385-0*); pap. text ed. 12.95 (*0-521-42447-X*) Cambridge U Pr.

***Theology of the Body According to John Paul II: Human Love in the Divine Plan.** John Paul II. 578p. (Orig.). 1997. pap. 19.95 (*0-8198-7394-2*) Pauline Bks.

Theology of the Book of Joel. Willem S. Prinsloo. (Beiheft zur Zeitschrift fuer die Alttestamentliche Wissenschaft Ser.: Vol. 163). viii, 136p. 1985. 70.00 (*3-11-010301-X*) De Gruyter.

Theology of the Book of Revelation. Richard J. Bauckham. LC 92-15805. (New Testament Theology Ser.). 168p. (C). 1993. text ed. 45.00 (*0-521-35610-5*); pap. text ed. 16.95 (*0-521-35691-1*) Cambridge U Pr.

Theology of the Cross: The Death of Jesus in the Pauline Letters. Charles B. Cousar. LC 90-31424. (Overtures to Biblical Theology Ser.). 192p. (Orig.). 1990. pap. 15.00 (*0-8006-1558-1*, 1-1558) Augsburg Fortress.

Theology of the Cross & Marx's Anthropology: A View from the Caribbean. Winston D. Persaud. LC 90-40423. (American University Studies: Theology & Religion: Ser. VII, Vol. 84). 298p. (C). 1991. text ed. 48.95 (*0-8204-1409-3*) P Lang Pubng.

Theology of the Early Greek Philosophers: The Gifford Lectures, 1936. Werner W. Jaeger. Tr. by Edward S. Robinson. LC 79-9940. vi, 259p. 1980. reprint ed. text ed. 62.50 (*0-313-21262-7*, JATH, Greenwood Pr) Greenwood.

***Theology of the English Reformers.** 3rd expanded rev. ed. Philip E. Hughes. LC 96-95429. 350p. (Orig.). 1997. pap. 17.99 (*0-9656563-0-6*) Horseradish.

***Theology of the First Christians.** Walter Schmithals. LC 97-23139. 1997. pap. text ed. 29.00 (*0-664-25615-5*) Westminster John Knox.

Theology of the Gospel of John. D. Moody Smith. LC 93-29256. (New Testament Theology Ser.). 210p. (C). 1995. 44.95 (*0-521-35514-1*); pap. text ed. 14.95 (*0-521-35776-4*) Cambridge U Pr.

Theology of the Gospel of Luke. Joel B. Green. (New Testament Theology Ser.). 172p. (C). 1995. 44.95 (*0-521-46529-X*); pap. text ed. 13.95 (*0-521-46932-5*) Cambridge U Pr.

Theology of the Gospel of Matthew. Ulrich Luz. Tr. by J. Bradford Robinson. (New Testament Theology Ser.). 180p. (C). 1995. text ed. 44.95 (*0-521-43433-5*) Cambridge U Pr.

Theology of the Gospel of Matthew. Ulrich Luz. Tr. by J. Bradford Robinson. (New Testament Theology Ser.). 180p. (C). 1995. pap. text ed. 13.95 (*0-521-43576-5*) Cambridge U Pr.

Theology of the Hammer. Millard Fuller. (Illus.). 160p. (Orig.). 1994. pap. 9.95 (*1-880837-92-7*) Smyth & Helwys.

Theology of the Icon, 2 vols. Leonid Ouspensky. Tr. by Anthony Gythiel & Elizabeth Meyendorff from FRE. LC 92-12323. (Illus.). 728p. (C). 1992. Set. pap. 25.95 (*0-88141-124-8*) St Vladimirs.

Theology of the Icon, 2 vols., 1. Leonid Ouspensky. Tr. by Anthony Gythiel & Elizabeth Meyendorff from FRE. LC 92-12323. (Illus.). 728p. (C). 1992. pap. 12.95 (*0-88141-122-1*) St Vladimirs.

Theology of the Icon, 2 vols., 2. Leonid Ouspensky. Tr. by Anthony Gythiel & Elizabeth Meyendorff from FRE. LC 92-12323. (Illus.). 728p. (C). 1992. pap. 13.95 (*0-88141-123-X*) St Vladimirs.

Theology of the Jewish-Christian Reality: A Christian Theology of the People Israel, Part 2. Paul M. Van Buren. 380p. 1995. reprint ed. pap. text ed. 44.80 (*0-8191-9970-2*) U Pr of Amer.

Theology of the Jewish-Christian Reality: Christ in Context, Part 3. Paul M. Van Buren. 332p. 1995. reprint ed. pap. text ed. 39.50 (*0-8191-9971-0*) U Pr of Amer.

Theology of the Jewish-Christian Reality: Discerning the Way, Part 1. Paul M. Van Buren. 220p. 1995. reprint ed. pap. text ed. 29.50 (*0-8191-9969-9*) U Pr of Amer.

Theology of the Johannine Epistles. Judith Lieu. (New Testament Theology Ser.). 148p. (C). 1991. text ed. 49.95 (*0-521-35246-0*); pap. text ed. 15.95 (*0-521-35806-X*) Cambridge U Pr.

Theology of the Laity. Hendrik Kraemer. 191p. 1994. reprint ed. pap. 17.95 (*1-57383-031-3*) Regent College.

Theology of the Later Pauline Letters. Andrew T. Lincoln & A. J. Wedderburn. LC 92-31674. (New Testament Theology Ser.). 175p. (C). 1993. text ed. 49.95 (*0-521-36460-4*); pap. text ed. 15.95 (*0-521-36721-2*) Cambridge U Pr.

Theology of the Letter to Hebrews. Barnabas Lindars. (New Testament Theology Ser.). 169p. 1991. pap. text ed. 16.95 (*0-521-35748-9*) Cambridge U Pr.

Theology of the Letter to Hebrews. Myeers. 1992. pap. write for info. (*0-521-35778-0*) Cambridge U Pr.

Theology of the Letter to the Hebrews. Barnabas Lindars. (New Testament Theology Ser.). 176p. (C). 1991. text ed. 49.95 (*0-521-35487-0*) Cambridge U Pr.

Theology of the Letters of James, Peter, & Jude. Andrew Chester & Ralph P. Martin. LC 93-33910. (New Testament Theology Ser.). 191p. (C). 1994. text ed. 49.95 (*0-521-35631-8*); pap. text ed. 15.95 (*0-521-35659-8*) Cambridge U Pr.

Theology of the Local Church in Relation to Migration see Pastoral Series

Theology of the New Testament. George B. Stevens. 636p. 1918. 47.95 (*0-567-07215-0*, Pub. by T & T Clark UK) Bks Intl VA.

Theology of the New Testament. rev. ed. George E. Ladd. Ed. by Donald A. Hagner. 740p. (C). 1993. pap. text ed. 35.00 (*0-8028-0680-5*) Eerdmans.

Theology of the Old Testament. Walther Eichrodt. Tr. by J. Baker. LC 61-11867. (Old Testament Library: Vol. 1). 542p. 1961. Vol. 1, 542p., 1961. 30.00 (*0-664-20352-3*, Westminster) Westminster John Knox.

Theology of the Old Testament. Walther Eichrodt. Tr. by J. Baker. (Old Testament Library: Vol. 2). 574p. 1967. Vol. 2, 574p., 1967. 30.00 (*0-664-20769-3*, Westminster) Westminster John Knox.

Theology of the Old Testament. John L. McKenzie. LC 86-9230. 336p. 1986. reprint ed. pap. text ed. 28.50 (*0-8191-5354-0*) U Pr of Amer.

***Theology of the Old Testament: Testimony, Dispute, Advocacy.** Walter Brueggemann. LC 97-21888. 1997. 48.00 (*0-8006-3087-4*, Fortress Pr) Augsburg Fortress.

Theology of the Pastoral Letters. Frances Young. LC 93-32146. (New Testament Theology Ser.). 186p. (C). 1994. text ed. 49.95 (*0-521-37036-1*); pap. text ed. 15.95 (*0-521-37931-8*) Cambridge U Pr.

Theology of the Pentateuch: Themes of the Priestly Narrative & Deuteronomy. Norbert Lohfink. 1994. pap. 24.00 (*0-8006-2593-5*, Fortress Pr) Augsburg Fortress.

Theology of the Program of Restoration of Ezekiel 40-48. Jon D. Levenson. LC 76-3769. (Harvard Semitic Monographs: No. 10). 186p. reprint ed. pap. 53.10 (*0-7837-5416-7*, 2045180) Bks Demand.

Theology of the Psalms. Hans-Joachim Kraus. Tr. by Keith R. Crim. LC 92-12739. 240p. (ENG & GER.). 1992. 32.00 (*0-8006-9506-2*, 1-9506, Fortress Pr) Augsburg Fortress.

Theology of the Reformers. Timothy George. LC 87-27759. (Illus.). (Orig.). 1988. pap. 24.99 (*0-8054-6573-1*, 4265-73) Broadman.

Theology of the Second Letter to the Corinthians. Jerome Murphy-O'Connor. (New Testament Theology Ser.). 168p. (C). 1991. text ed. 49.95 (*0-521-35379-3*); pap. text ed. 15.95 (*0-521-35898-1*) Cambridge U Pr.

Theology of the Shorter Pauline Letters. Karl P. Donfried & I. Howard Marshall. LC 92-41218. (New Testament Theology Ser.). 204p. (C). 1993. text ed. 49.95 (*0-521-36491-4*); pap. text ed. 15.95 (*0-521-36731-X*) Cambridge U Pr.

Theology of Time. Elijah Muhammad. 551p. (Orig.). 1992. pap. 24.95 (*1-56411-025-7*) Untd Bros & Sis.

Theology of Time. Elijah Muhammad. 551p. (Orig.). 1992. 49.95 (*1-56411-032-X*) Untd Bros & Sis.

***Theology of Time.** unabridged ed. Elijah Muhammad. Ed. by Nasir Hakim. 392p. 1997. 24.95 (*1-884855-30-X*) Secretarius.

Theology of Time, Vol. I. Elijah Muhammad. 170p. (Orig.). 1992. pap. 10.00 (*1-56411-028-1*) Untd Bros & Sis.

***Theology of Tongues: Why Did God Choose "Speaking with Tongues" As the Initial Sign of the Baptism of the Holy Spirit?** Douglas Stewart. 64p. (Orig.). 1996. pap. 6.00 (*0-9650904-1-8*, 2) Selah Pubns.

Theology of Uncreated Energies of God. George S. Maloney. LC 78-55049. (Pere Marquette Lectures). 1978. 15.00 (*0-87462-516-5*) Marquette.

Theology of Unity. Muhammad'Abduh. LC 79-52560. (Islam Ser.). 1980. reprint ed. lib. bdg. 19.95 (*0-8369-9267-9*) Ayer.

Theology of William Newton Clarke: Doctoral Dissertation. Claude L. Howe, Jr. Ed. by Edwin S. Gaustad. LC 79-52571. (Baptist Tradition Ser.). 1980. lib. bdg. 17.95 (*0-405-12440-6*) Ayer.

Theology of Word & Spirit: Authority & Method in Theology. Donald G. Bloesch. LC 92-20688. (Christian Foundations Ser.: Vol. 1). 400p. 1992. 24.99 (*0-8308-1411-6*, 1411) InterVarsity.

Theology on Its Way? Essays on Karl Barth. Richard H. Roberts. 256p. 1991. text ed. 43.95 (*0-567-09585-1*, Pub. by T & T Clark UK) Bks Intl VA.

Theology on the Way to Emmaus. Nicholas Lash. 256p. (C). 1986. pap. text ed. 18.95 (*0-334-02352-1*, SCM Pr) TPI PA.

Theology, Politics & Letters at the Crossroads of European Civilization. Gerald Cerny. 1987. lib. bdg. 146.00 (*90-247-3150-X*) Kluwer Ac.

Theology, Politics & Peace. Ed. by Theodore H. Runyon. LC 89-15977. 223p. 1989. reprint ed. pap. 63.60 (*0-7837-9838-5*, 2060567) Bks Demand.

Theology Primer. Robert C. Neville. LC 90-19636. 221p. (C). 1991. text ed. 44.50 (*0-7914-0849-3*); pap. text ed. 14.95 (*0-7914-0850-7*) State U NY Pr.

***Theology Through the Theologians.** Colin E. Gunton. 272p. 1996. 45.95 (*0-567-08527-9*, Pub. by T & T Clark UK) Bks Intl VA.

Theology Toward the Third Millennium: Theological Issues for the Twenty-First Century. Ed. by David G. Schultenover. LC 91-25518. (Toronto Studies in Theology: Vol. 56). 160p. 1991. lib. bdg. 69.95 (*0-7734-9747-1*) E Mellen.

Theology Without Boundaries: Encounters of Eastern Orthodoxy & Western Tradition. Carnegie S. Calian. 144p. (Orig.). 1992. pap. 15.00 (*0-664-25156-0*) Westminster John Knox.

Theology without Foundation. Stanley Hauerwas et al. 320p. (Orig.). 1994. pap. 19.95 (*0-687-00280-X*) Abingdon.

***Theology/Joseph Ratzinger.** Nichols. pap. 29.95 (*0-567-29148-0*, Pub. by T & T Clark UK) Bks Intl VA.

Theomatics II: God's Best Kept Secret Revealed. 2nd ed. Del Washburn. (Illus.). 664p. 1994. 24.95 (*0-8128-4023-2*, Scrbrough Hse) Madison Bks UPA.

Theomusicology. Ed. by Jon M. Spencer. 268p. 1994. pap. 10.00 (*0-8223-6422-0*) Duke.

Theon of Smyrna: Mathematics Useful for Understanding Plato or, Pythagorean Arithmetic, Music, Astronomy, Spiritual Disciplines. Theon Of Smyrna. Tr. by Robert Lawlor from GRE. LC 77-73716. (Secret Doctrine Reference Ser.). (Illus.). 200p. 1978. 16.00 (*0-913510-24-6*) Wizards.

Theonas. Jacques Maritain. LC 74-84325. (Essay Index Reprint Ser.). 1977. 19.95 (*0-8369-1095-8*) Ayer.

Theonome Anthropologie? F. Hammer. (Phaenomenologica Ser.: No. 45). 328p. 1972. lib. bdg. 82.50 (*90-247-1186-X*, Pub. by M Nijhoff NE) Kluwer Ac.

Theonomy: An Informed Response. Gary DeMar et al. LC 91-33321. 395p. 1991. 16.95 (*0-930464-59-1*) Inst Christian.

Theophane Venard: A Martyr of Vietnam. Christian Simonnet. Tr. by Cynthia Splatt from FRE. LC 87-83125. (Illus.). 179p. (Orig.). 1988. pap. 9.95 (*0-89870-186-4*) Ignatius Pr.

Theophanies: A Book of Verses (1916) Evelyn Underhill. 130p. 1996. reprint ed. pap. 16.95 (*1-56459-573-0*) Kessinger Pub.

Theophany. John Stahl. (Illus.). 24p. 1979. 45.00 (*0-945303-06-8*); 450.00 (*0-945303-05-X*) Evanescent Pr.

Theophany of Christ, Vol. 8. Monks of New Skete Staff. Tr. by Laurence Mancuso from GRE. (Liturgical Music Ser.: Vol. I). 96p. (Orig.). 1995. pap. 25.00 (*0-935129-17-0*) Monks of New Skete.

Theophany, Please. Cynthia B. Johnson. (Illus.). 96p. (Orig.). 1995. pap. 16.00 (*0-9648946-0-2*) C B Johnson.

Theophile Gautier. Maxime Du Camp. Tr. by J. E. Gordon. (Select Bibliographies Reprint Ser.). 1977. reprint ed. 20.95 (*0-8369-5732-6*) Ayer.

Theophile Gautier & the Fantastic. Albert B. Smith. LC 76-56455. (Romance Monographs: No. 23). 1977. 22.00 (*84-399-6137-5*) Romance.

Theophile Gautier's Short Stories. Theophile Gautier. Tr. by George B. Ives. LC 73-122710. (Short Story Index Reprint Ser.). 1977. 18.95 (*0-8369-3543-8*) Ayer.

Theophilus North. Thornton Wilder. 372p. 1988. pap. 4.95 (*0-88184-382-2*) Carroll & Graf.

Theophrastean Studies: On Natural Science, Physics & Metaphysics, Ethics, Religion & Rhetoric, Vol. III. Ed. by William W. Fortenbaugh. 384p. 1987. 54.95 (*0-88738-171-5*) Transaction Pubs.

Theophrastos' Schrift Uber Frommigkeit. Mit Bemerkungen Zu Porphyrios' Schrift Uber Enthaltsamkeit. Jacob Bernays. iv, 192p. 1979. reprint ed. 50.00 (*3-487-06826-5*) G Olms Pubs.

Theophrasts Methode in Seinen Botanischen Schriften. George Wohrle. (Studien zur antiken Philosophie: Band 13). 192p. 1985. 41.00 (*90-6032-257-6*, Pub. by Gruner NE) Benjamins North Am.

Theophrastus: Characters. R. G. Ussher. (Bristol Greek Texts Ser.). 1993. pap. 29.95 (*1-85399-188-0*, Pub. by Brstl Class Pr UK) Focus Pub-R Pullins.

Theophrastus: De Causis Plantarum, Vols. 2-3, Vol. 2. Theophrastus. Ed. by Benedict Einarson & George K. Link. Tr. by George K. Link from GER. LC 76-370781. (Loeb Classical Library: Nos. 474-475). 361p. 1990. text ed. 18.95 (*0-674-99523-6*) HUP.

Theophrastus: De Causis Plantarum, Vols. 2-3, Vol. 3. Theophrastus. Ed. by Benedict Einarson & George K. Link. Tr. by George K. Link from GER. LC 76-370781. (Loeb Classical Library: Nos. 474-475). 465p. 1990. text ed. 18.95 (*0-674-99524-4*) HUP.

Theophrastus: His Psychological, Doxographical, & Scientific Writings. Ed. by William W. Fortenbaugh & Dimitri Gutas. (Rutgers University Studies in Classical Humanities: Vol. 5). 350p. (C). 1991. text ed. 54.95 (*0-88738-404-8*) Transaction Pubs.

Theophrastus Vol. 1: De Causis Plantarum. Theophrastus. (Loeb Classical Library: No. 471). 430p. 1976. 18.95 (*0-674-99519-8*) HUP.

Theophrastus & the Greek Physiological Psychology Before Aristotle. G. M. Stratton. (Classical Studies Ser.). (ENG & GRE.). reprint ed. lib. bdg. 52.00 (*0-697-00017-6*) Irvington.

Theophrastus Bombastus von Hohenheim Called Paracelsus. John M. Stillman. LC 79-8625. (Illus.). viii, 184p. reprint ed. 34.50 (*0-404-18491-X*) AMS Pr.

An Asterisk (*) at the beginning of an entry indicates that the title is appearing in BIP for the first time.

Theophrastus Characters. Elizabeth A. Bobrick. (Greek Commentaries Ser.). 44p. (C). 1991. pap. text ed. 6.00 (*0-929524-69-1*) Bryn Mawr Commentaries.

Theophrastus. Characters Herodas. Mimes: Cercidas & the Choliambic Poets. 2nd ed. Ed. by Jeffrey Rusten et al. Tr. by I. C. Cunningham et al. (Loeb Classical Library: No. 225). 512p. 1993. text ed. 16.95 (*0-674-99244-X*) HUP.

Theophrastus of Eresus: On His Life & Work. Ed. by William W. Fortenbaugh. (Studies in Classical Humanities: Vol. II). 350p. (C). 1985. text ed. 54.95 (*0-88738-009-3*) Transaction Pubs.

Theophrastus of Eresus: Sources for His Life, Writings, Thought & Influence, 2 vols., Set. Ed. by William W. Fortenbaugh et al. Tr. by Pamela M. Huby et al. from ARA. LC 91-33945. (Philosophia Antiqua Ser.: No. 54). viii, 706p. 1993. reprint ed. 124.50 (*90-04-09440-7*) E J Brill.

Theophrastus of Eresus: Sources for His Life, Writings, Thought & Influence, Vol. 5. R. W. Sharples. (Human Physiology, Living Creatures, Botany Ser.). 284p. 1994. 90.00 (*90-04-10174-8*) E J Brill.

Theophylacht of Ochrid: Reading the Letters of a Byzantine Archbishop. Margaret Mullett. (Birmingham Byzantine & Ottoman Monographs: Vol. 2). 320p. Date not set. 72.50 (*0-86078-549-1*, Pub. by Variorum UK) Ashgate Pub Co.

Theophysical Glossary. Helena P. Blavatsky. 1975. lib. bdg. 250.00 (*0-87968-487-9*) Krishna Pr.

Theopompus & Fifth-Century Athens. Walter R. Connor. LC 68-14253. (Center for Hellenic Studies). 327p. reprint ed. 93.20 (*0-8357-9180-7*, 2016543) Bks Demand.

Theopompus Hellenika. Eduard Meyer. xii, 291p. 1966. reprint ed. write for info. (*0-318-70976-7*) G Olms Pubs.

***Theopompus of Chios: Historyb & Rhetoric in the Fourth Century BC.** Michael A. Flower. 264p. 1997. reprint ed. pap. 26.00 (*0-19-815243-4*) OUP.

Theopompus the Historian. Gordon S. Shrimpton. 360p. (C). 1991. text ed. 55.00 (*0-7735-0837-6*, Pub. by McGill CN) U of Toronto Pr.

Theorem Applique Bk. I: Abundant Harvest. Patricia B. Campbell & Mimi Ayars. Ed. by Janice P. Johnson. LC 94-31563. (Illus.). 40p. (Orig.). 1994. pap. 11.95 (*0-9622565-9-5*) Chitra Pubns.

Theorem Applique Bk. II: Summer Splendor. Patricia B. Campbell & Mimi Ayars. Ed. by Janice P. Johnson. LC 94-31563. (Illus.). 36p. (Orig.). 1995. pap. 11.95 (*1-885588-03-8*) Chitra Pubns.

Theorem Provers Circuit Design. 1995. 56.00 (*3-540-59047-1*) Spr-Verlag.

Theorem Provers in Circuit Design: Theory, Practice, & Experience: Proceedings of the Second International Conference, TPCD '94, Bad Herrenalb, Germany, September 26-28, 1994. Ed. by Ramayya Kumar & Thomas Kropf. LC 95-5971. (Lecture Notes in Computer Science Ser.: no. 901). 303p. 1995. 56.00 (*0-387-59047-1*) Spr-Verlag.

***Theorem Proving in Higher Order Logics: 9th International Conference, TPHOL 96, Turku, Finland, August 1996: Proceedings.** International Conference on Theorem Proving in Higher Order Logics Staff et al. LC 96-32853. (Lecture Notes in Computer Science Ser.: Vol. 1125). 447p. 1996. 75.00 (*3-540-61587-3*) Spr-Verlag.

Theorem Proving with Analytic Tableaux & Related Methods: Proceedings of the 4th International Workshop, TABIEAU-95, Held at Schlob Rheinfels, St. Goar, Germany, May 7-10, 1995. Fourth International Workshop on Theorem Proving with Analytic Tableaux & Related Methods Staff. Ed. by P. Baumgartner et al. (Lecture Notes in Computer Science; Lecture Notes in Artificial Intelligence Ser.: Vol. 918). 352p. 1995. 62.00 (*3-540-59338-1*) Spr-Verlag.

Theorem Proving with Analytic Tableux & Related Methods: Proceedings of the 5th International Workshop, Tableaux '96, Terrasini, Palermo, Italy, 15-17th, 1996. Ed. by P. Miglioli et al. LC 96-17235. (Lecture Notes in Artificial Intelligence Ser.: Vol. 107). 329p. 1996. pap. 56.00 (*3-540-61208-4*) Spr-Verlag.

Theoremes d'indices Gevrey pour les equations differentielles ordinaires. Jean-Pierre Ramis. LC 83-27157. (Memoirs Ser.: No. 48/296). 95p. 1984. pap. 17. 00 (*0-8218-2296-9*, MEMO/48/296) Am Math.

Theorems & Counterexamples in Mathematics. B. R. Gelbaum & J. M. Olmsted. Ed. by P. R. Halmos. (Problem Books in Mathematics). (Illus.). xxxiv, 305p. 1995. 54.95 (*0-387-97342-7*) Spr-Verlag.

Theorems & Problems in Functional Analysis. A. A. Kirillov & A. D. Gvishiani. (Problem Books in Mathematics). (Illus.). 352p. 1982. 59.95 (*0-387-90638-X*) Spr-Verlag.

Theorems on Regularity & Singularity of Energy Minimizing Maps. L. Simon. (Lectures in Mathematics). 160p. 1996. pap. 34.50 (*3-7643-5397-X*) Birkhauser.

Theorems on Regularity & Singularity of Energy Minimizing Maps. Leon Simon. LC 96-6193. (Lectures in Mathematics ETH Zurich Ser.). 152p. 1996. 34.50 (*0-8176-5397-X*) Birkhauser.

Theoretic Arithmetic of the Pythagoreans. Thomas Taylor. 248p. (Orig.). 1983. reprint ed. pap. 14.95 (*0-87728-558-6*) Weiser.

Theoretical Acoustics. Philip M. Morse & K. Uno Ingard. 960p. 1986. pap. text ed. 49.50 (*0-691-02401-4*) Princeton U Pr.

Theoretical Advancement in Chromatography & Related Separation Techniques. Ed. by Francesco Dondi & Georges Guiochon. LC 92-32221. 1992. lib. bdg. 306.00 (*0-7923-1991-5*) Kluwer Ac.

Theoretical Advances in Behavior Genetics, No. 2. Ed. by Joseph R. Royce & Leendert P. Mos. (NATO Advanced Study Institute Ser.). 722p. 1981. lib. bdg. 175.00 (*90-286-0569-X*) Kluwer Ac.

Theoretical Advances in Neural Computation & Learning. Ed. by Vwani P. Roychowdhury et al. LC 94-34334. 496p. (C). 1994. lib. bdg. 139.50 (*0-7923-9478-X*) Kluwer Ac.

Theoretical Aerodynamics. Louis M. Milne-Thomson. (Illus.). 430p. (C). 1973. reprint ed. pap. text ed. 10.95 (*0-486-61980-X*) Dover.

Theoretical Alchemy. A. Cockren. 1987. pap. 5.95 (*0-916411-67-2*) Holmes Pub.

Theoretical Analyses in Romance Linguistics: Selected Papers from the Symposium XIX, Ohio State University, April 21-23, 1989. Ed. by Christiane Laeufer & Terrell A. Morgan. LC 92-15113. (Current Issues in Linguistic Theory Ser.: No. 74). viii, 515p. 1992. 156.00 (*1-55619-130-8*) Benjamins North Am.

Theoretical & Applied Aspects of Health Psychology. L. R. Schmidt. xvi, 443p. 1990. text ed. 132.00 (*3-7186-5053-3*, Harwood Acad Pubs) Gordon & Breach.

Theoretical & Applied Econometrics: The Selected Papers of Phoebus J. Dhrymes. Phoebus J. Dhrymes. LC 94-48416. (Economists of the Twentieth Century Ser.). 672p. 1995. 90.00 (*1-85898-092-5*) E Elgar.

Theoretical & Applied Mechanics: Proceeding of the XVIIth International Congress of Theoretical & Applied Mechanics, Grenoble, France, 21-27 Aug., 1988. Ed. by P. Germain et al. 494p. 1989. 208.75 (*0-444-87302-3*, North Holland) Elsevier.

Theoretical & Applied Mechanics: Proceedings of the 21st Japan National Congress for Applied Mechanics, Held 1971, Tokyo, Japan, Vol. 21. Ed. by Japan National Congress for Applied Mechanics Staff. LC 84-644965. 528p. 1973. reprint ed. pap. 150.50 (*0-608-01219-X*, 2061908) Bks Demand.

Theoretical & Applied Mechanics: Proceedings of the 22nd Japan National Congress for Applied Mechanics, 1972. Japan National Congress for Applied Mechanics Staff. LC 84-644965. 538p. 1974. reprint ed. pap. 153.40 (*0-608-01261-0*, 2061949) Bks Demand.

Theoretical & Applied Mechanics: Proceedings of the 25th Japan National Congress for Applied Mechanics, 1975, Vol. 25. Japan National Congress for Applied Mechanics Staff. LC 84-644965. 737p. 1977. reprint ed. pap. 180.00 (*0-608-01592-X*, 2061979) Bks Demand.

Theoretical & Applied Mechanics: Proceedings of the 27th Japan National Congress for Applied Mechanics, 1977, Vol. 27. Japan National Congress for Applied Mechanics Staff. LC 84-644965. 588p. 1979. reprint ed. pap. 167.60 (*0-608-01594-6*, 2061985) Bks Demand.

Theoretical & Applied Mechanics: Proceedings of the 28th Japan National Congress for Applied Mechanics, 1978, Vol. 28. Japan National Congress for Applied Mechanics Staff. LC 84-644965. 589p. 1980. reprint ed. pap. 167.90 (*0-608-01595-4*, 2061970) Bks Demand.

Theoretical & Applied Mechanics: Proceedings of the 29th Japan National Congress for Applied Mechanics, 1979, Vol. 29. Japan National Congress for Applied Mechanics Staff. LC 84-644965. 497p. 1981. reprint ed. pap. 141.70 (*0-608-01596-2*, 2061971) Bks Demand.

Theoretical & Applied Mechanics: Proceedings of the 30th Japan National Congress for Applied Mechanics, 1980, Vol. 30. Japan National Congress for Applied Mechanics Staff. LC 84-644695. 537p. 1981. reprint ed. pap. 153.10 (*0-608-01597-0*, 2061972) Bks Demand.

Theoretical & Applied Mechanics: Proceedings of the 31st Japan National Congress for Applied Mechanics, 1981, Vol. 31. Japan National Congress for Applied Mechanics Staff. LC 84-644965. 481p. 1982. reprint ed. pap. 137.10 (*0-608-01598-9*, 2061973) Bks Demand.

Theoretical & Applied Mechanics: Proceedings of the 32nd Japan National Congress for Applied Mechanics, 1982, Vol. 32. Japan National Congress for Applied Mechanics Staff. LC 84-644965. 549p. 1984. reprint ed. pap. 156.50 (*0-608-01229-7*, 2061917) Bks Demand.

Theoretical & Applied Mechanics: Proceedings of the 33rd Japan National Congress for Applied Mechanics, 1983, Vol. 33. Japan National Congress for Applied Mechanics Staff. LC 84-644965. 477p. 1985. reprint ed. pap. 136.00 (*0-608-01230-0*, 2061918) Bks Demand.

Theoretical & Applied Mechanics: Proceedings of the 34th Japan National Congress for Applied Mechanics, 1984, Vol. 34. Japan National Congress for Applied Mechanics Staff. LC 84-644965. 431p. 1986. reprint ed. pap. 122.90 (*0-608-01231-9*, 2061919) Bks Demand.

Theoretical & Applied Mechanics: Proceedings of the 35th Japan National Congress for Applied Mechanics, 1985, Vol. 35. Japan National Congress for Applied Mechanics Staff. LC 84-644965. 451p. 1987. reprint ed. pap. 128.60 (*0-608-01599-7*, 2061963) Bks Demand.

Theoretical & Applied Mechanics: Proceedings of the 37th Japan National Congress for Applied Mechanics, 1987, Vol. 37. Japan National Congress for Applied Mechanics Staff. LC 84-644965. 407p. 1989. reprint ed. pap. 116.00 (*0-608-01205-X*, 2061894) Bks Demand.

Theoretical & Applied Mechanics: Proceedings of the 38th Japan National Congress for Applied Mechanics, Held 1988, Tokyo, Japan, Vol. 38. Ed. by Japan National Congress for Applied Mechanics Staff. LC 84-644965. 263p. 1989. reprint ed. pap. 75.60 (*0-608-01207-6*, 2061896) Bks Demand.

Theoretical & Applied Mechanics: Proceedings of the 39th Japan National Congress for Applied Mechanics, Held 1989, Tokyo, Japan, Vol. 39. Ed. by Japan National Congress for Applied Mechanics Staff. LC 84-644965. 355p. 1990. reprint ed. pap. 101.20 (*0-608-01208-4*, 2061897) Bks Demand.

Theoretical & Applied Mechanics: Proceedings of the 40th Japan National Congress for Applied Mechanics, Held 1990, Tokyo, Japan, Vol. 40. Ed. by Japan National Congress for Applied Mechanics Staff. LC 84-644965. 337p. 1991. reprint ed. pap. 96.10 (*0-608-01209-2*, 2061898) Bks Demand.

Theoretical & Applied Mechanics: Proceedings of the 41st Japan National Congress for Applied Mechanics, Held 1992, Tokyo, Japan, Vol. 41. Japan National Congress for Applied Mechanics Staff. Ed. by Motoo Hori & Genki Yagawa. LC 84-644965. 241p. 1992. reprint ed. pap. 68.70 (*0-608-01213-0*, 2061902) Bks Demand.

Theoretical & Applied Mechanics: Proceedings of the 42nd Japan National Congress for Applied Mechanics, Held 1993, Tokyo, Japan, Vol. 42. Ed. by Japan National Congress for Applied Mechanics Staff et al. LC 84-644965. 349p. 1993. reprint ed. pap. 99.50 (*0-608-01212-2*, 2061901) Bks Demand.

Theoretical & Applied Mechanics Vol. 26: Proceedings of the 26th Japan National Congress for Applied Mechanics, 1976, Vol. 26. Japan National Congress for Applied Mechanics Staff. LC 84-644965. 589p. 1978. reprint ed. pap. 167.90 (*0-608-01593-8*, 2061984) Bks Demand.

Theoretical & Applied Mechanics 1992. Ed. by S. R. Bodner et al. 492p. 1993. 221.00 (*0-444-88889-6*) Elsevier.

***Theoretical & Applied Perspectives, 2 vols.** Incl. Autobiographical Memory. Ed. by Charles P. Thompson et al. 300p. 1997. (*0-8058-2075-2*); Eyewitness Memory. Ed. by Charles P. Thompson et al. LC 97-8625. 300p. 1997. (*0-8058-2794-3*); LC 97-11841. write for info. (*0-8058-2795-1*) L Erlbaum Assocs.

Theoretical & Applied Rheology: Proceedings of the XIth International Congress on Rheology, Brussels, Belgium August 17-21, 1992. Ed. by P. Moldenaers & R. Keunings. LC 92-21902. 1020p. 1992. 437.75 (*0-444-89007-6*) Elsevier.

Theoretical & Computational Acoustics, 2 Vols. D. Lee et al. 1024p. 1994. text ed. 213.00 (*981-02-1695-5*) World Scientific Pub.

***Theoretical & Computational Acoustics '95.** 576p. 1996. lib. bdg. 90.00 (*981-02-2683-7*) World Scientific Pub.

Theoretical & Computational Approaches to Interface Phenomena. Harrell L. Sellers. LC 95-1410. 246p. (C). 1995. 85.00 (*0-306-44899-8*, Plenum Pr) Plenum.

Theoretical & Computational Dynamics of a Compressible Flow. Shih-I Pai & Shijun Luo. (Illus.). 740p. (gr. 13). 1991. text ed. 115.50 (*0-442-30310-6*) Chapman & Hall.

***Theoretical & Computational Methods in Genome Research: Proceedings of an International Symposium Held in Heidelberg, Germany, May 25-27, 1996.** Ed. by Sandor Suhai. (Illus.). 327p. (C). 95.00 (*0-306-45503-X*, Plenum Pr) Plenum.

Theoretical & Computational Models for Organic Chemistry. Ed. by Sebastiao J. Formosinho et al. (C). 1991. lib. bdg. 182.00 (*0-7923-1314-3*) Kluwer Ac.

Theoretical & Computational Radiation Hydrodynamics, Vol. 1: Radiation-Hydrodynamics Theoretical Considerations. G. C. Pomraning et al. LC 70-135085. 228p. 1969. 20.00 (*0-403-04529-0*) Scholarly.

Theoretical & Conceptual Issues in Hispanic Mental Health. Ed. by Robert G. Malgady & Orlando Rodriguez. LC 93-38655. 274p. 1994. 39.50 (*0-89464-839-X*) Krieger.

Theoretical & Critical Perspectives on Teacher Change. Ed. by Phyllis Kahaney et al. LC 93-22589. 1993. pap. 39.50 (*1-56750-059-5*); text ed. 73.25 (*0-89391-976-4*) Ablex Pub.

Theoretical & Empirical Advances in Community Mental Health. Ed. by Edward M. Bennett & Bruce Tefft. LC 85-21371. (Studies in Health & Human Services: Vol. 5). 280p. 1985. lib. bdg. 89.95 (*0-88946-131-7*) E Mellen.

Theoretical & Empirical Analysis of the Population Density Gradients of Urban Areas Characterized by Coast Lines Providing an Amenity to City Residents. Bruce H. Smith. (Illus.). 155p. (C). 1991. pap. text ed. 55.95 (*1-895583-00-4*) MAYA Pubs.

Theoretical & Experimental Analysis of Members of Earthquake Proof Frame Panel Buildings. M. A. Mardzhanishvili. (C). 1987. 28.50 (*0-8364-2121-3*, Pub. by Oxford IBH II) S Asia.

Theoretical & Experimental Analysis of Members of Earthquake-Proof Frame Panel Buildings. M. A. Mardzhanishvilli & L. Mardzhanishvilli. Tr. by K. Dhillon from RUS. 180p. (C). 1986. text ed. 90.00 (*90-6191-472-8*, Pub. by A A Balkema NE) Ashgate Pub Co.

Theoretical & Experimental Approaches to High Temperature Superconductivity. Ed. by L. C. Gupta. 810p. 1991. text ed. 165.00 (*1-56072-009-3*) Nova Sci Pubs.

Theoretical & Experimental Aspects of Valence Fluctuations & Heavy Fermions. Ed. by L. C. Gupta & S. K. Malik. LC 87-25816. 776p. 1987. 135.00 (*0-306-42763-X*, Plenum Pr) Plenum.

Theoretical & Experimental Base for Teaching Reading. Richard L. Venezky. (Janua Linguarum, Series Didactica: No. 9). (Illus.). 48p. 1976. pap. text ed. 13.10 (*90-279-3374-X*) Mouton.

Theoretical & Experimental Bases of the Behaviour Therapies. Ed. by M. Philip Feldman & Anne Broadhurst. LC 75-20000. 475p. reprint ed. pap. 135.40 (*0-317-07802-X*, 2020430) Bks Demand.

Theoretical & Experimental Biophysics, 1. Ed. by Arthur Cole. LC 66-29484. reprint ed. pap. 102.30 (*0-685-16344-X*, 2027124) Bks Demand.

Theoretical & Experimental Biophysics, 2. Ed. by Arthur Cole. LC 66-29484. reprint ed. pap. 89.30 (*0-685-16345-8*) Bks Demand.

Theoretical & Experimental Insights into Immunity. Ed. by Alan S. Perelson & Gerard Weisbuch. LC 92-27863. (NATO ASI Series H: Cell Biology: Vol. 95). xvii, 480p. 1992. 207.95 (*0-387-54614-6*) Spr-Verlag.

Theoretical & Experimental Investigation of Thermohydrologic Processes in a Partially Saturated, Fractured, Porous Medium. 1994. lib. bdg. 250.00 (*0-8490-8561-6*) Gordon Pr.

Theoretical & Experimental Investigations of Hadronic Few-Body Systems. Ed. by O. Benhar et al. (Few-Body Systems Ser.: Suppl. 1). (Illus.). 640p. 1986. 123.95 (*0-387-81983-5*) Spr-Verlag.

Theoretical & Experimental Methods of Heavy-Ion Physics. Ed. by Z. Wilhelmi & G. Szeflinska. (Nuclear Science Research Conference Ser.: Vol. 15). 276p. (C). 1988. pap. text ed. 129.00 (*3-7186-0485-X*) Gordon & Breach.

***Theoretical & Experimental Modal Analysis.** Manuel Mendes & J. M. Silva. LC 96-38057. (Mechanical Engineering Research Studies). 1997. write for info. (*0-86380-208-7*) Wiley.

Theoretical & Experimental Models of the Diffuse Radar Backscatter from Mars. Anthony W. England. (University of Michigan Reports: No. 027735-1-F). 166p. 1995. reprint ed. pap. 47.40 (*0-608-02394-9*, 2063035) Bks Demand.

***Theoretical & Mathematical Foundations of Human Health Risk Analysis: Biophysical Theory of Environmental Health Science.** Douglas J. Crawford-Brown. LC 97-2501. 1997. lib. bdg. 99.50 (*0-7923-9898-X*) Kluwer Ac.

Theoretical & Mathematical Physics: A Collection of Survey Papers, Part 3, on the 50th Anniversary of the Institute. V. Vladimorov. LC 88-22154. (Proceedings of the Steklov Institute of Mathematics Ser.: Vol. 175). 258p. 1988. pap. text ed. 135.00 (*0-8218-3119-4*, STEKLO/175) Am Math.

Theoretical & Methodological Issues in Human Resources Research. Ed. by Gerald R. Ferris & Kendrith M. Rowland. LC 90-4568. (Research in Personnel & Human Resources Management Ser.). 236p. 1990. pap. 25.75 (*1-55938-227-9*) Jai Pr.

***Theoretical & Observational Problems Related to Solar Eclipses.** Date not set. text ed. 220.00 (*0-7923-4619-X*) Kluwer Ac.

Theoretical & Physical Principles of Organic Reactivity. Addy Pross. LC 95-21389. 1995. text ed. 59.95 (*0-471-55599-1*) Wiley.

Theoretical & Policy-Oriented Aspects of the External Debt Economics. C. J. Czerkawski. Ed. by Dieter Bos et al. (Studies in Contemporary Economics). viii, 150p. 1991. 42.95 (*0-387-54282-5*) Spr-Verlag.

Theoretical & Practical Aspects of Allergic Disorders: Proceedings of the Collegium Internationale Allergologicum, 9th, London, Sept. 1972. Collegium Internationale Allergologicum Staff. Ed. by D. Parker et al. (International Archives of Allergy & Applied Immunology Ser.: Vol. 45, Nos. 1-2). (Illus.). 1973. reprint ed. pap. 62.50 (*3-8055-1605-3*) S Karger.

***Theoretical & Practical Phonetics.** Rogers Henry. (C). 1991. pap. text ed. write for info. (*0-7730-5038-8*) Addison-Wesley.

Theoretical & Practical Treatise on Dancing. Gennaro Magri. Tr. by Mary Skeaping & Irmgard Berry. (Illus.). 280p. 1980. text ed. 65.00 (*0-903102-99-4*, Pub. by Dance Bks UK) Princeton Bk Co.

Theoretical Anthropology. David Bidney. LC 53-12098. 506p. 1953. text ed. 85.00 (*0-231-01910-6*) Col U Pr.

Theoretical Anthropology. 2nd ed. David Bidney. LC 95-12862. 550p. (C). 1995. pap. text ed. 24.95 (*1-56000-832-6*) Transaction Pubs.

Theoretical Approaches. (Structure & Bonding Ser.: Vol. 68). 190p. 1987. 119.95 (*0-387-18058-3*) Spr-Verlag.

Theoretical Approaches in Neurobiology. Ed. by Werner E. Reichardt & Tomaso Poggio. (Illus.). 208p. 1980. 35.00 (*0-262-18100-2*) MIT Pr.

Theoretical Approaches to African Linguistics. Ed. by Akinlabi. 1995. per. 19.95 (*0-86543-463-8*) Africa World.

Theoretical Approaches to African Linguistics. Ed. by Akinbiyi Akinlabi. (Trends in African Linguistics Ser.: Vol. 1). 1995. 69.95 (*0-86543-462-X*) Africa World.

Theoretical Approaches to Obsessive-Compulsive Disorder. Ian Jakes. (Problems in the Behavioral Sciences Ser.: No. 14). (Illus.). 200p. (C). 1996. text ed. 59.95 (*0-521-46058-1*) Cambridge U Pr.

Theoretical Approaches to Personality. Barry D. Smith & Harold J. Vetter. (Illus.). 416p. (C). 1982. text ed. write for info. (*0-13-913491-3*) P-H.

Theoretical Approaches to Turbulence. Ed. by D. L. Dwoyer et al. LC 85-14765. (Applied Mathematical Sciences Ser.: Vol. 58). (Illus.). xii, 373p. 1985. 83.95 (*0-387-96191-7*) Spr-Verlag.

Theoretical Archaeology. K. R. Dark. LC 94-23209. 256p. 1995. 47.50 (*0-8014-3125-5*); pap. 19.95 (*0-8014-8252-6*) Cornell U Pr.

Theoretical Aspects of Band Structures & Electronic Properties of Psuedo-One-Dimensional Solids. Ed. by Hiroshi Kamimura. 1985. lib. bdg. 157.50 (*90-277-1927-6*) Kluwer Ac.

Theoretical Aspects of Bantu Grammar. Ed. by Sam A. Mchombo. LC 93-29496. (CSLI Lecture Notes Ser.: No. 38). 1993. 45.00 (*0-937073-73-3*); pap. 22.95 (*0-937073-72-5*) CSLI.

Theoretical Aspects of Computer Software: International Conference TACS '91 Sendai, Japan, September 24-27, 1991 Proceedings. Ed. by Takatoshi Ito et al. (Lecture Notes in Computer Science Ser.: Vol. 526). x, 772p. 1991. 79.95 (*0-387-54415-1*) Spr-Verlag.

Theoretical Aspects of Computer Software: International Symposium TACS '94, Sendai, Japan, April 19-22, 1994. Ed. by Masami Hagiya & John C. Mitchell. LC 94-7812. (Lecture Notes in Computer Science Ser.). 1994. write for info. (*3-540-57887-0*) Spr-Verlag.

Theoretical Aspects of Computer Software: International Symposium TACS '94, Sendai, Japan, April 19-22, 1994. Ed. by Masami Hagiya & John C. Mitchell. LC 94-7812. (Lecture Notes in Computer Science Ser.). 1995. 98.00 (*0-387-57887-0*) Spr-Verlag.

Theoretical Aspects of Fuzzy Control. Ed. by Hung T. Nguyen et al. LC 94-20867. 368p. 1995. text ed. 59.95 (*0-471-02079-6*) Wiley.

***Theoretical Aspects of Heterogeneous Catalysis.** J. Moffat. (VNR Catalysis Ser.). (Illus.). 616p. 1990. text ed. 126.95 (*0-442-20528-7*, Osprey Bks) Chapman & Hall.

Theoretical Aspects of Homogeneous Catalysis: Applications of Ab Initio Molecular Orbital Theory. Ed. by Piet W. Van Leeuwen & Keiji Morokuma. (Catalysis by Metal Complexes Ser.: 18). 216p. (C). 1995. lib. bdg. 109.00 (*0-7923-3107-9*) Kluwer Ac.

Theoretical Aspects of Industrial Design. Ed. by D. Field & Vadim Komkov. LC 92-7046. (Proceedings in Applied Mathematics Ser.: No. 58). ix, 133p. 1992. pap. 38.00 (*0-89871-291-2*) Soc Indus-Appl Math.

Theoretical Aspects of Kashaya Phonology & Morphology. Eugene Buckley. LC 93-8886. (Dissertations in Linguistics Ser.). 1993. 54.95 (*1-881526-03-8*); pap. 22.95 (*1-881526-02-X*) CSLI.

Theoretical Aspects of Mainly Low Dimensional Magnetic Systems. Hans C. Fogedby. (Lecture Notes in Physics Ser.: Vol. 131). 163p. 1980. 20.95 (*0-387-10238-8*) Spr-Verlag.

Theoretical Aspects of Memory Vol. 2. 2nd ed. Ed. by Peter Morris & Michael Gruneberg. 336p. (C). (gr. 13). 1994. text ed. 62.95 (*0-415-06957-2*, B7302) Routledge.

Theoretical Aspects of Memory Vol. 2. 2nd ed. Ed. by Peter Morris & Michael Gruneberg. 304p. (C). 1994. pap. 18.95 (*0-415-06958-0*, B3706) Routledge.

Theoretical Aspects of Neurocomputing. Ed. by M. Novak & E. Pelikan. 300p. (C). 1991. text ed. 118.00 (*981-02-0549-X*) World Scientific Pub.

Theoretical Aspects of Object-Oriented Programming: Types, Semantics, & Language Design. Ed. by Carl A. Gunter & John C. Mitchell. LC 93-28984. (Foundations of Computing Ser.). 480p. 1994. 50.00 (*0-262-07155-X*) MIT Pr.

Theoretical Aspects of Passivization in the Framework of Applicative Grammar. Jean-Pierre Descles et al. LC 85-26794. (Pragmatics & Beyond Ser.: VI-1). viii, 115p. (Orig.). 1986. pap. 41.00 (*0-915027-67-4*) Benjamins North Am.

Theoretical Aspects of Physical Organic Chemistry: Applications to the SN2 Transition State. Sason S. Shaik et al. LC 91-16855. 304p. 1991. text ed. 89.95 (*0-471-84041-6*) Wiley.

Theoretical Aspects of Reasoning about Knowledge: Proceedings of the Fourth Conference (TARK 1992), Monterey, California, March 22-25, 1992. Ed. by Yoram Moses. LC 92-12306. 329p. 1992. pap. 39.95 (*1-55860-243-7*) Morgan Kaufmann.

Theoretical Aspects of Reasoning about Knowledge: Proceedings of the Third Conference, Tark 1990. Ed. by Rohit Parikh. 1990. 39.95 (*1-55860-105-8*) Morgan Kaufmann.

Theoretical Aspects of Reasoning about Knowledge: Proceedings of the 1986 Conference. Ed. by Joseph Y. Halpern. LC 86-2755. (Illus.). 407p. (Orig.). 1986. 19.95 (*0-934613-04-4*) Morgan Kaufmann.

Theoretical Aspects of the Design of Fund-Supported Adjustment Programs: A Study by the Research Department of the IMF. (Occasional Paper Ser.: No. 55). v, 51p. 1987. pap. 7.50 (*0-939934-99-X*) Intl Monetary.

***Theoretical Aspects of Tip Relief.** R. E. Peterson. (Technical Papers). 1931. pap. text ed. 30.00 (*1-55589-179-9*) AGMA.

Theoretical Atomic Physics. H. Friedrich. (Illus.). ix, 316p. 1991. 54.95 (*0-387-54179-9*) Spr-Verlag.

***Theoretical Atomic Spectroscopy.** Zenonas Rudzikas. (Cambridge Monographs on Atomic, Molecular, & Chemical Physics Ser.: No. 7). (Illus.). 464p. (C). 1997. text ed. 110.00 (*0-521-44425-X*) Cambridge U Pr.

Theoretical Bases of Indo-European Languages. Lehmann. 336p. (C). 1996. pap. 24.95 (*0-415-13850-7*) Routledge.

Theoretical Basis of Occupational Therapy: An Annotated Bibliography of Applied Theory in the Professional Literature. Mary A. McColl et al. LC 93-24422. (Illus.). 344p. (C). 1993. pap. text ed. 23.00 (*1-55642-151-6*) SLACK Inc.

Theoretical Basis of the Living System. Jorge Macedo. LC 75-17399. (Illus.). 84p. 1979. 8.90 (*0-87527-158-8*) Green.

Theoretical Biochemistry & Molecular Biophysics: DNA; Proteins, 2 vols. Ed. by Beveridge & R. V. Lavery. (Illus.). 1990. Set. lib. bdg. 190.00 (*0-940030-28-4*) Adenine Pr.

Theoretical Biochemistry & Molecular Biophysics, Vol. 1: DNA. Ed. by Beveridge et al. (Illus.). 431p. 1990. lib. bdg. 95.00 (*0-940030-33-0*) Adenine Pr.

Theoretical Biochemistry & Molecular Biophysics, Vol. 2: Proteins. Ed. by Beveridge et al. (Illus.). 335p. 1990. lib. bdg. 95.00 (*0-940030-34-9*) Adenine Pr.

Theoretical Biology: Epigenetic & Evolutionary Order from Complex Systems. Ed. by Brian C. Goodwin & Peter Saunders. (Illus.). 244p. 1990. text ed. 70.00 (*0-85224-600-5*, Pub. by Edinburgh U Pr UK) Col U Pr.

Theoretical Biology: Epigenetic & Evolutionary Order from Complex Systems. Ed. by Brian Goodwin & Peter Saunders. LC 92-15373. 256p. 1992. reprint ed. pap. text ed. 18.50 (*0-8018-4519-X*) Johns Hopkins.

Theoretical Biology: Reprint of the 1935 Edition with a Preface, a Biographical & Critical Essay. E. S. Bauer. Ed. by J. Tigyi et al. 294p. (ENG & RUS.). (C). 1982. reprint ed. 42.00 (*963-05-3014-7*, Pub. by Akad Kiado HU) St Mut.

***Theoretical Challenges in the Dynamics of Complex Fluids: Lectures from the NATO Advanced Studies Institute Held at the Isaac Newton Institute for the Mathematical Sciences, Cambridge, U. K., March 1996.** Tom McLeish. LC 97-20158. (NATO ASI Series: Series E: Applied Sciences). 1997. write for info. (*0-7923-4607-6*) Kluwer Ac.

Theoretical Chemistry, Vol. 4. Royal Society of Chemistry Staff. 1988. 112.00 (*0-85186-784-7*) CRC Pr.

***Theoretical Comparison of Ball & Roller Bearings.** T. Barish. (Technical Papers). (Illus.). (Orig.). 1938. pap. text ed. 30.00 incl. audio compact disk (*1-55589-363-5*) AGMA.

Theoretical Computer Science: Proceedings - Third Italian Conference. C. Bohm et al. 436p. 1989. text ed. 113.00 (*981-02-0070-6*) World Scientific Pub.

Theoretical Computer Science: Proceedings, Dortmund, FRG, 1983. Ed. by A. B. Cremers & H. P. Kriegel. (Lecture Notes in Computer Science Ser.: Vol. 145). 367p. 1983. 35.00 (*0-387-11973-6*) Spr-Verlag.

Theoretical Computer Science: Proceedings of the GI Conference on Theoretical Computer Science, 3rd, Darmstadt, March 1977. Ed. by H. Tzschach & K. G. Waldshchimdt. (Lecture Notes in Computer Science Ser.: Vol. 48). 1977. pap. 25.00 (*3-540-08138-0*) Spr-Verlag.

Theoretical Computer Science: Proceedings of the 4th Italian Conference. A. Marchetti-Spaccamela et al. 372p. 1992. text ed. 121.00 (*981-02-1258-5*) World Scientific Pub.

***Theoretical Computer Science: Proceedings of the 5th Italian Conference.** 576p. 1996. lib. bdg. 104.00 (*981-02-2673-X*) World Scientific Pub.

Theoretical Computer Science Fifth Conference. Ed. by P. Deussen. (Lecture Notes in Computer Science Ser.: Vol. 104). 261p. 1981. 28.00 (*0-387-10576-X*) Spr-Verlag.

Theoretical Concepts. Raimo Tuomela. LC 73-80989. (Library of Exact Philosophy: Vol. 10). xiv, 254p. 1973. 67.95 (*0-387-81119-2*) Spr-Verlag.

Theoretical Concepts & Hypothetico-Inductive Inference. I. Niiniluoto & Raimo Tuomela. LC 73-83567. (Synthese Library: No. 53). 269p. 1973. lib. bdg. 104.50 (*90-277-0343-4*, D Reidel) Kluwer Ac.

Theoretical Criminology. 3rd ed. George B. Vold & Thomas J. Bernard. 388p. 1985. 36.00 (*0-19-503616-6*) OUP.

***Theoretical Criminology.** 4th ed. George B. Vold et al. (Illus.). 400p. (C). 1997. text ed. 48.00 (*0-19-507321-5*) OUP.

Theoretical Criminology: From Modernity to Post-Modernism. Wayne J. Morrison. 535p. 1995. 54.00 (*1-85941-221-1*, Pub. by Cavendish UK); pap. 34.00 (*1-85941-220-3*, Pub. by Cavendish UK) Gaunt.

***Theoretical Debates.** (Spanish American Literature Ser.). 350p. 1997. text ed. 75.00 (*0-8153-2676-9*) Garland.

Theoretical Dimensions of Henry James. John C. Rowe. LC 84-40158. (Wisconsin Project on American Writers Ser.: No. 2). 304p. 1985. pap. 14.95 (*0-299-09974-1*) U of Wis Pr.

Theoretical Ecosystem Ecology: Understanding Nutrient Cycles. Goran I. Ogren & Ernesto Bosatta. LC 96-18908. (Illus.). 245p. (C). 1997. text ed. 49.95 (*0-521-58022-6*) Cambridge U Pr.

Theoretical Elasticity. A. E. Green & Zerna W. Green. (Illus.). xv, 457p. 1992. reprint ed. pap. 11.95 (*0-486-67076-7*) Dover.

Theoretical Elasticity. Carl E. Pearson. LC 59-9283. 230p. reprint ed. pap. 65.60 (*0-317-08681-2*, 2001586) Bks Demand.

Theoretical Epidemiology: Principles of Occurrence Research in Medicine. Olli S. Miettinen. LC 85-3697. 354p. 1989. text ed. 49.95 (*0-8273-4313-2*) Delmar.

***Theoretical Evolution of International Political Economy: A Reader.** 2nd ed. Ed. by Geroge T. Crane & Abla M. Amawi. 352p. (C). 1997. pap. text ed. 19.95 (*0-19-509443-3*) OUP.

Theoretical Evolutionary Ecology. Michael Bulmer. LC 93-34424. (Illus.). 332p. (C). 1994. text ed. 65.00 (*0-87893-079-5*); pap. text ed. 37.95 (*0-87893-078-7*) Sinauer Assocs.

Theoretical Evolutions in Person-Centered - Experiential Therapy: Applications to Schizophrenic & Retarded Psychoses. Garry Prouty. LC 93-42143. 144p. 1994. text ed. 49.95 (*0-275-94543-X*, Praeger Pubs) Greenwood.

Theoretical, Experimental & Numerical Contributions to the Mechanics of Fluids & Solids: A Collection of Papers in Honor of Paul M. Naghdi. Ed. by James Casey & Marcel J. Crochet. LC 95-20143. (ZAMP Special Issue Ser.: Vol. 46). 847p. 1995. 365.00 (*0-8176-5139-X*) Birkhauser.

Theoretical Explorations in African Religion. Ed. by Wim M. Van Binsbergen & J. Matthew Schoffeleers. 330p. 1984. 65.00 (*0-7103-0049-2*) Routledge Chapman & Hall.

Theoretical Fables: The Pedagogical Dream in Contemporary Latin-American Literature. Alicia Borinsky. LC 93-26561. (Pennsylvania Studies in Contemporary American Fiction). 176p. (C). 1993. text ed. 31.50 (*0-8122-3234-8*) U of Pa Pr.

***Theoretical Fluid Dynamics.** 2nd ed. Bhimsen K. Shivamoggi. LC 97-10383. 576p. 1997. 69.95 (*0-471-05659-6*) Wiley.

Theoretical Foundation Engineering. B. M. Das. (Developments in Geotechnical Engineering Ser.: Vol. 47). 1987. 157.00 (*0-444-42860-7*) Elsevier.

Theoretical Foundation for Large-Scale Computations for Nonlinear Material Behavior. Nemat S. Nasser. 1984. lib. bdg. 171.00 (*90-247-3092-9*) Kluwer Ac.

Theoretical Foundation of Dendritic Function: Selected Papers of Wilfrid Rall. Ed. by Idam Segev et al. (Computional Neuroscience Ser.). 424p. 1994. 55.00 (*0-262-19356-6*, Bradford Bks) MIT Pr.

Theoretical Foundations *see* **Current Trends in Linguistics**

Theoretical Foundations of Behavior Therapy. Ed. by Hans J. Eysenck & I. Martin. LC 87-17168. (Perspectives on Individual Differences Ser.). 494p. 1987. 85.00 (*0-306-42634-X*, Plenum Pr) Plenum.

Theoretical Foundations of Cardiovascular Processes. Ed. by Dhanjoo N. Ghista et al. (Advances in Cardiovascular Physics Ser.: Vol. 1). (Illus.). 1978. 78.50 (*3-8055-2850-7*) S Karger.

Theoretical Foundations of Computer Graphics & CAD. Ed. by R. A. Earnshaw. (NATO Asi Series F: Vol. 40). 1270p. 1988. 264.95 (*0-387-19506-8*) Spr-Verlag.

Theoretical Foundations of Computer Sciences. Dino Mandrioli & Carlo Ghezzi. 504p. (C). 1992. reprint ed. lib. bdg. 59.95 (*0-89464-798-9*) Krieger.

Theoretical Foundations of Computer Vision. Ed. by W. G. Kropatsch et al. LC 95-45033. (Illus.). 256p. 1996. pap. 119.00 (*3-211-82730-7*) Spr-Verlag.

Theoretical Foundations of Cosmology: Introduction to the Global Structure of Space-Time. Michael Heller. 300p. (C). 1992. text ed. 45.00 (*981-02-0756-5*) World Scientific Pub.

Theoretical Foundations of Programming Methodology. Ed. by Manfred Broy & G. Schmidt. 1982. pap. text ed. 104.50 (*90-277-1462-2*); lib. bdg. 211.50 (*90-277-1460-6*) Kluwer Ac.

Theoretical Foundations of Radiation Chemistry. Jaroslav Bednar. 282p. 1990. lib. bdg. 162.50 (*90-277-2668-X*) Kluwer Ac.

Theoretical Foundations of VLSI Design. Ed. by K. McEvoy & J. V. Tucker. (Tracts in Theoretical Computer Science Ser.: No. 10). (Illus.). 250p. (C). 1991. text ed. 69.95 (*0-521-36631-3*) Cambridge U Pr.

Theoretical Framework for Monetary Analysis. Milton Friedman. LC 77-150319. (National Bureau of Economic Research, Occasional Paper Ser.: No. 112). (Illus.). 77p. reprint ed. pap. 25.00 (*0-317-09514-5*, 2051704) Bks Demand.

Theoretical Framework for Monetary Analysis. Milton Friedman. (Occasional Papers: No. 112). 77p. 1971. reprint ed. 20.00 (*0-685-61354-2*) Natl Bur Econ Res.

Theoretical Frameworks for Personal Relationships. Ed. by Ralph Erber & Robin Gilmour. 288p. 1994. text ed. 59.95 (*0-8058-0573-7*) L Erlbaum Assocs.

Theoretical Frameworks in the Sociology of Education. Blaine Mercer & Herbert C. Covey. 139p. 1980. pap. 11.95 (*0-87073-855-0*) Schenkman Bks Inc.

Theoretical Geochemistry: Applications of Quantum Mechanics in the Earth & Mineral Sciences. John A. Tossell & David J. Vaughan. (Illus.). 416p. 1992. 100.00 (*0-19-504403-7*) OUP.

Theoretical Geomorphology. 2nd ed. Adrian E. Scheidegger. LC 70-110153. (Illus.). 1970. 70.70 (*0-387-05005-1*) Spr-Verlag.

Theoretical Geomorphology. 3rd rev. ed. Adrian E. Scheidegger. (Illus.). 520p. 1991. 100.95 (*0-387-52510-6*) Spr-Verlag.

Theoretical Glaciology. Kolumban Hutter. 1983. lib. bdg. 281.50 (*90-277-1473-8*) Kluwer Ac.

Theoretical Heterogeneous Catalysis. R. A. Van Santen. (Lecture & Course Notes In Chemistry Ser.: Vol. 5). 408p. 1991. text ed. 86.00 (*981-02-0384-5*); pap. text ed. 46.00 (*981-02-0385-3*) World Scientific Pub.

Theoretical History. Joseph A. Uphoff, Jr. 38p. 1987. pap. text ed. 2.00 (*0-943123-12-7*) Arjuna Lib Pr.

Theoretical Hydrodynamics. 5th enl. rev. unabridged ed. Louis M. Milne-Thomson. (Illus.). 768p. reprint ed. pap. 20.95 (*0-486-68970-0*) Dover.

Theoretical Hydrodynamics. Ivan A. Kibel & N. E. Kochin. LC 63-23221. 583p. reprint ed. pap. 166.20 (*0-317-08587-5*, 2011961) Bks Demand.

Theoretical Immunology. Ed. by George I. Bell et al. LC 77-26655. (Immunology Ser.: No. 8). (Illus.). 660p. reprint ed. pap. 180.00 (*0-7837-3369-0*, 2043327) Bks Demand.

Theoretical Immunology, 2 vols., Vol. 2. Alan S. Perelson. (Santa Fe Institute Ser.). 420p. (C). 1988. 49.95 (*0-201-15687-3*) Addison-Wesley.

Theoretical Importance of Love. William J. Goode. (Reprint Series in Social Sciences). (C). 1993. reprint ed. pap. text ed. 1.00 (*0-8290-3792-6*, S-100) Irvington.

Theoretical Integration in the Study of Deviance & Crime: Problems & Prospects. Ed. by Steven F. Messner et al. LC 88-22441. (SUNY Series in Deviance & Social Control). 342p. 1989. text ed. 74.50 (*0-7914-0000-X*); pap. text ed. 24.95 (*0-7914-0001-8*) State U NY Pr.

Theoretical Issues & Practical Cases in Portuguese-English Translations. Ed. by Malcolm Coulthard & Pat O. De Baubeta. LC 95-26635. 144p. 1996. text ed. 69.95 (*0-7734-8806-5*) E Mellen.

Theoretical Issues in Development Economics. Ed. by Bhaskar Dutta et al. (Illus.). 312p. 1993. 32.00 (*0-19-563171-4*) OUP.

Theoretical Issues in Indian Archaeology. Dilip K. Chakrabarti. (C). 1989. 21.50 (*0-685-30706-9*, Pub. by Munshiram Manoharial II) S Asia.

Theoretical Issues in International Borrowing. Jeffrey Sachs. LC 84-10744. (Princeton Studies in International Finance Ser.: No. 54). 51p. reprint ed. pap. 25.00 (*0-317-28017-1*, 2025573) Bks Demand.

Theoretical Issues in Korean Linguistics. Young-Key Kim-Renaud. 571p. 1994. 55.00 (*1-881526-52-6*); pap. 29.95 (*1-881526-51-8*) CSLI.

Theoretical Issues in Language Acquisition: Continuity & Discontinuity in Development. Ed. by Juergen Weissenborn et al. 328p. 1991. pap. 32.50 (*0-8058-0380-7*); text ed. 69.95 (*0-8058-0379-3*) L Erlbaum Assocs.

Theoretical Issues in Literary History. David Perkins. (English Studies: Vol. No. 16). 303p. 1991. pap. 12.95 (*0-674-87913-9*) HUP.

Theoretical Issues in Literary History. Ed. by David D. Perkins. (English Studies: Vol. No. 16). 303p. (C). 1991. 29.95 (*0-674-87912-0*) HUP.

Theoretical Issues in Natural Language Processing. Ed. by Yorick Wilks. 264p. (C). 1989. pap. 27.50 (*0-8058-0184-7*); text ed. 49.95 (*0-8058-0183-9*) L Erlbaum Assocs.

Theoretical Issues in Policy Analysis. Mary E. Hawkesworth. LC 87-33629. (SUNY Series in Political Theory: Contemporary Issues). 287p. 1988. text ed. 67.50 (*0-88706-840-5*); pap. text ed. 24.95 (*0-88706-841-3*) State U NY Pr.

***Theoretical Issues in Psychology: An Introduction.** Sacha Bem & Huib L. De Jong. 192p. 1997. 69.95 (*0-8039-7826-X*) Sage.

***Theoretical Issues in Psychology: An Introduction.** Sacha Bem & Huib L. De Jong. 192p. 1997. pap. 22.95 (*0-8039-7827-8*) Sage.

Theoretical Issues in Reading Comprehension: Perspectives from Cognitive Psychology, Linguistics, Artificial Intelligence & Education. Ed. by Rand J. Spiro et al. LC 80-20716. 672p. 1981. text ed. 99.95 (*0-89859-036-1*) L Erlbaum Assocs.

Theoretical Issues in Sign Language Research, Vol. 1: Linguistics. Ed. by Susan D. Fischer & Patricia A. Siple. (Illus.). 352p. 1990. pap. text ed. 36.00 (*0-226-25150-0*) U Ch Pr.

Theoretical Issues in Sign Language Research, Vol. 1: Linguistics. Ed. by Susan D. Fischer & Patricia A. Siple. (Illus.). 352p. 1990. lib. bdg. 66.00 (*0-226-25149-7*) U Ch Pr.

Theoretical Issues in Sign Language Research, Vol. 2: Psychology. Ed. by Patricia A. Siple & Susan D. Fischer. LC 90-10997. (Illus.). 324p. 1991. pap. text ed. 36.00 (*0-226-25152-7*) U Ch Pr.

Theoretical Issues in Sign Language Research, Vol. 2: Psychology. Ed. by Patricia A. Siple & Susan D. Fischer. LC 90-10997. (Illus.). 324p. 1991. lib. bdg. 84.00 (*0-226-25151-9*) U Ch Pr.

***Theoretical Issues in Stimulus-Response Compatibility.** Bernhard Hommel & Wolfgang Prinz. LC 96-49378. (Advances in Psychology Ser.: Vol. 118). 430p. 1996. 150.00 (*0-444-82304-2*) Elsevier.

***Theoretical Kinematics.** O. Bottema & Roth. pap. 12.95 (*0-486-66346-9*) Dover.

Theoretical Linguistics & Grammatical Description: Papers in Honour of Hans-Heinrich Lieb on the Occasion of His 60th Birthday. Monika Budde. Ed. by Robin Sackmann. LC 96-27962. (Current Issues in Linguistics Theory Ser.: No. 138). x, 375p. 1996. lib. bdg. 79.00 (*1-55619-593-1*) Benjamins North Am.

Theoretical Logic in Sociology, Vol. 2: The Antimonies of Classical Thought: Marx & Durkheim. Jeffrey C. Alexander. LC 82-40096. 560p. 1982. 57.00 (*0-520-04481-9*); pap. 16.00 (*0-520-05613-2*) U CA Pr.

Theoretical Logic in Sociology, Vol. 3: The Classical Attempt at Theoretical Synthesis: Max Weber. Jeffrey C. Alexander. LC 75-17305. 224p. (C). 1983. pap. 16.00 (*0-520-05614-0*) U CA Pr.

Theoretical Logic in Sociology, Vol. 4: The Modern Reconstruction of Classical Thought: Talcott Parsons. Jeffrey C. Alexander. LC 75-17305. (C). 1984. 57.00 (*0-520-04483-5*); pap. 16.00 (*0-520-05615-9*) U CA Pr.

Theoretical Market Areas under Euclidean Distance. Pierre Hanjoul et al. (Monograph Ser.: No. 6). (Illus.). 162p. (Orig.). (C). 1988. pap. 15.95 (*1-877751-12-X*); pap. text ed. 15.95 (*1-877751-13-8*) Inst Math Geo.

Theoretical Mechanics. N. G. Chetave. 700p. 1990. 53.95 (*0-387-51379-5*) Spr-Verlag.

Theoretical Mechanics. Murray R. Spiegel. (Schaum's Outline Ser.). (C). 1967. pap. text ed. 14.95 (*0-07-060232-8*) McGraw.

Theoretical Mechanics. S. M. Targ. (Russian Monographs). (Illus.). 424p. 1967. text ed. 288.00 (*0-677-20370-5*) Gordon & Breach.

Theoretical Mechanics, 2 vols. Incl. 1. . G. S. Light & J. B. Higham. LC 74-81553. 93.00 (*0-317-27741-3*); 2. . G. S. Light & T. S. Kalsi. LC 74-81553. 110.00 (*0-317-27742-1*); LC 74-81553. reprint ed. write for info. (*0-318-59345-9*, 2025227) Bks Demand.

Theoretical Mechanics. Ted C. Bradbury. LC 80-23957. 656p. 1981. reprint ed. text ed. 56.50 (*0-89874-235-8*) Krieger.

Theoretical Mechanics of Biological Neural Networks. Ronald J. MacGregor. (Neural Networks: Foundations to Applications Ser.). (Illus.). 377p. 1993. text ed. 56.00 (*0-12-464255-1*) Acad Pr.

Theoretical Mechanics of Particles & Continua. Alexander L. Fetter & J. Dirk Walecka. (Illus.). 1980. text ed. write for info. (*0-07-020658-9*) McGraw.

Theoretical Methods for Atomic & Molecular Collisions: WS Lecture Notes in Physics, Vol. 14. J. Pascale & R. E. Olson. 450p. (C). 1993. text ed. 77.00 (*9971-5-0424-3*); pap. text ed. 37.00 (*9971-5-0425-1*) World Scientific Pub.

Theoretical Methods in Criminology. Ed. by Robert F. Meier. LC 84-27716. 247p. reprint ed. pap. 70.40 (*0-8357-4831-6*, 2037768) Bks Demand.

Theoretical Methods in the Physical Sciences: An Introduction to Problem Solving Using Maple V. William E. Baylis. xvii, 286p. 1994. 42.50 (*0-8176-3715-X*) Birkhauser.

An Asterisk (*) at the beginning of an entry indicates that the title is appearing in BIP for the first time.

Theoretical Methods of Texture Analysis: Proceedings of a Workshop. Ed. by H. J. Bunge. (Illus.). 452p. 1987. 85.00 (*3-88355-119-8*, Pub. by DGM Metallurgy Info GW) IR Pubns.

Theoretical Model for Crack Propagation & Arrest in Pressurized Pipelines. 80p. 1978. pap. 10.00 (*0-318-12721-0*, L00033) Am Gas Assn.

Theoretical Models & Personality Theory. Ed. by David Krech & George S. Klein. LC 68-29744. (Illus.). 142p. 1968. reprint ed. text ed. 49.75 (*0-8371-0134-4*, KRTM, Greenwood Pr) Greenwood.

Theoretical Models & Processes of Reading. 3rd ed. Ed. by Harry Singer & Robert B. Ruddell. LC 85-11858. 973p. reprint ed. pap. 180.00 (*0-7837-4582-6*, 2044301) Bks Demand.

Theoretical Models & Processes of Reading. 4th ed. Ed. by Robert B. Ruddell et al. 1296p. 1994. 99.95 (*0-87207-438-2*); pap. 75.00 (*0-87207-437-4*) Intl Reading.

Theoretical Models In Biology: The Original of Life, the Immune System, & the Brain. Glen W. Rowe. LC 93-40873. (Illus.). 440p. 1994. 65.00 (*0-19-859688-X*); pap. write for info. (*0-19-859687-1*) OUP.

***Theoretical Models of Skeletal Muscle.** M. Epstein & W. Herzog. text ed. write for info. (*0-471-96955-9*) Wiley.

Theoretical Morphology: Approaches in Modern Linguistics. Ed. by Michael T. Hammond & Michael P. Noonan. 394p. 1988. pap. text ed. 62.00 (*0-12-322046-7*) Acad Pr.

Theoretical Morphology of the French Verb. James Foley. (Linguisticae Investigationes Supplementa Ser.: No. 1). iv, 292p. 1979. 68.00 (*90-272-0502-7*, LIS 1) Benjamins North Am.

Theoretical Nuclear & Subnuclear Physics. John D. Walecka. (Illus.). 608p. (C). 1995. text ed. 73.50 (*0-19-507214-6*) OUP.

Theoretical Nuclear Physics. John M. Blatt & Victor F. Weisskopf. (Illus.). xiv, 864p. reprint ed. pap. 18.95 (*0-486-66827-4*) Dover.

Theoretical Nuclear Physics: Nuclear Reactions, 2 vols. Herman Feshbach. 1938p. 1993. text ed. 106.00 (*0-471-30442-5*) Wiley.

Theoretical Nuclear Physics Vol. 1: Nuclear Structure. Amos DeShalit. LC 73-17165. (Classics Library). 1008p. 1990. pap. text ed. 70.95 (*0-471-52366-6*) Wiley.

Theoretical Nuclear Physics Vol. 2: Nuclear Reactions, Vol. 2. Herman Feshbach. LC 91-4668. 959p. 1992. text ed. 260.00 (*0-471-05750-9*) Wiley.

Theoretical Nuclear Physics Vol. 2: Nuclear Reactions, Vol. 2. Herman Feshbach. 959p. 1993. pap. text ed. 81.00 (*0-471-57796-0*) Wiley.

***Theoretical Nursing: Development & Progress.** 3rd ed. Afaf I. Meleis. LC 96-36612. 688p. 1997. text ed. 37.95 (*0-397-55259-9*) Lppncott-Raven.

Theoretical Perspectives see Advances in Learning & Behavioral Disabilities

Theoretical Perspectives on Autobiographical Memory: Proceedings of the NATO Advanced Research Workshop, Grange-over-Sands, U. K. 4-12 July, 1991. Ed. by Martin A. Conway. (NATO Advanced Science Institutes Series C: Mathematical & Physical Sciences). 516p. (C). 1992. lib. bdg. 208.00 (*0-7923-1646-0*) Kluwer Ac.

Theoretical Perspectives on Cognitive Aging. Ed. by T. A. Salthouse. 448p. (C). 1991. pap. 39.50 (*0-8058-1170-2*); text ed. 89.95 (*0-8058-0424-2*) L Erlbaum Assocs.

Theoretical Perspectives on Language Deficits. Yosef Grodzinsky. (Biology of Language & Cognition Ser.). 280p. 1990. 27.50 (*0-262-07123-1*, Bradford Bks) MIT Pr.

Theoretical Perspectives on Native American Languages. Ed. by Donna B. Gerdts & Karin Michelson. LC 87-13226. (SUNY Series in Linguistics). (Illus.). 289p. 1989. text ed. 74.50 (*0-88706-642-9*); pap. text ed. 24.95 (*0-88706-643-7*) State U NY Pr.

Theoretical Perspectives on Planning Participation see Progress in Planning

Theoretical Perspectives on Sexual Difference. Ed. by Deborah L. Rhode. 326p. (C). 1992. reprint ed. pap. text ed. 17.00 (*0-300-05225-1*) Yale U Pr.

Theoretical Perspectives on Word Order in South Asian Languages. Ed. by Miriam J. Butt et al. (CSLI Lecture Notes Ser.). 1995. pap. 22.95 (*0-521-52649-3*) Cambridge U Pr.

Theoretical Perspectives on Word Order in South Asian Languages. Ed. by Tracy H. King et al. LC 94-28628. (Lecture Notes: No. 50). 1994. 45.00 (*1-881526-50-X*); pap. 22.95 (*1-881526-49-6*) CSLI.

Theoretical Philosophy, 1755-1770. Immanuel Kant. Ed. by David Walford. (Cambridge Edition of the Works of Immanuel Kant). 908p. (C). 1992. text ed. 95.00 (*0-521-39214-4*) Cambridge U Pr.

Theoretical Physics. Greiner. 1993. 101.95 (*0-387-56176-5*) Spr-Verlag.

Theoretical Physics. Gerhard A. Blass. LC 62-8896. (ACC Series in Physics). 465p. reprint ed. pap. 132.60 (*0-317-26225-4*, 2055682) Bks Demand.

Theoretical Physics. Georg Joos & Ira M. Freeman. xxiii, 885p. 1987. reprint ed. pap. 19.95 (*0-486-65227-0*) Dover.

Theoretical Physics: A Classical Approach. Josef Honerkamp & Hartmann Romer. Tr. by H. Pollack from GER. LC 92-42563. 584p. 1993. 89.95 (*0-387-56276-1*) Spr-Verlag.

Theoretical Physics: Classical & Modern Views. George H. Duffey. LC 79-23794. 704p. 1980. reprint ed. lib. bdg. 52.50 (*0-89874-062-2*) Krieger.

Theoretical Physics: Mechanics of Particles, Rigid & Elastic Bodies & Heat Flow. F. Woodbridge Constant. LC 78-14353. 296p. 1979. reprint ed. lib. bdg. 18.50 (*0-88275-738-5*) Krieger.

Theoretical Physics Vol. 1: Mechanics. 3rd ed. L. D. Landau et al. 1982. pap. text ed. 27.00 (*0-08-029141-4*, Prgamon Press) Buttrwrth-Heinemann.

Theoretical Physics & Philosophical Problems: Selected Writings. Ludwig Boltzmann. Ed. by Brian F. McGuinness. Tr. by Paul Foulkes from GER. LC 74-79571. (Vienna Circle Collection: No. 5). 296p. 1974. lib. bdg. 123.50 (*90-277-0249-7*, D Reidel) Kluwer Ac.

Theoretical Physics: Cosmology & Particle Physics: Proceedings of the XVII International GIFT Seminar, Peniscola, Spain, 2-7 June, 1986. Ed. by E. Alvarez et al. 300p. 1987. pap. 54.00 (*9971-5-0314-X*); text ed. 117.00 (*9971-5-0259-3*) World Scientific Pub.

Theoretical Physics in the Twentieth-Century: A Memorial Volume to Wolfgang Pauli. Ed. by Victor F. Weisskopf & Markus Fierz. LC 60-15886. 340p. reprint ed. pap. 96.90 (*0-317-08596-4*, 2007408) Bks Demand.

Theoretical Physics on the Personal Computer. E. W. Schmid et al. (Illus.). 245p. 1988. 49.50 (*0-387-18908-4*) Spr-Verlag.

Theoretical Physics on the Personal Computer. 2nd ed. E. W. Schmid et al. (Illus.). xiv, 213p. 1990. 69.95 incl. disk (*0-387-52243-3*) Spr-Verlag.

Theoretical Physics Three: Relativistic Quantum Mechanics: Wave Equations. Walter Greiner. (Illus.). xiv, 345p. 1994. 44.50 (*0-387-50986-0*) Spr-Verlag.

Theoretical Physics, Vol. 1: Text & Exercise Books. 2nd ed. LC 92-43256. 1993. write for info. (*3-540-56278-8*); 39.50 (*0-387-56278-8*) Spr-Verlag.

Theoretical Population Genetics. Jeff S. Gale. 320p. 1989. 90.00 (*0-04-575026-2*); pap. 37.00 (*0-04-575027-0*) Routledge Chapman & Hall.

Theoretical Population Geography. Robert Woods. LC 81-2842. (Illus.). 236p. reprint ed. pap. 67.30 (*0-8357-3567-2*, 2034473) Bks Demand.

Theoretical Principles in Astrophysics & Relativity. Norman Lebovitz et al. Ed. by William H. Reid & Peter O. Vandervoort. LC 76-25636. 272p. 1981. pap. text ed. 12.95 (*0-226-46990-5*) U Ch Pr.

Theoretical Principles of Distance Education. Ed. by Desmond J. Keegan. (Studies in Distance Education). 240p. (C). (gr. 13). 1993. text ed. 62.95 (*0-415-08942-5*, B2548) Routledge.

Theoretical Principles of Organic Chemistry. O. A. Reutov. Tr. by Mir Publishers Staff. 500p. (C). 1975. text ed. 35.00 (*0-8464-0919-4*) Beekman Pubs.

Theoretical Probability for Applications. Sidney C. Port. LC 93-114725. (Hilbert Space Methods in Reliability & Statistical Inference). 894p. 1993. text ed. 104.00 (*0-471-63216-3*) Wiley.

***Theoretical Problems in Cavity Nonlinear Optics.** Paul Mandel. LC 96-15181. (Cambridge Studies in Modern Optics: No. 21). (Illus.). 200p. (C). 1997. text ed. 59.95 (*0-521-55385-7*) Cambridge U Pr.

Theoretical Problems of Mathematical Statistics: Proceedings. Ed. by Jurii V. Linnik. LC 72-5245. (Proceedings of the Steklov Institute of Mathematics Ser.: No. 111). 316p. 1973. pap. 75.00 (*0-8218-3011-2*, STEKLO/111) Am Math.

Theoretical Problems of Typology & the Northern Eurasian Languages. Ed. by L. Dezso & P. Hajdu. 184p. 1970. 38.00 (*90-6032-062-X*) Benjamins North Am.

Theoretical Psychology: The Meeting of East & West. Anand C. Paranjpe. (PATH in Pathology Ser.). 344p. 1984. 75.00 (*0-306-41400-7*, Plenum Pr) Plenum.

Theoretical Research Programs: Studies in the Growth of Theory. Ed. by Joseph Berger & Morris Zelditch, Jr. LC 93-12907. 502p. (C). 1993. 57.50 (*0-8047-2230-7*) Stanford U Pr.

Theoretical Robotics: Redundancy & Optimization. Yoshihiko Nakamura. (Illus.). 240p. (C). 1990. text ed. write for info. (*0-318-66982-X*) Addison-Wesley.

Theoretical Roman Archaeology: Proceedings of the First Conference. Ed. by Eleanor Scott. (Worldwide Archaeology Ser.: Vol. 4). 200p. 1993. 55.95 (*1-85628-703-3*, Pub. by Avebury Pub UK) Ashgate Pub Co.

Theoretical Roman Archaeology: Second Conference Proceedings. Ed. by Peter Rush. 203p. (C). 1995. text ed. 59.95 (*1-85628-713-0*, Pub. by Avebury Pub UK) Ashgate Pub Co.

Theoretical Semics. Trevor Eaton. (De Proprietatibus Litterarum, Ser. Minor: No. 11). 1972. pap. text ed. 25.40 (*90-279-2116-4*) Mouton.

Theoretical Sensitivity: Advances in the Methodology of Grounded Theory. (Orig.). pap. 20.00 (*0-686-24892-9*) Sociology Pr.

Theoretical Sensitivity: Advances in the Methodology of Grounded Theory. Barney G. Glaser. 164p. 1978. pap. 28.00 (*1-884156-01-0*) Sociology Pr.

Theoretical Significance of Experimental Relativity. Robert H. Dicke. (Documents on Modern Physics Ser.). xii, 154p. (C). 1965. text ed. 195.00 (*0-677-00220-3*) Gordon & Breach.

Theoretical Sociology. Randall Collins. 565p. (C). 1988. text ed. 40.00 (*0-15-591474-X*) HB Coll Pubs.

Theoretical Solid State Physics, 2 vols. William Jones & Norman H. March. Incl. Vol. 1. Perfect Lattices in Equilibrium. 1985. pap. 16.95 (*0-486-65015-4*); Vol. 2. Non-Equilibrium & Disorder. 1985. pap. 16.95 (*0-486-65016-2*); 1301p. 1985. reprint ed. write for info. (*0-318-59237-1*) Dover.

Theoretical Solid State Physics: Non-Equilibrium & Disorder, Vol. 2. William Jones & Norman H. March. LC 75-324875. (Interscience Monographs & Texts in Physics & Astronomy: Vol. 27). 796p. reprint ed. pap. 180.00 (*0-317-08985-4*, 2015723) Bks Demand.

Theoretical Solid State Physics in 2 Volumes, Vol. 1. A. Haug & Harrie S. Massey. LC 78-129853. (International Series of Monographs in Natural Philosophy: Vol. 36). 1972. 229.00 (*0-08-015742-4*, Pub. by Pergamon Repr UK) Franklin.

Theoretical Solid State Physics in 2 Volumes, Vol. 2. A. Haug & D. Ter Haar. LC 78-129853. (International Series of Monographs in Natural Philosophy: Vol. 46: 2). 1972. 168.00 (*0-08-016636-9*, Pub. by Pergamon Repr UK) Franklin.

Theoretical Statistics. D. R. Cox & D. V. Hinkley. 528p. (gr. 13). 1986. pap. text ed. 41.95 (*0-412-16160-5*, 6069) Chapman & Hall.

***Theoretical Statistics.** 2nd ed. Cox. (C). (gr. 13 up). 1997. text ed. write for info. (*0-412-42860-1*) Chapman & Hall.

Theoretical Steam Rate Tables. LC 75-88047. 1969. pap. 15.00 (*0-685-06532-4*, 100003) ASME.

Theoretical Structures of Molecules, 22. Otfried Madelung & W. Martienssen. (Atomic & Molecular Physics Ser.: 22). 160p. 1994. 610.95 (*0-387-56332-6*) Spr-Verlag.

Theoretical Structures of Molecules, Subvol. A, Multiple Bonds see Crystal & Solid State Physics: Group III

Theoretical Studies in Islamic Banking & Finance. Ed. by Muhsin S. Khan & Abbas Mirakhor. 275p. 1987. 29.95 (*0-932625-07-X*); pap. 14.95 (*0-932625-06-1*) Inst Res Islam.

Theoretical Studies of Ecosystems: The Network Perspective. Ed. by Thomas P. Burns & M. Higashi. (Illus.). 300p. (C). 1991. 90.00 (*0-521-36138-9*) Cambridge U Pr.

Theoretical Studies on Sex Ratio Evolution. Samuel Karlin & Sabin Lessard. Ed. by Robert M. May. LC 85-43291. (Monographs in Population Biology: No. 22). (Illus.). 256p. 1986. text ed. 67.50 (*0-691-08411-4*); pap. text ed. 24.95 (*0-691-08412-2*) Princeton U Pr.

Theoretical Study of Milton's Art, Vol. 1. Mineo Moritani. 1986. 22.50 (*4-7952-6810-X*) World Univ AZ.

***Theoretical Study of Milton's Art: An Interpretation of Paradise Lost, Vol. 1.** Mineo Moritani. 338p. write for info. (*0-941902-03-X*) World Univ AZ.

***Theoretical Study of Milton's Art: An Interpretation of Paradise Lost, Vol. 2.** Mineo Moritani. 151p. pap. write for info. (*0-614-29775-3*) World Univ AZ.

Theoretical Study of the Generation of Infrasonic Waves in the Atmosphere. Walter E. Knabe. LC 70-136105. 105p. 1969. 19.00 (*0-403-04511-8*) Scholarly.

Theoretical Syntax 1980-1990: An Annotated & Classified Bibliography. Rosemarie Ostler. LC 91-42086. (Library & Information Sources in Linguistics: No. 21). viii, 192p. 1992. 53.00 (*1-55619-251-7*) Benjamins North Am.

Theoretical Systems in Biology: Hierarchial & Functional Integration, 3 vols. G. Chauvet. Tr. by K. Malkani from FRE. LC 95-30324. (Studies in Neurosciences: No. 13). 1800p. 1995. 384.75 (*0-08-041995-X*, Pergamon Pr) Elsevier.

Theoretical Time, The Industrial Renaissance. Carol J. Lick & Pam Peterson. 135p. (C). 1990. 23.50 (*0-9622176-6-2*) Air Acad Pr.

Theoretical Treatment of Large Molecules & Their Interactions, Pt. 4. Ed. by Z. B. Maksic. (Illus.). x, 458p. 1991. 244.00 (*0-387-52253-0*) Spr-Verlag.

Theoretical Treatment of Liquids & Liquid Mixtures. Ed. by C. Hoheisel. LC 92-34494. (Studies in Physical & Theoretical Chemistry: Vol. 80). 362p. 1992. 235.25 (*0-444-89835-2*) Elsevier.

***Theoretical Treatments of Hydrogen Bonding.** D. Hadzi. LC 97-11247. (Tutorial Series in Theoretical Chemistry). 1997. write for info. (*0-471-97395-5*) Wiley.

Theoretical Tunnel Mechanics. Ed. by Yoshui Matsumoto & Takashi Nishioka. 236p. 1992. 69.50 (*0-86008-482-5*, Pub. by U of Tokyo JA) Col U Pr.

Theoretical Welfare Economics. J. Graaff. 190p. reprint ed. pap. 54.20 (*0-685-16198-6*, 2027264) Bks Demand.

***Theoria - Praxis: How Jews, Christians, Muslims & Others Can Together Move from Theory to Practice.** Ed. by Leonard Swidler et al. 320p. 1997. pap. 34.95 (*90-390-0631-8*, Pub. by KOK Pharos NE) Eisenbrauns.

Theorica Musice see Monuments of Music & Music Literature in Facsimile

Theoricien Anglais Du Droit Public Au Xvlle Siecle. Renne Gadave. Ed. by J. P. Mayer. LC 78-67351. (European Political Thought Ser.). (FRE.). 1979. reprint ed. lib. bdg. 21.95 (*0-405-11698-5*) Ayer.

Theorie de la Deuxieme Microlocalisation dans le Domaine Complex. Yves Laurent. (Progress in Mathematics Ser.: No. 53). 311p. (C). 1985. 63.00 (*0-8176-3287-5*) Birkhauser.

Theorie de la Religion. Georges Bataille. (Tel Ser.). 159p. (FRE.). 1973. pap. 14.95 (*2-07-070577-3*) Schoenhof.

Theorie der Congruenzen. 2nd ed. Pafnuti L. Chebyshev. LC 71-113123. xvii, 366p. (GER.). 1972. text ed. 19.95 (*0-8284-0254-X*) Chelsea Pub.

Theorie der Konvexen Koerper. T. Bonnesen & W. Fenchel. LC 49-29452. 8.95 (*0-8284-0054-7*) Chelsea Pub.

Theorie der Laplace Transformation see Handbuch der Laplace Transformation

Theorie der Musischen Kunste der Hellenen, 3 vols. in 2. August Rossbach & Rudolf Westphal. cxii, 1783p. 1966. reprint ed. Set. write for info. (*0-318-71012-9*); reprint ed. Bd. I: Griechische Rhythmik. write for info. (*0-318-71013-7*); reprint ed. Bd. II: Griechische Harmonik und Melopoesie. write for info. (*0-318-71014-5*); reprint ed. Bd. III, 1: Allg. Theorie der Griechischen Metrik. write for info. (*0-318-71015-3*); reprint ed. Bd. III, 2: Griechische Metrik mit Besonderer Ruck Sicht auf die Strophengattungen und die Ubrigen M. write for info. (*0-318-71016-1*) G Olms Pubs.

Theorie der Theologie: Enzyklopadie als Methodenlehre. Friedrich Mildenberger. 164p. (GER.). 1972. 19.95 (*0-8288-6424-1*, M-7094) Fr & Eur.

Theorie des Exceptions. Phillipe Sollers. (Folio Essais Ser.: No. 28). (FRE.). pap. 11.95 (*2-07-032338-2*) Schoenhof.

Theorie des Fonctions Algebriques de Deux Variables Independantes, 2 vols. in 1. Emile Picard & G. Simart. LC 67-31156. 1971. 49.50 (*0-8284-0248-5*) Chelsea Pub.

Theorie Des Fonctions Algebriques et Leurs Integrales, Vol. 1. 3rd ed. Paul Appell et al. LC 72-114210. 1977. text ed. 49.50 (*0-8284-0285-X*) Chelsea Pub.

Theorie des Fonctions Algebriques et Leurs Integrales: Volume II. Paul Appell et al. LC 72-114210. text ed. 49.50 (*0-8284-0299-X*) Chelsea Pub.

Theorie Des Graphes et Structures Sociales. Claude Flament. (Mathematiques et Sciences de l'Homme Ser.: No. 2). 1968. pap. 20.80 (*90-279-6312-6*) Mouton.

Theorie des Kommunikativen Handelns see Theory of Communicative Action, Vol. I: Reason & the Rationalization of Society

Theorie des Operations Lineaires. 2nd ed. Stefan Banach. LC 63-21849. 14.95 (*0-8284-0110-1*) Chelsea Pub.

Theorie des Semi-Groupes de Markov. Jacques Neveu. LC 58-9788. (California University Publications in Statistics: Vol. 2 No. 14). 80p. reprint ed. pap. 25.00 (*0-317-08330-9*, 2021185) Bks Demand.

Theorie Elementaire des Fonctions Analytiques d'une ou Plusiers Variables Complexes see Elementary Theory of Analytic Functions of One or Several Complex Variables

Theorie et Politique see Saint-Simonisme et Pari pour l'Industrie, XIXe et XXe Siecles

Theorie Generale see Analyse Fonctionnelle

Theorie Generale des Surfaces, 4 Vols. 2nd ed. Gaston Darboux. LC 67-16997. 1968. Set. 150.00 (*0-8284-0216-7*) Chelsea Pub.

Theorie, la Pratique et L'art En Photographie Avec le Procede Au Gelatino Bromure D'argent. Frederic Dillaye. Ed. by Peter C. Bunnell & Robert A. Sobieszek. LC 76-23053. (Sources of Modern Photography Ser.). (Illus.). (FRE.). 1979. reprint ed. lib. bdg. 38.95 (*0-405-09618-6*) Ayer.

Theorie Platonicienne Des Idees et Des Nombres d'Apres Aristote. Leon Robin. xvii, 702p. 1984. reprint ed. write for info. (*3-487-00344-9*) G Olms Pubs.

Theorie Probabiliste du Controle des Diffusions. Jean-Michel Bismut. LC 75-41602. (Memoirs Ser.: No. 4/167). 130p. 1976. pap. 22.00 (*0-8218-1867-8*, MEMO/4/167) Am Math.

Theorie Quantique De la Liaison Chimique see Quantum Theory of the Chemical Bond

Theorie und Geschichte Des Photographischen Objecktivs. Moritz Von Rohr. Ed. by Peter C. Bunnell & Robert A. Sobieszek. LC 78-19592. (Sources of Modern Photography Ser.). (GER.). 1979. reprint ed. lib. bdg. 31.95 (*0-405-09869-3*) Ayer.

Theorie und Praxis der Linearen Integralaleichungen 4. Stefan Fenyo & Hans W. Stolle. 370p. (GER.). (C). 1984. text ed. 112.95 (*3-7643-1167-3*) Birkhauser.

Theorie und Praxis der Linearen Integralgleichungen: Vol. I. Stefan Fenyo & Hans W. Stolle. (LMW - MA Ser.: 74). 250p. (GER.). (C). 1982. 87.50 (*0-8176-1164-9*) Birkhauser.

Theorie und Praxis der Linearen Integralgleichungen: Vol. 2. Stefan Fenyo & Hans W. Stolle. 304p. (GER.). (C). 1983. 106.50 (*0-8176-1165-7*) Birkhauser.

Theorie und Praxis Des Lexikons. Ed. by Frank Beckmann & Gerhard Heyer. (Grundlagen der Kommunikation & Kognition (Foundations of Communication & Cognition) Ser.). viii, 348p. (GER.). (C). 1993. lib. bdg. 152.35 (*3-11-013502-7*) De Gruyter.

***Theorien und Gesellschaftliche Praxis Technischer Entwicklung: Soziale Verschrankungen in Modernen Technisierungsprozessen.** Richard Huisinga. (Technik Interdisziplinar Ser.). (GER.). 1996. text ed. 83.00 (*90-5708-003-6*); pap. text ed. 41.00 (*90-5708-004-4*) Gordon & Breach.

Theorien vom Ursprung der Sprache, 2 vols., Set. Ed. by Joachim Gessinger & Wolfert Von Rahden. (GER.). (C). 1989. lib. bdg. 453.85 (*3-11-010189-0*) De Gruyter.

Theories. Barry McLaughlin. 1995. text ed. 17.95 (*0-7131-6513-8*, Pub. by E Arnld UK) St Martin.

Theories & Analyses of Twentieth-Century Music. J. Kent Williams. 368p. (C). 1996. text ed. write for info. (*0-15-500316-X*) HB Coll Pubs.

Theories & Applications in the Detection of Deception. G. Ben-Shakhar & J. J. Furedy. xi, 169p. 1989. 79.95 (*0-387-97065-7*) Spr-Verlag.

Theories & Approaches to International Politics. 4th ed. Patrick M. Morgan. 314p. 1986. 39.95 (*0-88738-093-X*); pap. text ed. 24.95 (*0-88738-630-X*) Transaction Pubs.

Theories & Concepts in Comparative Industrial Relations. Intro. by Jack Barbash & Kate Barbash. 281p. 1989. text ed. 34.95 (*0-87249-580-9*) U of SC Pr.

Theories & Concepts of Politics. Ed. by Richard Bellamy. LC 93-9872. 309p. 1993. pap. 19.95 (*0-7190-3656-9*, Pub. by Manchester Univ Pr UK); text ed. 75.00 (*0-7190-3655-0*, Pub. by Manchester Univ Pr UK) St Martin.

Theories & Criticisms of Sir Henry Maine. Morgan O. Evans. viii, 93p. 1981. reprint ed. lib. bdg. 18.50 (*0-8377-0540-1*) Rothman.

Theories & Documents of Contemporary Art: A Sourcebook of Artists' Writings. Peter H. Selz. LC 94-46530. (California Studies in the History of Art: Vol. XXXV). (Illus.). 1003p. 1996. pap. 29.95 (*0-520-20253-8*) U CA Pr.

Theories & Documents of Contemporary Art: A Sourcebook of Artists' Writings. Peter H. Selz. LC 94-46530. (California Studies in the History of Art: Vol. XXXV). (Illus.). 1003p. (C). 1996. 60.00 (*0-520-20251-1*) U CA Pr.

T

Theories & Experiences for Real-Time System Development. Teodor Rus & Charles Rattray. (AMAST Computing Ser.). 444p. 1995. text ed. 99.00 (*981-02-1923-7*) World Scientific Pub.

Theories & Mechanism of Phase Transitions, Heterophase Polymerizations, Homopolymerizations, Addition Polymerization. (Advances in Polymer Science Ser.: Vol. 112). (Illus.). 320p. 1994. 174.95 (*0-387-57236-8*) Spr-Verlag.

Theories & Methods for Practice of Clinical Psychology. Malcolm H. Robertson & Robert H. Woody. LC 96-25085. 300p. 1997. 39.95 (*0-8236-6518-6*, BN06518) Intl Univs Pr.

Theories & Methods in Rural Community Studies. H. Mendras & I. Mihailescu. LC 82-16508. (Vienna Centre Ser.: No. 9). 304p. 1982. 139.00 (*0-08-025813-1*, Pub. by Pergamon Repr UK) Franklin.

Theories & Methods of Spatio-Temporal Reasoning in Geographic Space: International Conference GIS from Space to Territory: Theories & Methods of Spatio-Temporal Reasoning, Pisa, Italy, September 1992, Proceedings. Ed. by A. U. Frank et al. LC 92-30838. (Lecture Notes in Computer Science Ser.: Vol. 639). xi, 431p. 1992. 63.95 (*0-387-55966-3*) Spr-Verlag.

Theories & Narratives: Reflections on the Philosophy of History. Alex Callinicos. LC 94-24970. (Post-Contemporary Interventions Ser.). 264p. 1995. text ed. 45.00 (*0-8223-1631-5*); pap. text ed. 16.95 (*0-8223-1645-5*) Duke.

Theories & Observation in Science. Ed. by Richard E. Grandy. vii, 184p. (C). 1980. reprint ed. pap. text ed. 13.00 (*0-917930-19-3*); reprint ed. lib. bdg. 27.00 (*0-917930-39-8*) Ridgeview.

Theories & Practice of Harmonic Analysis. Gene J. Cho. LC 92-6539. 132p. 1992. pap. 19.95 (*0-7734-9917-2*) E Mellen.

Theories & Practice of Parliamentary Procedure in India. S. H. Belavadi. (C). 1989. 135.00 (*0-685-27942-1*) St Mut.

Theories & Principles of Occupational Therapy. Mary Young & Evie Quinn. (Illus.). 224p. (Orig.). 1992. pap. text ed. 29.95 (*0-443-04060-5*) Churchill.

***Theories & Programmes of the Late 20th Century.** Ed. by Charles Jencks & Karl Kropf. (Illus.). 200p. (Orig.). 1997. pap. 22.95 (*1-85490-407-8*) Academy Ed UK.

Theories & Strategies in Counseling & Psychotherapy. 3rd ed. Burl E. Gilliland et al. LC 93-16864. 1993. text ed. 67.00 (*0-205-14803-4*) Allyn.

***Theories & Strategies in Counseling & Psychotherapy.** 4th ed. Burl E. Gilliland & Richard K. James. LC 97-20362. 1998. 60.00 (*0-205-26832-3*) Allyn.

***Theories & Systems of Psychology.** 5th ed. Robert W. Lundin. 432p. (C). 1996. text ed. 59.16 (*0-669-35446-5*) HM College Div.

Theories & Things. Willard V. Quine. 225p. 1986. pap. 12.95 (*0-674-87926-0*) Belknap Pr.

Theories du Symbole. Tzvetan Todorov. (FRE.). 1985. pap. 19.95 (*0-7859-2702-6*) Fr & Eur.

Theories for Social Work with Groups. Robert W. Roberts & Helen Northen. LC 76-4967. 400p. 1976. text ed. 40.00 (*0-231-03885-2*) Col U Pr.

Theories in Intercultural Communication. Ed. by Young Y. Kim & William B. Gudykunst. (International & Intercultural Communication Ser.: Vol. 12). 320p. (C). 1988. text ed. 55.00 (*0-8039-3149-2*); pap. text ed. 24.95 (*0-8039-3150-6*) Sage.

Theories, Models & Methodology in Writing Research. Gert Rijlaarsdam et al. (Orig.). (C). 1995. pap. 65.00 (*90-5356-197-8*, Pub. by Amsterdam U Pr NE) U of Mich Pr.

Theories of Action in Conrad. Francis A. Hubbard. LC 84-8769. (Studies in Modern Literature: No. 40). 130p. reprint ed. pap. 37.10 (*0-8357-1588-4*, 2070555) Bks Demand.

***Theories of Action, Planning, & Robot Control: Bridging the Gap: Papers from the 1996 Workshop.** Ed. by Chitta Baral. (Technical Reports). (Illus.). 130p. 1996. spiral bd. 25.00 (*1-57735-021-9*) AAAI Pr.

Theories of Adolescence. 6th ed. Rolf E. Muuss et al. LC 95-41242. 1996. pap. text ed. write for info. (*0-07-044267-3*) McGraw.

Theories of Africans: Francophone Literature & Anthropology in Africa. Christopher L. Miller. (Black Literature & Culture Ser.). (Illus.). 338p. 1990. pap. text ed. 19.95 (*0-226-52802-2*) U Ch Pr.

Theories of Africans: Francophone Literature & Anthropology in Africa. Christopher L. Miller. (Black Literature & Culture Ser.). (Illus.). 352p. 1990. lib. bdg. 60.00 (*0-226-52801-4*) U Ch Pr.

Theories of Americanization: A Critical Study. Isaac B. Berkson. LC 77-87743. (American Education: Its Men, Institutions, & Ideas. Series 1). 1975. reprint ed. 18.95 (*0-405-01387-6*) Ayer.

Theories of Animal Memory: Animal Cognition. Ed. by Donald F. Kendrick et al. (Comparative Cognition & Neuroscience Bever-Alton Roeblatt Ser.). 224p. (C). 1986. pap. 29.95 (*0-89859-697-1*) L Erlbaum Assocs.

Theories of Art: From Plato to Winckelmann. Moshe Barasch. 352p. (C). 1985. pap. 18.50 (*0-8147-1061-1*); text ed. 44.00 (*0-8147-1060-3*) NYU Pr.

Theories of Authorship. Ed. by John Caughie. (BFI Readers in Film Ser.). (Illus.). 320p. 1981. pap. 15.95 (*0-7100-0650-0*, RKP) Routledge.

***Theories of Authorship: Reader.** J. Caughie. 318p. (C). 1981. pap. 17.95 (*0-415-02552-4*) Routledge.

Theories of Autism. Cheryl D. Seifert. 106p. (Orig.). (C). 1990. pap. text ed. 12.00 (*0-8191-7719-9*) U Pr of Amer.

Theories of Autism. Cheryl D. Seifert. 106p. (Orig.). (C). 1990. lib. bdg. 31.50 (*0-8191-7718-0*) U Pr of Amer.

Theories of Behavior Therapy: Exploring Behavior Change. Ed. by William O'Donohue & Leonard Krasner. 753p. 1995. text ed. 69.95 (*1-55798-265-1*) Am Psychol.

Theories of Carcinogenesis: Facts, Fashion, or Fiction? Olav H. Iversen. 327p. 1988. 94.95 (*0-89116-579-7*) Hemisp Pub.

Theories of Career Development. 4th ed. Samuel H. Osipow & Louise F. Fitzgerald. LC 95-9133. 1995. text ed. 64.00 (*0-205-18391-3*) Allyn.

Theories of Charges: A Study of Finitely Additive Measures. Bhaskara K. Rao. (Pure & Applied Mathematics Ser.). 1983. text ed. 149.00 (*0-12-095780-9*) Acad Pr.

Theories of Chemical Reactions Rates. Rudolphy A. Marcus. (Twentieth Century Chemistry Ser.). 400p. 1997. text ed. 109.00 (*981-02-1505-3*); pap. text ed. 53.00 (*981-02-1506-1*) World Scientific Pub.

Theories of Child Abuse & Neglect: Differential Perspectives, Summaries, & Evaluations. Oliver C. Tzeng et al. LC 90-46516. 392p. 1991. text ed. 65.00 (*0-275-93832-8*, C3832, Praeger Pubs) Greenwood.

Theories of Chromatic & Enharmonic Music in Late Sixteenth Century Italy. Karol Berger. LC 79-24734. (Studies in Musicology: No. 10). 187p. reprint ed. pap. 53.30 (*0-685-20822-2*, 2070037) Bks Demand.

Theories of Civil Violence. James B. Rule. 482p. 1988. pap. 14.00 (*0-520-06796-7*) U CA Pr.

Theories of Coalition Formation. James P. Kahan & Amnon Rapoport. (Basic Studies in Human Behavior). 381p. 1984. text ed. 89.95 (*0-89859-298-4*) L Erlbaum Assocs.

***Theories of Cognition in the Later Middle Ages.** Robert Pasnau. 380p. (C). 1997. 54.95 (*0-521-58368-3*) Cambridge U Pr.

Theories of Collective Action: Downs, Olson & Hirsch. David Reisman. LC 89-36477. 380p. 1990. text ed. 55.00 (*0-312-03595-0*) St Martin.

Theories of Comparative Analysis. Daniel S. Weld. Ed. by Brady, Bobrow & Davis Staff. (Artificial Intelligence Ser.). 200p. 1990. 32.50 (*0-262-23152-2*) MIT Pr.

Theories of Comparative Economic Growth. Kwang Choi. LC 83-284. (Illus.). 306p. 1983. reprint ed. pap. 87.30 (*0-608-00123-6*, 2060888) Bks Demand.

Theories of Comparative Politics: The Search for a Paradigm Reconsidered. 2nd ed. Ronald H. Chilcote. 417p. (C). 1994. pap. text ed. 24.95 (*0-8133-1017-2*) Westview.

Theories of Competition. L. G. Telser. 397p. 1988. 47.95 (*0-444-01248-6*) P-H.

***Theories of Computability.** Nicholas Pippenger. 240p. (C). 1997. text ed. 44.95 (*0-521-55380-6*) Cambridge U Pr.

Theories of Concepts: A History of the Major Philosophical Tradition. Morris Weitz. 344p. 1988. pap. text ed. 38.00 (*0-415-00180-3*) Routledge.

Theories of Contemporary Art. 2nd ed. Richard Hertz. 336p. 1993. pap. text ed. 33.33 (*0-13-012618-7*) P-H.

Theories of Counseling & Psychotherapy. 4th ed. C. H. Patterson. 608p. (C). 1990. pap. text ed. 63.00 (*0-06-045053-3*) Addson-Wesley Educ.

Theories of Counseling & Psychotherapy. 5th ed. C. H. Patterson & C. Edward Watkins, Jr. LC 95-17191. 560p. (C). 1996. text ed. 54.95 (*0-673-99103-2*) Addson-Wesley Educ.

Theories of Creativity. Ed. by Mark A. Runco & Robert S. Albert. (Focus Editions Ser.: Vol. 115). (Illus.). 320p. (C). 1990. pap. 24.95 (*0-8039-3545-5*) Sage.

Theories of Creativity. Ed. by Mark A. Runco & Robert S. Albert. LC 90-31971. (Sage Focus Editions Ser.: No. 115). 276p. 1990. reprint ed. pap. 78.70 (*0-608-01537-7*, 2059581) Bks Demand.

Theories of Crime. Daniel J. Curran & Claire M. Renzetti. LC 93-25394. 324p. 1993. pap. text ed. 29.00 (*0-205-14193-5*) Allyn.

***Theories of Culture: A Theological Assessment.** Kathryn Tanner. LC 97-22497. 1997. pap. text ed. 13.00 (*0-8006-3097-1*, Fortress Pr) Augsburg Fortress.

Theories of Delinquency: An Explanation of Delinquent Behavior. 3rd ed. Donald J. Shoemaker. (Illus.). 320p. (C). 1996. pap. 19.95 (*0-19-508731-3*) OUP.

Theories of Dependent Foreign Policy: The Case of Ecuador in the 1980s. Jeanne A. Hey. (Monographs in International Studies Latin America Ser.: No. 22). (Illus.). 280p. (Orig.). (C). 1995. pap. text ed. 22.00 (*0-89680-184-5*) Ohio U Pr.

Theories of Desire. Patrick Fuery. (Interpretations Ser.). 128p. pap. 19.95 (*0-522-84620-3*, Pub. by Melbourne Univ Pr AT) Paul & Co Pubs.

Theories of Developing: Proceedings of the 1993 Third World Symposium. Ed. by Yawsoon Sim. (Illus.). 70p. (Orig.). (C). 1994. pap. text ed. 20.00 (*0-7881-0884-0*) DIANE Pub.

Theories of Development. P. W. Preston. (International Library of Sociology). 300p. 1982. 29.50 (*0-7100-9055-2*, RKP) Routledge.

Theories of Development: Capitalism, Colonialism & Dependency. Jorge A. Larrain. (Illus.). 220p. (C). 1989. pap. text ed. 27.95 (*0-7456-0711-X*) Blackwell Pubs.

Theories of Development: Concepts & Applications. 3rd ed. William C. Crain. 384p. (C). 1991. pap. text ed. 36.80 (*0-13-913476-X*) P-H.

Theories of Development: Mode of Production or Dependency? Ed. by Ronald H. Chilcote & Dale L. Johnson. LC 82-19141. (Class, State & Development Ser.: No. 2). 256p. 1983. reprint ed. pap. 73.00 (*0-608-01509-1*, 2059553) Bks Demand.

Theories of Development Psychology. 3rd ed. Patricia H. Miller. LC 92-37252. (C). 1995. pap. text ed. write for info. (*0-7167-2309-3*) W H Freeman.

Theories of Deviance. 4th ed. Ed. by Stuart H. Traub & Craig B. Little. LC 92-61959. 632p. (C). 1993. pap. 42.00 (*0-87581-371-2*) Peacock Pubs.

Theories of Distributive Justice. John E. Roemer. LC 95-23768. (Illus.). 352p. 1996. 39.95 (*0-674-87919-8*) HUP.

Theories of Economic Growth & Development. Irma Adelman. viii, 164p. 1961. 29.50 (*0-8047-0083-4*); pap. 11.95 (*0-8047-0084-2*) Stanford U Pr.

Theories of Educational Management. 2nd ed. Troy Bush. 176p. 1995. 23.00 (*1-85396-283-X*, Pub. by Paul Chapman UK) Taylor & Francis.

Theories of Error in Indian Philosophy. Bijayananda Kar. 1978. 11.00 (*0-8364-0304-5*) S Asia.

Theories of Ethics. Ed. by Philippa R. Foot. (Oxford Readings in Philosophy Ser.). 192p. (C). 1976. pap. 18.95 (*0-19-875005-6*) OUP.

Theories of Ethnicity: A Classical Reader. Ed. by Werner Sollors. 496p. (C). 1996. 65.00 (*0-8147-8034-2*); pap. 22.50 (*0-8147-8035-0*) NYU Pr.

Theories of Ethnicity: A Critical Appraisal. Richard H. Thompson. LC 89-2120. (Contributions in Sociology Ser.: No. 82). 206p. 1989. text ed. 59.95 (*0-313-26636-0*, TTE/, Greenwood Pr) Greenwood.

Theories of Everything: The Quest for Ultimate Explanation. John D. Barrow. (Illus.). 336p. 1992. pap. 12.00 (*0-449-90738-4*, Columbine) Fawcett.

Theories of Everything: The Quest for Ultimate Explanation. John D. Barrow. (Illus.). 240p. 1991. 30.00 (*0-19-853928-2*, 12331) OUP.

Theories of Evidence: Bentham & Wigmore. William Twining. LC 85-50306. (Jurists: Profiles in Legal Theory Ser.). 272p. 1985. 42.50 (*0-8047-1285-9*) Stanford U Pr.

Theories of Explanation. Joseph C. Pitt. (Illus.). 234p. 1988. pap. text ed. 16.95 (*0-19-504971-3*) OUP.

Theories of Famine. Stephen Devereux. 288p. 1994. pap. text ed. 42.00 (*0-13-302217-X*) P-H.

Theories of General Education: A Critical Approach. Craig C. Howard. LC 90-30950. 144p. 1992. text ed. 39.95 (*0-312-04743-6*) St Martin.

Theories of Group Behavior. Ed. by B. Mullen & G. R. Geothals. (Social Psychology Ser.). (Illus.). 255p. 1986. 86.95 (*0-387-96351-0*) Spr-Verlag.

Theories of Group Processes. Ed. by Cary L. Cooper. LC 74-28089. 289p. reprint ed. pap. 82.40 (*0-317-09544-7*, 2051855) Bks Demand.

Theories of Heavy-Electron Systems. Ed. by P. A. Lee et al. (Journal Comments on Condensed Matter Physics). 65p. 1986. pap. text ed. 47.00 (*0-677-21460-X*) Gordon & Breach.

Theories of High Temperature Superconductivity. Ed. by J. Woods Halley. 272p. (C). 1988. 57.95 (*0-201-12008-9*, 12008, Adv Bk Prog) Addison-Wesley.

Theories of History. Ed. by Patrick L. Gardiner. LC 58-6481. 1959. 29.95 (*0-02-911210-9*, Free Press) Free Pr.

Theories of Homosexuality. Dannecker. 1995. per. 3.95 (*0-907040-05-5*, Pub. by Gay Mens Pr UK) LPC InBook.

Theories of Human Communication. 4th ed. Stephen W. Littlejohn. 417p. (C). 1992. text ed. 45.95 (*0-534-16134-0*) Wadsworth Pub.

Theories of Human Communication. 5th ed. Stephen W. Littlejohn. LC 95-4224. 399p. 1996. text ed. 55.95 (*0-534-26052-7*) Wadsworth Pub.

Theories of Human Communication. 5th ed. Stephen W. Littlejohn. (Speech & Theater Ser.). 1996. student ed., text ed. 17.95 (*0-534-26054-3*) Wadsworth Pub.

Theories of Human Development. 2nd ed. Neil J. Salkind. LC 84-19680. 270p. 1985. Net. pap. text ed. 27.50 (*0-471-80575-0*) Wiley.

Theories of Human Evolution: A Century of Debate, 1844-1944. Peter J. Bowler. LC 86-3029. (Illus.). 360p. 1986. text ed. 42.00 (*0-8018-3258-6*) Johns Hopkins.

Theories of Human Nature. Donald C. Abel. 448p. (C). 1992. pap. text ed. write for info. (*0-07-000050-6*) McGraw.

Theories of Human Nature. Peter Loptson. 220p. 1995. pap. 19.95 (*1-55111-061-X*) Broadview Pr.

Theories of Human Sexuality. Ed. by James H. Geer & William O'Donohue. (Perspectives in Sexuality Ser.). 426p. 1987. 80.00 (*0-306-42459-2*, Plenum Pr) Plenum.

Theories of Human Social Action. Charles V. Willie. LC 92-76214. 184p. (Orig.). 1994. text ed. 34.95 (*1-882289-09-9*); pap. text ed. 18.95 (*1-882289-08-0*) Gen Hall.

Theories of Hypnosis: Current Models & Perspectives. Ed. by Steven J. Lynn & Judith W. Rhue. LC 91-28531. (Guilford Clinical & Experimental Hypnosis Ser.). 634p. 1991. lib. bdg. 56.95 (*0-89862-343-X*) Guilford Pr.

Theories of Illness: A World Survey. George P. Murdock. LC 80-5257. 142p. 1980. pap. 40.50 (*0-7837-8545-3*, 2049360) Bks Demand.

Theories of Image Formation. David F. Marks. 1986. lib. bdg. 45.00 (*0-913412-18-X*) Brandon Hse.

Theories of Immune Networks. Ed. by H. Atlan & I. R. Cohen. (Synergetics Ser.: Vol. 46). (Illus.). 160p. 1989. 67.95 (*0-387-51678-6*) Spr-Verlag.

***Theories of Imperfectly Competitive Markets.** Luis C. Corchon. LC 96-27345. (Lecture Notes in Economics & Mathematical Systems Ser.: Vol. 442). 163p. 1996. 52.00 (*3-540-61553-9*) Spr-Verlag.

Theories of Imperialism. Wolfgang J. Mommsen. Tr. by P. S. Falla. LC 81-16091. 192p. (C). 1982. reprint ed. pap. text ed. 13.00 (*0-226-53396-4*) U Ch Pr.

Theories of Income Distribution. Ed. by Athanasios Asimakopulos. (C). 1987. lib. bdg. 83.50 (*0-89838-232-7*) Kluwer Ac.

Theories of Industrial Society. Richard J. Badham. LC 86-1742. 192p. 1986. text ed. 32.50 (*0-312-79640-4*) St Martin.

Theories of Inflation. Helmut Frisch. LC 83-1871. (Cambridge Surveys of Economic Literature Ser.). 256p. 1984. pap. text ed. 26.95 (*0-521-29512-2*) Cambridge U Pr.

Theories of Intergroup Relations: International Social Psychological Perspecctives. 2nd ed. Donald M. Taylor & Fathali M. Moghaddam. LC 93-30988. 256p. 1994. pap. text ed. 24.95 (*0-275-94635-5*, Praeger Pubs) Greenwood.

Theories of Intergroup Relations: International Social Psychological Perspectives. 2nd ed. Donald M. Taylor & Fathali M. Moghaddam. LC 93-30988. 256p. 1994. text ed. 65.00 (*0-275-94634-7*, Praeger Pubs) Greenwood.

***Theories of International Regimes.** Andreas Hasenclever et al. (Studies in International Relations: Vol. 55). 270p. (C). 1997. text ed. 59.95 (*0-521-59145-7*) Cambridge U Pr.

***Theories of International Regimes.** Andreas Hasenclever et al. (Studies in International Relations: Vol. 55). 270p. (C). 1997. pap. text ed. 18.95 (*0-521-59849-4*) Cambridge U Pr.

Theories of International Relations. Burchill & Scott Linklater. 280p. 1996. text ed. 49.95 (*0-312-16244-8*) St Martin.

Theories of International Relations. Frank M. Russell. LC 72-4297. (World Affairs Ser.: National & International Viewpoints). 658p. 1972. reprint ed. 44.95 (*0-405-04588-3*) Ayer.

Theories of International Relationship. Burchill. 1996. text ed. 19.95 (*0-312-16245-6*) St Martin.

Theories of Islamic Law. Imran A. Nyazee. 344p. (C). 1995. text ed. 21.95 (*0-934905-66-5*) Kazi Pubns.

Theories of Knowledge: With a New Preface. Reginald F. O'Neill. 242p. 1980. reprint ed. text ed. 29.50 (*0-8290-0227-8*); reprint ed. pap. text ed. 18.95 (*0-8290-0386-X*) Irvington.

Theories of Knowledge & Reality. 2nd ed. Cover & Garns. 1994. pap. text ed. write for info. (*0-07-013269-0*) McGraw.

Theories of Learning. 5th ed. Gordon H. Bower & Ernest J. Hilgard. (Illus.). 640p. 1980. text ed. 73.00 (*0-13-914432-3*) P-H.

Theories of Learning: A Historical Approach. John C. Malone. 342p. (C). 1991. text ed. 59.95 (*0-534-05760-8*) Brooks-Cole.

***Theories of Legal Arguments from the 19th Century to Contemporary Trends.** Robert Nozick. 400p. 1997. text ed. 75.00 (*0-8153-2658-0*) Garland.

Theories of Light from Descartes to Newton. A. I. Sabra. LC 81-6108. (Illus.). 380p. 1981. pap. 20.95 (*0-521-28436-8*) Cambridge U Pr.

Theories of Literary Genre. Ed. by Joseph P. Strelka. LC 76-41807. (Yearbook of Contemporary Criticism: Vol.8). 1978. text ed. 30.00 (*0-271-01243-9*) Pa St U Pr.

Theories of Literary Realism. Dario Villanueva. Tr. by Mihai I. Spariosu & Santiago G. Castanon from SPA. LC 96-23293. (SUNY Series, The Margins of Literature). 190p. (C). 1997. text ed. 39.50 (*0-7914-3327-7*); pap. text ed. 12.95 (*0-7914-3328-5*) State U NY Pr.

Theories of Literature in the Twentieth Century: Structuralism, Marxism, Aesthetics of Reception, Semiotics. 2nd ed. Douwe W. Fokkema & Elrud Ibsch. 219p. 1995. text ed. 17.95 (*0-312-12448-1*) St Martin.

Theories of Local Economic Development: Perspectives from Across the Disciplines. Richard D. Bingham & Robert Mier. (Illus.). 360p. (C). 1993. text ed. 62.00 (*0-8039-4867-0*); pap. text ed. 28.50 (*0-8039-4868-9*) Sage.

Theories of Love Development, Maintenance, & Dissolution: Octagonal Cycle & Differential Perspectives. Ed. by Oliver C. Tzeng. LC 91-41777. 336p. 1992. text ed. 69.50 (*0-275-94234-1*, C4234, Praeger Pubs) Greenwood.

Theories of Man & Culture. Elvin Hatch. LC 73-1250. 396p. 1974. pap. text ed. 21.00 (*0-231-03639-6*) Col U Pr.

Theories of Mass Communication. 5th ed. Melvin L. DeFleur & Sandra J. Ball-Rokeach. LC 81-8215. (Illus.). 288p. (C). 1989. pap. text ed. 40.95 (*0-582-99870-0*, 75295) Longman.

Theories of Mathematical Learning. Ed. by Leslie P. Steffe et al. 385p. 1996. pap. 39.95 (*0-8058-1662-3*); text ed. 99.95 (*0-8058-1661-5*) L Erlbaum Assocs.

Theories of Matter: A Festschrift for Professor Joseph Birman. Allan I. Solomon. 316p. 1994. text ed. 74.00 (*981-02-1759-5*) World Scientific Pub.

Theories of Migration. Ed. by Robin Cohen. LC 96-14469. (International Library of Studies on Migration: Vol. 1). 544p. (C). 1996. text ed. 160.00 (*1-85898-001-1*) E Elgar.

Theories of Mimesis. Arne Melberg. (Literature, Culture, Theory Ser.: No. 12). 196p. (C). 1995. text ed. 54.95 (*0-521-45225-2*) Cambridge U Pr.

Theories of Mimesis. Nicos A. Nicola et al. (Literature, Culture, Theory Ser.: No. 12). 196p. (C). 1995. pap. text ed. 17.95 (*0-521-45856-0*) Cambridge U Pr.

Theories of Modern Art: A Source Book by Artists & Critics. Herschel B. Chipp et al. (California Studies in the History of Art: No. XI). (Illus.). 680p. (C). 1968. pap. 17.95 (*0-520-05256-0*) U CA Pr.

Theories of Modern Art: A Source Book by Artists & Critics. Herschel B. Chipp. LC 68-12038. (California Studies in the History of Art: No. 11). 680p. reprint ed. pap. 180.00 (*0-685-17869-2*, 2029589) Bks Demand.

Theories of Modernity & Postmodernity. Ed. by Bryan S. Turner. (Theory, Culture & Society Ser.). 208p. (C). 1990. text ed. 45.00 (*0-8039-8370-0*); pap. text ed. 22.95 (*0-8039-8371-9*) Sage.

Theories of Moral Development. 2nd ed. John M. Rich & Joseph L. DeVitis. LC 94-21565. 164p. (C). 1994. pap. 22.95 (*0-398-06061-4*) C C Thomas.

Theories of Moral Development. 2nd ed. John M. Rich & Joseph L. DeVitis. LC 94-21565. 164p. (C). 1994. 34.95 (*0-398-05924-1*) C C Thomas.

T

An Asterisk (*) at the beginning of an entry indicates that the title is appearing in BIP for the first time.

Theories of Motivation: A Comparative Study of Modern Theories of Motivation. 4th ed. K. B. Madsen. LC 68-22338. 366p. reprint ed. pap. 104.40 (*0-317-10321-0*, 2050861) Bks Demand.

Theories of Muscle Contraction. William F. Harrington. Ed. by J. J. Head. LC 77-94953. (Carolina Biology Readers Ser.: No. 114). (Illus.). 32p. (YA). (gr. 10 up). 1981. pap. 3.00 (*0-89278-314-1*, 45-9714) Carolina Biological.

Theories of Musical Texture in Western History. John D. White. LC 95-3301. (Perspectives in Music Criticism & Theory Ser.: Vols. 1 & 1678). 431p. 1995. text ed. 70.00 (*0-8153-1187-7*, H1678) Garland.

***Theories of Myth: An Annotated Bibliography.** Thomas J. Sienkewicz. LC 97-25078. (Magill Bibliographies Ser.). 1997. write for info. (*0-8108-3388-3*) Scarecrow.

Theories of Myth: From Ancient Israel & Greece to Freud, Jung, Campbell & Levi-Strauss, 6 vols., Set. Ed. & Intro. by Robert A. Segal. 1996. 450.00 (*0-8153-2254-2*) Garland.

Theories of Nationalism. 2nd ed. Anthony D. Smith. LC 82-23216. 350p. (C). 1983. pap. text ed. 24.95 (*0-8419-0845-1*) Holmes & Meier.

Theories of Object Relations: Bridges to Self Psychology. Howard A. Bacal & Kenneth Newman. (Personality, Psychopathology & Psychotherapy: Theoretical & Clinical Perspectives Ser.). 312p. 1990. text ed. 39.50 (*0-231-06102-1*) Col U Pr.

Theories of Parallelism. William B. Frankland. LC 72-7224. (Select Bibliographies Reprint Ser.). 1977. reprint ed. 16.95 (*0-8369-6931-6*) Ayer.

Theories of Pastoral Poetry in England, 1684-1798. J. E. Congleton. LC 68-29735. (Studies in Poetry: No. 38). 1969. reprint ed. lib. bdg. 75.00 (*0-8383-0329-3*) M S G Haskell Hse.

Theories of Personality. David Lester. 200p. 1995. 59.50 (*1-56032-350-7*); pap. 29.50 (*1-56032-351-5*) Taylor & Francis.

Theories of Personality. Wallace. 1993. text ed. 72.00 (*0-205-14700-3*) Allyn.

Theories of Personality. 2nd ed. Jess Feist. (C). 1994. student ed., per. write for info. (*0-697-27662-7*) Brown & Benchmark.

Theories of Personality. 2nd ed. Barry D. Smith & Harold J. Vetter. 464p. (C). 1990. text ed. 60.00 (*0-13-913724-6*) P-H.

Theories of Personality. 2nd rev. ed. Jess Feist. (Illus.). 454p. (C). 1990. text ed. 46.75 (*0-03-027857-0*) HB Coll Pubs.

Theories of Personality. 3rd ed. Jess Feist. 818p. (C). 1994. text ed. write for info. (*0-697-27392-X*); student ed., per. write for info. (*0-697-27394-6*); per. write for info. (*0-697-27661-9*) Brown & Benchmark.

Theories of Personality. 3rd ed. Calvin S. Hall & Gardner Lindzey. 725p. 1978. Net. text ed. 47.50 (*0-471-34227-0*) Wiley.

***Theories of Personality.** 4th ed. Calvin S. Hall et al. LC 97-12707. 752p. 1997. text ed. write for info. (*0-471-30342-9*) Wiley.

Theories of Personality. 4th ed. Duane Schultz. LC 89-15744. 496p. (C). 1990. text ed. 49.95 (*0-534-12264-7*) Brooks-Cole.

***Theories of Personality.** 5th ed. Feist. Date not set. text ed. 42.84 (*0-697-36225-6*); wbk. ed., pap. text ed. 14.80 (*0-697-36227-2*) McGraw.

Theories of Personality. 5th ed. Richard M. Ryckman. LC 92-2646. 560p. (C). 1993. text ed. 43.25 (*0-534-16644-X*) Brooks-Cole.

Theories of Personality. 5th ed. Duane Schultz. LC 93-6486. 1994. text ed. 64.95 (*0-534-16650-4*) Brooks-Cole.

Theories of Personality. 6th ed. Richard M. Ryckman. (Psychology Ser.). 635p. (C). 1997. text ed. 50.95 (*0-534-33976-X*) Brooks-Cole.

Theories of Personality. 6th ed. Schultz. (Psychology Ser.). 1998. text ed. 53.95 (*0-534-34119-5*) Brooks-Cole.

***Theories of Personality.** 6th ed. Schultz. (Psychology Ser.). 1998. pap. 19.95 (*0-534-35015-1*) Brooks-Cole.

***Theories of Personality.** 7th ed. Richard M. Ryckman. (Psychology Ser.). Date not set. text ed. 47.95 (*0-534-34898-X*) Brooks-Cole.

Theories of Personality: Understanding Persons. 2nd ed. Susan C. Cloninger. LC 95-36896. 1995. text ed. 65.00 (*0-13-453227-9*) P-H.

Theories of Personality & Psychopathology. 3rd ed. Ed. by Theodore Millon. LC 82-25843. 452p. (C). 1983. text ed. 41.25 (*0-03-062629-3*) HB Coll Pubs.

Theories of Political Economy. James A. Caporaso & David P. Levine. (Illus.). 300p. (C). 1992. text ed. 59.95 (*0-521-41561-6*) Cambridge U Pr.

Theories of Political Economy. James A. Caporaso & David P. Levine. (Illus.). 300p. (C). 1992. pap. text ed. 18.95 (*0-521-42578-6*) Cambridge U Pr.

***Theories of Political Processes: A Bibliographic Guide to the Journal Literature, 1965-1995.** Ed. by Gregory G. Brunk. LC 96-52498. (Bibliographies & Indexes in Law & Political Science Ser.: Vol. 27). 272p. 1997. text ed. 79.50 (*0-313-30259-6*, Greenwood Pr) Greenwood.

***Theories of Population from Raleigh to Arthur Young: 1931 Edition.** James Bonar. 252p. 1996. reprint ed. write for info. (*1-85506-156-2*) Bks Intl VA.

Theories of Populations in Biological Communities. F. B. Christiansen & T. M. Fenchel. LC 76-49871. (Ecological Studies: Vol. 20). 1977. 39.00 (*3-540-08010-4*) Spr-Verlag.

***Theories of Preaching.** Lischer. pap. 26.75 (*0-8010-2025-5*) Baker Bks.

Theories of Preaching: Selected Readings in the Homiletical Tradition. Ed. by Richard Lischer. LC 87-3504. 384p. 1987. 30.00 (*0-939464-46-2*, Labyrinth); pap. 15.95 (*0-939464-45-4*, Labyrinth) Baker Bks.

Theories of Primitive Religion. Edward E. Evans-Pritchard. 140p. 1968. pap. 18.95 (*0-19-823131-8*) OUP.

Theories of Primitive Religion. Edward E. Evans-Pritchard. LC 85-22003. (Sir D. Owens Evan Lectures, 1962). 138p. 1985. reprint ed. text ed. 49.75 (*0-313-24978-4*, EPTP, Greenwood Pr) Greenwood.

***Theories of Programming Languages.** John C. Reynolds. 400p. (C). 1997. write for info. (*0-521-59414-6*) Cambridge U Pr.

***Theories of Psychotherapy: Origins & Evolution.** Ed. by Paul L. Wachtel & Stanley B. Messer. LC 97-20793. 304p. (Orig.). 1997. pap. 29.95 (*1-55798-435-2*, 431-6920) Am Psychol.

Theories of Psychotherapy & Counseling: Concepts & Cases. Richard S. Sharf. 1996. teacher ed. write for info. (*0-534-33970-0*) Brooks-Cole.

Theories of Psychotherapy & Counseling: Concepts & Cases. Richard S. Sharf. LC 95-23582. 720p. 1996. text ed. 62.95 (*0-534-21618-8*) Brooks-Cole.

Theories of Public Organization. 2nd ed. Robert B. Denhardt. 260p. (C). 1980. pap. text ed. 23.00 (*0-534-20070-2*) HarBrace.

Theories of Punishment. Ed. by Stanley E. Grupp. LC 73-165047. (Illus.). 407p. reprint ed. 116.00 (*0-8357-9247-1*, 2012998) Bks Demand.

Theories of Race & Ethnic Relations. Ed. by John Rex & David S. Mason. (Comparative Ethnic & Race Relations Ser.). (Illus.). 350p. 1988. pap. text ed. 20.95 (*0-521-36939-8*) Cambridge U Pr.

Theories of Rape: Recent Inquiries into the Causes of Sexual Aggression. Ed. by Lee Ellis. 175p. 1989. 47.95 (*0-89116-172-4*) Hemisp Pub.

Theories of Reading in Dialogue: An Interdisciplinary Study. Thomas W. McCormick. LC 88-20821. 410p. (Orig.). (C). 1988. pap. text ed. 33.00 (*0-8191-7169-7*); lib. bdg. 62.00 (*0-8191-7168-9*) U Pr of Amer.

Theories of Reading, Looking, & Listening. Ed. by Harry R. Garvin. LC 80-20475. (Bucknell Review Ser.: Vol. 26, No. 1). 192p. 1981. 22.00 (*0-8387-5007-9*) Bucknell U Pr.

Theories of Research. Maria Nowakowska. (Systems Inquiry Ser.). 580p. (Orig.). 1984. pap. text ed. 30.50 (*0-914105-20-5*) Intersystems Pubns.

Theories of Rhetoric in the 18th-Century Scottish Sermon. Ann Matheson. LC 93-42728. 308p. 1994. text ed. 99.95 (*0-7734-9413-8*) E Mellen.

Theories of Rights. Jeremy Waldron. LC 84-9648. (Oxford Readings in Philosophy Ser.). 216p. 1984. pap. 16.95 (*0-19-875063-3*) OUP.

Theories of Science. Struan Jacobs. (C). 1995. pap. 20.00 (*0-7300-1239-5*, Pub. by Deakin Univ AT) St Mut.

Theories of Science in Society. Ed. by Susan E. Cozzens & Thomas F. Gieryn. LC 89-45476. (Illus.). 272p. 1990. 27.50 (*0-253-31471-2*) Ind U Pr.

***Theories of Science in Society.** Ed. by Susan E. Cozzens & Thomas F. Gieryn. LC 89-45476. (Science, Technology, & Society Ser.). (Illus.). 264p. pap. 75.30 (*0-608-05013-X*, 2059674) Bks Demand.

Theories of Scientific Method: The Renaissance Through the Nineteenth Century, Vol. 2. R. M. Blake et al. (Classics in the History & Philosophy of Science Ser.: Vol. 2). 364, viiip. 1960. pap. text ed. 62.00 (*2-88124-351-7*) Gordon & Breach.

***Theories of Secession.** Percy B. Lehning. LC 97-24742. 1998. write for info. (*0-415-17192-X*) Routledge.

Theories of Social Change. Richard P. Appelbaum. LC 81-80801. (C). 1996. pap. 15.16 (*0-395-30558-6*) HM.

Theories of Social Change: A Critical Appraisal. Raymond Boudon. Tr. by J. C. Whitehouse. 1986. 50.00 (*0-520-05759-7*) U CA Pr.

Theories of Society. Ed. by Talcott Parsons. LC 61-9171. 1965. 60.00 (*0-02-924450-1*, Free Press) Free Pr.

Theories of Stress & Performance: A Short Overview. Bengt Bergstrom. 55p. (Orig.). (C). 1992. pap. text ed. 20.00 (*1-56806-046-7*) DIANE Pub.

Theories of Surplus & Transfer: Parasites & Producers in Economic Thought. Helen Boss. 300p. 1989. 55.00 (*0-04-330371-4*) Routledge Chapman & Hall.

Theories of Surplus & Transfer: Parasites & Producers in Economic Thought. Helen Boss. LC 89-9122. 300p. (C). 1989. pap. 29.95 (*0-04-330372-2*) Routledge Chapman & Hall.

Theories of Surplus Value, 3 vols. Karl Marx. 508p. 1970. Set. 135.00 (*0-8464-0920-8*) Beekman Pubs.

Theories of Technical Change & Investment: Riches & Rationality. Chidem Kurdas. LC 94-5973. 1994. text ed. 69.95 (*0-312-12181-4*) St Martin.

Theories of the Arts in China. Ed. by Susan Bush & Christian F. Murck. LC 83-42551. (Illus.). 474p. reprint ed. pap. 135.10 (*0-8357-4203-2*, 2036982) Bks Demand.

Theories of the Capitalist Economy. Ben Fine. LC 81-20187. 142p. 1982. pap. 16.50 (*0-8419-0786-2*) Holmes & Meier.

Theories of the Chakras. Hiroshi Motoyama. LC 81-51165. 350p. (Orig.). 1982. pap. 12.00 (*0-8356-0551-5*, Quest) Theos Pub Hse.

Theories of the Earth & Universe: A History of Dogma in the Earth Sciences. S. Warren Carey. LC 87-6433. (Illus.). 432p. 1988. 59.50 (*0-8047-1364-2*) Stanford U Pr.

Theories of the Evolution of Knowing, Vol. 4. Ed. by Gary Greenberg & Ethel Tobach. (T. C. Schneirla Conference Ser.: Vol. 4). 176p. 1990. text ed. 65.00 (*0-8058-0755-1*) L Erlbaum Assocs.

Theories of the Information Society. Frank Webster. LC 94-49029. (International Library of Sociology). 264p. (C). 1995. pap. 18.95 (*0-415-10574-9*) Routledge.

Theories of the Information Society. Frank Webster. LC 94-49029. (International Library of Sociology). 264p. (C). (gr. 13). 1995. text ed. 62.95 (*0-415-10573-0*) Routledge.

Theories of the Labor Movement. Ed. by Simeon Larson & Bruce Nissen. LC 86-32414. 408p. (C). 1987. text ed. 49.95 (*0-8143-1815-0*); pap. text ed. 19.95 (*0-8143-1816-9*) Wayne St U Pr.

Theories of the Middle Range. Herbert Poole. LC 84-28402. (Libraries & Information Science). 176p. 1985. text ed. 73.25 (*0-89391-257-3*) Ablex Pub.

Theories of the Mixed Economy, 10 vols. Ed. by David Reisman. 1995. 895.00 (*1-85196-213-1*, Pub. by Pickering & Chatto UK) Ashgate Pub Co.

Theories of the Self. Jerome D. Levin. LC 92-12864. 1992. 29.95 (*1-56032-260-8*); pap. 29.95 (*1-56032-261-6*) Hemisp Pub.

Theories of the Sign in Classical Antiquity. Giovanni Manetti. Tr. by Christine Richardson. LC 92-28924. (Advances in Semiotics Ser.). 220p. (ENG & ITA.). 1993. 35.00 (*0-253-33684-8*) Ind U Pr.

Theories of the State. Andrew Vincent. 224p. (Orig.). (C). 1987. pap. text ed. 26.95 (*0-631-14729-2*) Blackwell Pubs.

Theories of the State: The Politics of Liberal Democracy. Patrick Dunleavy & Brendan O'Leary. 368p. (C). 1989. reprint ed. pap. text ed. 19.95 (*0-941533-85-9*) New Amsterdam Bks.

Theories of the Symbol. Tzvetan Todorov. Tr. by Catherine Porter. LC 81-17420. (Illus.). 302p. 1984. 42.50 (*0-8014-1192-0*); pap. 15.95 (*0-8014-9288-2*) Cornell U Pr.

Theories of the Text. D. C. Greetham. 340p. 1997. 60.00 (*0-19-811993-3*) OUP.

Theories of the Theatre: A Historical & Critical Survey from the Greeks to the Present. Marvin Carlson. 560p. 1993. pap. 19.95 (*0-8014-8154-6*) Cornell U Pr.

Theories of the Trade Cycle. Alec L. Macfie. LC 78-119544. (Reprints of Economic Classics Ser.). ix, 198p. 1971. reprint ed. lib. bdg. 35.00 (*0-678-00699-7*) Kelley.

Theories of the Unconscious & Theories of the Self. Ed. by Raphael Stern. LC 85-26815. 296p. reprint ed. pap. 84.40 (*0-7837-4500-1*, 2044277) Bks Demand.

Theories of the Universe: From Babylonian Myth to Modern Science. Ed. by Milton K. Munitz. LC 57-6746. 438p. 1965. pap. 17.95 (*0-02-922270-2*, Free Press) Free Pr.

Theories of the World from Antiquity to the Copernican Revolution. Michael J. Crowe. 1990. pap. 6.95 (*0-486-26173-5*) Dover.

Theories of Theories of Mind. Ed. by Peter Carruthers & Peter K. Smith. (Illus.). 406p. (C). 1996. text ed. 59.95 (*0-521-55110-2*); pap. text ed. 19.95 (*0-521-55916-2*) Cambridge U Pr.

Theories of Translation: An Anthology of Essays from Dryden to Derrida. Ed. by John Biguenet & Rainer Schulte. 260p. 1992. pap. text ed. 13.95 (*0-226-04871-3*); lib. bdg. 32.00 (*0-226-04870-5*) U Ch Pr.

Theories of Truth. Ed. by Paul Horwich. (International Research Library of Philosophy). 532p. 1994. 129.95 (*1-85521-511-X*, Pub. by Dartmth Pub UK) Ashgate Pub Co.

Theories of Truth: A Critical Introduction. Richard L. Kirkham. (Illus.). 416p. 1995. pap. 17.50 (*0-262-61108-2*, Bradford Bks) MIT Pr.

Theories of Tyranny. Roger Boesche. LC 94-42591. 544p. 1995. 19.95 (*0-271-01458-X*) Pa St U Pr.

Theories of Tyranny. Roger Boesche. LC 94-42591. 544p. 1996. 55.00 (*0-271-01457-1*) Pa St U Pr.

Theories of Urban Politics. David Judge et al. 304p. 1995. text ed. 69.95 (*0-8039-8864-8*); pap. text ed. 25.95 (*0-8039-8865-6*) Sage.

Theories of Value & Distribution since Adam Smith. Maurice H. Dobb. LC 72-88619. (Illus.). 264p. 1973. 64.95 (*0-521-20100-4*) Cambridge U Pr.

Theories of Value & Distribution since Adam Smith. Maurice H. Dobb. LC 72-88619. (Illus.). 264p. 1975. pap. text ed. 24.95 (*0-521-09936-6*) Cambridge U Pr.

Theories of Vision from Al-kindi to Kepler. David G. Lindberg. LC 75-19504. 336p. 1981. reprint ed. pap. text ed. 16.95 (*0-226-48235-9*) U Ch Pr.

Theories of Visual Perception. Ian E. Gordon. 273p. 1991. pap. text ed. 60.00 (*0-471-92196-3*) Wiley.

***Theories of Visual Perception.** 2nd ed. Ian E. Gordon. LC 96-3081. 1997. pap. write for info. (*0-471-96825-0*); text ed. 65.95 (*0-471-96933-8*) Wiley.

Theories of Welfare Economics. U. Hla Myint. LC 65-16990. (Reprints of Economic Classics Ser.). (Illus.). xiii, 240p. 1965. reprint ed. 35.00 (*0-678-00069-7*) Kelley.

Theories of Women's Studies. Ed. by Gloria Bowles & Renate Duelli-Klein. 270p. (Orig.). 1983. pap. 13.95 (*0-415-04289-5*) Routledge.

Theories of Women's Studies. Gloria Bowles. (Orig.). 1983. pap. 15.95 (*0-7100-9488-4*) Routledge Chapman & Hall.

Theories on Distributed Feedback Lasers. F. K. Kneubuhl. LC 92-41425. (Laser Science & Technology Ser.: Vol. 4). 1993. pap. text ed. 50.00 (*3-7186-5350-8*) Gordon & Breach.

Theories on Drug Abuse: Selected Contemporary Perspectives. LC 67-11961. 1986. lib. bdg. 79.95 (*0-8490-3515-5*) Gordon Pr.

Theories, Practices & Training Systems of a Sufi School. Canon W. H. T. Gairdner. (Sufi Research Ser.). 1980. pap. 7.00 (*0-86304-003-9*, Pub. by Octagon Pr UK) ISHK.

Theorike & Practike of Moderne Warres. Robert Barret. LC 74-26523. (English Experience Ser.: No. 155). (Illus.). 247p. 1969. reprint ed. 65.00 (*90-221-0155-X*) Walter J Johnson.

***Theorising in International Relations: Contemporary Theorists & Their Critics.** Stephen Chan & Jarrod Wiener. LC 97-25258. 1997. write for info. (*0-7734-8640-2*) E Mellen.

***Theorising Textual Subjects: Agency & Oppression.** 233p. 1997. text ed. 54.95 (*0-521-57185-5*); pap. text ed. 17.95 (*0-521-57679-2*) Cambridge U Pr.

Theorising the Fantastic. Armitt. LC 96-21671. 1996. text ed. 59.95 (*0-340-67726-0*, Pub. by E Arnld UK) St Martin.

***Theorising Video Practice.** Wayne. 1997. pap. 18.50 (*0-85315-827-4*) NYU Pr.

Theorist Notebook - Calculus. 6th ed. Swokowski & Michael Olinick. (Mathematics Ser.). 1994. pap. 9.95 (*0-534-93636-9*) PWS Pubs.

Theorist Notebook - Precalculus. 7th ed. Earl W. Swokowski. (Mathematics Ser.). 1994. pap. 30.95 (*0-534-93712-8*) PWS Pubs.

Theorist, Student Edition. Prescience Corp. Staff. LC 93-6707. 1993. 26.95 (*0-534-20340-X*) PWS Pubs.

Theorists of Economic Growth from David Hume to the Present: With a Perspective on the Next Century. Walt W. Rostow. (Illus.). 768p. 1992. pap. 29.95 (*0-19-508043-2*) OUP.

***Theoritical Production Ecology Reflections & Prospects.** R. Rabbinge. 302p. 1992. pap. 163.00 (*81-7089-183-3*, Pub. by Intl Bks & Periodicals II) St Mut.

Theorizing a New Agenda for Architecture: An Anthology of Architectural Theory 1965-1995. Ed. by Kate Nesbitt. (Illus.). 608p. 1996. 50.00 (*1-56898-053-1*); pap. 34.95 (*1-56898-054-X*) Princeton Arch.

Theorizing American Literature: Hegel, the Sign, & History. Ed. by Bainard Cowan & Joseph G. Kronick. LC 90-49723. 320p. 1991. text ed. 38.50 (*0-8071-1628-9*) La State U Pr.

Theorizing Black Feminisms: The Visionary Pragmatism of Black Women. Ed. by Stanlie M. James & Abena P. Busia. LC 92-47346. 288p. (C). (gr. 13). 1993. pap. 17.95 (*0-415-07337-5*) Routledge.

Theorizing Black Feminisms: The Visionary Pragmatism of Black Women. Ed. by Stanlie M. James & Abena P. Busia. LC 92-47346. 288p. (C). (gr. 13). 1993. text ed. 59.95 (*0-415-07336-7*) Routledge.

Theorizing Citizenship. Ed. by Ronald S. Beiner. LC 94-10401. (SUNY Series in Political Theory: Contemporary Issues). 335p. (C). 1994. pap. text ed. 19.95 (*0-7914-2336-0*) State U NY Pr.

Theorizing Citizenship. Ed. by Ronald S. Beiner. LC 94-10401. (SUNY Series in Political Theory: Contemporary Issues). 335p. (C). 1995. text ed. 59.50 (*0-7914-2335-2*) State U NY Pr.

Theorizing Communication: A History. Dan Schiller. 296p. 1996. 39.95 (*0-19-510199-5*) OUP.

Theorizing Culture: An Interdisciplinary Critique after Postmodernism. Ed. by Barbara Adam & Stuart Allan. (Illus.). 288p. (C). 1995. 55.00 (*0-8147-0643-6*); pap. 19.50 (*0-8147-0644-4*) NYU Pr.

Theorizing Documentary. Ed. by Michael Renov. (AFI Film Readers Ser.). 256p. (C). 1993. pap. 17.95 (*0-415-90382-3*, A5181, Routledge NY) Routledge.

Theorizing Feminism: Parallel Trends in the Humanities & Social Sciences. Ed. by Anne G. Herrman & Abigail J. Stewart. LC 94-8994. (C). 1994. pap. text ed. 24.50 (*0-8133-8706-X*) Westview.

Theorizing Heterosexuality: Telling It Straight. Ed. by Diane Richardson. LC 96-12682. 204p. 1996. 85.00 (*0-335-19504-0*, Open Univ Pr); pap. 23.95 (*0-335-19503-2*, Open Univ Pr) Taylor & Francis.

Theorizing Masculinities. Ed. by Harry Brod & Michael Kaufman. LC 94-7490. (Research on Men & Masculinities Ser.: Vol. 5). 1994. 54.00 (*0-8039-4903-0*); pap. 24.95 (*0-8039-4904-9*) Sage.

Theorizing Modernism. Ed. by Steve Giles. LC 93-3001. (Nottingham Studies in Critical Theory). 224p. (C). (gr. 13). 1993. text ed. 79.95 (*0-415-07754-0*, B2283) Routledge.

Theorizing Modernism: Visual Art & the Critical Tradition. Johanna Drucker. LC 93-23718. (Illus.). 224p. 1994. 40.00 (*0-231-08082-4*) Col U Pr.

Theorizing Modernism: Visual Art & the Critical Tradition. Johanna Drucker. (Illus.). 224p. 1996. pap. 16.00 (*0-231-08083-2*) Col U Pr.

Theorizing Museums: Representing Identity & Diversity in a Changing World. Ed. by Sharon Macdonald & Gordon Fyfe. LC 96-6174. (Sociological Review Monograph: No. 43). 1996. pap. 20.95 (*0-631-20151-3*) Blackwell Pubs.

Theorizing Patriarchy. Sylvia Walby. (Illus.). 256p. 1990. pap. text ed. 25.95 (*0-631-14769-1*) Blackwell Pubs.

***Theorizing Revolutions: New Approaches from Across the Disciplines.** LC 96-40838. 296p. (C). 1997. pap. write for info. (*0-415-13568-0*); text ed. write for info. (*0-415-13567-2*) Routledge.

***Theorizing Social Life.** Alan Sica. Date not set. 22.95 (*0-465-08431-1*); pap. write for info. (*0-465-08432-X*) Basic.

Theorizing Social Movements. Joe Foweraker. (Pluto Latin American Studies). (C). 47.50 (*0-7453-0713-2*, Pub. by Pluto Pr UK); pap. 15.95 (*0-7453-0714-0*, Pub. by Pluto Pr UK) LPC InBook.

Theorizing the Fantastic. Lucie Armitt. LC 96-21671. (Interrogating Texts Ser.). 1996. text ed. 17.95 (*0-340-60587-1*, Pub. by E Arnld UK) St Martin.

Theorizing the Long Poem: The Contemporary Canadian Poet at the Edge of Genre. Smaro Kamboureli. (Theory - Culture Ser.). 256p. 1991. 45.00 (*0-8020-5908-2*); pap. 18.95 (*0-8020-6848-0*) U of Toronto Pr.

Theorizing the Moving Image. Noel Carroll. (Studies in Film). 480p. (C). 1996. text ed. 69.95 (*0-521-46049-2*) Cambridge U Pr.

Theorizing the Moving Image. Noel Carroll. (Studies in Film). 480p. (C). 1996. pap. text ed. 24.95 (*0-521-46607-5*) Cambridge U Pr.

Theory see Queueing Systems

T

Theory see Flame Emission & Atomic Absorption Spectrometry

Theory - Pedagogy - Politics: Texts for Change. Ed. by Donald Morton & Mas'ud Zavarzadeh. 264p. 1991. text ed. 29.95 (0-252-01761-7); pap. text ed. 12.50 (0-252-06157-8) U of Ill Pr.

Theory, Analysis & Meaning in Music. Ed. by Anthony Pople. (Illus.). 250p. (C). 1994. text ed. 54.95 (0-521-45236-8) Cambridge U Pr.

Theory & Aesthetic Evaluation of Literature. Mary F. Slattery. LC 88-43272. 128p. 1990. 28.50 (0-945636-08-3) Susquehanna U Pr.

Theory & an Econometric Model for Common Stock Purchase Warrants. Sheen T. Kassouf. LC 65-11090. 1967. 10.00 (0-9606348-1-9) Analytic Invest.

Theory & Analysis of Drama. Manfred Pfister. Tr. by John Halliday. (European Studies in English Literature). (Illus.). 360p. (C). 1991. pap. 19.95 (0-521-42383-X) Cambridge U Pr.

Theory & Analysis of Nonlinear Frames Structures. Yeong-Bin Yang. (Illus.). 450p. 1994. text ed. 79.00 (0-13-109224-3) P-H.

Theory & Application see Pharmaceutical Chemistry: Theory & Application

Theory & Application in Fish Feeding Ecology. Ed. by Deanna J. Stouder et al. (Illus.). 400p. (C). 1994. text ed. 45.00 (1-57003-013-8) U of SC Pr.

Theory & Application of Antenna Arrays. M. T. Ma. LC 73-15615. 429p. pap. 122.30 (0-317-09841-1, 2022491) Bks Demand.

Theory & Application of Apparel Construction Techniques: A Practical Guide to Traditional Sewing in an Industry Setting. Sharon B. Underwood & Cynthia L. Istook. 288p. (C). 1996. pap. 40.00 (1-888452-00-5) Ascot Publns.

Theory & Application of Apparel Construction Techniques: Full Size Patterns for Term Project. Sharon B. Underwood & Cynthia L. Istook. 150p. (C). 1996. lab manual ed., pap. text ed. 10.00 (1-888452-04-8) Ascot Publns.

Theory & Application of Apparel Construction Techniques: Half-Scale Patterns for Sample Construction. Sharon B. Underwood & Cynthia L. Istook. 150p. (C). 1996. lab manual ed., pap. text ed. 10.00 (1-888452-03-X) Ascot Publns.

Theory & Application of Cellular Automata. S. Wolfram. (Advanced Series on Complex Systems: Vol. 1). 560p. 1986. text ed. 108.00 (9971-5-0123-6); pap. text ed. 32.00 (9971-5-0124-4) World Scientific Pub.

Theory & Application of Differential Games: Proceedings of the NATO Advanced Study Institute, University of Warwick, Coventry England, August 27 - September 6, 1974. NATO Advanced Study Institute Staff. Ed. by J. D. Grote. LC 74-34041. (NATO Advanced Study Institutes Ser.: No. C13). 310p. 1975. lib. bdg. 104.50 (90-277-0581-X) Kluwer Ac.

Theory & Application of Image Analysis: Selected Papers from the 7th Scandinavian Conference on Image Analysis. Ed. by P. Johansen & S. Olsen. Vol. 2. 1992. write for info. (0-318-69312-7) World Scientific Pub.

Theory & Application of Infinite Series. Konrad Knopp. 1990. pap. 12.95 (0-486-66165-2) Dover.

Theory & Application of Kalman Filtering. Gary Minkler & Jing Minkler. (Illus.). 608p. (C). 1990. 72.00 (0-9621618-2-9) Magellan Bk.

Theory & Application of Laser Chemical Vapor Deposition. Jyoti Mazumder & Aravinda Kar. (Lasers, Photonics, & Electro-Optics Ser.). 400p. 1995. 89.50 (0-306-44936-6) Plenum.

Theory & Application of Morphological Analysis: Fine Particles & Surfaces. David W. Luerkens. Ed. by John K. Beddow. (Fine Particle Science & Technology Ser.). 336p. 1991. 118.00 (0-8493-6777-8, TA418) CRC Pr.

Theory & Application of Motor Learning. Mary E. Rudisill & Andrew S. Jackson. (Illus.). 175p. (C). 1992. write for info. (0-9634528-0-0) MacJR.

Theory & Application of Random Fields: Proceedings, Bangalore, India, 1982. Ed. by Gopinath Kallianpur. (Lecture Notes in Control & Information Sciences Ser.: Vol. 49). 290p. 1983. 29.95 (0-387-12232-X) Spr-Verlag.

Theory & Application of Statistical Energy Analysis. 2nd ed. Richard H. Lyon & Richard G. DeJong. 400p. 1994. 105.00 (0-7506-9111-5) Buttrwrth-Heinemann.

Theory & Application of the Interest Rate. Eli Schwartz. LC 92-28481. 192p. 1993. text ed. 59.95 (0-275-93630-9, C3630, Praeger Pubs) Greenwood.

Theory & Application of the Linear Model. Franklin A. Graybill. 704p. (C). 1976. text ed. 82.95 (0-87872-108-8) Wadsworth Pub.

Theory & Application of Tracers. David S. Schimel. LC 93-7462. (Isotopic Techniques in Plant, Soil, & Aquatic Biology Ser.). (Illus.). 119p. 1993. text ed. 29.95 (0-12-624650-5) Acad Pr.

***Theory & Applications of Additive Cellular Automata.** P. Pal Chaudhuri. LC 96-45234. 1997. write for info. (0-8186-7717-1) IEEE Standards.

Theory & Applications of Boundary Element Methods. Ed. by Qinghua Du & Masataka Tanaka. 495p. 1990. 139.95 (0-387-50703-5) Spr-Verlag.

Theory & Applications of Convolution Integral Equations. H. M. Srivastava & R. G. Buschman. LC 92-22560. 272p. (C). 1992. lib. bdg. 129.50 (0-7923-1891-9) Kluwer Ac.

Theory & Applications of Coupled Map Lattices. K. Kaneko. LC 92-24346. (Nonlinear Science: Theory & Applications Ser.). 192p. 1993. text ed. 119.00 (0-471-93741-X) Wiley.

Theory & Applications of Differentiable Functions of Several Variables. Ed. by S. M. Nikol'skii. LC 68-1677. (Proceedings of the Steklov Institute of Mathematics Ser.: Vol. 156). 284p. 1974. pap. 115.00 (0-8218-3017-1, STEKLO/117) Am Math.

Theory & Applications of Differentiable Functions of Several Variables. S. M. Nikol'skii. LC 68-1677. 293p. 1990. pap. 154.00 (0-8218-3131-3, STEKLO/181) Am Math.

Theory & Applications of Differentiable Functions of Several Variables. Ed. by S. M. Nikol'skii. LC 84-24501. (Proceedings of the Steklov Institute of Mathematics Ser.: Vol. 161). 253p. 1985. reprint ed. pap. text ed. 80.00 (0-8218-3083-X, STEKLO/161) Am Math.

Theory & Applications of Differentiable Functions of Several Variables: Proceedings. Ed. by S. M. Nikol'skii. (Proceedings of the Steklov Institute of Mathematics Ser.: No. 77). 212p. 1968. pap. 62.00 (0-8218-1877-5, STEKLO/77) Am Math.

Theory & Applications of Differentiable Functions of Several Variables, II: Proceedings. Ed. by S. M. Nikol'skii. (Proceedings of the Steklov Institute of Mathematics Ser.: No. 89). 290p. 1968. pap. 92.00 (0-8218-1889-9, STEKLO/89) Am Math.

Theory & Applications of Differentiable Functions of Several Variables, III: Proceedings. Ed. by S. M. Nikol'skii. LC 72-681. (Proceedings of the Steklov Institute of Mathematics Ser.: No. 105). 295p. 1971. pap. 62.00 (0-8218-9900-7, STEKLO/105) Am Math.

Theory & Applications of Differentiable Functions of Several Variables, V: Proceedings. Ed. by S. M. Nikol'skii. (Proceedings of the Steklov Institute of Mathematics Ser.: No. 131). 252p. 1975. pap. 82.00 (0-8218-3031-7, STEKLO/131) Am Math.

Theory & Applications of Differentiable Functions of Several Variables, VII. Ed. by S. M. Nikol'skii. LC 68-1677. (Proceedings of the Steklov Institute of Mathematics Ser.: Vol. 150). 336p. 1982. reprint ed. pap. 137.00 (0-8218-3047-3, STEKLO/150C) Am Math.

Theory & Applications of Differentiable Functions of Several Variables X. LC 87-11416. (Proceedings of the Steklov Institute of Mathematics Ser.: Vol. 170). 311p. 1987. pap. text ed. 147.00 (0-8218-3101-1, STEKLO/170) Am Math.

Theory & Applications of Differentiable Functions of Several Variables XI. LC 88-1272. (Proceedings of the Steklov Institute of Mathematics Ser.: Vol. 173). 290p. 1988. pap. text ed. 140.00 (0-8218-3117-8, STEKLO/173) Am Math.

Theory & Applications of Differentiable Functions of Several Variables, 6. Ed. by S. M. Nikol'skii. (Proceedings of the Steklov Institute of Mathematics Ser.: No. 140). 312p. 1979. pap. 113.00 (0-8218-3039-2, STEKLO/140) Am Math.

Theory & Applications of Differential Functions of Several Variable. LC 68-1677. (Proceedings of the Steklov Institute of Mathematics Ser.: Vol. 187). 261p. 1990. pap. 127.00 (0-8218-3135-6, STEKLO/187) Am Math.

Theory & Applications of Distance Geometry. 2nd ed. Leonard M. Blumenthal. LC 79-113117. 1970. text ed. 24.95 (0-8284-0242-6) Chelsea Pub.

Theory & Applications of Drilling Fluid Hydraulics. EXLOG Staff. LC 84-25172. (EXLOG Series of Petroleum Geology & Engineering Handbks.). (Illus.). 203p. 1985. text ed. 27.00 (0-88746-045-3) Intl Human Res.

Theory & Applications of Fourier Analysis. Ed. by C. Rees et al. (Pure & Applied Mathematics Ser.: Vol. 59). 423p. 1981. 160.00 (0-8247-6903-1) Dekker.

Theory & Applications of Holomorphic Functions on Algebraic Varieties over Arbitrary Ground Fields. Oscar Zariski. LC 52-42839. (Memoirs Ser.: No. 1/5). 90p. 1990. reprint ed. pap. 18.00 (0-8218-1205-X, MEMO/1/5) Am Math.

Theory & Applications of Image Analysis: Selected Papers from 7th Scandinavian Conference on Image Analysis. P. Johansen & S. Olsen. (World Scientific Series on Machine Perception & Artificial I). 360p. 1992. text ed. 109.00 (981-02-0945-2) World Scientific Pub.

Theory & Applications of Image Analysis II: Selected Papers from the 9th Scandinavian Conference on Image Analysis. Ed. by G. Borgefors. 400p. 1995. text ed. 72.00 (981-02-2448-6, REe-BR2920) World Scientific Pub.

Theory & Applications of Iteration Methods. Ferenc Szidarovsky & Ioannis K. Argyros. LC 93-7173. (Systems Engineering Ser.). 368p. 1993. 88.95 (0-8493-8014-6, QA297) CRC Pr.

Theory & Applications of Liquid Crystals. Ed. by David S. Kinderlehrer & J. L. Ericksen. (IMA Ser.: Vol. 5). (Illus.). 375p. 1987. 67.95 (0-387-96546-7) Spr-Verlag.

Theory & Applications of Nonlinear Operators of Accretive & Monotone Type. Ed. by Athanassios G. Kartsatos. (Lecture Notes in Pure & Applied Mathematics Ser.: Vol. 178). 336p. 1996. pap. 145.00 (0-8247-9721-3) Dekker.

Theory & Applications of Numerical Analysis. 2nd ed. G. M. Phillips & P. J. Taylor. (Illus.). 464p. 1996. boxed 39.95 (0-12-553560-0) Acad Pr.

Theory & Applications of Optical Remote Sensing. Asrar. LC 88-35182. (Remote Sensing & Image Processing Ser.). 734p. 1989. text ed. 178.00 (0-471-62895-6) Wiley.

***Theory & Applications of Partial Differential Equations.** P. Bassanini & A. R. Elcrat. (Mathematical Concepts & Methods in Science & Engineering Ser.: Vol. 45). 450p. (C). 1997. write for info. (0-306-45640-0, Plenum Pr) Plenum.

Theory & Applications of Partial Functional Differential Equations. J. Wu. LC 96-14763. (Applied Mathematical Sciences Ser.: Vol. 119). (Illus.). 448p. 1996. 59.95 (0-387-94771-X) Spr-Verlag.

Theory & Applications of Problem Solving. B. Zhang & L. Zhang. LC 92-13873. (Studies in Computer Science & Artificial Intelligence: Vol. 9). 234p. 1992. 128.00 (0-444-89565-5, North Holland) Elsevier.

Theory & Applications of Reaction Diffusion Equations: Patterns & Waves. 2nd ed. Peter Grindrod. (Oxford Applied Mathematics & Computing Science Ser.). (Illus.). 288p. 1996. 55.00 (0-19-850004-1) OUP.

Theory & Applications of Sequential Nonparametrics. Pranab K. Sen. LC 84-52332. (CBMS-NSF Regional Conference Series in Applied Mathematics: No. 49). vi, 100p. 1985. pap. text ed. 23.50 (0-89871-051-0) Soc Indus-Appl Math.

Theory & Applications of Some New Classes of Integral Equations. A. G. Ramm. 344p. 1980. pap. 31.50 (0-685-04732-6) Spr-Verlag.

***Theory & Applications of Spread Spectrum Systems.** Alex W. Lam & Sawasd Tantaratana. Ed. by Roman Zaputowycz & Svetislav Maric. 300p. 1994. student ed. 259.00 (0-7803-0374-1, HL4671) Inst Electrical.

Theory & Applications of Statistical Inference Functions. D. L. McLeish & C. S. Small. (Lecture Notes in Statistics Ser.: Vol. 44). (Illus.). vi, 124p. 1988. 52.95 (0-387-96720-6) Spr-Verlag.

Theory & Applications of Statistical Wave-Period Processing, 3 vols., Vol. 3. Albert A. Gerlach. 1434p. (C). Set. text ed. 923.00 (0-677-02510-6) Gordon & Breach.

***Theory & Applications of the Cluster Variation & Path Probability Methods: Proceedings of an International Workshop Held in Juan Teotihuacou, Mexico, June 19-23, 1995.** Ed. by J. L. Moran-Lopez & J. M. Sanchez. LC 96-35752. 427p. 1996. 129.50 (0-306-45461-0, Plenum Pr) Plenum.

Theory & Applications of the Poincare Group. Y. S. Kim & Marilyn E. Noz. 1986. lib. bdg. 165.50 (90-277-2141-6) Kluwer Ac.

Theory & Applications of Volterra Operators in Hilbert Space. I. C. Gohberg & M. G. Krein. Tr. by A. Feinstein. LC 71-120134. (Translations of Mathematical Monographs: Vol. 24). 430p. 1970. 87.00 (0-8218-1574-1, MMONO/24) Am Math.

Theory & Assessment of Stressful Life Events. Ed. by Thomas W. Miller. (Stress & Health Ser.: Monograph 6). 224p. 1996. 55.00 (0-8236-6521-6) Intl Univs Pr.

***Theory & Calculation of P-T-X: Multicomponent Phase Diagrams.** Muyu Zhao. (C). 1996. lib. bdg. 69.00 (1-56072-388-2) Nova Sci Pubs.

***Theory & Computer Simulation of Aggregation Phenomena in Complex Systems.** R. Mahnke. 1997. 70.00 (3-527-29354-X) Wiley.

Theory & Concepts in Qualitative Research: Perspectives from the Field. Ed. by David J. Flinders & Geoffery Mills. 264p. (C). 1993. text ed. 40.00 (0-8077-3290-7); pap. text ed. 18.95 (0-8077-3289-3) Tchrs Coll.

Theory & Control of Dynamical Systems: Applications to Systems in Biology, Huddinge, Stockholm, 4-10 August, 1991. Ed. by Stig I. Andersson et al. LC 92-10268. 340p. 1992. text ed. 93.00 (981-02-0895-2) World Scientific Pub.

Theory & Craft of American Law. Soia Mentschikoff & Irwin R. Stotzky. LC 80-70678. 1981. write for info. (0-8205-0211-1, 382) Bender.

Theory & Craft of the Scenographic Model. rev. ed. Darwin R. Payne. LC 84-5630. (Illus.). 192p. 1985. 29.95 (0-8093-1193-3); pap. 19.95 (0-8093-1194-1) S Ill U Pr.

Theory & Decision: Essays in Honor of Werner Leinfellner. Ed. by Gerald L. Eberlein & Hal Berghel. (C). 1987. lib. bdg. 143.00 (90-277-2519-5) Kluwer Ac.

Theory & Description in Generative Syntax: A Case Study in West Flemish. Liliane Haegeman. (Studies in Linguistics: Supplementary Volumes). (Illus.). 304p. (C). 1992. 69.95 (0-521-37005-1) Cambridge U Pr.

Theory & Design for Mechanical Measurements. Richard J. Figliola & Donald E. Beasley. 330p. 1991. teacher ed. 22.50 (0-471-53514-1) Wiley.

Theory & Design for Mechanical Measurements. 2nd ed. Richard J. Figliola & Donald E. Beasley. 624p. 1994. text ed. 72.95 (0-471-00089-2) Wiley.

Theory & Design in the First Machine Age. Reyner Banham. (Illus.). 340p. 1980. pap. 17.00 (0-7506-0718-1) MIT Pr.

Theory & Design in the First Machine Age. Reyner Banham. 340p. 1980. pap. 17.00 (0-262-52058-3) MIT Pr.

Theory & Design in the Second Machine Age. Martin Pawley. (Illus.). 1990. 38.95 (0-631-15828-6) Blackwell Pubs.

Theory & Design of Adaptive Filters. John R. Treichler et al. LC 87-6062. (Topics in Digital Signal Processing Ser.). 342p. 1987. text ed. 108.00 (0-471-83220-0) Wiley.

***Theory & Design of Air Cushion Craft.** Yun Liang & Alan Biaut. text ed. 110.00 (0-470-23621-3) Wiley.

Theory & Design of Bridges. Petros P. Xanthakos. LC 92-21520. 1443p. 1993. text ed. 175.00 (0-471-57097-4) Wiley.

Theory & Design of Broadband Matching Networks. Chen Wai-Kai. 360p. 1976. 211.00 (0-08-019702-7, Pub. by Pergamon Repr UK) Franklin.

Theory & Design of Charged Particle Beams. Martin Reiser. (Beam Physics & Accelerator Technology Ser.). 607p. 1994. text ed. 84.95 (0-471-30616-9) Wiley.

Theory & Design of Concrete Shells. B. K. Chatterjee. (C). 1988. 44.00 (81-204-0316-9, Pub. by Oxford IBH II) S Asia.

Theory & Design of Digital Computer Systems. 2nd ed. Douglas Lewin & David Noaks. LC 92-30621. 512p. (gr. 13). 1992. pap. text ed. 42.95 (0-412-42880-6) Chapman & Hall.

Theory & Design of Linear Active Networks. Sundaram Natarajan. 464p. 1987. write for info. (0-317-53615-X) Macmillan.

***Theory & Design of Loudspeaker Enclosures.** rev. ed. J. Ernest Benson. (Illus.). 256p. (C). 1996. reprint ed. pap. 19.95 (0-7906-1093-0) Prompt Publns.

Theory & Design of Plate Shell Structures. Maan H. Jawad. LC 93-48727. 423p. (gr. 13). 1994. text ed. 73.95 (0-412-98181-5) Chapman & Hall.

Theory & Design of Pressure Vessels. 2nd ed. John F. Harvey. (gr. 13). 1991. text ed. 79.95 (0-412-98651-5) Chapman & Hall.

Theory & Design of Surface Structures Slabs & Plates. Gustav Florin. (Structural Engineering Ser.: Vol. 2). (Illus.). 222p. (C). 1980. pap. 10.00 (0-87849-035-3, Pub. by Trans T Pub SZ) Enfield Pubs NH.

Theory & Design of the New Rational Combustion Engine. Ronald W. Satz. (Illus.). 459p. (C). 1978. pap. text ed. 85.00 (1-880845-01-6) Transpower.

Theory & Design of Wood & Fiber Composite Materials. Ed. by Benjamin A. Jayne. LC 72-1998. (Wood Science Ser.: No. 3). (Illus.). 464p. (C). 1972. text ed. 42.50 (0-8156-5031-0) Syracuse U Pr.

Theory & Detection of Magnetic Monopoles in Gauge Theories: A Collected Set of Lecture Notes. Ed. by Q. Sahfi et al. 512p. 1986. pap. text ed. 60.00 (9971-966-95-6) World Scientific Pub.

Theory & Detection of Magnetic Monopoles in Gauge Theories: A Collected Set of Lecture Notes. Ed. by Q. Shafi et al. 512p. 1986. text ed. 121.00 (9971-966-94-8) World Scientific Pub.

Theory & Empirical Analysis of Production. Ed. by Murray Brown. (Studies in Income & Wealth: No. 31). 525p. 1967. reprint ed. 136.50 (0-87014-486-3) Natl Bur Econ Res.

Theory & Estimation of Macroeconomic Rationing Models. H. R. Sneessens. (Lecture Notes in Economics & Mathematical Systems Ser.: Vol. 191). (Illus.). 138p. 1981. 15.95 (0-387-10837-8) Spr-Verlag.

Theory & Evaluation of Formation Pressures. EXLOG Staff. 231p. 1988. text ed. 36.00 (0-685-26606-0) P-H.

Theory & Evaluation of Formation Pressures: A Pressure Detection Reference Handbook. EXLOG Staff. Ed. by Alun Whittaker. LC 85-2287. (EXLOG Series of Petroleum Geology & Engineering Handbks.). (Illus.). 231p. 1985. text ed. 34.95 (0-88746-052-6) Intl Human Res.

Theory & Evidence. Clark N. Glymour. LC 79-3209. (Illus.). 396p. reprint ed. pap. 112.90 (0-8357-3568-0, 2052294) Bks Demand.

Theory & Evidence: The Development of Scientific Reasoning. Barbara Koslowski. (Learning, Development, & Conceptual Change Ser.). (Illus.). 360p. 1996. 40.00 (0-262-11209-4, Bradford Bks) MIT Pr.

Theory & Experiment: Recent Insights & New Perspectives on Their Relation. Ed. by Diderik Batens & Jean P. Van Dendegem. 296p. (C). 1988. lib. bdg. 116.50 (90-277-2645-0, D Reidel) Kluwer Ac.

Theory & Experiment in Gravitational Physics. rev. ed. Clifford M. Will. LC 92-29555. (Illus.). 380p. (C). 1993. pap. text ed. 44.95 (0-521-43973-6) Cambridge U Pr.

Theory & Experiment in Gravitational Physics. Clifford M. Will. LC 80-39642. 352p. reprint ed. pap. 100.40 (0-318-34674-5, 2031743) Bks Demand.

Theory & Experiment in Psychical Research. William G. Roll. LC 75-7398. (Perspectives in Psychical Research Ser.). (Illus.). 1975. 42.95 (0-405-07047-0) Ayer.

***Theory & Experimentation, Vol. 1.** Papadakis. 1993. 95.00 (0-312-08935-X) St Martin.

Theory & Experimentation: Architecture Ideas, No. 100. Academy Editions Staff. (Architectural Design Ser.). 1993. pap. 24.95 (1-85490-138-9) Academy Ed UK.

Theory & Experiments in Basic Electric Circuits. Sidney N. Sonsky. (Illus.). 244p. 1978. student ed. 19.95 (0-89529-050-2) Avery Pub.

Theory & Formal Methods: Proceedings of the First Imperial College Department of Computing Workshop on Theory & Formal Methods, Isle of Thorns Conference Centre, Chelwood Gate, Sussex, UK, March 1993. Ed. by Geoffrey Burn et al. LC 93-25444. (Workshops in Computing Ser.). 1993. 77.95 (0-387-19842-3) Spr-Verlag.

Theory & Formal Methods of Computing 94: Proceedings of the Second Imperial College Workshop. Ed. by C. Hankin et al. 450p. 1995. 61.00 (1-86094-003-X) World Scientific Pub.

Theory & Harmony for Everyone. L. Dean Bye. 1993. 7.95 (0-87166-882-3, 93790) Mel Bay.

***Theory & Harmony for the Contemporary Musician.** Arnie Berle. (Illus.). 112p. (Orig.). pap. 14.95 (0-8256-1499-6, AM931360, Amsco Music) Omnibus NY.

Theory & History of Bibliography. Georg Schneider. 1977. lib. bdg. 69.95 (0-8490-2741-1) Gordon Pr.

Theory & History of Folklore. Vladimir Propp. Ed. by Anatoly Liberman. Tr. by Ariadna Y. Martin & Richard P. Martin. LC 83-14840. (Theory & History of Literature Ser.: Vol. 5). (Illus.). 288p. (RUS.). 1984. pap. text ed. 17.95 (0-8166-1182-3) U of Minn Pr.

Theory & History of Ocean Boundary-Making. Douglas M. Johnston. 464p. 1988. 55.00 (0-7735-0624-1, Pub. by McGill CN) U of Toronto Pr.

Theory & Ideology in Indian Sociology: Essays in Honour of Professor Yogendra Singh. Ed. by Narendra K. Singhi. (C). 1996. 64.00 (0-614-13259-2, Pub. by Rawat II) S Asia.

An Asterisk (*) at the beginning of an entry indicates that the title is appearing in BIP for the first time.

Theory & Management of Tropical Multispecies Stock: A Review, with Emphasis on the Southeast Asian Demersal Fisheries. Daniel Pauly. (ICLARM Studies & Reviews: No. 1). (Illus.). 35p. 1983. pap. text ed. 6.50 (*0-89955-398-2*, Pub. by ICLARM PH) Intl Spec Bk.

Theory & Measurement. Henry E. Kyburg, Jr. LC 82-17905. (Studies in Philosophy). (Illus.). 280p. 1984. text ed. 75.00 (*0-521-24878-7*) Cambridge U Pr.

Theory & Measurement: Causality Issues in Milton Friedman's Monetary Economics. J. Daniel Hammond. (Historical Perspectives on Modern Economics Ser.). (Illus.). 240p. (C). 1996. text ed. 44.95 (*0-521-55205-2*) Cambridge U Pr.

Theory & Measurement for Economic Policy, 3 vols. Herbert G. Grubel. (Economists of the Twentieth Century Ser.). 1024p. 1993. Set. 215.00 (*1-85278-787-2*) E Elgar.

Theory & Measurement of Business Income. Edgar O. Edwards & Philip W. Bell. LC 95-30870. (New Works in Accounting History). 360p. 1995. text ed. 65.00 (*0-8153-2245-3*) Garland.

Theory & Measurement of Social Interest. James E. Crandall. LC 81-9973. 224p. 1981. text ed. 48.00 (*0-231-05256-1*) Col U Pr.

Theory & Measurement of Work Commitment. Paula C. Morrow. Ed. by Samuel B. Bacharach. LC 93-920. (Monographs in Organizational Behavior & Industrial Relations). 202p. 1993. 73.25 (*1-55938-523-5*) Jai Pr.

Theory & Method in Biblical & Cuneiform Law. B. M. Levinson. (Journal for the Study of the Old Testament Supplement Ser.: Vol. 181). 200p. 41.00 (*1-85075-498-5*, Pub. by Sheffield Acad UK) CUP Services.

Theory & Method in Religious Studies: Contemporary Approaches to the Study of Religion. Ed. by Frank Whaling. (C). 1995. pap. text ed. 24.95 (*3-11-014254-6*) Mouton.

Theory & Methodology of Training. 3rd ed. Bompa. 400p. (C). 1995. per. 32.49 (*0-8403-9061-0*) Kendall-Hunt.

Theory & Methods in Criminal Justice History see Crime & Justice in American History

Theory & Methods in Political Science. David Marsh & Gerry Stoker. LC 95-14920. 1995. text ed. 49.95 (*0-312-12761-8*); text ed. 19.95 (*0-312-12762-6*) St Martin.

Theory & Methods of Economic Evaluation of Health Care. Magnus Johannesson. (Developments in Health Economics & Public Policy Ser.: Vol. 4). 260p. (C). 1996. lib. bdg. 114.95 (*0-7923-4037-X*) Kluwer Ac.

Theory & Methods of Social Research. 2nd ed. Johan Galtung. LC 67-26343. (Illus.). 534p. (C). 1967. text ed. 65.00 (*0-231-03088-6*) Col U Pr.

Theory & Musicianship: Lessons with Worksheets & Supplements, Bk. 2, Pt. 2. Edith McIntosh. 62p. 1957. pap. 6.50 (*0-8258-0160-5*, 04012) Fischer Inc NY.

Theory & Numerical Modeling of Turbulent Gas-Particle Flows & Combustion. Zhou Lixinga. LC 92-38051. 200p. 1993. 73.00 (*0-8493-7721-8*, Q) CRC Pr.

Theory & Nursing Vol. 4: A Systematic Approach. 4th ed. Chinn. 256p. (C). (gr. 13). 1994. pap. text ed. 38.00 (*0-8016-7947-8*) Mosby Yr Bk.

Theory & Operation of Spectral Analysis Using ROBFIT. R. L. Coldwell & G. J. Bamford. 300p. 1991. 80.00 (*0-88318-929-1*); pap. 35.00 (*0-88318-941-0*) Am Inst Physics.

Theory & Philosophy of Art: Style, Artist, & Society, No. IV. Meyer Schapiro. LC 94-6626. (Selected Papers of Meyer Schapiro). (Illus.). 256p. 1994. 27.50 (*0-8076-1356-8*) Braziller.

Theory & Philosophy of Organisations: Critical Issues & New Perspectives. Ed. by John Hassard & Denis Pym. 244p. (C). 1994. pap. text ed. 22.95 (*0-415-06313-2*, B0198) Routledge.

Theory & Policy. Marquis. Date not set. teacher ed. write for info. (*0-314-06924-0*) West Pub.

Theory & Policy in Political Economy: Essays in Pricing, Distribution & Growth. Ed. by Philip Arestis & Yiannis Kitromilides. (New Directions in Modern Economics Ser.). (Illus.). 328p. 1990. text ed. 80.00 (*1-85278-205-6*) E Elgar.

Theory & Politics: Studies in the Development of Critical Theory. Hulmet Dubiel. Tr. by Benjamin Gregg from GER. (German Social Thought Ser.). (Illus.). 188p. 1985. 27.50 (*0-262-04080-8*) MIT Pr.

Theory & Practical Application of Adjuvants. Ed. by Duncan E. Stewart-Tull. LC 94-26748. 250p. 1995. text ed. 84.95 (*0-471-95170-6*) Wiley.

Theory & Practice. Rosa Luxemburg. Tr. by David Wolff from GER. (Illus.). 67p. (Orig.). 1980. pap. 2.00 (*0-914441-22-1*) News & Letters.

Theory & Practice. Nathan Rotenstreich. (Van Leer Jerusalem Foundation Ser.). 248p. 1977. pap. text ed. 82.50 (*90-247-2004-4*, Pub. by M Nijhoff NE) Kluwer Ac.

Theory & Practice. Jurgen Habermas. Tr. by John Viertel from GER. LC 72-6227. 310p. 1973. reprint ed. pap. 17.00 (*0-8070-1527-X*, BPA 21) Beacon Pr.

Theory & Practice: Essays Presented to Gene Weltfish. Ed. by Stanley Diamond. (Studies in Anthropology). 1979. text ed. 67.70 (*90-279-7958-8*) Mouton.

Theory & Practice: NOMOS XXXVII. Ed. by Ian Shapiro & Judith W. Decew. 487p. (C). 1995. 50.00 (*0-8147-8003-2*) NYU Pr.

Theory & Practice: NOMOS XXXVII. Ed. by Ian Shapiro & Judith W. Decew. 487p. (C). 1996. pap. 20.00 (*0-8147-8055-5*) NYU Pr.

Theory & Practice Estranged. Detine L. Bowers. Ed. by Graham Hodges. (Studies in African American History & Culture). 250p. 1996. text ed. 50.00 (*0-8153-2002-7*) Garland.

Theory & Practice in Adult Education: The Epistemological Debate. Ed. by Barry Bright. 288p. 1989. 49.95 (*0-415-02446-3*, A3534); pap. 18.50 (*0-415-03909-6*, A3538) Routledge.

Theory & Practice in Archaeology. Ian Hodder. 304p. (C). 1995. pap. 22.95 (*0-415-12777-7*, C0600) Routledge.

Theory & Practice in Behavior Therapy. Aubrey J. Yates. LC 74-30018. (Wiley-Interscience Publications). 261p. reprint ed. pap. 74.40 (*0-317-26094-4*, 2025176) Bks Demand.

Theory & Practice in British & Hungarian Geography: Proceedings of the 4th British-Hungarian Geographical Seminar, Nyiregyhaza, August 18-19, 1987. P. A. Compton & Marton Pecsi. (Studies in Geography in Hungary: No. 24). 351p. (C). 1989. 108.00 (*963-05-5589-1*, Pub. by Akad Kiado HU) St Mut.

Theory & Practice in Clinical Social Work. Brandell. 1997. 35.00 (*0-02-874116-1*) Free Pr.

Theory & Practice in Clinical Social Work. Brandell. LC 96-41714. 1997. 49.95 (*0-684-82765-4*) Free Pr.

Theory & Practice in Distributed Systems: International Workshop, Dagstuhl Castle, Germany, September 5-9, 1994: Selected Papers. Andre Schiper. LC 95-21873. (Lecture Notes in Computer Science Ser.: Vol. 938). x, 263p. 1995. pap. 49.00 (*3-540-60042-6*) Spr-Verlag.

Theory & Practice in Finite Element Structural Analysis: Proceedings of the 1973 Tokyo Seminar on Finite Element Analysis. Tokyo Seminar on Finite Element Analysis Staff. Ed. by Yoshiaki Yamada & Richard H. Gallagher. LC 75-306570. 753p. 1973. reprint ed. pap. 180.00 (*0-608-01566-0*, 2061983) Bks Demand.

Theory & Practice in Foreign Policy Making: National Perspectives on Academics & Professionals in International Relations. Ed. by Wolf-Dieter Eberwein et al. LC 94-15092. 1994. 55.00 (*1-85567-185-9*) St Martin.

Theory & Practice in Health & Social Welfare. Neil Thompson. 1995. write for info. (*0-335-19178-9*, Open Univ Pr); pap. write for info. (*0-335-19177-0*, Open Univ Pr) Taylor & Francis.

Theory & Practice in Listening. Dunkel. (College ESL Ser.). 1996. pap. 19.95 (*0-8384-5930-7*) Heinle & Heinle.

Theory & Practice in Medieval Persian Government. Ann K. Lambton. (Collected Studies: No. CS122). 332p. (C). 1980. reprint ed. lib. bdg. 89.95 (*0-86078-067-8*, Pub. by Variorum UK) Ashgate Pub Co.

Theory & Practice in Renaissance Textual Criticism: Beatus Rhenanus Between Conjecture & History. John F. D'Amico. 1988. 58.00 (*0-520-06199-3*) U CA Pr.

***Theory & Practice in Social Group Work: Creative Connections.** Ed. by Marie Weil et al. 282p. 1991. 39.95 (*1-56024-096-2*) Haworth Pr.

Theory & Practice in Social Services: SOC 120 Course Study Guide. California College for Health Sciences Staff. 172p. (C). 1992. ring bd. write for info. (*0-933195-20-6*) CA College Health Sci.

Theory & Practice in the History of European Expansion Overseas: Essays in Honour of R. E. Robinson. Ed. by A. Porter & R. Holland. (Illus.). 214p. 1988. text ed. 35.00 (*0-7146-3346-1*, Pub. by F Cass Pubs UK) Intl Spec Bk.

***Theory & Practice in the Organic Laboratory: With Microscale & Standard Scale Experiments.** 4th ed. John A. Landgrebe. teacher ed. write for info. (*0-534-16855-8*) Brooks-Cole.

Theory & Practice in the Organic Laboratory: With Microscale & Standard Scale Experiments. 4th ed. John A. Landgrebe. LC 92-32949. 573p. 1993. text ed. 64.95 (*0-534-16854-X*) Brooks-Cole.

Theory & Practice in the Teaching of Writing: Rethinking the Discipline. Ed. by Lee Odell. LC 92-40547. 352p. (C). 1993. 39.95 (*0-8093-1755-9*); pap. 19.95 (*0-8093-1947-0*) S Ill U Pr.

Theory & Practice in Voluntary Social Action. Chris L. Clark. (Avebury Studies of Care in the Community). 194p. 1991. text ed. 55.95 (*1-85628-113-2*, Pub. by Avebury Pub UK) Ashgate Pub Co.

Theory & Practice of Agricultural Policy. Teresa M. Curran. (EDI Policy Seminar Report Ser.: No. 23). 48p. 1990. 6.95 (*0-8213-1569-2*, 11569) World Bank.

Theory & Practice of American Literary Naturalism: Selected Essays & Reviews. Donald Pizer. LC 92-23398. 272p. (C). 1993. 34.95 (*0-8093-1847-4*) S Ill U Pr.

Theory & Practice of Autonomy. Gerald Dworkin. (Cambridge Studies in Philosophy). 176p. 1988. pap. text ed. 19.95 (*0-521-35767-5*) Cambridge U Pr.

Theory & Practice of Bank Book-Keeping & Joint Stock Accounts: Exemplified & Elucidated in a Complete Set of Bank Account Books. Christopher C. Marsh. Ed. by Richard P. Brief. LC 77-87278. (Development of Contemporary Accounting Thought Ser.). 1978. reprint ed. lib. bdg. 30.95 (*0-405-10906-7*) Ayer.

Theory & Practice of Bank-Owned Life Insurance. Warren T. Wamberg. (Illus.). 160p. 1995. 40.00 (*0-9647664-0-X*) T W O Pubng.

Theory & Practice of Brief Therapy. Simon H. Budman & Alan S. Gurman. LC 87-24847. 402p. 1988. lib. bdg. 44.95 (*0-89862-716-8*) Guilford Pr.

Theory & Practice of Central Banking, 1797-1913. Edward V. Morgan. 252p. 1965. 35.00 (*0-7146-1237-5*, Pub. by F Cass Pubs UK) Intl Spec Bk.

Theory & Practice of Challenge Education. Smith et al. 304p. 1992. pap. text ed. 30.00 (*0-8403-8042-9*) Kendall-Hunt.

***Theory & Practice of Classic Detective Fiction.** Ed. by Jerome H. Delamater & Ruth Prigozy. LC 97-1691. (Contributions to the Study of Popular Culture: Vol. 62). 1997. text ed. write for info. (*0-313-30462-9*, Greenwood Pr) Greenwood.

Theory & Practice of Community Social Work. Ed. by Samuel H. Taylor & Robert W. Roberts. 464p. 1985. text ed. 39.50 (*0-231-05368-1*) Col U Pr.

Theory & Practice of Constitutional Change in America: A Collection of Original Source Materials. Ed. by John R. Vile. LC 93-2514. (American University Studies: Vol. 42). 492p. 1993. write for info. (*0-8204-2193-6*) P Lang Pubng.

Theory & Practice of Construction Export Marketing. Low S. Pheng. 368p. 1996. 72.95 (*1-85972-304-7*, Pub. by Avebury Pub UK) Ashgate Pub Co.

Theory & Practice of Counseling & Psychotherapy. 4th ed. Ed. by Gerald Corey. LC 90-33124. (Counseling Ser.). 512p. (C). 1991. student ed., pap. 13.50 (*0-534-13316-9*); text ed. 43.25 (*0-534-13314-2*) Brooks-Cole.

Theory & Practice of Counseling & Psychotherapy. 5th ed. Gerald Corey. LC 95-15145. (Psychology-Counseling Ser.). 526p. 1996. text ed. 55.95 (*0-534-33856-9*) Brooks-Cole.

Theory & Practice of Counseling & Psychotherapy: HP 611. California College for Health Sciences Staff. 22p. (C). 1991. spiral bd. write for info. (*0-933195-35-4*) CA College Health Sci.

***Theory & Practice of Counsling & Psychot.** 6th ed. Corey. (Counseling Ser.). Date not set. pap. 53.95 (*0-534-34823-8*) Brooks-Cole.

***Theory & Practice of Cylinder Head Modification.** (Illus.). 174p. 19.95 (*0-85113-066-6*, Pub. by MRP Speedsport UK) Motorbooks Intl.

Theory & Practice of Dance: An Introduction for Students. Rickett Young. 1990. pap. 24.00 (*0-7463-0644-X*, Pub. by Northcote UK) St Mut.

Theory & Practice of Dental Health Education. Christina B. DeBiase. LC 90-13344. (Illus.). 314p. 1991. text ed. 36.00 (*0-8121-1366-7*) Williams & Wilkins.

Theory & Practice of Direct Methods in Crystallography. Ed. by M. F. Ladd & R. A. Palmer. LC 79-10566. (Illus.). 436p. 1980. 95.00 (*0-306-40223-8*, Plenum Pr) Plenum.

Theory & Practice of Distance Education. 2nd ed. Borje Holmberg. LC 94-20729. (Studies in Distance Education). 264p. (C). (gr. 13). 1995. text ed. 69.95 (*0-415-11292-3*, C0399, Routledge NY) Routledge.

Theory & Practice of Early Reading, Vol. 1. Ed. by Lauren B. Resnick & Phyllis A. Weaver. LC 79-22322. 416p. 1980. text ed. 79.95 (*0-89859-003-5*) L Erlbaum Assocs.

Theory & Practice of Early Reading, Vol. 2. Lauren B. Resnick & Phyllis A. Weaver. LC 79-23784. 368p. 1980. text ed. 79.95 (*0-89859-010-8*) L Erlbaum Assocs.

Theory & Practice of Early Reading, Vol. 3. Ed. by Lauren B. Resnick & Phyllis A. Weaver. 400p. 1980. text ed. 79.95 (*0-89859-011-6*) L Erlbaum Assocs.

Theory & Practice of Earth Reinforcement: Proceedings of the International Geotechnical Symposium on Theory & Practice of Earth Reinforcement, Fukuoka Kyushu, October 5-7, 1988. Ed. by N. Miura et al. (Illus.). xiv, 618p. 1988. text ed. 155.00 (*90-6191-820-0*, Pub. by A A Balkema NE) Ashgate Pub Co.

Theory & Practice of Econometrics. 2nd ed. George G. Judge et al. LC 84-7254. (Probability & Mathematical Statistics Ser.). 1019p. 1985. Net. text ed. 66.00 (*0-471-89530-X*) Wiley.

Theory & Practice of Eel Culture. Isao Matsui. Tr. by Alamelu Gopal from JPN. 141p. 1983. text ed. 60.00 (*90-6191-036-6*, Pub. by A A Balkema NE) Ashgate Pub Co.

Theory & Practice of Environmental Quality Analysis. Eric Hyman et al. (CPL Bibliographies Ser.: 27). 103p. 10.00 (*0-86602-027-6*, Sage Prdcls Pr) Sage.

Theory & Practice of Environmental Quality Analysis: Water Resources Management, Land Suitability Analysis, Economics & Aesthetics, No. 27. Eric Hyman et al. 103p. 1980. 15.00 (*0-317-00024-1*, Sage Prdcls Pr) Sage.

Theory & Practice of Error Control Codes. Richard E. Blahut. LC 82-11441. (Illus.). 512p. (C). 1983. text ed. 66.95 (*0-201-10102-5*) Addison-Wesley.

Theory & Practice of Ethical Decision Making in Social Work. Ann Conrad & Mary Joseph. 352p. (C). 1995. pap. write for info. (*0-02-324295-7*, Macmillan Coll) P-H.

Theory & Practice of Evaluation. Michael Scriven. 400p. 1987. pap. 12.50 (*0-918528-13-5*) Edgepress.

Theory & Practice of Events Research: Studies in Inter-Nation Actions & Interactions. Edward E. Azar & Joseph Ben-Dak. xvii, 304p. 1975. text ed. 241.00 (*0-677-15550-6*) Gordon & Breach.

Theory & Practice of Exchange in Germany. Frank C. Child. Ed. by Mira Wilkins. LC 78-3904. (International Finance Ser.). 1979. reprint ed. lib. bdg. 25.95 (*0-405-11209-2*) Ayer.

Theory & Practice of Feminist Literary Criticism. Ed. by Gabriela Mora & Karen S. Van Hooft. LC 81-67051. (Studies in Literary Analysis). 291p. (C). 1982. pap. 20.00 (*0-916950-22-0*); lib. bdg. 30.00 (*0-916950-23-9*) Biling Rev-Pr.

***Theory & Practice of Financial Stability.** Andrew Crockett. LC 97-5227. (Essays in International Finance Ser.). 1997. write for info. (*0-88165-110-9*) Princeton U Int Finan Econ.

Theory & Practice of Force Measurement. A. Bray et al. (Monographs in Physical Measurement). 380p. 1990. text ed. 135.00 (*0-12-128453-0*) Acad Pr.

Theory & Practice of Foundation Engineering. Louis J. Goodman & R. H. Karol. LC 68-12070. (Macmillan Series in Civil Engineering). (Illus.). 447p. reprint ed. pap. 127.40 (*0-317-10610-4*, 2010517) Bks Demand.

Theory & Practice of Futures Markets. Raymond M. Leuthold et al. LC 87-45248. 432p. 1989. 44.95 (*0-669-16260-4*) Free Pr.

Theory & Practice of Gamesmanship. Stephen Potter. 1993. reprint ed. lib. bdg. 18.95 (*1-56849-094-1*) Buccaneer Bks.

Theory & Practice of Geometric Modeling. Wolfgang Strasser. (Illus.). x, 547p. 1989. 122.95 (*0-387-51472-4*) Spr-Verlag.

Theory & Practice of Good Programming: ExaMaster Computerized 5.25 IBM Test Bank for Turbo Pascal. Gary W. Martin. (Illus.). 1995. write for info. (*0-15-592377-3*) OUP.

Theory & Practice of Good Programming: Turbo Pascal. Gary W. Martin. (Illus.). 416p. (C). 1992. teacher ed., pap. text ed. write for info. (*0-15-592376-5*) OUP.

***Theory & Practice of Grading Writing: Problems & Possibilities.** Ed. by Frances Zak & Christopher Weaver. 224p. (C). 1998. text ed. 59.50 (*0-7914-3669-1*) State U NY Pr.

***Theory & Practice of Grading Writing: Problems & Possibilities.** Ed. by Frances Zak & Christopher Weaver. 224p. (C). 1998. pap. text ed. 19.95 (*0-7914-3670-5*) State U NY Pr.

Theory & Practice of Group Counseling. 3rd ed. Gerald Corey. LC 89-7123. 590p. (C). 1989. text ed. 40.95 (*0-534-10284-0*) Brooks-Cole.

Theory & Practice of Group Counseling. 4th ed. Corey. (Counseling Ser.). 244p. 1995. student ed., pap. 17.95 (*0-534-24067-4*) Brooks-Cole.

Theory & Practice of Group Counseling. 4th ed. Gerald Corey. LC 94-1915. 506p. 1995. text ed. 49.95 (*0-534-24066-6*) Brooks-Cole.

Theory & Practice of Group Counseling. 4th ed. Gerald Corey. Incl. Student Manual for Theory & Practice of Counseling & Psychotherapy. LC 84-5026. 192p. 1984. pap. 8.50 (*0-685-08981-9*); 1995. Set teacher ed. write for info. (*0-534-24068-2*) Brooks-Cole.

***Theory & Practice of Group Counseling.** 5th ed. Corey. (Counseling Ser.). Date not set. pap. 14.95 (*0-534-34822-X*) Brooks-Cole.

***Theory & Practice of Group Counseling.** 5th ed. Corey. (Counseling Ser.). Date not set. pap. 39.95 (*0-534-34821-1*) Wadsworth Pub.

Theory & Practice of Group Psychotherapy. 4th ed. Irvin D. Yalom. LC 94-33555. 608p. 1995. 40.00 (*0-465-08448-6*) Basic.

Theory & Practice of Hell. Eugen Kogon. 1984. mass mkt. 6.99 (*0-425-07761-6*) Berkley Pub.

Theory & Practice of Histological Techniques. 3rd ed. Ed. by John D. Bancroft & Alan Stevens. (Illus.). 726p. 1990. text ed. 132.00 (*0-443-03559-8*) Churchill.

Theory & Practice of History. Leopold Von Ranke. Ed. by Georg G. Iggers & Konrad Von Moltke. Tr. by Wilma Iggers from GER. LC 79-167691. 500p. 1983. pap. text ed. 29.95 (*0-8290-1315-6*) Irvington.

Theory & Practice of Histotechnology. 2nd ed. Dezna C. Sheehan & Barbara B. Hrapchak. LC 87-17446. 493p. (C). 1987. text ed. 52.50 (*0-935470-39-5*) Battelle.

Theory & Practice of HIV Counselling: A Systemic Approach. Robert Bor et al. LC 92-48338. 208p. 1993. pap. text ed. 23.95 (*0-87630-717-9*) Brunner-Mazel.

Theory & Practice of Industrial Organizations. Peppall. (HU - Industrial Organization Ser.). Date not set. pap. 68.95 (*0-538-85948-2*) S-W Pub.

Theory & Practice of Industrial Pharmacy. 3rd ed. Ed. by Leon Lachman et al. LC 84-27806. (Illus.). 902p. 1986. text ed. 105.00 (*0-8121-0977-5*) Williams & Wilkins.

Theory & Practice of International Organization. 2nd ed. Samuel S. Chen. 133p. 1974. text ed. 29.75 (*0-8422-5139-1*); pap. text ed. 9.75 (*0-8422-0362-1*) Irvington.

Theory & Practice of International Trade Linkage Models. A. Italianer. 1986. lib. bdg. 146.00 (*90-247-3407-X*) Kluwer Ac.

Theory & Practice of Intra-Aortic Balloon Pump Therapy. Ed. by Gerald A. Maccioli. LC 96-14625. 206p. 1996. 39.95 (*0-683-05302-7*) Williams & Wilkins.

Theory & Practice of Investing. 5th ed. Goff. 1986. pap. 39.95 (*0-434-90663-8*) Buttrwrth-Heinemann.

Theory & Practice of Life-Style Assessment. 4th ed. Daniel Eckstein & Leroy G. Baruth. 296p. (C). 1996. per., pap. text ed. 26.19 (*0-7872-2369-7*) Kendall-Hunt.

Theory & Practice of Lubrication for Engineers. 2nd ed. Dudley D. Fuller. LC 83-27394. 682p. 1984. text ed. 150.00 (*0-471-04703-1*) Wiley.

Theory & Practice of Managed Competition in Health Care Finance: Lectures in Economics: Theory, Institutions, Policy, 9, 1988. Ed. by A. C. Enthoven. 162p. 1988. 108.25 (*0-444-70359-4*, North Holland) Elsevier.

Theory & Practice of Marriage at the Premier Institute of Marriage. Maureen K. Lambert. (Illus.). 80p. 1994. pap. 12.00 (*0-8059-3558-4*) Dorrance.

Theory & Practice of Meditation. 2nd ed. Himalayan Institute Staff. LC 86-9802. 150p. (Orig.). 1986. pap. 12.95 (*0-89389-075-8*) Himalayan Inst.

Theory & Practice of Midwifery. Smellie. 1974. text ed. 65.00 (*0-7020-0522-3*) HarBrace.

Theory & Practice of Missionary Identification 1860-1920. Jonathan Bonk. LC 88-32579. (Studies in History of Missions: Vol. 2). 384p. 1990. lib. bdg. 99.95 (*0-88946-071-X*) E Mellen.

Theory & Practice of Modem Design. John A. Bingham. LC 87-37262. 480p. 1988. text ed. 115.00 (*0-471-85108-6*) Wiley.

Theory & Practice of Modern Government. rev. ed. Herman Finer. LC 69-13895. (Illus.). xiv, 978p. 1971. reprint ed. text ed. 48.75 (*0-8371-1989-8*, FIMG, Greenwood Pr) Greenwood.

Theory & Practice of Multiparty Commercial Arbitration: With Special Reference to the UNCITRAL Framework. Isaak I. Dore. (C). 1990. lib. bdg. 114.50 (*1-85333-318-2*, Pub. by Graham & Trotman UK) Kluwer Ac.

T

Theory & Practice of Mysticism. Charles M. Addison. 1977. lib. bdg. 59.95 (*0-8490-2742-X*) Gordon Pr.

Theory & Practice of Observing Behavior. C. Fassnacht. (Behavioral Development Monographs). 1982. text ed. 108.00 (*0-12-249780-5*) Acad Pr.

Theory & Practice of Oncology: Historical Evolution & Present Principles. Ronald W. Raven. (History of Medicine Ser.). (Illus.). 366p. 1990. 95.00 (*1-85070-179-2*) Prthnon Pub.

Theory & Practice of Parallel Programming: International Workshop TPPP '94, Sendai, Japan, November 7-9, 1994. Proceedings. Ed. by Takatoshi Ito et al. (Lecture Notes in Computer Science Ser.: Vol. 907). viii, 485p. 1995. 75.00 (*3-540-59172-9*) Spr-Verlag.

Theory & Practice of Parallel Programming: Proceedings of the International Workshop TPPP '94, Sendai, Japan, November 7-9, 1994. Ed. by Takayasu Ito & Akinori Yonezawa. LC 95-10412. (Lecture Notes in Computer Science Ser.: Vol. 907). 1995. write for info. (*0-387-59172-9*) Spr-Verlag.

Theory & Practice of Parliamentary Procedure in India. S. H. Belavadi. (C). 1988. 135.00 (*0-685-36464-X*) St Mut.

Theory & Practice of Personnel Management. 7th ed. Maurice W. Cuming. 320p. 1993. pap. 45.95 (*0-7506-0713-0*) Buttrwrth-Heinemann.

Theory & Practice of Perspective. G. A. Storey. LC 74-174406. (Illus.). 284p. 1972. reprint ed. 18.95 (*0-405-09004-8*, Pub. by Blom Pubns UK) Ayer.

Theory & Practice of Piano Construction. William B. White. LC 74-78811. 160p. 1975. reprint ed. pap. 4.50 (*0-486-23139-9*) Dover.

Theory & Practice of Political Communication Research. Ed. by Mary E. Stuckey. LC 95-30117. (SUNY Series in Speech Communication). 236p. 1996. text ed. 59.50 (*0-7914-2899-0*); pap. text ed. 19.95 (*0-7914-2900-8*) State U NY Pr.

Theory & Practice of Poster Art. Duke Wellington. 1986. reprint ed. 5.00 (*0-911380-70-1*) ST Pubns.

Theory & Practice of Price Formation in the U. S. S. R. Bella Feygin. Ed. by Cynthia Corell. (Illus.). 118p. (Orig.). 1983. pap. text ed. 75.00 (*1-55831-008-8*) Delphic Associates.

***Theory & Practice of Program Development.** Derek Andrews. LC 97-19343. (Formal Approaches to Computing & Information Technology Ser.). 1997. pap. write for info. (*3-540-76162-4*) Spr-Verlag.

Theory & Practice of Propellers for Auxiliary Sailboats. John R. Stanton. LC 75-31778. (Illus.). 79p. reprint ed. pap. 25.00 (*0-8357-8346-4*, 2033967) Bks Demand.

***Theory & Practice of Psychiatric Care.** write for info. (*0-340-26564-7*, Pub. by E Arnold UK) Routledge Chapman & Hall.

Theory & Practice of Psychiatric Rehabilitation. Ed. by Fraser N. Watts & Douglas H. Bennett. 370p. 1984. text ed. 146.50 (*0-471-90147-4*) Wiley.

***Theory & Practice of Psychiatric Rehabilitation.** Ed. by Fraser N. Watts & Douglas H. Bennett. LC 83-1055. 418p. 1991. reprint ed. pap. 119.20 (*0-608-04004-5*, 2064741) Bks Demand.

Theory & Practice of Public Policy-Making in Canada: Metapolicymaking. Yvan Gagnon. LC 95-1882. (Canadian Studies: Vol. 9). (Illus.). 208p. 1995. text ed. 89.95 (*0-7734-8930-4*) E Mellen.

Theory & Practice of Pulse Plating. Jean-Claude Puippe & Frank Leaman. (Illus.). 250p. 1986. 57.00 (*0-936569-02-6*); pap. 47.00 (*0-936569-01-8*) Am Electro Surface.

Theory & Practice of Radiation Thermometry. William H. DeWitt. LC 88-14272. 1138p. 1988. text ed. 175.00 (*0-471-61018-6*) Wiley.

Theory & Practice of Real Estate Finance. Terrence M. Clauretie & James R. Webb. 726p. (C). 1993. text ed. 53.25 (*0-03-054062-3*) Dryden Pr.

Theory & Practice of Regional Geochemical Exploration. M. Foldvari-Vogi. 272p. (C). 1978. 80.00 (*963-05-1442-7*, Pub. by Akad Kiado HU) St Mut.

Theory & Practice of Rivers & New Poems. Jim Harrison. LC 88-63676. (Illus.). 88p. 1989. reprint ed. pap. 13.95 (*0-944439-10-1*) Clark City Pr.

Theory & Practice of Rivers & Other Poems. Jim Harrison. (Illus.). 64p. 1986. pap. 7.95 (*0-916947-06-8*) Winn Bks.

Theory & Practice of Rivers & Other Poems. deluxe limited ed. Jim Harrison. (Illus.). 64p. 1986. Signed Ltd. ed. write for info. (*0-916947-05-X*) Winn Bks.

Theory & Practice of Robots & Manipulators: Proceedings of RoManSy 10, the Tenth CISM-IFToMM Symposium. Ed. by A. Morecki et al. (International Centre for Mechanical Sciences Ser.: No.361). 427p. 1995. 110.95 (*3-211-82697-1*) Spr-Verlag.

Theory & Practice of Romance Etymology: Studies in Language, Culture & History. Yakov Malkiel. (Collected Studies: No. CS288). 348p. (C). 1989. lib. bdg. 98.95 (*0-86078-236-0*, Pub. by Variorum UK) Ashgate Pub Co.

Theory & Practice of Scintillation Counting. J. Birks & D. Fry. LC 63-19244. (International Series of Monographs in Electronics Instrumentation: Vol. 27). 1964. 303.00 (*0-08-010472-X*, Pub. by Pergamon Repr UK) Franklin.

Theory & Practice of Seamanship. 11th ed. Graham Danton. LC 96-14277. 560p. (C). 1996. pap. 35.00 (*0-415-15372-7*); text ed. 120.00 (*0-415-14200-8*) Routledge.

Theory & Practice of Self Psychology. Marjorie T. White & Marcella B. Weiner. LC 86-919. 240p. 1987. text ed. 32.95 (*0-87630-425-0*) Brunner-Mazel.

***Theory & Practice of Silvicultural.** Ram Parkash. 300p. 1991. pap. 88.00 (*81-7089-148-5*, Pub. by Intl Bks & Periodicals II) St Mut.

Theory & Practice of Silvicultural System. Ram Parkash. 256p. 1991. pap. 175.00 (*0-614-09778-9*, Pub. by Intl Bk Distr II) St Mut.

Theory & Practice of Silvicultural Systems. Ram Parkash. 256p. (C). 1983. text ed. 150.00 (*0-685-52006-4*, Pub. by Intl Bk Distr II) St Mut.

Theory & Practice of Silvicultural Systems. Ram Parkash. 256p. 1991. 195.00 (*81-7089-062-4*, Pub. by Intl Bk Distr II) St Mut.

Theory & Practice of Silvicultural Systems. Ram Parkash. 256p. (C). 1991. 260.00 (*0-685-61461-1*, Pub. by Intl Bk Distr II) St Mut.

Theory & Practice of Social Case Work. 2nd ed. Gordon Hamilton. LC 51-12493. 328p. 1951. text ed. 49.50 (*0-231-01862-2*) Col U Pr.

Theory & Practice of Social Planning. Alfred J. Kahn. LC 79-81406. 360p. 1969. 34.95 (*0-87154-430-X*) Russell Sage.

Theory & Practice of Sociocriticism. Edmond Cros. LC 87-21167. (Theory & History of Literature Ser.: Vol. 53). (Illus.). xviii, 275p. 1988. pap. text ed. 15.95 (*0-8166-1580-2*) U of Minn Pr.

***Theory & Practice of Static Headspace Gas Chromatography.** Bruno Kolb & Leslie S. Ettre. LC 96-27616. 1997. write for info. (*1-56081-696-1*, VCH) Wiley.

Theory & Practice of Tax Reform in Developing Countries. Ehtisham Ahmad & Nicholas Stern. (Illus.). 360p. (C). 1991. text ed. 80.00 (*0-521-26563-0*); pap. text ed. 29.95 (*0-521-39742-1*) Cambridge U Pr.

Theory & Practice of Teaching. David P. Page. LC 77-89216. (American Education: Its Men, Institutions, & Ideas. Series 1). 1970. reprint ed. 18.95 (*0-405-01455-4*) Ayer.

Theory & Practice of Text-Editing: Essays in Honour of James T. Boulton. Ed. by Ian Small & Marcus Walsh. 232p. (C). 1992. text ed. 59.95 (*0-521-40146-1*) Cambridge U Pr.

Theory & Practice of the Cine-Roman. W. F. Van Wert. LC 77-22912. 1978. lib. bdg. 29.95 (*0-405-10756-0*) Ayer.

Theory & Practice of the European Convention on Human Rights. 2nd ed. Pieter Van Dijk & F. Van Hoof. 1990. 100.00 (*90-6544-319-3*) Kluwer Law Tax Pubs.

Theory & Practice of the Photographic Art. W. Sparling. LC 72-9237. (Literature of Photography Ser.). 1973. reprint ed. 20.95 (*0-405-04942-0*) Ayer.

Theory & Practice of Therapeutic Touch. Jean Sayre-Adams & Stephen G. Wright. LC 95-7244. (Illus.). 1995. write for info. (*0-443-05227-1*) Churchill.

Theory & Practice of Thermally Stimulated Luminescence & Related Phenomena: Proceedings of the National Symposium Held in Ahmedabad, India, 8-10 February 1984. Ed. by A. K. Singhvi et al. (Illus.). 250p. 1986. pap. 62.00 (*0-08-032618-8*, Pub. by PPL UK) Elsevier.

Theory & Practice of Third World Solidarity. Darryl C. Thomas. LC 93-10900. 328p. 1995. text ed. 55.00 (*0-275-92843-8*, Praeger Pubs) Greenwood.

Theory & Practice of Vacuum Technology. Max Wutz et al. Tr. by Walter Stecklemacher from GER. xviii, 668p. 1989. 188.00 (*3-528-08908-3*, Pub. by Vieweg & Sohn GW) Informatica.

Theory & Practice of Virtue. Gilbert C. Meilaender, Jr. LC 83-40598. 208p. (C). 1984. pap. text ed. 13.00 (*0-268-01853-7*) U of Notre Dame Pr.

Theory & Practice of Water & Wastewater Treatment. Ronald L. Droste. LC 96-15477. 800p. 1996. text ed. 86.95 (*0-471-12444-3*) Wiley.

Theory & Practice of Wave Propagation & Diffraction in the U. S. S. R. Avgustin Tuzhilin. Ed. by Maureen Young. 157p. (Orig.). 1983. pap. text ed. 75.00 (*1-55831-053-3*) Delphic Associates.

Theory & Practice of Welcoming Converts to Judaism: Jewish Universalism. Lawrence J. Epstein. LC 92-10326. (Jewish Studies: Vol. 13). 176p. 1992. lib. bdg. 79.95 (*0-7734-9493-6*) E Mellen.

Theory & Practice Therapeutic Massage Curriculum Guide. Beck. (Cosmetology Ser.). 1982. 2.75 (*0-87350-372-4*) Van Nos Reinhold.

Theory & Principles of Tort see Foundations of Legal Liability: A Presentation of the Theory & Development of the Common Law

Theory & Problems of Industrial Psychology. Willard A. Kerr & Florence W. Dunbar. 411p. 1966. text ed. 10.00 (*0-317-11979-6*, William James) Psychometric.

Theory & Problems of Thermodynamics. Y. V. Rao. 1994. write for info. (*81-224-0659-9*, Pub. by Wiley Estrn II) Franklin.

Theory & Procedure of Scale Analysis with Applications in Political Research. Robert J. Mokken. (Methods & Models in the Social Sciences Ser.). 353p. 1971. text ed. 50.80 (*90-279-6882-9*) Mouton.

Theory & Processes of History. Frederick J. Teggart. 1976. pap. 14.00 (*0-520-03176-8*) U CA Pr.

***Theory & Progress in Social Science.** James B. Rule. (Illus.). 288p. (C). 1997. text ed. 54.95 (*0-521-57365-3*); pap. text ed. 17.95 (*0-521-57494-3*) Cambridge U Pr.

Theory & Reality: Federal Ideas in Australia, England & Europe. S. Rufus Davis. 240p. 1995. pap. 19.95 (*0-7022-2605-X*, Pub. by Univ Queensland Pr AT) Intl Spec Bk.

Theory & Reality in Foreign Policy Making: Nigeria after the Second Republic. Ibraham A. Gambari. LC 88-15884. 296p. (C). 1992. pap. 19.95 (*0-391-03743-9*) Humanities.

***Theory & Reality of Transition to a Market Economy.** Ed. by Shangquan Gao & Chi Fulin. 358p. 1995. 14.95 (*7-119-01816-7*, Pub. by Foreign Lang CH) China Bks.

Theory & Religious Understanding: A Critique of the Hermeneutics of Joachim Wach. Charles M. Wood. LC 75-26839. (American Academy of Religion. Dissertation Ser.: No. 12). 194p. reprint ed. pap. 55.30 (*0-7837-5473-6*, 2045238) Bks Demand.

Theory & Research in Behavioral Pediatrics, Vol. 1. Ed. by Hiram E. Fitzgerald et al. 308p. 1982. 65.00 (*0-306-40851-1*, Plenum Pr) Plenum.

Theory & Research in Behavioral Pediatrics, Vol. 2. Ed. by Hiram E. Fitzgerald et al. 266p. 1984. 75.00 (*0-306-41566-6*, Plenum Pr) Plenum.

Theory & Research in Behavioral Pediatrics, Vol. 3. Ed. by Hiram E. Fitzgerald et al. 226p. 1986. 75.00 (*0-306-42328-6*, Plenum Pr) Plenum.

Theory & Research in Behavioral Pediatrics, Vol. 4. Ed. by Hiram E. Fitzgerald et al. LC 82-646646. (Illus.). 282p. 1988. 75.00 (*0-306-42882-2*, Plenum Pr) Plenum.

Theory & Research in Behavioral Pediatrics, Vol. 5. Ed. by Hiram E. Fitzgerald et al. (Illus.). 246p. 1991. 75.00 (*0-306-43855-0*, Plenum Pr) Plenum.

Theory & Research in Conflict Management. Ed. by M. Afzalur Rahim. LC 90-31212. 256p. 1990. text ed. 55.00 (*0-275-93173-0*, C3173, Praeger Pubs) Greenwood.

Theory & Research in Mass Communication: Contexts & Consequences. David K. Perry. (LEA's Communication Ser.). 240p. 1996. pap. 19.95 (*0-8058-1924-X*); text ed. 39.95 (*0-8058-1923-1*) L Erlbaum Assocs.

Theory & Research in Small Group Communication: A Reader. Cragan & Wright. 1993. write for info. (*0-318-70336-X*) Burgess MN Intl.

Theory & Resistance in Education: A Pedagogy for the Opposition. Henry A. Giroux. LC 83-2698. 240p. 1983. text ed. 45.00 (*0-89789-031-0*, H031, Bergin & Garvey); pap. text ed. 19.95 (*0-89789-032-9*, G032, Bergin & Garvey) Greenwood.

Theory & Scholarship of Talcott Parsons to 1951: A Critical Theory. Bruce C. Wearne. (Illus.). 208p. (C). 1990. text ed. 54.95 (*0-521-37003-5*) Cambridge U Pr.

Theory & Science of Basketball. 2nd ed. John M. Cooper & Daryl Siedentop. LC 74-4376. (Health Education, Physical Education, & Recreation Ser.). (Illus.). 270p. reprint ed. pap. 78.40 (*0-685-23474-6*, 2056680) Bks Demand.

Theory & Strategy in Histochemistry: A Guide to the Selection & Understanding of Techniques. Ed. by H. Lyon. (Illus.). xviii, 591p. 1991. 107.00 (*0-387-19311-1*) Spr-Verlag.

Theory & System for Nonmonotonic Reasoning. James W. Goodwin. 175p. (C). 1990. pap. text ed. 180.00 (*0-273-08816-5*, Pub. by Pitman Pubng UK) St Mut.

Theory & Technique of Family Therapy. Charles P. Barnard & Ramon G. Corrales. (Illus.). 352p. 1981. pap. 32.95 (*0-398-06014-2*); text ed. 44.95 (*0-398-03859-7*) C C Thomas.

Theory & Technique of Latin-American Dancing. F. Borrows. (Ballroom Dance Ser.). 1986. lib. bdg. 250.00 (*0-8490-3389-6*) Gordon Pr.

Theory & Technique of Latin-American Dancing. F. Borrows. (Ballroom Dance Ser.). 1985. lib. bdg. 66.00 (*0-685-10688-8*) Revisionist Pr.

Theory & Technique of the Drown H. V. R. & Radio- Vision Instruments, Vol. 1. Ruth B. Drown. 152p. 1994. spiral bd. 31.00 (*0-7873-1235-5*) Hlth Research.

Theory & Technology of High Temperature Superconductors. Ed. by Yu I. Koptev. (Proceedings of the Lebedev Physics Institute Ser.: Vol. 210). 173p. 1993. lib. bdg. 125.00 (*1-56072-100-6*) Nova Sci Pubs.

Theory & Technology of Quenching: A Handbook. Ed. by B. Li i et al. (Illus.). 512p. 1992. 326.95 (*0-387-52040-6*) Spr-Verlag.

Theory & the Evasion of History. David Ferris. LC 92-22951. 320p. 1993. text ed. 45.00 (*0-8018-4504-1*) Johns Hopkins.

Theory & the Experimental Investigation of Social Structures. David Willer. xviii, 272p. 1987. text ed. 68.00 (*2-88124-156-5*) Gordon & Breach.

Theory & Therapy in Dynamic Psychiatry. Jules H. Masserman. LC 72-96926. 410p. 1986. 30.00 (*0-87668-067-8*) Aronson.

Theory & Therapy in Dynamic Psychiatry. Jules H. Masserman. LC 72-96926. 240p. 1995. pap. 25.00 (*1-56821-511-8*) Aronson.

Theory & Tradition in Eighteenth Century Studies. Ed. by Richard B. Schwartz. 224p. (C). 1990. text ed. 24.50 (*0-8093-1561-0*) S Ill U Pr.

Theory & Treatment of Anorexia Nervosa & Bulimia: Biomedical, Sociocultural, & Psychological Perspectives. Ed. by Steven W. Emmett. LC 84-29267. 352p. 1985. text ed. 49.95 (*0-87630-384-X*) Brunner-Mazel.

Theory Approximation Functions of a Real Variable. A. Timan & J. Berry. LC 62-22045. (International Series of Monographs on Pure & Applied Mathematics: Vol. 34). 1963. 278.00 (*0-08-009929-7*, Pub. by Pergamon Repr UK) Franklin.

Theory as a Prayerful Act: The Collected Essays of James B. Macdonald, Vol. 22. James B. MacDonald. Ed. by Bradley J. MacDonald. (Counterpoints Studies & Concepts in the Postmodern Theory of Education). 216p. (C). 1995. 29.95 (*0-8204-2792-6*) P Lang Pubng.

Theory As Practice: A Critical Anthology of Early German Romantic Writings. Ed. by Jochen Schulte-Sasse et al. Tr. by Haynes Horne et al. from GER. LC 96-17056. 456p. (C). 1997. text ed. 62.95 (*0-8166-2778-9*); pap. text ed. 24.95 (*0-8166-2779-7*) U of Minn Pr.

Theory as Practice: Ethical Inquiry in the Renaissance. Nancy S. Struever. LC 91-20446. 255p. 1992. 35.00 (*0-226-77742-1*) U Ch Pr.

Theory As Resistance: Politics & Culture after (Post) Structuralism. Mas'ud Zavarzadeh & Donald Morton. LC 93-41716. (Critical Perspectives Ser.). 256p. 1993. pap. 19.95 (*0-89862-421-5*) Guilford Pr.

Theory As Resistance: Politics & Culture after (Post) Structuralism. Mas'ud Zavarzadeh & Donald Morton. LC 93-41716. (Critical Perspectives Ser.). 256p. 1993. lib. bdg. 42.00 (*0-89862-414-2*) Guilford Pr.

Theory-Based Assessment, Treatment, & Prevention of Sexual Aggression. Gordon C. Hall. (Illus.). 264p. 1996. 39.95 (*0-19-509039-X*) OUP.

Theory Between the Disciplines: Authority, Vision, Politics. Ed. by Martin Kreiswirth & Mark A. Cheetham. LC 90-34588. (Illus.). 230p. 1990. text ed. 42.50 (*0-472-10165-X*) U of Mich Pr.

Theory Book: Level One. Morton Manus et al. (Basic Adult Piano Library). 64p. (Orig.). 1984. pap. text ed. 8.50 (*0-88284-635-3*, 2462) Alfred Pub.

Theory Building & Data Analysis in the Social Sciences. Ed. by Herbert B. Asher et al. LC 83-3458. 464p. 1984. pap. 20.00 (*0-87049-399-X*); text ed. 42.00 (*0-87049-398-1*) U of Tenn Pr.

Theory Building for Learning-How-to-Learn. Ed. by Robert M. Smith. LC 87-27618. 164p. reprint ed. pap. 46.80 (*0-7837-0609-X*, 2040957) Bks Demand.

Theory Building in Developmental Psychology. P. Van Geert. 500p. 1986. 180.00 (*0-444-70042-0*, North Holland) Elsevier.

Theory Building in Sociology: Assessing Theoretical Cumulation. Ed. by Jonathan H. Turner. LC 88-11349. (Key Issues in Sociological Theory Ser.: No. 3). 150p. reprint ed. pap. 42.80 (*0-7837-6721-8*, 2046348) Bks Demand.

Theory, Case, & Method in Comparative Politics. Nikolaos Zahariadis. 318p. (C). 1996. pap. text ed. write for info. (*0-15-503177-5*) HB Coll Pubs.

***Theory, Case, & Method in Comparative Politics.** Nikolaos Zahariadis. 318p. (C). 1996. pap. text ed. write for info. (*0-614-20960-9*) HB Coll Pubs.

Theory Change, Ancient Axiomatics, & Galileo's Methodology Vol. I: Proceedings of the 1978 Pisa, Italy, September 4-8, 1978 Conference on the History & Philosophy of Science. Ed. by Jaakko Hintikka et al. (Synthese Library: No. 145). 362p. 1980. lib. bdg. 129.50 (*90-277-1126-7*) Kluwer Ac.

Theory Change in Science: Strategies from Mendelian Genetics. Lindley Darden. (Monographs in the History & Philosophy of Biology). (Illus.). 328p. 1991. 49.95 (*0-19-506797-5*, 2394) OUP.

Theory, Complexity, Cinema & Evolution of the French Novel. Emily Zants. LC 96-3714. (Studies in French Literature: Vol. 25). 404p. 1996. 109.95 (*0-7734-8789-1*) E Mellen.

Theory, Construction & Calculations of Agricultural Machines, Vol. I. E. S. Bosoi et al. (C). 1987. 36.00 (*81-7087-021-6*, Pub. by Oxford IBH II) S Asia.

Theory, Construction & Calculations of Agricultural Machines, Vol. 2. E. S. Bosoi et al. (Russian Translation Ser.: No. 83). (Illus.). 510p. (C). 1990. text ed. 130.00 (*90-6191-999-1*, Pub. by A A Balkema NE) Ashgate Pub Co.

Theory, Construction & Calculations of Agricultural Machines, Vol. 1. E. S. Bosoi et al. (Russian Translation Ser.: No. 66). 325p. (C). 1988. text ed. 95.00 (*90-6191-914-2*, Pub. by A A Balkema NE) Ashgate Pub Co.

Theory Construction & Data Analysis in the Behavioral Sciences. Ed. by Samuel Shye. LC 78-62554. (Jossey-Bass Social & Behavioral Science Ser.). 448p. reprint ed. pap. 127.70 (*0-8357-6896-1*, 2037948) Bks Demand.

Theory Construction & Selection in Modern Physics. J. T. Cushing. (Illus.). 400p. (C). 1990. text ed. 105.00 (*0-521-38181-9*) Cambridge U Pr.

***Theory Construction & Testing.** Ed. by Margaret T. Beard. LC 95-60045. 328p. (C). 1996. pap. 45.95 (*0-923950-12-5*) Tucker IL.

Theory Control & Research Design. Schrieshe. write for info. (*0-275-90017-7*, C0017, Praeger Pubs) Greenwood.

Theory-Death of the Avant-Garde. Paul Mann. LC 90-49768. 160p. 1991. 29.95 (*0-253-33672-4*) Ind U Pr.

Theory, Design & Application of Electronic Devices & Circuits. Leslie E. Worden. (Illus.). 700p. text ed. write for info. (*0-89894-014-1*) Advocate Pub Group.

Theory, Determination & Control of Physical Properties of Food Materials. Ed. by Chokyun Rha. LC 74-76481. (Food Material Science Ser: No. 1). xi, 315p. 1975. lib. bdg. 182.50 (*90-277-0468-6*) Kluwer Ac.

Theory Development: What, Why, How? Jacqueline Fawcett et al. 86p. 1978. 12.95 (*0-88737-219-8*, 15-1708) Natl League Nurse.

Theory Development & Educational Administration. Ed. by Eddy J. Van Meter. 1973. pap. text ed. 12.95 (*0-8422-0297-8*) Irvington.

Theory-Directed Nursing Practice. Ed. by Shirley M. Ziegler. LC 92-2379. 280p. 1993. 37.95 (*0-8261-7630-5*) Springer Pub.

Theory Driven Evaluations. Huey-tsyh Chen. 336p. (C). 1990. pap. 25.00 (*0-8039-5899-4*); text ed. 52.00 (*0-8039-3532-3*) Sage.

Theory, Evidence, & Explanation. Ed. by Peter Lipton. (International Research Library of Philosophy: Vol. 11). (Illus.). 544p. 1995. 129.95 (*1-85521-633-7*, Pub. by Dartmth Pub UK) Ashgate Pub Co.

Theory for Everything: Essays & Short Fiction. J. Bernstein. LC 96-1553. 256p. 1996. 25.00 (*0-387-94700-0*) Spr-Verlag.

Theory for Nursing: Systems, Concepts & Process. Imogene M. King. LC 81-1996. 181p. 1989. text ed. 36.95 (*0-8273-4267-5*) Delmar.

Theory for Piano Students, Bk. 1. L. Benner. 56p. 1986. pap. 5.95 (*0-7935-5299-0*, 50330220) H Leonard.

Theory for Piano Students, Bk. 2. L. Benner. 56p. 1986. pap. 7.95 (*0-7935-5307-5*, 50330270) H Leonard.

Theory for Piano Students, Bk. 3. L. Benner. 56p. 1986. pap. 6.95 (*0-7935-3817-3*, 50330300) H Leonard.

Theory for Piano Students, Bk. 5. L. Benner. 56p. 1986. pap. 6.95 (*0-7935-3818-1*, 50331370) H Leonard.

An Asterisk (*) at the beginning of an entry indicates that the title is appearing in BIP for the first time.

Theory for Practice: Architecture in Three Discourses. Bill Hubbard, Jr. (Illus.). 192p. 1995. 22.50 (*0-262-08235-7*) MIT Pr.

Theory for Practice: Architecture in Three Discourses. Bill Hubbard. (Illus.). 192p. 1996. pap. 12.50 (*0-262-58145-0*) MIT Pr.

Theory for Reading Dramatic Texts: Selected Plays by Pirandello & Garcia Lorca. Catherine A. Parilla. (Currents in Comparative Romance Languages & Literatures Ser.: Vol. 24). 200p. (C). 1995. text ed. 44.95 (*0-8204-2368-8*) P Lang Pubng.

Theory for Social Work Practice. Ruth E. Smalley. LC 67-14290. 347p. reprint ed. pap. 98.90 (*0-8357-3725-X*, 2036447) Bks Demand.

Theory Formulations. Ed. by Williard E. Stone. LC 70-631270. (University of Florida Accounting Ser.: No. 6). 101p. reprint ed. pap. 28.80 (*0-7837-5010-2*, 2044677) Bks Demand.

Theory Groups & the Study of Language in North America: A Social History. Stephen O. Murray. LC 93-34835. (Studies in the History of the Language Sciences: No. 69). x, 598p. 1993. 110.00 (*1-55619-364-5*) Benjamins North Am.

Theory in Archaeology: A World Perspective. Ed. by Peter J. Ucko. LC 94-27877. (Illus.). 432p. (C). (gr. 13). 1995. text ed. 99.95 (*0-415-10677-X*, B4969) Routledge.

Theory in Educational Administration. English. (C). 1994. text ed. 60.95 (*0-06-500934-7*) Addson-Wesley Educ.

Theory in Industrial Design. H. Bradley Hammond. 216p. (C). 1993. pap. text ed. 22.00 (*1-57074-057-7*) Greyden Pr.

Theory in Its Feminist Travels: Conversations in U. S. Women's Movements. Katie King. LC 94-5612. 208p. 1995. 31.50 (*0-253-33138-2*); pap. 12.95 (*0-253-20905-6*) Ind U Pr.

Theory in Practice: Increasing Professional Effectiveness. Chris Argyris & Donald A. Schon. LC 74-3606. (Jossey-Bass Series in Higher Education). 240p. reprint ed. pap. 68.40 (*0-7837-2513-2*, 2042672) Bks Demand.

Theory in Practice: Increasing Professional Effectiveness. Chris Argyris & Donald A. Schon. LC 74-3606. (Classics Ser.). 260p. reprint ed. pap. 26.95 (*1-55542-446-5*) Jossey-Bass.

Theory in Practice: Tocqueville's New Science of Politics. Saguiv A. Hadari. LC 89-30920. 200p. 1989. 32.50 (*0-8047-1704-4*) Stanford U Pr.

Theory in Retailing: Traditional & Nontraditional Sources. Ronald W. Stampfl & Elizabeth C. Hirschman. LC 80-23919. (American Marketing Association, Proceedings Ser.). reprint ed. pap. 49.80 (*0-317-20072-0*, 20233354) Bks Demand.

Theory in the Classroom. Ed. by Cary Nelson. LC 85-16531. 288p. 1986. text ed. 29.95 (*0-252-01265-8*); pap. text ed. 13.95 (*0-252-01471-5*) U of Ill Pr.

Theory in the Practice of the Nicaraguan Revolution. Bruce E. Wright. (Monographs in International Studies Latin America Ser.: No. 24). (Illus.). 320p. (Orig.). (C). 1995. pap. text ed. 23.00 (*0-89680-185-3*) Ohio U Pr.

Theory into Practice: A Reader in Modern Literary Criticism. Ed. by Ken M. Newton. LC 92-4348. 256p. 1992. text ed. 45.00 (*0-312-07996-6*) St Martin.

Theory into Practice: A Reader in Modern Literary Criticism. Ed. by Ken M. Newton. LC 92-4348. 256p. 1992. pap. text ed. 16.95 (*0-312-07997-4*) St Martin.

Theory, Law, & Policy of Soviet Treaties. Jan F. Triska & Robert M. Slusser. LC 62-11989. (Hoover Institution Publications). 607p. reprint ed. pap. 173.00 (*0-7837-3946-X*, 2043775) Bks Demand.

Theory Linear Viscoelasticity. Ian N. Sneddon. LC 59-14489. (International Series of Monographs on Pure & Applied Mathematics: Vol. 10). 1960. 58.00 (*0-08-009316-7*, Pub. by Pergamon Repr UK) Franklin.

Theory Meets Experiment: Proceedings of the Johns Hopkins Workshop on Current Problems in Practice Theory. R. Casalbuoni & G. Domokos. 300p. 1995. text ed. 99.00 (*981-02-2235-1*) World Scientific Pub.

Theory, Method, & Practice in Social & Cultural History. Ed. by Peter Karsten & John Modell. (Problems in Method & Theory of Social History: The Pittsburgh Center Ser.). 256p. (C). 1991. text ed. 44.00 (*0-8147-4627-6*) NYU Pr.

Theory, Method, & Practice in Social & Cultural History. Ed. by Peter Karsten & John Modell. (Problems in Method & Theory of Social History: The Pittsburgh Center Ser.). 256p. (C). 1993. pap. 20.00 (*0-8147-4641-1*) NYU Pr.

Theory, Modeling, & Experience in the Management of Nonpoint-Source Pollution. Ed. by Clifford S. Russell & Jason F. Shogren. LC 92-36253. 368p. 1993. lib. bdg. 130.00 (*0-7923-9307-4*) Kluwer Ac.

Theory Notebook Complete. John Brimhall. 96p. (Orig.). 1985. pap. text ed. 9.95 (*0-8494-0028-7*, M465) Hansen Ed Mus.

Theory Now & Then. J. Hillis Miller. LC 90-44884. 420p. 1991. text ed. 54.95 (*0-8223-1112-7*) Duke.

Theory O: Creating an Ownership Style of Management. Karen M. Young. 120p. (Orig.). 1993. pap. 25.00 (*0-926902-25-3*) NCEO.

***Theory O at Work: A Collection of Participative Exercises.** 127p. 1997. ring bd. write for info. (*0-926902-33-4*) NCEO.

***Theory of a Higher-Order Sturm-Liouville Equation, Vol. 165.** Vladimir Kozlov & V. G. Mazia. LC 97-14884. (Lecture Notes in Mathematics Ser.). 1997. write for info. (*3-540-63065-1*) Spr-Verlag.

Theory of A. R. Luria: Functions of Spoken Language in the Development of Higher Mental Processes. Donna R. Vocate. (Functions of Spoken Language in the Development of Higher Mental Processes Ser.). 208p. 1986. text ed. 39.95 (*0-89859-709-9*) L Erlbaum Assocs.

Theory of Absence: Subjectivity, Signification, & Desire. Patrick Fuery. LC 94-47437. (Contributions in Philosophy Ser.: No. 55). 192p. 1995. text ed. 55.00 (*0-313-29588-3*, Greenwood Pr) Greenwood.

Theory of Absolute Space. George Junghanns. (Illus.). 100p. 1996. 10.00 (*1-881946-06-1*) Gauntlet Bks.
This revolutionary theory for the creation of the universe is a natural extension of Einstein's curved-space. For its basic idea of the "flash," which replaces the Big Bang's "fireball," a new mechanism is suggested, this being the gyroscopic effect on hydrogen atoms. Applying well-established mechanical principles, the creation of preformed galaxies through acceleration is suggested. Meanwhile, the payload develops positrons & electrons, which are compressed together into the "flash" when the peak acceleration is reached. This process, which explains the 3K background radiation quintessential to the Big Bang Theory, also answers the question why there is so little anti-matter in the universe today. Throughout, quantum mechanics is employed, not discredited. The argument is that its place as a tool subject was obfuscated into a cosmology. The current gridlock of issues in the Big Bang Theory is as much proof as anything else. The doors must be opened for some new thinking to take place, which is the ultimate hope of a theory. Here we look for guidance from the unresolved issues of classic physics. What with the promise of the Hubble telescope, & the success of quantum experimentation, no one should argue against the need for more options. ISBN 1-881946-06-1, 20 diagrams, 100 pages. Gauntlet Books, Box 499, Franklin, MA 02038. ***Publisher Provided Annotation.***

Theory of AC Circuits. Albert P. Malvino. (Illus.). 304p. (Orig.). (C). 1989. pap. text ed. 16.95 (*1-56048-302-4*, 302) Malvino Inc.

Theory of AC Circuits - Quik-Lab for AC Circuits: Conventional-Flow Version, 2 bks., Bks. 1 & 2. Albert P. Malvino. (IBM Package Ser.: No. 2). (Illus.). (Orig.). (C). 1989. Bk. 1: 304 pp., Feb., 1989; Bk. 2: 224 pp., March, 1989. pap. text ed. 24.95 incl. disk (*1-56048-383-0*, 3802C) Malvino Inc.

Theory of AC Circuits - Quik-Lab for AC Circuits: Electron-Flow Version, 2 bks., Bks. 1 & 2. Albert P. Malvino. (IBM Package Ser.: No. 2). (Illus.). (Orig.). (C). 1989. Bk. 1: 304 pp., Feb 1989; Bk. 2: 224 pp., March, 1989. pap. text ed. 24.95 incl. disk (*1-56048-382-2*, 3802E) Malvino Inc.

Theory of AC Circuits - Quik-Lab Two for AC Circuits: Electron-Flow Edition Package, 2 vols. Albert P. Malvino. (EGA - VGA - Hercules Graphics Ser.). (Illus.). 480p. (Orig.). (C). pap. text ed. 26.95 (*1-56048-399-7*, 3982); Bk. 1: 03/1989, 304p. write for info. (*0-318-68173-0*); Bk. 2: 1991, 176p. write for info. (*0-318-68174-9*) Malvino Inc.

Theory of AC Circuits - Quik-Lab(II) for AC Circuits Package: Conventional-Flow Edition, 2 bks. Albert P. Malvino. (CGA, Hercules, EGA - VGA Graphics Ser.). (Illus.). 492p. (Orig.). (C). 1991. Set. pap. text ed. 26.95 (*1-56048-397-0*, 3982C) Malvino Inc.

Theory of Accounting & Control. Sunder. (Miscellaneous/Catalogs Ser.). (C). 1997. pap. 20.95 (*0-538-86686-1*) S-W Pub.

Theory of Accounting Measurement, Vol. 10. Yuji Ijiri. (Studies in Accounting Research). 210p. 1975. 12.00 (*0-86539-022-3*) Am Accounting.

Theory of Accounts. Scott. LC 75-18482. (History of Accounting Ser.). (Illus.). 1978. reprint ed. 23.95 (*0-405-07564-2*) Ayer.

Theory of Accretion Disks: Proceedings of the NATO Advanced Research Workshop Held in Garching, FRG March 6-10, 1989. Ed. by Fredrich Meyer et al. (C). 1989. lib. bdg. 211.50 (*0-7923-0453-5*) Kluwer Ac.

Theory of Accretion Disks - 2: Proceedings of the NATO Advanced Research Workshop, Garching, Germany, March 16-22, 1993. Ed. by Wolfgang J. Duschl. LC 93-23735. (NATO Advanced Study Institutes Series C, Mathematical & Physical Sciences). 440p. 1993. lib. bdg. 222.00 (*0-7923-2609-1*) Kluwer Ac.

Theory of Achievement Motivation. Ed. by J. W. Atkinson & Norman T. Feather. LC 74-7064. 404p. 1974. reprint ed. 35.50 (*0-88275-166-2*) Krieger.

Theory of Action: Towards a New Synthesis Going Beyond Parsons. Richard Munch. 358p. (C). 1988. text ed. 67.50 (*0-7102-1218-6*, RKP) Routledge.

Theory of Action Identification. Robin R. Vallacher & Daniel M. Wegner. (Basic Studies in Human Behavior). 272p. (C). 1985. text ed. 49.95 (*0-89859-617-3*) L Erlbaum Assocs.

Theory of Advanced First Aid. J. A. Wood. 1986. lib. bdg. 61.00 (*0-85200-892-9*) Kluwer Ac.

Theory of Algebraic Integers. Richard Dedekind. (Cambridge Mathematical Library). 176p. (C). 1996. pap. text ed. 22.95 (*0-521-56518-9*) Cambridge U Pr.

Theory of Algebraic Invariants. David Hilbert. Ed. by Bernd Sturmfels. Tr. by Reinhard C. Laubenbacher. (Cambridge Mathematical Library). (Illus.). 200p. (C). 1993. pap. text ed. 21.95 (*0-521-44903-0*) Cambridge U Pr.

Theory of Algebraic Invariants. David Hilbert. Ed. by Bernd Sturmfels. Tr. by Reinhard C. Laubenbacher. (Cambridge Mathematical Library). (Illus.). 200p. (C). 1994. text ed. 49.95 (*0-521-44457-8*) Cambridge U Pr.

Theory of Alloy Phase Formation: Proceedings of a Symposium-Sponsored by the TMS-AIME Alloy Phases Committee & the Chemistry & Physics of Metals Committee at the 10th AIME Annual Meeting, New Orleans, La., February 19-20, 1979. Metallurgical Society of AIME Staff. Ed. by L. H. Bennett. LC 80-80305. 535p. reprint ed. pap. 152.50 (*0-317-26178-9*, 2024264) Bks Demand.

Theory of Almost Everything: A Scientific & Religious Quest for Ultimate Answers. Robert Barry. 208p. (Orig.). 1996. pap. 13.95 (*1-85168-123-X*) Onewrld Pubns.

Theory of Anisotropic Plates: Strength, Stability, & Vibrations. 2nd ed. S. E. Ambartsumyan. 1991. 198.00 (*0-89116-654-8*) Hemisp Pub.

Theory of Approximation. N. I. Achieser. x, 307p. 1992. reprint ed. pap. 8.95 (*0-486-67129-1*) Dover.

Theory of Approximation. Dunham Jackson. LC 30-32147. (Colloquium Publications: Vol. 11). 178p. 1930. reprint ed. pap. 38.00 (*0-8218-1011-1*, COLL/11) Am Math.

Theory of Approximation of Functions of a Real Variable. A. F. Timan. LC 93-33695. xii, 631p. 1993. reprint ed. pap. text ed. 14.95 (*0-486-67830-X*) Dover.

Theory of Architecture Concept. P. Johnson. 1994. pap. 44.95 (*0-442-01344-2*) Van Nos Reinhold.

Theory of Argumentation. Charles A. Willard. LC 88-27742. (Studies in Rhetoric & Communication). 336p. 1989. text ed. 39.95 (*0-8173-0427-4*) U of Ala Pr.

Theory of Art: Inexhaustibility by Contrast. Stephen D. Ross. LC 81-9027. (SUNY Series in Philosophy). 246p. (C). 1982. text ed. 59.50 (*0-87395-554-4*); pap. text ed. 19.95 (*0-87395-555-2*) State U NY Pr.

Theory of Art in the "Encyclopedie" Amy C. Simowitz. Ed. by Donald Kuspit. LC 83-4999. (Studies in the Fine Arts - Art Theory: No. 9). 148p. reprint ed. 41.90 (*0-8357-1433-0*, 2070474) Bks Demand.

Theory of Art, Tragedy & Culture: The Philosophy of Eliseo Vivas. Hugh Curtler. (World of Art Ser.). 224p. 1983. pap. text ed. 11.00 (*0-930586-15-8*) Haven Pubns.

Theory of Aspectuality: The Interaction Between Temporal & Atemporal Structure. Henk J. Verkuyl. LC 92-33563. (Studies in Linguistics: Vol. 64). (Illus.). 426p. (C). 1993. text ed. 65.00 (*0-521-44362-8*) Cambridge U Pr.

Theory of Aspectuality: The Interaction Between Temporal & Atemporal Structure. Henk J. Verkuyl. (Studies in Linguistics: No. 64). 411p. 1996. pap. text ed. 24.95 (*0-521-56452-2*) Cambridge U Pr.

Theory of Asymmetrical Elasticity. 2nd ed. Wojoiech K. Nowacki. 1986. 178.00 (*0-08-027584-2*, Pub. by Pergamon Repr UK) Franklin.

Theory of Atomic Nuclei: Quasi-Particles & Phonons. V. G. Soloviev. (Illus.). 352p. 1992. 176.00 (*0-7503-0131-7*) IOP Pub.

Theory of Atomic Spectra. E. U. Condon & George H. Shortley. 460p. (Orig.). (C). 1935. pap. text ed. 57.95 (*0-521-09209-4*) Cambridge U Pr.

Theory of Atomic Structure & Spectra. Robert D. Cowan. LC 81-4578. (Los Alamos Series in Basic & Applied Sciences: No. 3). 650p. 1981. 65.00 (*0-520-03821-5*) U CA Pr.

Theory of Auditing. Charles W. Schandl. LC 78-17862. 1978. text ed. 20.00 (*0-914348-23-X*) Scholars Bk.

Theory of Automata. Ian N. Sneddon. LC 71-76796. (International Series of Monographs on Pure & Applied Mathematics: Vol. 100). 1969. 119.00 (*0-08-013376-2*, Pub. by Pergamon Repr UK) Franklin.

Theory of Automatic Robot Assembly & Programming. Bartholomew O. Nnaji. LC 92-30586. 1992. write for info. (*0-442-31663-1*) Chapman & Hall.

***Theory of Automatic Robot Assembly & Programming.** Bartholomew O. Nnaji. (Illus.). 336p. (C). (gr. 13 up). Date not set. text ed. 62.95 (*0-412-39310-7*, Chap & Hall NY) Chapman & Hall.

Theory of Backmixing: The Design of Continuous Flow Chemical Plant with Backmixing. J. C. Mecklenburgh & S. Hartland. LC 74-32190. 529p. reprint ed. pap. 150.80 (*0-317-41980-3*, 2025977) Bks Demand.

Theory of Bad Faith. Sanford M. Gage. (ATLA Monograph Ser.). 60p. (Orig.). 1988. pap. 7.50 (*0-941916-46-4*) ATLA Pr.

Theory of Beats & Combination Tones, 1700-1863. V. Carlton Maley, Jr. LC 90-3350. (Harvard Dissertations in the History of Science Ser.). 184p. 1990. text ed. 15.00 (*0-8240-0040-4*) Garland.

Theory of Beauty in the Classical Aesthetics of Japan. Toshihiko Izutsu & Toyo Izutsu. 178p. 1981. lib. bdg. 82.50 (*90-247-2381-7*, Pub. by M Nijhoff NE) Kluwer Ac.

Theory of Bernoulli Shifts. Paul C. Shields. LC 73-85907. (Chicago Lectures in Mathematics). 128p. reprint ed. pap. 36.50 (*0-685-23834-2*, 2056615) Bks Demand.

Theory of Best Approximation & Functional Analysis. Ivan Singer. (CBMS-NSF Regional Conference Series in Applied Mathematics: No. 13). vii, 95p. (Orig.). 1974. pap. text ed. 21.50 (*0-89871-010-3*) Soc Indus-Appl Math.

Theory of Beta-Decay. C. Strachan. LC 72-86202. 1969. pap. 98.00 (*0-08-006508-2*, Pub. by Pergamon Repr UK) Franklin.

***Theory of Blackjack: The Compleat Card Counter's Guide to the Casino Game of 21.** 5th ed. Peter A. Griffin. 261p. (Orig.). 1996. pap. 11.95 (*0-929712-12-9*) Huntington Pr.

Theory of Box Girders. Vladimir Kristek. LC 78-8637. 371p. reprint ed. pap. 105.80 (*0-318-34896-9*, 2031293) Bks Demand.

Theory of Business Enterprise. Thorstein B. Veblen. 420p. 1978. pap. 24.95 (*0-87855-699-0*) Transaction Pubs.

Theory of Business Enterprise. Thorstein B. Veblen. LC 65-15957. (Reprints of Economic Classics Ser.). xx, 400p. 1965. reprint ed. 45.00 (*0-678-00056-5*) Kelley.

***Theory of Canonical Moments with Applications in Statistics, Probability & Analysis.** Holger Dette & William J. Studden. LC 96-53188. (Wiley Series in Probability & Statistics). 1997. write for info. (*0-471-10991-6*) Wiley.

Theory of Capital Reproduction & Accumulation. Shinzaburo Koshimura. Ed. by Jesse Schwartz. Tr. by Toshihiro Ataka from JPN. 1975. 14.95 (*0-8464-0921-6*) Beekman Pubs.

Theory of Capitalist Development. Paul M. Sweezy. LC 64-21234. 400p. 1968. reprint ed. pap. 18.00 (*0-85345-079-X*) Monthly Rev.

Theory of Capitalist Regulation: The U. S. Experience. Michel Aglietta. Tr. by David Fernbach from ITA. 390p. 1986. pap. text ed. 17.95 (*0-86091-850-5*, Pub. by Verso UK) Routledge Chapman & Hall.

***Theory of Carrier Adjusted DGPS Positioning Approach & Some Experimental Results.** Xin-Xiang Jin. (Illus.). 162p. (Orig.). 1996. pap. 43.50 (*90-407-1379-0*, Pub. by Delft U Pr NE) Coronet Bks.

Theory of Cataloguing. Krishan Kumar & Girija Kumar. 366p. (C). 1986. text ed. 35.00 (*0-7069-4067-9*, Pub. by Vikas II) S Asia.

Theory of Categories. F. C. Brentano. Tr. by Roderick M. Chisholm & Norbert Guterman. (Nijhoff International Philosophy Ser.: No. 8). 286p. 1981. lib. bdg. 104.50 (*90-247-2302-7*, Pub. by M Nijhoff NE) Kluwer Ac.

Theory of Celestial Influence. Rodney Collin. 1997. pap. 13.95 (*0-14-019365-0*, Arkana) Viking Penguin.

Theory of Celestial Influence: Man, the Universe, & Cosmic Mystery. Rodney Collin. 1984. pap. 10.95 (*0-394-72391-0*) Random.

Theory of Chattering Control with Applications to Astronautics, Robotics, Economics, & Engineering. V. F. Borisov & M. I. Zelikin. LC 93-51121. (Systems & Control: Foundations & Applications Ser.). (Illus.). 312p. 1994. 86.50 (*0-8176-3618-8*) Birkhauser.

Theory of Chemical Reaction Dynamics. Ed. by D. C. Clary. 1986. lib. bdg. 159.00 (*90-277-2202-1*) Kluwer Ac.

Theory of Chemical Reaction Dynamics, Vol. 1. Ed. by Michael Baer. 248p. 1985. 140.00 (*0-8493-6114-1*, CRC Reprint) Franklin.

Theory of Chemical Reaction Dynamics, Vol. IV. Ed. by Michael Baer. 264p. 1985. 216.00 (*0-8493-6117-6*) CRC Pr.

Theory of Chemical Reaction Dynamics, Vols. II, III, & IV. Ed. by Michael Baer. 1985. 719.80 (*0-8493-6113-3*, QD501) CRC Pr.

Theory of Chemisorption. Ed. by J. R. Smith. (Topics in Current Physics Ser.: Vol. 19). (Illus.). 280p. 1980. 52.95 (*0-387-09891-7*) Spr-Verlag.

***Theory of Choice.** M. Alzermant & F. Aleskerov. (Studies in Mechanical Engineering: Vol. 38). 324p. 1995. 145.75 (*0-444-82210-0*, North Holland) Elsevier.

Theory of Choice & Decision Making. I. Makarov & T. Vinogradskaia. 328p. (C). 1987. 80.00 (*0-685-46646-9*, Pub. by Collets) St Mut.

Theory of Cluster Sets. Edward F. Collingwood & A. J. Lohwater. LC 66-18115. (Cambridge Tracts in Mathematics & Mathematical Physics: No. 56). reprint ed. pap. 55.80 (*0-317-08574-3*, 2013053) Bks Demand.

Theory of CMOS Digital Circuits & Circuit Failures. Masakazu Shoji. (Illus.). 450p. 1992. text ed. 125.00 (*0-691-08763-6*) Princeton U Pr.

Theory of Cognitive Dissonance. Leon Festinger. xi, 291p. 1957. 39.50 (*0-8047-0131-8*) Stanford U Pr.

Theory of Coherent Atomic Excitation, 2 vols., Set. Bruce W. Shore. 2509p. 1990. text ed. 195.00 (*0-471-52417-4*) Wiley.

Theory of Coherent Atomic Excitation, Vol. 1. Shore. LC 88-33967. 774p. 1990. text ed. 142.00 (*0-471-61398-3*) Wiley.

Theory of Coherent Atomic Excitation, Vol. 2: Multilevel Atoms & Incoherence, Vol. 2. Bruce W. Shore. 1735p. 1990. text ed. 142.00 (*0-471-52416-6*) Wiley.

Theory of Collective Bargaining 1930-1975. W. H. Hutt. LC 80-36792. (Cato Papers: No. 14). 133p. 1980. reprint ed. pap. 1.00 (*0-932790-20-8*) Cato Inst.

***Theory of Coloration of Textiles.** 2nd ed. Ed. by Alan Johnson. 552p. (C). 1989. 72.00 (*0-901956-48-1*, Pub. by Textile Inst UK) St Mut.

Theory of Colours. Johann Wolfgang Von Goethe. Tr. by C. L. Eastlake. (Illus.). 428p. 1967. 35.00 (*0-7146-1107-7*, Pub. by F Cass Pubs UK) Intl Spec Bk.

Theory of Colours. Johann Wolfgang Von Goethe. 1970. pap. 18.50 (*0-262-57021-1*) MIT Pr.

***Theory of Combustion of Powder & Explosives.** Ed. by Aleksei Lipanov. (Illus.). 407p. (C). 1996. lib. bdg. 89.00 (*1-56072-398-X*) Nova Sci Pubs.

***Theory of Combustion of Powder & Explosives.** Ed. by Aleksei M. Lipanov. 407p. (C). 1996. lib. bdg. 89.00 (*0-614-21809-8*) Nova Sci Pubs.

Theory of Commodity Price Stabilization: A Study in the Economics of Risk. David M. Newberry & Joseph E. Stiglitz. (Illus.). 480p. 1981. pap. 38.00 (*0-19-828438-1*) OUP.

Theory of Communicative Action, Vol. I: Reason & the Rationalization of Society. Jurgen Habermas. Tr. & Intro. by Thomas McCarthy. LC 82-72506. Orig. Title: Theorie des Kommunikativen Handelns. 507p. 1985. 45.00 (*0-8070-1506-7*); pap. 21.00 (*0-8070-1507-5*, BP 687) Beacon Pr.

T

An Asterisk (*) at the beginning of an entry indicates that the title is appearing in BIP for the first time.

Theory of Communicative Action, Vol. II: Lifeworld & System: A Critique of Functionalist Reason. Jurgen Habermas. Tr. & Intro. by Thomas McCarthy. LC 87-47536. 468p. 1989. 40.00 (0-8070-1400-1); pap. 21.00 (0-8070-1401-X, BP833) Beacon Pr.

Theory of Commutative Fields. Masayoshi Nagata. LC 93-6503. (Translations of Mathematical Monographs: Vol. 125). 280p. 1993. 49.00 (0-8218-4572-1, MMONO/125) Am Math.

Theory of Commuting Nonselfadjoint Operators. M. S. Livsic. (Mathematics & Its Applications Ser.). 332p. (C). 1995. lib. bdg. 174.00 (0-7923-3588-0) Kluwer Ac.

Theory of Competing Risks. H. A. David & Melvin L. Moeschberger. 1978. 25.00 (0-85264-249-0) Lubrecht & Cramer.

Theory of Complex Functions. Reinhold Remmert. Tr. by R. B. Burckel from GER. (Graduate Texts in Mathematics Ser.: Vol. 122). (Illus.). xix, 453p. 1995. 64.95 (0-387-97195-5) Spr-Verlag.

Theory of Composites Design. Stephen W. Tsai. (Illus.). 225p. 1992. pap. 29.00 (0-9618090-3-5) Think Composites.

*Theory of Computation. Ed. by Meduna. (C). 1998. text ed. write for info. (0-321-01065-5) Addson-Wesley Educ.

*Theory of Computation. Bernard M. Moret. (C). 1998. pap. text ed. write for info. (0-201-25828-5) Addison-Wesley.

Theory of Computation. Derrick Wood. 450p. 1986. Net. text ed. 47.50 (0-471-60351-1) Wiley.

Theory of Computation. Walter S. Brainerd & Lawrence H. Landweber. LC 73-12950. reprint ed. pap. 89.30 (0-317-55578-2, 2056337) Bks Demand.

Theory of Computation: An Introduction. James L. Hein. LC 95-45894. (Math Ser.). 150p. (C). Date not set. text ed. 55.00 (0-86720-497-4) Jones & Bartlett.

Theory of Computation: Formal Languages, Automata & Complexity. J. Glenn Brookshear. Orig. Title: Introduction to Formal Languages, Computability & Complexity. (Illus.). 550p. (C). 1989. text ed. 56.95 (0-8053-0143-7) Benjamin-Cummings.

Theory of Computer Semiotics: Semiotic Approaches to Construction & Assessemnt of Computer Systems. Peter B. Andersen. (Series in Human-Computer Interaction). (Illus.). 238p. (C). 1991. text ed. 74.95 (0-521-39336-1) Cambridge U Pr.

Theory of Computer Semiotics: Semiotic Approaches to Construction & Assessment of Computer Systems. Peter B. Andersen. (Cambridge Series in Human-Computer Interaction: No. 3). 416p. 1997. pap. text ed. 29.95 (0-521-44868-9) Cambridge U Pr.

Theory of Computing & Systems: Israel Symposium ISTCS, Haifa, Israel, May 27-28, 1992, Proceedings. Ed. by D. Dolev et al. LC 92-11112. (Lecture Notes in Computer Science Ser.: Vol. 601). viii, 220p. 1992. 41.95 (0-387-55553-6) Spr-Verlag.

Theory of Computing & Systems, 3rd Israel Symposium On. LC 94-79253. 296p. 1995. pap. 60.00 (0-8186-6915-2) IEEE Comp Soc.

Theory of Computing Systems, 4th Israel Symposium on The: ISTCS 96. 248p. 1996. pap. 60.00 (0-8186-7610-8, PR07610) IEEE Comp Soc.

Theory of Conceptual Intelligence: Thinking, Learning, Creativity, & Giftedness. Rex Li. LC 95-37642. 256p. 1996. text ed. 55.00 (0-275-95326-2, Praeger Pubs) Greenwood.

Theory of Conjugation for Reflecting Prisms. Tongshu Lian. (International Academic Publishers Ser.). (Illus.). 500p. 1991. 115.00 (0-08-037935-4, Pub. by IAP UK) Elsevier.

Theory of Constraints. Eliyahu M. Goldratt. 162p. 1990. 25.00 (0-88427-085-8) North River.

*Theory of Constraints: Applications in Quality & Manufacturing. 2nd ed. Robert E. Stein. LC 96-52044. (Quality & Reliability Ser.: Vol. 50). 320p. 1997. 75.00 (0-8247-0064-3) Dekker.

Theory of Constraints & Its Implications for Management Accounting. Noreen et al. 1995. pap. 25.00 (0-88427-116-1) North River.

*Theory of Constraints Thinking Processes. Lisa Scheinkopf. 1997. 42.50 (1-57444-101-9) St Lucie Pr.

Theory of Consumer Behaviour & Welfare in Classical Paradigm. A. Ghosh. 1992. 22.50 (81-7040-417-7, Pub. by Himalaya II) Apt Bks.

Theory of Consumer's Demand. rev. ed. Ruby T. Norris. LC 75-39261. (Getting & Spending: The Consumer's Dilemma Ser.). (Illus.). 1976. reprint ed. 23.95 (0-405-08034-4) Ayer.

Theory of Consumption. Hazel Kyrk. LC 75-39253. (Getting & Spending: The Consumer's Dilemma Ser.). 1976. reprint ed. 25.95 (0-405-08026-3) Ayer.

Theory of Content & Other Essays. Jerry Fodor. 320p. 1990. 32.50 (0-262-06130-9) MIT Pr.

Theory of Content & Other Essays. Jerry A. Fodor. (Illus.). 282p. 1992. reprint ed. pap. 18.00 (0-262-56069-0, Bradford Bks) MIT Pr.

Theory of Contestable Markets: Applications to Regulatory & Antitrust Problems in the Rail Industry. William B. Tye. LC 89-25705. (Contributions in Economics & Economic History Ser.: No. 106). 160p. 1990. text ed. 47.95 (0-313-27337-5, TTC/, Greenwood Pr) Greenwood.

Theory of Continuous-Wave Chemical Lasers. A. A. Stepanov et al. 400p. 1996. boxed 130.00 (1-898326-36-3, Pub. by Cambdge Intl UK) Am Educ Systs.

Theory of Contracts in Islamic Law: A Comparative Analysis with Particular Reference to Modern Legislation in Kuwait, Bahrain & the U. A. E. Susan Rayner. 454p. (C). 1991. lib. bdg. 141.00 (1-85333-617-3, Pub. by Graham & Trotman UK) Kluwer Ac.

Theory of Convex Bodies. T. Bonnesen & W. Fenchel. Tr. by Leo F. Boron et al. from GER. LC 86-71997. (Illus.). 182p. (Orig.). 1987. pap. 30.00 (0-914351-02-8) BCS Assocs.

Theory of Convex Programming. E. G. Gol'Stein. Tr. by R. Tyrrell Rockafellar. LC 72-3180. (Translations of Mathematical Monographs: Vol. 36). 57p. 1972. 35.00 (0-8218-1586-5, MMONO/36) Am Math.

Theory of Convex Structures. M. L. Van de Vel. LC 93-8207. (Mathematical Library: Vol. 50). 556p. 1993. 187.25 (0-444-81505-8, North Holland) Elsevier.

Theory of Coping Systems: Change in Supportive Health Organizations. Francis D. Powell. 244p. 1975. boxed 34.95 (0-87073-029-0) Transaction Pubs.

Theory of Coronoid Hydrocarbons. S. J. Cyvin et al. (Lecture Notes in Chemistry Ser.: Vol. 54). (Illus.). 172p. 1991. 35.95 (0-387-53577-2) Spr-Verlag.

Theory of Coronoid Hydrocarbons II. S. J. Cyvin et al. LC 94-19284. (Lecture Notes in Chemistry Ser.: Vol. 62). 1994. 80.95 (0-387-58138-3) Spr-Verlag.

Theory of Corporate Finance. David Megginson. (C). 1995. teacher ed. write for info. (0-673-97137-6) Addson-Wesley Educ.

Theory of Corporate Finance. David Megginson. 416p. (C). 1997. text ed. 66.50 (0-673-99765-0) Addson-Wesley Educ.

Theory of Corporate Finance, 2 vols., Set. Ed. by Michael J. Brennan. LC 96-609. (International Library of Critical Writings in Financial Economics: Vol. 1). 1220p. 1996. 360.00 (1-85898-278-2) E Elgar.

Theory of Cosmic Grains. Fred Hoyle & Nalin C. Wickramasinghe. 320p. (C). 1991. lib. bdg. 108.50 (0-7923-1189-2) Kluwer Ac.

Theory of Counterfactuals. Igal Kvart. LC 84-22407. 512p. (C). 1986. pap. text ed. 19.00 (0-915145-64-2); lib. bdg. 35.00 (0-915145-63-4) Ridgeview.

Theory of Crime & Criminal Responsibility in Islamic Law: Shari'a. Nagaty Sanad. 108p. pap. 12.00 (0-942511-48-4) OICJ.

Theory of Criminal Justice. Jan Gorecki. LC 78-31559. 192p. 1979. text ed. 45.00 (0-231-04670-7) Col U Pr.

Theory of Critical Elections. V. O. Key, Jr. (Reprint Series in Social Sciences). (C). 1993. reprint ed. pap. text ed. 1.00 (0-8290-3104-9, PS-153) Irvington.

Theory of Critical Phenomena: An Introduction to the Renormalization Group. J. J. Binney et al. LC 92-8130. (Illus.). 416p. 1992. pap. 55.00 (0-19-851393-3, Clarendon Pr) OUP.

Theory of Criticism: A Reader. Seldon. 576p. (C). 1988. pap. text ed. 33.50 (0-582-00328-8, 70400) Longman.

Theory of Criticism: A Tradition & Its System. Murray Krieger. LC 75-36935. 271p. 1976. reprint ed. pap. 77.30 (0-608-00811-7, 2061599) Bks Demand.

Theory of Crystal Dislocations. A. H. Cottrell. (Documents on Modern Physics Ser.). 94p. 1964. pap. text ed. 106.00 (0-677-00175-4) Gordon & Breach.

Theory of Crystal Dislocations. F. R. Nabarro. (Illus.). 864p. 1987. reprint ed. pap. 19.95 (0-486-65488-5) Dover.

Theory of Crystal Space Groups & Lattice Dynamics: Infra-Red & Raman Optical Processes of Insulating Crystals. J. L. Birman. (Illus.). 570p. 1984. pap. 69.00 (0-387-13395-X) Spr-Verlag.

*Theory of Cubature Formulas. LC 97-17691. 1997. text ed. 350.00 (0-7923-4631-9) Kluwer Ac.

Theory of Cultural Value. Steven Connor. 1992. pap. text ed. 22.95 (0-631-18282-9) Blackwell Pubs.

Theory of Culture. Ed. by Richard Munch & Neil J. Smelser. 435p. 1994. 50.00 (0-520-07598-6); pap. 17.00 (0-520-07599-4) U CA Pr.

Theory of Culture. Raymond Tschumi. LC 74-81840. 296p. 1978. text ed. 21.95 (0-88357-003-3) NOK Pubs.

Theory of Culture Change: The Methodology of Multilinear Evolution. Julian H. Steward. LC 55-7372. 256p. (C). 1972. reprint ed. pap. text ed. 12.95 (0-252-00295-4) U of Ill Pr.

Theory of DC Circuits: Conventional-Flow Edition. Albert P. Malvino. (Illus.). 272p. (Orig.). (C). 1989. pap. text ed. 16.95 (1-56048-301-6, 301C) Malvino Inc.

Theory of DC Circuits: Electron-Flow Edition. Albert P. Malvino & Joanna M. Malvino. (Illus.). 272p. (Orig.). (C). 1989. pap. text ed. 16.95 (1-56048-300-8, 301E) Malvino Inc.

Theory of DC Circuits - Quik-Lab Two for DC Circuits: Electron-Flow Edition Package, 2 vols. Albert P. Malvino. (EGA - VGA - Hercules Graphics Ser.). (Illus.). 448p. (Orig.). (C). pap. text ed. 26.95 (1-56048-398-9, 3981); Bk. 1: 01/1989, 272p. write for info. (0-318-68171-4); Bk. 2: 1990, 176p. write for info. (0-318-68172-2) Malvino Inc.

Theory of DC Circuits - Quik-Lab(II) for DC Circuits Package: Conventional Flow Edition, 2 bks. Albert P. Malvino. (CGA, Hercules, EGA - VGA Graphics Ser.). (Illus.). 448p. (Orig.). (C). 1990. Set. pap. text ed. 26.95 (1-56048-396-2, 3981C) Malvino Inc.

Theory of Deductive Systems & Its Applications. S. Yu Maslov. Tr. by Michael Gelfond & Vladimir Lifschitz. 150p. 1987. 24.00 (0-262-13223-0) MIT Pr.

Theory of Degrees with Applications to Bifurcations & Differential Equations. Wieslaw Krazcewicz & Jianhong Wu. LC 96-33302. (Canadian Mathematical Society Ser& Advanced Texts). 328p. 1996. text ed. 89.95 (0-471-15740-6, Wiley-Interscience) Wiley.

Theory of Democracy Revisited, 2 vols. Giovanni Sartori. LC 86-31013. 560p. 1987. Set. text ed. 40.00 (0-934540-46-2) Chatham Hse Pubs.

Theory of Democracy Revisited, Vol. 1. Giovanni Sartori. LC 86-31013. 270p. 1987. pap. text ed. 19.95 (0-934540-47-0) Chatham Hse Pubs.

Theory of Democracy Revisited, Vol. 2. Giovanni Sartori. LC 86-31013. 295p. 1987. pap. text ed. 19.95 (0-934540-48-9) Chatham Hse Pubs.

Theory of Democratic Elitism: A Critique. Peter Bachrach. LC 80-5747. 125p. 1980. pap. text ed. 14.00 (0-8191-1185-6) U Pr of Amer.

Theory of Demonstration According to William Ockham. Damascene Webering. (Philosophy Ser.). xii, 186p. 1953. pap. 8.00 (1-57659-099-2) Franciscan Inst.

*Theory of Didactical Situations in Mathematics: Didactique des MathEmatiques, 1970-1990. Guy Brousseau & Nicolas Balacheff. LC 97-12155. (Mathematics Education Library). 1997. text ed. write for info. (0-7923-4526-6) Kluwer Ac.

Theory of Difference Equations: Numerical Methods & Applications. V. Lakshmikantham & D. Trigiante. (Mathematics in Science & Engineering Ser.). 242p. 1988. text ed. 80.00 (0-12-434100-4) Acad Pr.

Theory of Differential Equations with Unbounded Delay. V. Lakshmikantham. LC 94-27710. (Mathematics & Its Applications Ser.). 350p. (C). 1994. lib. bdg. 183.00 (0-7923-3003-X) Kluwer Ac.

Theory of Differentiation in Locally Convex Spaces. S. Yamamuro. LC 78-22099. (Memoirs Ser.: No. 17/212). 82p. 1981. reprint ed. pap. 21.00 (0-8218-2212-8, MEMO/17/212) Am Math.

Theory of Discourse. James L. Kinneavy. 496p. (C). 1980. reprint ed. pap. text ed. 11.95 (0-393-00919-X) Norton.

Theory of Discrete & Continuous Fourier Analysis. Weaver. LC 88-10820. 307p. 1989. text ed. 109.00 (0-471-62872-7) Wiley.

Theory of Dislocations. 2nd ed. John P. Hirth & Jens Lothe. LC 91-17004. 872p. 1991. reprint ed. text ed. 109.00 (0-89464-617-6) Krieger.

Theory of Distribution: A Nontechnical Introduction. Ian Richards & H. Youn. (Illus.). 157p. (C). 1990. text ed. 49.95 (0-521-37149-X) Cambridge U Pr.

Theory of Distributions. Al-Gwaiz. (Pure & Applied Mathematics Ser.: Vol. 159). 272p. 1992. 160.00 (0-8247-8672-6) Dekker.

Theory of Distributions: A Nontechnical Introduction. Ian Richards & Heekyung Youn. (Illus.). 160p. (C). 1995. pap. text ed. 20.95 (0-521-55890-5) Cambridge U Pr.

Theory of Distributions for Locally Compact Spaces. Leon Ehrenpreis. LC 52-42839. (Memoirs Ser.: No. 1/21). 80p. 1990. reprint ed. pap. 22.00 (0-8218-1221-1, MEMO/1/21) Am Math.

Theory of Dividends. Allen. (FB - Introduction to Finance Ser.). 1902. text ed. 62.95 (0-538-80270-7) S-W Pub.

Theory of Drama. Allardyce Nicoll. LC 66-29422. 1972. reprint ed. 23.95 (0-405-08818-3, Pub. by Blom Pubns UK) Ayer.

Theory of Drama: A Comparative Study of Aristotle & Bharata. R. N. Rai. (C). 1992. 29.50 (81-7054-155-7, Pub. by Classical Pub II) S Asia.

Theory of Duality & International Trade. Pasquale M. Sgro. LC 86-8575. 320p. (C). 1986. text ed. 40.00 (0-8147-7864-X) NYU Pr.

Theory of Duality in Mathematical Programming. M. Walk. (Illus.). 200p. 1989. 73.95 (0-387-82057-4) Spr-Verlag.

Theory of Dynamical Systems. D. J. Luo & L. B. Teng. (Advanced Series in Dynamical Systems). 280p. 1993. text ed. 61.00 (981-02-1268-2) World Scientific Pub.

Theory of Dynamical Systems & Its Applications to Nonlinear Problems. Ed. by H. Kawakami. 256p. 1984. 60.00 (9971-966-93-X) World Scientific Pub.

Theory of Earnings Distribution. Robert V. Weizsacker. 300p. (C). 1993. text ed. 59.95 (0-521-34294-5) Cambridge U Pr.

Theory of Earth Science. Wolf V. Engelhardt & Jorg Zimmermann. Tr. by Lenore Fischer. (Illus.). 384p. 1988. text ed. 105.00 (0-521-25989-4) Cambridge U Pr.

Theory of Econometrics: An Introductory Exposition of Econometric Methods. 2nd rev. ed. A. Koutsoyiannis. LC 76-53202. 681p. 1978. pap. 72.50 (0-389-20563-X, N6548) B&N Imports.

Theory of Economic Development: An Inquiry into Profits, Capital, Credit, Interest, & the Business Cycle. Joseph A. Schumpeter. Tr. by Redvers Opie. LC 34-38868. (Economic Studies: No. 46). 267p. 1934. 16.50 (0-674-87990-2) HUP.

Theory of Economic Development: An Inquiry into Profits, Capital, Credit, Interest & the Business Cycle. Joseph A. Schumpeter. Tr. by Redvers Opie. LC 79-67059. (Social Science Classics Ser.). 296p. 1983. pap. 24.95 (0-87855-698-2) Transaction Pubs.

Theory of Economic Dynamics: An Essay on Cyclical & Long-Run Changes in Capitalist Economy. 2nd ed. Michal Kalecki. LC 69-86244. (Illus.). 178p. 1969. 35.00 (0-678-06001-0) Kelley.

Theory of Economic Integration. Bela A. Balassa. LC 82-2971. (Irwin Series in Economics). xiv, 304p. 1982. reprint ed. text ed. 55.00 (0-313-23543-0, BATY, Greenwood Pr) Greenwood.

Theory of Economic Policy: Statics & Dynamics. A. J. Preston & A. R. Pagan. LC 81-10196. 400p. 1982. text ed. 80.00 (0-521-23366-6) Cambridge U Pr.

Theory of Education. Joseph D. Novak. LC 77-3123. 296p. 1986. pap. 15.95 (0-8014-9378-1) Cornell U Pr.

Theory of Education. Margaret Sutherland. (Effective Teacher Ser.). 192p. (Orig.). (C). 1988. pap. text ed. 14.36 (0-582-29722-2) Longman.

Theory of Education in Plato's Republic. (Works of John E. Adamson). xii, 258p. reprint ed. 44.00 (0-932051-56-1) Rprt Serv.

Theory of Education in the Republic of Plato. Richard L. Nettleship. LC 68-54676. (Classics in Education Ser.). 1968. pap. text ed. 6.00 (0-8077-1849-1) Tchrs Coll.

Theory of Education in the United States. Albert J. Nock. LC 72-89212. (American Education: Its Men, Institutions, & Ideas. Series 1). 1971. reprint ed. 16.95 (0-405-01451-1) Ayer.

Theory of Efficient Cooperation & Competition. Lester G. Telser. (Illus.). 320p. 1987. text ed. 80.00 (0-521-30619-1) Cambridge U Pr.

Theory of Elastic Stability. 2nd ed. Stephen P. Timoshenko & J. Gere. (Engineering Societies Monographs). (Illus.). 1961. text ed. write for info. (0-07-064749-6) McGraw.

Theory of Elasticity. V. Novozhilov & J. Lusher. LC 60-14992. 1961. 201.00 (0-08-009523-2, Pub. by Pergamon Repr UK) Franklin.

Theory of Elasticity. 3rd ed. L. D. Landau et al. Tr. by J. B. Sykes & W. H. Reid. (Course of Theoretical Physics Ser.: Vol. 7). (Illus.). 235p. 1986. pap. text ed. 37.00 (0-08-033916-6, Prgamon Press) Buttrwrth-Heinemann.

Theory of Elasticity. 3rd ed. Stephen P. Timoshenko & J. N. Goodier. LC 69-13617. (Engineering Societies Monographs). (Illus.). (C). 1970. text ed. write for info. (0-07-064720-8) McGraw.

Theory of Electric Polarization, Vol. 1: Dielectrics in Static Fields. 2nd ed. C. J. Bottcher et al. Ed. by P. Bordewijk & A. Rip. LC 72-83198. 378p. 1973. 255.75 (0-444-41019-8) Elsevier.

Theory of Electric Polarization, Vol. 2: Dielectrics in Time Dependent Fields. 2nd ed. C. J. Bottcher & P. Bordewijk. 562p. 1980. 334.00 (0-444-41579-3) Elsevier.

Theory of Electrical Filters. John D. Rhodes. LC 75-30767. 234p. reprint ed. pap. 66.70 (0-317-09071-2, 2022103) Bks Demand.

Theory of Electrical Transport in Semi-Conductors. B. R. Nag. 238p. 1972. 110.00 (0-08-016802-7, Pub. by Pergamon Repr UK) Franklin.

Theory of Electromagnetic Flow-Measurement. John A. Shercliff. (Cambridge Engineering Ser.). 158p. reprint ed. pap. 45.10 (0-317-09192-1, 2050749) Bks Demand.

Theory of Electromagnetic Wave Propagation. Charles H. Papas. 257p. 1988. reprint ed. pap. 6.95 (0-486-65678-0) Dover.

*Theory of Electromagnetic Waves. Hollis C. Chen. (Illus.). 467p. (C). 1992. reprint ed. text ed. 60.00 (1-878907-58-1) TechBooks.

Theory of Electromagnetism. Ian N. Sneddon. LC 62-19277. (International Series of Monographs on Pure & Applied Mathematics: Vol. 47). 1964. 355.00 (0-08-010090-2, Pub. by Pergamon Repr UK) Franklin.

Theory of Electron-Atom Collisions: Part 1: Potential Scattering. P. G. Burke & Charles J. Joachain. (Physics of Atoms & Molecules Ser.). 255p. 1994. 69.50 (0-306-44546-8, Plenum Pr) Plenum.

Theory of Elementary Gas Reaction Rates. D. Bunker & A. Dickenson. (International Encyclopedia of Physical Chemistry & Chemical Physics Ser.: Vol. 1, TP 19). 1966. 57.00 (0-08-011804-6, Pub. by Pergamon Repr UK) Franklin.

Theory of Energy Transfers & Conversions. Federico Grabiel. LC 67-23440. (Illus.). 231p. reprint ed. pap. 65.90 (0-317-07883-6, 2006350) Bks Demand.

Theory of English Lexicography 1530-1791. Tetsuro Hayashi. (Studies in the History of Linguistics: No. 18). xii, 168p. 1978. 43.00 (90-272-0959-6) Benjamins North Am.

Theory of Entire & Meromorphic Functions: Deficient & Asymptotic Values & Singular Directions. Kuan-hua Zhang. LC 93-43. (Translations of Mathematical Monographs: Vol. 122). 398p. 1993. 182.00 (0-8218-4589-6, MMONO/122) Am Math.

Theory of Environmental Policy. William J. Baumol & Wallace E. Oates. 288p. 1988. pap. text ed. 24.95 (0-521-31112-8) Cambridge U Pr.

Theory of Epistemic Rationality. Richard Foley. LC 86-31963. 352p. 1987. 52.50 (0-674-88276-8) HUP.

Theory of Error Correcting Codes, 2 Pts. in 1 vol. F. J. MacWilliams & N. J. Sloane. (Mathematical Library: Vol. 16). 782p. 1983. 82.00 (0-444-85193-3, North Holland) Elsevier.

Theory of Ethical Economy in the Historical School: Wilhelm Roscher, Lorenz von Stein, Gustav Schmoller, Wilhelm Dilthey & Contemporary Theory. Ed. by Peter Koslowski. LC 95-6437. (Studies in Economic Ethics & Philosophy). 1995. 107.00 (3-540-59070-6) Spr-Verlag.

Theory of Everything. Lisa Grunwald. 352p. 1992. reprint ed. pap. 9.99 (0-446-39368-1) Warner Bks.

Theory of Evolution. 3rd ed. John Maynard-Smith. LC 93-20358. (Canto Book Ser.). (Illus.). 368p. 1993. pap. text ed. 12.95 (0-521-45128-0) Cambridge U Pr.

Theory of Evolution & Dynamical Systems: Mathematical Aspects of Selection. J. Hofbauer & K. S. Sigmund. (London Mathematical Society Student Texts Ser.: No. 7). (Illus.). 350p. 1988. pap. text ed. 29.95 (0-521-35838-8) Cambridge U Pr.

Theory of Evolving Tonality. Joseph Yasser. (Illus.). 1932. 25.00 (0-8450-2599-6) Broude.

Theory of Evolving Tonality. Joseph Yasser. LC 74-34376. (Music Reprint Ser.). (Illus.). x, 381p. 1975. reprint ed. lib. bdg. 47.50 (0-306-70729-2) Da Capo.

Theory of Experiential Education. 3rd ed. Ed. by Karen Warren et al. 496p. 1994. 35.95 (0-7872-0262-2) Assn Exper Ed.

Theory of Externalities, Public Goods & Club Goods. Richard Cornes & Todd Sandler. (Illus.). 320p. 1986. 64.95 (0-521-30184-X); pap. text ed. 23.95 (0-521-31774-6) Cambridge U Pr.

An Asterisk (*) at the beginning of an entry indicates that the title is appearing in BIP for the first time.

Theory of Externalities, Public Goods & Club Goods. 2nd ed. Richard Cornes & Todd Sandler. LC 95-40500. (Illus.). 584p. (C). 1996. text ed. 69.95 (0-521-47148-6); pap. text ed. 27.95 (0-521-47718-2) Cambridge U Pr.

Theory of Extremal Problems for Univalent Functions of Class S, No. 101. K. I. Babenko. LC 74-23425. (Proceedings of the Steklov Institute of Mathematics Ser.). 327p. 1975. pap. 123.00 (0-8218-3001-5, STEKLO/101) Am Math.

***Theory of Film: The Redemption of Physical Reality.** Siegfried Kracauer. LC 97-23804. 1997. pap. text ed. 19.95 (0-691-03704-3) Princeton U Pr.

Theory of Film Language. Jerry L. Salvaggio. Ed. by Garth S. Jowett. LC 79-6684. (Dissertations on Film, 1980 Ser.). 1980. lib. bdg. 16.95 (0-405-12916-5) Ayer.

Theory of Film Practice. Noel Burch. Tr. by Helen R. Lane from FRE. LC 80-8676. (Illus.). 172p. (C). 1981. reprint ed. pap. text ed. 14.95 (0-691-00329-7) Princeton U Pr.

Theory of Finance. Eugene F. Fama & Merton H. Miller. 346p. (C). 1972. text ed. 52.00 (0-03-086732-0) Dryden Pr.

Theory of Finance. Martin. (C). 1988. teacher ed., pap. text ed. 36.75 (0-03-063856-9) HB Coll Pubs.

Theory of Finance: Being a Short Treatise on the Doctrine of Interest & Annuities-Certain. George King. Ed. by Richard P. Brief. LC 80-1506. (Dimensions of Accounting Theory & Practice Ser.). 1980. reprint ed. lib. bdg. 17.95 (0-405-13531-9) Ayer.

Theory of Finance: Evidence & Applications. John D. Martin et al. (Illus.). 656p. (C). 1988. text ed. 55.25 (0-03-063854-2) Dryden Pr.

Theory of Financial Decision Making. Jonathan E. Ingersoll, Jr. LC 86-1907. (Studies in Financial Economics). 496p. (C). 1987. 65.00 (0-8476-7359-6) Rowman.

Theory of Financial Management. Ezra Solomon. LC 63-8405. (Illus.). 1963. text ed. 37.50 (0-231-02604-8) Col U Pr.

Theory of Financial Markets & Information. J. A. Ohlson. 362p. 1987. 42.75 (0-444-01161-7) P-H.

Theory of Finite Linear Spaces: Combinatorics of Points & Lines. Lynn M. Batten & Albrecht Beutelspacher. 200p. (C). 1993. text ed. 52.95 (0-521-33317-2) Cambridge U Pr.

Theory of Fiscal Economics. Earl R. Rolph. LC 54-10435. (Publications of the Bureau of Business & Economic Research, University of California, California Library Reprint Ser.). (Illus.). 324p. reprint ed. pap. 92.40 (0-685-44495-3, 2031511) Bks Demand.

Theory of Fixed Point Classes. T. Kiang. (Illus.). xi, 175p. 1989. 94.95 (0-387-10819-X) Spr-Verlag.

Theory of Flight. Richard Von Mises. (Illus.). 629p. pap. 15.95 (0-486-60541-8) Dover.

Theory of Flight. Muriel Rukeyser. LC 74-144741. (Yale Series of Younger Poets: No. 34). reprint ed. 18.00 (0-404-53834-7) AMS Pr.

Theory of Flow & Transport in Porous Formations. Gedeon Dagan. (Illus.). 470p. 1989. 74.95 (0-387-51098-2) Spr-Verlag.

Theory of Forest Dynamics: The Ecological Implications of Forest Succession Models. Herman H. Shugart. (Illus.). 305p. 1984. 88.95 (0-387-96000-7) Spr-Verlag.

Theory of Formal Systems. R. M. Smullyan. 156p. 1985. pap. text ed. 29.95 (0-691-08047-X) Princeton U Pr.

***Theory of Fourier Series & Integrals.** Peter L. Walker. LC 85-17931. (Illus.). 200p. reprint ed. pap. 57.00 (0-608-05271-X, 2065809) Bks Demand.

Theory of Free Banking: A Study of the Supply of Money under Competitive Note Issue. George A. Selgin. 232p. 1988. 58.50 (0-8476-7578-5) Rowman.

Theory of Freedom. Stanley I. Benn. 448p. 1988. text ed. 85.00 (0-521-34260-0); pap. text ed. 36.95 (0-521-34802-1) Cambridge U Pr.

Theory of Full Employment. Y. S. Brenner & N. Brenner-Golomb. LC 95-42650. 232p. (C). 1996. lib. bdg. 89.95 (0-7923-9651-0) Kluwer Ac.

Theory of Function of Spaces. 1983. 129.00 (0-8176-1381-1) Spr-Verlag.

Theory of Function Spaces Two. Hans Triebel. (Monographs in Mathematics: Vol. 84). 380p. 1992. 149.50 (0-8176-2639-5) Spr-Verlag.

Theory of Functional Grammar, Pt. 1. Simon C. Dik. (Functional Grammar Ser.: No. 9). iv, 416p. 1989. pap. 29.95 (90-6765-432-9) Mouton.

Theory of Functions. 2nd ed. Edward C. Titchmarsh. 464p. 1976. 45.00 (0-19-853349-7) OUP.

Theory of Functions, 1. 2nd ed. Constantin Caratheodory. LC 60-16838. 22.95 (0-8284-0097-0) Chelsea Pub.

Theory of Functions, 2 vols, 1. Konrad Knopp. (Illus.). reprint ed. pap. 4.95 (0-486-60156-0) Dover.

Theory of Functions, 2. 2nd ed. Constantin Caratheodory. LC 60-16838. 24.95 (0-8284-0106-3) Chelsea Pub.

Theory of Functions, 2 vols, 2. Konrad Knopp. (Illus.). reprint ed. pap. text ed. 4.95 (0-486-60157-9) Dover.

Theory of Functions, 2 vols. in 1, Pts. I & II. unabridged ed. Konrad Knopp. Tr. by Frederick Bagemihl from GER. LC 96-12435. (Illus.). 320p. reprint ed. pap. text ed. 8.95 (0-486-69219-1) Dover.

Theory of Functions: Materials of the All-Union School on the Theory of Functions, Amberd, October 1987: Collection of Papers, Vol. 190. Steklov Institute of Mathematics Staff. 265p. 1992. pap. 195.00 (0-8218-3143-7, STEKLO/190) Am Math.

Theory of Functions & Its Applications. Ed. by Lev S. Pontryagin. LC 77-10017. (Proceedings of the Steklov Institute of Mathematics Ser.: No. 134). 458p. 1977. pap. 112.00 (0-8218-3034-1, STEKLO/134) Am Math.

Theory of Functions & Related Questions of Analysis. L. Kudryavtsev. LC 89-18114. (Proceedings of the Steklov Institute of Mathematics Ser.: Vol. 180). 283p. 1989. pap. 145.00 (0-8218-3128-3, STEKLO/180) Am Math.

Theory of Functions of a Complex Variable, 3 vols. in 1. 2nd ed. A. I. Markushevich. Tr. by Richard A. Silverman from RUS. LC 77-8515. 1977. text ed. 48.00 (0-8284-0296-5) Chelsea Pub.

Theory of Functions of a Real Variable. 2nd ed. R. L. Jeffery. (Mathematical Expositions Ser.: No. 6). 244p. reprint ed. pap. 69.60 (0-7837-0529-8, 2040857) Bks Demand.

Theory of Functions of a Real Variable. R. L. Jeffery. (Mathematics Ser.). 256p. 1985. reprint ed. pap. 6.95 (0-486-64781-1) Dover.

Theory of Functions on Complex Manifolds. Gennadi M. Henkin & Jurgen Leiterer. (Monographs in Mathematics). 240p. (C). 1983. text ed. 49.95 (3-7643-1477-X) Birkhauser.

Theory of Functions on Complexity. 1984. 127.50 (0-8176-1477-X) Birkhauser.

Theory of Fundamental Interactions. A. I. Aikhiezer & I. Yastrzhembsky. 500p. 1995. text ed. 82.00 (981-02-1666-1) World Scientific Pub.

Theory of Gambling & Statistical Logic. 2nd ed. Ed. by Richard A. Epstein. (Illus.). 465p. 1995. pap. text ed. 29.95 (0-12-240761-X) Acad Pr.

Theory of Games. Jianhua Wang. (Oxford Mathematical Monographs). (Illus.). 170p. 1988. 65.00 (0-19-853560-0) OUP.

Theory of Games & Economic Behavior. John Von Neumann & Oskar Morgenstern. LC 53-4426. 664p. 1953. pap. text ed. 29.95 (0-691-00362-9) Princeton U Pr.

Theory of Games & Statistical Decisions. David A. Blackwell & M. A. Girshick. 368p. (C). 1980. reprint ed. pap. 9.95 (0-486-63831-6) Dover.

***Theory of Games As a Tool for the Modern Philosopher Bound with an Empiricist's View of the Nature of Religious Belief: 1955 Edition.** R. B. Braithwaite. (Key Texts Ser.). 116p. 1996. reprint ed. pap. write for info. (1-85506-315-8) Bks Intl VA.

Theory of Games, Astrophysics, Hydrodynamics & Meteorology see Collected Works

Theory of Gauge Fields in Four Dimensions. H. Blaine Lawson, Jr. LC 85-441. (CBMS Regional Conference Series in Mathematics: No. 58). 101p. 1985. pap. text ed. 24.00 (0-8218-0708-0, CBMS/58) Am Math.

Theory of Gearing: The Mathematical Formulation & Theoretical Understanding of Spur, Helical, & Spiral Bevel Gears. 1991. lib. bdg. 88.95 (0-8490-4362-X) Gordon Pr.

Theory of Gene Frequencies see Evolution & the Genetics of Populations

Theory of General Economic Equilibrium. Andreu Mas-Colell. (Econometric Society Monographs). 369p. 1985. text ed. 74.95 (0-521-26514-2) Cambridge U Pr.

Theory of General Economic Equilibrium. Andreu Mas-Colell. (Econometric Society Monographs: No. 9). (Illus.). 398p. (C). 1990. pap. text ed. 32.95 (0-521-38870-8) Cambridge U Pr.

Theory of Generalized Spectral Operators, Vol. 9. I. Colojoara & C. Folias. LC 68-24488. (Mathematics & Its Applications Ser.). xvi, 232p. 1968. text ed. 287.00 (0-677-01480-5) Gordon & Breach.

Theory of Geostationary Satellites. Chong-Hung Zee. (C). 1989. lib. bdg. 171.50 (90-277-2636-1) Kluwer Ac.

Theory of German Word Order from the Renaissance to the Present. Aldo D. Scaglione. LC 80-16619. 241p. reprint ed. pap. 68.70 (0-7837-2920-0, 2057534) Bks Demand.

Theory of Global Random Search. Anatoly A. Zhiglijavsky. (C). 1991. lib. bdg. 178.50 (0-7923-1122-1) Kluwer Ac.

Theory of Graphs. Oystein Ore. LC 61-15687. (Colloquium Publications: Vol. 38). 270p. 1962. reprint ed. pap. 24.00 (0-8218-1038-3, COLL/38) Am Math.

Theory of Graphs & Its Applications. Claude Berg. Tr. by Alison Doig from FRE. LC 81-23719. x, 247p. 1982. reprint ed. text ed. 59.75 (0-313-23351-9, BETG, Greenwood Pr) Greenwood.

Theory of Grindability & the Communition of Binary Mixtures. K. Remenyi. 144p. (C). 1974. 30.00 (963-05-0231-3, Pub. by Akad Kiado HU) St Mut.

Theory of Ground Vehicles. 2nd ed. J. Y. Wong. LC 92-21523. 464p. 1993. text ed. 95.00 (0-471-52496-4) Wiley.

Theory of Ground Water Movement. P. Y. Polubarinova-Kochina. LC 62-12616. 635p. 1962. reprint ed. pap. 180.00 (0-7837-9328-6, 2060069) Bks Demand.

Theory of Group Representations. M. A. Naimark. (Illus.). 576p. 1982. 144.95 (0-387-90602-9) Spr-Verlag.

Theory of Group Representations & Applications. Asim O. Barut & R. Raczka. 740p. 1986. text ed. 99.00 (9971-5-0216-X); pap. text ed. 54.00 (9971-5-0217-8) World Scientific Pub.

Theory of Group Structures, 2 vols, Vol. 2. Mackenzie. 550p. 1976. Set. text ed. 164.00 (0-677-05330-4) Gordon & Breach.

Theory of Groups. 2nd ed. Marshall Hall, Jr. LC 75-42306. xiii, 434p. text ed. 19.95 (0-8284-0288-4) Chelsea Pub.

Theory of Groups. Ian D. MacDonald. LC 88-578. 262p. (C). 1988. reprint ed. lib. bdg. 29.50 (0-89464-287-1) Krieger.

Theory of Groups & Quantum Mechanics. Hermann Weyl. 1950. pap. text ed. 8.95 (0-486-60269-9) Dover.

Theory of Growth in a Corporate Economy: Management Preference, Research & Development & Economic Growth. Hiroyuki Odagiri. LC 80-23494. (Illus.). 256p. 1981. 69.95 (0-521-23132-9) Cambridge U Pr.

Theory of Hadrons & Light Front QCD, Light-Front Quantization & Non-Perturbative Dynamics. Stanislaw D. Glazek. 336p. 1995. text ed. 90.00 (981-02-2174-6) World Scientific Pub.

Theory of Harmony. Ernst Levy. LC 85-12604. (SUNY Series in Cultural Perspectives). (Illus.). 99p. 1985. text ed. 59.50 (0-87395-993-0); pap. text ed. 19.95 (0-87395-992-2) State U NY Pr.

Theory of Harmony. Arnold Schoenberg. Tr. by Roy E. Carter. 1983. pap. 19.95 (0-520-04944-6) U CA Pr.

Theory of Harmony. Matthew Shirlaw. LC 72-87348. (Music Reprint Ser.). 1969. reprint ed. lib. bdg. 49.50 (0-306-71658-5) Da Capo.

Theory of Heat. 3rd ed. James C. Maxwell. LC 77-173064. reprint ed. 29.50 (0-404-04277-5) AMS Pr.

Theory of Heat. 3rd ed. James C. Maxwell. LC 69-13993. 318p. 1970. reprint ed. text ed. 65.00 (0-8371-4097-8, MATH, Greenwood Pr) Greenwood.

Theory of Heat: Biomechanics, Biophysics, & Nonlinear Dynamics of Cardiac Function. Ed. by L. Glass et al. (Institute for Nonlinear Science Ser.). (Illus.). 656p. 1991. 69.95 (0-387-97483-0) Spr-Verlag.

Theory of Heat Radiation. Max Planck. (Illus.). 256p. reprint ed. pap. 7.95 (0-486-66811-8) Dover.

Theory of Heat Radiation - Waermestrahlung. Max Planck. Tr. by Morton Masius. (History of Modern Physics & Astronomy Ser.: No. 11). (Illus.). 224p. 1989. 45.00 (0-88318-597-0) Spr-Verlag.

Theory of Heavy Fermions & Valence Fluctuations. T. Kasuya & T. Saso. (Solid-State Sciences Ser.: Vol. 62). (Illus.). xii, 287p. 1985. 64.95 (0-387-15922-3) Spr-Verlag.

Theory of Hedge Investment. Brendan Brown. LC 82-5651. 240p. 1982. text ed. 29.95 (0-312-79783-4) St Martin.

Theory of Hegemonic Stability Changes in the International Economic Regimes. Robert O. Keohane. (CISA Working Papers: No. 22). 26p. (Orig.). 1980. pap. 15.00 (0-86682-021-3) Ctr Intl Relations.

Theory of History & Society. A. R. Gadolin. xx, 224p. 1987. pap. 72.00 (90-256-0906-6, Pub. by A M Hakkert NE) Benjamins North Am.

Theory of History in Ortega y Gasset: The Dawn of Historical Reason. John T. Graham. 392p. 1996. 44.95 (0-8262-1084-8) U of Mo Pr.

Theory of Holors: A Generalization of Tensors. Parry Moon & Domina E. Spencer. (Illus.). 330p. 1986. text ed. 100.00 (0-521-24585-0) Cambridge U Pr.

***Theory of Homogeneous Turbulence.** 197p. 1982. pap. text ed. 34.95 (0-521-04117-1) Cambridge U Pr.

Theory of Human Need. Len Doyal & Ian Gough. LC 91-18024. (Critical Perspectives Ser.). 365p. 1991. pap. 18.95 (0-89862-419-3) Guilford Pr.

Theory of Human Need. Len Doyal & Ian Gough. LC 91-18024. (Critical Perspectives Ser.). 365p. 1991. lib. bdg. 47.50 (0-89862-413-4) Guilford Pr.

Theory of Hydromagnetic Stability. Bhimsen K. Shivamoggi. x, 272p. 1986. text ed. 306.00 (2-88124-049-6) Gordon & Breach.

Theory of Implementation of Society. Corchon. 1996. text ed. 69.95 (0-312-15953-6) St Martin.

Theory of Impulsive Differential Equations. Ed. by V. Lakshmilcantham et al. 288p. (C). 1989. text ed. 74.00 (9971-5-0970-9) World Scientific Pub.

Theory of Incarnation. Bonnie Seefeldt. 17p. 1988. pap. 6.00 (1-884112-00-5) See More Bks.

Theory of Incentives in Regulation & Procurement. Jean-Jacques Laffont & Jean Tirole. (Illus.). 640p. 1993. 42.50 (0-262-12174-3) MIT Pr.

Theory of Income & Wealth Distribution. Ed. by Y. S. Brenner et al. LC 87-35308. 340p. 1988. text ed. 45.00 (0-312-01965-3) St Martin.

Theory of Incommensurate Crystals. V. L. Pokrovsky & A. L. Talapov. (Soviet Scientific Reviews, Section A, Physics Reviews Supplement Ser.: Vol. 1). 164p. 1984. text ed. 281.00 (3-7186-0134-6) Gordon & Breach.

Theory of Incompatibilities: A Conceptual Framework for Responding to the Educational Needs of Hispanic Americans. Jose A. Cardenas & Blandina Cardenas. 23p. (Orig.). 1977. pap. text ed. 2.50 (1-878550-06-3) Inter Dev Res Assn.

Theory of Incomplete Markets, Vol. 1. Michael Magill & Martine Quinzii. (Illus.). 504p. (C). 1996. 50.00 (0-262-13324-5) MIT Pr.

Theory of Indexing. Gerard Salton. (CBMS-NSF Regional Conference Series in Applied Mathematics: No. 18). v, 56p. (Orig.). 1975. pap. text ed. 16.00 (0-89871-015-4) Soc Indus-Appl Math.

Theory of Indian Music. Ram Avatar. (Illus.). 160p. 1980. 19.95 (0-940500-13-2) Asia Bk Corp.

Theory of Indian Music. Swarup Bishan. 233p. (C). 1987. 21.00 (0-8364-2081-0, Pub. by Mittal II) S Asia.

Theory of Indistinguishables: A Search for Explanatory Principles Below the Level of Physics. A. F. Parker-Rhodes. 230p. 1981. lib. bdg. 104.50 (90-277-1214-X, D Reidel) Kluwer Ac.

Theory of Individual Behavior. Robert Wichers. LC 96-26266. (Illus.). 209p. 1996. text ed. 49.95 (0-12-748450-7) Acad Pr.

Theory of Industrialism: Causal Analysis & Economic Plans. Johan Akerman. LC 80-21155. (Illus.). 332p. 1980. reprint ed. lib. bdg. 45.00 (0-87991-859-4) Porcupine Pr.

Theory of Inflation. Ed. by Michael Parkin. LC 94-13969. (International Library of Critical Writings in Economics Ser.: Vol. 41). 680p. 1994. 215.00 (1-85278-299-4) E Elgar.

***Theory of Inspiration.** Clark. LC 96-29805. 1997. text ed. 69.95 (0-7190-5064-2) St Martin.

Theory of Institutional Design. Ed. by Robert E. Goodin. (Theories of Institutional Design Ser.). (Illus.). 304p. (C). 1996. text ed. 49.95 (0-521-47119-2) Cambridge U Pr.

Theory of Instruction: Principles & Applications. rev. ed. S. Engelman & D. Carmine. LC 91-25887. (Illus.). 385p. (C). 1991. reprint ed. text ed. 40.00 (1-880183-80-3) ADI Pr.

Theory of Integro-Differential Equations. V. Lakshmikantham. 384p. 1995. text ed. 98.00 (2-88449-000-0) Gordon & Breach.

Theory of Intelligence: A Sensory-Rational View. Thorne Shipley. (Illus.). 116p. 1990. pap. 20.95 (0-398-06422-9) C C Thomas.

Theory of Intelligence: A Sensory-Rational View. Thorne Shipley. (Illus.). 116p. (C). 1990. text ed. 32.95 (0-398-05636-6) C C Thomas.

Theory of Inter-Sectoral Money Flows & Income Formation. John S. Chipman. LC 78-64212. (Johns Hopkins University. Studies in the Social Sciences. Thirtieth Ser. 1912: 2). 160p. 1982. reprint ed. 45.00 (0-404-61317-9) AMS Pr.

***Theory of Interacting Fermi System.** Philippe Nozieres. 1997. write for info. (0-201-32824-0) Addison-Wesley.

Theory of Interaction of Multilevel Systems with Quantized Fields. Ed. by V. I. Man'ko & M. A. Markov. (Proceedings of P. N. Lebedev Physics Institute Ser.: Vol. 209). 237p. (C). 1996. lib. bdg. 98.00 (1-56072-297-5) Nova Sci Pubs.

Theory of Interest. 2nd ed. Stephen G. Kellison. 448p. (C). 1991. text ed. 64.75 (0-256-09150-1) Irwin.

Theory of Interest & Life Contingencies, with Pension Applications: A Problem-Solving Approach. Michael M. Parmenter. LC 88-38947. (Illus.). 246p. (Orig.). 1988. pap. text ed. 47.50 (0-936031-04-2) Actex Pubns.

Theory of Intermolecular Forces. A. J. Stone. (International Series of Monographs on Chemistry: No. 32). (Illus.). 280p. 1996. 90.00 (0-19-855884-8) OUP.

Theory of International Law. G. I. Tunkin. Tr. by William E. Butler from RUS. LC 73-92258. 480p. 1974. 37.50 (0-674-88001-3) HUP.

***Theory of International Law at the Threshold of the 21st Century - Essays in Honour of Krzysztof Skubiszewski.** LC 96-54220. 1996. lib. bdg. 327.00 (90-411-0296-5) Kluwer Ac.

Theory of International Physical Education & Sports Studies for the Achievement of Peace. Noriaki Osada. 1991. 14.95 (0-533-09131-4) Vantage.

Theory of International Politics. Kenneth N. Waltz. (Illus.). 250p. (C). 1979. pap. text ed. write for info. (0-07-554852-6) McGraw.

Theory of International Prices: History, Criticism & Restatement. James W. Angell. LC 65-19644. (Reprints of Economic Classics Ser.). xiv, 571p. 1965. reprint ed. 57.50 (0-678-00094-8) Kelley.

Theory of International Trade. Avinash K. Dixit & V. D. Norman. (Cambridge Economic Handbook Ser.). 250p. 1980. pap. text ed. 24.95 (0-521-29969-1) Cambridge U Pr.

Theory of International Values. R. Parchure. 1994. write for info. (81-224-0664-5, Pub. by Wiley Estrn II) Franklin.

***Theory of Interplanetary Flights.** G. A. Gurzadyan. 1996. text ed. 120.00 (2-88449-074-4); pap. text ed. 44.00 (2-919875-15-9) Gordon & Breach.

Theory of Intuition in Husserl's Phenomenology. 2nd ed. Emmanuel Levinas. Tr. by Andre Orianne. LC 95-14655. (Studies in Phenomenology & Existential Philosophy). 163p. 1995. pap. text ed. 18.95 (0-8101-1281-7) Northwestern U Pr.

Theory of Intuition in Husserl's Phenomenology. Emmanuel Levinas. Tr. by Andre Orianne from FRE. (Studies in Phenomenology & Existential Philosophy). 163p. 1985. reprint ed. pap. 14.95 (0-8101-0708-2) Northwestern U Pr.

Theory of Investment Cycles in a Socialist Economy. Nikola Cobeljic & Radmila Stojanovic. Ed. by Jerzy Karcz. LC 68-14431. 174p. reprint ed. pap. 49.60 (0-317-41932-3, 2026140) Bks Demand.

Theory of Investment of the Firm. Friedrich A. Lutz & Vera C. Lutz. LC 69-13978. 253p. 1970. reprint ed. text ed. 59.75 (0-8371-1108-0, LUTI, Greenwood Pr) Greenwood.

***Theory of Investment Value.** John B. Williams. LC 97-60587. 648p. 1997. reprint ed. pap. 30.00 (0-87034-126-X) Fraser Pub Co.

Theory of Ionization of Atoms by Electron Impact. Raimonds Peterkops. Ed. by D. G. Hummer. Tr. by Elliot Aronson. LC 77-81310. (Illus.). 273p. reprint ed. pap. 77.90 (0-317-09233-2, 2012203) Bks Demand.

Theory of Irrationalities of the Third Degree. Boris N. Delone & D. K. Faddeev. Tr. by Emna Lehmer & Sue A. Walker from RUS. LC 63-21548. (Translations of Mathematical Monographs: Vol. 10). 531p. reprint ed. pap. 151.40 (0-7837-1634-6, 2041927) Bks Demand.

Theory of Island Biogeography. Roger H. MacArthur & Edward O. Wilson. (Monographs in Population Biology: Vol. 1). (Illus.). 218p. 1967. pap. text ed. 22.50 (0-691-08050-X) Princeton U Pr.

Theory of Jacobi Forms. Martin Eichler & Don Zagier. (Progress in Mathematics Ser.: No. 55). 154p. (C). 1985. 34.50 (0-8176-3180-1) Birkhauser.

Theory of Jets in an Ideal Fluid. Ian N. Sneddon. LC 66-17247. (International Series of Monographs on Pure & Applied Mathematics: Vol. 93). 1966. 185.00 (0-08-011706-6, Pub. by Pergamon Repr UK) Franklin.

Theory of Join Spaces: A Contemporary Approach to Convex Sets & Linear Geometry. W. Prenowitz & J. Jantosciak. (Undergraduate Texts in Mathematics Ser.). (Illus.). 1979. 54.95 (0-387-90340-2) Spr-Verlag.

Theory of Justice. John Rawls. LC 73-168432. (Illus.). 607p. 1971. 38.00 (0-674-88010-2); pap. text ed. 17.95 (0-674-88014-5) Belknap Pr.

Theory of Kinetics see Comprehensive Chemical Kinetics

Theory of Knowledge. Keith Lehrer. 212p. (C). 1990. pap. text ed. 22.50 (0-8133-0571-3) Westview.

Theory of Knowledge. 3rd ed. Roderick Chisholm. 144p. (C). 1988. pap. text ed. 16.80 (0-13-914177-4) P-H.

An Asterisk (*) at the beginning of an entry indicates that the title is appearing in BIP for the first time.

Theory of Knowledge. Leonard T. Hobhouse. LC 74-101094. reprint ed. 42.50 (0-404-03278-8) AMS Pr.

Theory of Knowledge. Charles A. Strong. LC 75-3405. reprint ed. 34.50 (0-404-59399-2) AMS Pr.

Theory of Knowledge: A Direct Realist Approach. Albert L. Hammond. Ed. by Gerald Hurwitz. LC 96-16487. (Illus.). 426p. 1996. lib. bdg. 54.00 (0-7618-0365-3) U Pr of Amer.

*Theory of Knowledge: A Thematic Introduction. Ed. by Paul K. Moser et al. 224p. (C). 1997. pap. text ed. 21.00 (0-19-509466-2) OUP.

*Theory of Knowledge: A Thematic Introduction. Ed. by Paul K. Moser et al. 224p. (C). 1997. text ed. 45.00 (0-19-509465-4) OUP.

Theory of Knowledge: Classical & Contemporary Readings. Louis P. Pojman. 556p. (C). 1993. text ed. 50.95 (0-534-17826-X) Wadsworth Pub.

Theory of Knowledge: The 1913 Manuscript. Bertrand Russell. Ed. by Elizabeth R. Eames & Kenneth Blackwell. 264p. (C). 1992. pap. 16.95 (0-415-08298-6, A7942) Routledge.

Theory of Knowledge: The 1913 Manuscript, Vol. 7. Elizabeth R. Eames & Kenneth Blackwell. (Collected Papers of Bertrand Russell). (Illus.). 314p. 1988. text ed. 171.50 (0-04-920073-9, A9415) Routledge Chapman & Hall.

*Theory of Knowledge: 1913 Manuscript, Vol. 7. Bertrand Russell. Ed. by Elizabeth Ramsden Eames. 314p. (C). 1988. text ed. 140.00 (0-415-10450-5) Routledge.

Theory of Knowledge & Existence. Walter T. Stace. LC 70-109852. 455p. 1970. reprint ed. text ed. 35.00 (0-8371-4343-8, STTK, Greenwood Pr) Greenwood.

Theory of Knowledge of Vital du Four. John E. Lynch. (Philosophy Ser.). 215p. 1972. pap. 17.00 (1-57659-103-4) Franciscan Inst.

Theory of Laminar Film Condensation. T. Fujii. (Illus.). 240p. 1991. 89.95 (0-387-97541-1) Spr-Verlag.

Theory of Laminar Flames. J. D. Buckmaster & G. S. Ludford. LC 81-21573. (Cambridge Monographs on Mechanics & Applied Mathematics). (Illus.). 250p. 1982. text ed. 80.00 (0-521-23929-X) Cambridge U Pr.

Theory of Language, Pts. 1 & 2. James Beattie. LC 78-147953. reprint ed. 61.50 (0-404-08201-7) AMS Pr.

*Theory of Language & Mind. Ermanno Bencivenga. LC 96-48498. 1997. write for info. (0-520-20791-2) U CA Pr.

Theory of Language, Culture & Human Behavior. Joe E. Pierce. 160p. 1972. 9.95 (0-913244-03-1) Hapi Pr.

Theory of Language Syntax: Categorical Approach. Urszula Wybraniec-Skardowska. (Nijhoff International Philosophy Ser.). 288p. 1991. lib. bdg. 113.50 (0-7923-1142-6, Pub. by Klwr Acad Pubs NE) Kluwer Ac.

Theory of Language. The Representational Function of Language. Karl Buhler. Tr. by Donald F. Goodwin from GER. LC 90-20219. (Foundations of Semiotics Ser.: Vol. 25). lxii, 508p. 1990. 148.00 (1-55619-200-2) Benjamins North Am.

Theory of Lattice-Ordered Groups. Michael R. Darnel. LC 94-35410. (Pure & Applied Mathematics Ser.: Vol. 187). 560p. 1994. 179.00 (0-8247-9326-9) Dekker.

Theory of Lattice-Ordered Groups. Valerii M. Kopytov. LC 94-37361. (Mathematics & Its Applications Ser.: Vol. 307). 416p. (C). 1994. lib. bdg. 194.00 (0-7923-3169-9) Kluwer Ac.

Theory of Latticed Plates & Shells, A plus IO. G. Ipshenichnov. (Advances in Mathematics Ser.). 324p. 1993. text ed. 74.00 (981-02-1049-3) World Scientific Pub.

Theory of Law. Philip Soper. LC 84-711. 200p. 1984. reprint ed. pap. 57.00 (0-7837-6092-2, 2059138) Bks Demand.

Theory of Learning: An Introduction. Julie Cotton. (The Theory of Training & Assessment Ser.). 128p. 1995. pap. 29.95 (0-7494-1479-0); pap. 29.95 (0-7494-1480-4) Taylor & Francis.

*Theory of Learning & Generalization: With Application to Neural Networks & Control Systems, Vol. XVIII. M. Vidyasagar. LC 96-49968. (Communications & Control Engineering Ser.). (Illus.). 393p. 1997. 79.95 (3-540-76120-9) Spr-Verlag.

Theory of Lebesgue Measure & Integration. S. Hartman & Jan Mikusinski. LC 60-14189. (International Series of Monographs on Pure & Applied Mathematics: Vol. 15). 1961. 76.00 (0-08-009525-9, Pub. by Pergamon Repr UK) Franklin.

Theory of Legal Argumentation. Robert W. Alexy. Tr. by D. Neil MacCormick & Ruth Adler. 344p. 1989. 85.00 (0-19-825503-9) OUP.

Theory of Legal Duties & Rights: An Introduction to Analytical Jurisprudence. William E. Hearn. viii, 401p. 1990. reprint ed. lib. bdg. 37.50 (0-8377-2244-6) Rothman.

Theory of Legal Science. Bert V. Roermund et al. 681p. 1984. lib. bdg. 204.50 (90-277-1834-2, D Reidel) Kluwer Ac.

Theory of Legislation. Jeremy Bentham. (Illus.). lii, 555p. 1987. reprint ed. 47.50 (0-8377-1947-X) Rothman.

Theory of Legislation: An Essay on the Dynamics of Public Mind. Elijah Jordan. LC 30-20688. 486p. reprint ed. pap. 138.60 (0-317-09406-8, 2011230) Bks Demand.

Theory of Lexical Phonology. K. P. Mohanan. 1986. pap. text ed. 57.00 (90-277-2124-6, Pub. by Klwr Acad Pubs NE) Kluwer Ac.

Theory of Lexical Phonology. K. P. Mohanan. 1986. lib. bdg. 118.50 (90-277-2226-9, Pub. by Klwr Acad Pubs NE) Kluwer Ac.

Theory of Lexical Phonology. K. P. Mohanan. 1987. pap. text ed. 23.00 (0-317-56507-9) Kluwer Ac.

Theory of Liberty: The Constitution & Minorities. H. N. Hirsch. LC 92-10561. (After the Law Ser.). 296p. (C). 1992. pap. 17.95 (0-415-90586-9, A7157, Routledge NY); text ed. 59.95 (0-415-90585-0, A7153, Routledge NY) Routledge.

Theory of Liberty, Legitimacy & Power: New Directions in the Intellectual & Scientific Legacy of Max Weber. Ed. & Contrib. by Vatro Murvar. (International Library of Sociology). 224p. 1985. 39.95 (0-7102-0355-1, RKP) Routledge.

Theory of Lie Groups. Claude C. Chevalley. (Mathematical Ser.: Vol. 8). 232p. 1946. text ed. 55.00 (0-691-08052-6) Princeton U Pr.

Theory of Limit Cycles. Yan-Qian et al. LC 86-14070. (Translations of Mathematical Monographs: Vol. 66). 435p. 1986. text ed. 175.00 (0-8218-4518-7, MMONO/66) Am Math.

*Theory of Linear Algebraic Equations with Random Coefficients. V. L. Girko. LC 96-28418. 1996. 120.00 (0-89864-078-4) Allerton Pr.

Theory of Linear & Integer Programming. Alexander Schrijver. LC 85-12314. (Discrete Mathematics Ser.). 471p. 1986. text ed. 298.00 (0-471-90854-1) Wiley.

Theory of Linear Economic Models. David Gale. (Illus.). xxii, 352p. 1989. pap. text ed. 17.95 (0-226-27884-0) U Ch Pr.

Theory of Linear Models. Bent Jorgensen. LC 93-7474. 232p. (gr. 13). 1993. text ed. 55.95 (0-412-04261-4) Chapman & Hall.

Theory of Linear Operations. Stefan Banach. (Mathematical Library: No. 38). 238p. 1987. 163.00 (0-444-70184-2, North Holland) Elsevier.

Theory of Linear Operators in Hilbert Space. N. I. Akhiezer & I. M. Glazman. Tr. by Merlynd Nestell from RUS. LC 93-6143. xiii, 365p. (ENG.). 1993. reprint ed. pap. 9.95 (0-486-67748-6) Dover.

Theory of Liquids. John G. Kirkwood. Ed. by B. Alder. (Documents on Modern Physics Ser.). (Illus.). 140p. (Orig.). (C). 1968. text ed. 178.00 (0-677-00350-1) Gordon & Breach.

Theory of Literary Production. Pierre Macherey. Tr. by Geoffrey Wall from FRE. 1978. pap. 15.95 (0-7100-0087-1) Routledge.

Theory of Literary Text. Antonio Garcia-Berrio. (Research in Text Theory Ser.: No. 17). x, 544p. (C). 1992. lib. bdg. 183.10 (3-11-012809-8, 39-92) De Gruyter.

Theory of Literature. rev. ed. Rene Wellek & Austin Warren. 375p. 1964. pap. 12.00 (0-15-689084-4, Harvest Bks) HarBrace.

Theory of Logical Calculi: Basic Theory of Consequence Operations. Ryszard Wojcicki. 492p. (C). 1988. lib. bdg. 162.50 (90-277-2785-6, Pub. by Klwr Acad Pubs NE) Kluwer Ac.

Theory of Lubrication: With Applications to Liquid- & Gas-Film Lubrication. Nicolae Tipei. Ed. by William A. Gross. xvi, 566p. 1962. 69.50 (0-8047-0028-1) Stanford U Pr.

Theory of Machines & Mechanisms, 2 Vols. 1979. Set. 40.00 (0-317-06827-X) ASME.

Theory of Machines & Mechanisms. Joseph E. Shigley & John J. Uiker. (Mechanical Engineering Ser.). (Illus.). 576p. 1980. text ed. write for info. (0-07-056884-7) McGraw.

Theory of Machines & Mechanisms. 2nd ed. Joseph E. Shigley & John J. Uicker. LC 94-19975. 1994. text ed. 68.13 (0-07-056930-4) McGraw.

Theory of Machines & Mechanisms, 2 Vols., Vol. 1. 1607p. 1979. 25.00 (0-685-73641-5, G00148) ASME.

Theory of Machines & Mechanisms, 2 Vols., Vol. 2. 1654p. 1979. 25.00 (0-685-73642-3, G00149) ASME.

Theory of Machines & Mechanisms: Solutions Manual. 2nd ed. Joseph E. Shigley & John J. Uicker. (Mechanical Engineering Ser.). 1994. pap. text ed. write for info. (0-07-056931-2) McGraw.

Theory of Macroscopic Systems. C. Ouwerkerk. (Illus.). 288p. 1991. pap. 34.00 (0-387-51575-5) Spr-Verlag.

Theory of Magnetic & Electric Susceptibilities for Optical Frequencies. Petar K. Anastasovski. 301p. (C). 1991. text ed. 125.00 (0-941743-83-7) Nova Sci Pubs.

Theory of Magnetic Neutron & Photon Scattering. Ewald Balcar & Stephen W. Lovesey. (Oxford Series on Neutron Scattering in Condensed Matter: No. 2). (Illus.). 236p. 1989. 65.00 (0-19-851006-3) OUP.

Theory of Magnetic Recording. H. Neal Bertram. (Illus.). 350p. (C). 1994. text ed. 85.00 (0-521-44512-4); pap. text ed. 38.95 (0-521-44973-1) Cambridge U Pr.

Theory of Magnetic Resonance. 2nd ed. Charles P. Poole & Horacio A. Farach. LC 86-11013. 359p. 1987. text ed. 145.00 (0-471-81530-6) Wiley.

Theory of Magnetically Confined Plasmas: Proceedings. Ed. by B. Coppi. (Commission of the European Communities Ser.: EUR 5737). (Illus.). 1979. pap. 236.00 (0-08-023434-8, Pub. by Pergamon Repr UK) Franklin.

Theory of Magnetism. Kei Yosida. LC 96-12857. (Solid-State Sciences Ser.: Vol. 122). 336p. 1996. 69.00 (3-540-60651-3) Spr-Verlag.

Theory of Magnetism I. D. C. Mattis. (Solid-State Sciences Ser.: Vol. 17). (Illus.). xv, 300p. 1988. 53.95 (0-387-18425-2) Spr-Verlag.

Theory of Magnetism II. D. C. Mattis. (Solid-State Sciences Ser.: Vol. 55). (Illus.). 190p. 1985. 69.00 (0-387-15025-0) Spr-Verlag.

Theory of Magnetism One: Statistics & Dynamics. (Solid-State Sciences Ser.: Vol. 17). (Illus.). 320p. 1981. 39.50 (0-387-10611-1) Spr-Verlag.

Theory of Magnetostatic Waves. Daniel D. Stancil. LC 92-38633. 232p. 1993. 59.95 (0-387-97969-7); write for info. (3-540-97969-7) Spr-Verlag.

Theory of Many-Particle Systems. I. P. Bazarov. Tr. by J. George Adashko. (AIP Translation Ser.). (Illus.). 312p. 1989. 75.00 (0-88318-601-2) Spr-Verlag.

Theory of Market Failure: A Critical Examination. Ed. by Tyler Cowen. 410p. (C). 1988. lib. bdg. 72.50 (0-913969-13-3, G Mason Univ Pr) Univ Pub Assocs.

Theory of Market Strategy. Richard J. Geruson. (Illus.). 272p. 1992. 45.00 (0-19-506800-9) OUP.

Theory of Markets. Michael Allingham. LC 89-29088. 128p. 1990. text ed. 45.00 (0-312-04062-8) St Martin.

Theory of Markets. Tun Thin. LC 60-5398. (Economic Studies: No. 114). (Illus.). 128p. 1960. 8.95 (0-674-88080-3) HUP.

Theory of Markets: Trade & Space-Time Patterns of Price Fluctuations: A Study in Analytical Economics. Bertrand M. Roehner. LC 95-5873. (Advances in Spatial & Network Economics Ser.). 1995. 125.00 (3-540-58815-9) Spr-Verlag.

Theory of Mathematical Structures. Jiri Adamek. 1983. lib. bdg. 182.50 (90-277-1459-2) Kluwer Ac.

Theory of Matrices. 2nd ed. Peter Lancaster & Miron Tismenetsky. (Computer Science & Applied Mathematics Ser.). (C). 1985. text ed. 77.00 (0-12-435560-9) Acad Pr.

Theory of Matrices. Sam Perlis. xiv, 237p. reprint ed. pap. 7.95 (0-486-66810-X) Dover.

Theory of Matrices, 2 Vols, 1. Felix R. Gantmacher. LC 59-11779. 27.50 (0-8284-0131-4) Chelsea Pub.

Theory of Matrices, 2 Vols, 2. Felix R. Gantmacher. LC 59-11779. 24.50 (0-8284-0133-0) Chelsea Pub.

Theory of Matrices in Numerical Analysis. Alston S. Householder. LC 74-83763. 288p. (C). 1975. reprint ed. pap. text ed. 7.95 (0-486-61781-5) Dover.

Theory of Matrix Structural Analysis. J. S. Przemieniecki. 480p. 1985. reprint ed. pap. 10.95 (0-486-64948-2) Dover.

Theory of Matroids. Ed. by Neil White. (Encyclopedia of Mathematics & Its Applications Ser.: No. 26). 448p. 1986. 69.95 (0-521-30937-9) Cambridge U Pr.

Theory of Measurements. Lucius Tuttle & John Satterly. 347p. reprint ed. pap. 98.90 (0-317-09118-2, 2014443) Bks Demand.

Theory of Mental Tests. Harold Gulliksen. 512p. (C). 1987. reprint ed. text ed. 89.95 (0-8058-0024-7) L Erlbaum Assocs.

Theory of Microwave Remote Sensing. 2nd ed. Jin A. Kong et al. LC 84-17397. (Remote Sensing & Image Processing Ser.). 613p. 1985. text ed. 129.95 (0-471-88860-5) Wiley.

Theory of Middle English Alliterative Meter with Critical Applications. Robert W. Sapora, Jr. LC 77-89927. 1977. 20.00 (0-910956-75-8, SAM1); pap. 12.00 (0-910956-61-8) Medieval Acad.

Theory of Military Compensation & Personnel Policy. Beth J. Asch & John T. Warner. LC 94-16956. 1994. pap. 15.00 (0-8330-1544-3, MR-439-OSD) Rand Corp.

Theory of Modelling & Simulation. Bernard P. Zeigler. LC 84-19443. 460p. (C). 1984. reprint ed. lib. bdg. 53.50 (0-89874-808-9) Krieger.

Theory of Modulation. Thorvald Otterstrom. LC 74-34379. (Music Reprint Ser.). (Illus.). viii, 162p. (ENG & GER.). 1975. reprint ed. lib. bdg. 29.50 (0-306-70721-7) Da Capo.

Theory of Moduli. Ed. by Edoardo Sernesi. (Lecture Notes in Mathematics Ser.: Vol. 1337). viii, 232p. 1988. 38.95 (0-387-50080-4) Spr-Verlag.

Theory of Molecular Relaxation: Applications in Chemistry & Biology. Francis K. Fong. LC 75-17814. (Illus.). 332p. reprint ed. pap. 94.70 (0-317-09104-2, 2017400) Bks Demand.

Theory of Monads. Herbert W. Carr. LC 75-3101. reprint ed. 32.50 (0-404-59098-5) AMS Pr.

Theory of Money. Jurg Niehans. LC 77-17247. (Illus.). 1980. text ed. 47.50 (0-8018-2055-3); pap. text ed. 16.95 (0-8018-2372-2) Johns Hopkins.

Theory of Money & Banks Investigated. George Tucker. LC 63-23038. (Reprints of Economic Classics Ser.). viii, 444p. 1964. reprint ed. 49.50 (0-678-00032-8) Kelley.

Theory of Money & Credit. Ludwig Von Mises. Tr. by H. E. Batson from GER. LC 79-25752. 544p. 1981. reprint ed. 20.00 (0-913966-70-3); reprint ed. pap. 10.00 (0-913966-71-1) Liberty Fund.

Theory of Money & Financial Institutions, Vol. 1. Martin Shubik. (Illus.). 600p. 1997. 50.00 (0-262-19344-2) MIT Pr.

Theory of Monopolistic Competition: A Re-Orientation of the Theory of Value. 8th ed. Edward H. Chamberlin. LC 63-649. (Economic Studies: No. 38). 410p. 1962. 27.50 (0-674-88125-7) HUP.

Theory of Moral Sentiments. 6th ed. Adam Smith. (C). 1986. reprint ed. pap. text ed. 14.95 (0-935005-67-6); reprint ed. lib. bdg. 24.95 (0-935005-66-8) Lincoln-Rembrandt.

Theory of Moral Sentiments: Glasgow Edition. Adam Smith. LC 81-23693. 422p. 1984. pap. 7.50 (0-86597-012-2) Liberty Fund.

Theory of Morality. Alan Donagan. LC 76-25634. 292p. 1979. pap. text ed. 12.95 (0-226-15567-6, P838) U Ch Pr.

Theory of Morals. Richard Hildreth. LC 69-16311. xix, 272p. 1971. reprint ed. 45.00 (0-678-00827-2) Kelley.

Theory of Morals. Richard Hildreth. (Notable American Authors Ser.). 1992. reprint ed. lib. bdg. 75.00 (0-7812-3126-4) Rprt Serv.

Theory of Moves. Steven J. Brams. (Illus.). 260p. (C). 1993. text ed. 49.95 (0-521-45226-0); pap. text ed. 18.95 (0-521-45867-6) Cambridge U Pr.

Theory of Multicodimensional (n plus l)-Webs. Vladislav V. Goldberg. (C). 1988. lib. bdg. 234.00 (90-277-2756-2) Kluwer Ac.

Theory of Multicultural Counseling & Therapy. Derald W. Sue et al. (Counseling Ser.). 265p. (C). 1996. text ed. 48.95 (0-534-34037-7) Brooks-Cole.

Theory of Multinational Enterprise. Jean-Francois Hennart. 208p. (C). 1982. text ed. 39.50 (0-472-10017-3) U of Mich Pr.

*Theory of Multinational Enterprises: The Selected Scientific Papers of Alan M. Rugman, Vol. 1. Alan M. Rugman. (Illus.). 320p. (C). 1996. 80.00 (1-85898-409-2) E Elgar.

Theory of Multiobjective Optimization. Yoshikazu Sawaragi et al. (Mathematics in Science & Engineering Ser.). 1985. text ed. 101.00 (0-12-620370-9) Acad Pr.

Theory of Multiparticle Production Processes. Yu P. Nikitin & I. L. Rosental. (Studies in High Energy Physics: Vol. 6). 344p. 1988. 366.00 (3-7186-4809-1) Gordon & Breach.

Theory of Multiphoton Processes. Farhad H. Faisal. (Physics of Atoms & Molecules Ser.). 410p. 1986. 105.00 (0-306-42317-0, Plenum Pr) Plenum.

Theory of Music. Franchino Gaffurio. Ed. by Claude V. Palisca. Tr. & Intro. by Walter K. Kreyszig. LC 92-33709. (Music Theory Translation Ser.). (Illus.). 240p. (C). 1993. text ed. 40.00 (0-300-05497-1) Yale U Pr.

Theory of Music for Young Musicians. M. Sharp. 57p. 1991. reprint ed. text ed. 59.00 (0-7812-9322-7) Rprt Serv.

Theory of Musical Semiotics. Eero Tarasti. LC 93-47889. (Advances in Semiotics Ser.). 368p. (C). 1994. 39.95 (0-253-35649-0) Ind U Pr.

*Theory of Nationhood. Heater. LC 97-13023. 1997. text ed. 59.95 (0-312-17596-5) St Martin.

Theory of Natural Monopoly. William W. Sharkey. LC 82-1136. (Illus.). 240p. 1982. pap. text ed. 26.95 (0-521-27194-0) Cambridge U Pr.

Theory of Nets: Flows in Networks. Chen Wai-Kai. LC 89-16721. 493p. 1990. text ed. 121.00 (0-471-85148-5) Wiley.

Theory of Neutralization & the Archiphoneme in Functional Phonology. Tsutomu Akamatsu. LC 87-28723. (Current Issues in Linguistic Theory Ser.: No. 43). xxi, 533p. (C). 1988. 130.00 (90-272-3537-6) Benjamins North Am.

Theory of Neutron Star Magnetospheres. F. Curtis Michel. (Theoretical Astrophysics Ser.). (Illus.). 532p. 1990. pap. text ed. 42.00 (0-226-52331-4); lib. bdg. 96.00 (0-226-52330-6) U Ch Pr.

Theory of NMR Parameters. Isal Ando & Graham A. Webb. 1984. text ed. 119.00 (0-12-056820-9) Acad Pr.

Theory of Nonlinear Age-Dependent Population Dynamics. Webb. (Pure & Applied Mathematics Ser.: Vol. 89). 312p. 1985. 145.00 (0-8247-7290-3) Dekker.

Theory of Nonlinear Lattices. 1988. 48.95 (0-387-18327-2) Spr-Verlag.

Theory of Nonlinear Lattices. Morikazu Toda. (Solid-State Sciences Ser.: Vol. 20). (Illus.). 220p. 1981. pap. 51.00 (0-387-10224-8) Spr-Verlag.

Theory of Nonstationary Quantum Oscillators: Proceedings of the Lebedev Physics Institute, Vol. 198. Ed. by M. A. Markov. (Proceedings of the Lebedev Physics Institute Ser.: Vol. 198). 181p. (C). 1992. lib. bdg. 125.00 (1-56072-076-X) Nova Sci Pubs.

Theory of Nuclear Magnetic Relaxation in Liquids. J. R. McConnell. (Illus.). 200p. 1987. text ed. 85.00 (0-521-32112-3) Cambridge U Pr.

Theory of Nuclear Reactions. Peter Frobrich & Richard Lipperheide. (Oxford Studies in Nuclear Physics: Vol. 18). (Illus.). 488p. 1996. 115.00 (0-19-853783-2) OUP.

Theory of Nuclear Reactions. Ed. by A. G. Sitenko & O. D. Kocherga. 636p. (C). 1990. text ed. 90.00 (9971-5-0481-2); pap. text ed. 44.00 (9971-5-0482-0) World Scientific Pub.

Theory of Nuclear Structure & Reactions: Proceedings of the Second La Rabida International Summer School on Nuclear Physics, Huelva, Spain, June 23-July 6, 1985. Ed. by M. Lozano & G. Madurga. 650p. 1986. text ed. 146.00 (9971-5-0074-4) World Scientific Pub.

*Theory of Nucleus: Nuclear Structure & Nuclear Interaction. A. G. Sitenko & V. K. Tartakovski. LC 96-52452. (Fundamental Theories of Physics Ser.). 1997. text ed. write for info. (0-7923-4423-5) Kluwer Ac.

Theory of Numbers. 2nd ed. George B. Mathews. LC 61-17958. 18.95 (0-8284-0156-X) Chelsea Pub.

Theory of Numbers. Pure Mathematics Symposium Staff. Ed. by A. L. Whiteman. LC 65-17382. (Proceedings of Symposia in Pure Mathematics Ser.: Vol. 8). 216p. 1965. reprint ed. pap. 38.00 (0-8218-1408-7, PSPUM/8) Am Math.

Theory of Numbers: A Text & Source Book of Problems. Andrew Adler & John E. Coury. LC 94-41865. 320p. 1995. 56.25 (0-86720-472-9) Jones & Bartlett.

Theory of Numbers, Mathematical Analysis & Their Applications. Ed. by N. N. Bogolyubov et al. LC 79-20552. (Proceedings of the Steklov Institute of Mathematics Ser.: No. 142). 289p. 1979. pap. 113.00 (0-8218-3042-2, STEKLO/142) Am Math.

Theory of Numbers, Mathematical Analysis & Their Applications. N. N. Bogolyubov & K. K. Mardzhanishvili. LC 83-22405. (Proceedings of the Steklov Institute of Mathematics Ser.: Vol. 157). 248p. 1983. pap. 96.00 (0-8218-3076-7, STEKLO/157) Am Math.

Theory of Objects. Martin Abadi & Luca Cardelli. LC 96-17038. (Monographs in Computer Science). 312p. 1996. 39.95 (0-387-94775-2) Spr-Verlag.

Theory of Oceanic Circulation As Developed in the U. S. S. R. over the Past Fifty Years. S. F. Grace. (Publications Scientifiques Ser.: No. 28). write for info. (0-614-17811-8) Intl Assoc Phys Sci Ocean.

An Asterisk (*) at the beginning of an entry indicates that the title is appearing in BIP for the first time.

Theory of Oligopoly with Multi-Product Firms. K. Okuguchi & Ferenc Szidarovszky. (Lecture Notes in Economics & Mathematical Systems Ser.: Vol. 342). v, 167p. 1990. 29.90 (*0-387-52567-X*) Spr-Verlag.

Theory of Operators. V. A. Sadovnichii. LC 90-40970. (Contemporary Soviet Mathematics Ser.). (Illus.). 364p. 1990. 105.00 (*0-306-11028-8*, Plenum Pr) Plenum.

Theory of Optical Communications. Alan R. Mickelson. 1992. text ed. write for info. (*0-442-00714-0*) Van Nos Reinhold.

***Theory of Optical Processes in Semiconductors: Bulk & Microstructures.** Prasanta K. Basu. (Semiconductor Science & Technology Ser.: No. 4). (Illus.). 480p. 1998. 125.00 (*0-19-851788-2*) OUP.

Theory of Optimal Designs. K. K. Shah & Bikas K. Sinha. (Lecture Notes in Statistics Ser.: Vol. 54). viii, 171p. 1989. 34.95 (*0-387-96991-8*) Spr-Verlag.

Theory of Optimal Search. 2nd rev. ed. Lawrence D. Stone. Ed. by John D. Kettelle. (Topics in Operations Research Ser.). xvii, 279p. 1989. 35.00 (*1-877640-03-4*) INFORMS.

Theory of Optimal Stopping. Y. S. Chow. 1991. pap. 6.95 (*0-486-66650-6*) Dover.

Theory of Optimization & Optimal Control for Nonlinear Evolution & Singular Operator Equations. Mieczyslaw Altman. 292p. (C). 1990. text ed. 48.00 (*981-02-0326-8*) World Scientific Pub.

Theory of Oral Composition: History & Methodology. John M. Foley. LC 87-45402. (Folkloristics Ser.). 186p. 1988. 35.00 (*0-253-34260-0*); pap. 11.95 (*0-253-20465-8*) Ind U Pr.

Theory of Orbits: Integrable Systems & Non-perturbative Methods. D. Boccaletti & G. Pucacco. (Astronomy & Astrophysics Library: Vol.1). 412p. 1996. 69.00 (*3-540-58963-5*) Spr-Verlag.

***Theory of Orbits: Perturbative & Geometrical Methods, Vol. 2.** D. Boccaletti. (Theory of Orbits Ser.). 1997. 69.00 (*3-540-60355-7*) Spr-Verlag.

Theory of Ordinary Differential Equations. John Charles Burkhill. LC 76-369325. (Longman Mathematical Texts Ser.). 130p. reprint ed. pap. 37.10 (*0-317-08520-4*, 2013563) Bks Demand.

Theory of Ordinary Differential Equations. Earl A. Coddington & Norman Levinson. LC 84-4438. 444p. (C). 1984. reprint ed. lib. bdg. 51.00 (*0-89874-755-4*) Krieger.

Theory of Organizational Structure. Marshall W. Meyer. LC 76-56415. (Studies in Sociology). 1977. pap. text ed. 3.95 (*0-672-61193-7*, Bobbs) Macmillan.

Theory of Orlicz Spaces. M. M. Rao & Z. D. Ren. (Pure & Applied Mathematics Ser.: Vol. 146). 472p. 1991. 199.00 (*0-8247-8478-2*) Dekker.

Theory of Oscillations. V. I. Zubov. (Series on Optimization). 550p. 1998. text ed. 86.00 (*981-02-0978-9*) World Scientific Pub.

Theory of Oscillators. Alexander Andronov et al. (Illus.). 1966. 370.00 (*0-08-009981-5*, Pub. by Pergamon Repr UK) Franklin.

Theory of Oscillators. Alexander Andronov & A. A. Vitt. LC 63-19610. 1966. 370.00 (*0-08-013729-6*, Pub. by Pergamon Repr UK) Franklin.

Theory of Oscillators. A. A. Andronov et al. xxxii, 815p. 1987. reprint ed. pap. 19.95 (*0-486-65508-3*) Dover.

Theory of Parody: The Teachings of Twentieth-Century Art Forms. Linda Hutcheon. (Illus.). 192p. (C). 1985. pap. 13.95 (*0-416-37090-X*, NO. 4091) Routledge Chapman & Hall.

***Theory of Partial Algebraic Operations.** LC 97-2589. 1997. text ed. 225.00 (*0-7923-4609-2*) Kluwer Ac.

Theory of Partial Coherence. Mark J. Beran & George B. Parrent. 207p. reprint ed. pap. 59.00 (*0-317-08514-X*, 2010137) Bks Demand.

Theory of Partial Differential Equations. Sigeru Mizohata. LC 72-83593. 350p. 1973. 79.95 (*0-521-08727-9*) Cambridge U Pr.

Theory of Particle Interactions. V. V. Belokurov & D. V. Shirov. Tr. by P. Millard from RUS. (Translation Ser.). (Illus.). 224p. 1990. 77.00 (*0-88318-715-9*) Am Inst Physics.

Theory of Particulate Processes: Analysis & Techniques of Continuous Crystallization. 2nd ed. Ed. by Alan D. Randolph & Maurice A. Larsen. 369p. 1988. text ed. 102.00 (*0-12-579652-8*) Acad Pr.

***Theory of Parties & Electoral Systems.** Richard S. Katz. LC 80-8019. 167p. 1980. reprint ed. pap. 47.60 (*0-608-03705-2*, 2064530) Bks Demand.

Theory of Party Competition. David B. Robertson. LC 74-23542. 220p. reprint ed. pap. 62.70 (*0-685-20753-6*, 2030394) Bks Demand.

Theory of Pay. Adrian Wood. LC 78-1038. 261p. reprint ed. pap. 74.40 (*0-685-20580-0*, 2030630) Bks Demand.

Theory of Peasant Cooperatives. Alexander V. Chayanov. 252p. 1991. 68.00 (*0-8142-0566-6*) Ohio St U Pr.

Theory of Peasant Economy. Alexander V. Chayanov. LC 85-40758. 400p. 1986. reprint ed. 32.50 (*0-299-10570-9*); reprint ed. pap. text ed. 17.50 (*0-299-10574-1*) U of Wis Pr.

Theory of Perceptions. Ed. by George Pitcher. LC 73-120759. 250p. reprint ed. pap. 71.30 (*0-317-10596-5*, 2011399) Bks Demand.

Theory of Performing Arts. Andre Helbo. LC 87-14584. (Critical Theory Ser.: No. 5). viii, 153p. (C). 1987. 48.00 (*1-55619-014-X*) Benjamins North Am.

Theory of Periodic Relativity: Treatise on Vedanta, Physics, & Cosmology. Vikram H. Zaveri. (Illus.). vi, 58p. (Orig.). (C). 1996. pap. text ed. 8.00 (*0-9652280-0-2*) Chamunda Bks.

Theory of Personality & Individual Differences: Factors, Systems, & Processes. Joseph R. Royce & D. Arnold Powell. (Illus.). 272p. (C). 1983. text ed. 46.00 (*0-13-914473-0*) P-H.

Theory of Personality Development. Luciano L'Abate. Ed. by Charles H. Bryson. LC 93-12795. (Personality Processes Ser.). 313p. 1993. text ed. 60.00 (*0-471-30303-8*) Wiley.

Theory of Phase Transition. Ya G. Sinai. 164p. 1982. 79.00 (*0-08-026469-7*, C111, D125, Pub. by Pergamon Repr UK) Franklin.

Theory of Photons & Electrons: Second Corrected Printing. 2nd rev. ed. J. M. Jauch & Fritz Rohrlich. LC 75-8890. (Texts & Monographs in Physics). (Illus.). 533p. 1985. 75.95 (*0-387-07295-0*) Spr-Verlag.

Theory of Phrase Markers & the Extended Base. Robert A. Chametzky. LC 95-26184. (SUNY Series in Linguistics). 206p. (C). 1996. text ed. 54.50 (*0-7914-2971-7*); pap. text ed. 17.95 (*0-7914-2972-5*) State U NY Pr.

***Theory of Physical & Technical Measurement.** J. Piotrowski. (Fundamental Studies in Engineering: Vol. 14). 306p. 1992. 195.25 (*0-444-98693-6*) Elsevier.

Theory of Physical Chemistry Processes at a Gas-Solid Interface. Yu K. Tovbin. 349p. 1991. 109.00 (*0-8493-7133-3*, Q) CRC Pr.

Theory of Piezoelectric Plates & Shells. Rogacheva. 272p. 1994. 159.95 (*0-8493-4459-X*) CRC Pr.

Theory of Planetary Atmospheres: An Introduction to Their Physics & Chemistry. 2nd ed. Joseph W. Chamberlain & Donald M. Hunten. (International Geophysics Ser.). 481p. 1989. reprint ed. pap. text ed. 59.00 (*0-12-167252-2*) Acad Pr.

Theory of Planning. John Sillince. 230p. 1986. text ed. 68.95 (*0-566-05231-8*, Pub. by Avebury Pub UK) Ashgate Pub Co.

Theory of Plasticity & Limit Design of Plates. Z. Sobotka. (Studies in Applied Mechanics: No. 18). 600p. 1989. 228.25 (*0-444-98907-2*) Elsevier.

Theory of Plates & Shells. 2nd ed. Stephen P. Timoshenko & S. Woinowsky-Krieger. (Engineering Societies Monographs). (Illus.). 1959. text ed. write for info. (*0-07-064779-8*) McGraw.

Theory of Poetry. Lascelles Abercrombie. LC 69-17712. 1969. reprint ed. 30.00 (*0-8196-0223-X*) Biblo.

Theory of Poetry. Lascelles Abercrombie. 1988. reprint ed. lib. bdg. 49.00 (*0-7812-0110-1*) Rprt Serv.

Theory of Poetry. Lascelles Abercrombie. LC 76-131602. 222p. 1924. reprint ed. 11.00 (*0-403-00489-6*) Scholarly.

Theory of Poetry in England: Its Development in Doctrines & Ideas from the 16th to the 19th Century. R. R. Cowl. LC 75-90366. 334p. 1970. reprint ed. 50.00 (*0-87753-009-2*) Phaeton.

Theory of Poetry in England from the 16th to the 19th Century. Richard P. Cowl. 1972. 59.95 (*0-8490-1190-6*) Gordon Pr.

Theory of Point Estimation. Lehmann. (Wadsworth & Brooks-Cole Advanced Books & Software). 528p. (C). 1991. text ed. 54.75 (*0-534-15978-8*) Chapman & Hall.

***Theory of Point Estimation.** Lehmann. (C). (gr. 13 up). 1991. text ed. 63.95 (*0-412-07231-9*) Chapman & Hall.

***Theory of Point Estimation.** E. L. Lehmann. LC 97-10650. 1997. write for info. (*0-387-98209-4*) Spr-Verlag.

Theory of Poker. 3rd ed. David Sklansky. 242p. 1994. pap. text ed. 29.95 (*1-880685-00-0*) Two Plus NV.

Theory of Political Choice Behavior. Bruce I. Newman & Jagdish N. Sheth. LC 86-15152. (Praeger Series in Public & Nonprofit Sector Marketing). 199p. 1987. text ed. 49.95 (*0-275-92187-5*, C2187, Praeger Pubs) Greenwood.

Theory of Political Coalitions. William H. Riker. 1962. 59.50 (*0-685-26647-8*) Elliots Bks.

Theory of Political Coalitions. William H. Riker. LC 84-684. xii, 300p. (C). 1984. reprint ed. text ed. 69.50 (*0-313-24299-2*, RITH, Greenwood Pr) Greenwood.

Theory of Political Decision Modes: Intraparty Decision Making in Switzerland. Jurg Steiner & Robert H. Dorff. LC 79-16390. 259p. reprint ed. pap. 73.90 (*0-7837-2455-1*, 2042608) Bks Demand.

Theory of Political Economy. 5th ed. William S. Jevons. LC 65-18334. (Reprints of Economic Classics Ser.). lxiv, 324p. 1965. reprint ed. 45.00 (*0-678-00084-0*) Kelley.

Theory of Political Economy. W. Stanley Jevons. 278p. 1986. reprint ed. pap. 13.95 (*0-935005-74-9*) Lincoln-Rembrandt.

Theory of Political Economy: Commentaries by Marshall, Cairnes, Newcomb, Cliffe Leslie & Wicksteed. W. Stanley Jevons. LC 95-78028. (Foundations of Mathematical Economics Ser.: Vol. 2). 248p. (C). 1996. 44.95 (*1-887585-02-8*) James & Gordon.

***Theory of Politics.** Kukathas. 1990. pap. text ed. write for info. (*0-582-86806-8*, Pub. by Longman UK) Longman.

Theory of Politics. Richard Hildreth. LC 69-16312. 274p. 1969. reprint ed. 45.00 (*0-678-00518-4*) Kelley.

Theory of Politics. Richard Hildreth. (Notable American Authors Ser.). 1992. reprint ed. lib. bdg. 75.00 (*0-7812-3128-0*) Rprt Serv.

Theory of Polymer Dynamics. M. Doi & S. F. Edwards. (International Series of Monographs on Physics). (Illus.). 408p. 1988. pap. 55.00 (*0-19-852033-6*) OUP.

Theory of Popular Elasticity: Proceedings of the CISM, Department of Mechanics of Deformable Bodies, 1970. CISM (International Center for Mechanical Sciences), Department for Mechanics of Deformable Bodies Staff. Ed. by Wojoiech K. Nowacki. (CISM Publications: No. 25). (Illus.). 286p. 1974. 47.95 (*0-387-81078-1*) Spr-Verlag.

Theory of Population Genetics & Evolutionary Ecology: An Introduction. Jonathan Roughgarden. LC 95-20698. 612p. (C). 1995. text ed. 55.00 (*0-13-441965-0*) P-H.

Theory of Potential & Spherical Harmonics. Wolfgang Sternberg & Turner L. Smith. LC 44-9717. (Mathematical Expositions Ser.: No. 3). 322p. reprint ed. pap. 91.80 (*0-317-09115-8*, 2014421) Bks Demand.

Theory of Povery & Social Exclusion. Bill Jordan. 280p. 1996. pap. 27.95 (*0-7456-1694-1*) Blackwell Pubs.

Theory of Povery & Social Exclusion. Bill Jordan. 280p. 1996. 57.95 (*0-7456-1693-3*) Blackwell Pubs.

***Theory of Predicates.** Farrell Ackerman & Gert Webelhuth. (Lecture Notes Ser.). 500p. (C). 1997. pap. text ed. 27.95 (*1-57586-086-4*) CSLI.

***Theory of Predicates.** Farrell Ackerman & Gert Webelhuth. (Lecture Notes Ser.). 500p. (C). 1997. text ed. 69.95 (*1-57586-087-2*) CSLI.

Theory of Price. 4th ed. George J. Stigler. (Illus.). 384p. (C). 1986. text ed. 89.00 (*0-02-417400-9*, Macmillan Coll) P-H.

Theory of Price Control: The Classic Account. John Kenneth Galbraith. 95p. 1980. 15.95 (*0-674-88170-2*) HUP.

Theory of Price Control & Black Markets. John Butterworth. 233p. 1994. 59.95 (*1-85628-601-0*, Pub. by Avebury Pub UK) Ashgate Pub Co.

Theory of Price Uncertainty, Production, & Profit. Clement A. Tisdell. LC 68-20881. 207p. 1968. reprint ed. pap. 59.00 (*0-7837-9462-2*, 2060204) Bks Demand.

Theory of Pricing & Monetary Economics. Ed. by R. N. Banerjee. (C). 1989. 40.00 (*0-89771-425-3*, Pub. by Current Dist II) St Mut.

***Theory of Probability.** 6th ed. Gnedenko. 1996. 69.00 (*2-88449-233-X*) Gordon & Breach.

***Theory of Probability.** 6th ed. Boris V. Gnedenko. Tr. by Igor A. Ushakov. 1996. text ed. 64.95 (*90-5699-585-5*) Gordon & Breach.

Theory of Probability: A Critical Introductory Treatment, 2 vols. B. DeFinetti. 675p. 1990. pap. text ed. 78.00 (*0-471-58882-2*) Wiley.

Theory of Probability: A Critical Introductory Treatment, Vol. 1. Bruno De Finetti. Tr. by Antonio Machi & Adrian Smith. LC 73-10744. (Wiley Series in Probability & Mathematical Statistics). (Illus.). 320p. reprint ed. pap. 91.20 (*0-8357-6297-1*, 2035058) Bks Demand.

Theory of Probability Vol. 1: A Critical Introductory Treatment. Bruno De Finetti. (Wiley Classics Library). 300p. 1990. pap. text ed. 64.95 (*0-471-92611-6*) Wiley.

Theory of Probability Vol. 2: A Critical Introductory Treatment. Bruno De Finetti. (Wiley Series in Probability & Mathematical Statistics). (Illus.). 393p. reprint ed. pap. 112.10 (*0-8357-8634-X*, 2035058) Bks Demand.

Theory of Probability Vol. 2: A Critical Introductory Treatment, Vol. 2. Ed. by Bruno De Finetti. (Wiley Classics Library). 375p. 1990. pap. text ed. 64.95 (*0-471-92612-4*) Wiley.

Theory of Probability - an Introduction. Ed. by P. Mukhopadhyay. (C). 1989. 60.00 (*0-89771-399-0*, Pub. by Current Dist II) St Mut.

Theory of Probability & the Elements of Statistics, with Answers to the Exercises. 5th ed. B. V. Gnedenko. Tr. by Bernard Seckler from RUS. LC 61-13496. 529p. (C). 1988. 23.95 (*0-8284-1132-8*, 132) Chelsea Pub.

Theory of Probability for Clinical Diagnostic Testing. Maxwell & Eiki Satake. 123p. (C). 1993. student ed. 13.84 (*1-56870-062-8*) RonJon Pub.

Theory of Process One: Prelude: Search for a Paradigm. Ed. by Joan L. Schleicher. (Broadside Editions Ser.). (Illus.). 51p. (Orig.). (C). 1991. pap. 5.95 (*0-931191-12-2*) Rob Briggs.

Theory of Process 2: Major Themes in the Reflexive Universe. Ed. by Joan L. Schleicher. (Broadside Editions Ser.). (Illus.). 51p. (Orig.). (C). 1991. pap. text ed. 5.95 (*0-931191-13-0*) Rob Briggs.

Theory of Production: A Long-Period Analysis. Heinz D. Kurz & Neri Salvadori. (Illus.). 592p. (C). 1995. text ed. 64.95 (*0-521-44325-3*) Cambridge U Pr.

***Theory of Production: A Long-Period Analysis.** Heinz D. Kurz & Neri Salvadori. 592p. 1997. pap. text ed. 24.95 (*0-521-58867-7*) Cambridge U Pr.

Theory of Production: Tasks, Processes, & Technical Practices. Roberto Scazzieri. LC 92-32577. (Illus.). 328p. (C). 1993. 65.00 (*0-19-828373-3*, Old Oregon Bk Store) OUP.

Theory of Production & Cost. Gunter U. Fandel. (Illus.). xv, 405p. 1991. 130.95 (*0-387-54342-2*) Spr-Verlag.

Theory of Production for the Financial Firm. Diana Hancock. 176p. (C). 1991. lib. bdg. 61.00 (*0-7923-9140-3*) Kluwer Ac.

Theory of Profit. Donald M. Lamberton. LC 70-1657. vii, 211p. 1965. 35.00 (*0-678-06259-5*) Kelley.

Theory of Profits. Adrian J. Wood. (Reprints of Economic Classics Ser.). (Illus.). viii, 184p. 1993. reprint ed. lib. bdg. 35.00 (*0-678-01469-8*) Kelley.

Theory of Projection in Syntax. Naoki Fukui. Ed. by Masayoshi Shibatani. LC 94-36031. (Studies in Japanese Linguistics). 160p. 1995. text ed. 49.95 (*1-881526-35-6*); pap. text ed. 24.95 (*1-881526-34-8*) CSLI.

Theory of Projection in Syntax. Naoki Fukui. 1995. pap. 29.95 (*0-521-52634-5*) Cambridge U Pr.

Theory of Property. Stephen R. Munzer. (Cambridge Studies in Philosophy & Law). (Illus.). 450p. (C). 1990. pap. text ed. 32.95 (*0-521-37886-9*) Cambridge U Pr.

Theory of Property Rights: With Application to the California Gold Rush. John R. Umbeck. LC 81-1141. (Illus.). 168p. 1981. reprint ed. pap. 47.90 (*0-608-00173-2*, 2060955) Bks Demand.

Theory of Prose. Viktor Shklovsky. Tr. by Benjamin Sher from RUS. LC 90-2714. 240p. 1991. pap. 14.95 (*0-916583-64-3*) Dalkey Arch.

Theory of Pseudo-Rigid Bodies. H. Cohen & R. G. Muncaster. (Tracts in Natural Philosophy Ser.: Vol. 33). (Illus.). 210p. 1988. 84.95 (*0-387-96635-8*) Spr-Verlag.

Theory of Psychoanalytic Technique. 2nd ed. Karl A. Menninger. LC 94-71264. 224p. 1995. pap. 40.00 (*1-56821-266-6*) Aronson.

Theory of Psychological Dispositions see Yale Psychological Studies, N.S.

Theory of Public Bureaucracy: Politics, Personality, & Organization in the State Department. Donald P. Warwick et al. LC 75-4907. 264p. 1979. pap. 14.50 (*0-674-88195-8*) HUP.

Theory of Public Bureaucracy: Politics, Personality, & Organization in the State Department. Donald P. Warwick et al. LC 75-4907. 264p. reprint ed. pap. 75.30 (*0-7837-3857-9*, 2043679) Bks Demand.

Theory of Public Choice, II. James M. Buchanan & Robert D. Tollison. 512p. (C). 1984. pap. text ed. 26.95 (*0-472-08041-5*) U of Mich Pr.

Theory of Public Opinion. Francis G. Wilson. LC 74-33748. 308p. 1975. reprint ed. text ed. 59.75 (*0-8371-7980-7*, WITP, Greenwood Pr) Greenwood.

Theory of Public Utility Pricing. Stephen Brown & David Sibley. 216p. 1986. text ed. 74.95 (*0-521-30626-4*) Cambridge U Pr.

Theory of Public Utility Pricing. Stephen Brown & David Sibley. 216p. 1986. pap. text ed. 23.95 (*0-521-31400-3*) Cambridge U Pr.

Theory of Quanta. Iwo Bialyncki-Birula et al. Tr. by Anna M. Furdyna. (Illus.). 448p. (C). 1992. text ed. 58.00 (*0-19-507157-3*) OUP.

***Theory of Quantaloids.** Kimmo I. Rosenthal. (Pitman Research Notes in Mathematics Ser.). 1996. pap. 37.48 (*0-582-29440-1*) Longman.

Theory of Quantum Liquids, Vol. 1. David Pines. (C). 1994. pap. 44.95 (*0-201-40774-4*) Addison-Wesley.

Theory of Quantum Liquids: Normal Fermi Liquids, Vol. I. David Pines & Philippe Nozieres. (Classics Ser.). (Illus.). 384p. (C). 1989. 49.95 (*0-201-09429-0*, Adv Bk Prog) Addison-Wesley.

Theory of Radiation Processes in Metal Solid Solutions. Yu V. Trushin. 257p. 1995. 79.00 (*1-56072-260-6*) Nova Sci Pubs.

Theory of Radicals. Ed. by L. Marki & R. Wiegandt. (Colloquia Mathematica Societatis Janos Bolyai Ser.: Vol. 61). 310p. 1993. 197.75 (*0-444-81528-7*, North Holland) Elsevier.

Theory of Random Determinants. V. L. Girko. (C). 1990. lib. bdg. 358.00 (*0-7923-0233-8*) Kluwer Ac.

Theory of Reading. Ed. by Frank Gloversmith. LC 84-280. 264p. 1984. 58.50 (*0-389-20467-6*, 08028) B&N Imports.

Theory of Real Time Computing. Ron Koymans. (C). 1992. text ed. write for info. (*0-201-56531-5*) Addison-Wesley.

Theory of Reasoned Action: Its Application to AIDS-Preventive Behavior. Ed. by Deborah J. Terry et al. LC 93-34087. (International Series in Experimental Social Psychology: No. 28). 362p. 1994. 59.95 (*0-08-041932-1*, Prgamon Press) Buttrwrth-Heinemann.

Theory of Reconstruction from Image Motion. Stephen Maybank. Ed. by T. S. Huang et al. LC 92-17979. (Information Sciences Ser.: Vol. 28). (Illus.). 264p. 1992. 75.95 (*0-387-55537-4*) Spr-Verlag.

Theory of Recursive Functions & Effective Computability. Hartley Rogers, Jr. 504p. (Orig.). 1987. pap. 23.50 (*0-262-68052-1*) MIT Pr.

Theory of Reflectance & Emittance Spectroscopy. Bruce Hapke. LC 92-40729. (Topics in Remote Sensing Ser.: No. 3). (Illus.). 300p. (C). 1993. text ed. 130.00 (*0-521-30789-9*) Cambridge U Pr.

***Theory of Relational Databases.** David Maier. LC 82-2518. 653p. 1983. reprint ed. pap. 180.00 (*0-608-03561-0*, AU00480) Bks Demand.

Theory of Relativity. Arnold Sommerfeld. xiv, 241p. 1981. reprint ed. pap. 6.95 (*0-486-64152-X*) Dover.

Theory of Relativity Based on Physical Reality. L. Janossy. 318p. (C). 1971. 57.00 (*963-05-8888-9*, Pub. by Akad Kiado HU) St Mut.

Theory of Religion. Georges Bataille. Tr. by Robert Hurley from FRE. LC 88-20591. 126p. 1989. 23.95 (*0-942299-08-6*); pap. 11.95 (*0-942299-09-4*) Zone Bks.

Theory of Religion. Rodney Stark & William S. Bainbridge. 388p. (C). 1996. pap. text ed. 17.95 (*0-8135-2330-3*) Rutgers U Pr.

Theory of Religious Thought: The Principles Underlying Forms of Knowledge, Behavior & Social Relationship in Traditional Society. K. S. Bose. 1991. text ed. 22.50 (*81-207-1325-7*, Pub. by Sterling Pubs II) Apt Bks.

Theory of Remainders. Andrea Rothbart. 1995. pap. 19.95 (*0-939765-82-9*, G168) Janson Pubns.

Theory of Republican Character & Related Essays. Wendell J. Coats, Jr. LC 93-29627. 1994. 33.50 (*0-945636-58-X*) Susquehanna U Pr.

Theory of Resonance Linear Accelerators, Vol. 5. I. M. Kapchinskiy. Tr. by S. J. Amoretty from RUS. (Accelerators & Storage Rings Ser.: Vol. 5). xiv, 398p. 1985. text ed. 499.00 (*3-7186-0233-4*) Gordon & Breach.

Theory of Resonances: Principles & Applications. V. I. Kukulin et al. (C). 1989. lib. bdg. 158.50 (*90-277-2364-8*) Kluwer Ac.

Theory of Retracts. Sze-Tsen Hu. LC 64-25182. 234p. reprint ed. 66.70 (*0-685-16216-8*, 2027597) Bks Demand.

Theory of Revolution in the Young Marx. Michael Lowy. (C). 1996. pap. 16.50 (*1-899438-20-3*, Pub. by Porcupine Bks UK) Humanities.

Theory of Rings. Nathan Jacobson. LC 43-15310. (Mathematical Surveys & Monographs: No. 2). 150p. 1943. reprint ed. pap. 42.00 (*0-8218-1502-4*, SURV/2) Am Math.

Theory of Robot Control. Carlso A. Canudas De Witt et al. LC 96-289. (Communications & Control Engineering Ser.). 392p. 1996. 89.50 (*3-540-76054-7*) Spr-Verlag.

Theory of Robotic Manipulators. Yoshihiko Nakamura. (Illus.). 224p. (C). 1991. text ed. 74.25 (*0-201-15198-7*) Addison-Wesley.

Theory of Role Strain. William J. Goode. (Reprint Series in Social Sciences). (C). 1993. reprint ed. pap. text ed. 1.00 (*0-8290-3745-4*, S-402) Irvington.

Theory of Rotating Diatomic Molecules. Masataka Mizushima. LC 74-34080. 543p. 1978. 42.50 (*0-471-61187-5*, Wiley) Krieger.

Theory of Rotating Fluids. rev. ed. Harvey P. Greenspan. LC 68-12058. (Illus.). 404p. 1990. reprint ed. 29.00 (*0-9626998-0-2*) Breukelen Pr.

Theory of Rotating Stars. Jean-Louis Tassoul. LC 78-51198. (Princeton Series in Astrophysics). 523p. 1978. reprint ed. pap. 149.10 (*0-7837-9291-3*, 2060030) Bks Demand.

Theory of S-R Compatibility. Ed. by Bernhard Hommel & W. Prinz. Date not set. write for info. (*0-614-17900-9*) Elsevier.

Theory of Satellite Geodesy & Gravity Field Determination. Ed. by Fernandno Sanso & Reiner Rummel. (Lecture Notes in Earth Sciences Ser.: Vol. 25). (Illus.). xii, 491p. 1989. 79.95 (*0-387-51528-3*) Spr-Verlag.

Theory of Science. George Gale. (Illus.). 1979. text ed. write for info. (*0-07-022680-6*) McGraw.

Theory of Scientific Method. rev. ed. William Whewell. LC 88-37200. (HPC Classics Ser.). 372p. (C). 1989. reprint ed. pap. 16.95 (*0-87220-082-5*); reprint ed. lib. bdg. 34.95 (*0-87220-083-3*) Hackett Pub.

Theory of Sediment. Steve McCaffery. 160p. 1991. pap. 13.95 (*0-88922-299-1*) SPD-Small Pr Dist.

Theory of Seismic Diffractions. Kamill Klem-Musator. Ed. by Larry Lines & Franta Hron. (Open File Publications: No. 1). (Illus.). 410p. 1994. pap. 94.00 (*1-56080-074-7*, 755) Soc Expl Geophys.

Theory of Seismic Imaging. John A. Scales. LC 95-7372. (Lecture Notes in Earth Sciences Ser.: Vol. 55). 1995. write for info. (*0-387-59051-X*) Spr-Verlag.

Theory of Seismic Imaging. A. Adolf Seilacher. (Lecture Notes in Earth Sciences Ser.: Vol. 55). (Illus.). xvi, 291p. 1995. 97.95 (*3-540-59051-X*) Spr-Verlag.

Theory of Semiotics. Umberto Eco. LC 74-22833. (Advances in Semiotics Ser.). 368p. 1976. 35.00 (*0-253-35955-4*) Ind U Pr.

Theory of Semiotics. Umberto Eco. LC 74-22833. (Advances in Semiotics Ser.). 368p. 1978. pap. 13.95 (*0-253-20217-5*, MB-217) Ind U Pr.

Theory of Sensitivity in Dynamic Systems: An Introduction. Mansour Eslami. LC 94-19386. 618p. 1994. 129.00 (*0-387-54761-4*) Spr-Verlag.

Theory of Sets. E. Kamke. Tr. by Frederick Bagemihl. 1950. pap. 6.95 (*0-486-60141-2*) Dover.

Theory of Sets of Points. 2nd ed. William H. Young & Grace C. Young. LC 75-184793. 330p. 1972. text ed. 19.50 (*0-8284-0259-0*) Chelsea Pub.

***Theory of Sex Allocation.** Eric L. Charnov. LC 82-47586. (Monographs in Population Biology: Vol. 18). 367p. 1982. reprint ed. pap. 104.60 (*0-608-03384-7*, 2063992) Bks Demand.

Theory of Sex Allocation: MPB. E. L. Charnov. 355p. 1982. pap. text ed. 26.95 (*0-691-08312-6*) Princeton U Pr.

Theory of Ship Wave Resistance for Unsteady Motion in Still Water. A. N. Shebalov. (University of Michigan, Dept. of Naval Architecture & Marine Engineering, Report Ser.: No. 67). 16p. reprint ed. pap. 25.00 (*0-317-28264-6*, 2022628) Bks Demand.

Theory of Simple Liquids. 2nd ed. J. P. Hansen & Ian R. McDonald. 556p. (C). 1990. reprint ed. pap. text ed. 69.00 (*0-12-323852-8*) Acad Pr.

Theory of Simple Liquids. 2nd ed. Jean P. Hansen & Ian R. McDonald. 547p. 1987. text ed. 195.00 (*0-12-323851-X*) Acad Pr.

Theory of Single & Multiple Interfaces: The Method of Surface Green Function Matching. F. Garcia-Moliner & V. R. Velasco. 500p. (C). 1992. text ed. 86.00 (*981-02-0818-9*) World Scientific Pub.

Theory of Singular Boundary Value Problems. Donal O'Regan. 168p. 1994. text ed. 48.00 (*981-02-1760-9*) World Scientific Pub.

Theory of Singular Perturbations. E.M. De Jager. 1996. write for info. (*0-614-17899-1*, North Holland) Elsevier.

***Theory of Singular Perturbations.** E. M. De Jager & Jiang Furu. LC 96-43440. (North-Holland Series in Applied Mathematics & Mechanics). 352p. 1996. 153.25 (*0-444-82170-8*) Elsevier.

Theory of Singularities & Its Applications. V. Arnol'd. LC 90-45636. (Advances in Soviet Mathematics Ser.: Vol. 1). 333p. 1990. 130.00 (*0-8218-4100-9*, ADVSOV/1) Am Math.

Theory of Singularities & Its Applications. V. I. Arnold. (Lezione Fermiane Ser.). (Illus.). 120p. (C). 1991. pap. text ed. 23.95 (*0-521-42280-9*) Cambridge U Pr.

Theory of Slow Atomic Collisions. E. E. Nikitin & S. Y. Umanskii. (Chemical Physics Ser.: Vol. 30). (Illus.). 440p. 1984. 103.95 (*0-387-12414-4*) Spr-Verlag.

Theory of Social Action. Raimo Tuomela. 544p. 1984. lib. bdg. 182.00 (*90-277-1703-6*, D Reidel) Kluwer Ac.

Theory of Social Action: The Correspondence of Alfred Schutz & Talcott Parsons. Ed. by Alfred Schutz. LC 77-15761. (Indiana University Studies in Phenomenology & Existential Philosophy). reprint ed. pap. 42.80 (*0-317-27818-5*, 2056036) Bks Demand.

***Theory of Social & Economic Organization.** Max Weber. 1997. pap. 19.95 (*0-684-83640-8*) Free Pr.

Theory of Social & Economic Organization. Max M. Weber. 1964. pap. 19.95 (*0-02-934930-3*, Free Press) Free Pr.

Theory of Social Integration. Peter M. Blau. (Reprint Series in Social Sciences). (C). 1993. reprint ed. pap. text ed. 1.00 (*0-8290-2704-1*, S-30) Irvington.

Theory of Social Interaction. Jonathan H. Turner. LC 87-32531. xiv, 225p. 1988. 42.50 (*0-8047-1463-0*); pap. 12.95 (*0-8047-1479-7*) Stanford U Pr.

Theory of Social Involvement: A Case Study in the Anthropology of Religion, State, & Society. Sunday A. Aigbe. LC 92-28390. 280p. (C). 1993. lib. bdg. 52.50 (*0-8191-8873-5*) U Pr of Amer.

Theory of Social Revolution. Brooks Adams. (Principle Works of Brooks Adams). 1989. reprint ed. lib. bdg. 79.00 (*0-7812-0285-X*) Rprt Serv.

Theory of Social Situations: A Game-Theoretic Approach. Joseph Greenberg. (Illus.). 197p. (C). 1990. text ed. 69.95 (*0-521-37425-1*); pap. text ed. 18.95 (*0-521-37689-0*) Cambridge U Pr.

Theory of Societal Constitutionalism: Foundations of a Non-Marxist Critical Theory. David Sciulli. (American Sociological Assn. Rose Monograph Ser.). (Illus.). 432p. (C). 1991. text ed. 65.00 (*0-521-41040-1*) Cambridge U Pr.

Theory of Solitons: The Inverse Scattering Method. S. P. Novikov et al. Ed. by V. E. Zakharov. LC 83-21051. (Contemporary Soviet Mathematics Ser.). 288p. 1984. 95.00 (*0-306-10977-8*, Consultants) Plenum.

Theory of Solitons in Inhomogeneous Media. Fatkhulla K. Abdullaev. LC 93-29288. (Series in Nonlinear Science). 182p. 1994. text ed. 87.95 (*0-471-94299-5*) Wiley.

Theory of Solutions. John G. Kirkwood. Ed. by Z. W. Salsburg & J. Poirier. (Documents on Modern Physics Ser.). 302p. (Orig.). (C). 1968. text ed. 276.00 (*0-677-01030-3*) Gordon & Breach.

Theory of Solutions & Stereo-Chemistry. Ed. by I. Bernard Cohen. LC 80-2103. (Development of Science Ser.). (Illus.). 1981. lib. bdg. 38.95 (*0-405-13868-7*) Ayer.

Theory of Sound, 2 vols., 1. Strutt Rayleigh. pap. 10.95 (*0-486-60292-3*) Dover.

Theory of Sound, 2 vols., 2. Strutt Rayleigh. pap. 10.95 (*0-486-60293-1*) Dover.

Theory of Space Plasma Microinstabilities. S. Peter Gary. (Cambridge Atmospheric & Space Science Ser.: No. 7). (Illus.). 250p. (C). 1993. text ed. 54.95 (*0-521-43167-0*) Cambridge U Pr.

Theory of Space, Time & Gravitation. 2nd ed. V. A. Fock. 1964. text ed. 206.00 (*0-08-010061-9*, Pub. by Pergamon Repr UK) Franklin.

Theory of Spectrochemical Excitation. Paul W. Boumans. LC 66-27686. 394p. reprint ed. pap. 112.30 (*0-317-27891-6*, 2055791) Bks Demand.

Theory of Speech & Language. Alan H. Gardiner. LC 79-4125. 348p. 1979. reprint ed. text ed. 38.50 (*0-313-20987-1*, GATS, Greenwood Pr) Greenwood.

Theory of Spencerian Penmanship. P. R. Spencer. 1985. pap. 4.99 (*0-88062-082-X*) Mott Media.

Theory of Spinors. Elie Cartan. 160p. (C). 1981. reprint ed. pap. 5.95 (*0-486-64070-1*) Dover.

Theory of Sprays & Finsler Spaces with Applications in Physics & Biology. P. L. Antonelli. LC 93-37463. (Fundamental Theories of Physics Ser.: Vol. 58). 324p. (C). 1993. lib. bdg. 163.00 (*0-7923-2577-X*) Kluwer Ac.

Theory of Stability of Colloids & Thin Films. B. V. Derjaguin. Tr. by Robert K. Johnston from RUS. (Illus.). 272p. 1989. 89.50 (*0-306-11022-9*, Consultants) Plenum.

Theory of Stability of Continuous Elastic Structures. Mario Como & Antonio Grimaldi. (CRC Press Library of Engineering Mathematics). 304p. 1995. 89.95 (*0-8493-8990-9*, 8990) CRC Pr.

Theory of Statistical Experiments. H. Heyer. (Series in Statistics). (Illus.). 289p. 1982. 65.95 (*0-387-90785-8*) Spr-Verlag.

Theory of Statistical Inference. Shelemyahu Zacks. LC 77-132227. (Wiley Probability & Mathematical Statistics Ser.). 625p. reprint ed. pap. 178.20 (*0-685-16172-2*, 2056297) Bks Demand.

Theory of Statistical Inference & Information. Igor Vajda. (C). 1989. lib. bdg. 269.00 (*90-277-2781-3*) Kluwer Ac.

Theory of Statistics. N. Wermuth & K. Krickeberg. (Springer Series in Statistics). (Illus.). 720p. 1996. 59.95 (*0-387-94546-6*) Spr-Verlag.

Theory of Stein Spaces. H. Grauert & Reinhold Remmert. LC 79-1430. (Grundlehren der Mathematischen Wissenschaften Ser.: Vol. 236). (Illus.). 1979. 98.00 (*0-387-90388-7*) Spr-Verlag.

Theory of Stellar Pulsation. J. P. Cox. LC 79-3198. (Astrophysics Ser.: No. 2). (Illus.). 400p. 1980. text ed. 85.00 (*0-691-08252-9*); pap. text ed. 29.95 (*0-691-08253-7*) Princeton U Pr.

Theory of Stellar Spectra. Charles R. Cowley. (Topics in Astrophysics & Space Physics Ser.). 260p. 1970. text ed. 253.00 (*0-677-02400-2*) Gordon & Breach.

Theory of Stochastic Processes. D. R. Fox. 408p. (gr. 13). 1984. pap. text ed. 47.50 (*0-412-15170-7*, NO. 6430) Chapman & Hall.

***Theory of Stochastic Processes & Random Vibrations.** Julius Solnes. text ed. 110.00 (*0-471-97191-X*); pap. text ed. 60.00 (*0-471-97192-8*) Wiley.

Theory of Stochastic Processes III. I. I. Giehman & A. V. Skorohod. (Grundlehren der Mathematischen Wissenschaften Ser.: Vol. 232). 1979. 144.95 (*0-387-90375-5*) Spr-Verlag.

Theory of Stock Speculation. Arthur Crump. LC 83-80982. 1983. reprint ed. pap. 12.00 (*0-87034-068-9*) Fraser Pub Co.

Theory of Story. Archibald C. Coolidge, Jr. LC 89-90740. 112p. (Orig.). 1989. pap. 9.95 (*0-944266-02-9*) Maecenas Pr.

Theory of Strata Mechanics. Ed. by H. Gil. (Developments in Geotechnical Engineering Ser.: No. 63). 296p. 1990. 138.25 (*0-444-98761-4*) Elsevier.

Theory of Stress & Accent. Shosuke Haraguchi. (Studies in Generative Grammar: No. 37). iv, 304p. (Orig.). (C). 1990. pap. 173.10 (*90-6765-427-2*) Mouton.

Theory of Strict Liability: Toward a Reformulation of Tort Law. Richard A. Epstein. (Cato Papers: No. 8). 141p. 1979. pap. 1.00 (*0-932790-08-9*) Cato Inst.

Theory of Structured Multiphase Mixtures. F. Dobran. (Lecture Notes in Physics Ser.: Vol. 372). vii, 223p. 1991. 31.95 (*0-387-53564-0*) Spr-Verlag.

Theory of Structures Vol. 43. S. Kalinszky & Gy Sebestyen. 144p. 1980. 30.00 (*963-05-1957-7*, Pub. by Akad Kiado HU) St Mut.

Theory of Subnormal Operators. J. Conway. LC 90-26659. (Mathematical Surveys & Monographs: Vol. 36). 436p. 1991. 133.00 (*0-8218-1536-9*, SURV/36) Am Math.

Theory of Subsonic Plane Flow. Leslie C. Woods. LC 61-4283. (Cambridge Aeronautical Ser.: No. 3). 616p. reprint ed. pap. 175.60 (*0-317-08679-0*, 2051464) Bks Demand.

Theory of Suicide. Maurice L. Farber. Ed. by Robert J. Kastenbaum. LC 76-19568. (Death & Dying Ser.). 1979. reprint ed. lib. bdg. 19.95 (*0-405-09564-3*) Ayer.

Theory of Superconductivity. M. Crisan. 312p. (C). 1989. text ed. 70.00 (*9971-5-0569-X*); pap. text ed. 36.00 (*9971-5-0997-0*) World Scientific Pub.

Theory of Superconductivity. J. Robert Schrieffer. (Frontiers in Physics Ser.). 296p. (C). 1964. text ed. write for info. (*0-8053-8502-9*, Adv Bk Prog) Addison-Wesley.

Theory of Superconductivity, Vol. 4. Ed. by N. N. Bogoliubov. (International Science Review Ser.). (Illus.). xiv, 356p. 1968. text ed. 226.00 (*0-677-00080-4*) Gordon & Breach.

Theory of Superconductivity: Frontiers in Physics, Vol. 20. J. Robert Schrieffer. 296p. 1964. 44.25 (*0-318-35465-9*); pap. 28.95 (*0-318-35466-7*) Addison-Wesley.

***Theory of Superconductivity in the High-TC Cuprate Superconductors.** P. W. Anderson. LC 96-43338. (Princeton Series in Physics). 352p. 1997. text ed. 49.50 (*0-691-04365-5*) Princeton U Pr.

Theory of Surfaces of Plow Bottoms. Ed. by L. V. Gyachev. Tr. by C. B. Malvadkar from RUS. 310p. (C). 1986. text ed. 140.00 (*90-6191-459-0*, Pub. by A A Balkema NE) Ashgate Pub Co.

Theory of Suspense. Arthur J. Komar. 1995. reprint ed. pap. 20.00 (*0-691-09111-0*) Ovenbird Pr.

Theory of Suspensions: A Study of Metrical & Pitch Relations in Tonal Music. Rthur J. Komar. (Illus.). 166p. (Orig.). (C). 1995. 20.00 (*1-886464-01-4*) Ovenbird Pr.

Theory of Syntax in Modern Linguistics. Olga Akhmanova & Galina Mikael'an. LC 69-13300. (Janua Linguarum, Ser. Minor: No. 68). (Orig.). 1969. pap. text ed. 52.35 (*90-279-0683-1*) Mouton.

Theory of Tables. Emmanuel Hocquard. Tr. by Michael Palmer. 128p. (Orig.). 1994. pap. 12.00 (*1-879645-07-6*) o-blek editions.

Theory of Target Compression by Longwave Laser Emission. G. V. Sklizkov. (Proceedings of the Lebedev Physics Institute Ser.: Vol. 170). 167p. (C). 1987. text ed. 120.00 (*0-941743-05-5*) Nova Sci Pubs.

Theory of Technical Systems. V. Hubka & W. E. Eder. (Illus.). 310p. 1988. 89.50 (*0-387-17451-6*) Spr-Verlag.

Theory of Technological Change & Economic Growth. Stanislaw Gomulka. 256p. (C). (gr. 13). 1990. pap. 29.95 (*0-415-05238-6*, A4627) Routledge.

Theory of Technology: Continuity & Change in Human Development. Thomas R. DeGregori. LC 85-11800. 278p. (Orig.). 1985. reprint ed. pap. 79.30 (*0-608-00027-2*, 2060793) Bks Demand.

***Theory of Textual Reconstruction in Indo-European Linguistics.** Ranko Matasovic. Ed. by Georg Holzer. (Schriften uber Sprachen und Texte Ser.: Vol. 2). 195p. (GER.). 1996. pap. 42.95 (*3-631-49751-2*) P Lang Pubng.

Theory of Textuality: The Logic & Epistemology. Jorge J. Gracia. LC 94-3613. 309p. (C). 1995. text ed. 64.50 (*0-7914-2467-7*); pap. text ed. 21.95 (*0-7914-2468-5*) State U NY Pr.

Theory of the Alternative Erechtheion: Premises, Definition, & Implications. Kristian Jeppesen. (Acta Jutlandica Ser.: No. 63, Pt. 1). (Illus.). 128p. (C). 1987. pap. 19.95 (*87-7288-094-5*, Pub. by Aarhus Univ Pr DK) David Brown.

Theory of the American Romance: An Ideology in American Intellectual History. William Ellis. LC 89-5139. 526p. 1991. 39.95 (*0-8357-1984-7*) Univ Rochester Pr.

Theory of the Avant-Garde. Peter Burger. Tr. by Michael Shaw from GER. LC 83-10549. (Theory & History of Literature Ser.: Vol. 4). 190p. (C). 1974. pap. text ed. 13.95 (*0-8166-1068-1*) U of Minn Pr.

Theory of the Avant-Garde. Renato Poggioli. (Belknap Ser.). 256p. 1981. pap. 15.95 (*0-674-88216-4*) HUP.

Theory of the Balance of Trade in England: A Study in Mercantilism. Bruno Suviranta. LC 67-28342. (Reprints of Economic Classics Ser.). iv, 171p. 1967. reprint ed. 35.00 (*0-678-00328-9*) Kelley.

Theory of the Budgetary Process. Otto A. Davis et al. (Reprint Series in Social Sciences). (C). 1993. reprint ed. pap. text ed. 1.90 (*0-8290-3376-9*, PS-375) Irvington.

Theory of the Chemostat: Dynamics of Microbial Competition. Hal L. Smith & Paul Waltman. (Studies in Mathematical Biology). (Illus.). 300p. (C). 1995. text ed. 64.95 (*0-521-47027-7*) Cambridge U Pr.

Theory of the Combination of Observations Least Subject to Error Pts. 1 & 2. Carl F. Gauss. Tr. by G. W. Stewart from LAT. LC 95-6589. (Classics in Applied Mathematics Ser.: Vol. 11). xi, 241p. 1995. suppl. ed., pap. 28.50 (*0-89871-347-1*) Soc Indus-Appl Math.

Theory of the Common Law. James M. Walker. vi, 130p. 1995. lib. bdg. 30.00 (*0-8377-2779-0*) Rothman.

Theory of the Consumption Function. Friedman. (General Ser.: No. 63). 260p. (C). 1957. text ed. 55.00 (*0-691-04182-2*) Princeton U Pr.

Theory of the Cost of Living Index. Robert A. Pollak. (Illus.). 224p. 1989. 65.00 (*0-19-505870-4*) OUP.

Theory of the Denjoy Integral & Some Applications. Ed. by V. G. Celidze & A. G. Davarseisvili. 334p. (C). 1989. text ed. 58.00 (*981-02-0021-8*) World Scientific Pub.

***Theory of the Derive: And Other Situationist Texts.** Guy Debord & Ivan Chetglov. 200p. 1997. pap. 22.00 (*84-89698-15-5*) Dist Art Pubs.

Theory of the Earth. Don Anderson. (Illus.). 384p. (C). 1989. reprint ed. pap. text ed. 49.95 (*0-86542-123-4*) Blackwell Sci.

Theory of the Earth, 2 vols. James Hutton. 1960. reprint ed. 95.00 (*3-7682-0025-6*) Lubrecht & Cramer.

***Theory of the Earth, Vol. 3.** fac. ed. James Hutton. 306p. 1996. 50.00 (*1-897799-78-0*, 364, Pub. by Geol Soc Pub Hse UK) AAPG.

Theory of the Evolution of Development. Wallace Arthur. LC 88-5628. 104p. 1988. text ed. 95.00 (*0-471-91974-8*) Wiley.

Theory of the Expenditure Budgetary Process. Douglas G. Hartle. LC 76-25827. (Ontario Economic Council Research Studies). 1976. pap. 6.95 (*0-8020-3341-5*) U of Toronto Pr.

Theory of the Expenditure Budgetary Process. Douglas G. Hartle. LC 76-25827. 108p. reprint ed. pap. 30.80 (*0-8357-3642-3*, 2036370) Bks Demand.

Theory of the Film: Character & Growth of a New Art. Bela Balazs. LC 71-169347. (Arno Press Cinema Program Ser.). (Illus.). 312p. 1978. reprint ed. 23.95 (*0-405-03910-7*) Ayer.

Theory of the Firm. Ed. by Mark Casson. LC 96-8724. (International Library of Critical Writings in Economics Ser.: Vol. 72). 768p. 1996. 240.00 (*1-85278-715-5*) E Elgar.

Theory of the Firm: Resource Allocation in a Market Economy. 2nd ed. Kalman J. Cohen & Richard M. Cyert. (Illus.). 640p. 1975. text ed. write for info. (*0-13-913798-X*) P-H.

Theory of the Firm in Economic Space. Melvin L. Greenhut. (Modern Revivals in Economics Ser.). 390p. 1992. 59.95 (*0-7512-0074-3*, Pub. by Gregg Revivals UK) Ashgate Pub Co.

Theory of the Foreign Exchanges. George J. Goschen. Ed. by Mira Wilkins. LC 78-3918. (International Finance Ser.). 1979. reprint ed. lib. bdg. 19.95 (*0-405-11221-1*) Ayer.

Theory of the Four Movements. Charles Fourier. Ed. by Ian J. Patterson & Gareth S. Jones. (Texts in the History of Political Thought Ser.). 275p. (C). 1992. pap. write for info. (*0-521-35839-6*) Cambridge U Pr.

Theory of the Four Movements. Ian J. Patterson. (Texts in the History of Political Thought Ser.). 275p. (C). 1992. write for info. (*0-521-35289-4*) Cambridge U Pr.

***Theory of the Garn System: A Unified Field Theory.** Luis R. Torres. (Illus.). 64p. (Orig.). 1997. pap. 12.95 (*0-9657379-0-X*) El Arte.

Theory of the General Strike from the French Revolution to Poland. Phil H. Goodstein. 337p. 1984. text ed. 61.00 (*0-88033-050-3*) East Eur Monographs.

***Theory of the Global Firm.** Vinay Bharat-Ram. (Illus.). 160p. 1997. 125.00 (*0-19-564183-3*) OUP.

Theory of the Growth of the Firm. Edith T. Penrose. 300p. 1995. pap. 19.95 (*0-19-828977-4*) OUP.

Theory of the Growth of the Firm. 3rd ed. Edith T. Penrose. 300p. 1995. 55.00 (*0-19-828978-2*) OUP.

Theory of the Growth of the Firm. Edith T. Penrose. LC 79-91109. 304p. reprint ed. 86.70 (*0-685-16342-3*, 2027623) Bks Demand.

Theory of the Inhomogeneous Electron Gas. Ed. by S. O. Lundqvist & Norman H. March. (Physics of Solids & Liquids Ser.). 426p. 1983. 115.00 (*0-306-41207-1*, Plenum Pr) Plenum.

***Theory of the Interaction of Strong Laser Pulses with Atoms & Molecules.** 250p. 1997. text ed. 26.00 (*981-02-3202-0*) World Scientific Pub.

Theory of the Judicial Process: The Establishment of Facts. Csaba S. Varga. 240p. 1995. 38.00 (*963-05-6869-1*, Pub. by A K HU) Intl Spec Bk.

Theory of the Labor Movement. Selig Perlman. LC 66-18323. (Reprints of Economic Classics Ser.). xii, 321p. 1966. reprint ed. 37.50 (*0-678-00025-5*) Kelley.

Theory of the Law of Evidence As Established in the United States & of the Conduct of the Examination of Witnesses. 3rd ed. William Reynolds. xix, 206p. 1983. reprint ed. lib. bdg. 22.50 (*0-8377-1039-1*) Rothman.

***Theory of the Leisure Class.** Thorstein B. Veblen. Date not set. lib. bdg. 28.95 (*0-8488-1659-5*) Amereon Ltd.

Theory of the Leisure Class. Thorstein B. Veblen. 1953. pap. 4.95 (*0-451-62591-9*, ME2345, Ment) NAL-Dutton.

Theory of the Leisure Class. Thorstein B. Veblen. 144p. 1994. pap. 10.95 (*0-14-018795-2*, Penguin Classics) Viking Penguin.

Theory of the Leisure Class. Thorstein B. Veblen. (Reprints of Economic Classics Ser.). 282p. (C). 1991. pap. text ed. 24.95 (*1-56000-562-9*) Transaction Pubs.

Theory of the Leisure Class. Thorstein B. Veblen. 1979. mass mkt. 5.95 (*0-14-005363-8*, Penguin Bks) Viking Penguin.

Theory of the Leisure Class. Thorstein B. Veblen. LC 93-42900. 256p. 1994. reprint ed. pap. 2.00 (*0-486-28062-4*) Dover.

Theory of the Linguistic Sign. J. W. Mulder & S. G. Hervey. (Janua Linguarum, Ser. Minor: No. 136). 70p. (Orig.). 1972. pap. text ed. 44.65 (*90-279-2187-3*) Mouton.

Theory of the Mixed Constitution in Antiquity: A Critical Analysis of Polybuis Political Ideas. Kurt Von Fritz. LC 75-7318. (Roman History Ser.). 1979. reprint ed. 44.95 (*0-405-07082-9*) Ayer.

An Asterisk (*) at the beginning of an entry indicates that the title is appearing in BIP for the first time.

Theory of the Modern Drama. Peter Szondi. Ed. by Michael Hays. LC 86-19302. (Theory & History of Literature Ser.: Vol. 29). 146p. (Orig.). 1987. text ed. 10.95 (*0-8166-1284-6*); pap. text ed. 10.95 (*0-8166-1285-4*) U of Minn Pr.

Theory of the Modern Stage. Ed. by Eric Bentley. 496p. 1976. pap. 8.95 (*0-14-020947-6*, Penguin Bks) Viking Penguin.

***Theory of the Modern Stage.** Eric Bentley. 1997. pap. text ed. 16.95 (*1-55783-279-X*) Applause Theatre Bk Pubs.

Theory of the Moral Life. John Dewey. 1992. pap. 14.95 (*0-8290-3150-2*) Irvington.

Theory of the Multinational Enterprise. Peter J. Buckley. (Studia Oeconomiae Negotiorum: No. 26). 64p. (Orig.). 1987. pap. 33.50 (*91-554-2025-7*, Pub. by Uppsala Univ Acta Univ Uppsaliensis SW) Coronet Bks.

Theory of the Novel. Georg Lukacs. Tr. by Anna Bostock from GER. 1974. pap. 11.95 (*0-262-62027-8*) MIT Pr.

Theory of the Novel. Georg Lukacs. Tr. by Anna Bostock. (C). 1971. pap. 15.00 (*0-85036-236-9*, Pub. by Merlin Pr UK) Humanities.

Theory of the Novel. Ed. by Philip Stevick. LC 67-25335. 1967. pap. 15.95 (*0-02-931490-9*, Free Press) Free Pr.

Theory of the Nuclear Shell Model. R. D. Lawson. (OSNP). (Illus.). 546p. (C). 1980. text ed. 125.00 (*0-19-851516-2*) OUP.

Theory of the Properties of Metals & Alloys. Nevill F. Mott & H. Jones. 1936. pap. 8.95 (*0-486-60456-X*) Dover.

Theory of the Riemann Zeta-Function. 2nd ed. Edward C. Titchmarsh. 380p. 1987. pap. 58.00 (*0-19-853369-1*) OUP.

Theory of the Secondary: Literature, Progress, & Reaction. Virgil Nemoianu. LC 88-83620. (Parallax: Re-Visions of Culture & Society Ser.). 272p. 1989. text ed. 42.50 (*0-8018-3731-6*) Johns Hopkins.

Theory of the State. Johann K. Bluntschli. LC 77-152975. (Select Bibliographies Reprint Ser.). 1977. reprint ed. 31.95 (*0-8369-5727-X*) Ayer.

Theory of the Steady State see Mathematical Theory of Diffusion & Reaction in Permeable Catalysts

Theory of the Striatum. Ed. by J. Wickens. LC 93-34358. (Studies in Neuroscience). 194p. 1993. 160.50 (*0-08-042278-0*, Pergamon Pr) Elsevier.

Theory of the Time-Energy Relationship: A Scientific Treatise. rev. ed. Robert G. Mertens. Ed. by Diana Weber. LC 95-81487. (Illus.). 350p. 1995. pap. 13.20 (*1-889398-01-2*); lib. bdg. 26.53 (*1-889398-00-4*) Gamma Publng.

***Theory of the Time-Energy Relationship: A Scientific Treatise.** 2nd ed. Robert G. Mertens. Ed. by Diana Weber. LC 96-77368. (Illus.). 350p. 1996. pap. 16.50 (*1-889398-03-9*); lib. bdg. 29.50 (*1-889398-02-0*) Gamma Publng.

Theory of the Unmagnetized Plasma. David C. Montgomery. (Illus.). 412p. 1971. 169.00 (*0-677-03350-8*) Gordon & Breach.

Theory of Therapy: Guidelines for Counseling Practice. Arthur W. Combs. LC 89-4295. 180p. reprint ed. pap. 51.30 (*0-7837-6585-1*, 2046150) Bks Demand.

Theory of Thermal-Neutron Nuclear Reactors, Pt. 2. A. D. Galanin. LC 58-22338. (Soviet Journal of Atomic Energy: Supplement Ser.: Nos. 2-3, 1957). (Illus.). 108p. reprint ed. pap. 30.80 (*0-317-09426-2*, 2020663) Bks Demand.

***Theory of Thermal Stresses.** Bruno A. Boley & Jerome H. Weiner. LC 96-49597. (Illus.). 502p. 1997. reprint ed. pap. text ed. 15.95 (*0-486-69579-4*) Dover.

Theory of Thermally Induced Gas Phase Reactions. Evengii Nikitin. Tr. by E. W. Schlag. LC 66-12733. 167p. reprint ed. pap. 47.60 (*0-317-09605-2*, 2050961) Bks Demand.

Theory of Thermoluminescence & Related Phenomena. R. Chen & S. W. McKeever. 300p. 1997. text ed. 54.00 (*981-02-2295-5*) World Scientific Pub.

Theory of Thin Shells: Proceedings of the International Union of Theoretical & Applied Mechanics Symposium, 2nd, Copenhagen, 1967. International Union of Theoretical & Applied Mechanics Staff. Ed. by F. I. Niordson. LC 68-26458. (Illus.). 1969. 92.95 (*0-387-04735-2*) Spr-Verlag.

Theory of Thin Walled Bars. Atle Gjelsvik. LC 80-26501. 260p. 1985. 42.95 (*0-471-08594-4*) Krieger.

Theory of Three-Dimensional Computer Graphics. Ed. by L. Szirmay-Kalos. (Technical Sciences - Advances in Electronics Ser.: Vol. 13). 421p. 1995. pap. 60.00 (*963-05-6911-6*, Pub. by Akadem Kiado HU) Intl Spec Bk.

Theory of Tokamak Plasmas. R. B. White. 372p. 1989. 160.00 (*0-444-87475-5*); pap. 106.25 (*0-444-87481-X*) Elsevier.

Theory of Topological Semigroups. Carruth et al. (Pure & Applied Mathematics Ser.: Vol. 75). 256p. 1983. 125.00 (*0-8247-1795-3*) Dekker.

Theory of Total Consonance. Paul Rosberger. LC 71-92560. (Illus.). 108p. 1975. 16.50 (*0-8386-7570-0*) Fairleigh Dickinson.

Theory of Trade & Protection. William P. Travis. LC 64-16070. (Economic Studies: No. 121). (Illus.). 306p. 1964. 20.00 (*0-674-88305-5*) HUP.

***Theory of Traditional Chinese Medicine.** Ed. by L. Yubin & L. Chengcai. LC 95-8084. (Traditional Chinese Medicine Ser.: Vol. 2). 280p. (YA). (gr. 12 up). Date not set. 70.00 (*90-5199-243-2*, 243-2) IOS Press.

Theory of Transactions. John R. Commons. LC 95-81035. (Frontiers of Economic Thought Ser.: Vol. 2). 200p. (C). 1996. text ed. 44.95 (*1-887585-34-6*) James & Gordon.

Theory of Transformation Groups. Katsuo Kawakubo. (Illus.). 384p. 1992. 98.00 (*0-19-853212-1*) OUP.

***Theory of Transnational Corporations.** Ed. by John H. Dunning. (Readings in Transnational Corporations Ser.). 272p. 1996. pap. 29.95 (*0-415-14106-0*) Routledge.

Theory of Transonic Astrophysical Flows. Sandip K. Chakrabarti. 212p. (C). 1990. text ed. 48.00 (*981-02-0204-0*) World Scientific Pub.

***Theory of Transport Properties of Semiconductor Nanostructures.** Scholl. (Illus.). 288p. 1997. text ed. write for info. (*0-412-73100-2*, Chap & Hall NY) Chapman & Hall.

Theory of Twilight. 2nd ed. Gary Short. Ed. by Tom Trusky. LC 93-72425. 60p. 1994. pap. 6.95 (*0-916272-58-3*) Ahsahta Pr.

Theory of U-Statistics. V. S. Koroljuk. (Mathematics & Its Applications Ser.). 564p. (C). 1993. lib. bdg. 310.50 (*0-7923-2608-3*) Kluwer Ac.

Theory of Ultra Filters. W. W. Comfort & S. Negrepontis. (Grundlehren der Mathematischen Wissenschaften Ser.: Vol. 211). 480p. 1974. 98.00 (*0-387-06604-7*) Spr-Verlag.

Theory of Ultraspherical Multipliers. W. C. Connett & Alan Lee Schwartz. LC 76-58958. (Memoirs Ser.: No. 9/183). 92p. 1977. pap. 21.00 (*0-8218-2183-0*, MEMO/9/183) Am Math.

Theory of Unitary Group Representation. G. W. Mackey. Ed. by Irving Kaplansky. LC 76-17697. (Chicago Lectures in Mathematics). 382p. 1976. pap. text ed. 12.00 (*0-226-50052-7*) U Ch Pr.

Theory of Unity. 223p. 1996. write for info. (*0-9638572-2-3*) Primary Nuclear.

Theory of Unity. Judith S. Stone. 83p. 1995. write for info. (*0-9646619-0-X*) Cosmogony Pubns.

Theory of Unity: The Final Theory. David E. Pressler. (Illus.). 162p. 1994. 39.95 (*0-9638572-0-7*) Primary Nuclear.

Theory of Valuation: Frontiers of Modern Financial Theory, Vol. 1. Sudipto Bhattacharya & George Constantinides. LC 87-32123. (Studies in Financial Economics). 368p. (Orig.). (C). 1988. pap. text ed. 39.50 (*0-8476-7487-8*) Rowman.

Theory of Valuations. O. F. Schilling. LC 50-12178. (Mathematical Surveys & Monographs: No. 4). 253p. 1950. reprint ed. pap. 49.00 (*0-8218-1504-0*, SURV/4) Am Math.

Theory of Value: An Axiomatic Analysis of Economic Equilibrium. Gerard Debreu. (Cowles Foundation Monograph Ser.: No. 17). 128p. 1972. reprint ed. pap. 12.00 (*0-300-01559-3*, Y-251) Yale U Pr.

Theory of Value & Obligation. Robin Attfield. 272p. 1987. lib. bdg. 45.00 (*0-7099-0572-6*, Pub. by Croom Helm UK) Routledge Chapman & Hall.

Theory of Value Before Adam Smith. Hannah R. Sewall. LC 65-26382. (Reprints of Economic Classics Ser.). 127p. 1968. reprint ed. 27.50 (*0-678-00279-7*) Kelley.

Theory of Value, Capital & Interest: A New Approach. Branko Horvat. 296p. 1995. 95.00 (*1-85898-055-0*) E Elgar.

Theory of Van der Waals Attraction. D. Langbein. LC 25-9130. (Tracts in Modern Physics Ser.: Vol. 72). (Illus.). 150p. 1974. 58.95 (*0-387-06742-6*) Spr-Verlag.

Theory of Vector Optimization. D. T. Luc. (Lecture Notes in Economics & Mathematical Systems Ser.: Vol. 319). viii, 173p. 1988. 30.70 (*0-387-50541-5*) Spr-Verlag.

Theory of Vibration, Vol. 2. 1991. 59.95 (*0-387-97384-2*) Spr-Verlag.

Theory of Vibration: An Introduction. 2nd ed. A. A. Shabana. Ed. by F. F. Ling. LC 95-8509. (Mechanical Engineering Ser.). (Illus.). 360p. 1995. 69.95 (*0-387-94524-5*) Spr-Verlag.

Theory of Vibration Vol. 1: An Introduction. A. A. Shabana. Ed. by M. Ling. (Mechanical Engineering Ser.). (Illus.). 296p. 1991. 49.50 (*0-387-97276-5*) Spr-Verlag.

Theory of Vibration Vol. 1: An Introduction. A. A. Shabana. (Mechanical Engineering Ser.). (Illus.). xiv, 289p. 1995. pap. text ed. 59.00 (*0-387-97985-9*) Spr-Verlag.

Theory of Vibration with Applications. 4th ed. William T. Thomson. 496p. 1992. text ed. 85.00 (*0-13-915323-3*) P-H.

***Theory of Vibrations with Applications.** 5th ed. Thomson & Marie D. Dahleh. (C). 1997. text ed. 85.00 (*0-13-651068-X*) P-H.

Theory of Vibratory Technology. enl. rev. ed. I. F. Goncharevich & K. V. Frolov. 350p. 1990. 181.00 (*0-89116-700-5*) Hemisp Pub.

Theory of Wages. Paul H. Douglas. LC 64-22237. (Reprints of Economic Classics Ser.). liv, 639p. 1964. reprint ed. 49.50 (*0-678-00062-X*) Kelley.

Theory of Wages in Classical Economics: A Study of Adam Smith, David Ricardo & Their Contemporaries. Antonella Stirati. 240p. 1994. text ed. 70.00 (*1-85278-710-4*) E Elgar.

Theory of War: A Novel. Joan Brady. 272p. 1994. reprint ed. pap. 11.00 (*0-449-90913-1*, Columbine) Fawcett.

Theory of Wave Scattering from Random Rough Surfaces. J. A. Ogilvy. (Illus.). 292p. 1991. 120.00 (*0-7503-0063-9*) IOP Pub.

Theory of Wealth Distribution & Accumulation. Mauro Baranzini. (Illus.). 288p. 1991. 75.00 (*0-19-823313-2*) OUP.

Theory of Weldability of Metals & Alloys. Ivan Hrivnak. LC 91-29084. (Materials Science Monographs: No. 74). 372p. 1992. 186.00 (*0-444-98707-X*, TS227) Elsevier.

Theory of Wing Sections. 620p. 13.95 (*0-614-13174-X*, 21-37117) EAA Aviation.

Theory of Wing Sections: Including a Summary of Airfoil Data. Ira H. Abbott & Albert E. Von Doenhoff. (Illus.). 687p. 1949. pap. 12.95 (*0-486-60586-8*) Dover.

Theory of Wire Rope. G. A. Costello. Ed. by Frederick F. Ling. (Mechanical Engineering Ser.). 120p. 1990. 69.00 (*0-387-97189-0*) Spr-Verlag.

***Theory of Wire Rope.** 2nd ed. G. A. Costello. LC 97-9273. (Mechanical Engineering Ser.). (Illus.). 152p. 1997. 59.95 (*0-387-98202-7*) Spr-Verlag.

Theory of X-Ray Diffraction in Crystals. unabridged ed. William H. Zachariasen. (Illus.). 272p. 1995. pap. text ed. 8.95 (*0-486-68363-X*) Dover.

***Theory of 6-Axis CNC Generation of Spiral Bevel & Hypoid Gears.** Robert N. Goldrich. (1989 Fall Technical Meeting). 1989. pap. text ed. 30.00 (*1-55589-548-4*) AGMA.

Theory on Gender. Paula England. (Social Institutions & Social Change Ser.). 389p. 1993. pap. text ed. 27.95 (*0-202-30438-8*); lib. bdg. 54.95 (*0-202-30437-X*) Aldine de Gruyter.

***Theory on the Relationship of Two Associated Variables: A New Mathematical Concept for Description of Two Related Variables.** Ralph W. Lai & Melisa W. Lai. (C). Date not set. pap. text ed. 19.95 (*0-614-29878-4*) Toshi Co.

***Theory on the Relationship of Two Associated Variables: A New Mathematical Concept for Description of Two Related Variables.** Ralph W. Lai & Melisa W. Lai. (C). Date not set. text ed. 49.95 (*0-9628526-4-3*) Toshi Co.

Theory P: A Premise for Improvement. Richard B. Doss. (Illus.). (Orig.). (C). pap. 19.50 (*0-9631680-0-2*) Human Side Pr.

Theory Papers, Bk. 4. Robert Pace. 48p. 1988. pap. 5.95 (*0-7935-3791-6*, 00372333) H Leonard.

Theory Piano Book: Level Two. Morton Manus et al. (Basic Adult Piano Library). 48p. (Orig.). 1985. pap. text ed. 6.95 (*0-88284-637-X*, 2118) Alfred Pub.

Theory + Experimentation: An Intellectual Extravaganza. Andreas Papasaki. 1993. 95.00 (*1-85490-157-5*) Academy Ed UK.

Theory, Policy, & Dynamics in International Trade. Ed. by Wilfred J. Ethier et al. LC 92-20680. 288p. (C). 1993. text ed. 59.95 (*0-521-43442-4*) Cambridge U Pr.

Theory, Policy & Dynamics in International Trade. Ed. by Wilfred J. Ethier et al. 308p. (C). 1995. pap. text ed. 18.95 (*0-521-55852-2*) Cambridge U Pr.

Theory, Politics & the Arab World. Hisham B. Sharabi. 272p. (C). 1991. pap. 17.95 (*0-415-90362-9*, A5168, Routledge NY) Routledge.

Theory, (Post) Modernity, Opposition: An "Other" Introduction to Literary & Cultural Theory. Mas'ud Zavarzadeh & Donald Morton. LC PN98.P67238. (Post Modern Positions Ser.: Vol. 5). 248p. (C). 1991. pap. text ed. 13.95 (*0-944624-12-X*); lib. bdg. 34.95 (*0-944624-11-1*) Maisonneuve Pr.

Theory, Practice, & the Education of the Person. Bohm Winfried. LC 94-36902. (Collection INTERAMER). 1994. write for info. (*0-8270-3423-7*) OAS.

Theory, Practice, & Trends in Human Services: An Overview of an Emerging Profession. Ed Neukrug. LC 93-20941. 350p. 1994. text ed. 55.95 (*0-534-22278-1*) Brooks-Cole.

Theory Practice Dilemmas: Gender, Knowledge, & Education. Lyn Yates. 153p. (C). 1995. pap. 40.00 (*0-7300-0000-1*, ESA841, Pub. by Deakin Univ AT) St Mut.

Theory R Management: How to Utilize Value of the Person Leadership Principles of Love, Dignity & Respect. Wayne T. Alderson & Nancy A. McDonnell. LC 94-12159. 239p. 1994. 20.00 (*0-8407-9148-8*) Value of the Person.

Theory, Tables & Data for Compressible Flow. Compiled by William B. Brower, Jr. (Illus.). 288p. 1990. 120.00 (*1-56032-065-6*) Hemisp Pub.

Theory, Text, Context: Issues in Greek Rhetoric & Oratory. Ed. by Christopher L. Johnstone. LC 95-51406. (SUNY Series in Speech Communication). 204p. (C). 1996. text ed. 54.50 (*0-7914-3107-X*); pap. text ed. 17.95 (*0-7914-3108-8*) State U NY Pr.

Theory Why: In Which the Boss Solves the Riddle of Quality. John Guaspari. LC 86-47593. 128p. 1986. 9.95 (*0-8144-5876-9*) AMACOM.

Theory Z: How American Business Can Meet the Japanese Challenge. William G. Ouchi. 1982. mass mkt. 5.99 (*0-380-59451-X*) Avon.

Theory Z: How American Business Can Meet the Japanese Challenge. William G. Ouchi. 256p. 1993. pap. 11.50 (*0-380-71944-4*) Avon.

Theoscopia, or the Highly Precious Gate of the Divine Intuition. Jacob Boehme. 1989. pap. 8.95 (*1-55818-112-1*, Sure Fire) Holmes Pub.

Theosophia: An Introduction. Lydia Ross & Charles J. Ryan. 57p. 1974. pap. 5.00 (*0-913004-13-8*) Point Loma Pub.

Theosophia: Hidden Dimensions of Christianity. Arthur Versluis. 160p. (Orig.). 1994. pap. 18.95 (*0-940262-64-9*) Lindisfarne Bks.

Theosophic Correspondence Between Louis Claude de Saint-Martin & Kirchberger, Baron de Liebistorf. Louis Claude de Saint-Martin. Tr. by Edward B. Penny from FRE. LC 82-61304. xxxii, 326p. 1991. reprint ed. 20.00 (*0-911500-62-6*) Theos U Pr.

Theosophical Articles: Articles by Wm. Q. Judge Reprinted from Nineteenth-Century Theosophical Periodicals, 2 vols. William Q. Judge. 1276p. 1980. Set. 25.00 (*0-938998-20-X*) Theosophy.

Theosophical Articles: Reprinted from the Theosophist, Lucifer & other Nineteenth-Century Journals, 3 vols. H. P. Blavatsky. 1692p. 1982. Set. 37.50 (*0-938998-26-9*) Theosophy.

Theosophical Articles & Notes. H. P. Blavatsky et al. 300p. 1985. reprint ed. 10.50 (*0-938998-29-3*) Theosophy.

Theosophical Enlightenment. Joscelyn Godwin. LC 94-1572. (SUNY Series in Western Esoteric Traditions). (Illus.). 448p. (C). 1994. pap. 19.95 (*0-7914-2152-X*) State U NY Pr.

Theosophical Enlightenment. Joscelyn Godwin. LC 94-1572. (SUNY Series in Western Esoteric Traditions). (Illus.). 448p. (C). 1994. text ed. 59.50 (*0-7914-2151-1*) State U NY Pr.

Theosophical Gleanings. 1994. pap. 3.25 (*0-8356-0226-5*, Quest) Theos Pub Hse.

Theosophical Glossary. Helena P. Blavatsky. LC 74-142546. 1971. reprint ed. 46.00 (*1-55888-235-9*) Omnigraphics Inc.

Theosophical Glossary: A Photographic Reproduction of the Original Edition, As First Issued at London, England, 1892. Helena P. Blavatsky. Ed. & Intro. by G. R. Mead. vi, 389p. 1930. reprint ed. 15.00 (*0-938998-04-8*) Theosophy.

Theosophical History Occasional Papers, Vol. 1. Ed. by James A. Santucci. (Theosophical History Occasional Papers). (Illus.). 60p. (Orig.). 1993. pap. text ed. 12.00 (*1-883279-00-3*) J Santucci.

Theosophical Movement, 1875-1950. rev. ed. xiii, 351p. 1951. 6.00 (*0-317-00028-4*) Cunningham Pr.

Theosophical Movement 1875-1950: Theosophy Company. xiii, 351p. 1951. 6.00 (*0-938998-14-5*) Theosophy.

Theosophical Society & Theosophy. H. B. Mitchell. 1988. pap. 3.00 (*0-936072-18-0*) Soc New Lang Study.

Theosophist: Oct. Eighteen Seventy-Nine to Sept. Eighteen Eighty. 2nd ed. Helena P. Blavatsky. (Secret Doctrine Reference Ser.). (Illus.). 320p. 1979. pap. 14.00 (*0-913510-31-9*) Wizards.

Theosophy. Robert Ellwood. LC 85-40843. (Illus.). 236p. (Orig.). (C). 1986. pap. 10.00 (*0-8356-0607-4*, Quest) Theos Pub Hse.

Theosophy. Rudolf Steiner. 230p. 1968. reprint ed. spiral bd. 8.50 (*0-7873-0825-0*) Hlth Research.

Theosophy: A Modern Revival of Ancient Wisdom. Alvin B. Kuhn. 381p. 1992. pap. 27.00 (*1-56459-175-1*) Kessinger Pub.

Theosophy: An Introduction to the Spiritual Processes in Human Life & in the Cosmos. Rudolf Steiner. Tr. by Catherine E. Creeger from GER. LC 93-35871. (Classics in Anthroposophy Ser.). 232p. 1994. pap. 12.95 (*0-88010-373-6*) Anthroposophic.

Theosophy: An Introduction to the Supersensible Knowledge of the World & the Destination of Man (1910) Rudolph Steiner. 250p. 1996. pap. 19.95 (*1-56459-806-3*) Kessinger Pub.

Theosophy: Or, Psychological Religion. Friedrich M. Mueller. LC 73-18830. (Gifford Lectures: 1892). reprint ed. 62.50 (*0-404-14460-8*) AMS Pr.

Theosophy: Religion & Occult Theosophy. Henry S. Olcott. 384p. 1993. reprint ed. pap. 24.95 (*1-56459-390-8*) Kessinger Pub.

Theosophy: The Path of the Mystic. 3rd rev. ed. Katherine Tingley. LC 77-82604. 170p. 1995. 12.00 (*0-911500-33-2*); pap. 7.00 (*0-911500-34-0*) Theos U Pr.

Theosophy & Christianity. rev. ed. Henry T. Edge. Ed. by W. Emmett Small & Helen Todd. (Theosophical Manual Ser.: No. 12). 80p. 1974. pap. 4.50 (*0-913004-17-0*) Point Loma Pub.

Theosophy & the Fourth Dimension. Alexander Horne. 110p. (Orig.). 1992. pap. 16.95 (*1-56459-114-X*) Kessinger Pub.

Theosophy I: The Inner Life of Theosophy. James R. Lewis. (Cults & New Religions Ser.: Vol. 6). 424p. 1990. reprint ed. text ed. 30.00 (*0-8240-4367-7*) Garland.

Theosophy II: Controversial & Polemical Pamphlets. Aidan Kelly. (Cults & New Religions Ser.: Vol. 7). 576p. 1990. reprint ed. text ed. 35.00 (*0-8240-4368-5*) Garland.

Theosophy in the Nineteenth Century: An Annotated Bibliography. Michael Gomes. LC 93-36932. 592p. 1994. text ed. 93.00 (*0-8240-8094-7*, SS532) Garland.

Theosophy: Key to Understanding see Life Your Great Adventure: A Theosophical View

Theosophy of the Rosicrucian. Rudolf Steiner. Tr. by Dorothy S. Osmond & Mabel Cotterell. 168p. (GER.). 1981. reprint ed. 18.95 (*0-85440-113-X*, Steinerbks); reprint ed. pap. 13.95 (*0-85440-401-5*, Steinerbks) Anthroposophic.

Theosophy Simplified. Irving S. Cooper. 1973. 59.95 (*0-8490-1191-4*) Gordon Pr.

Theosophy Simplified. rev. ed. Irving S. Cooper. 107p. (C). 1989. pap. 6.95 (*0-8356-0651-1*, Quest) Theos Pub Hse.

Theosophy under Fire: A Miniature Key to Theosophy As Recorded in a Legal Deposition. 2nd ed. Iverson L. Harris. 120p. (Orig.). 1970. pap. 6.00 (*0-913004-03-0*) Point Loma Pub.

Theotokos: A Theological Encyclopedia of Mary. Michael O'Carroll. LC 82-82382. 400p. 1982. pap. 24.95 (*0-8146-5268-9*) Liturgical Pr.

Theous Nomizein. Zum Problem der Anfange Des Atheismus Bei Den Griechen. Wilhelm Fahr. x, 211p. (GER.). 1969. write for info. (*0-318-70628-8*) G Olms Pubs.

Thera & the Aegean World, Vol. 1: Archaeology. Ed. by D. A. Hardy et al. 512p. write for info. (*0-9506133-4-7*, Pub. by Thera Fnd UK) DAP Assocs.

Therapeia: Plato's Conception of Philosophy. Robert E. Cushman. LC 76-6518. 322p. 1976. reprint ed. text ed. 67.50 (*0-8371-8879-2*, CUTP, Greenwood Pr) Greenwood.

Therapeutic Activities Specialist. Jack Rudman. (Career Examination Ser.: C-889). 1994. pap. 29.95 (*0-8373-0889-5*) Nat Learn.

Therapeutic Activities with Persons Disabled by Alzheimer's Disease & Related Disorders. Carol Bowlby. 432p. 1993. ring bd. 92.00 (*0-8342-0356-1*, 20356) Aspen Pub.

Therapeutic Activities with the Impaired Elderly. Phyllis M. Foster. LC 86-9945. (Activities, Adaptation & Aging Ser.: Vol. 8, Nos. 3 & 4). 204p. 1986. text ed. 39.95 (*0-86656-566-3*) Haworth Pr.

***Therapeutic Activity Intervention with the Elderly: Foundations & Practices.** Barbara A. Hawkins et al. LC 96-60329. 392p. 1996. text ed. 33.95 (*0-910251-81-9*, TIA85) Venture Pub PA.

Therapeutic Alliance. William W. Meissner. LC 96-13037. 100p. 1996. 37.50 (*0-300-06684-8*) Yale U Pr.

Therapeutic Alternatives in Management of Benign Prostatic Hyperplasia. Ed. by Flavio Castaneda et al. LC 92-49924. 1993. 99.00 (*0-86577-440-4*) Thieme Med Pubs.

Therapeutic & Adapted Recreational Services. Jay S. Shivers & Hollis F. Fait. LC 75-16377. (Health Education, Physical Education, & Recreation Ser.). (Illus.). 374p. reprint ed. pap. 106.60 (*0-318-39705-6*, 2056742) Bks Demand.

Therapeutic & Everyday Discourse As Behavior Change: Towards a Microanalysis in Psychotherapy Process Research. John Kaye et al. Ed. by Jurg Siegfried. LC 93-48581. 544p. 1995. text ed. 125.00 (*0-89391-919-5*) Ablex Pub.

Therapeutic & Surgical Equipment Markets: New Technologies Flourish Despite Slow FDA Approval & Reimbursement Issues. Market Intelligence Staff. 251p. 1993. 1,895.00 (*1-56753-427-9*) Frost & Sullivan.

Therapeutic Angiography. Ed. by C. A. Athanasoulis et al. (Illus.). 128p. 1981. 40.95 (*0-387-10526-3*) Spr-Verlag.

Therapeutic Antibodies. Ed. by J. Landon & T. Chard. LC 94-38225. (Illus.). 240p. 1994. 118.00 (*0-387-19722-2*) Spr-Verlag.

Therapeutic Apheresis: A Critical Look, Proceedings, Third International Symposium on Therapeutic Apheresis, 1984, Cleveland, Ohio. Paul S. Malchesky & Yukihiko Nose. 70.00 (*0-936022-19-1*); pap. 60.00 (*0-936022-18-3*) ICAOT Pr.

Therapeutic Application of Lasers. Boulds & Brown. Date not set. write for info. (*0-7506-1393-9*) Buttrwrth-Heinemann.

***Therapeutic Application of Ribozymes.** Ed. by Kevin J. Scanlon. (Methods in Molecular Medicine Ser.: Vol. 11). (Illus.). 352p. 1997. 69.50 (*0-89603-477-1*) Humana.

***Therapeutic Applications of Cytokines: Control of Inflammation, Growth & Differentiation.** Ed. by Johanna Schlegel. (Biomedical Library). 360p. 1996. pap. 795.00 (*1-57936-012-2*) IBC USA.

Therapeutic Applications of Interleukin-2. Atkins & Mier. (Basic & Clinical Oncology Ser.: Vol. 2). 520p. 1993. 215.00 (*0-8247-8809-5*) Dekker.

Therapeutic Applications of NSAIDs: Subpopulations & New Formulations. Ed. by J. P. Famaey & Harold E. Paulus. LC 92-17090. (Inflammatory Disease & Therapy Ser.: Vol. 10). 544p. 1992. 185.00 (*0-8247-8631-9*) Dekker.

Therapeutic Applications of Oligonucleotides. Ed. by Stanley T. Crooke. (Medical Intelligence Unit Ser.). 120p. 1995. text ed. 59.00 (*1-57059-190-3*) R G Landes.

***Therapeutic Applications of Prostaglandins.** write for info. (*0-340-56022-3*, Pub. by E Arnold UK) Routledge Chapman & Hall.

Therapeutic Approaches in Mental Health/Psychiatric Nursing. 4th ed. David S. Bailey & Deborah R. Bailey. LC 96-40370. (Illus.). 481p. (C). 1997. pap. text ed. 27.95 (*0-8036-0213-8*) Davis Co.

Therapeutic Approaches to Myocardial Infarct Size Limitation. Ed. by David J. Hearse & Derek M. Yellon. LC 84-13430. 271p. 1984. reprint ed. pap. 77.30 (*0-608-00361-1*, 2061078) Bks Demand.

Therapeutic Approaches to Women's Health: A Program of Exercise & Education. Julie A. Pauls. LC 95-19712. Date not set. ring bd. 159.00 (*0-8342-0564-5*) Aspen Pub.

Therapeutic Associates Rehabilitation Guidelines: Student Volume. Ed. by Carol Schunk & Kelly Reed. (C). Date not set. student ed., pap. text ed. write for info. (*1-888629-04-5*) Theraputic Assoc.

Therapeutic Associates Rehabilitation Guidelines: Volume 1 - Lower Extremity. Ed. by Carol Schunk & Kelly Reed. 180p. 1995. text ed. write for info. (*1-888629-01-0*) Theraputic Assoc.

Therapeutic Associates Rehabilitation Guidelines: Volume 2 - Spine & TMJ. Ed. by Carol Schunk & Kelly Reed. 150p. 1996. text ed. write for info. (*1-888629-02-9*) Theraputic Assoc.

Therapeutic Associates Rehabilitation Guidelines: Volume 3 - Upper Extremity. Ed. by Carol Schunk & Kelly Reed. 1996. text ed. write for info. (*1-888629-03-7*) Theraputic Assoc.

Therapeutic Astrology: Using the Birth Chart in Psychotherapy & Spiritual Counseling. Greg Bogart. (Illus.). 240p. (Orig.). 1996. pap. 17.95 (*0-9639068-6-0*) Dawn Mtn Pr.

Therapeutic Caregiving: A Practical Guide for Caregivers of Persons with Alzheimer's & Other Dementia Causing Diseases. rev. ed. Barbara J. Bridges. LC 95-94060. (Illus.). 256p. (Orig.). 1996. reprint ed. pap. 19.95 (*0-9645178-0-9*) BJB Pub.

Therapeutic Change: An Object Relations Perspective. Sidney J. Blatt & R. Q. Ford. (Applied Clinical Psychology Ser.). (Illus.). 250p. (C). 1994. 45.00 (*0-306-44601-4*, Plenum Pr) Plenum.

***Therapeutic Claims in Multiple Sclerosis: A Guide to Treatments.** 4th rev. ed. William A. Sibley. (Illus.). 213p. (Orig.). 1996. mass mkt., pap. 24.95 (*1-888799-08-0*) Demos Vermande.

Therapeutic Communication: A Guide to Effective Interpersonal Skills for Health Care Professionals. Tova Navarra et al. LC 88-43159. 158p. 1990. pap. 22.00 (*1-55642-075-7*) SLACK Inc.

Therapeutic Communication: Principles & Effective Practice. Paul L. Wachtel. LC 92-49431. 308p. 1993. lib. bdg. 35.00 (*0-89862-260-3*) Guilford Pr.

Therapeutic Communications for Allied Health Professions. Carol D. Tamparo & Wilburta Q. Lindh. 253p. 1993. text ed. 29.95 (*0-8273-4999-8*) Delmar.

Therapeutic Communities for Addictions: Readings in Theory, Research & Practice. George DeLeon & James T. Ziegenfuss, Jr. (Illus.). 282p. 1986. pap. 31.95 (*0-398-06087-8*) C C Thomas.

Therapeutic Communities for Addictions: Readings in Theory, Research & Practice. George DeLeon & James T. Ziegenfuss, Jr. (Illus.). 282p. (C). 1986. 46.95 (*0-398-05206-9*) C C Thomas.

***Therapeutic Communities for Offenders.** Eric Cullen et al. LC 96-30405. (The Wiley Series on Offender Rehabilitation). 1997. write for info. (*0-471-96980-X*); text ed. 65.00 (*0-471-96545-6*) Wiley.

Therapeutic Communities in Corrections. Hans Toch. LC 80-12158. 230p. (C). 1980. text ed. 55.00 (*0-275-90561-6*, C0561, Praeger Pubs) Greenwood.

Therapeutic Community: A Successful Approach for Treating Substance Abusers. Lewis Yablonsky. LC 87-19625. 1989. 27.95 (*0-89876-145-X*) Gardner Pr.

Therapeutic Community for Addicts: Intimacy, Parent Involvemement, & Treatment Success. Martien Kooyman. 252p. 1993. pap. 39.00 (*90-265-1358-5*) Swets.

Therapeutic Community Movement: Charisma & Routinisation. Nick Manning. (Therapeutic Communities Ser.). 256p. 1989. 49.50 (*0-415-02913-9*) Routledge.

Therapeutic Community with Chronic Mental Patients. J. Maller. (Bibliotheca Psychiatrica Ser.: No. 146). 1971. pap. 35.25 (*3-8055-1157-4*) S Karger.

Therapeutic Considerations for the Elderly. Ed. by Osa L. Jackson. (Clinics in Physical Therapy Ser.: Vol. 14). (Illus.). 316p. 1987. text ed. 37.95 (*0-443-08389-4*) Churchill.

Therapeutic Control of Inflammatory Diseases. Ed. by Ivan Otterness et al. LC 82-48972. (Advances in Inflammation Research Ser.: Vol. 7). 327p. 1984. reprint ed. pap. 93.20 (*0-608-00437-5*, 2061152) Bks Demand.

Therapeutic Conversations. Ed. by Stephen G. Gilligan & Reese E. Price. 250p. (C). 1993. 34.95 (*0-393-70145-X*) Norton.

Therapeutic Counseling & Psychotherapy. 6th ed. Lawrence M. Brammer et al. LC 92-26700. Orig. Title: Therapeutic Psychology. 400p. 1992. text ed. 64.00 (*0-13-912817-4*) P-H.

Therapeutic Crafts: A Practical Approach. Kathy Lobdell et al. LC 96-2755. (Illus.). 256p. (Orig.). 1996. pap. 26.00 (*1-55642-279-2*, 32792) SLACK Inc.

Therapeutic Dialogue: A Guide to Humane & Egalitarian Psychotherapy. Sohan L. Sharma. LC 95-9602. 376p. 1995. 30.00 (*1-56821-656-4*) Aronson.

Therapeutic Discourse & Socratic Dialogue: A Cultural Critique. Tullio Maranhao. LC 86-40056. (Rhetoric of the Human Sciences Ser.). 256p. 1986. text ed. 22.50 (*0-299-10920-8*) U of Wis Pr.

Therapeutic Drug Monitoring. Gerald E. Schumacher. (C). 1995. text ed. 65.00 (*0-8385-8946-4*) Appleton & Lange.

Therapeutic Drug Monitoring: A Guide to Clinical Application. Ed. by Mary H. Caviness et al. LC 85-71233. (Illus.). 438p. 1987. spiral bd. 35.00 (*0-9614903-1-4*, 9520-56) Abbott Laboratories.

Therapeutic Drug Monitoring & Toxicology by Liquid Chromatography. Wong. (Chromatographic Science Ser.: Vol. 32). 520p. 1985. 210.00 (*0-8247-7246-6*) Dekker.

Therapeutic Drugs. Ed. by Colin Dollery. (Illus.). 3000p. 1991. text ed. 450.00 (*0-443-02846-X*) Churchill.

Therapeutic Drugs, Supplement 1. Ed. by Colin Dollery. (Illus.). 272p. 1993. text ed. 225.00 (*0-443-04676-X*) Churchill.

Therapeutic Drugs, Supplement 2. Ed. by Colin Dollery et al. LC 93-36177. 1994. 235.00 (*0-443-04875-4*) Churchill.

***Therapeutic Drugs & the Quality of Life.** Ed. by Ivan K. Goldberg et al. 110p. (Orig.). 1997. pap. 17.95 (*0-930194-83-7*) Ctr Thanatology.

Therapeutic Effectiveness of Methadone Maintenance Programs in the U. S. A. S. S. Wilmarth & A. Avram. (Offset Publication Ser.: No. 3). 1974. pap. text ed. 17.00 (*92-4-170003-3*, 1120003) World Health.

Therapeutic Effects in Ocular Lesions Obtained by Systemic & Topical Administration of an Activator of the Oxygen Metabolism. Ed. by F. Menna. (Journal: Ophthalmologica: Vol. 180, Suppl. 1). (Illus.). vi, 92p. 1980. 26.50 (*3-8055-1686-X*) S Karger.

***Therapeutic Endoscopy: Color Atlas of Operative Techniques for the GI Tract.** N. Soehendra et al. (Illus.). 264p. 1997. 159.00 (*0-86577-638-5*) Thieme Med Pubs.

Therapeutic Environment. Robert J. Langs. LC 79-64458. 592p. 1979. 50.00 (*0-87668-385-5*) Aronson.

***Therapeutic Exercise.** Hall. 656p. 1998. text ed. write for info. (*0-397-55260-2*) Lppncott-Raven.

Therapeutic Exercise. 5th ed. John V. Basmajian & Steven Wolf. (Illus.). 608p. 1990. 49.00 (*0-683-00433-6*) Williams & Wilkins.

Therapeutic Exercise for Body Aligment and Function. 2nd ed. Lucille Daniels & Catherine Worthingham. LC 76-27058. (Illus.). 1977. pap. text ed. 33.95 (*0-7216-2873-7*) Saunders.

Therapeutic Exercise in Developmental Disabilities. 2nd ed. Ed. by Patricia C. Montgomery & Barbara Connolly. (Illus.). 244p. (Orig.). (C). 1993. pap. text ed. 34.95 (*1-879971-01-1*) Chattanga Grp.

Therapeutic Exercises: Foundations & Techniques. 3rd ed. Carolyn Kisner & Lynn A. Colby. 761p. (C). 1996. pap. text ed., spiral bd. 46.95 (*0-8036-0038-0*) Davis Co.

Therapeutic Exercises for Older Adults. Leonard Greninger & Mark Kinney. 158p. 1988. pap. text ed. 18.95 (*0-912855-81-9*) E Bowers Pub.

Therapeutic Exercises for Victimized & Neglected Girls: Applications for Individual, Family, & Group Psychotherapy. Pearl Berman. LC 94-15881. 178p. (Orig.). 1994. pap. 28.70 (*1-56887-003-5*, TEVBP, Prof Resc Pr) Pro Resource.

Therapeutic Exercises in Functional Kinetics: Analysis & Instruction of Individually Adaptable Exercise. S. Klein-Vogelbach. Tr. by L. Sloan-Ecker from GER. (Illus.). xvi, 375p. 1991. 54.00 (*0-387-52731-1*) Spr-Verlag.

Therapeutic Experience & Its Setting: A Clinical Dialogue. Leo Stone & Robert J. Langs. LC 80-667. 382p. 1980. 40.00 (*0-87668-405-3*) Aronson.

Therapeutic Experiencing: The Process of Change. Alvin R. Mahrer. (Professional Bks.). 1986. 34.95 (*0-393-70008-9*) Norton.

Therapeutic Gastrointestinal Endoscopy. Rosson & Bloom. 1991. write for info. (*0-8151-7399-7*, Yr Bk Med Pubs) Mosby Yr Bk.

Therapeutic Gastrointestinal Endoscopy. 2nd ed. Stephen E. Silvis. LC 89-15541. (Illus.). 400p. 1990. 115.00 (*0-89640-167-7*) Igaku-Shoin.

Therapeutic Group Analysis. Siegmund H. Foulkes. 328p. 1965. 47.50 (*0-8236-6480-5*) Intl Univs Pr.

Therapeutic Group Analysis. S. H. Foulkes. 320p. 1990. reprint ed. pap. text ed. 30.95 (*0-946439-09-5*, Pub. by Karnac Bks UK) Brunner-Mazel.

Therapeutic Heat & Cold. 4th ed. Justus F. Lehmann. (Rehabilitation Medicine Library). (Illus.). 752p. 1990. lib. bdg. 76.00 (*0-683-04908-9*) Williams & Wilkins.

Therapeutic Hemapheresis, 2 vols., Vol. 1. James L. MacPherson & Duke O. Kasprisin. LC 84-17637. 224p. 1985. 132.00 (*0-8493-6148-6*, RB173) Franklin.

Therapeutic Hemapheresis, 2 vols., Vol. 2. Ed. by Duke O. Kasprisin & James L. MacPherson. 208p. 1985. 117.00 (*0-8493-6149-4*) Franklin.

Therapeutic Hemapheresis in the 1990s. Ed. by U. E. Nydegger. (Current Studies in Hematology & Blood Transfusion: No. 57). (Illus.). viii, 282p. 1990. 232.25 (*3-8055-5166-5*) S Karger.

Therapeutic Hemorheology. A. M. Ehrly. 320p. 1991. 135.00 (*0-387-52263-8*) Spr-Verlag.

Therapeutic Humor with the Elderly. Ed. by Francis A. McGuire et al. LC 92-43465. (Activities, Adaptation & Aging Ser.: No. 17(1)). (Illus.). 116p. 1993. lib. bdg. 24.95 (*1-56024-310-4*) Haworth Pr.

Therapeutic Immunology. Ed. by K. Frank Austen et al. (Illus.). 650p. 1996. 175.00 (*0-86542-375-X*) Blackwell Sci.

***Therapeutic Implications & Mechanisms of Angiogenesis: Inhibitors & Stimulators.** Ed. by Wendy Hori. (Biomedical Library). 1996. pap. 795.00 (*1-57936-018-1*) IBC USA.

Therapeutic Index of Antihistamines. M. K. Church et al. 96p. 1992. 22.00 (*0-88937-082-6*) Hogrefe & Huber Pubs.

Therapeutic Insights: Earthly & Cosmic Laws. Rudolf Steiner. Tr. by May Laird-Brown et al. from GER. (Illus.). 91p. (Orig.). 1984. pap. 8.50 (*0-936132-66-3*) Merc Pr NY.

Therapeutic Intervention: Healing Strategies for Human Systems. Ed. by Uri Rueveni et al. LC 81-13501. 285p. 1982. 35.95 (*0-89885-086-X*) Human Sci Pr.

Therapeutic Interventions for the Person with Dementia. Ed. by Ellen D. Taira. LC 86-3123. (Physical & Occupational Therapy in Geriatrics Ser.: Vol. 4, No. 3). 143p. 1986. text ed. 39.95 (*0-86656-556-6*) Haworth Pr.

***Therapeutic Interventions in Alzheimer's Disease: A Program of Functional Communication Skills for Activities of Daily Living.** 2nd ed. Joan K. Glickstein. LC 96-45156. 1997. 58.00 (*0-8342-0930-6*) Aspen Pub.

Therapeutic Jurisprudence: The Law As a Therapeutic Agent. David B. Wexler. LC 89-62031. 408p. 1990. lib. bdg. 34.95 (*0-89089-374-8*) Carolina Acad Pr.

***Therapeutic Jurisprudence Applied: Essays on Mental Health Law.** Bruce J. Winick. LC 96-85954. 426p. 1997. boxed 50.00 (*0-89089-989-4*) Carolina Acad Pr.

Therapeutic Laser Endoscopy in Gastrointestinal Disease. Ed. by David Fleischer et al. 1983. lib. bdg. 117.50 (*0-89838-577-6*) Kluwer Ac.

Therapeutic Lasers: Theory & Practice. G. David Baxter & Costas. LC 93-14226. (Illus.). 192p. 1994. text ed. 39.95 (*0-443-04393-0*) Churchill.

Therapeutic Management of Metastatic Breast Cancer. Ed. by M. Kaufmann et al. (Consensus Development in Cancer Therapy Ser.: Vol. 1). viii, 88p. (C). 1989. lib. bdg. 79.25 (*3-11-012182-4*) De Gruyter.

***Therapeutic Management of the Complicated Patient with Reflux Disease.** Ed. by Chris Fellrier. Date not set. write for info. (*1-57130-021-X*) Medicine Grp USA.

***Therapeutic Massage.** Holey. 1997. pap. text ed. 50.00 (*0-7020-1923-2*, Bailliere-Tindall) Saunders.

Therapeutic Materials--Index of New Information & Medical Research Bible. David D. Zabarine. 150p. 1994. 44.50 (*0-7883-0092-X*); pap. 39.50 (*0-7883-0093-8*) ABBE Pubs Assn.

Therapeutic Medical Devices: Application & Design. Ed. by Albert M. Cook & John G. Webster. (Illus.). 656p. 1982. text ed. 72.00 (*0-13-914796-9*) P-H.

Therapeutic Metaphors. David Gordon. LC 78-58574. 1978. pap. 17.95 (*0-916990-04-4*) META Pubns.

Therapeutic Metaphors for Children & the Child Within. Joyce C. Mills & Richard J. Crowley. LC 86-9700. 288p. 1986. text ed. 29.95 (*0-87630-429-3*) Brunner-Mazel.

Therapeutic Modalities for Athletic Trainers. Chad Starkey. (Illus.). 313p. (C). 1993. text ed. 39.00 (*0-8036-8099-6*) Davis Co.

Therapeutic Modulation of Cytokines. Bodmer. 1993. write for info. (*0-318-70403-X*) CRC Pr.

Therapeutic Modulation of Cytokines. Ed. by Brian Henderson & Mark W. Bodmer. 352p. 1996. 131.95 (*0-8493-8381-1*, 8381) CRC Pr.

Therapeutic Narrative: Fictional Relationships & the Process of Psychological Change. Barbara Almond & Richard Almond. LC 96-550. 204p. 1996. text ed. 59.95 (*0-275-95362-9*, Praeger Pubs) Greenwood.

Therapeutic Narrative: Fictional Relationships & the Process of Psychological Change. Barbara Almond & Richard Almond. LC 96-550. 1996. write for info. (*0-614-13022-0*, Praeger Pubs); pap. text ed. 19.95 (*0-275-95579-6*, Praeger Pubs) Greenwood.

Therapeutic Nursery School. Ed. by Robert A. Furman & Anny Katan. LC 78-75187. 329p. 1969. 45.00 (*0-8236-6500-3*) Intl Univs Pr.

***Therapeutic Nutrition: A Practical Guide.** Pennington. (Illus.). 288p. (Orig.). (C). (gr. 13 up). 1991. pap. text ed. 43.50 (*0-412-29230-0*) Chapman & Hall.

***Therapeutic Opportunities in Alzheimer's Disease: Advances in Diagnostics & Drug Development.** Ed. by Katherine Emory. (Biomedical Library). 1996. pap. 795.00 (*1-57936-017-3*) IBC USA.

Therapeutic Paradox. Ed. by Michael L. Ascher. LC 89-11999. 385p. 1989. lib. bdg. 46.50 (*0-89862-393-6*) Guilford Pr.

Therapeutic Partnership: Ethical Concerns in Psychotherapy. Carl Goldberg. LC 94-72279. 290p. 1994. pap. 40.00 (*1-56821-325-5*) Aronson.

Therapeutic Peptides & Proteins: Assessing the New Technologies. Ed. by Daniel R. Marshak & Darrell T. Liu. (Banbury Reports: No. 29). (Illus.). 288p. 1988. text ed. 77.00 (*0-87969-229-4*) Cold Spring Harbor.

Therapeutic Peptides & Proteins: Formulation, Delivery & Targeting. Ed. by Daniel R. Marshak & Darrell T. Liu. (Current Communications in Molecular Biology Ser.). (Illus.). (Orig.). 1989. pap. text ed. 24.00 (*0-87969-328-2*) Cold Spring Harbor.

Therapeutic Peptides & Proteins: Formulation, Processing, & Delivery Systems. Ajay K. Banga. LC 95-61206. 340p. 1995. 99.95 (*1-56676-329-0*) Technomic.

Therapeutic Perspective: Medical Practice, Knowledge & Identity in America, 1820-1885. John H. Warner. LC 85-30235. (Illus.). 376p. 1986. 45.00 (*0-674-88330-6*) HUP.

***Therapeutic Perspective: Medical Practice, Knowledge & Identity in America, 1820-1885.** John H. Warner. 1997. pap. text ed. 19.95 (*0-691-01209-1*) Princeton U Pr.

Therapeutic Photomedicine. Ed. by H. Hoenigsmann & G. Stingl. (Current Problems in Dermatology Ser.: Vol. 15). (Illus.). viii, 308p. 1986. 184.00 (*3-8055-4151-1*) S Karger.

Therapeutic Plasmapheresis: Proceedings of the 4th International Congress of the World Apheresis Association, Sapporo, Japan, 1992. Ed. by T. Agishi et al. xxiv, 966p. 1993. 235.00 (*90-6764-151-0*) Coronet Bks.

Therapeutic Plasmapheresis (VII) Proceeding of the Seventh Symposium on Therapeutic Plasmapheresis, Tokyo, June 5-6, 1987. Ed. by T. Oda. LC 87-82168. 51.25 (*0-936022-32-9*) ICAOT Pr.

Therapeutic Play Activities for Hospitalized Children. Robyn H. Hart. 271p. (C). (gr. 13). 1992. spiral bd. 31.00 (*0-8016-1636-0*) Mosby Yr Bk.

***Therapeutic Potential of Melatonin: 2nd Locarno Meeting on Neuroendocrinoimmunology, Locarno, May 1996.** Ed. by Russell J. Reiter et al. (Frontiers of Hormone Research Ser.: Vol. 23, 1997). (Illus.). VIII, 178p. 1997. 172.25 (*3-8055-6439-2*) S Karger.

Therapeutic Powers of Play. Ed. by Charles E. Schaefer. LC 92-2849. 376p. 1993. 50.00 (*0-87668-454-1*) Aronson.

Therapeutic Powers of Play. Charles E. Schaefer. 1995. pap. text ed. 40.00 (*1-56821-794-3*) Aronson.

Therapeutic Practice in Behavioral Medicine: A Selective Guide to Assessment, Treatment, Clinical Issues, & Therapies for Specific Disorders. David I. Mostofsky & Ralph L. Piedmont. LC 84-43031. (Joint Publication in the Jossey-Bass Social & Behavioral Science Series & the Jossey-Bass Health Ser.). 380p. reprint ed. pap. 108.30 (*0-7837-2536-1*, 2042695) Bks Demand.

Therapeutic Principles in Practice: A Manual for Clinicians. Herbert S. Strean. LC 85-14338. (Sage Human Services Guides Ser.: No. 42). 151p. 1985. reprint ed. pap. 43.10 (*0-608-01510-5*, 2059554) Bks Demand.

Therapeutic Principles in Social Work Practice: A Primer for Clinicians. Herbert S. Strean. LC 93-31571. 152p. 1993. pap. 30.00 (*1-56821-137-6*) Aronson.

Therapeutic Process, the Self, & Female Psychology: Collected Psychoanalytic Papers. Helene Deutsch. Ed. by Paul Roazen. 376p. (C). 1991. text ed. 44.95 (*0-88738-429-3*) Transaction Pubs.

Therapeutic Program for the Patient with Arthritis. 3rd ed. Kenneth R. Wilske et al. 54p. 1980. pap. 5.00 (*0-9601944-3-6*) V Mason Clinic.

Therapeutic Progress in Ovarian Cancer, Testicular Cancer & Sarcomas. Ed. by A. T. Van Oosterom et al. (Boerhaave Series for Postgraduate Medical Education: No. 16). (Illus.). 516p. 1980. lib. bdg. 152.00 (*90-6021-452-8*) Kluwer Ac.

***Therapeutic Protein & Peptide Formulation & Delivery, Vol. 675.** American Chemical Society Staff & Zahra Shakrokh. LC 97-22244. (ACS Symposium Ser.). 1997. write for info. (*0-8412-3528-7*) Am Chemical.

An Asterisk (*) at the beginning of an entry indicates that the title is appearing in BIP for the first time.

Therapeutic Proteins: Pharmacokinetics & Pharmacodynamics. Ed. by Ada H. C. Kung et al. (Illus.). 368p. 1993. reprint ed. text ed. 90.00 (*0-7167-7011-3*) OUP.

Therapeutic Proteins Markets. (Market Research Reports: No. 361). 115p. 1993. 795.00 (*0-317-05021-4*) Theta Corp.

Therapeutic Psychology see Therapeutic Counseling & Psychotherapy

Therapeutic Radiology. 2nd ed. Mansfield. 1988. text ed. 105.00 (*0-8385-8947-2*) Appleton & Lange.

Therapeutic Recreation. 3rd ed. Gerald S. O'Morrow & Ronald P. Reynolds. 352p. 1988. text ed. 72.00 (*0-13-914896-5*) P-H.

Therapeutic Recreation: A Practical Approach. 2nd rev. ed. Marcia J. Carter et al. (Illus.). 593p. (C). 1995. text ed. 40.95 (*0-88133-822-2*) Waveland Pr.

Therapeutic Recreation: An Introduction. 2nd ed. David R. Austin & Michael E. Crawford. LC 95-50756. 1996. text ed. 50.50 (*0-13-110736-4*) Allyn.

Therapeutic Recreation: Cases & Exercises. Barbara C. Wilhite & M. Jean Keller. LC 91-68519. (Illus.). 263p. (C). 1992. pap. text ed. 22.95 (*0-910251-50-9*) Venture Pub PA.

Therapeutic Recreation: Processes & Techniques. 2nd ed. David R. Austin. LC 91-60385. 464p. (C). 1991. text ed. 37.95 (*0-915611-45-7*) Sagamore Pub.

Therapeutic Recreation: Processes & Techniques. 3rd rev. ed. David Austin. (Illus.). 464p. (C). 1996. text ed. 37.95 (*1-57167-032-7*) Sagamore Pub.

Therapeutic Recreation - the First Steps to Reimbursement: An Overview. Linda Hutchinson-Troyer & Ann Gillespie. 26p. 1991. ring bd. 24.95 (*1-889435-00-7*) Am Therapeutic.

Therapeutic Recreation for Chemically Dependent Adolescents & Adults: Programming & Activities. Agnes B. Rainwater. (Illus.). 196p. (Orig.). 1992. pap. text ed. 28.00 (*0-88314-523-5*, A5235) AAHPERD.

Therapeutic Recreation for Exceptional Children: Let Me in, I Want to Play. 2nd ed. Aubrey H. Fine & Nya M. Fine. LC 96-8263. (Illus.). 422p. 1996. text ed. 69.95 (*0-398-06661-2*); pap. text ed. 49.95 (*0-398-06662-0*) C C Thomas.

Therapeutic Recreation for Long Term-Care Facilities. Fred S. Greenblatt. LC 86-27697. 198p. 1988. 34.95 (*0-89885-356-7*) Human Sci Pr.

Therapeutic Recreation in the Nursing Home. Linda Buettner & Shelley Martin. LC 95-60609. (Illus.). 211p. (C). 1995. pap. text ed. 29.95 (*0-910251-76-2*, TRN78) Venture Pub PA.

Therapeutic Recreation Intervention: An Ecological Perspective. Roxanne Howe-Murphy & Becky Charboneau. (Illus.). 384p. (C). 1987. text ed. 72.00 (*0-13-914656-3*) P-H.

Therapeutic Recreation Program Design: Principles & Procedures. 2nd ed. Carol A. Peterson & Scout L. Gunn. (Illus.). 368p. 1984. text ed. 69.00 (*0-13-914839-6*) P-H.

Therapeutic Recreation Protocol for Treatment of Substance Addictions. Rozanne W. Faulkner. LC 90-71920. (Illus.). 259p. (C). 1991. 29.95 (*0-910251-37-1*) Venture Pub PA.

Therapeutic Recreation Service: Principles & Practices. 4th ed. Richard Kraus & John W. Shank. 416p. (C). 1992. boxed write for info. (*0-697-11026-5*) Brown & Benchmark.

Therapeutic Relationship. Petruska Clarkson. 400p. 1995. pap. 42.50 (*1-56593-595-0*, 1218) Singular Publishing.

Therapeutic Relationship & Its Impact. Carl R. Rogers. LC 76-14790. 625p. 1976. reprint ed. text ed. 62.50 (*0-8371-8358-8*, ROTR, Greenwood Pr) Greenwood.

Therapeutic Relationship in Behavioural Psychotherapy. Cas P. Schaap et al. LC 93-16587. (Psychotherapy & Counselling Ser.). 192p. 1993. text ed. 65.00 (*0-471-92458-X*) Wiley.

Therapeutic Relevance of Drug Assays. Ed. by Frederick A. DeWolff et al. (Boerhaave Series for Postgraduate Medical Education: No. 14). 1979. lib. bdg. 93.00 (*90-6021-443-9*) Kluwer Ac.

Therapeutic Riding I. rev. ed. Ed. by Barbara T. Engel. (Illus.). 500p. 1997. pap. text ed. write for info. (*0-9633065-5-3*) B E Therapy.

Therapeutic Riding II. rev. ed. Ed. by Barbara T. Engel. (Illus.). 400p. 1997. pap. text ed. write for info. (*0-9633065-6-1*) B E Therapy.

Therapeutic Riding Programs: Instruction & Rehabilitation: A Handbook for Instructors & Therapists on Riding with the Disabled Person. Ed. by Barbara T. Engel. LC 92-71597. 640p. (Orig.). (C). 1992. pap. 45.00 (*0-9633065-0-2*) B E Therapy.

Therapeutic Sarcogomy. Joseph R. Buchanan. 269p. 1993. reprint ed. spiral bd. 24.50 (*0-7873-0128-0*) Hlth Research.

Therapeutic Selectivity & Risk-Benefit Assessment of Hypolipidemic Drugs. Ed. by Giorgio Ricci et al. LC 81-40550. (Illus.). 351p. 1982. reprint ed. pap. 100.10 (*0-7837-9541-6*, 2060290) Bks Demand.

***Therapeutic State.** Nolan. 1998. 45.00 (*0-8147-5790-1*); pap. 18.95 (*0-8147-5791-X*) NYU Pr.

Therapeutic State: Psychiatry in the Mirror of Current Events. Thomas Szasz. LC 83-63057. 360p. 1984. 32.95 (*0-87975-239-4*); pap. 21.95 (*0-87975-242-4*) Prometheus Bks.

***Therapeutic Stories for Children in Foster Care.** Karen Lanners & Ken Schwartzenberger. (Illus.). x, 43p. (Orig.). (J). (ps-6). 1995. pap. 15.95 (*0-9652163-0-6*) Therapeutic Stories.

Therapeutic Stories That Teach & Heal. Nancy Davis & Marcella Marcey. (Illus.). 604p. 1996. ring bd. 69.00 (*0-9653088-1-2*, 002) Psychol Assocs.

Therapeutic Stories to Heal Abused Children. rev. ed. Nancy Davis et al. (Illus.). 516p. 1988. ring bd. 59.00 (*0-9653088-0-4*, 001) Psychol Assocs.

Therapeutic Studies. Kenneth L. Artiss. (C). 1986. text ed. 22.50 (*0-9615865-0-8*) Psych Bks.

Therapeutic Surgical & Electronic Device Markets: A Detailed Database on a 13 Billion Dollar Market. Market Intelligence Staff. 280p. 1992. 995.00 (*1-56753-081-8*) Frost & Sullivan.

Therapeutic Touch. Dolores K. Krieger. 176p. 1979. pap. 11.00 (*0-671-76537-X*, Fireside) S&S Trade.

Therapeutic Touch: A Practical Guide. Janet Macrae. LC 87-45444. (Illus.). 112p. 1988. pap. 10.00 (*0-394-75588-X*) Knopf.

Therapeutic Touch Inner Workbook: Ventures in Transpersonal Healing. Dolores K. Krieger. (Illus.). 224p. (Orig.). 1996. pap. 14.00 (*1-879181-39-8*) Bear & Co.

Therapeutic Trances: The Cooperation Principle in Ericksonian Hypnotherapy. Stephen G. Gilligan. LC 86-20706. 384p. 1986. text ed. 41.95 (*0-87630-442-0*) Brunner-Mazel.

Therapeutic Triangle: A Sourcebook on Marital Therapy. Carlfred B. Broderick. LC 82-23062. 184p. 1983. reprint ed. pap. 52.50 (*0-608-01507-5*, 2059551) Bks Demand.

Therapeutic Use of Child's Play. Charles E. Schaefer. LC 75-9556. 688p. 1990. reprint ed. 60.00 (*0-87668-209-3*) Aronson.

***Therapeutic Use of Stories.** Kedar N. Dwivedi. LC 97-8846. 1997. write for info. (*0-415-15070-1*); pap. write for info. (*0-415-15071-X*) Routledge.

Therapeutic Uses of Antioxidants for Health Improvements: Index of New Information with Authors, Subjects, & Bibliography. American Health Research Institute Staff. LC 95-16388. 1995. 47.50 (*0-7883-0468-2*); pap. 44.50 (*0-7883-0469-0*) ABBE Pubs Assn.

Therapeutic Uses of Music with Older Adults. Alicia A. Clair. LC 96-16282. (Illus.). 336p. (Orig.). 1996. pap. text ed. 29.95 (*1-878812-32-7*) Hlth Prof Pr.

***Therapeutic Uses of Trace Elements: Proceedings of the Fifth International Congress Held in Meribel, France, February 4-7, 1996.** Ed. by Jean Neve et al. LC 96-41996. 447p. 1997. 129.50 (*0-306-45485-8*) Plenum.

Therapeutic Uses of Vegetable Juices. Hugo Brandenberger. 1992. pap. 10.00 (*0-87983-578-8*) Keats.

***Therapeutic Uses of Writing.** Allan Hunter. 191p. 1996. lib. bdg. 59.00 (*1-56072-379-3*) Nova Sci Pubs.

Therapeutic Value of Music. Manly P. Hall. pap. 4.95 (*0-89314-815-6*) Philos Res.

Therapeutic Voice of Olga Silverstein. Bradford P. Keeney & Olga Silverstein. LC 86-18299. (Guilford Systemic Family Therapy in Practice Ser.). 193p. 1986. lib. bdg. 25.00 (*0-89862-350-2*) Guilford Pr.

Therapeutic Ways with Words. Kathleen W. Ferrara. (Oxford Studies in Sociolinguistics). (Illus.). 256p. (C). 1994. 52.00 (*0-19-508337-7*); pap. 22.00 (*0-19-508338-5*) OUP.

Therapeutics for Aggression: Psychological - Physical Crisis Intervention. Intro. by Michael Thackrey. 227p. 1986. 35.95 (*0-89885-305-2*) Human Sci Pr.

Therapeutics in Cardiology. Ed. by A. J. De Luna. (Developments in Cardiovascular Medicine Ser.). 700p. (C). 1988. lib. bdg. 269.50 (*0-89838-981-X*) Kluwer Ac.

Therapeutics in Respiratory Disease. Peter J. Barnes et al. LC 93-3749. 180p. 1993. text ed. 59.95 (*0-443-04134-2*) Churchill.

Therapeutics in Respiratory Diseases. Peter J. Barnes et al. 1994. 59.95 (*0-443-04234-9*) Churchill.

Therapeutics in Terminal Cancer Care. 2nd ed. Robert G. Twycross & Sylvia A. Lack. (Illus.). 237p. 1990. text ed. 39.95 (*0-443-04118-0*) Churchill.

Therapeutics in the Elderly. 2nd ed. Jeffrey C. Delafuenta & Ronald B. Stewart. viii, 572p. 1994. pap. 62.50 (*0-929375-11-4*) H W Bks.

Therapie der Zweierbeziehung see Dynamics of Couples Therapy

Therapie Urologischer Tumoren. R. Ackermann. (Illus.). 84p. 1991. pap. 35.00 (*3-8055-5294-7*) S Karger.

Therapies. Mark Dunster. 14p. (Orig.). (YA). (gr. 9-12). 1996. pap. 5.00 (*0-89642-329-8*) Linden Pubs.

Therapies for Adolescents: Current Treatments for Problem Behaviors. Michael D. Stein & J. Kent Davis. LC 81-20761. (Social & Behavioral Science Ser.). 418p. text ed. 38.95 (*0-87589-513-1*) Jossey-Bass.

Therapies for Adults. Howard L. Millman et al. LC 82-48064. (Jossey-Bass Social & Behavioral Science Ser.). 544p. reprint ed. pap. 155.10 (*0-7837-0184-5*, 2040480) Bks Demand.

Therapies for Children: A Handbook of Effective Treatments for Problem Behaviors. Charles E. Schaefer & Howard L. Millman. LC 77-79481. (Social & Behavioral Science Ser.). 524p. text ed. 90.00 (*0-87589-337-6*) Jossey-Bass.

Therapies for Psychosomatic Disorders in Children. Charles E. Schaefer et al. LC 94-30957. 380p. 1995. pap. 40.00 (*1-56821-375-1*) Aronson.

Therapies for Psychosomatic Disorders in Children. Ed. by Charles E. Schaefer et al. LC 79-88111. (Jossey-Bass Social & Behavioral Science Ser.). 384p. reprint ed. pap. 109.50 (*0-8357-6894-5*, 2037945) Bks Demand.

Therapies for School Behavior Problems: A Handbook of Practical Interventions. Howard L. Millman et al. LC 80-8318. (Social & Behavioral Science Ser.). 557p. text ed. 90.00 (*0-87589-483-6*) Jossey-Bass.

Therapist. Richard Alleman & Peter Garrett. 216p. 1989. 17.95 (*0-8027-5747-2*) Walker & Co.

Therapist. Ellen Plasil. 1988. pap. 3.95 (*0-317-65539-6*) St Martin.

Therapist As a Person: Life Crises, Life Choices, Life Experiences & Their Effects on Treatment. Ed. by Barbara Gerson. (Relational Perspectives Ser.: Vol. 6). 344p. 1996. 47.50 (*0-88163-178-7*) Analytic Pr.

***Therapist Driven Protocols.** George Burton. 547p. 1994. spiral bd. 175.00 (*1-879575-48-5*) Acad Med Sys.

Therapist Driven Protocols. Des Jardins & Burton. 240p. (gr. 13). 1996. wbk. ed., pap. text ed. 24.95 (*0-8151-1366-8*) Mosby Yr Bk.

Therapist Driven Protocols Course: RCP 302 Course. Volpe & Cronin. 206p. (C). 1994. spiral bd. write for info. (*0-933195-78-8*) CA College Health Sci.

Therapist Guide to the MMPI & MMPI-2: Providing Feedback & Treatment. G. Nelson et al. LC 89-81012. xii, 364p. 1990. 31.95 (*1-55959-006-8*) Accel Devel.

***Therapist Is the Therapy.** Louis B. Fierman. LC 96-43253. 248p. 1997. 40.00 (*0-7657-0047-6*) Aronson.

Therapist Techniques & Client Outcomes: Eight Cases of Brief Psychotherapy. Clara E. Hill. 352p. (C). 1989. text ed. 46.00 (*0-8039-3513-7*); pap. text ed. 22.95 (*0-8039-3514-5*) Sage.

Therapist Techniques & Client Outcomes: Eight Cases of Brief Psychotherapy. Clara E. Hill. LC 89-5893. 347p. 1989. reprint ed. pap. 98.90 (*0-7837-9903-9*, 2060629) Bks Demand.

Therapists at Risk: Perils of the Intimacy of the Therapeutic Relationship. Ed. by Lawrence E. Hedges et al. LC 96-11819. 344p. 1997. 40.00 (*1-56821-827-3*) Aronson.

Therapists' Dilemmas. Ed. by Wendy Dryden. 192p. 1988. 49.95 (*0-89116-775-7*) Hemisp Pub.

***Therapists' Dilemmas.** Ed. by Windy Dryden. 208p. 1997. 55.00 (*0-7619-5393-0*) Sage.

***Therapists' Dilemmas.** Ed. by Windy Dryden. 208p. 1997. pap. 19.95 (*0-7619-5394-9*) Sage.

Therapist's Guide to Art Therapy Assessments: Tools of the Trade. Stephanie L. Brooke. LC 96-11642. (Illus.). 164p. 1996. 32.95 (*0-398-06618-3*); pap. 22.95 (*0-398-06619-1*) C C Thomas.

***Therapist's Guide to Clinical Intervention: The 1-2-3s of Treatment Planning.** Sharon L. Johnson. LC 97-2832. (Illus.). 408p. 1997. pap. 39.95 (*0-12-386585-9*, AP Prof) Acad Pr.

Therapist's Guide to Pediatric Assessment. Linda King-Thomas. Ed. by Bonnie J. Hacker. 304p. (C). 1987. text ed. 38.95 (*0-316-49372-4*) Lppncott-Raven.

***Therapist's Handbook of Pediatric Disease & Disability.** 5th ed. Susan M. Porr et al. Ed. by Shelly J. Lane. (Pediatric Occupational Therapy Ser.). (Illus.). 200p. (C). 1997. pap. text ed. 18.00 (*0-8036-0259-6*) Davis Co.

Therapists in the Community: Changing the Conditions That Produce Psychopathology. Matthew Dumont. LC 94-37986. 200p. 1994. reprint ed. pap. text ed. 25.00 (*1-56821-405-7*) Aronson.

Therapists, Lawyers, & Divorcing Spouses. Mitchell S. Fisher. Ed. by Esther O. Fisher. LC 82-15515. (Journal of Divorce: Vol. 6, Nos. 1-2). 138p. 1982. text ed. 39.95 (*0-86656-169-2*) Haworth Pr.

Therapist's Manual for Cognitive Behavior Therapy in Groups. Lawrence I. Sank & Carolyn S. Shaffer. 230p. 1984. 55.00 (*0-306-41229-2*, Plenum Pr) Plenum.

Therapists on the Front Line: Psychotherapy with Gay Men in the Age of AIDS. Ed. by Stephen A. Cadwell et al. LC 93-46269. 608p. 1994. text ed. 59.95 (*0-88048-558-2*, 8558) Am Psychiatric.

Therapists on Therapy. Ed. by Bob Mullan. 275p. (C). 1996. 55.00 (*1-85343-329-2*) NYU Pr.

Therapists on Therapy. Ed. by Bob Mullan. 275p. (C). 1996. pap. 24.95 (*1-85343-331-4*) NYU Pr.

Therapist's Own Family: Toward the Differentiation of Self. Peter Titelman. 368p. 1995. pap. 40.00 (*1-56821-564-9*) Aronson.

Therapist's Own Family: Toward the Differentiation of Self. Ed. by Peter Titelman. LC 87-17128. 368p. 1992. reprint ed. 45.00 (*0-87668-921-7*) Aronson.

Therapist's Pregnancy: Intrusion in the Analytic Space. Sheri Fenster et al. 160p. 1994. reprint ed. pap. 24.95 (*0-88163-190-6*) Analytic Pr.

Therapist's Thesaurus: A Cartoon Guide. Robert Wilkins & Penny Loudon. LC 86-61879. (Illus.). 94p. (Orig.). 1987. pap. 16.95 (*0-914783-17-3*) Charles.

Therapist's View of Personal Goals. Carl R. Rogers. LC 60-11607. (Orig.). 1960. pap. 3.00 (*0-87574-108-8*) Pendle Hill.

Therapists Who Have Sex with Their Patients: Treatment & Recovery. Herbert S. Strean. LC 93-17864. 1993. pap. 21.95 (*0-87630-724-1*) Brunner-Mazel.

Theraplay: A New Treatment Using Structured Play for Problem Children & Their Families. Ann M. Jernberg. LC 79-88769. (Social & Behavioral Science Ser.). 486p. text ed. 48.00 (*0-87589-432-1*) Jossey-Bass.

Therapy. David Lodge. 336p. 1996. pap. 11.95 (*0-14-024900-1*, Penguin Bks) Viking Penguin.

Therapy. large type ed. David Lodge. LC 95-35734. 579p. 1996. 25.95 (*0-7862-0556-3*, Thorndike Lrg Prnt) Thorndike Pr.

Therapy: A Novel. Steven Schwartz. LC 93-40517. 1994. 22.95 (*0-15-100062-X*) HarBrace.

Therapy: A Novel. Steven Schwartz. LC 95-734. 1995. pap. 12.95 (*0-452-27431-1*, Plume) NAL-Dutton.

Therapy: Twelve Tales. Gregory M. Vogt. 96p. (Orig.). 1995. pap. 7.95 (*1-886805-27-X*) Talkingman Pr.

***Therapy A Message of Love about a Survivor.** Anne-Marie Chloe, pseud. (Illus.). xxv, 15p. (Orig.). 1996. pap. text ed. 9.88 (*0-9655557-9-8*) Anne-Maries Peaceful Connect.

***Therapy Abatement, Autonomy & Futility: Ethical Decisions at the Edge of Life.** David Lamb. 146p. (C). 1995. 51.95 (*1-85972-202-4*, Pub. by Avebury Pub UK) Ashgate Pub Co.

Therapy & Pathophysiology of End-Stage Renal Failure. Ed. by J. M. Scherbenske et al. (Journal: Vol. 13, No. 3-4, 1995). (Illus.). 122p. 1995. pap. 95.75 (*3-8055-6130-X*) S Karger.

Therapy & Prevention of Infections in Cancer Patients: Proceedings, Lausanne, 1978. European Organization for Research & Treatment of Cancer Staff & International Antimicrobial Therapy Group Staff. Ed. by M. Glauser & Jean Klastersky. (Illus.). 1979. pap. 41.00 (*0-08-024434-3*, Pergamon Pr) Elsevier.

***Therapy Answer Book: Getting the Most Out of Counseling.** Kathleen J. Papatola. 224p. 1997. pap. 12. 95 (*1-57749-048-7*) Fairview Press.

Therapy As Social Construction. Sheila McNamee & Kenneth J. Gergen. (Inquiries in Social Construction Ser.). 224p. (C). 1992. 59.95 (*0-8039-8302-6*); pap. 24.95 (*0-8039-8303-4*) Sage.

Therapy Dogs: Training Your Dog to Reach Others. Kathy D. Davis. (Illus.). 256p. 1992. pap. 25.95 (*0-87605-776-8*) Howell Bk.

Therapy for Adults Molested As Children: Beyond Survival. 2nd expanded rev. ed. John Briere. LC 96-8221. (Illus.). 256p. 1996. 36.95 (*0-8261-5641-X*) Springer Pub.

Therapy for Couples: A Clinician's Guide for Effective Treatment. Billie S. Ables & Jeffrey M. Brandsma. LC 76-50698. (Social & Behavioral Science Ser.). 380p. 70. 00 (*0-87589-312-0*) Jossey-Bass.

Therapy for Diabetes Mellitus & Related Disorders. American Diabetes Association Staff. 384p. 1994. pap. 34.50 (*0-945448-38-4*, PMTDRD2) Am Diabetes.

Therapy for Genetic Disease. Ed. by Theodore Friedmann. (Molecular Medicine Ser.). (Illus.). 127p. 1991. pap. 29. 95 (*0-19-261971-3*) OUP.

Therapy for Genitourinary Cancer. Ed. by Herbert Lepor & Russell K. Lawson. (Cancer Treatment & Research Ser.). 176p. (C). 1992. lib. bdg. 122.50 (*0-7923-1412-3*) Kluwer Ac.

Therapy for Stroke: Building on Experience. Margaret Johnstone. (Illus.). 106p. (Orig.). 1991. pap. text ed. 25. 00 (*0-443-04625-5*) Churchill.

Therapy for Stutterers, No. 10. Ed. by C. Woodruff Starkweather & Malcolm Fraser. LC 74-17097. 120p. 1974. pap. 2.00 (*0-933388-08-X*) Stuttering Fnd Am.

Therapy for the Burn Patient. Ed. by Leveridge. 182p. 1991. pap. 43.25 (*1-56593-013-4*, 0255) Singular Publishing.

Therapy for the Humerus: A Collection of Jokes Told by Nursing Home Residents to Their Therapists. 4th ed. Larry Cooper & Yvonne Harrison. 217p. 1992. spiral bd., pap. 10.00 (*1-885506-00-7*) Cooper & Harrison.

Therapy Fun with S & Z. Jean G. DeGaetano. 72p. 1991. pap. text ed. 26.00 (*1-886143-26-9*) Grt Ideas Tching.

Therapy Guide for Language & Speech Disorders, Vol. 1: A Selection of Stimulus Materials. Kathryn Kilpatrick et al. Orig. Title: Therapy Guide for the Adult with Language & Speech Disorders, Vol. 1. (Illus.). 429p. 1977. student ed. 37.00 (*1-880504-00-6*) Visit Nurse.

Therapy Guide for Language & Speech Disorders, Vol. 2: Advanced Stimulus Materials. rev. ed. Kathryn Kilpatrick. Orig. Title: Therapy Guide for the Adult with Language & Speech Disorders, Vol. 2. 254p. 1987. student ed. 30.00 (*1-880504-02-2*) Visit Nurse.

Therapy Guide for Language & Speech Disorders, Vol. 5: Reading Comprehension Materials. Kathryn Kilpatrick. 351p. 1987. student ed. 40.00 (*1-880504-05-7*) Visit Nurse.

Therapy Guide for the Adult with Language & Speech Disorders, Vol. 1 see Therapy Guide for Language & Speech Disorders, Vol. 1: A Selection of Stimulus Materials

Therapy Guide for the Adult with Language & Speech Disorders, Vol. 2 see Therapy Guide for Language & Speech Disorders, Vol. 2: Advanced Stimulus Materials

Therapy in Intermediate Care Facilities for the Mentally Retarded. Joan Burlingame & Tom Blaschko. (Illus.). 248p. 1991. pap. 25.00 (*0-939116-33-2*) Frontier OR.

Therapy in Motion. Ed. by Maureen N. Costonis. LC 77-9077. 298p. 1977. text ed. 29.95 (*0-252-00586-4*) U of Ill Pr.

Therapy in Nephrology-Hypertention. Brady. Date not set. text ed. write for info. (*0-7216-7149-7*) HarBrace.

Therapy in the Ghetto: Political Impotence & Personal Disintegration. Barbara Lerner. LC 74-186606. 256p. 1972. 40.00 (*0-8018-1373-5*) Johns Hopkins.

***Therapy, Inc. A Hands-On Guide to Developing, Positioning, & Marketing Your Mental Health Practice in the 1990s.** Linda L. Lawless. LC 96-35437. 304p. 1997. pap. text ed. 34.95 (*0-471-14760-5*) Wiley.

Therapy Kit for Language Disorders. Kathryn Kilpatrick. (Illus.). 230p. 1994. 70.00 (*1-880504-09-X*) Visit Nurse.

Therapy Made Easy with Computer Assistance: Index of New Information with Authors & Subjects. rev. ed. American Health Research Institute Staff. 149p. 1994. 47.50 (*0-7883-0398-8*); pap. 44.50 (*0-7883-0399-6*) ABBE Pubs Assn.

Therapy, Nudity, & Joy: The Therapeutic Use of Nudity Through the Ages. Aileen Goodson. Ed. by Keith Bancroft. LC 91-3717. 400p. 1991. 24.95 (*1-55599-028-2*) Elysium.

Therapy of Advanced Melanoma. Ed. by P. Ruemke. (Pigment Cell Ser.: Vol. 10). (Illus.). viii, 230p. 1990. 172.25 (*3-8055-5032-4*) S Karger.

Therapy of Angina Pectoris: A Comprehensive Guide for the Clinician. fac. ed. Ed. by Donald A. Weiner & William H. Frishman. LC 86-11452. (Basic & Clinical Cardiology Ser.: No. 8). 343p. reprint ed. pap. 97.80 (*0-7837-8327-2*, 2049114) Bks Demand.

Therapy of Anxiety & Chronic Worry: Index of New Information with Authors & Subjects. Dean A. Jobber. 180p. 1993. 47.50 (*1-55914-912-4*); pap. 44.50 (*1-55914-913-2*) ABBE Pubs Assn.

T

Therapy of Autoimmune Diseases. Ed. by J. M. Cruse & R. E. Lewis, Jr. (Concepts in Immunopathology Ser.: Vol. 7). (Illus.). viii, 216p. 1989. 153.75 (3-8055-4931-8) S Karger.

Therapy of Desire: Theory & Practice in Hellenistic Ethics. Martha C. Nussbaum. LC 93-6417. 464p. 1994. text ed. 45.00 (0-691-03342-0) Princeton U Pr.

Therapy of Desire: Theory & Practice in Hellenistic Ethics. Martha C. Nussbaum. 572p. (Orig.). (C). 1994. pap. text ed. 16.95 (0-691-00052-2) Princeton U Pr.

Therapy of Hematopoietic Neoplasia. Ed. by Emil Freireich & Hagop Kantarjian. (Hematology Ser.: No. 14). 456p. 1991. 210.00 (0-8247-8455-3) Dekker.

Therapy of Inflammatory Bowel Disease: New Medical & Surgical Approaches. Peppercorn. (Inflammatory Disease & Therapy Ser.: Vol. 2). 312p. 1989. 190.00 (0-8247-8169-4) Dekker.

Therapy of Lung Metastases. Ed. by P. Drings & I. Vogt-Moykopf. (Contributions to Oncology Ser.: Vol. 30). (Illus.). viii, 222p. 1988. 53.75 (3-8055-4749-8) S Karger.

Therapy of Malignant Brain Tumors. K. Jellinger. (Illus.). 500p. 1987. 190.00 (0-387-81946-0) Spr-Verlag.

Therapy of Parkinson's Disease. 2nd expanded rev. ed. Ed. by George Paulson & William C. Koller. (Neurological Disease & Therapy Ser.: No. 34). 632p. 1994. 165.00 (0-8247-9226-2) Dekker.

Therapy of Poetry. Molly Harrower. LC 95-33578. 132p. 1995. pap. 20.00 (1-56821-755-2) Aronson.

Therapy of Prostatis. Ed. by H. Weidner et al. (Clinical & Experimental Urology Ser.). (Illus.). 251p. 1986. text ed. 49.00 (3-88603-171-3, Pub. by W Zuckschwerdt GW) Scholium Intl.

Therapy of Renal Diseases & Related Disorders. 2nd ed. Ed. by Wadi N. Suki & Shaul G. Massry. (C). 1991. lib. bdg. 405.00 (0-7923-0676-7) Kluwer Ac.

***Therapy of Systemic Rheumatic Disorders.** Ed. by Van De Putte et al. 1160p. 1997. write for info. (0-8247-9516-4) Dekker.

Therapy of the Substance Abuse Syndromes. Henry J. Richards. LC 92-48826. 496p. 1994. 60.00 (0-87668-539-4) Aronson.

Therapy of Urological Cancer. R. Ackermann et al. (Illus.). viii, 178p. 1991. pap. 35.00 (3-8055-5369-2) S Karger.

Therapy or Theology: Religion & Mental Health. Joseoh Mauceri. (Orig.). 1995. pap. 8.00 (0-9626257-8-7) CBCCU Amer.

***Therapy Outcome Measures: Speech & Language Therapy.** Pam Enderby. 128p. (Orig.). 1997. pap. 49.95 (1-56593-807-0, 1578) Singular Publishing.

Therapy Physics Review Pt. 1: Basic Physics Examination & Study Guide. Bhudatt R. Paliwal. 65p. (Orig.). 1996. spiral bd. 24.95 (0-944838-67-7) Med Physics Pub.

Therapy-Resistant Depressions: Proceedings of the World Congress of Psychiatry, 6th, Honolulu, Hawaii, August-September, 1977. World Congress of Psychiatry Staff. Ed. by Cesar P. De Francisco. (Journal: International Pharmacopsychiatry: Vol. 14, No. 2). (Illus.). 1979. pap. 19.25 (3-8055-3055-2) S Karger.

Therapy Services: Organisation, Management & Autonomy. John Ovretveit. 222p. 1992. text ed. 61.00 (3-7186-5245-5, Harwood Acad Pubs); pap. text ed. 31.00 (3-7186-5246-3, Harwood Acad Pubs) Gordon & Breach.

***Therapy Sourcebook.** Francine Roberts. 256p. 1997. 25.00 (1-56565-793-4, Anodyne) Lowell Hse.

Therapy Through Handwriting. Helen Dinklage. (Illus.). 77p. (Orig.). 1978. pap. 10.00 (0-936132-41-8) Merc Pr NY.

Therapy Through Hypnosis. Ed. by Raphael H. Rhoades. 1976. pap. 5.00 (0-87980-162-X) Wilshire.

Therapy Wars: Contention & Convergence in Differing Clinical Approaches. Ed. by Nolan Saltzman & John C. Norcross. LC 90-4637. (Social & Behavioral Science Ser.). 312p. 34.95 (1-55542-259-4) Jossey-Bass.

Therapy with Botulinum Toxin. Ed. by Jankovic & Hallett. (Neurological Disease & Therapy Ser.: Vol. 25). 640p. 1994. 220.00 (0-8247-8824-9) Dekker.

Therapy with Couples. M. Crowe & J. Ridley. 432p. 1990. pap. 49.95 (0-632-02375-9) Blackwell Sci.

Therapy with Hydrogen Peroxide. 1991. lib. bdg. 79.00 (0-8490-5126-6) Gordon Pr.

Therapy with Stepfamilies. Emily B. Visher & John S. Visher. (Basic Principles into Practice Ser.: Vol. 6). 208p. 1996. pap. text ed. 23.95 (0-87630-799-3) Brunner-Mazel.

Therapy with Treatment Resistant Families: A Consultation-Crisis Intervention Model. William G. McCown et al. LC 93-35618. 328p. 1993. 59.95 (1-56024-244-2); pap. 19.95 (1-56024-245-0) Haworth Pr.

Therascribe: The Computerized Assistant to Psychotherapy Treatment Planning. Arthur E. Jongsma et al. LC 95-5061. 1996. 0.01 (0-471-12697-7) Wiley.

***Therascribe 3.0.** Jongsma. write for info. (0-471-17198-0) Wiley.

Theravada Buddhism. Reginald S. Copleston. Ed. by Harcharan S. Sobti. xxv, 206p. (C). 1993. reprint ed. 20.00 (81-85133-80-8, Pub. by Eastern Bk Linkers II) Nataraj Bks.

Theravada Buddhism: A Social History from Ancient Benares to Modern Colombo. Richard F. Gombrich. 240p. 1988. text ed. 55.00 (0-7100-9678-X, RKP); pap. text ed. 15.95 (0-7102-1319-0, RKP) Routledge.

Theravada Buddhism in Southeast Asia. Robert C. Lester. LC 71-185154. 1973. 17.95 (0-472-06184-4) U of Mich Pr.

Theravada Buddhist Ethics, with Special Reference to Visuddhimagga. Vyanjana. (C). 1992. 27.50 (81-85094-53-5, Pub. by Punthi Pus II) S Asia.

***There: In the Light & the Darkness of the Self & of the Other.** Etel Adnan. LC 96-52155. 70p. (Orig.). 1997. pap. 13.00 (0-942996-28-3) Post Apollo Pr.

There Ain't No Black in the Union Jack: The Cultural Politics of Race & Nation. Paul Gilroy. (Black Literature & Culture Ser.). 280p. 1991. pap. 14.95 (0-226-29427-7) U Ch Pr.

There Ain't No Such Animal & Other East Texas Tales. Bill Brett. LC 78-21777. (Illus.). 128p. 1987. 12.95 (0-89096-068-2) Tex A&M Univ Pr.

There & Back. Libby Hathorn. LC 92-27236. (Voyages Ser.). (J). 1993. 4.25 (0-383-03659-3) SRA McGraw.

There & Back. Roy Porter. Ed. by David Keller. (Bayou Press Ser.). (Illus.). 210p. 1991. write for info. (1-871478-30-8) Cassell.

There & Back. George MacDonald. (George MacDonald Original Works: Series I). 392p. 1992. reprint ed. 16.00 (1-881084-05-1) Johannesen.

There & Back: The Roy Porter Story. Roy Porter & David Keller. LC 91-18913. (Illus.). 216p. 1991. 24.95 (0-8071-1689-0) La State U Pr.

***There & Gone.** Thomas Weski. 1997. 45.00 (3-923922-49-3, Pub. by Nazraeli Pr GW) Dist Art Pubs.

***There & Now.** Linda L. Miller. 1997. mass mkt. 5.50 (1-55166-283-3, 1-66283-2, Mira Bks) Harlequin Bks.

There & Now. Linda L. Miller. (Special Ser.: No. 754). 1992. mass mkt. 3.39 (0-373-09754-9) Silhouette.

There & Then: A Vermont Childhood. Olive Pitkin, pseud. 160p. (Orig.). 1997. pap. 10.95 (1-56474-198-2) Fithian Pr.

There Are Babies to Adopt. Christine Adamec. 1996. pap. 12.00 (0-8217-5225-1) NAL-Dutton.

There Are Babies to Adopt. Christine A. Adamec. 272p. 1996. pap. 12.00 (1-57566-013-X) Kensgtn Pub Corp.

There Are Doors. Gene Wolfe. 320p. 1989. mass mkt. 4.95 (0-8125-0301-5) Tor Bks.

There Are Giants in the Sea: Monsters & Mysteries of the Depths Explored. Michael Bright. (Illus.). 224p. 1992. pap. 11.95 (0-86051-737-3, Robson-Parkwest) Parkwest Pubns.

***There Are Many Great Things You Can Do in the Snow.** Howard Hofherr. LC 96-36275. (Illus.). (J). 1997. write for info. (1-56763-308-0); pap. write for info. (1-56763-309-9) Ozark Pub.

There Are Men Too Gentle to Live among Wolves. James Kavanaugh. (Illus.). 1984. pap. 7.95 (0-06-250442-8, PL-4105, Torch) HarpC.

There Are Mountains to Climb. Jean M. Deeds. (Illus.). v, 200p. (Orig.). 1996. pap. 12.95 (0-9651487-1-8) Slvrwood Pr.

There Are No Accidents: A Magical Love Story. Jerry Stocking. Ed. by Sara Stamy & Jackie Stocking. (Illus.). 162p. 1995. pap. 11.95 (0-9629593-3-2) Moose Ear Pr.

***There Are No Accidents: Synchronicity and the Stories of Our Lives.** Robert H. Hopcke. LC 97-3853. 320p. 1997. 23.95 (1-57322-053-1, Riverhead Books) Putnam Pub Group.

There Are No Children Here: The Story of Two Boys Growing up in the Other America. Alex Kotlowitz. 332p. 1992. pap. 13.95 (0-385-26556-5, Anchor NY) Doubleday.

There Are No Electrons: Electronics for Earthlings. Kenn Amdahl. 330p. (Orig.). (C). 1991. pap. 12.95 (0-9627815-9-2) Clearwater Pub.

There Are No Ghosts in the Soviet Union. Reginald Hill. 224p. 1989. pap. 3.95 (0-380-70844-2) Avon.

There Are No Poets in the Yellow Pages. John Clark. LC 93-648. 100p. (Orig.). 1993. pap. 9.00 (1-882979-11-7) What the Heck.

There Are No Polar Bears down There. Trish Hart. LC 92-31949. (Voyages Ser.). (Illus.). (J). 1993. 3.75 (0-383-03597-X) SRA McGraw.

There Are No Problem Horses, Only Problem Riders. Mary Twelveponies. 1982. pap. 12.95 (0-395-33194-3) HM.

There Are No Secrets: Professor Cheng Man Ch'ing & His Ta Chi Chuan. Wolfe Lowenthal. 1991. pap. 14.95 (1-55643-112-0) North Atlantic.

"There Are No Slaves in France" The Political Culture of Race & Slavery in the Ancien Regime. Sue Peabody. (Illus.). 224p. 1996. 39.95 (0-19-510198-7) OUP.

There Are No Trees in the Prison. Joseph Bruchac. 1978. pap. 2.50 (0-942396-24-3) Blackberry ME.

***There Are Only Two Religions in the Whole World.** Akil. 1996. pap. 7.95 (1-56411-116-4) Untd Bros & Sis.

There Are Some Things More Important Than Baseball. Tony Huesman. LC 94-61470. (Illus.). 32p. (J). (gr. 3-6). 1994. pap. 4.95 (1-886165-21-1) TenderHearts.

There Are Some Things Worse Than Being over Forth. Wayne Allred. (Illus.). 24p. (Orig.). reprint ed. pap. 2.95 (1-885027-00-1) Willow T Bks.

There Are Talismans. Doris Radin. LC 91-16268. (Eileen W. Barnes Award Ser.). (Illus.). 64p. (Orig.). 1991. pap. 7.00 (0-938158-12-0) Saturday Pr.

There Are Those. rev. ed. Janet Levy & Nathan Levy. (Illus.). 40p. (J). (gr. 1-12). 1994. pap. 9.95 (1-878347-41-1) NL Assocs.

There Are Trolls. rev. ed. John F. Green. (Illus.). 24p. (J). (gr. k-3). 1975. pap. 5.00 (0-919566-38-3) Peguis Pubs Ltd.

There Are Two Errors in the the Title of This Book: A Sourcebook of Philosophical Puzzles, Problems, & Paradoxes. Robert M. Martin. 226p. (Orig.). 1992. pap. 15.95 (0-921149-98-0) Broadview Pr.

There Are Women & There Are Women. Luigi Faccenda. LC 92-74807. (Illus.). 158p. (Orig.). 1993. pap. text ed. 7.95 (0-9625953-2-2) Immaculata Pr.

There Be No Dragons: How to Cross a Big Ocean in a Small Sailboat. Reese Palley. (Illus.). 224p. 1996. 24.95 (1-57409-010-0) Sheridan.

There but for Fortune. large type ed. Alex Stuart. 384p. 1985. 25.99 (0-7089-1275-3) Ulverscroft.

There But for Fortune: A Life of Phil Ochs. Michael Schumacher. LC 96-6340. (Illus.). 400p. 1996. 24.95 (0-7868-6084-7) Hyperion.

***There But for Fortune: The Life of Phil Ochs.** Michael Schumacher. 1997. pap. text ed. 15.95 (0-7868-8288-3) Hyperion.

There Can Be Gods. Ed. & Tr. by Amnon Katz. 36p. 1989. pap. 10.00 (0-938245-09-0) Inverted-A.

There Comes a Time: A Challenge to the Two-Party System. Gerald J. Fresia. LC 86-12190. 225p. 1986. text ed. 55.00 (0-275-92095-X, C2095, Praeger Pubs) Greenwood.

There Goes Charlie. large type ed. Anne Fleming. (General Ser.). 400p. 1993. 25.99 (0-7089-2876-5) Ulverscroft.

There Goes Kafka. Johannes Urzidil. Tr. by Harold A. Basilius from GER. LC 68-21544. (Illus.). 238p. reprint ed. pap. 67.90 (0-7837-3581-2, 2043440) Bks Demand.

***There Goes Lowell's Party!** Esther Hershenhorn. LC 96-40168. (Illus.). (J). 1998. write for info. (0-8234-1313-6) Holiday.

There Goes Maine! A Sort of a History. John Gould. 1990. 18.95 (0-393-02834-8) Norton.

There Goes My Baby: A For Better or For Worse Collection. Lynn Johnston. (Illus.). 128p. (Orig.). 1993. pap. 9.95 (0-8362-1723-3) Andrews & McMeel.

There Goes the Neighborhood. Valeri Lupini. 112p. (YA). (gr. 10 up). 1995. pap. 7.95 (0-88995-128-4, Pub. by Red Deer CN) Orca Bk Pubs.

There Goes the Neighborhood. Jerry Van Amerongen. (Illus.). 152p. (Orig.). 1991. pap. 8.95 (0-8362-1874-4) Andrews & McMeel.

There Goes the Neighborhood: Cartoons on the Environment. Sidney Harris. LC 95-41977. (C). 1995. pap. text ed. 11.95 (0-8203-1805-1) U of Ga Pr.

There Goes the Shutout. Charles M. Schulz. LC 89-81386. (Illus.). 128p. 1990. pap. 7.95 (0-8050-1344-X, Owl) H Holt & Co.

There Hangs the Knife. Marcia Muller. 1993. mass mkt. 3.99 (0-373-83307-5, 1-83307-8) Harlequin Bks.

There Has Always Been One Baptism. rev. ed. Gerald Wright. 160p. 1993. reprint ed. pap. 6.95 (1-56794-029-3, C2289) Star Bible.

***There Have Always Been Puffins.** Ba Rea & C. J. Rea. (Illus.). 24p. (Orig.). (J). (gr. 4 up). 1997. pap. 7.95 (0-9657472-0-4) Bas Relief.

There He Keeps Them Very Well. Clare McNally. 368p. (Orig.). 1994. mass mkt. 4.99 (0-8125-3525-1) Tor Bks.

There I Was... Twenty Five Years. Bob Stevens. 304p. 1992. pap. 14.95 (0-8306-3831-8) McGraw-Hill Prof.

There I Was . . . Flat on My Back. Bob Stevens. (Illus.). 224p. pap. 12.95 (0-8306-8954-0, 28954, TAB-Aero) TAB Bks.

There I Was... Flat on My Back. Bob Stevens. 1985. pap. text ed. 13.95 (0-07-156054-8) McGraw.

There I Was...Flat on My Back. Bob Stevens. LC 75-25247. (Illus.). 224p. 1975. 13.95 (0-8168-8954-6, 28954, TAB-Aero) TAB Bks.

There I Was...25 Years. Bob Stevens. 304p. 1992. pap. text ed. 16.95 (0-07-061268-4) McGraw.

***There Is a Balm...** Ed. by Blair G. Meeks. (Liturgy Ser.). (Orig.). Date not set. pap. 10.95 (0-918208-76-9) Liturgical Conf.

There Is a Balm in Gilead. Sims. 1996. pap. 14.95 (0-8050-4411-6) H Holt & Co.

There Is a Balm in Gilead. Sims. 1997. 24.95 (0-8050-4410-8) H Holt & Co.

There Is a Balm in Gilead: The Cultural Roots of Martin Luther King, Jr. Lewis V. Baldwin. LC 90-13837. 352p. (Orig.). 1991. pap. 20.00 (0-8006-2457-2, 1-2457, Fortress Pr) Augsburg Fortress.

There Is a Carrot in My Ear & Other Noodle Tales. Alvin Schwartz. LC 80-8442. (Harper I Can Read Bk.). (Illus.). 64p. (J). (gr. k-3). 1982. lib. bdg. 14.89 (0-06-025234-0) HarpC Child Bks.

There Is a Carrot in My Ear & Other Noodle Tales. Alvin Schwartz. LC 80-8442. (Trophy I Can Read Bk.). (Illus.). 64p. (J). (gr. k-3). 1986. pap. 3.75 (0-06-444103-2, Trophy) HarpC Child Bks.

There Is a Child Hidden in This Picture. Muriel Cole. LC 91-8812. 160p. (Orig.). (C). 1991. pap. 7.95 (0-934678-35-9) New Victoria Pubs.

There Is a Choice. Marta Burleigh. LC 93-61661. 336p. 1994. pap. 12.95 (0-9639519-3-9) Whitewing Pr.

There Is a Cure for Arthritis. Paavo O. Airola. 204p. pap. 9.95 (0-13-914698-9) P-H.

There Is a Fortune to be Made in Software Maintenance: Opportunities in the 30 Billion Dollar Software AfterMarket. Girish Parikh. LC 84-51942. (Illus.). 402p. (Orig.). 1985. pap. 500.00 (0-932888-00-3, TFSM) Shetal Ent.

There Is a Fountain: The Autobiography of Conrad Lynn. rev. ed. Conrad Lynn. LC 92-29965. 288p. 1993. pap. 11.95 (1-55652-166-9) L Hill Bks.

There Is a Fountain: The Autobiography of Conrad Lynn. 2nd rev. ed. Conrad Lynn. LC 92-29965. 288p. 1993. 27.00 (1-55652-165-0) L Hill Bks.

***There Is a Future in the Past.** RoseMarie Clark. 155p. (YA). 1996. 20.00 (0-9655146-0-9) R M Clark.

***There Is a God!** Ron Sampson. (Illus.). 20p. (Orig.). (J). (ps-2). 1998. pap. 8.99 (1-55237-522-6, Pub. by Comnwlth Pub CN) Partners Pubs Grp.

There Is a Miracle in Your Mouth. John Osteen. pap. 1.99 (0-912631-14-7) J O Pubns.

There Is a Rainbow. Louis Gittner. (Illus.). 65p. (Orig.). 1981. pap. 7.95 (0-9605492-1-8) Touch Heart.

There Is a Rainbow Behind Every Dark Cloud. Gerald G. Jampolsky & Center for Attitudinal Healing Staff. LC 79-9453. (Illus.). 96p. (J). 1995. pap. 8.95 (0-89087-253-8) Celestial Arts.

There Is a Rainbow in the Moon. Lauren. 80p. 1985. 8.95 (0-911051-24-4) Plain View.

***There Is a Reason to Pray.** Janet Samolyk. LC 96-93023. 80p. (Orig.). 1997. pap. 10.00 (1-57502-381-4, PO1215) Morris Pubng.

***There Is a Redeemer.** 1987. pap. 1.20 (0-8341-9343-4) Lillenas.

There Is a River. Vincent Harding. 1993. pap. 14.00 (0-15-689089-5, Harvest Bks) HarBrace.

There Is a River. Thomas Sugrue. 453p. 1989. reprint ed. 19.95 (0-87604-235-3, 341) ARE Pr.

There Is a Season. Joan D. Chittister. LC 94-38523. 128p. 1995. 30.00 (1-57075-022-X) Orbis Bks.

There Is a Season: An Inspirational Journal. Robert F. Morneau. LC 84-11622. (Illus.). 175p. 1986. 18.95 (0-13-914755-1, Busn); 9.95 (0-13-914706-3, Busn) P-H.

There Is a Serpent in Eden. Robert Bloch. (Orig.). 1979. mass mkt. 2.25 (0-89083-514-4, Zebra Kensgtn) Kensgtn Pub Corp.

There Is a Singing Underneath: Meditations in Central Park. Thomas P. Coffey. 128p. 1985. pap. 4.95 (0-87193-217-2) Dimension Bks.

There Is a Spirit: The Nayles Sonnets. Kenneth E. Boulding. 1992. pap. 4.50 (0-87574-917-8) Pendle Hill.

There Is a Tide. Agatha Christie. 1989. 14.95 (0-396-09299-3) WC Stone PMA.

***There Is a Tomorrow.** David Nazar. Ed. by Gary Tucker. LC 96-83963. 265p. (Orig.). 1996. pap. 12.00 (0-9651566-0-5) Allastar.

There Is a Town. Gail Herman. LC 94-34991. (Early Step into Reading Ser.). (Illus.). (J). 1995. write for info. (0-679-86349-4); lib. bdg. write for info. (0-679-96349-9) Random.

There Is a Town. Gail Herman. (Step into Reading Ser.). (Illus.). (J). 1996. lib. bdg. 11.99 (0-679-96439-8) Random.

There Is a Town. Gail Herman. LC 94-34991. (Early Step Into Reading Ser.). (Illus.). (J). 1996. pap. 3.99 (0-679-86439-3) Random.

There Is a Tree More Ancient Than Eden. Leon Forrest. LC 87-71842. 214p. 1988. pap. 8.95 (0-9614644-5-3) Another Chicago Pr.

There Is a Way: Meditations for a Seeker. Stefan C. Nadzo. LC 80-66831. (Illus.). 129p. (Orig.). 1980. pap. 5.95 (0-937226-00-9) Laugh Cat.

There Is Always Something to Remind Me to Praise the Lord: DPK Inspirations. Dorothy P. Koger. Ed. by Senetta Pitts. (Illus.). 50p. 1993. pap. 4.00 (1-882821-00-9) DPK Pubns.

There Is an Answer. Leith Samuel. 1995. 6.99 (1-871676-06-1, Pub. by Christian Focus UK) Spring Arbor Dist.

There Is Confusion. Jessie R. Fauset. LC 73-18575. reprint ed. 23.50 (0-404-11386-9) AMS Pr.

There Is Confusion. Jessie R. Fauset. (Northeastern Library of Black Literature). 304p. 1989. reprint ed. pap. text ed. 15.95 (1-55553-066-4) NE U Pr.

There Is Greatness Within You My Son: A Collection of Poems from Blue Mountain Arts. LC 94-31218. 1994. pap. 7.95 (0-88396-396-5) Blue Mtn Pr CO.

There Is Hope. Doug Oldham & Laura L. Oldham. LC 96-21553. 192p. (gr. 10). 1996. 15.99 (0-8007-1727-9) Revell.

***There Is Hope: Learning to Live with HIV.** 3rd ed. Janice Ferri & Jill Schwendeman. LC 97-14113. 1997. pap. 15.00 (0-9639390-2-5) HIV Coalition.

There is Hope for a Tree. Pauline O'Regan. 200p. 1996. pap. 19.95 (1-86940-132-8, Pub. by Auckland Univ NZ) Paul & Co Pubs.

There Is Hope (Surviving Through Victimization) A Test of Faith. Dorothy Lewis-Brockington. Ed. by Hugh F. Brockington. (Illus.). (Orig.). 1996. pap. text ed. 5.95 (0-925783-06-4) Natl BIE Pub.

There Is Life after Bankruptcy: A Guide to Financial Recovery. Larry W. Smith. LC 95-92118. 185p. 1995. 24.95 (1-886944-00-8) On-Line Mktg Concepts.

There Is Life after Lettuce: Delicious Recipes for Heart Patients, Diabetics, Dieters, & Everyone Else. Carolyn Williamson et al. LC 93-9548. (Illus.). 1993. 15.95 (0-89015-891-6) Sunbelt Media.

There Is More Beyond: Selected Papers of Gardner Murphy. Lois Barclay Murphy. LC 89-42741. 311p. 1989. lib. bdg. 48.50 (0-89950-444-2) McFarland & Co.

There Is No Bad Truth. Charles Leviton. 288p. 1995. per., pap. text ed. 26.25 (0-7872-1093-5) Kendall-Hunt.

There is No Borges. Gerhard Kopf. Tr. by Leslie Willson from GER. LC 93-482. 200p. 1993. 18.50 (0-8076-1326-6) Braziller.

There Is No Choosing. large type ed. Marjorie Warby. 400p. 1992. 25.99 (0-7089-2617-7) Ulverscroft.

There Is No Death. 1991. write for info. (1-879605-25-2) U Sci & Philos.

There Is No Death. Betty Bethards. 94p. 1988. pap. 10.95 (0-918915-27-9) Inner Light Found.

There Is No Death. Florence Marryat. 1975. 69.95 (0-8490-1192-2) Gordon Pr.

There Is No Death: Inspirational Helps for Those Who Serve in Time of Sorrow. Lyman Madsen. LC 89-85212. 125p. 1990. 10.98 (0-88290-352-7) Horizon Utah.

There Is No Empty Space. Jan Van Rijckenborgh. 71p. (Orig.). 1986. pap. 6.50 (90-70196-50-6) Rosycross Pr.

***There Is No Falling.** Robert Hogg. 62p. 1993. pap. 12.00 (1-55022-198-1, Pub. by ECW Press CN) Genl Dist Srvs.

There Is No Friend Like a Sister. Mary Engelbreit. (Illus.). 48p. 1993. 4.95 (0-8362-4616-0) Andrews & McMeel.

There Is No Gene for Good Teaching: A Handbook on Lecture Skills for Medical Teachers. 3rd ed. Neal A. Whitman. 24p. 1986. reprint ed. pap. text ed. 10.00 (0-940193-00-0) Univ UT Sch Med.

An Asterisk (*) at the beginning of an entry indicates that the title is appearing in BIP for the first time.

There Is No Ithaca: Idylls of Seminis Kiai & Reminiscences. Jonas Megas. Tr. by Vyt Bakaitis. 181p. (Orig.). (ENG & LIT.). 1996. pap. 14.95 (*0-9628181-1-9*) Black Thistle Pr.

There Is No Joy in Gruntsville but There's Plenty to Learn. Ron Hostetler & Jeff Hostetler. 139p. (Orig.). 1995. pap. 13.00 (*0-937539-11-2*) Executive Bks.

There Is No Parting. Audrey Howard. 452p. 1995. pap. 10.95 (*0-340-59422-5*, Pub. by H & S UK) Trafalgar.

There Is No Parting. large type ed. Audrey Howard. (Charnwood Large Print Ser.). 800p. 1996. 27.99 (*0-7089-8913-6*) Ulverscroft.

There Is No Such Thing As a Poor American. William J. Owen, Sr. LC 96-90027. 1996. 16.95 (*0-533-11788-7*) Vantage.

There Is No Truce. Rudolph W. Chamberlain. LC 74-124229. (Select Bibliographies Reprint Ser.). 1977. 25.95 (*0-8369-5418-1*) Ayer.

There Is No Truer Truth: The Musical Aspect of Browning's Poetry. Nachum Schoffman. LC 91-4352. (Contributions to the Study of World Literature Ser.: No. 40). 200p. 1991. text ed. 45.00 (*0-313-27401-0*, STZ, Greenwood Pr) Greenwood.

There Is Nothing Like Having a Good Repository: An Introduction to the Massachusetts Historical Society. (Picture Bks.). 24p. 1984. pap. 4.00 (*0-934909-65-2*) Mass Hist Soc.

There Is Nothing Wrong with You: Going Beyond Self-Hate. Cheri Huber. (Illus.). 234p. (Orig.). 1993. pap. 12.00 (*0-9636255-0-0*) Keep it Simple.

There Is Only One God: A Social-Scientific & Theological Study of Popular Religion & Evangelization in Sukumaland, Northwest Tanzania. Frans J. Wijsen. (Church & Theology in Context Ser.: Vol. 22). 344p. 1993. pap. 29.75 (*90-390-0501-X*, Pub. by KOK Pharos NE) Eisenbrauns.

There Is Only One Nigeria. Peggy Watt. 203p. 1987. 49.00 (*0-7223-1913-4*, Pub. by A H S Ltd UK) St Mut.

There Is Only One Raffles. large type ed. Ilsa Sharp. 1991. 25.99 (*0-7089-2453-0*) Ulverscroft.

There Is Plenty of Love to Go Around for Everyone. Nancy L. Jensen. (Illus.). 32p. (Orig.). (J). (ps-6). 1995. pap. 6.25 (*0-9649196-1-3*) Heather Hill.

There Is Someone Out There. (Illus.). 382p. 1997. pap. 24.95 (*0-9649618-3-0*) Bks A-Hoy.

There Is Something. Kate Thompson. 44p. (Orig.). 1992. pap. write for info. (*0-936563-15-X*) Signpost.

There Is Something Wonderful Happening in Denmark. Arne Melchior. 1987. 14.95 (*0-8184-0429-9*) Carol Pub Group.

There Is Still Time: Thoughts of a Concerned Educator. Robert Smilovitz & Marge Des Groselliers. 200p. (C). 1993. reprint ed. pap. text ed. 14.00 (*0-9638858-0-4*) Horn of the Moon.

There Isn't Enough Toilet Paper in the World. Rino Pagnucco. (Orig.). 1996. pap. 10.95 (*0-533-11789-5*) Vantage.

There Might Have Been An Insane Heart: Selected Poems In Armenian Language. Sonia Balassanian. 80p. (Orig.). (ARM.). 1982. pap. 5.00 (*0-9608388-0-5*) S Balassanian.

There Must Be More to Love Than Death: Three Short Novels. Charles Newman. LC 76-17743. 217p. 1976. 12.95 (*0-89366-257-7*) Ultramarine Pub.

There Must Be Pony. Kirkwood. 1986. mass mkt. 3.95 (*0-671-63375-9*, Pocket Books) PB.

There Must Be Something for the Groom to Do: How to Plan Your Wedding Together. Paula Begoun & Stephanie Bell. 250p. 1995. pap. 12.95 (*1-877988-16-2*) Beginning Pr.

There Must Be 50 Ways to Tell Your Mother: Coming Out Stories. Lynn Sutcliffe. (Lesbian & Gay Studies). 160p. Date not set. write for info. (*0-304-33108-2*) Cassell.

There Must Be 50 Ways to Tell Your Mother: Coming Out Stories. Lynn Sutcliffe. (Lesbian & Gay Studies). 160p. 1996. pap. 12.95 (*0-304-33112-0*) Cassell.

There Never Was a Once upon a Time. Carmen Naranjo. Ed. by Yvette E. Miller. Tr. & Intro. by Linda Britt. LC 89-12822. (Illus.). 96p. 1989. pap. 11.50 (*0-935480-41-2*) Lat Am Lit Rev Pr.

There Never Was a Rose Without a Thorn. Carla Harryman. 180p. (Orig.). 1995. pap. 10.95 (*0-87286-301-8*) City Lights.

There Never Was a Time. Gail Link. 448p. (Orig.). 1995. mass mkt., pap. text ed. 4.99 (*0-505-52025-7*) Dorchester Pub Co.

There Once Was a Cook. Lora T. Spence et al. (Illus.). (J). (gr. k up). 1985. pap. 12.95 (*0-9614501-0-X*) Wesley Inst.

There Once Was a War: The Collected Color Photography of World War II. Photos by Jeffrey Ethell. (Illus.). 224p. 1995. pap. 29.95 (*0-670-86044-1*, Viking Studio) Studio Bks.

There Ought to Be a Bill of Rights: North Carolina Enters a New Nation. William S. Price, Jr. (Illus.). 19p. (Orig.). (YA). (gr. 8-12). 1991. pap. 4.00 (*0-86526-254-3*) NC Archives.

There Really Is a Devil! Basics for Spiritual Warfare. Arnold Prater. 202p. (Orig.). 1994. pap. 9.95 (*1-888874-00-7*) Marno Bks.

There Really is a Difference! A Comparison of Covenant & Dispensational Theology. Renald Showers. LC 90-80121. 1990. pap. 5.95 (*0-915540-50-9*) Frnds Israel.

There Shall Be Light: Treasury of Commentary on Sefer Bereishis. Yitzchak Goodman. 1992. 19.95 (*0-944070-89-2*) Targum Pr.

There Shall Be One Christ: A Collection of Essays on Teilhard de Chardin. Michael D. Meilach. (Spirit & Life Ser.). x, 85p. 1968. pap. 2.50 (*1-57659-095-X*) Franciscan Inst.

There She Blows: A Narrative of a Whaling Voyage, in the Indian & South Atlantic Oceans. Ben-Ezra S. Ely. LC 76-142726. (American Maritime Library: No. 3). 242p. reprint ed. pap. 69.00 (*0-8357-2791-2*, 2039917) Bks Demand.

There Shines Forth Christ. Julian Stead. LC 83-3382. 156p. 1983. pap. 6.95 (*0-932506-29-1*) St Bedes Pubns.

There Still Are Buffalo. Ann N. Clark. Ed. by Willard W. Beatty. LC 90-85645. (Illus.). 50p. (J). (gr. 2 up). 1992. reprint ed. pap. 8.95 (*0-941270-67-X*) Ancient City Pr.

There Stood Our Dog. Anne Houghton. LC 93-171. (J). 1994. write for info. (*0-383-03719-0*) SRA McGraw.

There to Breathe the Beauty: The Camping Trips of Henry Ford, Thomas Edison, Harvey Firestone & John Burroughs. Ed. by Nancy Kane. (Illus.). 234p. 1995. 75.00 (*0-9649996-0-9*) N Brauer.

There to Breathe the Beauty: The Camping Trips of Henry Ford, Thomas Edison, Harvey Firestone & John Burroughs. deluxe limited ed. Ed. by Nancy Kane. (Illus.). 234p. 1995. lthr. 500.00 (*0-9649996-1-7*) N Brauer.

There Was a Crooked Man. Illus. by Kevin O'Malley. (J). (ps). 1995. 9.95 (*0-671-89477-3*, Litl Simon S&S) S&S Childrens.

There Was a High Horse. Terry Page. (Illus.). 24p. (J). (gr. 2-6). 1997. pap. text ed. 4.00 (*1-887864-66-0*); lib. bdg. 7.00 (*1-887864-32-6*) Boo Bks.

There Was a High Horse Coloring Book. Terry Page. (Illus.). 32p. (J). (ps-5). 1997. pap. 3.00 (*1-887864-33-4*) Boo Bks.

There Was a Hill... Lark Carrier. LC 84-25536. (Illus.). 40p. (J). (ps up). 1991. pap. 15.95 (*0-907234-70-4*, Picture Book Studio) S&S Childrens.

There Was a Little Girl. Ed McBain. 352p. 1995. mass mkt. 6.50 (*0-446-60214-0*) Warner Bks.

There Was a Little Girl. large type ed. Ed McBain. 1995. 24.95 (*0-7838-1180-2*, GK Hall) Thorndike Pr.

There Was a Little Girl. large type ed. Ed McBain. 424p. 1995. pap. 19.95 (*0-7838-1181-0*, GK Hall) Thorndike Pr.

There Was a Man: The Saga of Gordon Kahl. Capstan Turner & A. J. Lowery. 264p. (Orig.). 1986. pap. 5.95 (*0-9614465-0-1*) Sozo Pub Co.

There Was a Man Named Job: Sixteenth Annual Spiritual Sword Lectureship. Ed. by Jim Laws. (Illus.). 416p. 1991. 24.00 (*0-9615751-6-6*) Getwell Church.

There Was a Mouse. Patricia Blanchard & Joanne Suhr. (Books for Young Learners). (Illus.). 16p. (Orig.). (J). (gr. k-2). 1997. pap. 5.00 (*1-57274-078-7*) R Owen Pubs.

There Was a River. Bruce Berger. 198p. (Orig.). 1994. 42.00 (*0-8165-1469-0*); pap. 17.95 (*0-8165-1493-3*) U of Ariz Pr.

There Was a Season. Theodore V. Olsen. 448p. 1994. reprint ed. mass mkt., pap. text ed. 4.99 (*0-8439-3652-5*) Dorchester Pub Co.

There Was a Tree. Cathy Beylon. (Window Bks.). (J). (ps). 1992. 4.95 (*1-56288-283-X*) Checkerboard.

There Was an Old Lady. (J). pap. 1.75 (*0-590-09992-2*) Scholastic Inc.

There Was an Old Lady. Illus. by Pam Adams. (Books with Holes Ser.). (FRE.). (J). 1972. pap. 6.99 (*0-85953-460-X*) Childs Play.

There Was an Old Lady. Illus. by Pam Adams. (Books with Holes Ser.). (ITA.). (J). 1989. pap. 6.99 (*0-85953-590-8*) Childs Play.

There Was an Old Lady Who Swallowed a Fly. (My Favorite Beanstalk Bks.). 24p. (J). 1996. write for info. (*1-57719-077-7*) GT Pubng Corp.

There Was an Old Lady Who Swallowed a Fly. Illus. by Pam Adams. LC 90-46921. (J). (ps-3). 1972. 13.99 (*0-85953-021-3*) Childs Play.

There Was an Old Lady Who Swallowed a Fly. Illus. by Pam Adams. LC 90-46921. (Books with Holes Ser.). 16p. (J). (ps-2). 1989. pap. 6.99 (*0-85953-018-3*, Pub. by Childs Play UK) Childs Play.

There Was an Old Lady Who Swallowed a Fly. Simms Taback. Orig. Title: I Know an Old Lady Who Swallowed a Fly. (J). 1997. pap. 14.99 (*0-670-86939-2*) Viking Child Bks.

There Was an Old Man: A Gallery of Nonsense Rhythms. Edward Lear. LC 93-46492. (Illus.). 80p. (J). 1994. 15.00 (*0-688-10788-5*, Morrow Junior) Morrow.

There Was an Old Man: A Gallery of Nonsense Rhythms, a Selection of Limericks. Edward Lear. LC 93-46492. (Illus.). 80p. (J). 1994. lib. bdg. 14.93 (*0-688-10789-3*, Morrow Junior) Morrow.

There Was an Old Woman. Dianne O. Burke. (Rhyme-along Book). (Illus.). 12p. (J). (ps). 1994. bds. 3.95 (*1-56565-095-6*) Lowell Hse Juvenile.

There Was an Old Woman. Kellogg. (J). 1998. pap. 16.00 (*0-689-81703-7*) S&S Childrens.

There Was an Old Woman. Retold by Steven Kellogg. LC 80-15293. (Illus.). 48p. (J). (ps-3). 1984. lib. bdg. 13.95 (*0-02-749780-1*, Four Winds Pr) S&S Childrens.

There Was an Old Woman: Nursery Crimes. Weiner. 272p. (J). 1995. mass mkt. 3.50 (*0-06-106240-5*, Harp PBks) HarpC.

There Was an Old Woman Who Lived in a Glove: A Picture Book. Bernard Lodge. LC 92-12967. (Illus.). 32p. (J). 1992. lib. bdg. 14.95 (*1-879085-55-0*) Whsprng Coyote Pr.

There Was Magic Inside. David Galchutt. LC 91-44107. (Illus.). 40p. (J). (ps-2). 1993. pap. 14.00 (*0-671-75978-7*, S&S Bks Young Read) S&S Childrens.

There Was No Jesus: Apollonius of Tyana & the New Testament. 1991. lib. bdg. 88.95 (*0-8490-4554-1*) Gordon Pr.

There Was No Jesus: The Teacher of the New Testament Was Apollonius of Tyana. Ed. by Jonathan N. Roberts & Gretta Spearman. reprint ed. spiral bd. 17.50 (*0-7873-0730-0*) Hlth Research.

There Was No Path So I Trod One: Poems by Edwina Gateley. Edwina Gateley. (Illus.). 120p. (Orig.). 1996. 8.95 (*0-940147-40-8*) Source Bks CA.

There Was So Much Laughter. Gary Morgan. 50p. 1984. pap. 2.95 (*0-942424-03-4*) W Anglia Pubns.

There We Sat Down: Talmudic Judaism in the Making. Jacob Neusner. pap. 11.95 (*0-87068-676-3*) Ktav.

There Were Also Strangers. Borden Deal. 280p. 1986. 15.95 (*0-88282-018-4*) New Horizon NJ.

There Were Days Like That. Harold P. Levy. Ed. by Beverley J. DeWitt. (Illus.). 164p. (Orig.). 1985. pap. 9.95 (*0-9615303-0-8*) Blue Whale Pr.

There Were Monkeys. Sheree Fitch. 1994. pap. 11.95 (*0-385-25496-2*) Doubleday.

There Were Monkeys in My Kitchen! Sheree Fitch. (Illus.). 32p. 1994. 4.95 (*0-385-25470-9*) Doubleday.

There Were Ten in the Bed. Illus. by Pam Adams. LC 90-45580. 24p. (J). (ps-2). 1979. 9.99 (*0-85953-095-7*, Pub. by Childs Play UK) Childs Play.

There Were Ten in the Bed. Illus. by Pam Adams. (GRE.). (J). 1979. 9.99 (*0-85953-826-5*) Childs Play.

There Were Ten in the Bed. Illus. by Pam Adams. (ITA.). (J). 1979. 9.99 (*0-85953-561-4*) Childs Play.

There Were These Two Guys. Jonathan Litter. (Orig.). 1988. pap. 3.50 (*0-945926-01-4*) Paradigm RI.

There Were Times When I Thought I Was Crazy: A Black Woman's Story of Incest. Vanessa Alleyne. 176p. Date not set. pap. 13.95 (*1-896705-08-1*, Pub. by Sis Vision Pr CN) LPC InBook.

There Were Two Trees in the Garden. Rick Joyner. 198p. 1994. mass mkt. 5.99 (*0-88368-326-1*) Whitaker Hse.

There Were Two Trees in the Garden. Rick Joyner. LC 97-16505. 1997. pap. write for info. (*0-88368-497-7*) Whitaker Hse.

There Were Two Trees in the Garden. rev. ed. Rick Joyner. 208p. 1992. reprint ed. pap. 9.95 (*1-878327-19-4*) Morning NC.

There Were Two Trees in the Garden. Rick Joyner. 136p. (C). reprint ed. pap. text ed. 5.95 (*1-878327-04-6*) Omega Pubns OR.

There Were Zulus at the Bottom of Our Garden. Margaret Heard. 204p. 1987. 29.00 (*0-7223-1910-X*, Pub. by A H S Ltd UK) St Mut.

There Will Be No Goodbyes. Laura D. Young. 240p. 1995. pap. 10.95 (*1-56280-103-1*) Naiad Pr.

There Will Be Time. Poul Anderson. 1993. mass mkt. 4.99 (*0-8125-2308-3*) Tor Bks.

There Will Be War. Ed. by Jerry Pournelle. 352p. 1990. pap. 3.95 (*0-8125-0900-5*) Tor Bks.

There Will Be War: After Armageddon, Vol. IX. Ed. by Jerry Pournelle. 1990. pap. 3.95 (*0-8125-4967-8*) Tor Bks.

There Will Be War: Armageddon, Vol. VIII. Ed. by Jerry Pournelle. 1989. pap. 3.95 (*0-8125-4965-1*) Tor Bks.

There Will Be War: Blood & Iron, Vol. III. Ed. by Jerry Pournelle. 384p. (Orig.). 1984. pap. 2.95 (*0-8125-4955-4*) Tor Bks.

There Will Be War: Call to Battle, Vol. VII. Ed. by Jerry Pournelle. 384p. 1988. pap. 3.95 (*0-8125-4963-5*) Tor Bks.

There Will Be War: Men of War, Vol. II. Ed. by Jerry Pournelle. 320p. (Orig.). 1990. pap. 3.95 (*0-8125-0902-1*) Tor Bks.

There Will Be Wolves. Karleen Bradford. LC 96-1399. 208p. (YA). (gr. 7 up). 1996. pap. 15.99 (*0-525-67539-6*, Lodestar Bks) Dutton Child Bks.

There Will I Sing: The Making of a Tenor: A Biography of Richard Lewis CBE. Richard Lewis. (Illus.). 152p. 1997. 24.95 (*1-871871-29-8*, Pub. by Open Gate Pr UK) Paul & Co Pubs.

There Will Never Be Another You. R. Weinreich. 1992. 17.99 (*0-89906-427-2*); pap. 14.99 (*0-89906-428-0*) Mesorah Pubns.

There Won't Be War. Ed. by Harry Harrison & Bruce McAllister. (Orig.). 1991. mass mkt. 3.99 (*0-8125-1941-8*) Tor Bks.

There You Are: Poems. Louis Simpson. 100p. (Orig.). 16.95 (*1-885266-15-4*); pap. 10.00 (*1-885266-17-0*) Story Line.

Therea & the Aegean World, Vol. 2: Earth Sciences. Ed. by D. A. Hardy et al. 488p. write for info. (*0-9506133-5-5*, Pub. by Thera Fnd UK) DAP Assocs.

Therea & the Aegean World, Vol. 3: Chronology. Ed. by D. A. Hardy & Colin Renfrew. 240p. write for info. (*0-9506133-6-3*, Pub. by Thera Fnd UK) DAP Assocs.

Thereafter Johnnie. Carolivia Herron. LC 91-51191. (Vintage Contemporaries Ser.). 1992. pap. 10.00 (*0-679-74188-7*, Vin) Random.

Thereby Hangs a Tale: Stories of Curious Word Origins. Charles E. Funk. 1993. pap. 9.00 (*0-06-272049-X*) HarpC.

Therefore, Choose Life. John Tallmadge. LC 91-50669. 32p. (Orig.). 1991. pap. 3.00 (*0-87574-300-5*) Pendle Hill.

Therefore Must Be Loved. large type ed. Theresa Charles. 320p. 1987. 25.99 (*0-7089-1723-2*) Ulverscroft.

Therefore Stand. Wilbur M. Smith. LC 81-81096. (Shepherd Illustrated Classics Ser.). 648p. 1988. pap. 9.95 (*0-8254-5320-8*, Kregel Class) Kregel.

Therein Goodness Stands You. Paul E. Barr. (Illus.). 184p. 1995. text ed. 17.00 (*0-8059-3738-2*) Dorrance.

Therein/Thereout. Mark Sonnenfeld. 52p. pap. 3.00 (*0-9632820-3-4*) M Sonnenfeld.

There'll Be Another. David W. McFadden. 1996. pap. text ed. 10.95 (*0-88922-361-0*) Genl Dist Srvs.

There's a Bat in Bunk Five. Paula Danziger. 160p. (J). (gr. 5-9). 1988. pap. 3.99 (*0-440-40098-8*, LE) Dell.

There's a Bat on the Balcony. Kim Caraher. LC 92-34260. (Voyages Ser.). (Illus.). (J). 1993. 4.25 (*0-383-03660-7*) SRA McGraw.

There's a Bat Wing in My Lunchbox. Ann Hodgman. 96p. (J). 1988. pap. 2.95 (*0-380-75426-6*, Camelot) Avon.

There's a Bear in the Bath! Nanette Newman. LC 93-12877. (Illus.). 32p. (J). (ps-3). 1994. 14.00 (*0-15-285512-2*) HarBrace.

There's a Bear in the Classroom. Nanette Newman. (Illus.). 32p. (J). (gr. 1-4). 1996. 19.95 (*1-85793-679-5*, Pub. by Pavilion UK) Trafalgar.

There's a Bear in the Woods. Louise Gikow. (J). (ps-3). 1993. pap. 3.50 (*0-307-11568-2*, Golden Pr) Western Pub.

There's a Bear in the Woods! Wishing Well Staff. (Peek-In Board Books Ser.). (Illus.). 10p. (J). (ps-k). 1995. 3.99 (*0-88705-740-3*, Wshng Well Bks) Joshua Morris.

There's a Beat That's Comin' A Poetic Journey Toward Self-Actualization. Andika. (Illus.). 128p. 1993. write for info. (*1-881441-54-7*); pap. write for info. (*1-881441-53-9*) Miss Link Comms.

There's a Blue Bear in the Bathtub & My Mother Is Mad. Sandra Potts. LC 93-93801. (Illus.). 64p. (Orig.). (J). 1994. pap. 5.00 (*1-56002-327-9*, Univ Edtns) Aegina Pr.

There's a Blue Square on My Brother's School Bus. Sally Craymer. LC 92-61768. (Illus.). 59p. (Orig.). (J). (gr. k-12). 1992. pap. 4.95 (*0-931563-12-7*) Wishing Rm.

There's a Boy in Here. Judy Barron & Sean Barron. 272p. 1994. mass mkt. 4.99 (*0-380-72292-5*) Avon.

There's a Boy in the Girl's Bathroom. (Reading Group Guides Ser.). (J). 1997. pap. write for info. (*0-676-76236-0*) Knopf Bks Yng Read.

There's a Boy in the Girl's Bathroom. Louis Sachar. LC 86-20100. 224p. (J). (gr. 5 up). 1987. lib. bdg. 13.99 (*0-394-98570-2*) Knopf Bks Yng Read.

There's a Boy in the Girls' Bathroom. Louis Sachar. LC 86-20100. 208p. (J). (gr. 3-7). 1988. reprint ed. pap. 3.99 (*0-394-80572-0*) Random.

There's a Bug in My Mug! Kent Salisbury. 1997. 6.99 (*1-56293-931-9*) McClanahan Bk.

There's a Building on Sixth Avenue. Rodney Rigby. LC 91-23097. (Illus.). 32p. (J). (ps-3). 1992. lib. bdg. 13.89 (*1-56282-156-3*) Hyprn Child.

There's a Cat in a Tree! Wishing Well Staff. (Peek-In Board Books Ser.). (Illus.). 10p. (J). (ps-k). 1995. 3.99 (*0-88705-742-X*, Wshng Well Bks) Joshua Morris.

There's a Cobweb on the Rocking Chair. Romaine Wismer. (Illus.). 96p. (Orig.). 1993. pap. 6.95 (*0-9617021-3-3*) R Wismer.

There's a Country in My Cellar. Russell Baker. 432p. 1991. pap. 8.95 (*0-380-71451-5*) Avon.

There's a Cow in the Road! Reeve Lindbergh. LC 92-34883. (Illus.). 32p. (J). (ps-2). 1993. pap. 13.99 (*0-8037-1335-5*) Dial Bks Young.

There's a Cricket in the Library. McKee Elementary School Fifth-Grade Students. (Kids Are Authors Ser.). (Illus.). 24p. (J). (gr. k-3). 1991. pap. 3.50 (*0-87406-568-2*) Willowisp Pr.

There's a Cupid in My Soup. Gail Hamilton. LC 96-95288. 192p. 1997. 17.95 (*0-8034-9188-3*, Avalon Bks) Bouregy.

There's a Dinosaur in My Bathtub! Olivia Long. (World of Dinosaurs Ser.). (Illus.). 32p. (J). (ps-4). Date not set. write for info. (*1-880042-11-8*) Shelf-Life Bks.

There's a Dinosaur in the Park! Rodney Martin. LC 86-42811. (Illus.). 31p. (J). (gr. 2-3). 1987. lib. bdg. 18.60 (*1-55532-151-8*) Gareth Stevens Inc.

There's a Dragon About: A Winter's Revel. Richard Schotter & Roni Schotter. LC 93-46421. (Illus.). 32p. (J). (ps-2). 1994. lib. bdg. 16.99 (*0-531-08708-5*) Orchard Bks Watts.

There's a Dragon About: A Winter's Revel. Richard Schotter & Roni Schotter. LC 93-46421. (Illus.). 32p. (J). (ps-2). 1994. 15.95 (*0-531-06858-7*) Orchard Bks Watts.

There's a Dragon at My School. Jenny Tyler. (Flap Bks.). (Illus.). 16p. (J). (ps up). 1997. pap. 6.95 (*0-7460-2818-0*, Usborne) EDC.

There's a Dragon in My Sleeping Bag. Howe. (J). 1998. mass mkt. 5.99 (*0-689-81922-6*) S&S Childrens.

There's a Dragon in My Sleeping Bag. James Howe. LC 93-26572. (Illus.). 40p. (J). (ps-2). 1994. text ed. 15.00 (*0-689-31873-1*, Atheneum Bks Young) S&S Childrens.

Theres a Dragon in My Sleeping Bag: Spanish, Vol 3. Howe. (J). 1996. 4.95 (*0-689-31955-X*, Atheneum Bks Young) S&S Childrens.

There's a Duck in My Closet! John Trent. LC 93-15707. (J). (gr. k-5). 1993. 12.99 (*0-8499-1037-4*) Word Pub.

There's a Fish in the Courthouse. 2nd rev. ed. Gary L. Wean. 1992. reprint ed. 29.95 (*0-685-58477-1*) Casitas Bks.

There's a Fox in Pinchot's Forest. Aileen S. Freeman. LC 96-83331. (Illus.). 278p. (Orig.). 1996. pap. 14.95 (*0-9644199-1-2*) Freeman Open Syst.

There's a Fungus Among Us. Carol Benanti. (Books & Stuff). (Illus.). 24p. (Orig.). (J). (gr. 3-7). 1996. pap. 8.95 (*0-448-41344-2*, G&D) Putnam Pub Group.

There's a Ghost in My House. Sarah Albee. (Illus.). 24p. (Orig.). (J). (ps-3). 1996. pap. 3.95 (*0-8167-4113-1*, Whistlstop) Troll Communs.

There's a Ghost in the Boys' Bathroom. Tom B. Stone. (Graveyard School Ser.: Vol. 10). 128p. (J). (gr. 3-7). 1996. pap. 3.50 (*0-553-48345-5*, Skylark BDD) BDD Bks Young Read.

There's a Ghost in the House. Daniel Cohen. 64p. (J). 1995. pap. 2.99 (*0-590-54333-4*) Scholastic Inc.

There's a Girl in My Hammerlock. Jerry Spinelli. LC 91-8765. 208p. (YA). (gr. 5-9). 1991. pap. 14.00 (*0-671-74684-7*, S&S Bks Young Read) S&S Childrens.

There's a Girl in My Hammerlock. Jerry Spinelli. LC 91-8765. 208p. (J). (gr. 5-9). 1993. pap. 4.50 (*0-671-86695-8*, Half Moon Paper) S&S Childrens.

There's a Good Girl: Gender Stereotyping in the First Three Years of Life. Marianne Grabrucker. 176p. pap. 13.95 (*0-7043-4090-9*, Pub. by Womens Press UK) Trafalgar.

T

There's a Hand in My Cupboard: A Story of Sharing & Caring. Doug Peterson. 32p. (J). pap. 5.99 (0-8066-2660-7) Augsburg Fortress.

There's a Hand in My Cupboard: A Story of Sharing & Caring. Doug Peterson. 32p. 1993. pap. 13.99 incl. audio (0-8066-2659-3) Augsburg Fortress.

There's a Healer in the House. Ed Dufresne. (Orig.). 1993. pap. 6.00 (0-940763-07-9) E Dufresne Minist.

***There's a Hearing Impaired Child in My Class: A Learning Packet about Hearing Loss for Public School Teachers.** Debra Nussbaum. (Into the Mainstream Ser.). 44p. Date not set. teacher ed., pap. text ed. 17.95 (0-88095-204-0) Gallaudet U Pre Coll.

There's a Hippopotamus under My Bed. Mike Thaler. (Illus.). 32p. (J). (gr. k-3). 1978. pap. 2.95 (0-380-40238-6, Camelot) Avon.

There's a Hole in My Chest: Healing & Hope for Adult Children Everywhere. William J. Jarema. (Illus.). 96p. 1995. pap. 9.95 (0-8245-1572-2) Crossroad NY.

There's a Hole in My Sidewalk. Portia Nelson. 128p. 1989. reprint ed. pap. 6.95 (0-9621159-0-8) Stonebarn.

There's a Hole in My Sidewalk: The Romance of Self-Discovery. Portia Nelson. LC 93-18380. 1993. pap. 7.95 (0-941831-87-6) Beyond Words Pub.

There's a Hole in the Roof! Wayne Walker. 24p. (J). 1994. pap. 2.99 (0-87406-706-5) Willowisp Pr.

There's a Light in the Gardibee House & Other Stories. Eugene J. Mahoney. 117p. (Orig.). 1985. pap. 2.95 (0-9615994-0-5) E J Mahoney.

There's a Lion in the Jungle! Wishing Well Staff. (Peek-In Board Books Ser.). (Illus.). 10p. (J). (ps-k). 1995. 3.99 (0-88705-743-8, Wshng Well Bks) Joshua Morris.

There's a Little Ambiguity over There among the Bluebells & Other Theater Poems. Ruth Krauss. LC 68-19709. (Illus.). 1968. 15.00 (0-89366-062-0) Ultramarine Pub.

There's a Lot More to Health Than Not Being Sick. Bruce Larson. 144p. 1991. write for info. (1-879989-00-X) New Hope Pub.

There's a Mastodon in My Living Room. Elaine Moore. 144p. (Orig.). (J). (gr. 3-7). 1996. pap. 3.95 (0-8167-4015-1) Troll Communs.

There's a Miracle in Your House. Tommy Barnett. 1993. pap. 9.99 (0-88419-330-6) Creation House.

There's a Missionary Loose in the Kitchen! Favorite Recipes from Around the World. Laurie Ingram & Becky Nelson. 198p. 1995. pap. text ed. 10.95 (1-56309-113-5, New Hope) Womans Mission Union.

***There's a Monster in My Bed!** Sue Inman. (Illus.). 24p. (J). (ps-3). 1997. 3.98 (1-85854-574-9) Brimax Bks.

***There's a Monster in My House.** Jenny Tyler. (Flap Bks.). (Illus.). 16p. (J). (ps up). 1997. pap. 6.95 (0-7460-2816-4, Usborne) EDC.

There's a Monster in the Tree. Rozanne L. Williams. (Emergent Reader Bks.). 16p. 1994. 2.49 (0-916119-66-1) Creat Teach Pr.

There's a Monster in the Tree. Rozanne L. Williams. (Emergent Reader Big Bks.). (Illus.). 16p. (Orig.). (J). (gr. k-2). 1995. pap. 11.98 (1-57471-078-8) Creat Teach Pr.

There's a Monster under My Bed. James Howe. LC 85-20026. (Illus.). 32p. (J). (ps-2). 1986. lib. bdg. 15.00 (0-689-31178-8, Atheneum Bks Young) S&S Childrens.

There's a Monster under My Bed. James Howe. LC 89-18664. (Illus.). 32p. (J). (gr. k-3). 1990. reprint ed. pap. 4.95 (0-689-71409-2, Aladdin Paperbacks) S&S Childrens.

***There's a Moose in My Juice.** Dr. Seuss. (J). 1997. 4.99 (0-679-88455-6) Random.

***There's a Moose in My Juice.** Ron Roy. (Wee Wubbulous Library). (J). 1997. pap. 4.99 (0-679-88755-5) Random Bks Yng Read.

There's a Mouse about the House. Richard Fowler. (Slot Bks.). (Illus.). 24p. (J). (ps-1). 1984. 10.95 (0-88110-154-0) EDC.

There's a New World Coming: An In-Depth Analysis of the Book of Revelation. Hal Lindsey. 288p. 1984. pap. 9.99 (0-89081-440-6) Harvest Hse.

There's a Nightmare in My Closet. Mercer Mayer. LC 68-15250. (Illus.). (J). (ps-3). 1968. pap. 15.99 (0-8037-8682-4) Dial Bks Young.

There's a Nightmare in My Closet. Mercer Mayer. LC 68-15250. (Illus.). (J). (ps-3). 1985. pap. 4.95 (0-8037-8574-7); lib. bdg. 14.89 (0-8037-8683-2); student ed. 17.99 (0-8037-0843-2) Dial Bks Young.

There's a Nightmare in My Closet. Mercer Mayer. (J). 1992. pap. 5.99 (0-14-054712-6, Puffin) Puffin Bks.

There's a Nightmare in My Closet - Una Pesadilla En Mi Armario. Mercer Mayer. (SPA.). (J). 7.50 (84-372-1754-7) Santillana.

There's a One-Armed Bandit in My Kitchen. Candy Coleman. (Illus.). 48p. (Orig.). 1980. pap. text ed. 3.00 (0-943768-03-9) C Coleman.

***There's a Party at Mona's Tonight.** Harry Allard. 1997. pap. 5.99 (0-440-91191-5) Dell.

***There's a Pharaoh in Our Bath!** large type ed. Jeremy Strong. (J). 1997. 16.95 (0-7451-6904-X, Galaxy Child Lrg Print) Chivers N Amer.

***There's a Pig in the Closet!** Kate Anderson & Bill Anderson. (Illus.). 32p. (J). (ps-3). 1997. 16.00 (0-9642979-3-0) New Energy Pr.

There's a Place I Go: A Fantasy Adventure for Children & Adults. Anne T. Lincoln. 40p. (J). (gr. 3-5). 1995. 24.95 incl. audio (0-9649730-2-2, TADCO TRIPLETT); audio 9.95 (0-9649730-1-4, TADCO TRIPLETT) TADCO.

There's a Place I Go: A Fantasy Adventure for Children & Adults. Anne T. Lincoln. 40p. (J). (gr. 3-5). 1997. 5.95 (0-9649730-0-6, TADCO TRIPLETT) TADCO.

There's a Rabbit in the Garden! Wishing Well Staff. (Peek-In Board Books Ser.). (Illus.). 10p. (J). (ps-k). 1995. 3.99 (0-88705-741-1, Wshng Well Bks) Joshua Morris.

There's a Rock in Your Coke. Armando B. Rico. 47p. (Orig.). (YA). 1987. pap. 2.50 (1-879219-02-6) Veracruz Pubs.

There's a Shark in the Swimming Pool Book 3, Bk. 3. George E. Stanley. (Scaredy Cats Ser.). (Illus.). 80p. (J). (gr. 2-5). 1996. pap. 3.99 (0-689-80859-3, Aladdin Paperbacks) S&S Childrens.

There's a Snake at Girls' Camp. Lael J. Littke. LC 94-751. (Bee There Ser.: No. 4). (Orig.). (J). (gr. 3-7). 1994. pap. 4.95 (0-87579-845-4) Deseret Bk.

There's a Snake in My Garden. Jill Briscoe. 205p. 1996. pap. 8.99 (0-87788-811-6) Shaw Pubs.

There's a Snake in the Toilet. Gisela T. Sherman. (J). (gr. 2-6). 1995. pap. 3.50 (0-671-87089-0, Minstrel Bks) PB.

There's a Spirit in the Kitchen. Jackie Dashiell & Wanda S. Parrott. LC 96-34493. 256p. (Orig.). 1996. pap. 16.95 (1-880090-25-2) Galde Pr.

There's a Spouse in the House! Get 'Em Out! 100 Plus Ways to Keep a Retired Spouse Busy! Patricia Schnepf. (Illus.). 112p. 1995. pap. 5.95 (0-9641919-5-4) Islewest Pub.

There's a Square: A Book about Shapes. Mary Serfozo. LC 95-9083. (Story Corner Ser.). (Illus.). 32p. (J). (ps). 1996. 6.95 (0-590-54426-8, Cartwheel) Scholastic Inc.

***There's a Star Spangled Banner Waving Somewhere.** Ed. by Carrie Neumann & Ginny Ballor. (Illus.). 40p. (Orig.). 1996. pap. 3.00 (1-882294-12-2) Green Gate.

***There's a Tarantula.** Susan Clymer. 1997. mass mkt. 2.99 (0-590-88025-X) Scholastic Inc.

There's a Troll in My Closet. Carol Ellis. (J). 1994. pap. 2.99 (0-671-87161-7, Minstrel Bks) PB.

There's a Troll in My Popcorn. Carol Ellis. (YA). 1994. pap. 3.50 (0-671-87162-5, Minstrel Bks) PB.

There's a Troll in My Sleeping Bag. Carol Ellis. Ed. by Ruth Ashby. (Illus.). 96p. (Orig.). 1994. pap. 3.50 (0-671-87163-3, Minstrel Bks) PB.

There's a Vulture Outside. Charles M. Schulz. LC 75-29871. 192p. 1976. pap. 4.95 (0-03-017481-3) H Holt & Co.

There's a Vulture Outside. Charles M. Schulz. (Peanuts Classics Ser.). 128p. 1991. pap. 7.95 (0-8050-1897-2, Owl) H Holt & Co.

There's a War to Be Won. Geoffrey Perret. 1992. mass mkt. 5.99 (0-345-37924-1) Ballantine.

***There's a War to Be Won.** Geoffrey Perret. 1997. pap. 14.00 (0-345-41909-X) Ballantine.

There's a Way Back to God. William MacDonald. 1986. reprint ed. pap. 3.00 (0-937396-42-7) Walterick Pubs.

There's a Wocket in My Pocket! Dr. Seuss. LC 74-5516. (Bright & Early Bks.). (Illus.). 36p. (J). (ps-1). 1974. 7.99 (0-394-82920-4); lib. bdg. 11.99 (0-394-92920-9) Random Bks Yng Read.

There's a Wocket in My Pocket! Dr. Suess's Book of Ridiculous Rhymes. 1996. 4.99 (0-679-88283-9) Random.

There's a Wolf in the Classroom! Bruce Weide & Patricia Tucker. LC 94-42673. (J). 1995. write for info. (0-87614-939-5, Carolrhoda) Lerner Group.

There's a Wolf in the Classroom. Bruce Weide. (J). 1995. pap. 8.95 (0-87614-958-1) Lerner Group.

***There's a Word for It.** Elster. 1997. pap. 14.00 (0-671-77858-7) PB.

There's a Word for It. Charles H. Elster. 192p. 1996. 22.00 (0-684-82455-8) S&S Trade.

There's a Worm in My Apple. Sheena Baker. (Illus.). 111p. 1985. pap. 6.95 (0-7737-5029-0) Genl Dist Srvs.

There's Always a Bull Market: Conservative Investing in Stocks, Bonds, & Gold. Robert Kinsman. 260p. 1989. 30.00 (1-55623-186-5) Irwin Prof Pubng.

There's Always Room for Sugar Free Jell-O Brand. (Favorite All Time Recipes Ser.). (Illus.). 96p. 1993. spiral bd. 3.50 (1-56173-543-4, 2014500) Pubns Intl Ltd.

There's an Alligator under My Bed. Mercer Mayer. LC 86-19944. (Illus.). 32p. (J). (ps-3). 1987. pap. 14.99 (0-8037-0374-0); lib. bdg. 14.89 (0-8037-0375-9) Dial Bks Young.

There's an Angel in My Locker. Mary L. Carney. (Herbie the Angel Ser.). 128p. (Orig.). (J). (gr. 7-9). 1986. pap. 6.99 (0-310-28471-6, 11341P) Zondervan.

There's an Angel on Your Shoulder: Angel Encounters in Everyday Life. Kelsey Tyler. 160p. (Orig.). 1994. pap. 10.00 (0-425-14369-4, Berkley Trade) Berkley Pub.

There's an Ant in Anthony. Bernard Most. LC 79-23089. (Illus.). 32p. (J). (gr. k-3). 1992. pap. 3.95 (0-688-11513-6, Morrow Junior) Morrow.

***There's an Awful Lot of Weirdos.** 2nd ed. Colin McNaughton. LC 97-538. (Illus.). 96p. (J). 1997. 16.99 (0-7636-0299-X) Candlewick Pr.

There's an Elephant in the Bathtub. Jo Albee. (Storytime Bks.). (Illus.). 24p. (Orig.). (J). (ps-2). 1992. pap. 1.29 (1-878624-39-3) McClanahan Bk.

There's an Old Southern Saying: The Wit & Wisdom of Dan May. Dan May. 130p. (Orig.). 1995. pap. 13.95 (0-9638911-0-3) Crabby Keys.

***There's an Orangutan in My Bathtub.** Mallory Tarcher. (J). 1997. pap. 2.95 (0-8167-4211-1) Troll Communs.

***There's an Owl in the Shower.** Jean C. George. (Illus.). 144p. (J). (gr. 2-5). 1997. pap. 4.50 (0-06-440682-2, Trophy) HarpC Child Bks.

***There's an Owl in the Shower.** Jean Craighead George. LC 94-38893. (Chapter Bk.). (Illus.). 128p. (J). (gr. 2-5). 1995. pap. 3.95 (0-06-442062-0, Trophy) HarpC Child Bks.

There's an Owl in the Shower. Jean Craighead George. LC 94-38893. (Illus.). 144p. (J). (gr. 2-5). 1995. 13.95 (0-06-024891-2); lib. bdg. 13.89 (0-06-024892-0) HarpC Child Bks.

There's Dynamite in Praise. Don Gossett. 128p. 1974. mass mkt. 4.99 (0-88368-048-3) Whitaker Hse.

There's Gotta Be a Better Way: Discipline That Works! rev. ed. Becky Bailey. Ed. by Penny Leggett & Keith McIntyre. (Illus.). 352p. (Orig.). 1996. pap. 19.95 (0-9638752-1-3) Loving Guidnce.

There's Hope after Divorce. Jeenie Gordon. 192p. (gr. 10). 1996. mass mkt. 5.99 (0-8007-8634-3, Spire) Revell.

***There's Hope for the Child That Says, "If I Grow Up..."** Fannie Butler. 146p. (Orig.). 1997. pap. 10.95 (0-9656774-2-7) Choice Pubng CA.

There's Hope for the Future. Richard G. Lee. LC 95-572. 192p. 1996. 16.99 (0-8054-6188-4, 4261-88) Broadman.

There's Hope for the Hurting. Richard Lee. LC 94-15731. (Illus.). 1994. pap. 8.99 (1-56507-164-6) Harvest Hse.

***There's Humor on the Other Side.** 225p. (Orig.). 1996. pap. 12.95 (0-9654226-0-7) L&E.

There's Magic in Discovery! John J. Pelizza. Ed. by Phillip Niles. (Illus.). 165p. 1993. pap. 11.95 (0-9614872-2-4) Pelizza & Assocs.

There's Math in Deviled Eggs. Agency for Instructional Technology Staff. 24p. (Orig.). 1993. pap. text ed. 4.00 (0-7842-0719-4); vhs write for info. (0-7842-0720-8) Agency Instr Tech.

There's Money Where Your Mouth Is: An Insider's Guide to a Career in Voice-overs. Elaine A. Clark. LC 95-17341. (Illus.). 208p. 1995. pap. 16.95 (0-8230-7703-9, Back Stage Bks) Watsn-Guptill.

There's More, Much More. Sue Alexander. LC 86-33632. (Illus.). 32p. (J). (ps-3). 1987. 13.00 (0-15-200605-2, Gulliver Bks) HarBrace.

There's More to Life Than Parsley. Maumee Valley Herb Society Staff et al. (Illus.). 192p. (Orig.). 1994. pap. 12.95 (0-9644350-0-4) Maumee Vall Herb Soc.

***There's More to Life Than Politics.** William P. Murchison, Jr. 1997. write for info. (0-9653208-3-9) Spence Pub.

There's More to Life Than Pumpkins, Drugs & Other False Gods. Kenneth G. Reiners. LC 80-50424. 64p. (Orig.). 1980. pap. 5.50 (0-934104-03-4) Woodland.

There's More to Me Than I've Used Yet. Frances Weaver. 140p. (Orig.). 1994. pap. 10.00 (0-9617930-6-6) Midlife Musings.

There's More to Musicals Than Music. Martha Eddins et al. (Illus.). 72p. 1980. pap. 7.95 (0-916642-13-5, 566) Somerset Pr IL.

There's More to Quitting Drinking Than Quitting Drinking. Paul O. 1995. pap. 14.95 (0-9644887-4-4) Sabrina Pub.

There's No Business. Charles Bukowski. LC 84-2977. (Illus.). 17p. 1995. reprint ed. 14.00 (0-87685-623-7); reprint ed. pap. 5.00 (0-87685-622-9) Black Sparrow.

***There's No Business Like Your Business: How to Turn Your Knowledge into Personal Profit.** Jack Nadel. 240p. (Orig.). 1996. pap. 14.95 (1-887697-03-9) Two Roads Pubng.

There's No Cure see Day at a Time

There's No One Quite Like You. Sue Schott. (Illus.). 20p. (J). (ps-2). 1995. 11.95 (1-885374-03-8) Global Blocks.

There's No Place Like Home. Marc Brown. LC 93-13040. (Parents Magazine Read Aloud Original Ser.). (J). lib. bdg. 17.27 (0-8368-0978-5) Gareth Stevens Inc.

There's No Place Like Home. Marc Brown. LC 84-4229. (Illus.). 48p. (J). (ps-3). 1984. 5.95 (0-8193-1125-1) Parents.

***There's No Place Like Home.** A. G. Cascone. (YA). (gr. 7 up). 1997. pap. 3.95 (0-8167-4222-7) Troll Communs.

There's No Place Like Home. Great Quotations Staff. 64p. 1995. 6.50 (1-56245-211-8) Great Quotations.

There's No Place Like Home. Dolah Saleh. 219p. (Orig.). 1996. pap. 12.95 (1-55197-234-4, Pub. by Comnwlth Pub CN) Partners Pubs Grp.

There's No Place Like Home: Anthropological Perspectives on Housing & Homelessness in the United States. Ed. by Anna L. Dehavenon. LC 96-10375. (Contemporary Urban Studies). 224p. 1996. text ed. 55.00 (0-89789-484-7, Bergin & Garvey) Greenwood.

There's No Place Like Home: Confessions of an Interior Designer. Carleton Varney. LC 80-1020. 228p. 1980. write for info. (0-672-51872-4) Macmillan.

There's No Sale Like Wholesale: A Directory to Wholesale & Factory Outlet Shopping in Southern California. Ann D. Ukrainetz & Michael W. King. (Illus.). 306p. (Orig.). 1992. pap. write for info. (0-9632080-0-4) Consumer Res.

There's No Such Place As Far Away. Richard Bach. (Illus.). 48p. 1990. 18.95 (0-385-30211-8) Delacorte.

There's No Such Thing As a Chanukah Bush, Sandy Goldstein. Susan Sussman. Ed. by Kathleen Tucker. LC 83-1291. (Illus.). 48p. (J). (gr. 3-7). 1983. lib. bdg. 8.95 (0-8075-7862-2) A Whitman.

There's No Such Thing As a Chanukah Bush, Sandy Goldstein. Susan Sussman. (J). (gr. 4-7). 1993. pap. 3.50 (0-8075-7863-0) A Whitman.

There's No Such Thing As a Ghost. Michael Teitelbaum. (Slightly Spooky Stories Ser.). (Illus.). (J). 1992. 2.98 (1-56156-091-X) Kidsbks.

There's No Such Thing As a Perfect Wedding: True Wedding Tales, Odd, Funny & Disastrous. Margaret G. Bigger. LC 91-71001. (Illus.). 90p. 1991. pap. 7.95 (1-878086-04-9) Down Home NC.

***There's No Such Thing As Coincidence.** Jan Wolterman. 136p. (Orig.). 1997. pap. 12.00 (0-9656221-0-X) Universal Pubns.

There's No Such Thing As Free Speech: And It's a Good Thing, Too. Stanley Fish. 348p. 1994. reprint ed. pap. 14.95 (0-19-509383-6) OUP.

There's No Such Thing As Too Much Love. Marty Links. LC 83-71146. (Illus.). 1984. 5.95 (0-915696-84-3) Determined Prods.

There's Nobody There: Community Care of Confused Older People. Anne Opie et al. (Studies in Health, Illness, & Caregiving). 232p. (Orig.). (C). 1992. pap. text ed. 19.95 (0-8122-1419-6) U of Pa Pr.

There's Not a Bathing Suit in Russia & Other Bare Facts. Will Rogers. Ed. by Joseph A. Stout, Jr. LC 73-89307. (Writings of Will Rogers Ser.: Ser. I, Vol. 2). (Illus.). 95p. 1973. pap. 5.95 (0-914956-03-5) Okla State Univ Pr.

***There's Nothing in the Middle of the Road But Yellow Stripes & Dead Armadillos.** Jim Hightower. 1997. 23.00 (0-06-018766-2) HarpC.

***There's Nothing Sweeter Than a Friend: Daybrighteners.** Garborg's Publishing Staff. 1997. 7.99 (1-881830-62-4) Garborgs.

There's Nothing to be Afraid Of. Marcia Muller. 224p. 1990. mass mkt. 5.50 (0-445-40901-0, Mysterious Paperbk) Warner Bks.

There's Nothing to Do! A Guide Full of Answers Right in Our Hometown. Ann N. Kowalski & Susan K. Donley. LC 92-62250. (Illus.). 200p. (Orig.). 1992. pap. 9.95 (0-9634794-0-7) Pittsbgh Fund.

There's One Thousand Things to Do! So Why Are You Watching TV? Melanie C. Ferguson. 116p. (Orig.). 1993. pap. 5.95 (0-9638202-9-X) New Moon CA.

There's Only One of Me Here Today. LC 92-90249. 1992. 9.95 (0-9632178-0-1) S M Brunsmann.

There's Only One Way to Win: Modern Success Principles, & the Colorful Style of an Old-Fashioned Coach. Dick DeVenzio. 224p. 1992. 17.95 (0-910305-02-1) Fool Court.

There's Something about the Nanny... Judy G. Gill. 1996. mass mkt. 3.50 (0-373-44007-3, 1-44007-2) Harlequin Bks.

There's Something at the Mail Slot. Jez Alborough. LC 94-22619. (Illus.). (J). (ps up). 1995. pap. 4.99 (1-56402-523-3) Candlewick Pr.

There's Something I Have to Tell You. Charles Foster. 1997. 25.00 (0-517-70730-6, Harmony) Crown Pub Group.

There's Something in a Sunday. Marcia Muller. 224p. 1990. mass mkt. 3.99 (0-445-40865-0, Mysterious Paperbk) Warner Bks.

There's Something in My Attic. Mercer Mayer. LC 86-32875. (Illus.). 32p. (J). (ps-3). 1988. lib. bdg. 11.89 (0-8037-0415-1) Dial Bks Young.

There's Something in My Attic. Mercer Mayer. (Illus.). 32p. (J). (ps-3). 1992. pap. 4.99 (0-14-054813-0, Puffin) Puffin Bks.

There's Something I've Been Meaning to Tell You: An Anthology about Lesbians & Gay Men Coming Out to Their Children. Ed. by Loralee MacPike. 288p. 1989. 16.95 (0-941483-54-1); pap. 9.95 (0-941483-44-4) Naiad Pr.

There's Something Seriously Wrong with Me. Craig Cotter. LC 91-13176. 68p. (Orig.). 1991. pap. 10.50 (0-941749-27-4) Black Tie Pr.

There's Something Weird in That Cave! Michael Teitelbaum. (Slightly Spooky Stories Ser.). (Illus.). (J). 1992. 2.98 (1-56156-092-8) Kidsbks.

***There's Still Time: The Success of the Endangered Species Act.** Mark Galan. 1997. 15.00 (0-7922-7092-4) Natl Geog.

There's This River... Grand Canyon Boatman Stories. Christa Sadler. (Illus.). 183p. 1994. pap. 14.95 (1-884546-01-3) Red Lake Bks.

There's Treasure Everywhere: A Calvin & Hobbes Collection. Bill Watterson. 176p. 1996. 19.95 (0-8362-1313-0); pap. 14.95 (0-8362-1312-2) Andrews & McMeel.

Theresa. Arthur Schnitzler. Tr. by William A. Drake. LC 70-175445. 460p. 1972. reprint ed. 37.50 (0-404-05617-2) AMS Pr.

Theresa Pollak: European Drawings. Marilyn A. Zeitlin. (Illus.). 48p. (Orig.). 1986. pap. text ed. write for info. (0-935519-05-X) Anderson Gal.

***Theresa's Diary.** Francis T. Vena. 64p. (Orig.). 1997. pap. 4.50 (1-56167-358-7) Am Literary Pr.

Therese. Dorothy Day. 178p. 1979. pap. 12.95 (0-87243-090-1) Templegate.

Therese. Francois Mauriac. Tr. by Gerard Hopkins. 400p. 1995. pap. 10.95 (0-14-018153-9, Penguin Classics) Viking Penguin.

Therese. Francois Mauriac. Date not set. pap. 9.95 (0-14-043486-0) Viking Penguin.

***Therese & Lisieux.** Pierre Descouvement. (Illus.). 336p. 1996. 60.00 (0-8028-3836-7) Eerdmans.

Therese & Pierrette & the Little Hanging Angel. Michel Tremblay. 262p. 1996. pap. text ed. 15.95 (0-88922-198-7) Genl Dist Srvs.

Therese Desqueyroux. Francois Mauriac. pap. 9.95 (0-686-55479-5) Fr & Eur.

Therese Desqueyroux. Francois Mauriac. (Coll. Diamant). (FRE.). 1955. 10.95 (0-8288-9868-5, F113170) Fr & Eur.

Therese, My Love. Shirley Dummer. 216p. (Orig.). 1987. pap. 8.00 (0-9633479-1-8) Dummer Pub.

Therese Neumann: Mystic & Stigmatist (1892-1962) Adalbert A. Vogl. LC 84-50403. (Illus.). 172p. 1994. reprint ed. pap. 13.00 (0-89555-241-8) TAN Bks Pubs.

***Therese of Lisieux.** Janice E. Leonard. (Illus.). 104p. (Orig.). 1997. pap. 8.95 (1-884454-50-X) Laudemont Pr.

Therese of Lisieux: A Biography. Patricia O'Connor. LC 83-63169. 168p. 1984. pap. 7.95 (0-87973-607-0, 607) Our Sunday Visitor.

Therese of Lisieux: A Discovery of Love: Selected Spiritual Writings. 3rd ed. Terence Carey. 144p. (Orig.). 1992. pap. 9.95 (1-56548-072-4) New City.

***Therese of Lisieux: A Life of Love.** Jean Chalon. Tr. by Anne C. Rehill from ENG. LC 97-9983. 288p. (Orig.). 1997. pap. 16.00 (0-7648-0111-2) Liguori Pubns.

Therese of Lisieux: A Vocation of Love. Marie-Pascale Ducrocq. LC 81-20512. 77p. (Orig.). 1982. pap. 3.95 (0-8189-0431-3) Alba.

An Asterisk (*) at the beginning of an entry indicates that the title is appearing in BIP for the first time.

***Therese of Lisieux & Marie of the Trinity: A Transformative Relationship.** Pierre Descouvemont & Joyce Ridick. Tr. by Alexandra Plettenberg-Serban from FRE. Orig. Title: Une Novice de Sainte Therese. (Illus.). 188p. (Orig.). 1997. pap. 14.95 (*0-8189-0732-0*) Alba.

Therese Raquin. Emile Zola. write for info. (*0-8488-0688-3*) Amereon Ltd.

Therese Raquin. Emile Zola. 335p. (FRE.). 1991. pap. 10.95 (*0-685-74011-0*, 2266036734) Fr & Eur.

Therese Raquin. Emile Zola. Ed. by Andrew Rothwell. (World's Classics Ser.). 272p. 1992. pap. 7.95 (*0-19-282653-0*) OUP.

Therese Raquin. Emile Zola. (Folio Ser.: No. 1116). 256p. (FRE.). 1970. 9.95 (*2-07-037116-6*) Schoenhof.

Therese Raquin. Emile Zola. Tr. by Leonard W. Tancock. (Classics Ser.). 265p. 1962. pap. 9.95 (*0-14-044120-4*, Penguin Classics) Viking Penguin.

Therese Raquin, Zola: Critical Monographs in English. Claude Schumacher. 96p. 1993. pap. 32.00 (*0-85261-263-X*, Pub. by Univ of Glasgow UK) St Mut.

Theresienstadt: Hitler's Gift to the Jews. Norbert Troller. Ed. by Joel Shatzky. Tr. by Susan E. Cernyak-Spatz from GER. LC 90-47029. (Illus.). xxxviii, 186p. (C). 1991. 24.95 (*0-8078-1965-4*) U of NC Pr.

***Therevidae (Insecta: Diptera)** L. Lyneborg. (Fauna of New Zealand Ser.: Vol. 24). (Illus.). 140p. 1992. pap. 34.95 (*0-477-02632-X*, Pub. by Manaaki Whenua NZ) Balogh.

***Theriault's Presents Barbie: 1959-1976.** Florence Theriault. (Illus.). 128p. 1996. pap. 27.00 (*0-614-23781-5*, N5165) Hobby Hse.

Theriodontia One: Phthinosuchia, Biarmosuchia, Eotitanosuchia, Gorgonopsia. Denise Sigogneau-Russell. (Encyclopedia of Paleoherpetology Ser.: Pt. 17 B-1). 127p. 1989. pap. 125.00 (*0-89574-292-6*, VCH) Wiley.

Theriodontia One: Phthinosuchia, Biarmosuchia, Eotitansuchia, Gorgonopsia - Encyclopedia of Paleoherpetology, Pt. 17 B/1. Denise Sigogneau-Russell. (Illus.). 127p. 1989. pap. text ed. 110.00 (*3-437-30487-9*, Pub. by G Fischer Verlag GW) Lubrecht & Cramer.

***Therma-Mechanical Processing Theory, Modelling, Practice.** 400p. 1997. 102.00 (*0-87170-612-1*, 6460) ASM.

Thermae Et Balnea: The Architecture & Cultural History of Roman Public Baths, 2 vols. Inge Nielsen. (Illus.). 400p. 1991. Set. 125.00 (*87-7288-212-3*) Coronet Bks.

Thermae et Balnea: The Architecture & Cultural History of Roman Public Baths, 2 vols., Set. 2nd ed. Inge Nielsen. (Illus.). 412p. (C). 1993. 100.00 (*87-7288-512-2*, Pub. by Aarhus Univ Pr DK) David Brown.

Thermal Accommodation & Adsorption Coefficients of Gases. S. C. Saxena & R. K. Joshi. (CINDAS Data Series on Material Properties: Vol. II-1). 412p. 1989. 154.00 (*0-89116-870-2*) Hemisp Pub.

Thermal Agents in Rehabilitation. 3rd ed. Ed. by Susan L. Michlovitz et al. (Contemporary Perspectives in Rehabilitation Ser.). (Illus.). 405p. (C). 1996. 39.00 (*0-8036-0044-5*) Davis Co.

Thermal Analysis. 3rd ed. Wesley W. Wendlandt. LC 85-12419. (Chemical Analysis Ser.). 814p. 1986. text ed. 235.00 (*0-471-88477-4*) Wiley.

Thermal Analysis, Vol. 1. 1980. 124.00 (*0-8176-0636-X*) Spr-Verlag.

Thermal Analysis, Vol. 2. 1980. 150.00 (*0-8176-0637-8*) Spr-Verlag.

Thermal Analysis, Vol. 3. 1980. 130.50 (*0-8176-0638-6*) Spr-Verlag.

Thermal Analysis: Fundamentals & Applications to Polymer Science Strategies. T. Hatakeyama & F. X. Quinn. LC 94-4641. 220p. 1994. text ed. 54.95 (*0-471-95103-X*) Wiley.

Thermal Analysis: Proceedings of the International Conference, 4th, Budapest, 1974, 3 vols. International Conference on Thermal Analysis Staff. Ed. by I. Buzas. LC 76-373658. reprint ed. Vol. 2- Organic & Macromolecular Chemistry. Earth Sciences. pap. 160.00 (*0-685-73719-5*); reprint ed. Vol. 3- Applied Sciences, Methodics, & Instrumentation. pap. 160.00 (*0-685-73720-9*) Bks Demand.

Thermal Analysis: Proceedings of the International Conference, 4th, Budapest, 1974, 3 vols., Vol. 1 - Theory Inorganic Chemistry. International Conference on Thermal Analysis Staff. Ed. by I. Buzas. LC 76-373658. reprint ed. Vol. 1- Theory Inorganic Chemistry. pap. 160.00 (*0-685-73718-7*, 2024032) Bks Demand.

Thermal Analysis: Proceedings of the International Conference, 5th, Kyoto, 1977. International Conference on Thermal Analysis Staff. Ed. by H. Chihara. LC 78-323070. 595p. reprint ed. pap. 169.60 (*0-317-29341-9*, 2024033) Bks Demand.

Thermal Analysis: Proceedings of the Seventh International Conference on Thermal Analysis, 2 vols., Vol. 1. International Conference on Thermal Analysis Staff. Ed. by Bernard Miller. LC 82-17517. 826p. reprint ed. pap. 180.00 (*0-8357-3099-9*, 2039356) Bks Demand.

Thermal Analysis: Proceedings of the Seventh International Conference on Thermal Analysis, 2 vols., Vol. 2. International Conference on Thermal Analysis Staff. Ed. by Bernard Miller. LC 82-17517. 771p. reprint ed. pap. 180.00 (*0-8357-3100-6*, 2039356) Bks Demand.

***Thermal Analysis Pt. C: Emanation Thermal Analysis & Other Radiometric Emanation Methods.** V. Balek & J. Tolgessy. (Comprehensive Analytical Chemistry Ser.: Vol. XII C). 304p. 1984. 196.50 (*0-444-99659-1*) Elsevier.

***Thermal Analysis Pt. D: Thermophysical Properties of Solids. Their Measurement & Theoretical Thermal Analysis.** J. Sestak. (Comprehensive Analytical Chemistry Ser.: Vol. XII D). 440p. 1984. 293.25 (*0-444-99653-2*) Elsevier.

Thermal Analysis & Control of Electronic Equipment. Allan D. Kraus & Avram Bar-Cohen. 680p. 1983. text ed. 79.95 (*0-07-035416-2*) McGraw.

Thermal Analysis in Clay Science, Vol. 3. Ed. by J. W. Stucki et al. (CMS Workshop Lectures). (Illus.). 192p. (Orig.). (C). 1990. pap. text ed. 15.00 (*1-881208-03-6*) Clay Minerals.

***Thermal Analysis in Metallurgy.** Ed. by Robert D. Shull & A. Joshi. LC 92-64195. (Illus.). 413p. 1992. reprint ed. pap. 117.80 (*0-608-02486-4*, 2063130) Bks Demand.

Thermal Analysis in the Geosciences. A. Adolf Seilacher. (Lecture Notes in Earth Sciences Ser.: Vol. 38). (Illus.). 392p. 1991. 79.95 (*0-387-54520-4*) Spr-Verlag.

Thermal Analysis of Liquid-Metal Fast Breeder. Tang et al. Ed. by Diane Wojciechowski. LC 77-14646. (Nuclear Science Technology Ser.). (Illus.). 1978. 46.00 (*0-89448-011-1*, 300013) Am Nuclear Soc.

Thermal Analysis of Materials. Robert F. Speyer. LC 93-25572. (Materials Engineering Ser.: Vol. 5). 304p. 1993. 125.00 (*0-8247-8963-6*, 6417U) Dekker.

Thermal Analysis of Pressurized Water Reactors. 2nd rev. ed. L. S. Tong & Joel Weisman. LC 79-54237. (Monograph Ser.). 1979. reprint ed. 45.00 (*0-89448-019-7*, 300015) Am Nuclear Soc.

Thermal Analysis of Pressurized Water Reactors. 3rd ed. L. S. Tong & Joel Weisman. LC 95-45359. 1996. write for info. (*0-89448-038-3*) Am Nuclear Soc.

Thermal Analysis of Pressurized Water Reactors, Study Guide 2. Joel Weisman. 26p. 20.00 (*0-89448-450-8*, 350006) Am Nuclear Soc.

Thermal Analysis of the Convective Three-Stream Heat Exchangers. J. Skladzien. 188p. (C). 1989. 75.00 (*0-685-36853-X*, Pub. by Collets) St Mut.

Thermal Analytical Techniques: Gasification Mechanisms; Production & Use of Carbon-Based Materials for Environmental Cleanup; Preprints of Papers Presented at the 211th ACS National Meeting, Held in New Orleans, Louisiana, March 24-28, 1996. American Chemical Society, Division of Fuel Chemistry Staff. (American Chemical Society, Division of Fuel Chemistry, Preprints of Papers: Vol. 41, No. 1). 527p. 1996. reprint ed. pap. 150.20 (*0-608-01766-3*, 2062424) Bks Demand.

Thermal & Chemical Welding of Plastics. EEMUA Staff. 1976. 135.00 (*0-85931-030-2*, Pub. by EEMUA UK) St Mut.

Thermal & Electrical Conductivity of Polymer Materials. Ed. by Y. K. Godovsky & V. P. Privalko. (Advances in Polymer Science Ser.: Vol. 119). 172p. 1995. 94.95 (*3-540-58502-8*) Spr-Verlag.

Thermal & Environmental Effects in Fatigue: Research-Design Interface. Ed. by C. E. Taske et al. (PVP Ser.: Vol. 71). 256p. 1983. pap. text ed. 12.00 (*0-317-02651-8*, H00257) ASME.

Thermal & Enzymatic Conversions of Precursors to Flavor Compounds: Developed from a Symposium Sponsored by the Divison of Agricultural & Food Chemistry at the Fourth Chemical Congress of North America, 202nd National Meeting of the American Chemical Society, New York, NY, August 25-30, 1991. Roy Teranishi et al. LC 92-10454. (ACS Symposium Ser.: Vol. 490). (Illus.). 281p. 1992. 64.95 (*0-8412-2222-3*) Am Chemical.

Thermal & Flow Design of Helium-Cooled Reactors. Melese & Katz. 432p. 1985. 59.00 (*0-89448-027-8*, 300019) Am Nuclear Soc.

Thermal & Mechanical Behavior of Metal Matrix & Ceramic Matrix Composites. Ed. by J. M. Kennedy et al. LC 90-669. (Special Technical Publication (STP) Ser.: STP 1080). (Illus.). 264p. 1990. text ed. 62.00 (*0-8031-1385-4*, 04-010800-33) ASTM.

***Thermal & Mechanical Test Methods & Behavior of Continuous-Fiber Ceramic Composites.** Ed. by Michael G. Jenkins et al. LC 97-1169. (STP Ser.: No. 1309). (Illus.). 325p. 1997. text ed. 65.00 (*0-8031-2033-8*, 04-01090-30) ASTM.

Thermal & Photostimulated Currents in Insulators: Proceedings of the Symposium. Symposium on Thermal & Photostimulated Currents in Insulators Staff. Ed. by Donald M. Smyth. LC 76-372145. (Illus.). 222p. 1976. pap. 63.30 (*0-7837-8992-0*, 2059257) Bks Demand.

Thermal & Statistical Physics Simulations. Harvey Gould et al. 156p. 1995. pap. text ed. 42.95 (*0-471-54886-3*) Wiley.

Thermal Anemometry 1993. Ed. by D. E. Stock et al. LC 87-71397. (FED Ser.: Vol. 167). 263p. 1993. pap. 45.00 (*0-7918-0975-7*, H00807) ASME.

Thermal Aspects of Fluid Film Tribology. Ed. by Oscar Pinkus. 515p. 1990. 94.00 (*0-7918-0011-3*, 800113) ASME Pr.

Thermal Balance in Health & Disease. Eduard Schonbaum et al. (Advances in Pharmacological Sciences Ser.). 540p. 1994. 145.50 (*0-8176-5054-7*) Birkhauser.

Thermal Balance in Health & Disease: Recent Basic Research & Clinical Progress. Edward Schonbaum & E. Zeisberger. Ed. by P. Lomax et al. LC 94-19416. 1995. 84.00 (*0-8176-5047-4*) Birkhauser.

Thermal Behaviour of Electrical Conductors: Steady, Dynamic & Fault-Current Ratings. Vincent T. Morgan. (Electronic & Electrical Engineering Research Ser.: No. 1744). 741p. 1991. text ed. 298.00 (*0-471-93071-7*) Wiley.

Thermal Characteristics of Polymetric Material. 2nd ed. Edith A. Turl. (C). 1997. text ed. 187.50 (*0-12-703781-0*) HarBrace.

Thermal Characteristics of Polymetric Materials. 2nd ed. Edith A. Turl. (C). 1997. text ed. 187.50 (*0-12-703782-9*) HarBrace.

Thermal Characteristics of Tumors: Applications in Detection & Treatment. Ed. by Rakesh K. Jain & Pietro M. Gullino. LC 80-13379. (Annals Ser.: Vol. 335). 542p. 1980. 97.00 (*0-89766-046-3*); pap. write for info. (*0-89766-047-1*) NY Acad Sci.

Thermal Characterization of Polymeric Materials. Ed. by Edith A. Turi. LC 81-17578. 1981. text ed. 187.00 (*0-12-703780-2*) Acad Pr.

Thermal Characterization of Polymeric Materials, 2 vols. 2nd ed. Ed. by Edith A. Turi. (Illus.). 2420p. 1997. boxed 375.00 (*0-12-703783-7*, AP Prof) Acad Pr.

Thermal Characterization Techniques. Ed. by Philip E. Slade, Jr. & Lloyd T. Jenkins. LC 79-114993. (Techniques & Methods of Polymer Evaluation Ser.: No. 2). (Illus.). 383p. reprint ed. pap. 109.20 (*0-7837-0935-8*, 2041240) Bks Demand.

Thermal Computations for Electronic Equipment. Gordon N. Ellison. LC 89-11066. 414p. (C). 1989. reprint ed. lib. bdg. 52.50 (*0-89464-401-7*) Krieger.

Thermal Conduction in Semiconductors. C. M. Bhandari & D. M. Rowe. (C). 1988. 26.00 (*81-224-0064-7*) S Asia.

Thermal Conduction in Semiconductors. J. Drabble & H. J. Goldsmid. LC 61-14037. (International Series of Monographs on Semiconductors: Vol. 4). 1961. 114.00 (*0-08-009541-0*, Pub. by Pergamon Repr UK) Franklin.

Thermal Conductivity, Vol. 19. Ed. by D. W. Yarbrough. (Illus.). 570p. 1988. 135.00 (*0-306-42787-7*, Plenum Pr) Plenum.

Thermal Conductivity, Vol. 20. Ed. by D. P. Hasselman & J. R. Thomas, Jr. (Illus.). 454p. 1989. 135.00 (*0-306-43097-5*, Plenum Pr) Plenum.

Thermal Conductivity, Vol. 21. Ed. by C. J. Cremers & H. A. Hine. LC 90-45242. (Illus.). 710p. 1990. 155.00 (*0-306-43672-8*, Plenum Pr) Plenum.

Thermal Conductivity & Viscosity Data of Fluid Mixtures. K. Stephen & T. Heckenberger. Ed. by R. Eckermann. (Dechema Chemistry Data Ser.: Vol. 10, Pt. 1). (Illus.). 550p. 1989. text ed. 305.00 (*3-921567-85-8*, Pub. by Dechema GW) Scholium Intl.

Thermal Conductivity of Building Materials. Frank B. Rowley & Axel B. Algren. LC 37-27901. (University of Minnesota Engineering Experimentation Bulletin Ser.: No. 12). 144p. reprint ed. pap. 41.10 (*0-317-29494-6*, 2055907) Bks Demand.

Thermal Conductivity of Uranium Dioxide. (Technical Reports: No. 59). 1966. pap. 15.00 (*92-0-145166-0*, IDC59, Pub. by IAEA AU) Bernan Associates.

Thermal Conductivity 22. Ed. by Timothy W. Tong. LC 94-60525. 1000p. 1994. text ed. 199.95 (*1-56676-172-7*) Technomic.

Thermal Constants of Substances, 10 vols. Ed. by V. P. Glushko & V. A. Medvedev. 2000p. 1984. Set. write for info. (*0-89116-537-1*) Begell Hse.

Thermal Contact Conductance. C. V. Madhusudana. Ed. by F. F. Ling. LC 95-19291. (Mechanical Engineering Ser.). (Illus.). 176p. 1995. 64.95 (*0-387-94534-2*) Spr-Verlag.

***Thermal Control of the Newborn: A Practical Guide.** 64p. 1997. pap. 9.00 (*0-615-11026-6*, 1931047) World Health.

***Thermal Conversion of Solid Wastes & Biomass.** Ed. by Jerry L. Jones & Shirley B. Radding. LC 80-14754. (ACS Symposium Ser.: Vol. 130). 765p. 1980. reprint ed. pap. 180.00 (*0-608-03065-1*, 2063518) Bks Demand.

Thermal Conversion Systems for Municipal Solid Waste. H. L. Hickman, Jr. et al. LC 84-16496. (Pollution Technology Review Ser.: No. 113). (Illus.). 746p. 1985. 56.00 (*0-8155-1001-2*) Noyes.

***Thermal Cracking in Concrete at Early Ages: Proceedings of the International Rilem Symposium.** Ed. by Springenschmid. (Rilem Proceedings Ser.). (Illus.). 496p. 1994. text ed. 125.95 (*0-419-18710-3*, E & FN Spon) Routledge Chapman & Hall.

Thermal Decomposition of Materials: Effect of Highly Intensive Heating. O. F. Shlensky et al. (Studies in Modern Thermodynamics: Vol. 12). 1991. 174.50 (*0-444-89041-6*, SMT 12) Elsevier.

Thermal Delight in Architecture. Lisa Heschong. 1979. 8.50 (*0-262-58039-X*) MIT Pr.

Thermal Design & Optimization. Adrian Bejan et al. LC 95-12071. 496p. 1995. text ed. 69.95 (*0-471-58467-3*) Wiley.

Thermal Design Considerations in Frozen Ground Engineering. Ed. by Thomas G. Krzewinski & Rupert G. Tart, Jr. 277p. 1985. 31.00 (*0-87262-500-1*) Am Soc Civil Eng.

Thermal Design of Heat Exchangers: A Numerical Approach - Direct Sizing & Stepwise Rating. Eric M. Smith. LC 95-54158. 1996. text ed. 75.00 (*0-471-96566-9*) Wiley.

Thermal Design of Nuclear Reactors. R. H. Winterton. LC 80-41187. (Illus.). 200p. 1981. 87.00 (*0-08-024215-4*, Pub. by Pergamon Repr UK) Franklin.

Thermal Design of Precast Concrete Buildings. 51p. 1985. pap. 18.00 (*0-318-19727-8*, JR-306) P-PCI.

Thermal Design of Underground Systems. 4th ed. Birron M. Weedy. LC 87-16078. 218p. 1988. text ed. 215.00 (*0-471-91673-0*) Wiley.

Thermal Desorption. W. C. Anderson. (Innovative Site Remediation Technology Ser.: Vol. 6). 130p. 1995. 59.95 (*3-540-59066-8*) Spr-Verlag.

***Thermal Desorption.** William Troxler et al. Ed. by William C. Anderson. (Innovative Site Remediation Technology Ser.: Vol. 5). (Illus.). 150p. 1997. 70.00 (*1-883767-21-0*) Am Acad Environ.

***Thermal Desorption: Design & Application.** W. Troxler et al. (Innovative Site Remediation Technology: Vol. 5). (Illus.). 200p. 1997. write for info. (*0-614-30718-X*) Am Acad Environ.

Thermal Destruction. W. C. Anderson. (Innovative Site Remediation Technology Ser.: Vol. 7). 110p. 1995. 75.95 (*3-540-59067-6*) Spr-Verlag.

***Thermal Destruction.** Francis W. Holm et al. Ed. by William C. Anderson. (Innovative Site Remediation Technology Ser.: Vol. 6). (Illus.). 200p. 1997. 70.00 (*1-883767-22-9*) Am Acad Environ.

***Thermal Destruction: Design & Application.** F. W. Holm et al. (Innovative Site Remediation Technology: Vol. 6). (Illus.). 180p. 1997. write for info. (*0-614-30719-8*) Am Acad Environ.

Thermal Diffusivity see Thermophysical Properties of Matter: The TPRC Data Series

Thermal Discharges at Nuclear Power Stations. (Technical Reports: No. 155). (Illus.). 155p. (Orig.). 1974. pap. 30.00 (*92-0-125274-9*, IDC155, Pub. by IAEA AU) Bernan Associates.

Thermal Ecology: Proceedings. Ed. by J. Whitfield Gibbons & Rebecca R. Sharitz. LC 74-600136. (AEC Symposium Ser.). 690p. 1974. 25.25 (*0-685-01484-3*, CONF-730505); fiche 9.00 (*0-87079-225-3*, CONF-730505) DOE.

Thermal Ecology II: Proceedings. Ed. by Gerald W. Esch & Robert W. McFarlane. LC 76-28206. (ERDA Symposium Ser.). 416p. 1976. pap. 18.25 (*0-87079-223-7*, CONF-750425); fiche 9.00 (*0-87079-224-5*, CONF-750425) DOE.

Thermal Effects in Concrete Bridge Superstructures. (National Cooperative Highway Research Program Report Ser.: No. 276). 99p. 1985. 9.60 (*0-309-03860-X*) Transport Res Bd.

Thermal Effects of Thin Igneous Intrusions on Diagenetic In A Tertiary Basin of Southwestern Washington. Kenneth J. Esposito & Gene Whitney. (Evolution of Sedimentary Basins--Cenozoic Sedimentary Basins in Southwest Washington & Northwest Oregon Ser.). 1995. write for info. (*0-615-00170-X*) US Geol Survey.

Thermal Effects of Thin Igneous Intrusions on Diagenetic Reactions in a Tertiary Basin of Southwestern Washington. Kenneth J. Esposito & Gene Whitney. (Evolution of Sedimentary Basins--Cenozoic Sedimentary Basins in Southwest Washington & Northwest Oregon Ser.). 1995. write for info. (*0-615-00169-6*) US Geol Survey.

Thermal Efficiency Construction. Richard P. Bentley. 1988. 15.75 (*0-317-68200-8*) R P Bentley.

Thermal Energy Storage. G. Beckmann & P. V. Gilli. (Topics in Energy Ser.). (Illus.). 240p. 1984. 69.95 (*0-387-81764-6*) Spr-Verlag.

Thermal Energy Storage. Ed. by Giogio Beghi. 1982. lib. bdg. 165.00 (*90-277-1428-2*) Kluwer Ac.

Thermal Energy Storage. Richard K. Miller & Marcia E. Rupnow. (Survey on Technology & Markets Ser.: No. 206). 50p. 1993. pap. text ed. 200.00 (*1-55865-237-X*) Future Tech Surveys.

Thermal Energy Storage for Commercial Applications: A Feasibility Study on Economic Storage Systems. F. Dinter et al. 400p. 1993. 103.95 (*0-387-53054-1*) Spr-Verlag.

Thermal Engineering for Global Environmental Protection. Ed. by Subrata Sengupta & Taeko Sano. LC 96-23723. 400p. 1996. 110.00 (*1-56700-055-X*) Begell Hse.

Thermal Engineering Joint Conference: Proceedings of the ASME-JSME, 4 vols., 1. Ed. by Y. Mori & W. Yang. 2005p. 1983. pap. text ed. 10.00 (*0-317-02653-4*, I00158A) ASME.

Thermal Engineering Joint Conference: Proceedings of the ASME-JSME, 4 vols., 2. Ed. by Y. Mori & W. Yang. 2005p. 1983. pap. text ed. 10.00 (*0-317-02654-2*, I00158B) ASME.

Thermal Engineering Joint Conference: Proceedings of the ASME-JSME, 4 vols., 3. Ed. by Y. Mori & W. Yang. 2005p. 1983. pap. text ed. 10.00 (*0-317-02655-0*, I00158C) ASME.

Thermal Engineering Joint Conference: Proceedings of the ASME-JSME, 4 vols., 4. Ed. by Y. Mori & W. Yang. 2005p. 1983. pap. text ed. 10.00 (*0-317-02656-9*, I00158D) ASME.

Thermal Engineering Joint Conference: Proceedings of the ASME-JSME, 4 vols., Set. Ed. by Y. Mori & W. Yang. 2005p. 1983. pap. text ed. 30.00 (*0-317-02652-6*, I00158) ASME.

Thermal Engineering (S. I. Unites) R. K. Purohit. (C). 1992. text ed. 145.00 (*81-7233-048-0*, Pub. by Scientific Pubs II) St Mut.

Thermal Environment. J. Longmore et al. (Technical Guide Ser.: No. 8). 84p. (C). 1992. 180.00 (*0-905927-38-9*, Pub. by H&H Sci Cnslts UK) St Mut.

***Thermal Environment.** A. Youle. Ed. by K. J. Collins et al. 114p. 1996. pap. 195.00 (*0-948237-29-5*, Pub. by H&H Sci Cnslts UK) St Mut.

***Thermal Environmental Engineering.** 3rd ed. Threlkeld & Kuehn. 1997. text ed. 90.00 (*0-13-917220-3*) P-H.

Thermal Evolution of the Tertiary Shimanto Belt, SW Japan: An Example of Ridge-Tranch Interaction. Ed. by M. B. Underwood. LC 92-43051. (Special Papers: No. 273). 1993. pap. 18.13 (*0-8137-2273-X*) Geol Soc.

Thermal Expansion: Proceedings, No. 17. American Institute of Physics. Ed. by R. E. Taylor & G. L. Denman. LC 73-94415. 1974. pap. 14.00 (*0-88318-116-9*) Am Inst Physics.

Thermal Expansion 1971: Proceedings of the Conference, Corning, NY, 1971, No. 3. American Institute of Physics. Ed. by M. G. Graham & H. E. Hagy. LC 72-76970. (AIP Conference Proceedings Ser.). 311p. 1972. 13.00 (*0-88318-102-9*) Am Inst Physics.

Thermal Fatigue in Heat Exchangers for Domestic Gas Furnaces. L. E. Hulbert et al. 180p. 1975. pap. 20.00 (*0-318-12722-9*, M60016) Am Gas Assn.

Thermal Fatigue of Materials & Components - STP 612. David A. Spera. 271p. 1977. 27.00 (*0-8031-0586-X*, 04-612000-30) ASTM.

An Asterisk (*) at the beginning of an entry indicates that the title is appearing in BIP for the first time.

Thermal Fatigue of Metals. Andrzej Weronski & Tadeusz Hejwowski. (Mechanical Engineering Ser.: Vol. 74). 384p. 1991. 175.00 (0-8247-7726-3) Dekker.

Thermal Field Theories: Proceedings of the Second Workshop, Tsukuba, Japan, 23-27 July, 1990. Ed. by Hiroshi Ezawa et al. (North-Holland Delta Ser.). 590p. 1991. 155.00 (0-444-88903-5, North Holland) Elsevier.

Thermal Field Theory. Michel Le Bellac. (Monographs on Mathematical Physics). (Illus.). 256p. (C). 1996. text ed. 69.95 (0-521-46040-9) Cambridge U Pr.

Thermal Generation of Aromas. Ed. by Chi-Tang Ho et al. LC 89-17796. (Symposium Ser.: No. 409). (Illus.). 560p. 1989. 109.95 (0-8412-1682-7) Am Chemical.

Thermal Geophysics. Ed. by A. M. Jessop. (Developments in Solid Earth Geophysics Ser.: No. 17). 316p. 1990. 201.25 (0-444-88309-6) Elsevier.

Thermal Hazards of Chemical Reactions. Theodor Grewer. LC 94-18030. (Industrial Safety Ser.: Vol. 4). 422p. 1994. 249.00 (0-444-89722-4) Elsevier.

Thermal History of Sedimentary Basins: Methods & Case Histories. Ed. by N. D. Naeser & T. H. McCullogh. (Illus.). 320p. 1988. 112.95 (0-387-96702-8) Spr-Verlag.

Thermal Hydraulic Design of Components for Steam Generation Plant. Cumo. 408p. 1990. 287.00 (0-8493-6792-1, TJ290) CRC Pr.

Thermal Hydraulics: Physical Properties & Characteristic Dimensions, Vol. 1. Maurizio Cumo & Antonio Naviglio. LC 87-15524. 176p. 1988. Vol. I, Physical Properties & Characteristic Dimensionless Groups, 176 pgs. 96.00 (0-8493-6789-1, TJ260, CRC Reprint) Franklin.

Thermal Hydraulics: Physical Properties & Characteristic Dimensions, 2 vols., Vol. II, Nucleate Boiling Heat Transfer. Maurizio Cumo & Antonio Naviglio. 160p. 1988. 90.00 (0-8493-6790-5, 6790, CRC Reprint) Franklin.

Thermal Hydraulics Division Proceedings, Chicago, IL, Nov. 15-20, 1992. 126p. 40.00 (0-89448-179-7, 700183) Am Nuclear Soc.

Thermal Hydraulics Division Proceedings, San Francisco, CA, November 14-19, 1993. 276p. 1994. 40.00 (0-89448-189-4, 700198) Am Nuclear Soc.

Thermal Hydraulics Division Proceedings, 1991: San Francisco, CA, Nov. 10-14, 1991. 363p. 40.00 (0-89448-170-3, 700171) Am Nuclear Soc.

T

Thermal-Hydraulics in Nuclear Power Technology: Presented at the 20th National Heat Transfer Conference, Milwaukee, Wisconsin, August 2-5, 1981. National Heat Transfer Conference Staff. Ed. by K. H. Sun et al. LC 81-65616. (HTD Ser.: Vol. 15). (Illus.). 92p. reprint ed. pap. 26.30 (0-8357-2815-3, 2039054) Bks Demand.

Thermal Hydraulics of a Boiling Water Nuclear Reactor. 2nd ed. R. T. Lahey & Frederick J. Moody. LC 93-12785. 1993. 65.00 (0-89448-037-5) Am Nuclear Soc.

Thermal Hydraulics of Advanced & Special Purpose Reactors. Ed. by F. B. Cheung & P. F. Peterson. (HTD Ser.: Vol. 209). 128p. 1992. 37.50 (0-7918-0799-1, G00693) ASME.

Thermal Hydraulics of Advanced Nuclear Reactors: 1994 International Mechanical Engineering Congress & Exposition, Chicago, Illinois - November 6-11, 1994. (HTD Ser.: Vol. 294). 56p. 1994. 40.00 (0-7918-1412-2, G00907) ASME.

Thermal Hydraulics of Advanced Steam Generators & Heat Exchangers: 1994 International Mechanical Engineering Congress & Exposition, Chicago, Illinois - November 6-11, 1994. (NE Ser.: Vol. 15). 104p. 1994. 48.00 (0-7918-1422-X, G00917) ASME.

Thermal Hydraulics of Nuclear Reactors, San Francisco, CA, Oct. 30-Nov. 3, 1983: Proceedings, 2 vols. 1525p. 1983. 98.00 (0-89448-110-X, 700081) Am Nuclear Soc.

Thermal Imaging Systems. Ed. by J. M. Lloyd. LC 75-9635. (Optical Physics & Engineering Ser.). 456p. 1975. 95.00 (0-306-30848-7, Plenum Pr) Plenum.

Thermal Infrared Characterization of Ground Targets & Backgrounds. Pieter A. Jacobs. LC 96-10613. (Tutorial Texts in Optical Engineering Ser.: No. TT26). 1996. pap. 42.00 (0-8194-2180-4) SPIE.

Thermal Insulation: Materials & Systems. Ed. by Frank J. Powell & Stanley L. Matthews. LC 87-27045. (Special Technical Publication Ser.: No. 922). (Illus.). 728p. 1987. text ed. 87.00 (0-8031-0493-6, 04-922000-10) ASTM.

Thermal Insulation - Environmental Acoustics see 1997 Annual Book of ASTM Standards: Construction, Section 4

Thermal Insulation Building Guide. William C. Turner. Ed. by Edwin F. Strother, IV. LC 82-16232. 512p. (C). 1990. 78.50 (0-88275-985-X) Krieger.

*Thermal Insulation Materials. 1996. lib. bdg. 251.95 (0-8490-6386-8) Gordon Pr.

Thermal Insulation of Industrial Buildings. EEMUA Staff. 1987. 125.00 (0-85931-045-0, Pub. by EEMUA UK) St Mut.

Thermal Insulation Performance - STP 718. Ed. by McElroy & Tye. 566p. 1981. 43.00 (0-8031-0794-3, 04-718000-10) ASTM.

Thermal Insulations Materials, & Systems for Energy Conservation in the '80s - STP 789. Ed. by F. A. Govan et al. LC 82-70616. 890p. 1983. text ed. 68.00 (0-8031-0230-5, 04-789000-10) ASTM.

Thermal Machining Processes. Society of Manufacturing Engineers Staff. LC 79-62917. (Manufacturing Update Ser.). 260p. reprint ed. pap. 74.10 (0-317-41891-2, 2026162) Bks Demand.

Thermal Management of Electronic Systems: Proceedings of the Eurotherm Seminar 29, 14-16 June 1993, Delft, The Netherlands. Ed. by C. J. Hoogendoorn et al. LC 94-7971. 348p. (C). 1994. lib. bdg. 169.00 (0-7923-2801-9) Kluwer Ac.

*Thermal Management of Electronics Systems II: Proceedings of Eurotherm Seminar 45, 20-22 September 1995, Leuven, Belgium. E. Seminar Beyne et al. LC 97-19915. 1997. write for info. (0-7923-4612-2) Kluwer Ac.

*Thermal Mass Handbook: Concrete & Masonry Design Provisions Using ASHRAE/IES 90.1 - 1989. 60p. 1994. 20.00 (0-614-25764-6, TMH-94) P-PCI.

*Thermal Measurements in Electronics Cooling. Kaveh Azar. LC 97-10722. 1997. write for info. (0-8493-3279-6) CRC Pr.

Thermal Mechanical Behavior of UO2 Nuclear Fuel, 4 vols. Ed. by R. Christensen. 1978. Set. 130.00 (0-938876-13-9) Entropy Ltd.

Thermal Mechanical Behavior of UO2 Nuclear Fuel, 4 vols., Vol. I. Ed. by R. Christensen. 240p. 1978. write for info. (0-318-51861-9) Entropy Ltd.

Thermal Mechanical Behavior of UO2 Nuclear Fuel, 4 vols., Vol. II. Ed. by R. Christensen. 121p. 1978. write for info. (0-318-51862-7) Entropy Ltd.

Thermal Mechanical Behavior of UO2 Nuclear Fuel, 4 vols., Vol. III. Ed. by R. Christensen. 321p. 1978. write for info. (0-318-51863-5) Entropy Ltd.

Thermal Mechanical Behavior of UO2 Nuclear Fuel, 4 vols., Vol. IV. Ed. by R. Christensen. 329p. 1978. write for info. (0-318-51864-3) Entropy Ltd.

Thermal Mechanical Behavior of UO2 Nuclear Fuel: Electrothermal Analysis, Vol. II. R. Christensen. x, 122p. 1978. 19.50 (0-938876-10-4) Entropy Ltd.

Thermal Mechanical Behavior of UO2 Nuclear Fuel: Multi-Cycle Test Description, Vol. IV. R. Christensen. xii, 329p. 1978. 49.50 (0-938876-12-0) Entropy Ltd.

Thermal Mechanical Behavior of UO2 Nuclear Fuel: Single Cycle Test Data Discriptions, Vol. III. R. Christensen. xii, 321p. 1978. 46.50 (0-938876-11-2) Entropy Ltd.

Thermal Mechanical Behavior of UO2 Nuclear Fuel: Statistical Analysis of Acoustic Emission Axial Elagation, & Crack Characteristics, Vol. I. R. Christensen. xi, 240p. 1978. 34.50 (0-938876-09-0) Entropy Ltd.

Thermal-Mechanical, Low-Cycle Fatigue of AISI 1010 Steel. C. E. Jaske et al. 51p. 1975. pap. 5.00 (0-318-12723-7, H54375) Am Gas Assn.

Thermal-Mechanical Modelling of the Flat Rolling Process. M. Pietrzyk & J. G. Lenard. Ed. by B. Ilschner & N. J. Grant. (Materials Research & Engineering Ser.). (Illus.). 216p. 1991. 94.95 (0-387-53316-8) Spr-Verlag.

Thermal Methods. James W. Dodd & Kenneth H. Tonge. Ed. by Brian R. Currell. LC 86-24548. (Analytical Chemistry by Open Learning Ser.). 337p. 1987. pap. text ed. 56.95 (0-471-91334-0) Wiley.

Thermal Methods in Petroleum Analysis. Heinz Kopsch. (Illus.). 500p. 1995. 170.00 (3-527-28740-X, VCH) Wiley.

*Thermal Methods of Analysis: Principles, Applications & Problems. Haines. (Illus.). 304p. (Orig.). 1994. pap. text ed. 47.95 (0-7514-0050-5, Pub. by Blackie Acad & Prof UK) Routledge Chapman & Hall.

Thermal Methods of Oil Recovery. Thomas C. Boberg. LC 87-22936. (Exxon Monographs). 411p. 1988. text ed. 169.00 (0-471-63300-3) Wiley.

Thermal Methods of Oil Recovery. Jacques Burger et al. (Illus.). 448p. (C). 1985. 665.00 (2-7108-0493-X, Pub. by Edits Technip FR) St Mut.

Thermal Modeling in Sedimentary Basins: 2nd, IFP Exploration & Production Research Conference, Carcans, 1985. Ed. by J. Burrus. (Illus.). 624p. (C). 1986. 725.00 (2-7108-0504-9, Pub. by Edits Technip FR) St Mut.

*Thermal Modeling of Petroleum Generation: Theory & Applications. LC 96-50381. (Developments in Petroleum Science Ser.). 526p. 1996. 187.50 (0-444-82030-2) Elsevier.

Thermal Movement, Bk. 5. H. T. Taylor & L. G. Bill. Ed. by K. Yandall. (C). 1989. 49.00 (0-85973-003-4, Pub. by S Thornes Pubs UK) St Mut.

Thermal Neutron Scattering Applied to Chemical & Solid State Physics. Ed. by H. G. Smith. (Transactions of the American Crystallographic Association Ser.: Vol. 3). 109p. 1967. pap. 25.00 (0-686-60374-5) Polycrystal Bk Serv.

Thermal Oxidation Stability of Aviation Turbine Fuels: Monograph 1. Ed. by Robert N. Hazlett. LC 91-36246. (Special Technical Publication Ser.). (Illus.). 160p. 1991. text ed. 49.00 (0-8031-1248-3, 31-001092-12) ASTM.

Thermal Phenomena aMolecular & Microscales & in Cryogenic Infrared Detectors. (HTD Ser.: Vol. 277). 96p. 1994. 35.00 (0-7918-1276-6, H00908) ASME.

Thermal Phenomena in Sedimentary Basins: 1st IPF Exploration & Production Research Conference, Bordeaux, 1983. B. Durand. (Illus.). 352p. 1984. 430.00 (2-7108-0481-6, Pub. by Edits Technip FR) St Mut.

Thermal Physics. C. B. Finn. (Student Physics Ser.). 320p. 1986. pap. text ed. 16.95 (0-7102-0660-7, RKP) Routledge.

Thermal Physics. Bruce Hoeneisen. LC 92-37924. (Illus.). 264p. 1993. pap. text ed. 39.95 (0-7734-1952-7) E Mellen.

Thermal Physics. Michael Sprackling. 370p. 1992. 65.00 (0-88318-919-4); pap. 45.00 (0-88318-920-8) Am Inst Physics.

Thermal Physics. 2nd ed. C. B. Finn. LC 92-35911. (Physics & Its Applications Ser.: Vol. 5). 272p. (gr. 13). 1993. pap. text ed. 27.95 (0-412-49540-6) Chapman & Hall.

Thermal Physics. 2nd ed. Charles Kittel & Herbert Kroemer. LC 79-16677. (Illus.). 473p. (C). 1995. text ed. write for info. (0-7167-1088-9) W H Freeman.

Thermal Physics Reviews, Vol. 1. Ed. by A. E. Scheindlin & V. E. Fortov. (Soviet Technology Reviews Ser.: Vol. 1). xv, 440p. 1987. text ed. 668.00 (3-7186-0404-3) Gordon & Breach.

Thermal Physics Reviews, Vol. 5. Ed. by A. E. Scheindlin. (Soviet Technology Reviews Ser.: Section B). 88p. 1994. pap. text ed. 122.00 (3-7186-5530-6) Gordon & Breach.

Thermal Physics Reviews, Vol. 5. Ed. by A. E. Scheindlin. (Soviet Technology Reviews Ser.: Section B). 95p. 1995. pap. text ed. 126.00 (3-7186-5473-3, Harwood Acad Pubs); pap. text ed. 119.00 (3-7186-5483-0, Harwood Acad Pubs) Gordon & Breach.

Thermal Physics Reviews. Part 5: Thermal Physics of, Vol. 5. A. E. Scheindlin & Fortov. (Soviet Technology Reviews Ser). 77p. 1995. pap. text ed. 35.00 (3-7186-5566-7, Harwood Acad Pubs) Gordon & Breach.

Thermal Physics Reviews Vol. 2, Pt. 5: Condensation of Supersaturated Vapor in a Field of Electromagnetic Radiation, Vol. 2. L. M. Biberman. (Soviet Technology Reviews Ser.: Section B). 48p. 1989. pap. text ed. 43.00 (3-7186-5002-9, Harwood Acad Pubs) Gordon & Breach.

Thermal Physics Reviews Vol. 3, Pt. 1: Thermohydrodynamic Models of Laser Irradiation of Metals, Vol. 3. R. V. Arutyunian. (Soviet Technology Reviews Ser.: Section B). 174p. 1990. text ed. 121.00 (3-7186-5071-1, Harwood Acad Pubs) Gordon & Breach.

Thermal Physics Reviews Vol. 3, Pt. 2: Universal Crossover Approach to Description of Thermodynamic Properties of Fluids & Fluid Mixtures, Vol. 3. Mikhail A. Anisimov. (Soviet Technology Reviews Ser.: Section B). 121p. 1992. pap. text ed. 84.00 (3-7186-5196-3, Harwood Acad Pubs) Gordon & Breach.

Thermal Physics Reviews Vol. 3, Pt. 3: The Equations of State & Macrokinetics of Decomposition of Solid Explosives in Shock & Detonation Waves, Vol. 3. G. Kanel. (Soviet Technology Reviews Ser.: Section B). 86p. 1992. pap. text ed. 89.00 (3-7186-5223-4, Harwood Acad Pubs) Gordon & Breach.

Thermal Physics Reviews Vol. 4, Pt. 2: Interaction of Intense Laser Radiation with Matter, Vol. 4. R. V. Arutyunian. (Soviet Technology Reviews Ser.: Section B). 65p. 1992. pap. text ed. 69.00 (3-7186-5216-1, Harwood Acad Pubs) Gordon & Breach.

Thermal Physics Reviews Vol. 4, Pt. 3.2: Techniques & Equipment for High Temperature Measurements in Physical Experiment, Vol. 4. M. Scheindlin. (Soviet Technology Reviews Ser.: Section B). 91p. 1992. pap. text ed. 141.00 (3-7186-5388-5, Harwood Acad Pubs) Gordon & Breach.

Thermal Physics Reviews Vol. 4, Pt. 4: Application of High-Current Charged Particle Beams in Dynamic High-Pressure Physics, Vol. 4. A. Akkerman. (Soviet Technology Reviews Ser.: Section B). 79p. 1992. pap. text ed. 122.00 (3-7186-5397-4, Harwood Acad Pubs) Gordon & Breach.

Thermal Physics Reviews Vol. 4, Pt. 5: Optical & Thermophysical Properties of Semitransparent Materials in the Calculation of Combines Radiation-Cond, Vol. 4. V. Petrov. (Soviet Technology Reviews Ser.: Section B). 79p. 1992. pap. text ed. 134.00 (3-7186-5445-8, Harwood Acad Pubs) Gordon & Breach.

Thermal Physics Reviews Vol. 5, No. 3, Vol. 5. Ed. by A. E. Scheindlin. (Soviet Technology Reviews Ser.: Section B). 80p. 1994. pap. text ed. 111.00 (3-7186-5512-8) Gordon & Breach.

Thermal Physiology. Ed. by J. R. Hales. LC 82-48991. 607p. 1984. reprint ed. pap. 173.00 (0-608-00438-3, 2061153) Bks Demand.

Thermal Plasma & New Materials Technology, Vol. 1. Ed. by O. P. Solonenko & M. F. Zhukov. 510p. (C). 1994. pap. 139.00 (1-898326-06-1, Pub. by Cambdge Intl UK) Am Educ Systs.

Thermal Plasma & New Materials Technology, Vol. 2. Ed. by O. P. Solonenko & M. F. Zhukov. 560p. (C). 1995. pap. 146.00 (1-898326-07-X, Pub. by Cambdge Intl UK) Am Educ Systs.

*Thermal Plasma Applications in Materials & Metallurgical Processing: Proceedings of an International Symposium Sponsored by TMS Process Fundamentals Committee Held at the 121st TMS Annual Meeting in San Diego, CA, March 1-5, 1992. Ed. by N. El-Kaddah. LC 91-68510. 377p. 1992. reprint ed. pap. 107.50 (0-608-03823-7, 2062785) Bks Demand.

Thermal Plasma Diagnostics. A. A. Ovsyannikov et al. 450p. 1995. boxed 130.00 (1-898326-23-1, Pub. by Cambdge Intl UK) Am Educ Systs.

Thermal Plasmas: Fundamentals & Applications, No. 1. M. I. Boulos et al. (Illus.). 420p. 1994. 85.00 (0-306-44607-3, Plenum Pr) Plenum.

*Thermal Plasmas for Hazardous Waste Treatment. 232p. 1996. 26.00 (981-02-2608-X) World Scientific Pub.

Thermal Pollution Analysis: Technical Papers from the Thermal Pollution Analysis Conference, May 1974. LC 75-2091. (Progress in Astronautics & Aeronautics Ser.: Vol. 36). 267p. reprint ed. pap. 76.10 (0-317-10991-X, 2011994) Bks Demand.

*Thermal Power Cycles. Cole. (Mechanical Engineering Ser.). 1993. pap. 40.95 (0-340-54522-4) Van Nos Reinhold.

*Thermal Problem of Enclosed Gear Drives. E. J. Wellauer. (Technical Papers). 1951. pap. text ed. 30.00 (1-55589-409-7) AGMA.

Thermal Problems in Biotechnology: Presented at the Winter Annual Meeting of ASME, New York, NY, December 3, 1968. American Society of Mechanical Engineers Staff. LC 68-58741. (Illus.). 132p. reprint ed. pap. 37.70 (0-317-08429-1, 2016822) Bks Demand.

Thermal Processing & Quality of Foods. Ed. by Peter Zeuthen. (Illus.). 935p. 1984. 89.00 (0-685-08302-0, Pub. by Elsevier Applied Sci UK) Elsevier.

Thermal Processing of Materials: Thermo-Mechanics, Controls & Composites: 1994 International Mechanical Engineering Congress & Exposition, Chicago, Illinois - November 6-11, 1994. (HTD Ser.: Vol. 289). 244p. 1994. 88.00 (0-7918-1407-6, G00902) ASME.

*Thermal Processing of Packaged Foods. D. Holdsworth. (Illus.). 320p. 1997. text ed. 138.00 (0-7514-0375-X, Pub. by Blackie Acad & Prof UK) Routledge Chapman & Hall.

*Thermal Properties & Some Miscellaneous Aspects of High Temperature Superconductors. Ed. by Anant Narlikar. (Studies of High Temperature Superconductors: Vol. 19). (Illus.). 262p. (C). 1996. lib. bdg. 89.00 (1-56072-393-9) Nova Sci Pubs.

*Thermal Properties & Temperature-Related Behavior of Rock/Fluid Systems. Wilbur H. Somerton. (Developments in Petroleum Science Ser.: Vol. 37). 258p. 1992. 167.50 (0-444-89001-7) Elsevier.

Thermal Properties of Food & Agricultural Materials. Nuri N. Mohsenin. 408p. 1980. text ed. 261.00 (0-677-05450-5) Gordon & Breach.

Thermal Radiation Heat Transfer. 3rd ed. Robert Siegel & John R. Howell. LC 92-10974. 950p. 1992. 76.95 (0-89116-271-2) Hemisp Pub.

Thermal Radiative Properties: Coatings see Thermophysical Properties of Matter: The TPRC Data Series

Thermal Radiative Properties: Metallic Elements & Alloys see Thermophysical Properties of Matter: The TPRC Data Series

Thermal Radiative Properties: Nonmetallic Solids see Thermophysical Properties of Matter: The TPRC Data Series

Thermal Radiative Transfer & Properties. M. Quinn Brewster. LC 91-12888. 568p. 1992. text ed. 95.00 (0-471-53982-1) Wiley.

*Thermal Radiative Transfer Properties. Quinn M. Brewster. 1991. pap. text ed. 25.00 (0-471-54922-3) Wiley.

*Thermal Rating of Gear Drives Balance Between Power Loss & Heat Dissipation. Bernd-Robert Hohn & Klaus Michaelis. (1996 Fall Technical Meeting Ser.: Vol. 8). 12p. 1996. pap. text ed. 30.00 (1-55589-675-8) AGMA.

Thermal Reactor Safety International Ans-ENS Topical Marketing: Proceedings in San Diego, CA February 2-6, 1986, 5 vols. 1604p. 1986. 125.00 (0-89448-121-5, 700106) Am Nuclear Soc.

Thermal Recovery. Michael Prats. 174p. 1982. 35.00 (0-89520-314-6) Soc Petrol Engineers.

Thermal Recovery Processes. (SPE Reprint Ser.). 480p. 1985. 21.30 (0-89520-325-1, 30554) Soc Petrol Engineers.

Thermal Regime of Santa Maria Province, California: Phosphorus Geochemistry, Diagnesis & Mass Balance of the Miocene Monterey Formation at Shell Beach, California. Gabriel M. Filippelli & Margaret L. Delaney. 1994. write for info. (0-615-00099-1) US Geol Survey.

Thermal Science Measurements. Amir Faghri. 152p. 1995. per. 24.09 (0-8403-6802-X) Kendall-Hunt.

Thermal Sensors. A. W. Van Herwaarden. Ed. by G. C. Meijer. (Sensors Ser.). (Illus.). 320p. 1994. 162.00 (0-7503-0220-8) IOP Pub.

Thermal Separation Processes: Principles & Design. Klaus Sattler & Hans J. Feindt. 1995. 135.00 (3-527-28622-5, VCH) Wiley.

Thermal Shock & Thermal Fatigue Behavior of Advanced Ceramics: Proceedings of the NATO Advanced Research Workshop, Schloss Ringberg - Munich, Germany, November 8-13, 1992. Ed. by Gerold A. Schneider & Gunter Petzow. LC 93-8337. (NATO Advanced Science Institutes Series C: Mathematical & Physical Sciences). 608p. (C). 1993. lib. bdg. 289.00 (0-7923-2361-0) Kluwer Ac.

Thermal Shutters & Shades. William A. Shurcliff. LC 80-11574. (Illus.). 238p. 1980. 19.95 (0-931790-08-5) Brick Hse Pub.

*Thermal Spray: Practical Solutions for Engineering Problems. Ed. by C. C. Berndt. 1050p. 1996. 161.00 (0-87170-583-4, 6485) ASM.

Thermal Spray Coating Applications in the Chemical Process Industries Pub. No. 42. NACE Staff. (Illus.). 252p. 1994. 85.00 (1-877914-59-2) NACE Intl.

*Thermal Spray Coatings. Hedges. (Illus.). 192p. 1997. text ed. write for info. (0-412-62200-9, Chap & Hall NY) Chapman & Hall.

Thermal Spray Coatings. Technical Association of the Pulp & Paper Industry Staff. Ed. by Vince Meringolo. 40p. reprint ed. pap. 25.00 (0-317-20542-0, 2022827) Bks Demand.

Thermal Spray Coatings: Research Design & Applications. Ed. by Christopher C. Berndt & Thomas F. Bernecki. LC 93-71173. 691p. 1993. 103.00 (0-87170-470-6, 6339) ASM.

*Thermal Spray Research & Applications: Proceedings of the Third National Thermal Spray Conference Held May 20-25, 1990, in Long Beach, CA. Ed. by Thomas F. Bernecki. LC 91-70802. (Illus.). 808p. 1991. reprint ed. pap. 180.00 (0-608-02629-8, 2063287) Bks Demand.

Thermal Spray Source Program. Heiman. 1995. 995.00 (0-8493-8639-X, TK) CRC Pr.

*Thermal Spray Technical Guide. (C). 1997. write for info. (0-614-26939-3) ASM.

Thermal Spraying: Practice, Theory, & Application. 185p. 1985. pap. 27.00 (0-87171-246-6, TSS) Am Welding.

Thermal Spraying: Twelfth International Conference, 2 vols., Set. Ed. by I. A. Bucklow. (Illus.). 726p. 1995. pap. 475.00 (1-85573-001-4, Pub. by Woodhead Pubng UK) Am Educ Systs.

An Asterisk (*) at the beginning of an entry indicates that the title is appearing in BIP for the first time.

Thermal Stability of Polymers, Vol. 1. Ed. by Robert T. Conley. LC 74-107753. (Monographs in Macromolecular Chemistry). 656p. reprint ed. pap. 180.00 (0-685-16355-5, 2027125) Bks Demand.

Thermal Storage & Heat Transfer in Solar Energy Systems. Ed. by F. Kreith et al. 1978. 4.00 (0-685-66812-6, H00126) ASME.

Thermal Stress & Strain in Microelectronics Packaging. Ed. by John H. Lau. LC 92-43285. 1993. text ed. 99.95 (0-442-01058-3) Van Nos Reinhold.

Thermal Stresses. Ed. by Richard B. Hetnarski. (Mechanics & Mathematical Methods Handbooks Ser.: Vol. 3). 574p. 1989. 285.75 (0-444-70447-7, North Holland) Elsevier.

Thermal Stresses, Vol. 4. Ed. by R. B. Hetnarski. (Mechanics & Mathematical Methods Ser.: Vol. B4). 554p. 1996. text ed. 274.75 (0-444-81571-6, North Holland) Elsevier.

Thermal Stresses & Strength of Turbines Calculation & Design. 2nd enl. ed. K. V. Frolov et al. Ed. by Richard B. Hetnarski. 320p. 1990. 170.00 (1-56032-103-2) Hemisp Pub.

Thermal Stresses & Thermal Fatigue. Ed. by D. J. Littler. LC 72-182668. (Proceedings of the International Conferences on Basement Tectonics Ser.). 586p. reprint ed. pap. 167.10 (0-317-41713-4, 2055831) Bks Demand.

Thermal Stresses I: Mechanics & Mathematical Methods, Vol. 1. Ed. by Richard B. Hetnarski. 548p. 1986. 127.75 (0-444-87728-2) Elsevier.

Thermal Stresses II. Ed. by Richard B. Hetnarski. (Mechanics & Mathematical Methods Ser.: No. 2). 452p. 1987. 228.25 (0-444-70046-3, North Holland) Elsevier.

Thermal Strike. (Super Bolan Ser.: No. 51). 1996. pap. 5.50 (0-373-61451-9, 1-61451-0, Wrldwide Lib) Harlequin Bks.

Thermal Structure of the Indian Ocean. J. G. Colborn. LC 75-17812. (International Indian Ocean Expedition. Oceanographic Monographs: No. 2). 181p. reprint ed. pap. 51.60 (0-7837-3986-9, 2043816) Bks Demand.

Thermal Surgical Lasers: A Technical Monograph. Terry A. Fuller. (Illus.). 55p. (Orig.). 1993. pap. 50.00 (1-883765-00-5) Surgical Laser.

Thermal Theory of Cyclones: A History of Meteorological Thought in the Nineteenth Century. Gisela Kutzbach. (Historical Monograph). (Illus.). 255p. 1979. 40.00 (0-933876-48-3) Am Meteorological.

Thermal Tissue Ablation. Ed. by M. Marberger. (Journal: European Urology: Vol. 23, Suppl. 1, 1993). (Illus.). iv, 72p. 1993. pap. 40.00 (3-8055-5799-X) S Karger.

Thermal Transmission Measurements of Insulation - STP 660. Ed. by R. P. Tye. 458p. 1979. 39.50 (0-8031-0589-4, 04-660000-10) ASTM.

Thermal Treatment of Hazardous Wastes. Ed. by Paul N. Cheremisinoff. (Encyclopedia of Environmental Control Technology Ser.: Vol. 1). (Illus.). 828p. 1989. 155.00 (0-87201-241-7) Gulf Pub.

***Thermal Vibrational Convection.** G. Z. Gershuni & D. V. Liubimov. 1997. write for info. (0-471-97385-8) Wiley.

Thermal Warriors: Strategies of Insect Survival. Bernd Heinrich. LC 96-1565. (Illus.). 332p. 1996. 27.00 (0-674-88340-3) HUP.

Thermally Generated Flavors: Maillard, Microwave, & Extrusion Processes. Ed. by Thomas H. Parliment et al. LC 93-36609. (ACS Symposium Ser.: No. 543). (Illus.). 492p. 1994. 109.95 (0-8412-2742-X) Am Chemical.

Thermally Stimulated Relaxation in Solids. Ed. by P. Braeunlich. (Topics in Applied Physics Ser.: Vol. 37). (Illus.). 1979. 93.95 (0-387-09595-0) Spr-Verlag.

Thermidorean Regime & the Directory, 1794-1799. Denis Woronoff. Tr. by Julian Jackson. LC 83-7672. (French Revolution Ser.: No. 3). 215p. 1984. 59.95 (0-521-24725-X); pap. 19.95 (0-521-28917-3) Cambridge U Pr.

Thermische Solaranlagen. 1995. 70.00 (0-387-58300-9) Spr-Verlag.

Thermistors. E. D. Macklen. 226p. 1980. 150.00 (0-901150-07-X) St Mut.

Thermo & Laser Anemometry. Ed. by A. F. Polyakov. 186p. 1988. 68.95 (0-89116-607-6) Hemisp Pub.

Thermo-Mechanical Aspects of Manufacturing & Materials Processing. Ed. by Ramesh K. Shah. 365p. 1991. 154.00 (0-89116-826-5) Hemisp Pub.

***Thermo-Mechanical Processing: Theory, Modelling, & Practice.** Ed. by B. Hutchinson et al. 400p. 1996. 102.00 (0-614-27207-6, 6460) ASM.

***Thermo-Mechanical Processing: Theory, Modelling, Practice.** 440p. 1996. 102.00 (0-614-24011-5, 6460) ASM.

Thermo-Mechanical Solar Power Plants: EURELIOS, the MWel Experimental Solar Thermal Electric Power Plant in the European Community. Ed. by J. Gretz et al. 1984. lib. bdg. 69.50 (90-277-1728-1) Kluwer Ac.

Thermo Using Mathcad. Anderson. (Miscellaneous/Catalogs Ser.). 1998. text ed. 20.95 (0-534-95105-8) Wadsworth Pub.

Thermoanalytical Techniques. Wesley W. Wendlandt. LC 74-187851. (Handbook of Commercial Scientific Instruments Ser.: Vol. 2). 248p. reprint ed. pap. 70.70 (0-685-15805-5, 2027810) Bks Demand.

Thermobacteriology in Food Processing. 2nd ed. C. R. Stumbo. (Food Science & Technology Ser.). 1973. text ed. 139.00 (0-12-675352-0) Acad Pr.

***Thermochemical & Chemical Kinetic Data for Fluorinated Hydrocarbons.** D. R. Burgess et al. (Illus.). 174p. (C). 1997. reprint ed. pap. text ed. 45.00 (0-7881-3783-2) DIANE Pub.

***Thermochemical Data of Pure Substances.** 3rd ed. I. Barin. 1995. text ed. 535.00 (0-471-18815-8) Wiley.

Thermochemical Kinetics. 2nd ed. Sidney W. Benson. 320p. 1976. text ed. 99.95 (0-471-06781-4) Wiley.

Thermochemical Methods in Silicate Investigation. Wilhelm Eitel. LC 52-3556. 140p. reprint ed. pap. 39.90 (0-317-08719-3, 2050515) Bks Demand.

Thermochemical Properties of Inorganic Substances, 2 vols. 2nd ed. Ed. by O. Knacke et al. 2500p. 1991. Set. 520.95 (0-387-54014-8) Spr-Verlag.

Thermochemical Properties of Inorganic Substances, 2 vols., Set. 2nd enl. rev. ed. O. Knacke et al. 2500p. 1995. 895.00 (3-514-00363-7, Pub. by Woodhead Pubng UK) Am Educ Systs.

Thermochemical Treatment of Metals & Alloys. L. S. Lyakhovich. 1986. 36.00 (81-205-0049-0, Pub. by Oxford IBH II) S Asia.

Thermochemistry & Equilibria of Organic Compounds. Ed. by Michael Frenkel. LC 93-4960. 584p. 1993. 150.00 (1-56081-559-0, VCH) Wiley.

Thermochemistry for Steelmaking, Vol. 2: Thermodynamic Transport Properties. J. Elliott & M. Gleiser. LC 60-7379. 1963. 248.00 (0-08-010050-3, Pub. by Pergamon Repr UK) Franklin.

Thermochemistry of Alloys. H. Brodowsky & H. J. Schaller. (C). 1989. lib. bdg. 238.00 (0-7923-0434-9) Kluwer Ac.

Thermocine. 1980. 79.50 (0-8176-0682-3) Spr-Verlag.

Thermocouples: Theory & Practice. Daniel D. Pollock. 350p. 1991. 115.95 (0-8493-4243-0, QC274) CRC Pr.

Thermocouples, Biology & Medicine, Geophysics & Space see Temperature: Its Measurement & Control in Science & Industry

***Thermodynam Chaos.** Berdichevsky. 1996. write for info. (0-582-08734-1, Pub. by Longman UK) Longman.

Thermodynamic Analysis of Combustion Engines. Ashley S. Campbell. LC 84-12203. 376p. (C). 1985. reprint ed. lib. bdg. 40.00 (0-89874-774-0) Krieger.

Thermodynamic Analysis of Vapor-Liquid Equilibria: Recommended Models & Standard Database. M. A. Gess et al. (Design Institute for Physical Property Data Ser.). 256p. 1991. text ed. 120.00 (0-8169-0559-2) Am Inst Chem Eng.

Thermodynamic & Optical Properties of Plasma of Metals & Dielectrics. Ed. by U. S. S. R., National Standard Reference Data Service Staff & Boyko. 200p. 1991. 115.00 (1-56032-110-5) Hemisp Pub.

Thermodynamic & Physical Property Data. Carl L. Yaws. (Library of Physico-Chemical Property Data). 220p. 1992. 75.00 (0-88415-031-3) Gulf Pub.

Thermodynamic & Transport Properties of Fluids: SI Units. 5th ed. G. F. Rogers. 30p. 1995. pap. 14.95 (0-631-19703-6) Blackwell Pubs.

Thermodynamic & Transport Properties of Steam. C. A. Meyer. LC 67-3043. 363p. reprint ed. pap. 103.50 (0-317-11072-1, 2011011) Bks Demand.

Thermodynamic & Transport Properties of Uranium Dioxide & Related Phases. (Technical Reports: No. 39). 1965. pap. 17.00 (92-0-145065-6, IDC39, Pub. by IAEA AU) Bernan Associates.

Thermodynamic Aspects. Hawley. 260p. (C). 1995. per., pap. text ed. 39.95 (0-7872-0615-6) Kendall-Hunt.

Thermodynamic Bases of Biological Processes: Physiological Reactiona & Adaptations. A. I. Zotin. xix, 293p. (C). 1990. lib. bdg. 292.35 (3-11-011401-1) De Gruyter.

Thermodynamic Bypass: Goto Log K. Wyatt. 1989. 11.00 (0-85186-313-2) CRC Pr.

Thermodynamic Cycles & Processes. Russel D. Hoyle & P. H. Clarke. LC 74-154749. (Introductory Engineering Ser.). 288p. reprint ed. pap. 82.10 (0-317-11043-8, 2006974) Bks Demand.

Thermodynamic Data: Systematics & Estimation. Ed. by Surendra K. Saxena. LC 91-31481. (Advances in Physical Geochemistry Ser.: Vol. 10). (Illus.). xiii, 368p. 1992. 144.95 (0-387-97696-5) Spr-Verlag.

Thermodynamic Data for Inorganic Sulphides, Selenides & Tellurides. K. C. Mills. LC 74-173939. 855p. reprint ed. pap. 180.00 (0-317-08901-3, 2051842) Bks Demand.

Thermodynamic Data on Metal Carbonates & Related Oxides. Y. Austin Chang & Nazeer Ahmad. LC 82-62692. (Technology of Metallurgy Ser.: No. 4). 241p. reprint ed. pap. 68.70 (0-8357-2522-7, 2052402) Bks Demand.

Thermodynamic Data on Oxides & Silicates: An Assessed Data Set Based on Thermochemistry & High Pressure Phase Equilibrium. Surendra K. Saxena et al. LC 93-28000. (Illus.). viii, 428p. 1993. 118.95 (0-387-56898-0) Spr-Verlag.

Thermodynamic Databases: Selected Papers from the First CODATA Symposium on Chemical Thermodynamic & Thermophysical Properties Databases, Paris, France, September 1985. Ed. by CODATA Staff. (CODATA Bulletin Ser.). 1986. pap. 15.00 (0-08-032487-8, Pub. by PPL UK) Elsevier.

Thermodynamic Design of the Stirling Cycle Machine. Allan J. Organ. (Illus.). 375p. (C). 1992. text ed. 135.00 (0-521-41363-X) Cambridge U Pr.

Thermodynamic Equilibria of Boiling Mixtures see Macroscopic & Technical Properties of Matter: Group IV

Thermodynamic Inequalities in Gases & Magnetoplasmas. L. C. Woods. LC 96-11159. 1996. text ed. 69.95 (0-471-96674-6) Wiley.

Thermodynamic, Loop Applications in Materials Systems: With Solutions Manual, 2 Vols., Set. G. B. Stracher. Ed. by Donald L. Johnson. (Illus.). 196p. 1995. text ed. 62.00 (0-87339-270-1, 2698) Minerals Metals.

Thermodynamic Modelling of Geological Materials: Minerals, Fluids, Melts. Ed. by E. S. Carmichael & H. P. Eugster. (Reviews in Mineralogy Ser.: Vol. 17). 499p. 1987. per. 25.00 (0-939950-21-9) Mineralogical Soc.

***Thermodynamic Optimization of Finite Time Processes.** R. S. Berry et al. LC 96-36799. 1997. write for info. (0-471-96752-1) Wiley.

Thermodynamic Properties - Individual Substances, Vol. 1, Pts. A & B. Gurvich. 1992. 235.95 (0-685-70443-2, 886760) CRC Pr.

***Thermodynamic Properties - Individual Substances Vol. 2, Pts. A & B.** Gurvich. 1992. 277.95 (0-685-70442-4) CRC Pr.

Thermodynamic Properties & Reduced Correlations for Gases. Lawrence N. Canjar & Francis S. Manning. LC 66-30022. 74p. reprint ed. 25.00 (0-8357-8347-2, 2032883); reprint ed. pap. 20.00 (0-685-08999-1) Bks Demand.

Thermodynamic Properties of a Lean Natural Gas at Cryogenic Conditions. D. P. Gregory et al. (Technical Reports: No. 11). xi, 83p. 1973. pap. 5.00 (0-317-56938-4) Inst Gas Tech.

Thermodynamic Properties of Air. Ed. by V. V. Sychev et al. Tr. by Dov B. Lederman from RUS. (National Standard Reference Data Service of the U. S. S. R.: A Series of Property Tables). 276p. 1987. 192.00 (0-89116-610-6) Hemisp Pub.

Thermodynamic Properties of Aqueous Inorganic Copper Systems. Columbia University Staff. 132p. 1977. write for info. (0-318-60399-3) Intl Copper.

Thermodynamic Properties of Aqueous Solutions of Organic Substances. V. P. Belousov. Tr. by Nicholas N. Bobrov from RUS. LC 93-8741. 384p. (ENG.). 1993. 201.95 (0-8493-9342-6, QD544) CRC Pr.

Thermodynamic Properties of Butane. V. V. Sychev et al. 261p. 1996. 117.50 (1-56700-049-5) Begell Hse.

Thermodynamic Properties of Copper & Its Inorganic Compounds. U. S. Bureau of Mines Staff. (INCRA Monograph). 257p. 1973. 20.00 (0-317-42833-0) Intl Copper.

Thermodynamic Properties of Copper-Base Alloys. Pennsylvania State University Staff. 134p. 1981. write for info. (0-318-60071-4, 245) Intl Copper.

Thermodynamic Properties of Copper-Slag Systems. University of Chile Staff. (INCRA Monograph). 178p. 1974. 20.00 (0-317-42839-X) Intl Copper.

***Thermodynamic Properties of Cryogenic Fluids.** Richard T. Jacobsen et al. LC 97-1550. (Volume in the International Cryogenics Monograph Ser.). (Illus.). 308p. (C). 95.00 (0-306-45522-6, Plenum Pr) Plenum.

Thermodynamic Properties of Ethylene. Ed. by V. V. Sychev et al. Tr. by Vladimir D. Azbel from RUS. (National Standard Reference Data Service of the U. S. S. R.: A Series of Property Tables). 1987. 192.00 (0-89116-612-2) Hemisp Pub.

Thermodynamic Properties of Gases: A Handbook. 4th rev. ed. C. L. Rivkin. 300p. 1988. 126.00 (0-89116-750-1) Hemisp Pub.

Thermodynamic Properties of Helium. Ed. by V. V. Sychev. Tr. by G. E. Slark from RUS. (National Standard Reference Data Service of the U. S. S. R.: A Series of Property Tables). 316p. 1987. 192.00 (0-89116-613-0) Hemisp Pub.

Thermodynamic Properties of Homogeneous Mixtures of Nitrogen & Water from 440 to 1000K, up to 100 MPA & 0.8 Mole Fraction N2. 1994. lib. bdg. 250.00 (0-8490-8426-1) Gordon Pr.

Thermodynamic Properties of Individual Substances, 2 vols. 3rd enl. rev. ed. Ed. by L. V. Gurvich. (Illus.). 830p. 1988. Set. 135.01 (0-08-027585-0, Pergamon Pr) Elsevier.

Thermodynamic Properties of Individual Substances, Vol. 1, Pts. 1 & 2. Veyts & L. V. Gurvich. LC 66-56649. 1100p. 1989. 262.00 (0-89116-760-9) Hemisp Pub.

Thermodynamic Properties of Individual Substances, Vol. 2. Ed. by Gurvitch & Veyts. Tr. by Henri A. Bronstein from RUS. 1990. 358.00 (0-89116-533-9) Hemisp Pub.

Thermodynamic Properties of Individual Substances, Vol. 3, Pt. 1. L. V. Gurvich. 720p. 1994. 297.00 (0-8493-9927-0, QC) CRC Pr.

Thermodynamic Properties of Individual Substances, Vol. 3, Pt. 2. L. V. Gurvich. 464p. 1994. 231.00 (0-8493-9928-9, QC) CRC Pr.

Thermodynamic Properties of Individual Substances, Vol. 4, Pt. 1. L. V. Gurvich. 1995. write for info. (0-8493-9930-0, QC) CRC Pr.

Thermodynamic Properties of Individual Substances, Vol. 4, Pt. 2. L. V. Gurvich. 1995. write for info. (0-8493-9931-9, QC) CRC Pr.

Thermodynamic Properties of Individual Substances, Vol. 5, Pt. 1. L. V. Gurvich. 1995. write for info. (0-8493-9933-5, QC) CRC Pr.

Thermodynamic Properties of Individual Substances, Vol. 5, Pt. 2. L. V. Gurvich. 1995. write for info. (0-8493-9934-3, QC) CRC Pr.

Thermodynamic Properties of Inorganic Materials: A Literature Database Covering the Period 1970-1987, 2 parts. B. Cheynet. (Physical Sciences Data Ser.: Vol. 38). 2402p. 1989. 1,191.50 (0-444-88036-4) Elsevier.

Thermodynamic Properties of Isomerization Reactions. M. L. Frenkel et al. 200p. 1992. 99.95 (1-56032-111-3) Hemisp Pub.

Thermodynamic Properties of Methane. Ed. by V. V. Sychev et al. Tr. by Dov B. Lederman from RUS. (National Standard Reference Data Service of the U. S. S. R.: A Series of Property Tables). 342p. 1987. 192.00 (0-89116-614-9) Hemisp Pub.

Thermodynamic Properties of Methane-Nitrogen Mixtures. O T. Bloomer et al. (Research Bulletin Ser.: No. 21). iv, 51p. 1955. pap. 3.50 (0-685-43365-X); suppl. ed., pap. 3.50 (0-685-11596-8) Inst Gas Tech.

Thermodynamic Properties of Multicomponent Systems, Multicomponent Phase Equilibria & Chemical Equilibria. Ed. by B. M. Goodwin. (AIChEMI Modular Instruction D Series: Vol. 3). 46p. 1982. pap. 44.00 (0-8169-0211-9, J-16) Am Inst Chem Eng.

Thermodynamic Properties of Nitrogen. O. T. Bloomer & K. N. Rao. (Research Bulletin Ser.: No. 18). iv, 28p. 1952. pap. 3.50 (0-317-56857-4); suppl. ed., pap. 3.50 (0-317-56858-2) Inst Gas Tech.

Thermodynamic Properties of Nitrogen. Ed. by V. V. Sychev et al. Tr. by Dov B. Lederman from RUS. (National Standard Reference Data Service of the U. S. S. R.: A Series of Property Tables). 342p. 1987. 192.00 (0-89116-615-7) Hemisp Pub.

***Thermodynamic Properties of Organic Compounds & Their Mixtures Subvolume B: Densities of Aliphatic Hydrocarbons: Alkanes.** Ed. by W. Martienssen & K. N. Marsh. (Landolt-Bornstein Numerical Data & Functosal Relationship in Science & Technology New Series: Vol. 8). (Illus.). x, 410p. 1996. 1,682.00 (3-540-61029-4) Spr-Verlag.

Thermodynamic Properties of Oxygen. Ed. by V. V. Sychev et al. Tr. by Dimitri Gokhman. (National Standard Reference Data Service of the U. S. S. R.: A Series of Property Tables). 308p. 1987. 192.00 (0-89116-616-5) Hemisp Pub.

Thermodynamic Properties of Propane. V. V. Sychev. 1991. 159.00 (0-89116-932-6) Hemisp Pub.

***Thermodynamic Properties of the Elements.** American Chemical Society Staff. Ed. by Industrial & Engineering Chemistry Staff. (Advances in Chemistry Ser.: No. 18). 240p. 1956. reprint ed. pap. 68.40 (0-608-03267-0, 2063786) Bks Demand.

Thermodynamic Properties of Water to 1,000 C & 10,000 Bars. C. Wayne Burnham et al. LC 73-96715. (Geological Society of America, Special Paper Ser.: No. 132). 104p. reprint ed. pap. 29.70 (0-318-34701-6, 2031866) Bks Demand.

Thermodynamic Relations in Open Systems. George Tunell. LC 77-80609. (Carnegie Institution of Washington Publication Ser.: No. 408a). 85p. reprint ed. pap. 25.00 (0-317-27755-3, 2015542) Bks Demand.

Thermodynamic Tables in SI (Metric) Units. 3rd ed. Ed. by R. W. Haywood. (Illus.). 56p. (C). 1990. pap. text ed. 18.95 (0-521-38693-4) Cambridge U Pr.

Thermodynamic Theory of Site-Specific Binding Processes in Biological Macromolecules. Enrico Di Cera. (Illus.). 320p. (C). 1996. text ed. 72.95 (0-521-41659-0) Cambridge U Pr.

***Thermodynamic Theory of the Evolution of Living Beings.** G. P. Gladyshev. 208p. 1997. lib. bdg. 79.00 (1-56072-457-9) Nova Sci Pubs.

Thermodynamic Values at Low Temperature for Natural Inorganic Materials. Terri Woods. 284p. 1986. 35.00 (0-19-504888-1) OUP.

***Thermodynamics.** ("Test Yourself" Testing Guides). Date not set. pap. 12.95 (0-8442-2378-6) NTC Pub Grp.

***Thermodynamics.** Muhammed Ali Rob Sharif. (Test Yourself Ser.). 1997. pap. 12.95 (0-614-27611-X) NTC Pub Grp.

Thermodynamics. Edward E. Anderson. LC 93-25647. 1994. text ed. 81.95 (0-534-93294-0) PWS Pubs.

Thermodynamics. Balmer. (West - Engineering Ser.). 1990. student ed., pap. 14.25 (0-534-93867-1) PWS Pubs.

Thermodynamics. Enrico Fermi. 1937. pap. 5.95 (0-486-60361-X) Dover.

Thermodynamics. P. C. Rakshit. 1985. 79.00 (0-317-38807-X, Pub. by Current Dist II) St Mut.

Thermodynamics. 2nd ed. Herbert B. Callen. LC 85-6387. 512p. 1985. text ed. 51.00 (0-471-86256-8) Wiley.

Thermodynamics. 2nd ed. R. G. Reddy & Nev A. Gokcen. LC 96-25897. 400p. 1996. 59.50 (0-306-45380-0) Plenum.

Thermodynamics. 3rd ed. Kenneth S. Pitzer. LC 94-26960. 1994. text ed. write for info. (0-07-050221-8) McGraw.

Thermodynamics. 4th ed. M. David Burghardt. (C). 1993. text ed. 84.68 (0-06-041049-3) Addson-Wesley Educ.

Thermodynamics. 4th rev. ed. Jack P. Holman. 832p. 1988. text ed. write for info. (0-07-029633-2) McGraw.

Thermodynamics. 5th ed. Kenneth Wark. 976p. 1988. text ed. write for info. (0-07-068286-0) McGraw.

Thermodynamics: A Rigorous Postulatory Approach. S. H. Chue. LC 76-44878. 286p. reprint ed. pap. 81.60 (0-685-20461-8, 2029857) Bks Demand.

Thermodynamics: A Self Instructional Problem Workbook. Louis Theodore. 248p. (C). 1992. pap. text ed. 50.00 (1-882767-04-7) ETS.

Thermodynamics: An Advanced Textbook for Chemical Engineers. G. Astarita. (Illus.). 456p. 1989. 79.50 (0-306-43048-7, Plenum Pr) Plenum.

Thermodynamics: An Advanced Treatment for Chemists & Physicists. E. A. Guggenheim. (North-Holland Personal Library). 390p. 1985. pap. 61.75 (0-444-86951-4, North Holland) Elsevier.

Thermodynamics: An Engineering Approach. 2nd ed. Unus Cengel & Michael A. Boles. 1994. pap. text ed. write for info. (0-07-011062-X) McGraw.

Thermodynamics: An Engineering Approach. 2nd ed. Yanus A. Cengel & Michael A. Boles. 1994. text ed. write for info. (0-07-011061-1) McGraw.

***Thermodynamics: An Engineering Approach.** 2nd ed. Yunus A. Cengel & Michael A. Boles. 1993. text ed. write for info. incl. 3.5 hd (0-07-911652-3) McGraw.

***Thermodynamics: An Engineering Approach.** 2nd ed. Yunus A. Cengel & Michael A. Boles. 1994. text ed. write for info. incl. 5.25 hd (0-07-911651-5) McGraw.

Thermodynamics: An Engineering Approach, 2 vols., Set. Yunis A. Cengel & Michael A. Boles. (Mechanical Engineering Ser.). 1989. text ed. write for info. (0-07-909389-2) McGraw.

Thermodynamics: English SI Version. 3rd ed. William Z. Black & James G. Hartley. LC 95-24455. (Illus.). 944p. (C). 1996. pap. text ed. 73.75 (0-673-99648-4) Addson-Wesley Educ.

Thermodynamics: From Concepts to Applications. 3rd ed. Arthur Shavit & Chaim Gutfinger. LC 94-29081. (C). 1995. pap. text ed. 49.00 (*0-13-288267-1*) P-H.

Thermodynamics: History & Philosophy - Facts, Trends & Debates. K. Martinas et al. 544p. 1991. text ed. 147.00 (*981-02-0464-7*) World Scientific Pub.

Thermodynamics: Principles & Applications. Frank C. Andrews. LC 77-150607. 300p. reprint ed. 85.50 (*0-8357-9993-X*, 2055278) Bks Demand.

***Thermodynamics: Principles & Practice.** Michel A. Saad. LC 96-3330. 1997. 87.00 (*0-13-490525-3*) P-H.

Thermodynamics: Second Law Analysis. Ed. by Richard A. Gaggioli. LC 80-10486. (ACS Symposium Ser.: No. 122). 1980. 38.95 (*0-8412-0541-8*) Am Chemical.

***Thermodynamics: Second Law Analysis.** Ed. by Richard A. Gaggioli. LC 80-10486. (ACS Symposium Ser.: Vol. 122). 312p. 1980. reprint ed. pap. 89.00 (*0-608-03060-0*, 2063513) Bks Demand.

Thermodynamics: SI Version. 3rd ed. William Z. Black & James G. Hartley. (Illus.). 864p. (C). 1996. text ed. 74. 68 (*0-673-99645-X*) Addson-Wesley Educ.

Thermodynamics: Tables & Charts. Anderson. (General Engineering Ser.). 1994. pap. 15.95 (*0-534-94262-8*) Wadsworth Pub.

Thermodynamics: The Application of Classical & Statistical Thermodynamics to the Prediction of Equilibrium Properties. G. Ali Mansoori. (Advances in Thermodynamics Ser.: Vol. 8). 300p. 1991. 41.00 (*0-8448-1681-7*, Crane Russak) Taylor & Francis.

***Thermodynamics Level 4.** (Longman Technician Ser.). Date not set. pap. text ed. write for info. (*0-582-41300-1*, Pub. by Longman UK) Longman.

Thermodynamics & Constitutive Equations. Ed. by G. Grioli. (Lecture Notes in Physics Ser.: Vol. 228). (Illus.). v, 257p. 1985. 33.95 (*0-387-15228-8*) Spr-Verlag.

Thermodynamics & Control of Biological Free-Energy Transduction. N. V. Westerhoff & K. Van Dam. 568p. 1987. 413.75 (*0-444-80783-7*) Elsevier.

Thermodynamics & Electrodynamics of Superconductors. Ed. by V. L. Ginzburg. (Proceedings of the Lebedev Physics Institute Ser.: Vol. 174, Supplemental Volume 1). 294p. 1988. text ed. 135.00 (*0-941743-18-7*) Nova Sci Pubs.

Thermodynamics & Fluid Mechanics of Turbomachinary, 2 vols. Ed. by A. S. Ucer et al. 1985. Set. lib. bdg. 401.50 (*90-247-3223-9*) Kluwer Ac.

Thermodynamics & Gas Dynamics of Internal-Combustion Engines, Vol. II. Ed. by J. H. Horlock & D. E. Winterbone. (Illus.). 668p. 1987. 140.00 (*0-19-856212-8*) OUP.

Thermodynamics & Heat Power. 4th ed. Kurt C. Rolle. (Illus.). 864p. (C). 1993. teacher ed. write for info. incl. disk (*0-318-69909-5*) Macmillan.

Thermodynamics & Heat Power. 4th ed. Kurt C. Rolle. (Illus.). 864p. (C). 1993. text ed. 96.00 (*0-02-403201-8*, Macmillan Coll) P-H.

Thermodynamics & Heat Power. 5th ed. Irving Granet. LC 95-4061. 796p. 1995. text ed. 96.00 (*0-13-432923-6*) P-H.

Thermodynamics & Its Application. 3rd ed. Michael Modell & Jefferson Tester. LC 96-3173. (C). 1996. text ed. 90.00 (*0-13-915356-X*) P-H.

Thermodynamics & Its Applications. 2nd ed. Michael Modell & Robert C. Reid. (Illus.). 512p. 1983. text ed. 99.00 (*0-13-915017-X*) P-H.

Thermodynamics & Kinetic Theory: Proceedings of the 5th Bilateral Polish-Italian Meeting. W. Kosinski et al. (Series on Advances in Mathematics for Applied Sciences: No. 12). 216p. 1992. text ed. 81.00 (*981-02-0930-4*) World Scientific Pub.

Thermodynamics & Kinetics of Diffusion of Solids. B. S. Bokshtein. (C). 1985. 37.50 (*81-205-0027-X*, Pub. by Oxford IBH II) S Asia.

Thermodynamics & Kinetics of Phase Transformations: Materials Research Society Symposium Proceedings, Vol. 398. Ed. by James S. Im et al. (MRS Symposium Proceedings Ser.: Vol. 398). 680p. 1996. 71.00 (*1-55899-301-0*, 398) Materials Res.

Thermodynamics & Pattern Formation in Biology. Ed. by I. Lamprecht & A. I. Zotin. xiii, 518p. (C). 1988. lib. bdg. 306.15 (*3-11-011368-6*) De Gruyter.

Thermodynamics & Physical Properties see Technical Engineering Training Series

Thermodynamics & Regulation of Biological Processes. Ed. by I. Lamprecht & A. I. Zotin. LC 84-23302. (Illus.). xiv, 573p. 1985. 207.70 (*3-11-009789-3*) De Gruyter.

***Thermodynamics & Rheology.** J. Ozsef Verhas. LC 96-40959. (Fluid Mechanics & Its Applications Ser.). 235p. (C). 1997. lib. bdg. 119.00 (*0-7923-4251-8*) Kluwer Ac.

Thermodynamics & Statistical Mechanics. Walter Greiner et al. LC 94-29072. (Classical Theoretical Physics Ser.). 1997. 49.00 (*0-387-94299-8*) Spr-Verlag.

Thermodynamics & Statistical Mechanics. Peter T. Landberg. 1990. pap. 12.95 (*0-486-66493-7*) Dover.

Thermodynamics & Statistical Mechanics. Arnold Sommerfeld. (Lectures on Theoretical Physics Ser.: Vol. 5). 1964. pap. text ed. 58.00 (*0-12-654682-7*) Acad Pr.

Thermodynamics & Statistical Mechanics: Proceeding of the XXII Winter Meeting on Statistical Physics. M. L. De Haro & C. Varea. 264p. 1994. text ed. 95.00 (*981-02-1527-4*) World Scientific Pub.

Thermodynamics & Statistical Mechanics, Lectures: Proceedings of the 21st Meeting in Statistical Physics. M. L. De Haro & C. Varea. 216p. 1992. text ed. 95.00 (*981-02-1221-6*) World Scientific Pub.

Thermodynamics & Statistical Mechanics, Lectures on: Seventeenth Winter Meeting on Statistical Physics. A. E. Gonzalez & C. Varea. 144p. 1988. text ed. 61.00 (*9971-5-0718-8*) World Scientific Pub.

Thermodynamics & Statistical Physics: Teaching Modern Physics, Badajoz, Spain July 1992. Ed. by M. G. Velarde & F. Cuadros. 310p. 1995. text ed. 86.00 (*981-02-2417-6*) World Scientific Pub.

Thermodynamics & the Design, Analysis & Improement of Energy Systems - 1995 Vol. 35: Proceedings of the ASME International Mechanical Engineering Congress & Exposition, 1995, San Francisco, CA. Ed. by D. L. O'Neal et al. (1995 ASME International Mechanical Engineering Congress & Exposition Ser.: AES-Vol. 35). 460p. 1995. 110.00 (*0-7918-1764-4*, H01045) ASME.

Thermodynamics & the Design, Analysis, & Improvement of Energy Systems. Ed. by R. F. Boehm. (AES Series, Vol. 27: HTD Ser.: Vol. 228). 392p. 1992. 67.50 (*0-7918-1073-9*, G00717) ASME.

Thermodynamics & the Design, Analysis, & Improvement of Energy Systems: 1994 International Mechanical Engineering Congress & Exposition, Chicago, Illinois - November 6-11, 1994. (Advanced Energy Systems Ser.: Vol. 33). 412p. 1994. 100.00 (*0-7918-1455-6*, G00950) ASME.

Thermodynamics & the Design, Analysis, & Improvement of Energy Systems 1993. Ed. by H. J. Richter. LC 93-73595. 435p. pap. 80.00 (*0-7918-1042-9*) ASME.

Thermodynamics & the Development of Order. Ed. by Emmett L. Williams. (Creation Research Society Monographs: No. 1). (Illus.). 141p. (Orig.). 1981. pap. 8.95 (*0-940384-01-9*) Creation Research.

***Thermodynamics, Combustion & Engines.** B. Milton. (Illus.). 392p. (Orig.). (C). (gr. 13 up). 1995. pap. text ed. 46.50 (*0-412-53840-7*, Chap & Hall NY) Chapman & Hall.

Thermodynamics Data for Biochemistry & Biotechnology. Ed. by H. J. Hinz. (Illus.). 480p. 1986. 310.95 (*0-387-16368-9*) Spr-Verlag.

Thermodynamics Exam File. Ed. by Stuart T. McComas. LC 84-24688. (Exam File Ser.). 250p. (Orig.). (C). 1985. pap. 15.50 (*0-910554-49-8*) Engineering.

Thermodynamics for Geologists. Kern & T. Weisbrod. 1967. pap. 35.00 (*0-87735-305-0*) Jones & Bartlett.

***Thermodynamics in Engineering & Physical Science: Heat-Power Conversion by Gas & Vapour Cycles.** G. H. Cole. 144p. 1997. pap. text ed. 29.95 (*1-898563-22-5*, Pub. by Albion Pubng UK) Paul & Co Pubs.

Thermodynamics in Geochemistry. Greg M. Anderson & David A. Crerar. (Illus.). 624p. 1993. 85.00 (*0-19-506464-X*) OUP.

Thermodynamics in Materials Science. R. T. DeHoff. LC 92-40109. (Series in Materials Science & Engineering). 1993. text ed. write for info. (*0-07-016313-8*) McGraw.

Thermodynamics Kinetic Theory & Statistical Mechanics. Herbert Goldstein. (C). 1997. text ed. write for info. (*0-201-18445-1*) Addison-Wesley.

***Thermodynamics of Alloy Formation.** Ed. by Y. A. Chang. (Illus.). 310p. 1997. 86.00 (*0-87339-355-4*, 3554) Minerals Metals.

Thermodynamics of Aqueous Systems with Industrial Applications. Ed. by Stephen A. Newman. LC 80-16044. (ACS Symposium Ser.: No. 133). 1980. 86.95 (*0-8412-0569-8*); suppl. ed. 14.95 (*0-8412-0590-6*) Am Chemical.

***Thermodynamics of Aqueous Systems with Industrial Applications.** Ed. by Stephen A. Newman. LC 80-16044. (ACS Symposium Ser.: No. 133). (Illus.). 783p. 1980. reprint ed. pap. 180.00 (*0-608-03235-2*, 2063754) Bks Demand.

Thermodynamics of Chaotic Systems: An Introduction. Christian Beck & Friedrich Schlogl. (Cambridge Nonlinear Science Ser.: No. 4). (Illus.). 250p. (C). 1993. text ed. 79.95 (*0-521-43367-3*) Cambridge U Pr.

Thermodynamics of Chaotic Systems: An Introduction. Christian Beck & Friedrich Schlogl. (Nonlinear Science Ser.: No. 4). (Illus.). 306p. (C). 1995. pap. text ed. 28.95 (*0-521-48451-0*) Cambridge U Pr.

Thermodynamics of Chemical Processes. Yu Zhorov. 518p. (C). 1987. 130.00 (*0-685-46653-1*, Pub. by Collets) St Mut.

Thermodynamics of Chemical Systems. Scott E. Wood & Rubin Battino. (Illus.). 528p. (C). 1990. text ed. 130.00 (*0-521-33041-6*) Cambridge U Pr.

Thermodynamics of Complex Systems. Ed. by L. Sertorio. 220p. (C). 1990. text ed. 48.00 (*9971-5-0978-4*) World Scientific Pub.

Thermodynamics of Crystals. Duane C. Wallace. LC 71-161495. (Illus.). 504p. reprint ed. pap. 143.70 (*0-317-09102-6*, 2017402) Bks Demand.

Thermodynamics of Electrical Phenomena in Metals & a Condensed Collection of Thermodynamic Formulas. P. W. Bridgman. (Illus.). 1990. 12.50 (*0-8446-1737-7*) Peter Smith.

Thermodynamics of Electrical Processes. Malcolm McChesney. LC 75-166417. 286p. reprint ed. pap. 81.60 (*0-317-10940-5*, 2016147) Bks Demand.

Thermodynamics of Extremes. Bernard H. Lavenda. 256p. 1996. 65.00 (*1-898563-24-1*, Pub. by Albion Pubng UK) Paul & Co Pubs.

Thermodynamics of Flowing Systems: With Internal Microstructure. Antony N. Beris & Brian J. Edwards. (Oxford Engineering Science Ser.: No. 36). (Illus.). 608p. (C). 1994. 120.00 (*0-19-507694-X*, 3804) OUP.

Thermodynamics of Fluids: An Introduction to Equilibrium Theory. Kwang-Chu Chao & R. A. Greenkorn. LC 75-13121. (Chemical Processing & Engineering Ser.: No. 4). (Illus.). 569p. reprint ed. pap. 162.20 (*0-7837-0968-4*, 2041273) Bks Demand.

Thermodynamics of Fluids: Measurement & Correlation. Stanislaw Malanowski. Ed. by Andrzej Anderko. 524p. (C). 1990. text ed. 113.00 (*981-02-0169-9*) World Scientific Pub.

Thermodynamics of Gases see Encyclopedia of Physics

***Thermodynamics of Irreversible Processes.** Rolf Haase. pap. 12.95 (*0-486-66356-6*) Dover.

Thermodynamics of Irreversible Processes. Bernard H. Lavenda. LC 93-3190. 182p. 1993. reprint ed. pap. 7.95 (*0-486-67576-9*) Dover.

Thermodynamics of Irreversible Processes in Fluid Mixtures. L. Samohyl. 176p. (C). 1987. 85.00 (*0-685-36852-1*, Pub. by Collets) St Mut.

Thermodynamics of Irreversible Processes with Applications to Diffusion & Rheology. G. D. C. Kuiken. 500p. 1994. text ed. 62.95 (*0-471-94844-6*) Wiley.

Thermodynamics of Light Energy Conversion. L. N. Bell & N. D. Gudkov. (Illus.). xvi, 204p. 1993. pap. 60.00 (*90-5103-081-9*, Pub. by SPB Acad Pub NE) Balogh.

Thermodynamics of Materials, 2 vols., Vol. 1. David A. Ragone. 336p. 1994. text ed. 52.00 (*0-471-30885-4*) Wiley.

Thermodynamics of Materials, 2 vols., Vol. 2. David V. Ragone. 256p. 1994. text ed. (*0-471-30886-2*) Wiley.

Thermodynamics of Materials: A Classical & Statistical Synthesis. John Hudson. LC 95-20224. 392p. 1996. text ed. 59.95 (*0-471-31143-X*) Wiley.

Thermodynamics of Membrane Receptors & Channels. Meyer B. Jackson. 448p. 1992. 127.00 (*0-8493-6908-8*, QH603) CRC Pr.

Thermodynamics of Molecular Species. Ernest Grunwald. LC 96-14103. 1996. text ed. 64.95 (*0-471-01254-8*, Wiley-Interscience) Wiley.

Thermodynamics of Natural Systems. G. M. Anderson. LC 95-23040. 382p. (C). 1995. text ed. 25.95 (*0-471-10943-6*) Wiley.

Thermodynamics of Nonequilibrium Processes. S. Wisniewski et al. LC 75-41486. 1976. lib. bdg. 135.00 (*90-277-0331-0*) Kluwer Ac.

Thermodynamics of Nuclear Materials: 1967. 890p. (ENG, FRE & RUS.). 1968. pap. 95.00 (*92-0-040068-X*, ISP162, Pub. by Stationery Ofc UK) Bernan Associates.

Thermodynamics of Nuclear Materials: 1974, Vols. 1 & 2. (Proceedings Ser.). (Illus.). 484p. 1975. Vol. 1. pap. 195. 00 (*92-0-040175-9*, ISP380-1 & 2, Pub. by Stationery Ofc UK) Bernan Associates.

Thermodynamics of Pizza. Harold J. Morowitz. 258p. (Orig.). 1992. reprint ed. pap. 14.95 (*0-8135-1774-5*) Rutgers U Pr.

Thermodynamics of Polymer Solutions. Michio Kurata. Tr. by Hiroshi Fujita from JPN. (MMI Press Polymer Monographs: Vol. 1). 294p. 1982. text ed. 321.00 (*3-7186-0023-4*) Gordon & Breach.

Thermodynamics of Polymer Solutions: Phase Equilibria & Critical Phenomena. K. Kamide. (Polymer Science Library: No. 9). 652p. 1990. 349.50 (*0-444-88184-0*, PSL 9) Elsevier.

Thermodynamics of Polymerization. Hideo Sawada. Ed. & Frwd. by Kenneth F. O'Driscoll. LC 76-12193. (Illus.). 419p. reprint ed. pap. 119.50 (*0-7837-3549-9*, 2043386) Bks Demand.

Thermodynamics of Rheology or (Inside the Thermodynamic Black Box) 3rd rev. ed. Harry H. Hull. (Illus.). 151p. 1995. 33.00 (*0-9606118-4-3*) Hull.

Thermodynamics of Seawater As a Multicomponent Electrolyte Solution, Pt. 1: Entropy, Volume, Expansibility, Compressibility. J. V. Leyendekkers. LC 76-18422. (Marine Science Ser.: No. 3). (Illus.). 510p. reprint ed. pap. 145.40 (*0-7837-0788-6*, 2041102) Bks Demand.

Thermodynamics of Silicates. V. I. Babushkin et al. Tr. by B. N. Frenkel & V. A. Terentyev from RUS. (Illus.). 470p. 1984. 287.95 (*0-387-12750-X*) Spr-Verlag.

Thermodynamics of Small Systems, 2 pts. in 1 vol. Terrell L. Hill. (Illus.). 416p. 1994. reprint ed. pap. 10.95 (*0-486-68109-2*) Dover.

Thermodynamics of Solids. 2nd ed. Richard A. Swalin. (Science & Technology of Materials Ser.). 387p. 1972. pap. text ed. 112.95 (*0-471-83854-3*) Wiley.

Thermodynamics of the Critical State of Individual Substances: Termodinamiia Kriticheskogo Sostoianiia Individual Nykh Veshchestv. S. I. Anisimov et al. LC 94-23466. Orig. Title: Termodinamika Kriticheskogo Sostoianiia Individualnykh Veshchestv. 182p. (ENG & RUS.). 1995. 240.00 (*0-8493-9901-7*, BB9901) CRC Pr.

Thermodynamics of the Future, 2 vols. Seymour Moskowitz. (Illus.). 257p. (C). 1989. reprint ed. Set. text ed. 300.00 (*0-9630456-2-8*); reprint ed. Set. pap. text ed. 275.00 (*0-9630456-5-2*) S Moskowitz.

Thermodynamics of the Future, Vol. 1. Seymour Moskowitz. (Illus.). 257p. (C). 1989. reprint ed. text ed. 160.00 (*0-9630456-0-1*); reprint ed. pap. text ed. 150.00 (*0-9630456-3-6*) S Moskowitz.

Thermodynamics of the Future, Vol. 2. Seymour Moskowitz. (Illus.). 257p. (C). 1989. reprint ed. text ed. 160.00 (*0-9630456-1-X*); reprint ed. pap. text ed. 150.00 (*0-9630456-4-4*) S Moskowitz.

Thermodynamics Problem Solver. rev. ed. Research & Education Association Staff. LC 84-61810. (Illus.). 892p. 1995. pap. text ed. 29.95 (*0-87891-555-9*) Res & Educ.

Thermodynamics, the Kinetic Theory of Gases & Statistical Mechanics. 3rd ed. Francis W. Sears & Gerhard L. Salinger. 464p. (C). 1975. text ed. 56.95 (*0-201-06894-X*) Addison-Wesley.

Thermodynamics with Disk. Balmer. (West - Engineering Ser.). 1990. text ed. 82.95 (*0-534-93811-6*) PWS Pubs.

Thermodynamique Structurale Des Alliages see Structural Thermodynamics of Alloys

Thermoelastic Crack Growth Analysis. A. Portela et al. 1995. ring bd. 460.00 incl. disk (*1-56252-269-8*, 3455) Computational Mech MA.

***Thermoelastic Deformations.** Dorin Iesan & A. Scalia. LC 96-27710. (Solid Mechanics & Its Applications Ser.). 320p. (C). 1996. lib. bdg. 147.00 (*0-7923-4230-5*) Kluwer Ac.

Thermoelastic Stress Analysis. Ed. by N. Harwood & W. M. Cummings. (Illus.). 256p. 1991. 130.00 (*0-7503-0075-2*) IOP Pub.

Thermoelasticity. 2nd enl. rev. ed. H. Parkus. 1976. 42.95 (*0-387-81375-6*) Spr-Verlag.

***Thermoelectric Materials - New Directions & Approaches: Materials Research Society Symposium Proceedings, Vol. 478.** Ed. by T. M. Tritt et al. 1997. text ed. 71.00 (*1-55899-382-7*) Materials Res.

***Thermofluids.** Keith Sherwin. (Illus.). 672p. (Orig.). 1995. pap. text ed. 34.50 (*0-412-59800-0*, Chap & Hall NY) Chapman & Hall.

Thermofluids: An Integrated Approach to Thermodynamics & Fluid Mechanics Principles. C. Marquand & D. Croft. 403p. 1994. pap. text ed. 60.00 (*0-471-94184-0*) Wiley.

Thermofluidynamics of Optimized Rocket Propulsions. Dieter Straub. 270p. 1989. 150.50 (*0-8176-2314-0*) Birkhauser.

Thermoforming. James L. Throne. 299p. (C). 1987. text ed. 65.00 (*1-56990-098-1*) Hanser-Gardner.

Thermoforming--a Plastics Processing Guide. G. Gruenwald. LC 87-50432. 224p. 1987. pap. 49.95 (*0-87762-526-3*) Technomic.

Thermographic Evidence of Soft Tissue Injury. 562p. 1987. text ed. 95.00 (*0-07-172008-1*) Shepards.

Thermographic Investigations into the Physiological Basis of Regional Anaesthesia. G. Sprotte. (Anaesthesiology & Intensive Care Medicine Ser.: Vol. 159). (Illus.). 65p. 1984. 56.95 (*0-387-12638-4*) Spr-Verlag.

Thermography: Proceedings of the European Congress on Thermography, 1st, Amsterdam, June 1974. European Congress on Thermography Staff. Ed. by N. J. Aarts. (Bibliotheca Radiologica Ser.: Vol. 6). (Illus.). xiv, 262p. 1975. pap. 78.50 (*3-8055-2134-0*) S Karger.

Thermoinelasticity: Proceedings of the International Union of Theoretical & Applied Mechanics Symposium, Glasgow, 1968. International Union of Theoretical & Applied Mechanics Staff. Ed. by Bruno A. Boley. LC 75-94050. (Illus.). 1970. 108.95 (*0-387-80961-9*) Spr-Verlag.

Thermoluminescence & Thermoluminescent Dosimetry, Vol. I. Ed. by Yigal S. Horowitz. 200p. 1984. 113.00 (*0-8493-5664-4*) Franklin.

Thermoluminescence & Thermoluminescent Dosimetry, Vol. II. Ed. by Yigal S. Horowitz. 232p. 1984. 146.00 (*0-8493-5665-2*, QC479) Franklin.

Thermoluminescence & Thermoluminescent Dosimetry, Vol. III. Ed. by Yigal S. Horowitz. 216p. 1984. 122.00 (*0-8493-5666-0*, QC479) Franklin.

Thermoluminescence Dosimetry. A. F. McKinlay. (Medical Physics Handbooks Ser.: No. 5). (Illus.). 170p. 1981. 19. 00 (*0-85274-520-6*) IOP Pub.

Thermoluminescence of Solids. S. W. McKeever. (Cambridge Solid State Science Ser.). (Illus.). 400p. 1985. text ed. 110.00 (*0-521-24520-6*) Cambridge U Pr.

Thermoluminescence of Solids. S. W. McKeever. (Cambridge Solid State Science Ser.). (Illus.). 400p. 1988. pap. text ed. 47.95 (*0-521-36811-1*) Cambridge U Pr.

Thermoluminescent Dosimetry. John R. Cameron & N. Suntharalingam. LC 68-16061. 256p. reprint ed. pap. 73. 00 (*0-317-11063-2*, 2012631) Bks Demand.

Thermomechanical Behavior of Advanced Structural Materials. Ed. by W. F. Jones. LC 93-73269. 193p. pap. 55.00 (*0-7918-1034-8*) ASME.

Thermomechanical Behavior of High-Temperature Composites: Presented at the Winter Annual Meeting of the American Society of Mechanical Engineers, Phoenix, Arizona, November 14-19, 1982. American Society of Mechanical Engineers Staff. Ed. by Julius Jortner. LC 82-73182. (AD Ser.: No. 04). (Illus.). 128p. reprint ed. pap. 36.50 (*0-8357-2909-5*, 2039146) Bks Demand.

Thermomechanical Fatigue Behavior of Materials. Huseyin Sehitoglu. LC 93-21663. (Special Technical Publication Ser.: Vol. 1186). (Illus.). 260p. 1993. 76.00 (*0-8031-1871-6*, 04-011860-30) ASTM.

Thermomechanical Fatigue Behavior of Materials, Vol. 2, No. 1263. Michael G. Castelli. Ed. by Michael J. Verrilli. LC 96-19174. (Special Technical Publication Ser.). (Illus.). 390p. text ed. 79.00 (*0-8031-2001-X*, 04-012630-30) ASTM.

Thermomechanical Processing & Transformation-Induced Plasticity: The Possible Achievement of Ultra-High Strength, Ductile Copper-Base Alloys. Stanford Research Institute Staff. 92p. 1972. 13.80 (*0-317-34554-0*, 135) Intl Copper.

Thermomechanical Processing of Aluminum Alloys: Processings of a Symposium Sponsored by the TMS-AIME Heat Treatment Committee at the TMS Fall Meeting in St. Louis, MO, October 18, 1978. AIME, Metallurgical Society Staff. Ed. by James G. Morris. LC 79-88848. 233p. reprint ed. pap. 66.50 (*0-685-16202-8*, 2056148) Bks Demand.

Thermomechanical Processing of Microalloyed Austenite: Proceedings of the International Conference on the Thermomechanical Processing of Microalloyed Austenite, 1981, Pittsburgh, PA. International Conference of the Thermomechanical Processing of Microalloyed Austenite Staff. Ed. by A. J. DeArdo et al. LC 82-61571. 696p. reprint ed. pap. 180.00 (*0-7837-2211-7*, 2052461) Bks Demand.

Thermomechanics of Evolving Phase Boundaries in the Plane. Morton E. Gurtin. LC 92-38016. (Oxford Mathematical Monographs). 160p. 1993. 75.00 (*0-19-853694-1*) OUP.

Thermomechanics of Magnetic Fluids, Vol. 2. B. M. Berkovsky & M. S. Krakov. (Thermal Physics Ser.: Vol. 2, Pt. 1). 102p. 1989. pap. text ed. 96.00 (*3-7186-4812-1*) Gordon & Breach.

An Asterisk (*) at the beginning of an entry indicates that the title is appearing in BIP for the first time.

Thermomechanics of Phase Transition in Classical Field Theory. A. Romano. (Advances in Mathematics for Applied Sciences Ser.). 272p. 1993. text ed. 48.00 (*981-02-1398-0*) World Scientific Pub.

Thermomechanics of Plasticity & Fracture. Gerard A. Maugin. (Cambridge Texts in Applied Mathematics Ser.: No. 7). (Illus.). 400p. (C). 1992. text ed. 100.00 (*0-521-39476-7*); pap. text ed. 39.95 (*0-521-39780-4*) Cambridge U Pr.

Thermometry. James F. Schooley. LC 86-6142. 336p. 1986. 147.00 (*0-8493-5833-7*, QC271, CRC Reprint) Franklin.

Thermomicroscopy in the Analysis of Pharmaceuticals. M. Kuhnert-Brandstatter. 424p. 1971. 185.00 (*0-08-006990-8*, Pub. by Pergamon Repr UK) Franklin.

***Thermonuclear Fusion in Stars.** James A. Green. LC 94-96185. (Physics Ser.: Vol. 4). (Illus.). 175p. 1997. 80.88 (*1-890121-14-2*, 02-04-01) Grnwd Resch.

***Thermonuclear Supernovae.** LC 96-52194. 1996. lib. bdg. 260.00 (*0-7923-4359-X*) Kluwer Ac.

Thermophilic Bacteria. Jakob K. Kristjansson. 224p. 1991. 179.95 (*0-8493-5239-8*, QR84) CRC Pr.

Thermophilic Microbes in Ethanol Production. Gary E. Slapack et al. LC 86-9597. 224p. 1987. 115.00 (*0-8493-5299-1*, QR151, CRC Reprint) Franklin.

***Thermophotovoltaic Generation of Electricity: 3rd NREL Conference.** Ed. by John P. Benner & Timothy J. Coutts. (Conference Proceedings: Vol. 401). (Illus.). 608p. 1997. 140.00 (*1-56396-734-0*, AIP) Am Inst Physics.

Thermophysical & Electrophysical Properties of Low-Temperature Plasma with Condensed Disperse Phase, Vol. 2. I. T. Yakubov & A. G. Khrapak. (Thermal Physics Ser.: Vol. 2, Pt. 4). 70p. 1989. pap. text ed. 67.00 (*3-7186-4909-8*) Gordon & Breach.

Thermophysical Aspects of Meteoroid Protection in Halley's Comet Project Vega, Vol. 2. S. I. Anisimov et al. (Thermal Physics Ser.: Vol. 2). 100p. 1989. pap. text ed. 72.00 (*3-7186-4910-1*) Gordon & Breach.

Thermophysical Properties: Proceedings of the Fifth Symposium , Newton MA, September 30-October 2, 1970, (Sponsored by Standing Committee on Thermophysical Properties, Heat Transfer Division , The American Society of Mechanical Engineers) 5th ed. Symposium on Thermophysical Properties. Ed. by C. F. Bonilla. LC 59-1391. 513p. reprint ed. pap. 146.30 (*0-685-15210-3*, 2056158) Bks Demand.

Thermophysical Properties: Proceedings of the Fourth Symposium, University of Maryland, College Park, Maryland, 1968. American Society of Mechanical Engineers Staff. Ed. by Jerzy R. Moszynski. LC 59-1391. 486p. reprint ed. pap. 138.60 (*0-317-29841-0*, 2051923) Bks Demand.

Thermophysical Properties: Proceedings of the 6th Symposium. Sponsored by Standing Committee on Thermophysical Properties, Heat Transfer Division, ASME, ...Atlanta, Georgia, August 6-8, 1973. Thermophysical Properties Symposium Staff. Ed. by Peter E. Liley. LC 59-1391. 415p. reprint ed. pap. 118.30 (*0-317-08104-7*, 2016833) Bks Demand.

Thermophysical Properties & Structure of Molten Metals under Extreme Conditions, Vol. 2. V. Y. Prokhorenko & V. E. Fortov. (Thermal Physics Ser.: Vol. 2, Pt. 2). 72p. 1989. pap. text ed. 62.00 (*3-7186-4908-X*) Gordon & Breach.

Thermophysical Properties for Industrial Process Design. Ed. by Theodore B. Selover et al. LC 93-39125. (Symposium Ser.: No. 298, Vol. 90). 190p. 1994. 75.00 (*0-8169-0630-0*) Am Inst Chem Eng.

***Thermophysical Properties of Fluids.** 372p. 1996. 33.00 (*1-86094-009-9*) World Scientific Pub.

Thermophysical Properties of Fluids: An Introduction to Their Prediction. Marc J. Assael et al. LC 96-22987. 372p. 1996. pap. write for info. (*1-86094-019-6*) World Scientific Pub.

Thermophysical Properties of Freons, Vol. 1. Ed. by V. V. Altunin. Tr. by Jamil I. Ghojel from RUS. (National Standard Reference Data Service of the U. S. S. R.: A Series of Property Tables). 200p. 1987. 192.00 (*0-89116-600-9*) Hemisp Pub.

Thermophysical Properties of Freons, Vol. 2. Ed. by V. V. Altunin. Tr. by Jamil I. Ghojel from RUS. (National Standard Reference Data Service of the U. S. S. R.: A Series of Property Tables). 243p. 1987. 192.00 (*0-89116-601-7*) Hemisp Pub.

Thermophysical Properties of Gases & Liquids. Viktor Abramovich Rabinovich. (Physical Constants & Properties of Substances Ser.: No. 1). 215p. reprint ed. pap. 61.30 (*0-317-08438-0*, 2004605) Bks Demand.

Thermophysical Properties of High Temperature Solid Materials, Vols. 1-6. Purdue University, Thermophysical Properties Research Center Staff. reprint ed. pap. write for info. (*0-318-63108-3*, 2056565) Bks Demand.

Thermophysical Properties of Liquid Crystals. A. L. Tsykalo. 420p. 1991. text ed. 345.00 (*2-88124-322-3*) Gordon & Breach.

Thermophysical Properties of Liquid in the Metastable Superheated State. V. P. Skripov et al. 286p. 1988. text ed. 360.00 (*2-88124-656-7*) Gordon & Breach.

Thermophysical Properties of Lithium Hydride, Deuteride, & Tritide & of Their Solutions with Lithium. E. E. Shpil'rain et al. Tr. by Stephen J. Amoretty. (AIP Translation Ser.). 225p. 1987. 65.00 (*0-88318-532-6*) Am Inst Physics.

Thermophysical Properties of Materials. G. Grimvall. (Selected Topics in Solid State Physics Ser.: Vol. 18). 348p. 1986. 182.25 (*0-444-86985-9*) Elsevier.

Thermophysical Properties of Matter: Specific Heat - Metallic Elements & Alloys. Purdue University, Thermophysical Properties Research Center Staff. LC 73-129616. (TPRC Data Ser.: Vol. 4). 814p. reprint ed. pap. 180.00 (*0-317-26282-3*, 2055697) Bks Demand.

Thermophysical Properties of Matter: Specific Heat Nonmetallic Liquids & Gases, Vol. 6. Purdue University, Thermophysical Properties Research Center Staff. LC 73-129616. 383p. reprint ed. pap. 109.20 (*0-317-27798-7*, 2055953) Bks Demand.

Thermophysical Properties of Matter: The TPRC Data Series, Vol. 1: Thermal Conductivity; Metallic Elements & Purdue University, Thermophysical Properties Research Center Staff. LC 73-129616. 1597p. reprint ed. pap. 180.00 (*0-317-28047-3*, 2055777) Bks Demand.

Thermophysical Properties of Matter: The TPRC Data Series, Vol. 6 Supplement: Specific Heat: Nonmetallic Liqu. Purdue University, Thermophysical Properties Research Center Staff. LC 73-129616. 169p. reprint ed. pap. 48.20 (*0-317-28042-2*, 2055778) Bks Demand.

Thermophysical Properties of Matter: The TPRC Data Series, 5 vols., Vols. 7-11. Purdue University, Thermophysical Properties Research Center Staff & Y. S. Touloukian. Incl. Vol. 7. Thermal Radiative Properties: Metallic Elements & Alloys. LC 73-129616. pap. 160.00 (*0-317-10946-4*); Vol. 8. Thermal Radiative Properties: Nonmetallic Solids. LC 73-129616. pap. 160.00 (*0-317-10947-2*); Vol. 9. Thermal Radiative Properties: Coatings. LC 73-129616. pap. 160.00 (*0-317-10948-0*); Vol. 10. Thermal Diffusivity. LC 73-129616. pap. 160.00 (*0-317-10949-9*); Vol. 11. Viscosity. LC 73-129616. pap. 160.00 (*0-317-10950-2*); LC 73-129616. reprint ed. Set pap. write for info. (*0-318-58069-1*, 2019412) Bks Demand.

Thermophysical Properties of Matter: The TPRC Data Series, Vol 12: Thermal Expansion: Metallic Elements & Alloys. Purdue University, Thermophysical Properties Research Center Staff. LC 73-129616. 1443p. reprint ed. pap. 180.00 (*0-317-07898-4*, 2022726) Bks Demand.

Thermophysical Properties of Matter: Thermal Conductivity - Nonmetallic Liquids & Gases. Purdue University, Thermophysical Properties Research Center Staff. LC 73-129616. (TPRC Data Ser.: Vol. 3). 707p. reprint ed. pap. 180.00 (*0-317-26375-7*, 2055696) Bks Demand.

Thermophysical Properties of Matter: Thermal Expansion-Nonmetallic Solids. Purdue University, Thermophysical Properties Research Center Staff & Y. S. Touloukian. LC 73-129616. (TPRC Data Ser.: Vol. 13). 1786p. reprint ed. pap. 180.00 (*0-317-26280-7*, 2055698) Bks Demand.

Thermophysical Properties of Organosilicon Compounds. P. F. Alekseev et al. 300p. 1996. 75.00 (*1-56700-037-1*) Begell Hse.

Thermophysical Properties of Polymers. Y. K. Godovsky. (Illus.). xvii, 300p. 1991. 181.95 (*0-387-54160-8*) Spr-Verlag.

Thermophysical Properties of Refrigerants. B. Platzer et al. (Illus.). 464p. 1990. 316.95 (*0-387-16112-0*) Spr-Verlag.

Thermophysical Properties of Some Key Solids: Heat Capacity, Thermal Expansion, Electrical Resistivity, Thermal Conductivity & Absolute Thermopower. Ed. by CODATA Staff. (CODATA Bulletin Ser.). (Illus.). 52p. 1986. pap. 15.00 (*0-08-032488-6*, Pub. by PPL UK) Elsevier.

Thermophysical Properties of Titanium & Its Alloys: A Handbook. V. E. Peletskii et al. 110p. 1990. 85.00 (*0-89116-752-8*) Begell Hse.

***Thermophysical Properties of Water Substance.** write for info. (*0-7131-3222-1*, Pub. by E Arnold UK) Routledge Chapman & Hall.

Thermophysical Properties, Proceedings of the Seventh Symposium, Gaithersburg, MD, May 10-12, 1977. Symposium on Thermophysical Properties Staff. Ed. by Ared Cezairliyan. LC 59-1391. 983p. reprint ed. pap. 180.00 (*0-8357-8766-4*, 2033626) Bks Demand.

Thermophysical Properties Research Literature Retrieval Guide, Bk. 1. 2nd ed. Purdue University, Thermophysical Properties Research Center Staff. Ed. by Y. S. Touloukian et al. LC 60-14226. reprint ed. pap. 160.00 (*0-317-10668-6*, 2022724) Bks Demand.

Thermophysical Properties Research Literature Retrieval Guide, Bk. 2. 2nd ed. Purdue University, Thermophysical Properties Research Center Staff. Ed. by Y. S. Touloukian et al. LC 60-14226. reprint ed. pap. 158.00 (*0-317-10669-4*) Bks Demand.

Thermophysical Properties Research Literature Retrieval Guide, Bk. 3. 2nd ed. Purdue University, Thermophysical Properties Research Center Staff. Ed. by Y. S. Touloukian et al. LC 60-14226. reprint ed. pap. 160.00 (*0-317-10670-8*) Bks Demand.

Thermophysical Properties Research Literature Retrieval Guide 1900-1980, Vol. 1: Elements. Ed. by J. F. Chaney et al. LC 81-15776. 804p. 1982. 175.00 (*0-306-67221-9*, IFI-Plenum) Plenum.

Thermophysical Properties Research Literature Retrieval Guide 1900-1980, Vol. 2: Inorganic Compounds. Ed. by J. F. Chaney et al. LC 81-15776. 1094p. 1982. 235.00 (*0-306-67222-7*, IFI-Plenum) Plenum.

Thermophysical Properties Research Literature Retrieval Guide 1900-1980, Vol. 3: Organic Compounds & Polymeric Materials. Ed. by J. F. Chaney et al. LC 81-15776. 630p. 1982. 150.00 (*0-306-67223-5*, IFI-Plenum) Plenum.

Thermophysical Properties Research Literature Retrieval Guide 1900-1980, Vol. 4: Alloys, Intermetallic Compounds & Ceramics. Ed. by J. F. Chaney et al. LC 81-15776. 736p. 1982. 160.00 (*0-306-67224-3*, IFI-Plenum) Plenum.

Thermophysical Properties Research Literature Retrieval Guide 1900-1980, Vol. 5: Oxide Mixtures & Minerals. Ed. by J. F. Chaney et al. LC 81-15776. 414p. 1982. 115.00 (*0-306-67225-1*, IFI-Plenum) Plenum.

Thermophysical Properties Research Literature Retrieval Guide 1900-1980, Vol. 6: Mixtures & Solutions. Ed. by J. F. Chaney et al. LC 81-155776. 498p. 1982. 125.00 (*0-306-67226-X*, IFI-Plenum) Plenum.

Thermophysical Properties Research Literature Retrieval Guide 1900-1980, Vol. 7: Coatings, Systems, Composites, Foods, Animal & Vegetable Products. Ed. by J. F. Chaney et al. LC 81-11653. 642p. 1982. 150.00 (*0-306-67227-8*, IFI-Plenum) Plenum.

Thermophysical Properties Research Literature Retrieval Guide 1900-1980, Vol. 7: Coatings, Systems, Composites, Foods, Animal & Vegetable Products, 7 vols., Set. Ed. by J. F. Chaney et al. LC 81-15776. 642p. 1982. 850.00 (*0-685-42429-4*, IFI-Plenum) Plenum.

Thermophysics of Glaciers. I. A. Zotikov. 1986. lib. bdg. 227.50 (*90-277-2163-7*) Kluwer Ac.

Thermophysics of Plasma Spraying & Related Technologies. O. P. Solonenko. 470p. 1995. boxed 133.00 (*1-898326-24-X*, Pub. by Cambdge Intl UK) Am Educ Systs.

Thermophysics of Translational Relaxation in Shock Waves in Gases, Vol. 4. A. P. Genich et al. 68p. 1992. text ed. 75.00 (*3-7186-5224-2*) Gordon & Breach.

Thermoplaste. 1989. 126.95 (*0-387-51104-0*) Spr-Verlag.

Thermoplaste. 1989. 316.95 (*0-387-51349-3*) Spr-Verlag.

Thermoplaste. 1989. 316.95 (*0-387-51350-7*) Spr-Verlag.

Thermoplastic Aromatic Polymer Composites: A Study of the Structure, Processing & Properties of Carbon Fibre Reinforced Polyetheretherketone & Related Materials. F. N. Cogswell. (Illus.). 289p. 1992. 99.95 (*0-7506-1086-7*, Pub. by Woodhead Pubng UK) Technomic.

Thermoplastic Composite Materials. Ed. by L. A. Carlsson. (Composite Materials Ser.: No. 7). 390p. 1991. 203.25 (*0-444-88118-2*) Elsevier.

Thermoplastic Elastomers. 122p. 1989. 1,950.00 (*0-89336-694-3*, P-026U) BCC.

Thermoplastic Elastomers. 2nd ed. Ed. by Geoffrey Holden et al. 620p. (C). 1996. text ed. 148.00 (*1-56990-205-4*) Hanser-Gardner.

Thermoplastic Elastomers: Selection, Processing, & Use Equals Profits: 1995 RETEC, September 26-27, 1995, Wilmington Hilton, Wilmington, DE. fac. ed. Society of Plastics Engineers Staff. 364p. 1995. reprint ed. pap. 103.80 (*0-608-00981-4*, 2061835) Bks Demand.

Thermoplastic Elastomers: U. S. Materials, Applications & Markets. 195p. 1993. pap. 199.95 (*1-56676-049-6*, 760496) Technomic.

Thermoplastic Elastometers: A Comprehensive Review. Norman R. Legge et al. 575p. (C). 1987. text ed. 125.00 (*1-56990-053-1*) Hanser-Gardner.

Thermoplastic Foams. James L. Throne. LC 94-10745. 1994. write for info. (*0-412-98671-X*) Chapman & Hall.

***Thermoplastic Insulated Wire & Cable for the Transmission & Distribution of Electrical Energy Plus Revision 1.** 43.00 (*0-614-18699-4*, S-61-402) Insulated Cable.

Thermoplastics Melt Rheology & Processing. Shenoy & Saini. (Plastics Engineering Ser.: Vol. 37). 480p. 1996. 175.00 (*0-8247-9723-X*) Dekker.

Thermoplastics Pipework & Ducting in Unplasticised Polyvinyl Chloride & Polythene. EEMUA Staff. 1965. 125.00 (*0-85931-046-9*, Pub. by EEMUA UK) St Mut.

Thermopylae. Philip Steele. LC 93-2645. (Great Battles & Sieges Ser.). (Illus.). 32p. (YA). (gr. 6 up). 1993. lib. bdg. 13.95 (*0-02-786887-7*, New Dscvry Bks) Silver Burdett Pr.

Thermopylae: The Battle for the West. Ernle Bradford. (Illus.). 256p. 1993. reprint ed. pap. 13.95 (*0-306-80531-6*) Da Capo.

Thermoradiotherapy & Thermochemotherapy Vol. 1: Biology, Physiology & Physics. Ed. by M. H. Seegenschmiedt et al. LC 95-11653. (Medical Radiology Ser.). 1995. write for info. (*3-540-57229-5*) Spr-Verlag.

Thermoradiotherapy & Thermochemotherapy Vol. 1: Biology, Physiology & Physics. Ed. by Michael H. Seegenschmiedt et al. (Medical Radiology Ser.: Diagnostic Imaging & Radiation Oncology). (Illus.). 416p. 1995. 210.00 (*0-387-57229-5*) Spr-Verlag.

Thermoradiotherapy & Thermochemotherapy Vol. 2: Clinical Applications. Ed. by M. H. Seegenschmiedt et al. (Medical Radiology, Diagnostic Imaging & Radiation Oncology Ser.). (Illus.). 400p. 1996. 189.00 (*0-387-57230-9*) Spr-Verlag.

***Thermoradiotherapy & Thermochemotherapy Vol. 2: Clinical Applications.** M. H. Seegenschmiedt et al. (Medical Radiology Ser.). (Illus.). 420p. 1996. 189.00 (*3-540-57230-9*) Spr-Verlag.

Thermoreception & Temperature Regulation. Ed. by J. Bligh & K. Voigt. (Illus.). 300p. 1990. 97.95 (*0-387-51711-1*) Spr-Verlag.

Thermoregulation: Pathology, Pharmacology & Therapy. P. Lomax & Edward Schonbaum. (International Encyclopedia of Pharmacology & Therapeutics Ser.). (Illus.). 692p. 1991. 206.25 (*0-08-036853-0*, Pub. by PPI UK) Elsevier.

Thermoregulation: Physiology & Biochemistry. rev. ed. Edward Schonbaum & P. Lomax. (International Encyclopedia of Pharmacology & Therapeutics Ser.). (Illus.). 528p. 1991. 165.00 (*0-08-036852-2*, Pub. by PPI UK) Elsevier.

Thermoregulation: Research & Clinical Applications: International Symposium on the Pharmacology of Thermoregulation, 7th, Odense, August, 1988. Ed. by Edward Schonbaum & P. Lomax. xiv, 250p. 1989. 127.25 (*3-8055-4921-0*) S Karger.

Thermoregulation: The Pathophysiological Basis of Clinical Disorders: Eighth International Symposium on the Pharmacology of Thermoregulation, Kananaskis, Alberta, August 1991. Ed. by P. Lomax & E. Schoenbaum. (Illus.). xiv, 200p. 1992. 135.75 (*3-8055-5513-X*) S Karger.

***Thermoregulation - Recent Progress & New Frontiers: Tenth International Symposium on the Pharmacology of Thermoregulation.** Ed. by Clark M. Blatteis. LC 97-329. 1997. 170.00 (*1-57331-088-3*) NY Acad Sci.

Thermoregulation of Sick & Low Birth Weight Neonates: Temperature Control, Temperature Monitoring, Thermal Environment. Ed. by Albert A. Okken & Jochim J. Koch. (Illus.). 256p. 1995. 104.00 (*3-540-60169-4*) Spr-Verlag.

Thermoregulatory Mechanisms & Their Therapeutic Implications: Symposium, 4th, Oxford, July-August, 1979. Ed. by B. Cox et al. (Illus.). 1979. 52.00 (*3-8055-0277-X*) S Karger.

Thermoreversible Gelation of Polymers & Biopolymers. Jean-Michel Guenet. (Illus.). 280p. 1992. text ed. 102.00 (*0-12-305380-3*) Acad Pr.

***Thermoreversible Networks: Viscoelastic Properties & Structure of Gels.** K. Nijenhuis. (Advances in Polymer Science Ser.: Vol. 130). (Illus.). 340p. 1997. 220.00 (*3-540-61857-0*) Spr-Verlag.

***Thermosense XIX: An International Conference on Thermal Sensing & Imaging Diagnostic Applications.** Ed. by Richard N. Winzbach & Douglas D. Burleigh. 1997. pap. 80.00 (*0-8194-2471-4*) SPIE.

***Thermoset Materials.** Monk. 1996. write for info. (*0-582-04071-X*, Pub. by Longman UK) Longman.

Thermoset Powder Coatings. FMJ Intl. Publ. Ltd. Staff. (C). 1989. 190.00 (*0-685-36805-X*, Pub. by Fuel Metallurgical Jrnl UK) St Mut.

Thermoset RETEC 1993: The Old & the New, March 8-10, 1993, Research Triangle Park, NC. Society of Plastics Engineers Staff. 228p. reprint ed. pap. 65.00 (*0-7837-5730-1*, 2045390) Bks Demand.

Thermoset Technologies: Design, Properties, Processing, Regulation: Regional Technical Conference. Society of Plastics Engineers Staff. (Illus.). 167p. reprint ed. pap. 47.60 (*0-318-39766-8*, 2033141) Bks Demand.

Thermoset Technology 86' Regional Technical Conference, March 19-21, 1986, Ramada Hotel O'Hare, Rosemont, IL. Society of Plastics Engineers Staff. 108p. pap. 30.80 (*0-317-58182-1*, 2029709) Bks Demand.

Thermoset Technology '95: Regional Technical Conference, March 13, 14 & 15, 1995, Sheraton Imperial Hotel & Convention Center, Research Triangle Park, NC. Society of Plastics Engineers Staff. (Illus.). 202p. 1995. reprint ed. pap. 57.60 (*0-7837-9710-9*, 2060441) Bks Demand.

Thermosets by Design: Regional Technical Conference Sponsored by the Chicago Section & the Thermose Division of SPE, Ramada, the O'Hare Inn, Des Plaines, Ill., March 7-9, 1984. Society of Plastics Engineers Staff. 74p. reprint ed. pap. 25.00 (*0-317-30375-9*, 2024724) Bks Demand.

Thermosets for the 21st Century: Regional Technical Conference, March 16, 17 & 18, 1994, Remada Hotel O'Hare, Rosemont, IL. Society of Plastics Engineers Staff. 208p. 1994. reprint ed. pap. 59.30 (*0-7837-9708-7*, 2060439) Bks Demand.

Thermosets Nineties, Meeting the Challenge: Regional Technical Conference, March 20-22, 1990, Ramada Hotel O'Hare, Rosemont, IL. Society of Plastics Engineers Staff. 294p. reprint ed. pap. 83.80 (*0-8357-2996-6*, 2039264) Bks Demand.

***Thermosphere-Ionosphere-Middle Atmosphere Coupling & Dynamics.** J. Rottger & V. B. Wickwar. (Advances in Space Research (RJ) Ser.: Vol. 18). 160p. 1995. 97.75 (*0-08-042667-0*, Pergamon Pr) Elsevier.

Thermostability of Enzymes. Ed. by M. N. Gupta. 200p. 1992. 109.00 (*0-387-56275-3*) Spr-Verlag.

Thermostable Proteins. D. Steel. (Life Chemistry Reports). 242p. 1991. pap. text ed. 224.00 (*3-7186-5226-9*, Harwood Acad Pubs) Gordon & Breach.

Thermostat Repairer. Jack Rudman. (Career Examination Ser.: C-3408). 1994. pap. 23.95 (*0-8373-3408-X*) Nat Learn.

Thermostatic Incubator: Raising Chickens by Hand. E. S. Renwick. 98p. 1883. pap. 25.00 (*0-87556-756-8*) Saifer.

Thermotherapy & BPH. Ed. by C. C. Schulman. (Journal: European Urology: Vol. 23, No. 2, 1993). (Illus.). 80p. 1993. pap. 69.75 (*3-8055-5781-7*) S Karger.

Thermothropic Liquid Crystals, Fundamentals. G. Vertegon & W. H. De Jeu. (Chemical Physics Ser.: Vol. 45). (Illus.). 330p. 1988. 115.95 (*0-387-17946-1*) Spr-Verlag.

Thermotolerance, 2 vols., Set. K. J. Henle. LC 87-6374. 1987. 215.00 (*0-8493-6453-1*, QP82, CRC Reprint) Franklin.

Thermotolerance, Vol. I. Henle. 192p. 1987. 112.00 (*0-8493-6459-0*) CRC Pr.

Thermotolerance Vol. 2: Mechanisms of Heat Resistance. K. J. Henle. LC 87-6374. 1987. 103.00 (*0-8493-6460-4*, QP82, CRC Reprint) Franklin.

Thermotropic Liquid Crystal Polymer Blends. Ed. by F. P. La Mantia. LC 92-61560. 190p. 1992. pap. text ed. 69.95 (*0-87762-960-9*) Technomic.

Thermotropic Liquid Crystals. Ed. by G. W. Gray. (Critical Reports on Applied Chemistry). 178p. 1987. text ed. 260.00 (*0-471-91504-1*) Wiley.

Therms of Political Discourse. William E. Connolly. 272p. (C). 1983. pap. text ed. 17.95 (*0-691-02223-2*) Princeton U Pr.

Thermus Species. Ed. by Richard Sharp & Ralph Williams. (Biotechnology Handbooks Ser.: Vol. 9). (Illus.). 230p. 1995. 75.00 (*0-306-44925-0*) Plenum.

Theron Came Later. Patricia L. Pilot. 210p. 1984. 7.45 (*0-89697-137-6*) Intl Univ Pr.

Theropithecus: The Life & Death of a Primate Genus. Ed. by Nina G. Jablonski. LC 92-10889. (Illus.). 550p. (C). 1993. text ed. 200.00 (*0-521-41105-X*) Cambridge U Pr.

Theros Ironfeld. Don Perrin. (Dragonlance Warrior Ser.: Vol. 4). 1996. pap. 5.99 (*0-7869-0481-X*) TSR Inc.

Thersites. John Heywood. LC 72-133744. (Tudor Facsimile Texts. Old English Plays Ser.: No. 31). reprint ed. 59.50 (*0-404-53331-0*) AMS Pr.

Thesauri Used in Online Databases: An Analytical Guide. Lois M. Chan & Richard Pollard. LC 88-10985. 284p. 1988. text ed. 59.95 (*0-313-25788-4*, CTI/, Greenwood Pr) Greenwood.

Thesaurus see Theilheimer's Synthetic Methods of Organic Chemistry: Synthetische Methoden der Organischen Chemie

Thesaurus Biomedical Francais-Anglais, 3 vols. Inserm-International Symposium Staff. 884p. (ENG & FRE.). 1986. Set. 555.00 (*0-8288-0563-6*, M1750) Fr & Eur.

Thesaurus de l'Education et de son Environment Socio-Economique: French-Arabic, Arabic-French. Conseil International de la Language Francaise Staff & Nouredine Abouriche. 105p. (ARA & FRE.). 1991. write for info. (*0-8288-7582-0*, 285319288) Fr & Eur.

Thesaurus Dictionary of the English Language. Francis A. March. (Illus.). 1994. reprint ed. lib. bdg. 48.00 (*0-7808-0011-7*) Omnigraphics Inc.

Thesaurus Dracularum Five: Eine Monographie der Gattung Dracula - A Monograph of the Genus Dracula. Carlyle A. Luer & Rodrigo R. Escobar. Tr. by Fritz Hamer. (Thesaurus Dracularum Ser.). (Illus.). 62p. (Orig.). (GER.). 1992. pap. 46.50 (*0-614-04648-3*) Miss Botan.

Thesaurus Dracularum Four: Eine Monographie der Gattung Dracula - A Monograph of the Genus Dracula. Carlyle A. Luer & Rodrigo R. Escobar. Tr. by Fritz Hamer. (Thesaurus Dracularum Ser.). (Illus.). 62p. (Orig.). (GER.). 1991. pap. 44.50 (*0-614-04647-5*) Miss Botan.

Thesaurus Dracularum One: Eine Monographie der Gattung Dracula - A Monograph of the Genus Dracula. Carlyle A. Luer & Rodrigo R. Escobar. Tr. by Fritz Hamer. (Thesaurus Dracularum Ser.). (Illus.). 62p. (Orig.). (GER.). 1988. pap. 41.50 (*0-614-04644-0*) Miss Botan.

Thesaurus Dracularum Seven: Eine Monographie der Gattung Dracula - A Monograph of the Genus Dracula. Carlyle A. Luer & Rodrigo R. Escobar. Tr. by Fritz Hamer. (Thesaurus Dracularum Ser.). (Illus.). v, 78p. (Orig.). (GER.). 1994. pap. 57.00 (*0-915279-28-2*) Miss Botan.

Thesaurus Dracularum Six: Eine Monographie der Gattung Dracula - A Monograph of the Genus Dracula. Carlyle A. Luer & Rodrigo R. Escobar. Tr. by Fritz Hamer. (Thesaurus Dracularum Ser.). (Illus.). 64p. (Orig.). (GER.). 1993. pap. 46.50 (*0-614-04649-1*) Miss Botan.

Thesaurus Dracularum Three: Eine Monographie der Gattung Dracula - A Monograph of the Genus Dracula. Carlyle A. Luer & Rodrigo R. Escobar. Tr. by Fritz Hamer. (Thesaurus Dracularum Ser.). (Illus.). 66p. (Orig.). (GER.). 1990. pap. text ed. 41.50 (*0-614-04646-7*) Miss Botan.

Thesaurus Dracularum Two: Eine Monographie der Gattung Dracula - A Monograph of the Genus Dracula. Carlyle A. Luer & Rodrigo R. Escobar. Tr. by Fritz Hamer. (Thesaurus Dracularum Ser.). (Illus.). 62p. (Orig.). (GER.). 1989. pap. 41.50 (*0-614-04645-9*) Miss Botan.

Thesaurus du CEMAGREF, 3 vols. Nicole Delherbe. Incl. Vol. 1. Liste Alphabetique Globale. 242p. 1992. pap. 75.00 (*0-7859-5654-9*, 2853623149); Vol. 2. Liste Thematique. 205p. 1992. pap. 75.00 (*0-7859-5655-7*, 2853623157); Vol. 3. Index Permute. 345p. 1992. pap. 75.00 (*0-7859-5656-5*, 2853623165); 792p. 1992. Set pap. 225.00 (*0-7859-5653-0*, 2853623130) Fr & Eur.

Thesaurus Eclas Part 4: Bilingual List of Descriptors English-French (New Edition/Nov. 1994) European Communities Staff. 255p. 1995. pap. text ed. 60.00 (*92-826-9471-2*, Pub. by Europ Com UK) Bernan Associates.

Thesaurus Eurovoc: Multilingual Version. European Commission Staff. 460p. 1995. pap. text ed. 55.00 (*92-77-86375-7*, FX0792003ENC, Pub. by Europ Com UK) Bernan Associates.

Thesaurus Eurovoc: Permuted Alphabetical Version, Vol. 1. European Commission Staff. 460p. 1995. pap. 105.00 (*92-77-86357-9*, FX-07-92-001ENC, Pub. by Europ Com UK) Bernan Associates.

Thesaurus Eurovoc: Subject-Oriented Version, Vol. 2. European Commission. 460p. 1995. pap. 55.00 (*92-77-86366-8*, FX-07-92-002ENC, Pub. by Europ Com UK) Bernan Associates.

***Thesaurus for Graphic Materials: Subject Terms & Genre & Physical Characteristic Terms.** (Illus.). 556p. 1995. per., pap. 34.00 (*0-8444-0889-1*) Lib Congress.

Thesaurus for Information Processing in Sociology. Jean Viet. 1971. pap. text ed. 60.80 (*90-279-6941-8*) Mouton.

Thesaurus for Kids. Evelyn Pesiri. (Illus.). 144p. (J). (gr. 3-7). 1993. pap. 7.95 (*1-56293-355-8*) McClanahan Bk.

Thesaurus for SoyaScan: Computerized Bibliographic Database on Soybeans & Soyfoods. 2nd rev. ed. William Shurtleff & Akiko Aoyagi. 34p. 1986. spiral bd. 14.95 (*0-933332-24-6*) Soyfoods Center.

***Thesaurus for Soyascan Database: With a Count for Each Subject Heading.** William Shurtleff & Akiko Aoyagi. LC 96-37965. 1996. write for info. (*0-933332-97-1*) Soyfoods Center.

***Thesaurus Hymnologicus.** Hermann A. Daniel. lxii, 1843p. (GER.). 1973. reprint ed. write for info. (*3-487-04912-0*) G Olms Pubs.

Thesaurus Larousse. Daniel Pechoin. 1146p. (FRE.). 1991. 125.00 (*0-8288-7369-0*, 2033201074) Fr & Eur.

***Thesaurus Linguae Gallicae.** Pierre-Henri Billy. 260p. (GER.). 1993. write for info. (*3-487-09746-X*) G Olms Pubs.

Thesaurus Linguae Graecae: Canon of Greek Authors & Works. 3rd ed. Ed. by Luci Berkowitz & Karl A. Squitier. (Illus.). 536p. 1990. 45.00 (*0-19-506037-7*) OUP.

Thesaurus Linguae Romanae Et Britannicae. Thomas Cooper. (Anglistica & Americana Ser.: No. 111). 1808p. 1975. reprint ed. 480.00 (*3-487-05439-6*) G Olms Pubs.

Thesaurus Linguae Tschuvaschorum, 2 vols., 1. Nikolaj I. Ashmarin. LC 68-64532. (Uralic & Altaic Ser.: Vol. 70, Bk. 1). 335p. 1968. pap. text ed. 13.00 (*0-87750-070-3*) Res Inst Inner Asian Studies.

Thesaurus Linguae Tschuvaschorum, 2 vols., 2. Nikolaj I. Ashmarin. LC 68-64532. (Uralic & Altaic Ser.: Vol. 70, Bk. 1). 335p. 1968. pap. 13.00 (*0-87750-071-1*) Res Inst Inner Asian Studies.

Thesaurus Linguae Tschuvaschorum, Vol. 70, Bks. 3 & 4. 2nd ed. Nikolaj I. Ashmarin. (Uralic & Altaic Ser.). 352p. (CHV & RUS.). 1969. pap. text ed. 13.00 (*0-87750-073-8*) Res Inst Inner Asian Studies.

Thesaurus of Abstract Musical Properties: A Theoretical & Compositional Resource. Jeffrey Johnson. LC 95-1402. (Music Reference Collection: Vol. 45). 344p. 1995. text ed. 79.50 (*0-313-29392-9*, Greenwood Pr) Greenwood.

Thesaurus of Agricultural Organisms, 2. Derwent. (Agriculture Ser.). 1991. text ed. 424.95 (*0-442-30422-6*) Van Nos Reinhold.

***Thesaurus of Botanical Literature.** G. A. Pritzel. 584p. 1995. reprint ed. 90.00 (*1-888262-60-5*) Martino Pubng.

Thesaurus of Engineering & Scientific Terms. rev. ed. Engineers Joint Council Editors. LC 68-6569. 1969. 125.00 (*0-87615-163-2*) AAES.

Thesaurus of English Traditional Metaphors. P. R. Wilkinson. LC 92-15338. 1024p. (C). (gr. 13). 1993. text ed. 199.95 (*0-415-07523-8*, A7982, Routledge NY) Routledge.

Thesaurus of English Words & Phrases. rev. ed. Peter M. Roget. Ed. by John L. Roget & Samuel R. Roget. 42.50 (*0-87559-049-7*); 47.50 (*0-87559-050-0*) Shalom.

Thesaurus of ERIC Descriptors. 13th ed. Ed. by James E. Houston. 744p. 1995. boxed 69.50 (*0-89774-788-7*) Oryx Pr.

Thesaurus of Information Sciences & Technologies. Canadian Workplace Automation Research Center, CWARC Staff. (ENG & FRE.). 1991. pap. 95.00 (*0-8288-9441-8*) Fr & Eur.

Thesaurus of Linguistic Indexing Terms. Ed. by Anita Colby. LC 92-62352. 97p. (C). 1992. 65.00 (*0-930710-10-X*) Soc Abstracts.

Thesaurus of Occupational Titles: With Current Employment by Occupation. Don E. Vander Vegt. 357p. 1992. 59.00 (*1-882642-00-7*) United Stat.

Thesaurus of Orchestral Devices. Gardner Read. LC 53-13253. 653p. 1953. reprint ed. pap. 180.00 (*0-608-00003-5*, AU00469) Bks Demand.

Thesaurus of Orchestral Devices. Gardner Read. LC 69-14045. 631p. 1969. reprint ed. text ed. 45.00 (*0-8371-1884-0*, REOD, Greenwood Pr) Greenwood.

Thesaurus of Photographic Science & Engineering Terms. Society of Photographic Scientists & Engineers Staff. LC 68-3006. 137p. reprint ed. pap. 39.10 (*0-317-10422-5*, 2003621) Bks Demand.

Thesaurus of Psychological Index Terms. 6th ed. 352p. 1991. 65.00 (*1-55798-111-6*) Am Psychol.

Thesaurus of Psychological Index Terms. 7th ed. Ed. by Alvin J. Walker. LC 93-44714. 343p. 1994. 75.00 (*1-55798-225-2*) Am Psychol.

***Thesaurus of Psychological Index Terms.** 8th ed. Alvin Walker. LC 97-3383. 408p. 1997. 75.00 (*1-55798-402-6*) Am Psychol.

Thesaurus of Pulp & Paper Terminology. rev. ed. 557p. 1991. write for info. (*0-318-68550-7*) Inst Paper Sci & Tech.

Thesaurus of Rock & Soil Mechanics Terms. Ed. by J. P. Jenkins & A. M. Smith. 72p. 1984. pap. 40.00 (*0-08-031632-8*, Pub. by Pergamon Repr UK) Franklin.

Thesaurus of Scales & Melodic Patterns. Nicolas Slonimsky. 243p. 1987. 55.00 (*0-02-611850-5*) Schirmer Bks.

Thesaurus of Scales & Melodic Patterns: Music Book Index. Nicolas Slonimsky. 243p. 1993. reprint ed. lib. bdg. 79.00 (*0-7812-9660-9*) Rprt Serv.

Thesaurus of Scientific, Technical & Engineering Terms. Hemisphere Staff. 1217p. 1987. 198.00 (*0-89116-794-3*) Hemisp Pub.

***Thesaurus of Slang.** expanded rev. ed. Esther Lewin. 1997. pap. text ed. 24.95 (*0-8160-3661-6*) Facts on File.

Thesaurus of Slang: Over 165,000 Uncensored Contemporary Slang Terms, Common Idioms, & Colloquialisms, Updated for the 1990's & Arranged for Quick & Easy Reference. Esther Lewin & Albert E. Lewis. LC 93-42890. 464p. 1994. 50.00 (*0-8160-2898-2*) Facts on File.

Thesaurus of Sociological Indexing Terms. 4th ed. Ed. by Barbara Booth. 350p. (C). 1996. 70.00 (*0-930710-13-4*) Soc Abstracts.

Thesaurus of Spanish Idioms. L. K. Brown. 155p. (ENG & SPA.). 1980. pap. 5.15 (*0-8288-2325-1*, S14394) Fr & Eur.

Thesaurus of Terms on Copper Technology. 7th ed. 407p. 40.00 (*0-318-17324-7*, 110/0) Copper Devel Assn.

Thesaurus of the Albanian Language: In Dictionary Form. Gasper Kici. 248p. (Orig.). (ALB.). 1992. 15.00 (*0-9606728-4-2*) G Kici.

Thesaurus of the Yiddish Language. Nahum Stutchkoff. lviv, 936p. (YID.). 1991. reprint ed. 30.00 (*0-914512-46-3*) Yivo Inst.

Thesaurus of University Terms. Jill M. Tatem & Jeffrey Rollison. 46p. (Orig.). 1986. pap. 8.00 (*0-931828-69-4*) Soc Am Archivists.

Thesaurus of Values: Comprehensive Index to Values That Strongly Influence People. C. Joseph Clawson. LC 96-94303. (Illus.). x, 283p. (Orig.). 1997. pap. 52.00 (*0-9646095-0-9*) Lake Arrowhead Pubns.

Thesaurus of Word Roots of the English Language. Horace G. Danner & Roger Noel. 788p. (Orig.). (C). 1992. lib. bdg. 75.00 (*0-8191-8666-X*) U Pr of Amer.

Thesaurus on Resource Recovery Terminology - STP 832. Ed. by H. I. Hollander. LC 83-72052. 279p. 1984. pap. 24.00 (*0-8031-0256-9*, 04-832000-16) ASTM.

Thesaurus Palaeohibernicus, 3 vols. Ed. by Whitley Stokes & John Strachan. LC 78-72646. (Celtic Language & Literature Ser.: Goidelic & Brythonic). reprint ed. Set. 150.00 (*0-404-17593-7*) AMS Pr.

Thesaurus Philosophicus Linguae Hebraicae et Veteris et Recentioris, 4 vols. Jacob Klatzkin. 1933. Set. write for info. (*0-318-71833-2*) G Olms Pubs.

Thesaurus Poeticus Linguae Latinae Ou Dictionnaire Prosodique et Poetique de la Langue Latine. Louis Quicherat. xx, 1251p. 1967. reprint ed. write for info. (*0-318-72070-1*) G Olms Pubs.

Thesaurus Poeticus Linguae Latine Ou Dictionnaire Prosodique et Poetique de la Langue Latine. Louis Quicherat. xx, 1251p. 1967. reprint ed. write for info. (*0-318-71206-7*) G Olms Pubs.

Thesaurus Poeticus Linguae Latine Ou Dictionnaire Prosodique et Poetique De la Langue Latine. Louis Quicherat. xx, 1251p. 1922. reprint ed. write for info. (*0-318-71395-0*) G Olms Pubs.

***Thesaurus Proverbiorum Medii Aevi: Lexikon der Sprichwoerter Romanisch-Germanischen Mittelalters, Vol. 3.** Ed. by Samuel Singer. iv, 496p. (GER, GRE & LAT.). (C). 1996. lib. bdg. 107.40 (*3-11-015108-1*) De Gruyter.

Thesaurus Proverbiorum Medii Aevi Vol. 2: Bisam-Erbauen: Lexikon der Sprichwoerter des Romanisch-Germanischen Mittelalters. Ed. by Samuel Singer. iv, 484p. (GER, GRE & LAT.). (C). 1996. lib. bdg. 207.40 (*3-11-014874-9*) De Gruyter.

***Thesaurus Proverbiorum Medii Aevi: Lexikon der Sprichwoerter des Romanisch-Germanischen Mittelalters Vol. 4: Freund-Gewoehnen.** Samuel Singer. iv, 496p. (GER.). (C). 1996. lib. bdg. 200.00 (*3-11-015202-9*) De Gruyter.

Thesaurus Proverbiorum medii aevi Quellenverzeichnis: Lexikon der Sprichwoerter des Romanisch-Germanischen Mittelalters. Ed. by Samuel Singer. iv, 249p. (GER, GRE & LAT.). (C). 1995. lib. bdg. 116.95 (*3-11-014761-0*) De Gruyter.

Thesaurus Pseudonymorum. Saul Chajes. xiv, 415p. 1967. reprint ed. 130.00 (*0-318-71891-X*) G Olms Pubs.

Thesaurus Symbolorum Ac Emblematum, I. E. Insignia Bibliopolarum et Typographorum. Friedrich Roth-Scholtz. 184p. reprint ed. write for info. (*0-318-71862-6*) G Olms Pubs.

Thesaurus Tenda: Dictionnaire Ethnolinguistique de Langues Senegalo-Guieenes Niyan (Bassari), Nik (Bedik), Mey (Konyagi), Vol. 1. Marie-Paul Ferry. 391p. (FRE.). 1991. pap. 79.95 (*0-7859-8183-7*, 2877230341) Fr & Eur.

Thesaurus Tenda: Dictionnaire Ethnolinguistique de Langues Senegalo-Guieenes Niyan (Bassari), Nik (Bedik), Mey (Konyagi), Vol. 3. Marie-Paul Ferry. 470p. (FRE.). 1991. pap. 79.95 (*0-7859-8184-5*, 2877230368) Fr & Eur.

Thesaurus Tenda Vol. 2: Dictionnaire Ethnolinguistique de Langues Senegalo-Guieenes Niyan (Bassari), Nik (Bedik), Mey (Konyagi) Marie-Paul Ferry. 414p. (FRE.). 1991. pap. 79.95 (*0-7859-8663-4*, 287723035x) Fr & Eur.

Thesaurus Woolwardiae Pt. 1: Orchids of the Marquis of Lothian: The Slipper Orchids. Phillip J. Cribb & Sandra Bell. Ed. & Frwd. by Carlyle A. Luer. (Thesaurus Woolwardiae Ser.). (Illus.). 78p. (Orig.). 1993. pap. 50.00 (*0-915279-14-2*) Miss Botan.

Thesaurus Woolwardiae Pt. 4: Orchids of the Marquis of Lothian: Miscellaneous Genera. Joyce Stewart. Ed. by Phillip J. Cribb & Carlyle A. Luer. (Thesaurus Woolwardiae Ser.). (Illus.). (Orig.). 1993. pap. 50.00 (*0-915279-17-7*) Miss Botan.

Thesaurus Woolwardiae Orchids of the Marquis of Lothian Pt. 2: Dendrobium. Jeffrey J. Wood. Ed. by Phillip J. Cribb & Carlyle A. Luer. (Thesaurus Woolwardiae Ser.). (Illus.). 64p. (Orig.). 1993. pap. 50.00 (*0-915279-15-0*) Miss Botan.

Thesaurus Woolwardiae Orchids of the Marquis of Lothian Pt. 3: Oncidium Alliance. Mark W. Chase. Ed. by Phillip J. Cribb & Carlyle A. Luer. (Thesaurus Woolwardiae Ser.). (Illus.). 64p. (Orig.). 1993. pap. 50.00 (*0-614-03697-6*) Miss Botan.

Thesaurus Woolwardiae Series: Orchids of the Marquis of Lothian, 4 vols. Jeffrey J. Wood et al. Ed. by Phillip J. Cribb & Carlyle A. Luer. (Illus.). 274p. (Orig.). 1993. Set. pap. 175.00 (*0-915279-18-5*) Miss Botan.

These. Charles Peguy. pap. 4.95 (*0-685-37043-7*) Fr & Eur.

These American Lands: Parks, Wilderness, & the Public Lands. Wilderness Society Staff & Dvan Zaslowsky. LC 86-3156. (Illus.). 384p. 1986. 22.95 (*0-8050-0084-4*) H Holt & Co.

These American Lands: Parks, Wilderness & the Public Lands. rev. ed. Dyan Zaslowsky & T. H. Watkins. LC 94-16293. 1994. pap. 22.00 (*1-55963-240-2*); text ed. 45.00 (*1-55963-239-9*) Island Pr.

These Are a Few of My Favorite Things. Joe Marcotte. 150p. 1995. pap. 10.95 (*0-9648807-1-7*) Spking With Insight.

***These Are My Christmas Wishes for You: A Special Holiday Collection by Collin McCarty.** Collin McCarty. LC 96-32025. (Illus.). 64p. (Orig.). 1996. pap. 7.95 (*0-88396-439-2*) Blue Mtn Pr CO.

These Are My Favorite Things. rev. ed. Alfredo D. Noble. 56p. (C). 1992. pap. 5.95 (*0-9622849-5-5*) Papito.

These Are My People. Mildred T. Howard. Ed. by Roger Bruckner. (English Skills for Christian Schools Ser.). (Illus.). 152p. (Orig.). (J). (gr. 3). 1984. pap. 9.17 (*0-89084-242-6*, 021782) Bob Jones Univ Pr.

These Are My Pets, Level 2. Mercer Mayer. (Little Critters Ser.). (Illus.). 32p. (J). (gr. 1-2). 1992. pap. 3.00 (*0-307-15962-0*, 15962, Golden Pr) Western Pub.

These Are My Rivers: New & Selected Poems 1955-1993. Lawrence Ferlinghetti. LC 93-10383. 320p. 1993. reprint ed. 16.95 (*0-8112-1252-1*) New Directions.

These Are My Rivers: New & Selected Poems 1955-1993. Lawrence Ferlinghetti. LC 93-10383. 320p. 1994. reprint ed. pap. 12.95 (*0-8112-1273-4*, NDP787) New Directions.

These Are My Shoes. Peter Money. 96p. (Orig.). 1991. pap. 6.95 (*0-9623193-8-4*) Boz Pub.

These Are Not Sweet Girls: An Anthology of Latin American Women Poets. Ed. by Marjorie Agosin. 1994. pap. 17.00 (*1-877727-38-5*) White Pine.

These Are our Children: Jewish Orphanages in the United States, 1880-1925. Reena S. Friedman. LC 93-36809. (Brandeis Series in American Jewish History, Culture, & Life). (Illus.). 314p. (C). 1994. text ed. 45.00 (*0-87451-665-X*) U Pr of New Eng.

These Are Our Lives. WPA Federal Writers' Project Staff. LC 69-18578. (American Negro: His History & Literature. Series 2). 1969. reprint ed. 22.95 (*0-405-01911-4*) Ayer.

These Are Our Voices: The Story of Oak Ridge, 1942-1970. Ed. by Jim Overholt. (Illus.). 535p. 1987. 19.95 (*0-9606832-4-0*) Chldrns Mus.

***These Are Successful Hands: An Anthology of Poetry from the Women of Huntington House.** Ed. by Janine P. Vega. (Illus.). 45p. (Orig.). 1994. pap. 7.00 (*0-937804-58-4*, Segue Books) Segue NYC.

These Are the Candles: Five Readings for Advent. Wayne Tilden. (Orig.). 1997. pap. write for info. (*0-7880-0844-7*) CSS OH.

These Are the Garments. Charles W. Slemming. 1992. pap. 4.95 (*0-87508-507-5*) Chr Lit.

These Are the People: Thoughts in Poetry & Prose. Bill Fenton. (Illus.). 88p. (Orig.). 1991. pap. 9.00 (*0-9630957-0-6*) Ah-tee-noh-eh.

***These Are the Rules.** Paul Many. LC 96-46324. 192p. (YA). (gr. 7 up). 1997. 15.95 (*0-8027-8619-7*) Walker & Co.

These Are the Sacraments. Anthony M. Coniaris. 1981. pap. 10.95 (*0-937032-22-0*) Light&Life Pub Co MN.

These Are the Voyages. Charles Kurts. (J). 1996. 35.00 (*0-671-55139-6*, PB Hardcover) PB.

These Bones Were Made for Dancin' A Smith & Wetzon Mystery. Annette Meyers. 336p. 1996. reprint ed. mass mkt. 5.50 (*0-553-56976-7*, Crimeline) Bantam.

These Branching Moments: Forty Odes. Jelaluddin Rumi. Tr. by Coleman Barks & John Moyne from PER. LC 87-36429. 52p. (Orig.). 1988. pap. 8.95 (*0-914278-50-9*) Copper Beech.

These "Colored" United States: African American Essays from the 1920s. Ed. by Tom Lutz & Susanna Ashton. LC 95-52258. (Illus.). 300p. (C). 1996. text ed. 50.00 (*0-8135-2305-2*); pap. text ed. 17.95 (*0-8135-2306-0*) Rutgers U Pr.

These Enchanted Woods. Allan Massie. 206p. 1994. 24.95 (*0-09-177411-X*, Pub. by Hutchnson UK) Trafalgar.

These Fallen Angels. Wendy Haley. 320p. (Orig.). 1995. mass mkt. 4.99 (*0-7865-0072-7*) Diamond.

These Foolish Things. Michael Sadleir. Ed. by Michael Levien. LC 87-60485. (Modern Romance Classics Ser.). 264p. 8600. reprint ed. 22.00 (*0-7206-0670-5*, Pub. by P Owen Ltd UK) Dufour.

These Fragment I Have Stored: Collage & Montage in Early Modernist Poetry. Andrew M. Clearfield. LC 84-57. (Studies in Modern Literature: No. 36). 162p. reprint ed. pap. 46.20 (*0-8357-1539-6*, 2070539) Bks Demand.

These Fringes of Time. Thelma Shaw. LC 89-34662. 64p. (Orig.). 1989. pap. 7.50 (*0-936784-78-4*) J Daniel.

These Gentle Hills. 4th ed. John Kollock. (Illus.). 96p. 1976. pap. 10.95 (*0-9633248-0-2*) Habersham Hse.

These Golden Days. Robert Funderburk. (Innocent Years Ser.: Bk. 2). 304p. 1995. pap. 8.99 (*1-55661-461-6*) Bethany Hse.

***These Hands.** Bradley. 1999. 14.89 (*0-7868-2320-8*) Hyperion.

***These Hands.** Bradley. (J). 1999. 14.95 (*0-7868-0370-3*) Hyprn Child.

These Hands Filled with Numbness. Simon Perchik. 24p. (Orig.). 1996. pap. 4.00 (*1-879259-08-7*) Dusty Dog.

These Happy Golden Years. rev. ed. Laura Ingalls Wilder. LC 52-7532. (Little House Bks.). (Illus.). 304p. (J). (gr. 3-7). 1953. 15.95 (*0-06-026480-2*); lib. bdg. 15.89 (*0-06-026481-0*) HarpC Child Bks.

These Happy Golden Years see Little House Books

These Harvest Years. Ed. by Janet H. Baird. LC 74-167308. (Essay Index Reprint Ser.). 1977. reprint ed. 20.95 (*0-8369-2581-5*) Ayer.

These Haunted Islands: A Story of Witchcraft in the Channel Islands. Lake. 1991. 35.00 (*0-318-68515-9*, Pub. by Aris & Phillips UK) David Brown.

These High, Green Hills. Jan Karon. (Mitford Years Ser.). 350p. 1996. 19.95 (*0-7459-3388-2*) Lion USA.

These High, Green Hills. Jan Karon. 1996. pap. write for info. (*0-670-87320-9*, Viking) Viking Penguin.

***These High Green Hills.** Jan Karon. (Mitford Years Ser.). 338p. 1997. pap. text ed. 11.95 (*0-7459-3741-1*, Lion) Chariot Victor.

***These High Green Hills.** Jan Karon. 1997. pap. 11.95 (*0-14-025793-4*) Viking Penguin.

***These High, Green Hills.** Jan Karon. 1997. pap. 11.95 (*0-614-27288-2*, Penguin Bks) Viking Penguin.

An Asterisk (*) at the beginning of an entry indicates that the title is appearing in BIP for the first time.

*These High, Green Hills. Jan Karon. 1997. pap. 16.95 (0-14-086598-5) Viking Penguin.
*These High, Green Hills. large type ed. Jan Karon. LC 96-42059. (Mitford Years Ser.). 1997. lib. bdg. 26.95 (1-57490-103-6, Beeler LP Bks) T T Beeler.
These High Green Hills: The Mitford Years. Jan Karon. 1995. 22.95 (0-614-96279-X, Viking) Viking Penguin.
These High, Green Hills: The Mitford Years. Jan Karon. 333p. 1996. pap. 22.95 (0-670-86934-1, Viking) Viking Penguin.
These Honored Dead: The Union Casualties at Gettysburg. 2nd ed. John W. Busey. (Illus.). 490p. 1996. 30.00 (0-944413-40-4) Longstreet Hse.
These Images Which Rain down into the Imaginary. Ron Burnett. LC 94-48674. 368p. 1995. 35.00 (0-253-32902-7); pap. 16.95 (0-253-20977-3) Ind U Pr.
These Lands Are Ours: Tecumseh's Fight for the Old Northwest. Kate Connell. LC 92-14417. (Stories of America Ser.). (Illus.). 96p. (J). (gr. 2-5). 1992. lib. bdg. 25.68 (0-8114-7227-2) Raintree Steck-V.
These Last Days: Angelic Messengers Reveal the Future. Dottie M. Goard. LC 94-10219. 239p. 1994. pap. 11.95 (0-932727-73-5); lib. bdg. 19.95 (0-932727-74-3) Hope Pub Hse.
These Last Four Centuries: A Romp Through Intellectual History. Christopher C. Faille. LC 88-1297. 404p. (Orig.). (C). 1988. pap. text ed. 24.00 (0-8191-6910-2); lib. bdg. 56.00 (0-8191-6909-9) U Pr of Amer.
These Lethal, Inexorable Laws: Rajiv, His Men & His Regime. Arun Shourie. (C). 1991. 22.00 (0-8364-2766-1, Pub. by Usha II) S Asia.
These Little Worlds. Fred Asnes. Ed. by Chuck Taylor. (Illus.). 82p. (Orig.). 1985. 10.95 (0-941720-23-3); pap. 4.95 (0-941720-22-5) Slough Pr TX.
These Live Tomorrow. 2nd ed. Clinton L. Scott. (Illus.). 228p. 1987. pap. 5.00 (0-933840-32-2, Skinner Hse Bks) Unitarian Univ.
*These Men Have Seen Hard Service: The First Michigan Sharpshooters in the Civil War. Raymond J. Herek. LC 97-24303. (Great Lakes Books Ser.). (Illus.). 680p. 1997. 34.95 (0-8143-2672-2) Wayne St U Pr.
These Men Shall Never Die. Lowell J. Thomas. LC 73-152217. (Essay Index Reprint Ser.). 1977. reprint ed. 38.95 (0-8369-2379-0) Ayer.
These Modern Nights: Poems. Richard Lyons. LC 87-26355. 80p. (Orig.). 1988. pap. 12.95 (0-8262-0672-7) U of Mo Pr.
These Modern Women: Autobiographical Essays from the Twenties. 2nd ed. Ed. by Elaine Showalter. LC 89-1153. 160p. (Orig.). 1989. pap. 8.95 (1-55861-007-3) Feminist Pr.
These Old Shades. Georgette Heyer. 372p. 1993. 24.95 (1-56723-058-X) Yestermorrow.
*These Old Stone Walls. unabridged ed. Phillips Russell. LC 73-151830. (Illus.). 154p. 1983. reprint ed. pap. 6.95 (0-940715-03-1) Chapel Hill Hist.
These Our Lives. William J. Fling. LC 90-72006. 108p. 1993. pap. 9.00 (1-56002-087-3, Univ Edtns) Aegina Pr.
These Places of Light. Patricia Gangas. 70p. (Orig.). 1995. pap. 9.95 (1-887312-02-1) P Gangas.
These Poems Are Not Pretty. Jan McLaughlin & Bruce Weber. 124p. 1992. pap. 7.95 (0-9615619-9-8) Palmetto.
*These Rare Lands: Images of America's National Parks. Stan Jorstad & Mark Strand. LC 97-16156. 1997. 40.00 (0-684-84112-6) S&S Trade.
These Rooms. Suzanne E. Berger. Ed. by Joan Norris & Michael Peich. LC 79-83711. 1979. 12.00 (0-915778-38-6); pap. 6.00 (0-915778-39-4) Penmaen Pr.
These Sad but Glorious Days: Dispatches from Europe, 1846-1850. Margaret Fuller. Ed. by Larry J. Reynolds & Susan B. Smith. (Illus.). 320p. 1992. 42.00 (0-300-05038-0) Yale U Pr.
These Same Long Bones. Gwendolyn M. Parker. LC 95-740. 1995. pap. 10.95 (0-452-27428-1, Plume) NAL-Dutton.
These Small Stones. Ed. by Norma Farber & Myra C. Livingston. LC 87-264. (Charlotte Zolotow Bk.). 128p. (J). (gr. 3-7). 1987. lib. bdg. 13.89 (0-06-024014-8) HarpC Child Bks.
These Splendid Priests. Compiled by James J. Walsh. LC 68-29252. (Essay Index Reprint Ser.). 1977. reprint ed. 19.95 (0-8369-0973-9) Ayer.
These Splendid Sisters. Compiled by James J. Walsh. LC 75-128326. (Essay Index Reprint Ser.). 1977. 20.95 (0-8369-1856-8) Ayer.
These Stones Will Shout. Mark Link. 297p. 1975. teacher ed., pap. 21.95 (0-89505-046-3, 21034) Tabor Pub.
These Stones Will Shout: A New Voice for the Old Testament. Mark Link. (Illus.). 236p. 1975. pap. text ed. 14.50 (0-89505-117-6, 21033) Tabor Pub.
These Things Are Mine. George Middleton. (American Autobiography Ser.). 448p. 1995. reprint ed. lib. bdg. 99.00 (0-7812-8594-1) Rprt Serv.
These Things Are Written: An Introduction to the Religious Ideas of the Bible. James M. Efird. LC 77-15749. 1986. pap. 12.00 (0-8042-0073-4, John Knox) Westminster John Knox.
These Things Have Been Written: Studies on the Fourth Gospel. Raymond F. Collins. (Louvain Theological & Pastoral Monographs). 270p. (Orig.). 1991. pap. 20.00 (0-8028-0561-2) Eerdmans.
These Things I Remember. J. Allen Easley. (Illus.). 332p. (Orig.). 1988. pap. write for info. (0-9621194-0-7) Stratford NC.
These Things I've Loved. Perry Tanksley. 5.95 (0-686-21184-7) Allgood Bks.
These Thousand Hills. A. B. Guthrie, Jr. LC 95-31060. 352p. 1995. pap. 11.95 (0-395-75520-4) HM.
These Thousand Hills. A. B. Guthrie, Jr. 1993. reprint ed. lib. bdg. 24.95 (1-56849-122-0) Buccaneer Bks.
*These Three Are One: The Practice of Trinitarian Theology. David S. Cunningham. (Challenges in Contemporary Theology Ser.: Vol. 2). 340p. 1998. text ed. 59.95 (1-55786-962-6) Blackwell Pubs.
*These Three Are One: The Practice of Trinitarian Theology. David S. Cunningham. (Challenges in Contemporary Theology Ser.: Vol. 2). 340p. 1998. pap. text ed. 29.95 (1-55786-963-4) Blackwell Pubs.
*These Three Balloons Are for Imogene Rottonbomb. Michael Deane. (Illus.). 30p. (Orig.). (J). (gr. k-12). 1997. pap. 10.00 (1-886383-32-4, Little Blue) Pride OH.
These Too Shall Be Heard, 5 Vols. Sam L. Vulgaris. (Illus.). 200p. (Orig.). 1992. Set. per. 54.95 (0-9620417-6-9) SA-DE Pubns.
These Too Shall Be Heard, Vol. 1. Ed. by Sam L. Vulgaris. LC 88-92826. (Illus.). 200p. (Orig.). 1989. pap. 14.95 (0-9620417-3-4) SA-DE Pubns.
These Too Shall Be Heard, Vol. 2. Ed. by Sam L. Vulgaris. LC 89-91597. (Illus.). 200p. (Orig.). 1940. pap. 14.95 (0-9620417-4-2) SA-DE Pubns.
These Too Shall Be Heard, 5 vols., Vol. III. Illus. by Sam L. Vulgaris. 200p. (Orig.). 1991. per. 15.95 (0-685-54323-4) SA-DE Pubns.
These Too Shall be Heard, Vol. 3. Ed. by Sam L. Vulgaris. (Illus.). 200p. (Orig.). 1991. per. 15.95 (0-685-39304-6) SA-DE Pubns.
These, Too, Shall Be Loved. 2nd ed. Flower A. Newhouse. LC 76-49246. 104p. 1976. pap. 9.00 (0-910378-11-8) Christward.
These Truths Can Change Your Life. Joseph Murphy. 280p. 1982. pap. 8.50 (0-87516-476-5) DeVorss.
These Truths Were Made for Walking. Martha Bolton. 1992. 8.99 (0-685-68451-2, MP-674) Lillenas.
*These Truths Were Made for Walking: Comedy Sketches about Walking the Talk. 64p. 1992. 8.99 (0-8341-9310-8) Lillenas.
These Twain. Arnold Bennett. LC 74-17052. (Collected Works of Arnold Bennett: Vol. 79). 1977. reprint ed. 45.95 (0-518-19160-5) Ayer.
These United States, 1. 6th ed. Brandon Falcone. 1995. student ed., pap. text ed. 20.20 (0-13-171505-4) P-H.
These United States, 2. 6th ed. Brandon Falcone. 1995. student ed., pap. text ed. 20.20 (0-13-172025-2) P-H.
These United States, Vol. 1. 5th ed. Claussen. 1991. student ed., pap. text ed. write for info. (0-13-914342-4) P-H.
These United States, Vol. 2. 5th ed. Claussen. 1991. student ed., pap. text ed. write for info. (0-13-914326-2) P-H.
These United States: Portraits of America from the 1920s. Ed. by Daniel H. Borus. LC 91-39031. (Illus.). 432p. 1992. 35.00 (0-8014-2747-9) Cornell U Pr.
These United States: The Questions of Our Past. 6th ed. Irwin Under & Debi Unger. LC 94-43671. (Illus.). 1022p. 1995. text ed. 62.67 (0-13-174079-2) P-H.
These United States: The Questions of Our Past, Vol. 1. 6th ed. Irwin Unger. (Illus.). 528p. 1995. pap. text ed. 49.00 (0-13-171463-5) P-H.
These United States: The Questions of Our Past, Vol. 2. 6th ed. Irwin Unger. (Illus.). 576p. (C). 1995. pap. text ed. 49.00 (0-13-172017-1) P-H.
These United States: The Questions of Our Past, Vols. I & II. 3rd ed. Irwin Unger. 960p. 1986. text ed. write for info. (0-13-915190-7) P-H.
These United States, First Series. Ed. by Ernest H. Gruening. LC 70-134088. (Essay Index Reprint Ser.). 1977. 24.95 (0-8369-2109-7) Ayer.
These United States, Second Series. Ed. by Ernest H. Gruening. LC 70-134088. (Essay Index Reprint Ser.). 1977. 26.95 (0-8369-2140-2) Ayer.
These United States, Vol. 2: The Questions of Our Past - Since 1865. 5th ed. Irwin Unger. 560p. (C). 1991. pap. text ed. 54.00 (0-13-914318-1) P-H.
These Upraised Hands. William B. Patrick. (American Poets Continuum Ser.: No. 34). 1995. 20.00 (1-880238-26-8); pap. 12.50 (1-880238-27-6) BOA Edns.
These Valiant Dead: Renewing the Past in Shakespeare's Histories. Robert C. Jones. LC 90-46586. 192p. (C). 1991. text ed. 28.95 (0-87745-308-X) U of Iowa Pr.
These Waves of Dying Friends. Michael Lynch. Ed. by Maurice Kenny & J. G. Gosciak. (Illus.). 80p. (Orig.). 1988. pap. 5.00 (0-936556-19-6) Contact Two.
These Were Actors: Extracts from a Newspaper Cutting Book, 1811-1833. James Agate. LC 72-91889. 1972. reprint ed. 17.95 (0-405-08195-2, Pub. by Blom Pubns UK) Ayer.
These Were My Children. Judith Green. 220p. (C). 1990. 45.00 (0-9589059-4-0, Pub. by Pascoe Pub AT) St Mut.
These Were My Days: A Welsh Boyhood in Portland, 1900-1919. Edward W. Coles. 95p. (Orig.). 1990. pap. 7.95 (1-880222-03-5) Red Apple Pub.
These Were the Greeks. H. D. Amos & A. G. Lang. LC 81-71846. (Illus.). 224p. (Orig.). (C). 9100. pap. 18.95 (0-8023-1275-6) Dufour.
These Were the Greeks. H. D. Amos & A. G. Lang. 224p. (Orig.). (C). 1979. pap. 35.00 (1-871402-04-2, Pub. by S Thornes Pubs UK) St Mut.
These Were the Greeks. H. D. Amos & G. P. Lang. (Orig.). (C). 1989. 130.00 (1-871402-05-0, Pub. by S Thornes Pubs UK) St Mut.
These Were the Romans. John Badcock & Graham I. Tingay. 240p. (C). 1989. pap. 35.00 (1-871402-03-4, Pub. by S Thornes Pubs UK) St Mut.
These Were the Romans. Stanley Thornes. (C). 1989. 65.00 (1-871402-00-X, Pub. by S Thornes Pubs UK) St Mut.
These Were the Romans. Graham I. Tingay & John Badcock. (YA). 1985. pap. 17.95 (0-7175-0591-X) Dufour.
These Were the Romans. Graham I. Tingay & John Badcock. LC 86-11654. (Illus.). 196p. (YA). (gr. 10-12). 8700. pap. 17.95 (0-8023-1280-2) Dufour.
These Were the Romans. 2nd ed. Graham I. Tingay & John Badcock. LC 88-7117. (Illus.). 240p. 9500. pap. 18.95 (0-8023-1285-3) Dufour.
These Were the Sioux. Mari Sandoz. LC 85-8914. (Illus.). 118p. (J). (gr. 6-12). 1985. reprint ed. pap. 5.95 (0-8032-9151-5, Bison Books) U of Nebr Pr.
These Women? Women Religious in the History of Australia: The Sisters of Mercy, Parramatta 1888-1988. Madeleine S. McGrath. 312p. 1990. 37.95 (0-86840-299-0, Pub. by New South Wales Univ Pr AT) Intl Spec Bk.
These Years of Promise. Nick Harrison & Kenneth Sollitt. LC 87-82630. (Ann of the Prairie Ser.: Vol. 3). 203p. (Orig.). 1988. pap. 6.95 (0-940652-05-6) Sunrise Bks.
These Yellow Sands. large type ed. Brenda H. English. (General Fiction Ser.). 368p. 1992. 25.99 (0-7089-2638-X) Ulverscroft.
These 50 Years Gone along with the Sorrow. Bern Porter. 20p. (Orig.). 1996. pap. 7.50 (0-614-13985-6) R Jackson.
Thesee. Andre Gide. (FRE.). 1981. pap. 10.95 (0-8288-3689-2, F48472) Fr & Eur.
Thesee. Andre Gide. (Folio Ser.: No. 1334). 116p. (FRE.). 1946. 8.95 (2-07-037334-7) Schoenhof.
Thesee. Jean-Baptiste Lully. Ed. by Theodore De Lajarte. (Chefs-d'oeuvre classiques de l'opera francaise Ser.: Vol. 26). (Illus.). 262p. (FRE.). 1970. reprint ed. pap. 35.00 (0-8450-1126-X) Broude.
*Theses & Dissertations: A Guide to Writing in the Social & Physical Sciences. Isadore Newman. LC 97-21779. 1997. write for info. (0-7618-0814-0); pap. write for info. (0-7618-0815-9) U Pr of Amer.
Theses & Dissertations on Black American Music. Eddie S. Meadows. LC 80-128580. (Front Music Publications: No. 1). ii, 19p. (Orig.). 1980. pap. 5.00 (0-934082-01-4) Theodore Front.
Theses & Dissertations on Virginia History: A Bibliography. Compiled by Richard R. Duncan. ix, 217p. 1986. pap. 10.00 (0-88490-136-X) Library of VA.
*Theses & Dissertations, 1941-1985, University of Hong Kong. 324p. 1986. pap. write for info. (962-7202-01-0, Pub. by Hong Kong Univ Pr HK) Coronet Bks.
Theses on Africa Accepted by Universities & Polytechnics in the United Kingdom & Ireland, 1976-1988. Ed. by Colin Hewson. LC 92-46745. 350p. 1993. 95.00 (1-873836-35-X, Pub. by H Zell Pubs UK) Bowker-Saur.
Theses on Asia Accepted by Universities in the United Kingdom & Ireland: 1877-1964. Ed. by B. C. Bloomfield. 127p. 1967. 35.00 (0-7146-1093-3, Pub. by F Cass Pubs UK) Intl Spec Bk.
Theses on Caribbean Topics, Seventeen Seventy-Eight to Nineteen Sixty-Eight. Ed. by Enid M. Baa. 146p. 1970. pap. 2.50 (0-8477-2000-4) U of PR Pr.
Theses on Islam, the Middle East & North-West Africa, 1880-1978: Accepted by Universities in the United Kingdom & Ireland. P. Sluglett. 160p. 1983. text ed. 85.00 (0-7201-1651-1, Mansell Pub) Cassell.
Theses on Worship: Notes Toward the Reformation of Worship. James B. Jordan. 123p. (Orig.). 1994. pap. 7.00 (1-883690-05-6) Transfig Pr.
Theseus. 1987. 69.95 (0-387-17538-5) Spr-Verlag.
*Theseus: Hero of the Maze. Laura Geringer. (Myth Men Ser.). (Illus.). (J). (ps-3). 1997. pap. 4.99 (0-614-29012-0) Scholastic Inc.
Theseus: The Deeds & Sufferings of the Greek Hero in Ancient Art & Literature. Frank Brommer. (Illus.). 208p. text ed. 50.00 (0-89241-438-3) Caratzas.
Theseus & Athens. Henry J. Walker. LC 93-44486. 256p. 1995. 45.00 (0-19-508908-1) OUP.
Theseus & the Minotaur. Illus. by Robert Baxter. LC 80-50067. 32p. (J). (gr. 4-8). 1980. pap. 3.95 (0-89375-367-X); lib. bdg. 13.95 (0-89375-363-7) Troll Communs.
Theseus & the Minotaur. Illus. & Retold by Leonard E. Fisher. LC 88-1970. 32p. (J). (gr. 1-4). 1988. lib. bdg. 15.95 (0-8234-0703-9) Holiday.
Theseus & the Minotaur. Illus. & Retold by Leonard E. Fisher. LC 88-1970. 32p. (J). (gr. 1-4). 1992. pap. 5.95 (0-8234-0954-6) Holiday.
Theseus & the Minotaur. Warwick Hutton. LC 88-26875. (Illus.). 32p. (J). (gr. 1-5). 1989. lib. bdg. 14.95 (0-689-50473-X, McElderry) S&S Childrens.
*Theseus, Tragedy, & the Athenian Empire. Sophie Mills. LC 97-14789. (Oxford Classical Monographs). 432p. 1997. 98.00 (0-19-815063-6) OUP.
*Thesis - The Winged Serpent: Ancient Mysteries & the Origin of Man. Tom Gilmore & T. Byron. (Illus.). 224p. (Orig.). 1997. pap. 17.95 (1-879352-50-8) Mini-Novel Pub.
Thesis & the Book. Ed. by Eleanor Harman & Ian Montagnes. LC 76-10704. 1976. pap. 12.95 (0-8020-6293-8) U of Toronto Pr.
Thesis Model for Typists - Pages-Modeles pour Dactylo. Thesis Model for Typists Staff. 50p. (ENG & FRE.). 1958. reprint ed. pap. 25.00 (0-608-02209-8, 2062880) Bks Demand.
Thesis Projects in Science & Engineering. Richard M. Davis. LC 78-65255. (Illus.). 1979. pap. 8.95 (0-312-79963-2) St Martin.
Thesmophoriazusae: The Comedies. Alan H. Sommerstein. (Classical Texts Ser.: Vol. 8). 49.95 (0-85668-558-5, Pub. by Aris & Phillips UK); pap. 24.95 (0-85668-559-3, Pub. by Aris & Phillips UK) David Brown.
Thespis: Ritual, Myth, & Drama in the Ancient Near East. 2nd rev. ed. Theodor H. Gaster. LC 75-15735. 515p. 1975. 75.00 (0-87752-188-3) Gordian.
Thessalonians. David P. Kuske. (People's Bible Ser.). 1984. pap. 8.99 (0-8100-0193-4, 15N0406) Northwest Pub.
Thessalonians. R. Reese. 1989. pap. 21.00 (0-86217-022-2, Pub. by Veritas IE) St Mut.
Thessalonians: Critical & Exegetical Commentary. James E. Frame. Ed. by Samuel R. Driver & Charles A. Briggs. (International Critical Commentary Ser.). 336p. 1912. 39.95 (0-567-05032-7, Pub. by T & T Clark UK) Bks Intl VA.
Thessalonians & Galatians. Stephen Doyle. (Read & Pray Ser.). 1980. pap. 1.00 (0-8199-0635-2, Frncscn Herld) Franciscan Pr.
Thessalonians & Pastoral: Thessalonians & Pastoral Epistles. Members of the Faculty of Theology of the University of Navarre. (Navarre Bible Ser.). 183p. 1992. pap. 14.95 (1-85182-077-9, Pub. by Four Cts Pr IE) Intl Spec Bk.
Thessalonians I-II. David P. Kuske. (People's Bible Commentary Ser.). 128p. (Orig.). 1994. pap. 7.99 (0-570-04656-4, 12-8021) Concordia.
Thessalonians I, II: Timothy I, II: Titus: Phelomon see Commentaries on the New Testament
*Thessalonica. Harry Turtledove. 416p. 1997. mass mkt. 5.99 (0-671-87761-5, Baen Books) Baen Bks.
Thessaly in the Fourth Century B.C. H. D. Westlake. (Illus.). viii, 248p. (C). 1993. text ed. 25.00 (0-89005-527-0) Ares.
Theta Device & Other Free Energy Patents. Compiled by Dan A. Davidson. 82p. 1991. pap. 15.00 (0-9626321-2-0) Rivas Pub.
Theta Function Conference-Bowdoin 1987, 2 pts. R. Gunning & L. Ehrenpries. LC 89-6723. (Proceedings of Symposia in Pure Mathematics Ser.: Vol. 49). 1094p. 1989. Set, 1094p. 173.00 (0-8218-1485-0, PSPUM/49) Am Math.
Theta Function Conference-Bowdoin 1987, 2 pts., Pt. 1. R. Gunning & L. Ehrenpries. LC 89-6723. (Proceedings of Symposia in Pure Mathematics Ser.: Vol. 49). 728p. 1989. 114.00 (0-8218-1483-4, PSPUM/49.1) Am Math.
Theta Function Conference-Bowdoin 1987, 2 pts., Pt. 2. R. Gunning & L. Ehrenpries. LC 89-6723. (Proceedings of Symposia in Pure Mathematics Ser.: Vol. 49). 366p. 1989. 67.00 (0-8218-1484-2, PSPUM/49.2) Am Math.
Theta Functions. Ed. by M. Ram Murty. LC 93-15008. (CRM Proceedings & Lecture Notes Ser.: Vol. 1). 174p. 1993. 58.00 (0-8218-6997-3, CRMP/1) Am Math.
Theta Functions, Kernel Functions, & Abelian Integrals. Dennis A. Hejhal. LC 72-6824. (Memoirs Ser.: No. 129). 112p. 1972. pap. 17.00 (0-8218-1829-5, MEMO/1/129) Am Math.
Thetis et Pelee Pascal Collasse see Chefs-d'Oeuvres Classiques de l'Opera Francais
Theurgy & the Soul: The Neoplatonism of Iamblichus. Gregory Shaw. LC 94-34076. 288p. 1995. 45.00 (0-271-01437-7) Pa St U Pr.
Theurgy, or the Hermetic Practice: A Treatise on Spiritual Alchemy. E. J. Gavstin. 1993. reprint ed. 35.00 (1-55818-221-7, First Impress) Holmes Pub.
Thex Ferns, 3 vols. F. O. Bower. (C). 1988. Set. 80.00 (0-685-22318-3) St Mut.
They: Three Parodies of H. Rider Haggard's She. Ed. by R. Reginald & Douglas Melville. LC 77-84277. (Lost Race & Adult Fantasy Ser.). (Illus.). 1978. lib. bdg. 54.95 (0-405-11015-4) Ayer.
They Aimed to Deliver. Charles F. Jackson, Sr. LC 96-84235. 160p. (Orig.). 1996. pap. 12.95 (0-9651797-0-2) Ashokan Bks.
They All Came to Pueblo: A Social History. Joanne W. Dodds. Ed. by Edwin L. Dodds. LC 94-35440. (Illus.). 1994. write for info. (0-89865-908-6) Donning Co.
They All Fall Down: Richard Nickel's Struggle to Save America's Architecture. Richard Cahan. LC 93-7613. (Illus.). 284p. 1995. text ed. 24.95 (0-471-14426-6) Wiley.
They All Laughed ... from Light Bulbs to Lasers: The Fascinating Stories Behind the Great Inventions That Have Changed Our Lives. Ira Flatow. LC 91-58336. (Illus.). 256p. 1993. pap. 11.00 (0-06-092415-2, PL) HarpC.
They All Ran after the Farmer's Wife. Veronica Frater. 220p. 1990. pap. 9.95 (0-85236-214-5, Pub. by Farming Pr UK) Diamond Farm Bk.
They All Ran Away. large type ed. Edward S. Aarons. (Linford Mystery Library). 352p. 1993. pap. 15.99 (0-7089-7425-2, Trailtree Bookshop) Ulverscroft.
They All Sang on the Corner: A Second Look at New York City's Rhythm & Blues Vocal Groups. rev. ed. Philip Groia. LC 83-61960. Orig. Title: They All Sang on the Corner: New York City's R&B Vocal Groups of the 1950's. (Illus.). 192p. 1995. pap. 20.00 (0-9612058-0-6) Phillie Dee Ent.
They All Sang on the Corner: New York City's R&B Vocal Groups of the 1950's see They All Sang on the Corner: A Second Look at New York City's Rhythm & Blues Vocal Groups
They All Sat Down: Pianists in Profile. 3rd ed. Leonice T. Kidd. (Illus.). 160p. (Orig.). 1995. pap. 9.95 (0-87718-000-8) Willis Music Co.
They All Want to Write: Written English in the Elementary School. 4th ed. Alvina T. Burrows et al. LC 84-15470. 238p. (C). 1984. pap. 25.00 (0-208-02043-8, Lib Prof Pubns) Shoe String.
They Also Flew: The Enlisted Pilot Legacy, 1912-1942. Lee Arbon. LC 91-32814. (Illus.). 288p. 1992. 32.00 (1-56098-108-3) Smithsonian.
*They Also Serve an Armorer's Life in World War II. John B. Henkels. (Illus.). 463p. 1997. 18.00 (0-8059-3998-9) Dorrance.
They Also Served. Bill Gilbert. 1994. 4.99 (0-517-09848-2) Random Hse Value.
They Also Served: American Women in World War II. Olga Gruhzit-Hoyt. (Illus.). 240p. 1995. 19.95 (1-55972-280-0, Birch Ln Pr) Carol Pub Group.

T

They Also Served: Citizen Soldiers of the Air Force Training & Service Commands. Edgar L. McCormick. LC 93-32304. (Illus.). 193p. (C). 1994. 19.95 (*0-942597-60-5*, Burd St Pr) White Mane Pub.

They Also Served: Texas Service Records from Headright Certificates. Gifford White. LC 91-76910. 185p. (C). 1991. pap. 25.00 (*0-911317-49-X*) Ericson Bks.

They Also Served: Twenty-Five Remarkable Alabama Women. Mildred G. Yelverton. 270p. 1993. 19.95 (*0-9638664-0-0*) Ampersand AL.

They Also Tried: Chasing the American Dream. M. C. Hamilton. 1994. 15.95 (*0-533-10854-3*) Vantage.

They Also Wrote for the Fan Magazines: Film Articles by Literary Giants from E. E. Cummings to Eleanor Roosevelt, 1920-1939. Ed. & Compiled by Anthony Slide. LC 92-50321. 158p. 1992. pap. 27.50 (*0-89950-753-0*) McFarland & Co.

They Always Call Us Ladies. Jean Harris. 320p. 1993. mass mkt. 4.99 (*0-8217-4314-7*, Zebra Kensgtn) Kensgtn Pub Corp.

They & We: Racial & Ethnic Relations in the United States. 4th ed. Peter I. Rose. 1990. pap. text ed. write for info. (*0-07-053640-6*) McGraw.

They & We: Racial & Ethnic Relations in the United States. 5th ed. Peter I. Rose. LC 96-24404. 1996. write for info. (*0-07-053971-5*); pap. text ed. write for info. (*0-07-053970-7*) McGraw.

They Answered God's Call. Kathleen D. Buehler. Ed. by Dan Harman. (Illus.). 1996. pap. 9.95 (*0-87162-690-X*) Warner Pr.

They Are Coming: The Conquest of Mexico. Jose L. Portillo y Pacheco. Tr. by Beatrice Berler from SPA. LC 92-3142. (Illus.). 375p. 1992. 34.50 (*0-929398-35-1*) UNTX Pr.

They Are in Earnest. Edward Yarnold. (C). 1988. 39.00 (*0-85439-212-2*, Pub. by St Paul Pubns UK) St Mut.

They Are Young Once but Indian Forever: A Summary & Analysis of Investigative Hearings on Indian Child Welfare, April 1980. American Indian Lawyer Training Program, Inc., Staff. Ed. & Frwd. by Joseph A. Myers. (Illus.). 207p. (Orig.). (C). 1981. pap. 6.00 (*0-939890-00-3*) Am Indian LTP.

***They Became Americans: How to Discover Your Family or Ancestors in Naturalization Records.** Dennis L. Szucs. LC 97-4. 200p. 1997. pap. 14.95 (*0-916489-71-X*) Ancestry.

They Bore the Wounds of Christ: The Mystery of the Sacred Stigmata. Michael Freze. LC 89-60271. (Illus.). (Orig.). 1989. pap. 14.95 (*0-87973-422-1*, 422) Our Sunday Visitor.

They Broke the Prairie. Earnest E. Calkins. (Prairie State Bks.). 480p. 1989. reprint ed. pap. text ed. 10.95 (*0-252-06094-6*) U of Ill Pr.

They Broke the Prairie: Being Some Account of the Settlement of the Upper Mississippi Valley by Religious & Educational Pioneers, Told in Terms of One City, Galesburg, & of One College, Knox. Earnest E. Calkins. LC 75-138103. 451p. (C). 1971. reprint ed. text ed. 38.50 (*0-8371-5679-3*, CABP) Greenwood.

They Brought Their Women. Edna Ferber. LC 70-110188. (Short Story Index Reprint Ser.). 1936. 3.95 (*0-8369-3339-7*) Ayer.

They Builded Better Than They Knew. Julius H. Cohen. LC 70-156633. (Essay Index Reprint Ser.). 1977. reprint ed. 23.95 (*0-8369-2350-2*) Ayer.

They Built Chicago: The Entrepreneurs Who Shaped a Great Cities Architecture. Miles Berger. (Illus.). 459p. 1992. 39.95 (*0-929387-76-7*) Bonus Books.

They Built for Eternity. Gustav-Adolf Gedat. Tr. by Roland H. Bainton. LC 72-167345. (Essay Index Reprint Ser.). 1977. reprint ed. 39.95 (*0-8369-2451-7*) Ayer.

They Built on Rock: The Story of the Celtic Christian Church. Diana Leathem. 1977. lib. bdg. 59.95 (*0-8490-2743-8*) Gordon Pr.

They Built the Capitol. Ihna T. Frary. LC 76-99660. (Select Bibliographies Reprint Ser.). 1977. 36.95 (*0-8369-5089-5*) Ayer.

They Built Utopia: The Jesuit Missions in Paraguay: 1610-1768. Frederick J. Reiter. (Illus.). x, 401p. 1995. 75.00 (*1-882528-11-5*) Scripta.

They Built with Faith: True Tales of God's Guidance in L. D.S. Chapel Building World-Wide. H. Dyke Walton. LC 79-89353. 125p. 1979. 8.98 (*0-88290-122-2*) Horizon Utah.

They Burn the Thistles: Memed My Hawk, Part II. Yashar Kemal. pap. 6.95 (*0-906495-47-4*) Writers & Readers.

They Bury Their Mistakes: How to Survive Your Hospitalization. Colleen O'Connor. 100p. (Orig.). 1994. pap. 10.95 (*0-9641088-3-6*) Valverde Pubns.

They Cage the Animals at Night. Jennings M. Burch. 1985. pap. 4.99 (*0-451-15941-1*, Sig) NAL-Dutton.

They Call Her Dana. Wilde. pap. 8.95 (*0-345-38660-4*) Ballantine.

They Call Her Pastor: A New Role for Catholic Women. Ruth A. Wallace. LC 91-15121. (SUNY Series in Religion, Culture & Society). 214p. (C). 1992. text ed. 44.50 (*0-7914-0925-2*); pap. text ed. 14.95 (*0-7914-0926-0*) State U NY Pr.

They Call Him Mr. Gacy: Selected Correspondence of John Wayne Gacy. John W. Gacy et al. (Illus.). 188p. (Orig.). 1989. pap. 14.95 (*1-878865-00-5*) C Bowley Consultants.

They Call Him the Buffalo Doctor. Jean Cummings. LC 73-147172. 320p. 1980. reprint ed. 7.00 (*0-8187-0035-1*) Harlo Press.

They Call Him the Walking Bible. 4th ed. Roger F. Campbell. 298p. 1977. pap. 9.00 (*0-934803-66-8*) J Van Impe.

They Call It Hypnosis. Robert A. Baker. (Illus.). 313p. (C). 1990. 27.95 (*0-87975-576-8*) Prometheus Bks.

They Call It Murder. large type ed. Peter Chambers. (Linford Mystery Library). 288p. 1993. pap. 15.99 (*0-7089-7389-2*, Linford) Ulverscroft.

They Call Me a Delinquent. Monty M. Stanley. 91p. (Orig.). (J). (gr. 5-12). 1989. 8.95 (*0-9622667-1-X*) Illini Pubns.

They Call Me Agnes: A Crow Narrative Based on the Life of Agnes Yellowtail Deernose. Fred W. Voget. LC 94-38872. (Illus.). 256p. 1995. 24.95 (*0-8061-2695-7*) U of Okla Pr.

They Call Me Assassin. 198p. reprint ed. pap. 4.50 (*0-9623579-0-1*) Angels Three.

They Call Me AWOL. Bob Hostetler. 160p. 1994. pap. 7.99 (*0-88965-113-2*, Pub. by Horizon Books CN) Chr Pubns.

***They Call Me Bill: Musings of an Enlightened Curmudgeon.** Bill Davis. 144p. 1997. 15.95 (*1-887750-56-8*) Rutledge Bks.

They Call Me Coach. John R. Wooden & Jack Tobin. (Illus.). 272p. (Orig.). 1988. pap. 14.95 (*0-8092-4591-4*) Contemp Bks.

They Call Me Father: Memoirs of Father Nicolas Coccola. Ed. by Margaret Whitehead. (Illus.). 231p. 1988. pap. 15.95 (*0-7748-0396-7*, Pub. by U BC Pr) U of Wash Pr.

They Call Me Hunter. Hunter Wells. (Illus.). 241p. 1984. 16.50 (*0-942078-09-8*) R Tanner Assocs Inc.

They Call Me Hunter. Hunter Wells. Ed. by G. Gail Gesell. (Illus.). 240p. 1993. write for info. (*0-942078-34-9*) R Tanner Assocs Inc.

They Call Me Kay: A Courtship in Letters. Kathleen W. Schad. Ed. by Nancy G. Anderson. LC 94-6585. (Illus.). 640p. 1994. 30.00 (*1-881320-16-2*, Black Belt) Black Belt Comm.

***They Call Me Mama Daktari.** Anne Spoerry. 224p. 1997. pap. 14.95 (*0-9697079-9-1*, Pub. by Moulin Pub CN) Genl Dist Srvs.

They Call Me the Bacon Priest. rev. ed. Werenfried Van Straaten & O. Praem. LC 89-81006. (Illus.). 241p. 1991. pap. text ed. 9.95 (*0-89870-276-3*) Ignatius Pr.

***They Call Themselves Queens.** Panja Juergens. (Transformation Ser.). 1996. 55.00 (*3-908162-38-6*, Pub. by Edit Stemmle SZ) Dist Art Pubs.

They Called Her Mrs. Doc. Janette Oke. (Women of the West Ser.: Vol. 5). 224p. 1992. pap. 8.99 (*1-55661-246-X*) Bethany Hse.

They Called Her Mrs. Doc. large type ed. Janette Oke. (Women of the West Ser.). 240p. 1992. pap. 10.99 (*1-55661-247-8*) Bethany Hse.

They Called Her Rebbe the Maiden of Ludmir. Gershon Winkler. Ed. by Marlene Greenspan & Reva S. Goldman. (Illus.). 200p. (Orig.). (YA). (gr. 9 up). 1990. 16.95 (*0-910818-83-5*); pap. 12.95 (*0-910818-90-8*) Judaica Pr.

They Called Her the Baroness: The Life of Catherine de Hueck Doherty. Lorene H. Duquin. LC 95-34825. (Illus.). 356p. 1995. 19.95 (*0-8189-0753-3*) Alba.

They Called Him Stonewall: A Life of Lt. General T. J. Jackson, C. S. A. Burke Davis. LC 87-32655. 1988. 10.99 (*0-517-66204-3*) Random Hse Value.

They Called Him Wild Bill. 2nd ed. Joseph G. Rosa. (Illus.). 1979. pap. 21.95 (*0-8061-1538-6*) U of Okla Pr.

They Called it Pilot Error: True Stories Behind General Aviation Accidents. Robert L. Cohn. LC 93-8267. 1993. 26.95 (*0-8306-4464-4*); pap. 16.60 (*0-8306-4463-6*) McGraw-Hill Prof.

They Called It Pilot Error: True Stories Behind General Aviation Accidents. Robert L. Cohn. 1994. text ed. 27.00 (*0-07-011605-9*); pap. text ed. 19.95 (*0-07-011606-7*) McGraw.

They Called It Prairie Light: The Story of Chilocco Indian School. K. Tsianina Lomawaima. LC 93-30255. (Illus.). xx, 215p. (C). 1994. pap. 12.00 (*0-8032-7957-4*, Bison Books) U of Nebr Pr.

They Called It the War Effort: Oral Histories from WWII, Orange, Texas. Louis Fairchild. 544p. 1993. 29.95 (*0-89015-919-X*) Sunbelt Media.

They Called Me Frau Anna. Chana Benat. LC 90-82060. (C). 1990. 17.95 (*1-56062-029-3*) CIS Comm.

They Called Me "Mr. Bonanza" Larry A. Ball. LC 90-63687. (Illus.). 321p. 1990. 39.95 (*0-911978-05-4*) Ball Pubns.

***They Called Me Slim.** James M. Leach. 1997. pap. write for info. (*1-57532-044-4*) Press-Tige Pub.

They Called Me Sweetgrass. Bernice Q. Estes. (Illus.). 80p. 1994. reprint ed. pap. 9.95 (*0-9644438-5-6*) Sweetgrass Pub.

They Called Them Greasers: Anglo Attitudes toward Mexicans in Texas, 1821-1900. Arnoldo De Leon. LC 82-24850. 167p. (C). 1983. pap. 9.95 (*0-292-78054-0*) U of Tex Pr.

They Called Us White Chinese: The Story of a Lifetime of Service to God & Mankind. Robert N. Tharp. Ed. by Judy Telfer & James Plessinger. LC 93-95018. (Illus.). 845p. (C). 1994. text ed. 34.95 (*0-9639425-0-6*) E E Tharp.

***They Calleth Me by the Thunder.** Beryl A. Khabeer. 100p. 1997. pap. 16.00 (*0-9632940-3-2*) Roots Act.

They Came Before Columbus: The African Presence in Ancient America. Ivan Van Sertima. 1977. 23.00 (*0-394-40245-6*) Random.

They Came Every Summer: Sorensen's Resort, from 1876 Alpine County, California. Arthur W. Ewart. LC 93-61127. (Illus.). 165p. (Orig.). 1993. pap. 16.95 (*0-9638545-0-X*) Hope Valley.

They Came from Babel, Vol. 1: Meet the Ancient Advanced Civilization That Dispersed to the Americas in 2000 B.C. S. A. Cranfill. (Biblical History of the Americas Ser.). (Illus.). 256p. (Orig.). 1994. write for info. (*0-9639202-1-9*) Write House.

They Came from Center Field. Dan Gutman. (J). (gr. 4-7). 1995. pap. 3.50 (*0-590-47975-X*) Scholastic Inc.

They Came from DNA: Mysteries of Science. Billy Aronson. LC 93-1038. (Illus.). (J). (gr. 4-9). 1995. text ed. 19.95 (*0-7167-9006-8*, Sci Am Yng Rdrs); pap. text ed. 13.95 (*0-7167-6526-8*, Sci Am Yng Rdrs) W H Freeman.

They Came from Everywhere Vol. 1: Census of Konawa & Avoca Townships, Oklahoma. 2nd ed. Arthur W. Kennedy. (They Came from Everywhere Ser.). 1995. 75.00 (*0-9640529-3-8*) A Kennedy.

They Came from Everywhere & Settled Here: Story of Konawa & Avoca Townships, Vol. II: Through 1930. Arthur W. Kennedy. (Illus.). 508p. 80.00 (*0-9640529-1-1*) A Kennedy.

They Came from Everywhere & Settled Here: Story of Konawa & Avoca Townships, Vol. III: 1930-1950. Arthur W. Kennedy. (Illus.). 500p. write for info. (*0-9640529-2-X*) A Kennedy.

***They Came from... Out of Noware.** Dann Gershon. (Out of Noware Ser.). (Illus.). 32p. (J). (ps-6). 1997. 6.50i (*0-9656985-0-5*) Noware Prodns.

They Came From the Fifties. Ed. by Mickie Villa. (Illus.). 100p. 1990. pap. 9.95 (*0-944735-45-2*) Malibu Comics Ent.

They Came in from the Road. Marjorie Starbuck & Elizabeth Platko. 319p. 1992. pap. text ed. 14.85 (*0-9632896-0-8*) Marbet Bks.

They Came in Ships. John P. Colletta. (Illus.). 108p. (Orig.). 1993. pap. 9.95 (*0-916489-42-6*) Ancestry.

***They Came in Ships Hotel Alantico.** J. G. Noll. Tr. by David Treece. 144p. 1997. pap. 16.95 (*1-899460-65-9*) Paul & Co Pubs.

They Came Like Swallows. William Maxwell. 1997. 14.50 (*0-679-60247-X*, Modern Lib) Random.

They Came Like Swallows. William Maxwell. LC 96-46880. 1997. pap. 12.00 (*0-679-77257-X*) McKay.

***They Came Searching: How Blacks Sought the Promised Land in Tulsa.** LC 96-48625. 1997. write for info. (*1-57168-146-9*, Eakin Pr) Sunbelt Media.

***They Came Searching: How Blacks Sought the Promised Land in Tulsa.** Eddy F. Gates. (Illus.). 356p. 1997. pap. 19.95 (*1-57168-145-0*, 145-0, Eakin Pr) Sunbelt Media.

***They Came Singing: Songs from California's History.** 3rd ed. Karen W. Arlen et al. (Illus.). ii, 110p. (J). (gr. 3-8). 1995. pap. 20.00 (*0-9648362-2-X*) Calicanto Assocs.

They Came This Way. J. H. Johnston, III. (Illus.). 252p. (C). 1988. 35.00 (*0-9621374-0-5*) J H Johnston.

They Came to Baghdad. Agatha Christie. 240p. 1984. pap. 5.50 (*0-425-06824-8*) Berkley Pub.

They Came to Baghdad. large type ed. Agatha Christie. (Agatha Christie Ser.). 359p. 1990. lib. bdg. 19.95 (*0-8161-4605-5*, GK Hall) Thorndike Pr.

They Came to Fish. Raymond A. Brighton. (Illus.). 912p. 1994. reprint ed. 35.00 (*0-914339-48-6*) P E Randall Pub.

They Came to Japan: An Anthology of European Reports on Japan, 1543-1640. Ed. by Michael Cooper. LC 95-41563. (Michigan Classics in Japanese Studies: No. 15). xviii, 439p. 1995. reprint ed. pap. 18.95 (*0-939512-73-4*) U MI Japan.

They Came to Louisiana: Letters of a Catholic Mission, 1854-1882. Ed. by Dorothea O. McCants. LC 72-96258. (Illus.). 287p. reprint ed. 81.80 (*0-8357-9392-3*, 2020997) Bks Demand.

They Came to Malaya: A Traveller's Anthology. Compiled & Intro. by J. M. Gullick. LC 92-45022. 1993. 28.00 (*0-19-588604-6*) OUP.

They Came to Pennsylvania Workshop. Lucille Wallower & Ellen J. Wholey. LC 76-14140. (J). (gr. 4-5). 1984. pap. 4.65 (*0-931992-02-8*) Penns Valley.

***They Came to Play: A Photographic History of Colorado Baseball.** Duane A. Smith & Mark S. Foster. LC 96-52683. (Illus.). 96p. (Orig.). 1997. pap. 14.95 (*0-87081-433-8*) Univ Pr Colo.

***They Came to See a Poet: Selected Poems.** Tadeusz Rozewicz & Adam Czerniawski. 232p. 1991. 34.95 (*0-85646-238-1*, Pub. by Anvil Press UK) Dufour.

They Came to Teach. Contrib. by Annabelle Raiche & Ann M. Biermaier. 300p. 1994. pap. 19.95 (*0-87839-088-X*) North Star.

They Came to the Mountain. Platt Cline. LC 76-10424. 384p. 1976. 24.95 (*0-87358-153-9*) Northland AZ.

They Came to the Smoky Hill: History of Three Generations. Frank Z. Glick. 660p. 1987. pap. 29.95 (*0-89745-092-2*) Sunflower U Pr.

They Can but They Don't: Helping Students Overcome Work Inhibition. Jerome H. Bruns. 240p. 1993. pap. 11.95 (*0-14-015229-6*, Penguin Bks) Viking Penguin.

They Can Sue Me? Jonathan Stevenson. 1987. pap. 21.20 (*1-55645-502-X*) Busn Legal Reports.

They Can't Talk, But Never Lie: The Making of a Zoo Vet. Theodore Zimmerman. Ed. by Elaine Zimmerman. (Illus.). 350p. 1996. 19.95 (*0-9643084-0-1*) Action Arts Pr.

They Carried the Torch: The Story of Oklahoma's Pioneer Newspapers. Elva S. Ferguson. Ed. by Molly L. Griffis. LC 89-80349. (Land We Belong to Is Grand Ser.: Bk. 8). (Illus.). 84p. (YA). (gr. 8 up). 1989. reprint ed. pap. 5.00 (*0-9618634-8-X*) Levite Apache.

They Changed Their Worlds: Nine Women of Asia - Based on Biographies Published by Ramon Magsaysay Award Foundation, Manila, Philippines. Ed. by Mae H. Esterline. LC 87-8208. (Illus.). 188p. (Orig.). (C). 1987. pap. text ed. 20.50 (*0-8191-6310-4*); lib. bdg. 44.50 (*0-8191-6309-0*) U Pr of Amer.

They Chose Life: Jewish Resistance in the Holocaust. Yehuda Bauer. LC 73-89085. (Illus.). 64p. (Orig.). 1973. pap. 2.00 (*0-87495-000-7*) Am Jewish Comm.

They Chose Minnesota: A Survey of the State's Ethnic Groups. Ed. by June D. Holmquist. LC 81-14124. (Illus.). xiii, 614p. (Orig.). 1981. pap. 24.95 (*0-87351-231-6*) Minn Hist.

They Chose the Star. William K. Sessions. (C). 1989. pap. 25.00 (*1-85072-073-8*, Pub. by W Sessions UK) St Mut.

They Chose This Valley. Virginia A. Pullen. Ed. by Charlotte Mills. LC 89-71479. (Illus.). 168p. (Orig.). 1991. pap. 8.95 (*0-9625483-0-8*) Dewey Pr.

They Chose to Live: The Racial Agony of an American Church. J. Herbert Gilmore. LC 72-75577. 206p. reprint ed. pap. 58.80 (*0-317-07872-0*, 2012911) Bks Demand.

***They Closed Their Schools: Prince Edward County, Virginia, 1951-1964.** Bob Smith. LC 96-78090. xxv, 281p. 1996. reprint ed. 24.95 (*0-9654106-1-7*); reprint ed. pap. 9.95 (*0-9654106-0-9*) M E Forrester.

They Come & Knock on the Door. Alfonso Q. Urias. Tr. by Claribel Alegria & Darwin J. Flakoll from SPA. LC 90-52758. 64p. 1991. 13.95 (*0-915306-99-9*) Curbstone.

They Come Out on Halloween Night. Michael P. Jones. (Illus.). 1984. write for info. (*0-318-58332-1*) Crumb Elbow Pub.

They Conquered AIDS: Case Histories of People Who Have Dealt Successfully with AIDS Without Drugs & Doctors. 1992. lib. bdg. 88.95 (*0-8490-8798-8*) Gordon Pr.

They Could Not Talk & So They Drew: Children's Styles of Coping & Thinking. Myra F. Levick. (Illus.). 240p. 1983. text ed. 53.95 (*0-398-04800-2*) C C Thomas.

They Could Not Talk & So They Drew: Children's Styles of Coping & Thinking. Myra F. Levick. (Illus.). 240p. 1983. pap. 38.95 (*0-398-06518-7*) C C Thomas.

***They Could Still Be Mountains.** Allan Fowler. LC 96-28292. (Rookie Read-about Science Ser.). (J). 1997. lib. bdg. write for info. (*0-516-20320-7*) Childrens.

***They Could Still Be Mountains.** Allan Fowler. (Rokie Read-About Science Ser.). 1997. pap. 4.95 (*0-516-26159-2*) Childrens.

They Counted Not the Cost: A History of the Memorial Union Corporation, 1919-1929. John J. Zimmerman. Ed. by Larry E. Anderson. (Illus.). 48p. 1982. pap. 5.00 (*0-934068-01-1*) Memorial Union.

They Cried to the Lord: The Form & Theology of Biblical Prayer. Patrick D. Miller. LC 94-10750. 1994. pap. 24.00 (*0-8006-2762-8*, Fortress Pr) Augsburg Fortress.

They Crossed Mountains & Oceans. Anisoaia Stan. (American Autobiography Ser.). 386p. 1995. reprint ed. lib. bdg. 89.00 (*0-7812-8646-8*) Rprt Serv.

They Dance in the Sky. Jean Guard & Ray A. Williamson. (Illus.). (J). (gr. 6 up). 1987. 15.00 (*0-395-39970-X*) HM.

They Dance in the Sky. Houghton Mifflin Company Staff. (Literature Experience 1993 Ser.). (J). (gr. 6). 1992. pap. 9.84 (*0-395-61832-0*) HM.

***They Dare to Speak Out.** Paul Findley. 390p. 1996. pap. 9.95 (*0-614-21500-5*, 1228) Kazi Pubns.

They Dare to Speak Out: People & Institutions Confront Israel's Lobby. 2nd rev. ed. Paul Findley. LC 84-28977. 408p. 1989. reprint ed. pap. 12.95 (*1-55652-073-5*) L Hill Bks.

They Dared to Live. Robert M. Bartlett. LC 76-90606. (Essay Index Reprint Ser.). 1977. 23.95 (*0-8369-1273-X*) Ayer.

***They Did Not Dwell Alone: Jewish Emigration from the Soviet Union, 1967-1990.** Piet Buwalda. LC 96-29951. 1997. write for info. (*0-8018-5616-7*) Johns Hopkins.

They Did Something about It. Robert M. Bartlett. LC 70-90607. (Essay Index Reprint Ser.). 1977. 19.95 (*0-8369-1243-8*) Ayer.

They Didn't Put That on the Huntley-Brinkley! A Vagabond Reporter Encounters the New South. Hunter James. LC 92-6569. 264p. 1993. 35.00 (*0-8203-1468-4*) U of Ga Pr.

They Didn't Use Their Heads. Jo A. Stover. (Pennant Ser.). (Illus.). 48p. (J). (ps). 1990. reprint ed. pap. 5.49 (*0-89084-546-8*, 050310) Bob Jones Univ Pr.

They Died Crawling...& Other Tales of Cleveland Woe: True Stories of the Foulest Crimes & Worst Disasters in Cleveland History. John S. Bellamy, II. (Illus.). 256p. (Orig.). 1995. pap. 12.95 (*1-886228-03-5*) Gray & Co Pubs.

They Died for King Coal. Lacy A. Dillon. (Illus.). 172p. (C). 1992. reprint ed. 12.95 (*0-9616811-0-1*) Coal Bks.

They Died in Silence: A Woman Steps Forward. James Casey. Ed. by Doug Gilliss. 400p. (Orig.). 1992. reprint ed. pap. text ed. 19.00 (*0-9633858-0-1*) Dillard Pub.

They Died in the Darkness. Lacy A. Dillon. (Illus.). 280p. (C). 1992. reprint ed. 14.95 (*0-87012-230-4*) Coal Bks.

They Died in the Spring. large type ed. J. Pullein-Thompson. (Linford Mystery Library). 1990. pap. 15.99 (*0-7089-6897-X*, Traiitree Bookshop) Ulverscroft.

They Died to Make Men Free: The 19th Michigan Infantry. rev. ed. William Anderson. (Illus.). 397p. 1994. 30.00 (*0-89029-322-8*) Morningside Bkshop.

***They Died Too Young: The Brief Lives & Tragic Deaths of the Mega-Star Legends of Our Times.** Smithmark Staff. 1996. 9.98 (*0-7651-9600-X*) Smithmark.

They Do It with Mirrors. large type ed. Agatha Christie. 1987. 16.95 (*0-7089-1737-2*) Ulverscroft.

***They Do It with Mirrors: A Romance of Faith & Love.** Geoffrey A. Todd. 120p. (Orig.). 1998. mass mkt. 6.99 (*1-58006-007-2*, Homage Pr) Sovereign.

They Do Remember: A Story of Soul Survival. Sandy Robins. 200p. (Orig.). 1996. pap. 13.95 (*0-9649105-0-0*) Home Ofc Pub.

They Don't Dance Much. James Ross. LC 74-23650. (Lost American Fiction Ser.). 308p. 1975. reprint ed. 14.95 (*0-8093-0714-6*) S Ill U Pr.

They Don't Get It, Do They: Closing the Communication Gap Between Women & Men in the, Vol. 1. Kathleen K. Reardon. 1995. 21.95 (*0-316-73641-4*) Little.

They Don't Get It, Do They? Communication in the Workplace - Closing the Gap Between Men & Women. Kathleen K. Reardon. 1996. pap. text ed. 12.95 (*0-316-73634-1*) Little.

An Asterisk (*) at the beginning of an entry indicates that the title is appearing in BIP for the first time.

They Don't Get It, Do They? Communication in the Workplace - Closing the Gap Between Women & Men. Kathleen K. Reardon. 1996. pap. 12.95 (*0-614-12585-5*) Little.

They Don't Have to Die: Home & Classroom Care for Small Animals. Jim Dunlap. LC 90-12685. (Illus.). 280p. (Orig.). 1990. pap. 12.95 (*1-55622-193-2*, Seaside Pr) Wordware Pub.

***They Don't Have to Die: Home & Classroom Care for Small Animals.** 2nd ed. Jim Dunlap. LC 96-44549. 288p. (Orig.). 1996. pap. 12.95 (*1-55622-533-4*, Seaside Pr) Wordware Pub.

They Don't Make 'Em Like That Anymore. Robert R. Knapp. 1994. 26.95 (*0-912736-30-5*) EDITS Pubs.

They Don't Make 'Em Like That Anymore. Robert R. Knapp & Dan Burger. (Illus.). 128p. 1994. pap. 17.95 (*0-912736-31-3*) EDITS Pubs.

***They Don't Play Stickball in Milwaukee.** Reed F. Coleman. 192p. 1997. 22.00 (*1-877946-95-8*) Permanent Pr.

They Don't Speak Russian in Alaska: A New Look at the History of Southern Alaska. David Wharton. LC 90-61086. 1991. 24.95 (*0-944109-08-X*) Margraf Pubns Grp.

***They Don't Teach That in Medical School: Sex with a Ball Bearing & Other Unusual Stories.** Mitch Cigielski. LC 96-72272. (Illus.). 304p. 1997. 26.95 (*1-56167-348-X*) Noble Hse MD.

They Don't Tell the Truth about the Wind: Hands-On Explorations in K-3 Science. Marilyn Fleer et al. LC 95-35550. 256p. 1996. pap. text ed. 29.50 (*0-435-08374-0*, 08374) Heinemann.

They Don't Wash Their Socks! Kathlyn Gay. 112p. (J). 1991. pap. 3.50 (*0-380-71302-0*, Camelot) Avon.

They Don't Wash Their Socks! Kathlyn Gay. (Illus.). (J). (gr. 4-7). 1990. 13.95 (*0-8027-6916-0*); lib. bdg. 14.85 (*0-8027-6917-9*) Walker & Co.

They Dreamed of Horses: Careers for Horse Lovers. Kay Frydenborg. LC 93-33023. (Illus.). 128p. (J). (gr. 4-6). 1994. 15.95 (*0-8027-8283-3*); lib. bdg. 16.85 (*0-8027-8284-1*) Walker & Co.

They Drivem Pickup Trucks They Shootem Shotguns. Renay. (Illus.). 40p. (Orig.). 1996. pap. 3.00 (*1-888431-06-7*) Small Garlic.

They Eat Dirt, Don't They? Christian Parenting Staff. Ed. by Colin Miller. LC 50-4017. (Illus.). 240p. (Orig.). 1993. pap. 6.99 (*0-7814-0144-5*, LifeJourney) Chariot Victor.

They Eat from Their Labor: Work & Social Change in Colonial Bolivia. Ann Zulawski. (Latin American Ser.). 304p. (C). 1994. 55.00 (*0-8229-1183-3*) U of Pittsburgh Pr.

They Eat Shit. Sue Williams. LC 93-85376. (Illus.). 28p. (Orig.). 1993. pap. write for info. (*0-930495-21-7*) San Fran Art Inst.

***They Finished Their Course.** James Anderson. 1996. pap. 14.99 (*0-946351-22-8*, Pub. by John Ritchie UK) Loizeaux.

***They Flash upon That Inward Eye: Poetry Recitation & American Readers.** Joan S. Rubin. 27p. 1997. pap. write for info. (*0-944026-76-1*) Am Antiquarian.

They Fly at Ciron. Samuel R. Delany. 150p. 1992. 25.00 (*0-9633637-0-0*) Incunabula WA.

They Fly at Ciron. Samuel R. Delany. mass mkt. write for info. (*0-614-08668-X*) Tor Bks.

They Fly at Ciron. Samuel R. Delany. 240p. 1996. mass mkt., pap. 6.99 (*0-8125-4317-3*) Tor Bks.

They Fly at Ciron. limited ed. Samuel R. Delany. 150p. 1992. write for info. (*0-9633637-1-9*) Incunabula WA.

They Followed His Call: Vocation & Asceticism. Adrienne Von Speyr. Tr. by Erasmo Leiva-Merikakis from GER. LC 86-80294. 137p. (Orig.). 1986. reprint ed. pap. 8.95 (*0-89870-100-7*) Ignatius Pr.

They Followed the Glory Trail. Roberta H. Green. (Illus.). 160p. (Orig.). 1989. pap. 10.00 (*0-9618656-0-1*) R H Green.

They Followed the Master. Cynthia S. Baker. 1994. pap. 5.95 (*1-55673-704-1*) CSS OH.

They Followed the Plume: The Story of J. E. B. Stuart & His Staff. Robert J. Trout. LC 91-41004. (Illus.). 400p. 1993. 24.95 (*0-8117-1760-7*) Stackpole.

They Followed the Rivers. Floyd Conn & Sadie Conn. (Illus.). 241p. 1981. 14.50 (*0-9607602-0-2*) Kiowa Pr.

They Followed Their Dreams. 169p. Date not set. 11.50 (*0-9618656-2-8*) R H Green.

They Forged the Signature of God: A Novel. Viriato Sencion. Tr. by Asa Zatz. 326p. (Orig.). 1996. pap. 14.95 (*1-880684-33-0*) Curbstone.

They Fought for the Union. Francis A. Lord. LC 81-6579. (Illus.). x, 375p. 1981. reprint ed. text ed. 89.50 (*0-313-22740-3*, LOTF, Greenwood Pr) Greenwood.

They Fought in the Creature Features: Interviews with 23 Classic Horror, Science Fiction, & Serial Stars. Tom Weaver. LC 94-48609. (Illus.). 328p. 1995. lib. bdg. 38.50 (*0-7864-0019-6*) McFarland & Co.

They Fought the Good Fight: Orestes Brownson & Father Feeney. Thomas M. Sennott. LC 88-71543. (Illus.). 440p. (Orig.). (C). 1988. pap. 12.95 (*0-9620994-0-6*) Cath Treas.

They Fought the Law: Rock & Roll's Most Famous Trials & Tribulations. Soocher. 1998. 30.00 (*0-02-864731-9*) Mac Lib Ref.

They Fought to Save. Jules Archer. 1998. pap. 16.99 (*0-670-87121-4*) Viking Penguin.

They Fought with What They Had: The Story of the Army Air Forces in the Southwest Pacific, Nineteen Forty-One to Nineteen Forty-Two. Walter D. Edmonds. 1981. reprint ed. 29.95 (*0-89201-068-1*) Zenger Pub.

They Found Gold: The Story of Successful Treasure Hunts. A. Hyatt Verrill. (Illus.). 296p. 1989. reprint ed. pap. 12.00 (*0-87380-166-0*) Rio Grande.

They Found Him Dead. Georgette Heyer. reprint ed. lib. bdg. 24.95 (*0-89190-647-9*, Rivercity Pr) Amereon Ltd.

They Found the Buried Cities: Exploration & Excavation in the American Tropics. Robert Wauchope. LC 65-24433. (Illus.). 390p. reprint ed. 111.20 (*0-8357-9658-2*, 2016986) Bks Demand.

They Found the Secret: Twenty Lives That Reveal a Touch of Eternity. V. Raymond Edman. 176p. 1984. reprint ed. pap. 10.99 (*0-310-24051-4*, 9564P) Zondervan.

They Glorified Mary: We Glorified Rice. Janet L. Martin & Suzann J. Nelson. 170p. 1994. pap. 6.95 (*0-9613437-4-5*) Redbird Prods.

They Grow in Silence: Understanding Deaf Children & Adults. 2nd ed. Ed. by Eugene D. Mindel & McCay Vernon. LC 90-21666. (Illus.). 204p. (C). 1987. reprint ed. pap. text ed. 29.00 (*0-89079-325-5*, 1744) PRO-ED.

They Had a Dream: The Civil Rights Struggle from Frederick Douglass to Marcus Garvey to Martin Luther King, Jr., & Malcolm X. Jules Archer. (Illus.). 272p. (YA). (gr. 5 up). 1996. pap. 5.99 (*0-14-034954-5*) Puffin Bks.

They Had a Dream: The Civil Rights Struggle from Frederick Douglass to Marcus Garvey to Martin Luther King, Jr., & Malcolm X. Jules Archer. (Epoch Biographies Ser.). (Illus.). 288p. (YA). (gr. 5 up). 1993. pap. 16.99 (*0-670-84494-2*) Viking Child Bks.

They Had Faces Then: Annabella to Zorina: the Superstars, Stars & Starlets of the 1930s. John Springer & Jack Hamilton. (Illus.). 384p. 1974. 19.95 (*0-8065-0300-9*, Citadel Pr) Carol Pub Group.

They Had Faces Then: Hollywood in the 30's - The Legendary Ladies. John Springer & Jack Hamilton. (Illus.). 352p. 1988. pap. 15.95 (*0-8065-1108-7*, Citadel Pr) Carol Pub Group.

They Had Stores...We Had Chores. Janet L. Martin & Suzann J. Nelson. 274p. 1995. pap. 6.95 (*0-9613437-7-X*) Redbird Prods.

They Hanged My Saintly Billy. rev. ed. Robert Graves. 312p. 1997. pap. 14.00 (*0-89733-029-3*) Academy Chi Pubs.

They Harvest Despair: The Migrant Farm Worker. Dale Wright. LC 65-13532. 174p. reprint ed. pap. 49.60 (*0-7837-0003-2*, AU00416) Bks Demand.

They Have Closed Their Eyes. Genni Tekiele. 64p. 1989. pap. 3.95 (*0-88144-132-5*) Christian Pub.

They Have Found a Faith. Marcus L. Bach. LC 74-134049. (Essay Index Reprint Ser.). 1977. reprint ed. 20.95 (*0-8369-2481-9*) Ayer.

They Have No Rights: Dred Scott's Struggle for Freedom. Walter Ehrlich. LC 78-22135. (Contributions in Legal Studies: No. 9). (Illus.). xvi, 266p. 1979. text ed. 55.00 (*0-313-20819-0*, ETH/, Greenwood Pr) Greenwood.

They Have Uncrowned Him. 3rd ed. Marcel Lefebvre. Tr. by Society of St. Pius X Staff from FRE. 261p. 1992. reprint ed. pap. text ed. 10.25 (*0-935952-05-5*) Angelus Pr.

They Heard Georgia Singing. Zell Miller. 272p. 1996. 24.95 (*0-86554-504-9*, MUP/H397) Mercer Univ Pr.

They Helped Shape Our City. Oliver M. Gale. (Illus.). 150p. (Orig.). 1992. pap. text ed. 25.00 (*0-9617747-1-1*) Cin Oral Hist Foun.

They "Knew" Billy the Kid: Interviews with Old-Time New Mexicans. Ed. by Robert F. Kadlec. LC 87-70295. (New Deal & Folk Culture Ser.). (Illus.). 136p. (Orig.). 1987. pap. 11.95 (*0-941270-36-X*) Ancient City Pr.

They Knew Franklin Pierce. Carl I. Bell. 1980. 8.95 (*0-917780-01-9*) April Hill.

They Knew Paul Bunyan. Earl C. Beck. Ed. by Richard M. Dorson. LC 80-789. (Folklore of the World Ser.). 1981. reprint ed. lib. bdg. 29.95 (*0-405-13328-6*) Ayer.

***They Knew Too Much about Flying Saucers.** Gray Barker. LC 96-46970. 256p. 1997. reprint ed. pap. 12.95 (*1-881532-10-0*) IllumiNet Pr.

They Led a Nation. Virginia D. Sneve. LC 75-254. (Illus.). 1975. pap. 5.95 (*0-88498-027-8*) Brevet Pr.

They Led the Way: Fourteen American Women. Johanna Johnston. 128p. (Orig.). (J). 1987. pap. 3.50 (*0-590-44431-X*) Scholastic Inc.

They Left No Monuments. Bob Bowman. 1991. 9.95 (*1-878096-18-4*) Best E TX Pubs.

***They Left Their Mark: Heros & Rogues of Arizona History.** Leo Banks. (Arizona Highways Wild West Ser.). 1997. pap. text ed. 7.95 (*0-916179-70-2*) Ariz Hwy.

They Left Their Mark: William Austin Burt & His Sons, Surveyors of the Public Domain. John S. Burt. (Illus.). 188p. 1987. 40.00 (*0-910845-31-X*, 977) Landmark Ent.

***They Left Their Tracks.** Copenha. Date not set. pap. text ed. 13.95 (*0-912299-46-0*) Stoneydale Pr Pub.

***They Like to Never Quit Praisin' God: The Role of Celebration in Preaching.** Frank A. Thomas. LC 97-212. 160p. (Orig.). 1997. pap. 15.95 (*0-8298-1181-8*) Pilgrim OH.

They Live on the Land: Life in an Open-Country Southern Community. Paul W. Terry & Verner M. Sims. LC 92-31416. (Library of Alabama Classics). 384p. 1993. reprint ed. pap. 24.95 (*0-8173-0587-4*) U of Ala Pr.

They Lived in Tubac. Elizabeth R. Brownell. LC 85-51587. (Illus.). 290p. 1987. 26.95 (*0-87026-061-8*) Westernlore.

They Lived with Dinosaurs. Houghton Mifflin Company Staff. (Literature Experience 1993 Ser.). (J). (gr. 4). 1992. pap. 9.16 (*0-395-61799-5*) HM.

They Lived with God: Life Stories of Some Devotees of Sri Ramakrishna. Swami Chetanananda. LC 88-5775. (Illus.). 434p. 1989. 17.95 (*0-916356-61-2*) Vedanta Soc St Louis.

They Looked for a City. LC 58-17705. 1955. pap. 4.95 (*0-915540-15-0*) Frnds Israel.

They Looked for a City. Lydia Buksbazen. 1976. pap. 8.95 (*0-87508-041-3*) Chr Lit.

They Looked for a City: A Comparative Analysis of the Ideal of Community in the Thought of Howard Thurman & Martin Luther King, Jr. Walter E. Fluker. LC 88-31335. 296p. (Orig.). (C). 1989. pap. text ed. 27.00 (*0-8191-7263-4*); lib. bdg. 46.00 (*0-8191-7262-6*) U Pr of Amer.

They Love a Man in the Country: Saints & Sinners in the South. Billy Bowles & Remer Tyson. (Illus.). 336p. 1989. 18.95 (*0-934601-67-4*) Peachtree Pubs.

They Loved Their Enemies: True Stories of African Christians. Marian Hostetler. LC 87-29696. (Peace & Justice Ser.: Vol. 3). 104p. (Orig.). 1988. pap. 6.99 (*0-8361-3456-7*) Herald Pr.

They Loved to Laugh. Kathryn Worth. LC 96-83480. (Young Adult Bookshelf Ser.). (Illus.). 254p. (YA). (gr. 8 up). 1996. reprint ed. pap. 11.95 (*1-883937-16-7*, 16-7) Bethlehem ND.

They Made History: A Biographical Dictionary. Geoffrey Wigoder. LC 93-25031. 1995. 60.00 (*0-13-915257-1*) S&S Trade.

They Made Their Own Law: Stories of Bolivar Peninsula. Melanie Wiggins. LC 90-53715. (Illus.). 220p. (C). 1991. 24.95 (*0-89263-307-7*); pap. 14.95 (*0-89263-308-5*) Tex A&M Univ Pr.

They Made Their Souls Anew: Ils Ont Refait Leur Ame. Andre Neher. Tr. by David Maisel. LC 89-38685. (SUNY Series in Modern Jewish Literature & Culture). 179p. 1990. text ed. 64.50 (*0-7914-0315-7*); pap. text ed. 21.95 (*0-7914-0316-5*) State U NY Pr.

***They Make Themselves: Work & Play among the Baining of Papua New Guinea.** Jane Fajans. LC 96-37641. 1996. pap. text ed. 19.95 (*0-226-23444-4*); lib. bdg. 50.00 (*0-226-23443-6*) U Ch Pr.

They Married Adventure: The Wandering Lives of Martin & Osa Johnson. Pascal J. Imperato & Eleanor M. Imperato. LC 92-4696. (Illus.). 350p. (C). 1992. 27.95 (*0-8135-1858-X*) Rutgers U Pr.

They Met at Gettysburg. 3rd ed. Edward J. Stackpole. LC 56-13070. (Illus.). 344p. 1982. pap. 14.95 (*0-8117-2089-6*) Stackpole.

They Met at Gettysburg. 40th anniversary ed. Edward J. Stackpole. (Illus.). 344p. 1995. 19.95 (*0-8117-1762-3*) Stackpole.

They Met at Perryville. 2nd rev. ed. Richard J. Reid. LC 95-94782. (Illus.). 94p. (Orig.). 1995. reprint ed. pap. 7.95 (*1-877713-07-4*) R J Reid.

They Met Jesus: Life-Changing Encounters. rev. ed. Marilyn Kunz & Catherine Schell. 56p. 1993. pap. 4.99 (*1-880266-02-4*) Neighborhood Bible.

They Must Be Represented: History & the Rhetoric of Gender in American Political Documentaries. Paula Rabinowitz. (Haymarket Ser.). (Illus.). 288p. (J). 1994. pap. text ed. 20.00 (*1-85984-025-6*, B4647, Pub. by Vrso UK) Norton.

They Must Be Represented: History & the Rhetoric of Gender in American Political Documentaries. Paula Rabinowitz. (Haymarket Ser.). (Illus.). 288p. (C). (gr. 13). 1994. text ed. 65.00 (*1-85984-925-3*, B4643, Pub. by Vrso UK) Norton.

***They Named Him Babi Yar.** Esther G. Johnson. 1997. 10.95 (*1-889279-05-6*) Best Small Pr.

They Never Came Home. Lois Duncan. 192p. (J). 1990. reprint ed. mass mkt. 4.50 (*0-440-20780-0*, LLL BDD) BDD Bks Young Read.

***They Never Gave Up: Adventures in Early Aviation.** Michael Wilkey. LC 97-65298. (Illus.). 120p. (Orig.). (J). (gr. 3-7). 1997. pap. 9.95 (*1-55143-077-0*) Orca Bk Pubs.

They Never Go Back to Pocatello: The Selected Essays of Richard Neuberger. Ed. by Steve Neal. (Illus.). 416p. 1988. 22.50 (*0-87595-201-1*) Oregon Hist.

***They Never Heard of the Tooth Fairy.** Marlene T. Brill. LC 97-14275. (Illus.). 1998. pap. write for info. (*0-88106-399-1*) Charlesbridge Pub.

***They Never Heard of the Tooth Fairy.** Marlene T. Brill. LC 97-14275. (Illus.). (J). 1998. write for info. (*0-88106-398-3*) Charlesbridge Pub.

They Never Knew: The Victims of Nuclear Testing. Glen Cheney. LC 96-14262. (Impact Ecology & Conservation Ser.). 144p. (YA). (gr. 9-12). 1996. lib. bdg. 22.70 (*0-531-11273-X*) Watts.

***They Never Rationed Courage: Letters.** Tom Patterson. pap. 17.50 (*1-55128-026-4*, Pub. by Mercury Pr CN) LPC InBook.

They Never Said It: A Book of Fake Quotes, Misquotes, & Misleading Attributions. Paul F. Boller, Jr. & John George. 192p. 1989. reprint ed. 22.00 (*0-19-505541-1*) OUP.

They Never Said It: A Book of Fake Quotes, Misquotes, & Misleading Attributions. Paul F. Boller, Jr. & John George. 192p. 1990. reprint ed. pap. 6.95 (*0-19-506469-0*) OUP.

They Never Surrendered: Bronco Apaches of the Sierra Madres, 1890-1935. Douglas V. Meed. (Great West & Indian Ser.: Vol. 59). (Illus.). 1993. 23.95 (*0-87026-086-3*) Westernlore.

They Never Want to Tell You: Children Talk about Cancer. David J. Bearison. LC 90-49945. 194p. 1991. text ed. 22.00 (*0-674-88370-5*, BEATHE) HUP.

They of the High Trails. Hamlin Garland. (Collected Works of Hamlin Garland). 1988. lib. bdg. 59.00 (*0-7812-1244-8*) Rprt Serv.

They of the High Trails see Collected Works of Hamlin Garland

***They Only Look Dead.** Dionne. LC 97-3713. 1997. pap. 13.00 (*0-684-82700-X*, Touchstone Bks) S&S Trade.

They Only Look Dead: Why Progressive Will Dominate the Next Political Era. E. J. Dionne, Jr. 352p. 1996. 24.00 (*0-684-80768-8*) S&S Trade.

They Oughta Be in Pictures: Your Kids on Camera. Kelly F. Kidwell & Ruth Devorin. LC 94-40936. 176p. (Orig.). 1995. pap. 12.95 (*0-942963-61-X*) Distinctive Pub.

They Painted from Their Hearts: Pioneer Asian American Artists. Ed. by Mayumi Tsutakawa. LC 94-36755. (Illus.). 92p. 1994. pap. 18.00 (*0-295-97430-3*) U of Wash Pr.

They Passed This Way. Esther Kreek. LC 93-710994. 37p. 1993. pap. 14.00 incl. audio (*1-884483-03-8*); pap. 12.00 incl. audio (*1-884483-02-X*) St Joseph Mus.

They Passed This Way: Mackays Rich Ethnic Heritage. 56p. Date not set. 7.50 (*0-614-04717-X*) R H Green.

They Played the Game: The Story of Baseball Greats. Harry Grayson. LC 77-167349. (Essay Index Reprint Ser.). 1977. reprint ed. 27.95 (*0-8369-2692-7*) Ayer.

They Raced Horses on Main Street: Recollections of an Era. limited ed. Anthony H. Coppola. Ed. by Peter A. Coppola. LC 90-93489. (Illus.). 235p. (Orig.). 1990. pap. 25.00 (*0-9627978-0-4*) C E Coppola.

***They Ran with the Ball: How Rugby Became Football.** Hickie. Date not set. pap. text ed. write for info. (*0-582-91062-5*, Pub. by Longman UK) Longman.

They Reached for the Stars. Ruth Turk. (Illus.). (J). (gr. 5-9). 1990. pap. 11.95 (*0-933025-20-3*) Blue Bird Pub.

They Refused to Name Names: The Freeway Hall Case Victory. Intro. by Clara Fraser. LC 95-70057. 48p. (Orig.). 1995. pap. 4.00 (*0-932323-02-2*) Red Letter Pr.

They Represent You, 1995-96. 1995. pap. 3.00 (*0-686-64779-3*) LWV NYC.

They Rest among the Known Black Defenders of America Who Have Responded to the Call of Taps. Robert E. Greene. LC 80-67671. (Illus.). 62p. 1982. write for info. (*0-9603320-1-4*) R E Greene.

***They Rode with Custer.** John M. Carroll. Date not set. lib. bdg. 27.95 (*0-8488-0236-5*, J M C & Co) Amereon Ltd.

They Rode with Custer. John M. Carroll. (Illus.). Date not set. pap. 17.95 (*0-8488-0237-3*, J M C & Co) Amereon Ltd.

They Rode with Forrest & Wheeler: A Chronicle of Five Tennessee Brothers' Service in the Confederate Western Cavalry. John E. Fisher. LC 95-10935. (Illus.). 320p. 1995. lib. bdg. 29.95 (*0-7864-0083-8*) McFarland & Co.

They Rose above It. Bob Considine. 1977. mass mkt. 1.75 (*0-449-23417-7*, Crest) Fawcett.

They Rose from the Valley. Lee Cavin. (Illus.). 1990. 9.95 (*1-879377-03-9*) Truax Print.

They Saddled the West. Lee M. Rice & Glenn R. Vernam. LC 75-5734. (Illus.). 202p. reprint ed. pap. 57.60 (*0-8357-4431-0*, 2037262) Bks Demand.

They Said about Islam. Imadudin Khalil. 504p. (ARA.). 1992. pap. write for info. (*1-882837-10-X*) W A M Y Intl.

They Said I Was Dead: The Complete Alternative Cure for Addiction. Anne McManus. 1993. pap. 15.50 (*1-85727-091-6*) LPC InBook.

They Said I Was Dead: The Complete Alternative Cure for Addiction. Anne McManus. 128p. 1994. 45.00 (*1-85727-086-X*) LPC InBook.

They Said It. Patrick Mcdonnell. 1990. pap. 5.95 (*0-8487-1028-2*) Oxmoor Hse.

They Said It Couldn't Be Done! Wallene T. Dockery & Steve Williford. LC 86-61416. (Motivational Ser.). 96p. 1987. 11.95 (*0-936169-03-6*) Dockery Enter.

They Sang for Horses: The Impact of the Horse on Navajo & Apache Folklore. fac. ed. LaVerne H. Clark. LC 66-18527. (Illus.). 247p. reprint ed. pap. 70.40 (*0-7837-6959-8*, 2046909) Bks Demand.

They Sang! They Danced! They Romanced! The Hollywood Musicals from the Advent of Sound Until. John Springer. 1991. pap. 16.95 (*0-8065-1254-7*, Citadel Pr) Carol Pub Group.

They Saw It Happen. Gordon Lindsay. 1972. 2.95 (*0-89985-010-3*) Christ for the Nations.

They Saw the Elephant: Women in the California Gold Rush. JoAnn Levy. LC 89-78223. (Illus.). xxii, 265p. (C). 1990. lib. bdg. 32.50 (*0-208-02273-2*, Archon Bks) Shoe String.

They Saw the Elephant: Women in the California Gold Rush. JoAnn Levy. LC 92-54146. (Illus.). 288p. 1992. reprint ed. pap. 12.95 (*0-8061-2473-3*) U of Okla Pr.

They Saw the Lord: The Resurrection Appearances. Bonnell Spencer. LC 83-61765. 235p. 1983. pap. 8.95 (*0-8192-1332-2*) Morehouse Pub.

***They Say I Broke the Rule. Helen O. Bradley. 128p. (Orig.). Date not set. pap. 25.00 (*0-9658140-0-9*) Bradleys Pub.**

THEY SAY I BROKE THE RULE is based on a true story. The actual character's names have been altered. This book is about a young girl whose life was full of love & happiness at her early years. Oh!, but as she was growing to become a young lady her life became a horror story. The rules she had hanging over her head was all a set up. The young girl ended up in a bloody battle with her family to keep herself out of a danger zone. After the bloody battle the young girl winds up in jail. All because of the lies her Mom used to protect her evil boyfriend Sid. Before it turned into a bloody battle the young girl grew into a rebellious state of mind. The young girl was delirious & couldn't trust no one but herself. She loved none but herself. Her relationship with her Mom was shattered beyond repair. The abuse the young girl suffered was tragic but it all ended well. After all the tragedy that happened the young girl & her Mom were able to patch things up. After reading this summary I bet you're all wondering what

T

happened during the abuse & how the abuse was inflicted. There are two mysteries unknown in this book. One mystery is who is the young girl?, the second mystery is what was so evil about the boyfriend Sid. Well folks you have to read the book in order to solve the mysteries. Order direct from Bradley's Publishing, Co., 15492 Cloverlawn Rd., Detroit, MI 48238. (313) 341-5591 call in orders. *Publisher Provided Annotation.*

They Say It Never Happened. David Ben Majer. Ed. by Jacqueline L. Gorman. 340p. 1993. pap. text ed. 30.00 (0-9639359-6-8) Koegel Ent.

*__They Say That I Am Two.__ Marcos M. Villatoro. LC 96-39828. 1997. 8.95 (1-55885-196-8) Arte Publico.

They Say You're Crazy: How the World's Most Powerful Psychiatrists Decide Who Is Normal. Paula J. Caplan. LC 94-39662. 355p. 1995. 22.00 (0-201-40758-2) Addison-Wesley.

They Say You're Crazy: How the World's Most Powerful Psychiatrists Decide Who's Normal. Paula J. Caplan. 384p. 1996. pap. 13.00 (0-201-48832-9) Addison-Wesley.

They Seek Me Early. Johnny Lawrence & James White. 42p. 1993. pap. 5.00 (0-916092-18-6) Tex Ctr Writers.

They Shall Be Heard: The Story of Susan B. Anthony & Elizabeth Cady Stanton. Kate Connell. LC 92-18088. (Stories of America Ser.). (Illus.). 85p. (J). (gr. 2-5). 1992. lib. bdg. 25.68 (0-8114-7228-0) Raintree Steck-V.

They Shall Be Mine. John Tallach. 128p. (YA). (gr. 9-12). 1981. pap. 8.50 (0-85151-320-4) Banner of Truth.

*__They Shall Inherit the Earth.__ Morley Callaghan. 1996. pap. text ed. 6.95 (0-7710-9881-2) McCland & Stewart.

*__They Shall Mount Up.__ Norma Richardson-Dade. LC 96-90190. (Orig.). 1996. pap. 14.95 (0-533-11926-X) Vantage.

They Shall Not Hurt: Human Suffering & Human Caring. Ed. by Rodney L. Taylor & M. Jean Watson. LC 89-904. 140p. (C). 1989. text ed. 24.95 (0-87081-201-7) Univ Pr Colo.

They Shall Not Pass: The Autobiography of La Pasionaria. Dolores Ibarruri. LC 66-25065. 360p. 1976. pap. 4.25 (0-7178-0468-2) Intl Pubs Co.

They Shall Take up Serpents: Psychology of the Southern Snake-Handling Cult. Weston La Barre. (Illus.). 208p. (C). 1992. reprint ed. pap. text ed. 10.95 (0-88133-663-7) Waveland Pr.

They Shaped the Game. William J. Jacobs. LC 94-14007. (J). 1994. text ed. 15.95 (0-684-19734-0) S&S Trade.

*__They Shoot Canoes, Vol. 1.__ P. McManus. (J). 1982. write for info. (0-03-062377-4) H Holt & Co.

They Shoot Canoes, Don't They? Patrick E. McManus. LC 80-24131. 288p. 1981. 18.95 (0-8050-0165-4) H Holt & Co.

They Shoot Canoes, Don't They? Patrick E. McManus. LC 80-24131. 288p. 1982. pap. 8.95 (0-8050-0030-5, Owl) H Holt & Co.

They Shoot Coaches, Don't They? Mark Heisler. 288p. 1996. 23.95 (0-02-860819-4) Macmillan.

They Shoot Horses, Don't They? 2nd ed. Horace McCoy. (Midnight Classics Ser.). 132p. 1995. pap. 9.99 (1-85242-401-X) Serpents Tail.

They Shoot Horses Don't They? Horace McCoy. 1993. reprint ed. lib. bdg. 19.95 (1-56849-241-3) Buccaneer Bks.

They Shoot Managers Don't They? Making Conflict Work in a Changing World. Terry L. Paulson. 192p. 1991. reprint ed. pap. 11.95 (0-89815-429-4) Ten Speed Pr.

They Shoot Managers, Don't They? Managing Yourself & Leading Others in a Changing World. Terry L. Paulson. (Illus.). 156p. (Orig.). pap. 10.95 (0-939007-15-0) Lee Canter & Assocs.

They Should Have Kept the Bear: The OK Miniature Engine Collector's Reference. Theodore R. Brebeck. (Illus.). 90p. 1995. pap. text ed. 19.95 (0-9628337-1-1) Caretaker.

They Should Have Served That Cup of Coffee: Seven Radicals Remember the '60s. Ed. by Dick Cluster. LC 78-68476. (Illus.). 268p. 1979. 30.00 (0-89608-083-8); pap. 14.00 (0-89608-082-X) South End Pr.

They Sleep Beneath the Mockingbird: Biographies & Burial Sites of Mississippi Confederate Generals. Harold Cross. 16.95 (0-9631963-9-1) So Herit Pr.

*__They Smell Like Sheep: Biblical Leadership for the Twenty-First Century.__ Lynn Anderson. 224p. 1997. 14.99 (1-878990-73-X) Howard Pub LA.

*__They Sought a Land: A Settlement in the Arkansas River Valley, 1840-1870.__ William O. Ragsdale. LC 97-17937. 1997. write for info. (1-55728-498-9) U of Ark Pr.

They Sought a New World: The Story of European Immigration to North America. William Kurelek & Margaret S. Engelhart. (Illus.). 48p. (J). (gr. 4 up). 1985. 16.95 (0-88776-172-0, U of Toronto Pr) Tundra Bks.

They Sought a New World: The Story of European Immigration to North America. William Kurelek & Margaret S. Engelhart. (Illus.). 48p. (J). (gr. 4 up). 1996. reprint ed. pap. 9.95 (0-88776-213-1) Tundra Bks.

They Speak with Other Tongues. John L. Sherill. LC 64-25003. 144p. (gr. 10). 1993. reprint ed. mass mkt. 4.99 (0-8007-8041-8, Spire) Revell.

They Spoke of Grace. Moody, Spurgeon, Whitefield, MacKay Staff. Ed. & Intro. by Bobby W. Austin. 190p. (Orig.). 1994. pap. write for info. (0-9639640-1-1) Grace Vision.

They Stay for Death. Sara Woods. 192p. 1988. mass mkt. 3.50 (0-380-70587-7) Avon.

They Still Call Me Assassin. Jack Tatum. 1989. 19.95 (0-9623579-1-X) Angels Three.

They Still Call Me Assassin - Here We Go Again. 260p. 1989. 19.95 (0-9623579-2-8) Angels Three.

They Still Call Me Junior: Autobiography of a Child Star; with a Filmography. Frank J. Coghlan. LC 92-50432. (Illus.). 383p. 1992. lib. bdg. 32.50 (0-89950-762-X) McFarland & Co.

They Still Shoot Models My Age. Susan Moncur. 1993. pap. 12.99 (1-85242-230-0) Serpents Tail.

They Still Speak: Readings for the Lesser Feasts. Ed. by J. Robert Wright. 256p. 1993. 27.95 (0-89869-208-3) Church Pub Inc.

They Stood in the Door. Don MacNaughtton. 413p. 1985. 24.00 (0-7223-1752-2, Pub. by A H S Ltd UK) St Mut.

They Taught Themselves: American Primitive Painters of the 20th Century. Sidney Janis. LC 83-45880. reprint ed. 72.50 (0-404-20134-2) AMS Pr.

They Tell Me You Danced. Irene Willis. LC 95-855. (University of Central Florida Contemporary Poetry Ser.). 88p. 1995. 19.95 (0-8130-1358-5); pap. 10.95 (0-8130-1371-2) U Press Fla.

They That Go down to the Sea: A Bicentennial Pictorial History of the United States Coast Guard. Paul A. Powers. LC 90-61231. (Illus.). vii, 208p. 1990. 35.00 (0-9626717-0-3) USCG CPO Assn.

They That Go down to the Sea: A Bicentennial Pictorial History of the United States Coast Guard. deluxe ed. Paul A. Powers. LC 90-61231. (Illus.). vii, 208p. 1990. 75.00 (0-9626717-1-1) USCG CPO Assn.

They That Walk in Darkness: Ghetto Tragedies. Israel Zangwill. LC 70-116969. (Short Story Index Reprint Ser.). 1977. 30.95 (0-8369-3473-3) Ayer.

They Thought They Saw Him. Craig K. Strete. LC 95-5465. (Illus.). 32p. (J). (ps up). 1996. 15.00 (0-688-14194-3); lib. bdg. 14.93 (0-688-14195-1) Greenwillow.

They Thought They Were Free: The Germans 1933-45. 2nd ed. Milton Mayer. LC 55-5137. 368p. 1966. pap. text ed. 16.50 (0-226-51192-8, P222) U Ch Pr.

They Tied a Label on My Coat. large type ed. Hilda Hollingsworth. 1993. 39.95 (0-7066-1029-6, Pub. by Remploy Pr CN) St Mut.

*__They Too Wore Pinstripes: Interviews with 20 Glory-Days New York Yankees.__ Brent P. Kelley. 1998. write for info. (0-7864-0355-1) McFarland & Co.

They Took My Father: A Story of Idealism & Betrayal. Mayme Sevander & Laurie Hertzel. LC 92-80225. 208p. (Orig.). 1992. pap. 12.95 (0-938586-64-5) Pfeifer-Hamilton.

They Took the Challenge: The Story of Rolling Meadows. Esther Perica. LC 79-14803. (Illus.). 167p. 1980. 9.75 (0-9602782-0-6) Rolling Meadows.

They Turned the War Around at Coral Sea & Midway. Stuart D. Ludlum. (World War II Historical Society Monograph Ser.). 156p. 1995. pap. 17.50 (1-57638-016-5) Merriam Pr.

They Used to Call Me Snow White... But I Drifted: Women's Strategic Use of Humor. Regina Barreca. LC 90-50511. 240p. 1992. pap. 11.95 (0-14-016835-4, Penguin Bks) Viking Penguin.

They Walked Before: The Indians of Washington State. rev. ed. Cecelia S. Carpenter. LC 89-91967. (Illus.). 75p. 1989. reprint ed. pap. 10.00 (0-9616969-1-5) Tahoma Pubns.

*__They Walked in the Spirit.__ Douglas M. Strong. 1997. pap. text ed. 25.00 (0-664-25706-2) Westminster John Knox.

They Walked the Earth. James H. Johnson, Jr. (Illus.). 112p. (Orig.). (J). (gr. 1-6). 1992. pap. 12.95 (0-9632717-0-9) P Q Pubns.

They Walked with God: Daily Readings from Moody Press Authors. Ed. by James S. Bell, Jr. 1993. text ed. 18.99 (0-8024-8349-6) Moody.

They Walked with Jesus: Past Life Experiences with Christ. 2nd ed. Dolores Cannon. 226p. (Orig.). 1994. pap. 11.95 (1-85860-007-3, Pub. by Gateway Books UK) ACCESS Pubs Network.

They Wanted to Win: Nineteen Eighty-Eight Notre Dame Football National Championship Review. Ed. by Pay Henderson & J. D. Rutledge. (Illus.). 142p. 1989. pap. 14.95 (1-879688-04-2) Host Comns Inc.

They Watch Me As They Watch This: Gertrude Stein's Metadrama. Jane P. Bowers. LC 91-9165. 160p. (C). 1991. text ed. 26.95 (0-8122-3057-4) U of Pa Pr.

They Went Thataway: Redefining Film Genres, a National Society of Film Critics Video Guide. Ed. by Richard T. Jameson. LC 93-15011. (National Society of Film Critics Video Guide Ser.). 392p. 1994. pap. 16.95 (1-56279-055-2) Mercury Hse Inc.

They Were - We Are: Allen-Gilchrist Scrapbook. Jean Cecil. (They Were - We Are Ser.: Vol. 1). (Illus.). 40p. (Orig.). 1993. pap. text ed. 32.50 (0-9636014-1-5) Jeans Write Shop.

*__They Were All Young Kids: The Story of Lieutenant Jim Flowers & the First Platoon, Company C, 712 Tank Battalion, on Hill 122.__ Aaron C. Elson. (Illus.). ix, 194p. (Orig.). 1997. pap. 17.95 (0-9640611-1-2) Chi Chi Pr.

*__They Were Children...Then: Holy Name Seminary (Madison, WI)__ Marje J. Brantmeyer. LC 96-90322. 1996. 17.95 (0-533-11997-9) Vantage.

They Were Considered Faithful. Roseanne Hilton. 104p. 1993. pap. 6.95 (0-939497-32-8) Promise Pub.

They Were Few. Alexander Bronowski. LC 91-21675. (Studies in the Shoah: Vol. 2). 218p. (C). 1992. text ed. 44.95 (0-8204-1629-0) P Lang Pubng.

They Were Giants. Charles R. Brown. LC 68-54332. (Essay Index Reprint Ser.). 1977. 20.95 (0-8369-0257-2) Ayer.

They Were Giants. Charles R. Brown. LC 68-54332. (Essay Index Reprint Ser.). 285p. 1982. reprint ed. lib. bdg. 17.00 (0-8290-0835-7) Irvington.

They Were San Franciscans. Miriam A. De Ford. LC 70-117781. (Essay Index Reprint Ser.). 1977. 24.95 (0-8369-1914-9) Ayer.

They Were Strangers: A Family History. Slovie S. Apple. 1994. 18.95 (0-533-11057-2) Vantage.

They Were Strong & Good. Robert Lawson. (Illus.). (J). (gr. 4-6). 1940. pap. 15.99 (0-670-69949-7) Viking Child Bks.

They Were There. Ed. by Curt Riess. LC 70-134127. (Essay Index Reprint Ser.). 1977. 37.95 (0-8369-2029-5) Ayer.

They Were Women Like Me: Women of the New Testament in Devotions for Today. Joy Jacobs. LC 85-7771. 224p. 1993. pap. 9.99 (0-87509-539-9) Chr Pubns.

They Were Women Like Me: Women of the New Testament in Devotions for Today. Joy Jacobs. 216p. 1985. 14.95 (0-13-917048-0) P-H.

They Were Women, Too. Joy Jacobs. LC 01-67319. 375p. 1981. pap. 10.99 (0-87509-304-3) Chr Pubns.

They Whisper. Robert Olen Butler. 352p. 1995. pap. 10.95 (0-14-024393-3, Penguin Bks) Viking Penguin.

They Who Tarry: A Doctrine of Translated Beings. R. Clayton Brough. 97p. 1976. 10.98 (0-88290-069-2) Horizon Utah.

They Who Would Be Free: Blacks' Search for Freedom, 1830-1861. Jane H. Pease & William H. Pease. (Blacks in the New World Ser.). 360p. 1990. pap. text ed. 14.95 (0-252-06143-8) U of Ill Pr.

They Won the War. Frank H. Simonds. LC 68-58813. (Essay Index Reprint Ser.). 1977. 17.95 (0-8369-0126-6) Ayer.

They Won't Demolish Me! Roch Carrier. Tr. by Sheila Fischman from FRE. 134p. 1974. reprint ed. pap. 7.95 (0-88784-328-X, Pub. by Hse of Anansi Pr CN) Genl Dist Srvs.

They Won't Love You If You Cry. Tr. by Sarah E. Sims. (Illus.). 300p. (C). 1989. write for info. (0-9621810-0-5) Tremont AL.

They Wore Garnet & Black. Don Barton. (Illus.). 330p. 1986. 14.95 (0-9615503-0-9) Spur Pubs.

They Work at the Same Place: Divorce Simulation. David W. Felder. 44p. 1996. pap. text ed. 8.95 (0-910959-93-5, B&G 18D) Wellington Pr.

They Work for Tomorrow. Robert M. Bartlett. LC 70-111813. (Essay Index Reprint Ser.). 1977. 19.95 (0-8369-1592-5) Ayer.

They Worked All Their Lives: Women of the Urban Poor in England, 1880-1939. Carl Chinn. LC 87-36701. 199p. 1989. text ed. 29.95 (0-7190-2437-4, Pub. by Manchester Univ Pr UK) St Martin.

They Would Never Be Friends. Lawrence Walsh & Suella Walsh. Ed. by Myrna Kemnitz. (Illus.). 158p. (Orig.). (J). (gr. 5-8). 1996. pap. 6.99 (0-88092-158-7) Royal Fireworks.

They Write Their Dreams on the Rock Forever: Rock Writings in the Stein River Valley of British Columbia. Annie York et al. (Illus.). 340p. 1994. pap. 36.95 (0-88922-331-9) Genl Dist Srvs.

They Write Their Own Sentences: The FBI Handwriting Analysis Manual. (Illus.). 56p. 1987. reprint ed. pap. 8.00 (0-87364-446-8) Paladin Pr.

They Wrote for Children Too: An Annotated Bibliography of Children's Literature by Famous Writers for Adults. Compiled by Marilyn F. Apseloff. LC 89-2194. (Bibliographies & Indexes in World Literature Ser.: No. 20). 216p. 1989. text ed. 59.95 (0-313-25981-X, ACL/) Greenwood.

They Wrote on Clay: The Babylonian Tablets Speak Today. Edward Chiera. Ed. by George G. Cameron. LC 38-27631. (Illus.). 251p. 1956. pap. text ed. 13.95 (0-226-10425-7, P2) U Ch Pr.

They Wrote Their Own Headlines: American Women Journalists. Nancy Whitelaw. LC 93-50818. (World Writers Ser.). (Illus.). 124p. (YA). (gr. 6 up). 1994. lib. bdg. 17.95 (1-883846-06-4) M Reynolds.

*__They'll Hang Billy for Sure.__ large type ed. Marshall Grover. (Linford Western Library). 288p. 1997. pap. 16.99 (0-7089-7987-4, Linford) Ulverscroft.

They're a Very Successful Family! The Vagaries & Vicissitudes of Upscaling It in the Suburbs. Joseph Farris. (Illus.). 112p. (Orig.). 1989. pap. 6.95 (0-930753-08-9) Spect Ln Pr.

They're All Afraid. Leonard Peterson. (Illus.). 161p. 1981. pap. 8.95 (0-7725-5032-8) Genl Dist Srvs.

They're All Crooks! A Guide to Auto & RV Buying. J. D. Gallant. 1994. 7.95 (1-884046-57-6) Quill Pubng.

*__They're Cows, We're Pigs.__ Carmen Boullosa. Tr. by Leland H. Chambers from SPA. LC 96-40086. 192p. 1997. 22.00 (0-8021-1610-8, Grove) Grove-Atltic.

*__They're Different: A Child's Book about Prejudice.__ Roxanne Heyl. (Illus.). 16p. (J). (gr. 1-5). 1996. pap. 16.00 (0-8059-3961-X) Dorrance.

They're Going to Kill My Son. Shirley Dicks. Ed. by Joan Dunphy. LC 92-60563. 297p. 1992. 22.95 (0-88282-112-1) New Horizon NJ.

They're Gonna Settle Out of Court, Herman. Jim Unger. (Herman Collection). (Illus.). 104p. (Orig.). 1989. pap. 6.95 (0-8362-1850-7) Andrews & McMeel.

They're Never Too Young for Books: A Guide to Children's Books Ages 1-8. Edythe M. McGovern & Helen D. Muller. 342p. 1994. pap. 14.95 (0-87975-858-9) Prometheus Bks.

They're Not Dumb, They're Different: Stalking the Second Tier. rev. ed. Sheila Tobias. 94p. (Orig.). 1990. pap. 5.95 (0-963504-0-4) Res Corp.

They're Off. Anne Alcock. 144p. 1990. pap. 35.00 (0-85131-299-3, Pub. by J A Allen & Co UK) St Mut.

They're Off! Horse Racing at Saratoga. Edward Hotaling. LC 95-7703. (Illus.). 360p. 1995. 45.00 (0-8156-0350-9) Syracuse U Pr.

They're Off! The Story of the Pony Express. Cheryl Harness. LC 95-43534. (Illus.). (J). (gr. 2-5). 1996. 16.00 (0-689-80523-3, S&S Bks Young Read) S&S Childrens.

*__They're Playing Our Song: Conversations with America's Classic Songwriters.__ 2nd ed. Max Wilk. LC 96-46835. (Illus.). 296p. 1997. reprint ed. pap. 14.95 (0-306-80746-7) Da Capo.

They're Playing Our Song: Vocal Selections. (Illus.). 040p. 1981. pap. 8.95 (0-88188-117-1, 00312430) H Leonard.

They're Torturing Teachers in Room 104. Jerry Piasecki. 144p. (YA). 1992. mass mkt. 3.50 (0-553-48024-3) Bantam.

They're Yodeling Rock & Roll Songs. Al Blair. 6p. 1988. pap. 3.95 (0-930366-51-4) Northcountry Pub.

They've Got Rockies in Their Heads! The Colorado Rockies' First Season...from the Fans' Point of View. Lew Cady. (Illus.). 296p. (Orig.). 1993. pap. 10.00 (0-9639257-0-9) Hindsight Hist.

Thiagaraja: A Great Musician Saint. M. S. Aiyar. 238p. 1986. reprint ed. 20.00 (0-8364-1766-6, Pub. by Usha II) S Asia.

Thialand's Turn: Profile of a New Dragon, Vol. 1. Elliott F. Kulick. 1994. text ed. 19.95 (0-312-12188-1) St Martin.

Thiamin: Twenty Years of Progress, Vol. 378. Ed. by Henry Z. Sable & Clark J. Gubler. 472p. 1982. 102.00 (0-89766-145-1); pap. 102.00 (0-89766-146-X) NY Acad Sci.

Thiamin Diphosphate & Its Catalytic Functions. L. O. Krampitz. LC 77-98063. (E. R. Squibb Lectures on Chemistry of Microbial Products: No. 1968). (Illus.). 77p. reprint ed. pap. 25.00 (0-7837-0858-0, 2041166) Bks Demand.

Thiamin Pyrophosphate Biochemistry: Fundamen Pyruvate Decarboxylas & Transketolase, 2 vols., Vol. I. Ed. by A. Schellenberger & R. L. Showen. LC 87-10367. 176p. 1988. 102.00 (0-8493-4682-7, QP772, CRC Reprint) Franklin.

Thiamin Pyrophosphate Biochemistry: Fundamen Pyruvate Decarboxylas & Transketolase, 2 vols., Vol. II. Ed. by A. Schellenberger & R. L. Showen. LC 87-10367. 192p. 1988. 105.00 (0-8493-4683-5, QP772, CRC Reprint) Franklin.

Thiamine. Ed. by Clark J. Gubler et al. LC 75-29485. 403p. reprint ed. pap. 114.90 (0-317-28657-9, 2055087) Bks Demand.

Thian Ti Hwui: The Hung-League. Gustave Schlegel. LC 73-12558. (Illus.). reprint ed. 53.00 (0-404-11218-8) AMS Pr.

Thibault, 5 tomes, 1. Roger Martin Du Gard. (Folio Ser.: Nos. 788, 140, 164, 165, & 189). (FRE.). 1959. pap. 12.95 (2-07-036788-6) Schoenhof.

Thibault, 5 tomes, 2. Roger Martin Du Gard. (Folio Ser.: Nos. 788, 140, 164, 165, & 189). (FRE.). 1959. pap. 10.95 (2-07-036140-3) Schoenhof.

Thibault, 5 tomes, 3. Roger Martin Du Gard. (Folio Ser.: Nos. 788, 140, 164, 165, & 189). (FRE.). 1959. pap. 9.95 (2-07-036164-0) Schoenhof.

Thibault, 5 tomes, 4. Roger Martin Du Gard. (Folio Ser.: Nos. 788, 140, 164, 165, & 189). (FRE.). 1959. 9.95 (2-07-036165-9) Schoenhof.

Thibault, 5 tomes, 5. Roger Martin Du Gard. (Folio Ser.: Nos. 788, 140, 164, 165, & 189). (FRE.). 1959. pap. 10.95 (2-07-036189-6) Schoenhof.

Thibault 1: Le Cahier Gris; Le Penitencier; La Belle Saison. Roger M. Du Gard. (FRE.). 1976. pap. 16.95 (0-7859-2885-5) Fr & Eur.

Thibault 2: La Consultation; La Sorelina; La Mort du Pere. Roger M. Du Gard. (FRE.). 1972. pap. 12.95 (0-7859-2859-6) Fr & Eur.

Thibault 3: L'Ete 1914, 3 vols., Pt. 1. Roger M. Du Gard. 1972. Part 1. pap. 12.95 (0-7859-2861-8) Fr & Eur.

Thibault 3: L'Ete 1914, 3 vols., Pt. 2. Roger M. Du Gard. 1972. Part 2. pap. 12.95 (0-7859-2862-6) Fr & Eur.

Thibault 3: L'Ete 1914, 3 vols., Pt. 3. Roger M. Du Gard. 1972. Part 3. pap. 12.95 (0-7859-2864-2) Fr & Eur.

Thibodeau, Health & Disease SG. Swisher. 335p. 1992. pap. 12.95 (0-8016-6409-8) Mosby Yr Bk.

Thibodeau, Structure & Function: Study Guide. 9th ed. Swisher. 288p. 1991. pap. 12.95 (0-8016-6407-1) Mosby Yr Bk.

Thibodeaux & Richard's Cajun Cookbook: Recipes since 1845. Elizabeth E. Thibodeaux. Ed. by Shannon Thorn. (Illus.). 120p. 12.50 (0-9643373-0-4) PTH.

Thick & Darksome Veil: The Rhetoric of Hawthorne's Sketches, Prefaces, & Essays. Thomas R. Moore. 192p. 1994. text ed. 37.50 (1-55553-184-9) NE U Pr.

Thick & Thin: Moral Argument at Home & Abroad. Michael Walzer. LC 93-43201. (Frank M. Covey, Jr., Loyola Lectures in Political Analysis). (C). 1996. pap. text ed. 10.00 (0-268-01897-9) U of Notre Dame Pr.

Thick & Thin Films in Microelectronics. 1993. 2,650.00 (0-89336-942-X, GB-128R) BCC.

Thick & Thin Films in Microelectronics. Business Communications Co., Inc. Staff. 151p. 1990. 2,650.00 (0-89336-729-X, GB-128) BCC.

Thick As Thieves. Franklin W. Dixon. (Hardy Boys Casefiles Ser.: No. 29). (Orig.). (YA). (gr. 6 up). 1991. pap. 3.50 (0-671-74663-4, Archway) PB.

Thick As Thieves. Tony Marchant. Incl. Dealt With. 1988. (0-318-57268-0); London Calling. 1988. (0-318-57269-9, Pub. by Methuen UK); 44p. (C). 1988. pap. 7.95 (0-413-51070-0, A0292, Pub. by Methuen UK) Heinemann.

Thick as Thieves. Patrick Quinn. LC 94-28424. 1995. 20.00 (0-517-70009-3, Crown) Crown Pub Group.

Thick As Thieves. Patrick Quinn. 288p. 1996. reprint ed. mass mkt. 5.99 (0-425-15259-6) Berkley Pub.

Thick Face, Black Heart: The Path to Thriving, Winning & Succeeding. Chin-Ning Chu. 400p. 1994. pap. 13.99 (0-446-67020-0) Warner Bks.

Thick Face, Black Heart: Thriving, Winning & Succeeding in Life's Every Endeavor. Chin-Ning Chu. 400p. 1992. 26.00 (0-929638-28-X) AMC Pub CA.

T

An Asterisk (*) at the beginning of an entry indicates that the title is appearing in BIP for the first time.

Thick Film Sensors. Ed. by M. Prudenziati. LC 94-29429. (Handbook of Sensors & Actuators Ser.: 1). 482p. 1994. 168.75 (0-444-89723-2) Elsevier.
Thick Plate Working (Two) 1990. 50.00 (0-685-05797-6) St Mut.
Thick Post-Devonian Sediment Cover over New York State: Evidence from Fluid-Inclusion, Organic Maturation, Clay Diagenesis, & Stable Isotope Studies. Golam Sarwar & Gerald M. Friedman. (Lecture Notes in Earth Sciences Ser.: Vol. 58). 1995. write for info. (0-387-59458-2) Spr-Verlag.
Thick Post-Devonian Sediment Cover over New York State: Evidence from Fluid-Inclusion, Organic Maturation, Clay Diagenesis, & Stable Isotope Studies. Golam Sarwar & Gerald M. Friedman. (Lecture Notes in Earth Sciences Ser.: Vol. 58). 1995. 54.95 (3-540-59458-2) Spr-Verlag.
Thick Seam Mining - Problems & Issues: Proceedings of the International Symposium 19-21 November 1992. Ed. by T. N. Singh & Bharat B. Dhar. (Illus.). 811p. (C). 1993. text ed. 95.00 (90-5410-244-6, Pub. by A A Balkema NE) Ashgate Pub Co.
Thick to Thin: Your Thirty-Day Diet Companion. Melissa Langston & Asunta Durso. (Orig.). 1992. pap. 2.95 (0-399-51703-0, Perigee Bks) Berkley Pub.
***Thickening & Gelling Agents for Food.** Ed. by Imeson. (Illus.). 272p. 1993. text ed. 162.95 (0-7514-0093-9, Pub. by Blackie Acad & Prof UK) Routledge Chapman & Hall.
Thickening Government. Paul C. Light. 217p. (C). 1995. 34.95 (0-8157-5250-4); pap. 14.95 (0-8157-5249-0) Brookings.
Thicker Than Blood. Alison Brooks. (Cyberpunk Ser.). 48p. 1993. pap. 9.00 (1-887801-40-5, Atlas Games) Trident MN.
Thicker Than Water. Linda Barlow & William G. Tapply. 416p. 1995. pap. 5.99 (0-451-40602-8, Sig) NAL-Dutton.
Thicker Than Water. Penelope Farmer. LC 92-53133. 208p. (J). (gr. 6-10). 1993. 16.95 (1-56402-178-5) Candlewick Pr.
Thicker Than Water. Penelope Farmer. LC 92-53133. (J). (gr. 6-10). 1995. pap. 4.99 (1-56402-519-5) Candlewick Pr.
Thicker Than Water. Hazel Sangster. 136p. 1996. pap. 11.95 (1-886028-17-6) Savage Pr.
Thicker Than Water: A Quinn Parker Mystery. Bruce Zimmerman. 368p. 1993. mass mkt. 4.50 (0-06-109026-3, Harp PBks) HarpC.
Thickhead. Haldun Taner. LC 88-82588. 172p. 8800. pap. 19.95 (0-948259-58-2) Dufour.
Thickhead: And Other Turkish Stories. Haldun Taner. Tr. by Geoffrey L. Lewis from TUR. LC 88-82588. 160p. (Orig.). 9100. pap. 21.00 (0-948259-59-0, Pub. by Forest Bks UK) Dufour.
Thickness Design: Asphalt Pavements for Air Carrier Airports. 3rd ed. (Illus.). 236p. 1987. 24.00 (0-318-23659-1, MS-11) Asphalt Inst.
Thickness Design: Asphalt Pavements for General Aviation. 3rd ed. (Illus.). 24p. 1987. 7.00 (0-318-23660-5, IS-154) Asphalt Inst.
Thickness Design: Asphalt Pavements for Heavy Wheel Loads. LC 85-73718. 76p. 1986. 14.00 (0-318-20069-4, MS-23) Asphalt Inst.
Thickness Design: Asphalt Pavements for Highways & Streets. 9th ed. 92p. 1990. 15.00 (0-318-13400-4, MS-1) Asphalt Inst.
***Thickness of Skin.** Clare McIntyre. 80p. (Orig.). 1996. pap. 13.95 (1-85459-350-1, Pub. by N Hern Bks UK) Theatre Comm.
Thidwick, the Big-Hearted Moose. Dr. Seuss. (Illus.). (J). (gr. k-3). 1962. lib. bdg. 15.99 (0-394-90086-3) Random Bks Yng Read.
Thidwick, the Big-Hearted Moose. Dr. Seuss. (Illus.). (J). (gr. k-3). 1966. 14.00 (0-394-80086-9) Random Bks Yng Read.
Thidwick the Big-Hearted Moose. Dr. Seuss. (Dr. Seuss Book & Cassette Classics Ser.). (Illus.). 48p. (J). (ps-6). 1993. 12.00 incl. audio (0-679-84338-8) Random Bks Yng Read.
***Thidwick's Paintbox Book.** 1997. pap. 2.75 (0-679-88514-5) Random Bks Yng Read.
***Thidwick's Rainbow.** Dr. Seuss. (Wubbulous Shaped Board Bks.). (J). 1997. pap. 4.99 (0-679-88610-9) Random Bks Yng Read.
Thiebaud Selects Thiebaud: A Forty-Year Survey from Private Collections. Stephen C. McGough. (Illus.). 56p. 1997. pap. 25.00 (1-884038-00-X) Crocker Art Mus.
Thief. Mark Dunster. 24p. (Orig.). 1983. pap. 4.00 (0-89642-097-3) Linden Pubs.
Thief. Megan W. Turner. LC 95-41040. 224p. (YA). (gr. 5 up). 1996. 15.00 (0-688-14627-9) Greenwillow.
Thief, Vol. 8. Nancy N. Rue. LC 96-8551. (Christian Heritage Ser.: Bk. 8). (J). 1996. pap. 5.99 (1-56179-479-1) Focus Family.
Thief: And Other Stories. Georg Heym. Tr. by Susan Bennett. 112p. 1994. 29.95 (1-870352-68-8, Pub. by Libris UK); pap. 9.95 (1-870352-48-3, Pub. by Libris UK) Paul & Co Pubs.
Thief see It's Your Choice
***Thief among Statues.** Donn Kushner. (Illus.). 72p. (J). (gr. 3-7). 1996. pap. 4.95 (1-55037-289-0, Pub. by Annick CN) Firefly Bks Ltd.
***Thief Among Us.** Golden Books Staff. (Aladdin Ser.). (J). 1997. pap. text ed. 2.29 (0-307-03445-3, Golden Books) Western Pub.
Thief & the Dogs. Naguib Mahfouz. 160p. 1989. pap. 11.95 (0-385-26462-3) Doubleday.
Thief & the Dogs: Les Wil Kelab. Naguib Mahfouz. (ARA.). 1976. pap. 9.95 (0-86685-158-5) Intl Bk Ctr.
Thief from Five Points. Lucille Travis. LC 94-27061. (Ben & Zack Ser.: Bk. 2). (Illus.). 168p. (Orig.). (J). (gr. 4-8). 1995. pap. 5.99 (0-8010-8916-6) Baker Bks.
Thief in the Green Van. Bob Wright. Tr. by Phyllis Bourne & Eugenia Tusquets. (Tom & Ricky Spanish-English Readers Ser.). (Illus.). 96p. (ENG & SPA.). (J). (gr. 1-5). 1988. pap. 4.95 (0-87879-666-5) High Noon Bks.
Thief in the Night. Sally Cheney. (Historical Ser.: No. 711). 1992. mass mkt. 3.99 (0-373-28712-7, 1-28712-7) Harlequin Bks.
Thief in the Night. A. R. Plumb. (Further Adventures of Aladdin Ser.: No. 1). (Illus.). 64p. (J). (gr. k-3). 1994. pap. 3.50 (0-7868-4016-1) Disney Pr.
Thief in the Night. William Sears. 320p. 1961. pap. 5.25 (0-85398-008-X) G Ronald Pub.
***Thief in the Night.** large type ed. Elizabeth Ferrars. LC 97-15409. 1997. write for info. (0-7838-8234-3) G K Hall.
Thief in the Village: And Other Stories of Jamaica. James Berry. 156p. (J). (gr. 4 up). 1990. pap. 4.99 (0-14-034357-1, Puffin) Puffin Bks.
Thief of Always. Clive Barker. 288p. 1993. mass mkt. 5.99 (0-06-109146-4, Harp PBks) HarpC.
***Thief of Always.** Clive Barker. 1997. pap. 3.99 (0-06-105769-X, Harp PBks) HarpC.
Thief of Bagdad. Achmed Abdullah. 248p. 1987. 55.00 (1-85077-900-7, Pub. by Darf Pubs Ltd UK) St Mut.
Thief of Bagdad. Illus. & Adapted by P. Craig Russell. 120p. 1987. pap. 12.95 (0-89865-523-4, Starblaze) Donning Co.
Thief of Bagdad. limited ed. Illus. & Adapted by P. Craig Russell. 120p. 1987. 40.00 (0-89865-525-0, Starblaze) Donning Co.
Thief of Dreams: A Novel. John Yount. LC 94-13620. 240p. 1994. reprint ed. pap. 10.95 (0-87074-375-9) SMU Press.
Thief of Hearts. Patricia Gaffney. 448p. 1996. mass mkt. 5.99 (0-8439-4075-1, Leisure Bks) Dorchester Pub Co.
Thief of Hearts. Tess Gerritsen. (Intrigue Ser.). 1995. mass mkt. 3.50 (0-373-22328-5, 1-22328-8) Harlequin Bks.
***Thief of Hearts.** Rita Herron. 1997. mass mkt. 1.78 (0-8217-5779-2) Kensgtn Pub Corp.
Thief of Hearts. Teresa Medeiros. 432p. 1994. mass mkt. 5.50 (0-553-56332-7) Bantam.
Thief of Hearts. Laurence Yep. LC 94-18703. 208p. (J). (gr. 5-9). 1995. 14.95 (0-06-025341-X, HarpT); lib. bdg. 14.89 (0-06-025342-8, HarpT) HarpC.
***Thief of Hearts.** Laurence Yep. LC 94-18703. 208p. (J). (gr. 5 up). 1997. pap. 4.95 (0-06-440591-5, Trophy) HarpC Child Bks.
Thief of Hearts. large type ed. Teresa Medeiros. LC 94-40173. 623p. 1995. lib. bdg. 20.95 (0-7862-0372-2) Thorndike Pr.
***Thief of Hermes.** Ru Emerson. (Xena Warrior Princess Ser.: No. 3). 1997. mass mkt. 5.99 (1-57207-237-7) Blvd Books.
***Thief of Hermes.** Ru Emerson. (Xena Warrior Princess Ser.). 1997. mass mkt. 5.99 (1-57297-232-7) Blvd Books.
Thief of Kalimar. Graham Diamond. 1979. mass mkt. 2.95 (0-449-14214-0, GM) Fawcett.
***Thief of Light.** David Ramus. 384p. 1997. mass mkt. 6.50 (0-06-109420-X, Harp PBks) HarpC.
Thief of Light. large type ed. David Ramus. 1996. pap. 22.95 (1-56895-304-6) Wheeler Pub.
Thief of Light: A Novel. David Ramus. LC 95-21754. 320p. 1995. 23.00 (0-06-017664-4, HarpT) HarpC.
Thief of Lives. Kit Reed. 192p. 1992. 24.95 (0-8262-0850-9) U of Mo Pr.
Thief of Love. Linda Walker. 208p. (Orig.). 1994. mass mkt. 3.99 (0-515-11355-7) Jove Pubns.
Thief of My Heart. Rexanne Becnel. 400p. 1991. mass mkt. 5.99 (0-440-20622-7) Dell.
Thief of Peirce: The Letters of Kenneth Laine Ketner & Walker Percy. Walker Percy & Kenneth L. Letner. Ed. by Patrick H. Samway. LC 95-14835. 350p. 1995. text ed. 45.00 (0-87805-810-9) U Pr of Miss.
Thief of Reason: Oscar Wilde & Modern Ireland. Richard Pine. LC 95-36425. 256p. 1995. text ed. 35.00 (0-312-15813-0) St Martin.
Thief of Souls. Darian North. LC 96-43645. 1997. pap. 23.95 (0-525-94200-9) NAL-Dutton.
Thief of the Deep. Jon Coon. LC 93-16853. 400p. (Orig.). 1993. pap. 11.95 (0-9623389-9-0) Aqua Quest.
Thief of Time. Tony Hillerman. LC 87-46147. 368p. 1990. reprint ed. mass mkt. 6.99 (0-06-100004-3, PL) HarpC.
Thief on Morgan's Plantation. Lisa Banim. (Mysteries in Time Ser.). (Illus.). 80p. (J). (gr. 4-6). 1995. lib. bdg. 13.95 (1-881889-62-9) Silver Moon.
Thief on Morgan's Plantation see Spy in the King's Colony; A Thief on Morgan's Plantation; An Art Bandit on Sugar Hill; A Conspiracy in Washington
Thief River Falls Run. David Robbins. (Endworld Ser.: No. 2). 256p. 1992. mass mkt., pap. text ed. 3.50 (0-8439-3106-X) Dorchester Pub Co.
Thief-Taker General: Jonathan Wild & the Emergence of Crime & Corruption As a Way of Life in Eighteenth-Century England. Gerald Howson. 338p. (C). 1985. 44.95 (0-88738-032-8) Transaction Pubs.
Thiefless City & the Contest Between Food & Throat: Four Eastern Turki Texts. Ed. & Tr. by Gunnar Jarring. (Scripta Minora Series, 1989-1990: No. 1). 87p. (Orig.). 1989. pap. 31.00 (91-22-01295-8) Coronet Bks.
Thief's Challenge 2. Terry K. Amthor. (Advanced Dungeons & Dragons, 2nd Edition: One-on-One Adventures Ser.). 1995. 6.95 (0-7869-0135-7) TSR Inc.
Thief's Daughter. Alan Marks. (J). (ps-3). 1994. 11.00 (0-374-37481-3) FS&G.
Thief's Journal. Jean Genet. Tr. by Bernard Frechtman from FRE. LC 87-12095. 272p. 1987. pap. 12.00 (0-8021-3014-3, Grove) Grove-Atltic.
Thief's Mistress. Gayle Feyrer. 400p. 1996. mass mkt. 5.99 (0-440-21778-4) Dell.
Thiem, Christoph & August-A Drean & a Promise. Marilyn Lind. LC 81-90330. (Illus.). 187p. (Orig.). 1981. text ed. 35.00 (0-937463-01-9); pap. text ed. 30.00 (0-937463-02-7) Linden Tree.
Thieme-Becker Lexicon, 37 vols. Set. 5,000.00 (0-317-54927-8) Apollo.
***Thieme Leximed: Dictionary, Vol. 1.** P. Reuter & C. Reuter. 400p. (ENG & GER.). 1995. 140.00 (3-13-100471-1, Pub. by G Thieme GW) Thieme Med Pubs.
***Thieme Leximed: Dictionary, Vol. 2.** P. Reuter & C. Reuter. 841p. (ENG & GER.). 1996. 140.00 (3-13-100491-6, Pub. by G Thieme GW) Thieme Med Pubs.
***Thiepval: Somme.** Michael Stedman. (Battleground Europe Ser.). 1997. pap. text ed. 14.95 (0-85052-473-3, Pub. by L Cooper Bks UK) Trans-Atl Phila.
Thiere Des Classischen Alterthums in Culturgeschichtlicher Beziehung. Otto Keller. (Illus.). 430p. 1887. write for info. (3-487-09424-X) G Olms Pubs.
Thiers, Seventeen Ninety-Seven to Eighteen Seventy-Seven: A Political Life. J. P. Bury & R. P. Tombs. 272p. 1986. text ed. 45.00 (0-04-944013-6) Routledge Chapman & Hall.
Thieves at Heart. Alina Adams. 192p. (Orig.). 1995. mass mkt. 3.99 (0-380-78293-6) Avon.
Thieves at Work: An Employer's Guide to Combating Workplace Dishonesty. LC 88-20806. (BNA Special Reports). 1988. 95.00 (1-55871-013-2) BNA Plus.
Thieves in the Schoolhouse. Lawrence Moores. LC 78-50636. 1979. 22.95 (0-87949-119-1) Ashley Bks.
Thieves Like Us: A Novel. Edward Anderson. LC 92-29959. 1993. 14.95 (0-8061-2503-4) U of Okla Pr.
***Thieves' Market.** A. I. Bezzerides. LC 97-18530. 1998. pap. write for info. (0-520-20746-7) U CA Pr.
Thieves of Tharbad. Rich Meyer. (Illus.). 36p. (J). (gr. 10-12). 1985. 7.00 (0-915795-35-3, 8050) Iron Crown Ent Inc.
Thieves of Tyburn Square: Elizabeth Fry. Dave Jackson & Neta Jackson. LC 95-43836. (Trailblazer Ser.). (Illus.). 144p. (Orig.). (J). (gr. 3-8). 1995. pap. 5.99 (1-55661-470-5) Bethany Hse.
Thieves on Wall Street: Survival Guide for the Investor. Gunther Karger. (Illus.). 228p. (Orig.). 1995. pap. 16.95 (0-9645979-1-8) Discov Grp.
Thieves' World. Claire Sterling. 1994. 23.00 (0-671-74997-8) S&S Trade.
Thieves' World, No. 2. Robert Asprin & Lynn Abbey. Ed. by Kay Reynolds & Laurie Sutton. LC 85-20471. (Thieves' World Graphics Ser.). (Illus.). 64p. pap. 3.95 (0-89865-416-5, Starblaze) Donning Co.
Thieves' World Graphics. Robert L. Asprin & Lynn Abbey. Ed. by Laurie Sutton. (Thieves' World Graphics Ser.: No. 6). (Illus.). 64p. (Orig.). 1987. pap. 4.95 (0-89865-522-6, Starblaze) Donning Co.
Thieves' World Graphics, No. 1. limited ed. Robert L. Asprin & Lynn Abbey. LC 86-4392. (Thieves' World Graphics Ser.). (Illus.). 184p. (Orig.). 1986. 40.00 (0-89865-478-5, Starblaze) Donning Co.
Thieves' World Graphics, No. 3. Robert L. Asprin & Lynn Abbey. (Thieves' World Graphics Ser.). (Illus.). 64p. (Orig.). 1986. pap. 3.95 (0-89865-457-2, Starblaze) Donning Co.
Thieves' World Graphics, No. 4. Robert L. Asprin & Lynn Abbey. (Thieves' World Graphics Ser.). (Illus.). 64p. (Orig.). 1986. pap. 3.95 (0-89865-458-0, Starblaze) Donning Co.
Thieves' World Graphics, No. 5. Robert L. Asprin & Lynn Abbey. (Thieves' World Graphics Ser.). (Illus.). 64p. (Orig.). 1987. pap. 3.95 (0-89865-521-8, Starblaze) Donning Co.
Thieving Magpie & Other Tales. Timur H. Uckun. 152p. 1995. pap. 12.95 (0-929968-41-7) Another Chicago Pr.
***Thighs to Die for.** Ann Piccirillo. LC 97-2162. 1997. pap. text ed. 12.95 (0-7611-0556-5) Workman Pub.
***Thighs to Die For: With Custom Exercise Pouch.** Ann Piccirillo. 1997. pap. text ed. 77.70 (0-7611-0892-0) Workman Pub.
Thigmotropism. Lee Pennington. Ed. by Mary E. O'Dell. (Green River Writers - Poetry Ser.). 54p. (Orig.). 1993. 17.50 (0-9623666-3-3); pap. 11.95 (0-9623666-4-1) Green Rvr Writers.
Thigmotropism. limited ed. Lee Pennington & Georgia Wallace. Ed. by Mary E. O'Dell. (Chapbook Ser.). 24p. (Orig.). 1996. pap. 6.00 (0-9623666-7-6) Green Rvr Writers.
Thilian Solution. Anthony Hodnett. 32p. (Orig.). 1993. pap. 3.95 (1-56411-058-3) Untd Bros & Sis.
Thimbelina & the Notion Parade. Cheryl Arrants & Dennis Arrants. (Sew Young Ser.). (Illus.). 32p. (Orig.). (J). (gr. k-4). 1983. pap. text ed. 2.50 (0-943704-03-0) Arrants & Assoc.
Thimble of Soil: A Woman's Quest for Land. Linda K. Hubalek. LC 96-83113. (Trail of Thread Ser.: Bk. 2). (Illus.). 120p. (Orig.). (J). (gr. 4-12). 1996. pap. 9.95 (1-886652-07-4) Butterfld Bks.
Thimble Summer. Elizabeth Enright. 144p. (J). (gr. k-6). 1987. pap. 3.99 (0-440-48681-5, YB BDD) BDD Bks Young Read.
Thimble Summer. Elizabeth Enright. LC 38-27586. (Illus.). 124p. (J). (gr. 6 up). 1938. 16.95 (0-8050-0306-1, Bks Young Read) H Holt & Co.
Thimbleberries Book of Quilts: Quilts of All Sizes Plus Decorative Accessories for Your Home. Lynette Jensen. LC 94-22955. 1994. 27.95 (0-87596-630-6) Rodale Pr Inc.
***Thimbleberries Book of Quilts: Quilts of All Sizes Plus Decorative Accessories for Your Home.** Lynette Jensen. (Illus.). 256p. 1998. pap. 15.95 (0-87596-963-1) Rodale Pr Inc.
***Thimbleberry Collection 1.** Rylant. 1998. write for info. (0-15-201081-5) HarBrace.
Thimbleriggers: The Law vs. Governor Marvin Mandel. Bradford Jacobs. LC 84-7879. 1984. 36.00 (0-8018-3170-9) Johns Hopkins.
Thimbles. Eleanor Johnson. 1989. pap. 25.00 (0-85263-619-9, Pub. by Shire UK) St Mut.
Thin Air. Greg Child. 320p. 1993. mass mkt. 5.99 (0-440-21450-5, LE) Dell.
Thin Air. Gerald Hammond. 144p. 1994. 17.95 (0-312-11339-0) St Martin.
Thin Air. Robert B. Parker. 1995. pap. 24.95 (0-7871-0277-6, Dove Bks) Dove Audio.
Thin Air. Robert B. Parker. 1995. 21.95 (0-399-14020-4, Putnam) Putnam Pub Group.
Thin Air. Robert B. Parker. 304p. 1996. reprint ed. mass mkt. 6.99 (0-425-15290-1) Berkley Pub.
Thin Air: A Spenser Novel. large type ed. Robert B. Parker. LC 95-15712. 1995. 26.95 (1-56895-212-0) Wheeler Pub.
Thin Black Lines Rides Again: General. Scott Sinclair et al. (General). 100p. (C). 1994. pap. 15.95 (0-85598-305-1, Pub. by Oxfam UK) Humanities.
Thin Blood. Zinsmeister. 22.95 (0-06-016806-4, HarpT) HarpC.
Thin Blue Line: International Peacekeeping & Its Future. Indar J. Rikhye et al. LC 74-79977. 387p. reprint ed. pap. 110.30 (0-8357-8348-0, 2033874) Bks Demand.
Thin Blue Lines: Cartoons for the United Nations: A Light-Hearted Look at Peace, Human Rights, the Environment & Poverty to Mark the 50th Anniversary of the U. N. Ed. by Mark Bryant. (Illus.). 82p. (Orig.). 1995. pap. 17.95 (0-85052-466-0, Pub. by L Cooper Bks UK) Trans-Atl Phila.
Thin Book. Jeane E. Westin. 1994. 7.98 (1-56731-030-3, MJF Bks) Fine Comms.
Thin Books: Strategies & Meditations for Fat Free, Guilt Free, Binge Free Living. Jeane E. Westin. Ed. by Betty Christiansen. 500p. 1996. pap. 15.95 (1-56838-108-5) Hazelden.
Thin Cats: The Community Development Credit Union Movement in the United States. John Isbister. (Illus.). 212p. (Orig.). (C). 1994. pap. 13.00 (1-885641-04-4, B4) U CA Ctr Cooperatives.
***Thin Clients: Web-Based Client/Server Architecture & Applications.** Travis Dewire. 1997. pap. text ed. 49.95 (0-07-016738-9) McGraw.
***Thin Dark Line.** Tami Hoag. LC 96-29690. 496p. 1997. 22.95 (0-553-09960-4, Fanfare) Bantam.
***Thin Dark Line.** Tami Hoag. LC 97-15915. 1997. write for info. (1-56895-450-6, Compass) Wheeler Pub.
Thin Dimes. Janet Lowery. (New Texas Poetry Sampler Ser.). 20p. 1992. pap. 10.00 (0-930324-19-6) Wings Pr.
Thin Disguise. Frank Minirth et al. 1996. mass mkt. 5.99 (0-7852-7716-1) Nelson.
Thin-Film & Depth-Profile Analysis. Ed. by H. Oechsner. (Topics in Current Physics Ser.: Vol. 37). (Illus.). 225p. 1984. 69.95 (0-387-13320-8) Spr-Verlag.
Thin Film Coating. Ed. by H. Benkreira. 218p. 1994. 94.00 (0-85186-695-6, Q) CRC Pr.
***Thin Film Colour Sensors.** Daniel P. Poenar. (Illus.). 236p. (Orig.). 1996. pap. 72.50 (90-407-1343-X, Pub. by Delft U Pr NE) Coronet Bks.
Thin Film Device Applications. Kasturi L. Chopra & I. Kaur. LC 83-9632. (Illus.). 312p. 1983. 85.00 (0-306-41297-7, Plenum Pr) Plenum.
Thin Film Diamonds. Ed. by A. Lettington & J. W. Steed. LC 93-33950. 168p. (gr. 13). 1993. text ed. 71.95 (0-412-49630-5, Chap & Hall NY) Chapman & Hall.
Thin Film Growth Techniques for Low-Dimensional Structures. Ed. by R. F. Farrow et al. LC 87-22766. (NATO ASI Series B, Physics: Vol. 163). 562p. 1987. 125.00 (0-306-42686-2, Plenum Pr) Plenum.
Thin Film Interfaces & Interactions: Proceedings of the Symposium. Symposium on Thin Film Interfaces & Interactions. Ed. by John E. Baglin & John M. Poate. LC 80-66386. (Electrochemical Society Proceedings Ser.: No. 80-2). 545p. reprint ed. pap. 155.40 (0-685-16435-7, 2027362) Bks Demand.
Thin Film Phenomena-Interfaces & Interactions: Proceedingins of the Symposium, Atlanta, 1977. Electrochemical Society, Thin Film Phenomena-Interfaces & Interactions Symposium Staff. Ed. by John E. Baglin & John M. Poate. LC 77-91607. (Electrochemical Society Proceedings Ser.: Vol. 78-2). 536p. reprint ed. pap. 152.80 (0-317-08747-9, 2051978) Bks Demand.
***Thin Film Processes.** Ed. by G. S. Mathad et al. Date not set. 66.00 (1-56677-183-8, PV97-30) Electrochem Soc.
Thin Film Processes. Ed. by John L. Vossen & Werner Kern. 1978. text ed. 99.00 (0-12-728250-5) Acad Pr.
Thin Film Processes Two. Ed. by John L. Vossen & Werner Kern. (Illus.). 866p. 1991. text ed. 78.00 (0-12-728251-3) Acad Pr.
Thin Film Processing & Characterization of High-Temperature Superconductors. Ed. by James M. Harper et al. LC 87-73420. (Conference Proceedings Ser.: No. 165). 488p. 1988. lib. bdg. 70.00 (0-88318-365-X) Am Inst Physics.
Thin Film Resistive Sensors. Ed. by P. Ciureanu & S. Middelhoek. (Sensors Ser.). (Illus.). 512p. 1992. 210.00 (0-7503-0173-2) IOP Pub.
Thin Film Sensors. Richard K. Miller & Terri C. Walker. LC 88-84057. (Survey on Technology & Markets Ser.: No. 61). 50p. 1989. pap. text ed. 200.00 (1-55865-107-1) Future Tech Surveys.
Thin Film Solar Cells. Kasturi L. Chopra & Sunhit R. Das. 600p. 1983. 135.00 (0-306-41141-5, Plenum Pr) Plenum.
***Thin-Film Solid Ionic Devices & Materials.** Ed. by J. B. Bates. (Illus.). 232p. 1996. 47.00 (1-56677-117-X, PV95-22) Electrochem Soc.

Thin Film Structures & Phase Stability Vol. 187: Symposium Proceedings Ser. Ed. by B. M. Clemens & W. L. Johnson. 341p. 1991. text ed. 30.00 (*1-55899-076-3*) Materials Res.

Thin Film Technology Handbook. Aicha Elshabini-Riad et al. LC 96-36938. (Illus.). 800p. 1997. text ed. 89.50 (*0-07-019025-9*) McGraw.

Thin Film Transistor Technologies: Second International Symposium. Y. Kuo. 420p. 1995. 64.00 (*1-56677-094-7*, PV 94-35) Electrochem Soc.

***Thin Film Transistor Technologies III.** Ed. by Y. Kuo et al. (Illus.). 404p. 1997. 71.00 (*1-56677-173-0*, PV96-23) Electrochem Soc.

Thin Film/Diamond Industry Review. Ed. by Robert Moran. 261p. 1996. 1,500.00 (*1-56965-342-9*, DTF95) BCC.

Thin Films. K. D. Leaver et al. LC 75-153871. (Wykeham Science Ser.: No. 17). 120p. (C). 1971. 18.00 (*0-8448-1119-X*, Crane Russak) Taylor & Francis.

Thin Films. K. D. Leaver et al. (Wykeham Science Ser.: No.17). 120p. 1971. pap. 18.00 (*0-85109-230-6*) Taylor & Francis.

Thin Films: Deposition & Applications. Donald L. Smith. 1995. text ed. 69.95 (*0-07-058502-4*) McGraw.

Thin Films: Stresses & Mechanical Properties III. Ed. by W. D. Nix et al. (Symposium Proceedings Ser.: Vol. 239). 723p. 1992. text ed. 30.00 (*1-55899-133-6*) Materials Res.

Thin Films: Stresses & Mechanical Properties IV. T. P. Weihs. (Symposium Proceedings Ser.: Vol. 308). 775p. 1993. text ed. 72.00 (*1-55899-204-9*) Materials Res.

Thin Films: Stresses & Mechanical Properties V. Ed. by Paul H. Townsend et al. (MRS Symposium Proceedings Ser.: Vol. 356). 901p. 1995. 75.00 (*1-55899-257-X*) Materials Res.

Thin Films: Stresses & Mechanical Properties VI. Ed. by W. W. Gerberich et al. (MRS Symposium Proceedings Ser.: Vol. 436). 1997. 68.00 (*1-55899-339-8*, 436) Materials Res.

Thin Films: The Relationship of Structure to Properties: Symposium Held April 15-17, 1985, San Francisco, California, U. S. A. Materials Research Society Staff. Ed. by Carolyn Aita & K. S. SreeHarsha. LC 85-21485. (Materials Research Society Symposia Proceedings Ser.: No. 47). (Illus.). 306p. reprint ed. pap. 87.30 (*0-7837-1927-2*, 2042142) Bks Demand.

T

Thin Films Vol. 20: Organic Thin Films & Surfaces: Directions for the Nineties, Vol. 20. Ed. by Abraham Ulman. (Physics & Thin Films Ser.). (Illus.). 392p. 1995. text ed. 84.95 (*0-12-523485-6*) Acad Pr.

Thin Films Vol. 21: Homojunction & Quantum-Well Infrared Detectors, Vol. 21. Ed. by Maurice Francombe & John Vossen. (Illus.). 387p. 1995. boxed 99.00 (*0-12-533021-9*) Acad Pr.

Thin Films - Stresses & Mechanical Properties Vol. 130: Materials Research Society Symposium Proceedings. Ed. by J. C. Bravman et al. 402p. 1989. text ed. 30.00 (*1-55899-003-8*) Materials Res.

Thin Films - Stresses & Mechanical Properties II Vol. 188: Symposium Proceedings. Ed. by W. C. Oliver et al. 365p. 1990. text ed. 17.50 (*1-55899-077-1*) Materials Res.

Thin Films--Interfaces & Phenomena: Symposium Proceedings, Vol. 54. Ed. by R. J. Nemanich et al. (Materials Research Society Symposium Proceedings Ser.). 1986. text ed. 17.50 (*0-931837-19-7*) Materials Res.

***Thin Films--Structure & Morphology.** Ed. by R. C. Cammarata et al. LC 97-21318. (Materials Research Society Symposium Proceedings Ser.: No. 441). 1997. text ed. 68.00 (*1-55899-345-2*) Materials Res.

Thin Films & Small Particles: 5th Latin American Symposium on Surface Physics. Ed. by M. Cardona. 450p. (C). 1989. text ed. 93.00 (*9971-5-0720-X*) World Scientific Pub.

Thin Films & Surfaces for Bioactivity & Biomedical Applications: Materials Research Society Symposium Proceedings, Vol. 414. Ed. by C. M. Cotell et al. 1996. 65.00 (*1-55899-317-7*) Materials Res.

Thin Films by Chemical Vapour Deposition. C. E. Morosanu. (Thin Films Science & Technology Ser.: Vol. 7). 718p. 1990. 296.50 (*0-444-98801-7*, TFS 7) Elsevier.

Thin Films for Integrated Optics Applications: Materials Research Society Symposium Proceedings, Vol. 392. Ed. by Bruce W. Wessels et al. (MRS Symposium Proceedings Ser.: Vol. 392). 290p. 1995. text ed. 74.00 (*1-55899-295-2*, 392) Materials Res.

Thin-Films for Microelectronics. Business Communications Co., Inc. Staff. 150p. 1987. 1,950.00 (*0-89336-569-6*, GB-100) BCC.

Thin Films for Optical Coatings. Ed. by Rolf Hummel & Karl H. Guenther. 384p. 1995. 99.95 (*0-8493-2484-X*) CRC Pr.

Thin Films for Optical Systems. Flory. (Optical Engineering Ser.: Vol. 49). 608p. 1995. 165.00 (*0-8247-9633-0*) Dekker.

Thin Films for Photovoltaic & Related Device Applications. Ed. by C. Eberspacher et al. (MRS Symposium Proceedings Ser.: Vol. 426). 1996. 70.00 (*1-55899-329-0*, 426) Materials Res.

Thin Films in Tribology: Proceedings of the 19th Leeds-Lyon Symposium on Tribology Held at the Institute of Tribology, University of Leeds, U. K., 8-11 September 1992. Ed. by Duncan Dowson et al. LC 93-5673. (Tribology Ser.: No. 25). 762p. 1993. 279.75 (*0-444-89789-5*) Elsevier.

Thin Films, Modelling of Film Deposition for Microelectronic Applications Vol. 22: Advances in Research & Development, Vol. 22. Ed. by Stephen Rossnagel et al. (Illus.). 290p. (C). 1996. boxed 120.00 (*0-12-533022-7*) Acad Pr.

Thin Fine Line. Michael C. Giammatteo. (Illus.). (Orig.). (C). 1975. pap. 8.95 (*0-918428-05-X*) Sylvan Inst.

Thin Fire. Nanci Little. LC 93-6312. 1993. pap. 9.95 (*0-9630822-4-8*) Madwoman Pr.

Thin Foil Preparation for Electron Microscopy. Ed. by Peter J. Goodhew & A. M. Glauert. (Practical Methods in Electron Microscopy Ser.: Vol. II). 206p. 1986. pap. 31.50 (*0-444-80699-7*) Elsevier.

Thin for Life: 10 Keys to Success from People Who Have Lost Weight & Kept It Off. Anne M. Fletcher. LC 93-40218. 352p. (Orig.). 1994. 24.95 (*1-881527-30-1*) Chapters Pub.

***Thin for Life Daybook: A Journal of Personal Progress - Inspiration & Keys to Success from People Who Have Lost Weight & Kept It Off.** Anne Fletcher. Ed. by Rux Martin. 224p. 1998. 13.00 (*1-57630-039-0*) HM.

Thin Ghost, & Others. Montague R. James. LC 74-167454. (Short Story Index Reprint Ser.). 1977. reprint ed. 13.95 (*0-8369-3980-8*) Ayer.

***Thin Ice.** Marsha Qualey. LC 97-2083. (J). 1997. write for info. (*0-385-32298-4*) Delacorte.

***Thin Ice: Coming of Age in Canada.** Bruce McCall. 256p. 1997. 24.00 (*0-679-44847-0*) Random.

Thin Ice & Other Poems. Marcia Muth. LC 85-27958. 48p. (Orig.). 1987. pap. 4.95 (*0-86534-081-1*) Sunstone Pr.

Thin Ice & Other Risks: Stories. Gary Eller. LC 93-83978. (Minnesota Voices Project Ser.). 160p. (Orig.). 1994. pap. 9.95 (*0-89823-155-8*) New Rivers Pr.

***Thin Is Just a Four-Letter Word: Living Fit - For All Shapes & Sizes.** Dee Hakala. 1997. 19.95 (*0-316-33911-3*) Little.

Thin Kids: The Proven, Healthy, Sensible Program for Children. Mindy Cohen et al. (Illus.). 256p. 1985. pap. 9.95 (*0-8253-0277-3*) Beaufort Bks NY.

***Thin-Layer Chromatographic R Values of Toxicologically Relevant Substances on Standardized Systems: Report XVII of the DFG Commission for Clinical-Toxicological Analysis.** 2nd enl. rev. ed. Ed. by International Association of Forensic Toxicologists Staff. (Commission Reports of the Deutsche Forschungsgemeinschaft). (Illus.). 308p. 1993. 92.00 (*3-527-27397-2*, VCH) Wiley.

Thin-Layer Chromatographic Rf Values of Toxicologically Relevant Substances on Standardized Systems. Ed. by D. F. De Zeeuw. 223p. 1987. 70.00 (*0-89573-665-9*, VCH) Wiley.

Thin-Layer Chromatographic RF Values of Toxicologically Relevant Substances on Standardized Systems. 2nd enl. rev. ed. Rokus A. De Zeeuw et al. Ed. by International Association of Forensic Toxicologists Staff. 250p. 1992. 92.00 (*1-56081-183-8*, 0930-7958, VCH) Wiley.

Thin Layer Chromatography. R. J. Hamilton. LC 86-32531. (Analytical Chemistry by Open Learning Ser.). 129p. 1987. pap. text ed. 49.95 (*0-471-91377-4*) Wiley.

Thin-Layer Chromatography: A CAMAG Bibliography. Ed. by Dieter Janchen. 54p. (Orig.). (C). 1993. pap. text ed. 30.00 (*1-56806-353-9*) DIANE Pub.

Thin-Layer Chromatography: A Laboratory Handbook. 2nd ed. Ed. by E. Stahl. Tr. by M. R. Ashworth. LC 69-14538. (Illus.). 1990. 224.00 (*0-387-04736-0*) Spr-Verlag.

Thin-Layer Chromatography: Techniques & Applications. 3rd ed. Joseph Sherma. LC 93-43297. (Chromatographic Science Ser.: Vol. 66). 464p. 1994. 185.00 (*0-8247-9171-1*) Dekker.

Thin-Layer Chromatography Vol. 1B: Reagents & Detection Methods. Hellmut Jork et al. 496p. 1994. 130.00 (*1-56081-103-X*, VCH) Wiley.

***Thin-Layer Chromatography Vol. 1B: Reagents & Detection Methods, Physical & Chemical Detection Methods, Activation Reactions, Reagent Series, Reagents II.** Hellmut Jork et al. (Illus.). xviii, 496p. 1994. 130.00 (*3-527-28205-X*, VCH) Wiley.

Thin-Layer Chromatography for Binding Media Analysis. Mary F. Striegel & Jo Hill. LC 96-19184. (Scientific Tools for Conservation Ser.). (Illus.). 184p. (Orig.). 1996. pap. 25.00 (*0-89236-390-8*, Getty Conservation Inst) J P Getty Trust.

Thin-Layer Chromatography with Flame Ionization Detection. M. Ranny. (C). 1987. lib. bdg. 115.50 (*90-277-1973-X*) Kluwer Ac.

***Thin Layer Deposition: Highlighting PVD.** (Report Ser.: No. GB-186B). 209p. 1996. 2,750.00 (*1-56965-237-6*) BCC.

***Thin Layer Deposition Technologies: Highlighting Implantation & Epitaxy, Plasma, Thermal & Ion.** (Report Ser.: No. GB-186C). 109p. 1996. 2,750.00 (*1-56965-238-4*) BCC.

***Thin Layer Deposition Technologies: Opportunities for the Future: Thin Layer Deposition: Highlighting CVD.** (Report Ser.: No. GB-186A). 157p. 1996. 2,750.00 (*1-56965-349-6*) BCC.

Thin Liquid Films. Ivanov. (Surfactant Science Ser.: Vol. 29). 1160p. 1988. 275.00 (*0-8247-7763-8*) Dekker.

Thin Man. Dashiell Hammett. 224p. 1989. pap. 9.00 (*0-679-72263-7*, Vin) Random.

Thin Man. Dashiell Hammett. 1992. pap. 9.00 (*0-394-23905-9*, Vin) Random.

Thin Man. Dashiell Hammett. 1992. pap. 9.00 (*0-679-74092-9*) Random.

Thin Man. Dashiell Hammett. 272p. 1994. 35.00 (*1-883402-70-0*) S&S Trade.

Thin Man. Dashiell Hammett. 736p. 1991. Not sold separately (*0-615-00023-1*) Random Hse Value.

Thin Meditations: Weight-loss for the Mind & Body. Brian Alman. 200p. (Orig.). 1995. teacher ed. 19.95 (*0-9644867-5-X*); pap. 19.95 (*0-9644867-3-3*); text ed. 19.95 (*0-9644867-2-5*); pap. text ed. 19.95 (*0-9644867-4-1*); lib. bdg. 19.95 (*0-9644867-1-7*) Longevity Educ.

Thin Meditations: Weight-loss for the Mind & Body. Brian Alman. 200p. (Orig.). 1995. 22.95 (*0-9644867-0-9*) Longevity Educ.

Thin Men of Haddam. C. W. Smith. LC 90-10848. (Texas Tradition Ser.: No. 15). 336p. 1990. reprint ed. pap. 15.95 (*0-87565-078-3*) Tex Christian.

Thin Moon & Cold Mist. Kathleen O'Neal Gear. 1996. mass mkt. 5.99 (*0-8125-3657-6*) Forge NYC.

Thin Moon & Cold Mist. large type ed. Kathleen O'Neal Gear. 1996. 23.95 (*0-7838-1636-7*, GK Hall) Thorndike Pr.

Thin Moon & Cold Mist: The First Women's West Novel. Kathleen O'Neal Gear. 384p. 1995. 22.95 (*0-312-85701-2*) Tor Bks.

Thin Needle Aspiration Biopsy. William J. Frable. (Major Problems in Pathology Ser.: Vol. 14). (Illus.). 384p. 1983. text ed. 115.00 (*0-7216-3835-X*) Saunders.

Thin Plate Working One. 1990. 50.00 (*0-85083-156-3*) St Mut.

Thin Plate Working Two. 1990. 50.00 (*0-685-05796-8*) St Mut.

***Thin Polymer & Phospholipid Films for Biosensors: Characterisation with Gravimetric, Electrochemical & Optical Methods.** Torbjorn Tjarnhage. (Illus.). 105p. (Orig.). (C). 1997. pap. 35.00 (*0-7881-3134-6*) DIANE Pub.

Thin Red Line. James Jones. 1985. 20.00 (*0-02-559780-9*) Macmillan.

Thin Red Line: Uniforms of the British Army Between 1751 & 1914. D. S. Fosten & B. K. Fosten. (Illus.). 128p. 1994. 69.95 (*1-872004-00-8*) Howell Pr VA.

Thin Reinforced Concrete Products & Systems. 156p. 1994. pap. 38.75 (*0-614-02516-8*, SP146BOW6) ACI.

Thin Reinforced Concrete Shells: Special Analysis Problems. Victor Gioncu. LC 78-10388. (Illus.). 516p. reprint ed. pap. 147.10 (*0-8357-8620-X*, 2035043) Bks Demand.

Thin Scars - Purple Leaves. Lise Couchot. (Rockbook Ser.: No. 10). 24p. (Orig.). 1981. pap. 3.00 (*0-930012-40-2*) J Mudfoot.

Thin-Section Fiber Reinforced Concrete & Ferrocement. 448p. 1990. 34.75 (*0-685-60171-4*, SP-124BOW6) ACI.

Thin Sets in Harmonic Analysis: Seminars Held at Institute Mittag-Leffler, 1969-70. Ed. by Lars-Ake Lindahl & F. Poulsen. LC 79-163310. (Lecture Notes in Pure & Applied Mathematics Ser.: No. 2). 197p. reprint ed. pap. 56.20 (*0-7837-3419-0*, 2052465) Bks Demand.

Thin-Shell Concrete Structures. 2nd ed. David P. Billington. (Illus.). 432p. 1982. text ed. write for info. (*0-07-005279-4*) McGraw.

Thin Shell Theory: New Trends & Applications. Ed. by W. Olszak. (CISM Courses & Lectures: Vol. 240). (Illus.). 301p. 1981. 50.95 (*0-387-81602-X*) Spr-Verlag.

Thin Shells: Theory & Problems. J. Ramachandran. 1993. text ed. 27.50 (*0-86311-272-2*, Pub. by Universities Pr II) Apt Bks.

Thin Skins. Taylor McCafferty. 1994. mass mkt. 4.99 (*0-671-79977-0*) PB.

Thin Taste Better: Control Your Food Triggers Without Feeling Deprived. 1996. mass mkt. 6.50 (*0-440-22231-1*) Dell.

***Thin Tastes Better.** Stephen P. Gullo. 1997. 5.99 (*0-517-17567-3*) Random Hse Value.

Thin Tastes Better: Six Step Weight Loss Program; The Successful Alternative to Dieting. Stephen Gullo. 1995. 22.00 (*0-517-70006-9*, Carol Southern Bks) Crown Pub Group.

Thin Thighs in Thirty Years. Cathy Guisewite. (Illus.). 128p. (Orig.). 1986. pap. 8.95 (*0-8362-2081-1*) Andrews & McMeel.

Thin-Walled Bars with Open Profiles. Morris Ojalvo. Ed. by Richard Straw. LC 90-60103. (Illus.). 208p. (C). 1990. lib. bdg. 27.50 (*0-9627025-0-1*) Olive Press.

Thin-Walled Structures with Structural Imperfections. Luis A. Godoy. 404p. 1996. text ed. 141.50 (*0-08-042266-7*, Pergamon Pr) Elsevier.

Thin Wing in a Compressible Flow. E. A. Krasilshchikova. Tr. by G. Leib from RUS. 248p. 1982. 69.50 (*0-306-10972-7*, Consultants) Plenum.

***Thin Within.** Judy Wardell. 1996. pap. 16.00 (*0-609-80054-X*) Random Hse Value.

Thin Woman. Dorothy A. Cannell. 304p. 1992. mass mkt. 5.50 (*0-553-29195-5*) Bantam.

***Thin Woman: Discourses of Anorexia & Gender.** Helen Malson. 1996. pap. text ed. 34.00 (*0-13-436700-6*) P-H.

***Thin Woman: Feminism, Post-Structuralism & the Social Psychology of Anorexia Nervosa.** LC 96-39930. (Women & Psychology Ser.). 224p. (C). 1997. text ed. write for info. (*0-415-16332-3*) Routledge.

***Thin Woman: Feminism, Post-Structuralism & the Social Psychology of Anorexia Nervosa.** LC 96-39930. (Women & Psychology Ser.). 224p. (C). 1997. pap. write for info. (*0-415-16333-1*) Routledge.

Thin You Within You. Abraham J. Twerski. LC 96-6984. 208p. 1997. 19.95 (*0-312-14433-4*) St Martin.

Thine Health, 3 vols., Set. Nicholas C. Eliopoulos. Ed. by Nicholas G. Phystiklakis. (Orig.). 1981. pap. 25.00 (*0-9605236-2-X*) Eliopoulos.

Thine in Storm & Calm: An Amanda McKittrick Ros Reader. Amanda M. Ros. LC 88-7510. 166p. 8900. pap. 12.95 (*0-85640-408-X*, Pub. by Blackstaff Pr IE) Dufour.

Thine Is the Kingdom. Leicester Chilton. LC 92-91196. 272p. (Orig.). 1994. pap. 12.00 (*1-56002-288-4*) Aegina Pr.

Thine Is the Kingdom: A Biblical Perspective on the Nature of Government & Politics Today. Paul Marshall. 160p. 1993. reprint ed. pap. 12.95 (*1-57383-007-0*) Regent College.

Thing: The Project Pegasus Saga. Mark Gruenwald et al. (Spiderman Ser.). (Illus.). 144p. 1988. pap. 8.95 (*0-87135-350-4*) Marvel Entmnt.

Thing about Language. Gerald Burns. 160p. (C). 1989. pap. 16.95 (*0-8093-1528-9*) S Ill U Pr.

Thing among Things, an Event among Events: Short Stories. Carolyn Bennett. (Illus.). 112p. (Orig.). 1993. pap. 12.00 (*0-913559-23-7*) Birch Brook Pr.

Thing Apart: Love & Reality in the Therapeutic Relationship. Irving Steingart. LC 94-41351. 318p. 1995. 40.00 (*1-56821-304-2*) Aronson.

Thing Divided: Representation in the Late Novels of Henry James. John Landau. 1995. write for info. (*0-614-96419-9*) Fairleigh Dickinson.

Thing Divided: Representation in the Late Novels of Henry James. John Landau. LC 95-53134. 192p. 1996. 32.50 (*0-8386-3626-8*) Fairleigh Dickinson.

Thing from Another World & Climate of Fear Collection. Chuck Pfarrer et al. (Illus.). 168p. 1993. pap. 15.95 (*1-878574-85-X*) Dark Horse Comics.

Thing from Somewhere. (J). pap. 25.33 (*0-590-21018-1*) Scholastic Inc.

Thing from Somewhere. (J). pap. 4.00 (*0-590-21019-X*) Scholastic Inc.

Thing from Somewhere. (J). pap. 6.00 (*0-590-21020-3*) Scholastic Inc.

Thing from Somewhere. (J). pap. 64.00 (*0-590-21120-X*) Scholastic Inc.

Thing from the Lake. Douglas A. Menville. LC 75-46281. (Supernatural & Occult Fiction Ser.). 1976. reprint ed. lib. bdg. 26.95 (*0-405-08140-5*) Ayer.

***Thing in the Closet.** Pike. (Spooksville Ser.: No. 17). (J). 1997. mass mkt. 3.99 (*0-671-00265-1*) PB.

Thing in the Gap-Stone Stile. Alice Oswald. 64p. (C). 1996. pap. 12.95 (*0-19-282513-5*) OUP.

Thing King. Charles E. Eaton. 104p. 1983. 9.95 (*0-8453-4743-8*, Cornwall Bks) Assoc Univ Prs.

Thing Never Taught Choral MTD. 16.95 (*0-7935-4212-X*, 08740014) H Leonard.

Thing of Beauty. (Flower Pop-up Gift Bks.). 1994. 5.99 (*0-8407-6964-4*) Nelson.

Thing of Beauty. Stephen Fried. Ed. by Jane Rosenman. 448p. 1994. reprint ed. pap. 6.50 (*0-671-70105-3*) PB.

***Thing of Beauty Is...** Ed. by Michael Petry. (Art & Design Ser.). (Illus.). 96p. (Orig.). 1997. pap. 29.95 (*1-85490-526-0*) Academy Ed UK.

Thing of It Is. John Callaway. 1994. 25.00 (*0-915463-65-2*) Jameson Bks.

Thing of State: A Novel. Allen Drury. LC 95-8857. 384p. 1995. 24.00 (*0-684-80702-5*) S&S Trade.

Thing or Two about Music. Nicolas Slonimsky. LC 72-156213. 304p. 1972. reprint ed. text ed. 79.50 (*0-8371-6163-0*, SLAM, Greenwood Pr) Greenwood.

Thing That Ate San Luis. Jerry James. (Illus.). 248p. (Orig.). 1993. pap. text ed. 10.00 (*0-9639347-0-8*) San Borja Pr.

Thing That Bothered Farmer Brown. Teri Sloat. LC 94-24873. (Illus.). 32p. (J). (ps-2). 1995. 15.95 (*0-531-06883-8*); lib. bdg. 16.99 (*0-531-08733-6*) Orchard Bks Watts.

***Thing That Is: New Poems.** Robert Lax. Ed. by Paul Spaeth. 96p. 1997. 19.95 (*0-87951-699-2*) Overlook Pr.

***Thing Under Marty's Bed.** Nubia Levon. (Illus.). 25p. (Orig.). (J). (ps-2). 1997. pap. 12.99 (*1-890254-37-1*) Innov Pub Concepts.

Thing under the Bed. (Sounds by Me Recordable Bks.). (Illus.). 20p. (YA). 1995. bds. 19.95 (*0-307-75900-8*, Golden Pr) Western Pub.

Thing under the Bed. (Bone Chillers Ser.: No. 13). 144p. (J). 1997. mass mkt. 3.99 (*0-06-106428-9*, Harp PBks) HarpC.

Thing Upstairs. Stephen Mooser. LC 93-50676. (Illus.). 144p. (J). (gr. 3-6). 1996. pap. 2.95 (*0-8167-3421-6*) Troll Communs.

Things. Mark Dunster. 12p. (Orig.). 1990. pap. text ed. 4.00 (*0-89642-182-1*) Linden Pubs.

Things. Stephen P. Martin. (Illus.). 1991. pap. 4.95 (*0-9623693-3-0*) Heaven Bone Pr.

***Things.** Mayfair Games Staff. Date not set. 16.00 (*0-923763-84-8*) Mayfair Games.

***Things, Bk. II.** Rodman Philbrick & Lynn Harnett. (Visitors Ser.). (J). (gr. 4-7). 1997. mass mkt. 3.99 (*0-590-97214-6*) Scholastic Inc.

Things: Four Metabletic Reflections. Jan H. Van Den Berg. LC 74-125033. 144p. 1970. pap. text ed. 12.50 (*0-8207-0192-0*) Duquesne.

Things about Life. Addie Johnson. (Orig.). 1996. pap. write for info. (*1-57553-211-5*) Watermrk Pr.

Things about the Guitar. Jose Ramirez, III. Tr. by Teresita. (Illus.). 230p. 1994. pap. 32.50 (*0-933224-88-5*, Pub. by Soneto Ediciones SP) Bold Strummer Ltd.

***Things Accomplished among Us: Prophetic Tradition in the Structural Pattern in Luke - Acts.** Rebecca I. Denova. (JSNTS Ser.: Vol. 141). 255p. 1997. write for info. (*1-85075-656-2*, Pub. by Sheffield Acad UK) CUP Services.

Thing's Ain't What They Used to Be. Al Young. LC 87-71146. 256p. (Orig.). 1987. pap. 8.95 (*0-88739-024-2*) Creat Arts Bk.

Things & A Man Asleep: Two Novels in One Volume. Georges Perec. Tr. by David Bellos & Andrew Leak from FRE. 1990. 19.95 (*0-87923-857-7*) Godine.

Things & Words. Fred Justus. (Early Education Ser.). 24p. (ps-1). 1978. student ed. 5.00 (*0-8209-0203-9*, K-5) ESP.

Things Are Looking Up: A for Better or for Worse Collection. Lynn Johnston. (Illus.). 128p. (Orig.). 1992. pap. 8.95 (*0-8362-1892-2*) Andrews & McMeel.

Things Are Out of Joint. Mario Mozzillo. 225p. 1995. 21.95 (*0-9644443-0-5*) Windsor House.

Things Are Seldom What They Seem. Sandy Asher. LC 82-72819. 144p. (J). (gr. 7-p). 1983. pap. 11.95 (*0-385-29250-3*) Delacorte.

An Asterisk (*) at the beginning of an entry indicates that the title is appearing in BIP for the first time.

Things Are Seldom What They Seem or Local Sculptors - Found Materials. Katy Kline. LC 86-63519. (Illus.). 10p. (Orig.). 1986. pap. 1.00 (*0-938437-16-X*) MIT List Visual Arts.

Things Around Us. (Child's First Library of Learning). (Illus.). 88p. (J). (gr. 1-4). 1989. 16.95 (*0-8094-4845-9*) Time-Life.

Things Around Us. (Child's First Library of Learning). (Illus.). 88p. (J). (ps-3). 1989. lib. bdg. 21.27 (*0-8094-4846-7*) Time-Life.

Things As They Are. James Mellow. 1998. pap. 29.95 (*0-670-86685-7*) Viking Penguin.

Things As They Are. Theodore Dwight. (Notable American Authors Ser.). 1992. reprint ed. lib. bdg. 75.00 (*0-7812-2728-3*) Rprt Serv.

Things As They Are: New Directions in Phenomenological Anthropology. Ed. by Michael Jackson. 400p. 1995. 39.95 (*0-253-33036-X*) Ind U Pr.

Things As They Are: New Directions in Phenomenological Anthropology. Ed. by Michael Jackson. 400p. 1996. pap. text ed. 19.95 (*0-253-21050-X*) Ind U Pr.

Things As They Are: Walker Evans Biography. James Mellow. 1996. write for info. (*0-201-62465-6*) Addison-Wesley.

Things As They Really Are. Neal A. Maxwell. LC 78-26077. 138p. 1992. reprint ed. boxed 7.95 (*0-87579-615-X*) Deseret Bk.

Things at Home. Eliot Humberstone. (Explainers Ser.). (J). (gr. 2-5). 1981. pap. 4.95 (*0-86020-501-0*, Usborne) EDC.

Things Banks & Other Lenders Won't Tell You: The National Handbook. James W. Hart, IV. (Money the Rules Ser.). 45p. (C). 1993. student ed. 15.00 (*0-9633209-1-2*) Smart Bks.

Things Bunny Sees. Cyndy Szekeres. (J). (ps-3). 1990. write for info. (*0-307-11591-7*) Western Pub.

Things Change. Troy Aikman. LC 95-5479. (Illus.). 40p. (J). 1995. 14.95 (*0-87833-888-8*) Taylor Pub.

Things Change. David Mamet & Shel Silverstein. (Illus.). 64p. 1988. pap. 7.95 (*0-8021-3047-X*, Grove) Grove-Atltic.

Things Change, Big bk. Phyllis M. Bourne. (Wonders! Ser.). (Illus.). 24p. (Orig.). (J). (gr. 1-3). 1992. pap. text ed. 29.95 (*1-56334-067-4*) Hampton-Brown.

Things Change, Small bk. Phyllis M. Bourne. (Wonders! Ser.). (Illus.). 24p. (Orig.). (J). (gr. 1-3). 1992. pap. text ed. 6.00 (*1-56334-073-9*) Hampton-Brown.

Things Chinese: Or Notes Connected with China. James D. Ball. 1972. lib. bdg. 250.00 (*0-87968-476-3*) Krishna Pr.

Things Chinese: Or Notes Connected with China. J. Dyer Ball. Ed. by Chalmers Werner. 1998. reprint ed. 56.00 (*1-55888-236-7*) Omnigraphics Inc.

***Things Common, Properly: Selected Poems, 1942-1980.** Peter Whigham. 114p. 1984. pap. 19.95 (*0-85646-091-5*, Pub. by Anvil Press UK) Dufour.

Things, Fail, People Fall. Deborah Brunt. Ed. by Cindy McClain. 129p. (Orig.). 1991. pap. text ed. 6.95 (*1-56309-014-7*, New Hope AL) Womans Mission Union.

Things Fall Apart. Chinua Achebe. 1995. 15.00 (*0-679-44623-0*) Knopf.

Things Fall Apart. Chinua Achebe. LC 59-7114. (C). 1959. 12.95 (*0-8392-1113-9*); pap. 7.95 (*0-8392-5006-1*) Astor-Honor.

Things Fall Apart. Chinua Achebe. LC 94-13429. 192p. 1994. pap. 6.95 (*0-385-47454-7*, Anchor NY) Doubleday.

Things Fall Apart. Joseph Claro. Ed. by J. Friedland & R. Kessler. (Novel-Ties Ser.). 1995. student ed., pap. text ed. 15.95 (*1-56982-324-3*) Lrn Links.

***Things Fall Apart.** Jon Margolis. Date not set. write for info. (*0-688-15323-2*) Morrow.

Things Fall Apart Notes. John Chua & Cliff Notes Staff. (Clifs Notes Ser.). (Illus.). 86p. (Orig.). 1996. pap. text ed. 4.25 (*0-8220-1276-6*) Cliffs.

Things for All Seasons see Story Books for We Can Read

Things for People to Do. Babette Katz. (Illus.). 64p. (Orig.). 1988. pap. 8.00 (*0-89822-054-8*) Visual Studies.

Things Happen When Women Care: Hospitality & Friendship in Today's Busy World. Emilie Barnes. LC 90-35983. (Orig.). 1990. pap. 8.99 (*0-89081-837-1*) Harvest Hse.

Things Hidden since the Foundation of the World. Rene Girard. Tr. by Stephen Bann & Michael Metteer from FRE. LC 86-63637. 479p. 1987. 55.00 (*0-8047-1403-7*) Stanford U Pr.

Things Hidden Since the Foundation of the World. Rene Girard. Tr. by Stephen Bann & Michael Metteer from FRE. 479p. (C). 1993. pap. 18.95 (*0-8047-2215-3*) Stanford U Pr.

Things I Can Make. Sabine Lohf. LC 93-40881. 128p. (J). (ps-3). 1994. 13.95 (*0-8118-0667-7*) Chronicle Bks.

Things I Couldn't Learn Alone. Debra Peterson. (Illus.). 122p. 40.00 (*0-9637375-1-1*) Pringle Pub.

Things I Did Last Summer. Erika Tamar. LC 93-32556. 256p. (YA). (gr. 7 up). 1994. 11.00 (*0-15-282490-1*); pap. 4.00 (*0-15-200020-8*) HarBrace.

Things I Don't Remember. Barbara J. Schaffer. (End of the Century Bks.). 48p. (Orig.). 1989. pap. 4.00 (*0-317-93353-1*) Bay Area Ctr Art & Tech.

Things I Hate! Harriet Wittels & Joan Greisman. LC 73-11053. (Illus.). 32p. (J). (ps-3). 1973. 16.95 (*0-87705-096-1*) Human Sci Pr.

Things I Have Learned: Chapel Talks. Bob Jones, Sr. 224p. 1944. pap. 8.25 (*0-89084-022-9*, 002337) Bob Jones Univ Pr.

Things I Learned after It Was Too Late. Charles M. Schulz. (Owl Bks.). 128p. 1989. pap. 7.95 (*0-8050-1202-8*) H Holt & Co.

Things I Learned after It Was Too Late: (& Other Minor Truths) Charles M. Schulz. LC 80-84137. (Illus.). 128p. 1981. 6.95 (*0-03-059264-X*, Owl) H Holt & Co.

Things I Like. Anthony Browne. LC 88-26632. (Illus.). 24p. (Orig.). (J). (ps-1). 1989. pap. 5.99 (*0-394-84192-1*); lib. bdg. 13.99 (*0-394-94192-6*) Knopf Bks Yng Read.

Things I Like about Grandma. Francine Haskins. (J). (gr. 4-7). 1994. pap. 6.95 (*0-89239-123-5*) Childrens Book Pr.

***Things I Like about Grandma: (African-American)** Francine Haskins. (Illus.). (J). (gr. 2-4). 1993. 19.90 (*0-516-80107-4*) Childrens.

***Things I Love.** Random House Staff. 1997. 6.99 (*0-679-88408-4*) Random Bks Yng Read.

Things I Really Want to Say. Edward R. Skane. 128p. 1994. 15.00 (*0-917655-03-6*) Dane Bks.

Things I Remember. Frederick T. Martin. LC 75-1859. (Leisure Class in America Ser.). (Illus.). 1975. reprint ed. 21.95 (*0-405-06925-1*) Ayer.

Things I Remember. Frederick T. Martin. (American Biography Ser.). 255p. 1991. reprint ed. lib. bdg. 69.00 (*0-7812-8272-1*) Rprt Serv.

Things I Should Have Said to My Father. Compiled by Joanna Powell. 144p. (Orig.). 1994. pap. 10.00 (*0-380-77348-1*) Avon.

Things I Want, Poems for Two Children. John M. Shaw. 1967. 5.00 (*0-9607778-7-3*) Friends Fla St.

***Things I Wish I'd Known Sooner: Personal Discoveries of a Mother of Twelve.** Jaroldeen Edwards. LC 96-45404. 1997. 16.00 (*0-671-55106-X*) PB.

***Things in a Small Town.** Mickey Taylor. 1996. mass mkt. 4.99 (*1-55197-142-9*, Pub. by Comnwlth Pub CN) Partners Pubs Grp.

Things in Corners. Ruth Park. Date not set. pap. 3.99 (*0-14-036331-9*, Viking) Viking Penguin.

Things in Heaven & Earth: The Life & Times of Wilford Woodruff, a Mormon Prophet. 2nd ed. Thomas G. Alexander. LC 91-21223. xvi, 456p. 1991. pap. 18.95 (*1-56085-045-0*) Signature Bks.

Things in Loops & Knots I Pick from the Ground Become a Small Italian Opera. Coco Gordon. (Intimate Ser.: No. 1). (Illus.). 88p. (Orig.). 1987. pap. 30.00 (*0-943375-00-2*) W Space.

Things in My House. Elisabeth Ivanovsky. (Picture-Word Boards Bks.). (Illus.). (J). (ps). 1985. bds. 3.98 (*0-517-47341-0*) Random Hse Value.

Things in Revolt. Lev Lunts. Tr. & Intro. by Gary Kern. Date not set. 29.95 (*0-88233-924-9*) Ardis Pubs.

***Things in Small Quantities Have Lasting Appeal.** Maureen A. Malloy. Ed. by Robert F. Soeder. (Illus.). 114p. (Orig.). 1996. pap. 12.95 (*0-9655355-0-9*) Academy Prods.

Things in the Saddle. George Norlin. LC 74-80393. (Essay Index Reprint Ser.). 1977. 20.95 (*0-8369-1047-8*) Ayer.

Things in This Mirror Are Closer Than They Seem. Charles W. Darling. LC 86-5127. 20p. (Orig.). 1986. pap. 4.00 (*0-916897-08-7*) Andrew Mtn Pr.

Things Irish. Anthony Bluett. 156p. 1995. pap. 13.95 (*1-85635-079-7*) Dufour.

Things I've Got Growing Deep down Inside. Jo Van Arkel. 96p. (Orig.). 1995. pap. 9.00 (*1-56002-401-1*, Univ Edtns) Aegina Pr.

Things I've Had to Learn Over & Over & Over. Charles M. Schulz. 128p. 1989. pap. 7.95 (*0-8050-1203-6*, Owl) H Holt & Co.

***Things Just Aren't the Same.** Catherine Brett. 100p. (YA). pap. 4.95 (*0-88961-115-7*, Pub. by Wmns Pr CN) LPC InBook.

Things Magical. La Rhue Finney. (Illus.). 22p. (Orig.). (J). (gr. 2-4). 1992. pap. text ed. 6.95 (*0-9635276-0-6*) Taffey Apple.

Things Mama Would Say. Darla Davenport-Powell. (Illus.). 60p. (Orig.). 1988. pap. write for info. (*0-945203-01-2*) Hi-Hopes Pub.

Things Maps Don't Tell Us: An Adventure into Map Interpretation. Armin K. Lobeck. (Illus.). xiv, 174p. (C). 1993. pap. text ed. 19.95 (*0-226-48877-2*) U Ch Pr.

Things Most Surely. pap. 2.49 (*0-87377-000-5*) GAM Pubns.

Things My Father Never Taught Me. Judy A. LeBlanc. 1994. 12.95 (*0-533-10817-9*) Vantage.

Things My Mother Said II. Toby Amirault. (Illus.). 48p. (Orig.). 1991. pap. 6.95 (*0-9625432-1-7*) Ivy Pr WA.

Things My Mother Tried to Teach Me. Vincent O'Neil. (Illus.). 89p. 1994. 9.95 (*0-9644938-0-2*) RVON Enter.

***Things My Sponsor Taught Me.** H. Paul. 1996. pap. 8.00 (*0-89486-444-0*) Hazelden.

Things Not Generally Known. J. Timbs. 1972. lib. bdg. 59.95 (*0-8490-1193-0*) Gordon Pr.

Things of Darkness: Economies of Race & Gender in Early Modern England. Kim F. Hall. (Illus.). 312p. 1996. 42.50 (*0-8014-3117-4*) Cornell U Pr.

Things of Man: Twenty-four Poems (1990-1991) Augustine Towey. 52p. 1991. pap. 12.95 (*0-7734-9474-X*) E Mellen.

***Things of the Soul.** Boyd K. Packer. 1996. 15.95 (*0-88494-951-6*) Bookcraft Inc.

Things Old & New: An Ecumenical Reflection on the Theology of John Henry Newman. Emmanuel Sullivan. 160p. 1993. 35.00 (*0-85439-438-9*, Pub. by St Paul Pubns UK) St Mut.

Things Old & New: Catholic Social Teaching Revisited. Ed. by Francis P. McHugh et al. LC 92-27123. 436p. (Orig.). (C). 1993. pap. text ed. 37.50 (*0-8191-8902-2*) U Pr of Amer.

Things Old & New: Catholic Social Teaching Revisited. Ed. by Francis P. McHugh et al. LC 92-27123. 436p. (Orig.). (C). 1993. lib. bdg. 72.50 (*0-8191-8901-4*) U Pr of Amer.

Things on the Net Newt Wouldn't Want You to See. B. Ballsey. (Illus.). 160p. (Orig.). 1996. pap. 8.95 (*1-887652-28-0*) Off Color Pr.

Things on Wheels. (Big Picture Paperbacks Ser.). (Illus.). 32p. (J). (gr. 1-3). 1994. pap. 4.95 (*1-56458-549-2*) DK Pub Inc.

Things Outdoors. Eliot Humberstone. (Explainers Ser.). (J). (gr. 2-5). 1981. pap. 4.95 (*0-86020-464-2*, Usborne) EDC.

Things People Do. (Ny First Sound Story Books). (Illus.). 14p. (J). 1995. bds. 12.95 (*0-307-74055-2*, Golden Pr) Western Pub.

Things People Do. Anne Civardi. (Illus.). 38p. (J). (ps-4). 1986. 12.95 (*0-86020-864-8*, Usborne) EDC.

Things Pleasing to God & the Things Not Pleasing to God in the Holy Scriptures. 11p. 1989. pap. 4.00 (*1-57277-017-1*) Script Rsch.

***Things Pondered: From the Heart of a Lesser Woman.** Beth Moore. LC 97-17520. 1997. write for info. (*0-8054-0166-0*) Broadman.

Things Remembered. Kelsey Roberts. 1994. mass mkt. 2.99 (*0-373-22294-7*, 1-22294-2) Harlequin Bks.

***Things Remembered: An Album of African Americans in Tampa.** Rowena F. Brady & Canter Brown. LC 96-51255. 1997. write for info. (*1-879852-53-5*) Univ Tampa.

Things Seen & Heard. Edgar J. Goodspeed. LC 68-29208. (Essay Index Reprint Ser.). 1977. reprint ed. 19.95 (*0-8369-0484-2*) Ayer.

Things Seen & Unseen: Discourse & Ideology in Tokugawa Nativism. Harry Harootunian. 510p. 1988. pap. text ed. 18.95 (*0-226-31707-2*) U Ch Pr.

Things Seen in Kashmir. Ernest F. Neve. (C). 1993. 18.00 (*81-7041-821-6*, Pub. by Anmol II) S Asia.

Things Shaped in Passing: More "Poets for Life" Writing from the AIDS Pandemic. Ed. by Michael Klein & Richard McCann. 304p. 1996. pap. 14.95 (*0-89255-217-4*) Persea Bks.

Things Stirring Together or Far Away. Larry Eigner. LC 73-23121. 120p. (Orig.). 1974. pap. 10.00 (*0-87685-187-1*) Black Sparrow.

Things Supernatural & Causeless: Shakespearean Romance. Marco Mincoff. LC 92-53580. 136p. 1992. 28.50 (*0-87413-456-0*) U Delaware Pr.

Things That Are: Poems. Alice Raphael. 1969. 4.95 (*0-8079-0155-5*); pap. 1.95 (*0-8079-0156-3*) October.

Things That are Better Than Money. John F. Avanzini. 98p. 1995. pap. 5.99 (*0-89274-781-1*, HH-781) Harrison Hse.

***Things That Are Broken or Unfinished: The Art of Doug Kenney.** Victor L. Davson et al. (Illus.). 48p. (Orig.). 1996. write for info. (*0-614-23698-3*) Aljira.

***Things That Are Most in the World.** Judi Barrett. LC 97-5155. (Illus.). (J). 1998. 16.00 (*0-689-81333-3*, Atheneum S&S) S&S Trade.

Things That Become Sound Doctrine: Doctrinal Studies of Fourteen Crucial Words of Faith. J. Dwight Pentecost. 160p. 1996. pap. 9.99 (*0-8254-3452-1*) Kregel.

Things That Come in Groups: Multiplication & Division. Cornelia Tierney et al. Ed. by Priscilla C. Samii et al. (Investigations in Number, Data, & Space Ser.). (Illus.). 134p. (Orig.). 1994. teacher ed., pap. 22.95 (*0-86651-801-0*, DS21239) Seymour Pubns.

***Things That Count.** 160p. 1983. kivar 7.99 (*0-8341-0830-5*) Nazarene.

***Things That Count.** Dr. Seuss. (J). 1997. 4.99 (*0-679-88456-4*) Random.

Things That Divide Us: Stories by Women. Ed. by Faith Conlon et al. LC 85-8290. 191p. (Orig.). 1985. pap. 10.95 (*0-931188-32-6*) Seal Pr WA.

Things That Float. A. Thomas. (Explainers Ser.). (Illus.). 24p. (J). (gr. 2-4). 1987. pap. 4.50 (*0-7460-0102-9*) EDC.

Things That Fly. (Information Activity Ser.). 24p. (J). 3.50 (*0-7214-3443-6*, Ladybrd) Penguin.

Things That Fly. Karen E. Little & A. Thomas. (Explainers Ser.). (Illus.). 24p. (J). (gr. 2-4). 1987. pap. 4.50 (*0-7460-0104-5*) EDC.

Things That Go. (Sesame Street Ser.: No. 12). (J). 1989. 1.49 (*0-553-18395-8*) Bantam.

Things That Go. (Little Bitty Ser.). (Illus.). 20p. (J). (ps). 1991. bds. 2.50 (*0-8120-6263-9*) Barron.

Things That Go. (Sticker Activity Ser.). (Illus.). 16p. (J). (ps-1). 1994. pap. 6.95 (*1-56458-523-9*) DK Pub Inc.

Things That Go. (Picture Bks.: No. S8817-1). (Illus.). (J). (ps). 3.95 (*0-7214-5140-3*, Ladybrd) Penguin.

Things That Go. (Little Book of Questions & Answers Ser.). (Illus.). 32p. (J). 1993. 4.98 (*1-56173-471-3*) Pubns Intl Ltd.

Things That Go. (Look, Find, & Listen Ser.). (Illus.). 24p. (J). 1993. 16.98 (*0-7853-0137-2*) Pubns Intl Ltd.

Things That Go. (My First Sound Story Bks.). (Illus.). 14p. (ESP.). (J). 1995. bds. 12.95 (*0-307-74050-1*, Golden Pr) Western Pub.

Things That Go. (First Little Landoll Ser.). 32p. (J). (ps-3). Date not set. text ed. 1.29 (*1-56987-375-5*) Landoll.

***Things That Go.** (J). 1989. 2.95 (*0-934593-03-5*) Wicklow Ltd.

Things That Go! Rachel Elliot. (I-See-You Ser.). (Illus.). 8p. (J). 1996. 3.50 (*1-56293-826-6*) McClanahan Bk.

Things That Go. Eliot Humberstone. (Explainers Ser.). (J). (gr. 2-5). 1981. pap. 4.95 (*0-86020-493-6*, Usborne) EDC.

***Things That Go.** Rosie McCormick. (Fun Finding Out Ser.). (Illus.). 32p. (J). (ps-1). 1997. pap. 7.95 (*0-7534-5072-0*) LKC.

***Things That Go.** Rosie McCormick. (Fun Finding Out Ser.). (Illus.). 32p. (J). (ps-1). 1997. 12.95 (*0-7534-5090-9*) LKC.

Things That Go. Judy Mullican. (Little Bks.). (Illus.). 8p. (Orig.). (J). (ps-k). 1995. pap. text ed. 10.95 (*1-57332-063-3*) HighReach Lrning.

Things That Go. Anne Rockwell. (J). 1995. pap. 4.99 (*0-14-054788-6*) Dutton Child Bks.

Things That Go. Anne Rockwell. LC 86-6199. (Unicorn Paperback Ser.). (Illus.). 24p. (J). (ps-1). 1991. pap. 3.95 (*0-525-44703-2*, Puffin) Puffin Bks.

Things That Go. Huck Scarry. (J). (ps-1). 1986. 3.98 (*0-685-16834-4*, 616556) Random Hse Value.

Things That Go. Harriet Ziefert. (Softies Bks.). (Illus.). 8p. (J). (ps). 1993. 4.95 (*0-694-00507-X*, Festival) HarpC Child Bks.

Things That Go: Paint Box Fun. Manny Campana. 32p. (J). (ps-3). 1993. pap. 1.95 (*0-590-46290-3*) Scholastic Inc.

Things That Go "Baa!" in the Night: Tales from a Country Kid. Roger Pond. (Illus.). 176p. (Orig.). 1992. pap. 11.95 (*0-9617766-2-5*) Pine Forest Pub.

Things That Go Bark in the Park. Mel Gilden. (Fifth Grade Monsters Ser.: No. 7). 96p. (J). 1989. pap. 2.75 (*0-380-75786-9*, Camelot) Avon.

Things That Go Board Shape Book. (Board Shape Bks.). (Illus.). (J). (ps). 1985. bds. 1.69 (*0-517-46322-9*) Random Hse Value.

Things That Go Bump in the Night. Louis C. Jones. (New York State Bks.). (Illus.). 208p. 1983. reprint ed. pap. 9.95 (*0-8156-0184-0*) Syracuse U Pr.

Things That Go Bump in Your Soup. Louise Hawes. (Tales from the Cafeteria Ser.: No. 2). 160p. (Orig.). (J). 1995. pap. 3.50 (*0-380-77791-6*, Camelot) Avon.

***Things That Go EEK on Halloween: Nickelodeon Real Monsters.** Andrew Clements. (Real Monsters Ser.). (J). 1997. pap. text ed. 5.99 (*0-689-81675-8*) S&S Childrens.

Things That Go! How to Make Toy Boats, Cars, & Planes. Judith Conaway. LC 86-7130. (Illus.). 48p. (J). (gr. 1-5). 1987. lib. bdg. 12.50 (*0-8167-0838-X*) Troll Communs.

Things That Go Snaps. (J). write for info. (*0-7894-0326-9*, 5-70677) DK Pub Inc.

Things That Grow. Snapshot Staff. (Tab Board Bks.). (Illus.). 10p. 1996. 3.95 (*0-7894-1134-2*) DK Pub Inc.

***Things That Happen Because They Should: A Teleological Approach to Action.** Rowland Stout. (Oxford Philosophical Monographs). 192p. 1996. 45.00 (*0-19-824063-5*) OUP.

***Things That Happen Once.** Jones. 1997. pap. 14.00 (*0-395-85601-9*) HM.

Things That Happen Once: New Poems. Rodney Jones. LC 95-44941. 86p. 1996. 19.95 (*0-395-77143-9*) HM.

Things That Have Interested Me: First Series. Arnold Bennett. LC 74-17049. (Collected Works of Arnold Bennett: Vol. 80). 1977. reprint ed. 30.95 (*0-518-19161-3*, 19161) Ayer.

T

Things That Have Interested Me: Second Series. Arnold Bennett. LC 74-17091. (Collected Works of Arnold Bennett: Vol. 81). 1977. reprint ed. 26.95 (*0-518-19162-1*) Ayer.

Things That Have Interested Me: Third Series. Arnold Bennett. LC 74-17074. (Collected Works of Arnold Bennett: Vol. 82). 1977. reprint ed. 25.95 (*0-518-19163-X*) Ayer.

Things That Last: Reflections on Faith, Hope, Love. Rubel Shelly. 154p. (Orig.). 1991. pap. 8.99 (*1-878990-19-5*) Howard Pub LA.

Things That Make Us Smart: Cognitive Artifacts As Tools for Thought. Donald A. Norman. (Illus.). 288p. 1993. 22.95 (*0-201-58129-9*) Addison-Wesley.

Things That Make Us Smart: Defending Human Attributes in the Age of the Machine. Donald Norman. 304p. 1994. pap. 15.00 (*0-201-62695-0*) Addison-Wesley.

Things That Matter. Hiasaura Rubenstein & Mary H. Block. 446p. (C). 1982. text ed. 57.00 (*0-02-404180-7*, Macmillan Coll) P-H.

***Things That Move Coloring Book.** (Illus.). (J). Date not set. pap. 3.95 (*0-910119-63-5*) SOCO Pubns.

Things That Sail. Huck Scarry. (J). (ps-1). 1986. 3.98 (*0-685-16828-X*, 616564) Random Hse Value.

Things That Surround Us. Muska Nagel. Ed. by Constance Hunting. 68p. (Orig.). 1987. pap. 8.95 (*0-913006-39-4*) Puckerbrush.

Things That Swim in Texas Waters Alphabetically Speaking: And in Other Coastal States of the Gulf of Mexico. Glenna Grimmer. Ed. by Edwin M. Eakin. (Illus.). 48p. (J). (gr. 4-6). 1989. 11.95 (*0-89015-694-8*) Sunbelt Media.

Things That Were Said of Them: Shaman Stories & Oral Histories of the Tikigaq People. Tr. by Tukummiq C. Omnik & Tom Lowenstein. 285p. 1992. 32.50 (*0-520-06569-7*) U CA Pr.

Things That Work in Community Service Learning Vol. I. Ed. by Lisa I. Laplante & Carol W. Kinsley. 160p. (Orig.). 1994. pap. 20.00 (*0-9644330-0-1*) Comm Srv Lrning.

Things the Manual Never Told You: Tips, Techniques, & Shortcuts from the Nation's Largest User Group. Compiled by Boston Computer Society Staff. write for info. (*0-318-59575-3*) Addison-Wesley.

Things They Carried. Tim O'Brien. (Contemporary American Fiction Ser.). 288p. 1991. pap. 11.95 (*0-14-014773-X*) Viking Penguin.

Things They Didn't Teach Me in Worship Leading School. Ed. by Tom Kraeuter. 276p. (Orig.). 1995. pap. 9.99 (*1-883002-31-1*) Emerald WA.

Things They Didn't Tell Me about Being a Minister of Music. C. Harry Causey. (Illus.). 234p. (Orig.). 1988. pap. 12.00 (*0-9620795-0-2*) Music Revelatn.

Things They Didn't Tell Me about Being a Minister of Music. C. Harry Causey. (Illus.). 234p. (Orig.). 1988. pap. 14.00 (*0-317-91233-X*) Music Revelatn.

Things They Never Taught You about Youth Ministry That You Really Need to Know. Todd Clark. LC 95-51052. 182p. 1996. pap. 8.99 (*0-89900-754-6*) College Pr Pub.

Things They Never Taught You in Seminary. Deborah Bushfield & James Bushfield. LC 93-36050. 160p. (Orig.). 1994. pap. 9.99 (*0-8361-3649-7*) Herald Pr.

An Asterisk (*) at the beginning of an entry indicates that the title is appearing in BIP for the first time.

Things They Never Tell You Before You Say "Yes" The Non-Musical Tasks of the Church Musician. Robin Knowles-Wallace. LC 94-11010. 96p. (Orig.). 1994. pap. 9.95 (0-687-28165-2) Abingdon.

Things They Never Told Me in Therapy School: Serious Problems - Surprising Solutions. Peg Blackstone. 256p. 1991. text ed. 19.95 (0-9630291-0-X) Port Gamble.

Things They Say Behind Your Back: Stereotypes & the Myths Behind Them. William B. Helmreich. 276p. (C). 1983. pap. 21.95 (0-87855-953-1) Transaction Pubs.

Things, Thoughts, Words, & Actions: The Problem of Language in Late Eighteenth Century British Rhetorical Theory. H. Lewis Ulman. LC 93-13709. 256p. (C). 1994. 24.95 (0-8093-1907-1) S Ill U Pr.

Things to Be Lost. Lionel Newton. 288p. 1996. pap. 10.95 (0-452-27148-7, Plume) NAL-Dutton.

***Things to Celebrate.** Benecia Aronwald. (J). 1998. write for info. (0-679-88286-3) Random Bks Yng Read.

Things to Come. Foster Bailey. 1974. pap. 9.00 (0-85330-129-8) Lucis.

Things to Come. Christopher Frayling. 84p. 1995. pap. 9.95 (0-85170-480-8, Pub. by British Film Inst UK) Ind U Pr.

Things to Come. John M. Murry. LC 70-93364. (Essay Index Reprint Ser.). 1977. 21.95 (0-8369-1337-X) Ayer.

Things to Come. J. Dwight Pentecost. 633p. 1965. 25.99 (0-310-30890-9, 6355) Zondervan.

Things to Come: An Illustrated History of the Science Fiction Film. Douglas A. Menville & R. Reginald. LC 83-8789. 212p. 1983. reprint ed. lib. bdg. 33.00 (0-89370-019-3) Borgo Pr.

Things to Come & Not to Come: Bible Prophecy & Modern Myths. 2nd rev. ed. Aaron L. Plueger. LC 90-70068. (Illus.). 110p. 1990. pap. 8.95 (0-9625719-0-3) Truth & Error.

Things to Cuddle. Debbie MacKinnon. (Learn-Along Board Bks.). (Illus.). 22p. (J). (ps up). 1994. 2.99 (0-553-09570-6, Litl Rooster) BDD Bks Young Read.

Things to Do. Gakken Co. Ltd Editors. Tr. by Time-Life Books Editors. (Child's First Library of Learning). 90p. (J). (gr. k-3). 1989. lib. bdg. write for info. (0-8094-4898-X) Time-Life.

Things to Do. Gakken Co. Ltd. Editors & Time-Life Books Editors. (Child's First Library of Learning). 88p. (J). (gr. 1-4). 1989. 14.95 (0-8094-4897-1) Time-Life.

Things to Do in Fort Wayne. Robert Novak. 1973. 4.00 (0-685-67934-9) Windless Orchard.

Things to Do in the Car. Linda Q. Hodgdon. (Illus.). 52p. (Orig.). (J). pap. write for info. (0-9616786-0-7) Quirk Roberts.

Things to Do in Zoobilee Zoo. Jan Carr. (Zoobilee Zoo Ser.). (Illus.). 32p. (J). (ps-3). 1988. pap. 1.95 (0-590-42116-6) Scholastic Inc.

Things to Do with Toddlers & Twos. Karen Miller. LC 92-184870. (Illus.). 168p. (C). 1984. pap. 14.95 (0-910287-04-X) TelShare Pub Co.

Things to Eat. (Treasure Hunt Board Bks.). 12p. (J). 1996. 4.95 (0-7894-0628-4) DK Pub Inc.

Things to Eat. Debbie MacKinnon. (Learn-Along Board Bks.). (Illus.). 22p. (J). (ps up). 1994. 2.99 (0-553-09568-4, Litl Rooster) BDD Bks Young Read.

Things to Know: Richard Scarry. Richard Scarry. (Illus.). 24p. (J). (ps). 1994. pap. 1.49 (0-307-11616-6, Golden Pr) Western Pub.

Things to Know about Americans: An Orientation for International Visitors. Janice C. Hepworth. (Illus.). 116p. (Orig.). (C). 1991. teacher ed., pap. text ed. 50.00 (1-881313-01-8) Univ Centers.

Things to Make: Arabic. (Ladybird Stories Ser.). (Illus.). (J). (gr. 5-12). 1987. 4.50 (0-86685-238-7) Intl Bk Ctr.

Things to Make & Do see Child Horizons

***Things to Make for Christmas.** (Activity Fun Packs Ser.). (Illus.). (YA). (gr. 6 up). 1996. pap. 6.95 (0-7894-1160-1) DK Pub Inc.

Things to Play With. (Picture Bks.: No. S8817-5). (Illus.). (J). (ps). 3.95 (0-7214-5144-6, Ladybrd) Penguin.

Things to Play With. Anne Rockwell. (Illus.). 24p. (J). (ps-1). 1994. pap. 3.99 (0-14-050308-0, Puff Unicorn) Puffin Bks.

Things to Translate & Other Poems: Selected Poems. Piotr Sommer. Tr. by E. Adams et al. from POL. (Illus.). 96p. (Orig.). 9100. pap. 13.95 (1-85224-155-1, Pub. by Bloodaxe Bks UK) Dufour.

Things to Wear. (Picture Bks.: No. S8817-4). (Illus.). (J). (ps). 3.95 (0-7214-5143-8, Ladybrd) Penguin.

Things to Wear. Debbie MacKinnon. (Learn-Along Board Bks.). (Illus.). 22p. (J). (ps up). 1994. 2.99 (0-553-09569-2, Litl Rooster) BDD Bks Young Read.

***Things to Wear.** Margot Richardson. LC 97-13923. (Design & Create Ser.). (J). 1998. write for info. (0-8172-4888-9) Raintree Steck-V.

Things to Worry about (in Case You Run Out) A Definitive Guide to the Ultimate in Worries, Phobias & Fears. Len Cella. (Illus.). 96p. (Orig.). 1987. pap. 6.95 (0-930753-03-8) Spect Ln Pr.

Things Undone. Max Childers. 279p. 1990. 16.95 (0-941711-10-2) Wyrick & Co.

Things Visible & Invisible: Images in the Spirituality of St. Catherine of Siena. Giuliana Cavallini. Tr. by Mary Jeremiah from ITA. LC 95-51322. 153p. (Orig.). 1996. pap. 5.50 (0-8189-0733-9) Alba.

Things We Adore. Judson Cornwall. 224p. 1991. 8.99 (1-56043-048-6) Destiny Image.

Things We Couldn't Say. James C. Schaap. LC 94-18828. (Illus.). 1994. 20.00 (0-8028-3763-8) Eerdmans.

Things We Couldn't Say. James C. Schaap. 44p. (Orig.). (YA). 1994. pap. 3.50 (1-57514-124-8, 1098) Encore Perform Pub.

Things We Do. (Key Words Readers Ser.: A Series, No. 641-4a). (Illus.). (J). (ps-5). 3.50 (0-7214-0540-1, Ladybrd) Penguin.

***Things We Do.** Ladybird Staff. (J). 1997. pap. 3.50 (0-7214-5768-1) Dutton Child Bks.

Things We Do, Ser. S705, No. 4. (Key Words Readers Ser.: A Series, No. 641-4a). (Illus.). (J). (ps-5). student ed. 1.95 (0-7214-3065-1, Ladybrd) Penguin.

Things We Don't Forget: Views from Real Life. Dianne Aprile. 364p. 1994. pap. 12.95 (0-9642802-0-5) Trout Lily Pr.

Things We Like. (Key Words Readers Ser.: A Series, No. 641-3a). (Illus.). (J). (ps-5). 3.50 (0-7214-0003-5, Ladybrd) Penguin.

***Things We Like.** Ladybird Staff. (J). 1997. pap. 3.50 (0-7214-5765-7) Dutton Child Bks.

Things We Like, Ser. S705, No. 3. (Key Words Readers Ser.: A Series, No. 641-3a). (Illus.). (J). (ps-5). student ed. 1.95 (0-7214-3064-3, Ladybrd) Penguin.

Things We Lose: Stories. Roland Sodowsky. LC 89-4835. 128p. (Orig.). 1989. pap. 12.95 (0-8262-0723-5) U of Mo Pr.

Things We Lost, Gave Away, Bought High & Sold Low. Deborah Navas. LC 92-53612. 152p. 1992. 16.95 (0-87074-336-8) SMU Press.

***Things We Said Today.** Geoffrey Giuliano & Brenda Giuliano. Date not set. pap. 12.95 (1-55850-800-7) Adams Media.

Things We Said Today: The Complete Lyrics & a Concordance to the Beatles' Songs, 1960-1970. Colin Campbell & Allan Murphy. LC 80-83203. (Rock & Roll Reference Ser.: No. 4). (Illus.). 430p. 1980. 45.00 (0-87650-104-8) Popular Culture.

Things We See & Know. Eva Phillips. LC 89-50580. 54p. 1990. pap. 4.95 (1-55523-230-2) Winston-Derek.

***Things We Use.** Sally Hewitt & Jane Rowe. LC 96-34733. (Have You Noticed? Ser.). (J). 1997. lib. bdg. 21.40 (0-8172-4601-0) Raintree Steck-V.

Things Were Different in Royce's Day: Royce S. Pitkin As Progressive Educator. A Perspective from Goddard College, 1950-1967. unabridged ed. Forest K. Davis. (Illus.). 325p. 1996. 35.00 (0-912362-17-0) Adamant Pr.

Things Which Are Done in Secret. Marlene Dixon. 296p. 1976. 19.95 (0-919618-68-5, Pub. by Black Rose Bks CN); pap. 9.95 (0-919618-92-8, Pub. by Black Rose Bks CN) Consort Bk Sales.

Things Which Soon Must Come to Pass: Commentary on Revelation. Philip Mauro. 1984. reprint ed. 17.99 (0-87377-056-0) GAM Pubns.

Things Will Be Different for My Daughter: A Practical Guide to Building Her Self-Esteem. Mindy Bingham et al. LC 94-18517. 1995. pap. 14.95 (0-14-024125-6, Penguin Bks) Viking Penguin.

Things with Wheels. Debbie MacKinnon. (Learn-Along Board Bks.). (Illus.). 22p. (J). (ps up). 1994. 2.99 (0-553-09571-4, Litl Rooster) BDD Bks Young Read.

Things with Wings. Carson Creagh. LC 96-15736. (Young Discoveries Ser.). (Illus.). 32p. (J). 1996. write for info. (0-7835-4838-9) Time-Life.

***Things with Wings.** Gregory Holch. LC 97-10679. (J). 1998. write for info. (0-590-93501-1) Scholastic Inc.

***Things Written Aforetime.** F. E. Stallan. 1996. 29.99 (0-946351-25-2, Pub. by John Ritchie UK) Loizeaux.

Things You Always Wanted to Know about Monsters: But Were Afraid to Ask. Tony Tallarico. (Illus.). 64p. (Orig.). (J). 1988. pap. 1.95 (0-942025-59-8) Kidsbks.

***Things You Can Be.** Benecia Aronwald. (J). 1998. write for info. (0-679-88284-7) Random Bks Yng Read.

Things You Can Do to Defend Your Gun Rights. Alan M. Gottlieb & David B. Kopel. 192p. (Orig.). 1994. pap. 9.95 (0-936783-10-9) Merril Pr.

Things You Can Do with a Useless Man. Scott Wilson. Ed. by Cliff Carle. 1994. pap. 5.95 (0-918259-69-X) CCC Pubns.

Things You Can Get for Free. 1994. lib. bdg. 263.95 (0-8490-5635-7) Gordon Pr.

***Things You Can Give.** Benecia Aronwald. 1998. 6.99 (0-679-88287-1) Random.

***Things You Know That Are Not So: A Digest of Erroneous Popular Wisdom.** David Moshinsky. LC 95-94457. (Illus.). 162p. (Orig.). 1995. pap. 12.95 (0-7880-0611-8) CSS OH.

Things You See When You Don't Have a Grenade! David L. Strauss et al. 120p. 1996. pap. 24.95 (0-9646426-6-2) Smart Art Pr.

***Things You Should Save.** Benecia Aronwald. 1998. 6.99 (0-679-88285-5) Random Hse Value.

Things You'll Learn If You Live Long Enough. Great Quotations Staff. 168p. (Orig.). 1992. pap. 5.95 (1-56245-054-9) Great Quotations.

Things You'll Learn If You Live Long Enough So You Might As Well Know Now. Illus. by McKee-Anderson Group Staff. 78p. (Orig.). 1989. pap. 7.95 (0-931089-81-6) Great Quotations.

Things Your Dad Always Told You but You Didn't Want to Hear. Carolyn Coats. 126p. 1988. 10.00 (1-878722-05-0) C Coats Bestsellers.

Things Your Family Should Know. Morton L. Paige. 88p. 1992. student ed. 14.95 (0-9635236-0-0) Paige Pub CA.

Things Your Father Never Taught You. Robert Masello. LC 95-12474. (Illus.). 1995. pap. 120.00 (0-399-52168-2, Perigee Bks) Berkley Pub.

Things Your Father Never Taught You. Robert Masello. LC 95-12474. (Illus.). 240p. 1995. pap. 12.00 (0-399-52167-4, Perigee Bks) Berkley Pub.

Things Your Mother Always Told You but You Didn't Want to Hear. Carolyn Coats. 126p. 1981. 10.00 (1-878722-01-8) C Coats Bestsellers.

Things Your Mother Always Told You, but You Didn't Want to Hear. Carolyn Coats. LC 93-38978. 1994. 7.99 (0-7852-8056-1) Nelson.

Things You's Never Hear a Southerner Say. Vic Henley. (Illus.). 80p. 1995. pap. 6.95 (1-56352-239-X) Longstreet Pr Inc.

Thingumajig Book of Manners. Irene Keller. (Illus.). 32p. (J). (ps-3). 1989. pap. 4.95 (0-8249-8346-7, Ideals Child) Hambleton-Hill.

Thinis. Patricia. (Illus.). 330p. (Orig.). 1980. spiral bd. 7.95 (0-935146-12-1) Morningland.

Think. Ed. by Mac Anderson. 77p. (Orig.). 1989. pap. 7.50 (1-880461-10-2) Celebrat Excell.

Think. Robert Anthony. 480p. 1985. pap. 4.50 (0-425-08747-6) Berkley Pub.

Think. Becky Daniel & Nancee McClure. 64p. teacher ed. 8.99 (0-86653-729-5, GA1451) Good Apple.

Think a Second Time. Dennis Prager. LC 95-37478. 288p. 1995. 24.00 (0-06-039157-X, HarpT) HarpC.

Think About: The Environment. Cathryn Jakobson. (Think Ser.). 160p. (YA). (gr. 7 up). 1992. pap. 9.95 (0-8027-7357-5); lib. bdg. 15.85 (0-8027-8105-5) Walker & Co.

Think about Drugs & Society: Responding to an Epidemic. Richard A. Hawley. LC 87-21681. 157p. (J). 1988. 14.85 (0-8027-6749-4); pap. 5.95 (0-8027-6750-8) Walker & Co.

Think about Editing: A Grammar Guide. Allen Ascher. 1993. pap. 27.95 (0-8384-3976-4) Heinle & Heinle.

Think about It. Nick Camus. 1996. pap. text ed. 8.95 (0-9645851-7-0) Pennhills.

Think about It! Ruth I. Dowell. (Illus.). 36p. (Orig.). (J). (ps-6). 1987. pap. 3.00 (0-945842-04-X) Pollyanna Prodns.

Think about It! Kindergarten. Imogene Forte. (Illus.). 80p. (J). (ps). 1981. pap. text ed. 9.95 (0-913916-96-X, IP-96X) Incentive Pubns.

Think about It! Middle Grades. Imogene Forte. (Illus.). 80p. (J). (gr. 4-6). 1981. pap. text ed. 9.95 (0-913916-98-6, IP 98-6) Incentive Pubns.

Think about It! Primary. Imogene Forte. (Illus.). 80p. (J). (gr. 1-3). 1981. pap. text ed. 9.95 (0-913916-97-8, IP 97-8) Incentive Pubns.

Think about It! Projects & Puzzles to Show You How People Think. Ian Horwarth. Ed. by Patrick Green. LC 96-6976. (Amazing Brain Ser.). (J). 1996. pap. 9.95 (0-382-39604-9, Julian Messner); lib. bdg. 15.95 (0-382-39603-0, Julian Messner) Silver Burdett Pr.

***Think about It: Reflections on Quality & the United Methodist Church.** Ezra E. Jones. 112p. pap. 12.95 (0-88177-148-1, DR148) Discipleship Res.

Think about Nuclear Arms Control: Understanding the Arms Race. Richard Smoke. (Think Ser.). (Illus.). 178p. (J). 1988. pap. 5.95 (0-8027-6762-1); lib. bdg. 14.85 (0-8027-6761-3) Walker & Co.

Think about Our Rights: Civil Liberties & the United States. Reginald Wilson. LC 87-22989. 123p. (J). 1988. 14.85 (0-8027-6751-6); pap. 5.95 (0-8027-6752-4) Walker & Co.

Think about Space: Where Have We Been? Where Are We Going? Isaac Asimov & Frank White. LC 88-36731. (Think Ser.). (Illus.). 120p. (YA). (gr. 6 up). 1989. pap. 5.95 (0-8027-6767-2); lib. bdg. 14.85 (0-8027-6766-4) Walker & Co.

Think about Terrorism: The New Warfare. Terrell E. Arnold & Moorhead Kennedy. LC 87-21158. (Think about Ser.). (Illus.). 153p. (YA). (gr. 9-12). 1988. pap. 5.95 (0-8027-6758-3); lib. bdg. 14.85 (0-8027-6757-5) Walker & Co.

Think about the Weather. Cynthia Rothman. Ed. by Janet Reed. (Newbridge Early Learning Program Ser.). 16p. (J). (ps-2). 1994. pap. 14.95 (1-56784-300-X) Newbridge Comms.

Think about the Weather: Mini Book. Cynthia Rothman. Ed. by Janet Reed. (Early Learning Program Ser.). (Illus.). 16p. (J). (ps-1). 1996. pap. 2.95 (1-56784-325-5) Newbridge Comms.

***Think about...Block Scheduling: It's Not a Question of Time.** Robin Fogarty. (Illus.). 24p. 1995. reprint ed. pap. 5.00 (1-57517-006-X, 1365) IRI-SkyLght.

Think about...Multiage Classrooms: An Anthology of Original Essays. Ed. by Robin Fogarty. LC 95-79280. (Illus.). 256p. (Orig.). 1995. pap. 16.95 (1-57517-003-5, 1345) IRI-SkyLght.

Think Again. Robert Anthony. 480p. 1986. pap. 4.50 (0-425-09572-X) Berkley Pub.

Think Aloud Method. Maarten Van Someren et al. (Knowledge Based Systems Ser.). 208p. 1994. text ed. 48.00 (0-12-714270-3) Acad Pr.

Think & Act: A Series of Articles Pertaining to Men & Women, Work & Wages, 2 Vols. Virginia Penny. LC 75-156420. (American Labor Ser.: No. 2). 1977. reprint ed. 26.95 (0-405-02938-1) Ayer.

***Think & Do.** Jo E. Moore. (Reading & Writing Ser.). (Illus.). 32p. (J). (ps-k). 1997. teacher ed., pap. 2.95 (1-55799-399-8, 4001) Evan-Moor Corp.

Think & Grow Rich. Napoleon Hill. 1987. pap. 16.95 (0-940687-00-3) St Martin.

***Think & Grow Rich.** Napoleon Hill. 1996. pap. 11.00 (0-449-91146-2) Fawcett.

***Think & Grow Rich.** D. Kimbro & N. Hill. 1997. pap. 11.00 (0-449-00108-3) Fawcett.

Think & Grow Rich: A Black Choice. Dennis Kimbro & Napoleon Hill. 384p. 1992. reprint ed. mass mkt. 5.99 (0-449-21998-4, Crest) Fawcett.

Think & Grow Rich: 13 Steps to Riche's. Napoleon Hill. 1987. mass mkt. 5.99 (0-449-21492-3, Crest) Fawcett.

Think & Grow Rich: 13 Steps to Riche's. Napoleon Hill. (C). 1989. write for info. (1-880369-00-1) N Hill Found.

Think & Grow Rich: 13 Steps to Riche's. Napoleon Hill. 1976. pap. 10.00 (0-87980-163-8) Wilshire.

Think & Grow Rich Action Pack. Napoleon Hill. (Illus.). 352p. 1988. pap. 13.95 (0-452-26660-2, Plume) NAL-Dutton.

Think & Read: Stories. Ed. by Roberta Koza. 47p. 1988. 2.50 (0-910307-19-9) Comp Pr.

Think & Read: Stories (Work-Text) Roberta Koza. 49p. 1988. student ed. 4.75 (0-910307-20-2) Comp Pr.

Think & Thank: A Tale. Samuel W. Cooper. LC 74-27975. (Modern Jewish Experience Ser.). 1975. reprint ed. 17.95 (0-405-06704-6) Ayer.

Think & Win. Robert Anthony. 80p. (Orig.). 1992. pap. 4.50 (0-425-13468-7) Berkley Pub.

Think & Write. Fred Justus. (Early Education Ser.). 24p. (gr. 1). 1982. student ed. 5.00 (0-8209-0220-9, K-22) ESP.

Think & Write: Activities for Grades 4-6. Hilarie N. Staton. (Illus.). 120p. (Orig.). (J). (gr. 4-6). 1984. pap. 12.95 (0-673-18028-X, GoodYrBooks) Addson-Wesley Educ.

***Think Anew, Act Anew: Lincoln on Slavery, Freedom & Union.** Brooks D. Simpson. 200p. (C). 1998. pap. 9.95 (0-88295-975-1) Harlan Davidson.

Think Away Tension. Richard Anglin. (Illus.). 110p. (Orig.). 1988. pap. 8.95 (0-317-91342-5) RDA Enter.

Think Before Measuring: Methodological Innovations for the Collection & Analysis of Statistical Data. Jean-Luc Dubois. (Social Dimensions of Adjustment in Sub-Saharan Africa Working Paper Ser.: No. 7). 59p. 1992. 6.95 (0-8213-1703-2, 11703) World Bank.

***Think Before You Act, 3 vols., Vol. 1.** Peter Favaro. LC 95-74695. 100p. 1996. lib. bdg. 11.95 (1-56875-185-0, 185-0) R & E Pubs.

Think Before You Eat: Smarter Food Choices for You & Your Family. Diane Olive. 13p. 1996. pap. text ed. 16.95 (1-888824-01-8) Bridgeport Bks.

Think Before You Speak: A Complete Guide to Strategic Negotiations. Roy J. Lewicki. LC 95-45411. (The Portable MBA Ser.). 288p. 1996. text ed. 27.95 (0-471-01321-8) Wiley.

Think Before You Speak: Complete Guide To Strategic Negotiations. Jim Schell. LC 95-53200. 256p. 1996. text ed. 34.95 (0-471-14841-5) Wiley.

Think Better, Feel Better. Carl Pacifico. LC 89-91280. 1990. 20.00 (0-87212-224-7) Libra.

Think Big. Richard L. Beals. (Orig.). 1992. pap. 9.00 (0-9632343-0-7) R L Beals.

Think Big. Ben Carson. 288p. 1993. mass mkt. 5.99 (0-06-104304-4, Harp PBks) HarpC.

Think Big. Martha Symonds. (Enrichment & Gifted Ser.). 76p. (J). (gr. 4-6). 1977. 8.95 (0-88160-024-5, LW 209) Learning Wks.

Think Big: Discovering Your Gift of Excellence. Ben Carson. 256p. 1992. 15.99 (0-310-57410-2) Zondervan.

Think Bigger. M. Symonds. (Enrichment & Gifted Ser.). 112p. (J). (gr. 4-6). 1993. 8.95 (0-88160-260-4, LW255) Learning Wks.

Think Black. 3rd ed. Don L. Lee. LC 70-882333. (YA). (gr. 12 up). 1969. pap. 3.00 (0-910296-03-0) Broadside Pr.

Think Book: Reproducible Problem-Solving Activities. Linda N. Brown. (Illus.). 240p. (Orig.). 1990. pap. text ed. 16.95 (0-86530-087-9, IP 190-1) Incentive Pubns.

Think Chinese, Speak Chinese. Allan B. Goldenthal. (Illus.). (C). (gr. 10-12). 1978. write for info. (0-318-55502-6); audio 45.00 (0-686-67814-1, 58687) Prentice ESL.

Think Chinese, Speak Chinese. Allan B. Goldenthal. (Illus.). (YA). (gr. 10-12). 1978. pap. text ed. 14.95 (0-88345-358-4, 18602) Prentice ESL.

Think Chinese, Speak Chinese. Allan B. Goldenthal. 1987. pap. text ed. 39.00 (0-13-917469-9) Prentice ESL.

Think, Choose, Act Healthy. ETR Staff. (Health Masters Book Ser.). 1996. 39.00 (1-56071-372-0, H329) ETR Assocs.

Think, Corrie, Think! A Brownie Girl Scout Book. Jane O'Connor. (Here Come the Brownies Ser.: No. 5). (Illus.). 64p. (J). (gr. 1-4). 1994. pap. 3.95 (0-448-40465-6, G&D) Putnam Pub Group.

Think Dog! An Owner's Guide to Canine Psychology. John Fisher. 160p. 1996. reprint ed. pap. 9.95 (1-57076-036-5, Trafalgar Sq Pub) Trafalgar.

Think! Draw! Write! Level One. Jean Marzollo & Katherine M. Widmer. (J). (gr. 1-3). 1982. pap. 6.99 (0-8224-6946-4) Fearon Teach Aids.

Think! Draw! Write! Level Two. Jean Marzollo & Karherine M. Widmer. 48p. (J). (gr. 4-6). 1982. 6.99 (0-8224-6947-2) Fearon Teach Aids.

***Think Fast! Race Driving from Novice to Expert: The Skip Barber Racing School Complete Racer's Reference.** Carl Lopez & Skip Barber Racing School Staff. LC 96-48026. 1996. write for info. (0-8376-0227-0) Bentley.

Think Fast! The ADD Experience. Ed. by Thom Hartmann & Janie Bowman. 256p. (Orig.). 1996. pap. 12.95 (1-887424-08-3) Underwood Bks.

Think Fast America. Lambert Schuyler. 1982. lib. bdg. 69.95 (0-87700-443-9) Revisionist Pr.

Think Fast, Mr. Peters. Stuart M. Kaminsky. 224p. 1988. 15.95 (0-317-64892-6, Thomas Dunne Bks) St Martin.

Think Fast, Mr. Peters. Stuart M. Kaminsky. 224p. 1996. mass mkt. 5.99 (0-446-40440-3, Mysterious Paperbk) Warner Bks.

***Think First: Self Study Guide.** Naunton. Date not set. pap. text ed. write for info. (0-582-55984-7, Pub. by Longman UK) Longman.

Think for Yourself. Robert P. Crawford. LC 64-8498. 250p. 1979. reprint ed. pap. 17.00 (0-87034-011-5) Fraser Pub Co.

Think Globally, Act Locally: The United Nations & the Peace Movements. Ken Coates. 168p. 1988. 44.50 (0-85124-503-X, Pub. by Spokesman Bks UK); pap. 24.00 (0-85124-504-8, Pub. by Spokesman Bks UK) Coronet Bks.

Think Green! A Retailer's Environmental Idea Book. Gary P. Rejebian. (Illus.). 50p. (Orig.). 1992. pap. 25.00 (1-885337-00-0) IL Retail Merchants.

Think Harmony with Horses. Ray Hunt. 100p. 1987. reprint ed. 14.95 (0-914330-15-2) Ag Access.

T

Think Hippo! Wendy Smith. (Carolrhoda Picture Bks.). (Illus.). 28p. (J). (ps-3). 1989. lib. bdg. 18.95 (*0-87614-372-9*, Carolrhoda) Lerner Group.

Think Home. Lisa Chinn. 1987. pap. 4.95 (*0-317-04077-4*) Intl Students Inc.

***Think It, Do It! Eliminating Fears.** Nina Craft. 60p. (Orig.). 1997. pap. 10.00 (*0-9652087-2-9*) VisionFocus.

***Think It, Do It! The Procrastinator's Guide to Action.** Nina Craft. 50p. 1993. pap. 10.00 (*0-9652087-0-2*) VisionFocus.

Think It Through. Martha A. Hayes & Kathy Faggella. Ed. by Lisa L. Durkin. (Illus.). 108p. 1986. pap. 10.95 (*0-9615005-2-2*) First Teacher.

Think Jazz, Bk. 1. B. Boyd. 88p. 1994. pap. 10.95 (*0-7935-2318-4*, 00290417) H Leonard.

Think Jewish: A Contemporary View of Judaism, a Jewish View of Today's World. Zalman I. Posner. LC 78-71323. 1979. 8.95 (*0-9602394-0-5*); pap. 4.95 (*0-9602394-1-3*) Kesher.

Think Light! Breaking Free from the Diet Prison. 4th ed. Greg Phillips & Gail Johnston. 126p. 1989. reprint ed. pap. 6.95 (*0-9625095-1-5*) Speaking Fitness.

***Think Like a Champion: A Guide to Championship Performance for Athletes in All Sports.** Dick DeVenzio. 416p. 1997. 24.95 (*0-614-29694-3*) Fool Court.

***Think Like a Dinosaur & Other Stories.** James P. Kelly. 288p. 1997. 22.95 (*0-9655901-9-4*) Golden Gryphon.

***Think Like a Genius.** Todd Siler. LC 97-17861. (Illus.). 304p. 1997. 23.95 (*0-553-10732-1*) Bantam.

***Think Like a Genius: Use Creativity in Ways That Will Enrich Your Life.** Todd Siler. (Illus.). 305p. 1996. pap. 14.95 (*0-9638696-1-2*); lib. bdg. 24.95 (*0-9638696-2-0*) Psi-Phi Communs.

***Think Like a Giraffe: A Reach for the Sky Guide in Creativity & Maximum Performance.** Stephen M. Gower. 176p. 1997. 20.00 (*1-880150-96-4*) Lectern Pub.

Think Like a Grandmaster: New Algebraic Edition. Alexander Kotov. (Illus.). 192p. 1996. pap. 17.95 (*0-7134-7885-3*, Pub. by Batsford UK) Trafalgar.

Think Like a Lawyer: How to Get What You Want by Using Advocacy Skills. Robert J. Dudley. LC 79-26488. 234p. 1980. 28.95 (*0-88229-571-3*) Nelson-Hall.

Think Like a Manager. Roger Fritz. 1991. pap. 14.95 (*1-55852-060-0*) Natl Pr Pubns.

Think Like a Manager. 2nd rev. ed. Roger Fritz. (Leadership Ser.). (Illus.). 261p. 1991. pap. 19.95 (*1-55852-052-X*) Natl Pr Pubns.

Think Like a Manager: Everything They Didn't Tell You When They Promoted You. 2nd ed. Roger Fritz. 316p. 1993. pap. 16.95 (*1-56414-102-0*) Career Pr Inc.

Think Like a Shrink: Solve Your Problems Yourself with Short-Term Therapy Techniques. Christ L. Zois. 272p. 1993. pap. 10.99 (*0-446-39256-1*) Warner Bks.

Think Like a Tycoon. 4th ed. Bill Greene. (Illus.). 253p. 1980. 29.95 (*0-936602-07-4*) J C Print.

Think Like a Winner! Walter D. Staples. LC 90-19985. 1991. 17.95 (*0-88289-833-7*) Pelican.

Think Like a Winner. Walter D. Staples. 1993. pap. 15.00 (*0-87980-433-5*) Wilshire.

Think Like an Eagle: At Work with a Wildlife Photographer. Kathryn Lasky. (Illus.). 48p. (J). (gr. 3 up). 1992. 15.95 (*0-316-51519-1*, Joy St Bks) Little.

Think Links: Fractions, Decimals, Percent. Paul J. Shoecraft. (Illus.). 61p. (J). (gr. 1-6). 1992. teacher ed. 12.95 (*0-941530-07-8*) Move It Math.

Think Links: Math-Language Arts. Paul J. Shoecraft. (Illus.). 80p. (J). (gr. 1-4). 1992. teacher ed. 14.95 (*0-941530-05-1*) Move It Math.

Think Links: Math-Reading Readiness. Lynne Shoecraft & Paul Shoecraft. (Illus.). 88p. (J). (gr. k-2). 1992. teacher ed. 14.95 (*0-941530-04-3*) Move It Math.

Think Links: Whole Number Arithmetic. Paul J. Shoecraft. 67p. (J). (gr. 1-4). 1992. teacher ed. 10.95 (*0-941530-06-X*) Move It Math.

***Think Locally, Act Globally! Linking Local & Global Communities Through Democracy & Environment.** Lorraine Dowler. (Active Learning Modules on the Human Dimensions of Global Change Ser.). (Illus.). 151p. (C). 1997. teacher ed., pap. 16.00 (*0-89291-237-5*) Assn Am Geographers.

***Think Locally, Act Globally! Linking Local & Global Communities Through Democracy & Environment.** Lorraine Dowler. (Active Learning Modules on the Human Dimensions of Global Change Ser.). (Illus.). 47p. (C). 1997. student ed., wbk. ed., pap. 7.00 (*0-89291-238-3*) Assn Am Geographers.

Think Math! Interactive Loops for Groups, Grades 4-10. Dale Bulla. LC 95-13799. 1995. pap. 29.00 (*1-56976-027-6*) Zephyr Pr AZ.

Think Neon. J. Greg Devlin. 1996. pap. text ed. 6.95 (*1-887654-12-7*) Premium Pr TN.

Think Neon Bk. I: Activities. J. Greg Devlin. (Illus.). 24p. (J). (ps-7). 1995. mass mkt. 6.95 incl. audio (*0-9649889-0-9*) Skedaddle.

Think of a Beaver. Karen Wallace. LC 92-53132. (Read & Wonder Bks.). (Illus.). 32p. (J). (ps up). 1993. 14.95 (*1-56402-179-3*) Candlewick Pr.

Think of a Beaver. Karen Wallace. LC 92-53132. (Read & Wonder Bks.). (J). (gr. k-4). 1995. pap. 5.99 (*1-56402-464-4*) Candlewick Pr.

Think of a Garden: And Other Plays. John Kneubuhl. LC 96-39137. (Talanoa Ser.). (Illus.). 272p. 1997. text ed. 39.00 (*0-8248-1773-7*); pap. text ed. 18.95 (*0-8248-1814-8*) UH Pr.

Think of a Number. Malcolm E. Lines. (Illus.). 172p. 1990. pap. 25.00 (*0-85274-183-9*) IOP Pub.

Think of an Eel. Karen Wallace. LC 92-53131. (Read & Wonder Bks.). (Illus.). 32p. (J). (ps up). 1993. 14.95 (*1-56402-180-7*) Candlewick Pr.

Think of an Eel. Karen Wallace. LC 92-53131. (Read & Wonder Bks.). (J). (ps up). 1995. pap. 5.99 (*1-56402-465-2*) Candlewick Pr.

***Think of Me.** Jane M. Choate. LC 97-93468. 192p. 1997. lib. bdg. 17.95 (*0-8034-9237-5*, Avalon Bks) Bouregy.

Think of One. P. Inman. 96p. (Orig.). 1986. pap. 7.50 (*0-937013-17-X*) Potes Poets.

Think of One Sextet. T. Monk. 1995. pap. text ed. 20.00 (*0-7935-4820-9*, 00000700) H Leonard.

Think of Something Quiet. Clare Cherry. LC 80-82981. (Early Childhood Library). (J). (ps-4). 1981. pap. 11.99 (*0-8224-6949-9*) Fearon Teach Aids.

***Think of Wind.** Catherine J. Mercury. Ed. by Dawn M. Stranges. (Illus.). 28p. (Orig.). 1996. pap. 14.95 (*0-9654447-1-6*) One Big Pr.

Think of Your Future. William MacDonald. 1956. pap. 3.00 (*0-937396-44-3*) Walterick Pubs.

Think On. Robert Anthony. 1988. pap. 4.50 (*0-425-11186-5*) Berkley Pub.

Think on New Levels. Robert G. Chaney. (Adventures in Esoteric Learning Ser.). 56p. 1963. pap. 4.95 (*0-918936-16-0*) Astara.

Think on These Things. 125p. 1981. pap. 4.50 (*0-87604-132-2*, 308) ARE Pr.

Think on These Things. Ernest H. Streets. LC 93-3723. (Illus.). 192p. (Orig.). 1993. pap. 12.00 (*1-880573-12-1*) Grace WI.

Think on These Things. 2nd ed. Joyce S. Hifler. 160p. 1995. reprint ed. pap. 10.95 (*0-933031-79-3*) Coun Oak Bks.

Think on These Things. Jiddu Krishnamurti. LC 89-45101. 265p. 1989. reprint ed. pap. 12.50 (*0-06-091609-5*, PL) HarpC.

Think on This. Gurani Anjali. (Illus.). 52p. (Orig.). Date not set. pap. write for info. (*0-933989-02-4*) Vajra Print & Pub.

Think on Your Feet. Dennis Matthies. (Illus.). 350p. (C). 1996. spiral bd. 35.00 (*1-887981-04-7*) Stanford Bookstore.

Think on Your Feet. L. Schwatrz. (Learning Works Creative Writing Ser.). (J). (gr. 4-8). 1989. 7.95 (*0-88160-172-1*, LW 283) Learning Wks.

Think or Else! Provocative Intellectual Essays. Maralene Wesner & Miles Wesner. 92p. (Orig.). 1988. pap. 4.95 (*0-936715-25-1*) Diversity Okla.

Think or Else! Provocative Spiritual Essays. Maralene Wesner & Miles Wesner. 140p. (Orig.). 1988. pap. 4.95 (*0-936715-28-6*) Diversity Okla.

Think Out of the Box. Mike Vance & Diane Deacon. 224p. 1995. 24.99 (*1-56414-186-1*) Career Pr Inc.

***Think Out of the Box.** Mike Vance & Diane Deacon. (Illus.). 224p. 1997. pap. 14.99 (*1-56414-278-7*) Career Pr Inc.

Think Pascal 4.0. Decker. (Computer Science Ser.). 1992. lab manual ed., pap. 21.95 (*0-534-16177-4*) PWS Pubs.

Think Patterns Consonants/Blends. Ann Wiebe. (Illus.). 42p. 1979. wbk. ed., pap. 10.95 (*1-878669-67-2*) Crea Tea Assocs.

Think Patterns Vowels. Ann Wiebe. (Illus.). 32p. (J). (gr. k-3). 1979. wbk. ed. 8.95 (*1-878669-66-4*) Crea Tea Assocs.

Think Pink. Olga Cossi. LC 93-5556. (Illus.). (J). 1994. 10. 95 (*0-88289-995-3*) Pelican.

Think Plus Science. Lori J. Bennett. (J). (gr. 4-8). 1993. pap. 9.95 (*1-878347-23-3*) NL Assocs.

Think Positive: Cope with Stress. Catherine Reef. LC 93-3973. (Good Health Guidelines Ser.). (Illus.). 64p. (J). (gr. 4-7). 1993. 15.98 (*0-8050-2443-3*) TFC Bks NY.

Think Quest Program 1. Sydney Tyler-Parker. (Think Quest Ser.). (Illus.). 128p. (Orig.). 1990. pap. 45.00 (*0-912781-14-9*) Thomas Geale.

Think Quest Program 2. Sydney Tyler-Parker. (Think Quest Ser.). (Illus.). 148p. (Orig.). 1990. pap. 45.00 (*0-912781-15-7*) Thomas Geale.

Think Quest Program 3. Sydney Tyler-Parker. (Think Quest Ser.). (Illus.). 136p. (Orig.). 1991. pap. 45.00 (*0-912781-17-3*) Thomas Geale.

Think Quest Program 4. Sydney Tyler-Parker. (Think Quest Ser.). (Illus.). 138p. (Orig.). 1992. pap. 45.00 (*0-912781-18-1*) Thomas Geale.

***Think, Read, React Plan for Writing.** 6th ed. Adams. (C). 1994. pap. write for info. (*0-15-500798-X*) HB Coll Pubs.

Think, Read, React, Plan, Write, Rewrite. 5th ed. W. Royce Adams. 368p. (C). 1986. teacher ed. write for info. (*0-318-69142-6*); pap. text ed. write for info. (*0-03-030819-4*) HB Coll Pubs.

Think Rugby. 2nd ed. Jim Greenwood. pap. 24.95 (*0-7136-3781-1*, 92983, Pub. by A&C Black UK) Talman.

Think Slim-Be Slim: A New 21-Day Plan for "Mental Dieting" That Can Give You Perfect Weight Control. rev. ed. Elsye Birkinshaw. LC 80-7115. 144p. (Orig.). 1981. pap. 7.95 (*0-912800-91-7*) Woodbridge Pr.

***Think Sociology.** Andrew Leach et al. 704p. (Orig.). 1997. pap. 59.50 (*0-7487-2563-6*, Pub. by Stanley Thornes UK) Trans-Atl Phila.

Think Space: A Low-Stress Behavior Management Technique, Especially for Early Childhood. Calvin M. Richert & Carolyn H. Richert. (Illus.). xvi, 177p. (Orig.). 1996. pap. 14.95 (*0-9651971-9-0*) Take V Publns.

Think Straight! Feel Great! Twenty-One Guides to Emotional Self-Control. Bill Borcherdt. LC 88-43055. 184p. (Orig.). 1989. pap. 18.20 (*0-943158-53-2*, TSFGPB) Pro Resource.

Think Tank Directory: A Guide to Nonprofit Public Policy Research Organizations. Ed. by Lynn Hellebust. 400p. 1996. pap. 125.00 (*1-879929-18-X*) Govt Res Serv.

***Think Tanks.** Day. Date not set. text ed. write for info. (*0-582-20905-6*, Pub. by Longman UK) Longman.

Think-Tanks of the New Right. Andrew Denham. LC 96-24901. (Illus.). 240p. 1996. text ed. 62.95 (*1-85521-868-2*, Pub. by Dartmth Pub UK) Ashgate Pub Co.

Think Thin. Murray J. Siegel & Dolores Van Keuren. LC 76-151435. 288p. 1981. reprint ed. pap. 15.95 (*0-8397-7993-3*) Eriksson.

***Think Think Think.** Brian Jones. LC 96-86541. (Illus.). 64p. (Orig.). (J). (gr. k). 1996. pap. 4.95 (*1-57733-005-6*) B Dolphin Pub.

Think ThinkC Programming for the Macintosh. Dan P. Sydow. 512p. (Orig.). 1993. pap. 39.95 incl. disk (*1-55958-388-6*) Prima Pub.

Think to Win. Don Alexander. (Illus.). 256p. 1994. pap. 19. 95 (*0-8376-0070-7*) Bentley.

Think to Win: The Strategic Dimension of Tennis. Allen Fox. LC 92-53397. (Illus.). 192p. 1993. pap. 12.00 (*0-06-098200-4*, PL) HarpC.

Think Together. Robert N. Anthony. 80p. (Orig.). 1995. pap. text ed. 4.50 (*0-425-15046-1*) Berkley Pub.

Think Twice: An Entertaining Collection of Choices. Paul Lowrie. 160p. 1996. pap. 5.95 (*0-9634251-2-9*) Questmarc Pub.

Think Twice: An Entertaining Collection of Choices. Paul Lowrie & Bret Nicholaus. 1996. pap. 5.95 (*0-9634251-3-7*) Questmarc Pub.

Think Twice: Communication Activities for Beginning to Intermediate Students. David Hover. (Illus.). 96p. 1986. pap. text ed. 13.95 (*0-521-27385-4*); teacher ed., pap. text ed. 15.95 (*0-521-27386-2*) Cambridge U Pr.

Think Twice: Medical Effects of Physical Punishment. Leslie Taylor & Adah Maurer. (Illus.). 80p. 1985. 5.95 (*0-932141-05-6*) End Violence.

Think up a Business. H. Hawkins & B. Bage. (C). 1989. text ed. 29.95 (*1-85631-002-7*, Pub. by Rosters Ltd) St Mut.

Think Visually! Handbook: Simple Techniques for Thinking, Planning & Problem Solving. 2nd ed. Yvonne M. Hansen. (Illus.). 160p. 1992. pap. 15.00 (*0-9625347-3-0*) Gemin-Ideas Pr.

Think Visually! Handbook: Using Simple Shapes for Thinking, Planning & Problem Solving. Yvonne M. Hansen. (Illus.). 156p. 1990. pap. 15.00 (*0-9625347-2-2*) Gemin-Ideas Pr.

Think Wealth: Put Your Money Where Your Mind Is! Judith L. Powell. LC 91-11420. 160p. 1997. pap. 12.95 (*1-56087-136-9*) Top Mtn Pub.

Think Young-Be Young! rev. ed. Elsye Birkinshaw. LC 86-28240. Orig. Title: Turn Off Your Age. 160p. (Orig.). 1988. pap. 8.95 (*0-88007-157-5*) Woodbridge Pr.

Think Yourself Slim. Bransby Clarke. 96p. (Orig.). 1995. pap. 7.95 (*0-572-01471-6*, Pub. by Foulsham UK) Assoc Pubs Grp.

***Think Yourself Thin: The Visualization Technique That Will Make You Lose Weight Without Diet or Exercise.** Debbie Johnson. audio 12.95 (*0-694-51729-1*) HarperAudio.

Think Yourself Thin: The Visualization Technique That Will Make You Lose Weight Without Diet or Exercise. Debbie Johnson. LC 95-24693. 256p. 1996. 16.95 (*0-7868-6222-X*) Hyperion.

***Think Yourself Thin: The Visualization Technique That Will Make You Lose Weight Without Diet or Exercise.** Debbie Johnson. 256p. 1997. pap. 9.95 (*0-7868-8247-6*) Hyperion.

Thinkability. Marco Meirovitz et al. 1995. teacher ed. write for info. (*1-57004-012-5*); wbk. ed. write for info. (*1-57004-028-1*) Lrning NJ.

Thinkability, Addtional Game Kits. Marco Meirovitz et al. 1995. 149.00 (*1-57004-018-4*) Lrning NJ.

Thinkability, 10 wkbks., Set. Marco Meirovitz et al. 1995. student ed., wbk. ed. 119.50 (*1-57004-017-6*); student ed., teacher ed. 239.00 (*1-57004-027-3*) Lrning NJ.

Thinkability: A Practical Program to Improve Thinking Skills Using Games. Marco Meirovitz et al. 1995. teacher ed. 89.00 (*0-570-04012-4*) L Erlbaum Assocs.

Thinkability: A Practical Program to Improve Thinking Skills Using Games, 10 wkbks., Set. Marco Meirovitz et al. 1995. student ed. 119.50 (*0-570-04017-5*); 149.00 (*0-570-04018-3*) L Erlbaum Assocs.

Thinkability: A Practical Program to Improve Thinking Skills Using Games, Set, incl. 10 wkbks. & 5 game kits. Marco Meirovitz et al. 1995. teacher ed. 239.00 (*0-570-04027-2*) L Erlbaum Assocs.

***Thinker As Artist: From Homer to Plato & Aristotle.** George Anastaplo. LC 97-2389. 400p. 1997. text ed. 49. 95 (*0-8214-1176-4*); pap. text ed. 24.95 (*0-8214-1184-5*) Ohio U Pr.

Thinker on Stage: Nietzsche's Materialism. Peter Sloterdijk. Tr. by Jamie O. Daniel. (Theory & History of Literature Ser.: Vol. 56). Orig. Title: Der Denker auf der Buhne Nietzsches Materialismus. 144p. (Orig.). 1989. pap. text ed. 12.95 (*0-8166-1765-1*) U of Minn Pr.

Thinker, Sailor, Brother, Spy. John E. Maher. 330p. (Orig.). 1995. pap. 10.00 (*0-9643121-0-7*) Maher & Maher.

Thinker Sheets. Becky Daniel & Charlie Daniel. 64p. (J). (gr. 2-6). 1978. 8.99 (*0-916456-23-4*, GA78) Good Apple.

Thinker Task Cards. Lisa Newsome. (Illus.). 128p. 1992. student ed. 12.99 (*0-86653-681-7*, 1415) Good Apple.

Thinkers. H. Newcomb Morse. 270p. (C). 1994. lib. bdg. 38.00 (*0-8191-9666-5*) U Pr of Amer.

Thinkers. Michael Pollard. Ed. by Rebecca Stefoff. LC 91-33296. (Pioneers in History Ser.). (Illus.). 48p. (J). (gr. 5-8). 1992. lib. bdg. 19.93 (*1-56074-036-1*) Garrett Ed Corp.

Thinkers & Feelers Mini Seminar Kit. William D. Murray & Rosalie R. Murray. (Type & Temperament Seminar Kits Ser.). 83p. 1989. 99.95 (*1-878287-13-3*, KTAF) Type & Temperament.

Thinkers & Teachers of Modern Judaism. Raphael Patai & Emanuel S. Goldsmith. LC 94-16063. 256p. 1995. 24.95 (*1-55778-701-8*) Paragon Hse.

Thinkers & Tinkers: Early American Men of Science. Silvio A. Bedini. (Illus.). 519p. 1983. reprint ed. 30.00 (*0-910845-19-0*, 901) Landmark Ent.

Thinkers' Chess. Stephan Gerzadowicz & Robert B. Long. (Illus.). 151p. (Orig.). 1995. pap. 17.95 (*0-938650-65-3*) Thinkers Pr.

***Thinker's Dictionary.** 1996. pap. text ed. write for info. (*0-07-066890-6*) McGraw.

Thinker's Guide to Recovery: A Rational Approach. Kenneth B. Peiser. 1993. pap. 9.95 (*0-8306-4218-8*) McGraw-Hill Prof.

Thinker's Guide to Ultrasonic Imaging. Raymond L. Powis & Wendy J. Powis. LC 83-21704. (Illus.). 430p. 1984. 55.00 (*0-683-06961-6*) Williams & Wilkins.

Thinker's Guide to Visual Basic. J. D. Evans, Jr. 1000p. (Orig.). 1996. pap. 59.95 (*1-881679-55-1*) ETN.

Thinker's Mother Goose. Nancy Polette. (Illus.). 32p. (J). 1983. pap. 3.95 (*0-913839-25-6*) Pieces of Lrning.

Thinkers of Indian Renaissance. Ed. by D. H. Bishop. 420p. 1986. 36.95 (*0-318-37041-7*) Asia Bk Corp.

Thinkers of the East. Idries Shah. 198p. 1971. 25.00 (*0-900860-46-4*, Pub. by Octagon Pr UK) ISHK.

Thinkers of the East. Idries Shah. 208p. 1972. mass mkt. 5.95 (*0-14-003410-2*, Penguin Bks) Viking Penguin.

Thinkers of the Twentieth Century. Elizabeth Devine & Michael Held. 635p. (C). 1987. 350.00 (*81-7002-026-3*, Pub. by Himalayan Bks II) St Mut.

Thinkers of the Twentieth Century. 2nd ed. Ed. by Roland Turner. 1987. 125.00 (*0-912289-83-X*) St James Pr.

Thinkers of the Twentieth Century: A Biographical, Bibliographical & Critical Dictionary. Ed. by Elizabeth Devine et al. 643p. 1984. 75.00 (*0-8103-1516-5*) Gale.

Thinkers of the Twenty Years' Crisis: Inter-War Idealism Reassessed. David Long & Peter C. Wilson. 368p. 1996. text ed. 74.00 (*0-19-827855-1*) OUP.

Thinkers Through Time: Reading Ethics with Literature. Mary B. Curran. LC 93-23843. 196p. 1993. pap. write for info. (*0-916078-31-0*) Iris Pr.

Thinker's Toolkit. Morgan Jones. 1997. 15.00 (*0-8129-2808-3*, Times Bks) Random.

Thinker's Toolkit: Fourteen Skills for Making Smarter Decisions in Business & in Life. Morgan D. Jones. 1995. 25.00 (*0-8129-2601-3*, Times Bks) Random.

Thinkertoys: A Handbook of Creativity in Business. Michael Michalko. (Illus.). 352p. (Orig.). 1991. pap. 17. 95 (*0-89815-408-1*) Ten Speed Pr.

Thinking. Gary Kirby & Jeff Goodpaster. LC 94-8445. 304p. 1994. pap. text ed. 30.40 (*0-13-030958-3*) P-H.

Thinking. Kathie B. Smith & Victoria Crenson. LC 87-5886. (Question Bks.). (Illus.). 24p. (J). (gr. k-3). 1988. lib. bdg. 11.89 (*0-8167-1016-3*) Troll Communs.

Thinking. Roxanne Vallet. (Illus.). 14p. (J). 1992. pap. 10.95 (*1-895583-39-X*) MAYA Pubs.

Thinking. Beth A. Wise. (Toddler Time Ser.). (Illus.). 16p. (J). 1992. student ed., pap. 2.95 (*1-56293-190-3*) McClanahan Bk.

Thinking, Vol. 1. Hannah Arendt. (Life of the Mind). 1978. 12.50 (*0-685-73339-4*) HarBrace.

Thinking: An Experimental & Social Study. Frederic C. Bartlett. LC 82-983. 203p. 1982. reprint ed. text ed. 55. 00 (*0-313-23412-4*, BART, Greenwood Pr) Greenwood.

Thinking: Directed, Undirected & Creative. 3rd ed. Ken Gilhooly. (Illus.). 304p. 1996. boxed 32.00 (*0-12-283485-2*) Acad Pr.

Thinking: From Association to Gestalt. Jean M. Mandler & George Mandler. LC 81-13347. (Perspectives in Psychology Ser.). x, 300p. 1982. reprint ed. text ed. 59. 75 (*0-313-23261-X*, MATK, Greenwood Pr) Greenwood.

Thinking: Skills for Success. Edward De Bono. 128p. (C). 1990. pap. text ed. 14.95 (*1-56118-048-3*) Paradigm MN.

Thinking: Studies of Covert Language Processes. Ed. by Frank J. McGuigan. LC 66-15745. (Century Psychology Ser.). (Illus.). 1966. pap. text ed. 16.95 (*0-89197-450-4*) Irvington.

Thinking: The Expanding Frontier. Ed. by William Maxwell. (Problem Solving Ser.). 304p. 1983. text ed. 59.95 (*0-89859-731-5*) L Erlbaum Assocs.

Thinking: The Second International Conference. Ed. by David Perkins et al. 552p. 1987. text ed. 110.00 (*0-89859-805-2*) L Erlbaum Assocs.

Thinking about American Higher Education. Edward L. Delaney et al. Ed. by J. Wade Gilley & George B. Vaughan. (ACE-Oryx Series on Higher Education). 224p. 1991. 27.95 (*0-02-897162-0*, ACE-Oryx) Oryx Pr.

Thinking about Answers: The Application of Cognitive Processes to Survey Methodology. Seymour Sudman et al. LC 95-16504. (Psychology Ser.). 320p. 33.95 (*0-7879-0120-2*) Jossey-Bass.

Thinking about Ants. Barbara Brenner. LC 95-45990. (Illus.). (J). 1996. write for info. (*1-57255-210-7*); pap. write for info. (*1-57255-209-3*) Mondo Pubng.

Thinking about Art. Edmund B. Feldman. (Illus.). 480p. (C). 1985. pap. text ed. 51.75 (*0-13-917493-1*) P-H.

Thinking about Art. Edward Lucie-Smith. 237p. 1968. 15. 95 (*0-7145-0552-8*) Dufour.

Thinking about Art: Conversations with Susan Hiller. Ed. by Barbara Einzig. LC 95-11073. 240p. 1996. text ed. 59.95 (*0-7190-4564-9*, Pub. by Manchester Univ Pr UK); text ed. 19.95 (*0-7190-4565-7*, Pub. by Manchester Univ Pr UK) St Martin.

Thinking about Basic Beliefs: An Introduction to Philosophy. Howard Kahane. 238p. (C). 1983. pap. 35. 95 (*0-534-01318-X*) Wadsworth Pub.

Thinking about Being: Aspects of Heidegger's Thought. Robert W. Shahan & J. N. Mohanty. LC 81-40297. 208p. 1984. 29.95 (*0-8061-1780-X*) U of Okla Pr.

Thinking about Being a Mathematics Teacher. Cooney. 1996. pap. text ed. 15.00 (*0-435-07107-6*) Heinemann.

Thinking about 'Beowulf' James W. Earl. LC 93-47132. xiv, 204p. 1995. 42.50 (*0-8047-1700-1*) Stanford U Pr.

***Thinking about "Beowulf"** James W. Earl. 1996. pap. text ed. 13.95 (*0-8047-2795-3*) Stanford U Pr.

Thinking about Biology: An Invitation to Current Theoretical Biology. Ed. by Francisco J. Varela & Wilfred D. Stein. LC 92-42853. (C). 1993. 39.95 (*0-201-62453-2*); pap. 24.95 (*0-201-62454-0*) Addison-Wesley.

***Thinking about Children.** Winnicott. 1996. pap. write for info. (*0-201-32794-5*) Addison-Wesley.

Thinking about Children. Donald W. Winnicott. 320p. (YA). 1996. 25.00 (*0-201-40700-0*) Addison-Wesley.

Thinking about Children: Sociology & Fertility in Post-War England. Joan Busfield & Michael Paddon. LC 76-22986. 324p. reprint ed. pap. 92.40 (*0-318-34765-2*, 2031625) Bks Demand.

Thinking about Crime. rev. ed. James Q. Wilson. 1985. pap. 13.00 (*0-394-72917-X*, Vin) Random.

Thinking about Development. Lisa Peattie. LC 81-15858. (Environment, Development, & Public Policy: Public Policy & Social Services Ser.). 208p. 1981. 45.00 (*0-306-40761-2*, Plenum Pr) Plenum.

Thinking about Development. Paul Streeten. (Raffaele Mattioli Lectures on the History of Economic Thought). (Illus.). 396p. (C). 1995. text ed. 49.95 (*0-521-48276-3*) Cambridge U Pr.

***Thinking about Development.** Paul Streeten. 425p. 1997. pap. text ed. 19.95 (*0-521-59973-3*) Cambridge U Pr.

Thinking about Education: Philosophical Issues & Perspectives. Ed. by Erskine S. Dottin et al. LC 89-33763. (Illus.). 218p. (C). 1990. lib. bdg. 34.50 (*0-8191-7504-8*) U Pr of Amer.

Thinking about Ethics. Richard L. Purtill. 160p. 1976. pap. text ed. 38.40 (*0-13-917716-7*) P-H.

Thinking about Exhibitions. Ed. by Reesa Greenberg et al. LC 95-14477. 376p. (C). 1996. pap. 22.95 (*0-415-11590-6*) Routledge.

Thinking about Exhibitions. Ed. by Reesa Greenberg et al. LC 95-14477. 376p. (C). (gr. 13). 1996. text ed. 79.95 (*0-415-11589-2*) Routledge.

***Thinking about God.** Ruqaiyyah W. Maqsood. 140p. 1996. pap. 9.95 (*0-614-21190-5*, 1495) Kazi Pubns.

Thinking about God. Susan McCaslin. (Illus.). 24p. (J). (ps-4). 1994. 7.95 (*0-89622-615-8*) Twenty-Third.

Thinking about God: An Introduction to Christian Theology. rev. ed. Fisher Humphreys. LC 94-41297. 1995. 19.00 (*0-914520-34-2*) Insight Pr.

Thinking about God: An Introduction to Theology. Dorothee Solle. Tr. by John Bowden from GER. LC 90-48834. 224p. (Orig.). (C). 1990. pap. 15.95 (*0-334-02476-5*) TPI PA.

Thinking about Growth: And Other Essays on Economic Growth & Welfare. Moses Abramovitz. (Studies in Economic History & Policy: The United States in the Twentieth Century). (Illus.). 406p. (C). 1989. text ed. 85.00 (*0-521-33396-2*) Cambridge U Pr.

Thinking about Growth: And Other Essays on Economic Growth & Welfare. Moses Abramovitz. (Studies in Economic History & Policy: The United States in the Twentieth Century). (Illus.). 406p. (C). 1991. pap. text ed. 20.95 (*0-521-40774-5*) Cambridge U Pr.

Thinking about Health. 3rd ed. Vestal. 1994. pap. text ed. 18.00 (*0-13-078619-5*) P-H.

Thinking about Health Access. 4th ed. Vestal. 1995. pap. text ed. 17.00 (*0-205-19919-4*) Allyn.

Thinking about Human Rights: Contending Approaches to Human Rights in U. S. Foreign Policy. Michael R. Fowler. Ed. by Kenneth W. Thompson. (Exxon Education Foundation Series on Rhetoric & Political Discourse: Vol. 6). (Orig.). (C). 1987. pap. text ed. 24.00 (*0-8191-5819-4*, Pub. by White Miller Center); lib. bdg. 46.00 (*0-8191-5818-6*, Pub. by White Miller Center) U Pr of Amer.

Thinking about Imps. Boeder. 12.95 (*0-939460-76-9*, 0795) Devyn Pr.

Thinking about Knowing. Alan Howard. 1985. pap. 4.95 (*0-916786-81-1*, Saint George Pubns) R Steiner Col Pubns.

Thinking About Law: Perspectives on the History, Philosophy & Sociology of Law. Ed. by Rosemary Hunter et al. 272p. 1996. pap. 29.95 (*1-86373-842-8*, Pub. by Allen & Unwin Aust Pty AT) Paul & Co Pubs.

Thinking about Law School: A Minority Guide. 1995. write for info. (*0-942639-52-9*) Law Schl Admission.

Thinking about Logic: An Introduction to the Philosophy of Logic. Stephen Read. 192p. 1995. pap. 17.95 (*0-19-289238-X*) OUP.

Thinking about Management. Theodore Levitt. 160p. 1990. 22.95 (*0-02-918605-6*, Free Press) Free Pr.

Thinking about Matter: Studies in the History of Chemical Philosophy. John H. Brooke. LC 95-10977. (Collected Studies: Vol. CS502). 304p. 1995. 87.50 (*0-86078-464-9*, Pub. by Variorum UK) Ashgate Pub Co.

Thinking about Music: An Introduction to the Philosophy of Music. Lewis Rowell. LC 82-21979. (Illus.). 304p. 1984. pap. text ed. 17.95 (*0-87023-461-7*) U of Mass Pr.

Thinking about Music: The Collected Writings of Rose Lee Finney. Ed. by Frederic Goossen. LC 90-11104. 224p. 1991. text ed. 34.95 (*0-8173-0521-1*) U of Ala Pr.

Thinking about Nature: An Investigation of Nature, Value, & Ecology. Andrew Brennan. LC 88-13977. 256p. 1988. 35.00 (*0-8203-1087-5*); pap. 17.00 (*0-8203-1088-3*) U of Ga Pr.

Thinking about Ordinary Differential Equations. Robert E. O'Malley, Jr. (Texts in Applied Mathematics Ser.: No. 18). (Illus.). 150p. (C). 1997. text ed. 69.95 (*0-521-55314-8*) Cambridge U Pr.

Thinking about Ordinary Differential Equations. Robert E. O'Malley, Jr. (Texts in Applied Mathematics Ser.: No. 18). (Illus.). 150p. (C). 1997. pap. text ed. 24.95 (*0-521-55742-9*) Cambridge U Pr.

Thinking about Our Kids: An Agenda for American Education. Harold Howe, III. LC 93-25789. 224p. 1993. 24.95 (*0-02-915294-1*, Free Press) Free Pr.

Thinking about Our Taxes: Myths & Morality. John L. Fremstad. 1989. pap. 5.00 (*1-55614-128-9*) U of SD Gov Res Bur.

Thinking about Police: Contemporary Readings. 2nd ed. Carl B. Klockars & Stephen D. Mastrofski. 1991. pap. text ed. write for info. (*0-07-035081-7*) McGraw.

Thinking about Political Corruption. Peter DeLeon. LC 93-4026. 256p. (gr. 13). 1993. text ed. 53.95 (*0-87332-838-8*); pap. text ed. 23.95 (*0-87332-839-6*) M E Sharpe.

Thinking about Politics: Comparisons of Experts & Novices. Ed. by Jon A. Krosnick. 158p. 1990. pap. text ed. 15.95 (*0-89862-441-X*) Guilford Pr.

Thinking about Population: An Introduction to Modern Demography. Ibtihaj S. Arafat & Donald E. Allen. LC 94-78415. 400p. (Orig.). 1995. text ed. 48.95 (*1-882289-28-5*); pap. text ed. 34.95 (*1-882289-27-7*) Gen Hall.

Thinking about Program Evaluation. Richard A. Berk & Peter H. Rossi. (Illus.). 128p. (C). 1990. text ed. 39.95 (*0-8039-3704-0*); pap. text ed. 17.50 (*0-8039-3705-9*) Sage.

Thinking about Religion: A Philosophical Introduction to Religion. Richard L. Purtill. 1978. pap. text ed. write for info. (*0-13-917724-8*) P-H.

Thinking about SDI. Stephen J. Hadley. (Orig.). (C). 1986. pap. text ed. 11.75 (*0-941700-21-6*) JH FPI SAIS.

Thinking about Social Problems. Richard L. Henshel. 292p. (C). 1990. pap. text ed. 18.75 (*0-15-591488-X*) HB Coll Pubs.

Thinking about Social Thinking. 2nd ed. Antony G. Flew. LC 94-39955. 278p. 1995. pap. 17.95 (*0-87975-954-2*) Prometheus Bks.

Thinking about Society: Theory & Practice. I. C. Jarvie. 520p. 1985. lib. bdg. 178.50 (*90-277-2068-1*, D Reidel) Kluwer Ac.

Thinking about the Earth: A History of Ideas in Geology. David R. Oldroyd. LC 95-48234. (Illus.). 488p. (C). 1996. 45.00 (*0-674-88382-9*) HUP.

Thinking about the Environment: Readings on Politics, Property, & the Physical World. Ed. by Matthew A. Cahn & Rory O'Brien. LC 96-10749. 224p. (C). (gr. 13). 1996. text ed. 62.95 (*1-56324-795-X*) M E Sharpe.

Thinking about the Environment: Readings on Politics, Property, & the Physical World. Ed. by Matthew A. Cahn & Rory O'Brien. LC 96-10749. 224p. (C). 1996. pap. text ed. 24.95 (*1-56324-796-8*) M E Sharpe.

Thinking about the Family: Views of the Parents & Children. Ed. by Richard D. Ashmore & David M. Brodzinsky. 336p. (C). 1986. text ed. 69.95 (*0-89859-693-9*) L Erlbaum Assocs.

***Thinking about the Holocaust: After Half a Century.** Alvin H. Rosenfeld. LC 97-3086. (Jewish Literature & Culture Ser.). 1997. write for info. (*0-253-33331-8*); pap. write for info. (*0-253-21137-9*) Ind U Pr.

Thinking about the Longstanding Problems of Virtue & Happiness: Essays, a Play, Two Poems & a Prayer. Tony Kushner. 276p. 1995. 25.95 (*1-55936-106-9*); pap. 13.95 (*1-55936-100-X*) Theatre Comm.

Thinking about the Playwright. Eric Bentley. 364p. 1987. pap. 15.95 (*0-8101-0733-3*) Northwestern U Pr.

Thinking about the Unthinkable in the Nineteen Eighties. Herman Kahn. 1985. 8.95 (*0-671-60449-X*) S&S Trade.

Thinking about the World: Building Geography Foundations. Lawrence Brown. (YA). 1993. pap. 16.00 (*0-201-45546-3*) Addison-Wesley.

Thinking about Thinking. Alan Howard. 1981. pap. 4.95 (*0-916786-51-X*, Saint George Pubns) R Steiner Col Pubns.

Thinking about Women. 4th ed. Margaret L. Andersen. 432p. 1996. pap. 35.00 (*0-205-17566-X*) Allyn.

Thinking about World Change: Specialists, Scientists & Historians Make Predictions about the Future of the World. 1992. lib. bdg. 88.95 (*0-8490-5493-1*) Gordon Pr.

Thinking Across Cultures: The Third International Conference on Thinking. Ed. by Donald M. Topping et al. (Third International Conference on Thinking Ser.). 512p. 1989. text ed. 110.00 (*0-89859-913-X*) L Erlbaum Assocs.

Thinking Across the American Grain: Ideology, Intellect, & the New Pragmatism. Giles Gunn. LC 91-23913. 288p. 1991. pap. text ed. 16.95 (*0-226-31077-9*) U Ch Pr.

***Thinking Activities for Books Children Love: A Whole Language Approach.** Carolyn Mohr et al. (Illus.). 221p. 1988. pap. text ed. 21.50 (*0-87287-697-7*) Teacher Ideas Pr.

Thinking Ahead: Preparing for Controversy. 1991. 11.85 (*0-917160-27-4*) Am Sch Health.

Thinking AIDS: The Social Response to the Biological Threat. Mary C. Bateson & Richard A. Goldsby. 1989. 12.95 (*0-685-22769-3*); pap. 7.95 (*0-685-22770-7*) Addison-Wesley.

Thinking Allowed: Conversations on the Leading Edge of Knowledge & Discovery. Jeffrey Mishlove. LC 91-77972. 372p. 1995. pap. 16.95 (*0-933031-64-5*) Coun Oak Bks.

Thinking Aloud. Richard Bates & Edward Kynaston. 444p. (C). 1983. 45.00 (*0-7300-0015-X*, Pub. by Deakin Univ AT) St Mut.

Thinking Aloud: Fragments of Autobiography. Peter Cotes. (Illus.). 208p. 9400. 35.00 (*0-7206-0900-3*, Pub. by P Owen Ltd UK) Dufour.

Thinking Aloud: Talks on Teaching the Alexander Technique. Walter Carrington. 176p. 1994. text ed. 22.00 (*0-9644352-0-9*) Mornum Time.

Thinking & Creativity Step by Step: Lateral & Vertical Thinking. 1991. lib. bdg. 250.00 (*0-8490-4640-8*) Gordon Pr.

Thinking & Deciding. Jonathan Baron. (Illus.). 500p. 1988. 74.95 (*0-521-34253-8*); pap. 34.95 (*0-521-34800-5*) Cambridge U Pr.

Thinking & Deciding. 2nd ed. Jonathan Baron. LC 93-46230. (Illus.). 510p. (C). 1994. text ed. 64.95 (*0-521-43131-X*); pap. text ed. 26.95 (*0-521-43732-6*) Cambridge U Pr.

Thinking & Destiny. 11th ed. Harold W. Percival. LC 47-1811. (Illus.). 1000p. (C). 1995. 29.95 (*0-911650-09-1*, 091); pap. 19.95 (*0-911650-06-7*) Word Foun.

***Thinking & Feeling.** Angela Royston. LC 96-29403. (Body Systems Ser.). (J). 1997. lib. bdg. write for info. (*1-57572-095-7*) Rigby Interact Libr.

Thinking & Learning: Matching Developmental Stages with Curriculum & Instruction. Lawrence F. Lowery. 101p. (Orig.). 1996. reprint ed. pap. 12.95 (*0-9624475-6-0*) Bks Educators.

Thinking & Learning Skills Vol. 2: Research & Open Questions. Ed. by S. F. Chipman et al. 640p. 1985. text ed. 99.95 (*0-89859-166-X*) L Erlbaum Assocs.

Thinking & Learning Skills, Vol. 1: Relating Instruction to Research. Ed. by Judith W. Segal et al. 568p. 1985. text ed. 89.95 (*0-89859-165-1*) L Erlbaum Assocs.

Thinking & Learning Together: Curriculum & Community in a Primary Classroom. Bobbi Fisher. LC 94-43728. 408p. 1995. pap. text ed. 26.00 (*0-435-08844-0*, 08844) Heinemann.

Thinking & Literacy: The Mind at Work. Ed. by Carolyn N. Hedley et al. 328p. 1995. pap. 32.50 (*0-8058-1548-1*); text ed. 69.95 (*0-8058-1547-3*) L Erlbaum Assocs.

Thinking & Living Skills: General Semantics for Critical Thinking. Created by Gregory Sawin. (Illus.). 255p. (Orig.). 1995. pap. 17.00 (*0-918970-42-3*) Intl Gen Semantics.

Thinking & Problem Solving. Ed. by Robert J. Sternberg. (Handbook of Perception & Cognition Ser.). (Illus.). 461p. 1994. text ed. 69.00 (*0-12-161952-4*) Acad Pr.

Thinking & Problem Solving Newsletter. Ed. by Julia S. Hough & Donald Woods. (Problem Solving Ser.). 385p. (C). 1984. pap. text ed. 69.95 (*0-89859-743-9*) L Erlbaum Assocs.

Thinking & Reading in the Philosophy of Religion. Dane Gorder. 314p. 1994. pap. 30.00 (*0-318-69372-0*) Haven Pubns.

Thinking & Reasoning. Alan Garnham & Jane Oakhill. (Illus.). 320p. 1994. pap. 24.95 (*0-631-17003-0*) Blackwell Pubs.

Thinking & Representation. H. H. Price. (Studies in Philosophy: No. 40). (C). 1977. lib. bdg. 24.95 (*0-8383-0117-7*) M S G Haskell Hse.

Thinking & Speaking: A Guide to Intelligent Oral Communication. 5th ed. Otis M. Walter & Robert L. Scott. 320p. (C). 1984. pap. write for info. (*0-02-424370-1*, Macmillan Coll) P-H.

Thinking & the Structure of the World - Das Denken & die Struktur der Welt: Hector-Neri Castaneda's Epistemic Ontology Presented & Criticised - Hector-Neri Castandas Epistemische Ontologie in Darstellung & Kritik. Ed. by Klaus Jacobi & Pape Helmut. (Foundations of Communication & Cognition Ser.). xiv, 537p. (C). 1990. lib. bdg. 183.10 (*3-11-011302-3*) De Gruyter.

Thinking & Writing about Literature. Michael Meyer. 208p. (C). 1995. pap. text ed. 13.50 (*0-312-11166-5*) St Martin.

Thinking & Writing about Psychology. Spencer A. Rathus. (C). 1993. pap. text ed. 11.50 (*0-15-500591-X*) HB Coll Pubs.

Thinking & Writing about Psychology. 2nd ed. Spencer A. Rathus. 168p. (C). 1996. pap. text ed. 10.75 (*0-15-504141-X*) HB Coll Pubs.

Thinking & Writing by Design: A Cross-Disciplinary Rhetoric & Reader. Allene Cooper. LC 95-36508. 1995. pap. text ed. 29.00 (*0-02-324702-9*, Macmillan Coll) P-H.

Thinking & Writing in College: A Naturalistic Study of Students in Four Disciplines. Barbara E. Walvoord & Lucille P. McCarthy. LC 91-18272. (Illus.). 281p. 1990. reprint ed. pap. 80.10 (*0-608-01624-1*, 2062209) Bks Demand.

Thinking & Writing Process: A Process for All Ages. Thea M. Holtan. (Writer's Guide Ser.: Level 1). 22p. (J). (gr. k-2). 1994. pap. text ed. 30.00 (*1-887071-00-8*) Thea-Thot.

Thinking & Writing Process: A Process for All Ages. Thea M. Holtan. (Writer's Guide Ser.: Level 2). 30p. (J). (gr. 3-4). 1994. pap. text ed. 40.00 (*1-887071-01-6*) Thea-Thot.

Thinking & Writing Process: A Process for All Ages. Thea M. Holtan. (Writer's Guide Ser.: Level 3). 40p. (YA). (gr. 5-12). 1994. pap. text ed. 50.00 (*1-887071-02-4*) Thea-Thot.

Thinking & Writing Process: A Process for All Ages. Thea M. Holtan. (Instructor's Guide Ser.). 336p. 1995. teacher ed. 105.00 (*1-887071-03-2*) Thea-Thot.

Thinking Ape: The Evolutionary Origins of Intelligence. Richard Byrne. (Illus.). 264p. (C). 1995. pap. text ed. 25.95 (*0-19-852265-7*) OUP.

Thinking Approach to Interdisciplinary Experience. Hope Irvine. (Illus.). 153p. 1993. teacher ed., pap. 10.00 (*0-89824-218-5*) Trillium Pr.

Thinking Back: The Perils of Writing History. C. Vann Woodward. LC 85-19692. x, 158p. 1986. 14.95 (*0-8071-1304-2*); pap. 11.95 (*0-8071-1377-8*) La State U Pr.

Thinking Bayonet. James K. Hosmer. (Notable American Authors Ser.). 1992. reprint ed. lib. bdg. 75.00 (*0-7812-3184-1*) Rprt Serv.

Thinking Between the Lines: Computers & the Comprehension of Casual Descriptions. Gary C. Borchardt. LC 93-36770. (Artificial Intelligence Ser.). (Illus.). 320p. 1994. 37.50 (*0-262-02374-1*) MIT Pr.

Thinking Beyond the Edge: Wisdom for the Ages. Ed. by Richard A. Kapnick & Aidan A. Kelly. (ISPE Collection). 500p. 1994. 30.00 (*1-883322-04-9*) Agamemnon Pr.

***Thinking Black.** Dewayne Wickham. 1997. pap. 14.00 (*0-609-80081-7*) Random Hse Value.

Thinking Black: Some of the Nation's Most Thoughtful & Provocative Black Columnists Speak Their Minds. Ed. by DeWayne Wickham. LC 95-34133. (Illus.). 256p. 1996. 23.00 (*0-517-59937-6*) Crown Pub Group.

Thinking Bodies. Ed. by Juliet F. MacCannell & Laura Zakarin. LC 93-34805. (Irvine Studies in the Humanities). 288p. 1994. 39.50 (*0-8047-2306-0*); pap. 15.95 (*0-8047-2304-4*) Stanford U Pr.

Thinking Body. Mabel E. Todd. 1991. lib. bdg. 250.00 (*0-8490-4646-7*) Gordon Pr.

Thinking Body: A Study of the Balancing Forces of Dynamic Man. Mabel E. Todd. LC 68-28048. (Illus.). 314p. 1968. reprint ed. pap. 17.95 (*0-87127-014-5*, Dance Horizons) Princeton Bk Co.

Thinking Body, Dancing Mind: Taosports for Extraordinary Performance in Athletics. Huang C. L. Al. 336p. 1994. pap. 13.95 (*0-553-37378-1*) Bantam.

Thinking Books. Susan Swan & Richard White. LC 94-4126. 1994. write for info. (*0-7507-0294-X*, Falmer Pr) Taylor & Francis.

Thinking Books. Ed. by Richard White & Susan Swan. 144p. 1994. pap. 21.95 (*0-7507-0295-8*, Falmer Pr) Taylor & Francis.

Thinking, Changing, Rearranging. Jill Anderson. 1985. reprint ed. student ed. 8.00 (*0-9608284-0-0*); reprint ed. teacher ed., pap. text ed. 17.00 (*0-9608284-1-9*) Timberline Pr.

Thinking, Changing, Rearranging: Improving Self Esteem in Young People. Jill Anderson. LC 88-2289. (Illus.). 80p. (J). (gr. 2). 1990. reprint ed. student ed., pap. 7.50 (*0-943920-30-2*) Metamorphous Pr.

Thinking Children & Education. Matthew Lipman. 768p. 1993. per. 42.95 (*0-8403-8584-6*) Kendall-Hunt.

Thinking Class: Sketches from a Cultural Worker. Joanna Kadi. LC 96-46462. 170p. 1996. 40.00 (*0-89608-548-1*); pap. 14.00 (*0-89608-547-3*) South End Pr.

Thinking Classroom: Learning & Teaching in a Culture of Thinking. Shari Tishman et al. LC 94-11003. 1994. pap. text ed. 25.00 (*0-205-16508-7*) Allyn.

Thinking Clearly. Douglass D. McFerran. 124p. 1993. per. 27.24 (*0-8403-9015-7*) Kendall-Hunt.

***Thinking Clearly: An Adventure in Mental Fitness.** 3rd rev. ed. Jerry Stocking. Ed. by Roger Anderson. (Illus.). 200p. 1997. pap. write for info. (*0-9629593-7-5*) Moose Ear Pr.

Thinking Clearly about Psychology, 2 vols. Ed. by Dante Cicchetti & William M. Grove. 864p. 1991. Set. text ed. 59.95 (*0-8166-1918-2*) U of Minn Pr.

Thinking Clearly about Psychology: Essays on Matters of Public Interest, Vol. 1. Ed. by William M. Grove & Dante Cicchetti. 320p. 1991. text ed. 39.95 (*0-8166-1891-7*) U of Minn Pr.

Thinking Clearly about Psychology Vol. 1: Essays on Matters of Public Interest, Vol. 2. Dante Cicchetti & William M. Grove. 320p. 1991. 44.95 (*0-8166-1892-5*) U of Minn Pr.

Thinking Computers & Virtual Persons: Essays on the Intentionality of Machines. Ed. by Eric Dietrich. (Illus.). 363p. 1994. pap. text ed. 59.95 (*0-12-215495-9*) Acad Pr.

Thinking Connections: Learning to Think & Thinking to Learn. David N. Perkins. (J). (gr. 4-7). 1993. pap. 24.95 (*0-201-81998-8*) Addison-Wesley.

Thinking Constructively about Science, Technology, & Society Education. Dennis W. Cheek. LC 91-9607. (SUNY Series in Curriculum Issues & Inquiries). (Illus.). 262p. (C). 1992. text ed. 21.50 (*0-7914-0939-2*) State U NY Pr.

Thinking Cop - Feeling Cop: A Study in Police Personalities. 3rd ed. Stephen M. Hennessy. 162p. 1996. pap. 9.95 (*1-887049-03-7*) Leader Scottsdale.

Thinking Course: How to Improve Your Thinking. 1991. lib. bdg. 250.00 (*0-8490-4645-9*) Gordon Pr.

Thinking Creatically: A Systematic, Interdisciplinary Approach to Creative-Critical Thinking. Pref. by Kenneth G. Johnson. 325p. 1991. pap. 15.95 (*0-910780-09-9*) Inst Gen Seman.

Thinking Creatively. Leona E. Tyler. LC 83-48166. (Jossey-Bass Social & Behavioral Science Ser.). 240p. reprint ed. pap. 68.40 (*0-8357-4925-8*, 2037855) Bks Demand.

Thinking Critically, 4 Vols. Chaffee. (C). 1994. teacher ed., pap. 3.96 (*0-395-69070-6*) HM.

Thinking Critically, 5 Vols. Chaffee. (C). 1996. pap. 34.36 (*0-395-83105-9*) HM.

Thinking Critically, 4 Vols. Chaffee. (C). 1993. pap. 34.36 (*0-395-67546-4*) HM.

Thinking Critically, 5 Vols. John Chaffee. (C). 1997. teacher ed., pap. 11.96 (*0-395-83106-7*) HM.

Thinking Critically: Techniques for Logical Reasoning. James H. Kiersky & Nicholas J. Caste. LC 94-34797. 448p. (C). 1995. pap. text ed. 36.50 (*0-314-04352-7*) West Pub.

Thinking Critically about Critical Thinking. 3rd ed. Diane F. Halpern. 1995. wbk. ed., pap. 37.50 (*0-8058-2040-X*); teacher ed., pap. write for info. (*0-8058-2177-5*) L Erlbaum Assocs.

An Asterisk (*) at the beginning of an entry indicates that the title is appearing in BIP for the first time.

Thinking Critically about Critical Thinking: An Exercise Book to Accompany Thought & Knowledge: an Introduction to Critical Thinking. 3rd ed. Diane F. Halpern. 216p. 1995. pap. 19.95 (*0-8058-2032-9*) L Erlbaum Assocs.

Thinking Critically about Ethical Issues. 3rd ed. Vincent R. Ruggiero. 188p. (C). 1991. pap. text ed. 20.95 (*1-55934-071-1*, 1071) Mayfield Pub.

Thinking Critically about Ethical Issues. 4th ed. Vincent R. Ruggiero. LC 96-7989. 224p. 1996. pap. text ed. 20.95 (*1-55934-654-X*, 1654) Mayfield Pub.

Thinking Critically about New Age Ideas. William D. Gray. 164p. (C). 1991. pap. 26.95 (*0-534-14394-6*) Wadsworth Pub.

Thinking Critically About Reading, Writing, & Study Skills. Orlando. (C). 1996. pap. text ed. write for info. (*0-15-501030-1*) HB Coll Pubs.

Thinking Critically about Reading, Writing & Study Skills. Orlando. (C). 1996. teacher ed., pap. text ed. write for info. (*0-15-501637-7*) HB Coll Pubs.

Thinking Critically about Research Methods. John G. Benjafield. LC 93-29724. 1993. pap. text ed. 26.00 (*0-205-13917-5*) Allyn.

Thinking Critically about Research on Sex & Gender. Paula J. Caplan & Jeremy B. Caplan. LC 93-22718. (C). 1994. text ed. 17.95 (*0-06-501621-1*) Addson-Wesley Educ.

Thinking Development. Fred Justus. (Early Education Ser.). 24p. (gr. k). 1981. student ed. 5.00 (*0-8209-0213-6*, K-15) ESP.

Thinking Divorce? Consider the Shocking Personal & Financial Realities. Daniel Z. Shapiro. LC 82-25113. 108p. (Orig.). 1983. pap. 7.95 (*0-930256-11-5*) Almar.

***Thinking Ecologically: An Agenda for the Next Generation Project.** Marian Chertow. LC 97-14996. 1998. pap. text ed. 16.00 (*0-300-07303-8*) Yale U Pr.

***Thinking Ecologically: An Agenda for the Next Generation Project.** Marian R. Chertow. LC 97-14996. 1998. 35.00 (*0-300-07301-1*) Yale U Pr.

***Thinking, Feeling & Being.** Ignacio Matte-Blanco. (New Library of Psychoanalysis Ser.: Vol. 5). 360p. (C). 1988. pap. text ed. 22.95 (*0-415-00678-3*) Routledge.

Thinking, Feeling & Being. Ignatio Matte-Blanco. 300p. 1987. text ed. 37.50 (*0-415-00677-5*) Routledge.

Thinking, Feeling, & Doing. Emil Oestereicher. Ed. by Patrick M. Hughes. 208p. (Orig.). 1992. pap. 10.00 (*0-9605008-9-8*) Hermes Hse.

Thinking, Feeling, Behaving: An Emotional Education Curriculum for Adolescents. Ann Vernon. LC 89-60736. 254p. (Orig.). 1989. pap. text ed. 25.95 (*0-87822-306-1*, 3182) Res Press.

Thinking, Feeling, Behaving: An Emotional Education Curriculum for Children. Ann Vernon. LC 89-60713. 252p. (Orig.). 1989. pap. text ed. 25.95 (*0-87822-305-3*, 3181) Res Press.

Thinking Feminist: Key Concepts in Women's Studies. Ed. by Diane Richardson & Vicki Robinson. LC 92-28106. 368p. 1993. lib. bdg. 45.00 (*0-89862-989-6*) Guilford Pr.

Thinking Feminist: Key Concepts in Women's Studies. Ed. by Diane Richardson & Vicki Robinson. LC 92-28106. 368p. 1993. pap. text ed. 21.95 (*0-89862-160-7*) Guilford Pr.

Thinking for a Change. Michael Gelb. 224p. 1996. 23.00 (*0-517-59824-8*) Crown Pub Group.

Thinking for a Living: Education & the Wealth of Nations. Ray Marshall & Marc Tucker. LC 91-58596. 304p. 1993. reprint ed. pap. 14.00 (*0-465-08557-1*) Basic.

Thinking for Orchestra: Practical Exercises in Orchestration. Rene Leibowitz. 240p. reprint ed. lib. bdg. 39.00 (*0-685-14890-4*) Rprt Serv.

Thinking for Themselves: Developing Strategies for Reflective Learning. Jeni Wilson & Jan L. Wing. LC 93-23457. 150p. (YA). 1993. pap. text ed. 21.00 (*0-435-08805-X*, 08805) Heinemann.

Thinking for Yourself. Cheryl S. Johnson & Richard L. Johnson. (Living Skills Ser.). 113p. 1993. teacher ed. 8.95 (*1-884245-16-1*); pap. text ed. 7.95 (*1-884245-15-3*) Life Choices.

Thinking for Yourself: Developing Critical Thinking Skills Through Reading & Writing. 4th ed. Marlys Mayfield. LC 96-8677. (Freshman English/Advanced Writing Ser.). (C). 1997. pap. text ed. 37.95 (*0-534-51858-3*) Wadsworth Pub.

Thinking for Yourself: Developing Critical Thinking Skills Through Writing. 2nd ed. Marlys Mayfield. 424p. (C). 1991. pap. 27.95 (*0-534-13812-8*) Wadsworth Pub.

Thinking Fragments: Psychoanalysis, Feminism, & Postmodernism in the Contemporary West. Jane Flax. 287p. 1991. pap. 15.95 (*0-520-07305-3*) U CA Pr.

Thinking Fragments: Psychoanalysis, Feminism, & Postmodernism in the Contemporary West. Jane Flax. LC 89-4797. 387p. reprint ed. pap. 110.30 (*0-7837-4804-3*, 2044451) Bks Demand.

Thinking from A-Z. LC 96-15068. 160p. (C). 1996. text ed. 49.95 (*0-415-09685-5*) Routledge.

Thinking from A-Z. Nigel Warburton. LC 96-15068. 160p. 1996. pap. 9.95 (*0-415-09686-3*) Routledge.

***Thinking from the Han: Self-Truth, & Transcendence in Chinese & Western Culture.** David L. Hall & Roger T. Ames. LC 97-24491. 320p. (C). 1998. text ed. 74.50 (*0-7914-3613-6*) State U NY Pr.

***Thinking from the Han: Self-Truth, & Transcendence in Chinese & Western Culture.** David L. Hall & Roger T. Ames. 320p. (C). 1998. pap. text ed. 24.95 (*0-7914-3614-4*) State U NY Pr.

Thinking Game: A Guide to Effective Study. Eugene J. Meehan. LC 88-4335. (Chatham House Studies in Political Thinking). (Illus.). 256p. (Orig.). (C). 1988. pap. text ed. 19.95 (*0-934540-64-0*) Chatham Hse Pubs.

***Thinking Games to Play with Your Child.** 2nd rev. ed. Cheryl Tuttle & Penny Paquette. 120p. 1997. pap. 12.00 (*1-56565-810-8*, Legcy) Lowell Hse.

Thinking Games to Play with Your Child: Easy Ways to Develop Creative & Critical Thinking Skills. Cheryl G. Tuttle & Penny Paquette. 120p. 1991. pap. 9.95 (*0-929923-49-9*) Lowell Hse.

Thinking German Translation: A Course in Translation Method, German-English. Sandor Hervey et al. LC 95-5794. 256p. (C). 1995. pap. 19.95 (*0-415-11638-4*) Routledge.

Thinking German Translation: A Course in Translation Method, German-English. Sandor Hervey et al. LC 95-5794. 256p. (C). (gr. 13). 1995. text ed. 74.95 (*0-415-11637-6*) Routledge.

***Thinking Globally.** Andrew J. Robson. 1997. pap. text ed. write for info. (*0-07-053398-9*) McGraw.

Thinking Globally...Acting Locally. League of Women Voters Education Fund Staff. 87p. 1988. pap. 5.00 (*0-89959-406-9*, 849) LWVUS.

Thinking Goes to School: Piaget's Theory in Practice with Additional Thoughts. Hans G. Furth & Harry Wachs. (Illus.). 316p. (C). 1975. pap. text ed. 14.95 (*0-19-501927-X*) OUP.

Thinking Green: My Home. Photos by Ann Bogart. (Thinking Green Ser.). (Illus.). 24p. (J). (ps). 1993. 3.98 (*0-8317-2530-3*) Smithmark.

Thinking Green: My Neighborhood. Photos by Ann Bogart. (Thinking Green Ser.). (Illus.). 24p. (J). (ps). 1993. 3.98 (*0-8317-2529-X*) Smithmark.

Thinking Green! Essays on Environmentalism, Feminism & Nonviolence. Petra K. Kelly. 167p. 1994. 18.00 (*0-938077-62-7*) Parallax Pr.

Thinking Healthy & Slim: A Recipe Journal. rev. ed. Bonnie Gene. 114p. 1994. student ed. 15.00 (*0-9641788-0-X*) Bonnie Gene.

***Thinking Heart: Best Canadian Essays.** Ed. by George Galt. 256p. 1991. pap. 18.95 (*1-55082-033-8*, Pub. by Quarry Pr CN) LPC InBook.

Thinking Heavenward. Lillian De Waters. 42p. 1968. reprint ed. spiral bd. 3.50 (*0-7873-0275-9*) Hlth Research.

Thinking Heavenward (1913) Lillian De Waters. 1996. pap. 9.95 (*1-56459-968-X*) Kessinger Pub.

Thinking in Art: A Philosophical Approach to Art Education. Charles M. Dorn. 180p. (Orig.). 1994. pap. 22.00 (*0-937652-69-5*) Natl Art Ed.

Thinking in C. Bruce Eckel. 1995. pap. 36.95 (*0-13-917709-4*) P-H.

Thinking in Complexity. Klaus Mainzer. 1995. 34.50 (*0-387-57597-9*) Spr-Verlag.

Thinking in Complexity: The Complex Dynamics of Matter, Mind & Mankind. 2nd enl. rev. ed. Klaus Mainzer. LC 95-53966. (Illus.). xii, 350p. 1996. 39.95 (*3-540-60637-8*) Spr-Verlag.

***Thinking in Complexity: The Complex Dynamics of Matter, Mind, & Mankind.** 3rd ed. Klaus Mainzer. LC 97-656. 1997. 39.95 (*3-540-62555-0*) Spr-Verlag.

Thinking in Context: Teaching Cognitive Processes across the Elementary School Curriculum. Arthur A. Hyde & Marilyn M. Bizar. 224p. (C). 1989. pap. text ed. 32.95 (*0-8013-0065-7*, 75729) Longman.

Thinking in Education. Matthew Lipman. 292p. (C). 1991. text ed. 59.95 (*0-521-40032-5*); pap. text ed. 20.95 (*0-521-40911-X*) Cambridge U Pr.

Thinking in English: Deep Immersion English for Foreigners. Anna H. Klimes. 120p. 1995. per., pap. text ed. 5.95 (*1-886304-03-3*) LearnWell Pr.

Thinking in Henry James. Sharon Cameron. LC 89-4707. 208p. 1989. 35.95 (*0-226-09230-5*) U Ch Pr.

Thinking in Henry James. Sharon Cameron. (Illus.). 208p. 1991. pap. text ed. 14.95 (*0-226-09231-3*) U Ch Pr.

Thinking in Jazz: The Infinite Art of Improvisation. Paul F. Berliner. LC 93-34660. (Chicago Studies in Ethnomusicology). (Illus.). 904p. (C). 1994. pap. 29.95 (*0-226-04381-9*) U Ch Pr.

Thinking in Jewish. Jonathan Boyarin. 200p. 1996. pap. text ed. 14.95 (*0-226-06927-3*); lib. bdg. 39.95 (*0-226-06926-5*) U Ch Pr.

Thinking in Logo: A Sourcebook for Teachers of Primary Students. Gina Shimabukuro. 1988. pap. text ed. 22.50 (*0-201-22124-1*) Addison-Wesley.

Thinking in Pascal: A Systematic Approach. Daniel Solow. LC 87-17521. (Illus.). 768p. (C). 1988. pap. text ed. 39. 75 (*0-201-12063-1*) Addison-Wesley.

Thinking in Pictures: And Other Reports from My Life with Autism. Temple Grandin. LC 95-8513. (Illus.). 224p. 1995. 22.95 (*0-385-47792-9*) Doubleday.

Thinking in Pictures: And Other Reports from My Life with Autism. Temple Grandin. LC 96-10737. 1996. reprint ed. pap. 12.00 (*0-679-77289-8*, Vin) Random.

Thinking in Pictures: Dramatic Structure in D. W. Griffith's Biograph Films. Joyce E. Jesionowski. LC 86-30793. (Illus.). 304p. 1987. 45.00 (*0-520-05776-7*); pap. 15.00 (*0-520-06792-4*) U CA Pr.

Thinking in Pictures: The Making of the Movie Matewan. John Sayles. LC 87-11881. 288p. 1987. pap. 14.95 (*0-395-45399-2*) HM.

Thinking in Poetry. Conrad Garcia. 65p. (Orig.). (YA). (gr. 10-12). 1988. pap. 7.50 (*0-9621124-0-2*) C Garcia.

Thinking in School & Society. Francis Schrag. (Philosophy of Education Research Library). 192p. 1988. text ed. 25. 00 (*0-415-00174-9*) Routledge.

Thinking in Story: Preaching in a Post-Literate Age. Richard A. Jensen. LC 92-38127. 1992. pap. 11.00 (*1-55673-573-1*, 9319) CSS OH.

Thinking in the Classroom: A Survey of Programs. Paul Chance. 165p. (Orig.). 1986. pap. text ed. 16.95 (*0-8077-2794-6*) Tchrs Coll.

***Thinking in the Future Tense.** James. 1997. pap. 12.00 (*0-684-83269-0*, Touchstone Bks) S&S Trade.

Thinking in the Future Tense: Leadership Skills for a New Age. Jennifer James. 256p. 1996. 23.00 (*0-684-81098-0*, S&S) S&S Trade.

Thinking in Time: The Uses of History for Decision Makers. Richard E. Neustadt & Ernest R. May. 350p. (Orig.). 1988. pap. 14.95 (*0-02-922791-7*, Free Press) Free Pr.

Thinking in Writing. 3rd ed. Robert Atwan & Donald McQuade. 544p. (C). 1988. pap. text ed. write for info. (*0-07-554637-X*) McGraw.

Thinking Is a Basic Skill: Creating Humanities Materials for the Adult New Reader. V. K. Lawson. 55p. 1988. pap. text ed. 5.00 (*0-930713-33-8*) Lit Vol Am.

Thinking Is Form: The Drawings of Joseph Beuys. Ann Temkin & Bernice Rose. LC 92-81535. (Illus.). 280p. 1993. 50.00 (*0-500-01547-3*) Phila Mus Art.

Thinking Is Form: The Drawings of Joseph Beuys. Ann Temkin & Bernice Rose. (Illus.). 280p. 1993. pap. 30.00 (*0-87633-089-8*) Phila Mus Art.

Thinking Is Good for the Mind. Angeline Bennett. 22p. (Orig.). 1981. 3.00 (*0-911826-33-5*, 5020) Am Atheist.

Thinking Is the Key: Questioning Makes the Difference. Nancy L. Johnson. (Illus.). 96p. (J). 1992. 10.95 (*1-880505-01-0*, CLC0144) Pieces of Lrning.

Thinking It Through: Facilitator's Guide. Richard M. Foxx & Ron G. Bittle. 48p. (Orig.). 1989. pap. text ed. 10.95 (*0-87822-297-9*, 2979) Res Press.

Thinking It Through: Teaching a Problem-Solving Strategy for Community Living (Curriculum for Adolescents with Emotional Problems) Richard M. Foxx & Ron G. Bittle. (Orig.). 1989. pap. text ed. 14.95 (*0-87822-301-0*, 2997) Res Press.

Thinking It Through: Teaching a Problem-Solving Strategy for Community Living (Curriculum for Individuals with Brain Injuries) Richard M. Foxx & Ron G. Bittle. (Orig.). 1989. pap. text ed. 14.95 (*0-87822-300-2*, 2996) Res Press.

Thinking It Through: Teaching a Problem-Solving Strategy for Community Living (Curriculum for Individuals with Chronic Mental Illness) Richard M. Foxx & Ron G. Bittle. (Orig.). 1989. pap. text ed. 14.95 (*0-87822-299-5*, 2995) Res Press.

Thinking It Through: Teaching a Problem-Solving Strategy for Community Living (Curriculum for Individuals with Developmental Disabilities) Richard M. Foxx & Ron G. Bittle. (Orig.). 1989. pap. text ed. 14.95 (*0-87822-298-7*, 2987) Res Press.

Thinking Like a Communist: State & Legitimacy in the Soviet Union, China & Cuba. Tony Smith. LC 86-21815. (C). 1987. pap. text ed. 7.95 (*0-393-95691-1*) Norton.

Thinking Like a Lawyer: An Introduction to Legal Reasoning. Kenneth J. Vandevelde. LC 95-48965. (New Perspectives on Law, Culture, & Society Ser.). 1996. text ed. 65.00 (*0-8133-2203-0*) Westview.

Thinking Like a Lawyer: An Introduction to Legal Reasoning. Kenneth J. Vandevelde. (New Perspectives on Law, Culture, & Society Ser.). 254p. (C). 1996. pap. text ed. 21.00 (*0-8133-2204-9*) Westview.

Thinking Like a Mountain: Aldo Leopold & the Evolution of an Ecological Attitude Toward Deer, Wolves, & Forests. Susan L. Flader. LC 94-18104. (Illus.). 306p. 1994. reprint ed. pap. 17.95 (*0-299-14504-2*) U of Wis Pr.

Thinking Like a Mountain: Aldo Leopold & the Evolution of an Ecological Attitude Toward Deer, Wolves, & Forests. Susan L. Flader. LC 94-18104. (Illus.). 306p. 1994. reprint ed. 52.00 (*0-299-14500-X*) U of Wis Pr.

Thinking Like a Mountain: Toward a Council of All Beings. John Seed et al. (Illus.). 128p. (Orig.). 1988. pap. 9.95 (*0-86571-133-X*); lib. bdg. 34.95 (*0-86571-132-1*) New Soc Pubs.

Thinking Like a Physicist: Physics Problems for Undergraduates. Ed. by N. Thompson. (Illus.). 160p. 1987. pap. 27.00 (*0-85274-513-3*) IOP Pub.

Thinking Like a Writer: A Lawyer's Guide to Effective Writing & Editing. Stephen V. Armstrong & Timothy P. Terrell. LC 92-15739. 1992. 29.95 (*0-87632-898-2*) Clark Boardman Callaghan.

Thinking Like Mathematicians: Putting the K-4 NCTM Standards into Practice. Thomas E. Rowan & Barbara Bourne. LC 93-43901. 134p. (YA). 1994. pap. text ed. 18.50 (*0-435-08343-0*, 08343) Heinemann.

Thinking Like Your Editor. S. Rabiner. Date not set. write for info. (*0-393-03892-0*) Norton.

Thinking Locally, Acting Globally: Congressman Jim Walsh & the NAFTA Vote. Mary E. Lovely. (Pew Case Studies in International Affairs). 50p. (C). 1994. pap. text ed. 3.50 (*1-56927-160-7*, GU Schl Foreign) Geo U Inst Dplmcy.

Thinking Logically: Basic Concepts for Reasoning. James B. Freeman. (Illus.). 352p. (C). 1988. pap. text ed. write for info. (*0-13-917733-7*) P-H.

Thinking Logically: Basic Concepts for Reasoning. 2nd ed. James R. Freeman. LC 92-14846. 336p. (C). 1992. pap. text ed. 46.00 (*0-13-905118-X*) P-H.

Thinking Machine. John K. Brierley. LC 72-14220. 195p. 1973. 18.50 (*0-8386-1364-0*) Fairleigh Dickinson.

Thinking Machine: Jacques Futrelle. Freddie Seymour & Bettina Kyper. (Illus.). 188p. (Orig.). 1995. pap. text ed. 12.00 (*0-9645193-0-5*) Seymour-Kyper.

***Thinking Machines: Understanding Computers.** Daniel Hillis. 176p. 1998. pap. write for info. (*0-465-02596-X*) Basic.

Thinking Makes a Difference. Lyn M. Butrick. Ed. by Baird Tate. LC 86-50146. (My Read & Think Ser.: Vol. III). (Illus.). 160p. (J). (gr. 4-8). 1986. student ed. 6.60 (*0-914127-19-5*) Univ Class.

Thinking Man Two: The Golden Guide to Handicapping, Racing, & Training. Katcha Goodwon. Ed. by Frank R. Di Fiore. 325p. (Orig.). 1990. pap. 12.95 (*0-932896-08-1*) Westcliff Pubns.

Thinking Manager's Guide to Effective Writing. Carl Stach. (Illus.). 135p. 1988. 37.95 (*0-916780-32-5*) CES Assocs.

Thinking Mathematically. John Mason et al. 240p. (C). 1982. pap. text ed. 9.95 (*0-201-10238-2*) Addison-Wesley.

Thinking Matter: Materialism in Eighteenth-Century Britain. John W. Yolton. LC 83-6507. 252p. reprint ed. pap. 71.90 (*0-7837-2903-0*, 2057552) Bks Demand.

Thinking Methodologically. Don L. Goldenberg. (C). 1992. text ed. 40.00 (*0-06-042382-X*) Addson-Wesley Educ.

Thinking Metric. 3rd ed. Thomas F. Gilbert & Marilyn B. Gilbert. 150p. 1992. pap. 15.00 (*0-87425-168-0*) HRD Press.

Thinking Muse: Feminism & Modern French Philosophy. Ed. by Jeffner Allen & Iris M. Young. LC 88-45388. 224p. 1989. 34.95 (*0-253-35980-5*); pap. 12.95 (*0-253-20502-6*, MB 502) Ind U Pr.

Thinking Numbers. Bob Bernstein. 96p. (J). (gr. 2-7). 1989. 9.99 (*0-86653-506-3*, GA1094) Good Apple.

Thinking of Rembrandt & ...Life: On the Canvas of Your Soul. Lena Allen-Shore. (Illus.). 104p. (C). 1988. pap. write for info. (*0-922351-00-7*) L Allen-Shore.

Thinking of Skins: New & Selected Poems. Carol Rumens. 160p. 9400. pap. 18.95 (*1-85224-280-9*, Pub. by Bloodaxe Bks UK) Dufour.

***Thinking of You.** (Tender Hearts Collection). 32p. 1997. 9.99 (*1-881830-27-6*, DS18409) Garborgs.

***Thinking of You.** Ed. by Helen Exley. 60p. 1997. 8.00 (*1-85015-777-4*) Exley Giftbooks.

***Thinking of You.** Dan Farrell. 70p. 1994. 8.95 (*0-921331-21-5*, Pub. by Tsunami Edits CN) SPD-Small Pr Dist.

Thinking of You. Elizabeth Lucas. Ed. by Mac Anderson. 78p. (Orig.). 1990. pap. 7.95 (*0-931089-87-5*) Great Quotations.

Thinking of You. Eve Merriam. (Illus.). 40p. 1991. lib. bdg. 7.95 (*0-8378-0372-1*) Gibson.

Thinking of You. St. Paul Publications Staff. (C). 1990. text ed. 29.00 (*0-85439-357-9*, Pub. by St Paul Pubns UK) St Mut.

***Thinking of You.** Ed. by Mark Water. (Words of Joy & Comfort Ser.). (Illus.). 92p. 1996. 4.95 (*0-8192-1661-5*) Morehouse Pub.

Thinking of You. Jim Wortham. LC 77-75911. 1977. pap. 2.95 (*0-915216-16-7*) Marathon Intl Bk.

Thinking of You: A Collection of Romantic Poetry. Dennis J. Gibbons. Ed. by J. C. Stathus. 102p. (Orig.). 1996. pap. 11.50 (*1-57502-124-2*) Morris Pubng.

***Thinking of You! Miniature Editions Pop-Up.** Illus. by Kate B. Hall. 14p. 1997. 4.95 (*0-7624-0109-5*, Running Pr Mini Edtns) Running Pr.

Thinking of You: Thinking of You. Pat C. Hinton & Adventure Publications Staff. (Enchanted Hearts Ser.). 48p. 1996. pap. 3.95 (*1-879127-67-9*) Lighten Up Enter.

Thinking of You the Whole Year 'Round. Jill Weber. 1992. pap. 2.50 (*1-878689-14-2*) Frajil Farms.

Thinking on Drinking: A New Look at an Old Question. Fred P. Miller. 32p. 1990. pap. 3.50 (*1-883116-04-X*) Moellerhaus.

Thinking on Paper. 3rd ed. Judy Markline. (C). 1995. teacher ed., pap. text ed. 33.75 (*0-15-501634-2*) HB Coll Pubs.

Thinking on Paper. 3rd ed. Judy Markline. (C). 1994. pap. text ed. 30.00 (*0-15-501120-0*) HB Coll Pubs.

Thinking on Paper. 4th ed. Judy Markline. (C). 1997. text ed. 26.25 (*0-15-505223-3*); teacher ed., text ed. 28.00 (*0-15-505224-1*) HarBrace.

Thinking on Paper: A Writing Process Workbook. Judy Markline et al. 256p. (C). 1991. pap. text ed. 22.00 (*0-03-052204-8*) HB Coll Pubs.

Thinking on Paper: Refine, Express & Actually Generate Ideas by Understanding the Processes of the Mind. V. A. Howard & J. H. Barton. LC 86-5270. 120p. 1988. pap. 9.00 (*0-688-07758-7*, Quill) Morrow.

Thinking on the Edge. Ed. by Richard A. Kapnick & Aidan A. Kelly. (ISPP Ser.). 448p. 1993. 25.00 (*1-883322-00-6*) Agamemnon Pr.

Thinking on Your Feet: How to Communicate under Pressure. 2nd rev. ed. Marian K. Woodall. LC 96-4533. 128p. 1996. pap. 11.95 (*0-941159-96-5*, 503.699.8482) Prof Busn Comns.

Thinking on Your Feet: Tools to Communicate Clearly & Convincingly. Marlene Caroselli. Ed. by Nina Pohl. LC 91-76252. (Fifty-Minute Ser.). (Illus.). 86p. (Orig.). 1992. pap. 10.95 (*1-56052-117-1*) Crisp Pubns.

Thinking on Your Feet in Negotiations. Jane Hodgson. 240p. (Orig.). 1996. pap. 42.50 (*0-273-62191-2*, Pub. by Pitman Pub Ltd UK) Trans-Atl Phila.

Thinking on Your Feet While Sitting on Your Butt: The College Success Guide. Chris Stockwell. (Illus.). 225p. (Orig.). Date not set. pap. 14.95 (*0-9648269-0-9*) Lrning Engine Pr.

***Thinking on Your Seat - For the Recruiting Professional: A Catalyst to Create Respect, Results & Revenue.** Russell Riendeau. Ed. by Sue Telingator. (Illus.). 228p. (Orig.). 1996. pap. 44.95 (*0-9654631-0-9*) R Riendeau.

***Thinking Option: For Improving Business Performance.** Roy Gilbert. 228p. pap. 19.95 (*0-13-618083-3*) P-H.

Thinking Organization: Dynamics of Organizational Social Cognition. Henry P. Sims, Jr. et al. LC 85-45913. (Joint Publication in the Jossey-Bass Management Series & the Jossey-Bass Social & Behavioral Science Ser.). 403p. reprint ed. pap. 114.90 (*0-7837-2546-9*, 2042705) Bks Demand.

Thinking Out Loud: An Essay on the Relation Between Thought & Language. Christopher Gauker. LC 93-50671. 344p. 1994. text ed. 39.50 (*0-691-03400-1*) Princeton U Pr.

Thinking Out Loud: On the Personal, the Political, the Public & the Private. Anna Quindlen. 320p. 1994. pap. 12.00 (*0-449-90905-0*, Columbine) Fawcett.

T

***Thinking Out of the Box: How to Market Your Company into the Future.** Kathy C. Yohalem. 256p. 1997. text ed. 24.95 (0-471-13916-5) Wiley.

Thinking Parent: Understanding & Guiding Your Child. Anne Stokes. LC 93-60401. 160p. (Orig.). 1993. pap. 9.95 (0-89622-568-2) Twenty-Third.

Thinking Passover: A Rabbi's Book of Holiday Values. Ben Kamin. LC 96-41987. 160p. 1997. pap. 16.95 (0-525-94131-2) NAL-Dutton.

Thinking Person's Guide to God: Overcoming Obstacles to Belief. Tom Harpur. 224p. 1996. boxed 20.00 (0-7615-0707-8) Prima Pub.

Thinking Person's Guide to OS-2 2.1. 2nd ed. Maria E. Tyne. 1993. pap. 24.95 (0-89435-467-1) Wiley.

Thinking Person's Guide to Perfect Health: The Transformation of Medicine. Ron Kennedy. (Orig.). 1996. pap. 19.95 (0-932654-13-4) Context Pubns.

Thinking Person's Guide to Permanent Weight Loss. Jon Perlow. LC 85-52342. 190p. (Orig.). 1986. pap. 9.95 (0-936877-02-2) Twining Pr.

***Thinking Person's Guide to Sobriety.** Bert Pluymen. 248p. (Orig.). 1996. pap. 14.95 (1-880092-40-9) Bright Bks TX.

Thinking Philosophically: An Introduction to Philosophy with Readings. Joseph J. Gusmano. 762p. (Orig.). (C). 1990. pap. text ed. 46.50 (0-8191-7884-5) U Pr of Amer.

Thinking Physics: Practical Lessons in Critical Thinking, Gedanken Physics. Lewis Carroll Epstein. (Illus.). 562p. 1995. pap. 27.95 (0-935218-06-8) Insight Pr CA.

Thinking Physics for Teaching: Proceedings of an International Conference on Thinking Science for Teaching: The Case of Physics Held in Rome, Italy, September 22-27, 1994. Ed. by Carlo Bernardini et al. (Illus.). 460p. (C). 1996. 115.00 (0-306-45192-1, Plenum Pr) Plenum.

***Thinking Politically: A Liberal in the Age of Ideology.** Raymond Aron. (Orig.). 1996. pap. 24.95 (0-614-20823-8) Transaction Pubs.

Thinking Politically: A Liberal in the Age of Ideology. Raymond Aron. LC 96-38935. 340p. (Orig.). 1996. pap. text ed. 24.95 (1-56000-934-9) Transaction Pubs.

Thinking Politics: Intellectuals & Democracy in Chile, 1973-1988. Jeffrey M. Puryear. LC 93-47402. (C). 1994. text ed. 42.50 (0-8018-4839-3); pap. text ed. 13.95 (0-8018-4841-5) Johns Hopkins.

***Thinking Politics: Perspectives in Ancient Modern & Postmodern Political Theory.** Leslie P. Thiel. LC 97-4769. (Studies in Political Thinking). (Illus.). 288p. (Orig.). (C). 1997. pap. text ed. 22.95 (1-56643-053-4) Chatham Hse Pubs.

Thinking Positive: Words of Inspiration, Encouragement & Validation for People with AIDS & Those Who Care for Them. Ashton Applewhite. LC 94-46729. 1995. Not sold separately (0-671-89436-6, Fireside) S&S Trade.

Thinking Positive: Words of Inspiration, Encouragement & Validation for People with AIDS & Those Who Care for Them. Ashton Applewhite. 1995. pap. 9.00 (0-684-80266-X, Fireside) S&S Trade.

Thinking Print: Books to Billboards, 1980-1995. Deborah Wye. (Illus.). 160p. 1996. 35.00 (0-8109-6164-4) Abrams.

***Thinking Print: Books to Billboards 1980-95.** Deborah Wye. (Illus.). 160p. 1996. 35.00 (0-87070-124-X, 0-8109-6164-4) Mus of Modern Art.

Thinking, Problem Solving, Cognition. 2nd ed. Richard E. Mayer. (C). 1995. pap. text ed. 28.95 (0-7167-2215-1) W H Freeman.

Thinking Pro/ENGINEER: Mastering Design Methodology. David Bigelow. (Illus.). 320p. 1995. pap. 49.95 (1-56690-065-4, 1910, OnWord Pr) High Mtn.

Thinking Reasonably: Reaching Emotional Peace Through Mental Toughness. Illus. by Dale R. Olen. 212p. (Orig.). 1992. pap. 5.95 (1-56583-004-0) JODA.

Thinking Recursively. Eric Roberts. 179p. 1986. Net. pap. text ed. 24.50 (0-471-81652-3) Wiley.

Thinking Reed. Rebecca West. LC 75-41294. reprint ed. 34.50 (0-404-14630-9) AMS Pr.

Thinking Reed: Intellectuals & the Soviet State from 1917 to the Present. Boris Kagarlitsky. Tr. by Brian Pearce. 364p. (C). 1988. pap. text ed. 23.00 (0-86091-961-7, Pub. by Vrso UK) Norton.

Thinking Revolutionary: Principle & Practice in the New Republic. Ralph Lerner. LC 87-5287. 256p. (C). 1987. 37.50 (0-8014-2007-5); pap. 13.95 (0-8014-9532-6) Cornell U Pr.

Thinking Rhapsody. John Rizzo. (Illus.). 350p. 1998. pap. 24.95 incl. cd-rom (0-12-589330-2, AP Prof) Acad Pr.

Thinking Riding, Bk. 2. Molly Siverwright. 319p. (C). 1990. 44.00 (0-85131-378-7, Pub. by J A Allen & Co UK) St Mut.

Thinking Riding Book. Molly Siverwright. 339p. (C). 1990. 52.00 (0-85131-321-3, Pub. by J A Allen & Co UK) St Mut.

Thinking Robots, an Aware Internet, & Cyberpunk Librarians: The 1992 LITA President's Program. Ed. by R. Bruce Miller. LC 92-30742. (LITA President's Ser.). (Illus.). 1992. 22.00 (0-8389-7625-5) Lib Info Tech.

***Thinking Self.** LC 97-21573. 1997. pap. write for info. (0-7618-0793-4) U Pr of Amer.

Thinking Self. Laurence L. Cassidy. 133p. (Orig.). 1993. pap. 28.00 (0-9626761-3-6) Al H Morrison.

Thinking Sideways. Paul Splittgerber. 128p. (Orig.). 1985. pap. 7.00 (0-9614321-3-6) Splittgerber.

Thinking Skills. pap. 15.95 (1-878571-05-2) Improvement Prod Intl.

Thinking Skills. Harry S. Dahlstrom. (Illus.). 50p. (Orig.). 1987. pap. text ed. 3.99 (0-940712-55-5) Dahlstrom & Co.

Thinking Skills. Joan Hoffman. (Get Ready! Bks.). (Illus.). 32p. (J). (ps). 1995. 1.99 (0-938256-68-8) Sch Zone Pub Co.

Thinking Skills. 2nd ed. Kysilka & Biraimah. 1993. pap. text ed. write for info. (0-07-035932-6) McGraw.

Thinking Skills: Research & Practice. Barbara Z. Presseisen. (What Research Says to the Teacher Ser.). 1986. pap. 3.95 (0-8106-1073-6) NEA.

Thinking Skills: Teaching English-Language Arts. Beau F. Jones et al. 104p. 1987. pap. 9.95 (0-8106-0204-0) NEA.

Thinking Skills: Teaching Social Studies. Karen Rosenblum-Cale. 48p. 1987. pap. 7.95 (0-8106-0205-9) NEA.

Thinking Skills for Success. Edward De Bono. 128p. (C). 1990. teacher ed., pap. 9.95 (1-56118-049-1) Paradigm MN.

Thinking Skills Instruction: Concepts & Techniques. Ed. by Marcia Heiman & Joshua Slomianko. 312p. 1987. pap. 16.95 (0-8106-0201-6) NEA.

Thinking Skills Resource Book. Lorene Reid. 94p. 1990. pap. 12.95 (0-936386-58-4) Creative Learning.

Thinking Skills Throughout the Curriculum: A Conceptual Design. Barbara Z. Presseisen. (Illus.). 109p. (Orig.). (C). pap. 8.95 (0-9618056-0-9) Pi Lambda Theta.

Thinking Skills Workbook: A Cognitive Skills Remediation Manual for Adults. 2nd ed. Lynn T. Carter et al. (Illus.). 234p. 1984. spiral bd., pap. 34.95 (0-398-04992-0) C C Thomas.

Thinking Smart: A Primer of the Talents Unlimited Model. Carol L. Schlichter. 1993. pap. 23.95 (0-936386-64-9) Creative Learning.

Thinking Smarter: Skills for Academic Success, Set. 2nd ed. Carla Crutsinger. (YA). (gr. 4 up). 1992. reprint ed. pap. 39.95 (0-944662-01-3) Brainworks Inc.

Thinking Sociologically. Nessmith. (C). 1994. student ed., pap. text ed. 21.00 (0-15-501864-7) HB Coll Pubs.

Thinking Sociologically. Nessmith. (C). 1994. pap. text ed. 47.75 (0-15-500830-7) HB Coll Pubs.

Thinking Sociologically. Nessmith. (C). 1994. teacher ed., pap. text ed. 33.75 (0-15-501870-1) HB Coll Pubs.

Thinking Sociologically. 5th ed. Ruggiero. 1990. pap. text ed. 2.00 (0-205-12702-9) Allyn.

Thinking Sociologically: An Introduction for Everyone. Zygmunt Bauman. 240p. (C). 1990. pap. text ed. 23.95 (0-631-16362-X) Blackwell Pubs.

Thinking Sociologically: Test Bank. Nessmith. (C). 1995. suppl. ed., teacher ed., pap. text ed. 11.50 (0-15-501871-X) HB Coll Pubs.

Thinking Socratically. Sharon Schwarze & Lape. (Illus.). 400p. (C). 1996. pap. text ed. 33.00 (0-13-438631-0) P-H.

Thinking Sound Music: The Life & Work of Robert Erickson. Charles Shere. LC 95-32686. (Fallen Leaf Monographs on Contemporary Composers: Vol. 2). (Illus.). xviii, 286p. 1996. audio, cd-rom 50.00 (0-914913-33-6) Fallen Leaf.

Thinking Spanish Translation: A Course in Translation Method, Spanish to English. Sandor Harvey et al. LC 95-17889. 240p. (ENG & SPA.). (C). (gr. 13). 1995. text ed. 74.95 (0-415-11658-9) Routledge.

Thinking Spanish Translation: A Course in Translation Method, Spanish to English. Sandor Hervey et al. LC 95-17889. 240p. (ENG & SPA.). (C). 1995. pap. 19.95 (0-415-11659-7) Routledge.

Thinking Speech: A Blueprint for Carryover. Roberta H. Fehling. 112p. (J). (gr. 3 up). 1991. 17.95 (0-937857-28-9, 1593) Speech Bin.

***Thinking Start-Ups.** Murray Suid. (Start-Up Ser.). (Illus.). 96p. (Orig.). (J). (gr. 3-6). 1997. pap. 10.95 (1-57612-004-X, MM2032) Monday Morning Bks.

Thinking Straight. Antony G. Flew. LC 76-56674. 127p. (C). 1977. pap. 14.95 (0-87975-088-X) Prometheus Bks.

Thinking Straight & Talking Sense: An Emotional Education Program. Mark Gerald & William Eyman. LC 78-71008. 1981. pap. 8.95 (0-917476-14-X) A Ellis Institute.

***Thinking Strategically.** Stephen J. Wall. LC 97-7894. (Special Report from Organizational Dynamics Ser.). 1997. write for info. (0-8144-6719-9) AMACOM.

Thinking Strategically: A Primer for Public Leaders. Susan M. Walter. LC 84-15544. 103p. 1984. 14.95 (0-934842-19-1) CSPA.

Thinking Strategically: For Innovation, Discovery & Problem Solving. Craig Loehle. LC 96-795. (Illus.). 212p. (C). 1996. pap. text ed. 16.95 (0-521-56841-2) Cambridge U Pr.

Thinking Strategically: For Innovation, Discovery & Problem Solving. Craig Loehle. LC 96-795. (Illus.). 212p. (C). 1996. text ed. 49.95 (0-521-56058-6) Cambridge U Pr.

Thinking Strategically: The Competitive Edge in Business, Politics & Everyday Life. Avinash Dixit & Barry J. Nalebuff. 416p. 1993. pap. 14.95 (0-393-31035-3) Norton.

Thinking Strategies. Larry Wood. 204p. 1985. 15.95 (0-13-918137-7) P-H.

Thinking Strategies for Clinical Practice. Marsha Fonteyn. LC 97-17478. 352p. 1997. pap. text ed. 29.95 (0-397-55274-2) Lppncott-Raven.

Thinking Student's Guide to College. Victor L. Cahn. LC 87-71926. 1988. pap. 6.95 (0-8158-0445-8) Chris Mass.

***Thinking Styles.** Robert J. Sternberg. 225p. (C). 1997. text ed. 21.95 (0-521-55316-4) Cambridge U Pr.

***Thinking Tarot.** Aviza. LC 97-10329. 1997. pap. 19.95 (0-684-82274-1) S&S Trade.

Thinking the Difference: For a Peaceful Revolution. Luce Irigaray. Tr. by Karin Montin. LC 93-40519. 132p. (C). 1994. text ed. 45.00 (0-415-90814-0) Routledge.

Thinking the Difference: For a Peaceful Revolution. Luce Irigaray. Tr. by Karin Montin. LC 93-40519. 132p. (C). (gr. 13). 1994. pap. 14.95 (0-415-90815-9) Routledge.

Thinking the Faith: Christian Theology in a North American Context. Douglas J. Hall. LC 88-8536. 464p. (Orig.). 1991. pap. 22.00 (0-8006-2545-5, 1-2545, Fortress Pr) Augsburg Fortress.

Thinking the Unthinkable: Meanings of the Holocaust. Roger S. Gottlieb. 1990. pap. 14.95 (0-8091-3172-2) Paulist Pr.

Thinking the World Visible. Valerie Wohlfeld. LC 94-1753. (Series of Younger Poets: Vol. 89). 1994. 17.00 (0-300-06018-1); pap. 10.00 (0-300-06020-3) Yale U Pr.

Thinking Theoretically About Soviet Nationalities. Ed. by Alexander J. Motyl. 288p. 1992. text ed. 49.50 (0-231-07512-X) Col U Pr.

Thinking Theoretically about Soviet Nationalities: History & Comparison in the Study of the U. S. S. R. Ed. by Alexander J. Motyl. LC 91-31877. (Studies of the Harriman Institute). 284p. (C). 1995. pap. 16.50 (0-231-07513-8) Col U Pr.

Thinking Theory Thoroughly: Coherent Approaches to an Incoherent World. James N. Rosenau & Mary Durfee. LC 95-1095. 218p. (C). 1995. pap. text ed. 21.00 (0-8133-2595-1) Westview.

Thinking Things Through: An Introduction to Philosophical Issues & Achievements. Clark Glymour. (Illus.). 400p. 1992. 42.00 (0-262-07141-X, Bradford Bks) MIT Pr.

***Thinking Things Through: An Introduction to Philosophical Issues & Achievements.** Clark Glymour. (Illus.). 400p. 1997. reprint ed. pap. 20.00 (0-262-57119-6, Bradford Bks) MIT Pr.

Thinking Things Through: Critical Thinking for Decisions You Can Live With. Dianne Romain. LC 96-8152. (Illus.). 376p. (Orig.). (C). 1996. pap. text ed. 32.95 (1-55934-175-0, 1175) Mayfield Pub.

***Thinking Things Through No. 2: Worship.** Michael Townsend. 112p. (Orig.). 1997. pap. 10.00 (0-7162-0513-0, Epworth Pr) TPI PA.

***Thinking Things Through Instructor's Manual: Critical Thinking for Decisions You Can Live With.** Dianne Romain. 185p. (C). 1996. pap. text ed. write for info. (1-55934-176-9, 1176) Mayfield Pub.

***Thinking Through: Essays on Feminism, Marxism & Anti-Racism.** Himani Bannerji. 192p. pap. 12.95 (0-88961-208-0, Pub. by Wmns Pr CN) LPC InBook.

Thinking Through Class Discussion: The Hilda Taba Approach. Mary Durkin. LC 93-60802. 115p. 1993. pap. text ed. 24.95 (1-56676-055-0) Technomic.

Thinking Through Communication: An Introduction to the Study of Human Communication. Sarah Trenholm. LC 94-40276. 1994. pap. text ed. 43.00 (0-13-486374-7) Allyn.

Thinking Through Confucius. Ed. by David L. Hall & Roger T. Ames. LC 87-6454. 393p. (C). 1987. text ed. 59.50 (0-88706-376-4); pap. text ed. 20.95 (0-88706-377-2) State U NY Pr.

Thinking Through Cultures: Expeditions in Cultural Psychology. Richard A. Shweder. LC 90-4796. (Illus.). 404p. 1991. 42.50 (0-674-88415-9, SHWTHI); pap. 18.95 (0-674-88416-7, SHWTHX) HUP.

Thinking Through Death, Vol. 1. Scott Kramer & Kuan-ming Wu. LC 87-29019. 184p. 1988. 26.00 (0-89464-220-0); pap. 19.50 (0-89464-337-1) Krieger.

Thinking Through Death, Vol. 2. Scott Kramer & Kuan-ming Wu. LC 87-29019. 272p. 1988. 33.50 (0-89464-294-4); pap. 26.50 (0-89464-338-X) Krieger.

Thinking Through English. P. Creber. 1990. pap. 27.00 (0-335-09360-4, Open Univ Pr) Taylor & Francis.

Thinking Through Literature & Film. Beiderwell. (C). 1996. pap. text ed. write for info. (0-15-501770-5) HB Coll Pubs.

Thinking Through Marx: Materialism & Political Identity. Robert Meister. 320p. (C). 1991. pap. text ed. 25.95 (0-631-17746-9) Blackwell Pubs.

Thinking Through Math Word Problems: Strategies for Intermediate Elementary School Students. Arthur Whimbey. (C). 1990. teacher ed. write for info. (0-8058-0912-0); pap. 16.50 (0-8058-0603-2) L Erlbaum Assocs.

Thinking Through Primary Practice. Ed. by Jill Bourne. LC 93-19473. 240p. (C). 1993. pap. 17.95 (0-415-10257-X) Routledge.

Thinking Through Stories: Predicting, Classifying, Building Vocabulary, Questioning, Storytelling, Discussing. Vicki Rothstein & Rhoda Z. Goldberg. (Language Lessons for the Curriculum Ser.). (gr. k-7). 1993. student ed., spiral bd. 31.95 (1-55999-253-0) LinguiSystems.

Thinking Through Technology: The Path Between Engineering & Philosophy. Carl Mitcham. LC 93-44581. 410p. 1994. pap. text ed. 17.95 (0-226-53198-8); lib. bdg. 49.95 (0-226-53196-1) U Ch Pr.

Thinking Through the Body. Jane Gallop. (Gender & Culture Ser.). (Illus.). 200p. 1990. pap. text ed. 15.50 (0-231-06611-2) Col U Pr.

Thinking Through the Body of the Law. Ed. by Pheng Cheah et al. LC 95-44549. (C). 1996. 55.00 (0-8147-1544-3); pap. 20.00 (0-8147-1545-1) NYU Pr.

Thinking Through the Energy Problem. Thomas C. Schelling. LC 79-4583. (CED Supplementary Paper). 63p. 1979. pap. 5.00 (0-87186-242-5) Comm Econ Dev.

***Thinking Through the Past: A Critical Thinking Approach to American History: To 1877.** John Hollitz. 352p. (C). 1997. pap. text ed. 21.56 (0-669-33487-1) HM College Div.

***Thinking Through the Past Vol. II: A Critical Thinking Approach to American History: From 1865.** John Hollitz. 352p. (C). 1997. pap. text ed. 21.56 (0-669-33488-X) HM College Div.

Thinking Through Theory: Vygotskian Perspectives on the Teaching of Writing. James Zebroski. LC 93-26406. 334p. 1994. text ed. 36.00 (0-86709-324-2, 0324) Boynton Cook Pubs.

Thinking Through Writing. Susan R. Horton. LC 81-18628. (Illus.). 217p. 1982. pap. 12.95 (0-8018-2717-5) Johns Hopkins.

Thinking Thru Writing. Chaffee. (C). Date not set. pap. 28.36 (0-395-73766-4) HM.

Thinking Thru Writing. Chaffee. (C). Date not set. pap. 11.96 (0-395-73767-2) HM.

Thinking to Go: Ready to Go, Ready to Teach Worksheets for Critical Thinking Skills, 5 bklts. Linda Zachman et al. 1987. Set, incl. vinyl folder. 31.95 (1-55999-078-3) LinguiSystems.

Thinking to Write. Watkins-Goffman & Berkowitz. 1990. pap. 26.95 (0-8384-3380-4) Heinle & Heinle.

Thinking to Write: A Work Journal Program. Frances R. Link & S. Almquist. 62p. (Orig.). 1987. pap. 2.50 (0-86631-120-3); teacher ed. 5.00 (0-317-62982-4) Curriculum Dev Assocs.

Thinking Tools. Lawrence A. Stevens. (Illus.). 73p. (Orig.). (J). (gr. 5-10). 1984. pap. text ed. 6.50 (0-89550-223-2) Stevens & Shea.

Thinking Tools. 2nd ed. Curtis Miles & Jane Rauton. Ed. by Katherine Savige. LC 87-219. (Illus.). 371p. (C). 1990. pap. text ed. 32.95 (0-943202-23-X) H & H Pub.

Thinking Translation: A Course in Translation Method. LC 91-33257. 256p. (C). 1992. pap. 19.95 (0-415-07816-4, A7128) Routledge.

Thinking Translation: A Course in Translation Method. LC 91-33257. 256p. (C). (gr. 13). 1992. text ed. 69.95 (0-415-07815-6, A7124) Routledge.

Thinking Translation: Teacher's Handbook & Cassette. Sandor Hervey & Ian Higgins. 112p. (C). 1992. pap. 39.95 incl. audio (0-415-07831-8, Routledge NY) Routledge.

Thinking Upside Down. Doris H. Metcalf. (Orig.). (J). (gr. 4-8). 1994. pap. text ed. 12.97 (0-937659-34-7) GCT.

Thinking Well Matters. Hole. Date not set. pap. text ed. 17.00 (0-314-02752-1) West Pub.

Thinking with a Pencil. Henning Nelms. (Illus.). 368p. 1986. pap. 14.95 (0-89815-052-3) Ten Speed Pr.

Thinking with Concepts. John Wilson. 182p. 1970. pap. text ed. 18.95 (0-521-09601-4) Cambridge U Pr.

***Thinking with Demons: The Idea of Witchcraft in Early Modern Europe.** Stuart Clark. (Illus.). 848p. 1997. 140.00 (0-19-820001-3) OUP.

Thinking with God see Pensando con Dios

Thinking with Horses. Henry Blake. (Illus.). 208p. 1993. pap. 11.95 (0-943955-79-3) Trafalgar.

***Thinking with Mathematical Models: Representing Relationships.** Glenda Lappan et al. Ed. by Catherine Anderson et al. (Connected Mathematics Ser.). (Illus.). 64p. (Orig.). 1997. pap. text ed. 5.95 (1-57232-178-4, 21473) Seymour Pubns.

***Thinking with Mathematical Models: Representing Relationships.** Glenda Lappan et al. Ed. by Catherine Anderson et al. (Connected Mathematics Ser.). (Illus.). 139p. (Orig.). 1997. teacher ed. 16.50 (1-57232-179-2, 21474) Seymour Pubns.

Thinking with Solomon. Benny B. Bristow. 1992. pap. 7.95 (0-89137-134-6) Quality Pubns.

Thinking with the Whole Brain: An Integrative Teaching & Learning Model (K-8). Jane K. Cooke & Mildred Haipt. 56p. 1986. pap. 6.95 (0-8106-0687-9); pap. 6.95 (0-8106-1831-1) NEA.

Thinking with Words. Carlos F. Navarro. Ed. by Judith Navarro. (Start Smart Ser.). 64p. 1990. student ed. 6.50 (1-878396-05-6) Start Smart Bks.

Thinking Without Thinking: Who's in Control of Your Mind. Eldon Taylor. Ed. by Janus Daniels. (Illus.). 438p. (Orig.). (C). 1995. pap. 27.95 (1-55978-033-9) R K Bks.

Thinking-Writing: An Introduction to the Writing Process for Students of ESL. Martha Rice & Jane Burns. (Illus.). 200p. (C). 1985. pap. text ed. 18.75 (0-13-918244-6) P-H.

Thinking-Writing: Fostering Critical Thinking Through Writing. Charles L. Olson. (C). 1991. text ed. 29.00 (0-673-46346-X) Addson-Wesley Educ.

Thinking Your Way Through English Grammar. Edmund Vitale. Ed. by Karen H. Davis. LC 91-75142. 179p. (C). 1992. pap. text ed. 14.95 (0-943202-36-1) H & H Pub.

Thinkpak. Michael Michalko. 1994. pap. 11.95 (0-89815-607-6) Ten Speed Pr.

Thinks. Edgar W. Nye. LC 74-104534. 181p. reprint ed. lib. bdg. 28.00 (0-8398-1354-6) Irvington.

Thinks. Edgar W. Nye. 181p. (C). 1986. reprint ed. pap. text ed. 6.95 (0-8290-2041-1) Irvington.

Thinkwork: Working, Learning, & Managing in a Computer-Interactive Society. Ed. by Fred Y. Phillips. LC 91-47085. 300p. 1992. text ed. 49.95 (0-275-93964-2, C3964, Praeger Pubs) Greenwood.

Thinlayer Chromatography Vol. 1A: Reagents & Detection Methods, Physical & Chemical Detection Methods, Fundamentals, Reagents I. Hellmut Jork et al. LC 89-16558. (Illus.). xv, 464p. 1989. text ed. 120.00 (3-527-27834-6, VCH) Wiley.

Thinner. Stephen King, pseud. 1996. mass mkt. 6.99 (0-451-19075-0, Sig) NAL-Dutton.

Thinner. Stephen King, pseud. 1996. pap. 34.95 (0-14-086266-8) Viking Penguin.

***Thinner.** Stephen King. 1997. pap. 34.95 (0-14-086629-9) Viking Penguin.

Thinner. Richard Bachman, pseud. 320p. 1985. reprint ed. pap. 6.99 (0-451-16134-3, Sig) NAL-Dutton.

Thinner at Last. Steven Lamm. 1997. pap. 13.00 (0-684-83035-3) S&S Trade.

Thinner at Last: The New Drugs That Release the Brains' Power to Bring about Permanent Weight Loss. Steven Lamm & Gerald S. Couzens. 1995. 23.00 (0-684-81368-8) S&S Trade.

An Asterisk (*) at the beginning of an entry indicates that the title is appearing in BIP for the first time.

Thinner Winners: The Complete All-in-One Guide to Lifetime Weight Control. Roseanne W. Strull & Howard A. Strull. LC 95-68218. (Illus.). 329p. (Orig.). 1996. pap. 19.95 (*0-9634934-3-4*) Rosecrest Pub.

Thinner Winners Workbook: Insights & Solutions for Lifetime Weight Control. Roseanne W. Strull & Howard A. Strull. (Illus.). 144p. (Orig.). 1996. wbk. ed., pap. 9.95 (*0-9634934-4-2*) Rosecrest Pub.

Thinnest Thread. Lynn Passek. 48p. (Orig.). Date not set. pap. 12.00 (*0-614-16391-9*) Em Pr.

Thinning Methodologies for Pattern Recognition. Ching Y. Suen. (Machine Perception & Artificial Intelligence Ser.). 352p. 1994. text ed. 99.00 (*981-02-1482-0*) World Scientific Pub.

Thinning of the Veil. Mary B. Wallace. 99p. 1967. reprint ed. spiral bd. 5.50 (*0-7873-0927-3*) Hlth Research.

Thinning the Predators. Jim Starlin & Daina Graziunas. 336p. 1996. 22.95 (*0-446-51985-5*) Warner Bks.

Thinning the Predators see Predators

Thinward Bound: Medical Management & Weight Loss. Mary J. Madden. Ed. by Donna Hoel. LC 82-17679. (Illus.). 112p. 1982. pap. text ed. 11.50 (*0-89303-228-X*) P-H.

***Thiocarbamate Pesticides: A General Introduction.** WHO Staff. (Environmental Health Criteria Ser.: No. 86). 49p. 1988. 15.00 (*92-4-154276-4*) World Health.

Thiophene & Its Derivatives. Howard D. Hartough. LC 51-13781. (Chemistry of Heterocyclic Compounds Ser.). 551p. reprint ed. pap. 157.10 (*0-317-08757-6*, 2007400) Bks Demand.

Thiophene & Its Derivatives, 4 pts., Vol. 44. Ed. by Salo Gronowitz. LC 84-15356. (Chemistry of Heterocyclic Compounds, a Series of Monographs: Vol. 44, Pt. 2). 906p. 1986. text ed. 520.00 (*0-471-83832-2*) Wiley.

Thiophene & Its Derivatives, 4 pts., Vol. 44. Ed. by Salo Gronowitz. (Chemistry of Heterocyclic Compounds, a Series of Monographs: Vol. 44, Pt. 3). 1272p. 1986. text ed. 635.00 (*0-471-83833-0*) Wiley.

Thiophene & Its Derivatives, Vol. 44. Ed. by Salo Gronowitz. (Chemistry of Heterocyclic Compounds, a Series of Monographs: Vol. 44, Pt. 4). 517p. 1991. text ed. 390.00 (*0-471-61221-9*) Wiley.

Thiophene & Its Derivatives, Vol. 44. Ed. by Salo Gronowitz. LC 84-15356. (Chemistry of Heterocyclic Compounds, a Series of Monographs: Vol. 44, Pt. 5). 944p. 1992. text ed. 470.00 (*0-471-52944-3*) Wiley.

Thiophene Derivatives of Group IV B Elements, Vol, 2. E. Lukevics et al. (Sulfur Reports: Vol. 2, No. 5). 38p. 1982. pap. text ed. 101.00 (*3-7186-0133-8*) Gordon & Breach.

***Thiopia: People of Thiopia, Dutch Edition.** Ed. by Gordon & Breach Publishing Group Staff. (DUT.). 1996. text ed. 75.00 (*90-5701-141-7*) Gordon & Breach.

***Thiopia: People of Thiopia, English Edition.** Ed. by Gordon & Breach Publishing Group Staff. 1998. text ed. 75.00 (*90-5701-151-4*) Gordon & Breach.

***Thiopia: People of Thiopia, French Edition.** Ed. by Gordon & Breach Publishing Group Staff. (FRE.). 1996. text ed. 75.00 (*90-5701-131-X*) Gordon & Breach.

***Thiopia: People of Thiopia, German Edition.** Ed. by Gordon & Breach Publishing Group Staff. (GER.). 1997. text ed. 75.00 (*90-5705-032-3*) Gordon & Breach.

***Thioredoxin & Glutaredoxin Systems: Structure & Function.** Ed. by Arne Holmgren et al. LC 85-23307. 429p. 1986. reprint ed. pap. 122.30 (*0-608-03416-9*, 2064115) Bks Demand.

3rd Aerospace Testing Seminar Proceedings, September 1976. LC 62-38584. (Illus.). 122p. 1977. pap. text ed. 75.00 (*0-915414-50-3*) Inst Environ Sci.

Third Age Careers: Meeting the Corporate Challenge. Barry Curnow & Jonh M. Fox. 200p. 1994. 48.95 (*0-566-07493-1*, Pub. by Gower UK) Ashgate Pub Co.

Third Age Miscellany. Elizabeth Wenzel. pap. 7.95 (*0-8488-0892-4*) Amereon Ltd.

Third Age Sampler. Elizabeth Wentzel. 7.95 (*0-8488-0891-6*) Amereon Ltd.

Third Americans: A Select Bibliography on Asians in America with Annotations. Te-Kong Tong & Robert Wu. 69p. 1980. pap. 6.95 (*0-937256-00-5*) Chinese Cult Serv.

Third & Goal: Great Football of the Twentieth Century, Reading Level 3-5. Mel Cebulash. LC 93-433. 1993. 9.95 incl. audio (*0-88336-900-1*); pap. 4.95 (*0-88336-743-2*) New Readers.

Third & Indiana. Steve Lopez. 320p. 1995. pap. 10.95 (*0-14-023945-6*, Penguin Bks) Viking Penguin.

Third & Oak: The Laundromat. Marsha Norman. 1980. pap. 3.25 (*0-8222-1132-7*) Dramatists Play.

Third & Oak: The Pool Hall. Marsha Norman. 1985. pap. 3.25 (*0-8222-1133-5*) Dramatists Play.

Third & Only Way: Reflections on Staying Alive. Helen S. Bevington. LC 96-14208. 224p. 1996. 21.95 (*0-8223-1850-4*) Duke.

Third & Possibly the Best Six Hundred & Thirty-Seven Things Anyone Ever Said. Robert Byrne. 192p. 1987. mass mkt. 5.99 (*0-449-21337-4*, Crest) Fawcett.

Third Angel. 458p. 1989. 19.95 (*0-9623579-3-6*) Angels Three.

Third Angel's Message of Righteousness by Faith & Its Present Rejection. 4th ed. Lowell Scarbrough. 116p. 1988. pap. 4.95 (*0-923309-11-X*) Hartland Pubns.

Third Annual ADR Digest 1992-1993. 27.50 (*0-685-62935-X*) Graduate Group.

Third Annual Bar Examination Fact Book. 1995. 27.50 (*0-685-68811-9*) Graduate Group.

Third Annual Binding Private Arbitration Panel (BPAP) Directory of Registered Arbitrators, 1992. 1992. 30.00 (*0-685-59616-8*) Graduate Group.

Third Annual BPAP Directory 1992-1993. 27.50 (*0-685-62936-8*) Graduate Group.

Third Annual Conference on African Linguistics. Ed. by Erhard Voeltz. (African Ser.: No. 7). 265p. 1974. pap. text ed. 20.00 (*0-87750-181-5*) Res Inst Inner Asian Studies.

Third Annual Directory of Alternative Dispute Resolutions in the United States, 1992. 1992. 30.00 (*0-685-59617-6*) Graduate Group.

Third Annual Directory of Graduate Law Programs. 1993. 27.50 (*0-685-67198-4*) Graduate Group.

Third Annual Directory of Graduate Law Programs in the United States. 1993. 27.50 (*0-685-62933-3*) Graduate Group.

Third Annual Global Directory of Schools of Law. 1997. 27.50 (*0-614-14949-5*) Graduate Group.

Third Annual Internships & Job Opportunities in N. Y. C. & Washington, D. C. 1991. 27.50 (*0-685-39162-0*) Graduate Group.

Third Annual Internships for College Students Interested in Law, Medicine & Politics. 125p. (C). 1991. pap. 27.50 (*0-317-58989-X*) Graduate Group.

Third Annual Internships for Two-Year College Students. 125p. (C). 1991. pap. 27.50 (*0-317-58991-1*) Graduate Group.

Third Annual Internships in Congress. 1994. 27.50 (*0-685-68812-7*) Graduate Group.

Third Annual Internships in New York City & Washington, D. C. 125p. (C). 1991. pap. 27.50 (*0-317-58990-3*) Graduate Group.

3rd Annual Japanese Symposium on Molecular Simulation. K. Nakanishik. 172p. 1991. pap. text ed. 426.00 (*2-88124-811-X*) Gordon & Breach.

Third Annual Judicial Clerkship Opportunities. 1997. 27.50 (*0-614-14950-9*) Graduate Group.

Third Annual Labor & Employment Law Institute: Labor & Employment Relations in the Age of the Robot, Computer & Foreign Competion. Ed. by Marlin M. Volz. LC 87-9725. (Illus.). viii, 352p. 1987. lib. bdg. 57.50 (*0-8377-1237-8*) Rothman.

Third Annual Litigation Management Supercourse. (Litigation & Administrative Practice Ser.). 767p. 1992. pap. text ed. 70.00 (*0-685-56926-8*, H4-5124) PLI.

Third Annual Outstanding Resumes of 2-Year College & College Graduates. 1997. 27.50 (*0-685-71245-1*) Graduate Group.

Third Annual Report of the Secretaries of Defense, 1989: Beyond the Cold War: New Threats to American Security. 1990. 5.00 (*0-685-34509-2*) Southern Ctr Intl Stud.

Third Annual Report of the Secretaries of State, 1985: The Summit, Latin America & Other Foreign Policy Challenges. 1990. 5.00 (*0-685-34500-9*) Southern Ctr Intl Stud.

Third Annual Technology Advancement Contractor Review Meeting Proceedings (Sept. 26-27, 1995) Compiled by South Coast Air Quality Management District Staff. (Electric Vehicle Information Ser.: Vol. 20). (Illus.). 54p. 1996. pap. 65.00 (*0-89934-279-5*, BT047); lib. bdg. 105.00 (*0-89934-280-9*, BT947) Bus Tech Bks.

Third Arkansas Union Cavalry. Desmond W. Allen. (Arkansas Union Regiment Ser.). 118p. 1987. pap. 15.00 (*0-941765-18-0*) Arkansas Res.

Third Arm. large type ed. Kenneth Royce. 416p. 1985. 25.99 (*0-7089-1332-6*) Ulverscroft.

Third Armored Division. Turner Publishing Company Staff. LC 90-71729. 144p. 1991. 48.00 (*1-56311-021-0*) Turner Pub KY.

Third Asia Pacific Physics Conference. Ed. by C. N. Yang et al. 1276p. 1988. pap. 71.00 (*9971-5-0690-4*); text ed. 154.00 (*9971-5-0651-3*) World Scientific Pub.

***Third Asian Fisheries Forum.** Ed. by L. M. Chou et al. 1135p. 1994. write for info. (*971-8709-64-9*, Pub. by ICLARM PH) Intl Spec Bk.

Third Asian-Pacific Regional Meeting of the International Astronomical Union, Kyoto, Japan, September 30 - October 6, 1984, 2 pts., Pt. 1. Ed. by M. Kitamura & E. Budding. 1986. lib. bdg. 223.50 (*90-277-1867-9*) Kluwer Ac.

Third Asian-Pacific Regional Meeting of the International Astronomical Union, Kyoto, Japan, September 30 - October 6, 1984, 2 pts., Pt. 2. Ed. by M. Kitamura & E. Budding. 1986. lib. bdg. 112.00 (*90-277-2210-2*) Kluwer Ac.

Third Assassin. large type ed. Howard C. Davis. (Linford Mystery Large Print Ser.). 1994. pap. 15.99 (*0-7089-7637-9*) Ulverscroft.

Third Assembling: An Annual of Otherwise Unpublishable Imaginative Work, No. 3. annuals Ed. by Richard Kostelanetz et al. (Illus.). 280p. (Orig.). 1972. pap. 26.00 (*0-915066-03-3*) Assembling Pr.

Third Assistant Engineer Through Chief Engineer. (USCG Examination Questions & Answers Ser.). 241p. (Orig.). 1990. pap. text ed. 49.95 (*0-932889-14-X*) Examco Inc.

Third Avenue Railway System in Manhattan. (Illus.). 64p. 1995. pap. write for info. (*0-934088-34-9*) NJ Intl Inc.

Third Avenue Railway System in Manhattan. (Illus.). 64p. 1996. 27.95 (*0-614-17865-7*, 7619) NJ Intl Inc.

Third Barnhart Dictionary of New English. Ed. by Robert K. Barnhart et al. 592p. 1990. 52.00 (*0-8242-0796-3*) Wilson.

Third Beis Hamikdash: The Third Temple. Shalom D. Steinberg. Tr. by Moshe L. Miller from HEB. 240p. 1993. 16.00 (*0-940118-80-7*) Moznaim.

Third Best Sport. Eleanor Bayer & Leo Bayer. 1959. pap. 5.25 (*0-8222-1134-3*) Dramatists Play.

Third Betrayal. large type ed. Michael Hartland. 384p. 1988. 25.99 (*0-7089-1787-9*) Ulverscroft.

Third Boat. large type ed. Leila Mackinlay. 1989. 25.99 (*0-7089-2106-X*) Ulverscroft.

Third Body Concept: Interpretation of Triboloal Phenomena: Proceedings of the 2nd Leeds-Lyon Symposium on Tribology, Lyon, France, 5-8 September 1995. Ed. by D. Dowson. LC 96-31165. (Tribology Ser.: Vol. 31). 780p. 1996. text ed. 287.25 (*0-444-82502-9*, North Holland) Elsevier.

Third Book of Horace's Odes. Horace. Tr. by Gordon Williams. 174p. 1969. pap. 18.95 (*0-19-912001-3*) OUP.

Third Book of Junior Authors. Ed. by Doris De Montreville & Donna Hill. LC 75-149381. (Illus.). 320p. 1972. 45.00 (*0-8242-0408-5*) Wilson.

Third Book of Lost Swords: Stonecutter's Story. Fred Saberhagen. 256p. 1989. mass mkt. 4.50 (*0-8125-5288-1*) Tor Bks.

Third Book of Lost Swords: Stonecutter's Story. Fred Saberhagen. 256p. 1995. 4.50 (*0-614-09357-0*) Tor Bks.

Third Book of Modern Verse. Ed. by Jessie B. Rittenhouse. LC 79-149114. (Granger Index Reprint Ser.). 1977. 23.95 (*0-8369-6239-7*) Ayer.

Third Book of Puzzle Adventures. Gaby Waters. (J). (gr. 4-7). 1994. pap. 9.95 (*0-7460-0512-1*, Usborne) EDC.

Third Book of Swords. Fred Saberhagen. 1988. pap. 3.95 (*0-8125-5345-4*) Tor Bks.

Third Book of Whimsey: Poignant Fragments, Serpentine Thoughts, & Other Things. Roberta Mendel. (Books for Browsers Ser.). 24p. (Orig.). 1994. pap. 9.00 (*0-936424-02-8*) Pin Prick.

Third Branch: Administrative Office of the U. S. Courts, 11 Vols. in 2 Bks, 1968-79. LC 76-39614. 1980. reprint ed. lib. bdg. 95.00 (*0-930342-35-6*, 107430) W S Hein.

Third Bridge Engineering Conference, 2 vols. (Transportation Research Record Ser.: No. 1290). 583p. 1991. Set. 70.00 (*0-309-05067-7*) Transport Res Bd.

3rd Brigade 101st Airborne Division (Air Assault) Desert Shield-Desert Storm History Book. Turner Publishing Company Staff. LC 91-67164. 100p. 1992. 19.95 (*1-56311-075-X*) Turner Pub KY.

Third British Empire. 3rd ed. Alfred E. Zimmern. LC 79-4333. 192p. 1979. reprint ed. text ed. 49.75 (*0-313-20990-1*, ZITB, Greenwood Pr) Greenwood.

Third California Islands Symposium: Recent Advances in Research on the California Islands. Ed. by F. G. Hochberg. LC 93-26463. 1993. 40.00 (*0-936494-05-0*) Santa B Museum.

Third Century Hoard of Tetradrachms from Gordion. D. H. Cox. (University Museum Monographs: No. 9). (Illus.). v, 20p. 1953. pap. 6.00 (*0-934718-01-6*) U PA Mus Pubns.

Third Century Iran see Persepolis, Third: The Royal Tombs & Other Monuments

Third Child: A Study in the Prediction of Fertility. Charles F. Westoff et al. LC 63-12672. 319p. 1963. reprint ed. pap. 91.00 (*0-7837-9477-0*, 2060219) Bks Demand.

Third Chimpanzee: The Evolution & Future of the Human Animal. Jared M. Diamond. LC 91-50455. (Illus.). 416p. 1992. pap. 13.50 (*0-06-098403-1*, PL) HarpC.

Third Choice. Robert Gregory. LC 78-54131. 1979. 22.95 (*0-87949-117-5*) Ashley Bks.

Third Christmas. Margot Early. (Superromance Ser.). 1994. mass mkt. 3.50 (*0-373-70625-1*, 1-70625-8) Harlequin Bks.

Third Coast: Contemporary Michigan Fiction. Ed. by James Tipton & Robert E. Wegner. LC 81-15936. (Illus.). 336p. 1982. pap. 15.95 (*0-8143-1695-6*) Wayne St U Pr.

Third Cold War. Walter LaFeber. LC 81-80739. (Charles Edmondson Historical Lectures). 42p. (Orig.). 1981. pap. 5.95 (*0-918954-25-8*) Baylor Univ Pr.

Third Colloquium in Biological Sciences: Cellular Signal Transduction. Pref. by Fleur L. Strand. (Annals Ser.: Vol. 594). 455p. 1987. 114.00 (*0-89766-383-7*) NY Acad Sci.

Third Component of Complement. Ed. by J. D. Lambris. (Current Topics in Microbiology & Immunology Ser.: Vol. 153). (Illus.). 248p. 1989. 123.00 (*0-387-51513-5*) Spr-Verlag.

Third Conference on Vitamin C. Ed. by John J. Burns et al. (Annals Ser.: Vol. 498). (Illus.). 537p. 1987. 134.00 (*0-89766-391-8*) NY Acad Sci.

Third Continuation see Continuations of the Old French Perceval of Chretien de Troyes

***Third Crown: A Study in World Government Exercised by the Popes.** Edmond P. Odescalchi. LC 96-40107. 190p. 1997. text ed. 32.50 (*0-7618-0669-5*) U Pr of Amer.

Third Cuckoo. Kenneth Gregory. 282p. 1985. 14.95 (*0-04-808054-3*) Routledge Chapman & Hall.

3rd Culprit. Cody et al. (Mystery Ser.). 1996. mass mkt. 5.99 (*0-373-26212-4*, Wrldwide Lib) Harlequin Bks.

Third Culprit: The Annual Anthology of the Crime Writer's Association. Liza Cody. 1994. 21.00 (*0-312-11736-1*) St Martin.

Third Culture. John Brockman. 416p. 1996. pap. 14.00 (*0-684-82344-6*, Touchstone Bks) S&S Trade.

Third Culture: Scientists on the Edge. John Brockman. LC 95-83. 1995. 27.50 (*0-684-80359-3*) S&S Trade.

***Third Culture Kids Profile.** David C. Pollack & Ruth Van Reken. 1997. pap. write for info. (*0-614-26093-0*) Intercult Pr.

Third Current of Revolution: Inside the "North American Front" of El Salvador's Guerrilla War. J. Michael Waller. 332p. (C). 1991. lib. bdg. 44.50 (*0-8191-8231-1*) U Pr of Amer.

***Third Date's the Charm.** Diane Pershing. 1997. pap. 3.50 (*0-373-52050-6*, 1-52050-1) Silhouette.

Third Day at Gettysburg & Beyond. Ed. by Gary W. Gallagher. LC 94-752. (Military Campaigns of the Civil War Ser.). (Illus.). 232p. 1994. 24.95 (*0-8078-2155-1*) U of NC Pr.

Third Deadly Sin. rev. ed. Lawrence Sanders. 416p. 1987. mass mkt. 6.99 (*0-425-10429-X*) Berkley Pub.

Third Decennial U. S. - U. S. S. R. Conference on SETI. G. Seth Shostak. (ASP Conference Series Proceedings: Vol. 47). 446p. 1993. 28.00 (*0-937707-66-X*) Astron Soc Pacific.

***Third Degree: A Cassidy James Mystery.** Kate Calloway. LC 97-10811. 256p. (Orig.). 1997. pap. 11.95 (*1-56280-185-6*) Naiad Pr.

Third Degree: Report to the National Commission on Law Observance & Enforcement. Zechariah Chafee, Jr. et al. LC 70-90169. (Mass Violence in America Ser.). 1973. reprint ed. 28.95 (*0-405-01304-3*) Ayer.

Third Department: The Establishment & Practices of the Political Police in the Russia of Nicholas I. Peter S. Squire. LC 69-10198. 288p. reprint ed. pap. 82.10 (*0-685-16249-4*, 2027272) Bks Demand.

Third Digest of Investigations in the Teaching of Science. Francis D. Curtis. LC 74-153694. 439p. reprint ed. pap. 125.20 (*0-317-42006-2*, 2026002) Bks Demand.

***Third Dimension.** O'Neill. Date not set. student ed., pap. text ed. write for info. (*0-582-03183-4*, Pub. by Longman UK) Longman.

***Third Dimension.** O'Neoill. Date not set. teacher ed., pap. text ed. write for info. (*0-582-01720-3*, Pub. by Longman UK) Longman.

Third Dimension in Organic Chemistry. Alan Bassindale. LC 84-166041. 256p. reprint ed. pap. 73.00 (*0-7837-3216-3*, 2043234) Bks Demand.

Third DOE-NARUC Nat'l Electricity Forum Proceedings. 1996. 35.00 (*0-614-14945-2*) NARUC.

Third Door. Ellen Tarry. LC 70-135613. 304p. (C). 1971. reprint ed. text ed. 38.50 (*0-8371-5200-3*, TTD&, Greenwood Pr) Greenwood.

Third Door: The Autobiography of an American Negro Woman. Ellen Tarry. LC 91-36037. (Library of Alabama Classics). 352p. (C). 1992. reprint ed. pap. 17.95 (*0-8173-0579-3*) U of Ala Pr.

Third Down & Forever. Brent Clark. LC 94-16791. 1994. pap. 12.95 (*0-312-11234-3*) St Martin.

***3rd Down & Forever.** J. Brent Clark. 1997. mass mkt. 5.99 (*0-312-96148-0*) St Martin.

Third Ear: On Listening to the World. Joachim-Ernst Berendt. 240p. (Orig.). 1992. pap. 13.95 (*0-8050-2007-1*, Owl) H Holt & Co.

Third Electoral System, 1853-1892: Parties, Voters, & Political Cultures. Paul Kleppner. LC 78-7949. xxi, 424p. 1979. 45.00 (*0-8078-1328-1*) U of NC Pr.

Third Encounter. G. Harry Stine. (Starsea Invaders Ser.). 304p. (Orig.). 1995. mass mkt. 4.99 (*0-451-45420-0*, ROC) NAL-Dutton.

Third Encounter. Sara Woods. 1986. pap. 3.50 (*0-380-69863-3*) Avon.

Third Essay: For Orchestra Full Score. S. Barber. 56p. 1991. pap. 25.00 (*0-7935-0934-3*, 50481210) H Leonard.

***Third European Research Roundtable Conference on Shortsea Shipping, Bergen, Norway: Conference Papers.** Ed. by F. A. Waals. (Illus.). 494p. (Orig.). 1996. pap. 77.50 (*90-407-1349-9*, Pub. by Delft U Pr NE) Coronet Bks.

Third Evil: Fear Street. R. L. Stine. Ed. by Patricia MacDonald. (Cheerleaders Ser.: No. 3). 176p. (Orig.). (J). (gr. 7 up). mass mkt. 3.99 (*0-671-75119-0*, Archway) PB.

Third Eye. Douglas M. Baker. (C). 1980. pap. 12.50 (*0-906006-59-7*, Pub. by Baker Pubns UK) New Leaf Dist.

Third Eye. Lois Duncan. 224p. (J). (gr. 6-12). 1991. mass mkt. 3.99 (*0-440-98720-2*, LLL BDD) BDD Bks Young Read.

Third Eye. Lois Duncan. (J). (gr. 7-p). 1984. 15.95 (*0-316-19553-7*) Little.

Third Eye. T. Lobsang Rampa. 1986. mass mkt. 5.99 (*0-345-34038-8*) Ballantine.

Third Eye: Bela Kalman - A Lifetime in Photography. Sally Eauclaire. (Illus.). 190p. 1994. 50.00 (*0-8263-1563-1*) U of NM Pr.

Third Eye: Race, Cinema, & Ethnographic Spectacle. Fatimah T. Rony. LC 96-13255. 328p. 1996. text ed. 49.95 (*0-8223-1834-2*); pap. text ed. 17.95 (*0-8223-1840-7*) Duke.

Third Eye: Supervision of Analytic Group. Ed. by Meg Sharpe. LC 94-10753. (International Library of Group Psychotherapy & Group Process). 208p. (C). 1994. pap. 17.95 (*0-415-10635-4*, B4430, Routledge NY) Routledge.

Third Eye: Supervision of Analytic Group. Ed. by Meg Sharpe. LC 94-10753. (International Library of Group Psychotherapy & Group Process). 192p. (C). (gr. 13). 1994. text ed. 62.95 (*0-415-10634-6*, B4698, Routledge NY) Routledge.

Third Eye & Other Animal Riddles. Les De Villiers & Andries De Villiers. (Illus.). 160p. 1992. pap. write for info. (*0-916673-08-1*) Business Bks CT.

Third Eye Theatre. Davydd A. Saille. LC 95-38648. 149p. (Orig.). 1996. pap. 8.95 (*1-887786-08-2*) Sky & Sage Bks.

Third-Eye Theology: Theology in Formation in Asian Settings. rev. ed. C. S. Song. LC 90-47639. 1991. pap. 18.00 (*0-88344-735-5*) Orbis Bks.

Third-Eye Theology: Theology in Formation in Asian Settings. Choan-Seng Song. LC 79-4208. 288p. reprint ed. pap. 82.10 (*0-317-26666-7*, 2025121) Bks Demand.

Third Federal Issue 1814 - 1817 & Other U. S. Embossed Revenue Stamped Paper 1791 - 1869. W. V. Combs. (Illus.). xvi, 224p. 1993. 27.50 (*0-945735-01-4*) Amer Revenue Assn.

Third Fiber Optics & Communications Exposition: FOC '80, San Francisco. 275p. 1980. 50.00 (*1-56851-020-9*, 133F04) Info Gatekeepers.

Third Five-Year Annotated Index to Media Report to Women: 1982-1986. 54p. 1987. 5.00 (*0-930470-10-9*) Womens Inst Free Press.

T

Third Force in Canada: The Cooperative Commonwealth Federation,1932-1948. Dean E. McHenry. LC 76-2061. 351p. 1976. reprint ed. text ed. 69.50 (*0-8371-8767-2*, MCTF, Greenwood Pr) Greenwood.

Third Force in Seventeenth-Century Thought. Richard H. Popkin. LC 91-10145. (Studies in Intellectual History: Vol. 22). vi, 377p. 1991. 109.50 (*90-04-09324-9*) E J Brill.

Third Force Psychology & the Study of Literature. Ed. by Bernard J. Paris. LC 85-47629. 344p. 1986. 45.00 (*0-8386-3263-7*) Fairleigh Dickinson.

Third French Republic, Eighteen-Seventy to Nineteen-Forty. Leslie Derfler. LC 82-177. (Anvil Ser.). 192p. (C). 1982. reprint ed. pap. text ed. 11.50 (*0-89874-480-6*) Krieger.

Third Garfield Treasury. Jim Davis. 112p. 1985. pap. 12.00 (*0-345-32635-0*, Ballantine Trade) Ballantine.

Third Generation. Chester Himes. 336p. 1989. reprint ed. pap. 14.95 (*0-938410-73-3*) Thunders Mouth.

Third Generation Greek Americans: A Study of Religious Attitudes. Alice Scourby. Ed. by Francesco Cordasco. LC 80-893. (American Ethnic Groups Ser.). 1981. lib. bdg. 18.95 (*0-405-13454-1*) Ayer.

Third Generation R & D: Managing the Link to Corporate Strategy. Philip A. Roussel et al. 224p. 1991. 29.95 (*0-87584-252-6*) Harvard Busn.

Third Generation R&D: Managing the Link to Corporate Strategy. Philip A. Roussel et al. 1991. text ed. 29.95 (*0-07-103284-3*) McGraw.

Third Generation World Organization. 217p. 1989. 40.00 (*92-1-157167-7*) UN.

Third George. large type ed. Jean Plaidy. (Shadows of the Crown Ser.). 1974. 25.99 (*0-85456-596-5*) Ulverscroft.

Third Girl: A Hercule Poirot Mystery. Agatha Christie. 272p. 1992. mass mkt. 5.50 (*0-06-100382-4*, Harp PBks) HarpC.

Third Globe: Symposium for the Reconstruction of the Globe Playhouse, Wayne State University, 1979. Symposium for the Reconstruction of the Globe Playhouse (1979: Wayne State University) Staff. Ed. by C. Walter Hodges et al. LC 81-3362. (Illus.). 268p. reprint ed. pap. 76.40 (*0-318-39790-0*, 2033192) Bks Demand.

***Third Gospel for the Third World Vol. 1: Preface & Infancy Narrative (Luke 1:1-2:52)** Herman Hendrickx. LC 96-3465. 280p. (Orig.). 1997. pap. text ed. 19.95 (*0-8146-5870-9*, M Glazier) Liturgical Pr.

Third Grade. B. K. Hixson. (Utah Core-Science Ser.). 95p. 1990. pap. text ed. 19.99 (*1-57156-014-9*) Wild Goose UT.

Third-Grade Book. Grace Burton et al. Ed. by Miriam A. Leiva. LC 91-34131. (Curriculum & Evaluation Standards for School Mathematics Addenda Ser.). (Illus.). 32p. (Orig.). (J). (gr. k-6). 1992. pap. 11.00 (*0-87353-313-5*) NCTM.

***Third Grade Bullies.** Elizabeth Levy. LC 96-49018. (J). 1997. 13.89 (*0-7868-2264-3*) Hyprn Child.

***Third Grade Bullies.** Elizabeth Levy. LC 96-49018. (J). 1998. pap. 3.95 (*0-7868-1214-1*) Hyprn Child.

Third Grade Detectives. Candice F. Ransom. LC 93-41364. (Tales from Third Grade Ser.). (Illus.). 128p. (J). (gr. 2-4). 1994. lib. bdg. 11.89 (*0-8167-2992-1*) Troll Communs.

Third Grade Dictionary Activity Book. Kaye Furlong. 1989. pap. 0.94 (*0-394-83406-2*) Random.

Third Grade Grammar. Frank Schaffer Publications, Inc. Staff. (Skill Builders Ser.). (Illus.). 128p. 1996. wbk. ed. 10.95 (*0-7647-0008-1*, FS-32077) Schaffer Pubns.

Third Grade Ideas & Whole Language Activities. Barbara Gruber. (Instant Idea Bks.). (Illus.). 64p. 1990. 7.95 (*0-86734-084-3*, FS-8322) Schaffer Pubns.

Third Grade Is Terrible. Barbara Baker. Ed. by Patricia MacDonald. 112p. (J). (gr. 2-5). 1991. reprint ed. mass mkt. 3.50 (*0-671-70379-X*, Minstrel Bks) PB.

Third Grade Math Review. Frank Schaffer Publications, Inc. Staff. (Skill Builders Ser.). (Illus.). 128p. 1996. wbk. ed. 10.95 (*0-7647-0004-9*, FS-32070) Schaffer Pubns.

Third Grade Math TAAS Instructional Packet. Patricia Enselek & Susan Griffin. (TAAS Instructional Packets (TIPs) Ser.). 72p. 1991. 19.95 (*1-883396-03-4*) Educ Etc.

Third Grade Reading & Writing TAAS Instructional Packet. Patricia Enselek & Susan Griffin. (TAAS Instructional Packets (TIPs) Ser.). 72p. 1991. 19.95 (*1-883396-02-6*) Educ Etc.

Third Grade Review. Frank Schaffer Publications, Inc. Staff. (Skill Builders Ser.). (Illus.). 128p. 1996. wbk. ed. 10.95 (*0-86734-914-X*, FS-32058) Schaffer Pubns.

Third Grade Stars: Tales from Third Grade. Candice F. Ransom. LC 93-7868. (Illus.). 128p. (J). (gr. 2-4). 1996. pap. 3.95 (*0-8167-2995-6*) Troll Communs.

Third Grade's Skinny Pig. Kathleen Duey. 80p. (Orig.). (J). (gr. 1). 1993. pap. 3.50 (*0-380-76730-9*, Camelot Young) Avon.

3rd Granada Lectures in Computational Physics: Proceedings of the III Granada Seminar on Computational Physics, Held at Granada, Spain, 5-10 September 1994. Ed. by Pedro L. Garrido et al. LC 95-12982. (Lecture Notes in Physics Ser.: Vol. 448). xiv, 346p. 1995. 92.95 (*3-540-59178-8*) Spr-Verlag.

Third Grave. David Case. LC 80-26818. (Illus.). 192p. 1981. 10.95 (*0-87054-089-0*) Arkham.

Third HGH Symposium Sorrento 1992, May, 1992. Ed. by J. Girard & J. S. Christiansen. (Hormone Research Journal: Vol. 38, Suppl. 1, 1992). (Illus.). vi, 118p. 1992. pap. 54.00 (*3-8055-5742-6*) S Karger.

Third Horizon. Frank Dossetor. 1985. 25.00 (*0-317-62218-8*) St Mut.

Third Horror. R. L. Stine. Ed. by Patricia MacDonald. (Ninety-Nine Fear Street: The House of Evil Ser.). 240p. (Orig.). 1994. pap. 3.99 (*0-685-71430-6*, Archway) PB.

Third Horror. R. L. Stine. (Ninety-Nine Fear Street; the House of Evil Ser.). (Orig.). (YA). (gr. 7 up). 1994. pap. 3.99 (*0-671-88564-2*, Archway) S&S Trade.

Third House: Lobbyists & Lobbying in the States. Alan Rosenthal. LC 92-28705. 242p. 1992. 34.95 (*0-87187-671-X*); pap. 20.95 (*0-87187-672-8*) Congr Quarterly.

***Third Hutton Symposium on the Origin of Granites & Related Rocks: Proceedings of a Symposium Held at the University of Maryland at College Park, 27 August to 2 September 1995.** Ed. by R. J. Walker et al. LC 96-30882. (Special Papers: No. 315). 1996. pap. 78.00 (*0-8137-2315-9*) Geol Soc.

Third IEEE International Workshop on Cellular Neural Networks & Their Applications Proceedings, 1994. LC 94-77701. 350p. 1994. pap. write for info. (*0-7803-2070-0*, 94TH0693-2) Inst Electrical.

Third IEEE International Workshop on Robot & Human Communications Proceedings, 1994. IEEE, Industrial Electronics Society Staff. Ed. by IEEE, Institute of Electrical & Electronics Engineers, Inc. Staff. LC 94-76919. 400p. 1994. pap. write for info. (*0-7803-2002-6*, 94TH0679-1); fiche write for info. (*0-7803-2003-4*) Inst Electrical.

Third IMA Conference on Control Theory. Ed. by J. E. Marshall et al. LC 81-67923. 1982. text ed. 210.00 (*0-12-473960-1*) Acad Pr.

Third Indo-China War. Deakin University Press Staff. 63p. (C). 1988. 30.00 (*0-7300-0602-6*, Pub. by Deakin Univ AT) St Mut.

Third Industrial Age: Strategy for Business Survival. Charles Tavel. LC 79-40199. (Illus.). 356p. 1980. 161.00 (*0-08-022506-3*, Pub. by Pergamon Repr UK) Franklin.

***Third Industrial Revolution.** Greenwood. 100p. (Orig.). 1997. pap. 9.95 (*0-8447-7093-0*) Am Enterprise.

Third Industrial Revolution. Lopez. 1995. pap. text ed. 24.95 (*0-07-031796-8*) McGraw.

Third Intermediate Period in Egypt (1100-650BC) 1100-650 BC, Incl. suppl. 2nd ed. K. A. Kitchen. (Illus.). 628p. 1996. reprint ed. pap. 49.95 (*0-85668-298-5*, Pub. by Aris & Phillips UK) David Brown.

Third International after Lenin. 4th ed. Leon Trotsky. LC 96-68845. 380p. 1996. reprint ed. pap. 25.95 (*0-87348-826-1*) Pathfinder NY.

***Third International after Lenin.** 4th ed. Leon Trotsky. LC 70-130578. 380p. 1996. reprint ed. lib. bdg. 60.00 (*0-87348-827-X*) Pathfinder NY.

Third International Conference on Computation in Electromegnetics, No. IC420. 422p. 1996. pap. 148.00 (*0-85296-657-1*) Inst Elect Eng.

Third International Conference on Data & Knowledge Bases. Ed. by C. Beeri et al. 400p. 1988. 29.95 (*0-934613-95-8*) Morgan Kaufmann.

Third International Conference on Facility Operations-Safeguards Interface: American Nuclear Society, San Diego, CA, November 29 to December 4, 1987. 502p. 50.00 (*0-89448-138-X*, 700132) Am Nuclear Soc.

Third International Conference on Industrial Fuzzy Control & Intelligent Systems, 1993. IEEE (Neural Networks Council) Staff. LC 93-80120. 275p. 1993. pap. write for info. (*0-7803-1485-9*, 93TH0594-2); fiche write for info. (*0-7803-1486-7*) Inst Electrical.

Third International Conference on Mathematical & Numerical Aspects of Wave Propagation. Ed. by Gary Cohen et al. LC 95-2390. (Proceedings in Applied Mathematics Ser.: Vol. 77). xiii, 808p. 1995. pap. 106.00 (*0-89871-350-1*) Soc Indus-Appl Math.

Third International Conference on Minority Languages: Celtic Papers. Ed. by E. Mac Oein et al. 1987. 59.00 (*0-905028-64-3*, Pub. by Multilingual Matters UK) Taylor & Francis.

Third International Conference on Minority Languages, Galway 1986: General Papers. Ed. by G. MacEoin et al. 240p. 1987. 59.00 (*0-905028-78-3*, MM31, Pub. by Multilingual Matters UK) Taylor & Francis.

Third International Conference on Nutrition in Cardio-Cerebrovascular Diseases. Ed. by Yasaburo Oike & Takemichi Kanazawa. LC 92-48405. (Annals Ser.: Vol. 676). 1993. write for info. (*0-89766-775-1*); pap. write for info. (*0-89766-776-X*) NY Acad Sci.

Third International Conference on Universal Personal Communications Record, 1994. IEEE, Communications Society Staff. Ed. by IEEE Staff. LC 93-81179. 1000p. 1994. pap. write for info. (*0-7803-1823-4*, 94TH0622-1); fiche write for info. (*0-7803-1824-2*) Inst Electrical.

Third International Congress of Neuroendocrinology, Budapest, July 1994: Abstracts. Ed. by I. Gerendai & B. Halasz. (Journal: Vol. 60, Suppl. 1, 1994). iv, 104p. 1994. pap. 67.00 (*3-8055-6012-5*) S Karger.

Third International Coral Reef Symposium: Proceedings, 1977, 2 Vols. 1300p. 1977. 44.00 (*0-930050-03-7*) Univ Miami A R C.

Third International Coral Reef Symposium: Proceedings, 1977, 2 Vols., 1. 1300p. 1977. write for info. (*0-930050-01-0*) Univ Miami A R C.

Third International Coral Reef Symposium: Proceedings, 1977, 2 Vols., 2. 1300p. 1977. write for info. (*0-930050-02-9*) Univ Miami A R C.

Third International Energy Efficiency & DSM Conference. 669p. (Orig.). 1994. pap. text ed. 175.00 (*1-883128-02-1*) SRC Intl.

Third International Exhibition of Holography. Ed. by Ed Wesly. (Illus.). 37p. 1988. pap. 10.00 (*0-910535-06-X*) Lake Forest.

***Third International Mathematics & Science Study Technical Report.** Ed. by Michael O. Martin. 250p. 1997. pap. write for info. (*1-889938-06-8*) Boston Coll.

***Third International Mathematics & Science Study Technical Report Vol. I: Design & Development.** Ed. by Michael O. Martin & Dana L. Kelly. LC 96-86397. (Illus.). 250p. (Orig.). 1996. pap. write for info. (*1-889938-00-9*) Boston Coll.

***Third International Mathematics & Science Study (TIMSS) Quality Assurance in Data Collection.** Ed. by Michael O. Martin & Ina V. Mullis. LC 96-71249. (Illus.). 220p. (Orig.). 1996. pap. write for info. (*1-889938-01-7*) Boston Coll.

***3rd International Meeting on Chemical SellSOrS, Cleveland OH.** 145.00 (*0-614-26524-X*, C90PRC) Info Gatekeepers.

Third International Meeting on Reactor Thermal Hydraulics: Proceedings in Newport, RI October 10-15, 1985. 1200p. 105.00 (*0-89448-122-3*, 700103) Am Nuclear Soc.

Third International Symposium on Flow-Induced Vibration & Noise, Vol. 1: FSI - FIV in Cylinder Arrays in Cross-Flow. Ed. by M. P. Paidoussis et al. (HTD Series, Vol. 230: NE: Vol. 9). 284p. 1992. 62.50 (*0-7918-1078-X*, G00722) ASME.

Third International Symposium on Flow-Induced Vibration & Noise, Vol. 2: Cross-Flow Induced Vibration of Cylinder Arrays. Ed. by M. P. Paidoussis et al. (PVP Ser.: Vol. 242). 356p. 1992. 65.00 (*0-7918-1079-8*, G00723) ASME.

Third International Symposium on Flow-Induced Vibration & Noise, Vol. 3: Flow-Structure & Flow-Sound Interactions. Ed. by T. M. Farabee & M. P. Paidoussis. (NCA Ser.: Vol. 13). 228p. 1992. 57.50 (*0-7918-1080-1*, G00724) ASME.

Third International Symposium on Flow-Induced Vibration & Noise, Vol. 4: Acoustical Effects in FSI. Ed. by M. P. Paidoussis & J. B. Sandifer. (PVP Ser.: Vol. 243). 164p. 1992. 45.00 (*0-7918-1081-X*, G00725) ASME.

Third International Symposium on Flow-Induced Vibration & Noise, Vol. 5: Axial & Annular Flow-Induced Vibrations & Instabilities. Ed. by M. P. Paidoussis & M. K. Au-Yang. (PVP Ser.: Vol. 244). 232p. 1992. 57.50 (*0-7918-1082-8*, G00726) ASME.

Third International Symposium on Flow-Induced Vibration & Noise, Vol. 6: Bluff-Body - Fluid & Hydraulic Machine Interactions. Ed. by M. P. Paidoussis et al. (FED Ser.: Vol. 138). 264p. 1992. 62.50 (*0-7918-1083-6*, G00727) ASME.

Third International Symposium on Flow-Induced Vibration & Noise, Vol. 7: Fundamental Aspects of Fluid-Structure Interactions. Ed. by M. P. Paidoussis et al. (AMD Series, Vol. 151: PVP: Vol. 247). 232p. 1992. 57.50 (*0-7918-1084-4*, G00728) ASME.

Third International Symposium on Flow-Induced Vibration & Noise, Vol. 8: Stability & Control of Pipes Conveying Fluid. Ed. by M. P. Paidoussis & N. S. Namachchivaya. (AMD Ser.: Vol. 152). 140p. 1992. 45.00 (*0-7918-1085-2*, G00729) ASME.

***Third International Symposium on Tilapia in Aquaculture.** Ed. by Daniel Pauly et al. (ICLARM Conference Proceedings Ser.: No. 41). 400p. Date not set. per. write for info. (*971-8709-42-8*, Pub. by ICLARM PH) Intl Spec Bk.

Third Joint Meeting of the European Society for Paediatric Endocrinology (ESPE) & the Lawson Wilkins Pediatric Endocrine Society (LWPES) Proceedings of the Plenary Lectures & Symposia, Jerusalem, October - November 1989. Ed. by Z. Laron. (Journal: Hormone Research: Vol. 33, No. 2-4, 1990). (Illus.). 116p. 1990. pap. 118.50 (*3-8055-5289-0*) S Karger.

Third Jungle Book. Pamela Jekel. LC 90-36410. (Illus.). 220p. (Orig.). 1992. 19.95 (*1-879373-22-X*) R Rinehart.

Third Kind of Knowledge: Memoirs & Selected Writings of Robert Fitzgerald. Robert Fitzgerald. Ed. by Penelope L. Fitzgerald. LC 88-1377. (Illus.). 320p. 1993. 24.95 (*0-8112-1056-1*) New Directions.

Third Leaders, Reprinted from the Times. London Times Staff. LC 68-16980. (Essay Index Reprint Ser.). 1977. 19.95 (*0-8369-0946-1*) Ayer.

Third Level. Jack Finney. 1994. lib. bdg. 27.95 (*1-56849-412-2*) Buccaneer Bks.

Third Lie. Agota Kristof. Tr. by Marc Romano from FRE. 144p. 1996. 20.00 (*0-8021-1583-7*, Grove) Grove-Atltic.

Third Life of Grange Copeland. Alice Walker. Ed. by Julie Rubenstein. 1991. pap. 6.99 (*0-671-74588-3*) PB.

Third Line: The Opera Performer As Interpreter. Daniel Helfgot & William O. Beeman. LC 93-12311. (Illus.). 272p. 1993. Alk. paper. 38.00 (*0-02-871036-3*) Schirmer Bks.

Third Line Medicine. Melvyn R. Werbach. 1988. pap. 10.95 (*0-14-019063-5*) Third Line Pr.

***Third Lion: A Novel about Talleyrand.** Floyd Kemske. LC 97-14171. 240p. 1997. 22.95 (*0-945774-37-0*, PS3561. E4226T48) Catbird Pr.

Third Man. Graham Greene. (Illus.). 120p. 1988. pap. 12.95 (*0-571-12634-0*) Faber & Faber.

***Third Man.** Graham Greene. lib. bdg. 17.95 (*0-8488-1875-X*) Amereon Ltd.

Third Man & the Fallen Idol. Graham Greene. 1981. mass mkt. 6.00 (*0-14-003278-9*, Penguin Bks) Viking Penguin.

Third Man & the Fallen Idol. Graham Greene. 160p. 1992. pap. 10.95 (*0-14-018533-X*, Penguin Classics) Viking Penguin.

Third Man Argument in the Parmenides. Gregory Vlastos. (Reprints in Philosophy Ser.). (C). 1991. reprint ed. pap. text ed. 1.00 (*0-8290-2602-9*, F-216) Irvington.

Third Man Out: A Donald Strachey Mystery. Richard Stevenson. LC 92-37743. (Stonewall Inn Mysteries Ser.). 1993. pap. 8.95 (*0-312-08906-6*) St Martin.

Third Man's Range. large type ed. Mark Donovan. (Linford Western Library). 240p. 1993. pap. 15.99 (*0-7089-7446-5*, Trailtree Bookshop) Ulverscroft.

Third Manual for the Calligraphic Arts. M. Jane Van Milligen et al. (Illus.). (Orig.). 1989. pap. text ed. 16.95 (*0-9617137-2-0*) Ctr Callig KS.

Third Marine Division. 15th ed. Robert Aurthur & Kenneth Cohlmia. (Elite Unit Ser.). (Illus.). 399p. 1989. reprint ed. 39.95 (*0-89839-110-5*) Battery Pr.

Third Mile: A Biblical View of Codependency. Omar K. Omland. 105p. (Orig.). 1992. pap. 8.95 (*0-943167-11-6*) Faith & Fellowship Pr.

Third Millenium: Living in the Posthistoric World. Ken Carey. LC 94-39494. 224p. 1996. pap. 12.00 (*0-06-251408-3*) Harper SF.

***Third Millenium: Small Business & Entrepreneurship in the 21st Century.** (Illus.). 68p. 1996. reprint ed. pap. 25.00 (*0-7881-3305-5*) DIANE Pub.

Third Millennium. Paul Meier. LC 93-18464. 320p. 1993. pap. 12.99 (*0-8407-7571-7*) Nelson.

***Third Millennium: A Catholic Perspective.** James P. Campbell. 76p. (Orig.). 1996. pap. 8.00 (*1-55833-173-5*) Natl Cath Educ.

Third Millennium Inscriptions Vol. 1: Cuneiform Inscriptions in the Collection of the Bible Lands Museum Jerusalem. Joan G. Westenholz. 1996. write for info. (*0-614-96307-9*, Pub. by Styx NE) Eisenbrauns.

Third-Millennium Legal & Administrative Texts in the Iraq Museum, Baghdad. Piotr Steinkeller & J. N. Postgate. LC 91-27938. (Mesopotamian Civilizations Ser.: Vol. 4). (Illus.). xv, 123p. 1992. 39.50 (*0-931464-60-9*) Eisenbrauns.

***Third Miracle.** Richard Vetere. LC 97-4261. 256p. 1997. 22.00 (*0-7867-0413-6*) Carroll & Graf.

Third Music. Ann R. Colton. LC 83-102627. (Illus.). 432p. 1982. 15.95 (*0-917187-00-8*) A R Colton Fnd.

***Third National Roundtable on Outcome Measures in Child Welfare Services: Summary of Proceedings.** Ed. by American Humane Association, Children's Division Staff. (Illus.). iii, 99p. 1996. pap. text ed. write for info. (*0-930915-03-8*, COM03) Am Humane Assn.

***Third Nuclear Simulation Symposium.** Ed. by Heller. 262p. 1993. 40.00 (*1-56555-058-7*, NSS-93) Soc Computer Sim.

Third of a Century with George Way Harley in Liberia. Winifred J. Harley. (Liberian Research Working Papers: No. 2). 1973. 8.00 (*0-317-00236-8*) Arden Assocs.

***III Olympiad, St. Louis 1904 & Athens 1906.** (Olympic Century Ser.). (Illus.). 1997. 21.95 (*1-888383-04-6*, Wrld Spt) Wld Sport Resch.

Third Opinion: An International Directory to Alternate Therapy Centers for the Treatment & Prevention of Cancer & Other Degenerative Diseases. 3rd ed. John M. Fink. 320p. 1996. pap. 15.95 (*0-89529-770-1*) Avery Pub.

Third Opinion: An International Directory to Alternative Therapy Centers for the Treatment & Prevention of Cancer. 2nd ed. John M. Fink. LC 91-41082. 256p. 1992. pap. 15.95 (*0-89529-503-2*) Avery Pub.

Third or Eighteen-Twenty Land Lotteries of Georgia. rev. ed. Silas E. Lucas, Jr. (Seven Land Lotteries of Georgia & Other Land Records Ser.). 382p. 1986. reprint ed. 35.00 (*0-89308-585-5*, GA 26) Southern Hist Pr.

Third-Order Linear Differential Equations. Michal Gregus. (Mathematics & Its Applications East European Ser.). 1987. lib. bdg. 134.00 (*90-277-2193-9*) Kluwer Ac.

Third Pandemic. Pierre Ouellette. 384p. 1996. 23.00 (*0-671-52534-4*, PB Hardcover) PB.

***Third Pandemic.** Pierre Ouellette. 1997. pap. 6.99 (*0-671-52536-0*) PB.

***Third Paradigm: God & Government in the 21st Century.** Mark A. Ludwig. (Illus.). 304p. (Orig.). 1997. pap. 14.95 (*0-929408-18-7*) Amer Eagle Pubns Inc.

Third Parent: Growth & Development of Indian Electronics Media. P. S. Deodhar. 123p. 1991. text ed. 18.95 (*0-7069-5801-2*) Advent Bks Div.

***Third Paris Cosmology Colloquium.** 436p. 1996. 61.00 (*981-02-2538-5*) World Scientific Pub.

Third Part of King Henry VI. William Shakespeare. Ed. by Michael Hattaway. (New Cambridge Shakespeare Ser.). (Illus.). 250p. 1993. text ed. 39.95 (*0-521-37331-X*); pap. text ed. 10.95 (*0-521-37705-6*) Cambridge U Pr.

Third Parties: Victims & the Criminal Justice System. Leslie Sebba. LC 95-50577. 448p. (C). 1996. 45.00 (*0-8142-0664-6*) Ohio St U Pr.

Third Parties in America. Steven J. Rosenstone et al. LC 83-43091. 266p. 1984. pap. 16.95 (*0-691-02225-9*) Princeton U Pr.

Third Parties in America: Citizen Response to Major Party Failure. 2nd expanded rev. ed. Steven J. Rosenstone. LC 96-510. 306p. 1984. pap. text ed. 16.95 (*0-691-02613-0*) Princeton U Pr.

Third Parties in Presidential Elections. Daniel A. Mazmanian. LC 74-281. (Studies in Presidential Selection). (Illus.). 175p. reprint ed. pap. 49.90 (*0-685-23664-1*, 2027969) Bks Demand.

***Third Partner.** William Devine. LC 97-21875. 1998. 25.00 (*0-517-70764-0*, Harmony) Crown Pub Group.

Third Party Billing for Special Education: Panacea or Mirage? Joy J. Rogers. LC 92-44211. 1993. pap. text ed. 27.95 (*0-914797-83-2*) Brookline Bks.

Third-Party Financing: Increasing Investment in Energy Efficient Industrial Projects. 122p. 4.00 (*0-317-01162-6*) Alliance Save Ener.

Third Party Footprints. James Youngdale. (Illus.). 1966. 10.00 (*0-87018-064-9*) Ross.

Third Party Payment for Funding Special Education & Related Services. Roberta A. Kreb. LC 90-23901. 190p. 1994. ring bd. 85.00 (*0-934753-47-4*) LRP Pubns.

Third Party Payments. J. Steve Strosnider & John D. Grad. LC 93-13262. (Legal Ser.: Vol. 9). 72p. 1993. pap. text ed. 12.95 (*1-55620-124-9*, 72309) Am Coun Assn.

Third Party Politics since Nineteen Forty-Five: The Politics of the Centre in Britain. John Stevenson. (Making Contemporary Britain Ser.). 160p. 1993. pap. 16.95 (*0-631-17127-4*) Blackwell Pubs.

Third Party Rape: The Conspiracy to Rob You of Health Care. C. Norman Shealy. LC 93-7684. (Illus.). 224p. (Orig.). 1993. pap. 12.95 (*1-880090-07-4*) Galde Pr.

Third Philippine Republic, 1946-1972. Lewis E. Gleeck, Jr. (Illus.). 429p. (Orig.). 1993. pap. 19.50 (*971-10-0473-9*, Pub. by New Day Pub PH) Cellar.

Third Pink Book: A Global View of Lesbian & Gay Liberation & Oppression. Ed. by Rob Tielman et al. 349p. (C). 1993. 33.95 (*0-87975-831-7*) Prometheus Bks.

Third Planet. (Voyage Through the Universe Ser.). (Illus.). 144p. 1989. 17.27 (*0-8094-6879-4*); lib. bdg. 24.60 (*0-8094-6880-8*) Time-Life.

Third Planet. Sally K. Ride & Tam O'Shaughnessy. LC 92-40609. (Illus.). 48p. (J). (gr. 3-7). 1994. 18.00 (*0-517-59361-0*); lib. bdg. 19.99 (*0-517-59362-9*) Crown Bks Yng Read.

Third Planet: An Introduction to Earth Science. Lemon. 608p. 1994. 39.95 (*0-8016-7470-0*) Mosby Yr Bk.

Third Poems, 1965-1978. David Galler. (QRL Poetry Bks.: Vol. XX). 1978. 20.00 (*0-614-06374-4*) Quarterly Rev.

Third Policeman. Flann O'Brien. 1976. pap. 12.95 (*0-452-25912-6*, Plume) NAL-Dutton.

Third Pos. Easy-Melodic Vln. Stephanie H. Swoveland. 4.95 (*0-7866-0075-6*, 95225) Mel Bay.

Third Power: Farmers to the Front (Fourth Edition) James A. Everitt. LC 74-30630. (American Farmers & the Rise of Agribusiness Ser.). (Illus.). 1975. reprint ed. 31.95 (*0-405-06799-2*) Ayer.

Third Prophecy. Clifton Bush. LC 94-90648. 1995. pap. 14.95 (*0-9643612-0-5*) FABCO Pubng.

***Third Protocol to the General Agreement on Trade in Services - Movement of Natural Revised Schedules of Commitments on Financial Services.** World Trade Organization Staff. 58p. 1997. pap. 125.00 (*92-870-0147-2*, G1472, Pub. by Wrld Trade SZ) Bernan Associates.

Third Rainbow Book of Adventures. Ed. by Jutta Kapfhammer & Philip S. Helm. (Illus.). 235p. (Orig.). 1987. pap. 11.95 (*0-932471-07-2*) Falsoft.

Third Reader see McGuffey's Revised Eclectic Readers

Third Reference Catalogue of Bright Galaxies, 3 vols. Gerard H. De Vaucouleurs et al. (Illus.). 1991. Set. 259.95 (*0-387-97552-7*); Vol. 1: Introduction, References, Notes, & Appendices, vi, 714p. 98.95 (*0-387-97549-7*) Spr-Verlag.

Third Reference Catalogue of Bright Galaxies, 3 vols., Vol. 2: Data for Galaxies Between 0h & 12h. Gerard H. De Vaucouleurs et al. (Illus.). viii, 723p. 1991. Vol. 2: Data for Galaxies Between 0h & 12h, viii, 723p. 109.95 (*0-387-97550-0*) Spr-Verlag.

Third Reference Catalogue of Bright Galaxies, 3 vols., Vol. 3: Data for Galaxies Between 12h & 24h. Gerard H. De Vaucouleurs et al. (Illus.). viii, 632p. 1991. 109.95 (*0-387-97551-9*) Spr-Verlag.

Third Reformation: Charismatic Movements & the Lutheran Tradition. Carter Lindberg. LC 83-11371. x, 346p. 1983. 24.95 (*0-86554-075-6*, MUP/H83) Mercer Univ Pr.

Third Reich. Klaus Hildebrand. Tr. by P. S. Falla from GER. (Illus.). 168p. 1984. 34.95 (*0-04-943033-5*); pap. 19.95 (*0-04-943032-7*) Routledge Chapman & Hall.

Third Reich. Klaus Hildebrand. (Illus.). 196p. (C). (gr. 13 up). 1986. pap. 22.95 (*0-415-07861-X*, Routledge NY) Routledge.

***Third Reich.** Eric Johnson. 288p. 25.00 (*0-465-08571-7*) Basic.

Third Reich. Henri Lichtenberger. Tr. by Koppel S. Pinson. LC 73-102249. (Select Bibliographies Reprint Ser.). 1977. 35.95 (*0-8369-5134-4*) Ayer.

Third Reich. Williamson. (C). 1982. pap. text ed. 12.50 (*0-582-35306-8*) Addison-Wesley.

Third Reich. 2nd ed. D. G. Williamson. LC 94-27052. (Seminar Studies in History). (C). 1995. pap. text ed. 13.50 (*0-582-20914-5*) Longman.

Third Reich: Politics & Propaganda. David Welch. (Illus.). 224p. (C). 1994. pap. 17.95 (*0-415-11910-3*, C0427) Routledge.

Third Reich & the Christian Churches. Ed. by Peter Matheson. 128p. 1981. pap. 19.95 (*0-567-29105-7*, Pub. by T & T Clark UK) Bks Intl VA.

Third Reich & the Palestine Question. Francis R. Nicosia. 335p. 1986. text ed. 35.00 (*0-292-72731-3*) U of Tex Pr.

Third Reich & Ukraine. Wolodymyr Kosyk. Tr. by Irene I. Rudnytzky from FRE. LC 92-31015. (Studies in Modern European History: Vol. 8). 670p. (C). 1993. text ed. 63.95 (*0-8204-1964-8*) P Lang Pubng.

Third Reich Daggers, 1933-45: A Guide to Identification, Reproduction Recognition & Values. J. A. Bowman. (Illus.). 496p. 1994. 65.00 (*1-884849-00-8*) R&R Bks.

Third Reich Edged Weapon Accouterments. 2nd ed. Thomas M. Johnson & Wilfred Bradach. LC 78-50089. (Illus.). 1978. pap. 25.00 (*0-9600906-5-7*) Johnson Ref Bks.

***Third Report on Nutrition Monitoring in the U. S., 2 vols., Set.** (Illus.). 600p. (Orig.). 1996. pap. text ed. 75.00 (*0-7881-2987-2*) DIANE Pub.

***Third Report on Nutrition Monitoring in the U. S. Executive Summary.** (Illus.). 40p. (Orig.). 1996. pap. 25.00 (*0-7881-2986-4*) DIANE Pub.

Third Republic. Raymond Recouly. Tr. by E. F. Buckley. LC 28-23849. (National History of France Ser.: No. 10). reprint ed. 45.00 (*0-404-50800-6*) AMS Pr.

Third Republic - Political Path of China. J. Q. Yan. 388p. 1992. pap. text ed. 13.00 (*1-879771-01-2*) Global Pub NJ.

Third Republic & the Centennial of 1789. Brenda Nelms. (Modern European History Ser.). 312p. 1987. text ed. 15.00 (*0-8240-8039-4*) Garland.

Third Republic from Its Origins to the Great War, 1871-1914. Jean-Marie Mayeur & Madeleine Reberioux. (Cambridge History of Modern France Ser.: No. 4). (Illus.). 412p. 1988. pap. text ed. 19.95 (*0-521-35857-4*) Cambridge U Pr.

Third Republic from 1870-1914. Robert Gildea. (C). 1988. pap. text ed. 13.50 (*0-582-35556-7*) Addison-Wesley.

Third Review of the Biological Weapons Convention: Issues & Proposals. (UNDIR Research Papers: No. 9). 79p. 1991. 12.00 (*92-9045-049-5*) UN.

Third Revolution: Population, Environment & a Sustainable World. Paul Harrison. 384p. 1993. pap. 13.95 (*0-14-014659-8*, Penguin Bks) Viking Penguin.

Third Revolution: Professional Society in International Perspective. Harold Perkin. LC 95-44146. 264p. (C). 1996. pap. 18.95 (*0-415-14338-1*); text ed. 65.00 (*0-415-14337-3*) Routledge.

Third Revolution Vol. 1: Popular Movements in the Revolutionary Era, Vol. 1. Murray Bookchin. (Global Issues Ser.). 384p. 1996. 85.00 (*0-304-33593-2*, Pub. by Cassell Pubng UK); pap. 19.95 (*0-304-33594-0*, Pub. by Cassell Pubng UK) LPC InBook.

Third Revolution in the Chinese Countryside. Ed. by Ross G. Garnaut et al. (Trade & Development Ser.). 304p. (C). 1996. text ed. 54.95 (*0-521-55409-8*) Cambridge U Pr.

Third Rider. large type ed. Barry Cord. (Linford Western Library). 240p. 1988. pap. 15.99 (*0-7089-6521-0*, Linford) Ulverscroft.

Third River Basin Management Conference: Proceedings of a Conference Held in York, 4-8 July 1983 & Incorporating the Workshop on Advances in the Application of Mathematical Modelling to Water Quality Management Held in London, July 11-12 1983. Ed. by D. H. Newsome & A. M. Edwards. (Illus.). 670p. 1984. pap. 130.00 (*0-08-031505-4*, Pergamon Pr) Elsevier.

***Third Rock from the Sun: The Official Tie-In.** Terry D. Turner. (Illus.). 160p. (Orig.). 1996. pap. 13.50 (*0-06-095228-8*, PL) HarpC.

***Third Secret: A Quest for the Truth Could Change the World.** Gil Court. 1997. mass mkt. 5.99 (*1-55197-408-8*, Pub. by Comnwlth Pub CN) Partners Pubs Grp.

Third Secret of Fatima. Brother Michael of the Holy Trinity. Tr. by Anne B. Gardiner from FRE. LC 91-65429. 53p. (Orig.). 1992. pap. 1.50 (*0-89555-435-6*) TAN Bks Pubs.

Third Sector: Comparative Studies of Nonprofit Organizations. Ed. by Helmut K. Anheier & Wolfgang Seibel. (Studies in Organization: No. 21). xiv, 413p. (C). 1990. lib. bdg. 69.95 (*3-11-011713-4*) De Gruyter.

Third Seed. Jane S. Bauld. (Illus.). 32p. (J). (gr. k-5). 1995. 16.95 (*1-885340-18-4*) Coming Age Pr.

Third Seminar on Advanced Vehicle System Dynamics: Proceedings of the Third ICTS Seminar Held at Amalfi, Italy, May 5-10, 1986. A. D. De Pater & Hans B. Pacejka. (Supplement to Vehicle System Dynamics Ser.: Vol. 16). x, 366p. 1987. pap. 57.25 (*90-265-0676-7*) Swets.

3rd Serving of Chicken Soup for the Soul: 101 More Stories to Open the Heart & Rekindle the Spirit. Ed. by Jack Canfield & Mark V. Hansen. (Chicken Soup for the Soul Ser.). 352p. 1996. pap. 12.95 (*1-55874-379-0*, 3901) Health Comm.

3rd Serving of Chicken Soup for the Soul: 101 More Stories to Open the Heart & Rekindle the Spirit. large type ed. Jack Canfield & Mark V. Hansen. (Chicken Soup for the Soul Ser.). 352p. 1996. 24.00 (*1-55874-380-4*); pap. 16.95 (*1-55874-400-2*, 4002) Health Comm.

Third Sex: The New Professional Woman. Patricia A. McBroom. 1994. pap. 14.95 (*1-56924-908-3*) Marlowe & Co.

Third Sex, Third Gender: Beyond Sexual Dimorphism in Culture & History. Ed. by Gilbert Herdt. LC 93-2276. (Illus.). 614p. 1994. 32.95 (*0-942299-81-7*) Zone Bks.

Third Sex, Third Gender: Beyond Sexual Dimorphism in Culture & History. Ed. by Gilbert Herdt. (Illus.). 614p. 1996. reprint ed. pap. 20.00 (*0-942299-82-5*) Zone Bks.

Third Siberian Winter School "Algebra & Analysis" Proceedings of the Third Siberian School, Irkutsk State University, Irkutsk, 1989. Ed. by Third Siberian School Staff et al. LC 94-40144. (American Mathematical Society Translations Series 2: Vol. 163). 1995. 95.00 (*0-8218-0286-0*, TRANS2/163) Am Math.

***Third Side of the Coin.** R. Mathews-Danzer. 780p. 1997. pap. 21.50 (*1-888417-00-5*) Dimefast.

Third Sikh War? Towards or Away from Khalistan? D. Butani. 150p. 1987. text ed. 75.00 (*0-7201-1893-X*, Mansell Pub) Cassell.

Third Sikh War - Towards or Away from Khalistan. D. H. Bhutani. 137p. 1986. 22.95 (*0-318-37216-9*) Asia Bk Corp.

Third Sikh War? Towards or Away from Khalistan? D. H. Butani. 137p. 1986. 25.00 (*81-85002-02-9*, Pub. by Promilla) S Asia.

Third Sister: A Sequel to Jane Austen's Sense & Sensibility. Julia Barrett. 256p. 1996. pap. 22.95 (*1-55611-496-6*, Dutton) D I Fine.

Third Solitudes: Tradition & Discontinuity in Jewish-Canadian Literature. Michael Greenstein. 240p. 1989. 49.95 (*0-7735-0675-6*, Pub. by McGill CN) U of Toronto Pr.

Third Sonata for Violin & Piano. Weins Bolcom. 48p. 1994. pap. 22.50 (*0-7935-3027-X*, 00008708) H Leonard.

Third Steps in Ballet: Basic Allegro Steps. Thalia Mara. LC 70-181475. (Illus.). 64p. (J). (gr. 6-9). 1987. reprint ed. pap. 6.95 (*0-916622-55-X*) Princeton Bk Co.

Third-Story Cat. Leslie Baker. (J). (ps-3). 1990. mass mkt. 4.95 (*0-316-07836-0*) Little.

Third Strike. Jerry Gray. (American Autobiography Ser.). 59p. 1995. reprint ed. lib. bdg. 69.00 (*0-7812-8539-9*) Rprt Serv.

***Third Summer.** Nancy Johnson. 176p. (J). (gr. 4-7). 1997. 14.95 (*0-89272-414-5*) Down East.

Third Supplement to the Cumulation of the Library Catalog Supplements of the New York State School of Industrial & Labor Relations, 2 vols. Cornell University, New York State School of Industrial & Labor Relations Staff. 1979. Set. 230.00 (*0-8161-0260-0*, Hall Library) G K Hall.

Third Symposium by the Seven Winners of the Grants from Sandoz Foundation for Gerontological Research, Annual Meeting of the Japan Gerontological Society, Yokohama, November 1991. Ed. by H. Orimo. (Journal: Gerontology: Vol. 38, Suppl. 1, 1992). (Illus.). vi, 50p. 1992. pap. 17.50 (*3-8055-5661-6*) S Karger.

Third Symposium on Respirable Dust in the Mineral Industries, 3rd. Ed. by R. L. Frantz & R. V. Ramani. LC 91-66952. (Illus.). 401p. 1991. 60.00 (*0-87335-098-7*) Penn St Environ.

***Third Term.** Darryl Nyznyk. LC 97-66088. 384p. 1997. 24.95 (*0-9656513-4-7*) Cross Dove.

Third Testament, Vol. One: Tales on the Evolution of God in Consciousness. John M. Fitzgerald. LC 88-70629. 145p. (C). 1988. 14.95 (*0-9620390-2-0*) Closet Pr.

Third Texas Cavalry in the Civil War. Douglas Hale. LC 92-54153. (Illus.). 384p. 1993. 29.95 (*0-8061-2462-8*) U of Okla Pr.

Third Third: Seeing the World Through Rose-Colored Bifocals. Claire Mitchel. LC 90-19246. 256p. 1991. 16.95 (*0-910155-17-8*) Bartleby Pr.

***Third Thunder Vol. I: The Fall of Etan - Orah, the Deathless Dancer.** MSI Staff. Ed. by Dharani Ishaya. LC 97-65521. (Illus.). 400p. (Orig.). 1997. pap. 17.95 (*0-931783-09-7*) SFA Pubns.

***Third Thunder Vol. II: The Fall of Etan - Shamara, the Oblation Bearer.** MSI Staff. Ed. by Dharani Ishaya. LC 97-65641. (Illus.). 400p. (Orig.). 1997. pap. 17.95 (*0-931783-10-0*) SFA Pubns.

***Third Thunder Vol. III: The Fall of Etan - Swayam, the Father of Time.** MSI Staff. Ed. by Dharani Ishaya. LC 97-65642. (Illus.). 400p. (Orig.). 1998. pap. 17.95 (*0-931783-11-9*) SFA Pubns.

Third Time Around: The BOC Challenge 1990-91. Tony Fairchild. (Illus.). 185p. 1992. 24.95 (*0-924486-24-4*) Sheridan.

Third Treasury of Kahlil Gibran. Kahlil Gibran. Ed. by Andrew D. Sherfan. 1978. reprint ed. pap. 12.95 (*0-8065-0648-2*, Citadel Pr) Carol Pub Group.

Third Treasury of the Familiar. Ralph L. Woods. (J). 1993. reprint ed. lib. bdg. 29.95 (*1-56849-106-9*) Buccaneer Bks.

Third Try at World Order. Harlan Cleveland. 3.95 (*0-686-25998-X*) Aspen Inst Human.

Third Try at World Order. Harlan Cleveland. 140p. 1977. pap. text ed. 14.50 (*0-8191-5901-8*, Aspen Inst for Humanistic Studies) U Pr of Amer.

***Third Twin.** Follett. 1997. mass mkt. 7.99 (*0-449-22742-1*, Crest) Fawcett.

Third Twin. Ken Follett. LC 96-32957. 416p. 1996. 25.95 (*0-517-70296-7*) Crown Pub Group.

Third Twin: A Novel. large type ed. Ken Follett. 672p. 1996. pap. 25.95 (*0-7838-1923-4*) Random Hse Lrg Prnt.

Third United Nations Conference on the Law of the Sea: Summary Records of Meetings, Vol. IV. 12.00 (*92-1-133228-1*, E.75.V.10) UN.

Third United Nations Conference on the Law of the Sea: Documents of the Conference, Vol. III. 14.00 (*92-1-133230-3*, E.75.V.5) UN.

Third United Nations Conference on the Law of the Sea: Documents of the Conference, Vol. VI. 13.00 (*92-1-133225-7*, E.77.V.2) UN.

Third United Nations Conference on the Law of the Sea: Official Records, Vol. XV. 1983. 23.00 (*92-1-133238-9*) UN.

Third United Nations Conference on the Law of the Sea: Official Records, Eighth Session, Vol. XI. 10.00 (*92-1-133222-2*, E.80.V.6) UN.

Third United Nations Conference on the Law of the Sea: Official Records, Seventh Session, Vol. X. 11.00 (*92-1-133223-0*, E.79.V.4) UN.

Third United Nations Conference on the Law of the Sea: Official Records, Summary of Meetings, Resumed Eighth Session, Vol. XII. 9.00 (*92-1-133221-4*, E.80.V.12) UN.

Third United Nations Conference on the Law of the Sea: Official Records, Summary Records of Meetings, Ninth Session, Vol. XIII. 12.00 (*92-1-133220-6*, E.81.V.5) UN.

Third United Nations Conference on the Law of the Sea: Summary Records of Meetings, Vol. I. 12.00 (*92-1-133205-2*, E.75.V.3) UN.

Third United Nations Conference on the Law of the Sea: Summary Records of Meetings, Vol. II. 19.00 (*92-1-133218-4*, E.75.V.4) UN.

Third United Nations Conference on the Law of the Sea: Summary Records of Meetings, Vol. V. 14.00 (*92-1-133227-3*, E.76.V.8) UN.

Third United Nations Conference on the Law of the Sea: Summary Records of Meetings, Vol. VII. 7.00 (*92-1-133226-5*, E.78.V.3) UN.

Third United Nations Conference on the Law of the Sea: Summary Records of Meetings, Vol. IX. 14.00 (*92-1-133224-9*, E.79.V.3) UN.

Third United Nations Conference on the Law of the Sea: Summary Records of Meetings & Documents, Resumed Ninth Session; Geneva, 28 July- 29 August 1980, Vol. XIV. 15.00 (*92-1-133219-2*, E.82.V.2) UN.

Third United Nations Conference on the Law of the Sea: Summary Records of Meetings & Documents, Resumed Ninth Session; Geneva, 28 July- 29 August 1980, Vol. XVII. 245p. 23.00 (*92-1-133333-4*, E.84.V.3) UN.

Third United Nations Conference on the Law of the Sea Series 1: Documents, 1973-1982, 18 vols. Ed. by Renate Platzoder. 1982. Set. lib. bdg. 1,800.00 (*0-379-20724-9*) Oceana.

Third United Nations Conference on the Law of the Sea Offical Records: Summary Records of Meetings & Documents, Eleventh Session; New York, 8 March- 30 April 1982, Vol. XVI. 281p. 27.00 (*92-1-133244-3*, E.84.V.2) UN.

Third United Nations Regional Cartographic Conference for the Americas, Vol. II: Technical Papers. 3rd ed. 362p. 42.00 (*92-1-002051-0*, EFS.88.I.19) UN.

***Third USENIX Conference on Object-Oriented Technologies & Systems (COOTS) Proceedings.** Ed. & Pref. by Steve Vinoski. 248p. (Orig.). 1997. pap. 30.00 (*1-880446-86-3*) USENIX Assn.

Third View of Tongues. K. Neill Foster. (Orig.). 1988. pap. 8.99 (*0-88965-051-9*, Pub. by Horizon Books CN) Chr Pubns.

Third Violet. Stephen Crane. (Works of Stephen Crane Ser.). 1990. reprint ed. lib. bdg. 79.00 (*0-685-44795-2*) Rprt Serv.

Third Virginia Cavalry. Thomas P. Nanzig. (Virginia Regimental Histories Ser.). (Illus.). 142p. 1989. 19.95 (*0-930919-85-8*) H E Howard.

Third Virginia Infantry. Lee A. Wallace. (Virginia Regimental Histories Ser.). (Illus.). 117p. 1986. 19.95 (*0-317-64927-2*) H E Howard.

Third Vow & Other Stories. Phanishwar N. Renu. Tr. by Kathryn Hansen. 1986. 18.50 (*81-7001-013-6*, Pub. by Chanakya II) S Asia.

Third Voyage of Captain Cook. Heinrich Zimmerman. 1988. 29.95 (*0-87770-165-2*) Ye Galleon.

Third Wave. Alvin Toffler. 576p. (Orig.). 1984. mass mkt. 7.99 (*0-553-24698-4*) Bantam.

Third Wave: Democratization in the Late Twentieth Century. Samuel P. Huntington. LC 90-50690. (Julian J. Rothbaum Distinguished Lectures: Vol. 4). (Illus.). 384p. 1993. pap. 18.95 (*0-8061-2516-0*) U of Okla Pr.

Third Wave: Feminist Perspectives on Racism. Ed. by M. Jacqui Alexander et al. 1997. pap. 19.95 (*0-913175-25-0*); lib. bdg. 39.95 (*0-913175-26-9*) Kitchen Table.

Third Wave: The New Russian Poetry. Ed. by Kent Johnson & Stephen M. Ashby. 272p. (C). 1992. text ed. 44.50 (*0-472-09415-7*); pap. text ed. 17.95 (*0-472-06415-0*) U of Mich Pr.

***Third Wave Agenda: Being Feminist, Doing Feminism.** Leslie Heywood & Jennifer Drake. LC 97-20301. 1997. write for info. (*0-8166-3004-6*); pap. write for info. (*0-8166-3005-4*) U of Minn Pr.

Third Wave & the Local Church. Dennis M. Davis & Steve Clapp. 175p. (Orig.). 1983. pap. 8.00 (*0-914527-54-1*) C-Four Res.

Third Wave & West Virginia. Lyle Sattes. Ed. by Carla McClure. (Illus.). x, 116p. (Orig.). 1996. pap. 6.00 (*0-938985-14-0*) Mntn Memories Bks.

Third Wave of Asbestos Disease, Exposure to Asbestos in Place: Public Health Control. Ed. by Philip J. Landrigan & Homayoun Kazemi. LC 92-6138. (Annals Ser.: Vol. 643). 628p. 1992. pap. 190.00 (*0-89766-678-X*, Q11) NY Acad Sci.

***Third Wave of Modernization in Latin America: Cultural Perspectives on Neoliberalism.** Lynne Phillips. LC 97-22853. (Jaguar Books on Latin America Ser.). 1997. write for info. (*0-8420-2606-1*); write for info. (*0-8420-2608-8*) Scholarly Res Inc.

Third Wave Processing: Database Machines & Decision Support Systems. William H. Inmon. 207p. 1993. pap. text ed. 59.95 (*0-471-56790-6*) Wiley.

Third Way. Paul M. Lederach. LC 80-18041. 160p. 1980. pap. 7.99 (*0-8361-1934-7*) Herald Pr.

Third Way. Jean Warmbold. LC 89-91097. 240p. 1990. 22.00 (*0-932966-92-6*) Permanent Pr.

Third Way: Marxist-Leninist Theory & Modern Industrial Society. Ota Sik. Tr. by Marian Sling. LC 76-8032. 431p. 1976. reprint ed. pap. 122.90 (*0-7837-9942-X*, 2060669) Bks Demand.

Third Way: New Directions in Platonic Studies. Ed. by Francisco J. Gonzalez. LC 95-30779. 272p. (C). 1995. pap. text ed. 21.95 (*0-8476-8114-9*); lib. bdg. 46.00 (*0-8476-8113-0*) Rowman.

Third Wedding. Costas Taktsis. Tr. by Leslie Finer. 1979. pap. 8.95 (*0-87376-048-4*) Red Dust.

Third Williams College Alumni Loan Exhibition: Two Hundred Years of American Art: June 12 - November 28, 1993, Williams College Museum of Art. Contrib. by Linda Shearer et al. LC 93-27081. 1993. write for info. (*0-913697-17-6*) Williams Art.

Third Woman: Minority Woman Writers of the United States. Dexter Fisher. LC 79-87863. (C). 1980. pap. 40.76 (*0-395-27707-8*) HM.

3rd Workshop, Actinides under Pressure. U. Benedict. 150p. 1990. text ed. 184.00 (*2-88124-778-4*) Gordon & Breach.

Third World. Ed. by Naton Leslie & Jim Villani. LC 88-60726. (Pig Iron Ser.: No. 15). (Illus.). 96p. (Orig.). 1988. pap. 8.95 (*0-917530-23-3*) Pig Iron Pr.

Third World. Peter Worsley. LC 74-124639. (Nature of Human Society Ser.). 390p. 1973. pap. text ed. 12.00 (*0-226-90753-8*) U Ch Pr.

Third World: Exploring U. S. Interests. John W. Sewell & John A. Mathieson. (Headline Ser.: No. 259). (Illus.). 64p. (gr. 11-12). 1982. pap. 5.95 (*0-87124-076-9*) Foreign Policy.

T

Third World: Opposing Viewpoints. rev. ed. (Opposing Viewpoints Ser.). (Illus.). 288p. 1995. pap. text ed. 12.96 (*1-56510-249-5*, 2495) Greenhaven.

Third World: Opposing Viewpoints. rev. ed. David Bender et al. (Opposing Viewpoints Ser.). (Illus.). 288p. 1995. lib. bdg. 20.96 (*1-56510-250-9*, 2509) Greenhaven.

Third World: Premises of U. S. Policy. 2nd rev. ed. Ed. by W. Scott Thompson et al. LC 83-8426. 319p. 1983. pap. text ed. 21.95 (*0-917616-57-X*) Transaction Pubs.

Third World: Problems, Conflicts & Solutions: Symposium at Grambling State University, 1991 (Proceedings) (Illus.). 50p. (Orig.). (C). 1993. pap. text ed. 20.00 (*0-7881-0183-8*) DIANE Pub.

Third World: States of Mind & Being. Ed. by Jim Norwine & Alfonso Gonzalez. (Illus.). 320p. 1988. text ed. 55.00 (*0-04-910106-4*) Routledge Chapman & Hall.

Third World: States of Mind & Being. Ed. by Jim Norwine & Alfonso Gonzalez. (Illus.). 320p. (C). 1988. pap. 22.95 (*0-04-910121-8*) Routledge Chapman & Hall.

Third World: States of Mind & Being. 2nd ed. Ed. by Alfonso Gonzalez & Jim Norwine. 320p. 1996. 69.00 (*0-8133-2250-2*) Westview.

Third World: States of Mind & Being. 2nd ed. Ed. by Alfonso Gonzalez & Jim Norwine. 320p. 1996. pap. 19.95 (*0-8133-2251-0*) Westview.

Third World Vol. 4: (Incl. 1993-1994 Supplement) Ed. by Eleanor C. Goldstein. (Resources Ser.). 1995. suppl. ed. 76.00 (*0-89777-185-0*) Sirs Inc.

Third World & Peace: Some Aspects of Problems of the Inter-Relationship of Interdevelopment & International Security. Marion Mushkat. LC 82-774. 356p. 1983. text ed. 32.50 (*0-312-80039-8*) St Martin.

***Third World & Prospectrs for Development in a Changing International Environment.** Ed. by Harold Isaacs. (Journal of Third World Studies: Vol. XI, No. 1). 666p. 1994. pap. 23.00 (*0-931971-19-5*) Assn Third Wld.

***Third World & Prospects for Development in a Changing International Environment.** Ed. by Harold Isaacs. (Journal of Third World Studies: Vol. XI, No. 1). (Orig.). pap. 23.00 (*0-614-30671-X*) Assn Third Wld.

Third World & South Africa: Post-Apartheid Challenges. Richard J. Payne. LC 92-8847. (Contributions in Political Science Ser.: No. 304). 224p. 1992. text ed. 47.95 (*0-313-28542-X*, PTW, Greenwood Pr) Greenwood.

Third World & the Rich Countries: Proposals to Combat the Global Economic Crisis. Angelos Angelopoulos & Melvin Fagen. 158p. (C). 1993. pap. text ed. 23.50 (*0-8191-9256-2*); lib. bdg. 48.00 (*0-8191-9240-6*) U Pr of Amer.

Third World & the Rich Countries: Prospects for the Year 2000. Angelos Angelopoulos. LC 72-75694. (Special Studies in International Economics & Development). 1972. text ed. 46.50 (*0-275-28608-8*) Irvington.

Third World at an Impasse. Paul Bairoch. LC 96-9061. 1995. pap. 52.00 (*0-13-434275-5*) P-H.

Third World at the Crossroads. Ed. by Sheikh R. Ali. LC 88-28834. 232p. 1989. text ed. 55.00 (*0-275-93057-2*, C3057, Praeger Pubs) Greenwood.

Third World Atlas. Ben Crow et al. 76p. 1984. 62.00 (*0-335-15015-2*, Open Univ Pr); pap. 29.00 (*0-335-10259-X*, Open Univ Pr) Taylor & Francis.

***Third World Atlas.** Alan Thomas et al. 80p. 1994. 40.00 (*0-335-19077-4*, Open Univ Pr) Taylor & Francis.

***Third World Atlas.** 2nd ed. Alan Thomas et al. 80p. 1994. pap. 12.99 (*0-335-19076-6*, Open Univ Pr) Taylor & Francis.

Third World Atlas. 2nd ed. Ed. by Alan Thomas & Ben Crow. LC 94-4713. 1994. 72.95 (*1-56032-322-1*); pap. 26.95 (*1-56032-323-X*) Hemisp Pub.

Third World Attitudes Toward International Law: An Introduction. Frederick Snyder & Sathirathai Surakiart. LC 86-5383. 1987. lib. bdg. 299.00 (*0-89838-914-3*) Kluwer Ac.

Third World Century. Charles S. Goodwin. 188p. (C). 1994. lib. bdg. 37.50 (*0-8191-9534-0*) U Pr of Amer.

Third World Cities: Problems, Policies, & Prospects. John D. Kasarda & Allan M. Parnell. (Focus Editions Ser.: Vol. 148). (Illus.). 320p. (C). 1992. 54.00 (*0-8039-4484-5*); pap. 24.95 (*0-8039-4485-3*) Sage.

Third World Cities in Global Perspective: The Political Economy of Uneven Urbanization. David Smith. (C). 1996. pap. text ed. 21.95 (*0-8133-2998-1*) Westview.

Third World City. David Drakakis-Smith. (Introductions to Development Ser.). 160p. 1987. pap. text ed. 9.95 (*0-416-91970-7*) Routledge Chapman & Hall.

***Third World City.** David Drakakis-Smith. (Routledge Introductions to Development Ser.). 116p. (C). 1987. pap. 13.95 (*0-415-05895-3*) Routledge.

Third World Colonias: Lower Rio Grande Valley, Texas. Robert K. Holz & Christopher S. Davies. (Working Paper Ser.: No. 72). 148p. 1993. pap. 5.50 (*0-89940-555-X*) LBJ Sch Pub Aff.

Third World Conference on Engineering: Innovation, Teaching & Management, Vol. 2. LC 92-81951. 586p. 1992. 181.00 (*1-56252-119-5*, 1916) Computational Mech MA.

Third World Conference on Engineering Education: Industrial Links, Vol. 3. LC 92-81951. 610p. 1992. 187.00 (*1-56252-120-9*, 1924) Computational Mech MA.

Third World Conference on Engineering Education: International Quality & Environmental Issues, Vol. 1. LC 92-81951. 590p. 1992. 181.00 (*1-56252-118-7*, 1908) Computational Mech MA.

Third World Conference on Engineering Education: Proceedings of the Third Major World Conference on Engineering Education Held at the Guildhall in Portsmith, England, September 20-24, 1992, 3 vols. Ed. by T. Duggan. LC 92-81591. 1992. Set. 492.00 (*1-56252-117-9*, 1894) Computational Mech MA.

Third-World Conflict & International Security. Ed. by Christoph Bertram. LC 81-19036. 121p. (C). 1982. 28.50 (*0-208-01957-X*, Archon Bks) Shoe String.

***Third World Congress on Biosensors Abstracts.** pap. 133.50 (*1-85617-242-2*) Elsevier.

Third World Conundrum: A Call to Christian Partnership. Max Peberdy. 188p. 1986. pap. 7.50 (*0-85364-463-2*, Pub. by Paternoster UK) Attic Pr.

Third World Cooperation: The Group of 77 in UNCTAD. Marc Williams. 250p. 1991. text ed. 69.95 (*0-312-05725-3*) St Martin.

Third World Coups D'Etat & International Security. Steven R. David. LC 86-45451. 192p. 1986. text ed. 32.50 (*0-8018-3307-8*) Johns Hopkins.

***Third World Crises.** Ed. by Harold Isaacs. (Journal of Third World Studies: Vol. XI, No. 2). (Orig.). pap. 23.00 (*0-614-30672-8*) Assn Third Wld.

***Third World Crises.** Ed. by Harold Isaacs. (Journal of Third World Studies: Vol. XI, No. 2). 758p. 1994. pap. 23.00 (*0-931971-20-9*) Assn Third Wld.

Third World Debt: How Sustainable Are Current Strategies & Solutions? Ed. by Helen O'Neill. 1990. text ed. 32.00 (*0-7146-3409-3*, Pub. by F Cass Pubs UK) Intl Spec Bk.

Third World Debt: The Next Phase. Ed. by Edward R. Fried & Philip H. Trezise. (Dialogues on Public Policy Ser.). 120p. (Orig.). 1989. pap. text ed. 10.95 (*0-8157-2977-4*) Brookings.

Third World Debt: The Search for a Solution. Ed. by Graham Bird. (Illus.). 256p. 1989. text ed. 80.00 (*1-85278-162-9*) E Elgar.

Third World Debt & Financial Innovation: The Experiences of Chile & Mexico. OECD Staff. 148p. (Orig.). 1991. pap. 31.00 (*92-64-13496-4*) OECD.

Third World Debt & International Public Policy. Seamus O'Cleireacain. LC 89-16019. 262p. 1990. text ed. 59.95 (*0-275-92520-X*, C2520, Praeger Pubs) Greenwood.

***Third World Development.** Ed. by Harold Isaacs. (Journal of Third World Studies: Vol. VI, No. 2). (Orig.). pap. 11.25 (*0-614-30662-0*) Assn Third Wld.

***Third World Development.** Ed. by Harold Isaacs. (Journal of Third World Studies: Vol. VI, No. 2). 367p. 1989. pap. 11.25 (*0-931971-10-1*) Assn Third Wld.

Third World Development: A Basic Needs Approach. Ed. by Pradip K. Ghosh. LC 83-26681. (International Development Resource Bks.: No. 13). (Illus.). xv, 436p. 1984. text ed. 89.50 (*0-313-24149-X*, GTW/, Greenwood Pr) Greenwood.

Third-World Development: Aspects of Political Legitimacy & Viability. Tri Q. Nguyen. LC 87-45959. (Illus.). 224p. 1989. 35.00 (*0-8386-3327-7*) Fairleigh Dickinson.

Third World Development Experience - Tanzania. S. Chandrasekhar. (C). 1990. 13.00 (*81-7035-092-1*, Pub. by Daya Pub Hse II) S Asia.

***Third World Diversity Change Independence.** 2nd ed. Barke. 1991. pap. text ed. write for info. (*0-05-004485-0*) Addison-Wesley.

Third World Economic Handbook. 198p. 1983. 80.00 (*0-903706-85-7*, Pub. by Euromonitor Pubns UK) Gale.

Third World Economic Handbook. Stuart W. Sinclair. 224p. 1985. 150.00 (*0-686-83129-2*, Pub. by Euromonitor Pubns UK) St Mut.

Third World Economic Handbook. 2nd ed. Stuart Sinclair. 1986. 80.00 (*0-86338-163-4*, Pub. by Euromonitor Pubns UK) Gale.

***Third World Education: Quality & Equality.** Anthony R. Welch. Ed. by Edward R. Beauchamp. (Reference Books in International Education). Date not set. text ed. 37.50 (*0-8153-1394-2*) Garland.

Third World Film Making & the West. Roy Armes. (Orig.). (C). 1987. pap. 21.00 (*0-520-05690-6*) U CA Pr.

Third World Guide Facts, Figures & Opinions, 89-90: The World As Seen by the Third World. Third World Editors & Robert R. Bissio. 625p. 1989. Spanish. pap. text ed. 59.95 (*950-99264-0-X*) Neal-Schuman.

Third World Handbook. Guy Arnold. LC 90-63741. (Illus.). 221p. 1991. 59.95 (*1-55862-149-0*) St James Pr.

Third World Handbook. 2nd ed. Guy Arnold. (Reference Ser.). (Illus.). 224p. 1994. pap. 21.95 (*0-304-32835-9*) Cassell.

Third World Handbook. 2nd ed. Guy Arnold. (Illus.). 400p. 1994. lib. bdg. 45.00 (*1-884964-12-5*) Fitzroy Dearborn.

Third World Housing in Social & Spatial Development: The Case of Jakarta Housing in Social & Spatial Development. Lars Marcussen. 205p. 1990. text ed. 68.95 (*1-85628-085-3*, Pub. by Avebury Pub UK) Ashgate Pub Co.

Third World Ideology & Western Reality: Manufacturing Political Myth. Carlos Rangel. 180p. 1986. pap. 24.95 (*0-88738-601-6*) Transaction Pubs.

Third World in Film & Video: 1984-1990. Helen W. Cyr. LC 90-25883. 256p. 1991. 29.50 (*0-8108-2380-2*) Scarecrow.

Third World in Global Environmental Politics. Marian A. Miller. LC 94-36484. 182p. 1995. pap. text ed. 17.95 (*1-55587-423-1*); lib. bdg. 40.00 (*1-55587-422-3*) Lynne Rienner.

***Third World in Global Environmental Politics.** Marian A. Miller. 224p. 1995. 42.50 (*0-335-19501-6*, Open Univ Pr); pap. 13.99 (*0-335-19500-8*, Open Univ Pr) Taylor & Francis.

Third World in the First: Development & Aboriginal Peoples of Remote Canada Australia. Elspeth Young. LC 94-11463. (Illus.). 336p. (C). 1995. pap. 22.95 (*0-415-11673-2*, B0212) Routledge.

Third World in the First: Development & Aboriginal Peoples of Remote Canada Australia. Elspeth Young. LC 94-11463. (Illus.). 336p. (C). (gr. 13). 1995. text ed. 79.95 (*0-415-05543-1*, B0208) Routledge.

***Third World in the Post-Cold War Era: Problems & Possible Solutions.** Ed. by Harold Isaacs. (Journal of Third World Studies: Vol. X, No. 1). (Orig.). pap. 18.25 (*0-614-30669-8*) Assn Third Wld.

***Third World in the Post-Cold War Era: Problems & Prospects.** Ed. by Harold Isaacs. (Journal of Third World Studies: Vol. X, No. 1). 636p. 1993. pap. 23.00 (*0-931971-17-9*) Assn Third Wld.

***Third World in the 1990s: Prospects & Problems.** Ed. by Harold Isaacs. (Journal of Third World Studies: Vol. IX, No. 1). (Orig.). pap. 16.25 (*0-614-30667-1*) Assn Third Wld.

***Third World in the 1990s: Prospects & Problems.** Ed. by Harold Isaacs. (Journal of Third World Studies: Vol. IX, No. 1). 392p. 1992. pap. 16.25 (*0-931971-15-2*) Assn Third Wld.

Third World in World Economy. Pierre Jalee. Tr. by Mary Klopper from FRE. LC 70-81791. 224p. 1971. pap. 10.00 (*0-85345-177-X*) Monthly Rev.

Third World Industrialisation in the 1980's: Open Economies in a Closing World. Ed. by Raphael Kaplinsky. 142p. 1984. 32.00 (*0-7146-3240-6*, Pub. by F Cass Pubs UK) Intl Spec Bk.

Third World Instability: The Case of Central America. Ed. by Andrew J. Pierre. 128p. (C). 1985. text ed. 24.00 (*0-8147-6594-7*) NYU Pr.

Third World Law Directory. Ed. by J. C. Forbes. (C). 1988. 295.00 (*0-685-61455-7*, Pub. by Royston Ltd) St Mut.

Third World Law Directory. Ed. by J. C. Forbes. 1988. 110.00 (*0-946706-27-1*, Pub. by Royston Ltd) St Mut.

Third World Liberation Theologies: A Reader. Ed. by Deane W. Ferm. LC 85-15302. 400p. (Orig.). reprint ed. pap. 114.00 (*0-7837-5505-8*, 2045275) Bks Demand.

Third World Liberation Theologies: An Introductory Survey. Deane W. Ferm. LC 85-15534. 160p. reprint ed. pap. 45.60 (*0-7837-6975-X*, 2046786) Bks Demand.

Third World Lives of Struggle. Ed. by Hazel Johnson & Henry Bernstein. 271p. (Orig.). (C). 1983. pap. text ed. 22.50 (*0-435-96130-6*, 96130) Heinemann.

Third World Mass Media & Their Search for Modernity: The Case of Commonwealth Caribbean, 1717-1976. John A. Lent. LC 75-39110. 405p. 1978. 45.00 (*0-8387-1896-5*) Bucknell U Pr.

Third World Militarization: A Challenge to Third World Diplomacy. Ed. by Jagat S. Mehta. LC 85-50860. (Tom Slick World Peace Ser.). 295p. 1985. pap. 8.00 (*0-89940-006-X*) LBJ Sch Pub Aff.

Third World Military Expenditure: A Political Economy Approach. Robert Mckinlay. 250p. 1992. 49.00 (*0-86187-721-7*) St Martin.

Third-World Military Expenditure & Arms Production. Robert E. Looney. LC 88-4465. 242p. 1988. text ed. 59.95 (*0-312-02034-1*) St Martin.

Third World Multinationals: The Rise of Foreign Investment from Developing Countries. Louis T. Wells, Jr. 272p. 1983. 27.50 (*0-262-23113-1*) MIT Pr.

***Third World Nationalism.** Ed. by Harold Isaacs. (Journal of Third World Studies: Vol. V, No. 2). (Orig.). pap. 11.25 (*0-614-30660-4*) Assn Third Wld.

***Third World Nationalism.** Ed. by Harold Isaacs. (Journal of Third World Studies: Vol. V, No. 2). 336p. 1988. pap. 11.25 (*0-931971-08-X*) Assn Third Wld.

Third World Novel of Expatriation: A Study of Emigre Fiction by Indian, West African & Caribbean Writers. Viney Kirpal. 208p. 1989. text ed. 25.00 (*81-207-0904-7*, Pub. by Sterling Pubs II) Apt Bks.

Third World of Theory. Gates. 96p. 1992. 15.95 (*0-226-28432-8*) U Ch Pr.

***Third World on the Eve of the 21st Century: Perspectives, Problems, & Prospects.** Ed. by Harold Isaacs. (Journal of Third World Studies: Vol. XII, No. 1). (Orig.). pap. 23.00 (*0-614-30673-6*) Assn Third Wld.

***Third World on the Eve of the 21st Century: Perspectives, Problems, & Prospects.** Ed. by Harold Isaacs. (Journal of Third World Studies: Vol. XII, No. 1). 538p. 1995. pap. 23.00 (*0-931971-21-7*) Assn Third Wld.

Third World Out! Tim Adams. Ed. by A. L. Hardy. LC 78-74429. 1978. pap. 14.00 (*0-686-23919-9*) Central FL Voters.

Third World Peasantry: A Continuing Saga of Deprivation, 2 vols. R. P. Misra. 1986. text ed. 75.00 (*81-207-0158-5*, Pub. by Sterling Pubs II) Apt Bks.

Third World Policies of Industrialized Nations. Ed. by Phillip Taylor & Gregory A. Raymond. LC 81-13308. (Contributions in Political Science Ser.: No. 76). (Illus.). xix, 282p. 1982. text ed. 59.95 (*0-313-22730-6*, TTW/, Greenwood Pr) Greenwood.

***Third World Political Ecology: An Introduction.** Raymond L. Bryant & Sinead Bailey. LC 96-43170. 224p. (C). 1997. pap. write for info. (*0-415-12744-0*); text ed. write for info. (*0-415-12743-2*) Routledge.

***Third World Political, Economic, & Intellectual Developments.** Ed. by Harold Isaacs. (Journal of Third World Studies: Vol. XIII, No. 2). (Orig.). pap. 23.00 (*0-614-30676-0*) Assn Third Wld.

***Third World Political, Economic, & Intellectual Developments.** Ed. by Harold Isaacs. (Journal of Third World Studies: Vol. XIII, No. 2). 407p. 1997. pap. 23.00 (*0-931971-24-1*) Assn Third Wld.

***Third World Political Systems.** Ed. by Harold Isaacs. (Journal of Third World Studies: Vol. IV, No. 1). (Orig.). pap. 7.00 (*0-614-30657-4*) Assn Third Wld.

***Third World Political Systems.** Ed. by Harold Isaacs. (Journal of Third World Studies: Vol. IV, No. 1). 228p. 1987. pap. 7.00 (*0-931971-05-5*) Assn Third Wld.

Third World Politics: A Comparative Introduction. 2nd ed. Paul A. Cammack et al. LC 93-13687. 320p. (C). 1993. text ed. 48.00 (*0-8018-4750-8*); pap. text ed. 17.95 (*0-8018-4751-6*) Johns Hopkins.

Third World Politics: A Concise Introduction. Jeff Haynes. LC 96-6453. 220p. (C). 1996. 54.95 (*0-631-19777-X*); pap. 18.95 (*0-631-19778-8*) Blackwell Pubs.

Third World Politics: An Introduction. Christopher Clapham. 256p. 1985. pap. text ed. 13.50 (*0-299-10334-X*) U of Wis Pr.

Third World Politics: China & the Afro-Asian People's Solidarity Organization, 1957-1967. Charles Neuhauser. LC 76-2492. (East Asian Monographs: No. 27). 107p. 1968. pap. 11.00 (*0-674-88455-8*) HUP.

***Third World Politics at the Crossroads.** Mark Kesselman et al. 471p. (C). 1996. pap. text ed. 33.16 (*0-669-33201-1*) HM College Div.

***Third World Problems.** Ed. by Harold Isaacs. (Journal of Third World Studies: Vol. II, No. 2). 95p. 1985. pap. 7.00 (*0-931971-02-0*) Assn Third Wld.

***Third World Problems & Issues.** Ed. by Harold Isaacs. (Journal of Third World Studies: Vol. X, No. 2). (Orig.). pap. 23.00 (*0-614-30670-1*) Assn Third Wld.

***Third World Problems & Issues.** Ed. by Harold Isaacs. (Journal of Third World Studies: Vol. X, No. 2). 608p. 1993. pap. 23.00 (*0-931971-18-7*) Assn Third Wld.

***Third World Problems, Issues, & Developments.** Ed. by Harold Isaacs. (Journal of Third World Studies: Vol. VI, No. 1). (Orig.). pap. 11.25 (*0-614-30661-2*) Assn Third Wld.

***Third World Problems, Issues, & Developments.** Harold Isaacs. (Journal of Third World Studies: Vol. VI, No. 1). 381p. 1989. pap. 11.25 (*0-931971-09-8*) Assn Third Wld.

***Third World Professionals & Development Education in Europe: Personal Narratives, Global Conversations.** Shanti George. LC 97-14486. 1997. write for info. (*0-8039-9387-0*) Sage.

Third World Proletariat? Peter C. Lloyd. (Controversies in Sociology Ser.: No. 11). 144p. 1982. pap. text ed. 11.95 (*0-04-301141-1*) Routledge Chapman & Hall.

Third World Radical Regimes: U. S. Policy under Carter & Reagan. Anthony Lake. LC 85-81057. (Headline Ser.: No. 272). (Illus.). 56p. (Orig.). 1985. pap. 5.95 (*0-87124-099-8*) Foreign Policy.

***Third World Religious & Cultural Influences.** Ed. by Harold Isaacs. (Journal of Third World Studies: Vol. VIII, No. 2). (Orig.). pap. 16.25 (*0-614-30666-3*) Assn Third Wld.

***Third World Religious & Cultural Influences.** Ed. by Harold Isaacs. (Journal of Third World Studies: Vol. VIII, No. 2). 375p. 1991. pap. 16.25 (*0-931971-14-4*) Assn Third Wld.

Third World Resource Directory. Ed. by Thomas P. Fenton & Mary J. Heffron. LC 83-6783. 306p. 1984. reprint ed. pap. 87.30 (*0-8357-2674-6*, 2040210) Bks Demand.

Third World Resource Directory: 1994-1995. Thomas P. Fenton & Mary J. Heffron. LC 94-1601. 800p. (Orig.). 1994. pap. 62.00 (*0-88344-941-2*) Orbis Bks.

***Third World Revolutions.** Ed. by Harold Isaacs. (Journal of Third World Studies: Vol. III, No. 2). (Orig.). pap. 7.00 (*0-614-30656-6*) Assn Third Wld.

***Third World Revolutions.** Ed. by Harold Isaacs. (Journal of Third World Studies: Vol. III, No. 2). 171p. 1986. pap. 7.00 (*0-931971-04-7*) Assn Third Wld.

Third World-Second Sex, Vol. 1: Women's Struggles & National Liberation. Ed. by Miranda E. Davies. (Illus.). (C). 1983. pap. 17.50 (*0-86232-029-1*, Pub. by Zed Bks Ltd UK); text ed. 49.95 (*0-86232-017-8*, Pub. by Zed Bks Ltd UK) Humanities.

Third World Security in the Post-Cold War Era. Ed. by Thomas G. Weiss & Meryl A. Kessler. LC 91-3672. (Emerging Global Issues Ser.). 185p. 1991. lib. bdg. 35.00 (*1-55587-264-6*) Lynne Rienner.

Third World Security Predicament: State Making, Regional Conflict, & the International System. Mohammed Ayoob. LC 94-27603. (Emerging Global Issues Ser.). 1995. pap. text ed. 18.95 (*1-55587-576-9*); lib. bdg. 43.00 (*1-55587-552-1*) Lynne Rienner.

Third World Strategy: Economic & Political Cohesion in the South. Ed. by Altaf Gauhar. 238p. 1983. 38.50 (*0-275-90985-9*, C0985, Praeger Pubs) Greenwood.

***Third World-Superpower Relations.** Ed. by Harold Isaacs. (Journal of Third World Studies: Vol. VII, No. 2). (Orig.). pap. 11.25 (*0-614-30664-7*) Assn Third Wld.

Third World Tour of Kirpal Singh. Ed. by Russell Perkins. (Illus.). 1974. pap. 2.50 (*0-89142-008-8*) Sant Bani Ash.

Third World Tropical Diet Health Maintenance & Medical Management Program. Alcena. 112p. 1992. pap. 8.25 (*0-8403-8223-5*) Kendall-Hunt.

Third World Urbanization. Ed. by Janet L. Abu-Lughod & Richard Hay, Jr. 1980. pap. 12.95 (*0-416-60141-3*, NO. 2866) Routledge Chapman & Hall.

Third World Voices for Children. Ed. by Robert E. McDowell & Edward Lavitt. LC 71-169091. (Odarkai Book Ser.). (Illus.). 156p. (J). (gr. 5-9). 1981. 7.95 (*0-89388-020-5*, Odakai) Okpaku Communications.

Third World, Vol. 3: (Incl. 1988-1992 Supplements) Ed. by Eleanor C. Goldstein. (Social Issues Resource Ser.). 1993. 95.00 (*0-89777-095-1*) Sirs Inc.

Third World Without Superpowers: The Collected Documents of the Group of 77, 21 vols. including index, Set. Karl P. Sauvant. LC 80-29266. 1981. lib. bdg. 1,260.00 (*0-379-00969-2*) Oceana.

Third World Without Superpowers: The Collected Documents of the Non-Aligned Countries, 13 vols. including index. Ed. by Karl P. Sauvant & Odette Jankowitsch. 1978. Vols. 1-9. lib. bdg. 692.50 (*0-379-00965-X*) Oceana.

Third World Women & the Politics of Feminism. Ed. by Chandra T. Mohanty et al. LC 90-43510. (Illus.). 352p. 1991. 39.95 (*0-253-33873-5*); pap. 15.95 (*0-253-20632-4*, MB-632) Ind U Pr.

An Asterisk (*) at the beginning of an entry indicates that the title is appearing in BIP for the first time.

Third World Women's Literatures: A Dictionary & Guide to Materials in English. Barbara Fister. LC 95-7479. 408p. 1995. text ed. 75.00 (*0-313-28988-3*, Greenwood Pr) Greenwood.

Third World Worker in the Multinational Corporation: A Bibliography. Ed. by Joan Nordquist. (Contemporary Social Issues: A Bibliographic Ser.: No. 30). 64p. (Orig.). 1993. pap. 15.00 (*0-937855-58-8*) Ref Rsch Serv.

Third Worlds. Deagan. 288p. (C). 1996. pap. 19.95 (*0-415-12219-8*); text ed. 65.00 (*0-415-12218-X*) Routledge.

***Third-Year Follow-Up of the Section 130 Tribally Operated Vocational Rehabilitation Projects.** G. L. Lonetree. 55p. 1992. pap. text ed. write for info. (*1-888557-18-4*, 100099) No Ariz Univ.

Third Year Latin. Robert J. Henle. (Henle Latin Ser.). 480p. (ENG & LAT.). 1958. 12.95 (*0-8299-0115-9*, HLAT3) Loyola Pr.

Third Year Latin. 5th ed. Charles Jenny. 1989. 25.00 (*0-13-918814-2*) P-H.

Thirds. Charles Rossiter et al. LC 85-70935. (Illus.). 64p. (Orig.). 1985. pap. 3.95 (*0-9614525-0-1*) Distant Pr.

Thirdspace: Expanding the Geographical Imagination. Edward W. Soja. LC 95-26474. (Illus.). 320p. (C). 1996. text ed. 69.95 (*1-55786-674-0*); pap. text ed. 22.95 (*1-55786-675-9*) Blackwell Pubs.

Photovoltaics Program Review: Proceedings, NREL Photovoltaics Program Review, 13th, Lakewood, CO, 1995. Ed. by Harin S. Ullal & C. Edwin Witt. LC 95-80662. (AIP Conference Proceedings Ser.: Vol. 353). (Illus.). 652p. 1995. 165.00 (*1-56396-510-0*, TK2960) Am Inst Physics.

Thirst. Stephen Amidon. LC 92-36963. 1993. 18.95 (*0-88001-296-X*) Ecco Pr.

Thirst. Mike Cecilione. 480p. 1999. mass mkt. 5.99 (*0-8217-5143-3*, Zebra Kensgtn) Kensgtn Pub Corp.

Thirst. Pyotyr Kurtinski. 352p. (Orig.). 1995. mass mkt., pap. text ed. 4.99 (*0-8439-3826-9*) Dorchester Pub Co.

***Thirst.** Ed. by D. J. Ramsay & D. A. Booth. (Illus.). 509p. 1991. 75.00 (*3-540-19641-2*, 196412) Spr-Verlag.

Thirst: The Desert Trilogy. Shulamith Hareven. Tr. by Hillel Halkin from HEB. LC 96-5152. 186p. (Orig.). 1996. pap. 16.95 (*1-56279-088-9*) Mercury Hse Inc.

Thirst for Growth: Water Agencies As Hidden Government in California. Robert Gottlieb & Margaret FitzSimmons. LC 90-20184. (Illus.). 286p. 1991. 45.00 (*0-8165-1134-9*) U of Ariz Pr.

Thirst for Growth: Water Agencies As Hidden Government in California. Robert Gottlieb & Margaret FitzSimmons. LC 90-20184. 286p. 1994. reprint ed. pap. 20.95 (*0-8165-1418-6*) U of Ariz Pr.

Thirst for Love: My True Life Story. D. Pal Jain. 160p. 1995. 14.95 (*0-9635307-4-7*) First Prsn Pr.

Thirst for Wholeness. Jay E. Adams. 136p. Date not set. pap. 8.95 (*0-9643556-9-8*) Timeless Texts.

Thirst for Wholeness: Attachment, Addiction, & the Spiritual Path. Christina Grof. LC 92-54616. 304p. 1994. reprint ed. pap. 13.00 (*0-06-250315-4*) Harper SF.

Thirst Like This: Poems. John Repp. 64p. 1990. 18.95 (*0-8262-0762-6*); pap. 10.95 (*0-8262-0765-0*) U of Mo Pr.

Thirst of Annihilation: George Bataille & Virulent Nihilism. Nick Land. LC 91-36365. 248p. (C). 1992. pap. text ed. 29.95 (*0-415-05608-X*, Routledge NY) Routledge.

Thirst of the Salt Mountain: A Trilogy of Plays. Marin Sorescu. Tr. by Andrea Deletant & Brenda Walker. LC 85-70248. 112p. 9000. reprint ed. pap. 16.95 (*0-9509487-5-6*, Pub. by Forest Bks UK) Dufour.

Thirst of the Vampire. T. Lucien Wright. 352p. 1992. mass mkt. 4.50 (*1-55817-649-7*, Pinncle Kensgtn) Kensgtn Pub Corp.

Thirsting for Peace in a Raging Century: Selected Poems, 1961-1985. Edward Sanders. LC 87-10237. (Selected Works). 248p. (Orig.). 1987. 19.95 (*0-918273-25-0*); pap. 9.95 (*0-918273-24-2*) Coffee Hse.

Thirsty. M. T. Anderson. LC 96-30744. (YA). (gr. 9-12). 1997. 17.99 (*0-7636-0048-2*) Candlewick Pr.

Thirsty Day & Permanent Wave. Kathleen Aguero & Miriam Goodman. LC 76-55615. 88p. 1977. pap. 3.95 (*0-914086-17-0*) Alicejamesbooks.

Thirsty Evil. Gore Vidal. LC 72-140345. (Short Story Index Reprint Ser.). 1977. 13.95 (*0-8369-3737-6*) Ayer.

Thirsty Evil: Seven Short Stories. deluxe limited ed. Gore Vidal. 128p. 1981. reprint ed. Signed, Specially Bound. 50.00 (*0-917342-97-6*) Gay Sunshine.

Thirsty Evil: Seven Short Stories. Gore Vidal. 128p. 1981. reprint ed. pap. 7.95 (*0-917342-84-4*); reprint ed. lib. bdg. 20.00 (*0-917342-83-6*) Gay Sunshine.

Thirsty for God: A Brief History of Christian Spirituality. Bradley P. Holt. LC 93-17863. 160p. 1993. pap. 10.99 (*0-8066-2640-2*, 9-2640, Augsburg) Augsburg Fortress.

Thirsty Land: The Story of the Central Valley Project. Robert W. De Roos. LC 48-10963. 120p. reprint ed. pap. 30.00 (*0-317-27233-0*, 2025083) Bks Demand.

Thirsty Seagull Bar & Grille. Jill C. Brady. 136p. 1995. pap. 9.95 (*0-8059-3618-1*) Dorrance.

Thirsty Sword: Sirat Antar & the Arabic Popular Epic. Peter Heath. 400p. 1996. 50.00 (*0-87480-515-5*) U of Utah Pr.

Thirteen. (J). Date not set. pap. 2.75 (*0-590-43459-4*) Scholastic Inc.

Thirteen. Remy Charlip. (J). 1994. pap. text ed. 4.95 (*0-689-71860-8*, Aladdin Paperbacks) S&S Childrens.

Thirteen. Ursule Molinaro. LC 89-31186. 128p. 1989. 16.00 (*0-929701-02-X*); pap. 9.00 (*0-929701-01-1*) McPherson & Co.

Thirteen. Ed. by Tonya Pines. 352p. (YA). (gr. 7-9). 1991. pap. 4.99 (*0-590-45256-8*, Point) Scholastic Inc.

Thirteen. Candice F. Ransom. 192p. (Orig.). (J). (gr. 4-6). 1990. pap. 2.95 (*0-590-43742-9*) Scholastic Inc.

Thirteen: A Journey into the Number. Jonathan Cott. LC 96-16062. 192p. 1996. 15.95 (*0-385-41798-5*) Doubleday.

Thirteen: The Apollo Flight That Failed. Henry S. Cooper, Jr. 208p. 1995. pap. 13.00 (*0-8018-5097-5*) Johns Hopkins.

Thirteen - A Romantic Novel of the Sea. Leroy F. Oates. LC 95-91040. 1996. 16.95 (*0-533-11830-1*) Vantage.

13 Alabama Ghosts & Jeffrey. Kathryn T. Windham & Margaret G. Figh. LC 71-94443. (Illus.). 120p. (YA). (gr. 6 up). 1987. reprint ed. pap. 13.00 (*0-8173-0376-6*) U of Ala Pr.

Thirteen Ballroom Dances. Dance Educators of America. (Ballroom Dance Ser.). 1986. lib. bdg. 79.95 (*0-8490-3313-6*) Gordon Pr.

Thirteen Ballroom Dances. Dance Educators of America Staff. (Ballroom Dance Ser.). 1985. lib. bdg. 74.00 (*0-87700-846-9*) Revisionist Pr.

Thirteen Bells of Boglewood. Max Bush. (Orig.). (J). (gr. k-3). 1987. pap. 5.00 (*0-87602-272-7*) Anchorage.

Thirteen Blessings of the Twelve Steps: As Lived by Dee Frances. Dee Frances. 193p. (Orig.). 1994. pap. 10.95 (*0-9635341-9-X*) DDDD Pubns.

Thirteen-Book "Prelude", 2 vol. set. William Wordsworth. Ed. by Mark L. Reed. LC 89-99997. (Cornell Wordsworth Ser.). (Illus.). 2384p. 1992. 300.00 (*0-8014-2184-5*) Cornell U Pr.

Thirteen by Shanley: The Collected Plays, Vol. I. John P. Shanley. (Contemporary Masters Ser.). 384p. 1992. 27.95 (*1-55783-129-7*); pap. 14.95 (*1-55783-099-1*) Applause Theatre Bk Pubs.

Thirteen C-NMR of Natural Products, Vol. 1: Monoterpenes & Sesquiterpenes. Ed. by A. Ur-Rahman & V. U. Ahmad. (Illus.). 830p. 1992. 135.00 (*0-306-43897-6*, Plenum Pr) Plenum.

Thirteen C-NMR of Natural Products, Vol. 2: Diterpenes. Ed. by A. Ur-Rahman & V. U. Ahmad. (Illus.). 676p. 1992. 125.00 (*0-306-43898-4*, Plenum Pr) Plenum.

Thirteen C-NMR Spectroscopy: A Working Manual with Exercises. Eberhard Breitmaier & Gerhard Bauer. Tr. by Bruce K. Cassels from GER. (MMI Press Polymer Monographs). 431p. pap. text ed. 79.00 (*3-7186-0473-6*) Gordon & Breach.

Thirteen Clocks. James Thurber. 128p. (J). (gr. 4-7). 1992. pap. 3.50 (*0-440-40582-3*, YB BDD) BDD Bks Young Read.

***13 Clocks.** James Thurber. lib. bdg. 17.95 (*0-8488-2116-5*) Amereon Ltd.

Thirteen Clocks. James Thurber. (Illus.). 124p. 1992. reprint ed. lib. bdg. 19.95 (*0-89968-314-2*, Lghtyr Pr) Buccaneer Bks.

***Thirteen Coins & a Ring.** Salcedo. 1996. 28.95 (*0-8050-4466-3*) St Martin.

***Thirteen Coins & a Ring.** Salcedo. 1996. pap. 16.95 (*0-8050-4467-1*) St Martin.

Thirteen Colonies. Dennis B. Fradin. LC 88-11827. (New True Bks.). (Illus.). 48p. (J). (gr. k-4). 1988. pap. 5.50 (*0-516-41157-8*); lib. bdg. 19.00 (*0-516-01157-X*) Childrens.

Thirteen Colonies. Harry Knill. (J). (gr. 1-9). 1992. pap. 3.95 (*0-88388-103-9*) Bellerophon Bks.

Thirteen Colonies: A History Picture Book. Betsy Warren & Martha Ingerson. (Illus.). 32p. (Orig.). (J). (gr. 3 up). 1992. reprint ed. pap. 3.50 (*0-9618660-3-9*) Ranch Gate Bks.

***Thirteen Coptic Acrostic Hymns: From MS 5574 of the Pierpont Morgan Library.** Ed. by K. H. Kuhn & H. J. Tait. 176p. 1996. 60.00 (*0-900416-66-1*, Pub. by Aris & Phillips UK) David Brown.

13 Days. Robert F. Kennedy. Date not set. pap. 8.95 (*0-452-27391-9*, Plume) NAL-Dutton.

Thirteen Days. large type ed. L. D. Tetlow. (Linford Western Library). 272p. 1995. pap. 15.99 (*0-7089-7706-5*, Linford) Ulverscroft.

Thirteen Days: A Memoir of the Cuban Missile Crisis. Robert F. Kennedy. 192p. 1969. pap. 4.99 (*0-451-62794-6*, Ment) NAL-Dutton.

Thirteen Days: A Memoir of the Cuban Missile Crisis. Robert F. Kennedy. Ed. by Richard Neustadt & Graham T. Allison. (C). 1971. pap. text ed. 6.95 (*0-393-09896-6*) Norton.

Thirteen Days - Ninety Miles: The Cuban Missile Crisis. Norman H. Finkelstein. LC 93-29425. (J). 1994. lib. bdg. 14.95 (*0-671-86622-2*, Julian Messner) Silver Burdett Pr.

***Thirteen Days of Terror: The Rufus Buck Gang in Indian Territory.** Glenn Shirley. LC 96-32089. (Illus.). 109p. 1996. 22.95 (*0-935269-22-3*, Barbed Wire Pr) Western Pubns.

13 Days to Glory: The Siege of the Alamo. Lon Tinkle. LC 85-40043. (Southwest Landmark Ser.: Vol. 2). (Illus.). 256p. (C). 1996. reprint ed. 22.95 (*0-89096-238-3*); reprint ed. pap. 12.95 (*0-89096-707-5*) Tex A&M Univ Pr.

Thirteen Desperate Days. John M. Potter. 1964. 12.95 (*0-8392-1114-7*) Astor-Honor.

***Thirteen Detectives.** Gilbert K. Chesterton. Date not set. lib. bdg. 23.95 (*0-8488-1658-7*) Amereon Ltd.

Thirteen Essays on Photography. Canadian Museum of Contemporary Photography Staff. (Illus.). 258p. 1992. pap. 39.95 (*0-88884-557-X*) U Ch Pr.

13 Fatal Errors Managers Make: And How You Can Avoid Them. W. Steven Brown. 224p. 1987. mass mkt. 5.99 (*0-425-09644-0*) Berkley Pub.

13 Fatal Errors Managers Make: And How You Can Avoid Them. W. Steven Brown. LC 85-8245. 192p. 1919. audio 9.95 (*0-88749-056-5*) Revell.

13 Fatal Errors Managers Make: And How You Can Avoid Them. W. Steven Brown. LC 85-8245. 160p. (gr. 13). 1989. 15.99 (*0-8007-1423-7*) Revell.

Thirteen Folksongs: Voice/Piano. P. Grainger. 88p. 1991. otabind 12.95 (*0-7935-1197-6*, 50488975) H Leonard.

Thirteen for Corwin: Estimates of Radio's Foremost Writer-Director-Producer. Ray Bradbury et al. LC 92-38802. 112p. 1992. pap. 7.95 (*0-942637-89-5*) Barricade Bks.

Thirteen for Luck. Date not set. pap. 1.95 (*0-590-05211-X*) Scholastic Inc.

1341 Royal Inquest in Lincolnshire. Ed. by Bernard W. McLane. (Lincoln Record Society Ser.: No. 78). 224p. 1989. 39.00 (*0-901503-51-7*) Boydell & Brewer.

13 Georgia Ghosts & Jeffrey. Kathryn T. Windham. LC 73-87004. (Illus.). 160p. (YA). (gr. 6 up). 1987. reprint ed. pap. 13.00 (*0-8173-0377-4*) U of Ala Pr.

Thirteen Going on Seven. Marilyn Sachs. LC 92-44427. 112p. (J). (gr. 5-9). 1993. pap. 14.99 (*0-525-45096-3*) Dutton Child Bks.

Thirteen Going on Seven. Marilyn Sachs. 144p. (J). (gr. 3-7). 1995. pap. 3.99 (*0-14-037436-1*) Puffin Bks.

Thirteen Gun Salute. Patrick O'Brian. 1991. 22.50 (*0-393-02974-3*) Norton.

Thirteen Gun Salute. Patrick O'Brian. 336p. 1992. pap. 12.95 (*0-393-30907-X*) Norton.

Thirteen Hours of Halloween. Dian C. Regan. LC 92-41207. (Illus.). (J). 1993. lib. bdg. 14.95 (*0-8075-7876-2*) A Whitman.

Thirteen-Hundred Sixty-Nine. H. Lee Bell. Ed. by Stephen Bilheimer. LC 92-81201. 350p. (Orig.). 1992. 29.69 (*0-9632869-1-9*); pap. 16.69 (*0-9632869-0-0*) Halo Pr AR.

Thirteen Is a Good Age to Think about God. Eli Siegel. 15p. 1967. pap. 2.50 (*0-911492-09-7*) Aesthetic Realism.

***13 Is My Lucky Number.** Mary Scrima. Ed. by Ann Kinsey. 138p. (Orig.). 1996. pap. 4.95 (*1-57502-335-0*, PO1117) Morris Pubng.

Thirteen Is My Lucky Number: The Dramatic True Story of a Polish Resistance Fighter. B. C. Biega. (Illus.). 328p. 1996. 21.95 (*1-57087-204-X*) Prof Pr NC.

Thirteen Kalmyk-Oirat Tales from the Bewitched Corpse Cycle. Compiled by John R. Krueger. (Mongolia Society Special Papers: No. 7). 1978. spiral bd. 10.00 (*0-910980-27-6*) Mongolia.

Thirteen Keys: Thirteen Keys to the Thirteen Horned Beast of Revelation Thirteen. Thomas B. Windham. (Illus.). 50p. 1988. pap. 6.00 (*0-317-90597-X*) Lamp Trimmers.

Thirteen Keys to the Presidency. Allan J. Lichtman & Ken DeCell. 464p. 1992. pap. 14.95 (*0-8191-8751-8*) Madison Bks UPA.

Thirteen Keys to Winning the Presidency: A Radically New System for Determining the Winners & Losers of American Presidential Elections. Allan J. Lichtman & Ken DeCell. 456p. 1990. pap. 24.95 (*0-8191-7008-9*) Madison Bks UPA.

Thirteen Lectures on Fermant's Last Theorem. Paulo Ribenboim. 1995. 59.95 (*0-387-90432-8*) Spr-Verlag.

Thirteen Lessons in Christian Doctrine. 16th ed. Denver Sizemore. 172p. 1992. 8.99 (*0-89900-136-X*) College Pr Pub.

Thirteen Lessons on Galatians. Kenneth L. Boles. (Bible Student Study Guides Ser.). 84p. (C). 1978. pap. 4.99 (*0-89900-158-0*) College Pr Pub.

Thirteen Lessons on Grace. Jack Cottrell. 104p. 1988. reprint ed. teacher ed. 4.99 (*0-89900-316-8*); reprint ed. pap. 8.99 (*0-89900-312-5*) College Pr Pub.

Thirteen Lessons on James & Jude. Donald Fream. (Bible Student Study Guides Ser.). 104p. (C). 1979. pap. 4.99 (*0-89900-161-0*) College Pr Pub.

Thirteen Lessons on Missions. Richard Hostefter. LC 88-70220. 112p. 1988. pap. 5.99 (*0-89900-223-4*) College Pr Pub.

Thirteen Lessons on Missions. Richard Hostefter. 1991. teacher ed. 2.99 (*0-89900-248-X*) College Pr Pub.

Thirteen Lessons on Restoration History. Morris M. Womack. LC 88-71154. 156p. (Orig.). 1988. teacher ed. 2.99 (*0-89900-317-6*); pap. 5.99 (*0-89900-303-6*) College Pr Pub.

Thirteen Lessons on Romans, Vol. I. Sherwood Smith. LC 79-55509. (Bible Student Study Guides Ser.). 114p. (C). 1980. pap. 4.95 (*0-89900-164-5*) College Pr Pub.

Thirteen Lessons on Romans, Vol. II. Sherwood Smith. LC 81-65030. (Bible Student Study Guides Ser.). 114p. (C). 1981. pap. 4.99 (*0-89900-170-X*) College Pr Pub.

Thirteen Lessons on Timothy & Titus. John Pommert. (Bible Student Study Guides Ser.). 92p. (C). 1978. 4.99 (*0-89900-162-9*) College Pr Pub.

Thirteen Lessons on...Second Corinthians. Wallace Wartick. (Bible Student Study Guides Ser.). 96p. (C). 1977. pap. 4.99 (*0-89900-155-6*) College Pr Pub.

***13 Los Angeles Poets.** Ed. by Jack Grapes. LC 95-83261. (Onthebus Poets Ser.: No. 1). 160p. 1997. per. 13.95 (*0-941017-47-8*) Bombshelter Pr.

Thirteen Masterpieces of Mexican Archaeology. Antonio Caso. 1976. lib. bdg. 59.95 (*0-8490-1194-9*) Gordon Pr.

Thirteen Mathematics SAT Sample Tests. rev. ed. Max Tuchman. 87p. 1988. reprint ed. pap. text ed. 10.00 (*0-9626715-0-9*) Tuchman Tutoring.

Thirteen Men. William A. Fraser. LC 72-4423. (Short Story Index Reprint Ser.). 1977. reprint ed. 23.95 (*0-8369-4176-4*) Ayer.

Thirteen Miles From Suncrest: A Novel. Donald Davis. LC 94-12998. 1994. 22.95 (*0-87483-379-5*) August Hse.

Thirteen Miles from Suncrest: A Novel. Donald Davis. 1996. pap. text ed. 14.95 (*0-87483-455-4*) August Hse.

13 Mississippi Ghosts & Jeffrey. Kathryn T. Windham. LC 74-15509. (Illus.). 152p. (YA). (gr. 6 up). 1988. reprint ed. pap. 13.00 (*0-8173-0379-0*) U of Ala Pr.

***13 Monsters Who Should Be Avoided.** Kevin Shortsleeve. LC 97-11838. (Illus.). (J). 1998. write for info. (*1-56145-146-0*) Peachtree Pubs.

Thirteen Months Coinage of Hieronymos of Syracuse. R. Ross Holloway. (Illus.). (C). 1969. 35.40 (*3-11-002537-X*) De Gruyter.

Thirteen Months of Pregnancy: A Guide for the Pregnant Father. Bill M. Atalla & Stephen Beitler. LC 92-60038. (Illus.). 128p. 1992. 19.95 (*0-9631754-5-9*) Oddly Enough.

Thirteen Moons. Robert M. Chute. 72p. 1982. 12.95 (*0-920806-29-5*, Pub. by Penumbra Pr CN); pap. 7.95 (*0-920806-23-6*, Pub. by Penumbra Pr CN) U of Toronto Pr.

***Thirteen Moons on Turtle's Back: A Native American Year of Moons.** Joseph Bruchac & Jonathan London. LC 91-3961. (Illus.). 32p. (Orig.). (J). (ps up). 1997. pap. 5.95 (*0-698-11584-8*, Paperstar) Putnam Pub Group.

Thirteen Moons on Turtle's Back: A Native American Year of Moons. Ed. by Jonathan London. (Illus.). 32p. (J). (ps-8). 1992. lib. bdg. 15.95 (*0-399-22141-7*, Philomel Bks) Putnam Pub Group.

Thirteen Mystical Treasures: The Tools of Welsh Witchcraft. Rhuddlwm Gawr. LC 85-73756. (Illus.). 176p. (Orig.). 1989. reprint ed. 14.95 (*0-931760-42-9*, CP 10120); reprint ed. pap. 10.95 (*0-931760-20-8*) Camelot GA.

Thirteen New Mormon Temples: Counted Cross-Stitch Patterns of Temples of the Church of Jesus Christ of Latter-Day Saints. Jean D. Crowther & Bill Crowther. 1992. 7.98 (*0-88290-429-9*, 2809) Horizon Utah.

Thirteen NMR Spectroscopy, Vol. 3. E. Breitmeier et al. (MMI Press Polymer Monographs). 356p. 1984. text ed. 321.00 (*3-7186-0022-6*) Gordon & Breach.

Thirteen O'Clock. Stephen Vincent Benet. 1993. reprint ed. lib. bdg. 18.95 (*0-89968-390-8*, Lghtyr Pr) Buccaneer Bks.

Thirteen O'Clock, Stories of Several Worlds. Stephen Vincent Benet. LC 78-152935. (Short Story Index Reprint Ser.). 1977. reprint ed. 26.95 (*0-8369-3793-7*) Ayer.

Thirteen Original Clan Mothers: Your Sacred Path to Discovering the Gifts, Talents, & Abilities of the Feminine Through the Ancient Teachings of the Sisterhood. Jamie Sams. LC 92-53910. 320p. 1994. reprint ed. pap. 16.00 (*0-06-250756-7*) Harper SF.

Thirteen Papers in Algebra. L. Dmitirev et al. LC 86-17254. (Translations Ser.: Series 2, Vol. 132). 104p. 1986. 51.00 (*0-8218-3107-0*, TRANS2/132) Am Math.

Thirteen Papers in Algebra & Number Theory. Zhuk et al. LC 83-30651. (AMS Translations Ser.: Series 2, Vol. 128). 122p. 1986. 62.00 (*0-8218-3097-X*, TRANS2/128) Am Math.

Thirteen Papers in Algebra, Functional Analysis, Topology, & Probability. (Translations Ser.: Series 2, Vol. 149). 220p. 1991. 119.00 (*0-8218-3137-2*, TRANS2/149) Am Math.

Thirteen Papers in Analysis. R. R. Suncheleev et al. LC 86-26455. (Translations Ser.: Series 2, Vol. 133). 122p. 1986. 59.00 (*0-8218-9904-X*, TRANS2/133C) Am Math.

Thirteen Papers on Algebra & Analysis. B. L. Golinskii et al. (Translations Ser.: Series 2, Vol. 76). 263p. 1969. 49.00 (*0-8218-1776-0*, TRANS2/76) Am Math.

Thirteen Papers on Algebra, Topology, Complex Variables, & Linear Programming. I. E. Bazilevic et al. (Translations Ser.: Series 2, Vol. 71). 236p. 1968. 44.00 (*0-8218-1771-X*, TRANS2/71) Am Math.

Thirteen Papers on Analysis. B. M. Gagaev et al. LC 51-5559. (Translations Ser.: Series 2, Vol. 10). 409p. 1958. reprint ed. 44.00 (*0-8218-1710-8*, TRANS2/10) Am Math.

Thirteen Papers on Differential Equations. V. M. Alekseev et al. (Translations Ser.: Series 2, Vol. 89). 300p. 1970. 49.00 (*0-8218-1789-2*, TRANS2/89) Am Math.

Thirteen Papers on Functional Analysis. Z. S. Agranovic et al. (Translations Ser.: Series 2, Vol. 90). 253p. 1970. 44.00 (*0-8218-1790-6*, TRANS2/90) Am Math.

Thirteen Papers on Functional Analysis & Differential Equations. V. I. Arnol'd et al. LC 51-5559. (Translations Ser.: Series 2, Vol. 79). 269p. 1969. 49.00 (*0-8218-1779-5*, TRANS2/79) Am Math.

Thirteen Papers on Functional Analysis & Partial Differential Equations. M. S. Brodskii et al. LC 51-5559. (Translations Ser.: Series 2, Vol. 47). 299p. 1965. 36.00 (*0-8218-1747-7*, TRANS2/47) Am Math.

Thirteen Papers on Functions of Real & Complex Variables. V. S. Azarin et al. (Translations Ser.: Series 2, Vol. 80). 278p. 1969. 50.00 (*0-8218-1780-9*, TRANS2/80) Am Math.

Thirteen Papers on Group Theory, Algebraic Geometry & Algebraic Topology. A. N. Andrianov et al. (Translations Ser.: Series 2, Vol. 66). 272p. 1968. 49.00 (*0-8218-1766-3*, TRANS2/66) Am Math.

Thirteen Papers Translated from the Russian. Tr. by S. Berman et al. LC 89-15010. (Translations Ser.: Series 2, Vol. 144). 140p. 1989. 70.00 (*0-8218-3125-9*, TRANS2/144) Am Math.

Thirteen Perspectives on Regulatory Simplification. Ed. by Annette Kolis. LC 79-65686. (ULI Research Reports: No. 29). 152p. reprint ed. pap. 43.40 (*0-685-20357-3*, 2029806) Bks Demand.

Thirteen Petalled Rose. Adin Steinsaltz. LC 79-3077. 184p. 1985. pap. 13.50 (*0-465-08561-X*) Basic.

Thirteen Petalled Rose. Adin Steinsaltz. LC 91-44053. 200p. 1997. 30.00 (*0-87668-450-9*) Aronson.

Thirteen Pieces: Life with a Multiple. Mary Locke. 272p. (Orig.). 1993. pap. 10.00 (*0-9635966-0-8*) Atlan St Pub.

Thirteen Plays of Bhasa. Alred C. Woolner & Lakshman Sarup. 400p. 1986. reprint ed. 20.00 (*0-317-53537-4*, Pub. by Motilal Banarsidass II) S Asia.

Thirteen Poems. David Hosburgh. (Writers Workshop Redbird Ser.). 1975. 8.00 (*0-88253-658-3*); pap. text ed. 4.00 (*0-88253-657-5*) Ind-US Inc.

Thirteen Principles of Faith: A Chasidic Viewpoint. Noson Gurary. LC 95-36646. 264p. 1996. 30.00 (*1-56821-532-0*) Aronson.

Thirteen Problems. Agatha Christie. 224p. 1985. mass mkt. 5.50 (*0-425-08903-7*) Berkley Pub.

Thirteen Propositions for Piano Solo. Ridgway Banks. (Contemporary Keyboard Ser.: No. 4). i, 9p. 1990. pap. text ed. 10.00 (*1-56571-017-7*) PRB Prods.

***13 Proven Ways to Get Your Message Across: The Essential Reference for Teachers, Trainers, Presenters, & Speakers.** Ernest W. Brewer. LC 97-22291. 96p. 1997. text ed. 49.95 (*0-8039-6641-5*) Corwin Pr.

***13 Proven Ways to Get Your Message Across: The Essential Reference for Teachers, Trainers, Presenters, & Speakers.** Ernest W. Brewer. LC 97-22291. 96p. 1997. pap. 19.95 (*0-8039-6642-3*) Corwin Pr.

Thirteen Questions: Reframing Education's Conversation. Ed. by Joe L. Kincheloe & Shirley R. Steinberg. LC 92-3894. 301p. (Orig.). (C). 1992. pap. text ed. 29.95 (*0-8204-1924-9*) P Lang Pubng.

Thirteen Questions: Reframing Education's Conversation. 2nd rev. ed. Ed. by Joe L. Kincheloe & Shirley R. Steinberg. 344p. (C). 1995. pap. text ed. 29.95 (*0-8204-2769-1*) P Lang Pubng.

Thirteen Questions in Ethics. G. Lee Bowie et al. 800p. (C). 1992. pap. text ed. 26.75 (*0-15-591744-7*) HB Coll Pubs.

***Thirteen Questions in Ethics.** 2nd ed. Bowie. (C). 1997. pap. text ed. 38.00 (*0-15-503684-X*) HB Coll Pubs.

Thirteen Satires of Juvenal, 2 Vols. Juvenal. Ed. by W. R. Connor. LC 78-67141. (Latin Texts & Commentaries Ser.). (ENG & LAT.). 1979. reprint ed. lib. bdg. 61.95 (*0-405-11610-1*) Ayer.

***13 Secrets of Power Performance.** Roger Dawson. 1997. pap. text ed. 14.95 (*0-13-671497-8*) P-H.

Thirteen Songs: High Voice & Piano. L. Hoiby. 72p. 1990. pap. 9.95 (*0-7935-4384-3*, 50480727) H Leonard.

Thirteen Spits. John M. Bennett. 1986. pap. 2.00 (*0-935350-91-8*) Luna Bisonte.

Thirteen Stories. Robert B. Graham. LC 78-103511. (Short Story Ipdex Reprint Ser.). 1977. 19.95 (*0-8369-3253-6*) Ayer.

Thirteen Stories. Eudora Welty. Ed. by Ruth M. Vande Kieft. LC 65-14703. 243p. (Orig.). 1965. pap. 9.00 (*0-15-689969-8*, Harvest Bks) HarBrace.

Thirteen Stories & Thirteen Epitaphs. William T. Vollmann. LC 94-790. 256p. 1994. pap. 12.00 (*0-8021-3395-9*, Grove) Grove-Atltic.

Thirteen Tales of Terror. Jack London. 23.95 (*0-8488-0096-6*) Amereon Ltd.

13 Tennessee Ghosts & Jeffrey. Kathryn T. Windham. LC 73-87004. (Illus.). 160p. (YA). (gr. 6 up). 1988. reprint ed. pap. 13.00 (*0-8173-0378-2*) U of Ala Pr.

Thirteen Things Not to Tell a Parent. Patricia Hermes. (Cousins' Club Ser.: No. 3). (J). 1995. mass mkt. 3.99 (*0-671-87968-5*) PB.

Thirteen Things You Gotta Know: To Make It As a Christian. Josh McDowell & Bob Hostetler. LC 92-33490. (YA). 1992. pap. 6.99 (*0-8499-3413-3*) Word Pub.

Thirteen Things You Gotta Know to Keep Your Love Life Alive & Well. Josh McDowell. 1994. pap. 6.99 (*0-8499-3534-2*) Word Pub.

Thirteen Thinkers-Plus: A Sampler of Great Philosophers. rev. ed. Gerald F. Kreyche. 172p. (C). 1984. pap. text ed. 11.50 (*0-8191-3889-4*); lib. bdg. 35.50 (*0-8191-3888-6*) U Pr of Amer.

***13,012 Questionable Doctors, 3 vols.** 3rd ed. Sidney M. Wolfe et al. 2968p. 1996. pap. 250.00 (*0-937188-05-0*) Pub Citizen Inc.

13 to 19. Wendy Grant. 1996. pap. 12.95 (*1-85230-862-1*) Element MA.

Thirteen to Nineteen: Discovering the Light Conversations with Parents. Julian Sleigh. 120p. 1990. pap. 8.95 (*0-86315-078-0*, 1344, Pub. by Floris Books UK) Anthroposophic.

Thirteen Uncanny Stories. Hans H. Jahnn. Tr. by Gerda Jordan from GER. LC 84-47544. (American University Studies: Germanic Languages & Literature: Ser. I, Vol. 20). 196p. (Orig.). (C). 1984. pap. text ed. 16.95 (*0-8204-0114-5*) P Lang Pubng.

Thirteen Uncollected Stories by John Cheever. John Cheever. Ed. by Franklin Dennis. 240p. 1994. 19.95 (*0-89733-405-1*) Academy Chi Pubs.

***Thirteen Ways: Theoretical Investigations in Architecture.** Robert Harbison. LC 96-44542. (Contemporary Architectural Discourse Ser.). 1997. 20.00 (*0-262-08256-X*) MIT Pr.

***Thirteen Ways of Looking at a Black Man.** Henry L. Gates, Jr. 22.00 (*0-614-26977-6*) Random.

***13 Ways of Looking at a Black Man.** Henry Louis Gates, Jr. LC 96-33138. 1997. 22.00 (*0-679-45713-5*) Random.

Thirteen Ways of Looking at a Blackbird. Lukas Foss. 1979. pap. 7.50 (*0-8258-0064-1*, PCB114) Fischer Inc NY.

Thirteen Ways of Looking at a Crow. Dennis Lucas. 32p. (Orig.). 1992. pap. 9.00 (*1-880516-05-5*) Left Hand Bks.

***Thirteen Ways of Looking for a Poem: A Guide to Writing Poetry.** Ed. by Bishop. (C). 1998. text ed. write for info. (*0-321-01130-9*) Addson-Wesley Educ.

Thirteen Ways to Confident Faith: A Study in 1 John 4: 7 - 5: 21. large type ed. Edward A. Friess. 136p. 1997. spiral bd. 12.95 (*0-9643297-7-8*) E A Friess.

***13 Ways to Look at a Black Man.** Henry L. Gates, Jr. 1998. pap. write for info. (*0-679-77666-4*, Vin) Random.

Thirteen Ways to Sink a Sub. Jamie Gilson. (Illus.). (J). (gr. 3-7). 1982. 16.00 (*0-688-01304-X*) Lothrop.

Thirteen Ways to Sink a Sub. Jamie Gilson. (J). Date not set. mass mkt. 3.50 (*0-671-72958-6*) PB.

Thirteen Weeks: A Guide to Teaching College Writing. Irvin Y. Hashimoto. LC 90-2089. 263p. (gr. 13). 1990. pap. text ed. 24.00 (*0-86709-261-0*, 0261) Boynton Cook Pubs.

Thirteen Worthies. Llewelyn Powys. LC 67-22112. (Essay Index Reprint Ser.). 1977. 18.95 (*0-8369-0799-X*) Ayer.

Thirteen Worthies. Llewelyn Powys. 1985. 35.00 (*0-317-38814-2*, Pub. by Redcliffe Pr Ltd) St Mut.

***Thirteen Years: 1936-1949.** George Paulikas. (Illus.). 120p. 1997. pap. 12.00 (*0-8059-4105-3*) Dorrance.

Thirteen Years at the Russian Court a Personal Record of the Last Years & Death of the Czar Nicholas Second & His Family. Pierre Gilliard. LC 75-115539. (Russia Observed, Series I). 1976. reprint ed. 38.95 (*0-405-03029-0*) Ayer.

13th Aerospace Testing Seminar Proceedings: Proceedings of the 13th Space Simulation Conference. 396p. (Orig.). 1991. 100.00 (*1-877862-12-6*) Inst Environ Sci.

Thirteenth Air Force Story. Kenn Rust. (Illus.). 72p. 1993. pap. text ed. 15.95 (*0-911852-90-5*) Aviation Heritage.

Thirteenth Airborne Division. Thirteenth Airborne Division Staff. LC 89-50491. 450p. 1989. reprint ed. 48.00 (*0-938021-43-5*) Turner Pub KY.

***Thirteenth Annual IEEE Semiconductor Thermal Measurement & Management Symposium, 1997.** IEEE, Components, Packaging & Manufacturing Technology Society Staff. Ed. by Institute of Electrical & Electronics Engineers, Inc. Staff. 200p. 1997. pap. text ed. write for info. (*0-7803-3793-X*, 97CH36031); lib. bdg. write for info. (*0-7803-3794-8*, 97CH36031); fiche write for info. (*0-7803-3795-6*, 97CH36031) Inst Electrical.

13th Annual Institute on Municipal Finance. (Real Estate Law & Practice Course Handbook Ser.). 968p. 1994. pap. 99.00 (*0-614-17222-5*, N4-4588) PLI.

13th Annual Insurance, Excess & Reinsurance Coverage Disputes. (Litigation & Administrative Practice Course Handbook, 1983-84 Ser.). Date not set. pap. 99.00 (*0-614-17270-5*, H4-5228) PLI.

Thirteenth Annual Review, NC 1993. Wake Forest University School of Law Continuing Legal Education Staff. 757p. 1993. suppl. ed., pap. 90.00 (*0-942225-69-4*) Wake Forest Law.

Thirteenth Assembling Annual. Ed. by Charles Doria et al. (Illus.). 100p. (Orig.). 1987. pap. 50.00 (*0-915066-56-4*) Assembling Pr.

Thirteenth Avenue. Miriam Friedman. 272p. 1995. 17.95 (*1-56871-056-9*) Targum Pr.

Thirteenth Biennial Color Aerial Photography in the Plant Sciences & Related Fields. 240p. 1992. 20.00 (*0-944426-82-4*) ASP & RS.

Thirteenth Biennial Conference Proceedings. ICHCA Staff. (C). 1977. 100.00 (*0-685-37349-5*, Pub. by ICHCA UK) St Mut.

Thirteenth Candle. T. Lobsang Rampa. 1994. lib. bdg. 23.95 (*1-56849-437-8*) Buccaneer Bks.

Thirteenth Census of the United States Taken in the Year 1910. U. S. Bureau of the Census Staff. LC 75-22857. (America in Two Centuries Ser.). 1976. reprint ed. 46.95 (*0-405-07724-6*) Ayer.

Thirteenth-Century Church at St. Denis. Caroline A. Bruzelius. LC 85-3354. 256p. 1986. 35.00 (*0-300-03190-4*) Yale U Pr.

Thirteenth Century England Four: Proceedings of the Newcastle upon Tyne Conference 1991. Ed. by P. R. Coss & S. D. Lloyd. 230p. (C). 1993. 71.00 (*0-85115-325-9*) Boydell & Brewer.

Thirteenth-Century England I: Proceedings of the Newcastle-Upon-Tyne Conference 1985. Ed. by P. R. Ross & S. D. Lloyd. 202p. 1986. 79.00 (*0-85115-452-2*) Boydell & Brewer.

Thirteenth-Century England II: Proceedings of the Newcastle upon Tyne Conference 1987. Ed. by P. R. Coss & S. D. Lloyd. (Illus.). 190p. 1989. 79.00 (*0-85115-513-8*) Boydell & Brewer.

Thirteenth-Century England III: Proceedings of the Newcastle upon Tyne Conference, 1989. Ed. by P. R. Coss & S. D. Lloyd. (Illus.). 224p. 1991. 79.00 (*0-85115-548-0*) Boydell & Brewer.

Thirteenth Century England V: Proceedings of the Newcastle upon Tyne Conference 1993. Ed. by P. R. Coss & S. D. Lloyd. (Illus.). 240p. (C). 1995. 71.00 (*0-85115-565-0*) Boydell & Brewer.

***Thirteenth Century England VI: Proceedings of the Durham Conference, 1995.** Ed. by Michael Prestwich et al. (Illus.). 256p. 1997. 71.00 (*0-85115-674-6*) Boydell & Brewer.

Thirteenth-Century Life of Charlemagne. Ed. & Tr. by Robert Levine. LC 91-13581. (Library of Medieval Literature: Vol. 80A). 170p. 1991. text ed. 15.00 (*0-8153-0397-1*) Garland.

Thirteenth-Century Minstrel's Chronicle (Recits d'un Menestrel de Reims) A Translation & Introduction. Minstrel of Reims. Tr. by Robert Levine from FRE. (Studies in French Civilization: Vol. 4). 256p. 1990. lib. bdg. 89.95 (*0-88946-623-8*) E Mellen.

Thirteenth Child. large type ed. Antonia Ridge. 1978. 25.99 (*0-7089-0181-6*) Ulverscroft.

Thirteenth Clue. Ann Jonas. LC 91-34586. (Illus.). 32p. (J). (ps-6). 1992. 16.00 (*0-688-09742-1*); lib. bdg. 15.93 (*0-688-09743-X*) Greenwillow.

Thirteenth Conference Proceedings. ICHCA Staff. (C). 1977. 60.00 (*0-685-46485-7*, Pub. by ICHCA UK) St Mut.

Thirteenth Disciple: Sermons of a Psychic Evangelist! Walker H. Wescott. LC 41-920. 200p. (Orig.). 1989. pap. write for info. (*0-9624691-7-3*) Wescott & MacMillan.

Thirteenth District: A Story of a Candidate. Brand Whitlock. 1993. reprint ed. lib. bdg. 89.00 (*0-7812-5415-9*) Rprt Serv.

***13th Floor: A Ghost Story.** Sid Fleischman. (Illus.). 144p. (J). 1997. pap. 3.99 (*0-440-41243-9*, YB BDD) BDD Bks Young Read.

13th Floor: A Ghost Story. Sid Fleischman. LC 94-42806. (Illus.). 144p. (J). (gr. 3 up). 1995. 15.00 (*0-688-14216-8*) Greenwillow.

Thirteenth Gen: Abort, Retry, Ignore, Fail? William Strauss et al. LC 92-56350. (Illus.). 240p. 1993. pap. 12.00 (*0-679-74365-0*, Vin) Random.

Thirteenth Hour. Barbara Sofer. LC 96-17108. 352p. 1996. pap. 24.95 (*0-525-94181-9*) NAL-Dutton.

Thirteenth House. Adam Zameenzad. 1989. 15.95 (*0-394-57561-X*) Random.

Thirteenth International Complement Workshop, San Diego, Calif., September 1989 Abstracts. Ed. by N. R. Cooper. (Journal: Complement & Inflammation: Vol. 6, No. 5). 128p. 1990. pap. 36.75 (*3-8055-5089-8*) S Karger.

13th International Conference on Fluidized Bed Combustion: Proceedings: (13th: 1995: Orlando, FL), 2 vols., Set. Ed. by Kay J. Heinschel. LC 87-70969. (FBC-Technology of Choice Ser.). 1548p. 1995. 300.00 (*0-7918-1305-3*, HX0937) ASME.

13th International Conference on NOE in the Nuclear & Pressure Vessel Industries. Ed. by K. Iida et al. 494p. 1995. 110.00 (*0-87170-548-6*, 6573) ASM.

Thirteenth International Conference on Numerical Methods in Fluid Dynamics: Proceedings of the Conference Held at the Consiglio Nazionale Delle Ricerche, Rome, Italy, 6-10 July 1992. Ed. by M. Napolitano et al. (Lecture Notes in Physics Ser.: Vol. 414). xiv, 541p. 1993. 101.95 (*0-387-56394-6*) Spr-Verlag.

Thirteenth International Conference on Raman Spectroscopy. Ed. by W. Kiefer et al. LC 92-18039. 1130p. 1992. text ed. 524.00 (*0-471-93335-X*) Wiley.

Thirteenth International Conference on Thermoelectrics. Ed. by B. Mathiprakasam & Patrick Heenan. (AIP Conference Proceedings Ser.: No. 316). (Illus.). 359p. 1995. text ed. 140.00 (*1-56396-444-9*, AIP) Am Inst Physics.

Thirteenth International Congress on Thrombosis, Bilbao, Spain, June 1994 Abstracts. Ed. by J. A. Iriarte et al. (Journal: Haemostasis Ser.: Vol. 24, Suppl. 1, 1994). viii, 410p. 1994. pap. 127.00 (*3-8055-6020-6*) S Karger.

Thirteenth International Seaweed Symposium. Ed. by Sandra C. Lindstrom & P. W. Gabrielson. (Developments in Hydrobiology Ser.). (C). 1990. 630.00 (*0-7923-0763-1*) Kluwer Ac.

13th Juror. John T. Lescroart. 560p. 1995. mass mkt. 6.50 (*0-440-22079-3*, Island Bks) Dell.

Thirteenth Juror at the Lawrencia Bembenek Murder Trial. B. Roddick. 1982. pap. 4.95 (*0-937816-23-X*) Tech Data.

Thirteenth Labor. Belluomini Ronald. LC 85-70532. (Living Poets' Library). 1985. pap. 5.00 (*0-934218-32-3*) Dragons Teeth.

Thirteenth Man: A Reagan Cabinet Memoir. Terrel H. Bell. 300p. 1988. 35.00 (*0-02-902351-3*, Free Press) Free Pr.

Thirteenth Member. Molly Hunter. (J). (gr. 6-9). 1988. 19.75 (*0-8446-6362-X*) Peter Smith.

Thirteenth National Passive Solar Conference Proceedings, 1988: Solar 88. Ed. by M. J. Coleman. (Illus.). 523p. (Orig.). (C). 1988. per. 50.00 (*0-89553-204-2*) Am Solar Energy.

Thirteenth Pearl. Carolyn Keene. LC 78-57931. (Nancy Drew Ser.: Vol. 56). (Illus.). 180p. (J). (gr. 3-7). 1978. 5.95 (*0-448-09556-4*, G&D) Putnam Pub Group.

Thirteenth Penguin Book of The Times Crosswords. Ed. by John Grant. 114p. 1991. pap. 6.50 (*0-14-012113-7*, Penguin Bks) Viking Penguin.

Thirteenth Process Technology Conference: Continuous Casting, Vol. XIII. LC 82-197229. 468p. 1995. 90.00 (*1-886362-01-7*) Iron & Steel.

***Thirteenth Sign.** Lisa Kent. Ed. by Charles G. Gee. 1997. text ed. 22.95 (*1-889936-05-7*) Skyline Pubs Inc.

Thirteenth Sign No. 7. Ellen Steiber. 1996. pap. 3.99 (*0-679-87944-7*) Random Bks Yng Read.

Thirteenth Summer. Mary Brown. 120p. (Orig.). 1996. mass mkt. 4.99 (*1-55197-047-3*, Pub. by Comnwlth Pub CN) Partners Pubs Grp.

Thirteenth Summer. Jose L. Olaizola. Tr. by Susan Ouriou. 288p. 1993. pap. 12.95 (*0-88995-094-6*, Pub. by Red Deer CN) Orca Bk Pubs.

Thirteenth Summer. Stephen Roos. 112p. (J). (gr. 4-7). 1992. pap. 2.95 (*0-8167-1840-7*) Troll Communs.

***Thirteenth Summer: An Adirondack Adventure.** Gerald Cashion. (Illus.). 156p. (Orig.). (J). (gr. 5-8). 1996. pap. 11.50 (*0-9654280-0-1*) Sunset Ent.

Thirteenth Symposium on Nucleic Acids Chemistry. Ed. by Ken-ichi Tomita. (Nucleic Acids Symposium Ser.: No. 16). 308p. 1985. pap. 59.00 (*0-947946-43-8*, IRL Pr) OUP.

Thirteenth Trick. Russell Braddon. LC 73-665. 168p. 1973. 5.95 (*0-393-08375-6*) Norton.

Thirteenth Virginia Cavalry. Daniel T. Balfour. (Virginia Regimental Histories Ser.). (Illus.). 115p. 1986. 19.95 (*0-930919-29-7*) H E Howard.

Thirteenth Virginia Infantry. David F. Riggs. (Virginia Regimental Histories Ser.). (Illus.). 158p. 1988. 19.95 (*0-930919-65-3*) H E Howard.

***Thirteenth Window.** George Yelcich. 151p. (Orig.). 1997. mass mkt. 4.99 (*1-55237-160-3*, Pub. by Comnwlth Pub CN) Partners Pubs Grp.

Thirties. (Warner - Chappell Golden Decade Ser.). 160p. (Orig.). 1995. pap. 16.95 (*0-89724-040-5*, VF1916) Warner Brothers.

Thirties America: Prints from the Milwaukee Art Museum. Terrence L. Marvel. (Illus.). 30p. (Orig.). 1991. pap. 12.00 (*0-944110-30-4*) Milwauk Art Mus.

Thirties Poets. Jem Poster. LC 92-45681. (Open Guides to Literature Ser.). 1993. 75.00 (*0-335-09664-6*, Open Univ Pr); pap. 18.00 (*0-335-09663-8*, Open Univ Pr) Taylor & Francis.

Thirtieth Anniversary Exhibition of the Magnes Museum. Ed. by Marni Welch & Paula Friedman. (Illus.). 32p. 1992. pap. write for info. (*0-943376-56-4*) Magnes Mus.

Thirtieth Anniversary Salute to GI Joe. Vincent Santelmo. LC 93-75299. (Illus.). 192p. 1994. 34.95 (*0-87341-301-6*, JL01) Krause Pubns.

Thirtieth Battalion Virginia Sharpshooters. Michael West. (Virginia Regimental Histories Ser.). (Illus.). 321p. 1995. 19.95 (*1-56190-081-8*) H E Howard.

30th Infantry. Thirtieth Infantry Association Staff. LC 90-70160. (Illus.). 128p. 1990. 45.00 (*0-938021-86-9*) Turner Pub KY.

Thirtieth Piece of Silver. Lilian Hayes. LC 70-125217. (Short Story Index Reprint Ser.). 1977. 31.95 (*0-8369-3584-5*) Ayer.

30th Publication Design Annual No. 30. Compiled by Society of Publication Designers Staff. 240p. 1995. 49.99 (*1-56496-165-6*) Rockport Pubs.

Thirtieth Virginia Infantry. Robert K. Krick. (Virginia Regimental Histories Ser.). (Illus.). 143p. 1983. 19.95 (*0-930919-03-3*) H E Howard.

Thirtieth Year. Ingeborg Bachmann. Tr. by Michael Bullock from GER. LC 87-14846. (Modern German Voices Ser.). 200p. 1987. 19.95 (*0-8419-1068-5*) Holmes & Meier.

Thirtieth Year. Ingeborg Bachmann. Tr. by Michael Bullock from GER. LC 87-14846. (Portico Paperbacks Ser.). 200p. 1995. pap. 11.95 (*0-8419-1069-3*) Holmes & Meier.

Thirtieth Year to Heaven: New American Poets. LC 80-22063. (Bree Bks.: No. 2). 1980. 15.95 (*0-917492-09-9*) Jackpine Pr.

***30 - Deal with It.** Jan B. King. Ed. by Cliff Carle. (Illus.). 64p. (Orig.). 1997. pap. 5.95 (*1-57644-037-0*) CCC Pubns.

***Thirty Acres.** Ringuet. 1996. pap. text ed. 7.95 (*0-7710-9995-9*) McCland & Stewart.

30 Activities for Internal Customer Care. Echelon Learning Staff. 405p. 1996. ring bd. 189.95 (*0-566-07643-8*, Pub. by Gower UK) Ashgate Pub Co.

Thirty an' Seen a Lot. Evangelina Vigil. LC 81-68073. 88p. (Orig.). 1982. pap. 7.00 (*0-934770-13-1*) Arte Publico.

Thirty Ancestors of Richard Henry Koch (Koch, Neufang, Bock, Bolich, Beck, et al) R. H. Koch. (Illus.). 327p. 1993. reprint ed. pap. 49.50 (*0-8328-3771-7*); reprint ed. lib. bdg. 59.50 (*0-8328-3770-9*) Higginson Bk Co.

***Thirty & Terminal: Cancer Survival.** John R. Wagner. LC 96-78123. 160p. (Orig.). 1997. pap. 12.95 (*0-9651590-0-0*) Infnty Pub.

Thirty at Athens. fac. ed. Peter Krentz. LC 81-70697. 167p. 1982. reprint ed. pap. 47.60 (*0-608-01017-0*, 2061875) Bks Demand.

Thirty Bible Reasons Why Christ Heals Today. Gordon Lindsay. 1968. 2.95 (*0-89985-031-6*) Christ for the Nations.

30 Bicycle Tours in New Hampshire: A Guide to Selected Backcountry Roads through the Granite State. 3rd rev. ed. Adolphe Bernotas et al. LC 91-7546. (Bicycle Tours Ser.). 192p. 1991. pap. 13.00 (*0-88150-192-1*, Backcountry) Countryman.

***30 Bicycle Tours in New Jersey: Almost 1000 Miles of Scenic Pleasures & Historic Treasures.** 2nd ed. Arline Zatz. LC 97-20176. (Bicycle Tour Ser.). (Illus.). 212p. 1997. pap. 14.95 (*0-88150-368-1*, Backcountry) Countryman.

30 Bicycle Tours in Wisconsin: Lakes, Forests, & Glacier-Carved Countryside. Jane E. Hall & Scott D. Hall. (Bicycle Tours Ser.). (Illus.). 256p. (Orig.). 1994. pap. 14.00 (*0-88150-286-3*, Backcountry) Countryman.

Thirty Birds That Will Build in Bird Houses. Illus. by R. B. Layton. LC 77-81805. 1977. pap. 10.95 (*0-912542-05-5*) Nature Bks Pubs.

Thirty Caprices for the Clarinet. Ernesto Cavallini. 64p. 1909. pap. 10.95 (*0-8258-0238-5*, 0106) Fischer Inc NY.

Thirty Changing Meter Duets for Treble Clef Instruments. James Meyer. 41p. 1984. pap. 9.95 (*0-938170-05-8*) Wimbledon Music.

Thirty Classic Boat Designs: The Best of the Good Boats. Roger C. Taylor. (Illus.). 256p. 1992. pap. 25.95 (*0-87742-329-6*, 60317) Intl Marine.

Thirty Classic Boat Designs: The Best of the Good Boats. Roger C. Taylor. 1992. pap. text ed. 24.95 (*0-07-063004-6*) McGraw.

***30 Classic Cakes.** Smithmark Staff. 1996. 6.98 (*0-7651-9766-9*) Smithmark.

Thirty Classic Patchwork Patterns. Dorothy H. Welch. (Illus.). 96p. (Orig.). pap. 7.95 (*0-486-28967-2*) Dover.

Thirty Country Road Loop Trips in Northern California: North of Sacramento. Gilbert W. Davies & Florice M. Frank. LC 94-76970. (Illus.). 220p. (Orig.). (C). 1995. pap. 14.95 (*0-9634413-7-X*) HiSt Ink Bks.

***Thirty Creative Containers: Inspirational Ideas for Making & Decorating Containers.** Smithmark Staff. (Thrifty Projects Ser.). 1996. 6.98 (*0-7651-9452-X*) Smithmark.

***30 Cross Stitch Designs.** Smithmark Staff. 1996. 6.98 (*0-7651-9767-7*) Smithmark.

Thirty Day Action Guide to Big Money Selling. William E. Edwards. 1972. 49.50 (*0-13-918698-0*) Exec Reports.

Thirty Day Body Purification: How to Cleanse Your Inner Body & Experience the Joys. Lewis Harrison. 1994. pap. text ed. 12.95 (*0-13-917303-X*) P-H.

Thirty-Day Diarrhea Diet Plan. Kurt Brecht. 86p. (Orig.). (C). 1989. pap. 4.00 (*1-879188-01-5*) Dirty Rotten Pr.

30-Day Evangelism Plan: Developing the Habit of Loving People. Len Andyshak. (PathFinder Pamphlets Ser.). 32p. (Orig.). 1986. pap. 3.99 (*0-87784-218-3*, 218) InterVarsity.

Thirty-Day Forcasting: A Review of a Ten-Year Experiment. Jerome Namias. (Meteorological Monograph: Vol. 2, No. 6). (Illus.). 83p. (Orig.). 1953. pap. 17.00 (*0-933876-01-7*) Am Meteorological.

An Asterisk (*) at the beginning of an entry indicates that the title is appearing in BIP for the first time.

Thirty-Day Mental Diet. Willis H. Kinnear. 144p. 1990. reprint ed. pap. 13.95 (*0-87516-624-5*) DeVorss.

30 Day Turn Around. John Lambert. 144p. 1995. per., pap. text ed. 16.95 (*0-7872-1490-6*) Kendall-Hunt.

Thirty Days at the Foot of the Cross. Ed. by Thomas Jones & Sheila Jones. (Daily Power Ser.). 120p. 1993. pap. 5.99 (*1-884553-12-5*) Discipleshp.

Thirty Days at the Foot of the Cross-Trente Jours Au Pied De la Croix. Ed. by Thomas Jones & Sheila Jones. Tr. by Franck Descotes. 44p. (FRE.). 1994. 5.99 (*1-884553-13-3*) Discipleshp.

Thirty Days Has September: Calendar Trivia & Activities for Kids. Carole Marsh. (Quantum Leap Ser.). (J). (gr. 3-9). 1994. 29.95 (*0-7933-0015-0*); pap. 19.95 (*0-7933-0016-9*); disk 29.95 (*0-7933-0017-7*) Gallopade Pub Group.

Thirty Days on the Planet Thebel: Theories, Ideas, Hypotheses. N. Vardy. LC 95-90933. 1996. pap. 15.95 (*0-533-11758-5*) Vantage.

Thirty Days Prayer to the Sacred Heart. Veritas Publications Staff. 1989. pap. 15.00 (*0-86217-234-9*, Pub. by Veritas IE) St Mut.

***30 Days Smart Family Look.** P. Lewis. 1997. pap. 4.99 (*0-310-21588-9*) Zondervan.

Thirty Days to a Better Life. John W. Adams. 1988. pap. 3.00 (*0-9602166-4-2*) Golden Key.

30 Days to a Better Memory. Carol A. Turkington. 1996. pap. 10.00 (*0-671-51729-5*) S&S Trade.

30 Days to a Happier Marriage. Jay Gale & Lia Taurone. 192p. (Orig.). 1995. pap. text ed. 5.50 (*0-425-15056-9*) Berkley Pub.

Thirty Days to a More Powerful Vocabulary. Wilfred Funk & Norman Lewis. 256p. mass mkt. 5.50 (*0-671-74349-X*, 80003) PB.

30 Days to a Sexier You. Paula P. Coxe & Jessica Daniels. LC 95-23995. (Illus.). 128p. (Orig.). 1995. pap. 6.95 (*1-57071-054-6*) Sourcebks.

***30 Days to a Smart Family: A Powerful Way to Make Your Family Dreams a Reality.** Paul Lewis & Thomas Black. LC 96-47821. 128p. 1997. 15.99 (*0-310-21585-4*) Zondervan.

Thirty Days to Beautiful Legs. Marc Selner. 1985. pap. 3.00 (*0-87980-407-6*) Wilshire.

Thirty Days to Better English. N. Lewis. 1985. mass mkt. 4.99 (*0-451-16191-2*) NAL-Dutton.

Thirty Days to Better English. Norman Lewis. 208p. 1985. pap. 4.95 (*0-451-15702-8*, Sig) NAL-Dutton.

***30 Days to Effective Speaking.** Paul Sorvino. Date not set. write for info. (*0-688-06470-1*) Morrow.

30 Days to Finding a Good Job. Hal Geiseking. 176p. 1994. pap. 10.00 (*0-671-88127-2*, Fireside) S&S Trade.

30 Days to Happiness: Setting Yourself up to Win at Life. Liah Kraft-Kristaine. 130p. (Orig.). 1987. pap. 9.95 (*1-878095-21-8*) LMI Prodns.

Thirty Days to Metric Mastery: For People Who Hate Math. Don C. Steinke. (Illus.). (Orig.). 1981. pap. 6.95 (*0-9605344-0-7*) Steinke.

***30 Days to Swimsuit Lean.** Cliff Sheats & Maggie Greenwood-Robinson. Ed. by Margaret Allyson. (Illus.). 176p. (Orig.). 1997. pap. 19.95 (*0-9653970-1-7*) Magnolia Media.

***30 Days to the GMAT.** Mark A. Stewart & Frederick J. O'Toole. (Illus.). 240p. 1997. pap. 11.95 (*0-02-861834-3*, Arco) Macmillan Gen Ref.

30 Days to the GRE. Rajvin N. Rimal. 240p. 1996. 11.95 (*0-02-861261-2*) Macmillan.

***30 Days to the GRE.** 2nd ed. Rajiv N. Rimal. 1998. pap. 11.95 (*0-02-862180-8*) Macmillan.

***30 Days to the LSAT.** Frederick J. O'Toole. 1998. pap. 11.95 (*0-02-862176-X*) Macmillan.

***30 Days to the LSAT.** Mark A. Stewart & Frederick J. O'Toole. (Illus.). 240p. 1997. pap. 11.95 (*0-02-861835-1*, Arco) Macmillan Gen Ref.

30 Days to the SAT. Rajiv N. Rimal & Peter Z. Orton. LC 96-16204. 240p. 1996. pap. write for info. (*0-02-861262-0*) Macmillan.

30 Days to Understanding the Bible. rev. ed. M. Anders. 1994. pap. 12.99 (*0-8499-3575-X*) Word Pub.

Thirty Degrees North, One Sixty Fifth East. Paul J. Stam. 1978. mass mkt. 1.75 (*0-380-01965-5*) Avon.

30 Designs for Small Gardens. Ed. by Tony Laryea. LC 95-83719. (Illus.). 128p. 1996. pap. 16.95 (*0-563-37122-6*, BBC-Parkwest) Parkwest Pubns.

***Thirty Dough Craft Creations: Inspirational Projects with Salt Dough.** Smithmark Staff. (Thirty Projects Ser.). 1996. 6.98 (*0-7651-9453-8*) Smithmark.

***30 Dried Flower Designs.** Smithmark Staff. 1996. 6.98 (*0-7651-9768-5*) Smithmark.

38 Activities for Handling Difficult Situations. Jacqueline Stewart & David Couper. 336p. 1995. ring bd. 169.95 (*0-566-07635-7*, Pub. by Gower UK) Ashgate Pub Co.

Thirty-Eight Basic Joseki. Six-Dan Kosugi Kiyoshi & James Davies. (Elementary Go Ser.: Vol. 2). 1973. pap. 14.95 (*4-87187-011-1*, G11) Ishi Pr Intl.

Thirty-Eight Basic Speech Experiences. Clark Carlile. 1993. 21.33 (*0-931054-25-7*); teacher ed., pap. 6.67 (*0-931054-26-5*) Clark Pub.

Thirty-Eight Basic Speech Experiences. Clark Carlile & Dana Hensley. 1993. pap. 15.67 (*0-931054-29-X*) Clark Pub.

38 Most Common Fiction Writing Mistakes & How to Avoid Them. Jack Bickham. 118p. 1992. 12.99 (*0-89879-503-6*, Wrtrs Digest Bks) F & W Pubns Inc.

Thirty-Eight Latin Stories Designed to Accompany Frederick M. Wheelock's Latin: An Introductory Course Based on Ancient Authors. 3rd ed. Anne H. Groton & James M. May. LC 86-71229. 110p. (ENG & LAT.). 1989. reprint ed. pap. 10.00 (*0-86516-289-1*) Bolchazy-Carducci.

***38 Most Common Fiction Writing Mistakes.** Jack M. Bickham. 1997. pap. text ed. 12.99 (*0-89879-821-3*, Wrtrs Digest Bks) F & W Pubns Inc.

Thirty-Eight North Yankee. Ed Ruggero. Ed. by Paul McCarthy. 480p. 1991. reprint ed. mass mkt. 5.99 (*0-671-70022-7*) PB.

Thirty-Eight Short Stories: An Introductory Anthology. 2nd ed. Ed. by Michael Timko. 1978. pap. text ed. write for info. (*0-07-553610-2*) McGraw.

***38 Short Stories by American Women Writers, Set.** Dover Staff. boxed, pap. 6.00 (*0-486-29459-5*) Dover.

.38 Special & a Broken Heart. Jonis Agee. LC 94-48076. (Coffee-to-Go-Short-Short Story Ser.). 128p. (Orig.). 1995. pap. 10.95 (*1-56689-032-2*) Coffee Hse.

Thirty-Eight State U. S. A. G. Etzel Pearcy. LC 73-83685. (Monographs: No.2). (Illus.). 1973. 4.95 (*0-916434-09-5*) Plycon Pr.

Thirty-Eight, Twenty-Two, Thirty-Six Conceptual Statistics for Beginners. 4th ed. Isadore Newman & Carole Newman. 207p. 1977. pap. text ed. 5.50 (*0-917180-06-2*) I Newman.

Thirty-Eight Years: Poetry & Prose of a Writer's Life. Mark Grover. Ed. by Denise Broms. 54p. pap. 9.95 (*0-9640114-3-3*) Noble Crown.

Thirty-Eighth Arkansas Confederate Infantry. Desmond W. Allen. (Illus.). 73p. 1988. pap. 16.00 (*0-941765-37-7*) Arkansas Res.

38th Stapp Car Crash Conference Proceedings. 1994. pap. 85.00 (*1-56091-543-9*, P279) Soc Auto Engineers.

Thirty-Eighth Virginia Infantry. G. Howard Gregory. (Virginia Regimental Histories Ser.). (Illus.). 137p. 1988. 19.95 (*0-930919-58-0*) H E Howard.

Thirty-Eighth Western New York Exhibition. LC 80-50571. (Illus.). 43p. 1980. pap. 5.50 (*0-914782-33-9*) Buffalo Fine-Albrght-Knox.

Thirty English Songs: High - Renaissance to Baroque. pap. 12.95 (*0-7935-4632-X*, 00740018) H Leonard.

Thirty English Songs: Low - Renaissance to Baroque. pap. 12.95 (*0-7935-4633-8*, 00740019) H Leonard.

Thirty Epigrams. Illus. by Richard O'Connell. 1971. pap. 6.00 (*0-685-62619-9*) Atlantis Edns.

30 Family Christmas Favorites: Arranged for Easy Piano by Dan Coates. Ed. by Carol Cuellar. 80p. (Orig.). 1995. pap. text ed. 10.95 (*0-89724-884-8*, AF9539) Warner Brothers.

Thirty Famous One-Act Plays. Ed. by Bennett Cerf & Van H. Cartmell. LC 49-9032. 1979. 16.00 (*0-394-60473-3*, Modern Lib) Random.

Thirty Favorite Novenas. 31p. 1994. reprint ed. pap. 0.75 (*0-89555-105-5*) TAN Bks Pubs.

***Thirty Fiddle Tunes from the Manuscript Collection of William Sidney Mount.** Ed. by Alan Buechner & Bill Shull. (Orig.). 1995. pap. 16.95 (*0-9637812-3-5*) MO St Old Time.

35th Annual Advanced Antitrust Seminar: Distribution & Marketing. (Corporate Law & Practice Course Handbook, 1985-86 Ser.). Date not set. pap. 99.00 (*0-614-17213-6*, B4-7134) PLI.

Thirty-Fifth Battalion Virginia Cavalry. John E. Divine. (Virginia Regimental Histories Ser.). (Illus.). 112p. 1985. 19.95 (*0-930919-19-X*) H E Howard.

Thirty-Fifth Biennial of American Painting. (Illus.). 1977. 5.00 (*0-686-20555-3*) Corcoran.

35th Infantry History Book. Turner Publishing Company Staff. LC 94-61441. 112p. 1994. 48.00 (*1-56311-169-1*) Turner Pub KY.

35th International Symposium on Neuromedical Chemistry. Povl Krogsgaard-Larsen. 160p. 1992. pap. text ed. 299.00 (*3-7186-5367-2*, Harwood Acad Pubs) Gordon & Breach.

Thirty-Fifth International Conference Proceedings. 720p. 1992. 35.00 (*1-55822-095-X*) Am Prod & Inventory.

Thirty-First Annual International Conference Proceedings. (Illus.). 788p. (Orig.). 1988. pap. 35.00 (*1-55822-007-0*) Am Prod & Inventory.

Thirty-First Annual Meeting of the European Society for Paediatric Endocrinology (ESPE) Abstracts, Zaragoza, September, 1992. Ed. by A. Ferrandez Longas. (Journal: Hormone Research: Vol. 37, Suppl. 4, 1992). viii, 76p. 1992. pap. 36.75 (*3-8055-5666-7*) S Karger.

31st Infantry. Turner Publishing Company Staff. LC 94-61889. 96p. 1995. 48.00 (*1-56311-176-4*) Turner Pub KY.

Thirty-First of February. Nelson S. Bond. LC 78-121524. (Short Story Index Reprint Ser.). 1977. 21.95 (*0-8369-3480-6*) Ayer.

Thirty-First of February. Julian Symons. 190p. 1987. pap. 3.50 (*0-88184-317-2*) Carroll & Graf.

31st of February. Julian Symons. 192p. 1995. 18.50 (*0-7451-8672-6*, Black Dagger) Chivers N Amer.

Thirty-First Virginia Infantry. John M. Ashcraft, Jr. (Virginia Regimental Histories Ser.). (Illus.). 171p. 1988. 19.95 (*0-930919-59-9*) H E Howard.

Thirty-Five & Counting. James C. Schaap. 300p. 1986. pap. 7.95 (*0-932914-11-X*) Dordt Coll Pr.

Thirty-Five Best Ghost Towns. Bob Bowman. 1991. 16.95 (*1-878096-12-5*) Best E TX Pubs.

Thirty-Five Checklists for Human Resource Development. Ian MacKay. (Illus.). 179p. 1989. text ed. 79.95 (*0-566-02823-9*, Pub. by Gower UK) Ashgate Pub Co.

35 Classic Hits. 176p. 1994. otabind 12.95 (*0-7935-3129-2*, 00311654) H Leonard.

35 Days to Gettysburg: The Campaign Diaries of Two American Enemies. Mark V. Nesbitt. LC 92-13397. (Illus.). 208p. 1992. 19.95 (*0-8117-1757-7*) Stackpole.

***35 for Two: Original Comedy Scenes.** Ken Friedman. 100p. (Orig.). 1997. pap. 9.95 (*0-9641946-1-9*) Wagon Pr.

***35 Golden Keys about Who You Are & Why You're Here.** Linda C. Anderson. LC 96-46477. (Orig.). 1997. pap. 11.00 (*1-57043-118-3*) ECKANKAR.

35 Hiking Trails Columbia River Gorge. Don Lowe & Roberta Lowe. (Illus.). 96p. 1995. pap. 15.95 (*1-57188-010-0*) F Amato Pubns.

Thirty Five Hiking Trails, Columbia River Gorge. 2nd ed. Don Lowe & Roberta Lowe. Ed. by Oral Bullard. (Illus.). 80p. (Orig.). 1988. pap. 7.95 (*0-911518-77-0*) Touchstone Oregon.

Thirty-Five Lesson Formats: A Sourcebook of Instructional Alternatives. Paul Lyons. LC 91-45289. 160p. (Orig.). 1992. pap. 24.95 (*0-87778-244-X*) Educ Tech Pubns.

Thirty-Five Letters of Cicero. Marcus Tullius Cicero. Ed. by David Stockton. 274p. 1969. pap. 16.95 (*0-19-912005-6*) OUP.

Thirty-Five Millimeter Camera Handbook. Book Sales, Inc. Staff. 1994. 17.98 (*0-7858-0019-0*) Bk Sales Inc.

Thirty-Five Millimeter Film Source Book. Marc Levey. (Illus.). 248p. 1992. 47.95 (*0-240-80125-3*, Focal) Buttrwrth-Heinemann.

Thirty-Five Miniatures & Other Pieces for Organ. Flor Peeters. 64p. (Orig.). (gr. 7-12). 1975. pap. text ed. 10.95 (*0-87487-602-8*) Summy-Birchard.

Thirty-Five mm Planetary Cameras (Top Light) - Procedures for Determining Illumination Uniformity of Microfilming Engineering Drawings: ANSI-AIIM MS26-1990. Association for Information & Image Management Staff. 1990. pap. 33.00 (*0-89258-187-5*, MS26) Assn Inform & Image Mgmt.

Thirty-Five Oriental Philosophers. Diane Collinson & Robert Wilkinson. LC 93-26262. 216p. (C). 1994. 69.95 (*0-415-02596-6*, Routledge NY) Routledge.

Thirty-Five Papers on Statistics & Probability. G. A. Ambarcumjan et al. LC 61-9803. (Selected Translations in Mathematical Statistics & Probability Ser.: Vol. 4). 387p. 1963. 44.00 (*0-8218-1454-0*, STAPRO/4) Am Math.

35 Plus Diet for Women. Jean P. Spodnick. 1990. mass mkt. 5.99 (*0-671-73213-7*, PB Trade Paper) PB.

Thirty-Five Practical Ways to Improve Your Health: A Common Sense Approach for Wholesome Living. Reid E. Lassonde. LC 91-68336. (Illus.). 142p. (Orig.). 1992. pap. 9.95 (*0-9631846-7-9*) Real-Life Pubns.

Thirty-Five Receipts from "The Larder Invaded" William W. Weaver. 91p. (Orig.). 1986. pap. 8.95 (*0-914076-69-8*) Lib Co Phila.

Thirty-Five Scientific Communications from the All-Union Conference on Functional Analysis & Its Applications & Five Papers on Analysis. (Translations Ser.: Series 2, Vol. 16). 479p. 1960. 50.00 (*0-8218-1716-7*, TRANS2/16) Am Math.

Thirty-Five Simple Studies on the Book of Revelation. M. R. De Hann. 304p. 1988. pap. 17.99 (*0-310-23441-7*, 9500P) Zondervan.

Thirty-Five Sundays. Lyn Lifshin. (Offset Offshoot Ser.: No. 3). 56p. 1979. pap. 4.00 (*0-317-06439-8*) Ommation Pr.

35,000 Baby Names. Bruce Lansky. 272p. 1995. pap. 5.95 (*0-671-51975-1*) Meadowbrook.

35,000+ Baby Names. Bruce Lansky. LC 95-10295. 1995. pap. write for info. (*0-88166-216-X*) Meadowbrook.

Thirty-Five Thousand Tennessee Marriage Records & Bonds, 3 vols. Ed. by Silas E. Lucas, Jr. 1981. Set. 135.00 (*0-89308-226-0*); Vol. 1, (a-f), 604pp. write for info. (*0-89308-223-6*); Vol. 2, (g-n), 610pp. write for info. (*0-89308-224-4*); Vol. 3, (o-z), 580pp. write for info. (*0-89308-225-2*) Southern Hist Pr.

Thirty-Five Thousands Palabras. M. Villamizar et al. 1985. text ed. 8.96 (*0-07-067456-6*) McGraw.

***Thirty-Five Years at Crown Point Press: Making Prints, Doing Art.** Ruth Fine et al. (Illus.). 1997. pap. 29.95 (*0-520-21061-1*) U CA Pr.

Thirty-Five Years in Russia. George Hume. LC 79-115548. (Russia Observed Ser.). (Illus.). 1971. reprint ed. 23.95 (*0-405-03082-7*) Ayer.

Thirty-Five Years of Luther Research. Johann M. Reu. LC 79-13505. (Illus.). reprint ed. 36.50 (*0-404-05284-3*) AMS Pr.

Thirty-Five Years of Newspaper Work. Henry L. Mencken. LC 94-2077. 1994. 34.95 (*0-8018-4791-5*) Johns Hopkins.

Thirty-Five Years of Newspaper Work: A Memoir by H. L. Mencken. Henry L. Mencken. (Maryland Paperback Bookshelf Ser.). (Illus.). 416p. (C). 1996. reprint ed. pap. 16.95 (*0-8018-5380-X*) Johns Hopkins.

Thirty Florida Shipwrecks. William L. Trotter & Kevin M. McCarthy. LC 91-47020. (Illus.). 128p. 1992. pap. 17.95 (*1-56164-007-7*) Pineapple Pr.

34 Activities for Recruitment & Selection. Debbie Widdop & Dee Jones. 332p. 1996. ring bd. 169.95 (*0-566-07548-2*, Pub. by Gower UK) Ashgate Pub Co.

Thirty-Four Biographies of Canadian Composers. Canadian Broadcasting Corp. Staff. 1988. reprint ed. lib. bdg. 49.00 (*0-7812-0748-7*) Rprt Serv.

Thirty-Four Biographies of Canadian Composers. Canadian Broadcasting Corporation Staff. LC 75-166224. 1964. reprint ed. 39.00 (*0-403-01351-8*) Scholarly.

Thirty-Four Mountain Bike Routes, Northern Oregon Cascades. Don Lowe & Roberta Lowe. Ed. by Oral Bullard. (Illus.). 80p. (Orig.). 1991. pap. 9.95 (*0-911518-82-7*) Touchstone Oregon.

34 Useful, Inexpensive Electronic Projects That Help You Unlock Your Instrument's Potential: Do-it-Yourself Projects for Guitarists. Craig Anderton. (Illus.). 170p. 1995. pap. 19.95 (*0-87930-359-X*) Miller Freeman.

34th Annual Advanced Antitrust Seminar: Distribution & Marketing. (Corporate Law & Practice Course Handbook, 1985-86 Ser.). 816p. 1994. pap. 99.00 (*0-614-17178-4*, B4-7085) PLI.

Thirty-Fourth Annual Antitrust Law Institute. (Corporate Law & Practice Course Handbook, 1985-86 Ser.: Vols. 813 & 814). 1972p. 1993. 80.00 (*0-685-69723-1*, B4-7035) PLI.

Thirty-Fourth Battalion Virginia Cavalry. Scott C. Cole. (Virginia Regimental Histories Ser.). (Illus.). 183p. 1993. 19.95 (*0-685-74824-3*) H E Howard.

Thirty-Fourth Bombardment Group (H) Turner Publishing Company Staff. LC 88-50049. 128p. 1988. 48.00 (*0-938021-61-3*) Turner Pub KY.

Thirty-Fourth Infantry Division. Turner Publishing Company Staff. LC 88-51837. 88p. 1989. 48.00 (*0-938021-30-3*) Turner Pub KY.

Thirty-Fourth International Conference Proceedings. 800p. 1991. 35.00 (*1-55822-085-2*) Am Prod & Inventory.

Thirty-Fourth Stapp Car Crash Proceedings (P-236) 380p. 1991. pap. text ed. 39.00 (*1-56091-075-5*) Soc Auto Engineers.

Thirty-Fourth Street & Other Poems. Carlota Caulfield. Tr. by Chris Allen. LC 87-80166. (Poetry Ser.). 56p. (Orig.). (ENG & SPA.). 1987. pap. 5.00 (*0-932367-08-9*) Ed El Gato Tuerto.

Thirty-Fourth World's Fair Exposition Scrapbook. Clayton Cottrell. Ed. by Barry M. Nord. (Illus.). 55p. (Orig.). 1982. pap. 10.95 (*0-935656-06-5*, 101F) Nords Studio.

***30 Fresh Flower Displays.** Smithmark Staff. 1996. 6.98 (*0-7651-9769-3*) Smithmark.

Thirty Games for the Timex-Sinclair Computer. Bill L. Behrendt. 1983. write for info. (*0-318-57970-7*) P-H.

***30 Great Cities to Start Out In.** 1997. 17.95 (*0-02-861522-0*, Arco) Macmillan Gen Ref.

Thirty Happens. Herbert I. Kavet. 1991. pap. 5.95 (*0-88032-408-2*) Ivory Tower Pub.

***Thirty Herbal Gifts: Enchanting Gift Ideas with Fresh & Dried Herbs.** Smithmark Staff. (Thirty Projects Ser.). 1996. 6.98 (*0-7651-9454-6*) Smithmark.

30 Hit Season. D. Michael Tomkins. LC 94-68378. 1995. mass mkt. 5.99 (*0-89716-523-3*) P B Pubng.

Thirty International Short Stories: For ESL Students. Raja T. Nasr. LC 94-48843. 1995. pap. 16.50 (*0-8191-9864-1*) U Pr of Amer.

Thirty Keys to Success in Real Estate. Jack L. Gale. Ed. by Pat Allen. LC 81-10746. 88p. (Orig.). 1981. 11.00 (*0-913652-29-6*, 151) Realtors Natl.

30 Low-Fat Meals in 30 Minutes. Faye Levy. 208p. (Orig.). 1995. pap. 9.99 (*0-446-67059-6*) Warner Bks.

***30 Low-Fat Vegetarian Meals in 30 Minutes.** Faye Levy. 176p. (Orig.). 1997. pap. 11.99 (*0-446-67211-4*) Warner Bks.

Thirty Miles from J-Town. Amy Uyematsu. (Roerich Poetry Prize Winner Ser.). 107p. 1992. pap. 11.95 (*0-934257-92-2*) Story Line.

Thirty Million Texans? Leon F. Bouvier & Dudley L. Poston. LC 92-75793. (Illus.). 113p. (Orig.). 1993. pap. 9.95 (*1-881290-20-4*) Ctr Immigrat.

***30 Minute Kosher Cookbook.** Judy Zeidler. Date not set. write for info. (*0-688-15533-2*) Morrow.

Thirty-Minute Light Gourmet. Lulu Grace. LC 89-71365. (Illus.). 312p. 1990. 18.95 (*0-87833-617-6*) Taylor Pub.

Thirty Minute Meals. rev. ed. Susan D. Brown. 1991. pap. 12.95 (*1-55788-015-8*, HP Books) Berkley Pub.

Thirty Minute Menus. 1992. spiral bd. 6.99 (*0-517-05671-2*) Random Hse Value.

30-Minute Vegetarian Recipes. Better Homes & Gardens Editors. (Illus.). 96p. 1996. text ed. 12.95 (*0-696-20615-3*) Meredith Bks.

30-Minute Writer. Connie Emerson. 256p. 1996. pap. 14.99 (*0-89879-760-8*, Wrtrs Digest Bks) F & W Pubns Inc.

Thirty Minutes to Financial Freedom. 3rd ed. Adrian Day. 91p. 1989. 19.95 (*0-945332-15-7*) Agora Inc MD.

Thirty Modern Monologues. Roger Karshner. 4.95 (*0-573-60078-3*) French.

Thirty Modern Scenes. Roger Karshner. 4.95 (*0-573-60079-1*) French.

Thirty More Planes for the Paper Pilot. Peter Vollheim. 1988. pap. 8.95 (*0-671-65810-7*) PB.

Thirty Most Common Problems in Management & How to Solve Them. William A. Delaney. LC 81-69375. 192p. reprint ed. pap. 54.80 (*0-317-19939-0*, 2023569) Bks Demand.

***Thirty Myths about Lee's Surrender.** 5th rev. ed. Patrick A. Schroeder. (Illus.). 32p. (YA). (gr. 7 up). 1996. pap. 4.00 (*1-889246-05-0*) P A Schroeder.

30 Nail Designs. Susan Tumblety. (Cosmetology Ser.). 144p. 1996. text ed. 24.95 (*1-56253-268-5*) Milady Pub.

Thirty New Studies in Technics Opus 849/Etudes of Mecanisme. Carl Czerny. 56p. 1986. pap. 7.95 (*0-7935-5293-1*) H Leonard.

Thirty New Studies in Technique for Piano, Op. 849. Carl Czerny. (Carl Fischer Music Library: No. 487). 56p. (J). 1907. pap. 8.95 (*0-8258-0127-3*, L 487) Fischer Inc NY.

Thirty-Nine Av Melachoth of Shabbath. Barvch Chait. 1992. 22.50 (*0-87306-586-7*); 29.95 (*0-685-74443-4*) Feldheim.

Thirty-Nine Av Melachoth of Shabbath. deluxe ed. Barvch Chait. 1992. 37.50 (*0-685-59620-6*) Feldheim.

Thirty-Nine Blossoms. Elizabeth S. Lamb. 28p. 1982. pap. 2.00 (*0-913719-59-5*) High-Coo Pr.

Thirty-Nine Blows on a Gone Trumpet. Johnny Dolphin. 194p. 1985. pap. 5.95 (*0-907791-07-7*) Synerg AZ.

39 Dollar Man. William Gleason. 1976. pap. 3.00 (*0-87129-214-9*, T21) Dramatic Pub.

Thirty-Nine Easy Animal Biology Experiments. Robert W. Wood. (Science for Kids Ser.). (Illus.). 160p. (J). (gr. 3-8). 1991. pap. 9.95 (*0-8306-3594-7*) McGraw-Hill Prof.

Thirty-Nine Easy Animal Biology Experiments. Robert W. Wood. (Science for Kids Ser.). (Illus.). 160p. (J). (gr. 3-8). 1991. 9.70 (*0-8306-6594-3*, 3594) TAB Bks.

Thirty-Nine Easy Astronomy Experiments. Robert W. Wood. (Science for Kids Ser.). (Illus.). 160p. (J). 1991. pap. 9.95 (*0-8306-3597-1*) McGraw-Hill Prof.

Thirty-Nine Easy Astronomy Experiments. Robert W. Wood. (Science for Kids Ser.). (Illus.). 160p. (J). 1991. 16.95 (*0-8306-7597-3*, 3597) TAB Bks.

Thirty-Nine Easy Chemistry Experiments. Robert W. Wood. (Science for Kids Ser.). (Illus.). 160p. (J). 1991. pap. 9.95 (0-8306-3596-3) McGraw-Hill Prof.

Thirty-Nine Easy Chemistry Experiments. Robert W. Wood. (Science for Kids Ser.). (Illus.). 160p. (J). 1991. 16.95 (0-8306-7596-5, 3596) TAB Bks.

Thirty-Nine Easy Geography Activities. Robert W. Wood. (J). 1991. 16.95 (0-8306-2493-7); pap. 9.95 (0-8306-2492-9) McGraw-Hill Prof.

Thirty-Nine Easy Geology Experiments. Robert W. Wood. (Science for Kids Ser.). (Illus.). 160p. (J). (gr. 3-8). 1991. pap. 9.95 (0-8306-3598-X) McGraw-Hill Prof.

Thirty-Nine Easy Geology Experiments. Robert W. Wood. (Science for Kids Ser.). (Illus.). 160p. (J). (gr. 3-8). 1991. 16.95 (0-8306-6598-6, 3598) TAB Bks.

Thirty-Nine Easy Meteorology Experiments. Robert W. Wood. (Science for Kids Ser.). (Illus.). 160p. (J). (gr. 3-8). 1991. pap. 9.95 (0-8306-3595-5) McGraw-Hill Prof.

Thirty-Nine Easy Meteorology Experiments. Robert W. Wood. (Science for Kids Ser.). (Illus.). 160p. (J). (gr. 3-8). 1991. 16.95 (0-8306-6595-1, 3595) TAB Bks.

Thirty-Nine Easy Plant Biology Experiments. Robert W. Wood. (Science for Kids Ser.). 160p. (YA). 1991. 16.95 (0-8306-1941-0, 5003); pap. 9.95 (0-8306-1935-6) McGraw-Hill Prof.

Thirty-Nine Progressive Solos for Classical Guitar, Bk. 2. Ben Bolt. pap. 14.95 incl. audio (0-89524-688-0); pap. 17.95 incl. cd-rom (0-89524-742-9) Cherry Lane.

Thirty-Nine Progressive Solos for Classical Guitar, Bk. 1. Ben Bolt. pap. 14.95 incl. audio (0-89524-682-1); pap. 17.95 incl. cd-rom (0-89524-741-0) Cherry Lane.

Thirty-Nine Steps. (Fiction Ser.). (YA). 1993. pap. text ed. 7.50 (0-582-08467-9, 79834) Longman.

***Thirty-Nine Steps.** (Nelson Readers Ser.). (J). Date not set. pap. text ed. write for info. (0-17-557053-1) Addison-Wesley.

Thirty-Nine Steps. 1995. pap. 5.25 (0-19-421677-2) OUP.

***Thirty-Nine Steps.** Buchan. 1967. pap. text ed. write for info. (0-582-53752-5, Pub. by Longman UK) Longman.

Thirty-Nine Steps. John Buchan. LC 93-26287. (Pocket Classics Ser.). 1993. 7.00 (0-7509-0482-8, Pub. by Sutton Pubng UK) Bks Intl VA.

Thirty-Nine Steps. John Buchan. LC 93-9414. (World's Classics Ser.). 160p. 1994. 6.95 (0-19-282991-2) OUP.

Thirty-Nine Steps. John Buchan. 128p. 1991. pap. 6.95 (0-14-001130-7, Penguin Bks) Viking Penguin.

Thirty-Nine Steps. unabridged ed. John Buchan. 96p. 1994. pap. text ed. 1.00 (0-486-28201-5) Dover.

Thirty-Nine Steps. John Buchan. 1976. reprint ed. lib. bdg. 19.95 (0-89190-243-0, Rivercity Pr) Amereon Ltd.

Thirty-Nine Steps. John Buchan. 1990. reprint ed. lib. bdg. 21.95 (0-89968-487-4) Buccaneer Bks.

Thirty-Nine Steps. John Buchan. LC 89-46194. 160p. 1991. reprint ed. pap. 6.95 (0-87923-838-0) Godine.

39 Ways to Open Your Heart. Arlene G. Levine. (Illus.). 96p. 1996. 12.95 (0-943233-90-9) Conari Press.

Thirty-Nine Ways to Sell Your Car Fast! Timothy Johnson. LC 92-83935. (Illus.). 100p. (Orig.). 1993. pap. 8.95 (1-880782-49-9) Spirit Dance.

***Thirty-Ninth International Conference Proceedings: Harmonize Business Solutions & All That Jazz New Orleans.** 374p. (Orig.). 1996. pap. 35.00 (1-55822-127-1) Am Prod & Inventory.

Thirty-One Banana Leaves. Winifred K. Vass. (Illus.). 64p. 1994. pap. 8.95 (1-881576-39-6) Providence Hse.

31-Day Prayer Venture. Dennis Gorton. 36p. 1995. pap. 3.99 (0-87509-543-7) Chr Pubns.

Thirty-One Days of Blessings. Max Lucado. 32p. 1995. pap. 2.99 (0-8499-5127-5) Word Pub.

Thirty One Days of Praise: Enjoying God Anew. Ruth Myers. 160p. 1994. Spiral bdg. 9.99 (0-88070-634-1, Multnomah Bks) Multnomah Pubs.

Thirty-One Days of Praise: Prayer Journal Edition. Ruth Myers. 192p. 1996. 12.99 (0-88070-898-0, Multnomah Bks) Multnomah Pubs.

***31 Days of Prayer Journal.** Ruth Myers. LC 97-20963. 176p. 1997. 12.99 (1-57673-099-9, Multnomah Bks) Multnomah Pubs.

***31 Days to High Self-Esteem: How to Change Your Life So You Have Joy, Bliss, & Abundance.** Terry Bragg. (Illus.). 220p. (Orig.). 1997. pap. 19.95 (0-9654663-0-2) Peacemakers Trng.

***31 Days with the Master Fisherman: A Daily Devotional on Bringing Others to Christ.** R. Larry Moyer. LC 96-2940. 1997. pap. 5.99 (0-8254-3178-6) Kregel.

Thirty-One Financial Secrets. Paul D. Catchings. LC 85-50642. (Illus.). 274p. (C). 1985. 59.95 (0-9614410-1-1) WITT Pasadena.

Thirty One Hymns to the Star Goddess. Frater Achad. 1987. pap. 5.95 (0-916411-63-X, Sure Fire) Holmes Pub.

Thirty-One Invited Addresses (Eight in Abstract) at the International Congress of Mathematicians in Moscow 1966. M. A. Aizerman et al. (Translations Ser.: Series 2, Vol. 70). 266p. 1968. 49.00 (0-8218-1770-1, TRANS2/70) Am Math.

Thirty-One Kings: Or Victory over Self. A. B. Simpson. (Heritage Ser.). 26p. (Orig.). 1992. pap. 1.49 (0-87509-471-6) Chr Pubns.

Thirty-One New Atari Computer Programs for Home, School & Office. Alan North. (Illus.). 96p. (Orig.). 1982. pap. 8.95 (0-86668-018-7) ARCsoft.

Thirty-One Quick & Easy Meals. Donna C. Watson. 1987. 7.95 (0-939035-03-0) Watson Pub Hse.

***Thirty-One Sonnets.** Richard Eberhart. LC 67-14530. 1967. 20.00 (0-614-30640-X) Eakins.

Thirty One Ways to Spend a Romantic Evening: Put Romance Back in Your Relationship. David L. Timmons. LC 91-90511. (Illus.). 68p. (Orig.). 1991. pap. 9.95 (0-9630385-0-8) Snowy Owl.

31 Wedding Solos: Flute. 6.95 (0-7935-4065-8, 00849001) H Leonard.

31 Wedding Solos: Piano Accompaniment. 10.95 (0-7935-4066-6, 00849000) H Leonard.

31 Wedding Solos: Trumpet. 6.95 (0-7935-4062-3, 00849002) H Leonard.

***30 Origami Projects.** Smithmark Staff. 1996. 6.98 (0-7651-9770-7) Smithmark.

***30 Papercraft Creations.** Smithmark Staff. 1996. 6.98 (0-7651-9771-5) Smithmark.

***Thirty Papier Mache Projects: Fantastic Step-by-Step Creations from Papier-Mache.** Smithmark Staff. (Thirty Projects Ser.). 1996. 6.98 (0-7651-9455-4) Smithmark.

***30 Party Cakes.** Smithmark Staff. 1996. 6.98 (0-7651-9772-3) Smithmark.

Thirty Passages: Comprehension Practice for High Intermediate & Advanced Students. Donn Byrne, Jr. & Edwin T. Cornelius. (English As a Second Language Bk.). (Illus.). 1978. pap. text ed. 10.95 (0-582-79704-7, 74972) Longman.

Thirty Percent Solution: The Diet Doctor's Plan for Life Long Weight Control. Robert Stark. LC 90-80607. 112p. (Orig.). 1990. pap. 14.95 (0-9618415-5-9) AZ Bariatric Phy.

Thirty Pieces for Children Opus 27: Piano. D. Kabalevsky. 68p. 1986. per. 7.95 (0-7935-3627-8, 50331530) H Leonard.

***Thirty Pieces of Silver: A Kayla Montgomery Mystery.** Amy C. Laundrie. 156p. (Orig.). (YA). (gr. 6 up). 1996. pap. 6.99 (0-88092-364-4) Royal Fireworks.

Thirty Plants That Can Save Your Life. Douglas Schar. LC 92-38634. 134p. (Orig.). 1993. pap. 12.95 (1-880216-09-4, Elliott Clark) Black Belt Comm.

***Thirty Plays from Favorite Stories.** Ed. by Sylvia K. Burack. LC 97-1039. (Orig.). (J). 1997. pap. 15.95 (0-8238-0306-6) Plays.

Thirty Plus Games to Get Ready to Read: Teaching Kids at Home & in School. Toni S. Gould. 156p. (Orig.). 1994. pap. 12.95 (0-8027-7432-6) Walker & Co.

Thirty Poems. William C. Bryant. (Works of William Cullen Bryant). 1989. reprint ed. lib. bdg. 79.00 (0-7812-2131-5) Rprt Serv.

Thirty Poems from the Carmina Burana. P. G. Walsh. 148p. 1993. 16.95 (0-7049-0525-6, Pub. by Brstl Class Pr UK) Focus Pub-R Pullins.

Thirty Popular Tunes Easy Rec. 2. Ellen Cranitch. 8.75 (0-7866-1586-9, 95171WW) Mel Bay.

Thirty Pound Rails. Kelly Choda. LC 57-17961. (Wild & Woolly West Ser., No. 1). (Illus.). (Orig.). 1956. pap. 4.00 (0-910584-01-X) Filter.

Thirty Progressive Studies: For Two Soprano (or Tenor) Recorders or Oboes. Joseph F. Garnier. Ed. by Peter Hedrick & Elizabeth Hedrick. 1977. 5.00 (0-913334-37-5, CM1041) Consort Music.

Thirty Questions. Robert Whitelaw. pap. 1.49 (0-87377-115-X) GAM Pubns.

Thirty Reasons Not to Buy or Start a Business. 2nd ed. David Z. O'Brian. 201p. 1994. pap. 12.95 (1-881385-00-0) New Cent Pubns.

Thirty Scripts for Relaxation, Imagery & Inner Healing. Julie T. Lusk. 192p. (Orig.). 1992. pap. 19.95 (0-938586-69-6) Whole Person.

Thirty Scripts for Relaxation, Imagery & Inner Healing, Vol. 2. Julie T. Lusk. LC 92-80231. 192p. (Orig.). 1993. pap. 19.95 (0-938586-76-9) Whole Person.

Thirty-Second Annual Advanced Antitrust Seminar: Distribution, Marketing, & Joint Ventures. (Corporate Law & Practice Course Handbook, 1985-86 Ser.: Vol. 801). 810p. 1993. 70.00 (0-685-65502-4, B4-7025) PLI.

Thirty-Second Annual Denver X-ray Conference: Summer Meeting, Snowmass, CO. American Crystallographic Association Staff. (American Crystallographic Association Program & Abstracts Ser. 2: Vol. 11, No. 2). 72p. 1983. pap. 10.00 (0-317-03259-3) Polycrystal Bk Serv.

Thirty-Second Commute: Home-Based Small Business Strategies for the 90s. Don Terp & Carole Terp. LC 92-96990. (Small Business Strategies Book Ser.). 272p. (Orig.). 1992. pap. 19.95 (1-881070-01-8) Read Mtn Pr.

Thirty-Second International Conference Proceedings. (Orig.). 1989. pap. 35.00 (1-55822-021-6) Am Prod & Inventory.

Thirty-Second Politics: Political Advertising in the Eighties. Montague Kern. LC 88-34250. 249p. 1989. text ed. 45.00 (0-275-93194-3, C3194, Praeger Pubs); pap. text ed. 22.95 (0-275-93195-1, B3195, Praeger Pubs) Greenwood.

Thirty-Second SICE Annual Conference, 1993. IEEE (Industrial Electronics Society) Staff. 558p. 1993. pap. write for info. (0-7803-1403-4, 93TH0575-1); fiche write for info. (0-7803-1404-2) Inst Electrical.

Thirty-Second Virginia Infantry. Les Jensen. (Virginia Regimental Histories Ser.). (Illus.). 218p. 1990. 19.95 (1-56190-006-0) H E Howard.

Thirty Seconds over Tokyo. Ted W. Lawson. 290p. 1992. reprint ed. lib. bdg. 25.95 (0-89966-886-0) Buccaneer Bks.

Thirty Seconds with Your Bible: Learn How to Chart Your Horoscope, Predict Your Destiny, Luck, Fortune... Donatus O. Enyi. LC 86-70272. (Illus.). 80p. 1986. 9.95 (0-937171-00-X); pap. 6.95 (0-937171-01-8) D Enyi.

Thirty Secrets of Happily Married Couples. Paul Coleman. 240p. (Orig.). 1992. pap. 7.95 (1-55850-166-5) Adams Media.

30 "Secrets" to Saving Money on Your Auto Insurance. Chris A. Newbold. (Illus.). (Orig.). 1995. pap. text ed. 9.95 (0-9646190-0-8) Newbold Ins.

Thirty-Seven More Things Every Black Man Needs to Know. Errol Smith. 128p. (Orig.). 1994. pap. 10.00 (0-9625578-4-6); text ed. 17.00 (0-9625578-3-8) St Clair Rene Pub.

Thirty-Seven Papers Presented at the Twentieth Anniversary of the New York Botanical Garden. Ed. by M. A. Howe. (Memoirs Ser.: Vol. 6). 592p. 1915. pap. 10.00 (0-89327-025-3) NY Botanical.

***Thirty-Seven Practices of Bodhisattvas.** Geshe S. Rinchen. Tr. by Ruth Sonam from TIB. 110p. (Orig.). 1997. pap. 12.95 (1-55939-068-9) Snow Lion Pubns.

Thirty Seven Quick & Easy Tips You Can Use to Keep Your Customers. 1990. 12.50 (1-878604-03-1) Comn Pubns & Resources.

***Thirty-Seven Sermons & Twelve Poems by a Layman.** Floyd Barton. 208p. 1997. pap. 15.00 (0-8059-4084-7) Dorrance.

37 Super Hits of the Superstars. (Piano-Vocal-Guitar Ser.). 224p. 1991. otabind 14.95 (0-7935-1067-8, 00311539) H Leonard.

Thirty-Seven Things Every Black Man Needs to Know. Errol Smith. LC 91-176884. 136p. (Orig.). 1991. pap. text ed. 10.00 (0-9625578-1-1, 53) St Clair Rene Pub.

Thirty-Seven Timex-Sinclair 1000 ZX-81 Computer Programs for Home, School & Office. Edward Page. (Illus.). 96p. (Orig.). 1982. pap. 8.95 (0-86668-021-7) ARCsoft.

37 to One: Living As an Integrated Multiple. Phoenix J. Hocking. Ed. by Euan Bear. 76p. (Orig.). 1996. wbk. ed., pap. text ed. 12.00 (1-884444-22-9) Safer Soc.

Thirty Seven Violin Pieces You Like to Play with Piano Accompaniment. 184p. 1987. pap. 16.95 (0-7935-3851-3, 50327830) H Leonard.

37th Annual Antitrust Law Institute, 2 vols., Set. (Corporate Law & Practice Course Handbook, 1985-86 Ser.). Date not set. pap. 149.00 (0-614-17209-8, B4-7128) PLI.

37th Mandala. Marc Laidlaw. 384p. 1996. 23.95 (0-312-13021-X) St Martin.

Thirty-Seventh Stapp Car Crash Conference Proceedings. 294p. 1993. pap. 74.00 (1-56091-408-4, P-269) Soc Auto Engineers.

Thirty-Seventh Virginia Infantry. Thomas M. Rankin. (Virginia Regimental Histories Ser.). (Illus.). 150p. 1987. 19.95 (0-930919-44-0) H E Howard.

Thirty Seventh Western New York Exhibition. Albright-Knox Art Gallery Staff. LC 78-53046. (Illus.). 1978. 3.50 (0-914782-18-5) Buffalo Fine-Albrght-Knox.

***36 Activities of Developing Managerial Competencies.** Mike Woodcock & Dave Francis. 300p. 1997. 215.95 (0-566-07932-1, Pub. by Gower UK) Ashgate Pub Co.

Thirty-Six Best Christmas Party Ideas. Marty Sprague. 1994. pap. 12.95 (1-56530-142-0) Summit TX.

Thirty Six Biggest Mistakes Salesmen Make & How to Correct Them. George N. Kahn. 1986. 9.95 (0-13-918979-3) P-H.

Thirty-Six Biggest Mistakes Salesmen Make & How to Correct Them. George N. Kahn. 224p. 1988. 7.95 (0-13-918939-4) P-H.

Thirty Six Billion Dollar Bargain. A. F. Organski. 315p. 1991. pap. text ed. 17.00 (0-231-07197-3) Col U Pr.

Thirty-Six Billion Dollar Bargain: Strategy & Politics in U. S. Assistance to Israel. A. F. Organski. 1990. text ed. 49.50 (0-231-07196-5) Col U Pr.

Thirty-Six Caprices or Etudes for Violin. F. Fiorillo. Ed. by Edmund Singer. (Carl Fischer Music Library: No. 582). 1964. pap. 7.50 (0-8258-0075-7, L582) Fischer Inc NY.

Thirty-Six Cats of Marie Tatin. Sylvie Chausse. (Illus.). (J). (gr. 2). 1996. pap. 5.95 (0-382-39283-3, Silver Pr NJ) Silver Burdett Pr.

Thirty-Six Cats of Marie Tatin. Sylvie Chausse. (Illus.). 32p. (J). 1996. lib. bdg. 13.95 (0-382-39282-5, Silver Pr NJ) Silver Burdett Pr.

Thirty-Six Children. Herbert R. Kohl. 1988. pap. 7.95 (0-452-26155-4, Plume); pap. 10.95 (0-452-26463-4, Plume) NAL-Dutton.

Thirty-Six Complete Church Dinner Programs: Menus, Recipes, Decorations, Biblical Themes, Seasonal Celebrations, Special Occasions. Adell Harvey & Mari Gonzalez. 176p. (Orig.). 1992. pap. 6.48 (0-687-41885-2) Abingdon.

Thirty-Six Dramatic Situations. Georges Polti. LC 77-8343. 1988. pap. 8.95 (0-87116-109-5) Writer.

Thirty-Six Eight Measure Vocalises: Opus 93 for Mezzo-Soprano. F. Sieber. 20p. 1986. pap. 4.95 (0-7935-5347-4) H Leonard.

Thirty-Six Elementary & Progressive Studies: Complete Violin Opus 20. H. E. Kayser. 52p. 1986. pap. 5.95 (0-7935-5434-9) H Leonard.

36 Exposures. Kevin Major. 160p. 1994. pap. 10.95 (0-385-25464-4) Doubleday.

Thirty-Six Hour Day. Nancy L. Mace & Peter V. Rabins. (C). 1989. 45.00 (0-340-37012-2, Pub. by Age Concern Eng UK) St Mut.

Thirty-Six Hour Day: A Family Guide to Caring for Persons with Alzheimer's Disease, Related Dementing Illnesses & Memory Loss in Later Life. rev. ed. Nancy L. Mace & Peter V. Rabins. LC 90-49523. 352p. (Orig.). 1991. pap. 11.95 (0-8018-4034-1) Johns Hopkins.

Thirty-Six Hour Day: A Family Guide to Caring for Persons with Alzheimer's Disease, Related Dementing Illnesses & Memory Loss in Later Life. rev. ed. Nancy L. Mace & Peter V. Rabins. 448p. (Orig.). 1992. reprint ed. mass mkt. 6.50 (0-446-36104-6) Warner Bks.

Thirty-Six Hour Day: A Family Guide to Caring for Persons with Alzheimer's Disease, Related Dementing Illnesses & Memory Loss in Later Life. 2nd rev. ed. Nancy L. Mace & Peter V. Rabins. LC 90-49523. 352p. (Orig.). 1991. text ed. 38.95 (0-8018-4033-3) Johns Hopkins.

Thirty-Six Hours of Hell. E. N. Coons. 160p. 1988. 12.95 (0-685-29173-1) E N Coons.

***36 Hours of Hell.** 2nd ed. E. N. Coons. (Illus.). 162p. 1988. reprint ed. 14.00 (0-9624037-0-9) E N Coons.

Thirty-Six Hours to Live: The Diary of a Teenage Suicide. Craig Franklin & Gary Hutchison. 150p. (YA). (gr. 8 up). 1994. pap. 20.00 (1-885631-04-9) G F Hutchison.

Thirty-Six Immortal Women Poets. Andrew J. Pekarik. (Illus.). 192p. 1991. 45.00 (0-8076-1256-1); pap. 24.95 (0-8076-1257-X) Braziller.

Thirty-Six Programs for Unit Study & Workshop Leaders: Compiled from NAP Training Guides. National Association of Parliamentarians Staff. 198p. (Orig.). 1995. pap. 25.00 (1-884048-12-9) Natl Assn Parliamentarians.

Thirty-Six Small Business Mistakes & How to Avoid Them. Mark Stevens. 1986. 7.95 (0-13-918920-3, Reward) P-H.

Thirty-Six Strange Little Animals Waiting to Eat: With Simple Little Recipes to Make. Roz Denny. LC 92-358. (Illus.). 32p. (J). 1992. 6.50 (1-55670-272-8) Stewart Tabori & Chang.

Thirty-Six Texas Instruments T1 99-4A Programs for Home, School & Office. Len Turner. 96p. 1983. 8.95 (0-86668-024-1) ARCsoft.

Thirty-Six Thousand Dollars a Year in Your Own Home Merchandising Business. Barry Z. Masser. (Illus.). 1978. 14.95 (0-13-918987-4, Parker Publishing Co) P-H.

Thirty-Six Top Hits: Easy Guitar. 112p. 1988. pap. 9.95 (0-7935-3239-6, 00699776) H Leonard.

36 Views of Mount Fuji: On Finding Myself in Japan. Cathy N. Davidson. 320p. 1994. pap. 11.95 (0-452-27240-8, Plume) NAL-Dutton.

Thirty-Six Years of All-Star Rookies. Merritt Clifton. 64p. 1994. pap. text ed. 8.00 (0-614-01212-0) Samisdat.

Thirty-SixE Dessous. Pierre Daninos. (FRE.). 1990. pap. 10.95 (0-7859-3054-X, 2253000973) Fr & Eur.

Thirty-Sixth & Thirty-Seventh Battalion Virginia Cavalry. J. L. Scott. (Virginia Regimental Histories Ser.). (Illus.). 104p. 1986. 19.95 (0-930919-25-4) H E Howard.

36th Annual Antitrust Law Institute, 2 vols., Set. (Corporate Law & Practice Course Handbook, 1985-86 Ser.). 2004p. 1994. pap. 149.00 (0-614-17184-9, B4-7098) PLI.

36th Infantry. Turner Publishing Company Staff. LC 95-60493. 360p. 1995. 48.00 (1-56311-201-9) Turner Pub KY.

Thirty-Sixth International Conference Proceedings. 768p. 1993. 35.00 (1-55822-104-2) Am Prod & Inventory.

Thirty-Sixth Stapp Car Crash Conference Proceedings: Twenty-Six Papers. 288p. 1992. 39.00 (1-56091-292-8, P-261) Soc Auto Engineers.

Thirty-Sixth Virginia Infantry. J. L. Scott. (Virginia Regimental Histories Ser.). (Illus.). 116p. 1987. 19.95 (0-930919-36-X) H E Howard.

Thirty, Sixty, Hundredfold: The Laws of the Financial Harvest. John F. Avanzini. 192p. (Orig.). 1989. pap. 8.99 (0-89274-596-7) Harrison Hse.

Thirty Songs, for High Voice. Franz Liszt. Ed. by Carl Armbruster. 1979. 11.75 (0-8446-5502-3) Peter Smith.

Thirty Songs for High Voice. Franz Liszt. Ed. by Carl Armbruster. LC 75-17172. 160p. 1975. reprint ed. pap. 7.95 (0-486-23197-6) Dover.

Thirty Sons, Thirty Donkeys, Thirty Towns: Is this Any Way to Run a Church. Jerald Johnson. 88p. 1992. pap. 5.99 (0-8341-1416-X) Beacon Hill.

Thirty Spirituals: Voice Piano. 84p. 1986. pap. 9.95 (0-7935-4803-9, 50328310) H Leonard.

30 Steps to Becoming a Writer & Getting Published. Scott Edelstein. 176p. 1993. 16.99 (0-89879-545-1, Wrtrs Digest Bks) F & W Pubns Inc.

Thirty Strange Stories. H. G. Wells. LC 72-103531. (Short Story Index Reprint Ser.). 1977. 30.95 (0-8369-3274-9) Ayer.

***Thirty Strange Stories.** H. G. Wells. 416p. 1998. pap. 12.95 (0-7867-0488-8) Carroll & Graf.

***30 Strategies for High Profit Investment Success.** Donald L. Cassidy. 270p. (Orig.). 1998. pap. 18.95 (0-7931-2680-0, 5680-5901) Dearborn Finan.

Thirty Tales & Sketches. Robert B. Graham. LC 76-125213. (Short Story Index Reprint Ser.). 1977. reprint ed. 23.95 (0-8369-3580-2) Ayer.

***30-Tegn Fra Doves Tegnsprog.** Elisabeth Engberg-Pedersen & Annegrethe Pedersen. (DAN.). write for info. (87-981812-4-6, DAC) Ctr Sutton Movement.

Thirty-Third & Last Degree: Masonry or Politics? J. D. Buck. 1992. pap. 7.00 (1-56459-208-1) Kessinger Pub.

Thirty-Third Annual Meeting of the European Society for Paediatric Endocrinology (ESPE), Maastricht, June 1994, Abstracts: Hormone Research. Ed. by J. L. Van Den Brande & M. Jansen. (Journal: Vol. 41, No. 2-4, 1994). viii, 104p. 1994. pap. 68.75 (3-8055-6011-7) S Karger.

Thirty-Third Biennial Exhibition of Art, Venice, 1966. American Federation of Arts Staff. (Illus.). 1966. 5.00 (0-8079-0123-7); pap. 2.00 (0-8079-0124-5) October.

Thirty-Third International Conference Proceedings. (Illus.). 713p. 1990. pap. 35.00 (1-55822-027-5) Am Prod & Inventory.

Thirty-Third Virginia Infantry. Lowell Reidenbaugh. (Virginia Regimental Histories Ser.). (Illus.). 151p. 1987. 19.95 (0-930919-37-8) H E Howard.

Thirty-Thirty Three. Ed. by Francine Ringold. 146p. 1987. pap. 5.50 (0-318-32887-9) Art & Human Council Tulsa.

Thirty Thousand Bequest. Mark Twain, pseud. (Works of Mark Twain). 1988. reprint ed. lib. bdg. 59.00 (0-7812-1129-8) Rprt Serv.

***$30,000 Bequest & Other Stories (1906)** Shelley F. Fishkin. (Oxford Mark Twain). 624p. 1997. lib. bdg. 30.00 (0-19-511423-X) OUP.

$30,000 Solution. Robert R. Schutz. 160p. (Orig.). 1996. pap. 12.95 (1-56474-150-8) Fithian Pr.

Thirty Thousand Gods Before Jehovah. H. H. Stein. 1991. lib. bdg. 79.95 (0-8490-4552-5) Gordon Pr.

An Asterisk (*) at the beginning of an entry indicates that the title is appearing in BIP for the first time.

Thirty Thousand Gods Before Jehovah. Henry B. Stein. 50p. 1959. reprint ed. spiral bd. 9.00 (0-7873-1125-1) Hlth Research.

Thirty Thousand on the Hoof. Zane Grey. 288p. 1990. mass mkt. 3.99 (0-06-100085-X, Harp PBks) HarpC.

30,638 Burials in Georgia. Jeannette H. Austin. 708p. 1995. 50.00 (0-8063-1454-0) Genealog Pub.

Thirty-Three. Marjorie Fletcher. LC 75-32642. 72p. 1976. pap. 3.95 (0-914086-12-X) Alicejamesbooks.

Thirty-Three & Mortgage Free. Maureen Jones-Ryan. 71p. 1978. pap. 11.95 (0-87073-919-0) Schenkman Bks Inc.

Thirty-Three by Arthur Conan Doyle. Arthur Conan Doyle. 1986. 6.98 (0-685-16821-2, 625431) Random Hse Value.

Thirty-Three Chronological Events Connected with the Life of the Lord Jesus Christ. (Walk with Jesus Ser.). 36p. 1992. pap. 5.00 (1-57277-406-1) Script Rsch.

33 Days Hath September: A Travel Adventure Cookbook on Alaska's Yukon River. Lisa A. Valore. (Illus.). 100p. 1992. pap. 9.95 (0-940055-74-0) Vanessapress.

Thirty-Three Fingers: A Collection of Modern American Koans. Michael Wenger. LC 94-71376. (Illus.). 63p. (Orig.). 1994. pap. 10.00 (0-931425-35-2) Clear Glass.

Thirty-Three Fun & Easy Weekend Electronics Project. Andres Guzman. LC 87-13883. (Illus.). 140p. 1987. 14.95 (0-8306-0261-5, 2861); pap. 8.95 (0-8306-2861-4) McGraw-Hill Prof.

33 Major Doctrinal Errors Found in Churches Today: Layman's Reference Guide. Fred Kerr. 1995. write for info. (0-9649862-0-5) Life Call.

Thirty-Three Major Gospels of the Lord God of Israel. (Walk with Jesus Ser.). 72p. 1987. pap. 10.00 (1-57277-601-3) Script Rsch.

33 Model Memos for Tough Situations. Prentice Hall Editorial Staff. 1995. pap. text ed. 5.95 (0-13-461914-5) P-H.

Thirty-Three Multicultural Tales to Tell. Illus. by Joe Shlichta. LC 93-1824. 126p. 1993. 25.00 (0-87483-265-9); pap. 15.00 (0-87483-266-7) August Hse.

Thirty-Three Profitable Part-Time Businesses. Income Opportunities Editors. LC 92-20295. 1992. pap. text ed. 12.95 (0-13-919044-9) P-H.

***33 Short Stories.** Wilhelm Dittrich. 134p. 1963. 9.80 (3-296-50800-7, Pub. by Weidmann GW) Lubrecht & Cramer.

***33 Simple Weekend Projects for the Ham, the Student, & the Experimenter.** Dave Ingram. LC 97-67120. (Illus.). 156p. (Orig.). 1997. mass mkt. 15.95 (0-943016-17-7) CQ Commns Inc.

Thirty-three Sonnets of Guido Cavalcanti. limited ed. Guido Cavalcanti. Tr. by Ezra Pound. (Illus.). 1991. 650.00 (0-685-56699-4) Arion Pr.

***33 Things Every Girl Should Know.** Tonya Bolden. 1997. 18.00 (0-517-70936-8, Crown) Crown Pub Group.

Thirty-Three Ways to Ease Work - Family Tensions: An Employer's Checklist. (National Report on Work & Family Ser.: Special Report No. 2). 32p. 1988. 35.00 (0-87179-958-8) BNA Plus.

Thirty-Three Years among the Indians: The Story of Mary Sagatoo. Mary Sagatoo. Ed. & Intro. by Donna Winters. (Bigwater Classics Ser.). 224p. 1994. pap. 9.95 (0-923048-50-2) Bigwater Pub.

Thirty to One: A Practical Guide to Personal Holiness & Mission. Phil Stevenson. (Illus.). 80p. 1990. pap. 6.95 (0-89827-078-2, HA283) Wesleyan Pub Hse.

Thirty Top Hits: Alto Saxophone. 40p. 1993. pap. 4.95 (0-7935-2132-7, 00847214) H Leonard.

Thirty Top Hits: Clarinet. 40p. 1993. pap. 4.95 (0-7935-2131-9, 00847216) H Leonard.

Thirty Top Hits: Flute. 40p. 1993. pap. 4.95 (0-7935-2130-0, 00847215) H Leonard.

Thirty Top Hits: Trombone. 40p. 1993. pap. 4.95 (0-7935-2134-3, 00847212) H Leonard.

Thirty Top Hits: Trumpet. 40p. 1993. pap. 4.95 (0-7935-2133-5, 00847213) H Leonard.

***32 Activities on Coaching & Mentoring.** Mike Whittaker & Ann Cartwright. 300p. 1997. ring bd. 215.95 (0-566-07757-4, Pub. by Gower UK) Ashgate Pub Co.

Thirty-Two Basic Steps into Hindi Vocubulary: A Vocabulary Workbook. Harinder J. Dhillon. (Illus.). 143p. (Orig.). (HIN.). 1986. 15.00 (0-9617188-0-3); audio 14.95 (0-685-14680-4) H J Dhillon.

Thirty Two Basic Steps into Panjabi Vocubulary: A Vocabulary Workbook. Harinder J. Dhillon. (Illus.). 143p. (Orig.). (PAN.). 1986. Gurmukhi Script. pap. 15.00 (0-9617188-1-1); audio 14.95 (0-317-54405-5) H J Dhillon.

Thirty-Two Basic Steps into Panjabi Vocubulary: A Vocabulary Workbook. Harinder J. Dhillon. (Illus.). 143p. (Orig.). (PAN.). 1986. Persian script. pap. 15.00 (0-9617188-2-X); audio 14.95 (0-685-37382-7) H J Dhillon.

Thirty Two Basic Steps into Urdu Vocubulary: A Vocabulary Workbook. Harinder J. Dhillon. (Illus.). 143p. (Orig.). (URD.). 1986. pap. 15.00 (0-9617188-3-8); audio 14.95 (0-317-54404-7) H J Dhillon.

***32 Bible Learning Activities for Kids.** Connie Hodges. 32p. (J). (gr. 2-4). 3.99 (0-570-04022-1, 61-1021) Concordia.

Thirty-Two-Bit Architecture & OS-2 Applications. (Illus.). 30p. (Orig.). (C). 1993. pap. text ed. 20.00 (1-56806-409-8) DIANE Pub.

32 Bit Microprocessor, Vol. 17. Lab-Volt Systems, Inc. Staff. (F.A.C.E.T. Ser.). (Illus.). 496p. (Orig.). (C). 1995. student ed., pap. text ed. write for info. (0-86657-079-9, TM90876-00) Lab-Volt.

32 Bit Microprocessor, Vol. 17. Lab-Volt Systems, Inc. Staff. (F.A.C.E.T. Ser.). (Illus.). 165p. (Orig.). (C). 1995. teacher ed., pap. text ed. write for info. (0-86657-089-6, TM90876-10) Lab-Volt.

32-Bit Microprocessors. 2nd ed. Mitchell. 1991. 66.00 (0-8493-7713-7) CRC Pr.

Thirty-Two-Bit Microprocessors: A Primer Plus. Stephen J. Menconi. (AT&T Advanced Technology Ser.: Vol. 1). (Illus.). 568p. (C). 1988. text ed. 24.95 (0-932764-10-X, 311-027) AT&T Customer Info.

32-Bit Operating Systems: Upgrading the Desktop. Computer Technology Research Corp. Staff. LC 95-2241. (Illus.). 170p. (Orig.). 1995. pap. 275.00 (1-56607-043-0) Comput Tech Res.

***32-Bit Processors Reach High-Volume Price Points.** Jim Turley. 61p. 1996. spiral bd. 295.00 (1-885330-08-1) MicroDes Res.

32 Cadillacs. Joe Gores. 352p. 1992. 18.95 (0-89296-298-4) Mysterious Pr.

32 Cadillacs. Joe Gores. 352p. 1993. mass mkt. 5.50 (0-446-40360-1, Mysterious Paperbk) Warner Bks.

Thirty Two Canons for Keyboard Instruments. Robert Donahue. 1975. pap. 5.95 (0-934286-57-4) Kenyon.

Thirty-Two Cantigas d'Amigo of Dom Diniz: Typology of a Portuguese Renunciation. Rip Cohen. (Portuguese Ser.: No. 1). 1987. 12.50 (0-942260-55-4) Hispanic Seminary.

Thirty-Two Days to a Thirty-Two Inch Waist. Ellington Darden. LC 89-71364. (Illus.). 152p. 1990. pap. 8.95 (0-685-35024-X) Easi-Bild.

Thirty-Two Days to a Thirty-Two Inch Waist. Ellington Darden. LC 89-71364. 160p. 1990. pap. 8.95 (0-87833-710-5) Taylor Pub.

Thirty-Two Earth Worlds Speak to Planet Earth. Ruth E. Norman. (Tesla Speaks Ser.: Vol. 4, Pt. 1). (Illus.). 621p. 1974. Part 1. 17.00 (0-932642-23-3) Unarius Acad Sci.

Thirty-Two Earth Worlds Speak to Planet Earth. Ruth E. Norman. (Tesla Speaks Ser.: Vol. 4, Pt. 3). (Illus.). 410p. 1974. Part 3. 17.00 (0-932642-25-X) Unarius Acad Sci.

32 Easy Piano Great Hits of Today. 176p. 1992. otabind 12.95 (0-7935-1091-0, 00222539) H Leonard.

32 Errors & How to Avoid Them. Beason. 1996. pap. text ed. 15.00 (0-312-13359-6) St Martin.

Thirty-Two Gun Frigate Essex: Building A Plank-On-Frame Model. Portia Takakjian. (Illus.). 80p. (Orig.). 1985. 9.95 (0-9615021-0-X) Phoen Pubns.

Thirty Two Million Judges: Analysis of 1977 Lok Sabha & State Elections in India. G. G. Mirchandani. 1977. 12.00 (0-8364-0052-6) S Asia.

Thirty-Two Papers on Statistics & Probability. M. Arato & A. G. Kusnirenko. LC 61-9803. (Selected Translations in Mathematical Statistics & Probability Ser.: Vol. 10). 314p. 1972. 50.00 (0-8218-1460-5, STAPRO/10) Am Math.

Thirty-Two Piano Sonatas of Ludvig Van Beethoven, 2 Vols. Ed. by Arthur Schnabel. 1983. pap. write for info. (0-318-57258-3) S&S Trade.

Thirty-Two Picture Postcards of Old Philadelphia. Ed. by Robert F. Looney. (Postcard Ser.). (Illus.). (Orig.). 1977. pap. 3.95 (0-486-23421-5) Dover.

Thirty-Two Short Views of Mazo De La Roche. Daniel Bratton. 200p. 1996. pap. text ed. 9.95 (1-55022-274-0, Pub. by ECW Pr CN) LPC InBook.

Thirty-Two Sonatas for the Pianoforte, 2 Vols. Ludwig van Beethoven. Ed. by Arthur Schnabel. 1935. Set. pap. 15.00 (0-686-66528-7, Fireside) S&S Trade.

Thirty-Two Sonatas for the Pianoforte, 2 Vols, 1. Ludwig van Beethoven. Ed. by Arthur Schnabel. 1935. pap. 7.50 (0-685-73425-0, 07100, Fireside) S&S Trade.

Thirty-Two Sonatas for the Pianoforte, 2 Vols, 2. Ludwig van Beethoven. Ed. by Arthur Schnabel. 1935. pap. 7.50 (0-685-73426-9, 07110, Fireside) S&S Trade.

Thirty-Two Votes Before Breakfast. 350p. 1974. 20.00 (0-07-062299-X) McGraw.

***32 Ways to Be a Great Sunday School Teacher.** Delia Halverson. 1997. pap. text ed. 14.95 (0-687-01787-4) Abingdon.

Thirty Velocity Studies for Trumpet. Claude Gordon. (FRE, GER & SPA.). 1981. pap. 6.95 (0-8258-0213-X, 05092) Fischer Inc NY.

Thirty Vital Years: The Positive Experience of Ageing. Francis Macnab. LC 93-40291. 306p. 1994. pap. text ed. 50.00 (0-471-94333-9) Wiley.

Thirty Walks in New Jersey. enl. rev. ed. Kevin Dann & Gordon Miller. LC 91-38199. (Illus.). 240p. (C). 1992. pap. 14.95 (0-8135-1812-1); text ed. 25.00 (0-8135-1811-3) Rutgers U Pr.

Thirty Ways to Make Money in Franchising. J. Johnson. (C). 1989. text ed. 40.00 (0-948032-48-0, Pub. by Rosters Ltd) St Mut.

Thirty Ways to Make Money in Property. J. Johnson & G. Gill. (C). 1989. text ed. 40.00 (0-948032-43-X, Pub. by Rosters Ltd) St Mut.

Thirty Ways to Make Money in Teaching. H. Holyoak. (C). 1989. text ed. 40.00 (0-948032-98-7, Pub. by Rosters Ltd) St Mut.

Thirty Ways to Make Money in Writing. H. Hawthorne. (C). 1989. text ed. 40.00 (0-948032-53-7, Pub. by Rosters Ltd) St Mut.

Thirty Wild & Wonderful Math Stories to Develop Problem-Solving Skills. Dan Greenberg. 1992. pap. text ed. 15.95 (0-590-49169-5) Scholastic Inc.

Thirty Wooden Boats. WoodenBoat Magazine Editors. 1987. pap. 8.95 (0-07-155821-7) McGraw.

Thirty Wooden Boats: A Second Catalog of Building Plans. WoodenBoat Magazine Editors. (Illus.). 80p. 1988. pap. 12.95 (0-937822-15-9) WoodenBoat Pubns.

Thirty Word My First Series, 6 bks. Julia Allen. (Illus.). (J). (gr. k-3). 1987. Set. 59.70 (0-89868-236-3); Set. pap. 27.30 (0-89868-237-1) ARO Pub.

***30 Wreath & Garland Projects.** Smithmark Staff. 1996. 6.98 (0-7651-9773-1) Smithmark.

Thirty-Year History of Programs Carried on National Radio Networks in the United States, 1926-1956. Ed. by Harrison B. Summers. LC 78-161155. (History of Broadcasting: Radio to Television Ser.). 1980. reprint ed. 26.95 (0-405-03572-1) Ayer.

***Thirty Years: Tweed Museum of Art.** Steven Klindt. (Illus.). 72p. (Orig.). 1988. pap. 10.00 (1-889523-05-4) Tweed Mus.

Thirty Years a Detective: A Thorough & Comprehensive Expose of Criminal Practices of All Grades & Classes. Allan Pinkerton. (Criminology, Law Enforcement, & Social Problems Ser.: No. 154). (Illus.). 1975. reprint ed. Witn Intro. Essay & Index Added. 28.00 (0-87585-154-1) Patterson Smith.

Thirty Years a Slave. Louis Hughes. LC 79-89404. (Black Heritage Library Collection). 1977. 24.95 (0-8369-8607-5) Ayer.

Thirty Years a Slave: From Bondage to Freedom. Louis Hughes. LC 75-92431. 1896. 14.00 (0-403-00164-1) Scholarly.

30 Years a Watch Tower Slave. William J. Schnell. (Direction Bks.). 1971. mass mkt. 5.99 (0-8010-7933-0) Baker Bks.

Thirty Years After: An Artist's Memoir of the Civil War. Illus. by Edwin Forbes. LC 93-11083. xxx, 344p. 1993. 65.00 (0-8071-1877-X) La State U Pr.

Thirty Years after Brown. Jennifer L. Hochschild. LC 84-29739. 55p. (Orig.). 1985. pap. 13.50 (0-941410-49-8) Jt Ctr Pol Studies.

***Thirty Years after Sharkovskii's Theorem: New Perspectives.** 188p. 1996. 22.00 (981-02-2504-0) World Scientific Pub.

Thirty Years after the War. S. J. Leonard. LC 92-61970. 104p. (Orig.). 1994. pap. 9.00 (1-56002-217-5, Univ Edtns) Aegina Pr.

Thirty Years Ago: Or, the Memoirs of a Water-Drinker. William Dunlap. (Notable American Authors Ser.). 1992. reprint ed. lib. bdg. 75.00 (0-7812-2721-6) Rprt Serv.

Thirty Years Ago: 1849-1879: Gold Rush Memories of a Daguerreotype Artist. George D. Dornin. Ed. & Intro. by Peter Palmquist. LC 95-78477. (Illus.). 64p. 1995. pap. 14.95 (1-887694-00-5) C Mautz Pubng.

Thirty Years among the Dead. Carl A. Wickland. 466p. 1963. reprint ed. spiral bd. 14.00 (0-7873-0965-6) Hlth Research.

Thirty Years & Still Training for Safety: Proceedings of the 30th Annual Meeting Corporate Aviation Safety Seminar, April 14-16 ,1985, AMFAC Hotel & Resort, Dallas - Fort Worth International Airport. Corporate Aviation Safety Seminar Staff. 224p. reprint ed. pap. 63.90 (0-317-42279-0, 2025797) Bks Demand.

Thirty Years at Sea. Edward Shippen. Ed. by Richard H. Kohn. LC 78-22396. (American Military Experience Ser.). 1980. reprint ed. lib. bdg. 28.95 (0-405-11872-4) Ayer.

Thirty Years at the Mansion. Intro. by Liza Ashley & Bill Clinton. LC 84-73313. (Illus.). 176p. 1985. 24.95 (0-935304-88-6) August Hse.

Thirty Years' Battle with Crime: Or, the Crying Shame of New York, As Seen under the Broad Glare of an Old Detective's Lantern. John H. Warren, Jr. LC 73-112582. (Rise of Urban America Ser.). (Illus.). 1974. reprint ed. 28.95 (0-405-02484-3) Ayer.

Thirty Years CINP. Ed. by T. A. Ban & H. Hippius. (Illus.). xviii, 138p. 1988. 34.00 (0-387-50117-7) Spr-Verlag.

***Thirty Years in a Red House: A Memoir of Childhood & Youth in Communist China.** Zhu X. Di. LC 97-15886. (Illus.). 320p. 1998. 34.95 (1-55849-112-0) U of Mass Pr.

Thirty Years in Australia. Ada Cambridge. 251p. 1989. pap. 19.95 (0-86840-020-3, Pub. by New South Wales Univ Pr AT) Intl Spec Bk.

***Thirty Years in Central Banking.** Erik Hoffmeyer. (Occasional Papers: Vol. 48). 42p. (Orig.). 1994. pap. 10.00 (1-56708-044-8) Grp of Thirty.

Thirty Years in Hell: From Darkness to Light. Bernard Fresenborg. 126p. 1961. reprint ed. spiral bd. 10.00 (0-7873-0336-4) Hlth Research.

Thirty Years in Hell: Or, the Confessions of a Drug Fiend. D. F. Macmartin. Ed. by Gerald N. Grob. LC 80-1256. (Addiction in America Ser.). 1981. reprint ed. lib. bdg. 27.95 (0-405-13606-4) Ayer.

Thirty Years in the Arctic Regions. John Franklin. LC 88-14329. 494p. 1988. reprint ed. pap. 140.80 (0-7837-8864-9, 2049575) Bks Demand.

Thirty Years Later: The Shore Line. Ed. by Norman Carlson. LC 85-72307. (NS-300 Ser.). (Illus.). 32p. (Orig.). 1985. pap. 6.00 (0-915348-00-4, NS-300) Central Electric.

Thirty Years' Musical Recollections, 2 vols. Henry F. Chorley. LC 83-7558. (Music Reprint Ser.). 1983. reprint ed. Set. lib. bdg. 65.00 (0-306-76216-1) Da Capo.

Thirty Years' Musical Recollections, 2 vols., Vol. I. Henry F. Chorley. 312p. 1983. reprint ed. lib. bdg. write for info. (0-318-56917-5) Da Capo.

Thirty Years' Musical Recollections, 2 vols., Vol. II. Henry F. Chorley. 323p. 1983. reprint ed. lib. bdg. write for info. (0-318-56918-3) Da Capo.

Thirty Years of American Zionism, Vol.1. Louis Lipsky. Ed. by Moshe Davis. LC 77-70718. (America & the Holy Land Ser.). 1977. reprint ed. lib. bdg. 29.95 (0-405-10263-1) Ayer.

Thirty Years of Army Life on the Border. Comprising Descriptions of the Indian Nomads of the Plains, Explorations... Randolph B. March. (American Biography Ser.). 442p. 1991. reprint ed. lib. bdg. 89.00 (0-7812-8265-9) Rprt Serv.

Thirty Years of Buddhist Studies: Selected Essays. Edward Conze. 274p. 1967. 69.50 (0-614-01821-8) Elliots Bks.

Thirty Years of Championship Golf. Gene Sarazen & Herbert W. Wind. 1987. 28.00 (0-940889-13-7) Classics Golf.

Thirty Years of European Monetary Integration from the Wener Plan to EMU. Ed. by Alfred Steinherr. LC 94-4963. (C). 1994. text ed. 66.50 (0-582-24357-2) Longman.

Thirty Years of European Monetary Integration from the Wener Plan to EMU. Ed. by Alfred Steinherr. LC 94-4963. (C). 1995. pap. text ed. 37.50 (0-582-24401-3) Longman.

Thirty Years of Honesty: Honest to God Then & Now. Ed. by John Bowden. 112p. (Orig.). (C). 1993. pap. 9.50 (0-334-02362-9, SCM Pr) TPI PA.

Thirty Years of Life & Labor, 1859-1889. rev. ed. Terence V. Powderly. LC 66-21692. (Reprints of Economic Classics Ser.). 372p. 1967. reprint ed. 49.50 (0-678-00249-5) Kelley.

Thirty Years of Linguistic Evolution: Studies in Honor of Rene Dirven on the Occasion of His 60th Birthday. Ed. by Martin Putz. LC 92-22941. xi, 632p. 1992. 106.00 (1-55619-462-5); pap. 39.95 (1-55619-463-3) Benjamins North Am.

Thirty Years of Lynching in the United States, 1889-1918. National Association for the Advancement of Colored People Staff. LC 73-94142. (American Negro: His History & Literature. Series 3). 1970. reprint ed. 18.95 (0-405-01932-7) Ayer.

Thirty Years of Lynching in the United States, 1889-1918. National Association for the Advancement of Colored People Staff. LC 72-89046. (Illus.). 105p. 1970. reprint ed. text ed. 35.00 (0-8371-1950-2, LYU&, Greenwood Pr) Greenwood.

Thirty Years of Musical Life in London. Hermann Klein. LC 78-2565. (Music Reprint Ser.: 1978). (Illus.). 1978. reprint ed. lib. bdg. 49.50 (0-306-77586-7) Da Capo.

Thirty Years of New York Politics, Up-to-Date. Matthew P. Breen. LC 73-19132. (Politics & People Ser.). (Illus.). 918p. 1974. reprint ed. 70.95 (0-405-05857-8) Ayer.

Thirty Years of Parity Nonconservation: A Symposium Honoring T. D. Lee. Ed. by Robert Novick. 220p. 1987. 54.00 (0-8176-3375-8) Birkhauser.

Thirty Years of Prestressed Concrete Railroad Bridges. (PCI Journal Reprints Ser.). 36p. 1983. pap. 20.00 (0-318-19796-0, JR285) P-PCI.

Thirty Years of Progress in Mitochondrial Bioenergetics & Molecular Biology. Ed. by Ferdinando Palmieri et al. (Progress in Cell Research Ser.: Vol. 5). 278p. 1995. 217.50 (0-444-82235-6) Elsevier.

Thirty Years of Psychical Research: Being a Treatise on Metaphysics. Charles Richet. Tr. by Stanley De Brath from FRE. LC 75-7397. (Perspectives in Psychical Research Ser.). (Illus.). 1975. reprint ed. 54.95 (0-405-07046-2) Ayer.

Thirty Years of Shire Publications: A Bibliography for Collectors of Shire Books. 96p. 1989. pap. 25.00 (0-7478-0170-3, Pub. by Shire UK) St Mut.

Thirty Years of the American Neptune. Ed. by Ernest S. Dodge. LC 72-82988. (Illus.). 313p. reprint ed. pap. 89.30 (0-7837-4460-9, 2057990) Bks Demand.

Thirty Years of the Communist Party of China. Chi'Iai-Mu Hu. 1976. lib. bdg. 59.95 (0-8490-2744-6) Gordon Pr.

Thirty Years of the Freedom Charter. Ed. by Jeremy Cronin & Raymond Suttner. (Illus.). 266p. 1987. pap. text ed. 15.95 (0-86975-299-5, Pub. by Ravan Pr ZA) Ohio U Pr.

30 Years of the Landau Institute - Selected Papers. Isaac M. Khalatnikov & V. P. Mineev. (Series on 20th Century Physics: Vol. 11). 700p. 1996. text ed. 97.00 (981-02-2253-X) World Scientific Pub.

Thirty Years of Yugoslav Literature: 1945-1975. Thomas Eekman. LC 78-53535. (Joint Committee on Eastern Europe Publication Ser.: No. 5). 1978. 15.00 (0-930042-21-2) Mich Slavic Pubns.

Thirty Years on the Line. Leo D. Stapleton. 272p. 1987. mass mkt. 3.95 (0-380-70327-0) Avon.

***Thirty Years over the Top: Scandinavian Airlines System Polar Flights, Seattle-Copenhagen, 1966-1996.** Junius Rochester & SAS Staff. 33p. (Orig.). 1996. pap. write for info. (0-9648950-1-3) Tommie Pr.

Thirty Years Passed among the Players in England & America. Arthur H. Saxon. LC 78-26796. (Popular Entertainments Ser.). (Illus.). viii, 103p. (C). 1979. reprint ed. 25.00 (0-208-01778-X, Archon Bks) Shoe String.

Thirty Years' Review of China's Science & Technology (1949-1979) 322p. 1982. text ed. 100.00 (9971-950-48-0) World Scientific Pub.

Thirty Years That Shook Physics: The Story of Quantum Theory. George Gamow. 240p. 1985. reprint ed. pap. 5.95 (0-486-24895-X) Dover.

Thirty Years War. David W. Felder. 56p. 1996. pap. text ed. 8.95 (0-910959-75-7, B&G 26A) Wellington Pr.

Thirty Years War. Stephen J. Lee. LC 91-16159. (Lancaster Pamphlets Ser.). 80p. (C). 1991. pap. 9.95 (0-415-06027-3, A6684) Routledge.

Thirty Years War. Geoffrey Parker. (Illus.). 320p. 1985. 47.50 (0-7100-9788-3, RKP) Routledge.

Thirty Years' War. Ed. by Geoffrey Parker. 384p. (C). 1988. pap. text ed. 15.95 (0-7102-1181-3, RKP) Routledge.

Thirty Years' War. Geoffrey Parker. 1988. pap. 16.95 (0-415-02534-6) Routledge.

Thirty Years' War. Henrik Tikkanen. Tr. by George Blecher & Lone T. Blecher. LC 86-8740. (Modern Scandinavian Literature in Translation Ser.). (Illus.). vi, 158p. 1987. pap. 8.95 (0-8032-9407-7, Bison Books) U of Nebr Pr.

Thirty Years War. C. V. Wedgewood. 542p. 1981. pap. 15.95 (0-416-32020-1, NO. 3578) Routledge Chapman & Hall.

An Asterisk (*) at the beginning of an entry indicates that the title is appearing in BIP for the first time.

Thirty Years War. C. V. Wedgwood. 1990. pap. 15.95 (0-415-04574-6) Routledge.

***Thirty Years' War.** 2nd ed. Ed. by Geoffrey Parker. 384p. (C). 1997. pap. 19.95 (0-415-12883-8); text ed. 79.95 (0-415-15458-8) Routledge.

Thirty Years' War. 2nd ed. Ed. by Theodore K. Rabb. LC 80-6215. (Illus.). 190p. 1981. reprint ed. pap. text ed. 16.50 (0-8191-1747-1) U Pr of Amer.

Thirty Years' War: Dispatches & Diversions of a Radical Journalist, 1965-1994. Andrew Kopkind. 1995. 28.00 (1-85984-902-4, Pub. by Vrso UK) Norton.

***Thirty Years War: Dispatches & Diversions of a Radical Journalist, 1965-1994.** Andrew Kopkind. Date not set. pap. 20.00 (1-85984-096-5, Pub. by Verso UK) Routledge Chapman & Hall.

Thirty Years War: The Politics of the Sixties Generation. Thomas A. Pauken. 238p. 1995. write for info. (0-614-14595-3) Jameson Bks.

***Thirty Years' War - Dispatches & Diversions of a Radical Journalist.** Andrew Kopkind. Date not set. 27.50 (0-8446-6913-X) Peter Smith.

Thirty Years War for Wild Life. William T. Hornaday. LC 71-125768. (American Environmental Studies). 1974. reprint ed. 21.95 (0-405-02675-7) Ayer.

Thirty Years' War, Sixteen Eighteen to Sixteen Forty-Eight. Samuel R. Gardiner. LC 69-13901. 233p. 1970. reprint ed. text ed. 59.75 (0-8371-2171-X, GATY, Greenwood Pr) Greenwood.

***Thirty Years War, 1618 to 1648.** Asch. LC 96-41029. 1997. text ed. 49.95 (0-312-16584-6); pap. text ed. 19.95 (0-312-16585-4) St Martin.

Thirty Years' War, 1618-1648. Samuel Gardiner. LC 68-25233. (British History Ser.: No. 30). (Illus.). 1968. reprint ed. lib. bdg. 75.00 (0-8383-0940-2) M S G Haskell Hse.

Thirty Years War, 1618-1648. Samuel R. Gardiner. LC 70-131717. 260p. 1972. reprint ed. 15.00 (0-403-00604-X) Scholarly.

Thirty Years with Computers: And Other Narrow Opinions. John T. Benton. Ed. by Virginia McCullough. (Illus.). 176p. (Orig.). 1991. pap. write for info. (0-9629271-0-4) Exec Info Dev.

***Thirtysomething: A Patchwork Pattern.** Gayle Bong. (Illus.). 60p. (Orig.). 1997. pap. 19.00 (0-9654580-1-6) P L Publns.

Thirtysomething Soundtrack. 88p. 1991. otabind 12.95 (0-7935-0957-2, 00311536) H Leonard.

This above All. Barbara Faith. (Special Edition Ser.). 1993. mass mkt. 3.39 (0-373-09812-X, 5-09812-4) Silhouette.

This above All. Eric M. Knight. 1977. reprint ed. lib. bdg. 26.95 (0-89244-047-3) Queens Hse-Focus Serv.

This Accursed Land. large type ed. Lennard Bickel. 1991. 25.99 (0-7089-2457-3) Ulverscroft.

This Action of Our Death: The Performance of Death in English Renaissance Drama. Michael C. Andrews. LC 88-45743. 216p. 1989. 38.50 (0-87413-354-8) U Delaware Pr.

This Adventure Called Life: Healing from Breast Cancer Naturally. Peny Goodson-Kjome. LC 95-68183. (Illus.). 128p. (Orig.). 1995. pap. 14.00 (0-9615743-8-0) SunShine CO.

This Affair Is Over! Nanette J. Miner & Sandi Terri. 56p. (Orig.). 1996. pap. text ed. 6.95 (0-9650666-1-4) BVC Pubng.

This Affair of Louisiana. Alexander DeConde. LC 76-12468. (Illus.). 347p. 1976. reprint ed. pap. 98.90 (0-7837-9879-2, 2060605) Bks Demand.

This Aging Society. 2nd ed. William C. Cockerham. LC 96-41176. 288p. (C). 1996. pap. text ed. 33.33 (0-13-651092-2) P-H.

This Ain't Hell, but You Can See It from Here: A Gulf War Sketchbook. Barry McWilliams. 256p. 1992. pap. 9.95 (0-89141-443-6) Presidio Pr.

This Alien...Native Land. Asif Currimbhoy. 12.00 (0-89253-796-5); 6.75 (0-89253-527-X) Ind-US Inc.

This & That. Julie Sykes. LC 95-21259. (Illus.). 32p. (J). (gr. k-2). 1996. 14.00 (0-374-37492-9) FS&G.

This & That: Selected Poems of Two Sisters. Elizabeth M. Minier & Dorothy M. Field. 32p. 1990. pap. 5.95 (1-880404-00-1) Bkwrights.

This & That & the Other. Hilaire Belloc. LC 68-22903. (Essay Index Reprint Ser.). 1977. reprint ed. 23.95 (0-8369-0193-2) Ayer.

This & That Bread. Houghton Mifflin Company Staff. (Literature Experience 1991 Ser.). (J). 1990. pap. write for info. (0-395-55027-0) HM.

This & That Bread. Houghton Mifflin Company Staff. (J). 1993. pap. 4.00 (0-395-62578-5) HM.

***This Angry Land.** large type ed. Terence Strong. (Magna Large Print Ser.). 656p. 1996. 25.99 (0-7505-1009-9, Pub. by Magna Print Bks UK) Ulverscroft.

***This Awakening Generation.** John Osteen. Date not set. mass mkt. 2.99 (0-912631-15-5) J O Pubns.

This Band of Heroes: Grandbury's Texas Brigade, C. S. A. James M. McCaffrey. LC 96-3005. (Illus.). 272p. 1996. reprint ed. pap. 16.95 (0-89096-727-X) Tex A&M Univ Pr.

This Bastard Planet: Another Crib Death. Clifford L. Meth. 80p. (Orig.). 1995. pap. write for info. (1-57502-026-2) Morris Pub.

***This Big Sky.** Pat Mora. LC 97-7285. (Illus.). (J). 1998. write for info. (0-590-37120-7); pap. write for info. (0-590-37121-5) Scholastic Inc.

This Bird of Dawning Singeth All Night Long: One Act Acting Edition. Phillip H. Dean. 1971. pap. 3.25 (0-8222-1135-1) Dramatists Play.

This Bittersweet Soil: The Chinese in California Agriculture, 1860-1910. Sucheng Chan. 1986. 55.00 (0-520-05376-1) U CA Pr.

This Bittersweet Soil: The Chinese in California Agriculture, 1860-1910. Sucheng Chan. 1986. pap. 17.00 (0-520-06737-1) U CA Pr.

This Blessed Plot. M. R. Meek. (Worldwide Library Mystery: No. 93). 1992. mass mkt. 3.99 (0-373-26093-8, 1-26093-4) Harlequin Bks.

This Bloody Deed: The Magruder Incident. Ladd Hamilton. (Illus.). 280p. (Orig.). 1994. pap. 18.95 (0-87422-107-2) Wash St U Pr.

This Body She's Entered: A Collection of Poems. Mary K. Rummel. 1990. pap. 6.00 (0-89823-115-9) New Rivers Pr.

***This Book Belongs to Eva.** Stephen Gardner. 32p. 1996. pap. 5.00 (1-889806-12-9) Devils Millhopper.

This Book Doesn't Make Sense: Living & Learning with Dyslexia. Jean Augur. 130p. 1995. pap. 34.95 (1-56593-605-1, 1256) Singular Publishing.

This Book Is about Time. Marilyn Burns. LC 78-6614. (Brown Paper School Bks.). (Illus.). (YA). (gr. 5 up). 1978. pap. 11.95 (0-316-11750-1) Little.

This Book Is Mine: The Harmony Feeding System. Milo E. Yergin. 1972. reprint ed. spiral bd. 9.50 (0-7873-1133-2) Hlth Research.

This Book Is Not Required. 2nd rev. ed. Inge Bell. (Illus.). 271p. (C). 1990. pap. text ed. write for info. (1-878020-04-8) Small Pr CA.

This Book of Starres: Learning to Read George Herbert. James B. White. LC 93-46407. (C). 1995. 19.95 (0-472-08337-6) U of Mich Pr.

***This Book Won't Help You!** Craig Rypstat. 120p. 1997. pap. 7.95 (0-9654436-2-0) Honey Creek WI.

This Bookish Inclination: The Story of the Arlington Heights Memorial Library, 1887-1987. Margery Frisbie. (Illus.). 240p. 1987. 10.00 (0-9617830-0-1) Friends Mem Libr.

This Boundless Mist. Robert F. Mainone. (Haiku Series: Vol. 4). (Illus.). 60p. (Orig.). 1984. pap. 7.00 (1-888693-04-5) Wnderlnd MI.

This Boy's Life: A Memoir. Tobias Wolff. 1990. pap. 11.00 (0-06-097277-7, PL) HarpC.

This Bread, This Cup: An Introduction to the Eucharist. Anna D. Gulick. LC 92-16685. 72p. (Orig.). 1992. pap. 4.95 (0-8192-1591-0) Morehouse Pub.

This Breast Gothic. Ruth Krauss. (Illus.). 48p. (YA). (gr. 7 up). 1973. pap. 8.00 (0-912846-02-X) Bookstore Pr.

This Bridge Called My Back: Writings by Radical Women of Color. Ed. by Cherrie Moraga & Gloria Anzaldua. (Illus.). 261p. (Orig.). (C). 1983. reprint ed. 23.95 (0-913175-18-8); reprint ed. pap. 11.95 (0-913175-03-X) Kitchen Table.

***This Bright Field: Speculations on the East End of London.** William Taylor. 1997. pap. text ed. 19.95 (1-897959-34-6, Pub. by Serif UK) LPC InBook.

This Bright Mantle. large type ed. Paula Lindsay. 1990. 25.99 (0-7089-2141-8) Ulverscroft.

This Britain. Ed. by Newton Branch. LC 79-90612. (Essay Index Reprint Ser.). 1977. 39.95 (0-8369-1549-6) Ayer.

***This Broad's Life.** Carlson. 1997. pap. 14.00 (0-671-52304-X, PB Trade Paper) PB.

This Broad's Life: Raucous Riveting Autobiography of the Most Outrageous Radio Talk-Show Host. Barbara Carlson & Jess Cagle. (Illus.). 320p. 1996. 23.00 (0-671-52305-8) S&S Trade.

This Business Has Legs: The Inside Story of the Infomercial Entrpreneur Who Turned the Thigh-Master into a Household Name. Peter Bieler & Suzanne Costas. LC 96-18232. 256p. 1996. text ed. 24.95 (0-471-14749-4) Wiley.

This Business Is Murder. Joyce Christmas. 1993. mass mkt. 4.50 (0-449-14800-9) Fawcett.

***This Business of Artist Management.** Xavier M. Frascogna & H. Lee Hetherington. LC 96-52598. 1997. write for info. (0-8230-7705-5, Billboard Bks) Watsn-Guptill.

***This Business of Books: An Overview of the Industry from Concept Through Sales.** 3rd ed. Claudia Suzanne. LC 96-60760. 256p. 1996. per. 19.95 (0-963829-1-0) Wambtac.

This Business of Boxing & Its Secrets. Gregory J. Reed. 300p. 1981. text ed. 20.00 (1-882806-03-4); pap. text ed. 20.00 (1-882806-04-2) New Natl Pub.

This Business of Celebrity Estates. Gregory J. Reed. 1992. text ed. 25.00 (1-882806-06-9); pap. text ed. 19.50 (1-882806-05-0) New Natl Pub.

This Business of Communicating. 5th ed. Roy M. Berko et al. 416p. (C). 1992. per. write for info. (0-697-12913-6) Brown & Benchmark.

This Business of Communicating. 5th ed. Roy M. Berko et al. 416p. (C). 1992. write for info. (0-697-21252-1) Brown & Benchmark.

This Business of Entertainment & Its Secrets. Gregory J. Reed. 295p. 1985. text ed. 25.50 (1-882806-01-8); pap. text ed. 19.50 (1-882806-02-6) New Natl Pub.

This Business of Glass: The Complete Guide for Artists, Craftspeople & Retailers. Loretta Radeschi. Ed. by Joe Porcelli. (Illus.). 320p. 1993. pap. 19.95 (0-9629053-3-X) Glass Pr.

This Business of Music: A Practical Guide to the Music Industry for Publishers, Writers, Record Companies, Producers, Artists, Agents. 7th enl. rev. ed. M. William Krasilovsky & Sidney Shemel. 736p. 1995. 29.95 (0-8230-7755-1, Billboard Bks) Watsn-Guptill.

This Business of Television. Howard J. Blumenthal & Oliver Goodenough. 672p. 1991. 32.50 (0-8230-7762-4, Billboard Bks) Watsn-Guptill.

This Business of Writing. Gregg Levoy. 224p. 1992. 19.95 (0-89879-505-2, Wrtrs Digest Bks) F & W Pubns Inc.

This Calder Range see Stands A Calder Man

This Calder Sky. Janet Dailey. 1993. pap. 6.99 (0-671-87518-3) PB.

This Caldor Sky see Stands A Calder Man

This Candescent World. Cliff Dweller. 32p. (Orig.). 1993. pap. 5.00 (0-926935-87-9) Runaway Spoon.

This Can't Be Happening at MacDonald Hall. Gordon Korman. 128p. (J). 1990. pap. 3.50 (0-590-44213-9) Scholastic Inc.

***This Can't Be My Last Flight: A Nurse-Pilot's Personal Account of His Heart Attack & Recovery.** unabridged ed. David A. Hopkins. Ed. & Photos by Pamela J. Hopkins. 80p. (Orig.). 1997. pap. 7.95 (0-9658175-0-4) Breezy Pub.

This Changing South. John M. Maclachlan & Joe S. Floyd, Jr. LC 56-12858. 166p. reprint ed. pap. 47.40 (0-8357-6720-5, 2035355) Bks Demand.

This Child Is Mine. Trisha Alexander. 1995. mass mkt. 3.75 (0-373-09989-4, 1-09989-4) Silhouette.

***This Child Is Mine.** large type ed. Henry Denker. (Charnwood Large Print Ser.). 464p. 1997. 29.50 (0-7089-8929-2, Charnwood) Ulverscroft.

This Child Is Mine: A Novel. Henry Denker. LC 94-32360. 1995. 23.00 (0-688-14125-0) Morrow.

***This Child Is the One.** 1996. pap. 1.35 (0-8341-9484-8) Lillenas.

This Child Must Die. Anne Ruck. 148p. (Orig.). 1991. pap. write for info. (981-3009-01-2) OMF Bks.

This Child Shall Be Lent Unto the Lord. C. M. Ward. (Illus.). 32p. 1967. pap. 0.85 (0-88243-822-0, 02-0822) Gospel Pub.

This Child's Gonna Live. Sarah E. Wright. LC 86-25786. 304p. (C). 1986. reprint ed. pap. 10.95 (0-935312-67-6) Feminist Pr.

This Chosen Generation: Armed with the Gifts of God. Margaret M. Pope. 160p. 1994. 12.98 (0-88290-483-3, 1968) Horizon Utah.

***This Chosen Place: The 4UR Ranch.** Max Evans. 256p. 1997. 29.95 (0-87081-437-0) Univ Pr Colo.

This Christmas. Laura Abbot. 1996. pap. 3.99 (0-373-70721-5, 1-70721-5) Harlequin Bks.

This City, This Man: The Cookingham Era in Kansas City. Bill Gilbert. LC 78-13401. (Illus.). 276p. 1978. 21.00 (0-87326-021-X) Intl City-Cnty Mgt.

This Close to the Earth. Enid Shomer. LC 91-45530. 80p. 1992. 20.00 (1-55728-255-2); pap. 12.00 (1-55728-256-0) U of Ark Pr.

This Common Inheritance: The Third Year Report. HMSO Staff. (Command Papers: No. 2549). 192p. 1994. pap. 40.00 (0-10-125492-X, HM5492X, Pub. by Stationery Ofc UK) Bernan Associates.

This Complicated Form of Life: Essays on Wittgenstein. Newton Garver. 338p. 1994. 44.95 (0-8126-9252-7); pap. 19.95 (0-8126-9253-5) Open Court.

This Confident Church: Catholic Leadership & Life in Chicago, 1940-1965. Steven M. Avella. LC 91-51121. (C). 1992. text ed. 34.50 (0-268-01879-0) U of Notre Dame Pr.

This Crazy Thing Called Love. Susan Braudy. 1993. mass mkt. 5.99 (0-312-95145-0) St Martin.

This Crud's for You: Chemicals & How to Use Them. James F. Willenbecher. 25p. 1993. pap. text ed. 3.50 (0-9632514-2-2) Crossfire Eng.

This Culture of Ours: Intellectual Transitions in T'ang & Sung China. Peter K. Bol. LC 91-16004. 532p. 1992. 57.50 (0-8047-1920-9) Stanford U Pr.

This Culture of Ours: Intellectual Transitions in T'ang & Sung China. Peter K. Bol. (Transitions in T'ang & Sun China). xii, 520p. 1994. pap. 22.50 (0-8047-2361-3) Stanford U Pr.

This Curious Country Badlands National Park. limited ed. Mary Durant & Michael Harwood. (Illus.). 64p. 1988. pap. 14.00 (0-912410-08-6) Badlands Natl Hist.

This Damn House! Mt Subcontract with America. Margo Kaufman. LC 95-22708. 240p. 1996. 21.00 (0-679-42840-2, Villard Bks) Random.

***This Damn House: My Subcontract with America.** Margo Kaufman. 1997. pap. 11.95 (0-440-50796-0) Dell.

This Dancing Ground of Sky: The Selected Poetry of Peggy Pond Church. Peggy P. Church. LC 92-32298. 216p. 1993. pap. 12.95 (1-878610-28-7) Red Crane Bks.

This Dangerous Menace: Dundee & the River Tay at War. Andrew Jeffrey. (Illus.). 190p. 1992. 34.95 (1-85158-492-7, Pub. by Mnstream UK) Trafalgar.

This Daniel. Harold S. Paisley. 190p. (Orig.). 1991. pap. text ed. 10.95 (0-9631200-1-8) Gospel Folio CT.

***This Dark Embrace.** Paul Stuewe. 15.95 (1-55128-037-X, Pub. by Mercury Pr CN) LPC InBook.

This Dark Paradise. Wendy Haley. 1994. mass mkt. 4.99 (0-7865-0000-X) Diamond.

This Dawning Land. Tony Matthews. 116p. (C). 1990. 45.00 (0-86439-010-6, Pub. by Boolarong Pubns AT) St Mut.

This Day All Gods Die: The Gap into Ruin. Stephen R. Donaldson. LC 95-21037. (Gap Ser.: No. 5). 608p. 1996. 22.95 (0-553-07180-7, Spectra) Bantam.

This Day All Gods Die: The Gap into Ruin. Stephen R. Donaldson. (Gap Ser.: No. 5). 720p. 1997. mass mkt. 6.99 (0-553-57328-4) Bantam.

This Day & Age. Mike Nicol. LC 92-53054. 1995. pap. 11.00 (0-679-74200-X) Random.

This Day in African-American Music. Ted Holland. LC 93-5840. (Illus.). 176p. 1993. 30.00 (1-56640-571-8) Pomegranate Calif.

This Day in American History. Ed. by Ernest Gross. 450p. (Orig.). 1990. 49.95 (1-55570-046-2) Neal-Schuman.

This Day in Baptist History: Three Hundred Sixty-Six Daily Devotions Drawn from the Baptist Heritage. E. Wayne Thompson & David L. Cummins. LC 93-32398. 1995. pap. 23.95 (0-89084-709-6, 070656) Bob Jones Univ Pr.

This Day in Oregon. James Cloutier. LC 80-83719. (Illus.). 128p. (J). 1981. pap. 6.95 (0-918966-06-X) Image West.

This Day in Religion. Ed. by Ernest Gross. 294p. (Orig.). 1989. 45.00 (1-55570-045-4) Neal-Schuman.

This Day in Rock: Day by Day Record of Rock's Biggest News Stories. John Tobler. (Illus.). 384p. 1993. pap. text ed. 19.50 (0-685-66700-6); pap. text ed. 19.50 (0-88184-860-3) Carroll & Graf.

***This Death by Drowning.** William Kloefkorn. LC 96-53543. 144p. 1997. 22.00 (0-8032-2736-1) U of Nebr Pr.

This Desert Now. Yves Prefontaine. Tr. by Judith Cowan from FRE. (Essential Poets Ser.: No. 52). 64p. 1994. pap. 8.00 (0-920717-66-7) Guernica Editions.

This Destructive War: The British Campaign in the Carolinas, 1780-1782. John S. Pancake. LC 83-5025. 320p. 1992. pap. 17.95 (0-8173-0688-9) U of Ala Pr.

This Difficult Individual: Ezra Pound. Eustace C. Mullins. LC 78-64049. (Des Imagistes: Literature of the Imagist Movement Ser.). reprint ed. 31.00 (0-404-17081-1) AMS Pr.

This Doesn't Feel Like Love: Trusting God When Bad Things Happen. Roger Lamb & Marcia Lamb. 210p. 1996. pap. 10.99 (1-884553-82-6) Discipleshp.

This Dog for Hire: A Rachel Alexander & Dash Mystery. Carol L. Benjamin. LC 96-26066. (Rachel Alexander & Dash Mystery Ser.). 224p. 1996. 20.95 (0-8027-3292-5) Walker & Co.

This Dog'll Hunt. Wallace O. Chariton. (Regional Bks.). (Illus.). 300p. (Orig.). 1989. pap. 12.95 (1-55622-125-8, Rep of TX Pr) Wordware Pub.

This Drinking Nation. Jonathan Harris. (Illus.). 208p. (YA). (gr. 5 up). 1994. lib. bdg. 15.95 (0-02-742744-7, Four Winds Pr) S&S Childrens.

***This Dynamic Earth: The Story of Plate Tectonics.** 1996. lib. bdg. 252.99 (0-8490-6061-3) Gordon Pr.

***This Dynamic Earth: The Story of Plate Tectonics.** W. Jacquelyne Klous & Robert I. Tilling. (Illus.). 77p. (Orig.). 1996. pap. 35.00 (0-7881-3318-7) DIANE Pub.

This Dynamic Universe. Smith & Trew. 1994. pap. 5.95 (0-8356-0232-X, Quest) Theos Pub Hse.

This Earth, My Brother... Kofi Awoonor. (African Writers Ser.). 183p. (C). 1972. pap. 8.95 (0-435-90108-7, 90108) Heinemann.

This Earth of Mankind. Pramoedya A. Toer. Tr. by Max Lane. 368p. 1993. pap. 10.00 (0-380-71974-6) Avon.

This Ecstasy. John Squadra. (Illus.). 96p. 1996. pap. 8.95 (0-9651372-0-1) Hermes Pr.

This Edifice Is Colossal: 19th Century Architectural Photography. Robert A. Sobieszek. 88p. 1986. pap. 15.95 (0-935398-14-7) G Eastman Hse.

This Emigrating Company: The Eighteen Forty-Four Oregon Trail Journal of Jacob Hammer. Jacob Hammer. Ed. by Thomas A. Rumer. LC 89-62715. (American Trails Ser.: No. XVI). (Illus.). 274p. 1991. 35.50 (0-87062-196-3) A H Clark.

This Error Is the Sign of Love: Poems. Lewis Hyde. LC 87-63533. 64p. (Orig.). 1988. pap. 6.95 (0-915943-29-8) Milkweed Ed.

This Family of Women. large type ed. Peck. (Charnwood Large Print Ser.). 1984. 27.99 (0-7089-8214-X, Charnwood) Ulverscroft.

This Far. Joan Aleshire. (QRL Poetry Bks.: Vol. XXVII). 1987. 35.00 (0-614-06421-X) Quarterly Rev.

This Far by Faith. Gwen Main. LC 91-33130. 105p. 1992. pap. 8.95 (0-944350-21-6) Friends United.

This Far by Faith: Readings in African-American Women's Religious Biography. Judith Weisenfeld & Richard Newman. LC 95-31000. 288p. (C). 1995. pap. 17.95 (0-415-91312-8) Routledge.

This Far by Faith: Readings in African-American Women's Religious Biography. Ed. by Judith Weisenfeld & Richard Newman. LC 95-31000. 288p. (C). (gr. 13). 1995. text ed. 59.95 (0-415-91311-X) Routledge.

***This Far, No Further.** John Wessel. 1997. mass mkt. 6.99 (0-440-22490-X, Island Bks) Dell.

This Far, No Further. John Wessel. LC 96-8034. 336p. 1996. 23.00 (0-684-81463-3) S&S Trade.

***This Far, No Further.** large type ed. John Wessel. LC 97-3569. (Large Print Book Ser.). 1997. 24.95 (1-56895-418-2) Wheeler Pub.

***This Far North.** Tony Curtis. 74p. 9400. pap. 11.95 (1-873790-62-7) Dufour.

This Farm Is a Mess. Leslie McGuire. LC 94-11354. (Parents Magazine Whole Language Library). (Illus.). (J). (gr. 1 up). lib. bdg. 17.27 (0-8368-0983-1) Gareth Stevens Inc.

This Farm Is a Mess. Leslie McGuire. LC 80-25811. (Illus.). 48p. (J). (ps-3). 1981. 5.95 (0-8193-1045-X); lib. bdg. 5.95 (0-8193-1046-8) Parents.

This Fascinating Oil Business. Max W. Ball et al. LC 64-15660. (Illus.). 1979. reprint ed. pap. write for info. (0-672-52584-4) Macmillan.

This Fast I Choose. Friendship Press Editors. (Orig.). 1990. pap. 5.95 (0-377-00201-1) Friendship Pr.

This Father Knows Best. Anthony Good. Ed. by Patrick J. Canter. 175p. 1994. pap. 14.95 (0-937816-87-6) Tech Data.

This Favored Place: The Texas Hill Country. Elroy Bode. (Illus.). 124p. 1983. 13.95 (0-940672-09-X) Shearer Pub.

This Fellow with the Fabulous Smile: A Tribute to Brendan Kennelly. Ed. by Ake Persson. 128p. 1996. pap. 17.95 (1-85224-367-8, Pub. by Bloodaxe Bks UK) Dufour.

This Female Man of God: Women & Spiritual Power in the Patristic Age, 350-450. Gillian Cloke. LC 94-16028. 256p. (C). 1994. text ed. 62.95 (0-415-09469-0, A9992) Routledge.

This Female Man of God: Women & Spiritual Power in the Patristic Age, 350-450. Gillian Cloke. LC 94-16028. 256p. (C). 1995. pap. 17.95 (0-415-09470-4, A9996) Routledge.

This Fierce Loving. Judith E. French. 384p. (Orig.). 1994. mass mkt. 4.99 (0-380-77704-5) Avon.

An Asterisk (*) at the beginning of an entry indicates that the title is appearing in BIP for the first time.

This Fine Place So Far from Home: Voices of Academics from the Working Class. Ed. by C. L. Dews & Carolyn L. Law. LC 94-28730. 384p. (Orig.). (C). 1995. pap. text ed. 22.95 (*1-56639-291-8*); lib. bdg. 59.95 (*1-56639-290-X*) Temple U Pr.

This Fish Is Loaded! The Book of Surreal Humor. Ed. by Alastair Brotchie & Richard G. Jones. 256p. (Orig.). 1991. 17.95 (*0-8065-1262-8*, Citadel Pr); pap. 10.95 (*0-8065-1270-9*, Citadel Pr) Carol Pub Group.

This Fissured Land: An Ecological History of India. Madhav Gadgil & Ramachandra Guha. (Oxford India Paperbacks Ser.). 340p. 1994. pap. 8.95 (*0-19-563341-5*) OUP.

This Fissured Land: An Ecological History of India. Madhav Gadgil & Ramachandra Guha. LC 92-29904. 1993. 40.00 (*0-520-07621-4*); pap. 15.00 (*0-520-08296-6*) U CA Pr.

This for That: A Tonga Tale. Illus. by Victoria Chess. LC 93-32309. (J). 1997. pap. 14.99 (*0-8037-1553-6*); pap. 14.89 (*0-8037-1554-4*) Dial Bks Young.

This for That: A Treasury of Savy Substitutions for the Creative Cook. 3rd ed. Meryl Nelson. Ed. by Shirley Sing & Frances Thoman. LC 90-62126. (Illus.). 112p. 1991. pap. 6.95 (*0-88247-847-8*) R & E Pubs.

This for That: A Treasury of Savy Substitutions for the Creative Cook. 4th ed. Meryl Nelson. Ed. by Shirley Sing & Frances Thoman. (Illus.). 130p. 1996. pap. 7.95 (*1-56875-184-2*) R & E Pubs.

This Fragile Eden. Barbara B. Robinson. (Illus.). 1978. pap. 8.95 (*0-916630-11-0*) Pr Pacifica.

This Fragile Land: A Natural History of the Nebraska Sandhills. Paul A. Johnsgard. LC 94-36409. (Illus.). xv, 256p. 1995. 35.00 (*0-8032-2578-4*) U of Nebr Pr.

This Functional Family. Jimmy D. Evans. Ed. by Glenda Lowery & Kimberly Fritts. 1996. 10.00 (*0-9647435-9-0*) Majestic Media.

This Game of Artist Management: The Success Attitude. Walt F. Goodridge. LC 94-70567. (Game of...Ser.: No. 2). (Illus.). 256p. 1994. pap. 45.00 (*0-9629202-3-1*) Co Called W.

This Game of Ghosts. Joe Simpson. 1995. pap. 14.95 (*0-89886-460-7*) Mountaineers.

***This Game's the Best! So Why Don't They Quit Screwing with It?** George Karl & Don Yaeger. LC 97-2354. 1997. 23.95 (*0-312-15671-5*) St Martin.

This Gift of Water: The Theology & Practice of Baptism among Methodists in America. Gayle Felton. 224p. (Orig.). 1993. pap. 19.95 (*0-687-33327-X*) Abingdon.

This Gifted Age: Science & Technology at the Millennium. John H. Gibbons. LC 96-51110. (Masters of Modern Physics Ser.). (Illus.). 300p. 1996. 29.95 (*1-56396-129-6*) Am Inst Physics.

This Gilded African: Toussaint L'Ouverture. Wenda Parkinson. 12.95 (*0-7043-2187-4*, Pub. by Quartet UK) Charles River Bks.

This Good Food: Contemporary French Vegetarian Recipes from a Monastery Kitchen. Victor-Antoine D'Avila-Latourrette. (Illus.). 222p. 1994. reprint ed. pap. 13.95 (*0-87951-551-1*) Overlook Pr.

This Good Food: French Vegetarian Recipes from a Monastery Kitchen. Victor-Antoine D'Avila-Latourrette. LC 92-25544. (Illus.). 240p. 1993. 22.95 (*0-87951-483-3*) Overlook Pr.

This Gospel...Shall Be Preached vol.2: A History & Theology of Assemblies of God Foreign Missions Since 1959, 2 vols., Vol. 2. Gary B. McGee. LC 86-80015. (Illus.). 358p. (Orig.). (C). 1989. kivar 12.95 (*0-88243-673-2*, 02-0673) Gospel Pub.

***This Great Calamity: The Irish Famine 1845-52.** Christine Kinealy. 472p. 1997. pap. 16.95 (*1-57098-140-X*) R Rinehart.

This Great Calamity: The Irish Famine 1845-52. rev. ed. Christine Kinealy. (Illus.). 472p. (C). 1995. text ed. 24.95 (*1-57098-034-9*) R Rinehart.

***This Great Epoch of Our Lives No. 33: Susanna Moodie's Roughing It in the Bush.** Michael Peterman. (Canadian Fiction Studies). pap. 14.95 (*1-55022-182-5*, Pub. by ECW Press CN) Genl Dist Srvs.

This Great Harbour Scapa Flow. W. S. Hewison. (C). 1986. 85.00 (*0-907618-11-1*, Pub. by Orkney Pr UK) St Mut.

This Great Harbour Scapa Flow. Ed. by Maritime Books Staff. (C). 1986. text ed. 200.00 (*0-685-38771-2*, Pub. by Maritime Bks UK) St Mut.

***This Great House Vol. 1: The Story of This Home.** David W. Stackhouse. (Illus.). 66p. (Orig.). 1996. pap. 14.95 (*0-9654221-0-0*) Half-High Hill.

This Great Salvation: Unmerited Favor, Unmatched Joy. Robin Boisvert & C. J. Mahaney. 112p. (Orig.). 1992. pap. 6.50 (*1-881039-01-3*) People of Destiny.

This Great Stage: Image & Structure in King Lear. Robert B. Heilman. LC 75-31365. 339p. 1976. reprint ed. text ed. 37.50 (*0-8371-8523-8*, HEGS, Greenwood Pr) Greenwood.

This Green. Barry Grimes. 96p. (Orig.). 1993. pap. 10.00 (*0-911287-15-9*) Blue Begonia.

This Handful of Dust. Feroz Ahmed-Ud-Din. (Redbird Ser.). 31p. 1975. 8.00 (*0-88253-835-7*); pap. 4.80 (*0-88253-836-5*) Ind-US Inc.

***This Happened Everywhere: Selected Poems of Remco Campert.** Remco Campert. Tr. by Manfred Wolf from DUT. 84p. (Orig.). 1997. pap. 12.00 (*1-879594-20-X*) Androgyne Bks.

This Happy Land: The Jews of Colonial & Antebellum Charleston. James W. Hagy. LC 92-12171. (Judaic Studies). 440p. 1993. text ed. 49.95 (*0-8173-0576-9*) U of Ala Pr.

This Harmonica Is for "You", No. 1. Charles Potter. Ed. by Philana Potter. (Illus.). 52p. 1995. pap. 10.17 (*0-9646765-0-8*) Charles Publns.

This Heart of Mine. Bertrice Small. (Orig.). 1988. mass mkt. 5.95 (*0-345-35673-X*) Ballantine.

This Heart of Stone. Rowan Edwards. (Rainbow Romances Ser.). 160p. 1995. 14.95 (*0-7090-5489-0*, 920, Hale-Parkwest) Parkwest Pubns.

This Heart of Stone. large type ed. Rowan Edwards. 288p. 1995. pap. 15.99 (*0-7089-7791-X*, Linford) Ulverscroft.

This Hebrew Lord. John S. Spong. LC 92-53898. 1993. pap. 14.00 (*0-06-067520-9*) Harper SF.

This Hell of Stories: A Hegelian Approach to the Novels of Samuel Beckett. Hans J. Schulz. LC 72-94504. (De Proprietatibus Litterarum, Ser. Practica: No. 63). 117p. 1973. pap. text ed. 21.35 (*90-279-2471-6*) Mouton.

This Hemisphere of Liberty: A Philosophy of the Americas. Michael Novak. 150p. 1990. 24.75 (*0-8447-3735-6*, AEI Pr) Am Enterprise.

This Hemisphere of Liberty: A Philosophy of the Americas. Michael Novak. 168p. 1990. pap. 12.95 (*0-8447-3736-4*) Am Enterprise.

This High Name: Public Relations & the U. S. Marine Corps. Robert G. Lindsay. LC 57-5238. (Illus.). 126p. reprint ed. pap. 36.00 (*0-317-08238-8*, 2021140) Bks Demand.

This Hill, This Valley. Hal Borland. 1990. pap. 13.95 (*0-8018-4020-1*) Johns Hopkins.

This Holler Is My Home. Alyce F. Bragg. 182p. (Orig.). 1993. 12.95 (*0-941092-26-7*) Mtn St Pr.

***This Holy Place: On the Sanctity of the Synagogue During the Greco-Roman Period.** Steven Fine. LC 97-25833. (Christianity & Judaism in Antiquity Ser.). 1998. write for info. (*0-268-04205-5*) U of Notre Dame Pr.

This Horn for Hire: Pee Wee Erwin. Warren W. Vache, Sr. LC 87-4842. (Studies in Jazz: No. 5). (Illus.). 453p. 1987. 45.00 (*0-8108-1945-7*) Scarecrow.

This House Had Windows. David S. Blackhall. 1962. 12.95 (*0-8392-1115-5*) Astor-Honor.

This House Is Filled with Cracks: Poems. Madelyn Camrud. LC 93-83976. (Minnesota Voices Project Ser.: Vol. 61). 72p. (Orig.). 1994. pap. 7.95 (*0-89823-153-1*) New Rivers Pr.

This House Is Made of Mud-Esta Casa Esta Hecha de Lodo. Ken Buchanan. LC 93-45711. (Illus.). 32p. (ENG & SPA.). (J). (ps up). 1994. pap. 6.95 (*0-87358-593-3*); lib. bdg. 14.95 (*0-87358-580-1*) Northland AZ.

This House, My Ghetto. Mike Jenkins. 64p. 1996. pap. 15.95 (*1-85411-140-X*, Pub. by Seren Bks UK) Dufour.

This House of Sky: Landscapes of a Western Mind. Ivan Doig. LC 79-18783. 314p. 1980. pap. 8.95 (*0-15-689982-5*, Harvest Bks) HarBrace.

This House of Sky: Landscapes of a Western Mind. Ivan Doig. 1992. 24.95 (*0-15-190055-8*) HarBrace.

This House of Sky: Landscapes of a Western Mind. Ivan Doig. 1990. 21.00 (*0-8446-6218-6*) Peter Smith.

This House on Fire: The Story of the Blues. Craig Awmiller. (African-American Experience Ser.). (Illus.). 144p. (YA). (gr. 9-12). 1996. lib. bdg. 22.70 (*0-531-11253-5*) Watts.

This House on Fire: The Story of the Blues. Craig Awmiller. (African-American Experience Ser.). (Illus.). 176p. (YA). (gr. 9-12). 1996. pap. 8.00 (*0-531-15797-0*) Watts.

This How-to Book Is Classified! Using Classified Ads for Profit. Gary Bryant. 62p. 1992. pap. 6.95 (*1-881442-01-2*) New Legends Pub.

This Human World. rev. ed. Allen K. Philbrick. (Illus.). 500p. (C). 1986. reprint ed. pap. text ed. 39.95 (*1-877751-39-1*) Inst Math Geo.

This I Ask of You. Pat Warren. (Special Edition Ser.). 1993. mass mkt. 3.39 (*0-373-09815-4*, 5-09815-7) Silhouette.

This I Believe. Charles T. Crabtree. LC 81-84913. 160p. (Orig.). 1982. pap. 4.95 (*0-88243-758-5*, 02-0758) Gospel Pub.

This I Believe. Donald D. Day. 224p. 1972. pap. 1.95 (*0-9600500-1-9*) Three D Pubs.

***This I Believe.** Kenneth D. Wells. LC 96-37245. 90p. 1997. pap. 15.95 (*1-877633-36-4*) Luthers.

This I Believe: Documents of American Jewish Life. Jacob R. Marcus. LC 90-33814. 304p. 1990. 30.00 (*0-87668-782-6*) Aronson.

This I Believe: Documents of American Jewish Life. Jacob R. Marcus. LC 90-33814. 304p. 1997. pap. 24.95 (*1-56821-968-7*) Aronson.

This I Can Believe. Alfred G. Walton. LC 79-142708. (Essay Index Reprint Ser.). 1977. 20.95 (*0-8369-2207-7*) Ayer.

This I Cannot Forget: The Memoirs of Nikolai Bukharin's Widow. Anna Larina. 408p. 1994. pap. 15.00 (*0-393-31234-8*) Norton.

This, I Do for Me. Marjory A. Spraycar. 128p. boxed 12.95 (*1-882626-23-0*) Impress Ink.

***This I Know: Poetry Across Black Cultures.** Arlene H. Mitchell & Darwin L. Henderson. LC 96-40409. (J). 1998. write for info. (*0-590-45119-7*); pap. write for info. (*0-590-45120-0*) Scholastic Inc.

This I Remember. Karl Geiringer. LC 92-36717. (Illus.). 272p. 1993. 24.95 (*1-56474-045-5*) Fithian Pr.

This I Remember. Peter G. Treves. 230p. 1990. write for info. (*0-918367-34-4*) Elite.

This I Remember. Eleanor Roosevelt. LC 74-11884. (Illus.). 387p. 1975. reprint ed. text ed. 85.00 (*0-8371-7702-2*, ROTI, Greenwood Pr) Greenwood.

This I Remember: From War to Peace. George Dolnikowski. LC 94-12609. 60p. 1994. 9.95 (*0-87178-849-7*, 8497) Brethren.

This I Remember: Growing up in Schenectady. Larry Hart. (Illus.). 180p. (Orig.). 1994. pap. text ed. 15.00 (*0-932035-15-9*) Old Dorp Bks.

This Imagined Permanence. Nathalie Stephens. 104p. 1996. pap. 8.95 (*1-896356-05-2*, Pub. by Gutter Pr CN) Dist Art Pubs.

This Immortal People: A Short History of the Jewish People. Emil B. Cohn. LC 84-62563. 180p. (Orig.). 1985. pap. 5.95 (*0-8091-2693-1*) Paulist Pr.

This Indecision Is Final: 32 Management Secrets of Albert Einstein, Billie Holiday & a Bunch of Other People Who Never Worked 9 to 5. Barry J. Gibbons. 192p. 1996. per. 21.95 (*0-7863-0838-9*) Irwin Prof Pubng.

This India. Shahana Dasgupta. (C). 1993. 14.00 (*81-7167-159-4*, Pub. by Rupa II) S Asia.

This Infinite Fraternity of Feeling: Gender, Genre & Homoerotic Crisis in Hawthorne's The Blithedale Romance & Melville's Pierre. Mokika Mueller. LC 96-4204. 232p. 1996. 37.50 (*0-8386-3650-0*) Fairleigh Dickinson.

This Inventive Century. Norm Bezane. 1994. pap. text ed. 18.95 (*1-55989-580-2*) Underwrtrs Labs.

This Invisible Riot of the Mind: Samuel Johnson's Psychological Theory. Gloria S. Gross. LC 91-39482. 216p. (C). 1992. text ed. 29.95 (*0-8122-3146-5*) U of Pa Pr.

This Irritating World We Live In. Richard A. Mosman. (Illus.). 1989. pap. write for info. (*0-318-65828-3*) R A Mosman.

This Is a Great Place for a Hot Dog Stand. large type ed. Barney Saltzberg. LC 94-22503. (Illus.). 32p. (J). (gr. k-3). 1995. 14.95 (*0-7868-0070-4*) Hyprn Child.

This Is a Pair of Levi's Jeans: The Official History of the Levi's Brand. Lynn Downey et al. Ed. by Steve Goldstein. (Illus.). 318p. 1995. 75.00 (*0-9617460-1-7*) Gingko Press.

This Is a Penny. Anne T. Perkins. (Big Books - Mini Bks.). (Illus.). 8p. (J). (gr. k). 1995. 12.00 (*1-884204-15-5*) Teach Nxt Door.

This Is a Printing Office: Broadsheet. Ed. by Albert Sperisen. (California Broadsheet Ser.: No. 1). 1984. 105.00 (*0-520-05360-5*) U CA Pr.

This Is a Test. Stephen Gregg. 1988. 3.00 (*0-87129-442-7*, T73) Dramatic Pub.

This Is a "Thriller" An Episode Guide, History & Analysis of the Classic 1960s Television Series. Alan Warren. LC 96-32736. (Illus.). 215p. 1996. lib. bdg. 45.00 (*0-7864-0256-3*) McFarland & Co.

This Is about Incest. Margaret Randall. LC 87-412. (Illus.). 72p. (Orig.). 1987. pap. 8.95 (*0-932379-29-X*); lib. bdg. 18.95 (*0-932379-30-3*) Firebrand Bks.

***This Is about Vision: Interviews with Southwestern Writers.** Ed. by William Balassi et al. LC 89-70428. 210p. 1990. reprint ed. pap. 59.90 (*0-608-04145-9*, 2064878) Bks Demand.

This Is Adam. Brainard Cheney. 1958. 12.95 (*0-8392-1116-3*) Astor-Honor.

This Is AISC. 1990. (*0-318-68353-9*, G442) Am Inst Steel Construct.

This Is Alabama. 3rd rev. ed. Merle T. Carroll. (Illus.). 336p. (J). (gr. 4). 1993. reprint ed. text ed. 14.50 (*0-9632262-0-7*) J Y Carroll.

This is Alabama: Teacher's Guide - Student Activity Book. 3rd ed. Merle T. Carroll. (Illus.). 116p. 1993. pap. text ed. 6.95 (*0-9632262-1-5*) J Y Carroll.

***This Is All I Ask.** Lynn Kurland. 432p. 1997. mass mkt. 5.99 (*0-515-12139-8*) Jove Pubns.

This Is Always Finished (David Dunlap) M. Jessica Rowe. LC 89-81319. (Illus.). 42p. (Orig.). 1989. pap. 12.00 (*0-9614615-9-4*) Edmundson.

This Is-Asi Es San Antonio. rev. ed. Carlos Freymann & Bud Shannon. Ed. by Freymann & Associates, Inc. Staff. LC 82-90967. (Illus.). 172p. (ENG & SPA.). 1986. reprint ed. pap. 19.95 (*0-317-93922-X*) Freymann & Assocs.

This Is-Asi Es San Antonio. 3rd rev. ed. Carlos Freymann & Bud Shannon. Ed. by Freymann & Associates, Inc. Staff. LC 82-90967. (Illus.). 172p. (ENG & SPA.). 1986. reprint ed. 26.95 (*0-317-93921-1*) Freymann & Assocs.

This Is Ballroom Dance. L. Ellfeldt. (Ballroom Dance Ser.). 1986. lib. bdg. 79.95 (*0-8490-3281-4*) Gordon Pr.

This Is Ballroom Dance. L. Ellfeldt. (Ballroom Dance Ser.). 1985. lib. bdg. 79.00 (*0-87700-825-6*) Revisionist Pr.

This Is Baseball. Margaret Blackstone. LC 92-22921. (Illus.). 32p. (J). (ps). 1993. 14.95 (*0-8050-2390-9*, Bks Young Read) H Holt & Co.

***This Is Baseball.** Margaret Blackstone. 1997. pap. text ed. 5.95 (*0-8050-5169-4*) H Holt & Co.

***This Is Basketball, Vol. 1.** Blackstone. 1995. pap. 14.95 (*0-8050-3387-4*) St Martin.

This is Bear. Houghton Mifflin Company Staff. (Literature Experience 1991 Ser.). (J). 1990. pap. 5.44 (*0-395-53888-2*) HM.

This Is Betsy. Gunilla Wolde. LC 75-7566. (Betsy Bks.). (Illus.). 24p. (J). (ps). 1990. 4.95 (*0-394-83161-6*) Random Bks Yng Read.

***This is Biology: The Science of the Living World.** Ernst Mayr. 1997. 29.95 (*0-614-28203-9*) HUP.

***This Is Biology: The Science of the Living World.** Ernst W. Mayr. LC 96-42192. 1997. 29.95 (*0-674-88468-X*) Belknap Pr.

This Is Birmingham: The Founding & Growth of an American City. John C. Henley, Jr. (Illus.). 1960. 9.95 (*0-87651-008-X*); pap. 6.95 (*0-87651-009-8*) Southern U Pr.

This Is Boat Interior Construction. Michael Naujok. (Illus.). 138p. 1993. 39.95 (*0-7136-3612-2*) Sheridan.

This Is Charleston. rev. ed. Samuel G. Stoney. (Illus.). 139p. (Orig.). reprint ed. pap. text ed. 6.95 (*0-910326-04-5*) Carolina Art.

This Is Christianity. Maxie Dunnam. LC 94-12639. 160p. (Orig.). 1994. pap. 7.95 (*0-687-00256-7*) Abingdon.

This Is Christianity. Jack Van Impe. 50p. 1986. pap. 2.00 (*0-934803-55-2*) J Van Impe.

This is Christmas: Singers Edition. T. Jennings. 12p. 1989. pap. 1.25 (*0-931205-43-3*) H Leonard.

This is Coffee Point, Go Ahead: A Mother's Story of Fishing & Survival at Alaska's Bristol Bay. Wilma Williams. Ed. by Diane F. Wood. (Alaska Pioneer Ser.: No. 2). 200p. (Orig.). 1996. pap. 15.95 (*1-886921-03-2*) Alaska Pr.

This Is Cruising. 2nd ed. Des Sleightholme. (This Is...Ser.). (Illus.). 160p. 1989. 24.95 (*0-911378-88-X*) Sheridan.

This Is Diving. 2nd ed. Duilio Marcante. Tr. by Mike Busuttili from ITA. (This Is...Ser.). (Illus.). 160p. 1989. 24.95 (*0-911378-96-0*) Sheridan.

This Is Earth Calling. United Nations Population Fund Staff. (Illus.). 1993. text ed. 15.95 (*81-220-0299-4*, Pub. by Konark Pubs II) Advent Bks Div.

This Is Figure Skating. Margaret Blackstone. LC 94-45695. (Illus.). (J). (gr. k-2). 1996. 15.95 (*0-8050-3706-3*, Bks Young Read) H Holt & Co.

This Is for You. Compiled by William S. Lord. LC 78-121926. (Granger Index Reprint Ser.). 1977. 19.95 (*0-8369-6167-6*) Ayer.

This Is for You. V. Lind Shipe. LC 92-80785. 117p. 1993. pap. 6.95 (*1-55523-530-1*) Winston-Derek.

This Is Germany. C. Domville-Fife. 1972. 59.95 (*0-8490-1195-7*) Gordon Pr.

This Is Germany. Ed. by Arthur Settel. LC 70-156715. (Essay Index Reprint Ser.). 1977. reprint ed. 28.95 (*0-8369-2427-4*) Ayer.

This Is God's World, 4 bks., Set. Charlotte Stowell. (Illus.). 22p. (J). 1994. boxed 10.99 (*1-56476-358-7*, 6-3358, Victor Bks) Chariot Victor.

This Is Gold Country. Bob Utecht. LC 77-91022. (Illus.). 1977. pap. 10.00 (*0-87832-041-5*) Piper.

This Is Hawaii Color/Sticker Book. 4th ed. Bernard O. Atkins. (Illus.). 20p. (J). (ps-6). 1995. pap. 4.95 (*0-9642050-2-5*) Great Creations.

This Is How I Love You. Selene De Medeiros. 67p. (YA). (gr. 9-12). 1990. per. 6.00 (*0-916418-76-6*) Lotus.

This Is How It Was. William J. Laubenstein. (Illus.). vi, 132p. 1971. pap. 4.95 (*0-913228-03-6*) Dillon-Liederbach.

This is How it Was: History of the 485th Bomb Group. Sam Schneider. Ed. by Byron L. Kennedy, 3rd. (Illus.). 328p. (C). 1995. text ed. 39.95 (*0-941072-15-0*) Southern Herit.

This Is How Seventy Looks: Stories of My Life. Constance Lindemann. 147p. (Orig.). 1993. pap. 9.50 (*0-9637014-0-1*) Compage Pr.

This Is How They Were Placed for Us: A Poem. Lucy Tapahonso. Ed. by Gloria V. Hickok. 6p. (Orig.). 1994. pap. 2.50 (*1-884235-01-8*) Helicon Nine Eds.

This Is How We Live: Listening to the Poorest Families. International Movement & Fourth World Staff. Tr. by Fourth World Movement Staff from FRE. 145p. (Orig.). 1995. pap. 12.00 (*0-934199-02-7*) New Fourth Wrld.

This Is Illyria, Lady. Constance Pilgrim. 179p. (C). 1989. text ed. 59.00 (*1-872795-21-8*, Pub. by Pentland Pr UK) St Mut.

This Is Insanity! No Dieting-No Exercising-No Counseling-No Results. Beth Donahue. Ed. by Mike Towle. (Illus.). 224p. (Orig.). 1994. pap. 9.95 (*1-56530-153-6*) Summit TX.

This Is Iowa. Marquis Childs & Paul Engel. Ed. by Clarence A. Andrews. LC 82-61137. (Illus.). 320p. 1982. lib. bdg. 14.95 (*0-934582-04-1*) Midwest Heritage.

This Is It. Alan W. Watts. 1973. pap. 9.00 (*0-394-71904-2*, Vin) Random.

***This Is Jamaica - Reggae - & Rastafari: The Book of Truths - Eye on Jamaica.** Ras Cardo & Gartie Dennis. (Reggae Family Ser.). (Illus.). 200p. (Orig.). Date not set. pap. write for info. (*1-883427-92-4*, RAS9949-A) Crnerstone GA.

This Is Jest for You. Skip Wilson. LC 85-1399. (Orig.). 1986. pap. 12.95 (*0-87949-261-9*) Ashley Bks.

This Is Jim Rockford: The Rockford Files. Ed Robertson. (Illus.). 176p. (Orig.). 1995. pap. 19.95 (*0-938817-36-1*) Pomegranate Pr.

This Is Just to Say. Bill Deemer. Tr. by Stefan Hyner from ENG. (Orig.). (GER.). 1981. pap. 4.00 (*0-940556-03-0*) Coyote.

This Is Kendo. Junzo Sasamori. 14.95 (*0-685-22139-3*) Wehman.

This Is Kendo: The Art of Japanese Fencing. Gordon Warner & Junzo Sasamori. LC 64-22900. 160p. 1964. pap. 16.95 (*0-8048-1607-7*) C E Tuttle.

This Is Lagos & Other Stories. Flora Nwapa. 140p. 1992. 24.95 (*0-86543-320-8*); pap. 9.95 (*0-86543-321-6*) Africa World.

This Is Life. S. L. Chin. 172p. 1990. pap. text ed. 7.00 (*0-9625118-2-X*) World Scientific Pub.

This Is Liquid Sugar (Including Supplement) P. X. Hoynak & G. N. Bollenback. 1966. text ed. 14.50 (*0-934636-04-4*) Key Bk Serv.

This Is Living. Constant S. Kaczmarek. (Illus.). 325p. (YA). 1990. text ed. 75.00 (*0-9626041-0-0*) C Kaczmarek.

This Is Living: How I Found Health & Happiness. Lynn Redgrave. 400p. 1992. pap. 5.99 (*0-451-17307-4*, Sig) NAL-Dutton.

This Is Logging & Sawmilling - Documentary. Bert Webber & Margie Webber. LC 96-12172. (Illus.). (Orig.). 1996. pap. 19.95 (*0-936738-18-9*) Webb Research.

This is Maine. Margaret Blackstone & Segal. (J). 1995. 15.95 (*0-8050-2800-5*, Bks Young Read) H Holt & Co.

***This Is Me.** (Richard Scarry's First Little Learners Ser.). (Illus.). 24p. (J). (gr. k-2). 1995. write for info. (*1-56144-725-0*, Honey Bear Bks) Modern Pub NYC.

This Is Me. Lenore Blegvad. LC 85-61671. (Chunky Bks.). (Illus.). 28p. (J). (ps). 1986. 3.99 (*0-394-87816-7*) Random Bks Yng Read.

This Is Me. 2nd rev. ed. Hazel Neitzke. LC 96-84632. (Illus.). 32p. (J). (gr. 2-3). 1996. pap. write for info. (*0-942495-58-6*) Amherst Pr.

This Is Me: A Collection of Poems & Things. 2nd ed. Gabrielle David. (Illus.). 30p. 1994. reprint ed. pap. 5.00 (*1-889033-00-6*, 01-941996) Chimeara Communs.

This Is Me - Block Book. Snapshot Staff. 22p. (J). 1996. 3.95 (*0-7894-0625-X*) DK Pub Inc.

This Is Me & My Two Families: An Awareness Scrapbook - Journal for Children Living in Stepfamilies. Marla D. Evans. (Illus.). 88p. (J). (gr. 2-6). 1988. pap. 14.95 (*0-945354-06-1*) Magination Pr.

This Is Me, Answering Your Last Letter. Kevin Asher et al. (Illus.). 24p. 1995. 17.50 (*0-9650548-0-2*) K Asher.

This Is Me, Laughing. Lynea Bowdish. LC 95-13860. (Illus.). 32p. (J). (gr. k-3). 1996. 16.00 (*0-374-37489-9*) FS&G.

This Is Milwaukee. Robert Wells. LC 78-71508. 1978. reprint ed. 17.50 (*0-932476-00-7*) Renaiss Bks.

This Is Mine. Ellen Stephenson. (C). 1989. text ed. 40.00 (*1-872795-62-5*, Pub. by Pentland Pr UK) St Mut.

This Is Mohan. Ella Grove. (Jewel Bks.). 1989. pap. 2.15 (*0-317-02026-9*) Rod & Staff.

This Is Music: A Guide to the Pleasures of Listening. rev. ed. David Randolph. 236p. 1997. pap. 12.50 (*0-88739-110-9*) Creat Arts Bk.

This Is My Beloved. Walter Benton. 1949. 20.00 (*0-394-40458-0*) Knopf.

This Is My Beloved: Psalms of Communion. Lucy Brown. LC 88-71798. (Illus.). 196p. (Orig.). (C). 1988. pap 8.95 (*0-9620560-0-6*) Cedargarden.

This Is My Beloved Son - Listen to Him, Vol. 1. Anthony M. Coniaris. 1987. pap. 15.95 (*0-937032-55-7*) Light&Life Pub Co MN.

This is My Beloved Son - Listen to Him, Vol. 2. Anthony M. Coniaris. 1988. pap. 15.95 (*0-937032-50-6*) Light&Life Pub Co MN.

This Is My Body. Ian Petit. 96p. (Orig.). 1993. pap. 5.95 (*0-8146-2133-3*) Liturgical Pr.

This Is My Body. Terry Song. 56p. 1994. pap. 7.95 (*0-931122-77-5*) West End.

This Is My Body: An Evangelical Discovers the Real Presence. Mark P. Shea. 64p. (Orig.). 1993. pap. 3.95 (*0-931888-48-4*) Christendom Pr.

This Is My Body: Creativity, Clay, & Change. Marjory Z. Bankson. LC 92-35244. (Illus.). 192p. (Orig.). 1993. pap. 14.95 (*0-931055-94-6*) Innisfree Pr.

This is My Body, This is My Blood: Miracles of the Eucharist. Bob Lord & Penny Lord. (Illus.). 192p. (Orig.). 1986. pap. 8.95 (*0-926143-02-6*) Journeys Faith.

***This Is My Body, This Is My Blood, Miracles of the Eucharist, Vol. 2.** Bob Lord & Penny Lord. (Illus.). 272p. 1994. pap. 12.95 (*0-926143-33-6*, BT-2) Journeys Faith.

This Is My Century: New & Collected Poems. Margaret Walker. LC 88-8016. 232p. 1989. 30.00 (*0-8203-1134-0*); pap. 14.95 (*0-8203-1135-9*) U of Ga Pr.

This Is My Child. Lucy Gordon. (Desire Ser.). 1996. mass mkt. 3.50 (*0-373-05982-5*, 1-05982-3) Silhouette.

***This Is My Church.** rev. ed. Robert D. Troutman. 40p. 1988. pap. 1.99 (*0-8341-1264-7*); teacher ed., pap. 1.99 (*0-8341-1265-5*) Beacon Hill.

This Is My Country. Jacobs & Raye. (Piano-Vocal-Guitar Ser.). 4p. 1981. pap. 3.95 (*0-7935-0689-1*, 00355305) H Leonard.

This is My Country. Houghton Mifflin Social Studies Staff. 1993. text ed. 43.88 (*0-395-54891-8*) HM.

This Is My Destiny. large type ed. Juliet Gray. 288p. 1992. pap. 15.99 (*0-7089-7291-8*, Trailtree Bookshop) Ulverscroft.

This is My Family. Gina Mayer & Mercer Mayer. (Little Golden Bks.). (Illus.). 24p. (J). (ps-2). 1992. bds. 1.49 (*0-307-00137-7*, 312-02, Golden Books) Western Pub.

This Is My Friend. Mercer Mayer. (Golden Easy Reader Ser.: Level 2). (Illus.). 40p. (J). (gr. k-2). 1989. write for info. (*0-307-11685-9*) Western Pub.

This Is My God. large type ed. Herman Wouk. (Large Print Jewish Classics Ser.). 395p. 1991. reprint ed. pap. 15.95 (*0-8027-2643-7*) Walker & Co.

This Is My God, Vol. 1. Herman Wouk. 1988. 17.95 (*0-316-95507-8*) Little.

This Is My God: The Jewish Way of Life. Herman Wouk. (Illus.). 358p. 1992. 10.95 (*0-316-95514-0*) Little.

***This Is My House.** (Richard Scarry's First Little Learners Ser.). (Illus.). 24p. (J). (gr. k-2). 1995. write for info. (*1-56144-726-9*, Honey Bear Bks) Modern Pub NYC.

This is My House. Arthur Dorros. (Illus.). 32p. (J). (ps). 1992. 15.95 (*0-590-45302-5*, 019, Scholastic Hardcover) Scholastic Inc.

This Is My House. Tiziano Sclavi. (Wire-O-Board Bks.). (Illus.). 24p. (J). (gr. 3 up). 1994. 7.95 (*1-55550-993-2*) Universe.

This Is My Life. Carol McConnell. 128p. (Orig.). 1996. pap. 15.95 (*1-886094-29-2*) Chicago Spectrum.

This Is My Life. Bonnie F. Phillips. LC 93-73817. (Illus.). 362p. (Orig.). 1993. pap. write for info. (*0-938041-18-5*) Arc Pr AR.

This Is My Life. Agnes Hunt. Ed. by William R. Phillips & Janet Rosenberg. LC 79-6013. (Physically Handicapped in Society Ser.). 1980. reprint ed. lib. bdg. 24.95 (*0-405-13116-X*) Ayer.

This Is My Life: A Youth Genealogy Starter Kit. Duane S. Crowther. LC 78-52406. 76p. 1995. pap. 9.98 (*0-88290-582-1*, 1505) Horizon Utah.

***This Is My Life: Life Stories of David Carter As Told to Wanda Kay Steele.** David W. Carter. LC 96-97106. (Illus.). xix, 83p. (Orig.). 1996. pap. 10.00 (*0-9655009-0-X*) D Carter.

***This Is My Life: Never Give Up - There Is Hope in God.** Ennis B. Song. 80p. (Orig.). 1997. pap. 11.99 (*0-9633356-8-5*) Harvest Time.

This Is My Opinion about... Linda P. Silbert & Alvin J. Silbert. (Little Twirps Creative Thinking Workbook Ser.). (Illus.). (J). (gr. 5-12). 1977. 4.98 (*0-89544-020-2*, 020) Silbert Bress.

This Is My Song! A Collection of Gospel Music for the Family. Vy Higgenson. LC 93-34303. (Illus.). 96p. (J). (gr. 1 up). 1995. 25.00 (*0-517-59492-7*); lib. bdg. 26.99 (*0-517-59493-5*) Crown Pub Group.

This Is My Story. Candi Suswell. 1995. pap. 9.95 (*1-56229-422-9*) Pneuma Life Pub.

This Is My Story: Perspectives on the Use of Oral Sources. Tr. by Shelley Schreiner & Diana Bell. 132p. 1992. pap. 30.00 (*0-7300-1435-5*, Pub. by Deakin Univ AT) St Mut.

This Is My Story - This Is My Song. Frances Cardone. 192p. 1994. lib. bdg. 14.95 (*1-883928-05-2*) Longwood.

This Is My Wish for You. Charles L. Snell. (Illus.). 48p. 1992. 18.95 (*0-9621131-4-X*) Blue Lantern Studio.

This Is New Jersey. John T. Cunningham. 1978. pap. 16.95 (*0-8135-0862-2*) Rutgers U Pr.

This Is New Jersey. rev. ed. John T. Cunningham. (Illus.). 285p. (C). 1994. reprint ed. pap. 15.95 (*0-8135-2141-6*) Rutgers U Pr.

This Is New Jersey. 3rd ed. John T. Cunningham. LC 78-5884. (Illus.). 301p. 1978. reprint ed. pap. 85.80 (*0-7837-9214-X*, 2049964) Bks Demand.

This Is New Jersey. 4th rev. ed. John T. Cunningham. (Illus.). 285p. (C). 1994. reprint ed. text ed. 35.00 (*0-8135-2140-8*) Rutgers U Pr.

This Is No Book: A Gay Reader. Gergory Woods. 112p. (Orig.). 1995. pap. 14.90 (*0-907123-26-0*, Pub. by Five Leaves UK) AK Pr Dist.

This Is Not a Photograph: Twenty Years of Photography, 1966-1986. Joseph Jacobs. LC 86-80681. 110p. 1987. pap. 30.00 (*0-916758-23-0*) Ringling Mus Art.

This Is Not a Pipe: Illustrations & Letters by Rene Magritte. Michel Foucault. Tr. by James Harkness. LC 80-26627. (Quantum Bks.: No. 24). (Illus.). 112p. 1982. pap. 12.95 (*0-520-04916-0*) U CA Pr.

This Is Not a Pipe Dream (Playscript) Barry Kornhauser. (Orig.). (YA). 1993. pap. 5.00 (*0-87602-316-2*) Anchorage.

This Is Not a Place to Sing. Christina Pacosz. 48p. (Orig.). (C). 1987. pap. 4.95 (*0-931122-47-3*) West End.

This Is Not a Story & Other Stories. Denis Diderot. Tr. & Intro. by P. N. Furbank. LC 92-26850. (World's Classics Ser.). 176p. 1993. 7.95 (*0-19-282958-0*) OUP.

This Is Not a Story & Other Stories. Dennis Diderot. Tr. & Intro. by P. N. Furbank. 176p. 1991. text ed. 27.50 (*0-8262-0815-0*) U of Mo Pr.

This Is Not America, Either. Balazs Czeizel. (Illus.). 96p. (Orig.). 1993. pap. 25.00 (*0-89822-107-2*) Visual Studies.

This Is Not Another Poet. Ethel D. Smith. 48p. (Orig.). pap. text ed. 9.95 (*0-9622820-2-2*) Dee & P Pr.

This Is Not for You. Jane Rule. 304p. 1982. reprint ed. pap. 8.95 (*0-930044-25-8*) Naiad Pr.

This Is Not Goodbye...It's Halo: Awakening the Angelsoul Within. Victoria L. Feldman. Ed. by Sara Patton. (Illus.). 120p. (Orig.). 1994. pap. 10.95 (*0-9642697-0-8*) Angelsoul Pr.

This Is Not Just Another Poet. 1990. write for info. (*0-318-67250-2*) Dee & P Pr.

This Is Not My Child. Mel C. Thompson. 46p. (Orig.). 1990. pap. 3.95 (*1-879665-01-8*) Cyborg Prods.

This Is Not Surrealism. Dennis Saleh. Ed. by Douglas A. Conner. 24p. (Orig.). 1992. pap. 5.50 (*0-9627791-2-1*) Willamette Bks OR.

This Is Not the Honeymoon I Anticipated. Richard Hafer. Ed. by Christianson. (Illus.). 80p. (Orig.). 1996. per. 8.95 (*0-89024-302-6*, 12183) Kalmbach.

This Is Not Your Father's Stock. Derrick Niederman. 1997. pap. write for info. (*0-8129-2862-8*, Times Bks) Random.

This Is Not Your Father's Stockpicking Book. Derrick Neiderman. LC 95-2485. 1995. 25.00 (*0-8129-2216-6*) Random.

This Is Not Your Father's Stockpicking Book. Derrick Niederman. Date not set. write for info. (*0-8129-2832-6*, Times Bks) Random.

This Is Nothing Special. Martha Doherty. (Illus.). (Orig.). (J). (gr. 1-4). 1996. pap. 6.95 (*0-533-11729-1*) Vantage.

This Is Our Child: How Parents Experience the Medical World. Antonya Cooper & Valerie Harpin. 160p. 1991. pap. 14.95 (*0-19-261899-7*, 12169) OUP.

This Is Our Earth. Laura L. Benson. LC 93-11936. (Illus.). 32p. (J). (ps-3). 1994. 15.95 (*0-88106-445-9*); pap. 6.95 (*0-88106-447-5*) Charlesbridge Pub.

***This Is Our Earth.** Laura L. Benson. LC 93-11936. (Illus.). 32p. (J). (ps-4). 1997. reprint ed. pap. 6.95 (*0-88106-839-X*) Charlesbridge Pub.

***This Is Our Earth.** Laura L. Benson. LC 93-11936. (Illus.). 32p. (J). (ps-4). 1997. reprint ed. 15.95 (*0-88106-838-1*) Charlesbridge Pub.

This Is Our Faith... A Catholic Catechism for Adults. Michael F. Pennock. LC 88-82681. 288p. (Orig.). 1989. pap. 8.95 (*0-87793-389-8*) Ave Maria.

This Is Our House. Michael Rosen. LC 95-36137. (Illus.). 32p. (J). (ps up). 1996. 15.99 (*1-56402-870-4*) Candlewick Pr.

This Is Our Land, Vol. 1. Val J. McClellan. LC 77-151749. (Illus.). 902p. 1977. 17.95 (*0-533-02248-7*, 77-151749) Western Pubs NC.

This Is Our Land, Vol. 2. Val J. McClellan. LC 77-151749. (Illus.). 927p. 1979. 17.95 (*0-9602218-0-8*) Western Pubs NC.

This Is Our Mass. Thomas Coyle. LC 89-50155. 160p. 1989. pap. 7.95 (*0-89622-394-9*) Twenty-Third.

This Is Our St. Rose Church in Proctor Minnesota. Claire W. Schumacher. LC 76-22312. (Illus.). 100p. 1976. pap. 10.00 (*0-917378-02-4*) Zenith City.

***This Is Our Work: The Legacy of Sir William Osler.** Ted Grant. 249p. 1994. text ed. 117.00 (*0-9698568-0-6*) Amer Coll Phys.

This Is Pearl: The United States & Japan, 1941. Walter Millis. LC 77-138594. (Illus.). 384p. 1971. reprint ed. text ed. 65.00 (*0-8371-5795-1*, MITP, Greenwood Pr) Greenwood.

This Is PR: The Realities of Public Relations. 5th ed. Doug Newsom et al. LC 92-10718. 615p. (C). 1993. text ed. 47.75 (*0-534-17262-8*) Wadsworth Pub.

This Is PR: The Realities of Public Relations. 6th ed. Doug Newsom et al. LC 92-10718. (C). 1996. text ed. 69.95 (*0-534-22890-9*) Wadsworth Pub.

This is Ragtime. Terry Waldo. (Quality Paperbacks Ser.). (Illus.). 256p. 1991. reprint ed. pap. 12.95 (*0-306-80439-5*) Da Capo.

This Is Reading. Frank G. Jennings. LC 82-361. 210p. (C). 1982. reprint ed. 37.50 (*0-306-40990-9*, Plenum Pr); reprint ed. pap. 19.95 (*0-306-40992-5*, Plenum Pr) Plenum.

This Is Really a Great City. J. P. Fennell. 1991. pap. 7.95 (*0-8065-9980-4*, Citadel Pr) Carol Pub Group.

This Is Rhythm. Ella Jenkins. (Illus.). 96p. (J). (ps-5). 1993. pap. 14.95 (*1-881322-02-5*) Sing Out.

This Is San Francisco: A Classic Portrait of the City. Robert O'Brien. LC 94-4578. (Illus.). 372p. 1994. pap. 12.95 (*0-8118-0578-6*) Chronicle Bks.

This Is San Quentin. Peek. (Illus.). 50p. (Orig.). 1991. pap. 3.95 (*0-9630115-0-2*) San Quentin Mus.

***This Is Soccer, Vol. 1.** Blackstone. 1996. 14.95 (*0-8050-2801-3*) St Martin.

This Is South Dakota. (Orig.). pap. text ed. write for info. (*1-56944-091-3*) Terrell Missouri.

This is South Dakota. Date not set. text ed. write for info. (*1-56944-107-3*) Terrell Missouri.

This Is the Abyssinian Cat. Kate Faler. (Illus.). 160p. 1983. 35.95 (*0-87666-866-X*, PS-783) TFH Pubns.

This Is the Alaskan Malamute. Joan M. Brearley. (Illus.). 415p. 1975. 24.95 (*0-87666-650-0*, PS-737) TFH Pubns.

This Is the American Earth. Ansel Adams & Nancy Newhall. (Illus.). 96p. 1995. 50.00 (*0-8212-2182-5*) Bulfinch Pr.

This Is the American Pit Bull Terrier. Richard F. Stratton. (Illus.). 1976. 24.95 (*0-87666-660-8*, PS-613) TFH Pubns.

***This Is the Baby.** Eldon Weisheit. (Illus.). 32p. (J). (ps-2). 1996. 5.99 (*0-570-04808-7*, 56-1823) Concordia.

This Is the Bear. Sarah Hayes. LC 92-53421. (Bear Hugs Ser.). (Illus.). 32p. (J). (ps up). 1993. 4.95 (*1-56402-253-6*) Candlewick Pr.

This Is the Bear. Sarah Hayes. LC 92-53421. (Illus.). 32p. (J). (ps up). 1994. pap. 4.99 (*1-56402-270-6*) Candlewick Pr.

***This Is the Bear.** Sarah Hayes. (Little Book Cards Ser.). (Illus.). (J). 1997. pap. 3.29 (*0-7636-0219-1*) Candlewick Pr.

This Is the Bear & the Bad Little Girl. Sarah Hayes. LC 95-10699. (Illus.). (J). (ps up). 1995. 14.99 (*1-56402-648-5*) Candlewick Pr.

***This Is the Bear & the Bad Little Girl.** Sarah Hayes. LC 95-10699. (Illus.). 32p. (J). (ps-2). 1997. reprint ed. pap. 5.99 (*0-7636-0297-3*) Candlewick Pr.

This Is the Bear & the Picnic Lunch. Sarah Hayes. (Illus.). 32p. (J). (ps-1). 1989. 12.95 (*0-316-35248-9*, Joy St Bks) Little.

This Is the Bear Big Book. Sarah Hayes. LC 92-53421. (Illus.). (J). 1995. bds. 19.99 (*1-56402-494-6*) Candlewick Pr.

This Is the Bichon Frise. Joan McD. Brearley & Anna K. Nicholas. (Illus.). 1973. 24.95 (*0-87666-247-5*, PS-700) TFH Pubns.

This Is the Bird. George Shannon. LC 94-28974. (Illus.). (J). 1997. 15.95 (*0-395-72037-0*) HM.

This Is the Book That I Borrowed. June Loves. LC 92-31955. (Voyages Ser.). (Illus.). (J). 1993. 4.25 (*0-383-03598-8*) SRA McGraw.

This Is the Bread I Baked for Ned. Crescent Dragonwagon. LC 88-22619. (Illus.). 32p. (J). (gr. k-3). 1989. lib. bdg. 14.95 (*0-02-733220-9*, Mac Bks Young Read) S&S Childrens.

This Is the British Forces Network... The Story of Forces Broadcasting in Germany. Alan Grace. (Illus.). 224p. 1996. 26.95 (*0-7509-1105-0*, Pub. by Sutton Pubng UK) Bks Intl VA.

This Is the Child. Terry Pringle. LC 91-52776. 208p. 1992. reprint ed. pap. 10.95 (*0-87074-332-5*); reprint ed. text ed. 19.95 (*0-87074-335-X*) SMU Press.

This Is the Day. Llewellyn McKernan. (Stardust Ser.). (Illus.). 24p. 1994. 4.50 (*0-8378-7690-7*) Gibson.

This Is the Day. Elaine Rendler. Ed. by Bari Colombari. 255p. 1995. pap. text ed. 11.95 (*0-915531-42-9*) OR Catholic.

This Is the Day: The Biblical Doctrine of the Christian Sunday in it's Jewish & Early Church Setting. Roger T. Beckwith & Wilfrid Scott. 392p. 1978. 12.00 (*0-551-05568-5*) Attic Pr.

This Is the End...My Only Friend: Living & Dying with Jim Morrison. Judy Huddleston. 1991. 18.95 (*1-56171-038-5*) Sure Seller.

This Is the Farmer. Nancy Tafuri. LC 92-30082. (Illus.). 24p. (J). (ps up). 1994. 15.00 (*0-688-09468-6*); lib. bdg. 14.93 (*0-688-09469-4*) Greenwillow.

This Is the Hat. Nancy Van Laan. LC 94-26624. (Illus.). 32p. (J). (ps-2). 1995. pap. 4.95 (*0-7868-1030-0*) Hyprn Child.

This Is the Hat: Book Pack, 8 Bks., Level 2. Nancy Van Laan. LC 94-26624. (Early Readers Ser.). (Illus.). 32p. (J). (ps-2). 1995. pap. 16.95 (*0-7868-1052-1*) Hyprn Child.

This Is the Hat Level 1: Book Pack, 8 bks., Level 1. Nancy Van Laan. LC 94-26624. (Illus.). 32p. 1995. pap. 16.95 (*0-7868-1051-3*) Hyprn Child.

This Is the House That Jack Built. Illus. by Pam Adams. LC 90-46922. (Books with Holes Ser.). 16p. (Orig.). (J). (ps-2). 1977. pap. 6.99 (*0-85953-075-2*, Pub. by Childs Play UK) Childs Play.

This is the House that Jack Built. Pam Adams. LC 90-46922. (J). 1972. 13.99 (*0-85953-076-0*) Childs Play.

***This Is the House That Jack Built.** Illus. by Pam Adams. (Books with Holes Ser.). (ITA.). (J). 1977. pap. 6.99 (*0-85953-593-2*) Childs Play.

This Is the House Where Jack Lives. Joan Heilbroner. LC 62-7311. (Harper I Can Read Bk.). (Illus.). 64p. (J). (gr. k-3). 1962. lib. bdg. 14.89 (*0-06-022286-7*) HarpC Child Bks.

This Is the Just Cause: Breaking the Silence: Testimony of the Panamanian People, Resulting from the U. S. A. Invasion. 2nd ed. Commission for the Defence of Human Rights in Central America Staff. (Illus.). 80p. (Orig.). 1991. pap. 9.95 (*0-945257-39-2*) Apex Pr.

This Is the King! A Service for Palm - Passion Sunday. Cynthia E. Cowen. 1992. pap. 3.25 (*1-55673-568-5*, 9315) CSS OH.

This Is the Life. Goodspeed. (gr. 7-12). 1981. text ed. 15.40 (*0-02-665910-7*) Glencoe.

This Is the Life. Joseph O'Neill. 224p. 1991. 18.95 (*0-374-27590-4*) FS&G.

This Is the Life Story of John Konjak. John Konjak. 24p. 1996. pap. 6.00 (*0-8059-3741-2*) Dorrance.

***This Is the Love.** write for info. (*0-929917-05-7*) Magnolia PA.

This Is the Maine Coon Cat. Sharon P. Bass. (Illus.). 128p. 1983. 23.95 (*0-86622-096-8*, H-1057) TFH Pubns.

This Is the Newfoundland. K. Drury. 23.95 (*0-87666-340-4*, PS-666) TFH Pubns.

This Is the Night. Llewellyn McKernan. (Stardust Ser.). (Illus.). 24p. 1994. 4.50 (*0-8378-7691-5*) Gibson.

This is the One I Want. Linda G. Richman. (Illus.). 172p. 1987. spiral bd. 24.00 (*0-9609160-3-2*) Mayer-Johnson.

This Is the Ordinance for the Quenes Swannes see Proclamations II, Chronological Series

This Is the Path: The 12 Steps in a Jewish Context. Rami M. Shapiro. 68p. (Orig.). 1993. pap. 9.95 (*0-911511-01-6*) Light House.

This Is the Place. Will Bagley. LC 95-40502. (Illus.). 32p. (J). (gr. 2-8). 1996. pap. 9.95 (*1-885628-25-0*) Buckaroo Bks.

***This Is the Place.** Peter Rock. LC 96-33606. 240p. 1997. pap. 12.00 (*0-385-48598-0*, Anchor NY) Doubleday.

This Is the Place: Brigham Young & the New Zion. Ed. by Ernest H. Taves. (Illus.). 299p. (C). 1991. 28.95 (*0-87975-628-4*) Prometheus Bks.

***This Is the Place: The Story of the Mormon Trail.** William E. Hill & Jan C. Hill. (Illus.). 40p. (Orig.). (J). (ps-4). 1996. pap. 4.50 (*0-9636071-2-X*) HillHouse Pub.

This Is the Place for Me. Joanna Cole. (Illus.). 32p. (Orig.). (J). (gr. k-3). 1986. pap. 2.99 (*0-590-33996-6*) Scholastic Inc.

***This Is the Place for Me.** Joanna Cole & William Van Horn. (FRE.). (J). pap. 6.99 (*0-590-71919-X*); pap. 13.99 incl. audio (*0-614-28373-6*) Scholastic Inc.

This Is the Plate. 2nd ed. Alan Trussell-Cullen. (Let Me Read Ser.). (Illus.). 8p. (J). (ps). 1995. pap. 2.95 (*0-673-36234-5*, GoodYrBooks) Addson-Wesley Educ.

This Is the Prophet Jesus. Fred Howes. LC 82-72741. 276p. 1983. pap. 8.95 (*0-87516-497-8*) DeVorss.

***This Is the Pumpkin.** Abby Levine. LC 97-6156. (Illus.). 24p. (J). (ps-1). 1997. lib. bdg. 13.95 (*0-8075-7886-X*) A Whitman.

This Is the Seed, Level 2. Alan Trussell-Cullen. (Let Me Read Ser.). (J). 1996. 2.95 (*0-673-36339-2*, GoodYrBooks) Addson-Wesley Educ.

This Is the Shih Tzu. rev. ed. Allan Easton. 1969. 23.95 (*0-87666-389-7*, PS661) TFH Pubns.

This is the Sound: The Best of Alternative Rock. Randi Reisfeld. (Illus.). 128p. (YA). (gr. 7 up). 1996. pap. 7.99 (*0-689-80670-1*, Aladdin Paperbacks) S&S Childrens.

This Is the South. Ed. by Robert W. Howard. LC 77-167357. (Essay Index Reprint Ser.). 1977. reprint ed. 31.95 (*0-8369-2507-6*) Ayer.

This Is the Star. Joyce Dunbar. (Illus.). 36p. (J). 1996. 16.00 (*0-15-200851-9*) HarBrace.

This Is the Torah. Alfred J. Kolatch. LC 87-33624. 364p. 1988. 25.00 (*0-8246-0333-8*) Jonathan David.

This Is the Torah. Alfred J. Kolatch. 364p. 1994. pap. 15.00 (*0-8246-0377-X*) Jonathan David.

This Is the Town of Bethlehem. Evelyn O. Jensen. 28p. 1995. pap. 7.50 (*0-9644772-0-3*, Triple J) Triple J Prod.

This Is the Way I Pass My Time. Ellen J. Gehret et al. LC 84-62851. (Pennsylvania German Folklore Ser.: Vol. 18). (Illus.). 292p. 1985. 45.00 (*0-911122-48-6*) Penn German Soc.

This Is the Way I See Aesthetic Realism. Chaim Koppelman. (Illus.). 33p. 1969. pap. 3.50 (*0-911492-11-9*) Aesthetic Realism.

This Is the Way the World Ends. James Morrow. LC 85-24773. 1995. pap. 11.00 (*0-15-600208-6*) HarBrace.

This Is the Way We Eat Our Lunch: A Book about Children Around the World. Edith Baer. LC 94-9753. (Illus.). 40p. (J). (gr. 2-5). 1995. 14.95 (*0-590-46887-1*, Scholastic Hardcover) Scholastic Inc.

This Is the Way We Go to School. Edith Baer. (Illus.). 40p. (J). (ps-1). 1992. reprint ed. pap. 4.99 (*0-590-43162-5*, Blue Ribbon Bks) Scholastic Inc.

This Is the Way We Go to School - Asi Vamos a la Escuala. Edith Baer. 40p. (ENG & SPA.). (J). (ps-3). 1994. pap. 4.99 (*0-590-49443-0*) Scholastic Inc.

This Is the Way We Make a Face. Jo Lodge. (J). (ps). 1996. 5.95 (*0-8120-6607-3*) Barron.

This Is the Way We Make Our Baskets. Dorothy Titus & Matthew Titus. (Illus.). 28p. 1991. pap. 5.00 (*0-933769-06-7*) Alaska Native.

This Is the Will of God. John H. Barker. pap. 4.99 (*0-88019-116-3*) Schmul Pub Co.

This Is Thumb Book. Rosemary Callahan. LC 92-56931. (Illus.). 35p. (J). (gr. k-3). 1993. pap. 5.95 (*1-55523-571-9*) Winston-Derek.

This Is True: Deputy Kills Man with Hammer: And 500 Other Bizarre-but-True Stories & Headlines from the World's Press. Randy Cassingham. (This Is True Ser.: Vol. 1). 160p. (Orig.). 1995. pap. 11.00 (*0-935309-21-7*) Freelance Comm.

This Is True: Glow-in-the-Dark Plants Could Help Farmers: And over 500 Other Bizarre-but True Stories & Headlines from the World's Press. Randy Cassingham. (This Is True Ser.: Vol. 2). 160p. (Orig.). 1996. pap. 11.00 (*0-935309-22-5*) Freelance Comm.

This Is Truth about the Self. 3rd ed. Ann Davies. 1984. 2.50 (*0-938002-03-1*) Builders of Adytum.

This Is Vermont. Vermont Historical Society Staff & George Merkle. (Illus.). 100p. 1965. pap. 1.98 (*0-911868-14-3*, C14) Carstens Pubns.

***This Is What I Call Cooking.** Klarissa Kochen. 74p. 1997. pap. 14.95 (*1-890634-00-X*) Hugelwilhelm Pub.

This Is What I Remember: A Boy's Life in Louisiana & Texas 1862-1869 - the Reminiscences of John Allen Tippit. Ed. by Clifton Caldwell & Mary Crawford. 96p. 1989. 17.95 (*0-685-50776-9*) State House Pr.

This Is What Was Down That Road! What's Down That Road? rev. ed. Harriet U. Fish. (Illus.). 44p. 1993. reprint ed. lib. bdg. write for info. (*0-9612344-1-5*) H U Fish.

This Is What We Have to Do - Are You Okay? (DINROO) Nurses Speech with Elderly Nursing Home Residents. Heather Gibb. (Research Monographs: No. 1). (C). 1991. pap. 21.00 (*0-7300-1444-4*, Pub. by Deakin Univ AT) St Mut.

***This Is Where I Love: A Journal by Appalachian Women.** Ed. by Lilith Quinlan et al. (Common Ground Ser.: Vol. IX). (Illus.). 110p. (Orig.). 1997. pap. 10.00 (*1-884478-08-5*) Common Grnd.

This Is Wisdom. Satguru S. Keshavadas. (Illus.). 96p. (Orig.). 1975. pap. 8.00 (*0-942508-07-6*) Vishwa.

This Is Women's Work: An Anthology of Women's Poetry, Prose & Graphics. Ed. by Susan Efros. LC 74-19118. (Illus.). 160p. 1974. pap. 6.95 (*0-915572-02-8*) Panjandrum.

This Is Wrestling. George J. Napolitano. (Illus.). 64p. 1995. 9.98 (*0-8317-8016-9*) Smithmark.

This Is Wyoming: Read 'n Color Book. Tony Elliott. LC 89-469. (Illus.). (J). (gr. 3-6). 1989. pap. 4.50 (*0-914565-39-7*, 39-7, Timbertrails) Capstan Pubns.

This Is You, America: The Constitution Explained. Barbara Lamm. (Illus.). 227p. (Orig.). 1996. pap. 18.95 (*1-56072-326-2*) Nova Sci Pubs.

***This Is Your Day.** Lisa Weiss. 1998. write for info. (*0-375-75017-7*, Villard Bks) Random.

This Is Your Day. Edward Newhouse. LC 74-2800. (Labor Movement in Fiction & Non-Fiction Ser.). reprint ed. 45.00 (*0-404-58456-X*) AMS Pr.

This Is Your Day for a Miracle. Benny Hinn. 192p. 1996. 16.99 (*0-88419-391-8*) Creation House.

This Is Your Final Warning! Thom Metzger. 181p. Date not set. 7.00 (*0-936756-88-8*) Autonomedia.

***This Is Your Garden.** Maggie Smith. (J). 1998. write for info. (*0-517-70992-9*); lib. bdg. write for info. (*0-517-70993-7*) Crown Bks Yng Read.

This Is Your Georgia. 1981. write for info. (*0-932659-00-4*) Viewpoint Pubns.

This Is Your Georgia. 1986. write for info. (*0-932659-01-2*) Viewpoint Pubns.

This Is Your Law. 2nd ed. Communications Library Staff. 70p. 1987. pap. text ed. 25.00 (*0-934339-87-2*) Comm Lib.

This Is Your Life! M. Frazier Keables. LC 98-83426. 64p. (Orig.). 1993. pap. 6.95 (*0-9630779-4-5*) PPC Bks.

This Is Your Life. Mimi Tate. 1986. pap. 3.95 (*0-89137-815-4*) Quality Pubns.

This Island Earth: The Original Shooting Script. Philip J. Riley & Robert Skotak. LC 89-63448. (Universal Filmscript Series: Classic Science Fiction: Vol. 1). (Illus.). 184p. 1995. pap. 19.95 (*1-882127-27-7*) Magicimage Filmbooks.

This Island Earth from the Viewpoint of the Apollo Spacecraft. 1994. lib. bdg. 260.95 (*0-8490-6400-7*) Gordon Pr.

This Island Isn't Big Enough for the Four of Us! Gary Greer & Robert Ruddick. LC 86-47750. (Trophy Bk.). 160p. (J). (gr. 3-7). 1989. reprint ed. pap. 3.95 (*0-06-440203-7*, Trophy) HarpC Child Bks.

This Isn't Exactly What I Had in Mind, God: How to Get Your Life Back on Course. Hal Larson. (Illus.). 200p. (Orig.). 1996. pap. 14.95 (*1-879904-17-9*) Halo Bks.

***This Isn't the Company I Joined.** Carol K. Goman. 300p. 1997. text ed. 24.95 (*0-442-02582-3*) Van Nos Reinhold.

This Isn't What I Expected: Overcoming Postpartum Depression. Karen R. Kleiman & Valerie D. Raskin. LC 93-44769. 320p. 1994. pap. 12.95 (*0-553-37075-8*) Bantam.

This Issue Commemorating the 70th Birthday of Dr. Josiah L. Lowe. Clark T. Rogerson. LC 66-6394. (Memoirs Ser.: Vol. 28, No. 1). 231p. 1976. pap. 10.00 (*0-89327-004-0*) NY Botanical.

This Jesus: Martyr, Lord, Messiah. Markus Bockmuehl. 256p. 1994. pap. text ed. 19.95 (*0-567-29250-9*, Pub. by T & T Clark UK) Bks Intl VA.

This Jesus: Martyr, Lord, Messiah. Markus Bockmuehl. LC 96-11251. 252p. (Orig.). 1996. pap. 17.99 (*0-8308-1875-8*) InterVarsity.

This Job Should Be Fun. Bob Basso & Judi Klossek. 280p. 1991. pap. 12.95 (*1-55850-015-4*) Adams Media.

This Kind of War: The Classic Korean War History. T. R. Fehrenbach. (Association of the U. S. Army Book Ser.). (Illus.). 483p. 1994. 28.00 (*0-02-881113-5*) Brasseys Inc.

This Kind of Woman: Ten Stories by Japanese Women Writers, 1960-1976. Ed. by Yukiko Tanaka & Elizabeth Hanson. LC 81-51332. 320p. 1982. 39.50 (*0-8047-1130-5*) Stanford U Pr.

This Kind of Woman: Ten Stories by Japanese Women Writers, 1960-1976. Ed. by Yukiko Tanaka & Elizabeth Hanson. Tr. by Mona Nagai et al. LC 94-29159. (Michigan Classics in Japanese Studies: No. 12). xxv, 287p. 1994. reprint ed. pap. text ed. 15.95 (*0-939512-66-1*) U MI Japan.

This Knot of Life. 1991. pap. 20.00 (*0-932499-32-5*) Lapis Pr.

This Land Is My Land. George Littlechild. (Illus.). 32p. (J). (gr. 3-8). 1993. 16.95 (*0-89239-119-7*) Childrens Book Pr.

***This Land Is My Land: (Native American)** George Littlechild. (Illus.). (J). (gr. 2-4). 1993. lib. bdg. 22.60 (*0-516-80119-8*) Childrens.

This Land Is Our Land: A Guide to Multicultural Literature for Children & Young Adults. Alethea K. Helbig & Agnes R. Perkins. LC 94-16124. 416p. 1994. text ed. 49.95 (*0-313-28742-2*, Greenwood Pr) Greenwood.

This Land Is Our Land: How to End the War on Private Property. Richard Pombo. LC 96-20254. 224p. 1996. 22.95 (*0-312-14747-3*) St Martin.

This Land Is Sacred: A Teacher's Activity Guide to Environmental Ethics. Jane Krupnick. (Orig.). pap. text ed. 4.50 (*0-9628949-3-1*); All Things Are Connected. vhs 20.00 (*0-9628949-2-3*) NC Wildlife.

***This Land Is Your Land.** Marilyn Bridges. 1997. 45.00 (*0-89381-604-3*) Aperture.

***This Land Is Your Land.** Woody Guthrie. LC 96-54628. (Illus.). (J). 1998. write for info. (*0-316-39215-4*) Little.

This Land Is Your Land: The American Conservation Movement. Sylvia Whitman. LC 94-3099. (Illus.). 88p. (YA). (gr. 5 up). 1994. lib. bdg. 19.95 (*0-8225-1729-9*, Lerner Publctns) Lerner Group.

This Land of Legend. Ruth Couch. LC 90-62573. 71p. 1992. per. 18.00 (*0-914546-88-0*) Rose Pub.

This Land of Liberty: A History of America's Jews. Mia Simmons & John Simmons. 216p. 1995. teacher ed., pap. 14.95 (*0-87441-421-0*) Behrman.

***This Land This Love.** Sole. Date not set. write for info. (*0-312-18195-7*) St Martin.

This Land, This South: An Environmental History. Albert E. Cowdrey. LC 95-36831. (New Perspectives on the South Ser.). (Illus.). 256p. 1995. pap. 14.95 (*0-8131-0851-9*) U Pr of Ky.

This Land, This South: An Environmental History. rev. ed. Albert E. Cowdrey. LC 95-36831. (New Perspectives on the South Ser.). (Illus.). 272p. 1995. 32.95 (*0-8131-1933-2*) U Pr of Ky.

This Land, This South: An Environmental History. Albert E. Cowdrey. LC 82-20154. (New Perspectives on the South Ser.). 250p. reprint ed. pap. 71.30 (*0-7837-5807-3*, 2045473) Bks Demand.

This Land, This Time, 4 vols., Set. Dobrica Cosic. Tr. by Muriel Heppell. Incl. Into the Battle. 1983. pap. 8.95 (*0-15-644991-9*, Harvest Bks); 1983. reprint ed. Set pap. 29.95 (*0-15-690026-2*, Harvest Bks) HarBrace.

This Land Was Theirs: A Study of North American Indians. 5th ed. Wendell H. Oswalt & Sharlotte Neely. LC 95-40687. (Illus.). 510p. (C). 1995. pap. text ed. 37.95 (*1-55934-375-3*, 1375) Mayfield Pub.

***This Law of Ours.** Muhammad Asad. 195p. 1996. 21.95 (*0-614-21449-1*, 1229) Kazi Pubns.

This Law of Ours. Muhammad Asad. 196p. 1987. reprint ed. 20.00 (*0-939660-09-1*, Pub. by Dar Al-Andalus SP) Threshold VT.

This Lie Called Evil. Denise Breton. LC 82-80906. 130p. (Orig.). 1983. pap. 12.00 (*0-942958-02-0*) Kappeler Inst Pub.

This Life Is a Test. Ted Gibbons. 171p. (Orig.). 1991. pap. write for info. (*0-929985-81-8*) Jackman Pubng.

This Life I've Led. Babe D. Zaharias. 1994. lib. bdg. 24.95 (*1-56849-390-8*) Buccaneer Bks.

This Light Will Spread: Selected Poems Nineteen Sixty to Nineteen Seventy-Five. deluxe ed. Paul Mariah. 15.00 (*0-686-25740-5*) Man-Root.

This Light Will Spread: Selected Poems Nineteen Sixty to Nineteen Seventy-Five. limited ed. Paul Mariah. pap. 8.95 (*0-686-25741-3*) Man-Root.

***This Lime Tree Bower.** Conor McPherson. 96p. (Orig.). 1996. pap. 14.95 (*1-85459-299-8*, Pub. by N Hern Bks UK) Theatre Comm.

This Literary Life. Peter Van Straaten. LC 91-4969. (Illus.). 144p. (Orig.). 1991. pap. 7.50 (*0-918273-92-7*) Coffee Hse.

***This Little Baby.** Joyce Sullivan. 1997. mass mkt. 3.75 (*0-373-22436-2*, 1-22436-9) Harlequin Bks.

***This Little Bit of Earth: Fiction & Poetry by Chico Area Writers.** Chico Area Writers. 104p. 1997. pap. 12.00 (*0-9656222-0-7*) Valley Oaks.

This Little Inventor Went to the Patent Office: Phase I & Phase II (Under One Cover) 2nd ed. William J. Nasset. Ed. by Liz Brooks. (Illus.). 107p. 1996. lib. bdg. 59.90 (*1-889285-00-5*) Little Inventor.

This Little Land. Menke Katz. Ed. by Stanley H. Barkan. Tr. by Aaron Kramer et al. (Review Jewish Writers Chapbook Ser.: No. 1). 48p. (ENG & YID.). 1991. 15.00 (*0-89304-325-7*); pap. 5.00 (*0-89304-326-5*) Cross-Cultrl NY.

This Little Land, Mini bk. Menke Katz. Ed. by Stanley H. Barkan. Tr. by Aaron Kramer et al. (Review Jewish Writers Chapbook Ser.: No. 1). 48p. (ENG & YID.). 1991. 15.00 (*0-89304-327-3*); pap. 5.00 (*0-89304-328-1*) Cross-Cultrl NY.

This Little Light of Mine. 128p. Date not set. pap. 7.99 (*1-56292-151-7*, HB-151) Honor Bks OK.

This Little Light of Mine: The Life of Fannie Lou Hamer. Kay Mills. (Illus.). 400p. 1994. pap. 14.95 (*0-452-27052-9*, Plume) NAL-Dutton.

This Little Measure. Sara Woods. (Anthony Maitland Detective Ser.). 192p. 1986. mass mkt. 2.95 (*0-380-69862-5*) Avon.

This Little Pig. Janette Oke. (Illus.). 145p. (Orig.). (J). (gr. 3 up). pap. 4.99 (*0-934998-43-4*) Bethel Pub.

This Little Piggy. (My First Golden Board Bks.). (Illus.). (J). (ps). 1991. write for info. (*0-307-06136-1*, Golden Pr) Western Pub.

This Little Piggy. Heather S. Buchanan. LC 92-11895. (J). 1993. pap. 14.00 (*0-671-79351-9*, S&S Bks Young Read) S&S Childrens.

This Little Piggy. Cynthia Gaskill. (Illus.). 32p. 1992. 16.95 (*0-912823-28-3*) Gold Horse.

***This Little Piggy.** Golden Books Satff. (Golden Board Bks.). (J). 1997. 2.29 (*0-307-06166-3*, Golden Books) Western Pub.

This Little Piggy. Nicholas Heller. LC 95-976. (Illus.). 24p. (J). 1997. 15.00 (*0-688-14049-1*) Greenwillow.

This Little Piggy. Nicholas Heller. LC 95-976. (Illus.). 24p. (J). 1997. lib. bdg. 14.93 (*0-688-15175-2*) Greenwillow.

This Little Piggy. Illus. by Moira Kemp. 10p. (J). (ps). 1991. pap. 4.99 (*0-525-67326-1*, Lodestar Bks) Dutton Child Bks.

This Little Piggy. Illus. by Moira Kemp. LC 93-18683. 12p. (J). (ps). 1994. pap. 2.99 (*0-525-67446-2*, Lodestar Bks) Dutton Child Bks.

***This Little Piggy.** Illus. by Jane Manning. 10p. (J). (ps). 1997. 6.95 (*0-694-01000-6*, Festival) HarpC Child Bks.

This Little Piggy. Anne Shufflebotham. (J). (gr. 4 up). 1991. 6.99 (*0-85953-445-6*) Childs Play.

***This Little Piggy.** unabridged ed. Heather Collins. (Illus.). 12p. (J). 1997. bds. 3.95 (*1-55074-404-6*, Pub. by Kids Can Pr CN) Genl Dist Srvs.

This Little Piggy Went to Murder. Ellen Hart. (Midwest Mysteries Ser.). 230p. (Orig.). 1994. mass mkt. 4.99 (*0-345-38189-0*) Ballantine.

This Living Mirror: Reflections on Clare of Assisi. Sister Frances Teresa. LC 95-10029. 144p. (Orig.). 1995. pap. 10.95 (*1-57075-023-8*) Orbis Bks.

***This Longing.** Tr. by Coleman Books & John Moyne. 96p. 1996. pap. 9.00 (*0-614-21371-1*, 1230) Kazi Pubns.

This Longing - Poetry, Teaching Stories, & Selected Letters of Jelaluddin Rumi. Tr. by Coleman Barks & John Moyne. LC 88-40221. 133p. (Orig.). 1988. pap. 10.00 (*0-939660-29-6*) Threshold VT.

This Love We Share: Daily Devotions to Bring Wholeness to Your Marriage. Harry Griffith & Emily Griffith. 380p. 1995. pap. 11.99 (*0-8423-7161-3*) Tyndale.

This Loving Land. Dorothy Garlock. 288p. (Orig.). 1996. mass mkt. 5.99 (*0-446-36525-4*) Warner Bks.

This Mac Is Mine. John Pivovarnick. LC 92-10937. 1992. write for info. (*0-201-63206-3*) Addison-Wesley.

This Mac Is Mine: Twelve Terrific Tools to Customize Your Macintosh. John Pivovarnick. 1992. pap. 19.95 incl. disk (*0-201-63267-5*) Addison-Wesley.

This Mad Masquerade: Stardom & Masculinity in the Jazz Age. Gaylyn Studlar. LC 95-47557. (Film & Culture Ser.). (Illus.). 320p. (C). 1996. pap. 17.50 (*0-231-10321-2*) Col U Pr.

This Mad Masquerade: Stardom & Masculinity in the Jazz Age. Gaylyn Studlar. LC 95-47557. (Film & Culture Ser.). 320p. (C). 1996. 39.50 (*0-231-10320-4*) Col U Pr.

***This Magic Moment.** Beattie. pap. 10.00 (*0-06-251118-1*) HarpC.

This Magic Moment. Langston O. Harris. LC 92-70183. (Illus.). 469p. 1992. pap. 10.00 (*0-9631730-1-4*) DRL Bks.

This Magic Moment. Nora Roberts. (NR Flowers Ser.: No. 24). 1993. mass mkt. 3.59 (*0-373-51024-1*, 5-51024-3) Silhouette.

This Magic Moment: Musical Reflections of A Generation. Harry Turner. 195p. 1994. 18.95 (*0-9640761-0-1*); pap. 14.95 (*0-9640761-1-X*) A G M Ent.

***This Man & Others: The Personal Memoirs of Samuel H. Zorian.** Samuel H. Zorian. (Illus.). 94p. (Orig.). 1996. pap. 15.00 (*0-9651712-0-5*) Mihran & Azniv.

This Man & This Woman. Lucy Gordon. (Romance Ser.). 1995. mass mkt. 2.99 (*0-373-19079-4*, 1-19079-2) Silhouette.

This Man Bernardin. Eugene Kennedy. LC 96-7997. (Illus.). 180p. (C). 1996. 34.95 (*0-8294-0909-2*) Loyola Pr.

This Man Cries: Permission to Grieve. Henry P. Hosey, 2nd. LC 95-95150. 120p. (Orig.). 1996. pap. 7.95 (*0-9648216-0-5*) Brown Basket Pubns.

This Man from Lebanon. Barbara Young. (Illus.). 1950. 18.95 (*0-394-44848-0*) Knopf.

This Man I Love. large type ed. W. E. Ross. (Romance Ser.). 320p. 1995. pap. 15.99 (*0-7089-7665-4*, Linford) Ulverscroft.

This Man...This Cause...This Hour. Ruth Paxton. pap. 0.10 (*1-56632-079-8*) Revival Lit.

***This Matter of Marriage.** Debbie Macomber. 1997. mass mkt. 6.99 (*1-55166-260-4*, 1-66260-0, Mira Bks) Harlequin Bks.

This Meadow of Time: A Provence Journal. Frederick Smock. Ed. by John S. Moremen. (Illus.). 114p. 1995. 15.95 (*0-9624086-7-0*) Sulgrave Pr.

***This Means Mischief.** large type ed. Anne Fleming. (Ulverscroft Large Print Ser.). 336p. 1997. 27.50 (*0-7089-3807-8*) Ulverscroft.

This Means War: The Official Strategy Guide. Told to Mark Dultz. 1996. pap. text ed. 19.95 (*0-7615-0176-2*) Prima Pub.

This Mess. Pam Conrad. (Illus.). 32p. (J). (ps-3). 1998. 14.95 (*0-7868-0159-X*); lib. bdg. 14.89 (*0-7868-2131-0*) Hyprn Child.

This Metal. Joseph Bathanti. 136p. (Orig.). 1996. pap. 10.95 (*1-879934-30-2*) St Andrews NC.

This Mighty Dream: Social Protest Movements in the United States. Madeleine Adamson & Seth Borgos. (Illus.). 128p. 1984. pap. 10.95 (*0-7102-0042-0*, RKP) Routledge.

This Mighty Sum of Things: Wordsworth's Theme of Benevolent Necessity. Thomas J. Rountree. LC 65-12244. reprint ed. 27.00 (*0-8357-9621-3*, 2103214) Bks Demand.

This Migrant Earth. Tomas Rivera. Tr. by Rolando Hinojosa from SPA. LC 85-73354. 160p. (Orig.). 1986. pap. 9.00 (*0-934770-55-7*) Arte Publico.

This Mind in You: Studies in Philippians. Bramwell H. Tillsley. (Illus.). 150p. (Orig.). 1990. pap. 5.95 (*0-86544-056-5*) Salv Army Suppl South.

This Modern Music. John T. Howard, Jr. LC 68-58796. (Essay Index Reprint Ser.). 1977. 18.95 (*0-8369-0018-9*) Ayer.

This Moment: Tea Ceremony Kaiku. Margaret Chula. 32p. 1995. pap. 6.00 (*0-9638551-7-4*) Katsura Pr.

This Montana Home. Sherry Lewis. (Superromance Ser.). 1996. mass mkt. 3.99 (*0-373-70692-8*, 1-70692-8) Harlequin Bks.

This Morning with God. Ed. by Carol Adeney. LC 68-28080. 512p. 1978. pap. 16.99 (*0-87784-870-X*, 870) InterVarsity.

This Morning's Mockingbird. George Swede. 16p. 1980. pap. 2.00 (*0-913719-45-5*) High-Coo Pr.

This Mortal Coil. Jill Solnicki. 72p. 1990. pap. 9.95 (*0-921254-23-7*, Pub. by Penumbra Pr CN) U of Toronto Pr.

This Moste Highe Prince - John of Gaunt. Anil De Silva-Vigier. 452p. (C). 1989. text ed. 85.00 (*1-872795-47-1*, Pub. by Pentland Pr UK) St Mut.

This Must Be My Brother. LeAnn Thieman & Carol Dey. 200p. 1995. 12.99 (*1-56476-383-8*, 6-3383, Victor Bks) Chariot Victor.

This Mystical Life of Ours. Ralph W. Trine. 190p. 1996. pap. 17.00 (*0-89540-279-3*, SB-279) Sun Pub.

This N' That: Handwriting from a Wounded Heart 1991-1993. Radomir V. Luza, Jr. 66p. 1993. pap. 6.00 (*0-9643783-1-0*) R Luza.

This Nervous Breakdown Is Driving Me Crazy. Annie Reiner. 192p. 1996. pap. 19.95 (*0-7871-0707-7*, Dove Bks) Dove Audio.

This Nest of Vipers: McCarthyism & Higher Education in the Mundel Affair, 1951-52. Charles H. McCormick. LC 88-29592. (Illus.). 248p. 1989. text ed. 24.95 (*0-252-01614-9*) U of Ill Pr.

This Never Happened: A Novel. E. W. Summers. LC 97-9677. 1998. 22.00 (*0-679-45148-X*) Fodors Travel.

This New Day. (Gifts of Growth Ser.). 386p. (Orig.). 1985. pap. 6.95 (*0-934391-02-5*) Quotidian.

This New Land. G. Clifton Wisler. LC 87-17749. (J). (gr. 5 up). 1987. 13.95 (*0-8027-6726-5*); lib. bdg. 14.85 (*0-8027-6727-3*) Walker & Co.

This New Life Together: An Anthology of Wedding Meditations. LC 93-43014. 64p. 1994. pap. 6.75 (*1-55673-597-9*, 9418) CSS OH.

This New World - Birth. Frank Jakubowsky. 170p. (Orig.). 1990. pap. 19.95 (*0-932588-15-8*) Jesus Bks.

This New Yet Unapproachable America: Essays after Emerson after Wittgenstein. Stanley Cavell. 108p. 1989. 19.95 (*0-945953-01-1*); pap. 9.95 (*0-945953-00-3*) Living Batch Bks.

***This Noble Land.** James A. Michener. 1997. mass mkt. 12.95 (*0-449-22611-5*, Crest) Fawcett.

This Noble Land: My Vision for America. James A Michener. LC 96-17912. 288p. 1996. 23.00 (*0-679-45152-8*) Random.

This Ol' Drought Ain't Broke Us Yet: Stories from the American West. Jim Garry. LC 92-12629. 240p. 1996. reprint ed. pap. 14.95 (*1-55566-170-X*) Johnson Bks.

This Ol' Drought Ain't Broke Us Yet (But We're All Bent Pretty Bad) Stories of the American West. Jim Garry. LC 92-12629. (Library of the American West). 1992. 18.00 (*0-517-58814-5*, Orion Bks) Crown Pub Group.

***This Ol' Sack of Spuds Ain't No Netted Gem & Other Postcards from Potato Land: Postcards from Potato Land.** Marianne Love. (Illus.). 184p. (Orig.). 1997. pap. 9.95 (*1-56044-538-6*, Skyhse) Falcon Pr MT.

***This Old Barn.** This Old Barn Magazine Staff. 1997. 19.95 (*0-89821-175-1*) Reiman Pubns.

This Old Bill. Loren D. Estleman. 1990. mass mkt. 3.95 (*1-55817-422-2*, Pinncle Kensgtn) Kensgtn Pub Corp.

This Old Bill. Loren D. Estleman. LC 83-20766. 203p. 1984. 25.00 (*0-385-19165-0*) Ultramarine Pub.

This Old Boat. Don Casey. (Illus.). 480p. 34.95 (*0-87742-262-1*, 60233) Intl Marine.

This Old Boat. Don Casey. 1991. text ed. 34.95 (*0-07-157993-1*) McGraw.

This Old Boat: Powerboat Edition. Don Casey. 1996. text ed. 34.95 (*0-07-013241-0*) McGraw.

This Old Heart of Mine: The Best of Merrill Joan Gerber's Redbook Stories. Merrill J. Gerber. LC 93-79663. 240p. 1993. 18.95 (*1-56352-091-5*) Longstreet Pr Inc.

This Old House. Karen Ackerman. LC 91-20449. (Illus.). 40p. (J). (ps-1). 1992. lib. bdg. 14.95 (*0-689-31741-7*, Atheneum Bks Young) S&S Childrens.

This Old House. Ed. by Florence Theriault. (Illus.). 32p. 1989. 13.00 (*0-912823-03-8*) Gold Horse.

This Old House. Linda R. Wisdom. (American Romance Ser.: No. 443). 1992. mass mkt. 3.39 (*0-373-16443-2*, 1-16443-3) Harlequin Bks.

T

This Old House: Restoring, Rehabilitating & Renovating. Bob Vila & Jane Davison. (Illus.). 336p. 1980. pap. 24.95 (*0-316-17702-4*) Little.

This Old House Bathrooms: A Guide to Design & Renovation. Steve Thomas & Philip Langdon. LC 92-25218. 1992. pap. 24.95 (*0-316-84110-2*) Little.

This Old House Heating, Ventilation, & Air Conditioning: A Guide to the Invisible Comforts of Your Home. Richard Trethewey & Don Best. LC 93-20584. 1994. pap. 24.95 (*0-316-85272-4*) Little.

This Old House Kitchens: A Guide to Design & Renovation. Steve Thomas. 1992. pap. 24.95 (*0-316-84107-2*) Little.

***This Old House Sourcebook: Where to Find & How to Use the Tools & Materials You Need to Maintain.** This Old House Magazine Staff. 1997. pap. text ed. 24.95 (*0-316-83958-2*) Little.

This Old Man. (Little Golden Sound Story Bks.). (Illus.). 24p. (J). 1995. bds. 6.95 (*0-307-74828-6*, Golden Pr) Western Pub.

This Old Man. 1995. pap. 1.50 (*0-7214-5536-0*, Ladybrd) Penguin.

This Old Man. Illus. by Pam Adams. LC 90-34327. (Books with Holes Ser.). 16p. (Orig.). (J). (ps-2). 1974. pap. 6.99 (*0-85953-026-4*, Pub. by Childs Play UK) Childs Play.

***This Old Man.** Illus. by Pam Adams. (Books with Holes Ser.). (FRE.). (J). 1974. pap. 6.99 (*0-85953-462-6*) Childs Play.

***This Old Man.** Illus. by Pam Adams. (Books with Holes Ser.). (ITA.). (J). 1974. pap. 6.99 (*0-85953-591-6*) Childs Play.

This Old Man. Carol Jones. (Illus.). 48p. (J). (gr. k-3). 1990. 14.95 (*0-395-54699-0*) HM.

This Old Man. Tony Ross. 12p. (J). (ps-1). 1990. text ed. 9.95 (*0-689-71386-X*, Aladdin Paperbacks) S&S Childrens.

This Old Man. Harriet Ziefert. (J). 1995. 8.95 (*0-689-80054-1*, Litl Simon S&S) S&S Childrens.

***This Old Man - Este Viejito.** Ed. by Sarah Barchas. Tr. by Marilyn McClure & Anne D. Woolfolk. (Singing Your Way to English & Spanish Ser.). (Illus.). 32p. (Orig.). (ENG & SPA.). (J). (ps-2). 1997. pap. 9.95 incl. audio (*0-9632621-9-X*) High Haven Mus.

***This Old Man - Este Viejito.** Ed. by Sarah Barchas. Tr. by Marilyn McClure & Anne D. Woolfolk. (Singing Your Way to English & Spanish Ser.). (Illus.). 32p. (Orig.). (ENG & SPA.). (J). (ps-2). 1997. pap. 3.95 (*1-889686-01-8*) High Haven Mus.

This Old Monmouth of Ours. William S. Hornor. LC 73-89903. 1974. 30.00 (*0-686-11780-8*) Morris Genealog Lib.

This Old New House. Sheila. McGraw. (Illus.). 32p. (J). (ps-8). 1989. pap. 4.95 (*1-55037-034-0*, Pub. by Annick CN) Firefly Bks Ltd.

This Old PC. Dale Lewallen. 640p. 1993. pap. 29.95 incl. disk (*1-56276-108-0*, Ziff-Davis Pr) Que.

This Once: New & Selected Poems, 1965-1978. David Gitin. LC 79-1108. (Selected Works Ser.: No. 3). 1979. 29.95 (*0-912652-48-9*); pap. 10.95 (*0-912652-49-7*) Blue Wind.

This Once: New & Selected Poems, 1965-1978. deluxe ed. David Gitin. LC 79-1108. (Selected Works Ser.: No. 3). 1979. 49.95 (*0-912652-50-0*) Blue Wind.

***This Once: Poems 1976-1996.** Nick Bozanic. LC 96-80111. 96p. (Orig.). 1997. pap. 10.00 (*0-938078-49-6*) Anhinga Pr.

This or a That. Ralph F. Parkison. Ed. by Marion O. Withrow. (Illus.). 53p. (Orig.). (J). (gr. 2-8). 1988. pap. write for info. (*0-318-63999-8*) Little Wood Bks.

***This Ordinary World.** Ed. by Carrie Neumann & Ginny Ballor. 40p. (C). Date not set. pap. text ed. 3.00 (*1-882294-24-6*) Green Gate.

This Other Eden. Ben Elton. Ed. by Claire Zion. 1995. reprint ed. pap. 12.00 (*0-671-89702-0*) PB.

This Other Kind of Doctors: Traditional Medical Systems in Black Neighborhoods in Austin, Texas. Suzanne J. Terrell. LC 88-35024. (Immigrant Communities & Ethnic Minorities in the U. S. & Canada Ser.: No. 50). 1990. 34.50 (*0-404-19460-5*) AMS Pr.

This Other Ocean, 2 vols. Vincent Ferrini. (Know Fish Ser.). 235p. 1991. Set. pap. 12.95 (*0-685-56980-2*) Univ Conn Lib.

This Our Caesar: A Study of Bernard Shaw's "Ceasar & Cleopatra" Gordon W. Couchman. 1973. pap. text ed. 36.95 (*90-279-2601-8*) Mouton.

This Our Church: The People and Events That Shaped It. William A. Herr. (Basics of Christian Thought Ser.). 1986. pap. 16.95 (*0-88347-271-6*) Res Christian Liv.

***This, Our Lofty Scene.** John Andrews. 1998. pap. 19.95 (*0-670-83313-4*) Viking Penguin.

This Pair of Hands. Dallas Mucci. 152p. (Orig.). 1988. pap. 7.99 (*0-8341-1239-6*) Beacon Hill.

This Particular Earthly Scene. Margaret Lloyd. LC 92-38198. 80p. (Orig.). 1993. pap. 9.95 (*0-914086-99-5*) Alicejamesbooks.

This Particular Web: Essays on Middlemarch. Ed. by Ian Adam. LC 75-15844. 137p. reprint ed. pap. 39.10 (*0-8357-3628-8*, 2036356) Bks Demand.

This Path I Follow. Kenneth L. Hardin. (Illus.). 224p. (Orig.). 1994. pap. 6.00 (*0-9619153-4-X*) K L Hardin.

This Path of Scattered Glass: A Collection of Poems. Tom Miller. LC 92-84067. (Illus.). 96p. (Orig.). (YA). (gr. 7 up). 1993. pap. 6.95 (*1-878893-39-4*) Telcraft Bks.

This Path We Travel: Celebrations of Contemporary Native American Creativity. Smithsonian Institution, National Museum of American Art Staff. (Illus.). 128p. 1994. 10.99 (*1-55591-205-2*); pap. 8.99 (*1-55591-208-7*) Fulcrum Pub.

This People's Navy: The Making of American Sea Power. Kenneth J. Hagan. 434p. 1992. pap. 17.95 (*0-02-913471-4*, Free Press) Free Pr.

This Perfect Life. Kate K. Johnson. (Miami University Press Poetry Ser.: Vol. 3). 65p. (C). 1993. 15.95 (*1-881163-04-0*); pap. 9.95 (*1-881163-05-9*) Miami Univ Pr.

This Pilgrim's Progress: A Correspondence with Joel Goldsmith. Barbara M. Muhl. 364p. (Orig.). 1991. pap. 24.95 (*1-880863-25-1*) Christus Pub. COMMENTS FROM READERS: "Joel's consciousness was oozing off the pages. I understand him now in a way I would not have thought possible."--R.W., Rancho Mirage, CA. "I felt the love. I cried & I laughed. The book has changed me."--E.W., Newhall, CA. "This wonderful book will put at ease the students like me who thought they had to be 'good' to go to God."--T.H., New York, NY. "A gold mine for all serious students. Love & integrity shine through the book."--C.S., Long Beach, Miss. "Thanks so much for your honesty & doggedness. I feel experienced getting to know & love Joel as he REALLY is!"--A.C., Canyon Country, CA. "I now have a better grasp of the nature of the teacher/student relationship. The teacher's role is loving, but impersonal."--A.L., Valencia, CA. To order write, phone or FAX: Christus Publishing, P.O. Box 802649, Santa Carita, CA 91380-2649. U.S.A. Order line: 805-296-7836, FAX: 805-296-2182. ***Publisher Provided Annotation.***

***This Place Accursed.** Mojmir Nemecek. 168p. (Orig.). (YA). 1998. mass mkt. 5.99 (*1-55237-395-9*, Pub. by Comnwlth Pub CN) Partners Pubs Grp.

This Place Called Kentucky. J. E. Pearce. Ed. by John S. Moremen & Amy Spears. (Illus.). 138p. 1994. 29.95 (*0-9624086-6-2*) Sulgrave Pr.

***This Place Called Saint Martin's, 1895-1995: A Centennial History of Saint Martin's College & Abbey, Lacey, Washington.** John C. Scott. LC 96-36891. 1997. write for info. (*0-89865-982-5*) Donning Co.

This Place for Me. Joanna Cole. (J). 1993. 19.95 (*0-590-71917-3*) Scholastic Inc.

This Place Has No Atmosphere. Paula Danziger. 160p. (J). (gr. k-12). 1987. mass mkt. 3.99 (*0-440-98726-1*, LLL BDD) BDD Bks Young Read.

This Place Has No Atmosphere. Paula Danziger. 160p. (J). (gr. k-6). 1989. pap. 3.99 (*0-440-40205-0*, YB BDD) BDD Bks Young Read.

This Place Is Cold. Vicki Cobb. (Imagine Living Here Ser.). (Illus.). (J). (gr. 2-4). 1989. 14.95 (*0-8027-6852-0*); lib. bdg. 13.85 (*0-8027-6853-9*) Walker & Co.

This Place Is Cold. Vicki Cobb. (Imagine Living Here Ser.). (Illus.). 32p. (J). (gr. 2-5). 1990. pap. 7.95 (*0-8027-7340-0*) Walker & Co.

This Place Is Crowded. Vicki Cobb. (Imagine Living Here Ser.). (Illus.). 32p. (J). (gr. 4-7). 1993. pap. 6.95 (*0-8027-7407-5*) Walker & Co.

This Place Is Crowded: Japan. Vicki Cobb. 32p. (J). (gr. 2-4). 1992. 14.95 (*0-8027-8145-4*); lib. bdg. 15.85 (*0-8027-8146-2*) Walker & Co.

This Place Is Dry. Vicki Cobb. (Imagine Living Here Ser.). (Illus.). (J). (gr. 2-4). 1989. 12.95 (*0-8027-6854-7*); lib. bdg. 13.85 (*0-8027-6855-5*) Walker & Co.

This Place Is Dry. Vicki Cobb. (Imagine Living Here Ser.). (Illus.). 32p. (J). (gr. 2-5). 1993. pap. 6.95 (*0-8027-7400-8*) Walker & Co.

This Place Is High. Vicki Cobb. (Imagine Living Here Ser.). (Illus.). 32p. (J). (gr. 2-4). 1989. 12.95 (*0-8027-6882-2*); lib. bdg. 13.85 (*0-8027-6883-0*) Walker & Co.

This Place Is High. Vicki Cobb. (Imagine Living Here Ser.). (Illus.). 32p. (J). (gr. 4-7). 1993. pap. 7.95 (*0-8027-7406-7*) Walker & Co.

This Place Is Lonely: The Australian Outback. Vicki Cobb. (Imagine Living Here Ser.). (Illus.). 32p. (Orig.). (J). (gr. 2-5). 1994. 13.95 (*0-8027-6959-4*); pap. 6.95 (*0-8027-7415-6*); lib. bdg. 14.85 (*0-8027-6960-8*) Walker & Co.

This Place Is Wet. Vicki Cobb. (Imagine Living Here Ser.). (Illus.). 32p. (J). (gr. 2-4). 1989. 12.95 (*0-8027-6880-6*); lib. bdg. 13.85 (*0-8027-6881-4*) Walker & Co.

This Place Is Wet. Vicki Cobb. (Imagine Living Here Ser.). (Illus.). 32p. (J). (gr. 2-5). 1993. pap. 6.95 (*0-8027-7399-0*) Walker & Co.

This Place Is Wet. 95th ed. HB Staff. (J). (gr. 4). 1995. text ed., lib. bdg. 8.00 (*0-15-305216-3*) HB Coll Pubs.

***This Place Is Wild: East Africa.** Vicki Cobb. LC 97-25454. (Imagine Living Here Ser.). (Illus.). 1998. write for info. (*0-8027-8632-4*) Walker & Co.

***This Place Is Wild: East Africa.** Vicki Cobb, Vicki. LC 97-25454. (Imagine Living Here Ser.). (Illus.). 1998. lib. bdg. write for info. (*0-8027-8633-2*) Walker & Co.

This Place of Memory: A Texas Perspective. Ed. by Joyce G. Roach. LC 92-6890. (Illus.). 161p. (Orig.). 1992. pap. 8.95 (*0-929398-32-7*) UNTX Pr.

This Place on Earth: Home & the Practice of Permanence. Alan T. Durning. LC 96-20592. 302p. 1996. 22.95 (*1-57061-040-1*) Sasquatch Bks.

***This Place on Earth: Home & the Practice of Permanence.** Alan T. Durning. 336p. 1997. reprint ed. pap. 14.95 (*1-57061-127-0*) Sasquatch Bks.

This Planet Is Mine. Dianna Dee. (J). 1994. pap. 14.95 (*0-590-48794-9*) Scholastic Inc.

This Planet Is Mine: Teaching Environmental Awareness & Appreciation to Children. Mary Metzger & Cinthya P. Whittaker. 256p. (Orig.). 1991. 17.00 (*0-671-74817-3*, Fireside) S&S Trade.

This Pony Is Dangerous. Diana Pullein-Thompson. 174p. (C). 1990. pap. 29.00 (*0-85131-520-8*, Pub. by J A Allen & Co UK) St Mut.

This Popular Engine: New England Newspapers During the American Revolution, 1775-1789. Carol S. Humphrey. LC 90-50938. (Illus.). 208p. 1992. 38.50 (*0-87413-430-7*) U Delaware Pr.

This Precipice Garden. James DePriest. 60p. 1987. reprint ed. 15.00 (*0-940869-00-4*); reprint ed. pap. 8.00 (*0-940869-01-2*) Univ Portland Pr.

This Present Darkness. Frank E. Peretti. LC 86-70282. 416p. 1986. pap. 12.99 (*0-89107-390-6*) Crossway Bks.

***This Present Darkness.** Frank E. Peretti. LC 92-35902. 1990. audio 15.99 (*0-89107-597-6*, Crossway Audio) Crossway Bks.

This Present Darkness. large type ed. Frank E. Peretti. LC 92-35902. (General Ser.). 1993. lib. bdg. 23.95 (*0-8161-5698-0*, GK Hall) Thorndike Pr.

***This Present Darkness: Live! A Case Study.** Daniel Ryder & Liz Ryder. LC 96-92224. 74p. (Orig.). 1996. pap. 6.95 (*0-7880-0680-0*) CSS OH.

This Present Darkness: 10th Anniversary. anniversary limited ed. Frank E. Peretti. 384p. 1996. 25.00 (*0-89107-919-X*) Crossway Bks.

This Present Darkness & Piercing the Darkness, 2 vols. Frank E. Peretti. 816p. (Orig.). 1991. Set. boxed, pap. 25.98 (*0-89107-640-9*) Crossway Bks.

***This Present Darkness/Piercing the Darkness: Two Bestselling Novels Complete in One Volume.** Frank E. Peretti. 1997. 14.99 (*0-88486-178-3*, Inspirational Pr) Arrowood Pr.

This Present Victory: Discover the Phenomenal Rewards & Favor of Overcoming Bitterness, Hurt & Rejection. Lawrence Kennedy. Ed. by Margaret J. Kinney. 160p. (Orig.). 1993. pap. 9.95 (*1-880563-01-0*) FAME Pub.

This Present World. Dale M. Yocum. pap. 7.99 (*0-88019-194-5*) Schmul Pub Co.

***This Promiscuous Light: Young Women Poets of San Antonio.** Victoria Garcia-Galaviz et al. Ed. & Intro. by Bryce Milligan. (Illus.). 126p. 1996. pap. 12.00 (*0-930324-34-X*) Wings Pr.

This Promised Land. Robert Easton. (Saga of California Ser.). 368p. (Orig.). 1996. reprint ed. mass mkt., pap. text ed. 4.99 (*0-8439-3955-9*) Dorchester Pub Co.

This Promised Land. Robert Easton. (Saga of California Ser.: Vol. 1). 328p. (C). 1988. reprint ed. lib. bdg. 35.00 (*0-8095-4050-9*) Borgo Pr.

This Property Is Mine. Grace C. Johnson. 350p. (Orig.). 1992. pap. 12.95 (*0-9630762-0-5*) Enrobialc.

This Prophecy Merlin Shall Make. Eric Felderman. LC 90-29171. (Illus.). 101p. 1991. 38.95 (*0-945942-14-1*); pap. 16.95 (*0-945942-15-X*) Portmanteau Editions.

This Psychic Prophetic Age. Pam Vinnett. 1994. pap. text ed. 10.00 (*0-927936-65-8*) Vincom Inc.

This Quarter: The Surrealist Number. Ed. by Edward Titus. LC 71-88578. 1969. reprint ed. 15.95 (*0-405-00740-X*) Ayer.

This Queendom Come. V. S. Chochezi & Staajabu. 77p. 1994. pap. 7.00 (*0-9642340-0-9*) Straight Out.

This Quiet Dust: And Other Writings. William Styron. 304p. 1982. 17.50 (*0-394-50934-X*) Random.

This Quiet Dust & Other Writings. William Styron. LC 92-56372. 1993. reprint ed. pap. 14.00 (*0-679-73596-8*, Vin) Random.

This Quiet Lady. Charlotte Zolotow. LC 90-38485. 24p. (J). (ps up). 1992. 14.00 (*0-688-09305-1*); lib. bdg. 13.93 (*0-688-09306-X*) Greenwillow.

This Ravished Land. large type ed. Pamela Oldfield. 595p. 1995. 25.99 (*0-7505-0620-2*) Ulverscroft.

***This Raw Land.** Wayne Short. LC 68-14509. 203p. 1995. reprint ed. pap. 13.95 (*0-9644980-6-5*) Devils Thumb.

This Realm of England. John A. Marriott. LC 78-140368. (Select Bibliographies Reprint Ser.). 1977. reprint ed. 23.95 (*0-8369-5611-7*) Ayer.

***This Realm of England 1399-1688.** 7th ed. Lacey B. Smith. 384p. (C). 1996. pap. text ed. 24.76 (*0-669-39717-2*) HM College Div.

This Rebellious House: American History & the Truth of Christianity. Steven J. Keillor. 368p. (Orig.). 1996. pap. 24.99 (*0-8308-1877-4*, 1877) InterVarsity.

This Reckless Breed of Men: The Trappers & Fur Traders of the Southwest. Robert G. Cleland. LC 92-13879. (Illus.). xvi, 404p. 1992. reprint ed. pap. 13.95 (*0-8032-6354-6*, Bison Books) U of Nebr Pr.

***This Religion of Islam.** Sayyid Qutb. 110p. (Orig.). 1996. pap. 4.00 (*0-614-21450-5*, 1231) Kazi Pubns.

This Religion of Islam. Sayyid Qutb. 104p. (Orig.). 1977. pap. 2.95 (*0-939830-08-6*, Pub. by IIFSO KW) New Era Publns MI.

***This Rimy River: Vaughn Oliver & V23.** Vaughn Oliver. Ed. by Vulva O'Reighan. (Illus.). 72p. 1994. reprint ed. pap. 49.95 (*0-9524216-0-7*) Gingko Press.

This River of Courage: Generations of Women's Resistance & Action. Pam McAllister. (Barbara Deming Memorial Ser.). 240p. 1991. pap. 12.95 (*0-86571-198-4*); lib. bdg. 39.95 (*0-86571-197-6*) New Soc Pubs.

This River the Muskoka. Gary Long. (Illus.). 184p. 35.00 (*1-55046-012-9*, Pub. by Boston Mills Pr CN) Genl Dist Srvs.

This Road since Freedom. C. Eric Lincoln. 92p. (Orig.). 1990. 17.50 (*0-932112-30-7*); pap. 10.00 (*0-932112-31-5*) Carolina Wren.

This Romance, a Further Notebook on Rural Life, Building, Love & a Son. Bob Arnold. Ed. by Cid Corman. LC 91-46046. 112p. (Orig.). 1992. pap. 8.00 (*0-9620575-2-5*) Origin Pr.

This Rough Magic. large type ed. Mary Stewart. LC 91-34684. 493p. 1992. reprint ed. lib. bdg. 21.95 (*1-56054-290-X*) Thorndike Pr.

This Rough Magic: The Life of Teaching. Daniel A. Lindley. LC 93-25009. 160p. 1993. text ed. 52.95 (*0-89789-363-8*, G366, Bergin & Garvey); pap. text ed. 15.95 (*0-89789-366-2*, H363, Bergin & Garvey) Greenwood.

This Rough Magic Vol. 13: Technology in Latin American Fiction. Jane Robinett. LC 92-17509. (Worcester Polytechnic Institute Studies in Science, Technology & Culture: Vol. 13). 284p. (C). 1994. text ed. 53.95 (*0-8204-1889-7*) P Lang Pubng.

This Rough New Land. rev. ed. Kenneth Sollitt. LC 85-63052. (Ann of the Prairie Ser.: Vol. 1). Orig. Title: Remember the Days. 190p. 1985. reprint ed. pap. 6.95 (*0-940652-03-X*) Sunrise Bks.

This Royal Breed. large type ed. Judith A. Saxton. 774p. 1992. 25.99 (*0-7505-0302-5*) Ulverscroft.

This Ruth. Harold S. Paisley. (Illus.). 175p. 1996. 14.99 (*0-9631200-2-6*) OlivePr CT.

This Sacred Earth: Religion, Nature, Environment. Ed. by Roger S. Gottlieb. LC 95-11986. 500p. (C). 1995. pap. 24.95 (*0-415-91233-4*, Routledge NY); text ed. 74.95 (*0-415-91232-6*, Routledge NY) Routledge.

This Sacred Earth & Other Poems. Elaine L. Kleiner. LC 96-26026. 76p. 1997. pap. 12.95 (*0-7734-2710-4*, Mellen Poetry Pr) E Mellen.

This Same Sky. Selected by Naomi S. Nye. (Illus.). 232p. (YA). (gr. 5 up). 1996. pap. 8.99 (*0-689-80630-2*, Aladdin Paperbacks) S&S Childrens.

This Same Sky: A Collection of Poems from Around the World. Naomi S. Nye. LC 92-11617. (Illus.). 224p. (YA). (gr. 5 up). 1992. lib. bdg. 17.00 (*0-02-768440-7*, Four Winds Pr) S&S Childrens.

This Savage Land. large type ed. Johnny M. Bride. (Western Ser.). 1994. pap. 15.99 (*0-7089-7596-8*, Linford) Ulverscroft.

This Savage Race. Douglas C. Jones. 512p. 1994. mass mkt. 4.50 (*0-06-100770-6*) HarpC.

This Savage Race. large type ed. Douglas C. Jones. LC 93-11694. 1993. lib. bdg. 23.95 (*0-7862-0030-8*) Thorndike Pr.

This Season's People: A Book of Spiritual Teachings. Stephen Gaskin. LC 86-159636. (Illus.). 168p. 1976. pap. 5.95 (*0-913990-05-1*) Book Pub Co.

This Seething Ocean, That Damned Eagle. Caleb Powell. LC 93-807018. 127p. (Orig.). 1993. pap. text ed. 9.95 (*1-878815-04-0*) Reflected Images.

This Sex Which Is Not One. Luce Irigaray. Tr. by Catherine Porter & Carolyn Burke from FRE. LC 84-23013. 208p. (C). 1985. 39.95 (*0-8014-1546-2*); pap. 15.95 (*0-8014-9331-5*) Cornell U Pr.

This Shakespeare Industry. Ivor Brown & George Fearon. LC 70-92951. (Studies in Shakespeare: No. 24). 1970. reprint ed. lib. bdg. 62.95 (*0-8383-1063-X*) M S G Haskell Hse.

This Shakespeare Industry: Amazing Monument. Ivor J. Brown & George Fearon. LC 77-98824. 332p. 1970. reprint ed. text ed. 59.75 (*0-8371-2850-1*, BRSI, Greenwood Pr) Greenwood.

This Sheba, Self: The Conceptualization of Economic Life in Eighteenth-Century America. J. E. Crowley. LC 73-19334. (Johns Hopkins University Studies in Historical & Political Science: Series 92, No. 2). 176p. reprint ed. pap. 50.20 (*0-8357-6910-0*, 2037968) Bks Demand.

This Shining Place: A Meditation. Vince Clemente. 16p. (Orig.). (C). 1992. pap. 5.00 (*1-878173-25-1*) Birnham Wood.

This Shining Woman: Mary Wollstonecraft. M. Bowen. 1972. lib. bdg. 59.95 (*0-8490-1196-5*) Gordon Pr.

This Side of Cooperstown: An Oral History of Major League Baseball in the 1950s. Larry Moffi. LC 95-23761. (Illus.). 282p. 1996. 24.95 (*0-87745-521-X*) U of Iowa Pr.

This Side of Crazy: Lessons on Living from Someone Who Should Know Better but Keeps Messing up Anyway. Allen Johnson. 163p. (Orig.). 1990. pap. 9.95 (*0-9626600-0-0*); audio 39.95 (*0-9626600-1-9*) Rnssnce Pub Hse.

This Side of Glory. Gwen Bristow. 278p. 1979. reprint ed. lib. bdg. 25.95 (*0-89966-026-6*) Buccaneer Bks.

This Side of Glory: The Autobiography of David Hilliard & the Story of the Black Panther Party. David Hilliard & Lewis Cole. 1994. pap. 12.95 (*0-316-36421-5*) Little.

This Side of Harlem, Short Stories about Us. Taiwo Ogunade. 85p. 1995. lib. bdg. 4.95 (*1-881549-08-9*) Oluweri Pubns.

This Side of Heaven. Karen Robards. 448p. 1991. mass mkt. 5.99 (*0-440-20827-0*) Dell.

***This Side of Heaven.** large type ed. Juliet Gray. (Linford Romance Large Print Ser.). 272p. 1997. pap. 16.99 (*0-7089-5114-7*, Linford) Ulverscroft.

This Side of Innocence. Taylor Caldwell. 1994. lib. bdg. 39.95 (*1-56849-489-0*) Buccaneer Bks.

This Side of Judgement. J. R. Dunn. LC 93-23696. 1994. 21.95 (*0-15-100076-X*) HarBrace.

This Side of Judgment. J. R. Dunn. 368p. 1995. mass mkt. 5.99 (*0-451-45486-3*, ROC) NAL-Dutton.

This Side of Paradise. F. Scott Fitzgerald. (Hudson River Editions Ver.). 288p. 1978. 30.00 (*0-684-15601-6*) S&S Trade.

This Side of Paradise. F. Scott Fitzgerald. 24.95 (*0-89190-603-7*) Amereon Ltd.

This Side of Paradise. F. Scott Fitzgerald. 336p. 1996. mass mkt. 5.95 (*0-553-21453-5*, Bantam Classics) Bantam.

This Side of Paradise. F. Scott Fitzgerald. 7288p. 1988. pap. 6.95 (*0-02-019920-1*) Macmillan.

This Side of Paradise. F. Scott Fitzgerald. 268p. 1996. pap. 9.95 (*0-14-018976-9*, Modern Lib) Random.

This Side of Paradise. F. Scott Fitzgerald. 288p. 1996. pap. 11.00 (*0-684-71765-4*, SL60, Modern Lib) Random.

An Asterisk (*) at the beginning of an entry indicates that the title is appearing in BIP for the first time.

This Side of Paradise. F. Scott Fitzgerald. 288p. 1996. 15.00 (*0-679-44723-7*, Modern Lib); 15.50 (*0-679-60206-2*, Modern Lib); write for info. (*0-679-60043-4*, Modern Lib) Random.

This Side of Paradise. F. Scott Fitzgerald. 1995. pap. 10.00 (*0-684-80072-1*) S&S Trade.

This Side of Paradise. F. Scott Fitzgerald. LC 96-15673. 1996. 25.00 (*0-684-83046-9*) S&S Trade.

This Side of Paradise. F. Scott Fitzgerald. Ed. & Intro. by Patrick O'Donnell. LC 9[illegible]7. (Twentieth-Century Classics Ser.). 1996. pap. [illegible] for info. (*0-14-018077-X*, Penguin Bks) Viking Penguin.

This Side of Paradise. F. Scott Fitzgerald. Ed. by James L. West, III. (Cambridge Edition of the Works of F. Scott Fitzgerald). (Illus.). 407p. (C). 1996. text ed. 34.95 (*0-521-40234-4*) Cambridge U Pr.

This Side of Paradise. F. Scott Fitzgerald. 288p. 1996. mass mkt., pap. 5.95 (*0-451-52610-4*, Sig Classics) NAL-Dutton.

This Side of Paradise. F. Scott Fitzgerald. (YA). (gr. 9 up). 1996. mass mkt. 4.99 (*0-8041-1480-3*) Ivy Books.

This Side of Paradise. F. Scott Fitzgerald. 320p. 1995. mass mkt. 5.50 (*0-671-53555-2*, WSP) PB.

***This Side of Paradise.** large type ed. F. Scott Fitzgerald. LC 96-32267. (Perennial Ser.). 416p. 1996. 23.95 (*0-7838-1924-2*, Thorndike Lrg Prnt) Thorndike Pr.

This Side of Paradise. large type ed. F. Scott Fitzgerald. 420p. 1996. lib. bdg. 24.00 (*0-939495-90-2*) North Bks.

This Side of Paradise. large type ed. Kay Thorpe. (Linford Romance Library). 320p. 1985. pap. 15.99 (*0-7089-6057-X*) Ulverscroft.

This Side of Paradise. F. Scott Fitzgerald. 1995. reprint ed. lib. bdg. 24.95 (*1-56849-586-2*) Buccaneer Bks.

This Side of Paradise. F. Scott Fitzgerald. LC 95-49134. 208p. 1996. reprint ed. pap. text ed. 2.00 (*0-486-28999-0*) Dover.

This Side of Paradise As Bildungsroman. Jack Hendriksen. LC 92-13242. (American University Studies: American Literature: Ser. XXIV, Vol. 35). 147p. (C). 1993. text ed. 41.95 (*0-8204-1852-8*) P Lang Pubng.

This Side of Peace. Hanan Ashrawi. 320p. 1996. pap. 13.00 (*0-684-82342-X*, Touchstone Bks) S&S Trade.

This Side of Peace: A Personal Account. Hanan Ashrawi. LC 95-1793. (Illus.). 318p. 1995. 25.00 (*0-684-80294-5*) S&S Trade.

This Side of Reality: Modern Czech Short Stories. Ed. by Alexandra Buchler. (Contemporary European Short Stories Ser.). 256p. (Orig.). 1996. pap. 14.99 (*1-85242-378-1*) Serpents Tail.

This Side of Resurrection: Meditations on the Way of the Cross for Our Daily Lives. Mary J. Tully. 72p. (Orig.). 1989. pap. 2.50 (*0-87973-361-6*, 361) Our Sunday Visitor.

This Side of the Stars. L. B. Burgess. 1950. 15.95 (*0-87505-356-4*) Borden.

This Side the Other Side. Minh D. Trinh. LC 80-81781. (Illus.). 1980. 10.00 (*0-911050-48-5*) Occidental.

This Side Up: Spatial Determination in the Early Development of Animals. Robert Wall. (Developmental & Cell Biology Monographs: No. 23). (Illus.). 450p. (C). 1990. text ed. 130.00 (*0-521-36115-X*) Cambridge U Pr.

This So Remote Frontier: The Chattahoochee Country of Alabama & Georgia. Mark E. Fretwell. (Illus.). 369p. 1987. 14.50 (*0-945477-04-X*) Hist Chattahoochee.

This Soil of Sand. Mark Raney. (Illus.). 26p. 1978. 20.00 (*0-933272-01-4*) Hurricane Co.

This Solemn Mockery. John Whitehead. (Illus.). 22.50 (*0-89979-044-5*) British Am Bks.

This Song's for You. Reva Griffith. LC 92-74144. (Illus.). 240p. (Orig.). (YA). (gr. 9-12). 1993. pap. 14.95 (*0-923687-23-8*) Celo Valley Bks.

This Special Place: North Central College. Helen S. Strehlow. 112p. 1994. write for info. (*0-9641418-0-9*) H S Strehlow.

This Species of Property: Slave Life & Culture in the Old South. Leslie H. Owens. LC 75-38110. 291p. 1977. pap. 12.95 (*0-19-502245-9*) OUP.

This Sporting Life: Contemporary American Poems about Sports & Games. Ed. by Emilie Buchwald & Ruth Roston. (Illus.). 176p. (Orig.). 1997. pap. 14.95 (*1-57131-404-0*) Milkweed Ed.

This Stage Play World: English Literature & Its Background, 1580-1625. Julia Briggs. LC 82-22473. 234p. (C). 1983. pap. 17.95 (*0-19-289134-0*) OUP.

This State of Wonders: The Letters of an Iowa Frontier Family, 1858-1861. Ed. by John K. Folmar. LC 86-7012. (Illus.). 186p. reprint ed. pap. 53.10 (*0-8357-3841-8*, 2036573) Bks Demand.

This State of Wonders: The Letters of an Iowa Frontier Family, 1858-1861. Ed. by John K. Folmar. LC 86-7012. (Bur Oak Bk.). (Illus.). 186p. 1986. reprint ed. pap. 13.95 (*0-87745-341-1*) U of Iowa Pr.

This Stinging Exultation. Mary B. Treudley. (Asian Folklore & Social Life Monographs: No.42). 310p. 1972. 16.00 (*0-89986-041-9*) Oriental Bk Store.

This Strange Joy: Selected Poems of Sandro Penna. Sandro Penna. Tr. by W. S. Di Piero from ITA. LC 81-22288. 154p. 1982. 22.50 (*0-8142-0328-0*) Ohio St U Pr.

This Strange New Feeling. Julius Lester. 172p. (YA). (gr. 7-9). 1985. pap. 2.75 (*0-590-44047-0*) Scholastic Inc.

This Strange Old World & Other Book Reviews by Katherine Anne Porter. Katherine Anne Porter. Ed. by Darlene H. Unrue. LC 90-20486. 192p. 1991. 30.00 (*0-8203-1331-9*) U of Ga Pr.

This Strange Society of Women: Reading the Letters & Lives of the Women's Commonwealth. Sally L. Kitch. LC 92-12216. (Helen Hooven Santmyer Prize in Women's Studies). (Illus.). 352p. 1993. 45.00 (*0-8142-0579-8*) Ohio St U Pr.

This Stranger, My Father. Robert Hawks. 240p. (J). (gr. 4). 1990. mass mkt. 2.95 (*0-380-70739-X*, Flare) Avon.

This Stubborn Quantum: Sixty Poems. Jeremy Ingalls. LC 82-74424. 100p. 1983. 10.00 (*0-9610662-0-2*) Capstone Edns.

This Stubborn Soil. William A. Owens. 312p. 1992. 19.95 (*0-941130-19-3*) Lyons & Burford.

This Stubborn Soil. William A. Owens. 1989. pap. 8.95 (*0-679-72227-0*, Vin) Random.

This Sucks, Change It! Larry Doyle. (MTV's Beavis & Butthead Ser.: No. 3). 1995. 20.00 (*0-671-53633-8*) PB.

This Sweet & Bitter Earth. Alexander Cordell. 1996. 24.00 (*0-7278-4950-6*) Severn Hse.

This Terrible Fragility. Robert Jaeger. 60p. 1988. pap. 7.00 (*0-912549-22-X*) Bread & Butter.

***This Terrible Sound: The Battle of Chickamauga.** write for info. (*0-252-06594-8*) U of Ill Pr.

This Terrible Sound: The Battle of Chickamauga. Peter Cozzens. (Illus.). 688p. (C). 1992. 39.95 (*0-252-01703-X*) U of Ill Pr.

This, That & the Other Thing. Reginald T. Townsend. LC 75-84344. (Essay Index Reprint Ser.). 1977. 18.95 (*0-8369-1112-1*) Ayer.

***This They Believed: A Brief History of Doctrine in the Cumberland Presbyterian Church.** 800p. 1997. write for info. (*0-9656815-0-5*) J B Irby.

This Thing Called Christianity: How to Get a Life That Makes a Difference. Brad Humphrey. 1996. spiral bd. 9.99 (*0-8024-6876-4*) Moody.

This Thing Called Gangs: A Guide to Recognizing the Danger Signs. Darryln Johnson. (Illus.). 48p. (Orig.). 1992. pap. 5.95 (*0-943861-20-9*) Lone Tree.

***This Thing Called Life.** Ernest Holmes. (New Thought Library). 160p. 1997. reprint ed. 16.95 (*0-87477-867-0*, Tarcher Putnam) Putnam Pub Group.

This Thing Called Love. Marvin L. Smith. LC 92-73950. 66p. (Orig.). 1993. pap. text ed. 4.95 (*0-9625115-9-5*) Campbell Rd Pr.

This Thing Called Love: Thoughts of an Out-of-Step Romantic. Steven Schnur. 208p. 1993. reprint ed. pap. 8.00 (*0-380-71713-1*) Avon.

***This Thing Called You.** Ernest Holmes. (New Thought Library). 160p. 1997. reprint ed. 16.95 (*0-87477-868-9*, Tarcher Putnam) Putnam Pub Group.

This Thing of Darkness: A Sociology of the Enemy. James A. Aho. LC 94-12015. (Illus.). 224p. 1994. 22.50 (*0-295-97355-2*) U of Wash Pr.

This, This, a Thousand Times This: The Very Essence of Zen. Rajneesh Osho Staff. Ed. by Mahasattva S. Govind. (Zen Ser.). (Illus.). 288p. 1988. 12.95 (*3-89338-013-2*, Pub. by Rebel Hse GW) Osho America.

This Thousand Years. L. B. Brooks. LC 94-71926. 392p. (Orig.). 1994. pap. 10.95 (*0-88270-711-6*) Bridge-Logos.

This Time. Mary S. Plowman. Ed. by Pamela R. Goodfellow. 384p. (Orig.). 7.99 (*0-9639882-1-2*) Goodfellow Pr.

This Time for Keeps. John P. MacCormac. LC 72-4584. (Essay Index Reprint Ser.). 1977. reprint ed. 20.95 (*0-8369-2962-4*) Ayer.

This Time, For Sure. large type ed. Cathy Christopher. (Romance Ser.). 272p. 1995. pap. 15.99 (*0-7089-7675-1*, Linford) Ulverscroft.

This Time Forever. Margaret Chittenden. (Harlequin Dreamscape Ser.: No. 1). 1990. mass mkt. 3.25 (*0-373-79001-5*) Harlequin Bks.

This Time Forever. Kathleen Eagle. 400p. (Orig.). 1992. mass mkt. 4.99 (*0-380-76688-4*) Avon.

***This Time Forever.** Vickie Moore. 400p. (Orig.). 1996. mass mkt. 3.99 (*1-85487-721-6*, Pub. by Scarlet Bks UK) London Bridge.

This Time I Promise It'll Be: Different Short Stories. Makarand Paranjape. (C). 1994. 7.50 (*81-85944-46-6*, Pub. by UBS Pubs Dist II) S Asia.

This Time It's Me: For Teens Who Have Just Found out They're Pregnant. Mary Vondra & Lisa Vondra. (Illus.). 24p. (Orig.). (YA). 1985. pap. 3.10 (*1-56123-042-1*) Centering Corp.

This Time Let's Not Eat the Bones: Bill James Without the Numbers. Bill James. 1989. 22.50 (*0-394-57714-0*, Villard Bks) Random.

This Time, Tempe Wick? Patricia L. Gauch. (Illus.). 48p. (J). (gr. 1-4). 1992. 13.95 (*0-399-21880-7*, Putnam) Putnam Pub Group.

This Time, This Place. Dennis Vannatta. 1991. pap. 10.00 (*1-877727-01-6*) White Pine.

***This Time Together.** Susan L. Liepitz. (Time Passages Ser.). 352p. 1996. mass mkt. 5.99 (*0-515-11981-4*) Jove Pubns.

This Time We Knew: Western Responses to Genocide in Bosnia. Ed. by Thomas Cushman & Stjepan G. Mestrovic. 320p. (C). 1996. pap. 18.95 (*0-8147-1535-4*) NYU Pr.

This Time We Knew: Western Responses to Genocide in Bosnia. Ed. by Thomas Cushman & Stjepan G. Mestrovic. 320p. (C). 1996. 50.00 (*0-8147-1534-6*) NYU Pr.

This Time Yesterday. Antonio M. Allego. 109p. (Orig.). 1983. pap. 7.50 (*971-10-0152-7*, Pub. by New Day Pub PH) Cellar.

This Time You've Gone Too Far! A Sick & Twisted Cartoon Collection. National Lampoon Editors. (Illus.). 128p. 1995. pap. 8.95 (*0-8092-3567-6*) Contemp Bks.

This Timeless Moment: A Personal View of Aldous Huxley. Laura Huxley. LC 90-49560. (Illus.). 352p. 1991. reprint ed. pap. 10.95 (*0-916515-95-8*) Mercury Hse Inc.

This Time...Marriage. (Harlequin Promo Ser.). 1996. mass mkt. 4.99 (*0-373-83314-8*, 1-83314-4) Harlequin Bks.

This, Too, is for the Best - Simon Kramer & His Stories. Julia W. Kramer. xvii, 433p. 1989. 52.00 (*0-8204-1086-1*) P Lang Pubng.

This Too Is Music. Rena Upitis. LC 90-4791. 151p. 1990. pap. text ed. 19.50 (*0-435-08539-5*, 08539) Heinemann.

***This Too Shall Pass.** 1996. pap. 1.20 (*0-8341-9503-8*) Lillenas.

This Too Shall Pass: Encouragement for Parents Who Sometimes Doubt Their Teens Were Created in the Image of God. Kel Groseclose. 160p. 1995. pap. 9.00 (*0-687-00610-4*) Dimen for Liv.

This Too Shall Pass: Leader's Guide. 48p. 1996. 6.95 (*0-687-49670-5*) Abingdon.

This Torch of Freedom: Speeches & Addresses. Stanley Baldwin. LC 73-157962. (Essay Index Reprint Ser.). 1977. reprint ed. 23.95 (*0-8369-2213-1*) Ayer.

This Treatise Concernynge the Fruytfull Saynges of Davyd.. Was Made & Compyled by..John Fyssher..Bysshop of Rochester. John Fisher. LC 79-84106. (English Experience Ser.: No. 925). 296p. 1979. reprint ed. lib. bdg. 28.00 (*90-221-0925-9*) Walter J Johnson.

This Tremendous Lover. rev. ed. M. Eugene Boylan. 373p. 1947. pap. 8.95 (*0-87061-138-0*, 6981) Chr Classics.

This Troubled World. John Drinkwater. 1977. 17.95 (*0-8369-0392-7*) Ayer.

This Ugly Civilization. Ralph Borsodi. LC 74-2668. (American Utopian Adventure Ser.). (Illus.). viii, 468p. 1972. reprint ed. lib. bdg. 49.50 (*0-87991-025-9*) Porcupine Pr.

This Unfriendly Soil: The Loyalist Experience in Nova Scotia, 1783-1791. Neil MacKinnon. 244p. (C). 1989. pap. text ed. 22.95 (*0-7735-0719-1*, Pub. by McGill CN) U of Toronto Pr.

This Universe of Men. Greg Logan. (Illus.). 150p. 1992. pap. 10.95 (*0-943383-04-8*) FirstHand Ltd.

This Valentines Day, I Promise You All My Love. Ed. by Blue Mountain Arts Staff. LC 95-36006. 1995. 16.95 (*0-88396-421-X*) Blue Mtn Pr CO.

***This Very Moment: A Brief Introduction to Buddhism & Zen for Unitarian Universalists.** James I. Ford. 128p. (Orig.). 1996. pap. 10.00 (*1-55896-347-2*, 5323, Skinner Hse Bks) Unitarian Univ.

This Waking Unafraid: Poems. David Swanger. 64p. (C). 1995. pap. 12.95 (*0-8262-0987-4*) U of Mo Pr.

This Wanting to Sing: Asian in South America. Ed. by Jaime Jacinto et al. (Illus.). 40p. (Orig.). 1988. reprint ed. pap. 4.00 (*0-936556-17-X*) Contact Two.

This War Is an Awful Thing: Civil War Letters of the National Guards, the 19th & 90th Pennsylvania Volunteers. James Durkin. (Illus.). 300p. 1994. 27.50 (*0-9631314-1-9*) J M S Civil War.

This Was America: True Accounts of People & Places, Manners & Customs, As Recorded by European Travelers to the Western Shore in the 18th, 19th & 20th Centuries. Ed. by Oscar Handlin. LC 49-7940. 616p. 1949. 42.50 (*0-674-88470-1*) HUP.

This Was Andersonville. John McElroy. (Illus.). 1957. 29.95 (*0-8392-1117-1*) Astor-Honor.

This Was Chesapeake Bay. Robert H. Burgess. LC 63-20545. (Illus.). 218p. 1963. 24.95 (*0-87033-125-6*, Tidewtr Pubs) Cornell Maritime.

This Was Corporate America. Chauncey Hare. 1984. 15.00 (*0-910663-40-8*) ICA Inc.

This Was Estes Park: Historical Vignettes. 3rd ed. Ruth Stauffer. Ed. by Sybil Barnes. (Illus.). 64p. (Orig.). 1990. reprint ed. pap. 4.95 (*0-9626381-1-0*) Estes Pk Area Hist Mus.

This Was Issaquah. Harriet U. Fish et al. (Illus.). 144p. 1987. pap. 11.95 (*0-9612344-4-X*) H U Fish.

This Was Issaquah. Harriet U. Fish. (Illus.). 144p. 1987. 11.95 (*0-685-60790-9*) WASPC.

This Was Jackson's Hole: Incidents & Profiles from the Settlement of Jackson Hole. Fern K. Nelson. LC 94-25082. (Illus.). 384p. 1994. pap. 15.95 (*0-931271-25-8*) Hi Plains Pr.

This Was Logging: Drama in the Northwest Timber Country. Ralph W. Andrews. (Illus.). 157p. 1985. reprint ed. pap. 9.95 (*0-88740-035-3*) Schiffer.

This Was My Daddy. Walter G. Slappey. 75p. 9.95 (*0-930061-02-0*) Interspace Bks.

This Was My Newport. Maud H. Elliott. LC 75-1842. (Leisure Class in America Ser.). (Illus.). 1975. reprint ed. 28.95 (*0-405-06911-1*) Ayer.

This Was New York: The Nation's Capital in 1789. Frank Monaghan & Marvin Lowenthal. LC 70-117884. (Select Bibliographies Reprint Ser.). 1977. reprint ed. 29.95 (*0-8369-5337-1*) Ayer.

This Was Our Valley. Earl K. Pollon & Shirley S. Matheson. (Illus.). 403p. (Orig.). 1989. pap. 17.95 (*0-920490-91-3*) Temeron Bks.

This Was Our Valley. Earl K. Pollon & Shirley S. Matheson. (Illus.). 1989. 26.95 (*0-920490-92-1*) Temeron Bks.

This Was Sawmilling. Ralph W. Andrews. LC 93-87502. (Illus.). 176p. 1993. pap. 15.95 (*0-88740-594-0*) Schiffer.

This Was Their Time. Florence E. Sherfey. (Illus.). 206p. 1975. 14.95 (*0-87770-146-6*) Ye Galleon.

This Was Tomorrow. Elswyth Thane. 1994. lib. bdg. 28.95 (*1-56849-478-5*) Buccaneer Bks.

This Was Toscanini. Samuel Antek. 1980. 34.50 (*0-8149-0018-6*) Random.

***This Was Wheat Farming.** Kirby Brumfield. LC 68-22356. (Illus.). 192p. (YA). (gr. 10 up). 1997. pap. 19.95 (*0-7643-0188-8*) Schiffer.

This Way for the Gas, Ladies & Gentlemen. Tadeusz Borowski. 1976. pap. 8.95 (*0-14-004114-1*, Penguin Bks) Viking Penguin.

This Way for the Gas, Ladies & Gentlemen. Tadeusz Borowski. Tr. by Barbara Vedder. 192p. 1992. pap. 11.95 (*0-14-018624-7*, Penguin Classics) Viking Penguin.

This Way Madness Lies. Thomas W. Simpson. 448p. 1993. mass mkt. 4.99 (*0-446-36390-1*) Warner Bks.

This Way, That Way, Set 1. Emily Dickinson et al. (Illus.). 1990. Best Friends. pap. 6.88 (*0-8123-6215-2*); My Little Chickadees. pap. 6.88 (*0-8123-6216-0*); Ice Cream & Plums. pap. 6.88 (*0-8123-6217-9*); Counting to 100. pap. 6.88 (*0-8123-6218-7*); With Flowers. pap. 6.88 (*0-8123-6219-5*) McDougal-Littell.

This Way, That Way, Set 2. Emily Dickinson et al. (Illus.). 1990. Tracey's Tree. pap. 8.80 (*0-8123-6220-9*); Castles on the Ground. pap. 8.80 (*0-8123-6221-7*); Clockwork. pap. 8.80 (*0-8123-6222-5*); The Wind & the Rain. pap. 8.80 (*0-8123-6223-3*) McDougal-Littell.

***This Way to Bethlehem.** pap. 3.70 (*0-687-41740-6*) Abingdon.

This Way to Books. Caroline Feller Bauer. LC 82-19985. 378p. 1983. 45.00 (*0-8242-0678-9*) Wilson.

This Way to Foster Parenting. Barbara Kendrick & Carol Ertl. 292p. (Orig.). 1979. pap. 9.00 (*1-55719-109-3*) U NE CPAR.

***This Way to Happiness: Meeting Your Basic Emotional Needs Leads to Lasting Happiness.** 2nd rev. ed. Clyde M. Narramore. 176p. 1997. pap. text ed. write for info. (*0-9658067-0-7*) C Narramore.

This Way to My Heart. large type ed. Kathleen Treves. 336p. 1989. 25.99 (*0-7089-1983-9*) Ulverscroft.

This Way Up. Charles Hunter & Frances Hunter. 1978. pap. 6.95 (*0-917726-23-5*) Hunter Bks.

This Way Up: Legal & Business Essentials for Nonprofits. Ed. by Barry H. Slinker. 84p. 1988. pap. 14.95 (*0-917103-11-4*) Vol Lawyers Arts.

This We Believe. (ENG & GER.). 1980. pap. 0.95 (*0-8100-0004-0*, 04-0622) Northwest Pub.

This We Believe. National Middle School Association Staff. 40p. 1992. 6.00 (*1-56090-019-9*) Natl Middle Schl.

This We Believe. James Waltner. LC 68-20281. 1968. pap. 5.95 (*0-87303-845-2*) Faith & Life.

This We Believe: An Overview of the Teachings of Seventh-Day Adventists. Leo R. Van Dolson, pseud. LC 92-39733. 1993. pap. 10.99 (*0-8163-1138-2*) Pacific Pr Pub Assn.

This We Believe This We Proclaim. 1971. pap. 3.50 (*0-87162-986-0*) Warner Pr.

This Well-Wooded Land: Americans & Their Forests from Colonial Times to the Present. Thomas R. Cox et al. LC 85-1141. (Illus.). 365p. reprint ed. pap. 104.10 (*0-7837-7048-0*, 2046859) Bks Demand.

This Wheel's on Fire: Levon Helm & the Story of the Band. Levon Helm. (Illus.). 352p. 1995. pap. 12.00 (*0-688-14070-X*, Quill) Morrow.

This Widowed Land. Kathleen O'Neal Gear. 448p. 1994. mass mkt. 5.99 (*0-8125-8307-8*) Tor Bks.

***This Wild Darkness.** Brodkey. 1997. pap. 12.00 (*0-8050-5511-8*) H Holt & Co.

This Wild Darkness: The Story of My Death. Harold Brodkey. 224p. 1996. 20.00 (*0-8050-4831-6*) H Holt & Co.

This Woman: Poetry of Love & Change. Barbara O'Mary. LC 72-95283. (Illus.). 64p. (Orig.). 1973. pap. 3.25 (*0-87810-024-5*) Times Change.

This Woman Called Mother. Grace Freeman. 59p. Date not set. pap. 7.95 (*1-879934-03-5*) St Andrews NC.

This Woman in Particular: Contexts for the Biographical Image of Emily Carr. Stephanie K. Walker. (Illus.). xvi, 212p. (C). 1996. 34.95 (*0-88920-263-X*) Wilfrid Laurier.

This Won't Change Your Life: (But It Might Help!) Elizabeth Pitman. 140p. 1990. pap. 19.95 (*1-873150-00-8*, Pub. by Multilingual Matters UK) Taylor & Francis.

This Wood Sang Out: A Collection of Poetry & Prose by Western Massachusetts Writers Presented by the Literacy Project. Rachel Ferris-Jenkins et al. Ed. by Amy Dryansky et al. LC 95-81622. 120p. (Orig.). 1995. pap. 10.00 (*1-884540-15-5*) Haleys.

This Word. Henry G. Fischer. (Illus.). 54p. (Orig.). 1992. pap. 2.00 (*0-926935-72-0*) Runaway Spoon.

This Working Day World: A Social, Political, & Cultural History of Women's Lives, 1914-1945. Ed. by Sybil Oldfield & June Purvis. LC 93-41225. (Gender & society Series: Feminist Perspectives on the Past & Present). 224p. 1994. 75.00 (*0-7484-0107-5*, Pub. by Tay Francis Ltd UK); pap. 27.50 (*0-7484-0108-3*, Pub. by Tay Francis Ltd UK) Taylor & Francis.

***This World.** 1996. pap. 1.20 (*0-8341-9483-X*) Lillenas.

This World & Nearer Ones. Brian Aldiss. 262p. 1981. pap. 14.95 (*0-938075-41-1*) Ocean View Bks.

This World & That: An Analytical Study of Psychic Communication. Phoebe D. Bendit & Laurence J. Bendit. 1969. pap. 1.75 (*0-8356-0413-6*, Quest) Theos Pub Hse.

This World & the Next One. Aiello. 113p. (Orig.). 1993. pap. 9.95 (*0-929385-44-6*) Light Tech Comns Servs.

***This World Is Not My Home.** Date not set. pap. 1.20 (*0-8341-9423-6*) Lillenas.

This World, Other Worlds: Sickness, Suicide, Death, & the Afterlife among the Vaqueiros De Alzada of Spain. Maria Catedra. Tr. by William A. Christian, Jr. (Illus.). 402p. 1992. pap. text ed. 22.00 (*0-226-09716-1*); lib. bdg. 69.00 (*0-226-09715-3*) U Ch Pr.

This World Playground or Battleground? Aiden W. Tozer. LC 88-93033. 1989. pap. 8.99 (*0-87509-420-1*) Chr Pubns.

This World We Must Leave. Jacques Camatte. 256p. Date not set. 8.00 (*1-57027-020-1*) Autonomedia.

This Year I Plan to Go Elsewhere. Frances Weaver. LC 88-31458. 102p. 1989. pap. 9.95 (*1-55591-032-7*) Fulcrum Pub.

This Year in Jerusalem. Mordecai Richler. LC 94-10455. 1994. 23.00 (*0-679-43610-3*) Knopf.

This Year in School Science 1989: Scientific Literacy. Ed. by Audrey B. Champagne et al. 190p. 1989. pap. 15.95 (*0-87168-359-8*, 89-30S) AAAS.

An Asterisk (*) at the beginning of an entry indicates that the title is appearing in BIP for the first time.

This Year in School Science 1991: Technology for Teaching & Learning. Ed. by Shirley M. Malcom et al. 212p. 1991. 15.95 (*0-87168-428-4*, 91-37S) AAAS.

***This Year It Will Be Different.** large type ed. Maeve Binchy. 1996. 25.95 (*1-56895-381-X*, Compass) Wheeler Pub.

This Year It Will Be Different: And Other Stories. Maeve Binchy. 240p. 1996. 15.95 (*0-385-31503-1*) Delacorte.

***This Year It Will Be Different: And Other Stories.** Maeve Binchy. 1997. mass mkt. 6.99 (*0-440-22357-1*, Dell Trade Pbks) Dell.

***This Year Next Year.** Norah Harding. LC 97-124292. 1997. pap. text ed. 11.95 (*0-88754-546-7*, Pub. by Playwrights CN Pr CN) Theatre Comm.

This Year's Garden. Cynthia Rylant. LC 84-10974. (Illus.). 32p. (J). (gr. k-3). 1984. lib. bdg. 15.00 (*0-02-777970-X*, Bradbury S&S) S&S Childrens.

This Year's Garden. Cynthia Rylant. LC 86-22224. (Illus.). 32p. (J). (ps-3). 1987. reprint ed. pap. 4.95 (*0-689-71122-0*, Aladdin Paperbacks) S&S Childrens.

This You Can Believe: Participant. John Brokhoff. (Orig.). 1987. pap. 2.75 (*0-89536-893-5*, 7879) CSS OH.

This Young World. Wisdom O. Ogbor. (Wisdom's Writings Ser.). 250p. (Orig.). 1985. write for info. (*0-933889-01-1*) Ashiedu Pubns.

This'll Kill Ya: And Other Dangerous Stories. Harry Willson. (Illus.). 184p. (Orig.). 1991. pap. 6.00 (*0-9622937-2-5*) III Pub.

This'll Kill You. Peter Chambers. 200p. 1994. 18.50 (*0-7451-8631-9*, Black Dagger) Chivers N Amer.

This...Seasonal Journal (...) Todd Baron. 44p. (Orig.). 1992. pap. 5.00 (*0-945926-25-1*) Paradigm RI.

Thistle. Walter Wangerin, Jr. LC 82-47717. (Illus.). (J). 1995. 15.99 (*0-8066-2837-5*) Augsburg Fortress.

Thistle & Co. see Foundlings

Thistle & Rose: A Study of Hugh MacDiamid's Poetry. Ann E. Boutelle. LC 81-65859. 259p. 1981. 35.00 (*0-8387-5023-0*) Bucknell U Pr.

***Thistle & the Grail.** Robin Jenkins. 1994. pap. 18.00 (*0-7486-6193-X*, Pub. by Polygon UK) Subterranean Co.

Thistle & the Rose. May McGoldrick. 384p. 1995. pap. 4.99 (*0-451-40626-5*) NAL-Dutton.

Thistle Greens & Mistletoe: Edible & Poisonous Plants of Northern California. 2nd ed. James Wiltens. LC 88-40003. (Illus.). 160p. 1988. pap. 6.95 (*0-89997-090-7*) Wilderness Pr.

Thistle Hill: The History & the House. Judy Alter. LC 87-10251. (Illus.). 88p. (Orig.). 1988. pap. 5.95 (*0-87565-074-0*) Tex Christian.

Thistle in Her Hand. Margarita T. Diddel. (Illus.). 424p. (Orig.). 1988. pap. 14.95 (*1-55787-035-7*, MA20064, Windswept Books) Hrt of the Lakes.

***Thistle Journal: And Other Essays on Building a House.** Daniel Minock. (First Series). 192p. (Orig.). 1998. pap. 14.00 (*0-922811-34-2*) Mid-List.

***Thistle Princess.** Vivian French. LC 97-14669. (Illus.). (J). 1998. write for info. (*0-7636-0307-4*) Candlewick Pr.

Thistle Worth: Poetry to Read Aloud. Carole Marsh. (Illus.). (Orig.). (gr. 2-12). 1994. pap. 19.95 (*0-935326-60-X*) Gallopade Pub Group.

Thistledown. S. Grey Brewer. (Illus.). 83p. (Orig.). 1993. pap. 8.00 (*1-879025-07-8*) Christopher-Burghardt.

Thistles & Bluebonnets. Ethel L. Evey. LC 95-12779. (Illus.). 128p. (J). (gr. 4-7). 1996. 14.95 (*1-57168-037-3*, Eakin Pr) Sunbelt Media.

Thistles & Daffodils. Beulah D. Fabris. LC 95-67163. (Illus.). 464p. (Orig.). 1996. pap. 16.95 (*0-936029-42-0*) Western Bk Journ.

Thistlewood Plot. J. G. Jeffries. 192p. 1987. 15.95 (*0-8027-5678-6*) Walker & Co.

Thit. Mark Dunster. 14p. (Orig.). 1992. pap. 4.00 (*0-89642-207-0*) Linden Pubs.

Thody Bros. Unusual Window Cleaners: An illustrated Children's Book for Adults. Tom Slack. 61p. (C). 1988. 39.00 (*1-85200-024-4*, Pub. by United Writers Pubns UK) St Mut.

Thom Bohnert: Six Experiments in Sculpture. Christopher R. Young. LC 85-82504. (Illus.). 29p. (Orig.). 1986. pap. 3.50 (*0-939896-07-9*) Flint Inst Arts.

Thom Duncan's Guide to Netware Shareware. Thom Duncan. 1994. pap. 29.95 (*1-55958-514-5*) Prima Pub.

Thomae Dempsteri Historia Ecclesiastica Gentis Scotorum: Sive, De Scriptoribus Scotis, 2 Vols. Thomas Dempster. Ed. by David Irving. LC 72-163685. (Bannatyne Club, Edinburgh. Publications: No. 21). reprint ed. Set. 125.00 (*0-404-52725-6*) AMS Pr.

***Thomas.** Shelly Mydans. lib. bdg. 27.95 (*0-8488-2105-X*) Amereon Ltd.

***Thomas.** Bonnie Pryor. (Illus.). (J). Date not set. write for info. (*0-688-15669-X*, Morrow Junior) Morrow.

Thomas A. Dorsey & the Rise of Gospel Music. Michael W. Harris. (Illus.). 320p. 1992. 48.00 (*0-19-506376-7*) OUP.

Thomas A. Edison: A Streak of Luck. Robert Conot. (Series in Science). (Illus.). 608p. 1986. pap. 15.95 (*0-306-80261-9*) Da Capo.

Thomas A. Edison: Young Inventor. Sue Guthridge. LC 86-10862. (Childhood of Famous Americans Ser.). (Illus.). 192p. (Orig.). (J). (gr. 2-6). 1986. reprint ed. pap. 4.95 (*0-02-041850-7*) Macmillan.

***Thomas A. Edison Album.** Lawrence A. Frost. 39.95 (*0-8488-1718-4*, Am Repr) Amereon Ltd.

***Thomas A. Edison Album.** Lawrence A. Frost. Date not set. pap. 20.95 (*0-8488-1719-2*) Amereon Ltd.

Thomas A. Edison & His Kinetographic Motion Pictures. Charles Musser. LC 93-96. 1993. Alk. paper. 12.95 (*0-9634879-0-6*) Frnds of Edison.

Thomas A. Edison & His Kinetoscopic Motion Pictures. Charles Musser. (Illus.). 70p. (C). 1995. pap. 14.95 (*0-8135-2210-2*) Rutgers U Pr.

Thomas A. Edison & the Modernization of America. Martin V. Melosi. (Library of American Biography). 224p. reprint ed. pap. 15.95 (*1-886746-27-3*, 93480) Talman.

Thomas A. Jaggar Museum Guidebook. Darcy Bevens & Thomas L. Wright. (Illus.). 34p. (Orig.). 1992. pap. 6.95 (*0-940295-10-5*) HI Natural Hist.

Thomas a Kempis: On the Love of God. rev. ed. S. Abhayananda. (Classics of Mystical Literature Ser.). 160p. (Orig.). 1992. pap. 7.95 (*0-914557-00-9*) Atma Bks.

Thomas A. R. Nelson of East Tennessee. Thomas B. Alexander. LC 56-63418. 224p. reprint ed. pap. 63.90 (*0-317-26107-X*, 2024383) Bks Demand.

Thomas A. Sebek Bibliography 1942-1995. 144p. 1995. pap. 26.00 (*0-614-10762-8*) Eurolingua.

Thomas Abthorpe Cooper: America's Premier Tragedian. Geddeth Smith. LC 96-6028. (Illus.). 384p. 1996. 52.50 (*0-8386-3659-4*) Fairleigh Dickinson.

Thomas Alexander Tefft: American Architecture in Transition, 1845-1860. Ed. by Kathleen Curran. LC 87-72847. (Illus.). 288p. (Orig.). 1988. pap. 20.00 (*0-933519-12-5*) D W Bell Gallery.

Thomas Alva Edison: Great Inventor. David A. Adler. LC 89-77507. (Illus.). 48p. (J). (gr. 2-5). 1990. lib. bdg. 15.95 (*0-8234-0820-5*) Holiday.

Thomas Alva Edison: Inventing the Electric Age. Gene Adair. (Oxford Scientists Ser.). (Illus.). 144p. (YA). (gr. 7 up). 1996. lib. bdg. 20.00 (*0-19-508799-2*) OUP.

***Thomas Alva Edison: Inventing the Electric Age.** Gene Adair. (Oxford Portraits in Science). (Illus.). 144p. (J). 1997. pap. 12.95 (*0-19-511981-9*) OUP.

Thomas Alva Edison: Persistent Dreamer & Doer. AESOP Enterprises, Inc. Staff & Gwendolyn J. Crenshaw. (Heroes & Sheroes Ser.). 14p. (J). (gr. 3-12). 1991. pap. write for info. incl. audio (*1-880771-13-6*) AESOP Enter.

Thomas Alva Edison: The King of Inventors. David C. King. LC 95-68767. (Scientists & Inventors Ser.). (Illus.). 88p. (Orig.). (J). (gr. 5-12). 1995. pap. 5.95 (*1-878668-55-2*) Disc Enter Ltd.

Thomas Alva Edison: Young Inventor. Louis Sabin. LC 82-15889. (Illus.). 48p. (J). (gr. 4-6). 1983. lib. bdg. 12.95 (*0-89375-841-8*) Troll Communs.

Thomas Alva Edison: Young Inventor. Louis Sabin. LC 82-15889. (Illus.). 48p. (J). (gr. 4-6). 1996. pap. 3.95 (*0-89375-842-6*) Troll Communs.

Thomas Alva Edison, Great Inventor. Nancy S. Levinson. (J). (gr. 3-7). 1996. mass mkt. 3.50 (*0-590-52767-3*) Scholastic Inc.

***Thomas & Bertie.** 1997. 5.99 (*0-679-88682-6*) Random Bks Yng Read.

Thomas & Beulah. Dove. 1987. pap. 11.95 (*0-88748-021-7*) Carnegie-Mellon.

Thomas & Bonaventure: A Septicentenary Commemoration. Ed. by George F. McLean. LC 75-319639. (Proceedings of the American Catholic Philosophical Association Ser.: Vol. 48). 1974. pap. 20.00 (*0-918090-08-3*) Am Cath Philo.

Thomas & Elizabeth Savage. Sue Hart. LC 95-75726. (Western Writers Ser.: No. 119). (Illus.). 50p. (C). 1995. pap. 4.95 (*0-88430-118-4*) Boise St U W Writ Ser.

Thomas & Launia - Their Ancestors & Descendants: A History of One Branch of the Lincoln County, West Virginia, McClures. Drollene P. Brown. Ed. by Sharon E. Reynolds. LC 94-20856. (Illus.). 192p. (Orig.). 1994. pap. 24.95 (*0-9641216-0-3*) RitAmelia Pr.

Thomas & the Bulldozer. Sally Passantino. (Illus.). 64p. (Orig.). (J). 1994. pap. text ed. 7.50 (*1-56002-395-3*, Univ Edtns) Aegina Pr.

Thomas & the Freight Train. W. Awdry. LC 90-62371. (Chunky Shape Bks.). (Illus.). 22p. (J). (ps). 1991. 3.99 (*0-679-81599-6*) Random Bks Yng Read.

Thomas & the Giant. Tank Thomas. 1995. pap. 4.99 (*0-679-87754-1*) Random.

Thomas & the Helicopter Rescue: A Revolving Picture Book with Flaps. Christopher Awdry. LC 95-67485. (J). (ps-3). 1995. 15.00 (*0-679-87690-1*) Random.

Thomas & the Hide-&-Seek Animals: A Thomas the Tank Engine Flap Book. W. Awdry. LC 90-62114. (Flap Bks.). (Illus.). 24p. (J). (ps-1). 1991. 10.95 (*0-679-81316-0*) Random Bks Yng Read.

Thomas & the Lost Cat. Tank Thomas. 1995. pap. 4.99 (*0-679-87753-3*) Random.

Thomas & the Physics of Nineteen Fifty-Eight: A Confrontation. Henry Margenau. LC 58-9679. (Aquinas Lectures). 1958. 15.00 (*0-87462-123-2*) Marquette.

Thomas & the Warlock. Mollie Hunter. (Illus.). 1990. 17.00 (*0-8446-6243-7*) Peter Smith.

***Thomas & the Weather.** W. Awdry. (J). 1998. 4.99 (*0-679-89004-1*) Random Bks Yng Read.

Thomas Anshutz, Artist & Teacher. Ed. by Randall C. Griffin. LC 94-77597. (Illus.). 146p. (Orig.). 1994. pap. 22.50 (*0-295-97413-3*) Heckscher Mus.

Thomas Aquinas: International Bibliography, 1977-1990. Ed. by Richard Ingardia. (Bibliographies of Famous Philosophers Ser.). 492p. 1993. 57.00 (*0-912632-92-5*) Philos Document.

Thomas Aquinas: Preacher & Friend. Mary A. Fatula. (Way of the Christian Mystics Ser.: No. 15). 320p. (Orig.). 1992. pap. text ed. 17.95 (*0-8146-5031-7*, M Glazier) Liturgical Pr.

Thomas Aquinas: Spiritual Master. Robert Barron. LC 95-34303. (Spiritual Legacy Ser.). 180p. 1996. pap. 14.95 (*0-8245-2507-8*) Crossroad NY.

Thomas Aquinas - Gifts of the Spirit: Selected Spiritual Writings. 2nd ed. Ed. by Thomas Ashley. Tr. by Matthew Rzeczkoski. (Profiles Ser.). 144p. (Orig.). 1995. pap. 8.95 (*1-56548-071-6*) New City.

Thomas Aquinas & Gabriel Biel: Interpretations of St Thomas Aquinas in German Nominalism on the Eve of the Reformation. John L. Farthing. LC 87-27431. (Monographs in Medieval & Renaissance Studies). x, 275p. 1988. text ed. 35.95 (*0-8223-0806-1*) Duke.

Thomas Aquinas & His Legacy. Ed. by David A. Gallagher. LC 93-25825. (Studies in Philosophy & the History of Philosophy: No. 28). 246p. 1994. 59.95 (*0-8132-0790-8*) Cath U Pr.

Thomas Aquinas & Karl Barth: Sacred Doctrine & the Natural Knowledge of God. Eugene F. Rogers, Jr. LC 94-42830. (Revisions: A Series of Books on Ethics: Vol. 13). (C). 1996. text ed. 34.95 (*0-268-01889-8*) U of Notre Dame Pr.

Thomas Aquinas & Radical Aristotelianism. Fernand Van Steenberghen. LC 80-10137. 124p. reprint ed. pap. 35.40 (*0-7837-4636-9*, 2044360) Bks Demand.

Thomas Aquinas the Literal Exposition of Job: A Scriptual Commentary Concerning Providence. Tr. by Anthony Damico. LC 88-31855. (American Academy of Religion, Classics in Religious Studies). 496p. 1989. 62.95 (*1-55540-291-7*, 01-05-07); pap. 41.95 (*1-55540-292-5*) Scholars Pr GA.

***Thomas Aquinas Theologian.** Thomas F. O'Meara. LC 96-26438. 368p. 1997. text ed. 36.00 (*0-268-01898-7*); pap. text ed. 16.95 (*0-268-04201-2*) U of Notre Dame Pr.

Thomas Attwood: The Biography of a Radical. David J. Moss. 400p. 1990. text ed. 55.00 (*0-7735-0708-6*, Pub. by McGill CN) U of Toronto Pr.

Thomas B. Reed. Samuel W. McCall. Ed. by John T. Morse, Jr. LC 74-128950. (American Statesmen Ser.: No. 35). reprint ed. 45.00 (*0-404-50885-5*) AMS Pr.

Thomas B. Reed, Parliamentarian. William A. Robinson. (History - United States Ser.). 423p. 1992. reprint ed. lib. bdg. 99.00 (*0-7812-6200-3*) Rprt Serv.

Thomas Bailey Aldrich. Charles E. Samuels. (Twayne's United States Authors Ser.). 1965. pap. 10.95 (*0-8084-0297-8*, T94) NCUP.

***Thomas Bailey Aldrich: Great American Short Stories III.** Illus. by James Balkovek. LC 95-76745. (Classic Short Stories Ser.). 80p. (YA). (gr. 6-12). 1995. pap. 5.95 (*0-7854-0595-X*, 40081) Am Guidance.

Thomas Barker Talks about Divorce & Separation. Teresa M. Schmidt. (Building Trust, Making Friends Ser.). 236p. (J). (gr. 6-8). 1991. pap. 59.95 (*1-56246-022-6*, P162) Johnsn Inst.

Thomas Barnes of the Times. Derek Hudson. Ed. by Harold Child. LC 70-138623. (Illus.). 196p. 1973. reprint ed. text ed. 65.00 (*0-8371-5735-8*, HUTB, Greenwood Pr) Greenwood.

Thomas Bartlett Sears, Jr. (1834-1925), the Journals of a Plymouth Seaman. Ed. by Marian S. Chaffin. 58p. 1989. pap. 5.00 (*0-940628-50-3*) Pilgrim Soc.

Thomas Basson 1555-1613: English Printer at Leiden. Jan A. Van Dorsten. (Illus.). x, 126p. 1961. text ed. 29.50 (*0-317-55883-8*, Pub. by B De Graaf NE) Coronet Bks.

Thomas Bayrle: Big Book. Thomas Bayrle. (Illus.). 432p. 1991. pap. 40.00 (*3-88375-170-7*, Pub. by Walther Konig GW) Dist Art Pubs.

Thomas Becket. Frank Barlow. 384p. 1990. pap. 16.00 (*0-520-07175-1*) U CA Pr.

Thomas Becket. David Knowles. LC 77-143785. xi, 183p. 1971. 24.50 (*0-8047-0766-9*) Stanford U Pr.

Thomas Becket dans la Tradition Historique et Hagiographique. Raymonde Foreville. (Collected Studies: No. CS130). (Illus.). 348p. (FRE.). (C). 1981. reprint ed. lib. bdg. 105.00 (*0-86078-076-7*, Pub. by Variorum UK) Ashgate Pub Co.

Thomas Beddoes M. D., Seventeen Sixty to Eighteen Eight: Chemist, Physician, Democrat. Dorothy A. Stansfield. (Chemists & Chemistry Ser.: Vol. 3). 1984. lib. bdg. 149.00 (*90-277-1686-2*) Kluwer Ac.

Thomas Begbie's Edinburgh. Joe Rock & David Patterson. 200p. (C). 1996. 90.00 (*0-85976-337-4*, Pub. by J Donald UK) St Mut.

Thomas Bell-Military Pension Record: The Bell Family History. George E. Bell. Ed. by Jean P. Bell. (Illus.). 200p. (C). 1989. text ed. write for info. (*0-9623275-0-6*) Wayne Ridge.

Thomas Benton Catron & His Era. Victor Westphall. LC 73-75304. 472p. reprint ed. pap. 134.60 (*0-317-28048-1*, 2025556) Bks Demand.

Thomas Bernhard & His Grandfather Johannes Freumbichler: Our Grandfathers Are Our Teachers. Caroline Markolin. Tr. by Petra Hartweg. LC 92-38175. (Studies in Austrian Literature, Culture & Thought; Translation Ser.). 1993. 27.50 (*0-929497-51-1*) Ariadne CA.

Thomas Berry & the New Cosmology: In Dialogue with Gregory Baum, Margaret Brennan, Stephen Dunn, James Farris, Caroline Richards, Donald Senior, & Brian Swimme. Ed. by Anne Lonergan & Caroline Richards. LC 87-40528. 120p. (Orig.). (C). 1987. pap. 7.95 (*0-89622-337-X*) Twenty-Third.

Thomas Betterton. Robert W. Lowe. LC 77-144652. reprint ed. 37.50 (*0-404-04038-1*) AMS Pr.

Thomas Betterton & the Management of Lincoln's Inn Fields, 1695-1708. Judith Milhous. LC 78-21017. 318p. 1979. 29.95 (*0-8093-0906-8*) S Ill U Pr.

Thomas Betts, (1618-1688) & His Descendants. Charles W. Betts & Frederick Betts. (Illus.). 136p. 1988. reprint ed. pap. 27.50 (*0-8328-0247-6*); reprint ed. lib. bdg. 35.50 (*0-8328-0246-8*) Higginson Bk Co.

***Thomas Bewick (1753-1828) Selected Work.** Ed. by Robyn Marsack. pap. write for info. (*0-85635-780-4*, Pub. by Carcanet Pr UK) Paul & Co Pubs.

Thomas Bewick's Birds: Watercolours & Engravings. Thomas Bewick. (Illus.). 52p. 1982. 9.95 (*0-262-02176-5*) MIT Pr.

Thomas Birch Seventeen Seventy-Nine to Eighteen Fifty-One: Paintings & Drawings. Philadelphia Maritime Museum Staff. (Illus.). 64p. 1966. pap. 2.00 (*0-913346-06-3*) Indep Seaport.

Thomas Book: Giving the Genealogies of Sir Rhys ap Thomas, K. G., the Thomas Family Descended from Him, & of Some Allied Families. Lawrence B. Thomas. (Illus.). 627p. 1994. pap. 43.00 (*0-7884-0030-4*) Heritage Bk.

Thomas Book, Giving the Genealogy of Sir Rhy of Thomas, K. G., the Thomas Family Descended from Him & Some Allied Families. L. B. Thomas. (Illus.). 648p. 1989. reprint ed. pap. 97.00 (*0-8328-1163-7*); reprint ed. lib. bdg. 105.00 (*0-8328-1162-9*) Higginson Bk Co.

Thomas Boyden & His Descendants. Wallace C. Boyden et al. (Illus.). 267p. 1988. reprint ed. pap. 40.00 (*0-8328-0297-2*); reprint ed. lib. bdg. 48.00 (*0-8328-0296-4*) Higginson Bk Co.

Thomas Bradwardine: A View of Time & a Vision of Eternity in Fourteenth Century Thought. Edith W. Dolnikowski. LC 95-2091. (Studies in the History of Christian Thought: Vol. 65). 250p. 1995. 92.00 (*90-04-10226-4*) E J Brill.

Thomas Bray's Grand Design: Libraries of the Church of England in America, 1695-1785. Charles T. Laugher. LC 73-16332. (ACRL Publications in Librarianship: No. 35). 125p. reprint ed. pap. 35.70 (*0-317-29444-X*, 2024224) Bks Demand.

Thomas Buckingham & the Contingency of Futures: The Possibility of Human Freedom. Bartholomew R. De la Torre. LC 86-40336. (Mediaeval Studies: No. 25). 328p. 1987. text ed. 46.00 (*0-268-01861-8*) U of Notre Dame Pr.

Thomas Bullock Journal. Thomas Bullock & Greg R. Knight. 101p. 1994. 39.95 (*0-910523-09-6*) Grandin Bk Co.

Thomas Burnett, Seventeen Fifty-Five to Seventeen Eighty, of VA & NC. Frances Gass. LC 64-25445. 250p. reprint ed. 40.00 (*0-916497-10-0*); reprint ed. fiche 6.00 (*0-916497-01-1*) Burnett Micro.

Thomas Burt's "Bellvale Rising Star Newspaper", 1889. Orange County Genealogical Society Staff. 1986. pap. text ed. 3.50 (*0-937135-18-6*) Orange County Genealog.

Thomas Butler & His Descendants, 1674-1886: A Genealogy of the Descendants of Thomas & Elizabeth Butler of Butler's Hill. G. H. Butler. 199p. 1989. reprint ed. pap. 30.00 (*0-8328-1295-1*); reprint ed. lib. bdg. 38.00 (*0-8328-1294-3*) Higginson Bk Co.

Thomas Campion. David Lindley. (Medieval & Renaissance Authors Ser.: Vol. 7). xii, 242p. 1986. 60.75 (*90-04-07601-8*) E J Brill.

***Thomas Campion (1567-1620) Ayres & Observations.** Ed. by Joan Hart. pap. write for info. (*0-85635-099-0*, Pub. by Carcanet Pr UK) Paul & Co Pubs.

Thomas Cantimpratensis: Liber De Natura Rerum. Editio Princeps Secundum Codices Manuscriptos, 2pts, Pt. 1. (C). 1973. 173.10 (*3-11-003789-0*) De Gruyter.

Thomas Carlyle. Ian Campbell. (C). 1994. pap. 39.95 (*0-85411-052-6*, Pub. by Saltire Soc) St Mut.

Thomas Carlyle. D. Lammond. LC 73-18127. (Studies in Thos. Carlyle: No. 53). 1974. lib. bdg. 49.95 (*0-8383-1740-5*) M S G Haskell Hse.

Thomas Carlyle. Gilbert K. Chesterton. LC 73-9601. (Studies in Thos. Carlyle: No. 53). 1973. reprint ed. lib. bdg. 75.00 (*0-8383-1705-7*) M S G Haskell Hse.

Thomas Carlyle. Moncure D. Conway. (Works of Moncure Daniel Conway Ser.). 1990. reprint ed. lib. bdg. 79.00 (*0-7812-2336-9*) Rprt Serv.

Thomas Carlyle. Edwin P. Hood. LC 71-116795. (English Biography Ser.: No. 31). 1970. reprint ed. lib. bdg. 67.95 (*0-8383-1037-0*) M S G Haskell Hse.

Thomas Carlyle. John Nichol. Ed. by John Morley. LC 68-58391. (English Men of Letters Ser.). reprint ed. lib. bdg. 27.50 (*0-404-51723-4*) AMS Pr.

Thomas Carlyle: A Bibliography of English-Language Criticism, 1824-1974. Rodger L. Tarr. LC 76-10837. 309p. reprint ed. pap. 88.10 (*0-8357-7055-9*, 2033296) Bks Demand.

Thomas Carlyle: A Biography. Fred Kaplan. LC 83-5364. (Illus.). 640p. 1983. 59.95 (*0-8014-1508-X*) Cornell U Pr.

Thomas Carlyle: A Biography. Fred Kaplan. LC 92-24439. 1993. 17.95 (*0-520-08200-1*) U CA Pr.

Thomas Carlyle: A Descriptive Bibliography. Rodger L. Tarr. LC 89-30016. (Series in Bibliography). (Illus.). 568p. 1990. 110.00 (*0-8229-3607-0*) U of Pittsburgh Pr.

Thomas Carlyle: A History of His Life in London, 2 vols. James A. Froude. (BCL1-PR English Literature Ser.). 1992. reprint ed. Set. lib. bdg. 150.00 (*0-7812-7488-5*) Rprt Serv.

Thomas Carlyle: A History of His Life in London, 2 vols. James A. Froude. 1971. reprint ed. Set. 59.00 (*0-403-00191-9*) Scholarly.

Thomas Carlyle: A History of the First Forty Years of His Life, 2 vols. James A. Froude. (BCL1-PR English Literature Ser.). 1992. reprint ed. Set. lib. bdg. 150.00 (*0-7812-7489-3*) Rprt Serv.

Thomas Carlyle: Study of His Apprenticeship. William S. Johnson. LC 79-122993. (English Biography Ser.: No. 31). 1970. reprint ed. lib. bdg. 55.95 (*0-8383-1126-1*) M S G Haskell Hse.

Thomas Carlyle: The Life & Ideas of a Prophet. Julian Symons. LC 76-126261. (Select Bibliographies Reprint Ser.). 1977. 20.95 (*0-8369-5488-2*) Ayer.

Thomas Carlyle see Victorian Thinkers

Thomas Carlyle's Apprenticeship. John Muir. LC 79-116797. (English Biography Ser.: No. 31). 1970. reprint ed. lib. bdg. 49.95 (*0-8383-1039-7*) M S G Haskell Hse.

An Asterisk (*) at the beginning of an entry indicates that the title is appearing in BIP for the first time.

Thomas Carlyle's Moral & Religious Development. E. Flugel. LC 74-116793. (Studies in Philosophy: No. 40). 1970. reprint ed. lib. bdg. 56.95 (*0-8383-1035-4*) M S G Haskell Hse.

Thomas Carlyle's Writing of Oliver Cromwell's Letters & Speeches. D. J. Trela. LC 91-47614. (Studies in British History: Vol. 30). 220p. 1992. lib. bdg. 89.95 (*0-7734-9451-0*) E Mellen.

Thomas Cave Wilson: Reminiscences of a Nevada Advertising Man, 1930-1980, Or Half a Century of Very Hot Air, Or I Wouldn't Believe It If I Hadn't Been There. Intro. by Mary E. Glass. 753p. 1982. Set. lib. bdg. 94.50 (*1-56475-228-3*); Set. fiche write for info. (*1-56475-229-1*) U NV Oral Hist.

Thomas Chalmers McCorvey: Teacher, Poet, Historian. George B. Johnston. LC 85-51715. (Illus.). 252p. 1986. 20.00 (*0-9616760-1-9*); pap. 5.00 (*0-9616760-2-7*) White Rhino Pr.

Thomas Chalmers Works on Economics & Social Welfare, 8 vols., Set. 2nd ed. Ed. by David Gladstone & University of Bristol. (Pioneers In Social Welfare Ser.). 4005p. (C). (gr. 13 up). 1995. text ed. 925.00 (*0-415-12208-2*, Routledge NY) Routledge.

Thomas Chaloner's in Laudem Henrici Octavi. Ed. by John B. Gabel & Carl C. Schlam. 112p. 1979. 10.00 (*0-87291-135-7*) Coronado Pr.

Thomas Chandler Haliburton & His Works. Stan McMullin. (Canadian Author Studies). 50p. (C). 1989. pap. text ed. 9.95 (*1-55022-047-0*, Pub. by ECW Press CN) Genl Dist Srvs.

Thomas Chandler Haliburton, "Sam Slick" Victor L. Chittick. LC 24-29336. reprint ed. 42.50 (*0-404-01525-5*) AMS Pr.

Thomas Charles' Spiritual Counsels. Thomas Charles. 477p. 1993. reprint ed. text ed. 23.99 (*0-85151-656-4*) Banner of Truth.

Thomas Chatterton. Charles E. Russell. LC 70-130258. (English Literature Ser.: No. 33). 1970. reprint ed. lib. bdg. 62.95 (*0-8383-1162-8*) M S G Haskell Hse.

Thomas Chatterton: Early Sources & Responses, 6 vols., Set. 1568p. (C). (gr. 13 up). 1993. boxed, text ed. 460.00 (*0-415-09255-8*, Routledge NY) Routledge.

***Thomas Chatterton (1752-1770) Selected Poems.** Ed. by Grevel Lindop. pap. write for info. (*0-902145-54-1*, Pub. by Carcanet Pr UK) Paul & Co Pubs.

Thomas Chaucer. Martin B. Ruud. LC 78-174797. reprint ed. 21.50 (*0-404-05469-2*) AMS Pr.

Thomas Chaucer. Martin B. Ruud. (BCL1-PR English Literature Ser.). 131p. 1992. reprint ed. lib. bdg. 69.00 (*0-7812-7176-2*) Rprt Serv.

Thomas Chimes. Contrib. by Marian Locks. LC 90-60705. (Orig.). 1990. pap. text ed. 15.00 (*0-9623799-2-1*) Locks Gallery.

Thomas Chimes: The Hermes Cycle. Contrib. by Jane Livingston. (Illus.). 52p. 1992. pap. 15.00 (*1-879173-11-5*) Locks Gallery.

Thomas Christy's Road Across the Plains. limited ed. Ed. by Robert H. Becker. 1969. 50.00 (*0-912094-13-3*) Old West.

Thomas, Churdonis & Allied Family Lines. Berwyn B. Thomas. (Illus.). 117p. 1991. 30.00 (*0-935693-13-0*) Mason Cty Hist.

Thomas Clarkson: A Biography. Ellen G. Wilson. LC 89-78518. 288p. 1990. text ed. 45.00 (*0-312-04637-5*) St Martin.

Thomas Clarkson: A Monograph: Being a Contribution Towards the History of the Abolition of the Slave Trade & Slavery. James Elmes. LC 76-89414. (Black Heritage Library Collection). 1977. 30.95 (*0-8369-8569-9*) Ayer.

Thomas Clarkson: The Friend of Slaves. Earl L. Griggs. LC 75-107476. 210p. 1970. reprint ed. text ed. 45.00 (*0-8371-3754-3*, GRC&, Greenwood Pr) Greenwood.

Thomas Coke: The Foreign Minister of Methodism. 3rd ed. Warren T. Smith. 24p. 1976. reprint ed. pap. 1.00 (*1-880927-03-9*) Gen Comm Arch.

Thomas Cole. Matthew Baigell. (Great Artists Ser.). (Illus.). 84p. 1988. pap. 16.95 (*0-8230-0648-4*, Watsn-Guptill) Watsn-Guptill.

Thomas Cole. Earl A. Powell, III. (Illus.). 144p. 1990. 49.50 (*0-8109-3158-3*) Abrams.

Thomas Cole: Landscape into History. Ed. by William H. Truettner & Allan Wallach. LC 93-33272. 185p. (C). 1994. pap. 29.95 (*0-937311-11-1*) Natl Mus Amer Art.

Thomas Cole: Landscape into History. Ed. by William H. Truettner & Allan Wallach. LC 93-33272. (Illus.). 185p. (C). 1994. 50.00 (*0-300-05850-0*) Yale U Pr.

Thomas Cole's Paintings of Eden. Franklin Kelly. LC 94-12139. 72p. 1994. pap. 17.95 (*0-88360-083-8*) Amon Carter.

Thomas Cole's Poetry: The Collected Poems of America's Foremost Painter of the Hudson River School, Reflecting His Feelings for Nature & the Romantic Spirit of the 19th Century. Thomas Cole. Ed. by Marshall B. Tymn. LC 72-7843. (Illus.). 1972. boxed 25.00 (*0-87387-057-3*) Shumway.

Thomas Cook European Airport's Directory. Thomas Cook. 1994. pap. 15.95 (*0-8442-9039-4*, Passport Bks) NTC Pub Grp.

Thomas Cook European Travel Phrasebook. Thomas Cook Editors. 352p. (Orig.). 1996. pap. 6.95 (*0-8442-9004-1*, Passport Bks) NTC Pub Grp.

***Thomas Cook International Air Travel Handbook: A Guide to the World's Major Airports, Their Facilities & Transport Connections.** 208p. 1997. pap. 24.95 (*0-8442-9188-9*) NTC Pub Grp.

Thomas Cooke of Rhode Island: A Genealogy of Thomas Cooke Alias Butcher of Netherbury, Dorsetshire, England, Who Came to Taunton, Massachusetts, in 1637 & Settled in Portsmouth, Rhode Island in 1643, 2 vols. Jane F. Fiske. (Illus.). xxv, 980p. 1987. 68.00 (*0-9615790-0-5*) J F Fiske.

Thomas Cornell Paintings: The Birth of Nature. Illus. by Thomas Cornell. LC 89-64317. 32p. (Orig.). 1990. pap. 15.00 (*0-916606-20-1*) Bowdoin Coll.

Thomas Couture & the Eclectic Vision. Albert Boime. LC 79-23507. (Illus.). 707p. reprint ed. pap. 180.00 (*0-7837-4529-X*, 2080199) Bks Demand.

Thomas Cramner: Churchman & Scholar. Ed. by Paul Ayris & David Selwyn. (Illus.). 371p. (C). 1993. 63.00 (*0-85115-549-9*) Boydell & Brewer.

Thomas Cranmer: A Life. Diarmaid MacCulloch. LC 95-49593. (Illus.). 704p. (C). 1996. 35.00 (*0-300-06688-0*) Yale U Pr.

Thomas Cranmer & the English Reformation, 1849-1556. Albert F. Pollard. LC 83-45587. reprint ed. 42.50 (*0-404-19905-4*) AMS Pr.

Thomas Crosby & the Tsimshian: Small Shoes for Feet Too Large. Clarence R. Bolt. 160p. 1992. 35.95 (*0-7748-0430-0*, Pub. by U BC Pr) U of Wash Pr.

Thomas Daniel of Col. VA: And Eight Generations of His Descendants. Kevin W. Daniel. (Illus.). 341p. (Orig.). 1995. pap. 25.00 (*0-7884-0235-8*) Heritage Bk.

Thomas d'Aquin: Sa Vision de Theologie et de l'Eglise. Yves Congar. (Collected Studies: No. CS190). 334p. (ENG, FRE & LAT.). (C). 1984. reprint ed. text ed. 109.95 (*0-86078-138-0*, Pub. by Variorum UK) Ashgate Pub Co.

Thomas David Duane, MD: Wills Eye Hospital & Thomas Jefferson Medical College. Thomas D. Duane. (Ophthalmology Oral History Ser.). (Illus.). (Orig.). 1989. 35.00 (*0-926866-03-6*) FAAO.

Thomas Davis. Eileen Sullivan. Ed. by James F. Carens. LC 72-482. (Irish Writers Ser.). 90p. 1979. 8.50 (*0-8387-1234-7*); pap. 1.95 (*0-8387-1237-1*) Bucknell U Pr.

Thomas Davis, Selections from His Prose & Poetry. Thomas Davis. LC 75-28810. (Illus.). 392p. reprint ed. 57.50 (*0-404-13803-9*) AMS Pr.

Thomas De Quincey: Bicentenary Studies. Ed. & Intro. by Robert L. Snyder. LC 85-40487. (Illus.). 416p. 1986. 39.95 (*0-8061-1849-0*) U of Okla Pr.

Thomas De Quincey: His Life & Writings, 2 vols. Alexander H. Japp. (BCL1-PR English Literature Ser.). 1992. reprint ed. Set. lib. bdg. 150.00 (*0-7812-7509-1*) Rprt Serv.

Thomas De Quincey, Literary Critic. John E. Jordan. LC 70-189248. 301p. 1973. reprint ed. 50.00 (*0-87752-160-3*) Gordian.

Thomas Dekker. George R. Price. LC 68-17241. (Twayne's English Authors Ser.). 1969. pap. text ed. 5.95 (*0-8290-2006-3*); lib. bdg. 17.95 (*0-8057-1148-1*) Irvington.

Thomas Dekker: A Study. Mary L. Hunt. (BCL1-PR English Literature Ser.). 213p. 1992. reprint ed. lib. bdg. 79.00 (*0-7812-7240-8*) Rprt Serv.

Thomas Dewey: The Upset Presidential Candidate of 1948. Gerald Kurland. Ed. by D. Steve Rahmas. LC 70-185659. (Outstanding Personalities Ser.: No. 3). 32p. 1972. lib. bdg. 7.25 (*0-87157-503-5*) SamHar Pr.

***Thomas Dolby's Guide to Web Site Sound Design.** Thomas Dolby Robertson & Chris Van Rensburg. 400p. 1997. 34.99 (*1-56276-547-7*, Ziff-Davis Pr) Que.

Thomas Dongan, Governor of New York (1682-1688) John H. Kennedy. LC 73-3564. (Catholic University of America. Studies in Romance Languages & Literatures: No. 9). reprint ed. 31.50 (*0-404-57759-8*) AMS Pr.

Thomas Dorman of Topsfield, MA (1600-1670) Twelve Generations of Descendants. Franklin A. Dorman. (Illus.). 733p. (Orig.). 1995. pap. text ed. 46.50 (*0-7884-0108-4*) Heritage Bk.

Thomas E. Watson Revisited: The Saga of a Great Southern Populist. Thomas H. Irwin. 1984. lib. bdg. 79.95 (*0-87700-601-6*) Revisionist Pr.

Thomas Eakins, 2 vols. Lloyd Goodrich. (Ailsa Mellon Bruce Studies in American Art). (Illus.). 368p. 1982. text ed. 90.00 (*0-674-88490-6*) HUP.

Thomas Eakins. Ed. by John Wilmerding. LC 93-85709. (Illus.). 212p. 1993. 55.00 (*1-56098-313-2*) Smithsonian.

Thomas Eakins: His Life & Art. William I. Homer. LC 92-10163. (Illus.). 276p. 1992. 95.00 (*1-55859-281-4*) Abbeville Pr.

Thomas Eakins: The Heroism of Modern Life. Elizabeth Johns. (Illus.). 227p. 1991. pap. text ed. 35.00 (*0-691-00288-6*) Princeton U Pr.

Thomas Eakins: The Rowing Pictures. Helen Cooper et al. Ed. by Shelia Schwartz. LC 96-15716. (Illus.). 139p. (C). 1996. pap. 20.95 (*0-89467-076-X*) Yale Art Gallery.

Thomas Eakins: The Rowing Pictures. Helen A. Cooper. LC 96-15716. 1996. pap. write for info. (*0-89467-077-8*) Yale Art Gallery.

Thomas Eakins: The Rowing Pictures. Helen A. Cooper. (Illus.). 144p. 1996. 30.00 (*0-300-06939-1*) Yale U Pr.

Thomas Eakins & the Swimming Picture. Doreen Bolger et al. LC 95-45967. (Illus.). 176p. 1996. pap. 30.00 (*0-88360-085-4*) Amon Carter.

Thomas Eakins Collection of the Hirshhorn Museum & Sculpture Garden. Smithsonian Institution Staff. LC 79-10081. 154p. 1979. lib. bdg. 39.00 incl. fiche (*0-226-69102-0*) U Ch Pr.

***Thomas Eakins Rediscovered: Charles Bregler's Thomas Eakins Collection at the Pennsylvania Academy of the Fine Arts.** Kathleeen A. Foster & Mark Bockrat. LC 97-8253. 1997. write for info. (*0-300-06174-9*) Yale U Pr.

Thomas Edison. Kelly C. Anderson. LC 93-14156. (Importance of Ser.). 112p. (J). (gr. 5-8). 1994. lib. bdg. 17.96 (*1-56006-041-7*) Lucent Bks.

Thomas Edison. Paul Joseph. (Inventors Ser.). (J). 1996. lib. bdg. 13.98 (*1-56239-634-X*) Abdo & Dghtrs.

***Thomas Edison.** Haydn Middleton. (What's Their Story?). (Illus.). (J). 1997. lib. bdg. 12.95 (*0-19-521401-3*) OUP.

Thomas Edison. Nicholas Nirgiotis. LC 93-37028. (Cornerstones of Freedom Ser.). (Illus.). 32p. (J). (gr. 3-6). 1994. lib. bdg. 18.00 (*0-516-06676-5*) Childrens.

Thomas Edison. Nicholas Nirgiotis. (Cornerstones of Freedom Ser.). (J). (gr. 3-6). 1994. pap. 4.95 (*0-516-46676-3*) Childrens.

Thomas Edison: A Study. Elbert Hubbard. 1979. pap. 2.00 (*0-932282-45-8*) Caledonia Pr.

Thomas Edison: Great American Inventor. Shelly Bedik. 32p. (J). (ps-3). 1995. pap. 2.50 (*0-590-48357-9*) Scholastic Inc.

Thomas Edison - Alexander Graham Bell. Naunerle C. Farr. (Pendulum Illustrated Biography Ser.). (Illus.). (J). (gr. 4-12). 1979. student ed. 1.25 (*0-88301-381-9*); pap. text ed. 2.95 (*0-88301-357-6*) Pendulum Pr.

Thomas Edison & Electricity see Science Discoveries

Thomas Edison & the Modernization of America. Martin V. Melosi. (C). 1990. pap. text ed. 16.95 (*0-673-39625-8*) Addson-Wesley Educ.

Thomas Edison Book of Easy & Incredible Experiments. James G. Cook. LC 88-20669. (Science Editions Ser.). 146p. 1988. pap. text ed. 14.95 (*0-471-62090-4*) Wiley.

Thomas Edison, Chemist. Byron M. Vanderbilt. LC 75-172526. 1971. 14.95 (*0-8412-0129-3*); pap. 9.95 (*0-8412-0534-5*) Am Chemical.

Thomas Edison on Money & Banking. Thomas Edison. 1992. lib. bdg. 75.00 (*0-8490-8727-9*) Gordon Pr.

Thomas Elfe: Cabinetmaker. Samuel A. Humphrey. (Illus.). 128p. (Orig.). 1995. pap. 24.95 (*0-941711-15-3*) Wyrick & Co.

Thomas Erskine: Advocate for the Character of God. Donald F. Winslow. 154p. (Orig.). (C). 1992. pap. text ed. 23.50 (*0-8191-8837-9*); lib. bdg. 48.00 (*0-8191-8836-0*) U Pr of Amer.

Thomas Erskine of Linlathen: His Life & Theology, 1788-1837. Nicholas R. Needham. LC 92-7135. (Rutherford Studies in Historical Theology). 452p. 1992. reprint ed. lib. bdg. 109.95 (*0-7734-1645-5*) E Mellen.

Thomas F. McManus & the American Fishing Schooners: An Irish-American Success Story. W. M. Dunne. (American Maritime Library Ser.: Vol. XIV). (Illus.). xi, 406p. 1994. 39.95 (*0-913372-69-2*) Mystic Seaport.

Thomas Florschuetz. John P. Jacob & Christoph Tannert. 32p. (Orig.). 1988. 7.50 (*0-935519-08-4*) Anderson Gal.

Thomas Francis Meagher: An Irish Revolutionary in America. Robert G. Athearn. LC 76-6321. (Irish Americans Ser.). (Illus.). 1976. reprint ed. 18.95 (*0-405-09318-7*) Ayer.

Thomas Francis Roberts, 1860-1919. David Williams. 48p. pap. 6.95 (*0-7083-0167-3*) Bks Intl VA.

Thomas Frognall Dibdin: Horae Bibligraphicae Cantabrigienses: A Facsimile of Dibdin's Cambridge Notebook, 1823. Thomas F. Dibdin. (Illus.). 80p. 1989. 185.00 (*0-938768-15-8*) Oak Knoll.

Thomas Gainsborough: A Biography. Isabelle Worman. 148p. (C). 1988. 70.00 (*0-900963-69-7*, Pub. by T Dalton UK) St Mut.

Thomas Gambier Parry (1816-1888) As Artist & Collector. Ed. by Dennis Farr. (Illus.). 80p. (C). 1993. pap. 25.00 (*0-904563-09-X*, Pub. by Lund Humphries UK) Antique Collect.

Thomas Gardner, Planter, Cape Ann, 1623-1626, Salem, 1626-1674 & Some of His Descendants. F. A. Gardner. (Illus.). 347p. 1989. reprint ed. pap. 52.00 (*0-8328-0586-6*); reprint ed. lib. bdg. 60.00 (*0-8328-0585-8*) Higginson Bk Co.

Thomas George-A Retrospective: Paintings & Works on Paper. Intro. by Churchill Lathrop & Rowland Elzea. (Illus.). 32p. (Orig.). 1987. pap. 7.50 (*0-938766-04-X*) NJ State Mus.

Thomas Gets Bumped. W. Awdry. LC 93-23326. (Thomas the Tank Engine & Friends Ser.). (Illus.). 32p. (J). 1994. 3.50 (*0-679-86045-2*) Random Bks Yng Read.

Thomas Gets Tricked & Other Stories. W. Awdry. (Thomas the Tank Engine & Friends Book & Cassette Ser.). (Illus.). 32p. (Orig.). (J). (ps-2). 1991. 7.95 incl. audio (*0-679-80108-1*) Random Bks Yng Read.

Thomas Gets Tricked & Other Stories: Based on the Railway Series. W. Awdry. LC 89-8502. (Thomas the Tank Engine Picturebacks Ser.). (Illus.). 32p. (J). (ps-3). 1989. pap. 3.25 (*0-679-80100-6*) Random Bks Yng Read.

Thomas Girtin (1775-1802) Susan Morris. LC 85-51651. (Illus.). 79p. (Orig.). 1986. pap. 12.00 (*0-930606-50-7*) Yale Ctr Brit Art.

Thomas Gray: The Progress of a Poet. B. Eugene McCarthy. LC 96-25906. 1997. write for info. (*0-8386-3715-9*) Fairleigh Dickinson.

Thomas Gray & Literary Authority: A Study in Ideology & Poetics. Suvir Kaul. LC 91-67134. 280p. (C). 1993. 37.50 (*0-8047-2027-4*) Stanford U Pr.

Thomas Gray in Copenhagen: In Which the Philosopher Cat Meets the Ghost of Hans Christian Andersen. Philip J. Davis. LC 95-13243. (Illus.). 192p. 1995. 16.00 (*0-387-94493-1*) Spr-Verlag.

Thomas Gray, Philosopher Cat. Philip J. Davis. (HBJ-Boston Bk.). (Illus.). 100p. 1988. 10.95 (*0-15-188100-6*) HarBrace.

***Thomas Gray (1716-1771) Selected Poems.** Ed. by John Heath-Stubbs. pap. write for info. (*0-85635-317-5*, Pub. by Carcanet Pr UK) Paul & Co Pubs.

Thomas Grocery Register, 3 vols. 2431p. 1988. Set. 125.00 (*0-937200-44-1*) Thomas Pubng.

Thomas Grocery Register, 3 vols., 1. 2431p. 1988. write for info. (*0-937200-45-X*) Thomas Pubng.

Thomas Grocery Register, 3 vols., 2. 2431p. 1988. write for info. (*0-937200-46-8*) Thomas Pubng.

Thomas Grocery Register, 3 vols., 3. 2431p. 1988. write for info. (*0-937200-47-6*) Thomas Pubng.

Thomas H. Benton. Theodore Roosevelt. Ed. by John T. Morse, Jr. LC 79-128972. (American Statesmen Ser.: No. 23). reprint ed. 45.00 (*0-404-50873-1*) AMS Pr.

Thomas H. Huxley. James R. Ainsworth-Davis. LC 70-158236. (English Men of Science Ser.: No. 2). reprint ed. 39.50 (*0-404-07892-3*) AMS Pr.

Thomas Halsey of Hertfordshire, England & Southampton, Long Island, 1591-1679. J. L. Halsey & E. D. Halsey. (Illus.). 550p. 1989. reprint ed. pap. 53.00 (*0-8328-6585-0*); reprint ed. lib. bdg. 90.50 (*0-8328-0632-3*) Higginson Bk Co.

Thomas Hardy. Charles Lock. LC 92-22237. (Criticism in Focus Ser.). 1992. text ed. 29.95 (*0-312-08604-0*) St Martin.

Thomas Hardy. McDowall. 1972. 59.95 (*0-8490-1197-3*) Gordon Pr.

***Thomas Hardy.** Edward Neill. (LCENG Ser.). Date not set. write for info. (*1-57113-194-9*) Camden Hse.

Thomas Hardy. Henry Tomlinson. LC 70-160129. (Studies in Thomas Hardy: No. 14). 1971. lib. bdg. 50.95 (*0-8383-1283-7*) M S G Haskell Hse.

***Thomas Hardy.** Peter Widdowson. (Writers & Their Works). 113p. (Orig.). 1996. pap. 22.50 (*0-7463-0756-X*, Pub. by Northcote House UK) Trans-Atl Phila.

Thomas Hardy, 2 vols. R. E. Zachrisson. 1972. 500.00 (*0-8490-1198-1*) Gordon Pr.

Thomas Hardy. Douglas Brown. LC 79-19057. (Illus.). 196p. 1980. reprint ed. text ed. 35.00 (*0-313-22105-7*, BRTH, Greenwood Pr) Greenwood.

Thomas Hardy. H. Child. LC 72-3631. (Studies in Thomas Hardy: No. 14). 1972. reprint ed. lib. bdg. 45.95 (*0-8383-1584-4*) M S G Haskell Hse.

Thomas Hardy. Annie Macdonell. LC 77-148276. reprint ed. 36.00 (*0-404-08885-6*) AMS Pr.

Thomas Hardy. Henry W. Nevinson. LC 72-2084. (Studies in Thomas Hardy: No. 14). 1972. reprint ed. lib. bdg. 39.95 (*0-8383-1466-X*) M S G Haskell Hse.

Thomas Hardy: A Literary Life. James Gibson. (Literary Lives Ser.). 224p. 1996. text ed. 29.95 (*0-312-15945-5*) St Martin.

Thomas Hardy: A Study of the Wessex Novels, the Poems, & the Dynasts. Henry C. Duffin. LC 77-17945. 356p. 1978. reprint ed. text ed. 37.50 (*0-313-20109-9*, DUTH, Greenwood Pr) Greenwood.

***Thomas Hardy: A Textual Study of the Short Stories.** Martin Ray. LC 97-15585. (Nineteenth Century Ser.). 372p. (C). 1997. text ed. 68.95 (*1-85928-202-4*) Ashgate Pub Co.

Thomas Hardy: An Annotated Bibliography of Writings about Him, Vol. I. Ed. by Helmut E. Gerber & W. Eugene Davis. LC 72-7514. (Annotated Secondary Bibliography Series on English Literature in Transition, 1880-1920). 841p. 1973. 52.00 (*0-87580-039-4*) N Ill U Pr.

Thomas Hardy: An Annotated Bibliography of Writings about Him, Vol. II. Ed. by W. Eugene Davis & Helmut E. Gerber. LC 72-7514. (Annotated Secondary Bibliography Series on English Literature in Transition, 1880-1920). 735p. 1983. 52.00 (*0-87580-091-2*) N Ill U Pr.

Thomas Hardy: An Autobiography in Verse. Thomas Hardy. Ed. by Elaine Wilson. (Illus.). 160p. 1985. 25.00 (*0-85683-073-9*, Pub. by Shepheard-Walwyn Pubs UK) Paul & Co Pubs.

Thomas Hardy: Critical Assessments, 4 vols., Set. Ed. by Grahm Clarke. (Critical Assessments of Writers in English Ser.). (Illus.). 1900p. (C). (gr. 13 up). 1993. boxed, text ed. 495.00 (*1-873403-08-9*, Routledge NY) Routledge.

***Thomas Hardy: Great British & Irish Short Stories I.** Illus. by James McConnell. LC 94-75355. (Classic Short Stories Ser.). 80p. 1994. pap. 5.95 (*0-7854-0636-0*, 40045) Am Guidance.

Thomas Hardy: His British & American Critics. D. J. Winslow. 1972. 59.95 (*0-8490-1199-X*) Gordon Pr.

Thomas Hardy: His Career As a Novelist. Michael Millgate. LC 94-9494. 1994. text ed. 19.95 (*0-312-12233-0*) St Martin.

Thomas Hardy: His Life & Friends. Frank B. Pinion. LC 91-38715. 396p. 1992. text ed. 39.95 (*0-312-07570-7*) St Martin.

Thomas Hardy: Novelist or Poet. Alfred E. Newton. LC 70-160428. (Studies in Thomas Hardy: No. 14). 1971. reprint ed. lib. bdg. 32.95 (*0-8383-1298-5*) M S G Haskell Hse.

Thomas Hardy: Poet & Novelist. Samuel C. Chew. 1973. 59.95 (*0-8490-1200-7*) Gordon Pr.

Thomas Hardy: Selected Poems. Tim Armstrong. LC 92-44541. (Annotated Texts Ser.). 1994. pap. 26.95 (*0-685-72541-3*, 79857) Longman.

Thomas Hardy: Selected Poems. annot. ed. Tim Armstrong. (Annotated Texts Ser.). (C). 1994. pap. text ed. 35.95 (*0-582-04061-2*) Longman.

Thomas Hardy: Selected Poetry. Thomas Hardy. 1996. text ed. 39.95 (*0-312-16193-X*) St Martin.

Thomas Hardy: The "Dream-Country" of His Fiction. Anne Alexander. (Critical Studies). 260p. 1987. 50.00 (*0-389-20712-8*, N8270) B&N Imports.

Thomas Hardy: The Forms of Tragedy. Dale Kramer. LC 74-17084. 191p. reprint ed. pap. 54.50 (*0-7837-3598-7*, 2043463) Bks Demand.

Thomas Hardy: The Return of the Repressed; a Study of the Major Fiction. Perry Meisel. LC 77-182211. (Yale College Ser.: No. 12). 189p. reprint ed. pap. 53.90 (*0-8357-8349-9*, 2033824) Bks Demand.

Thomas Hardy: Three Complete Novels. Thomas Hardy. 1995. 12.99 (*0-517-12419-X*) Random.

Thomas Hardy: Three Great Novels: Far from the Madding Crowd, The Mayor of Casterbridge, Tess of the D'Urbervilles. Thomas Hardy. (World's Classics Ser.). (Illus.). 848p. 1994. pap. 14.95 (*0-19-282286-1*) OUP.

Thomas Hardy: Towards a Materialist Criticism. George Wotton. LC 85-749. 240p. 1985. 52.00 (*0-389-20564-8*, N8125) B&N Imports.

Thomas Hardy see Later 19th Century Novelists: Critical Heritage

Thomas Hardy see Modern Critical Views Series

Thomas Hardy, a Critical Study. Lascelles Abercrombie. (BCL1-PR English Literature Ser.). 224p. 1992. reprint ed. lib. bdg. 79.00 (*0-7812-7549-0*) Rprt Serv.

***Thomas Hardy & Paradoxes of Love.** H. M. Daleski. LC 97-15472. 1997. write for info. (*0-8262-1125-9*) U of Mo Pr.

Thomas Hardy & the Church. Jan Jedrzejewski. LC 95-8582. 1996. text ed. 49.95 (*0-312-12702-2*) St Martin.

Thomas Hardy & the Cosmic Mind: A New Reading of "the Dynasts" J. O. Bailey. LC 77-24118. 223p. 1977. reprint ed. text ed. 55.00 (*0-8371-9743-0*, BATH, Greenwood Pr) Greenwood.

Thomas Hardy & the Proper Study of Mankind. Simon Gatrell. LC 92-24349. (Victorian Literature & Culture Ser.). 195p. (C). 1993. text ed. 29.50 (*0-8139-1435-3*) U Pr of Va.

Thomas Hardy & Visual Structures: Framing, Disruption, Process. Sheila Berger. 232p. (C). 1990. text ed. 40.00 (*0-8147-1142-1*) NYU Pr.

Thomas Hardy & Women: Sexual Ideology & Narrative Form. Penny Boumelha. LC 84-49663. 192p. 1985. pap. 11.95 (*0-299-10244-0*) U of Wis Pr.

Thomas Hardy As a Man, Writer & Philosopher. R. E. Zachrisson. (Studies in Thomas Hardy: No. 14). 1970. reprint ed. pap. 39.95 (*0-8383-0104-5*) M S G Haskell Hse.

Thomas Hardy Dictionary. Ed. by F. B. Pinion. 256p. (C). 1989. text ed. 44.00 (*0-8147-6610-2*) NYU Pr.

Thomas Hardy Dictionary. Ed. by F. B. Pinion. 256p. (C). 1993. pap. text ed. 16.00 (*0-8147-6621-8*) NYU Pr.

Thomas Hardy Dictionary. F. Outwin Saxelby. (BCL1-PR English Literature Ser.). 238p. 1992. reprint ed. lib. bdg. 79.00 (*0-7812-7555-5*) Rprt Serv.

Thomas Hardy England. John Fowles. 1984. 25.00 (*0-316-28989-2*) Little.

Thomas Hardy from Serial to Novel. Mary E. Chase. (BCL1-PR English Literature Ser.). 210p. 1992. reprint ed. lib. bdg. 79.00 (*0-7812-7550-4*) Rprt Serv.

Thomas Hardy in Maine. Carl Weber. LC 75-22203. (Studies in Thomas Hardy: No. 14). 1975. lib. bdg. 40.95 (*0-8383-2077-5*) M S G Haskell Hse.

***Thomas Hardy in Our Time.** Robert Langbaum. 256p. 1996. pap. 18.95 (*0-312-16409-2*) St Martin.

Thomas Hardy, O.M. C. Holland. LC 68-952. (Studies in Thomas Hardy: No. 14). 1969. reprint ed. lib. bdg. 75.00 (*0-8383-0570-9*) M S G Haskell Hse.

Thomas Hardy on Stage. Keith Wilson. LC 93-39874. 1995. text ed. 65.00 (*0-312-12053-2*) St Martin.

Thomas Hardy, Poet & Novelist. Samuel C. Chew. (BCL1-PR English Literature Ser.). 196p. 1992. reprint ed. lib. bdg. 69.00 (*0-7812-7551-2*) Rprt Serv.

***Thomas Hardy's Christmas.** Compiled by John Chandler. (Illus.). 128p. 1997. pap. 17.95 (*0-7509-1434-3*, Pub. by Sutton Pubng UK) Bks Intl VA.

Thomas Hardy's Epic-Drama: A Study of the Dynasts. Harold Orel. LC 69-14022. 122p. 1969. reprint ed. text ed. 45.00 (*0-8371-0602-8*, ORTD, Greenwood Pr) Greenwood.

Thomas Hardy's Heroines: A Chorus of Priorities. Pamela L. Jekel. LC 85-51934. 233p. 1986. 22.50 (*0-87875-309-5*) Whitston Pub.

Thomas Hardy's Jude the Obscure see Modern Critical Interpretations

***Thomas Hardy's Major Novels: An Annotated Bibliography.** Julie Sherrick. (Magill Bibliographies Ser.). 192p. 1998. 36.00 (*0-8108-3382-4*) Scarecrow.

Thomas Hardy's Personal Writings: Prefaces - Literary Opinions - Reminiscences. Thomas Hardy. Ed. by Harold Orel. 307p. 1990. text ed. 45.00 (*0-312-03234-X*) St Martin.

Thomas Hardy's Poetry. John P. Ward. LC 92-14301. (Open Guides to Literature Ser.). 1992. 75.00 (*0-335-09991-2*, Open Univ Pr); pap. 22.00 (*0-335-09990-4*, Open Univ Pr) Taylor & Francis.

Thomas Hardy's Studies, Specimens &c. Notebook. Thomas Hardy. Ed. by Pamela Dalziel & Michael Millgate. (Illus.). 208p. 1994. 45.00 (*0-19-811757-4*) OUP.

Thomas Hardy's Tess of the D'Urbervilles see Bloom's Notes

Thomas Hardy's Tess of the D'Urbervilles see Modern Critical Interpretations

Thomas Hardy's Tess of the D'Urbervilles see Bloom's Notes

Thomas Hardy's Tragic Poetry: The Lyrics & "The Dynasts" Katherine K. Maynard. LC 91-15975. 247p. 1991. text ed. 32.95 (*0-87745-344-6*) U of Iowa Pr.

Thomas Hardy's Twilight View of Life. R. E. Zachrisson. (Studies in Thomas Hardy: No. 14). 1970. pap. 39.95 (*0-8383-0105-3*) M S G Haskell Hse.

Thomas Hardy's Universe: A Study of a Poet's Mind. E. Brennecke. LC 68-689. (Studies in Thomas Hardy: No. 14). 1969. reprint ed. lib. bdg. 75.00 (*0-8383-0651-9*) M S G Haskell Hse.

Thomas Hardy's Wessex. H. Lea. 1972. 35.00 (*0-8490-1201-5*) Gordon Pr.

***Thomas Harriot, Science Pioneer.** Ralph Staiger. LC 96-41842. 1997. 17.00 (*0-395-67296-1*, Clarion Bks) HM.

Thomas Hart Benton. Theodore Roosevelt. LC 68-24995. (American Biography Ser.: No. 32). 1969. reprint ed. lib. bdg. 52.95 (*0-8383-0275-0*) M S G Haskell Hse.

Thomas Hart Benton: Artist, Writer & Intellectual. Ed. by R. Douglas Hurt & Mary K. Dains. LC 90-187299. (Illus.). 244p. (Orig.). (C). 1989. pap. 22.95 (*0-9622891-0-8*) SHS MO.

Thomas Hart Benton: Drawing from Life. Henry Adams. LC 89-37316. (Illus.). 208p. 1990. pap. 24.95 (*1-55859-071-4*) Abbeville Pr.

Thomas Hearne & His Landscape. David Morris. (Illus.). 160p. 1990. text ed. 50.00 (*0-295-97040-5*) U of Wash Pr.

Thomas Hennell: Countryman, Artist, & Writer. Michael MacLeod. (Illus.). 256p. (C). 1989. text ed. 69.95 (*0-521-33124-2*) Cambridge U Pr.

Thomas Henry Huxley. Leonard Huxley. LC 76-102247. (Select Bibliographies Reprint Ser.). 1977. 20.95 (*0-8369-5132-8*) Ayer.

Thomas Henry Huxley. Edward Clodd. LC 75-30018. reprint ed. 32.50 (*0-404-14023-8*) AMS Pr.

Thomas Henry Huxley: Communicating for Science. J. Vernon Jensen. LC 89-40762. 256p. 1991. 38.50 (*0-87413-379-3*) U Delaware Pr.

Thomas Henry Huxley's Place in Science & Letters: Centenary Essays. Ed. by Alan P. Barr. LC 96-13705. 1997. 50.00 (*0-8203-1865-5*) U of Ga Pr.

Thomas Herzog: Design Center Linz. Friedrich Aschleitner et al. 132p. 1995. pap. 45.00 (*3-7757-0524-4*) Dist Art Pubs.

Thomas Heywood. Thomas Heywood. 1977. text ed. 23.95 (*0-8369-8185-5*, 8323) Ayer.

Thomas Heywood. Merchant. 304p. 1996. text ed. 79.95 (*0-7190-2221-5*, Pub. by Manchester Univ Pr UK) St Martin.

Thomas Heywood. Frederich S. Boas. LC 75-15587. 159p. 1974. reprint ed. 40.00 (*0-87753-056-4*) Phaeton.

Thomas Heywood, Dramatic Works, with a Life & Remarks on His Writing by J. P. Collier, 2 vols. Thomas Heywood. Incl. First & Second Parts of King Edward IV: The Fair Maid of the Exchange: Fortune by Land & Sea: The First & Second Parts of the Fair Maid. 1974. reprint ed. (*0-318-58695-9*); Royal King & Loyal Subject: A Woman Skilled with Kindness: Two Historical Plays on the Life & Reign of Queen Elizabeth: The Golden & Silver Ages: An Apology for Actors. 1974. (*0-318-58696-7*); (Shakespeare Society of London Publications Ser.: Vol. 5). 1974. reprint ed. Set. pap. (*0-8115-0165-5*) Periodicals Srv.

Thomas Hildreth: Early California Cattle Baron. Brenda B. Preston. LC 95-73061. (Illus.). 75p. (Orig.). 1995. pap. 9.95 (*0-9645475-5-4*) Rio Del Mar Pr.

Thomas Hill & Rebecca Miles: Ancestors & Descendants. rev. ed. Mary L. Donnelly. LC 84-247052. (Illus.). 911p. 1984. 49.00 (*0-939142-09-0*) M L Donnelly.

Thomas Hill Green & the Development of Liberal-Democratic Thought. I. M. Greengarten. LC 81-156441. 163p. reprint ed. pap. 46.50 (*0-8357-8350-2*, 2034074) Bks Demand.

***Thomas Hobbes.** Aloysius P. Martinich. 1997. text ed. 39.95 (*0-312-16493-9*); text ed. 18.95 (*0-312-16494-7*) St Martin.

Thomas Hobbes: A Reference Guide. Charles H. Hinnant. LC 79-28134. 1980. 50.00 (*0-8161-8173-X*, Hall Reference) Macmillan.

Thomas Hobbes: Critical Assessments, 4 vols., Set. Ed. by Preston King. 1600p. (C). (gr. 13). 1992. boxed, text ed. 695.00 (*0-415-02004-2*, A7401) Routledge.

Thomas Hobbes: Political Ideas in Historical Context. Johann P. Sommerville. LC 92-3442. 256p. 1992. text ed. 49.95 (*0-312-07966-4*); pap. text ed. 19.95 (*0-312-07967-2*) St Martin.

Thomas Hobbes: Skepticism, Individuality & Chastened Politics. Richard E. Flathman. (Modernity & Political Thought Ser.: Vol. 2). 160p. (C). 1993. text ed. 42.00 (*0-8039-4080-7*); pap. text ed. 18.95 (*0-8039-4081-5*) Sage.

Thomas Hobbes & Political Theory. Ed. by Mary G. Dietz. LC 89-37242. x, 214p. 1990. pap. 14.95 (*0-7006-0519-3*) U Pr of KS.

Thomas Hobbes & the Natural Law Tradition. Norberto Bobbio. Tr. by Daniela Gobetti. 246p. (C). 1993. pap. text ed. 16.95 (*0-226-06248-1*) U Ch Pr.

Thomas Hobbes & the Science of Moral Virtue. David Boonin-Vail. (Illus.). 272p. (C). 1994. text ed. 59.95 (*0-521-46209-6*) Cambridge U Pr.

Thomas Hobbes Collected Works, 12 vols. Ed. by William Molesworth. 5206p. (C). (gr. 13). 1993. Set. text ed. 925.00 (*0-415-08811-9*, B0740) Routledge.

Thomas Hobbes in His Time. Ed. by Ralph G. Ross et al. LC 74-83134. 160p. reprint ed. pap. 45.60 (*0-318-39663-7*, 2033232) Bks Demand.

Thomas Hobbes' Theory of Obligation: A Modern Interpretation. Ralph P. Forsberg. LC 89-32633. 300p. 1990. 35.00 (*0-89341-574-X*, Longwood Academic) Hollowbrook.

Thomas Hoccleve. J. A. Burrow. (Authors of the Middle Ages Ser.: No. 4). 64p. 1994. pap. 15.00 (*0-86078-419-3*, Pub. by Variorum UK) Ashgate Pub Co.

Thomas Hoccleve: A Study in Early Fifteenth-Century English Poetic. Jerome Mitchell. LC 67-21855. (Illus.). 165p. reprint ed. 47.10 (*0-685-07757-8*, 2014938) Bks Demand.

Thomas Hodgkin: Morbid Anatomist & Social Activist. Louis Rosenfeld. LC 92-28528. (Illus.). 356p. 1992. 24.95 (*0-8191-8633-3*) Madison Bks UPA.

Thomas Hollis of Lincoln's Inn: A Whig & His Books. W. H. Bond. (Sandars Lectures in Bibliography). 160p. (C). 1991. text ed. 69.95 (*0-521-39091-5*) Cambridge U Pr.

Thomas Holme, 1624-1695: Surveyor General of Pennsylvania. Irma Corcoran. LC 91-76987. (Memoirs Ser.: Vol. 200). (Illus.). 414p. (C). 1992. 40.00 (*0-87169-200-7*, M200-COI) Am Philos.

Thomas Hood: His Life & Times. Walter Jerrold. LC 68-24911. (English Biography Ser.: No. 31). (Illus.). 1969. reprint ed. lib. bdg. 75.00 (*0-8383-0209-2*) M S G Haskell Hse.

Thomas Hood: His Life & Times. Walter C. Jerrold. (BCL1-PR English Literature Ser.). 420p. 1992. reprint ed. lib. bdg. 99.00 (*0-7812-7563-6*) Rprt Serv.

***Thomas Hood (1799-1845) Selected Poems.** Ed. by Joy Flint. pap. write for info. (*0-85635-957-2*, Pub. by Carcanet Pr UK) Paul & Co Pubs.

Thomas Hooker: Preacher, Founder, Democrat. George L. Walker. 1972. reprint ed. lib. bdg. 19.00 (*0-8422-8120-7*) Irvington.

Thomas Hooker: The Soules Exaltation see Library of American Puritan Writings. The Seventeenth Century: The Seventeenth Century

Thomas Hooker: The Soules Humiliation see Library of American Puritan Writings. The Seventeenth Century: The Seventeenth Century

Thomas Hooker: The Soules Implantation see Library of American Puritan Writings. The Seventeenth Century: The Seventeenth Century

Thomas Hooker: The Soules Preparation for Christ see Library of American Puritan Writings. The Seventeenth Century: The Seventeenth Century

Thomas Hooker, 1586-1647. Frank Shuffelton. LC 76-45912. 337p. 1977. reprint ed. pap. 96.10 (*0-7837-9446-0*, 2060188) Bks Demand.

Thomas Hornsby Ferril & the American West. Ed. by Robert C. Baron et al. 160p. 1996. pap. 17.95 (*1-55591-334-2*) Fulcrum Pub.

***Thomas Hornsby Ferril & the American West.** aut. limited num. ed. Ed. by Robert C. Baron et al. 160p. 1996. 85.00 (*1-55591-339-3*) Fulcrum Pub.

Thomas Howell & the School at Llandaff. J. E. McCann. 260p. (C). 1989. 39.00 (*0-685-61445-X*, Pub. by D Brown & Sons Ltd UK) St Mut.

Thomas Hucker. Peter D. Slatin et al. (Illus.). (Orig.). 1992. pap. text ed. write for info. (*0-9628849-5-2*) P J Gallery.

Thomas Hunt Morgan: Pioneer of Genetics. Ian B. Shine. LC 76-9519. (Kentucky Bicentennial Bookshelf Ser.). 172p. 1976. reprint ed. pap. 49.10 (*0-608-02127-X*, 2062776) Bks Demand.

Thomas Hutchinson & His Contemporaries. (Picture Bks.). 1974. pap. 4.00 (*0-934909-57-1*) Mass Hist Soc.

Thomas International Photo Directory of Antique Cameras. Douglas B. Thomas. (Illus.). 356p. 1983. 27.50 (*0-9612128-0-2*) Thomas Intl DC.

Thomas J. Stieltjes , Oeuvres Completes, Vols. 1-2: Collected Papers, 2 vols. G. Van Dijk. 1332p. 1993. reprint ed. 295.00 (*0-387-55560-9*) Spr-Verlag.

Thomas James Wise & the Trial Book Fallacy. Roger C. Lewis. (Illus.). 260p. 1994. 76.95 (*1-85928-036-6*, Pub. by Scolar Pr UK) Ashgate Pub Co.

Thomas Jefferson. Roger Bruns. (World Leaders - Past & Present Ser.). (Illus.). 112p. (YA). (gr. 5 up). 1986. pap. 8.95 (*0-7910-0644-1*); lib. bdg. 19.95 (*0-87754-583-9*) Chelsea Hse.

Thomas Jefferson. Jim Hargrove. LC 86-9658. (Encyclopedia of Presidents Ser.). (Illus.). 100p. (J). (gr. 3 up). 1986. lib. bdg. 22.00 (*0-516-01385-8*) Childrens.

Thomas Jefferson. Jenkinson & Burns. Date not set. pap. write for info. (*0-679-44718-0*) Random.

***Thomas Jefferson.** John T. Morse. LC 96-50448. (American Statesmen Ser.). 1997. write for info. (*0-7910-4545-5*, Am Art Analog) Chelsea Hse.

Thomas Jefferson. Don Nardo. LC 92-43913. (Importance of Ser.). (Illus.). 112p. (J). (gr. 5-8). 1993. lib. bdg. 17.96 (*1-56006-037-9*) Lucent Bks.

***Thomas Jefferson.** Wendie C. Old. LC 97-7273. (United States Presidents Ser.). (Illus.). 128p. (YA). (gr. 5 up). 1997. lib. bdg. 18.95 (*0-89490-837-5*) Enslow Pubs.

Thomas Jefferson. Norman K. Risjord. LC 94-6614. (American Profiles Ser.). 1994. 28.95 (*0-945612-38-9*); pap. text ed. 14.95 (*0-945612-39-7*) Madison Hse.

Thomas Jefferson. Laurence Santrey. LC 84-2579. (Illus.). 32p. (J). (gr. 3-6). 1985. pap. text ed. 3.50 (*0-8167-0177-6*) Troll Communs.

Thomas Jefferson. Kathie B. Smith & Pamela Z. Bradbury. (Great Americans Ser.). (Illus.). 32p. (J). (ps up). 1989. pap. 2.25 (*0-671-64768-7*, Litl Simon S&S) S&S Childrens.

***Thomas Jefferson.** T. M. Usel. (Read-&-Discover Biographies Ser.). (Illus.). 24p. (J). (gr. k-3). 1996. 13.25 (*0-516-20122-0*) Childrens.

Thomas Jefferson. Wade. (Presidential Read along Ser.). (J). (gr. 4-12). 1993. pap. 1.95 (*0-87386-084-5*); lib. bdg. 8.49 (*0-87386-035-7*) Jan Prods.

Thomas Jefferson. John T. Morse, Jr. LC 77-128975. (American Statesmen Ser.: No. 11). reprint ed. 45.00 (*0-404-50861-8*) AMS Pr.

Thomas Jefferson. John S. Williams. LC 13-9744. reprint ed. 34.50 (*0-404-06985-1*) AMS Pr.

Thomas Jefferson: A Brief Biography. Dumas Malone. (Monticello Monographs). (Illus.). 48p. (Orig.). 1993. reprint ed. pap. 4.95 (*1-882886-00-3*) T J Mem Fnd.

Thomas Jefferson: A Life with Letters. C. Cullen & M. Briggs. (Illus.). 80p. 1993. pap. 10.00 (*0-685-70215-4*) Newberry.

Thomas Jefferson: A Picture Book Biography. James C. Giblin. LC 93-23340. (Illus.). 48p. (J). 1994. 16.95 (*0-590-44838-2*) Scholastic Inc.

Thomas Jefferson: A Strange Case of Mistaken Identity. Alf J. Mapp, Jr. 512p. 1989. 24.95 (*0-8191-5782-1*); pap. 17.95 (*0-8191-7454-8*) Madison Bks UPA.

Thomas Jefferson: America's Philosopher-King. Max Lerner. 115p. 1996. text ed. 29.95 (*1-56000-262-X*) Transaction Pubs.

Thomas Jefferson: An Intimate History. Fawn M. Brodie. 832p. 1981. mass mkt. 7.99 (*0-553-27335-3*, Bantam Classics) Bantam.

Thomas Jefferson: Author, Inventor, President. Carol Greene. LC 91-16363. (Rookie Biographies Ser.). (Illus.). 48p. (J). (gr. k-3). 1991. pap. 4.95 (*0-516-44224-4*); lib. bdg. 18.30 (*0-516-04224-6*) Childrens.

Thomas Jefferson: Farmer. Barbara McEwan. LC 91-52748. 232p. 1991. lib. bdg. 35.00 (*0-89950-633-X*) McFarland & Co.

Thomas Jefferson: His Words & Vision. Ed. by Nick Beilenson. (Illus.). 64p. 1986. 7.99 (*0-88088-347-2*, 883472) Peter Pauper.

***Thomas Jefferson: Man on a Mountain.** Natalie Bober. (J). 1997. pap. 12.00 (*0-689-81523-9*, Aladdin Paperbacks) S&S Childrens.

Thomas Jefferson: Mini-Play & Activities. (President's Choice Ser.). (YA). (gr. 8 up). 1979. 6.50 (*0-89550-338-7*) Stevens & Shea.

Thomas Jefferson: Passionate Pilgrim - the Presidency, the Founding of the University, & the Private Battle. Alf J. Mapp, Jr. (Illus.). 472p. 1991. 24.95 (*0-8191-8053-X*) Madison Bks UPA.

Thomas Jefferson: Statesman of Science. Silvio A. Bedini. (Illus.). 604p. 1990. 35.00 (*0-02-897041-1*) Macmillan.

Thomas Jefferson: The Philosopher President. John W. Selfridge. (Great Lives Biography Ser.). (Illus.). 128p. (Orig.). 1991. pap. 4.00 (*0-449-90379-6*, Columbine) Fawcett.

Thomas Jefferson: The Revolutionary Aristocrat. Milton Meltzer. LC 91-15943. (Non-Fiction Ser.). (Illus.). 160p. (YA). (gr. 9-12). 1991. lib. bdg. 25.80 (*0-531-11069-9*) Watts.

Thomas Jefferson: 3rd President of the United States. Rebecca Stefoff. Ed. by Richard G. Young. LC 87-32818. (Presidents of the United States Ser.). (Illus.). (J). (gr. 5-9). 1988. lib. bdg. 17.26 (*0-944483-07-0*) Garrett Ed Corp.

Thomas Jefferson - Passionate Pilgrim: The Presidency & the Founding of the University. Alf J. Mapp. 1993. pap. 16.95 (*1-56833-020-0*) Madison Bks UPA.

Thomas Jefferson Abroad: An Original Collection. Thomas Jefferson. Ed. by Douglas Wilson. 496p. 1997. 19.00 (*0-679-60186-4*) Random.

Thomas Jefferson, American Humanist. Karl Lehmann. LC 85-13479. xviii, 273p. 1985. reprint ed. pap. text ed. 16.50 (*0-8139-1078-1*) U Pr of Va.

Thomas Jefferson & American Democracy. Max Beloff. (History - United States Ser.). 271p. 1993. reprint ed. lib. bdg. 79.00 (*0-7812-4828-0*) Rprt Serv.

Thomas Jefferson & Bolling v. Bolling: Law & the Legal Profession in Pre-Revolutionary America. Bernard Schwartz. (Illus.). 316p. (Orig.). 1997. 50.00 (*0-87328-158-6*) Huntington Lib.

Thomas Jefferson & Education in a Republic. Ed. by Charles F. Arrowood. LC 79-136406. (BCL Ser.: No. 1). reprint ed. 20.00 (*0-404-00406-7*) AMS Pr.

Thomas Jefferson & Education in a Republic. Charles F. Arrowood. 1988. reprint ed. lib. bdg. 49.00 (*0-7812-0210-8*) Rprt Serv.

Thomas Jefferson & Education in a Republic. Ed. by Charles F. Arrowood. (History - United States Ser.). 184p. 1992. reprint ed. lib. bdg. 69.00 (*0-7812-6141-4*) Rprt Serv.

Thomas Jefferson & Education in a Republic. Ed. by Charles F. Arrowood. LC 70-131611. 1970. reprint ed. 49.00 (*0-403-00498-5*) Scholarly.

Thomas Jefferson & His Copying Machines. Silvio A. Bedini. LC 81-7288. (Illus.). 239p. 1984. text ed. 28.50 (*0-8139-1025-0*) U Pr of Va.

Thomas Jefferson & His Family Paper Dolls in Full Color. Tom Tierney. (Illus.). (J). (gr. k-3). 1992. pap. 3.00 (*0-486-27068-8*) Dover.

Thomas Jefferson & His Unknown Brother. Ed. by Bernard Mayo & James A. Bear. LC 80-25272. 59p. 1981. text ed. 10.00 (*0-8139-0890-6*) U Pr of Va.

Thomas Jefferson & His Unknown Brother. Thomas Jefferson. LC 80-25272. 69p. reprint ed. pap. 25.00 (*0-7837-2052-1*, 2042327) Bks Demand.

***Thomas Jefferson & Sally Hemings: An American Controversy.** Annette Gordon-Reed. LC 96-34550. 305p. 1997. 29.95 (*0-8139-1698-4*) U Pr of Va.

Thomas Jefferson & the American Ideal. Russell Shorto. (Henry Steele Commager's Americans Ser.). (Illus.). 144p. (J). (gr. 3-6). 1987. pap. 6.95 (*0-8120-3918-1*) Barron.

Thomas Jefferson & the Bible. Thomas Jefferson. 1992. lib. bdg. 79.95 (*0-8490-5444-3*) Gordon Pr.

***Thomas Jefferson & the Changing West: From Conquest to Conservation.** James P. Ronda. LC 96-25330. 1997. 29.95 (*0-8263-1775-8*) U of NM Pr.

***Thomas Jefferson & the Changing West: From Conquest to Conservation.** James P. Ronda. LC 96-25330. 1997. pap. 16.95 (*0-8263-1801-0*) U of NM Pr.

***Thomas Jefferson & the Creation of America.** Douglas Miller. LC 96-29803. (Makers of America Ser.). 1997. write for info. (*0-8160-3393-5*) Facts on File.

Thomas Jefferson & the Law. Edward Dumbauld. LC 78-5742. (Illus.). 1978. 39.95 (*0-8061-1441-X*) U of Okla Pr.

Thomas Jefferson & the National Capital. Thomas Jefferson. Ed. by Saul K. Padover. LC 83-45441. reprint ed. 76.00 (*0-404-20135-0*) AMS Pr.

Thomas Jefferson & the New Nation: A Biography. Merrill D. Peterson. LC 70-110394. (Illus.). 1104p. 1986. reprint ed. pap. 26.00 (*0-19-501909-1*) OUP.

Thomas Jefferson & the Sciences: An Original Anthology. Ed. by I. Bernard Cohen. LC 79-7970. (Three Centuries of Science in America Ser.). (Illus.). 1980. 63.95 (*0-405-12552-6*) Ayer.

Thomas Jefferson & the Stony Mountains: Exploring the West from Monticello. Donald Jackson. LC 80-10546. (Illus.). 351p. 1981. text ed. 29.95 (*0-252-00823-5*) U of Ill Pr.

An Asterisk (*) at the beginning of an entry indicates that the title is appearing in BIP for the first time.

Thomas Jefferson & the Stony Mountains: Exploring the West from Monticello. Donald Jackson. LC 92-32562. 1993. reprint ed. pap. 17.95 (0-8061-2504-7) U of Okla Pr.

Thomas Jefferson, Architect: Original Designs in the Collection of Thomas Jefferson Coolidge. Thomas Jefferson. (BCL1 - U. S. History Ser.). 205p. 1992. reprint ed. lib. bdg. 79.00 (0-7812-6143-0) Rprt Serv.

Thomas Jefferson As Political Leader. Dumas Malone. LC 78-21568. 75p. 1979. reprint ed. text ed. 35.00 (0-313-20730-5, MATJ, Greenwood Pr) Greenwood.

Thomas Jefferson, Landscape Architect. Frederick D. Nichols & Ralph E. Griswold. LC 77-10601. (Illus.). ix, 196p. 1981. pap. text ed. 8.95 (0-8139-0899-X) U Pr of Va.

Thomas Jefferson, Lawyer. Frank L. Dewey. LC 85-26571. 184p. 1986. text ed. 29.50 (0-8139-1079-X) U Pr of Va.

***Thomas Jefferson Treats Himself: Herbs, Physicke, & Nutrition in Early America.** John M. Holmes. Ed. by Ann A. Hunter. (Illus.). 136p. 1997. 24.95 (0-9630797-3-5) Loft Pr.

Thomas Jefferson University: Tradition & Heritage. Frederick B. Wagner. LC 88-8338. (Illus.). 1120p. 1989. text ed. 120.00 (0-8121-1210-5) Williams & Wilkins.

Thomas Jefferson University Hospital Nutrition Manual. Department of Nutrition & Dietetics Staff. LC 93-2824. 650p. 1993. Loose leaf. ring bd. 196.00 (0-8342-0335-9) Aspen Pub.

Thomas Jefferson, 1981-1990: An Annotated Bibliography. Frank Shuffelton. LC 92-6846. 270p. 1992. text ed. 45.00 (0-8240-5347-8, H1217) Garland.

Thomas Jefferson's Abridgement of the Words of Jesus of Nazareth. Ed. by Mark A. Beliles. 80p. 1993. pap. 5.95 (1-887456-04-X) Providence Found.

Thomas Jefferson's Academical Village: The Creation of an Architectural Masterpiece. Ed. by Richard G. Wilson. LC 93-21324. (Illus.). 93p. (Orig.). (C). 1994. pap. text ed. 24.95 (0-8139-1511-2) U Pr of Va.

Thomas Jefferson's Cook Book. Marie Kimball. LC 76-22698. 1987. reprint ed. 12.95 (0-8139-0706-3) U Pr of Va.

Thomas Jefferson's European Travel Diaries. Thomas Jefferson. Ed. by James M. Morris & Persephone Weene. LC 87-9991. (Illus.). 144p. 1987. pap. 7.95 (0-9615964-3-0) Seven Locks Pr.

Thomas Jefferson's 'Ferme Ornee' at Monticello. Rudy J. Favretti. (Illus.). 12p. (Orig.). 1993. pap. 7.50 (0-944026-44-3) Am Antiquarian.

Thomas Jefferson's Flower Garden at Monticello. 3rd ed. Edwin M. Betts & Hazlehurst B. Perkins. LC 86-5613. (Illus.). xiv, 96p. 1986. pap. 10.95 (0-8139-1087-0) U Pr of Va.

Thomas Jefferson's Freethought Legacy: A Saying Per Day by the Sage of Monticello. Roger E. Greeley. LC 95-31633. 138p. 1995. 21.95 (1-57392-008-8) Prometheus Bks.

Thomas Jefferson's Garden Book. Ed. by Edwin M. Betts. (Memoirs Ser.: Vol. 22). (Illus.). 1981. reprint ed. 35.00 (0-87169-022-5, M022-BEE) Am Philos.

Thomas Jefferson's Human Jesus. LC 68-27400. 152p. 1968. 20.00 (0-87130-010-9) Eakins.

Thomas Jefferson's Library. 1995. lib. bdg. 251.95 (0-8490-6768-5) Gordon Pr.

Thomas Jefferson's Library: A Catalog with the Entries in His Own Order. Ed. by James Gilreath & Douglas L. Wilson. LC 88-607928. 149p. 1989. 19.00 (0-8444-0634-1, 030-001-00130-0) Lib Congress.

***Thomas Jefferson's Monticello: A Photographic Portrait.** Robert C. Lautman. (Illus.). 1997. 35.00 (0-614-28246-2) Monacelli Pr.

Thomas Jefferson's Paris. Howard C. Rice, Jr. (Illus.). 166p. 1991. pap. text ed. 16.95 (0-691-00776-4) Princeton U Pr.

Thomas Jefferson's Paris. Howard C. Rice. LC 75-30203. (Illus.). 168p. reprint ed. pap. 47.90 (0-8357-3569-9, 2034649) Bks Demand.

Thomas Jefferson's Travels in Europe, 1784-1789. George G. Shackelford. LC 94-34705. (Illus.). 240p. 1995. 34.95 (0-8018-4843-1) Johns Hopkins.

Thomas Jefferson's Views on Public Education. John C. Henderson. LC 76-137239. reprint ed. 45.00 (0-404-03236-2) AMS Pr.

Thomas John Welsh, Architect 1845-1915: A Journey of Discovering by His Great-Grandaughter. Patricia A. Welsh. (Illus.). 80p. (Orig.). 1995. pap. 21.95 (1-884620-13-2) PAW Prods.

Thomas John Welsh, Architect, 1845-1918: A Journey of Discovery by his Great-Granddaughter. Patricia A. Welsh. 80p. 1993. lib. bdg. write for info. (1-884620-08-6) PAW Prods.

Thomas Joplin & Classical Macroeconomics: A Re-Appraisal of Classical Monetary Thought. D. P. O'Brien. 304p. 1993. 85.00 (1-85278-676-0) E Elgar.

Thomas Joshua Cooper: Dreaming the Gokstadt. (Illus.). 64p. 1988. 50.00 (0-948274-02-6, Pub. by Graeme Murray UK) Dist Art Pubs.

Thomas K. Beecher: Minister to a Changing America, 1824-1900. Myra C. Glenn. LC 95-43390. (Contributions to the Study of Religion Ser.: Vol. 47). 256p. 1996. text ed. 59.95 (0-313-29862-9, Greenwood Pr) Greenwood.

Thomas Kelly As I Remember Him. T. Canby Jones. LC 89-60506. (Orig.). 1989. pap. 3.00 (0-87574-284-X) Pendle Hill.

Thomas Keneally. Peter Quartermaine. (Modern Fiction Ser.). 128p. 1991. pap. 10.95 (0-340-51826-X, A6318, Pub. by E Arnold UK) Routledge Chapman & Hall.

Thomas Killigrew, Cavalier Dramatist. Alfred Harbage. LC 67-23854. 1972. reprint ed. 21.95 (0-405-08597-4) Ayer.

Thomas Kinkade: Painter of Radiant Light. Thomas Kinkade & Philippa Reed. LC 95-34334. (Illus.). 236p. 1996. 50.00 (0-7892-0082-1) Abbeville Pr.

***Thomas Kinkade: Paintings of Radiant Light.** Thomas Kinkade & Philippa Reed. (Illus.). 236p. 1997. 24.98 (0-89660-087-4, Artabras) Abbeville Pr.

Thomas Kinsella. Badin. 1996. lib. bdg. 26.95 (0-8057-7047-X, Twayne) Scribnrs Ref.

Thomas Knew There Were Pirates Living in the Bathroom. Beth Parker. (Illus.). 28p. (J). (ps-3). 1990. 12.95 (0-88753-224-1, Pub. by Black Moss Pr CN); pap. 4.95 (0-88753-201-2, Pub. by Black Moss Pr CN) Firefly Bks Ltd.

Thomas Lawrence: Complete Edition of the Paintings. Kenneth Garlick. (Illus.). 320p. (C). 1989. text ed. 172.00 (0-8147-3022-1) NYU Pr.

Thomas Lawson Sixteen Thirty to Sixteen Ninety-One: North Country Botanist, Quaker & Schoolmaster. E. J. Whittaker. (Illus.). 250p. (C). 1989. pap. 21.00 (1-85072-003-7, Pub. by W Sessions UK) St Mut.

Thomas Legge: Complete Plays, 2 vols., Set. Ed. by Dana F. Sutton. LC 91-42125. (American University Studies: Classical Languages & Literature: Ser. XVII, Vols. 13 & 14). (C). 1992. text ed. 138.95 (0-8204-1826-9) P Lang Pubng.

Thomas Lester: His Lace & the East Midlands Industry. Anne Buck. 1981. 15.00 (0-903585-09-X) Robin & Russ.

Thomas L'Imposteur: Roman. Jean Cocteau. (FRE.). 1971. 10.95 (0-8288-9133-8, M3311) Fr & Eur.

Thomas L'Imposteur: Roman. Jean Cocteau. (Folio Ser.: No. 480). (FRE.). 1971. pap. 6.95 (2-07-036480-1) Schoenhof.

Thomas Lodge. Wesley D. Rae. LC 67-25185. (Twayne's English Authors Ser.). 1967. pap. text ed. 5.95 (0-8290-2007-1); lib. bdg. 17.95 (0-89197-964-6) Irvington.

Thomas Lord Cromwell. LC 76-133745. (Tudor Facsimile Texts. Old English Plays Ser.: No. 97). reprint ed. 49.50 (0-404-53397-3) AMS Pr.

Thomas Love Peacock. Olwen W. Campbell. LC 73-157327. (Select Bibliographies Reprint Ser.). 1977. reprint ed. 17.95 (0-8369-5787-3) Ayer.

Thomas Love Peacock. John B. Priestley. (BCL1-PR English Literature Ser.). 215p. 1992. reprint ed. lib. bdg. 79.00 (0-7812-7617-9) Rprt Serv.

Thomas Love Peacock. John B. Priestly. LC 74-131808. 1970. reprint ed. 49.00 (0-403-00695-3) Scholarly.

Thomas Lovell Beddoes. R. Snow. 1972. 59.95 (0-8490-1202-3) Gordon Pr.

Thomas Macaulay: Sculptural Views on Perceptual Ambiguity, 1968-1986. Betty Collings & Donald Kuspit. LC 86-61901. 71p. (Orig.). 1986. pap. text ed. 14.95 (0-937809-00-4) Dayton Art.

Thomas MacDonagh: A Critical Biography. Johann A. Norstedt. LC 78-31320. (Illus.). 175p. 1980. text ed. 19.50 (0-8139-0786-1) U Pr of Va.

***Thomas MacDonagh, a Critical Biography.** Johann A. Norstedt. LC 78-31320. 187p. 1980. reprint ed. pap. 53.30 (0-608-04238-2, 2064994) Bks Demand.

Thomas Mann. Ed. by Michael Minden. (Modern Literatures in Perspective Ser.). 264p. (C). 1996. text ed. 78.50 (0-582-21678-8, Pub. by Longman UK) Longman.

Thomas Mann. Martin Travers. LC 91-31847. (Modern Novelists Ser.). 160p. 1992. text ed. 35.00 (0-312-07206-6) St Martin.

Thomas Mann: A Biography. Ronald Hayman. (Illus.). 632p. 1995. 35.00 (0-684-19319-1) S&S Trade.

Thomas Mann: A Critical Study. R. J. Hollingdale. LC 79-161509. 204p. 1971. 32.50 (0-8387-1004-2) Bucknell U Pr.

Thomas Mann: A Life. Donald A. Prater. (Illus.). 554p. 1995. 39.95 (0-19-815861-0) OUP.

Thomas Mann: A Study. Martin Swales. 117p. 1980. pap. 21.00 (0-8476-6270-5) Rowman.

Thomas Mann: Eros & Literature. Anthony Heilbut. (Illus.). 688p. 1996. 40.00 (0-394-55633-X) Knopf.

***Thomas Mann: Eros & Literature.** Anthony Heilbut. LC 96-34572. (Illus.). 1997. pap. 16.95 (0-520-20911-7) U CA Pr.

Thomas Mann: The Uses of Tradition. 2nd ed. T. J. Reed. (Illus.). 488p. 1996. pap. 29.95 (0-19-815915-3) OUP.

Thomas Mann see Modern Critical Views Series

Thomas Mann - Felix Bertaux: Correspondence 1923-1948. Ed. by Biruta Cap. LC 93-26886. (Studies in Modern German Literature: Vol. 49). 216p. (C). 1994. text ed. 49.95 (0-8204-1842-0) P Lang Pubng.

Thomas Mann in Context: Proceedings of the Centennial Colloquium on Thomas Mann, Clark University, 1975. Centennial Colloquium on Thomas Mann Staff. Ed. by Kenneth Hughes. LC 77-26366. 138p. reprint ed. pap. 39.40 (0-317-27753-7, 2015545) Bks Demand.

Thomas Mann, the Ironic German: A Study (1958) Erich Heller. 314p. 1958. 15.00 (0-911858-29-6) Appel.

Thomas Mann, 1875-1955. Theodore J. Ziolkowski et al. (Illus.). 62p. 1975. pap. 10.00 (0-87811-021-6) Princeton Lib.

Thomas Mann's "Doctor Faustus" A Novel at the Margin of Modernism. Herbert Lehnert. Ed. by Peter Pfeiffer. (GERM Ser.: Vol. 49). (Illus.). xii, 226p. 1991. 65.00 (0-938100-73-4) Camden Hse.

Thomas Mann's Doctor Faustus: The Sources & Structure of the Novel. Gunilla U. Bergsten. LC 69-14483. 254p. reprint ed. pap. 72.40 (0-317-29848-8, 2020031) Bks Demand.

Thomas Mann's FIORENZA. Alba Amoia. (American University Studies: Theatre Arts: Ser. XXVI, Vol. 3). 201p. (C). 1989. text ed. 30.00 (0-8204-1091-8) P Lang Pubng.

Thomas Mann's "Goethe & Tolstoy" otes & Sources. Thomas Mann. Ed. & Tr. by Clayton Koelb. Tr. by Alcyone Scott. LC 82-13497. 267p. 1984. pap. 76.10 (0-7837-8388-4, 2059199) Bks Demand.

Thomas Mann's Short Fiction: An Intellectual Biography. Esther H. Leser. LC 87-45369. 352p. 1989. 47.50 (0-8386-3319-6) Fairleigh Dickinson.

Thomas Mante Writer, Soldier, Adventurer. Richard C. Cole. LC 93-25230. (American University Studies: Vol. 148). 213p. (C). 1994. text ed. 39.95 (0-8204-2259-2) P Lang Pubng.

Thomas Mayhew, Patriarch to the Indians, 1593-1682. Lloyd C. Hare. LC 76-104347. (Illus.). reprint ed. 39.50 (0-404-03108-0) AMS Pr.

Thomas Mayhew, Patriarch to the Indians, 1593-1682. Lloyd C. Hare. LC 76-145070. 231p. 1932. reprint ed. 49.00 (0-403-01012-8) Scholarly.

Thomas McGrath: Life & the Poem. Ed. by Reginald Gibbons & Terrence Des Pres. 248p. 1991. text ed. 29.95 (0-252-01852-4); pap. text ed. 12.95 (0-252-06177-2) U of Ill Pr.

Thomas McKean. John M. Coleman. LC 74-19952. 1975. 16.95 (0-912834-07-2) Am Faculty Pr.

Thomas McKean: The Shaping of an American Republicanism. Gail S. Rowe. LC 77-94085. (Illus.). 517p. reprint ed. pap. 147.40 (0-8357-5500-2, 2035115) Bks Demand.

Thomas McKnight: Windows on Paradise. Thomas McKnight. (Illus.). 200p. 1990. 75.00 (1-55859-126-5) Abbeville Pr.

***Thomas McKnight: Windows on Paradise.** Thomas McKnight. (Illus.). 200p. 1997. 29.98 (0-89660-088-2, Artabras) Abbeville Pr.

Thomas Mellon & His Times. Thomas Mellon. (Illus.). 560p. (C). 1996. pap. 22.95 (0-8229-5572-5) U of Pittsburgh Pr.

Thomas Mellon & His Times. 2nd rev. ed. Thomas Mellon. (Illus.). 560p. (C). 1994. 35.00 (0-8229-3777-8) U of Pittsburgh Pr.

Thomas Merton. Thomas Merton. (Modern Spirituality Ser.). 96p. 1990. pap. 4.95 (0-87243-174-6) Templegate.

Thomas Merton: A Bibliography. enl. rev. ed. Frank Dell'Isola. LC 74-79148. (Serif Series: Bibliographies & Checklists: No. 31). 238p. reprint ed. pap. 67.90 (0-8357-5570-3, 2035197) Bks Demand.

Thomas Merton: Contemplative Critic. Henri J. Nouwen. LC 90-47991. 168p. 1991. reprint ed. pap. 9.95 (0-89243-508-9, Triumph Books) Liguori Pubns.

Thomas Merton: Monk & Artist. Victor A. Kramer. 1988. pap. 10.95 (0-87907-602-X) Cistercian Pubns.

Thomas Merton: Poet, Prophet, Priest. Jennifer F. Bryant. LC 96-2783. (Illus.). 150p. (YA). (gr. 7 up). 1997. pap. 8.00 (0-8028-5140-1, Eerdmans Bks) Eerdmans.

Thomas Merton: Poet, Prophet, Priest. Jennifer F. Bryant. LC 96-2783. (Illus.). 150p. (YA). (gr. 7 up). 1997. 15.00 (0-8028-5109-6, Eerdmans Bks) Eerdmans.

Thomas Merton: Preview of the Asian Journey. Intro. by Walter Capps. 120p. 1991. reprint ed. pap. 8.95 (0-8245-1124-7) Crossroad NY.

Thomas Merton: Social Critic: A Study. James T. Baker. LC 76-132827. 183p. reprint ed. pap. 52.20 (0-685-44498-8, 2031521) Bks Demand.

Thomas Merton: Spiritual Master: The Essential Writings. Intro. by Lawrence S. Cunningham. LC 92-9072. 464p. 1992. pap. 14.95 (0-8091-3314-8) Paulist Pr.

Thomas Merton: The Development of a Spiritual Theologian. Donald Grayston. LC 84-27299. (Toronto Studies in Theology: Vol. 20). 225p. 1985. lib. bdg. 89.95 (0-88946-758-7) E Mellen.

Thomas Merton: The Hermitage Years. John H. Griffin. 176p. 1994. pap. 40.00 (0-86012-214-X, Pub. by Srch Pr UK) St Mut.

Thomas Merton: The Poet & the Contemplative Life. Compiled by Patrick T. Lawlor. 64p. 1990. pap. 12.50 (0-9607862-2-8) Columbia U Libs.

***Thomas Merton & James Laughlin: Selected Letters.** Ed. by David D. Cooper. LC 96-39819. 320p. (C). 1997. 35.00 (0-393-04069-0) Norton.

Thomas Merton & the Education of the Whole Person. Thomas Del Prete. LC 89-27775. 195p. (Orig.). 1990. pap. 14.95 (0-89135-074-8) Religious Educ.

Thomas Merton as Writer & Monk: A Cultural Study, 1915-1951. Peter Kountz. LC 91-25223. (Chicago Studies in the History of American Religion Ser.: Vol. 11). 250p. 1991. 50.00 (0-926019-48-1) Carlson Pub.

***Thomas Merton, Brother Monk: The Quest for True Freedom.** Basil A. Pennington. 208p. 1997. pap. text ed. 15.95 (0-8264-1012-X) Continuum.

Thomas Merton in Alaska: Prelude to the Asian Journal. Thomas Merton. LC 87-24028. (Illus.). 224p. 1989. 19.95 (0-8112-1048-0); pap. 9.95 (0-8112-1038-3, NDP652) New Directions.

Thomas Merton in Search of His Soul: A Jungian Perspective. Robert G. Waldron. LC 93-74198. 160p. (Orig.). 1994. pap. 7.95 (0-87793-524-6) Ave Maria.

Thomas Merton Monk. enl. rev. ed. Patrick Hart. 1974. pap. 10.95 (0-87907-752-2) Cistercian Pubns.

Thomas Merton, My Brother: His Journey into Freedom, Compassion, & Final Integration. 2nd ed. M. Basil Pennington. LC 95-34530. 208p. 1996. pap. 10.95 (1-56548-039-2) New City.

Thomas Merton on Nuclear Weapons. Ronald E. Powaski. LC 87-31108. 187p. (C). 1988. pap. 2.50 (0-8294-0586-0) Loyola Pr.

Thomas Merton Reader. Thomas Merton. Ed. by Thomas P. McDonnell. LC 74-29. 528p. 1974. pap. 12.95 (0-385-03292-7, Image Bks) Doubleday.

***Thomas Merton's American Prophecy.** Robert Inchausti. LC 97-19155. 192p. (C). 1998. text ed. 59.50 (0-7914-3635-7) State Univ of New York.

***Thomas Merton's American Prophecy.** Robert Inchausti. LC 97-19155. 192p. (C). 1998. pap. text ed. 19.95 (0-7914-3636-5) State Univ of New York.

Thomas Merton's Art of Denial: The Evolution of a Radical Humanist. David D. Cooper. LC 88-17230. 320p. 1989. 40.00 (0-8203-1094-8) U of Ga Pr.

Thomas Merton's Rewriting: The Five Versions of Seeds-New Seeds of Contemplation as A Key to the Development of His Thought. Donald Grayston. LC 89-38907. (Studies in Art & Religious Interpretation: Vol. 8). 490p. 1987. lib. bdg. 109.95 (0-88946-559-2) E Mellen.

Thomas Middleton, 2 vols. Havelock Ellis. 1988. reprint ed. Set. lib. bdg. 75.00 (0-7812-0477-1) Rprt Serv.

Thomas Middleton: A Game At Chess. Ed. by Trevor H. Howard-Hill. (Revels Plays Ser.). (Illus.). 240p. 1993. text ed. 74.95 (0-7190-1546-4, Pub. by Manchester Univ Pr UK) St Martin.

Thomas Middleton: Best Plays of Old Dramatists, 2 vols. Havelock Ellis. reprint ed. Set. lib. bdg. 79.00 (0-403-00123-4) Scholarly.

Thomas Middleton: With an Introduction by Algernon Charles Swinburne, 2 vols. Thomas Middleton. (BCL1-PR English Literature Ser.). 1992. reprint ed. lib. bdg. 150.00 (0-7812-7253-X) Rprt Serv.

Thomas Middleton: With an Introduction by Algernon Charles Swinburne, 2 vols. Thomas Middleton. (BCL1-PR English Literature Ser.). 1992. reprint ed. Set. lib. bdg. 150.00 (0-7812-7265-3) Rprt Serv.

Thomas Middleton & the New Comedy Tradition. George E. Rowe. LC 79-4289. 252p. reprint ed. pap. 71.90 (0-7837-6179-1, 2045901) Bks Demand.

Thomas Middleton Revisited. Jowett. 1997. 26.95 (0-8057-7036-4, Twayne) Scribnrs Ref.

Thomas Moffet: The Silkewormes & Their Flies: A Facsimile (1599) Ed. by Victor Houliston. (Renaissance Triumphs & Magnificences, Medieval & Renaissance Texts & Studies: Vol. 56). 144p. 1989. 22.00 (0-86698-040-7, MR56) MRTS.

***Thomas Moran.** Nancy K. Anderson et al. LC 97-23435. 1997. pap. write for info. (0-89468-225-3) Natl Gallery Art.

***Thomas Moran.** Nancy K. Anderson. LC 97-23435. 1997. 60.00 (0-300-07325-9) Yale U Pr.

Thomas Moran: The Field Sketches, 1856-1923, Vol. 4. Anne Morand. LC 94-49719. (Illus.). 325p. 1996. 75.00 (0-8061-2704-X) U of Okla Pr.

Thomas Moran & the Surveying of the American West. Joni L. Kinsey. LC 91-23705. (New Directions in American Art Ser.). (Illus.). 247p. (Orig.). (C). 1992. pap. text ed. 34.95 (1-56098-170-9) Smithsonian.

Thomas Moran, Artist of the Mountains. Thurman Wilkins. LC 65-11235. (Illus.). 387p. reprint ed. pap. 110.30 (0-317-10416-0, 2005062) Bks Demand.

Thomas Moran in Utah. Gaell Lindstrom. 21p. 1983. pap. 1.00 (0-87421-146-8) Utah St U Pr.

Thomas Moran's Journey to the Tetons in 1879. Fritiof Fryxell. 12p. (C). 1988. reprint ed. lib. bdg. 25.00 (0-8095-6108-5) Borgo Pr.

Thomas More. Daniel Sargent. LC 71-119963. (Select Bibliographies Reprint Ser.). 1977. 21.95 (0-8369-5406-8) Ayer.

***Thomas More.** Anne Murphy. Ed. by Peter Vardy. LC 96-52493. (Great Christian Thinkers Ser.). 112p. 1997. reprint ed. pap. 9.00 (0-7648-0117-1, Triumph Books) Liguori Pubns.

Thomas More: A Portrait of Courage. Gerard B. Wegemer. LC 95-15747. 307p. 1995. 24.95 (0-933932-84-7) Scepter Pubs.

Thomas More: The King's Good Servant. Dorothy Smith. (Illus.). (J). 1990. pap. 2.95 (0-8091-6595-3) Paulist Pr.

Thomas More: The Search for the Inner Man. Louis L. Martz. (Illus.). 128p. (C). 1992. reprint ed. pap. 10.00 (0-300-05668-0) Yale U Pr.

Thomas More & Erasmus. Ernest E. Reynolds. LC 65-26739. (Illus.). 278p. reprint ed. pap. 79.30 (0-7837-5582-1, 2045370) Bks Demand.

Thomas More on Statesmanship. Gerard B. Wegemer. LC 95-12682. 262p. 1996. 49.95 (0-8132-0836-X) Cath U Pr.

Thomas More's Prayer Book: A Facsimile Reproduction of the Annotated Pages. Thomas More. Tr. by Louis L. Martz & Richard S. Sylvester. LC 69-15454. (Elizabethan Club Ser.: No. 4). (Illus.). (ENG & LAT.). 1969. 45.00 (0-300-00179-7) Yale U Pr.

Thomas Morley's First Book of Consort Lessons, 6 vols. Ed. by William Casey. LC 81-80729. 1982. spiral bd. 45.00 (0-918954-27-4) Baylor Univ Pr.

Thomas Morris Chester, Black Civil War Correspondent: His Dispatches from the Virginia Front. R. J. Blackett. LC 89-30169. (Illus.). 376p. 1989. text ed. 45.00 (0-8071-1516-9) La State U Pr.

Thomas Morris Chester, Black Civil War Correspondent: His Dispatches from the Virginia Front. Thomas M. Chester. (Quality Paperbacks Ser.). (Illus.). 375p. 1991. reprint ed. pap. 13.95 (0-306-80453-0) Da Capo.

Thomas Morrow: Pioneer of Alabama & Texas. David C. Morrow. 18p. (Orig.). 1994. pap. 18.00 (0-9641836-1-7) Textar Media.

Thomas Muentzer, a Destroyer of the Godless: The Making of a Sixteenth-Century Religious Revolutionary. Abraham Friesen. LC 90-32488. (Illus.). 3320p. 1990. 48.00 (0-520-06761-4) U CA Pr.

Thomas Munro & the Development of Administrative Policy in Madras, 1792-1818: The Origins of the Munro System. T. H. Beaglehole. LC 65-17209. 193p. reprint ed. pap. 55.10 (0-317-26048-0, 2024419) Bks Demand.

Thomas Muntzer: Apocalyptic Mystic & Revolutionary. Hans-Jurge Goertz. Tr. by Jocelyn Jaquiery from GER. 256p. 1993. text ed. 44.95 (0-567-09606-8, Pub. by T & T Clark UK) Bks Intl VA.

Thomas Muntzer: Herkunft und Bildung. Ulrich Bubenheimer. LC 89-31185. (Studies in Medieval & Reformation Thought: Vol. XLVI). xx, 359p. (GER.). 1989. text ed. 99.75 (*90-04-08850-4*) E J Brill.

Thomas Muntzer: Theology & Revolution in the German Reformation. Tom Scott. LC 88-28183. 160p. 1989. text ed. 35.00 (*0-312-02679-X*) St Martin.

Thomas Murner & the Eucharist. Jason Miskuly. 200p. 1990. pap. 10.00 (*1-57659-115-8*) Franciscan Inst.

Thomas, Naogeorg, Werke, Vol. 1: Tragoedia Nova Pammachius, Mit der Deutschen Uebersetzung des Johann Tyrolff. Ed. by Hans-Gert Roloff. (Ausgaben Deutscher Literatur des XV bis XVIII Jahrhunderts Ser.). (C). 1974. 426.95 (*3-11-004074-3*) De Gruyter.

Thomas Nashe's Summer's Last Will & Testament: A Critical Modern-Spelling Edition. Patricia Posluszny. LC 89-34168. (American University Studies: English Language & Literature: Ser. IV, Vol. 108). 214p. 1990. text ed. 36.95 (*0-8204-1110-8*) P Lang Pubng.

***Thomas Nast: Cartoonist & Illustrator.** David Shirley. LC 97-8323. (Book Report Biography Ser.). (J). 1998. write for info. (*0-531-11372-8*) Watts.

***Thomas Nast: His Period & His Pictures.** Albert B. Paine. 1997. 44.95 (*0-7910-4537-4*) Chelsea Hse.

Thomas Nast: His Period & His Pictures. Albert B. Paine. LC 78-177504. (Illus.). 1972. reprint ed. 30.95 (*0-405-08831-0*) Ayer.

Thomas Nast's Christmas Drawings. Thomas Nast. (Illus.). 1978. pap. 5.95 (*0-486-23660-9*) Dover.

Thomas Nelson Page. Theodore L. Gross. (Twayne's United States Authors Ser.). 1967. pap. 13.95 (*0-8084-0298-6*, T111) NCUP.

Thomas Nelson Page: A Memoir of a Virginia Gentleman, by His Brother. Rosewell Page. (BCL1-PS American Literature Ser.). 210p. 1992. reprint ed. lib. bdg. 79.00 (*0-7812-6916-4*) Rprt Serv.

Thomas Norton: The Parliament Man. Michael A. Graves. 400p. 1994. 67.95 (*0-631-16799-4*) Blackwell Pubs.

Thomas O. Larkin: A Life of Patriotism & Profit in Old California. Harlan Hague & David J. Langum. LC 90-50234. (Illus.). 352p. 1995. pap. 14.95 (*0-8061-2733-3*) U of Okla Pr.

Thomas of Britain: Tristan. Stewart Gregory. LC 91-13487. (Library of Medical Literature: No. A 78). 230p. 1991. text ed. 11.00 (*0-8240-4034-1*) Garland.

Thomas of Erceldoune. Ed. by James A. Murray. (EETS, OS Ser.: No. 61). 1974. reprint ed. 40.00 (*0-527-00055-8*) Periodicals Srv.

Thomas of Woodstock: An English History Play of Shakespeare's Time. Ed. by George Parfitt & Simon Shepherd. (C). 1989. 35.00 (*0-907839-36-3*, Pub. by Brynmill Pr Ltd UK) St Mut.

***Thomas "Old Tom" Higgins, 1790-1836, Illinois Mounted Ranger, War of 1812: Research of Higgins & Related Families.** Cleo M. Alward. LC 97-72837. (Illus.). xxiii, 190p. 1997. pap. 16.50 (*0-9658670-0-5*) C M Alward.

Thomas Onetwo. Ernest M. Robson. (Illus.). 1971. 6.95 (*0-87110-074-6*) Primary Pr.

Thomas Onetwo. Ernest M. Robson. (Illus.). 1971. 20.00 (*0-89366-258-5*) Ultramarine Pub.

Thomas Paine. Karin C. Farley. LC 92-17662. (American Troublemakers Ser.). (Illus.). 128p. (J). (gr. 7-10). 1992. lib. bdg. 27.11 (*0-8114-2329-8*) Raintree Steck-V.

Thomas Paine. John Vail. (World Leaders - Past & Present Ser.). (Illus.). 112p. (YA). (gr. 5 up). 1990. lib. bdg. 19.95 (*1-55546-819-5*) Chelsea Hse.

Thomas Paine: Apostle of Freedom. Jack Fruchtman, Jr. LC 94-22790. (Illus.). 576p. 1994. 30.00 (*0-941423-94-8*) FWEW.

Thomas Paine: Apostle of Freedom. Jack Fruchtman, Jr. LC 94-22790. (Illus.). 416p. 1996. pap. 17.00 (*1-56858-063-0*) FWEW.

***Thomas Paine: Life & Works, 6 vols.** Michael Foot. 2872p. (C). 1997. text ed. 465.00 (*0-415-14762-X*) Routledge.

Thomas Paine: Social & Political Thought. Gregory Claeys. LC 89-16531. 256p. (C). 1989. pap. 22.95 (*0-04-445090-7*) Routledge Chapman & Hall.

Thomas Paine: Social & Political Thought. Gregory Claeys. LC 89-16531. 256p. (C). (gr. 13). 1989. text ed. 79.95 (*0-04-445089-3*) Routledge Chapman & Hall.

Thomas Paine & the Religion of Nature. Jack Fruchtman, Jr. LC 92-40586. 232p. (C). 1993. text ed. 37.00 (*0-8018-4571-8*) Johns Hopkins.

Thomas Paine Collection of Richard Gimbel in the Library of the American Philosophical Society. Compiled & Pref. by Hildegard Stephans. LC 76-49800. 265p. 1976. lib. bdg. 60.00 (*0-8420-2108-6*) Scholarly Res Inc.

Thomas Paine, Liberator. Frank Smith. 1993. reprint ed. lib. bdg. 89.00 (*0-7812-5834-0*) Rprt Serv.

Thomas Paine Portfolio. Carl Shapiro et al. 1976. 10.00 (*0-914937-05-7*) Ind Pubns.

Thomas Paine, Prophet & Martyr of Democracy. Mary A. Best. 1972. 59.95 (*0-8490-1203-1*) Gordon Pr.

Thomas Paine Reader. Thomas Paine. Ed. by Isaac Kramnick & Michael Foot. 544p. 1987. pap. 12.95 (*0-14-044496-3*, Penguin Classics) Viking Penguin.

Thomas Paine's American Idealogy. A. Owen Aldridge. LC 83-40239. 328p. 1984. 45.00 (*0-87413-260-6*) U Delaware Pr.

Thomas Percy: A Scholar-Cleric in the Age of Johnson. Bertram H. Davis. LC 88-38842. (Illus.). 346p. (C). 1989. text ed. 46.95 (*0-8122-8161-6*) U of Pa Pr.

Thomas Pownall: British Defender of American Liberty: A Story of Anglo-American Relations in the Eighteenth Century. John A. Schutz. LC 85-21309. 340p. 1985. reprint ed. lib. bdg. 35.00 (*0-89370-864-X*) Borgo Pr.

Thomas Pradzynski: Collector's Edition Book I: Galerie Du Midi. Oliver Caldwell et al. LC 93-72847. (Illus.). 176p. 1993. 1,500.00 (*1-884495-01-X*) Caldwell Snyder.

***Thomas Pradzynski: Collector's Edition Book I: Galerie Du Midi. Includes Serigraph.** deluxe ed. Oliver Caldwell et al. LC 93-72847. (Illus.). 176p. 1993. 1,700.00 (*1-884495-06-0*) Caldwell Snyder.

Thomas Pradzynski: Collector's Edition Book II: Le Bistrot. Oliver Caldwell et al. LC 93-72847. (Illus.). 176p. 1993. 850.00 (*1-884495-02-8*) Caldwell Snyder.

***Thomas Pradzynski: Collector's Edition Book II: Le Bistrot. Includes Serigraph.** deluxe ed. Oliver Caldwell et al. LC 93-72847. (Illus.). 176p. 1993. 1,050.00 (*1-884495-07-9*) Caldwell Snyder.

Thomas Pradzynski: Collector's Edition Book III: Librairie St. Germain. Oliver Caldwell et al. LC 93-72847. (Illus.). 176p. 1993. 850.00 (*1-884495-03-6*) Caldwell Snyder.

***Thomas Pradzynski: Collector's Edition Book III: Librairie St. Germain. Includes Serigraph.** deluxe ed. Oliver Caldwell et al. (Illus.). 175p. 1993. 1,050.00 (*1-884495-08-7*) Caldwell Snyder.

Thomas Pradzynski: Modern Realist. Oliver Caldwell et al. LC 93-72847. (Illus.). 176p. 1993. 75.00 (*1-884495-00-1*) Caldwell Snyder.

Thomas Pynchon. Joseph W. Slade. (Worcester Polytechnic Institute Studies in Science, Technology, & Culture). 241p. (C). 1990. text ed. 39.00 (*0-8204-1031-4*) P Lang Pubng.

Thomas Pynchon. Tony Tanner. (Contemporary Writers Ser.). 96p. 1982. pap. 8.50 (*0-416-31670-0*, NO. 3602) Routledge Chapman & Hall.

Thomas Pynchon: A Bibliography of Primary & Secondary Materials. Clifford S. Mead. LC 88-30415. (Illus.). 176p. 1989. 39.95 (*0-916583-37-6*) Dalkey Arch.

Thomas Pynchon: The Art of Allusion. David Cowart. LC 79-20157. (Crosscurrents-Modern Critiques, New Ser.). 168p. 1980. 19.95 (*0-8093-0944-0*) S Ill U Pr.

Thomas Raccoon's Fantastic Airshow. Shintaro Maeda. Ed. by Nancy R. Thatch. (Books for Students by Students). (Illus.). 29p. (J). (gr. k-3). 1994. lib. bdg. 14.95 (*0-933849-51-6*) Landmark Edns.

Thomas Randall & His Works. Alan Young. (Canadian Author Studies). 44p. (C). 1990. pap. text ed. 9.95 (*1-55022-031-4*, Pub. by ECW Press CN) Genl Dist Srvs.

Thomas Register Guide to the Microfilm Collection,1905-1938. 26p. 1982. 30.00 (*0-89235-072-5*) Primary Srce Media.

Thomas Reid. Keith Lehrer. 400p. 1989. 49.95 (*0-415-03886-3*, A3536) Routledge.

Thomas Reid. Keith Lehrer. 324p. (C). 1991. pap. text ed. 19.95 (*0-415-06390-6*, A5714) Routledge.

***Thomas Reid: 1898 Edition.** Alexander C. Fraser. 176p. 1996. reprint ed. write for info. (*1-85506-205-4*) Bks Intl VA.

***Thomas Reid, an Inquiry into the Human Mind: On the Principles of Common Sense.** Thomas Reid & Derek R. Brookes. LC 97-16293. 1997. write for info. (*0-271-01741-4*) Pa St U Pr.

Thomas Reid & "The Way of Ideas" Roger D. Gallie. (Philosophical Studies: No. 45). 312p. 1989. lib. bdg. 114.50 (*0-7923-0390-3*, Pub. by Klwr Acad Pubs NE) Kluwer Ac.

Thomas Reid on Freedom & Morality. William L. Rowe. LC 90-55715. 208p. 1991. 32.50 (*0-8014-2557-3*) Cornell U Pr.

Thomas Reid on the Animate Creation: Papers Relating to the Life Sciences. Ed. by Paul Wood. 1996. 55.00 (*0-271-01571-3*) Pa St U Pr.

***Thomas Reid's An Inquiry into the Human Mind on the Principles of Common Sense.** Derek R. Brookes. 340p. 1997. write for info. (*0-271-01702-3*) Pa St U Pr.

Thomas Reid's 'Inquiry' The Geometry of Visibles & the Case for Realism. Norman Daniels. LC 88-60488. (Series in Philosophy). 196p. 1989. reprint ed. 39.50 (*0-8047-1504-1*); reprint ed. pap. 14.95 (*0-8047-1712-5*) Stanford U Pr.

Thomas Ritchie: A Study in Virginia Politics. Charles H. Ambler. (Law, Politics & History Ser.). 1970. reprint ed. lib. bdg. 39.50 (*0-306-70092-1*) Da Capo.

***Thomas Robert Malthus: Critical Assessments, Vol. 14.** Ed. by John C. Wood. (Critical Assessments of Leading Economists Ser.). 1424p. (C). 1986. text ed. 660.00 (*0-415-09908-0*) Routledge.

Thomas Robert Malthus, 1766-1834 & John Stuart Mill, 1806-1873. Ed. by Mark Blaug. (Pioneers in Economics Ser.: No. 16). 400p. 1991. text ed. 140.00 (*1-85278-478-4*) E Elgar.

Thomas Rogers: Leicester's Ghost. Ed. by Franklin B. Williams, Jr. (Renaissance English Text Society Ser.: Vol. 4). 124p. 1972. 20.00 (*0-685-56250-6*, MRET4, Renaiss Eng Text Soc) MRTS.

Thomas S. Buechner. Rachael Sadinsky. LC 95-15106. 1995. pap. 10.95 (*1-877885-07-X*) Arnot Art.

Thomas Saga Erkibyskups: A Life of Archbishop Thomas Becket, in Icelandic, with English Translation, Notes & Glossary, 2 vols. M. Eirikr Magnusson. (Rolls Ser.: No. 65). 1974. reprint ed. Set. 140.00 (*0-8115-1133-2*) Periodicals Srv.

Thomas Sankara Speaks: The Burkina Faso Revolution, 1983-87. Thomas Sankara. Ed. by Samantha Anderson. LC 88-61827. 260p. (Orig.). 1988. reprint ed. pap. 18.95 (*0-87348-526-2*); reprint ed. lib. bdg. 50.00 (*0-87348-527-0*) Pathfinder NY.

Thomas Satterwhite Noble, 1835-1907. James D. Birchfield et al. (Illus.). 156p. 1989. pap. text ed. 18.00 (*0-929007-00-X*) Univ KY Art Mus.

Thomas Say: Early American Naturalist. Harry B. Weiss & Grace M. Ziegler. Ed. by Keir B. Sterling. LC 77-81137. (Biologists & Their World Ser.). (Illus.). 1978. reprint ed. lib. bdg. 26.95 (*0-405-10737-4*) Ayer.

Thomas Say, New World Naturalist. Patricia T. Stroud. LC 92-4528. (Illus.). 362p. (C). 1992. 27.95 (*0-8122-3103-1*) U of Pa Pr.

***Thomas Schutte.** Thomas Schutte. (Illus.). 160p. 1998. pap. 29.95 (*0-7148-3714-8*, Pub. by Phaidon Press UK) Chronicle Bks.

Thomas Shadwell: His Life & Comedies. Albert S. Borgman. LC 68-56540. 1972. reprint ed. 24.95 (*0-405-08289-4*, Pub. by Blom Pubns UK) Ayer.

Thomas Shadwell's Bury-Fair: A Critical Edition. Thomas Shadwell. Ed. by John C. Ross. LC 94-43031. (Renaissance Imagination Ser.). 203p. 1995. text ed. 61.00 (*0-8153-1740-9*) Garland.

Thomas Shadwell's The Woman-Captain: A Critical Old-Spelling Edition. Thomas Shadwell. Ed. by Judith B. Slagle. LC 93-30105. (Renaissance Imagination Ser.). 200p. 1993. text ed. 54.00 (*0-8153-1528-7*) Garland.

Thomas Skyler: Foothills Preacher. Ralph Connor. Ed. by Michael R. Phillips. LC 87-82629. (Stories of Yesteryear Ser.: Vol. 2). Orig. Title: The Sky Pilot. 169p. 1988. pap. 6.95 (*0-940652-07-2*) Sunrise Bks.

Thomas' Snowsuit. Robert Munsch. 24p. (J). (gr. k-3). 1985. pap. 5.95 (*0-920303-33-1*, Pub. by Annick CN); lib. bdg. 15.95 (*0-920303-32-3*, Pub. by Annick CN) Firefly Bks Ltd.

Thomas Southerne: Dramatist. John W. Dodds. LC 78-91179. (Yale Studies in English: No. 81). iv, 232p. (C). 1970. reprint ed. lib. bdg. 33.50 (*0-208-00912-4*, Archon Bks) Shoe String.

Thomas Spence & His Connections. Olive D. Rudkin. LC 65-26376. (Reprints of Economic Classics Ser.). 256p. 1966. reprint ed. 37.50 (*0-678-00178-2*) Kelley.

Thomas Spry, Lawyer & Physician: The First Attorney Admitted to Practice under English Law in the Delaware River Settlements Now Included in the States of Pennsylvania, New Jersey & Delaware. John F. Lewis. ix, 126p. 1996. reprint ed. 40.00 (*1-56169-209-3*) Gaunt.

Thomas Starkey: A Dialogue Between Pole & Lupset. T. F. Mayer. (Camden Fourth Ser.: No. 37). 172p. 27.00 (*0-86193-119-X*) David Brown.

Thomas Starkey & the Commonweal: Humanist Politics & Religion in the Reign of Henry VIII. Thomas F. Mayer. (Cambridge Studies in Early Modern British History). 328p. (C). 1989. text ed. 69.95 (*0-521-36104-4*) Cambridge U Pr.

Thomas Starr King. Robert Monzingo. (Illus.). 1991. pap. 12.50 (*0-940168-20-0*) Boxwood.

Thomas Stearns Eliot: A Study. Thomas McGreevey. LC 74-164026. (Studies in T. S. Eliot: No. 11). 1971. reprint ed. lib. bdg. 75.00 (*0-8383-1327-2*) M S G Haskell Hse.

Thomas Stearns Eliot: Poet. 2nd ed. A. David Moody. 420p. (C). 1995. pap. 19.95 (*0-521-46750-0*) Cambridge U Pr.

Thomas Stearns Eliot: Poet. 2nd ed. A. David Moody. 420p. (C). 1995. 59.95 (*0-521-46186-3*) Cambridge U Pr.

Thomas Stowage. ICHCA Staff. (C). 1988. 558.00 (*0-685-46495-4*, Pub. by ICHCA UK) St Mut.

***Thomas' Stowage.** 3rd ed. O. O. Thomas et al. (Illus.). 388p. (C). 1996. text ed. 120.00 (*0-85174-625-X*) Sheridan.

Thomas Struth: Photographs. Benjamin Buchloh. (Illus.). 1990. pap. 30.00 (*0-941548-19-8*) Ren Soc U Chi.

Thomas Struth: Strangers & Friends Photographs 1986-1992. Thomas Struth. (Illus.). 108p. 1994. 45.00 (*0-262-19357-4*) MIT Pr.

Thomas Szasz: Primary Values & Major Contentions. Ed. by Richard E. Vatz & Lee S. Weinberg. LC 82-62083. 253p. 1982. 28.95 (*0-87975-187-8*); pap. 21.95 (*0-87975-188-6*) Prometheus Bks.

***Thomas Taggart: Public Servant, Political Boss, 1856-1929.** James P. Fadely. LC 96-29072. (Illus.). 1996. 27.95 (*0-87195-115-0*) Ind Hist Soc.

Thomas Telford. Rhoda M. Pearce. 1989. pap. 30.00 (*0-85263-410-2*, Pub. by Shire UK) St Mut.

***Thomas, the Doubting Disciple.** Arch Books Staff. 1997. pap. text ed. 1.99 (*0-570-07531-9*) Concordia.

Thomas the Obscure. Maurice Blanchot. Tr. & Afterword by Robert Lamberton. 128p. 1988. reprint ed. 15.95 (*0-88268-077-3*); reprint ed. pap. 8.95 (*0-88268-076-5*) Station Hill Pr.

Thomas the Rhymer. Ellen Kushner. 1991. mass mkt. 3.99 (*0-8125-1445-9*) Tor Bks.

***Thomas the Tank.** Random House Value Publishing Staff. 1997. 19.99 (*0-517-18786-8*) Random Hse Value.

Thomas the Tank Engine - Colors. Illus. by Pam Posey. (Thomas the Tank Engine Toddler Board Bks.). 12p. (J). (ps). 1991. 2.50 (*0-679-81646-1*) Random Bks Yng Read.

Thomas the Tank Engine - Shapes & Sizes. Illus. by Deborah C. Borgo. (Thomas the Tank Engine Toddler Board Bks.). 14p. (J). (ps). 1991. 2.50 (*0-679-81643-7*) Random Bks Yng Read.

Thomas the Tank Engine ABC: (Just Right for 2's & 3's) W. Awdry. LC 89-10605. (Just Right Bks.). (Illus.). 24p. (J). (ps). 1990. 6.99 (*0-679-80352-1*) Random Bks Yng Read.

Thomas the Tank Engine & the Great Race. W. Awdry. (Illus.). 7p. (J). (ps). 1989. spiral bd. 7.00 (*0-679-80000-X*) Random Bks Yng Read.

Thomas the Tank Engine & the School Trip. W. Awdry. LC 92-33711. (Step into Reading Bks.: Step 1). (Illus.). 32p. (J). (ps-1). 1993. pap. 3.99 (*0-679-84365-5*) Random Bks Yng Read.

Thomas the Tank Engine & the Tractor. W. Awdry. LC 91-67969. (Thomas the Tank Engine Little Pops Ser.). (Illus.). 12p. (J). (ps-1). 1992. 3.99 (*0-679-83452-4*) Random Bks Yng Read.

Thomas the Tank Engine Catches a Thief. Christopher Awdry. LC 94-66489. 1995. 4.50 (*0-679-86994-8*) Random.

***Thomas the Tank Engine Colors.** Random House Staff. (Board Bks.). 1997. 2.50 (*0-679-88888-8*) Random Bks Yng Read.

***Thomas the Tank Engine Coming & Going.** Random House Staff. (Board Bks.). (J). 1997. 2.50 (*0-679-88880-2*) Random Bks Yng Read.

Thomas the Tank Engine Counts to Ten. Illus. by Deborah C. Borgo. (Thomas the Tank Engine Toddler Board Bks.). (J). (ps). 1991. 2.50 (*0-679-81644-5*) Random Bks Yng Read.

***Thomas The Tank Engine Counts to Ten.** Random House Staff. (Board Bks.). 1997. 2.50 (*0-679-88879-9*) Random Bks Yng Read.

Thomas the Tank Engine Says Goodnight. Illus. by Owain Bell. (Cuddle Cloth Bks.). 12p. (J). (ps). 1990. 4.99 (*0-679-80791-8*) Random Bks Yng Read.

***Thomas the Tank Engine Shapes & Sizes.** Random House Staff. (Board Bks.). 1997. 2.50 (*0-679-88887-X*) Random Bks Yng Read.

Thomas the Tank Engine Storybook. Photos by David Mitton & Terry Permane. LC 92-35915. (Illus.). (J). 1993. 8.00 (*0-679-84465-1*) Random Bks Yng Read.

Thomas the Tank Engine Visits a Farm. W. Awdry. (Bathtime Bks.). (Illus.). 10p. (J). (ps). 1991. 4.99 (*0-679-81580-5*) Random Bks Yng Read.

Thomas the Tank Engine's Big Lift-&-Look Book. W. Awdry. (Great Big Flap Book). 1996. 11.99 (*0-679-88072-0*, Bullseye Bks) Random Bks Yng Read.

Thomas the Tank Engine's Noisy Trip. W. Awdry. LC 89-60089. (Chunky Bks.). (Illus.). 28p. (J). 1989. 3.99 (*0-679-80083-2*) Random Bks Yng Read.

Thomas Theodor Heine: Fin-de Siecle-Munich & the Origins of Simplicissimus, Vol. 9. Timothy W. Hiles. LC 94-36245. (Literature & the Visual Arts Ser.). 264p. (C). 1995. 49.95 (*0-8204-2689-X*) P Lang Pubng.

Thomas Tomkins, Fifteen Seventy-Two to Sixteen Fifty-Six. D. Stevens. (Illus.). 1990. 8.75 (*0-8446-3010-1*) Peter Smith.

Thomas Tooke. Arie Arnon. LC 90-35606. 226p. (C). 1990. text ed. 49.50 (*0-472-10199-4*) U of Mich Pr.

***Thomas Tooke: Pioneer of Monetary Theory.** Arie Arnon. 224p. 1990. 70.00 (*1-85278-204-8*) E Elgar.

Thomas Tooke (1774-1858), Mountifort Longfield (1802-1884), Richard Jones (1790-1855) Ed. by Mark Blaug. (Pioneers in Economics Ser.: No. 18). 384p. 1991. text ed. 135.00 (*1-85278-480-6*) E Elgar.

***Thomas Traherne: Select Meditation.** Ed. & Intro. by J. J. Smith. 208p. 1997. pap. 24.95 (*1-85754-308-4*, Pub. by Carcanet Pr UK) Paul & Co Pubs.

***Thomas Traherne (1637?-1674) Selected Writings.** Ed. by Dick Davis. pap. write for info. (*0-85635-231-4*, Pub. by Carcanet Pr UK) Paul & Co Pubs.

Thomas Troward, the Man & His Work. Harry Gaze. 145p. 1993. reprint ed. pap. 8.95 (*0-87516-654-7*) DeVorss.

Thomas Tuttle Just in Time. Becky T. Lindberg. LC 93-38606. (Illus.). (J). (gr. 4-7). 1994. lib. bdg. 12.95 (*0-8075-7898-3*) A Whitman.

Thomas Untitled. Thomas. LC 97-524. (J). 1997. 16.00 (*0-689-80958-1*) S&S Childrens.

Thomas Vaughan at Oxford. Mary J. Skrine. 1990. pap. text ed. 4.95 (*1-55818-128-8*) Holmes Pub.

Thomas W. Martin: A Biography. William M. Murray, Jr. LC 77-85483. (Illus.). 276p. 1978. 6.50 (*0-940824-01-9*) S Res Inst.

Thomas W. Nason: New England Virtues Aged in Wood. Charles Price. (Illus.). 61p. (Orig.). 1993. pap. 13.95 (*1-880897-03-2*) Lyme Hist.

Thomas W. Salmon: Psychiatrist. Earl D. Bond & Paul O. Komora. Ed. by Gerald N. Grob. LC 78-22550. (Historical Issues in Mental Health Ser.). (Illus.). 1980. reprint ed. lib. bdg. 19.95 (*0-405-11904-6*) Ayer.

Thomas W. Talley's Negro Folk Rhymes. Thomas W. Talley. LC 90-12561. (Illus.). 360p. 1991. 38.00 (*0-87049-673-5*) U of Tenn Pr.

Thomas Ware, a Spectator at the Christmas Conference: A Miscellany on Thomas Ware & the Christmas Conference. Ed. by William R. Phinney et al. LC 84-70457. (Illus.). 320p. (Orig.). 1984. reprint ed. 8.95 (*0-914960-48-2*) Academy Bks.

Thomas Waterman Wood, PNA, 1823-1903. William C. Lipke. (Illus.). 1970. pap. 4.00 (*0-89073-032-6*) Boston Public Lib.

Thomas Watson's "Amyntas" (1585) & Fraunce's Translation "The Lamentations of Amyntas" (1587) Ed. by Franklin M. Dickey & Walter F. Staton, Jr. (Renaissance English Text Society Ser.: Vol. 2). 122p. 1967. 20.00 (*0-685-58833-5*, MRET2, Renaiss Eng Text Soc) MRTS.

Thomas Weelkes. David Brown. LC 79-10068. 1979. reprint ed. lib. bdg. 32.50 (*0-306-79523-X*) Da Capo.

Thomas Wentworth Higginson: The Story of His Life. Mary T. Higginson. LC 76-37886. (Select Bibliographies Reprint Ser.). 1977. reprint ed. 30.95 (*0-8369-6723-2*) Ayer.

Thomas Wharton's Adenographia. Thomas Wharton. Tr. by Stephen Freer from LAT. (Illus.). 752p. (C). 1996. text ed. 149.50 (*0-19-854788-9*, Clarendon Pr) OUP.

Thomas William Robertson: His Plays & Stagecraft. Maynard Savin. LC 50-4959. (Brown University Studies: Vol. 13). 160p. reprint ed. 45.60 (*0-685-15773-3*, 2027522) Bks Demand.

Thomas Wingfold, Curate. George MacDonald. 1989. 29.50 (*0-940652-57-9*) Sunrise Bks.

Thomas Wingfold, Curate. George MacDonald. (George MacDonald Original Works: Series VIII). 518p. 1997. reprint ed. 20.00 (*1-881084-53-1*) Johannesen.

Thomas Wolfe. Herbert J. Muller. 1976. 21.95 (*0-8488-1435-5*) Amereon Ltd.

Thomas Wolfe: A Bibliography. George R. Preston, Jr. LC 74-12760. (Illus.). 1979. reprint ed. text ed. 65.00 (*0-8371-7750-2*, PRTW, Greenwood Pr) Greenwood.

An Asterisk (*) at the beginning of an entry indicates that the title is appearing in BIP for the first time.

Thomas Wolfe: A Biography. Elizabeth Nowell. LC 72-7507. 456p. 1973. reprint ed. text ed. 38.50 (*0-8371-6519-9*, NOTW, Greenwood Pr) Greenwood.

Thomas Wolfe: A Checklist. Elmer D. Johnson. LC 74-626233. (Serif Series: Bibliographies & Checklists: No. 12). 292p. reprint ed. pap. 83.30 (*0-8357-5572-X*, 2035199) Bks Demand.

Thomas Wolfe: A Descriptive Bibliography. Carol Johnston. LC 86-16192. (Series in Bibliography). (Illus.). 320p. 1987. 100.00 (*0-8229-3546-5*) U of Pittsburgh Pr.

Thomas Wolfe: A Harvard Perspective. Ed. & Intro. by Richard S. Kennedy. LC 83-2050. (Illus.). 108p. 1983. 12.95 (*0-912348-10-0*) Croissant & Co.

Thomas Wolfe: An Annotated Critical Bibliography. John E. Bassett. (Scarecrow Author Bibliographies Ser.: Vol. 96). 456p. 1996. 54.50 (*0-8108-3146-5*) Scarecrow.

Thomas Wolfe: Memoir of a Friendship. Robert Reynolds. LC 65-23163. 173p. reprint ed. pap. 49.40 (*0-8357-7717-0*, 2036074) Bks Demand.

Thomas Wolfe & His Editors: Establishing a True Text for the Posthumous Publications. Leslie Field. LC 87-40207. (Illus.). 240p. 1988. 24.95 (*0-8061-2095-9*) U of Okla Pr.

***Thomas Wolfe As I Knew Him & Other Essays.** Vardis Fisher. 166p. 1963. write for info. (*0-614-22027-0*) Idaho Ctr Bk.

Thomas Wolfe Companion. John L. Idol, Jr. LC 87-268. 227p. 1987. text ed. 55.00 (*0-313-23829-4*, ITW/, Greenwood Pr) Greenwood.

Thomas Wolfe Interviewed, 1929-1938. Ed. by Aldo P. Magi & Richard Walser. LC 84-25083. (Southern Literary Studies). (Illus.). viii, 135p. 1985. text ed. 25.00 (*0-8071-1229-1*) La State U Pr.

Thomas Wolfe Our Friend 1933-1938. Clayton Hoagland & Kathleen Hoagland. Ed. by Aldo P. Magi. (Illus.). 21p. 1979. 25.00 (*0-912348-03-8*) Croissant & Co.

Thomas Wolfe's Letters to His Mother, Julia Elizabeth Wolfe. Thomas Wolfe. Ed. by John S. Terry. LC 83-45870. 1943. 36.00 (*0-404-20292-6*, PS3545) AMS Pr.

Thomas Wolfe's Pennsylvania. Richard Walser. (Illus.). 20p. 1994. pap. 5.95 (*0-912348-09-7*) Croissant & Co.

Thomas Woolner, R. A,, Sculptor & Poet: His Life & Letters. Amy Woolner. LC 70-158614. reprint ed. 52.50 (*0-404-07030-2*) AMS Pr.

***Thomas Woolston: Madman & Deist?** William H. Trapnell. 240p. 1994. write for info. (*1-85506-227-5*) Bks Intl VA.

Thomas Wright's Political Songs of England: From the Reign of John to That of Edward II. Ed. by Peter Coss. (Camden Classic Reprints Ser.: No. 2). 464p. (C). 1996. text ed. 69.95 (*0-521-55466-7*); pap. text ed. 24.95 (*0-521-55587-6*) Cambridge U Pr.

Thomas Wyatt see Renaissance Poets: Critical Heritage

Thomas Young: Forgotten Genius. Daniel L. Kline. (Illus.). 210p. (Orig.). 1993. pap. text ed. 10.95 (*0-9635046-0-6*) Vidan Pr.

Thomasina. Paul Gallico. LC 88-82349. 299p. 1988. reprint ed. pap. 5.95 (*0-930330-93-5*, Lib Crime Classics) Intl Polygonics.

Thomasina & the Tommyknocker. Juanita K. Browne. LC 93-13732. (Illus.). viii, 85p. (Orig.). (J). (gr. 4-7). 1993. pap. 8.75 (*0-9636621-0-4*) Browne Bks.

Thomas's Big Railway Pop-up Book. W. Awdry. (Illus.). 14p. (J). (ps up). 1992. 13.00 (*0-679-83465-6*) Random Bks Yng Read.

***Thomas's Sheep & the Great Geography Test.** Steven L. Layne. LC 97-15816. (Illus.). (J). 1998. write for info. (*1-56554-274-6*) Pelican.

Thomas's Sitter. Jean Richardson. LC 90-13799. (Illus.). 32p. (J). (ps-1). 1991. lib. bdg. 13.95 (*0-02-776146-0*, Four Winds Pr) S&S Childrens.

***Thomassy's Trial.** Sol Stein. Date not set. write for info. (*0-688-05621-0*) Morrow.

***Thomaston Register, 1904 (Town History & Directory)** Mitchell & Gastonguay. 102p. 1997. reprint ed. pap. 17.00 (*0-8328-5916-8*) Higginson Bk Co.

Thomism & Aristotelianism: A Study of the Commentary by Thomas Aquinas on the Nicomachean Ethics. Harry V. Jaffa. LC 78-21520. 230p. 1979. reprint ed. text ed. 45.00 (*0-313-21149-3*, JATA, Greenwood Pr) Greenwood.

Thomism & Modern Thought. Ed. by Harry R. Klocker. LC 62-9414. 1962. 32.50 (*0-89197-451-2*) Irvington.

Thomist Spectrum. Helen J. John. LC 66-23619. (Orestes Brownson Series on Contemporary Thought & Affairs: No. 5). 208p. reprint ed. pap. 59.30 (*0-7837-0452-6*, 2040775) Bks Demand.

Thomistic Bibliography, 1940-1978. Compiled by Terry L. Miethe & Vernon J. Bourke. LC 80-1195. xxii, 318p. 1980. text ed. 49.95 (*0-313-21991-5*, MTH/, Greenwood Pr) Greenwood.

Thomistic Papers, No. I. Ed. by Victor B. Brezik. LC 83-73623. 176p. 1984. 20.95 (*0-685-31936-9*); pap. 10.95 (*0-685-31937-7*) Ctr Thomistic.

Thomistic Papers, No. I. Ed. by Victor B. Brezik. LC 85-18508. 176p. 1984. text ed. 24.50 (*0-268-01850-2*); pap. text ed. 13.00 (*0-268-01851-0*) U of Notre Dame Pr.

Thomistic Papers II. Ed. by Leonard A. Kennedy & Jack C. Marler. LC 83-73623. (Center for Thomistic Studies). 160p. 1986. 20.95 (*0-268-01860-X*); pap. 13.00 (*0-268-01859-6*) Ctr Thomistic.

Thomistic Papers III, Vol. III. Ed. by Leonard A. Kennedy. LC 83-73623. 150p. 1987. 24.50 (*0-268-01864-2*); pap. 13.00 (*0-268-01865-0*) Ctr Thomistic.

Thomistic Papers IV, Vol. IV. Ed. by Leonard A. Kennedy. LC 83-73623. 217p. 1988. 15.00 (*0-268-01867-7*); pap. 15.00 (*0-268-01868-5*) Ctr Thomistic.

Thomistic Papers V, Vol. V. Ed. by Thomas A. Russman. LC 83-73623. 104p. (C). 1990. 24.50 (*0-268-01875-8*); pap. 13.00 (*0-268-01876-6*) Ctr Thomistic.

Thomistic Papers VI, Vol. VI. Ed. by John F. Knasas. LC 83-73623. (Center for Thomistic Studies). 292p. (C). 1994. 31.00 (*0-268-01886-3*); pap. 18.50 (*0-268-01887-1*) Ctr Thomistic.

Thompson & Thompson: Genetics in Medicine. 5th ed. Thompson et al. (Illus.). 368p. 1991. pap. text ed. 41.00 (*0-7216-2817-6*) Saunders.

Thompson & Thompson Genetics in Medicine. 6th ed. Willard. 1998. pap. text ed. write for info. (*0-7216-6902-6*) Saunders.

Thompson & West History of Nevada, 1881. Ed. by Myron F. Angel. (Illus.). 900p. 1958. 175.00 (*0-913814-52-0*) Nevada Pubns.

Thompson Chain-Reference Bible Companion. Howard A. Hanke. (Illus.). 1995. 29.95 (*0-88707-174-0*); 34.95 (*0-88707-200-3*) Kirkbride Bible.

***Thompson Chemical Pathol Meth.** 1989. lib. bdg. write for info. (*0-7462-0054-4*) Kluwer Ac.

Thompson Common Sense Geriatric. 1900. lib. bdg. write for info. (*0-7462-0070-6*) Kluwer Ac.

***Thompson Haskell-The Craft of Functional Programming.** 2nd ed. Simon Thompson. (C). 1998. pap. text ed. write for info. (*0-201-34275-8*) Addison-Wesley.

Thompson Indians of British Columbia. James A. Teit. Ed. by Franz Boas. LC 73-3513. (Jesup North Pacific Expedition. Publications: No. 1, Pt. 4). reprint ed. 59.50 (*0-404-58115-3*) AMS Pr.

Thompson Language. Laurence C. Thompson & M. Terry Thompson. LC 91-65825. 1992. pap. 20.00 (*1-879763-08-7*) U MT UMOPL.

Thompson on Real Property, Thomas Edition, 15 vols., Set. David A. Thomas. 1994. 1,195.00 (*1-55834-156-0*) MICHIE.

Thompson River, BC. Arthur J. Lingren. (River Journal Ser.: Vol. 2, No. 3). (Illus.). 48p. 1994. pap. 14.95 (*1-878175-47-5*) F Amato Pubns.

Thompson River Salish Dictionary. Laurence C. Thompson & M. Terry Thompson. LC 96-60021. (University of Montana Occasional Papers in Linguistics). xxvii, 1411p. 1996. 45.00 (*1-879763-12-5*) U MT UMOPL.

Thompson Submachine Guns. 1986. lib. bdg. 79.95 (*0-8490-3580-5*) Gordon Pr.

Thompson/Center Contender Pistol: How to Tune, Time, Load, & Shoot for Accuracy. Charles Stephens. (Illus.). 64p. 1996. pap. 12.00 (*0-87364-885-4*) Paladin Pr.

Thompson's Core Textbook of Anatomy. 2nd ed. Akesson et al. (Illus.). 586p. 1989. spiral bd. 39.95 (*0-397-50849-2*) Lppncott-Raven.

Thompson's Mountain. G. Clifton Wisler. 448p. 1987. mass mkt. 3.95 (*0-8217-2042-2*, Zebra Kensgtn) Kensgtn Pub Corp.

***Thompson's Pediatric Nursing: An Introductory Text.** 7th ed. Elizabeth Schulte et al. Ed. by Ilze Rader. 512p. 1997. pap. text ed. 29.95 (*0-7216-4239-X*) Saunders.

***Thompson's Pediatric Nursing: An Introductory Text.** 7th ed. Elizabeth Schulte et al. (Illus.). 1997. teacher ed. write for info. (*0-7216-4258-6*) Saunders.

***Thompson's Resource Guide for Aging: The Caregivers Choice.** Loretto Thompson & Sherry Fleckenstein. 12.95 (*1-58409-644-6*) Meyer Enter.

Thom's Irish Who's Who. Thom. (Biographical Reference Work Ser.). 266p. reprint ed. 39.00 (*0-932051-30-8*) Rprt Serv.

Thomson: Descendants of John Thomson, Pioneer Scotch Covenanter: Genealogical Notes on All Known Descendants of John Thomson of Scotland, Ireland & Pennsylvania, with Biographical Sketches. A. S. McAllister. (Illus.). 357p. 1993. reprint ed. pap. 59.50 (*0-8328-3423-8*); reprint ed. lib. bdg. 69.50 (*0-8328-3422-X*) Higginson Bk Co.

***Thomson ACH Participant Directory, Fall 1996.** 1996. pap. 119.00 (*1-56310-163-7*) Thomson Fin Pub.

***Thomson ACH Participant Directory, Spring 1997.** 1997. pap. 119.00 (*1-56310-186-6*) Thomson Fin Pub.

***Thomson Bank Directory.** Thomson. 1996. 395.00 (*1-56310-154-8*) Amer Bank Bond Buyer.

Thomson Bank Directory, 3 vols. Ed. by Thomson Financial Directory Staff. 1991. Set. 265.00 (*1-56310-010-X*) Amer Bank Bond Buyer.

Thomson Bank Directory, 3 vols. Ed. by Thomson Financial Publishing Staff. 1996. Set. write for info. (*1-56310-018-5*) Thomson Fin Pub.

Thomson Bank Directory, 3 vols., 3. Ed. by Thomson Financial Directory Staff. 1991. 190.00 (*1-56310-009-6*) Amer Bank Bond Buyer.

Thomson Bank Directory, 3 vols., 3. Ed. by Thomson Financial Publishing Staff. 1996. write for info. (*1-56310-017-7*) Thomson Fin Pub.

Thomson Bank Directory, 3 vols., Set, Vols. 1 & 2. Ed. by Thomson Financial Directory Staff. 1991. 245.00 (*1-56310-008-8*) Amer Bank Bond Buyer.

Thomson Bank Directory, 3 vols., Vols. 1-2. Ed. by Thomson Financial Publishing Staff. 1996. write for info. (*1-56310-016-9*) Thomson Fin Pub.

Thomson Bank Directory: July-November 1993, 3 vols. Thomson Financial Publishing Inc. Staff. 1993. Set. 738.00 (*1-56310-042-8*) Amer Bank Bond Buyer.

Thomson Bank Directory: July-November 1993, 3 vols., 3. Thomson Financial Publishing Inc. Staff. 1993. 199.00 (*1-56310-040-1*) Amer Bank Bond Buyer.

Thomson Bank Directory: July-November 1993, 3 vols., Vols. 1 & 2. Thomson Financial Publishing Inc. Staff. 1993. Vol. 1 & 2. 269.00 (*1-56310-039-8*) Amer Bank Bond Buyer.

***Thomson Bank Directory, Dec. 1996-May 1997, 2 vols.** Incl. Vol. 1-4. . 1996. (*1-56310-173-4*); Vol. 5. . 1996. (*1-56310-174-2*); write for info. (*1-56310-175-0*) Thomson Fin Pub.

***Thomson Bank Directory, June-November 1997, 3 vols.** Incl. Vol. 1-2. . 1997. 285.00 (*1-56310-197-1*); Vol. 3-4. . 1997. 285.00 (*1-56310-198-X*); Vol. 5. . 1997. 129.00 (*1-56310-199-8*); 475.00 (*1-56310-200-5*) Thomson Fin Pub.

***Thomson Credit Union Directory, January-June 1997, Vol. 11, No. 1.** 1996. pap. 149.00 (*1-56310-182-3*) Thomson Fin Pub.

***Thomson Credit Union Directory, July-December 1996.** 1996. pap. 149.00 (*1-56310-156-4*) Thomson Fin Pub.

***Thomson Credit Union Directory, July-December 1997.** 1997. pap. 149.00 (*1-56310-204-8*) Thomson Fin Pub.

Thomson Credit Union Directory, 1996. Ed. by Thomson Financial Publishing Staff. 1996. 139.00 (*1-56310-021-5*) Thomson Fin Pub.

Thomson Empire. Susan Goldenberg. 272p. 1985. 16.95 (*0-8253-0259-5*) Beaufort Bks NY.

Thomson Multimedia Resource, 1996. Thomson Technology Services Group Staff. (C). 1996. pap. 44.95 (*0-534-50719-0*) Wadsworth Pub.

***Thomson National Directory of Mortgage Brokers, December 1996, Vol. 1, No. 2.** 1996. pap. 295.00 (*1-56310-181-5*) Thomson Fin Pub.

***Thomson National Directory of Mortgage Brokers, June 1996.** 1996. pap. 295.00 (*1-56310-159-9*) Thomson Fin Pub.

***Thomson National Directory of Mortgage Brokers, June 1997.** 1997. pap. 295.00 (*1-56310-203-X*) Thomson Fin Pub.

Thomson Regulation CC Directory: July-December 1993. Thomson Financial Publishing Inc. Staff. 1993. pap. 65.00 (*1-56310-048-7*) Amer Bank Bond Buyer.

Thomson Regulation CC Directory, Jan.-June 1996. Ed. by Thomson Financial Publishing Staff. 1996. 170.00 (*1-56310-014-2*) Thomson Fin Pub.

***Thomson Regulation CC Directory, January-June 1997.** 1996. pap. 79.00 (*1-56310-180-7*) Thomson Fin Pub.

***Thomson Regulation CC Directory, July-December 1997.** 1997. pap. 79.00 (*1-56310-202-1*) Thomson Fin Pub.

***Thomson Risk Management Directory, November 1996, Vol. 1, No. 3.** 1996. pap. write for info. (*1-56310-176-9*) Thomson Fin Pub.

Thomson Same-Day Settlement Presentment Point Directory, April 1994. Thomson Financial Publishing Inc. Staff. 1994. pap. 275.00 (*1-56310-079-7*) Amer Bank Bond Buyer.

***Thomson Saving Directory.** Thomson. 1997. 1.95 (*5-556-73598-0*) ZZZ Bks.

***Thomson Saving Directory July-December.** Thomson Staff. 1996. 195.00 (*1-56310-155-6*) Thomson Fin Pub.

Thomson Savings Directory. Ed. by Thomson Financial Publishing Staff. 1991. 155.00 (*1-56310-005-3*) Amer Bank Bond Buyer.

Thomson Savings Directory: July-Nov. 1993. Thomson Financial Publishing Inc. Staff. 1993. 185.00 (*1-56310-038-X*) Amer Bank Bond Buyer.

***Thomson Savings Directory, January-June 1997.** 1996. pap. 199.00 (*1-56310-183-1*) Thomson Fin Pub.

***Thomson Savings Directory, July-December 1997.** 1997. pap. 199.00 (*1-56310-205-6*) Thomson Fin Pub.

Thomson's Blue Book of Bank Suppliers: The Complete Buyer's Guide to Products & Services for Financial Institutions. 1996. pap. write for info. (*1-56310-055-X*) Thomson Fin Pub.

Thomson's Blue Book of Bank Suppliers: The Complete Buyer's Guide to Products & Services for Financial Institutions. Thomson Financial Publishing Inc. Staff. 1993. pap. 20.00 (*1-56310-041-X*); Free with purchase of Thomson Bank Directory. write for info. (*0-318-71305-5*) Amer Bank Bond Buyer.

***Thomson's Bluebook: The Banker's Guide to Product & Service Providers, 1997.** 1997. pap. 40.00 (*1-56310-187-4*) Thomson Fin Pub.

Thomson's China: Travels & Adventures of a Nineteenth-Century Photographer. John Thomson. (Oxford in Asia Hardback Reprints Ser.). (Illus.). 276p. 1994. 45.00 (*0-19-585741-0*) OUP.

Thomson's English-Spanish - Spanish-English Illustrated Agricultural Dictionary. Robert P. Rice, Jr. 160p. 1993. pap. 27.95 (*0-913702-56-0*) Thomson Pubns.

Thomson's Special Veterinary Pathology, Vol. 2. 2nd ed. Carlton & McGavin. 656p. (C). (gr. 13). 1995. text ed. 99.00 (*0-8016-7968-0*) Mosby Yr Bk.

Thones: Thirty-Four Calligraphic Meditations from a Westerner's Pen. Kathryn Cihak. 34p. (Orig.). 1994. pap. 10.95 (*0-9631750-3-3*) Muse Pubns.

***Thonet: Classic Furniture.** Vegesack. Date not set. 50.00 (*0-8478-2040-8*) Rizzoli Intl.

Thonet Bentwood & Other Furniture: The 1904 Illustrated Catalogue & Supplements. Thonet Company Staff. (Illus.). 154p. 1980. pap. 11.95 (*0-486-24024-X*) Dover.

Thong Tree. Richard T. Haynes. LC 90-70508. (Illus.). 64p. (J). (gr. 3-7). 1990. 11.95 (*0-929146-02-6*) Voyageur Pub.

Thongs. Alexander Trocchi. 1993. pap. 9.95 (*0-922233-11-X*) Blast Bks.

Thonk. 19.95 (*0-7935-3397-X*, 00694924) H Leonard.

Thonner's Analytical Key to the Families of Flowering Plants. R. Geesink. 253p. (C). 1991. text ed. 250.00 (*0-89771-624-8*, Pub. by Intl Bk Distr II) St Mut.

Thoor Ballylee: Home of William Butler Yeats. Mary Hanley & Liam Miller. (Illus.). 32p. 1984. pap. 8.95 (*0-85105-300-9*, Pub. by Colin Smythe Ltd UK) Dufour.

***Thoor Ballylee, Home of William Butler Yeats.** 3rd ed. Mary Hanley & Liam Miller. 32p. 9500. pap. 8.95 (*0-85105-511-7*, Pub. by Colin Smythe Ltd UK) Dufour.

Thor. David D. Duncan. LC 93-2163. (Illus.). 96p. 1993. 27.95 (*1-55821-237-X*) Lyons & Burford.

Thor. Wayne Smith. 1994. reprint ed. mass mkt. 5.99 (*0-345-38455-5*) Ballantine.

Thor: Alone Against the Celestials. Tom DeFalco et al. 64p. 1992. 5.95 (*0-87135-934-0*) Marvel Entmnt.

Thor: Ballad of Beta Ray Bill. Walter Simonson. 96p. 1989. pap. 9.95 (*0-87135-614-7*) Marvel Entmnt.

Thor: I Whom the Gods Destroy. Shooter et al. 64p. 1987. 5.95 (*0-87135-268-0*) Marvel Entmnt.

Thor Bridge: A Play. Mark Dunster. 1989. 4.00 (*0-89642-178-3*) Linden Pubs.

Thor Conspiracy. Larry Burkett. LC 94-23593. 336p. 1995. 16.99 (*0-8407-7801-5*) Nelson.

***Thor Conspiracy: The Seventy-Hour Countdown to Disaster.** Larry Burkett. 1996. pap. text ed. 12.99 (*0-7852-7200-3*) Nelson.

Thor Heyerdahl & the Kon-Tiki Voyage. Philip Steele. LC 93-9335. (Great Twentieth Century Expeditions Ser.). (Illus.). 32p. (J). (gr. 4-6). 1993. lib. bdg. 13.95 (*0-87518-533-9*, Dillon Silver Burdett) Silver Burdett Pr.

Thor, the Last of the Sperm Whales. Robert M. McClung. LC 87-26090. (Animal Life Cycle Ser.). 64p. (J). (gr. 3-7). 1988. reprint ed. lib. bdg. 16.50 (*0-208-02186-8*, Linnet Bks) Shoe String.

Thoracic Anesthesia. 2nd ed. Ed. by Joel A. Kaplan. (Illus.). 769p. 1991. text ed. 99.50 (*0-443-08712-1*) Churchill.

Thoracic Anesthesia. Ed. by Joel A. Kaplan. LC 82-12809. 778p. reprint ed. pap. 180.00 (*0-7837-1377-0*, 2041525) Bks Demand.

Thoracic Lumbar Spine & Spinal Cord Injuries. Ed. by P. Harris. (Advances in Neurotraumatology Ser.: Vol. 2). (Illus.). 230p. 1987. 96.00 (*0-387-81928-2*) Spr-Verlag.

Thoracic Oncology. 2nd ed. Jack Roth et al. LC 94-26869. (Illus.). 608p. 1995. text ed. 139.00 (*0-7216-4769-3*) Saunders.

Thoracic Oncology. Ed. by Noah C. Choi & Hermes C. Grillo. LC 79-63971. (Illus.). 384p. 1983. reprint ed. pap. 109.50 (*0-608-00596-7*, 2061183) Bks Demand.

Thoracic Organ Transplantation - Routine As a Challenge: Proceedings of the Third International Symposium Held in Bad Oeynhausen, 9-11 September, 1993. Ed. by Michael M. Korner et al. LC 94-3686. (Proceedings of the Third International Symposium). 350p. 1994. 201.25 (*0-444-81687-9*) Elsevier.

Thoracic Outlet Syndrome: A Common Sequela of Neck Injuries. Richard J. Sanders & Craig E. Haug. (Illus.). 348p. 1991. text ed. 79.50 (*0-397-51097-7*) Lppncott-Raven.

Thoracic Outlet Syndrome: Diagnosis & Treatment. Erich W. Pollak. (Illus.). 248p. 1986. 39.50 (*0-87993-246-5*) Fairleigh Dickinson.

Thoracic Radiology. Ed. by John D. Newell, Jr. & Robert D. Tarver. LC 92-49207. 192p. 1993. text ed. 100.00 (*0-88167-983-6*) Lppncott-Raven.

Thoracic Radiology - the Requisites. McLoud. 384p. (C). (gr. 13). 1997. text ed. 79.00 (*0-8016-6354-7*) Mosby Yr Bk.

Thoracic Spine. Ed. by Edward C. Benzel & Charles B. Stillerman. (Illus.). 400p. 1996. 145.00 (*0-942219-75-9*) Quality Med Pub.

***Thoracic Surgery.** A. G. Casson & M. R. Johnston. (Key Topics Ser.). 304p. 1997. pap. 21.95 (*1-85996-155-X*, Pub. by Bios Scientific UK) Coronet Bks.

Thoracic Surgery. Ed. by F. Griffin Pearson et al. LC 94-42025. 1995. write for info. (*0-443-08798-9*) Churchill.

Thoracic Surgery. Ed. by H. Pichelmaier & F. W. Schildberg. (Illus.). 480p. 1989. 477.00 (*0-387-18464-3*) Spr-Verlag.

Thoracic Surgical Oncology. Edward J. Beattie et al. (Illus.). 405p. 1992. text ed. 115.00 (*0-443-08589-7*) Churchill.

Thoracic Surgical Techniques. Wells & Milstein. (Illus.). 480p. 1990. text ed. 235.00 (*0-7020-1239-4*, Bailliere-Tindall) Saunders.

Thoracic Transplantation. R. Sibly & P. Calow. 512p. 1995. 125.00 (*0-86542-285-0*) Blackwell Sci.

Thoracic Trauma. R. Maurice Hood & A. W. Boyd. 448p. 1989. text ed. 147.00 (*0-7216-2353-0*) Saunders.

Thoracolumbar Spine Fractures. Ed. by Yizhar Floman et al. LC 92-48559. 528p. 1993. text ed. 136.50 (*0-7817-0049-3*) Lppncott-Raven.

Thoracolumbar Spine Fractures Without Neurologic Deficit. E. S. Stauffer. 96p. 1993. pap. 35.00 (*0-89203-100-X*) Amer Acad Ortho Surg.

Thoracoscopic Surgery. Ed. by Larry R. Kaiser & Thomas M. Daniel. LC 93-16239. (Illus.). 192p. 1993. 195.00 (*0-316-48218-8*) Little.

Thoracoscopic Surgery. Doug Wood & Thomas Marchioro. 1995. text ed. 150.00 (*0-07-071638-2*) McGraw.

Thoracoscopy for Surgeons: Diagnostic & Therapeutic. Ed. by Raymond A. Dieter, Jr. LC 94-29082. (Illus.). 271p. 1995. 98.50 (*0-89640-269-X*) Igaku-Shoin.

Thorax. Jean-Pierre Barral. LC 90-85570. (Illus.). 186p. (C). 1991. text ed. 44.00 (*0-939616-12-2*) Eastland.

Thorax. 2nd expanded rev. ed. Roussos. (Lung Biology in Health & Disease Ser.: Vol. 85, Pt. A). 1080p. 1995. 165.00 (*0-8247-9504-0*) Dekker.

Thorax. 2nd expanded rev. ed. Roussos. (Lung Biology in Health & Disease Ser.: Vol. 85, Pt. B). 1995. 165.00 (*0-8247-9600-4*) Dekker.

Thorax. 2nd expanded rev. ed. Roussos. (Lung Biology in Health & Disease Ser.: Vol. 85, Pt. C). 1144p. 1995. 165.00 (*0-8247-9601-2*) Dekker.

Thorax, Pt. A. Ed. by Charis Roussos & Peter T. Macklem. LC 85-25254. (Lung Biology in Health & Disease Ser.: No. 29). 655p. reprint ed. Part A, 655p. pap. 176.90 (*0-7837-0322-8*, 2040642) Bks Demand.

Thorax, Pt. B. Ed. by Charis Roussos & Peter T. Macklem. LC 85-25254. (Lung Biology in Health & Disease Ser.: No. 29). 955p. reprint ed. Part B, 955p. pap. 180.00 (*0-7837-0323-6*) Bks Demand.

Thoreau: A Century of Criticism. Walter R. Harding. LC 55-116. 217p. reprint ed. pap. 61.90 (*0-317-28189-5*, 2022784) Bks Demand.

Thoreau: A Chronology. V. Munoz. Tr. by W. Scott Johnson. (Libertarian & Anarchist Chronology Ser.). 1979. lib. bdg. 59.95 (*0-8490-3021-8*) Gordon Pr.

Thoreau: A Glimpse. Samuel A. Jones. LC 72-3174. (American Literature Ser.: No. 49). (Illus.). 1972. reprint ed. lib. bdg. 39.95 (*0-8383-1516-X*) M S G Haskell Hse.

Thoreau: A Naturalist's Liberty. John Hildebidle. 192p. 1983. 23.50 (*0-674-88640-2*) HUP.

Thoreau: His Home, Friends & Books. Annie R. Marble. 1972. 59.95 (*0-8490-1204-X*) Gordon Pr.

Thoreau: His Home, Friends & Books. Annie R. Marble. LC 73-85906. reprint ed. 34.50 (*0-404-04185-X*) AMS Pr.

Thoreau: His Home, Friends & Books. Annie R. Marble. (BCL1-PS American Literature Ser.). 343p. 1992. reprint ed. lib. bdg. 89.00 (*0-7812-6884-2*) Rprt Serv.

Thoreau: His Life & Aims. H. A. Page. 1972. 59.95 (*0-8490-1205-8*) Gordon Pr.

Thoreau: His Life & Aims. H. A. Page. LC 72-3653. (American Literature Ser.: No. 49). 1972. reprint ed. lib. bdg. 59.95 (*0-8383-1585-2*) M S G Haskell Hse.

Thoreau: Political Writings. Henry David Thoreau. Ed. by Nancy L. Rosenblum. (Texts in the History of Political Thought Ser.). 212p. (C). 1996. text ed. 39.95 (*0-521-47090-0*); pap. text ed. 14.95 (*0-521-47675-5*) Cambridge U Pr.

Thoreau: The Poet-Naturalist. William E. Channing, II. (Works of William Ellery Channing II). 1990. reprint ed. lib. bdg. 79.00 (*0-685-27613-9*) Rprt Serv.

Thoreau & the American Indians. Robert F. Sayre. LC 76-45910. 260p. reprint ed. pap. 74.10 (*0-8357-2555-3*, 2040246) Bks Demand.

Thoreau & the Wild Appetite. Kenneth A. Robinson. LC 80-2682. (Thoreau Ser.). (Illus.). reprint ed. 29.50 (*0-404-19079-0*) AMS Pr.

Thoreau, As Seen By His Contemporaries. Walter Harding. 1990. pap. 6.95 (*0-486-26160-3*) Dover.

Thoreau As Seen by His Contemporaries. Ed. by Walter Harding. 1991. 19.25 (*0-8446-6465-0*) Peter Smith.

Thoreau As World Traveler. John A. Christie. (Special Publication Ser.: No. 37). (Illus.). 358p. 1965. 18.00 (*0-318-12736-9*) Am Geographical.

Thoreau Centennial: Papers Marking the Observance of the 100th Anniversary of the Death of Henry David Thoreau. Ed. by Walter R. Harding. LC 65-19729. 119p. 1964. text ed. 21.50 (*0-87395-015-1*) State U NY Pr.

Thoreau Chronology. Leonard F. Kleinfeld. 1980. lib. bdg. 69.95 (*0-87700-306-8*) Revisionist Pr.

Thoreau in the Human Community. Mary E. Moller. LC 79-22549. 224p. 1980. lib. bdg. 30.00 (*0-87023-293-2*) U of Mass Pr.

Thoreau Log: A Documentary Life of Henry David Thoreau, 1817-1862. Ed. by Raymond R. Borst. (Reference Ser.). 300p. 1992. 80.00 (*0-8161-8985-4*, Hall Reference) Macmillan.

Thoreau Log: A Documentary Life of Henry David Thoreau 1817-1862. Raymond R. Borst. 1995. 24.95 (*0-7838-1399-6*) Macmillan.

Thoreau MacDonald's Notebooks. Thoreau MacDonald. Ed. by John Flood. 224p. 1980. 14.95 (*0-920806-05-8*, Pub. by Penumbra Pr CN) U of Toronto Pr.

Thoreau on Birds. Henry David Thoreau. Ed. by Francis H. Allen. LC 92-30469. (Concord Library). (Illus.). 448p. 1993. 25.00 (*0-8070-8520-0*) Beacon Pr.

Thoreau on the Art of Writing. Franklin W. Hamilton. 1967. pap. 2.00 (*0-911938-01-X*) Walden Pr.

Thoreau, Poet-Naturalist. enl. ed. William E. Channing. Ed. by Franklin B. Sanborn. LC 65-27095. (Illus.). 1902. 32.00 (*0-8196-0173-X*) Biblo.

Thoreau's Comments on the Art of Writing. Richard Dillman. 66p. (Orig.). 1987. pap. text ed. 14.00 (*0-8191-6601-4*) U Pr of Amer.

Thoreau's Complex Weave: The Writing of "A Week on the Concord & Merrimack Rivers", with the Text of the First Draft. Linck C. Johnson. LC 85-17859. xxii, 490p. 1986. text ed. 45.00 (*0-8139-1063-3*) U Pr of Va.

Thoreau's Complex Weave: The Writing of a Week on the Concord & Merrimack Rivers, with the Text of the First Draft. Linck C. Johnson. LC 85-17859. 512p. 1986. reprint ed. pap. 146.00 (*0-608-01437-0*, 2062199) Bks Demand.

***Thoreau's Fable of Inscribing.** Frederick Garber. LC 90-44497. 238p. 1991. reprint ed. pap. 67.90 (*0-608-02581-X*, 2063227) Bks Demand.

Thoreau's Garden: Native Plants for the American Landscape. Peter H. Loewer. (Illus.). 192p. 1996. 22.95 (*0-8117-1728-3*) Stackpole.

Thoreau's Guide to Cape Cod. Henry David Thoreau. Ed. by Alexander B. Adams. (Illus.). 1962. 14.50 (*0-8159-6904-X*) Devin.

Thoreau's Indian of the Mind. Elizabeth I. Hanson. LC 91-44967. (Studies in American Literature: Vol. 4). 148p. 1992. lib. bdg. 69.95 (*0-88946-170-8*) E Mellen.

Thoreau's Library. Walter R. Harding. LC 80-2507. reprint ed. 27.50 (*0-404-19055-3*) AMS Pr.

Thoreau's Maine Woods: Yesterday & Today. Cheryl Seal. (Illus.). 192p. 1992. 24.95 (*0-89909-314-0*, 80-951-8) Yankee Bks.

Thoreau's Minnesota Journey: Two Documents. Henry David Thoreau. Ed. by Walter Harding. LC 80-2524. (Thoreau Ser.). (Illus.). 80p. 1981. reprint ed. 31.50 (*0-404-19072-3*) AMS Pr.

Thoreau's Morning Work: Memory & Perception in a Week on the Concord & Merrimack Rivers, the Journal & Walden. H. Daniel Peck. 208p. (C). 1990. text ed. 30.00 (*0-300-04823-8*) Yale U Pr.

Thoreau's Morning Work: Memory & Perception in A Week on the Concord & Merrimack Rivers, the Journal, & Walden. H. Daniel Peck. 208p. 1994. pap. 14.00 (*0-300-06104-8*) Yale U Pr.

Thoreau's Nature: Ethics, Politics & the Wild. Jane Bennett. (Modernity & Political Thought Ser.: Vol. 7). 203p. 1994. 42.00 (*0-8039-3868-3*) Sage.

Thoreau's Nature: Ethics, Politics & the Wild. Jane Bennett. (Modernity & Political Thought Ser.: Vol. 7). 1994. pap. 18.95 (*0-8039-3869-1*) Sage.

Thoreau's Philosophy of Life, with Special Consideration of the Influence of Hindoo Philosophy. Helena A. Snyder. LC 80-2518. (Thoreau Ser.). 104p. reprint ed. 32.50 (*0-404-19066-9*) AMS Pr.

Thoreau's Reading: A Study in Intellectual History with Bibliographical Catalogue. Robert Sattelmeyer. 400p. 1988. text ed. 60.00 (*0-691-06745-7*) Princeton U Pr.

Thoreau's Redemptive Imagination. Frederick Garber. LC 77-73031. (Gotham Library). 229p. (C). 1977. text ed. 40.00 (*0-8147-2965-7*); pap. text ed. 16.00 (*0-8147-2966-5*) NYU Pr.

Thoreau's Seasons. Richard Lebeaux. LC 83-17982. 432p. 1984. 40.00 (*0-87023-401-3*) U of Mass Pr.

Thoreau's Wild Rhetoric. Henry Golemba. 320p. (C). 1990. text ed. 40.00 (*0-8147-3036-1*) NYU Pr.

Thoreau's World & Ours: A Natural Legacy. Ed. by Robert Baron & Edmund Schofield. LC 93-12848. (Illus.). 429p. 1993. 26.95 (*1-55591-903-0*) Fulcrum Pub.

Thorgal: The Archers. Jean Van Hamme. Tr. by Chris Tanz & Jean-Paul Bierny. (Illus.). 48p. 1988. pap. 5.95 (*0-9617885-2-6*) Ink Pub AZ.

Thorgal: The Sorceress Betrayed. Jean Van Hamme. Tr. by Chris Tanz & Jean-Paul Bierny. Orig. Title: La Magicienne Trahie & L'ile des mers gelees. (Illus.). 104p. 1988. pap. 12.95 (*0-9617885-1-8*) Ink Pub AZ.

Thorium. (Metals & Minerals Ser.). 1993. lib. bdg. 240.95 (*0-8490-8978-6*) Gordon Pr.

Thorium. 1955. 370.00 (*0-387-93227-5*) Spr-Verlag.

Thorium & Gas Cooled Reactors. J. P. Howe & G. Melese-D'Hospital. 1978. pap. 63.00 (*0-08-024208-1*, Pergamon Pr) Elsevier.

Thorium Fuel Cycle. Compiled by E. Roth. (Bibliographical Ser.: No. 39). 462p. 1972. pap. 60.00 (*92-0-054070-8*, ISP21 39, Pub. by IAEA AU) Bernan Associates.

Thorium Fuel Cycle: Proceedings. Ed. by Raymond G. Wymer. LC 67-62083. (AEC Symposium Ser.). 834p. 1968. pap. 29.25 (*0-87079-228-8*, CONF-660524); fiche 9.00 (*0-87079-229-6*, CONF-660524) DOE.

Thorium-232 & Uranium-238 see Toxicology of Radioactive Substances

Thorn. Fred Saberhagen. 1990. mass mkt. 4.95 (*0-8125-0316-3*) Tor Bks.

***Thorn & the Thistle.** Julie Moffett. 368p. (Orig.). 1997. mass mkt. 5.50 (*0-8439-4263-0*, Leisure Bks) Dorchester Pub Co.

Thorn Birds. Colleen Mccullough. 704p. 1978. mass mkt. 6.99 (*0-380-01817-9*) Avon.

Thorn-Fruit. Clifford Lanier. 1973. reprint ed. lib. bdg. 35.00 (*0-8490-1206-6*) Gordon Pr.

Thorn in Paradise. large type ed. Cathy Williams. (Harlequin Romance Ser.). 288p. 1995. lib. bdg. 18.95 (*0-263-14104-7*, Pub. by Mills & Boon UK) Thorndike Pr.

Thorn in the Chrysanthemum: Suicide & Economic Success in Modern Japan. Mamoru Iga. 286p. 1986. 45.00 (*0-520-05648-5*) U CA Pr.

Thorn in the Starfish: The Immune System & How It Works. Robert S. Desowitz. (Illus.). 1988. pap. 9.95 (*0-393-30556-2*) Norton.

Thorn of Arimathea. Frank Slaughter. 24.95 (*0-89190-288-0*) Amereon Ltd.

Thorn Witch: Biscuit, Buttons, & Pickles. E. J. Taylor. LC 91-58807. (Illus.). (J). (gr. 1-4). 1992. 12.95 (*1-56402-151-3*) Candlewick Pr.

Thornbeck. Lynda Trent. (Historical Ser.). 1994. mass mkt. 3.99 (*0-373-28832-8*, 1-28832-3) Harlequin Bks.

Thornburn's Birds of Prey. Archibald Thornburn. (C). 1990. 350.00 (*0-9516546-0-8*, Pub. by Greyfriars UK) St Mut.

Thorndike: Descendants of John Thorndike. M. H. Stafford. 349p. 1991. reprint ed. pap. 54.00 (*0-8328-2186-1*); reprint ed. lib. bdg. 64.00 (*0-8328-2185-3*) Higginson Bk Co.

***Thorndike & Nelson: A Monster Story.** Jean Jackson. (Illus.). 32p. (J). (ps-k). 1997. 15.95 (*0-7894-2452-5*) DK Pub Inc.

Thorndike-Barnhart Children's Dictionary. Ed. by Linda Cunningham. (Illus.). 832p. 1996. 15.95 (*0-06-270162-2*, Harper Ref) HarpC.

Thorndike-Barnhart Junior Dictionary. Ed. by Linda Cunningham. (Illus.). 1152p. 1996. 17.00 (*0-06-270161-4*, Harper Ref) HarpC.

Thorndike-Barnhart Student's Dictionary. Ed. by Linda Cunningham. (Illus.). 1280p. 1996. 18.00 (*0-06-270160-6*, Harper Ref) HarpC.

Thorndike Encyclopedia of Banking & Financial Tables. David Thorndike. LC 87-50721. 1792p. boxed 165.00 (*0-88712-883-1*) Warren Gorham & Lamont.

Thorndike Encyclopedia of Banking & Financial Tables. David Thorndike. LC 87-50721. 1792p. 1991. Supplement, 1991. suppl. ed. 79.00 (*0-7913-0801-4*) Warren Gorham & Lamont.

Thorne in the Flesh. Rhona Petrie. 200p. 1996. 18.50 (*0-7451-8678-5*, Black Dagger) Chivers N Amer.

Thorne Mere & the Old River Don: Illustrated Historical & Geographic Research into Much-Changed South Yorkshire River System. Martin Taylor. (C). 1989. pap. 31.00 (*1-85072-012-6*, Pub. by W Sessions UK) St Mut.

Thornes & Thrones. B. J. Hoff. 1991. pap. 9.95 (*0-87162-602-0*, D7520) Warner Pr.

***Thorne's Cove.** James C. Harper. 211p. (Orig.). 1998. mass mkt. 4.99 (*1-55237-474-2*, Pub. by Comnwlth Pub CN) Partners Pubs Grp.

Thorne's Guide to Herbal Extracts: A Compilation of Historical Uses, Vol. I. Terry Thorne. LC 93-193110. 129p. 1992. spiral bd., pap. 15.00 (*0-9643661-0-X*) Wisteria Pr.

Thorne's Guide to Herbal Extracts: A Compilation of Historical Uses, Vol. II. Terry Thorne. LC 93-193110. 127p. 1994. spiral bd., pap. 15.00 (*0-9643661-1-8*) Wisteria Pr.

Thorne's Way. Joan Hohl. 1996. mass mkt. 4.99 (*1-55166-081-4*, 1-66081-0, Mira Bks) Harlequin Bks.

***Thorne's Wife.** Joan Hohl. (Born in the U. S. A. Ser.). 1997. 4.50 (*0-373-47188-2*, 1-47188-7) Harlequin Bks.

Thorngumbald. G. S. Skeggs. (C). 1989. text ed. 35.00 (*0-948929-35-9*) St Mut.

Thorns. Shirley Buettner. (Juniper Book Ser.: No. 61). 34p. (Orig.). 1995. pap. 8.00 (*0-614-03104-4*) Juniper Pr.

Thorns among the Sagebrush. Elaine V. Bercik. 189p. 1984. 7.95 (*0-89697-161-9*) Intl Univ Pr.

Thorns & Angel Wings. Donna Laughlin. LC 91-75212. 55p. 1992. pap. 6.95 (*1-55523-462-3*) Winston-Derek.

***Thorns & Arabesques: Contexts for Conrad's Fiction.** William W. Bonney. LC 80-13308. 256p. 1980. reprint ed. pap. 73.00 (*0-608-03641-2*, 2064467) Bks Demand.

Thorns & Roses. Robert P. Clayton. (Orig.). 1996. pap. write for info. (*1-57553-116-X*) Watermrk Pr.

Thorns & Thistles: Diplomacy Between Henry VIII & James V - 1528-1542. C. Patrick Hotle. LC 96-21503. 234p. 1996. lib. bdg. 39.50 (*0-7618-0405-6*) U Pr of Amer.

Thorns & Thistles: Juvenile Delinquents in the United States, 1825-1940. Robert M. Mennel. LC 72-95187. 259p. reprint ed. pap. 73.90 (*0-317-41775-4*, 2025640) Bks Demand.

Thorns Are Green My Friend. Lourdes G. Franca & Pablo Cano. LC 88-80862. (Coleccion Arte). (Illus.). 54p. 1990. text ed. 39.00 (*0-89729-480-7*) Ediciones.

Thorns in the Heart: A Christian's Guide to Dealing with Pain. Steven Stiles. 174p. (Orig.). 1994. pap. 6.50 (*0-88243-347-4*, 02-0347) Gospel Pub.

Thorns of Resistance. Deane A. Tack & Elmer Berger. LC 93-90051. 320p. 1993. pap. 15.00 (*0-9635982-0-1*); text ed. 20.00 (*0-9635982-1-X*) Destra Pubs.

Thorns of the Sun. Marilyn Brown. 1996. pap. 9.95 (*1-55503-394-6*, 01111051) Covenant Comms.

***Thorns on the Laurel.** Catherine T. Gonzalez. 103p. 1996. 10.95 (*0-9653328-1-0*) Duckworth Pr.

Thorns, Thistles & Chrome. Joe E. Pierce. 160p. 1984. pap. 6.95 (*0-913244-63-5*) Hapi Pr.

Thornton Dial: Images of the Tiger. Amiri Baraka & Thomas McEvilley. LC 93-15002. 1993. 45.00 (*0-8109-3217-2*) Abrams.

Thornton Guide to Hong Kong Companies. (Illus.). 529p. 1995. write for info. (*962-7982-05-9*, Pub. by Edinburgh Finan HK) Am Educ Systs.

Thornton Guide to the Companies of Singapore & Malaysia. (Illus.). 758p. 1995. write for info. (*0-614-17581-X*, Pub. by Edinburgh Finan HK) Am Educ Systs.

Thornton Guide to the Companies of Thailand. 431p. 1996. write for info. (*962-7982-08-3*, Pub. by Edinburgh Finan HK) Am Educ Systs.

Thornton Romances: The Early English Metrical Romances of Perceval, Isumbras, Eglamour & Degravant. Ed. by James O. Halliwell-Phillipps. LC 73-177456. reprint ed. 85.00 (*0-404-50130-3*) AMS Pr.

Thornton Wilder: A Bibliographical Checklist of Work by & about Thornton Wilder. Compiled by Richard H. Goldstone & Gary Anderson. LC 79-6273. (Studies in Modern Literature: No. 7). 120p. 1982. 34.50 (*0-404-18046-9*) AMS Pr.

Thornton Wilder: A Reference Guide. Claudette M. Walsh. (Reference Ser.). 250p. 1993. 55.00 (*0-8161-8790-8*, Hall Reference) Macmillan.

Thornton Wilder & His Public. Amos N. Wilder. LC 79-26564. 102p. reprint ed. pap. 29.10 (*0-685-23665-X*, 2029113) Bks Demand.

***Thornton Wilder Reader.** Thornton Wilder. 1997. 20.00 (*0-679-60256-9*, Modern Lib) Random.

Thornton's Medical Books, Libraries & Collectors. Ed. by Alain Besson. (Illus.). 450p. 1990. text ed. 89.95 (*0-566-05481-7*, Pub. by Gower UK) Ashgate Pub Co.

Thorny Gates of Learning in Sung China: A Social History of Examinations. John Chaffee. LC 94-18315. 280p. 1995. pap. text ed. 19.95 (*0-7914-2424-3*) State U NY Pr.

Thorny Gates of Learning in Sung China: A Social History of Examinations. John W. Chaffee. LC 94-18315. 280p. 1995. text ed. 59.50 (*0-7914-2423-5*) State U NY Pr.

***Thorny Rose of Texas.** Mike Shropshire & Frank Schaefer. 272p. 4.98 (*0-8317-7026-0*) Smithmark.

Thorny Rose of Texas: An Intimate Portrait of Governor Ann Richards. Mike Shropshire & Frank Schaefer. LC 93-42170. 1994. 19.95 (*1-55972-232-0*) Carol Pub Group.

Thornyhold. Mary Stewart. 1989. mass mkt. 5.99 (*0-449-21712-4*, Crest) Fawcett.

***Thorold Dickinson & the British Cinema.** Jeffrey Richards. (Filmmakers Ser.: No. 54). (Illus.). 256p. 1997. 49.00 (*0-8108-3279-8*) Scarecrow.

Thorough & Fair: Creating Routes to Success for Mexican-American Students. Alicia Sosa. 63p. (Orig.). 1993. pap. 10.00 (*1-880785-10-2*) ERIC-CRESS.

Thorough-Bass Accompaniment According to Johann David Heinichen. rev. ed. George Buelow. LC 92-16780. (Illus.). xviii, 462p. 1992. pap. text ed. 25.00 (*0-8032-6106-3*, Bison Books) U of Nebr Pr.

Thorough Earth. Louis D. Brodsky. LC 89-50805. 52p. 1989. 18.95 (*1-877770-03-5*); pap. 12.50 (*1-877770-04-3*); pap. 19.95 incl. audio (*1-877770-06-X*); audio 12.95 (*1-877770-05-1*) Time Being Bks.

Thorough View Of The Body Of Christ. Witness Lee. 57p. 2.25 (*0-87083-512-2*, 08030001) Living Stream Ministry.

Thoroughbred Handicapping As an Investment. Dick Mitchell. 300p. 1986. text ed. 39.95 (*0-9614168-3-1*) Cynthia Pub Co.

Thoroughbred Handicapping the Computer Way. Howard Berenbon. LC 95-68650. 65p. 1995. pap. 19.95 (*0-9646207-0-7*) Soft Exchange.

Thoroughbred Hookers I Have Known (Items to Make You Chuckle) Don McAnally. 72p. 1991. pap. 5.95 (*0-9630282-1-9*) McAnally & Assocs.

***Thoroughbred Horse.** (Learning about Horses Ser.). (Illus.). 48p. (J). (gr. 3-7). 1995. 18.40 (*0-516-35245-8*) Childrens.

Thoroughbred Horse. Gail B. Stewart. (Learning about Horses Ser.). 48p. (J). (gr. 3-4). 1994. lib. bdg. 17.80 (*1-56065-245-4*) Capstone Pr.

Thoroughbred Horses. Janet L. Gammie. LC 95-1508. (Horses Ser.). (J). 1995. lib. bdg. 13.98 (*1-56239-437-1*) Abdo & Dghtrs.

Thoroughbred Pedigrees Simplified. Miles Napier. 76p. 1990. pap. 21.00 (*0-85131-351-5*, Pub. by J A Allen & Co UK) St Mut.

Thoroughbred Prequel: Ashleigh's Hope. Joanna Campbell. 192p. 1996. mass mkt. 3.99 (*0-06-106395-9*, Harp PBks) HarpC.

Thoroughbred Super: Ashleigh's Christmas Miracle. Joanna Campbell. 256p. (J). (gr. 4-7). 1994. mass mkt. 3.99 (*0-06-106249-9*) HarpC Child Bks.

Thoroughly Efficient Navy. William W. Kaufmann. LC 87-11596. (Studies in Defense Policy). 123p. 1987. pap. 10.95 (*0-8157-4845-0*) Brookings.

Thoroughly Fit: How to Make a Lifestyle Change in 90 Days: A Motivational Devotional Journal. Becky Tirabassi & Candice Copeland-Brooks. 208p. 1993. pap. 12.99 (*0-310-40301-4*) Zondervan.

Thoroughly Modern Grandma: Quaint She Ain't. Ed. by Louise Wollman. LC 89-63622. (Illus.). 64p. 1990. 7.99 (*0-88088-211-5*) Peter Pauper.

Thorp: The Whitehall Nightmare. Aubrey. 1993. pap. 11.95 (*1-897766-07-6*, Pub. by Jon Pubng UK) LPC InBook.

Thorpe's Dictionary of Applied Chemistry, 11 vols. 4th enl. rev. ed. Incl. A-Bl. Jocelyn F. Thorpe & M. A. Whiteley. LC 37-28650. pap. 160.00 (*0-317-10765-8*); Vol. 2. Bl - Chemical Analysis. Jocelyn F. Thorpe & M. A. Whiteley. LC 37-28650. pap. 160.00 (*0-317-10766-6*); Vol. 3. Chemical Calculations - Diffusion. Jocelyn F. Thorpe & M. A. Whiteley. LC 37-28650. pap. 158.00 (*0-317-10767-4*); Vol. 4. Digallic Acid - Feeding Stuffs. Jocelyn F. Thorpe & M. A. Whiteley. LC 37-28650. reprint ed. pap. 156.80 (*0-317-10768-2*); Vol. 5. Feh - Glass. Jocelyn F. Thorpe & M. A. Whiteley. LC 37-28650. reprint ed. pap. 156.00 (*0-317-10769-0*); Vol. 6. Glau - Inv (Index to Vols. I-VI). Jocelyn F. Thorpe & M. A. Whiteley. LC 37-28650. reprint ed. pap. 155.80 (*0-317-10770-4*); Vol. 7. Iodazide - Metegallic Acid. Jocelyn F. Thorpe & M. A. Whiteley. LC 37-28650. reprint ed. pap. 160.00 (*0-317-10771-2*); Vol. 8. . Jocelyn F. Thorpe. Ed. by M. A. Whiteley. LC 37-28650. reprint ed. pap. 160.00 (*0-317-10772-0*); Vol. 9. Oils, Fatty -Pituitary Body. Jocelyn F. Thorpe & M. A. Whiteley. LC 37-28650. reprint ed. pap. 160.00 (*0-317-10773-9*); Vol. 10. Plagioclase - Sodium. Jocelyn F. Thorpe & M. A. Whiteley. LC 37-28650. reprint ed. pap. 160.00 (*0-317-10774-7*); Vol. 12. General Index. LC 37-28650. 191p. reprint ed. pap. 54.50 (*0-317-10775-5*, 2005892); LC 37-28650. reprint ed. Set pap. write for info. (*0-318-58066-7*, 2004549) Bks Demand.

Thor's Home. Rodney Nelson. (Kestrel Ser.: No. 8). 28p. 1983. pap. 3.00 (*0-914974-40-8*) Holmgangers.

Thorsby. large type ed. Joan Hessayon. 352p. 1989. 25.99 (*0-7089-2037-3*) Ulverscroft.

Thorson's Encyclopedia Dictionary: Homeopath. Harald Gaier. 1992. 55.00 (*0-7225-1823-4*) Thorsons SF.

Thorsons Guide to Amino Acids. Leon Chaitow. 208p. (Orig.). 1991. pap. 13.00 (*0-7225-2492-7*) Thorsons SF.

Thorsons Introductory Guide to Herbalism. Christopher Robbins. 1994. pap. 8.00 (*0-7225-2791-8*) Thorsons SF.

Thorsons Introductory Guide to Homeopathy: A Patient's Guide. Anne Clover. (Illus.). 1992. pap. 8.00 (*0-7225-2529-X*) Thorsons SF.

Thorsons Introductory Guide to Kinesiology: Touch for Health. Maggie La Tourelle & Anthea Courtenay. 1993. pap. 8.00 (*0-7225-2699-7*) Thorsons SF.

Thorsons Introductory Guide to Reflexology: A Patient's Guide. Nicola M. Hall. (Illus.). 128p. 1996. pap. 8.00 (*0-7225-2528-1*) Thorsons SF.

Thorsons Introductory Guide to the Alexander Technique. Jonathan Drake. 1993. pap. 8.00 (*0-7225-2779-9*) Thorsons SF.

Thorstein Veblen. rev. ed. David Riesman. 248p. (C). 1994. pap. 24.95 (*1-56000-776-1*) Transaction Pubs.

Thorstein Veblen: A Critical Reappraisal-Lectures & Essays Commemorating the Hundredth Anniversary of Veblen's Birth. Ed. by Douglas F. Dowd. LC 77-9623. 328p. 1977. reprint ed. text ed. 35.00 (*0-8371-9714-7*, DOTV, Greenwood Pr) Greenwood.

Thorstein Veblen: Critical Assessments, 4 vols. Ed. by John C. Wood. LC 93-16581. (Critical Assessments of Leading Economists Ser.). 2048p. (C). (gr. 13). 1993. Set. boxed, text ed. 545.00 (*0-415-07487-8*, B0759) Routledge.

Thorstein Veblen: The Carleton College Veblen Seminar Essays. Ed. by Carlton C. Qualey. LC 68-28400. 170p. 1968. text ed. 45.00 (*0-231-03111-4*) Col U Pr.

Thorstein Veblen & His America. Joseph Dorfman. LC 64-7662. (Reprints of Economic Classics Ser.). (Illus.). 572p. 1992. reprint ed. 49.50 (*0-678-00007-7*) Kelley.

Thorstein Veblen & His Critics, 1891-1963: Conservative, Liberal, & Radical Perspectives. Rick Tilman. 388p. 1992. text ed. 49.50 (*0-691-04286-1*) Princeton U Pr.

An Asterisk (*) at the beginning of an entry indicates that the title is appearing in BIP for the first time.

Thorstein Veblen & the Institutionalists: A Study in the Social Philosophy of Economics. David W. Seckler. LC 73-91642. 176p. reprint ed. pap. 50.20 (*0-8357-5498-7*, 2035112) Bks Demand.

Thorstein Veblen & the Persistence of Capitalism: Work, Consumption, Patriotism & Social Integration. Stephen Edgell. (Studies in Institutional Economics). 224p. (C). 1997. pap. text ed. 24.95 (*1-56324-117-X*) M E Sharpe.

Thorstein Veblen & the Persistence of Capitalism: Work, Consumption, Patriotism & Social Integration. Stephen Edgell. (Studies in Institutional Economics). 224p. (C). (gr. 13). 1997. text ed. 50.00 (*1-56324-116-1*) M E Sharpe.

Thorstein Veblen, 1857-1929. Ed. by Mark Blaug. (Pioneers in Economics Ser.: Vol. 32). 352p. 1992. 125.00 (*1-85278-495-4*) E Elgar.

Thorstein Veblen's Social Theory. Arthur K. Davis. Ed. by Harriet Zuckerman & Robert K. Merton. LC 79-8989. (Dissertations on Sociology Ser.). 1980. lib. bdg. 46.95 (*0-405-12961-0*) Ayer.

Thoscanello de la Musica. fac. ed. Pietro Aaron. (Monuments of Music & Music Literature in Facsimile Ser., Series II: Vol. 69). 1969. lib. bdg. 42.50 (*0-8450-2269-5*) Broude.

Those Amazing Ants. Patricia B. Demuth. LC 93-1769. (Illus.). 32p. (J). 1994. text ed. 14.95 (*0-02-728467-0*, Mac Bks Young Read) S&S Childrens.

Those Amazing Dinosaur Mazes. John Cartwright. (J). 1989. pap. 1.50 (*0-8167-1220-4*) Troll Communs.

Those Amazing Methodists. Aiden W. Tozer. (Heritage Ser.). pap. 1.99 (*0-87509-609-3*) Chr Pubns.

Those Amazing Tables: Teaching Multiplication Through Patterns & Color Strips. Joe Lieberman. (J). (gr. 4-7). 1983. pap. 11.95 (*0-201-48019-0*) Addison-Wesley.

Those Amazing Tables: Teaching Multiplication Through Patterns & Color Strips. Joe Lieberman. 64p. (J). (gr. 3-8). 1983. pap. text ed. 11.95 (*0-914040-98-7*) Cuisenaire.

Those Annoying Post Bros. Disturb the Neighbors. Matt Howarth. (Illus.). 96p. (Orig.). 1995. pap. 9.99 (*1-883847-15-X*) MU Press.

Those Annoying Post Brothers in Das Loot. Matt Howarth & Lou Stathis. (Illus.). 160p. (Orig.). 1994. pap. write for info. (*1-883847-06-0*) MU Press.

Those Baby Blues. Helen Conrad. (Hometown Reunion Ser.). 1997. mass mkt. 4.50 (*0-373-82553-6*, 1-82553-8) Silhouette.

Those Banded & Coherent. Angela Kelly. 1994. pap. 6.95 (*0-685-72050-0*) Pudding Hse Pubns.

***Those Barren Leaves.** Aldous Huxley. LC 97-25220. 320p. 1998. reprint ed. pap. 13.95 (*1-56478-169-0*) Dalkey Arch.

Those Bicentennials...from American Rails. G. R. Cockle. LC 78-50294. (Illus.). 1986. 35.00 (*0-916160-04-1*) G R Cockle.

Those Billington Boys: A Pilgrim Story. Janice Glover. (Illus.). 40p. (Orig.). (J). (gr. 3-6). 1994. pap. text ed. 10.00 (*1-883613-02-7*) Byte Size.

Those Black Diamond Men. William F. Gibbons. LC 74-22785. (Labor Movement in Fiction & Non-Fiction Ser.). reprint ed. 47.50 (*0-404-58431-4*) AMS Pr.

Those Bloomin' Books: A Handbook for Extending Thinking Skills. Carol S. Kruise. LC 86-27862. xii, 217p. 1986. pap. text ed. 22.00 (*0-87287-548-2*) Libs Unl.

Those Born at Koona. John Smyly & Carolyn Smyly. (Illus.). 120p. pap. 12.95 (*0-88839-101-3*) Hancock House.

Those Buried Texans, No Stone Unturned. Tom Allen. LC 80-82288. (Illus.). 192p. (Orig.). (J). (gr. 4 up). 1980. pap. 6.95 (*0-937460-00-1*) Hendrick-Long.

Those Calculating Crows! A. Wakefield & C. Hale. (J). 1996. 16.00 (*0-689-80483-0*) S&S Childrens.

Those Can-Do Pigs. David McPhail. LC 96-14689. (Illus.). 32p. (J). (ps-4). 1996. pap. 14.99 (*0-525-45495-0*) Dutton Child Bks.

Those Celadon Blues. rev. ed. Robert Tichane & W. G. Lawrence. LC 83-62553. (Oriental Glaze Ser.). (Illus.). 214p. 1983. 22.00 (*0-914267-03-5*) NYS Inst Glaze.

***Those Courageous Women of the Civil War.** Karen Zeinert. LC 97-21485. (J). 1998. lib. bdg. write for info. (*0-7613-0212-3*) Millbrook Pr.

Those Crazy Ladies in the House on the Corner. Pat Cook. 1993. pap. 5.00 (*0-87129-301-3*, T94) Dramatic Pub.

Those Crazy Wonderful Years: When We Ran Warner Brothers. Stuart Jerome. (Illus.). 256p. 1983. 14.95 (*0-8184-0343-8*) Carol Pub Group.

Those Damn Islands: Quemoy, Matsu & Nuclear Brinkmanship, 1945-58. Pruessen. 1994. 22.95 (*0-02-925475-2*) S&S Trade.

***Those Damn Republicans: Let's Give 'em Hell.** Mo H. Trueman. 128p. 1995. pap. text ed. write for info. (*0-9648863-6-7*) Progress Products.

Those Darn Dithers. Sid Hite. 160p. (YA). (gr. 7 up). 1996. 15.95 (*0-8050-3838-8*, B Martin BYR) H Holt & Co.

Those Devils in Baggy Pants. Ross S. Carter. 1976. 24.95 (*0-8488-1265-4*) Amereon Ltd.

Those Devils in Baggy Pants. Ross S. Carter. 192p. 1987. reprint ed. lib. bdg. 25.95 (*0-89966-613-2*) Buccaneer Bks.

Those Earnest Victorians. Esme Wingfield-Stratford. 1990. 14.50 (*0-8446-0966-8*) Peter Smith.

Those Elegant Decorums: The Concept of Propriety in Jane Austen's Novels. Jane Nardin. LC 73-4821. 168p. 1973. text ed. 29.50 (*0-87395-236-7*) State U NY Pr.

Those Episkopols. rev. ed. Dennis R. Maynard. LC 94-92277. Orig. Title: Episcopalians: Following in the Way of Jesus. 70p. (Orig.). 1994. pap. 8.00 (*1-885985-02-9*) Dionysus Pubns.

Those Europeans. Sisley Huddleston. LC 79-90647. (Essay Index Reprint Ser.). 1977. 21.95 (*0-8369-1218-7*) Ayer.

Those Extra Chances in Bridge. Terence Reese & Roger Trezel. (Master Class Ser.). (Illus.). 128p. 1987. pap. 7.95 (*0-575-02634-0*, Pub. by V Gollancz UK) Trafalgar.

Those Fabulous Fifties at WKU. Turner Publishing Company Staff. LC 89-50832. 96p. 1989. 39.95 (*0-938021-47-8*) Turner Pub KY.

Those Fabulous Frogs. Melvin Berger. Ed. by Janet Reed. (Ranger Rick Science Spectacular Ser.). 16p. (J). (gr. 2-4). 1994. pap. 14.95 (*1-56784-208-9*) Newbridge Comms.

Those Fabulous Frogs: Student Book. Melvin Berger. Ed. by Janet Reed. (Ranger Rick Science Spectacular Ser.). (Illus.). 16p. (Orig.). (J). (gr. 2-4). 1996. pap. write for info. (*1-56784-233-X*) Newbridge Comms.

***Those Fabulous Frogs: Theme Pack.** Melvin Berger. Ed. by Janet Reed. (Ranger Rick Science Spectacular Ser.). (Illus.). (Orig.). (J). (gr. 2-4). 1996. pap. write for info. (*1-56784-268-2*) Newbridge Comms.

Those Fabulous Serial Heroines. Buck Rainey. (Illus.). 523p. 1990. pap. text ed. 29.95 (*0-936505-10-9*) World Yesterday.

Those Fabulous Serial Heroines: Their Lives & Films. Buck Rainey. LC 88-11369. (Illus.). 537p. 1990. 62.50 (*0-8108-1911-2*) Scarecrow.

Those Fascinating Little Lamps. John F. Solverson. 1988. pap. 7.98 (*0-915410-42-7*) Antique Pubns.

Those Fascinating Little Lamps Price Guide. John F. Solverson. 1988. 5.98 (*0-915410-46-X*) Antique Pubns.

Those Fascinating Paper Dolls: An Illustrated Handbook for Collectors. Marion Howard. (Illus.). 320p. 1981. pap. 10.95 (*0-486-24055-X*) Dover.

***Those Fiendish Years: Interview with a Sex Fiend.** Pete McKenna. (Illus.). 128p. (Orig.). 1997. pap. 26.95 (*1-898927-55-3*, Pub. by S T Pubng UK) AK Pr Dist.

Those Fragile Years. large type ed. Rose Franken. 528p. 1983. 25.99 (*0-7089-0957-4*) Ulverscroft.

Those Glittering Years. Alida Harvie. (Illus.). 232p. (C). 1988. 40.00 (*0-7212-0597-6*, Pub. by Regency Press UK) St Mut.

Those Glorious Days: Louisville As Georgia's Capital 1796-1807. Y. Lynn Holmes. LC 96-30440. (Illus.). 128p. (Orig.). 1996. pap. 15.95 (*0-86554-527-8*, MUP/P149) Mercer Univ Pr.

***Those Glorious Days: Louisville As Georgia's Capital 1796-1807.** Y. Lynn Holmes. (Illus.). 128p. (Orig.). 1996. 24.95 (*0-86554-540-5*, MUP/H414) Mercer Univ Pr.

Those Glorious Glamour Years. Margaret Bailey. 1983. pap. 19.95 (*0-8065-0860-4*, Citadel Pr) Carol Pub Group.

Those Glorious Glamour Years: The Great Hollywood Costume Designs of the Thirties. Margaret J. Bailey. (Illus.). 352p. 1982. 25.00 (*0-8065-0784-5*, Citadel Pr) Carol Pub Group.

Those Good Old Days in the Black Hills. George Moses. 120p. (Orig.). 1991. pap. text ed. write for info. (*0-913062-01-4*) Fenwyn Pr.

Those Great Cowboy Sidekicks. David Rothel. LC 84-10513. 338p. 1984. 45.00 (*0-8108-1707-1*) Scarecrow.

Those Green Things. Kathy Stinson. (Illus.). 32p. (J). (ps-2). 1995. pap. 4.95 (*1-55037-376-5*, Pub. by Annick CN); lib. bdg. 15.95 (*1-55037-377-3*, Pub. by Annick CN) Firefly Bks Ltd.

Those Having Torches. Mount Holyoke College Staff. LC 68-57335. (Essay Index Reprint Ser.). 1977. 18.95 (*0-8369-0716-7*) Ayer.

Those Hours Spent Outdoors: Reflections on Hunting & Fishing. William G. Tapply. 224p. 1990. pap. 7.95 (*0-380-70820-5*) Avon.

Those I Guard. Karl Kirchwey. LC 93-12729. 1993. 18.95 (*0-15-190170-8*); pap. write for info. (*0-15-190120-1*); pap. 10.95 (*0-15-690120-X*) HarBrace.

***Those Icky Sticky Smelly Cavity-Causing but--Invisible Germs.** Illus. by Julie Stricklin. (J). 1997. write for info. (*1-884834-30-2*) Redleaf Pr.

Those Incomparable Bonanzas. 9th ed. Larry A. Ball. LC 73-187284. (Illus.). 219p. 1971. reprint ed. 39.95 (*0-9641514-1-3*) Ball Pubns.

Those Incredible B2FDC-B2J4C's! see Bicentennial Two Dollar Bill Cancellations

Those Incredible Christians. Hugh J. Schonfield. 266p. 1910. pap. 14.95 (*0-906540-71-2*) Element MA.

Those Incredible Women of World War II. Karen Zeinert. LC 94-2579. (Illus.). 112p. (YA). (gr. 7 up). 1994. lib. bdg. 17.90 (*1-56294-434-7*) Millbrook Pr.

Those Inner Cities: Reconciling the Social & Economic Aims of Urban Policy. Brian Robson. (Illus.). 264p. 1989. 65.00 (*0-19-874148-0*) OUP.

***Those Irrepressible Toys.** Darlene Arden. LC 97-15941. 1997. pap. 14.95 (*0-87605-649-4*) Howell Bk.

Those Kings & Queens of Old Hawaii: A Mele to Their Memory. Paul Bailey. LC 75-259. (Illus.). 381p. 1975. 31.95 (*0-87026-035-9*) Westernlore.

Those Legendary Men of the Wild West. Phyllis Zauner. (Western Mini-Histories Ser.). (Illus.). 64p. (Orig.). 1991. pap. 5.95 (*0-936914-24-6*) Zanel Pubns.

Those Lips, Those Eyes. Edward Z. Epstein & Lou Valentino. (Illus.). 128p. 1992. 35.00 (*1-55972-142-1*, Birch Ln Pr) Carol Pub Group.

***Those Loving Ducks: Coloring Book.** Delphine Siggers-Williams & George A. Harley. (Illus.). iv, 30p. (Orig.). (J). (ps-6). 1996. wbk. ed., spiral bd., pap. 10.95 (*0-9656591-0-0*) D Siggers-Williams.

***Those Magical Red Sneaks.** Jack Dyville & Lawrence Wankel. (Orig.). pap. 4.50 (*0-614-23028-4*) I E Clark.

***Those Magical Red Sneaks.** Jack Dyville. (Illus.). 51p. (Orig.). 1996. pap. 4.50 (*0-88680-429-9*) I E Clark.

Those Magical Years: The Making of Nigerian Literature: 1948-1966. Robert M. Wren. 140p. (Orig.). 1991. 22.00 (*0-89410-655-4*, Three Contnts); pap. 14.00 (*0-89410-656-2*, Three Contnts) Lynne Rienner.

Those Magnificent Cowgirls. Milt Riske. LC 83-71805. (Illus.). 130p. 1984. pap. 15.00 (*0-913701-00-9*) Wyoming Pub.

Those Magnificent Men in Flying Machines. John Burke. 20.95 (*0-8488-0374-4*) Amereon Ltd.

Those Magnificent Old Steam Fire Engines. W. Fred Conway. LC 96-83534. (Illus.). 304p. 1996. 29.95 (*0-925165-19-0*) Fire Buff Hse.

Those Magnificent Trains: An American Anthology. rev. ed. Charles E. Ditlefsen. (Illus.). 104p. 1997. pap. 17.95 (*1-55912-154-8*) CEDCO Pub.

Those Many-Splendored Faraway Places. J. Paul Werner. (Illus.). 304p. 1976. lib. bdg. 8.95 (*0-9601368-1-9*, 3455) J P Werner.

***Those Mean Nasty Dirty Downright Disgusting but--Invisible Germs.** Judith Rice. LC 97-9060. (J). 1997. write for info. (*1-884834-31-0*) Redleaf Pr.

Those Move Easiest Who Have Learned to Dance: Collections of Poems by Writers in Delaware, Maryland, Virginia, & the District of Columbia. Compiled by Joseph D. Adams. (Poet's Domain Ser.: 10). 160p. (Orig.). 1994. pap. text ed. 7.50 (*1-880016-15-X*) Road Pubs.

Those Mysterious Dinosaurs. Gina Ingoglia. (Golden Little Look-Look Bks.). (Illus.). 24p. (J). (ps-3). 1989. pap. write for info. (*0-307-11747-2*, Golden Books) Western Pub.

Those Mysterious Dinosaurs: A Biblical Approach for Children, Their Parents & Their Teachers. 2nd ed. Norma A. Whitcomb. (Illus.). 125p. (J). (gr. 4 up). 1993. reprint ed. pap. text ed. 11.99 (*0-9635049-0-8*); reprint ed. Spiral bdg. spiral bd. 7.20 (*0-685-67781-8*) Whitcomb Minist.

Those Mysterious Dinosaurs see Esos Dinosaurios Misteriosos

Those Navy Guys & Their PBYs: The Aleutian Solution. Elmer Freeman. 1992. 18.95 (*0-9632463-0-5*) Kedging Pub.

Those Not Elect. Leonie Adams. (BCL1-PS American Literature Ser.). 50p. 1992. reprint ed. lib. bdg. 59.00 (*0-7812-6913-X*) Rprt Serv.

Those Nut-Cracking Elizabethans. W. J. Lawrence. LC 74-98684. (Studies in Drama: No. 39). 1970. reprint ed. lib. bdg. 49.95 (*0-8383-0988-7*) M S G Haskell Hse.

Those of Little Note: Gender, Race, & Class in Historical Archaeology. Ed. by Elizabeth M. Scott. (Illus.). 240p. (Orig.). 1994. pap. text ed. 24.95 (*0-8165-1499-2*) U of Ariz Pr.

Those of the Forest. Wallace B. Grange. 1990. pap. 9.95 (*1-55971-083-7*) NorthWord.

Those of the Forest. Wallace B. Grange. Ed. by Chuck Petrie. (Illus.). 336p. (YA). (gr. 6 up). 1989. reprint ed. 19.50 (*0-932558-49-6*, 1485) Willow Creek Pr.

Those of the Gray Wind: The Sandhill Cranes. Paul A. Johnsgard. LC 86-4292. (Illus.). xii, 116p. 1986. reprint ed. pap. 6.00 (*0-8032-7566-8*, Bison Books) U of Nebr Pr.

Those Old Yellow Dog Days: Frontier Journalism in Arizona, 1859-1912. William H. Lyon. LC 93-49523. (Illus.). 272p. 1994. 29.95 (*0-910037-32-9*) AZ Hist Soc.

Those Other People. Alice Childress. LC 88-10309. 144p. (YA). (gr. 8 up). 1989. 14.95 (*0-399-21510-7*, Putnam) Putnam Pub Group.

Those Other Religions in Your Neighborhood: Loving Your Neighbor When You Don't Know How. Terry C. Muck. LC 92-14188. 176p. 1992. pap. 10.99 (*0-310-54041-0*) Zondervan.

Those People: Humorous Drawings by Jeff Foxworthy. Illus. by Jeff Foxworthy. 1996. pap. 7.95 (*1-56352-297-7*) Longstreet Pr Inc.

Those People: The Subculture of a Housing Project. Colette Petonnet. Tr. by Rita Smidt from FRE. LC 72-825. (Contributions in Sociology Ser.: No. 10). 293p. 1973. text ed. 55.00 (*0-8371-6393-5*, PTP/, Greenwood Pr) Greenwood.

Those People at That Church: The St. Francis Lutheran Cookbook. Compiled by Wayne A. Strei. (Illus.). 256p. 1994. pap. 18.95 (*0-9642337-1-1*) St Francis Luth Church.

***Those Playful Bunnies.** (J). Date not set. pap. 4.95 (*0-448-40902-X*) Putnam Pub Group.

Those Powerful Years: The South Coast & Los Angeles 1887-1917. 2nd ed. Joseph S. O'Flaherty. LC 92-81270. (Illus.). 357p. 1992. 29.95 (*0-914421-06-9*) Hist Soc So CA.

Those Preachin' Women, Vol. 1. Ed. by Ella P. Mitchell. 128p. 1985. pap. 11.00 (*0-8170-1073-4*) Judson.

***Those Preaching Women, Vol. 3.** Ed. by Ella P. Mitchell. 128p. (Orig.). 1996. pap. 11.00 (*0-8170-1249-4*) Judson.

Those Preaching Women: More Sermons by Black Women Preachers, Vol. 2. Ed. by Ella P. Mitchell. 112p. 1988. pap. 11.00 (*0-8170-1131-5*) Judson.

Those Professionals. Frank Kubic. LC 94-65545. 288p. 1994. pap. 15.00 (*0-9636320-1-9*) Nuggets Wisdom.

Those Pullman Blues: An Oral History of the African American Railroad Attendant. David Perata. 250p. 1996. pap. 28.95 (*0-8057-4520-3*) Macmillan.

Those Puzzling Parables. Jack B. Scott. (Orig.). 1987. teacher ed. 3.95 (*0-934688-28-1*); pap. text ed. 5.95 (*0-934688-27-3*) Great Comm Pubns.

***Those Remarkable Mooneys.** Larry A. Ball. (Illus.). 320p. 1997. 39.95 (*0-9641514-9-9*) Ball Pubns.

Those Remarkable Women of the American Revolution. Karen Zeinert. LC 95-47609. (Illus.). 96p. (YA). (gr. 7 up). 1996. lib. bdg. 20.90 (*1-56294-657-9*) Millbrook Pr.

Those Southern Milners: A Collection of Record Abstracts for the Southern States Between 1606 & 1850 with Biographical & Historical Sketches, Family Records, & Genealogies up to 1900. Virginia S. Hershey. (Illus.). 426p. 1980. 40.00 (*0-9605320-0-5*, TX-578-128) Hershey.

Those Spirited Women of the Early West. Phyllis Zauner. LC 89-50594. (Western Mini-Histories Ser.). (Illus.). 64p. (Orig.). 1989. pap. 5.95 (*0-936914-21-1*) Zanel Pubns.

Those Strange Louisiana Names. Codman Parkerson. 1969. pap. 3.95 (*1-57980-038-6*) Claitors.

Those Strenuous Dames of the Colorado Prairie. Nell B. Propst. (Illus.). 310p. 1994. reprint ed. pap. 15.95 (*0-9634839-6-X*) Tamarack Bks.

Those Summer Girls I Never Met. Richard Peck. 192p. (J). (gr. k up). 1989. pap. 3.50 (*0-440-20457-7*, LLL BDD) BDD Bks Young Read.

Those Summers. Aliki. LC 95-1195. (Illus.). 40p. (J). (ps-3). 1996. 14.95 (*0-06-024937-4*); lib. bdg. 14.89 (*0-06-024938-2*) HarpC Child Bks.

Those Swinging Years: The Autobiography of Charlie Barnet. Charlie Barnet & Stanley Dance. (Illus.). 245p. 1992. reprint ed. pap. 12.95 (*0-306-80492-1*) Da Capo.

Those Terrible Carpetbaggers. Richard N. Current. (Illus.). 494p. 1988. 35.00 (*0-19-504872-5*) OUP.

Those Terrible Toy Breakers. (Parents Magazine Press Read-Aloud Library). (Illus.). 42p. (J). (ps-3). 1992. lib. bdg. 17.27 (*0-8368-0889-4*) Gareth Stevens Inc.

Those Terrible Toy-Breakers. David McPhail. LC 80-10450. (Illus.). 48p. (J). (ps-3). 1980. 5.95 (*0-8193-1019-0*); lib. bdg. 5.95 (*0-8193-1020-4*) Parents.

Those That Be in Bondage: A Tale of Indian Indentures & Sunlit Western Waters. A. R. Webber. LC 88-71567. 254p. 1988. pap. 13.95 (*0-911565-05-1*) Calaloux Pubns.

Those that Mattered. Barbara Angle. LC 94-6828. 1994. 22.00 (*0-517-59799-3*) Crown Pub Group.

***Those That Mattered.** Barbara Angle. 1997. 3.99 (*0-517-17461-8*) Random Hse Value.

Those Times & These. Irvin S. Cobb. LC 72-5862. (Short Story Index Reprint Ser.). 1977. reprint ed. 23.95 (*0-8369-4201-9*) Ayer.

Those Tremendous Mountains: The Story of the Lewis & Clark Expeditions. David F. Hawke. (Illus.). 288p. 1985. reprint ed. pap. 8.95 (*0-393-30289-X*) Norton.

Those Twentieth Century Blues: An Autobiography. Michael Tippett. (Illus.). 290p. 1995. pap. 19.95 (*0-7126-6059-3*, Pub. by Pimlico) Trafalgar.

***Those United States, Vol. 1.** Greenfield. (C). Date not set. pap. text ed. write for info. (*0-15-508258-2*) HB Coll Pubs.

***Those United States, Vol. 2.** Greenfield. (C). Date not set. pap. text ed. write for info. (*0-15-508259-0*) HB Coll Pubs.

Those Upland Meadows. Margaret B. Waters. 97p. (Orig.). 1994. pap. 9.95 (*0-9624949-1-7*) M B Waters.

Those Vulgar Tubes: External Sanitary Accommodations Aboard European Ships of the Fifteenth Through Seventeenth Centuries. Joe J. Simmons, III. (Studies in Nautical Archaeology). (Illus.). 93p. 1996. pap. 9.95 (*1-879735-00-8*) TX A&M Naut Arch.

***Those Vulgar Tubes: External Sanitary Accomodations Aboard European Ships of the Fifteenth Through Seventeenth Centuries.** Joe J. Simmons, 3rd. (Studies in Nautical Archaeology: No. 1). (Illus.). 112p. 1997. pap. 15.95 (*0-89096-788-1*) Tex A&M Univ Pr.

Those Walled Garrisons. Suskind. 1997. 24.95 (*0-684-19315-9*) S&S Trade.

Those Well Beloved Hills. Stephen Kirby. (C). 1989. text ed. 35.00 (*0-948929-02-2*) St Mut.

Those Were the Days. limited ed. R. Sand. (Illus.). 294p. 1992. boxed 100.00 (*0-940143-72-0*) Safari Pr.

Those Were the Days. 2nd rev. ed. Mark A. Savage. Ed. by Roland W. Tapp. LC 93-91381. (Illus.). 134p. 1993. reprint ed. per., pap. 9.95 (*1-878455-08-7*) Markas Pub.

Those Were the Days: Landmarks of Old Goleta. Gary B. Coombs et al. LC 86-81698. (Illus.). 1986. 15.00 (*0-911773-08-8*); pap. 8.50 (*0-911773-09-6*) Inst Am Res.

Those Were the Days, My Friend. M. Emmett Ratts. (Illus.). 208p. 1996. 25.00 (*0-8059-3837-0*) Dorrance.

Those Were the Days, My Friend: My Life in Hollywood with David O. Selznick & Others. Paul Macnamara. LC 93-32129. (Filmmakers Ser.: No. 35). (Illus.). 207p. 1993. 29.50 (*0-8108-2694-1*) Scarecrow.

Those Were the Days Through. Wendell Trogdon. 1986. pap. 8.95 (*0-913617-02-4*) Highlander Pr.

Those Were the Nights. James Agate. LC 77-91890. 1972. reprint ed. 20.95 (*0-405-08196-0*, Pub. by Blom Pubns UK) Ayer.

Those Who Blink. Novel. William Mills. LC 85-24160. 177p. 1986. 14.95 (*0-8071-1270-4*) La State U Pr.

Those Who Came Before: Southwestern Archaeology in the National Park System: Featuring Photographs from the George A. Grant Collection & a Portfolio by David Muench. Robert H. Lister & Florence C. Lister. LC 83-60100. (Illus.). 184p. reprint ed. pap. 52.50 (*0-8357-3617-2*, 2036148) Bks Demand.

Those Who Came Before: Southwestern Archeology in the National Park System. 2nd ed. Robert H. Lister & Florence C. Lister. Ed. by T. J. Priehs & Sandra Scott. LC 93-86265. (Illus.). 238p. 1994. pap. 16.95 (*1-877856-38-X*) SW Pks Mnmts.

Those Who Can. Robin Wilson. 352p. 1996. pap. 13.95 (*0-312-14139-4*) St Martin.

Those Who Can: Undergraduate Programs to Prepare Arts & Science Majors for Careers in Teaching. Joseph S. Johnston, Jr. et al. (Illus.). viii, 175p. 1989. pap. text ed. 18.00 (*0-911696-47-4*) Assn Am Coll.

Those Who Can: Undergraduate Programs to Prepare Arts & Sciences Majors for Teaching. Joseph S. Johnston, Jr. et al. LC 89-216403. 183p. 1989. reprint ed. pap. 52.20 (*0-608-01791-4*, 2062444) Bks Demand.

Those Who Can, Teach, 7 Vols. Kevin Ryan. (C). 1994. pap. 60.36 (*0-395-71242-4*) HM.

An Asterisk (*) at the beginning of an entry indicates that the title is appearing in BIP for the first time.

Those Who Died Youngcult Heroes of the 20th Century. Marianne Sinclair. 1994. per. 14.95 (*0-85965-023-5*, Pub. by Plexus UK) Publishers Group.

Those Who Do, Can: Teachers Writing, Writers Teaching. National Council of Teachers of English Staff. Ed. by Robert L. Root, Jr. & Michael Steinberg. LC 96-22113. 206p. 1996. pap. 26.95 (*0-8141-1860-7*) NCTE.

Those Who Favor Fire. Lauren Wolk. 1998. write for info. (*0-679-44849-7*) Random.

Those Who Follow. Jan Huesgen. 1992. 2.50 (*0-941127-11-7*) Dacotah Terr Pr.

Those Who Fought. Peter F. Speed. LC 96-4607. (Illus.). 256p. (Orig.). 1996. pap. 17.50 (*0-934977-39-9*) Italica Pr.

Those Who Have Vanished: An Introduction to Prehistory. Ronald L. Wallace. 527p. (C). 1983. pap. 39.95 (*0-534-10876-8*) Wadsworth Pub.

Those Who Hear You, Hear Me: A Resource for Bishops & Diocesan Education-Catechetical Leaders. National Catholic Education Association Staff & National Conference of Catechetical Leadership, & U. S. Catholic Conference Dept. of Education Staff. 44p. (Orig.). 1995. pap. text ed. 5.95 (*1-55586-051-6*) US Catholic.

Those Who Hunt the Night. Barbara Hambly. 352p. 1989. mass mkt. 5.99 (*0-345-36132-6*, Del Rey) Ballantine.

***Those Who Knew Him: Inspirational Verse.** Gilbert Morris. LC 96-53602. (Illus.). 96p. (gr. 10). 1997. 19.99 (*0-8007-7155-9*) Revell.

***Those Who Listen Hear His Voice: An Awareness Journal.** Thecia Merlo. 256p. spiral bd. 9.50 (*0-8198-7378-0*) Pauline Bks.

Those Who Love the Game. Glenn Rivers. (Trophy Nonfiction Bk.). (Illus.). 240p. (YA). (gr. 5 up). 1995. pap. 4.95 (*0-06-446174-2*, Trophy) HarpC Child Bks.

Those Who Love the Game: Glenn "Doc" Rivers on Life in NBA & Elsewhere. Glenn Rivers & Bruce Brooks. (Illus.). 176p. (YA). (gr. 6 up). 1994. 15.95 (*0-8050-2822-6*, Bks Young Read) H Holt & Co.

Those Who Move with God. Elbert Willis. 1977. 1.95 (*0-89858-006-4*) Fill the Gap.

Those Who Perish. Edward Dahlberg. LC 75-41070. reprint ed. 37.50 (*0-404-14528-0*) AMS Pr.

Those Who Prayed. Ed. by Peter Speed. (Illus.). 256p. (Orig.). 1997. pap. 17.50 (*0-934977-41-0*) Italica Pr.

Those Who Remain. Charles R. Taylor. (Illus.). 104p. (Orig.). 1980. pap. 2.95 (*0-937682-02-0*) Today Bible.

Those Who Ride the Night Winds. Nikki Giovanni. LC 82-20811. 64p. 1984. pap. 6.95 (*0-688-02653-2*, Quill) Morrow.

***Those Who Saw Her: Apparitions of Mary.** rev. ed. Catherine M. Odell. 264p. 1996. pap. 11.95 (*0-614-22129-3*) Our Sunday Visitor.

Those Who Stayed Behind: Rural Society in Nineteenth-Century New England. Hal S. Barron. LC 83-26354. (Illus.). 212p. 1984. text ed. 59.95 (*0-521-25784-0*) Cambridge U Pr.

Those Who Stayed Behind: Rural Society in Nineteenth-Century New England. Hal S. Barron. LC 83-26354. (Illus.). 212p. 1988. pap. text ed. 16.95 (*0-521-34777-7*) Cambridge U Pr.

***Those Who Touch Our Lives.** Andrews & McMeel Staff. 1997. 4.95 (*0-8362-3741-2*) Andrews & McMeel.

***Those Who Trespass: A Novel of Television & Murder.** Bill O'Reilly. 320p. (Orig.). 1998. pap. 19.95 (*0-9631246-8-4*) Bancroft MD.

Those Who Wait: Learning How to Wait on the Lord in an Impatient World. Rosemary McKnight. 140p. 1990. pap. 6.99 (*0-89225-365-7*) Gospel Advocate.

Those Who Walk Away. Patricia Highsmith. LC 88-26301. 264p. 1988. reprint ed. pap. 12.00 (*0-87113-259-1*, Atlntc Mnthly) Grove-Atltic.

Those Who Were There: Eyewitness Accounts of the War in Southeast Asia, 1956-1975, & Aftermath; Annotated Bibliography of Books, Articles, & Topic-Related Magazines, Covering Writings Both Factual & Imaginative. Ed. by Merritt Clifton et al. LC 83-25434. (American Dust Ser.: No. 15). 297p. 1984. 12.95 (*0-913218-97-9*) Dustbooks.

Those Who Won't & Those Who Will. Darlene Loomis. (Illus.). 12p. (Orig.). 1977. pap. 1.00 (*0-686-36278-0*) Drain Enterprise.

Those Who Worked. Ed. by Peter Speed. LC 97-12493. (Illus.). 256p. (Orig.). 1997. pap. 17.50 (*0-934977-40-2*) Italica Pr.

Those Whose Names Were Terrible. Carole Marsh. (Lost Colony Collection). (Illus.). (Orig.). (J). (gr. 4-8). 1994. pap. 19.95 (*0-935326-48-0*) Gallopade Pub Group.

***Those Wild Fuel Altereds: Drag Racing in the Sixties.** Don Montgomery. (Illus.). 192p. 1997. 33.95 (*0-9626454-5-1*) D Montgomery.

Those Women. Nor Hall. LC 88-4676. (Illus.). 84p. (Orig.). 1988. pap. 12.50 (*0-88214-333-6*) Spring Pubns.

Those Women in White. Elaine A. Masters. (Illus.). 386p. 1989. 40.00 (*0-685-26798-9*) E A Masters.

Those Wonderful Chriscraft Speedboats. Anthony Mollica & Bill Northup. (Coloring the Classics Ser.). (Illus.). 28p. (J). 1992. student ed. 3.95 (*1-883029-02-3*) CHP NY.

Those Wonderful, Colorful & Exciting Carnival Trains. Robert J. Goldsack. (Illus.). 120p. 1991. pap. 24.95 (*1-880545-00-4*) Midway Mus.

Those Wonderful Garwood Speedboats. Tony Mollica & Bill Northup. (Coloring the Classics Ser.). (Illus.). 28p. (J). 1992. student ed. 3.95 (*1-883029-01-5*) CHP NY.

Those Wonderful Old Racing Boats. Tony Mollica & Bill Northup. (Coloring the Classics Ser.). (Illus.). 28p. (J). 1992. student ed. 3.95 (*1-883029-00-7*) CHP NY.

Those Wonderful, Terrible Years: George Heller & the American Federation of Television & Radio Artists. Rita M. Harvey. LC 95-34321. 232p. 1996. pap. 19.95 (*0-8093-2023-1*); text ed. 34.95 (*0-8093-2022-3*) S Ill U Pr.

Those Wonderful Unauthorized Accessories for Model A Ford. Ed. by Murray Fahnestock. LC 73-164930. (Illus.). 256p. 1971. pap. 13.95 (*0-911160-27-2*) Post Group.

Those Wonderful Women in Their Flying Machines: The Unknown Heroines of World War II. rev. ed. Sally V. Keil. LC 90-84246. (Illus.). 418p. 1990. 24.95 (*0-9627659-0-2*) Four Directions.

Those Wonderful Yard-Long Prints & More. William D. Keagy et al. (Illus.). 112p. 1989. 8.50 (*0-9633922-0-4*) W D Keagy.

Thoth: The Hermes of Egypt. P. Boylan. 215p. 1979. pap. 20.00 (*0-89005-280-8*) Ares.

Thou Art a Wonderful God. Lowell E. Eason. (Illus.). (J). (gr. k-6). 1957. 5.99 (*3-901170-06-5*) CEF Press.

Thou Dost Open up My Life. Rufus M. Jones. LC 63-11819. (Orig.). 1963. pap. 3.00 (*0-87574-127-4*) Pendle Hill.

Thou Givest... They Gather. Amy Carmichael. 1991. pap. 5.95 (*0-87508-083-9*) Chr Lit.

Thou Holdest My Right Hand: On Pastoral Care of the Dying. D. Los. Tr. by Theodore Plantinga from DUT. (Pastoral Perspectives Ser.: No. 2). 141p. Date not set. pap. 8.90 (*0-921100-45-0*) Inhtce Pubns.

Thou Shall Not Covet. Megan Kaufmunn. LC 96-90111. 1996. 17.95 (*0-533-11909-X*) Vantage.

Thou Shall Not Kill. Antoine Reboul. Tr. by Stephanie Craig. LC 77-77312. Orig. Title: Tu Ne Tueras Point. (J). (gr. 5-8). 1969. 24.95 (*0-87599-161-0*) S G Phillips.

Thou Shalt Call His Name. (Illus.). 102p. 1975. pap. 2.50 (*0-915952-00-9*) Lords Line.

Thou Shalt Kill: Revolutionary Terrorism in Russia, 1894-1917. Anna Geifman. LC 92-46314. (Illus.). 392p. 1993. text ed. 49.50 (*0-691-08778-4*) Princeton U Pr.

Thou Shalt Kill: Revolutionary Terrorism in Russia, 1894-1917. Anna Geifman. 388p. (C). 1993. pap. text ed. 18.95 (*0-691-02549-5*) Princeton U Pr.

Thou Shalt Not Be Aware: Society's Betrayal of the Child. Alice Miller. 1986. pap. 8.95 (*0-452-00801-8*, Plume) NAL-Dutton.

Thou Shalt Not Be Aware: Society's Betrayal of the Child. Alice Miller. LC 85-32084. 336p. 1991. pap. 12.95 (*0-452-00929-4*, Mer) NAL-Dutton.

Thou Shalt Not Kill. Hilda M. McMahand. 1995. 10.95 (*0-533-11564-7*) Vantage.

Thou Shalt Not Kill. Mary S. Ryzuk. 1990. mass mkt. 4.95 (*0-445-21043-5*) Warner Bks.

***Thou Shalt Not Kill, But Stop Nazi Germany! A Syndicated Story of Young American Men, W W II Europe.** (Illus.). 1997. write for info. (*1-885170-07-6*) Walden Press.

Though I Be Crushed. LC 85-61194. 130p. 1985. pap. 9.95 (*0-912624-04-3*) Nembutsu Pr.

***Though Justice Sleeps: African Americans 1880-1900.** Barbara Bair. (The Young Oxford History of African Americans Ser.). (C). (gr. 12 up). 1997. 21.00 (*0-614-25378-0*) OUP.

Though Lions Roar: The Story of Helen Roseveare. Mary B. Lagerborg. 124p. (Orig.). (YA). (gr. 9-11). 1995. mass mkt. 4.95 (*0-87508-663-2*, 663) Chr Lit.

Though Times May Change. large type ed. Mary L. Temple. (Linford Romance Library). 288p. 1993. pap. 15.99 (*0-7089-7402-3*, Linford) Ulverscroft.

***Thoughest Houseplants.** Gary M. Spahl. (Indoor Gardening for Brown Thumbs Ser.). (Illus.). 96p. (Orig.). 1997. pap. 8.95 (*1-55867-178-1*) Bristol Pub Ent CA.

Thought. Julian J. Joyce. 106p. (Orig.). 1987. pap. 5.00 (*0-944851-00-2*) Earth Star.

Thought. Gilbert Harman. LC 72-4044. 209p. reprint ed. pap. 59.60 (*0-8357-3311-4*, 2039534) Bks Demand.

Thought, Vol. 36. Colin Baerman. 100p. (Orig.). 1994. pap. write for info. (*1-880764-01-6*) Northwind NJ.

***Thought: From the Skin to the Thinking Ego.** Didier Anzieu. 160p. 1996. pap. 32.95 (*1-85302-401-5*, Pub. by J Kingsley Pubs UK) Taylor & Francis.

***Thought: The Greatest Power.** Hector Amezquita. 140p. (Orig.). 1997. pap. 8.95 (*0-87516-708-X*) DeVorss.

Thought, Action & Intuition As a Symposium on the Philosophy of Benedetto Croce. Benedetto Croce. Ed. by L. M. Palmer & H. S. Harris. vii, 363p. 1976. lib. bdg. 70.00 (*3-487-05860-X*) Lubrecht & Cramer.

Thought, An Intention, a Review & Journal. Paul S. Mushala. Ed. by Gary Mease. (Illus.). 320p. 1996. pap. 12.95 (*0-9647776-0-6*) Mushala Hse Pub.

Thought & Action. Stuart Hampshire. LC 81-19834. (C). 1981. pap. text ed. 13.00 (*0-268-01847-2*) U of Notre Dame Pr.

Thought & Character: The Rhetoric of Democratic Education. Frederick J. Antczak. LC 85-2430. (Illus.). 250p. 1985. reprint ed. pap. 71.30 (*0-608-00026-4*, 2060792) Bks Demand.

Thought & Character of William James. Ralph B. Perry. LC 96-32306. (Vanderbilt Library of American Philosophy). 424p. 1996. reprint ed. pap. 21.95 (*0-8265-1279-8*) Vanderbilt U Pr.

Thought & Choice in Chess. 2nd ed. Adriaan D. De Groot. (Psychological Studies: No. 4). 1978. text ed. 89.25 (*3-11-000286-8*) Mouton.

Thought & Emotion: Developmental Perspectives. Ed. by David J. Bearison & Herbert Zimiles. (Jean Piaget Society Ser.). 256p. (C). 1985. text ed. 49.95 (*0-89859-530-4*) L Erlbaum Assocs.

Thought & Experience. Peter H. Hess. 202p. (C). 1988. text ed. 32.50 (*0-8020-5788-8*) U of Toronto Pr.

Thought & Faith in the Philosophy of Hegel. Ed. by John Walker. 204p. (C). 1991. lib. bdg. 121.50 (*0-7923-1234-1*, Pub. by Klwr Acad Pubs NE) Kluwer Ac.

Thought & Knowledge: An Introduction to Critical Thinking. 2nd ed. Diane F. Halpern. 536p. 1989. teacher ed., pap. 29.95 (*0-8058-0295-9*); text ed. 89.95 (*0-8058-0294-0*) L Erlbaum Assocs.

Thought & Knowledge: An Introduction to Critical Thinking. 3rd ed. Diane F. Halpern. 440p. 1995. text ed. 89.95 (*0-8058-1493-0*) L Erlbaum Assocs.

Thought & Knowledge: An Introduction to Critical Thinking. 3rd ed. Diane F. Halpern. 440p. 1995. pap. 29.95 (*0-8058-1494-9*) L Erlbaum Assocs.

Thought & Language. Julius M. Moravcsik. (Problems of Philosophy Series; Their Past & Present). 304p. (C). 1992. pap. 18.95 (*0-415-07105-4*, A7121) Routledge.

Thought & Language. rev. ed. Lev S. Vygotsky. Ed. by Alex Kozulin. 256p. 1986. pap. 16.00 (*0-262-72010-8*) MIT Pr.

Thought & Language - Language & Reading. Ed. by Maryanne Wolf et al. LC 79-89713. (Reprint Ser.: No. 14). 732p. 1980. 16.95 (*0-916690-15-6*) Harvard Educ Rev.

Thought & Letters in Western Europe, A. D. 500-900. Max L. Laistner. 1972. 59.95 (*0-8490-1207-4*) Gordon Pr.

Thought & Meditation. Kahlil Gibran. 1993. 4.98 (*1-55521-894-6*) Bk Sales Inc.

Thought & Nature: Studies in Rationalist Philosophy. Arthur W. Collins. LC 84-4023. 272p. (C). 1986. pap. 15.00 (*0-268-01857-X*); text ed. 33.50 (*0-268-01856-1*) U of Notre Dame Pr.

Thought & Reference. Kent Bach. 320p. 1988. 75.00 (*0-19-824983-7*) OUP.

Thought & Reference. Kent Bach. 320p. 1994. reprint ed. pap. 21.00 (*0-19-824077-5*) OUP.

Thought & Style in the Works of Leon Bloy. M. Rosalie Brady. LC 70-94176. (Catholic University of America. Studies in Romance Languages & Literatures: No. 30). reprint ed. 37.50 (*0-404-50330-6*) AMS Pr.

Thought & the Brain. Henri Pieron. LC 73-2981. (Classics in Psychology Ser.). 1980. reprint ed. 25.95 (*0-405-05153-0*) Ayer.

Thought, & the Glory of Thinking. unabridged ed. Torkom Saraydarian. LC 92-61034. 700p. 1996. 48.00 (*0-929874-28-5*); pap. 38.00 (*0-929874-27-7*) TSG Pub Found.

Thought & Things: A Study of the Development & Meaning of Thought or Genetic Logic, 3 vols., Set. James M. Baldwin. LC 75-3029. (Philosophy in America Ser.). reprint ed. 275.00 (*0-404-59025-X*) AMS Pr.

Thought & Things: Study of the Development & Meaning of Thought or Genetic Logic, 4 Vols. James M. Baldwin. LC 74-21397. (Classics in Child Development Ser.). 1975. reprint ed. 103.95 (*0-405-06451-9*) Ayer.

Thought & Vision: A Critical Reading of H. D.'s. Angela D. Pace-Fritz. LC 87-13193. 245p. 1988. reprint ed. pap. 69.90 (*0-7837-9119-4*, 2049920) Bks Demand.

Thought & Wisdom. C. West Churchman. (Systems Inquiry Ser.). 150p. 1982. pap. text ed. 10.95 (*0-914105-03-5*) Intersystems Pubns.

Thought As a System. David Bohm. LC 93-46728. 256p. (C). 1994. pap. 16.95 (*0-415-11030-0*, B4699, Routledge NY) Routledge.

Thought As a System. David Bohm. 272p. (C). 1994. text ed. 59.95 (*0-415-11980-4*) Routledge.

Thought Brigade. Roger W. Stuart. 1963. 10.95 (*0-8392-1118-X*) Astor-Honor.

***Thought Collector & Nature Talks.** Bettina Howitz. 1997. 8.95 (*0-533-12142-6*) Vantage.

Thought, Consciousness, & Reality: Psychiatry & the Humanities, Vol. 2. Ed. by Joseph H. Smith. LC 77-77350. 1977. 45.00 (*0-300-02138-0*) Yale U Pr.

Thought Contagion: How Belief Spreads Through Society. Aaron Lynch. 256p. 1996. 25.00 (*0-465-08466-4*) Basic.

Thought Control & Technological Slavery in America. (Analysis Ser.: No. 1). 1982. pap. 10.00 (*0-686-42834-X*) Inst Analysis.

Thought Control & Technological Slavery in America: Illustration & Selected Correspondence. (Analysis Ser.). 75p. 1983. pap. 20.00 (*0-686-42852-8*) Inst Analysis.

Thought Control in America: A New Technology Analysis. Charles W. Lachenmeyer. 140p. 1982. pap. 10.00 (*0-938526-04-9*) Inst Analysis.

Thought Crimes Against Old Glory. Scott Preston. 12p. 1991. pap. 3.00 (*0-915214-22-9*) Current.

Thought Dial. Sydney Omar. 1975. pap. 7.00 (*0-87980-164-6*) Wilshire.

Thought Experiments. Roy A. Sorensen. (Illus.). 352p. 1992. 55.00 (*0-19-507422-X*) OUP.

Thought Experiments in Science & Philosophy. Ed. by Tamara Horowitz & Gerald J. Massey. 352p. (C). 1991. text ed. 57.50 (*0-8476-7706-0*) Rowman.

Thought for Rosh Hashonoh. Charles B. Chavel. 64p. 1980. pap. 3.50 (*0-88328-029-9*) Shilo Pub Hse.

Thought for the Day. M. K. Gandhi. 595p. 1982. 24.95 (*0-318-36639-8*) Asia Bk Corp.

***Thought for the Week, Vol. 2.** 2nd ed. Menachem M. Schneerson. Tr. by Y. M. Kagan from HEB. 118p. (Orig.). 1973. reprint ed. pap. 6.00 (*0-8266-0474-9*) Kehot Pubn Soc.

***Thought for the Week, Vol. 8.** Menachem M. Schneerson. Tr. by Y. M. Kagan from HEB. 120p. (Orig.). 1977. pap. 6.00 (*0-8266-0480-3*) Kehot Pubn Soc.

Thought for Yom Kippur. Charles B. Chavel. 64p. 1980. pap. 3.50 (*0-88328-028-0*) Shilo Pub Hse.

Thought-Force in Business & Everyday Life. William W. Atkinson. 92p. 1996. pap. 12.95 (*1-56459-933-7*) Kessinger Pub.

Thought Force in Business & Everyday Life. William W. Atkinson. 91p. 1967. reprint ed. spiral bd. 7.00 (*0-7873-0061-6*) Hlth Research.

Thought Forces. Prentice Mulford. 172p. 1984. pap. 17.00 (*0-89540-144-4*, SB-144) Sun Pub.

Thought Forms. Besant. 1994. 9.95 (*0-8356-7187-9*) Theos Pub Hse.

Thought Forms. abr. ed. Annie Besant & Charles W. Leadbeater. (Illus.). 88p. 1969. pap. 13.00 (*0-8356-0008-4*, Quest) Theos Pub Hse.

***Thought from Outside: The Art & Artefacts of John Heward.** James D. Campbell. 160p. 1996. pap. 20.00 (*1-55022-276-7*, Pub. by ECW Press CN) Genl Dist Srvs.

Thought Fugues: An Introduction to Knowledge & Reality. Valerie Hardcastle. 614p. (C). 1996. pap. text ed. 42.99 (*0-7872-2504-5*) Kendall-Hunt.

***Thought Gang.** Tibor Fischer. LC 96-51544. 1997. pap. 12.00 (*0-684-83079-5*, Scribners PB Fict) S&S Trade.

***Thought Gang.** Tibor Fischer. 1994. 18.00 (*0-7486-6160-3*, Pub. by Polygon UK) Subterranean Co.

Thought Gang: A Novel. Tibor Fischer. 320p. 1995. 18.95 (*1-56584-286-3*) New Press NY.

Thought in the Young Child. Ed. by William Kessen & Clementina Kuhlmann. (SRCD M Ser.: Vol. 27, No. 2). 1962. 25.00 (*0-527-01593-8*) Periodicals Srv.

Thought into Speech: The Psychology of a Language. James Deese. (Century Psychology Ser.). (Illus.). 160p. 1984. text ed. 40.00 (*0-13-919944-6*) P-H.

Thought, Language & Reality in Logic. Katalin G. Havas. 210p. (C). 1992. 70.00 (*963-05-6332-0*, Pub. by Akad Kiado HU) St Mut.

***Thought Leaders.** Kurtzman. 1997. 25.00 (*0-7879-3903-X*) S&S Trade.

Thought Museum. Paul Schroeder. 32p. (Orig.). 1995. pap. 6.00 (*0-9644333-1-1*) CrossplusRds.

Thought Objects. Ed. by Barbara Ess. (Illus.). 142p. 1987. pap. 15.00 (*0-939784-17-3*) CEPA Gall.

Thought Objects: Just Another Asshole No. 7. Ed. by Barbara Ess & Glenn Branca. 11.95 (*0-317-59114-2*) Just Another.

Thought of Chang Tsai. Ira E. Kasoff. (Cambridge Studies in Chinese History, Literature & Institutions). 250p. 1984. text ed. 69.95 (*0-521-25549-X*) Cambridge U Pr.

Thought of Contemporary Spanish Essayists. Ed. by Donald W. Bleznick. LC 92-24203. 146p. (Orig.). (C). 1992. lib. bdg. 39.50 (*0-8191-8860-3*) U Pr of Amer.

Thought of Contemporary Spanish Essayists. Ed. & Tr. by Donald W. Bleznick from SPA. LC 92-24203. 146p. (Orig.). (C). 1992. pap. text ed. 23.50 (*0-8191-8861-1*) U Pr of Amer.

Thought of God. Maurice Roberts. 232p. 1993. pap. 8.99 (*0-85151-658-0*) Banner of Truth.

Thought of Gregory the Great. G. R. Evans. (Cambridge Studies in Medieval Life & Thought: No. 2). 160p. 1986. 54.95 (*0-521-30904-2*) Cambridge U Pr.

Thought of Gregory the Great. G. R. Evans. (Cambridge Studies in Medieval Life & Thought: No. 2). 160p. 1988. pap. text ed. 17.95 (*0-521-36826-X*) Cambridge U Pr.

Thought of Jacques Ellul: A Systematic Exposition. Darrell J. Fasching. LC 81-22529. (Toronto Studies in Theology: Vol. 7). 232p. (C). 1981. lib. bdg. 89.95 (*0-88946-961-X*) E Mellen.

***Thought of Karl Marx.** 3rd ed. David McLellan. 268p. 1995. pap. 26.50 (*0-333-63948-0*, Pub. by Papermac UK) Trans-Atl Phila.

Thought of Lucien Goldmann: A Critical Study. Aidan Donaldson. LC 96-16094. (Problems in Contemporary Philosophy Ser.: Vol. 35). 348p. 1996. text ed. 99.95 (*0-7734-8742-5*) E Mellen.

Thought of Mao Tse-Tung. Stuart R. Schram. 275p. 1989. text ed. 64.95 (*0-521-32549-8*); pap. text ed. 22.95 (*0-521-31062-8*) Cambridge U Pr.

Thought of Mikhail Bakhtin: From Word to Culture. David K. Danow. LC 90-46988. 110p. 1991. text ed. 16.95 (*0-312-05609-5*) St Martin.

Thought of Moses Maimonides: Philosophical & Legal Studies. Ed. by Ira Robinson et al. (Studies in the History of Philosophy: Vol. 17). 424p. (ENG & FRE.). 1991. lib. bdg. 109.95 (*0-88946-286-0*) E Mellen.

Thought of St. Paul: A Commentary on the Pauline Epistles. William G. Most. 301p. (Orig.). 1994. pap. 14.95 (*0-931888-56-5*) Christendom Pr.

Thought of the Evangelical Leaders: John Newton, Thomas Scott, Charles Simeon, Etc. Ed. by Josiah Pratt. 1978. 29.99 (*0-85151-270-4*) Banner of Truth.

Thought of the Heart & the Soul of the World. James Hillman. LC 92-13675. 130p. (Orig.). 1992. pap. 14.00 (*0-88214-353-0*) Spring Pubns.

Thought of Their Heart: On Devotion to the Sacred Heart & the Holy Rosary. 158p. (Orig.). 1994. pap. 10.50 (*1-883511-04-6*) Veritas Pr CA.

Thought of Thomas Aquinas. Brian Davies. 408p. 1993. reprint ed. pap. 24.95 (*0-19-826753-3*) OUP.

Thought Power: Its Control & Culture. Annie Besant. LC 73-7644. 1967. pap. 9.00 (*0-8356-0312-1*, Quest) Theos Pub Hse.

Thought Power: Its Control & Culture (1905) Annie Besant. 146p. 1996. pap. 16.95 (*1-56459-713-X*) Kessinger Pub.

Thought Power, Its Control & Culture. Annie Besant. 145p. 1971. reprint ed. spiral bd. 7.00 (*0-7873-0105-1*) Hlth Research.

Thought Power: Think Better, Feel Better, Act Better: An Emotional Health Program for Children, Adolescents, Teachers & Parents. Robert F. Chapman. 110p. (Orig.). (YA). (gr. 5 up). 1994. teacher ed. 19.95 (*0-9644000-6-5*); pap. 14.95 (*0-9644000-5-7*) Cypress Trail Pr.

Thought Provokers. Doug Rohrer. 57p. (YA). (gr. 9-12). 1993. pap. 9.95 (*1-55953-065-0*) Key Curr Pr.

Thought-Reader's Thoughts: Being the Impressions & Confessions of Stuart Cumberland. Stuart Cumberland. LC 75-7373. (Perspectives in Psychical Research Ser.). 1975. reprint ed. 28.95 (*0-405-07024-1*) Ayer.

T

Thought Reform & the Psychology of Totalism: A Study of "Brainwashing" in China. Robert J. Lifton. LC 88-40534. xiv, 510p. (C). 1989. reprint ed. pap. 19.95 (0-8078-4253-2) U of NC Pr.
Thought Signs: The Semiotics of Symbols - Western Ideograms. C. Liungman. LC 94-79555. 660p. (gr. 12). 1994. 49.00 (90-5199-197-5) IOS Press.
Thought Styles & Everyday Life: The Gamut from Rude to Elegant. Mary Douglas. (C). 1996. 65.00 (0-8039-7655-0); pap. 19.95 (0-8039-7656-9) Sage.
Thought to Be Rehearsed: Aphorism in Wallace Steven's Poetry. Beverly Coyle. LC 83-5778. (Studies in Modern Literature: No. 9). (Illus.). 130p. reprint ed. pap. 37.10 (0-8357-1414-4, 2070541) Bks Demand.
Thought Tracking Level 1: Simple Phrases. Kitty Wehrli. (J). (gr. 2). 1976. student ed. 12.00 (0-87879-739-4, Ann Arbor Div) Acad Therapy.
Thought Tracking Level 2: Sequential Phrases. Kitty Wehrli. (J). (gr. 2). 1976. student ed. 12.00 (0-87879-740-8, Ann Arbor Div) Acad Therapy.
Thought Tracking Level 3: Simple Sentences. Kitty Wehrli. (J). (gr. 2). 1976. student ed. 12.00 (0-87879-741-6, Ann Arbor Div) Acad Therapy.
Thought Tracking Level 4: Questions & Answers. Kitty Wehrli. (J). (gr. 2 up). 1976. student ed. 12.00 (0-87879-742-4, Ann Arbor Div) Acad Therapy.
***Thought Tracks.** Drumbeat Publishing Staff. Date not set. pap. text ed. write for info. (0-582-78560-X, Pub. by Longman UK) Longman.
Thought Vibration: The Law of Attraction in the Thought Word. William W. Atkinson. 112p. 1966. reprint ed. spiral bd. 7.00 (0-7873-0060-8) Hlth Research.
Thought Vibration of the Law of Attraction in the Thought World (1906) William W. Atkinson. 142p. 1996. pap. 16.95 (1-56459-660-5) Kessinger Pub.
Thought Viruses. Donald Lofland. 1997. pap. write for info. (0-517-88742-8) Random Hse Value.
Thought Viruses: Powerful Ways to Change Your Thought Patterns & Get What You Want in Life. Donald Lofland. LC 97-869. 1997. 23.00 (0-517-70577-X) Random.
Thought Wheel Tm: Uplifting Thoughts, Bk. II. Ed. by Mary Glaub & Sonny Helmkampf. 366p. 1985. pap. 8.50 (0-685-22583-6) Sonshine Unltd.
Thought Wheel Tm, Bk. 1: Uplifting Thoughts. Ed. by Mary Glaub & Sonny Helmkampf. 366p. 1981. pap. 8.50 (0-317-93235-7) Sonshine Unltd.
Thought Wheels Tm: Motivating Thoughts. Ed. by Mary Glaub & Sonny Helmkampf. 366p. 1983. pap. 8.50 (0-685-22582-8) Sonshine Unltd.
Thoughtful Art of Discipline: Teaching Responsibility When Your Child Misbehaves. Dale R. Olen. (Life Skills Parenting Ser.). (Illus.). 195p. (Orig.). 1994. pap. 8.95 (1-56583-014-8) JODA.
Thoughtful Economic Man: Essays on Rationality, Moral Rules & Benevolence. Ed. by J. Gay Meeks. (Illus.). 160p. (C). 1991. text ed. 34.95 (0-521-32574-9) Cambridge U Pr.
Thoughtful Faith: Essays on Belief by Mormon Scholars. Ed. by Philip L. Barlow. LC 86-71882. 310p. 1986. 16.95 (0-939651-00-9) Canon Pr.
Thoughtful Foragers: A Study of Prehistoric Decision Making. Steven Mithen. (New Studies in Archaeology). (Illus.). 220p. (C). 1990. text ed. 89.95 (0-521-35570-2) Cambridge U Pr.
Thoughtful Passions. Jean-Paul Sartre. 1986. 25.00 (0-02-606830-3) Macmillan.
***Thoughtful Reader.** Fjeldst. (C). 1994. pap. write for info. (0-15-500782-3) HB Coll Pubs.
Thoughtful Reader. Danuta Fjellestad. (C). 1994. teacher ed., pap. text ed. 33.75 (0-15-501553-2) HB Coll Pubs.
Thoughtful Soul: Reflections from Swedenborg. rev. ed. Emanuel Swedenborg. Ed. by George F. Dole. 184p. 1995. pap. 11.95 (0-87785-148-4) Swedenborg.
Thoughtful Teacher's Guide to Thinking Skills. G. A. Woditsch. 296p. (C). 1990. pap. 39.95 (0-8058-0290-8) L Erlbaum Assocs.
Thoughtful Teacher's Guide to Thinking Skills. G. A. Woditsch. 296p. (C). 1991. text ed. 79.95 (0-8058-0289-4) L Erlbaum Assocs.
Thoughtful Teachers Thought. 2nd ed. Editorial Projects in Education Staff. 1995. pap. text ed. 14.00 (0-205-18496-0) P-H.
Thoughtful Teaching. Christopher M. Clark. 160p. (C). 1995. pap. text ed. 17.95 (0-8077-3502-7) Tchrs Coll.
Thoughtful Word, a Healing Touch: A Guide for Visiting the Sick. Joseph M. Champlin & Susan C. Taylor. 40p. (Orig.). 1995. pap. 2.95 (0-89622-637-9) Twenty-Third.
Thoughtology. Thomas A. Hughes. (Illus.). 32p. (Orig.). 1985. pap. 4.95 (0-9614866-0-0, 866-0) TA Hughes Pubns.
Thoughts. James Alberione. (C). 1988. 39.00 (0-85439-233-5, Pub. by St Paul Pubns UK) St Mut.
Thoughts. Arvalene Hitchens. 28p. (Orig.). 1994. pap. 4.00 (1-886467-03-X) WJM Press.
Thoughts. Ainslie Meares. 62p. (Orig.). 1994. pap. 7.95 (0-85572-116-2, Pub. by Hill Content Pubng AT) Seven Hills Bk.
Thoughts. Ed. by Shirley Morris. (C). 1989. 30.00 (0-7223-2352-2, Pub. by A H S Ltd UK) St Mut.
Thoughts. Keith Peeler. (Orig.). 1996. pap. write for info. (1-57553-215-8) Watermrk Pr.
Thoughts. Frances E. Tolson. (Orig.). 1996. pap. write for info. (1-57553-173-9) Watermrk Pr.
Thoughts: Based on the Teaching of Robert Burton. Girard Haven. 88p. (Orig.). 1995. pap. 12.00 (0-9645782-0-4) Ulysses Bks.
Thoughts: Education for Peace & One World. Irene Taafaki. (Illus.). 336p. 1986. pap. text ed. 18.50 (0-85398-222-8) G Ronald Pub.
Thoughts: Etcetera...Etcetera. Bette J. Poisson. (Illus.). 96p. (Orig.). 1994. pap. 12.95 (1-879260-21-2) Evanston Pub.
Thoughts: On Apparitions, Chastisements, the Church. William A. Reck. LC 93-83447. 92p. (Orig.). 1993. pap. 2.00 (1-877678-23-6) Riehle Found.
Thoughts: Reflections in a Search for Meaning. Edward Lazar. Ed. by Francine Banwarth & Michael Lembeck. LC 89-91041. (Illus.). 138p. (Orig.). 1989. pap. 6.00 (0-9622548-0-0) JZ Redman Pubs.
Thoughts: Reflections in the Search for Meaning. Edward Lazar. Ed. by Sheilah Tobin & Francine Banwarth. 144p. 1989. write for info. (0-318-64896-2) JZ Redman Pubs.
Thoughts - Shackles of the Mind. Ophelia S. Parker. (Illus.). (Orig.). 1986. 14.95 (0-937895-01-6); pap. 12.95 (0-937895-00-8) By Faith Direct.
Thoughts about Architecture. J. B. Bakema. Ed. by Marianne Grey. (Academy Architecture Ser.). (Illus.). 160p. 1982. pap. 14.95 (0-312-80190-4) St Martin.
Thoughts about Children. Johann C. Blumhardt & Christopher F. Blumhardt. Tr. by Hutterian Society of Brothers Staff from GER. LC 79-24844. 77p. 1980. pap. 1.50 (0-87486-224-8) Plough.
Thoughts about Jesus & Mary. Harry O. Nawroth. 109p. pap. 4.95 (1-883537-50-9) Nawroth Pub.
Thoughts about the City of St. Louis. John Hogan. (Notable American Authors Ser.). 1992. reprint ed. lib. bdg. 75.00 (0-7812-3139-6) Rprt Serv.
Thoughts along the Way. David Graham. 224p. (Orig.). 1996. pap. 9.95 (1-887750-15-0) Rutledge Bks.
Thoughts among the Ruins: Collected Essays on Europe & Beyond. George Lichtheim. 524p. 1986. reprint ed. pap. 44.95 (0-88738-657-1) Transaction Pubs.
Thoughts & Aphorisms. Sri Aurobindo. 1979. pap. 2.00 (0-89744-927-4) Auromere.
Thoughts & Aphorisms of George Sand. George Sand, pseud. 1991. lib. bdg. 75.00 (0-8490-4147-3) Gordon Pr.
Thoughts & Expressions. Delton Jessee. (Orig.). 1995. pap. write for info. (1-57553-055-4) Watermrk Pr.
Thoughts & Feelings: The Art of Cognitive Stress Intervention. Matthew McKay et al. 218p. 1981. pap. 17.95 (0-934986-03-7) New Harbinger.
***Thoughts & Feelings: The Art of Cognitive Stress Reduction.** 2nd rev. ed. Matthew McKay et al. 224p. 1997. pap. 17.95 (1-57224-093-8) New Harbinger.
Thoughts & Glimpses. Sri Aurobindo. 30p. 1987. pap. 1.50 (81-7058-150-8, Pub. by SAA II) Aurobindo Assn.
Thoughts & Meditations. Kahlil Gibran. Tr. by Anthony R. Ferris. 128p. 1984. pap. 5.95 (0-8065-0916-3, 240, Citadel Pr) Carol Pub Group.
Thoughts & Meditations on Life & Being. Jalal I. Griffith. 1993. 17.95 (0-533-10395-9) Vantage.
Thoughts & Reflections of Iqbal. Syed Abdul Vahid. 380p. 1985. 19.95 (1-56744-402-4) Kazi Pubns.
Thoughts & Thinkers. Anthony Quinton. LC 81-13372. 350p. 1982. 54.50 (0-8419-0772-2); pap. 29.50 (0-8419-0773-0) Holmes & Meier.
Thoughts & Visions: Poems of the Heart & the Imagination. Anne M. Cusmano. 50p. (Orig.). 1995. pap. 7.50 (0-9645160-0-4) Dutchess Angel.
Thoughts Are Free: A Quaker Youth in Nazi Germany. Anna S. Halle. LC 85-61843. (Orig.). 1985. pap. 3.00 (0-87574-265-3) Pendle Hill.
Thoughts Are Things. Ernest Holmes. Ed. by Willis H. Kinnear. 95p. 1967. pap. 7.95 (0-911336-33-8) Sci of Mind.
Thoughts Are Things. Prentice Mulford. 1991. lib. bdg. 79.95 (0-8490-4293-3) Gordon Pr.
Thoughts Are Things. Prentice Mulford. 176p. 1996. pap. 17.95 (1-56459-673-7) Kessinger Pub.
Thoughts Are Things. Prentice Mulford. 171p. 1993. pap. 16.00 (0-89540-232-7, SB-232) Sun Pub.
***Thoughts Are Things.** R. C. Van Meter. LC 96-84625. 110p. (Orig.). 1996. pap. 10.00 (0-9653899-0-1, 1001) Digi Print.
Thoughts Are Things. Edward Walker. pap. text ed. 4.00 (0-911662-18-9) Yoga.
***Thoughts Are Things.** Edward Walker. 72p. 1997. pap. 5.95 (0-614-29650-1) Shiloh Press.
***Thoughts Are Things.** Edward Walker. Date not set. write for info. (1-889868-01-9) Shiloh Press.
Thoughts Are Things. Prentice Mulford. 171p. 1977. reprint ed. spiral bd. 7.00 (0-7873-0629-0) Hlth Research.
Thoughts As a Child. Penny L. Sanders. 32p. (Orig.). (YA). (gr. 7 up). 1994. pap. write for info. (1-56167-161-4) Am Literary Pr.
Thought's Ego in Augustine & Descartes. Gareth B. Matthews. LC 92-52767. 240p. (C). 1992. 29.95 (0-8014-2775-4) Cornell U Pr.
Thoughts for a Bad Hair Day. Mary E. Edmunds. LC 94-47393. 128p. (Orig.). 1995. pap. 7.95 (0-87579-952-3) Deseret Bk.
Thoughts for a Sunny Day. Ariel Books Staff. (Illus.). 16p. 1994. 4.95 (0-8362-3056-6) Andrews & McMeel.
***Thoughts for All Time Vol. 1: Selections from the Works of Frederick Douglass.** 4th rev. ed. Frederick Douglass. (Illus.). 32p. 1996. pap. 3.95 (1-887878-04-1) Pks & Hist.
Thoughts for Joint Commanders. John H. Cushman. 64p. (C). 1993. pap. text ed. write for info. (0-9637932-0-9) J H Cushman.
Thoughts for Living Wisely. Ted O'Krent. 132p. Date not set. pap. write for info. (0-9649275-0-0) Heirloom TX.
Thoughts for Meditation: A Way to Recovery from Within. N. Gangulee & T. S. Eliot. 1972. 59.95 (0-8490-1208-2) Gordon Pr.
Thoughts for Men on the Move. Warren W. Wiersbe. 1988. pap. 10.99 (0-8024-8781-5) Moody.
Thoughts for My Secret Pal: 101 Thoughts for You. Brownlow. (Easelette Miniatures Ser.). (Illus.). 1995. spiral bd. 4.99 (1-57051-008-3) Brownlow Pub Co.
***Thoughts for My Secret Pal: 101 Thoughts for You.** Brownlow Publishing Staff. 1996. pap. text ed. 4.99 (1-57051-113-6) Brownlow Pub Co.
Thoughts for Religious. Gerald Mackrell. (C). 1988. 39.00 (0-85439-234-3, Pub. by St Paul Pubns UK) St Mut.
***Thoughts for Scouts Own.** Judy McGorray. 35p. (YA). (gr. 6-12). 1997. pap. text ed. write for info. (1-888200-08-1) JayMac Commun.
***Thoughts for Sunday.** Handley C. Moule. (Walk in the Word Ser.). 400p. 1997. 24.99 (0-89957-216-2) AMG Pubs.
***Thoughts for the Day.** John T. Ferrier. 52p. Date not set. pap. text ed. 6.00 (0-900235-68-3) Order Of The Cross.
***Thoughts for the Free Life: Lao Tsu to the Present.** 3rd ed. Lao Tsu et al. Ed. & Illus. by Cicely Buckley. 128p. (Orig.). 1997. pap. 12.95 (1-882291-56-5) Oyster River Pr.
Thoughts for the Moment Only Or Just Words. Joseph R. Forte & Joe Forte. (Illus.). 256p. (Orig.). 1988. pap. 20.00 (0-685-29456-0) Ashleigh Face Pr.
Thoughts for the Quiet Hour. Dwight L. Moody. 256p. 1993. mass mkt. 5.99 (0-88368-247-8) Whitaker Hse.
Thoughts for the Throne: The Ultimate Bathroom Book of Useless Information. Donald A. Voorhees. (Illus.). 208p. 1995. pap. 8.95 (0-8065-1650-X, Citadel Pr) Carol Pub Group.
Thoughts for Young Men. rev. ed. J. C. Ryle. 96p. (YA). (gr. 9 up). 1993. pap. 5.95 (1-879737-09-4) Calvary Press.
Thoughts from Inside. Mark A. Adams. 48p. (Orig.). 1996. pap. write for info. (0-9652761-0-4) Kat & Mouse.
Thoughts from My Rocking Chair. Naomi H. Larsen & Lisa A. Windham. (Illus.). 39p. (Orig.). 1994. pap. 7.95 (1-884498-00-0) CompuVisuals.
Thoughts from the Berkshires: Poems. Helen E. Scott. Ed. by M. A. Myers. LC 91-75435. 58p. (Orig.). 1991. pap. text ed. 7.95 (1-879183-10-2) Bristol Banner.
***Thoughts from the Garden Gate.** Brownlow Publishing Company Staff. (Ribbons of Love Ser.). 1997. pap. text ed. 7.99 (1-57051-130-6) Brownlow Pub Co.
Thoughts from the Heart. Ed. by Mac Anderson. 78p. (Orig.). 1991. pap. 7.95 (1-56245-016-6) Great Quotations.
Thoughts from the Mount of Blessing. Ellen G. White. LC 56-7170. 172p. 1956. 8.99 (0-8163-0047-X, 20401-6) Pacific Pr Pub Assn.
Thoughts from the Seat of the Soul. Gary Zukav. 256p. 1994. pap. 10.95 (0-671-88769-6, Fireside) S&S Trade.
Thoughts from the Spirit Side. Marlene Shepherd. (Illus.). 70p. (Orig.). 1991. pap. 6.50 (0-9629013-1-8) Feather Prodns.
Thoughts from the Teachings of Agni Yoga. 1977. reprint ed. 0.75 (0-933574-20-7) Agni Yoga Soc.
Thoughts from the World's Great Religions: A Guide to the Understanding of the Fundamental Unity Underlying the Great Living Religions of the World. Compiled by O. P. Ghai. LC 94-8243. 128p. (Orig.). 1995. pap. 12.95 (1-56087-053-2) Top Mtn Pub.
Thoughts from the World's Great Religions: A Guide to the Understanding of the Fundamental Unity Underlying the Great Living Religions of the World. O. P. Ghai. LC 94-8243. 128p. 1995. boxed 21.95 (1-56087-048-6) Top Mtn Pub.
Thoughts in a Dry Season: A Miscellany. Gerald Brenan. LC 78-4508. 185p. reprint ed. pap. 52.80 (0-685-20627-0, 2030582) Bks Demand.
Thoughts in Rhyme. Jeanie Robertson. 128p. (Orig.). 1992. pap. 9.95 (0-9632312-0-0) Thoughts Rhyme.
Thoughts in Solitude. Thomas Merton. 124p. 1976. pap. 7.00 (0-374-51325-2, Noonday) FS&G.
Thoughts in Solitude. Thomas Merton. 114p. 1994. pap. 21.00 (0-86012-017-1, Pub. by Srch Pr UK) St Mut.
Thoughts in Solitude. Thomas Merton. LC 92-50736. 168p. 1993. reprint ed. pap. 6.00 (0-87773-920-X, Sham Pocket Class) Shambhala Pubns.
Thoughts in Solitude: A Guide to Your Inner Journey. Rosemarie Ludwig. 120p. (Orig.). 1993. pap. 17.95 (1-879046-01-6) Jacaranda AZ.
Thoughts in Time. limited ed. Frwd. by Frederick L. Carlson. (Illus.). 61p. 1984. 20.00 (0-89904-006-3) Crumb Elbow Pub.
Thoughts into Words. Bruce C. Johnson. 1974. pap. 3.00 (0-686-10568-0) Goranson Pr.
***Thoughts Matter: The Practice of the Spiritual Life.** Mary M. Funk. 1998. 14.95 (0-8264-1063-4) Continuum.
***Thoughts Of...** Susan Chiucarello. (Orig.). 1996. pap. write for info. (1-57553-398-7) Watermrk Pr.
***Thoughts of a Boy Growing Up, Vol. 1.** Kenneth E. Nelson. LC 96-86565. 96p. 1997. 11.95 (0-8158-0525-X) Chris Mass.
Thoughts of a Modern Mystic. Charles C. Massey. 1972. 59.95 (0-8490-1209-0) Gordon Pr.
Thoughts of a Philosophical Fighter Pilot. Jim Stockdale. 245p. (Orig.). (C). 1995. 25.95 (0-8179-9391-6); pap. 15.95 (0-8179-9392-4) Hoover Inst Pr.
Thoughts of Being Human. Donna B. Cheney. LC 83-82480. (Illus.). 160p. (Orig.). (C). 1984. 5.50 (0-87527-332-7) Green.
Thoughts of Blaise Pascal. Blaise Pascal. LC 78-12814. 320p. 1978. reprint ed. text ed. 65.00 (0-313-20530-2, PATH, Greenwood Pr) Greenwood.
Thoughts of Christmas: Childrens Christmas Party. Ed. by E. McFadden & Dawn Rogers. (Illus.). 56p. (Orig.). (J). (gr. 3-6). 1994. pap. 4.99 (0-9640168-1-8) Pirate Writings.
***Thoughts of Gandhi & Vinoba.** K. S. Bharathi. (C). 1995. 18.00 (81-7022-543-4, Pub. by Concept II) S Asia.
***Thoughts of God.** Michael Kanaly. (Orig.). 1997. pap. 12.00 (0-614-27308-0) Ace Bks.
***Thoughts of God: A Novel.** Michael Kanaly. 320p. 1997. pap. 12.00 (0-441-00466-0) Ace Bks.
Thoughts of Gold: Wisdom for Living from the Book of Proverbs. Leroy Brownlow. (Illus.). 1974. 9.99 (0-915720-13-2) Brownlow Pub Co.
Thoughts of Gold: Wisdom for Living from the Book of Proverbs. deluxe ed. Leroy Brownlow. (Illus.). 1974. 9.99 (0-915720-45-0) Brownlow Pub Co.
***Thoughts of Home.** Beautiful House Editors. Date not set. write for info. (0-688-13689-3) Hearst Bks.
Thoughts of Home: Reflections on Families, Houses, & Homelands From the Pages of House Beautiful Magazine. Ed. by Elaine Green. LC 95-14551. 256p. 1995. 25.00 (0-688-14383-0) Hearst Bks.
Thoughts of Lloyd. Lloyd F. Brubaker. (Orig.). 1996. pap. write for info. (1-57553-245-X) Watermrk Pr.
Thoughts of Love. Ed. by Helen Exley. (Heart Shaped Bks.). (Illus.). 32p. 1992. pap. 3.99 (1-85015-294-2) Exley Giftbooks.
Thoughts of Love. Ed. by Susan P. Schutz. LC 82-72630. (Illus.). 64p. (Orig.). 1982. pap. 7.95 (0-88396-181-4) Blue Mtn Pr CO.
Thoughts of P. R. Sarkar. Prabhat Rainjan Sarkar. Ed. by Avadhutika Ananda Mitra Acarya. 214p. (Orig.). (C). 1981. pap. text ed. 4.95 (0-88476-016-2) Ananda Marga.
Thoughts of Power & Love. Susan Jeffers. Ed. by Jill Kramer. LC 94-38171. 176p. (Orig.). 1995. pap. 7.95 (1-56170-122-X, 165) Hay House.
Thoughts of St. Therese: The Little Flower of Jesus Carmelite of the Monastery of Lisieux, 1873-1897. St. Therese of Lisieux. LC 88-50745. 180p. 1988. reprint ed. pap. 6.00 (0-89555-344-9) TAN Bks Pubs.
Thoughts of the Cure d'Ars. St. John Vianney. LC 84-50404. 79p. 1984. reprint ed. pap. 2.00 (0-89555-240-X) TAN Bks Pubs.
Thoughts of the Day. A. S. Ahmed. 24p. 1986. pap. 30.00 (0-7223-2052-3, Pub. by A H S Ltd UK) St Mut.
Thoughts of the Emperor: Marcus Aurelius Antoninus. George Long. 195p. 1995. pap. 25.00 (0-87556-785-1) Saifer.
Thoughts of the Seasons: A Journey Through the Colors. Shay Thoelke. (Winning Colors Ser.). 158p. 1996. spiral bd. 15.00 (1-880830-28-0) AEON-Hierophant.
Thoughts on African Colonization. William L. Garrison. LC 68-28997. (American Negro: His History & Literature. Series 1). (Illus.). 1974. reprint ed. 28.95 (0-405-01816-9) Ayer.
Thoughts on Architecture. D. N. Dhar. 142p. 1987. text ed. 25.00 (81-207-0646-3, Pub. by Sterling Pubs II) Apt Bks.
Thoughts on Art Education. Rudolf Arnheim. LC 89-26831. (Occasional Paper Ser.: Vol. 2). (Illus.). 68p. 1990. pap. 10.00 (0-89236-163-8, Getty Educ Inst) J P Getty Trust.
Thoughts on Being at Peace. Ed. by Helen Exley. (Thoughts Ser.). (Illus.). 60p. 1995. 8.00 (1-85015-647-6) Exley Giftbooks.
Thoughts on Being Happy. Ed. by Helen Exley. (Thoughts Ser.). (Illus.). 60p. 1996. 8.00 (1-85015-646-8) Exley Giftbooks.
***Thoughts on Courage: Thoughts & Reflections from History's Great Thinkers.** Forbes Magazine Editors. (Forbes Leadership Library). (Illus.). 192p. (Orig.). 1997. 12.95 (1-57243-182-2) Triumph Bks.
Thoughts on Culture. Lula K. Murphy. LC 86-50664. 65p. 1986. 5.95 (1-55523-021-0) Winston-Derek.
Thoughts on Death & Immortality: From the Papers of a Thinker, along with an Appendix of Theological Satirical Epigrams, Edited by One of His Friends. Ludwig Feuerbach. Tr. by James A. Massey from GER. LC 80-25259. 263p. 1980. pap. 11.00 (0-520-04062-7) U CA Pr.
Thoughts on Education. Vinoba Bhave. Ed. by Marjorie Sykes. 288p. (Orig.). 1983. pap. 12.00 (0-934676-47-X) Greenlf Bks.
Thoughts on Family Worship. James W. Alexander. 260p. 1990. reprint ed. 16.95 (1-877611-18-2) Soli Deo Gloria.
Thoughts on Freedom: Two Essays. Lorin McMackin. LC 81-23297. 111p. 1982. 12.50 (0-8093-1076-7) S Ill U Pr.
Thoughts on Heidegger. Joan Stambaugh. 170p. (C). 1991. lib. bdg. 52.00 (0-8191-8334-2) U Pr of Amer.
Thoughts on Hunting. Peter Beckford. 254p. 1990. 60.00 (0-85131-367-1, Pub. by J A Allen & Co UK) St Mut.
Thoughts on Indian Mysticism. V. Patanjali. 226p. 1989. 14.95 (0-318-36391-7) Asia Bk Corp.
Thoughts on Industrial Policy & Corporate Strategy: The Swedish Case. Bo Ekman. 52p. (Orig.). 1991. pap. text ed. 11.50 (0-8191-5835-6, Aspen Inst for Humanistic Studies) U Pr of Amer.
Thoughts on Leadership: A Treasury of Quotations. William D. Hitt. LC 91-15106. 330p. 1992. 29.95 (0-935470-66-2); pap. 19.95 (0-935470-61-1) Battelle.
Thoughts on Leadership: A Treasury of Quotations, Gift Edition. William D. Hitt. LC 91-15106. 330p. 1992. 34.95 (0-935470-91-3) Battelle.
Thoughts on Leadership: Thoughts & Reflections from History's Great Thinkers. Forbes Magazine Editors. (Forbes Leadership Library). (Illus.). 160p. 1995. 12.95 (1-57243-076-1) Triumph Bks.
Thoughts on Leadership: Thoughts & Reflections from History's Greatest Thinkers. Ed. by Forbes Magazine Staff. (Forbes Leadership Library). (Illus.). 160p. (Orig.). 1995. pap. 9.95 (1-57243-058-3) Triumph Bks.
Thoughts on Listening to God. Charles Stanley. LC 92-40248. (Itty Bitty Bk.). 1993. 4.99 (0-8407-9209-3) Nelson.
Thoughts on Machiavelli. Leo Strauss. 348p. 1995. pap. text ed. 16.95 (0-226-77702-2) U Ch Pr.
Thoughts on Man, His Nature, Productions, & Discoveries. William Godwin. LC 68-55719. vi, 471p. 1969. reprint ed. 57.50 (0-678-00442-0) Kelley.
Thoughts on Paper. Mark Tunik. 1995. 8.95 (0-533-11544-2) Vantage.

T

An Asterisk (*) at the beginning of an entry indicates that the title is appearing in BIP for the first time.

Thoughts on Popery. William Nevins. Ed. by Gerald Grob. LC 76-46093. (Anti-Movements in America Ser.). 1977. reprint ed. lib. bdg. 19.95 (*0-405-09966-5*) Ayer.

Thoughts on Preaching. J. W. Alexander. 332p. 1975. 16.99 (*0-85151-210-0*) Banner of Truth.

Thoughts on Prosperity: Thoughts & Reflections from History's Great Thinkers. Forbes Magazine Editors. (Forbes Leadership Library). (Illus.). 160p. 1996. 12.95 (*1-57243-107-5*) Triumph Bks.

Thoughts on Psalm 119. Ken Clegg. 20p. 1997. pap. 2.50 (*1-880573-28-8*) Grace WI.

Thoughts on Religious Experience. Archibald Alexander. 1978. 19.99 (*0-85151-080-9*) Banner of Truth.

Thoughts on School Reform: Edited Remarks. LC 89-62048. (Dialogue Ser.: No. 1). 60p. 1989. pap. 5.00 (*0-929930-01-0*) Pioneer Inst.

Thoughts on Some Questions Relating to Women: 1860-1908. Emily Davies. LC 73-14557. reprint ed. 34.50 (*0-404-56741-X*) AMS Pr.

Thoughts on Spiritual Life. Bhuteshananda. pap. 4.95 (*0-87481-241-0*) Vedanta Pr.

Thoughts on Stewardship, Vol. 2. Rodney M. Howard-Browne. 76p. 1995. pap. text ed. 5.00 (*1-884662-02-1*) Revival Minst Intl.

Thoughts on Success: Thoughts & Reflections from History's Great Thinkers. Forbes Magazine Editors. (Forbes Leadership Library). (Illus.). 160p. 1995. 12.95 (*1-57243-075-3*) Triumph Bks.

Thoughts on Success: Thoughts & Reflections from History's Greatest Thinkers. Ed. by Forbes Magazine Staff. (Forbes Leadership Library). (Illus.). 160p. (Orig.). 1995. pap. 9.95 (*1-57243-059-1*) Triumph Bks.

Thoughts on the American Flintlock Pistol. S. E. Dyke. LC 74-24435. (Illus.). 52p. 1974. pap. 15.00 (*0-87387-070-0*) Shumway.

Thoughts on the Business of Life. Forbes Magazine Editors. (Forbes Leadership Library). 574p. 1995. 19.95 (*1-57243-092-3*) Triumph Bks.

Thoughts on the Death Penalty. Charles C. Burleigh. LC 82-45657. (Capital Punishment Ser.). 1983. reprint ed. 37.50 (*0-404-62404-9*) AMS Pr.

Thoughts on the East. Thomas Merton. LC 95-5377. (New Directions Bibelot Ser.). 96p. (Orig.). 1995. pap. 6.00 (*0-8112-1293-9*, NDP802) New Directions.

Thoughts on the Education of Daughters. Mary Wollstonecraft. LC 94-5545. (Revolution & Romanticism, 1789-1834 Ser.). 1994. 48.00 (*1-85477-195-7*, Pub. by Woodstock Bks UK) Cassell.

***Thoughts on the Education of Daughters: 1787 Edition.** Mary Wollstonecraft. Ed. by Marie M. Roberts. (For Her Own Good Ser.). 192p. 1996. reprint ed. pap. write for info. (*1-85506-381-6*) Bks Intl VA.

Thoughts on the Funding System & Its Effects. Piercy Ravenstone. LC 66-28961. (Reprints of Economic Classics Ser.). 80p. 1966. reprint ed. 25.00 (*0-678-00192-8*) Kelley.

Thoughts on the Future Civil Policy of America. John W. Draper. (Notable American Authors Ser.). 1992. reprint ed. lib. bdg. 75.00 (*0-7812-2701-1*) Rprt Serv.

Thoughts on the Meaning & Use of Pre-Hispanic Mexican Sellos. Frederick V. Field. LC 67-31521. (Studies in Pre-Columbian Art & Archaeology: No. 3). (Illus.). 48p. 1967. pap. 6.00 (*0-88402-017-7*) Dumbarton Oaks.

Thoughts on the Nature of Things. Francis Bacon. 50p. 1996. pap. 9.95 (*1-56459-642-7*) Kessinger Pub.

Thoughts on the Present Collegiate System in the United States. Francis Wayland. LC 74-89250. (American Education: Its Men, Institutions, & Ideas. Series 1). 1978. reprint ed. 17.95 (*0-405-01488-0*) Ayer.

Thoughts on the Spiritual Life. Tr. by Jacob Behman & Charlotte A. Rainy. 87p. 1972. reprint ed. spiral bd. 5.50 (*0-7873-0086-1*) Hlth Research.

Thoughts on the Spiritual Life (1896) Jacob Boehme. Tr. by Charlotte A. Rainy. 88p. 1996. pap. 14.95 (*1-56459-905-1*) Kessinger Pub.

Thoughts on the Study of Political Economy: With an Appendix: Drydocks. Loammi Baldwin. 105p. 1968. 37.50 (*0-678-00374-2*) Kelley.

Thoughts on the Suzuki Piano School. Kyoko I. Selden. (About Suzuki Ser.). 48p. (Orig.). 1985. pap. text ed. 5.95 (*0-87487-297-9*, Suzuki Method) Summy-Birchard.

Thoughts on the Tabernacle. J. Denham Smith. LC 86-27631. 304p. 1987. pap. 12.99 (*0-8254-3756-3*, Kregel Class) Kregel.

Thoughts on Thinking. Norma Brody. (Orig.). (SPA.). (YA). (gr. 11 up). 1991. pap. 7.95 (*0-925360-09-0*) Geste Pub.

Thoughts on Tintern Abbey. Andrew Digby. (Broadside Ser.: No. 13). 1987. 20.00 (*0-937035-23-8*) Stone Hse NY.

Thoughts on U.S. Foreign Policy Toward the People's Republic of China. Ramon H. Myers. LC 94-5583. (Essays in Public Policy Ser.: No. 47). 1994. pap. text ed. 5.00 (*0-8179-5522-4*) Hoover Inst Pr.

Thoughts on Virtue: Thoughts & Reflections from History's Great Thinkers. Forbes Magazine Editors. (Forbes Leadership Library). (Illus.). 160p. 1996. 12.95 (*1-57243-106-7*) Triumph Bks.

***Thoughts on Wisdom: Thoughts & Reflections from History's Great Thinkers.** Forbes Magazine Editors. (Forbes Leadership Library). (Illus.). 192p. 1997. 12.95 (*1-57243-183-0*) Triumph Bks.

Thoughts on Women & Society. Eleanor M. Aveling & Edward Aveling. LC 86-27203. Orig. Title: The Woman Question. (Illus.). 100p. (Orig.). 1987. pap. 4.95 (*0-7178-0648-0*) Intl Pubs Co.

Thoughts Out of Season, 2 vols. Friedrich Wilhelm Nietzsche. 1974. lib. bdg. 600.00 (*0-87968-202-7*) Gordon Pr.

Thoughts, Pictures, & Words. Karla Kuskin. LC 95-1290. (Meet the Author Ser.). (Illus.). 32p. (J). (gr. 2-5). 1995. 13.95 (*1-878450-41-7*) R Owen Pubs.

Thoughts Silenced-Thoughts Secrets: And Thoughts Not Taught to Blacks, Et Al. Abd-Salaam. LC 94-9696. 1995. pap. 10.00 (*0-9627854-5-8*) Writers Inc.

Thoughts Through the Year. R. D. Kernohan. 1985. 40.00 (*0-946270-16-3*, Pub. by Pentland Pr UK) St Mut.

Thoughts to Be Added To... How One Successful Entrepreneur Thinks. C. J. Bailey. (Illus.). 93p. (Orig.). 1987. pap. 3.95 (*0-9619857-0-4*) Entrprnr Projects.

Thoughts to Build On. M. R. Kopmeyer. LC 72-122340. 336p. 1970. 17.95 (*0-913200-01-8*) Success Found.

Thoughts to Consider with Love. Jodi Hershey. 50p. 1992. 14.95 (*0-9634555-0-8*) Chldrns Inn.

Thoughts to Dwell On. Alwyn R. Morrison. LC 94-69160. 125p. 1995. pap. 9.95 (*0-9643939-0-5*) Shepard Edge.

Thoughts to Hold Onto: Just for Teenagers. Peter A. Pactor. 48p. (Orig.). (YA). 1995. pap. 5.95 (*0-9638569-1-X*) P A Pactor.

Thoughts to Live By: A Collection of Meaningful Quotes from the Experiences of Three Generations. Ed. by Erwin Boschmann. (Illus.). 72p. 1987. pap. 4.95 (*0-930116-05-4*) Sci Ent.

Thoughts to Make You Think & Feel Better. John J. Pelizza. 87p. 1988. pap. 11.95 (*0-9614872-1-6*) Pelizza & Assocs.

***Thoughts to Ponder, Vol. 1.** Cathy D. Johnson. 18p. (Orig.). 1996. pap. 7.95 (*0-9654480-0-2*, 100) Gam-Jam Pub.

Thoughts to Sell By: A Collection of over 100 Quotes from Personal Selling Power. Gerhard Gschwandtner. LC 95-6400. 1995. 5.95 (*0-939613-07-7*) Personal Selling.

Thoughts to Think About. Lucile N. Osgood. (Orig.). 1996. pap. write for info. (*1-57553-128-3*) Watermrk Pr.

Thoughts Turn to Actions. Carol Crook. 7p. (Orig.). (YA). (gr. 5 up). 1989. pap. 1.50 (*0-939399-10-5*) Bks of Truth.

Thoughts Wander Through. Jose Carrasco. LC 88-63603. (Poetry Ser.). 1989. pap. 15.95 (*0-944109-05-5*) Margraf Pubns Grp.

Thoughts When Caught Between a Rock & a Hard Place. Caldwell Van Roden. 40p. (Orig.). 1988. spiral bd. 5.00 (*0-940844-61-3*) Wellspring.

Thoughts While Swinging a Wild Child in a Green Mesh Hammock: Poems of Rebirth from the Bootheels of Appalachia. Allison Thorpe. 60p. (Orig.). 1991. pap. 9.00 (*0-9629142-0-7*) Janze Pubns.

Thoughts without a Thinker: Psychotherapy from a Buddhist Perspective. Mark Epstein. 240p. 1995. 22.00 (*0-465-03931-6*) Basic.

Thoughts without a Thinker: Psychotherapy from a Buddhist Perspective. Mark Epstein. LC 94-38063. 256p. 1996. pap. 13.00 (*0-465-08585-7*) Basic.

Thoughts, Words & Deeds: Poems, Vol. 1. Andrew Dickson. LC 94-18616. 64p. 1995. pap. 12.95 (*0-7734-0009-5*, Mellen Poetry Pr) E Mellen.

***Thoughtware: Change the Thinking & the Organization Will Change Itself.** J. Philip Kirby & David Hughes. LC 97-13605. (Illus.). 265p. 1997. 35.00 (*1-56327-106-0*) Prod Press.

Thousand Acres. Jane Smiley. 384p. 1992. pap. 12.00 (*0-449-90748-1*, Columbine) Fawcett.

***Thousand Acres.** Jane Smiley. 1996. mass mkt. 6.99 (*0-8041-1576-1*) Ivy Books.

***Thousand Acres.** Jane Smiley. 1997. mass mkt. 9.50 (*0-8041-9717-2*) Ivy Books.

Thousand Acres. large type ed. Jane Smiley. LC 91-52. 670p. 1992. lib. bdg. 24.95 (*1-56054-361-2*) Thorndike Pr.

***Thousand Afternoons.** Date not set. 25.00 (*0-8464-0924-0*) Beekman Pubs.

Thousand & More Feature Story Ideas. rev. ed. Clark. 1994. 2.00 (*0-318-19214-4*) Quill & Scroll.

Thousand & One Afternoons in Chicago. Ben Hecht. (Illus.). 290p. 1992. pap. 17.95 (*0-226-32279-3*) U Ch Pr.

Thousand & One Chickens. Seymour Rossel. LC 95-32230. (Illus.). (J). 1995. pap. 10.00 (*0-8074-0541-8*, 123940) UAHC.

Thousand & One Churches. W. M. Ramsay & Gertrude L. Bell. (Illus.). xvi, 580p. reprint ed. lib. bdg. 100.00 (*0-89241-121-X*) Caratzas.

Thousand & One Coffee Mornings: Scenes from Saudi Arabia. Miranda Miller. LC 89-81667. 142p. 9000. 28.00 (*0-7206-0761-2*, Pub. by P Owen Ltd UK) Dufour.

Thousand & One Cookie Recipes: The Ultimate A-Z Collection of Bars, Drops, Crescents, Snaps... Gregg R. Gillespie. 464p. 1995. 19.98 (*1-884822-35-5*) Blck Dog & Leventhal.

Thousand & One Delights Cookbook. Nahda Salah. 29.95 (*0-86685-549-1*) Intl Bk Ctr.

Thousand & One Formulas. 1996. lib. bdg. 299.75 (*0-8490-5638-1*) Gordon Pr.

***Thousand & One Nights, 4 vols.** (ARA.). 59.95 (*0-86685-708-7*, LDL829, Pub. by Librairie du Liban FR) Intl Bk Ctr.

Thousand & One Nights. Muhsin Mahdi. LC 95-3212. 1995. pap. 24.00 (*90-04-10204-3*) E J Brill.

***Thousand & One Nights.** Muhsin Mahdi. 278p. 1996. pap. 19.95 (*0-614-21658-3*, 1362) Kazi Pubns.

Thousand & One Nights (Alf Layla Wa-Layla) From Earliest Known Sources, Vol. 3. Ed. by Muhsin Mahdi. 396p. (ARA & ENG.). 1994. 135.00 (*90-04-10106-3*) E J Brill.

Thousand & One Nights in Arabic, 4 vols. 1975. 60.00 (*0-86685-326-X*) Intl Bk Ctr.

***Thousand & One Nights in Arabic Literature & Society.** Ed. by Richard C. Hovannisian & Georges Sabagh. (Levi Della Vida Symposia Ser.: No. 12). 128p. (C). 1997. text ed. 49.95 (*0-521-57397-1*) Cambridge U Pr.

Thousand & One Nights of Opera. Frederick H. Martens. LC 77-25416. (Music Reprint Ser.: 1978). 1978. reprint ed. lib. bdg. 49.50 (*0-306-77565-4*) Da Capo.

Thousand & One Notable Nativities: Astrologer's "Who's Who" 4th ed. Alan Leo. 130p. 1978. reprint ed. spiral bd. 8.50 (*0-7873-0551-0*) Hlth Research.

***Thousand & One-Second Stories.** Taruho Inagaki. Tr. by Tricia Vita from JPN. (Sun & Moon Classics Ser.: Vol. 138). 150p. 1997. pap. 12.95 (*1-55713-361-1*) Sun & Moon CA.

1,001 Secrets of Great Cooks. Jean Anderson. LC 95-3. 272p. (Orig.). 1995. pap. 12.00 (*0-399-52153-4*, Perigee Bks) Berkley Pub.

Thousand Armed Avalokitesvara. Lokesh Chandra. (C). 1988. 80.00 (*81-7017-247-0*, Pub. by Abhinav II) S Asia.

1,000 AutoCAD Tips & Tricks: For Release 13. 4th ed. George O. Head & Jan D. Head. (Illus.). 648p. 1995. 34.95 (*1-56604-141-4*) Ventana Communs.

***Thousand Blunders: The Grand Pacific Railway & Northern British Columbia.** Frank Leonard. (Illus.). 355p. 1995. pap. 24.95 (*0-7748-0552-8*, Pub. by U BC Pr) U of Wash Pr.

***Thousand Blunders: The Grand Trunk Pacific Railway & Northern British Columbia.** Frank Leonard. (Illus.). 355p. 1995. 49.95 (*0-7748-0532-3*, Pub. by U BC Pr) U of Wash Pr.

Thousand Bridges: A Novel. Michael McKinney. LC 92-15737. 153p. 1992. 19.95 (*0-8027-1223-1*) Walker & Co.

Thousand Campfires: A Scouter's Story. James T. Henderson. (Illus.). 204p. (Orig.). 1991. 17.95 (*0-9631648-0-5*); pap. 10.95 (*0-9631648-1-3*) Ambush Pub.

***Thousand Cities.** Harry Turtledove. (Time of Troubles Ser.: Bk. 3). (Orig.). 1997. mass mkt. 6.99 (*0-345-38049-5*, Del Rey) Ballantine.

Thousand Cousins: Poems of Family Life. David L. Harrison. LC 94-79158. (Illus.). 32p. (J). (gr. 2-5). 1996. 14.95 (*1-56397-131-3*, Wordsong) Boyds Mills Pr.

Thousand Cranes. Yasunari Kawabata. Tr. by Edward G. Seidensticker. 1996. pap. 11.00 (*0-679-76265-5*) Random Hse Value.

Thousand Cranes. Kathryn Miller. 28p. 1990. pap. 5.00 (*0-87129-004-9*, T80) Dramatic Pub.

Thousand Cups of Rice: Surviving the Death Railway. Kyle Thompson. LC 94-22388. 1994. 19.95 (*0-89015-990-4*) Sunbelt Media.

Thousand Days. Arthur M. Schlesinger, Jr. 968p. 1984. mass mkt. 6.95 (*0-449-30021-8*) Fawcett.

Thousand Days of Indo-U. S. Diplomacy: The Kennedy-Nehru Era. Meenu Roy. (C). 1993. 20.00 (*81-7100-580-2*, Pub. by Deep II) S Asia.

Thousand Days of Magic: Dressing Jacqueline Kennedy for the White House. Oleg Cassini. (Illus.). 224p. 1995. 42.50 (*0-8478-1900-0*) Rizzoli Intl.

Thousand Deaths. Jack London. (Illus.). 40p. 1984. pap. 1.95 (*0-932458-22-X*) Star Rover.

Thousand Delights. Joseph S. Salzburg. 115p. 1972. 5.00 (*0-682-47253-0*) Sovereign MD.

Thousand Dollar Fish. Paul Hutchens. (Sugar Creek Gang Ser.: 13). (J). (gr. 2-7). 1966. mass mkt., pap. 3.99 (*0-8024-4815-1*) Moody.

Thousand Dollar Yacht. Anthony Bailey. (Illus.). 214p. 1996. pap. 14.95 (*1-57409-011-9*) Sheridan.

Thousand Eyes for an Eye. Dom Martin. (Illus.). 125p. (Orig.). 1994. pap. 15.00 (*0-9616078-1-5*) Trans Gala Pubns.

Thousand Faces: Lon Chaney's Unique Artistry in Motion Pictures. Michael F. Blake. 398p. 1995. pap. 19.95 (*1-879511-21-5*) Madison Bks UPA.

Thousand Faces of the Virgin Mary. George H. Tavard. 280p. (Orig.). 1996. pap. 19.95 (*0-8146-5914-4*, M Glazier) Liturgical Pr.

***Thousand Frightening Fantasies: Understanding & Healing Scrupulosity & Obsessive Compulsive Disorder.** William Van Ornum. (Orig.). 1997. pap. 17.95 (*0-614-27642-X*) Crossroad NY.

***Thousand Frightening Fantasies: Understanding & Healing Scrupulosity & Obsessive Compulsive Disorder.** William E. Van Ornum. LC 96-29581. 240p. (Orig.). 1997. pap. 17.95 (*0-8245-1605-2*) Crossroad NY.

Thousand Generation Covenant: Dutch Reformed Covenant Theology & Group Identity in Colonial South Africa, 1652-1814. Jonathan N. Gerstner. LC 90-22416. (Studies in the History of Christian Thought: No. 44). xi, 280p. 1991. 96.50 (*90-04-09361-3*) E J Brill.

Thousand Graceful Subtleties: Rhetoric in the Poetry of Robinson Jeffers. Terry Beers. LC 94-21930. (Studies in Modern Poetry: Vol. 3). 128p. (C). 1995. text ed. 38.95 (*0-8204-2592-3*) P Lang Pubng.

Thousand Holy Temples in the Earth! Clyde E. Weeks, Jr. (Illus.). 160p. 1994. pap. 24.95 (*0-9643423-0-8*) Magnif Mormon.

***Thousand Honey Creeks Later: My Life in Music from Basie to Motown - & Beyond.** Preston Love. (Illus.). 288p. 1997. text ed. 45.00 (*0-8195-6318-8*, Wesleyan Univ Pr) U Pr of New Eng.

***Thousand Honey Creeks Later: My Life in Music from Basie to Motown - & Beyond.** Preston Love. (Illus.). 288p. 1997. pap. 19.95 (*0-8195-6320-X*, Wesleyan Univ Pr) U Pr of New Eng.

Thousand Journeys. Helen Fahrbach. (Illus.). 64p. (Orig.). 1989. pap. 11.95 (*0-929682-01-7*) Perin Pr.

Thousand Journeys: The Biography of Lama Anagarika Govinda. Ken Winkler. 1993. pap. 14.95 (*1-85230-149-X*) Element MA.

Thousand Leagues of Blue: The Sierra Club Book of the Pacific. Selected by John A. Murray. LC 93-23196. 488p. (Orig.). 1994. pap. 16.00 (*0-87156-452-1*) Sierra.

***Thousand Lights.** Hope Benton. LC 96-92560. (Illus.). 95p. (J). (gr. 3-8). 1996. 14.95 (*1-888927-03-8*, ATLB); pap. 4.50 (*1-888927-81-X*, ATLB) Open Minds.

***Thousand Lights: Teacher & Parent Guide.** Beatrice H. Benton-Borghi et al. LC 96-92556. (Illus.). 60p. (Orig.). 1996. teacher ed., pap. 14.95 (*1-888927-28-3*, ATLG) Open Minds.

Thousand Luna Moths. Albert Kausch. 64p. 1994. pap. 5.00 (*0-614-04112-0*) Hozomeen Pr.

Thousand Marriages: A Medical Study of Sex Adjustment. Robert L. Dickinson & Lura Beam. LC 76-95093. 1970. reprint ed. text ed. 69.50 (*0-8371-3085-9*, DIMA, Greenwood Pr) Greenwood.

Thousand-Mile Summer. Colin Fletcher. 1989. pap. 10.00 (*0-679-72326-9*, Vin) Random.

Thousand-Mile Walk to the Gulf. John Muir. (Illus.). 256p. 1981. pap. 14.00 (*0-395-31542-5*) HM.

Thousand-Mile Walk to the Gulf. John Muir. (BCL1 - United States Local History Ser.). 219p. 1991. reprint ed. lib. bdg. 79.00 (*0-7812-6291-7*) Rprt Serv.

Thousand-Mile Walk to the Gulf. John Muir. LC 91-30471. (John Muir Library). (Illus.). 160p. 1992. reprint ed. pap. 10.00 (*0-87156-591-9*) Sierra.

Thousand Mile Walk to the Gulf. John Muir. LC 90-47830. (Illus.). 246p. 1990. reprint ed. 24.95 (*0-87797-193-5*) Cherokee.

Thousand-Mile Walk to the Gulf. Frederick W. Turner. (Nature Library). 240p. 1992. reprint ed. pap. 12.00 (*0-14-017017-0*, Penguin Bks) Viking Penguin.

Thousand-Mile War: World War II in Alaska & the Aleutians. Brian Garfield. LC 95-39358. 1995. reprint ed. 35.95 (*0-912006-82-X*); reprint ed. pap. 24.95 (*0-912006-83-8*) U of Alaska Pr.

Thousand Miles from Nowhere: Trucking Two Continents. Graham Coster. LC 94-43040. 224p. 1995. 20.00 (*0-86547-489-3*, North Pt Pr) FS&G.

Thousand Miles from Wall Street: Tony Gray's A Commonsense Guide to Picking Stocks. Tony Gray. LC 95-3843. 1995. pap. 21.95 (*0-02-545167-7*) Macmillan.

1,000 Miles in 12 Days: Pro Cyclists on Tour. David Hautzig. LC 94-33809. (Illus.). 32p. (J). (gr. 1-5). 1995. 15.95 (*0-531-06896-X*); lib. bdg. 16.99 (*0-531-08746-8*) Orchard Bks Watts.

Thousand Miles of Miracle: A Personal Record of God's Delivering Power in China. A. E. Glover. 191p. 1991. 11.95 (*9971-972-95-6*) OMF Bks.

Thousand Miles of Miracles in China. Archibald Glover. 1990. pap. 8.99 (*0-88019-263-1*) Schmul Pub Co.

Thousand Miles up the Nile. Amelia Edwards. 499p. (Orig.). (C). 1993. 125.00 (*1-85077-227-4*, Pub. by Darf Pubs Ltd UK) St Mut.

Thousand Months to Remember: An Autobiography. Joseph M. Dawson. 306p. 1964. 4.95 (*0-918954-03-7*) Baylor Univ Pr.

Thousand Mountains, a Million Hills: Creating the Rock Work of Japanese Gardens. David H. Engel. (Illus.). 144p. 1995. 29.00 (*0-87040-969-7*) Japan Pubns USA.

Thousand Mountains, A Million Hills: Creating the Rock Work of Japanese Gardens. David H. Engel. 144p. 29.00 (*1-56836-969-7*) FS&G.

Thousand Names of Vishnu. Eknath Easwaran. LC 87-28225. 1987. pap. 12.00 (*0-915132-46-X*); pap. 22.00 (*0-915132-47-8*) Nilgiri Pr.

Thousand Nights & One Night, Vol. 1. J. C. Mardrus. 644p. 1986. pap. 21.00 (*0-415-04539-8*) Routledge.

Thousand Nights & One Night Vol. 2. J. C. Mardrus. 1986. pap. 14.95 (*0-415-04540-1*) Routledge Chapman & Hall.

Thousand Nights & One Night Vol. 3. J. C. Mardrus. 1986. pap. 13.75 (*0-415-04541-X*) Routledge Chapman & Hall.

Thousand Nights & One Night Vol. 4. J. C. Mardrus. 1987. pap. 13.75 (*0-415-04542-8*) Routledge Chapman & Hall.

1,001 Bright Ideas to Stretch Your Dollars: Pinch Your Pennies, Hoard Your Quarters, & Collar Your Dollars. Cynthia G. Yates. 235p. 1995. pap. 9.99 (*0-89283-899-X*, Vine Bks) Servant.

Thousand Peaks: Korean Zen - Tradition & Teachers. 2nd ed. Mu S. Soeng. 243p. Date not set. reprint ed. pap. 15.95 (*0-942795-02-4*) Primary Point Pr.

Thousand Pieces of Gold. Ruthanne L. McCunn. LC 88-47881. (Asian Voices Ser.). 312p. 1989. pap. 12.00 (*0-8070-8317-8*) Beacon Pr.

Thousand Plateaus: Capitalism & Schizophrenia. Gilles Deleuze & Felix Guattari. LC 87-18623. 629p. 1987. pap. 19.95 (*0-8166-1402-4*); text ed. 49.95 (*0-8166-1401-6*) U of Minn Pr.

Thousand Rainy Days. Jody Wallace. (Illus.). 96p. (Orig.). (C). 1988. pap. 6.95 (*1-882021-00-2*) Salt River Pr.

Thousand Recipe Chinese Cookbook. Gloria B. Miller. 944p. 1984. pap. 20.00 (*0-671-50993-4*, Fireside) S&S Trade.

Thousand Shall Fall. Bodie Thoene. (Shiloh Legacy Ser.: Vol. 2). 432p. (Orig.). 1992. pap. 12.99 (*1-55661-190-0*) Bethany Hse.

Thousand Shall Fall. large type ed. Bodie Thoene. LC 92-46711. (General Ser.). (Orig.). 1993. lib. bdg. 22.95 (*0-8161-5718-9*, GK Hall) Thorndike Pr.

Thousand Steps & More: Selected Poems & Prose 1964-1984. Yoshimasu Gozo. Ed. by Thomas Fitzsimmons. Tr. by Richard Arno et al. from JPN. LC 86-27349. (Asian Poetry in Translation: Japan Ser.: No. 8). (Illus.). 184p. (Orig.). 1987. pap. 14.95 (*0-942668-10-3*) Katydid Bks.

Thousand Teachings: The Upadesasahasri of Sankara. Ed. by Sengaku Mayeda & John M. Koller. Tr. by John M. Koller. LC 91-9641. 265p. (C). 1992. text ed. 48.50 (*0-7914-0943-0*); pap. text ed. 16.95 (*0-7914-0944-9*) State U NY Pr.

Thousand Tears Falling: The True Story of a Vietnamese Family Torn Apart by War, Communism, & the CIA. Yung Krall. (Illus.). 414p. 1995. 22.00 (*1-56352-231-4*) Longstreet Pr Inc.

T

An Asterisk (*) at the beginning of an entry indicates that the title is appearing in BIP for the first time.

Thousand Thousands Served Him: Exegesis & the Naming of Angels in Ancient Judaism. Saul M. Olyan. (Texte und Studien zum Antiken Judentum: No. 36). 148p. 1993. 97.50 (*3-16-146063-4*, Pub. by J C B Mohr GW) Coronet Bks.
Thousand Times & Other Poems. Pat Sweeney. 47p. (Orig.). 1994. pap. 10.00 (*0-9630164-8-2*) Canios Edit.
Thousand to One. Rosemary Aubert. LC 96-96136. 192p. 1996. 17.95 (*0-8034-9173-5*) Bouregy.
Thousand Voices: The Story of Nashville's Union Station. Joe Sherman. LC 87-9700. 125p. 1995. pap. text ed. 19.95 (*1-55853-378-8*) Rutledge Hill Pr.
Thousand Winds May Make a Storm: Poems & Aphorisms. Hasan Dewran. Tr. by Hans W. Panthel. LC 90-6215. (Studies in Germanic Language & Literature: Vol. 4). 120p. (ENG & GER.). 1990. lib. bdg. 59.95 (*0-88946-582-7*) E Mellen.
***Thousand Wings.** T. Huo. 1998. pap. 23.95 (*0-525-94280-7*) NAL-Dutton.
***Thousand Words for Stranger.** Julie Czernada. 1997. mass mkt. 5.99 (*0-88677-769-0*) DAW Bks.
Thousand-Yard Model, Or the Earth As a Peppercorn. (Illus.). 1989. pap. 5.00 (*0-934546-21-5*) Univ Wrkshop.
***Thousand Yards of Sea.** Compiled by Laura Cecil. (Illus.). (J). 4.98 (*0-8317-3498-1*) Smithmark.
Thousand Yards of Sea. Illus. by Emma C. Clark. LC 91-35687. 80p. (J). (ps up). 1993. 18.00 (*0-688-11437-7*) Greenwillow.
Thousand Year Gamble, the World Awaits. Donald E. LeBlond. LC 89-81711. 1991. pap. 8.95 (*0-8158-0457-1*) Chris Mass.
Thousand Year Reign of Christ. Nathaniel West. LC 93-4549. 496p. 1993. pap. 16.99 (*0-8254-4000-9*) Kregel.
***Thousand Years in East Africa.** John Sutton. (Illus.). 112p. 1990. pap. 15.00 (*1-872566-00-6*, Pub. by Brit Inst Estrn Africa UK) David Brown.
Thousand Years in Sicily: From the Arabs to the Bourbons. Giuseppe Quatriglio. Tr. by Justin Vitiello. (Illus.). 228p. Date not set. pap. 16.00 (*0-921252-17-X*) LEGAS.
Thousand Years of Christianity in Ukraine: An Encyclopedic Chronology. Ed. by Andrew Sorokowski. LC 88-61255. 312p. 1988. 49.75 (*0-914834-58-4*) Smoloskyp.
Thousand Years of Czech Culture: Riches from the National Museum in Prague. Vladimir Boych et al. LC 96-8564. (Illus.). 180p. (Orig.). 1996. pap. 39.95 (*1-879704-02-1*) Old Salem NC.
Thousand Years of Faith in Russia. Alceste Santini. (C). 1988. 50.00 (*0-85439-274-2*, Pub. by St Paul Pubns UK) St Mut.
Thousand Years of Hungarian Masterpieces. D. Keresztury. (Illus.). 404p. (C). 1988. text ed. 460.00 (*0-685-40247-9*, Pub. by Collets) St Mut.
***Thousand Years of Nonlinear History.** Manuel De Landa. LC 96-38752. 288p. 1998. 24.50 (*0-942299-31-0*) Zone Bks.
Thousand Years of Peace, Vol. 8 of 9. Gordon Lindsay. (End of the Age Ser.: Vol. 8). 1974. 1.95 (*0-89985-074-X*) Christ for the Nations.
Thousand Years of Stained Glass. Catherine Brisac. 1994. 24.98 (*0-7858-0169-3*) Bk Sales Inc.
Thousand Years of the Bible. Ranee Katzenstein & David S. Zeidberg. (Illus.). 102p. 1991. pap. 11.95 (*0-89236-193-X*, J P Getty Museum) J P Getty Trust.
Thousand Years of Yesterday. 22th ed. H. Spencer Lewis. LC 20-9068. 156p. 1920. 15.95 (*0-912057-01-7*, 501630) RO AMORC.
Thousands & Thousands of Words see Miles & Miles de Palabras
Thousands of Practical Hints & Tips. (Illus.). 576p. 1993. 19.98 (*1-56173-735-6*, 3314600) Pubns Intl Ltd.
Thousands of Words You Already Know in Spanish-Miles De Palabras Que Usted Ya Conoce en Ingles: 3024 Common, Useful, Spanish Nouns, Verbs, & Adjectives Already in Your Vocabulary-3024 Nombres, Verbos y Adjetivos en Ingles de Uso Comun y Util, Que Usted Ya Tiene en Su Vocabulario. Ed. by Richard Kirschman & Doris Ober. LC 93-60854. (Words You Already Know Ser.). 128p. (Orig.). (ENG & SPA.). 1994. pap. 6.95 (*1-883843-11-1*) Villca Qutu.
Thracian Glosses: Contribution to the Study of the Thracian Vocabulary. Zivka Veklkova. 150p. 1986. pap. 52.00 (*90-256-0864-7*, Pub. by A M Hakkert NE) Benjamins North Am.
Thracian Horses. Maurice Valency. 1963. pap. 5.25 (*0-8222-1136-X*) Dramatists Play.
Thracians. R. F. Hoddinott. LC 80-51906. (Ancient Peoples & Places Ser.). (Illus.). 192p. 1981. 19.95 (*0-500-02099-X*) Thames Hudson.
Thraker im Karpatenbecken. Mikulas Dusek. (Publications of the Henri Frankfort Foundation: No. 4). xiv, 210p. 1978. pap. 35.00 (*90-6032-108-1*, Pub. by Gruner NE) Benjamins North Am.
Thrales of Streatham Park. Mary Hyde. (Illus.). 368p. 1977. 32.50 (*0-674-88746-8*) HUP.
***Thrand of Gotu.** George Johnston. 144p. 1994. pap. 14.95 (*0-88984-180-2*, Pub. by Porcupines Quill CN) Genl Dist Srvs.
Thrash Time - Five of the Best: Play-It-Like-It-Is-Guitar. pap. 8.95 (*0-89524-529-9*) Cherry Lane.
Thrasyllan Platonism. Harold Tarrant. LC 93-18778. 272p. (C). 1993. 37.50 (*0-8014-2719-3*) Cornell U Pr.
Thrasymachus: New Greek Course. C. W. Peckett & A. R. Munday. 326p. 1965. reprint ed. 25.95 (*0-86292-139-2*, Pub. by Brstl Class Pr UK) Focus Pub-R Pullins.
***Thrawn Trilogy Sourcebook.** (Star Wars Ser.). pap. 25.00 (*0-87431-280-9*, 40131) West End Games.
Thread: A Mathematical Yarn. Philip J. Davis. 1989. pap. 10.95 (*0-15-690140-4*, Harvest Bks) HarBrace.
***Thread Magic: The Enchanted World of Ellen Anne Eddy.** Ellen A. Eddy. Ed. by Laura M. Resintatler. LC 97-6040. (Illus.). 112p. (Orig.). 1997. pap. 29.95 (*1-56477-189-X*, B303) That Patchwork.
Thread of Ariadne. Ed. by Priscilla J. Umphrey. LC 88-30860. (Illus.). 200p. 1988. pap. 11.95 (*0-936609-14-1*) QED Ft Bragg.
Thread of Belonging. Nancy Talmage. 128p. (Orig.). 1990. pap. 19.95 (*0-685-28909-5*) St Johann Pr.
Thread of Blood: Colonialism, Revolution, & Gender on Mexico's Northern Frontier. Ana M. Alonso. LC 95-32475. (Hegemony & Experience Ser.). (Illus.). 303p. 1995. 46.00 (*0-8165-1511-5*); pap. 19.95 (*0-8165-1574-3*) U of Ariz Pr.
Thread of Blue: A Journey Through Loss, Faith & Renewal. Judy Belsky. 95p. 1992. 12.95 (*0-944070-77-9*) Targum Pr.
Thread of Discourse. 3rd ed. Roy E. Grimes. LC 74-78506. (Janua Linguarum, Series Minor: No. 207). 408p. (Orig.). 1984. pap. text ed. 29.95 (*90-279-3164-X*) Mouton.
Thread of Gold: Journeys Towards Reconciliation. Albert H. Friedlander. Tr. by John Bowden from GER. LC 90-39231. 160p. (Orig.). (C). 1990. pap. 12.95 (*0-334-02467-6*) TPI PA.
Thread of Gold, an Anthology of Poetry. Ed. by Eleanor Graham. LC 75-99030. (Granger Index Reprint Ser.). 1977. 16.95 (*0-8369-6104-8*) Ayer.
Thread of Life. Richard Wollheim. (William James Lectures). 304p. 1984. 22.50 (*0-685-08576-7*) HUP.
Thread of Life. Richard Wollheim. (William James Lectures). 304p. 1986. pap. text ed. 11.95 (*0-674-88758-1*) HUP.
Thread of Life. Richard Wollheim. 304p. 1984. 33.95 (*0-674-88757-3*) HUP.
Thread of Life: Symbolism of Miniature Art from Ecuador. Johannes Wilbert. Bd. with Further Exploration of the Rowe Chavin Seriation & Its Implications for North Central Coast Chronology. Peter Roe. LC 74-16851.; Man & a Feline in Mochica Art. Elizabeth P. Benson. LC 74-16851. LC 74-16851. (Studies in Pre-Columbian Art & Archaeology: Nos. 12-14). (Illus.). 1974. 20.00 (*0-88402-061-4*) Dumbarton Oaks.
Thread of Life: The Smithsonian Looks at Evolution. Roger Lewin. LC 82-16834. (Illus.). 256p. (C). 1989. 35.00 (*0-89599-010-5*, Norton) Smithsonian.
Thread of Life: The Story of Genes & Genetic Engineering. Susan Aldridge. (Illus.). 272p. (C). 1996. text ed. 24.95 (*0-521-46542-7*) Cambridge U Pr.
Thread of Life: Toraja Reflections on the Life Cycle. Douglas W. Hollan & Jane C. Wellenkamp. LC 96-18316. (Illus.). 256p. 1996. text ed. 40.00 (*0-8248-1771-0*); pap. text ed. 18.95 (*0-8248-1839-3*) UH Pr.
Thread of Life: Twelve Old Italian Tales. Illus. by Mary GrandPre. LC 93-29497. 80p. 1995. lib. bdg. 21.99 (*0-517-59595-8*) Crown Bks Yng Read.
Thread of Life: Twelve Old Italian Tales. Illus. by Mary GrandPre. LC 93-29497. 80p. (J). 1995. 20.00 (*0-517-59594-X*) Crown Bks Yng Read.
Thread of the Silkworm. Iris Chang. LC 95-20890. (Illus.). 480p. 1995. 27.50 (*0-465-08716-7*) Basic.
Thread of the Silkworm. Iris Chang. 480p. 1996. pap. 16.00 (*0-465-00678-7*) HarpC.
***Thread of Years.** John Lukacs. LC 97-25045. 1998. write for info. (*0-300-07188-4*) Yale U Pr.
Thread That Binds the Bones. Nina K. Hoffman. 320p. (Orig.). 1993. mass mkt. 4.99 (*0-380-77253-1*, AvoNova) Avon.
Thread That Runs So True. Jesse Stuart. 107p. 1958. pap. 5.00 (*0-87129-677-2*, T24) Dramatic Pub.
Thread That Runs So True. Jesse Stuart. 304p. 1950. pap. 9.95 (*0-684-71904-5*) S&S Trade.
Thread That Runs So True. Jesse Stuart. 336p. 1977. 40.00 (*0-684-15160-X*) S&S Trade.
Thread That Runs So True. Jesse Stuart. 24.95 (*0-8488-0638-7*) Amereon Ltd.
***Thread the Needle Bk. 1.** Booth. (J). (gr. 5). 1990. pap. text ed. 36.25 (*0-03-927203-6*) HR&W Schl Div.
Thread Time: A Multi-Threaded Programming Guide. Mark Dipasquale & Hewlett-Packard Staff. (C). 1996. pap. text ed. 48.00 (*0-13-190067-6*) P-H.
Thread to Hold: The Story of Ojai Valley School. Patricia L. Fry. (Illus.). 232p. 1996. 24.95 (*1-56474-149-4*) Fithian Pr.
Threadbear. Christophe Gallaz. (Illus.). 40p. (J). (ps-3). 1993. 14.95 (*1-56846-085-6*) Creative Ed.
Threadbear. Christophe Gallaz. (Illus.). 40p. (J). (ps-3). 1995. 14.95 (*0-15-200929-9*) HarBrace.
***Threadbear: A Story of Christian Healing for Adult Survivors of Sexual Abuse.** Tilda Norberg. (Illus.). 120p. 1997. pap. 12.00 (*0-9658707-0-7*) Penn Hse Pr.
Threadgill's Cookbook. Eddie Wilson. (Illus.). 1996. 21.95 (*1-56352-277-2*) Longstreet Pr Inc.
Threading My Way: Twenty-Seven Years of Autobiography. Robert D. Owen. LC 67-18582. 360p. 1967. reprint ed. 45.00 (*0-678-00261-4*) Kelley.
Threading the Maze. Janine Pommy-Vega. LC 92-56590. 1992. pap. 6.95 (*1-880636-04-2*) Cloud Mtn.
Threading the Maze. Janine P. Vega. Ed. by Alan Drake & Mikhail Horowitz. LC 92-56590. (Illus.). 56p. (Orig.). 1992. pap. 6.95 (*1-880636-09-3*) Cloud Mtn.
***Threading the Maze: A Collection of Seven Modern Japanese Poets.** Ed. & Tr. by Robert Epp from JPN. LC 96-61098. 370p. 1997. 25.00 (*1-880276-87-9*) Yakusha.
***Threadplay with Libby Lehman: Mastering Machine Embroidery Techniques.** Libby Lehman. Ed. by Ursula Reikes. (Illus.). 96p. (Orig.). 1997. pap. 24.95 (*1-56477-202-0*, B313) That Patchwork.
Threads. Jonathan Bolt. 1982. pap. 5.25 (*0-8222-1137-8*) Dramatists Play.
Threads: Insights by Women Architects. Ed. by Celine Pinet & Kimberly Devlin. (Publications in Architecture & Urban Planning: No. R91-1). (Illus.). 53p. 1991. 12.50 (*0-938744-73-9*) U of Wis Ctr Arch-Urban.
Threads & Ties That Bind: Exquisite Quilts from Tie Fabrics. Jean Johnson. (Illus.). 144p. 1996. pap. 24.95 (*0-8442-2625-4*) Quilt Digest Pr.
Threads Cable-Strong: William Faulkner's Go Down, Moses. Dirk Kuyk, Jr. LC 81-72030. 192p. 1983. 29.50 (*0-8387-5037-0*) Bucknell U Pr.
***Thread's End.** LaJoyce Martin. Ed. by Bethany Martin. 180p. (Orig.). 1997. pap. 7.99 (*1-57502-419-5*, PO1289) Morris Pubng.
Threads from Our Tapestry: Benedictine Women in Central Minnesota. Iomogene Blatz & Alard Zimmer. LC 94-8627. 1994. pap. 14.95 (*0-87839-085-5*) North Star.
Threads in the Genealogical Tapestry. Ed. by Nita Neblock. (Illus.). 38p. 1990. pap. 5.00 (*0-913233-18-8*) AFRA.
Threads of Arctic Prehistory: Papers in Honour of William E. Taylor, Jr. Ed. by David A. Morrison & Jean-Luc Pilon. (Mercury Ser.: No. 149). (Illus.). 434p. 1994. pap. 29.95 (*0-660-50751-X*, Pub. by Can Mus Civil CN) U of Wash Pr.
Threads of Blue & Gold: Poems from the First Century of Graceland College. Ed. by Mary K. Kenworthy. 208p. (Orig.). 1995. pap. 14.95 (*0-9636457-2-2*) Gracelnd Coll.
Threads of Circumstance. Ruby Dymond. 206p. 1987. 30.00 (*0-7212-0733-2*, Pub. by Regency Press UK) St Mut.
Threads of Death. Hillary Wolfe. 1995. pap. 3.99 (*0-8217-4850-5*) NAL-Dutton.
Threads of Destiny. Sara Wood. 1996. 3.50 (*0-373-11802-3*, 1-11802-5) Harlequin Bks.
***Threads of Evidence.** Silverstein. 1996. write for info. (*0-8050-5280-1*) H Holt & Co.
Threads of Experience: Fabric & Thread Images. Deidre Scherer. Ed. by Sandra H. Martz. LC 95-51733. (Illus.). 64p. 1996. 19.95 (*0-918949-92-0*) Papier-Mache Press.
Threads of Honor. Gordon Ryan. LC 96-33821. xv, 80p. (Orig.). 1996. pap. 6.95 (*1-57345-169-X*) Deseret Bk.
***Threads of Identity: Embroidery & Adornment of the Nomadic Rabaris.** Judy Frater. (Illus.). 216p. 75.00 (*81-85822-08-5*, Pub. by Mapin Pubng II) Antique Collect.
Threads of Identity: Maya Costume of the 1960s in Highland Guatemala. Patricia Altman & Caroline West. LC 92-72523. (Illus.). 192p. (C). 1992. 45.00 (*0-930741-23-4*); pap. 27.00 (*0-930741-24-2*) UCLA Fowler Mus.
Threads of Lace from Source to Sink. Pat Earnshaw. (Illus.). 108p. 1989. 27.00 (*0-9513891-1-4*, Pub. by Gorse Pubns UK) Lacis Pubns.
Threads of Life Vol. 1: A History of Kerrs Creek Baptist Church. unabridged ed. Alfred C. Miller. (Illus.). 301p. 1996. pap. 20.00 (*0-9624215-5-3*) A C Miller.
Threads of Light. David Kherdian. (Farm Poems Ser.: Bks. III & IV). (Illus.). 76p. 1985. 10.00 (*0-89756-014-0*) Two Rivers.
Threads of Love. large type ed. Ellen Randolph. (Romance Ser.). 288p. 1993. 25.99 (*0-7089-2993-1*) Ulverscroft.
***Threads of Magic.** Mike Jefferies. Date not set. mass mkt. write for info. (*0-06-105760-6*, HarperPrism) HarpC.
Threads of Memory: A Memoir of the 1920s. Margaret O. Onerheim. LC 93-12733. (Iowa Heritage Collection). (Illus.). 146p. (Orig.). 1993. pap. 14.95 (*0-8138-0902-9*) Iowa St U Pr.
Threads of Paradise: In the Fabric of Everyday Life. Christopher De Vinck. 192p. 1996. 12.99 (*0-310-49931-3*) Zondervan.
Threads of Public Policy: A Study in Policy Leadership. Robert Eyestone. LC 79-106638. (Urban Governor Ser.). 1971. pap. 5.95 (*0-672-61142-2*, Bobbs) Macmillan.
Threads of Public Policy: A Study in Political Leadership. Robert Eyestone. 216p. reprint ed. pap. text ed. 14.95 (*0-8290-0325-8*) Irvington.
***Threads of Silver, Cords of Gold.** Beverly McCoy. 300p. (Orig.). 1997. pap. 21.95 (*1-881636-21-6*) Windsor Hse Pub Grp.
Threads of Solidarity: Women in South African Industry, 1900-1980. Iris Berger. LC 91-23112. (Illus.). 384p. 1992. text ed. 45.00 (*0-253-31173-X*); pap. text ed. 8.95 (*0-253-20700-2*) Ind U Pr.
Threads of the Covenant: Growing up Jewish in Small Town America. Harley L. Sachs. LC 95-68799. 272p. 1995. pap. 18.00 (*0-914615-03-3*) I Nathan Pub Co.
***Threads of Time.** 160p. 1997. 19.96 (*1-57367-094-4*) Needlecrft Shop.
Threads of Time. Sheena Coupe & Barbara Scanlan. 1985. pap. text ed. 16.65 (*0-582-66342-3*, 74669) Longman.
Threads of Time. Nancy J. Martin. (Orig.). 1993. pap. 9.95 (*0-486-27418-7*) Dover.
Threads of Time. Jean B. Swengel. 182p. (Orig.). 1993. pap. 7.95 (*1-56043-776-6*) Destiny Image.
Threads of Time. 2nd ed. Sheena Coupe. (J). 1993. pap. text ed. 25.32 (*0-8013-1041-5*) Addison-Wesley.
Threads of Time. 2nd ed. Sheena Coupe. (J). 1993. pap. text ed. 26.60 (*0-8013-1045-8*) Addison-Wesley.
***Threads of Time: The Autobiography of Peter Brook.** Peter Brook. 1997. 29.50 (*1-887178-35-X*) Counterpt DC.
Threads of Tradition & Culture along the Gulf Coast (1986) Ed. by Ronald V. Evans. (Gulf Coast History & Humanities Conference Publications Ser.: Vol. X). 15.00 (*0-940836-18-1*) U of W Fla.
Threads Primer: A Guide to Solaris Multithreaded Programming. Bil Lewis. 1995. pap. text ed. 36.00 (*0-13-443698-9*) P-H.
Threadsuns. Paul Celan. Tr. & Intro. by Pierre Joris. (Classics Ser.: No. 140). 220p. 1996. pap. 13.95 (*1-55713-294-1*) Sun & Moon CA.
Threadsuns. Paul Celan. Tr. by Pierre Joris from GER. (Classics Ser.: No. 140). 220p. 1997. 21.95 (*1-55713-295-X*) Sun & Moon CA.
Threat. large type ed. Richard Jessup. 432p. 1982. 27.99 (*0-7089-8085-6*) Ulverscroft.
Threat: Inside the Soviet Military Machine. Andrew Cockborn. 333p. 1983. 16.95 (*0-394-52402-0*) Random.
***Threat: The Secret Alien Agenda.** David M. Jacobs. 1998. 23.00 (*0-684-81484-6*, S&S) S&S Trade.
Threat at Home: Confronting the Toxic Legacy of the U. S. Military. Seth Shulman. 272p. 1994. pap. 15.00 (*0-8070-0417-0*) Beacon Pr.
Threat Case. J. C. Pollock. 368p. 1992. mass mkt. 5.99 (*0-440-21204-9*) Dell.
Threat-Formulae in Ancient Egypt. Scott Morschauser. xvi, 268p. (Orig.). 1991. pap. 72.00 (*0-9613805-5-1*) Halgo Inc.
Threat from the Past. Diana Hamilton. (Presents Ser.). 1994. mass mkt. 2.99 (*0-373-11641-1*, 1-11641-7) Harlequin Bks.
Threat from the Past. large type unabridged ed. (Harlequin Ser.). 1994. lib. bdg. 18.95 (*0-263-13587-X*, Pub. by Mills & Boon UK) Thorndike Pr.
Threat of False Doctrine. Gerald F. Mundfrom. 144p. (Orig.). 1988. pap. 5.00 (*0-9615494-2-4*) Mercy & Truth.
Threat of International Chaos. Francis Neilson. 1979. lib. bdg. 39.95 (*0-685-96641-0*) Revisionist Pr.
***Threat of Leisure.** George B. Cutten. Date not set. write for info. (*0-8434-0435-3*, Pub. by McGrath NH) Ayer.
Threat of Life: Sermons on Pain, Power & Weakness. Walter Brueggemann. Ed. by Charles Campbell. 160p. 1996. pap. 15.00 (*0-8006-2975-2*, Fortress Pr) Augsburg Fortress.
Threat of Love. Charlotte Lamb. (Presents Ser.: No. 435). 1992. pap. 2.79 (*0-373-11435-4*, 1-11435-4) Harlequin Bks.
Threat of Love. large type ed. Charlotte Lamb. 1991. reprint ed. lib. bdg. 18.95 (*0-263-12623-4*) Thorndike Pr.
Threat of Managed Trade to Transforming Economics. Sylvia Ostry. (Orig.). 1993. pap. text ed. write for info. (*1-56708-088-X*) Grp of Thirty.
Threat Perception in International Crisis. Raymond Cohen. LC 79-3964. 239p. 1979. reprint ed. pap. 68.20 (*0-608-01944-5*, 2062599) Bks Demand.
Threat Perceptions in Asia & the Role of the Major Powers: A Workshop Report. 37p. (Orig.). (C). 1993. pap. text ed. 20.00 (*1-56806-775-5*) DIANE Pub.
Threat to Genesis. Rudolf Wittenberg. LC 76-15750. (Living Poets' Library). 1976. pap. 3.50 (*0-686-17002-4*) Dragons Teeth.
Threat to the Cosmic Order: Psychological, Social & Health Implications of Richard Wagner's Ring of the Nibelung. Peter F. Ostwald & Leonard S. Zegans. LC 96-24652. (Mental Health Library Series). 1997. 32.50 (*0-8236-6528-3*) Intl Univs Pr.
Threatened & Endangered Animals: An Extended Case Study for the Investigation & Evaluation of Issues Surrounding Threatened & Endangered Animals of the United States. David Hagengruber & Harold R. Hungerford. (Illus.). 189p. (Orig.). 1993. teacher ed., spiral bd. 20.80 (*0-87563-484-2*); spiral bd. 9.80 (*0-87563-480-X*) Stipes.
Threatened Birds of Africa & Related Islands: The ICBP/IUCN Red Data Book, Pt. 1. N. J. Collar & S. N. Stuart. (Illus.). 761p. 1993. text ed. 50.00 (*1-56098-266-7*) Smithsonian.
Threatened Birds of the Americas: The ICBP/IUCN Red Data Book, Pt. 2. 3rd ed. N. J. Collar et al. 1150p. (C). 1993. text ed. 75.00 (*1-56098-267-5*) Smithsonian.
***Threatened Cacti of Mexico.** E. F. Anderson et al. (Succulent Plant Research Ser.: Vol. 2). 135p. 1994. pap. 36.00 (*0-947643-69-9*, Pub. by Royal Botnic Grdns UK) Balogh.
***Threatened Cacti of Mexico.** E. F. Anderson et al. (Succulent Plant Research Ser.: Vol. 2). 135p. 1994. 66.00 (*0-947643-70-2*, Pub. by Royal Botnic Grdns UK) Balogh.
Threatened Children: Rhetoric & Concern about Child-Victims. Joel Best. LC 89-48508. (Illus.). xii, 244p. (C). 1993. pap. text ed. 12.95 (*0-226-04426-2*) U Ch Pr.
Threatened Cultures. Virginia Tulling. (World Issues Ser.). (Illus.). 48p. (J). (gr. 5 up). 1990. lib. bdg. 18.60 (*0-86592-096-6*); lib. bdg. 13.95 (*0-685-36381-3*) Rourke Corp.
Threatened Florida Black Bear. Margaret G. Clark. LC 94-48532. (Illus.). 64p. (J). (gr. 4-7). 1995. pap. 15.99 (*0-525-65196-9*, Cobblehill Bks) Dutton Child Bks.
Threatened Medical Identity of Psychiatry: The Winds of Change. Theodore Pearlman. (American Series in Behavioral Science & Law). 292p. (C). 1992. text ed. 51.95 (*0-398-05768-0*) C C Thomas.
Threatened Oceans. Jenny E. Tesar. (Our Fragile Planet Ser.). (Illus.). 128p. (YA). (gr. 7-12). 1992. lib. bdg. 18.95 (*0-8160-2494-4*) Facts on File.
Threatened People. Michael Teitelbaum. (C). Date not set. pap. text ed. write for info. (*0-393-96944-4*) Norton.
Threatened Peoples, Threatened Borders: World Migration & U. S. Policy. Ed. by Michael S. Teitelbaum & Myron Weiner. 300p. 1995. 25.00 (*0-393-03777-0*) Norton.
Threatened Primates of Africa. IUCN Conservation Monitoring Centre Staff et al. (IUCN Red Data Book Ser.). (Illus.). 153p. 1988. 24.00 (*2-88032-955-8*, Pub. by IUCN SZ) Island Pr.
Threatened Primates of Africa: The IUCN Red Data Book. IUCN Conservation Monitoring Centre Staff et al. 174p. 1989. 30.00 (*0-685-27045-9*) St Martin.

T

Threatened Swallowtail Butterflies of the World. N. Mark Collins & Michael G. Morris. (IUCN Red Data Book Ser.). (Illus.). 401p. 1985. 36.00 (*2-88032-603-6*, Pub. by IUCN SZ) Island Pr.

Threatened with Resurrection (Amenazado de Resurreccion) Poems of an Exiled Guatemalan. 2nd ed. Julia Esquivel. Tr. by Anne Woehrli from SPA. LC 93-44941. 128p. 1994. pap. 10.95 (*0-87178-851-9*, 8519) Brethren.

Threateners. Donald Hamilton. 1992. mass mkt. 5.99 (*0-449-14681-2*, GM) Fawcett.

Threatening Eye. large type ed. Lesley Grant-Adamson. 1991. 25.99 (*0-7089-2518-9*) Ulverscroft.

Threatening Youth: State Policy & the Containment of the Young. Bernard Davies. LC 86-12588. 192p. 1986. 85.00 (*0-335-15392-5*, Open Univ Pr); pap. 32.00 (*0-335-15391-7*, Open Univ Pr) Taylor & Francis.

Threats: A Shadowrun Sourcebook. Diane Piron-Gelman et al. (Shadowrun Ser.). (Illus.). 128p. (Orig.). 1996. suppl. ed., pap. 18.00 (*1-55560-290-8*, 7121) FASA Corp.

Threats & Promises. Barbara Delinsky. (Best of the Best Ser.). 1993. mass mkt. 4.50 (*0-373-83262-1*, 1-83262-5) Harlequin Bks.

Threats of Opposite. Mark Waid. Ed. by Spencer Selby. 36p. (Orig.). 1989. pap. 5.00 (*0-9623806-1-X*) SINK Pr.

***Threats Pending, Fuses Burning: Managing Workplace Violence.** Dennis A. Davis. LC 96-40266. 176p. 1997. 22.95 (*0-89106-102-9*, 7750) Davies-Black.

Threats to Optimal Development: Integrating Biological, Psychological, & Social Risk Factors: The Minnesota Symposia on Child Psychology, Vol. 29. Ed. by Charles A. Nelson. (Minnesota Symposium on Child Psychology Ser.). 360p. 1994. text ed. 69.95 (*0-8058-1510-4*) L Erlbaum Assocs.

Threats to Security in East Asia-Pacific. Ed. & Intro. by Charles E. Morrison. 221p. (C). 1983. text ed. 27.95 (*0-317-91349-2*) Pac Forum.

Threats to the International Civil Service: Past Pressures & New Trends. Yves Beigbeder. 220p. 1988. text ed. 54.00 (*0-86187-953-8*) St Martin.

Threats to Wildlife & the Platte River. C. Safira et al. (Environmental Policy Analysis Department Reports). (Orig.). 1989. 5.00 (*0-930698-30-4*) Natl Audubon.

Threats Without Enemies: Facing Environmental Insecurity. Gwyn Prins. 192p. (Orig.). 1992. 19.95 (*1-85383-157-3*, Pub. by Erthscan Pubns UK) Island Pr.

3DO Games Guide: Book 2. Zach Meston & Doug Arnold. (Illus.). 1995. pap. 16.95 (*1-884364-20-9*) Sandwich Islands.

Three: An Unfinished Woman, Pentimento, Scoundrel Time. Lillian Hellman. 1980. 19.95 (*0-316-35514-3*) Little.

Three: Collection of Poetry. 84p. 1981. pap. 9.00 (*0-935090-06-1*) Almanac Pr.

3-A Dairy & Egg Sanitary Standards. 1996. 120.00 (*0-317-02824-3*) Intl Assn Milk.

Three A. M. Meditations for the Middle of the Night. Richard A. Wing. LC 21-786068. 144p. (Orig.). 1985. pap. 9.95 (*0-934849-00-5*) Arthur Pub.

Three Across: The Great Air Race of 1927. Finklestein. Date not set. 15.95 (*0-689-80537-3*) S&S Childrens.

Three Across, the Great Air Race of 1927. Finkelstei. (J). 1996. 15.95 (*0-684-19740-5*, Atheneum Bks Young) S&S Childrens.

Three Act Tragedy. Agatha Christie. 240p. 1986. pap. text ed. 5.50 (*0-425-09180-5*) Berkley Pub.

Three-Acylcyclopentenes & Five-Acylbiyclo (2.1.0) Pentanes: Photochemical & Thermal Isomerizations. Kenneth F. Schaffner. 1976. pap. 15.50 (*0-08-020476-7*, Pergamon Pr) Elsevier.

Three Adventure Novels: One in Thine Hand; Leverage Point; The Alliance, 3 bks., Set. Gerald N. Lund. LC 94-71451. 875p. 1994. 15.95 (*0-87579-861-6*) Deseret Bk.

Three Aesop Fox Fables. Miriam Chaikin. (J). (gr. 4-7). 1992. pap. 10.00 (*0-395-61580-1*, Clarion Bks) HM.

Three Against Hitler. Rudi Wobbe & Jerry Borrowman. Orig. Title: Before the Blood Tribunal. 1992. pap. 9.95 (*1-55503-396-2*, 01111019) Covenant Comms.

Three Against Hitler. Rudi Wobbe & Jerry Borrowman. Orig. Title: Before the Blood Tribunal. 1996. pap. 9.95 (*1-55503-803-4*, 01111876) Covenant Comms.

Three Against the Third Republic: Sorel, Barres & Maurras. Michael Curtis. LC 76-26140. 313p. 1976. reprint ed. text ed. 59.75 (*0-8371-9048-7*, CUTR, Greenwood Pr) Greenwood.

Three Against the Wilderness. large type ed. Eric Collier. 559p. 1969. 25.99 (*0-85456-560-4*) Ulverscroft.

***Three Against Time.** Margaret Taylor. LC 97-65301. 176p. (Orig.). (J). (gr. 3-7). 1997. pap. 6.95 (*1-55143-067-3*) Orca Bk Pubs.

***Three Ages Cave.** John Long. (YA). 1997. pap. 9.95 (*1-86368-164-7*, Pub. by Fremantle Arts AT) Intl Spec Bk.

Three Ages of Musical Thought: Essays on Ethics & Aesthetics. Eric Werner. LC 80-28330. (Music Reprint Ser.). iv, 368p. 1981. reprint ed. 45.00 (*0-306-76032-0*) Da Capo.

Three Ages of the Italian Renaissance. Robert S. Lopez. LC 75-94759. 137p. reprint ed. 39.10 (*0-8357-9819-4*, 2011465) Bks Demand.

Three Ages of Zen: Samurai, Feudal & Modern. Trevor P. Leggett. 192p. 1993. pap. 12.95 (*0-8048-1898-3*) C E Tuttle.

Three Alternative Histories of Chinese Painting. James Cahill. (Franklin D. Murphy Lectures: No. 9). (Illus.). 112p. 1990. 12.00 (*0-913689-28-9*) Spencer Muse Art.

Three American Architects: Richardson, Sullivan, & Wright, 1865-1915. James F. O'Gorman. LC 90-10957. (Illus.). 190p. 1992. pap. 14.95 (*0-226-62072-7*) U Ch Pr.

Three American Composers. Edith Borroff. (Illus.). 310p. (Orig.). 1986. lib. bdg. 48.50 (*0-8191-5371-0*) U Pr of Amer.

Three American Indian Women: Pocahontas, Sacajawea & Sarah Winnemucca. Grace Woodward et al. (Illus.). 1995. 12.98 (*1-56731-089-3*, MJF Bks) Fine Comms.

Three American Literatures: Essays in Chicano, Native American, & Asian-American Literature for Teachers of American Literature. Ed. by Houston A. Baker, Jr. LC 82-63420. iii, 265p. 1982. pap. 19.75 (*0-87352-353-9*, B103P) Modern Lang.

Three American Modernist Painters. Incl. Max Weber. Alfred H. Barr, Jr. LC 70-86440. 1970. (*0-318-50899-0*); Maurice Stern. Horace M. Kallen. LC 70-86440. 1970. (*0-318-50900-8*); Stuart Davis. James J. Sweeney. LC 70-86440. 1970. (*0-318-50901-6*); LC 70-86440. (Museum of Modern Art Publications in Reprint). (Illus.). 152p. 1970. reprint ed. 13.00 (*0-685-22839-8*) Ayer.

Three American Modernist Painters: Max Weber, with an Introduction by Alfred H. Barr, Jr.; Maurice Sterne by H. M. Kallen, with a Note by the Artist; Stuart Davis by James Johnson Sweeney. New York City Museum of Modern Art Max Weber, Retrospective Exhibition, 1907-1930, 1969 Staff et al. 1969. reprint ed. 20.95 (*0-405-01528-3*, 15554) Ayer.

Three American Moralists: Mailer, Bellow, Trilling. Nathan A. Scott. LC 73-11558. 238p. 1973. reprint ed. pap. 67.90 (*0-608-00887-7*, 2061681) Bks Demand.

Three American Originals: John Ford, William Faulkner, & Charles Ives. Joseph W. Reed. LC 83-23349. (Illus.). 255p. 1984. pap. 15.95 (*0-8195-6186-X*, Wesleyan Univ Pr); text ed. 35.00 (*0-8195-5101-5*, Wesleyan Univ Pr) U Pr of New Eng.

Three American Purists: Mason - Miles - Von Wiegand. (Illus.). 18p. 1975. 2.00 (*0-916746-54-2*) Springfield Lib & Mus.

Three American Romantic Painters. Incl. Charles Burchfield, Early Watercolor. Alfred H. Barr, Jr. LC 74-86441. 1970. (*0-318-50902-4*); Florine Stettheimer. Henry McBride. LC 74-86441. 1970. (*0-318-50903-2*); Franklin Watkins. Andrew C. Ritchie. LC 74-86441. 1970. (*0-318-50904-0*); LC 74-86441. (Museum of Modern Art Publications in Reprint). 132p. 1970. reprint ed. 13.00 (*0-685-22840-1*) Ayer.

Three American Romantic Painters: Burchfield, Stettheimer, Watkins. New York City Museum Of Modern Art Staff & Henry McBride. 1969. 18.95 (*0-405-01538-0*, 15564) Ayer.

Three American Travellers in England. Robert C. Le Clair. (BCL1-PS American Literature Ser.). 223p. 1993. reprint ed. lib. bdg. 79.00 (*0-7812-6571-1*) Rprt Serv.

Three American Travellers in England: James Russell Lowell, Henry Adams, Henry James. Robert C. Le Clair. LC 77-19341. 222p. 1978. reprint ed. text ed. 55.00 (*0-313-20190-0*, LETA, Greenwood Pr) Greenwood.

Three Americas Railway. Hinton R. Helper. (Notable American Authors Ser.). 1992. reprint ed. lib. bdg. 75.00 (*0-7812-3079-9*) Rprt Serv.

Three & Half Powers: The New Balance in Asia. Harold C. Hinton. LC 74-23956. 320p. reprint ed. pap. 91.20 (*0-317-11160-4*, 2055230) Bks Demand.

***Three & Many Wishes of Jason Reid.** Hazel Hutchins. (Young Novels Ser.). (Illus.). 80p. (J). (gr. 3-7). 1996. pap. 5.95 (*0-920236-61-8*, Pub. by Annick CN) Firefly Bks Ltd.

Three & One: Poems by David Lloyd Whited. David L. Whited. Ed. & Illus. by Marion Kimes. 72p. 1993. pap. 9.00 (*0-9638199-0-9*) Red Sky Pr.

Three & One Half Years Related to the Ministry of Jesus of Nazareth. (Walk with Jesus Ser.). 20p. 1993. pap. 5.00 (*1-57277-409-6*) Script Rsch.

***Three Anglo-Irish Plays.** Rudolf Stamm. 114p. 1970. 12.95 (*0-8369-8205-3*) Ayer.

Three Apples from Heaven: Armenian Folk Tales. O. Sheohmelian. Ed. by Arra Avakian et al. Tr. by O. Sheohmelian from ARM. (Illus.). 150p. (Orig.). 1982. pap. 6.95 (*0-933706-23-5*) Ararat Pr.

Three Approaches to Electron Correlation in Atoms. Keith A. Brueckner & Oktay Sinanoglu. LC 76-89666. (Yale Series in the Sciences). (Illus.). 398p. reprint ed. pap. 113.50 (*0-317-09328-2*, 2022039) Bks Demand.

Three-Arched Bridge. Ismail Kadare. Tr. by John Hodgson. 184p. 1997. 21.95 (*1-55970-368-7*) Arcade Pub Inc.

***Three-Arched Bridge.** Ismail Kadare. 1998. pap. write for info. (*0-375-70094-3*, Vin) Random.

Three Arthurian Romances: Poems from Medieval France. Ed. & Tr. by Ross G. Arthur. (Everyman Paperback Classics Ser.). 288p. (Orig.). (C). 1996. pap. 7.50 (*0-460-87577-9*, Everyman's Classic Lib) C E Tuttle.

Three Articles of Faith. Carver Collins. 96p. 1995. pap. 9.00 (*0-8059-3770-6*) Dorrance.

Three Artists (Three Women) Modernism & the Art of Hesse, Krasner, & O'Keeffe. Anne M. Wagner. LC 96-14058. (Ahmanson Murphy Fine Arts Bk.). (Illus.). 384p. (C). 1997. 35.00 (*0-520-20608-8*) U CA Pr.

Three Aspects of Labor Dynamics. Wladimir S. Woytinsky. LC 73-16650. (Illus.). 249p. 1974. reprint ed. text ed. 65.00 (*0-8371-7215-2*, WOLD, Greenwood Pr) Greenwood.

Three Aspects of the Cross see Cross & Sanctification

Three Aspects of the Late Alfred Lord Tennyson. John M. Moore. LC 79-185968. (Studies in Tennyson: No. 27). vi, 144p. 1972. reprint ed. lib. bdg. 55.95 (*0-8383-1387-6*) M S G Haskell Hse.

***** Michael Brodsky. LC 93-40969. 350p. 1994. 25.95 (*1-56858-000-2*) FWEW.

****** Michael Brodsky. 350p. 1994. pap. 13.95 (*1-56858-001-0*) FWEW.

Three Astronauts. Umberto Eco. (Illus.). (J). (gr. 1 up). 1989. 15.00 (*0-15-286383-4*, HB Juv Bks) HarBrace.

Three at Sea. Timothy Bush. LC 93-3677. (Illus.). 32p. (J). (ps-2). 1994. 14.00 (*0-517-59299-1*) Crown Bks Yng Read.

Three at Wolfe's Door. Rex Stout. 240p. 1995. mass mkt. 4.99 (*0-553-23803-5*, Crimeline) Bantam.

Three Autobiographical Fragments. Isaiah Thomas. 1962. pap. 4.50 (*0-912296-32-1*) Am Antiquarian.

***Three Avante-Vaudeville Monologues +** Philip-Dimitri Galas. (Illus.). 64p. (Orig.). 1995. pap. 7.95 (*1-884923-00-3*) Dimitri Pubns.

Three Avenues of Spiritual Development. Robert V. Dodd. 1990. pap. 6.50 (*1-877871-05-2*, 3337) Ed Ministries.

Three Axioms for a Theory of Conduct: Philosophy, & the Humanistic Science of Psychology. Louis Carini. 108p. (Orig.). (C). 1984. pap. text ed. 13.50 (*0-8191-3971-8*) U Pr of Amer.

Three-Axle Streetcars: From Robinson to Rathgeber, Vol. 1. Henry Elsner, Jr. (Illus.). 180p. (Orig.). 1995. pap. 29.95 (*0-934088-29-2*, 7614) NJ Intl Inc.

Three-Axle Streetcars: From Robinson to Rathgeber, Vol. 2. Henry Elsner, Jr. (Illus.). (Orig.). 1995. pap. 31.95 (*0-934088-31-4*, 7616) NJ Intl Inc.

Three Baby Chicks. Ellen Patrick. (Easter Ornament Bks.). (J). 1996. 2.95 (*0-689-80785-6*) S&S Childrens.

Three Bags Full. Ragnhild Scamell. LC 92-50882. (Illus.). 32p. (J). (ps-1). 1993. 14.95 (*0-531-05486-1*) Orchard Bks Watts.

Three Ball Digest: All You'll Ever Need to Know about Juggling Three Balls. Plus !!! Mastering the Headroll. Dick Franco. LC 89-11769. (Illus.). 150p. (Orig.). 1989. 21.95 (*0-917643-05-4*); pap. 17.95 (*0-917643-04-6*) B Dube.

***Three Battle Grounds.** Francis Frangipane. Tr. by Jei-In Lee. 158p. (Orig.). (KOR.). 1992. pap. 4.11 (*1-890209-00-7*) New Name.

Three Battlegrounds. Francis Frangipane. 153p. 1989. pap. 6.50 (*0-9629049-0-2*, FF1-001) Arrow Publications.

Three Battlegrounds. Francis Frangipane. 118p. (SPA.). 1991. pap. text ed. 5.00 (*0-9629049-2-9*, FFS-001) Arrow Publications.

***Three Battlegrounds.** Francis Frangipane. 160p. 1996. reprint ed. 14.50 (*1-886296-13-8*, FF1-022) Arrow Publications.

Three Bears. (FRE.). (J). (gr. k-3). 4.25 (*0-685-28449-2*) Fr & Eur.

Three Bears. (Read Along With Me Ser.). 24p. (J). (ps-3). 1988. 2.25 (*1-56288-150-7*) Checkerboard.

Three Bears. (Picture Tales Ser.). (Illus.). 32p. (J). (ps-1). 1985. 2.49 (*0-517-46239-7*) Random Hse Value.

Three Bears. (Cherished Fairytale Ser.). 32p. (J). (ps-3). Date not set. spiral bd. 4.95 (*1-56987-235-X*) Landoll.

Three Bears. 1996. pap. 7.95 (*0-937306-14-2*) Creat Res NC.

Three Bears. Illus. & Retold by Byron Barton. LC 90-43151. 32p. (J). (ps-1). 1991. 15.00 (*0-06-020423-0*); lib. bdg. 14.89 (*0-06-020424-9*) HarpC Child Bks.

***Three Bears.** Byron Barton. (Illus.). 32p. (J). (ps). 1997. bds. 6.95 (*0-694-00998-9*, Festival) HarpC Child Bks.

Three Bears. Charlotte B. Chorpenning. 50p. (Orig.). (J). 1949. 5.00 (*0-87602-208-5*) Anchorage.

Three Bears. Kathleen D. Duchak. (Illus.). 28p. (J). (ps). 1994. 15.00 (*0-9640865-0-6*) Family Pubng.

Three Bears. Charl Fromme. (Storytime Classics Ser.). (Illus.). 24p. (J). (ps-2). 1995. pap. 1.29 (*1-56293-556-9*) McClanahan Bk.

Three Bears. Ed. & Illus. by Paul Galdone. LC 78-158833. 32p. (J). (ps-3). 1979. 14.95 (*0-395-28811-8*, Clarion Bks) HM.

Three Bears. Paul Galdone. LC 78-158833. (Illus.). 32p. (J). (ps-3). 1985. pap. 5.95 (*0-89919-401-X*, Clarion Bks) HM.

Three Bears. Margaret Hillert. (Illus.). (J). (ps). 1963. pap. 5.10 (*0-8136-5515-3*, TK2367); lib. bdg. 7.95 (*0-8136-5015-1*, TK2366) Modern Curr.

Three Bears. Hanna Hutchinson. (Illus.). 24p. (J). (gr. 1-2). 1995. pap. 2.95 (*0-922852-41-3*) Another Lang Pr.

Three Bears. Gina Ingoglia. (Illus.). (J). (ps-3). 1990. write for info. (*0-307-11594-1*, Golden Books) Western Pub.

Three Bears. Little Golden Books Staff. (Illus.). (J). (ps-3). 1987. pap. 1.59 (*0-307-02140-8*, Golden Books) Western Pub.

Three Bears. Little Golden Books Staff. (FIrst Little Golden Bks). (Illus.). 24p. (J). (ps). 1995. bds. 1.19 (*0-307-10147-9*, Golden Books) Western Pub.

Three Bears. Illus. by Yuri Salzman. (Golden Super Shape Bks.). 24p. (J). (ps-3). 1987. pap. 1.95 (*0-307-10050-2*, Golden Books) Western Pub.

Three Bears. Cindy West. (Illus.). 24p. (J). (ps-3). 1993. pap. 1.49 (*0-307-11544-5*, Golden Books) Western Pub.

Three Bears: A Forties Fable. Terry Beal. 24p. (Orig.). (J). (gr. 3 up). 1993. pap. 3.00 (*1-57514-265-1*) Encore Perform Pub.

Three Bears: Cut & Tell Cutouts. Jean Warren. Ed. by Kathleen Cubley. (Nursery Tales Ser.). (Illus.). 8p. (Orig.). (J). (ps). 1994. pap. 2.95 (*0-911019-85-5*, WPH 2203) Warren Pub Hse.

Three Bears: Richard Scarry. Richard Scarry. (Little Nugget Bks.). (Illus.). 28p. (J). (ps). 1993. bds. 3.25 (*0-307-12524-6*, 12524, Golden Pr) Western Pub.

Three Bears see Tres Osos

Three Bears see Tri Ursoj

Three Bears see Tova Lous Yo

Three Bears see Tres Ursi

Three Bears see Dubu Watatu

Three Bears - Little Red Riding Hood. J. Vreeman. (Illus.). 16p. (Orig.). (J). 1985. pap. 3.95 (*0-918789-03-6*) FreeMan Prods.

3 Bears: And Other Great Stories with Hats. Susan Pagnucci & Franco Pagnucci. (Illus.). 64p. (Orig.). (J). (ps-3). 1995. pap. 8.99 (*0-929326-12-1*) Bur Oak Pr Inc.

Three Bears Big Book. Illus. & Retold by Byron Barton. LC 91-34151. (Trophy Picture Bk.). 32p. (J). (ps-1). 1994. pap. 19.95 (*0-06-443380-3*, Trophy) HarpC Child Bks.

Three Bears Holiday Rhyme Book. Jane Yolen. LC 93-17252. (Illus.). 32p. (J). (ps-3). 1995. 15.00 (*0-15-200932-9*, J Yolen Bks) HarBrace.

Three Bears in the Ministry. Beverly C. Burgess. 32p. (Orig.). (J). (ps). 1982. pap. 4.98 (*0-89274-252-6*) Harrison Hse.

Three Bears Rhyme Book. Jane Yolen. LC 86-19514. (Illus.). 32p. (J). (ps-3). 1987. 14.95 (*0-15-286386-9*, HB Juv Bks) HarBrace.

***Three Bears Rhyme Book.** Jane Yolen. (J). 1997. pap. write for info. (*0-15-201564-7*) HarBrace.

Three Bears, Three Sizes, Vol. 4: Pasitos English Language Development Books. Darlyne F. Schott. (Pasitos Hacia la Lectura Ser.). 24p. (J). (gr. k-1). 1990. pap. text ed. 11.00 (*1-56537-063-5*) D F Schott Educ.

Three Bedrooms, One Corpse. Charlaine Harris. 256p. 1994. 20.00 (*0-684-19643-3*) S&S Trade.

Three Bedrooms, One Corpse. Charlaine Harris. 1995. mass mkt. 3.99 (*0-373-26177-2*) Harlequin Bks.

Three Bedtime Stories. (Illus.). (J). (ps-1). 1985. 2.98 (*0-517-46989-8*) Random Hse Value.

Three Beginnings Vol. 5: Revolution, Rights & the Liberal State. Ed. by Stephen F. Englehart & John A. Moore, Jr. LC 93-41632. (Comparative Cultures & Literatures Ser.: Vol. 5). 219p. (C). 1994. text ed. 51.95 (*0-8204-2343-2*) P Lang Pubng.

Three Behaim Boys: Growing up in Early Modern Germany. Ed. by Steven Ozment. (Illus.). 312p. (C). 1991. reprint ed. pap. text ed. 18.00 (*0-300-05133-6*) Yale U Pr.

Three Behaim Boys: Growing Up in Early Modern Germany - A Chronicle of Their Lives. Steven Ozment. LC 89-27312. 312p. (C). 1990. 32.00 (*0-300-04670-7*) Yale U Pr.

Three Berlin Artists of the Weimar Era: Hannah Hoch, Kathe Kollowitz, Jeanne Mammen. Louise R. Noun. LC 94-71498. (Illus.). 48p. 1993. pap. 20.00 (*1-879003-10-4*) Edmundson.

Three Best-Loved Tales: A Second Volume Featuring the Art of Gustaf Tenggren. (Little Golden Bks.). (Illus.). 72p. (J). (ps-1). 1993. 8.95 (*0-307-15636-2*, 15636, Golden Pr) Western Pub.

Three Bible Churches. Vernon A. Schutz. 52p. 3.50 (*0-89814-047-1*) Grace Publns.

***Three Big Bangs.** Dauber. (C). 1997. pap. 13.00 (*0-201-15495-1*) Addison-Wesley.

Three Big Bangs: Comet Crashes, Exploding Stars & the Creation of the Universe. Philip M. Dauber & Richard A. Muller. 192p. (C). 1996. 25.00 (*0-201-40752-3*) Addison-Wesley.

Three Big Pigs. Carmen Van Horne. LC 92-91035. (Illus.). 48p. (Orig.). (J). (ps-3). 1993. 12.95 (*1-882643-00-3*); pap. 7.95 (*1-882643-01-1*) V H Visionarts.

Three Big Pigs. Carmen Van Horne. LC 92-91035. (Illus.). 32p. (Orig.). (J). (ps-3). 1993. lib. bdg. 13.95 (*1-882643-04-6*) V H Visionarts.

Three Big Words. Kenneth E. Hagin. 1983. pap. 0.75 (*0-89276-258-6*) Hagin Ministries.

***Three Billy Goats.** Paul Galdone. (J). 1987. pap. 8.95 incl. audio (*0-89919-688-8*) Ticknor & Flds Bks Yng Read.

***Three Billy Goats Gruff.** (Little Reader Ser.). (J). 1997. pap. 2.49 (*0-395-88293-1*) HM.

Three Billy-Goats Gruff. (Ladybird Stories Ser.). (Illus.). (ARA.). (J). (gr. 5-8). 1987. 4.50 (*0-86685-239-5*) Intl Bk Ctr.

Three Billy-Goats-Gruff. (Picture Tales Ser.). (Illus.). 32p. (J). (ps-1). 1985. 2.49 (*0-517-46241-9*) Random Hse Value.

Three Billy Goats Gruff. (Book & Cassette Favorites Ser.). (J). (gr. 3-4). 1987. 6.95 incl. audio (*0-317-64578-1*) HM.

Three Billy Goats Gruff. (Square Format Fairy Tales Ser.: No. S874-4). (Illus.). 28p. (J). (ps up). 1987. 3.95 (*0-7214-5031-8*, Ladybrd) Penguin.

Three Billy Goats Gruff. (Read Along With Me Ser.: No. 2). 24p. (Orig.). (J). (ps). 1989. 2.25 (*1-56288-162-0*) Checkerboard.

Three Billy Goats Gruff. (Fairy Tale Fun Ser.). (J). 3.95 (*0-7214-5430-5*, Ladybrd) Penguin.

Three Billy Goats Gruff. (Illus.). 32p. (J). (ps-2). 1996. pap. 2.50 (*0-7214-5624-3*, Ladybrd) Penguin.

Three Billy-Goats Gruff. Ellen Appleby. (Easy to Read Folktales Ser.). (Illus.). 32p. (J). (gr. k-2). 1985. pap. 2.99 (*0-590-41121-7*) Scholastic Inc.

Three Billy-Goats Gruff. Ellen Appleby. (J). 1993. 19.95 (*0-590-71393-0*) Scholastic Inc.

***Three Billy Goats Gruff.** Ellen Appleby. (FRE.). (J). pap. 6.99 (*0-590-71770-7*) Scholastic Inc.

Three Billy Goats Gruff. Illus. & Retold by Tim Arnold. LC 92-23992. 32p. (J). (ps-3). 1993. lib. bdg. 14.95 (*0-689-50575-2*, McElderry) S&S Childrens.

***Three Billy Goats Gruff.** Peter C. Asbjornsen. LC 96-42349. (Illus.). (J). 1998. write for info. (*0-694-01033-2*) HarpC.

***Three Billy Goats Gruff.** Carolyn S. Bailey. (Children's Thrift Classics Ser.). (J). pap. 1.00 (*0-486-28021-7*) Dover.

Three Billy-Goats Gruff. Val Biro. (J). write for info. (*0-19-272280-8*) OUP.

Three Billy Goats Gruff. Ted Dewan. 32p. (J). (ps-3). 1995. pap. 4.95 (*0-590-20515-3*) Scholastic Inc.

Three Billy Goats Gruff. Illus. & Retold by Paul Galdone. LC 72-85338. 32p. (J). (ps-3). 1979. 14.95 (*0-395-28812-6*, Clarion Bks) HM.

Three Billy Goats Gruff. Paul Galdone. (Illus.). 32p. (J). (ps-3). 1981. pap. 5.95 (*0-89919-035-9*, Clarion Bks) HM.

An Asterisk (*) at the beginning of an entry indicates that the title is appearing in BIP for the first time.

Three Billy Goats Gruff. Golden Books Staff. (First Little Golden Bks.). (Illus.). 24p. (J). 1995. 1.09 (*0-307-10117-7*, Golden Pr) Western Pub.

Three Billy Goats Gruff. Illus. by David Jorgensen. (Rabbit Ears Storybook Classics Ser.). 32p. (J). (ps up). 1993. boxed write for info. incl. audio (*0-307-14329-5*, 14329, Golden Pr) Western Pub.

Three Billy Goats Gruff. Illus. by David Jorgensen. (J). (ps up). 1995. 10.95 incl. audio (*0-689-80060-6*) S&S Trade.

Three Billy Goats Gruff. Jonathan Langley. LC 92-4842. (Illus.). 32p. (J). (ps-3). 1998. 15.00 (*0-06-021224-1*); lib. bdg. 14.89 (*0-06-021474-0*) HarpC Child Bks.

Three Billy Goats Gruff. Illus. by Loretta Lustig. (Children's Classics Ser.). 32p. (J). 1991. 6.95 (*0-8362-4913-5*) Andrews & McMeel.

Three Billy Goats Gruff. Illus. by David Pace. (Fairy Tale Pop-ups Ser.). 16p. (J). 1994. 3.95 (*0-7214-9418-8*, Ladybrd) Penguin.

Three Billy Goats Gruff. Illus. by Ed Parker. LC 78-18068. 32p. (J). (gr. k-3). 1979. lib. bdg. 11.89 (*0-89375-121-9*); audio 9.95 (*0-685-04953-1*) Troll Communs.

Three Billy Goats Gruff. Illus. by Ed Parker. LC 78-18068. 32p. (J). (gr. k-3). 1997. pap. 3.95 (*0-89375-099-9*) Troll Communs.

Three Billy Goats Gruff. Tom Roberts. LC 93-6678. (J). (ps-6). 1993. 9.95 (*0-88708-319-6*, Picture Book Studio) S&S Childrens.

Three Billy Goats Gruff. Illus. & Retold by Glen Rounds. LC 92-23951. 32p. (J). (ps-3). 1993. lib. bdg. 15.95 (*0-8234-1015-3*) Holiday.

Three Billy Goats Gruff. Illus. & Retold by Glen Rounds. LC 92-23951. 32p. (J). (ps-3). 1994. pap. 5.95 (*0-8234-1136-2*) Holiday.

Three Billy Goats Gruff. Janet Stevens. LC 86-33512. (Illus.). 32p. (J). (ps-3). 1990. pap. 6.00 (*0-15-286397-4*, Voyager Bks) HarBrace.

Three Billy Goats Gruff. Illus. & Retold by Janet Stevens. LC 86-33512. 32p. (J). (ps-3). 1995. pap. 20.00 (*0-15-200233-2*, Red Wagon Bks) HarBrace.

Three Billy Goats Gruff. Harriet Ziefert. LC 94-4987. (Illus.). 32p. (J). (ps up). 1995. 9.95 (*0-688-13259-6*, Tambourine Bks) Morrow.

Three Billy Goats Gruff. Peter C. Asbjornsen & J. E. Moe. LC 57-5265. (Illus.). 32p. (J). (ps-3). 1991. reprint ed. pap. 6.00 (*0-15-690150-1*) HarBrace.

***Three Billy Goats Gruff, Big Bk.** Ellen Appleby. (FRE.). (J). 29.99 (*0-590-71769-3*) Scholastic Inc.

Three Billy Goats Gruff: A Folktale Play for Children. Martha Mutz. (Illus.). 57p. (Orig.). (J). (gr. k-3). 1996. pap. 16.00 (*1-889397-23-7*, 023) Curiosity Canyon.

Three Billy Goats Gruff: Cut & Tell Cutouts. Jean Warren. Ed. by Kathleen Cubley. (Nursery Tales Ser.). (Illus.). 8p. (Orig.). (J). (ps). 1994. pap. 2.95 (*0-911019-87-1*, WPH 2204) Warren Pub Hse.

Three Billy Goats Gruff: Just a Friendly Old Troll. Alvin Granowsky. LC 90-9605. (Another Point of View Ser.). (Illus.). (J). 1995. pap. 5.95 (*0-8114-6635-3*) Raintree Steck-V.

Three Billy Goats Gruff: Just a Friendly Old Troll. Alvin Granowsky. LC 90-9605. (Another Point of View Ser.). (Illus.). 48p. (J). (gr. k-2). 1996. lib. bdg. 22.83 (*0-8114-7128-4*) Raintree Steck-V.

Three Billy Goats Gruff & Other Read-Aloud Stories. Ed. by Carolyn S. Bailey. LC 93-33492. (Children's Thrift Stories Ser.). (Illus.). 96p. (Orig.). (J). 1994. pap. 1.00 (*0-685-75328-X*) Dover.

Three Birds: A Story for Children about the Loss of a Loved One. Marinus Van den Berg. LC 93-38211. (Books to Help Children Ser.). (Illus.). 32p. (J). (ps up). 1994. lib. bdg. 18.60 (*0-8368-1072-4*) Gareth Stevens Inc.

Three Birds: A Story for Children about the Loss of a Loved One. Marinus Van den Berg. LC 93-38734. (Illus.). 24p. (J). (ps-3). 1994. pap. 8.95 (*0-945354-59-2*) Magination Pr.

Three Birds: A Story for Children about the Loss of a Loved One, 11 vols., Set. Marinus Van Den Berg. (Books to Help Children Ser.). (Illus.). 32p. (J). (ps up). 1994. lib. bdg. 204.60 (*0-8368-1096-1*) Gareth Stevens Inc.

Three Birds Alighting on a Field. Timberlake Wertenbaker. 1993. pap. 5.95 (*0-87129-273-4*, T90) Dramatic Pub.

Three Birds Alighting on a Field. Timberlake Westenbaker. 96p. (Orig.). 1992. pap. 8.95 (*0-571-16105-7*) Faber & Faber.

Three Black Pennys. Joseph Hergesheimer. 1993. reprint ed. lib. bdg. 89.00 (*0-7812-5468-X*) Rprt Serv.

Three Blind Mice. Ed McBain. 1990. 18.95 (*0-685-36235-3*) Little.

Three Blind Mice. Ed McBain. 1991. mass mkt. 4.99 (*0-446-40035-1*, Mysterious Paperbk) Warner Bks.

Three Blind Mice. Nicola Smee. (Finger Puppet Board Bks.). (Illus.). 12p. (J). (ps). 1995. bds. 6.95 (*0-590-22486-7*, Cartwheel) Scholastic Inc.

Three Blind Mice. large type ed. Ed McBain. (General Ser.). 396p. 1991. lib. bdg. 21.95 (*0-8161-5169-5*, GK Hall) Thorndike Pr.

Three Blind Mice: How the TV Networks Lost Their Way. Ken Auletta. LC 92-50105. 1992. pap. 18.00 (*0-679-74135-6*, Vin) Random.

Three Blind Mice: Two Novels. Carol Hebald. 200p. 1989. 19.95 (*0-87775-215-X*) Unicorn Pr.

Three Blind Mice & Other Stories. Agatha Christie. 224p. 1984. pap. text ed. 5.50 (*0-425-06806-4*) Berkley Pub.

Three Blind Mice & Other Stories. large type ed. Agatha Christie. (Popular Author Ser.). 338p. 1988. lib. bdg. 19.95 (*0-8161-4461-3*, GK Hall) Thorndike Pr.

Three Blind Mice Mystery. Stephen Krensky. (Illus.). 48p. (J). (ps-2). 1995. 13.95 (*0-385-32131-7*, YB BDD) BDD Bks Young Read.

Three Blind Mice Mystery. Stephen Krensky. LC 94-32511. (Illus.). 48p. (J). (ps-2). 1995. pap. 3.99 (*0-440-41082-7*, YB BDD) BDD Bks Young Read.

Three Blind Mice Mystery. Stephen Krensky. LC 94-32511. (Illus.). (J). 1995. write for info. (*0-440-41085-1*) Dell.

Three Blind Mice Sextet. C. Fuller. 1995. pap. text ed. 20.00 (*0-7935-4822-5*, 00000504) H Leonard.

Three Blondes & Death: A Novel. Yuriy Tarnawsky. 451p. 1993. 21.95 (*0-932511-68-6*); pap. 10.95 (*0-932511-69-4*) Fiction Coll.

Three Bob Day see Stichus

Three-Body Problem. C. Marchal. (Studies in Astronautics: No. 4). 576p. 1990. 256.25 (*0-444-87440-2*) Elsevier.

Three Booklets in One Volume. M. Tartani. Ed. by Mary Caroland. LC 90-71226. 55p. 1991. pap. 8.95 (*1-55523-377-5*) Winston-Derek.

Three Books. Joe Illing. (Illus.). 85p. (Orig.). 1995. pap. 10.00 (*1-57637-000-3*) Blck Hills.

Three Books: Body Rags; Mortal Acts, Mortal Words; the Past. Galway Kinnell. 1993. pap. 18.95 (*0-395-68088-3*) HM.

3 Books for Baby: Bedtime, Bathtime, Playtime. Emma Books Ltd. Staff. (J). 1995. 10.95 (*0-689-80127-0*, Litl Simon S&S) S&S Childrens.

Three Books of Embassies, Vol. 2, No. 12. Alberico Gentili. LC 95-77090. (Classics in International Law Reprint Ser.: No. 12). 1995. 95.00 (*1-57588-256-6*, 310230) W S Hein.

Three Books of Khepra, Bks. I & II. Ahmad Azzahir. 180p. 1992. write for info. (*1-881421-00-7*) Intl Khepran Inst.

Three Books of Known Space. Larry Niven. 608p. 1996. pap. 12.95 (*0-345-40448-3*) Ballantine.

Three Books of Occult Philosophy. Henry C. Agrippa. Ed. by Donald Tyson. Tr. by James Freake. LC 92-33147. (Llewellyn's Sourcebook Ser.). 1010p. 1994. pap. 39.95 (*0-87542-832-0*) Llewellyn Pubns.

Three Books of Occult Philosophy or Magic. Henry C. Agrippa. 288p. 1992. pap. 24.95 (*1-56459-199-9*) Kessinger Pub.

Three Books of Occult Philosophy or Magic. Heinrich C. Agrippa von Nettesheim. LC 79-8222. (Illus.). reprint ed. 39.50 (*0-404-18401-4*) AMS Pr.

Three Books of Polydore Vergil's English History, Comprising the Reigns of Henry Sixth, Edward Fourth, & Richard Third. Polydorus Vergilius. Ed. by Henry Ellis. (Camden Society, London. Publications, First Ser.: No. 29). reprint ed. 72.00 (*0-404-50129-X*) AMS Pr.

Three Books of the Potter's Art. Cipriano Piccolpasso. 1980. 212.95 (*0-85967-452-5*, Pub. by Scolar Pr UK) Ashgate Pub Co.

Three Books on Fishing: Associated with the Complete Angler by Izaac Walton. LC 62-7054. 1962. reprint ed. 50.00 (*0-8201-1017-5*) Schol Facsimiles.

Three Books on the Law of War, Vol. 2. Alberico Gentili. LC 95-77181. (Classics in International Law Reprint Ser.: No. 16). 1995. reprint ed. 125.00 (*1-57588-260-4*, 310320) W S Hein.

Three Boxes of Life: And How to Get Out of Them. Richard N. Bolles. LC 78-17000. (Illus.). 480p. 1981. pap. 18.95 (*0-913668-58-3*) Ten Speed Pr.

***Three Branches of India's Life-Tree: Commentaries on the Vedas, the Upanishads, & the...** Sri Chinmoy. 1997. pap. text ed. 13.95 (*0-88497-113-9*) Aum Pubns.

Three Brass Monkeys. Bonnie Pike. LC 88-9331. 96p. (Orig.). 1988. pap. 7.95 (*0-932419-11-9*) Cherokee.

Three Brave Men: Level Two. Lavaun Linde & Mary Quishenberry. (Bible Stories for Early Readers Ser.: Bk. 3). (Illus.). 32p. (Orig.). (J). (gr. 1). 1988. pap. text ed. 4.99 (*0-945107-07-2*) Bradshaw Pubs.

Three Brave Women. C. L. Martin. LC 89-77770. (Illus.). 32p. (J). (gr. k-3). 1991. lib. bdg. 15.00 (*0-02-762445-5*, Mac Bks Young Read) S&S Childrens.

***Three Brides, No Groom.** Macomber. 1997. mass mkt. 6.99 (*0-373-48352-X*) Harlequin Bks.

Three Brontes. May Sinclair. (BCL1-PR English Literature Ser.). 296p. 1992. reprint ed. lib. bdg. 79.00 (*0-7812-7452-4*) Rprt Serv.

Three Bucketeers: Commander, Thinker, Player. Mike Epperley. (Buckethead Ser.). (Illus.). 48p. (Orig.). (J). (gr. k-6). 1994. pap. 6.98 (*1-882183-22-3*) Computer Pr.

Three Bullets Sealed His Lips. Bruce A. Rubenstein & Lawrence E. Ziewacz. (Illus.). 200p. 1987. pap. 15.95 (*0-87013-252-0*) Mich St U Pr.

Three Burlesque Plays of Thomas Duffett. Ed. by Ronald E. Dilorenzo. LC 72-81173. 319p. 1973. 37.95 (*0-87745-033-1*) U of Iowa Pr.

Three by Annie Dillard: Pilgrim at Tinker Creek, an American Childhood, & the Writing Life. Annie Dillard. LC 90-55495. 640p. 1990. reprint ed. pap. 19.00 (*0-06-092064-5*, PL) HarpC.

Three by Cain: Serenade, Love's Lovely Counterfeit, & The Butterfly. James M. Cain. 1989. pap. 14.00 (*0-679-72323-4*, Vin) Random.

Three by Finney. Jack Finney. 432p. 1987. pap. 12.00 (*0-671-64048-8*, Fireside) S&S Trade.

Three by Flannery O'Connor: Wise Blood, the Violent Bear It Away, a Good Man Is Hard to Find. Flannery O'Connor. 1986. pap. 4.95 (*0-451-52101-3*, Sig Classics) NAL-Dutton.

***Three by Fulghum.** Robert Fulghum. 1997. 19.95 (*0-375-50075-8*, Villard Bks) Random.

Three by Harry Barba. Harry Barba. LC 67-27073. (Orig.). 1967. pap. 35.00 (*0-911906-00-2*) Harian Creative Bks.

Three by O'Connor. Flannery O'Connor. 1986. pap. 6.95 (*0-451-52514-0*, Sig Classics) NAL-Dutton.

Three By Szekely: Three Books in One Volume, Book of Vitamins, Book of Minerals & Book of Herbs. Edmond B. Szekely. LC 83-47674. 200p. (Orig.). 1983. pap. 7.95 (*0-87983-342-4*) Keats.

Three by Tennessee Williams. Incl. Sweet Bird of Youth. Tennessee Williams. 1976. pap. (*0-318-54501-2*); Rose Tattoo. (*0-318-54502-0*); Night of the Iguana. (*0-318-54503-9*); 1976. pap. 6.95 (*0-451-52149-8*, Sig Classics) NAL-Dutton.

Three by the Sea. Edward Marshall. (Easy-to-Read Ser.: Level 2, Red). (Illus.). (J). (gr. k-3). 1994. pap. 3.50 (*0-14-037004-8*) Puffin Bks.

Three-by-Three. Linda A. Crist. LC 92-524579. 41p. (C). 1991. pap. text ed. 25.00 (*0-9620289-1-6*) Crist Pubns.

Three by Three: Barba, Bond, Hamalian. Harry Barba et al. LC 77-78963. 115p. (Orig.). 1969. 30.00 (*0-911906-01-0*) Harian Creative Bks.

Three by Three: Masterworks of the Southern Gothic. Doris Betts et al. LC 85-61992. 568p. (Orig.). 1985. 22.95 (*0-931948-80-0*) Peachtree Pubs.

Three by Three: Short Stories. Anne Dandurand et al. Tr. & Selected by Luise Von Flotow. (Prose Ser.: No. 18). 122p. 1994. pap. 10.00 (*0-920717-69-1*) Guernica Editions.

***Three by Three, Bloom Blood, After Uelsmann, The Edge of Heaven.** Roy Bentley et al. Ed. by Larry Smith. (Ohio Writers Ser.: Nos. 9, 10 & 11). (Illus.). 108p. (Orig.). 1988. pap. 7.95 (*0-933087-11-X*) Bottom Dog Pr.

***3 by 3 from Hungary.** Vasif Kortun et al. (Illus.). 40p. (Orig.). Date not set. write for info. (*0-941276-19-8*) Bard Coll Pubns.

Three Byzantine Literatures: A Layman's Guide. Ihor Sevcenko. (Nichola E. Kulukundis Lectures in History of Hellenism). 26p. 1985. pap. 2.50 (*0-917653-13-0*) Holy Cross Orthodox.

Three Byzantine Military Treatises. Ed. by George T. Dennis. LC 84-26053. (Dumbarton Oaks Texts: Vol. 9). (Illus.). 400p. (ENG & GRE.). 1985. 28.00 (*0-88402-140-8*) Dumbarton Oaks.

Three Byzantine Saints. Tr. by Elizabeth Dawes & Norman H. Baynes from GRE. LC 96-31502. 275p. 1996. pap. 13.95 (*0-913836-44-3*) St Vladimirs.

Three California Artists: Kim Abeles, Judy Fiskin, Anne Scott Plummer, 3 bks., Set. Ed. by William S. Bartman & Lucinda Barnes. (Illus.). 102p. 1992. Boxed set. boxed 34.95 (*0-923183-10-8*) ART Pr CA.

Three Came Home. large type ed. Agnes N. Keith. 1975. 25.99 (*0-85456-339-3*) Ulverscroft.

Three-Career Couple. Marcia Byalick & Linda Saslow. LC 93-360. (Illus.). 248p. 1993. pap. 12.95 (*1-56079-239-6*) Petersons.

Three Case Histories: The "Wolf Man," the "Rat Man," & the Psychotic Doctor Schreber. Sigmund Freud. 282p. (C). 1993. pap. 12.00 (*0-02-050988-X*) Macmillan.

***Three Case Studies: The "Wolf Man", the "Rat Man" & the Psychotic Doctor Schreber.** Sigmund Freud. 1996. pap. 12.00 (*0-684-82945-2*) S&S Trade.

Three Catholic Afro-American Congresses. Congress of Colored Catholics of the United States. 1978. 21.95 (*0-405-10863-X*, 11829) Ayer.

Three Catholic Reformers of the Fifteenth Century. Mary H. Allies. LC 73-38755. (Essay Index Reprint Ser.). 1977. reprint ed. 16.95 (*0-8369-2633-1*) Ayer.

Three Cautionary Tales. Virginia Christian et al. 153p. (Orig.). 1993. pap. 14.00 (*0-9630164-3-1*) Canios Edit.

Three Centuries & the Island: A Historical Geography of Settlement & Agriculture in Prince Edward Island, Canada. Andrew H. Clark. LC 59-2157. 300p. reprint ed. pap. 85.50 (*0-317-27978-5*, 2055817) Bks Demand.

Three Centuries of Accounting in Massachusetts. William Holmes et al. Ed. by Richard P. Brief. LC 77-87295. (Development of Contemporary Accounting Thought Ser.). 1978. lib. bdg. 30.95 (*0-405-10922-9*) Ayer.

Three Centuries of American Furniture see Four Centuries of American Furniture

Three Centuries of American Music Vol. 1: A Collection of Sacred & Secular Music: Solo Song to 1865. Tawa Nicholas. 400p. (C). 1989. 100.00 (*0-8161-0542-1*) G K Hall.

Three Centuries of American Music Vol. 2: A Collection of Sacred & Secular Music: Solo Song, 1866-1910. Tawa Nichols. 400p. (C). 1989. Catalog. 100.00 (*0-8161-0543-X*) G K Hall.

Three Centuries of American Music Vol. 3: A Collection of Sacred & Secular Music: Keyboard Music Through 1865. Ed. by Sam Dennison et al. 425p. 1990. 100.00 (*0-8161-0544-8*) G K Hall.

Three Centuries of American Music Vol. 4: A Collection of Sacred & Secular Music: Keyboard Music 1866 Through 1910. Ed. by Sam Dennison et al. 425p. 1990. 100.00 (*0-8161-0545-6*) G K Hall.

Three Centuries of American Music Vol. 5: A Collection of Sacred & Secular Music: Opera. Ed. by Martha F. Schleifer. 425p. 1990. 100.00 (*0-8161-0546-4*) G K Hall.

Three Centuries of American Music Vol. 6: A Collection of Sacred & Secular Music: Opera. Ed. by Martha F. Schleifer. 425p. (C). 1990. 100.00 (*0-8161-0547-2*) G K Hall.

Three Centuries of American Music Vol. 7: A Collection of Sacred & Secular Music: Choral Music. Phillip Vandermeer. 400p. 1991. Catalog. 100.00 (*0-8161-0548-0*) G K Hall.

Three Centuries of American Music Vol. 8: A Collection of Sacred & Secular Music. Ed. by Graziano et al. 425p. (C). 1991. 100.00 (*0-8161-0549-9*) G K Hall.

Three Centuries of American Music Vol. 9: A Collection of Sacred & Secular Music: Orchestra. Sam Dennison. 1992. 100.00 (*0-8161-0550-2*) G K Hall.

Three Centuries of American Music Vol. 10: A Collection of Sacred & Secular Music: Orchestra. Sam Dennison. 1992. 100.00 (*0-8161-0551-0*) G K Hall.

Three Centuries of American Music Vol. 11: A Collection of Sacred & Secular Music: Orchestra. Sam Dennison. 1992. 105.00 (*0-8161-0552-9*) G K Hall.

Three Centuries of American Music Vol. 12: A Collection of Sacred & Secular Music: Wind & Percussion. Camus. 1992. 100.00 (*0-8161-0553-7*, Hall Library) G K Hall.

Three Centuries of Architectural Craftsmanship. Ed. by Colin Amery. (Illus.). 221p. 1978. pap. 61.95 (*0-7506-0301-1*) Buttrwrth-Heinemann.

Three Centuries of Ballingers in America. Emma B. Reeves. LC 75-27993. (Illus.). 614p. 1977. lib. bdg. 20.00 (*0-911013-02-4*) E B Reeves.

Three Centuries of English Church Music. W. H. Parry. 1977. lib. bdg. 59.95 (*0-8490-2745-4*) Gordon Pr.

Three Centuries of English Essays: From Francis Bacon to Max Beerbohm. Ed. by Vere H. Collins. LC 67-26727. (Essay Index Reprint Ser.). 1977. 13.95 (*0-8369-0327-7*) Ayer.

Three Centuries of French Domestic Silver: Its Makers & Its Marks: The Metropolitan Museum of Art, 2 vols. Faith Dennis. (Illus.). 1993. reprint ed. Set, Vol. 1, 382p. Vol. 2, 224p. 295.00 (*1-55660-175-1*) A Wofsy Fine Arts.

Three Centuries of German Life in America. Rudolf Cronau. 1972. 59.95 (*0-8490-1210-4*) Gordon Pr.

Three Centuries of Harpsichord Making. Frank T. Hubbard. LC 65-12784. (Illus.). 470p. 1965. 35.50 (*0-674-88845-6*) HUP.

Three Centuries of Harvard. Samuel E. Morison. 520p. 1986. pap. 19.95 (*0-674-88891-X*) Belknap Pr.

***Three Centuries of Italian Sculpture: Masterpieces from the Museo Nazionale del Palazzo di Venezia: Georgia Museum of Art, October 5-November 24, 1996.** Museo di Palazzo Venezia Staff et al. LC 96-36152. 1996. write for info. (*0-915977-29-X*) Georgia Museum of Art.

Three Centuries of Maryland Architecture. (Illus.). 91p. 1982. 5.00 (*1-878399-15-2*) Div Hist Cult Progs.

Three Centuries of New Haven, 1638-1938. Rollin G. Osterweis. LC 52-12064. (Illus.). 559p. reprint ed. pap. 159.40 (*0-8357-8351-0*, 2033849) Bks Demand.

Three Centuries of Poor Law Administration: A Study of Legislation in Rhode Island. Margaret Creech. 21.95 (*0-405-19031-X*) Ayer.

Three Centuries of Science in America Series, 66 bks. Ed. by I. Bernard Cohen. (Illus.). 1980. Set. lib. bdg. 2,939.00 (*0-405-12525-9*) Ayer.

Three Centuries of Women's Dress Fashions: A Quantitative Analysis. fac. ed. A. L. Kroeber & J. Richardson. Ed. by Robert H. Lowie et al. (University of California Publications: No. 5:2). 48p. (C). 1940. reprint ed. pap. 4.35 (*1-55567-082-2*) Coyote Press.

Three Chances. Annie L. Fincher. LC 94-90895. 200p. (Orig.). 1996. pap. 7.00 (*1-56002-545-X*, Univ Edtns) Aegina Pr.

Three Chanteys for Violin, Clarinet & Piano. Ridgway Banks. (Contemporary Instrumental Ser.: No. 2). i, 19p. 1989. pap. text ed. 10.00 (*1-56571-019-3*) PRB Prods.

Three Chapters from the Samadhirajasutra. Tr. by Constantin Regamey from SAN. 112p. 1984. reprint ed. lib. bdg. 19.50 (*0-88181-003-7*) Canon Pubns.

Three Chapters of Letters Relating to the Suppression of Monasteries. Ed. by Thomas Wright. LC 72-74268. (Camden Society, London. Publications, First Ser.: No. 26). reprint ed. 80.00 (*0-404-50126-5*) AMS Pr.

Three Chapters on Courtly Love in Arthurian France & Germany. Hermann J. Weigand. LC 56-58693. (North Carolina. University. Studies in the Germanic Languages & Literatures: No. 17). reprint ed. 27.00 (*0-404-50917-7*) AMS Pr.

Three Cheers: International Edition. (YA). 1994. pap. 3.50 (*0-553-24385-3*) Bantam.

Three Cheers for Civilization. Peter Lyssiotis. 96p. (C). 1990. 120.00 (*0-685-52924-X*, Pub. by Pascoe Pub AT) St Mut.

Three Cheers for Keisha. Teresa Reed. (Magic Attic Club Ser.). (Illus.). 72p. (Orig.). (J). (gr. 2-6). 1995. 12.95 (*1-57513-008-4*); pap. 5.95 (*1-57513-009-2*) Magic Attic.

3 Cheers for Ostric. Francesca Simon. 1998. pap. 14.99 (*0-8037-1955-8*); pap. 14.89 (*0-8037-1956-6*) Dial Bks Young.

Three Cheers for Tacky. Helen Lester. LC 93-14342. (Illus.). (J). 1994. 14.95 (*0-395-66841-7*) HM.

Three Cheers for Tacky. Helen Lester. LC 93-14342. (Illus.). 32p. (J). (ps-3). 1996. pap. 4.95 (*0-395-82740-X*) HM.

Three Cheers for the Unemployed: Government & Unemployment Before the New Deal. Udo Sautter. (Illus.). 368p. (C). 1992. text ed. 69.95 (*0-521-40041-4*) Cambridge U Pr.

Three Cheers for You, Cassie. Katy Hall & Lisa Eisenberg. Ed. by Lisa Clancy. (Paxton Cheerleaders Ser.). 160p. (Orig.). (J). (gr. 3-6). 1994. pap. 3.50 (*0-671-89789-6*, Minstrel Bks) PB.

Three Children: Orphan Survivors in Israel. Rachel Araten. 152p. 1993. pap. 8.95 (*965-229-091-2*, Pub. by Gefen Pub Hse IS) Gefen Bks.

Three Children in the Furnace. Susan Crowder. (Illus.). 37p. (Orig.). (J). 1984. pap. 2.50 (*0-912927-11-9*, X011) St John Kronstadt.

Three Children's Novels. Christopher P. Cranch. Ed. by Joel Myerson. LC 92-24894. (Illus.). 200p. (J). (gr. 4 up). 1993. 35.00 (*0-8203-1507-9*) U of Ga Pr.

Three Children's Plays: The Poet & the Rent; The Frog Prince; The Revenge of the Space Pandas or Binky Rudich & the Two-Speed Clock. David Mamet. LC 86-45245. 144p. (J). (gr. 3-7). 1986. pap. 8.95 (*0-8021-5173-6*, Grove) Grove-Atltic.

Three Chinese Love Songs: For Voice Viola & Piano. B. Sheng. 16p. 1995. pap. 7.95 (*0-7935-4510-2*, 50482387) H Leonard.

Three Choirs: A History of the Festival Gloucester - Hereford - Worcester. Anthony Boden. (Illus.). 320p. 1992. 42.00 (*0-7509-0082-2*, Pub. by Sutton Pubng UK) Bks Intl VA.

T

Three Chord Favorites. (Easy Play Ser.: Vol. 313). 1990. pap. 4.95 (*0-7935-0173-3*, 00001384) H Leonard.

Three Chord Songbook: Traditional. Russ Shipton. (Illus.). 48p. 1983. pap. 5.95 (*0-7119-0412-X*, AM34414) Music Sales.

***Three Chords & the Truth.** Laurence Leamer. 1997. 26.00 (*0-614-27995-X*) HarpC.

***Three Chords & the Truth: Hope, Heartbreak & Changing Fortunes in Nashville.** Laurence Leamer. LC 97-5070. 480p. 1997. 25.00 (*0-06-017505-2*) HarpC.

Three Christian Capitals: Topography & Politics. Richard Krautheimer. (Una's Lectures: No. 4). 168p. 1983. pap. 17.00 (*0-520-06034-2*) U CA Pr.

***Three Christmas Bears.** Illus. by Linda Worrall. (Toddlers' First Stories Ser.). 12p. (J). (ps up). 1997. bds. 2.98 (*1-85854-747-4*) Brimax Bks.

***Three Christmas Programs - Elementary.** (J). 4.85 (*0-687-41884-4*) Abingdon.

Three Chronicles of the Reign of Edward the Fourth. Intro. by Keith Dockray. LC 89-36197. 224p. 1989. 35.00 (*0-86299-568-X*, Pub. by Sutton Pubng UK) Bks Intl VA.

Three City Blocks: CB Score. J. Harbison. 96p. 1995. pap. 25.00 (*0-7935-4512-9*, 50482273) H Leonard.

Three Civilizations, Two Cultures, One State: Canada's Political Traditions. Douglas V. Verney. LC 85-25313. (Duke University Center for International Studies Publications). (Illus.). xiii, 454p. 1986. text ed. 46.95 (*0-8223-0654-9*) Duke.

Three Classic African-American Novels. Ed. by William L. Andrews. 1990. pap. 6.99 (*0-451-62788-1*, Ment) NAL-Dutton.

Three Classic African-American Novels. Ed. by Henry Louis Gates, Jr. LC 89-40704. 1990. pap. 16.00 (*0-679-72742-6*, Vin) Random.

Three Classic Silent Screen Comedies Starring Harold Lloyd. Donald W. McCaffrey. LC 74-4993. (Illus.). 264p. 1976. 35.00 (*0-8386-1455-8*) Fairleigh Dickinson.

Three Classical Poets: Sappho, Catullus & Juvenal. Richard Jenkyns. 254p. 1982. 32.00 (*0-674-88895-2*) HUP.

Three Classics in the Aesthetic of Music. Claude Debussy et al. pap. 5.95 (*0-486-20320-4*) Dover.

Three Clean Fuels from Coal: Technology & Economics: Synthetic Natural Gas, Methanol, Medium Btu Gas. A. Kasem. LC 79-20745. (Series of Special Reports: No. 2). (Illus.). 208p. reprint ed. pap. 59.30 (*0-7837-0682-0*, 2041015) Bks Demand.

Three Clerks. Anthony Trollope. Ed. by Graham Handley. (World's Classics Ser.). (Illus.). 648p. 1990. pap. 9.95 (*0-19-281829-5*) OUP.

Three Clerks, 3 Vols. Anthony Trollope. Ed. by N. John Hall. LC 80-1876. (Selected Works of Anthony Trollope). 1982. reprint ed. lib. bdg. 115.95 (*0-405-14126-2*) Ayer.

Three Clerks. Anthony Trollope. 497p. 1981. reprint ed. pap. 8.95 (*0-486-24099-1*) Dover.

Three Clerks (1858) Anthony Trollope. 576p. 1993. pap. 8.95 (*0-14-043805-X*, Penguin Classics) Viking Penguin.

Three Clicks Left. Katerina Gogou. Tr. by Jack Hirschman from GRE. LC 82-63186. (Literature Ser.: No. 2). 64p. 1983. pap. 4.50 (*0-941842-01-0*) Night Horn Books.

Three Club Juggling: An Introduction. Dick Franco. Ed. by Brian Dube et al. LC 87-30370. (Illus.). 128p. 1987. 16. 95 (*0-917643-03-8*); pap. 12.95 (*0-917643-02-X*) B Dube.

Three Coffins. John Dickson Carr. 1989. lib. bdg. 16.95 (*0-89966-048-7*) Buccaneer Bks.

Three Coffins. John Dickson Carr. LC 79-690. 306p. 1979. reprint ed. 25.00 (*0-89366-259-3*) Ultramarine Pub.

Three Coffins for Nino Lencho. Armando B. Rico. 332p. 1987. lib. bdg. 12.00 (*1-879219-01-8*) Veracruz Pubs.

Three Collections of Poetry: Joggin Erlong; Lyrics Sunshine & Shadow; Majors & Minors. Paul L. Dunbar. (Illus.). (C). 1991. 43.95 (*0-88143-122-2*) Ayer.

Three Comedies. Ben Jonson. Ed. by Michael Jameison. (English Library). 496p. 1966. pap. 10.95 (*0-14-043013-X*, Penguin Classics) Viking Penguin.

Three Comedies: Love's Labor Lost, The Two Gentlemen of Verona, & The Merry Wives of Windsor. William Shakespeare. Ed. by Arthos et al. 1989. pap. 4.95 (*0-451-52026-2*) NAL-Dutton.

Three Comedies: Miles Gloriosus - Pseudolus - Rudens. Plautus. LC 90-41383. (Masters of Latin Literature Ser.). 320p. 1991. 42.50 (*0-8014-2355-4*); pap. 13.95 (*0-8014-9594-6*) Cornell U Pr.

Three Comedies: Mine Hostess, the Boors, & the Fan. Carlo Goldoni. Tr. by Clifford Bax et al. from ITA. LC 79-4666. 293p. 1979. reprint ed. text ed. 35.00 (*0-313-21259-7*, GOTC, Greenwood Pr) Greenwood.

Three Comedies: The Birds, the Clouds, the Wasps. Aristophanes. Ed. by William Arrowsmith. (Illus.). 400p. 1969. pap. 13.95 (*0-472-06153-4*, 153, Ann Arbor Bks) U of Mich Pr.

***Three Comedies by Aristophanes: Lysistrata, Clouds, Acharnians.** Jeffrey Henderson & Aristophanes. (Classical Library). 200p. (C). 1997. pap. text ed. 8.95 (*0-941051-58-7*) Focus Pub-R Pullins.

Three Companions. Rabindranath Tagore. Tr. by Sujit Mukherjee. 1993. text ed. 15.95 (*0-86311-298-6*, Pub. by Sangam Bks II) Apt Bks.

Three Complete Civil War Novels. Heather X. Graham. 1995. 13.99 (*0-517-14888-9*, Wings Books) Random.

Three Complete Novels. Pat Booth. LC 93-41487. 1994. 6.99 (*0-517-10065-7*) Random Hse Value.

Three Complete Novels. Barbara Cartland. LC 94-17427. 1994. 7.99 (*0-517-11928-5*) Random Hse Value.

Three Complete Novels. William J. Caunitz. LC 94-8401. 1994. 6.99 (*0-517-11844-0*) Random Hse Value.

Three Complete Novels. Shirley Conran. LC 94-6606. 1994. 6.99 (*0-517-10073-8*) Random Hse Value.

Three Complete Novels. Janet Dailey. LC 94-17966. 1994. 13.99 (*0-517-11822-X*) Random Hse Value.

***Three Complete Novels.** W. E. B. Griffin. LC 96-46327. 1997. 12.98 (*0-399-14238-X*) Putnam Pub Group.

Three Complete Novels. J. A. Jance. LC 95-23560. 1996. 13.99 (*0-517-14764-5*, Wings Books) Random.

Three Complete Novels. Michael Palmer. 1996. 13.99 (*0-517-14959-1*, Wings Books) Random.

Three Complete Novels, 3 vols. Robert B. Parker. Incl. Godwulf Manuscript. LC 95-15248. 1995. Not sold separately (*0-615-00743-0*); God Save the Child. LC 95-15248. 1995. Not sold separately (*0-615-00744-9*); Mortal Stakes. LC 95-15248. 1995. Not sold separately (*0-615-00745-7*); LC 95-15248. 1995. 13.99 (*0-517-14802-1*) Random.

Three Complete Novels. Rosamunde Pilcher. 1995. 13.99 (*0-517-12190-5*, Wings Books) Random.

Three Complete Novels: A Night of Gaiety; A Duke in Danger; Secret Harbor. Barbara Cartland. LC 94-17415. 1994. 7.99 (*0-517-11929-3*) Random Hse Value.

***Three Complete Novels: Acceptable Risk; Fatal Cure; Terminal.** Robin Cook. LC 97-6480. 832p. 1997. 12.98 (*0-399-14319-X*) Putnam Pub Group.

Three Complete Novels: Bygones, November of the Heart, Family Blessings. LaVyrle Spencer. LC 94-22682. 720p. 1996. 12.98 (*0-399-14181-2*, Putnam) Putnam Pub Group.

***Three Complete Novels: Come to Grief; Decider; Wild Horses.** Dick Francis. 720p. 1997. 12.98 (*0-399-14306-8*) Putnam Pub Group.

Three Complete Novels: Indemnity Only; Blood Shot; Burn Marks. Sara Paretsky. LC 95-10833. 1995. 13.99 (*0-517-14801-3*) Random.

***Three Complete Novels: McNally's Secret; McNally's Luck; McNally's Risk.** Lawrence Sanders. 576p. 1997. 12.98 (*0-399-14307-6*) Putnam Pub Group.

Three Complete Novels: Morning Glory; Vows; The Gamble. LaVyrle Spencer. 784p. 1994. pap. 11.98 (*0-399-13923-0*, Putnam) Putnam Pub Group.

Three Complete Novels: Outbreak; Mortal Fear; Mutation. Robin Cook. LC 93-3230. 720p. 1993. 11.98 (*0-399-13876-5*, Putnam) Putnam Pub Group.

Three Complete Novels: Patriot Games; Clear & Present Danger, The Sum of All Fears. Tom Clancy. LC 93-31270. 1456p. 1994. pap. 14.98 (*0-399-13935-4*, Putnam) Putnam Pub Group.

Three Complete Novels: Rules of Prey, Shadows of Prey, Eyes of Prey. John Sandford. 752p. 1995. 11.98 (*0-399-14007-7*, Putnam) Putnam Pub Group.

Three Complete Novels: Semper Fi; Call to Arms; Counterattack. W. E. B. Griffin. LC 93-31937. 816p. 1994. pap. 11.98 (*0-399-13913-3*, Putnam) Putnam Pub Group.

Three Complete Novels: Silent Prey, Winter Prey, Night Prey. John Sandford. LC 96-7278. 752p. 1996. 12.98 (*0-399-14191-X*, Putnam) Putnam Pub Group.

Three Complete Novels: The Anderson Tapes, the Tenth Commandment, the Fourth Deadly Sin. Lawrence Sanders. LC 96-7270. 752p. 1996. 12.98 (*0-399-14182-0*, Putnam) Putnam Pub Group.

Three Complete Novels: The Cat Who Saw Red; The Cat Who Played Brahms; The Cat Who Played Post Office: Omnibus Edition. Lilian Jackson Braun. LC 93-632. 608p. 1993. 11.98 (*0-399-13885-4*, Putnam) Putnam Pub Group.

***Three Complete Novels: The Cat Who Talked to Ghosts; The Cat Who Knew a Bishop; The Cat Who Lived High.** Lilian Jackson Braun. 512p. 1997. 12.98 (*0-399-14258-4*, Putnam) Putnam Pub Group.

Three Complete Novels: The First Deadly Sin; The Secondly Deadly Sin, The Third Deadly Sin. Lawrence Sanders. LC 93-18769. 896p. 1993. 11.98 (*0-399-13877-3*, Putnam) Putnam Pub Group.

Three Complete Novels: The Lilac Bus; Firefly Summer; Silver Wedding. Maeve Binchy. LC 95-10831. 1995. 13. 99 (*0-517-14864-1*) Random.

Three Complete Novels: The Postman Always Rings Twice; Double Indemnity; Mildred Pierce. James M. Cain. LC 94-17117. 1994. 6.99 (*0-517-11858-0*) Random.

Three Complete Novels: The Two Mrs. Grenvilles - People Like Us - An Inconvenient Woman. Dominick Dunne. LC 94-18339. 1994. 13.99 (*0-517-11916-1*) Random Hse Value.

Three Complete Novels: Years; Twice Loved; Spring Fancy, 3 bks. in 1. LaVyrle Spencer. LC 92-39606. 704p. 1993. 11.98 (*0-399-13842-0*, Putnam) Putnam Pub Group.

Three Complete Novels of Courtly Love: The Prude & the Prodigal - Lies for Love - From Hate to Love. Barbara Cartland. 1996. 7.99 (*0-517-18238-6*, Wings Books) Random.

Three Complete Novels of Earls & Their Ladies. Barbara Cartland. 1996. 7.99 (*0-517-14772-6*, Wings Books) Random.

Three Complete Novels of Royalty & Romance. Barbara Cartland. LC 95-21906. 1995. pap. 7.99 (*0-517-14678-9*, Wings Books) Random.

Three Complete Novels of Royalty & Romance. Barbara Cartland. LC 95-21906. 1996. 7.99 (*0-517-15045-X*, Wings Books) Random.

***Three Comrades.** Eric M. Remarque. 1998. pap. 12.00 (*0-449-91242-6*) Fawcett.

Three Concepts of Time. Kenneth G. Denbigh. 160p. 1981. 50.95 (*0-387-10757-6*) Spr-Verlag.

***Three Connecticut Composers: The Collected Works of Oliver Brownson, Alexander Gillet, & Solomon Chandler.** Ed. by Karl Kroeger. (Music of the New American Nation Ser.: Vol. 2). 200p. 1997. text ed. 78. 00 (*0-8153-2779-X*) Garland.

Three Consort Songs, for Soprano & Treble, Tenor & Bass Viols. Sarah Michael. (Contemporary Consort Ser.: No. 6). 22p. 1994. pap. text ed. 12.00 (*1-56571-094-0*) PRB Prods.

Three Contemporary Brazilian Plays in Bilingual Edition. Plinio Marcos et al. Ed. by Elzbieta Szoka & Joe Bratcher. Tr. by Lydia Marques & Lelina Pinto from POR. (Illus.). 525p. (Orig.). (C). 1988. pap. 20.00 (*0-924047-00-3*) Host Pubns.

Three Contributions to the Development of Accounting Thought. Ed. by Maurice Moonitz & Richard P. Brief. LC 77-87315. (Development of Contemporary Accounting Thought Ser.). 1978. lib. bdg. 37.95 (*0-405-10928-8*) Ayer.

OS/23 Warp Presentation Manager API. Joel L. Barnum. LC 95-1222. 512p. 1995. pap. text ed. 29.95 (*0-471-03873-3*) Wiley.

Three Cool Kids. Rebecca Emberley. LC 93-40113. (J). 1995. 15.95 (*0-316-23666-7*) Little.

Three-Cornered Hat. Pedro A. De Alarcon. 23.95 (*0-8488-0903-3*) Amereon Ltd.

Three-Cornered Hat. A. R. Tulloch. 224p. (Orig.). 1995. pap. 7.95 (*0-460-87614-7*, Everyman's Classic Lib) C E Tuttle.

Three Cornered World. Natsume Suseki. LC 67-28480. 184p. 1989. pap. 8.95 (*0-89526-768-3*) Regnery Pub.

***3 Corporate Design Systems.** Phiitgraphic Book Company Staff. 1987. 39.95 (*0-688-07248-8*) Morrow.

Three Costume Plays for Women. Norman Holland et al. LC 95-22404. 1995. pap. 7.00 (*0-88734-914-5*) Players Pr.

Three Count Hustle. (Ballroom Dance Ser.). 1985. lib. bdg. 70.00 (*0-87700-724-1*) Revisionist Pr.

Three Count Hustle. Earl Atkinson. (Ballroom Dance Ser.). 1986. lib. bdg. 250.00 (*0-8490-3642-9*) Gordon Pr.

Three Court Dances of the Early Renaissance. Ingrid Brainard & Ray Cook. (Illus.). 34p. 1977. reprint ed. pap. text ed. 9.95 (*0-932582-10-9*, Pub. by Dance Bks UK) Princeton Bk Co.

***Three Cousins (1847)** Fanny Trollope. (Pocket Classics Ser.). 368p. 1997. pap. 12.95 (*0-7509-1412-2*, Pub. by Sutton Pubng UK) Bks Intl VA.

Three Criminal Law Reformers: Beccaria, Bentham, Romilly. Coleman Phillipson. LC 77-17157. (Criminology, Law Enforcement, & Social Problems Ser.: No. 113). 1970. reprint ed. 25.00 (*0-87585-113-4*); reprint ed. pap. 14.00 (*0-87585-904-6*) Patterson Smith.

Three Criticisms of Locke. Edward Stillingfleet. (Anglistica & Americana Ser.: No. 97). 394p. 1987. reprint ed. lib. bdg. 76.70 (*3-487-06391-3*) G Olms Pubs.

Three Crosses. Leonard Peusch. 1978. pap. 1.00 (*0-8199-0723-5*, Frncscn Herld) Franciscan Pr.

Three Crowns: Structures of Communal Politics in Early Rabbinic Jewry. Stuart A. Cohen. 280p. (C). 1990. text ed. 80.00 (*0-521-37290-9*) Cambridge U Pr.

3 Crucial Questions about Jesus. Murray J. Harris. LC 93-46097. 128p. (Orig.). (C). 1994. pap. 11.99 (*0-8010-4388-3*) Baker Bks.

***Three Crucial Questions about Spiritual Warfare.** Clinton E. Arnold. LC 97-8642. 240p. 1997. pap. 11.99 (*0-8010-5784-1*) Baker Bks.

3 Crucial Questions about the Bible. Ed. by Grant R. Osborne & Richard J. Jones. LC 87-28910. (Three Crucial Questions Ser.). 176p. (C). 1995. pap. 11.99 (*0-8010-5273-4*) Baker Bks.

Three Crucial Questions about the Holy Spirit. Craig S. Keener. 176p. (YA). (gr. 10). 1996. pap. 11.99 (*0-8010-5592-X*) Baker Bks.

Three C's: Children, Computers & Communication. Tom Stonier & Cathy Conlin. 218p. 1985. pap. text ed. 72.00 (*0-471-90828-2*) Wiley.

Three Cubic Meter Biogas Plant. (Illus.). 28p. 1979. 8.25 (*0-86619-069-4*) Vols Tech Asst.

Three Cuckolds. Leon Katz. (Commedia in Performance Ser.: Vol. 1). 96p. (Orig.). 1986. pap. 6.95 (*0-936839-06-6*) Applause Theatre Bk Pubs.

Three Cultures: Science, the Humanities & Religious Values. Joseph M. Zycinski. (Philosophy in Science Library: Vol. 4). 96p. (Orig.). 1990. pap. 9.95 (*0-88126-727-9*) Pachart Pub Hse.

Three-D. Hannah Tofts. LC 89-27416. (J). (ps-3). 1990. pap. 4.95 (*0-671-70371-4*, S&S Bks Young Read) S&S Childrens.

3-D Action Gamers Bible: Strategies, Secrets & Cheats Most 3D. Mike Van Mantgem. 352p. 1996. per. 19.99 incl. disk (*0-7615-0766-3*) Prima Pub.

Three-D Action Kit. Three-D, Inc. Staff. 1991. 25.95 (*1-55725-024-3*) Paraclete MA.

***3-D & Shaded Alphabets.** Dan X. Solo. (Illus.). pap. 7.95 (*0-486-24246-3*) Dover.

Three-D & the MAFIA Club. Kenneth L. Lindsay. viii, 228p. (Orig.). 1981. pap. 10.00 (*0-943980-00-3*) AIGA Pubns.

Three-D Art Projects That Teach. Lynn Brisson. (Illus.). 80p. (J). (gr. k-6). 1989. pap. text ed. 8.95 (*0-86530-084-4*, IP 166-1) Incentive Pubns.

3D Basics. John Wilson. LC 97-6037. (Auto Cad Visual Approach Ser.). (Illus.). 288p. 1996. spiral bd. 15.00 (*0-8273-6901-8*) Delmar.

Three-D Bible Stories. Mary Ruberry. 64p. 1994. pap. text ed. 15.95 (*0-9641811-4-2*) Three-D Revel.

3D Body Adventure. pap. 35.00 (*1-56997-091-2*) Knowldge Adv.

3 - D Books: Outerspace. (J). 1997. 11.95 (*0-689-80909-3*) S&S Childrens.

3-D Book of Angels: A Collection. Mary Ruberry. Ed. by Norma Collins. (Illus.). 32p. (YA). (gr. 12). 1995. text ed. 12.95 (*0-9641811-8-5*) Three-D Revel.

Three-D CAD Principles & Applications. Ed. by H. Toriya & H. Chiyokura. Tr. by Hiromi Yaguchi. LC 93-5665. (Computer Science Workbench Ser.). (Illus.). vi, 282p. 1993. 103.95 (*0-387-56507-8*) Spr-Verlag.

Three-D Cake Cartooning. Roland A. Winbeckler. (Illus.). 35p. (Orig.). 1984. pap. 10.95 (*0-930113-02-0*) Winbeckler.

Three-D Castle Book. (Illus.). (J). (ps). 10.00 (*1-56021-226-8*) W J Fantasy.

Three-D-Computation of Incompressible Internal Flows: Proceedings of the GAMM-Workshop Held in EPFL, 13-15 September 1989, Lausanne, Switzerland. Ed. by Gabriel Sottas & Inge L. Ryhming. (Notes on Numerical Fluid Mechanics Ser.: Vol. 39). viii, 233p. 1993. 63.00 (*3-528-07639-9*, Pub. by Vieweg & Sohn GW) Informatica.

Three-D Computer Graphics. Mark A. Willis. 140p. 1983. pap. text ed. 16.95 (*0-87567-041-5*) Entelek.

Three-D Computer Graphics. 2nd ed. Alan Watt. (C). 1993. text ed. 49.50 (*0-201-63186-5*) Addison-Wesley.

Three D Computer Graphics: A User's Guide for Artists & Designers. 2nd ed. Andrew S. Glassner. (Illus.). 240p. 1996. pap. 26.95 (*1-55821-305-8*) Lyons & Burford.

Three-D Computing: Modeling, Image Processing, & Visualization. Richard K. Miller & Terri C. Walker. 246p. 1991. 285.00 (*0-89671-130-7*) SEAI Tech Pubns.

3-D Conformal Radiotherapy: A New Era in the Irradiation of Cancer. Ed. by John L. Meyer & James A. Purdy. (Frontiers of Radiation Therapy & Oncology Ser.: Vol. 29). (Illus.). x, 278p. 1996. 259.25 (*3-8055-6161-X*) S Karger.

Three-D Constructions. James Rizzi. (Illus.). 119p. 1988. 50.00 (*0-936598-02-6*) J Szoke Graphics.

Three D Dinosaurs. Three D Office & Computer Art Laboratories Staff. 1994. write for info. (*1-886316-00-7*, Sunny Pubns USA) Oregon Vocations.

***3D Draughting Using AutoCAD.** Robert McFarlane. 234p. 1996. pap. 69.95 incl. disk (*0-470-23732-5*) Wiley.

Three D-Dynamic Scene Analysis: A Stereo Based Approach. Zhengyou Zhang & Olivier Faugeras. Ed. by T. S. Hunag et al. LC 92-11015. (Information Sciences Ser.: Vol. 27). (Illus.). xi, 300p. 1992. 59.95 (*0-387-55429-7*); write for info. (*3-540-55429-7*) Spr-Verlag.

Three-D Electrodynamic Wave Simulator. C. Hafner & L. Bomholt. LC 92-39166. 368p. 1993. 518.00 (*0-471-93847-5*); text ed. 550.00 (*0-471-93812-2*) Wiley.

Three-D Electromagnetic Field Analysis. Ed. by T. Nakata. (Illus.). 322p. (Orig.). (C). 1990. 110.00 (*0-907383-51-3*, Pub. by J & J Sci Pubs UK) Bks Intl VA.

3D File Formats. Keith. (C). 1996. pap. text ed. 39.95 (*0-201-48835-3*) Addison-Wesley.

3-D Fun. Oliver Fuhrer. (Illus.). 36p. 1996. write for info. (*1-57215-183-8*) World Pubns.

3-D Geometric Origami. Rona Gurkewitz & Bennett Arnstein. 1995. pap. write for info. (*0-486-28863-3*) Dover.

3D Geoscience Modeling: Computer Techniques for Geological Characterization. Simon Houlding. LC 94-36000. 1994. write for info. (*3-540-58015-8*) Spr-Verlag.

3D Geoscience Modeling: Computer Techniques for Geological Characterization. Simon Houlding. LC 94-36000. (Illus.). 328p. 1995. 108.95 (*0-387-58015-8*) Spr-Verlag.

Three-D Graphics. (Illus.). 224p. 1994. 69.95 (*4-938586-49-5*, Pub. by PIE Bks JA) Bks Nippan.

***3-D Graphics & Animation: From Starting Up to Standing Out.** Mark Giambruno. LC 96-46693. 600p. 1997. 44. 99 (*1-56205-698-0*) Mac Comp Pub.

Three-D Graphics in Pascal. G. Bielig-Schulz & Chi Schulz. 163p. 1990. pap. text ed. 44.95 (*0-471-92451-2*) Wiley.

3D Graphics Programming for Windows. Nigel Thompson. 1996. pap. text ed. 39.95 incl. cd-rom (*1-57231-345-5*) Microsoft.

3-D Graphics Programming in Windows. Phillip Taylor. 896p. 1994. pap. 49.95 (*0-201-60882-0*) Addison-Wesley.

3D Graphics Programming with QuickDraw 3D. Apple Computer, Inc. Staff. 496p. 1995. pap. 39.95 incl. cd-rom (*0-201-48926-0*) Addison-Wesley.

Three-D Greeting Cards: A Collection from Around the World. Takenobu Igarashi. (Illus.). 160p. 1994. pap. 49. 95 (*4-7661-0754-3*, Pub. by Graphic Sha JA) Bks Nippan.

Three-D Hidden Pictures Activity Book. Illus. by Carol Russo. 16p. (J). 1991. pap. write for info. (*1-56156-012-X*) Kidsbks.

3-D Horror. Roger Kean & Oliver Frey. (Illus.). 36p. 1996. write for info. (*1-57215-184-6*) World Pubns.

3-D Illustration Awards Annual V. 1995. 39.99 (*1-56496-132-X*) Rockport Pubs.

3-D Imaging & Animation with Infini-D. Lisa Cresson. 272p. 1996. pap. 45.00 incl. cd-rom (*1-56830-222-3*) Hayden.

Three-D Imaging in Medicine. Ayaram Udupa & Gabor T. Herman. (Illus.). 368p. 1991. 133.00 (*0-8493-4294-5*, L4294BK, CRC Reprint) Franklin.

3-D Kid. Illus. by Robert Margulies. (J). (ps-7). 1996. text ed. 19.95 (*0-7167-6615-9*) W H Freeman.

Three-D-Light: A Handbook Laboratory in the Rendering of the Universal Mesh. David R. Wheeler. LC 76-21441. (Illus.). 1976. pap. 12.95 (*0-918562-01-5*) Biohydrant.

***3-D Look at Ocean Life.** Keith Faulkner. (Illus.). (J). (gr. k-4). 1997. 11.95 (*0-614-29103-8*, Litl Simon S&S) S&S Childrens.

***3-D Look at Outer Space.** Keith Faulkner. (Illus.). (J). (gr. k-4). 1997. 11.95 (*0-614-29104-6*, Litl Simon S&S) S&S Childrens.

Three-D Machine Vision. 215p. 190.00 (*0-317-65581-7*) TBC Inc.

An Asterisk (*) at the beginning of an entry indicates that the title is appearing in BIP for the first time.

3-D Mazes. Larry Evans. (Troubador Funbooks). 32p. (J). (gr. 2 up). 1995. pap. 3.50 (*0-8431-3888-2*) Price Stern Sloan.

Three-D Model Recognition from Stereoscopic Cues. Ed. by John E. Mayhew & John P. Frisby. (Artificial Intelligence Ser.). (Illus.). 350p. 1991. 50.00 (*0-262-13243-5*) MIT Pr.

3-D Modeling Technology in Oral & Maxillofacial Surgery. J. Thomas Lambrecht. LC 94-48366. (Illus.). 160p. 1995. text ed. 140.00 (*0-86715-287-7*, B2877) Quint Pub Co.

***3-D Movies.** 1991. 58.00 (*1-55862-164-4*, 00010677) St James Pr.

3-D Movies: A History & Filmography of Stereoscopic Cinema. R. M. Hayes. LC 89-42720. (Illus.). 430p. 1989. lib. bdg. 55.00 (*0-89950-407-8*) McFarland & Co.

Three-D Night Before Christmas. Clement C. Moore. 32p. (J). 1994. pap. text ed. 7.95 (*0-9641811-5-0*) Three-D Revel.

Three-D Oscilloscope: A Practical Manual & Guide. Homer B. Tilton. 288p. 1987. 27.95 (*0-13-920240-4*, Busn) P-H.

3-D Outrageous Reptiles. Ian Boyd. (Illus.). 24p. (Orig.). (J). (ps-3). 1996. pap. 4.95 (*0-8167-4142-5*) Troll Communs.

Three-D Paper Ornaments & Calendars. Bennett Arnstein. 1988. pap. 9.95 (*0-9620058-0-0*) B Arnstein.

3-D Photon Beam Treatment Planning. Ed. by Alfred R. Smith & James A. Purdy. (Illus.). 256p. 1991. 63.00 (*0-08-041180-0*, Pergamon Pr) Elsevier.

3-D Puzzles. Roger Kean & Oliver Frey. (Illus.). 36p. 1996. write for info. (*1-57215-185-4*) World Pubns.

***3D QSAR in Drug Design Theory Methods & Applications.** Date not set. text ed. 515.00 (*90-72199-14-6*) Kluwer Ac.

Three-D Salvation: Decision, Discipline & Direction. Maralene Wesner & Miles Wesner. LC 88-51804. 100p. (Orig.). 1989. pap. 4.95 (*0-936715-20-0*) Diversity Okla.

3-D Seismic & Well Log Data Set: Fluvial Reservoir Systems-Stratton Field, South Texas. Compiled by R. A. Levey et al. 30p. 1994. pap. text ed. 40.00 incl. audio, 3.5 hd (*0-614-01872-2*) Bur Econ Geology.

3-D Seismic Case History Evaluating Fluvially Deposited Thin-Bed Reservoirs in a Gas-Producing Property. B. A. Hardage et al. (Geological Circular Ser.: No. 95-1). 1995. pap. 5.50 (*0-614-06193-8*) Bur Econ Geology.

Three-D SEM-Atlas of Insect Morphology, Vol. 1: Heteroptera, Report 7. Ed. by Werner Nachtigall et al. 1991. pap. text ed. 45.00 (*1-56081-310-5*, Pub. by G Fischer Verlag GW) Lubrecht & Cramer.

Three-D Shapes. A. G. Smith. 1989. pap. 2.95 (*0-486-25931-5*) Dover.

3-D Sound for Virtual Reality & Multimedia Applications. Durand R. Begault. (Illus.). 293p. 1994. text ed. 53.00 (*0-12-084735-3*, AP Prof) Acad Pr.

Three D Stress Analysis of Spur & Helical Gears: An Integrated System Based on the P-FEM Approach. Carlo Baret et al. (Fall Technical Meeting Papers 88FTM7). (Illus.). 22p. 1988. pap. text ed. 30.00 (*1-55589-512-3*) AGMA.

3D Studio. Autodesk, Inc. Staff. (General Engineering Ser.). 1996. pap. 5.95 (*0-534-95376-X*) PWS Pubs.

3D Studio. Autodesk, Inc. Staff. (General Engineering Ser.). 1996. cd-rom 79.50 (*0-534-95382-4*) PWS Pubs.

3D Studio - Educational Version: Reference Manual. Autodesk, Inc. Staff. (General Engineering Ser.). 1996. suppl. ed., pap. 31.75 (*0-534-95370-0*) PWS Pubs.

3D Studio - Educational Version: Tutorial Guide. Autodesk, Inc. Staff. (General Engineering Ser.). 1996. suppl. ed., pap. 31.75 (*0-534-95364-6*) PWS Pubs.

Three D Studio Applied. Nancy Fulton. LC 93-73784. (Illus.). 430p. 1993. pap. 39.95 incl. cd-rom (*0-929870-24-7*) Advanstar Commns.

Three-D Studio Applied Release 4 Supplement. Nancy Fulton. LC 94-73308. (Illus.). 150p. 1994. pap. 14.95 (*0-929870-28-X*) Advanstar Commns.

3-D Studio Architectural Rendering. Rowlell et al. 272p. 1996. 45.00 (*1-56205-565-8*) New Riders Pub.

3-D Studio for Beginners. Steven Elliott & Phillip Miller. (Illus.). 497p. (Orig.). 1995. pap. text ed. 40.00 (*1-56205-419-8*) New Riders Pub.

***3D Studio 4: Level 1.** New Riders Publishing Staff. 1997. pap. text ed. write for info. (*1-56205-542-9*) New Riders Pub.

3-D Studio Hollywood & Gaming Effects. New Riders Development Group Staff. (Illus.). 272p. (Orig.). 1995. pap. 50.00 incl. cd-rom (*1-56205-430-9*) New Riders Pub.

3D Studio Plug-in Reference. New Riders Development Group Staff & Tim Forcade. (Illus.). 304p. (Orig.). 1995. pap. text ed. 55.00 (*1-56205-431-7*) New Riders Pub.

***3-D Studio Max: Tutorials from the Masters.** Michele Bousquet. 400p. 1996. text ed. 36.95 (*0-8273-8391-6*) Delmar.

3D Studio Max Applied. Nancy Fulton & Andrew Clayton. LC 96-84479. 575p. (Orig.). 1996. pap. 44.95 (*0-929870-40-9*) Advanstar Commns.

***3D Studio Max Clay Sculpture, Digitizing, & Motion Capture.** Stephanie Reese. 1997. pap. text ed. 49.99 (*1-57610-150-9*) Coriolis Grp.

3D Studio Max Design Guide. Friedel Potts et al. 1996. pap. 39.99 incl. cd-rom (*1-883577-83-7*) Coriolis Grp.

3-D Studio Max Fundamentals. Todd Peterson. LC 96-19479. 528p. 1996. pap. text ed. 45.00 incl. cd-rom (*1-56205-625-5*) New Riders Pub.

***3D Studio Max Magic: Expert Edition.** Bijan Tehrani. 1997. 60.00 (*1-56830-379-3*) Hayden.

3D Studio Secrets. Andy Reese. 1996. pap. 49.99 (*1-56884-829-3*) IDG Bks.

3-D Studio Special Effects. New Riders Publishington Staff. 233p. 1994. 50.00 (*1-56205-303-5*) New Riders Pub.

3D Studio Unleashed. 1996. 49.99 (*0-672-30671-9*, Bobbs) Macmillan.

Three-D Summertime Fun Book. (Illus.). (J). 1992. pap. 2.95 (*1-56156-107-X*) Kidsbks.

***3D Talking Globe.** 1996. pap. text ed. 34.95 (*1-882807-18-9*, G1021) Now What Sftware.

Three-D Teaching Aids. Lynn Brisson. (Illus.). 64p. (J). (gr. k-6). 1989. pap. text ed. 8.95 (*0-86530-072-0*, IP 166-2) Incentive Pubns.

3-D Viewer: Oceans. (J). 1997. 11.95 (*0-689-80910-7*) S&S Childrens.

3-D Visual Dictionary of Computing. Maran Graphics Staff. 224p. 1995. pap. 19.99 (*1-56884-678-9*) IDG Bks.

3-D Wings: Fabulous Flying Machines. Rick Sammon. (Illus.). 28p. (YA). (gr. 6-12). 1995. 11.95 (*1-56566-087-0*) Lickle Pubng.

3D with HOOPS: Build Interactive 3D Graphics into Your C++ Applications. William Leler & Jim Merry. LC 95-37454. 546p. (C). 1996. pap. text ed. 45.95 (*0-201-87025-8*) Addison-Wesley.

Three-D Wizardry: Design in Papier Mache, Plaster & Foam. George Wolfe. (Illus.). 172p. 1995. 23.95 (*0-87192-294-0*) Davis Mass.

Three Dales Way Guide: Riverside Walk Thorugh Wharfedale, Wensleydale & Swaledale. Richard Hayward. (British Footpath Guides Ser.: No. 6). (Illus.). 100p. (Orig.). 1995. pap. 6.95 (*1-880848-16-3*) Brit Footpaths.

Three Dance Portraits. Weins Bolcom. 24p. 1991. pap. 8.95 (*0-7935-0969-6*, 00009642) H Leonard.

Three Daughters of Madam Liang. Pearl S. Buck. (Oriental Novels of Pearl S. Buck Ser.). 316p. 1991. reprint ed. pap. 8.95 (*1-55921-040-0*) Moyer Bell.

Three Day Break. David Hegarty. 200p. 1989. pap. 7.95 (*0-685-25876-9*, Pub. by Poolbeg Pr IE) Dufour.

Three Day Break. David Hegarty. 220p. 1989. pap. 7.95 (*1-85371-024-5*) Dufour.

Three Day Diet to Improve Your Relationship with Just about Everyone. 2nd ed. Debbie Gallagher. (Illus.). 50p. 1991. reprint ed. pap. 4.95 (*1-878131-01-X*) Brght Ideas Make Diff.

***3-Day Energy Fast: Cleanse Your Body, Clear Your Mind & Claim Your Spirit.** Pamela Serure. LC 96-47957. 224p. 1997. 24.00 (*0-06-017491-9*) HarpC.

Three Day Promise: A Korean Soldier's Memoirs. Donald K. Chung. (Illus.). 434p. 1989. text ed. 20.00 (*0-942407-06-7*) Father & Son.

Three-Day Traffic Jam. John Keefauver. LC 91-30583. 80p. (J). (gr. 4-8). 1992. pap. 13.00 (*0-671-75599-4*, S&S Bks Young Read) S&S Childrens.

Three-Day Week-Offshoot of an EDP Operation. M. C. Dobelis. (Illus.). 1976. reprint ed. pap. 0.50 (*0-918230-04-7*) Barnstable.

Three Days. Clayton E. Krug. 1981. pap. 0.79 (*0-8100-0138-1*, 15N0381) Northwest Pub.

Three Days: Parish Prayer in the Paschal Triduum. rev. ed. Gabe Huck. LC 91-43792. (Illus.). 206p. 1992. pap. 11.95 (*0-929650-51-4*, 3D-R) Liturgy Tr Pubns.

Three Days & Three Nights Reconsidered. Ralph E. Woodrow. 64p. 1993. pap. 5.00 (*0-916938-11-5*) R Woodrow.

***Three Days at Gettysburg: Turning Point of the Civil War, July 1863.** Rod Gragg. (Civil War Ser.). (Illus.). 32p. (Orig.). 1997. pap. 4.95 (*1-890099-02-3*, Travel Time) Lawson Mardon.

Three Days for Emeralds. Mignon G. Eberhart. LC 87-42668. 272p. 1988. 14.95 (*0-394-56108-2*) Random.

Three Days in July. Etienne Poirier. 258p. (Orig.). 1996. mass mkt. 4.99 (*1-55197-271-9*, Pub. by Comnwlth Pub CN) Partners Pubs Grp.

Three Days in Sedona: A Personal Harmonic Convergence. Alan Klevit. 150p. (Orig.). (C). 1989. pap. text ed. 9.95 (*0-317-93749-9*) Stardust Pubns.

***Three Days of Darkness, Vol. 1.** rev. ed. Louis W. Barta. (Illus.). 24p. (Orig.). 1989. pap. 2.95 (*0-9655050-7-3*) L W Barta Pubns.

Three Days on a River in a Red Canoe. Vera B. Williams. LC 80-23893. (Illus.). 32p. (J). (gr. k-3). 1981. 16.00 (*0-688-80307-5*); lib. bdg. 15.93 (*0-688-84307-7*) Greenwillow.

Three Days on a River in a Red Canoe. Vera B. Williams. LC 80-23893. (Illus.). 32p. (J). (ps up). 1984. reprint ed. pap. 5.95 (*0-688-04072-1*, Mulberry) Morrow.

Three Days Scene at the Temple in Jerusalem. 2nd ed. Jakob Lorber. Tr. by Dr. Nordewin & Hildegard Von Koerber from GER. LC 82-83492. 116p. 1981. pap. 10.00 (*0-934616-10-8*) Valkyrie Pub Hse.

Three Days to Love No. 150: Camfield. Barbara Cartland. (Camfield Ser.: No. 150). 176p. (Orig.). 1996. mass mkt. 4.50 (*0-515-11812-5*) Jove Pubns.

Three Days Tournament: Study in Romance & Folk-Lore. Jessie L. Weston. LC 65-26456. (Studies in Comparative Literature: No. 35). 1969. reprint ed. lib. bdg. 52.95 (*0-8383-0643-8*) M S G Haskell Hse.

Three Days' Tournament, a Study in Romance & Folklore. Jessie L. Weston. LC 76-144538. (Grimm Library: No. 15). reprint ed. 27.50 (*0-404-53558-5*) AMS Pr.

Three Days with Joyce. Gisele Freund. Tr. by Peter St. J. Ginna from FRE. (Illus.). 80p. 1985. 17.95 (*0-89255-096-1*) Persea Bks.

Three Days with Joyce. Gisele Freund. Tr. by Peter St. John Ginna from FRE. LC 86-131351. (Illus.). 80p. 1990. pap. 11.95 (*0-89255-142-9*) Persea Bks.

Three Decadent Poets: Ernest Dowson, John Gray, Lionel Johnson - An Annotated Bibliography. George A. Cevasco. LC 89-23712. 412p. 1990. text ed. 60.00 (*0-8240-3149-0*, H968) Garland.

Three Decades & Two Kings (Nineteen Sixty to Nineteen Ninety) Eclipse of Nepal's Partyless Monarchic Rule. Rishikesh Shaha. 160p. 1990. text ed. 25.00 (*81-207-1217-X*, Pub. by Sterling Pubs II) Apt Bks.

Three Decades & Two Kings (1960-1990) Rishikesh Shah. (C). 1991. text ed. 65.00 (*0-7855-0162-2*, Pub. by Ratna Pustak Bhandar) St Mut.

Three Decades of British Art, 1740-1770. Ellis K. Waterhouse. LC 65-23431. (American Philosophical Society, Philadelphia. Memoirs Ser.: Vol. 63). (Illus.). 91p. reprint ed. pap. 26.00 (*0-317-10474-8*, 2015020) Bks Demand.

Three Decades of Exploration: Homage to Leo Castelli. Ed. by Ruth A. Matinko-Wald. LC 87-62753. 16p. (Orig.). 1987. pap. write for info. (*0-942461-02-9*) Mus Art Fl.

Three Decades of Federal Legislation 1855 to 1885. Samuel S. Cox. LC 75-114870. (Select Bibliographies Reprint Ser.). 1977. 58.95 (*0-8369-5275-8*) Ayer.

Three Decades of Mathematical System Theory. Ed. by H. Nijmeijer & J. M. Schumacher. (Lecture Notes in Control & Information Sciences Ser.: Vol. 135). (Illus.). vi, 562p. 1989. 103.95 (*0-387-51605-0*) Spr-Verlag.

Three Decades of Palestine: Speeches & Papers on the Upbuilding of the Jewish National Home. Arthur Ruppin. LC 70-97301. (Illus.). 342p. 1975. reprint ed. text ed. 38.50 (*0-8371-2629-0*, RUPA, Greenwood Pr) Greenwood.

Three Decades of Peace Education Around the World: An Anthology. Robin J. Burns & Robert Aspeslagh. LC 95-25440. (Reference Books in International Education, Vol. 27, Reference Library of Social Science: Vol. 24). 413p. 1996. text ed. 86.00 (*0-8240-5549-7*, SS600) Garland.

***Three Decades of Rhythm & Blues Classics.** Ed. by Carol Cuellar. 152p. (Orig.). 1997. pap. text ed. 14.95 (*1-57623-888-1*, 5202A) Warner Brothers.

Three Decades of Television: A Catalog of Television Programs Acquired by the Library of Congress, 1949-1979. Ed. by Katharine Loughney. LC 86-20098. 688p. 51.00 (*0-8444-0544-2*, 030-000-00185-1) Lib Congress.

Three Decades of Television: A Catalogue, 1949-1979, 2 vols. 1991. Set. lib. bdg. 175.95 (*0-8490-4331-X*) Gordon Pr.

Three-Dee Mouse Mazes. Dan Nevins. (Illus.). 48p. (Orig.). (J). (gr. 8-11). 1989. pap. 2.95 (*0-8431-1883-0*) Price Stern Sloan.

Three Degrees & Great Symbols of Masonry. Joseph F. Newton. 112p. 1992. reprint ed. pap. 12.95 (*1-56459-045-3*) Kessinger Pub.

Three Degrees West: A Walk Through Britain's Local & Natural History. Ed. by Stephen Sankey. 200p. (C). 1989. text ed. 45.00 (*0-85976-299-8*, Pub. by J Donald UK) St Mut.

Three Deltas: Accumulation & Poverty in Rural Burma, Bengal & South India. Willem Van Schendel. (Indo-Dutch Studies on Development Alternatives: No. 8). 352p. (C). 1991. 35.00 (*0-8039-9681-0*) Sage.

Three Designs: For Three Timpani - Opus 11, No. 2. R. Muczynski. 1987. pap. 3.95 (*0-7935-5575-2*, 50353570) H Leonard.

Three Determinants of Attention-Seeking in Young Children. Jacob L. Gewirtz. (Society for Research in Child Development Monographs: Vol. 19, No. 2). 1954. pap. 25.00 (*0-527-01561-X*) Periodicals Srv.

Three Devils: Luther's, Milton's & Goethe's. David Masson. LC 78-128340. reprint ed. 36.00 (*0-404-04247-3*) AMS Pr.

Three Diagnostic Scorings for the Thurstone Personality Schedule. Edmund S. Conklin. LC 37-28256. (Science Study Ser.: No. 6). 25p. reprint ed. pap. 25.00 (*0-317-08001-6*, 2055229) Bks Demand.

Three Dialogues *see* **Empiricists**

Three Dialogues Between Hylas & Philonous. George Berkeley. Ed. by John Perry. 138p. (C). 1994. pap. text ed. 5.95 (*0-941736-05-9*) Arete Pr.

Three Dialogues Between Hylas & Philonous. George Berkeley. Ed. by Robert M. Adams. LC 79-65276. (HPC Classics Ser.). 138p. (C). 1979. pap. text ed. 4.95 (*0-915144-61-1*); lib. bdg. 21.95 (*0-915144-62-X*) Hackett Pub.

Three Dialogues Between Hylas & Philonous. George Berkeley. (Great Books in Philosophy). 110p. (C). 1988. pap. 4.95 (*0-87975-499-0*) Prometheus Bks.

Three Dialogues Between Hylas & Philonous: Berkeley. Ed. by Colin M. Turbayne. 144p. (C). 1954. pap. text ed. 5.33 (*0-02-421670-4*, Macmillan Coll) P-H.

Three Dialogues on Knowledge. Paul K. Feyerabend. 192p. (C). 1991. pap. 22.95 (*0-631-17918-6*) Blackwell Pubs.

Three Diamonds. Gerard Malanga. LC 91-23551. (Illus.). 220p. (Orig.). 1991. 20.00 (*0-87685-838-8*); pap. 12.50 (*0-87685-837-X*) Black Sparrow.

Three Diamonds, signed ed. deluxe ed. Gerard Malanga. LC 91-23551. (Illus.). 220p. (Orig.). 1991. 30.00 (*0-87685-839-6*) Black Sparrow.

Three Different Worlds: Women, Men, & Children in an Industrializing Community. Frances A. Rothstein. LC 82-6216. (Contributions in Family Studies: No. 7). (Illus.). xii, 148p. 1982. text ed. 45.00 (*0-313-22594-X*, RTW/, Greenwood Pr) Greenwood.

Three-Dimension Computer Animation. John Vince. LC 92-26697. (C). 1992. pap. text ed. 45.25 (*0-201-62756-6*) Addison-Wesley.

Three Dimension Models of Basic Crystal Forms: 111 Crystal Models. Construction Kit. A. J. Gude. 1948. pap. 15.00 (*0-686-47211-X*) Polycrystal Bk Serv.

Three Dimension Models of Simple Crystal Forms: 15 Crystal Models Construction Kit. A. J. Gude. 1957. pap. 7.50 (*0-686-47218-7*) Polycrystal Bk Serv.

Three Dimensional Analysis of Crack Growth. Y. Mi. (Topics in Engineering Ser.). 230p. 1996. 104.00 (*1-56252-355-4*, 4451) Computational Mech MA.

***Three-Dimensional Analysis of Human Locomotion.** P. Allard et al. LC 97-11505. 1997. text ed. write for info. (*0-471-96949-4*) Wiley.

Three-Dimensional Analysis of Human Movement. Ed. by Paul Allard et al. LC 93-37710. (Illus.). 384p. 1994. text ed. 45.00 (*0-87322-623-2*, BALL0623) Human Kinetics.

Three Dimensional Analysis of Spinal Deformities. M. D'Amico & G. C. Santambrogio. LC 94-77521. (Studies in Health Technology & Informatics: Vol. 15). 550p. (gr. 12). 1995. 130.00 (*90-5199-181-9*) IOS Press.

Three-Dimensional Applications in G. I. S. Ed. by Jonathan Raper. 260p. 1989. 75.00 (*0-85066-776-3*) Taylor & Francis.

Three Dimensional Applique. Jodie Davis. LC 92-56582. 160p. 1993. pap. 16.95 (*0-8019-8353-3*) Chilton.

Three-Dimensional Applique & Embroidery Embellishment: Techniques for Today's Album Quilt. Anita Shackelford. 1994. pap. 24.95 (*0-89145-819-0*) Collector Bks.

Three-Dimensional Biomedical Imaging, Vol. I. Robert A. Robb. 184p. 1985. 85.00 (*0-8493-5264-9*, RC78, CRC Reprint) Franklin.

Three-Dimensional Biomedical Imaging, Vol. II, incl. poster. Robert A. Robb. 160p. 1985. Vol. II, 160 p. 85.00 (*0-8493-5265-7*, CRC Reprint) Franklin.

Three-Dimensional Biomedical Imaging: Principles & Practice. Richard A. Robb. LC 94-38015. 1994. 145.00 (*1-56081-570-1*, VCH) Wiley.

Three-Dimensional Bulletin Boards. Sally D. Sharpe. (Illus.). 80p. 1988. pap. text ed. 8.95 (*0-86530-164-6*, IP 28-4) Incentive Pubns.

Three-Dimensional Chemical Similarity Searching. C. A. Pepperell. LC 93-39096. (Computers & Chemical Structure Information Ser.: Vol. 3). 304p. 1994. text ed. 98.00 (*0-471-94238-3*) Wiley.

Three-Dimensional Chemical Structure Handling. Peter Willett. LC 91-19729. 241p. 1991. text ed. 110.00 (*0-471-93108-X*) Wiley.

Three-Dimensional Children's Bulletin Covers. Patt Ensing. (ReproBooks Ser.). (Illus.). 304p. (Orig.). (J). (gr. 10). 1995. pap. 24.99 (*0-8010-3231-8*) Baker Bks.

Three-Dimensional Coastal Ocean Models. Ed. by Norman S. Heaps. (Coastal & Estuarine Sciences Ser.: Vol. 4). (Illus.). 224p. 1987. 30.00 (*0-87590-253-7*) Am Geophysical.

Three-Dimensional Computer Vision. Olivier Faugeras. (Illus.). 805p. 1993. 70.00 (*0-262-06158-9*) MIT Pr.

Three-Dimensional Computer Vision. Y. Shirai. (Symbolic Computation - Computer Graphics Ser.). 375p. 1987. 132.95 (*0-387-15119-2*) Spr-Verlag.

Three-Dimensional Confocal Microscopy: Volume Investigation of Biological Specimens. Ed. by John K. Stevens et al. (Cell Biology Ser.). (Illus.). 507p. 1994. text ed. 89.00 (*0-12-668330-1*) Acad Pr.

Three-Dimensional Continuum Computer Programs for Structural Analysis: Presented at the Winter Annual Meeting of the American Society of Mechanical Engineers, New York, NY, November 26-30, 1972. Ed. by Thomas A. Cruse & Donald S. Griffin. LC 72-92593. 54p. reprint ed. pap. 25.00 (*0-317-10641-4*, 2022061) Bks Demand.

Three-Dimensional CT Angiography. Hideo Adachi & Jun Nagai. LC 95-3482. 248p. 1995. text ed. 149.95 (*0-316-00701-3*) Lppncott-Raven.

***Three-Dimensional Decoupage.** Vivien Crook. (Illus.). 48p. 1996. pap. 25.00 (*0-85532-808-8*, 7936X, Pub. by Search Pr UK) A Schwartz & Co.

***Three Dimensional Decoupage.** Letty Oates. (Illus.). 128p. (Orig.). 1997. pap. 19.95 (*0-8019-9049-1*, THRDE) Krause Pubns.

Three-Dimensional Design. Katie Pasquini. Ed. by Randi Loft. LC 88-70657. (Illus.). 80p. (Orig.). 1988. pap. text ed. 16.95 (*0-914881-19-1*, 10024) C & T Pub.

Three-Dimensional Electron Microscopy of Macromolecular Assemblies. Joachim Frank. LC 95-30893. (Illus.). 342p. 1996. boxed 85.00 (*0-12-265040-9*) Acad Pr.

Three-Dimensional Facies Architecture of Terrigenous Clastic Sediments & Its Implications for Hydrocarbon Discovery & Recovery. Ed. by Andrew D. Miall & Noel Tyler. (Concepts in Sedimentology & Paleontology Ser.: No. 52). (Illus.). 310p. 1992. pap. 95.00 (*0-918985-94-3*) SEPM.

***Three-Dimensional Geometry & Topology.** William P. Thurston & Silvio Levy. LC 96-45578. (Princeton Mathematical Ser.). 320p. 1997. text ed. 39.50 (*0-691-08304-5*) Princeton U Pr.

Three-Dimensional Ground-Water Modeling in Depositional Systems, Wilcox Group, Oakwood Salt Dome Area, East Texas. G. E. Fogg et al. (Report of Investigations Ser.: RI 133). (Illus.). 55p. 1983. pap. 3.25 (*0-318-03289-9*) Bur Econ Geology.

***3-Dimensional Illustration.** Rockport Staff. 1991. 59.95 (*0-688-10371-5*) Morrow.

Three-Dimensional Illustration: Designing with Paper, Clay, Casts, Wood, Assemblage, Plastics, Fabric, Metal, & Food. Ellen Rixford. LC 92-11619. (Illus.). 176p. 1992. 55.00 (*0-8230-5367-9*, Watsn-Guptill) Watsn-Guptill.

3-Dimensional Illustration Awards Annual IV: The Best in 3-D Advertising & Publishing Worldwide. Ed. by Rockport Publishers Editorial Staff. (Illus.). 256p. 1993. 59.99 (*1-56496-058-7*, 30556) Rockport Pubs.

Three-Dimensional Illustrator's Awards Annual, Vol. 3. Ed. by Rockport Publishers Editorial Staff. (Illus.). 256p. 1993. 59.99 (*1-56496-024-2*, 30456) Rockport Pubs.

Three-Dimensional Image Reconstruction in Radiology & Nuclear Medicine. Pierre Grangeat & Jean-Louis Amans. LC 96-25828. (Computational Imaging & Vision Ser.). 315p. 1996. lib. bdg. 143.00 (*0-7923-4129-5*) Kluwer Ac.

Three-Dimensional Imaging. Fishman. Date not set. write for info. (*0-7506-9544-7*) Buttrwrth-Heinemann.

Three-Dimensional Integrated Circuit Layout. A. C. Harter. (Distinguished Dissertations in Computer Science Ser.: No. 2). (Illus.). 200p. (C). 1991. text ed. 57.95 (0-521-41630-2) Cambridge U Pr.

***Three-Dimensional Kinematics of the Eye, Head & Limb Movements.** Ed. by Michael Fetter et al. 480p. 1997. 135.00 (90-5702-148-X, Harwood Acad Pubs) Gordon & Breach.

***3-Dimensional Lateral Logic Mazes.** Larry Evans. LC 96-48270. 1997. 5.95 (0-8069-9624-2) Sterling.

***Three-Dimensional Link Theory & Invariants of Plane Curve Singularities.** David Eisenbud & Walter Neumann. LC 85-545. (Annals of Mathematics Studies: Vol. 110). reprint ed. pap. 51.60 (0-608-04590-X, 2065360) Bks Demand.

Three Dimensional Living, Version 1. Aaron H. Shovers. 49p. 1986. pap. 9.00 (0-685-27135-8) Three Dimensional.

Three Dimensional Living, Version 2. rev. ed. Aaron H. Shovers. (Illus.). 174p. (C). 1989. pap. 18.00 (0-9613613-6-0); audio 21.00 (0-9613613-5-2) Three Dimensional.

Three-Dimensional Magnetic Resonance Imaging: An Integrated Clinical Update of 3D-Imaging & 3D-Postprocessing: Proceedings of a Joint Meeting in Obergurgl, Austria, 23-27 March 1992. Ed. by F. Aichner et al. LC 94-20996. 300p. 1994. 110.00 (0-86542-800-X) Blackwell Sci.

Three-Dimensional Magnetosphere: Proceedings of the D3.1 Symposium of COSPAR Scientific Commission D. Ed. by J. Buchner. (Advances in Space Research Ser.: Vol. 18). 326p. 1996. pap. text ed. 92.75 (0-08-042674-3, Pergamon Pr) Elsevier.

Three-Dimensional Models of Marine & Estuarine Dyanmics. Ed. by J. C. Nihoul & B. M. Jamart. 630p. 1987. 264.25 (0-444-42794-5) Elsevier.

***3-D Human Modeling & Animation.** Ratnerp. (Design & Graphic Design Ser.). 1998. pap. 49.95 (0-442-02508-4) Van Nos Reinhold.

Three-Dimensional Object Recognition from Range Images. Minsoo Suk & Suchendra M. Bhandarkar. LC 92-34454. (Computer Science Workbench Ser.). 1992. 109.00 (0-387-70107-9) Spr-Verlag.

Three-Dimensional Object Recognition Systems. Ed. by Anil K. Jain & Patrick J. Flynn. LC 93-16947. (Advances in Image Communication Ser.: Vol. 1). 480p. 1993. 190.75 (0-444-89797-6) Elsevier.

Three-Dimensional Pieced Quilts. Jodie Davis. 144p. 1995. pap. 19.95 (0-8019-8390-8) Chilton.

3-Dimensional Process Simulation. Ed. by J. Lorenz. 200p. 1995. 70.95 (3-211-82741-2) Spr-Verlag.

Three Dimensional Projection Drawing. P. J. Booker. pap. 6.00 (0-85344-082-4) Apple Blossom.

Three-Dimensional Seismic Exploration. Ursin. (Handbook of Geophysical Exploration Ser.). Date not set. write for info. (0-08-037221-X, Pergamon Pr) Elsevier.

Three-Dimensional Shapes. David L. Stienecker. LC 96-10860. (Discovering Shapes Ser.). (Illus.). (J). (gr. 3 up). 1996. lib. bdg. 14.95 (0-7614-0463-5, Benchmark NY) Marshall Cavendish.

***Three Dimensional Simulation of Fabric Draping: Development & Application.** Otto K. Bergsma. (Illus.). xvi, 137p. (Orig.). 1996. pap. 52.50 (90-407-1351-0, Pub. by Delft U Pr NE) Coronet Bks.

Three-Dimensional Simulation of Semiconductor Devices. R. Kircher & W. Bergner. (Progress in Numerical Simulation for Microelectronics Ser.: Vol. 1). x, 114p. 1991. 91.00 (0-8176-2644-1) Spr-Verlag.

Three-Dimensional Structure of Wood: A Scanning Electron Microscope Study. B. A. Meylan & B. G. Butterfield. (Illus.). 80p. (C). 1972. pap. text ed. 34.50 (0-8156-5030-2) Syracuse U Pr.

Three Dimensional Surface Topography: Measurement & Interpretation. Kenneth J. Stout et al. 220p. 1993. 95.00 (1-85718-004-6) Taylor & Francis.

Three-Dimensional Systems. Ed. by Henry E. Kandrup et al. LC 95-17287. (Annals of the New York Academy of Sciences Ser.: Vol. 751). 1995. write for info. (0-89766-925-8); pap. write for info. (0-89766-926-6) NY Acad Sci.

Three Dimensional Tolerancing of Mechanical Systems: Theory & Practice. Andre Clement. (C). 1997. pap. text ed. 36.95 (0-201-63484-8) Addison-Wesley.

Three-Dimensional Turbulent Boundry Layers, Berlin FRG 1982: Proceedings. Ed. by H. Fernholz & E. Krause. (International Union of Theoretical & Applied Mechanics Symposia Ser.). (Illus.). 389p. 1982. 70.95 (0-387-11772-5) Spr-Verlag.

Three Dimensional Turbulent Shear Flows: Presented at 1982 AIAA-ASME Joint Fluids, Plasma, Thermophysics, & Heat Transfer Conference, St. Louis, Missouri, June 7-11, 1982. AIAA-ASME Joint Fluids, Plasma Thermophysics, & Heat Transfer Conference Staff. Ed. by S. Carmi et al. LC 82-71168. (Illus.). 166p. reprint ed. pap. 47.40 (0-8357-2875-7, 2039111) Bks Demand.

***Three-Dimensional Ultrasound.** Ed. by K. Baba & D. Jurkovic. LC 96-51892. (Progress in Obstetric & Gynecological Sonography Ser.). (Illus.). 150p. 1997. 78.00 (1-85070-619-0) Prthnon Pub.

***Three-Dimensional Velocity & Vorticity Measuring & Image Analysis Techniques: Lecture Notes from the Short Course Held in Zurich, Switzerland, 3-6 September 1996.** Ed. by T. A. Dracos. LC 96-42043. (ERCOFTAC Ser.). 310p. (C). 1996. lib. bdg. 150.00 (0-7923-4256-9) Kluwer Ac.

***Three Dimensions & Impossible Solids.** Allan Wiltshire. 64p. (J). (gr. 4-12). pap. 12.50 (1-871098-17-3, Pub. by Claire Pubns UK) Parkwest Pubns.

Three Dimensions of Hindu-Muslim Confrontation. A. K. Vakil. 1982. 6.00 (0-8364-0844-6) S Asia.

Three Diminutive Pigs. James Magorian. LC 88-71605. (Illus.). 20p. (J). (gr. 1-4). 1988. pap. 3.00 (0-930674-30-8) Black Oak.

***Three Discourses: A Critical Modern Edition of Newley Identified Work of the Young Hobbes.** Thomas Hobbes. 1997. pap. text ed. 12.95 (0-226-34546-7) U Ch Pr.

Three Discourses on Imagined Occasions. Soren Kierkegaard. Ed. by Edna H. Hong. Tr. by Howard V. Hong & Edna H. Hong. LC 92-36382. (Kierkegaard's Writings: Vol. 10). 176p. (C). 1993. text ed. 37.50 (0-691-03300-5) Princeton U Pr.

***Three Discovery Plays.** Gil Vicente. Ed. & Tr. by A. J. Lappin. (Hispanic Classics Ser.). 300p. 1997. text ed. 49.95 (0-85668-665-4, Pub. by Aris & Phillips UK); pap. text ed. 25.00 (0-85668-666-2, Pub. by Aris & Phillips UK) David Brown.

Three Discussions on the Conflict of Laws: Three & Comments on Fundamental Principles. G. O. Sunderstrom. (Acta Instituti Upsaliensis Jurisprudentiae Comparative: No. 11). 149p. (Orig.). 1970. pap. 53.00 (0-317-65787-9) Coronet Bks.

Three Distinct Knocks: On the Door of the Most Ancient Freemasonry; Being a Universal Description of All Its Branches from Its First Rite to This Present Time. Samuel Pritchard. 73p. 1992. reprint ed. pap. 9.00 (1-56459-247-2) Kessinger Pub.

Three Dog Winter. Elizabeth Van Steenwyk. (J). (gr. 4-9). 1987. 13.95 (0-8027-6718-4) Walker & Co.

Three-Dollar Day see Rope & Other Plays

Three-Dollar Mule. Clyde R. Bulla. (Illus.). (J). 1995. lib. bdg. 11.50 (0-8167-3711-8, Little Rainbow) Troll Communs.

Three-Dollar Mule. Clyde R. Bulla. LC 94-18508. (Illus.). 96p. (J). (gr. 1-3). 1995. pap. 2.50 (0-8167-3598-0) Troll Communs.

Three Doors to Death. Rex Stout. 240p. 1995. mass mkt. 4.99 (0-553-25127-9) Bantam.

Three Double King Pawn Openings. Yakov B. Estrin. Tr. by Jim Marfia from RUS. (Illus.). 86p. (Orig.). 1982. pap. 6.00 (0-931462-19-3) Chess Ent.

Three Ducks Went Wandering. Paul Galdone. 1987. pap. 4.80 (0-89919-494-X) Ticknor & Fields.

Three Duos Concertants Opus 57 for 2 Violins. C. Deberiot. 28p. 1986. pap. 6.95 (0-7935-5134-X) H Leonard.

Three Dwarfs. (Fun Time Pop-Up Ser.). (Illus.). (J). (ps-1). pap. 2.49 (0-517-46823-9) Random Hse Value.

Three Dynamite Authors: Derek Walcott (Nobel 1992), Naguib Mahfouz (Nobel 1988), & Wole Soyinka (Nobel 1986) Ed. by D. Herdeck. 1995. 24.00 (0-89410-773-9, Three Contnts); pap. 16.00 (0-89410-774-7, Three Contnts) Lynne Rienner.

Three Early Ballets for Piano: Centennial Edition. Igor Stravinsky. 192p. 1995. pap. 17.95 (0-7935-4425-4) H Leonard.

Three Early Books of Poems, 1965-1969: The Easy Philosopher, "A Hard Coming of It" & Other Poems, & the Foul Rag-&-Bone Shop. Louis D. Brodsky. Ed. by Sheri L. Vandermolen. LG 96-17150. 205p. 1997. pap. 16.95 (1-56809-031-5) Time Being Bks.

Three Early Books of Poems, 1965-1969: The Easy Philosopher, "A Hard Coming of It" & Other Poems, & the Foul Rag-&-Bone Shop. Ed. by Sheri L. Vandermolen. LC 96-17150. 205p. 1997. 25.00 (1-56809-030-7) Time Being Bks.

Three Early Comedies: Love's Labor Lost, The Merry Wives of Windsor, Two Gentlemen of Verona. William Shakespeare. (Classics Ser.). 448p. 1988. mass mkt. 4.95 (0-553-21282-6, Bantam Classics) Bantam.

Three Early English Metrical Romances. Ed. by John Robson. (Camden Society, London. Publications, First Ser.: No. 18). reprint ed. 42.50 (0-404-50118-4) AMS Pr.

Three Easy Pieces. Wright Morris. LC 93-35699. 328p. (Orig.). (C). 1993. 25.00 (0-87685-924-4); pap. 15.00 (0-87685-923-6) Black Sparrow.

Three Easy Pieces, signed ed. deluxe ed. Wright Morris. LC 93-35699. 328p. (Orig.). (C). 1993. 35.00 (0-87685-925-2) Black Sparrow.

Three Economic Commandments. Hans F. Sennholz. 47p. 1990. pap. 4.95 (0-910884-24-2) Libertarian Press.

Three-Edged Sword: Being Ill in America. Maureen A. Potts. 128p. (C). 1992. lib. bdg. 37.00 (0-8191-8669-4) U Pr of Amer.

Three Edwards. Thomas B. Costain. 1994. reprint ed. lib. bdg. 37.95 (1-56849-370-3) Buccaneer Bks.

Three Edwards: War & State in England, 1272-1377. Michael Prestwich. LC 92-19386. 352p. (C). (gr. 13). 1992. pap. 17.95 (0-415-05133-9, A9854) Routledge.

Three Eighty Six SX Microprocessor Hardware Reference Manual. 224p. 1990. 25.95 (1-55512-105-5, 240332-001) Intel Corp.

Three Elegies of Chu: An Introduction to the Traditional Interpretation of the Chu Tzu. Geoffrey R. Waters. LC 84-40505. 245p. 1985. reprint ed. pap. 69.90 (0-608-01867-8, 2062519) Bks Demand.

Three Eleventh-Century Anglo-Latin Saints' Lives: Vita S. Birini, Vita et Miracula S. Kenelmi, & Vita S. Rummoldi. Ed. & Tr. by Rosalind C. Love. (Oxford Medieval Texts Ser.). 344p. 1996. text ed. 85.00 (0-19-820524-4) OUP.

Three Elizabethan Fencing Manuals: True Arte of Defence; His Practice; Paradoxes of Defence. Giacomo Di Grassi et al. Ed. by James L. Jackson. LC 72-6321. 640p. 1972. reprint ed. 75.00 (0-8201-1107-4) Schol Facsimiles.

Three Elizabethan Pamphlets. Ed. by George R. Hibbard. LC 74-80622. (Select Bibliographies Reprint Ser.). 1977. 21.95 (0-8369-5034-8) Ayer.

Three English Brothers: Sir T. Sheley His Travels, Sir A. Sherley His Ambassage to the Christian Princes, Master R. Sheley His Wars Against the Turkes. Anthony Nixon. LC 72-26473. (English Experience Ser.: No. 270). 80p. 1970. reprint ed. 30.00 (90-221-0270-X) Walter J Johnson.

Three English Epics: Studies of Troilus & Criseyde, The Faerie Queen, & Paradise Lost. Thomas E. Maresca. LC 79-1080. 238p. reprint ed. pap. 67.90 (0-7837-6022-1, 2045834) Bks Demand.

***Three English Kings.** Nelson U. K. Staff. 1991. pap. text ed. write for info. (0-00-370128-X) Addison-Wesley.

Three English Statesmen: A Course of Lectures on the Political History of England. Goldwin A. Smith. LC 72-4587. (Essay Index Reprint Ser.). 1977. reprint ed. 23.95 (0-8369-2979-9) Ayer.

Three Entertainments. Graham Greene. 624p. 1994. pap. 15.00 (0-14-017363-3, Penguin Bks) Viking Penguin.

Three Episodes in Massachusetts History. Charles F. Adams, Jr. (Works of Charles Francis Adams Jr. (1835-1915)). 1989. reprint ed. lib. bdg. 79.00 (0-7812-1410-6) Rprt Serv.

***Three Eras of Political Change in Eastern Europe.** Gale Stokes. 272p. (C). 1996. text ed. 37.00 (0-19-510481-1); pap. text ed. 16.95 (0-19-510482-X) OUP.

Three Essays. Albrecht B. Ritschl. Tr. & Intro. by Philip Hefner. LC 72-75654. 309p. reprint ed. pap. 88.10 (0-685-15486-6, 2026887) Bks Demand.

Three Essays: On Reading the Gospel, on Reading the Holy Fathers, on Shunning Reading of Books Containing False Teachings. Ignatius Brianchianinov. pap. 0.50 (0-89981-103-5) Eastern Orthodox.

Three Essays "Father Vincent McNabb"; "A Modern Hand-Printer: Edward Walters"; & "Voyage to a Beginning"; the Introduction to Colin Wilson's Autobiography. Brocard Sewell. (Aylesford Review Essays Ser.: No. 1). 23p. (C). 1990. reprint ed. pap. 15.00 (0-946650-05-5); reprint ed. lib. bdg. 25.00 (0-8095-6754-7) Borgo Pr.

Three Essays on Lingusitic Diversity in the Spanish-Speaking World: The U. S. Southwest & the River Plate Area. Ed. by Jacob Ornstein. (Janua Linguarum, Ser Practica: No. 174). (Illus.). (Orig.). 1976. pap. text ed. 24.65 (90-279-3167-4) Mouton.

Three Essays on Religion. John Stuart Mill. LC 76-130995. reprint ed. 23.45 (0-404-04325-9) AMS Pr.

***Three Essays on Religion: 1878 Edition.** John S. Mill. (Key Texts Ser.). 314p. 1996. reprint ed. pap. write for info. (1-85506-218-6) Bks Intl VA.

Three Essays on Style. Erwin Panofsky. Ed. by Irving Lavin. (Illus.). 132p. 1995. 30.00 (0-262-16151-6) MIT Pr.

***Three Essays on Style.** Erwin Panofsky. (Illus.). 149p. 1997. reprint ed. pap. 15.00 (0-262-66103-9) MIT Pr.

Three Essays on the State Economic Science. Tjalling C. Koopmans. LC 90-35120. (Reprints of Economic Classics Ser.). ix, 231p. 1991. reprint ed. lib. bdg. 35.00 (0-678-01397-7) Kelley.

Three Essays on the Theory of Sexuality. Sigmund Freud. Tr. by James Strachey. LC 62-11202. 164p. 1976. pap. 16.00 (0-465-08606-3) Basic.

Three Essays on Thucydides. John H. Finley. LC 67-17308. (Loeb Classical Monographs). 212p. reprint ed. pap. 60.50 (0-7837-3863-3, 2043685) Bks Demand.

Three Essays, 1793-1795: The Tubingen Essay, Berne Fragments, The Life of Jesus. G. W. Hegel. Ed. by Peter Fuss & John Dobbins. LC 83-40599. 192p. 1984. text ed. 25.50 (0-268-01854-5) U of Notre Dame Pr.

***Three Etruscan Painted Sarcophagi.** Frank B. Tarbell. LC 17-28742. (Field Museum of Natural History Anthropological Ser.: Vol. 6, No. 4). (Illus.). 29p. 1917. reprint ed. pap. 25.00 (0-608-02708-1, 2063373) Bks Demand.

Three Evenings: Stories. James Lasdun. 192p. 1992. 18.00 (0-374-20887-5) FS&G.

***Three Evil Wishes.** R. L. Stine. (R. L. Stine's Ghosts of Fear Street Ser.). (J). (gr. 3-6). 1997. pap. 3.99 (0-671-00189-2, Minstrel Bks); mass mkt. 3.99 (0-671-57531-7, Minstrel Bks) PB.

Three Exemplary Novels. Miguel de Unamuno. Tr. by Angel Flores from SPA. LC 86-33606. 228p. 1987. pap. 7.95 (0-8021-5153-1, Grove) Grove-Atltic.

Three Exemplary Novels. Miguel de Cervantes Saavedra. Tr. by Samuel Putnam. LC 81-20235. Orig. Title: Novelas Ejemplares. (Illus.). xxi, 232p. 1982. reprint ed. text ed. 38.50 (0-313-23346-2, CETN, Greenwood Pr) Greenwood.

Three Extraordinary Ambassadors. Harold Acton. LC 83-50109. (Walter Neurath Memorial Lectures). (Illus.). 64p. 1984. 12.95 (0-500-55015-8) Thames Hudson.

Three Eyes on the Past: Exploring New York State Folk Life. Louis C. Jones. LC 82-7334. (New York State Bks.). (Illus.). 194p. (Orig.). 1982. pap. 13.95 (0-8156-0179-4) Syracuse U Pr.

Three Fables. Mary Barnard. LC 83-19719. 56p. 1984. 10.00 (0-932576-20-6); pap. 4.95 (0-932576-21-4) Breitenbush Bks.

Three Faces of Being: Toward an Existential Clinical Psychology. Ernest Keen. LC 78-128900. (Century Psychology Ser.). (Orig.). (C). 1970. 39.50 (0-89197-452-0); pap. text ed. 16.95 (0-89197-453-9) Irvington.

Three Faces of Berkeley: Competing Ideologies in the Wheeler Era, 1899-1919. Henry F. May. Ed. by Carroll Brentano & Sheldon Rothblatt. LC 93-30444. (Chapters in the History of the University of California Ser.: No. 1). 53p. (Orig.). 1994. pap. 10.00 (0-87772-342-7) UCB IGS.

Three Faces of Discipline for Early Childhood: Empowering the Teacher & Students. Charles H. Wolfgang & Mary E. Wolfgang. LC 94-981. 1994. pap. text ed. 39.95 (0-205-15649-5, Longwood Div) Allyn.

Three Faces of Discipline for the Elementary School Teacher: A Pathway of Power to Effective Discipline & Classroom Management. Charles H. Wolfgang. LC 95-47108. 1996. pap. text ed. 38.50 (0-205-15647-9) Allyn.

Three Faces of Eve. rev. ed. Corbett Thigpen & Hervey M. Cleckley. LC 56-12526. 309p. 1992. reprint ed. 30.00 (0-911238-51-4) Three Faces Eve.

Three Faces of Imperialism. Philip Darby. LC 86-24665. 256p. 1987. text ed. 37.50 (0-300-03748-1) Yale U Pr.

Three Faces of Jesus. Josef Imbach. 151p. 1992. pap. 12.95 (0-87243-194-0) Templegate.

Three Faces of Love. Paul A. Hauck. LC 83-10468. 174p. 1984. pap. 12.00 (0-664-24486-6, Westminster) Westminster John Knox.

Three Faces of Love. large type ed. Peggy Gaddis. LC 93-40512. 192p. 1994. lib. bdg. 19.95 (0-7862-0151-7) Thorndike Pr.

Three Faces of Mind: Developing Your Mental, Emotional & Behavioral Intelligences. Elaine De Beauport & Aura S. Diaz. LC 96-22709. (Illus.). 1996. 24.95 (0-8356-0748-8, Quest) Theos Pub Hse.

***Three Faces of Molly Brant.** Earle Thomas. 1997. pap. 14.95 (1-55082-176-8, Pub. by Quarry Pr CN) LPC InBook.

Three Faces of Power. Kenneth E. Boulding. 264p. (C). 1989. pap. 25.00 (0-8039-3862-4); text ed. 52.00 (0-8039-3554-4) Sage.

***Three Faces of Richard Nixon: A Psychobiography.** Vamik D. Volkan et al. LC 97-3477. 1997. write for info. (0-231-10854-0); pap. write for info. (0-231-10855-9) Col U Pr.

Three Faces of the River. Janet Pellam. 67p. (Orig.). 1994. pap. write for info. (1-879294-06-0) Warm Spring Pr.

Three Faces of Vietnam. Richard L. Wormser. LC 93-11099. (America Past & Present Ser.). (Illus.). 160p. (YA). (gr. 7-12). 1993. lib. bdg. 22.70 (0-531-11142-3) Watts.

Three Fairy Godmothers. Jerry L. Twedt. 88p. 1967. pap. 3.00 (0-87129-163-0, T25) Dramatic Pub.

***Three Faiths/One God: A Jewish, Christian, Muslim Encounter.** Ed. by John Hick. 240p. 1996. 22.50 (0-614-21686-9, 1233) Kazi Pubns.

Three Famous Alchemists: Raymund Lully, Cornelius Agrippa, Theophrastus Paracelsus. Arthur E. Waite et al. 186p. 1992. pap. 16.95 (0-922802-84-X) Kessinger Pub.

3 Famous Artists-Naturalists of the Colonial Period: John Abbot: William Bartram: Mark Catesby: A Coloring Book for All Ages. Susan C. Smith. (Illus.). 20p. 1994. pap. 6.00 (0-937543-05-5) Sacrum Pr.

Three Famous Mystics: Saint-Martin, Jacob Boehme, Swedenborg. Arthur E. Waite & W. P. Swainson. 192p. 1992. pap. 16.95 (0-922802-85-8) Kessinger Pub.

Three Famous Occultists: Dr. John Dee, Franz Anton Mesmer & Thomas Lake Harris. R. B. Hort & W. P. Swaison. 190p. 1993. reprint ed. spiral bd. 10.50 (0-7873-0419-0) Hlth Research.

Three Famous Occultists: Dr. John Dee, Franz Anton Mesmer, Thomas Lake Harris. G. M. Hort et al. 190p. 1992. pap. 16.95 (0-922802-86-6) Kessinger Pub.

Three Famous Plays: A Month in the Country, A Provincial Lady, A Poor Gentleman. Ivan S. Turgenev. Tr. by Constance Garnett from RUS. LC 75-41276. reprint ed. 29.50 (0-404-14619-8) AMS Pr.

Three Famous Short Novels. Incl. Spotted Horses. William Faulkner. 1958. pap. (0-318-55474-7); Old Man. (0-318-55475-5); Bear. (0-318-55476-3); 316p. 1958. pap. 10.00 (0-394-70149-6, V-149, Vin) Random.

***Three Fantasies for Five Viols.** John Milton. Ed. by Rita Morey. i, 27p. (Orig.). 1997. pap. text ed. 15.00 (1-56571-145-9) PRB Prods.

Three Fantastic Dances, Opus 5. Shostakovich. 8p. 1985. pap. 3.95 (0-7935-3370-8, 00121240) H Leonard.

Three Farmers on Their Way to a Dance. Richard Powers. LC 92-52617. 352p. 1992. pap. 12.00 (0-06-097509-1, PL) HarpC.

Three Farms: Making Milk, Meat, & Money from the American Soil. Mark Kramer. LC 87-12327. 300p. reprint ed. pap. 85.50 (0-7837-5934-7, 2045733) Bks Demand.

Three Fates. Francis M. Crawford. (Works of Francis Marion Crawford Ser.). 1990. reprint ed. lib. bdg. 79.00 (0-7812-2540-X) Rprt Serv.

Three Feathers. Jacob W. Grimm & Wilhelm K. Grimm. (Creative's Collection of Fairy Tales). (Illus.). 32p. (J). (gr. 4 up). 1984. lib. bdg. 13.95 (0-87191-941-9) Creative Ed.

Three Festivals: SFAS EMES. Yosef Stern. 1993. 22.99 (0-89906-429-9); pap. 19.99 (0-89906-430-2) Mesorah Pubns.

***Three Festive Pieces for Christmastide.** Ed. by Dale Tucker. 16p. (Orig.). (C). 1997. pap. text ed. 6.95 (0-7692-0078-8) Warner Brothers.

Three Fifty-Six Porsche: A Restorer's Guide to Authenticity. 2nd ed. Brett Johnson. LC 89-85080. (Illus.). 160p. 1991. pap. 24.95 (0-929758-08-0) Beeman Jorgensen.

Three Films of W.C. Fields. W. C. Fields. (Classic Screenplay Ser.). (Illus.). 208p. (Orig.). 1990. pap. 11.95 (0-571-14385-7) Faber & Faber.

Three Films of Woody Allen: Broadway Danny Rose, Zelig, the Purple Rose of Cairo. Woody Allen. 1987. 16.00 (0-394-75304-6, Vin) Random.

***Three Fin-de-Siecle Farces.** Tr. by David Willinger from FRE. (Belgian Francophone Library: Vol. 5). 280p. (C). 1996. text ed. 50.95 (0-8204-3041-2) P Lang Pubng.

Three Finger Pickin' Banjo Songbook. 9.95 (0-87166-959-5, 93612) Mel Bay.

Three Finger Pickin' Banjo Songbook. 1993. audio 9.95 (1-56222-591-X, 93612C) Mel Bay.

An Asterisk (*) at the beginning of an entry indicates that the title is appearing in BIP for the first time.

*Three Finger Pickin' Banjo Songbook.** Mike Bailey. 18.95 incl. audio (0-7866-0919-2, 93612P) Mel Bay.

Three Fingers: The Mountain, the Men & the Lookout. Malcolm S. Bates. (Illus.). 159p. 1987. pap. 12.95 (0-938567-03-9) Cloudcap.

Three-Five-Seven Minute Talks on Freemasonry. 9th ed. Elbert Bede. xii, 116p. 1993. reprint ed. pap. 6.50 (0-88053-048-0, M-306) Macoy Pub.

Three Flags over Pittsburgh: A History Coloring Book. Linda Steiner. 1992. pap. 3.95 (0-910042-62-4) Allegheny.

Three Flights Up. Beth Stahlecker. LC 94-71636. (Stahlecker Ser.). 48p. 1996. pap. 11.95 (1-884800-04-1) Four Way Bks.

Three Flute Notes. Jeannie Ebner. Tr. & Afterword by Lowell A. Bangerter. LC 92-44547. (Studies in Austrian Literature, Culture, & Thought. Translation Ser.). 1993. pap. 21.50 (0-929497-62-7) Ariadne CA.

*Three Folk Tales.** (Nelson Readers Ser.). (J). Date not set. pap. text ed. write for info. (0-17-557041-8) Addison-Wesley.

*Three for a Wedding.** Neels. 1997. mass mkt. 3.99 (0-373-83339-3) Harlequin Bks.

*Three for Brighton.** Martha Kirkland. 224p. 1998. mass mkt. 4.99 (0-8217-5852-7, Zebra Kensgtn) Kensgtn Pub Corp.

Three for Space. William F. Nolan. 1992. 19.95 (0-936071-32-X); pap. 9.95 (0-936071-33-8) Gryphon Pubns.

Three for the Bobcat. Ron Olson. LC 84-70024. 187p. (Orig.). 1984. pap. 2.95 (0-916027-00-7) Bannack Pub Co.

Three for the Road. Shannon Waverly. (Superromance Ser.). 1995. mass mkt. 3.75 (0-373-70660-X, 1-70660-5) Harlequin Bks.

Three for the Third Day: Three Easter Sunrise Services. Mary L. Warstler. 48p. (Orig.). 1995. pap. 5.75 (0-7880-0331-3) CSS OH.

Three Founders: Charles K. Stillman, Carl C. Cutler, Edward E. Bradley. Marion Dickerman. (Illus.). 42p. 1965. pap. 4.00 (0-913372-18-8) Mystic Seaport.

Three Fountains. large type ed. Patricia Toms. 320p. 1987. 25.99 (0-7089-1707-0) Ulverscroft.

Three Freckles Past a Hair: A Grandfather's Legacy of Love. P. K. Hallinan. LC 94-31747. (P. K. Hallinan - Personal Values Ser.). (Illus.). 32p. (J). 1996. lib. bdg. 14.95 (1-56674-105-X) Forest Hse.

Three French Comedies. Ed. by C. B. Coleman. Tr. & Intro. by James Magruder. 1996. 30.00 (0-300-06275-3); pap. write for info. (0-300-06276-1) Yale U Pr.

Three French Moralists & the Gallantry of France. Edmund W. Gosse. LC 67-23223. (Essay Index Reprint Ser.). 1977. 18.95 (0-8369-0489-3) Ayer.

Three French Short Verse Satirists: Marot, Magny, & Du Bellay. Ed. by William F. Panici. LC 90-3800. (Studies in Comparative Literature). 152p. 1990. reprint ed. 15.00 (0-8240-0010-2) Garland.

Three Friends. Jeanne Bonnette. (J). (ps-2). 1982. pap. 4.95 (0-89992-066-7) Coun India Ed.

*Three Friends.** Jim Boulden & Joan Boulden. Ed. by JoAnn Farness. (Illus.). 32p. 1996. pap. 5.95 (1-878076-77-9) Boulden Pub.

Three Friends. Robert Kraus. (J). (gr. k-3). 1975. pap. 2.95 (0-525-62346-9, Dutton) NAL-Dutton.

Three Friends: Bedichek, Dobie, Webb. A Personal History. William A. Owens. LC 70-82957. 335p. 1975. pap. 7.95 (0-292-78012-5) U of Tex Pr.

Three Friends/Tres Amigos: A Counting Book/Un Cuento Para Contar. Maria C. Brusca & Tona Wilson. LC 94-44648. (Illus.). 32p. (ENG & SPA.). (J). (ps-3). 1995. 14.95 (0-8050-3707-1) H Holt & Co.

3 from Baltimore. (Illus.). 24p. 1982. pap. 5.00 (0-932718-10-8) Kohler Arts.

Three from the Gorilla Theatre: Gorilla My Dreams I Love You, Plutography in the Slave Trade & Mixed Blood. Aubrey Hampton & Susan Hussey. (Illus.). (Orig.). 1990. pap. 8.95 (0-939157-07-1) Organica Pr.

Three Frontiers: Family, Land, & Society in the American West, 1850-1900. Dean L. May. LC 93-43560. (Interdisciplinary Perspectives on Modern History Ser.). (Illus.). 352p. (C). 1994. text ed. 47.95 (0-521-43499-8) Cambridge U Pr.

*Three Frontiers: Family, Land, & Society in the American West, 1850-1900.** Dean L. May. (Interdisciplinary Perspectives on Modern History Ser.). (Illus.). 329p. 1997. pap. text ed. 17.95 (0-521-58575-9) Cambridge U Pr.

*Three Generals of Later Han.** Gregory Young. (Faculty of Asian Studies Monographs: Vol. 6). 116p. 1997. pap. text ed. 20.00 (0-86784-526-0, Pub. by Aust Nat Univ AT) UH Pr.

Three Generations: Riding the Waves of Change in Your Church. Gary L. McIntosh. LC 94-44012. 224p. (Orig.). (gr. 13). 1995. pap. 9.99 (0-8007-5544-8) Revell.

Three Generations in Twentieth Century America: Family, Community, & Nation. 2nd rev. ed. John G. Clark et al. 515p. (C). 1982. pap. 45.95 (0-534-10503-3) Wadsworth Pub.

Three Generations of Chilean Cuisine. Mirtha Umana-Murray. 240p. 1996. pap. 26.00 (1-56565-467-6) Lowell Hse.

*Three Generations of Chilean Cuisine.** 2nd ed. Mirtha Umana-Murray. 304p. 1997. reprint ed. pap. 16.00 (1-56565-817-5, Global Gourmet) Lowell Hse.

Three Generations, Two Languages, One Family: Language Choice & Language Shift in a Chinese Community in Britain. Li Wei. LC 94-9959. (Multilingual Matters Ser.: Vol. 104). 1994. 55.00 (1-85359-241-2, Pub. by Multilingual Matters UK); pap. 34.95 (1-85359-240-4, Pub. by Multilingual Matters UK) Taylor & Francis.

Three Generations West. John A. Gjevre. (Saga of the Soo Ser.: Vol. II). (Illus.). 224p. 1995. 45.00 (0-9646134-0-9) Agassiz Pubns.

*Three Genres.** 6th ed. Minot. 1997. pap. text ed. 28.00 (0-13-491929-7) P-H.

Three Genres: The Writing of Poetry, Fiction, & Drama. 5th ed. Stephen Minot. LC 92-20807. 384p. (C). 1993. pap. text ed. 32.80 (0-13-918467-8) P-H.

Three Genres & the Interpretation of Lyric. William E. Rogers. LC 82-12293. 288p. reprint ed. pap. 82.10 (0-7837-1936-1, 2042151) Bks Demand.

Three George Rogers Clark Lectures. Russell F. Weigley et al. (Illus.). 84p. (C). 1991. lib. bdg. 29.00 (0-8191-8142-0) U Pr of Amer.

Three German Classics: A Village Romeo & Juliet - Gottfried Keller, Immensee - Theodore Storm, Lenz - Georg Buchner. (Orig.). 1980. pap. 7.95 (0-7145-0561-7) Riverrun NY.

*Three Gifts & Other Stories.** Ed. by David S. Pape. (Illus.). (J). (gr. 3-9). 1997. 13.95 (0-922613-68-0) Hachai Pubns.

Three Girls in Blue. Ludmila Petrushevskaya. Tr. by Stephen Mulrine. 1991. 5.95 (0-87129-403-6, T87) Dramatic Pub.

*Three Go Back.** Grassic L. Gibbon. 1996. pap. 16.00 (0-7486-6203-0, Pub. by Polygon UK) Subterranean Co.

Three Go Searching. Patricia M. St. John. (Patricia St. John Bks.). (Illus.). (YA). (gr. 9-12). 1977. mass mkt. 5.99 (0-8024-8748-3) Moody.

Three Go Searching see Tres en Busca de Aventuras

Three Goat Songs. Michael Brodsky. LC 90-49706. 166p. 1991. 18.95 (0-941423-46-8); pap. 9.95 (0-941423-47-6) FWEW.

Three Goats. Margaret Hillert. (Illus.). (J). (ps). 1963. pap. 5.10 (0-8136-5554-4, TK2369); lib. bdg. 7.95 (0-8136-5054-2, TK2368) Modern Curr.

Three Gold Bricks. Chen Li. (Asian Folk Tales Ser.). (Illus.). 24p. (J). 1995. 9.95 (983-9808-63-X, Pub. by Delta Edits MY) Weatherhill.

Three Gold Pieces: A Greek Folk Tale (Mexico) Aliki. (Trophy Picture Bk.). (Illus.). 32p. (J). (ps-3). 1994. pap. 5.95 (0-06-443386-2, Trophy) HarpC Child Bks.

Three Golden Apples. Nathaniel Hawthorne. (YA). (gr. 5 up). 1992. lib. bdg. 17.95 (0-88682-517-2); lib. bdg. 39.95 (1-56846-007-4) Creative Ed.

Three Golden Apples. Nathaniel Hawthorne. 56p. 1995. 39.95 (0-15-201058-0, Red Wagon Bks) HarBrace.

Three Golden Keys. Peter Sis. LC 94-6743. (Illus.). 64p. (J). 1994. 22.50 (0-385-47292-7) Doubleday.

*Three Golden Looms.** 128p. (J). 1997. write for info. (0-7459-3816-7, Lion) Chariot Victor.

*Three Golden Looms.** Julia Duin. (Illus.). 128p. (J). 1997. 12.99 (0-7814-0013-9, Chariot Bks) Chariot Victor.

Three Golden Oranges. Ada. 1997. 17.00 (0-689-80775-9, S&S Bks Young Read) S&S Childrens.

Three Golden Pearls on a String: The Esoteric Teachings of Karate - Do. 2nd ed. Thomas White. Orig. Title: Three Golden Pearls on a String: the Warrior Priest. 112p. 1991. pap. 9.95 (1-55643-107-4) North Atlantic.

Three Golden Pearls on a String: the Warrior Priest see Three Golden Pearls on a String: The Esoteric Teachings of Karate - Do

Three Good Events. Ilyon. Tr. by Edward B. Adams from KOR. (Children's Stories from Korean History Ser.: Vol. 4). (Illus.). 30p. (J). (gr. 5). 1986. 8.95 (0-00-000009-4, Pub. by Seoul Intl Tourist KO) C E Tuttle.

*Three Gospels.** Reynolds Price. 1997. pap. 12.00 (0-684-83281-X, Touchstone Bks) S&S Trade.

Three Gospels. large type ed. Reynolds Price. 392p. 1996. lib. bdg. 22.95 (0-7838-1854-8, GK Hall) Thorndike Pr.

Three Gospels: The Good News According to Mark, The Good News According to John, an Honest Account of a Memorable Life. Reynolds Price. 288p. 1996. 23.00 (0-684-80336-4) S&S Trade.

*Three Gospels Reading Group Guide.** 1997. pap. write for info. (0-684-00295-7, Touchstone Bks) S&S Trade.

Three Gothic Novels. Incl. Castle of Otronto. Horace Walpole. 1968. (0-318-55101-2); Vathek. William Bockford. 1968. (0-318-55102-0); Frankenstein. Mary Wollstonecraft Shelley. (0-318-55103-9); (English Library). 512p. (Orig.). 1968. pap. 9.95 (0-14-043036-9, Penguin Classics) Viking Penguin.

Three Graces. Timothy Clifford et al. (Illus.). 112p. Date not set. pap. 25.00 (0-903598-59-0, Pub. by Natl Galleries UK) Antique Collect.

Three Great Friday Sermons & Other Theological Discourses. Apostolos Makrakis. Ed. by Orthodox Christian Educational Society Staff. Tr. by Denver Cummings. 107p. (Orig.). 1952. pap. 6.95 (0-938366-48-3) Orthodox Chr.

Three Great Gothic Novels. E. F. Bieler. 25.95 (0-8488-0060-5) Amereon Ltd.

Three Great Hoaxes of the War: Blessed Are Those Who Have Not Seen & Yet Have Believed. Aleister Crowley. 1993. reprint ed. pap. 5.95 (1-55818-264-0) Holmes Pub.

Three Great Irishmen: Shaw, Yeats, Joyce. Arland Ussher. LC 68-54235. 1953. 28.00 (0-8196-0222-1) Biblo.

Three Great Islamic Movements: In the Arab World of the Recent Past. Maryam Jameelah. 46p. (Orig.). 1985. pap. 3.00 (1-56744-403-2) Kazi Pubns.

Three Great Jewish Plays. Ed. & Tr. by Joseph C. Landis from YID. 272p. 1986. pap. 8.95 (0-936839-04-X) Applause Theatre Bk Pubs.

Three Great Novels: The Woman in White - The Moonstone - The Law & the Lady. Wilkie Collins. LC 93-37406. 1168p. 1994. pap. 16.95 (0-19-282333-7) OUP.

Three Great Novels World War II. Marc Jaffe. 1996. 13.99 (0-517-15038-7) Random.

Three Great Plays. Euripides. 1958. pap. 9.95 (0-452-01040-3, Mer) NAL-Dutton.

Three Great Plays of Euripides. R. Ware. pap. 2.50 (0-452-00672-4, Mer) NAL-Dutton.

Three Great Plays of Euripides. Tr. by R. Ware. 1989. pap. 3.95 (0-452-00919-7) NAL-Dutton.

Three Great Plays of Shakespeare. William Shakespeare. (Classics Ser.). (YA). (gr. 4-7). 1991. pap. text ed. 7.49 (0-582-03586-4, 79122) Longman.

Three Great Thrillers. Buchan. 1994. 12.00 (0-19-521094-8) OUP.

Three Great Works: Lord Jim - Heart of Darkness - Nostromo. Joseph Conrad. LC 93-41828. 656p. 1994. pap. 14.95 (0-19-282336-1) OUP.

*Three Greatest Prayers.** St. Thomas Aquinas. LC 87-12661. 209p. 1997. reprint ed. pap. 14.95 (0-918477-52-2) Sophia Inst Pr.

Three Greek Romances. Incl. Daphnis & Chloe. Longus. LC 53-10378. (0-318-51124-X); Ephesian Tale. Xenophon. LC 53-10378. 1964. (0-318-51125-8); Hunters of Euboia. Dio Chrysoston. LC 53-10378. 1964. (0-318-51126-6); LC 53-10378. 1964. write for info. (0-318-51123-1, LLA201) Macmillan.

Three Greek Romances. Ed. & Tr. by Moses Hadas from GRE. LC 53-10378. 1964. text ed. 29.50 (0-8290-2405-0) Irvington.

Three Grooms & a Wedding. Joann Ross. (Temptation Ser.). 1995. mass mkt. 3.25 (0-373-25645-0, 1-25645-2) Harlequin Bks.

Three Guineas. Virginia Woolf. LC 38-27681. 188p. 1963. pap. 6.95 (0-15-690177-3, Harvest Bks) HarBrace.

*Three Guns for Guadla.** large type ed. John Renwick. (Dales Large Print Ser.). 195p. 1997. pap. 18.99 (1-85389-687-X) Ulverscroft.

Three-Guy Weekend. Alexis Page. (Love Stories Ser.: No. 14). 192p. 1996. mass mkt. 3.99 (0-553-57044-7) Bantam.

Three Gymnopedies for the Piano. Erik Satie. 12p. 1986. pap. 4.95 (0-7935-2590-X, 50262410) H Leonard.

Three Habitations of Devils. Lester Sumrall. 64p. (Orig.). 1990. pap. text ed. 1.95 (0-937580-22-8) LeSEA Pub Co.

Three Habitations of Devils. Lester Sumrall. 64p. 1993. mass mkt. 3.99 (0-88368-293-1) Whitaker Hse.

Three Hairs: Adapted from a Haitian Folktale. (Step into a Story Bk.). 20p. (Orig.). 1996. pap. 3.50 (1-889238-03-1) Papa Joes.

Three Halves of Ino Moxo: Teachings of the Wizard of the Upper Amazon. Cesar Calvo. Tr. by Kenneth Symington. LC 94-30522. 1994. pap. 14.95 (0-89281-519-1) Inner Tradit.

Three-Hand Jax & Other Spells. Staszek. (Illus.). 170p. 1996. pap. 9.95 (1-882633-08-3) Permeable.

Three Hand Reel: Three One Act Plays Based on Short Stories by Frank O'Connor. adapted ed. Frank O'Connor. 1967. pap. 5.25 (0-8222-1138-6) Dramatists Play.

Three Hands of God. Barbara B. Van Noord. 104p. 1995. pap. 12.00 (0-941895-13-0) Amherst Wri Art.

Three Hannahs. Hannah H. Taylor. 108p. (C). 1989. pap. 21.00 (1-85072-044-4, Pub. by W Sessions UK) St Mut.

Three Happy Birthdays. Judith Caseley. LC 92-24583. 40p. (J). (gr. 1 up). 1993. pap. 4.95 (0-688-11699-X, Mulberry) Morrow.

Three Happy Days. Edith Witmer. (Jewel Bks.). 1989. pap. 2.15 (0-317-02027-7) Rod & Staff.

Three Hat Day. Laura Geringer. LC 85-42640. (Illus.). 32p. (J). (ps-3). 1985. lib. bdg. 14.89 (0-06-021989-0) HarpC Child Bks.

Three Hat Day. Laura Geringer. LC 85-42640. (Trophy Picture Bk.). (Illus.). 32p. (J). (ps-3). 1987. pap. 4.95 (0-06-443157-6, Trophy) HarpC Child Bks.

Three Hearts & Three Lions. Poul Anderson. 256p. 1993. mass mkt. 4.99 (0-671-72186-0) Baen Bks.

Three Hearts & Three Lions. Poul Anderson. 1993. reprint ed. lib. bdg. 18.95 (0-89968-389-4, Lghtyr Pr) Buccaneer Bks.

Three Hinged-Arch Storage Building in Precast Prestressed Concrete. (PCI Journal Reprints Ser.). 8p. 1969. pap. 10.00 (0-686-40022-4, JR81) P-PCI.

Three Homes: Recollections of Childhood. Virginia O. Earle. LC 92-4246. (Illus.). 1992. 18.00 (0-87233-103-2) Bauhan.

Three Hostages. John Buchan. 284p. reprint ed. lib. bdg. 23.95 (0-89190-245-7, Rivercity Pr) Amereon Ltd.

Three Hotels: Plays & Monologues. Jon R. Baitz. LC 93-51492. 1994. pap. 8.95 (1-55936-085-2) Theatre Comm.

Three Hour Meditation. Herbert L. Beierle. 1995. pap. 2.00 (0-940480-29-8) UNI Press.

Three Hours for Lunch: The Life & Times of Christopher Morley. Helen M. Oakley. LC 75-39492. 1976. 12.00 (0-88370-005-0) Watermill Pubs.

Three Hours to Live. W. A. Fagel. 64p. 1981. pap. 0.49 (0-317-00062-4) Pacific Pr Pub Assn.

*Three Houses.** Angela Thirkell. LC 97-22319. 134p. 1998. 19.95 (1-55921-215-2) Moyer Bell.

Three Houses: New South Wales, Australia 1974-84 Glenn Murcutt. E. M. Farrelly. (Architecture in Detail Ser.). (Illus.). 60p. (C). 1993. pap. 29.95 (0-7148-2875-0, Pub. by Phaidon Press UK) Chronicle Bks.

Three Hundred Affordable Home Plans: Home Designs under 2,650 Square Feet. LC 92-70534. (Home Plans Ser.). 256p. 1994. pap. 8.95 (1-880029-10-3) Creative Homeowner.

Three Hundred & Fifty Secondary Diseases-Disorders to Alcoholism. LC 85-73319. 45p. 1985. pap. 3.55 (0-88270-610-1) Bridge-Logos.

*344th Bomb Group (M) "Silver Streaks" History & Remembrances World War II.** Ed. by Lambert D. Austin. 358p. 1996. 39.95 (0-941072-20-7) Southern Herit.

*301 Ways to Have Fun at Work.** David Hemsath & Leslie Yerkes. LC 97-10609. (Illus.). 200p. (Orig.). 1997. pap. 14.95 (1-57675-019-1) Berrett-Koehler.

Three Hundred & Sixty Degrees of the Zodiac. Adriano Carelli. 208p. 1982. write for info. (0-86690-063-2, C1032-014) Am Fed Astrologers.

Three Hundred & Sixty-Five Cookies & Brownies. Joanne L. Hayes. 256p. 1996. mass mkt. 5.99 (0-06-109442-0) HarpC.

Three Hundred & Sixty-Five Days of Creative Play for Children Two Years & Up. rev. ed. Sheila Ellison & Judith Gray. (Illus.). 400p. 1990. spiral bd. 14.95 (0-9620467-8-7) Forward March.

Three Hundred & Sixty-Five Easy Italian Recipes. Rick M. O'Connell. 256p. 1994. mass mkt. 5.99 (0-06-109345-9, Harp PBks) HarpC.

Three Hundred & Sixty-Five Easy Italian Recipes. Rick M. O'Connell. 256p. 1996. 12.95 (0-06-018661-5) HarpC.

Three Hundred & Sixty-Five Easy Low-Calorie Recipes. Sylvia Schur. 224p. 1995. mass mkt. 5.99 (0-06-109407-2, Harp PBks) HarpC.

Three Hundred & Sixty-Five Easy Low Calorie Recipes. Sylvia Schur. 224p. 1996. 12.95 (0-06-018660-7) HarpC.

Three Hundred & Sixty-Five Easy One Dish Meals. Natalie H. Haughton. 288p. 1996. 12.95 (0-06-018662-3) HarpC.

Three Hundred & Sixty-Five Foods Kids Love to Eat. Sheila Ellison & Judith Gray. 430p. 1989. spiral bd. 14.95 (0-9620467-5-2) Forward March.

365 Four-Star Videos You (Probably) Haven't Seen. Leslie Hamilton. 384p. 1996. pap. 11.00 (0-8092-3219-7) Contemp Bks.

Three Hundred & Sixty-Five Great Barbecue & Grilling Recipes. Lonnie Gandara. 224p. 1993. mass mkt. 5.99 (0-06-109133-2, Harp PBks) HarpC.

Three Hundred & Sixty-Five Great Barbecue & Grilling Recipes. Lonnie Gandara. 224p. 1996. 12.95 (0-06-018656-9) HarpC.

Three Hundred & Sixty-Five Great Chocolate Desserts. Natalie H. Naughton. 288p. 1996. 12.95 (0-06-018665-8) HarpC.

Three Hundred & Sixty-Five Meditations for Teachers. Greg H. Quinn. 384p. 1995. pap. 4.95 (0-590-25508-8) Scholastic Inc.

Three Hundred & Sixty-Five Meditations for Women. Burrjis Abernethy et al. LC 89-194. 352p. 1989. pap. 12.00 (0-687-41886-0) Abingdon.

Three Hundred & Sixty-Five Quick & Easy Microwave Recipes. Thelma Pressman. 192p. 1996. 12.95 (0-06-018657-7) HarpC.

Three Hundred & Sixty-Five Snacks, Hors D'Oevres & Appetizers. Lonnie Gandara. 256p. 1996. 12.95 (0-06-018659-3) HarpC.

Three Hundred & Sixty-Five Ways to Cook Chicken. Cheryl Sedeker. 1996. 12.95 (0-06-018664-X) HarpC.

Three-Hundred & Sixty-Five Ways to Cook Pasta. Marie Simmons. 240p. 1995. mass mkt. 5.99 (0-06-109416-1, Harp PBks) HarpC.

Three Hundred & Sixty-Five Ways to Cook Pasta. Marie Simmons. 240p. 1996. 12.95 (0-06-018663-1) HarpC.

Three Hundred & Sixty-Five Ways to Wok. Linda Drachman. 256p. 1996. 12.95 (0-06-018658-5) HarpC.

Three Hundred & Three Dumb Spelling Mistakes & What You Can Do about Them. David Downing. 128p. 1994. pap. 5.95 (0-8442-5475-4, Natl Textbk) NTC Pub Grp.

Three Hundred & Twenty-Five Francs. Roger Vailland. Ed. by David Nott. 224p. (C). 1990. pap. text ed. 17.95 (0-415-01710-6) Routledge.

Three Hundred & Twenty-Five Prompts for Personal Journals. Scholastic Books Staff. 48p. 1993. pap. 10.95 (0-590-49350-7) Scholastic Inc.

Three Hundred Art Nouveau Designs & Motifs in Full Color. Ed. by Carol B. Grafton. (Illus.). 48p. reprint ed. pap. 7.95 (0-486-24354-0) Dover.

Three-Hundred Calorie One-Dish Meal Cookbook. Nancy S. Hughes. 176p. 1992. pap. 11.95 (0-8092-3956-6) Contemp Bks.

300 Christian & Inspirational Patterns for Scroll Saw Woodworking. Tom Zieg. 152p. 1995. pap. 14.95 (1-56523-063-9) Fox Chapel Pub.

388th Tactical Fighter Wing: At Korat Royal Thai Air Force Base. Don Logan. LC 95-67627. (Illus.). 128p. 1995. 29.95 (0-88740-798-6) Schiffer.

381st Bomb Group. Ron MacKay. (Fighter Groups - Squadrons Ser.). (Illus.). 64p. 1994. pap. 10.95 (0-89747-314-0) Squad Sig Pubns.

*381 Old-Fashioned Holiday Vignettes in Color.** Carol B. Grafton. pap. 5.95 (0-486-27686-4) Dover.

Three Hundred Eighty-Seven DX User's Manual Programmer's Reference. Intel Corporation Staff. 304p. (Orig.). 1990. pap. 20.00 (1-55512-107-1, 231917-002) Intel Corp.

Three Hundred Eminent Personalities. Mildred G. Goertzel et al. LC 78-1149. (Joint Publication in the Jossey-Bass Series in Social & Behavioral Science & in Higher Education). 461p. reprint ed. pap. 131.40 (0-8357-4977-0, 2037910) Bks Demand.

300 Extraordinary Plants: For Home & Garden. Jack Kramer. LC 93-41471. (Illus.). 228p. 1994. 29.98 (1-55859-382-9) Abbeville Pr.

*300 Extraordinary Plants for Home & Garden.** Jack Kramer. 1997. 19.98 (0-89660-081-5, Artabras) Abbeville Pr.

*350th Fighter Group in the Mediterranean Campaign: 2 November 1942 to 2 May 1945.** fac. ed. (Illus.). 80p. 1997. reprint ed. pap. 19.95 (0-7643-0220-5) Schiffer.

Three Hundred Fifty Fabulous Writing Prompts: Thought-Provoking Springboards for Creative... Jacqueline Sweeney. 1996. pap. text ed. 8.95 (0-590-59933-X) Scholastic Inc.

T

An Asterisk (*) at the beginning of an entry indicates that the title is appearing in BIP for the first time.

*357th over Europe: The 357th Fighter Group in World War II. Merle C. Olmsted. 164p. 1997. reprint ed. pap. 24.95 (0-933424-73-6) Specialty Pr.
356 Carrera: Four Cam Production Car. Cole R. Scrogham. (Illus.). 120p. 1996. 29.95 (0-929758-13-7) Beeman Jorgensen.
356 Porsche Technical & Restoration Guide. Ed. by Three-Fifty-Six Registry Editorial Staff. (Illus.). 400p. (Orig.). 1994. pap. 19.95 (0-929758-10-2) Beeman Jorgensen.
350 Tested Strategies to Prevent Crime: A Resource Book for Municipal Agencies & Community Groups. Theresa Kelly & Jean O'Neil. Ed. by Judy Kirby. 400p. (Orig.). 1995. lib. bdg. 39.95 (0-934513-05-8, M50) Natl Crime DC.
300 First Words - Palabras Primeras. Betty Root. 156p. (ENG & SPA.). (J). (ps). 1993. 9.95 (0-8120-6358-9) Barron.
Three Hundred Five Authentic Art Nouveau Jewelry Designs. Maurice Dufrene. 48p. 1985. reprint ed. pap. 6.95 (0-486-24904-2) Dover.
*345 Solved Seismic Design Problems. 3rd ed. Majid Baradar. LC 97-11469. 126p. 1997. pap. 26.95 (1-888577-16-9) Prof Pubns CA.
Three Hundred Forty-Seven Patrons De Decoupage Sur Bois. FC&A Staff. Tr. by Roberta DelPrince from ENG. (Illus.). 160p. (FRE.). 1992. pap. text ed. 11.95 (0-915099-44-6) FC&A Pub.
Three Hundred Golf Solutions. Kelli A. Kostick. LC 95-42645. 157p. 1996. pap. 14.95 (1-56072-275-4) Nova Sci Pubs.
Three Hundred Important Combinations: Indian Astrology. Bangalore V. Raman. (C). 1991. reprint ed. 12.50 (81-208-0843-6, Pub. by Motilal Banarsidass II) S Asia.
300 Medical Data Interpretation Questions for MRCP. 3rd ed. Nick Sawyer et al. 231p. 1995. student ed., pap. text ed. 32.50 (0-7506-1396-3) Buttrwrth-Heinemann.
3000 Mile Garden. Leslie Land. 1997. pap. 13.95 (0-14-025447-1) Viking Penguin.
*300 Three Minute Games. Jackie Silberg. LC 96-37864. (Illus.). 1997. pap. 12.95 (0-87659-182-9) Gryphon Hse.
Three Hundred New Ways to Get a Better Job. Eleanor Baldwin. 384p. 1991. pap. 7.95 (1-55850-016-2) Adams Media.
390th Bomb Group. Turner Publishing Company Staff. LC 94-60144. 144p. 1994. 48.00 (1-56311-137-3) Turner Pub KY.
Three Hundred Ninety-Nine Kansas Characters. Dave Webb. LC 92-73654. (Illus.). 320p. (Orig.). 1992. 27.95 (1-882404-04-1) KS Herit Ctr.
Three Hundred Ninety-Nine Kansas Characters. rev. ed. Dave Webb. LC 94-18325. (Illus.). (Orig.). 1995. pap. 22.95 (1-882404-07-6) KS Herit Ctr.
Three Hundred Ninety-Seven Chairs. Ed. by Arthur C. Danto. 1988. 34.95 (0-8109-1698-3) Abrams.
390 Traditional Stained Glass Designs. Hywel G. Harris. LC 95-35801. (Pictorial Archive Ser.). (Illus.). 80p. Date not set. pap. 6.95 (0-486-28964-8) Dover.
*301 Do-It-Yourself Marketing Ideas from America's Most Innovative Small Companies. Inc. Magazine Editors. Ed. by Sam Decker. 345p. 1997. pap. 14.95 (1-880394-30-8) Inc Pub MA.
*301 Great Customer Service Ideas from America's Most Innovative Small Companies. Ed. by Nancy Artz. 345p. 1997. pap. 14.95 (1-880394-33-2) Inc Pub MA.
301 Great Management Ideas from America's Most Innovative Small Companies. rev. ed. Ed. by Leslie Brokaw. 347p. 1995. pap. 14.95 (1-880394-21-9) Inc Pub MA.
Three Hundred One Great Management Ideas from America's Most Innovative Small Companies. Ed. by Sara P. Noble. 360p. (Orig.). 1991. 24.95 (0-9626146-5-3) Inc Pub MA.
301 Legal Forms & Agreements. Ed. by Sondra Servais. LC 93-72019. 378p. 1993. pap. 24.95 (1-56382-301-2) E-Z Legal.
Three Hundred One Plus Plus Ways to Get Ahead--Business Success from Home. Susan Klopfer & Fred Klopfer. (Illus.). 240p. (Orig.). 1994. pap. 19.95 (0-9638715-0-1) Vanatech Systs.
301 Random Acts of Kindness: A User's Guide to a Giving Life. Mary K. Colf & Len Oszustowicz. 128p. (Orig.). 1994. pap. 7.95 (1-56530-135-8) Summit TX.
*301 Startling Proofs & Prophecies: Proving That God Exists. Peter Lalonde & Paul Lalonde. 1997. pap. 6.99 (0-9680758-1-9) Prophecy Partners.
Three Hundred One Venison Recipes. rev. ed. Deer & Deer Hunting Staff. LC 92-74074. 128p. 1992. 10.95 (0-87341-227-3) Krause Pubns.
Three Hundred Questions DREs Are Asking about People & Programs. Gail T. McKenna. 1990. pap. 8.95 (0-8091-3185-4) Paulist Pr.
Three-Hundred Sermon Outlines from the Old Testament. Ed. by William H. Smitty. LC 81-67996. 120p. 1982. pap. 5.99 (0-8054-2242-0, 4222-42) Broadman.
*307 Feet of Silence. Roland W. Hodgdon. LC 97-93113. (Illus.). 121p. (Orig.). 1996. pap. 10.00 (0-9656631-0-8) R W Hodgdon.
Three Hundred Seventy-Five Meatless Recipes: Century 21 Cookbook. Ed. by Ethel R. Nelson. LC 91-61582. 164p. (Orig.). 1993. spiral bd. 7.95 (0-945383-41-X) Teach Servs.
377 Simple Ways You Can Make a Difference: Practical Suggestions for Busy People. Marie Angnardo. LC 94-75099. 224p. (Orig.). 1994. pap. 6.95 (0-9640406-0-3) Help Hand Pubs.
Three Hundred Seventy-Six Decorative Allover Patterns from Historic Tilework & Textiles. Charles Cahier & Arthur Martin. (Illus.). 256p. 1989. pap. 9.95 (0-486-26146-8) Dover.
Three Hundred Seventy-Six Embedded Processor Programmer's Reference Manual. Intel Corporation Staff. 384p. (Orig.). (C). 1988. pap. 23.00 (1-55512-040-7, 240314-001) Intel Corp.
Three Hundred Sixty Brilliant & Instructive End Games. Aleksei A. Troitzky. LC 68-12938. Orig. Title: Chess Handbook of Three Hundred Sixty Brilliant & Instructive End Games. (Illus.). 1968. reprint ed. pap. 7.95 (0-486-21959-3) Dover.
360 Degree Feedback. Edwards. 1995. 24.95 (0-02-909235-3) S&S Trade.
360 Degree Feedback: The Powerful New Model for Employee Assessment & Performance Improvement. Mark R. Edwards & Ann J. Ewen. 247p. 1996. 27.95 (0-8144-0326-3) AMACOM.
Three Hundred Sixty-Eight Animal Illustrations from Buffon's "Natural History" Georges-Louis Leclerc. LC 93-3708. (Pictorial Archive Ser.). (Illus.). 1993. write for info. (0-486-27703-8) Dover.
*360 Feedback: Strategies, Tatics & Techniques for Developing Leaders. John E. Jones. LC 96-20420. 1996. pap. text ed. 29.95 (0-87425-356-X) HRD Press.
365 Things You Should Know About Investing 1998. Williamson. 1997. 9.95 (0-684-82231-8) S&S Trade.
Never Throw Out a Banana Again: And 364 Other Ways to Save Money at Home Without Knocking Yourself Out. Darcie Sanders & Martha M. Bullen. LC 94-20942. 1995. pap. 9.00 (0-517-88233-7, Crown) Crown Pub Group.
Three Hundred Sixty-Five Affirmations for Hopeful Living. Patricia D. Brown. LC 92-18261. 384p. (Orig.). 1992. pap. 10.00 (0-687-41889-5) Dimen for Liv.
*365 Afterschool Activities. Sheila Ellison. 1997. pap. text ed. 12.95 (1-57071-205-0) Sourcebks.
365 Afterschool Activities: TV-Free Fun Anytime for Kids Ages 7-12. Sheila Ellison & Judith Gray. LC 95-23996. (365 Parenting Ser.). (Illus.). 416p. (Orig.). (J). (gr. 1 up). 1995. otabind, pap. 12.95 (1-57071-080-5) Sourcebks.
*365 All American Favorites. Sarah Reynolds. LC 96-28422. 288p. 1997. 113.70 (0-06-018775-1) HarpC.
*365 All-American Favorites. Sarah Reynolds. LC 96-28422. 288p. 1997. 18.95 (0-06-017294-0) HarpC.
*365 Amazing Days in Sports: A Day-by-Day Look at Sports History. David Fiscner. Ed. by Jill Satro. (Illus.). 208p. (Orig.). (J). (gr. 4-7). 1995. pap. 5.95 (1-886749-33-7, Spts Illus Kids) Little.
*365 Amazing Scientific Facts, Breakthroughs & Discoveries. Sharon B. McGrayne. LC 96-33303. 288p. (Orig.). 1997. pap. text ed. 14.95 (0-471-14575-0) Wiley.
*365 Art & Craft Activities. Donna Shyrer. (Craft & Project Books for Children). (Illus.). 240p. (J). (ps-6). 1996. lib. bdg. 24.95 (1-56674-175-0, HTS Bks) Forest Hse.
*365 Asian Recipes. John Boswell. 288p. Date not set. 17.95 (0-06-017292-4) HarpC.
365 Bible Promises for Busy Dads. Ken R. Canfield. (Living Bks.). 1996. mass mkt., pap. 5.99 (0-8423-2502-6) Tyndale.
365 Bible Promises for Busy People. Alice Chapin. LC 92-18468. 205p. 1992. mass mkt. 4.99 (0-8423-7048-X) Tyndale.
*365 Bible Stories. Random House Value Publishing Staff. 1998. 5.99 (0-517-18820-1) Random Hse Value.
Three Hundred Sixty-Five Children's Prayers. Compiled by Carol Watson. (Illus.). 160p. (J). 1989. text ed. 12.95 (0-7459-1454-3) Lion USA.
Three Hundred Sixty-Five Creative Party Ideas. Sheila Ellison & Nancy Maley. (Illus.). 400p. 1991. spiral bd. 14.95 (0-9620467-7-9) Forward March.
*365 Daily Meditations for Women: Meditations to Enrich a Woman's Daily Faith Journey. Mary R. Howes. 1997. pap. text ed. 12.00 (0-687-01733-5) Abingdon.
Three Hundred Sixty-Five Day Devotional Commentary. Larry Richards. 1216p. 1990. text ed. 37.99 (0-89693-503-5, 6-1503, Victor Bks) Chariot Victor.
Three Hundred Sixty-Five Days. Ronald J. Glasser. LC 77-156599. 292p. 1971. pap. 12.95 (0-8076-0995-1) Braziller.
365 Days a Year with D. L. Moody. D. L. Moody. 240p. (gr. 10). 1996. pap. 12.99 (0-8007-5590-1) Revell.
Three Hundred Sixty-Five Days from Genesis Through Revelation. J. Ellsworth Kalas. LC 93-3742. 352p. (Orig.). 1993. pap. 11.95 (0-687-46626-1) Abingdon.
365 Days of Baby Love: Playing, Growing & Exploring with Babies from Birth to Age 2. Sheila Ellison & Susan Ferdinandi. LC 96-33707. (365 Parenting Ser.). (Illus.). 408p. (Orig.). 1996. otabind, pap. 12.95 (1-57071-110-0) Sourcebks.
365 Days of Christmas: Keeping the Wonder of It All Ever Green. William J. Byron. LC 96-16618. 88p. 1996. 9.95 (0-8091-0481-4) Paulist Pr.
365 Days of Creative Play: For Children 2 Yrs. & Up. Sheila Ellison & Judith Gray. LC 95-3261. (365 Parenting Ser.). (Illus.). 384p. (J). (ps up). 1995. otabind, pap. 12.95 (1-57071-029-5) Sourcebks.
Three Hundred Sixty-Five Days of Creative Play for Children 2-6 Years. Sheila Ellison & Judith Gray. (Illus.). 400p. (Orig.). spiral bd. 14.95 (0-9620467-0-1) Forward March.
Three Hundred Sixty-Five Days of Gardening. C. Allison. 1995. 17.95 (0-06-017032-8, HarpT) HarpC.
365 Days of Gifts for Your Love: A Daily Guide to Creative Giving. Tomima Edmark. 1996. 9.95 (1-56530-211-7) Summit TX.
*365 Days of Health. Patricia Telesco. (Through-the-Year Ser.: Bk. III). 370p. (Orig.). 1997. pap. 5.95 (1-881542-33-5) Blue Star Prodns.
365 Days of Life in the Stress Lane. Sherrie Weaver. 366p. (Orig.). 1994. spiral bd., pap. 8.95 (1-56245-168-5) Great Quotations.
*365 Days of Luck. Patricia Telesco. (Through-the-Year Ser.: Bk. II). 370p. (Orig.). 1997. pap. 5.95 (1-881542-32-7) Blue Star Prodns.
*365 Days of Prosperity. Patricia Telesco. (Through-the-Year Ser.: Bk. I). 370p. (Orig.). 1997. pap. 5.95 (1-881542-31-9) Blue Star Prodns.
*On This Day. Robert J. Morgan. LC 97-8956. 1997. 14.99 (0-7852-1162-4) Nelson.
365 Devotions 1996-97. Ed. by Eileen Wilmoth. 384p. 1996. pap. text ed. 5.99 (0-7847-0482-1, 03097) Standard Pub.
365 Devotions 1996-97. large type ed. Ed. by Eileen Wilmoth. 384p. 1996. 10.99 (0-7847-0483-X, 04097) Standard Pub.
*365 Devotions 1997-98. Ed. & Compiled by Eileen Wilmoth. 384p. 1997. pap. 5.99 (0-7847-0622-0, 11-03098) Standard Pub.
*365 Devotions 1997-98. large type ed. Ed. & Compiled by Eileen Wilmoth. 384p. 1997. pap. 10.99 (0-7847-0623-9, 11-04098) Standard Pub.
*365 Easy One-Dish Meals. Natalie H. Haughton. 1997. mass mkt. 5.99 (0-06-109582-6, Harp PBks) HarpC.
365 Excuses for Being Late to Work. Andy Sharpe. 1996. pap. text ed. 5.95 (1-55850-635-7) Adams Media.
Three Hundred Sixty-Five Family Activities: Reaching Love & Respect Together. Sheila Ellison & Barbara A. Barnett. (Illus.). 400p. 1993. spiral bd. 16.98 (0-9620467-9-5) Forward March.
365 Foods Kids Love to Eat: Fun, Nutritious & Kid-Tested! Sheila Ellison & Judith Gray. LC 95-3310. (365 Parenting Ser.). (Illus.). 416p. 1995. otabind, pap. 12.95 (1-57071-030-9) Sourcebks.
Three Hundred Sixty-Five Fun Facts for Catholic Kids. Bernadette M. Snyder. LC 89-84983. 144p. (Orig.). (J). (gr. 4-12). 1989. pap. 6.95 (0-89243-309-4) Liguori Pubns.
365 Funniest Golf Jokes. Fred Gefen. (Illus.). 160p. 1995. pap. 7.95 (0-8065-1688-7, Citadel Pr) Carol Pub Group.
Three Hundred Sixty Five Good Health Hints. David J. Pine. Ed. by Jill Kramer. LC 94-16934. 192p. (Orig.). 1994. pap. 5.95 (1-56170-099-1, 162) Hay House.
*365 Good Reasons to Be a Vegetarian. Victor Parachin. 1997. pap. 5.95 (0-89529-813-9) Avery Group Inc.
*365 Great Cakes & Pies. Date not set. mass mkt. write for info. (0-06-101230-0, Harp PBks) HarpC.
*365 Great Chocolate Desserts. Natalie H. Haughton. 288p. mass mkt. 5.99 (0-06-101225-4, Harp PBks) HarpC.
Three Hundred Sixty-Five Health Hints: Quick, Practical Ways to Protect Your Health, Maintain Your Well-Being, & Feel Better Than Ever - Everyday. American Institute for Preventive Medicine Staff & Don R. Powell. 400p. 1991. pap. 8.95 (0-671-73167-X, Fireside) S&S Trade.
366 Healthful Ways to Cook Leafy Greens. Linda R. Leahy. LC 96-47951. 360p. 1997. pap. 16.95 (0-452-27511-3, Plume) NAL-Dutton.
*365 Healthful Rice Recipes. Andrea Chesman. LC 97-24289. 1998. pap. 15.95 (0-452-27654-3, Plume) NAL-Dutton.
*365 Jewish Recipes. John Boswell. 288p. 1997. 17.95 (0-06-017295-9) HarpC.
Three Hundred Sixty-Five Kids' Confessions: Making God's Word Personal in Little Lives. Virginia G. Kite. (Illus.). 224p. (J). (gr. k-7). 1990. 12.95 (0-942847-02-4) Nugget Truth Minist.
365 Life Lessons from Bible People: A Life Application Devotional. Ed. by Michael Kendrick & Daryl J. Lucas. LC 95-45518. (Illus.). 1996. pap. 10.99 (0-8423-3799-7) Tyndale.
*365 Main-Dish Salads. Carol Foster. LC 96-44782. 1997. write for info. (0-06-017293-2) HarpC.
*365 Mary: A Daily Guide to Mary's Wisdom & Comfort. Woodeene Koenig-Bricker. 1997. pap. 14.00 (0-06-064744-2) Harper SF.
365 Meditations for Teachers. Anne M. Drew. 336p. 1996. pap. 12.00 (0-687-01025-X) Dimen for Liv.
365 Meditations for Mothers of Teens. Garlinda M. Burton. LC 96-19805. 336p. 1996. pap. 12.00 (0-687-10921-3) Dimen for Liv.
Three Hundred Sixty-Five Meditations for Grandmothers. Gloria Gaither et al. LC 94-11026. 336p. (Orig.). 1994. pap. 12.00 (0-687-41893-3) Dimen for Liv.
Three Hundred Sixty-Five Meditations for Mothers of Young Children. LC 92-44072. 352p. (Orig.). 1993. pap. 12.00 (0-687-41890-9) Dimen for Liv.
Three Hundred Sixty-Five Meditations for Mothers of Young Children. Patricia Brown. 352p. (Orig.). 1993. pap. 12.00 (0-687-01246-5) Dimen for Liv.
*365 Meditations on Pregnancy. Frances Stone. 1998. pap. 9.95 (0-14-025529-X) Viking Penguin.
*365 Moments to Cherish. Robert Strand. 400p. 1997. 14.95 (0-89221-360-4) New Leaf.
Three Hundred Sixty-Five More Meditations for Women. LC 91-33363. 352p. (Orig.). 1992. pap. 12.00 (0-687-41888-7) Dimen for Liv.
365 More Ways to Cook Chicken. Melanie Barnard. LC 96-14265. 288p. 1996. 12.95 (0-06-017139-1) HarpC.
Three Hundred Sixty-Five One Minute Golf Lessons. Robin McMillan. LC 94-4834. 400p. 1994. 19.95 (0-06-017087-5, HarpT) HarpC.
Three Hundred Sixty-Five Outdoor Activities You Can Do with Your Child. Steve Bennett & Ruth Bennett. 480p. 1993. pap. 6.95 (1-55850-260-2) Adams Media.
Three Hundred Sixty-Five Questions & Answers. 1988. 7.99 (0-517-64979-9) Random Hse Value.
Three Hundred Sixty-Five Quick & Easy Microwave Recipes. Thelma Pressman. 192p. 1995. mass mkt. 5.99 (0-06-109462-5, Harp PBks) HarpC.
365 Reasons to Eat Chocolate. Sherrie Weaver. 366p. 1995. spiral bd., pap. 6.50 (1-56245-180-4) Great Quotations.
Three Hundred Sixty-Five Reasons Workbook: How to Find a Reason to Be Happy Every Day. Reba Karp. 376p. 1991. pap. 10.95 (1-878901-06-0) Hampton Roads Pub Co.
*365 Reflections on Sisters. Date not set. pap. 6.95 (1-55850-810-4) Adams Media.
*365 Reflections on Grandmothers. Date not set. pap. 6.95 (1-55850-811-2) Adams Media.
*365 Reflections on Daughters. Date not set. pap. 6.95 (1-55850-812-0) Adams Media.
*365 Reflections on Love & Friendship. Date not set. pap. 6.95 (1-55850-813-9) Adams Media.
*365 Romantic Gifts for Your Love: A Daily Guide to Creative Giving. Tomima Edmark. 1998. write for info. (1-56530-238-9) Summit TX.
365 Saints: Your Daily Guide to the Wisdom & Wonder of Their Lives. Woodeene Koenig-Bricker. LC 95-17827. 400p. 1995. pap. 13.00 (0-06-067594-2) Harper SF.
*365 Saints: Your Daily Guide to the Wisdom & Wonder of Their Lives. Woodeene Koenig-Bricker. pap. write for info. (0-06-064781-7) HarpC.
*365 Science Projects & Activities. Illus. by Ellen J. Sasaki et al. (Craft & Project Books for Children). 240p. (J). (ps-6). 1996. lib. bdg. 24.95 (1-56674-176-9, HTS Bks) Forest Hse.
*365 Simple Science Experiments with Everyday Materials. Frances W. Zweifel et al. (Illus.). 352p. (J). (gr. 2 up). 1997. reprint ed. 12.98 (1-884822-67-3) Blck Dog & Leventhal.
Three Hundred Sixty-Five Stories for Bedtime. (Illus.). (J). (ps-1). 1985. 5.98 (0-517-46715-1) Random Hse Value.
Three Hundred Sixty-Five Tao: Daily Meditations. Deng Ming-Dao. LC 91-55332. (Illus.). 384p. 1992. pap. 15.00 (0-06-250223-9) Harper SF.
365 Great Things about Atlanta. Kim Bixler & Jon Gordon. (Illus.). 96p. (Orig.). 1996. pap. 5.95 (0-9652426-0-9) Clue Guides.
365 Things Every Couple Should Know. Doug Fields. 1993. pap. 5.99 (1-56507-072-0) Harvest Hse.
365 Things I Learned in College. Robert Sherfield & Dan Moody. 1995. pap. 6.95 (0-205-19574-1) Allyn.
*365 Things Your Kids Can Do Instead of Watching TV. large type ed. Susan M. Fischer. 184p. (Orig.). (J). 1996. 9.95 (0-9656416-0-0) Miss Muffet Pr.
365 TV-Free Activities You Can Do with Your Child. 2nd ed. Steve Bennett & Ruth Bennett. (Illus.). 480p. 1996. pap. 7.95 (1-55850-585-7) Adams Media.
Three Hundred Sixty-Five Wacky, Wonderful Ways to Get Your Children to Do What You Want. Elizabeth Crary. (Tools for Everyday Parenting Ser.). (Illus.). 104p. (Orig.). 1995. pap. 9.95 (0-943990-79-3); lib. bdg. 18.95 (0-943990-80-7) Parenting Pr.
365 Ways: Retirees' Resource Guide for Productive Lifestyles. American Association for International Aging Staff & Hansan Group Staff. Ed. by Helen K. Kerschner & John E. Hansan. LC 96-28187. 215p. 1996. text ed. 35.00 (0-313-30196-4, Greenwood Pr) Greenwood.
Three Hundred Sixty-Five Ways to Bless Your Wife. Glenn Egli & Jennifer Carrell. LC 94-70065. 174p. 1994. pap. 9.95 (0-88270-665-9) Bridge-Logos.
Three Hundred Sixty Five Ways to Build Your Child's Self-Esteem. Cheri Fuller. LC 94-67031. 160p. (Orig.). 1994. pap. 6.00 (0-89109-855-0) Pinon Press.
*365 Ways to Cook Chicken. Cheryl Sedaker. 224p. mass mkt. write for info. (0-06-109413-7, Harp PBks) HarpC.
365 Ways to Cook Chicken: Simply the Best Chicken Recipes You'll Find Anywhere. Cheryl Sedeker. LC 85-45231. (365 Ways Ser.). 240p. 1986. 17.95 (0-06-015539-6, HarpT) HarpC.
365 Ways to Cook Eggs. Elaine Corn. 288p. 1996. pap. 18.95 (0-06-017138-3) HarpC.
365 Ways to Cook Hamburger & Other Ground Meats. Rick Rodgers. LC 91-50445. (365 Ways Ser.). 256p. 1992. 17.95 (0-06-016535-9, HarpT) HarpC.
Three Hundred Sixty-Five Ways to Cook Hamburger: And Other Meats. Rick Rodgers. 288p. 1994. mass mkt. 5.99 (0-06-109331-9) HarpC.
365 Ways to Cook Pasta: For Every Season, For Every Reason, A Pasta Lover's Paradise. Marie Simmons. LC 87-46171. (365 Ways Ser.). (Illus.). 224p. 1988. 17.95 (0-06-015865-4, HarpT) HarpC.
365 Ways to Date Your Love: A Daily Guide to Creative Romance. Tomima Edmark. 1995. 9.95 (1-56530-174-9) Summit TX.
*365 Ways to Date Your Love: A Daily Guide to Creative Romance. Tomima Edmark. 1997. write for info. (1-56530-200-1) Summit TX.
Three Hundred Sixty Five Ways to Develop Your Child's Values. Cheri Fuller. LC 94-67030. 160p. (Orig.). 1994. pap. 6.00 (0-89109-856-9) Pinon Press.
365 Ways to Fix Up Your Place. M. Buller & D. Sanders. 1998. pap. write for info. (0-517-88722-3) Random.
*365 Ways to Help Your Children Grow. Sheila Ellison & Barbara A. Barnett. 416p. 1996. pap. text ed. 12.95 (1-57071-122-4) Sourcebks.
Three Hundred Sixty Five Ways to Help Your Child Learn & Achieve. Cheri Fuller. LC 94-67029. 160p. (Orig.). 1994. pap. 6.00 (0-89109-854-2) Pinon Press.
365 Ways to Improve Your Sex Life: From the Files of the Playboy Advisor. James R. Petersen. 320p. 1996. pap. 13.95 (0-452-27576-8, Plume) NAL-Dutton.
365 Ways to Kiss Your Love: A Daily Guide to Creative Kissing. Tomima Edmark. 128p. 1993. 9.95 (1-56530-028-9) Summit TX.
365 Ways to Love Your Lover. D. S. Love. LC 95-21438. 1995. 6.99 (0-517-14872-2, Wings Books) Random.
365 Ways to Love Your Child. Alex J. Packer. LC 94-48755. 144p. 1995. pap. 8.95 (0-440-50590-9) Dell.

An Asterisk (*) at the beginning of an entry indicates that the title is appearing in BIP for the first time.

Three Hundred Sixty-Five Ways to Love Your Child. Caryl W. Krueger. LC 93-44083. 144p. (Orig.). 1994. pap. 3.89 (*0-687-41891-7*) Abingdon.

365 Ways to Make Love. Lori Salkin & Rob Spery. Ed. by Amy Einhorn. 128p. 1996. 10.00 (*0-671-53632-X*, PB Hardcover) PB.

Three Hundred Sixty-Five Ways to Manage the Business Called Private Practice. James Davis. 125p. 1990. 24.95 (*1-878487-10-8*) Practice Mgmt Info.

365 Ways to Prepare for Christmas. David E. Monn. LC 92-56214. (365 Ways Ser.). 288p. 1993. 16.95 (*0-06-017048-4*, HarpT) HarpC.

365 Ways to Prepare for Christmas. David E. Monn. 288p. 1996. mass mkt. 5.99 (*0-06-109330-0*, Harp PBks) HarpC.

365 Ways to Simplify Your Work Life. Odette Pollar. LC 96-22812. 224p. (Orig.). 1996. pap. 8.95 (*0-7931-2281-3*, 56144801) Dearborn Finan.

365 Women Who Made a Difference. Adams Publishing Staff. 1996. pap. text ed. 6.95 (*1-55850-641-1*) Adams Media.

365 Women's Reflections on Men. Adams Publishing Staff. 1996. pap. text ed. 6.95 (*1-55850-642-X*) Adams Media.

***365 Words of Well-Being for Women.** Rachel Snyder. LC 96-36776. 1997. pap. write for info. (*0-8092-3079-8*) Contemp Bks.

Three Hundred Sixty Most Guarded Secrets of Executive Success. National Institute of Business Management Staff. 381p. 1990. write for info. (*1-880024-00-4*) Natl Inst Busn.

Three Hundred Sixty-Seventh Fighter Group in World War Two. Peter R. Moody. (Illus.). 75p. (Orig.). 1979. pap. 24.95 (*0-89126-080-3*) MA-AH Pub.

Three Hundred Sixty Six & More Things to Know. 1991. 7.99 (*0-517-06023-X*) Random Hse Value.

***366 Days of Wisdom & Inspiration: With America's Success Coach.** Tommy Newberry. LC 96-95187. 192p. 1997. 12.00 (*1-886669-08-2*) T Newberry.

***366 Emergency Ideas.** Ferguson & Durkin. Date not set. pap. text ed. write for info. (*0-05-004603-9*) Addison-Wesley.

***366 Delicious Ways to Cook Pasta with Vegetables.** Dolores Riccio. LC 97-17697. 1997. pap. 16.95 (*0-452-27727-2*, Plume) NAL-Dutton.

366 Healthful Ways to Cook Tofu & Other Meat Alternatives. Robin Robertson. LC 95-41517. 396p. 1996. pap. 15.95 (*0-452-27597-0*, Plume) NAL-Dutton.

Three Hundred Sixty-Six Low-Fat Brand Name Recipes in Minutes. M. J. Smith. 385p. 1994. pap. 12.95 (*1-56561-050-4*) Chronimed.

366 Healthful Recipes for Soy Milk. Robin Robertson. 1997. pap. 16.95 (*0-452-27623-3*, Plume) NAL-Dutton.

***366 Thoughts for Home.** Lighten Up Enterprises Staff. (Add-A-Thought Series Feature). 1997. pap. text ed. 6.99 (*1-879127-85-7*) Lighten Up Enter.

***366 Thoughts for Teachers.** Lighten Up Enterprises Staff. (Ass-A-Thought Series Feature). 1997. pap. text ed. 6.99 (*1-879127-84-9*) Lighten Up Enter.

***366 Thoughts for the Office.** Lighten up Enterprises Staff. (Add-A-Thought Series Feature). Date not set. pap. text ed. 6.99 (*1-879127-82-2*) Lighten Up Enter.

***366 Thoughts of Friendship.** Lighten Up Enterprises Staff. (Add-A-Thought Series Feature). 1997. pap. text ed. 6.99 (*1-879127-83-0*) Lighten Up Enter.

Three Hundred Thirty-Five Crucial Questions on Christian Unity. Thomas B. Warren. 48p. 1984. pap. 1.50 (*0-934916-06-3*) Natl Christian Pr.

***330 Reasons to Love the Corps: Silly, Serious & Revealing Reasons to Love the U. S. Marine Corps.** Chris Lawson. LC 96-78537. 160p. (Orig.). 1996. pap. 7.95 (*9964-79-241-7*) Army Times Pubng.

Three Hundred Thirty-Three: A Bibliography of the Science Fantasy Novel. Joseph H. Crawford et al. LC 74-15959. (Science Fiction Ser.). 82p. 1975. reprint ed. 17.95 (*0-405-06324-5*) Ayer.

Three Hundred Thirty-Three More Science Tricks & Experiments. Robert J. Brown. 1984. pap. text ed. 10.95 (*0-07-156204-4*) McGraw.

Three Hundred Thirty-Three More Science Tricks & Experiments. Robert J. Brown. (Illus.). 208p. 1984. pap. 10.95 (*0-8306-1835-X*, 1835) McGraw-Hill Prof.

Three Hundred Thirty-Three Science Tricks & Experiments. Robert J. Brown. (Orig.). 1984. pap. text ed. 11.95 (*0-07-156080-7*) McGraw.

Three Hundred Thirty-Three Science Tricks & Experiments. Robert J. Brown. (Illus.). 208p. (Orig.). 1984. 15.95 (*0-8306-0825-7*); pap. 9.95 (*0-8306-1825-2*, 1825) McGraw-Hill Prof.

Three Hundred Three CD-ROMs to use in Your Library: Descriptions, Evaluations, & Practical Advice. Patrick R. Dewey. (One Hundred One Micro Ser.). 238p. (Orig.). 1995. pap. 30.00 (*0-8389-0666-4*, 0666-4-2045) ALA.

303 Great Ideas for Families: Most Cost Less Than 99 Cents. Phyllis P. Good & Merle Good. LC 96-48861. 96p. (Orig.). 1996. pap. 6.95 (*1-56148-211-0*) Good Bks PA.

303 Off-the-Wall Ways to Get a Job. Brandon Toropov. 312p. (Orig.). 1995. pap. 12.99 (*1-56414-199-3*) Career Pr Inc.

303 Tips for Detailing Model Railroad Scenery & Structures. Dave Frary. 1995. per. 16.95 (*0-89024-243-7*, 12153) Kalmbach.

Three Hundred Twenty Desert Watering Places in Southeastern California & Southwestern Nevada. W. C. Mendenhall. 104p. 1982. 14.95 (*0-913814-62-8*) Nevada Pubns.

325 Teaching Hints for Professional Cosmetologists Instructors. Jacob J. Yahm. (Cosmetology Ser.). 1969. pap. 21.50 (*0-87350-353-8*) Van Nos Reinhold.

Three Hundred Twenty-One Quick Tips to Create Better Results. A. D. Jeary. 20p. 1993. pap. write for info. (*1-883454-01-8*) TPG Inc.

Three Hundred Ways to Make Your Business Even More Successful. Allan Smith. 24p. 1988. 4.00 (*0-931113-13-X*) Success Publ.

Three Hundred Years: Historical Highlights of Nevada & Vernon County, Missouri. Patrick Brophy. (Illus.). 350p. (Orig.). 1993. pap. 12.95 (*0-9614944-2-5*) DGL InfoWrite.

Three Hundred Years at the Keyboard: A Piano Sourcebook from Bach to the Moderns. Patricia Fallows-Hammond. LC 83-23056. 312p. 1984. pap. 19.95 (*0-89496-043-1*) Ross Bks.

Three Hundred Years at the Point: A History of Sommers Point, New Jersey. William E. Kelly. 1994. 15.00 (*1-882127-34-X*) Magicimage Filmbooks.

300 Years in Eastern Virginia: Descendants of Arthur Jones (1630-1692) Anthony M. Lowe. LC 95-1161. 1995. write for info. (*0-89865-934-5*) Donning Co.

Three Hundred Years of American Art in the Chrysler Museum. Dennis R. Anderson. LC 75-42583. (Illus.). 270p. 1976. pap. 10.00 (*0-940744-11-2*) Chrysler Museum.

Three Hundred Years of Carolina Cooking. LC 76-124563. (Illus.). 318p. 1970. 9.95 (*0-9608172-0-4*) Greenville SC Jr League.

Three Hundred Years of Education in South Africa. Edward G. Pells. LC 71-90156. 152p. 1970. reprint ed. text ed. 52.50 (*0-8371-2217-1*, PEEA, Greenwood Pr) Greenwood.

Three Hundred Years of French Architecture, 1494-1794. Reginald T. Blomfield. LC 70-124233. (Select Bibliographies Reprint Ser.). 1977. 18.95 (*0-8369-5414-9*) Ayer.

Three Hundred Years of Gravitation. Ed. by Stephen W. Hawking & Werner Israel. (Illus.). 704p. 1989. pap. text ed. 57.95 (*0-521-37976-8*) Cambridge U Pr.

Three Hundred Years of Housekeeping Collectibles. Linda C. Franklin. (Illus.). 416p. 1992. 22.95 (*0-89689-093-7*) Bks Americana.

300 Years of Joseph Olin & His Descendants, Vol. 1. Warren G. Olin. Ed. by A. Joyce Olin Powell. LC 96-68406. (Illus.). 700p. 1996. write for info. (*0-9651495-0-1*) Type-O-Graphics.

***300 Years of Kitchen Collectibles: Identification & Value Guide.** 4th ed. Linda C. Franklin. (Illus.). 640p. 1997. pap. 24.95 (*0-89689-112-7*, KIT04) Krause Pubns.

Three Hundred Years of Kitchen Collectibles. 3rd ed. Linda C. Franklin. 640p. (Orig.). 1991. 22.95 (*0-89689-077-5*) Bks Americana.

Three Hundred Years of Lloyd's: A Lloyd's List Special Supplement. Antony Brown. 1988. pap. 43.00 (*1-85044-188-X*) LLP.

Three Hundred Years of Psychiatry, 1535-1860. Richard Hunter & Ida Macalpine. LC 82-73004. xxvi, 1107p. 1982. reprint ed. 125.00 (*0-910177-00-7*) Carlisle Pub.

***Three Hundred Years of Quincy, 1625-1925: Historical Retrospective of Mt. Wollaston, Braintree & Quincy, with a Chronicle of the Tercentenary Celebration.** David M. Wilson & Timothy J. Collins. (Illus.). 455p. 1997. reprint ed. lib. bdg. 47.00 (*0-8328-5961-3*) Higginson Bk Co.

Three Hundred Years of the American Newspaper. John B. Hench et al. 108p. 1991. pap. 13.95 (*0-944026-29-X*, 37006) Am Antiquarian.

Three Hungarian Folk Songs: A Capella. Seiber & Lloyd. 12p. 1986. pap. 1.25 (*0-7935-5496-9*, 50307930) H Leonard.

Three-Hydroxy-Three-Methylglutaryl Coenzyms a Reductase. John R. Sabine. 288p. 1984. 160.00 (*0-8493-6551-1*, QP603, CRC Reprint) Franklin.

Three Imperial Mathematicians. Edward Rosen. 367p. 1986. 25.00 (*0-89835-242-8*) Abaris Bks.

Three Impostors. rev. ed. Arthur Machen. Ed. by David Trotter. (Everyman Paperback Classics Ser.). 320p. (C). 1995. pap. 6.95 (*0-460-87718-6*, Everyman's Classic Lib) C E Tuttle.

Three Impresarios: Tom Maguire, Yankee Robinson, M. B. Leavitt. Lawrence Estavan. Ed. by Paul D. Seldis. (Clipper Studies in the Theatre). (Illus.). pap. write for info. (*0-89370-465-2*); lib. bdg. write for info. (*0-89370-365-6*) Borgo Pr.

Three in a Bed. Deborah Jackson. 1992. pap. 9.00 (*0-380-76579-9*) Avon.

Three in a Bed: Fiction, Morals, & Politics. Nadine Gordimer. (Chapbooks in Literature Ser.). 1991. pap. 5.00 (*1-878603-03-5*) Bennington Coll.

***Three in Love.** Foster. pap. 12.00 (*0-06-251296-X*) HarpC.

***Three in Love: Menages a Trois from Ancient to Modern Times.** Barbara Foster. 1997. 25.00 (*0-06-251295-1*) Harper SF.

***Three in One: A Picture of God.** Joanne Marxhausen. (Illus.). 48p. (J). (gr. k-4). 1978. 4.99 (*0-570-07790-7*, 56-1314) Concordia.

***3-in-1 Book of Less Fat & Sugar & Breads.** (Illus.). 60p. pap. 8.75 (*0-614-28387-6*) G Pitzers.

***Three in the Back, Two in the Head.** Jason Sherman. LC 95-218622. 1997. pap. text ed. 11.95 (*0-88754-534-3*, Pub. by Playwrights CN Pr CN) Theatre Comm.

***Three in Time: White Wolf Rediscovery Trio.** Ed. by Jack Dann et al. 1997. reprint ed. pap. 14.99 (*1-56504-985-3*, 10041) White Wolf.

Three-Inch Golden Lotus: A Novel on Foot Binding. Feng Jicai. Tr. by David Wakefield from CHI. LC 93-44402. (Fiction from Modern China Ser.). 208p. (C). 1994. pap. 12.95 (*0-8248-1606-4*) UH Pr.

Three Incredible Weeks with Meher Baba. Malcolm Schloss & Charles Purdom. Ed. by Filis Frederick. LC 80-109542. (Illus.). 165p. 1979. pap. 7.95 (*0-913078-36-0*) Sheriar Pr.

Three Indespensable Words. Sergio Franco. 20p. 1987. pap. 2.00 (*0-8341-1211-6*) Beacon Hill.

Three Indian Campaigns. Wesley Merritt. 24p. reprint ed. pap. 3.95 (*0-8466-4037-6*, 137) Shorey.

Three Indian Poets: Nissim Ezekiel, A. K. Ramanujan, & Dom Moraes. Bruce King. (Oxford India Paperbacks Ser.). 160p. 1991. pap. 10.95 (*0-19-562598-6*) OUP.

Three Ingredient Cookbook. Pat Pexton. (Illus.). 76p. 1982. spiral bd. 8.00 (*0-9624039-1-1*) DeBry-Pexton.

Three Ingredient Cookbook, Vol. I. Ruthie Wornall. (Illus.). 20p. 1988. reprint ed. spiral bd. 6.95 (*0-9624467-0-X*) Wornall Pub.

Three Ingredient Cookbook, Vol. II. Ruthie Wornall. (Illus.). 63p. 1990. spiral bd. 6.95 (*0-9624467-1-8*) Wornall Pub.

Three Ingredient Cookbook, Vol. III. Ruthie Wornall. (Illus.). 69p. 1991. spiral bd. 6.95 (*0-9624467-2-6*) Wornall Pub.

Three-Ingredient Cookbook: Fast, Flavorful Flood in a Jiffy. Andrew Schloss. 224p. 1996. 17.00 (*0-06-017375-0*) HarpC.

***Three Ingredient Low Fat Cookbook.** Ruthie Wornall. 1997. 14.95 (*0-614-30632-9*) Wornall Pub.

Three Ingredient Main Dish Cookbook, Vol. VI. Ruthie Wornall. (Illus.). 60p. 1993. spiral bd. 6.95 (*0-9624467-5-0*) Wornall Pub.

Three Ingredient Party Cookbook, Vol. V. Ruthie Wornall. (Illus.). 60p. 1992. spiral bd. 5.95 (*0-9624467-4-2*) Wornall Pub.

Three Inner Voices: Uncovering the Spiritual Roots of Addiction & Recovery. Richard G. Hartnett. LC 94-92282. (Illus.). 128p. (Orig.). 1994. pap. 10.95 (*1-885909-20-9*) Serenity NY.

Three Installations by Xu Bing. Britta Erickson. (Illus.). (Orig.). 1992. pap. 10.00 (*0-932900-31-3*) Elvejhem Mus.

Three Instances of Injustice. K. R. Eissler. LC 93-21078. 265p. 1993. 39.50 (*0-8236-6530-5*) Intl Univs Pr.

Three Introductory Lectures on the Science of Thought. F. Max Muller. (C). 1988. reprint ed. 11.50 (*81-206-0423-7*, Pub. by Asian Educ Servs II) S Asia.

Three Irish Bardic Tales: Being Metrical Versions of the Three Tales Known As the Three Sorrows of Story-Telling. John Todhunter. LC 75-28845. reprint ed. 32.50 (*0-404-13829-2*) AMS Pr.

Three Irish Glossaries. Ed. by Whitley Stokes. LC 78-72647. (Celtic Language & Literature Ser.: Goidelic & Brythonic). reprint ed. 37.50 (*0-404-17597-X*) AMS Pr.

Three Irish Plays. Incl. Land of Heart's Desire. William Butler Yeats. 1962. (*0-318-51182-7*); Twisting of the Rope. Douglas Hyde. 1962. (*0-318-51183-5*); Riders to the Sea. John Millington Synge. 1962. (*0-318-51184-3*); 1962. pap. 5.95 (*0-8283-1457-8*, Intl Pocket Lib) Branden Pub Co.

Three Iron Mining Towns: A Study in Cultural Change. Paul H. Landis. LC 72-112555. (Rise of Urban America Ser.). 1974. reprint ed. 16.95 (*0-405-02462-2*) Ayer.

Three Italian Chronicles. Stendhal. Tr. by C. K. Scott-Moncrieff from FRE. LC 90-35325. (New Directions Classics Ser.). 208p. 1991. pap. 9.95 (*0-8112-1150-9*, NDP704) New Directions.

Three Ivans Choreography Nijinska. Ray G. Cook. (Illus.). 30p. (Orig.). (C). 1988. ring bd. 20.00 (*0-9602002-8-2*) Ray Cook.

Three Jacobean Tragedies. Incl. White Devil. John Webster. (*0-318-55104-7*); Revenger's Tragedy. Cyril Tourneur. (*0-318-55105-5*); Changeling. Thomas Middleton. 1965. (*0-318-55106-3*); (English Library). 368p. 1965. pap. 10.95 (*0-14-043006-7*, Penguin Classics) Viking Penguin.

Three Japanese Plays from the Traditional Theatre. Ed. by Earle Ernst. 200p. 1959. 19.95 (*0-910278-86-5*) Boulevard.

Three Jewels: A Study & Translation of Minamoto Tamenori's Sanboe. Edward Kamens. LC 87-30940. (Michigan Monographs in Japanese Studies: No. 2). xii, 446p. 1988. 29.95 (*0-939512-34-3*) U MI Japan.

Three Jewels: An Introduction to Buddhism. 2nd ed. Sangharakshita. 293p. 1996. reprint ed. pap. 18.00 (*0-904766-49-7*) Windhorse Pubns.

***Three Jewish Physicians of the Renaissance: The Marriage of Science & Ethics.** Aaron Feingold. LC 96-85973. (Illus.). 63p. 1996. 18.00 (*0-9653735-0-9*) Amer Frnds.

Three Jolly Stories Include - Three Jollys, Jollys Visit L. A., Jolly Gets Mugged: An ESL Adult-Child Reader. Valerie H. Weisberg. (Jolly Ser.). (Illus.). 76p. (Orig.). (J). (gr. 4 up). 1985. pap. text ed. 6.95 (*0-9610912-4-X*) V H Pub.

Three Jovial Huntsmen. Susan Jeffers. LC 88-32708. (Illus.). 32p. (J). (ps-2). 1989. reprint ed. pap. 3.95 (*0-689-71309-6*, Aladdin Paperbacks) S&S Childrens.

3K: The Cosmic Microwave Background Radiation. R. B. Partridge. (Astrophysics Ser.: Vol. 25). (Illus.). 416p. (C). 1995. text ed. 95.00 (*0-521-35254-1*) Cambridge U Pr.

Three Kentucky Presidents: Lincoln, Taylor, Davis. Holman Hamilton. LC 77-92922. (Kentucky Bicentennial Bookshelf Ser.). (Illus.). 96p. 1978. 12.95 (*0-8131-0246-4*) U Pr of Ky.

Three Kentucky Tragedies. Richard Taylor. LC 91-29438. 64p. 1991. pap. text ed. 4.50 (*0-8131-0907-8*) U Pr of Ky.

Three Keys to Positive Confession. Frederick K. Price. 71p. (Orig.). 1994. pap. 5.99 (*1-883798-05-1*) Faith One.

***Three Kids & a Cowboy.** Natalie Patrick. (Romance Ser.: No. 1235). 1997. mass mkt. 3.25 (*0-373-19235-5*, 1-19235-0) Silhouette.

3 Kids Dreamin' Linda Egland. (Illus.). (J). (gr. 2-5). 1997. 16.00 (*0-689-80866-6*, McElderry) S&S Childrens.

Three Kilos of Coffee: An Autobiography. Manu Dibango & Danielle Rouard. Tr. by Beth G. Raps. LC 93-44597. 158p. 1994. pap. 13.95 (*0-226-14490-9*); lib. bdg. 32.00 (*0-226-14491-7*) U Ch Pr.

Three Kind Mice. Vivian Sathre. (J). 1997. 13.00 (*0-15-201266-4*) HarBrace.

Three Kinds of Love see IVP Booklets

Three Kinds of Love - Chinese Edition. Masumi Toyotome. Tr. by Peter Chiu. 28p. (CHI.). 1991. 1.00 (*1-56582-069-X*) Christ Renew Min.

Three Kingdoms: A Historical Novel. Luo Guanzhong. 1994. pap. 40.00 (*0-520-08930-8*) U CA Pr.

Three Kingdoms on the Roof of the World: Bhutan, Nepal, Ladakh. Robert Z. Apte. LC 90-7710. (Illus.). 130p. 1990. 35.00 (*0-938077-33-3*) Parallax Pr.

Three Kings. Hyman E. Goldin. 144p. 1929. 4.95 (*0-88482-737-2*) Hebrew Pub.

Three Kings of Cologne. Joannes Of Hildesheim. Ed. by C. Horstmann. (EETS, OS Ser.: No. 85). 1974. reprint ed. 55.00 (*0-527-00083-3*) Periodicals Srv.

Three Ladies of Bagdad. Mark Dunster. 24p. (Orig.). 1989. pap. 5.00 (*0-89642-175-9*) Linden Pubs.

Three Ladies of London. Robert Wilson. LC 78-133767. (Tudor Facsimile Texts. Old English Plays Ser.: No. 55). reprint ed. 59.50 (*0-404-53355-8*) AMS Pr.

Three Language Dictionary of Fruit & Vegetable Processing. Florin. 455p. (ENG, FRE & GER.). 1987. 175.00 (*0-8288-7747-5*) Fr & Eur.

Three Language Formula: An Educational Problem. Santosh Aggarwal. (C). 1991. 28.00 (*81-212-0336-8*, Pub. by Gian Publng Hse II) S Asia.

Three Languages. Jacob W. Grimm & Wilhelm K. Grimm. (Creative's Collection of Fairy Tales). (Illus.). 32p. (J). (gr. 4 up). 1984. lib. bdg. 13.95 (*0-87191-940-0*) Creative Ed.

Three Last Plays. Isabella A. Gregory. 1988. reprint ed. lib. bdg. 49.00 (*0-7812-0284-1*) Rprt Serv.

Three Last Plays. Isabella A. Gregory. (BCL1-PR English Literature Ser.). 280p. 1992. reprint ed. lib. bdg. 79.00 (*0-7812-7543-1*) Rprt Serv.

Three Last Plays. Isabella A. Gregory. 1971. reprint ed. 59.00 (*0-403-00615-5*) Scholarly.

Three Last Plays for Reading. Tom Bowie. 367p. 1991. 22.95 (*0-932508-09-X*) Seven Oaks.

Three Late Medieval Morality Plays: Mankind, Everyman & Mundis et Infans. Ed. by G. A. Lesker. (New Mermaid Ser.). (C). 1984. pap. text ed. 7.95 (*0-393-90054-1*) Norton.

Three Late Plays. Arthur Schnitzler. Tr. & Afterword by G. J. Weinberger. (Studies in Austrian Literature, Culture, & Thought. Translation Ser.). 349p. (Orig.). (C). 1992. pap. 25.00 (*0-929497-52-X*) Ariadne CA.

Three Latin American Sociologists: Gino Germani, Pablo Gonzales Casanova, Fernando Henrique Cardoso. 2nd ed. Joseph A. Kahl & Peter B. Evans. 240p. 1987. 39.95 (*0-88738-169-3*); pap. 21.95 (*0-88738-700-4*) Transaction Pubs.

Three Laws. John Bale. LC 78-133637. (Tudor Facsimile Texts. Old English Plays Ser.: No. 23). reprint ed. 59.50 (*0-404-53323-X*) AMS Pr.

Three Laws & the Golden Rule. Morgan Robertson. LC 70-86152. (Short Story Index Reprint Ser.). 1977. 20.95 (*0-8369-3058-4*) Ayer.

Three Layer Model Curves for Geoelectrical Curves for Geoelectrical Measurements: Schlumberger Array Log Cycle 83,33mm. E. Mundry & J. Homilius. (Illus.). (ENG & GER.). 1980. spiral bd. 110.50 (*0-945345-07-0*, Pub. by Schweizerbartsche GW) Lubrecht & Cramer.

Three Lectures. K. K. Mathew. 75p. 1983. 105.00 (*0-317-54568-X*) St Mut.

Three Lectures on Aesthetic. Bernard Bosanquet. Ed. by Ralph G. Ross. LC 63-22370. (Orig.). 1963. pap. 1.70 (*0-672-60376-4*, LLA154, Bobbs) Macmillan.

Three Lectures on Bio-Dynamics. H. H. Koepf. (Bio-Dynamics Ser.: No. 88). 50p. pap. 1.60 (*0-938250-06-X*) Bio-Dynamic Farm.

Three Lectures on Chinese Folklore. R. Jameson. 1972. lib. bdg. 79.95 (*0-87968-527-1*) Krishna Pr.

Three Lectures on the Mystery Dramas. Rudolf Steiner. Tr. by Ruth Pusch from GER. 101p. (Orig.). 1983. pap. 8.95 (*0-88010-060-5*) Anthroposophic.

Three Lectures on the Rate of Wages. 2nd ed. Nassau W. Senior. LC 65-25863. (Reprints of Economic Classics Ser.). xix, 57p. 1966. reprint ed. 25.00 (*0-678-00126-X*) Kelley.

Three Lectures on the Value of Money: Delivered Before the University of Oxford in 1829. Nassau W. Senior. LC 75-41245. reprint ed. 29.50 (*0-404-14779-8*) AMS Pr.

Three-Legged Cat. Margaret Mahy. (Illus.). 32p. (J). (ps-3). 1993. pap. 14.99 (*0-670-85015-2*) Viking Child Bks.

Three-Legged Cat. Margaret Mahy. (Illus.). 32p. (J). (ps-3). 1995. pap. 4.99 (*0-14-055331-2*) Puffin Bks.

Three Legged Chair. James McNeilus. 476p. 1988. reprint ed. 16.75 (*0-9620256-0-7*) J McNeilus.

Three Legged Dog. James Ward. LC 90-740. (Target Poetry Ser.). 57p. 1991. pap. 6.50 (*0-933532-67-9*) BkMk.

Three Lessons of Mr. Markew: How to Turn Dull Talks into Sparkling Sermons. Graham Fysh. LC 91-90056. (Illus.). 64p. 1991. pap. 9.95 (*0-9628987-0-8*) Lifetime Creat.

Three Letters from Africa. Edgar H. Brookes. LC 65-12948. (Orig.). 1965. pap. 3.00 (*0-87574-139-8*) Pendle Hill.

Three Letters from the Andes. 2nd large type ed. Patrick L. Fermor. (Illus.). 148p. 1993. 18.95 (*1-85695-200-2*, Pub. by ISIS UK) Transaction Pubs.

T

Three Letters to the Duke of Wellington on the Fourth Report of the Select Committee of the House of Commons, Appointed in 1828 to Enquire into the Public Income & Expenditure of the United Kingdom. James M. Lauderdale. LC 64-7668. (Reprints of Economic Classics Ser.). 138p. 1965. reprint ed. 35.00 (0-678-00089-1) Kelley.

Three-Level Gas System & Their Interaction with Radiation see Progress in Quantum Electronics

Three Levels of Our Rising. Will Ali. LC 90-86327. 134p. (Orig.). (C). 1991. pap. 12.95 (1-879625-00-8) Families Fam.

Three Levels of Spiritual Perception: An Oral Commentary on the Three Visions (Nang Sum) of Ngorchen Konchong Lhundrub. Deshung K. Rinpoche. Ed. by Victoria R. Scott. Tr. by Jared Rhoton. LC 95-1490. (Illus.). 620p. (ENG & TIB.). 1995. 24.95 (0-86171-101-7) Wisdom MA.

Three Literary Letters. Dionysius of Halicarnassus. Tr. & Comment by William R. Roberts. xi, 233p. 1901. write for info. (0-318-70913-9) G Olms Pubs.

Three Little Africans. Alhaji Obaba Abdullahi Muhammad. (Illus.). 36p. (Orig.). (J). (gr. k-4). 1978. pap. 2.50 (0-916157-00-8) African Islam Miss Pubns.

Three Little Bears. Max Bolliger. (Illus.). (J). (ps-3). 1987. 12.95 (1-55774-006-2) Hemed Bks.

Three Little Bunnies. Nicola Smee. (Illus.). 12p. (J). (ps). 1994. bds. 6.95 (0-590-48078-2, Cartwheel) Scholastic Inc.

Three Little Chaperones. Helen R. Myers. (Romance Ser.: No. 861). 1992. pap. 2.69 (0-373-08861-2, 5-08861-2) Silhouette.

Three Little Chicks. Kathy Feczko. LC 84-8629. (Giant First Start Reader Ser.). (Illus.). 32p. (J). (gr. k-2). 1985. lib. bdg. 12.95 (0-8167-0355-8) Troll Communs.

Three Little Chicks. Nicola Smee. (Illus.). 12p. (J). (ps). 1994. bds. 6.95 (0-590-48079-0, Cartwheel) Scholastic Inc.

Three Little Hawaiian Pigs & the Magic Shark. Donivee M. Laird. LC 81-67047. (Illus.). 40p. (J). (ps-3). 1981. 8.95 (0-940350-25-4) Barnaby Bks.

Three Little Indians see Books for Young Explorers

Three Little Javelinas. Susan Lowell. LC 92-14232. (Illus.). 32p. (J). (ps up). 1992. lib. bdg. 14.95 (0-87358-542-9) Northland AZ.

Three Little Kittens. (Read Along With Me Ser.). (Illus.). (J). (ps-1). 1985. 2.99 (0-517-47898-6) Random Hse Value.

Three Little Kittens. (Golden Fuzzy Wuzzy Bks.). (Illus.). (J). (ps-3). 1991. write for info. (0-307-15703-2, Golden Books) Western Pub.

Three Little Kittens. Ed. by Kathleen Cubley. (Cut & Tell Cutout Ser.). (Illus.). 8p. (J). (ps). 1995. 2.95 (1-57029-034-2, WPH 2224, Totline Bks) Warren Pub Hse.

Three Little Kittens. Paul Galdone. LC 86-2655. (Illus.). 32p. (J). (ps-2). 1986. 14.95 (0-89919-426-5, Clarion Bks) HM.

Three Little Kittens. Paul Galdone. LC 86-2655. (Illus.). 32p. (J). (ps-2). 1988. pap. 5.95 (0-89919-796-5, Clarion Bks) HM.

Three Little Kittens. Paul Galdone. (J). 1989. pap. 8.95 incl. audio (0-395-51999-3) Ticknor & Fields.

Three Little Kittens. Illus. by Tracey Moroney. (My First Nursery Rhyme Books Ser.). 12p. (J). (ps). 1995. 3.99 (0-88705-780-2, Wshng Well Bks) Joshua Morris.

Three Little Kittens. Lee Randall. (Storyshapes Ser.). (Illus.). 24p. (J). (ps-1). 1996. pap. 2.25 (1-56293-891-6) McClanahan Bk.

Three Little Kittens. Illus. by Jerry Smath. (Take-a-Look Bks.). 14p. (J). (ps-3). 1995. bds. 3.95 (0-307-12470-3, Golden Books) Western Pub.

Three Little Kittens. Nicola Smee. (Finger Puppet Board Bks.). (Illus.). 12p. (J). (ps). 1995. bds. 6.95 (0-590-22496-4, Cartwheel) Scholastic Inc.

***Three Little Kittens.** Linda J. Smith. (Illus.). 32p. (J). 1991. pap. write for info. (1-85479-003-X, Pub. by M OMara UK) Assoc Pubs Grp.

Three Little Kittens. Stephanie St. Pierre. (Pudgy Pop-up Board Bks.). (Illus.). 12p. (J). (ps). 1994. bds. 4.95 (0-448-40459-1, G&D) Putnam Pub Group.

Three Little Kittens, Vol. 1. Judith S. Hannant. (J). 1995. 12.95 (0-316-34413-3) Little.

Three Little Kittens in the Enchanted Forest: A Pop-up Adventure. Hilary Aaron. LC 94-79230. (Illus.). 16p. (J). (ps-2). 1995. 18.95 (0-7868-0137-9) Hyprn Child.

Three Little Kittens Paper Dolls in Full Color. Tom Tierney. (J). 1986. pap. 3.50 (0-486-25065-2) Dover.

***Three Little Miracles.** Rebecca Winters. (Romance Ser.). 1997. 3.25 (0-373-03443-1, 1-03443-8) Harlequin Bks.

Three Little Mousies. Joseph A. White. LC 93-70959. 20p. (J). (gr. k-3). 1993. pap. 5.95 (0-9636278-0-5) White DEI.

Three Little Pigs. (FRE.). (J). (gr. k-3). 4.25 (0-685-28448-4) Fr & Eur.

Three Little Pigs. (First Fairy Tales Ser.: No. S852-2). (Illus.). (J). (ps-2). 3.95 (0-7214-5059-8, Ladybrd) Penguin.

Three Little Pigs. (Read Along With Me Ser.). (Illus.). (J). (ps-1). 1985. 1.98 (0-517-47899-4) Random Hse Value.

Three Little Pigs. (J). 1988. 2.98 (0-671-10041-6) S&S Trade.

Three Little Pigs. (J). 1989. 2.98 (0-671-06785-0) S&S Trade.

Three Little Pigs. (Illus.). 16p. (Orig.). (J). 1991. write for info. incl. audio (1-880459-02-7) Arrow Trad.

Three Little Pigs. (Fun-to-Read Fairy Tales Series II). (Illus.). 24p. (Orig.). (J). (gr. k-3). 1992. pap. 2.50 (1-56144-173-2, Honey Bear Bks) Modern Pub NYC.

Three Little Pigs. (Classic Fairytales Pop-Ups Ser.). (Illus.). (Orig.). (J). (ps-1). 1.98 (0-517-39466-9) Random Hse Value.

Three Little Pigs. (Picture Tales Ser.). (Illus.). 32p. (Orig.). (J). (ps-1). 1985. 2.49 (0-517-46242-7) Random Hse Value.

Three Little Pigs. (Little Golden Sound Story Bks.). (Illus.). 24p. (Orig.). (J). (ps-3). 1992. 6.95 (0-307-74807-3, 64807, Golden Books) Western Pub.

Three Little Pigs. (Fairy Tale Fun Ser.). (J). 3.95 (0-7214-5431-3, Ladybrd) Penguin.

Three Little Pigs. (J). 1.59 (0-307-01028-7, Golden Pr) Western Pub.

Three Little Pigs. (Paint with Water Fairy Tales Ser.). (Illus.). 32p. (Orig.). (J). (gr. k-2). 1994. pap. write for info. (1-56144-488-X, Honey Bear Bks) Modern Pub NYC.

3 Little Pigs. (J). pap. write for info. (0-590-31818-7) Scholastic Inc.

3 Little Pigs. (J). pap. write for info. (0-590-31819-5) Scholastic Inc.

Three Little Pigs. (Illus.). 32p. (J). (ps-2). 1996. pap. 2.50 (0-7214-5618-9, Ladybrd) Penguin.

Three Little Pigs. (Little Landoll Fairytale Ser.). 32p. (J). (ps-3). Date not set. text ed. 1.29 (1-56987-227-9) Landoll.

Three Little Pigs. (Favorite Fairy Tale Classics Ser.). 24p. (J). (ps-3). Date not set. text ed. 3.50 (1-56987-202-3) Landoll.

Three Little Pigs. (Every Day Pop-Up Bks.). (Illus.). 12p. (J). (ps-3). Date not set. text ed. 7.95 (1-56987-422-0) Landoll.

Three Little Pigs. (Spanish Fairytale Ser.). 24p. (SPA.). (J). (ps-3). Date not set. text ed. write for info. (1-56987-255-4) Landoll.

Three Little Pigs. Addison-Wesley Staff. (ESL Ser.). 16p. (J). (gr. k-2). 1988. text ed. 31.75 (0-201-19322-1) Addison-Wesley.

Three Little Pigs. Addison-Wesley Staff. (ESL Ser.). 16p. (J). (gr. k-2). 1989. pap. 16.00 (0-201-19066-4) Addison-Wesley.

Three Little Pigs. Harry Bornstein. (Signed English Ser.). 44p. (J). (ps-3). 1972. pap. 6.50 (0-913580-09-0, Pub. by K Green Pubns) Gallaudet Univ Pr.

Three Little Pigs. Beverly C. Burgess. (Illus.). 30p. (Orig.). 1982. pap. 4.99 (0-89274-283-6) Harrison Hse.

Three Little Pigs. Illus. by Lynne Byrnes. (Happytime Storybks.). 24p. (J). (ps-1). 1991. pap. 1.25 (0-7214-5305-8, S9016-6 SER., Ladybrd) Penguin.

***Three Little Pigs.** Richard Caudle & Brad Caudle. (Rock 'N Learn Ser.). (Illus.). 20p. (J). (gr. 1 up). 1996. pap. 7.95 (1-878489-67-4) Rock n Learn.

Three Little Pigs. Illus. by Debbie Dieneman. (Children's Classics Ser.). 32p. (J). 1991. 6.95 (0-8362-4904-6) Andrews & McMeel.

Three Little Pigs. Paul Galdone. LC 75-123456. (Illus.). (J). (ps-3). 1979. 14.95 (0-395-28813-4, Clarion Bks) HM.

Three Little Pigs. Paul Galdone. (Book & Cassette Favorites Ser.). (J). (gr. 1 up). 1987. 6.95 incl. audio (0-317-64579-X, Clarion Bks) HM.

Three Little Pigs. Paul Galdone. LC 75-123456. (Illus.). 40p. (Orig.). (J). (ps-3). 1984. pap. 5.95 (0-89919-275-0, Clarion Bks) HM.

***Three Little Pigs.** Paul Galdone. (J). 1987. 8.95 incl. audio (0-89919-683-7) Ticknor & Flds Bks Yng Read.

***Three Little Pigs.** Marie-Louise Gay. 1997. pap. text ed. 5.95 (0-88899-299-8, Pub. by Groundwood-Douglas & McIntyre CN) Firefly Bks Ltd.

Three Little Pigs. Dara Goldman. (Illus.). 32p. (Orig.). (J). (ps-3). 1996. pap. 2.95 (0-8167-4130-1, Whistlstop) Troll Communs.

Three Little Pigs. Illus. by Eileen Grace. LC 80-27483. 32p. (J). (gr. k-2). 1981. pap. 3.95 (0-89375-463-3) Troll Communs.

Three LIttle Pigs. Illus. by Gill Guile. (Once Upon a Time Ser.). 24p. (J). (ps-1). 1996. 3.98 (1-85854-414-9) Brimax Bks.

***Three Little Pigs.** Illus. by Jim Harris. 32p. 1995. 10.95 (0-939251-94-9) Accord CO.

Three Little Pigs. Margaret Hillert. (Illus.). (J). (ps). 1963. pap. 5.10 (0-8136-5535-8, TK2371); lib. bdg. 7.95 (0-8136-5035-6, TK2370) Modern Curr.

Three Little Pigs. Illus. by Tony Hutchings. (Storytime PlaySet Ser.). 14p. (J). 1994. 7.95 (0-307-16325-3) Western Pub.

Three Little Pigs. Illus. by David Jorgensen. LC 92-36277. (J). 1993. 4.95 (0-88708-298-X, Rabbit) S&S Childrens.

***Three Little Pigs.** Steven Kellogg. LC 96-34434. (J). 1999. 16.00 (0-688-08731-0, Morrow Junior); lib. bdg. write for info. (0-688-08732-9, Morrow Junior) Morrow.

***Three Little Pigs.** Ladybird Staff. (J). 1997. pap. 3.50 (0-7214-5786-X, Ladybrd) Penguin.

Three Little Pigs. Jonathan Langley. (Nursery Pop-Up Bks.). 10p. (J). 1996. 4.95 (0-8120-6571-9) Barron.

Three Little Pigs. Little Golden Books Staff. (First Little Golden Bks). (Illus.). 24p. (J). (ps). 1995. bds. 1.19 (0-307-10173-8, Golden Books) Western Pub.

Three Little Pigs. John Malam. (Story Stickers Ser.). 16p. (J). (ps-2). 1995. pap. 1.95 (1-56293-563-1) McClanahan Bk.

Three Little Pigs. Carrie Mapes & Judith Gold. (Folktale Theme Ser.: Vol. 3). (Illus.). 64p. (J). (gr. k-2). 1995. teacher ed., pap. text ed. 6.95 (1-55799-374-2, EMC 526) Evan-Moor Corp.

Three Little Pigs. Illus. & Retold by James Marshall. LC 88-33411. (J). (ps-3). 1989. pap. 15.99 (0-8037-0591-3); lib. bdg. 12.89 (0-8037-0594-8) Dial Bks Young.

Three Little Pigs. Retold by James Marshall. (Illus.). 32p. (J). (ps-3). 1996. pap. 4.99 (0-14-055742-3, Puffin) Puffin Bks.

Three Little Pigs. David McPhail. LC 93-43991. (David McPhail's Favorite Tales Ser.). (Illus.). 32p. (J). (ps-k). 1995. bds. 4.95 (0-590-48118-5, Cartwheel) Scholastic Inc.

***Three Little Pigs.** Miles. LC 97-16007. (J). 1998. mass mkt. 3.99 (0-689-81789-4) S&S Childrens.

Three Little Pigs. Illus. by David Pace. (Fairy Tale Pop-ups Ser.). 16p. (J). 1994. 3.95 (0-7214-9419-6, Ladybrd) Penguin.

Three Little Pigs. Random House Staff. 1995. 4.50 (0-679-84914-9) Random.

Three Little Pigs. Tom Roberts. LC 89-70097. (Illus.). 32p. (J). (ps up). 1991. pap. 19.95 incl. audio (0-88708-133-9, Rabbit) S&S Childrens.

Three Little Pigs. Illus. & Retold by Yuri Salzman. LC 87-81773. (Golden Super Shape Bks.). 24p. (J). 1988. pap. 1.95 (0-307-10099-5, Golden Pr) Western Pub.

Three Little Pigs. Eric Suben. (Storytime Classics Ser.). (Illus.). 24p. (J). (ps-2). 1995. pap. 1.29 (1-56293-543-7) McClanahan Bk.

Three Little Pigs. Illus. by Terri Super. (Pudgy Pal Board Bks.). 18p. (J). (ps-1). 1984. bds. 3.95 (0-448-10214-5, G&D) Putnam Pub Group.

Three Little Pigs. Margot Zemach. LC 87-73488. (Michael di Capua Bks.). (Illus.). 32p. 1988. 14.00 (0-374-37527-5) FS&G.

Three Little Pigs. Margot Zemach. (Illus.). 32p. (J). (ps up). 1991. pap. 3.95 (0-374-47717-5, Sunburst Bks) FS&G.

Three Little Pigs. Harriet Ziefert. (J). 1995. pap. 3.50 (0-14-037624-0) Puffin Bks.

Three Little Pigs. Tom Roberts. (Illus.). 64p. (J). 1993. reprint ed. 9.95 incl. audio (0-88708-299-8, Rabbit) S&S Childrens.

***Three Little Pigs.** Margot Zemach. (J). (gr. k-3). 1997. reprint ed. pap. 4.95 (0-614-28744-8, Sunburst Bks) FS&G.

Three Little Pigs, 6 bks., Set. Margaret Fanning & Linda Bak. (Theatre Phonics Ser.). 24p. (J). (gr. k-1). 1992. pap. text ed. 18.00 (1-882063-22-8) Cottage Pr MA.

Three Little Pigs: A Book to Read & Color. rev. ed. (J). 1996. pap. 1.25 (0-8167-0875-4) Troll Communs.

***Three Little Pigs: A Classic Fairy Tale.** Illus. by Agnes Mathieu. LC 97-23044. (Little Pebbles Ser.). (J). 1998. write for info. (0-7892-0423-1) Abbeville Pr.

Three Little Pigs: As It Was Originally Passed into English Folklore in 1620. Craig Pleasants. (Illus.). 16p. (Orig.). (J). (gr. 3 up). 1994. pap. 5.00 (0-9638129-2-0) Gates of Heck.

Three Little Pigs: Cut & Tell Cutout. Jean Warren. Ed. by Kathleen Cubley. (Nursery Tales Ser.). (Illus.). 8p. (Orig.). (J). (ps). 1994. pap. 2.95 (0-911019-89-8, WPH 2206) Warren Pub Hse.

Three Little Pigs: Full-Color Sturdy Book. Valeri Gorbachev. LC 95-7168. (Little Activity Bks.). (Illus.). 16p. (Orig.). (J). 1996. pap. text ed. 1.00 (0-486-28691-6) Dover.

Three Little Pigs: Includes Book & Night Light. Illus. by Jim Harris. (J). 1995. 15.95 (0-939251-57-4) Accord CO.

***Three Little Pigs: Interactive Storybook.** (Illus.). 8p. (J). (ps-6). 1997. 12.50 (1-890647-01-2) Lrning Curve.

Three Little Pigs: Lamb Chop's Play-along Fairy Tales. Shari Lewis. (Illus.). 32p. (J). (ps-3). 1994. pap. 2.99 (0-553-37387-0) Bantam.

Three Little Pigs: Pop-up Book. Illus. by Mike Peterkin. LC 93-70940. 10p. (J). (ps-3). 1993. 11.95 (1-56282-513-5) Disney Pr.

Three Little Pigs: Richard Scarry. Richard Scarry. (Little Nugget Bks.). (Illus.). 28p. (J). (ps). 1993. bds. 3.25 (0-307-12521-1, 12521, Golden Pr) Western Pub.

Three Little Pigs & Other Favorite Nursery Stories. Illus. & Retold by Charlotte Voake. LC 91-58759. 96p. (J). (ps up). 1992. 19.95 (1-56402-118-1) Candlewick Pr.

Three Little Pigs & Other Favorite Nursery Stories. Illus. & Retold by Charlotte Voake. LC 91-58759. 96p. (J). (gr. k-2). 1996. reprint ed. pap. 9.99 (1-56402-957-3) Candlewick Pr.

3 Little Pigs: And Other Great Stories with Masks. Susan Pagnucci & Franco Pagnucci. (Illus.). 64p. (Orig.). (J). (ps-3). 1994. pap. 8.99 (0-929326-11-3) Bur Oak Pr Inc.

Three Little Pigs & the Big Bad Wolf. Illus. & Retold by Glen Rounds. LC 91-18173. 32p. (J). (ps-3). 1992. lib. bdg. 15.95 (0-8234-0923-6) Holiday.

Three Little Pigs & the Big, Bad Wolf: Three Little Rottweilers & the Big, Bad German Shepherd. G. A. Bradley. (Illus.). 34p. (J). (gr. 2-4). 1995. 29.95 (1-886123-05-5) Geyers Garten.

Three Little Pigs & the Fox. Hooks & Schindler. (J). 1997. 5.99 (0-689-80962-X, S&S Bks Young Read) S&S Childrens.

Three Little Pigs Go to Greasy Pete's. David Adams. (Illus.). 40p. (J). (ps-3). 1994. pap. 5.95 (0-9638421-8-8); lib. bdg. 14.95 (0-9638421-9-6) Flatland Tales.

Three Little Pigs Little Book. Addison-Wesley Staff. (ESOL Elementary Supplement Ser.). (Illus.). 16p. (J). (gr. k-3). 1989. ring bd. 4.33 (0-201-19058-3) Addison-Wesley.

Three Little Pigs Play Set: Pop-up with Press-Out Figures. Stephanie St. Pierre. 1992. pap. 5.99 (0-8431-3421-6) Price Stern Sloan.

Three Little Pigs-Sticker Book. 1990. 3.99 (0-517-69692-4) Random Hse Value.

***Three Little Pigs Sticker Storybook.** Thea Kliros. (Illus.). 16p. (Orig.). (J). 1997. pap. text ed. 1.00 (0-486-29542-7) Dover.

Three Little Puppies. Nicola Smee. (Finger Puppet Board Bks.). (Illus.). 12p. (J). (ps). 1995. bds. 6.95 (0-590-22485-9, Cartwheel) Scholastic Inc.

Three Little Teddy Bears. Nicola Smee. (Finger Puppet Board Bks.). (Illus.). 12p. (J). (ps). 1995. bds. 6.95 (0-590-22487-5, Cartwheel) Scholastic Inc.

Three Little Witches. Sharon Gordon. (Illus.). 32p. (J). (gr. k-2). 1997. pap. 2.50 (0-89375-290-8) Troll Communs.

Three Little Witches & the Fortune-Teller's Curse. Debra Hess. (Three Little Witches Ser.: No. 6). 96p. (J). (gr. 4-7). 1992. mass mkt. 2.99 (0-06-106117-4, Harp PBks) HarpC.

Three Little Wolves & the Big Bad Pig. Eugene Trivizas. LC 92-24829. (Illus.). 32p. (J). (gr. k-5). 1993. lib. bdg. 17.00 (0-689-50569-8, McElderry) S&S Childrens.

***Three Little Wolves & the Big Bad Pig.** Eugene Trivizas. (J). 1997. pap. text ed. 5.99 (0-689-81528-X, Atheneum Bks Young) S&S Childrens.

***Three Little Words.** Don C. France. 300p. (Orig.). 1998. mass mkt. 7.99 (1-889501-99-9, Appaloosa) Sovereign.

Three Little Words: A, An, & The: A Foreign Student's Guide to English Articles. Elizabeth Claire. (Illus.). 62p. (Orig.). (C). 1988. pap. text ed. 9.95 (0-937354-46-5) Delta Systems.

Three Lives. Gertrude Stein. 23.95 (0-8488-0634-4) Amereon Ltd.

Three Lives. Gertrude Stein. 1958. pap. 10.00 (0-394-70153-4, Vin) Random.

Three Lives. Gertrude Stein. (Classics Ser.: No. 192). 280p. 1997. pap. 12.95 (1-55713-215-1) Sun & Moon CA.

Three Lives. Gertrude Stein. 1990. reprint ed. lib. bdg. 25.95 (0-89966-711-2) Buccaneer Bks.

Three Lives. Gertrude Stein. LC 93-34478. (Thrift Editions Ser.). 176p. reprint ed. pap. 2.00 (0-486-28059-4) Dover.

Three Lives. Gertrude Stein. (Classics Ser.). 320p. 1990. reprint ed. pap. 9.95 (0-14-018184-9, Penguin Classics) Viking Penguin.

Three Lives of Elizabeth. Shirley Seifert. 1976. reprint ed. lib. bdg. 23.95 (0-89190-139-6, Rivercity Pr) Amereon Ltd.

Three Lives of Harris Harper. Lynn Cullen. 160p. (J). (gr. 5-7). 1996. 14.95 (0-395-73680-3, Clarion Bks) HM.

***Three Lives of Littleton Blue, Vol. 1.** Doug Bowman. 1996. mass mkt. 4.99 (0-8125-3454-9) Forge NYC.

Three Lives of Lucie Cabrol. Theatre De Complicite Staff. 1996. pap. 11.95 (0-413-69690-1, Pub. by Methuen UK) Heinemann.

Three Lives to Live. Anne M. Lindbergh. (J). (gr. 3-6). 1995. reprint ed. pap. 3.50 (0-671-86732-6, Minstrel Bks) PB.

Three Lords of London. Robert Wilson. LC 71-133768. (Tudor Facsimile Texts. Old English Plays Ser.: No. 57). reprint ed. 59.50 (0-404-53357-4) AMS Pr.

Three Loves: Philosophy, Theology & World Religions: Essays in Honour of Joseph C. McLelland. Ed. by Robert C. Culley & William Klempa. LC 94-30658. (McGill Studies in Religion). 218p. 1994. pap. 35.95 (0-7885-0029-5, 650002) Scholars Pr GA.

Three Macabre Stories. Rosaleen Norton. Ed. by Keith Richmond. (Illus.). 48p. 1996. 45.00 (0-930126-50-5) Typographeum.

Three Magic Flip Books. Martha Alexander. Incl. Magic Hat. 1984. (0-318-58158-2); Magic Picture. 1984. (0-318-58159-0); Magic Box. 1984. (0-318-58160-4); (Illus.). (J). (ps-k). 1984. Three bks. in a shrink-wrapped slipcase. pap. 5.95 (0-8037-0051-2, 0578-170) Dial Bks Young.

Three Magic Words. Uell S. Andersen. 323p. 1977. pap. 10.00 (0-87980-165-4) Wilshire.

Three Magic Words. U. S. Anderson. 10.00 (0-685-70722-9) Wehman.

Three Magics. Ed. by John Caddy. (Illus.). 176p. (Orig.). 1987. pap. 7.50 (0-927663-03-1) COMPAS.

Three Major New Ways to Improve Language & Reading Skills. Win Wenger. (Illus.). 88p. (Orig.). 1987. pap. 12.00 (0-931865-18-2) Psychegenics.

***Three Malay Villages: A Sociology of Paddy Growers in West Malaysia.** Ed. by Masuo Kuchiba et al. Tr. by Peter Hawkes & Stephanie Hawkes. LC 79-573. (Monographs of the Center for Southeast Asian Studies, Kyoto University: No. 14). (Illus.). 378p. 1979. reprint ed. pap. 107.80 (0-608-04388-5, 2065169) Bks Demand.

Three-Manifolds. John Hempel. LC 76-3027. (Annals of Mathematics Studies: No. 86). 204p. 1911. pap. text ed. 57.50 (0-691-08178-6) Princeton U Pr.

Three-Manifolds Which Are End One-Movable. M. Brin & T. Thickstun. LC 89-15146. (Memoirs Ser.: Vol. 81/411). 73p. 1989. pap. 17.00 (0-8218-2474-0, MEMO/81/411) Am Math.

Three Marion Motets (a Three) Gregor Aichinger. Ed. by William E. Hettrick. (Renaissance Recorder Ser.: No. 6). 1975. 2.75 (0-913334-25-1, CM1026) Consort Music.

Three Marios, 2 vols., Set. Jose Corrales. Tr. by Presbyter's Peartree Staff from SPA. 103p. 1993. pap. text ed. 7.90 (1-885901-06-2) Presbyters Peartree.

Three Marios Vol. I: Circus Maximus, Corpus Delicti. Jose Corrales. Tr. by Presbyter's Peartree Staff from SPA. 60p. 1993. pap. text ed. 3.95 (1-885901-07-0) Presbyters Peartree.

Three Marios Vol. II: In Absentia. Jose Corrales. Tr. by Presbyter's Peartree Staff from SPA. 43p. 1993. pap. text ed. 3.95 (1-885901-08-9) Presbyters Peartree.

Three Marshals of France: Leadership after Trauma. Anthony Clayton. (Illus.). 229p. 1992. 41.00 (0-08-040707-2, Pub. by Brasseys UK) Brasseys Inc.

Three Martian Novels. Edgar Rice Burroughs. Incl. Thuvia, Maid of Mars. reprint ed. pap. (0-318-51773-6); Chessmen of Mars. reprint ed. pap. (0-318-51774-4); Master Mind of Mars. reprint ed. pap. (0-318-51775-2); vi, 499p. pap. 9.95 (0-486-20039-6) Dover.

Three Marys. Moody K. Stuart. 1984. pap. 9.99 (0-85151-381-6) Banner of Truth.

Three Masks of American Tragedy. Dan Vogel. LC 73-90865. 194p. reprint ed. pap. 55.30 (0-317-28669-2, 2055304) Bks Demand.

An Asterisk (*) at the beginning of an entry indicates that the title is appearing in BIP for the first time.

***Three Masquerades: Essays on Equality, Work Hu(man) Rights.** Marilyn Waring. 205p. 1996. 45.00 (*0-8020-4230-9*) U of Toronto Pr.

***Three Masquerades: Essays on Equality, Works & Human Rights.** Marilyn Waring. 1997. pap. text ed. 19.95 (*0-8020-8076-6*) U of Toronto Pr.

Three-Masted Schooner James Miller: A History & Model Maker's Source Book. William S. Quincy. (Illus.). 48p. 1986. pap. 9.95 (*0-913372-37-4*) Mystic Seaport.

Three Master Builders, & Another: Studies in Modern Revolutionary & Liberal Statesmanship. Pelham H. Box. LC 68-22904. (Essay Index Reprint Ser.). 1977. 23.95 (*0-8369-0234-3*) Ayer.

Three Master Masons. Milton A. Pottenger. 402p. 1972. reprint ed. spiral bd. 12.50 (*0-7873-0672-X*) Hlth Research.

Three Master Masons: A Scientific & Philosophical Explanation of the Emblems of Masonry Proving It to Be the Great Constructive Principle of the World (1916) Milton A. Pottenger. 410p. 1996. pap. 29.95 (*1-56459-792-X*) Kessinger Pub.

Three Masters of Landscape: Fragonard, Robert, & Boucher. Pinkney L. Near. LC 81-16180. (Illus.). 56p. 1981. pap. 1.50 (*0-917046-11-0*) Va Mus Arts.

Three Maya Relief Panels at Dumbarton Oaks. Michael D. Coe & Elizabeth P. Benson. LC 66-30016. (Studies in Pre-Columbian Art & Archaeology: No. 2). (Illus.). 1966. pap. 6.00 (*0-88402-014-2*) Dumbarton Oaks.

Three Meals a Day: A Collection of Valuable & Reliable Recipes in All Classes of Cookery. Maud C. Cooke. 560p. 1989. reprint ed. pap. 14.95 (*0-685-28907-9*) St Johann Pr.

Three Mean Alligators. Joy Vaughan-Brown. Ed. by Eric H. Brown. LC 96-90318. (Illus.). 32p. (Orig.). (J). (ps-5). 1996. pap. text ed. 12.95 (*1-889306-00-2*) Hilton A Vaughan.

Three Medieval Centuries of Literature in England, 1100-1400. Charles S. Baldwin. LC 68-58890. 274p. (C). 1968. reprint ed. 50.00 (*0-87753-003-3*) Phaeton.

Three Medieval Greek Romances: Velthandros & Chrysandza, Kallimachos & Chrysorroi, Livistros & Rodamni. Tr. by Gavin Betts. LC 94-32655. (Library of Medieval Literature: Vol. 98B). 240p. 1995. text ed. 38.00 (*0-8153-1279-2*) Garland.

Three Medieval Views of Women: "La Contenance des Fames," "Le Bien des Fames," "Le Blasme des Fames" Gloria K. Fiero. LC 88-37431. 184p. (C). 1989. pap. 14.00 (*0-300-04442-9*); text ed. 35.00 (*0-300-04441-0*) Yale U Pr.

Three Melodramas. Pietro Metastasio. Tr. by Joseph G. Fucilla. LC 80-51017. (Studies in Romance Languages: No. 24). 164p. 1981. 18.00 (*0-8131-1400-4*) U Pr of Ky.

***Three Men for Julie: A Novel.** Elaina. LC 97-9938. 1997. pap. write for info. (*1-55618-163-9*) Brunswick Pub.

Three Men in a Boat. 1991. pap. 5.25 (*0-19-421654-3*) OUP.

Three Men in a Boat. 1995. pap. 5.25 (*0-19-586321-6*) OUP.

Three Men in a Boat. Jerome K. Jerome. 1976. 19.95 (*0-8488-1388-X*) Amereon Ltd.

Three Men in a Boat. Jerome K. Jerome. (Jerome K. Jerome Ser.). (Illus.). 224p. (J). (gr. 6-9). 1989. 22.00 (*0-86299-569-8*, Pub. by Sutton Pubng UK); pap. 8.00 (*0-86299-028-9*, Pub. by Sutton Pubng UK); pap. 18.00 (*0-7509-0062-8*, Pub. by Sutton Pubng UK) Bks Intl VA.

Three Men in a Boat. Jerome K. Jerome. (Illus.). 192p. 1991. pap. 6.95 (*0-460-87028-9*, Everyman's Classic Lib) C E Tuttle.

Three Men in a Boat. Jerome K. Jerome. 192p. 1978. pap. 6.95 (*0-14-001213-3*, Penguin Bks) Viking Penguin.

Three Men in a Boat. Jerome K. Jerome. 1986. reprint ed. lib. bdg. 18.95 (*0-89966-541-1*) Buccaneer Bks.

Three Men in the Fiery Furnace: Daniel 3:1-30. Teresa Olive. (Arch Bks.). (Illus.). 24p. (J). (ps-3). 1994. pap. 1.99 (*0-570-09043-1*, 59-1466) Concordia.

Three Men of Boston: Leadership & Conflict at the Start of the American Revolution. John R. Galvin. (Association of the U. S. Army Book Ser.). 344p. 1996. reprint ed. pap. 23.95 (*1-57488-111-6*) Brasseys Inc.

Three Men of the Beagle. Richard L. Marks. 272p. 1992. pap. 11.00 (*0-380-71838-3*) Avon.

Three Men on a Horse. George Abbott. 1935. pap. 5.25 (*0-8222-1139-4*) Dramatists Play.

***Three Men on an Island.** James MacIntyre. 150p. 9700. 39.95 (*0-85640-582-5*, Pub. by Blackstaff Pr IE) Dufour.

Three Men on the Bummel. Jerome K. Jerome. (Jerome K. Jerome Ser.). (Illus.). 240p. 1991. pap. 8.00 (*0-86299-029-7*, Pub. by Sutton Pubng UK) Bks Intl VA.

Three Mennonite Poets. Jean Janzen et al. LC 86-81460. 177p. (Orig.). 1986. 13.95 (*0-934672-38-5*); pap. 8.95 (*0-934672-40-7*) Good Bks PA.

Three Merchants: And Other Stories. Shaindel Weinbach. (ArtScroll Youth Ser.). (Illus.). 160p. (YA). (gr. 6-12). 1983. 14.99 (*0-89906-768-9*) Mesorah Pubns.

Three Messengers for One God. Roger Arnaldez. Tr. by Gerald W. Schlabach et al. from FRE. LC 93-42512. (C). 1995. text ed. 34.50 (*0-268-01885-5*) U of Notre Dame Pr.

Three Middle English Charlemagne Romances. Ed. by Alan Lupack. (TEAMS Middle English Text Ser.). 1991. pap. 7.00 (*0-918720-44-3*) Medieval Inst.

Three Middle English Religious Poems. Ed. by Robert H. Bowers. LC 63-63267. (University of Florida Humanities Monographs: No. 12). 72p. reprint ed. pap. 25.00 (*0-7837-5017-X*, 2044684) Bks Demand.

Three Mile an Hour God: Biblical Reflections. Kosuke Koyama. LC 79-24785. 156p. reprint ed. pap. 44.50 (*0-7837-6411-1*, 2046391) Bks Demand.

Three Mile Island: A Reader's Guide to Selected Government Publications & Government-Sponsored Research Publications. Peggy M. Hassler. LC 88-10086. 222p. 1988. 27.50 (*0-8108-2118-4*) Scarecrow.

Three Mile Island: A Selectively Annotated Bibliography. Ed. by Suzanne M. Shultz. LC 87-37547. (Bibliographies & Indexes in Science & Technology Ser.: No. 3). 328p. 1988. text ed. 65.00 (*0-313-25573-3*, WTE/, Greenwood Pr) Greenwood.

Three Mile Island Accident: Diagnosis & Prognosis. Ed. by L. M. Toth et al. LC 85-26852. (ACS Symposium Ser.: No. 293). (Illus.). ix, 297p. 1986. 60.95 (*0-8412-0948-0*) Am Chemical.

***Three Mile Island Accident: Diagnosis & Prognosis.** Ed. by Louis M. Toth et al. LC 85-26852. (ACS Symposium Ser.: Vol. 293). 312p. 1986. reprint ed. pap. 89.00 (*0-608-03921-7*, 2064368) Bks Demand.

Three Mile Island Crisis: Psychological, Social, & Economic Impacts on the Surrounding Population. Peter S. Houts et al. LC 87-43186. (Penn State Studies: No. 49). (Illus.). 131p. (Orig.). 1988. pap. 14.50 (*0-271-00633-1*) Pa St U Pr.

Three Military Leaders: Togo, Yamamoto, Yamashita. Edwin P. Hoyt. Ed. by Pockell. LC 93-24515. (Biographies Ser.). (Illus.). 176p. 1994. pap. 10.00 (*4-7700-1737-5*) Kodansha.

Three Military Posts in Northeastern California 1849-1863. Norris A. Bleyhl. (ANCRR Occasional Publications: No. 9). 57p. 1984. 6.00 (*0-614-05677-2*) Assn NC Records.

Three Minute Aesop's Fables. Ed. by Gina Phillips. (Three Minute Bks.). (Illus.). 24p. (J). 1991. 2.98 (*1-56156-088-X*) Kidsbks.

Three Minute Bedtime Stories. Ed. by Gina Phillips. (Three Minute Bks.). (Illus.). 24p. (J). 1991. 2.98 (*1-56156-087-1*) Kidsbks.

Three-Minute Bible Stories. Judy Leale. (Illus.). 32p. (J). 1992. 9.95 (*1-56156-152-5*) Kidsbks.

3 Minute Bible Stories. Dave Senterfitt. Date not set. 9.95 (*0-86653-760-0*) Good Apple.

Three Minute Declamations for College Men. H. C. Davis & J. C. Bridgeman. LC 68-58819. (Granger Index Reprint Ser.). 1977. 20.95 (*0-8369-6013-0*) Ayer.

***3-Minute Dieting: The Holistic Approach to Permanent Weight Loss.** Ted Natt. LC 613.25. (Illus.). 248p. (Orig.). 1996. spiral bd., pap. 29.97 (*0-9654658-0-2*) Light Inc.

Three-Minute Dramas for Worship. Karen Patitucci. LC 89-30342. 272p. (C). 1989. pap. 11.95 (*0-89390-143-1*) Resource Pubns.

Three Minute Meditator: 30 Simple Ways to Unwind Your Mind While Enhancing Your Emotional Intelligence. 3rd ed. David Harp & Nina Feldman. LC 96-67942. Orig. Title: The New Three Minute Meditator. 208p. 1996. pap. 12.95 (*1-57224-054-7*) New Harbinger.

***Three Minute Therapy: Change Your Thinking, Change Your Life.** Michael R. Edelstein & David R. Steele. LC 96-78374. 210p. 1997. 21.95 (*0-944435-42-4*) Glenbridge Pub.

Three-Minute Thrillers: The Oozing Eyeball & Other Hasty Horrors. Eric Elfman. (Illus.). 96p. (J). (gr. 4-7). 1994. pap. 4.95 (*1-56565-138-3*) Lowell Hse Juvenile.

***Three-Minute Timings for Typing.** 84p. 1983. teacher ed. 6.95 (*0-89420-243-X*) Natl Book.

Three-Minute Timings for Typing. 2nd ed. George S. Rhodes. Ed. by Calfrey C. Calhoun. 81p. 1983. pap. text ed. 5.95 (*0-89420-228-6*, 296951) Natl Book.

Three Miseries of Barbary: Plague, Famine, Civill Warre. George Wilkins. LC 77-26339. (English Experience Ser.: No. 178). 32p. 1969. reprint ed. 20.00 (*90-221-0178-9*) Walter J Johnson.

Three Modern Italian Poets: Saba, Ungaretti, Montale. 2nd ed. Joseph Cary. LC 93-12940. 400p. 1993. pap. text ed. 16.95 (*0-226-09527-4*) U Ch Pr.

Three Modern Novelists: Soseki, Tanizaki, Kawabata. Van C. Gessel. Ed. by Brase. (Biographies Ser.). (Illus.). 176p. (Orig.). 1993. pap. 10.00 (*4-7700-1652-2*) Kodansha.

Three Modern Seers. Havelock Ellis. 1972. 59.95 (*0-8490-1211-2*) Gordon Pr.

Three Month Curriculum for the Beginning Synchronized Swimming Class. Charlotte Davis & Dawn Bean. 55p. (Orig.). pap. text ed. 10.00 (*0-911543-08-2*) US Synch Swim.

Three Months in a Workshop: A Practical Study. Paul Gohre. LC 74-38277. (Evolution of Capitalism Ser.). 236p. 1972. reprint ed. 28.95 (*0-405-04121-7*) Ayer.

Three Months in the Southern States: April - June 1863. Arthur J. Fremantle. LC 90-46246. (Illus.). xxix, 329p. 1991. reprint ed. pap. 12.95 (*0-8032-6875-0*, Bison Books) U of Nebr Pr.

Three Months in the Southern States: April to June, 1863. Arthur J. Fremantle. LC 72-107514. 309p. 1970. reprint ed. text ed. 35.00 (*0-8371-3761-6*, FTM&, Greenwood Pr) Greenwood.

Three Months in the Southern States: The 1863 War Diary of an English Soldier. Arthur J. Fremantle. 1991. 24.95 (*0-9616844-7-X*) Greenhouse Pub.

Three Months' Residence at Nablus: And an Account of the Modern Samaritans. John Mills. LC 77-87610. reprint ed. 37.50 (*0-404-16434-X*) AMS Pr.

Three More Novels: Vainglory, Inclinations, & Caprice. Ronald Firbank. LC 86-2363. (New Directions Classics Ser.). 448p. 1986. pap. 9.95 (*0-8112-0975-X*, NDP614) New Directions.

Three More Plays for Reading. Tom Bowie. 1988. 22.95 (*0-932508-08-1*) Seven Oaks.

Three More Schools of Education. Ed. by Erwin V. Johanningmeier. (Monograph Ser.). 1986. 3.00 (*0-933669-37-2*) Soc Profs Ed.

Three Mormon Classics. deluxe ed. Compiled by Preston Nibley. 9.95 (*0-88494-049-7*) Bookcraft Inc.

Three Mothers & a Cradle: Rock-a-Bye Baby; Cradle Song; Beginnings. Debbie Macomber et al. (Silhouette Promo Ser.). 1995. mass mkt. 4.99 (*0-373-48335-X*, 1-48335-3) Harlequin Bks.

Three Mothers, Three Daughters: Palestinian Women's Stories. Michael Gorkin & Rafiqa Othman. LC 95-43324. (Illus.). 263p. (C). 1996. 24.95 (*0-520-20329-1*) U CA Pr.

Three Motives for Murder. large type ed. Roy Winsor. 1978. 25.99 (*0-7089-0087-9*) Ulverscroft.

Three Murders & It's Only Monday. Pat Cook. 71p. 1990. pap. 5.00 (*0-87129-068-5*, T82) Dramatic Pub.

Three Musicians. Rod Townley. LC 77-826861. (Illus.). 96p. (Orig.). 1978. pap. 6.00 (*0-912292-43-1*) Smith.

***Three Muskateers.** Alexandre Dumas. Ed. by Malvina Vogel. (Great Illustrated Classics Ser.: Vol. 15). (Illus.). 240p. (J). (gr. 3-6). 1990. 9.95 (*0-86611-966-3*) Playmore Inc.

Three Musketeers. (Classics Ser.). 56p. (J). 3.50 (*0-7214-1753-1*, Ladybrd) Penguin.

***Three Musketeers.** (Classics Illustrated Study Guides Ser.). (Illus.). (Orig.). 1997. mass mkt. write for info. (*1-57840-029-5*) Acclaim Bks.

Three Musketeers. Alexander Dumas. (Illus.). 56p. (J). (gr. 2-4). 1996. pap. 2.99 (*0-7214-5610-3*, Ladybrd) Penguin.

Three Musketeers. Alexandre Dumas. LC 93-71247. (Junior Novel Ser.). (J). (gr. 4-7). 1993. pap. 3.50 (*1-56282-590-9*) Disney Pr.

Three Musketeers. Alexandre Dumas. (Airmont Classics Ser.). (J). (gr. 8 up). 1966. mass mkt. 3.95 (*0-8049-0127-9*, CL-127) Airmont.

Three Musketeers. Alexandre Dumas. 1976. 29.95 (*0-8488-1295-6*) Amereon Ltd.

Three Musketeers. Alexandre Dumas. 1993. mass mkt. 5.95 (*0-451-52594-9*, Sig Classics) NAL-Dutton.

Three Musketeers. Alexandre Dumas. (Classics Ser.). 1987. pap. 3.50 (*0-14-035054-3*, Puffin) Puffin Bks.

Three Musketeers. Alexandre Dumas. (Illustrated Junior Library). (Illus.). (J). (gr. 4-6). 1953. 15.95 (*0-448-06024-8*, G&D) Putnam Pub Group.

***Three Musketeers.** Peter Glassman. (J). Date not set. write for info. (*0-688-14583-3*, Morrow Junior) Morrow.

Three Musketeers. abr. ed. Alexandre Dumas. (Puffin Classics Ser.). 224p. (YA). (gr. 5 up). 1995. pap. 3.99 (*0-14-036747-0*) Puffin Bks.

Three Musketeers. adapted ed. Alexandre Dumas. 1976. pap. 5.25 (*0-8222-1140-8*) Dramatists Play.

Three Musketeers: Acting Edition. Alexander Dumas. Tr. by Lord Sudley. 720p. 1982. pap. 8.95 (*0-14-044025-9*, Penguin Classics) Viking Penguin.

***Three Musketeers: Acting Edition.** Alexandre Dumas. (Illustrated Classics Collection 2). 64p. 1994. pap. 4.95 (*0-7854-0675-1*, 40421) Am Guidance.

Three Musketeers: Acting Edition. Alexandre Dumas. (Illus.). 96p. 1994. pap. text ed. 1.00 (*0-486-28326-7*) Dover.

Three Musketeers: Acting Edition. Alexandre Dumas. (World's Classics Ser.). 696p. 1992. pap. 7.95 (*0-19-282751-0*) OUP.

Three Musketeers: Acting Edition. Alexandre Dumas. (Regents Illustrated Classics Ser.). 62p. (YA). (gr. 7-12). 1987. pap. text ed. 3.75 (*0-13-920463-6*, 20533) Prentice ESL.

Three Musketeers: Acting Edition. Alexandre Dumas. LC 93-42782. (Bullseye Step into Classics Ser.). 108p. (J). (gr. 2-6). 1994. pap. 3.99 (*0-679-86017-7*, Bullseye Bks) Random Bks Yng Read.

Three Musketeers: Acting Edition. Alexandre Dumas. (J). 1994. mass mkt. 4.99 (*0-8125-3602-9*) Tor Bks.

Three Musketeers: Acting Edition. abr. ed. Alexandre Dumas. Tr. & Rev. by Eleanor Hochman. 608p. (J). (gr. 7). 1991. reprint ed. pap. 5.95 (*0-451-52547-7*, W8107, Sig Classics) NAL-Dutton.

Three Musketeers: Acting Edition. unabridged ed. Alexandre Dumas. Tr. by Lowell Bair from FRE. 560p. (J). 1984. mass mkt. 5.95 (*0-553-21337-7*, Bantam Classics) Bantam.

Three Musketeers: Acting Edition. Alexandre Dumas. 1984. reprint ed. lib. bdg. 28.95 (*0-89968-148-4*, Lghtyr Pr) Buccaneer Bks.

Three Musketeers: Student Activity Book. Marcia Sohl & Gerald Dackerman. (Now Age Illustrated Ser.). (Illus.). (J). (gr. 4-10). 1976. student ed. 1.25 (*0-88301-197-2*) Pendulum Pr.

Three Musketeers Notes. James L. Roberts. 86p. (Orig.). 1989. pap. text ed. 3.95 (*0-8220-1300-2*) Cliffs.

***Three Musketeers Readalong.** Alexandre Dumas. (Illustrated Classics Collection 2). 64p. 1994. pap. 14.95 incl. audio (*0-7854-0691-3*, 40423) Am Guidance.

Three Muslim Sages. Seyyed H. Nasr. LC 75-14430. 192p. (C). 1976. reprint ed. pap. text ed. 15.00 (*0-88206-500-9*) Caravan Bks.

Three Mysteries of Jesus. Glenn Clark. 1978. 1.95 (*0-910924-85-6*) Macalester.

Three Names. Patricia MacLachlan. LC 90-4444. (Charlotte Zolotow Bk.). (Illus.). 32p. (J). (gr. k-4). 1991. 14.95 (*0-06-024035-0*); lib. bdg. 14.89 (*0-06-024036-9*) HarpC Child Bks.

Three Names. Patricia MacLachlan. LC 90-4444. (Illus.). 32p. (J). (gr. k-4). 1994. pap. 5.95 (*0-06-443360-9*, Trophy) HarpC Child Bks.

Three Nanny Goats Gruff. Carol Kaplan & Sandi Becker. (Illus.). 33p. (J). (ps). 1989. 17.00 (*0-88734-409-7*) Players Pr.

Three Napoleonic Battles. Harold T. Parker. LC 82-21082. (Illus.). xxiii, 235p. 1983. reprint ed. pap. text ed. 17.95 (*0-8223-0547-X*) Duke.

Three Native American Learning Stories: Who Speaks for Wolf; Winter White & Summer Gold; & Many Circles, Many Paths, 3 bks., Set. Paula Underwood. Ed. by Jeanne L. Slobod. (Illus.). 172p. (Orig.). (C). 1995. boxed, pap. 28.00 (*1-879678-12-8*) Tribe Two Pr.

Three Nativity Plays for Christmas. Linda Aranda. 25p. (Orig.). 1994. pap. 6.95 (*1-57514-233-3*, 6004) Encore Perform Pub.

Three NBs of Julian Drew. James M. Deem. LC 93-39306. (J). 1994. 15.95 (*0-395-69453-1*) HM.

3 NBs of Julian Drew. James M. Deem. 176p. (YA). 1996. mass mkt. 4.50 (*0-380-72587-8*, Flare) Avon.

Three Negro Classics. Incl. Up from Slavery. Booker T. Washington. 1976. (*0-318-50971-7*); Souls of Black Folk. W. E. B. Du Bois. (*0-318-50972-5*); Autobiography of an Ex-Colored Man. James Weldon Johnson. (*0-318-50973-3*); 1976. mass mkt. 5.99 (*0-380-01581-1*) Avon.

Three Nephites: Substance & Significance of the Legend in Folklore. Lee H. Hector. Ed. by Richard M. Dorson. LC 77-70608. (International Folklore Ser.). 1977. reprint ed. lib. bdg. 17.95 (*0-405-10105-8*) Ayer.

Three New Mexico Chronicles. Incl. Exposicion. Pedro B Pino. LC 67-24722. 1967. (*0-318-50905-9*); Ojeada. Antonio Barreiro. LC 67-24722. 1967. (*0-318-50906-7*); Addition. Jose A. De Escudero. LC 67-24722. 1967. (*0-318-50907-5*); LC 67-24722. (Quivira Society Publications). 342p. 1967. reprint ed. 19.95 (*0-405-00085-5*) Ayer.

Three New Species of Centrolenid Frogs from the Pacific Versant of Ecuador & Colombia. William E. Duellman. (Occasional Papers: No. 88). 9p. 1981. 1.00 (*0-317-04856-2*) U KS Nat Hist Mus.

Three New Species of Darters (Percidae, Etheostoma) of the Subgenus Nanostoma from Kentucky & Tennessee. Lawrence M. Page & Brooks M. Burr. (Occasional Papers: No. 101). (Illus.). 20p. 1982. 1.00 (*0-317-04835-X*) U KS Nat Hist Mus.

Three New York Composers: The Collected Works of Lewis Edson, Lewis Edson Jr., & Nathaniel Billings. Ed. by Karl Kroeger. LC 95-32688. (Music of the New American Nation Ser.: Vol. 3). (Illus.). 176p. 1995. text ed. 75.00 (*0-8153-2170-8*) Garland.

Three Nigerian Emirates: A Study in Oral History. Victor N. Low. LC 74-176163. 328p. reprint ed. pap. 93.50 (*0-317-27770-7*, 2015424) Bks Demand.

Three Northumbrian Poems. Ed. by A. H. Smith. (Old English Ser.). 1968. pap. text ed. 4.95 (*0-89197-571-3*) Irvington.

Three Northumbrian Poems. Ed. by A. H. Smith. 66p. 1978. pap. text ed. 10.95 (*0-85989-078-3*, Pub. by Univ Exeter Pr UK) Northwestern U Pr.

Three Notelets on Shakespeare. W. J. Thoms. LC 72-3737. (Studies in Shakespeare: No. 24). 1972. reprint ed. lib. bdg. 49.95 (*0-8383-1570-4*) M S G Haskell Hse.

Three Notes on Longfellow. Carl L. Johnson. (American Literature Ser.: No. 49). 1970. reprint ed. pap. 39.95 (*0-8383-0047-2*) M S G Haskell Hse.

Three Novellas. Eliza Haywood. Ed. by Earla A. Wilputte. (Early Women Writers 1650-1800 Ser.: Vol. 5). 150p. 1995. pap. 14.95 (*0-937191-58-2*) Colleagues Pr Inc.

***Three Novellas.** Eliza Haywood. Ed. by Earla A. Wilputte. (Early Women Writers 1650-1800 Ser.: Vol. 5). 150p. 1995. pap. 14.95 (*0-87013-428-0*) Colleagues Pr Inc.

Three Novellas. Laura McGhee et al. Ed. by Philip Miller. 178p. (Orig.). 1993. pap. 10.00 (*0-939391-17-1*) B Woodley Pr.

***Three Novellas.** Richard Plant et al. (Texas Review Southern & Southwestern Breakthrough Ser.). 160p. (Orig.). 1997. pap. 10.00 (*1-881515-10-9*) TX Review Pr.

Three Novellas: A Truth Lover - Pegan's Pilgrimage Clapperton. John Herdman. LC 87-63146. 200p. (Orig.). 8800. pap. 10.95 (*0-948275-37-5*) Dufour.

Three Novels. V. S. Naipaul. LC 82-47819. 1982. 18.95 (*0-394-52847-6*) Knopf.

Three Novels: Hordubal, Meteor, an Ordinary Life. Karel Capek. Tr. by M. Weatherall & R. Weatherall from CZE. LC 89-23957. 480p. 1990. reprint ed. pap. 13.95 (*0-945774-08-7*, PG5038.C2A28) Catbird Pr.

Three Novels: Molloy; Malone Dies; The Unnamable. Samuel Beckett. LC 59-13886. 422p. 1955. reprint ed. pap. 14.00 (*0-8021-5091-8*, Grove) Grove-Atltic.

Three Novels: Uncle Tom's Cabin; The Minister's Wooing; Oldtown Folks. Harriet Beecher Stowe. Ed. by Kathryn K. Sklar. LC 81-18629. 1478p. 1982. 40.00 (*0-940450-01-1*) Library of America.

***Three Novels & a Story.** William Mulvihill. 450p. 1995. pap. write for info. (*0-9645875-6-4*) Brickiln Pr.

***Three Novels & a Story: Sagaponack, Ava, Speakeasy, Wrackline.** William Mulvihill. Ed. by D. Zebrowski. 447p. (Orig.). 1996. pap. 16.00 (*0-9645875-0-5*) Brickiln Pr.

Three Novels of F. Scott Fitzgerald. F. Scott Fitzgerald. Bd. with Great Gatsby.; Tender is the Night. F. Scott Fitzgerald. ; Last Tycoon. F. Scott Fitzgerald. 634p. 1979. Set pap. text ed. write for info. (*0-02-337980-4*, Macmillan Coll) P-H.

Three Novels of Old New York. Edith Wharton. 1995. pap. 11.00 (*0-02-038314-2*) Macmillan.

Three Novels of Old New York, 3 bks in 1. Edith Wharton. 1994. 11.99 (*0-517-11828-9*) Random Hse Value.

***Three Novels of Old New York.** Edith Wharton. 1997. pap. 16.95 (*0-14-018984-X*) Viking Penguin.

Three Novels of the Snopes Family: The Hamlet, The Town, The Mansion. William Faulkner. 1088p. 1994. 22.00 (*0-679-60092-2*) Random.

Three Number Author Tables. G. C. Makkar. 200p. 1974. 6.00 (*0-88065-153-9*, Messers Today & Tomorrow) Scholarly Pubns.

Three O'Clock. large type ed. Doris Howe. 448p. 1989. 25.99 (*0-7089-2026-8*) Ulverscroft.

An Asterisk (*) at the beginning of an entry indicates that the title is appearing in BIP for the first time.

***3:00 to 6:00 P.M. Planning Programs for Young Adolescents.** Gayle Dorman. 351p. 1985. ring bd. 150.00 (*1-57482-809-6*) Search Inst.

Three Odes of Keats. E. L. Marilla. (Essays & Studies on English Language & Literature: Vol. 24). (Orig.). 1962. pap. 25.00 (*0-8115-0222-8*) Periodicals Srv.

Three of a Kind. (J). 1985. pap. 1.95 (*0-590-33706-8*) Scholastic Inc.

Three of a Kind, No. 1: With Friends Like These, Who Needs Enemies. Marilyn Kaye. 144p. (J). (gr. 4-7). 1994. mass mkt. 3.50 (*0-06-106001-1*, Harp PBks) HarpC.

***3 of 10: Poems.** Hank Lazer. LC 96-3079. 1996. write for info. (*0-925904-18-X*) Chax Pr.

Three of the Best. J. D. Lewis. (C). 1989. 23.00 (*0-7223-2331-X*, Pub. by A H S Ltd UK) St Mut.

Three of Us. Samantha Day. (Romance Ser.). 1994. mass mkt. 2.99 (*0-373-03297-8*, 1-03297-8) Harlequin Bks.

Three Old English Elegies. Ed. by Leslie. 108p. 1988. pap. text ed. 13.95 (*0-85989-184-4*, Pub. by Univ Exeter Pr UK) Northwestern U Pr.

Three Old English Prose Texts. Ed. by S. Rypins. (EETS, OS Ser.: No. 161). 1974. reprint ed. 45.00 (*0-527-00158-9*) Periodicals Srv.

***Three on Community.** Wendell Berry et al. 68p. (Orig.). 1996. pap. 25.00 (*0-931659-27-2*) Limberlost Pr.

***Three on Community.** deluxe limited ed. Wendell Berry et al. 68p. (Orig.). 1996. 175.00 (*0-931659-28-0*) Limberlost Pr.

Three on Technology: New Photographs by Robert Cumming. Leo Marx & Alan Trachtenberg. LC 88-2678. (Illus.). 72p. 1988. pap. 15.00 (*0-938437-21-6*) MIT List Visual Arts.

Three One Act Plays by Jason Miller. Jason Miller. 1972. pap. 5.25 (*0-8222-0759-1*) Dramatists Play.

Three Orations in Favour of the Olynthians with Fower Orations Against King Philip. Demosthenes. Tr. by Thomas Wilson. LC 68-54637. (English Experience Ser.: No. 54). 200p. 1968. reprint ed. 27.50 (*90-221-0054-5*) Walter J Johnson.

Three Orchestral Works in Full Score. Johannes Brahms. 1984. pap. 8.95 (*0-486-24637-X*) Dover.

Three Orders: Feudal Society Imagined. Georges Duby. Tr. by Arthur Goldhammer. LC 80-13158. 392p. 1982. pap. text ed. 19.95 (*0-226-16772-0*) U Ch Pr.

Three Orphan Kittens. Margaret Wise Brown. LC 94-71790. (Illus.). 32p. 1995. 13.95 (*0-7868-3020-4*) Disney Pr.

Three Orphan Kittens. Margaret Wise Brown. LC 94-71790. (Illus.). 32p. 1995. lib. bdg. 13.89 (*0-7868-5010-8*) Disney Pr.

Three Othellos. Daniel Amneus. 1986. 15.00 (*0-9610864-2-4*); pap. 10.00 (*0-9610864-3-2*) Primrose Pr.

Three Out of Four Like Spaghetti: Data & Fractions. Mary Berle-Carman et al. Ed. by Ann Marie Brennan et al. (Investigations in Number, Data, & Space Ser.). (Illus.). 79p. (Orig.). 1994. teacher ed., pap. 22.95 (*0-86651-818-5*, DS21256) Seymour Pubns.

***Three Out of Four Like Spaghetti: Data & Fractions.** rev. ed. Mary Berle-Carman et al. Ed. by Catherine Anderson & Beverly Cory. (Investigations in Number, Data, & Space Ser.). (Illus.). 81p. (YA). (gr. 4 up). 1997. pap. text ed. 22.95 (*1-57232-753-7*, 47000) Seymour Pubns.

***3 Packaging Design Systems.** Photographic Book Company Staff. 1987. 19.95 (*0-688-07249-6*) Morrow.

***Three Painters of America.** Date not set. 26.95 (*0-405-01546-1*) Ayer.

Three Palladins. Harold Lamb. 1977. 12.00 (*0-686-27901-8*) D M Grant.

Three Pamphlets on the Jacobean Antifeminist Controversy. LC 78-5847. 1978. reprint ed. 50.00 (*0-8201-1307-7*) Schol Facsimiles.

Three Pandas Planting: Counting down to Help the Earth. Megan Halsey. LC 93-22971. (Illus.). 40p. (J). (ps-2). 1994. lib. bdg. 14.95 (*0-02-742035-3*, Bradbury S&S) S&S Childrens.

Three Papers on Algebras & Their Representations. V. N. Gerasimov et al. LC 93-20884. (Translations Ser.: Series 2, Vol. 156). 216p. 1993. 98.00 (*0-8218-7503-5*, TRANS2/156) Am Math.

Three Papers on Dynamical Systems. A. G. Kusnirenko et al. LC 81-4981. (Translations Ser.: Series 2, Vol. 116). 169p. 1981. 51.00 (*0-8218-3066-X*, TRANS2/116) Am Math.

Three Papers on the History & Language of the Hittites see Mediterranean Studies

Three-Part Airs for Two Treble Viols or Violins, Bass Viol & Continuo, Vol. I. John Jenkins. Ed. by Andrew Ashbee. (Viol Consort Ser.: No. 17). i, 34p. 1993. pap. text ed. 18.00 (*1-56571-071-1*, VC017) PRB Prods.

Three-Part Airs for Two Treble Viols or Violins, Bass Viol & Continuo, Vol. II. John Jenkins. Ed. by Andrew Ashbee. (Viol Consort Series: No. 21). 35p. 1997. pap. text ed. 18.00 (*1-56571-102-5*) PRB Prods.

Three Part Conductus in Related Sources. Ed. by Gordon A. Anderson. (Gesamtausgaben - Collected Works Ser.: Vol. X, Pt. 9). 160p. 1986. lib. bdg. 107.00 (*0-931902-24-X*) Inst Mediaeval Mus.

Three Partners, & Other Tales. Bret Harte. LC 76-37547. (Short Story Index Reprint Ser.). 1977. reprint ed. 25.95 (*0-8369-4106-3*) Ayer.

Three Paths to Glory: A Season on the Hardwood with Duke, N. C. State & N. Carolina. Jacobs. 1994. pap. 13.95 (*0-02-052291-6*) Mac Lib Ref.

Three Paths to Leadership: A Study of Women on the Minnesota Supreme Court. Christine Krueger. (Illus.). 20p. (Orig.). (C). 1994. pap. 8.00 (*0-9633686-4-8*) Hamline Univ.

Three Paths to the Lake. Ingeborg Bachmann. Tr. by Mary F. Gilbert & Mark Anderson from GER. LC 88-21243. (Modern German Voices Ser.). Orig. Title: Simultan. 212p. (C). 1989. 29.95 (*0-8419-1070-7*) Holmes & Meier.

Three Paths to the Lake. Ingeborg Bachmann. Tr. by Mary F. Gilbert from GER. LC 96-53686. (Portico Paperback Ser.). Orig. Title: Simultan. 212p. (C). 1997. reprint ed. pap. 14.00 (*0-8419-1071-5*) Holmes & Meier.

Three Penny Lane. Fielding Dawson. LC 80-27344. 150p. (Orig.). 1981. pap. 5.00 (*0-87685-446-3*) Black Sparrow.

Three Penny Lane. deluxe ed. Fielding Dawson. LC 80-27344. 150p. (Orig.). 1981. 20.00 (*0-87685-447-1*) Black Sparrow.

Three Penny Opera, Baal & the Mother, Vol. 1. Bertolt Brecht. Tr. by Ralph Manheim et al. from GER. LC 93-16334. 248p. (C). 1993. pap. 11.95 (*1-55970-188-9*) Arcade Pub Inc.

Three People. Isabel Alden. (Grace Livingston Hill Ser.: Vol. 4). 1995. pap. 5.99 (*0-8423-3178-6*) Tyndale.

Three Per Cent Solution & the Future of NATO. Foreign Policy Research Institute Staff. LC 80-27824. (Western Security Studies Program). 134p. reprint ed. pap. 38.20 (*0-7837-1782-2*, 2041980) Bks Demand.

Three Percent Solution & the Future of NATO. Foreign Policy Research Institute Staff. LC 80-27824. 118p. (Orig.). 1981. pap. 6.95 (*0-910191-02-6*) For Policy Res.

***Three Perfect Men.** Evelyn Palfrey. LC 96-94883. 310p. (Orig.). 1997. pap. 10.95 (*0-9654190-0-2*) Moon Child.

Three "Perfect Novels" - & What They Have in Common. limited ed. Louis Auchincloss. 1981. 20.00 (*0-89723-025-6*) Bruccoli.

Three Perfect Peaches: A French Folktale. Cynthia DeFelice & Mary DeMarsh. LC 94-24872. 32p. (J). (gr. k-3). 1995. 15.95 (*0-531-06872-2*); lib. bdg. 16.99 (*0-531-08722-0*) Orchard Bks Watts.

Three Perfections: Chinese Painting, Poetry & Calligraphy. Michael Sullivan. LC 80-18189. (Illus.). 64p. 1980. pap. 11.95 (*0-8076-0997-8*) Braziller.

***Three Perils of Man: War, Women & Witchcraft.** James Hogg. 600p. 1997. pap. 14.95 (*0-86241-646-9*, Pub. by Canongate Bks UK) Interlink Pub.

Three Perils of Woman. James Hogg. Ed. by David Groves et al. (Collected Works of James Hogg). 480p. 1995. 50.00 (*0-7486-0477-4*, Pub. by Edinburgh U Pr UK) Col U Pr.

Three-Personed God: The Trinity As a Mystery of Salvation. William J. Hill. LC 81-18012. 354p. 1988. reprint ed. pap. 16.95 (*0-8132-0676-6*) Cath U Pr.

Three Perspectives on Kundalini. Gopi Krishna. (C). 1994. 8.00 (*81-86112-16-2*, Pub. by UBS Pubs Dist II) S Asia.

Three-Phase Cage Induction Motors: Formerly OCMA Specification Number Elec. 1. EEMUA Staff. 1988. 125.00 (*0-85931-137-6*, Pub. by EEMUA UK) St Mut.

Three-Phase Electrical Machine Systems: Computer Simulation. John R. Smith & Meng-Jen Chen. (Electronic & Electrical Engineering Research Ser.). 268p. 1993. text ed. 106.00 (*0-471-94053-4*) Wiley.

Three-Phase Electricity. Wolfgang Weiske. (Siemens Programmed Instruction Ser.: 15). 64p. reprint ed. pap. 25.00 (*0-317-27748-0*, 2052091) Bks Demand.

Three-Phase Motor Winding Data from Simple Measurements. 3rd ed. Samuel Heller. (Illus.). 55p. (Orig.). 1961. pap. 61.00 (*0-911740-00-7*) Datarule.

Three-Phase Power & Its Measurements. Hans-Joachim Gaus. (Siemens Programmed Instruction Ser.: 16). 67p. reprint ed. pap. 25.00 (*0-317-27745-6*, 2052092) Bks Demand.

***Three-Phase Sparged Reactors.** Nigam & Schumpa. (Topics in Chemical Engineering Ser.). 1996. text ed. 250.00 (*2-88124-909-4*) Gordon & Breach.

Three Phases of Ease. Jerry Buchanan. 1993. pap. 4.95 (*0-930668-09-X*) Towers Club.

Three Phases of Matter. 2nd ed. Alan J. Walton. (Illus.). 494p. 1983. pap. 35.00 (*0-19-851953-2*) OUP.

Three Phi Beta Kappa Addresses. Charles F. Adams, Jr. (Works of Charles Francis Adams Jr. (1835-1915)). 1989. reprint ed. lib. bdg. 79.00 (*0-7812-1415-7*) Rprt Serv.

Three Philippine Ethnic-Hero Plays. Mig A. Enriquez. viii, 145p. (Orig.). (C). 1991. pap. text ed. 10.75 (*971-10-0448-8*, Pub. by New Day Pub PH) Cellar.

Three Philosophers: Lavoisier, Priestley & Cavendish. Wallace R. Aykroyd. LC 77-98808. 227p. 1970. reprint ed. text ed. 59.75 (*0-8371-2890-0*, AYTB, Greenwood Pr) Greenwood.

Three Philosophies of Life: Ecclesiastes: Life as Vanity, Job: Life as Suffering, Song of Songs: Life as Love. Peter Kreeft. LC 89-84054. 141p. (Orig.). 1989. pap. text ed. 9.95 (*0-89870-262-3*) Ignatius Pr.

Three Physico-Theological Discourses: Primitive Chaos, & Creation of the World, the General Deluge, Its Causes & Effects. John Ray. Ed. by Claude C. Albritton, Jr. LC 77-6538. (History of Geology Ser.). 1978. reprint ed. lib. bdg. 37.95 (*0-405-10457-X*) Ayer.

Three Piano Works. Cecile Chaminade. Incl. Sonata in C Minor, Opus 21. LC 79-1501. 1979. (*0-318-51598-9*); Etude Symphonique, Opus 28. LC 79-1501. 1979. (*0-318-51599-7*); Six Concert Etudes, Opus 35. LC 79-1501. 1979. (*0-318-51600-4*); LC 79-1501. (Women Composers Ser.: No. 2). 1979. reprint ed. 27.50 (*0-306-79551-5*) Da Capo.

Three Pieces. Ntozake Shange. 160p. 1992. pap. 10.95 (*0-312-07872-2*) St Martin.

Three Pieces for Flute, Clarinet & Bassoon 1926. W. Piston. 1986. pap. text ed. 18.50 (*0-7935-2205-6*) H Leonard.

Three Pieces for Flute Solo. 8p. pap. 5.95 (*0-7935-5022-X*, 50482257) H Leonard.

Three Pieces from Schindler's List for Itzhak Perlman: Violin & Piano. J. Williams. 20p. 1994. pap. 12.95 (*0-7935-3584-0*, 00849954) H Leonard.

Three Pies Hot! A Race to Nowhere. Robert P. Welsh. LC 93-79284. 288p. 1993. pap. 10.95 (*0-9637639-0-3*) Glass Onion.

***Three Pillars.** (Vampire). (Illus.). (Orig.). 1997. pap. 18.00 (*1-56504-288-3*, 2809) White Wolf.

***Three Pillars of Judaism: A Search for Faith & Values.** Jonathan Wittenberg. 112p. (Orig.). 1996. pap. 17.00 (*0-334-02665-2*, SCM Pr) TPI PA.

Three Pillars of Liberty: Securing Political Rights & Freedom in the United Kingdom. Francesca Klug et al. (Democratic Audit of the United Kingdom Ser.). 400p. 1996. pap. 24.95 (*0-415-09642-1*); text ed. 74.95 (*0-415-09641-3*) Routledge.

Three Pillars of Zen. Roshi P. Kapleau. 430p. 1989. pap. 12.95 (*0-385-26093-8*, Anchor NY) Doubleday.

Three Pioneer Rapides Families. G. M. Stafford. 1968. 32.50 (*0-87511-631-0*) Claitors.

Three Pioneer Tennessee Documents: Donelson's Journal, Cumberland Compact, Minutes of Cumberland Court. LC 64-64789. 52p. reprint ed. pap. 25.00 (*0-317-26104-5*, 2024382) Bks Demand.

Three Places in New Inkland. David Cole et al. LC 77-72826. 1977. pap. 5.95 (*0-9605610-1-3*) P Zelevansky.

Three Plays. Incl. Father. (*0-318-55107-1*); Miss Julie. August Strindberg. Ed. by Peter Watts. (Orig.). 1958. (*0-318-55108-X*); Easter. (*0-318-55109-8*); (Classics Ser.). 176p. 1958. pap. 9.95 (*0-14-044082-8*, Penguin Classics) Viking Penguin.

Three Plays. Incl. Miss Julie. August Strindberg. (Orig.). pap. (*0-318-51185-1*); Outlaw. (*0-318-51186-X*); Stronger. August Strindberg. pap. (*0-318-51187-8*); pap. 5.95 (*0-8283-1458-6*) Branden Pub Co.

Three Plays. Kobo Abe. 1993. 32.50 (*0-231-08280-0*) Col U Pr.

Three Plays. John Ashbery. 1978. 15.00 (*0-915990-12-1*); pap. 7.50 (*0-915990-13-X*) Z Pr.

Three Plays. Sebastian Barry & O'Toole. 1996. pap. 15.95 (*0-413-69890-4*, Pub. by Methuen UK) Heinemann.

Three Plays. Nissim Ezekiel. (Writers Workshop Bluebird Ser.). 95p. 1975. pap. text ed. 4.00 (*0-88253-659-1*) Ind-US Inc.

Three Plays. John Ford. Ed. & Intro. by Keith Sturgess. (Classics Ser.). 416p. 1971. pap. 10.95 (*0-14-043059-8*, Penguin Classics) Viking Penguin.

***Three Plays.** Arthur Kopit. LC 97-7532. 1997. pap. text ed. 13.00 (*0-8090-1595-1*) Hill & Wang.

Three Plays. Paul Metcalf. LC 92-85260. 138p. 1993. pap. 11.95 (*0-933598-46-7*) NC Wesleyan Pr.

Three Plays. M. J. Molloy. 1975. 10.00 (*0-912262-30-3*) Proscenium.

Three Plays. Mother. 101p. (Orig.). 1989. pap. 3.95 (*0-317-99973-7*, Pub. by Sri Aurob Ashram Trust II) Auromere.

Three Plays. Eugene O'Neill. 1995. pap. 11.00 (*0-679-76396-1*) Random.

Three Plays. Gwyn Thomas. 240p. 1990. pap. 15.95 (*1-85411-017-9*, Pub. by Seren Bks UK) Dufour.

Three Plays. Mario Vargas Llosa. Tr. by David Graham-Young. 1990. pap. 11.95 (*0-374-52265-0*, Noonday) FS&G.

Three Plays. Mario Vargas Llosa. 1990. 30.00 (*0-8090-9367-7*) Hill & Wang.

Three Plays. John Webster. (English Library). 464p. 1973. pap. 11.95 (*0-14-043081-4*, Penguin Classics) Viking Penguin.

Three Plays. Thornton Wilder. Bd. with Our Town. Ed. by Thornton Wilder. LC 85-42603.; Skin of Our Teeth. Thornton Wilder. LC 85-42603.; Matchmaker. LC 85-42603. LC 85-42603. 416p. (C). 1985. Set pap. 14.00 (*0-06-091293-6*, PL 1293, PL) HarpC.

Three Plays. limited ed. Paul Metcalf. LC 92-85260. 138p. 1993. pap. 20.00 (*0-933598-47-5*) NC Wesleyan Pr.

Three Plays. George Gordon Byron. LC 90-19523. 456p. 1990. reprint ed. 65.00 (*1-85477-038-1*, Pub. by Woodstock Bks UK) Cassell.

Three Plays. Noel Leslie. LC 79-50026. (One-Act Plays in Reprint Ser.). 1980. reprint ed. 20.00 (*0-8486-2050-X*) Roth Pub Inc.

Three Plays. Joyce Carol Oates. LC 80-20210. 157p. 1980. reprint ed. 12.95 (*0-86538-001-5*); reprint ed. pap. 7.95 (*0-86538-002-3*) Ontario Rev NJ.

Three Plays. David Pinski. Tr. by Isaac Goldberg from YID. LC 74-29513. (Modern Jewish Experience Ser.). 1975. reprint ed. 23.95 (*0-405-06739-9*) Ayer.

Three Plays: 'Enrico IV', 'Sei Personaggi in Cerca d'Autore', 'La Giara' Luigi Pirandello. Ed. by Felicity Firth. (Italian Texts Ser.). 308p. (ITA.). (C). 1988. text ed. 17.95 (*0-7190-0346-6*, Pub. by Manchester Univ Pr UK) St Martin.

Three Plays: "The Broken Calabash," "Parables for a Season," & "The Reign of Wazobia" Tess A. Onwueme. LC 92-47582. (African American Life Ser.). 174p. 1993. text ed. 29.95 (*0-8143-2444-4*); pap. text ed. 16.95 (*0-8143-2445-2*) Wayne St U Pr.

Three Plays: A Moment in Orbit; Move & Counter-Move; What do You Mean by That? Henry Kitt. 104p. 1991. pap. 6.50 (*0-924694-14-9*) Capricornis.

Three Plays: Absurd Person Singular; Absent Friends; Bedroom Farce. Alan Ayckbourn. LC 78-20339. 230p. 1989. pap. 9.95 (*0-8021-3157-3*, Grove) Grove-Atltic.

***Three Plays: Bagdad Saloon, Beyond Mozambique, Ramona & the White Slaves.** George F. Walker. 200p. Date not set. 13.95 (*0-88910-078-0*, Pub. by Talonbooks CN) Genl Dist Srvs.

Three Plays: Blithe Spirit; Hay Fever; Private Lives. Noel Coward. LC 79-52122. 254p. 1965. reprint ed. pap. 11.95 (*0-8021-5108-6*, E742, Grove) Grove-Atltic.

Three Plays: Blood Wedding; Yerma; The House of Bernarda Alba. Federico Garcia Lorca. Tr. by Michael Dewell & Carmen Zapata. (Illus.). 192p. 1993. pap. 16.00 (*0-374-52332-0*) FS&G.

Three Plays: Juno & the Paycock, The Shadow of a Gunman, & The Plough & the Stars. Sean O'Casey. 218p. 1969. pap. 7.95 (*0-312-80290-0*, Papermac) St Martin.

Three Plays: Naga-mandala; Hayavadana; Tughalaq. Girish Karnad. 228p. (C). 1996. pap. 8.95 (*0-19-563765-8*) OUP.

Three Plays: Naga-Mandala; Hayavadana; Tughlaq. Girish Karnad. 240p. 1994. 24.95 (*0-19-563331-8*) OUP.

Three Plays: Phaedra, Andromache, Britannicus. Jean-Baptiste Racine. Tr. by George Dillon. LC 61-15938. 199p. 1961. pap. text ed. 11.95 (*0-226-15077-1*, P76) U Ch Pr.

Three Plays: Procession, Bhoma, Stale News. Badal Sircar. 1983. pap. 8.00 (*0-8364-0964-7*, Pub. by Seagull Bks II) S Asia.

Three Plays: Striptease, Repeat Performance, the Prophets. Slawomir Mrozek. Tr. by Lola Gruenthal et al. from POL. 168p. (Orig.). 1986. pap. 5.95 (*0-936839-49-X*) Applause Theatre Bk Pubs.

Three Plays: The Black Maskers. The Life of Man. The Sabine Woman. Leonid Andreyev. Tr. by C. Meador & F. Scott from RUS. LC 88-7108. xxvi, 214p. 1989. reprint ed. lib. bdg. 35.00 (*0-86527-388-X*) Fertig.

Three Plays: The Gauntlet, Beyond Our Power, The New System. Bjornstjerne Bjornson. Tr. by Edwin Bjorkman from NOR. LC 87-38139. vi, 280p. 1989. reprint ed. lib. bdg. 35.00 (*0-86527-383-9*) Fertig.

Three Plays: The Weavers, Hannele & the Beaver Coat. Gerhart Hauptmann. Tr. by Horst Frenz & Miles Waggoner from GER. 218p. (C). 1991. reprint ed. pap. text ed. 9.95 (*0-88133-540-1*) Waveland Pr.

Three Plays by Armand Salacrou: The World Is Round, When the Music Stops, Marguerite. Armand Salacrou. LC 67-28877. (Minnesota Drama Editions Ser.: No. 4). 229p. reprint ed. pap. 65.30 (*0-317-29491-1*, 2055909) Bks Demand.

Three Plays by David Garrick. David Garrick. Ed. by Elizabeth P. Stein. LC 67-23858. 1972. reprint ed. 12.95 (*0-405-08556-7*) Ayer.

Three Plays by Eduardo Pavlovsky: Slow Motion, Potestad - Paternity, Pablo. Eduardo Pavlovsky. Ed. by Hilma O. Carter. Tr. & Adapted by Paul Verdier. (Illus.). 160p. (Orig.). 1994. pap. 12.95 (*0-9642024-0-9*) Stages Theatre.

Three Plays by Emmanuel Robles: Plaidoyer Pour un Rebelle (Case for a Rebel), L'Horloge (the Clock), & Porfirio. Emmanuel Robles. Tr. by James A. Kilker from FRE. LC 77-24662. (Illus.). 223p. 1977. 19.95 (*0-8093-0822-3*) S Ill U Pr.

Three Plays by Isaac Chocron, Vol. 4. Isaac E. Chocron. Tr. by Barbara Younoszai & Rossi Irausquin-Johnson. LC 94-17357. (Taft Memorial Fund & University of Cincinnati Studies in Latin American, Chicano, & U. S. Latino Theatre: Vol. 4). 256p. (C). 1995. 39.95 (*0-8204-2320-3*) P Lang Pubng.

Three Plays by Kaufman & Hart: Once in a Lifetime; You Can't Take It with You; The Man Who Came to Dinner. George S. Kaufman & Moss Hart. 240p. 1995. pap. 10.95 (*0-8021-5064-0*, Grove) Grove-Atltic.

***Three Plays by Kobo Abe.** Kobo Abe. 1997. pap. text ed. 16.00 (*0-231-08281-9*) Col U Pr.

***Three Plays by Mae West: Sex the Drag & Pleasure Man.** Ed. by Lillian Schlissel. 256p. 1997. pap. 16.95 (*0-415-90933-3*, Routledge NY) Routledge.

***Three Plays by Mae West: Sex, the Drag & Pleasure Man.** Ed. by Lillian Schlissel. 256p. (C). 1997. text ed. 65.00 (*0-415-90932-5*, Routledge NY) Routledge.

***Three Plays by Mae West: Sex, the Drag, the Pleasure Man.** Mae West & Lillian Schlissel. LC 97-24425. 1997. write for info. (*0-04-159032-5*); pap. write for info. (*0-04-159033-3*) Routledge.

3 Plays by Mart Crowley. Mart Crowley. LC 96-13206. 224p. (Orig.). 1996. pap. text ed. 13.95 (*1-55583-357-8*) Alyson Pubns.

Three Plays by Moreto & Their Adaptation in France, Vol. II. Hilda Rissel. LC 93-40940. (Iberica Ser.). 176p. (C). 1995. 42.95 (*0-8204-2364-5*) P Lang Pubng.

Three Plays by Plautus. Paul Roche. 1984. pap. 7.00 (*0-86516-035-X*) Bolchazy-Carducci.

Three Plays by Terrence McNally. Terrence McNally. 256p. 1990. pap. 11.95 (*0-452-26425-1*, Plume) NAL-Dutton.

Three Plays Crime Criminal. Kinsley. mass mkt. 5.50 (*0-671-67248-7*, WSP) PB.

Three Plays for a Gay Theater. Richard Hall. LC 82-12099. 188p. (Orig.). 1983. pap. 6.95 (*0-912516-73-9*) Grey Fox.

Three Plays for Puritans. George Bernard Shaw. 96p. 1991. pap. 11.95 (*0-14-045028-9*) Viking Penguin.

Three Plays for Reading. Tom Bowie. LC 79-64092. 1979. 22.95 (*0-932508-04-9*) Seven Oaks.

Three Plays of Euripides. Incl. Alcestis. (*0-318-54694-9*); Medea. (*0-318-54695-7*); Bacchae. Euripides. Ed. by Paul Roche. 1974. pap. text ed. (*0-318-54696-5*); 126p. (C). 1974. pap. text ed. 6.95 (*0-393-09312-3*) Norton.

3 Plays: Our Town; The Skin of Our Teeth; The Matchmaker. Thornton Wilder. 416p. 1994. lib. bdg. 37.00 (*0-8095-9149-9*) Borgo Pr.

Three Plays with an Exit. Linda P. Willaims. LC 94-18617. 1995. pap. 12.95 (*0-7734-0007-9*, Mellen Poetry Pr) E Mellen.

Three Plots for Asey Mayo. Phoebe Atwood Taylor. (Asey Mayo Cape Cod Mystery Ser.). 320p. reprint ed. pap. 6.95 (*0-88150-205-7*) Countryman.

Three Poems. John Ashbery. 1989. pap. 8.95 (*0-88001-227-7*) Ecco Pr.

Three Poems. St. Gregory of Nazianzus. Tr. by Denis Meehan from GRE. LC 86-6821. (Fathers of the Church Ser.: Vol. 75). 142p. 1987. 26.95 (*0-8132-0075-X*) Cath U Pr.

Three Poems: Dolphin Skull, Rare Angel & Dark Brown. Michael McClure. LC 94-47326. 256p. 1995. pap. 14.95 (*0-14-058709-8*, Penguin Bks) Viking Penguin.

Three Poems by W. H. Davies: Song Set. Dorothy C. Raemsch. (Illus.). 12p. (Orig.). 1994. pap. 4.00 (*0-9605398-3-2*) D C Raemsch.

Three Poems of Robert Frost. E. Carter. 1987. pap. 8.95 (*0-7935-1326-X*) H Leonard.

Three Poems Osip Mandelstam. E. Firsova. 24p. 1991. pap. 8.95 (*0-7935-1108-9*) H Leonard.

Three Poets. Romulus Linney. 1990. pap. 5.25 (*0-8222-1141-6*) Dramatists Play.

***Three Point Field Goal Offense for Men's & Women's Basketball.** Harry L. Harkins & Jerry Krause. 1997. 15.00 (*1-57167-138-2*) Sagamore Pub.

***3 Points of Purchase.** Retail Reporting Staff. 1995. 55.00 (*0-688-14259-1*) Morrow.

Three Portraits: Hitler, Mussolini, Stalin. Emil Ludwig. LC 78-63689. (Studies in Fascism: Ideology & Practice). 128p. reprint ed. 37.50 (*0-404-16905-8*) AMS Pr.

Three Postcards. rev. ed. Craig Lucas & Craig Carnelia. 1995. pap. 6.00 (*0-8222-1477-6*) Dramatists Play.

Three Pound Universe: Revolutionary Discoveries about the Brain from the Chemistry of Mind to the New Frontiers of the Soul. Judith Hooper & Dick Teresi. (Illus.). 432p. 14.95 (*0-87477-650-3*, Tarcher Putnam) Putnam Pub Group.

***Three Pre-Surrealist Plays.** Maurice Maeterlinck et al. Tr. & Intro. by Maya Slater. (The World's Classics Ser.). (Illus.). 272p. 1997. pap. 11.95 (*0-19-283217-4*) OUP.

Three Predatory Women. Sydney Loch. LC 70-125230. (Short Story Index Reprint Ser.). 1977. 19.95 (*0-8369-3597-7*) Ayer.

***Three Presents for Baby Jesus.** (Arch Bks.). (Illus.). (J). (ps-4). 1996. 1.99 (*0-570-07524-6*, 59-1497) Concordia.

Three Presidents & Their Books: The Readings of Jefferson, Lincoln, & F. D. Roosevelt. Arthur E. Bestor et al. LC 54-12305. (Fifth Annual Windsor Lectures Ser.). 141p. reprint ed. pap. 40.20 (*0-317-28792-3*, 2020219) Bks Demand.

Three Princes: A Middle Eastern Tale. Illus. by Leonard E. Fisher. LC 93-25862. 32p. (J). (ps-3). 1994. lib. bdg. 15.95 (*0-8234-1115-X*) Holiday.

Three Principles of the Divine Essence. Jacob Behem. 1978. reprint ed. 16.50 (*0-911662-65-0*) Yoga.

Three Prize Essays on American Slavery. Richard B. Thurston et al. 1977. 15.95 (*0-8369-8620-2*, 8504) Ayer.

Three Problem Plays: All's Well That Ends Well, Measure for Measure, Troilus & Cressida. William Shakespeare. (Classics Ser.). 496p. 1988. mass mkt. 4.95 (*0-553-21287-7*, Bantam Classics) Bantam.

Three Problems. Chen Li. (Asian Folk Tales Ser.). (Illus.). 24p. (J). 1995. 9.95 (*983-9808-66-4*, Pub. by Delta Edits MY) Weatherhill.

***Three Programs & Ten Criteria: Evaluating & Improving Acquisition Program Management & Oversight Processes Within the Department of Defense.** Robert V. Johnson et al. LC 96-32483. (Illus.). 109p. (Orig.). 1997. pap. 15.00 (*0-8330-2436-1*, MR-758-OSD) Rand Corp.

***Three Prophetic Novels: When the Sleeper Wakes, A Story of the Day to Come, The Time Machine.** H. G. Wells. 1960. 21.00 (*0-8446-3151-5*) Peter Smith.

Three Prophetic Novels of H. G. Wells. H. G. Wells. Ed. by E. F. Bleiler. pap. 6.95 (*0-486-20605-X*) Dover.

Three Prophets of Religious Liberalism. Ed. by Conrad Wright. 1994. pap. 10.00 (*0-933840-20-9*, Skinner Hse Bks) Unitarian Univ.

Three Proud Princesses. Janet E. Cooper. LC 93-36897. (Illus.). 64p. (J). 1995. 16.95 (*0-913720-86-0*) Beil.

Three P's in Recovery. 2nd ed. J. B. Brown. 24p. 1984. pap. write for info. (*0-318-58107-8*) H & H Pubs.

Three Psychologies: Perspectives from Freud, Skinner & Rogers. 4th ed. Robert D. Nye. LC 91-8546. 176p. (Orig.). (C). 1991. pap. 21.95 (*0-534-16224-X*) Brooks-Cole.

Three Psychologies: Perspectives from Freud, Skinner, & Rogers. 5th ed. Robert D. Nye. LC 94-42256. 192p. 1996. pap. 14.95 (*0-534-26616-9*) Brooks-Cole.

Three Pups. Angela F. Aymerich. (ESL Theme Links Ser.). (Illus.). (Orig.). 1993. teacher ed., ring bd. 99.50 incl. audio (*1-56334-292-8*); 35.00 (*1-56334-291-X*); audio 10.50 (*1-56334-290-1*) Hampton-Brown.

Three Pups: Big Book, Big bk. Angela F. Aymerich. (ESL Theme Links Ser.). (Illus.). 16p. (Orig.). (J). (gr. 1-3). 1991. pap. text ed. 29.95 (*1-56334-049-6*) Hampton-Brown.

Three Pups: Small Book, Small bk. Angela F. Aymerich. (ESL Theme Links Ser.). (Illus.). 16p. (Orig.). (J). (gr. 1-3). 1991. pap. text ed. 6.00 (*1-56334-055-0*) Hampton-Brown.

Three Pups: Teacher's Guide. (ESL Theme Links Ser.). (Illus.). 1993. 15.00 (*1-56334-342-8*) Hampton-Brown.

Three Pure Land Sutras: The Larger Sutra on Amitayus; the Smaller Sutra on Amitayus; the Sutra on Contemplation of Amitayus. Numata Center for Buddhist Translation & Research Staff. Ed. by Hanayama Shoyu et al. Tr. & Pref. by Hisao Inagaki. LC 94-73930. (BDK English Tripitaka Ser.: Vols. 12-II, III, & IV). 173p. (C). 1995. 30.00 (*1-886439-01-X*) Numata Ctr.

Three-Quarter Time: The Life & Music of the Strauss Family of Vienna. Jerome Pastene. LC 76-91768. (Illus.). 307p. 1971. reprint ed. text ed. 38.50 (*0-8371-3991-0*, PATQ, Greenwood Pr) Greenwood.

Three Quest Plays. JoAnne James. 55p. (Orig.). 1996. pap. 17.00 (*0-88734-682-0*) Empire Pub Srvs.

Three Questions. Leo Tolstoy. LC 83-71787. (Creative's Classic Short Stories Ser.). 32p. (J). (gr. 4 up). 1983. lib. bdg. 13.95 (*0-87191-962-1*) Creative Ed.

"Three Rabbis in a Row Boat..." The World's Best Jewish Humor. A. Stanley Kramer. 192p. 1996. pap. 9.95 (*0-8065-1775-1*, Citadel Pr) Carol Pub Group.

Three Radical Women Writers: Class & Gender in Meridel le Sueur, Tillie Olsen, & Josephine Herbst. Nora R. Roberts. LC 95-43538. (Gender & Genre in Literature Ser.: Vol. 06). (Illus.). 224p. 1996. text ed. 40.00 (*0-8153-0330-0*, H1452) Garland.

Three Rastell Plays: Four Elements, Calisto & Melebea, Gentleness & Nobility. Ed. by Richard Axton. (Tudor Interludes Ser.: No. I). (Illus.). 175p. 1979. 59.00 (*0-85991-047-4*) Boydell & Brewer.

***Three Really Nasty Plays.** unabridged ed. Ronald M. Chambers. Ed. by William-Alan Landes. LC 97-22595. 224p. 1997. pap. 17.00 (*0-88734-928-5*) Players Pr.

Three Realms of Ethics: Individual, Institutional, Societal. John W. Glaser. 160p. (Orig.). 1994. pap. 17.95 (*1-55612-722-7*, LL1722) Sheed & Ward MO.

Three Reformation Catechisms: Catholic, Anabaptist, Lutheran. Ed. by Denis Janz. LC 82-20799. (Texts & Studies in Religion: Vol. 13). viii, 224p. (C). 1982. lib. bdg. 89.95 (*0-88946-800-1*) E Mellen.

Three Reformers: Luther-Descartes-Rousseau. Jacques Maritain. LC 78-98780. 234p. 1970. reprint ed. text ed. 35.00 (*0-8371-2825-0*, MATR, Greenwood Pr) Greenwood.

Three Religious Rebels: Founding Fathers of the Cistercians. M. Raymond. LC 88-6992. 407p. 1992. reprint ed. pap. 9.95 (*0-8198-7340-3*) Pauline Bks.

Three Remarkable Women. Harold Balyoz. 285p. 1986. pap. 14.95 (*0-9609710-1-7*) Altai Pub.

Three Renaissance Comedies. Ed. by Christopher Cairns. LC 91-42459. (Illus.). 366p. 1991. lib. bdg. 99.95 (*0-7734-9450-2*) E Mellen.

Three Renaissance Pastorals: Tasso, Guarini, Daniel. Ed. by Elizabeth S. Donno. LC 92-16043. (Medieval & Renaissance Texts & Studies: Vol. 102). 278p. 1993. 20.00 (*0-86698-118-7*, MR102) MRTS.

Three Renaissance Travel Plays, Vol. 1. A. N. Parr. 1995. text ed. 79.95 (*0-7190-3746-8*, Pub. by Manchester Univ Pr UK) St Martin.

Three Responses to Christmas. Mark Hitchcock. 27p. (Orig.). 1994. pap. 2.50 (*1-879366-68-1*) Hearthstone OK.

Three Restoration Comedies: Etherege: The Man of Mode; Wycherley: the Country Wife; Congreve: Love for Love. Ed. by Garmini Salgado. (English Library). 368p. 1976. pap. 10.95 (*0-14-043027-X*, Penguin Classics) Viking Penguin.

Three Ring Circus. Curtis E. Rickels. 289p. 1992. pap. write for info. (*0-9637087-0-8*) Sunrise Track.

Three Ring Circus: Poems from a Life. Ruth M. Kempher. 80p. 1982. pap. 4.95 (*0-935684-04-2*) Plumbers Ink Bks.

Three-Ring Psychus. John Shirley. (Orig.). 1990. mass mkt. 3.95 (*0-8217-3286-2*, Zebra Kensgtn) Kensgtn Pub Corp.

Three Rival Versions of Moral Enquiry: Encyclopaedia, Genealogy, & Tradition. Alasdair MacIntyre. LC 89-29275. 256p. (C). 1990. text ed. 29.00 (*0-268-01871-5*) U of Notre Dame Pr.

Three Rival Versions of Moral Enquiry: Encyclopaedia, Genealogy, & Tradition. Alasdair MacIntyre. LC 89-29275. (C). 1991. pap. text ed. 15.00 (*0-268-01877-4*) U of Notre Dame Pr.

***Three River Junction: A Story of an Alaskan Bald Eagle Preserve.** Saranne D. Burnham. (Illus.). 32p. (J). (gr. 1-4). 1997. 14.95 (*1-56899-441-9*); 19.95 incl. digital audio (*1-56899-443-5*); pap. 5.95 (*1-56899-442-7*) Soundprints.

***Three River Junction: A Story of an Alaskan Bald Eagle Preserve, Incl. plush toy.** Saranne D. Burnham. (Illus.). 36p. (J). (gr. 1-4). 1997. 24.95 (*1-56899-444-3*); write for info. incl. digital audio (*1-56899-445-1*) Soundprints.

***Three River Junction: A Story of an Alaskan Bald Eagle Preserve, Incl. toy.** Saranne D. Burnham. (Illus.). 36p. (J). (gr. 1-4). 1997. pap. 14.95 (*1-56899-446-X*); pap. write for info. incl. digital audio (*1-56899-447-8*) Soundprints.

Three Rivers Cookbook, Vol. One. Ed. by Norma Sproull & Ann H. Garrett. (Illus.). 254p. (Orig.). 1973. pap. 12.95 (*0-9607634-0-6*) T Rivers Cookbook.

Three Rivers Cookbook, Vol. Three. Ed. by Jane Birnie. (Illus.). 254p. 1990. vinyl bd. 12.95 (*0-9607634-2-2*) T Rivers Cookbook.

Three Rivers Cookbook, Vol. Two. Ed. by Carolyn S. Hammer & Doris H. Paul. (Illus.). 254p. (Orig.). 1981. pap. 12.95 (*0-9607634-1-4*) T Rivers Cookbook.

Three Rivers of France. Freda White. (Illus.). 224p. 1989. 29.95 (*1-55970-014-9*) Arcade Pub Inc.

Three Rivers of France. Photos by Freda White. (Illus.). 224p. 1996. pap. 22.95 (*1-85145-754-2*, Pub. by Pavilion UK) Trafalgar.

Three Rivers of France. 2nd ed. Freda White. (Illus.). 232p. 1984. pap. 10.95 (*0-571-13386-X*) Faber & Faber.

Three Rivers Ten Years. Ed. by Gerald Costanzo. 1983. 20.95 (*0-915604-84-1*); pap. 11.95 (*0-915604-85-X*) Carnegie-Mellon.

Three Robbers. 2nd ed. Tomi Ungerer. LC 91-246. (Illus.). 40p. (J). (gr. k-3). 1991. reprint ed. pap. 4.95 (*0-689-71511-0*, Aladdin Paperbacks) S&S Childrens.

Three Robeson Township Cemeteries. Donald D. DeTemple. 223p. 1995. pap. 19.95 (*1-55856-188-9*) Closson Pr.

Three Robots. LC 80-84356. (Illus.). (J). (gr. k-7). 1981. pap. 3.95 (*0-9601334-4-5*) Growth Unltd.

Three Robots & the Sandstorm. Art Fettig. LC 82-90993. (Illus.). 96p. (J). (gr. k-7). 1983. pap. 3.95 (*0-9601334-3-7*) Growth Unltd.

Three Robots Discover Their Pos-Abilities: A Lesson in Goal Setting. Art Fettig. LC 84-81461. (Illus.). (J). (gr. k-7). 1984. pap. 3.95 (*0-916927-00-8*) Growth Unltd.

Three Robots Find a Grandpa. Art Fettig. LC 84-80378. (Illus.). 96p. (Orig.). (J). (gr. k-7). 1984. pap. 5.95 incl. audio (*0-9601334-8-8*) Growth Unltd.

Three Robots Learn about Drugs. Art Fettig. LC 86-83041. (Illus.). 96p. (J). (gr. k-7). 1987. pap. 3.95 (*0-916927-04-0*) Growth Unltd.

Three Rode South. Jake Foster. 1990. mass mkt. 2.95 (*1-55817-351-X*, Pinncle Kensgtn) Kensgtn Pub Corp.

Three Roman Plays: Coriolanus, Julius Caesar, Antony & Cleopatra. William Shakespeare. (Classics Ser.). 672p. 1995. pap. 11.95 (*0-14-043461-5*, Penguin Classics) Viking Penguin.

Three Roman Poets: Plautus, Catullus, Ovid. Frederick A. Wright. 1977. lib. bdg. 250.00 (*0-8490-2746-2*) Gordon Pr.

Three R's: Grades K-3, 3 vols. & poster. Ruth Beechick. 96p. 1986. Set (incl. poster). pap. 12.00 (*0-940319-06-3*) Arrow Press.

Three R's at Home. Howard B. Richman & Susan P. Richman. LC 88-90813. 228p. (Orig.). 1988. pap. 7.95 (*0-929446-00-3*) PA Homeschoolers.

Three R's for Dancing, Vol. II. Nadia Chilkovsky. 32p. 1956. pap. text ed. 9.95 (*0-932582-61-3*, Pub. by Dance Bks UK) Princeton Bk Co.

Three R's for Dancing, Vol. III. Nadia Chilkovsky. (Illus.). 32p. 1961. pap. text ed. 9.95 (*0-932582-62-1*, Pub. by Dance Bks UK) Princeton Bk Co.

Three R's for the Gifted-Component: Card Catalog. Judy Williams. (J). (gr. 4-9). 1993. pap. text ed. 6.97 (*0-937659-14-2*) GCT.

Three R's for the Gifted-Component No. 1: Almanacs. Judy Williams. (J). (gr. 4-9). 1993. pap. text ed. 6.97 (*0-937659-12-6*) GCT.

Three R's for the Gifted-Component No. 2: Atlases. Judy Williams. (J). (gr. 4-9). 1993. pap. text ed. 6.97 (*0-937659-13-4*) GCT.

Three R's for the Gifted-Component No. 4: Dictionary. Judy Williams. (J). (gr. 4-9). 1994. pap. text ed. 6.97 (*0-937659-15-0*) GCT.

Three R's for the Gifted-Component No. 5: Encyclopedia. Judy Williams. (J). (gr. 4-9). 1993. pap. text ed. 6.97 (*0-937659-16-9*) GCT.

Three R's for the Gifted-Component No. 6: Magazines & Journals. Judy Williams. (J). (gr. 4-9). 1994. pap. text ed. 6.97 (*0-937659-17-7*) GCT.

Three R's for the Gifted-Component No. 7: Newspaper. Judy Williams. (J). (gr. 4-9). 1993. pap. text ed. 6.97 (*0-937659-18-5*) GCT.

Three R's for the Gifted-Component No. 8: Readers Guide. Judy Williams. (J). (gr. 4-9). 1994. pap. text ed. 6.97 (*0-937659-19-3*) GCT.

Three R's for the Gifted-Component No. 9: Telephone Book. Judy Williams. (J). (gr. 4-9). 1994. pap. text ed. 6.97 (*0-937659-20-7*) GCT.

Three R's for the Gifted-Component No. 10: Who's Who. Judy Williams. (J). (gr. 4-9). 1994. pap. text ed. 6.97 (*0-937659-21-5*) GCT.

Three R's for the Gifted-Component No. 11: Business People. Judy Williams. (J). (gr. 4-9). 1994. pap. text ed. 6.97 (*0-937659-22-3*) GCT.

Three R's for the Gifted-Component No. 12: College & Vocational Personnel. Judy Williams. (J). (gr. 4-9). 1986. pap. text ed. 6.97 (*0-937659-23-1*) GCT.

Three R's for the Gifted-Component No. 13: Courthouse. Judy Williams. (J). (gr. 4-9). 1994. pap. text ed. 6.97 (*0-937659-24-X*) GCT.

Three R's for the Gifted-Component No. 14: Government Resources. Judy Williams. (J). (gr. 4-9). 1994. pap. text ed. 6.97 (*0-937659-25-8*) GCT.

Three R's for the Gifted-Component No. 15: Historical Sites. Judy Williams. (J). (gr. 4-9). 1994. pap. text ed. 6.97 (*0-937659-26-6*) GCT.

Three R's for the Gifted-Component No. 16: Indigenous Resources. Judy Williams. (J). (gr. 4-9). 1994. pap. text ed. 6.97 (*0-937659-27-4*) GCT.

Three R's for the Gifted-Component No. 17: Museums. Judy Williams. (J). (gr. 4-9). 1994. pap. text ed. 6.97 (*0-937659-28-2*) GCT.

Three R's for the Gifted-Component No. 18: Public Officials. Judy Williams. (J). (gr. 4-9). 1994. pap. text ed. 6.97 (*0-937659-29-0*) GCT.

Three R's for the Gifted-Component No. 19: Teachers. Judy Williams. (J). (gr. 4-9). 1994. pap. text ed. 6.97 (*0-937659-30-4*) GCT.

Three R's for the Gifted-Component No. 20: Teacher's Manual. Judy Williams. (J). (gr. 4-9). 1994. teacher ed., pap. text ed. 6.97 (*0-937659-31-2*) GCT.

Three "R's" of Calvary. Vernelle B. Allen. 85p. 1994. pap. write for info. (*1-885984-05-7*) Wings of Healing.

3 Rs of E-Mail: Risks, Rights, & Responsibilities. Diane B. Hartman & Karen S. Nantz. LC 95-74725. (On-Line Ser.). 153p. (Orig.). 1995. pap. 12.95 (*1-56052-378-6*) Crisp Pubns.

***Three Rules for Writing a Novel: A Writer's Guide to Story Development.** abr. ed. William Noble. 384p. 1997. pap. 17.95 (*0-8397-8050-8*) Eriksson.

Three Russian Lyric Folk Song Meters. James Bailey. 429p. 1993. 27.95 (*0-89357-237-3*) Slavica.

Three Sacks of Truth: A Story from France. Illus. by Robert Rayevsky. 32p. (J). (ps-3). 1993. lib. bdg. 15.95 (*0-8234-0921-X*) Holiday.

Three Saints' Lives by Nicholas Bozon. M. Amelia Klenke. (History Ser.). 1xxvii, 123p. 1947. pap. 3.50 (*1-57659-082-8*) Franciscan Inst.

Three Sarahs: Documents of Antebellum Black College Women. Ellen N. Lawson. LC 84-18914. (Studies in Women & Religion: Vol. 13). (Illus.). 350p. 1984. lib. bdg. 99.95 (*0-88946-536-3*) E Mellen.

Three Satirists of Snobbery: Thackeray, Meredith, Proust. Margaret M. Goodell. 1972. 59.95 (*0-8490-1212-0*) Gordon Pr.

Three Satyric Plays of Albert Tallman. Albert Tallman. LC 75-28897. (Illus.). 1975. pap. 15.00 (*0-87423-019-5*) Westburg.

Three Saviours Are Here. 2nd ed. George King. LC 86-204666. 96p. 1982. pap. 7.95 (*0-937249-06-8*) Aetherius Soc.

Three Schools of Education: Approaches to Institutional History. Ed. by Ayers Bagley. (SPE Monographs). 1984. 3.00 (*0-933669-25-9*) Soc Profs Ed.

Three Scientists & Their Gods: A Search for Meaning in an Age of Information. Robert Wright. 320p. 1988. 18.95 (*0-8129-1328-0*, Times Bks) Random.

***Three Score & Ten: A History of Christ School 1900-1970 - Arden NC.** David W. McCullough. LC 96-61366. (Illus.). 302p. 1996. 24.95 (*1-56664-104-7*) WorldComm.

***Three Scottish Carmelite Friaries.** Ed. by J. A. Stone. (Illus.). 175p. 1989. pap. 44.00 (*0-903903-06-7*) David Brown.

Three Screen Comedies by Samson Raphaelson: Trouble in Paradise, The Shop Around the Corner, Heaven Can Wait. Samson Raphaelson. LC 81-50948. 512p. 1983. 13.95 (*0-299-08780-8*) U of Wis Pr.

***Three Screenplays.** Edward Burns. LC 97-15616. 256p. 1997. pap. 15.95 (*0-7868-8272-7*) Hyperion.

Three Screenplays for Reading. Tom Bowie. 1992. 22.95 (*0-932508-10-3*) Seven Oaks.

Three Seals. Sean McMahon. 181p. (Orig.). (J). (gr. 7-9). 1991. pap. 7.95 (*1-85371-148-9*, Pub. by Poolbeg Pr IE) Dufour.

Three Seas: A Christopher Columbus Counting Book. Hap Preston. LC 92-80784. (Illus.). 44p. (J). (ps-3). 1992. pap. 5.95 (*1-55523-529-8*) Winston-Derek.

Three Seasons at Askrigg. large type ed. Clare Rossiter. 288p. 1996. 25.99 (*0-7089-3508-7*) Ulverscroft.

***Three Seasons of Bloom.** Ed. by Time-Life Book Editors. LC 96-47271. (Time-Life Complete Gardener Ser.). 1997. write for info. (*0-7835-4117-1*) Time-Life.

***Three Sections of Poems.** Philip Holmes. Date not set. 14.95 (*0-900977-75-2*, Pub. by Anvil Press UK) Dufour.

Three Sermons: The Benefit of Contentation, the Affinitie of the Faithful, the Lost Sheep Is Found. Henry Smith. LC 76-57418. (English Experience Ser.: No. 832). 1977. reprint ed. lib. bdg. 25.00 (*90-221-0832-5*) Walter J Johnson.

Three Sets of Tables: Expected Sizes of a Selected Subset in Paired Comparison Experiments; Tables of Admissible & Optimal Balanced Treatment Incomplete Block (BTIB) Designs for Comparing Treatments with a Control; Expected Values & Variances & Covariances of Order Statistics for a Family of Symmetric Distributions. B. J. Trawinski et al. LC 74-6283. (Selected Tables in Mathematical Statistics Ser.: Vol. 8). 270p. 1985. 42.00 (*0-8218-1908-9*, TABLES/8) Am Math.

Three Sevens. William Phelon & Mira M. Phelon. Ed. by R. Swinburne Clymer. 212p. 1977. 7.95 (*0-932785-47-6*) Philos Pub.

***Three Sherlock Holmes Adventures.** Doyle & Gonan. Date not set. pap. text ed. write for info. (*0-17-557037-X*) Addison-Wesley.

Three Ships Come Sailing. Gilchrist Waring. 1948. pap. 6.00 (*0-87517-013-7*) Dietz.

Three Ships for Columbus. Eve Spencer. LC 92-14401. (Stories of America Ser.). (Illus.). 32p. (J). (gr. 2-5). 1992. lib. bdg. 22.83 (*0-8114-7212-4*) Raintree Steck-V.

***Three Short Novels: Bartleby, Benito Cereno, Billy Budd.** large type ed. Herman Melville. 381p. 1997. reprint ed. lib. bdg. 24.00 (*0-939495-20-1*) North Bks.

Three Short Novels: The Crazy Hunter, The Bridegroom's Body, Decision. Kay Boyle. LC 90-47955. (New Directions Classics Ser.). 272p. 1991. pap. 10.95 (*0-8112-1149-5*, NDP703) New Directions.

Three Short Novels from Papua New Guinea. Incl. Fires of Dawn. Benjamin Umba. 1976. (*0-318-55934-X*, Three Contnts); Flight of a Villager. August Kituai. 1976. (*0-318-55935-8*, Three Contnts); 140p. 1976. 20.00 (*0-582-71437-0*, Three Contnts) Lynne Rienner.

Three Short Novels of Mystery & Suspense. large type ed. Sheridan Le Fanu et al. (Large-Print Ser.). 542p. 1992. reprint ed. lib. bdg. 24.00 (*0-939495-41-4*) North Bks.

Three Short Plays: Manuscript Edition. Archibald Macleish. 1961. pap. 13.00 (*0-8222-0600-5*) Dramatists Play.

Three Short Plays: Minions of the Race, Incident at the Great Wall, The Actor in Search of His Mask. Intro. by Mario Fratti. (Illus.). 176p. 1994. pap. 14.95 (*0-918680-36-0*) Bagehot Council.

Three Short Plays by Christopher Durang. Christopher Durang. 1979. pap. 5.25 (*0-8222-0341-3*) Dramatists Play.

Three Short Plays by Elinor Jones: Number 6: 15 on the 104 - If You Were My Wife I'd Shoot Myself - under Control. Elinor Jones. 1989. pap. 5.25 (*0-8222-1036-3*) Dramatists Play.

Three Short Plays by Jonathan Marc Sherman. Jonathan M. Sherman. 1995. pap. 5.25 (*0-8222-1372-9*) Dramatists Play.

Three Short Plays for the Teaching of German. Christiane Ullmann. 83p. 1990. 10.95 (*0-533-08608-6*) Vantage.

Three Short Romances. Carol A. Phelps. (Illus.). 1977. boxed 12.00 (*0-87770-195-4*) Ye Galleon.

Three Short Works on Japanese Americans. Ed. by Roger Daniels. LC 78-3223. (Asian Experience in North America Ser.). 1979. lib. bdg. 29.95 (*0-405-11291-2*) Ayer.

Three Shots in the Night. Sonny Carbone. Ed. by Literacy Volunteers of New York City Staff. (New Writers' Voices Ser.). (Illus.). 64p. (Orig.). 1992. pap. text ed. 3.50 (*0-929631-63-3*, Signal Hill) New Readers.

Three Sillies. Walter J. De La Mare. (Classic Short Stories Ser.). (J). 1991. lib. bdg. 13.95 (*0-88682-467-2*) Creative Ed.

Three Sillies. Illus. by Arthur Friedman. LC 80-27636. 32p. (J). (gr. k-4). 1997. pap. 3.95 (*0-89375-487-0*) Troll Communs.

Three Silver Coins: A Story from Tibet. Veronica Leo & Tashi Daknewa. Tr. by Nina Aberg. LC 94-39648. (Illus.). 165p. (J). (gr. 5-8). 1995. pap. 12.95 (*1-55939-040-9*) Snow Lion Pubns.

Three Simple Principles of Trade Policy. Douglas A. Irwin. 36p. (Orig.). 1996. pap. 9.95 (*0-8447-7079-5*, AEI Pr) Am Enterprise.

Three Simple Steps to Flatten Your Belly. Chet Cunningham. LC 94-60412. (Illus.). 176p. (Orig.). 1995. pap. 14.95 (*0-9614924-8-1*) United Res CA.

Three Singing Pigs. Kaye Umansky. (J). pap. 15.95 (*0-7136-3804-4*, 93116, Pub. by A&C Black UK) Talman.

Three Sisters. Anton P. Chekhov. Ed. by R. Nelson. 1991. pap. 5.95 (*0-88145-098-7*) Broadway Play.

***Three Sisters.** Anton P. Chekhov. 55p. 1996. pap. 7.00 (*0-88734-705-3*) Players Pr.

Three Sisters. Kenward Elmslie. LC 85-52101. 72p. (Orig.). 1986. pap. 9.00 (*0-915990-27-X*) Z Pr.

Three Sisters. adapted ed. Anton P. Chekhov. Tr. by Lanford Wilson from RUS. 1984. pap. 5.25 (*0-8222-1144-0*) Dramatists Play.

Three Sisters. Anton P. Chekhov. LC 93-10454. (Thrift Editions Ser.). 64p. 1993. reprint ed. pap. 1.00 (*0-486-27544-2*) Dover.

Three Sisters: A Drama in Four Acts. rev. ed. Anton P. Chekhov. 1995. pap. 5.25 (*0-8222-1451-2*) Dramatists Play.

Three Sisters: A Play. Anton P. Chekhov. LC 91-12802. 112p. 1991. reprint ed. pap. 10.95 (*0-8021-3276-6*, Grove) Grove-Atltic.

***Three Sisters: After Chekhov.** Brian Friel. 124p. 9200. pap. 14.95 (*0-904011-26-7*) Dufour.

Three Sisters: Three Sisters (Tri Sewiry) Anton P. Chekhov. Tr. by Lanford Wilson from RUS. (Great Translations for Actors Ser.). 82p. 1994. pap. 11.95 (*1-880399-28-8*) Smith & Kraus.

Three Sisters: Three Sisters (Tri Sewiry) Anton P. Chekhov. Tr. by Paul Schmidt from RUS. LC 92-11369. (TCG Translations Ser.). 112p. 1992. 21.95 (*1-55936-056-9*); pap. 8.95 (*1-55936-055-0*) Theatre Comm.

Three Sisters see Plays

Three Sisters Cookbook: Recipes & Remembrances. Carol Harner. (Illus.). 164p. (Orig.). (YA). (gr. 12). 1989. pap. 9.95 (*0-685-26082-8*) Harner Pubns.

Three Sisters: Three Sisters (Tri Sewiry) see Six Great Modern Plays

Three Sitwells: A Biographical & Critical Study. Rodolphe L. Megroz. LC 79-145174. 1971. reprint ed. 29.00 (*0-403-01102-7*) Scholarly.

Three-Six-Seven: Memoirs of a Very Important Man. Peter Vansittart. 236p. 8300. 27.00 (*0-7206-0602-0*) Dufour.

Three, Sixteen: Bible Texts Illuminated. Donald E. Knuth et al. LC 90-44038. (Illus.). 272p. (Orig.). 1990. pap. 29.95 (*0-89579-252-4*) A-R Eds.

Three Sixteenth Century Comedies: Roister Doister, Gammer Gurton's Needle & the Old Wife's Tale. Ed. by Charles Whitworth. (New Mermaid Ser.). (C). 1984. pap. text ed. 7.95 (*0-393-90051-7*) Norton.

Three Sleep: A Historomance. Richard Blevins. LC 91-77166. 118p. (Orig.). 1992. pap. text ed. 10.00 (*0-9627891-3-5*) Igneus Pr.

Three Smaller Wisdom Books: Lao Zi's Dao De Jing, the Great Learning (Da Zue), & the Doctrine of the Mean (Zhong Yong) Tr. by Patrick E. Moran from CHI. 310p. (Orig.). (C). 1993. pap. text ed. 28.50 (*0-8191-9215-5*); lib. bdg. 51.50 (*0-8191-9214-7*) U Pr of Amer.

Three Smart Pals. Joanne Rocklin. (Hello Reader! Ser.). (Illus.). 48p. (J). (gr. 2-3). 1994. pap. 3.99 (*0-590-47431-6*, Cartwheel) Scholastic Inc.

Three Smiths in the Wind: Low Man on a Totem Pole, Life in a Putty Knife Factory, Lost in Horse Latitudes. Harry A. Smith. LC 73-112330. 218p. 1971. reprint ed. text ed. 65.00 (*0-8371-4719-0*, SMSW, Greenwood Pr) Greenwood.

***Three Social Plays of the Black Experience.** Eddie Abner, Jr. LC 79-50129. 316p. (Orig.). (C). 1996. pap. text ed. 35.00 (*0-9602508-0-8*) Wildcat Pub.

Three Socialist Plays: Lear, Roots, Sergeant Musgrave's Dance. Robert Shaughnessy. (Open Guides to Literature Ser.). 128p. 1992. 75.00 (*0-335-09607-7*, Open Univ Pr); pap. 22.00 (*0-335-09606-9*, Open Univ Pr) Taylor & Francis.

***Three Soldiers.** John R. Dos Passos. 1997. mass mkt. 5.95 (*0-553-21456-X*, Bantam Classics) Bantam.

Three Soldiers. John R. Dos Passos. 433p. 1988. pap. 9.95 (*0-88184-413-6*) Carroll & Graf.

***Three Soldiers.** John R. Dos Passos. 1997. pap. 5.95 (*0-451-52645-7*, Sig Classics) NAL-Dutton.

***Three Soldiers.** John R. Dos Passos. LC 97-18911. 1997. pap. 9.95 (*0-14-118027-7*) Viking Penguin.

Three Some Poems. Jeannine Dobbs et al. LC 75-23819. 88p. 1976. pap. 3.95 (*0-914086-11-1*) Alicejamesbooks.

Three Songs & Other Poems. 3rd ed. Richard L. West. LC 78-64347. (Illus.). 188p. 1994. 15.00 (*0-9648597-0-X*) West Wind MO.

Three Songs Opus 45 Low Voice & Piano. S. Barber. 20p. 1995. pap. 8.95 (*0-7935-3837-8*, 50333030) H Leonard.

Three Sons of Han. Jim H. Reed. 390p. (Orig.). 1994. pap. 13.50 (*1-885411-00-6*) Columbia Lit.

***Three South Etrurian Churches.** Ed. by Neil Christie. (British School at Rome Archaeological Monographs). (Illus.). 374p. 1991. pap. 99.00 (*0-904152-17-0*, Pub. by British Schl Rome UK) David Brown.

3 Southwest Mysteries. Olga G. Holt & Rochelle L. Holt. (Illus.). 100p. (Orig.). 1996. pap. 15.00 (*0-934536-60-0*) Rose Shell Pr.

Three Southwest Plays. LC 70-111115. (Play Anthology Reprint Ser.). 1977. 22.95 (*0-8369-8208-8*) Ayer.

Three Spanish American Poets: Pellicer, Neruda, Andrade. Pablo Neruda et al. Ed. by Lloyd Mallan. Tr. by Mary Wicker. 1977. lib. bdg. 59.95 (*0-8490-2747-0*) Gordon Pr.

Three Special Journeys, 3 bks. Sally L. Jones. (J). (ps). 1993. Set. 9.99 (*0-7847-0075-3*, 03645) Standard Pub.

Three Spinning Fairies. Miriam Biskin. 24p. 1973. pap. 3.00 (*0-87129-180-0*, T26) Dramatic Pub.

Three Squirt Dog. Rick Ridgway. 176p. (Orig.). 1994. pap. 12.95 (*0-312-11079-0*) St Martin.

Three-Stage Model of Course Design. John F. Feldhusen. Ed. by Danny G. Langdon. LC 79-26576. (Instructional Design Library). 96p. 1980. 27.95 (*0-87778-159-1*) Educ Tech Pubns.

Three Stalks of Corn. Leo Politi. LC 93-19737. (Illus.). 32p. (J). (gr. k-3). 1994. reprint ed. pap. 4.95 (*0-689-71782-2*, Aladdin Paperbacks) S&S Childrens.

Three-Star Billy. Pat Hutchins. LC 93-26517. 32p. (J). 1994. 15.00 (*0-688-13078-X*); lib. bdg. 14.93 (*0-688-13079-8*) Greenwillow.

Three Stars of Ingaar. Jean Leturgie & Phillipe Luguy. Tr. by Dwight R. Decker from FRE. (Percevan Ser.). (Illus.). 48p. (Orig.). (YA). (gr. 5 up). 1996. pap. 8.95 (*1-887911-53-7*) Fantsy Flight.

Three Steps Forward Two Steps Back. Charles R. Swindoll. 192p. 1985. mass mkt. 5.99 (*0-553-27334-5*) Bantam.

Three Steps Forward, Two Steps Back. large type ed. Charles R. Swindoll. 320p. 1985. reprint ed. pap. 11.95 (*0-8027-2506-6*) Walker & Co.

Three Steps on the Ladder of Writing. Helene Cixous. Tr. by Sarah Cornell & Susan Sellers from FRE. LC 92-38009. 160p. (C). 1993. 21.50 (*0-231-07658-4*) Col U Pr.

Three Steps on the Ladder of Writing. Helene Cixous. 1994. pap. 12.00 (*0-231-07659-2*) Col U Pr.

Three Steps, One Bow. Bhikshu Hung Ju & Bhikshu Hung Yo. (Illus.). 160p. (Orig.). 1977. pap. 5.00 (*0-917512-18-9*) Buddhist Text.

Three Steps to a Strong Family. Linda Eyre. 240p. 1994. 19.50 (*0-671-88728-9*) S&S Trade.

Three Steps to a Strong Family. Linda Eyre. 1995. pap. 12.00 (*0-684-80288-0*, Fireside) S&S Trade.

Three Steps to a Strong Family. Richard Eyre. 1994. 19.50 (*0-671-99728-9*) S&S Trade.

Three Steps to Answered Prayer. Peter Popoff. Ed. by Don Tanner. LC 81-70342. 92p. 1981. pap. 2.00 (*0-938544-10-1*) Faith Messenger.

***Three Steps to Chess Mastery.** Suetin. 1997. pap. 22.95 (*1-85744-109-5*, Pub. by Cadogan Books UK) Macmillan.

Three Steps to Chess Mastery. A. S. Suetin. Tr. by Kenneth P. Neat from RUS. (Russian Chess Ser.). (Illus.). 204p. 1982. 25.95 (*0-08-024139-5*, Pergamon Pr); pap. 19.90 (*0-08-024138-7*, Pergamon Pr) Elsevier.

Three Steps to Fiduciary Responsibility. John Carver. LC 96-10046. (CarverGuide Series on Effective Board Governance: Vol. 3). 1996. pap. write for info. (*0-7879-0298-5*) Jossey-Bass.

Three Steps to Infinity. L. Gordon Plummer. 1994. 10.00 (*0-913004-81-2*) Point Loma Pub.

Three Steps to Sanctity. Albert J. Shamon. LC 93-71836. 45p. (Orig.). 1993. pap. 1.00 (*1-880033-06-2*) Faith Pub OH.

Three Steps to Success. James M. Carroll. 86p. (Orig.). 1984. pap. 4.95 (*0-89826-011-6*) Natl Paperback.

3 Steps to Your Right Career: LifePlan "Professional Fulfillment" Guide. Gary Joseph. (Illus.). 136p. (Orig.). 1996. pap. 16.95 (*0-9651553-0-7*, 001) LifePlan.

Three Stigmata of Palmer Eldritch. Philip K. Dick. LC 91-50091. 208p. 1991. pap. 11.00 (*0-679-73666-2*, Vin) Random.

Three Stooges see Pop Culture Legends

Three Stooges Book of Scripts. Joan H. Maurer. LC 84-17614. (Illus.). 256p. 1984. 19.95 (*0-8065-0933-3*) Carol Pub Group.

Three Stooges Book of Scripts, Vol. II. Joan H. Maurer & Norman Maurer. (Illus.). 256p. 1987. 19.95 (*0-8065-1018-8*, Citadel Pr) Carol Pub Group.

Three Stooges in Full Color. Ed. by Chris Ulm et al. (Illus.). 48p. 1991. pap. 5.95 (*0-944735-92-4*) Malibu Comics Ent.

Three Stooges in Three-D! Ed. by Tom Mason. 32p. 1991. pap. 3.95 (*0-944735-91-6*) Malibu Comics Ent.

***Three Stooges Party Book.** Matt Kavet. (Illus.). 64p. (Orig.). 1997. pap. 5.99 (*1-889647-18-7*) Boston Am.

Three Stooges Scrapbook. Joan H. Maurer et al. (Illus.). 256p. 1985. reprint ed. pap. 16.95 (*0-8065-0946-5*, Citadel Pr) Carol Pub Group.

Three Stooges, Vol. 1: The Knuckleheads Return. Ed. by Tom Mason. (Illus.). 141p. 1989. pap. 14.95 (*0-944735-20-7*) Malibu Comics Ent.

Three Stories. Raymond Carver. 95.00 (*0-939489-09-0*) Engdahl Typo.

Three Stories. R. V. Cassill. LC 82-82012. 75p. (Orig.). 1982. pap. 4.50 (*0-9605008-1-2*) Hermes Hse.

Three Stories. Mahendranath Gooljar. LC 96-90140. 1996. 16.95 (*0-533-11903-0*) Vantage.

Three Stories. Pati Hill. 12p. (Orig.). 1979. pap. 3.00 (*0-917061-03-9*) Top Stories.

Three Stories. Gordon C. Wilson. LC 80-21609. 1980. pap. 2.00 (*0-933292-06-6*) Arts End.

Three Stories: Snow, Smoke, The Missing Piece. John Moat. (Illus.). 60p. 1995. 40.00 (*0-930126-47-5*) Typographeum.

Three Stories & Ten Poems. Ernest Hemingway. 1977. 30.00 (*0-89723-005-1*) Bruccoli.

Three Stories from India. Illus. by Meg Wright. (J). (gr. 1-8). 1984. pap. text ed. 10.00 (*0-86508-166-2*) BCM Pubn.

Three Stories High: The First Big Bungalo Boys Book. John Bianchi. (Illus.). 72p. (J). (ps-2). 1995. pap. 8.95 (*0-921285-42-6*, Pub. by Bungalo Bks CN); lib. bdg. 18.95 (*0-921285-43-4*, Pub. by Bungalo Bks CN) Firefly Bks Ltd.

Three Stories Scandinavian Kings & Queens. Selma O. Lagerlof. 80p. 1996. pap. 10.95 (*1-57216-023-3*) Penfield.

Three Stories You Can Read to Your Cat. Sara S. Miller. LC 96-51. (Illus.). (J). 1997. 13.95 (*0-395-78831-5*) HM.

Three Stories You Can Read to Your Dog. Sara S. Miller. LC 93-38856. (Illus.). 48p. (J). 1995. 13.95 (*0-395-69938-X*) HM.

***Three Stories You Can Read to Your Dog.** Sara S. Miller. 1997. pap. 5.95 (*0-395-86135-7*) HM.

Three Storytellers of Or: A Flexible-Thinking Book. Time-Life Books Editors. Ed. by Neil Kagan & Elizabeth Ward. (Early Learning Program Ser.). (Illus.). 64p. (J). (ps-2). 1991. write for info. (*0-8094-9283-0*); lib. bdg. write for info. (*0-8094-9284-9*) Time-Life.

Three Strands in the Braid: A Guide for Enablers of Learning. 3rd rev. ed. Paula Underwood. Ed. by Jeanne L. Slobod & Sarah A. Robertson. LC 91-65523. (Three Learning Stories Ser.). (Illus.). 78p. 1994. reprint ed. pap. 12.00 (*1-879678-00-4*) Tribe Two Pr.

Three Strikes & You're Out. (Illus.). (J). (ps-2). 1991. pap. 5.10 (*0-8136-5585-4*); lib. bdg. 7.95 (*0-8136-5085-2*) Modern Curr.

Three Strikes & You're Out: Estimated Benefits & Costs of California's New Mandatory-Sentencing Law. Allan Abrahamse et al. LC 94-37970. 1994. pap. text ed. 13.00 (*0-8330-1597-4*, MR-509-RC) Rand Corp.

Three Strikes & You're Out: Vengeance As Social Policy. David Shichor & Dale K. Sechrest. LC 96-10039. 256p. 1996. 46.00 (*0-7619-0004-7*); pap. 21.95 (*0-7619-0005-5*) Sage.

Three Strikes & You're Out!...A Promise to Kimber: The Chronicle of America's Toughest Anti-Crime Law. Mike Reynolds et al. (Illus.). 272p. 1996. 24.95 (*1-884956-12-2*) Quill Driver.

3 Strikes, You're Dead: Adventure Mystery for Kids Ages 8-12. Dennis Harrington. (Spider Tales Ser.). (Orig.). (J). (gr. 3-7). 1995. 14.00 (*0-922242-77-1*) Bepuzzled.

Three Strong Women. Claus Stamm. (Illus.). 32p. (J). (gr. 2-5). 1990. pap. 12.95 (*0-670-83323-1*) Viking Child Bks.

Three Studies: Masolino & Masaccio, Caravaggio & His Forerunners, Carlo Braccesco. abr. ed. Robert Longhi. Tr. by David Tabbat & David Jacobson from ITA. LC 96-16974. (Illus.). 245p. 1996. text ed. 28.95 (*1-878818-51-1*) Sheep Meadow.

Three Studies in Current Philosophical Questions. Arthur O. Lovejoy. LC 75-3249. reprint ed. write for info. (*0-404-59237-6*) AMS Pr.

Three Studies in Locality & Case. Alexander Grosu. LC 93-49751. (Theoretical Linguistics Ser.). 272p. (C). (gr. 13). 1994. text ed. 85.00 (*0-415-10827-6*, B4431) Routledge.

Three Studies in Medieval Religious & Social Thought: The Interpretation of Mary & Martha, the Ideal of the Imitation of Christ, the Orders of Society. Giles Constable. (Illus.). 300p. (C). 1995. text ed. 59.95 (*0-521-30515-2*) Cambridge U Pr.

Three Studies in Mineral Economics. Orris C. Herfindahl. LC 77-86399. 64p. reprint ed. 37.50 (*0-404-60335-1*) AMS Pr.

Three Studies in Minerals Economics. Orris C. Herfindahl. LC 61-9336. 69p. reprint ed. pap. 25.00 (*0-7837-3129-9*, 2042858) Bks Demand.

Three Studies in Modern French Literature: Proust, Gide, & Mauriac. J. M. Cocking et al. 1960. pap. 39.50 (*0-685-26713-X*) Elliots Bks.

Three Studies in Twentieth Century Obscurity. Francis Russell. 1973. lib. bdg. 200.00 (*0-87968-046-6*) Gordon Pr.

Three Studies in Twentieth Century Obscurity: Joyce, Kafka, Gertrude Stein. Frances Russell. LC 68-658. (Studies in Comparative Literature: No. 35). (C). 1969. reprint ed. lib. bdg. 75.00 (*0-8383-0678-0*) M S G Haskell Hse.

Three Studies on Charles Robert Maturin. Henry W. Hinck. Ed. by Devendra P. Varma. LC 79-8458. (Gothic Studies & Dissertations). 1980. lib. bdg. 24.95 (*0-405-12647-6*) Ayer.

Three Studies on Egyptian Feasts & Their Chronological Implications. Anthony Spalinger. 75p. (Orig.). (C). 1992. pap. 36.00 (*0-9613805-6-X*) Halgo Inc.

Three Studies on National Integration in the Arab World. C. Farah et al. (Information Papers: No. 12). 34p. (Orig.). 1974. pap. text ed. 1.00 (*0-937694-28-2*) Assn Arab-Amer U Grads.

Three Stuffed Owls, 2 vols. large type ed. Robertson. (J). (gr. 6-7). reprint ed. Set. 10.00 (*0-318-65701-5*) NAVH.

Three Styles in the Study of Kinship. J. A. Barnes. LC 74-142057. 1972. 45.00 (*0-520-01879-6*) U CA Pr.

***Three Summers.** Margarita Liberaki. Tr. by Karen Van Dyck. (Modern Greek Writers Ser.). 320p. pap. 19.95 (*960-04-0948-X*, Pub. by Kedros Pubs GR) Paul & Co Pubs.

Three Suns of Vina. Roger Leloup. Tr. by Dwight Decker from FRE. (Adventures of Yoko, Vic & Paul Ser.). (Illus.). 49p. 1989. pap. 6.95 (*0-87416-076-6*, Comcat Comics) Catalan Communs.

Three Swahili Women: Life Histories from Mombasa, Kenya. Ed. by Sarah Mirza & Margaret Strobel. LC 88-45093. (Illus.). 176p. 1989. pap. 10.95 (*0-253-28854-1*) Ind U Pr.

Three Swahili Women: Life Histories from Mombasa, Kenya. Ed. by Margaret Strobel & Sarah M. Mirza. LC 88-45093. (Illus.). 176p. 1989. 27.50 (*0-253-36012-9*) Ind U Pr.

Three Swiss Painters: Cuno Amiet, Giovanni Giacometti, Augusto Giacometti: Exhibition Catalogue. George Mauner. (Illus.). 166p. 1973. pap. 7.50 (*0-911209-02-6*) Palmer Mus Art.

Three Swiss Realists: Gotthelf, Keller, & Meyer. Robert Godwin-Jones & Margaret T. Peischl. LC 88-5778. 264p. (C). 1988. lib. bdg. 45.00 (*0-8191-6965-X*) U Pr of Amer.

Three Tales. Gustave Flaubert. (Orig.). 1976. 20.95 (*0-8488-0486-4*) Amereon Ltd.

Three Tales. Gustave Flaubert. Tr. by Walter J. Cobb. (Orig.). 1989. mass mkt. 4.95 (*0-452-01002-0*, Mer) NAL-Dutton.

Three Tales. Gustave Flaubert. Tr. & Intro. by Alban J. Krailsheimer. (World's Classics Ser.). 142p. (Orig.). 1991. pap. 5.95 (*0-19-282226-8*) OUP.

Three Tales. Gustave Flaubert. Tr. by Robert Baldick. Incl. Simple Heart. 1961. pap. (*0-318-55110-1*); Legend of Saint Julian Hospitator. 1961. pap. (*0-318-55111-X*); Herodias. 1961. pap. (*0-318-55112-8*); (Classics Ser.). 128p. (Orig.). 1961. pap. 9.95 (*0-14-044106-9*, Penguin Classics) Viking Penguin.

Three Tales from Japan. Robin Hall. (J). (gr. 1-9). 1973. 5.00 (*0-87602-209-3*) Anchorage.

Three Talks & a Few Words. Richard Usborne et al. 52p. 1995. reprint ed. 18.50 (*0-87008-103-9*) JAS Heineman.

Three Tall Women. Edward Albee. 1994. pap. 5.25 (*0-8222-1420-2*) Dramatists Play.

Three Tall Women. Edward Albee. 128p. 1995. pap. 9.95 (*0-452-27400-1*, Plume) NAL-Dutton.

Three Tall Women: A Play in Two Acts. Edward Albee. LC 94-23234. 128p. 1995. pap. 17.95 (*0-525-93960-1*, Dutton) NAL-Dutton.

Three Taxes, Law of Wealth, Gift & Expenditure Tax, 2 vols. Ed. by K. Chaturvedi & M. K. Pithisaria. (C). 1989. Set. 660.00 (*0-685-36454-2*) St Mut.

Three Terrible Trins. Dick King-Smith. (Illus.). 128p. (J). (gr. 2-7). 1994. 15.00 (*0-517-59828-0*); lib. bdg. 16.99 (*0-517-59829-9*) Crown Bks Yng Read.

***Three Terrible Twins.** Dick King-Smith. (J). 1997. pap. 4.99 (*0-679-88552-8*) Knopf.

Three Texas Poets. Charles Behlen et al. (Illus.). 80p. (Orig.). (C). 1986. pap. 8.95 (*0-317-43327-X*); lib. bdg. 12.95 (*0-317-43326-1*) Prickly Pear.

Three-Text Hamlet: Parallel Texts of the First & Second Quartos & First Folio. William Shakespeare. Ed. by Bernice W. Kliman & Paul Bertram. LC 90-21317. (Studies in the Renaissance: No. 30). 1991. 64.50 (*0-404-62330-1*) AMS Pr.

Three the Lost Ant. Diana Stoneberg. (Illus.). 18p. (J). (gr. k-3). 1995. write for info. (*0-9642796-1-4*) Snapping Turtle.

Three Theban Plays. Sophocles. Ed. by Constantine A. Trypanis. (Classical Texts Ser.). 1986. pap. 17.50 (*0-85668-375-2*, Pub. by Aris & Phillips UK) David Brown.

Three Theban Plays. Sophocles. Tr. by Robert Fagels. 1992. reprint ed. lib. bdg. 24.95 (*0-89968-265-0*, Lghtyr Pr) Buccaneer Bks.

***Three Theban Plays: Antigone, Oedipus the King, Oedipus at Colonus.** Tr. by Theodore H. Harold. 144p. 1956. pap. 12.95 (*0-19-501059-0*) OUP.

Three Theban Plays: Antigone, Oedipus the King, Oedipus at Colonus. Sophocles. Tr. by Robert Fagles. (Classics Ser.). 432p. 1984. pap. 9.95 (*0-14-044425-4*, Penguin Classics) Viking Penguin.

Three Thinkers of Thay-Lee. D. L. Pape. LC 68-56828. (Sound Ser.). (Illus.). 48p. (J). (gr. 2-5). 1968. lib. bdg. 10.95 (*0-87783-040-1*) Oddo.

Three Thirteenth Century Dances. Ed. by Peter Hedrick. 1975. 4.00 (*0-913334-26-X*, CM1034) Consort Music.

Three Thirty-Four. Thomas M. Disch. 248p. 1987. pap. 3.95 (*0-88184-340-7*) Carroll & Graf.

Three Thirty-One Last Processes in Radiation Chemistry: International Symposium on Fast Processes in Radiation Chemistry. Y. Tabata. 1983. pap. 50.00 (*0-08-029155-4*, Pergamon Pr) Elsevier.

Three Thousand & Eight Hundred Early Advertising Cuts. Deberny T. Foundry. (Pictorial Archive Ser.). (Illus.). 192p. (Orig.). 1991. pap. 8.95 (*0-486-26658-3*) Dover.

Three Thousand Five Hundred Good Jokes for Speakers. Gerald F. Lieberman. LC 74-29354. 480p. 1975. pap. 7.95 (*0-385-00545-8*, Dolp) Doubleday.

Three Thousand Five Hundred Good Quotes for Speakers. Gerald F. Lieberman. LC 81-43552. 288p. 1987. pap. 7.95 (*0-385-17769-0*) Doubleday.

Three Thousand Futures: The Next Twenty Years for Higher Education: Final Report. Carnegie Council on Policy Studies in Higher Education Staff. LC 79-9675. (Carnegie Council Ser.). (Illus.). 461p. reprint ed. pap. 131.40 (*0-8357-4873-1*, 2037805) Bks Demand.

3000 Mile Garden: An Exchange of Letters on Gardening, Food, & the Good Life. Roger Phillips & Leslie Land. LC 95-24621. (Illus.). 320p. 1996. pap. 24.95 (*0-670-86714-4*, Viking) Viking Penguin.

***3001: The Final Odyssey.** Arthur C. Clarke. LC 96-49490. 263p. 1997. 25.00 (*0-345-31522-7*, Del Rey) Ballantine.

***3001: The Final Odyssey.** large type ed. Arthur C. Clarke. LC 97-10818. 1997. 25.95 (*0-7838-8190-8*) G K Hall.

An Asterisk (*) at the beginning of an entry indicates that the title is appearing in BIP for the first time.

Three Thousand One Questions & Answers. A. R. Harding. 395p. pap. 6.00 (*0-936622-22-9*) A R Harding Pub.
Three Thousand Problems in Chemistry. David E. Goldberg. (Schaum's Solved Problems Ser.). 1987. pap. 19.95 (*0-07-023665-8*) McGraw.
3,000 Quotations from the Writings of Matthew Henry: Arranged Topically & Indexed Biblically. 2nd ed. Matthew Henry. LC 89-48222. 356p. (gr. 10). 1995. pap. 14.99 (*0-8007-5564-2*) Revell.
3000 Quotations from the Writings of George MacDonald. George MacDonald. 368p. (YA). (gr. 10). 1996. pap. 15.99 (*0-8007-5606-1*) Revell.
Three Thousand Six Hundred Ghanian Proverbs (from the Asante & Fante Language) J. G. Christaller. Tr. by Kofi R. Lange. LC 89-28424. (Studies in African Literature: Vol. 2). 323p. 1990. lib. bdg. 99.95 (*0-88946-234-8*) E Mellen.
Three Thousand Solved Problems in Biology. Ruth Bernstein. (Schaum's Solved Problems Ser.). 1988. pap. text ed. 16.95 (*0-07-005022-8*) McGraw.
Three Thousand Solved Problems in Physics. Alvin Halpern. (Schaum's Solved Problems Ser.). 1988. pap. text ed. 20.95 (*0-07-025734-5*) McGraw.
Three Thousand Solved Problems in Precalculus Mathematics. Philip A. Schmidt. (Schaum's Solved Problems Ser.). 3840p. 1989. pap. text ed. 16.95 (*0-07-055365-3*) McGraw.
Three Thousand Three Hundred Keyboard Chords. Brimhall. (Keyboard Chords Ser.). 1990. 7.95 (*0-685-32020-0*, P030) Hansen Ed Mus.
Three Thousand Transducers Varriable of Temperature, Heat Flux, Magnetic Qualities, Humidity & Moisture, Electromagnetic & Nuclear Radiation see ISA Transducer Compendium
3285 Bible Questions & Answers. Emily Filipi. 1994. 8.99 (*0-517-02748-8*) Random Hse Value.
Three Thousand Years in Glass: Treasures from The Walters Art Gallery. Robert P. Bergman et al. Ed. by Carol Strohecker. (Illus.). 16p. (Orig.). 1982. pap. 3.95 (*0-911886-24-9*) Walters Art.
***Three Thousand Years of Chinese Painting.** Hsin Yang. LC 97-11152. (Culture & Civilization of China Ser.). 1997. write for info. (*0-300-07013-6*) Yale U Pr.
Three Thousand Years of Educational Wisdom: Selections from Great Documents. 2nd enl. ed. Ed. by Robert Ulich. 668p. 1954. pap. 23.50 (*0-674-89072-8*) HUP.
Three Thousand Years of Espionage. Kurt Singer. 27.95 (*0-8488-0357-4*) Amereon Ltd.
***Three Thousand Years of Espionage: An Anthology of the World's Greatest Spy Stories.** Kurt D. Singer. 384p. 1970. 23.95 (*0-8369-8049-2*) Ayer.
Three, Three'-Dichlorobenzidine: Three, Three'-Dichloro-biphenyl-4, 4'-Dyldiamine. GDCh-Advisory Committee on Existing Chemicals of Environmental Relevance Staff. Tr. by M. J. Blumich from GER. LC 93-2637. (BUA Reports: Vol. 30). 79p. (ENG & GER.). 1993. pap. 32.00 (*3-527-28590-3*, VCH) Wiley.
Three-Three Point: Modern Opening Strategy. Nine-Dan Cho Chikun. Tr. by Stuart Dowsey from JPN. (Illus.). 216p. (Orig.). 1991. pap. 12.95 (*4-87187-044-8*, G44) Ishi Pr Intl.
Three, Three, the Rivals. Anthea Fraser. 1995. 18.95 (*0-312-11902-X*, Thomas Dunne Bks) St Martin.
***Three, Three, the Rivals.** Anthea Fraser. 1992. pap. 13.99 (*0-00-232380-X*) Collins SF.
Three, Three, the Rivals. large type ed. Anthea Fraser. (Mystery Ser.). 368p. 1993. 25.99 (*0-7089-2984-2*) Ulverscroft.
Three Tibetan Mysteries. H. I. Woolf. (Illus.). 268p. 1989. reprint ed. pap. 25.00 (*957-9482-22-5*) Oriental Bk Store.
Three Tibetan Mysteries: Tchrimekundan, Nansal, Djroazanmo. J. Bacot. (C). 1990. reprint ed. 21.00 (*81-85326-42-8*, Pub. by Vintage II) S Asia.
Three Tibetan Mysteries: Tchrimekundan, Nansal, Djroazanmo, As Performed in the Tibetan Monasteries. Jacques Bacot. Tr. by H. I. Woolf from FRE. LC 78-72375. (Illus.). reprint ed. 49.50 (*0-404-17225-3*) AMS Pr.
***Three-Tier Client/Server at Work: Ten of the World's Most Demanding Mission Critical Applications.** Jen Edwards & Jeri Edwards. 224p. 1997. pap. 22.99 (*0-471-18443-8*) Wiley.
Three Times a Bride. Catherine Spencer. (Presents Ser.). 1996. mass mkt. 3.50 (*0-373-11842-2*, 1-11842-1) Harlequin Bks.
Three Times a Bride. large type ed. Catherine Spencer. 288p. 1996. 21.50 (*0-263-14511-5*, Pub. by M & B UK) Ulverscroft.
Three Times a Woman: Chicana Poetry. Alicia Gaspar de Alba et al. LC 88-64101. 168p. 1989. pap. 16.00 (*0-916950-91-3*) Biling Rev-Pr.
Three Times Three. Paul Metcalf et al. LC 88-62647. 96p. (Orig.). 1989. pap. 10.00 (*0-933598-11-4*) NC Wesleyan Pr.
3 X 3 Eyes, Bk. 1. Yuzo Takada. (Illus.). 160p. 1995. pap. 12.95 (*1-56971-059-7*) Dark Horse Comics.
***Three to Get Deadly.** Janet Evanovich. 1997. 24.00 (*0-684-82265-2*, Scribners PB Fict) S&S Trade.
***Three to Get Deadly.** large type ed. Janet Evanovich. LC 97-9695. (Large Print Book Ser.). 1997. 25.95 (*1-56895-429-8*) Wheeler Pub.
Three to Get Married. Fulton J. Sheen. 216p. 1996. reprint ed. pap. 9.95 (*0-933932-87-1*) Scepter Pubs.
***Three to Get Ready: Premarital Counseling Manual.** Howard A. Eyrich. 228p. Date not set. reprint ed. pap. 14.95 (*1-885904-16-9*) Focus Pubng.
***Three to Get Ready: The Education of a White Family in Inner City Schools.** Lois M. Stalvey. LC 96-44854. Orig. Title: Getting Ready. 328p. 1996. pap. 16.95 (*0-299-15394-0*) U of Wis Pr.
3 to 1. Jim Coyne. Ed. by Maryann Dec. (Jim Coyne Ser.). 215p. (Orig.). (YA). 1996. 20.00 (*0-9648228-3-0*); pap. 11.00 (*0-614-16680-2*) Elysium Pubng.
3:00 to 6:00 P. M. Young Adolescents at Home & in the Community. Leah Lefstein et al. 92p. (Orig.). 1982. reprint ed. pap. 7.00 (*1-57482-714-6*) Search Inst.
Three to Win. James E. Adams. LC 77-72255. (Radiant Life Ser.). 125p. 1977. pap. 3.95 (*0-88243-906-5*, 02-0906); teacher ed., pap. 5.50 (*0-88243-176-5*, 32-0176) Gospel Pub.
Three Tomato Four: Pick, Cook & Store. Virginia B. Elliott. 44p. 1991. pap. write for info. (*1-883782-00-7*) Best Image.
Three Tombs & Other Stories. Domingo F. Nolasco. 97p. (Orig.). (C). 1992. pap. 6.75 (*971-10-0325-2*, Pub. by New Day Pub PH) Cellar.
Three Tours Through London in the Years 1748, 1776, 1797. Wilmarth S. Lewis. LC 77-104252. (Illus.). 135p. 1971. reprint ed. lib. bdg. 49.75 (*0-8371-3977-5*, LETL, Greenwood Pr) Greenwood.
***Three Tragedies: Blood Wedding, Yerma & House of Bernarda Alba.** Federico Garcia Lorca. Tr. by Richard L. O'Connell & James Graham-Lujan. LC 77-11626. 1956. pap. 9.95 (*0-8112-0092-2*, NDP52) New Directions.
Three Tragedies: Blood Wedding, Yerma, Bernarda Alba. Federico Garcia Lorca. Tr. by Richard L. O'Connell & James Graham-Lujan from SPA. LC 77-3056. 212p. 1977. reprint ed. text ed. 55.00 (*0-8371-9578-0*, LOTT, Greenwood Pr) Greenwood.
Three Tragedies: Trojan Women, Medea & Phaedra. Lucius A. Seneca. LC 86-47632. (Masters of Latin Literature Ser.). 272p. 1986. 47.50 (*0-8014-1664-7*) Cornell U Pr.
Three Tragic Actresses: Siddons, Rachel, Ristori. Michael R. Booth et al. (Illus.). 200p. (C). 1996. text ed. 49.95 (*0-521-41115-7*) Cambridge U Pr.
Three Transcendentalists: Kant, Thoreau, & Contemporary. Richard S. Hoehler. LC 71-185781. (Illus.). 432p. 1972. 20.00 (*0-930590-00-7*) R Hoehler Pub.
Three Transcriptions: Violin/Piano Great Performers Edition. N. Milstein. 1986. pap. 7.50 (*0-7935-5463-2*, 50333740) H Leonard.
3-Transposition Groups. Michael Aschbacher. (Tracts in Mathematics Ser.: No. 124). (Illus.). 224p. (C). 1996. text ed. 49.95 (*0-521-57196-0*) Cambridge U Pr.
***Three Trapped Tigers.** Guillermo C. Infante. 1997. pap. text ed. 14.95 (*1-56924-713-7*) Marlowe & Co.
Three Trapped Tigers. G. Cabrera Infante. 487p. 1993. reprint ed. pap. 10.95 (*0-571-15370-4*) Faber & Faber.
Three Treatises. rev. ed. Martin Luther. LC 73-114753. 320p. 1970. pap. 12.00 (*0-8006-1639-1*, 1-1639, Fortress Pr) Augsburg Fortress.
Three Treatises on Man: A Cistercian Anthropology. Ed. by Bernard McGinn. LC 77-184906. (Cistercian Fathers Ser.: No. 24). 1977. 13.95 (*0-87907-024-2*) Cistercian Pubns.
Three Treatises on the Nature of Science. Galen. Ed. by Michael Frede & R. Walzer. Tr. by R. Walzer from GRE. LC 84-19826. (HPC Classics Ser.). 148p. (C). 1985. pap. text ed. 10.95 (*0-915145-92-8*); lib. bdg. 34.95 (*0-915145-91-X*) Hackett Pub.
Three Trials. William H. Rehnquist. Date not set. pap. write for info. (*0-679-44661-3*) McKay.
Three Tudor Classical Interludes: Thersites, Jacke Jugeler, Horestes. Ed. by Marie Axton. (Tudor Interludes Ser.: No. III). (Illus.). 247p. 1977. 59.00 (*0-85991-096-2*) Boydell & Brewer.
Three Tudor Dialogues. LC 78-14887. 1979. 50.00 (*0-8201-1319-0*) Schol Facsimiles.
***3 Tunes & a Vibe.** Frank J. Valentino. (Illus.). 25p. (Orig.). 1997. pap. text ed. 5.00 (*1-880764-10-5*) Northwind NJ.
3" Tutor - Intermediate Macroeconomics. Auerbach. (HB - Economics Ser.). 1995. 14.95 (*0-538-84275-X*) S-W Pub.
Three Types of Religious Philosophy. 2nd ed. Gordon H. Clark. Ed. & Intro. by John W. Robbins. 155p. 1989. pap. 6.95 (*0-940931-21-4*) Trinity Found.
Three Uneasy Pieces. Patrick White. (C). 1990. 45.00 (*0-947087-13-3*, Pub. by Pascoe Pub AT); pap. 24.00 (*0-685-52921-5*, Pub. by Pascoe Pub AT) St Mut.
Three Unique Letters to Alexander Humboldt by Peter S. P. Pallas & Wilhelm H. Abich. fac. ed. Ed. by Karel B. Absolon. (Illus.). 24p. (C). 1994. pap. 14.50 (*0-614-04352-2*) Kabel Pubs.
Three up a Tree. James Marshall. LC 86-2163. (Easy-to-Read Bks.). (Illus.). 48p. (J). (ps-3). 1986. pap. 9.95 (*0-8037-0328-7*); lib. bdg. 9.89 (*0-685-13452-0*) Dial Bks Young.
Three up a Tree Level 2, Red. James Marshall. LC 86-2163. (Illus.). (J). (gr. k-3). 1994. pap. 3.50 (*0-14-037003-X*) Puffin Bks.
Three Urgent Messages: (From the Book of Revelation) Kingdom Quotes Staff. pap. write for info. (*0-930179-15-3*) Johns Enter.
Three Uses of Christian Discourse in John Henry Newman: An Example of Nonreductive Reflection on the Christian Faith. Jouett L. Powell. LC 75-29423. (American Academy of Religion. Dissertation Ser.: No. 10). 242p. reprint ed. pap. 69.00 (*0-7837-5487-6*, 2045252) Bks Demand.
***Three Uses of the Knife: On the Nature & Purpose of Drama.** David Mamet. LC 97-23606. 1998. 19.95 (*0-231-11088-X*) Col U Pr.
Three Vehicles of Buddhist Practice. G. Rabjam & Abbot of Rumtek Monastery. Tr. by Ken Holmes. (C). 1995. 15.00 (*81-7030-457-1*, Pub. by Sri Satguru Pubns II) S Asia.
Three Victorian Detective Novels. Ed. by E. F. Bleiler. 1978. pap. 8.95 (*0-486-23668-4*) Dover.
Three Victorian Telephone Directories. Ed. & Intro. by David S. Thomas. 1970. 24.95 (*0-678-05678-1*) Kelley.
Three Victorians in the New World: Interpretations of America in the Works of Frances Trollope, Charles Dickens, & Anthony Trollope. Helen K. Heineman. (American University Studies: Ser. IV, Vol. 106). 298p. (C). 1990. text ed. 44.95 (*0-8204-0967-7*) P Lang Pubng.
Three Viennese Comedies. Johann Nestroy. Tr. by Robert Harrison & Katharina M. Wilson from GER. LC 85-71916. (GERM Ser.: Vol. 21). (Illus.). viii, 264p. 1986. 29.00 (*0-938100-37-8*) Camden Hse.
Three Viewings. Jeffrey Hatcher. 1996. pap. 5.25 (*0-8222-1494-6*) Dramatists Play.
Three Views of the Internet. Ed. by Ann M. Cunningham & Wendy Wicks. (Report Series, 1993: No. 3). 128p. (Orig.). (C). 1993. pap. 60.00 (*0-942308-42-5*) NFAIS.
Three Views on the Rapture: Pre-, Mid-, or Post-Tribulation ? Gleason L. Archer. LC 96-22775. (Counterpoints Ser.). 272p. 1996. pap. 14.99 (*0-310-21298-7*) Zondervan.
Three Virginia Frontiers. Thomas P. Abernethy. 1962. 14.50 (*0-8446-1001-1*) Peter Smith.
***Three Visitors for Jesus.** Carol Wehrheim. (Word & Picture Bks.: Set 2). (Illus.). 12p. (J). (gr. k). 1997. bds. 4.95 (*0-8298-1194-X*) Pilgrim OH.
***Three Visitors to Early Plymouth.** John Pory et al. 96p. 1997. reprint ed. pap. 9.95 (*1-55709-463-2*) Applewood.
Three-Voice Mass in the Later Fifteenth & Early Sixteenth Centuries: Style, Distribution, & Case Studies. rev. ed. Andrew Kirkman. LC 94-43504. (Outstanding Dissertations in Music from British Universities Ser.). (Illus.). 378p. 1995. text ed. 93.00 (*0-8153-1871-5*) Garland.
Three Voices: An Invitation to Poetry Across the Curriculum. Bernice Cullinan et al. (Illus.). 152p. (Orig.). (C). 1995. pap. text ed. 18.50 (*1-57110-015-6*) Stenhse Pubs.
Three Voices of Art Therapy: Image, Client, Therapist. Tessa Dalley et al. LC 93-16768. (Illus.). 192p. (C). 1993. pap. 17.95 (*0-415-07796-6*, B0888); text ed. 69.95 (*0-415-07795-8*, B0884) Routledge.
Three Vows. Gerald Epstein. 1997. write for info. (*0-517-70549-4*) Random.
Three Waifs & a Daddy. Margot Dalton. (Superromance Ser.: No. 480). 1991. mass mkt. 3.29 (*0-373-70480-1*) Harlequin Bks.
Three Wartons. Ed. by Eric Partridge. LC 71-128881. (Select Bibliographies Reprint Ser.). 1977. reprint ed. 19.95 (*0-8369-5501-3*) Ayer.
Three-Way Scaling & Clustering. Phipps Arabie et al. (Quantitative Applications in the Social Sciences Ser.: Vol. 65). 92p. (C). 1987. pap. text ed. 9.95 (*0-8039-3068-2*) Sage.
Three-Way Split. Rebecca Brown. LC 77-8993. (Illus.). 1978. pap. 4.00 (*0-916382-14-1*) Telephone Bks.
Three Way Street: Strategic Reciprocity in World Politics. Joshua S. Goldstein & John R. Freeman. LC 90-10812. (Illus.). xiv, 254p. 1990. pap. text ed. 13.95 (*0-226-30159-1*); lib. bdg. 36.00 (*0-226-30158-3*) U Ch Pr.
Three Wayfarers. Thomas Hardy. LC 44-3618. 1979. reprint ed. lib. bdg. 50.00 (*0-8201-1206-2*) Schol Facsimiles.
Three Ways of the Spiritual Life. Reginald Garrigou-Lagrange. 1977. reprint ed. pap. 6.00 (*0-89555-017-2*) TAN Bks Pubs.
Three Ways of Thought in Ancient China. Arthur Waley. xv, 216p. 1939. reprint ed. pap. 10.95 (*0-8047-1169-0*) Stanford U Pr.
Three Weddings & a Kiss. Kathleen E. Woodiwiss et al. 400p. 1995. mass mkt. 5.99 (*0-380-78122-0*) Avon.
Three Weddings & a Kiss. large type ed. Kathleen E. Woodiwiss et al. 571p. 1996. 24.95 (*0-7862-0614-4*) Thorndike Pr.
Three-Week Trance Diet. Jane Piirto. 240p. (Orig.). 1985. pap. 12.50 (*0-914140-14-0*) Carpenter Pr.
Three Weeks in October: The Great Earthquake Series of '89. Ron Fimrite et al. Ed. by Laurence J. Hyman. (Illus.). 132p. (Orig.). 1990. 29.95 (*0-942627-10-5*) Woodford Pubng.
***Three Weeks to Better Kids: Making Rules That Stick, & Discipline with a Smile.** George J. Downing. 210p. (Orig.). 1996. pap. 19.95 (*1-889565-06-7*, 996) Omnipr.
Three White Swans. large type ed. Cloete Stuart. 1991. 25.99 (*0-7089-2497-2*) Ulverscroft.
Three Who Dared: Prudence Crandall, Margaret Douglass, Myrtilla Miner-Champions of Antebellum Black Education. Philip S. Foner & Josephine F. Pacheco. LC 83-12830. (Contributions in Women's Studies: No. 47). xviii, 234p. 1984. text ed. 42.95 (*0-313-23584-8*, FTH/) Greenwood.
Three Who Made a Revolution. Bertram D. Wolfe. 37.95 (*0-8488-1225-5*) Amereon Ltd.
Three Who Made a Revolution. Bertram D. Wolfe. 1986. pap. 14.95 (*0-8128-6212-0*, Scrbrough Hse) Madison Bks UPA.
Three Why's of the Russian Revolution. Richard Pipes. LC 96-46857. 1997. pap. 11.00 (*0-679-77646-X*) Random.
Three Windows. Greg Evason. (Illus.). 48p. (Orig.). 1988. pap. 3.00 (*0-926935-04-6*) Runaway Spoon.
Three Windows. Abby Niebauer. (Illus.). 60p. (Orig.). 1980. 140.00 (*0-940592-05-3*) Heyeck Pr.
Three Winter Poems. Ardyth Bradley et al. (Illus.). 1985. pap. 20.00 (*0-318-41021-4*) Abattoir.
Three Wise Men. Regine Schindler. (Illus.). (C). 1989. 35.00 (*0-85439-304-8*, Pub. by St Paul Pubns UK) St Mut.
Three Wise Men & a Baby. Jenna McKnight. 1996. pap. 3.75 (*0-373-16660-5*, 1-16660-2) Harlequin Bks.
Three Wise Men Dream Book. Zonite. pap. 4.00 (*0-685-48421-1*) Wehman.
3 Wise Men Dream Book 1995. Sneaky Pete Group, Inc. Staff & Calvin P. Kline. 80p. pap. 4.95 (*0-944149-08-1*) Sneaky Pete.
***3 Wishes.** 1997. pap. write for info. (*0-8289-1010-3*) Viking Penguin.
Three Wishes. Lucille Clifton. (Illus.). 32p. (J). (ps-3). 1994. pap. 4.99 (*0-440-40921-7*) Dell.
Three Wishes. M. Jean Craig. (Easy to Read Folktales Ser.). (Illus.). 32p. (Orig.). (J). (gr. k-3). 1986. pap. 2.99 (*0-590-41744-4*) Scholastic Inc.
Three Wishes. Jaymi Cristol. (Lucky in Love Ser.: No. 28). 304p. 1993. mass mkt. 3.50 (*0-8217-4114-4*, Zebra Kensgtn) Kensgtn Pub Corp.
***Three Wishes.** Barbara Delinsky. LC 97-15217. 1997. 23.00 (*0-684-84507-5*) S&S Trade.
Three Wishes. Charles Perrault. LC 78-18060. (Illus.). 32p. (J). (gr. k-3). 1979. pap. 3.95 (*0-89375-107-3*); lib. bdg. 11.89 (*0-89375-129-4*) Troll Communs.
***Three Wishes.** Judith B. Stamper & Wiley Blevins. LC 97-14517. (Hello Reader! Ser.). (Illus.). (J). 1997. write for info. (*0-590-76266-4*) Scholastic Inc.
Three Wishes. Harriet Ziefert. (Hello Reading! Ser.). (Illus.). 32p. (J). (ps-3). 1993. pap. 3.50 (*0-14-054556-5*) Puffin Bks.
Three Wishes. Harriet Ziefert. (Illus.). 32p. 1996. pap. 3.50 (*0-14-038323-9*) Viking Penguin.
Three Wishes: An Old Story. Margot Zemach. LC 86-80956. (Illus.). 32p. (J). (ps up). 1986. 16.00 (*0-374-37529-1*) FS&G.
Three Wishes: An Old Story. Margot Zemoch. (J). (ps-3). 1993. pap. 4.95 (*0-374-47728-0*) FS&G.
Three Wishes: Puerto Rican Story Pak. Retold by K. Hollenbeck. (Graphic Learning Literature Program Series: Folk Tales). (Illus.). (ENG & SPA.). 1992. 43.00 (*0-87746-271-2*) Graphic Learning.
Three Wishes for Jamie. Charles O'Neal. 1976. 22.95 (*0-8488-0184-9*) Amereon Ltd.
Three Wishes for Jamie. large type ed. Charles O'Neal. LC 93-42059. 1994. lib. bdg. 17.95 (*0-7862-0140-1*) Thorndike Pr.
Three Wishes for Jamie. Charles O'Neal. LC 79-66116. 256p. 1980. reprint ed. 22.00 (*0-933256-08-6*); reprint ed. pap. text ed. 16.00 (*0-933256-09-4*) Second Chance.
Three with a Bullet. Arthur Lyons. LC 84-4598. 240p. 1986. pap. 3.95 (*0-03-008539-X*, Owl) H Holt & Co.
Three Wogs: A Novel. Alexander Theroux. LC 96-30743. 224p. 1997. pap. 14.00 (*0-8050-4459-0*) H Holt & Co.
Three Women. Marie Hanson. LC 85-71032. 190p. (Orig.). 1985. pap. 7.95 (*0-933753-01-2*) Canterbury.
Three Women. March Hastings. 240p. 1989. pap. 8.95 (*0-941483-43-6*) Naiad Pr.
Three Women. Anne McCaffrey. 1992. mass mkt. 5.99 (*0-8125-0587-5*) Tor Bks.
***Three Women: Touching the Boundaries of Life.** Mark Saba et al. LC 96-31424. 212p. 1996. pap. 29.95 (*0-7734-2704-X*, Mellen Poetry Pr) E Mellen.
***Three Women at the Water's Edge, Vol. 1.** Nancy Thayer. 1996. mass mkt. 6.99 (*0-312-96064-6*) St Martin.
Three Women in the House. large type ed. Estelle Thompson. 1979. 25.99 (*0-7089-0366-5*) Ulverscroft.
Three Women K. Helke Sander. LC 90-60277. 1991. pap. 13.95 (*1-85242-171-1*) Serpents Tail.
Three Women of Herat. Veronica Doubleday. (Illus.). 256p. (Orig.). 1990. pap. 14.95 (*0-292-78112-1*) U of Tex Pr.
Three Women of Herat. large type ed. Veronica Doubleday. (Orig.). 1990. 25.99 (*0-7089-2201-5*) Ulverscroft.
Three Women Poets: Poems by Louise Labe, Gaspara Stampa, & Sor Juana Ines de la Cruz. Ed. by Frank J. Warnke. LC 84-46104. (Illus.). 136p. 1987. 32.50 (*0-8387-5089-3*) Bucknell U Pr.
Three Women Prophets: Ellen Gould White see Millennium in America: From the Puritan Migration to the Civil War
Three Women Prophets: Harriet Livermore see Millennium in America: From the Puritan Migration to the Civil War
Three Women Prophets: Phoebe Palmer see Millennium in America: From the Puritan Migration to the Civil War
Three Wonder Plays: The Dragon, Aristotle's Bellows, The Jester. Isabella A. Gregory. (BCL1-PR English Literature Ser.). 290p. 1992. reprint ed. lib. bdg. 79.00 (*0-7812-7544-X*) Rprt Serv.
Three Words a Day for Kids: A Fun & Helpful Calendar Journal. 366p. (J). (gr. 1-6). 1993. spiral bd. 8.50 (*1-882835-21-2*) STA-Kris.
Three Words a Day for Teachers: A Helpful & Stimulating Calendar Journal. 366p. (Orig.). 1992. spiral bd. 8.50 (*1-882835-08-5*) STA-Kris.
OS/23 Warp Workplace Shell API. Mindy Pollack. 480p. 1995. pap. text ed. 29.95 (*0-471-03872-5*) Wiley.
Three Works. Morris. (C). 1968. pap. 15.00 (*0-85315-170-9*, Pub. by Lawrence & Wishart UK) NYU Pr.
Three Works. William Morris. Ed. by A. L. Morton. 404p. 1987. reprint ed. pap. 4.95 (*0-7178-0202-7*) Intl Pubs Co.
Three Works of Ancient Jewish Magic. G. Gaster & D. Daiches. 156p. (C). 1988. text ed. 95.00 (*0-948366-03-6*, Pub. by Chthonios Bks UK) St Mut.
Three World Surveys by the Food & Agriculture Organization of the United Nations: An Original Anthology. LC 75-27639. (World Food Supply Ser.). (Illus.). 1976. 23.95 (*0-405-07779-3*) Ayer.
Three Worlds: Plan of Redemption. Nelson H. Barbour. 199p. 1985. reprint ed. pap. 7.95 (*1-883858-30-5*) Witness CA.
***Three Worlds According to King Ruang: A Thai Buddhist Cosmology.** Ed. by Frank E. Reynolds & Mani B. Reynolds. (Berkeley Buddhist Studies). (Illus.). 383p. 1982. 30.00 (*0-87725-314-5*) U of Cal IAS.
Three Worlds of Bali. J. Stephen Lansing. LC 83-4117. (Illus.). 188p. 1983. text ed. 37.50 (*0-275-91720-7*, C1720, Praeger Pubs) Greenwood.

T

Three Worlds of Culture & World Development. Peter Worsley. LC 84-2609. 424p. 1984. pap. 20.95 (*0-226-90755-4*) U Ch Pr.

Three Worlds of Economics. Lloyd G. Reynolds. LC 71-151588. (Studies in Comparative Economics: No. 12). 358p. reprint ed. pap. 102.10 (*0-8357-8352-9*, 2033870) Bks Demand.

Three Worlds of Labor Economics. Ed. by Garth L. Mangum & Peter Philips. LC 87-26423. 392p. (C). 1988. pap. text ed. 29.95 (*0-87332-456-0*) M E Sharpe.

Three Worlds of Labor Economics. Ed. by Garth L. Mangum & Peter Philips. LC 87-26423. 392p. (C). (gr. 13). 1988. text ed. 62.95 (*0-87332-455-2*) M E Sharpe.

Three Worlds of Larissa. Larissa Kotyeva. LC 93-71552. (Illus.). 290p. (Orig.). 1993. pap. 16.50 (*1-879418-08-8*) Biddle Pub.

Three Worlds of Medicine: Stories of Hope & Courage. Herbert Chasis. Ed. by Roger E. Egan, Sr. (Illus.). 160p. (Orig.). pap. 21.95 (*0-9632687-4-0*) PenRose Pub.

***Three Worlds of Paul of Tarsus.** Richard Wallace & Wynne Williams. LC 97-15856. 1998. write for info. (*0-415-13591-5*); pap. write for info. (*0-415-13592-3*) Routledge.

Three Worlds of Welfare Capitalism. Gosta Esping-Andersen. 240p. 1990. pap. text ed. 16.95 (*0-691-02857-5*) Princeton U Pr.

Three Writers in Exile: Eliot, Pound & Joyce. Doris L. Eder. LC 84-51739. 108p. 1985. 12.50 (*0-87875-292-7*) Whitston Pub.

Three Writers of Victorian Canada. Carole Gerson. 62p. (C). 1983. pap. text ed. 9.95 (*0-920763-42-1*, Pub. by ECW Press CN) Genl Dist Srvs.

Peter I Island 1994 Expedition. Robert W. Schmieder. (Illus.). 240p. (Orig.). 1994. pap. 20.00 (*0-9626013-5-7*) Cordell Expeditions.

Three-Year Garden Journal. Joanne Lawson & Louise Carter. (Illus.). 208p. 1989. 27.95 (*0-912347-36-8*) Fulcrum Pub.

***Three-Year MENU Planner: (Efficient, Wall-Hanging, Week-by-Week Design)** Lucia Jewel. (Illus.). 170p. 1997. vinyl bd. 18.50 (*1-886197-10-5*) Joy Books.

Three Years: The Life of Christ Between Baptism & Ascension. Emil Bock. 290p. 1990. 27.50 (*0-86315-060-8*, 1307, Pub. by Floris Books UK) Anthroposophic.

Three Years among Indians in Dakota. J. H. Drips. 1976. 22.95 (*0-8488-0220-9*, J M C & Co) Amereon Ltd.

Three Years among the Comanches: The Narrative of Nelson Lee, the Texas Ranger. Nelson Lee. LC 57-11197. (Western Frontier Library: Vol. 9). 200p. 1991. pap. 10.95 (*0-8061-2339-7*) U of Okla Pr.

Three Years among the Indians & Mexicans. Thomas James. LC 83-23440. 197p. reprint ed. pap. 56.20 (*0-7837-1838-1*, 2042039) Bks Demand.

Three Years among the Indians & Mexicans. Thomas James. (American Biography Ser.). 130p. 1991. reprint ed. lib. bdg. 59.00 (*0-7812-8213-6*) Rprt Serv.

Three Years among the Working-Classes in the United States During the War. James D. Burn. LC 74-22735. reprint ed. 39.50 (*0-404-58487-X*) AMS Pr.

Three Years at the East-West Divide. Max M. Kampelman. Ed. by Leonard R. Sussman. LC 83-82249. (Perspectives on Freedom Ser.: No. 2). xix, 133p. 1983. 18.00 (*0-932088-04-X*); pap. 18.25 (*0-932088-05-8*) Freedom Hse.

Three Years Behind Barbed Wire: The Diary of a British Internee in Schloss Wurzach Germany 1942-1945. Coles. (Jersey Heritage Editions Ser.). 1991. 40.00 (*0-86120-008-X*, Pub. by Aris & Phillips UK) David Brown.

Three Years' Cruize in the Mozambique Channel: For the Suppression of the Slave Trade. F. L. Barnard. LC 79-149863. (Black Heritage Library Collection). 1977. 27.95 (*0-8369-8745-4*) Ayer.

Three Years in a Mantrap. Timothy S. Arthur. (Works of Timothy Shay Arthur). 1989. reprint ed. lib. bdg. 79.00 (*0-7812-1804-7*) Rprt Serv.

Three Years in America: 1859-1862, 2 Vols. Israel B. Benjamin. Tr. by Charles Reznikoff from GER. LC 74-27962. (Modern Jewish Experience Ser.). 1975. reprint ed. 57.95 (*0-405-06693-7*) Ayer.

Three Years in California. Walter Colton. Ed. by Carlos E. Cortes. LC 76-1221. (Chicano Heritage Ser.). (Illus.). 1977. reprint ed. 39.95 (*0-405-09496-5*) Ayer.

Three Years in California. Walter Colton. 1992. reprint ed. lib. bdg. 75.00 (*0-7812-5016-1*) Rprt Serv.

Three Years in California: William Perkins' Journal of Life at Sonora, 1849-1852. (With an Introduction & Annotations by Dale L. Morgan & James P. Scobie) William Perkins. LC 64-21141. (Illus.). 442p. reprint ed. pap. 126.00 (*0-685-23666-8*, 2029059) Bks Demand.

Three Years in North America, 2 Vols. James Stuart. LC 73-13151. (Foreign Travelers in America, 1810-1935 Ser.). 676p. 1974. reprint ed. 50.95 (*0-405-05474-2*) Ayer.

Three Years in the Army of the Cumberland. James A Connolly. Ed. by Paul M Angle. 1996. pap. text ed. 14.95 (*0-253-21073-9*) Ind U Pr.

Three Years in the Holy City see Prince of the House of David

Three Years in the Libyan Desert. J. C. Falls. 460p. 1990. 150.00 (*1-85077-080-8*, Pub. by Darf Pubs Ltd UK) St Mut.

Three Years in the Rocky Mountains. David L. Brown. 28p. 1975. pap. 4.95 (*0-87770-151-2*) Ye Galleon.

Three Years in Tibet. Ed. by Ekai Kawaguchi. 748p. (C). 1979. 175.00 (*0-89771-104-1*, Pub. by Ratna Pustak Bhandar) St Mut.

Three Years of H Cl Therapy. W. Roy Huntsman. 159p. 1976. reprint ed. spiral bd. 19.00 (*0-7873-0459-X*) Hlth Research.

Three Years of War in East Africa. Angus Buchanan. LC 72-90108. 247p. 1970. reprint ed. text ed. 35.00 (*0-8371-2026-8*, BUY&, Greenwood Pr) Greenwood.

Three Years Rings. John Perlman. 1972. 16.00 (*0-685-27715-1*); pap. 8.00 (*0-685-27716-X*) Elizabeth Pr.

Three Years' Service with the Thirty-Third Massachusetts Infantry 1862-1865. Adin B. Underwood. (Illus.). 420p. 1993. reprint ed. 30.00 (*0-9628866-8-8*) Blue Acorn Pr.

Three Years with Grant: As Recalled by War Correspondent Sylvanus Cadwallader. Sylvanus Cadwallader. Ed. & Intro. by Benjamin P. Thomas. LC 96-30286. xxxi, 362p. 1996. pap. 15.00 (*0-8032-6369-4*, Bison Books) U of Nebr Pr.

Three Years with Quantrell. John McCorkle. Ed. by D. S. Barton. LC 67-6851. (American Biography Ser.: No. 32). 1970. lib. bdg. 75.00 (*0-8383-1107-5*) M S G Haskell Hse.

Three Years with Quantrill: A True Story Told by His Scout. John McCorkle & O. S. Barton. LC 92-54158. (Western Frontier Library: Vol. 60). (Illus.). 240p. 1992. 19.95 (*0-8061-2451-2*) U of Okla Pr.

Three Years with the Poets. Ed. by Bertha Hazard. LC 70-108583. (Granger Index Reprint Ser.). 1977. 19.95 (*0-8369-6111-0*) Ayer.

***Three Yellow Dogs.** Caron L. Cohen. 1997. pap. 3.95 (*0-688-15286-4*, Mulberry) Morrow.

Three Yoruba Divination Systems & Ebo. Apena Taiyewo Ogunade. LC 94-67072. (Illus.). 84p. (Orig.). 1996. pap. 14.50 (*1-881549-05-4*) Oluweri Pubns.

Three Young Pilgrims. Cheryl Harness. LC 91-7289. (Illus.). 40p. (J). (gr. k-5). 1992. lib. bdg. 16.00 (*0-02-742643-2*, Bradbury S&S) S&S Childrens.

Three Young Pilgrims. Cheryl Harness. (J). 1995. pap. 5.95 (*0-689-80208-0*, Aladdin Paperbacks) S&S Childrens.

Three Zen Masters: Ikkyu, Hakuin, Ryokan. John Stevens. Ed. by Brase. (Biographies Ser.). (Illus.). 176p. (Orig.). 1993. pap. 10.00 (*4-7700-1651-4*) Kodansha.

Three Z's. Gordon Korman. LC 93-30421. 128p. (J). 1994. 13.95 (*0-590-47501-0*) Scholastic Inc.

***3D Contrast MR Angiography.** M. R. Prince et al. LC 97-6972. 1997. pap. write for info. (*3-540-62577-1*) Spr-Verlag.

3D Graphics: Tips, Tricks, & Techniques. David Kalwick. (Illus.). 478p. 1996. pap. 34.95 incl. cd-rom (*0-12-394970-X*) Acad Pr.

***3D Graphics File Formats.** Keith Rule. 1996. 39.95 (*0-614-20262-0*) Addison-Wesley.

3D Java. Chris Laurel. Date not set. pap. text ed. 50.00 (*1-56205-597-6*) New Riders Pub.

3D Radiation Treatment Planning & Conformal Therapy. Ed. by James Purdy & Bahman Emami. LC 95-80190. (Illus.). 465p. (C). 1996. pap. text ed. 98.95 (*0-944838-51-0*) Med Physics Pub.

3D Studio Max F/X. Jon Bell. 1996. pap. text ed. 49.99 incl. cd-rom (*1-56604-427-8*) Ventana Communs.

3D Studio 4 for Level 1. NRP Staff. 1996. wbk. ed. 30.00 (*1-56205-539-9*) New Riders Pub.

3DO Game Guide. Rusel DeMaria. 1995. pap. 16.95 (*1-55958-462-9*) Prima Pub.

3DO Game Secrets. J. Douglas Arnold & Zach Meston. (Gaming Mastery Ser.). (Illus.). 256p. (Orig.). 1995. pap. 14.95 (*1-884364-17-9*) Sandwich Islands.

Threefold Garland: The World's Salvation in Mary's Prayer. Hans U. Von Balthasar. Tr. by Erasmo Leiva-Merikakis & Erasmo Leiva from GER. LC 81-83569. 146p. (Orig.). 1982. pap. 9.95 (*0-89870-015-9*) Ignatius Pr.

Threefold Life of Man: The High & Deep Searching Out of the Three Principles. Jacob Boehme. Tr. by John Sparrow. 670p. 1992. pap. 33.00 (*1-56459-224-3*) Kessinger Pub.

Threefold Lotus Sutra: Sutra of Innumerable Meanings, Sutra of the Lotus Flower of the Wonderful Law, Sutra of Meditation on the Bodhisattva Universal Virtue. Tr. by Bunno Kato et al. from CHI. 404p. 1986. pap. 14.95 (*4-333-00208-7*, Pub. by Kosei Pub Co JA) C E Tuttle.

Threefold Method for Understanding the Seven Rays & Other Essays in Esoteric Psychology. Kurt Abraham. LC 84-81567. 120p. (Orig.). 1984. pap. 8.50 (*0-9609002-1-7*) Lampus Pr.

Threefold Paradise of Cotton Mather: An Edition of Triparadisus. Cotton Mather. Ed. by Reiner Smolinski. LC 92-29850. 520p. 1995. 75.00 (*0-8203-1519-2*) U of Ga Pr.

Threefold State. Rudolph Steiner. 201p. 1993. reprint ed. spiral bd. 8.50 (*0-7873-0843-9*) Hlth Research.

Threefold State: The True Aspect of the Social Question. Rudolph Steiner. 216p. 1996. pap. 19.95 (*1-56459-784-9*) Kessinger Pub.

3i: Fifty Years of Investing in Industry. Richard Coopey & Donald Clarke. (Illus.). 350p. 1995. 39.95 (*0-19-828944-8*) OUP.

***Threepenny Opera.** Bertolt Brecht. (Orig.). Date not set. lib. bdg. 17.95 (*0-8488-1668-4*) Amereon Ltd.

Threepenny Opera. Bertolt Brecht. Tr. by Desmond Vesey from FRE. LC 64-8478. 128p. (Orig.). 1983. pap. 5.95 (*0-8021-5039-X*, Grove) Grove-Atltic.

Threepenny Opera. Bertolt Brecht. Ed. by John Willett & Ralph Manheim. Tr. by Ralph Manheim from GER. 144p. (Orig.). (C). 1994. pap. 8.95 (*1-55970-252-4*) Arcade Pub Inc.

Threepenny Opera: Vocal Selections. Ed. by Carol Cuellar. 60p. (Orig.). (C). 1984. pap. text ed. 11.95 (*0-943351-70-7*, SF0137) Astor Bks.

3.Quik-Lab for AC Circuits - Conventional-Flow Version: A Whole-Brain Learning System. Albert P. Malvino. (IBM (MS-DOS) Ser.: No. 2). (Illus.). 2p. (C). 1989. wbk. ed. 16.45 incl. disk (*1-56048-812-3*, 802C) Malvino Inc.

Three's a Crowd. Judy Baer. (Cedar River Daydreams Ser.: Bk. 22). 144p. (YA). (gr. 7-10). 1994. mass mkt. 4.99 (*1-55661-526-4*) Bethany Hse.

Three's a Crowd. Doris M. Disney. 240p. 1987. mass mkt. 2.95 (*0-8217-2079-1*, Zebra Kensgtn) Kensgtn Pub Corp.

Three's a Crowd. Jordan Horowitz. (Cabbage Patch Kids Ser.). (Illus.). 32p. (J). (ps-3). 1992. pap. 2.50 (*0-590-45459-5*) Scholastic Inc.

Three's a Crowd. Francine Pascal. (Sweet Valley Twins Ser.: No. 7). 112p. (J). 1987. pap. 3.50 (*0-553-15661-6*) Bantam.

Three's a Crowd. large type ed. Jamie Suzanne. (Sweet Valley Twins Ser.: No. 7). 105p. (YA). (gr. 7-12). 1990. reprint ed. 9.95 (*1-55905-070-5*) Grey Castle.

Threescore. Sarah N. Cleghorn. Ed. by Annette K. Baxter. LC 79-8783. (Signal Lives Ser.). (Illus.). 1980. reprint ed. lib. bdg. 37.95 (*0-405-12831-2*) Ayer.

Threescore & Ten: Essays in Honor of Rabbi Seymour J. Cohen on the Occasion of His Seventieth Birthday. Ed. by Abraham J. Karp et al. 39.50 (*0-88125-386-3*) Ktav.

Three...Two...One Lift Off. Thomas Buckingham. (Readers Ser.). 1987. pap. text ed. 3.50 (*0-13-920455-5*) Prentice ESL.

***Threnody & Other Memories: 17 Chronicles.** Joseph Napoli. 350p. (Orig.). 1995. pap. 20.00 (*1-886166-02-1*) Marna Pr.

Thresher see Krause Trio

Thresher Sharks. Sarah Palmer. (Shark Discovery Library). (Illus.). 24p. (J). (gr. k-5). 1988. lib. bdg. 11.94 (*0-86592-460-0*); lib. bdg. 8.95 (*0-685-58313-9*) Rourke Corp.

Threshers. Andrew Morland & Robert A. Pripps. (Farm Tractor Color History Ser.). (Illus.). 128p. 1992. pap. 19.95 (*0-87938-617-7*) Motorbooks Intl.

***Threshers at Work.** Hans Halberstadt. LC 96-50418. (Illus.). 96p. 1997. pap. 14.95 (*0-7603-0133-6*) Motorbooks Intl.

Thresher's Labour & the Woman's Labour. Intro. by Moira Ferguson. LC 92-554. (Augustan Reprints Ser.: No. 230). 1985. reprint ed. 14.50 (*0-404-70230-9*) AMS Pr.

Threshers Labour-Womans Labour: Two Eighteenth Century Poems. Ed. by E. P. Thompson & Marian Sugden. (Illus.). 56p. (C). 1989. text ed. 9.95 (*0-85036-375-6*, Pub. by Merlin Pr UK) Humanities.

Threshing Floor. Barbara Burford. LC 87-7411. 214p. (Orig.). 1987. pap. 7.95 (*0-932379-27-3*); lib. bdg. 16.95 (*0-932379-28-1*) Firebrand Bks.

***Threshing Floor: An Interpretation of the Old Testament.** John F. Sheehan. LC 72-81574. 220p. 1985. reprint ed. pap. 62.70 (*0-608-04198-X*, 2064933) Bks Demand.

Threshing Time: A Tribute to James Hearst. Wayne Lanter. LC 96-67071. 55p. (Orig.). 1996. pap. 10.00 (*0-9650764-0-7*) River King.

Threshold! Astara. LC 96-92177. 112p. 1996. pap. 11.95 (*1-885226-11-X*) StarLineage.

Threshold. Ben Mezrich. LC 96-6362. 320p. 1996. 24.00 (*0-06-017302-5*) HarpC.

***Threshold.** Ben Mezrich. 352p. 1997. mass mkt. 6.99 (*0-446-60521-2*) Warner Bks.

Threshold. Janet Morris & Chris Morris. 256p. 1991. pap. 5.50 (*0-451-45084-1*, ROC) NAL-Dutton.

***Threshold.** Bill Myers. 304p. 1997. pap. 12.99 (*0-310-20120-9*) Zondervan.

Threshold. Zofia Pytowska. 176p. 1982. 18.95 (*0-87073-518-7*); pap. 14.95 (*0-87073-519-5*) Schenkman Bks Inc.

Threshold: African Art on the Verge. Allen F. Roberts. (Illus.). 96p. 1994. pap. 19.95 (*3-7913-1369-X*) Mus African Art.

Threshold: Cambridge Pre-GED Program in Interpreting Literature & the Arts. 2nd ed. Cambridge Staff. 224p. (C). 1992. pap. text ed. 7.25 (*0-13-111097-7*) P-H.

Threshold: Cambridge Pre GED Program in Math Two. Cambridge Staff. 288p. 1993. pap. text ed. 7.25 (*0-13-917600-4*, 640803) P-H.

Threshold: Cambridge Pre-GED Program in Mathematics. Cambridge Staff. 256p. 1992. pap. text ed. 7.25 (*0-13-110966-9*) P-H.

Threshold: Cambridge Pre-GED Program in Science. Cambridge Staff. 256p. (C). 1992. pap. text ed. 7.25 (*0-13-116419-8*) P-H.

Threshold: Cambridge Pre-GED Program in Social Studies. Cambridge Staff. 224p. 1994. pap. text ed. 7.25 (*0-13-111089-6*) P-H.

Threshold: Cambridge Pre-GED Program in Writing. Cambridge Staff. LC 93-5349. (C). 1993. pap. text ed. 7.25 (*0-13-110958-8*) P-H.

***Threshold Competitor: A Management Simulation.** 2nd ed. Philip H. Anderson & David A. Beveridge. (C). 1997. pap. text ed. 26.00 (*0-13-675539-9*) P-H.

Threshold Graphs & Related Topics. N. V. Mahadev & U. N. Peled. LC 95-24781. (Annals of Discrete Mathematics Ser.: Vol. 56). 558p. 1995. 162.50 (*0-444-89287-7*) Elsevier.

Threshold Is High: The Brethren in Christ in Japan. Doyle C. Book. Ed. by Ray M. Zercher. (Illus.). 208p. (Orig.). 1986. pap. 7.95 (*0-916035-15-8*) Evangel Indiana.

Threshold Level for Modern Language Learning in Schools. Jan A. Van Ek. (Applied Linguistics & Language Ser.). 1978. pap. text ed. 11.75 (*0-582-55700-3*) Longman.

Threshold Limit Values for Chemical Substances & Physical Agents & Biological Exposure Indices, 1996. (Illus.). (C). 1996. pap. text ed. 11.00 (*1-882417-13-5*) Am Conf Govt Indus Hygienist.

Threshold of a New Age. Wilbur Von Fange. Ed. by Ruth Von Fange. (Illus.). 268p. (Orig.). 1982. pap. 6.95 (*0-9607900-0-4*) W H Von Fange.

Threshold of a New World: Intellectuals & the Exile Experience in Paris, 1830-1848. Lloyd S. Kramer. LC 87-19899. 320p. 1988. 39.95 (*0-8014-1939-5*) Cornell U Pr.

Threshold of Anglo Saxon. Alfred J. Wyatt. LC 75-41302. reprint ed. 29.50 (*0-404-14634-1*) AMS Pr.

***Threshold of Empire: Battle for Manila 1898-1899.** James H. Nelson. 288p. (Orig.). 1997. pap. 19.95 (*1-884570-71-2*) Research Triangle.

Threshold of Eternity see Science & Religion Series

Threshold of Fire. Hella Haasse. Tr. by Anita Miller & Nini Blinstrub from DUT. 230p. 1993. 19.95 (*0-89733-390-X*) Academy Chi Pubs.

Threshold of Fire: A Novel of Fifth Century Rome. Hella Haasse. 255p. 1996. pap. text ed. 13.95 (*0-89733-426-4*) Academy Chi Pubs.

Threshold of Religion. Robert R. Marett. LC 76-44755. reprint ed. 34.50 (*0-404-15950-8*) AMS Pr.

Threshold of the Millennium: A Worldview Journal. 2nd ed. Barbara Scott et al. (Illus.). 216p. (Orig.). 1992. pap. text ed. 25.00 (*0-9631458-0-0*) Scott Grp.

***Threshold of the New.** Henry Sloss. 90p. 1997. 15.95 (*1-57003-234-3*) U of SC Pr.

***Threshold of the New.** Henry Sloss. 90p. 1997. pap. 9.95 (*1-57003-235-1*) U of SC Pr.

Threshold of the Spiritual World. Rudolf Steiner. 41p. 1994. reprint ed. spiral bd. 4.50 (*0-7873-1295-9*) Hlth Research.

Threshold of the Visible World. Kaja Silverman. 1995. pap. 17.95 (*0-415-91039-0*) Routledge.

Threshold of the Visible World. Kaja Silverman. (Illus.). (C). (gr. 13 up). 1995. text ed. 62.95 (*0-415-91038-2*, Routledge NY) Routledge.

Threshold of War: Franklin D. Roosevelt & the American Entry into World War II. Waldo H. Heinrichs, Jr. (Illus.). 302p. 1990. pap. 11.95 (*0-19-506168-3*) OUP.

Threshold Pressure in Gas Storage. American Gas Association, Pipeline Research Committee et al. 309p. 1971. 6.00 (*0-318-12724-5*, L20170) Am Gas Assn.

Threshold to Tomorrow. Ruth Montgomery. 1985. mass mkt. 5.99 (*0-449-20847-8*) Fawcett.

***Thresholds.** David P. Beavers. 1997. pap. text ed. 12.95 (*1-873741-28-6*, Pub. by Millvres Bks UK) LPC InBook.

Thresholds: A Study of Proust. Gerda Blumenthal. 112p. 1984. 13.95 (*0-917786-49-1*) Summa Pubns.

***Thresholds: Literature-Based Composition.** J. Sterling Warner. 632p. (C). 1996. pap. text ed. 27.50 (*0-15-501977-5*) HB Coll Pubs.

Thresholds: Near-Life Experiences. Ed. by Gabriel B. Millar. (Illus.). 192p. 1995. pap. 18.95 (*1-869890-68-X*, Pub. by Hawthorn Press UK) Anthroposophic.

Thresholds: Umbrales: Poems. Claribel Alegria. Tr. by Darwin J. Flakoll from SPA. LC 96-21329. 80p. 1996. pap. 10.95 (*1-880684-36-5*) Curbstone.

Thresholds & Testimonies: Recovering Order in Literature & Criticism. Frederic Will. LC 88-145. 184p. 1988. 29.95 (*0-8143-1943-2*) Wayne St U Pr.

***Thresholds in Feminist Geography: Difference, Methodology, Representation.** Ed. by John P. Jones, 3rd et al. LC 96-46790. (Illus.). 400p. 1997. 64.95 (*0-8476-8436-9*); pap. 21.95 (*0-8476-8437-7*) Rowman.

Thresholds in Precision Engineering - Abstracts & Agenda. 44p. 1986. pap. write for info. (*1-887706-00-3*) Am Soc Prec Engr.

Thresholds in Reading. Low. (College ESL Ser.). 1995. pap. 6.95 (*0-8384-5337-6*) Heinle & Heinle.

Thresholds in Reading. Martha Low. 224p. 1995. pap. 21.95 (*0-8384-5336-8*) Heinle & Heinle.

Thresholds of Change in African Literature: The Emergence of a Tradition. Kenneth W. Harrow. (Studies in African Literature). 371p. (C). 1993. pap. 25.00 (*0-435-08082-2*, 08082) Heinemann.

Thresholds of Desire: Authority & Transgression in the Rougon-Macquart. Ilona Chessid. LC 92-30423. (Reading Plus Ser.: Vol. 12). 145p. (C). 1994. text ed. 45.95 (*0-8204-2037-9*) P Lang Pubng.

Thresholds of Difference: Feminists Critique, Native Women's Writings, Postcolonial Theory. Julia V. Emberley. LC 92-95726. 202p. 1993. 21.00 (*0-8020-7729-3*) U of Toronto Pr.

Thresholds of Motivation: Nurturing Human Growth in the Organization. V. S. Mahesh. 1995. text ed. 27.95 (*0-07-462232-3*) McGraw.

Thresholds to Adult Living. rev. ed. Craig. 1982. teacher ed. 9.32 (*0-02-665950-6*) Glencoe.

Thresholds to Adult Living. rev. ed. Craig. (gr. 9-12). 1982. text ed. 26.00 (*0-02-665940-9*) Glencoe.

Thresholds to Thriving: A Power Pack of Practial Rx's. Arlene Taylor & Lorna Lawrence. 160p. 1995. pap. 12.00 (*1-887307-97-4*) Success Res Intl.

Thresor des Propheties de l'Univers: Manuscrit Publie avec une Introduction & des Notes par Francois Secret. Guillaume Postel. (International Archives of the History of Ideas Ser.: No. 27). 276p. 1969. lib. bdg. 70.50 (*90-247-0203-8*, Pub. by M Nijhoff NE) Kluwer Ac.

Thrice Chosen. Edouard Roditi. LC 81-9946. 135p. (Orig.). (C). 1981. pap. 5.00 (*0-87685-350-5*) Black Sparrow.

Thrice Familiar. Caroline Burnes. (Intrigue Ser.). 1993. mass mkt. 2.99 (*0-373-22256-4*, 1-22256-1) Harlequin Bks.

Thrice Greatest Hermes, 3 vols. G. R. Mead. 1986. reprint ed. Set. spiral bd. 70.00 (*0-7873-0604-5*) Hlth Research.

Thrice Greatest Hermes: Studies in Hellenistic Theosophy & Gnosis Being a Translation of the Extant Sermons & Fragments of the Trismegistic Literature with Prolegomena, Commentaries, & Notes. G. R. Mead. 864p. 1992. pap. 39.95 (*1-56459-186-7*) Kessinger Pub.

Thrice in Time: A Novel of the Savior's Love. James T. Walker. 208p. 1994. 15.98 (*0-88290-481-7*, 1980) Horizon Utah.

An Asterisk (*) at the beginning of an entry indicates that the title is appearing in BIP for the first time.

Thrice-Told Tale: Feminism, Postmodernism, & Ethnographic Responsibility. Margery Wolf. LC 91-24593. 168p. (C). 1992. 35.00 (0-8047-1979-9); pap. 11.95 (0-8047-1980-2) Stanford U Pr.

***Thrice upon a Time.** Genni Gunn. 232p. 1990. pap. 12.95 (0-919627-81-1, Pub. by Quarry Pr CN) LPC InBook.

Thrice upon a Time. James P. Hogan. 1984. mass mkt. 5.99 (0-345-32386-6, Del Rey) Ballantine.

Thrift Book Index. Bibliotheca Press Staff. LC 82-70344. 100p. (C). 1982. ring bd. 28.95 (0-939476-45-2) Prosperity & Profits.

Thrift Book-Possibilities for Saving & Budgeting Plus Work Pages. Bibliotheca Press Staff. 70p. 1991. ring bd. 24.95 (0-939476-09-6) Prosperity & Profits.

Thrift Financing Devices. C. Thomas Long & Thomas P. Vartanian. 246p. write for info. (0-318-60936-3) HarBrace.

Thrift Institution Automation Survey. 247p. 1987. 150.00 (0-318-35253-2) Finan Mgrs Soc.

Thrift Reform Act & the Future of the Thrift Industry, 1990. (Commercial Law & Practice Course Handbook Ser.). 786p. 1990. 17.50 (0-685-69504-2) PLI.

***Thrift Score: The Stuff, the Method, the Madness!** Al Hoff. 1997. pap. 12.50 (0-06-095209-1, PL) HarpC.

Thrift Shop Maniac's Guide: To the Delaware Valley & the Universe, Vol. II, 1993-1994. Nancy L. Berman. 128p. 1993. pap. 9.95 (0-9639533-0-3) Thrift Shop.

Thrift Shopping in England. Nancy E. Carlberg & Pamela T. Jenkins. 175p. (Orig.). 1992. pap. 15.00 (0-944878-21-0) Carlberg Pr.

Thrift Store Prospecting. Megan Moore. (Illus.). 95p. 1994. reprint ed. pap. 29.95 (1-879878-13-5) Penultimate Pr.

Thrift Stores & Resale Shops - Suggestive Ideas for Specialized Thrift Shops: A Business Workbook. rev. ed. Center for Self-Sufficiency Staff. (Illus.). 128p. 1992. ring bd. 29.95 (0-910811-46-6) Ctr Self Suff.

Thrifty Decorator: A DIY Guide to Style on a Shoe-String. Jocasta Innes. (Illus.). 192p. 1994. 22.95 (1-85029-560-3, Pub. by Conrad Octopus) Trafalgar.

Thrifty Decorator: A Do-It-Yourself Guide to Style on a Shoe-String. Jocasta Innes. (Illus.). 192p. 1996. pap. 17.95 (1-85029-741-X, Pub. by Conran Octopus UK) Trafalgar.

Thrifty Gourmet: Guide to Fine Dining in Santa Barbara for Under Seven Dollars. David Wyatt. LC 81-53014. (Illus.). 60p. (Orig.). 1981. pap. 5.95 (0-941428-00-1) Queen Missions.

Thrifty Meals for Two: Making Food Dollars Count. Mary D. Evans & Linda E. Cleveland. (Home & Garden Bulletin Ser.: No. 244). (Illus.). 69p. 1986. pap. 2.50 (0-16-000046-7, S/N 001-000-04459-1) USGPO.

***Thrifty Meals for Two: Making Food Dollars Count.** (Illus.). 69p. 1996. reprint ed. pap. 15.00 (0-7881-3335-7) DIANE Pub.

Thrill. Robert Byrne. 224p. 1995. 19.95 (0-7867-0199-4) Carroll & Graf.

Thrill. Wolff Ryp. (Midnight Secrets Ser.: No. 02). (YA). 1996. pap. 3.50 (0-8167-3543-3) Troll Communs.

Thrill. Patricia Wallace. 1990. mass mkt. 4.50 (0-8217-3142-4, Zebra Kensgtn) Kensgtn Pub Corp.

Thrill City. Jean Stine. 1996. reprint ed. mass mkt. 6.95 (1-56333-411-9, Rhinoceros) Masquerade.

Thrill Club. R. L. Stine. Ed. by Patricia MacDonald. (Fear Street Ser.). 160p. (Orig.). (YA). (gr. 7 up). 1994. mass mkt. 3.99 (0-671-78581-8, Archway) PB.

Thrill Is Gone: Your Relationship May Be in Trouble If... Joe Hobby. (Illus.). 80p. (Orig.). 1996. pap. 7.95 (1-886049-05-X) Best Times Inc.

Thrill Kill. William Vanderberg. 1994. pap. 5.99 (1-56171-352-X) Sure Seller.

Thrill of Anarchy. Kay Sturdivant. 23p. (Orig.). 1989. pap. 6.65 (0-685-29967-8) Geanie.

Thrill of Faith. C. S. Lovett. 1960. pap. 4.95 (0-938148-21-4) Prsnl Christianity.

Thrill of Fear: Two-Hundred & Fifty Years of Scary Entertainment. Walter Kendrick. LC 91-11495. 292p. 1992. pap. 12.95 (0-8021-3246-4, Grove) Grove-Atltic.

Thrill of the Grass. W. P. Kinsella. (Fiction Ser.). 196p. 1985. pap. 10.00 (0-14-007386-8, Penguin Bks) Viking Penguin.

Thrill of the Grill: Techniques, Recipes & Down Home Barbecue. Chris Schlesinger & John Willoughby. LC 89-77522. (Illus.). 416p. 1990. 25.00 (0-688-08832-5) Morrow.

***Thrill of the Grill Recipeasel.** Chris Schlesigner. 1997. pap. 14.95 (0-8118-1672-9) Chronicle Bks.

Thrill of Victory. Sandra Brown. 1994. mass mkt. 4.99 (0-373-48296-5, 5-48296-3) Harlequin Bks.

Thrill of Victory. Sandra Brown. 1995. mass mkt. 4.99 (1-55166-025-3, 1-66025-7, Mira Bks) Harlequin Bks.

Thrill of Victory: A Summer Olympic Games Mega Sticker Activity Book. 20p. (J). (gr. 1-6). 1996. pap. 4.99 (0-7214-5644-8, Ladybrd) Penguin.

Thrill Ride! Eric Weiner. (Cliffhangers Ser.). 1996. pap. text ed. 3.99 (0-425-14985-4) Berkley Pub.

Thrill Show Nurse. large type ed. Jane Converse. (Linford Romance Library). 288p. 1994. pap. 15.99 (0-7089-7505-4, Linford) Ulverscroft.

Thrill Sports in the Great Lakes Region. Bill Bailey. 1994. pap. 12.95 (1-881139-10-7) Glovebox Guidebks.

Thriller Talkers. (J). 1995. pap. write for info. (0-590-28646-3) Scholastic Inc.

Thrillers: Seven Decades of Classic Film Suspense. John McCarty. (Illus.). 256p. 1992. pap. 17.95 (0-8065-1339-X, Citadel Pr) Carol Pub Group.

Thrilling Adventures of Daniel Ellis. Daniel Ellis. LC 76-37303. (Black Heritage Library Collection). 1977. reprint ed. 37.95 (0-8369-8940-6) Ayer.

Thrilling Adventures of Daniel Ellis: The Great Union Guide of East Tennessee for a Period of Nearly Four Years During the Great Southern Rebellion. Daniel Ellis. (Illus.). 438p. 1989. reprint ed. 19.95 (0-932807-44-5) Overmountain Pr.

Thrilling Bug Stories. Stuart et al. (Thrilling Tales Ser.). (Illus.). 21p. (Orig.). (J). (gr. 4-8). 1994. pap. 2.95 (0-9639985-0-1) Fat Cat Pr.

Thrilling Days in Army Life. George A. Forsyth. LC 94-18457. (Illus.). xxii, 227p. 1994. reprint ed. pap. 8.95 (0-8032-6873-4, Bison Books) U of Nebr Pr.

Thrilling Escapes by Night. Albert Lee. 296p. 1968. 8.75 (0-686-05596-9) Rod & Staff.

Thrilling Events: The Life of Henry Starr. deluxe ed. Henry Starr. LC 82-2431. (Early West Ser.). (Illus.). 96p. reprint ed. 19.95 (0-932702-21-X) Creative Texas.

Thrilling Narrative of the Adventures, Sufferings & Starvation of Pike's Peak Gold Seekers on the Plains of the West in the Winter & Spring of 1859. Daniel Blue. 23p. 1968. reprint ed. pap. 4.95 (0-87770-032-X) Ye Galleon.

***Thrilling Number 3: Amazing Facts about the Number Three.** Kitty Higgins. (Birthday Book Ser.). 1998. 6.95 (0-8362-3222-4) Andrews & McMeel.

Thrilling Planet Tales. Ed. by Bill Black. (Illus.). 68p. (Orig.). 1991. pap. 9.95 (1-56225-001-9) A C Comics.

Thrills & Regressions. Michael Balint. 148p. (Orig.). 1959. 27.50 (0-8236-6540-2) Intl Univs Pr.

Thrills, Chills & Spills: A Photographic History of Early Aviation on the World's Most Bizarre Airport - The Beach at Daytona Beach, Florida - 1906-1929. Dick Punnett & Yvonne Punnett. LC 90-42545. (Illus.). 120p. (Orig.). 1990. write for info. (1-877633-10-0); pap. text ed. 17.95 (1-877633-09-7) Luthers.

Thrinaxodon: Digital Atlas of the Skull. William Carlson et al. (Illus.). 1995. 35.00 (0-292-77072-3) U of Tex Pr.

Thrips & Gall Dynamics. T. N. Ananthakrishnan & A. Raman. (C). 1989. 31.00 (81-204-0412-2, Pub. by Oxford IBH II) S Asia.

***Thrips As Crop Pests.** Trevor Lewis. LC 97-24320. 1997. write for info. (0-85199-178-5) CAB Intl.

Thrips Biology & Management: Proceedings of a NATO ARW on Thysanoptera: Toward Understanding Thrips Management, Held at the University of Vermont, Burlington, September 28-30, 1993. Ed. by Bruce L. Parker et al. LC 95-16545. (NATO ASI Ser.: Series A, Life Sciences: Vol. 276). 630p. (C). 1995. 145.00 (0-306-45013-5) Plenum.

Thrips of Central & South America: An Introduction (Insecta: Thysanoptera) Laurence A. Mound & Rita Marullo. Ed. by Virendra K. Gupta. LC 96-1387. (Memoirs on Entomology, International Ser.: No. 6). (Illus.). 1996. 65.00 (1-56665-061-5) Assoc Pubs FL.

Thrips Palmi: A Literature Survey with Annotated Bibliography. Ed. by D. J. Girling. (CAB International Publication). 44p. 1992. pap. 29.95 (0-85198-838-5) CAB Intl.

Thrival! - a Guide to Soaring with Your Spirit: Six Essential Steps to Thriving. Paul O. Radde. 21.95 (0-9625872-1-4) Thriving Pubns.

***Thrive! You Have a Right to Thrive...Not Just Survive.** Hope Sinclair. LC 95-82069. 300p. 1997. pap. 12.95 (0-9649014-5-5) Millennia CA.

Thrive as an Employer Without the Employee Headaches. T. Joe Willey. (Illus.). 44p. (Orig.). 1994. pap. 8.95 (0-944308-16-3) Aegis Consulting.

***Thriving.** Robert Ivker. 1998. pap. write for info. (0-609-80192-9) Crown Pub Group.

***Thriving: The New Mind-Body Approach to Optimal Health & Fitness for Men.** Robert Ivker. 1997. 23.00 (0-517-70460-9, Crown) Crown Pub Group.

Thriving After Surviving. Barry M. Richards. LC 88-84104. 128p. (Orig.). 1989. pap. 9.95 (0-9622787-0-X) Hartley Commns.

Thriving As a Working Woman. Gwen Ellis. LC 94-4237. 256p. 1995. pap. 8.99 (0-8423-4598-1) Tyndale.

Thriving in an Age of Change: Practical Strategies for Health Care Leaders. Donald N. Lombardi. LC 96-6417. (Management Ser.). (Illus.). 1996. 36.00 (1-56793-043-3, 0978) Health Admin Pr.

Thriving in Transition: Effective Living in Times of Change. Marcia Perkins-Reed. LC 95-25479. (Illus.). 224p. 1996. pap. 12.00 (0-684-81189-8, Touchstone Bks) S&S Trade.

***Thriving on Change.** Ed. by Rick Crandall. 380p. 1997. pap. 7.95 (0-9644294-5-4) Select Pr.

Thriving on Change: The Art of Using Change to Your Advantage. Nate Booth. (Illus.). 300p. 1996. 24.95 (0-9649500-0-6) Harrison Acorn.

Thriving on Chaos: Handbook for a Management Revolution. Tom Peters. LC 87-45575. 561p. 1987. 30.00 (0-394-56784-6) Knopf.

Thriving on Chaos: Handbook for a Management Revolution. Tom Peters. LC 88-45121. 736p. 1989. pap. 16.00 (0-06-097184-3, PL) HarpC.

Thriving on Reform: Meeting Tomorrow's Healthcare Challenges Today. E. Preston Gee. 1994. text ed. 27.50 (1-55738-618-8) Irwin Prof Pubng.

Thriving on Stress for Success. Walter H. Gmelch & Wilbert Chan. LC 93-37724. 152p. 1994. 42.95 (0-8039-6111-1); pap. 18.95 (0-8039-6112-X) Corwin Pr.

Thriving on Thrift: A Common Sense Guide to Feeding Your Family for Less. Cynthia Hillson. Ed. by Jan Teel. (Illus.). 96p. (Orig.). 1995. pap. 14.95 (0-9649267-0-9) Up on the Hill.

Thriving on Thrift: 101 Thrifty Christmas Ideas. Cynthia Hillson. Ed. by Jan Teel. (Illus.). 96p. (Orig.). 1996. pap. 16.95 (0-9649267-1-7) Up on the Hill.

Thro' the Vision of the Night: A Study of Source, Evolution & Structure in Tennyson's "Idylls of the King" J. M. Gray. 189p. 1980. 44.95 (0-7735-0519-9, Pub. by McGill CN) U of Toronto Pr.

Thro' the Vision of the Night: A Study of Source, Evolution, & Structure in Tennyson's Idylls of the King. James M. Gray. LC 80-153744. 189p. reprint ed. pap. 53.90 (0-7837-6935-0, 2046764) Bks Demand.

Throal: The Dwarf Kingdom. Robin Laws. (Illus.). 200p. 1996. pap. 20.00 (1-55560-296-7) FASA Corp.

Throat. Peter Straub. 800p. 1994. pap. 6.99 (0-451-17918-8, Sig) NAL-Dutton.

Throat of Feathers. Beverly Lawn. 1979. 6.00 (0-918870-07-0); pap. 3.00 (0-918870-08-9) Pleasure Dome.

Throat of the Peacock: Japanese Senryu on Filial Devotion. Tr. by Harold J. Isaacson. (Bhaisajaguru Ser.). 1977. pap. 5.95 (0-87830-557-2, Thtre Arts Bks) Routledge.

Throbbing Dark. large type ed. Frank Arthur. 1990. pap. 15.99 (0-7089-6993-3, Trailtree Bookshop) Ulverscroft.

Throbbing Modems: How to Find Romance & Adventure on Your Personal Computer. Joshua Bagby. LC 95-81298. (Illus.). 300p. (Orig.). 1995. pap. 17.95 (1-56866-088-X) Index Pub Grp.

Throckmorton, TX 76083. Barry Corbin. 1984. pap. 5.25 (0-8222-1145-9) Dramatists Play.

Thrombin, 2 vols., Vol. I. Ed. by Raymond Machovich. 176p. 1984. 104.00 (0-8493-6186-9, QP93, CRC Reprint) Franklin.

Thrombin, 2 vols., Vol. II. Ed. by Raymond Machovich. 128p. 1984. 76.00 (0-8493-6187-7, QP93, CRC Reprint) Franklin.

Thrombin: Its Key Role in Thrombogenesis-Implications for Its Inhibition. Ed. by Michael R. Buchanan et al. LC 94-26483. 256p. 1994. 159.95 (0-8493-7649-1, 7649) CRC Pr.

Thrombin: Structure & Function. Ed. by Lawrence J. Berliner. (Illus.). 365p. 1992. 105.00 (0-306-43991-3, Plenum Pr) Plenum.

***Thromboembolic Complications in Children.** Maureen Andrew. 1996. 89.95 (1-55009-036-4, Pub. by B C Decker CN) Blackwell Sci.

Thrombolysis: The Dawn of a New Era? Ed. by P. Sleight & D. A. Chamberlain. 168p. (C). 1990. 395.00 (1-85271-098-5, Pub. by IBC Tech Srvs UK) St Mut.

Thrombolysis & Acute Myocardial Infarction: Early & Late Effects on Clinical Status, Left Ventricular Function & Exercise Capacity. T. Brzostek. No. 39. 134p. (Orig.). 1991. pap. 32.50 (90-6186-441-0, Pub. by Leuven Univ BE) Coronet Bks.

Thrombolysis & Adjunctive Therapy for Acute Myocardial Infarction. Ed. by Eric R. Bates. LC 92-49831. (Fundamental & Clinical Cardiology Ser.: Vol. 10). 528p. 1992. 125.00 (0-8247-8664-5) Dekker.

Thrombolysis in Cardiovascular Disease. Julian et al. 480p. 1989. 150.00 (0-8247-8147-3) Dekker.

***Thrombolytic Properties of Recombinent Staphylokinase in Experimental Animal Models & Clinical Trials.** Steven Vanderschueren. (Acta Biomedica Lovaniensia Ser.: No. 133). (Illus.). 104p. (Orig.). 1996. pap. 34.50 (90-6186-752-5, Pub. by Leuven Univ BE) Coronet Bks.

Thrombolytic Therapy in Acute Ischemic Stroke III. Ed. by T. Yamaguchi et al. (Illus.). 376p. 1996. 115.00 (0-387-70139-7) Spr-Verlag.

Thrombolytic Therapy in Acute Myocardial Infarction. Ed. by G. J. Taylor. (Illus.). 256p. 1992. pap. 32.95 (0-86542-200-1) Blackwell Sci.

Thrombolytic Therapy in Vascular Disease. Ed. by Anthony J. Comerota. (Illus.). 400p. 1994. text ed. 89.50 (0-397-51343-7) Lppncott-Raven.

Thrombomodulin, Thrombin, & the Control of Hemostasis. Ed. by John C. Giddings. (Medical Intelligence Unit Ser.). 113p. 1994. 89.95 (1-57059-117-2, LN9117) R G Landes.

Thromboplastin Calibration & Oral Anticoagulant Control. Ed. by A. Van Den Besselaar et al. (Development in Hematology & Immunology Ser.). 1984. lib. bdg. 122.50 (0-89838-637-3) Kluwer Ac.

Thrombopoiesis & Thrombopoietins: Molecular, Cellular, Preclinical, & Clinical Biology. Ed. by David Kuter et al. LC 96-44461. (Illus.). 456p. 1996. 150.00 (0-89603-379-1) Humana.

Thrombosis: Directory of Authors of New Medical & Scientific Reviews with Subject Index. Science & Life Consultants Association Staff. 160p. 1995. 47.50 (0-7883-0616-2); pap. 44.50 (0-7883-0617-0) ABBE Pubs Assn.

Thrombosis & Atherosclerosis. Ed. by Nils U. Bang. LC 81-11708. (Illus.). 484p. reprint ed. pap. 138.00 (0-8357-7606-9, 2056929) Bks Demand.

Thrombosis & Coronary Heart Disease: Proceedings of the Paavo Nurmi Symposium, 1st, Finland, 1969. Paavo Nurmi Symposium Staff. Ed. by P. I. Halonen & A. Louhija. (Advances in Cardiology Ser.: Vol. 4). 1970. 72.00 (3-8055-0727-5) S Karger.

Thrombosis & Hemorrhage. J. Loscalzo & A. Schafer. (Illus.). 1360p. 1993. 245.00 (0-86542-263-X) Blackwell Sci.

Thrombosis & Its Management. Ed. by Leon Poller & Jean M. Thomson. (Illus.). 272p. (Orig.). 1993. pap. text ed. write for info. (0-443-04797-9) Churchill.

Thrombosis & Thrombolysis. Ed. by Eugene I. Chazov & V. N. Smirnov. LC 86-20472. 444p. 1986. 115.00 (0-306-10989-1, Consultants) Plenum.

***Thrombosis in Cardiovascular Disorders.** Ed. by Valentin Fuster & Marc Verstraete. (Illus.). 586p. 1992. write for info. (0-7216-4012-5) Saunders.

Thrombospondin. O. Lahay. 320p. 1993. 195.00 (0-8493-4929-X, QP552) CRC Pr.

Thrombospondin Gene Family. Josephine C. Adams et al. LC 95-38427. (Molecular Biology Intelligence Unit Ser.). 187p. 1995. 89.00 (1-57059-308-6) R G Landes.

Throne & Mandarins: China's Search for a Policy During the Sino-French Controversy, 1880-1885. Lloyd E. Eastman. LC 67-12098. (Historical Studies: No. 79). 267p. 1967. 20.00 (0-674-89115-5) HUP.

Throne Carrier of God: The Life & Thought of 'Ala' ad-dawla as-Simnani. Jamal J. Elias. LC 94-37174. 255p. 1995. text ed. 49.50 (0-7914-2611-4); pap. text ed. 16.95 (0-7914-2612-2) State U NY Pr.

***Throne Carrier of God: The Life & Thought of Ala ad-Dawla As-Simnani.** Jamal J. Elias. 271p. 1996. pap. 16.95 (0-614-21372-X, 1486); pap. 16.95 (0-614-21560-9, 1486) Kazi Pubns.

Throne, Falcon, Eye: Poems. 2nd deluxe ed. Hugh Seidman. (ZerOX Editions Ser.). (Illus.). 69p. (C). reprint ed. lib. bdg. 24.95 (0-934450-15-3) Unmuzzled Ox.

Throne, Falcon, Eye: Poems. 2nd ed. Hugh Seidman. (ZerOX Editions Ser.). (Illus.). 69p. (C). reprint ed. pap. 9.95 (0-934450-53-6) Unmuzzled Ox.

Throne of Council. Artemis OakGrove. 151p. (Orig.). 1991. reprint ed. pap. 8.95 (1-55583-308-X) Alyson Pubns.

***Throne of Evil Game.** Mayfair Games Staff. Date not set. pap. 7.00 (0-912771-24-0) Mayfair Games.

Throne of Fools: The Omaran Saga, Bk. 2. Adrian Cole. 384p. 1990. pap. 3.95 (0-380-75840-7) Avon.

Throne of Gold: The Mighty Khans: Descendants of Mohammed. Anne Edwards. LC 94-32359. 346p. 1996. 25.00 (0-688-08838-4) Morrow.

Throne of Grace. Ernest L. Green. 60p. 1979. 1.50 (0-89814-041-2) Grace Publns.

Throne of Isis. Judith Tarr. 416p. 1995. 5.99 (0-8125-2079-3) Tor Bks.

Throne of Scone. Patricia Kennealy. (Tale of Aeron Ser.: Bk. 3). 384p. 1987. pap. 5.50 (0-451-45051-5, ROC) NAL-Dutton.

Throne of Tara. John Desjarlais. LC 90-80614. 256p. (Orig.). 1990. pap. 8.95 (0-89107-574-7) Crossway Bks.

Throne of the Gods: An Account of the First Swiss Expedition to the Himalayas. Arnold Heim & August Gansser. (C). 1995. reprint ed. 82.00 (81-7303-012-X, Pub. by Book Faith II) S Asia.

Throne of the Third Heaven: Poems Collected & New. Denis Johnson. 240p. 1996. pap. 12.00 (0-06-092696-1) HarpC.

Throne of Wisdom: Wood Sculptures of the Madonna in Romanesque France. Ilene H. Forsyth. LC 72-166372. 309p. reprint ed. pap. 88.10 (0-317-41726-6, 2052061) Bks Demand.

***Throope. WIlliam Throope & Adrian Scrope: The Family Tradition, History of the Scrope Family & Barony of Bolton (Etc.), with Addendum.** Evelyn F. Knudson. (Illus.). 81p. 1996. reprint ed. pap. 16.00 (0-8328-5226-0) Higginson Bk Co.

***Throope. William Throope & Adrian Scrope: The Family Tradition, History of the Scrope Family & Barony of Bolton (Etc.), with Addendum.** Evelyn F. Knudson. (Illus.). 81p. 1996. reprint ed. lib. bdg. 26.00 (0-8328-5225-2) Higginson Bk Co.

Throttled Street & Other Stories. Gangadhar Gadgil. (C). 1994. pap. text ed. 9.00 (81-7154-774-5, Pub. by Popular Prakashan II) S Asia.

Through a Brief Darkness. Richard Peck. 144p. (J). (gr. 7 up). 1989. pap. 3.25 (0-440-98809-8, LLL BDD) BDD Bks Young Read.

Through a Dark Mist. Marsha Canham. 480p. 1991. mass mkt. 5.50 (0-440-20611-1) Dell.

Through a Dark Tunnel: The Story of Titus Brandsma. Boniface Hanley. 1989. pap. 21.00 (0-86217-209-8, Pub. by Veritas IE) St Mut.

Through a Darkening Glass: Philosophy, Literature & Cultural Change. Dewi Z. Philips. LC 81-40456. 206p. 1982. reprint ed. pap. 58.80 (0-608-00888-5, 2061682) Bks Demand.

Through a Fiery Trial: Building Washington, 1790-1800. Bob Arnebeck. (Illus.). 732p. 1991. 29.95 (0-8191-7832-2) Madison Bks UPA.

Through a Fiery Trial: Building Washington, 1790-1800. Bob Arnebeck. 1994. pap. 16.95 (1-56833-027-8) Madison Bks UPA.

Through a Freudian Lens Deeply: A Psychoanalysis of Cinema. Daniel Dervin. LC 85-1430. 256p. reprint ed. pap. 73.00 (0-8357-2736-X, 2039845) Bks Demand.

Through a Glass Clearly: Finding, Evaluating, & Using Business Information from the Soviet Union. Karen Anderson & Jonathan J. Halperin. (Occasional Papers). 50p. 1992. 25.00 (0-87111-385-6) SLA.

Through a Glass, Darkly. Beij Beltrisi. (Illus.). 82p. (Orig.). 1990. pap. text ed. 5.00 (0-9626890-2-5) Dark West Pub.

Through a Glass Darkly. Janice Braud. LC 94-70817. (Illus.). 64p. 1994. lib. bdg. 10.00 (1-878149-26-1) Counterpoint Pub.

Through a Glass Darkly. Deb K. Das. (Writers Workshop Redbird Ser.). 53p. 1975. 8.00 (0-89253-519-9); pap. 3.00 (0-88253-723-7) Ind-US Inc.

Through a Glass, Darkly. David Hunter. 160p. (Orig.). 1984. pap. 5.76 (0-915153-06-8) Gold Star Pr.

Through a Glass Darkly. Karleen Koen. 768p. 1987. mass mkt. 6.99 (0-380-70416-1) Avon.

***Through a Glass Darkly.** Christopher Kubasik. 352p. 1997. mass mkt. 4.99 (0-06-105673-1, HarperPrism) HarpC.

Through a Glass Darkly. E. L. Risden. LC 95-8693. 68p. 1997. pap. 12.95 (0-7734-2731-7, Mellen Poetry Pr) E Mellen.

Through a Glass Darkly. Maralene Wesner & Miles Wesner. LC 85-90504. 134p. 1986. pap. 4.95 (0-936715-01-4) Diversity Okla.

Through a Glass Darkly: A Spiritual Psychology of Faith. Mary J. Meadow. LC 95-13753. 144p. 1995. pap. 14.95 (0-8245-1510-2) Crossroad NY.

Through a Glass Darkly: Essays in the Religious Imagination. John C. Hawley. xi, 300p. (Orig.). 1996. 35.00 (*0-8232-1636-5*); pap. 18.00 (*0-8232-1637-3*) Fordham.

Through a Glass Darkly: Ethnic Semiosis in American Literature. William Boelhower. 154p. 1987. pap. 13.95 (*0-19-504195-X*) OUP.

Through a Glass Darkly: Milton's Reinvention of the Mythological Tradition. John Mulryan. LC 96-9980. (Language & Literature Ser.: Vol. 21). (Illus.). 350p. (C). 1996. text ed. 48.00 (*0-8207-0267-6*) Duquesne.

***Through a Glass Darkly: Reflections on Personal Identity in Early America.** Ronald Hoffman et al. LC 96-52036. 480p. (C). (gr. 13). 1997. text ed. 49.95 (*0-8078-2336-8*) U of NC Pr.

***Through a Glass Darkly: Reflections on Personal Identity in Early America.** Ronald Hoffman et al. LC 97-9888. 448p. (C). (gr. 13). 1997. pap. text ed. 24.95 (*0-8078-4645-7*) U of NC Pr.

***Through a Glass Darkly: Reflections on Personal Identity in Early America.** Ed. by Ronald Hoffman & Mechal Sobel. 480p. 1997. pap. text ed. 19.95 (*0-8078-4644-9*) U of NC Pr.

Through a Glass Darkly: The Story of Eleanor of Aquitaine. Carol P. Cooke. LC 90-91897. (Illus.). 220p. 1990. pap. 9.95 (*0-9628114-0-8*) MHI.

Through a Glass Darkly: Thirteen Tales of Wine & Crime. Ed. by Barry Woelfel. 1984. 16.95 (*0-8253-0197-1*) Beaufort Bks NY.

Through a Glass Lightly. Joe Wise. 80p. (Orig.). 1987. pap. 4.95 (*0-944736-00-9*) Fontaine Hse Inc.

Through a Glass Lightly. John J. Timmerman. LC 87-2977. 198p. (Orig.). reprint ed. pap. 56.50 (*0-8357-4369-1*, 2037198) Bks Demand.

***Through a Gold Eagle.** Miriam G. Monfredo. 384p. 1997. mass mkt. 5.99 (*0-425-15898-5*, Prime Crime) Berkley Pub.

Through a Lens Darkly. James Cohen. 256p. 1993. mass mkt. 4.99 (*0-446-36340-5*) Warner Bks.

Through a Miner's Eye... Diana M. Aikens. 60p. (J). (gr. 3-6). 1992. pap. 2.00 (*1-886182-01-9*) Heritage Edits.

Through a Mirror: A Guide to Evaluating Programs. Louise K. Stevens. 186p. 1993. write for info. (*0-9630540-1-5*) ArtsMarket.

Through a Reporter's Eyes: The Life of Stefan Banach. Roman Kaluza. Ed. by Wojbor Woyczynski & Ann S. Kostant. Tr. by Ann S. Kostant. LC 95-25811. (Illus.). 176p. 1996. 24.50 (*0-8176-3772-9*) Birkhauser.

Through a Ruby Window: A Martha's Vineyard Childhood. Susan Klein. (American Storytelling Ser.). 224p. 1995. 19.95 (*0-87483-416-3*) August Hse.

Through a Speculum That Shines: Vision & Imagination in Medieval Jewish Mysticism. Elliot R. Wolfson. LC 94-18186. 464p. 1995. text ed. 49.50 (*0-691-07343-0*) Princeton U Pr.

***Through a Speculum That Shines: Vision & Imagination in Medieval Jewish Mysticism.** Elliot R. Wolfson. 1997. pap. text ed. 23.95 (*0-691-01722-0*) Princeton U Pr.

Through a Stone Wall: A Writer's Handbook & Literary Autobiography. Ardath Mayhar. Ed. by J. Richards. LC 95-76457. 200p. (Orig.). 1995. pap. 9.98 (*1-887303-07-3*) Blu Lantern Pub.

Through a Stranger's Eyes. Tom Fallon. 54p. (Orig.). 1978. pap. 4.95 (*0-9616146-0-9*) Small-Small Pr.

***Through a Termite City.** Rod Theodorou & Carole Telford. LC 97-13744. (Amazing Journeys Ser.). 1997. lib. bdg. write for info. (*1-57572-155-4*) Rigby Interact Libr.

Through a Universe Darkly. Marcia Bartusiak. 400p. 1995. pap. 12.50 (*0-380-72420-0*) Avon.

Through a Window: My Thirty Years with the Chimpanzees of Gombe. Jane Goodall. 320p. 1991. pap. 14.00 (*0-395-59925-3*) HM.

Through a Woman's Eye: Pioneering Photographers in Rural Upstate. Diane Galusha. LC 93-74182. (Illus.). 200p. (Orig.). 1993. pap. 19.95 (*1-883789-00-1*) Blk Dome Pr.

Through a Woman's I: An Annotated Bibliography of American Women's Autobiographical Writings, 1946-1976. Patricia K. Addis. LC 82-10813. 621p. 1983. 42.50 (*0-8108-1588-5*) Scarecrow.

Through African Eyes: Teaching Strategies, Vol. 1. Leon E. Clark. 81p. 1989. pap. 9.95 (*0-938960-32-6*) CITE.

***Through African Eyes: The Past: The Road to Independence.** 2nd rev. ed. Leon E. Clark. (Illus.). 288p. (C). (gr. 11 up). 1994. text ed. 39.50 (*0-938960-44-X*) CITE.

Through African Eyes Vol. 1: The Past: The Road to Independence. Leon E. Clark. (Illus.). 288p. (YA). (gr. 11 up). 1988. pap. text ed. 19.95 (*0-938960-27-X*) CITE.

Through African Eyes, Vol. 2: Teaching Strategies. Leon E. Clark. 81p. 1997. pap. 9.95 (*0-938960-33-4*) CITE.

Through African Eyes, Vol. 2: The Present: Tradition & Change. Leon E. Clark. (Illus.). 292p. (Orig.). (YA). (gr. 11 up). 1994. pap. text ed. 19.95 (*0-938960-28-8*) CITE.

Through African Eyes, Vol. 2: The Present: Tradition & Change. Leon E. Clark. (Illus.). 292p. (Orig.). (YA). (gr. 11 up). 1997. lib. bdg. 28.95 (*0-938960-45-8*) CITE.

Through Afro-America. William Archer. (Works of William Archer). xvi, 295p. reprint ed. 49.00 (*0-932051-75-8*) Rprt Serv.

Through Alchemy to Chemistry. John Read. 206p. 1992. reprint ed. pap. 19.95 (*1-56459-013-5*) Kessinger Pub.

Through Alchemy to Chemistry: A Procession of Ideas & Personalities. John Read. LC 79-8623. (Illus.). reprint ed. 37.50 (*0-404-18489-8*) AMS Pr.

Through Algeria. 384p. 1985. 250.00 (*1-85077-037-9*, Pub. by Darf Pubs Ltd UK) St Mut.

Through All the Displacements: Poems by Edgar Gabriel Silex. Edgar G. Silex. 78p. (Orig.). 1995. pap. 10.95 (*1-880684-25-X*) Curbstone.

Through All the Years. large type ed. Essie Summers. (General Ser.). 400p. 1993. 25.99 (*0-7089-2870-6*) Ulverscroft.

Through Amazonian Eyes: The Human Ecology of Amazonian Populations. Emilio F. Moran. LC 93-1148. (Illus.). 252p. 1993. pap. 12.95 (*0-87745-418-3*); text ed. 34.95 (*0-87745-417-5*) U of Iowa Pr.

Through America: Nine Months in the United States. Walter G. Marshal. LC 73-13143. (Foreign Travelers in America, 1810-1935 Ser.). (Illus.). 490p. 1974. reprint ed. 35.95 (*0-405-05466-1*) Ayer.

Through America: Or, Nine Months in the United States. W. G. Marshall. LC 72-3388. (Essay Index Reprint Ser.). 1977. reprint ed. 39.95 (*0-8369-2913-6*) Ayer.

Through & Through: Toledo Stories. Joseph Geha. (Short Fiction Ser.). 180p. (Orig.). (C). 1990. pap. 7.95 (*1-55597-135-0*) Graywolf.

***Through Another Lens: My Years with Edward Weston.** Charis Wilson. 1998. 40.00 (*0-86547-521-0*, North Pt Pr) FS&G.

Through Asian Eyes. (Through Eyes Ser.). write for info. (*0-614-02970-8*) Amer Forum.

Through Bible Lands: Notes on Travel in Egypt, the Desert, & Palestine. Philip Schaff. Ed. by Moshe Davis. LC 77-70740. (America & the Holy Land Ser.). 1977. reprint ed. lib. bdg. 33.95 (*0-405-10286-0*) Ayer.

Through Blood & Fire: Selected Civil War Papers of Major General Joshua Chamberlain. Joshua Chamberlain. LC 95-25430. (Illus.). 240p. 1996. 19.95 (*0-8117-1750-X*) Stackpole.

Through Bosnia & the Herzegovina on Foot During the Insurrection August & September 1875. Arthur J. Evans. LC 73-135804. (Eastern Europe Collection). 1971. reprint ed. 34.95 (*0-405-02746-X*) Ayer.

***Through Brief Darkness.** Richard Peck. 1997. pap. 3.99 (*0-14-038557-6*) Penguin.

Through Canada with a Kodak: The Countess of Aberdeen. Ed. & Intro. by Marjory Harper. (Reprints in Canadian History Ser.). (Illus.). 286p. 1994. pap. 24.95 (*0-8020-7765-X*) U of Toronto Pr.

Through Caribbean Eyes: Reflections on an Era of Independence. Clement B. London. LC 89-84287. 491p. pap. 12.95 (*0-938818-18-X*) ECA Assoc.

Through Central Borneo: An Account of Two Years' Travel in the Land of the Head-Hunters Between the Years 1913 & 1917, 2 vols., Set. Karl S. Lumholtz. LC 77-87504. (Illus.). reprint ed. 53.00 (*0-404-16760-8*) AMS Pr.

Through Chinese Eyes: Revolution & Transformation. Peter J. Seybold. (Through Eyes Ser.). (C). 1988. teacher ed., pap. 9.90 (*0-614-02973-2*) Amer Forum.

Through Chinese Eyes: Revolution & Transformation. rev. ed. Peter J. Seybolt. Ed. by Leon E. Clark. (Illus.). 280p. (YA). (gr. 11 up). 1988. reprint ed. pap. text ed. 19.95 (*0-938960-29-6*) CITE.

Through Christ's Word: A Festschrift for Philip E. Hughes. Ed. by W. Robert Godfrey & Jesse L. Boyd, III. 272p. (Orig.). 1985. pap. 10.99 (*0-87552-274-2*, Pub. by Evangelical Pr) Presby & Reformed.

Through Cities & Prairie Lands. Mary Hardy. LC 73-13137. (Foreign Travelers in America, 1810-1935 Ser.). 354p. 1974. reprint ed. 26.95 (*0-405-05459-9*) Ayer.

***Through Corridors of Power: Institutions & Civil-Military Relations in Argentina.** David Pion-Berlin. LC 96-48046. 1997. 45.00 (*0-271-01705-8*) Pa St U Pr.

***Through Corridors of Power: Institutions & Civil-Military Relations In Argentina.** David Pion-Berlin. LC 96-48046. 1997. pap. 17.95 (*0-271-01706-6*) Pa St U Pr.

Through Crisis to Freedom. William Cane. LC 79-89874. 144p. (Orig.). 1980. pap. 4.95 (*0-914070-14-2*, 109) ACTA Pubns.

Through Dakota Eyes: Narrative Accounts of the Minnesota Indian War of 1862. Alan R. Woolworth. Ed. by Gary C. Anderson. LC 87-28954. (Illus.). 316p. (Orig.). 1988. pap. 11.95 (*0-87351-216-2*) Minn Hist.

Through Darkest Resnick with Gun & Camera. Mike Resnick. 200p. 1990. 35.00 (*0-9621725-1-0*) Washington Sci Fiction.

Through Death to Life: Preparing to Celebrate the Funeral Mass. rev. ed. Joseph M. Champlin. LC 86-71916. 128p. 1990. pap. 3.25 (*0-87793-347-2*) Ave Maria.

Through Death to Rebirth. James S. Perkins. LC 61-13301. (Illus.). 124p. 1974. pap. 4.25 (*0-8356-0451-9*, Quest) Theos Pub Hse.

Through Death's Gate: A Guide to Selfless Dying. Joel. LC 95-46744. 83p. (Orig.). 1996. pap. 6.95 (*0-9620387-1-7*) Ctr Sacred Sciences.

Through Different Colored Glasses: The World as Seen Through the Left & Right Hemispheres of the Brain. Ellen R. Lopez. (Illus.). 60p. 1989. pap. write for info. (*0-318-64915-2*) McDonald & Hezlep.

Through Different Eyes: The Cultural Identity of Young Chinese in Britain. Ed. by David Parker. (Research in Ethnic Relations Ser.). 285p. 1995. 63.95 (*1-85628-923-0*, Pub. by Avebury Pub UK) Ashgate Pub Co.

Through Divided Minds. Robert S. Mayer. 304p. 1992. mass mkt. 4.99 (*0-380-71920-7*) Avon.

Through Divided Minds: Probing the Mysteries of Multiple Personalites - A Doctor's First-Person Story. Robert S. Mayer. 304p. 1990. pap. 8.95 (*0-380-70905-8*) Avon.

Through Ebony Eyes. Detroit Black Writers Guild Staff. 105p. 1987. pap. 6.00 (*0-9613078-6-2*) Detroit Black.

Through Elegant Eyes: Stories of Austro & the Men Who Know Everything. R. A. Lafferty. Ed. by Ira M. Thornhill. LC 83-72190. (Illus.). 240p. 1983. 20.00 (*0-911169-01-6*) Corroboree Pr.

Through Emotions to Maturity: Psychological Readings of Fairy Tales. Verena Kast. Tr. by Douglas Whitcher from GER. LC 93-33193. (Psychology Ser.). 208p. 1993. 19.95 (*0-88064-205-X*); pap. 11.95 (*0-88064-206-8*) Fromm Intl Pub.

Through Family Times: A Conversational Prayerbook for Today's World. Ginger Farry. LC 93-15069. 96p. 1993. pap. 4.95 (*0-8091-3392-X*) Paulist Pr.

Through Fascism to World Power: A History of the Revolution in Italy. Ion S. Munro. 1976. lib. bdg. 50.00 (*0-8490-2748-9*) Gordon Pr.

Through Fascism to World Power: History of the Revolution in Italy. Ion S. Munro. LC 73-164618. (Select Bibliographies Reprint Ser.). 1977. reprint ed. 36.95 (*0-8369-5912-4*) Ayer.

Through Fire & Water: An Overview of Mennonite History. Carol Duerksen et al. (Illus.). 320p. (Orig.). 1996. pap. 14.99 (*0-8361-9015-7*) Herald Pr.

Through Fire & Water: The Life of Reb Noson of Breslov. Chaim Kramer. Ed. by Avraham Greenbaum. 777p. 1992. 30.00 (*0-930213-44-0*) Breslov Res Inst.

Through Five Hundred Years: A Popular History of the Moravian Church. rev. ed. Allen W. Schattschneider. LC 89-69833. 144p. 1996. pap. 5.00 (*1-878422-01-4*) Moravian Ch in Amer.

Through Forbidden Tibet. Harrison Forman. 1984. lib. bdg. 90.00 (*0-8490-3240-7*) Gordon Pr.

Through Foreign Eyes: Western Attitudes Toward North Africa. Ed. by Alf A. Heggoy et al. LC 81-43474. 200p. (Orig.). 1982. pap. text ed. 24.50 (*0-8191-2182-7*); lib. bdg. 50.50 (*0-8191-2181-9*) U Pr of Amer.

Through Formosa. Owen Rutter. (Illus.). 288p. 1989. reprint ed. 30.00 (*957-9482-15-2*) Oriental Bk Store.

Through French Windows: An Introduction to France in the Nineties. James Corbett. LC 93-41808. (Illus.). 320p. (C). 1994. text ed. 49.50 (*0-472-09469-6*); pap. text ed. 20.95 (*0-472-06469-X*) U of Mich Pr.

Through Garden Gates. Ed. by Garden Club of Savannah Book Committee. (Illus.). 28p. (Orig.). 1984. pap. 4.75 (*0-317-11351-8*) Garden Club Sav.

Through Gates of Splendor. Elisabeth Elliot. 274p. 1981. mass mkt. 4.99 (*0-8423-7151-6*) Tyndale.

Through Gates of Splendor. rev. ed. Elisabeth Elliot. LC 85-51792. 274p. 1986. pap. 9.99 (*0-8423-7152-4*) Tyndale.

Through Gateway of Death. Geoffrey Hodson. LC 61-13301. (Illus.). 124p. 1986. pap. 4.50 (*81-7059-038-8*, Quest) Theos Pub Hse.

Through Glacier Park in 1915. Mary R. Rinehart. LC 83-60777. 102p. 1983. pap. 6.95 (*0-911797-06-8*) R Rinehart.

Through Glass. Henry Alley. LC 79-21296. (American Land Ser.: Vol. 1). 191p. (Orig.). 1979. pap. 7.95 (*0-916078-07-8*) Iris Pr.

***Through Grandpa's Eyes.** Patricia MacLachlan & Deborah K. Ray. (Illus.). (J). (gr. 2-5). 13.89 (*0-06-024044-X*, 595015) HarpC Child Bks.

Through Grandpa's Eyes. Patricia MacLachlan. LC 79-2019. (Trophy Picture Bk.). (Illus.). 48p. (J). (gr. k-3). 1983. pap. 4.95 (*0-06-443041-3*, Trophy) HarpC Child Bks.

Through Grandpa's Eyes. Patricia MacLachlan. LC 79-2019. (Illus.). 48p. (J). (gr. 2-4). 1980. lib. bdg. 14.89 (*0-06-024043-1*) HarpC.

Through Greek Eyes. 2nd ed. Ed. by Roger Nichols & Kenneth McLeish. (Illus.). 144p. (C). 1991. pap. text ed. 14.95 (*0-521-37756-0*) Cambridge U Pr.

Through Green-Colored Glasses: Environmentalism Reconsidered. Wilfred Beckerman. LC 96-30858. 1996. 21.95 (*1-882577-35-3*); pap. text ed. 11.95 (*1-882577-36-1*) Cato Inst.

Through Harsh Winters: The Life of a Japanese Immigrant Woman. Akemi Kikumura. LC 81-15534. 176p. (C). 1981. pap. 12.95 (*0-88316-543-0*) Chandler & Sharp.

Through Hell & High Water: The Wartime Memories of a Junior Combat Infantry Officer. Leslie W. Bailey. 1994. 16.95 (*0-533-10942-6*) Vantage.

Through Him, With Him, In Him. Ruth Burrows. (Illus.). 1982. pap. 9.95 (*0-87193-261-X*) Dimension Bks.

***Through Hubble's Eyes: The Birth, Life, & Violent Death of Stars.** Robert Naeye. (Illus.). 112p. 1997. write for info. (*0-913135-34-8*, 18550, Kalmbach Books) Kalmbach.

Through Indian Country to California: John P. Sherburne's Diary of the Whipple Expedition, 1853-1854. Ed. by Mary M. Gordon. LC 88-2152. (Illus.). 304p. 1988. 37.50 (*0-8047-1447-9*) Stanford U Pr.

Through Indian Eyes: Our Nations Past as Experienced by Native Americans. Reader's Digest Editors. LC 95-34273. (Illus.). 400p. 1996. 40.00 (*0-89577-819-X*) RD Assn.

Through Indian Eyes: Teaching Strategies. Ed. by Leon E. Clark. 81p. 1995. pap. text ed. 9.95 (*0-938960-40-7*) CITE.

Through Indian Eyes: The Living Tradition. 3rd ed. Donald J. Johnson et al. LC 92-16585. (Illus.). 356p. (Orig.). 1992. pap. text ed. 21.95 (*0-938960-39-3*); lib. bdg. 44.00 (*0-938960-38-5*) CITE.

Through Innocent Eyes: Teenagers' Impressions of WW2 Internment Camp Life. Ed. by Vincent Tajiri. (Illus.). 120p. (Orig.). 1990. 49.50 (*0-9624450-0-2*); pap. 29.50 (*0-9624450-1-0*); audio 15.00 (*1-878385-00-3*) Keiro Services.

Through Iran in Disguise. Sarah Hobson. (Illus.). 1979. 20.00 (*0-89733-013-7*) Academy Chi Pubs.

Through Iran in Disguise. Sarah Hobson. (Illus.). 189p. 1982. pap. 9.00 (*0-89733-024-2*) Academy Chi Pubs.

Through Isaac's Eyes: Crossing of Cultures, Coming of Age & the Healing Between a Father & Son. Daniel B. Peters. LC 95-20912. 208p. 1996. pap. 10.99 (*0-310-20376-7*) Zondervan.

Through Israeli Eyes: Attitudes Toward Judaism, American Jewry, Zionism & the Arab-Israeli Conflict. Mina Zemach. LC 87-71754. 52p. 1987. pap. 5.00 (*0-87495-094-5*) Am Jewish Comm.

Through It All. Ruth A. Marks. LC 87-73017. 1990. 11.95 (*0-8158-0448-2*) Chris Mass.

Through It All. Gary O. McKean. 8p. 1994. pap. text ed. 3.00 (*0-944561-25-X*) Chr Legal.

Through Italy with the Poets. Compiled by Robert H. Schauffler. LC 78-39397. (Granger Index Reprint Ser.). 1977. reprint ed. 26.95 (*0-8369-6351-2*) Ayer.

Through Japanese Eyes. 3rd rev. ed. Richard H. Minear. Ed. by Leon E. Clark. LC 94-298338. (Illus.). 360p. 1994. pap. text ed. 21.95 (*0-938960-36-9*); lib. bdg. 44.00 (*0-938960-34-2*) CITE.

Through Japanese Eyes: Teaching Strategies. Leon E. Clark & Jack Strauss. (Illus.). 179p. (Orig.). 1995. teacher ed., pap. text ed. 11.95 (*0-938960-37-7*) CITE.

Through Jaundiced Eyes: How the Media View Organized Labor. William J. Puette. 240p. (Orig.). 1992. 39.95 (*0-87546-184-0*, ILR Press); pap. 16.95 (*0-87546-185-9*, ILR Press) Cornell U Pr.

Through Jungle & Desert, Travels in E. Africa. William A. Chanler. 1896. 59.00 (*0-403-00438-1*) Scholarly.

***Through Krista's Eyes.** Lee Erickson. LC 96-96979. (Illus.). vi, 170p. (Orig.). 1996. pap. 11.95 (*0-9654147-1-X*) Erickson Ctr.

Through Language to Reality: Studies on Medieval Semantics & Metaphysics. Lambertus M. De Rijk. Ed. by E. P. Bos. (Collected Studies: No. CS302). 334p. (ENG, FRE & GER.). (C). 1989. reprint ed. 94.95 (*0-86078-250-6*, Pub. by Variorum UK) Ashgate Pub Co.

Through Lent to Resurrection. Flower A. Newhouse. Ed. by Melodie N. Bengtson. LC 77-77088. (Illus.). 72p. 1977. pap. 9.00 (*0-910378-13-4*) Christward.

Through Life Inverse. Carol A. Vercz. 1985. pap. 4.50 (*0-910119-19-8*) SOCO Pubns.

Through Life's Window. Carl G. Carlozzi. 96p. 1989. 12.95 (*0-89869-207-5*) Church Pub Inc.

***Through Loona's Door: A Tammy & Owen Adventure with Carter G. Woodson.** Tonya Bolden. LC 94-69224. (America's Family Bks.). (Illus.). 48p. (J). (gr. k-5). 1997. 15.95 (*1-885053-00-2*) Corp Cult Lit.

Through Los Alamos, 1945: Memoirs of a Nuclear Physicist. Hugh T. Richards. (Illus.). 106p. (Orig.). 1993. pap. 15.00 (*0-9637521-1-1*) Arlington Pl.

***Through Many Bridges.** Fletcher. 1997. pap. 12.95 (*1-887650-07-5*) Factor Pr.

Through Many Dangers: The Story of John Newton. Brian H. Edwards. 1985. pap. 4.99 (*0-85234-250-0*, Pub. by Evangelical Pr) Presby & Reformed.

***Through Many Dangers Toils & Snares.** rev. ed. Merlene Pitre. (Illus.). 300p. 1997. reprint ed. pap. 19.95 (*1-57168-165-5*, 165-5, Eakin Pr) Sunbelt Media.

***Through Mary's Eyes: Reflections of Her Life & Times.** Francis C. Bernardo. LC 97-25008. 1997. write for info. (*0-8091-3745-3*) Paulist Pr.

Through Masailand with Joseph Thomson. Ed. by Roland Young. 218p. 1962. 45.00 (*0-89771-010-X*) St Mut.

***Through Mathematical Eyes: Exploring Functional Relationships in Math & Science.** LC 97-5389. (Moving Middle Schools Ser.). 1997. pap. text ed. write for info. (*0-435-07217-X*, 07217) Heinemann.

Through Measurement to Knowledge: The Selected Papers of Heike Hamerlingh Onnes, 1853-1926. Keike K. Onnes. Ed. by Kostas Gavroglu & Yorgos Goudaroulis. 688p. (C). 1990. lib. bdg. 210.00 (*0-7923-0825-5*, Pub. by Klwr Acad Pubs NE) Kluwer Ac.

Through Middle Eastern Eyes. Robert P. Pearson. (Through Eyes Ser.). (Orig.). (C). 1993. teacher ed., pap. 8.95 (*0-614-02977-5*) Amer Forum.

Through Middle Eastern Eyes. 3rd ed. Robert P. Pearson & Leon E. Clark. LC 92-44505. (Illus.). 352p. (Orig.). 1993. lib. bdg. 44.00 (*0-938960-43-1*) CITE.

Through Middle Eastern Eyes. 3rd rev. ed. Robert P. Pearson & Leon E. Clark. LC 92-44505. (Illus.). 352p. (Orig.). 1993. pap. text ed. 21.95 (*0-938960-41-5*) CITE.

Through Middle Eastern Eyes: Teaching Strategies. Robert P. Pearson. 110p. (C). 1993. pap. text ed. 8.95 (*0-938960-42-3*) CITE.

Through Moon & Stars & Night Skies. Ann Turner. LC 87-35044. (Charlotte Zolotow Bk.). (Illus.). 32p. (J). (ps-3). 1990. 13.95 (*0-06-026189-7*); lib. bdg. 13.89 (*0-06-026190-0*) HarpC Child Bks.

Through Moon & Stars & Night Skies. Ann Turner. LC 87-35044. (Charlotte Zolotow Bk.: A Trophy Picture Bk.). (Illus.). 32p. (J). (ps-3). 1992. pap. 4.95 (*0-06-443308-0*, Trophy) HarpC Child Bks.

Through Moon & Stars & Night Skies. Ann Turner. LC 87-35044. (Illus.). 32p. (J). (ps-3). 1995. 7.95 incl. audio (*0-694-70013-4*) HarperAudio.

Through Music to the Self: How to Appreciate & Experience Music Anew. Peter M. Hamel. (Illus.). 240p. 1993. pap. 14.95 (*1-85230-136-8*) Element MA.

Through Muslim Eyes: M. Rashid Rida & the West. Emad E. Shahin. LC 93-24081. (Dissertations Ser.: No. 1). (Orig.). 1993. 15.00 (*1-56564-141-8*); pap. 7.50 (*1-56564-142-6*) IIIT VA.

Through My Day with the 'L' Sound. Linda S. Messick. (Illus.). 120p. (Orig.). (J). (gr. k-6). 1975. pap. text ed. 6.95 (*0-87015-212-2*) Pacific Bks.

Through My Day with the 'S' Sound. Linda S. Messick. (Illus.). 120p. (Orig.). (J). (gr. k-6). 1975. pap. text ed. 6.95 (*0-87015-214-9*) Pacific Bks.

Through My Day with the 'SH' Sound. Linda S. Messick. (Illus.). 112p. (Orig.). (J). (gr. k-6). 1975. pap. text ed. 6.95 (*0-87015-215-7*) Pacific Bks.

***Through My Eyes.** 320p. 1997. write for info. (*1-56476-636-5*, Victor Bks) Chariot Victor.

An Asterisk (*) at the beginning of an entry indicates that the title is appearing in BIP for the first time.

Through My Eyes. Barbara Delinsky. 1995. mass mkt. 4.99 (*1-55166-039-3*, 1-66039-8, Mira Bks) Harlequin Bks.

Through My Eyes. large type ed. Helen R. Myers. 214p. 1992. reprint ed. lib. bdg. 18.95 (*1-56054-308-6*) Thorndike Pr.

Through My Eyes - A Teenage Look at Life. Penny Zito. Ed. by Sherri York. LC 87-50257. (Illus.). 152p. (YA). (gr. 7 up). 1987. 7.95 (*1-55523-075-X*) Winston-Derek.

Through My Eyes - From My Heart. Tina Ray. (Orig.). 1996. pap. write for info. (*1-57553-287-5*) Watermrk Pr.

Through My Eyes the Amish Way, Vol. 1. Phyllis K. Kult. (Illus.). 54p. 1986. pap. 6.49 (*0-9648495-0-X*) Elijah Pubng.

***Through My Glasses: Reflections on This & That in Essays & Stories.** Ruby Phillipy. (Illus.). 55p. (Orig.). 1996. pap. 10.95 (*0-9644370-6-6*) Dryden Publ.

***Through My Kitchen Window.** Emily. 1997. 12.95 (*0-533-12334-8*) Vantage.

Through My Looking Glass: A Personal Journey into Vaster States of Awareness. Winafred Blake. 290p. 1995. write for info. (*1-882530-03-9*) Deep Forest Pr.

Through My Looking Glass: A View from the Beach. Jan Bond. Ed. by Penny Lent. LC 95-80731. 192p. (Orig.). 1995. pap. 9.95 (*1-885371-14-4*) Kldoscope Pr.

Through My Monacle. George R. Cregan. 480p. 1991. pap. 24.95 (*0-614-15840-0*) McClain.

Through My Own Eyes: A Personalized Look at the U. S. Justice System: Videotape & Instructors Manual. Kathleen M. Sampson. 32p. 1994. pap. 12.00 (*0-938870-64-5*) Am Judicature.

***Through My Own Eyes: Single Mothers & the Cultures of Poverty.** Susan Holloway. LC 97-25240. 1997. 35.00 (*0-674-89122-8*) HUP.

Through My Picture Window. Robert B. Phillips. LC 88-90639. (Illus.). 256p. (YA). (gr. 9-12). 1988. 9.95 (*0-9620577-1-1*) R B Phillips Pub.

Through Nature to Eternity: Chaucer's Legend of Good Women. Donald W. Rowe. LC 87-5993. 228p. 1988. reprint ed. pap. 65.00 (*0-608-02132-6*, 2062801) Bks Demand.

Through Nature to God. John Fiske. 211p. 1996. reprint ed. pap. 17.95 (*1-56459-579-X*) Kessinger Pub.

Through Nature to God. John Fiske. (Notable American Authors Ser.). 1992. reprint ed. lib. bdg. 75.00 (*0-7812-2859-X*) Rprt Serv.

***Through Navajo Eyes: An Exploration in Film Communication & Anthropology.** Sol Worth & John Adair. LC 96-3019. 1996. pap. 24.95 (*0-8263-1771-5*) U of NM Pr.

Through Old Rose Glasses, & Other Stories. Mary T. Earle. LC 70-128732. (Short Story Index Reprint Ser.). 1977. 17.95 (*0-8369-3623-X*) Ayer.

Through One Administration. Frances Hodgson Burnett. LC 67-29260. reprint ed. pap. text ed. 6.95 (*0-89197-965-4*); reprint ed. lib. bdg. 16.50 (*0-8398-0181-5*) Irvington.

***Through One Tear: Poems.** Edward Nobles. 80p. 1997. 22.00 (*0-89255-227-1*) Persea Bks.

Through Open Doors. Emma Mariane. 1990. 13.95 (*0-533-08832-1*) Vantage.

Through Open Eyes. Glen W. Gouder. Ed. by Sharon J. Gouder. 87p. 1996. lib. bdg. 7.00 (*0-614-97213-2*) Osage Bend Pub.

***Through Otis' Eyes.** Kennedy. 1997. 12.95 (*0-87605-473-4*) Howell Bk.

Through Our Eyes Only: A Journey into Animal Consciousness. Marian S. Dawkins. LC 92-32995. 1995. text ed. write for info. (*0-7167-4501-1*) W H Freeman.

Through Paediatrics to Psychoanalysis: Collected Papers. Donald W. Winnicott. LC 92-26889. 350p. 1992. reprint ed. pap. text ed. 37.95 (*0-87630-703-9*) Brunner-Mazel.

Through Paphlagonia with a Donkey: An Adventure in the Turkish Isfendyars. David Beasley. (Illus.). 235p. 1983. pap. 9.95 (*0-915317-00-1*) Davus Pub.

Through Parisian Eyes: Reflections on Contemporary French Arts & Culture. Melinda C. Porter. (Illus.). 256p. 1993. reprint ed. pap. 13.95 (*0-306-80540-5*) Da Capo.

Through Peter's Eyes. Ed. by Hazel Morgan. (C). 1990. pap. 24.00 (*0-85305-305-7*, Pub. by J Arthur Ltd UK) St Mut.

Through "Poverty's Vale" A Hardscrabble Boyhood in Upstate New York, 1832-1862. Henry Conklin. Ed. by Wendell Tripp. LC 73-19980. (Illus.). 280p. 1974. 19.95 (*0-8156-0098-4*) Syracuse U Pr.

Through "Poverty's Vale" A Hardscrabble Boyhood in Upstate New York, 1832-1862. Henry Conklin. Ed. by Wendell Tripp. LC 73-19980. (Illus.). 280p. 1975. pap. 12.95 (*0-8156-0117-4*) Syracuse U Pr.

Through Preservice Teachers' Eyes. J. Gary Knowles. 400p. (C). 1994. pap. text ed. 37.00 (*0-02-365371-X*, Macmillan Coll) P-H.

Through Prism of Difference. Baca Zinn & Hondagneu Sot. LC 96-43746. 600p. 1997. pap. 38.00 (*0-205-26415-8*) Allyn.

Through Rose Colored Glasses: The Drawings & Illustrations of Rose Cecil O'Neill. Greg C. Thielen. LC 85-50464. (Illus.). 64p. (Orig.). 1985. pap. text ed. 7.00 (*0-934306-05-2*) Springfield.

Through Russia: From St. Petersburg to Astrakhan & the Crimea. Katherine B. Guthrie. LC 73-115541. (Russia Observed Ser., No. 1). 1970. reprint ed. 35.95 (*0-405-03030-4*) Ayer.

Through Russia on a Mustang. Thomas Stevens. LC 78-115588. (Russia Observed, Series I). 1970. reprint ed. 23.95 (*0-405-03065-7*) Ayer.

Through Science & Philosophy to Religion. F. R. Ansari. pap. 2.00 (*0-933511-76-0*) Kazi Pubns.

Through Seasons of the Heart. John Powell. (Illus.). 384p. 1989. reprint ed. pap. 14.95 (*0-88347-343-7*, 7343) Res Christian Liv.

Through Siberia. Henry Lansdell. LC 75-115555. (Russia Observed, Series I). 1970. reprint ed. 46.95 (*0-405-03042-8*) Ayer.

Through Siberia: The Land of the Future. Fridtjof Nansen. Tr. by A. G. Chater from NOR. LC 73-115568. (Russia Observed Ser.). (Illus.). 1971. reprint ed. 39.95 (*0-405-03087-8*) Ayer.

Through Stone. Evangeline Paterson. LC 93-13725. 22p. 1993. pap. 4.00 (*0-940895-10-2*) Cornerstone IL.

Through Streets Broad & Narrow. Gabriel Fielding. LC 86-11244. (Phoenix Fiction Ser.). viii, 346p. 1986. reprint ed. pap. 11.95 (*0-226-24844-5*) U Ch Pr.

Through Streets Broad & Narrow: A Woman Pacifist's 17-Year Sojourn in the Bruderhof Communities. Belinda Manley. Ed. by Gertrude E. Huntington. LC 96-83706. (Women from Utopia Ser.). (Illus.). 270p. (Orig.). 1996. pap. 17.00 (*1-882260-05-8*) Carrier Pigeon.

***Through Students' Eyes: Combating Racism in United States Schools.** Karen B. Donaldson. LC 96-10432. 184p. 1996. pap. text ed. 18.95 (*0-275-95818-3*, Praeger Pubs) Greenwood.

Through Students' Eyes: Combating Racism in United States Schools. Karen B. Mclean-Donaldson. LC 96-10432. 184p. 1996. text ed. 49.95 (*0-275-95478-1*, Praeger Pubs) Greenwood.

Through Sunshine & Shadow: The Woman's Christian Temperance Union, Evangelicalism... Sharon Anne Cook. 1995. 39.95 (*0-7735-1305-1*, Pub. by McGill CN) U of Toronto Pr.

Through Switzerland with Turner: Ruskin's First Selection from the Turner Bequest. Ian Warrell. (Illus.). 160p. 1996. pap. 35.00 (*1-85437-151-7*, Pub. by Tate Gallery UK) U of Wash Pr.

Through Tears. Samuel Huber. (Illus.). 376p. (J). 1996. 10.00 (*0-614-17640-9*, 2440) Rod & Staff.

Through Tears to Triumph: God's Gracious Help Through Grief & Sorrow. John W. Stephenson. LC 96-4075. (Illus.). 106p. (Orig.). 1996. pap. 7.95 (*0-87227-189-7*, RBP5227) Reg Baptist.

Through the Ages in Palestinian Archaeology: An Introductory Handbook. Walter E. Rast. LC 92-33156. 240p. 1992. pap. 15.95 (*1-56338-055-2*) TPI PA.

Through the Air: A Narrative of Forty Years' Experience As an Aeronaut. John S. Wise. LC 79-169444. (Literature & History of Aviation Ser.). 1972. reprint ed. 44.95 (*0-405-03787-2*) Ayer.

Through the Arc of the Rain Forest. Karen T. Yamashita. LC 90-40471. 212p. (Orig.). (YA). (gr. 11-12). 1990. pap. 12.95 (*0-918273-82-X*) Coffee Hse.

Through the Awakening Eye, Poems. Elbridge Anderson. (Illus.). 1976. pap. 4.00 (*0-915242-08-7*) Pygmalion Pr.

Through the Bible, Vol I. Steve Clapp & Sue I. Mauck. (C-Four Youth Bible Materials Ser.). (Illus.). 138p. (Orig.). 1982. pap. 10.00 (*0-914527-15-0*) C-Four Res.

Through The Bible: A Complete Old & New Testament Bible Study. Patricia J. David. (Illus.). 253p. (Orig.). 1994. wbk. ed., spiral bd. 14.95 (*0-89827-130-4*, BKC77) Wesleyan Pub Hse.

Through The Bible: A Comprehensive, Sequential Bible Survey Study & Reference Resource. Patricia J. David. (Illus.). 385p. 1995. 24.95 (*0-89827-131-2*, BKC78) Wesleyan Pub Hse.

Through the Bible Book by Book Pt. 2: Job to Malichi, Vol. 2. Myer Pearlman. 112p. 1935. pap. 4.50 (*0-88243-661-9*, 02-0661) Gospel Pub.

Through the Bible Book by Book Pt. 3: Matthew to Acts, Vol. 3. Myer Pearlman. 96p. 1935. pap. 4.50 (*0-88243-662-7*, 02-0662) Gospel Pub.

Through the Bible Book by Book Pt. 4: Romans to Revelation, Vol. 4. Myer Pearlman. 128p. 1935. pap. 4.50 (*0-88243-663-5*, 02-0663) Gospel Pub.

Through the Bible Book by Book Vol. 1: Genesis to Ester. Myer Pearlman. 99p. 1935. pap. 4.50 (*0-88243-660-0*, 02-0660) Gospel Pub.

Through the Bible Commentary: Psalms, Vol. 1. J. Vernon McGee. LC 90-41340. 1991. pap. 9.99 (*0-8407-3268-6*) Nelson.

Through the Bible Commentary: Psalms, Vol. 2. J. Vernon McGee. LC 90-41340. 1995. pap. 9.99 (*0-7852-1019-9*) Nelson.

Through the Bible Commentary: Psalms, Vol. 3. J. Vernon McGee. LC 90-41340. 1991. pap. 9.99 (*0-8407-3270-8*) Nelson.

Through the Bible in One Year. Alan Stringfellow. 238p. 1978. ring bd. 22.99 (*1-56322-000-8*) V Hensley.

Through the Bible in One Year. Alan Stringfellow. 238p. 1990. pap. text ed. 16.99 (*1-56322-014-8*) V Hensley.

***Through the Bible in One Year.** Alan Stringfellow. 238p. (SPA.). 1990. pap. 16.99 (*1-56322-061-X*) V Hensley.

Through the Black Hole. Edward Packard. (Choose Your Own Adventure Ser.: No. 97). 128p. (J). 1990. pap. 3.50 (*0-553-28440-1*) Bantam.

Through the Black Hole, Vol. 97. large type ed. Edward Packard. LC 95-21015. (Choose Your Own Adventure Ser.: Vol. 97). (Illus.). 128p. (J). (gr. 4 up). 1995. lib. bdg. 15.93 (*0-8368-1408-8*) Gareth Stevens Inc.

Through the Box-Office Window. William H. Leverton. LC 79-8069. (Illus.). reprint ed. 26.50 (*0-404-18379-4*) AMS Pr.

Through the Brazilian Wilderness. Theodore Roosevelt. (Classics of American Sport Ser.). (Illus.). 448p. 1994. pap. 16.95 (*0-8117-2569-3*) Stackpole.

Through the Brick Wall. Kate Wendleton. 1992. 12.95 (*0-679-41229-8*) McKay.

Through the Brick Wall: How to Job Hunt in a Tight Market. Kate Wendleton. 1993. pap. 13.00 (*0-679-74498-3*, Villard Bks) Random.

Through the Brick Wall: Resume Builder for Hunters & Career Changers. Kate Wendleton. (Illus.). 176p. (Orig.). 1994. pap. 13.00 (*0-944054-07-2*) Five Oclock.

***Through the Catechism with Fr. Champlin: A Question-&-Answer Guide.** Joseph M. Champlin. LC 95-82113. 80p. (Orig.). 1996. pap. 3.95 (*0-89243-907-6*) Liguori Pubns.

Through the Centuries. Iu. V. Belichko & V. O. Pidgora. 336p. 1982. 155.00 (*0-317-57469-8*) St Mut.

Through the Chinese Revolution. Fernand Farjenel. LC 72-79820. (China Library). 1972. reprint ed. 31.00 (*0-8420-1381-4*) Scholarly Res Inc.

Through the Collector's Eye: Oriental Rugs from New England Private Collections. Ed. by Susan A. Hay. LC 91-66142. (Illus.). 127p. 1991. pap. 30.00 (*0-911517-59-6*) Mus of Art RI.

***Through the Cracks.** (Shatterzone Ser.). 15.00 (*0-87431-241-8*, 21023) West End Games.

Through the Cracks. Carolyn Sollman. LC 93-74011. 56p. 1994. 19.95 (*0-87192-293-2*) Davis Mass.

Through the Cracks: Horrendous Child Abuse & Murder. Patti A. Bell & Debbie Leonard. 1995. 13.95 (*0-533-11310-5*) Vantage.

Through the Curtain. 2nd ed. Viola P. Neal & Shafica Karagulla. LC 83-71171. 360p. 1993. reprint ed. pap. 13.95 (*0-87516-517-6*) DeVorss.

***Through the Custom-House: Nineteenth-Century American Fiction & Modern Theory.** John C. Rowe. LC 81-20866. 235p. 1982. reprint ed. pap. 67.00 (*0-608-03747-8*, 2064572) Bks Demand.

Through the Customer's Eyes: Improving Your Company's Results with the CORe Method. Lindsay Geddes. 224p. 1993. 24.95 (*0-8144-5070-9*) AMACOM.

Through the Dark Continent: Or the Sources of the Nile Around the Great Lakes of Equatorial Africa & Down the Livingstone River to the Atlantic Ocean, 2 vols., I. Henry M. Stanley. (Illus.). 960p. 1988. reprint ed. pap. 10.95 (*0-486-25667-7*) Dover.

Through the Dark Continent: Or the Sources of the Nile Around the Great Lakes of Equatorial Africa & Down the Livingstone River to the Atlantic Ocean, 2 vols., II. Henry M. Stanley. (Illus.). 960p. 1988. reprint ed. pap. 10.95 (*0-486-25668-5*) Dover.

***Through the Dark Labyrinth.** Gordon Bowker. 1997. 29.95 (*0-312-17225-7*) St Martin.

Through the Darkest Hour. Larry Hart. (Illus.). 144p. (Orig.). 1990. pap. text ed. 11.95 (*0-932035-11-6*) Old Dorp Bks.

Through the Darkness. Adolfo Quezada. LC 92-74491. 260p. 1993. 7.95 (*0-87029-256-0*) Abbey.

***Through the Deadfall.** Kennedy. 1997. pap. 14.95 (*0-385-25605-1*) Doubleday.

Through the Doors of the Mission Inn. Joan H. Hall. 232p. 1996. pap. text ed. 12.00 (*0-9631618-2-2*) Highgrove Pr.

Through the Doors of Truth, Find Thyself. Deborah Morea. 1978. 5.50 (*0-9603022-0-4*) Davida Pubns.

***Through the Dutch & Belgian Canals.** Philip Bristow. (Illus.). 200p. 1996. pap. 24.50 (*0-7136-5760-X*) Sheridan.

Through the Earth. Clement Fezandie. 238p. 1971. reprint ed. spiral bd. 16.50 (*0-7873-0323-2*) Hlth Research.

***Through the Earth Darkly: Female Spirituality in Comparative Perspective.** Jordan Paper. LC 97-23307. 1997. pap. text ed. 29.50 (*0-8264-1050-2*) Continuum.

Through the Eighties: Thinking Globally, Acting Locally. Ed. by Frank Feather. 1980. 12.50 (*0-930242-11-4*) World Future.

Through the Eye of a Needle. Board of St. Paul Editorial Staff. (C). 1989. 40.00 (*0-85439-313-7*, Pub. by St Paul Pubns UK) St Mut.

Through the Eye of a Needle: Judeo-Christian Roots of Social Welfare. Ed. by Carter Lindberg. (Illus.). 264p. (C). 1994. lib. bdg. 51.00 (*0-943549-17-5*) TJU Pr.

Through the Eye of the Feather: Native American Visions. Gail Tuchman. (Illus.). 112p. 1994. 29.95 (*0-87905-641-X*, Peregrine Smith); pap. 19.95 (*0-87905-597-9*) Gibbs Smith Pub.

Through the Eye of the Needle. William Dean Howells. (Notable American Authors Ser.). 1992. reprint ed. lib. bdg. 75.00 (*0-7812-3259-7*) Rprt Serv.

Through the Eye of the Needle: A Romance. William Dean Howells. LC 78-9572. reprint ed. 34.00 (*0-404-11548-9*) AMS Pr.

Through the Eye of the Needle: Immigrants & Enterprise in the New York Garment Trade. Roger D. Waldinger. LC 86-12451. 256p. (C). 1986. 50.00 (*0-8147-9212-X*) NYU Pr.

Through the Eye of the Needle: Immigrants & Enterprise in the New York Garment Trade. Roger D. Waldinger. LC 86-12451. 256p. (C). 1989. pap. 17.50 (*0-8147-9234-0*) NYU Pr.

Through the Eyes & Mind of a Storyteller. William C. McKelvey. LC 92-81942. (Illus.). 110p. (Orig.). 1992. pap. 10.95 (*0-9633719-0-8*) Eclipse Pub.

Through the Eyes of a Child. Mildred Caughey. 83p. 1979. 8.50 (*0-87770-224-1*) Ye Galleon.

Through the Eyes of a Child. 4th ed. Donna E. Norton. LC 94-4485. 784p. (C). 1994. text ed. 64.00 (*0-02-388313-8*, Macmillan Coll) P-H.

Through the Eyes of a Dolphin: An Inner Journey Which Can Only Be Approached in the Imagination, Beyond the Mind, Experienced in the Heart & Recognized by the Soul. Liliana Saca. (Illus.). 128p. (Orig.). 1996. pap. 9.95 (*0-9650530-8-3*) VISIGRAF.

Through the Eyes of a Loon: Impressions of the Northwoods. Laura Hanson et al. (Illus.). xv, 76p. (Orig.). 1996. pap. 10.95 (*0-9652772-0-8*) Summer Winds.

Through the Eyes of a Poet: A Collection of Philosophical Poems. John J. Layden. 70p. (Orig.). (YA). (gr. 9-12). 1995. pap. write for info. (*1-57502-028-9*) Morris Pub.

Through the Eyes of a Wheelchair: The Tommy Neal Story. Robert J. Walker & Tommy Neal. 111p. (Orig.). 1996. pap. 7.95 (*0-9642553-2-4*) In His Name.

Through the Eyes of a Young Heart. Pamela K. Costa. LC 94-93835. 108p. (YA). (gr. 8-12). 1994. pap. 9.95 (*0-9643002-0-6*) Costa Pubng.

Through the Eyes of an Adoptee Vol. 1: One Man's Compelling Search for His Beginnings. Frank Law. LC 96-94346. (Illus.). 130p. (Orig.). 1996. pap. 10.95 (*0-9652437-3-7*) Gann Pubng.

Through the Eyes of Children: Liberty & Justice for All. Ed. by Libby Post. (Illus.). 48p. (Orig.). (J). 1989. pap. write for info. (*0-318-65750-3*) NY State Alliance.

Through the Eyes of Faith. John Powell. (Illus.). 156p. (Orig.). 1995. reprint ed. pap. 9.50 (*0-88347-330-5*, 7330) Res Christian Liv.

***Through the Eyes of Gabriel.** Virginia S. Fair. (Illus.). 130p. (YA). 1997. pap. 12.95 (*0-9655035-8-5*) Threesie Pubns.

***Through the Eyes of Jesus.** Carver A. Ames. 153p. 1996. pap. 8.00 (*1-890137-00-6*) One Hund-One Fnd.

***Through the Eyes of Jesus.** Carver A. Ames. 157p. 1997. pap. text ed. 8.00 (*1-890137-03-0*) One Hund-One Fnd.

Through the Eyes of Jesus. Mack Thomas. LC 95-40220. (Illus.). 64p. (J). 1995. 14.99 (*0-88070-803-4*, Gold & Honey) Multnomah Pubs.

Through the Eyes of Others: Why Everyone Is So Stressed Out & Depressed. Ricardo A. Scott. (Ras Cardo Speaks Ser.). (Illus.). 70p. (Orig.). Date not set. pap. write for info. (*1-883427-72-X*) Crnerstone GA.

Through the Eyes of Social Science. 5th rev. ed. Ed. by Frank Zulke. (Illus.). 538p. (C). 1995. pap. text ed. 20.95 (*0-88133-816-8*) Waveland Pr.

Through the Eyes of Spirit: As a Bridge Between This World & the Spirit World, Jenny Brings Us Proof of Life Beyond Death. Jenny Crawford. LC 96-30461. 128p. (Orig.). 1996. pap. 11.00 (*0-931892-32-5*) B Dolphin Pub.

***Through the Eyes of the Children.** Johnston & Garrity. LC 97-9284. 1997. pap. 16.95 (*0-684-83703-X*) S&S Trade.

Through the Eyes of the Dead. Melisa C. Michaels. 192p. 1989. 17.95 (*0-8027-5718-9*) Walker & Co.

Through the Eyes of the Explorers: Minds-On Math & Mapping. (J). (gr. 5-9). 1994. 16.95 (*1-881431-48-7*, 1314) AIMS Educ Fnd.

Through the Eyes of the Goddess: How to Give Life to the Spirit of Aphrodite in You. S. Kathena Mosich. (Illus.). 167p. (Orig.). 1990. pap. 12.99 (*0-9634361-0-4*) Shapes of Spirit.

Through the Eyes of Two Enemies. Anthony Muscarella. 120p. (Orig.). 1995. pap. 12.00 (*0-9641970-1-4*) Freedom Press.

Through the Eyes of Women: Insights for Pastoral Care the Handbook of Womencare. Ed. by Jeanne S. Moessner. 352p. 1996. pap. 22.00 (*0-8006-2928-0*, Fortress Pr) Augsburg Fortress.

***Through the Eyes of Women of the 20th Century.** Ed. & Intro. by Jacqueline J. Pliskin. (Illus.). 378p. (Orig.). 1997. pap. 19.95 (*0-9647480-1-0*) Words & Pict.

Through the Fairy Door - Only I Am. Rob Brown. (Illus.). 48p. (J). (gr. k-3). 1995. 14.95 (*1-56313-744-5*) BrownTrout Pubs Inc.

***Through the Fields: A Journey Through Life Seasoned with Prayer.** Laura R. Hess. (Illus.). 80p. 1996. pap. text ed. 9.95 (*0-9629755-5-9*) Wingborne-Diaconal.

Through the Fire. Emma Pertz. (Folktales for Children Ser.). 58p. (J). (gr. 6-8). 1994. pap. 7.95 (*1-882427-18-1*) Aspasia Inc.

Through the Fire: A Collection of Poems. Dennis L. Markin. 1996. 8.95 (*0-533-10148-4*) Vantage.

Through the Fire: The True Story of a Romanian Pastor Facing Communist Persecution. Dumitru Duduman. 120p. 1991. pap. 8.95 (*1-879913-00-3*) Christ Creator.

Through the Fire Without Burning. Dumitru Duduman. (Illus.). 198p. (Orig.). 1992. pap. 9.95 (*0-9635055-0-5*); disk write for info. (*0-9635055-1-3*) Hand of Help.

Through the First Antarctic Night, 1898-1899: A Narrative of the Voyage of the "Belgica" among Newly Discovered Lands & over an Unknown Sea about the South Pole. Frederick A. Cook. LC 81-129738. 582p. reprint ed. pap. 165.90 (*0-7837-1043-7*, 2041354) Bks Demand.

Through the Flower: My Struggle As a Woman Artist. Judy Chicago. LC 93-19313. (Illus.). 248p. 1993. pap. 13.95 (*0-14-023122-6*, Penguin Bks) Viking Penguin.

Through the Fourth Wall. William A. Darlington. LC 68-16925. (Essay Index Reprint Ser.). 1977. 19.95 (*0-8369-0363-3*) Ayer.

Through the French Canals. 8th ed. Philip Bristow. pap. 20.95 (*0-7136-3844-3*, 93171, Pub. by A&C Black UK) Talman.

Through the Gap: An Anthology of Contemporary Kentucky Poetry. Ed. by Scot Brannon et al. 118p. (Orig.). 1991. pap. 9.00 (*0-9628089-0-3*) Free Pr.

Through the Garden Gate. Elizabeth Lawrence. Ed. by Bill Neal. LC 89-27890. xiv, 256p. (C). 1990. 22.50 (*0-8078-1907-7*) U of NC Pr.

Through the Garden Gate. Elizabeth Lawrence. Ed. by Bill Neal. LC 89-27890. (Chapel Hill Bks.). 256p. 1995. pap. 14.95 (*0-8078-4519-1*) U of NC Pr.

Through the Gate of Good. James Allen. 66p. 1992. pap. 6.00 (*0-89540-216-5*, SB-216) Sun Pub.

Through the Gateless Gate. Catherine De Vinck. LC 96-84270. 170p. (Orig.). 1996. pap. 10.75 (*0-911726-62-4*, TGG) Alleluia Pr.

Through the Gates of Gold: A Fragment of Thought. Mabel Collins. 151p. 1967. reprint ed. spiral bd. 9.00 (*0-7873-1229-0*) Hlth Research.

***Through the German Waterways.** Philip Bristow. (Illus.). 158p. 1996. pap. 24.50 (*0-7136-5770-7*) Sheridan.

***Through the Glass Darkly.** Kevin Hassall & Kevin Siembieda. Ed. by Alex Marciniszyn & James Osten. (Nightbane Worldbook Ser.: Vol. 3). (Illus.). 152p. (Orig.). (YA). (gr. 8 up). 1997. pap. 16.95 (*1-57457-004-8*, 733) Palladium Bks.

Through the Glass of Soviet Literature: Views, of Russian Society. Ed. & Intro. by Ernest J. Simmons. LC 72-337. (Essay Index Reprint Ser.). 1977. reprint ed. 23.95 (*0-8369-2827-X*) Ayer.

Through the Glass Window Shines the Sun: An Anthology of Medieval Poetry & Prose. Pamela Norris. 128p. 1995. 18.95 (*0-8212-2206-6*) Bulfinch Pr.

***Through the Global Lens.** Strada. 1997. pap. text ed. 46.67 (*0-13-614538-8*) P-H.

Through the Goddess: A Woman's Way of Healing. Patricia Reis. 240p. 1995. pap. text ed. 15.95 (*0-8264-0856-7*) Continuum.

Through the Goddess: A Woman's Way of Healing. Patricia Reis. 225p. 1991. 24.95 (*0-8245-1343-6*) Crossroad NY.

Through the Green: The Mind & Art of a Professional Golfer. Sal Maiorana. (Illus.). 272p. 1993. 21.95 (*0-312-09363-2*) St Martin.

Through the Green Fire: Personal Essays, Prose Poems & Poetry. James Grabil. 120p. (Orig.). (C). 1995. pap. text ed. 10.95 (*0-930100-60-3*) Holy Cow.

Through the Green Fuse. Michael Dudley. 32p. 1983. pap. 3.50 (*0-913719-23-4*) High-Coo Pr.

Through the Habitrails. 2nd rev. ed. Jeff Nicholson. (Illus.). 144p. (Orig.). 1996. pap. 14.95 (*1-885047-03-7*) Bad Habit.

Through the Hebrew Looking-Glass: Arab Stereotypes in Children's Literature. Fouzi El-Asmar. (Illus.). 150p. 1986. 17.95 (*0-915597-39-X*); pap. 9.95 (*0-915597-37-3*) Amana Bks.

Through the Hoop. Ed. by Tema Okun & Peter Wood. (Southern Exposure Ser.). (Illus.). 128p. (Orig.). (C). 1979. pap. 4.00 (*0-943810-07-8*) Inst Southern Studies.

***Through the Hourglass.** Ed. by Diana Zeiger. 1996. 69.95 (*1-57553-069-4*) Watermrk Pr.

Through the Ice. Piers Anthony & Robert Kornwise. 1992. mass mkt. 5.99 (*0-671-72113-5*) Baen Bks.

Through the Inner Eye: Awakening to the Creative Spirit. Jan Groenemann. 96p. 1994. pap. 19.95 (*0-9641919-0-3*) Islewest Pub.

Through the Interface: A Human Activity Approach to User Interface Design. Susanne Bodker. 192p. (C). 1990. pap. 32.50 (*0-8058-0571-0*); text ed. 65.00 (*0-8058-0570-2*) L Erlbaum Assocs.

Through the Ivory Gate. large type ed. Dia Orridge. (Romance Ser.). 1989. 25.99 (*0-7089-2062-4*) Ulverscroft.

Through the Ivory Gate: A Novel. Rita Dove. LC 92-4456. 272p. 1992. 21.00 (*0-679-41604-8*) Pantheon.

Through the Ivory Gate: A Novel. Rita Dove. LC 93-10509. (Vintage Contemporaries Ser.). 288p. 1993. pap. 12.00 (*0-679-74240-9*, Vin) Random.

***Through the Kitchen Window: Women Explore the Intimate Meaning of Food & Cooking2.** Arlene V. Avakian. LC 96-46130. 1997. 25.00 (*0-8070-6508-0*) Beacon Pr.

Through the Laughter & the Tears. Michael B. Devlin. 60p. (Orig.). Date not set. write for info. (*0-614-08589-6*) Watermrk Pr.

Through the Laughter & the Tears. Michael B. Devlin. (Orig.). 1995. pap. write for info. (*1-57553-024-4*) Watermrk Pr.

Through the Leaves & Other Plays. Franz X. Kroetz. Tr. by Roger Downey from GER. (TCG Translations Ser.). 162p. 1992. 24.95 (*1-55936-044-5*); pap. 12.95 (*1-55936-043-7*) Theatre Comm.

Through the Lens of the Reader: Explorations of European Narrative. Lilian R. Furst. LC 90-19546. (SUNY Series, The Margins of Literature). 186p. 1991. pap. text ed. 21.95 (*0-7914-0808-6*) State U NY Pr.

Through the Lens of the Reader: Explorations of European Narrative. Lilian R. Furst. LC 90-19546. (SUNY Series, The Margins of Literature). 186p. 1991. text ed. 64.50 (*0-7914-0807-8*) State U NY Pr.

Through the Leper-Squint. Anthony Weymouth. LC 75-23769. (Illus.). reprint ed. 37.50 (*0-404-13395-9*) AMS Pr.

Through the Light Continent: The United States in 1877-1878. William Saunders. LC 73-13148. (Foreign Travelers in America, 1810-1935 Ser.). 432p. 1974. reprint ed. 33.95 (*0-405-05472-6*) Ayer.

Through the Light Hole: A Saga of Adirondack Mines & Men. Patrick F. Farrell. LC 94-38137. write for info. (*0-615-00282-X*) North Country.

Through the Loneliness: A Woman's Spiritual Journal. Antonia J. van den Beld. 144p. 1987. pap. 8.95 (*0-8091-2913-2*) Paulist Pr.

***Through the Looking Glass.** Dana Becker. (New Directions in Theory & Psychology Ser.). 1997. text ed. 65.00 (*0-8133-3309-1*) Westview.

***Through the Looking Glass.** Dana Becker. (New Directions in Theory & Psychology Ser.). (C). 1997. pap. text ed. 21.00 (*0-8133-3310-5*) Westview.

Through the Looking Glass. Lewis Carroll. 1994. 16.95 incl. audio (*1-883049-41-5*); lib. bdg. 18.95 incl. audio (*1-883049-47-4*) Commuters Lib.

Through the Looking Glass. Lewis Carroll. 176p. (YA). (gr. 5 up). 1996. pap. 3.99 (*0-14-036709-8*) Puffin Bks.

Through the Looking-Glass. Lewis Carroll & Kyle Baker. (Classics Illustrated Ser.). (Illus.). 52p. (YA). pap. 4.95 (*1-57209-002-2*) Classics Int Ent.

Through the Looking-Glass. Lewis Carroll. (Illus.). (J). 1990. pap. 3.75 (*0-425-12022-8*) First Classics.

Through the Looking Glass. Elizabeth Wilson & Lou Taylor. (Illus.). 236p. 1991. pap. 17.95 (*0-563-21441-4*, BBC-Parkwest) Parkwest Pubns.

Through the Looking Glass. Tom Wolfe. LC 91-67011. (Illus.). 64p. 1992. pap. 12.95 (*0-88740-380-8*) Schiffer.

Through the Looking-Glass. abr. ed. Lewis Carroll. (Illus.). 128p. (J). (gr. 2 up). 1993. reprint ed. lib. bdg. 16.95 (*0-689-31863-4*, Atheneum Bks Young) S&S Childrens.

Through the Looking Glass. 2nd ed. David Carlson & Vaughn Bryant, Jr. 1994. pap. text ed. write for info. (*0-07-009980-4*) McGraw.

Through the Looking Glass. Lewis Carroll. 1981. reprint ed. lib. bdg. 15.95 (*0-89966-419-9*) Buccaneer Bks.

Through the Looking Glass. Lewis Carroll. (Illus.). 224p. (J). 1977. reprint ed. 14.95 (*0-312-80374-5*) St Martin.

Through the Looking Glass, 2 cassettes, Set. (Read-Along Ser.). (YA). student ed. 34.95 incl. audio (*0-88432-971-2*, S23946) Audio-Forum.

Through the Looking Glass: A Dialogue of Soviet Jewish Immigrants & American Jews. Ed. by Gerald L. Showstack. (Illus.). 67p. (Orig.). 1990. pap. text ed. 7.50 (*1-879083-00-0*) Brandeis U Hornstein Prog.

Through the Looking Glass: Breast Cancer Stories of Northern Native Women. Colomeda. LC 96-18865. 180p. 1996. pap. 17.95 (*0-88737-682-7*) Natl League Nurse.

Through the Looking Glass: Issues of Psychological Well-Being in Captive Nonhuman Primates. Ed. by Melinda A. Novak & Andrew J. Petto. 285p. 1991. text ed. 39.95 (*1-55798-087-X*) Am Psychol.

Through the Looking Glass: Observations in the Early Childhood Classroom. Sheryl A. Nicolson & Susan G. Shipstead. 448p. (C). 1993. pap. text ed. 36.00 (*0-02-387491-0*, Macmillan Coll) P-H.

***Through the Looking Glass: Readings in Anthropology.** David L. Carlson & Vaughn M. Bryant. 1996. pap. text ed. write for info. (*0-07-011884-1*) McGraw.

Through the Looking Glass: Seminars in Psychological Astrology, Vol. 5. Richard Idemon. LC 91-43165. 195p. 1992. pap. 14.95 (*0-87728-721-X*) Weiser.

Through the Looking Glass: The American Family on Television. Garth Jowett & William Douglas. (C). 1995. pap. text ed. 15.95 (*0-8133-1991-9*) Westview.

Through the Looking Glass see Alice's Adventures in Wonderland

Through the Looking Glass & Back: Your Passport to Identity-Self-Image. Susan G. Bondow & Paul Kelm. LC 93-84288. 96p. 1993. 9.99 (*0-8100-0489-5*, 15N2000) Northwest Pub.

Through the Looking Glass & What Alice Found There. Lewis Carroll. (Illus.). 127p. (J). 1991. 7.99 (*0-517-00233-7*) Random Hse Value.

Through the Looking Glass & What Alice Found There. Lewis Carroll. LC 92-20642. (Books of Wonder). (Illus.). 240p. (J). (gr. 1 up). 1993. 16.00 (*0-688-12049-0*, Morrow Junior) Morrow.

Through the Looking Glass & What Alice Found There (Playscript) Rosemary Nursey-Bray. (Orig.). (J). (ps up). 1988. 5.50 (*0-87602-276-X*) Anchorage.

Through the Looking Glasses II. Faye Clark. LC 93-80576. 72p. 1993. pap. 8.95 (*0-9639110-0-7*) Lavender Lady.

***Through the Magic.** rev. ed. Anthony Browne. (J). Date not set. lib. bdg. write for info. (*0-688-10726-5*) Greenwillow.

Through the Media Looking Glass: Decoding Bias & Blather in the News. Jeff Cohen & Norman Solomon. 272p. 1995. text ed. 29.95 (*1-56751-049-3*) Common Courage.

Through the Media Looking Glass: Decoding Bias & Blather in the News. Jeff Cohen & Norman Solomon. 272p. 1995. pap. text ed. 13.95 (*1-56751-048-5*) Common Courage.

Through the Medicine Cabinet. Dan Greenburg. LC 96-7107. (Zack Files Ser.: No. 2). (Illus.). 64p. (J). (gr. 2-5). 1996. pap. 3.95 (*0-448-41262-4*, G&D); lib. bdg. 11.99 (*0-448-41291-8*, G&D) Putnam Pub Group.

Through the Middle Ages: Chapters 1-11 see Societies & Cultures in World History

***Through the Mill Door & Beyond: Trail Guide to Babcock State Park.** Emily Grafton. LC 97-72799. (Illus.). 96p. (Orig.). 1997. pap. 8.95 (*0-929915-19-4*) Headline Bks.

Through the Mind's Eye. Ralph M. Lewis. LC 81-84954. 371p. 1982. 18.95 (*0-912057-32-7*, 501890) RO AMORC.

Through the Mist of Time. R. Hall. 1994. 9.95 incl. reel tape (*0-87249-990-1*) U of SC Pr.

Through the Mist of Time: An Alpine Memory. Martha M. Burt. (Illus.). 64p. (Orig.). 1994. pap. write for info. (*0-942495-40-3*) Amherst Pr.

Through the Mists of Darkness. Bonnie Robinson. (YA). 1996. pap. 8.95 (*1-55503-693-7*, 01111728) Covenant Comms.

Through the Molecular Maze. 3rd ed. John V. Basmajian et al. (Illus.). (C). 1991. pap. text ed. 7.95 (*1-879336-00-6*) Bio-Venture.

Through the Moral Maze: Searching for Absolute Values in a Pluralistic World. Robert Kane. LC 96-4562. 272p. (C). 1996. pap. 17.50 (*1-56324-866-2*, N Castle) M E Sharpe.

Through the Moral Maze: Searching for Absolute Values in a Pluralistic World. Robert H. Kane. LC 92-36927. 1993. 27.95 (*1-55778-601-1*) Paragon Hse.

***Through the Mousehole: A Journey in Faith.** Jane Segerstrom. 138p. 1996. pap. 9.95 (*0-936740-20-5*) Triad Pr TX.

Through the Narrow Gate. Karen Armstrong. 1994. pap. 10.95 (*0-312-11903-8*) St Martin.

Through the Narrow Gate. large type ed. Karen Armstrong. 544p. 1983. 25.99 (*0-7089-0941-8*) Ulverscroft.

Through the Narrow Gate: The Mythological Consciousness of Russell Hoban. Christine Wilkie. LC 87-46419. 136p. 1989. 32.50 (*0-8386-3339-0*) Fairleigh Dickinson.

Through the Needle's Eye. Jon Milos. Tr. by B. Walker from RUM. 112p. (Orig.). 9000. pap. 19.95 (*0-948259-61-2*, Pub. by Forest Bks UK) Dufour.

Through the Night. Aylesworth. LC 97-7281. (J). 1998. 16.00 (*0-689-80642-6*) S&S Childrens.

Through the Night Raptly. Mohinder Monga. 8.00 (*0-89253-778-7*); text ed. 4.80 (*0-89253-779-5*) Ind-US Inc.

Through the Northern Gate Vol. 6: Childhood & Growing up in British Fiction, 1719-1901. Jacqueline Banerjee. (Studies in Nineteenth Century British Literature). 280p. (C). 1996. text ed. 49.95 (*0-8204-3010-2*) P Lang Pubng.

***Through the Pages of Daily Racing Form.** John McEvoy. (Illus.). 102p. Date not set. pap. 19.95 (*0-9648493-4-8*) Daily Racing.

Through the Pale Door: A Guide to & Through the American Gothic. Frederick S. Frank. LC 90-31733. (Bibliographies & Indexes in American Literature Ser.: No. 11). 384p. 1990. text ed. 59.95 (*0-313-25900-3*, FGF, Greenwood Pr) Greenwood.

Through the Path of Echoes - Por el Camino de Ecos: Contemporary Art in Mexico. Elizabeth Ferrer & Alberto M. Ruy-Sanchez. LC 90-71025. (ENG & SPA.). 1990. 13.00 (*0-916365-29-8*) Ind Curators.

Through the Path of Grace: An Extraordinary Journey for an Ordinary Woman. Bonnie Chen. 291p. 1994. pap. write for info. (*0-9631789-7-0*) Evan Formosan.

Through the Patient's Eyes: Understanding & Promoting Patient-Centered Care. Ed. by Margaret Gerteis et al. LC 93-51. (Health-Management Ser.). 347p. text ed. 31.95 (*1-55542-544-5*) Jossey-Bass.

Through the Porthole. (Illus.). 1965. pap. 5.00 (*0-914412-25-6*) Inst for the Arts.

Through the Rainbow Canyon: A Personal Narrative of the People, Places & Events, from Caliente to Carp, Nevada. Walter Averett. (Illus.). 192p. 1995. 20.00 (*0-87062-237-4*) A H Clark.

Through the Reversal of Time. Emilio A. Jamarron. Ed. by Malvin Wald. LC 86-9644. 400p. (Orig.). 1986. pap. 18.95 (*0-317-47445-6*) Blue Lagoon.

Through the Roof! (J). (gr. 2-5). 1991. audio 10.95 (*0-687-41912-3*) Abingdon.

***Through the Roof! A Musical Story Based on Luke 5:17-26: PreviewPak.** Terry Kirkland. 1995. pap. 6.00 incl. audio (*0-687-07595-5*) Abingdon.

Through the Roof! Accompaniment. (J). (gr. 2-5). 1991. audio 29.95 (*0-687-41913-1*) Abingdon.

Through the Roof! Intro Pak - Both Books & Listening Tape. Terry Kirkland. (J). (gr. 2-5). 1991. pap. 19.95 (*0-687-41915-8*) Abingdon.

Through the Roof: Jesus Heals a Paralyzed Man. Mary M. Simon. LC 93-36193. (Hear Me Read Ser.: Level 2). (Illus.). 32p. (Orig.). (J). (gr. 1-3). 1994. pap. 3.99 (*0-570-04734-X*, 56-1691) Concordia.

Through the Roof! Leader/Accompanist Edition. 64p. (J). (gr. 2-5). 1991. teacher ed., spiral bd. 14.95 (*0-687-41911-5*) Abingdon.

Through the Roof! Singer's Edition. 16p. (J). (gr. 2-5). 1991. pap. 2.95 (*0-687-41914-X*) Abingdon.

Through the Rosary with Fra Angelico. Domenico Marcucci. Tr. by Edmund C. Lane from ITA. (Illus.). 48p. (Orig.). 1989. pap. 2.50 (*0-8189-0557-3*) Alba.

Through the Russian Prism: Essays on Literature & Culture. Joseph Frank. 224p. (C). 1990. text ed. 45.00 (*0-691-06821-6*); pap. text ed. 14.95 (*0-691-01456-6*) Princeton U Pr.

Through the Saloon Doors (Anthology) Caroline Ehlers et al. LC 92-50828. 208p. 1982. pap. 7.50 (*0-9609062-0-7*) WA Expatriates Pr.

Through the Scriptures. A. P. Gibbs. 1935. pap. 9.95 (*0-937396-45-1*) Walterick Pubs.

Through the Shattering Glass: Cervantes & the Self-Made World. Nicholas Spadaccini & Jenaro Talens. LC 92-14158. 8p. (C). 1992. pap. text ed. 16.95 (*0-8166-2263-9*) U of Minn Pr.

Through the Sky in the Lake: Sayings & Photographs. Sid Gershgoren. LC 90-41194. (Seeing Double Collaborative Book). 80p. (Orig.). 1990. pap. 9.95 (*0-915943-60-3*) Milkweed Ed.

Through the Spyglass: A Sailor Looks at Cruising & Tells What & Why. Anne M. Hays. 176p. (Orig.). 1995. pap. 14.95 (*1-56167-228-9*) Am Literary Pr.

Through the Stalks Exposing. M. J. Bender. 40p. (Orig.). 1990. pap. 3.00 (*0-685-29033-6*) Landside Pr.

Through the Storm: A Polio Story. Robert F. Hall. LC 90-36783. 160p. 1990. pap. 12.95 (*0-87839-059-6*) North Star.

Through the Storm of an Affair: Collected True Stories. Anna Chen et al. 278p. 1994. pap. write for info. (*1-885216-01-7*) Evan Formosan.

Through the Storybook. Greg Atkins. (Illus.). 24p. (Orig.). (J). (ps-4). 1988. pap. 3.25 (*0-88680-306-3*); 7.50 (*0-88680-307-1*) I E Clark.

***Through the Straits, at Large.** Anca Vlasopolos. 44p. (Orig.). 1997. pap. text ed. 8.00 (*1-56439-053-5*) Ridgeway.

Through the Straits of Armageddon: Arms Control Issues & Prospects. Ed. by Paul F. Diehl & Loch K. Johnson. LC 86-30813. 304p. 1987. 40.00 (*0-8203-0946-X*) U of Ga Pr.

***Through the Sunlit Year.** Ralph W. Trine. 250p. 1997. pap. 23.00 (*0-89540-350-1*) Sun Pub.

Through the Tears: Caring for the Sexually Abused Child. Karen C. Johnson & M. C. Fritzemeier. LC 92-18651. (Orig.). 1993. pap. 8.99 (*0-8054-6062-4*, 4260-62) Broadman.

Through the Telescope: A Guide for the Amateur Astronomer. Michael R. Porcellino. 1989. pap. text ed. 21.95 (*0-07-156226-5*) McGraw.

Through the Telescope: A Guide for the Amateur Astronomer. Michael R. Porcellino. (Discovering Earth Science Ser.). (Illus.). 272p. 1989. 22.95 (*0-8306-1459-1*); pap. 19.95 (*0-8306-3159-3*) McGraw-Hill Prof.

Through the Tiger's Eyes. Stanley Breeden & Belinda Wright. (Illus.). 192p. (Orig.). 1996. pap. 24.95 (*0-89815-847-8*) Ten Speed Pr.

Through the Tunnel. Doris Lessing. (Creative Short Stories Ser.). (YA). (gr. 4-12). 1989. 13.95 (*0-88682-346-3*, 97224-098) Creative Ed.

Through the Tunnel: A Traveler's Guide to Spiritual Rebirth. Diane Goble. 150p. (Orig.). 1994. pap. 12.00 (*0-9638606-0-7*) D Goble.

Through the Turf Smoke. Seumas Macmanus. LC 72-81273. (Short Story Index Reprint Ser.). 1977. 20.95 (*0-8369-3025-8*) Ayer.

***Through the Valley.** Suzanne Hellman. 260p. Date not set. 9.99 (*1-56476-718-3*, Victor Bks) Chariot Victor.

Through the Valley. Nancy Morris. LC 91-66013. 85p. 1992. pap. 6.95 (*1-55523-453-4*) Winston-Derek.

Through the Valley. Marjorie Oliver. 96p. (Orig.). 1995. pap. 6.99 (*1-56043-251-9*) Destiny Image.

Through the Valley. Frances M. Swan. LC 78-73254. (Illus.). (Orig.). 1978. pap. 5.00 (*0-9602126-1-2*) F M Swan.

Through the Valley... Prayers for Violent Times. Margaret A. Huffman. 200p. 1996. pap. 13.50 (*0-8170-1238-9*) Judson.

Through the Valley of the Shadow: A Guide for the Care of the Dying & Their Loved Ones. L. Richard Batzler. LC 83-11282. 1983. 10.95 (*0-935710-05-1*) Hid Valley MD.

***Through the Veil.** Peter Paddon. (Illus.). (Orig.). 1997. pap. 22.95 (*1-898307-49-0*) Holmes Pub.

Through the Waiting Room. Henry Kitt. 110p. 1992. 7.50 (*0-924694-15-7*) Capricornis.

Through the Wall. 1,909th ed. Cleveland Moffett. LC 75-32768. (Literature of Mystery & Detection Ser.). (Illus.). 1976. reprint ed. 34.95 (*0-405-07887-0*) Ayer.

Through the Water, Through the Fire. Ron McRay. 64p. 1992. per. 3.95 (*0-9631167-0-3*) R McRay.

Through the Waters: Baptism & the Christian Life. David S. Hamilton. 160p. 1990. pap. 24.95 (*0-567-29178-2*, Pub. by T & T Clark UK) Bks Intl VA.

Through the Wilderness of Loneliness. Tim Hansel. 1991. pap. 8.99 (*1-55513-744-X*, LifeJourney) Chariot Victor.

Through the Window & Beyond. Lynne Edwards. Ed. by Sharon Rose & Barbara Weiland. (Illus.). 80p. (Orig.). 1995. pap. 19.95 (*1-56477-100-8*, B217) That Patchwork.

Through the Window of the Past Abstracts of the Washington Reporter: August 1, 1814-December 30, 1816. Bonnie Malmat. 222p. 1993. pap. text ed. 19.95 (*1-55856-151-X*) Closson Pr.

Through the Woods. Carroll Arnett. 1971. 10.00 (*0-685-00984-X*); pap. 5.00 (*0-685-00985-8*) Elizabeth Pr.

Through the Woods: The English Woodland - April to April. H. E. Bates. (Illus.). 144p. 1995. 27.50 (*0-7112-0992-8*, Pub. by F Lincoln UK) Trafalgar.

***Through the Woods & over the Mountains.** Etta D. Martin. (Illus.). 122p. (Orig.). 1997. pap. write for info. (*1-57502-477-2*, P01431) Morris Pubng.

Through the Year see Aguas Refrescantes

Through the Year with - Prairie Dogs. Caroline Arnold. LC 92-38283. (Illus.). 32p. (J). 1993. pap. 3.95 (*0-590-46946-0*) Scholastic Inc.

***Through the Year with Feelings.** Ed. by Carole J. Heffley. (Illus.). 124p. (Orig.). 1996. pap. text ed. 21.95 (*1-883331-20-X*) Anderie Poetry.

Through the Year with Francis of Assisi: Daily Meditations from his Words & Life. Murray Bodo. 240p. 1993. pap. 7.95 (*0-86716-196-5*) St Anthony Mess Pr.

Through the Year with Fulton Sheen: Inspiration Selections for Each Day of the Year. Fulton J. Sheen. 215p. 1985. pap. 10.99 (*0-89283-236-3*) Servant.

Through the Year with the Church Fathers. Emily Harakas. 1985. pap. 10.95 (*0-937032-37-9*) Light&Life Pub Co MN.

Through the Year with the DRE: A Seasonal Guide for Christian Educators. Gail T. McKenna. 128p. (Orig.). 1987. pap. 7.95 (*0-8091-2860-8*) Paulist Pr.

Through the Year with William Barclay. Ed. by William Barclay. (C). 1990. pap. 35.00 (*0-85305-252-2*, Pub. by J Arthur Ltd UK) St Mut.

Through the Year with Words of Comfort. Daniel P. Cronin. 208p. (C). 1990. 49.00 (*0-85439-344-7*, Pub. by St Paul Pubns UK) St Mut.

Through the Year with Words of Encouragement. Daniel P. Cronin. 206p. (C). 1990. 49.00 (*0-85439-422-2*, Pub. by St Paul Pubns UK) St Mut.

Through the Year with Words of Wisdom. Daniel P. Cronin. 170p. (C). 1990. 49.00 (*0-85439-284-X*, Pub. by St Paul Pubns UK) St Mut.

Through the Years. Eugene C. Chorosinski. 80p. (Orig.). 1995. pap. write for info. (*1-57553-011-2*) Watermrk Pr.

Through the Years: Light out of Darkness, 1867-1977. M. H. Crockett & Barbara C. Dease. (Illus.). 473p. (Orig.). 1991. pap. 30.00 (*1-882133-03-X*) Barefoot Pr.

Through the Years: Memoirs of Elsie Penner Pankratz. Elsie P. Pankratz. LC 93-61427. (Illus.). xiv, 149p. (Orig.). 1993. pap. 12.00 (*0-945530-10-2*) Wordsworth KS.

Through the Years: My Life in Pictures. Cilla Black. 160p. 1994. 34.95 (*0-7472-0918-9*, Pub. by Headline UK) Trafalgar.

***Through the Years: Poems by M. M. Moore.** M. M. Moore. 64p. (Orig.). 1996. pap. write for info. (*0-9639290-2-X*) Good Times.

Through the Years in Old Winnsboro. Katharine T. Obear. LC 80-23314. xx, 258p. 1980. reprint ed. 20.00 (*0-87152-344-2*) Reprint.

Through the Years with Fulton Sheen. large type ed. Fulton J. Sheen. (Large Print Inspirational Ser.). 400p. 1987. pap. 15.95 (*0-8027-2572-4*) Walker & Co.

An Asterisk (*) at the beginning of an entry indicates that the title is appearing in BIP for the first time.

***Through the Yellowstone Park on Horseback.** George W. Wingate. LC 96-29682. (Idaho Yesterdays Ser.). 1997. write for info. (0-89301-205-X) U of Idaho Pr.

***Through the Yellowstone Park on Horseback.** George W. Wingate. LC 96-29682. (Idaho Yesterdays Ser.). 1998. write for info. (0-89301-208-4) U of Idaho Pr.

Through Their Eyes: Memories of Berkeley Hillel. Ida Frank. (Illus.). 300p. 1993. pap. 19.95 (0-943376-53-X) Magnes Mus.

Through Their Eyes, Intermediate Level: A Sequentially Developed Art Program, Grades 4-6. Rebecca Brooks et al. Ed. by Ann F. Crawford. (Illus.). 288p. 1989. suppl. ed., ring bd. 99.92 (0-87443-087-9) Benson.

Through Their Eyes, Primary Level: A Sequentially Developed Art Program, Grades 1-3. Rebecca Brooks et al. Ed. by Ann F. Crawford. (Illus.). 280p. 1989. suppl. ed., ring bd. 99.92 (0-87443-086-0) Benson.

Through These Doors: Discovering Oakland at Preservation Park. Helaine K. Prentice. 1996. pap. text ed. 12.95 (0-9650265-0-7) Preserv Pk.

Through These Eyes. Lauren A. Isaacson. 334p. 1991. lib. bdg. write for info. (0-9628196-0-3) M K Isaacson.

Through These Eyes: My Ministry to the Mentally Ill. Otis D. Thomas. 1996. pap. text ed. 12.95 (1-886049-06-8) Best Times Inc.

Through These Fires. Grace L. Hill. (Grace Livingston Hill Ser.: Vol. 46). 1992. pap. 4.99 (0-8423-7095-1) Tyndale.

Through These Men: Some Aspects of Our Passing History. John M. Brown. LC 71-167318. (Essay Index Reprint Ser.). 1977. reprint ed. 23.95 (0-8369-2756-7) Ayer.

Through These Portals: From Immigrant to University President. Rolf A. Weil. (Illus.). 146p. 1991. 16.95 (0-9632567-0-X) Roosevelt U.

***Through Thick & Thin: Young Women Talk Relationships.** Ed. by Jane Waghorn. (Livewire Ser.). 154p. (YA). (gr. 7-11). 1997. pap. 6.95 (0-7043-4940-X, Pub. by Womens Press UK) Trafalgar.

Through Thick & Thin "An Adventure in Whole Food Cooking" Kay Huberty. LC 81-85960. (Illus.). 300p. 1982. spiral bd. 9.95 (0-686-32819-1) Through Thick & Thin.

Through-Thickness Tension Testing of Steel- STP 794. Ed. by R. J. Glodowski. LC 82-72887. 152p. 1983. text ed. 21.00 (0-8031-0232-1, 04-794000-02) ASTM.

Through This Window: Views on Traumatic Brain Injury. Ed. by Patricia I. Felton. (Illus.). 278p. (Orig.). 1992. pap. text ed. 19.50 (0-9634461-0-X) EBTS.

Through Time, Across Continents: A Hundred Years of Archaeology & Anthropology at the University Museum. Dilys P. Winegrad. LC 92-36824. (Illus.). xviii, 226p. (C). text ed. 80.00 (0-924171-16-2) U PA Mus Pubns.

Through Time & Culture: Introductory Readings in Philosophy. A. Pablo Iannone. LC 93-23864. 520p. (C). 1993. text ed. 49.00 (0-13-920620-5) P-H Gen Ref & Trav.

Through Time & the Valley. John R. Erickson. LC 95-8925. (Illus.). 230p. 1995. reprint ed. 24.95 (0-929398-95-5) UNTX Pr.

Through Time into Healing. Brian L. Weiss. 224p. 1992. audio 16.00 (0-671-79269-5) S&S Trade.

Through Time into Healing. Brian L. Weiss & Raymond A. Moody. 208p. 1993. pap. 11.00 (0-671-86786-5, Fireside) S&S Trade.

Through Transport Security. Paul Elliott. 70p. 1991. 140.00 (1-85609-011-6, Pub. by Witherby & Co UK) St Mut.

Through Travellers' Eyes Vol. 7: Proceedings of the 1989 Groningen Achaemenid History Workshop. Ed. by Heleen Sancisi-Weerdenburg & Jan W. Drijvers. (Achaemenid History Ser.: Vol. 7). xi, 223p. 1991. text ed. 75.75 (90-6258-407-1, Pub. by Netherlands Inst NE) Eisenbrauns.

Through Trials & Triumphs: A History of Augustana College. Donald Sneen. LC 85-62800. 192p. 1985. 9.95 (0-931170-29-X) Ctr Western Studies.

Through Turkish Arabia. H. Cowper. 512p. 1987. 350.00 (1-85077-170-7, Pub. by Darf Pubs Ltd UK) St Mut.

Through Twisted Thorns. J. Remy Theberge. Ed. by R. Moisan. LC 85-80145. (Illus.). 360p. (Orig.). 1985. 12.95 (0-918862-02-7) Golden Gambit.

Through Two Wars & Beyond: A Study of Gulf Cooperation Council. Gulshan Dietl. xii, 312p. 1991. 40.00 (81-7095-024-4) Advent Bks Div.

Through Unexplored Texas. W. B. Parker. LC 84-80800. 242p. 1990. reprint ed. 21.95 (0-87611-064-2); reprint ed. pap. 12.95 (0-87611-065-0) Tex St Hist Assn.

Through Unknown African Countries: The First Expedition from Somaliland to Lake Lamu. Smith. (American Biography Ser.). 471p. 1991. reprint ed. lib. bdg. 89.00 (0-7812-8357-4) Rprt Serv.

Through Values to Social Interpretation: Essays on Social Contexts, Actions, Types & Prospects. Howard P. Becker. LC 69-10068. 341p. 1968. reprint ed. text ed. 35.00 (0-8371-0014-3, BESI, Greenwood Pr) Greenwood.

Through Welsh Border Country. Mark Richards. (C). 1988. pap. 29.00 (0-904110-53-2, Pub. by Thornhill Pr UK) St Mut.

Through Welsh Doorways. Jeannette A. Marks. LC 78-167463. (Short Story Index Reprint Ser.). 1977. reprint ed. 20.95 (0-8369-3989-1) Ayer.

Through Wood & Nails. 1987. 25.00 incl. lp (0-317-89960-0, Pub. by Wild Goose Pubns UK); audio 30.00 (0-317-89961-9, Pub. by Wild Goose Pubns UK) St Mut.

Through Writing to Reading: Classroom Strategies for Supporting Literacy. Brigid Smith. LC 93-34387. 192p. (C). 1994. pap. 17.95 (0-415-09614-6, B3605, Routledge NY); text ed. 59.95 (0-415-09613-8, B3601, Routledge NY) Routledge.

***Through Your Heart over the Fence: The Inspiring Story of the Famous People Players.** Diane Dupuy. (Illus.). 192p. (Orig.). 1997. pap. 26.95 (1-55013-814-6, Pub. by Key Porter Bks CN) Firefly Bks Ltd.

Throughout Cities & Prairie Lands: Sketches of an American Tour by Lady Duffus Hardy. Mary M. Hardy. (American Biography Ser.). 338p. 1991. reprint ed. lib. bdg. 79.00 (0-7812-8168-7) Rprt Serv.

Throughout Your Generations Forever: Sacrifice, Religion, & Paternity. Nancy Jay. (Illus.). 192p. 1992. 30.50 (0-226-39572-3) U Ch Pr.

Throughout Your Generations Forever: Sacrifice, Religion, & Paternity. Nancy Jay. LC 91-33085. (Illus.). xxviii, 222p. 1993. pap. text ed. 13.95 (0-226-39573-1) U Ch Pr.

Throw a Hungry Loop. Dona Schenker. LC 89-35496. 160p. (J). (gr. 7 up). 1990. 12.95 (0-679-80332-7) Knopf Bks Yng Read.

Throw-Away Generation. Jill C. Wheeler. Ed. by Stuart A. Kallen. LC 91-73071. (We Can Save the Earth Ser.). 202p. (J). 1991. lib. bdg. 12.94 (1-56239-030-9) Abdo & Dghtrs.

Throw-Away Pets. Betsy Duffey. (Pet Patrol Ser.: No. 3). (Illus.). 80p. (J). (gr. 2-6). 1995. pap. 3.99 (0-14-034999-5) Puffin Bks.

***Throw Away the Textbook & Be a Better Manager: When Good Management Clashes with Bad Theory.** 2nd ed. Fred Jordan. (Illus.). 184p. 1996. reprint ed. pap. 21.95 (0-9653245-0-8) Mgmt Tech.

Throw Away Your Glasses. Harper West. (Illus.). 96p. 1994. pap. 7.95 (0-9641719-0-2) Avalanche Pub.

Throw Away Your Resume. 3rd ed. Robert M. Hochheiser. LC 95-12666. (Educational Ser.). (Illus.). 200p. 1995. 10.95 (0-8120-9334-8) Barron.

Throw Away Your Scale. Daniel L. Sister. LC 95-5246. 160p. 1995. 4.95 (0-87983-677-6) Keats.

Throw Darts at a Cheesecake. Denise Dietz. LC 92-12607. 211p. 1992. 19.95 (0-8027-1237-1) Walker & Co.

"Throw Down" on Drugs. William Goodman. (Illus.). 80p. (Orig.). 1987. pap. 4.99 (0-8341-1192-6) Beacon Hill.

Throw Down the Box: Treasure Tales from Gilmer & Salisbury the Western Stagecoach King. George A. Thompson. (Illus.). 128p. 1989. 15.95 (0-942688-73-2) Dream Garden.

***Throw It to the River.** Nice Rodriguez. (International Connections Ser.). 156p. pap. 9.95 (0-88961-187-4, Pub. by Wmns Pr CN) LPC InBook.

Throw Me a Bone: What Happens When You Marry an Archaeologist. Eleanor B. Lothrop. (American Biography Ser.). 234p. 1991. reprint ed. lib. bdg. 69.00 (0-7812-8251-9) Rprt Serv.

Throw Me Somethin' Mistuh! The Mardi Gras Book. Brod Bagert & Charlie Smith. (Illus.). (Orig.). 1996. pap. 14.95 (1-887746-02-1) Juliahouse Pubs.

Throw of the Dice: The Life of Stephane Mallarme. Gordon Millan. LC 93-40180. 1994. 35.00 (0-374-27707-9) FS&G.

Throw of Vertically Discharged Warm Air Jets. M. J. Holmes. 1976. 60.00 (0-86022-026-5, Pub. by Build Servs Info Assn UK) St Mut.

***Throw Out the Lifeline.** Asa Benveniste. Date not set. pap. 17.95 (0-85646-098-2, Pub. by Anvil Press UK) Dufour.

Throw the Rascals Out: Here's the Real McCoy. Otis Carney. 1992. 14.95 (1-881649-02-4); pap. 9.95 (1-881649-01-6) Genl Pub Grp.

***Throwaway Angels.** Nancy Richler. 264p. 1996. pap. 12.95 (0-88974-062-3, Pub. by Press Gang CN) LPC InBook.

***Throwaway Sensors: Ultra-Low Cost Sensors Key to Smart Products, Smarter Manufacturing.** (Emerging Technologies Ser.: Vol. 64). 100p. 1996. spiral bd., vinyl bd. 1,775.00 (1-56217-030-9) Tech Insights.

Throwaway Society: I Know That We're a Throwaway Society...But This Is Ridiculous. Dick Hafer. LC 88-22550. (Illus.). 144p. (Orig.). 1989. pap. 5.95 (0-942803-00-0) Freedomlight Pubns.

Throwaways: Work Culture & Consumer Education. Evan Watkins. LC 93-19270. 248p. (C). 1993. 39.50 (0-8047-2249-8); pap. 14.95 (0-8047-2250-1) Stanford U Pr.

Throwback. Frank C. Strunk. 320p. 1996. 20.00 (0-06-101057-X, Harp PBks) HarpC.

***Throwback.** Frank C. Strunk. 1997. pap. 6.50 (0-06-101058-8, Harp PBks) HarpC.

Throwed Away: Failures of Progress in Eastern North Carolina. Linda Flowers. LC 89-28167. (Illus.). 264p. 1990. pap. 15.95 (0-87049-767-7) U of Tenn Pr.

Throwing Away the Compass. Harry Humes. Ed. by Rodger Moody. 24p. 1986. 4.00 (0-9610508-5-3) Silverfish Rev Pr.

Throwing Away the Key: Indefinite Political Detention in Syria. Ed. by Human Rights Watch Staff. 72p. (Orig.). 1992. pap. 7.00 (1-56432-087-1) Hum Rts Watch.

Throwing Events see Modern Drills for Track & Field

Throwing Firecrackers out the Window While the Ex-Husband Drives By. Mary N. Korte. 38p. 1991. 4.00 (1-879082-03-9) Rainy Day CA.

Throwing Heat. Nolan Ryan & Harvey Frommer. 288p. 1990. mass mkt. 5.99 (0-380-70826-4) Avon.

Throwing Like a Girl & Other Essays in Feminist Philosophy & Social Theory. Iris M. Young. LC 89-46002. (Illus.). 224p. 1990. 31.50 (0-253-36857-X); pap. text ed. 15.95 (0-253-20597-2, MB-597) Ind U Pr.

***Throwing Like a Girl & Other Essays in Feminist Philosophy & Social Theory.** Iris M. Young. LC 89-46002. (Illus.). 213p. pap. 60.80 (0-608-05047-4, 2059708) Bks Demand.

Throwing Pots. Phil Rogers. (Illus.). 128p. (Orig.). 1995. pap. 22.95 (1-889250-04-X) Gentle Br.

Throwing Roses. Elizabeth Ridley. LC 92-34344. 131p. 1993. 22.00 (1-877946-29-X) Permanent Pr.

Throwing Shadows. E. L. Konigsburg. (J). 1994. 18.00 (0-8446-6768-4) Peter Smith.

Throwing Shadows. E. L. Konigsburg. 168p. (YA). (gr. 7 up). 1988. reprint ed. pap. 4.50 (0-02-044140-1) Macmillan.

"Throwing the Emperor from His Horse" Portrait of a Village Leader in China, 1923-1995. Peter J. Seybold. 8p. (C). 1996. pap. text ed. 19.95 (0-8133-3131-5) Westview.

"Throwing the Emperor from His Horse" Portrait of a Village Leader in China, 1923-1995. Peter J. Seybolt. 8p. 1996. text ed. 49.95 (0-8133-3130-7) Westview.

Throwing the Scabbard Away: Byron's Battle Against the Censors of Don Juan. Robinson Blann. LC 90-19402. (American University Studies: English Language & Literature: Ser. IV, Vol. 126). 179p. (C). 1991. text ed. 34.95 (0-8204-1437-9) P Lang Pubng.

Thrown among Strangers: John Henry Newman in Ireland. Louis McRedmond. 223p. (Orig.). 1990. pap. 16.95 (1-85390-180-6, Pub. by Veritas Publns IE) Ignatius Pr.

Thrown among Strangers: The Making of Mexican Culture in Frontier California. Douglas Monroy. LC 89-49035. (Illus.). 288p. 1990. 32.50 (0-520-06914-5) U CA Pr.

Thrown Among Strangers: The Making of Mexican Culture in Frontier California. Douglas Monroy. 1993. pap. 15.95 (0-520-08275-3) U CA Pr.

***Thrown Away Child.** Adcock. 1997. mass mkt. 5.99 (0-671-51984-0) S&S Trade.

Thrown Away Child. Thomas Adcock. 266p. 1996. 21.00 (0-671-51985-9, PB Hardcover) PB.

***Throws.** 4th ed. Ed. by Jess Jarver. (Contemporary Theory, Technique & Training Ser.). (Illus.). 136p. 1994. pap. 16.00 (0-911521-35-6) Tafnews.

***Throws Manual.** 2nd ed. George Dunn, Jr. & Kevin McGill. (Orig.). 1994. pap. 16.50 (0-911521-39-9) Tafnews.

Throy. Jack Vance. (Cadwal Chronicles Ser.: Bk. 3). 256p. 1994. mass mkt. 4.99 (0-8125-1140-9) Tor Bks.

Thru-Hiker's Handbook 1996: #1 Guide for Long-Distance Hikes on the Appalachian Trail. Dan W. Bruce. (Illus.). 204p. 1996. pap. 10.95 (0-9636342-5-9) Ctr AT Studies.

Thru-Hiker's Planning Guide (Workbook Edition) A Detailed Manual for Planning End-to-End Appalachian Trail Hikes. Dan W. Bruce. LC 94-70565. (Illus.). 125p. (Orig.). 1994. pap. 11.95 (0-9636342-3-2) Ctr AT Studies.

Thru My Soul. Joseph A. Whittington. 1996. 8.95 (0-533-11565-5) Vantage.

***Thru One Orphan's Eyes: The Girard Story.** unabridged ed. John H. Anderson. LC 96-96316. (Illus.). 400p. (YA). (gr. 10 up). 1996. 25.00 (0-9654295-0-4) Pocono.

Thru the Bible, 5 vols. J. Vernon McGee. Incl. Thru the Bible with J. Vernon McGee Vol. 1: Genesis-Deuteronomy. , 5 vols. LC 81-3930. 640p. 1983. 34.99 (0-8407-4973-2); Thru the Bible with J. Vernon McGee Vol. 2: Joshua-Psalms. , 5 vols. LC 81-3930. 896p. 1983. 34.99 (0-8407-4974-0); Thru the Bible with J. Vernon McGee Vol. 3: Proverbs-Malachi. , 5 vols. LC 81-3930. 1040p. 1983. 34.99 (0-8407-4975-9); Thru the Bible with J. Vernon McGee Vol. 4: Matthew-Romans. , 5 vols. LC 81-3930. 768p. 1983. 34.99 (0-8407-4976-7); Thru the Bible with J. Vernon McGee Vol. 5: Corinthians-Revelation. , 5 vols. LC 81-3930. 1088p. 1983. 34.99 (0-8407-4977-5); LC 81-3930. 1984. 174.99 (0-8407-4957-0) Nelson.

***Thru the Bible: Ecclesiastes, Song of Solomon 21.** J. Vernon McGee. Date not set. pap. text ed. 9.99 (0-7852-1022-9) Nelson.

Thru the Bible Commentary: Acts, Vol. 1. J. Vernon McGee. LC 90-41340. 1991. pap. 9.99 (0-8407-3291-0) Nelson.

Thru the Bible Commentary: Acts, Vol. 1. J. Vernon McGee. 1995. pap. text ed. 9.99 (0-7852-1043-1) Nelson.

Thru the Bible Commentary: Amos & Obadiah. J. Vernon McGee. LC 90-41340. 1991. pap. 9.99 (0-8407-3279-1) Nelson.

Thru the Bible Commentary: Deuteronomy. J. Vernon McGee. 1995. pap. 9.99 (0-7852-1009-1) Nelson.

Thru the Bible Commentary: Ephesians. J. Vernon McGee. LC 90-41340. 1995. pap. 9.99 (0-7852-1051-2) Nelson.

Thru the Bible Commentary: Ezekiel. J. Vernon McGee. LC 90-41340. 1995. pap. 9.99 (0-7852-1026-1) Nelson.

Thru the Bible Commentary: Galatians. J. Vernon McGee. LC 90-41340. 1991. pap. 9.99 (0-8407-3298-8) Nelson.

Thru the Bible Commentary: Genesis, Vol. 1. J. Vernon McGee. 1995. pap. 9.99 (0-7852-1001-6) Nelson.

Thru the Bible Commentary: Genesis, Vol. 2. J. Vernon McGee. 1995. pap. 9.99 (0-7852-1002-4) Nelson.

Thru the Bible Commentary: Hebrews, Vol. 1. J. Vernon McGee. LC 90-41340. 1996. pap. 9.99 (0-7852-1055-5) Nelson.

Thru the Bible Commentary: I & II Chronicles. J. Vernon McGee. LC 90-41340. 1991. pap. 9.99 (0-8407-3264-3) Nelson.

Thru the Bible Commentary: I & II Kings. J. Vernon McGee. LC 90-41340. 1991. pap. 9.99 (0-8407-3263-5) Nelson.

Thru the Bible Commentary: I & II Samuel. J. Vernon McGee. LC 90-41340. 1991. pap. 9.99 (0-8407-3262-7) Nelson.

Thru the Bible Commentary: I & II Thessalonians. J. Vernon McGee. LC 90-41340. 1995. pap. 9.99 (0-7852-1053-9) Nelson.

Thru the Bible Commentary: I & II Timothy, Titus, Philemon. J. Vernon McGee. LC 90-41340. 1995. pap. 9.99 (0-7852-1054-7) Nelson.

Thru the Bible Commentary: I Corinthians. J. Vernon McGee. LC 90-41340. 1991. pap. 9.99 (0-8407-3295-3) Nelson.

Thru the Bible Commentary: I John. J. Vernon McGee. LC 90-41340. 1995. pap. 9.99 (0-7852-1062-8) Nelson.

Thru the Bible Commentary: I Peter. J. Vernon McGee. LC 90-41340. 1995. pap. 9.99 (0-7852-1059-8) Nelson.

Thru the Bible Commentary: II Corinthians. J. Vernon McGee. LC 90-41340. 1991. pap. 9.99 (0-7852-1049-0) Nelson.

Thru the Bible Commentary: Isaiah, Vol. 1. J. Vernon McGee. LC 90-41340. 1995. pap. 9.99 (0-7852-1023-7) Nelson.

Thru the Bible Commentary: Isaiah, Vol. 2. J. Vernon McGee. LC 90-41340. 1995. pap. 9.99 (0-7852-1024-5) Nelson.

Thru the Bible Commentary: Job. J. Vernon McGee. 1991. pap. 9.99 (0-8407-3267-8) Nelson.

Thru the Bible Commentary: Job. J. Vernon McGee. LC 90-41340. 1995. pap. 9.99 (0-7852-1017-2) Nelson.

Thru the Bible Commentary: John, Vol. 1. J. Vernon McGee. LC 90-41340. 1995. pap. 9.99 (0-7852-1041-5) Nelson.

Thru the Bible Commentary: Leviticus, Vol. 1. J. Vernon McGee. 1995. pap. 9.99 (0-7852-1006-7) Nelson.

Thru the Bible Commentary: Leviticus, Vol. 2. J. Vernon McGee. LC 90-41340. 1995. pap. 9.99 (0-7852-1007-5) Nelson.

Thru the Bible Commentary: Luke. J. Vernon McGee. LC 90-41340. 1995. pap. 9.99 (0-7852-1040-7) Nelson.

***Thru the Bible Commentary: Malachi 33.** Vernon Mcgee. Date not set. pap. text ed. 8.99 (0-7852-1036-9) Nelson.

Thru the Bible Commentary: Mark. J. Vernon McGee. LC 90-41340. 1995. pap. 9.99 (0-7852-1039-3) Nelson.

Thru the Bible Commentary: Matthew, Vol. 1. J. Vernon McGee. LC 90-41340. 1995. pap. 9.99 (0-7852-1037-7) Nelson.

Thru the Bible Commentary: Matthew, Vol. 2. J. Vernon McGee. LC 90-41340. 1995. pap. 9.99 (0-7852-1038-5) Nelson.

Thru the Bible Commentary: Nahum, Habakkuk. J. Vernon McGee. LC 90-41340. 1995. pap. 9.99 (0-7852-1033-4) Nelson.

Thru the Bible Commentary: New Testament Complete, 27 vols. J. Vernon McGee. LC 90-41340. (Thru the Bible Commentary Ser.). 1995. pap. 242.73 (0-7852-1137-3) Nelson.

Thru the Bible Commentary: Numbers. J. Vernon McGee. LC 90-41340. 1995. pap. 9.99 (0-7852-1008-3) Nelson.

Thru the Bible Commentary: Old Testament Complete, 33 vols. J. Vernon McGee. LC 90-41340. (Thru the Bible Commentary Ser.). 1995. pap. 296.67 (0-7852-1136-5) Nelson.

Thru the Bible Commentary: Philippians/Colossians. J. Vernon McGee. LC 90-41340. 1995. pap. 9.99 (0-7852-1052-0) Nelson.

Thru the Bible Commentary: Proverbs. J. Vernon McGee. LC 90-41340. 1995. pap. 9.99 (0-7852-1021-0) Nelson.

Thru the Bible Commentary: Revelation, Vol. 1. J. Vernon McGee. LC 90-41340. 1995. pap. 9.99 (0-7852-1064-4) Nelson.

Thru the Bible Commentary: Revelation, Vol. 3. J. Vernon McGee. LC 90-41340. 1995. pap. 9.99 (0-7852-1066-0) Nelson.

Thru the Bible Commentary: Ruth. J. Vernon McGee. LC 90-41340. (Thru the Bible Commentary Ser.). 1991. pap. 9.99 (0-8407-3261-9) Nelson.

Thru the Bible Commentary: Zachariah. J. Vernon McGee. LC 90-41340. 1996. pap. 9.99 (0-7852-1035-0) Nelson.

***Thru The Bible Commentary No. 46: Galatians.** J. Vernon McGee. 1996. pap. 8.99 (0-7852-1050-4) Nelson.

***Thru the Bible Commentary I Corinthians Number 44.** J. Vernon McGee. Date not set. pap. text ed. 9.99 (0-7852-1048-2) Nelson.

Thru the Bible Commentary Series. Contrib. by J. Vernon McGee. Date not set. 242.73 (0-8407-6751-X) Nelson.

Thru the Bible with J. Vernon McGee, Vol. 1, Genesis-Deuteronomy see Thru the Bible

Thru the Bible with J. Vernon McGee, Vol. 2, Joshua-Psalms see Thru the Bible

Thru the Bible with J. Vernon McGee, Vol. 3, Proverbs-Malachi see Thru the Bible

Thru the Bible with J. Vernon McGee, Vol. 4, Matthew-Romans see Thru the Bible

Thru the Bible with J. Vernon McGee, Vol. 5, Corinthians-Revelation see Thru the Bible

Thru the Grapevine. Junior League of Elmira, Inc. Staff. Ed. by Margaret Morse. LC 82-83914. (Illus.). 368p. 1983. 14.95 (0-9609980-1-2) Jr League Elmira.

***Thru the Looking Glass.** 2nd ed. Nicolson & Shipstead. LC 97-16725. 1997. pap. text ed. 36.00 (0-13-651993-8) P-H.

Thru the Looking Glass & What Alice Found There. Lewis Carroll. 24p. (Orig.). (J). (gr. 3-8). 1993. pap. 3.00 (1-57514-234-1, 1071) Encore Perform Pub.

Thru the Numbers: Aquarius. Paul Rice & Valeta Rice. 195p. 1983. pap. 3.95 (0-87728-575-6) Weiser.

Thru the Numbers: Aries. Paul Rice & Valeta Rice. 195p. 1983. pap. 3.95 (0-87728-565-9) Weiser.

Thru the Numbers: Cancer. Paul Rice & Valeta Rice. 195p. 1983. pap. 3.95 (0-87728-568-3) Weiser.

Thru the Numbers: Capricorn. Paul Rice & Valeta Rice. 195p. 1983. pap. 3.95 (0-87728-574-8) Weiser.

Thru the Numbers: Gemini. Paul Rice & Valeta Rice. 195p. 1983. pap. 3.95 (0-87728-567-5) Weiser.

Thru the Numbers: Leo. Paul Rice & Valeta Rice. 195p. 1983. pap. 3.95 (0-87728-569-1) Weiser.

Thru the Numbers: Libra. Paul Rice & Valeta Rice. 195p. 1983. pap. 3.95 (0-87728-571-3) Weiser.

Thru the Numbers: Pisces. Paul Rice & Valeta Rice. 195p. 1983. pap. 3.95 (0-87728-576-4) Weiser.

Thru the Numbers: Sagittarius. Paul Rice & Valeta Rice. 195p. 1983. pap. 3.95 (0-87728-573-X) Weiser.

Thru the Numbers: Scorpio. Paul Rice & Valeta Rice. 195p. 1983. pap. 3.95 (*0-87728-572-1*) Weiser.

Thru the Numbers: Taurus. Paul Rice & Valeta Rice. 195p. 1983. pap. 3.95 (*0-87728-566-7*) Weiser.

Thru the Numbers: Virgo. Paul Rice & Valeta Rice. 195p. 1983. pap. 3.95 (*0-87728-570-5*) Weiser.

Thru the Smoky End Boards: Canadian Poetry about Sport & Games. Kevin Brooks & Sean Brooks. 248p. (Orig.). 1996. pap. 14.95 (*1-896095-15-1*, Pub. by Polestar Bk Pubs CN) Orca Bk Pubs.

Thrums. Faithe S. Nunneley. Ed. by Seymour Bress. (Illus.). 149p. 1991. pap. 14.95 (*0-9620543-3-X*) Flower Valley Pr.

***Thrush Green.** Read. Date not set. lib. bdg. 21.95 (*0-8488-1692-7*) Amereon Ltd.

Thrush Green. Miss Read. 1982. reprint ed. lib. bdg. 21.95 (*0-89966-435-0*) Buccaneer Bks.

Thrust for Flight: The Propulsion Element of Aircraft Flight. 2nd ed. W. Thomson. (Illus.). 200p. 1992. pap. 37.50 (*0-582-08280-3*, Pub. by Longman Group UK) Trans-Atl Phila.

Thrust for Freedom. Andrew J. Galambos. 1991. reprint ed. 6.50 (*0-88078-003-7*) Univ Sci Publns.

***Thrust in the Sickle.** Walter C. Lanyon. 224p. 1983. reprint ed. pap. 8.00 (*1-889870-01-3*) Union Life.

Thrust in the Sickle & Reap. Earl Paulk. 141p. (Orig.). 1986. pap. 5.95 (*0-917595-11-4*) Kingdom Pubs.

***Thrust Plate Hip Prosthesis.** Arnold H. Huggler & Hilaire A. Jacob. LC 96-34374. 1996. 98.00 (*3-540-61506-7*) Spr-Verlag.

Thrust Tectonics. Ed. by Ken McClay. (Illus.). 428p. (C). (gr. 13). 1992. pap. text ed. 58.95 (*0-412-43900-X*, A8208) Chapman & Hall.

Thrymsas & Sceattas in the Ashmolean Museum, Vol. 1. D. M. Metcalf. (Illus.). 208p. 1993. 42.00 (*1-85444-047-0*, 047-1, Pub. by Ashmolean Mus UK) A Schwartz & Co.

Thrymsas & Sceattas in the Ashmolean Museum, Vol. 2. D. M. Metcalf. (Illus.). 152p. 1994. 42.00 (*1-85444-066-7*, 066-7, Pub. by Ashmolean Mus UK) A Schwartz & Co.

Thrymsas & Sceattas in the Ashmolean Museum, Vol. 3. D. M. Metcalf. (Illus.). 436p. 1995. 65.00 (*1-85444-067-5*, 067-5, Pub. by Ashmolean Mus UK) A Schwartz & Co.

Thucydides. W. Robert Connor. LC 83-43066. 256p. 1984. pap. text ed. 18.95 (*0-691-10239-2*) Princeton U Pr.

***Thucydides.** Simon Hornblower. LC 87-4213. 240p. 1987. reprint ed. pap. 68.40 (*0-608-03691-9*, 2064516) Bks Demand.

Thucydides, Bk. I. E. C. Marchant. (Bristol Greek Texts Ser.). 334p. (GRE.). 1982. reprint ed. 27.95 (*0-86292-027-2*, Pub. by Brstl Class Pr UK) Focus Pub-R Pullins.

Thucydides, Bk. II. Ed. by E. C. Marchant & T. Wiedmann. (Bristol Greek Texts Ser.). 281p. (GRE.). 1978. pap. 27.95 (*0-906515-20-3*, Pub. by Brstl Class Pr UK) Focus Pub-R Pullins.

Thucydides, Bk. 7. Thucydides & Kenneth J. Dover. 1965. write for info. (*0-19-831829-4*) OUP.

Thucydides: Athens & Corcyra. Ed. by J. Wilson. (Bristol Greek Texts Ser.). 152p. (GRE.). 1987. pap. 20.95 (*0-86292-196-1*, Pub. by Brstl Class Pr UK) Focus Pub-R Pullins.

Thucydides Bks. 1-11.65: A Companion to the Penguin Translation. Thomas Wiedemann. (Classics Companions Ser.). 94p. 1985. pap. 14.95 (*0-86292-170-8*, Pub. by Brstl Class Pr UK) Focus Pub-R Pullins.

Thucydides Bks. III-V: A Companion to the Penguin Translation. N. K. Rutter. (Classics Companions Ser.). 1996. pap. 14.95 (*1-85399-438-3*, Pub. by Brstl Class Pr UK) Focus Pub-R Pullins.

Thucydides Bks. VI & VII: A Companion to the Penguin Translation. N. K. Rutter. (Classics Companions Ser.). 80p. 1991. pap. 14.95 (*1-85399-055-8*, Pub. by Brstl Class Pr UK) Focus Pub-R Pullins.

Thucydides & Athenian Imperialism. Jacqueline De Romilly. Ed. by Gregory Vlastos. Tr. by Philip Thody from ENG. LC 78-19381. (Morals & Law in Ancient Greece Ser.). 1979. reprint ed. lib. bdg. 33.95 (*0-88143-072-2*) Ayer.

***Thucydides & the Ancient Simplicity: The Limits of Political Realism.** LC 96-29615. 1997. write for info. (*0-520-20789-0*) U CA Pr.

***Thucydides & the Peloponnesian War.** George Cawkwell. LC 96-37755. 224p. (C). 1997. pap. write for info. (*0-415-16552-0*); text ed. write for info. (*0-415-16430-3*) Routledge.

***Thucydides & the Tradition of Funeral Speeches at Athens.** John E. Ziolowski. Date not set. write for info. (*0-88143-023-4*) Ayer.

Thucydides & the Tradition of Funeral Speeches at Athens. rev. ed. John E. Ziolkowiski. Ed. by W. R. Connor. LC 80-2674. (Monographs in Classical Studies). 1981. lib. bdg. 25.00 (*0-405-14057-6*) Ayer.

Thucydides Book Six Commentary. Cynthia W. Shelmerdine. (Greek Commentaries Ser.). 35p. (Orig.). (C). 1988. pap. text ed. 4.00 (*0-929524-35-7*) Bryn Mawr Commentaries.

Thucydides History. Robert B. Strassler. 1998. pap. 15.00 (*0-684-82790-5*) Free Pr.

Thucydides History. Robert B. Strassler. 1996. pap. 15.00 (*0-02-913395-5*, Free Press) Free Pr.

Thucydides History of Pelopennesia Wars. Robert B. Strassler. 1996. 45.00 (*0-02-928215-2*, Free Press) Free Pr.

Thucydides, Hobbes, & the Interpretation of Realism. Laurie M. Johnson. LC 92-34016. 245p. (C). 1993. lib. bdg. 32.00 (*0-87580-175-7*) N Ill U Pr.

Thucydides' Pentekontaetia & Other Essays. W. Kendrick Pritchett. (Archaia Hellas Ser.: Vol. 1). viii, 280p. 1995. lib. bdg. 60.00 (*90-5063-487-7*, Pub. by Gieben NE) Benjamins North Am.

***Thud Ridge.** Jack Broughton. 286p. 1996. reprint ed. pap. 9.99 (*1-888237-09-0*) Baxter Pr.

Thudding Drums. Compiled by G. M. Miller. LC 79-76948. (Granger Index Reprint Ser.). 1977. 19.95 (*0-8369-6030-0*) Ayer.

Thueson's Guide to Over-the-Counter Drugs: A Symptom-by-Symptom Handbook of the Best Nonprescription Drugs. David O. Thueson. LC 94-73922. 242p. (Orig.). 1995. pap. 13.95 (*1-57224-005-9*) New Harbinger.

Thukydides, Bd. 2. Ed. by Johannes Classen & Julius Steup. iv, 334p. 1982. 80.00 (*3-296-15802-2*) G Olms Pubs.

Thukydides, Bd. 3. Ed. by Johannes Classen & Julius Steup. iv, 285p. 1977. 80.00 (*3-296-15803-0*) G Olms Pubs.

Thukydides, Bd. 4. Ed. by Johannes Classen & Julius Steup. iv, 316p. 1966. 80.00 (*3-296-15804-9*) G Olms Pubs.

Thukydides, Bd. 5. Ed. by Johannes Classen & Julius Steup. vii, 290p. 1979. 80.00 (*3-296-15805-7*) G Olms Pubs.

Thukydides, Bd. 6. Ed. by Johannes Classen & Julius Steup. iv, 299p. 1975. 80.00 (*3-296-15806-5*) G Olms Pubs.

Thukydides, Bd. 7. Ed. by Johannes Classen & Julius Steup. iv, 286p. 1967. 80.00 (*3-296-15807-3*) G Olms Pubs.

Thukydides, Bd. 8. Ed. by Johannes Classen & Julius Steup. viii, 302p. 1982. 80.00 (*3-296-15808-1*) G Olms Pubs.

Thukydides, Bd. 1: Einleitung. Ed. by Johannes Classen & Julius Steup. iv, 474p. 1977. 105.00 (*3-296-15801-4*) G Olms Pubs.

Thukydides-Studien. Hans Drexler. (Altertumswissenschaftliche Texte und Studien: No. 5). 288p. 1976. write for info. (*3-487-05945-2*) G Olms Pubs.

Thule Expedition, Fifth, 1921-1924: Reports of the Danish Ethnographical Expedition to Arctic America, 27 vols., Set, Vols. 1-10. (Illus.). reprint ed. Set. write for info. (*0-404-58300-8*) AMS Pr.

Thumb: The Hand & Upper Limb. Ed. by James W. Strickland. (Illus.). 240p. 1994. 115.00 (*0-443-03337-4*) Churchill.

Thumb Basics on Electric Bass. Jonas Hellborg. (Illus.). 36p. 1984. pap. 11.95 (*0-7119-0503-7*, AM36765) Music Sales.

Thumb Impression Identification & Expert Evidence. Y. C. Jain. (C). 1988. 100.00 (*0-685-27905-7*) St Mut.

Thumbelina. (Fun-to-Read Fairy Tales Series III). (Illus.). 24p. (J). (gr. k-3). 1993. pap. 2.50 (*1-56144-298-4*, Honey Bear Bks) Modern Pub NYC.

Thumbelina. (Read Along With Me Ser.). (Illus.). (J). (ps-1). 1989. 2.99 (*0-517-69214-7*) Random Hse Value.

Thumbelina. (Little Golden Story Book 'n' Tape Ser.). (Illus.). 24p. (J). (ps-3). 5.95 incl. audio (*0-307-14453-4*, 14453) Western Pub.

Thumbelina. (Pocket Play Bks.). (Illus.). 24p. (J). (ps-2). 1996. 9.95 (*0-8362-0956-7*) Andrews & McMeel.

Thumbelina. (Illus.). 32p. (J). (ps-2). 1996. pap. 2.50 (*0-7214-5617-0*, Ladybrd) Penguin.

Thumbelina. (Little Landoll Fairytale Ser.). 32p. (J). (ps-3). Date not set. text ed. 1.29 (*1-56987-228-7*) Landoll.

Thumbelina. (Favorite Fairy Tale Classics Ser.). 24p. (J). (ps-3). Date not set. text ed. 3.50 (*1-56987-205-8*) Landoll.

Thumbelina. (Spanish Fairytale Ser.). 24p. (SPA.). (J). (ps-3). Date not set. text ed. write for info. (*1-56987-256-2*) Landoll.

Thumbelina. Hans Christian Andersen. LC 79-50146. (Children's Classics Ser.). (Illus.). 32p. (J). (ps-3). 1992. 6.95 (*0-8362-4926-7*) Andrews & McMeel.

Thumbelina. Hans Christian Andersen. Tr. by Erik C. Haugaard. LC 95-53284. (Illus.). (J). 1997. write for info. (*0-385-32251-8*, DD Bks Yng Read) BDD Bks Young Read.

Thumbelina. Hans Christian Andersen. LC 79-50146. (Pied Piper Bks.). (Illus.). 32p. (J). (ps-3). 1985. pap. 5.95 (*0-8037-0232-9*) Dial Bks Young.

Thumbelina. Hans Christian Andersen. LC 89-8484. (Illus.). 32p. (J). (gr. 1 up). 1991. pap. 14.95 (*0-88708-113-4*, Rabbit) S&S Childrens.

Thumbelina. Hans Christian Andersen. LC 79-50146. 32p. (J). 1992. pap. 2.99 (*0-8125-2318-0*) Tor Bks.

Thumbelina. Hans Christian Andersen. LC 78-18080. (Illus.). 32p. (J). (gr. k-4). 1979. pap. 3.95 (*0-89375-119-7*); lib. bdg. 11.89 (*0-89375-141-3*) Troll Communs.

Thumbelina. Hans Christian Andersen. LC 79-50146. (J). 1994. pap. 5.99 (*0-14-054714-2*) Viking Penguin.

Thumbelina. Hans Christian Andersen. 1994. 7.98 (*1-57042-086-6*) Warner Bks.

Thumbelina. Hans Christian Andersen. LC 79-50146. 32p. (J). (gr. k-3). 1993. pap. 2.99 (*0-87406-663-8*) Willowisp Pr.

Thumbelina. Ed. by Janet L. Bolinske. LC 87-61669. (Children's Classics Ser.). (Illus.). 32p. (Orig.). (J). (gr. 1-3). 1987. pap. text ed. 4.95 (*0-88335-576-0*); spiral bd. 14.95 (*0-88335-546-9*) Milliken Pub Co.

Thumbelina. Rebecca Bondor. (Storytime Classics Ser.). (Illus.). 24p. (J). (ps-2). 1995. pap. 1.29 (*1-56293-559-3*) McClanahan Bk.

Thumbelina. Falloon & Clark. 1997. 16.00 (*0-689-81181-0*) S&S Childrens.

Thumbelina. Golden Books Staff. (Little Golden Bks.). (Illus.). 24p. (J). (ps-2). 1995. 1.49 (*0-307-03001-6*, Golden Pr) Western Pub.

***Thumbelina.** Ladybird Books Staff. (J). 1997. pap. 3.50 (*0-7214-5787-8*, Ladybrd) Penguin.

Thumbelina. Illus. by Jerry Smath. (Pudgy Pal Board Bks.). 18p. (J). 1995. bds. 3.95 (*0-448-40855-4*, G&D) Putnam Pub Group.

Thumbelina: A Musical. Gail Erwin. 34p. (Orig.). (J). (gr. 1-7). 1995. pap. 3.00 (*1-57514-131-0*, 0024) Encore Perform Pub.

Thumbelina: A Retold Story. Fred Crump. LC 88-51223. (Illus.). 44p. (J). (gr. k-2). 1989. pap. 6.95 (*1-55523-191-8*) Winston-Derek.

Thumbelina: Mini Book. Hans Christian Andersen. LC 79-50146. (Illus.). 64p. (J). 1992. reprint ed. Mini-bk. 9.95 incl. audio (*0-88708-256-4*, Rabbit) S&S Childrens.

Thumbelina: Story Pak. Retold by K. Hollenbeck. (Graphic Learning Literature Program Series: Folk Tales). (Illus.). (ENG & SPA.). 1992. 43.00 (*0-87746-235-6*) Graphic Learning.

Thumbeline. Hans Christian Andersen. LC 85-12062. (Illus.). 28p. (J). (gr. 1 up). 1991. pap. 16.00 (*0-88708-006-5*, Picture Book Studio) S&S Childrens.

Thumbnail Sketches of Famous Arizona Desert Riders, 1538-1946. Frank C. Lockwood. LC 73-148224. (Biography Index Reprint Ser.). 1977. 16.95 (*0-8369-8071-9*) Ayer.

Thumbprint Critters, Level 1. Sarah Tatler. (Let Me Read Ser.). (J). 1996. 2.95 (*0-673-36336-8*, GoodYrBooks) Addson-Wesley Educ.

***Thumbs down Mama.** D. K. Toteras. (Orig.). 1998. pap. write for info. (*0-9644122-1-7*) Nine Muses Pr.

Thumbs Up: A Pentagram - a Pantacle to Win the War. Aleister Crowley. 1993. reprint ed. pap. 5.95 (*1-55818-255-1*) Holmes Pub.

Thumbs Up! Teaching Interdependence to Grades 3 & 4. Linda Bessom. Ed. by Jane P. Keegan. (Illus.). 32p. (Orig.). 1989. teacher ed. 5.00 (*0-941395-03-0*) Maryknoll Miss.

Thumbs Up, Rico! Maria Testa. (Illus.). (J). (gr. 3-7). 1994. lib. bdg. 14.95 (*0-8075-7906-8*) A Whitman.

***Thumbs up/Thumbs Down.** 24p. 1996. reprint ed. pap. write for info. (*0-915708-45-0*) Cheever Pub.

Thumbscrew & Rack. rev. ed. George E. Macdonald. (Illus.). 26p. 1991. reprint ed. 6.00 (*0-910309-68-X*, 5232) Am Atheist.

Thump & Plunk. Janice M. Udry. LC 80-8443. (Illus.). 32p. (J). (ps-3). 1981. lib. bdg. 14.89 (*0-06-026150-1*) HarpC Child Bks.

Thump, Bump. Janet Craig. LC 87-10933. (Illus.). 32p. (J). (gr. k-2). 1988. lib. bdg. 12.95 (*0-8167-1077-5*) Troll Communs.

Thump, Bump. Janet Craig. LC 87-10933. (Illus.). 32p. (J). (gr. k-2). 1997. pap. 3.95 (*0-8167-1078-3*) Troll Communs.

Thump, Thump, Rat-a-Tat-Tat. Gene Baer. LC 88-28469. (Charlotte Zolotow Bk.). (Illus.). 32p. (J). (ps-1). 1991. pap. 4.95 (*0-06-443265-3*, Trophy) HarpC Child Bks.

Thump, Thump, Rat-a-Tat-Tat. Gene Baer. LC 88-28469. (Illus.). 32p. (J). (ps). 1996. bds. 6.95 (*0-694-00813-3*, Festival) HarpC Child Bks.

Thump, Thump, Rat-a-Tat-Tat Big Book. Gene Baer. LC 88-28469. (Illus.). 32p. (J). (ps-1). 1992. 21.95 (*0-694-00386-7*) HarpC Child Bks.

Thumper's Little Sisters, Vols. 2 & 19: Road to Reading, Set. Walt Disney Productions Staff. (Illus.). 44p. (J). (gr. 1-6). 1986. reprint ed. 3.49 (*1-885222-32-7*) Advance Pubs.

Thumpity Thump Gets Dressed. Cyndy Szekeres. LC 83-83284. (Golden Naptime Tales Series - A Jim Henson Muppet Press Bk.). (Illus.). 16p. (J). (ps). 1991. 4.95 (*0-307-12203-4*, 12233) Western Pub.

Thumri in Historical & Stylistic Perspectives. Peter Manuel. 1989. 47.50 (*81-208-0673-5*, Pub. by Motilal Banarsidass II) S Asia.

Thunder Alley. Mack Maloney. 432p. 1988. mass mkt. 3.95 (*0-8217-2405-3*, Zebra Kensgtn) Kensgtn Pub Corp.

Thunder along the Mississippi: The River Battles That Split the Confederacy. Jack D. Coombe. LC 96-18422. (Illus.). 304p. 1996. 24.95 (*1-885119-25-9*) Sarpedon.

Thunder & Lightening. (Information Ser.). 32p. (J). 3.50 (*0-7214-1749-3*, Ladybrd) Penguin.

Thunder & Lightning: Poems on African American Life & Love. rev. ed. Esmo Woods. (Illus.). 1993. pap. 14.00 (*0-9641636-1-6*) New Pontiac.

Thunder & Lightning: Spooky Beasts. Karen Wallace. (J). (ps-3). 1996. pap. text ed. 3.50 (*0-8120-9629-0*) Barron.

Thunder & Mud: A Pioneer Childhood on the Prairie. Julia B. Tobias. (Illus.). 176p. (Orig.). 1996. pap. 11.95 (*0-931271-29-0*) Hi Plains Pr.

Thunder & Roses. Mary J. Putney. 384p. (Orig.). 1993. pap. 4.99 (*0-451-40367-3*, Topaz) NAL-Dutton.

***Thunder & Roses Vol. IV: The Complete Stories of Theodore Sturgeon.** Theodore Sturgeon. Ed. by Paul Williams. (The Complete Stories of Theodore Sturgeon Ser.: Vol. 4). 250p. 1997. 25.00 (*1-55643-252-6*) North Atlantic.

Thunder & Silence: The Mass Media in Africa. Dhyana Ziegler & Molefi K. Asante. 212p. 1992. 45.00 (*0-86543-250-3*); pap. 12.95 (*0-86543-251-1*) Africa World.

Thunder & Trumpets: The Millerites Dissenting Religion in Upstate New York, 1800-1850. David Rowe. (American Academy of Religion, Studies in Religion: No. 38). 188p. 1985. pap. 24.95 (*0-89130-769-9*, 01 00 38) Scholars Pr GA.

Thunder at Dawn. large type ed. Alan Evans. 400p. 1980. 25.99 (*0-7089-0541-2*) Ulverscroft.

Thunder at Dawn. Alan Evans. 256p. 1995. reprint ed. 20.00 (*0-7278-4755-4*) Severn Hse.

Thunder at Gettysburg. Patricia Gauch. 64p. (J). 1990. mass mkt. 3.50 (*0-440-41075-4*) Dell.

Thunder at Gettysburg. Patricia L. Gauch. (Illus.). 48p. (J). (gr. 3-6). 1990. 14.95 (*0-399-22201-4*, Putnam) Putnam Pub Group.

Thunder at Gettysburg. Barbara Reeves. Ed. by J. Friedland & R. Kessler. (Novel-Ties Ser.). 1993. student ed., pap. text ed. 15.95 (*0-88122-881-8*) Lrn Links.

Thunder at Hampton Roads. Adolph A. Hoehling. (Illus.). 268p. 1993. reprint ed. pap. 13.95 (*0-306-80523-5*) Da Capo.

Thunder Bay. Michael E. Degregorio. Tr. by Jiro Hanaue from JPN. LC TXU-686-966. (Illus.). 327p. (Orig.). (J). (ps-12). 1995. pap. 17.75 (*0-9649417-7-5*) Degregorio.

***Thunder Before the Dawn: Stories of the Early Settlers & Warriors in Clermont County, Ohio.** Richard Crawford. Ed. by John M. Spafford. (Illus.). 154p. (Orig.). pap. 15.00 (*1-890538-17-5*) Rhiannon Pubns.

***Thunder Below! Revolutionizes Submarine Warfare in World War II.** Date not set. 18.95 (*0-252-06670-7*) U of Ill Pr.

Thunder Below! The USS Barb Revolutionizes Submarine Warfare in World War II. Eugene B. Fluckey. (Illus.). 466p. (C). 1992. 34.95 (*0-252-01925-3*) U of Ill Pr.

Thunder Bunny. Rodney A. Greenblat. LC 95-5811. (Joanna Cotler Bks.). (Illus.). 40p. (J). (ps-3). 1997. 14.95 (*0-06-026424-1*); lib. bdg. 14.89 (*0-06-026434-9*) HarpC Child Bks.

***Thunder Cake.** Patricia Polacco. (Illus.). 32p. (Orig.). (J). (ps-3). 1997. pap. 5.95 (*0-698-11581-3*, Paperstar) Putnam Pub Group.

Thunder Cave. Roland Smith. LC 94-19714. (Illus.). 288p. (YA). (gr. 5 up). 1997. 16.89 (*0-7868-2055-1*) Hyprn Child.

***Thunder Cave.** Roland Smith. LC 94-19714. (YA). (gr. 5 up). 1997. pap. 5.95 (*0-7868-1159-5*) Hyprn Ppbks.

Thunder Dragon Kingdom: A Mountaineering Expedition to Bhutan. Steven K. Berry. (Illus.). 176p. 1988. 29.95 (*0-938567-07-1*) Cloudcap.

Thunder Dreamer. Ron Robinson. LC 96-21302. 252p. (Orig.). 1996. pap. 12.95 (*0-929925-33-5*) Ex Machina.

Thunder Egg. Jack Little. LC 77-94288. (J). (gr. 5 up). 1978. pap. 5.00 (*0-934768-01-3*) Altair Pr.

Thunder Falls: Dinotopia Digest Novel. Scott Ciencin. (YA). 1997. pap. 3.99 (*0-679-88256-1*, Bullseye Bks) Random Bks Yng Read.

***Thunder, Flush & Thomas Crapper: An Encyclopedia.** Adam Hart-Davis. (Illus.). 162p. 1997. 11.95 (*1-57076-081-0*, Trafalgar Sq Pub) Trafalgar.

Thunder Foot. Geri K. Strigenz. LC 91-37548. (History's Children Ser.). (Illus.). 48p. (J). (gr. 4-5). 1992. lib. bdg. 21.36 (*0-8114-3500-8*) Raintree Steck-V.

Thunder from a Clear Sky. Marcia Sewall. LC 95-2120. (Illus.). 64p. (J). (gr. 2 up). 1995. 17.00 (*0-689-31775-1*, Atheneum Bks Young) S&S Childrens.

Thunder from Above: The War in the Air Through 1968. Ed. by Robert Manning. (Vietnam Experience Ser.). (Illus.). 192p. 1984. 16.30 (*0-201-11265-5*) Addison-Wesley.

Thunder from the Bayous: Huey P. Long & the Great Depression. Glen Jeansonne. LC 92-15963. (C). 1993. text ed. 16.95 (*0-06-500162-1*) Addison-Wesley Educ.

Thunder from the Mountains: Poems & Songs from the Mau Mau. Ed. by Kinyatti. per. 9.95 (*0-86543-185-X*) Africa World.

***Thunder from the Mountains: Poems & Songs from the Mau Mau.** Maina W. Kinyatti. 1996. 29.95 (*0-86543-184-1*) Africa World.

Thunder from the Mountains: The Ten Commandments Today. John A. Stroman. 1990. pap. 8.95 (*0-687-61186-5*) Abingdon.

Thunder Heights. Phyllis A. Whitney. 23.95 (*0-89190-534-0*) Amereon Ltd.

Thunder Heights. Phyllis A. Whitney. 224p. 1994. mass mkt. 4.99 (*0-06-100215-1*, Harp PBks) HarpC.

Thunder Hooves: History's Greatest Racehorses. Frederick Gomez. LC 95-61445. (Illus.). iii, 139p. (Orig.). 1995. pap. 12.00 (*0-9651405-0-4*) Riders Up.

***Thunder Ice.** Alison Acheson. 143p. (Orig.). (J). (gr. 3-6). 1996. pap. 6.95 (*1-55050-105-4*, Pub. by Coteau CN) Genl Dist Srvs.

Thunder in Gemini. Michael O. Wise. (Journal for the Study of the Pseudepigrapha Supplement Ser.: No. 15). 265p. 52.00 (*1-85075-460-8*, Pub. by Sheffield Acad UK) CUP Services.

Thunder in Heaven. Armine Von Tempski. LC 89-78472. 368p. 1990. reprint ed. 27.50 (*0-918024-75-7*); reprint ed. pap. 14.95 (*0-918024-74-9*) Ox Bow.

Thunder in Montana. large type ed. Jim Bowden. (Linford Western Library). 288p. 1993. pap. 15.99 (*0-7089-7369-8*, Linford) Ulverscroft.

Thunder in the Dawn. Earl P. Murray. 416p. 1994. mass mkt. 4.99 (*0-8125-1319-3*) Tor Bks.

Thunder in the East. Mack Maloney. (Wingman Ser.: No. 4). 432p. 1988. mass mkt. 3.95 (*0-8217-2453-3*, Zebra Kensgtn) Kensgtn Pub Corp.

***Thunder in the East.** Mack Maloney. 1997. mass mkt. 4.99 (*0-7860-0428-2*) Kensgtn Pub Corp.

Thunder in the East. Mike Roarke. 1993. mass mkt. 4.50 (*0-312-95192-2*) St Martin.

Thunder in the Heartland: A Chronicle of Outstanding Weather Events in Ohio. Thomas W. Schmidlin & Jeanne A. Schmidlin. LC 96-5626. (Illus.). 528p. 1996. 45.00 (*0-87338-549-7*) Kent St U Pr.

Thunder in the Heavens: Classic American Aircraft of World War II. Martin Bowman. LC 93-37287. (Illus.). 144p. 1994. 16.98 (*0-8317-8297-8*) Smithmark.

Thunder in the Hills: Sturgis at 50. Miguel L. Fairbanks. Ed. by Ted Wood. LC 91-90271. (Illus.). 100p. (Orig.). 1991. pap. 19.95 (*0-9629521-0-9*) Off the Edge Pr.

Thunder in the Mountains: The Story of the Nez Perce War. Ronald K. Fisher. Ed. by Merle Wells. LC 91-76063. (Illus.). 345p. (Orig.). 1992. pap. 12.95 (*0-941734-02-1*) Alpha Om ID.

Thunder in the Mountains: The West Virginia Mine Wars, 1920-21. Lon K. Savage. LC 89-39087. (Illus.). 216p. 1990. reprint ed. 29.95 (*0-8229-3634-8*); reprint ed. pap. 14.95 (*0-8229-5426-5*) U of Pittsburgh Pr.

Thunder in the Sky. William Sarabande. (First Americans Ser.: No. 6). 464p. 1992. pap. 5.99 (*0-553-29106-8*) Bantam.

Thunder in the Sky: Secrets on the Acquisition & Exercise of Power. Tr. by Thomas Cleary. LC 94-9613. 1994. pap. 10.00 (*1-57062-027-X*) Shambhala Pubns.

An Asterisk (*) at the beginning of an entry indicates that the title is appearing in BIP for the first time.

Thunder in the Southwest: Echoes from the Wild Frontier. Oren Arnold. LC 52-4324. 246p. reprint ed. pap. 70.20 (*0-317-28707-9*, 2055508) Bks Demand.

Thunder in the Valley. Kristi Lorene. (Young Reader's Christian Library). 224p. (J). 1994. pap. text ed. 1.39 (*1-55748-551-8*) Barbour & Co.

Thunder in the Valley. Jim R. Woolard. 256p. (Orig.). 1995. mass mkt. 4.99 (*0-515-11630-0*) Jove Pubns.

Thunder Lake Narrow Gauge. 2nd rev. ed. Harvey Huston. Ed. by Ondre H. Andrews & Ondre N. Huston. LC 82-82291. 168p. 1982. pap. 20.00 (*0-9600048-3-1*) Huston.

Thunder Monsters over Europe: A History of the 405th Fighter Group in WWII. Reginald G. Nolte. (Illus.). 160p. 1986. pap. 18.95 (*0-89745-075-2*) Sunflower U Pr.

***Thunder Moon.** Larry V. Franklin. 300p. (Orig.). 1998. mass mkt. 7.99 (*1-889501-20-4*, Sunset Trails) Sovereign.

Thunder Moon & the Sky People. Max Brand. LC 95-43104. vii, 212p. 1996. text ed. 25.00 (*0-8032-1264-X*) U of Nebr Pr.

Thunder Mountain. Zane Grey. 320p. 1991. mass mkt. 3.99 (*0-06-100216-X*, Harp PBks) HarpC.

Thunder Mountain. Uncle River. LC 95-82041. 194p. 1996. pap. 11.00 (*1-883821-10-X*) Mother Bird.

Thunder Mountain Snowmobile. Leland Mansuetti & Keith Weidkamp. (C). 1994. 28.50 incl. 3.5 hd (*0-256-17251-X*); 26.95 incl. 5.25 hd (*0-256-17252-8*) Irwin.

Thunder Nation. David Seals, pseud. (7 Council Fires of Sweet Medicine Ser.: Vol. 3). 750p. 1996. 26.00 (*1-887786-13-9*) Sky & Sage Bks.

Thunder of Erebus. Payne Harrison. 1993. mass mkt. 5.99 (*0-8041-0877-3*) Ivy Books.

Thunder of Justice: The Warning, the Miracle, the Chastisement, the Era of Peace. Ted Flynn & Maureen Flynn. Ed. by Ted Bruchalski. Orig. Title: The Signs of All Time: The Warning, the Miracle, the Chastisement, the Era of Peace. (Illus.). 399p. (Orig.). 1993. pap. 15.95 (*0-9634307-0-X*) MaxKol Communs.

Thunder of Silence. Joel S. Goldsmith. LC 91-58902. 1993. reprint ed. pap. 11.00 (*0-06-250342-1*) Harper SF.

Thunder of the Captains: A Bard's Tale. Holly Lisle & Aaron Allston. 1996. mass mkt., pap. 5.99 (*0-671-87731-3*) Baen Bks.

***Thunder of the Mustangs.** Mark Spragg. LC 97-16759. 1997. 30.00 (*0-87156-974-4*) Sierra.

***Thunder of War.** Peter Tsouras. 1997. write for info. (*0-8069-9650-1*) Sterling.

Thunder on Sycamore Street. Reginald Rose. 1986. pap. 5.00 (*0-87129-325-0*, T27) Dramatic Pub.

***Thunder on the Dnepr: Zhukov, Stalin, & the Defeat of Hitler's Blitzkrieg.** Bryan I. Fugate & Lev Dvoretsky. LC 96-51177. 416p. 1997. 27.95 (*0-89141-529-7*) Presidio Pr.

Thunder on the Left. Christopher D. Morley. (Classics Ser.: No. 68). 276p. 1995. 21.95 (*1-55713-013-2*) Sun & Moon CA.

Thunder on the Left. Christopher D. Morley. (Sun & Moon Classics Ser.: No. 68). 280p. 1995. pap. 12.95 (*1-55713-190-2*) Sun & Moon CA.

Thunder on the Left. Christopher D. Morley. LC 83-45821. reprint ed. 27.00 (*0-404-20185-7*) AMS Pr.

Thunder on the Plains. F. Rosanne Bittner. 576p. 1992. mass mkt. 5.99 (*0-553-29015-0*) Bantam.

Thunder on the Reef. Sara Craven. (Presents Plus Ser.). 1995. pap. 3.25 (*0-373-11761-2*) Harlequin Bks.

Thunder on the Reef. large type ed. Sara Craven. 288p. 1995. 21.50 (*0-263-14210-8*, Pub. by M & B UK) Ulverscroft.

Thunder on the St. Johns. Lee Gramling. LC 94-12984. 260p. 1994. 14.95 (*1-56164-064-6*); pap. 8.95 (*1-56164-080-8*) Pineapple Pr.

Thunder on the Steppe: Volga German Folklife in a Changing Russia. Timothy J. Kloberdanz & Rosalinda Kloberdanz. LC 93-72234. (Illus.). 300p. (Orig.). 1993. pap. 26.00 (*0-914222-25-2*) Am Hist Soc Ger.

Thunder on the Tennessee. G. Clifton Wisler. (J). 1995. pap. 3.99 (*0-14-037612-7*) Puffin Bks.

***Thunder on the Tennessee.** G. Clifton Wisler. (J). (gr. 5-9). Date not set. 17.75 (*0-8446-6904-0*) Peter Smith.

Thunder One. Ryne D. Pearson. 384p. 1994. reprint ed. mass mkt. 5.50 (*0-380-72037-X*) Avon.

Thunder Out of China. Theodore H. White & Annalee Jacoby. LC 74-31228. (China in the 20th Century Ser.). vi, 331p. 1975. reprint ed. lib. bdg. 32.50 (*0-306-70699-7*) Da Capo.

Thunder Out of China. Theodore H. White & Annalee Jacoby. (Quality Paperbacks Ser.). 345p. 1980. reprint ed. pap. 12.95 (*0-306-80128-0*) Da Capo.

Thunder over Europe. E. Alexander Powell. 1972. 250.00 (*0-8490-1213-9*) Gordon Pr.

Thunder over New England: Benjamin Bonnell, the Loyalist. Paul J. Bunnell. LC 86-71836. 1988. 12.95 (*0-8158-0436-9*) Chris Mass.

Thunder over Scotland: George Wishart, Mentor of John Knox, James William Baird. James W. Baird. LC 82-81516. (Illus.). 206p. 1982. pap. 9.95 (*0-938462-04-0*) Green Leaf CA.

Thunder over the Door: The Ships, Shores, & Woods of Wisconsin's Door Peninsula. Robert D. Murray. LC 91-16418. (Illus.). (Orig.). 1991. 19.95 (*0-940473-22-4*) Wm Caxton.

Thunder over the Ochoco, Vol. I, Pts. 1 & 2. Andrew G. Ontko. LC 93-18698. (Illus.). 400p. (Orig.). 1993. pap. 16.95 (*0-89288-232-8*) Maverick.

Thunder over the Ochoco: Distant Thunder, Vol. II. Gale Ontko. 400p. 1994. pap. 16.95 (*0-89288-248-4*) Maverick.

Thunder Point. Jack Higgins. Date not set. 5.98 (*0-8317-6524-0*) Smithmark.

Thunder Point. Jack Higgins. 368p. 1994. reprint ed. pap. text ed. 6.99 (*0-425-14357-0*) Berkley Pub.

Thunder Point. Jack Higgins. 1995. reprint ed. lib. bdg. 26.95 (*1-56849-594-3*) Buccaneer Bks.

Thunder Rides a Black Horse: Mescalero Apaches & the Mythic Present. 2nd ed. Claire R. Farrer. (Illus.). 124p. (Orig.). (C). 1996. pap. text ed. 9.95 (*0-88133-897-4*) Waveland Pr.

Thunder Road: Chris Curry's Terrifying & Hilarious Vision of the Apocalypse. Chris Curry. 1995. mass mkt. 5.99 (*0-671-89737-3*) PB.

Thunder Road Electrical Guide. Bill Sinclair. (Illus.). 140p. (C). 1995. 19.95 (*0-9631350-4-X*) Thund Rd Mot Wks.

Thunder Road Flathead. 3rd ed. Bill Sinclair. 84p. (Orig.). 1989. 19.95 (*0-9631350-2-3*, TXU366-252) Thund Rd Mot Wks.

Thunder Rock. Robert Ardrey. 1946. pap. 5.25 (*0-8222-1146-7*) Dramatists Play.

Thunder Rolling in the Mountains. Scott O'Dell. 144p. (J). 1993. pap. 4.99 (*0-440-40879-2*) Dell.

Thunder Rolling in the Mountains. Scott O'Dell & Elizabeth Hall. (Illus.). 144p. (J). (gr. 5-9). 1992. 15.95 (*0-395-59966-0*) HM.

Thunder Rolls. Bethany Campbell. (Crystal Creek Ser.). 1993. mass mkt. 3.99 (*0-373-82520-X*, 1-82520-7) Harlequin Bks.

Thunder-Root: Traditional & Contemporary N-A Verse. J. Ivaloo Volborth. (Native American Literature Ser.). 51p. 1978. pap. 5.00 (*0-935626-24-7*) U Cal AISC.

***Thunder Rumbling at My Heels: Tracing Ingeborg Bachmann.** Gundrun Brokoph-Mauch. LC 97-13187. (Studies in Austrian Literature, Culture & Thought). 1997. write for info. (*1-57241-043-4*) Ariadne CA.

Thunder Valley. Lauran Paine. 198p. 1993. 19.95 (*0-8027-1235-5*) Walker & Co.

***Thunder Valley.** Gary Paulsen. (Gary Paulsen World of Adventure Ser.: No. 16). 96p. (Orig.). (J). (gr. 3-7). 1998. pap. 3.99 (*0-440-41220-X*) BDD Bks Young Read.

Thunder Valley. large type ed. John R. Fearn. (Linford Western Library). 301p. 1993. pap. 15.99 (*0-7089-7447-3*, Trailtree Bookshop) Ulverscroft.

Thunder Valley. large type ed. Lauran Paine. LC 93-1385. 1993. lib. bdg. 18.95 (*1-56054-720-0*) Thorndike Pr.

Thunder Valley. large type ed. Cole Shelby. (Linford Western Library). 272p. 1992. pap. 15.99 (*0-7089-7256-X*, Trailtree Bookshop) Ulverscroft.

Thunder Voice. S. W. Brouwer. (Ghost Rider Ser.). 312p. 1995. pap. 9.99 (*1-56476-426-5*, 6-3426, Victor Bks) Chariot Victor.

Thunder Wagon. James Reasoner. (Wind River Ser.: No. 2). 304p. 1994. mass mkt. 3.50 (*0-06-100772-2*) HarpC.

***Thunder Wonder: A Drop in Our Bucket of Mystery.** Bryce W. Yourd. LC 96-90659. 85p. (Orig.). 1996. pap. 8.95 (*0-9627285-2-7*) B W Yourd.

Thunderball. Ian Fleming. (James Bond Ser.). 1994. 6.98 (*1-56731-048-6*, MJF Bks) Fine Comms.

Thunderball. Ian Fleming. pap. 9.95 (*0-685-11597-6*); pap. 9.95 (*0-685-11598-4*) Fr & Eur.

Thunderbird. Marilyn Sachs. LC 84-21252. (Skinny Bks.). (Illus.). 88p. (J). (gr. 7 up). 1985. pap. 10.95 (*0-525-44163-8*, 01063-320) Dutton Child Bks.

Thunderbird. Jay Schleifer. LC 93-17241. (Cool Classics Ser.). (Illus.). 48p. (YA). (gr. 6 up). 1994. lib. bdg. 13.95 (*0-89686-816-8*, Crstwood Hse) Silver Burdett Pr.

Thunderbird. Jay Schleifer. LC 93-17241. (Cool Classics Ser.). (Illus.). 48p. (YA). (gr. 6 up). 1994. pap. 7.95 (*0-382-24811-2*, Crstwood Hse) Silver Burdett Pr.

Thunderbird! An Illustrated History of the Ford T-Bird. Ray Miller & Glenn Embree. LC 73-75630. (Ford Road Ser.: Vol. 4). (Illus.). 300p. 1973. 44.95 (*0-913056-04-9*) Evergreen Pr.

***Thunderbird: An Odyssey in Automotive Design.** William P. Boyer. LC 86-13426. 1987. 25.00 (*0-517-56475-0*) Crown Pub Group.

Thunderbird: The High-Flying Ford. Linda Craven & Jerry Craven. LC 93-219. (J). 1993. write for info. (*0-86593-254-9*) Rourke Corp.

***Thunderbird Gold.** Nat Reed. LC 96-45496. (J). 1997. pap. 6.49 (*0-89084-919-6*, 103325) Bob Jones Univ Pr.

Thunderbird Guide to International Business Resources on the World Wide Web. Candance Deans et al. LC 96-23146. 142p. 1996. pap. text ed. 21.94 (*0-471-16016-4*) Wiley.

Thunderbird Remembered: Maynard Dixon, the Man & the Artist. Daniel Dixon et al. Ed. by John P. Langellier. (Illus.). 112p. (Orig.). (C). 1994. pap. write for info. (*1-882880-01-3*) G Autry Wstrn.

Thunderbird Remembered: Maynard Dixon, the Man & the Artist. Dorothea Lange et al. LC 94-75152. (Gene Autry Western Heritage Museum Ser.). (Illus.). 112p. 1994. pap. 19.95 (*0-295-97388-9*) U of Wash Pr.

***Thunderbird Restoration Guide 1958-1966.** William Wonder. LC 97-12554. (Authentic Restoration Ser.). (Illus.). 240p. 1997. pap. 29.95 (*0-7603-0390-8*) Motorbooks Intl.

Thunderbird Spirit. Sigmund Brouwer. LC 95-19410. (Lightning on Ice Ser.: Bk. 3). 128p. 1996. pap. 5.99 (*0-8499-3639-X*) Word Pub.

Thunderbird, 1955-1966. Alan Tast. (American Classics Ser.). (Illus.). 160p. 1996. pap. 21.95 (*0-7603-0098-4*) Motorbooks Intl.

***Thunderbirds & Thunderbeings.** Olivia Long. (Our Precious Planet Ser.). (Illus.). 32p. (J). (ps-4). Date not set. write for info. (*1-880042-10-X*) Shelf-Life Bks.

Thunderbolt: Learning about Lightning. Jonathan D. Kahl. LC 92-45177. (J). (gr. 4 up). 1993. lib. bdg. 19.95 (*0-8225-2528-3*, Lerner Publctns) Lerner Group.

Thunderbolt: Republic P-47. Photos by Dan Patterson. (Living History Ser.). (Illus.). 64p. 1996. pap. 15.95 (*1-57427-053-2*) Howell Pr VA.

Thunderbolt: The History of the Eleventh Armored Division. (Divisional Ser.: No. 17). (Illus.). 1980. reprint ed. 39.95 (*0-89839-041-9*) Battery Pr.

Thunderbolt in Blue: History of 1st Minnesota Regiment of Volunteers. William Haiber & Robert Haiber. (Illus.). 300p. (Orig.). 1994. per. 24.99 (*0-944089-21-6*) Info Devels.

Thunderbolt Odyssey: P-47 War in Europe. Kemal Saied. LC 89-51511. 160p. (Orig.). 1990. pap. 16.95 (*0-9624084-0-9*) Stonewood Pr.

Thunderbolt Thinking: Transform Your Insights & Options into Powerful Business Results. Grace McGartland. 1993. 26.95 (*0-9632785-1-7*); pap. 16.95 (*0-9632785-0-9*) Bernard-Davis.

Thundercake. Patricia Polacco. (Illus.). 32p. (J). (ps-3). 1990. 15.95 (*0-399-22231-6*, Philomel Bks) Putnam Pub Group.

***Thunderfeet: Alaska's Dinosaurs & Other Prehistoric Critters.** Shelley R. Gill. Date not set. audio 5.95 (*0-934007-16-0*) Paws Four Pub.

***Thunderfeet: Alaska's Dinosaurs & Other Prehistoric Critters.** Shelley R. Gill. 19.95 incl. audio (*0-934007-15-2*) Paws Four Pub.

Thunderfeet: Alaska's Dinosaurs & Other Prehistoric Critters. Shelley R. Gill. (Illus.). 36p. (J). (gr. 1-6). pap. 8.95 (*0-934007-19-5*) Paws Four Pub.

Thunderfeet: Alaska's Dinosaurs & Other Prehistoric Critters. Shelley R. Gill. (Illus.). 36p. (J). (gr. k-4). 1988. pap. 14.95 incl. audio (*0-934007-03-9*) Paws Four Pub.

Thunderfeet: Alaska's Dinosaurs & Other Prehistoric Critters. Shelley R. Gill. (Illus.). 36p. (J). (gr. 1-6). 1988. 15.95 (*0-934007-04-7*) Paws Four Pub.

Thunderhead. Mary O'Hara. LC 87-45653. 320p. (YA). (gr. 7 up). 1988. reprint ed. pap. 7.50 (*0-06-080903-5*, P-903, PL) HarpC.

Thunderheart. Lowell Charters. 1992. mass mkt. 4.50 (*0-380-76881-X*) Avon.

Thunderherd. Kathi Appelt. (Illus.). (J). 1996. 16.00 (*0-688-13263-4*, Morrow Junior); lib. bdg. 15.93 (*0-688-13264-2*, Morrow Junior) Morrow.

Thunderhoof. Syd Hoff. LC 75-129855. (Harper Early I Can Read Bk.). (Illus.). (J). (gr. k-3). 1971. lib. bdg. 14.89 (*0-06-022560-2*) HarpC Child Bks.

***Thunderhoof.** Syd Hoff. (Illus.). (J). (ps-3). 1971. 16.12 (*0-06-022559-9*, 451983) HarpC.

Thundering Herd: The Authorized Edition. Zane Grey. LC 96-17286. (Illus.). vii, 402p. 1996. pap. 16.00 (*0-8032-7065-8*, Bison Books) U of Nebr Pr.

Thundering Hooves: A Collection of Horse Stories. Illus. by Victor Ambrus. (Story Library). 224p. (J). (gr. 4-9). 1996. pap. 6.95 (*1-85697-675-0*, Kingfisher LKC) LKC.

Thundering Silence. N. Morrison. 1996. pap. text ed. 14.95 (*1-880404-10-9*, Shoji Bks) Bkwrights.

Thundering Silence: Sutra on Knowing the Better Way to Catch a Snake. Thich Nhat Hanh. Tr. by Annabel Laity. LC 93-31387. 59p. 1993. pap. 7.00 (*0-938077-64-3*) Parallax Pr.

Thundering Steel: The Role-Playing - Combat Game of Warfare in the Near Future. Edwin M. Dyer, III. (Illus.). 200p. (Orig.). 1991. pap. 28.95 (*0-9631504-0-5*) Minds In One Prods.

Thundering Trail. large type ed. Norman A. Fox. 242p. 1996. 18.95 (*0-7862-0584-9*) Thorndike Pr.

Thunderland. D. Parkinson. 1989. pap. 3.95 (*0-8217-3031-2*) NAL-Dutton.

Thunderland. Dan Parkinson. 368p. 1987. mass mkt. 3.50 (*0-8217-1991-2*, Zebra Kensgtn) Kensgtn Pub Corp.

Thunder's Grace: Autobiography of a Sun Dancer. Mary E. Thunder. 1995. pap. 16.95 (*0-88268-166-4*) Station Hill Pr.

***Thunderscape: Indomitable Thunder.** Mark Acres. 240p. 1996. mass mkt. 5.50 (*0-06-105458-5*, Harp PBks) HarpC.

Thunderscape: The World of Aden. Peter Olafson. 1995. pap. text ed. 19.95 (*0-7615-0312-9*) Prima Pub.

Thunderscape Vol. 2: Darkfall. Shane L. Hensley. 320p. 1996. mass mkt. 4.99 (*0-06-105459-3*, HarperPrism) HarpC.

Thunderstick. Don Coldsmith. 240p. 1994. 4.99 (*0-553-29466-0*) Bantam.

***Thunderstone.** Pj Belanger. iv, 210p. (Orig.). 1996. pap. 5.99 (*0-9613180-1-5*) Jason Pub.

Thunderstones & Shooting Stars: The Meaning of Meteorites. Robert S. Dodd. (Illus.). 208p. 1988. reprint ed. pap. text ed. 12.95 (*0-674-89138-4*) HUP.

Thunderstorm! Nathaniel Tripp. LC 93-4612. (Illus.). (J). 1994. pap. 15.99 (*0-8037-1365-7*); pap. 15.89 (*0-8037-1366-5*) Dial Bks Young.

Thunderstorm. 3rd ed. Yu Tsao. Tr. by Tso-Liang Wang et al. from CHI. (Illus.). 151p. (C). 1978. 9.95 (*0-917056-74-4*, Pub. by Foreign Lang Pr CH) Cheng & Tsui.

Thunderstorm in Church: The Life of Martin Luther. Louise A. Vernon. 134p. (J). (gr. 4-8). 1993. reprint ed. pap. 7.95 (*1-882514-08-4*) Greenleaf TN.

Thunderstorm in Human Affairs. enl. rev. ed. Ed. by Edwin Kessler. LC 83-47836. (Illus.). 200p. 1988. pap. 19.95 (*0-8061-2153-X*) U of Okla Pr.

Thunderstorm Morphology & Dynamics. 2nd rev. ed. Ed. by Edwin Kessler. LC 85-8450. (Illus.). 432p. 1992. pap. text ed. 37.95 (*0-8061-2434-2*) U of Okla Pr.

Thunderstorm of Words. Kidship Associates Staff. (Illus.). (Orig.). (J). (gr. 4-6). 1994. pap. text ed. 3.50 (*0-685-71423-3*) Kidship Assoc.

Thunderstorms & Rainbows: Poetic Reflections on the Magic of Love. Beverly L. Gray. 1995. 12.95 (*0-533-11124-2*) Vantage.

Thunderweapon in Religion & Folklore. C. Blinkenberg. 1977. lib. bdg. 250.00 (*0-8490-2749-7*) Gordon Pr.

Thunderweapon in Religion & Folklore. C. Blinkenberg. xii, 122p. (C). 1987. reprint ed. lib. bdg. 30.00 (*0-89241-205-4*) Caratzas.

Thunderwith. Libby Hathorn. (YA). 1991. 15.95 (*0-316-35034-6*) Little.

Thunderwoman. Nancy Wood. 1998. pap. 16.99 (*0-525-45498-5*) Viking Penguin.

Thurber: A Biography. Burton Bernstein. 1996. pap. 16.00 (*0-688-14772-0*, Quill) Morrow.

Thurber Carnival. James Thurber. 1975. pap. 12.00 (*0-06-090445-3*, CN445, PL) HarpC.

Thurber Carnival. James Thurber. LC 93-29575. (Illus.). 462p. 1994. 16.50 (*0-679-60089-2*, Modern Lib) Random.

Thurber on Crime. James Thurber. Ed. by Robert Lopresti. LC 91-8174. (Illus.). 224p. 1991. 18.95 (*0-89296-450-2*) Mysterious Pr.

Thurber, Texas: The Life & Death of a Company Coal Town. John S. Spratt, Sr. Ed. by Harwood P. Hinton. (Personal Narratives of the West Ser.). (Illus.). 176p. 1986. 22.50 (*0-292-78067-2*) U of Tex Pr.

Thurber's Anatomy of Confusion. Catherine M. Kenney. LC 84-465. xii, 235p. (C). 1984. lib. bdg. 32.50 (*0-208-02050-0*, Archon Bks) Shoe String.

Thurber's Dogs - Voices from the Gallery. Peter Schickele et al. (Illus.). 64p. 1996. 19.99 incl. audio compact disk (*0-9642066-2-5*, DND 1010-2) MK Prods.

Thurcroft: A Village & the Miners Strike, an Oral History. Ed. by Peter Gibbon & David Steyne. (Illus.). 276p. 1986. 57.50 (*0-85124-441-6*, Pub. by Spokesman Bks UK); pap. 24.00 (*0-85124-442-4*, Pub. by Spokesman Bks UK) Coronet Bks.

***Thurgood Marshall.** Roger Goldman & David Gallen. 13.95 (*0-7867-0965-0*) Carroll & Graf.

***Thurgood Marshall.** Thurgood Marshall. LC 96-40129. (Importance of Ser.). (Illus.). (YA). (gr. 4-12). 1997. lib. bdg. 17.96 (*1-56006-061-1*) Lucent Bks.

Thurgood Marshall. Juan Williams. 1992. write for info. (*0-8129-2028-7*, Times Bks) Random.

Thurgood Marshall: A Dream of Justice for All. Stuart A. Kallen. LC 93-8333. (I Have a Dream Ser.). 1993. lib. bdg. 15.98 (*1-56239-258-1*) Abdo & Dghtrs.

Thurgood Marshall: A Life for Justice. James Haskins. (Illus.). 172p. (J). (gr. 4-7). 1995. pap. 7.95 (*0-8050-4256-3*) H Holt & Co.

Thurgood Marshall: Champion of Civil Rights. Elizabeth Krug. (Great Lives Biography Ser.). 160p. (Orig.). (J). 1993. pap. 4.00 (*0-449-90731-7*, Columbine) Fawcett.

Thurgood Marshall: Champion of Justice. G. S. Prentzas. LC 92-34222. (Junior Black Americans of Achievement Ser.). (Illus.). 80p. (J). (gr. 3-6). 1993. pap. 4.95 (*0-7910-1969-1*); lib. bdg. 15.95 (*0-7910-1769-9*) Chelsea Hse.

Thurgood Marshall: Civil Rights Champion. D. J. Herda. LC 94-31224. (Justices of the Supreme Court Ser.). (Illus.). 112p. (YA). (gr. 6 up). 1995. lib. bdg. 18.95 (*0-89490-557-0*) Enslow Pubs.

Thurgood Marshall: Fight for Justice. Rae Bains. LC 92-37302. (Illus.). 48p. (J). (gr. 4-6). 1993. 12.95 (*0-8167-2827-5*) Troll Communs.

Thurgood Marshall: Fight for Justice. Rae Bains. LC 92-37302. (Illus.). 48p. (J). (gr. 4-6). 1997. teacher ed., pap. 3.95 (*0-8167-2828-3*) Troll Communs.

Thurgood Marshall: First Black Supreme Court Justice. Carol Greene. LC 91-4798. (Rookie Biographies Ser.). (Illus.). 48p. (J). (gr. k-3). 1991. pap. 4.95 (*0-516-44225-2*); lib. bdg. 18.30 (*0-516-04225-4*) Childrens.

Thurgood Marshall: Justice for All. Roger Goldman & David Gallen. (Illus.). 512p. 1993. pap. 13.95 (*0-88184-965-0*) Carroll & Graf.

Thurgood Marshall: Supreme Court Justice. Lisa Aldred. Ed. by Nathan I. Huggins. (Black Americans of Achievement Ser.). (Illus.). 128p. (YA). (gr. 5 up). 1990. pap. 8.95 (*0-7910-0245-4*); lib. bdg. 19.95 (*1-55546-601-X*) Chelsea Hse.

Thurgood Marshall: Supreme Court Justice. Joseph Nazel. (Black American Ser.). (Illus.). 192p. (YA). 1993. mass mkt. 3.95 (*0-87067-584-2*, Melrose Sq) Holloway.

Thurgood Marshall: The Fight for Equal Justice. Debra Hess. Ed. by Richard Gallin. (History of the Civil Rights Movement Ser.). (Illus.). 128p. (J). (gr. 5 up). 1990. lib. bdg. 12.95 (*0-382-09921-4*) Silver Burdett Pr.

Thurgood Marshall: The Fight for Equal Justice. Debra Hess. Ed. by Richard Gallin. (History of the Civil Rights Movement Ser.). (Illus.). 128p. (YA). (gr. 5 up). 1990. pap. 7.95 (*0-382-24058-8*) Silver Burdett Pr.

Thurgood Marshall: Warrior at the Bar, Rebel on the Bench. Michael D. Davis & Hunter R. Clark. (Illus.). 304p. 1992. 22.00 (*1-55972-133-2*, Birch Ln Pr) Carol Pub Group.

Thurgood Marshall: Warrior at the Bar, Rebel on the Bench. Michael D. Davis & Hunter R. Clark. LC 93-44236. 1994. pap. 16.95 (*0-8065-1494-9*, Citadel Pr) Carol Pub Group.

Thurgood Marshall & Equal Rights. Seamus Cavan. LC 92-12995. (Gateway Civil Rights Ser.). (Illus.). 32p. (J). (gr. 2-4). 1993. pap. 4.95 (*1-56294-793-1*); lib. bdg. 15.40 (*1-56294-277-8*) Millbrook Pr.

***Thurgood Marshall & the Supreme Court.** Deborah Kent. LC 96-9865. (Cornerstones of Freedom Ser.). (J). 1997. lib. bdg. 18.00 (*0-516-20297-9*) Childrens.

***Thurgood Marshall & the Supreme Court.** Deborah Kent. 1997. pap. 4.95 (*0-516-26139-8*) Childrens.

Thurgood Marshall, Supreme Court Justice. Garnet N. Jackson. (Illus.). (J). (gr. 1-4). 1994. pap. 4.95 (*0-8136-5243-X*); lib. bdg. 9.95 (*0-8136-5237-5*) Modern Curr.

Thurlow Weed. Glyndon G. Van Deusen. LC 73-87698. (American Scene Ser.). 1969. reprint ed. lib. bdg. 42.50 (*0-306-71693-3*) Da Capo.

An Asterisk (*) at the beginning of an entry indicates that the title is appearing in BIP for the first time.

***Thurman Runs Away from Home.** (Little Twirps: Understanding People Storybooks: No. 62). 40p. (J). (gr. k-5). 1996. pap. 4.98 (*0-89544-062-8*) Silbert Bress.

Thurman Thomas: Star Running Back. Jeff Savage. LC 93-2557. (Sports Reports Ser.). (Illus.). 104p. (J). (gr. 4-10). 1994. lib. bdg. 18.95 (*0-89490-445-0*) Enslow Pubs.

Thurmond's Partisan Rangers & Swann's Battalion of Virginia Cavalry. Jeffrey C. Weaver. (Virginia Regimental Histories Ser.). (Illus.). 159p. 1994. 19.95 (*1-56190-055-9*) H E Howard.

Thursday & the Lady. Patricia Mathews. 408p. 1987. mass mkt. 4.50 (*0-373-97047-1*) Harlequin Bks.

Thursday at Noon. William F. Brown. 384p. 1988. reprint ed. pap. 4.50 (*0-373-97080-3*) Harlequin Bks.

Thursday Club. Vincent Murano & Richard Hammer. Ed. by Julie Rubenstein. 288p. 1994. reprint ed. mass mkt. 5.50 (*0-671-73864-X*) PB.

Thursday Is Pot Luck: From Hearty Casseroles to Stir-Fries to Main-Course Salads. Time-Life Books Editors. LC 95-18646. (Everyday Cookbooks Ser.). 128p. 1995. 14.95 (*0-8094-9189-3*) Time-Life.

Thursday-Night Poker: Understand, Enjoy, Win. Peter O. Steiner. LC 95-8485. (Illus.). 464p. 1996. pap. 16.00 (*0-679-76020-2*) Random.

Thursday Night Tarot. Jason C. Lotterhand. 379p. 1989. pap. 14.95 (*0-87877-147-6*) Newcastle Pub.

***Thursday Rides Again.** Michael Bond. 128p. (J). 1994. pap. write for info. (*1-85479-942-8*, Pub. by M OMara UK) Assoc Pubs Grp.

Thursday the Rabbi Walked Out. Harry Kemelman. 1986. mass mkt. 4.99 (*0-449-21157-6*) Fawcett.

Thursday's Child. Kat Adams. (Desire Ser.). 1993. pap. 2.89 (*0-373-05773-3*, 5-05773-2) Silhouette.

Thursdays Child. Bane. Date not set. 24.95 (*0-02-901785-8*, Free Press) Free Pr.

Thursday's Child. Francis C. Gray. 64p. (Orig.). 1994. pap. text ed. 14.95 (*1-883218-11-X*) Vande Vere.

***Thursday's Child.** Judy McGorray. 129p. 1997. pap. text ed. write for info. (*1-888200-07-3*) JayMac Commun.

***Thursday's Child.** Steven E. Swerdfeger. LC 96-96340. (Illus.). 312p. (J). (gr. 5-9). 1996. pap. 8.95 (*0-9651835-0-5*) Cloudbank Creations.

Thursday's Child. Rose Weite. 300p. 1996. per. 10.95 (*0-9636043-2-5*) Clementine Bks.

Thursday's Child. Teri White. 304p. 1992. mass mkt. 4.99 (*0-446-40092-0*, Mysterious Paperbk) Warner Bks.

Thursday's Child. large type ed. Joyce Stranger. 480p. 1995. 25.99 (*0-7089-3354-8*) Ulverscroft.

Thursday's Child: Trends & Patterns in Contemporary Children's Literature. Sheila A. Egoff. LC 81-8066. 340p. reprint ed. pap. 96.90 (*0-7837-5905-3*, 2045703) Bks Demand.

Thursday's Season. Zephr Jans, pseud. 60p. 1950. pap. 75.00 (*0-913844-17-9*) Am Canadian.

Thurston Genealogy, Sixteen Sixty-Five to Eighteen Ninety-Two. 2nd ed. B. Thurston. (Illus.). 760p. 1989. reprint ed. pap. 114.00 (*0-8328-1165-3*); reprint ed. lib. bdg. 122.00 (*0-8328-1164-5*) Higginson Bk Co.

Thurston House. Danielle Steel. 512p. 1984. mass mkt. 6.50 (*0-440-18532-7*) Dell.

Thus Be Their Destiny: The Personality Development of Negro Youth in Three Communities. Jesse H. Atwood et al. LC 71-155631. reprint ed. 24.50 (*0-404-00135-1*) AMS Pr.

Thus Far by Faith: Mount Pilgrim Baptist Church 1893-1993. Ruby R. Ennis. LC 92-62806. (Illus.). 112p. 1993. 14.00 (*0-9635196-0-3*) Mt Pilgrim BC.

Thus Have I Heard. Geoffrey Hodson. 115p. 1973. reprint ed. spiral bd. 5.50 (*0-7873-0413-1*) Hlth Research.

Thus Have I Heard: A Book of Spiritual & Occult Gleanings from the Teachings of the Great. Ed. by Geoffrey F. Hudson. 1991. lib. bdg. 79.95 (*0-8490-5010-3*) Gordon Pr.

Thus I Have Heard: A Book of Spiritual & Occult Gleanings from the Teachings of the Great (1929) Geoffrey Hodson. 120p. 1996. pap. 16.95 (*1-56459-878-0*) Kessinger Pub.

Thus I Hear: Essays & Collected Sermons. Masami Fujitani. Ed. by Calvin Steimetz. 132p. 1989. text ed. 12.00 (*1-877604-00-3*) Pure Land.

Thus It Is. Martin Exeter. 238p. 1989. 12.95 (*0-935427-23-6*) Foundation Hse.

Thus Ruled Emir Abbas: Selected Cases from the Records of the Emir of Kano's Judicial Council. Ed. by Allan Christelow. (African Historical Sources Ser.: Vol. 5). 285p. (C). 1994. 28.00 (*0-87013-309-8*) Mich St U Pr.

Thus Saith the Lord: Giddyap!: Metapsychiatric Commentaries on Human Experience & Spiritual Growth. Ann T. Linthorst. 106p. (Orig.). 1986. pap. 10.00 (*0-913105-18-X*) PAGL Pr.

Thus Saith the Lord: The Autobiography of God. Charles C. Wise, Jr. LC 84-60414. 293p. (Orig.). 1984. pap. 7.95 (*0-917023-07-2*) Magian Pr.

Thus Says the Lord: The Message of the Prophets. James M. Ward. LC 90-28590. 1991. pap. 18.95 (*0-687-41902-6*) Abingdon.

Thus Shalt Thou Live. Sebastian Kneipp. 389p. 1966. reprint ed. spiral bd. 24.50 (*0-7873-0504-9*) Hlth Research.

Thus Shalt Thou Serve. Charles W. Slemming. 1992. pap. 4.95 (*0-87508-508-3*) Chr Lit.

Thus Spake Bhisma. M. M. Thakur. (C). 1992. text ed. 14.00 (*81-208-0938-6*) S Asia.

Thus Spake Library: Teachings of Vivekananda, Ramakrishna, Sri Sarada Devi, Rama, Krishna, Buddha, Christ, Muhammad, Shankara & Guru Nanak, the Vedas. Swami Vivekananda et al. pap. 0.75 (*0-87481-444-8*) Vedanta Pr.

Thus Spake Master Chuang: A Structural Exegesis of Taoist Philosophy. Stephen Lukashevich. (American University Studies: Philosophy: Ser. V, Vol. 25). 170p. (C). 1987. text ed. 35.00 (*0-8204-0390-3*) P Lang Pubng.

Thus Spake the Moguls. Yale Magrass. 274p. 1981. text ed. 22.95 (*0-87073-578-0*); pap. text ed. 15.95 (*0-87073-579-9*) Schenkman Bks Inc.

Thus Spake Zarathustra. Friedrich Wilhelm Nietzsche. 1974. lib. bdg. 300.00 (*0-87968-206-X*) Gordon Pr.

Thus Spake Zarathustra. Friedrich Wilhelm Nietzsche. (Great Books in Philosophy). 341p. 1993. pap. 9.95 (*0-87975-861-9*) Prometheus Bks.

Thus Spake Zarathustra. Friedrich Wilhelm Nietzsche. Tr. by Thomas Common. LC 83-42947. 1982. 14.50 (*0-394-60808-9*, Modern Lib) Random.

Thus Speaks Germany. Ed. by W. W. Kulski. LC 72-180394. reprint ed. 36.00 (*0-404-56115-2*) AMS Pr.

Thus Speaks the Body: Attempts Toward a Personology from the Point of View of Respiration & Postures. Bjorn Christiansen. LC 72-342. (Body Movement Perspectives in Research Ser.). 246p. 1980. reprint ed. 24.95 (*0-405-03141-6*) Ayer.

Thus Spoke Zarathustra. Friedrich W. Nietzsche. 352p. 1961. pap. 11.95 (*0-14-044118-2*, Penguin Classics) Viking Penguin.

Thus Spoke Zarathustra. Friedrich W. Nietzsche. LC 95-15383. 364p. 1995. 15.50 (*0-679-60175-9*, Modern Lib) Random.

Thus Spoke Zarathustra. Friedrich Wilhelm Nietzsche. Tr. by Walter Kaufmann. 352p. 1978. pap. 11.95 (*0-14-004748-4*, Penguin Classics) Viking Penguin.

Thus They Lived. Joseph W. Schmitz. 1993. reprint ed. lib. bdg. 75.00 (*0-685-62349-1*) Rprt Serv.

Thus Was Adonis Murdered. Sarah Caudwell. 320p. 1994. mass mkt. 4.99 (*0-440-21231-6*) Dell.

Thus We Are Men. Walter Langdon-Brown. LC 79-86768. (Essay Index Reprint Ser.). 1977. 23.95 (*0-8369-1148-2*) Ayer.

Thus Wrote 'Onchsheshonqy: An Introductory Grammar of Demotic. 2nd rev. ed. J. H. Johnson. LC 91-66151. (Studies in Ancient Oriental Civilization: No. 45). vii, 126p. 1991. 18.00 (*0-918986-76-1*) Orient Inst.

Thuvia, Maid of Mars see Three Martian Novels

Thuykdides und die Hippokratische Medizin. Georg Rechenauer. (Spudasmata Ser.: Bd. XLVII). xii, 396p. (GER.). 1991. write for info. (*3-487-09226-3*) G Olms Pubs.

Thw Wholesome Family Life. Nikkyo Niwano. Tr. by Joy Alexander from JPN. Orig. Title: Ningen o Sodateru Kokoro. 182p. 1982. pap. 6.95 (*4-333-01026-8*, Pub. by Kosei Pub Co JA) C E Tuttle.

Thwart the Gremlins in Real Computing! Error Prevention in Scientific Calculations. Forman S. Acton. LC 95-10606. 1995. write for info. (*0-691-03663-2*) P-H.

Thwarted: Effort to Destroy the Unarius Mission. Ruth E. Norman. 404p. (Orig.). (C). 1984. pap. 9.00 (*0-932642-89-6*) Unarius Acad Sci.

Thwarting Anger: A View of Anger. Jim Cole. 1985. pap. 5.50 (*0-9601200-5-X*) Growing Images.

Thwarting Anger: A View of How We Keep Anger Alive. Jim Cole. (Illus.). 1985. pap. 5.50 (*0-88310-007-X*) Publishers Consult.

Thwarting Enemies at Home & Abroad: How to Be a Counterintelligence Officer. William R. Johnson. Ed. by David A. Phillips. (Self Confidence - Self Competence Ser.). 200p. (Orig.). 1987. pap. 11.95 (*0-932123-04-X*) Stone Trail Pr.

Thwarting of Saplace's Demon: Arguments Against the Mechanistic World-View. Richard Green. LC 94-43401. 229p. 1995. text ed. 55.00 (*0-312-12472-4*) St Martin.

Thwonk. Joan Bauer. 224p. (YA). (gr. 7 up). 1996. mass mkt. 3.99 (*0-440-21980-9*, LLL BDD) BDD Bks Young Read.

Thwonk. Joan Bauer. LC 94-20293. 224p. (J). 1995. 14.95 (*0-385-32092-2*) Delacorte.

Thy Brothers Blood: The Orthodox Response During the Holocaust. David Kranzler & Isaac Lewin. (ArtScroll Judaicascope Ser.). (Illus.). 338p. 1987. 19.99 (*0-89906-858-8*); pap. 16.99 (*0-89906-859-6*) Mesorah Pubns.

Thy Brother's Wife. Andrew M. Greeley. 1985. 4.50 (*0-446-34035-9*) Warner Bks.

Thy Daily Bread: Sharing Bread, Country Memories, Recipes & Prayer. Linda Kastner. LC 92-7140. (Illus.). 64p. (Orig.). 1992. spiral bd. 14.95 (*1-879560-15-1*) Harbor Hse West.

Thy Friend, Obadiah. Brinton Turkle. (Illus.). 40p. (J). (gr. k-3). 1982. pap. 4.99 (*0-14-050393-5*, Puffin) Puffin Bks.

Thy Gentle Call. Joe Combs. 140p. (Orig.). 1996. pap. 6.00 (*1-57502-195-1*, P0823) Morris Pubng.

Thy God Reigneth. R. Edward Miller. 58p. (YA). (gr. 12). 1964. pap. 3.95 (*0-945818-02-5*) Peniel Pubns.

Thy Hand, Great Anarch! India Nineteen Twenty-One to Nineteen Fifty-Two. Nirad C. Chaudhuri. 1008p. 1988. 28.95 (*0-201-15577-X*) Addison-Wesley.

Thy Hand, Great Anarch! India, 1921-1952. Nirad C. Chaudhuri. 1989. pap. 19.18 (*0-201-19606-9*) Addison-Wesley.

Thy Hand Hath Provided: A History of the Louisville Conference of the United Methodist Church. R. Kenneth Lile. (Illus.). 480p. 1996. text ed. 29.95 (*1-881576-92-2*) Providence Hse.

Thy Hidden Ones. Jessie Penn-Lewis. 210p. Date not set. pap. text ed. 6.95 (*0-87508-735-3*) Chr Lit.

Thy Kingdom Come. Johann C. Blumhardt & Christopher F. Blumhardt. Ed. by Vernard Eller. LC 80-19328. (Blumhardt Reader Ser.). 200p. 1980. text ed. 1.00 (*0-8028-3544-9*) Plough.

Thy Kingdom Come. J. Dwight Pentecost. 360p. 1995. pap. 13.99 (*0-8254-3450-5*) Kregel.

***Thy Kingdom Come.** Geraldine Sistrunk. 80p. (Orig.). 1996. pap. 7.99 (*1-57502-267-2*, PO954) Morris Pubng.

Thy Kingdom Come: A Biblical Introduction to the Baha'i Faith. Thomas Tai-Seale. LC 93-6484. 1993. pap. 14.95 (*0-933770-93-6*) Kalimat.

Thy Kingdom Come: Psychoanalytic Perspectives on the Messiah & the Millennium. William W. Meissner. 256p. (Orig.). 1995. pap. 29.95 (*1-55612-750-2*) Sheed & Ward MO.

***Thy Kingdom Come: Woman in the Wilderness.** John F. Floyd. 374p. (Orig.). 1996. pap. 12.95 (*1-56794-104-4*, C-2404) Star Bible.

***Thy Kingdom Come - White Man: When the Invention Turns Against the Inventor.** Ricardo A. Scott. (Ras Cardo Speaks Ser.). (Illus.). 110p. (Orig.). Date not set. pap. write for info. (*1-883427-94-0*) Crnerstone GA.

Thy Love Is Better Than Wine. Raymond S. Nelson. LC 93-81210. (Illus.). 96p. (Orig.). 1994. pap. 9.95 (*1-882420-11-X*, 1-882420-11-X) Hearth KS.

Thy Rod & Thy Creel. Odell Shepard. LC 84-60996. 128p. 1984. pap. 8.95 (*0-8329-0364-7*) Lyons & Burford.

Thy Sons & Daughters Ever: A History of the University of New Hampshire Alumni Association. 1994. write for info. (*0-615-00133-5*) P E Randall Pub.

Thy Strong Word: The Enduring Legacy of Martin Franzmann. Richard N. Brinkley. LC 93-28284. 1993. 9.95 (*0-570-01347-X*, 99-1480) Concordia.

***Thy Will Be Done.** Michael J. Freeman. iii, 45p. (Orig.). 1995. pap. 4.99 (*1-890255-00-9*) Truth Pubns PA.

Thy Will Be Done: A Guide to Wills, Taxation, & Estate Planning for Older Persons. 2nd ed. Eugene J. Daly. LC 94-4962. (Golden Age Books - Perspectives on Aging Ser.). 234p. (C). 1994. pap. 17.95 (*0-87975-903-8*) Prometheus Bks.

Thy Will Be Done: A Spiritual Portrait of Terence Cardinal Cooke. Benedict J. Groeschel & Terrence L. Weber. LC 90-917. 296p. (Orig.). 1990. 16.95 (*0-8189-0591-3*) Alba.

Thy Will Be Done: How to Organize Your Estate, & How to Be an Executor. Mary G. Thompson. LC 95-76518. (Illus.). 69p. 1995. pap. 19.95 (*0-9646420-0-X*) Ascot Pub OH.

Thy Will Be Done: Letters to Persons in the World. St. Francis de Sales. LC 95-13475. 264p. 1995. pap. 12.95 (*0-918477-29-8*) Sophia Inst Pr.

Thy Will Be Done: The Conquest of the Amazon: Nelson Rockefeller & Evangelism in the Age of Oil. Gerard Colby & Charlotte Dennett. (Illus.). 960p. 1996. pap. 20.00 (*0-06-092723-2*) HarpC.

Thy Word is Truth: Some Thoughts on the Biblical Doctrine of Inspiration. Edward J. Young. 274p. 1963. reprint ed. pap. 16.99 (*0-85151-172-4*) Banner of Truth.

***Thyestes.** Lucius A. Seneca. LC 57-14639. 1957. pap. 1.95 (*0-672-60258-X*) Macmillan.

Thyestes. Lucius A. Seneca. 60p. Date not set. pap. 12.95 (*1-85459-213-0*, Pub. by N Hern Bks UK) Theatre Comm.

Thyestes see Anthology of Roman Drama

Thyme & Monet. Ed. by Krasl Art Center Staff. (Illus.). 1990. write for info. (*0-318-65789-9*) Krasl Art Ctr.

Thyme & the River Too Cookbook. 1993. 22.95 (*1-55868-155-8*) Gr Arts Ctr Pub.

Thyme for All Seasons. 4th ed. (Illus.). 298p. 1992. 13.95 (*0-9634926-0-8*) Jr Leag Duluth.

Thyme in a Bottle: Recipes from Ingrid Croce's San Diego Cafes. Ingrid Croce. LC 95-48280. (Illus.). 256p. 1996. 25.00 (*0-06-258624-6*) Harper SF.

Thyme of Death. Susan W. Albert. 1994. mass mkt. 5.99 (*0-425-14098-9*) Berkley Pub.

Thyme on My Hands. Eric Grissell. (Illus.). 182p. 1987. 14.95 (*0-88192-042-8*) Timber.

Thyme on My Hands. Eric Grissell. LC 94-37137. (Illus.). 182p. 1995. pap. 14.95 (*0-88192-310-9*) Timber.

Thymes Remembered: A Lifetime of Treasured Recipes. Junior League of Tallahassee, Inc. Staff. (Illus.). 280p. 1988. 17.95 (*0-9620166-0-8*) Jr League Tallahassee.

Thymic Hormones & Lymphokines: Basic Chemistry & Clinical Applications. Ed. by Allan L. Goldstein. LC 84-9995. (GWUMC Department of Biochemistry Annual Spring Symposia Ser.). 684p. 1984. 135.00 (*0-306-41649-2*, Plenum Pr) Plenum.

Thymic Tumors. Ed. by R. Sarrazin et al. (Illus.). viii, 172p. 1989. 135.25 (*3-8055-4800-1*) S Karger.

Thymopentin in Experimental & Clinical Medicine. Ed. by E. Sundal. (Journal: Survey of Immunologic Research: Vol. 4, Suppl. 1, 1985). (Illus.). iv, 156p. 1985. pap. 38.50 (*3-8055-4153-8*) S Karger.

Thymus: Diagnostic Imaging, Functions, & Pathologic Anatomy. W. Richard Webb. (Medical Radiology, Diagnostic Imaging & Radiation Oncology Ser.). (Illus.). xvi, 224p. 1992. 262.00 (*0-387-52547-5*) Spr-Verlag.

Thymus: In Focus. M. Ritter & N. Crisp. (In Focus Ser.). (Illus.). 80p. (C). 1992. pap. text ed. 17.95 (*0-19-963144-1*, IRL Pr) OUP.

Thymus Chakra Handbook: Channeled from the Christ & Kwan Yin. Brenda Montgomery. pap. 9.95 (*1-880666-35-9*) Oughten Hse.

Thymus Factors in Immunity. Ed. by Herman Friedman. (Annals Ser.: Vol. 249). 547p. 1975. 65.00 (*0-89072-003-7*) NY Acad Sci.

Thymus in Immunotoxicology, 4, Vol. 4. Ed. by Marion D. Kendall. (Thymus Update Ser.: Vol. 4). 360p. 1991. text ed. 176.00 (*3-7186-5113-0*, Harwood Acad Pubs) Gordon & Breach.

Thymus Involvement in Immunity & Disease. W. D. Biggar et al. LC 72-13558. (Illus.). 220p. (C). 1973. text ed. 29.50 (*0-8422-7068-X*) Irvington.

Thymus, Lymph Nodes, Spleen & Lymphatics. 3rd ed. Ed. by K. Henry & W. S. Symmers. (Systemic Pathology Ser.). (Illus.). 1042p. 1992. text ed. 210.00 (*0-443-03429-X*) Churchill.

Thymus Manganese, & Myasthenia Gravis. Emanuel Josephson. (Natural Health Ser.). 124p. 1958. 7.50 (*0-686-29293-6*, Chedney); pap. 12.00 (*0-686-29294-4*, Chedney) A-albionic Res.

Thymus, Myasthenia Gravis & Manganese. Emanuel M. Josephson. 1979. 250.00 (*0-685-96470-1*) Revisionist Pr.

Thymus Update Series, 4 vols., Vol. 4. Ed. by Marion D. Kendall. 1317p. 1994. text ed. 259.00 (*3-7186-5073-8*) Gordon & Breach.

Thymus Vulgaris: A One-Act Play. Lanford Wilson. 1982. pap. 3.25 (*0-8222-1147-5*) Dramatists Play.

Thynne on Speght's Edition of Chaucer, A. D. 1599. Ed. by G. Kingsley & F. J. Furnivall. (ETS, OS Ser.: Vol. 9). 1974. reprint ed. 30.00 (*0-8115-3344-1*) Periodicals Srv.

Thyra: A Romance of the Polar Pit. Robert A. Bennet. 258p. 1974. spiral bd. 11.00 (*0-7873-1208-8*) Hlth Research.

Thyra: A Romance of the Polar Pit. Robert A. Bennet. Ed. by R. Reginald & Douglas Melville. LC 77-84199. (Lost Race & Adult Fantasy Ser.). (Illus.). 1978. reprint ed. lib. bdg. 29.95 (*0-405-10957-1*) Ayer.

Thyrde & Last Parte of the Secretes of Maister Alexis of Piemont. Allesio Piemontese. Tr. by W. Warde. LC 77-6844. (English Experience Ser.: No. 840). 1977. reprint ed. lib. bdg. 20.00 (*90-221-0840-6*) Walter J Johnson.

Thyristor & Phase Control Circuits. Buck Engineering Staff. Ed. by Buck Engineering Tech. Writers. (F. A. C. E. T. Ser.: Vol. 11). (Illus.). 100p. 1989. teacher ed., pap. text ed. 11.00 (*0-86657-029-2*); ring bd. 13.00 (*0-86657-028-4*) Lab-Volt.

Thyristor Book: With 49 Projects. Delton T. Horn. (Illus.). 220p. 1990. 26.95 (*0-8306-8307-0*); pap. 16.95 (*0-8306-3307-3*) McGraw-Hill Prof.

Thyristor Book: With 49 Projects. Delton T. Horn. 1990. pap. 16.95 (*0-07-155294-4*) McGraw.

Thyristor Control of Electric Drives. Vempa Subramaniam. 500p. 1988. text ed. write for info. (*0-07-460341-8*) McGraw.

Thyristor DC Drives. P. C. Sen. 330p. (C). 1991. reprint ed. lib. bdg. 49.50 (*0-89464-608-7*) Krieger.

Thyristor Networks for the Transfer of Energy Between Superconducting Coils. Robert L. Kustom. LC 79-5410. 135p. reprint ed. pap. 38.50 (*0-7837-6665-3*, 2046277) Bks Demand.

Thyroglobulin: The Prothyroid Hormone. fac. ed. Ed. by Margaret C. Eggo & Gerard N. Burrow. LC 84-24870. (Progress in Endocrine Research & Therapy Ser.: No. 2). (Illus.). 359p. pap. 102.40 (*0-7837-7524-5*, 2046981) Bks Demand.

Thyroid. 2nd ed. Sudha R. Kini. LC 95-25633. (Guides to Clinical Aspiration Biopsy Ser.). (Illus.). 536p. 1996. 98.50 (*0-89640-303-3*) Igaku-Shoin.

***Thyroid: Fine-Needle Biopsy & Cytological Diagnosis of Thyroid Lesions.** Svante R. Orell & Jeanette Philips. LC 96-53276. (Monographs in Clinical Cytology Ser.: Vol. 14, 1997). (Illus.). X, 206p. 1997. 97.50 (*3-8055-6383-3*) S Karger.

Thyroid & Antithyroid Preparations to Vinyl Polymers see Encyclopedia of Chemical Technology

Thyroid & Its Diseases. 5th ed. Leslie J. DeGroot et al. LC 83-27411. 907p. (C). 1984. 82.00 (*0-471-88688-2*) Churchill.

Thyroid & Its Diseases. 6th rev. ed. Leslie J. DeGroot et al. LC 95-36116. 793p. 1995. 145.00 (*0-443-08895-0*) Churchill.

Thyroid Autoimmunity. A. Pinchera et al. LC 87-29258. (Illus.). 654p. 1987. 120.00 (*0-306-42762-1*, Plenum Pr) Plenum.

Thyroid Autoimmunity. David Rayner. Ed. by B. R. Champion. LC 95-24720. (Medical Intelligence Unit Ser.). 238p. 1995. 89.95 (*1-57059-301-9*) R G Landes.

Thyroid Axis & Psychiatric Illness. Ed. by Russell T. Joffe & Anthony J. Levitt. 339p. 1993. text ed. 49.95 (*0-88048-364-4*, 8364) Am Psychiatric.

Thyroid Book: What Goes Wrong & How to Treat It. Martin I. Surks. 224p. 1993. 24.95 (*0-89043-584-7*) Consumer Reports.

Thyroid Disease. M. H. Wheeler & J. H. Lazarus. (Illus.). 360p. (gr. 13). 1993. text ed. 121.95 (*0-412-43030-4*) Chapman & Hall.

***Thyroid Disease: Endocrinology, Surgery, Nuclear Medicine, & Radiotherapy.** 2nd ed. Stephen A. Falk. LC 96-47104. 800p. 1997. text ed. 139.00 (*0-397-51705-X*) Lppncott-Raven.

Thyroid Disease in Clinical Practice. I. Ross McDougall. (Illus.). 344p. 1992. 88.50 (*0-19-520936-2*) OUP.

Thyroid Diseases. Ed. by C. Beckers. 236p. 1983. 56.25 (*0-08-027094-8*, Pergamon Pr) Elsevier.

Thyroid Diseases: Clinical Fundamentals & Therapy. Fabrizio Monaco. 688p. 1993. 265.00 (*0-8493-4821-8*, RC655) CRC Pr.

Thyroid Diseases: Clinical Fundamentals & Therapy. Ed. by Fabrizio Monaco et al. 1993. 249.95 (*0-8439-4821-3*, RC655) CRC Pr.

Thyroid Diseases: Clinical Fundamentals & Therapy. Luigi Troncone. 416p. 1993. 254.00 (*0-8493-4820-X*, RC655) CRC Pr.

Thyroid Eye Disease. 2nd ed. Devron H. Char. (Illus.). 402p. 1990. text ed. 85.00 (*0-443-08682-6*) Churchill.

***Thyroid Eye Disease.** 3rd ed. Devron H. Char. LC 96-50467. 304p. 1997. 95.00 (*0-7506-9893-4*) Buttrwrth-Heinemann.

Thyroid Function & Disease. Burrow et al. (Illus.). 352p. 1989. text ed. 99.00 (*0-7216-2190-2*) Saunders.

Thyroid Gland. Ed. by Michel De Visscher. LC 78-55803. (Comprehensive Endocrinology Ser.). (Illus.). 551p. reprint ed. pap. 157.10 (*0-7837-7089-8*, 2046903) Bks Demand.

T

An Asterisk (*) at the beginning of an entry indicates that the title is appearing in BIP for the first time.

***Thyroid Gland.** Ed. by Monte A. Greer. LC 90-8682. (Comprehensive Endocrinology Ser.). 608p. 1990. reprint ed. pap. 173.30 (*0-608-03412-6*, 2064111) Bks Demand.

Thyroid Gland, 2 vols., I. Ed. by Rosalind Pitt-Rivers & W. R. Trotter. LC 64-9966. (Illus.). reprint ed. pap. 114.00 (*0-317-41693-6*, 2025714) Bks Demand.

Thyroid Gland, 2 vols., II. Ed. by Rosalind Pitt-Rivers & W. R. Trotter. LC 64-9966. (Illus.). reprint ed. pap. 84.30 (*0-317-41694-4*) Bks Demand.

Thyroid Hormone Metabolism. Hennemann. (Basic & Clinical Endocrinology Ser.: Vol. 8). 648p. 1986. 225.00 (*0-8247-7475-2*) Dekker.

Thyroid Hormone Metabolism: Molecular Biology & Alternate Pathways. Ed. by Sing-Yung Wu & Theo J. Visser. LC 94-15571. 266p. 1994. 138.95 (*0-8493-4774-2*) CRC Pr.

Thyroid Hormones. F. M. McNabb. 356p. 1992. text ed. 84.00 (*0-13-921123-3*) P-H.

Thyroid Hormones & Brain Development. Ed. by Gilman D. Grave. LC 76-52899. (Illus.). 392p. reprint ed. pap. 111.80 (*0-7837-7126-6*, 2046955) Bks Demand.

Thyroid Nodule. Hans Heeneman et al. (Self-Instructional Package Ser.). (Illus.). 68p. (Orig.). (C). 1993. pap. text ed. 25.00 (*1-56772-009-9*) AAO-HNS.

***Thyroid Pathology.** Kurt W. Schmid & W. Bocker. LC 96-38761. (Current Topics in Pathology Ser.: Vol. 91). (Illus.). 160p. 1996. 175.00 (*3-540-61623-3*) Spr-Verlag.

Thyroid Sourcebook. M. Sara Rosenthal. 228p. 1995. pap. 12.95 (*1-56565-215-0*) Lowell Hse.

Thyroid Sourcebook: Everything You Need to Know. M. Sara Rosenthal. LC 93-10425. 228p. 1993. 23.95 (*1-56565-087-5*, Legcy) Lowell Hse.

Thyroid Sourcebook: Everything You Need to Know. M. Sara Rosenthal. 224p. 1996. pap. 16.00 (*1-56565-482-X*) Lowell Hse.

Thyroid Testing. Milton W. Hamolsky. LC 77-152025. (Medical Technology Ser.). (Illus.). 109p. reprint ed. 31.10 (*0-8357-9423-7*, 2014551) Bks Demand.

Thyroid Tumors. Ed. by O. Clark & H. D. Roeher. (Progress in Surgery Ser.: Vol. 19). (Illus.). viii, 228p. 1988. 152.00 (*3-8055-4713-7*) S Karger.

Thyroid Tumours. D. Wynford-Thomas & E. D. Williams. (Illus.). 176p. 1989. text ed. 98.00 (*0-443-03568-7*) Churchill.

Thyroiditis. Virginia A. Livolsi & Paul Logerfo. 224p. 1981. 126.00 (*0-8493-5705-5*, RC657, CRC Reprint) Franklin.

Thyrotropin: Ultrasensitive TSH Measurement in Clinical Research & Diagnostics. A. Passath & H. Hoefler. Ed. by G. Leb et al. (Illus.). x, 361p. (C). 1987. 113.85 (*0-89925-209-5*) De Gruyter.

Thyrotropin Releasing Hormone. fac. ed. Ed. by E. C. Griffiths & G. W. Bennett. LC 81-40370. (Illus.). 416p. pap. 118.60 (*0-7837-7210-6*, 2047088) Bks Demand.

Thyrsus II. Ed. by Gail Burnett. 1990. pap. 12.00 (*0-685-60195-1*) Aegis Pub Co.

Thyrsus-Poems. Ed. by Gail Burnett. 1985. pap. 6.00 (*0-318-03122-1*) Aegis Pub Co.

Thyrza: A Tale. George R. Gissing. Ed. by Jacob Korg. 495p. 24.50 (*0-8386-1544-9*) Fairleigh Dickinson.

Thyrza: A Tale, 3 Vols. in 1. George Gissing. LC 72-75984. reprint ed. 30.00 (*0-404-02789-X*) AMS Pr.

Thysanopteren Europas. H. Priesner. 1963. reprint ed. 77.00 (*90-6123-121-3*) Lubrecht & Cramer.

Thystram's Collectanea. Stephan M. Sechi. (Talislanta Ser.). (Illus.). 160p. (Orig.). 1993. pap. 15.00 (*1-880992-07-8*) Wizards Coast.

Th1 & Th2 Cells in Health & Disease. Sergio Romagnani. (Chemical Immunology Ser.: Vol. 63, 1996). (Illus.). xii, 222p. 1996. 224.50 (*3-8055-6241-1*) S Karger.

Th1-Th2 Paradigm & Transplantation Tolerance: Exploring the Microcosm of Transplantation-Of What Is Past, Passing, & to Come. Robin P. Lowry & Takumi Takeuchi. (Medical Intelligence Unit Ser.). 118p. 1994. 89.95 (*1-57059-108-3*, LN9108) R G Landes.

***Th1-Th2 Paradigm in Disease.** Sergio Romagnani. LC 96-43792. (Molecular Biology Intelligence Unit Ser.). 196p. 1996. 89.95 (*1-57059-409-0*) R G Landes.

Ti Basic. Haskell et al. 1985. 19.95 (*0-13-921115-2*) P-H.

Ti Liv Konpreyansyon. Oreste R. Joseph & Rita Parisse. (Illus.). 70p. (Orig.). (CRP.). (J). (gr. 3-4). 1996. wbk. ed. 5.95 (*1-885566-13-1*) Oresjozef.

Ti Nv Eivai Bei Aristoteles. Curt Arpe. Bd. with Logische Regeln der Platonischen Schule in der Aristotelischen Topik. LC 75-13254. LC 75-13254. (History of Ideas in Ancient Greece Ser.). (GER.). 1976. reprint ed. 21.95 (*0-405-07292-9*) Ayer.

TI-59 & HP-41CV Instrument Engineering Programs. Stanley W. Thrift. LC 82-20920. 384p. 1983. reprint ed. pap. 109.50 (*0-608-01578-4*, 2061998) Bks Demand.

***TI-8x & CBL Lab: Applications in Biology & Chemistry.** 2nd ed. Sconzo et al. 156p. 1997. spiral bd. 28.95 (*0-7872-3778-7*) Kendall-Hunt.

***TI-82 & CBL Lab: Applications.** Penny Sconzo. 154p. 1996. pap. text ed., spiral bd. 28.95 (*0-7872-2042-6*) Kendall-Hunt.

TI-82 Companion to Elementary Statistics. Larry A. Morgan. Ed. by Julia Berrisford. (C). 1996. pap. text ed. 9.50 (*0-201-87002-9*) Addison-Wesley.

TI-82 Graphing Calculator Activities for Middle School Math. Charles Lund. (Illus.). 200p. 1995. pap. text ed. 18.95 (*0-9623629-6-4*) MathWare.

***TI-83 Enhanced Statistics.** Ray Barton & John Diehl. 140p. (YA). (gr. 9-12). 1997. spiral bd. 25.00 (*1-886018-10-3*) Venture Pubng.

TI-85 Reference Guide. Nelson G. Rich & Lawrence G. Gilligan. (Illus.). 112p. (Orig.). 1993. pap. 18.95 (*0-9626661-6-5*) Gilmar Pub.

TI 99-4A, Vol. 1. Tammy Buxton. (Thinking-Learning-Creating: TLC for Growing Minds Ser.). 54p. (J). (gr. 4-12). 1983. pap. text ed. 11.95 (*0-88193-051-2*) Create Learn.

TI 99-4A, Vol. 2. Tammy Buxton. (Thinking-Learning-Creating: TLC for Growing Minds Ser.). 53p. (J). (gr. 4-12). 1983. pap. text ed. 11.95 (*0-88193-052-0*) Create Learn.

TI 99-4A, Vol. 3. Marilyn Buxton & Tammy Buxton. (Thinking-Learning-Creating: TLC for Growing Minds Ser.). 65p. (J). (gr. 5-12). 1983. pap. text ed. 11.95 (*0-88193-053-9*) Create Learn.

TI 99-4A, Vol. 4. Marilyn Buxton & Tammy Buxton. (Thinking-Learning-Creating: TLC for Growing Minds Ser.). 45p. (J). (gr. 5-12). 1983. pap. text ed. 11.95 (*0-88193-054-7*) Create Learn.

TI 99-4A in Bits & Bytes. Remo A. Loreto. Ed. by Robert Wartman. (Illus.). (Orig.). 1983. pap. 14.99 (*0-914209-01-9*) R A Loreto.

TIA International Travel News Directory. Ed. by Robin Longman. (Illus.). 98p. (Orig.). 1988. pap. 140.00 (*0-685-23260-3*) Travel Ind Assoc.

Tia Julia y el Escribidor. 7th ed. Mario Vargas Llosa. (SPA.). 1992. pap. 17.95 (*0-7859-0543-X*, 8432230251) Fr & Eur.

Tia Tula. Miguel De Unamuno. (Nueva Austral Ser.: Vol. 144). (SPA.). 1991. pap. text ed. 13.95 (*84-239-1944-7*) Elliots Bks.

Tia Tula, No. 122. Miguel De Unamuno. 149p. (SPA.). 1980. 11.95 (*0-8288-8578-8*) Fr & Eur.

Tian Wen: A Chinese Book of Origins. Tr. by Stephen Field from CHI. LC 86-12737. 128p. (Orig.). 1986. 22.95 (*0-8112-1010-3*); pap. 8.95 (*0-8112-1011-1*, NDP624) New Directions.

Tiananmen: China's Struggle for Democracy - Its Prelude, Development, Aftermath, & Impact. Ed. by Winston L. Yang & Marsha L. Wager. 1990. 14.00 (*0-925153-08-7*) Occasional Papers.

Tiananmen Diary: Thirteen Days in June. Harrison E. Salisbury. 1989. 18.95 (*0-316-80904-7*); pap. 10.95 (*0-316-80905-5*) Little.

Tiananmen Square. Scott Simmie et al. (Illus.). 224p. 1989. pap. 16.95 (*0-295-96950-4*) U of Wash Pr.

***Tiananmen to Tiananment: China under Communism 1947-1996: After Delusion & Disillusionment, a Nation at the Crossroads, No. 1, 1997.** (Occasional Papers/Reprints Series in Contemporary Asian Studies: Vol. 138). 361p. (Orig.). 1997. pap. 35.00 (*0-925153-52-4*) Occasional Papers.

***Tiananmen to Tiananment: China under Communism 1947-1996: After Delusion & Disillusionment, a Nation at the Crossroads, No. 1, 1997.** (Occasional Papers/Reprints Series in Contemporary Asian Studies: Vol. 138). 361p. (Orig.). 1997. 45.00 (*0-925153-53-2*) Occasional Papers.

Tianna, the Terrible. Karen Rispin. LC 92-19294. (Anika Scott Ser.: No. 2). (J). (gr. 3-7). 1992. 4.99 (*0-8423-2031-8*) Tyndale.

Tiara: An Insider's Guide to Choosing & Winning Pageants. Barbara T. Howell. 336p. 1992. pap. 19.95 (*0-9633530-0-4*) Tiara NJ.

***Tia's Valentine.** Jenna Jones. 320p. 1997. mass mkt. 4.99 (*0-8217-5576-5*, Zebra Kensgtn) Kensgtn Pub Corp.

Tiazhelye Zvezdy. Ivan Elagin. LC 86-32761. 364p. (RUS.). 1987. text ed. 21.95 (*0-938920-86-3*) Hermitage.

Tib. Mark Dunster. (Holiday Ser.: Pt. 6: Easter). 77p. (Orig.). 1981. pap. 5.00 (*0-89642-077-9*) Linden Pubs.

***Tibaldo & the Hole in the Calendar.** Abner Shimony. LC 97-2157. (Copernicus Ser.). (Illus.). 120p. 1997. 20.00 (*0-387-94935-6*) Spr-Verlag.

Tibbetts: Henry Tibbetts of Dover, NH & Some of His Descendants. M. T. Jarvis. (Illus.). 821p. 1991. reprint ed. pap. 117.00 (*0-8328-1834-8*); reprint ed. lib. bdg. 127.00 (*0-8328-1833-X*) Higginson Bk Co.

***Tibbits' Boys: A History of the 21st New York Cavalry.** Thomas J. Reed. LC 96-52016. 368p. 1997. 62.50 (*0-7618-0688-1*); pap. 42.50 (*0-7618-0689-X*) U Pr of Amer.

***Tibblestone Hundred: A Journey Through an English Village.** Fred Archer. (Illus.). 160p. 1996. 26.95 (*0-7509-1256-1*, Pub. by Sutton Pubng UK) Bks Intl VA.

Tibby. DeeDee Reilly. LC 95-78544. (Illus.). 44p. (J). (gr. k-4). 1997. 8.95 (*1-55523-759-2*) Winston-Derek.

Tiber Afire. Fabio Della Seta. Tr. by Frances Frenaye from ITA. LC 90-60882. 192p. 1992. pap. 10.95 (*0-910395-72-1*) Marlboro Pr.

Tiberi: The Uncrowned Champion. Andy Ecrole. 1993. 25.00 (*0-89802-598-2*) Beautiful Am.

Tiberian Hebrew Phonology. Joseph L. Malone. LC 92-43400. x, 204p. 1993. 55.00 (*0-931464-75-7*) Eisenbrauns.

Tiberius & the Roman Empire. Charles E. Smith. LC 42-23574. 286p. reprint ed. pap. 81.60 (*0-317-28662-5*, 2055315) Bks Demand.

Tiberius Caesar. David Shotter. LC 92-13934. (Lancaster Pamphlets Ser.). (Illus.). 112p. (C). 1992. pap. 9.95 (*0-415-07654-4*, A9787) Routledge.

Tiberius Caesar & the Roman Constitution. Olive Kuntz. 1974. lib. bdg. 250.00 (*0-87968-391-0*) Gordon Pr.

Tiberius Claudius Maximus: The Cavalryman. Peter Connolly. (Rebuilding the Past Ser.). (Illus.). 32p. (J). (gr. 5-9). 1989. bds. 19.95 (*0-19-917106-8*) OUP.

Tiberius the Politician. Barbara Levick. (Classical Lives Ser.). (Illus.). 256p. 1986. reprint ed. pap. 16.95 (*0-7099-4132-3*, Pub. by Croom Helm UK) Routledge Chapman & Hall.

Tiberius to Commodus see Roman Silver Coins

Tibet. 1991. pap. 9.95 (*0-8442-9812-3*, Passport Bks) NTC Pub Grp.

Tibet. Elizabeth Booz. (Illus.). 228p. 1992. pap. 12.95 (*0-8442-9806-9*, Passport Bks) NTC Pub Grp.

Tibet. Bobbie Kalman. (Lands, Peoples, & Cultures Ser.). (Illus.). 32p. (J). (gr. 4-5). 1990. pap. 7.95 (*0-86505-293-X*); lib. bdg. 19.16 (*0-86505-213-1*) Crabtree Pub Co.

Tibet. Pietro F. Mele. (Illus.). 222p. 1988. 14.95 (*0-937938-63-7*) Snow Lion Pubns.

***Tibet.** Kazuyoshi Nomachi. LC 97-3533. 1997. 55.00 (*1-57062-256-6*) Shambhala Pubns.

Tibet. John R. Pinfold. (World Bibliographical Ser.). 1991. lib. bdg. 66.00 (*1-85109-158-0*) ABC-CLIO.

Tibet. Tr. by Maureen Walker. LC 95-17240. (Tintin's Travel Diaries Ser.). (Illus.). 80p. (FRE.). (J). 1995. 11.95 (*0-8120-6504-2*) Barron.

Tibet. Tr. by Maureen Walker. LC 95-17240. (Tintin's Travel Diaries Ser.). (Illus.). 80p. (FRE.). (J). 1995. pap. 6.95 (*0-8120-9237-6*) Barron.

Tibet. 3rd ed. Thomas Cook. (Illustrated Travel Guides from Thomas Cook Ser.). 1994. pap. 16.95 (*0-8442-9455-1*, Passport Bks) NTC Pub Grp.

Tibet: A Bibliography of Its Culture, History & Religion. 1989. lib. bdg. 250.00 (*0-87700-880-9*) Revisionist Pr.

Tibet: A Political History. 3rd ed. Tsepan W. Shakabpa. 369p. 1984. reprint ed. pap. write for info. (*0-9611474-1-5*) Potala.

Tibet: A Reality. M. G. Chitkara. xviii, 162p. (C). 1994. 18.00 (*81-7024-639-3*, Pub. by Ashish Pub Hse II) Nataraj Bks.

***Tibet: A Sourcebook.** Ed. by Anand Kumar. 1995. 30.00 (*81-7027-213-0*, Pub. by Radiant Pubs II) S Asia.

***Tibet: Abode of the Gods, Pearl of the Motherland.** Barbara Erickson. LC 97-2611. 250p. 1997. 29.95 (*1-881896-16-1*) Pacific View Pr.

Tibet: Enactment of the World. Ann Heinrichs. LC 96-12389. 128p. (J). (gr. 6-9). 1996. lib. bdg. 30.00 (*0-516-20155-7*) Childrens.

Tibet: Endurance of the National Ideal. Stephen R. Bowers & Eva M. Neterowicz. (Journal of Social, Political & Economic Studies: No. 23). 1995. pap. text ed. 15.00 (*0-930690-52-4*) Coun Soc Econ.

Tibet: Harvest of the Spirit. Robert Apte et al. LC 97-21948. (Illus.). 150p. 1997. 34.95 (*1-57416-001-X*) Clear Light.

***Tibet: Journey to the Forbidden City.** Tiziana Baldizzone & Gianni Baldizzone. (Illus.). 160p. 1997. 40.00 (*1-55670-511-5*) Stewart Tabori & Chang.

Tibet: One Second to Live. unabridged ed. H. J. McCallum. Ed. by Charles L. Tracy. Tr. by Lesley Needham. (Illus.). 339p. (Orig.). 1995. pap. 17.50 (*0-9651610-0-5*, 001) H J McCallum.

Tibet: Past & Present. Charles A Bell. 1975. lib. bdg. 250.00 (*0-87968-483-6*) Krishna Pr.

Tibet: Reflections from the Wheel of Life. Carroll Dunham. (Illus.). 204p. 1993. 55.00 (*1-55859-218-0*) Abbeville Pr.

Tibet: Survival in Question. Pierre-Antoine Donnet. Tr. by Tica Broch. (Politics in Contemporary Asia Ser.). (Illus.). 256p. (C). 1994. pap. 25.00 (*1-85649-130-7*, Pub. by Zed Bks Ltd UK); text ed. 59.95 (*1-85649-129-3*, Pub. by Zed Bks Ltd UK) Humanities.

Tibet: The Issue Is Independence. Ed. by Ed Lazar. 92p. 1994. pap. 7.00 (*0-938077-75-9*) Parallax Pr.

Tibet: The Position of International Law. Ed. by Robert McCorquodale & Nicholas Orosz. (Illus.). 238p. 1995. pap. 25.00 (*0-906026-34-2*, Pub. by Serindia UK) Weatherhill.

Tibet: The Sacred Realm, Photographs 1880-1950. Dalai Lama & Lobsang P. Lhalungpa. (Illus.). 159p. 1997. 39.95 (*0-89381-109-2*) Aperture.

***Tibet: The Sacred Realm, Photographs 1880-1950.** Dalai Lama & Lobsang P. Lhalungpa. (Illus.). 159p. 1997. pap. 27.50 (*0-89381-121-1*) Aperture.

Tibet: Travel Survival Kit. 3rd ed. Chris Taylor. (Illus.). 256p. 1995. pap. 14.95 (*0-86442-289-X*) Lonely Planet.

Tibet see Cultures of the World - Group 12

Tibet - Cutting off the Serpent's Head: Tightening Control in Tibet, 1994-1995. Human Rights Watch Asia Staff & Tibet Information Network Staff. 208p. (Orig.). 1996. pap. 15.00 (*1-56432-166-5*) Hum Rts Watch.

***Tibet - My Story: An Autobiography.** Jetsun Pema. 1997. 24.95 (*1-86204-124-5*) Element MA.

Tibet & Nepal Painted & Described. A. H. Landor. (C). 1994. 48.50 (*81-206-0852-6*, Pub. by Asian Educ Servs II) S Asia.

Tibet & the Chinese People's Republic. 1991. lib. bdg. 87.95 (*0-8490-4504-5*) Gordon Pr.

Tibet Handbook: A Pilgrimage Guide. Victor Chan. (Illus.). 1103p. (Orig.). 1994. pap. 30.00 (*0-918373-90-5*) Moon Trvl Hdbks.

Tibet in Pictures: A Journey into the Past, 2 vols., Set. Gotami G. Li. LC 79-21352. 210p. 1980. 85.00 (*0-913546-57-7*) Dharma Pub.

Tibet Is My Country: Autobiography of Thubten Jigme Norbu, Brother of the Dalai Lama. Thubten J. Norbu. Tr. by Edward Fitzgerald from GER. (Tibet Book - Yellow Ser.). 276p. 1986. pap. 16.95 (*0-86171-045-2*) Wisdom MA.

Tibet-Land of Mystery. Ed. by Sun Jie. (Illus.). 158p. 1990. 49.95 (*0-8351-2443-6*) China Bks.

Tibet Past & Present. Charles Bell. (Illus.). 340p. 1990. reprint ed. 36.50 (*0-317-99944-3*, Pub. by M Manoharial II) Coronet Bks.

Tibet Past & Present: Featuring Personal Sacred Objects of His Holiness the Dalai Lama. Glenn H. Mullin. 1996. 27.00 (*1-56352-352-3*) Longstreet Pr Inc.

Tibet Past & Present: Featuring Personal Sacred Objects of His Holiness the Dalai Lama. Glenn H. Mullin. 1996. pap. text ed. 16.95 (*1-56352-353-1*) Longstreet Pr Inc.

***Tibet, the Mysterious.** Thomas H. Hodich. 1996. reprint ed. 44.00 (*81-206-1146-2*, Pub. by Asian Educ Servs II) S Asia.

Tibet Through China. A. E. Pratt. (C). 1987. 28.50 (*0-8364-2348-8*, Pub. by Mittal II) S Asia.

Tibet Through Dissident Chinese Eyes: Essays on Self-Determination. James D. Seymour. 160p. (C). (gr. 13). 1997. text ed. 48.95 (*1-56324-922-7*, East Gate Bk) M E Sharpe.

Tibet Travel Companion. 3rd ed. Robert Strauss. 1996. pap. text ed. 16.95 (*0-9520900-6-6*) Hunter NJ.

Tibetan: Language Survival Kit. 2nd ed. Sandup Tsering. (Illus.). 160p. 1996. pap. 4.95 (*0-86442-346-2*) Lonely Planet.

Tibetan see Mother of Knowledge: The Enlightenment of Ye-shes Mtsho-Rgyal

***Tibetan Art of Healing.** Ian A. Baker. 1997. 50.00 (*0-8118-1897-7*); pap. text ed. 29.95 (*0-8118-1871-3*) Chronicle Bks.

***Tibetan Art of Parenting: From Before Conception Through Early Childhood.** Anne H. Maiden & Edie Farwell. LC 97-17055. 1997. write for info. (*0-86171-129-7*) Wisdom MA.

Tibetan Arts of Love. Gedun Chopel. Ed. & Tr. by Jeffrey Hopkins. 225p. (Orig.). 1992. pap. 14.95 (*0-937938-97-1*) Snow Lion Pubns.

***Tibetan Astrology.** Philippe Cornu. LC 96-39527. 368p. 1997. 30.00 (*1-57062-217-5*) Shambhala Pubns.

***Tibetan Book of Days: A Journal with Thoughts from Sogyal Rinpoche.** Sogyal Rinpoche. 1997. 14.95 (*0-00-649174-X*) HarpC.

Tibetan Book of Healing. Lopsang Rapgay. (Illus.). 208p. (Orig.). 1997. per., pap. 12.95 (*1-878423-21-5*) Morson Pub.

Tibetan Book of Living & Dying: A New Spiritual Classic from One of the Foremost Interpreters of Tibetan Buddhism to the West. Sogyal Rinpoche. LC 90-56214. 444p. 1994. reprint ed. pap. 15.00 (*0-06-250834-2*) Harper SF.

Tibetan Book of the Dead. Jean-Claude Van Itallie. 1983. pap. 4.75 (*0-8222-1148-3*) Dramatists Play.

Tibetan Book of the Dead. Ed. by W. Y. Evans-Wentz. (Illus.). 334p. 1960. reprint ed. pap. 8.95 (*0-19-500223-7*) OUP.

Tibetan Book of the Dead: The Great Book of Natural Liberation Through Understanding in the Between. Tr. by Robert A. Thurman. LC 93-2891. 304p. 1994. pap. 13.95 (*0-553-37090-1*) Bantam.

Tibetan Book of the Dead: The Great Liberation Through Hearing in the Bardo. Tr. by Francesca Fremantle & Chogyam Trungpa from TIB. LC 74-29615. (Dragon Editions Ser.). (Illus.). 120p. 1988. pap. 10.00 (*0-87773-074-1*) Shambhala Pubns.

Tibetan Book of the Dead: The Great Liberation Through Hearing in the Bardo. Tr. by Francesca Fremantle & Chogyam Trungpa. LC 91-50798. (Pocket Classics Ser.). 288p. (TIB.). 1992. pap. 7.00 (*0-87773-675-8*) Shambhala Pubns.

Tibetan Book of the Great Liberation. Ed. by W. Y. Evans-Wentz. (Illus.). 328p. 1968. reprint ed. pap. 13.95 (*0-19-500293-8*) OUP.

Tibetan Buddhism: Reason & Revelation. Ed. by Steven D. Goodman & Ronald M. Davidson. LC 90-49077. (SUNY Series in Buddhist Studies). 215p. (C). 1992. text ed. 59.50 (*0-7914-0785-3*); pap. text ed. 19.95 (*0-7914-0786-1*) State U NY Pr.

Tibetan Buddhism from the Ground Up: A Practical Approach for Modern Life. B. Alan Wallace. Ed. by Steven Wilhelm. LC 93-15120. 228p. (Orig.). 1993. pap. 14.00 (*0-86171-075-4*) Wisdom MA.

Tibetan Buddhism in Western Perspective. rev. ed. Herbert V. Guenther. LC 76-47758. (Illus.). 274p. 1989. pap. 14.95 (*0-913546-50-X*) Dharma Pub.

Tibetan Buddhism with Its Mystic Cults Symbolism & Mythology, & in Its Relation to Indian Buddhism. Austine Waddell. (Illus.). 598p. 1972. reprint ed. pap. 12.95 (*0-486-20130-9*) Dover.

Tibetan Buddhist Medicine & Psychiatry: The Diamond Healing. Terry Clifford. LC 82-61872. (Illus.). 288p. 1990. pap. 12.95 (*0-87728-710-4*) Weiser.

Tibetan Civilization. R. A. Stein. Tr. by J. E. Driver. (Illus.). 334p. 1972. 47.50 (*0-8047-0806-1*); pap. 15.95 (*0-8047-0901-7*) Stanford U Pr.

***Tibetan Coins.** O. D. Cresswell. 67p. 1977. pap. 4.00 (*1-889172-08-1*) Numismatic Intl.

Tibetan Empire in Central Asia: A History of the Struggle for Great Power among Tibetans, Turks, Arabs, & Chinese during the Early Middle Ages. Christopher I. Beckwith. 290p. 1987. pap. text ed. 18.95 (*0-691-02469-3*) Princeton U Pr.

Tibetan-English Compact Dictionary with Sanskrit Synonyms. S. C. Das. 1353p. 1989. 35.00 (*81-206-0455-5*) IBD Ltd.

Tibetan-English Dictionary. Sarat C. Das. 1987. 75.00 (*0-8288-1759-6*, F63570) Fr & Eur.

Tibetan-English Dictionary. Sarat C. Das. 1353p. (C). 1987. 220.00 (*0-89771-085-1*, Pub. by Ratna Pustak Bhandar) St Mut.

Tibetan-English Dictionary. H. A. Jaschke. (ENG & TIB.). 1987. 49.95 (*0-8288-1142-3*, M14106) Fr & Eur.

Tibetan-English Dictionary. rev. ed. Sarat C. Das. 1353p. 1985. reprint ed. text ed. 40.00 (*0-86590-722-6*, Pub. by Gaurav Pub Hse II) Apt Bks.

Tibetan-English Dictionary. Sarat C. Das. (C). 1983. reprint ed. 44.00 (*0-8364-2194-9*, Pub. by Motilal Banarsidass II) S Asia.

Tibetan-English Dictionary. H. A. Jaschke. (C). 1987. reprint ed. 21.00 (*81-208-0321-3*, Pub. by Motilal Banarsidass II) S Asia.

Tibetan-English Dictionary: Compact Edition. Sarat C. Das. 1987. 80.00 (*0-7855-0290-4*) St Mut.

Tibetan-English Dictionary of Buddhist Terminology. Tsepak Rigzin. (ENG & TIB.). 1987. 95.00 (*0-8288-2319-7*, F 140705) Fr & Eur.

T

Tibetan-English Dictionary of Modern Tibetan. Melvyn C. Goldstein. 1987. 75.00 (*0-8288-1760-X*, M15609) Fr & Eur.

Tibetan-English Dictionary of Modern Tibetan. Ed. by Melvyn C. Goldstein. 1234p. (C). 1983. 275.00 (*0-89771-113-0*, Pub. by Ratna Pustak Bhandar) St Mut.

Tibetan Environment & Development News - Compilation. Ed. by John Ackerly. pap. 5.00 (*1-879245-07-8*) Intl Campaign Tibet.

***Tibetan Family.** Stephen Chicoine. LC 97-12645. (Journey Between Two Worlds Ser.). (J). 1998. lib. bdg. write for info. (*0-8225-3408-8*, Lerner Publctns) Lerner Group.

Tibetan Folk Tales. Albert L. Shelton. LC 78-63220. (Folktale Ser.). (Illus.). 192p. reprint ed. 41.50 (*0-404-16157-X*) AMS Pr.

Tibetan for Beginners & Travellers. Melvyn C. Goldstein. 1988. 30.00 (*0-7855-0289-0*, Pub. by Ratna Pustak Bhandar) St Mut.

Tibetan for Beginners & Travellers. Melvyn C. Goldstein. 62p. (C). 1988. 45.00 (*0-89771-084-3*, Pub. by Ratna Pustak Bhandar) St Mut.

Tibetan Frontiers Question: From Curzon to the Colombo Conference. Frederic A. Greenhut, II. (Illus.). 178p. 1982. 24.95 (*0-940500-71-X*) Asia Bk Corp.

Tibetan Frontiers Question from Curzon to the Colombo Conference: An Unresolved Factor in Indo-Sinic Relations. Frederic A. Greenhutt, II. 192p. 1986. 45.00 (*0-317-52160-8*, Pub. by S Chand II) St Mut.

Tibetan Historical Literature. A. I. Vostrikov. (C). 1945. text ed. 55.00 (*0-7007-0267-9*, Pub. by Curzon Press UK) UH Pr.

Tibetan Kung-Fu: The Way of the Monk. Michael P. Staples. LC 80-106130. (Illus.). 80p. 1976. pap. 5.95 (*0-86568-004-3*, 203) Unique Pubns.

Tibetan Literature: Studies in Genre. Jose I. Cabezon & Roger R. Jackson. (Studies in Indo-Tibetan Buddhism). 45p. 1995. 45.00 (*1-55939-031-X*); pap. 29.95 (*1-55939-044-1*) Snow Lion Pubns.

Tibetan Mandalas. Raghu Vira & Lokesha Chandra. (C). 1995. 94.00 (*81-86471-01-4*, Pub. by Aditya Prakashan II) S Asia.

Tibetan Mastiff: Legendary Guardian of the Himalayas. Ann Rohrer & Cathy J. Flamholtz. LC 89-3377. (Illus.). 160p. (Orig.). 1989. 16.95 (*0-940269-02-3*) OTR Pubns.

Tibetan Medical Paintings: Illustrations of the Blue Beryl Treatise of Sangye Gyamtso (1653-1705), Set, Vols. I & II. Ed. by Yuri Parfionovitch et al. (Illus.). (gr. 13). 1992. Set. 195.00 (*0-8109-3861-8*) Mosby Yr Bk.

Tibetan Medicine: Illustrated in Original Text. Ed. & Tr. by Ven R. Rechung. 346p. 1973. reprint ed. pap. 16.00 (*0-520-03048-6*) U CA Pr.

***Tibetan Medicine & Healing.** Namgyal Qusar & Jean Sergen. 320p. Date not set. pap. 15.00 (*0-465-08481-8*) Basic.

***Tibetan Nation: A History of Tibetan Nationalism And Sino-Tibetan Relations.** Warren W. Smith. 4p. (C). 1997. pap. text ed. 29.95 (*0-8133-3280-X*) Westview.

Tibetan New Words Dictionary. Thomas Creamer. 1996. write for info. (*1-881265-30-7*) Dunwoody Pr.

Tibetan Newspaper Reader. Michael Lempert & Tenzing Sangpo. Ed. by Paul Hackett. LC 96-83390. 1996. 44.00 (*1-881265-40-4*) Dunwoody Pr.

Tibetan Nomads. Schuyler Jones. LC 95-61962. (Carlsberg Nomad Ser.). (Illus.). 400p. 1996. 50.00 (*0-500-23720-4*) Thames Hudson.

Tibetan on Tibet. 2nd ed. G. A. Combe. LC 88-23854. (Illus.). 238p. 1989. reprint ed. pap. 12.95 (*0-943389-02-X*) Snow Lion-SLG Bks.

Tibetan on Tibet. G. A. Combe. (C). 1994. reprint ed. text ed. 28.50 (*81-7305-036-8*, Pub. by Aryan Bks Intl II) S Asia.

Tibetan Paintings. George N. Roerich. (Illus.). 176p. 1986. 49.95 (*0-318-36347-X*) Asia Bk Corp.

Tibetan Phrasebook. Andrew Bloomfield & Yanki Tshering. LC 87-12989. 218p. (Orig.). 1987. pap. 8.95 (*0-937938-54-8*) Snow Lion Pubns.

Tibetan Pilgrimage. Peter Gold. LC 87-12998. (Illus.). 175p. (Orig.). 1988. pap. 14.95 (*0-937938-52-1*) Snow Lion Pubns.

Tibetan Portrait: The Power of Compassion. Phil Borges et al. LC 95-49939. (Illus.). 96p. 1996. 27.50 (*0-8478-1957-4*) Rizzoli Intl.

***Tibetan Power Yoga: The Essence of All Yogas - A Tibetaan Exercise for Physical Vitality & Mental Power.** Jutta Mattausch. (Illus.). 112p. (Orig.). 1997. pap. 9.95 (*0-914955-30-6*) Lotus Light.

Tibetan Religious Dances. Rene De Nebesky-Wojkowitz. Ed. by Christoph Von Furer-Haimendorf. (Religion & Society Ser.: No. 2). 1976. text ed. 69.25 (*90-279-7621-X*) Mouton.

Tibetan-Sanskrit Dictionary. L. Chandra. 1987. 250.00 (*0-8288-1761-8*, M14101) Fr & Eur.

Tibetan-Sanskrit Dictionary Supplementary Volume. I. Lokesh Chandra. (Sata-Pitaka Series Indo-Asian Literature: Vol. 369). (C). 1992. 54.00 (*81-85689-11-3*, Pub. by Aditya Prakashan II) S Asia.

Tibetan Spaniel: A Gift from the Roof of the World. Susan W. Miccio. LC 96-13302. (Illus.). 256p. 1996. 39.95 (*0-940269-12-0*) OTR Pubns.

Tibetan Spaniel Champions, 1984-1986. Camino E. E. & Bk. Co. Staff. (Illus.). 46p. 1987. pap. 24.95 (*0-940808-41-2*) Camino E E & Bk.

Tibetan Studies. Sarat C. Das. Ed. by Alaka Chattopadhyay. 1985. 24.00 (*0-8364-1501-9*, Pub. by KP Bagchi IA) S Asia.

Tibetan Studies: Being a Reprint of the Articles Contributed to the Journal of the Asiatic Society of Bengal. Sandor K. Csoma. Ed. by E. Denilson. LC 78-72400. reprint ed. 47.50 (*0-404-17259-8*) AMS Pr.

Tibetan, Survival, 2 cassettes, Set. Andrew Bloomfield & Yanki Tshering. 145p. (YA). 1991. pap. 34.95 incl. audio (*0-88432-738-8*, AFTB10) Audio-Forum.

Tibetan Tales: Derived from Indian Sources. Tr. by F. Anton Von Schiefner & W. R. Ralston from GER. (Bibliotheca Indo-Buddhica Ser.: No. 52). (C). 1988. text ed. 21.00 (*81-7030-165-3*) S Asia.

Tibetan Tales: Derived from Indian Sources. Tr. by F. Anton Von Schiefner. (C). 1991. 28.00 (*81-85326-43-6*, Pub. by Vintage II) S Asia.

Tibetan Tales Derived from Indian Sources. W. R. Ralston. 368p. 1989. reprint ed. pap. 30.00 (*957-9482-21-7*) Oriental Bk Store.

Tibetan Terrier. Anne Keleman. (Illus.). 192p. 1993. 9.95 (*0-86622-758-X*, KW230) TFH Pubns.

***Tibetan Terrier: AKC Rank #91.** Anne Keleman. (Rare Breed Ser.). (Illus.). 96p. 1997. 19.95 (*0-7938-0782-4*, RX-132) TFH Pubns.

Tibetan Terrier Book. 2nd ed. Jane Reif. (Illus.). 272p. (Orig.). 1996. pap. 42.00 (*0-913337-28-5*) Southfarm Pr.

Tibetan Terrier Champions, 1973-1986. Camino E. E. & Bk. Co. Staff. (Illus.). 119p. 1988. pap. 36.95 (*0-940808-70-6*) Camino E E & Bk.

Tibetan Terrier Champions, 1988-1994. Camino E. E. & Bk. Co. Staff. (Illus.). 90p. 1997. pap. 32.95 (*1-55893-045-0*) Camino E E & Bk.

Tibetan Tripitaka, 72 vols. Ed. by A. W. Barber. (TIB.). 1991. write for info. (*957-9482-42-X*, TBT001, Pub. by SMC Pub CC) Oriental Bk Store.

Tibetan Voices: A Traditional Memoir. Brian Harris. LC 96-26458. (Illus.). 144p. 1996. pap. 31.95 (*0-7649-0004-8*) Pomegranate Calif.

Tibetan Way of Living & Dying. Sogyal Rinpoche. LC 90-56214. 1992. 26.00 (*0-06-250793-1*) Harper SF.

Tibetan Yoga & Secret Doctrines. Ed. by W. Y. Evans-Wentz. (Illus.). 432p. 1967. reprint ed. pap. 15.95 (*0-19-500278-4*) OUP.

Tibetan Yoga & Secret Doctrines: Or Seven Books of Wisdom of the Great Path. Ed. by Walter Y. Wentz. LC 78-70140. reprint ed. 49.50 (*0-404-17413-2*) AMS Pr.

***Tibetans: Exile in India.** Carol Barker. (Illus.). 50p. (J). 1996. pap. 17.95 (*0-85692-205-6*, Pub. by Gallery Chldrns UK) Assoc Pubs Grp.

Tibeto-Burman Tonology: A Comparative Analysis. Alfons Weidert. LC 87-5140. (Current Issues in Linguistic Theory Ser.: Vol. 5). xvii, 512p. 1987. 124.00 (*90-272-3548-1*) Benjamins North Am.

Tibet's Great Yogi, Milarepa. 2nd ed. Ed. by W. Y. Evans-Wentz. (Illus.). 353p. 1969. reprint ed. pap. 13.95 (*0-19-500301-2*) OUP.

***Tibet's Hidden Wilderness: Wildlife & Nomads of the Chang Tang Reserve.** George B. Schaller. LC 97-821. 1997. write for info. (*0-8109-3893-6*) Abrams.

Tibia and Fibula. Charles Court-Brown & Dietmar Pennig. (Musculoskeletal Trauma Ser.). 208p. Date not set. write for info. (*0-7506-0529-4*) Buttrwrth-Heinemann.

Tibial Nonunion: Diagnosis & Treatment. Ed. by John F. Connolly. LC 91-4558. 71p. 1991. pap. 35.00 (*0-89203-048-8*) Amer Acad Ortho Surg.

Tibial Plateau Fractures. H. Mason Hohl. Ed. by Richard Lampert. 224p. 1997. text ed. 125.00 (*0-7216-7015-6*) Saunders.

Tibull-Studien. Mauriz Schuster. vii, 203p. 1968. reprint ed. write for info. (*0-318-71224-5*) G Olms Pubs.

Tibulle et les Auteurs Du Corpus Tibullianum. Augstin Cartault. 260p. 1981. reprint ed. 55.00 (*3-487-07131-2*) G Olms Pubs.

Tibullus: A Commentary. Michael C. Putnam. (American Philological Association Ser.: Vol. 3). 222p. 1979. pap. 15.95 (*0-8061-1560-2*) U of Okla Pr.

Tibullus: Elegies I. Ed. by P. Murgatroyd. (Bristol Latin Texts Ser.). 348p. (LAT.). 1980. pap. 29.95 (*1-85399-175-9*, Pub. by Brstl Class Pr UK) Focus Pub-R Pullins.

***Tiburones.** (Eyewitness Bks.). (SPA.). (J). 1997. 19.99 (*84-372-3770-X*) Random.

Tiburones. Norman S. Barrett. LC 90-70892. (Biblioteca Grafica Ser.). (Illus.). 32p. (SPA.). (J). (gr. k-4). 1990. lib. bdg. 18.60 (*0-531-07910-4*) Watts.

Tibyan: Memoirs of Abd Allah b. Buluggin, Last Zirid Amir of Granada. Translated from the Emended Arabic Text & Provided with Introduction, Notes & Comments. Amin T. Tibi. (Medieval Iberian Peninsula Ser.: Vol. 5). xiii, 291p. 1986. 64.50 (*90-04-07669-7*) E J Brill.

***Tic-Tac-Toe: Three in a Row.** Judith B. Stamper et al. LC 97-12852. (Hello Math Reader Ser.). (Illus.). (J). 1998. write for info. (*0-590-39963-2*) Scholastic Inc.

TICCIT. M. David Merrill et al. Ed. by Danny G. Langdon. LC 79-24448. (Instructional Design Library). 144p. 1980. 27.95 (*0-87778-160-5*) Educ Tech Pubns.

Ticino Guide. Gerardo Brown-Manrique. LC 89-3635. (Illus.). 192p. (Orig.). 1989. pap. 19.95 (*0-910413-46-0*) Princeton Arch.

Tick. Clay S. Griffith. 160p. (J). (gr. 4-7). 1994. pap. 3.50 (*0-553-48301-3*) Bantam.

***Tick: Mighty Blue Justice!** Greg Hyland. 160p. 1997. pap. 12.00 (*1-57297-250-5*) Blvd Books.

***Tick: Mighty Blue Justice!** Greg Hyland & Chris McCulloch. (Orig.). 1997. pap. 12.00 (*0-614-27408-7*) Blvd Books.

***Tick: Raw Justice.** Acclaim Comics Staff. 1997. mass mkt. 4.50 (*1-57840-085-6*) Acclaim Bks.

Tick: The Naked City. Ben Edlund. (Illus.). 221p. (Orig.). 1996. pap. 14.95 (*1-56924-828-1*) Marlowe & Co.

Tick-Borne Encephalitis & Haemorrhagic Fever with Renal Syndrome in Europe. (EURO Reports & Studies: No. 104). 79p. 1986. pap. text ed. 8.00 (*92-890-1270-6*, 1330104) World Health.

Tick Creek Cave: An Archaic Site in the Gasconade River Valley of Missouri. Ralph G. Roberts. Ed. by Robert T. Bray. (Missouri Archaeologist Ser.: Vol. 27, No. 2). (Illus.). 52p. (Orig.). 1965. pap. 2.00 (*0-943414-44-X*) MO Arch Soc.

Tick-i-ty Ted Joins the Circus. Jane Norman & Frank Beazley. (Adventures of Tick-i-ty Ted Ser.). 24p. (J). (ps-3). 1993. pap. write for info. (*1-883585-01-5*) Pixanne Ent.

Tick-i-ty Ted Meets the Rude Rabbits. Jane Norman & Frank Beazley. (Adventures of Tick-i-ty Ted Ser.). 24p. (J). (ps-3). 1993. pap. write for info. (*1-883585-09-0*) Pixanne Ent.

***Tick Special 1.** Acclaim Comics Staff. 1997. mass mkt. 4.50 (*1-57840-071-6*) Acclaim Bks.

***Tick Tock.** Lena Anderson. LC 97-12075. (J). 1998. write for info. (*0-385-32554-1*, DD Bks Yng Read) BDD Bks Young Read.

Tick-Tock. Eileen Browne. LC 93-927. (Illus.). 32p. (J). (ps up). 1994. 14.95 (*1-56402-300-1*) Candlewick Pr.

Tick-Tock. Dean R. Koontz. 1997. mass mkt. 7.99 (*0-345-38430-X*) Ballantine.

Tick-Tock. large type ed. Dean R. Koontz. LC 95-36490. 1997. pap. 20.00 (*0-679-75873-9*) Random.

Tick Tock. limited ed. Russell Edson. (Illus.). 32p. (Orig.). 1992. 50.00 (*0-918273-72-2*) Coffee Hse.

Tick-Tock. Eileen Browne. LC 93-927. (Illus.). 32p. (J). (gr. k-4). 1996. reprint ed. pap. 5.99 (*1-56402-608-6*) Candlewick Pr.

Tick Tock Clock. Sharon Gordon. LC 81-11393. (J). 1982. pap. 3.50 (*0-89375-677-6*); lib. bdg. 12.95 (*0-89375-676-8*) Troll Communs.

***Tick Tock Clock.** John J. Ollivier. (Wisdom Series for Children). (Illus.). 13p. (Orig.). (J). (gr. k-1). 1996. pap. 5.49 (*1-888995-00-9*) MI GALS.

Tick Tock of Oz. L. Frank Baum. 20.95 (*0-8488-0708-1*) Amereon Ltd.

Tick Tock Tales. Margaret Mahy. (Illus.). 96p. (J). (gr. k-4). 1994. lib. bdg. 16.95 (*0-689-50604-X*, McElderry) S&S Childrens.

Tick Tock the Giant Who Hates Time. Donna R. Davis. 20p. (J). (gr. k-5). 1995. pap. text ed. 9.95 (*0-9644890-0-7*) Spirit Bks.

Tick Tock, You're Dead! R. L. Stine. (Give Yourself Goosebumps Ser.: No. 2). (J). 1995. pap. 3.99 (*0-590-56645-8*) Scholastic Inc.

Tick Vector Biology: Medical & Veterinarian Aspects. Ed. by B. Fifaz et al. (Illus.). 228p. (C). 1993. 120.00 (*0-387-54045-8*) Spr-Verlag.

Tick Vector Biology: Medical & Veterinary Aspects. Ed. by B. Fivaz et al. LC 92-7684. 1992. write for info. (*3-540-54045-8*) Spr-Verlag.

Ticker Symbol Book: 1997 Edition. Standard & Poors Staff. 368p. 1996. pap. text ed. 8.95 (*0-07-052409-2*) McGraw.

***Ticker Symbol Book, 1998.** Standard & Poor's Staff. 1997. pap. text ed. 8.95 (*0-07-052623-0*) McGraw.

Ticker Tape Parade. David O. Blizzard. Ed. by Helon Fife. 390p. (Orig.). 1991. pap. 11.00 (*0-9631324-0-7*) Blizz Bks.

Ticker Tapes. Leah Paransky. 64p. 1978. pap. 3.95 (*0-931642-01-9*) Lintel.

***Ticket: A Fifty-Year Sports Odyssey.** Jack Newcomb. Ed. by John Perry. LC 96-71357. (Illus.). 248p. 1997. 24.00 (*1-887654-25-9*) Premium Pr TN.

Ticket Agent. Jack Rudman. (Career Examination Ser.: C-808). 1994. pap. 23.95 (*0-8373-0808-9*) Nat Learn.

Ticket for a Seamstitch. Mark Harris. LC 84-25627. xxiv, 143p. 1985. reprint ed. pap. 7.95 (*0-8032-7224-3*, Bison Books) U of Nebr Pr.

Ticket That Exploded. William S. Burroughs. LC 86-33486. 217p. 1971. pap. 9.95 (*0-8021-5150-7*, Grove) Grove-Atltic.

Ticket to Canada. Celia B. Lottridge. LC 95-10697. (Illus.). 144p. (J). (gr. 1-4). 1995. 11.95 (*0-382-39144-6*) Silver Burdett Pr.

Ticket to Canada. Celia B. Lottridge. LC 95-10697. (Illus.). 144p. (YA). (gr. 5 up). 1995. pap. 7.95 (*0-382-39146-2*); lib. bdg. 13.95 (*0-382-39145-4*) Silver Burdett Pr.

***Ticket to France.** pap. 10.95 (*0-8442-9161-7*, Passport Bks) NTC Pub Grp.

Ticket to Freedom. Elliot Tiber. 1995. 29.95 (*0-9641806-2-6*) Fest Conserv.

***Ticket to Germany.** pap. 10.95 (*0-8442-9162-5*, Passport Bks) NTC Pub Grp.

Ticket to Harmony. William M. Ross. 94p. (Orig.). (J). (gr. 4-9). 1993. pap. 4.95 (*1-883787-00-9*, Baker & Taylor) Trolley Car.

Ticket to Harmony, Set. William M. Ross. 94p. (Orig.). (J). (gr. 4-9). 1993. teacher ed., pap. 7.95 (*1-883787-01-7*) Trolley Car.

***Ticket to Italy.** pap. 10.95 (*0-8442-9163-3*, Passport Bks) NTC Pub Grp.

Ticket to Life. Esther Whitehead. (Poetry Collection). 69p. (Orig.). 1988. pap. 4.95 (*0-9620688-0-2*) Simonds Pr.

***Ticket to Prague.** James Watson. 192p. 1997. pap. 8.95 (*0-575-06443-9*, Pub. by V Gollancz UK) Trafalgar.

Ticket to Ride. Dennis Potter. 1989. pap. 6.95 (*0-679-72353-6*, Vin) Random.

Ticket to Ride: The Extraordinary Diary of the Beatle's Last Tour. Barry Tashian. (Illus.). 160p. 1996. 19.95 (*0-9646452-4-6*) Dowling Pr.

***Ticket to Spain.** 10.95 (*0-8442-9160-9*, Passport Bks) NTC Pub Grp.

***Ticket to Tallinn.** Hare. 1993. pap. text ed. write for info. (*0-17-556293-8*) Addison-Wesley.

Ticket to the Boneyard. Lawrence Block. 352p. 1991. reprint ed. mass mkt. 5.99 (*0-380-70994-5*) Avon.

Ticket to the Future. Carolyn M. Deckelman. LC 85-72041. 240p. (Orig.). 1985. pap. 1.95 (*0-9615639-0-7*) Callwyn.

Ticket to the Opera: Discovering & Exploring 100 Famous Works, History, Lore & Singers. Phil Goulding. 640p. 1996. 25.00 (*0-449-90900-X*) Fawcett.

Ticket to Toltec: A Mile by Mile Guide for the Cumbres & Toltec Scenic Railroad. Doris B. Osterwald. (Illus.). 128p. 1992. pap. 9.95 (*0-931788-26-9*) Western Guideways.

Ticketing Series: Basic Ticketing; Prepaid Ticketing; Special Ticketing. 4th ed. Barbara A. Krygel. (Illus.). 124p. 1994. pap. text ed. 28.95 (*0-917063-04-X*) Travel Text.

Tickets & Passes of Great Britain & Ireland. W. J. Davis & A. W. Waters. 1977. 40.00 (*0-685-51520-6*) S J Durst.

Tickets for a Prayer Wheel. Annie Dillard. LC 85-45629. 1988. pap. 11.00 (*0-06-091542-0*, PL) HarpC.

Tickets for a Prayer Wheel. Annie Dillard. LC 73-86759. (Breakthrough Bks.). 128p. 1974. reprint ed. 18.95 (*0-8262-0156-3*) U of Mo Pr.

Tickets to Health: Your Healthy Living Calendar. Marshall W. Kreuter et al. 320p. 1995. 9.95 (*0-9646430-0-6*) Hlth TwoThousand.

Tickets to Success. Jim Fay. (Illus.). 112p. (Orig.). 1994. pap. 7.95 (*0-944634-02-8*, Love & Logic Pr) Cline-Fay Inst.

Tickets to the Devil. Powell. 5.95 (*0-910791-41-4*, 0670) Devyn Pr.

Ticking Bombs: Defusing Violence in the Workplace. Michael Mantell. LC 93-44770. 300p. 1994. text ed. 27.00 (*0-7863-0189-9*) Irwin Prof Pubng.

Ticking Time Bombs: The New Conservative Assaults on Democracy. Robert L. Kuttner. 320p. 1996. pap. text ed. 14.00 (*1-56584-346-0*) New Press NY.

Tickle Day: Poems from Father Goose. Charles Ghigna. LC 93-40847. (Illus.). 40p. (J). (ps-2). 1994. 14.95 (*0-7868-0015-1*); lib. bdg. 14.89 (*0-7868-2010-1*) Hyprn Child.

***Tickle Me Big Bird.** Sesame Street Staff. (Lift-&-Peek-a-Board Bks.). (J). 1997. 4.99 (*0-679-88798-9*) Random Bks Yng Read.

***Tickle Me, Elmo.** Stephanie St. Pierre. (J). 1997. 4.99 (*0-679-88754-7*) Random Bks Yng Read.

Tickle My Funny Bone. H. Palmer. (J). 1993. pap. 9.95 incl. audio (*0-7935-2274-9*, 00330600); pap. 12.95 incl. audio compact disk (*0-7935-2292-7*, 00330602) H Leonard.

***Tickle Stories.** Jean Van Leeuwen. (C). 1998. write for info. (*0-8037-2048-3*) Dial Bks Young.

***Tickle Stories.** Jean Van Leeuwen. LC 97-22107. (Illus.). (J). 1998. lib. bdg. write for info. (*0-8037-2049-1*) Dial Bks Young.

Tickled To Death. large type ed. Joan Hess. 1994. pap. 19.95 (*1-56895-079-9*) Wheeler Pub.

Tickled to Death: A Claire Malloy Mystery. Joan Hess. 304p. 1995. mass mkt. 4.99 (*0-451-40550-1*, Onyx) NAL-Dutton.

***Tickled to Death to Go: The Memoirs of a Cavalryman in World War I.** Ed. by Richard Van Emden. (Illus.). 208p. 1996. 34.95 (*1-873376-55-3*, Pub. by Spellmnt Pubs UK) Howell Pr VA.

Tickleoctopus. Audrey Wood. LC 93-26868. (Illus.). 46p. (J). (ps-3). 1994. 15.00 (*0-15-287000-8*) HarBrace.

Tickle's Tale. Stephen Cosgrove. LC 89-60565. (Serendipity Ser.). (Illus.). 32p. (J). (ps-4). 1995. pap. 3.95 (*0-8431-3826-2*) Price Stern Sloan.

Tickles You. (J). 1993. pap. 8.98 (*1-879496-35-6*) Lightyear Entrtnmnt.

Tickley Tiger. Garnett T. Bond. LC 95-70940. (Illus.). 12p. (Orig.). (J). 1995. pap. 9.95 (*1-886225-05-2*) Dageforde Pub.

Tickling Catfish: A Texan Looks at Culture from Amarillo to Borneo. Jerry Craven. LC 96-25540. (Illus.). 160p. (Orig.). 1996. pap. 14.95 (*0-89096-728-8*) Tex A&M Univ Pr.

***Tickling the Dragon's Tail & Yarns of the Cold War Era.** Frank J. Willig. LC 96-90693. (Orig.). 1997. pap. 12.95 (*0-533-12230-9*) Vantage.

Tickling Tigers. Anna Currey. (Educational Ser.). (J). 1996. pap. 5.95 (*0-8120-9594-4*) Barron.

Tickling Tigers. Anna Currey. (J). (ps-3). 1996. 12.95 (*0-8120-6594-8*) Barron.

***Ticklish Tales for Tellers: 99 Jokes & Riddles about Storytellers.** Iva P. Andriddle. Ed. by Christine P. Kallevig. (Illus.). 32p. 1997. pap. 4.99 (*0-9628769-5-X*) Storytime Ink.

***Ticklish Timmy.** (Little Monsters Ser.). (J). 1997. write for info. (*0-614-21792-X*, Pub. by Splash UK) Assoc Pubs Grp.

***Ticks.** Patrick Merrick. LC 96-47082. (Nature Bks.). 32p. (J). (gr. 1-5). 1997. lib. bdg. 22.79 (*1-56766-384-2*) Childs World.

Ticks: And What You Can Do about Them. Roger Drummond. LC 90-12236. (Illus.). 60p. (Orig.). 1990. pap. 4.95 (*0-89997-116-4*) Wilderness Pr.

Tick...Tick...Tick... Suspenseful Tale of Outrageous Medical Ignorance. Roberta Crawford. Ed. by Alan Britt. LC 94-61928. 375p. 1995. 16.95 (*0-9632547-2-3*) Vida Pub.

***Ticktock.** Dean R. Koontz. (Orig.). 1997. mass mkt. 7.99 (*0-614-27714-0*) Ballantine.

***Ticky-Tacky Doll.** Cynthia Rylant. LC 97-20281. (Illus.). (J). 1920. write for info. (*0-15-201078-5*) HarBrace.

Ticlopidine, Platelets, & Vascular Disease. Ed. by William K. Hass & J. Donald Easton. LC 92-48386. 1993. 83.00 (*0-387-94009-X*) Spr-Verlag.

Ticlopidine, Platelets, & Vascular Disease. Ed. by William K. Hass & J. Donald Easton. LC 92-48386. 1994. write for info. (*3-540-94009-X*) Spr-Verlag.

***Ticonderoga: Tales of an Enchanted Yacht.** Jack A. Somer. LC 97-16311. (Illus.). 264p. 1997. 60.00 (*0-393-04613-3*) Concepts Pub.

An Asterisk (*) at the beginning of an entry indicates that the title is appearing in BIP for the first time.

Tics, Tics & Tics: Figures, Syllogismes, Recit Dans les Chants de Maldoror. Ora Avni. LC 84-81849. (French Forum Monographs: No. 54). 186p. (Orig.). 1984. pap. 13.45 (*0-917058-54-2*) French Forum.

Tidal Current Tables, Atlantic Coast of North America, 1983. (Illus.). 235p. 1991. pap. text ed. 20.00 (*1-879778-31-9*, BK-518) Marine Educ.

Tidal Current Tables 1996: Pacific Coast of North America & Asia. National Oceanic & Atmospheric Administration Staff. 1995. pap. text ed. 12.95 (*0-07-046125-2*) McGraw.

Tidal Current Tables 1997: Atlantic Coast of North America. National Oceanic & Atmospheric Administration Staff. 216p. 1996. pap. text ed. 13.95 (*0-07-047084-7*) McGraw.

Tidal Current Tables 1997: Pacific Coast of North America & Asia. National Oceanic & Atmospheric Administration Staff. 224p. 1996. pap. text ed. 13.95 (*0-07-047085-5*) McGraw.

Tidal Energy: or Time & Tide Wait for No Man. G. F. Duff. (Illus.). 40p. 1984. 14.00 (*0-917853-02-4*, IO15) Am Assn Physics.

Tidal Estuaries: Manual of Sampling & Analytical Procedures. K. L. Kramer et al. (Illus.). 314p. (C). 1994. text ed. 75.00 (*90-5410-601-8*, Pub. by A A Balkema NE) Ashgate Pub Co.

Tidal Flat Ecology. K. Reise. (Ecological Studies: Vol. 54). (Illus.). 210p. 1985. 93.95 (*0-387-15447-7*) Spr-Verlag.

Tidal Flat Estuaries. Ed. by J. W. Baretta & P. Ruardij. (Ecological Studies: Vol. 71). (Illus.). 360p. 1988. 158.95 (*0-387-19323-5*) Spr-Verlag.

Tidal Friction & the Earth's Rotation, Bielefeld, FRG, 1981: Proceedings. Ed. by F. Brosche & J. Suendermann. (Illus.). 345p. 1982. 54.95 (*0-387-12011-4*) Spr-Verlag.

Tidal Havens of the Wash & Humber. Henry Irving. 66p. 1983. 65.00 (*0-685-09793-5*, Pub. by Imray Laurie Norie & Wilson UK) St Mut.

Tidal Havens of the Wash & Humber. 4th rev. ed. Ed. by Henry Irving. 72p. (C). 1991. 90.00 (*0-85288-159-2*, Pub. by Imray Laurie Norie & Wilson UK) St Mut.

Tidal Havens of Wash & Humber. Imray, Laurie, Norie & Wilson Ltd. Staff. 66p. (C). 1988. pap. 50.00 (*0-685-40207-X*, Pub. by Imray Laurie Norie & Wilson UK) St Mut.

Tidal Hydrodynamics. Ed. by Bruce B. Parker. LC 91-16603. 912p. 1991. text ed. 145.00 (*0-471-51498-5*) Wiley.

Tidal Instrumentation & Predictions of Tides Symposium: Proceedings, Paris, 1965. (Publications Scientifique Ser.). 242p. 1967. write for info. (*0-318-14528-6*) Intl Assoc Phys Sci Ocean.

Tidal Marsh Plants. Lionel N. Eleuterius. LC 90-6718. (Illus.). 160p. (C). 1990. 27.50 (*0-88289-795-0*) Pelican.

Tidal Marshes of Long Island Sound: Ecology, History & Restoration. Ed. by Glenn D. Dreyer & William A. Niering. (Connecticut College Arboretum Bulletin Ser.: No. 34). (Illus.). 73p. (Orig.). 1995. pap. 5.00 (*1-878899-05-8*) CT Coll Arboretum.

Tidal Mixing & Plankton Dynamics. Ed. by M. J. Bowman et al. (Lecture Notes on Coastal & Estuarine Studies: Vol. 17). (Illus.). x, 502p. 1986. 128.95 (*0-387-96346-4*) Spr-Verlag.

***Tidal Models.** John Birtwhistle. Date not set. pap. 14.95 (*0-85646-052-4*, Pub. by Anvil Press UK) Dufour.

Tidal News. John Curl. 108p. (Orig.). 1982. pap. 5.00 (*0-938392-02-6*) Homeward Pr.

***Tidal Phenomena.** Helmut Wilhelm et al. LC 97-20660. (Lecture Notes in Earth Sciences Ser.). 1997. pap. write for info. (*3-540-62833-9*) Spr-Verlag.

Tidal Power: Symposium Proceedings. 338p. 1987. 79.00 (*0-7277-0390-0*) Am Soc Civil Eng.

Tidal Power & Estuary Management. Ed. by R. T. Severn et al. (Colston Paper Ser.: No. 30). (Illus.). 296p. 1979. 65.00 (*0-85608-023-3*) Transatl Arts.

Tidal Signatures in Modern & Ancient Sediments. Ed. by B. W. Flemming & A. Bartholoma. (International Association of Sedimentologists Special Publication: No. 24). 1995. 75.00 (*0-86542-978-2*) Blackwell Sci.

Tidal Swings of the Stock Market. Scribner Browne. LC 92-74294. 120p. (C). 1992. reprint ed. pap. 12.00 (*0-87034-106-5*) Fraser Pub Co.

Tidal Waterways of Arnhem Bay: Darwarunga, Habgood, Baralminer, Gobalpa, Coromuro, Cato, Peter John & Burungbirinung Rivers see Surveys of Tidal River Systems in the Northern Territory & Their Crocodile Populations

Tidal Waterways of Castlereagh Bay & Hutchinson & Cadell Straits: Bennett, Darbitla, Djigaglia Djabura, Ngandadauda Creeks & the Glyde & Woolen Rivers see Surveys of Tidal River Systems in the Northern Territory & Their Crocodile Populations

Tidal Waterways of the Van Diemen Gulf: Ilamary; River, Iwalg, Saltwater & Minimini: Creeks & Coastal Arms on Cobourg Peninsula. Resurveys of the Alligator Region Rivers see Surveys of Tidal River Systems in the Northern Territory & Their Crocodile Populations

Tidal Waterways on the South-Western Coast of the Gulf of Carpentaria: Limmen Bight Towns, Roper, Phelp & Wilson Rivers; Nayarupi, Wungguliyanga, Painnyilatya, Mangkurdurrungku & Yiwapa Creeks see Surveys of Tidal River Systems in the Northern Territory & Their Crocodile Populations

Tidal Waterways on the Southern Coast of the Gulf of Carpentaria: Calvert, Robinson, Wearyan & McArthur Rivers & Some Intervening Creeks see Surveys of Tidal River Systems in the Northern Territory & Their Crocodile Populations

Tidal Wave. Werner Reichhold. (Illus.). 170p. (Orig.). 1989. pap. 14.00 (*0-944676-12-X*) AHA Bks.

Tidal Wave: A Disaster Book. Christopher Lampton. (J). (gr. 4-7). 1992. pap. 6.52 (*0-395-62464-9*) HM.

Tidal Waves of School Reform: Types of Reform, Government Controls, & Community Advocates. Samuel Mitchell. LC 96-16281. 224p. 1996. text ed. 55.00 (*0-275-95644-X*, Praeger Pubs) Greenwood.

Tidbits for Thought: From the Journal of Willis F. Cox. Willis F. Cox. LC 83-90752. (Illus.). (Orig.). 1983. pap. 6.95 (*0-9610758-0-5*) W F Cox.

Tidbits for Young Doctors & Their Patients: Journal of a Country Doctor, Pt. II. Donald L. Martin. (Orig.). 1993. pap. 9.95 (*1-55673-528-6*) CSS OH.

Tidbits Treasury of Trivia & Compendium of Miscellany: Odd & Obscure, Amazing & Amusing Facts, Stories, & Statistics. J. Spencer. (Tidbits Ser.: Vol. One). (Illus.). 155p. (Orig.). 1995. pap. 10.00 (*0-9645583-0-0*, TBVI) Jes Pr.

Tide & Continuities: Last & First Poems, 1995-1938. Peter Viereck. LC 95-20274. 400p. 1995. 42.00 (*1-55728-313-3*) U of Ark Pr.

Tide & Continuities: Last & First Poems, 1995-1938. Peter Viereck. LC 95-20274. 400p. 1995. pap. 24.00 (*1-55728-314-1*) U of Ark Pr.

Tide & Current: Fishponds of Hawai'i. Carol A. Wyban. LC 92-10426. (Illus.). 1992. text ed. 28.00 (*0-8248-1396-0*, Kolowalu Bk) UH Pr.

Tide, Distance & Speed Tables. Brown, Son & Ferguson Ltd. Staff. (C). 1987. 30.00 (*0-85174-544-X*, Pub. by Brwn Son Ferg) St Mut.

Tide-Drift Shells of the Monterey Bay Region. Hulda H. McLean. LC 92-81082. (Illus.). 72p. (Orig.). 1992. pap. 9.95 (*0-9632480-0-6*) Santa Cruz Mus Assn.

Tide Is Right. Hugo Charteris. LC 90-14062. (Illus.). x, 145p. 1991. 19.95 (*0-916583-71-6*) Dalkey Arch.

Tide Is Right. Hugo Charteris. (Illus.). 145p. 1992. reprint ed. pap. 9.95 (*0-916583-78-3*) Dalkey Arch.

Tide Lines. Larry Charrier. 190p. 1994. pap. 6.95 (*0-9640637-0-0*) Great Wave AK.

***Tide of Chariots.** large type ed. Henry Chesham. (Linford Mystery Library). 384p. 1996. pap. 15.99 (*0-7089-7934-3*) Ulverscroft.

***Tide of Destiny.** Betty Z. Watson. Date not set. write for info. (*1-885181-01-9*) Watson Pubns.

Tide of Life. Catherine Cookson. 512p. 1993. mass mkt. 7.99 (*0-552-10630-5*) Bantam.

Tide of Victory. William Reed. (Soldiers of War Ser.: No. 03). 1991. mass mkt. 3.50 (*0-373-63403-X*) Harlequin Bks.

Tide Pool. Christiane Gunzi. LC 92-52823. (Look Closer Ser.). (Illus.). 32p. (J). (gr. 1-4). 1992. 9.95 (*1-56458-131-4*) DK Pub Inc.

Tide Pools. Jason Cooper. LC 92-16074. (Sea Discovery Library). (J). 1992. 12.67 (*0-86593-234-4*); lib. bdg. 9.50 (*0-685-59716-4*) Rourke Corp.

Tide Pools & Coral Reefs: A Thematic Unit. Jeanne King. Ed. by Patricia M. Sima. (Thematic Units Ser.). (Illus.). 80p. 1993. student ed. 9.95 (*1-55734-249-0*) Tchr Create Mat.

Tide Pools of Southern California: An Illustrated Guide to 100 Locations. Linda Tway. (Illus.). 160p. (C). 1991. reprint ed. lib. bdg. 41.00 (*0-8095-4082-7*) Borgo Pr.

Tide-Race. Brenda Chamberlain. (Illus.). 228p. 9600. pap. 14.95 (*0-907476-65-1*, Pub. by Seren Bks UK) Dufour.

Tide Race. Brian Morris. (C). 1976. pap. 20.00 (*0-85088-420-9*, Pub. by Gomer Pr UK) St Mut.

Tide Tables, East Coast of North & South America, 1983. (Illus.). 285p. 1991. pap. text ed. 22.00 (*1-879778-30-0*, BK-517) Marine Educ.

Tide Tables 1996: East Coast of North America & South America, Including Greenland. National Oceanic & Atmospheric Administration Staff. 1995. pap. text ed. 13.95 (*0-07-046122-8*) McGraw.

Tide Tables 1997: East Coast of North & South America. National Oceanic & Atmospheric Administration Staff. 320p. 1996. pap. text ed. 14.95 (*0-07-047087-1*) McGraw.

Tide Tables 1997: West Coast of North & South America. National Oceanic & Atmospheric Administration Staff. 304p. 1996. pap. text ed. 14.95 (*0-07-047086-3*) McGraw.

***Tide Tables 1998: East Coast of North & South America, Including Greenland.** 1997. pap. text ed. 13.95 (*0-07-047119-3*) McGraw.

***Tide Tables 1998: Europe & West Coast of Africa, including the Mediterranean Sea.** Noaa. 1997. pap. text ed. 25.95 (*0-07-047116-9*) McGraw.

Tide Tarrieth No Man. George Wapull. LC 77-133756. (Tudor Facsimile Texts. Old English Plays Ser.: No. 50). reprint ed. 59.50 (*0-404-53350-7*) AMS Pr.

Tideaway Torment. Ed. by Hilbert Hardy. 176p. (C). 1988. 35.00 (*0-7212-0810-X*, Pub. by Regency Press UK) St Mut.

Tidecraft: The Boats of South Carolina, Georgia, & Northeastern Florida, 1550-1950. 2nd ed. William E. Fleetwood, Jr. LC 94-60888. (Illus.). 1995. 47.50 (*0-9642519-0-6*) WBG Marine Pr.

Tideland Treasure. Todd Ballantine. (Illus.). 222p. 1991. reprint ed. pap. 15.95 (*0-87249-795-X*) U of SC Pr.

Tidelands Oil Controversy. Ernest R. Bartley. Ed. by Stuart Bruchey. LC 78-53555. (Development of Public Land Law in the U. S. Ser.). 1979. reprint ed. lib. bdg. 25.95 (*0-405-11368-4*) Ayer.

***Tidelog 1997: Chesapeake Tidewater Edition.** Mark A. Brown. (Illus.). 144p. 1996. 12.95 (*0-936521-60-0*) Pac Pubs.

***Tidelog 1997: Long Island Sound Edition.** Mark A. Born. (Illus.). 144p. 1996. 12.95 (*0-936521-59-7*) Pac Pubs.

***Tidelog 1997: MidAtlantic Edition.** Mark A. Born. (Illus.). 144p. 1996. 12.95 (*0-936521-58-9*) Pac Pubs.

***Tidelog 1997: Northern California Edition.** Mark A. Born. (Illus.). 144p. 1996. 12.95 (*0-936521-53-8*) Pac Pubs.

***Tidelog 1997: Northern New England Edition.** Mark A. Born. (Illus.). 128p. 1996. 12.95 (*0-936521-56-2*) Pac Pubs.

***Tidelog 1997: Puget Sound Edition.** Mark A. Born. (Illus.). 160p. 1996. 12.95 (*0-936521-55-4*) Pac Pubs.

***Tidelog 1997: Southeastern Edition.** Mark A. Born. (Illus.). 144p. 1996. 12.95 (*0-936521-61-9*) Pac Pubs.

***Tidelog 1997: Southern California Edition.** Mark A. Born. (Illus.). 128p. 1996. 12.95 (*0-936521-54-6*) Pac Pubs.

***Tidelog 1997: Southern New England Edition.** Mark A. Born. (Illus.). 128p. 1996. 12.95 (*0-936521-57-0*) Pac Pubs.

Tidemarsh Guide. Mervin F. Roberts. LC 79-63522. (Tidemarsh Guides Ser.). (Illus.). 240p. 1985. 5.95 (*0-933614-19-5*) M Roberts.

Tidemarsh Guide to Fishes. Mervin F. Roberts. LC 85-90364. (Tidemarsh Guides Ser.). (Illus.). 370p. (Orig.). 1985. 10.95 (*0-9615047-0-6*) M Roberts.

Tidepool & Nearshore Fishes of California. John E. Fitch & Robert J. Lavenberg. (California Natural History Guides Ser.: No. 38). (Illus.). 1975. pap. 7.95 (*0-520-02845-7*) U CA Pr.

Tidepool & Reef. Rick M. Harbo. (Illus.). 56p. 1988. pap. 6.95 (*0-88839-039-4*) Hancock House.

Tidepools: The Bright World of the Rocky Shoreline. rev. ed. Diana Barnhart & Vicki Leon. LC 94-31822. (Close up: A Focus on Nature Ser.). (Illus.). 48p. (YA). (gr. 5 up). 1994. pap. 7.95 (*0-382-24867-8*); lib. bdg. 14.95 (*0-382-24865-1*) Silver Burdett Pr.

Tidepools of Southern California: An Illustrated Guide. Linda Tway. LC 90-19864. (Illus.). 176p. 1991. pap. 15.95 (*0-88496-322-5*) Capra Pr.

Tides. Philippe Van Rjndt. LC 87-47889. 560p. 1988. 18.95 (*0-318-32612-4*) Bantam.

Tides. George W. Bunton. LC 67-2157. (Bernice P. Bishop Museum Special Publications: No. 54). (Illus.). 24p. reprint ed. pap. 25.00 (*0-685-20291-7*, 2030324) Bks Demand.

Tides Vol. III: An Anthology, Creative Works of Women in the Second Half of Life. 109p. 1995. pap. write for info. (*0-9647558-0-7*) WRCUR.

***Tides & Ceremonies.** Lorne Patterson. LC 97-13833. 64p. 1997. pap. 12.95 (*0-7734-2820-8*, Mellen Poetry Pr) E Mellen.

Tides & Currents. David Arnold. 64p. (C). 1990. text ed. 59.00 (*0-906754-24-0*, Pub. by Fernhurst Bks UK) St Mut.

Tides in the Affairs of Men. Edgar L. Smith. LC 89-85656. 178p. 1989. reprint ed. pap. 15.00 (*0-87034-090-5*) Fraser Pub Co.

Tides in Time. Douglas I. Busch. LC 96-92051. (Illus.). 56p. (Orig.). 1996. 40.00 (*0-88496-413-2*) Capra Pr.

***Tides in Time.** deluxe limited ed. Douglas I. Busch. LC 96-3015. (Illus.). 56p. (Orig.). 1996. 250.00 (*0-88496-414-0*) Capra Pr.

Tides of Change: A Guide to the Harraseeket District of Freeport, Maine. Bruce Jacobson et al. (Illus.). 88p. (Orig.). 1985. pap. 6.95 (*0-9613259-0-9*) Freeport Hist.

Tides of Change: Faces of the Northwest Coast. Sheryl McFarlane. (Illus.). 32p. (J). (gr. k-4). 1995. 14.95 (*1-55143-040-1*) Orca Bk Pubs.

Tides of Ecstasy. Luanne Walden. 1981. mass mkt. 3.25 (*0-89083-769-4*, Zebra Kensgtn) Kensgtn Pub Corp.

Tides of Empire: Discussions on the Expansion of Britain Overseas. Gerald Graham. LC 72-82242. 120p. reprint ed. pap. 34.20 (*0-317-26049-9*, 2023840) Bks Demand.

***Tides of History.** Louis Lavoie. LC 96-95301. (Illus.). 350p. (Orig.). 1997. pap. 14.95 (*1-57502-385-7*, P01220) Morris Pubng.

Tides of History: The Pacific Islands in the Twentieth Century. Ed. by K. R. Howe et al. LC 93-34015. (C). 1994. pap. text ed. 22.00 (*0-8248-1597-1*) UH Pr.

***Tides of Influence.** Stella Humphreys. Ed. & Tr. by Betsy Whitmore. (Illus.). 88p. 1996. pap. 12.95 (*0-9654037-0-X*) B W W Pub.

***Tides of Loon Island.** Martha D. Peterson. 1996. mass mkt. 4.99 (*1-55197-123-2*, Pub. by Comnwlth Pub CN) Partners Pubs Grp.

Tides of Love. large type ed. Helen McCabe. (Linford Romance library). 224p. 1996. pap. 15.99 (*0-7089-7890-8*, Linford) Ulverscroft.

Tides of Migration: A Study of Migration Decision-Making & Social Progress in Sao Miguel, Azores. Francis W. Chapin. LC 89-6507. (Immigrant Communities & Ethnic Minorities in the U. S. & Canada Ser.: No. 64). 1989. 64.50 (*0-404-19474-5*) AMS Pr.

Tides of Mont St. Michel. Roger Vercel. Tr. by Warre B. Wells. LC 78-100213. 305p. 1971. reprint ed. text ed. 35.00 (*0-8371-4052-8*, VEMM, Greenwood Pr) Greenwood.

Tides of Morning. Mei Mei Evans et al. 95p. 1987. 7.00 (*0-914221-05-1*) Vanessapress.

***Tides of Reform: Making Government Work, 1945-1995.** Paul C. Light. LC 96-38557. 1997. write for info. (*0-300-06987-1*) Yale U Pr.

Tides of the Heart. large type ed. Diana Bachmann. Orig. Title: Janthina. 560p. 1987. 27.99 (*0-7089-8444-4*, Charnwood) Ulverscroft.

Tides of the Planet Earth. 2nd ed. P. Melchoir. LC 82-16567. (Illus.). 648p. 1983. 284.00 (*0-08-026248-1*, Pub. by Pergamon Repr UK) Franklin.

Tides of War. Peter Vine & Michael McKinnon. 192p. (C). 1995. 54.00 (*0-907151-65-5*, Pub. by IMMEL Pubng UK) St Mut.

Tides of War: World News Reporting 1931-1945. Robert W. Desmond. LC 84-2504. (World News Reporting Ser.: Vol. IV). 608p. 1984. text ed. 75.00 (*0-87745-125-7*) U of Iowa Pr.

Tides of Youth. large type ed. Nelle M. Scanlan. 608p. 1982. 25.99 (*0-7089-0849-7*) Ulverscroft.

***Tide's Table: Maritime Cooking from Inn on the Cove.** Ross Mavis & Willa Mavis. (Illus.). 184p. 1996. pap. 16.95 (*0-86492-208-6*, Pub. by Goose Ln Edits CN) Genl Dist Srvs.

Tidewater Bobber Fishing for Chinook Salmon. Gene Martin. (Illus.). 32p. 1993. pap. 6.95 (*1-878175-54-8*) F Amato Pubns.

Tidewater by Steamboat: A Saga of the Chesapeake. David C. Holly. LC 90-27826. (Illus.). 352p. 1991. 34.95 (*0-8018-4168-2*) Johns Hopkins.

Tidewater Fishing: The Complete Guide to Eastern Virginia Waters. Skip Miller. LC 93-9061. 256p. 1993. pap. 11.95 (*1-56943-007-1*, Tribune) Contemp Bks.

Tidewater Lover. Janet Dailey. 1992. mass mkt. 3.59 (*0-373-89896-7*, 1-89896-4) Harlequin Bks.

Tidewater Morning. William Styron. 1994. pap. 10.00 (*0-679-75449-0*, Vin) Random.

Tidewater Morning. limited ed. William Styron. 1993. Ltd. ed. 100.00 (*0-679-42963-8*) Random.

Tidewater Morning: Three Tales from Youth. William Styron. LC 93-3639. 1993. 17.00 (*0-679-42742-2*) Random.

Tidewater Morning: Three Tales from Youth. large type ed. William Styron. LC 93-43829. 1993. 21.95 (*1-56895-048-9*) Wheeler Pub.

Tidewater on the Half Shell: Fine Virginia Recipes. Junior League of Norfolk, Virginia Beach, Inc. Staff. LC 85-60705. 354p. 1985. 16.95 (*0-9614767-0-2*) Jr League Norfolk.

Tidewater Place: Portrait of the Willapa Ecosystem. Edward C. Wolf. (Illus.). 48p. (Orig.). 1993. pap. 9.95 (*0-89886-400-3*) Mountaineers.

Tidewater Seduction. Anne Mather. (Presents Plus Ser.). 1993. mass mkt. 2.99 (*0-373-11591-1*, 1-11591-4) Harlequin Bks.

Tidewater Seduction. large type ed. Anne Mather. (Harlequin Ser.). 1993. 19.95 (*0-263-13356-7*, Pub. by Mills & Boon UK) Thorndike Pr.

Tidewater Tales: A Novel. John Barth. 656p. 1988. pap. 15.00 (*0-449-90293-5*, Columbine) Fawcett.

***Tidewater Tales: A Novel.** John Barth & Mary Johnston. (Maryland Paperback Bookshelf Ser.). (Illus.). 656p. 1997. reprint ed. pap. 16.95 (*0-8018-5556-X*) Johns Hopkins.

Tidewater Time Capsule: History Beneath the Patuxent. Donald G. Shomette. LC 94-39900. (Illus.). 384p. 1995. 29.95 (*0-87033-463-8*, Tidewtr Pubs) Cornell Maritime.

Tidewater Virginia with Children: Where to Go & What to Do in Williamsburg, Jamestown, Yorktown, Hampton & Newport News. Barbara M. Wohlford & Mary L. Eley. LC 96-6883. (Illus.). 240p. (Orig.). 1996. pap. 9.95 (*0-940159-38-4*) Camino Bks.

Tidings. James Broughton. 70p. 1965. boxed 10.00 (*0-931757-03-7*) Pterodactyl Pr.

***Tidings.** Nick Mezins. 540p. (Orig.). 1997. mass mkt. 6.99 (*1-55237-357-6*, Pub. by Comnwlth Pub CN) Partners Pubs Grp.

Tidings from the Eighteenth Century. Beth Gilgun. Ed. by Linda C. Scurlock. LC 93-84593. (Illus.). 277p. 1993. pap. 24.95 (*1-880655-04-7*) Scurlock Pub.

***Tidings of Comfort & Joy.** T. Davis Bunn. LC 97-24436. (Illus.). 128p. 1997. 12.99 (*0-7852-7203-8*) Nelson.

***Tidings of Great Joy.** Sandra Brown. 240p. 1997. 17.95 (*0-553-10403-9*) Bantam.

Tidings of the King: A Translation & Ethnohistorical Analysis of the Rayavacakamu. Phillip B. Wagoner. LC 93-18879. (Illus.). 256p. (C). 1993. text ed. 38.00 (*0-8248-1495-9*) UH Pr.

Tidings of the Resurrection & Tidings of Doomsday. Ed. & Tr. by Whitley Stokes from IRI. 1996. pap. 10.00 (*0-89979-082-8*) British Am Bks.

Tidings to a Tick, Vol. 1. Carolyn E. Cardwell. (Illus.). 225p. (Orig.). 1988. pap. 10.95 (*0-916395-17-0*, TT-1) Hieroglyphics.

Tidoon. Robert L. Olivier. LC 70-18934. 83p. 1972. 12.95 (*0-911116-62-1*) Pelican.

Tidy Bowl Man Lives & Jiffy John: Two Comic Novellas. Douglas H. Young. 368p. 21.95 (*0-9606510-0-4*) Writers Pub Hse.

Tidy Lady. Anne M. Lindbergh. LC 88-10905. (Illus.). 32p. (J). (ps-3). 1989. 14.00 (*0-15-287150-0*) HarBrace.

Tidy Titch. Pat Hutchins. LC 90-38483. (Illus.). 32p. (J). (ps up). 1991. 16.00 (*0-688-09963-7*); lib. bdg. 15.93 (*0-688-09964-5*) Greenwillow.

Tidy Titch. Pat Hutchins. LC 90-38483. (Illus.). 32p. (J). (ps up). 1995. reprint ed. pap. 4.95 (*0-688-13648-6*, Mulberry) Morrow.

***Tidy Universe of Islands.** William Peck. Ed. by Franz Broswimmer. (Illus.). 196p. 1996. pap. 14.95 (*1-56647-117-6*) Mutual Pub HI.

***Tidy-Up Spider.** Monique Hagen & Hans Hagen. LC 97-23385. (Illus.). (J). 1997. write for info. (*1-57379-027-3*) High-Scope.

***Tidy up, Trevor.** Rob Lewis. (Illus.). 28p. (J). 3.98 (*0-8317-0014-9*) Smithmark.

Tidy's Physiotherapy. 12th ed. A. M. Thompson et al. (Illus.). 448p. 1991. pap. 50.00 (*0-7506-1346-7*, Pub. by John Wright UK) Buttrwrth-Heinemann.

Tie a Bow, Ben Bunny: A Lacing Book with Step-by-Step Instructions. Mavis Smith. 24p. (J). (ps-1). 1996. 9.95 (*0-590-87188-9*, Cartwheel) Scholastic Inc.

Tie a String Around Your Finger: The History & Lore of Knots. Ellen Jackson. LC 93-41042. (Illus.). (J). 1996. 14.95 (*0-395-68710-1*) Ticknor & Fields.

Tie-Dye, Back by Popular Demand. Virginia Gleser. (Illus.). 48p. (J). (gr. 2 up). 1995. pap. text ed. write for info. (*0-9647247-0-7*) Harmony Enter.

Tie Dying. Celia Buchanan. 1995. (*0-7858-0315-7*) Bk Sales Inc.

T

Tie Fighter: Defender of the Empire: Official Secrets & Solutions. Rusel Demaria. 1995. pap. text ed. 12.95 (0-7615-0142-8) Prima Pub.

TIE Fighter Collector's CD-ROM: The Official Strategy Guide. Rusel Demaria. 1996. pap. 19.99 (0-7615-0276-9) Prima Pub.

Tie Fighter, the Official Strategy Guide. Rusel DeMaria. 1994. pap. 19.95 (1-55958-519-6) Prima Pub.

Tie Man's Miracle. Steven Schnur. LC 94-39854. (Illus.). 32p. (J). (gr. k up). 1995. lib. bdg. 15.93 (0-688-13464-5, Morrow Junior) Morrow.

Tie Man's Miracle. Steven Schnur. (Illus.). 1995. 16.00 (0-614-06505-4, Morrow Junior) Morrow.

Tie Man's Miracle: A Chanukah Tale. Steven Schnur. LC 94-39854. (Illus.). 32p. (J). (gr. k up). 1995. 16.00 (0-688-13463-7, Morrow Junior) Morrow.

Tie Me up with Rainbows: A Guide to Beauty & Color for You & Your Home. Bernice Kentner. (Illus.). 205p. (C). 1980. 14.95 (0-941522-02-4, 788-156) Ken Kra Pubs.

Tie My Bones to Her Back. Robert F. Jones. 256p. 1996. 23.00 (0-374-27759-1) FS&G.

***Tie My Bones to Her Back.** Robert F. Jones. LC 96-43983. 412p. 1997. 22.95 (0-7838-1986-2, GK Hall) Thorndike Pr.

Tie That Binds. Winnie Corley. LC 83-61020. (Illus.). 155p. 1983. 14.95 (0-9611478-0-6) Evans Pubns.

Tie That Binds. Kent Haruf. 256p. 1991. pap. 9.95 (0-8050-1869-7, Owl) H Holt & Co.

Tie That Binds: A Collection of Writings about Fathers & Daughters - Mothers & Sons. 2nd ed. Ed. by Sandra H. Martz. (Illus.). 165p. 1992. 18.00 (0-918949-20-3); pap. 10.00 (0-918949-19-X) Papier-Mache Press.

Tie That Binds: Harvey United with Lake, Bridgewater, Clark, Smith, Carter, Dotterer, Other Families. Marilyn L. Landreth & Roy H. Smith. (Illus.). 224p. (Orig.). 1996. pap. 25.00 (0-9649896-0-3, 750) Muddy Water.

Tie the Moon to Your Car: My Cancer, My Way. Marcia C. Rolof. 1994. 10.95 (0-533-10890-X) Vantage.

Tie up the Strong Man. Carson Reed. 50p. 1989. pap. 6.95 (0-912549-14-9) Bread & Butter.

Tie Your Shoes! Sue Hendra. LC 96-24576. (J). 1997. 12.99 (0-517-70953-8) Crown Pub Group.

Tiebacks for Bulkheads. Ed. by Donald R. McMahon. (Sessions Proceedings, Geotechnical Special Publication Ser.: No. 4). 90p. 1986. 13.00 (0-317-60383-3, 525-1) Am Soc Civil Eng.

Tiebreaker. Jack Bickham. 320p. 1990. pap. 4.99 (0-8125-0050-4) Tor Bks.

Tieck Ludwig: Kritische Schriften Zum Ersten Malgesammelt und Mit Einer Vorrede Herausgegeben Von Ludwig Tieck, 4 vols. 1433p. (C). 1974. reprint ed. 215.40 (3-11-002348-2) De Gruyter.

***Tied Flies: The Fisherman's Companion.** Ariel Books Staff. (Tiny Tomes Ser.). 128p. 1997. 3.95 (0-8362-2665-8, Arie Bks) Andrews & McMeel.

Tied to Masonic Apron Strings. Stewart M. Pollard. Ed. by Lewis C. Cook. vi, 121p. 1991. pap. 6.00 (0-88053-059-6, M-322) Macoy Pub.

Tied to the Land: Living Conditions of Labourers on Large Farms in Trans Nzioa District Kenya. Ed. by Dick Foeker & Nina Tellegen. 172p. 1995. 38.95 (1-85628-913-3, Pub. by Avebury Pub UK) Ashgate Pub Co.

Tied Together: Topics & Thoughts for Introducing Children's Books. Charlotte Leonard. LC 80-11135. 261p. 1980. lib. bdg. 29.50 (0-8108-1293-2) Scarecrow.

***Tied up in Knots.** Carl Sommer. LC 96-22014. (Another Sommer-Time Story Ser.). (Illus.). 48p. (J). (gr. 1-4). 1997. lib. bdg. 14.95 (1-57537-050-6) Advance Pub.

Tiefkuhl Lexikon. G. Doring & Rudolphi Doring. 19.95 (0-8288-7713-0, M7666) Fr & Eur.

Tiefkuhl Lexikon. G. Doring & Rudolphi. 239p. (GER.). 19.95 (3-87150-020-8, M-7666) Fr & Eur.

Tiempo. National Science Resources Center Staff. Tr. by DTS Language Services Staff. (Science & Technology for Children Ser.). (Illus.). 16p. (Orig.). (SPA.). (J). (gr. 1). 1995. wbk. ed., pap. text ed. write for info. (0-89278-715-5) Carolina Biological.

Tiempo. 2nd ed. Ana M. Ausejo. 264p. (SPA.). 1991. pap. 17.95 (0-7859-4994-1) Fr & Eur.

Tiempo: Spanish Take-Home Parent Pack, Set. (Take-Home Parent Packs Ser.). (Illus.). (Orig.). (SPA.). 1993. student ed., teacher ed., pap. 11.95 (1-56334-388-6) Hampton-Brown.

Tiempo al Tiempo. Isaac Goldemberg. 172p. (SPA.). 1983. pap. 10.00 (0-910061-18-1, 1111) Ediciones Norte.

Tiempo Artesano. Mireya Robles. 85p. (SPA.). 1973. pap. 7.00 (0-317-46767-0, 3402) Ediciones Norte.

Tiempo Congelado: Poemario De una Isla Ausente. Jose Sanchez-Boudy. LC 79-50631. (Coleccion Espejo de Paciencia). (Illus.). 131p. (SPA.). 1979. pap. 6.00 (0-89729-224-3) Ediciones.

Tiempo de Silencio. Luis Martin-Santos. (SPA.). 1989. 19.95 (0-8288-2569-6) Fr & Eur.

Tiempo En Perspectiva. Georges Delacre. 171p. (C). 1975. pap. 4.00 (0-8477-0505-6) U of PR Pr.

Tiempo es el Diablo. Ricardo Bofill. (Biblioteca Cubana Contemporanea Ser.). 106p. (Orig.). (SPA.). 1985. pap. 6.00 (84-359-0397-4) Ediciones.

Tiempo Falto. Jorge Luis Borges. 44p. 1989. pap. 7.95 (0-912159-02-2) Center Pr CA.

Tiempo Inagotado de Irene Marquina. Josefina Leyva. 255p. (Orig.). (SPA.). 1994. pap. 14.95 (1-882721-05-5) Edit Ponce de Leon.

Tiempo Mismo. Teresa Sansirene. LC 95-62023. (Coleccion Espejo de Paciencia). 72p. (Orig.). (SPA.). 1996. pap. 9.00 (0-89729-787-3) Ediciones.

***Tiempo Para Cada Casa.** R. Ricker. (SPA.). 1.50 (0-8297-1097-3) Life Pubs Intl.

Tiempo Pasado de la Palabra de Dios. Kenneth Hagin, Jr. (SPA.). 1983. pap. 0.75 (0-89276-176-8) Hagin Ministries.

Tiempo Theme Pack: Spanish Level 2, 14 bks. (Que Maravilla! Ser.). (Illus.). (Orig.). (SPA.). 1992. teacher ed., pap. 159.00 (1-56334-211-1) Hampton-Brown.

Tiempo y Asentamiento en Xochicalco. Kenneth G. Hirth & Ann C. Guillen. 206p. 1988. pap. 11.50 (968-36-0345-9, UN008) UPLAAP.

***Tiempo y Clima - Weather & Climate.** (Enciclopedia Ilustrada de Ciencia y Naturaleza - Understanding Science & Nature Ser.). (Illus.). 152p. (SPA.). (YA). (gr. 6 up). 17.95 (0-7835-3366-7) Time-Life.

Tiempo y los Margenes: Europa como Utopia y como Amenaza en la Literatura Espaola, Vol. 253. Jesus Torrecilla. 260p. (C). 1997. lib. bdg. 27.50 (0-8078-9257-2) U of NC Pr.

Tiempo y Yo: Articulos Ensayos, Cronicas. Alvarez A. Martinez. (UPREX, Ensayo Ser.: No. 5). 317p. (C). 1972. pap. 1.50 (0-8477-0005-4) U of PR Pr.

Tiempos de Riesgo. Jeanne Blake. LC 89-40728. 196p. 1993. pap. 5.95 (1-56305-436-1, 3436) Workman Pub.

Tiempos Dificiles No Perduran, Pero Las Personas Fuertes Si! Tough Times Never Last, But Tough People Do. Robert H. Schuller. Ed. by Frank Callaghan. Tr. by Daniel Darling from ENG. 300p. (Orig.). 1991. pap. 5.95 (0-945201-35-4) Gannam-Kubat.

Tiempos Duros: Tight Times. Barbara S. Hazen. (Illus.). 32p. (J). (ps-3). 1993. pap. 12.99 (0-670-84841-7) Viking Child Bks.

Tien-T'ai Buddhism & Early Madhyamika. Ng Yu-Kwan. LC 93-23160. 1993. text ed. 37.00 (0-8248-1560-2); pap. text ed. 21.95 (0-8248-1561-0) UH Pr.

***Tiene Cuidado.** (Serie Pensamientos de Vida - Thoughts of Life Ser.: Vol. 3). 24p. (SPA.). 1986. pap. write for info. (0-614-27034-0) Editorial Unilit.

***Tiene Cuidado - Someone Who Cares.** (Serie Pensamientos de Vida - Thoughts of Life Ser.: No. 3). 24p. (SPA.). 1986. write for info. (0-614-24364-5) Editorial Unilit.

Tiens Bon, Charlie Brown. Charles M. Schulz. (Peanuts Ser.). (FRE.). (J). 1985. 4.95 (0-8288-4527-1) Fr & Eur.

Tiens Bon la Rampe. Jim Davis. (Garfield Ser.). (FRE.). (J). 1989. 18.95 (0-8288-4589-1) Fr & Eur.

Tiepin Eros - Typing Errors: New & Selected Poems. Tom Pickard. 160p. 9400. pap. 16.95 (1-85224-130-6, Pub. by Bloodaxe Bks UK) Dufour.

Tiepolo. Text by William L. Barcham. (Masters of Art Ser.). (Illus.). 128p. 1992. 22.95 (0-8109-3858-8) Abrams.

Tiepolo - Heaven on Earth: Masterpieces in the Wurzburg Palace. Peter O. Kruckmann. (Illus.). 144p. 1996. 39.95 (3-7913-1728-8, Pub. by Prestel GW) te Neues.

***Tiepolo & His Circle: Drawings in American Collections.** Bernard Aikema. Tr. by Andrew McCormick. (Illus.). 347p. (Orig.). 1996. pap. 39.95 (0-916724-90-5) Harvard Art Mus.

Tiepolo & His Circle: Drawings in American Collections. Bernard J. Aikema. LC 96-17795. 1996. write for info. (0-87598-115-1) Pierpont Morgan.

Tiepolo & the Pictorial Intelligence. Svetlana Alpers & Michael Baxandall. LC 94-13926. (Illus.). 1994. 55.00 (0-300-05978-7) Yale U Pr.

Tiepolo & the Pictorial Intelligence. Svetlana Alpers. 1996. pap. 27.50 (0-300-06817-4) Yale U Pr.

Tiepolo Drawings: Forty-Four Plates. Giovanni B. Tiepolo. (Art Library). 48p. (Orig.). 1987. pap. 3.95 (0-486-25366-X) Dover.

***Tiepolo in Holland: Works by Giambattista Tiepolo & His Circle in Dutch Collections.** Bernard Aikema & Marguerite Tuijn. (Illus.). 232p. 1997. pap. 40.00 (90-6918-171-1, Pub. by Mus Boymans-van Beuningen NE) U of Wash Pr.

Tiepolo in Venice: A Guide to Paintings in Original Settings. Terisio Pignatti. (Illus.). 160p. (Orig.). 1996. pap. 19.95 (88-86502-18-4, Pub. by Canal & Stamperia UK) Antique Collect.

Tier 2 Guidance Manual for Risk-Based Corrective Action. John A. Connor et al. (Illus.). (Orig.). 1996. pap. 75.00 (1-882713-03-6) Grndwater Srv.

Tiere der Urwelt *see* **From Dinosaurs to Fossils**

Tiergeographische Undokologische Beitrag Zur Okologischen Landschaftsforschung. Jurgen H. Jungbluth. (Biogeographica Ser.: No. 13). 1978. lib. bdg. 141.50 (90-6193-214-9) Kluwer Ac.

Tierleben Im Sprichwort der Griechen und Romer. Carl S. Kohler. viii, 221p. 1967. reprint ed. write for info. (0-318-70775-6) G Olms Pubs.

Tierlexikon, 5 vols. H. Smolik. (GER.). 1968. pap. 75.00 (0-8288-6665-1, M-7667) Fr & Eur.

***Tierna Pasion - Tender Passion, Vol. 201.** Beverly Barton. (Silhouette Deseo). (SPA.). 1997. mass mkt. 3.50 (0-373-35201-8, 1-35201-2) Harlequin Bks.

Tiernan & Other Families. C. B. Tiernan. (Illus.). 466p. 1990. reprint ed. pap. 68.50 (0-8328-1549-7); reprint ed. lib. bdg. 76.50 (0-8328-1548-9) Higginson Bk Co.

Tiernan & Other Families. Charles B. Tiernan. (Illus.). 466p. 1989. reprint ed. pap. 68.50 (0-8328-1404-0); reprint ed. lib. bdg. 74.50 (0-8328-1403-2) Higginson Bk Co.

Tiernan Family in Maryland. C. B. Tiernan. (Illus.). 222p. 1991. reprint ed. pap. 33.50 (0-8328-1946-8); reprint ed. lib. bdg. 43.50 (0-8328-1945-X) Higginson Bk Co.

Tierra: Contemporary Short Fiction of New Mexico. Ed. by Rudolfo Anaya. LC 89-91054. 258p. (Orig.). 1989. pap. 12.95 (0-938317-09-1) Cinco Puntos.

Tierra Amarilla: Stories of New Mexico. Sabine R. Ulibarri et al. Tr. by Thelma C. Nason from SPA. LC 93-1882. (Paso por Aqui Ser.). (Illus.). 195p. (ENG.). 1993. pap. 13.95 (0-8263-1438-4) U of NM Pr.

Tierra de Extranos. Jose A. Albertini. LC 82-8440. (Coleccion Caniqui). 160p. (Orig.). (SPA.). 1983. pap. 9.95 (0-89729-327-4) Ediciones.

***Tierra de Neustros Antepasados: Estudio de la Herencia y la Tenencia de la Tierra en el Altiplano de Guatemala.** Shelton H. Davis. Tr. by C. Margarita Valladares. (Serie Monografica: Vol. 8). (Illus.). 279p. (Orig.). (SPA.). 1997. pap. 20.00 (0-910443-13-0) CIRMA.

Tierra del Sur. Luis I. Larcada. Ed. by Editorial Arcos, Inc., Staff. (Arcos Poetica Ser.: No. 3). (Illus.). 44p. (SPA.). 1993. lib. bdg. 6.00 (0-937509-09-4) Edit Arcos.

Tierra Dulce: The Jesse Nusbaum Papers. Rosemary Nusbaum. LC 80-18365. (Illus.). 128p. 1980. pap. 7.95 (0-913270-83-0) Sunstone Pr.

Tierra Metalizada (Poemas) Alberto Muller & Manuel L. Suarez. LC 85-82279. 62p. (Orig.). (SPA.). 1986. pap. 6.95 (0-89729-385-1) Ediciones.

Tierra Norte: A Collection of Works from North Tejas. Ed. by Teri Aquilar et al. 39p. (Orig.). 1994. pap. 5.00 (0-913983-12-8) M & A Edns.

Tierra Primitiva. John C. Whitcomb. Orig. Title: The Early Earth. 176p. (SPA.). 1993. pap. 7.99 (0-8254-1868-2, Edit Portavoz) Kregel.

Tierra y Libertad: Photographs of Mexico 1900-1935. Intro. by Enrigue Florescano. (Illus.). 120p. 1985. pap. 32.00 (0-905836-51-0, Pub. by Museum Modern Art UK) St Mut.

Tierra Zia. Gary David. (Illus.). 40p. (Orig.). 1996. pap. 8.00 (1-878888-19-6) Nine Muses.

Tierreich - The Animal Kingdom: A Characterization & Compilation of All Current Animal Groups: Dermaptera Catadermaptera I, Pt. 106. Ed. by M. Fischer & H. Wermuth. xx, 558p. (C). 1989. lib. bdg. 630.75 (3-11-010612-4) De Gruyter.

Tierreich - The Animal Kingdom, Pt. 108: Dermaptura Eudermaptera II, a Characterization & Compilation of All Current Animal Groups. Ed. by H. Wermuth & M. Fischer. (Illus.). xxii, 711p. (ENG & GER.). (C). 1993. lib. bdg. 846.15 (3-11-012298-7) De Gruyter.

Tierreich (The Animal Kingdom) Eine Zusammenstellung der Rezenten Tierformen (A Characterization & Compilation of All Current Animal Groups) Ed. by H. Wermuth & M. Fischer. (Teilband: Richard L. Hoffman, Myriapoda 4, Polydesmida: Oxydesmidae Ser.: Pt. 107). (Illus.). xvi, 512p. (C). 1990. lib. bdg. 611.55 (3-11-012234-0) De Gruyter.

Tiers Livre. Francois Rabelais. Ed. by Pierre Michel. 1973. 4.95 (0-686-54704-7) Fr & Eur.

Tiers Livre. Francois Rabelais. Ed. by A. M. Screech. 474p. (FRE.). 1991. pap. 11.95 (0-7859-4557-1) Fr & Eur.

Tiers Livre (Original) Francois Rabelais. (Folio Ser.: No. 462). (FRE.). pap. 9.25 (2-07-036462-3) Schoenhof.

Tiers of Survival: Selected Poems. Jean Orizet. Tr. by Aletha DeWees from FRE. Orig. Title: Niveaux de Survie. 120p. (Orig.). 1984. pap. 8.00 (0-939378-03-5) Mundus Artium.

Ties: A Play in Two Acts. Jeffrey Sweet. 1982. pap. 5.25 (0-8222-1149-1) Dramatists Play.

Ties & Attachments: Italian-Americans in the West. Ed. by David A. Taylor & John A. Williams. LC 92-11572. (Studies in American Folklife: No. 5). 1992. write for info. (0-8444-0753-4) Lib Congress.

Ties & Tensions: The 1986 Survey of American Jewish Attitudes Toward Israel & Israelis. Steven M. Cohen. LC 87-70839. 114p. (Orig.). 1987. pap. 7.50 (0-87495-088-0) Am Jewish Comm.

Ties Beyond Trade: Labor & Environmental Issues under the NAFTA. Ed. by Jonathan Lemco & William B. Robson. 162p. (Orig.). 1993. pap. text ed. 14.95 (0-89068-120-1, CAC 61(NPA 265)) Natl Planning.

Ties of Blood. Gillian Slovo. 704p. 1991. reprint ed. mass mkt. 5.95 (0-380-70902-3) Avon.

Ties of Common Blood: A History of Maine's Northeast Boundary Dispute with Great Britain, 1783-1842. Geraldine T. Scott. (Illus.). 469p. (Orig.). 1992. pap. 25.50 (1-55613-541-6) Heritage Bk.

Ties of Later Life. Ed. by Jon Hendricks. LC 94-19532. 234p. 1995. pap. 21.95 (0-89503-166-3) Baywood Pub.

Ties of the Past: The Gettysburg Diaries of Salome Myers Stewart 1854-1922. Sarah S. Rodgers. (Illus.). 300p. (Orig.). 1996. pap. text ed. 14.95 (0-939631-91-1) Thomas Publications.

Ties That Bind. 1990. text ed. 34.95 (0-86861-700-8) Routledge Chapman & Hall.

***Ties That Bind.** Vanessa Duries. (Orig.). Date not set. mass mkt. 6.50 (1-56333-510-7) Masquerade.

Ties That Bind. Bonnie J. Jones. (Illus.). 153p. 1988. 24.95 (0-9619804-0-0) B J Jones.

Ties That Bind. Jayne Ann Krentz. 1993. mass mkt. 4.50 (0-373-83269-9, 1-83269-0) Harlequin Bks.

Ties That Bind. Leigh Michaels. (Romance Ser.). 1993. pap. 2.89 (0-373-03263-3, 1-03263-0) Harlequin Bks.

Ties That Bind. Dave Sargent. 188p. (YA). 1992. write for info. (0-318-69582-0) Ozark Pub.

Ties That Bind. Regina Taylor. 1995. 5.25 (0-87129-519-9, T22) Dramatic Pub.

Ties That Bind. Sherryl Woods. 256p. 1991. mass mkt. 4.99 (0-446-36117-8) Warner Bks.

Ties That Bind. large type ed. Barbara Nickolae. LC 93-29304. (Orig.). 1993. lib. bdg. 19.95 (0-8161-5885-1, GK Hall) Thorndike Pr.

Ties That Bind: A Social History of the Iranian Carpet. Leonard M. Helfgott. (Illus.). 368p. 1996. pap. text ed. 19.95 (1-56098-726-X) Smithsonian.

Ties That Bind: African American Consciousness of Africa. 2nd ed. Bernard M. Magubane. LC 86-70980. 250p. (C). 1990. 35.00 (0-86543-036-5); pap. 12.95 (0-86543-037-3) Africa World.

Ties That Bind: Communities in American History. LC 94-40704. (Illus.). 40p. 1992. pap. 4.95 (0-911333-93-2) National Archives & Recs.

Ties That Bind: Family & Community. Rebecca Clay. Ed. by Bruce Glassman. LC 94-46632. (Our Human Family Ser.). (Illus.). 80p. (YA). (gr. 5 up). 1995. lib. bdg. 21.95 (1-56711-126-2) Blackbirch.

Ties That Bind: Folk Art in Contemporary American Culture. Eugene W. Metcalf. (Illus.). 84p. 1986. pap. 12.95 (0-917562-45-3) Contemp Arts.

Ties That Bind: Intelligence Co-operation Between the UKUSA Countries. Jeffrey T. Richelson & Desmond J. Ball. (Illus.). 420p. 1986. text ed. 34.95 (0-04-327092-1) Routledge Chapman & Hall.

Ties That Bind: Intelligent Cooperation Between the Ukusa Countries. rev. ed. Jeffrey T. Richelson & Desmond J. Ball. 420p. (C). 1990. text ed. 49.95 (0-685-54061-8) Routledge Chapman & Hall.

Ties That Bind: Law, Marriage & the Reproduction of Patriarchal Relations. Carol Smart. 256p. (Orig.). 1984. pap. 12.95 (0-7100-9832-4, RKP) Routledge.

Ties That Bind: Life Together in the Baptist Vision. Gary Furr. 256p. (Orig.). 1994. pap. 14.95 (1-880837-77-3) Smyth & Helwys.

Ties That Bind: Mainstream Foundations for a Healing Theology of Baptist Unity. Craig Skinner. 143p. 1993. 29.95 (1-883255-08-2, Cath Scholar Pr); pap. 17.95 (1-883255-01-5, Cath Scholar Pr) Intl Scholars.

Ties That Bind: Men's & Women's Social Networks. Ed. by Laura Lein & Marvin B. Sussman. LC 82-23230. (Marriage & Family Review Ser.: Vol. 5, No. 4). 111p. 1983. text ed. 29.95 (0-86656-161-7) Haworth Pr.

Ties That Bind: Remaining Happy As a Couple after the Wedding. Victor M. Parachin. LC 92-32942. 80p. (Orig.). 1993. pap. 7.99 (0-8272-3630-1) Chalice Pr.

Ties that Bind: The Interdependence of Generations. Eric R. Kingson et al. 176p. 1986. pap. 9.95 (0-685-13899-2) Gerontological Soc.

Ties That Bind: The SM - Leather - Fetish Erotic Style Issues, Commentaries & Advice. Guy Baldwin. Ed. by Joseph Bean. LC 93-70930. 244p. (Orig.). 1993. pap. 14.95 (1-881943-09-7) Daedalus Pub.

Ties That Bind, Ties That Divide: 100 Years of Hungarian Experience in the U. S. Julianna Puskas. LC 96-18828. (Ellis Island Ser.). 375p. (C). 1997. 40.00 (0-8419-1320-X) Holmes & Meier.

***Ties That Blind: Neckties, 1945-1975.** Michael J. Goldberg. LC 97-15392. 1997. pap. write for info. (0-88740-982-2) Schiffer.

Ties That Blind in Canadian-American Relations: The Politics of News Discourse. Ed. by Richard L. Barton. (Communication Ser.). 240p. (C). 1990. text ed. 69.95 (0-8058-0743-8) L Erlbaum Assocs.

Ties That Bound: Peasant Families in Medieval England. Barbara A. Hanawalt. LC 85-3112. (Illus.). 364p. 1989. reprint ed. pap. 12.95 (0-19-504564-5) OUP.

Ties That No Longer Bind: Russians & Americans Talk to Each Other. Ed. by Jill O'Hora & Anna Varga. (West & the Wider World: Vol. 1). (Illus.). 250p. (Orig.). 1996. pap. 21.95 (0-940121-37-9, P305) Cross Cultural Pubns.

Ties That Stress: The New Familiy Imbalance. David Elkind. 272p. 1994. 19.95 (0-674-89149-X, ELKTIE) HUP.

Ties That Stress: The New Family Inbalance. David Elkind. 260p. (Orig.). (C). 1995. pap. 12.95 (0-674-89150-3) HUP.

Ties Ties Ties. Janet Elwin. 80p. 1996. pap. 15.95 (0-89145-864-6, 4598, Am Quilters Soc) Collector Bks.

Ties to the Past: A Family Collection of Favorite Recipes. Joann E. Gonzales. (Illus.). 212p. (Orig.). 1995. pap. 14.95 (0-9643885-0-2) Personal Profiles.

Tieta. Jorge Amado. 688p. 1988. pap. 9.95 (0-380-75477-0, Bard) Avon.

Tietz Fundamentals of Clinical Chemistry. 4th rev. ed. Carl A. Burtis & Edward R. Ashwood. LC 95-5400. (Illus.). 880p. 1995. text ed. 62.95 (0-7216-3763-9) Saunders.

Tietz Textbook of Clinical Chemistry. 2nd ed. Carl A. Burtis & Edward R. Ashwood. LC 93-22596. (Illus.). 1952p. 1993. text ed. 147.00 (0-7216-4472-4) Saunders.

***TIF Discovering Computers.** Simkin. 1990. pap. text ed. 25.20 (0-697-07487-0) McGraw.

Tifaifai & Quilts of Polynesia. Joyce D. Hammond. LC 86-6897. (Illus.). 136p. 1986. pap. text ed. 19.00 (0-8248-0975-0) UH Pr.

Tiff & His Bone *see* **Phonics Is My Way Series**

Tiffany. Joyce Ellis. (Springsong Bks.). 176p. (Orig.). (YA). (gr. 7 up). 1996. mass mkt. 4.99 (1-55661-734-8, Hampshire MN) Bethany Hse.

***Tiffany.** Mirabella. Date not set. 18.95 (0-7893-0119-9) Universe.

Tiffany: Thirty Postcards. Metropolitan Museum of Art Staff. (Illus.). 30p. 1991. 8.95 (0-8212-1880-8) Bulfinch Pr.

Tiffany Address Book. New York Metropolitan Museum of Art Staff. (Illus.). 128p. 1991. 18.95 (0-8212-1878-6) Bulfinch Pr.

Tiffany Christmas. John Loring. LC 96-13534. (Illus.). 208p. 1996. 60.00 (0-385-48585-9, DD Bks Yng Read) BDD Bks Young Read.

Tiffany Collection from the Chrysler Museum at Norfolk. Paul E. Doros. LC 77-4768. (Illus.). 160p. 1977. pap. 10.00 (0-940744-13-9) Chrysler Museum.

Tiffany Dino Works Out. Marjorie W. Sharmat. LC 94-32995. (J). (gr. k-4). 1995. 15.00 (0-689-80309-5, Mac Bks Young Read) S&S Childrens.

***Tiffany Favrile Art Glass.** Moise S. Steeg, Jr. LC 96-71098. (Illus.). 192p. 1997. 59.95 (0-7643-0207-8) Schiffer.

Tiffany Fortune: And Other Chronicles of a Connecticut Family. Alfred M. Bingham. LC 96-1360. (Illus.). 448p. 1996. 35.00 (0-9650357-1-9) Abeel & Leet.

An Asterisk (*) at the beginning of an entry indicates that the title is appearing in BIP for the first time.

*Tiffany Meisterwerke. Alastair Duncan et al. Tr. by W. Auffhammer. (Illus.). 160p. (ENG & GER.). (C). 1989. 84.00 (3-8170-2017-1, Pub. by Knstvrlag Weingrtn GW) Intl Bk Import.

Tiffany Silver. rev. ed. Charles Carpenter, Jr. (Illus.). 288p. 1997. 95.00 (1-55660-243-X) A Wofsy Fine Arts.

Tiffany-Style Stained Glass Lampshades: With Full-Size Templates for 11 Designs. Connie C. Eaton. LC 93-12325. 1993. pap. 5.95 (0-486-27589-2) Dover.

Tiffany, the Disaster. Janice Harrell. Ed. by Ruth Ashby. 112p. (Orig.). (J). (gr. 3-6). 1992. pap. 2.99 (0-671-72860-1, Minstrel Bks) PB.

Tiffany's Table Manners for Teenagers. Walter Hoving. LC 88-23964. (Illus.). 96p. (J). (gr. 5 up). 1989. reprint ed. 15.00 (0-394-82877-1) Random Bks Yng Read.

*Tiffany's 20th Century: A Portrait of American Style. John Loring. LC 97-8128. 1997. write for info. (0-8109-3887-1) Abrams.

Tiffin Glass, 1914-1940. Gerry Gallagher & Leslie Pia. (Illus.). 160p. 1996. 29.95 (0-7643-0102-0) Schiffer.

*Tiffin Modern: Mid-Century Art Glass. Ruth Hemminger et al. LC 97-11399. 1997. write for info. (0-7643-0320-1) Schiffer.

Tiffky Doofky. William Steig. (Sunburst Ser.). (Illus.). (J). (ps up). 1987. pap. 3.95 (0-374-47748-5) FS&G.

Tig & Plasma Welding: Process Techniques, Recommended Practices & Applications. W. Lucas. 112p. 1995. pap. 69.95 (1-85573-005-7, Pub. by Woodhead Pubng UK) Am Educ Systs.

TIG & Related Processes in Welding Automation. J. Cornu. (Advanced Welding Systems Ser.: Vol. 3). (Illus.). 350p. 1989. 111.95 (0-387-50484-2) Spr-Verlag.

Tig Welding. Richard Hunter. (Series 905). (Orig.). 1983. student ed., pap. 6.00 (0-8064-0377-2, 905); audio, vhs 439.00 (0-8064-0378-0) Bergwall.

TIGA Interface User's Guide. Texas Instruments Engineering Staff. 500p. 1991. 19.95 (0-685-62514-1, SPVU015C) Tex Instr Inc.

Tigana. Guy G. Kay. 688p. 1991. pap. 6.99 (0-451-45115-5, ROC) NAL-Dutton.

Tigana. Guy G. Kay. LC 89-40657. 640p. 1999. pap. 22.95 (0-670-83333-9, Viking) Viking Penguin.

Tiger. (Animal World Bks.). 28p. (J). (gr. 2-5). 1997. pap. 3.50 (0-8167-1571-8) Troll Communs.

Tiger. Judy Allen. LC 91-58760. 32p. (J). (ps-3). 1994. pap. 4.99 (1-56402-284-6) Candlewick Pr.

Tiger. Mark Dunster. (Holiday Ser.: Pt. 4: New Years Eve). 79p. (Orig.). 1980. pap. 4.00 (0-89642-068-X) Linden Pubs.

Tiger. Mary Hoffman. LC 84-15120. (Animals in the Wild Ser.). (Illus.). 24p. (J). (gr. k-5). 1984. pap. 3.95 (0-8114-6890-9) Raintree Steck-V.

Tiger. Kwok Man-Ho. LC 93-48006. (Chinese Horoscopes Library). (Illus.). 48p. 1994. pap. 8.95 (1-56458-611-1) DK Pub Inc.

Tiger. Anna L. Lorenzen. (Illus.). 22p. (Orig.). (J). (gr. 1-2). 1989. pap. text ed. 2.95 (0-9626133-0-4) ALL Ventura Pub.

Tiger. Witter Bynner. LC 77-70352. (One-Act Plays in Reprint Ser.). 1977. reprint ed. 16.00 (0-8486-2013-5) Roth Pub Inc.

Tiger, Reading Level 3-4. Nadine Saunier. (World Animal Library). (Illus.). 28p. (J). (gr. 2-5). 1983. lib. bdg. 16.67 (0-86592-866-5); lib. bdg. 12.50 (0-685-58827-0) Rourke Corp.

*Tiger: A Biography of Tiger Woods. John Strege. 256p. 1997. 25.00 (0-553-06219-0) Broadway BDD.

Tiger: A True Champion. Wayne Memmer. LC 91-62540. 56p. 1993. 6.95 (0-944957-32-3) Rivercross Pub.

*Tiger: Reflections on a Champion. Ed. by David LaFontaine. Date not set. pap. 5.95 (0-7871-1622-X, Dove Bks) Dove Audio.

Tiger! Stories of Old Korea. Carol Farley. LC 93-49674. (J). Date not set. write for info. (0-688-13676-1); lib. bdg. write for info. (0-688-13677-X) Lothrop.

Tiger: Symbol of Freedom. Nicholas Courtney. (Illus.). 128p. 1981. 25.00 (0-7043-2245-5, Pub. by Quartet UK) Charles River Bks.

Tiger: The Rise & Fall of Tammany Hall. Oliver E. Allen. (Illus.). 1993. 24.95 (0-201-62463-X) Addison-Wesley.

Tiger! Vol. 1. Simon Barnes. 1994. 24.95 (0-312-11544-X) St Martin.

Tiger - the Making of a Sports Car. Mike Taylor. (Illus.). 240p. 1988. 29.95 (0-85429-774-X, Pub. by G T Foulis Ltd) Haynes Pubns.

Tiger Ace: The Life Story of Panzer Commander Michael Wittmann. Gary Simpson. LC 93-84858. (Illus.). 346p. 1994. 35.00 (0-88740-526-6) Schiffer.

Tiger & the Brahmin. Brian Gleeson. (We All Have Tales Ser.). (Illus.). 40p. (J). (gr. k up). 1992. 19.95 incl. audio (0-88708-233-5, Rabbit) S&S Childrens.

Tiger & the Children: Fidel Castro & the Judgment of History. Roberto L. Escalona. Tr. by Manuel A. Tellechea. LC 91-46477. 212p. (C). 1992. 34.95 (1-56000-027-9); pap. 21.95 (1-56000-593-9) Transaction Pubs.

Tiger & the Millionaire. Roger Hall. LC 93-28932. (Voyages Ser.). (Illus.). (J). 1994. 4.25 (0-383-03786-7) SRA McGraw.

Tiger & the Shark: Empirical Roots of Wave-Particle Dualism. Bruce R. Wheaton. LC 82-22069. (Illus.). 352p. 1983. text ed. 69.95 (0-521-25098-6) Cambridge U Pr.

Tiger & the Shark: Empirical Roots of Wave-Particle Dualism. Bruce R. Wheaton. (Illus.). 355p. 1991. pap. text ed. 23.95 (0-521-35892-2) Cambridge U Pr.

Tiger Beetles of Ohio: (Coleoptera - Cicindelidae) Robert C. Graves & David W. Brzoska. Ed. by Veda M. Cafazzo. LC 90-62740. (Bulletin New Ser.: Vol. 8, No. 4). (Illus.). vi, 42p. (Orig.). (C). 1991. pap. 10.00 (0-86727-109-4) Ohio Bio Survey.

Tiger Beetles of the Genus Cicindela in Arizona: Coleoptera: Cicindelidae. Judy Bertholf. (Special Publications: No. 19). (Illus.). 44p. 1983. pap. 7.00 (0-89672-110-8) Tex Tech Univ Pr.

Tiger Bridge: Nine Days on a Bend of the Nauranala. Barbara C. Horton. 80p. (Orig.). 1993. pap. 9.00 (1-880284-01-4) J Daniel.

Tiger Bridge Revisited. Freddie North & Jeremy Flint. 152p. 1991. pap. 12.95 (1-85744-502-3, Maxwell Macmillan) Macmillan.

Tiger Burning Bright. Marion Zimmer Bradley et al. LC 95-1763. 1995. 23.00 (0-688-14360-1, AvoNova) Avon.

Tiger Burning Bright. Marion Zimmer Bradley et al. 512p. 1996. mass mkt. 6.50 (0-380-77512-3, AvoNova) Avon.

Tiger, Burning Bright: More Myths Than Truths about Korean Tigers. Kathleen J. Crane Foundation Staff. (Illus.). 240p. 1993. 19.95 (1-56591-003-6, Pub. by Hollym Bks SK); pap. 14.95 (1-56591-004-4, Pub. by Hollym Bks SK) Weatherhill.

Tiger Butte. Jack Cummings. 1992. mass mkt. 3.50 (1-55817-583-0, Pinncle Kensgtn) Kensgtn Pub Corp.

Tiger Butte. Jack Cummings. LC 85-20288. 178p. 1986. 14.95 (0-8027-4055-3) Walker & Co.

Tiger by the Tail: Reorienting Biodiversity Conservation & Development in Indonesia. Charles V. Barber et al. (Illus.). 150p. (Orig.). 1995. pap. 14.95 (1-56973-043-1) World Resources Inst.

*Tiger by the Tale: A Celebration of Tiger Woods. Mark Stewart. 1997. pap. text ed. 14.95 (0-9658048-0-1) Hoofbeat Pubns.

Tiger Called Thomas. rev. ed. Charlotte Zolotow. LC 86-20878. (Illus.). 40p. (J). (ps-3). 1988. lib. bdg. 12.88 (0-688-06697-6) Lothrop.

Tiger-Crane Form of Hung Gar Kung-Fu. Bucksam Kong. LC 83-60126. (Chinese Arts Ser.). (Illus.). (Orig.). 1983. pap. 14.95 (0-89750-087-3, 424) Ohara Pubns.

Tiger Cub Chants & Poems, 8 bks., Set. rev. ed. Marlene J. McCracken & Robert A. McCracken. (Tiger Cub Bks.). (Illus.). (J). (gr. k-3). 1988. 20.00 (0-920541-66-6) Peguis Pubs Ltd.

Tiger Cub Readers, 8 bks., Set. rev. ed. Marlene J. McCracken & Robert A. McCracken. (Tiger Cub Bks.). (Illus.). (J). (gr. k-1). 1988. 20.00 (0-920541-62-3) Peguis Pubs Ltd.

Tiger Cub Songs, 8 bks., Set. rev. ed. Marlene J. McCracken & Robert A. McCracken. (Tiger Cub Bks.). (Illus.). (J). (gr. k-2). 1988. 20.00 (0-920541-68-2) Peguis Pubs Ltd.

Tiger Cub Stories, 8 bks., Set. rev. ed. Marlene J. McCracken & Robert A. McCracken. (Tiger Cub Bks.). (Illus.). (J). (gr. k-2). 1988. 20.00 (0-920541-64-X) Peguis Pubs Ltd.

Tiger Cub's Surprise. Stewart Cowley. LC 94-67213. (Magic Window Bks.). (Illus.). 22p. (J). (ps-k). 1995. 6.99 (0-89577-640-5) RD Assn.

Tiger Dance. Jillian Hunter. 400p. (Orig.). 1991. mass mkt. 4.50 (0-380-76095-9) Avon.

Tiger Eyes. Judy Blume. 224p. (YA). (gr. 7 up). 1982. 4.50 (0-440-98469-6, LLL BDD) BDD Bks Young Read.

*Tiger Eyes. Judy Blume. (YA). (gr. 8-12). 14.95 (0-87888-185-9, 128826, Bradbury S&S) S&S Childrens.

Tiger Eyes. Judy Blume. LC 81-6152. 256p. (YA). (gr. 7 up). 1982. lib. bdg. 16.00 (0-02-711080-X, Bradbury S&S) S&S Childrens.

Tiger Eyes. Robyn Donald. (Presents Ser.). 1995. mass mkt. 3.25 (0-373-11755-8, 1-11755-5) Harlequin Bks.

Tiger Eyes. large type ed. Robyn Donald. 1995. lib. bdg. 18.95 (0-263-13966-2) Thorndike Pr.

Tiger Family of Tanks. Horst Scheibert. LC 89-84178. (Illus.). 48p. 1989. pap. 8.95 (0-88740-187-2) Schiffer.

Tiger for Malgudi. R. K. Narayan. 160p. 1994. pap. 8.95 (0-14-018545-3, Penguin Classics) Viking Penguin.

*Tiger Garden: A Book of Writers' Dreams. Ed. by Nicholas Doyle. LC 96-69726. 272p. (Orig.). (C). 1997. pap. text ed. 14.99 (1-85242-533-4) Serpents Tail.

Tiger Handbook: Stories, Stats, & Stuff about Missouri Basketball. Dennis Dodd. (Illus.). 160p. (Orig.). 1995. pap. 9.95 (1-880652-48-X) Wichita Eagle.

*Tiger Heart. William Mulvihill. 126p. 1997. pap. 12.00 (0-9645875-7-2) Brickiln Pr.

Tiger in a Lion's Den: Adventures in LSU Basketball. Dale Brown & Don Yaeger. (Illus.). 192p. 1994. 22.95 (0-7868-6044-8) Hyperion.

Tiger in Action. Bruce Culver. (Armor in Action Ser.). (Illus.). 50p. 1989. pap. 7.95 (0-89747-230-6, 2027) Squad Sig Pubns.

Tiger in His Pocket. Sandra Clayton. 80p. (J). (gr. 1-5). 1995. pap. 6.95 (1-86373-699-9, Pub. by Allen & Unwin Aust Pty AT) IPG Chicago.

Tiger in His Time: Hal Newhouser & the Burden of Wartime Ball. David M. Jordan. LC 90-43187. (Illus.). 1991. 19.95 (0-912083-49-2) Diamond Communications.

Tiger in the Barbed Wire: An American in Vietnam. Howard R. Simpson. Ed. by Philip Turner. 304p. 1994. pap. 16.00 (1-56836-025-8) Kodansha.

Tiger in the Grass. Harriet Doerr. 224p. 1996. pap. 10.95 (0-14-025148-0) Viking Penguin.

Tiger in the Grass: Stories & Other Inventions. Harriet Doerr. LC 95-32391. 208p. 1995. pap. 19.95 (0-670-86471-4, Viking) Viking Penguin.

*Tiger in the Grass: Stories & Other Inventions. large type ed. Harriet Doerr. LC 96-31685. (Large Print Bks.). 1996. 23.95 (1-56895-358-5, Compass) Wheeler Pub.

Tiger in the House. 3rd unabridged ed. Carl Van Vechten. LC 95-45906. (Illus.). 416p. 1996. reprint ed. pap. text ed. 8.95 (0-486-29129-4) Dover.

Tiger in the Kitchen, & Other Strange Stories. Villy Sorensen. Tr. by Maureen Neiiendam. LC 74-87737. (Short Story Index Reprint Ser.). 1977. 19.95 (0-8369-3060-6) Ayer.

Tiger in the Mountain Pass. Jinye Lorenz. LC 95-81447. (Illus.). 45p. (Orig.). (J). 1995. pap. 9.95 (1-888350-00-8) Lighted Lamp.

Tiger in the Rain: Rogue's Gallery. Parker. 1995. pap. 3.75 (0-373-07663-0) Harlequin Bks.

Tiger in the Smoke. Margery Allingham. 21.95 (0-89190-198-1) Amereon Ltd.

Tiger in the Smoke. Margery Allingham. 1994. lib. bdg. 17.95 (1-56849-459-9) Buccaneer Bks.

Tiger in the Smoke. Margery Allingham. 232p. 1995. mass mkt. 4.95 (0-7867-0225-7) Carroll & Graf.

Tiger in the Tiger Pit. Janette T. Hospital. 1996. pap. 12.95 (0-8050-3294-0) H Holt & Co.

*Tiger Inside. David Alderton. 1998. pap. 19.95 (0-87605-611-7) Howell Bk.

Tiger Is a Scaredy Cat: A Step One Book. Joan Phillips. LC 85-19673. (Step into Reading Bks.). (Illus.). 32p. (J). (ps-1). 1986. pap. 3.99 (0-394-88056-0) Random Bks Yng Read.

Tiger Island. 2nd ed. Jack Ritchie. 1987. 4.95 (0-932310-09-5) U of Wis-Stevens Point.

*Tiger Killers, Vol. 2. Shi Naian. (The Marshes of Mount Liang Ser.). 1997. pap. text ed. 32.50 (962-201-751-7, Pub. by Chinese U Pr CA) Cheng & Tsui.

*Tiger Lil. Ellen Archer. 288p. 1997. mass mkt. 4.99 (0-8217-5644-3, Zebra Kensgtn) Kensgtn Pub Corp.

Tiger Lilies: An American Childhood. Fielding Dawson. LC 84-4170. vi, 213p. 1984. text ed. 29.95 (0-8223-0593-3) Duke.

Tiger Lilies & Other Beastly Plants. Elizabeth Ring. LC 84-7499. (Illus.). 32p. (J). (gr. 3 up). 1985. 9.95 (0-8027-6540-8) Walker & Co.

Tiger Lilies & Other Beastly Plants. Elizabeth Ring. (J). 1996. pap. 6.95 (0-8027-7454-7) Walker & Co.

Tiger Lilies & Southern Prose see Centennial Edition of the Works of Sidney Lanier

Tiger Lily. Shirlee Busbee. 464p. 1985. mass mkt. 5.50 (0-380-89499-8) Avon.

Tiger Lily & Other Stories. Julia Schayer. LC 70-98593. (Short Story Index Reprint Ser.). 1977. 19.95 (0-8369-3167-X) Ayer.

Tiger Man. Max Brand. 1996. reprint ed. mass mkt., pap. text ed. 4.50 (0-8439-3957-5) Dorchester Pub Co.

*Tiger Man, Elvis '68. Joseph A. Tunzi. LC 97-93609. (Illus.). 128p. (Orig.). 1997. pap. 54.95 (1-888464-02-X) JAT Pub.

Tiger Moon. Fiona Sunquist & Mel Sunquist. (Illus.). xii, 188p. 1988. 29.95 (0-226-78001-5) U Ch Pr.

Tiger Moon. Fiona Sunquist & Mel Sunquist. (Illus.). xii, 200p. 1990. pap. 15.95 (0-226-78002-3) U Ch Pr.

Tiger Moth, CT-4, Wackett & Winjeel in Australian Service. Stewart Wilson. (Australian Service Ser.). (Illus.). 197p. 1995. pap. 25.95 (1-875671-16-1, Pub. by Australian Aviation AT) Motorbooks Intl.

Tiger of Mysore: Story of the War with Tippoo Saib. G. A. Henty. (C). 1995. reprint ed. 27.00 (81-206-1034-2, Pub. by Asian Educ Servs II) S Asia.

Tiger on Spreads: The Spread Trader's Manual. Philip E. Tiger. 1996. text ed. 55.00 (0-471-15651-5) Wiley.

Tiger on the Road: The Life of Vardis Fisher. Tim Woodward. LC 89-25400. (Illus.). (Orig.). 1989. 19.95 (0-87004-338-2); pap. 14.95 (0-87004-333-1) Caxton.

Tiger on Your Couch: What the Big Cat Can Teach You about Living in Harmony with Your House Cat. Bill Fleming. 1994. pap. 12.00 (0-688-13508-0, Quill) Morrow.

Tiger One. Hilary Doyle & Tom Jentz. (New Vanguard Ser.). (Illus.). 48p. 1993. pap. 12.95 (1-85532-337-0, 9340, Pub. by Osprey UK) Stackpole.

Tiger I. Horst Scheibert. Tr. by Edward Force from GER. LC 91-62746. (Illus.). 48p. 1991. pap. 8.95 (0-88740-352-2) Schiffer.

Tiger I & Stormtiger in Detail. Bruce Culver & Uwe Feist. (Illus.). (YA). 40.00 (0-9633824-0-3) Ryton Pub.

Tiger I & Tiger II Profile. R. Ehninger & David Johnston. 48p. (ENG & GER.). (C). (gr. 13). 1996. 13.00 (0-88740-925-3) Schiffer.

Tiger Orchard. Joyce Sweeney. 240p. (YA). 1995. mass mkt. 3.99 (0-440-21927-2) Dell.

Tiger Orchids on Mount Mayon: A Novella. Paulino Lim, Jr. 94p. (Orig.). (C). 1990. pap. 10.00 (971-10-0410-0, Pub. by New Day Pub PH) Cellar.

Tiger Prince. Sandra Brown. 1994. mass mkt. 4.99 (0-373-48295-7, 5-48295-5) Silhouette.

Tiger Prince. Sandra Brown. 1994. pap. 4.99 (1-55166-023-7, 1-66023-2, Mira Bks) Harlequin Bks.

Tiger Prince. Iris Johansen. 512p. 1993. mass mkt. 5.99 (0-553-29968-9) Bantam.

Tiger Ride. Mildred P. Walter. LC 92-40281. (Illus.). 32p. (J). 1995. lib. bdg. 17.00 (0-02-792303-7, Mac Bks Young Read) S&S Childrens.

Tiger Rugs of Tibet. Ed. by Mimi Lipton. LC 88-51136. (Illus.). 1989. 60.00 (0-500-97369-5) Thames Hudson.

Tiger Scroll of the Koga Ninja. Jay Sensei. (Illus.). 96p. 1985. pap. 12.00 (0-87364-313-5) Paladin Pr.

Tiger Scrolls of the Koga Ninja. Jay Sensei. pap. 8.95 (0-901764-70-1, 93348) Talman.

Tiger Sharks! Wallace H. Little & Charles Goodman. (Illus.). 246p. 1987. pap. 17.95 (0-916693-08-2) Castle Bks.

Tiger Sharks. John F. Prevost. LC 95-2749. (Sharks Ser.). (J). (gr. k-3). 1995. lib. bdg. 13.99 (1-56239-468-1) Abdo & Dghtrs.

Tiger Sharks. Anne Welsbacher. (Animals & the Environment Ser.). 48p. (J). (gr. 3-9). 1995. lib. bdg. 17.80 (1-56065-269-1) Capstone Pr.

*Tiger Sharks. Anne Welsbacher. (Sharks Ser.). (Illus.). 48p. (J). (gr. 3-7). 1995. 18.40 (0-516-35269-5) Childrens.

Tiger Sharks & Other Dangerous Animals. Anita Ganeri. LC 95-6103. (Illus.). 40p. (J). (gr. 3-5). 1995. pap. 6.95 (1-85697-576-2, Kingfisher LKC) LKC.

Tiger Sleeps. Fela D. Scott. 368p. (Orig.). 1993. mass mkt., pap. text ed. 4.50 (0-8439-3529-4) Dorchester Pub Co.

Tiger Soup: An Anansi Story from Jamaica. Frances Temple. LC 93-48834. (Illus.). 32p. (J). (ps-2). 1994. 15.95 (0-531-06859-5); lib. bdg. 16.99 (0-531-08709-3) Orchard Bks Watts.

*Tiger Stalk. 1997. mass mkt. 3.75 (0-373-64220-2, 1-64220-6, Wrldwide Lib) Harlequin Bks.

Tiger, Take off Your Hat. Linda P. Silbert & Alvin J. Silbert. (Little Twirps Understanding People Bks.). (Illus.). (J). (gr. k-4). 1978. pap. 4.98 (0-89544-051-2) Silbert Bress.

*Tiger Tales. Leverne J. Moldrem. LC 96-86705. 456p. 29.95 (0-9649498-5-7) Flying M Pr.

*Tiger Tales: An Anecdotal History of the Flying Tiger Line. rev. ed. Leverne J. Moldrem. 455p. 1996. write for info. (0-614-28316-7) Flying M Pr.

Tiger Talk. Vanessa Vargo. (J). (ps-3). 1992. pap. 5.99 (0-85953-397-2) Childs Play.

Tiger Tanks. Michael Green. (Warbird History Ser.). (Illus.). 128p. 1995. pap. 19.95 (0-87938-954-0) Motorbooks Intl.

Tiger Tanks: Tiger & King Tiger Tanks & Their Variants. Walter J. Spielberger. (Illus.). 220p. 1991. 54.95 (0-85429-841-X) Haynes Pubns.

Tiger! Tiger! James Gunn. (Booklet Ser.: No. 17). 55p. (Orig.). 1984. pap. 2.25 (0-936055-14-6) C Drumm Bks.

*Tiger, Tiger. Dee Lillegard. Date not set. 15.95 (0-399-22633-8) Putnam Pub Group.

Tiger, Tiger. Les Martin. (X-Files Ser.: Vol. 3). Orig. Title: Untitled X-Files No. 4. 112p. (YA). (gr. 5 up). 1995. pap. 3.95 (0-06-440626-1, Trophy) HarpC Child Bks.

Tiger, Tiger. large type ed. Philip Caveney. 576p. 1985. 27.99 (0-7089-8294-8) Ulverscroft.

Tiger, Tiger. large type ed. George Goodchild. (Linford Mystery Library). 464p. 1996. pap. 15.99 (0-7089-7867-3, Linford) Ulverscroft.

Tiger, Tiger. large type ed. Frank Ryan. 1990. 25.99 (0-7089-2287-2) Ulverscroft.

Tiger, Tiger Burning Bright. Peter S. Feibleman. LC 63-18585. 148p. 1963. 16.95 (0-910278-98-9) Boulevard.

Tiger, Tiger, Burning Bright. Ronald Koertge. 179p. (J). 1995. pap. 3.99 (0-380-72474-X, Camelot) Avon.

Tiger, Tiger, Burning Bright. Ronald Koertge. 192p. (YA). (gr. 5 up). 1994. 16.95 (0-531-06840-4); lib. bdg. 17.99 (0-531-08690-9) Orchard Bks Watts.

Tiger Trek. Ted Lewin. LC 89-12710. (Illus.). 40p. (J). (gr. 1-5). 1990. lib. bdg. 14.95 (0-02-757381-8, Mac Bks Young Read) S&S Childrens.

*Tiger under My Bed! Lieneke Dijkzeul. LC 97-23392. (J). 1997. write for info. (1-57379-069-9) High-Scope.

*Tiger Walks. Kenneth Anderson. 1997. pap. text ed. 16.95 (1-887269-29-0) J Culler & Sons.

Tiger Who Lost His Stripes. 2nd ed. Anthony Paul. LC 95-15472. (Illus.). 32p. (J). (gr. 2-5). 1995. 15.00 (0-15-200992-2, HB Juv Bks) HarBrace.

Tiger Who Was a Roaring Success. Don Conroy et al. 77p. (J). (gr. 1-4). 1995. pap. 0.95 (0-86278-371-2) Dufour.

Tiger Who Wore White Gloves: Or What You Are You Are. Gwendolyn Brooks. LC 74-75589. (J). 1974. pap. 6.95 (0-88378-031-3) Third World.

Tiger with Wings: The Great Horned Owl. Barbara J. Esbensen. LC 90-23034. (Illus.). 32p. (J). (gr. 2-4). 1991. 16.95 (0-531-05940-5) Orchard Bks Watts.

Tiger with Wings: The Great Horned Owl. Barbara J. Esbensen. LC 90-23034. (Illus.). 32p. (J). (gr. 2-4). 1996. pap. 5.95 (0-531-07071-9) Orchard Bks Watts.

Tiger Woman. Laurence Yep. LC 93-38685. (Illus.). 32p. (J). (gr. k-3). 1995. pap. 15.95 (0-8167-3464-X) BrdgeWater.

Tiger Woman. Laurence Yep. LC 93-38685. (Illus.). 32p. (J). (gr. k-3). 1996. pap. 4.95 (0-8167-3465-8) BrdgeWater.

Tiger Woman. Betty May. (Illus.). 1993. reprint ed. 45.00 (1-55818-225-X, First Impress) Holmes Pub.

*Tiger Woods. (Black Americans of Achievement Ser.). 96p. (YA). (gr. 3 up). 1997. lib. bdg. 19.95 (0-7910-4651-6) Chelsea Hse.

*Tiger Woods. (Black Americans of Achievement Ser.). 96p. (YA). (gr. 3 up). 1997. pap. 8.95 (0-7910-4687-7) Chelsea Hse.

*Tiger Woods. Aaron Boyd. LC 97-2980. (Great Athletes Ser.). (Illus.). 64p. (J). (gr. 3 up). 1997. lib. bdg. 17.95 (1-883846-19-6) M Reynolds.

*Tiger Woods. William Durbin. (Golf Legends Ser.). (Illus.). 64p. (YA). (gr. 7 up). 1997. lib. bdg. 15.95 (0-7910-4563-3) Chelsea Hse.

*Tiger Woods. Gutman. (J). 1997. mass mkt. 3.99 (0-671-88737-8) PB.

*Tiger Woods. Paul Joseph. LC 97-24866. (Awesome Athletes Ser.). 1998. write for info. (1-56239-841-5) Abdo & Dghtrs.

*Tiger Woods. S. A. Kramer. 1998. pap. 3.99 (0-679-88849-7); lib. bdg. 11.99 (0-679-98849-1) Random Bks Yng Read.

*Tiger Woods. Richard Rambeck. LC 97-2519. (J). 1997. write for info. (1-56766-407-5) Childs World.

*Tiger Woods. Sports Illustrated Staff. 1997. pap. 10.95 (0-684-84462-1) S&S Trade.

*Tiger Woods, Vol. 1. Rosaforte. 1997. mass mkt. 5.99 (0-312-96437-4) St Martin.

*Tiger Woods: Golfing to Greatness. S. A. Kramer. LC 97-16974. 1997. pap. 3.99 (0-679-88969-8) Random.

*Tiger Woods: Golfing to Greatness. S. A. Kramer. LC 97-16974. 1997. lib. bdg. 11.99 (0-679-98969-2) Random.

T

An Asterisk (*) at the beginning of an entry indicates that the title is appearing in BIP for the first time.

***Tiger Woods: Golf's Shining Young Star.** Bill Gutman. LC 97-25906. (Millbrook Sports World Ser.). 1998. pap. write for info. (0-7613-0329-4); lib. bdg. write for info. (0-7613-0309-X) Millbrook Pr.

***Tiger Woods: King of the Course.** Jeff Savage. LC 97-5451. (J). 1997. write for info. (0-8225-3655-2, Lerner Publctns); pap. write for info. (0-8225-9811-6, Lerner Publctns) Lerner Group.

Tiger Woods: Lion on the Links. Jill C. Wheeler. LC 95-17423. (Reaching for the Stars Ser.). (J). 1995. lib. bdg. 13.98 (1-56239-498-3) Abdo & Dghtrs.

***Tiger Woods: The Making of a Champion.** Tim Rosaforte. 1996. 21.95 (0-312-15672-3) St Martin.

***Tiger Woods: The Making of a Champion.** Sports Illustrated Writers Staff. LC 96-52835. 96p. 1996. 20.00 (0-684-84226-2) S&S Trade.

***Tiger Woods an American Master.** Greg Quinn. 1997. pap. text ed. 3.99 (0-590-76777-1) Scholastic Inc.

***Tiger Woods Way.** John Andrisani. 1997. pap. write for info. (0-609-80139-2) Random Hse Value.

***Tiger Woods Way.** John Andrisani. LC 97-6083. 1997. 18.00 (0-609-60094-X) Random Hse Value.

***Tiger Woods' Way: Secrets of Tiger Woods' Power Swing Technique.** John Andrisani. (Illus.). 1997. 18.00 (0-614-28177-6) Berkley Pub.

Tiger X: The Adventure Begins. Benn Dunn. (Illus.). 101p. 1989. pap. 9.95 (0-944735-26-6) Malibu Comics Ent.

Tigerati: A Dictionary of Clemson Humor, Heros & Hindsight. Blaine Tate. 183p. 1991. pap. 11.95 (1-880529-00-9) Pat Back.

Tigerbone Wine. Hilary Tham. 1992. 18.00 (0-89410-727-5, Three Contnts); pap. 10.00 (0-89410-728-3, Three Contnts) Lynne Rienner.

Tigers. Timothy L. Biel. (Zoobooks Ser.). 24p. (J). (gr. 4). 1989. lib. bdg. 14.95 (0-88682-266-1) Creative Ed.

Tigers. Lesley A. DuTemple. (Early Bird Nature Bks.). (J). 1996. lib. bdg. 18.95 (0-8225-3010-4, Lerner Publctns) Lerner Group.

Tigers. Roland Edwards. LC 91-40098. (Illus.). 32p. (J). (ps-2). 1992. 15.00 (0-688-11685-X, Tambourine Bks); lib. bdg. 14.93 (0-688-11686-8, Tambourine Bks) Morrow.

Tigers. Amanda Harman. (Endangered! Ser.). 32p. (J). (gr. 3-5). 1995. lib. bdg. 14.95 (0-7614-0215-2, Benchmark NY) Marshall Cavendish.

Tigers. Highlights for Children Editors. (Highlights Animal Bks.). (Illus.). 32p. (Orig.). (J). (gr. 2-5). 1993. pap. 3.95 (1-56397-287-5) Boyds Mills Pr.

Tigers. Jenny Markert. (Nature Bks.). 32p. (J). (gr. 2-6). 1991. lib. bdg. 22.79 (0-89565-722-8) Childs World.

Tigers. L. Martin. (Wildlife in Danger Ser.). (Illus.). 24p. (J). (gr. k-5). 1988. lib. bdg. 11.94 (0-86592-995-5); lib. bdg. 8.95 (0-685-58307-4) Rourke Corp.

Tigers. Peter Murray. (Baby Zoobks.). (Illus.). 32p. (YA). (gr. 3 up). 1998. lib. bdg. write for info. (0-88682-839-2) Creative Ed.

Tigers. John Seidensticker. LC 95-43477. (WorldLife Library). (Illus.). 72p. 1996. pap. 14.95 (0-89658-295-7) Voyageur Pr.

Tigers. L. Stone. (Big Cat Discovery Library). (Illus.). 24p. (J). (gr. k-5). 1989. lib. bdg. 11.94 (0-86592-504-6); lib. bdg. 8.95 (0-685-58632-4) Rourke Corp.

Tigers. Two Can Publishing Ltd. Staff. (Animal Bks.). (Illus.). 32p. (J). (gr. 2-7). 1991. pap. 2.95 (0-87534-212-4) Highlights.

Tigers. Wildlife Education, Ltd. Staff. (Illus.). 20p. (Orig.). (J). (gr. k-12). 1985. pap. 2.75 (0-937934-35-6) Wildlife Educ.

Tigers. Jean-Pierre Zwaerepoel. Ed. by Nion McEvoy. (Illus.). 80p. 1992. 19.95 (0-8118-0136-5); pap. 12.95 (0-8118-0143-8) Chronicle Bks.

***Tigers: Leaders of the New Asia-Pacific.** Greg Sheridan. 344p. 1997. pap. 29.95 (1-86448-153-6, Pub. by Allen Unwin AT) Paul & Co Pubs.

Tigers Are Better-Looking. Jean Rhys. 1996. pap. 11.95 (0-14-018346-9) Viking Penguin.

***Tigers Are Better-Looking.** Jean Rhys. lib. bdg. 21.95 (0-8488-1885-7) Amereon Ltd.

Tiger's Breakfast. Jan Mogensen. LC 91-3606. (Illus.). 32p. (J). (ps-3). 1991. 14.95 (0-940793-83-0, Crocodile Bks) Interlink Pub.

Tigers Burning. Crabbe Evers. 272p. 1995. mass mkt. 4.99 (0-380-71866-9) Avon.

Tigers by Night. Sandra Canfield. (Superromance Ser.: No. 419). 1990. pap. 2.95 (0-373-70419-4) Harlequin Bks.

***Tigers Can't Tap Dance, but They Know How to Tango: And Other Things You May Not Know about Big Cats.** Yalerre Wurst. (Illus.). 48p. (Orig.). (J). 1997. pap. text ed. 12.95 (0-9657290-0-1) Destiny Pub NV.

Tiger's Cave: And Translations of Other Zen Writings. Trevor P. Leggett. 1995. pap. 9.95 (0-8048-2021-X) C E Tuttle.

Tiger's Child. Torey Hayden. 272p. 1996. mass mkt. 5.99 (0-380-72544-4) Avon.

Tiger's Child: The Story of a Gifted, Troubled Child & the Teacher Who Refused to Give Up... Torey Hayden. 1995. 21.00 (0-02-549150-4) S&S Trade.

Tiger's Daughter. Bharati Mukherjee. 1992. mass mkt. 5.99 (0-449-22100-8, Crest) Fawcett.

***Tiger's Daughter.** Bharati Mukherjee. 1996. pap. 11.00 (0-449-91270-1) Fawcett.

Tiger's Den. Andrea Davidson. (Intrigue Ser.). 1992. pap. 2.89 (0-373-22203-3, 1-22203-3) Harlequin Bks.

Tiger's Destiny. Valmik Thapar. (Illus.). 176p. 1994. pap. 22.95 (1-85626-142-5) Trafalgar.

Tiger's Eye. Karen Robards. 400p. (Orig.). 1989. mass mkt. 5.99 (0-380-75555-6) Avon.

Tiger's Eye. large type ed. Madeleine Ker. 1990. reprint ed. lib. bdg. 18.95 (0-263-12264-6, Pub. by Mills & Boon UK) Thorndike Pr.

***Tiger's Eye, the Bird's Fist: A Beginner's Guide to the Martial Arts.** Louise Rafkin. (Illus.). (YA). (gr. 3 up). 1997. 12.95 (0-614-28844-4) Little.

***Tiger's Eye, the Bird's Fist: Mastering the Self.** Louise Rafkin & Leslie Mcgrath. LC 96-35407. 1997. pap. 12.95 (0-316-73464-0) Little.

Tiger's Heart. Lauren W. Douglas. (Caitlin Reece Mystery Ser.: No. 4). 240p. 1992. pap. 9.95 (1-56280-018-3) Naiad Pr.

Tiger's Heart. Lewis Orde. 720p. 1987. mass mkt. 4.50 (0-8217-2086-4, Zebra Kensgtn) Kensgtn Pub Corp.

Tiger's Heart: What Really Happened in the "Groat's-worth of Wit" Controversy of 1592. Jay Hoster. LC 93-92606. 96p. (Orig.). 1993. pap. 10.00 (0-9630946-9-6) Ravine Bks.

Tigers in a Tea Cup: Collected Haiku. rev. ed. Jane Reichhold. (Illus.). 344p. 1988. pap. 12.95 (0-944676-07-3) AHA Bks.

Tigers in the Dark: A Call to Courage & Christian Maturity. Thomas L. Butts. 110p. 1994. reprint ed. pap. text ed. 7.95 (0-940882-19-1) HB Pubns.

***Tigers Must Prey.** Susan Nagelsen & Charles Huckelbury. 248p. (Orig.). 1998. mass mkt. 4.99 (1-55237-442-4, Pub. by Comnwlth Pub CN) Partners Pubs Grp.

***Tiger's New Car.** Illus. by Terry Burton. (My Big Little Fat Bks.). 20p. (J). (ps up). 1997. bds. 3.49 (1-85854-599-4) Brimax Bks.

***Tiger's New Cowboy Boots.** Irene Morck. (Illus.). 32p. (J). (gr. k-3). 1996. 15.95 (0-88995-153-5, Pub. by Red Deer CN) Orca Bk Pubs.

Tiger's New Prey. Nelson A. Ossorio et al. (Wildlife among Us Ser.). (Illus.). 48p. (J). (gr. 4-6). 1994. pap. 6.95 (1-56721-074-0) Twenty-Fifth Cent Pr.

Tigers of Lanka: From Boys to Guerrillas. M. R. Narayan. (C). 1995. reprint ed. 36.00 (81-220-0386-9, Pub. by Konark Pubs II) S Asia.

Tigers of the Night. large type ed. Vicky Martin. 592p. 1986. 25.99 (0-7089-1448-9) Ulverscroft.

Tigers of the Sea: Hawaii's Deadly Sharks. Jim Borg. 88p. 1993. pap. 12.95 (1-56647-048-X) Mutual Pub HI.

Tigers of the Snow & Other Virtual Sherpas. Vincanne Adams. LC 95-4618. 296p. 1996. text ed. 49.50 (0-691-03441-9) Princeton U Pr.

Tigers of the Snow & Other Virtual Sherpas: An Ethnography of Himalayan Encounters. Vincanne Adams. 296p. (C). 1996. pap. text ed. 16.95 (0-691-00111-1) Princeton U Pr.

Tigers of the World: The Biology, Biopolitics, Management, & Conservation of an Endangered Species. Ed. by Ronald Tilson & Ulysses S. Seal. LC 87-12204. (Illus.). 510p. 1988. 64.00 (0-8155-1133-7) Noyes.

***Tigers of '68: Baseball's Last Real Champions.** George Cantor. LC 96-29580. (Illus.). 256p. 1997. 22.95 (0-87833-928-0) Taylor Pub.

Tigers on the Tenth Day & Other Stories. Zakaria Tamer. Tr. by Denys Johnson-Davies. 128p. 1993. 14.95 (0-7043-2465-2, Pub. by Quartet UK) Interlink Pub.

***Tigers, Rice, Silk, & Silt: Environment & Economy in Late Imperial South China.** Robert B. Marks. (Studies in Environment & History). (Illus.). 300p. (C). 1997. text ed. 59.95 (0-521-59177-5) Cambridge U Pr.

Tiger's Tail. Gus Lee. 288p. 1996. 24.00 (0-679-43855-6) Knopf.

Tiger's Tail. Gus Lee. (Illus.). 1997. mass mkt. 6.99 (0-8041-1326-2) Ivy Books.

***Tiger's Tale: The Indian Tiger's Struggle for Survival in the Wild.** Anup Shah & Manoj Shah. (Illus.). 144p. 1997. 39.95 (0-86343-391-X, Pub. by Fountain Pr UK) Fisher Bks.

***Tiger's Tale of Twirptown.** (Little Twirps: Understanding People Storybooks: No. 61). 40p. (J). (gr. k-5). 1996. pap. 4.98 (0-89544-061-X) Silbert Bress.

Tiger's Vacation. Ann J. Mooney. 1994. pap. text ed. 7.95 (0-9631035-2-0) Jamondas Pr.

Tiger's Whisker: And Other Tales from Asia, the Pacific, & the Middle East. Harold Courlander. LC 95-15322. (Illus.). (J). 1995. pap. 10.95 (0-8050-3512-5) H Holt & Co.

Tigerskin. Joel M. Levin. 14p. (Orig.). 1981. pap. text ed. 0.75 (1-879594-05-6) Androgyne Bks.

Tigger: Story of a Mayan Ocelot. Bunny. LC 66-12746. (Illus.). (J). (gr. k-2). 1974. 6.95 (0-87208-009-9) Shoeless Pub.

Tigger & the Apple Tree. Walt Disney Productions Staff. (Mickey's Young Readers Library Ser.: Vol. 8). (Illus.). (J). (gr. 1-6). reprint ed. 3.49 (1-885222-41-6) Advance Pubs.

***Tigger Bounce.** Oyster. Date not set. 14.95 (0-7868-2786-6) Disney Pr.

Tigger Bounces Back. Disney Studios Staff. (Winnie the Pooh Ser.). (Illus.). 10p. (J). (ps-3). 1994. 6.98 (1-57082-095-3) Mouse Works.

Tigger Has Breakfast. A. A. Milne. (Illus.). 24p. (J). 1996. pap. 3.50 (0-525-45529-9) Dutton Child Bks.

***Tigger Tales.** Mouse Works. (J). 1997. 5.98 (1-57082-693-5) Mouse Works.

Tiggy Primary Academics (ps-12) A Reproducible Social Studies Through Literature Mini Program & Reproducible Student Storybook: Tiggy & Me & Butterfly, Too! Joan Barrie. Tr. by T. Blanco et al. LC 92-23008. (Illus.). 330p. (ENG, JPN & SPA.). 1993. Incl. 3 ring binder, 3 hole punch manuscript, tchr's. man., pupil's text, 50 p. wkbk. teacher ed., ring bd. 19.95 (0-936788-14-3) Evrst Cultural.

***Tight & Taut Submanifolds.** Ed. by Thomas E. Cecil & Shiling-Shen Chern. (Mathematical Sciences Research Institute Publications: Vol. 32). 200p. (C). 1997. write for info. (0-521-62047-3) Cambridge U Pr.

Tight & Trim Buns & Thighs. Karen Amen. 128p. 1996. pap. 16.00 (0-517-88621-9) Crown Pub Group.

***Tight As a Tick.** Toni L. Kelner. 320p. 1998. write for info. (1-57566-242-6, Knsington) Kensgtn Pub Corp.

***Tight Buns, Trim Thighs.** Karen Amen. 1997. pap. 3.99 (0-517-17566-5) Random Hse Value.

Tight Closure & Its Applications. Craig L. Huneke. LC 96-4965. (Conference Board of the Mathematical Sciences Ser.: No. 88). (Illus.). 137p. 1996. 29.00 (0-8218-0412-X, CBMS/88) Am Math.

Tight Corner. Ken Grundy & Mallett. (Illus.). 96p. 1995. pap. 7.95 (0-8362-0422-0) Andrews & McMeel.

Tight Corner. large type ed. Basil Copper. (Linford Mystery Library). 304p. 1994. pap. 15.99 (0-7089-7564-X, Linford) Ulverscroft.

Tight Cornered. Ken Grundy. LC 96-84109. (Tight Corner Collection). (Illus.). 96p. (Orig.). 1996. pap. 8.95 (0-8362-2124-9) Andrews & McMeel.

Tight End. Matt Christopher. (J). (gr. 4-6). 1986. write for info. (0-318-61361-1); mass mkt. 3.95 (0-316-14054-6) Little.

***Tight-Fittin' Jeans.** Mary L. Baxter. (Desire Ser.). 1997. mass mkt. 3.50 (0-373-76057-4, 1-76057-8) Silhouette.

Tight Junction. Marcelino Cereijido. (Illus.). 384p. 1991. 189.00 (0-8493-8850-3, QH603) CRC Pr.

Tight Lines. large type ed. Bill Walsh. (Mystery Library). 368p. 1995. pap. 15.99 (0-7089-7651-4, Linford) Ulverscroft.

Tight Money Timing: The Impact of Interest Rates & the Federal Reserve on the Stock Market. Wilfred R. George. LC 81-12131. 256p. 1982. text ed. 55.00 (0-275-91708-8, C1708, Praeger Pubs) Greenwood.

Tight Polyhedral Submanifolds & Tight Triangulations, Vol. VII. Wolfgang Kuhnel. Ed. by A. Dold & F. Takens. (Lecture Notes in Mathematics Ser.: Vol. 1612). 122p. 1995. 29.95 (3-540-60121-X) Spr-Verlag.

Tight Rein. Bonnie Bryant. (Saddle Club Ser.: No. 57). 144p. (J). (gr. 4-7). 1996. pap. 3.99 (0-553-48370-6, Skylark BDD) BDD Bks Young Read.

Tight Ships Don't Sink: Profit Secrets from a No-Nonsense CEO. Gary Sutton & Brian S. Tracy. LC 93-4454. 1993. pap. text ed. 14.95 (0-13-035973-4) P-H.

Tight Times. Barbara S. Hazen. (Illus.). 32p. (J). (ps-3). 1983. pap. 4.99 (0-14-050442-7, Puffin) Puffin Bks.

Tight White Collar. John L'Heureux. LC 93-13352. 224p. 1993. pap. 10.00 (0-14-015526-0, Penguin Bks) Viking Penguin.

Tighten Your Helmet Strings in the Hour of Victory. Ed. by Douglass Hubbard. (Illus.). 1990. pap. 2.00 (0-934841-11-X) Adm Nimitz Foun.

Tightening the Circle over Eel Country. Elisavietta Ritchie. LC 74-17130. 110p. 1974. pap. 4.95 (0-87491-390-X) Signal Bks.

Tightening the Knot: Couple-Tested Ideas to Keep Your Marriage Strong. Susan A. Yates & Allison Y. Gaskins. LC 95-67771. 160p. 1995. pap. 6.00 (0-89109-905-0) Pinon Press.

Tightening the Reins of Justice in America: A Comparative Analysis of the Criminal Jury Trial in England & the United States. Michael H. Graham. LC 82-12029. (Contributions in Legal Studies: No. 26). (Illus.). xiii, 341p. 1983. text ed. 55.00 (0-313-23598-8, GJA/) Greenwood.

Tightrope. Don Pendleton. (Super Bolan Ser.: No. 15). 352p. (Orig.). 1989. mass mkt. 3.95 (0-373-61415-2) Harlequin Bks.

Tightrope for Three. Marian Babson. 192p. 1990. 16.95 (0-8027-5750-2) Walker & Co.

Tightrope for Three. large type ed. Marian Babson. LC 93-8879. (Nightingale Ser.). 1993. lib. bdg. 16.95 (0-8161-5255-1, GK Hall) Thorndike Pr.

***Tightrope to Tomorrow: Pensions, Productivity, & Public Education.** Morton J. Marcus. 152p. (C). 1997. text ed. 24.98 (0-7842-0866-2, 401-BK) Agency Instr Tech.

***Tightrope Walk: Identity, Survival & the Corporate World in African American Literature.** James R. Saunders. LC 97-47867. 168p. 1997. lib. bdg. 28.50 (0-7864-0358-6) McFarland & Co.

Tightrope Walker. Dorothy Gilman. 1986. mass mkt. 5.99 (0-449-21177-0, Crest) Fawcett.

***Tightrope Walker.** Francisco Pittau. (J). 0009. lib. bdg. write for info. (0-688-12380-5) Lothrop.

Tightrope Walker: Autobiographical Writings of Anne Wilkinson. Ed. by Joan Coldwell. 288p. 1992. 35.00 (0-8020-5745-4) U of Toronto Pr.

***Tightrope Walkers.** large type ed. Daphne Wright. (Charnwood Large Print Ser.). 544p. 1996. 27.99 (0-7089-8904-7) Ulverscroft.

Tightrope Walkers: A Greenwood Archival Edition. Giorgio Melchiori. LC 73-14036. 277p. 1974. reprint ed. text ed. 65.00 (0-8371-7141-5, METW, Greenwood Pr) Greenwood.

***Tightwad Gazette, Vol. 3.** Amy Dacyczyn. 1997. pap. 12.99 (0-679-77766-0, Villard Bks) Random.

Tightwad Gazette: Promoting Thrift As a Viable Alternative Lifestyle. Amy Dacyczyn. LC 92-22876. 1993. 9.95 (0-679-74403-7, Villard Bks); pap. 12.99 (0-679-74388-X, Villard Bks) Random.

Tightwad Gazette II. Amy Dacyczyn. LC 94-12490. (Illus.). 1995. pap. 12.99 (0-679-75078-9, Villard Bks) Random.

***Tightwad 20-Year Road to Riches Budget Book.** Michael Greene, Jr. (Illus.). 168p. 1997. vinyl bd. 21.00 (1-886197-13-X) Joy Books.

***Tightwad's Guide to Free Email & Other Cool Internet Stuff.** David Ebner & Henry Mullish. LC 97-13880. 200p. 1997. pap. 19.95 (1-56690-140-5, OnWord Pr) High Mtn.

Tiglath Pileser Third. Abraham S. Anspacher. LC 70-158263. (Columbia University. Contributions to Oriental History & Philology Ser.: No. 5). reprint ed. 39.50 (0-404-50535-X) AMS Pr.

Tigran Petrosian - World Champion. A. O. De Galway. 1965. 64.00 (0-08-011013-4, Pergamon Pr); pap. 45.00 (0-08-011012-6, Pergamon Pr) Elsevier.

Tigre Grammar & Texts. S. Raz. LC 81-71735. (Afroasiatic Dialects Ser.: Vol. 4). 163p. (C). 1983. pap. 24.50 (0-89003-097-9) Undena Pubns.

Tigre Juan, el Curandero de su Honra. Ramon Perez De Ayala. Ed. by Miguel A. Lozano Marcos. (Nueva Austral Ser.: Vol. 122). (SPA.). 1991. pap. text ed. 24.95 (84-239-1922-6) Elliots Bks.

Tigrela: & Other Stories. Lygia F. Telles. (Latin American Ser.). 160p. 1986. pap. 3.95 (0-380-89627-3, Bard) Avon.

Tigresa. Helen Cowcher. Tr. by Aida E. Marcuse. 32p. (SPA.). (J). (gr. 4-8). 1993. pap. 5.95 (0-374-47779-5) FS&G.

Tigresa: Tigress. Helen Cowcher. (J). (ps-3). 1993. 16.00 (0-374-37565-8, Mirasol) FS&G.

Tigress. Jennifer Blake. 1996. mass mkt. 4.99 (0-449-14954-4) Fawcett.

Tigress. Helen Cowcher. (Illus.). 32p. (J). (ps up). 1991. bds. 14.95 (0-374-37567-4) FS&G.

Tigress. Helen Cowcher. (J). (ps-3). 1993. pap. 5.95 (0-374-47781-7) FS&G.

***Tigress.** Helen Cowcher. (Illus.). 34p. (J). 3.98 (0-8317-2263-0) Smithmark.

***Tigress.** large type ed. Jennifer Blake. LC 96-32353. 1996. 25.95 (1-56895-361-5, Compass) Wheeler Pub.

Tigrinya Grammar. Ed. by John Mason. LC 95-26821. (ENG & TIR.). 1996. 35.00 (0-932415-20-2); pap. 12.95 (0-932415-21-0) Red Sea Pr.

Tiguas: Pueblo Indians of Texas. Bill Wright. LC 92-62200. 161p. 1993. 40.00 (0-87404-229-1) Tex Western.

***Tihkal: A Continuation.** Ann Shulgin & Alexander Shulgin. (Illus.). (Orig.). 1997. pap. 24.50 (0-9630096-9-9, 02) Transform Pr.

Tijuana: Stories on the Border. Federico Campbell. Tr. by Debra A. Castillo. LC 94-9498. (ENG & SPA.). 1995. 30.00 (0-520-08946-4); pap. 13.00 (0-520-08603-1) U CA Pr.

Tijuana: The History of a Mexican Metropolis. abr. ed. T. D. Proffitt, III. 426p. (C). 1993. pap. text ed. 29.50 (0-916304-90-6); lib. bdg. 66.00 (1-879691-01-9) SDSU Press.

Tijuana: Urbanization in a Border Culture. John A. Price. LC 72-1264. (Illus.). 217p. 1973. reprint ed. pap. 61.90 (0-608-00889-3, 2061683) Bks Demand.

***Tijuana Bibles.** Merkin. 1997. 24.00 (0-684-83461-8, S&S Editions) S&S Trade.

Tijuana Handbook & Souvenir Guide. Bob McPhail. 48p. 1996. reprint ed. pap. text ed. 3.00 (0-9646406-0-0) CF Pub CA.

Tijuana Sunday. Leigh Weiner. 263p. 1990. 40.00 (0-9619146-1-0); pap. 24.95 (0-9619146-2-9) Seventy Four Ten.

Tijuanenses. Federico Campbell. (SPA.). 1996. pap. 12.50 (0-679-76846-7, Vin) Random.

Tik-Tok of Oz. L. Frank Baum. (Illus.). 304p. (J). (gr. 3-6). 1996. 22.00 (0-688-13355-X, Morrow Junior) Morrow.

Tik-Tok of Oz. L. Frank Baum. (J). pap. 4.95 (0-8167-2895-X) Troll Communs.

Tik-Tok of Oz. L. Frank Baum. LC 93-37906. (Illus.). 304p. (J). reprint ed. pap. 6.95 (0-486-28002-0) Dover.

Tika the Tiger. Kathy Quigley. (Friends of the Forest Adventure Bks.). (Illus.). (J). (ps-8). 1995. 16.95 (0-9641742-8-6) Pequot Pubng.

Tikal: A Novel about the Maya. Daniel Peters. LC 83-3273. 422p. 1983. 16.95 (0-394-53278-3) Random.

Tikal Report: No. 31, The Graffiti of Tikal. Helen W. Trik & Michael E. Kampen. Ed. by William R. Coe. (University Museum Monographs: No. 57). (Illus.). 128p. 1983. text ed. 30.00 (0-934718-56-3) U PA Mus Pubns.

Tikal Report, No. 13: The Settlement Survey of Tikal. Dennis E. Puleston. (University Museum Monographs: No. 48). (Illus.). 136p. 1983. text ed. 30.00 (0-934718-47-4) U PA Mus Pubns.

Tikal Report, No. 14: Excavations in the Great Plaza, North Terrace & North Acropolis of Tikal. William R. Coe. (Monographs: No. 61). (Illus.). 1100p. 1990. text ed. 395.00 (0-934718-66-0) U PA Mus Pubns.

Tikal Report, No. 19: Excavations in Small Residential Groups of Tikal, Group 4F-1 & 4F-2. William A. Haviland. Ed. by William R. Coe. (University Museum Monographs: No. 58). (Illus.). xvi, 200p. 1985. text ed. 75.00 (0-934718-58-X) U PA Mus Pubns.

Tikal Report No. 25A Ceramics of Tikal. Patrick T. Culbert. LC 93-14674. (University Museum Monographs: Vol. 81). (C). text ed. 65.00 (0-924171-20-0) U PA Mus Pubns.

Tikal Reports, Nos. 1-11: Facsimile Reissue of Original Reports Published 1958-1961. Edwin M. Shook et al. (University Museum Monographs: No. 64). (Illus.). xiv, 401p. 1986. 29.00 (0-934718-75-X); text ed. 39.00 (0-934718-74-1) U PA Mus Pubns.

Tikal y Uaxactun en el Preclasico. Ed. by Juan P. Laporte & Juan A. Valdes. 126p. 1993. pap. 9.20 (968-36-2673-4, UN010) UPLAAP.

Tiki: Spirit Unbroken. Charlotte B. Reid. LC 94-90588. (Illus.). 144p. (Orig.). 1995. pap. 11.95 (0-9643061-3-1) Egret Press.

***Tiki Doll of Doom.** Betsy Haynes. 144p. 1997. mass mkt. 3.99 (0-06-106447-5, Harp PBks) HarpC.

Tikip Santakki Mala Basmu... Eine Festschrift Fur Rykle Borger Zu Seinem 65. Geburtstag am 24. Mai 1994. Ed. by Stefan M. Maul. 1996. write for info. (0-614-96308-7, Pub. by Styx NE) Eisenbrauns.

Tikki Tikki Tembo. Illus. by Blair Lent. LC 68-11839. 48p. (J). (ps-2). 1989. pap. 5.95 (0-8050-1166-8, Bks Young Read) H Holt & Co.

An Asterisk (*) at the beginning of an entry indicates that the title is appearing in BIP for the first time.

Tikki Tikki Tembo. Arlene Mosel. LC 68-11839. (Illus.). 48p. (J). (ps-2). 1968. 15.95 (*0-8050-0662-1*, Bks Young Read) H Holt & Co.

Tikki Tikki Tembo. Arlene Mosel. Tr. by Liwayway Alonso. LC 68-11839. (Illus.). 48p. (J). 1994. 14.95 (*1-880507-13-7*) Lectorum Pubns.

Tikki Tikki Tembo: Big Book. Arlene Mosel. LC 68-11839. (Illus.). 32p. (J). (ps-2). 1992. pap. 19.95 (*0-8050-2345-3*, Bks Young Read) H Holt & Co.

Tikkun: To Heal, Repair & Transform the World. Michael Lerner. 1992. 39.95 (*0-935933-03-4*); pap. 16.95 (*0-935933-04-2*) Inst Labor & Mental.

***Tikkun Olam: Social Responsibility in Jewish Thought & Law.** Ed. by David Shatz et al. LC 96-28578. 1997. pap. 40.00 (*0-7657-5951-9*) Aronson.

Tikla. George P. Lewnes. (Illus.). 229p. (C). 1988. reprint ed. 13.95 (*0-9623211-0-9*); reprint ed. lib. bdg. 10.00 (*0-685-26168-9*) T Lewnes Pub.

Tikopia Songs: Poetic & Musical Art of a Polynesian People of the Solomon Islands. Raymond Firth & Mervyn McClean. (Studies in Oral & Literate Culture: No. 20). (Illus.). 336p. (C). 1991. text ed. 80.00 (*0-521-39129-6*) Cambridge U Pr.

Tikoun Haklali. Rabbi Nachman. Tr. by Alon Dimermanas from HEB. 125p. (FRE.). 1986. pap. text ed. 3.00 (*0-930213-24-6*) Breslov Res Inst.

Tikoun Haklali. rev. ed. Nachman. Ed. & Tr. by A. Dimermanas. 115p. (FRE.). 1989. pap. text ed. 7.00 (*0-930213-34-3*) Breslov Res Inst.

Tiktala. Margaret Shaw-MacKinnon. (Illus.). (J). (gr. k-3). 1996. 15.95 (*0-8234-1221-0*) Holiday.

Tikta'Liktak. Houghton Mifflin Company Staff. (Literature Experience 1993 Ser.). (J). (gr. 5). 1992. pap. 9.16 (*0-395-61812-6*) HM.

Tikta'liktak. James R. Houston. LC 89-32473. (Inuit-Eskimo Legend Ser.). (Illus.). 64p. (J). (gr. 3-7). 1990. pap. 10.00 (*0-15-287748-7*) HarBrace.

***Tikun Olam: Fixing the World.** Anne L. Fenton. LC 97-24607. (Illus.). 32p. (YA). (gr. 3 up). 1997. 17.95 (*1-57129-049-4*) Brookline Bks.

Tikune Zohar: Hebrew Text, 3 vols., 1. Yehuda Brandwein. 850p. 1973. write for info. (*0-943688-27-2*) Res Ctr Kabbalah.

Tikune Zohar: Hebrew Text, 3 vols., 2. Yehuda Brandwein. 850p. 1973. write for info. (*0-943688-28-0*) Res Ctr Kabbalah.

Tikune Zohar: Hebrew Text, 3 vols., 3. Yehuda Brandwein. 850p. 1973. write for info. (*0-924457-53-8*) Res Ctr Kabbalah.

Tikvah Means Hope. Patricia Polacco. (Illus.). 48p. (J). (ps-3). 1994. 15.95 (*0-385-32059-0*) Doubleday.

Tikvah Means Hope. Patricia Polacco. (Illus.). 48p. (J). (ps-3). 1996. pap. 5.99 (*0-440-41229-3*, Picture Yearling) BDD Bks Young Read.

Til All the Stars Have Fallen: A Collection of Poems for Children. Illus. by Kady M. Denton. 96p. (J). (ps-3). 1994. pap. 6.99 (*0-14-034438-1*) Puffin Bks.

Til Death. Ed McBain. (Eighty-Seventh Precinct Mysteries Ser.). 176p. 1989. mass mkt. 4.50 (*0-451-15891-1*, Sig) NAL-Dutton.

***Til Death Do Us Part.** Lurlene McDaniel. (J). 1997. mass mkt. 4.50 (*0-553-57085-4*) BDD Bks Young Read.

Til Death Do Us Part: A Basic Education in Total Health: How to Keep Body & Soul Happily Together. Martin P. Cornelius, III. 256p. (Orig.). (C). 1981. pap. 15.00 (*0-9607142-0-0*) Health Ed & Life Exp Res.

Til Death Do Us Part: A Study & Guide to Long-Term Marriage. Jeanette C. Lauer & Robert H. Lauer. LC 86-22735. (Marriage & Family Review Ser.: Supp. No. 1). 192p. 1986. pap. text ed. 14.95 (*0-918393-32-9*) Harrington Pk.

Til Death Do Us Part: How Couples Stay Together. Jeanette C. Lauer & Robert H. Lauer. LC 86-22735. (Supplement to Marriage & Family Review Ser.: No. 1). 192p. 1986. text ed. 39.95 (*0-86656-601-5*) Haworth Pr.

***Til Golf Do Us Part: The Trials & Tribulations of Golf Widows in Coping with Their Obsessed Golfers.** Fred H. Thomas. (Illus.). 112p. 1997. pap. 8.95 (*0-930753-23-2*) Spect Ln Pr.

Til Healing Comes. Ken Dignan. 164p. (Orig.). 1993. pap. 8.95 (*1-883928-00-1*) Longwood.

Til I Come Marching Home: A Brief History of American Women in World War II. C. Kay Larson. LC 95-81150. (Illus.). (Orig.). 1995. pap. 10.00 (*0-9634895-2-6*) Minerva Ctr.

Til Judgment Day. Harry L. Graham. 236p. 1994. pap. 14.00 (*0-9644857-0-2*) Wrds & Pict Pr.

Til Love's Known. Linda Bairstow. LC 94-73493. 1995. pap. 12.00 (*0-87212-263-8*) Libra.

Til Politics Do Us Part: A Political Wife's Declaration of Independence. Paula Blanchard. 240p. 1990. 18.95 (*1-878005-01-4*) Northmont Pub.

Til the Fat Lady Sings: Classic Texas Sports Quotes. Alan Burton. (Illus.). 192p. (Orig.). 1994. pap. 9.95 (*0-89672-339-9*) Tex Tech Univ Pr.

Til the Real Thing Comes Along. Iris Rainer Dart. 416p. (Orig.). 1995. mass mkt. 6.50 (*0-446-60123-3*) Warner Bks.

'Til Tomorrow. Sandra Marton. 384p. 1996. mass mkt. 4.99 (*0-7860-0229-8*, Pinncle Kensgtn) Kensgtn Pub Corp.

Til We Meet Again. John McQuarrie. 1992. 34.95 (*0-07-551301-3*, Pub. by McGrw-Hill Ryerson CN) Howell Pr VA.

Til We Meet Again. Helen Mittermeyer. (Loveswept Ser.: No. 621). 1993. pap. 3.50 (*0-553-44243-0*, Loveswept) Bantam.

Til We Meet Again. Kimberly Raye. (Shadows Ser.). 1996. mass mkt. 3.50 (*0-373-27060-7*, 1-27060-2) Silhouette.

Til What Do We Part? A Wedding Planner to the Etiquette Impaired. Tom Carey & Greg Schnem. (Illus.). 128p. (Orig.). 1996. pap. 7.95 (*1-877590-84-3*) DE Pr IL.

Tilak & Gokhale: A Comparative Study. Mohammad S. Khan. xii, 376p. 1992. 39.00 (*81-7024-478-1*, Pub. by Ashish Pub Hse II) Nataraj Bks.

Tilapia Genetic Resources for Aquaculture. Ed. by Roger S. Pullin. (Conference Proceedings Ser.: No. 16). 108p. 1988. pap. 7.40 (*971-10-2244-3*, Pub. by ICLARM PH) Intl Spec Bk.

Tilbury Score: Centennial Edition. E. A. Robinson. 1987. reprint ed. pap. 5.00 (*0-912156-05-8*) Masterwork Pr.

Tilden & Tennis in the Twenties. Arthur Voss. LC 84-51651. 194p. 1985. 15.00 (*0-87875-291-9*) Whitston Pub.

Tildy. large type ed. Sara Fraser. (Magna General Fiction Ser.). 1992. 19.95 (*0-7505-0432-3*, Pub. by Magna Print Bks UK) Ulverscroft.

***Tildy: Invincible Woman.** Sara Fraser. 445p. write for info. (*0-7505-0926-0*, Pub. by Magna Print Bks UK) Ulverscroft.

Tildy: Nursing Woman. large type ed. Sara Fraser. 398p. 1994. 25.99 (*0-7505-0600-8*) Ulverscroft.

Tildy- Pointing Woman. large type ed. Sara Fraser. 1995. 25.99 (*0-7505-0726-8*, Pub. by Magna Print Bks UK) Ulverscroft.

Tile. Jill Hebers. LC 96-21062. (Illus.). 192p. 1996. 35.00 (*1-885183-29-1*) Artisan.

***Tile Decorating Book: Practical Ideas for Creating & Designing with Tiles.** Marion Elliot. (Illus.). 160p. 1997. 27.50 (*1-85967-529-8*, Lorenz Bks) Anness Pub.

Tile Floors. 2nd ed. Dan Ramsey. (Illus.). 164p. 1991. pap. 13.95 (*0-8306-3535-1*) McGraw-Hill Prof.

Tile Floors. 2nd ed. Dan Ramsey. (Illus.). 164p. 1991. 22.95 (*0-8306-7535-3*, 3535) TAB Bks.

Tile Panels of Spain, 1500-1650. Alice W. Frothingham. (Illus.). 1969. 30.00 (*0-87535-110-7*) Hispanic Soc.

Tile Roofs of Alfred: A Clay Tradition in Alfred, NY. Susan Tunick et al. 12p. (Orig.). pap. 7.00 (*0-9636061-1-5*) Frnds of TC.

***Tile Style Pattern Guide.** Jill Blake. 160p. 1996. 24.95 (*1-57715-006-6*) Knckerbocker.

Tiled Furniture. Hans Van Lemmen. 1989. pap. 25.00 (*0-7478-0046-4*, Pub. by Shire UK) St Mut.

Tiler's Afternoon. Lars Gustafsson. Tr. by Tom Geddes from SWE. LC 93-16457. 128p. (Orig.). 1993. pap. 8.95 (*0-8112-1240-8*, NDP761) New Directions.

Tiles. Olivia B. Buehl. 1996. 40.00 (*0-517-79976-6*, C P Pubs) Crown Pub Group.

Tiles: A Collector's Guide. rev. ed. Hans Van Lemmen. (Illus.). 144p. 1990. pap. 18.95 (*0-285-62957-3*) Intl Spec Bk.

Tiles: One Thousand Years of Architectural Decoration. Hans Van Lemmen. LC 93-7308. 1993. 60.00 (*0-8109-3867-7*) Abrams.

Tilesetting: Workbook. California Department of Education Staff. (Apprenticeship Instructional Materials Ser.). (Illus.). 254p. 1986. pap. 16.00 (*0-8011-0490-4*) Calif Education.

Tilesetting, Testbook. California Department of Education Staff. (Apprenticeship Instructional Materials Ser.). 104p. 1986. pap. 5.50 (*0-8011-0491-2*) Calif Education.

Tilford Trails. Pearl O. Smith. 278p. 1991. 19.00 (*0-685-71952-9*) Weeks Pubs.

Tilghman Expression Emotion. 1970. pap. text ed. 41.50 (*90-247-5011-3*, Pub. by M Nijhoff NE) Kluwer Ac.

Tilghman-Tillman Family 1225-1945. Stephen F. Tillman. (Illus.). 473p. 1994. reprint ed. pap. 69.50 (*0-8328-3988-4*); reprint ed. lib. bdg. 79.50 (*0-8328-3987-6*) Higginson Bk Co.

Tilings & Patterns. Geoffrey C. Shephard. LC 86-2007. (Illus.). 700p. (C). 1995. text ed. write for info. (*0-7167-1193-1*); pap. text ed. write for info. (*0-7167-1194-X*) W H Freeman.

Till a Hundred & Twenty Years: A Memoir. Jo-Ann Middleman. LC 95-94698. 224p. 1995. pap. 12.95 (*0-9647771-0-X*) EMESS Pr.

Till Armageddon see Hasta el Armagedon

Till Armageddon - Chinese Edition. Billy Graham. Tr. by Violet W. Chen. 309p. (CHI.). 1993. pap. 8.00 (*1-56582-043-6*) Christ Renew Min.

Till Death Do Us Part. Katharine H. Fryer. 320p. 1994. pap. write for info. (*0-9640468-0-6*) K H Fryer.

Till Death Do Us Part. Carolyn Keene. (Nancy Drew Files Ser.: No. 24). (Orig.). (J). 1988. pap. 2.95 (*0-318-35168-4*) PB.

Till Death Do Us Part. Rochelle M. Krich. 304p. (Orig.). 1992. mass mkt. 4.99 (*0-380-76533-0*) Avon.

***Till Death Do Us Part.** Lurlene McDaniel. (J). 1997. write for info. (*0-614-29176-3*, Starfire BDD) BDD Bks Young Read.

Till Death Do Us Part. John Dickson Carr. 224p. 1989. reprint ed. pap. 5.95 (*1-55882-017-5*, Lib Crime Classics) Intl Polygonics.

***Till Death Do Us Part: A Multicultural Anthology on Marriage.** Ed. by Sandra L. Browning & R. Robin Miller. (Contemporary Studies in Sociology: Vol. 14). 1998. 73.25 (*0-7623-0263-1*) Jai Pr.

***Till Death Do Us Part: The Ultimate Divorce Guide.** F. A. Forester. 1997. pap. text ed. 17.95 (*1-880231-16-6*) Intelligence.

***Till Death Do Us Part: What the Bible Really Says about Marriage & Divorce.** 3rd expanded rev. ed. Joseph A. Webb. (Illus.). 274p. 1996. per., pap. 12.95 (*0-9632226-2-7*) Webb Minist.

***Till Death or Whatever Do Us Part.** Garry M. Kluger. Ed. by William-Alan Landes. LC 96-47435. 68p. (Orig.). 1996. pap. 6.00 (*0-88734-706-1*) Players Pr.

Till Death Us Do Part: (43 Light St.) Rebecca York. (Intrigue Ser.). 1995. mass mkt. 3.50 (*0-373-22318-8*, 1-22318-9) Harlequin Bks.

Till Debt Do Us Part: Who Wins, Who Loses, & Who Pays for the International Debt Crisis. Alfred J. Watkins. LC 85-40999. 108p. (Orig.). 1986. pap. text ed. 13.50 (*0-8191-5176-9*); lib. bdg. 34.50 (*0-8191-5175-0*) U Pr of Amer.

Till Debt Due Us Part: The Step-by-Step Guide to Getting Out of Debt & Managing Your Money. Derek A. Marquis. 1993. pap. 16.95 (*1-883163-23-4*) DC Pubs & Mgmt.

Till Divorce Do Us Part: A Practical Guide for Women in Troubled Marriages. Beverly J. Grottkau & Eva A. Rumpf. LC 95-80541. 230p. 1996. 22.95 (*0-944435-39-4*) Glenbridge Pub.

Till Eulenspiegel: His Adventures. Tr. by Paul J. Oppenheimer. (World's Classics Ser.). (Illus.). 256p. 1995. pap. 8.95 (*0-19-282343-4*) OUP.

***Till Eulenspiegel & Emerging Views of the Late Medieval Period.** William C. McDonald. (LCGERM Ser.). Date not set. 59.95 (*1-57113-052-7*) Camden Hse.

***Till Freedom Cried Out: Memories of Texas Slave Life.** Ed. by T. Lindsay Baker & Julie P. Baker. LC 96-38575. (Clayton Wheat Williams Texas Life Ser.: Vol. 6). (Illus.). 192p. (C). 1997. text ed. 29.95 (*0-89096-736-9*) Tex A&M Univ Pr.

Till He Come. (Spurgeon Collection). 1995. 8.99 (*1-871676-00-2*, Pub. by Christian Focus UK) Spring Arbor Dist.

Till He Come. Charles H. Spurgeon. 1978. mass mkt. 8.00 (*1-56186-342-4*) Pilgrim Pubns.

Till Hope Creates. Ray Smith. 1981. 2.00 (*0-686-31823-4*) Kirk Pr.

Till I Find Myself: Selected Poems. Sunita Jain. 112p. 1987. text ed. 18.95 (*81-207-0615-3*, Pub. by Sterling Pubs II) Apt Bks.

Till Jesus Comes: Origins of Christian Apocalyptic Expectation. Charles Holman. 190p. 1996. pap. 12.95 (*0-943575-74-5*) Hendrickson MA.

Till Morning Breaks: A Story of the Millerite Movement & the Great Disappointment. Elaine Egbert. LC 93-13806. 1993. pap. 6.97 (*0-8163-1164-1*) Pacific Pr Pub Assn.

Till Murder Do Us Part. Ernest Volkman & John Cummings. 376p. 1994. 5.50 (*0-451-40429-7*, Onyx) NAL-Dutton.

Till September. Ginger Chambers. 1994. mass mkt. 3.50 (*0-373-70601-4*, 1-70601-9) Harlequin Bks.

Till the Bell Rings. 1981. pap. 2.95 (*0-590-49061-3*, Scholastic Hardcover) Scholastic Inc.

Till the Boys Come Home: The Picture Postcard of the First World War. Toni Holt & Valmai Holt. (Illus.). 192p. 1986. 18.95 (*0-913782-08-4*) Deltiologists Am.

Till the Butchers Cut Him Down. Marcia Muller. 1995. pap. write for info. (*0-446-40034-3*, Mysterious Paperbk); mass mkt. 5.99 (*0-446-60302-3*, Mysterious Paperbk) Warner Bks.

***Till the End of Time.** Patti Berg. 1997. mass mkt. 5.99 (*0-380-78339-8*) Avon.

Till the End of Time. Suzanne Elizabeth. 256p. 1995. mass mkt. 4.99 (*0-06-108408-5*, Harp PBks) HarpC.

Till the End of Time. Elise Title. (American Romance Ser.: No. 377). 1991. pap. 2.95 (*0-373-16377-0*) Harlequin Bks.

Till the Leaves Change. Erin Flanagan. 128p. (Orig.). (J). 1996. pap. 3.99 (*0-380-77850-5*, Camelot) Avon.

Till the Old Men Die. Janet Dawson. (Orig.). 1993. mass mkt. 4.50 (*0-449-22133-4*) Fawcett.

***Till There Was You.** Elizabeth A. Michaels. 320p. 1998. mass mkt. 4.99 (*0-8217-5821-7*, Zebra Kensgtn) Kensgtn Pub Corp.

Till Victory Is Won: Black Soldiers in the Civil War. Zak Mettger. (Illus.). 96p. (J). (gr. 5-9). 1994. pap. 16.99 (*0-525-67412-8*, Lodestar Bks) Dutton Child Bks.

***Till Victory Is Won: Black Soldiers in the Civil War.** Zak Mettger. 1997. pap. 8.99 (*0-14-038727-7*) Puffin Bks.

Till War Do Us Part. Frank Bogart & Mary Bogart. LC 95-68068. (Illus.). 160p. (Orig.). 1995. pap. 17.00 (*0-913337-24-2*) Southfarm Pr.

Till We Have Faces: A Myth Retold. C. S. Lewis. LC 79-24272. (Illus.). 320p. 1980. pap. 11.00 (*0-15-690436-5*, Harvest Bks) HarBrace.

Till We Meet Again. Judith Krantz. 608p. 1989. mass mkt. 7.50 (*0-553-28014-7*) Bantam.

***Till We Meet Again.** Penelope J. Stokes. LC 96-45608. (Faith on the Home Front Ser.: No. 2). 1997. pap. 10.99 (*0-8423-0852-0*) Tyndale.

Till Year's Good End. W. Nikola-Lisa. LC 95-45822. (J). 1997. 16.00 (*0-689-80020-7*, Atheneum Bks Young) S&S Childrens.

Till You Love Me. Burr & Dipiero. (Piano-Vocal-Guitar Ser.). 6p. 1994. pap. 3.95 (*0-7935-4286-3*, 00120024) H Leonard.

Tillage. rev. ed. Ed. by Deere & Company Staff. (Fundamentals of Machine Operation Ser.). (Illus.). 118p. 1993. student ed., pap. text ed. 21.95 (*0-86691-196-0*, FMO11603W) Deere & Co.

Tillage. 3rd ed. Ed. by Deere & Company Staff. (Fundamentals of Machine Operation Ser.). (Illus.). 232p. 1993. teacher ed., pap. text ed. 79.95 incl. trans. (*0-86691-195-2*, FMO11503T) Deere & Co.

Tillage. 3rd rev. ed. Ed. by Deere & Company Staff. (Fundamentals of Machine Operation Ser.). (Illus.). 172p. 1993. pap. text ed. 29.95 (*0-86691-180-4*, FMO11103B) Deere & Co.

***Tillage.** 3rd rev. ed. Ed. by Deere & Company Staff. (Fundamentals of Machine Operation Ser.). 148p. 1993. sl. 148.95 (*0-614-24207-X*, FMO11203S) Deere & Co.

***Tillage Systems for Soil & Water Conservation.** 296p. 1984. 35.00 (*92-5-102154-6*, F2730, Pub. by FAO IT) Bernan Associates.

Tillamook Burn Country: A Pictorial History. Ellis Lucia. LC 83-18164. (Illus.). (Orig.). 1983. pap. 14.95 (*0-87004-296-3*) Caxton.

Tillamook Light. James A. Gibbs. LC 79-65015. (Illus.). 145p. 1995. pap. 11.95 (*0-8323-0344-5*) Binford Mort.

Tillandsioideae (Bromeliaceae) Lyman B. Smith & Robert J. Downs. LC 76-55104. (Flora Neotropica Monographs: Vol. 14, No. 2). (Illus.). 830p. (Orig.). 1988. reprint ed. pap. 49.50 (*0-89327-297-3*) NY Botanical.

***Tille Hoyuk Vol. 1: The Medieval Period.** John Moore. (Illus.). 205p. 1993. 80.00 (*1-898249-00-8*, Pub. by Brit Inst Arch UK) David Brown.

***Tille Hoyuk Vol. 4: The Late Bronze Age & the Iron Age Transition.** G. D. Summers. (Illus.). 203p. 1993. 72.00 (*1-898249-01-6*, Pub. by Brit Inst Arch UK) David Brown.

Tiller & the Pen: A Collection of Sailors' Stories. Michael Badham et al. Ed. by John Ellsworth. LC 94-90405. (Illus.). 192p. (Orig.). 1994. pap. 12.00 (*0-9642853-0-4*) Eighth Moon.

Tillers: An Oral History of Family Farms in California. Ann F. Scheuring. LC 83-4179. (Illus.). 300p. 1983. text ed. 49.95 (*0-275-91076-8*, C1076, Praeger Pubs) Greenwood.

Tillers of a Myth: Southern Agrarians As Social & Literary Critics. Alexander Karanikas. LC 66-11802. 263p. 1996. reprint ed. pap. 75.00 (*0-608-02100-8*, 2023714) Bks Demand.

Tillers of the Cultural Soil: Scholar Printers. Ronald Lieberman. (Orig.). pap. write for info. (*0-934630-19-4*) Family Album.

***Tilley the Trolley.** Rachel S. Spector. (Illus.). 20p. (Orig.). (J). (ps-3). 1996. pap. write for info. (*0-9655887-0-X*) R S S Pub.

Tilli Comes to Texas. (J). (gr. k up). 1987. lib. bdg. 15.95 incl. audio (*0-937460-57-5*); audio 6.95 (*0-937460-56-7*) Hendrick-Long.

Tilli Comes to Texas. Evelyn Oppenheimer. LC 86-3089. (Illus.). 40p. (J). (gr. k up). 1986. lib. bdg. 9.95 (*0-937460-21-4*) Hendrick-Long.

Tillie & the Wall. Leo Lionni. LC 88-9316. (Illus.). 32p. (J). (ps-2). 1989. 12.95 (*0-394-82155-6*); lib. bdg. 13.99 (*0-394-92155-0*) Knopf Bks Yng Read.

Tillie Olsen: A Study of the Short Fiction. Joanne Frye. LC 94-49320. (Twayne's Studies in Short Fiction: Vol. 60). 1995. 23.95 (*0-8057-0863-4*, Twayne) Scribnrs Ref.

Tilling the Good Earth. Dan P. Logan. LC 89-83521. 185p. 1989. pap. 7.95 (*0-944419-08-9*) Everett Cos Pub.

Tilling the Land: Poems. John J. Brugaletta. LC 92-22418. (Illus.). 68p. 1992. pap. 12.95 (*0-7734-0022-2*, Mellen Poetry Pr) E Mellen.

Tilling the Soul. Wingate Paine. 215p. 1984. pap. 10.95 (*0-943358-20-5*) Aurora Press.

Tillite Occurrence on the Canadian Shield, Vol. 1. Curt Teichert. LC 76-21824. (Thule Expedition, 5th, 1921-1924 Ser.: No. 6). reprint ed. 32.50 (*0-404-58306-7*) AMS Pr.

Tillman Movement in South Carolina. Francis B. Simkins. 1964. 14.50 (*0-8446-1408-4*) Peter Smith.

Tillman Movement in South Carolina. Francis B. Simkins. (BCL1 - United States Local History Ser.). 274p. 1991. reprint ed. lib. bdg. 79.00 (*0-7812-6299-2*) Rprt Serv.

***Tillman's Treehouse.** large type ed. Meredith B. Olson. LC 97-93132. (Illus.). 56p. (Orig.). (J). (gr. 3-4). 1997. pap. 6.95 (*0-9657061-4-1*) Glenhaven.

***Tillman's Treehouse.** large type ed. Meredith B. Olson. LC 97-93132. (Illus.). 56p. (Orig.). (J). (gr. 3-4). 1997. 11.95 (*0-9657061-5-X*) Glenhaven.

***Tills & Glaciotectonics: Proceedings of the INQUA Meeting on Genesis & Lithology of Glacial Deposits, Amsterdam, 1986.** Ed. by J. M. Van der Meer. 280p. (C). 1987. text ed. 85.00 (*90-6191-731-X*, Pub. by A A Balkema NE) Ashgate Pub Co.

Tills & Reltated Deposits - Genesis, Petrology, Applications, Stratigraphy: Proceedings of the INQUA Symposia on the Genesis & Lithology of Quaternary Deposits, USA, 1981 - Argentina, 1982. C. Schluchter. 464p. (C). 1983. text ed. 130.00 (*90-6191-511-2*, Pub. by A A Balkema NE) Ashgate Pub Co.

Till's Christmas. Nola Thacker. 144p. (J). (gr. 4-6). 1991. 13.95 (*0-590-43542-6*, Scholastic Hardcover) Scholastic Inc.

Till's Christmas. Nola Thacker. 144p. (J). (gr. 4-6). 1992. 2.95 (*0-590-43543-4*, Apple Paperbacks) Scholastic Inc.

Tilly. Frank E. Peretti. LC 88-70700. 128p. 1988. pap. 7.99 (*0-89107-496-1*) Crossway Bks.

Tilly. Frank E. Peretti. 112p. (FRE.). 1990. pap. 2.95 (*0-8297-1468-5*) Life Pubs Intl.

***Tilly the Sea Turtle.** Sharon Groce. (Illus.). (J). 1992. write for info. (*1-880258-05-6*) Thriftecon.

Tilly the Turtle. Annie Kubler. (J). 1995. pap. 7.99 (*0-85953-720-X*) Childs Play.

Tilly Trotter Wed. Catherine Cookson. 352p. 1989. mass mkt. 7.99 (*0-552-11960-1*) Bantam.

Tilly Witch. Don Freeman. (Picture Puffins Ser.). (J). (ps). 1978. pap. 4.99 (*0-14-050262-9*, Puffin) Puffin Bks.

Tillyloss Scandal. James M. Barrie. LC 77-98560. (Short Story Index Reprint Ser.). 1977. 19.95 (*0-8369-3134-3*) Ayer.

Tilman C. Cothran: Second Generation Sociologist. Gordon D. Morgan. 225p. (C). 1995. text ed. 39.95 (*1-55605-252-9*); pap. text ed. 29.95 (*1-55605-251-0*) Wyndham Hall.

Tilmann Riemenschneider: His Life & Work. fac. ed. Justus Bier. LC 80-5171. (Illus.). 142p. 1982. pap. 40.50 (*0-7837-7588-1*, 2047341) Bks Demand.

***Tiln & Other Plays.** Michael Cook. 13.95 (*0-88922-107-3*, Pub. by Talonbooks CN) Genl Dist Srvs.

Tilson. Michael Compton & Marco Livingstone. LC 93-61597. (Illus.). 184p. 1994. 45.00 (*0-500-97410-1*) Thames Hudson.

Tilson Genealogy from Edmund Tilson at Plymouth, New England, 1638-1911: Also Brief Account of Waterman, Murdock, Bertlett, Turner, Winslow, Sturtervant Keith & Parrir Family. M. Tilson. (Illus.). 610p. 1989. reprint ed. pap. 91.50 (*0-8328-1167-X*); reprint ed. lib. bdg. 99.50 (*0-8328-1166-1*) Higginson Bk Co.

Tilson Grist Mill. Pat Alderman. (Illus.). 49p. 1981. pap. 3.95 (*0-932807-07-0*) Overmountain Pr.

Tilt. Gillian McCain. 88p. 1996. pap. 10.00 (*0-935724-75-3*) Figures.

***Tilt.** Gillian McCain. 1996. pap. text ed. 10.00 (*1-889097-04-7*) Hard Pr MA.

***Tilt the World Towards Tolerance.** Glenda G. Thomson-Daniel. Ed. by Yvonne McCall. (Illus.). 100p. 1997. pap. text ed. 21.95 (*1-887003-49-5*) Dancng Jester.

Tilt-up Building: Methods & Marketing. 36p. 1988. pap. 11.95 (*0-924659-28-9*, 3990) Aberdeen Group.

Tilt-up Concrete Structures. 46p. 1992. 46.75 (*0-685-62964-3*, 551-92BOW6) ACI.

Tilt-up Construction. 80p. 1980. 22.50 (*0-317-32094-7*, C-4BOW6) ACI.

Tilt-Up Design & Construction Manual. Hugh Brooks. (Illus.). 263p. 1989. ring bd. 87.50 (*0-9623910-1-8*) HBA Pubns.

Tilt-Up Design & Construction Manual. Hugh Brooks. (Illus.). 324p. 1994. ring bd. 92.00 (*0-9623910-3-4*) HBA Pubns.

***Tilt-Up Design & Construction Manual.** 4th ed. Hugh Brooks. (Illus.). 382p. 1997. ring bd. 92.00 (*0-9623910-5-0*) HBA Pubns.

Tilt-up Load Bearing Walls: A Design Aid. rev. ed. 28p. 1994. pap. 12.00 (*0-89312-120-7*, EB074D) Portland Cement.

Tiltable Book: How to Turn the Tables on Your Railroad. Ray Matthews. (Illus.). 96p. (Orig.). 1996. pap. 14.95 (*1-884570-48-8*) Research Triangle.

Tiltawhirl John. Gary Paulsen. 1992. 17.75 (*0-8446-6535-5*) Peter Smith.

Tiltawhirl John. Gary Paulsen. (J). 1990. pap. 3.99 (*0-14-034312-1*, Puffin) Puffin Bks.

Tilted Cross. Hal Porter. 266p. 1989. reprint ed. pap. 14.95 (*0-7022-2183-X*, Pub. by Univ Queensland Pr AT) Intl Spec Bk.

Tilted Nose Defense. Denny Marcin. (Art & Science of Coaching Ser.). (Illus.). 150p. (Orig.). 1996. pap. 15.00 (*1-57167-062-9*) Sagamore Pub.

***Tilting at Matilda.** Ed. by Dennis Haskell. 219p. 1994. pap. 19.95 (*1-86368-105-1*, Pub. by Fremantle Arts AT) Intl Spec Bk.

***Tilting at Mortality: Narrative Strategies in Joseph Heller's Fiction.** David M. Craig. LC 96-44560. (Humor in Life & Letters Ser.). (Illus.). 240p. 1997. text ed. 34.95 (*0-8143-2653-6*) Wayne St U Pr.

Tilting at Windmills. Charles Peters. 1990. pap. 12.95 (*0-201-52415-5*) Addison-Wesley.

Tilting at Windmills: An Autobiography. Charles Peters. Ed. by Washington Monthly Staff. LC 87-35903. 1988. 18.22 (*0-201-05657-7*) Addison-Wesley.

***Tilting at Windmills: New Welsh Short Fiction.** Ravi Pawar. 144p. 1995. pap. 9.95 (*0-9521558-1-8*) Dufour.

Tilting in Abelian Categories & Quasitilted Algebras. Dieter Happel et al. (Memoirs of the American Mathematical Society Ser.: Vol. 575). 1996. pap. 35.00 (*0-8218-0444-8*, MEMO/120/575) Am Math.

Tilting the Balance. Harry Turtledove. (Worldwar Ser.). 1996. mass mkt. 6.99 (*0-345-38998-0*) Ballantine.

Tilting the Tower: Lesbians, Teaching, Queer Subjects. Ed. by Linda Garber. LC 94-8048. 256p. (C). 1994. pap. 16.95 (*0-415-90841-8*, Pub. by Tavistock UK) Routledge Chapman & Hall.

Tily. Frank E. Peretti. 128p. (SPA.). 1989. pap. 1.50 (*0-8297-0739-5*) Life Pubs Intl.

Tim. Mark Dunster. (Rin Ser.: Pt. 20). 25p. (Orig.). 1987. pap. 4.00 (*0-89642-145-7*) Linden Pubs.

Tim. Colleen McCullough. 288p. 1990. mass mkt. 6.99 (*0-380-71196-6*) Avon.

Tim. large type ed. Colleen McCullough. 362p. 1992. 22.95 (*1-85089-362-4*, Pub. by ISIS UK) Transaction Pubs.

Tim: A Story of School Life. Howard O. Sturgis. LC 78-63996. (Gay Experience Ser.). reprint ed. 32.50 (*0-404-61514-7*) AMS Pr.

Tim: An Ordinary Boy. Colin Parry & Wendy Parry. (Illus.). 240p. 1995. 29.95 (*0-340-61789-6*, Pub. by H & S UK) Trafalgar.

Tim, a Little Kitten with a Big Heart. Fred R. Toothman. (Illus.). 14p. (Orig.). (J). (gr. 1 up). 1995. pap. 3.49 (*0-9617545-6-7*) F R Toothman.

Tim All Alone. Edward Ardizzone. (Illus.). 48p. (J). (ps-7). 1990. pap. 6.95 (*0-19-272125-9*) OUP.

***Tim Allen: Comedian/Performer.** John Wukovits. (Overcoming Adversity Ser.). 1997. lib. bdg. 19.95 (*0-7910-4696-6*) Chelsea Hse.

***Tim Allen: Comedian/Performer.** John Wukovits. (Overcoming Adversity Ser.). 1997. pap. 8.95 (*0-7910-4697-4*) Chelsea Hse.

Tim Allen Laid Bare: Unauthorized. Michael Arkush. (Orig.). 1995. mass mkt. 5.99 (*0-380-78260-X*) Avon.

Tim & Charlotte. Edward Ardizzone. (Illus.). 48p. (J). (ps-6). 1987. pap. 6.95 (*0-19-272118-6*) OUP.

Tim & Ginger. Edward Ardizzone. (Illus.). 48p. (J). (ps-3). 1987. reprint ed. pap. 6.95 (*0-19-272113-5*) OUP.

Tim & His Lamp. Fern Stubblefield. 52p. (J). (gr. k-6). pap. 0.40 (*0-686-29170-0*); pap. 1.00 (*0-686-29171-9*) Faith Pub Hse.

Tim & Pete. James R. Baker. (Contemporary American Fiction Ser.). 256p. 1994. pap. 9.95 (*0-14-023493-4*, Penguin Bks) Viking Penguin.

Tim Avery's Secret. Hilda Stahl. LC 85-70271. (Wren House Mystery Ser.). 128p. (J). (gr. 4-6). 1986. pap. 3.99 (*0-89636-213-2*, Chariot Bks) Chariot Victor.

Tim Boxer's Jewish Celebrity Anecdotes. Tim Boxer. LC 96-17366. 276p. 1996. pap. 19.95 (*0-8246-0391-5*) Jonathan David.

Tim Bunker Paper, or Yankee Farming. William Clift. LC 72-137727. (American Fiction Reprint Ser.). 1977. 23.95 (*0-8369-7026-8*) Ayer.

Tim Burton's Nightmare Before Christmas: The Film, the Art, the Vision. Frank Thompson. (Illus.). 192p. 1993. 24.95 (*1-56282-774-X*) Hyperion.

Tim Burton's Nightmare Before Christmas: The Film, the Art, the Vision. Frank Thompson. (Illus.). 192p. 1994. pap. 15.95 (*0-7868-8066-X*) Hyperion.

Tim Burton's Nightmare Before Christmas Jr. Novel. Daphne Skinner. LC 93-78835. 80p. (J). (gr. 2-6). 1993. pap. 3.50 (*1-56282-592-5*) Hyprn Child.

Tim Burton's the Nightmare Before Christmas. (Piano-Vocal Ser.). (Illus.). 96p. (Orig.). 1993. pap. 16.95 (*0-7935-2827-5*, HL00312488) H Leonard.

***Tim Egan Library, 3 Vols.** Cra. 1996. 29.95 (*0-395-86507-7*) HM.

Tim Holt. David Rothel. (Illus.). 290p. 1994. text ed. 30.00 (*0-944019-13-7*) Empire NC.

***Tim Horton Tribute Book.** Tim Griggs. 1997. pap. text ed. 22.95 (*1-55022-319-4*, Pub. by ECW Press CN) Genl Dist Srvs.

Tim in Tibet. Herge. (Illus.). 62p. (GER.). (J). pap. 19.95 (*0-8288-5083-6*) Fr & Eur.

Tim Kitten & the Red Cupboard. Jan Wahl. (J). 1990. pap. 2.25 (*0-671-70296-3*, S&S Bks Young Read) S&S Childrens.

***Tim McGraw - Not a Moment Too Soon.** Ed. by Carol Cuellar. 52p. (Orig.). (C). 1994. pap. text ed. 14.95 (*0-910957-66-5*, P1077SMX) Warner Brothers.

Tim McKernan Barrelman. McKernan-Cramer, Inc. Staff. 144p. 1995. pap. text ed. 15.95 (*0-7872-1042-0*) Kendall-Hunt.

Tim O'Brien. Herzog. LC 97-25478. 1997. 22.95 (*0-8057-7825-X*, Twayne) Scribnrs Ref.

Tim O'Toole & the Wee Folk. Gerald McDermott. (Illus.). 32p. (J). (ps-3). 1992. pap. 4.99 (*0-14-050675-6*) Puffin Bks.

Tim Page's Nam. Tim Page. LC 94-61398. (Illus.). 120p. 1995. pap. 19.95 (*0-500-27280-8*) Thames Hudson.

Tim Prythero. Intro. by Robert Creeley. LC 90-62109. (Illus.). 16p. 1990. pap. 7.00 (*0-935037-34-9*) G Peters Gallery.

Tim Rollins & K. O. S. The Red Badge of Courage. Tim Rollins et al. Ed. by Nancy H. Margolis. (Illus.). 1994. 8.00 (*0-9611560-4-X*) SEC Contemp Art.

Tim Rollins & K.O.S. (Parkett Art Magazine Ser.: No. 20). (Illus.). 200p. 1989. 19.50 (*3-907509-70-6*, Pub. by Parkett Pubs SZ) Dist Art Pubs.

***Tim Testa's Computer Improvement.** Tim Testa. 1997. 24.99 (*0-7897-0808-6*) Macmillan.

Tim, the Peacemaker. Uwe Friesel. LC 72-145822. (Illus.). 32p. (J). (ps-3). 8.95 (*0-87592-052-7*) Scroll Pr.

Tim Tidies Up. Anne-Marie Chaponton. (Child's World Library). (Illus.). 32p. (J). (gr. k-5). 1991. lib. bdg. 18.50 (*0-89565-750-3*) Childs World.

Tim und der Haifschsee. Herge. (Illus.). 62p. (GER.). (J). pap. 19.95 (*0-8288-5084-4*) Fr & Eur.

Tim und die Picaros. Herge. (Illus.). 62p. (GER.). (J). pap. 19.95 (*0-8288-5085-2*) Fr & Eur.

Timachides: Chronicum Lindium. C. Blinkenberg. 80p. 1980. pap. 10.00 (*0-89005-353-7*) Ares.

Timaeus: Plato. Benjamin E. Jowett. 96p. (C). 1959. pap. text ed. 6.00 (*0-02-360790-4*, Macmillan Coll) P-H.

Timaeus & Critias. Plato. Tr. & Intro. by Desmond Lee. (Classics Ser.). 176p. 1972. pap. 9.95 (*0-14-044261-8*, Penguin Classics) Viking Penguin.

Timaeus, Critias, Cleitophon, Menexenus, Epistolae, Vol. IX. Plato. (Loeb Classical Library: No. 234). 644p. 1929. text ed. 18.95 (*0-674-99257-1*) HUP.

Timaeus of Plato. Plato. vii, 358p. write for info. (*0-318-71000-5*) G Olms Pubs.

Timaeus of Plato. Plato. vii, 358p. (GER.). 1988. write for info. (*0-318-70539-7*) G Olms Pubs.

Timaeus of Plato. Plato. Ed. by R. D. Archer-Hind. LC 72-9281. (Philosophy of Plato & Aristotle Ser.). (ENG & GRE.). 1977. reprint ed. 27.95 (*0-405-04832-7*) Ayer.

Timaios of Locri, on the Nature of the World & the Soul. Thomas H. Tobin. (Society of Biblical Literature Texts & Translations Ser.: No. 26). 93p. (C). 1986. pap. 15.95 (*0-89130-742-7*, 06 02 26) Scholars Pr GA.

Timarion. Tr. & Intro. by Barry Baldwin. LC 84-10426. 172p. 1984. 24.95 (*0-8143-1771-5*) Wayne St U Pr.

Timbal Gulch Trail. Max Brand. 224p. 1995. mass mkt., pap. text ed. 3.99 (*0-8439-3828-5*) Dorchester Pub Co.

Timbal Gulch Trail. large type ed. Max Brand. LC 95-13693. 353p. 1995. 20.95 (*0-7862-0480-X*) Thorndike Pr.

Timber: A Novel of Pacific Northwest Loggers. Roderick Haig-Brown. LC 93-6737. (Northwest Reprints Ser.). (Illus.). 448p. 1993. reprint ed. pap. 15.95 (*0-87071-515-1*); reprint ed. text ed. 27.95 (*0-87071-514-3*) Oreg St U Pr.

Timber: From Trees to Wood Products. William Jaspersohn. LC 95-25194. (Illus.). 32p. (J). (gr. 3-7). 1996. 16.95 (*0-316-45825-2*) Little.

Timber: Loggers Challenge the Great Northwest Forests. Ralph W. Andrews. (Illus.). 182p. 1985. reprint ed. pap. 12.95 (*0-88740-036-1*) Schiffer.

Timber: Or Discoveries. Ben Jonson. Ed. by Ralph S. Walker. LC 76-7990. 135p. 1976. reprint ed. text ed. 35.00 (*0-8371-8882-2*, WABJ, Greenwood Pr) Greenwood.

Timber: Problems, Prospects, & Policies. Timber Supply Policy Conference Staff. Ed. by William A. Duerr. LC 72-1160. (Illus.). 276p. 1973. reprint ed. pap. 78.70 (*0-608-00055-8*, 2060821) Bks Demand.

Timber: Structure, Properties, Conversion, & Use. 7th rev. ed. H. E. Desch. 1996. 49.95 (*1-56022-861-X*) Haworth Jrnl Co-Edits.

Timber & Iron: Houses in North Queensland Mining Settlements 1861-1920. Peter Bell. (Illus.). 1985. 49.95 (*0-7022-1714-X*, Pub. by Univ Queensland Pr AT) Intl Spec Bk.

***Timber & Iron Reinforcement in Early Buildings.** R. P. Wilcox. (Illus.). 112p. 1982. pap. 15.98 (*0-85431-227-7*, Pub. by Soc Antiquaries UK) David Brown.

Timber & Men: The Weyerhaeuser Story. Ralph Hidy et al. LC 63-7450. 752p. reprint ed. pap. 180.00 (*0-317-42049-6*, 2056093) Bks Demand.

Timber & Prayer: The Indian Pond Prayers. Michael S. Weaver. LC 94-43085. (Poetry Ser.). 134p. 1995. 29.95 (*0-8229-3873-1*); pap. 15.95 (*0-8229-5554-7*) U of Pittsburgh Pr.

Timber Bubble That Burst: Government Policy & the Bailout of 1984. Joe P. Mattey. (Illus.). 120p. 1990. 38.00 (*0-19-506275-2*) OUP.

Timber Building in Britain. R. W. Brunskill. (Illus.). 256p. 1985. 55.00 (*0-575-05611-8*, Pub. by V Gollancz UK) Trafalgar.

Timber Bulkheads. Ed. by James Graham. 96p. 1987. 14.00 (*0-87262-593-1*) Am Soc Civil Eng.

Timber Castles. Robert Higham & Philip Barker. LC 94-19557. (Illus.). 390p. 1995. 40.00 (*0-8117-1747-X*) Stackpole.

Timber City Masks: A Royce Madison Mystery. Kieran York. LC 93-14628. 232p. (Orig.). 1993. pap. 9.95 (*1-879427-13-3*) Third Side Pr.

Timber Colony: A Historical Geography of Early Nineteenth Century New Brunswick. Graeme Wynn. 248p. 1980. pap. 15.95 (*0-8020-6407-8*) U of Toronto Pr.

Timber Construction for Developing Countries: Applications & Examples. (General Studies). 111p. 1995. pap. 20.00 (*92-1-106296-9*) UN.

Timber Construction for Developing Countries: Strength Characteristics & Design. (General Studies). 160p. 1995. pap. 25.00 (*92-1-106297-7*) UN.

Timber Construction for Developing Countries: Structural Timber & Related Products. (General Studies). 179p. 1995. pap. 25.00 (*92-1-106286-1*) UN.

Timber Construction Manual. 4th ed. American Institute of Timber Construction Staff. 904p. 1994. text ed. 89.95 (*0-471-30970-2*) Wiley.

Timber Country. Lynn M. Stone. LC 93-4522. (Back Roads Ser.). (Illus.). (J). 1993. write for info. (*0-86593-305-7*) Rourke Corp.

Timber Country Revisited: Managing Our Renewable Resource. Roberge. 1991. 39.95 (*0-9631295-0-3*) WA Contract Log.

Timber Cutting Practices. 3rd ed. Steve Conway. LC 78-53017. (Forest Industries Book). (Illus.). 192p. 1978. pap. 35.00 (*0-87930-021-3*) Miller Freeman.

***Timber Design for the Civil & Structural Professional Engineering Exams.** 4th ed. Robert H. Kim & Jai B. Kim. LC 96-47550. (Illus.). 216p. 1997. pap. 29.95 (*1-888577-00-2*) Prof Pubns CA.

Timber Design Review Manual. Frank Talania. (Illus.). 400p. 1995. pap. 37.50 (*0-929176-14-6*) Burdick & Landreth Co.

Timber Designer's Manual. 2nd ed. J. A. Baird & E. C. Ozelton. (Illus.). 656p. 1984. text ed. 110.00 (*0-246-12375-3*, Pub. by Granada UK) Sheridan.

Timber-Drying System Fuelled by Sawdust. Ed. by A. P. Robinson et al. 1993. pap. 25.00 (*0-85954-328-5*, Pub. by Nat Res Inst UK) St Mut.

Timber Economy of Puritan New England. Charles F. Carroll. LC 73-7122. 235p. reprint ed. pap. 67.00 (*0-7837-2619-8*, 2042954) Bks Demand.

Timber Engineering for Developing. 230p. 1990. 32.00 (*92-1-106241-1*, 90.III.E.4) UN.

Timber Engineering for Developing Countries: Introduction to Wood & Timber Engineering. (General Studies). 1992. 10.00 (*92-1-106278-0*) UN.

Timber Engineering for Developing Countries, Pt. 3: Durability & Fire Resistance of Timber. 155p. 1990. 21.00 (*92-1-106240-3*, 90.III.E.3) UN.

Timber Engineering for Developing Countries, Pt. 3: Introduction to Wood & Timber Engineering. 131p. 1990. 19.00 (*92-1-106237-3*, 90.III.E.1) UN.

Timber Engineering for Developing Countries, Pt. 3: Structural Timber & Products. 267p. 1990. 39.00 (*92-1-106238-1*, 90.III.E.2) UN.

Timber Engineering for Developing Countries, Pt. 5: Applications & Construction. 138p. 1990. 20.00 (*92-1-106243-8*, 90.III.E.5) UN.

Timber Frame Construction: All About Post-&-Beam Building. Jack A. Sobon. LC 83-48972. (Illus.). 208p. 1984. pap. 18.95 (*0-88266-365-8*, Garden Way Pub) Storey Comm Inc.

Timber-Frame Houses. Fine Homebuilding Magazine Staff. (Illus.). 160p. 1996. pap. text ed. 17.95 (*1-56158-150-X*) Taunton.

Timber Frame Houses in the Scottish Countryside. HMSO Staff. 72p. 1994. pap. 25.00 (*0-11-495191-8*, HM51918, Pub. by Stationery Ofc UK) Bernan Associates.

Timber Framing Book. Elliott Wallas. 1977. pap. 25.00 (*0-918238-01-3*) Housesmiths.

Timber Harvesting. 4th ed. American Pulpwood Association Staff. 306p. 1988. 37.25 (*0-8134-2775-4*) Interstate.

***Timber in Buildings: Decay, Treatment & Conservation.** B. Ridout. (Illus.). 250p. 1997. text ed. 47.00 (*0-419-18820-7*, E & FN Spon) Routledge Chapman & Hall.

Timber Lake "The Gem of Piedmont, Virginia" Doug Washington. LC 95-62191. (Illus.). 199p. 1996. 25.00 (*0-9638455-6-X*) Warwick Hse.

Timber Line. Gene Fowler. 1981. reprint ed. lib. bdg. 17.95 (*0-89966-424-5*) Buccaneer Bks.

Timber Management: A Quantitative Approach. Jerome L. Clutter et al. LC 92-11878. 352p. (C). 1992. reprint ed. lib. bdg. 51.50 (*0-89464-747-4*) Krieger.

***Timber Management for Small Woodlands.** 3rd rev. ed. Gary R. Goff et al. (Information Bulletin Ser.). (Illus.). 57p. (Orig.). 1995. pap. 5.50 (*1-57753-032-2*, 1471B180) Corn Coop Ext.

***Timber Plantations in the Humid Tropics of Africa.** 199p. 1993. 25.00 (*92-5-103020-0*, F0200, Pub. by FAO IT) Bernan Associates.

***Timber Production & Biodiversity Conservation in Tropical Rain Forests.** Andrew G. Johns. LC 96-46907. (Studies in Applied Ecology & Resource Management). (Illus.). 283p. (C). 1997. text ed. 69.95 (*0-521-57282-7*) Cambridge U Pr.

Timber Reduced Energy Efficient Home. Ed Paschich & Paula Hendricks. Ed. by James C. Smith, Jr. LC 93-35704. (Illus.). 128p. (Orig.). 1993. pap. 17.95 (*0-86534-208-3*) Sunstone Pr.

Timber Resources for America's Future: Forest Resource Report No. 14. U. S. Department of Agriculture Forest Service Staff. LC 72-2872. (Use & Abuse of America's Natural Resources Ser.). 728p. 1972. reprint ed. 45.95 (*0-405-04538-7*) Ayer.

***Timber Solutions Manual.** David Duquette. LC 96-93136. (Illus.). 360p. (Orig.). (C). 1997. pap. text ed. 49.95 (*0-9656181-0-2*) Argulus Pub.

Timber Supply, Land Allocation, & Economic Efficiency. William F. Hyde. LC 80-8021. 224p. 1980. 21.00 (*0-8018-2489-3*) Resources Future.

Timber, Talus & Tundra: Hiking Trails & Mountain Peaks of the Gunnison Basin. Mary A. Tarr. Ed. by Susan Lebow et al. LC 96-90018. (Illus.). 200p. (Orig.). 1996. pap. 19.95 (*0-9650842-0-5*) Uncompahgre.

***Timber Tourists & Temples: Conservation & Development in the Maya Forest of Belize.** Richard B. Primack. 420p. 1997. pap. text ed. 35.00 (*1-55963-542-8*) Island Pr.

***Timber, Tourists & Temples: Conservation & Development in the Maya Forest of Belize, Guatemala & Mexico.** Ed. by Richard B. Primack & David Bray. 420p. 1997. text ed. 55.00 (*1-55963-541-X*) Island Pr.

Timber Trade: An Introduction to Commercial Aspects. J. H. Leigh. LC 79-42776. 115p. 1980. 63.00 (*0-08-024917-5*, Pub. by Pergamon Repr UK) Franklin.

***Timber Trees: Major Commercial Timbers.** Ed. by I. Soerianegara & R. H. Lemmens. (PROSEA Ser.: No. 5.1). (Illus.). 610p. 1993. 282.00 (*90-220-1033-3*, Pub. by Backhuys Pubs NE) Balogh.

***Timber Trees: Major Commercial Timbers.** Ed. by I. Soerianegara & R. H. Lemmens. (PROSEA Ser.: No. 5.1). (Illus.). 610p. 1993. pap. 123.00 (*979-8316-17-7*, Pub. by Backhuys Pubs NE) Balogh.

***Timber Trees: Minor Commercial Timbers.** Ed. by R. H. Lemmens et al. (PROSEA Ser.: No. 5.2). (Illus.). 655p. 1995. 175.00 (*90-73348-44-7*, Pub. by Backhuys Pubs NE) Balogh.

Timber Trees of India & of Eastern & Southern Asia, 1870. E. Balfour. 370p. (C). 1988. 80.00 (*0-685-22313-2*, Pub. by Scientific UK) St Mut.

Timber Trends & Prospects for North America. 68p. 1990. 32.00 (*92-1-116468-0*, 90.II.E.4) UN.

Timber Wars. Judy Bari. 300p. (Orig.). 1994. pap. 14.95 (*1-56751-026-4*); lib. bdg. 29.95 (*1-56751-027-2*) Common Courage.

Timber Wolf. Paul Hutchens. (Sugar Creek Gang Ser.: Vol. 23). (J). (gr. 3-7). 1965. mass mkt., pap. 3.99 (*0-8024-4823-2*) Moody.

Timber Wolf: Hands-on Activities for Elementary Teachers. Two Herons Staff. 112p. 1996. teacher ed., pap. text ed. 18.95 (*0-7872-2243-7*) Kendall-Hunt.

Timber Wolf in Wisconsin: The Death & Life of a Majestic Predator. Richard P. Thiel. LC 93-3577. (North Coast Bks.). (Illus.). 320p. (Orig.). (C). 1994. pap. 17.95 (*0-299-13944-1*); lib. bdg. 45.00 (*0-299-13940-9*) U of Wis Pr.

Timberdoodle: A Guide to Woodcock. Frank Woolner. (Illus.). 192p. 1994. reprint ed. text ed. 18.95 (*0-941130-52-5*, 52-5) Lyons & Burford.

Timberdoodle Tales: Adventures of a Minnesota Woodcock Hunter. Tom F. Waters. 1993. 45.00 (*0-9637616-0-9*) Riparian Pr.

***Timberdoodle Tales: Adventures of a Minnesota Woodcock Hunter.** Tom F. Waters. 1997. 30.00 (*1-57157-057-8*) Safari Pr.

Timbered Lives: Selected Poems of 1979-1986. Coral Crosman. 112p. (Orig.). 1994. pap. text ed. 13.95 (*0-913884-05-7*) Porphyrion Pr.

Timberlake Wertenbaker Plays 1 Plays 1: New Anatomies; The Grace of Mary Trverse; Our Country's Good... Timberlake Wertenbaker. 400p. (Orig.). 1996. pap. text ed. 13.95 (*0-571-17743-3*) Faber & Faber.

***Timberland Vengeance.** large type ed. Jack Greer. (Dales Large Print Ser.). 224p. 1996. pap. 17.99 (*1-85389-660-8*, Dales) Ulverscroft.

Timberline. Deborah Bedford. 352p. 1996. mass mkt. 4.99 (*0-06-108358-5*) HarpC.

Timberline. large type ed. Lauran Paine. LC 94-45642. (Western Ser.). 177p. 1995. 17.95 (*0-7862-0398-6*) Thorndike Pr.

Timberline: Mountain & Arctic Forest Frontiers. Stephen F. Arno. LC 84-14844. (Illus.). 304p. (Orig.). 1984. pap. 16.95 (*0-89886-085-7*) Mountaineers.

Timberline Lodge: A Love Story. Ed. by Judith A. Rose. LC 86-82136. (Illus.). 128p. 1986. 29.50 (*0-932575-24-2*) Gr Arts Ctr Pub.

Timberline Lodge Cookbook: The Northwest Cuisine. Contrib. by Leif E. Benson. 1988. 29.50 (*0-932575-86-2*) Gr Arts Ctr Pub.

T

An Asterisk (*) at the beginning of an entry indicates that the title is appearing in BIP for the first time.

Timberline Tailings: Tales of Colorado's Ghost Towns & Mining Camps. Muriel S. Wolle. LC 92-28343. (Illus.). xii, 337p. 1993. reprint ed. pap. 24.95 (*0-8040-0963-5*) Swallow.

Timbers of Commerce & Their Identification. H. Stone. (Illus.). 311p. 1986. pap. 225.00 (*81-7089-044-6*, Pub. by Intl Bk Distr II) St Mut.

Timbers of Commerce & Their Identification. H. Stone. (Illus.). 311p. (C). 1989. 250.00 (*0-685-21823-6*, Pub. by Intl Bk Distr II) St Mut.

Timbers of the New World. Samuel J. Record & Robert W. Hess. LC 73-140611. (Use & Abuse of America's Natural Resources Ser.). (Illus.). 718p. 1975. reprint ed. 63.95 (*0-405-02806-7*) Ayer.

***Timbertoes ABC Alphabet Book.** Highlights Staff. LC 95-83423. (Illus.). 32p. (J). (ps-1). 1997. 7.95 (*1-56397-604-8*) Boyds Mills Pr.

***Timbertoes 1 2 3 Counting Book.** Highlights Staff. LC 96-84146. (Illus.). 32p. (J). (ps-1). 1997. 7.95 (*1-56397-627-7*) Boyds Mills Pr.

Timbre Composition in Electroacoustic Music. Ed. by Simon Emmerson. (Contemporary Music Review Ser.). 239p. 1994. pap. text ed. 46.00 (*3-7186-5572-1*, Harwood Acad Pubs) Gordon & Breach.

Timbre Composition in Electroacoustic Music. Ed. by Simon Emmerson. (Contemporary Music Review Ser.). 368p. 1995. text ed. 93.00 (*3-7186-5576-4*, Harwood Acad Pubs) Gordon & Breach.

Timbuctoo the Mysterious. Felix Dubois. Tr. by Diana White. LC 70-94475. (Illus.). 377p. 1970. reprint ed. text ed. 35.00 (*0-8371-2372-0*, DTI&, Greenwood Pr) Greenwood.

Time. (Sticker Activity Ser.). (Illus.). 16p. (J). (ps-1). 1993. pap. 6.95 (*1-56458-398-8*) DK Pub Inc.

Time. (My First Learning Ser.). (Illus.). 24p. (J). (gr. k-2). 1995. text ed. write for info. (*1-56144-739-0*) Modern Pub NYC.

Time. Christopher Carrie. (Crayola Kinder Art BKs.). (Illus.). 12p. (Orig.). (J). (gr. 3-6). 1987. pap. 4.70 (*0-86696-207-7*) Binney & Smith.

***Time.** Andrew Haslam et al. (Make It Work! Ser.). (Illus.). (J). 16.99 (*0-590-24914-2*) Scholastic Inc.

***Time.** Andrew Haslam et al. (Make It Work! Ser.). (Illus.). (J). pap. 7.99 (*0-590-24915-0*) Scholastic Inc.

Time. Sally Hewitt. LC 95-18464. (Take off With Ser.). (J). 1996. lib. bdg. 21.40 (*0-8172-4111-6*) Raintree Steck-V.

***Time.** Evan Kimble. (Illus.). (J). 1997. pap. 3.95 (*0-8069-9752-4*) Sterling.

Time. Werner Kirst & Ulrich Diekmeyer. (Illus.). 1977. 14.95 (*0-8464-0928-3*) Beekman Pubs.

Time. Kosta Kontoyiannaki. (Illus.). 12p. (J). (gr. k-3). 1992. pap. 10.95 (*1-895583-22-5*) MAYA Pubs.

Time. Photos by Stephen Oliver. LC 90-8576. (My First Look At Ser.). (Illus.). 24p. (J). (ps-k). 1991. 7.00 (*0-679-81164-8*) Random Bks Yng Read.

Time. Jan Pienkowski. (Nursery Board Bks.). (Illus.). 24p. (J). (ps). 1991. pap. 2.95 (*0-671-72847-4*, Litl Simon S&S) S&S Childrens.

Time. Henry Pluckrose. (Math Counts Ser.). 32p. (J). 1995. lib. bdg. 17.80 (*0-516-05459-7*) Childrens.

Time. Henry Pluckrose. (Math Counts Ser.). (J). 1995. pap. 4.95 (*0-516-45459-5*) Childrens.

Time. Pamela J. Schroeder & Jean M. Donisch. LC 96-714. (What's the Big Idea Ser.). (Illus.). (J). 1996. write for info. (*0-86625-578-8*) Rourke Pubns.

Time. Robert Snedden. LC 94-41165. (Science Horizons Ser.). 48p. (J). 1995. lib. bdg. 16.95 (*0-7910-3026-1*) Chelsea Hse.

Time. Mark Travis. 1995. pap. 7.95 (*0-533-11531-0*) Vantage.

Time. J. Tyler. (First Learning Ser.). 1989. pap. 3.95 (*0-7460-0266-1*, Usborne) EDC.

Time. Brenda Walpole. LC 95-21855. (Measure up with Science Ser.). (Illus.). (J). 1995. lib. bdg. 18.60 (*0-8368-1364-2*) Gareth Stevens Inc.

Time. Ed. by Jonathan Westphal & Carl Levenson. LC 93-14608. (Readings in Philosophy Ser.). 192p. (Orig.). (C). 1993. pap. text ed. 7.95 (*0-87220-206-2*); lib. bdg. 24.95 (*0-87220-207-0*) Hackett Pub.

Time: A Bibliographic Guide. Samuel L. Macey. LC 91-25934. (Reference Books on Sociology & Science Ser.). 448p. 1991. text ed. 66.00 (*0-8153-0646-6*, H1506) Garland.

Time: A Critical Analysis for Children. Warren Shibles. LC 77-93811. (Teaching Young People to Be Critical Ser.). (J). (gr. 4-12). 1978. pap. 6.50 (*0-912386-17-7*) Language Pr.

Time: A Philosophical Analysis. T. Chapman. 178p. 1982. lib. bdg. 82.50 (*90-277-1465-7*, D Reidel) Kluwer Ac.

Time: A Philosophical Treatment. Keith Seddon. 176p. 1987. lib. bdg. 47.50 (*0-7099-5424-7*, Pub. by Croom Helm UK) Routledge Chapman & Hall.

***Time: A Temporal Hypothesis.** G. Motte Martin. LC 96-90750. (Orig.). 1997. pap. 8.95 (*0-533-12160-4*) Vantage.

Time: Histories & Ethnologies. Ed. by Diane O. Hughes & Thomas R. Trautmann. LC 95-15095. (Comparative Studies in Society & History). 1995. 57.50 (*0-472-09579-X*); pap. text ed. 24.95 (*0-472-06579-3*) U of Mich Pr.

Time: Its Structure & Role in Physical Theories. Peter Kroes. (Synthese Library: No. 179). 252p. 1984. lib. bdg. 101.50 (*90-277-1894-6*) Kluwer Ac.

Time: Man's Cosmic Locator. Robert V. Gerard. LC 95-17206. 17p. 1995. pap. 4.50 (*1-880666-49-9*) Oughten Hse.

Time: Months, Holidays, Seasons, & Telling Time, 5 bks. Cynthia Muller et al. (Apples for Teachers Ser.). 96p. Time. 9.99 (*0-8224-0458-3*, FE0458) Fearon Teach Aids.

Time: Night. Ludmilla Petrushevskaya. 1995. pap. 11.00 (*0-679-75768-6*) Random.

Time: Now!: The Political Ideas of Salvador de Madariaga. Robert D. Judy. 64p. (C). 1992. 8.95 (*0-9627383-3-6*, BK3) RDJ Assocs.

Time: Past, Present & Future. Zdzislaw Augustynek. (Nijhoff International Philosophy Ser.). 146p. 1991. lib. bdg. 108.50 (*0-7923-0270-2*, Pub. by Klwr Acad Pubs NE) Kluwer Ac.

Time: Patterns of Flow & Return. Marie-Louise Von Franz. (Art & Imagination Ser.). (Illus.). 1979. pap. 14.95 (*0-500-81016-8*) Thames Hudson.

Time: Portraits of a Journey Home: Poems & Photographs by Esther Iverem. LC 93-30709. (Illus.). 96p. 1994. 24.95 (*0-86543-405-0*); pap. 9.95 (*0-86543-406-9*) Africa World.

Time: Reaching for Tomorrow. Linda Schinke-Llano. 160p. 1994. pap. 23.95 (*0-8442-0774-8*, Natl Textbk) NTC Pub Grp.

Time: Reaching for Tomorrow. Linda Schinke-Llano. 160p. 1995. pap. 39.95 incl. audio (*0-8442-0773-X*) NTC Pub Grp.

Time: Statistical Methods: Games & Songs. Turkan Kumbaraci & George H. Gardenier. LC 89-90944. (Gardenier Math-Stat Ser.). (Illus.). 19p. (J). (gr. 1-8). 1989. 20.00 (*0-685-29041-7*, 0005) Teka Trends.

Time: The Modern & Postmodern Experience. Helga Nowotny. LC 94-27880. 179p. 1995. 33.95 (*0-7456-0892-2*) Blackwell Pubs.

Time: The Ultimate Energy: An Exploration of the Scientific, Psychological & Metaphysical Aspects of Time. Murry Hope. (Illus.). 224p. 1993. pap. 14.95 (*1-85230-237-2*) Element MA.

Time: Towards a Consistent-Theory, 65. C. K. Raju. LC 94-32856. (Fundamental Theories of Physics Ser.). 272p. (C). 1994. lib. bdg. 130.00 (*0-7923-3103-6*, Pub. by Klwr Acad Pubs NE) Kluwer Ac.

Time: We the People. Linda Schinke-Llano. 176p. 1995. boxed 39.95 (*0-8442-7447-X*, Natl Textbk) NTC Pub Grp.

Time a Cloud Came into the Cabin (A Mountain Tale for Boys) Jacquelyn Smyers. LC 86-50627. (Illus.). 12p. (Orig.). (J). (ps-6). 1986. pap. 3.98 (*0-9615130-3-9*) Very Idea.

Time a Cloud Came into the Cabin (A Mountain Tale for Girls) Jacquelyn Smyers. LC 86-50626. (Illus.). 12p. (Orig.). (J). (ps-6). 1986. pap. 3.98 (*0-9615130-4-7*) Very Idea.

Time, Action & Cognition Towards Bridging the Gap: Proceedings of the NATO Advanced Research Workshop, Held in St. Malo, France, 22-25 October, 1991. Ed. by Francoise Macar et al. LC 92-10966. (NATO Advanced Study Institutes Series D, Behavioural & Social Sciences: No. 66). 432p. (C). 1992. lib. bdg. 180.50 (*0-7923-1783-1*, Pub. by Klwr Acad Pubs NE) Kluwer Ac.

Time after Time. Karl Alexander et al. 1983. 5.00 (*0-87129-423-0*, T55) Dramatic Pub.

Time after Time. Antoinette Stockenberg. 432p. 1995. mass mkt. 5.50 (*0-440-21676-1*) Dell.

Time after Time, the Photographs of Alice Wells. Ed. by Susan E. Cohen. (Illus.). 60p. 1990. pap. 10.00 (*0-89822-065-3*) Visual Studies.

Time Alone with God Notebook. rev. ed. Barry St. Clair. 128p. (YA). 1994. pap. 5.99 (*1-56476-143-6*, 6-3143, Victor Bks) Chariot Victor.

Time Alterations: An Astonishing Phenomenon of Natural Law with Applications Ranging from Health Maintenance to the Eradication of Terminal Illness, 6 vols., I. August N. Alonzo. Ed. by Word for Word, Inc. Staff. LC 89-50550. 147p. (Orig.). (C). 1989. write for info. (*0-9622698-0-8*) Taqua Pub.

Time Alterations: An Astonishing Phenomenon of Natural Law with Applications Ranging from Health Maintenance to the Eradication of Terminal Illness, 6 vols., II. August N. Alonzo. Ed. by Word for Word, Inc. Staff. LC 89-50550. 147p. (Orig.). (C). 1989. write for info. (*0-9622698-1-6*) Taqua Pub.

Time Alterations: An Astonishing Phenomenon of Natural Law with Applications Ranging from Health Maintenance to the Eradication of Terminal Illness, 6 vols., III. August N. Alonzo. Ed. by Word for Word, Inc. Staff. LC 89-50550. 147p. (Orig.). (C). 1989. write for info. (*0-9622698-3-2*) Taqua Pub.

Time Alterations: An Astonishing Phenomenon of Natural Law with Applications Ranging from Health Maintenance to the Eradication of Terminal Illness, 6 vols., IV. August N. Alonzo. Ed. by Word for Word, Inc. Staff. LC 89-50550. 147p. (Orig.). (C). 1989. write for info. (*0-9622698-4-0*) Taqua Pub.

Time Alterations: An Astonishing Phenomenon of Natural Law with Applications Ranging from Health Maintenance to the Eradication of Terminal Illness, 6 vols., Set. August N. Alonzo. Ed. by Word for Word, Inc. Staff. LC 89-50550. 147p. (Orig.). (C). 1989. pap. 39.95 (*0-9622698-9-1*) Taqua Pub.

Time Alterations: An Astonishing Phenomenon of Natural Law with Applications Ranging from Health Maintenance to the Eradication of Terminal Illness, 6 vols., V. August N. Alonzo. Ed. by Word for Word, Inc. Staff. LC 89-50550. 147p. (Orig.). (C). 1989. write for info. (*0-9622698-6-7*) Taqua Pub.

Time Alterations: An Astonishing Phenomenon of Natural Law with Applications Ranging from Health Maintenance to the Eradication of Terminal Illness, 6 vols., VI. August N. Alonzo. Ed. by Word for Word, Inc. Staff. LC 89-50550. 147p. (Orig.). (C). 1989. write for info. (*0-9622698-7-5*) Taqua Pub.

Time Alterations: An Option to Live. August N. Alonzo. Ed. by Barbara Wohlstadter. LC 90-70502. (Illus.). 125p. (Orig.). 1990. pap. 9.95 (*0-9622698-2-4*) Taqua Pub.

Time among the Maya: Travels in Belize, Guatemala, & Mexico. Ronald Wright. 464p. 1991. pap. 15.95 (*0-8050-1470-5*, Owl) H Holt & Co.

Time among the Navajo: Traditional Lifeways on the Reservation. Kathy E. Hooker. (Illus.). 98p. 1991. pap. text ed. 19.95 (*0-89013-221-6*) Museum NM Pr.

Time & a Season. Curtiss A. Matlock. (Men Made in America Ser.). 1995. mass mkt. 3.99 (*0-373-45186-5*, 1-45186-3) Harlequin Bks.

Time & Again. Jack Finney. (Illus.). 400p. 1995. pap. 12.00 (*0-684-80105-1*, Scribners PB Fict) S&S Trade.

Time & Again. Jack Finney. 1995. 25.00 (*0-684-80117-5*) S&S Trade.

Time & Again. Kathryn Jensen. (Intimate Moments Ser.). 1996. mass mkt. 3.75 (*0-373-07685-1*, 1-07685-0) Silhouette.

Time & Again. Beverly Sommers. 256p. 1987. mass mkt. 3.95 (*0-373-97042-0*) Harlequin Bks.

Time & Again. large type ed. Jack Finney. LC 95-9439. 512p. 1995. 25.95 (*0-7838-1386-4*, GK Hall) Thorndike Pr.

Time & Again. Jack Finney. 1993. reprint ed. lib. bdg. 31.95 (*0-89968-403-3*, Lghtyr Pr) Buccaneer Bks.

Time & Again: Broadway Edition. Jack Finney. 1997. pap. 11.00 (*0-684-83594-0*) S&S Trade.

Time & Anthony Powell: A Critical Study. Robert L. Selig. LC 89-46409. 176p. 1991. 31.50 (*0-8386-3405-2*) Fairleigh Dickinson.

***Time & Behaviour: Psychological & Neurobehavioral Analyses.** C. M. Bradshaw & E. Szabadi. (Advances in Psychology Ser.: Vol. 120). 1997. write for info. (*0-444-82449-9*) Elsevier.

Time & Cause: Essays Presented to Richard Taylor. Ed. by Peter Van Inwagen. (Philosophical Studies in Philosophy: No. 19). 323p. 1980. lib. bdg. 88.00 (*90-277-1048-1*, D Reidel) Kluwer Ac.

Time & Chance. Alan Brennert. 1990. mass mkt. 4.95 (*0-8125-3188-4*) Tor Bks.

Time & Chance. large type ed. Anne Weale. (Charnwood Library). 1991. 27.99 (*0-7089-8586-6*, Trail West Pubs) Ulverscroft.

***Time & Chance.** 2nd ed. Herman Wilson, II. v, 82p. 1997. pap. write for info. (*1-890667-00-5*) Introspect Bks.

***Time & Chance.** 2nd ed. Herman Wilson, II. v, 82p. 1997. lib. bdg. write for info. (*1-890667-05-6*) Introspect Bks.

***Time & Chance: Gerald Ford's Appointment with History.** James M. Cannon. (C). 1997. reprint ed. pap. 19.95 (*0-472-08482-8*) U of Mich Pr.

Time & Change. John Burroughs. (Works of John Burroughs). 1989. reprint ed. lib. bdg. 79.00 (*0-7812-2196-X*) Rprt Serv.

Time & Change: Short but Different Philosophies. E. H. Chacalos. LC 88-63739. 367p. (C). 1989. text ed. 24.95 (*0-917262-03-4*) Potomac Pr Cir.

***Time & Commodity Culture.** John Frow. 224p. 1997. text ed. 65.00 (*0-19-815947-1*) OUP.

***Time & Commodity Culture: Essays on Cultural Theory & Postmodernity.** John Frow. 224p. 1997. pap. 18.95 (*0-19-815948-X*) OUP.

Time & Community: Studies in Liturgical History & Theology. Ed. by J. Neil Alexander. (NPM Studies in Church Music & Liturgy). 468p. (Orig.). 1990. pap. 34.95 (*0-912405-66-X*) Pastoral Pr.

Time & Cosmology: Creation & Expansion of Our Universe. Charles B. Leffert. LC 95-78202. (Illus.). 255p. 1996. 49.95 (*0-9647745-6-9*) Anoka Pubng.

Time & Dancing Image. Deborah Jowitt. 184p. 1989. pap. 18.95 (*0-520-06627-8*) U CA Pr.

Time & Dose Dependent Risk Assessment - Urethane Carcinogen. Salmon & Zeise. 1991. 79.95 (*0-685-48462-9*, CRC Reprint) Franklin.

Time & Duration: A Philosophical Study by S. V. Keeling. Stanley V. Keeling. Ed. by Gerald Rochelle. LC 91-11365. (Problems in Contemporary Philosophy Ser.: Vol. 31). 116p. 1991. lib. bdg. 59.95 (*0-7734-9767-6*) E Mellen.

Time & Eastern Man. Joseph Needham. LC 65-29667. (Royal Anthropological Institute, Occasional Paper Ser.: No. 21). 62p. reprint ed. pap. 25.00 (*0-317-28751-6*, 2055492) Bks Demand.

Time & Eternal Change. John M. Malville. 128p. 1991. text ed. 25.00 (*81-207-1288-9*, Pub. by Sterling Pubs II) Apt Bks.

Time & Eternity. Ananda K. Coomaraswamy. 107p. 1991. text ed. 25.00 (*81-85503-00-1*, Pub. by Sterling Pubs II) Apt Bks.

Time & Eternity. Brian Leftow. LC 90-55890. (Cornell Studies in the Philosophy of Religion). 352p. 1991. 47.50 (*0-8014-2459-3*) Cornell U Pr.

Time & Eternity. 2nd ed. Ananda K. Coomaraswamy. (C). 1990. 14.00 (*0-685-59777-6*, Pub. by Usha II) S Asia.

Time & Eternity. 2nd rev. ed. Ananda K. Coomaraswamy. (C). 1989. 18.50 (*0-8364-2488-3*) S Asia.

Time & Eternity. Ananda K. Coomaraswamy. 1993. reprint ed. 12.00 (*81-215-0059-1*, Pub. by Munshiram Manoharial II) S Asia.

Time & Eternity, 10 vols., Set. Seiichi Hatano. Tr. by Ichiro Suzuki. (Documentary Reference Collections). 1988. 395.00 (*0-318-35979-0*, CMJ/, Greenwood Pr) Greenwood.

Time & Eternity, 10 vols., Vol. 4. Seiichi Hatano. Tr. by Ichiro Suzuki. LC 88-21949. (Documentary Reference Collections). 181p. 1988. text ed. 42.95 (*0-313-26557-7*, CMJ04, Greenwood Pr) Greenwood.

Time & Eternity: An Essay in the Philosophy of Religion. Walter T. Stace. LC 69-14094. 169p. 1970. reprint ed. text ed. 35.00 (*0-8371-1867-0*, STTE, Greenwood Pr) Greenwood.

Time & Eternity - Chinese Edition. Moody Institute of Science Staff. Tr. by CRM Staff. 15p. (CHI.). 1977. 0.40 (*1-56582-060-6*) Christ Renew Min.

Time & Experience. Peter K. McInerney. 224p. 1991. 44.95 (*0-87722-752-7*) Temple U Pr.

Time & Experience. Peter K. McInerney. 296p. 1992. pap. 22.95 (*1-56639-010-9*) Temple U Pr.

Time & Exteriority: Aristotle, Heidegger, Derrida. John Protevi. LC 93-49860. 1994. 38.50 (*0-8387-5229-2*) Bucknell U Pr.

Time & Free Will: An Essay on the Immediate Data of Consciousness. Henri Bergson. 277p. 1996. reprint ed. pap. 24.95 (*1-56459-593-5*) Kessinger Pub.

Time & Frequency Representation of Signals & Systems. Ed. by G. Longo & Bernard Picinbono. (CISM Courses & Lectures: Vol. 309). (Illus.). vii, 175p. 1989. 50.95 (*0-387-82143-0*) Spr-Verlag.

Time & Ginger. Ronald Alexander. 1980. pap. 5.25 (*0-8222-1151-3*) Dramatists Play.

Time & History in Contemporary Philosophy. H. Wildon Carr. 1970. reprint ed. pap. 39.95 (*0-8383-0120-7*) M S G Haskell Hse.

Time & History in Contemporary Philosophy with Special Reference to Bergson & Croce. H. Wildon Carr. 1974. lib. bdg. 59.95 (*0-8490-2750-0*) Gordon Pr.

Time & Human Cognition: A Life-Span Perspective. Ed. by I. Levin & D. Zakay. (Advances in Psychology Ser.: No. 59). 412p. 1989. 192.00 (*0-444-87379-1*, North Holland) Elsevier.

Time & Human Interaction: Toward a Social Psychology of Time. Joseph E. McGrath & Janice R. Kelly. LC 86-396. (Guilford Social Psychology Ser.). 183p. 1986. lib. bdg. 30.00 (*0-89862-111-9*) Guilford Pr.

***Time & Imperishability: Essays on the Capricorn Hieroglyph.** Patrizia Norelli-Bachelet. 210p. (Orig.). 1997. pap. 9.00 (*0-945747-90-X*) Aeon Bks.

Time & Information Management That Really Works. Kathleen R. Allen & Office Depot Staff. (Small Business Solutions Ser.). 128p. (Orig.). 1995. pap. 13.95 (*0-8442-2998-9*, NTC Busn Bks) NTC Pub Grp.

Time & Information Management That Really Works! Organization for the 90s. Kathleen R. Allen. Ed. by Peter H. Engel. (Office Depot's Small Business Solutions Ser.). (Illus.). 128p. (Orig.). 1995. pap. 13.95 (*1-886111-22-7*) Affinity CA.

Time & Its Use: A Self-Management Guide for Teachers. Charles C. Drawbaugh. LC 84-8578. (Illus.). 144p. 1984. reprint ed. pap. 41.10 (*0-7837-8877-0*, 2049588) Bks Demand.

Time & Learning in the Special Education Classroom. Libby Goodman. LC 89-29353. (SUNY Series in Special Education). 255p. 1990. text ed. 64.50 (*0-7914-0371-8*); pap. text ed. 21.95 (*0-7914-0372-6*) State U NY Pr.

Time & Light. William Bornefeld. (Illus.). (C). 1996. pap. 5.99 (*1-56504-914-4*, 13352, Borealis) White Wolf.

Time & Logic: A Computational Approach. Ed. by Leonard Bolc & Andrzej Szalas. 367p. 1994. 70.00 (*1-85728-233-7*, Pub. by UCL Pr UK) Taylor & Francis.

Time & Man. L. R. Elton & Harry Messel. LC 76-26511. (Illus.). 114p. 1978. text ed. 62.00 (*0-08-021332-4*, Pub. by Pergamon Repr UK) Franklin.

Time & Man. Georgios I. Mantzaridis. Tr. by Julian Vulliamy from GRE. LC 96-11015. 1996. write for info. (*1-878997-54-8*) St Tikhons Pr.

Time & Mankind: An Historical & Philosophical Study of Mankind's Attitude to the Phenomena of Change. S. G. Brandon. 1977. lib. bdg. 250.00 (*0-8490-2751-9*) Gordon Pr.

Time & Meaning in History. Nathan Rotenstreich. (Boston Studies in the Philosophy of Science: No. 101). 228p. (C). 1987. lib. bdg. 118.50 (*90-277-2467-9*, D Reidel) Kluwer Ac.

Time & Mind. Ed. by J. T. Fraser. (Study of Time Ser.: No. VI). 320p. 1990. 45.00 (*0-8236-6542-9*) Intl Univs Pr.

Time & Mind. Hede Helfrich. LC 96-8729. 209p. 1996. 38.00 (*0-88937-173-3*) Hogrefe & Huber Pubs.

Time & Mind in Wordsworth's Poetry. Jeffrey Baker. LC 80-11947. 214p. 1980. 34.95 (*0-8143-1655-7*) Wayne St U Pr.

Time & Modality. Arthur N. Prior. LC 78-26696. (Illus.). 148p. 1979. reprint ed. text ed. 35.00 (*0-313-20911-1*, PRTI, Greenwood Pr) Greenwood.

***Time & Money.** Ed. by Janet Bruno. (Child-Centered Math Ser.: Vol. 10). (Illus.). 80p. (Orig.). 1997. pap. 4.98 (*1-57471-243-8*, 2660) Creat Teach Pr.

Time & Money. William Matthews. 76p. 1996. pap. 12.95 (*0-395-82526-1*) HM.

Time & Money: New Poems. William Matthews. 69p. 1995. 19.95 (*0-395-71134-7*) HM.

Time & Money: The Making of Consumerist Modernity. Gary Cross. LC 92-28020. 256p. (C). 1993. pap. 18.95 (*0-415-08855-0*, B0016, Routledge NY) Routledge.

Time & Money: Using Time Value Analysis in Financial Planning. Robert Crowe. 160p. 1987. per. 7.50 (*1-55623-051-6*) Irwin Prof Pubng.

Time & Money: Using Time Value Analysis in Financial Planning. 2nd ed. Robert M. Crowe. 176p. 1990. text ed. 35.00 (*1-55623-421-X*) Irwin Prof Pubng.

Time & Money Time Value of Money Templates. Robert Crowe. 1987. text ed. 15.00 (*1-55623-059-1*) Irwin Prof Pubng.

Time & Myth. John S. Dunne. LC 74-32289. 128p. 1975. reprint ed. pap. 9.50 (*0-268-01828-6*) U of Notre Dame Pr.

Time & Narrative, Vol. 1. Paul Ricoeur. Tr. by Kathleen Blamey & David Pellauer. LC 83-17995. 286p. 1990. pap. 13.95 (*0-226-71332-6*) U Ch Pr.

Time & Narrative, Vol. 2. Paul Ricoeur. Tr. by Kathleen McLaughlin & David Pellauer. viii, 216p. 1986. lib. bdg. 30.00 (*0-226-71333-4*) U Ch Pr.

Time & Narrative, Vol. 2. Paul Ricoeur. Tr. by Kathleen Blamey & David Pellauer. LC 83-17995. 216p. 1990. pap. 13.95 (*0-226-71334-2*) U Ch Pr.

Time & Narrative, Vol. 3. Paul Ricoeur. Tr. by Kathleen Blamey & David Pellauer. 362p. 1988. lib. bdg. 36.00 (*0-226-71335-0*) U Ch Pr.

Time & Narrative, Vol. 3. Paul Ricoeur. Tr. by Kathleen Blamey & David Pellauer. LC 83-17995. vi, 362p. 1990. pap. 16.95 (*0-226-71336-9*) U Ch Pr.

Time & Narrative in Stendhal. Benjamin M. Amoss, Jr. LC 91-18323. (South Atlantic Modern Language Association Award Study). 200p. 1992. 40.00 (*0-8203-1400-5*) U of Ga Pr.

Time & Order in Metropolitan Vienna: A Seizure of Schedules. Robert Rotenberg. LC 91-32894. (Series in Ethnographic Inquiry). (Illus.). 224p. (C). 1992. text ed. 35.00 (*1-56098-103-2*) Smithsonian.

Time & Place. M. W. Beresford. 420p. (C). 1985. text ed. 60.00 (*0-907628-39-7*) Hambledon Press.

Time & Place. Bryan Woolley. LC 84-8797. (Texas Tradition Ser.: No. 2). 246p. (C). 1985. reprint ed. 16.95 (*0-912646-98-5*); reprint ed. pap. 9.95 (*0-912646-99-3*) Tex Christian.

***Time & Place: Fifty Years of Santa Cruz Studio Ceramics.** (Illus.). 152p. (Orig.). 1997. pap. 32.00 (*0-945952-02-3*) Mus Art Hist.

Time & Place in Deuteronomy. J. Gordon McConville & J. G. Millar. (Journal for the Study of the Old Testament Supplement Ser.: Vol. 179). 155p. 37.50 (*1-85075-494-2*, Pub. by Sheffield Acad UK) CUP Services.

Time & Place in Joliet: Essays on the Geographical Evolution of the City. fac. ed. Ed. by Michael P. Conzen. LC 86-6108. (Studies on the Illinois & Michigan Canal Corridor: No. 2). (Illus.). 221p. 1988. reprint ed. pap. 63.00 (*0-7837-8041-9*, 2047591) Bks Demand.

Time & Probability in Formal Design of Distributed Systems. Hans A. Hansson. LC 94-29186. (Real-Time Safety Critical Systems Ser.: Vol. 1). 330p. 1994. 149.50 (*0-444-89940-5*) Elsevier.

Time & Process: Interdisciplinary Issues. Ed. by J. T. Fraser & Lewis Rowell. LC 92-973. (Study of Time Ser.: Vol. 7). 320p. (C). 1993. 47.00 (*0-8236-6544-5*) Intl Univs Pr.

Time & Psychological Explanation. Brent D. Slife. LC 92-21062. (SUNY Series, Alternatives in Psychology). 343p. (C). 1993. text ed. 64.50 (*0-7914-1469-8*); pap. text ed. 21.95 (*0-7914-1470-1*) State U NY Pr.

Time & Public Policy. T. Alexander Smith. LC 87-36554. 312p. 1989. text ed. 34.00 (*0-87049-574-7*) U of Tenn Pr.

Time & Quality in Graduate Work Education: Report of the Special Committee to Study the Length of Graduate Education Social Work Education. 1972. 2.00 (*0-318-35377-6*) Coun Soc Wk Ed.

Time & Reality. John E. Boodin. LC 75-3064. (Philosophy in America Ser.). reprint ed. 39.50 (*0-404-59063-2*) AMS Pr.

Time & Reality: Spacetime Physics & the Objectivity of Temporal Becoming. Mauro Dorato. 238p. 1996. pap. 24.00 (*88-8091-172-4*) Paul & Co Pubs.

Time & Reality see Study in Reaction Time & Movement

Time & Reality in American Philosophy. Bertrand P. Helm. LC 85-8583. 264p. 1986. 30.00 (*0-87023-493-5*) U of Mass Pr.

Time & Reality in the Thought of the Maya. Miguel Leon-Portilla. Tr. by Charles L. Boiles & Fernando Horcasitas from SPA. LC 88-40207. (Civilization of the American Indian Ser.: Vol. 190). (Illus.). 256p. 1990. pap. 14.95 (*0-8061-2308-7*) U of Okla Pr.

Time & Revolution: Marxism & the Design of Soviet Institutions. Stephen E. Hanson. LC 96-13723. 312p. (C). 1997. text ed. 45.00 (*0-8078-2305-8*) U of NC Pr.

Time & Revolution: Marxism & the Design of Soviet Institutions. Stephen E. Hanson. LC 96-13723. 312p. (C). 1997. pap. 18.95 (*0-8078-4615-5*) U of NC Pr.

Time & School Learning: Theory, Research & Practice. Ed. by Lorin W. Anderson. LC 83-11009. 240p. 1984. text ed. 29.95 (*0-312-80505-5*) St Martin.

Time & Schools: The Impact of Time Use on the Quality of Education. 58p. 1991. 7.50 (*1-56452-038-2*) NY Boards Assoc.

Time & Self: Phenomenological Explorations. Paul Brockelman. (American Academy of Religion, Studies in Religion). 83p. (C). 1985. 27.95 (*0-89130-779-6*, 01-00-39); pap. 16.95 (*0-89130-780-X*) Scholars Pr GA.

Time & Sense: Proust & the Experience of Literature. Julia Kristeva. Tr. by Ross Guberman. LC 95-36160. (European Perspectives Ser.). (Illus.). 407p. 1996. 32.50 (*0-231-10250-X*) Col U Pr.

Time & Social Structure & Other Essays. Meyer Fortes. (London School of Economics Monographs on Social Anthropology: No. 40). 290p. (C). 1970. text ed. 38.50 (*0-485-19540-2*, Pub. by Athlone Pr UK) Humanities.

Time & Social Theory. Barbara Adam. 250p. 1990. 39.95 (*0-87722-788-8*) Temple U Pr.

Time & Space. John R. Gribbin & Mary Gribbin. LC 93-44285. (Eyewitness Science Ser.). (Illus.). 64p. (J). (gr. 7 up). 1994. 15.95 (*1-56458-478-X*) DK Pub Inc.

Time & Space. Time-Life Books Editors. Ed. by Jim Hicks. (Mysteries of the Unknown Ser.). (Illus.). 144p. 1990. 14.95 (*0-8094-6396-2*); lib. bdg. 23.27 (*0-8094-6397-0*) Time-Life.

Time & Space: A Basic Reader. Jean Sims & Michael Connelly. (Illus.). 176p. (C). 1982. pap. text ed. write for info. (*0-13-922005-4*) P-H.

Time & Space: A Beginning Reader. 2nd ed. Michael Connelly & Jean Sims. 224p. (C). 1990. pap. text ed. 19.80 (*0-13-922014-3*) P-H.

Time & Space: The Treasure Map. Kurt A. Feger. (Illus.). 87p. (C). 1989. pap. write for info. (*0-9622661-0-8*) K A Feger.

Time & Space in Chinese Culture. Erik J. Zurcher. LC 95-20958. (Sinica Leidensia Ser.: No. 33). (Illus.). 416p. 1995. 125.50 (*90-04-10287-6*) E J Brill.

Time & Space in Euripides & Racine: The Hippolytos of Euripides & Racine's Phedre. Mary Pittas-Hershbach. LC 89-29820. (American University Studies: Comparative Literature: Ser. III, Vol. 32). 344p. (C). 1990. text ed. 53.95 (*0-8204-1182-5*) P Lang Pubng.

Time & T. S. Eliot: His Poetry, Plays & Philosophy. Jitendra K. Sharma. viii, 212p. 1985. text ed. 25.00 (*0-86590-556-8*) Apt Bks.

Time & Teamwork Manager. LC 86-73017. 1987. 14.50 (*0-938485-01-6*) Beverly Found.

Time & Temporality in Samkhya-Yoga & Abhidharma Buddhism. Braj M. Sinha. (C). 1983. text ed. 13.00 (*0-8364-2837-4*, Pub. by Manohar II) S Asia.

Time & the Art of Living. Robert Grudin. 256p. 1988. pap. 12.00 (*0-89919-789-2*) Ticknor & Fields.

Time & the Artist in Shakespeare's English Histories. John W. Blanpied. LC 82-40387. 280p. 1983. 38.50 (*0-87413-230-4*) U Delaware Pr.

Time & the Clock Mice, Etcetera. Peter Dickinson. LC 93-11434. (Illus.). 128p. (J). 1994. 16.95 (*0-385-32038-8*) Delacorte.

Time & the Crystal: Studies in Dante's "Rime Petrose" Robert Durling & Ronald L. Martinez. 1990. 60.00 (*0-520-06488-7*) U CA Pr.

Time & the Earth's Rotation. Ed. by Dennis D. McCarthy & John D. Pilkington. (International Astronomical Union Symposia Ser.: No. 82). 1979. pap. text ed. 70.50 (*90-277-0893-2*); lib. bdg. 104.50 (*90-277-0892-4*) Kluwer Ac.

Time & the Erotic in Horace's Odes. Ronnie Ancona. LC 93-46913. 208p. 1994. text ed. 39.95 (*0-8223-1476-2*) Duke.

Time & the Flying Snow. Gordon Bok. LC 77-80648. 88p. 1977. pap. 10.95 (*0-938702-03-3*) Folk-Legacy.

Time & the Gods. Edward J. Dunsany. LC 76-113659. (Short Story Index Reprint Ser.). 1977. 18.95 (*0-8369-3388-5*) Ayer.

Time & the Highland Maya. rev. ed. Barbara Tedlock. LC 91-44651. (Illus.). 311p. 1992. pap. 15.95 (*0-8263-1358-2*) U of NM Pr.

***Time & the Hour.** Kerslake. Date not set. text ed. 39.50 (*1-86064-154-7*, Pub. by I B Tauris UK) St Martin.

***Time & the Island.** Sean Dunne. 62p. 1996. pap. 12.95 (*1-85235-180-2*) Dufour.

***Time & the Maiden.** Matthew Piepenburg. LC 97-72256. 256p. 1997. pap. 15.95 (*1-882897-15-3*) Lost Coast.

Time & the Novel: The Genealogical Imperative. Patricia D. Tobin. LC 78-52486. 248p. 1978. reprint ed. pap. 70.70 (*0-7837-9463-0*, 2060205) Bks Demand.

Time & the Other. Johannes Fabian. LC 42-19751. 224p. 1983. pap. text ed. 19.50 (*0-231-05591-9*) Col U Pr.

Time & the Other. Emmanuel Levinas. Tr. & Intro. by Richard A. Cohen. LC 87-6900. 149p. (C). 1990. reprint ed. pap. text ed. 17.95 (*0-8207-0233-1*) Duquesne.

Time & the Place. Naguib Mahfouz. 192p. 1992. pap. 8.95 (*0-385-26472-0*, Anchor NY) Doubleday.

Time & the River. Ed. by Geoff W. Kite. 375p. 1995. boxed 58.00 (*0-918334-97-7*, TAR) WRP.

Time & the Seasons. Bobbie Kalman. (In My World Ser.). (Illus.). 32p. (J). (gr. 2-3). 1986. 19.16 (*0-86505-072-4*); pap. 6.95 (*0-86505-094-5*) Crabtree Pub Co.

***Time & the Soul: Where Has All the Meaningful Time Gone? & How to Get It Back.** Jacob Needleman. 112p. 1997. 16.00 (*0-385-48177-2*, Currency) Doubleday.

Time & the Town: A Provincetown Chronicle. Mary H. Vorse. LC 90-81455. (Provincetown Classics in History, Literature, & Art Ser.: No. 4). 372p. 1990. pap. 20.00 (*0-945135-04-1*); pap. 12.95 (*0-945135-03-3*) Cape Cod Pilgrim.

Time & the Town: A Provincetown Chronicle. Mary H. Vorse. 372p. (C). 1991. reprint ed. pap. 14.95 (*0-8135-1752-4*); reprint ed. text ed. 45.00 (*0-8135-1751-6*) Rutgers U Pr.

Time & the Tuolumne Landscape: Continuity & Change in the Yosemite High Country. Thomas R. Vale & Geraldine R. Vale. LC 93-21700. (Illus.). 224p. (C). 1994. text ed. 50.00 (*0-87480-429-9*) U of Utah Pr.

Time & the Verb: A Guide to Tense & Aspect. Robert I. Binnick. (Illus.). 584p. 1991. 75.00 (*0-19-506206-X*) OUP.

Time & the White Tigress. Mary Barnard. LC 85-31353. (Illus.). 96p. 1986. 19.95 (*0-932576-31-1*) Breitenbush Bks.

Time & the Wind. Erico Verissimo. Tr. by L. L. Barrett. LC 78-88995. 624p. 1970. reprint ed. text ed. 75.00 (*0-8371-2111-6*, VETW, Greenwood Pr) Greenwood.

Time & the Work of Anthropology: Critical Essays 1971-1991. Johannes Fabian. (Studies in Anthropology & History). Date not set. pap. text ed. 24.00 (*3-7186-5222-6*, Harwood Acad Pubs) Gordon & Breach.

Time & the Work of Anthropology: Critical Essays 1971-1991. Johannes Fabian. (Studies in Anthropology & History). 1991. text ed. 64.00 (*3-7186-5179-3*, Harwood Acad Pubs) Gordon & Breach.

***Time & Tide.** Bosker et al. 1997. 30.00 (*0-684-82422-1*) S&S Trade.

Time & Tide. Eve Gladstone. 1994. mass mkt. 2.99 (*0-373-22295-5*, 1-22295-9) Harlequin Bks.

Time & Tide. Edna O'Brien. 1992. 21.00 (*0-374-27776-1*) FS&G.

Time & Tide. Edna O'Brien. 336p. 1993. pap. 10.99 (*0-446-39510-2*) Warner Bks.

Time & Tide: The Transformation of Bear River, Nova Scotia. Stephen J. Hornsby. (Northeast Folklore Ser.: No. 31). (Illus.). 70p. (Orig.). 1996. pap. 15.00 (*0-943197-23-6*) ME Folklife Ctr.

Time & Tide: Tyne International Exhibition of Contemporary Art. (Art & Design Ser.: No. 32). (Illus.). 96p. 1993. pap. 26.95 (*1-85490-215-6*) Academy Ed UK.

Time & Tide Wait for No Man: The Changing European Geopolitical Landscape. Karel De Gucht & Stephan Keukeleire. LC 91-9196. 256p. 1991. text ed. 55.00 (*0-275-94062-4*, C4062, Praeger Pubs) Greenwood.

Time & Time Again. Dennis Danvers. LC 94-11965. 1994. 22.00 (*0-671-78800-0*) S&S Trade.

Time & Time Again. Dennis Danvers. 1995. mass mkt. 5.99 (*0-671-53448-3*, Pocket Books) PB.

Time & Time Again. Catherine Ennis. 224p. (Orig.). 1996. pap. 10.95 (*1-56280-145-7*) Naiad Pr.

Time & Time Again. Lee Jenkins. Ed. by Mary Laycock. (Illus.). 72p. (Orig.). (J). (gr. 1-6). 1985. pap. text ed. 7.95 (*0-918932-85-8*, AE-1038) Activity Resources.

Time & Time Again. large type ed. B. M. Gill. 232p. 1990. 21.95 (*1-85089-339-X*, Pub. by ISIS UK) Transaction Pubs.

Time & Time Again: Two Immigrant Groups. Hary Monroe. (Illus.). 1985. 3.00 (*0-615-00718-X*) Balch IES Pr.

Time & Timelessness: A Psychoanalytic Exploration of the Varieties of Temporal Experience. Peter Hartocollis. LC 83-237. 261p. 1984. 40.00 (*0-8236-6545-3*) Intl Univs Pr.

Time & Times & Half a Time: Historical Consciousness in the Jewish Literature of the Persian & Hellenistic Eras. Ida Frohlich. (Journal for the Study of the Pseudepigrapha Supplement Ser.: No. 19). 300p. 1996. 58.50 (*1-85075-566-3*, Pub. by Sheffield Acad UK) CUP Services.

Time & Transcendence: Secular History, the Catholic Reaction, & the Rediscovery of the Future. Gabriel Motzkin. LC 92-10249. (Philosophical Studies in Contemporary Culture: Vol. 1). 320p. (C). 1992. lib. bdg. 137.50 (*0-7923-1773-4*, Pub. by Klwr Acad Pubs NE) Kluwer Ac.

Time & Transcendence: The Deeper Insight of the Jewish Calender. Rabbi Dalfin. (Illus.). 100p. (Orig.). 1996. pap. 12.95 (*1-880880-13-X*) Israeli Trad.

Time & Western Man. Wyndham Lewis. Ed. & Intro. by Paul Edwards. LC 93-1568. 617p. (Orig.). (C). 1993. 30.00 (*0-87685-879-5*); pap. 17.50 (*0-87685-878-7*) Black Sparrow.

Time & Western Man. deluxe ed. Wyndham Lewis. Ed. & Intro. by Paul Edwards. LC 93-1568. 617p. (Orig.). (C). 1993. 35.00 (*0-87685-880-9*) Black Sparrow.

Time & Western Man. Wyndham Lewis. LC 78-64042. (Des Imagistes: Literature of the Imagist Movement Ser.). (Orig.). reprint ed. 36.00 (*0-404-17125-7*) AMS Pr.

Time Apart: An Experiment in International Living. Richard S. Case. (Illus.). 224p. 1995. pap. text ed. 14.00 (*0-8059-3824-9*) Dorrance.

Time Apart: Dealing with Family Separation. Bonnie S. Linder. LC 94-92271. (Children in the Military Ser.). 18p. (J). (ps-4). 1994. pap. text ed. 4.95 (*0-9643966-1-0*) Sylvan Crest.

Time Apart: Reflection Models for Parish Ministers. Center for Learning Network Staff. 120p. 1992. teacher ed., spiral bd. 15.95 (*1-56077-207-7*) Ctr Learning.

Time As a Factor in Groupwork: Time-Limited Group Experiences. Ed. by Albert Alissi & Max Casper. LC 85-7636. (Social Work with Groups Ser.: Vol. 8, No. 2). 160p. 1985. text ed. 39.95 (*0-86656-409-8*); pap. text ed. 19.95 (*0-86656-438-1*) Haworth Pr.

Time as a Metaphor of History: Early India. A. Thapar. (Illus.). 64p. (C). 1996. pap. 5.95 (*0-19-563798-4*) OUP.

Time As Conflict: A Scientific & Humanistic Study. J. T. Fraser. (Science & Culture Ser.: No. 35). 356p. 1980. 66.50 (*0-8176-0950-4*) Birkhauser.

Time As History. George Grant. Ed. & Intro. by William Christian. 120p. 1995. 35.00 (*0-8020-0640-X*); pap. 14.95 (*0-8020-7593-2*) U of Toronto Pr.

***Time at the Lake: A Minnesota Album.** William Allard. LC 97-21099. (Illus.). 1997. pap. 19.95 (*1-57025-133-9*) Pfeifer-Hamilton.

Time-Barred Actions. 2nd ed. F. Berlingieri. (International Maritime Law Ser.). 256p. 1993. boxed 110.00 (*1-85044-525-7*) LLP.

Time-Based Competition: The Next Battle Ground in American Manufacturing. Joseph C. Blackburn. (APICS Ser.). 240p. 1990. text ed. 50.00 (*1-55623-321-3*) Irwin Prof Pubng.

Time-Based Manufacturing. Joseph A. Bockerstette & Richard L. Shell. LC 92-41480. 336p. 1993. 49.95 (*0-89806-126-1*) Eng Mgmt Pr.

Time-Based Reality: Toward the Simplest Technical Description of Nature. Norm Buske. LC 86-62803. (Illus.). 52p. 1987. pap. 9.00 (*0-932975-02-X*) N Buske.

Time Before Deception: Truth in Communication, Culture & Ethics. Thomas W. Cooper. LC 94-43547. (Illus.). 330p. (C). 1997. 24.95 (*0-940666-59-6*) Clear Light.

***Time Before Deception: Truth in Communication Culture & Ethics.** Thomas W Cooper. (Illus.). 244p. (C). 1997. pap. text ed. 14.95 (*0-940666-89-8*) Clear Light.

Time Before History. Colin Tudge. 1997. pap. 14.00 (*0-684-83052-3*) S&S Trade.

Time Before History: 5 Million Years of Human Impact. Colin Tudge. 384p. 1996. 27.50 (*0-684-80726-2*) S&S Trade.

Time Before Space: An Airman's Odyssey...from Biplanes to Rockets. Elton H. Rowley. (Illus.). 238p. 1994. 33.95 (*0-89745-178-3*); pap. 25.95 (*0-89745-174-0*) Sunflower U Pr.

Time Before Time: Prehistory & Archaeology in the Lake Sonoma Area. fac. ed. Suzanne B. Stewart. (Illus.). 73p. (C). 1985. reprint ed. pap. 6.85 (*1-55567-583-2*) Coyote Press.

Time Began in a Garden. Emilie Barnes & Anne C. Buchanan. (Illus.). (Orig.). 1995. 15.99 (*1-56507-368-1*) Harvest Hse.

Time Being. Don Cupitt. 208p. (Orig.). 1992. pap. 18.50 (*0-334-02522-2*, SCM Pr) TPI PA.

***Time Being.** Mary Meigs. 176p. 1997. pap. 12.95 (*0-88922-374-2*, Pub. by Talonbooks CN) Genl Dist Srvs.

***Time Benders.** Gary Paulsen. (World of Adventure Ser.: No. 14). 1997. mass mkt. 3.99 (*0-440-41214-5*) Dell.

***Time Between Hosanna & Alleluia.** Kathy Kirkpatrick. 36p. 1994. pap. 7.50 (*1-877871-59-1*, 6220) Ed Ministries.

Time Bind: When Work Becomes Home & Home Becomes Work. Arlie R. Hochschild. LC 97-3411. (Illus.). 316p. 1997. 22.50 (*0-8050-4470-1*) H Holt & Co.

Time-Binding: The General Theory. Alfred Korzybski. 60p. 1979. pap. 5.95 (*0-910780-01-3*) Inst Gen Seman.

***Time Blender No. 1.** Michael Dorn. 1997. mass mkt. 5.99 (*0-06-105682-0*, HarperPrism) HarpC.

***Time Blender No. 2.** 288p. mass mkt. write for info. (*0-06-105683-9*, HarperPrism) HarpC.

***Time Blender No. 3.** 288p. mass mkt. write for info. (*0-06-105684-7*, HarperPrism) HarpC.

Time Bomb. Jonathan Kellerman. 496p. 1991. mass mkt. 6.99 (*0-553-29170-X*) Bantam.

Time Bomb: How Terrorists & the Russian Mafia Threaten the World with a Nuclear Nightmare. Joel Seidman & Patricia F. Allingham. (Illus.). 300p. 1995. 23.95 (*1-882605-29-2*) Natl Pr Bks.

***Time Bombs.** Nancy Herndon. 320p. 1997. mass mkt. 5.99 (*0-425-15965-5*, Prime Crime) Berkley Pub.

Time Book. John Cassidy. 32p. (J). (ps-8). 1991. spiral bd. 10.95 (*1-878257-08-0*) Klutz Pr.

Time Burial. Howard Wandrei. Ed. & Intro. by D. H. Olson. (Illus.). 368p. 1995. 29.00 (*1-878252-22-4*) Fedogan & Bremer.

Time by Distance. William L. Fox. Ed. by Kirk Robertson. (Windriver Ser.). (Illus.). 64p. (Orig.). 1985. pap. 6.00 (*0-916918-28-9*) Duck Down.

Time by Distance. deluxe ed. William L. Fox. Ed. by Kirk Robertson. (Windriver Ser.). (Illus.). 64p. (Orig.). 1985. 20.00 (*0-916918-29-7*) Duck Down.

***Time Capsule.** Pat Lowther. 200p. 1997. 19.95 (*1-896095-25-9*, Pub. by Polestar Bk Pubs CN) Orca Bk Pubs.

Time Capsule: A Concise Encyclopedia by Women Artists. Robin Kahn. (Illus.). 400p. 1995. pap. 19.95 (*1-881616-33-9*) Dist Art Pubs.

Time Capsules. F. Marino. 1988. 9.95 (*0-7935-1586-6*, 06620615) H Leonard.

Time Capsules: For Head & Heart. William I. Gorden. 96p. (Orig.). 1995. pap. 5.95 (*0-9643860-0-3*) Wego Bks.

Time Cat. Lloyd Alexander. 192p. (J). (gr. 3-7). 1996. pap. 3.99 (*0-14-037827-8*) Puffin Bks.

Time, Causality & the Quantum Theory, 2 vols. Henry Mehlberg. Tr. by Paul Benecerraf from FRE. Incl. Vol. 1. Essay on the Causal Theory of Time. 322p. 1980. lib. bdg. 104.50 (*90-277-0721-9*, D Reidel); (Boston Studies in the Philosophy of Science: No. 19). 1980. write for info. (*0-318-53991-8*) Kluwer Ac.

Time, Chance, & Organizations: Natural Selection in a Perilous Environment. 2nd ed. Herbert Kaufman. LC 91-11731. 224p. (C). 1991. pap. text ed. 19.95 (*0-934540-93-4*) Chatham Hse Pubs.

Time Change. Lynne H. DeCourcy. LC 91-73699. 80p. 1992. pap. 10.00 (*0-935331-13-1*) Ampersand RI.

***Time Change: An Alternative View of the History of Dallas.** Kevin Shay & Roy Williams. (Orig.). 1997. pap. 16.95 (*0-9650505-2-1*) CGS Communs.

Time Change: An Alternative View of the History of Dallas. Roy H. Williams & Kevin J. Shay. LC 91-67434. (Illus.). 186p. (Orig.). 1991. pap. 9.95 (*1-881365-03-4*) To Be Pub.

Time Change & Freedom: An Introduction to Metaphysics. L. Nathan Oaklander & Quentin Smith. (Illus.). 224p. (C). 1995. pap. 17.95 (*0-415-10249-5*, B7018) Routledge.

Time Change & Freedom: An Introduction to Metaphysics. L. Nathan Oaklander & Quentin Smith. LC 94-34474. (Illus.). 224p. (C). (gr. 13). 1995. text ed. 59.95 (*0-415-10248-0*, B7014) Routledge.

Time Changes in Canada & Mexico. Doris C. Doane. 80p. 1980. 10.00 (*0-86690-075-6*, D1070-014) Am Fed Astrologers.

Time Changes in the U. S. A. Doris C. Doane. 200p. 1981. 12.00 (*0-86690-076-4*, D1071-014) Am Fed Astrologers.

Time Changes in the World. Doris C. Doane. 112p. 1980. 12.00 (*0-86690-077-2*, D1072-014) Am Fed Astrologers.

Time Chart Concerning the Return of Israel's Messiah: Daniel's 70 Weeks. 10p. 1989. pap. 4.50 (*1-57277-015-5*) Script Rsch.

Time Charters. 4th rev. ed. M. Wilford et al. 582p. 1995. 250.00 (*1-85044-185-5*) LLP.

Time-Conscious Psychological Therapy: A Life Stage to Go Through. Jenifer E. Wilson. LC 95-9188. 208p. (C). 1996. pap. 18.95 (*0-415-11458-6*); text ed. 59.95 (*0-415-11457-8*) Routledge.

Time-Constrained Evaluation: A Practical Approach for LEAS & Schools. Brian Wilcox. LC 91-20993. (Educational Management Ser.). 224p. (C). (gr. 13). 1992. text ed. 85.00 (*0-415-06968-8*, A6587) Routledge.

Time-Constrained Evaluation: Practical Approach for Schools. Brian Wilcox. (Educational Management Ser.). 240p. (C). 1992. pap. text ed. 17.95 (*0-415-06969-6*, Routledge NY) Routledge.

Time-Constrained Memory: A Reader-Based Approach to Text Comprehension. Jean-Pierre Corriveau. 424p. 1995. pap. 39.95 (*0-8058-1712-3*); text ed. 79.95 (*0-8058-1711-5*) L Erlbaum Assocs.

An Asterisk (*) at the beginning of an entry indicates that the title is appearing in BIP for the first time.

***Time-Constrained Transaction Management: Real-Time Constraints in Database Transaction Systems.** Mandit R. Soparkar et al. LC 96-9935. (International Series on Advances in Database Systems). 160p. (C). 1996. lib. bdg. 88.00 (*0-7923-9752-5*) Kluwer Ac.

Time Cop. Steve Perry. 208p. (Orig.). 1994. mass mkt. 4.99 (*0-425-14652-9*) Berkley Pub.

Time, Creation, & the Continuum: Theories in Antiquity & the Early Middle Ages. Richard Sorabji. LC 82-48714. 474p. 1983. 65.00 (*0-8014-1593-4*) Cornell U Pr.

Time Crunch: What to Do When You Can't Do It All. Greg Asimakoupoulos et al. 156p. 1993. 15.99 (*0-88070-555-8*, Multnomah Bks) Multnomah Pubs.

Time, Culture, & Identity: An Interpretative Archaeology. Julian Thomas. LC 95-37250. (Illus.). 208p. (C). 1996. text ed. 59.95 (*0-415-11861-1*) Routledge.

Time Dancer: A Novel of Gypsy Magic. Zelda L. Gatuskin. LC 91-72033. 245p. (Orig.). 1991. pap. 10.00 (*0-938513-12-5*) Amador Pubs.

Time, Death, & Eternity: Reflecting on Augustine's Confessions in Light of Heidegger's Being & Time. Richard J. Severson. LC 95-7904. (ATLA Monographs: No. 36). 178p. 1995. 34.50 (*0-8108-3012-4*) Scarecrow.

Time-Delay Systems: Analysis, Optimization & Applications. M. Malek-Zavarei & Mohammad Jamshidi. (Systems & Control Ser.: No. 9). 500p. 1987. 160.00 (*0-444-70204-0*, North Holland) Elsevier.

Time Dependent & Vibration Problems. Ed. by C. A. Brebbia. (Topics in Boundary Elements Ser.: Vol. 2). 271p. 1985. 64.00 (*1-56252-138-1*) Computational Mech MA.

***Time Dependent Behavior of High Strength Concrete.** Ningxu Han. (Illus.). 315p. (Orig.). 1996. pap. 67.50 (*90-407-1398-7*, Pub. by Delft U Pr NE) Coronet Bks.

Time-Dependent Effects in Disordered Materials. Ed. by Roger Pynn & Tormod Riste. LC 87-28562. (NATO ASI Series B, Physics: Vol. 167). (Illus.). 518p. 1988. 110.00 (*0-306-42782-6*, Plenum Pr) Plenum.

Time-Dependent Failure Mechanisms & Assessment Methodologies: Proceedings of the 35th Meeting of the Mechanical Failures Prevention Group, National Bureau of Standards, Gaithersburg, MD, April 20-22, 1982. Mechanical Failures Prevention Group, Meeting (35th: 1982: National Bureau of Standards) Staff. Ed. by James G. Early et al. LC 82-19892. 331p. reprint ed. pap. 94.40 (*0-318-34782-2*, 2031643) Bks Demand.

Time-Dependent Failure of Polymers: Experimental Studies. Ed. by V. H. Kenner. (AMD Ser.: Vol. 155). 80p. 1992. 30.00 (*0-7918-1130-1*, G00774) ASME.

Time Dependent Fracture. A. S. Krausz. 1985. lib. bdg. 112.00 (*90-247-3132-1*) Kluwer Ac.

Time Dependent Hartree-Fock & Beyond, Bad Honnef, FRG, 1982 Proceedings. K. Goeke & P. G. Reinhard. (Lecture Notes in Physics Ser.: Vol. 171). 426p. 1982. 42.95 (*0-387-11950-7*) Spr-Verlag.

Time-Dependent Methods for Quantum Dynamics. K. C. Kulander. (Computer Physics Communications Ser.: Vol. 63 1-3). 548p. 1991. 465.00 (*0-444-89199-4*, North Holland) Elsevier.

***Time-Dependent NonLinear Convection.** Ed. by P. A. Tyvand. (Advances in Fluid Mechanics Ser.). 250p. 1997. text ed. 117.00 (*1-85312-521-0*, 5210) Computational Mech MA.

Time Dependent Problems & Difference Methods. Bertil Gustafsson et al. LC 94-44176. (Pure & Applied Mathematics Ser.). 642p. 1996. text ed. 79.95 (*0-471-50734-2*) Wiley.

Time-Dependent Processes see Statistical Mechanics

Time-Dependent Quantum Molecular Dynamics. Ed. by J. Broeckhove & L. Lathouwers. LC 92-28749. (NATO ASI Series B, Physics: Vol. 299). 1992. 125.00 (*0-306-44305-8*, Plenum Pr) Plenum.

Time-Dependent Structure & Control of Arterial Blood Pressure. Ed. by Francesco Portaluppi & Michael H. Smolensky. LC 96-7856. (Annals of the New York Academy of Sciences Ser.: Vol. 783). 1996. write for info. (*1-57331-008-5*); pap. write for info. (*1-57331-009-3*) NY Acad Sci.

Time, Desire, & Horror: Towards a History of the Senses. Alain Corbin. Tr. by Jean Birrell from FRE. 224p. 1995. 47.95 (*0-7456-1131-1*, Pub. by Polity Pr UK) Blackwell Pubs.

Time, Details of a Tree. Larry Eigner. 1979. 12.00 (*0-686-59677-3*); pap. 5.00 (*0-686-59678-1*) Elizabeth Pr.

Time Detectives. Brian Fagan. 1995. 24.00 (*0-671-79385-3*) S&S Trade.

***Time Detectives: Clues from Our Past.** Donalda Badone. (Illus.). 100p. (YA). (gr. 5 up). 1996. pap. 12.95 (*1-55037-240-8*, Pub. by Annick CN) Firefly Bks Ltd.

Time Detectives: How Archeologists Use Technology to Recapture the Past. Brian Fagan. (Illus.). 288p. 1996. pap. 14.00 (*0-684-81828-0*, Touchstone Bks) S&S Trade.

Time Dimension. A. E. Wilder-Smith. (Orig.). 1993. pap. 7.99 (*0-936728-45-0*) Word for Today.

Time Dimension: An Interdisciplinary Guide. Compiled by T. K. Das. LC 90-31137. 368p. 1990. text ed. 59.95 (*0-275-92681-8*, C2681, Praeger Pubs) Greenwood.

***Time Discounting & Future Generations: The Harmful Effects of an Untrue Economic Theory.** Erhun Kula. LC 96-46714. 224p. 1997. text ed. 59.95 (*1-56720-090-7*, Quorum Bks) Greenwood.

Time, Discounting, & Value. Colin Price. LC 92-36108. 1993. pap. 28.95 (*0-631-17986-0*) Blackwell Pubs.

Time, Distance, & Speed. Marion Smoothey. LC 92-36225. (Let's Investigate Ser.). (J). (gr. 4 up). 1993. lib. bdg. 17.95 (*1-85435-467-1*) Marshall Cavendish.

Time Distortion in Hypnosis: An Experimental & Clinical Investigation. 2nd ed. Linn F. Cooper & Milton H. Erickson. LC 82-663. (Illus.). 206p. 1982. reprint ed. text ed. 29.50 (*0-8290-0702-4*) Irvington.

Time Diversification Revisited. William Reichenstein & Dovalee Dorsett. 82p. (Orig.). 1995. pap. text ed. 30.00 (*0-943205-30-1*) ICFARF.

Time Dog. Mark Neville. Ed. by Edward Mycue. (Took Modern Poetry in English Ser.: No. 16). (Illus.). 32p. (Orig.). 1991. pap. 4.00 (*1-879457-15-6*) Norton Coker Pr.

Time Domain in Surface & Structural Dynamics. Ed. by Gary J. Long & Fernande Grandjean. (C). 1988. lib. bdg. 247.50 (*90-277-2688-4*) Kluwer Ac.

Time Domain Optics of Ultrashort Waveforms. A. B. Shvartsburg. (Oxford Series in Optical & Imaging Sciences: Vol. 8). (Illus.). 208p. 1996. 90.00 (*0-19-856509-7*, Clarendon Pr) OUP.

Time-Domain Response of Multiconductor Transmission Lines. A. R. Djordjevic et al. (Microwave Software Library). 150p. (C). 1989. student ed. 300.00 incl. disk (*0-89006-356-7*) Artech Hse.

Time, Dose & Fractionation in the Radiation Therapy of Cancer: A Frontier Revisited. Ed. by J. M. Vaeth & J. Meyer. (Frontiers of Radiation Therapy & Oncology Ser.: Vol. 22). (Illus.). x, 194p. 1988. 143.25 (*3-8055-4654-8*) S Karger.

Time Dust, James Rosenquist: Complete Graphics, 1962-1992. Constance W. Glenn. LC 92-40160. (Illus.). 192p. 1993. 50.00 (*0-8478-1709-1*) Rizzoli Intl.

Time-Effective Psychotherapy: Maximizing Outcomes in an Era of Minimized Resources. Steven Friedman. 224p. 1996. 41.95 (*0-205-26119-1*) Allyn.

Time Effects in Concrete Structures. R. I. Gilbert. (Developments in Civil Engineering Ser.: No. 23). 321p. 1988. 167.50 (*0-444-70473-6*) Elsevier.

***Time Effects in Rock Mechanics.** N. Cristescu & U. Hunsche. text ed. 115.00 (*0-471-95517-5*) Wiley.

Time Element Referred to in the Gospel of John. (Walk with Jesus Ser.). 12p. 1993. pap. 5.00 (*1-57277-627-7*) Script Rsch.

Time, Energy & Stone Tools. Ed. by Robin Torrence. (New Directions in Archaeology Ser.). (Illus.). 130p. (C). 1989. text ed. 74.95 (*0-521-25350-0*) Cambridge U Pr.

Time, Energy & the Psychology of Healing. Helen Graham. 300p. 1990. 34.00 (*1-85302-066-4*) Taylor & Francis.

Time Enough. Emily Kimbrough. (Illus.). 220p. 1984. pap. 15.00 (*0-910258-19-8*) Book & Tackle.

***Time Enough? States Respond to Term Limits.** Intro. by Daniel M. Fox & William Pound. 32p. (Orig.). 1997. pap. write for info. (*1-887748-12-1*) Milbank Memorial.

Time Enough for Drums. Ann Rinaldi. 249p. (J). 1989. pap. 3.95 (*0-8167-1269-7*) Troll Communs.

***Time Enough for Love.** Suzanne Brockmann. (Loveswept Ser.: Vol. 858). 1997. mass mkt. 3.50 (*0-553-44597-9*, Loveswept) Bantam.

Time Enough for Love. Robert A. Heinlein. 1987. mass mkt. 6.99 (*0-441-81076-4*) Ace Bks.

Time Enough for the World, Vol. 1. Ed. by Rich Ives. 127p. (Orig.). 1986. pap. 7.00 (*0-937669-24-5*) Owl Creek Pr.

Time Enough for the World, Vol. 2. Ed. by Rich Ives. 191p. (Orig.). 1987. pap. text ed. 7.00 (*0-937669-28-8*) Owl Creek Pr.

Time, Existence & Destiny. Howard A. Slaatte. (Contemporary Existentialism Ser.: Vol. 1). 201p. (C). 1989. text ed. 38.50 (*0-8204-0655-4*) P Lang Pubng.

Time, Expectations & Uncertainty in Economics: Selected Essays of G. L. S. Shackle. G. L. Shackle. Ed. by J. L. Ford. 288p. 1990. text ed. 80.00 (*1-85278-362-1*) E Elgar.

Time Expired. Susan Dunlap. (Jimmy Flannery Mystery Ser.). 304p. 1994. mass mkt. 4.99 (*0-440-21683-4*) Dell.

Time Exposure. William H. Jackson. (Illus.). 359p. 1994. pap. 16.95 (*1-880397-08-0*) Patrice Pr.

Time Exposure: A Photographic Record of the Dinosaur Age. Jane Burton & Dougal Dixon. (Illus.). 96p. 1984. 14.95 (*0-8253-0217-X*) Beaufort Bks NY.

Time Falling Bodies Take to Light. William I. Thompson. (Illus.). 280p. 1982. pap. 10.95 (*0-312-80512-8*) St Martin.

Time Falling Bodies Take to Light: Mythology, Sexuality, & the Origins of Culture. William I. Thompson. LC 96-549. 280p. 1996. pap. 13.95 (*0-312-16062-3*, Griffin) St Martin.

Time, Family & Community: Perspectives on Family & Community History. Michael Drake. (Illus.). 352p. (C). 1994. pap. 25.95 (*0-631-19237-9*); text ed. 67.95 (*0-631-19236-0*) Blackwell Pubs.

***Time Famine.** Lance Olsen. 328p. (Orig.). 1996. pap. 12.95 (*1-882633-15-6*) Permeable.

***Time Far Past.** Le Luu. Ed. by Ngo V. Hai et al. Tr. by Nguyen B. Chung et al. from VIE. LC 96-47787. 296p. 1997. 24.95 (*1-55849-085-X*) U of Mass Pr.

Time Flies. Bill Cosby. 192p. 1988. mass mkt. 5.99 (*0-553-27724-3*) Bantam.

Time Flies. Eric Rohmann. LC 93-28200. (Illus.). 32p. (J). (ps-4). 1994. 17.00 (*0-517-59598-2*); lib. bdg. 17.99 (*0-517-59599-0*) Crown Bks Yng Read.

***Time Flies.** Eric Rohmann. (J). 1997. write for info. (*0-614-29248-4*) Knopf Bks Yng Read.

Time Flies - Stuart Netsky. Judith Tannenbaum. (Illus.). 32p. 1993. pap. 15.00 (*0-88454-072-3*) U of Pa Contemp Art.

Time Flies When You're Alive: A Love Story. Paul Linke. LC 92-37589. 1993. 16.95 (*1-55972-183-9*, Birch Ln Pr) Carol Pub Group.

Time Flowers. L. Sanina. 126p. 1984. pap. 7.00 (*0-935090-11-8*) Almanac Pr.

Time for a Better Marriage. Don Dinkmeyer, Sr. & Jon Carlson. 1985. pap. 14.95 (*0-394-73394-0*) Random.

Time for a Change. Richard Bandler. LC 93-84505. 1993. 19.95 (*0-916990-28-1*) META Pubns.

Time for a Change. Marcia Cebulska. (Literacy Volunteers of America Readers Ser.). 32p. (Orig.). 1988. pap. text ed. 3.00 (*0-8428-9606-6*) Cambridge Bk.

Time for a Change? A Field's Eye View on Donor Agency Support for Nutrition. Julia Tagwireyi. LC 95-5689. (Martin J. Forman Memorial Lectures: Vol. 7). 1995. 7.50 (*0-915173-32-8*) Helen Keller Intl.

Time for a Change: The Re-Entry & Re-Career Workbook. Kent B. Banning & Ardelle F. Friday. LC 95-2573. 192p. 1995. pap. 9.95 (*0-8442-4396-5*, VGM Career Bks) NTC Pub Grp.

***Time for a Checkup.** Alice L. Cullinan. 30p. (Orig.). 1995. teacher ed., wbk. ed. 2.95 (*0-87508-717-5*, 717) Chr Lit.

Time for a Checkup. Alice R. Cullinan. 128p. (Orig.). 1994. pap. 5.95 (*0-87508-739-6*) Chr Lit.

***Time for a Checkup.** Alice R. Cullinan. (Illus.). 15p. (Orig.). 1995. student ed., wbk. ed., pap. 2.95 (*0-87508-718-3*, 718) Chr Lit.

Time for a Second Opinion, 1986. Kenna Farris. write for info. (*0-318-60953-3*) Port Love Intl.

Time for Action. Robert Close. (Brassey Bks.). 170p. 1984. text ed. 33.00 (*0-08-028344-6*, Pergamon Pr); pap. text ed. 19.25 (*0-08-028345-4*, Pergamon Pr) Elsevier.

Time for Action: Report of the West Indian Commission. Ed. by West Indian Commission Staff. 592p. 1994. reprint ed. 30.00 (*0-9643624-0-6*) Intl Develop Options.

Time for America: Hamilton Watch, 1892-1992. Don Sauers. LC 92-12460. (Illus.). 320p. 1992. 39.95 (*0-915010-36-4*) Sutter House.

Time for Andrew: A Ghost Story. Mary D. Hahn. LC 93-2877. (J). 1994. 15.00 (*0-395-66556-6*, Clarion Bks) HM.

Time for Andrew: A Ghost Story. Mary D. Hahn. 176p. (J). (gr. 5). 1995. pap. 4.50 (*0-380-72469-3*, Camelot) Avon.

Time for Another Dream. large type ed. Van der Zee. 1995. 25.99 (*0-7505-0778-0*, Pub. by Magna Print Bks UK) Ulverscroft.

Time for Assessment: Evaluation Tips with Six New Learning Centers. Dana McMillan. Ed. by Judy Mitchell. (Illus.). 144p. (Orig.). 1996. teacher ed., pap. 13.95 (*1-57310-046-3*) Teachng & Lrning Co.

Time for Babies. Ron Hirschi. LC 92-21409. (How Animals Live Bk.). (Illus.). 32p. (J). (ps-3). 1993. pap. 13.99 (*0-525-65095-4*, Cobblehill Bks) Dutton Child Bks.

***Time for Bed.** Fox. 1997. pap. write for info. (*0-15-201066-1*) HarBrace.

Time for Bed. Mem Fox. LC 92-19771. (Illus.). 32p. (J). (ps-1). 1993. 15.00 (*0-15-288183-2*, Gulliver Bks) HarBrace.

***Time for Bed.** Illus. by Gill Guile. (Toddlers' First Words Ser.). 12p. (J). (ps). 1997. bds. 2.98 (*1-85854-522-6*) Brimax Bks.

Time for Bed. Ruth Huddleston & Wendy Madgwick. (Illus.). 18p. (J). (ps). 1995. 12.99 (*1-881445-41-0*) Sandvik Pub.

Time for Bed. Ruth Huddleston & Wendy Madgwick. LC 95-40553. (Illus.). 24p. (J). 1996. 12.95 (*0-7613-0476-2*, Copper Beech Bks) Millbrook Pr.

Time for Bed? Leslie McGuire. LC 93-85491. (Action Pop-Up Bks.). (Illus.). (J). (ps). 1994. 11.95 (*0-89577-572-7*) Rdrs Dgst Yng Fam.

Time For Bed: Big Book. Mem Fox. (J). 1997. pap. 22.00 (*0-15-201014-9*) HarBrace.

***Time for Bed: Signed Copy.** Fox. 1993. 15.00 (*0-15-201758-5*) HarBrace.

Time for Bed, the Babysitter Said. Peggy P. Anderson. LC 86-27388. (J). (ps). 1987. 14.95 (*0-395-41851-8*) HM.

Time for Bed, the Babysitter Said. Peggy P. Anderson. (Illus.). 32p. (J). (ps-k). 1995. pap. 4.95 (*0-395-74511-X*, Sandpiper) HM.

Time for Being: Images of Beginning & Ending. Ed. by Billy L. Skinner. (Illus.). 112p. 1996. pap. write for info. (*0-9652411-0-6*) B L Skinner.

Time for Building: The Third Migration. Gerald Sorin. (Jewish People in America Ser.). (Illus.). 336p. 1992. 35.00 (*0-8018-4345-6*) Johns Hopkins.

Time for Change: A New Approach to Environment & Development. Ed. by Hal Kane & Linda Starke. LC 91-41029. 141p. (Orig.). 1992. 20.00 (*1-55963-156-2*); pap. 11.95 (*1-55963-155-4*) Island Pr.

Time for Christmas. A. J. Wood. 24p. (J). 1996. 12.95 (*0-7613-0521-1*, Copper Beech Bks) Millbrook Pr.

Time for Consideration: A Scholarly Appraisal of the Unification Church. 2nd ed. M. Darrol Bryant & Herbert W. Richardson. LC 78-61364. (Symposium Ser.: Vol. 3). xi, 332p. 1978. lib. bdg. 99.95 (*0-88946-954-7*) E Mellen.

Time for Dancing. Davida L. Hurwin. LC 95-7169. 257p. (YA). (gr. 7 up). 1995. 15.95 (*0-316-38351-1*) Little.

***Time for Dancing.** Davida L. Hurwin. LC 97-15201. (J). 1997. pap. 4.99 (*0-14-038618-1*) Viking Penguin.

Time for Death of a King. Ann Dukthas. 1995. mass mkt. 4.99 (*0-312-95613-4*) St Martin.

Time for Dialogue & Healing: A Pastoral Reflection on United States - Vietnam Relations. United States Catholic Conference Staff. 60p. (Orig.). 1989. pap. 3.25 (*1-55586-287-X*) US Catholic.

Time for Dignity: Police (Response to) & Domestic Abuse of the Elderly. Martha R. Plotkin. LC 88-62067. 112p. (Orig.). (C). 1988. pap. 11.50 (*1-878734-05-9*) Police Exec Res.

Time for Drama. Roma Burgess & Pamela Gaudry. LC 86-12672. (English, Language & Education Ser.). 288p. 1986. pap. 27.00 (*0-335-15249-X*, Open Univ Pr) Taylor & Francis.

Time for Dying. Barney G. Glaser & Anselm L. Strauss. LC 67-17601. 285p. 1968. lib. bdg. 34.95 (*0-202-30027-7*) Aldine de Gruyter.

Time for Every Purpose: Life Stories of Foster Grandparents. Edith S. Stein. (Illus.). 300p. (Orig.). 1994. pap. 20.00 (*1-879198-11-8*) Knwldg Ideas & Trnds.

Time for Faith: Adventures in Triumph over Trial. Ernest H. Thomas. (Illus.). 229p. (Orig.). 1990. pap. 7.95 (*0-9626754-0-7*) PMP Pub Co.

Time for Flowers. Dale L. Rohman. LC 82-14362. (Illus.). 140p. 1983. 50.00 (*0-935284-26-5*) Patrice Pr.

Time For Friends: Level 8. Evertts. 1986. 29.75 (*0-03-002342-4*) HB Schl Dept.

Time for Friends: Level 8. E. Evertts. (J). 1983. wbk. ed., pap. 14.75 (*0-03-061432-5*) HB Schl Dept.

***Time for Friends Level 8.** Evertts. 1986. wbk. ed., pap. text ed. 13.00 (*0-03-002344-0*) HR&W Schl Div.

***Time for Fun.** (Illus.). 24p. (J). (gr. k-2). 1995. pap. write for info. (*1-56144-366-2*, Honey Bear Bks) Modern Pub NYC.

Time for Gathering: The Second Migration, 1820-1880. Hasia R. Diner. (Jewish People in America Ser.). (Illus.). 344p. 1992. 35.00 (*0-8018-4344-8*) Johns Hopkins.

***Time for Giving.** Evelyn Wright. 76p. 1994. pap. 9.50 (*1-56770-308-9*) S Scheewe Pubns.

Time for Glory...& Hate: The American Civil Rights Movement. Nelson G. Alston. Ed. by Murial Hayden. (Illus.). 96p. (Orig.). 1993. pap. 8.95 (*0-9632202-0-9*) Alpha Bk Pr.

Time for Hanging. large type ed. Bill Crider. LC 90-34619. 339p. 1990. lib. bdg. 14.95 (*1-56054-002-8*) Thorndike Pr.

Time for Healing, Vol. 1. Anne Skaggs. Ed. by Kay Turner. 62p. 1992. 7.95 (*0-9635322-0-0*) A Skaggs.

Time for Healing: Adult Resource for 1991 Reunions. Shirley VanRiette. 120p. 1991. pap. 2.00 (*0-8309-0586-3*) Herald Hse.

Time for Healing: American Jewry since World War II. Edward S. Shapiro. (Jewish People in America Ser.). (Illus.). 344p. 1992. 35.00 (*0-8018-4347-2*) Johns Hopkins.

Time for Healing: Overcoming the Perils of Ministry. Jody Seymour. 128p. 1995. pap. 12.00 (*0-8170-1235-4*) Judson.

Time for Healing: The Journey to Wholeness. Eddie Shaprio & Debbie Shapiro. 228p. (Orig.). 1996. pap. text ed. 12.95 (*0-7499-1346-0*, Pub. by Piatkus Bks UK) London Brdge.

Time for Horatio. Penelope C. Paine. Ed. by Sandy Stryker. LC 89-18304. (Illus.). 48p. (J). (ps up). 1990. 14.95 (*0-911655-33-6*) Advocacy Pr.

Time for Joy: Daily Affirmations. Ruth Fishel. (Illus.). 375p. 1988. pap. 6.95 (*0-932194-82-6*) Health Comm.

Time for Joy (Christmas), Vol. 3. Shirley A. Barone. (Illus.). 44p. (Orig.). (J). (ps-2). 1989. pap. write for info. (*0-318-66613-8*) Toad Hse Bks.

Time for Joy Daily Journal: A Pocket-Book of Affirmations. Ruth Fishel. 380p. (Orig.). 1990. pap. 8.95 (*1-55874-063-5*) Health Comm.

Time for Learning Colors. Matthew V. Smith. (Illus.). 12p. (J). (gr. k-3). 1993. pap. 10.95 (*1-895583-55-1*) MAYA Pubs.

***Time for Life: The Surprising Ways Americans Use Their Time.** John P. Robinson & Geoffrey Godbey. LC 96-52500. 1997. 24.95 (*0-271-01652-3*) Pa St U Pr.

***Time for Love.** Wendy P. AcRish. 202p. (Orig.). 1997. mass mkt. 4.99 (*1-55237-035-6*, Pub. by Comnwlth Pub CN) Partners Pubs Grp.

Time for Love. Amanda Browning. (Presents Ser.). 1993. mass mkt. 2.99 (*0-373-11566-0*, 1-11566-6) Harlequin Bks.

Time for Love, Vol. 18. Hilda Stahl. (Elizabeth Gail Ser.: Vol. 18). 128p. (J). 1989. pap. 5.99 (*0-8423-0813-X*) Tyndale.

Time for Love: Assisted Living Viewed by One of the Very Old. Janet C. Chandler. LC 95-43611. (Illus.). 120p. (Orig.). 1996. pap. 10.00 (*0-918949-91-2*) Papier-Mache Press.

Time for Loving. large type ed. Kathleen Treves. (Linford Romance Library). 352p. 1984. pap. 15.99 (*0-7089-6015-4*) Ulverscroft.

Time for Me. Pat Farrell. (Everyday Ser.). (Illus.). 26p. (Orig.). 1983. pap. 3.00 (*0-915517-01-9*) Everyday Ser.

Time for Meaning: Crafting Literate Lives in Middle & High School. Randy Bomer. LC 95-12089. 234p. 1995. pap. text ed. 22.50 (*0-435-08849-1*, 08849) Heinemann.

Time for Memories. Denise Hemingway. 64p. 1994. pap. 8.95 (*0-8059-3365-4*) Dorrance.

Time for My Soul: A Treasury of Jewish Stories for Our Holy Days. Annette Labovitz & Eugene Labovitz. LC 86-32243. 448p. 1987. 30.00 (*0-87668-954-3*) Aronson.

Time for My Soul: A Treasury of Jewish Stories for Our Holy Days. Annette Labovitz & Eugene Labovitz. LC 86-32243. 448p. 1996. pap. 30.00 (*1-56821-924-5*) Aronson.

Time for Peace: Biblical Meditations for Advent. William F. Maestri. LC 83-22399. 94p. 1983. pap. 4.95 (*0-8189-0463-1*) Alba.

Time for Peace: Daily Meditations for Twelve-Step Living. Mary Y. Nilsen. Ed. by R. Cheryl Friedman. LC 90-90177. (Illus.). 416p. (Orig.). 1990. pap. 8.95 (*0-9627147-0-4*) Zion Pub.

Time for Peace: The Ecclesiastes of Erasmus. Judith T. Wozniak. (European History Ser.: No. 1). (Orig.). 1996. pap. text ed. 49.95 (*1-889431-00-1*) Univ Pr South.

Time for Peace Between Muslims & the West. Judith Shadzi. Ed. by Diane Parker. LC 93-37239. 252p. (Orig.). 1994. pap. 14.95 (*1-56875-068-4*) R & E Pubs.

Time for Planting: The First Migration, 1654-1820. Eli Faber. (Jewish People in America Ser.). (Illus.). 224p. 1992. 35.00 (*0-8018-4343-X*) Johns Hopkins.

Time for Playing. Ron Hirschi. LC 93-36773. (Illus.). (J). (ps-3). 1994. pap. 13.99 (*0-525-65159-4*, Cobblehill Bks) Dutton Child Bks.

Time for Prayer: Daily Prayer Journal. Edd Anthony. (Illus.). 212p. 1993. student ed. 10.95 (*1-881586-05-7*) Canticle Cass.

T

Time for Reflection. Paul J. Burt. LC 93-49349. (Poetry Ser.: Vol. 21). 64p. 1995. pap. 12.95 (0-7734-2724-4, Mellen Poetry Pr) E Mellen.

Time for Reflection. Ed. by Lois L. Kaufman. (Petites Ser.). (Illus.). 80p. 1991. 4.95 (0-88088-744-3) Peter Pauper.

Time for Reflection. abr. ed. Helen Steiner Rice. (Thumbprint Bks.). (Illus.). 92p. (gr. 10). 1995. 4.99 (0-8007-7144-3) Revell.

Time for Remembrance: Poems. Dorothy H. Moffatt. LC 94-15047. 1994. pap. 8.95 (0-87233-115-6) Bauhan.

Time for Retirement: Comparative Studies of the Decreasing Age of Exit from the Labour Force. Ed. by Martin Kohli et al. (Illus.). 400p. (C). 1991. text ed. 69.95 (0-521-40053-8); pap. text ed. 34.95 (0-521-42364-3) Cambridge U Pr.

Time for Rhyme: Stories, Poems, Games, Art Projects, Fun Sheets. Illus. by Rochelle Valdivia. (Topics for Preschool Ser.). 64p. (J). (ps). 1988. pap. text ed. 8.95 (0-943129-02-8) Chatterbox Pr.

Time for Roses. Elaine Coffman. 472p. (Orig.). 1995. mass mkt. 5.99 (0-449-14862-9, GM) Fawcett.

***Time for School.** Dugald Steer. LC 96-37252. (Illus.). 24p. (J). (ps-k). 1997. 12.95 (0-7613-0278-6) Millbrook Pr.

Time for School, Little Dinosaur. Gail Herman. LC 89-70331. (Pictureback Ser.). (Illus.). 24p. (Orig.). (J). (ps-2). 1990. pap. 2.25 (0-679-80789-6) Random Bks Yng Read.

Time for School, Nathan! Lulu Delacre. (Illus.). 32p. (J). (ps-2). 1991. pap. 2.50 (0-590-45688-1) Scholastic Inc.

Time for Searching: Entering the Mainstream, 1920-1945. Henry L. Feingold. (Jewish People in America Ser.). (Illus.). 368p. 1992. 35.00 (0-8018-4346-4) Johns Hopkins.

Time for Seasons & Holidays: A Creative with Words Celebration. Ed. by Brigitta Geltrich. (Thematic Anthologies Ser.). (Illus.). 76p. (Orig.). 1992. pap. text ed. 10.00 (0-936945-20-6) Creat with Wds.

Time for Singing. Thomas D. Mangelsen. LC 93-36772. (Illus.). 32p. (J). (ps-3). 1994. pap. 13.99 (0-525-65096-2, Cobblehill Bks) Dutton Child Bks.

Time for Sleeping. Ron Hirschi. LC 92-21408. (How Animals Live Bk.). (Illus.). 32p. (J). (ps-3). 1993. pap. 13.99 (0-525-65128-4, Cobblehill Bks) Dutton Child Bks.

Time for Speech: Festschrift on the Occasion of Klaus Kohler's 60th Birthday. A. Simpson. (Journal: Phonetica Ser.: Vol. 52, No. 3, 1995). (Illus.). 148p. 1995. pap. 75.00 (3-8055-6217-9) S Karger.

Time for Success: A Goal-Getter's Strategy. R. Alec Mackenzie. 192p. 1991. pap. text ed. 9.95 (0-07-044656-3) McGraw.

Time for Tea: Conversations with English Women. Michele Rivers. LC 93-42375. 1995. 22.00 (0-517-59219-3, Crown) Crown Pub Group.

***Time for Tea with Mary Engelbreit.** Mary Engelbreit. LC 96-52595. (Illus.). 112p. 1997. 16.95 (0-8362-2770-0) Andrews & McMeel.

Time for Telling Truth Is Running Out: Conversations with Zhang Shenfu. Vera Schwarcz. (Illus.). 256p. (C). 1992. text ed. 35.00 (0-300-05009-7) Yale U Pr.

Time for the Death of a King. Ann Dukthas. 1995. mass mkt. 4.99 (0-614-15605-X) St Martin.

Time for the Stars: Astronomy in the 1990's. Alan P. Lightman. 144p. 1994. mass mkt. 6.99 (0-446-67024-3) Warner Bks.

Time for Thoughtfulness: A Daily Guide to Filling the World with Love, Care & Compassion. Ruth Fishel. (Illus.). 380p. (Orig.). 1994. pap. 7.95 (1-55874-322-7, 3227) Health Comm.

Time for Training Wheels: Family Devotions for Three to Seven Year Olds. Mary-Lynn Chambers. (Illus.). 87p. (J). (ps-2). 1995. pap. 11.95 (0-921788-22-3) Kindred Prods.

***Time for Transformation: How to Awaken to Your Soul's Purpose & Claim Your Power.** Diana Cooper. 170p. (Orig.). 1996. pap. 12.95 (0-7499-1556-0, Pub. by Piatkus Bks UK) London Brdge.

Time for Treason. Doug Everett. 352p. (Orig.). 1994. pap. 4.99 (0-451-17921-8, Sig) NAL-Dutton.

***Time for Trumpets: The Untold Story of the Battle of the Bulge.** Charles B. MacDonald. (Illus.). 720p. 1997. reprint ed. pap. 17.00 (0-688-15157-4, Quill) Morrow.

Time for Trust. Penny Jordan. (Presents Ser.: No. 1339). 1991. pap. 2.50 (0-373-11339-0) Harlequin Bks.

Time for Truth. Asaraf Pahlavi. Ed. by Tomi Keitlen. LC 95-76051. (Illus.). 224p. 1995. pap. 14.95 (1-886966-00-1) In Print.

Time for Us. Richard J. Beckmen. LC 92-6666. 1993. 8.99 (0-8407-9189-5) Nelson.

Time for Us. Alex N. Holland. (Illus.). 19p. (J). (gr. k-3). 1994. pap. 11.95 (1-895583-70-5) MAYA Pubs.

***Time for Us.** Cheryl F. Smith. 400p. 1997. mass mkt. 4.99 (0-7860-0417-7, Pinncle Kensgtn) Kensgtn Pub Corp.

***Time for Us.** large type ed. Josephine Cox. (Charnwood Large Print Ser.). 496p. 1997. 29.50 (0-7089-8960-8, Charnwood) Ulverscroft.

Time for Voices: Selected Poems 1960-1990. Brendan Kennelly. LC 89-82483. 160p. 9000. 35.00 (1-85224-096-2, Pub. by Bloodaxe Bks UK); pap. 19.95 (1-85224-097-0, Pub. by Bloodaxe Bks UK) Dufour.

Time for War. Terry M. Crist, Jr. 64p. (Orig.). (C). 1989. student ed. 10.00 (0-9623768-1-7) T Crist Ministries.

***Time for War.** Gilbert Morris. (American Odyssey Ser.: Bk. 5). 304p. (YA). (gr. 10). 1997. pap. 10.99 (0-8007-5610-X) Revell.

***Time for War: The United States & Vietnam, 1941-1975.** Robert D. Schulzinger. (Illus.). 432p. 1997. 35.00 (0-19-507189-1) OUP.

Time for Yesterday. A. C. Crispin. (Star Trek Ser.: No. 39). 288p. 1989. mass mkt. 5.50 (0-671-70094-4) PB.

Time, Form & Style in Boswell's Life of Johnson. David L. Passler. LC 70-151585. (Yale Studies in English: No. 155). 180p. reprint ed. 51.30 (0-8357-9591-8, 2013384) Bks Demand.

Time, Forward! Valentin Kataev. Tr. by Charles Malamuth. (European Classics Ser.). 345p. 1995. pap. 15.95 (0-8101-1247-7) Northwestern U Pr.

Time Frames. James Rush. 304p. 1988. 16.95 (0-8065-1083-8, Citadel Pr) Carol Pub Group.

Time, Freedom, & the Common Good: An Essay in Public Philosophy. Charles M. Sherover. LC 89-4337. (SUNY Series in Systematic Philosophy). 314p. 1989. text ed. 59.50 (0-7914-0178-2); pap. text ed. 19.95 (0-7914-0179-0) State U NY Pr.

Time Frequency Analysis: Theory & Applications. Leon Cohen. 320p. 1994. text ed. 60.00 (0-13-594532-1) P-H.

***Time-Frequency & Wavelets in Biomedical Signal Processing.** Ed. by Metin Akay. LC 97-19866. 700p. 1997. 129.95 (0-7803-1147-7, PC5619) Inst Electrical.

***Time Frequency Signal Analysis.** Boashash. Date not set. pap. text ed. write for info. (0-582-71286-6, Pub. by Longman UK) Longman.

Time-Frequency Signals Analysis: Methods & Applications. Boualem Boashash. LC 91-32658. 547p. 1992. text ed. 104.00 (0-470-21821-5) Halsted Pr.

Time Game: Two Views of a Prison. Anthony J. Manocchio & Jimmy Dunn. 1970. pap. 19.95 (0-8039-0920-9) Sage.

***Time Game: Two Views of a Prison.** Anthony J. Manocchio & Jimmy Dunn. LC 77-85238. 272p. pap. 77.60 (0-608-05072-5, 2065627) Bks Demand.

Time Garden. Edward Eager. (Illus.). 208p. (J). (gr. 3-7). 1990. pap. 6.00 (0-15-288193-X, Odyssey) HarBrace.

Time Gate: Hurtling Backward Through History. Charles R. Pellegrino. LC 84-23955. 1985. pap. 16.95 (0-8306-1863-5, 1863P) McGraw-Hill Prof.

Time Gatherer: El Greco & the Sacred Theme. Patrick Pye. (Illus.). 126p. 1991. 25.00 (1-85182-084-1, Pub. by Four Cts Pr IE) Intl Spec Bk.

Time Gatherers: Writings from Prison. Gertrude Katz. LC 70-143613. 120p. reprint ed. pap. 34.20 (0-7837-7003-0, 2046817) Bks Demand.

Time Ghost. Ed. by Welwyn W. Katz. LC 94-29208. (J). (gr. 1-8). 1995. 16.00 (0-689-80027-4, Mac Bks Young Read) S&S Childrens.

Time Gives It Proofe: Paradox in the Late Music of Beethoven. Sylvia Imeson. (American University Studies XX: Vol. 29). 256p. (C). 1996. 44.95 (0-8204-3029-3) P Lang Pubng.

***Time Goes on Forever.** Katherine M. Marko. LC 96-29749. (First Bk.). (J). 1997. write for info. (0-531-20316-6) Watts.

Time, Goods, & Well-Being. Ed. by F. Thomas Juster & Frank P. Stafford. LC 85-10818. (Illus.). 560p. 1985. 48.00 (0-87944-293-X) Inst Soc Res.

Time Happens: You Could Not Have Picked a Better Time to Be Fiftysomething. H. Samm Coombs. LC 94-34061. 248p. (Orig.). 1995. pap. 13.95 (1-879904-13-6) Halo Bks.

Time-Harmonic Electromagnetic Fields. Roger F. Harrington. (Electronic & Electrical Engineering Ser.). 1961. text ed. write for info. (0-07-026745-6) McGraw.

Time-Harmonic Electromagnetic Fields in Chiral Media. Akhlesh Lakhtakia et al. (Lecture Notes in Physics Ser.: Vol. 335). vii, 121p. 1989. 34.95 (0-387-51317-5) Spr-Verlag.

Time Has Come. Xavier C. Dicks. LC 95-90487. (Illus.). 260p. 1995. 19.95 (0-9647003-0-1) Farry Bell.

Time Has Come: An Autobiography of a Texas Woman. Gene C. Hackerman. LC 94-38292. 1994. 21.95 (0-89015-954-8, Eakin Pr) Sunbelt Media.

Time Heals. Susan Collier. 400p. (Orig.). 1995. mass mkt., pap. text ed. 5.99 (0-505-52030-3, Love Spell) Dorchester Pub Co.

Time Heals No Wounds. Jack Lenninger. (Orig.). 1993. mass mkt. 5.99 (0-8041-0916-8) Ivy Books.

Time, Health & Medicine. Ronald Frankenberg. 176p. (C). 1992. text ed. 49.95 (0-8039-8678-5) Sage.

Time Holds the Mirror: A Study of Knowledge in Euripides' Hippolytus. C. A. Luschnig. (Mnemosyne Ser.: Supplement 102). 1988. pap. 34.50 (90-04-08601-3) E J Brill.

Time-Honored Friends: The Best Is Yet to Come. John P. Beilenson. (Keepsakes with Ribbons Ser.). (Illus.). 56p. 1995. 7.99 (0-88088-888-1) Peter Pauper.

Time Honored Norwegian Recipes. Erna O. Xan. 128p. 1988. pap. 12.95 (0-941016-76-5) Penfield.

Time Horizons of Pension Fund Managers. Employee Benefit Research Institute Staff. LC 92-70834. 36p. 1993. pap. 18.00 (0-910586-87-X, 092-93) Finan Exec.

Time, Illusion, Light & the Ever-Flowing: The World of the Riverman. Rachel C. Edwards. LC 92-97530. (Illus.). 1993. 35.00 (1-883033-00-4) Flats Pub.

Time Immemorial: Archaic History & Its Sources in Christian Chronography from Julius Africanus to George Syncellus. William Adler. LC 88-13942. (Dumbarton Oaks Studies: Vol. 26). 200p. 1989. 19.50 (0-88402-176-9) Dumbarton Oaks.

***Time In: Loving Connections That Build Responsible Behavior.** Jean I. Clarke. 1997. 18.95 (1-884734-29-4); pap. text ed. 11.95 (1-884734-28-6) Parenting Pr.

Time in a Quantized Universe, Vol. 2. Henry Mehlberg. Tr. by Paul Benecerraf. (Boston Studies in the Philosophy of Science). 296p. 1980. pap. text ed. 52.00 (90-277-1076-7, D Reidel) Kluwer Ac.

Time in a Quantized Universe, Vol. 2. Henry Mehlberg. Tr. by Paul Benecerraf. (Boston Studies in the Philosophy of Science). 296p. 1980. lib. bdg. 88.00 (90-277-1075-9, D Reidel) Kluwer Ac.

Time in a Teardrop. Sam. (Illus.). 76p. 1993. pap. 12.95 (1-880163-05-5) Firefly Pub.

Time in a Vacuum: A Collection of Short Stories. Susan Darby. LC 93-93767. 104p. (Orig.). 1994. pap. 8.00 (1-56002-303-1, Univ Edtns) Aegina Pr.

Time in Contemporary Musical Thought. Jonathan D. Kramer. 249p. 1993. pap. text ed. 47.00 (3-7186-5364-8, Harwood Acad Pubs) Gordon & Breach.

Time in Dynamic Geometry. Paul H. Fejer. Ed. by Bernadette Meier. (Illus.). 70p. (C). 1984. text ed. 65.00 (0-9607422-2-0, TX-1-315-232) P H Fejer.

Time in Economics. George L. Shackle. LC 83-1758. (Professor Dr. F. De Vries Lectures). 111p. (C). 1983. reprint ed. text ed. 55.00 (0-313-23969-X, SHTI, Greenwood Pr) Greenwood.

Time in Ezra Pound's Work. William Harmon. LC 77-5958. 179p. reprint ed. pap. 51.10 (0-8357-4411-6, 2037231) Bks Demand.

Time in Geographic Information Systems. Gail Langran. (Technical Issues in GIS Ser.). 180p. 1992. 90.00 (0-7484-0003-6, Pub. by Tay Francis Ltd UK); pap. 39.95 (0-7484-0059-1, Pub. by Tay Francis Ltd UK) Taylor & Francis.

Time in God's World. Beverly Beckmann. (In God's World Ser.). (Illus.). 24p. (J). (gr. 2-5). 1985. 6.99 (0-570-04128-7, 56-1539) Concordia.

Time in Gold, Wristwatches. Gerald Viola & Gisbert Brunner. LC 88-61466. (Illus.). 256p. 1988. 79.95 (0-88740-137-6) Schiffer.

Time in History: Views of Time from Prehistory to the Present Day. G. J. Whitrow. (Illus.). 240p. 1989. pap. 12.95 (0-19-285211-6) OUP.

Time in Indian Philosophy: A Collection of Essays. Ed. by Hari S. Prasad. (C). 1992. 58.00 (81-7030-267-6) S Asia.

Time in India's Development Programmes. Robert C. Repetto. LC 71-143230. (Economic Studies: No. 137). (Illus.). 249p. 1971. 16.50 (0-674-89180-5) HUP.

Time in Language. Wolfgang Klein. LC 93-37452. (Germanic Linguistics Ser.). 264p. (C). (gr. 13). 1994. text ed. 69.95 (0-415-10412-2, B3740) Routledge.

Time in Language: Temporal Adverbial Constructions in Czech, Russian & English. Henry Kucera & Karla Trnka. LC 75-16785. (Michigan Slavic Materials Ser.: Bno. 12). 1975. pap. 10.00 (0-930042-05-0) Mich Slavic Pubns.

Time in Many Places. Nels Olson. 218p. 1980. 9.00 (0-87839-036-7) North Star.

Time in Mind. Kathlyn S. Starbuck. 320p. 1996. mass mkt. 5.50 (0-06-105444-5, HarperPrism) HarpC.

Time in New England. limited ed. Ed. by Nancy Newhall & Paul Metcalf. (Illus.). 256p. 1980. 350.00 (0-89381-061-4) Aperture.

Time in Overdrive. Mark Schultz. Ed. by Dave Schreiner. (Cadillacs & Dinosaurs Ser.: Vol. 3). (Illus.). 128p. (J). (gr. 3 up). 1994. 19.95 (0-87816-266-6) Kitchen Sink.

Time in Overdrive. limited ed. Mark Schultz. LC 93-23952. 1993. 29.95 (0-87816-213-5) Kitchen Sink.

Time in Rome. Elizabeth Bowen. 1992. 19.00 (0-8446-6537-1) Peter Smith.

Time in the Air. Thomas Reiter. Ed. by Ron Ellis. 36p. (Orig.). 1990. pap. write for info. (0-9624746-1-4) Woodhenge.

Time in the Air. Rachel Wyatt. 171p. 1985. pap. 9.95 (0-88784-146-5, Pub. by Hse of Anansi Pr CN) Genl Dist Srvs.

Time in the Black Experience. Ed. by Joseph K. Adjaye. LC 93-35843. (Contributions in Afro-American & African Studies: No. 167). 248p. 1994. text ed. 59.95 (0-313-29118-7, Greenwood Pr) Greenwood.

***Time in the Life of Israel Szapiro: # 129564.** 2nd ed. Ed. by Howard Shaff & Audrey K. Shaff. 155p. (Orig.). 1988. pap. 8.95 (0-932195-07-5) Permelia Pub.

Time in the Performance of Contracts. 2nd ed. K. E. Lindgren. 1982. Australia. 62.00 (0-409-30390-9, A.T.) MICHIE.

Time in the Play of "Hamlet" Edward P. Vining. Bd. with Communication. James O. Halliwell-Phillipps. LC 70-169825.; Once Used Words in Shakespeare. James D. Butler. LC 70-169825. LC 70-169825. (Shakespeare Society of New York. Publications: Nos. 5 & 6). reprint ed. 29.50 (0-404-54205-0) AMS Pr.

Time in the Southwest Postcards. Judith Vejvoda. 48p. 1995. pap. 9.95 (0-89815-741-2) Ten Speed Pr.

Time in, Time Out, Time Enough: A Time Management Guide for Women. 2nd ed. Pat R. Materka. (Illus.). 222p. 1993. pap. 11.95 (0-9635113-0-0) Leap Frog.

***Time in Transit.** David Sanders. 50p. 1995. 14.95 (0-937692-12-3) Litrary Hse Pr.

Time, Inflation & Growth: Some Macroeconomic Themes in an Indian Perspective. Prabhat Patnaik. (R C Dutt Lectures). 56p. (C). 1988. pap. 4.95 (0-86131-878-1, Pub. by Orient Longman Ltd II) Apt Bks.

Time, Internal Clocks & Movement, Vol. 115. Ed. by Maria A. Pastor & Julio Artieda. LC 96-18161. (Advances in Psychology Ser.: Vol. 115). 324p. 1996. text ed. 142.00 (0-444-82114-7, North Holland) Elsevier.

Time Investment Register. Josef G. Lowder. (What in the World Are You Doing with Your Life Ser.: No. 2). 32p. 1986. pap. 1.50 (0-935597-02-6, 8507-02); disk 29.95 (0-935597-03-4) Comm Architects.

Time Is a Lover. Barbara Allen. 288p. 1988. pap. 3.95 (0-317-67262-2) Bantam.

***Time Is a River.** Anthony J. Daniels. (Illus.). 176p. (Orig.). 1996. pap. 12.95 (1-56167-333-1) Am Literary Pr.

Time Is All We Have. Barnaby Conrad. 1992. 9.95 (0-918684-37-4) Cameron & Co.

Time Is an Illusion. Chris Griscom. 224p. 1988. pap. 10.00 (0-671-66334-8) S&S Trade.

Time Is at Hand: The Rosicrucian Nature of Goethe's Fairy Tale of the Green Snake & the Beautiful Lily & the Mystery Dramas of Rudolf Steiner. Marshall Allen et al. LC 95-46451. (Illus.). 192p. (Orig.). 1996. pap. 24.95 (0-88010-400-7) Anthroposophic.

Time Is Day. Cal Roy. (Illus.). (J). (gr. k-3). 1968. 9.95 (0-8392-3065-6) Astor-Honor.

Time Is Fulfilled. F. F. Bruce. 1979. pap. 9.00 (0-8028-1756-4) Eerdmans.

Time Is Life. Avi Shulman. (Dynamics of Personal Achievement Ser.). 96p. (Orig.). 1985. pap. 4.95 (0-87306-927-7) Feldheim.

***Time is Money.** Ambrose Clancy. Date not set. write for info. (0-688-04467-0) Morrow.

Time Is Money: A Million-Dollar Investment Plan for Today's Twenty & Thirty-Somethings. Frances Leonard. LC 95-17911. 1996. pap. 12.00 (0-201-40962-3) Addison-Wesley.

Time Is Money: Save It. Lothar J. Seiwert. Tr. by Edward J. Zajac. 250p. 1989. text ed. 30.00 (1-55623-185-7) Irwin Prof Pubng.

***Time Is Money: Save It.** Lothar J. Seiwert. (Business & Management Ser.). 1991. pap. 15.95 (0-7494-0460-4) Kogan Page Ltd.

Time Is Not Linear: A Collection of Poetry & Prose. Cindi St. Germain. 40p. (Orig.). 1995. pap. text ed. 6.00 (1-56439-046-2) Ridgeway.

***Time Is Not Yet Ripe.** Ed. by Ying Bian. 382p. 1991. 9.95 (7-119-00742-4, Pub. by Foreign Lang CH) China Bks.

***Time Is Now.** 1995. pap. 1.20 (0-8341-9356-6) Lillenas.

Time Is Now. Miguel Algarin. LC 83-72575. 80p. (Orig.). (ENG & SPA.). (C). 1985. pap. 7.00 (0-934770-33-6) Arte Publico.

Time Is Now for a Better Life & a Better World. Hua-Ching Ni. LC 92-50854. 136p. (Orig.). 1993. pap. 10.95 (0-937064-63-7) SevenStar Comm.

***Time Is of the Essence: Learning in Schools.** Sarah H. Huyvaert. LC 97-24730. 1997. 34.95 (0-205-17150-8) Allyn.

Time Is Running Short. Sid Roth. 238p. (Orig.). 1991. pap. 9.99 (1-56043-030-3) Destiny Image.

Time Is the Longest Distance. Ed. by Ruth Gordon. LC 90-4947. (Charlotte Zolotow Bk.). 96p. (YA). (gr. 7 up). 1991. 13.95 (0-06-022297-2) HarpC Child Bks.

Time It Never Rained. Elmer Kelton. 432p. 1994. 4.99 (0-553-56320-3) Bantam.

Time It Never Rained. Elmer Kelton. LC 84-157. (Chisholm Trail Ser.: No. 2). 378p. (C). 1984. reprint ed. 16.95 (0-912646-91-8); reprint ed. pap. 9.95 (0-912646-89-6) Tex Christian.

Time Kept Promises. Constance O'Day-Flannery. 1988. mass mkt. 4.95 (0-8217-3554-3, Zebra Kensgtn) Kensgtn Pub Corp.

***Time Killers.** Albertus Bille. LC 96-60702. 260p. (Orig.). 1996. pap. 10.00 (0-938711-38-5) Tecolote Pubns.

Time, Labor, & Social Domination: A Reinterpretation of Marx's Critical Theory. Moishe Postone. 500p. (C). 1993. text ed. 59.95 (0-521-39157-1) Cambridge U Pr.

Time, Labor & Social Domination: A Reinterpretation of Marx's Critical Theory. Moishe Postone. 438p. 1996. pap. text ed. 19.95 (0-521-56540-5) Cambridge U Pr.

Time Lags in Biological Models. N. MacDonald. (Lecture Notes in Biomathematics Ser.: Vol. 27). (Illus.). 1978. pap. 23.00 (0-387-09092-4) Spr-Verlag.

Time Lapse: An Anna Peters Mystery. Janice Law. 199p. 1992. 19.95 (0-8027-3221-6) Walker & Co.

Time-Life Book of Annuals. James U. Crocket et al. LC 85-27287. 176p. 1986. pap. 12.95 (0-03-008524-1, Owl) H Holt & Co.

Time-Life Book of Foliage House Plants. Time-Life Books Editors & James U. Crockett. (Illus.). 160p. 1986. pap. 12.95 (0-8050-0123-9) H Holt & Co.

Time-Life Book of Perennials. James U. Crocket et al. LC 85-27327. 160p. 1986. pap. 12.95 (0-03-008523-3, Owl) H Holt & Co.

Time-Life Book of Shade Gardens. James U. Crocket et al. LC 85-27289. (Illus.). 160p. 1986. pap. 12.95 (0-03-008519-5, Owl) H Holt & Co.

Time Life Books: Estate Planning. Mare Robinson. 1996. 4.95 (0-7835-4791-9) Time-Life.

Time-Life Books: The Old West. Time-Life Books Editors. (Illus.). 432p. 1990. 39.95 (0-685-54071-5) P-H.

Time-Life Books Complete Home Improvement & Renovation Manual. Time-Life Books Editors. 480p. 1991. 27.95 (0-13-921883-1) P-H.

Time Life Complete Home Repair Manual. Time-Life Books Editors. (Illus.). 480p. 1987. 25.00 (0-671-76542-6) S&S Trade.

Time-Life Edition of Discipline of Market Leaders. Treacy. 1996. pap. write for info. (0-201-55419-4) Addison-Wesley.

Time Life Fix It Yourself Manual. Time-Life Books Editors. 448p. 1989. 25.00 (0-671-76541-8) S&S Trade.

Time Life Gardening & Landscaping: Gaardener's Guide. Time life Gardener's Guide Editors. (Illus.). 584p. 1991. 30.00 (0-671-76842-5) S&S Trade.

***Time-Life How-To Garden Designs: Simple Steps to Beautiful Flower Gardens.** Time-Life Books Editors. LC 96-34319. (Illus.). 144p. 1997. write for info. (0-7835-4866-4) Time-Life.

***Time-Life How-To Gardening Basics: Everything You Need to Know to Get Started.** Time-Life Books Editors. LC 96-33440. (Illus.). 144p. 1997. write for info. (0-7835-4864-8) Time-Life.

***Time-Life How-To Landscaping Basics: Everything You Need to Know to Get Started.** Time-Life Books Editors. LC 96-33439. (Illus.). 144p. 1997. write for info. (0-7835-4865-6) Time-Life.

An Asterisk (*) at the beginning of an entry indicates that the title is appearing in BIP for the first time.

***Time-Life How-To Landscaping Projects: Simple Steps to Enhance Your Home & Yard.** Time-Life Books Editors. LC 96-34320. (Illus.). 144p. 1997. write for info. (0-7835-4867-2) Time-Life.

Time-Life Old-Fashioned Christmas Cookbook. Time-Life Books Editors. LC 96-17861. (Illus.). 224p. 1996. 24.95 (0-7835-4831-1) Time-Life.

***Time Like a River.** Randy Perrin et al. 130p. (YA). (gr. 5 up). 1997. 14.95 (1-57143-061-X, Wetlands Pr) RDR Bks.

***Time-Limited Counselling.** Colin Feltham. (Professional Skills for Counselors Ser.). 160p. 1996. 45.00 (0-8039-7974-6); pap. 18.95 (0-8039-7975-4) Sage.

Time-Limited Day Treatment for Personality Disorders: Integration of Research & Practice in a Group Program. William E. Piper. LC 96-20928. 360p. 1996. 49.95 (1-55798-370-4) Am Psychol.

Time-Limited Dynamic Psychotherapy: A Guide to Clinical Practice. Hanna Levenson. LC 95-13934. 256p. 1995. 37.00 (0-465-08651-9) Basic.

Time-Limited, Intermittent Therapy with Children & Families. Thomas Kreilkamp. LC 88-30229. 264p. 1989. text ed. 32.95 (0-87630-532-X) Brunner-Mazel.

Time-Limited Psychotherapy. James Mann. LC 72-96631. (Commonwealth Fund Publications). 212p. 1980. pap. 16.95 (0-674-89191-0) HUP.

Time Line: A Guidebook to Help You Give Solid Answers about Your Past, Present, Future... Elizabeth R. Walters & Barbara J. Dickman. LC 91-67070. 144p. 1991. ring bd. 24.95 (0-9631223-4-7) Paragon MI.

Time Line Display of Jewish History: Poster Edition. 1982. 8.00 (0-686-46792-2) T Black.

Time Line of Culture in the Nile Valley & Its Relationship to Other World Cultures. Metropolitan Museum of Art Staff. 1994. 10.95 (0-8109-6474-0) Abrams.

Time Line Therapy. LC 87-63197. 1988. pap. 21.95 (0-916990-21-4) META Pubns.

Time Lines on File. Diagram Group Staff. 300p. 1988. ring bd. 155.00 (0-8160-1897-9) Facts on File.

Time Longer Than Rope: A History of the Black Man's Struggle for Freedom in South Africa. 2nd ed. Edward Roux. 488p. 1967. pap. 7.95 (0-299-03204-3) U of Wis Pr.

Time Machine. Created by Harcourt Brace Staff. 1990. student ed., pap. 10.00 (0-15-348525-6) HR&W Schl Div.

Time Machine. Created by Harcourt Brace Staff. 1990. student ed., teacher ed., pap. 22.75 (0-15-348531-0) HR&W Schl Div.

***Time Machine.** Intro. by Michael Moorcock. 144p. 1993. pap. 3.95 (0-460-87735-6, Everyman's Classic Lib) C E Tuttle.

Time Machine. H. G. Wells. (Airmont Classics Ser.). (J). (gr. 7 up). 1964. mass mkt. 3.95 (0-8049-0044-2, CL-44) Airmont.

Time Machine. H. G. Wells. 128p. 1984. 3.95 (0-553-21351-2) Bantam.

Time Machine. H. G. Wells. 1997. pap. 2.95 (0-89375-345-9) Troll Communs.

Time Machine. H. G. Wells. 1988. mass mkt. 3.99 (0-441-80263-X) Ace Bks.

Time Machine. H. G. Wells. 144p. 1993. pap. 3.95 (0-460-87300-8, Everyman's Classic Lib) C E Tuttle.

Time Machine. H. G. Wells. Ed. by Otto Binder. LC 73-75467. (Now Age Illustrated Ser.). (Illus.). 64p. (J). (gr. 5-10). 1973. pap. 2.95 (0-88301-102-6) Pendulum Pr.

Time Machine. H. G. Wells. LC 81-4097. (Short Classics Ser.). (Illus.). 48p. (J). (gr. 4 up). 1983. lib. bdg. 24.26 (0-8172-1675-8) Raintree Steck-V.

Time Machine. H. G. Wells. LC 89-39506. (Bullseye Step into Classics Ser.). (Illus.). 96p. (J). (gr. 2-6). 1990. pap. 3.99 (0-679-80371-8) Random Bks Yng Read.

Time Machine. H. G. Wells. 144p. 1992. pap. 2.50 (0-8125-0504-2) Tor Bks.

Time Machine. H. G. Wells. Ed. by Raymond James. LC 92-5804. (Illustrated Classics Ser.). (Illus.). 48p. (J). (gr. 3-6). 1992. pap. 5.95 (0-8167-2873-9); lib. bdg. 14.95 (0-8167-2872-0) Troll Communs.

Time Machine. H. G. Wells. Bd. with Invisible Man. 320p. 1984. Set pap. 4.95 (0-451-52238-9, Sig Classics) NAL-Dutton.

Time Machine. H. G. Wells. LC 94-32659. (Thrift Editions Ser.). 80p. 1995. pap. text ed. 1.00 (0-486-28472-7) Dover.

Time Machine. H. G. Wells. 128p. (J). (gr. 5-8). 1995. pap. 2.50 (0-87406-726-X) Willowisp Pr.

Time Machine. H. G. Wells. (H. G. Wells Ser.). 1994. 16.95 incl. audio (1-883049-06-7) Commuters Lib.

Time Machine. H. G. Wells. 1994. lib. bdg. 18.95 incl. audio (1-883049-25-3) Commuters Lib.

***Time Machine.** H. G. Wells. (Illustrated Classics Collection 1). 64p. 1994. pap. 4.95 (0-7854-0670-0, 40355) Am Guidance.

***Time Machine.** H. G. Wells. Ed. by Malvina Vogel. (Great Illustrated Classics Ser.: Vol. 32). (Illus.). 240p. (J). (gr. 3-6). 1993. 9.95 (0-86611-983-3) Playmore Inc.

Time Machine. large type ed. H. G. Wells. 1995. 37.50 (0-614-09612-X, L-81886-00) Am Printing Hse.

Time Machine. H. G. Wells. 1992. reprint ed. 18.95 (0-89968-283-9, Lghtyr Pr) Buccaneer Bks.

Time Machine. H. G. Wells. LC 71-183141. 128p. 1971. reprint ed. lib. bdg. 14.00 (0-8376-0403-6) Bentley.

Time Machine: Based on the H. G. Wells Classic Tale. Bill Spangler. 77p. (Orig.). 1991. pap. 9.95 (0-944735-93-2) Malibu Comics Ent.

Time Machine: Duck for Hire. Terry Page. (Illus.). 24p. (J). (gr. 2-6). 1997. pap. text ed. 4.00 (1-887864-67-9); lib. bdg. 7.00 (1-887864-34-2) Boo Bks.

Time Machine: The Modern Girls. Joan Hinds & Jean Becker. (Illus.). 80p. (Orig.). 1994. per., pap. 24.50 (0-9636287-2-0) Fancywrk & Fashion.

***Time Machine: The Modern Girls.** Joan Hinds & Jean Becker. (Illus.). 78p. (Orig.). 1996. pap. 24.95 (0-614-23848-X, N4883) Hobby Hse.

Time Machine: War of the Worlds. H. G. Wells. 288p. 1986. mass mkt. 5.99 (0-449-30043-9) Fawcett.

Time Machine - An Invention: A Critical Text of the 1895 London First Edition, with an Introduction & Appendices. H. G. Wells. Ed. by Leon Stover. LC 95-43023. (Annotated H. G. Wells Ser.: No. 1). 270p. 1996. lib. bdg. 45.00 (0-7864-0124-9) McFarland & Co.

***Time Machine & Other Cases.** Seymour Simon. LC 96-41765. (Einstein Anderson, Science Detective Ser.). (Illus.). (J). Date not set. 14.00 (0-688-14441-1, Morrow Junior) Morrow.

Time Machine & The Chef: Tribute to Orson Wells & Son. Baker. Ed. & Illus. by Joan Abell. (Orig.). (YA). (gr. 8 up). 1992. pap. 28.00 (1-56611-041-6); lib. bdg. 32.00 (1-56611-014-9) Jones.

Time Machine & The Island of Doctor Moreau. H. G. Wells & Patrick Parrinder. (World's Classics Ser.). 280p. (C). 1996. pap. 7.95 (0-19-282825-8) OUP.

Time Machine Coloring Book: Duck for Hire. Terry Page. (Illus.). 32p. (J). (ps-5). 1997. pap. 3.00 (1-887864-35-0) Boo Bks.

***Time Machine Readalong.** H. G. Wells. (Illustrated Classics Collection 1). 64p. 1994. pap. 14.95 incl. audio (0-7854-0711-1, 40357) Am Guidance.

***Time Machines.** Ed. by Bill Adler, Jr. 400p. 1997. 24.00 (0-7867-0493-4) Carroll & Graf.

Time Machines: Time Travel in Physics, Metaphysics, & Science Fiction. Paul J. Nahin. LC 92-75255. 1993. 40.00 (0-88318-935-6) Spr-Verlag.

Time Machines: Time Travel in Physics, Metaphysics, & Science Fiction. Paul J. Nahin. LC 92-75255. (Illus.). 408p. 1994. pap. 15.95 (1-56396-371-X) Spr-Verlag.

Time Magazine: We the People. Selected by Linda Schinke-Llano. 176p. 1995. pap. 21.95 (0-8442-7461-5, Natl Textbk) NTC Pub Grp.

Time Manage Your Reading. Shirley Rudd. 173p. 1990. text ed. 34.95 (0-566-02762-3, Pub. by Gower UK); pap. text ed. 23.95 (0-566-02976-6, Pub. by Gower UK) Ashgate Pub Co.

Time-Managed Group Psychotherapy: Effective Clinical Applications. K. Roy MacKenzie. 466p. 1997. text ed. 67.50 (0-88048-863-8, 8863) Am Psychiatric.

Time Management. Kenneth R. Finn. (Simulation Game Ser.). 1975. pap. 50.00 (0-89401-092-1) Didactic Syst.

Time Management. Robert M. Hochheiser. (Business Success Ser.). 96p. 1992. pap. 4.95 (0-8120-4792-3) Barron.

***Time Management.** Walt Lacey. 1992. ring bd. 49.95 incl. audio (1-57052-071-2) Chrch Grwth VA.

Time Management: A Manual for Trainers. John Richards. Ed. by John Adair. 255p. (C). 1989. ring bd. 285.00 (0-85171-088-3, Pub. by IPM Hse UK) St Mut.

Time Management for Business People. Allan H. Smith. 210p. (Orig.). 1988. pap. 7.00 (0-931113-28-8) Success Publ.

***Time Management for Busy People.** Roberta Roesch. 1998. pap. text ed. 16.95 (0-07-053406-3) McGraw.

Time Management for Claims Professionals. rev. ed. Kevin M. Quinley. 176p. 1997. reprint ed. 21.95 (0-9634957-1-2) Insuranceweek.

Time Management for Dummies: A Reference for the Rest of Us. Jeffrey J. Mayer. 274p. 1995. pap. 16.99 (1-56884-360-7) IDG Bks.

Time Management for Dummies: Briefcase Edition. Jeffrey J. Mayer. 1995. pap. 9.99 (1-56884-973-7) IDG Bks.

Time Management for Educators. Charles E. Kozoll. LC 81-86309. (Fastback Ser.: No. 175). 50p. (Orig.). 1982. pap. 3.00 (0-87367-175-9) Phi Delta Kappa.

Time Management for Engineers & Constructors. Ray G. Helmer. LC 91-24919. 110p. 1991. pap. text ed. 17.00 (0-87262-793-4) Am Soc Civil Eng.

Time Management for Executives. Lauren R. Januz. 1992. pap. 15.95 (0-9623414-4-4) Smith Collins.

Time Management for High School Students. Raymond W. Meliza. (Illus.). 8p. (YA). 1995. pap. 2.50 (0-9626591-9-3, AO402) Energeia Pub.

Time Management for Teachers: Essential Tips & Techniques. Scott Purdy. (Orig.). (C). 1995. pap. 10.00 (0-9641366-3-5) Write Time.

Time Management for Teachers: Practical Techniques & Skills That Give You More to Teach. Cathy Collins. 312p. 1987. pap. text ed. 22.95 (0-13-921701-0) P-H.

Time Management for Teams. Merrill E. Douglass & Donna N. Douglass. LC 92-22118. 192p. 1992. pap. 17.95 (0-8144-7804-2) AMACOM.

Time Management for Unmanageable People. Ann McGee-Cooper & Duane Trammell. LC 93-47683. 272p. 1994. pap. 12.95 (0-553-37071-5) Bantam.

Time Management Forms. (Easy-to-Make Photocopier Bks.). (Orig.). 1984. pap. 19.95 (0-87280-032-6, 779, Asher-Gallant) Caddylak Systs.

Time Management Handbook. Pref. by James J. Messina. (Professional Handbook Ser.). 37p. (Orig.). 1982. pap. text ed. 7.00 (0-931975-15-8) Advanced Dev Sys.

Time Management Handbook for Librarians. J. Wesley Cochran. LC 91-17120. (Library Management Collection). 160p. 1991. text ed. 42.95 (0-313-27842-3, CTG) Greenwood.

Time Management in the Small Library. Andrew Berner. 1988. student ed. 75.00 (0-87111-392-9) SLA.

Time Management Made Easy. Peter Turla & Kathleen L. Hawkins. 206p. 1994. pap. 15.95 (0-452-27202-5) NAL-Dutton.

Time Management Skillbook. Educational Foundation of the National Restaurant Association Staff. (Management Skills Program Ser.). 36p. (Orig.). 1993. pap. 10.95 (0-915452-41-3) Educ Found.

Time Management Skills: Leadership Skills for Women. Debbie Lloyd. Ed. by Judith Edwards. 72p. (Orig.). 1994. pap. text ed. 5.95 (1-56309-102-X, New Hope) Womans Mission Union.

Time Management Skills see Productive Supervisor: A Program of Practical Managerial Skills

***Time Management So What? So Help Me!** Kathleen R. Wood. 112p. (J). (gr. 1-6). 1986. pap. 14.95 (1-878347-45-4) NL Assocs.

Time Management Study Guide: A Manual to Accompany the Coaches Guide to Time Management. Stephen C. Jefferies. (Illus.). 1985. ring bd. 26.00 (0-931250-98-6, ACEP0201) Human Kinetics.

Time Management Survival Guide for Dummies. Jeffrey J. Mayer. 202p. 1995. pap. 12.99 (1-56884-972-9) IDG Bks.

***Time Management Techniques.** Raymond W. Meliza. (Illus.). 8p. (Orig.). 1997. pap. 2.50 (0-9626591-3-4, SPS0341) Energeia Pub.

***Time Marching: A Step-by-Step Guide to a Flow Solver.** Michael Lobo. 160p. 1996. 68.95 (0-291-39826-X, Pub. by Avebury Technical UK) Ashgate Pub Co.

***Time Masters: Secrets of Successful Time Managers.** Jan Yager. (Illus.). 228p. 1998. 28.95 (1-889262-05-6) Hannacroix.

Time Mastery: The Beginner's Book, Vol. 5. Tisziji Munoz. (Illus.). (Orig.). (C). 1987. pap. 15.00 (0-945174-02-0) Illum Soc Pubns.

Time, Measurement, & Money. Lea Rangel-Ribeiro. Ed. by Susan Evento. (Macmillan Early Skills Program - Conversion Ser.). 64p. (J). (ps-2). 1995. pap. 9.95 (1-56784-509-6) Newbridge Comms.

Time, Memory & Society. Franco Ferrarotti. LC 89-27370. (Contributions in Sociology Ser.: No. 91). 168p. 1990. text ed. 45.00 (0-313-26828-2, FTC/, Greenwood Pr) Greenwood.

Time, Mind & Behavior. J. A. Michon & J. L. Jackson. (Illus.). 340p. 1985. 105.00 (0-387-15444-2) Spr-Verlag.

Time Mine. Duane E. Patterson. LC 95-90792. 1996. 19.95 (0-533-11717-8) Vantage.

Time, Money & Fractions. Lorie DeYoung. Ed. by Joan Hoffman. (I Know It! Bks.). (Illus.). 32p. (J). (gr. 1-2). 1993. student ed. 1.99 (0-938256-44-0) Sch Zone Pub Co.

Time, Money, & Measurement. (Step Ahead Plus Workbooks). (Illus.). 64p. (J). (gr. 2-3). 1995. pap. 3.50 (0-307-03661-8, Golden Pr) Western Pub.

Time, Money, & Measurement. Frank Schaffer Publications, Inc. Staff. (Homework Helpers Ser.). (Illus.). 56p. (J). (gr. 1-2). 1996. wbk. ed. 2.29 (0-86734-945-X, FS-11059) Schaffer Pubns.

Time, Money, & Measurement. Frank Schaffer Publications, Inc. Staff. (Homework Helpers Ser.). (Illus.). 56p. (J). (gr. 2-3). 1996. wbk. ed. 2.29 (0-86734-946-8, FS-11060) Schaffer Pubns.

Time, Money, & Measurement. Frank Schaffer Publications, Inc. Staff. (Skill Builders Ser.). (Illus.). 128p. 1996. wbk. ed. 10.95 (0-7647-0010-3, FS-32079) Schaffer Pubns.

Time Museum Catalogue of Astrolabes & Related Instruments. Anthony J. Turner. (Illus.). xviii, 270p. 1986. 115.00 (0-912947-02-0) Time Museum.

Time Museum Catalogue of Chronometers. Anthony G. Randall. Ed. by Bruce Chandler. (Illus.). x, 366p. 1992. 139.00 (0-912947-03-9) Time Museum.

Time Museum Catalogue of Water-Clocks, Fire-Clocks, Sand-Glasses Vol. I. Anthony J. Turner. (Illus.). xvi, 184p. 1985. 95.00 (0-912947-01-2) Time Museum.

Time Museum Historical Catalogue of American Pocket Watches. Donald R. Hoke. Ed. by Bruce Chandler. (Illus.). xiv, 330p. 1991. 79.95 (0-912947-04-7) Time Museum.

Time Must Have a Stop. Aldous Huxley. 1976. 23.95 (0-8488-0536-4) Amereon Ltd.

Time, Narrative, & History. David Carr. LC 85-45742. (Studies in Phenomenology & Existential Philosophy). 200p. 1986. 29.95 (0-253-36024-2) Ind U Pr.

Time, Narrative, & History. David Carr. LC 85-45742. (Studies in Phenomenology & Existential Philosophy). 200p. 1991. pap. 13.95 (0-253-20603-0, MB 603) Ind U Pr.

Time No Longer. Taylor Caldwell. Date not set. reprint ed. lib. bdg. 25.95 (0-88411-161-X, Aeonian Pr) Amereon Ltd.

Time Not Here, the Mississippi Delta: Photographs by Norman Mauskapf. Randall Kenan. (Illus.). 112p. 1996. 50.00 (0-944092-43-8) Twin Palms Pub.

Time of Agony, Time of Destiny: The Upsurge of Popular Protest in South Africa. Martin Murray. 272p. 1987. 39.95 (0-86091-146-2, Pub. by Verso UK); pap. 14.95 (0-86091-857-2, Pub. by Verso UK) Schocken.

Time of Angels. Karen Hesse. LC 95-4461. 224p. (J). (gr. 5-9). 1995. 15.95 (0-7868-0087-9); lib. bdg. 15.89 (0-7868-2072-1) Hyprn Child.

***Time of Angels.** Karen Hesse. 224p. (J). (gr. 5-9). 1997. pap. 4.95 (0-7868-1209-5) Hyprn Ppbks.

Time of Apprenticeship: The Fiction of Young James Joyce. Marvin Magalaner. LC 70-140366. (Select Bibliographies Reprint Ser.). 1977. reprint ed. 18.95 (0-8369-5609-5) Ayer.

Time of Awakening: The Young Christian Worker Story in the United States, 1938-1970. Mary I. Zotti. LC 90-24689. (Values & Ethics Ser.: Vol. 2). (Illus.). 338p. (C). 1991. 6.50 (0-8294-0716-2) Loyola Pr.

***Time of Champions.** TSR Inc. Staff. 1997. pap. 5.99 (0-7869-0755-X) TSR Inc.

Time of Change: Awakening to Womanhood. rev. ed. (Illus.). 68p. (ENG & SPA.). (C). pap. text ed. 20.00 (0-7881-2511-7) DIANE Pub.

Time of Change - De Nina a Mujer. (Illus.). 34p. (Orig.). (SPA.). (C). 1995. pap. text ed. 20.00 (0-7881-2402-1) DIANE Pub.

Time of Christ: A Chronology of the Incarnation. Ormond Edwards. 208p. 1990. 37.95 (0-86315-030-6, 1080, Pub. by Floris Books UK) Anthroposophic.

Time of Darkness: Local Legends & Volcanic Reality in Papua New Guinea. R. J. Blong. LC 81-11484. (Illus.). 270p. 1982. 30.00 (0-295-95880-4) U of Wash Pr.

Time of Decision with Rudolf Steiner: Experience & Encounter. Friedrich Hiebel. Tr. by Maria St. Goar from GER. 420p. (Orig.). 1989. pap. 19.95 (0-88010-274-8) Anthroposophic.

Time of Exile. Katharine Kerr. 432p. 1992. mass mkt. 5.99 (0-553-29813-5, Spectra) Bantam.

Time of Fear. Kate Chester. (Hear No Evil Ser.: No. 3). (YA). 1996. mass mkt. 3.99 (0-590-67328-9) Scholastic Inc.

Time of Feasting. Mick Farren. LC 96-22943. 1996. 23.95 (0-312-86213-X) St Martin.

***Time of Fire.** Robert Westall. LC 96-37259. (J). 1997. 15.95 (0-590-47746-3) Scholastic Inc.

Time of Flight Diffraction at Pulsed Neutron Sources, Vol. 29. Y. D. Jorgensen et al. 117p. pap. text ed. 30.00 (0-937140-38-4) Am Crystallographic.

Time-of-Flight Mass Spectrometry. Ed. by Robert J. Cotter. LC 93-23638. 233p. 1994. 59.95 (0-8412-2771-3) Am Chemical.

***Time-of-Flight Mass Spectrometry: Instrumentation & Applications in Biological Research.** Robert J. Cotter. LC 97-3734. (Professional Reference Bks.). 1997. write for info. (0-8412-3474-4) Am Chemical.

Time-of-Flight Mass Spectrometry & Its Applications. Ed. by E. W. Schlag. 422p. 1994. pap. 140.75 (0-444-81875-8) Elsevier.

Time of Friendship. Paul Bowles & Vittorio Santoro. (Illus.). 68p. 1996. 40.00 (3-9520497-2-7, 610201, Pub. by Memory-Cage SZ) Dist Art Pubs.

Time of Gathering: Native Heritage in Washington State. Ed. by Robin K. Wright. LC 90-1341. (Illus.). 256p. 1992. pap. 35.00 (0-295-96820-6) U of Wash Pr.

Time of Gifts. Patrick L. Fermor. 1990. 22.50 (0-8446-6264-X) Peter Smith.

Time of Gifts. Patrick L. Fermor. (Travel Library). 304p. 1984. mass mkt. 6.95 (0-14-009513-6, Penguin Bks) Viking Penguin.

Time of Gifts. Patrick L. Fermor. 1988. pap. 11.95 (0-14-004947-9, Penguin Bks) Viking Penguin.

Time of Gifts. large type ed. Patrick L. Fermor. (Mainstream Ser.). 424p. 1988. reprint ed. 16.95 (1-85089-192-3, Pub. by ISIS UK) Transaction Pubs.

Time of Grace: One Family's Experience with Chronic Care. Daniel Donovan. 1990. pap. 5.95 (0-8091-3164-1) Paulist Pr.

Time of Her Life: Menopause, Health & Well Being. Myra Hunter & Jean Coope. 192p. 1995. pap. 12.95 (0-563-36759-8, Pub. by BBC UK) Parkwest Pubns.

Time of Hope. C. P. Snow. 1977. 20.00 (0-684-15315-7) S&S Trade.

Time of Hope. large type ed. Susan Kelly. 346p. 1993. 25.99 (0-7505-0487-0) Ulverscroft.

Time of Horses, Cattle & Sheep. Don Jordan. Ed. by Renae Crippen. 112p. 1993. reprint ed. 12.95 (0-9636762-0-2) Juniper Mtn.

Time of Illusion. Jonathan Schell. 1975. pap. 4.76 (0-685-02841-0) Knopf.

Time of Illusion. Jonathan Schell. 1976. pap. 8.76 (0-394-72217-5, 72217, Vin) Random.

Time of Little Choice: The Disintegration of Tribal Culture in the San Francisco Bay Area 1769-1810. Randall Milliken. Ed. by Thomas C. Blackburn. (Ballena Press Anthropological Papers: No. 43). 400p. 1995. pap. 24.95 (0-87919-131-7) Ballena Pr.

Time of Little Choice: The Disintegration of Tribal Culture in the San Francisco Bay Area 1769-1810. Randall Milliken. Ed. by Thomas C. Blackburn. (Ballena Press Anthropological Papers: No. 43). 400p. (C). 1995. 32.95 (0-87919-132-5) Ballena Pr.

Time of Love. Eleanor M. Howard. (Illus.). 209p. 1992. 21.95 (0-9633869-7-2) Eleanor M Howard.

Time of Miracles. Jeff Lahr. 40p. 1991. pap. 2.95 (0-87227-170-6, RBP5202) Reg Baptist.

Time of Miracles: A Legend. Borislav Pekic. Tr. by Lovett F. Edwards from SER. LC 93-45889. (Writings from an Unbound Europe). 332p. (C). 1994. reprint ed. pap. 13.95 (0-8101-1117-9) Northwestern U Pr.

Time of Murder at Mayerling. Ann Dukthas. LC 96-25616. 224p. 1996. 20.95 (0-312-14676-0) St Martin.

***Time of Murder at Mayerling, Vol. 1.** Dukthas. 1997. mass mkt. write for info. (0-312-96338-6) St Martin.

Time of Music: New Meanings, New Temporalities, New Listening Strategies. Jonathan D. Kramer. 493p. 1988. 44.00 (0-02-872590-5) Schirmer Bks.

Time of My Life. Alan Ayckbourn. 98p. (Orig.). 1993. pap. 8.95 (0-571-16990-2) Faber & Faber.

Time of My Life. Gertrude S. Legendre. LC 87-50640. (Illus.). 235p. 1987. 18.95 (0-941711-02-1) Wyrick & Co.

Time of My Life. Jack Leonard & Sid Shapira. (Illus.). 189p. 1993. 14.95 (0-9639900-0-4) Drumalee.

Time of My Life. Thomas Yoseloff. 8.95 (0-8453-1761-X, Cornwall Bks) Assoc Univ Prs.

Time of My Life: An Autobiography. Willard Van Orman Quine. (Illus.). 384p. 1985. 35.00 (0-262-17003-5, Bradford Bks) MIT Pr.

Time of My Life: Memoirs of a Government Agent. Adrian Swain. Ed. by Marsha P. Raymond & Karen L. Jacob. LC 91-77659. 640p. (Orig.). 1995. pap. 16.95 (0-936417-41-2) Axelrod Pub.

Time of Omens. Katharine Kerr. 432p. 1993. mass mkt. 5.99 (0-553-29011-8) Bantam.

***Time of Our Lives.** Adler. 1970. write for info. (0-8050-4785-9) St Martin.

Time of Our Lives: The Ethics of Common Sense. rev. ed. Mortimer J. Adler. xxiv, 360p. 1996. 29.95 (*0-8232-1669-1*); pap. 18.00 (*0-8232-1670-5*) Fordham.

*__Time of Paradox: America in the 20th Century.__ Ed. by Jeansonne. (C). Date not set. text ed. write for info. (*0-673-99688-3*) Addison-Wesley.

*__Time of Paradox: America in the 20th Century, 1945 to Present, Vol. 1.__ Ed. by Jeansonne. (C). 1901. text ed. write for info. (*0-673-99689-1*) Addison-Wesley.

Time of Personal Regeneration. Richard J. Aschwanden & Maria Aschwanden. Ed. by Charles R. Aschwanden. 60p. 1984. pap. 3.40 (*0-913071-00-5*, TX1-202-40) Rama Pub Co.

Time of Renaissance see Literary History of the English People

Time of Silence. Luis Martin-Santos. Tr. by George Leeson. 247p. 1989. text ed. 52.50 (*0-231-06984-7*); pap. text ed. 14.50 (*0-231-06985-5*) Col U Pr.

Time of Terror. James Cameron. 207p. 1994. 22.00 (*0-933121-45-8*); pap. 14.95 (*0-933121-44-X*) Black Classic.

*__Time of the Aces: Marine Pilots in the Solomons, 1942-1944.__ Peter B. Mersky. (Illus.). 41p. 1996. reprint ed. pap. 25.00 (*0-7881-3521-X*) DIANE Pub.

Time of the Angels. Iris Murdoch. 240p. 1988. pap. 10.95 (*0-14-002848-X*, Penguin Bks) Viking Penguin.

Time of the Assassins: A Study of Rimbaud. Henry Miller. LC 55-12452. 1962. pap. 8.95 (*0-8112-0115-5*, NDP115) New Directions.

Time of the Buffalo. Tom McHugh. LC 78-24261. (Illus.). xxiv, 383p. 1979. reprint ed. pap. 16.95 (*0-8032-8105-6*, Bison Books) U of Nebr Pr.

Time of the Butcherbird. Alex La Guma. LC 79-670199. (African Writers Ser.). 119p. (C). 1979. pap. 9.95 (*0-435-90758-1*, 90758) Heinemann.

Time of the Cranes. Norma Johnston. LC 89-39818. 176p. (YA). (gr. 7 up). 1990. lib. bdg. 14.95 (*0-02-747713-4*, Four Winds Pr) S&S Childrens.

Time Of The Cross. Watchman Nee. 21p. 1.00 (*0-87083-607-2*, 07034001) Living Stream Ministry.

*__Time of the Dark.__ Barbara Hambly. (The Darwath Trilogy Ser.). 1997. mass mkt. 5.99 (*0-345-91168-7*, Del Rey) Ballantine.

Time of the Dark, No. 1. Barbara Hambly. 272p. 1984. mass mkt. 5.99 (*0-345-31965-6*, Del Rey) Ballantine.

Time of the Dinosaurs. Ann Packard & Shirley Stafford. (Learning Experiences for Young Children Ser.). 92p. (J). (ps-3). 1981. write for info. (*0-9607580-1-1*) S Stafford.

Time of the Doves. Merce Rodereda. Tr. by David H. Rosenthal from CAT. LC 85-80976. 201p. 1986. reprint ed. pap. 12.00 (*0-915308-75-4*) Graywolf.

Time of the French in the Heart of North America, 1673-1818. Charles J. Balesi. (Illus.). (Orig.). (C). 1992. pap. text ed. 17.00 (*1-881370-00-3*) Alliance Francaise.

Time of the Generals: Latin American Professional Militarism in World Perspective. Frederick M. Nunn. LC 91-39896. xvi, 340p. 1992. text ed. 55.00 (*0-8032-3334-5*) U of Nebr Pr.

Time of the Ghost. Diana W. Jones. LC 95-36155. 256p. (YA). (gr. 5 up). 1996. 15.00 (*0-688-14598-1*) Greenwillow.

*__Time of the Ghost.__ Diana W. Jones. (J). Date not set. pap. 4.95 (*0-688-15492-1*, Beech Tree Bks) Morrow.

Time of the Great Freeze. Robert Silverberg. 224p. 1988. pap. 2.95 (*0-8125-5469-8*) Tor Bks.

Time of the Gypsies. Michael Stewart. LC 97-9001. (Studies in Ethnographic Imagination). 1997. text ed. 26.00 (*0-8133-3198-6*) Westview.

Time of the Gypsies. Michael Stewart. LC 97-9001. (Studies in Ethnographic Imagination). (C). 1998. pap. text ed. 19.95 (*0-8133-3199-4*) Westview.

Time of the Hero. Mario Vargas Llosa. Tr. by Lysander Kemp. 412p. 1986. pap. 15.00 (*0-374-52021-6*) FS&G.

Time of the Hunter's Moon. Victoria Holt. 384p. 1985. mass mkt. 5.99 (*0-449-20511-8*, Crest) Fawcett.

Time of the Kingfishers. David Watmough. 1995. pap. 14.95 (*1-55152-008-7*) LPC InBook.

Time of the Leonids. Christine Bruckner. Tr. by Marlies I. Comjean from GER. Orig. Title: Die Zeit Von Den Leoniden. 160p. 13.95 (*0-89182-040-X*) Charles River Bks.

*__Time of the Messiah.__ Kelley Varner. 210p. (Orig.). 1996. pap. 8.99 (*1-56043-177-6*) Destiny Image.

Time of the Pheasant. Otto F. Walter. Tr. by Lelia Vennewitz from GER. LC 91-3929. Orig. Title: Zeit des Fasans. 428p. 1991. 21.95 (*0-88064-129-0*) Fromm Intl Pub.

Time of the Rose. Bonita Clifton. 400p. (Orig.). 1994. mass mkt., pap. text ed. 4.99 (*0-505-51922-4*, Love Spell) Dorchester Pub Co.

Time of the Sign: A Semiotic Interpretation of Modern Culture. Dean MacCannell & Juliet F. MacCannell. LC 81-47960. (Advances in Semiotics Ser.). 221p. reprint ed. pap. 63.90 (*0-685-23890-3*, 2056709) Bks Demand.

Time of the Singing of Birds, No. 23. Grace L. Hill. (Grace Livingston Hill Ser.: Vol. 23). 288p. 1995. mass mkt., pap. 4.99 (*0-8423-7209-1*) Tyndale.

Time of the Spirit. Ed. by George Every et al. LC 84-10696. 256p. (Orig.). 1984. pap. text ed. 10.95 (*0-88141-035-7*) St Vladimirs.

Time of the Thunderer: Mikhail Katkov, Russian Nationalist Extremism & the Failure of the Bimarkian System, 1871-1887. Karel Durman. 609p. 1988. text ed. 99.00 (*0-88033-134-8*) East Eur Monographs.

Time of the Transference. Alan Dean Foster. (Spellsinger Ser.). 1986. 17.00 (*0-932096-43-3*) Phantasia Pr.

Time of the Tribes: The Decline of Individualism in Mass Societies. Michel Maffesoli. (Theory, Culture & Society Ser.). 224p. 1996. 69.95 (*0-8039-8473-1*); pap. 23.95 (*0-8039-8474-X*) Sage.

Time of the Trolley: The Street Railway from Horsecar to Light Rail, Vol. 1. William D. Middleton. LC 87-21112. (Illus.). 240p. 1987. 42.95 (*0-87095-098-3*) Gldn West Bks.

Time of the Twins, Vol. 1. Margaret Weis & Tracy Hickman. (Dragon Lance Legends Ser.: Vol. III). 1995. pap. 5.99 (*0-7869-0262-0*) TSR Inc.

*__Time of the Wild.__ A. B. Curtiss. (Illus.). 40p. (J). (gr. 4-8). 1998. lib. bdg. 18.95 (*0-932529-55-0*) Oldcastle.

Time of the Witch. Mary D. Hahn. 176p. (YA). 1991. pap. 3.99 (*0-380-71116-8*, Camelot) Avon.

*__Time of the Wolf.__ William D. Blankenship. 1998. pap. 22.95 (*1-55611-528-8*) D I Fine.

Time of Their Lives: The Dionne Tragedy. Stuart Nihmey. 240p. 1994. mass mkt. 6.99 (*0-7704-2621-2*) Bantam.

Time of Theory: A History of Tel Quel, 1960-1983. Patrick Ffrench. 320p. 1996. 65.00 (*0-19-815897-1*) OUP.

Time of Tigers. Elmer E. Haynes. LC 85-61329. (Illus.). 300p. (Orig.). 1986. pap. 16.00 (*0-931571-02-2*) Lifetime Pr.

Time of Transition: The Growth of Families Headed by Women. Heather L. Ross & Isabel V. Sawhill. 233p. (Orig.). 1975. pap. text ed. 24.00 (*0-87766-148-0*) Urban Inst.

Time of Transition: Women in Science: History of Sigma Delta Epsilon - Graduate Women in Science, Inc., 1979-1986 Supplement. Ruth S. Dickie. LC 88-61097. (Orig.). 1988. pap. 2.00 (*0-9620513-3-0*) Sigma Delta Epsilon.

Time of Triumph & of Sorrow: Spanish Politics During the Reign of Alfonso XII, 1874-1885. Earl R. Beck. LC 78-23282. 320p. 1979. 29.95 (*0-8093-0902-5*) S Ill U Pr.

Time of Troubles. Sami. 1995. pap. 6.95 (*0-395-72085-0*) HM.

Time of Troubles. R. G. Skrynnikov. Ed. by Hugh Graham. 1987. 29.00 (*0-87569-097-1*); pap. 12.50 (*0-685-43865-1*) Academic Intl.

Time of Troubles: A Historical Study of the Internal Crisis & Social Struggles in Sixteenth & Seventeenth-Century Muscovy. Sergei F. Platonov. Tr. by John T. Alexander. LC 79-97029. xviii, 198p. (C). 1970. pap. 7.95 (*0-7006-0062-0*) U Pr of KS.

Time of Troubles in the Low Countries: The Chronicles & Memoirs of Pasquier de le Barre of Tournai, 1559-1567. Charlie R. Steen. Ed. by Eckhard Bernstein. (Renaissance & Baroque Studies & Texts: Vol. 1). 280p. 1989. 49.95 (*0-8204-0852-2*) P Lang Pubng.

*__Time of Troubles, the Diary of Iurii Vladimirovich Gote: Moscow, July 8, 1917 to July 23, 1922.__ Iurii V. Gote. Ed. & Tr. by Terence Emmons. LC 87-33017. 550p. 1988. reprint ed. pap. 156.80 (*0-608-03304-9*, 2064016) Bks Demand.

Time of Use Rates: Pennsylvania Public Utility Commission. 52p. (Orig.). (C). 1993. pap. text ed. 20.00 (*1-56806-699-6*) DIANE Pub.

Time of Vampires. Ed. by P. N. Elrod. 1996. pap. 5.50 (*0-88677-693-7*) DAW Bks.

Time of War. Michael Peterson. 1996. mass mkt., pap. 6.50 (*0-671-56787-X*) PB.

Time of War: Air Force Diaries & Pentagon Memos, 1943-45. James G. Cozzens. Ed. by Matthew J. Bruccoli. 1984. 45.00 (*0-89723-043-4*) Bruccoli.

Time of Wonder. Robert McCloskey. (Illus.). 64p. (J). (gr. k-3). 1989. pap. 5.99 (*0-14-050201-7*, Puffin) Puffin Bks.

Time of Wonder. Robert McCloskey. (Illus.). (J). (gr. k-3). 1957. pap. 16.99 (*0-670-71512-3*) Viking Child Bks.

Time of Your Life. (Dr. Who Missing Adventures Ser.). (Illus.). 1995. pap. 5.95 (*0-426-20438-7*, Pub. by Virgin Pub UK) London Brdge.

*__Time of Your Life.__ Mary C. McGuinness. (Impact Ser.). 16p. 1996. 1.95 (*1-55612-852-5*, LL1852) Sheed & Ward MO.

Time of Your Life. Mark Porter. 1988. pap. 7.00 (*0-937396-71-0*) Walterick Pubs.

Time of Your Life. Jack H. Smith. 1994. reprint ed. 16.95 (*0-940375-04-4*) WindRiver Pub.

Time of Your Life: Self-Time Management for Pastors. Robert L. Randall. LC 93-45856. 144p. (Orig.). 1994. pap. 8.37 (*0-687-37137-6*) Abingdon.

*__Time of Your Own.__ Carlos Blanco-Aguinaga. Tr. by Agnes Moncy from SPA. 1997. pap. text ed. 10.00 (*0-9629903-3-7*) Jahbone Pr.

Time off from Good Behavior. Susan Sussman. Ed. by Jane Chelius. 320p. 1992. reprint ed. mass mkt. 5.50 (*0-671-68517-1*, Pocket Star Bks) PB.

Time off from Work: Using Sabbaticals to Enhance Your Life While Keeping Your Career on Track. Lisa Angowski. 224p. 1994. pap. text ed. 14.95 (*0-471-31067-0*) Wiley.

Time on Earth. Vilhelm Moberg. 1994. reprint ed. lib. bdg. 29.95 (*1-56849-314-2*) Buccaneer Bks.

Time on Fire. Evan Handler. LC 97-1750. 1997. pap. 12.95 (*0-8050-5067-1*) H Holt & Co.

Time on Fire: My Comedy of Terrors. Evan Handler. LC 95-2913. 286p. 1996. 21.95 (*0-316-34409-5*) Little.

*__Time on Ice: An Overwinter Voyage to Antarctica.__ Deborah Shapiro. 1997. 27.95 (*0-07-006399-0*) McGraw.

*__Time on My Hands: A Novel with Photographs.__ Peter Delacorte. 1997. 23.00 (*0-684-82651-8*) S&S Trade.

*__Time on Target: The 945th Field Artillery Battalion in World War II.__ William M. Cosgrove, III. (Illus.). 225p. 1997. 35.00 (*0-9656892-0-4*) W Cosgrove.

Time on the Cross: The Economics of American Negro Slavery. Robert W. Fogel & Stanley L. Engerman. 304p. 1995. pap. 11.95 (*0-393-31218-6*) Norton.

Time on the Cross: The Economics of American Negro Slavery. Robert W. Fogel & Stanley L. Engerman. (Illus.). 304p. 1985. reprint ed. pap. text ed. 26.00 (*0-8191-4331-6*) U Pr of Amer.

Time on the Line: An Integrated Activity Unit. Bev McKay. (Illus.). 32p. 1993. pap. text ed. 4.95 (*0-86530-235-9*) Incentive Pubns.

Time on Their Hands: A Report on Leisure, Recreation, & Young People. C. Gilbert Wrenn & D. L. Harley. LC 74-1718. (Children & Youth Ser.: Vol. 11). (Illus.). 1974. reprint ed. 28.95 (*0-405-05993-0*) Ayer.

Time One-Thousand Action Words. Valerie Barth. (Illus.). 110p. (Orig.). (J). (gr. 2-6). 1992. pap. 11.95 (*981-01-0383-2*, Pub. by Europ Lang Inst IT) Midwest European Pubns.

*__Time, Order, Chaos.__ J. T. Fraser et al. LC 97-11412. (Study of Time Ser.). 1997. write for info. (*0-8236-6547-X*) Intl Univs Pr.

Time, Organization & the Administration of Education. Peter Watkins. 106p. (C). 1986. 60.00 (*0-7300-0372-8*, Pub. by Deakin Univ AT) St Mut.

Time Out. Dawn Fergut. Ed. by John P. Schumake. (Orig.). 1992. pap. 13.95 (*0-9616789-3-3*) Earnest Pubns.

Time Out! Janet H. McHenry. (Golden Rule Duo Ser.). (Illus.). 48p. (Orig.). (J). (gr. 2-5). 1995. pap. 2.99 (*0-7814-0173-9*) Chariot Victor.

Time Out: A Guide for Parents & Teachers Using Popular Discipline Methods to Empower & Encourage Children. 2nd ed. Jane Nelsen & H. Stephen Glenn. Ed. by Cheryl Erwin. 111p. 1992. pap. 6.95 (*0-9606896-8-0*, B105) Empowering People.

Time Out: A Peace Corps Volunteer's Story. June Woods. LC 88-90457. (Illus.). 154p. (Orig.). 1988. pap. 8.95 (*0-9621922-0-1*) June Woods.

Time Out! Devotions for Athletes. J. Patrick Street. LC 96-68107. 104p. (Orig.). (YA). 1996. pap. write for info. (*0-936497-18-1*) Seven Worlds.

Time Out: How to Take a Year (or More or Less) off Without Jeopardizing Your Job, Your Family or Your Bank Account. Bonnie M. Rubin. 1987. pap. 12.95 (*0-393-30510-4*) Norton.

Time Out! Restoring Your Passion for Life, Love & Work. Philip Johnson. 1994. 12.95 (*0-7737-5491-1*) Genl Dist Srvs.

Time Out: Time Management Strategies for the Real Estate Professional. John Ravage. 144p. 1991. 19.95 (*0-7931-0210-3*, 27031101) Dearborn Finan.

*__Time Out Amsterdam.__ 4th ed. Time Out Magazine Staff. 1997. pap. 14.95 (*0-14-025715-2*) Viking Penguin.

Time Out Amsterdam Guide. 244p. 1991. pap. 14.95 (*0-14-013338-0*, Penguin Bks) Viking Penguin.

Time Out Amsterdam Guide. (Illus.). 288p. 1993. pap. 16.00 (*0-14-017915-1*, Penguin Bks) Viking Penguin.

Time Out Barcelona 1. Time Out Magazine Staff. 1997. pap. 14.95 (*0-14-025972-4*) Viking Penguin.

Time Out Berlin Guide. Penguin Staff. (Illus.). 296p. 1993. pap. 14.00 (*0-14-023042-4*, Penguin Bks) Viking Penguin.

Time Out Berlin Guide. 2nd ed. (Time Out Ser.). (Illus.). 296p. 1995. pap. 13.95 (*0-14-023759-3*, Penguin Bks) Viking Penguin.

Time Out Brussels 1. Time Out Magazine Staff. 1997. pap. 14.95 (*0-14-025971-6*) Viking Penguin.

Time Out Budapest. (Time Out Ser.). (Illus.). 356p. 1996. pap. 14.95 (*0-14-025416-1*, Penguin Bks) Viking Penguin.

Time Out Film. 5th ed. Time Out Magazine Staff. 1997. pap. 21.95 (*0-14-026132-X*) Viking Penguin.

Time Out Film Guide. Ed. by Tom Milne. (Illus.). 784p. 1990. pap. 14.95 (*0-14-012700-3*, Penguin Bks) Viking Penguin.

Time Out Film Guide. Ed. by Tom Milne. 784p. (Orig.). 1992. pap. 15.00 (*0-14-014592-3*, Penguin Bks) Viking Penguin.

Time Out Film Guide: The Definitive, A-Z Directory of over 10,000 Films. 3rd ed. Ed. by Tom Milne. 992p. 1994. pap. 20.00 (*0-14-017513-X*, Penguin Bks) Viking Penguin.

Time-Out for Children: A Simple Solution to Discipline Problems. Barbara A. Hill. 128p. 1996. mass mkt. 4.95 (*0-89529-772-8*) Avery Pub.

Time Out for Coffee. Jeanette Lockerbie. (Quiet Time Books for Women). 1978. pap. 4.99 (*0-8024-8759-9*) Moody.

Time Out for Ginger. Ronald Alexander. 1953. pap. 3.25 (*0-8222-1152-1*) Dramatists Play.

Time-Out for January: An Activity for Every Day. Becky Daniel. (Illus.). 48p. (J). (gr. 1-4). 1994. 6.99 (*0-86653-828-3*, GA1520) Good Apple.

Time Out for Love. Linda D. Miller. 150p. 1996. mass mkt. 5.00 (*0-9634431-5-1*) C Y Pub Grp.

Time Out for the Family-1989. Bill Maynard. 1989. pap. 6.25 (*0-89137-119-2*) Quality Pubns.

Time Out for Toddlers. James W. Varni & Carni. 1991. pap. 10.00 (*0-425-12943-8*, Berkley Trade) Berkley Pub.

Time out for War. Ed C. Cury. LC 87-43321. (Illus.). 272p. (Orig.). 1988. pap. 15.50 (*0-935834-59-1*) Rainbow Books.

Time-Out Leadership: Daily Reflections to Maximize Your Leadership Effectiveness. Donald Luce. LC 95-40762. 368p. 1995. 16.99 (*0-7852-7565-7*) Nelson.

Time Out London Guide. 1992. pap. 14.00 (*0-14-014863-9*, Penguin Bks) Viking Penguin.

Time Out London Guide. Time Out Magazine Staff. (Illus.). 356p. 1996. pap. 14.95 (*0-14-024873-0*) Viking Penguin.

*__Time Out London 5.__ Time Out Staff. 1997. pap. 14.95 (*0-14-026440-X*) Viking Penguin.

Time Out Los Angeles 1. Time Out Magazine Staff. (Time Out Ser.). 1997. pap. 14.95 (*0-14-025974-0*, Penguin Bks) Viking Penguin.

*__Time Out Madrid.__ 2nd ed. Time Out Magazine Staff. 1997. pap. 14.95 (*0-14-025717-9*) Viking Penguin.

Time Out New York. 4th ed. (Time Out Ser.). (Illus.). 346p. 1996. pap. 14.95 (*0-14-024872-2*, Pelican Bks) Viking Penguin.

Time Out New York Guide. 1992. pap. 14.00 (*0-14-017452-4*, Penguin Bks) Viking Penguin.

Time Out New York Guide. Compiled by Time Out Magazine Staff. (Illus.). 260p. 1990. pap. 12.95 (*0-14-012703-8*, Penguin Bks) Viking Penguin.

Time Out of Joint. Philip K. Dick. 263p. 1987. reprint ed. pap. 4.95 (*0-88184-352-0*) Carroll & Graf.

Time Out of Mind. Kelly Cherry. Ed. by Robert Bixby. 21p. 1993. pap. 6.00 (*1-882983-08-4*) March Street Pr.

Time out of Mind. Joan M. Grant. 1980. 23.95 (*0-405-11792-2*) Ayer.

Time out of Mind. Marc Robertson. 44p. 1972. 8.00 (*0-86690-220-1*, R1405-014) Am Fed Astrologers.

Time out of Mind: The Story of Simon McDonald. Hugh Anderson. 153p. 1989. 12.95 (*0-909470-16-2*) Legacy Books.

Time out of Mind: Trekking the Hindu Kush. Lynda W. Schmidt. LC 79-90967. (Illus.). viii, 158p. (Orig.). 1979. pap. 5.95 (*0-931474-11-6*) TBW Bks.

Time Out of Time: Essays on the Festival. Ed. by Alessandro Falassi. LC 86-30804. 321p. reprint ed. pap. 91.50 (*0-7837-5850-2*, 2045569) Bks Demand.

Time Out Paris Guide. 1992. pap. 14.00 (*0-14-014865-5*, Penguin Bks) Viking Penguin.

Time Out Paris Guide. Compiled by Time Out Magazine Staff. (Illus.). 260p. 1990. pap. 12.95 (*0-14-012701-1*, Penguin Bks) Viking Penguin.

Time Out Paris Guide. 3rd ed. Time Out Magazine Staff. (Time Out Ser.). (Illus.). 292p. 1994. pap. 13.95 (*0-14-023040-8*, Penguin Bks) Viking Penguin.

Time Out Paris Guide. 4th ed. Time Out Magazine Staff. (Illus.). 356p. 1996. pap. 14.95 (*0-14-024874-9*) Viking Penguin.

*__Time Out Paris 5.__ Time Out Staff. 1997. pap. 14.95 (*0-14-025975-9*) Viking Penguin.

*__Time Out Prague.__ 2nd ed. Time Out Magazine Staff. 1997. pap. 14.95 (*0-14-025716-0*) Viking Penguin.

Time-Out Prescription: A Parent's Guide to Positive & Loving Discipline. Donna G. Corwin. LC 96-13811. (Illus.). 144p. 1996. pap. 11.95 (*0-8092-3235-9*) Contemp Bks.

Time Out Rome. 2nd ed. (Time Out Ser.). (Illus.). 356p. 1996. pap. 14.95 (*0-14-024875-7*, Penguin Bks) Viking Penguin.

Time Out Rome Guide. 1994. 13.95 (*0-14-023317-2*, Penguin Bks) Viking Penguin.

Time Out San Francisco. (Time Out Ser.). (Illus.). 356p. 1996. pap. 14.95 (*0-14-025417-X*, Penguin Bks) Viking Penguin.

Time Out Sydney 1. Time Out Magazine Staff. (Time Out Ser.). 1997. pap. 14.95 (*0-14-025973-2*, Penguin Bks) Viking Penguin.

Time Out Together. Jan Brennan. 171p. (Orig.). 1990. pap. 14.95 (*0-87483-103-2*) August Hse.

Time-Out Trivia. annuals Becky Daniel. teacher ed. 49.99 (*1-56417-688-6*, GA1581) Good Apple.

Time-Out Trivia for April: An Activity for Every Day. Becky Daniel. (Illus.). 48p. (J). (gr. 1-4). 1994. 6.99 (*0-86653-787-2*, GA1481) Good Apple.

Time-Out Trivia for December: An Activity for Every Day. Becky Daniel. (Illus.). 48p. (J). (gr. 1-4). 1994. 6.99 (*0-86653-827-5*, GA1519) Good Apple.

Time-Out Trivia for February: An Activity for Every Day. Becky Daniel. (Illus.). 48p. (J). (gr. 1-4). 1994. 6.99 (*0-86653-829-1*, GA1521) Good Apple.

Time-Out Trivia for June/Summer. Becky Daniel. 48p. 1996. teacher ed. 6.99 (*1-56417-724-6*, GA1543) Good Apple.

Time-Out Trivia for May: An Activity for Every Day. Becky Daniel. (Illus.). 48p. (J). (gr. 1-4). 1994. 6.99 (*0-86653-788-0*, GA1482) Good Apple.

Time-Out Trivia for November. Becky Daniel. 48p. 1996. teacher ed. 6.99 (*1-56417-723-8*, GA1542) Good Apple.

Time-Out Trivia for October. Becky Daniel. 48p. 1996. teacher ed. 6.99 (*1-56417-722-X*, GA1541) Good Apple.

Time-Out Trivia for September. Becky Daniel. 48p. 1996. teacher ed. 6.99 (*1-56417-721-1*, GA1540) Good Apple.

Time out with Jesus: 52 Devotions for Christian Teachers. Jacqueline L. Loontjer. LC 93-2986. 1993. pap. 8.99 (*0-570-04611-4*, 12-3196) Concordia.

Time Out...for Parents: A Compassionate Approach to Parenting. Cheri Huber & Melinda Guyol. (Illus.). 94p. (Orig.). 1994. pap. 12.00 (*0-9614754-4-7*) Zen Med Ctr.

Time Outs. Nancy Holt. LC 85-51128. (Artist's Bks.). (Illus.). 64p. (Orig.). 1985. pap. 10.00 (*0-89822-043-2*) Visual Studies.

Time Outworn. Val Mulkerns. 9.95 (*0-8159-6905-8*) Devin.

Time Passages. Randy Ball. (Illus.). 60p. (Orig.). 1992. pap. 5.00 (*0-9631936-1-9*) R Ball Photo.

Time Passages: Collective Memory & American Popular Culture. George Lipsitz. 323p. 1990. pap. text ed. 17.95 (*0-8166-1806-2*) U of Minn Pr.

Time Past. Marie Scheikevitch. Tr. by Francoise Delisle. LC 70-142691. (Essay Index Reprint Ser.). 1977. 23.95 (*0-8369-2073-2*) Ayer.

Time Past, Time Future: An Historical Study of Catholic Moral Theology. John A. Gallagher. LC 89-48607. 288p. 1990. pap. 12.95 (*0-8091-3142-0*) Paulist Pr.

Time Patrol. Poul Anderson. 464p. 1994. pap. 14.95 (*0-312-85636-9*) Tor Bks.

Time Payment. Kerry Tomlinson. LC 77-93227. 60p. 1978. 10.00 (*0-930012-05-4*); pap. 3.50 (*0-930012-04-6*) J Mudfoot.

Time Pieces. Paul Henry. 58p. (Orig.). 1991. pap. 14.95 (*1-85411-058-6*, Pub. by Seren Bks UK) Dufour.

*__Time Pieces.__ Rella Lossy. (Illus.). 160p. (Orig.). 1996. 24.95 (*1-57143-059-8*) RDR Bks.

*__Time Pieces: A Collection of Poetry, 1944-1996.__ Rella Lossy. (Illus.). 160p. (Orig.). 1996. pap. 16.95 (*1-57143-060-1*) RDR Bks.

An Asterisk (*) at the beginning of an entry indicates that the title is appearing in BIP for the first time.

*__Time Pieces: Reflections on the Jewish Year.__ Aaron Lopiansky. 295p. 1995. 18.95 (*1-56871-091-7*) Targum Pr.

Time Pieces: Word & Image. Wright Morris. (Writers & Artists on Photography Ser.). (Illus.). 126p. 1989. 35.00 (*0-89381-381-8*); pap. 14.95 (*0-89381-382-6*) Aperture.

Time Pioneers: Flexible Working Time & New Lifestyles. Karl H. Horning et al. Ed. by Sue Leigh. Tr. by Anthony Williams from GER. LC 95-36048. 220p. (C). 1995. 57.95 (*0-7456-1076-5*, Pub. by Polity Pr UK) Blackwell Pubs.

Time, Place, & Circumstance: Neo-Weberian Studies in Comparative Religious History. Ed. by William H. Swatos, Jr. LC 89-37501. (Contributions to the Study of Religion Ser.: No. 24). 232p. 1990. text ed. 59.95 (*0-313-26892-4*, STQ/, Greenwood Pr) Greenwood.

Time Plots: Plain & Simple. Joiner Assocs., Inc. Staff. Ed. by Sue Reynard. (Illus.). 156p. (Orig.). 1995. wbk. ed. 19.95 (*1-884731-05-8*) Joiner Assoc.

Time, Politics, & Policies: A Legislative Year. Burdett A. Loomis. LC 93-29050. (Studies in Government & Public Policy). 200p. 1994. 29.95 (*0-7006-0621-1*); pap. 12.95 (*0-7006-0622-X*) U Pr of KS.

Time Present, Time Past. Bill Bradley. 1996. 27.50 (*0-614-13228-2*) Knopf.

Time Present, Time Past: A Memoir. Bill Bradley. 400p. 1996. 26.00 (*0-679-44488-2*) Knopf.

*__Time Present, Time Past: A Memoir.__ Bill Bradley. 1997. pap. 13.00 (*0-679-76815-7*, Vin) Random.

Time Present, Time Past: A Memoir. large type ed. Bill Bradley. LC 96-14353. 757p. 1996. 25.95 (*0-7862-0726-4*, Thorndike Lrg Prnt) Thorndike Pr.

Time Pressure & Stress in Human Judgment & Decision Making. Ed. by Olga Svenson & A. J. Maule. (Illus.). 340p. (C). 1994. 59.50 (*0-306-44426-7*, Plenum Pr) Plenum.

Time Projection Chamber: AIP Conference Proceedings, TRIUMF, Vancover, 1983, No. 108. Ed. by J. A. Macdonald. LC 83-83445. 264p. 1984. lib. bdg. 39.00 (*0-88318-307-2*) Am Inst Physics.

Time Raid. Charles Upton. LC 68-26903. (Writing Ser.: No. 19). 40p. (Orig.). 1969. pap. 2.00 (*0-87704-009-5*) Four Seasons Foun.

Time Raider. R. L. Stine. 96p. (J). (gr. 4-6). 1995. pap. 2.99 (*0-590-48555-5*) Scholastic Inc.

Time Rambler. Kim Hansen. (American Romance Ser.). 1994. mass mkt. 3.50 (*0-373-16548-X*, 1-16548-9) Harlequin Bks.

Time Rations. Benjamin Friedlander. LC 90-63841. 60p. 1991. 7.50 (*1-882022-05-X*) O Bks.

Time Regained - Guide to Proust, Vol. 6. Marcel Proust. (In Search of Lost Time Ser.: No. 6). 770p. 1993. 18.50 (*0-679-42476-8*, Modern Lib) Random.

Time Release. John M. Bennett. 1978. pap. 4.00 (*0-935350-92-6*) Luna Bisonte.

*__Time Release.__ Martin J. Smith. 352p. 1997. mass mkt. 5.99 (*0-515-12028-6*) Jove Pubns.

Time Release. deluxe ed. John M. Bennett. 1978. pap. 5.00 (*0-935350-93-4*) Luna Bisonte.

Time, Religion & Social Experience in Rural Greece. Laurie K. Hart. 1991. pap. 24.50 (*0-8476-7752-4*) Rowman.

*__Time Remembered.__ Elizabeth Crane. 448p. 1997. mass mkt. 5.50 (*0-505-52223-3*, Love Spell) Dorchester Pub Co.

Time Remembered. Richard Walker. 136p. (C). 1987. 21.00 (*0-86383-310-1*, Pub. by Gomer Pr UK) St Mut.

Time Remembered. large type ed. Ralph L. Finn. 400p. 1996. 25.99 (*0-7089-3515-X*) Ulverscroft.

Time Remembered. large type ed. Lucy Gillen. (Romance Ser.). 304p. 1992. 25.99 (*0-7089-2676-2*) Ulverscroft.

Time Remembered: A Journal for Survivors. Earl A. Grollman. LC 86-47753. 98p. 1987. 18.00 (*0-8070-2704-9*) Beacon Pr.

Time Remembered After Pere Lachaise. Vyvyan B. Holland. LC 79-8064. reprint ed. 32.50 (*0-404-18375-1*) AMS Pr.

Time Research: 1172 Studies. Joseph W. Sprug. LC 74-14970. 253p. 1974. 25.00 (*0-8108-0768-8*) Scarecrow.

*__Time-Resolved Diffraction.__ John R. Helliwell & P. M. Rentzepis. (Illus.). 456p. 1997. 140.00 (*0-19-850032-7*) OUP.

Time-Resolved Laser Raman Spectroscopy. Ed. by David Phillips & George H. Atkinson. 180p. 1987. text ed. 150.00 (*3-7186-0343-8*) Gordon & Breach.

Time-Resolved Laser Spectroscopy in Biochemistry III. Ed. by Joseph R. Lakowicz. 1992. 20.00 (*0-8194-0786-0*, 1640) SPIE.

Time-Resolved Macromolecular Crystallography: Proceedings of a Royal Society Discussion Meeting, Held on 29 & 30 January 1992. Ed. by John R. Helliwell & L. N. Johnson. LC 92-26790. 186p. 1993. 65.00 (*0-19-855781-7*) OUP.

Time Resolved Spectroscopy, Vol. 18. Ed. by R. J. Clark & R. E. Hester. LC 89-5310. 406p. 1989. text ed. 554.00 (*0-471-92293-5*) Wiley.

Time-Resolved Vibrational Spectroscopy: Proceedings of the JSPS-NSF Symposium Held in Honolulu, Hawaii, November 18-22, 1985. Ed. by George H. Atkinson. 432p. 1987. text ed. 164.00 (*2-88124-191-3*) Gordon & Breach.

Time Resolved Vibrational Spectroscopy V: Proceedings of the 5th International Conference on Time-Resolved Vibrational Spectroscopy, Tokyo, Japan, June 3-7, 1991. Ed. by H. Takahashi. LC 92-20872. (Proceedings in Physics Ser.: Vol. 68). (Illus.). 348p. 1992. 86.95 (*0-387-55473-4*) Spr-Verlag.

Time-Resolved Vibrational Spectroscopy VI: Proceedings of the Sixth International Conference on Time-Resolved Vibrational Spectroscopy, Berlin, Germany, May 23-28, 1993. Ed. by A. Lau et al. LC 93-40610. (Proceedings in Physics Ser.: Vol. 74). 1994. 86.95 (*0-387-57573-1*) Spr-Verlag.

Time Returned: A Pictorial History of Obion County, Tennessee. Bill Threlkeld & Charlene Threlkeld. LC 94-16397. 1994. write for info. (*0-89865-898-5*) Donning Co.

Time Returns. Alexandra Ripley. 400p. 1996. mass mkt. 6.50 (*0-446-60258-2*) Warner Bks.

Time Reversal: An Autobiography. Anatole Abragam. (Illus.). 384p. 1989. 55.00 (*0-19-853926-6*) OUP.

Time Reversal: The Arthur Rich Memorial Symposium Proceedings of the Conference Held in Ann Arbor, October 1991. Ed. by M. Skalsey et al. (AIP Conference Proceedings Ser.: No. 270). (Illus.). 224p. 1993. pap. text ed. 95.00 (*1-56396-105-9*, AIP) Am Inst Physics.

Time Reversal Invariance & Parity Violation in Neutron Reactions: Proceedings of the International Conference. A. R. Gould et al. 250p. 1994. text ed. 95.00 (*981-02-1575-4*) World Scientific Pub.

Time Rides the River. Bob Mills. Ed. by Carol Spelius & Wayne Spelius. 75p. 1993. pap. 7.95 (*0-941363-27-9*) Lake Shore Pub.

Time, Roles & Self in Old Age. Ed. by Jaber F. Gubrium. LC 74-12131. 363p. 1976. 45.95 (*0-87705-230-1*); pap. 24.95 (*0-87705-350-2*) Human Sci Pr.

Time-Sampling Studies of Child Behavior see Differential Forecasts of Achievement & Their Use in Educational Counseling

Time-Saver Details for Exterior Wall Designs. Fred Nashed. LC 95-34805. 1996. text ed. 55.00 (*0-07-046082-5*) McGraw.

Time-Saver Details for Retail Planning & Design. Vilma Baarr & Charles E. Broudy. 1995. text ed. 45.50 (*0-07-004386-8*) McGraw.

Time-Saver Details for Roof Design. Steve Hardy. LC 97-15253. (Illus.). 400p. 1997. text ed. 49.50 (*0-07-026368-X*) McGraw.

Time-Saver Standards for Architectural Design Data. 6th ed. John H. Callender. 1982. text ed. 150.00 (*0-07-009663-5*) McGraw.

*__Time-Saver Standards for Architectural Design Data.__ 7th rev. ed. John H. Callender et al. (Illus.). 1024p. 1997. text ed. 150.00 (*0-07-068506-1*) McGraw.

Time-Saver Standards for Building Types. 3rd ed. Joseph De Chiara. 1440p. 1990. text ed. 119.50 (*0-07-016279-4*) McGraw.

Time-Saver Standards for Housing & Residential Development. 2nd ed. Ed. by Joseph De Chiara et al. LC 94-5366. 1994. text ed. 119.50 (*0-07-016301-4*) McGraw.

Time-Saver Standards for Interior Design & Space PLanning. J. De Chiara. 1104p. 1991. text ed. 109.50 (*0-07-016299-9*) McGraw.

Time-Saver Standards for Landscape Architecture. Cyril M. Harris. 896p. 1988. text ed. 119.50 (*0-07-026725-1*) McGraw.

*__Time-Saver Standards for Landscape Architecture.__ 2nd rev. ed. Nicholas T. Dines & Charles W. Harris. (Illus.). 960p. 1997. text ed. 125.00 (*0-07-017027-4*) McGraw.

Time-Saving Gourmet Cookbook. Janis Wicks. 189p. 1990. pap. 6.95 (*1-55867-011-4*, Nitty Gritty Ckbks) Bristol Pub Ent CA.

Time-Saving Sermon Outlines. Russell E. Spray. (Sermon Outline Ser.). 48p. (Orig.). 1981. pap. 4.99 (*0-8010-8193-9*) Baker Bks.

Time-Saving Techniques for Architectural Construction Drawings. Fred Nashed. LC 92-18922. 1993. text ed. 52.95 (*0-442-00951-8*) Van Nos Reinhold.

Time Saving Tips for Teachers. Barbara Gruber. (Instant Idea Bks.). (Illus.). 64p. 1983. 7.95 (*0-86734-047-9*, FS-8301) Schaffer Pubns.

*__Time-Saving Tips for Teachers.__ Joanne C. Strohmer & Clare Carhart. LC 96-51289. (Illus.). 112p. 1997. 49.95 (*0-8039-6614-8*); pap. 21.95 (*0-8039-6607-5*) Corwin Pr.

*__Time-Saving Tools.__ Sally Bell. Ed. by Jane Sovndal. (Thinking Skills Library). (Illus.). 108p. (Orig.). (J). (gr. 2-5). 1997. teacher ed., pap. 9.95 (*1-56784-708-0*) Newbridge Comms.

*__Time-Saving Training for Multisport Athletes: How to Fit Workouts into Workdays.__ Richard Niles. LC 96-31260. (Illus.). 192p. (Orig.). 1996. pap. 16.95 (*0-88011-538-6*, PNIL0538) Human Kinetics.

Time Scales of Biological Responses to Water Contraints: The Case of Mediterranean Biota. J. Roy et al. 242p. 1995. 85.00 (*90-5103-107-6*, Pub. by SPB Acad Pub NE) Balogh.

Time, Science & Society in China & the West: The Study of Time V. Ed. by J. T. Fraser et al. LC 79-640956. (Illus.). 288p. 1986. lib. bdg. 35.00 (*0-87023-495-1*) U of Mass Pr.

Time Scout. Robert L. Asprin & Linda Evans. 1995. mass mkt. 5.99 (*0-671-87698-8*) Baen Bks.

Time, Self & Social Being: Temporality Within a Sociological Context. Patrick Baert. (Avebury Series in Philosophy). 172p. 1992. 63.95 (*1-85628-286-4*, Pub. by Avebury Pub UK) Ashgate Pub Co.

Time Series, 2 vols. Ed. by Andrew Harvey. (International Library of Critical Writings in Economics Ser.: Vol. 5). 928p. 1994. 285.00 (*1-85278-662-0*) E Elgar.

*__Time Series.__ 3rd ed. write for info. (*0-340-59327-X*, Pub. by E Arnold UK) Routledge Chapman & Hall.

Time-Series. 3rd ed. Maurice Kendall & J. Keith Ord. (Charles Griffin Book). 312p. 1990. 70.00 (*0-19-520706-8*) OUP.

Time Series: A Biostatistical Introduction. Peter J. Diggle. (Oxford Statistical Science Ser.: No. 5). (Illus.). 272p. 1990. pap. 45.00 (*0-19-852226-6*) OUP.

Time Series: Data Analysis & Theory. David R. Brillinger. Ed. by Richard Wallis. 540p. (C). 1981. text ed. write for info. (*0-07-007852-1*) Gregg-McGraw.

Time Series: Theory & Methods. P. J. Brockwell & R. A. Davis. (Series in Statistics). (Illus.). 520p. 1986. 49.00 (*0-387-96406-1*) Spr-Verlag.

Time Series: Theory & Methods. 2nd ed. P. J. Brockwell & R. A. Davis. 1989. disk 24.00 (*0-387-14204-5*) Spr-Verlag.

Time Series: Theory & Methods. 2nd ed. P. J. Brockwell & R. A. Davis. (Series in Statistics). xvi, 577p. 1993. write for info. (*3-540-97429-6*) Spr-Verlag.

Time Series: Theory & Methods. 2nd ed. P. J. Brockwell et al. Ed. by J. O. Berger et al. (Series in Statistics). (Illus.). 544p. 1996. 54.95 (*0-387-97429-6*) Spr-Verlag.

Time Series Analysis. James Hamilton. 600p. 1994. text ed. 59.50 (*0-691-04289-6*) Princeton U Pr.

Time Series Analysis: A Comprehensive Introduction for Social Scientists. John M. Gottman. LC 80-25644. (Illus.). 368p. 1982. text ed. 57.95 (*0-521-23597-9*) Cambridge U Pr.

Time Series Analysis: Forecasting & Control. 3rd ed. George E. Box et al. LC 93-34620. 1994. text ed. 71.00 (*0-13-060774-6*) P-H.

Time Series Analysis: Nonstationary & Noninvertible Distribution Theory. Katsuto Tanaka. LC 95-46270. (Series in Probability & Statistics). 1996. text ed. 89.95 (*0-471-14191-7*) Wiley.

Time Series Analysis: Proceedings of the International Conference, Held in Houston, Texas, August, 1980. Ed. by O. D. Anderson & M. R. Perryman. 1981. 128.25 (*0-444-86177-7*) Elsevier.

Time Series Analysis: Regression Techniques. 2nd ed. Charles W. Ostrom, Jr. (Quantitative Applications in the Social Sciences Ser.: Vol. 9). (Illus.). 96p. (C). 1990. pap. 9.95 (*0-8039-3135-2*) Sage.

Time Series Analysis: Theory & Practice, No. 2. O. D. Anderson. 1983. 92.50 (*0-444-86536-5*) Elsevier.

Time Series Analysis: Theory & Practice, No. 4. Ed. by O. D. Anderson. 352p. 1983. 97.50 (*0-444-86731-7*, I-253-83) Elsevier.

Time Series Analysis: Univariate & Multivariate Methods. William Wei & David P. Reilly. (Illus.). 478p. (C). 1990. text ed. 60.25 (*0-201-15911-2*, Adv Bk Prog) Addison-Wesley.

Time Series Analysis & Applications. Robinson. 621p. 1988. text ed. 59.00 (*0-13-921677-4*) P-H.

Time Series Analysis & Macroeconometric Modelling: The Collected Papers of Kenneth F. Wallis. Kenneth F. Wallis. LC 95-13217. (Economists of the Twentieth Century Ser.). 456p. 1995. 85.00 (*1-85278-821-6*) E Elgar.

Time Series Analysis by Higher Order Crossings. Intro. by Benjamin Kedem. (Illus.). 336p. (C). 1994. text ed. 79.95 (*0-87942-299-8*, PC02949) Inst Electrical.

Time Series Analysis, Forecasting & Control. rev. ed. George E. Box & Gwilym Jenkins. LC 76-8713. 500p. 1976. text ed. 59.95 (*0-8162-1104-3*) Holden-Day.

Time Series Analysis, Identification & Adaptive Filtering. 2nd ed. Daniel Graupe. LC 88-14048. 438p. (C). 1989. lib. bdg. 57.50 (*0-89464-315-0*) Krieger.

Time Series Analysis in Water Resources. Ed. by Keith W. Hipel. (AWRA Monograph Ser.: No. 4). 231p. reprint ed. pap. 65.90 (*0-8357-7928-9*, 2036354); reprint ed. pap. 62.40 (*0-8357-3174-X*, 2039437) Bks Demand.

Time Series Analysis Theory & Practice, No. 3. Ed. by O. D. Anderson. 302p. 1983. 97.50 (*0-444-86625-6*, I-117-83, North Holland) Elsevier.

Time Series Analysis, Theory & Practice: Proceedings of the Conference, Nottingham, March 1983, Vol. 5. Ed. by O. D. Anderson. 1984. 97.50 (*0-444-87568-9*, I-438-84, North Holland) Elsevier.

Time Series & Dynamic Models. Christian Gourieroux & Alain Monfort. (Themes in Modern Econometrics Ser.). (Illus.). 500p. (C). 1996. text ed. 74.95 (*0-521-41146-7*) Cambridge U Pr.

Time Series & Dynamic Models. Christian Gourieroux & Alain Monfort. (Themes in Modern Econometrics Ser.). (Illus.). 500p. (C). 1997. pap. text ed. 29.95 (*0-521-42308-2*) Cambridge U Pr.

Time Series & Linear Systems. Ed. by S. Bittanti. (Lecture Notes in Control & Information Sciences Ser.: Vol. 86). xvii, 243p. 1986. 40.95 (*0-387-16903-2*) Spr-Verlag.

Time Series & System Analysis with Applications. S. M. Wu. 606p. 1993. 79.50 (*0-89464-844-6*) Krieger.

Time-Series-Based Econometrics: Unit Roots & Co-Integrations. Michio Hatanaka. (Advanced Texts in Econometrics Ser.). (Illus.). 312p. 1996. 72.00 (*0-19-877352-8*); pap. 29.95 (*0-19-877353-6*) OUP.

*__Time Series Forcasting.__ Christopher Chatfield. (Illus.). 256p. 1997. text ed. 49.95 (*0-412-57600-7*, Chap & Hall NY) Chapman & Hall.

Time Series in Psychology. Robert A. Gregson. 456p. (C). 1983. text ed. 89.95 (*0-89859-250-X*) L Erlbaum Assocs.

Time Series in the Time Domain. Ed. by E. J. Hannan et al. (Handbook of Statistics Ser.: Vol. 5). 490p. 1985. 170.00 (*0-444-87629-4*, North Holland) Elsevier.

Time Series Modelling of Water Resources & Environmental Systems. Keith W. Hipel & A. I. McLeod. (Developments in Water Science Ser.: Vol. 45). 1013p. 1994. 264.25 (*0-444-89270-2*) Elsevier.

Time Series Models. 2nd ed. Andrew Harvey. (Illus.). 310p. 1993. 44.00 (*0-262-08224-1*) MIT Pr.

*__Time Series Models, Causality & Exogeneity.__ Ed. by Omar F. Hamouda & J. C. Rowley. (Foundations of Probability, Econometrics & Economic Games Ser.: Vol. 8). 544p. 1997. 170.00 (*1-85898-440-8*) E Elgar.

Time Series Models in Econometrics, Finance & Other Fields. D. Cox et al. 256p. (gr. 13). 1996. text ed. 54.95 (*0-412-72930-X*) Chapman & Hall.

Time Series Prediction: Forecasting the Future & Understanding the Past. Andreas S. Weigend & Neil A. Gershenfeld. (Santa Fe Institute Ser.). (C). 1993. pap. 32.95 (*0-201-62602-0*) Addison-Wesley.

Time Series Techniques for Economists. Terence C. Mills. 381p. (C). 1991. pap. text ed. 22.95 (*0-521-40574-2*) Cambridge U Pr.

Time Shall Reap. large type ed. Doris Davidson. (Magna Large Print Ser.). 1994. 25.99 (*0-7505-0654-7*, Pub. by Magna Print Bks UK) Ulverscroft.

Time-Share Condominiums: To Buy or Not to Buy. Michael Strauss. 1994. 14.95 (*0-533-11038-6*) Vantage.

Time Sharing: A New Way of Life. Larry J. Tracy. LC 76-50231. 1977. 4.95 (*0-933984-01-4*) Tracy Pub.

Time Sharing: Computer Programs & Applications in Accounting. Elbert B. Greynolds, Jr. (Research Monograph: No. 57). 291p. 1974. spiral bd. 30.00 (*0-88406-021-7*) GA St U Busn Pr.

Time Shifting: Creating More Time to Enjoy Your Life. Stephan Rechtschaffen. LC 95-48148. 224p. 1996. 22.95 (*0-385-47849-6*) Doubleday.

Time Shot & Other Stories. Judith Green. 128p. (C). 1993. pap. text ed. 5.00 (*0-13-600090-8*) P-H.

Time Song. Rozanne L. Williams. (Emergent Reader Bks.). (Illus.). 16p. (Orig.). (J). (gr. k-2). 1995. pap. 2.49 (*1-57471-004-4*) Creat Teach Pr.

Time Song. Rozanne L. Williams. (Emergent Reader Big Bks.). (Illus.). 16p. (Orig.). (J). (gr. k-2). 1996. pap. 11.98 (*1-57471-114-8*) Creat Teach Pr.

Time, Space, & Atoms. Richard T. Cox. LC 33-6773. 170p. reprint ed. pap. 48.50 (*0-317-29503-9*, 2055962) Bks Demand.

Time, Space & Knowledge: A New Vision of Reality. Tarthang Tulku. LC 77-19224. (Illus.). 357p. 1977. pap. 15.95 (*0-913546-08-9*) Dharma Pub.

Time, Space, & Man. Alfred A. Maske. 1995. 14.95 (*0-533-11438-1*) Vantage.

Time, Space & Philosophy. Christopher Ray. (Philosophical Issues in Science Ser.). (Illus.). 288p. (C). 1991. pap. 18.95 (*0-415-03222-9*, A5754); text ed. 69.95 (*0-415-03221-0*, A5750) Routledge.

Time, Space, & Society: Geographical Societal Perspectives. Aharon Kellerman. (C). 1989. lib. bdg. 92.00 (*0-7923-0123-4*) Kluwer Ac.

Time, Space & Things. 3rd ed. B. K. Ridley. (Canto Book Ser.). (Illus.). 200p. (C). 1995. pap. text ed. 9.95 (*0-521-48486-3*) Cambridge U Pr.

Time, Space & Transition in Anasazi Prehistory. Michael S. Berry. LC 82-11102. (Illus.). 159p. reprint ed. pap. 45.40 (*0-8357-4374-8*, 2037203) Bks Demand.

Time-Space Transcendence. Paul Philips. LC 84-71711. 72p. (Orig.). 1984. pap. 8.95 (*0-930149-00-9*) AAP Calif.

Time-Span Quilts: New Quilts from Old Tops. Becky Herdle. 1995. pap. 16.95 (*0-89145-845-X*) Collector Bks.

*__Time-Spun Treasure.__ Thomasina Ring. 368p. 1997. mass mkt. 5.50 (*0-505-52214-4*, Love Spell) Dorchester Pub Co.

Time Station: London. David Evans. 1996. mass mkt. 5.99 (*0-441-00364-8*) Ace Bks.

*__Time Station No. 2: Paris.__ David Evans. (Time Station Ser.). 272p. 1997. mass mkt. 5.99 (*0-441-00441-5*) Ace Bks.

*__Time Station No. 3: Berlin.__ David Evans. 272p. 1997. mass mkt. 5.99 (*0-441-00473-3*) Ace Bks.

Time Steals Softly. rev. ed. Virginia J. Harper. (Illus.). 224p. 1992. 16.95 (*0-8059-3257-7*) Dorrance.

Time Storm. Gordon R. Dickson. 432p. 1992. mass mkt. 4.99 (*0-671-72148-8*) Baen Bks.

Time Strategies. LC 93-47488. (Teacher to Teacher Ser.). 1994. pap. 12.95 (*0-8106-2902-X*) NEA.

*__Time Stress.__ David C. Rainham. (Illus.). 16p. (Orig.). 1997. pap. 3.00 (*1-884241-67-0*, EHO540) Energeia Pub.

Time Structures: Formal Description & Algorithmic Representation. Elzbieta Hajnicz. LC 96-10637. (Lecture Notes in Artificial Intelligence: No. 1047). ix, 244p. 1996. pap. 49.00 (*3-540-60941-5*) Spr-Verlag.

Time Tabler 3. Keith Johnson. (C). 1989. 80.00 (*0-7487-1077-9*) St Mut.

Time Tactics of Very Successful People. B. Eugene Griessman. 1994. pap. text ed. 14.95 (*0-07-024644-0*) McGraw.

Time-Temperature Indicators. Ed. by Peter Allen. 200p. 1988. 1,750.00 (*0-941285-17-0*) FIND-SVP.

*__Time, Temporality, Now: Experiencing Time & Concepts of Time in an Interdisciplinary Perspective.__ Harald Atmanspacher & Eva Ruhnau. LC 97-7812. 1997. write for info. (*3-540-62486-4*) Spr-Verlag.

*__Time, Tense, & Causation.__ Michael Tooley. 416p. 1997. 45.00 (*0-19-823579-8*) OUP.

Time, the Familiar Stranger. J. T. Fraser. LC 87-10865. (Illus.). 408p. (C). 1987. 40.00 (*0-87023-576-1*) U of Mass Pr.

Time, the Hour, the Solitariness of the Place. Louis Phillips. LC 85-62684. 88p. (Orig.). 1985. 13.95 (*0-930501-05-5*); pap. 8.95 (*0-930501-02-0*) Swallows Tale Pr.

Time, the Physical Magnitude. Olivier Costa de Beauregard. 344p. (C). 1987. lib. bdg. 146.00 (*90-277-2444-X*, D Reidel) Kluwer Ac.

Time, the Refreshing River. Joseph Needham. 280p. 1986. reprint ed. 57.50 (*0-85124-429-7*, Pub. by Spokesman Bks UK); reprint ed. pap. 26.50 (*0-85124-439-4*, Pub. by Spokesman Bks UK) Coronet Bks.

Time There Was: Memories of Rural Life in Sussex. Phoebe Somers. LC 93-26282. 1993. 14.00 (*0-7509-0385-6*, Pub. by Sutton Pubng UK) Bks Intl VA.

Time Ticks On. Helen B. Cook. (Illus.). 144p. (Orig.). 1990. pap. 19.95 (*0-940151-17-0*) Statesman-Exam.

T

***Time, Tide, & Tempest: A Study of Shakespeare's Romances.** Douglas L. Peterson. LC 72-94155. 275p. 1973. reprint ed. pap. 78.40 (*0-608-03175-5*, 2063628) Bks Demand.

Time To... Illus. by Tony Tallarico. (Tiny Bks.). 28p. (J). (ps-1). 1984. bds. 2.95 (*0-448-48823-X*, Tuffy) Putnam Pub Group.

Time to Act. Archibald MacLeish. LC 71-117820. (Essay Index Reprint Ser.). 1977. 20.95 (*0-8369-1713-8*) Ayer.

Time to Act: The Report of the Commission on Jewish Education in North America. Commission on Jewish Education in North America Staff. 97p. (Orig.). (C). 1991. pap. text ed. 16.00 (*0-8191-8104-8*); lib. bdg. 39.00 (*0-8191-8105-6*) U Pr of Amer.

Time to Be. Shirley Ho. LC 93-43930. (J). 12.95 (*1-879965-10-0*) Polychrome Pub.

Time to Be a Friend. Karen E. Lansing. LC 92-13010. 96p. (J). (gr. 4-8). 1993. pap. 5.99 (*0-8361-3614-4*) Herald Pr.

Time To Be A Teen Series, 3 vols., Set. Mary Bowman-Kruhm & Claudine G. Wirths. (Illus.). 64p. (J). (gr. 5-8). 1994. lib. bdg. 44.94 (*0-8050-3458-7*) TFC Bks NY.

Time to Be Bold. Michael W. Smith. 176p. 1997. pap. 10.99 (*0-8499-3336-6*) Word Pub.

Time to Be Born. Gilbert Morris. LC 93-26089. (American Odyssey Ser.: Bk. 1). 320p. (Orig.). (YA). (gr. 10). 1994. pap. 10.99 (*0-8007-5497-2*) Revell.

Time to Be Born. Dawn Powell. 334p. 1996. pap. 14.00 (*1-883642-41-8*) Steerforth Pr.

Time to Be Born. Bonnie Shullenberger. 120p. 1996. pap. 9.95 (*1-56101-131-2*) Cowley Pubns.

Time to Be Born. Dawn Powell. LC 83-45842. reprint ed. 30.00 (*0-404-20206-3*, PS3531) AMS Pr.

***Time to Be Born: Jewish Birth Customs & Traditions.** Michele Klein. LC 97-2518. (Illus.). 316p. 1997. 34.95 (*0-8276-0608-7*) JPS Phila.

Time to Be Born - A Time to Die: A Study of the Age of Accountability. Kent A. Field. 1984. pap. text ed. 5.50 (*0-9623100-1-8*) KAF Minsts.

Time to Be Born, a Time to Die. teacher ed. 2.00 (*0-686-99692-5*); pap. 3.50 (*0-686-96060-2*) USCJE.

Time to Be Born, a Time to Die. Rasa Gustaitis & Ernle W. Young. LC 85-26804. 1986p. 1986. 18.22 (*0-201-11555-7*) Addison-Wesley.

Time to be Born & a Time to Die: The Ethics of Choice. Ed. by Barry S. Kogan. 277p. 1991. pap. text ed. 26.95 (*0-202-30389-6*); lib. bdg. 49.95 (*0-202-30388-8*) Aldine de Gruyter.

Time to Be Free: Three Hundred Sixty-Five Meditations for Enhancing Your Self-Esteem. 432p. 1991. pap. 9.95 (*0-553-35203-2*) Bantam.

Time to Be Holy: Reflecting on Daily Life. Sivananda Radha. LC 96-14329. (Illus.). 320p. 1996. 29.95 (*0-931454-84-0*); pap. 19.95 (*0-931454-81-6*) Timeless Bks.

Time to Be Old a Time to Flourish: The Special Needs of the Elderly-at-Risk. 136p. 1988. pap. 6.00 (*0-87125-151-5*, 235) Cath Health.

Time to Be Re-Born: A Biblical Journey Through Lent. William F. Maestri. LC 82-24336. 157p. (Orig.). 1983. pap. 5.95 (*0-8189-0447-X*) Alba.

Time to Be Silent: What "Taking Time to Be Still" Will Do for You. Anne Sandberg. LC 94-70899. (Orig.). 1994. pap. 7.95 (*0-9624398-9-4*) Abel II Pub.

Time to Be Young. Martin Yoseloff. 4.50 (*0-8453-6445-6*, Cornwall Bks) Assoc Univ Prs.

Time to Begin. rev. ed. Frances Clark & Louise Goss. 72p. 1993. reprint ed. pap. text ed. 7.95 (*0-87487-685-0*) Summy-Birchard.

Time to Begin: Teacher's Handbook. Frances Clark & Louise Goss. 25p. 1993. reprint ed. pap. text ed. 3.95 (*0-87487-954-X*) Summy-Birchard.

Time-to-Build. 1995. 59.00 (*3-540-58809-4*) Spr-Verlag.

***Time to Build.** Gilbert Morris. (American Odyssey). 320p. Date not set. pap. 10.99 (*0-8007-5645-2*) Revell.

Time-to-Build: Interrelated Investments & Labour Demand Modelling with Applications to Six OECD Countries. Marga Peeters. LC 94-43958. (Lecture Notes in Economics & Mathematical Systems Ser.: Vol. 420). 1995. write for info. (*0-387-58809-4*) Spr-Verlag.

Time to Build Joseph Breuer, 2. 1982. 8.95 (*0-87306-734-7*) Feldheim.

Time to Care. Future Studies, Secretariat, Stockholm, Sweden. LC 83-8331. (Illus.). 296p. 1984. text ed. 95.75 (*0-08-028929-0*, Pergamon Pr) Elsevier.

Time to Care. large type ed. E. A. Webster. (Linford Romance Library). 1990. pap. 15.99 (*0-7089-6832-5*) Ulverscroft.

Time to Celebrate: Holiday & Seasonal Messages. Maralene Wesner & Miles Wesner. LC 88-51864. 75p. 1988. pap. 4.95 (*0-936715-10-3*) Diversity Okla.

Time to Chant: The Soka Gakkai Buddhists in Britain. Bryan R. Wilson & Karel Dobbelaere. LC 93-24507. (Illus.). 280p. (C). 1994. 60.00 (*0-19-827915-9*, Clarendon Pr) OUP.

***Time to Chant: The Soka Gakkai Buddhists in Britain.** Bryan Wilson & Karel Dobbelaere. (Illus.). 280p. 1997. reprint ed. pap. 19.95 (*0-19-829314-3*) OUP.

***Time to Check Out.** Michaels. LC 97-8807. 1997. pap. 11.95 (*0-312-15673-1*) St Martin.

Time to Check Out: A Stan Kraychik Mystery. Grant Michaels. LC 96-6870. 272p. 1996. 21.95 (*0-312-14434-2*) St Martin.

Time to Cherish. Robin J. Gunn. (Christy Miller Ser.: Vol. 10). 150p. 1994. pap. 5.99 (*1-56179-219-5*) Focus Family.

Time to Choose. Martha Attema. 176p. (Orig.). (YA). 1995. pap. 6.95 (*1-55143-045-2*) Orca Bk Pubs.

Time to Choose: America at the Crossroads of School Choice Policy. Amy S. Wells. LC 93-15080. 1993. 12.00 (*0-8090-1563-3*) Hill & Wang.

Time to Choose Life: Women, Abortion & Human Rights. Ed. by Ian Gentles. 256p. 1990. pap. 16.95 (*0-7737-5366-4*) Genl Dist Srvs.

Time to Consider. Mildred Cousens. 1990. 12.95 (*0-87233-099-0*) Bauhan.

Time to Dance: A Novel. Walter Sullivan. LC 94-37394. 195p. 1995. 22.95 (*0-8071-1985-7*) La State U Pr.

Time to Dance: An Invitation. Barbara Knoll. 111p. (Orig.). 1991. pap. 7.99 (*1-56043-703-0*) Destiny Image.

Time to Decide, a Time to Heal. 4th ed. Molly A. Minnick. LC 90-91478. 118p. 1994. 6.95 (*1-878526-39-1*) Pineapple MI.

Time to Depart. Lindsey Davis. 416p. 1997. 23.00 (*0-89296-626-2*) Warner Bks.

***Time to Depart.** Lindsey Davis. 432p. 1998. pap. 6.50 (*0-446-40528-0*, Mysterious Paperbk) Warner Bks.

***Time to Depart.** large type ed. Lindsey Davis. LC 96-49065. 674p. 1997. 24.95 (*0-7862-0962-3*, Thorndike Lrg Prnt) Thorndike Pr.

Time to Destroy-To Discover. Lawrence Fixel. 1972. 4.00 (*0-915572-09-5*) Panjandrum.

Time to Destroy-To Discover. deluxe limited ed. Lawrence Fixel. 1972. 10.00 (*0-915572-58-3*) Panjandrum.

Time to Die. Gilbert Morris. LC 93-36519. (American Odyssey Ser.: No. 2). 296p. (Orig.). (YA). (gr. 10). 1994. pap. 10.99 (*0-8007-5521-9*) Revell.

Time to Die. Wilbur Smith. 480p. 1991. mass mkt. 6.99 (*0-449-14761-4*, GM) Fawcett.

Time to Die. Wilbur Smith. 1990. 19.95 (*0-394-58475-9*) Random.

Time to Die. large type ed. Wilbur Smith. 1990. 27.99 (*0-7089-8537-8*, Trail West Pubs) Ulverscroft.

Time to Die: The Attica Prison Revolt. Tom Wicker. LC 93-44409. (Illus.). xiii, 362p. 1994. reprint ed. pap. 12.95 (*0-8032-9756-4*, Bison Books) U of Nebr Pr.

Time to Dream. Ruth Glover. 192p. 1995. per., pap. 9.99 (*0-8341-1572-7*) Beacon Hill.

Time to Dream. Penny Jordan. (Presents Ser.). 1993. pap. 2.89 (*0-373-11529-6*, 1-11529-4) Harlequin Bks.

Time to Dream. large type ed. Penny Jordan. 285p. 1992. reprint ed. lib. bdg. 18.95 (*0-263-12837-7*) Thorndike Pr.

***Time to Eat! A Shake-N-Move Book about Colors.** Dawn Bentley. (Shake-N-Move Ser.). (J). 1997. 5.99 (*0-689-81408-9*, Litl Simon S&S) S&S Childrens.

Time to Eat: Animals Who Hide & Save Their Food. Marilyn Baillie. (Amazing Things Animals Do Ser.). (Illus.). 32p. (J). (ps up). 1995. pap. 5.95 (*1-895688-30-2*, Pub. by Owl Bks CN); text ed. 14.95 (*1-895688-36-1*, Pub. by Owl Bks CN) Firefly Bks Ltd.

Time to Embrace. Linda Shands. (Seasons Remembered Ser.: Vol. 2). 232p. (Orig.). 1995. pap. 9.99 (*0-8308-1932-0*, 1932) InterVarsity.

Time to Fantasize. May K. Davenport. LC 80-69294. (Illus.). 130p. (Orig.). (gr. 5-12). 1980. pap. 3.50 (*0-9603118-7-4*) Davenport.

Time to Favor Zion: The Ecology of Religion & School Development on the Urban Frontier, Cincinnati, 1830-1870. F. Michael Perko. (Illus.). 276p. (Orig.). 1987. pap. 11.95 (*0-934328-05-6*) Educ Studies Pr.

***Time to Favor Zion Has Come.** Richard Booker. 47p. (Orig.). 1996. pap. 5.95 (*0-9615302-5-1*) Sounds of Trumpet Inc.

Time to Fight, a Time to Serve. Gregory Boratgis. 88p. 1995. pap. 10.00 (*0-8059-3715-3*) Dorrance.

Time to Fight Back: True Stories of Wartime Resistance. Jane Pettit. LC 95-34381. 176p. (J). (gr. 5-9). 1996. 14.95 (*0-395-76504-8*) HM.

***Time to Fish & a Time to Dry Nets.** Alvin Johnston. (Illus.). 259p. (Orig.). 1996. 22.00 (*1-886895-03-1*); pap. 12.00 (*1-886895-04-X*) Poetry Harbor.

Time to Fly. Karen E. Lansing. LC 91-14393. 104p. (Orig.). (J). (gr. 4-8). 1991. pap. 5.99 (*0-8361-3560-1*) Herald Pr.

Time to Fly: From Fear to Freedom. Ellie Janow. 128p. (Orig.). 1990. pap. 24.95 incl. audio (*1-878563-01-7*) Sky Pkwy Pub.

Time to Forget. large type ed. Ann Redmayne. (Linford Romance Library). 1989. pap. 15.99 (*0-7089-6791-4*) Ulverscroft.

Time to Gather: Selected Poems. Catherine De Vinck. LC 67-28572. (Illus.). 72p. 1987. reprint ed. pap. 6.75 (*0-911726-02-0*, CODE ATG) Alleluia Pr.

Time to Gather Stones. Vladimir Soloukhin. Tr. & Intro. by Valerie Nollan. 276p. 1993. 29.95 (*0-8101-1127-6*) Northwestern U Pr.

Time to Get out of the Bath, Shirley. John Burningham. LC 76-58503. (Illus.). 32p. (J). (gr. k-2). 1978. 13.95 (*0-690-01378-7*, Crowell Jr Bks); lib. bdg. 13.89 (*0-690-01379-5*, Crowell Jr Bks) HarpC Child Bks.

Time to Get Serious: Daily Devotions to Keep You Close to God. Tony Evans. LC 95-37964. 352p. 1995. 15.99 (*0-89107-866-5*) Crossway Bks.

Time to Go. Stephen Dixon. LC 83-22624. 192p. 1984. 17.95 (*0-8018-3234-9*) Johns Hopkins.

Time to Go. Beverly Fiday & David J. Fiday. (Illus.). 32p. (J). (ps-3). 1990. 15.00 (*0-15-200608-7*, Gulliver Bks) HarBrace.

***Time to Go.** Marion D. Owens. 160p. (Orig.). 1995. pap. 4.95 (*1-56794-085-4*, C-2381) Star Bible.

Time to Go. large type ed. Renee Shann. 414p. 1981. 25.99 (*0-7089-0677-X*) Ulverscroft.

Time to Go: Three Plays on Death & Dying, with Commentary on End-of-Life Issues. Ed. by Anne H. Hawkins & James O. Ballard. 136p. (Orig.). 1995. pap. text ed. 14.95 (*0-8122-1519-2*) U of Pa Pr.

***Time to Go Home.** Ruth Huddleston. (Illus.). 24p. (J). (ps-k). 1997. 12.95 (*0-7613-0286-7*) Millbrook Pr.

Time to Go Home. G. M. Thompson. 1995. 3.00 (*0-87129-550-4*, T97) Dramatic Pub.

Time to Go Home: Turning the Hearts of the Fathers to Their Children. Paul H. Heidebrecht. 168p. 1991. pap. write for info. (*0-934688-63-X*) Great Comm Pubns.

Time to Go House. Walter D. Edmonds. (Illus.). 144p. (J). 1994. reprint ed. pap. 9.95 (*0-8156-0293-6*) Syracuse U Pr.

Time to Grieve: Help & Hope from the Bible. Carol Lynn. (Inspirational Library). 256p. 1995. pap. text ed. 4.97 (*1-55748-645-X*) Barbour & Co.

Time to Grieve: Loss a Universal Human Experience. Bertha G. Simos. LC 75-27964. 1979. pap. 19.95 (*0-87304-153-4*) Families Intl.

Time to Grieve: Meditations for Healing after the Death of a Loved One. Carol Staudacher. LC 93-33318. 240p. 1994. pap. 13.00 (*0-06-250845-8*) Harper SF.

Time to Grow. George MacDonald. (George McDonald Classic Devotionals Ser.). 128p. (Orig.). 1991. pap. 6.99 (*1-55661-202-8*) Bethany Hse.

Time to Grow: A Study Guide for the Televised Course. Glenda Riddick & Mary Weir. 1992. pap. text ed. write for info. (*0-07-052892-6*) McGraw.

Time to Harvest. George MacDonald. Ed. by Michael Phillips. (George MacDonald Classic Devotionals Ser.: Bk. 2). 128p. (Orig.). 1991. pap. 6.99 (*1-55661-207-9*) Bethany Hse.

Time to Harvest: The Farm Paintings of Franklin Halverson. Bob Barnard. LC 93-78987. 112p. 1993. 24.95 (*1-883953-04-9*) Midwest Trad.

Time to Heal. Marcia Kamien. Date not set. write for info. (*0-345-40225-1*) Ballantine.

Time to Heal. Marcia Kamien. Date not set. pap. write for info. (*0-345-40226-X*) Ballantine.

Time to Heal. Chana S. Rubin. 235p. (C). 1991. 15.95 (*1-56062-067-6*) CIS Comm.

***Time to Heal: John Perkins, Community Development & Racial Reconciliation.** Stephen E. Berk. LC 97-11672. 400p. (Orig.). 1997. pap. 17.99 (*0-8010-5756-6*) Baker Bks.

Time to Heal: The Road to Recovery for Adult Children of Alcoholics. Timmen L. Cermak. 240p. 1989. pap. 10.00 (*0-380-70722-5*) Avon.

Time to Hear, a Time to Help: Listening to People with Cancer. Daniel Rosenblum. 250p. 1993. text ed. 27.95 (*0-02-927105-3*, Free Press) Free Pr.

Time to Hear & Answer: Essays for the Bicentennial Season. Robert P. Warren et al. LC 75-31774. (Franklin Lectures in the Sciences & Humanities Ser.: No. 4). 232p. 1977. pap. 66.20 (*0-7837-8414-7*, 2059225) Bks Demand.

Time to Keep. Curtiss A. Matlock. 1994. 3.59 (*0-373-45166-0*) Harlequin Bks.

Time to Keep. Linda Shands. LC 94-28135. (Seasons Remembered Ser.: Vol. 1). 192p. (Orig.). 1994. pap. 8.99 (*0-8308-1931-2*, 1931) InterVarsity.

Time to Keep: The Tasha Tudor Book of Holidays. Tasha Tudor. (J). 1996. 18.00 (*0-689-81162-4*) S&S Childrens.

Time to Keep Silent. Gloria Whelan. 124p. (J). (gr. 5-7). 1993. pap. 6.00 (*0-8028-0118-8*) Eerdmans.

***Time to Kill.** Margaret Bingley. (Crime & Passion Ser.). (Orig.). 1997. mass mkt. 5.95 (*0-7535-0164-3*, Pub. by Virgin Pub UK) London Brdge.

Time to Kill. M. T. Dykes. LC 82-6811. 1989. pap. 12.95 (*0-87949-223-6*) Ashley Bks.

Time to Kill. John Grisham. 528p. 1992. mass mkt. 7.50 (*0-440-21172-7*) Dell.

Time to Kill. John Grisham. LC 93-32545. 496p. 1993. 23.50 (*0-385-47081-9*) Doubleday.

Time to Kill. John Grisham. LC 92-36474. 1993. write for info. (*0-8161-5590-9*) G K Hall.

Time to Kill. Douglas Skelton. (Illus.). 192p. 1996. pap. 17.95 (*1-85158-721-7*, Pub. by Mnstream UK) Trafalgar.

Time To Kill. large type ed. Roger Ormerod. (Linford Mystery Library). 320p. 1993. pap. 15.99 (*0-7089-7420-1*, Linford) Ulverscroft.

***Time to Know Them: A Longitudinal Study of Writing & Learning at the College Level.** Marilyn S. Sternglass. 224p. 1997. write for info. (*0-8058-2722-6*) L Erlbaum Assocs.

***Time to Know Them: A Longitudinal Study of Writing & Learning at the College Level.** Marilyn S. Sternglass. 224p. 1997. pap. write for info. (*0-8058-2723-4*) L Erlbaum Assocs.

Time to Laugh. Ed. by Christopher H. Cooke. (C). 1990. pap. text ed. 24.00 (*0-85305-308-1*, Pub. by J Arthur Ltd UK) St Mut.

Time to Laugh. Gilbert Morris. LC 95-14699. (American Odyssey Ser.: Bk. 3). 304p. (Orig.). (YA). (gr. 10). 1995. pap. 9.99 (*0-8007-5566-9*) Revell.

Time to Laugh: Funny Stories for Children. Ed. by Sara Corrin. (Illus.). 142p. (J). (ps). 1991. pap. 3.95 (*0-571-15499-9*) Faber & Faber.

Time to Laugh: The Holy Laughter Phenomenon Examined. B. J. Oropeza. 208p. 1995. pap. 12.95 (*1-56563-183-8*) Hendrickson MA.

Time to Learn Our ABC's. Alex N. Holland. (Illus.). 10p. (J). (gr. k-3). 1992. pap. 8.95 (*1-895583-14-4*) MAYA Pubs.

Time to Let Go. Lurlene McDaniel. 176p. (J). (gr. 5 up). 1991. pap. 3.99 (*0-553-28350-2*, Starfire BDD) BDD Bks Young Read.

Time to Listen: Preventing Youth Suicide. Patricia Hermes. 144p. (YA). (gr. 7 up). 1987. 14.00 (*0-15-288196-4*, HB Juv Bks) HarBrace.

***Time to Live.** Jim Brogan. 235p. (Orig.). Date not set. pap. 13.95 (*1-879194-22-8*) GLB Pubs.

Time to Live. Chana S. Rubin. 269p. (YA). (gr. 9-12). 1988. 14.95 (*0-935063-48-X*) CIS Comm.

***Time to Live: A Journal of the Chilcotin.** Will Jenkins. 240p. 1997. pap. 14.95 (*0-614-27185-1*) Hancock House.

Time to Live: Graduation & Youth Messages. Maralene Wesner & Miles Wesner. LC 88-51870. 78p. 1988. pap. 4.95 (*0-936715-12-X*) Diversity Okla.

***Time to Live: Seven Tasks of Creative Aging.** Robert Raines. LC 96-39771. 1997. pap. 20.95 (*0-525-94283-1*) NAL-Dutton.

Time to Live a Time to Die: Important Concerns When Death Draws Near. Beatrice M. Ash. 80p. Date not set. pap. 7.99 (*0-8066-2664-X*) Augsburg Fortress.

Time to Look Back & a Time to Look Ahead: ASI Oral History. Dorothy Thomas. 40p. (Orig.). 1995. pap. 15.00 (*0-936547-29-4*) Am Soc Index.

Time to Lose: Representing Kansas in Brown v. Board of Education. Paul E. Wilson. LC 94-41098. (Illus.). 320p. 1995. 24.95 (*0-7006-0709-9*) U Pr of KS.

Time to Love. Barbara Delinsky. 256p. 1996. mass mkt. 5.99 (*0-06-101100-2*, Harp PBks) HarpC.

Time to Love. Brid Mahon. 484p. 1992. pap. 13.95 (*1-85371-221-3*, Pub. by Poolbeg Pr IE) Dufour.

***Time to Love.** large type ed. Barbara Delinsky. LC 97-9212. (Large Print Book Ser.). 1997. pap. 22.95 (*1-56895-433-6*) Wheeler Pub.

Time to Love. Helen M. Hostetler. LC 89-33683. (Illus.). 231p. 1989. reprint ed. pap. 65.90 (*0-608-01750-7*, 2062408) Bks Demand.

Time to Love Again. Flora M. Speer. 448p. (Orig.). 1993. mass mkt., pap. text ed. 4.99 (*0-505-51900-3*, Love Spell) Dorchester Pub Co.

***Time to Love Again.** Flora M. Speer. 336p. (Orig.). 1997. mass mkt. 5.50 (*0-505-52196-2*) Dorchester Pub Co.

***Time to Love & a Time to Die.** Eric M. Remarque. 1998. pap. write for info. (*0-449-91250-7*) Fawcett.

***Time to Love & a Time to Kill.** Ed. by Pamela Muzoleski. (Orig.). 1997. pap. 11.95 (*1-57532-039-8*) Press-Tige Pub.

Time to Market: Reducing Product Lead Time. Cyril Charney. LC 90-72145. (Illus.). 260p. 1991. 50.00 (*0-87263-396-9*) SME.

Time to Meet. Marcus Braybrooke. LC 90-30880. 192p. (Orig.). (C). 1990. pap. 13.95 (*0-334-02447-1*) TPI PA.

Time to Mend: An Irish-American Republican Solution. Robert E. Connolly. 145p. (Orig.). 1990. pap. 7.00 (*0-9614659-5-6*) Cuchullain Pubns.

***Time to Mourn.** Debene. 5.95 (*0-687-61196-2*) Abingdon.

Time to Mourn. Jack D. Spiro. LC 67-30744. 160p. 1985. pap. text ed. 8.95 (*0-8197-0497-0*) Bloch.

Time to Mourn: Growing Through the Grief Process. Verena Kast. 156p. 1995. pap. 16.95 (*3-85630-509-2*, Pub. by Daimon Pubs SZ) Continuum.

Time to Mourn: Recovering from the Death of a Loved One. Ron DelBene et al. 24p. 1988. pap. 3.95 (*0-8358-0577-8*) Upper Room Bks.

Time to Mourn - A Time to Comfort. Ron Wolfson. Ed. by Joel L. Grishaver. (Art of Jewish Living Ser.). (Illus.). 300p. (Orig.). 1993. pap. 16.95 (*0-935665-07-2*) Fed Jewish Mens Clubs.

Time to Mourn, a Time to Comfort. Ron Wolfson. LC 96-46453. 320p. 1996. pap. text ed. 16.95 (*1-879045-96-6*) Jewish Lights.

Time to Mourn, a Time to Dance: The Expression of Grief & Joy in Israelite Religion. Gary A. Anderson. 152p. 1991. 28.50 (*0-271-00729-X*) Pa St U Pr.

Time to Murder & Create. Lawrence Block. 192p. 1991. mass mkt. 5.99 (*0-380-76365-6*) Avon.

Time to Murder & Create: The Contemporary Novel in Crisis. John W. Aldridge. LC 79-39113. (Essay Index Reprint Ser.). 1980. reprint ed. 29.95 (*0-8369-2682-X*) Ayer.

Time to Plant - Creation to Salvation, Fall. Herb Woodward & Hazel Woodward. 1989. pap. 4.50 (*0-89137-821-9*) Quality Pubns.

Time to Plant - Creation to Salvation, Spring. Herb Woodward & Hazel Woodward. 1989. pap. 4.50 (*0-89137-823-5*) Quality Pubns.

Time to Plant - Creation to Salvation, Summer. Herb Woodward & Hazel Woodward. 1989. pap. 4.50 (*0-89137-824-3*) Quality Pubns.

Time to Plant - Creation to Salvation, Winter. Herb Woodward & Hazel Woodward. 1989. pap. 4.50 (*0-89137-822-7*) Quality Pubns.

Time to Play. Levinson. 1996. bds. write for info. (*0-15-201262-1*) HarBrace.

***Time to Play! A Shake-N-Move Book about Opposites.** Dawn Bentley. (Shake-N-Move Ser.). (J). 1997. 5.99 (*0-689-81407-0*, Litl Simon S&S) S&S Childrens.

***Time to Play House.** Dugald Steer. (Illus.). (J). (ps-k). 1997. 16.95 (*0-7613-0289-1*) Millbrook Pr.

Time to Pray. Rebera E. Foston. Ed. by Cynthia E. Garnett. 96p. (Orig.). Date not set. pap. 12.00 (*0-9641709-7-3*) Foston Adolescent.

Time to Pray. Rose Goldstein. LC 72-91792. 10.00 (*0-87677-141-X*) Hartmore.

Time to Pray: Prayers, Psalms & Readings for Personal Devotion. Ed. by George T. Cobbett. 175p. 1981. 7.95 (*0-89869-073-0*) Church Pub Inc.

Time to Pray God's Way: Changing Your World Through Prayer. Evelyn Christenson. 192p. 1996. pap. 9.99 (*1-56507-300-2*) Harvest Hse.

Time to Prepare: A Practical Guide for Individuals & Families in Determining One's Wishes for Extraordinary Medical Treatment & Financial Arrangements. Ed. by Richard F. Address. 54p. (Orig.). 1994. pap. 6.95 (*0-8074-0534-5*, 243871) UAHC.

Time to Prepare the Way in the Wilderness: Papers on the Qumran Scrolls. Fellows of the Institute for Advanced Studies of the Hebrew University, Jerusalem, 1989-90. Ed. by Devorah Dimant & Lawrence H. Schiffman. (Studies on the Text of the Desert of Judah: Vol. 16). 1994. 61.50 (*90-04-10225-6*) E J Brill.

Time to Reap: The Middle Age of Women in Five Israeli Subcultures. Nancy Datan et al. LC 80-26776. 208p. (C). 1981. text ed. 32.50 (*0-8018-2516-4*) Johns Hopkins.

An Asterisk (*) at the beginning of an entry indicates that the title is appearing in BIP for the first time.

Time to Remember. Jack Parsonson. Ed. by Tom Frisque. (Illus.). 127p. (Orig.). 1994. pap. 17.95 (*0-9623080-4-8*) Aviation Usk.

Time to Remember. Stanley Shapiro. LC 85-30061. 224p. 1986. 16.95 (*0-394-55031-5*) Random.

Time to Remember. Maude F. Zimmer. 8.95 (*0-8315-0005-0*) Speller.

***Time to Remember: A Biography of St. Andrew's School from the 1950s to the 1980s.** William H. Amos. LC 96-72586. (Illus.). 400p. 1997. 45.00 (*0-9656434-0-9*) Saint Andrews Schl.

Time to Remember: A Portrait of African American Life in Mount Vernon, New York. Larry H. Spruill. Ed. by Michael C. Gillespie. (Illus.). 350p. (Orig.). 1994. pap. 25.00 (*0-9625473-0-1*) Afro-Amer Workshop.

***Time to Remember: Commerce City Area Memories.** Dorothy Miller. LC 97-93248. (Illus.). (Orig.). 1997. pap. 7.00 (*0-9657329-1-6*) Homespun Pubns.

Time to Remember: Growing up in New York Before the Great War. Marie Jastrow. 1979. 10.95 (*0-393-85001-3*) Norton.

Time to Remember: The Autobiography of a Chemist. Alexander Todd. LC 83-5172. 257p. 1984. text ed. 49.95 (*0-521-25593-7*) Cambridge U Pr.

Time to Rend: An Essay on the Decision for American Independence. John M. Head. LC 68-63548. 1968. 7.50 (*0-87020-042-9*) State Hist Soc Wis.

Time to Rend, A Time to Sew. Rachel Pomerantz. 1995. 23.95 (*0-87306-743-6*); pap. 19.95 (*0-87306-744-4*) Feldheim.

Time to Retire. Bruce Cochran. 10p. 1995. write for info. (*1-886386-30-7*) Trisar.

Time to Rhyme. Martha Holmes. (Illus.). 52p. (J). (gr. k-1). 1990. lib. bdg. 17.95 (*0-89796-042-4*) New Dimens Educ.

***Time to Rhyme: A Rhyming Dictionary.** Marvin Terban. LC 93-60242. (Illus.). 96p. (J). (gr. 2-7). 1997. pap. 7.95 (*1-56397-630-7*, Wordsong) Boyds Mills Pr.

Time to Rock: A Social History of Rock 'n' Roll. David P. Szatmary. LC 96-7915. 400p. 1996. 22.00 (*0-02-864670-3*) Schirmer Bks.

Time to Say Good-Bye: Moving Beyond Loss. Mary M. Goulding. LC 95-26563. 168p. (Orig.). 1996. 25.00 (*0-918949-75-0*); pap. 14.00 (*0-918949-74-2*) Papier-Mache Press.

Time to Search. Linda Shands. LC 95-8897. (Seasons Remembered Ser.: Vol. 3). 180p. (Orig.). 1995. pap. 9.99 (*0-8308-1933-9*, 1933) InterVarsity.

Time to Seek God. Francis Frangipane. (Love & Devotion Ser.). 53p. (Orig.). 1994. pap. 2.50 (*1-886296-00-6*, FF1-021) Arrow Publications.

***Time to Share.** Joyce B. McDonald. 175p. (Orig.). 1997. mass mkt. 4.99 (*1-55237-193-X*, Pub. by Comnwlth Pub CN) Partners Pubs Grp.

Time to Sing Songs. Alex N. Holland. (Illus.). 13p. (J). (gr. k-3). 1992. pap. 12.95 (*1-895583-10-1*) MAYA Pubs.

***Time to Sleep.** Fleming. (J). 1996. pap. 15.95 (*0-8050-3762-4*) St Martin.

Time to Sleep, Little Lamb. Nicola Baxter. (J). 1996. pap. 14.95 (*0-689-80782-1*, Atheneum S&S) S&S Trade.

Time to Sow & a Time to Reap. Paul Link. (Illus.). 178p. 1990. pap. text ed. write for info. (*0-318-66612-X*) P Link.

Time to Sow & a Time to Reap. rev. ed. Paul Link. 182p. 1991. pap. text ed. write for info. (*0-9625216-1-2*) P Link.

Time to Spare. Lorraine H. Bailey. (Gregg-McGraw-Hill Series for Independent Living). 1978. text ed. 13.20 (*0-07-003223-8*) McGraw.

Time to Speak. Helen Lewis. 144p. 1994. 16.95 (*0-7867-0068-8*) Carroll & Graf.

Time to Speak. Helen Lewis. 132p. 1993. pap. 15.95 (*0-85640-491-8*, Pub. by Blackstaff Pr IE) Dufour.

***Time to Speak.** Helen Lewis. 144p. 1998. pap. 9.95 (*0-7867-0486-1*) Carroll & Graf.

Time to Speak. Linda Shands. LC 95-48941. (Seasons Remembered Ser.: No. 4). 239p. (Orig.). 1996. pap. 9.99 (*0-8308-1934-7*, 1934) InterVarsity.

***Time to Speak.** large type ed. Judith A. Salisbury. LC 97-93415. (Illus.). v, 134p. 1997. spiral bd. 24.95 (*0-9657678-0-9*) Logos Present.

Time to Speak: A Brief History of the Afro-Americans of Bloomington, Indiana 1865 - 1965. Frances V. Gilliam. LC 85-51626. xiii, 162p. 1985. 12.95 (*0-9615771-0-X*) Pinus.

Time to Speak: The Autobiography of the Reverend Jesse Jackson. Jesse Jackson. 304p. 1988. 17.45 (*0-671-62299-4*) S&S Trade.

Time to Speak: The Evangelical-Jewish Encounter. Ed. by A. James Rudin & Marvin R. Wilson. LC 87-16770. 218p. (Orig.). reprint ed. pap. 62.20 (*0-7837-3187-6*, 2042791) Bks Demand.

Time to Stand. Walter Lord. LC 78-8708. (Illus.). 271p. 1978. reprint ed. pap. 9.95 (*0-8032-7902-7*, Bison Books) U of Nebr Pr.

Time to Stop & Think, Vol. 1. Michael Wharton. 1981. 23.00 (*0-7223-1422-1*, Pub. by A H S Ltd UK) St Mut.

Time to Stop Pretending: A Mother's Story of Domestic Violence, Homelessness & Escape. Stephanie Rodriguez. LC 93-8299. 192p. 1994. 19.95 (*0-8397-8060-5*) Eriksson.

Time to Surrender. large type ed. Margaret A. Carr. (Linford Romance Library). 288p. 1993. pap. 15.99 (*0-7089-7317-5*, Linford) Ulverscroft.

Time to Take Control: The Impact of Change on Corporate Computer Systems. Tony Johnson. 250p. 1996. pap. 29.95 (*0-7506-2462-0*) Buttrwrth-Heinemann.

Time to Take Control: The Impact of Change on Corporate Computer Systems. Tony Johnson. LC 96-27819. 253p. 1996. pap. 24.95 (*0-7506-9863-2*) Buttrwrth-Heinemann.

Time to Talk: Poems of Friendship. Myra C. Livingston. LC 91-42234. 128p. (YA). (gr. 7 up). 1992. lib. bdg. 14.00 (*0-689-50558-2*, McElderry) S&S Childrens.

Time to Tell. David Hacohen. Tr. by Menachem Dagut. LC 84-45243. 256p. 1985. 18.50 (*0-8453-4789-6*, Cornwall Bks) Assoc Univ Prs.

Time to Tell Time. Shereen G. Rutman. (Illus.). (J). (ps-1). 1996. 4.99 (*0-614-15638-6*, Golden Books) Western Pub.

***Time to Tell Time.** Shereen G. Rutman & John Speirs. 1992. write for info. (*0-307-14019-9*) Western Pub.

Time to Think. Raymond Beshara & Leontine D. Scott. (Illus.). 1989. pap. text ed. 7.95 (*0-9623161-0-5*) ERN Inc.

***Time to Trust.** Jill Sheldon. 400p. (Orig.). 1997. mass mkt. 3.99 (*1-85487-926-X*, Pub. by Scarlet Bks UK) London Brdge.

Time to Trust. Isobel Stewart. (Rainbow Romances Ser.). 160p. 1995. 14.95 (*0-7090-5530-7*, 931, Hale-Parkwest) Parkwest Pubns.

Time to Turn...the Paschal Experience: The Paschal Experience. Anita M. Constance. LC 95-35390. 96p. (Orig.). 1996. pap. 5.95 (*0-8091-3613-9*) Paulist Pr.

Time to Vegetate. Rose M. Hill. (Illus.). 112p. (Orig.). 1993. pap. 12.75 (*0-9633071-3-4*) S A Griffiths.

Time to Wake Up. Levinson. 1996. bds. write for info. (*0-15-201261-3*) HarBrace.

Time to Wake Up! Marisabina Russo. LC 93-18185. (Illus.). 24p. (J). (ps up). 1994. 14.00 (*0-688-04599-5*) Greenwillow.

Time to Wake Up! Leith Samuel. 1992. pap. 8.99 (*0-85234-296-9*, Pub. by Evangelical Pr) Presby & Reformed.

Time to Weep. Gilbert Morris. LC 96-6950. (American Odyssey Ser.: Bk. 4). 320p. (Orig.). (gr. 10). 1996. pap. 9.99 (*0-8007-5576-6*) Revell.

Time to Weep. Laibel Resnick. LC 93-72409. 200p. 1993. write for info. (*1-56062-211-3*); pap. write for info. (*1-56062-212-1*) CIS Comm.

***Time to Weep: Discover the Supernatural Power of Repentance that Sparked the Brownsville Revival.** Steven Hill. 1997. pap. text ed. 9.99 (*0-88419-459-0*) Creation House.

Time to Weep: Funeral & Grief Messages. Maralene Wesner & Miles Wesner. LC 88-51867. 67p. 1988. pap. 4.95 (*0-936715-11-1*) Diversity Okla.

***Time to Weep: The Lang.** Stephen Hill. Ed. by Scott Sawyer & Tom Davidson. 258p. (Orig.). 1996. pap. 10.00 (*0-9637090-3-8*) Together Harvest.

Time to Wonder: Level 13. Evertts. 1983. 52.25 (*0-03-061396-5*) HB Schl Dept.

Time to Wonder: Level 13. Evertts. 1986. pap. 43.25 (*0-03-002378-5*) HB Schl Dept.

Time to Wonder: Level 13. E. Evertts. (J). 1983. wbk. ed., pap. 16.75 (*0-03-061438-4*) HB Schl Dept.

Time to Wonder 1986: Level 13. Evertts. (J). 1986. wbk. ed., pap. 13.75 (*0-03-002383-1*) HB Schl Dept.

Time to Write: The Influence of Time & Culture on Learning to Write. John S. Lofty. LC 91-21447. (SUNY Series, Literacy, Culture, & Learning: Theory & Practice). (Illus.). 292p. 1992. text ed. 64.50 (*0-7914-0901-5*); pap. text ed. 21.95 (*0-7914-0902-3*) State U NY Pr.

Time-Together Before Bedtime. Carole Gesme & Douglas Pearson. (Time-Together Ser.). (J). (gr. k-6). 1995. wbk. ed. 9.95 (*1-888384-01-8*) Time-Together.

Time-Together Communicating. Carole Gesme & Douglas Pearson. (Time-Together Ser.). (J). (gr. k-6). 1995. wbk. ed. 9.95 (*1-888384-00-X*) Time-Together.

Time Together Learning about Family Values. Carole Gesme & Douglas Pearson. (Time-Together Ser.). (J). (gr. k-6). wbk. ed. 9.95 (*1-888384-02-6*) Time-Together.

Time Too Late. Doris R. Meredith. 448p. 1993. mass mkt. 4.99 (*0-06-100566-5*, Harp PBks) HarpC.

Time, Tradition & Society in Greek Archaeology: Bridging the Great Divide. Ed. by Nigel Spencer. LC 94-44388. (TAG Ser.). 208p. (C). (gr. 13). 1995. text ed. 62.95 (*0-415-11412-8*, C0069) Routledge.

Time Train. Paul Fleischman. LC 90-27357. (Charlotte Zolotow Bk.). (Illus.). 32p. (J). (gr. k-4). 1991. 15.00 (*0-06-021709-X*) HarpC Child Bks.

Time Train. Paul Fleischman. LC 90-27357. (Charlotte Zolotow Bks.). (Illus.). 32p. (J). (gr. k-4). 1994. pap. 4.95 (*0-06-443351-X*, Trophy) HarpC Child Bks.

Time Train to Ancient Rome. Gaby Waters. (Puzzle Adventures Ser.). (Illus.). 48p. (J). (gr. 3-5). 1988. pap. 5.50 (*0-7460-0153-3*); lib. bdg. 13.95 (*0-88110-302-0*) EDC.

Time Trap. Peter H. Barnett. LC 79-57447. (Illus.). 50p. 1980. pap. 5.00 (*0-915066-37-8*) Assembling Pr.

Time Trap. Edgar P. Jacobs. Tr. by Jean-Jacques Surbeck from FRE. (Adventures of Blake & Mortimer Ser.). (Illus.). 49p. (Orig.). (YA). (gr. 12 up). 1989. pap. 8.95 (*0-87416-066-9*, Comcat Comics) Catalan Communs.

***Time Trap: The Classic Book on Time Management.** 3rd ed. Alec R. Mackenzie. LC 97-20780. 240p. 1997. pap. 17.95 (*0-8144-7926-X*) AMACOM.

Time Trap: The New Version of the Classic Book on Time Management. Alec R. Mackenzie. LC 89-46217. 176p. 1991. pap. 14.95 (*0-8144-7760-7*) AMACOM.

***Time Travel.** Paul J. Nahin. LC 96-30080. (Science Fiction Writing Ser.). (Illus.). 208p. 1997. pap. 16.99 (*0-89879-748-9*, Wrtrs Digest Bks) F & W Pubns Inc.

***Time Travel: A New Perspective.** J. H. Brennan. (Illus.). 224p. (Orig.). 1997. pap. 12.95 (*1-56718-085-X*) Llewellyn Pubns.

Time Travel: Do-It-Yourself Past Life Journey Handbook. Shelley L. Stockwell. 178p. 1995. pap. 19.95 (*0-912559-19-5*) Creativity Unltd Pr.

Time Travel & Other Mathematical Bewilderments. M. Gardner. 295p. 1995. pap. text ed. write for info. (*0-7167-1925-8*) W H Freeman.

***Time-Travel Christmas.** Megan Daniel et al. 448p. 1997. mass mkt. 5.50 (*0-505-52241-1*, Love Spell) Dorchester Pub Co.

Time-Travel Christmas. Flora M. Speer et al. 448p. (Orig.). 1993. mass mkt., pap. text ed. 4.99 (*0-505-51912-7*, Love Spell) Dorchester Pub Co.

***Time-Travel Christmas.** Flora M. Speer et al. 448p. (Orig.). 1996. mass mkt. 5.99 (*0-505-52186-5*, Love Spell) Dorchester Pub Co.

Time Travel Chronological Discoveries. Steven Gibbs. (Illus.). 110p. 1994. 20.00 (*1-57179-016-0*) Intern Guild ASRS.

Time Travel Machines. Steven Gibbs. (Illus.). 110p. 1994. 20.00 (*1-57179-018-7*) Intern Guild ASRS.

Time Travel Physics. Steven Gibbs. (Illus.). 110p. 1994. 20.00 (*1-57179-014-4*) Intern Guild ASRS.

Time Travelers. Jan Peck. 18p. (J). (ps-2). 1993. 10.95 (*1-879680-16-3*) About You.

Time Travelers & Other People. Calvin Richens. (Illus.). 69p. (Orig.). 1993. pap. 9.95 (*1-882892-01-1*) Creat Energies.

Time Travelers Compendium. Steven Gibbs. Ed. by Thorguard Templar. (Illus.). 105p. 1994. 20.00 (*1-57179-020-9*) Intern Guild ASRS.

***Time Travelers First Adventure - Wild West Vol. 4: With Buffalo Biff & Farley's Raiders.** large type unabridged ed. Joe Loesch. Ed. by Cheryl J. Hutchinson. (Backyard Adventure Ser.: Vol. 4). (Illus.). 60p. (Orig.). (J). (gr. 3-6). 1996. 14.95 incl. audio (*1-887729-14-3*); 16.95 incl. digital audio (*1-887729-15-1*) Toy Box Prods.

Time Traveller's Book. J. Hindley et al. (Time Traveller Ser.). (Illus.). 32p. (J). 1977. text ed. 19.95 (*0-86020-222-4*) EDC.

Time Traveller's Guide. Peter Haining. 1989. pap. 12.95 (*0-86379-188-3*, Univ Books) Carol Pub Group.

***Time-Travellers' Guide.** Peter Haining. (Dr. Who Ser.). pap. 19.95 (*0-86369-927-8*, Pub. by Virgin Pub UK) London Brdge.

***Time Travels: A Collection of Poetry & Essays.** Maia S. Bass. (Illus.). (Orig.). 1997. pap. write for info. (*0-614-29839-3*) Shango Prodn Co.

Time Tree. Enid Richemont. (J). (gr. 3-7). 1990. 12.95 (*0-316-74452-2*) Little.

Time Trekkers Visit the Dinosaurs. Kate Needham. LC 95-14023. (Time Trekkers Ser.). (Illus.). 32p. (J). (gr. 2-4). 1995. pap. 5.95 (*1-56294-196-8*, Copper Beech Bks); lib. bdg. 15.40 (*1-56294-942-X*, Copper Beech Bks) Millbrook Pr.

Time Trekkers Visit the Middle Ages. Kate Needham. (Time Trekkers Ser.). (Illus.). 32p. (J). (gr. 2-4). 1996. lib. bdg. 15.40 (*0-7613-0481-9*, Copper Beech Bks) Millbrook Pr.

Time Trekkers Visit the Romans. Antony Mason. (Time Trekkers Ser.). (Illus.). 32p. (J). (gr. 2-4). 1995. pap. 5.95 (*1-56294-936-5*, Copper Beech Bks); lib. bdg. 15.40 (*1-56294-910-1*, Copper Beech Bks) Millbrook Pr.

Time Trekkers Visit the Stone Age. Antony Mason. (Time Trekkers Ser.). (Illus.). 32p. (J). (gr. 2-4). 1996. pap. 5.95 (*0-7613-0480-0*, Copper Beech Bks); lib. bdg. 15.40 (*0-7613-0479-7*, Copper Beech Bks) Millbrook Pr.

Time Trends in Cancer Incidence & Mortality. P. Damiecki. Ed. by M. Coleman et al. (IARC Scientific Publications: No. 121). (Illus.). 800p. 1993. 195.00 (*92-832-2121-4*) OUP.

Time Trilogy: A Wrinkle in Time; A Wind in the Door; A Swiftly Tilting Planet, 3 vols., Set. Madeleine L'Engle. 710p. (J). (gr. 5 up). 1979. boxed 47.85 (*0-374-37592-5*) FS&G.

Time Trip. Lee Mountain. (Attention Span Stories Ser.). (Illus.). 48p. (Orig.). 1978. pap. text ed. 8.65 (*0-89061-145-9*, 581) Jamestown Pubs.

Time Tunnel. Art L'Hommedieu. (J). (ps-3). 1995. 10.99 (*0-85953-940-7*) Childs Play.

***Time Twist, No. 2.** 144p. (J). 1996. write for info. (*0-7814-0288-3*, Lion) Chariot Victor.

***Time Twist, No. 3.** 144p. (J). 1996. write for info. (*0-7814-0289-1*, Lion) Chariot Victor.

Time under Control: Efficient Self Management in & out of the Office. Ivan W. Fitzwater. LC 87-72603. (Illus.). 175p. 1987. pap. 12.00 (*0-931722-63-2*) Corona Pub.

Time Unguarded. Edmund Ironside. Ed. by Roderick Macleod & Denis Kelly. LC 74-64. (Illus.). 434p. 1974. reprint ed. text ed. 59.75 (*0-8371-7369-8*, IRTG, Greenwood Pr) Greenwood.

Time Value of Money Rules under the 1984 Tax Act. Mortimer M. Caplin. LC 85-136473. 35.00 (*0-685-13481-4*) HarBrace.

Time-Variant Systems & Interpolation. Ed. by I. Gohberg. LC 92-11450. (Operator Theory Ser.: Vol. 56). 308p. 1992. 74.50 (*3-7643-2738-3*, Pub. by Birkhauser Vlg SZ); 105.00 (*0-8176-2738-3*, Pub. by Birkhauser Vlg SZ) Birkhauser.

Time Varying Discrete Linear Systems: Input-OutPut Operators. Aristide Halanay & Vlad Ionescu. LC 94-1011. 228p. 1994. 111.00 (*0-8176-5012-1*) Birkhauser.

Time-Varying Discrete Linear Systems: Input-Output Operators, Riccati Equations, Disturbance Attenuation. Aristide Halanay & Vlad Ionescu. LC 94-1011. (Operator Theory, Advances & Applications Ser.: Vol. 68). 240p. 1994. 94.00 (*3-7643-5012-1*) Birkhauser.

***Time-Varying Image Processing & Moving Object Recognition: Proceedings of the 5th International Workshop, Florence, Italy, September 5-6, 1996.** Vito Cappellini. LC 97-23533. 1997. write for info. (*0-444-82307-7*) Elsevier.

Time-Varying Image Processing & Moving Object Recognition, No. 2: Proceedings of the 3rd International Workshop, Florence, Italy, 29-31 May, 1989. Ed. by Vito Cappellini. 340p. 1990. 142.00 (*0-444-88559-5*) Elsevier.

Time-Varying Image Processing & Moving Object Recognition, No 4. Ed. by V. Cappellini. 1997. write for info. (*0-614-17887-8*) Elsevier.

Time-Varying Processing & Moving Object Recognition, No. 3: Proceedings of the 4th International Workshop, Florence, Italy, June 1993. Ed. by V. Cappellini. (Illus.). 444p. 1994. 194.50 (*0-444-81467-1*) Elsevier.

Time, Wait. Hannah Kahn. LC 83-12565. (University of Central Florida Contemporary Poetry Ser.). 76p. 1984. 14.95 (*0-8130-0775-5*) U Press Fla.

Time Walker. James Conlan. 1994. 10.95 (*0-533-11009-2*) Vantage.

Time Warp: Golden Mini Play Lights. (Illus.). 14p. (J). (ps-3). 1993. 10.95 (*0-307-75400-6*, Golden Pr) Western Pub.

***Time Warp Trio, XYZ.** Jon Scieszka. 1998. pap. 10.99 (*0-670-84831-X*) Viking Penguin.

Time Warp Tunnel. Stephen Bly. (Making Choices Ser.). (Illus.). 160p. (J). (gr. 3-6). 1995. pap. 4.99 (*0-7814-0187-9*) Chariot Victor.

***Time Warp Virus.** Clive Gifford. (Science Puzzle Adventures Ser.). (Illus.). 48p. (J). (gr. 4 up). 1997. pap. 5.50 (*0-7460-2395-2*, Usborne); lib. bdg. 13.95 (*0-88110-908-8*, Usborne) EDC.

Time Warps, String Edits & Macromolecules: The Theory & Practice of Sequence Comparison. David Sankoff & Joseph P. Kruskal. LC 83-11874. (Illus.). 400p. 1983. write for info. (*0-201-07809-0*) Addison-Wesley.

Time Warrior. 1993. pap. 5.95 (*0-426-20023-3*, Dr Who) Carol Pub Group.

Time Warriors: Messengers for the Future. Ann Valentin. (Galactic Awakening Ser.). 100p. 1995. 14.95 (*0-9635703-1-5*) Gate Way Pubs.

Time Wars. Ed. by Poul Anderson. 384p. (Orig.). 1990. pap. 3.95 (*0-8125-1311-8*) Tor Bks.

Time Was: When Life Was Simple, Faith & Friendship Strong. Claudette H. Howell. LC 87-51388. 215p. (Orig.). 1987. pap. 10.50 (*0-9619794-0-2*) C H Howell.

Time Was Right: A History of the Buffalo & Erie County Public Library, 1940-1975. Joseph B. Rounds. Ed. by Michael C. Mahaney. (Illus.). x, 172p. 1986. 11.95 (*0-9615896-0-4*) Grosvenor Soc.

***Time Was, She Declares: Selected Poems.** Adrienne M. Bond. LC 96-35540. 84p. 1996. 19.95 (*0-86554-538-3*, MUP/H411) Mercer Univ Pr.

Time Wasters - Time Savers: Sixty-One Ways to Beat the Clock. Richard G. Neal. 88p. 1994. pap. 16.00 (*0-910170-64-9*) Assn Sch Busn.

Time, Water & Development. Henry D. Molumphy. (Illus.). 16p. 1986. 1.00 (*0-918397-02-2*) Foster Parents.

Time We Knew: Images of Yesterday in the Basque Homeland. Photos by William A. Allard. LC 90-12259. (Basque Ser.). (Illus.). 120p. 1990. 34.95 (*0-87417-157-1*) U of Nev Pr.

Time Well Spent: Family Hiking in the Smokies. rev. ed. Hal Hubbs et al. 95p. 1993. pap. text ed. 6.95 (*0-9630682-3-7*) Panther TN.

Time Well Spent, Business & Stress Planner. Larry Tobin. 208p. 1989. pap. 14.95 (*0-941831-37-X*) Beyond Words Pub.

Time, Will, & Mental Process. Jason W. Brown. (Cognition & Language Ser.). (Illus.). 250p. (C). 1996. 42.50 (*0-306-45231-6*, Plenum Pr) Plenum.

Time Will Darken It. William Maxwell. LC 82-81311. 320p. 1983. pap. 11.95 (*0-87923-448-2*) Godine.

Time Will Darken It, Vol. 1. William Maxwell. 1997. pap. 13.00 (*0-679-77258-8*) McKay.

Time Will Not Wait. large type ed. Hannah Cooper. (Linford Romance Library). 304p. 1993. pap. 15.99 (*0-7089-7395-7*, Linford) Ulverscroft.

Time Will Tell. Jamina Marcus. 384p. (Orig.). 1996. pap. 8.25 (*0-9649465-0-5*) Humming Wrds.

Time Will Tell. large type ed. June Barraclough. (General Ser.). 592p. 1993. 25.99 (*0-7089-2871-4*) Ulverscroft.

Time Windows. Kathryn Reiss. 272p. (J). (gr. 3-7). 1991. 17.00 (*0-15-288205-7*, HB Juv Bks) HarBrace.

Time Winds. Alfred Kisubi. 79p. 1994. pap. 10.00 (*0-933532-95-4*) BkMk.

Time Wipe-Off Book. 24p. (J). (ps-3). 1992. pap. 1.95 (*0-590-45693-8*) Scholastic Inc.

Time with Jesus: Twenty Guided Meditations for Youth. Thomas F. Catucci. LC 93-71891. 160p. (Orig.). (YA). (gr. 9-12). 1993. pap. 13.95 (*0-87793-499-1*) Ave Maria.

Time with Our Children: Stories for Use in Worship, Year A. Dianne E. Deming. LC 92-31638. 208p. (Orig.). 1992. pap. 9.95 (*0-8298-0941-4*) Pilgrim OH.

Time with Our Children: Stories for Use in Worship, Year B. Dianne E. Deming. LC 92-31638. (Illus.). 200p. (Orig.). 1993. pap. 9.95 (*0-8298-0952-X*) Pilgrim OH.

Time with Our Children: Stories for Use in Worship, Year C. rev. ed. Dianne E. Deming. LC 92-31638. (Illus.). 168p. (Orig.). 1993. pap. 9.95 (*0-8298-0953-8*) Pilgrim OH.

Time Without End. Linda L. Miller. 368p. (Orig.). 1995. mass mkt. 5.99 (*0-425-15042-9*, Berkley Trade) Berkley Pub.

Time Without Shadows. Ted Allbeury. 304p. 1992. mass mkt. 4.99 (*0-446-40090-4*, Mysterious Paperbk) Warner Bks.

Time Without Shadows. large type ed. Ted Allbeury. LC 91-8486. 516p. 1991. reprint ed. lib. bdg. 21.95 (*1-56054-158-X*) Thorndike Pr.

Time Without Work: People Who Are Not Working Tell Their Stories, How They Feel, What They Do, How They Survive. Walli F. Leff & Marilyn G. Haft. LC 83-61477. 403p. 1983. pap. 9.00 (*0-89608-185-0*) South End Pr.

Time, Work, & Culture in the Middle Ages. Jacques Le Goff. Tr. by Arthur Goldhammer. LC 79-25400. xvi, 400p. (C). 1982. pap. 22.50 (*0-226-47081-4*) U Ch Pr.

Time Wreck. Vivien Alcock. LC 96-1209. (J). 1997. 15.95 (*0-395-81660-2*) HM.
Time Zones: Your Key to Control. Philip S. Berg. 256p. 1990. 12.95 (*0-924457-00-7*); pap. 12.95 (*0-924457-01-5*) Res Ctr Kabbalah.
Time Zones: Your Key to Control. Philip S. Berg. 256p. (SPA.). 1991. 12.95 (*0-924457-59-7*); 12.95 (*0-924457-54-6*); pap. 12.95 (*0-924457-60-0*); pap. 12.95 (*0-924457-55-4*); pap. 13.95 (*0-924457-74-0*) Res Ctr Kabbalah.
Time Zones: Your Key to Control. Philip S. Berg. 14p. (HEB.). 1994. pap. 11.95 (*0-924457-76-7*) Res Ctr Kabbalah.
Timebends. Arthur Miller. 1995. pap. 16.95 (*0-14-086306-0*) Viking Penguin.
Timebends: A Life. Arthur Miller. (Illus.). 656p. 1995. pap. 14.95 (*0-14-024917-6*, Penguin Bks) Viking Penguin.
Timecode: A User's Guide. John Ratcliff. (Illus.). 272p. 1993. 32.95 (*0-240-51334-7*, Focal) Buttrwrth-Heinemann.
Timecode: A User's Guide. 2nd ed. John Ratcliff. (Illus.). 272p. 1996. pap. 47.95 (*0-240-51404-1*, Focal) Buttrwrth-Heinemann.
Timed Boolean Functions: A Unified Formalism for Exact Timing Analysis. William K. Lam & Robert K. Brayton. LC 94-8519. (International Series in Engineering Computer Science, Computer Architecture & Digital Signal Processing Ser.). 296p. (C). 1994. lib. bdg. 110.50 (*0-7923-9454-2*) Kluwer Ac.
Timed Readings, 10 bks. 3rd ed. Edward Spargo et al. Incl. Timed Readings Bk. 1. 3rd ed. 120p. 1989. 13.97 (*0-89061-503-9*, 901); Timed Readings Bk. 2. 3rd ed. 120p. 1989. 13.97 (*0-89061-504-7*, 902); Timed Readings Bk. 3. 3rd ed. 120p. 1989. 13.97 (*0-89061-505-5*, 903); Timed Readings Bk. 4. 3rd ed. 120p. 1989. 13.97 (*0-89061-506-3*, 904); Timed Readings Bk. 5. 3rd ed. 120p. 1989. 13.97 (*0-89061-507-1*, 905); Timed Readings Bk. 6. 3rd ed. 120p. 1989. 13.97 (*0-89061-508-X*, 906); Timed Readings Bk. 7. 3rd ed. 120p. 1989. 13.97 (*0-89061-509-8*, 907); Timed Readings Bk. 8. 3rd ed. 120p. 1989. 13.97 (*0-89061-510-1*, 908); Timed Readings Bk. 9. 3rd ed. 120p. 1989. 13.97 (*0-89061-511-X*, 909); Timed Readings Bk. 10. 3rd ed. 120p. 1989. 13.97 (*0-89061-512-8*, 910); 1989. 6.75 (*0-685-74378-0*) Jamestown Pubs.
Timed Readings, Bk. 2. 3rd ed. Ed. by Jamestown Publishers Staff. 1989. pap. 12.66 (*0-8092-0090-2*) Jamestown Pubs.
Timed Readings, Set. 3rd ed. Ed. by Jamestown Publishers Staff. 1989. pap. 82.25 (*0-8092-0009-0*) Jamestown Pubs.
Timed Readings, Vol. 10. 3rd ed. Ed. by Jamestown Publishers Editors. 1989. pap. 12.66 (*0-8092-0091-0*) Jamestown Pubs.
Timed Readings, Bk. 1 see Timed Readings
Timed Readings, Bk. 10 see Timed Readings
Timed Readings, Bk. 2 see Timed Readings
Timed Readings, Bk. 3 see Timed Readings
Timed Readings, Bk. 4 see Timed Readings
Timed Readings, Bk. 5 see Timed Readings
Timed Readings, Bk. 6 see Timed Readings
Timed Readings, Bk. 7 see Timed Readings
Timed Readings, Bk. 8 see Timed Readings
Timed Readings, Bk. 9 see Timed Readings
Timed Readings in Literature, 10 bks. Edward Spargo et al. Incl. Timed Readings in Literature. 1989. 13.97 (*0-89061-514-4*, 911); Timed Readings in Literature Bk. 2. 1989. 13.97 (*0-89061-515-2*, 912); Timed Readings in Literature Bk. 3. 1989. 13.97 (*0-89061-516-0*, 913); Timed Readings in Literature Bk. 4. 1989. 13.97 (*0-89061-517-9*, 914); Timed Readings in Literature Bk. 5. 1989. 13.97 (*0-89061-518-7*, 915); Timed Readings in Literature Bk. 6. 1989. 13.97 (*0-89061-519-5*, 916); Timed Readings in Literature Bk. 7. 1989. 13.97 (*0-89061-520-9*, 917); Timed Readings in Literature Bk. 8. 1989. 13.97 (*0-89061-521-7*, 918); Timed Readings in Literature Bk. 9. 1989. 13.97 (*0-89061-522-5*, 919); Timed Readings in Literature Bk. 10. 1989. 13.97 (*0-89061-523-3*, 920); 120p. 1989. 6.75 (*0-685-74379-9*); 13.97 (*0-89061-514-4*, 911) Jamestown Pubs.
Timed Readings in Literature see Timed Readings in Literature
Timed Readings in Literature, Bk. 10 see Timed Readings in Literature
Timed Readings in Literature, Bk. 2 see Timed Readings in Literature
Timed Readings in Literature, Bk. 3 see Timed Readings in Literature
Timed Readings in Literature, Bk. 4 see Timed Readings in Literature
Timed Readings in Literature, Bk. 5 see Timed Readings in Literature
Timed Readings in Literature, Bk. 6 see Timed Readings in Literature
Timed Readings in Literature, Bk. 7 see Timed Readings in Literature
Timed Readings in Literature, Bk. 8 see Timed Readings in Literature
Timed Readings in Literature, Bk. 9 see Timed Readings in Literature
Timed Writings about Careers. 3rd ed. Clayton. (TA - Typing/Keyboarding Ser.). 1985. text ed. 17.95 (*0-538-20790-6*) S-W Pub.
Timed Writings About Careers: Template D. 3rd ed. Clayton. (TA - Typing/Keyboarding Ser.). 1985. 104.95 (*0-538-20795-7*) S-W Pub.
Timeframe: The Illustrated History of Doctor Who. (Illus.). 1993. 24.95 (*1-85227-427-1*, Dr Who) Carol Pub Group.
***Timegates.** Jack Dann & Gardner Dozois. 256p. 1997. mass mkt. 5.99 (*0-441-04288-0*) Ace Bks.
***Timegates.** Ed. by Jack Dann & Gardner Dozois. pap. 5.99 (*0-441-00428-8*) Ace Bks.
***Timekeeper.** Trevor Ferguson. 256p. (Orig.). 1997. pap. 14.00 (*0-00-648112-4*) HarperColl Wrld.
Timekeeper. Anna Riphahn. Ed. by Nancy R. Thatch. LC 96-12957. (Books for Students by Students). (Illus.). 29p. (J). (gr. 2-4). 1996. lib. bdg. 14.95 (*0-933849-62-1*) Landmark Edns.
Timekeeper. Jack Rudman. (Career Examination Ser.: C-3485). 1994. pap. 23.95 (*0-8373-3485-3*) Nat Learn.
Timekeeping. Rodney Dale. LC 92-21661. (Discoveries & Inventions Ser.). 64p. (J). 1993. 18.00 (*0-19-520968-0*) OUP.
Timelapse: Ancient Civilizations: The Official Strategy Guide. Rick Barba. 264p. 1996. per. 19.99 (*0-7615-0497-4*) Prima Pub.
Timeless. Jasmine Cresswell. 384p. (Orig.). 1994. pap. 4.99 (*0-451-40460-2*, Topaz) NAL-Dutton.
Timeless. Deloras Scott. 1994. mass mkt. 3.99 (*0-373-28825-5*, 1-28825-7) Harlequin Bks.
Timeless Bouquets: Decorate & Design with Dried Flowers. Mil Farjon. 128p. 1994. pap. 18.95 (*0-8019-8610-9*) Chilton.
Timeless Christian. Erik Von Kuehnelt-Leddihn. LC 73-10604. 220p. 1976. 4.50 (*0-8199-0416-3*, Frncscn Herld) Franciscan Pr.
Timeless Christmas. Patricia Chandler. (American Romance Ser.). 1994. mass mkt. 3.50 (*0-373-16564-1*, 1-16564-6) Harlequin Bks.
***Timeless Design.** Bo Niles. LC 96-49986. 1997. 34.95 (*0-86636-543-5*); pap. write for info. (*0-86636-544-3*) PBC Intl Inc.
***Timeless Designs.** PBC International Staff. Date not set. 34.95 (*0-688-15375-5*) Morrow.
Timeless Documents of the Soul. Helmuth Jacobsohn. LC 68-15329. (Studies in Jungian Thought). 275p. reprint ed. pap. 78.40 (*0-317-08260-4*, 2010268) Bks Demand.
Timeless Earth. Peter Kolosimo. Ed. by Paul Stevenson. (Illus.). 270p. 1974. 7.95 (*0-8216-0209-8*, Univ Bks) Carol Pub Group.
Timeless Earth: Journey Across India. Gianni Baldizzone. 1996. 45.00 (*0-944142-72-9*, Pub. by Mapin Pubng II) Antique Collect.
***Timeless Face.** Elinwood. LC 97-11480. 1997. pap. 14.95 (*0-312-15674-X*) St Martin.
Timeless Fashions. Ed. by Pam Aulson. (Illus.). 72p. (Orig.). 1981. pap. 2.00 (*0-918178-25-8*) Simplicity.
Timeless Gift of Love: An Intimate Glimpse into Famous Love Affairs. 160p. (Orig.). 1996. pap. 7.95 (*1-889116-05-X*) Penbrooke Pub.
***Timeless Healing.** Benson. LC 96-49270. 1997. pap. 13.00 (*0-684-83146-5*, Fireside) S&S Trade.
Timeless Healing: The Power & Biology of Belief. Herbert Benson. 352p. 1996. 24.00 (*0-684-81441-2*) S&S Trade.
***Timeless Healing: The Power & Biology of Belief.** large type ed. Herbert Benson & Marg Stark. LC 96-2763. 1996. 24.95 (*1-56895-366-6*, Compass) Wheeler Pub.
Timeless Images. Bob Dyer. 176p. 1990. 39.95 (*0-916179-27-3*) Ariz Hwy.
Timeless Interlude at Wounded Knee: A Novella of Love & Savage Revenge. Barry Brierley. 1995. 14.95 (*0-933025-34-3*) Blue Bird Pub.
Timeless Jewish Songs. Tr. by Martha R. Birnbaum from HEB. 31p. (Orig.). (C). pap. 10.00 (*1-878617-14-1*) Leyerle Pubns.
Timeless Leader. John K. Clemens & Steven Albrecht. 272p. 1995. 22.95 (*1-55850-483-4*) Adams Media.
Timeless Leader. John K. Clemens. 272p. 1997. pap. text ed. 12.95 (*1-55850-657-8*) Adams Media.
Timeless Love. Judith Arnold. 1995. mass mkt. 3.25 (*0-373-25665-5*, 1-25665-0) Harlequin Bks.
***Timeless Love.** Jeanne Savery. 304p. 1997. mass mkt. 4.99 (*0-8217-5574-9*, Zebra Kensgtn) Kensgtn Pub Corp.
Timeless Moment. Annette Daniels. 1995. pap. 4.99 (*0-7860-0114-3*) Kensgtn Pub Corp.
Timeless Moment. Annette Daniels. 1996. mass mkt. 4.99 (*0-8217-5330-4*, Zebra Kensgtn) Kensgtn Pub Corp.
Timeless Myths. Alexander Eliot. LC 97-15649. 1997. pap. 10.95 (*0-452-01126-4*, Mer) NAL-Dutton.
Timeless Myths: How Ancient Legends Influence the World Around Us. Alexander Eliot. 156p. 1995. 19.95 (*0-8264-0869-9*) Continuum.
Timeless Ornaments. Leisure Arts Staff. 1995. 24.95 (*0-942237-66-8*) Leisure AR.
Timeless Passion. Constance O'Day-Flannery. 1986. mass mkt. 4.99 (*0-8217-3683-3*, Zebra Kensgtn) Kensgtn Pub Corp.
***Timeless Patterns for Today's Quilter: The Best of Traditional Quiltworks & Quilting Today Magazines.** 10th ed. Chitra Publications Staff. Ed. by Kent Ward. LC 96-49567. (Illus.). 32p. (Orig.). 1997. pap. 12.95 (*1-885588-14-3*) Chitra Pubns.
Timeless Patterns in Time, Vol. 1. Menachem M. Schneerson. Ed. by Uri Kaploun. Tr. by Eliyahu Touger. 184p. 1993. 17.00 (*0-8266-0531-1*) Kehot Pubn Soc.
Timeless Patterns in Time, Vol. 2. Menachem M. Schneerson. Ed. by Uri Kaploun. Tr. by Eliyahu Touger. 188p. 1994. 17.00 (*0-8266-0532-X*) Kehot Pubn Soc.
Timeless Piano Standards, Bk. 1. Warner. 1994. pap. 9.95 (*0-7604-0081-4*, F3457P9X) Warner Brothers.
Timeless Piano Standards, Bk. 2. Warner. 1994. pap. 9.95 (*0-7604-0082-2*, F3458P9X) Warner Brothers.
Timeless Piano Standards, Bk. 3. Warner. 1994. pap. 9.95 (*0-7604-0083-0*, F3459P9X) Warner Brothers.
***Timeless Storyteller: A Study of the Parables in the Gospels.** Evelyn F. Capel. 160p. 1995. pap. write for info. (*0-904693-74-0*, Pub. by Temple Ldge Pub UK) Anthroposophic.
Timeless Techniques for Better Oil Paintings. Tom Browning. (Illus.). 144p. 1994. 27.99 (*0-89134-513-2*, 30553, North Lght Bks) F & W Pubns Inc.
Timeless Tennesseans. James A. Crutchfield. (Illus.). 200p. 1983. 19.95 (*0-87397-186-8*, Strode Pubs) Circle Bk Service.
Timeless Themes: Complete Program for Grades 3 & 4. Ed. by UUA Staff. 1993. pap. 50.00 (*0-614-06535-6*) Unitarian Univ.
Timeless Travels of J. J. & Kelly: The London Adventure. Jan Lawrence & Linda Raskin. 78p. (Orig.). (J). (gr. 6-9). 1994. pap. 5.00 (*0-88092-085-8*) Royal Fireworks.
Timeless Treasure: The Art of Stephen Gjertson. Annette LeSueur. LC 93-70682. (Illus.). 64p. (Orig.). 1993. pap. 29.95 (*0-9636180-0-8*) AS Class Realism.
Timeless Treasures. (Illus.). 160p. 1996. 19.96 (*1-57367-053-7*) Needlecrft Shop.
Timeless Treasures: Landmarks of Southern Cuisine. Valdosta Staff. 1993. 16.95 (*0-9635249-0-9*) Valdosta JSL.
Timeless Treasures: The Charm & Romance of Cherished Memories. Emilie Barnes & Anne Buchanan. 84p. 1996. bds. 15.99 (*1-56507-428-9*) Harvest Hse.
***Timeless Treasures Journal.** Illus. by Sandy L. Clough. 128p. 1996. 8.99 (*1-56507-509-9*) Harvest Hse.
Timeless Trees: The U. S. National Bonsai Collection. Photos by Peter L. Bloomer. (Illus.). 109p. 1986. 44.95 (*0-87358-415-5*) Horizons West.
Timeless Tribute. Contrib. by Marilynn Ham. 1986. 8.99 (*0-8341-9177-6*, MB-568) Lillenas.
Timeless Trinity. Roy H. Lanier, Sr. 1974. 11.95 (*0-89137-551-1*) Quality Pubns.
Timeless Tripod. G. Bald. 1993. 16.99 (*0-89906-131-1*); pap. 12.99 (*0-89906-132-X*) Mesorah Pubns.
Timeless Truth for Twentieth Century Times. Fred M. Barlow. 123p. 1970. 3.25 (*0-87398-838-8*) Sword of Lord.
Timeless Truths, Priceless Promises. Ed. by Linda G. Smith. 1984. 12.95 (*0-89952-082-0*) Littlebrook.
Timeless Walks in San Francisco: A Historical Walking Guide to the City. 2nd ed. Michelle Brant. 104p. (Orig.). 1996. pap. 8.95 (*0-9611346-1-5*) Brant.
Timeless Warrior. Georgina Gentry. 1990. mass mkt. 5.50 (*0-8217-5283-9*, Zebra Kensgtn) Kensgtn Pub Corp.
Timeless Way of Building. Christopher Alexander. 568p. 1979. 45.00 (*0-19-502402-8*) OUP.
Timeless Wedding Standards, Bk. 3. rev. ed. Ed. by Carol Cuellar. 144p. (Orig.). 1997. pap. 10.95 (*0-89724-545-8*, MF9516A) Warner Brothers.
Timeless Wisdom: Thoughts on Life...The Way It Should Be. rev. ed. Gary W. Fenchuk. 177p. 1995. per. 9.95 (*0-9644902-1-8*) E W Realty.
Timelessness of God. John C. Yates. 368p. (Orig.). (C). 1990. lib. bdg. 56.00 (*0-8191-7937-X*) U Pr of Amer.
Timeline: The Police. Elizabeth Campling. (Weighing up the Evidence Ser.). (Illus.). 64p. (YA). (gr. 7-10). 1989. 19.95 (*0-85219-789-6*, Pub. by Batsford UK) Trafalgar.
Timeline: Women & Power. Susan Mayfield. (Weighing up the Evidence Ser.). (Illus.). 64p. (YA). (gr. 7-9). 1989. 19.95 (*0-85219-768-3*, Pub. by Batsford UK) Trafalgar.
Timeline Book of the Arts. George Ochoa & Melinda Corey. (Illus.). 464p. (Orig.). 1995. pap. 12.00 (*0-345-38264-1*) Ballantine.
Timeline for Ancient Egypt: A Companion to the Greenleaf Guide to Ancient Egypt. Trina Dofflemyer. 8p. (Orig.). (J). (gr. 2 up). 1997. pap. 4.95 (*1-882514-21-1*) Greenleaf TN.
Timeline for Ancient Greece: A Companion to the Greenleaf Guide to Greece. Trina Dofflemyer. 8p. (Orig.). (J). (gr. 3 up). 1995. pap. 4.95 (*1-882514-22-X*) Greenleaf TN.
Timeline for Ancient Rome: A Companion to the Greenleaf Guide to Rome. Trina Dofflemyer. 8p. (Orig.). (J). (gr. 3 up). 1995. pap. 4.95 (*1-882514-23-8*) Greenleaf TN.
Timeline for Old Testament History: A Companion to the Greenleaf Guide to Old Testament History. Trina Dofflemyer. 8p. (Orig.). (J). (gr. 1 up). 1996. pap. 4.95 (*1-882514-20-3*) Greenleaf TN.
Timeline for the Middle Ages: A Companion to the Greenleaf Guide to the Middle Ages. Trina Dofflemyer. 8p. (Orig.). (J). (gr. 4 up). 1996. pap. 4.95 (*1-882514-24-6*) Greenleaf TN.
Timeline for the Renaissance & Reformation: A Companion to the Greenleaf Guide to the Renaissance. Trina Dofflemyer. 8p. (Orig.). (J). (gr. 5-12). 1997. pap. 4.95 (*1-882514-25-4*) Greenleaf TN.
Timeline of Dinosaurs: Tracing the Evolution of the World's Most Incredible Creatures. (J). 1993. 12.98 (*0-88394-974-1*) Promntory Pr.
Timeline of Discovery & Invention: Tracing the Development of Knowledge from Toolmaking. (J). 1993. 12.98 (*0-88394-973-3*) Promntory Pr.
Timeline of World History: Tracing 6000 Years of the History of Mankind. (J). 1993. 12.95 (*0-88394-972-5*) Promntory Pr.
***Timeline Wars: Crux of Battle, Vol. 1.** John Barnes. 352p. 1997. mass mkt. 5.99 (*0-06-105659-6*, HarperPrism) HarpC.
Timelines. Paul Dickson. 1991. pap. 10.95 (*0-201-56753-9*) Addison-Wesley.
Timelines & Rhythm Patterns: Representing Time. Tracey Wright et al. Ed. by Catherine Anderson et al. (Investigations in Number, Data, & Space Ser.). (Illus.). 103p. (J). (gr. 2). 1996. teacher ed. 22.95 (*1-57232-221-7*, DS21652) Seymour Pubns.
***Timelines & Rhythm Patterns: Representing Time.** rev. ed. Tracey Wright et al. Ed. by Catherine Anderson & Beverly Cory. (Investigations in Number, Data, & Space Ser.). (Illus.). 105p. (J). (gr. 2 up). 1997. pap. text ed. 22.95 (*1-57232-660-3*, 43807) Seymour Pubns.
***Timelines Information.** Purkiss. 1993. pap. text ed. write for info. (*0-582-22771-2*, Pub. by Longman UK) Longman.
Timelines Native American History. Carl Waldman. (Illus.). 36p. 1994. 22.00 (*0-671-88992-3*) P-H Gen Ref & Trav.
Timelines of African-American History: Five Hundred Years of Black Achievement. Tom Cowan. Ed. by Jack Maguire et al. 368p. (Orig.). 1994. pap. 15.00 (*0-399-52127-5*, Perigee Bks) Berkley Pub.
Timelines of American Women's History. Sue Heinemann. LC 95-23067. 400p. (Orig.). 1996. pap. 15.00 (*0-399-51986-6*, Perigee Bks) Berkley Pub.
***Timelines of Native American History: Through the Centuries with Mother Earth & Father Sky.** Susan Hazen-Hammond. LC 96-36559. 352p. 1997. pap. 16.00 (*0-399-52307-3*, Perigee Bks) Berkley Pub.
Timelines of the Twentieth Century: A Chronology of over 7,500 Key Events, Works, Discoveries, & People That Shaped Our Century. David M. Brownstone & Irene Franck. 1996. 29.95 (*0-316-11406-5*) Little.
***Timelines of the Twentieth Century: A Chronology of 7, 500 People That Shaped the Century.** David Brownstone & Irene Franck. 512p. 1997. pap. 19.95 (*0-316-11501-0*) Little.
Timelines of War: A Chronology of Warfare from 100,000 B.C. to the Present. David Brownstone & Irene Franck. 1996. pap. 19.95 (*0-316-11447-2*) Little.
Timelines of War: Chronology of Warfare from the Earliest Times to the Present. David Brownstone & Irene Franck. LC 94-203. 1994. pap. 19.95 (*0-685-71375-X*) Little.
***Timelock.** McRobbie. (Clipper Fiction Ser.). 1993. pap. text ed. write for info. (*0-582-91190-7*, Pub. by Longman UK) Longman.
Timelocke. large type ed. Jack Barnao. LC 92-314. 325p. 1992. reprint ed. lib. bdg. 20.95 (*1-56054-394-9*) Thorndike Pr.
Timeloop. C. Carew. (Spirals Ser.). (C). 1989. 23.00 (*0-09-149091-X*, Pub. by S Thornes Pubs UK) St Mut.
TimeLords. Greg Porter. (Illus.). 124p. (Orig.). (C). 1987. pap. 12.95 (*0-943891-00-0*) Blacksburg Tactical.
Timely & Profitable Help for Troubled Americans. 3rd enl. rev. ed. Hans J. Schneider & Inger M. Schneider. Orig. Title: Help for Troubled Americans. (Illus.). 320p. (Orig.). 1996. pap. 24.95 (*0-930294-14-9*) World Wide OR.
***Timely & Timeless.** Jakobvits. 27.50 (*0-85303-189-4*, Pub. by Vallentine Mitchell UK) Intl Spec Bk.
Timely & Untimely Virtues. Bernard Haring. (C). 1988. 39.00 (*0-85439-245-9*, Pub. by St Paul Pubns UK) St Mut.
Timely Articles on Slavery. Samuel Hopkins. LC 70-81121. (Black Heritage Library Collection). 1977. 13.95 (*0-8369-8603-2*) Ayer.
***Timely Death.** large type ed. Janet Neel. LC 97-9881. 382p. 1997. pap. 21.95 (*0-7838-8140-1*, GK Hall) Thorndike Pr.
***Timely Death: A Francesca Wilson Mystery.** Janet Neel. LC 96-44847. 1996. 21.95 (*0-312-15223-X*) St Martin.
Timely Homilies: The Wit & Wisdom of an Ordinary Pastor. William J. Bausch. LC 89-52152. 176p. (Orig.). 1990. pap. text ed. 9.95 (*0-89622-426-0*) Twenty-Third.
Timely Jewish Questions, Timeless Rabbinic Answers. J. Simcha Cohen. LC 90-33511. 376p. 1991. 35.00 (*0-87668-784-2*) Aronson.
Timely, Low-Cost Evaluation in the Public Sector. Ed. by Christopher G. Wye & Harry P. Hatry. LC 85-644749. (New Directions for Evaluation Ser.: No. PE 38). 1988. 19.00 (*1-55542-925-4*) Jossey-Bass.
Timely Matrimony. Kasey Michaels. (Silhouette Romance Ser.). 1994. pap. 2.75 (*0-373-19030-1*, 1-19030-5) Harlequin Bks.
Timely Meditations: Martin Heidegger & Postmodern Politics. Leslie P. Thiele. LC 94-43133. 280p. 1995. text ed. 49.50 (*0-691-08659-1*); pap. text ed. 14.95 (*0-691-04336-1*) Princeton U Pr.
Timely Pearl Vol. 1: A 12th Century Tangut-Chinese Glossary. Luc Kwanten. LC 82-62332. (Uralic & Altaic Ser.: Vol. 142). 265p. 1982. 15.00 (*0-933070-10-1*) Res Inst Inner Asian Studies.
Timely Reading: Between Exegesis & Interpretation. Susan Noakes. LC 87-47862. 288p. 1988. 39.95 (*0-8014-2144-6*) Cornell U Pr.
Timely Reflections. Marsha Sampson-Gilliam. (Poetry Ser.). 70p. 1995. pap. text ed. write for info. (*0-9645445-0-4*) M Sampson-Gilliam.
Timely Reflections & Examples of Saints for Our Times. Ed. by Gustavo Solimeo & Antonio A. Machado. Tr. by Foundation for a Christian Civilization, Inc. Staff from POR. (Illus.). 418p. (Orig.). (C). 1989. pap. 11.95 (*1-877905-21-6*) Am Soc Defense TFP.
Timely Rhymes. Henry Fischer. 64p. (Orig.). 1993. pap. 6.50 (*1-880286-30-0*) Singular Speech Pr.

Timely Tales. Stephen Wagshel. LC 91-71656. 170p. (Orig.). 1992. pap. 9.95 (*1-879629-02-X*) Galaxy Pub CO.
A book comprised of short stories that are both timely in nature & easy to read. "Lifting the Spirit" is about a high-tech exec who is haunted by the memory of a girl whom he might have pushed to suicide. "Kristen Karlsen", the second story, is about a former stewardess forced to live her life exiled in a small mountain town. "Meander", takes place long ago, focusing on the desert wanderings of a nomadic tribe seeking to regain its ancient birthright. "Eastern Analogy" is about a love affair between two people who meet in the office of a war criminal turned psychiatrist. The essay "Time, One Cycle", is also in. Here are a few lines from it - In discussing Real Time, we are referring to that time that a person can comprehend with their senses & not merely calculate intellectually....beyond the time

An Asterisk (*) at the beginning of an entry indicates that the title is appearing in BIP for the first time.

period required for all possible living experiences to transpire, occurs or what we call a full revolution in time; there is no longer any ability on the part of the individual to comprehend a greater time period. ***Publisher Provided Annotation.***

Timely Tips & Treats for the Tenderfoot Homemaker. R. Helen Van Tuyle. (Illus.). 108p. (Orig.). (YA). 1987. student ed. 9.95 (*0-9617816-0-2*) R H Van Tuyle.
Timely Tips for Travelers. 2nd ed. John R. Terry. 132p. 1991. pap. 12.50 (*0-933704-91-7*) Dawn Pr.
Timely Tips for Travellers. John R. Terry. 132p. 1990. pap. 9.95 (*0-933704-81-X*) Dawn Pr.
Timely Topics. Aquilina. 1993. pap. 25.95 (*0-8384-4200-5*) Heinle & Heinle.
Timely Topics. George N. Schlesinger. 256p. 1994. text ed. 55.00 (*0-312-12078-8*) St Martin.
Timely Torah Twinkles. I. Nathan Bamberger. LC 88-43161. 110p. 1988. pap. 8.95 (*0-88400-131-8*) Shengold.
Timely Truths from the Book of Mormon. Allan K. Burgess. 1995. pap. 8.95 (*1-57008-199-9*) Bookcraft Inc.
Timemaster. Robert L. Forward. 320p. 1993. mass mkt. 5.99 (*0-8125-1644-3*) Tor Bks.
Timenglish: The Words of Time. Ed. by George Kurian. 123p. (Orig.). 1993. pap. 12.95 (*0-685-64941-5*) G Kurian.
***Timepiece.** Evans. 1997. mass mkt. 5.99 (*0-671-00897-8*) PB.
***Timepiece.** Richard P. Evans. 1996. 15.95 (*0-684-83798-6*) S&S Trade.
Timepiece. Richard Paul Evans. 1996. 18.00 (*0-684-81576-1*) S&S Trade.
Timepiece. Jane Flanders. LC 87-25191. (Poetry Ser.). 72p. (C). 1988. 19.95 (*0-8229-3573-2*); pap. 10.95 (*0-8229-5399-4*) U of Pittsburgh Pr.
Timepiece. large type ed. Richard Paul Evans. 1996. 20.00 (*0-684-82346-2*) S&S Trade.
Timepiece: Extending & Enhancing Learning Time. Ed. by Loren W. Anderson & Herbert J. Walberg. 56p. (Orig.). (C). 1993. pap. text ed. 9.00 (*0-88210-280-X*) Natl Assn Principals.
***Timepieces 5-Year Daily Journal.** John S. Williams, 3rd. (Illus.). 240p. 1997. vinyl bd. 25.50 (*1-886197-05-9*) Joy Books.
Timequake. Kurt Vonnegut. LC 97-14508. 320p. 1997. 22.95 (*0-399-13737-8*) Putnam Pub Group.
Times Alone: Selected Poems of Antonio Machado. Antonio Machado. Tr. by Robert Bly. LC 83-6955. (Wesleyan Poetry in Translation Ser.). 187p. (ENG & SPA.). 1983. pap. 14.95 (*0-8195-6081-2*, Wesleyan Univ Pr) U Pr of New Eng.
Times & Appetites of Toulouse-Lautrec: A Play with Songs. Jeff Wanshel. 1986. pap. 5.25 (*0-8222-1153-X*) Dramatists Play.
Times & Places see Corridors of Time: New Haven & London, 1927-1956
Times & Places for Literature see Foreign Languages: Reading, Literature, Requirements
Times & Places, Home & Away: A Life of Freelancing in the Outdoors. Charles F. Waterman. LC 87-82428. (Illus.). 272p. 1988. 17.95 (*0-9609842-8-3*) GSJ Press.
Times & Seasons: Homilies for the Church Year. Sergio P. Negro. LC 94-76370. (Illus.). 200p. 1994. pap. 15.00 (*0-9641404-9-7*, WordWrks) Sixth St Pr.
Times & Tendencies. Agnes Repplier. LC 71-128297. (Essay Index Reprint Ser.). 1977. 21.95 (*0-8369-2028-7*) Ayer.
Times & Triumphs of American Woman. Ed. by Elaine Scott. (Illus.). 79p. (J). (gr. 4-9). 1986. pap. text ed. 8.00 (*0-9610622-1-5*) Natl Wmns Hall Fame.
Times Are Never So Bad. Andre Dubus. LC 82-48703. 192p. 1986. pap. 11.95 (*0-87923-641-8*) Godine.
Time's Arrow. Martin Amis. LC 91-5112. 1992. pap. 11.00 (*0-679-73572-0*, Vin) Random.
Time's Arrow: Origins of Thermodynamic Behavior. 2nd ed. M. C. Mackey. (Illus.). 190p. 1993. write for info. (*3-540-94093-6*) Spr-Verlag.
Time's Arrow: Origins of Thermodynamic Behavior. M. C. Mackey. (Illus.). 192p. 1994. reprint ed. 39.95 (*0-387-94093-6*) Spr-Verlag.
Time's Arrow: The Origin of Thermodynamic Behavior. M. C. Mackey. (Illus.). 150p. 1991. 49.00 (*0-387-97702-3*) Spr-Verlag.
Time's Arrow - Time's Cycle: Myth & Metaphor in the Discovery of Geological Time. Stephen J. Gould. 240p. 1988. reprint ed. pap. text ed. 12.00 (*0-674-89199-6*) HUP.
Time's Arrow & Archimedes' Point: New Directions for the Physics of Time. Huw Price. 320p. 1996. 25.00 (*0-19-510095-6*) OUP.
***Time's Arrow & Archimedes' Point: New Directions for the Physics of Time.** Huw Price. (Illus.). 320p. 1997. reprint ed. pap. 14.95 (*0-19-511798-0*) OUP.
Time's Arrow & Evolution. 3rd ed. Harold F. Blum. LC 68-31676. 250p. reprint ed. pap. 71.30 (*0-8357-2786-6*, 2039912) Bks Demand.
Time's Arrow, or, the Nature of the Offense. Martin Amis. LC 91-51128. 1992. pap. 7.00 (*0-679-74170-4*, Vin) Random.
Time's Arrow, Time's Cycle: Myth & Metaphor in the Discovery of Geological Time. Stephen J. Gould. LC 86-29485. 240p. 1987. 23.50 (*0-674-89198-8*) HUP.
Time's Arrows & Quantum Measurement. L. S. Schulman. LC 95-47482. (Illus.). 256p. (C). 1997. text ed. 90.00 (*0-521-56122-1*); pap. text ed. 29.95 (*0-521-56775-0*) Cambridge U Pr.
Time's Arrows Today: Recent Physical & Philosophical Work on the Direction of Time. Ed. by Steven F. Savitt. (Illus.). 326p. (C). 1995. text ed. 52.95 (*0-521-46111-1*) Cambridge U Pr.
***Time's Arrows Today: Recent Physical & Philosophical Work on the Direction of Time.** Ed. by Steven F. Savitt. 344p. 1997. pap. text ed. 24.95 (*0-521-59945-8*) Cambridge U Pr.
Times Atlas of the Bible. Random House Value Pubns. Staff. 1996. 39.99 (*0-517-16022-6*) Random Hse Value.
Times Atlas of the World. New York Times Staff. 1995. 100.00 (*0-8129-2604-8*) Random.
Times Atlas of the World. 7th rev. ed. LC 85-675126. (Illus.). 520p. 1985. 149.95 (*0-8129-1298-5*, Times Bks) Random.
Times Atlas of the World. 8th ed. New York Times Staff. (Illus.). 1990. 159.95 (*0-8129-1874-6*, Times Bks) Random.
Times Atlas of the World. 9th ed. LC 92-53672. 514p. 1992. 175.00 (*0-8129-2077-5*, Times Bks) Random.
***Times Atlas of the World.** 10th ed. New York Times Staff. 1997. write for info. (*0-8129-2945-4*, Times Bks) Random.
Times Atlas of World History. 4th ed. Ed. by Geoffrey Barraclogh. LC 93-23944. 360p. 1994. 95.00 (*0-7230-0534-6*) Hammond Inc.
Times Atlas Second World War. RH Value Publishing Staff & John Keegan. 1995. 29.99 (*0-517-12377-0*) Random.
Times Between. Wyatt Prunty. LC 81-13724. (Poetry & Fiction Ser.). 80p. 1982. pap. 9.95 (*0-8018-2407-9*); text ed. 14.95 (*0-8018-2403-6*) Johns Hopkins.
Times Books World Weather Guide. enl. ed. E. A. Pearce & Gordon Smith. (Illus.). 1990. pap. 17.95 (*0-8129-1881-9*, Times Bks) Random.
Times Change: The Minimum Wage & the New York Times. Richard B. McKenzie. LC 94-15800. 1994. 19.95 (*0-936488-76-X*) PRIPP.
Times Chinese-English Dictionary. Commercial Press Staff. 564p. (CHI & ENG.). 1980. pap. 14.95 (*0-8288-1602-6*, M9273) Fr & Eur.
Times Concise Atlas of World History. 4th ed. Ed. by Geoffrey Barraclough. 1995. pap. text ed. 31.95 (*0-7230-0674-1*) Hammond Inc.
***Times Concise Atlas of World History.** 4th rev. ed. Geoffrey Barraclough. LC 82-50111. (Illus.). 192p. 1995. pap. 31.95 (*0-8437-1147-7*) Hammond Inc.
Times Cookbook. Frances Bissell. (Illus.). 654p. 1996. pap. 24.95 (*0-7011-6366-6*, Pub. by Chatto & Windus UK) Trafalgar.
Time's Covenant: The Essays & Sermons of William Clancy. Ed. by Eugene Green. LC 86-19517. xviii, 232p. 1987. 19.95 (*0-8229-3545-7*) U of Pittsburgh Pr.
Time's Dipstick. John M. Bennett. 1976. pap. 2.00 (*0-935350-94-2*) Luna Bisonte.
Time's Discipline: The Eight Beatitudes & Nuclear Resistance. Daniel Berrigan et al. (Illus.). 286p. (Orig.). 1989. pap. 14.95 (*1-879175-02-9*) Fortkamp.
Time's Disinherited Children: Childhood, Regression & Sacrifice in the Plays of Henrik Ibsen. Robin Young. 200p. 8800. pap. 23.00 (*1-870041-06-2*, Pub. by Norvik Pr UK) Dufour.
Time's Enemy: Invasion. L. A. Graf. (Star Trek: Deep Space Nine Ser.). 1996. mass mkt. 5.99 (*0-671-54150-1*) PB.
Time's Fancy. Ronald Wallace. (Poetry Ser.). 96p. (C). 1994. 22.95 (*0-8229-3868-5*); pap. 10.95 (*0-8229-5548-2*) U of Pittsburgh Pr.
***Times Flies.** Eric Rohmann. 1997. pap. write for info. (*0-517-88555-7*) Crown Pub Group.
Time's Flotsam: Overseas Collections of California Indian Material Culture. Thomas C. Blackburn & Travis Hudson. LC 90-308. (Anthropological Papers: No. 35). (Illus.). 225p. 1990. 34.95 (*0-87919-117-1*); pap. 24.95 (*0-87919-116-3*) Ballena Pr.
Time's Fool: A Story in Sonnets Based on Those of Shakespeare. Judson Jerome. LC 91-47950. 128p. (Orig.). 1992. pap. 10.00 (*0-936784-98-9*) J Daniel.
Times for Learning. John R. Bergan et al. (Illus.). 237p. (Orig.). 1994. pap. 21.95 (*1-888639-01-6*, TFL) Assessmnt Tech.
Time's Glory: Original Essays on Robert Penn Warren. Ed. by James A. Grimshaw, Jr. (Illus.). 126p. 1997. 19.95 (*0-9615143-2-9*) Pelican.
Times Guide to the Middle East: The Arab World & Its Neighbors. Marion Farouk-Sluglett. Ed. by Peter Sluglett. (C). 1996. pap. text ed. 24.00 (*0-8133-2788-1*) Westview.
Times Guide to World Organizations: Their Role & Reach in the New World Order. Richard Owen. (C). 1996. text ed. 35.00 (*0-8133-6967-3*) Westview.
Time's Healing Heart. Marti Jones. 400p. (Orig.). 1994. mass mkt., pap. text ed. 4.99 (*0-505-51954-2*, Love Spell) Dorchester Pub Co.
Times I Like the Best. Les Wilson. LC 95-62231. (Illus.). 24p. (Orig.). (J). (ps). 1995. pap. 7.95 (*0-9650393-0-7*) Tootetti Pubng.
Times Illustrated History of Europe. Felipe Fernandez-Armesto. (Illus.). 192p. 1996. 40.00 (*0-7230-0724-1*) HarperColl Wrld.
Times Illustrated History of the World. 3rd ed. E. Ehrlich. (Illus.). 1995. 40.00 (*0-06-270010-3*, HarpT) HarpC.
Times in Review: New York Times Decade Book 1920, Vol. 5. Date not set. 55.95 (*0-405-00375-7*) Ayer.
Times in Review: New York Times Decade Books, 5 Vols. Incl. Vol. 1. Nineteen Twenty-Nineteen Twenty Nine. 50.00 (*0-685-73169-3*); Vol. 2. Nineteen Thirty-Nineteen Thirty Nine. 50.00 (*0-685-73170-7*); Vol. 3. Nineteen Forty-Nineteen Forty Nine. 50.00 (*0-685-73171-5*); Vol. J. Nineteen Fifty-Nineteen Fifty Nine. 50.00 (*0-685-73172-3*); Vol. 5. Nineteen Sixty-Nineteen Sixty Nine. 50.00 (*0-685-73173-1*); (Illus.). write for info. (*0-318-50909-1*) Ayer.
Times I've Seen. Ulick O'Connor. (Illus.). 1964. 19.95 (*0-8392-1119-8*) Astor-Honor.
Time's Last Gift. Philip Jose Farmer. 256p. 1991. pap. 3.95 (*0-8125-1440-8*) Tor Bks.
Time's Noblest Name: (L-O) see Names & Titles of Jesus Christ
Times of Joshua & the Judges. (Bible Adventure Bks.). (J). (gr. 4-6). 1995. 2.19 (*0-89636-112-8*, JB 1B) Accent CO.
Times of Our Lives: A Guide to Writing Autobiography & Memoir. 3rd ed. Mary J. Moffat. 64p. (Orig.). 1996. pap. 8.95 (*1-880284-18-9*) J Daniel.
Times of Refreshing: A Practical Theology of Revival for Today. Mark Stibbe. 1995. pap. 11.99 (*0-551-02959-5*, Pub. by M Pickering UK) Zondervan.
Times of Refreshing Cycle B: Sermons for Lent-Easter: First Lesson Texts. E. Carver McGriff. LC 96-6867. 111p. (Orig.). 1996. pap. 9.25 (*0-7880-0773-4*) CSS OH.
Times of Surrender: Selected Essays. Robert Coles. LC 87-30221. 292p. 1988. 28.95 (*0-87745-188-5*) U of Iowa Pr.
Times of the Rebellion in the West. Henry Howe. (Notable American Authors Ser.). 1992. reprint ed. lib. bdg. 75.00 (*0-7812-3209-0*) Rprt Serv.
Times of the Trinity: A Proposal for Theistic Cosmology, Vol. 17. Duane H. Larson. LC 94-37760. (Worcester Polytechnic Institute Studies in Science, Technology & Culture: Vol. 17). 224p. (C). 1995. 45.95 (*0-8204-2706-3*) P Lang Pubng.
Times of Time: A New Perspective in Systemic Therapy & Consultation. Luigi Boscolo & Paola Bertrando. 352p. (C). 1993. 35.00 (*0-393-70163-8*) Norton.
Times of Turmoil: A Collection of Stories. Felix Rozinier et al. Tr. by Arkady Yanishevsky from RUS. LC 93-40496. (Illus.). 176p. (Orig.). 1994. pap. 12.00 (*1-55779-065-5*) Hermitage.
Times of Used to Be. Denvil Mullins. 188p. 1993. pap. 9.95 (*1-57072-001-0*) Overmountain Pr.
Times of War & Peace: Dealing with Kids' Concerns. Susan Goldberg. 88p. 1992. pap. 6.95 (*1-55037-202-5*, Pub. by Annick CN) Firefly Bks Ltd.
Times of Your Life. Ralph Kamhi. 8p. (J). (gr. 6-12). 1989. write for info. (*0-9627292-0-5*) Extra NY.
Times One-Thousand Mots En Images. Ed. by European Language Institute Staff. (Illus.). 92p. (Orig.). (FRE.). (J). (gr. 2-6). 1992. pap. 11.95 (*88-85148-52-2*, Pub. by Europ Lang Inst IT) Midwest European Pubns.
Times One-Thousand Mots Pour Parler. Kathleen Lloyd. (Illus.). 95p. (Orig.). (FRE.). (J). (gr. 2-6). 1992. pap. 9.95 (*88-85148-54-9*, Pub. by Europ Lang Inst IT) Midwest European Pubns.
Times One-Thousand Words Dictionary. Myra Ellis. (Illus.). 120p. (Orig.). (J). (gr. 2-6). 1992. pap. 11.95 (*981-01-0381-6*, Pub. by Europ Lang Inst IT) Midwest European Pubns.
Times One-Thousand Words in Pictures. Ed. by Federal Publications Staff. (Illus.). 92p. (Orig.). (J). (gr. 2-6). 1987. pap. 11.95 (*981-01-0010-8*, Pub. by Europ Lang Inst IT) Midwest European Pubns.
Times One-Thousand Words to Talk About. Kathleen Lloyd. (Illus.). 95p. (Orig.). (J). (gr. 2-6). 1992. pap. 11.95 (*981-01-0384-0*, Pub. by Europ Lang Inst IT) Midwest European Pubns.
Times One-Thousand Worter in Bildern. European Language Institute Staff. (Illus.). 92p. (Orig.). (GER.). (J). (gr. 2-6). 1992. reprint ed. pap. 11.95 (*88-85148-53-0*, Pub. by Europ Lang Inst IT) Midwest European Pubns.
Times One-Thousand Worter Zum Sprechen. Kathleen Lloyd. (Illus.). 95p. (Orig.). (GER.). (J). (gr. 2-6). 1992. reprint ed. pap. 11.95 (*88-85148-55-7*, Pub. by Europ Lang Inst IT) Midwest European Pubns.
Times Past. Ed. by Glenda Hadley. (Illus.). (Orig.). 1982. pap. write for info. (*0-9607910-0-0*) Golden Aires.
Time's Pickpocket. Roy Shepard. LC 92-91119. 74p. 1993. pap. 8.00 (*1-56002-262-0*, Univ Edtns) Aegina Pr.
Time's Power: Poems 1985-1988. Adrienne Rich. 1989. pap. 9.95 (*0-393-30575-9*) Norton.
Time's Purpled Masquers: Stars & the Afterlife in Renaissance English Literature. Alastair Fowler. 184p. (C). 1996. 52.00 (*0-19-818340-2*, Clarendon Pr) OUP.
Time's Reasons: Philosophies of History Old & New. Leonard Krieger. LC 88-29407. 214p. 1989. 39.00 (*0-226-45300-6*) U Ch Pr.
Times Recalled: Tales from an Extraordinary Man in OSS, Fred Farris. Ed. by Helen M. Copeland. 92p. (Orig.). 1989. per., pap. 16.00 (*0-9624737-2-3*) S P-Persephone Pr.
Times Seventeen: The Amazing Story of the Zodiac Murders in California & Massachusetts, 1966-1981. Gareth Penn. (Illus.). 380p. 1987. pap. 25.00 (*0-9618494-0-1*) Foxglove Pr.
Time's Silent Stealth: A Tribute to Jane. F. Smith Fussner. LC 94-71585. 260p. (Orig.). 1994. pap. 19.95 (*0-940121-28-X*, P215, Cross Roads Bks) Cross Cultural Pubns.
Times, Spaces & Places: A Chronogeographic Perspective. Don Parkes & Nigel Thrift. LC 79-40523. 543p. reprint ed. pap. 154.80 (*0-318-34960-4*, 2030757) Bks Demand.
Times Square Bossa Nova. (Ballroom Dance Ser.). 1986. lib. bdg. 64.95 (*0-8490-3279-2*) Gordon Pr.
Times Square Bossa Nova. (Ballroom Dance Ser.). 1985. lib. bdg. 250.00 (*0-87700-824-8*) Revisionist Pr.
Times Square Gym. Photos by John Goodman. (Illus.). 96p. 1996. pap. 29.95 (*1-886212-06-6*, 620081) Amilus.
Times Square Hustler: Male Prostitution in New York City. Robert P. McNamara. LC 94-21689. 168p. 1994. text ed. 52.95 (*0-275-95003-4*, Praeger Pubs); pap. text ed. 17.95 (*0-275-95186-3*, Praeger Pubs) Greenwood.
***Times Square Rabbi: Finding the Hope in Lost Kids' Lives.** LC 96-53665. 1997. 14.95 (*1-56838-145-X*) Hazelden.
Time's Stop in Savannah: Conrad Aiken's Inner Journey. Ted R. Spivey. LC 96-37749. 184p. 1996. text ed. 32.00 (*0-86554-533-2*, MUP/H408) Mercer Univ Pr.
Times Survey of the Foreign Ministries of the World. Ed. by Zara S. Steiner. 624p. 1982. text ed. 95.00 (*0-313-28129-7*, SZU/, Greenwood Pr) Greenwood.
Times Table Secrets. James A. Davis. (Illus.). 12p. (J). (gr. 3-5). 1994. 10.00 (*0-9634088-1-X*) Simp Solns.
Times Tables. David Clemson & Wendy Clemson. LC 95-44393. (J). 1996. write for info. (*0-7894-0472-9*) DK Pub Inc.
***Times Tables!** Wendy Clemson & David Clemson. (Illus.). (J). 11.99 (*0-590-24755-7*) Scholastic Inc.
***Times Tables.** Dorling Kindersley Staff. (My Math Sticker Work Bk.). (Illus.). 16p. (J). 1997. pap. 6.95 (*0-7894-1516-X*) DK Pub Inc.
Times Tables. Rebecca Treays. (Math Skills Ser.). (Illus.). 32p. (J). (gr. 1-5). 1996. pap. 5.95 (*0-7460-2399-5*, Usborne) EDC.
Times Tables the Fun Way Book for Kids: A Picture Method of Learning the Multiplication Facts. 2nd enl. rev. ed. David Rodriguez & Judy Rodriguez. LC 93-79769. (Illus.). 86p. (J). (gr. 2-8). 1994. spiral bd. 19.95 (*1-883841-26-7*) Key Pubs UT.
***Times Tables the Fun Way Book for Kids Parent's Set: A Picture Method of Learning the Multiplication Facts, Incl. Flash Cards & Student Workbook.** 2nd enl. rev. ed. Dave Rodriguez et al. (Illus.). 86p. (J). (gr. 2-8). 1994. spiral bd. 33.85 (*1-883841-40-2*) Key Pubs UT.
***Times Tables the Fun Way Book for Kids Starter Set: A Picture Method of Learning the Multiplication Facts, Incl. Flash Cards.** 2nd enl. rev. ed. Dave Rodriguez & Judy Rodriguez. (Illus.). 86p. (J). (gr. 2-8). 1994. spiral bd. 25.90 (*1-883841-39-9*) Key Pubs UT.
Time's Tapestry. Joan E. Overfield. 304p. 1996. mass mkt. 4.99 (*0-8217-5381-9*, Zebra Kensgtn) Kensgtn Pub Corp.
***Time's Tapestry: Four Generations of a New Orleans Family.** Leta W. Marks. LC 97-25816. (Illus.). 200p. 1997. 24.95 (*0-8071-2205-X*) La State U Pr.
Times That Prove People's Principles: Civil War Georgia. Ed. by Mills Lane. (Documentary History Ser.). 276p. 1993. 35.00 (*0-88322-017-2*) Beehive GA.
Times, the Chronicle & the Observer. Douglas Blau. (Illus.). 64p. 1990. pap. 20.00 (*1-878607-25-1*) Kent Gallery.
Times, the Man, the Company see Ford
Times, Thoughts...Words. R. D. Peters. LC 93-93900. 160p. (Orig.). 1994. pap. 10.00 (*1-56002-339-2*, Univ Edtns) Aegina Pr.
Times to Come. Noel Tyl. LC 73-19910. (Principles & Practice of Astrology Ser.: Vol. 12). (Illus.). 197p. (Orig.). 1975. pap. 3.95 (*0-87542-811-8*) Llewellyn Pubns.
Times to Remember. Rose F. Kennedy. LC 73-79682. 1994. reprint ed. lib. bdg. 29.95 (*1-56849-567-6*) Buccaneer Bks.
Time's Up: Mystery Jigsaw Puzzle Thriller. Al Carusone. (Spider Tales Ser.). (Orig.). (J). (gr. 3-7). 1996. pap. 13.50 (*1-57561-010-8*, 00906TUP) Bepuzzled.
Times We Had. Marion Davies. 1985. mass mkt. 6.99 (*0-345-32739-X*) Ballantine.
Times Were a Changin' Irwin Unger. 1998. write for info. (*0-517-70590-7*) Random Hse Value.
Times Were Strange & Stirring: Methodist Preachers & the Crisis of Emancipation. Reginald F. Hildebrand. LC 94-46758. 240p. 1995. text ed. 45.95 (*0-8223-1627-7*); pap. text ed. 17.95 (*0-8223-1639-0*) Duke.
Time's Winged Chariot. Heald T. Bernard. 136p. 1985. 55.00 (*0-907033-26-1*) St Mut.
Time's Witness. Michael Malone. Ed. by Jane Rosenman. 562p. 1994. pap. 10.00 (*0-671-87527-2*, WSP) PB.
Times Witness. Michael Malone. Ed. by Sally Peters. 592p. 1991. reprint ed. mass mkt. 5.95 (*0-671-70318-8*) PB.
Time's Witness: Historical Representation in English Poetry, 1603- 1660. Gerald M. MacLean. LC 89-40532. (Illus.). 336p. (C). 1990. pap. text ed. 17.50 (*0-299-12394-4*) U of Wis Pr.
Timesaving Aid to Virginia-West Virginia Ancestors, Vol. 1. Patrick G. Wardell. vii, 170p. (Orig.). 1985. pap. 10.00 (*0-935931-01-5*) Iberian Pub.
Timesaving Aid to Virginia-West Virginia Ancestors, Vol. 2. Patrick G. Wardell. vii, 182p. (Orig.). 1986. pap. 10.00 (*0-935931-28-7*) Iberian Pub.
Timesaving Aid to Virginia-West Virginia Ancestors, Vol. 3. Patrick G. Wardell. vi, 142p. (Orig.). 1987. pap. 10.00 (*0-935931-34-1*) Iberian Pub.
Timesaving Aid to Virginia-West Virginia Ancestors: A Genealogical Index of Surnames from Published Sources. Patrick G. Wardell. iv, 429p. 1990. pap. 36.00 (*0-935931-52-X*) Borgo Pr.
Timesaving Aid to Virginia-West Virginia Ancestors: A Genealogical Index of Surnames from Published Sources. Patrick G. Wardell. iv, 429p. (C). 1990. reprint ed. Vol. 4. lib. bdg. 66.00 (*0-8095-8241-4*) Borgo Pr.
Timesaving Sewing. Cy DeCosse Incorporated Staff. LC 87-649. (Singer Sewing Reference Library). (Illus.). 128p. 1987. 18.95 (*0-86573-215-9*); pap. 16.95 (*0-86573-216-7*) Cowles Creative.
Timescale. Nigel Calder. pap. 8.95 (*0-14-006342-0*, Penguin Bks) Viking Penguin.
Timescales in Geomorphology. Ed. by R. A. Cullingford et al. LC 79-40517. (Illus.). 370p. reprint ed. pap. 105.50 (*0-8357-3075-1*, 2039332) Bks Demand.
Timescales of Environmental Change. Ed. by Chapman. 288p. (C). 1996. pap. 22.95 (*0-415-13253-3*); text ed. 75.00 (*0-415-13252-5*) Routledge.
Timescape. Gregory Benford. 512p. 1992. mass mkt. 6.50 (*0-553-29709-0*) Bantam.
Timescapes of John Fowles. H. W. Fawkner. LC 82-48606. 180p. 1984. 32.50 (*0-8386-3175-4*) Fairleigh Dickinson.
***Timeshadow Rider.** Ann Maxwell. 320p. 1997. mass mkt. 5.99 (*0-7860-0368-5*, Pinncle Kensgtn) Kensgtn Pub Corp.
***Timeshare: Do You Believe in Yesterday?** Joshua Dann. 256p. 1997. mass mkt. 5.99 (*0-441-00457-1*) Ace Bks.

Timeshare Financing Manual. 1985. 38.50 (*0-318-19150-4*); 28.50 (*0-318-19151-2*) ARDA.

Timeshare Lenders Survey. 125.00 (*0-318-03347-X*) ARDA.

Timeshare Property Assessment & Taxation. Kathleen Conroy & James DiChiara. Ed. by Jeanette E. Smith. (Illus.). (Orig.). (C). 1983. 31.00 (*0-318-04658-X*) ARDA.

Timeshare Purchasers: Who They Are, Why They Buy, 1993. (Industry Issues Ser.). 88p. 1993. 75.00 (*0-614-04628-9*, 21300) ARDA.

Timesharing: What's in It for You. Robert MacBride. LC 76-10858. 26p. reprint ed. pap. 25.00 (*0-317-08635-9*, 2004617) Bks Demand.

Timeshift: On Video Culture. Sean Cubitt. (Illus.). 200p. 1991. 49.95 (*0-685-50225-2*, A5097, Comedia) Routledge.

Timeshift: On Video Culture. Sean Cubitt. (Illus.). 200p. (C). 1991. pap. 19.95 (*0-415-01678-9*, A5101, Comedia) Routledge.

Timeshift: The Experience of Dimensional Change. Janet I. Sussman. LC 95-6002. (Illus.). 210p. (Orig.). 1996. pap. text ed. 12.95 (*0-9643535-0-4*) Time Portal.

***Timeshifting: Creating More Time to Enjoy Your Life.** Stephan Rechtschaffen. 256p. 1996. pap. 12.95 (*0-385-48390-2*, Main St Bks) Doubleday.

***Timeslips: New & Selected Poems.** Anne Cluysenaar. 144p. 1997. pap. 16.95 (*1-85754-267-3*, Pub. by Carcanet Pr UK) Paul & Co Pubs.

Timeswept Bride. Eugenia Riley. 416p. (Orig.). 1995. mass mkt. 5.50 (*0-380-77157-8*) Avon.

Timeswept Brides. Mary Balogh et al. 352p. 1996. mass mkt. 5.99 (*0-515-11891-5*) Jove Pubns.

Timeswept Lovers. Constance O'Day-Flannery. 496p. 1987. mass mkt. 3.95 (*0-8217-2057-0*, Zebra Kensgtn) Kensgtn Pub Corp.

Timeswept Lovers. Oday-Flannry. 1993. pap. 4.99 (*0-8217-4552-2*) NAL-Dutton.

***Timeswept Passion.** Joyce Carlow. 320p. 1997. mass mkt. 4.99 (*0-8217-5567-6*, Zebra Kensgtn) Kensgtn Pub Corp.

Timeswept Rogue. Amy J. Fetzer. 416p. 1996. mass mkt. 5.50 (*0-8217-5456-4*, Zebra Kensgtn) Kensgtn Pub Corp.

Timetable of Computers: A Chronology of the Most Important People & Events in the History of Computers. Donald D. Spencer. LC 95-3766. 1997. pap. 34.95 (*0-89218-302-0*) Camelot Pub.

Timetable of Life. Louise Fimlaid. 244p. 1990. 17.95 (*0-86690-385-2*, AFA NO. F3081-0) Am Fed Astrologers.

Timetable of Life: You Chose It! Now Do the Best with What You've Got. Louise Fimlaid. (Illus.). 256p. 1990. 17.95 (*0-9630409-2-8*, TX2921085) Galaxy Pub.

Timetable of Mathematics: A Chronology of the Most Important People & Events in the History of Mathematics. Donald D. Spencer. LC 95-3767. 1998. pap. 34.95 (*0-89218-303-9*) Camelot Pub.

TimeTabler 3. Keith Johnson. 216p. (C). 1994. 75.00 (*0-7478-1077-X*, Pub. by Stanley Thornes UK) Trans-Atl Phila.

Timetables: Structuring the Passage of Time in Hospital Treatment & Other Careers. Julius A. Roth. (Orig.). 1963. pap. 4.95 (*0-672-60851-0*, Bobbs) Macmillan.

Timetables of African-American History: A Chronology of the Most Important People & Events in African-American History. Sharon Harley. LC 94-22571. (Illus.). 400p. 1995. 35.00 (*0-671-79524-4*) S&S Trade.

Timetables of African American History: Chronology Important People & Events. Sharon Harley. (Illus.). 400p. 1996. pap. 21.00 (*0-684-81578-8*, Touchstone Bks) S&S Trade.

Timetables of American History. Ed. by Laurence Urdang. 480p. 1983. pap. 20.00 (*0-671-25246-1*, Touchstone Bks) S&S Trade.

Timetables of American History. rev. ed. Laurence Urdang. LC 96-18446. 512p. 1996. pap. 21.00 (*0-684-81420-X*, Touchstone Bks) S&S Trade.

Timetables of History: A Horizontal Linkage of People & Events. rev. ed. Bernard Grun. (Illus.). 688p. 1991. pap. 20.00 (*0-671-74271-X*, Touchstone Bks) S&S Trade.

Timetables of Jewish History: A Chronology of the Most Important People & Events in Jewish History. Judah Gribetz et al. 752p. 1994. pap. 20.00 (*0-671-88577-4*, Touchstone Bks) S&S Trade.

Timetables of Science: A Chronology of the Most Important People & Events in the History of Science. Alexander Hellemans & Bryan Bunch. 672p. 1991. pap. 20.00 (*0-671-73328-1*, Touchstone Bks) S&S Trade.

Timetables of Sports History: Football. William Jarrett. (Illus.). 96p. (YA). (gr. 6 up). 1989. 17.95 (*0-8160-1919-3*) Facts on File.

Timetables of Sports History: The Olympic Games. William Jarrett. (Illus.). 96p. (YA). 1990. 17.95 (*0-8160-1921-5*) Facts on File.

Timetables of Technology. Bryan Bunch & Alexander Hellemans. 512p. 1994. pap. 20.00 (*0-671-88767-X*, Touchstone Bks) S&S Trade.

Timetables of Technology: A Chronology of the Most Important People & Events in the History of Technology. Alexander Hellemans & Brian Bunch. LC 93-27734. 512p. 1993. 35.00 (*0-671-76918-9*) S&S Trade.

Timetables of Women's History. Karen Greenspan. (Illus.). 464p. 1996. pap. 21.00 (*0-684-81579-6*, Touchstone Bks) S&S Trade.

Timetables of Women's History: A Chronology of the Most Important People & Events in Women's History. Karen Greenspan. 528p. 1995. 35.00 (*0-671-67150-2*) S&S Trade.

Timetabling. Ed. by J. Johnson. (C). 1989. 130.00 (*0-09-141630-2*, Pub. by S Thornes Pubs UK) St Mut.

Timetrap. David Dvorkin. (Star Trek Ser.: No. 40). 288p. (Orig.). 1988. pap. 4.95 (*0-671-64870-5*) PB.

Timewalkers: The Prehistory of Global Colonization. Clive Gamble. LC 93-28825. 319p. 1994. text ed. 24.95 (*0-674-89202-X*) HUP.

Timewalkers: The Prehistory of Global Colonization. Clive Gamble. (Illus.). 320p. 1996. pap. 15.95 (*0-674-89203-8*) HUP.

***Timewankers.** Stephen Sullivan. (Eros Graphic Novel Ser.: No. 13). 120p. pap. 16.95 (*1-56097-211-4*) Fantagraph Bks.

Timewatch: The Social Analysis of Time. Barbara Adam. 224p. (C). 1995. pap. text ed. 22.95 (*0-7456-1461-2*) Blackwell Pubs.

Timex-Sinclair Computer Games Programs. Edward Page. 96p. 1983. 7.95 (*0-86668-026-8*) ARCsoft.

Timex TS 2000: Your Personal Computer. Ian McLean. (Illus.). 240p. 1984. pap. text ed. 12.95 (*0-13-921974-9*) P-H.

Timid Dragon. Tim Kelly. 1968. pap. 3.00 (*0-87129-077-4*, T30) Dramatic Pub.

Timing Analysis of Real-Time Software: A Practical Approach to the Specification & Design of Real-Time. Leo Motus & Michael G. Rodd. LC 94-28551. 1994. text ed. 125.00 (*0-08-042026-5*, Pergamon Pr); pap. text ed. 51.25 (*0-08-042025-7*, Pergamon Pr) Elsevier.

Timing & Patterns of Molt in Microtus Breweri. Carol Rowsemitt et al. (Occasional Papers: No. 34). 11p. 1975. pap. 1.00 (*0-317-04913-5*) U KS Nat Hist Mus.

Timing & the De-Escalation of International Conflicts. Ed. by Louis Kriesberg & Stuart J. Thorson. LC 91-9810. (Studies on Peace & Conflict Resolution). 256p. (C). 1991. text ed. 39.95 (*0-8156-2521-9*); pap. text ed. 15.95 (*0-8156-2523-5*) Syracuse U Pr.

Timing & Time Perception. Intro. by John Gibbon & Lorraine Allan. (Annals Ser.: Vol. 423). 654p. 1984. lib. bdg. 144.00 (*0-89766-240-7*) NY Acad Sci.

Timing Chain. Douglas Woolf. 140p. (Orig.). 1985. pap. 7.00 (*0-939180-36-7*) Tombouctou.

Timing Chain. limited ed. Douglas Woolf. 140p. (Orig.). 1985. 35.00 (*0-939180-37-5*) Tombouctou.

Timing Is Everything. Denis Waitley. 1996. pap. 6.50 (*0-671-88102-7*) PB.

Timing Manipulations. James Hamilton. 1974. pap. 4.50 (*0-918845-00-9*) Am Watchmakers.

Timing Neutron Stars. Edward P. Van Den Heuvel, pseud. (C). 1989. lib. bdg. 299.00 (*0-7923-0101-3*) Kluwer Ac.

Timing of Aneurysm Surgery. Ed. by L. M. Auer & N. Kassel. (Illus.). xiv, 685p. 1985. 176.95 (*3-11-010156-4*) De Gruyter.

Timing of Events: Electional Astrology. Bruce Scofield. (Illus.). 144p. (Orig.). 1986. pap. 9.95 (*0-87199-039-3*) Astrolabe SW.

Timing of Toxicological Studies to Support Clinical Trials: Proceedings: C. M. R. Discussion Meeting on the Timing of Toxicological Studies (1994: Nutfield, U. K.) Ed. by Christopher Parkinson. 150p. 1995. lib. bdg. 82.50 (*0-7923-8872-0*) Kluwer Ac.

Timing of Voicing in British English Obstruents. Gerard J. Docherty. LC 91-42837. (Netherlands Phonetic Archives Ser.: No. 9). x, 289p. (C). 1992. lib. bdg. 129.25 (*3-11-013408-X*) Mouton.

Timing Signals in the Futures Market: The Trader's Definitive Guide to Buy-Sell Indictators. Jake Bernstein. 1990. 45.00 (*1-55738-155-0*) Irwin Prof Pubng.

Timing the Heart. Gina Schien. 1996. pap. text ed. 10.95 (*1-875243-20-8*, Pub. by Blackwattle AT) LPC InBook.

Timing the Market: How to Profit in Bull & Bear Markets with Technical Analysis. 2nd rev. ed. Curtis M. Arnold. 250p. 1995. text ed. 24.95 (*1-55738-496-7*) Irwin Prof Pubng.

Timing the Stock Market for Maximum Profits. Stanley S. Huang. 1987. 34.95 (*0-930233-16-6*) Windsor.

Timing to Negotiating to Win. 1996. 12.99 (*1-56761-647-X*, Alpha Ref) Macmillan Gen Ref.

Timing to Selling (Just about) Anything. 1997. 12.99 (*1-56761-644-5*, Alpha Ref) Macmillan Gen Ref.

Timing to Time Management. 1997. 12.99 (*1-56761-646-1*, Alpha Ref) Macmillan Gen Ref.

***Timing Zero.** (Illus.). 80p. 1997. pap. 12.95 (*4-89444-044-X*, Pub. by PIE Bks JA) Bks Nippan.

Timings for Typing. Carl W. Salser. 1973. 7.15 (*0-89420-013-5*, 296955) Natl Book.

Timken Museum of Art: European Works of Art, American Paintings & Russian Icons in the Putnam Foundation Collection. Timken Museum of Art Staff. Ed. by Hal Fischer & Fronia Simpson. LC 96-33970. (Illus.). 240p. 1997. pap. text ed. 25.00 (*1-879067-01-3*) Putnam Found.

Timlick Family History: The Timlick, Timleck, Timlake, Timlock Family. deluxe ed. Ivan A. Conger & Dorothy S. Conger. (Illus.). 544p. 1990. 40.00 (*0-9626440-0-5*) I A Conger.

Timman's Select Games. Jan Timman. 1996. pap. 19.95 (*1-85744-121-4*) Macmillan.

Timmerman's Lectures on Catholicism. S. F. Timmerman, Jr. 1952. 3.95 (*0-88027-085-3*) Firm Foun Pub.

Timmins: The Porcupine Country. Michael Barnes. (Illus.). 144p. 1995. 28.00 (*1-55046-050-1*) Genl Dist Srvs.

Timmon. Mark Dunster. 22p. (Orig.). 1996. pap. 5.00 (*0-89642-296-8*) Linden Pubs.

Timms of Waterloo County. Barbara T. Arndt. (Illus.). 100p. (Orig.). 1991. pap. 45.00 (*0-9623606-1-9*) B E Arndt.

Timmy the Turtle. unabridged ed. Mae O. Ra'Oof & Jum Ra'Oof. (Five Friends of Rainbow Forest Ser.). (Illus.). 65p. (Orig.). (J). (gr. 3-5). 1995. pap. 8.95 (*1-888527-10-2*) New Wrld Ent.

Timmy the Turtle. unabridged ed. Mae O. Ra'Oof & Jum Ra'Oof. (Five Friends of Rainbow Forest Ser.). (Illus.). 54p. (Orig.). (J). (ps-2). 1995. pap. 7.95 (*1-888527-04-8*) New Wrld Ent.

Timmy Tiger & the Butterfly Net. Katherine Oana. LC 80-82954. (Timmy Tiger Ser.). (Illus.). 32p. (J). (ps-4). 1981. lib. bdg. 9.95 (*0-87783-160-2*) Oddo.

Timmy Tiger & the Elephant. Rae Oetting. LC 73-108730. (Timmy Tiger Ser.). (Illus.). 32p. (J). (ps-2). 1970. lib. bdg. 9.95 (*0-87783-041-X*); audio 7.94 (*0-87783-277-3*) Oddo.

Timmy Tiger & the Elephant. deluxe ed. Rae Oetting. LC 73-108730. (Timmy Tiger Ser.). (Illus.). 32p. (J). (ps-2). 1970. pap. 3.94 (*0-87783-111-4*) Oddo.

Timmy Tiger & the Masked Bandit. Katherine Oana. LC 80-82955. (Timmy Tiger Ser.). (Illus.). 32p. (J). (ps-4). 1981. lib. bdg. 9.95 (*0-87783-161-0*) Oddo.

Timmy Tiger Series, 6 vols. (Illus.). (J). (ps-4). 1981. audio 31.76 (*0-87783-228-5*) Oddo.

Timmy Tiger Series, 6 vols., Set. (Illus.). (J). (ps-4). 1981. lib. bdg. 59.70 (*0-87783-166-1*) Oddo.

Timmy Tiger Series, 4 vols., Set. deluxe ed. (Illus.). (J). (ps-4). 1981. pap. 15.76 (*0-87783-167-X*) Oddo.

Timmy Tiger to the Rescue. Rae Oetting. LC 70-108733. (Timmy Tiger Ser.). (Illus.). 32p. (J). (ps-4). 1970. lib. bdg. 9.95 (*0-87783-043-6*); audio 7.94 (*0-87783-229-3*) Oddo.

Timmy Tiger to the Rescue. deluxe ed. Rae Oetting. LC 70-108733. (Timmy Tiger Ser.). (Illus.). 32p. (J). (ps-4). 1970. pap. 3.94 (*0-87783-112-2*) Oddo.

Timmy Tiger's New Coat. Rae Oetting. LC 74-108734. (Timmy Tiger Ser.). (Illus.). 32p. (J). (ps-2). 1970. lib. bdg. 9.95 (*0-87783-044-4*); audio 7.94 (*0-87783-230-7*) Oddo.

Timmy Tiger's New Coat. deluxe ed. Rae Oetting. LC 74-108734. (Timmy Tiger Ser.). (Illus.). 32p. (J). (ps-2). 1970. pap. 3.94 (*0-87783-113-0*) Oddo.

Timmy Tiger's New Friend. Rae Oetting. LC 77-108732. (Timmy Tiger Ser.). (Illus.). (J). (ps-2). 1970. lib. bdg. 9.95 (*0-87783-042-8*); audio 7.94 (*0-87783-231-5*) Oddo.

Timmy Tiger's New Friend. deluxe ed. Rae Oetting. LC 77-108732. (Timmy Tiger Ser.). (Illus.). (J). (ps-2). 1970. pap. 3.94 (*0-87783-114-9*) Oddo.

Timmy's Gift: Precious Moments of Christmas. Samuel Butcher. (Illus.). 64p. (J). (ps-3). 1991. 9.95 (*0-307-15506-4*) Western Pub.

Timnah: A Biblical City in the Sorek Valley. George L. Kelm & Amihai Mazar. LC 95-21534. (Illus.). xx, 186p. 1995. text ed. 29.50 (*0-931464-97-8*) Eisenbrauns.

Timoleon. Herman Melville. 1972. 35.00 (*0-8490-1215-5*) Gordon Pr.

Timoleon & the Revival of Greek Sicily, 344-317 B. C. Richard J. Talbert. LC 74-16854. (Cambridge Classical Studies). 242p. reprint ed. pap. 69.00 (*0-317-27982-3*, 2025596) Bks Demand.

Timolol Ophthalmic Solution in the Treatment of Glaucoma. D. Dausch & H. Honegger. LC 78-72505. 1978. 3.00 (*0-911910-95-6*) Merck-Sharp-Dohme.

Timon, a Play. Ed. by Alexander Dyce. LC 75-16481. reprint ed. 29.50 (*0-404-02229-4*) AMS Pr.

Timon of Athens. William Shakespeare. (BBC Television Plays Ser.). 1981. pap. 4.95 (*0-563-17872-8*, Pub. by BBC UK) Parkwest Pubns.

Timon of Athens. William Shakespeare. Ed. by Louis B. Wright & Virginia A. La Mar. (Folger Library). 256p. 1988. pap. 2.95 (*0-671-66935-4*, WSP) PB.

Timon of Athens. William Shakespeare. Ed. by G. R. Hibbard. (New Penguin Shakespeare Ser.). 272p. 1981. pap. 5.95 (*0-14-070721-2*, Penguin Classics) Viking Penguin.

***Timon of Athens.** 3rd ed. William Shakespeare. (English Texts Ser.). 1963. pap. 9.95 (*0-415-02705-5*) Routledge.

Timon of Athens. 3rd ed. William Shakespeare. Ed. by H. J. Oliver. (Arden Shakespeare Ser.). 1969. reprint ed. pap. 8.95 (*0-416-27860-4*, NO. 2493) Routledge Chapman & Hall.

***Timon of Athens.** 3rd ed. William Shakespeare. (English Ser.). (C). Date not set. pap. 9.95 (*0-17-443536-3*); text ed. 45.00 (*0-17-443569-X*) Wadsworth Pub.

***Timon of Athens.** 3rd ed. William Shakespeare. (English Ser.). (C). 1997. pap. 9.95 (*0-17-443476-6*) Wadsworth Pub.

Timon of Athens: Modern Text with Introduction. Ed. by A. L. Rowse. LC 86-23380. 116p. (Orig.). (C). 1987. pap. text ed. 3.45 (*0-8191-3939-4*) U Pr of Amer.

Timon of Athens: Shakespeare's Pessimistic Tragedy. Rolf Soellner. LC 78-10884. (Illus.). 255p. 1979. 50.00 (*0-8142-0292-6*) Ohio St U Pr.

Timon of Athens see also Titus Andronicus

Timor. I. Rowland. (World Bibliographical Ser.). 1992. lib. bdg. 67.50 (*1-85109-159-9*) ABC-CLIO.

Timor Mortis. Will Harriss. 192p. 1986. 15.95 (*0-8027-5643-3*) Walker & Co.

Timor Problem: A Geographical Interpretation of an Underdeveloped Island. Ferdinand J. Ormeling. LC 77-86997. (Illus.). 296p. reprint ed. 57.50 (*0-404-16769-1*) AMS Pr.

Timor's Anschluss: Indonesian & Australian Policy in East Timor, 1974-76. Sue R. Roff. (Illus.). 142p. 1992. lib. bdg. 69.95 (*0-7734-9500-2*) E Mellen.

Timoteo-Tito. Charles Erdman. 175p. (SPA.). 1987. reprint ed. pap. 5.95 (*0-939125-29-3*) Evangelical Lit.

***Timoteo Va A La Escuela.** Rosemary Wells. (SPA.). (J). 1995. pap. text ed. 6.75 (*84-372-1751-2*) Santillana.

Timoteo y Tito - Obreros Aprobados: Studies in Timothy & Titus. James D. Crane. 160p. (Orig.). (SPA.). 1990. pap. 7.50 (*0-311-04364-X*) Casa Bautista.

Timotheus Persae: A Commentary. T. H. Janssen. vii, 183p. 1989. pap. 64.00 (*90-256-0845-0*, Pub. by A M Hakkert NE) Benjamins North Am.

Timothy - Nez Perce Chief, Life & Times, 1800-1891. Rowena Alcorn. 72p. 1996. pap. 9.95 (*0-87770-362-0*) Ye Galleon.

Timothy Abbott Conrad, with Particular Reference to His Work in Alabama One Hundred Years Ago. H. E. Wheeler. (Illus.). 158p. 1977. reprint ed. 10.00 (*0-87710-375-5*) Paleo Res.

Timothy & the Blanket Fairy. Nita Clarke. (J). (gr. k-6). 1981. 6.95 (*0-933184-06-9*); pap. 4.95 (*0-933184-16-6*) Flame Intl.

Timothy & the Night Noises. Jeffrey Dinardo. LC 86-9383. (J). 11.95 (*0-671-66807-2*, Litl Simon S&S) S&S Childrens.

Timothy & the Night Noises. Jeffrey Dinardo. LC 86-9383. (J). 1990. pap. 3.25 (*0-671-70298-X*, Litl Simon S&S) S&S Childrens.

Timothy & Titus. Michael Griffiths. LC 96-46092. (Baker Bible Guides Ser.). 192p. (gr. 10). 1996. pap. 9.99 (*0-8010-5733-7*) Baker Bks.

Timothy & Titus: Counsels to Young Pastors for Struggling Churches. Charles E. Bradford. LC 93-50863. (Abundant Life Bible Amplifier Ser.). 1994. 17.99 (*0-8163-1213-3*); pap. 12.99 (*0-8163-1215-X*) Pacific Pr Pub Assn.

Timothy Cole, Wood-Engraver: Illustrated with Nineteen of Timothy Cole's Finest Wood-Engravings. Alphaeus P. Cole & Margaret W. Cole. LC 92-24170. (Illus.). 1992. reprint ed. pap. 18.50 (*0-87233-106-7*) Bauhan.

Timothy Crump's Ward: The New Years Loan & What Became of It. Horatio Alger, Jr. 188p. 1977. reprint ed. 30.00 (*0-686-37023-6*) G K Westgard.

Timothy Duck: The Story of the Death of a Friend. Lynn B. Blackburn. Ed. by Joy Johnson. (Illus.). 24p. (Orig.). (J). (gr. 1-6). 1989. pap. 3.60 (*1-56123-013-8*) Centering Corp.

Timothy Dwight: Selected Writings see Millennium in America: From the Puritan Migration to the Civil War

Timothy Dwight (1752-1817) Anabelle S. Wenzke. LC 88-38616. (Studies in American Religion: Vol. 38). 250p. 1989. lib. bdg. 89.95 (*0-88946-681-5*) E Mellen.

Timothy Dwight, 1752-1817: A Biography. Charles E. Cuningham. LC 75-41069. reprint ed. 34.50 (*0-404-14746-1*) AMS Pr.

Timothy Eaton & the Rise of His Department Store. Joy L. Santink. 352p. 1990. 40.00 (*0-8020-2720-2*) U of Toronto Pr.

Timothy Files. Lawrence Sanders. 1988. mass mkt. 6.99 (*0-425-10924-0*) Berkley Pub.

Timothy Findley: An Annotated Bibliography. Carol Roberts. 150p. (C). 1990. text ed. 30.00 (*1-55022-112-4*, Pub. by ECW Press CN) Genl Dist Srvs.

Timothy Findley: Stories from a Life. Carol Roberts. (Illus.). 180p. 1994. pap. 9.95 (*1-55022-195-7*, Pub. by ECW Pr CN) LPC InBook.

Timothy, First & Second, Titus. Carl Spain. 1970. 12.95 (*0-915547-33-3*) Abilene Christ U.

Timothy Flint. James K. Folsom. (Twayne's United States Authors Ser.). 1965. pap. 13.95 (*0-8084-0301-X*, T83) NCUP.

Timothy Goes to School. Rosemary Wells. LC 80-20785. (Pied Piper Bks.). (Illus.). 32p. (J). (ps-2). 1981. pap. 15.99 (*0-8037-8948-3*); lib. bdg. 11.89 (*0-8037-8949-1*) Dial Bks Young.

Timothy Goes to School. Rosemary Wells. 1992. pap. 5.99 (*0-14-054715-0*) NAL-Dutton.

Timothy-James. Raymond Brown. (Bible Study Commentaries Ser.). 1983. pap. 4.95 (*0-87508-174-6*) Chr Lit.

Timothy of the Cay. Theodore Taylor. 160p. (YA). (gr. 6 up). 1995. pap. 4.50 (*0-380-72522-3*, Camelot) Avon.

Timothy of the Cay: A Prequel-Seque. Theodore Taylor. 0380776049p. (YA). (gr. 5 up). 1994. mass mkt. 4.50 (*0-380-72119-8*, Flare) Avon.

Timothy of the Cay: A Prequel-Seque. Theodore Taylor. 176p. (J). (gr. 5-9). 1993. 14.00 (*0-15-288358-4*, HB Juv Bks) HarBrace.

Timothy of the Cay: A Prequel-Seque. large type ed. Theodore Taylor. 1994. 41.00 (*0-614-09809-2*, L-04435-00) Am Printing Hse.

Timothy O'Toole: Irish Stories for Little Folk. Paradise C. Rose. LC 93-94368. (Illus.). 136p. (J). 1994. 14.95 (*1-56002-431-3*, Univ Edtns) Aegina Pr.

Timothy Philbrick: New Furniture. Peter T. Joseph & Richard Gruber. (Illus.). (Orig.). 1992. pap. text ed. 15.00 (*0-9628849-7-9*) P J Gallery.

Timothy Pickering & the Age of the American Revolution. David McLean. 1981. 60.95 (*0-405-14098-3*) Ayer.

Timothy Pickering & the American Republic. Gerard H. Clarfield. LC 79-24326. 328p. 1980. reprint ed. pap. 93.50 (*0-608-00901-6*, 2061695) Bks Demand.

Timothy Pickering As the Leader of New England Federalism, 1800-1815. Hervey P. Prentiss. LC 71-124882. (American Scene Ser.). (Illus.). 118p. 1972. reprint ed. lib. bdg. 22.50 (*0-306-71052-8*) Da Capo.

Timothy, Titus & Philemon. William Barclay. 304p. 1993. pap. 21.00 (*0-7152-0281-2*, Pub. by St Andrew UK) St Mut.

Timothy Toad. (Choices & Decisions Ser.). (J). (gr. k-1). 1991. 35.24 (*0-8123-6717-0*); pap. 5.28 (*0-8123-6718-9*); 84.56 (*0-8123-6712-X*); 29.08 (*0-8123-6849-5*); audio 7.92 (*0-8123-6720-0*) McDougal-Littell.

Timothy Too! Charlotte Zolotow. (J). (ps-3). 1986. 13.95 (*0-395-39378-7*) HM.

Timothy Walker: Antebellum Lawyer. Walter T. Hitchcock. LC 90-39466. (Distinguished Studies in American Legal & Constitutional History: Vol. 12). 255p. 1990. reprint ed. text ed. 15.00 (*0-8240-0033-1*) Garland.

***Timothy's Five-City Tour.** Gare Thompson. LC 97-23085. (Illus.). (J). 1998. write for info. (*0-8172-7280-1*) Raintree Steck-V.

An Asterisk (*) at the beginning of an entry indicates that the title is appearing in BIP for the first time.

Timothy's Game. Lawrence Sanders. 352p. 1989. mass mkt. 6.99 (*0-425-11641-7*) Berkley Pub.

Timothy's Numbers. Harriet Ziefert. (Fundamentals Ser.). (Illus.). 12p. (J). (ps). 1997. 8.95 (*0-7894-0589-X*) DK Pub Inc.

Timothy's Shapes. Harriet Ziefert. (Fundamentals Ser.). (Illus.). 12p. (J). (ps). 1997. 8.95 (*0-7894-0588-1*) DK Pub Inc.

Timoyo: The Cosmic Tree. Dibinga W. Said. LC 95-92458. (Unity of Thought in Kaffric, Kushanic, Ani & Kemetic Civilizations Ser.: No. 006, Pt. 1). 50p. (Orig.). (C). 1995. pap. text ed. 5.00 (*0-943324-75-0*) Omenana.

***Timpani.** Steven Houghton & George Nishigomi. Ed. by Joe Testa. (Percussion Recital Ser.). (Illus.). 24p. (Orig.). 1996. pap. text ed. 19.95 (*1-57623-683-8*, PERC9615CD) Warner Brothers.

Timpani. Bruce Pearson. (Standard of Excellence Ser.: Bk. 3). 1996. 6.45 (*0-8497-5992-7*, W23TM) Kjos.

Timpani & Auxiliary Percussion. (Standard of Excellence Ser.: Bk. 1). 1993. 6.45 (*0-8497-5946-3*, W21TM) Kjos.

Timpani & Auxiliary Percussion. (Standard of Excellence Ser.: Bk. 2). 1994. 6.45 (*0-8497-5971-4*, W22TM) Kjos.

Timpanogas-Lone Peak-Nebo, UT. rev. ed. Ed. by Trails Illustrated Staff. (Illus.). 1992. 8.99 (*0-925873-64-0*) Trails Illustrated.

Timpanogos Cave: A Window into the Earth. Stephen A. Trimble. Ed. by T. J. Priehs & Barnard Fontana. LC 82-61192. (Illus.). 48p. (Orig.). 1983. pap. 3.50 (*0-911408-64-9*) SW Pks Mnmts.

***Timpson's Book of Curious Days: A Year of English Oddities.** John Timpson. 1997. 29.95 (*0-7117-0861-4*, Pub. by Jarrold Pub UK) Seven Hills Bk.

Timpson's England: A Look Beyond the Obvious. John Timpson. (Illus.). 264p. (Orig.). 1994. pap. 18.95 (*0-7117-0324-8*) Seven Hills Bk.

Timpson's English Country Inns. John Timpson. (Illus.). 216p. 1996. 35.00 (*0-7472-0826-3*, Pub. by Headline UK) Trafalgar.

***Timpson's English Country Inns.** John Timpson. (Illus.). 216p. 1997. pap. 22.95 (*0-7472-7770-2*, Pub. by Headline UK) Trafalgar.

Timpson's English Villages. John Timpson. (Illus.). 192p. 1993. 45.00 (*0-7472-0586-8*, Pub. by Headline UK) Trafalgar.

Timpson's English Villages. John Timpson. (Illus.). 192p. 1994. pap. 24.95 (*0-7472-7877-6*, Pub. by Headline UK) Trafalgar.

Timpson's Other England: A Look at the Unusual & the Definitely Odd. John Timpson. (Illus.). 224p. 1994. 27.95 (*0-7117-0645-X*, Pub. by Jarrold Pub UK) Seven Hills Bk.

Tim's Friend Towser. Edward Ardizzone. (Illus.). 48p. (J). (ps-3). 1987. reprint ed. pap. 6.95 (*0-19-272112-7*) OUP.

***Tim's Place.** Judith I. Fringuello. (Illus.). vii, 205p. (Orig.). 1997. pap. 8.99 (*0-9657764-3-3*) Nu Leaf.

Timucua. Jerald T. Milanich. LC 95-40082. (Peoples of America Ser.). (Illus.). 256p. (C). 1996. 29.95 (*1-55786-488-8*) Blackwell Pubs.

Timurid Architecture in Khurasan. Bernard O'Kane. LC 85-43494. (Islamic Art & Architecture Ser.: Vol. 3). (Illus.). 520p. 1987. lib. bdg. 55.00 (*0-939214-35-0*) Mazda Pubs.

Tin. (Metals & Minerals Ser.). 1993. lib. bdg. 250.95 (*0-8490-8994-8*) Gordon Pr.

Tin. J. W. Price & R. Smith. (Handbook of Analytical Chemistry Ser.: Vol. 4, Pt. 3, Section A, Y). (Illus.). 1978. 117.95 (*0-387-08234-4*) Spr-Verlag.

Tin: Its Mining, Production, Technology, & Applications. 2nd ed. Charles L. Mantell. LC 29-22211. (ACS Monograph: No. 51). 1949. 47.95 (*0-8412-0257-5*) Am Chemical.

Tin: Its Production & Marketing. William Robertson. LC 82-9269. (Contributions in Economics & Economic History Ser.: No. 51). (Illus.). 212p. 1982. text ed. 55.00 (*0-313-23637-2*, RTN/, Greenwood Pr) Greenwood.

Tin: The Working of a Commodity Agreement. William Fox. 1977. 75.00 (*0-685-87560-1*) St Mut.

Tin - International Strategic Minerals Inventory Summary Report. David M. Sutphin et al. (Illus.). 52p. (Orig.). (C). 1992. pap. text ed. 30.00 (*0-941375-62-5*) DIANE Pub.

Tin & Malignant Cell Growth. J. J. Zuckerman. 256p. 1988. 141.00 (*0-8493-4714-9*, RC271, CRC Reprint) Franklin.

***Tin & Organotin Compounds: A Preliminary Review.** (Environmental Health Criteria Ser.: No. 5). 109p. 1980. pap. text ed. 12.00 (*92-4-154075-3*, 1160015) World Health.

***Tin & Solder Plating in the Semiconductor Industry.** Tan. (Illus.). 326p. 1992. text ed. 115.50 (*0-412-48240-1*, Chap & Hall NY) Chapman & Hall.

Tin & Tin-Alloy Plating. J. W. Price. 1982. 240.00 (*0-686-81702-8*) St Mut.

Tin & Tin Mining. R. L. Atkinson. 1989. pap. 25.00 (*0-85263-733-0*, Pub. by Shire UK) St Mut.

Tin Angel. Kathy Lawrence. 352p. (Orig.). 1989. mass mkt. 3.95 (*0-380-75735-4*) Avon.

Tin As a Vital Nutrient: Implications in Cancer Prophylaxis & Other Physiological Processes. Ed. by Nate F. Cardarelli. 336p. 1986. 138.00 (*0-8493-6579-1*, RC271, CRC Reprint) Franklin.

Tin-Based Antitumour Drugs. Ed. by Marcel Gielen. (NATO ASI Series H: Vol. 37). (Illus.). 240p. 1990. 83.00 (*0-387-50417-6*) Spr-Verlag.

Tin Box & What It Contained. Horatio Alger, Jr. (Works of Horatio Alger Jr.). 1989. reprint ed. lib. bdg. 79.00 (*0-685-27550-7*) Rprt Serv.

Tin Can. William J. Smith. (Chapbook Ser.: No. 3). 1988. 30.00 (*0-937035-10-6*) Stone Hse NY.

***Tin Can Man.** Larry Incollingo. 1993. pap. 10.50 (*0-9619795-6-9*) Reunion Bks.

Tin Can Man. Emory J. Jernigan. LC 92-43163. (Illus.). 206p. 1993. 19.95 (*0-918339-23-5*) Vandamere.

Tin Can Papermaking: Recycle for Earth & Art. Arnold E. Grummer. (Illus.). 80p. (Orig.). (J). (gr. 1 up). 1992. pap. 7.95 (*0-938251-01-5*) G Markim.

Tin Can Sailor: Life Aboard the USS Sterett, 1939-1945. Charles R. Calhoun. LC 93-14743. 198p. 1993. 24.95 (*1-55750-108-4*) Naval Inst Pr.

***Tin Can Tree.** Anne Tyler. 1996. pap. 11.00 (*0-449-91189-6*) Fawcett.

Tin Cans & Other Ships. Joseph A. Donahue. (Illus.). 1979. 7.50 (*0-8158-0378-8*) Chris Mass.

***Tin-Coated Hob: A Link Between the High-Speed & the Carbide Hob.** A. Schmidthammer. (Technical Papers). 29p. 1983. pap. text ed. 30.00 (*1-55589-073-3*) AGMA.

Tin Craft: A Workbook. 2nd rev. ed. Fern-Rae Abraham. LC 93-46615. (Illus.). 32p. 1994. pap. 5.95 (*0-86534-098-6*) Sunstone Pr.

***Tin Dog, Damper & Dust: A Shearer's Life.** Don Munday. pap. 16.95 (*1-875560-06-8*, Pub. by Univ of West Aust Pr AT) Intl Spec Bk.

Tin Dream Machines: German Tin Toy Cars & Motorcycles of the 1950-1960. Gerhard Walter. (Illus.). 224p. 1997. pap. text ed. 39.95 (*1-872727-13-1*) Pincushion Pr.

Tin Drum. Gunter Grass. Tr. by Ralph Manheim. 1990. pap. 15.00 (*0-679-72575-X*, Vin) Random.

Tin Drum. Gunter Grass. LC 92-54295. 1993. 20.00 (*0-679-42033-9*, Everymans Lib) Knopf.

Tin Drum. Gunter Grass. 1992. 24.00 (*0-8446-6519-3*) Peter Smith.

Tin Drum Country. Sabine Wichert. 80p. 9600. pap. 14.95 (*1-897648-29-4*, Pub. by Poolbeg Pr IE) Dufour.

***Tin Flute.** Gabrielle Roy. 1996. pap. text ed. 7.95 (*0-7710-9860-X*) McCland & Stewart.

Tin for Sale. John Manca & Vincent Cosgrove. 320p. 1993. reprint ed. mass mkt. 4.99 (*0-380-71034-X*) Avon.

Tin Glazed Earthenware. Daphne Carnegy. (Illus.). 176p. 1993. reprint ed. 34.95 (*0-9650786-8-X*) Gentle Br.

Tin-Glazed Earthenware: Majolica, Faience, & Delftware. Daphne Carnegy. 160p. 1993. 34.95 (*0-8019-8487-4*) Chilton.

Tin Heart. Karen Ackerman. LC 89-6528. (Illus.). 32p. (J). (gr. 1-3). 1990. lib. bdg. 13.95 (*0-689-31461-2*, Atheneum Bks Young) S&S Childrens.

Tin in Antiquity. R. D. Penhallurick. 272p. 1986. pap. 62.90 (*0-904357-81-3*, Pub. by Inst Materials UK) Ashgate Pub Co.

Tin in the World Economy. John T. Thoburn. (Commodities in the International Community Ser.). 256p. 1995. 50.00 (*0-7486-0516-9*, Pub. by Edinburgh U Pr UK) Col U Pr.

***Tin Islands.** Kenneth Martin. 300p. 1996. pap. text ed. 14.95 (*1-873741-27-8*, Pub. by Millvres Bks UK) LPC InBook.

Tin Mill Products. LC 92-75013. 50p. 1992. 17.00 (*0-932897-73-8*) Iron & Steel.

Tin Mung Cho Ban. Charles Brock. 28p. (VIE.). pap. 1.00 (*1-885504-08-X*) Church Gwth.

Tin Pan Alley: The Complete Popular Song Companion, Set. Ken Bloom. LC 95-31913. 1996. 225.00 (*0-8160-2583-5*) Facts on File.

***Tin Pan Alley: The Complete Popular Song Companion, 3 vols.** Ken Bloom. 1997. 225.00 (*0-614-28252-7*) Facts on File.

Tin Pan Alley: The Complete Popular Song Companion, Vol. Ken Bloom. LC 95-31913. 1996. write for info. (*0-8160-3473-7*) Facts on File.

Tin Pan Alley: The Complete Popular Song Companion, Vol. 2. Ken Bloom. LC 95-31913. 1996. write for info. (*0-8160-3474-5*) Facts on File.

Tin Pan Alley: The Complete Popular Song Companion, Vol. 3. Ken Bloom. LC 95-31913. 1996. write for info. (*0-8160-3475-3*) Facts on File.

Tin-Pan Man. P. A. Bechko. LC 96-43957. (Five Star Ser.). 246p. 1997. 17.95 (*0-7862-0736-1*, Five Star) Mac Lib Ref.

Tin-Pan Man. large type ed. P.A. Bechko. Date not set. 20.00 (*0-7862-0759-0*, Thorndike Lrg Prnt) Thorndike Pr.

Tin-Pots & Pirate Ships: Canadian Naval Forces & German Sea Raiders, 1880-1918. Michael L. Hadley & Roger Sarty. (Illus.). 424p. (C). 1991. text ed. 44.95 (*0-7735-0778-7*, Pub. by McGill CN) U of Toronto Pr.

Tin Princess. Philip Pullman. LC 93-38305. 304p. (YA). (gr. 9-12). 1994. pap. write for info. (*0-679-84756-1*) Knopf Bks Yng Read.

Tin Princess. Philip Pullman. LC 93-38305. 304p. (YA). (gr. 9-12). 1994. 16.00 (*0-679-84757-X*) Knopf Bks Yng Read.

Tin Princess. Philip Pullman. 304p. (J). 1996. pap. 4.99 (*0-679-87615-4*) Random.

Tin, Pt. C. Planck, Max, Society for the Advancement of Science, Gmelin Institute for Inorganic Chemistry Staff. (Gmelin Handbuch der Anorganischen Chemie Ser.). (Illus.). 206p. 1975. 330.00 (*0-387-93284-4*) Spr-Verlag.

Tin Roofs & Palm Trees: A Report on the New South Seas. Robert Trumbull. LC 76-49164. (Illus.). 344p. 1977. 30.00 (*0-295-95544-9*) U of Wash Pr.

Tin Soldier. Temple Bailey. 1975. lib. bdg. 19.10 (*0-89966-011-8*) Buccaneer Bks.

Tin Star. large type ed. M. Duggan. (Western Ser.). 1994. pap. 15.99 (*0-7089-7598-4*, Linford) Ulverscroft.

Tin Tuba. Terry Page. (Illus.). 24p. (J). (gr. 2-6). 1977. pap. text ed. 4.00 (*1-887864-63-6*) Boo Bks.

Tin Tuba. Terry Page. (Illus.). 24p. (J). (gr. 2-6). 1997. lib. bdg. 7.00 (*1-887864-26-1*) Boo Bks.

Tin Tuba Coloring Book. Terry Page. (Illus.). 32p. (J). (ps-5). 1997. pap. 3.00 (*1-887864-27-X*) Boo Bks.

Tin Whistle Tune Book: Thirty-Eight Tunes Appropriate for Tin Whistler Fife, Flute, or Violin. William E. White. LC 79-26872. 27p. 1980. pap. 3.25 (*0-87935-051-2*) Colonial Williamsburg.

Tin Whistle Tutor, Vol. 2. Pat Conway. 6.95 (*0-7866-1592-3*, 95177WW) Mel Bay.

Tin Woodman of Oz. L. Frank Baum. (Illus.). 272p. 1985. mass mkt. 4.99 (*0-345-33436-1*, Del Rey) Ballantine.

Tin Woodsman of Oz. L. Frank Baum. 20.95 (*0-8488-0709-X*) Amereon Ltd.

***Tin Woodsman of Oz.** Peter Glassman. (J). Date not set. write for info. (*0-688-14976-6*, Morrow Junior) Morrow.

Tina. Herman Bang. Tr. by Paul Christopherson. LC 84-12286. 224p. (C). 1984. text ed. 18.95 (*0-485-11254-X*, Pub. by Athlone Pr UK) Humanities.

Tina: Autobiography & Genealogy. Justina E. Smith. (Illus.). 218p. 1988. 15.00 (*0-9620249-1-0*); pap. 12.00 (*0-9620249-0-2*) Broadblade Pr.

Tina: The Really Rascally Red Fox. VeraLee Wiggins. LC 95-52409. (Illus.). (J). 1996. pap. 5.99 (*0-8163-1321-0*) Pacific Pr Pub Assn.

Tina la Tortuga y Carlos el Conejo see Bilingual Fables & Folk Tales

Tina Modotti: A Fragile Life. Mildred Constantine. LC 93-1154. 200p. 1993. pap. 18.95 (*0-8118-0502-6*) Chronicle Bks.

Tina Modotti: Photographer & Revolutionary. Margaret Hooks. (Illus.). 320p. 1995. pap. 22.00 (*0-04-440925-7*) Harper SF.

Tina Modotti: Photographs. Sarah M. Lowe. LC 95-889. (Illus.). 160p. 1995. 45.00 (*0-8109-4280-1*) Abrams.

Tina the Tiger. John Storms. (World of Animals Ser.). (Illus.). 24p. (J). (gr. k up). 1995. pap. 4.95 (*0-89346-814-2*) Heian Intl.

Tina Trapp's Guide to Craps. Ed. by Larry Edell. LC 96-76520. 120p. 1996. pap. 14.95 (*0-9652215-0-4*) LEAF Press.

Tina Turner Experience. Chris Welch. (Illus.). 208p. 1995. pap. 15.95 (*0-86369-816-6*, Pub. by Virgin Pub UK) London Brdge.

Tina's Diner. Adinolfi. (J). 1997. 16.00 (*0-689-80634-5*) S&S Childrens.

Tina's Island Home. J. Van Walsum-Quispel. LC 71-99920. (Illus.). 36p. (J). (gr. k-5). 7.95 (*0-87592-053-5*) Scroll Pr.

Tina's Science Adventures. Tina DeCloux. Ed. by Rosanne Werges. (Illus.). 80p. (J). (ps-3). 1992. spiral bd. 12.95 (*0-9615903-3-5*) Symbiosis Bks.

Tina's Science Notebook. Tina DeCloux & Rosanne Werges. (Illus.). 80p. (J). (gr. k-3). 1985. pap. 12.95 (*0-9615903-0-0*) Symbiosis Bks.

Tinbergen Lectures. Ed. by A. Knoester & A. H. Wellink. LC 93-15948. 170p. 1993. 102.50 (*0-444-81569-4*, North Holland) Elsevier.

Tinbergen Lectures in Organization Theory. 2nd rev. ed. Martin J. Beckmann. (Texts & Monographs in Economics & Mathematical Systems). 280p. 1988. 49.95 (*0-387-18515-1*) Spr-Verlag.

Tinbergen Legacy. Ed. by M. S. Dawkins et al. (Illus.). 208p. (gr. 13). 1991. text ed. 70.95 (*0-412-39120-1*, A6373) Chapman & Hall.

Tincture of Tears & Laughter. Cheryl D. Zimmerman. LC 95-75678. (Illus.). 90p. (Orig.). 1995. pap. 15.00 (*0-9639838-1-4*) Little Treasure.

Tincture of the Philosophers. Paracelsus. Tr. by A. E. Waite from LAT. 1984. reprint ed. pap. 3.95 (*0-916411-45-1*) Holmes Pub.

Tincture of Time: The Story of 150 Years of Medicine in Atlanta. Martin Moran. 140p. 1995. 45.00 (*0-9647461-0-7*) Med Assn Atlanta.

***Tincup in the Storm Country.** Lewis B. Patten. (Western Ser.). 296p. 1997. 18.95 (*0-7862-0903-8*) Thorndike Pr.

Tincup in the Storm Country. large type ed. Lewis B. Patten. (Five-Star Western Ser.). 200p. 1996. 16.95 (*0-7862-0593-8*) Thorndike Pr.

Tindel's Blue Door. 2nd ed. Beatrice Tallarico & S. C. Stone. (Weeuns Ser.). (Illus.). 19p. (J). (gr. 2-8). 1986. pap. 2.95 (*0-936191-14-7*) Tallstone Pub.

Tinder Box. LC 89-48014. (J). 1991. pap. 14.95 (*0-671-70546-6*, S&S Bks Young Read) S&S Childrens.

Tinder Box. Michael Bedard. (Illus.). (J). (gr. k-3). 1995. 12.95 (*0-19-540767-9*, Pub. by Stoddart Pubng CN) Genl Dist Srvs.

Tinder-Box Criminal Aggression: Neuropsychology, Demography, Phenomenology. James Hennessy. 401p. 1996. text ed. 44.95 (*1-56000-253-0*) Transaction Pubs.

Tinderbox. Hans Christian Andersen. LC 88-9206. (Illus.). 32p. (J). (gr. 1 up). 1988. lib. bdg. 14.95 (*0-689-50458-6*, McElderry) S&S Childrens.

Tinderbox. Brandis. 1995. mass mkt. 4.95 (*0-88984-154-3*, Pub. by Porcupines Quill CN) Genl Dist Srvs.

***Tinderbox.** Marianne Brandis. 160p. 1982. pap. 8.95 (*0-88984-064-4*, Pub. by Porcupines Quill CN) Genl Dist Srvs.

***Tinderbox.** Marianne Brandis. 224p. 1994. mass mkt. 4.95 (*0-88984-153-5*, Pub. by Porcupines Quill CN) Genl Dist Srvs.

Tineid Genera of Australia. Gaden S. Robinson & Ebbe S. Nielsen. (Monographs on Australian Lepidoptera: Vol. 2). (C). 1993. 80.00 (*0-643-05025-6*, Pub. by CSIRO AT) Aubrey Bks.

Ting Shao Kuang. Anna M. Macdonnell. (Illus.). 192p. 1989. text ed. 100.00 (*0-685-27816-6*) Segal Fine Art.

Ting Shao Kuang Serigraphs. Ed. by Charles Liu. (Illus.). 110p. 1991. 30.00 (*0-9623747-4-1*) Segal Fine Art.

Ting Tang Mine & Other Plays. Nick Darke. (Methuen Theatrescripts Ser.). 70p. (C). 1988. pap. 9.95 (*0-413-17930-3*, A0296, Pub. by Methuen UK) Heinemann.

Ting Wen-Chiang: Science & China's New Culture. Charlotte Furth. LC 78-95920. (Harvard East Asian Ser.: No. 42). 314p. reprint ed. pap. 92.40 (*0-7837-4148-0*, 2057996) Bks Demand.

Tingalayo. Illus. by Kate Duke. (Raffi Songs to Read Ser.). (J). (ps-2). 1988. 9.95 (*0-517-56926-4*) Crown Bks Yng Read.

Tingaling. Pam Adams. (J). (gr. 4 up). 1981. 9.99 (*0-85953-328-X*) Childs Play.

Tinged with Gold: Hop Culture in the United States. Michael A. Tomlan. LC 90-46389. (Illus.). 272p. 1992. 40.00 (*0-8203-1313-0*) U of Ga Pr.

Tinglatar: Socio-Economic Relationship of a Brahmin Village in Eastern Nepal. Peter H. Prindle. 1983. 75.00 (*0-7855-0237-8*, Pub. by Ratna Pustak Bhandar); 70.00 (*0-7855-0322-6*, Pub. by Ratna Pustak Bhandar) St Mut.

Tinglatar: Socio-Economic Relationship of a Brahmin Village in Eastern Nepal. Ed. by Peter H. Prindle. 157p. (C). 1989. 125.00 (*0-89771-126-2*, Pub. by Ratna Pustak Bhandar) St Mut.

Tingleberries, Tuckertubs & Telephones. Margaret Mahy. (Illus.). 96p. (J). (gr. 3-7). 1996. pap. 12.99 (*0-670-86331-9*) Viking Child Bks.

Tingley Family, Being an Account of the Descendants of Samuel Tingley of Malden, Massachusetts. R. M. Tingley. 894p. 1989. reprint ed. pap. 134.00 (*0-8328-1169-6*); reprint ed. lib. bdg. 142.00 (*0-8328-1168-8*) Higginson Bk Co.

Tingo Tango Mango Tree. Marcia K. Vaughan. (Animal Fair Ser.). (Illus.). 32p. (J). 1994. 10.95 (*0-382-24077-4*); lib. bdg. 14.95 (*0-382-24071-5*) Silver Burdett Pr.

Tingo Tango Mango Tree. Marcia K. Vaughan. (Animal Fair Ser.). (Illus.). 32p. (J). (ps-3). 1994. pap. 4.95 (*0-382-24452-4*) Silver Burdett Pr.

Tingo Tango Mango Tree. Marcia K. Vaughn. LC 93-44867. (Animal Fair Ser.). (Illus.). (J). 1994. write for info. (*0-382-24605-5*); pap. write for info. (*0-382-24454-0*) Silver.

Tings an Times. Linton K. Johnson. 64p. (Orig.). 9200. pap. 14.95 (*1-85224-168-3*, Pub. by Bloodaxe Bks UK) Dufour.

Tinh-Yeu Trong Doi Thuong. Hoang D. Mai. 104p. pap. text ed. 7.50 (*1-885550-03-0*) Du-Sinh St Joseph.

Tinhorn Murder Case: Larry & Stretch. large type ed. Marshall Grover. (Western Ser.). 1994. pap. 15.99 (*0-7089-7599-2*, Linford) Ulverscroft.

Tinies ABC Pop-Up Book. (Pop-Up Bks.). (Illus.). (J). (ps-1). 1.49 (*0-517-43893-3*) Random Hse Value.

Tiniest Hippo. (Language of Mathematics Ser.). 1989. 35.92 (*0-8123-6500-3*); pap. 5.36 (*0-8123-6501-1*); audio 7.92 (*0-8123-6503-8*) McDougal-Littell.

***Tiniest Humans: Based on Interviews with Professor Jerome Lejeune & Professor Sir Albert William.** 2nd rev. ed. Robert L. Sassone et al. LC 77-76811. 119p. 1995. pap. 6.00 (*1-890712-17-5*, EG5) Amer Life League.

***Tiniest Miracle: Angel of Grace.** Mark Patrick. 1997. mass mkt. 5.99 (*0-380-78442-4*) Avon.

Tinisima. Elena Poniatowska. Tr. by Katherine Silver. LC 96-33810. 256p. 1996. 25.00 (*0-374-27785-0*) FS&G.

***Tinisima.** Elena Poniatowska. 1998. pap. 11.95 (*0-14-026876-6*) Viking Penguin.

Tinka: A Day in a Little Girl's Life. Carol Batdorf. (Illus.). 32p. (Orig.). (J). (gr. 1-6). 1990. pap. 5.95 (*0-88839-249-4*) Hancock House.

Tinker & a Poor Man: John Bunyan & His Church, 1628-1688. Christopher Hill. 1990. pap. 10.95 (*0-393-30662-3*) Norton.

***Tinker & Tom & the Star Baby.** LC 96-45439. (J). 1997. 14.95 (*0-316-56349-8*) Little.

Tinker Autumn. Wil Denson. 1987. pap. 3.45 (*0-87129-008-1*, T78) Dramatic Pub.

Tinker Family: Ancestors & Descendants of Joseph Wescot Tinker, Ellsworth, Maine, 1791-1868, a Descendant of John Tinker of Boston. Frederick J. Libbie. 36p. 1994. reprint ed. pap. 7.50 (*0-8328-4065-3*) Higginson Bk Co.

Tinker Guide to Latin American & Caribbean Policy & Scholarly Resources in Metropolitan New York. Ed. by Ronald G. Hellman & Beth K. Pfannl. LC 88-8186. 217p. 1989. 27.95 (*0-929972-00-7*); pap. 13.95 (*0-929972-01-5*) Bildner Ctr.

Tinker Jim. Paul Coltman. (J). (ps-3). 1992. 15.00 (*0-374-37611-5*) FS&G.

***Tinker Library.** R. F. Metzdorf. 556p. 1995. reprint ed. 75.00 (*1-888262-66-4*) Martino Pubng.

***Tinker of Toledo.** Nellie McCaslin. 55p. (Orig.). 1996. pap. 5.00 (*0-88734-456-9*) Players Pr.

***Tinker, Tailor, Missionary?** Michael Griffiths. 112p. pap. 8.99 (*0-8308-5474-6*) InterVarsity.

***Tinker Tailor Soldier.** John Lecarre. Date not set. 14.95 (*0-559-35018-X*) Putnam Pub Group.

Tinker, Tailor, Soldier, Spy. John Le Carre. 1974. 25.00 (*0-394-49219-6*) Knopf.

Tinker, Tailor, Soldier, Spy. John Le Carre. 384p. 1985. mass mkt. 6.99 (*0-553-26778-7*) Bantam.

Tinker, Tiller, Technical Change. Matthew Gamser. 288p. (Orig.). 1990. pap. 19.50 (*0-942850-31-9*) Bootstrap Pr.

Tinker vs. Desmoines: Student Protest. Leah Farish. LC 96-25704. (Landmark Supreme Court Cases Ser.). (Illus.). 128p. (YA). (gr. 6 up). 1997. lib. bdg. 18.95 (*0-89490-859-6*) Enslow Pubs.

***Tinkerbell Jerusalem.** Bonnie K. Kaback. Ed. & Photos by Vi Goldsberry. (Illus.). 192p. 1996. 18.95 (*1-889430-01-3*); pap. 12.95 (*1-889430-02-1*) Three Monkeys.

Tinkering Toward Utopia: A Century of Public School Reform. David B. Tyack. LC 94-47545. (Illus.). 192p. (C). 1995. 22.50 (*0-674-89282-8*) HUP.

***Tinkering Toward Utopia: A Century of Public School Reform.** David B. Tyack. 1997. pap. text ed. 14.00 (*0-674-89283-6*) HUP.

Tinker's Daughter. Sheila Hayes. 153p. (J). (gr. 5-9). 1995. pap. 14.99 (*0-525-67497-7*, Lodestar Bks) Dutton Child Bks.

Tinker's Girl. Catherine Cookson. 384p. 1996. mass mkt. 7.99 (*0-552-14038-4*) Bantam.

Tinker's Journey Home. Bryant. (J). 11.95 (*0-671-75182-4*, S&S Bks Young Read) S&S Childrens.

T

Tinker's Journey Home. Devony Lehner. Ed. by P. Dennis Maloney. (Illus.). 34p. (J). (ps-6). 12.95 (*0-940305-00-3*) P D Maloney.

Tinker's Wedding see Complete Plays of John M. Synge

Tinkertoy Computer & Other Machinations: Computer Recreations from the Pages of Scientific American & Algorithm. A. K. Dewdeny. LC 93-10478. 1995. text ed. write for info. (*0-7167-2489-8*) W H Freeman.

Tinkertoy Computer & Other Machinations: Computer Recreations from the Pages of Scientific American & Algorithm. A. K. Dewdeny. LC 93-10478. 1995. pap. text ed. write for info. (*0-7167-2491-X*) W H Freeman.

Tinkling. Stephen Cosgrove. (Treasure Trolls Ser.). (Illus.). 32p. (J). (gr. k-5). 1993. lib. bdg. 12.95 (*1-56674-045-2*, HTS Bks) Forest Hse.

Tinkling. Stephen Cosgrove. (J). (ps-3). 1992. pap. 3.95 (*0-307-13451-2*) Western Pub.

Tinkling Cymbals & Sounding Brass: The Art of Telling Tales about Joseph Smith & Brigham Young. Hugh Nibley. LC 91-11539. (Collected Works of Hugh Nibley: Vol. 11). xxii, 741p. 1991. 29.95 (*0-87579-516-1*) Deseret Bk.

Tinkling Symbol. Phoebe Atwood Taylor. (Asey Mayo Cape Cod Mystery Ser.). 288p. pap. 6.50 (*0-88150-263-4*) Countryman.

Tinnemaha. J. R. Alcorn. (Illus.). 155p. 1991. 24.95 (*0-9620221-1-X*) Fairview West Pub.

***Tinner's Bride.** large type ed. Irene Northan. (Large Print Ser.). 320p. 1996. 25.99 (*0-7089-3639-3*) Ulverscroft.

***Tinner's Daughter.** Rosemary Aitken. 375p. 1997. 27.00 (*1-85797-637-1*, Pub. by Orion Bks UK) Trafalgar.

Tinnirello's Dilemmas: Case Studies for the Software Manager. Paul C. Tinnirello. 64p. 1993. pap. text ed. 35.00 (*1-884521-00-2*) Software Maint.

Tinnitus. Masaaki Kitahara. LC 99-12777. (Illus.). 140p. 1988. 66.00 (*0-89640-174-X*) Igaku-Shoin.

Tinnitus. CIBA Foundation Staff. LC 81-25761. (CIBA Foundation Symposium: New Ser.: No. 85). 333p. reprint ed. pap. 95.00 (*0-8357-7056-7*, 2033612) Bks Demand.

Tinnitus: Diagnosis-Treatment. Abraham Shulman et al. LC 90-5759. (Illus.). 571p. 1991. text ed. 99.50 (*0-8121-1121-4*) Williams & Wilkins.

Tinnitus: Facts, Theories, & Treatments. National Research Council Staff. 150p. (C). 1982. pap. text ed. 14.95 (*0-309-03328-4*) Natl Acad Pr.

Tinnitus - New Hope for a Cure. Paul V. Valkenburgh. (Illus.). 128p. (Orig.). (C). 1995. pap. 14.95 (*0-9617425-2-6*) Van Valkenburgh.

Tinnitus Handbook: A Self-Help Guide. Bill Habets. (Illus.). 240p. (Orig.). 1997. pap. 14.95 (*1-887053-06-9*) United Res CA.

Tinnitus-Hilfe: Ein Arbeitsbuch Fuer Patienten und Ihre Aerztlichen und Nichtaerztlichen Helfer. B. Kellerhals & R. Zogg. (Illus.). xii, 88p. 1996. pap. 28.00 (*3-8055-6291-8*) S Karger.

***Tinnitus-Hilfe: Ein Arbeitsbuch Fuer Patienten und Ihre Aerztlichen und Nichtaerztlichen Helfer.** 2nd rev. ed. Bernhard Kellerhals & Regula Zogg. (Illus.). xii, 90p. 1997. pap. 28.00 (*3-8055-6527-5*) S Karger.

Tinnitus, 1991: Proceedings of the Fourth International Tinnitus Seminar, Bordeaux, France, August 27-30, 1991. Ed. by J. M. Aran & R. Dauman. LC 92-49982. (Illus.). 575p. 1992. lib. bdg. 184.50 (*90-6299-087-8*, Pub. by Kugler NE) Kugler Pubns.

Tino. C. A. Ramsay. (Illus.). 188p. 1996. write for info. (*0-9650882-0-0*) Ramsay Property.

Tino Di Comaino, a Sienese Sculptor of the Fourteenth Century. Wilhelm R. Valentiner. Tr. by R. H. Boothroyd. LC 73-143366. (Illus.). 107p. reprint ed. write for info. (*0-87817-085-5*) Hacker.

Tinonc: Son of the Cajun Teche. Robert L. Olivier. (Illus.). 122p. 1974. 12.95 (*0-88289-054-9*) Pelican.

Tinplate Toys: From Schuco, Bing, & Other Companies. Jurgen Franzke. Tr. by Edward Force from GER. LC 95-35254. (Illus.). 136p. (Orig.). 1996. pap. 24.95 (*0-88740-863-X*) Schiffer.

Tinrin Grammar. Midori Osumi. (Oceanic Linguistics Special Publications: No. 25). 340p. (C). 1994. pap. text ed. 35.00 (*0-8248-1629-3*) UH Pr.

Tinseltown Murders: A Mac Slade Mystery. John Blumenthal. 1985. pap. 2.95 (*0-671-55539-1*, Fireside) S&S Trade.

Tinseltowns, U. S. A. John Kremer. (Illus.). 144p. (Orig.). 1988. 13.95 (*0-912411-21-X*); pap. 6.95 (*0-912411-18-X*) Open Horizons.

Tinsmith's Helper & Pattern Book. H. K. Vosburgh. (Illus.). 120p. 1994. pap. 13.50 (*1-879335-56-5*) Astragal Pr.

***Tintin, Vol. 6.** Herge. 1997. 16.95 (*0-316-35724-3*) Little.

***Tintin, Vol. 7.** Herge. 1997. 16.95 (*0-316-35727-8*) Little.

Tintin & the Broken Ear. Herge. (Illus.). 62p. (J). 19.95 (*0-8288-5086-0*) Fr & Eur.

Tintin & the Golden Fleece. Herge. (J). (gr. 3-8). 19.95 (*0-8288-5087-9*) Fr & Eur.

Tintin & the Lake of Sharks. Herge. (Illus.). 62p. (J). 19.95 (*0-416-78950-1*) Fr & Eur.

Tintin & the Picaros. Herge. (Illus.). 62p. (J). 19.95 (*0-8288-5089-5*) Fr & Eur.

Tintin & the Picaros. Herge. 1978. pap. 8.95 (*0-316-35849-5*, Joy St Bks) Little.

Tintin & the World of Herge: An Illustrated History. Benoit Peeters. (Illus.). 160p. (YA). (gr. 5 up). 1992. 45.00 (*0-316-69752-4*, Joy St Bks) Little.

Tintin au Congo. Herge. (Illus.). (FRE.). (J). (gr. 7-9). 19.95 (*0-8288-5090-9*) Fr & Eur.

Tintin au Pays de L'or Noir. Herge. (FRE.). (J). (gr. 7-9). 19.95 (*0-8288-5091-7*) Fr & Eur.

Tintin au Pays des Mots: Dictionnaire Illustre English-French, French-English. Helene Houssemaine-Florent. 429p. (ENG & FRE.). 1990. 75.00 (*0-7859-8590-5*, 0245549617) Fr & Eur.

Tintin Au Tibet. Herge. (J). (gr. 7-9). ring bd. 19.95 (*0-8288-5092-5*) Fr & Eur.

Tintin en America. Herge. (Illus.). 62p. (SPA.). (J). 19.95 (*0-8288-5094-1*) Fr & Eur.

Tintin en Amerique. Herge. (Illus.). 62p. (FRE.). (J). 19.95 (*0-8288-5093-3*) Fr & Eur.

Tintin en el Congo. Herge. (Illus.). 62p. (SPA.). (J). 19.95 (*0-8288-5095-X*) Fr & Eur.

Tintin en el Pais del Oro Negro. Herge. (Illus.). 62p. (SPA.). (J). 19.95 (*0-8288-4995-1*) Fr & Eur.

Tintin en el Tibet. Herge. (Illus.). 62p. (SPA.). (J). 19.95 (*0-8288-4996-X*) Fr & Eur.

Tintin et la Mystere de la Toison d'Or. (J). (gr. 7-9). 15.95 (*0-685-33970-X*) Fr & Eur.

Tintin et les Picaros. Herge. (Illus.). 62p. (FRE.). (J). 19.95 (*0-8288-4997-8*) Fr & Eur.

Tintin Games Book, Vol. 1. Herge. (J). 1990. mass mkt. 6.95 (*0-316-35858-4*) Little.

Tintin im Amerika. Herge. (Illus.). 62p. (GER.). (J). pap. 19.95 (*0-8288-4999-4*) Fr & Eur.

Tintin im Kongo. Herge. (Illus.). 62p. (GER.). (J). pap. 19.95 (*0-8288-4998-6*) Fr & Eur.

Tintin in America. Herge. (Illus.). 62p. (J). 19.95 (*0-8288-5000-3*) Fr & Eur.

Tintin in America. Herge. LC 79-64865. (Adventures of Tintin Ser.). 1979. pap. 8.95 (*0-316-35852-5*) Little.

Tintin in the Land of the Soviets. Herge. 116p. 1992. 39.95 (*0-7859-0978-8*, 2203020016) Fr & Eur.

Tintin in the New World: A Romance. Frederic Tuten. 1993. 22.00 (*0-688-12314-7*) Morrow.

Tintin in the New World: A Romance. Frederic Tuter. LC 95-21689. 240p. 1996. pap. 12.00 (*1-57322-529-0*, Riverhd Trade) Berkley Pub.

Tintin in Tibet. Herge. (Illus.). 62p. (J). 19.95 (*0-8288-5001-1*) Fr & Eur.

Tintin in Tibet. Herge. LC 74-21621. (Adventures of Tintin Ser.). (J). (gr. k up). 1975. pap. 8.95 (*0-316-35839-8*, Joy St Bks) Little.

Tintin y los Picaros. Herge. (Illus.). 62p. (SPA.). (J). 19.95 (*0-8288-5002-X*) Fr & Eur.

Tintinnids: A Taxon-Vertical Distributional Study of Settling Assemblages from the Panama Basin. Hsin Yi Ling. (Ocean Biocoenosis Ser.: No. 4). 21p. 1992. pap. text ed. 10.00 (*1-880224-03-8*) Woods Hole Ocean.

Tintoretto. Eric Newton. LC 70-110275. (Illus.). 250p. 1972. reprint ed. text ed. 35.00 (*0-8371-4501-5*, NETI, Greenwood Pr) Greenwood.

Tinware: Yesterday & Today. (Americana Bks.). (Illus.). 1974. 3.00 (*0-911410-36-8*) Applied Arts.

Tinwhistle Basic. R. Martin Helick. LC 93-176696. 112p. 1992. spiral bd. 29.50 incl. disk (*0-912710-34-9*) Regent Graphic Serv.

Tinwhistle for Beginners. Dona Gilliam & Mizzy McCaskill. 1993. 3.95 (*0-87166-891-2*, 93821) Mel Bay.

Tinwhistle Legends-T. Walsh. Sean Potts et al. 10.95 (*0-7866-1604-0*, 95189WW) Mel Bay.

Tinwhistle Tutor, Vol. 1. Pat Conway. 6.95 (*0-7866-1591-5*, 95176WW) Mel Bay.

Tinwork. Marion Elliot. 96p. 1996. 14.95 (*1-85967-143-8*, Lorenz Bks) Anness Pub.

Tiny Alice. Edward Albee. 1965. pap. 5.25 (*0-8222-1154-8*) Dramatists Play.

Tiny Amish Traditions. Sylvia T. Voudrie. Ed. by Janice P. Johnson. LC 94-29993. (Illus.). 64p. (Orig.). 1994. pap. 9.95 (*0-9622565-8-7*) Chitra Pubns.

Tiny Angel. Elizabeth Koda-Callan. LC 91-50386. (Illus.). 40p. (J). (ps-3). 1991. 12.95 (*1-56305-120-6*, 3120) Workman Pub.

Tiny Bible Promises. Ed. & Compiled by Dan Penwell. 1995. kivar 1.09 (*0-529-10387-7*, TBP3); kivar 1.09 (*0-529-10388-5*, TBP3BL3); kivar 1.09 (*0-529-10389-3*, TBP3G); kivar 1.09 (*0-529-10390-7*, TBP3W); kivar 1.09 (*0-529-10391-5*, TBP3R) World Publng.

Tiny Bible Tales, 4 bks., Set. Anne Gill. (Illus.). (J). (ps-2). 1996. pap. 19.95 (*0-8167-3317-1*) BrdgeWater.

Tiny Book of Tiny Houses. Lester Walker. (Illus.). 96p. 1993. 12.95 (*0-87951-510-4*) Overlook Pr.

Tiny Christmas Elf. Sharon Peters. LC 86-30849. (Illus.). 32p. (J). (gr. k-2). 1988. lib. bdg. 9.79 (*0-8167-0988-2*) Troll Communs.

Tiny Christmas Elf. Sharon Peters. LC 86-30849. (Illus.). 32p. (J). (gr. k-2). 1997. pap. 2.50 (*0-8167-0989-0*) Troll Communs.

Tiny Church in a Big Church World. Richard P. Thompson. 72p. 1992. pap. 5.99 (*0-8341-1399-6*) Beacon Hill.

Tiny Dinos Fun at the Beach: A Book of Actions. Guy Gilchrist. LC 87-40337. (Tiny Dinos Concept Bks.). (Illus.). (J). (ps-1). 1988. 4.95 (*1-55782-013-9*, Warner Juvenile Bks) Little.

Tiny Feelings: Tips for Shy People. Janice Krasnow. LC 96-8266. 1995. pap. 9.95 (*0-88268-193-1*) Station Hill Pr.

Tiny Footprints. B. Kliban. LC 77-94068. (Illus.). 160p. 1978. pap. 5.95 (*0-89480-031-0*, 186) Workman Pub.

Tiny Goes to the Doctor. Jeannette N. Hafford. 48p. (Orig.). (J). (gr. 3-8). 1990. pap. write for info. (*0-318-68017-3*) Tinys Self Help Bks.

Tiny Houses. Lester Walker. LC 86-21736. (Illus.). 208p. 1987. 29.95 (*0-87951-271-7*) Overlook Pr.

Tiny Houses: How to Build Them. 1991. lib. bdg. 250.00 (*0-8490-4672-6*) Gordon Pr.

Tiny Kite of Eddie Wing. Maxine Trottier. LC 96-3100. (Illus.). 32p. (J). (ps-3). 1996. 13.95 (*0-916291-66-9*) Kane-Miller Bk.

Tiny Kittens. Lesley A. Ivory. 4p. 1990. 10.95 (*1-55859-124-9*, Abbeville Kids) Abbeville Pr.

Tiny Little Story. Nancy Yeager & Doug Yeager. 32p. (J). (ps). 1993. pap. write for info. (*1-879911-01-9*) Rams Horn Bks.

Tiny Miracle. Richard M. Wainwright. (Illus.). 40p. (J). 1986. reprint ed. 18.00 (*0-9619566-0-7*) Family Life.

***Tiny Monkey Can, Too!** Muff Singer & Risa S. Gordon. (Tiny Hugs Ser.). (Illus.). 9p. (J). (ps-k). 1997. bds. 4.99 (*1-57584-154-1*) Rdrs Dgst Yng Fam.

Tiny Parents. Ellen Weiss & Mel Friedman. LC 88-23103. 96p. (Orig.). (J). (gr. 3-7). 1989. pap. 2.95 (*0-394-82418-0*) Knopf Bks Yng Read.

***Tiny Penguin's Flying Lesson.** Muff Singer & Risa S. Gordon. (Tiny Hugs Ser.). (Illus.). 9p. (J). (ps-k). 1997. bds. 4.99 (*1-57584-155-X*) Rdrs Dgst Yng Fam.

***Tiny Perfect Dinosaur Book, Bones & Egg: Velociraptor.** Ed. by Somerville House Staff. (Illus.). 32p. (Orig.). (J). 1997. pap. 12.95 (*0-8362-3195-3*) Andrews & McMeel.

Tiny Perfect Dinosaur Book, Bones, Egg & Poster: Presenting Leptoceratops. Dale A. Russell & John Acorn. (Illus.). 32p. (Orig.). (J). 1991. pap. 10.95 (*0-8362-4213-0*) Andrews & McMeel.

Tiny Perfect Dinosaur Book, Bones, Egg, & Poster: Stegosaurus. Dale A. Russell & Jennifer Glossup. (Illus.). 32p. (J). 1995. pap. 12.95 (*0-8362-0646-0*) Andrews & McMeel.

Tiny Perfect Dinosaur, Book, Bones, Egg, & Poster: Triceratops. Somerville House Staff. (Illus.). 32p. (Orig.). (J). 1996. pap. 12.95 (*0-8362-2107-9*) Andrews & McMeel.

Tiny Perfect Dinosaur Book, Bones, Egg & Poster Kits: Presenting Brachiosaurus. Dale A. Russell & John Acorn. 32p. (J). 1994. pap. 12.95 (*0-8362-4234-3*) Andrews & McMeel.

***Tiny Pig's Big Adventure, Incl. toy.** Muff Singer & Risa S. Gordon. (Tiny Hugs Ser.: Vol. 4). (Illus.). 9p. (J). (ps up). 1997. bds. 4.99 (*1-57584-176-2*) Rdrs Dgst Yng Fam.

Tiny Rowland: The Ugly Face of Neocolonialism in Africa. EIR Investigative Team Staff. 146p. (Orig.). 1993. pap. 10.00 (*0-943235-08-1*) Exec Intel Review.

Tiny Seed. Eric Carle. LC 86-2534. (Illus.). 32p. (J). (gr. k up). 1991. pap. 16.00 (*0-88708-015-4*, Picture Book Studio) S&S Childrens.

Tiny Seed. 2nd ed. Eric Carle. LC 86-2534. (Pixies Ser.). (Illus.). 36p. (J). (gr. k up). 1991. reprint ed. pap. 4.95 (*0-88708-155-X*, Picture Book Studio) S&S Childrens.

Tiny Seedlings: ...Their Journey. June F. Esparza. LC 95-90501. (Illus.). 264p. (Orig.). 1998. 14.95 (*0-9647161-2-7*) Thgts in Motion.

Tiny Sheep. Bunshu Iguchi. 24p. (J). (ps up). 1986. 10.00 (*0-8170-1108-0*) Judson.

Tiny Shiny: A Christmas Story. Lloyd Funchess, Jr. (J). 1964. 5.95 (*0-87511-052-5*) Claitors.

Tiny Star. Arthur Ginolfi. (Illus.). 32p. (J). 1989. 6.95 (*1-56288-134-5*) Checkerboard.

***Tiny Star.** rev. ed. Art Ginolfi. LC 97-19109. (Illus.). 32p. (J). (ps-2). 1997. 7.99 (*0-8499-1510-4*) Tommy Nelson.

Tiny Steps of Faith Series. Lois J. Haas. (ENG & SPA.). (J). 1985. pap. text ed. 3.50 (*0-86508-010-0*) BCM Pubn.

***Tiny Stories.** Dennis Ciscel. (Illus.). 100p. Date not set. 11.95 (*0-911051-62-7*) Plain View.

Tiny Tale of Peter Rabbit. (J). 1985. pap. 3.95 (*0-671-52695-2*, Litl Simon S&S) S&S Childrens.

Tiny Talks: A Book of Devotions for Small Children. Robert J. Morgan. (Illus.). 160p. (J). 1996. 10.99 (*0-7852-7562-2*) Nelson.

Tiny Tappers Level 1: Book One. Bonnie Nemeth. (Timeless Tap Ser.). 72p. (J). (ps-k). 1995. pap. 12.00 (*1-888199-50-4*) Dance Innovators.

Tiny Taste of the Southwest. Karen Price. 128p. 1993. pap. write for info. (*0-9637591-0-8*) KAP Ent.

Tiny Taxman. M. Hencher. 2.99 (*1-871676-57-6*, Pub. by Christian Focus UK) Spring Arbor Dist.

***Tiny Tea, a Friendship Gift.** Dee Appel. (Illus.). 22p. (Orig.). 1996. pap. 6.95 (*0-9654957-0-1*) Heartfelt Lines-Mailbox Memories.

Tiny Textiles: The Bedroom, Pt. I. Mary E. Erf. 52p. 1992. 20.00 (*0-9632828-9-1*); pap. text ed. 20.00 (*0-9632828-5-9*) Treadle One.

***Tiny Tiger.** Barbara DeRubertis. LC 96-53272. (Illus.). 32p. (Orig.). (J). (ps-2). 1997. pap. 4.95 (*1-57565-024-X*); pap. 7.95 incl. audio (*1-57565-034-7*) Kane Pr.

Tiny Tim Is Dead. Barbara Lebow. 1993. pap. 5.25 (*0-8222-1363-X*) Dramatists Play.

Tiny Timothy Turtle. Anna Leditschke. (Illus.). 32p. (J). (ps-2). 1991. lib. bdg. 18.60 (*0-8368-0667-0*) Gareth Stevens Inc.

Tiny Tina, Messy Maggie, & Perfect Pal. Louise Kantenwein. (J). 1992. 7.95 (*0-533-10174-3*) Vantage.

Tiny Toes. large type ed. Donna Jakob. LC 93-40846. (Illus.). 32p. (J). (ps-1). 1995. 13.95 (*0-7868-0013-5*); lib. bdg. 13.89 (*0-7868-2009-8*) Hyprn Child.

Tiny Toon Adventures: A Clubhouse Built for Toons. Carol A. Hanshaw. (Comes to Life Bks.). 16p. (J). (ps-2). 1994. write for info. (*1-883366-37-2*) YES Ent.

Tiny Toon Adventures: The Big Race. (Golden Easy Readers Ser.: Level 2). (J). (gr. k-2). 1991. write for info. (*0-307-11698-0*, Golden Pr) Western Pub.

Tiny Toon Adventures: This Way to Wackyland. Susan R. Simms. (Travel Traxx Ser.). 10p. (J). (ps-2). 1994. write for info. (*1-883366-55-0*) YES Ent.

Tiny Tot Tunes. JTG of Nashville Staff. (J). (ps-3). 1996. 18.95 (*1-884832-75-X*) JTG Nashville.

Tiny Tots Bible Story Book. John Walton & Kim Walton. LC 50-2503. (Illus.). 432p. (J). (ps). 1993. 15.99 (*0-7814-0834-2*, Chariot Bks) Chariot Victor.

***Tiny Tots Bible Storybook.** (J). 1994. write for info. (*0-7814-1544-6*, Chariot Bks) Chariot Victor.

Tiny Tots Fruits. Western Promotional Books Staff. (Tiny Tots Bks.). (Illus.). 10p. (J). (ps). 1993. bds. 2.95 (*0-307-16225-7*, Golden Books) Western Pub.

Tiny Tots Jesus Storybook. John Walton & Kim Walton. (Illus.). 128p. (J). 1996. 10.99 (*0-7814-0271-9*) Chariot Victor.

Tiny Tots Pets. Western Promotional Books Staff. (Illus.). 10p. (J). (ps). 1993. bds. 2.95 (*0-307-16226-5*, Golden Books) Western Pub.

Tiny Tot's Speaker. Lizzie J. Rook & E. J. Goodfellow. LC 73-160907. (Granger Index Reprint Ser.). (YA). (gr. 7 up). 1977. reprint ed. 17.95 (*0-8369-6271-0*) Ayer.

Tiny Tots Things. Western Promotional Books Staff. (Illus.). 10p. (J). (ps). 1993. bds. 2.95 (*0-307-16227-3*, Golden Books) Western Pub.

Tiny Tots Toys. Western Promotional Books Staff. (Illus.). 10p. (J). (ps). 1993. bds. 2.95 (*0-307-16228-1*, Golden Books) Western Pub.

***Tiny Tow Truck.** Robert Kraus. (Sticker 'n' Shapes Bks.). (J). (ps-2). 1997. 3.99 (*0-614-29115-1*, Litl Simon S&S) S&S Childrens.

Tiny Town Tale. Christopher Carrie. (Crayola Coloring Storybks.). (Illus.). 32p. (Orig.). (J). (ps). 1990. 1.99 (*0-86696-237-9*) Binney & Smith.

Tiny Traditions. Sylvia T. Voudrie. Ed. by Patti L. Bachelder. LC 92-16803. (Illus.). 66p. (Orig.). 1992. pap. 9.95 (*0-9622565-2-8*) Chitra Pubns.

Tiny Treasure Bible Gems: New International Version. 1993. text ed. 4.99 (*0-310-96258-7*) Zondervan.

Tiny Treasures: The Wonderful World of a Jewish Child. Dina Rosenfeld. (Illus.). 26p. (J). 1988. reprint ed. 10.00 (*0-8266-0365-3*, Merkos LInyonei Chinuch) Kehot Pubn Soc.

***Tiny Treasury of Friendship.** Andrews & McMeel Staff. (Tiny Tomes Ser.). (J). 1997. 3.95 (*0-8362-3634-3*) Andrews & McMeel.

Tiny Troll Treasury: Lucky Rainbow; Magic Hair; The Enchanted Frog; The Sword & the Troll; The Princess Troll; The Littlest Troll, 6 bks., Set. (Illus.). 24p. (J). 1993. boxed 9.98 (*0-7853-0019-8*) Pubns Intl Ltd.

Tiny Tunes: A New & Practical Approach to Reading Piano Music. 52p. 1994. spiral bd., pap. 8.00 (*1-880571-08-0*) Decision Pt.

***Tiny Tyrannosaurus & Her Fierce Teeth, Incl. toy.** Paul Flemming. (Snappy Fun Bks.). (Illus.). 13p. (J). (gr. k-2). 1997. bds. 4.99 (*1-57584-171-1*) Rdrs Dgst Yng Fam.

Tinyburg Tales. Robert J. Hastings. LC 83-71167. 168p. (Orig.). 1983. pap. 7.99 (*0-8054-5218-4*, 4252-18) Broadman.

***Tiny's Hat.** Ann Grifalconi. LC 96-42555. (J). Date not set. write for info. (*0-06-027654-1*); lib. bdg. write for info. (*0-06-027655-X*) HarpC.

Tiny's Self Help Books for Children. Jeanette N. Hafford. Orig. Title: Help Mates for Your Playmates. (Illus.). 18p. (Orig.). (J). (gr. k-5). 1986. pap. 4.22 (*0-685-14506-9*) Tinys Self Help Bks.

Tio Armando. Florence P. Heide & Roxanne H. Pierce. LC 93-37434. (Illus.). (YA). (gr. 5 up). Date not set. write for info. (*0-688-12107-1*); lib. bdg. write for info. (*0-688-12108-X*) Lothrop.

Tio Kingdom of the Middle Congo, 1880-1892. Jan Vansina. LC 73-164033. 608p. reprint ed. pap. 173.30 (*0-8357-6976-3*, 2039036) Bks Demand.

Tioga Tales: The Eighth Northwoods Reader. 2nd ed. Cully Gage. (Illus.). 130p. 1993. 10.95 (*0-932212-80-8*) Avery Color.

Tip Lewis & His Lamp. Isabella Alden. (Grace Livingston Hill Ser.: Vol. 8). 1996. mass mkt., pap. 4.99 (*0-8423-3184-0*) Tyndale.

Tip Lewis & His Lamp. rev. ed. 208p. 1987. 7.30 (*0-318-41781-2*) Rod & Staff.

Tip of the Iceberg: Hemingway & the Short Story. Kenneth G. Johnston. (Illus.). 315p. 1987. lib. bdg. 30.00 (*0-913283-19-3*) Penkevill.

***Tip of the Scales.** Darlene Pelletier. 64p. 1997. pap. 7.00 (*0-8059-4190-8*) Dorrance.

Tip Reporting Alternative Commitment: Market Segment Understanding with the Food Service Industry. 13p. 1995. pap. 11.00 (*1-57402-320-9*) Athena Info Mgt.

T.I.P. Resource Guide. 350p. 1995. 150.00 (*0-614-06057-5*) Bureau Style.

Tip, Tap, Toe: The Great Tapdancers. William C. Lane. write for info. (*0-318-58990-7*) World Pr Ltd.

Tip-Toe Tappers. Bonnie Nemeth. Ed. by Wolf Nemeth & Debby Bouldin. (Timeless Tap Ser.: Level 2, Bk. 2, Vol. 2). (Illus.). 72p. (Orig.). (J). (ps-1). 1996. pap. 12.00 (*1-888199-52-0*) Dance Innovators.

Tip-Top Tappers. Bonnie Nemeth. Ed. by Wolf Nemeth & Debby Bouldin. (Timeless Tap Ser.: Level 5, Bk.5, Vol. 5). (Illus.). 72p. (Orig.). (YA). (gr. 8 up). 1996. pap. 12.00 (*1-888199-55-5*) Dance Innovators.

Tip up Shotguns from Hopkins & Allen Arms Company. Charles E. Carder. 60p. 1994. pap. text ed. 13.95 (*0-9635451-1-6*) Aero Print.

Tipis & Yurts: Authentic Design for Circular Shelters. Blue Evening Star Staff. Ed. by Leslie Dierks. LC 95-6219. (Illus.). 128p. 1995. 24.95 (*0-937274-88-7*) Lark Books.

***Tipitaka Men Sanyaka Sambuddha: Introduction to the Tipitaka.** S. N. Goenka. 254p. 1996. 14.95 (*81-7414-026-3*) Vipassana Res.

Tippecanoe & Trinkets Too: The Material Culture of American Presidential Campaigns, 1828-1984. Roger A. Fischer. LC 86-30924. (Illus.). 336p. 1988. text ed. 34.95 (*0-252-00960-6*) U of Ill Pr.

Tipper Gore. Julie S. Bach. LC 93-15326. (Leading Ladies Ser.). (Illus.). (J). 1993. lib. bdg. 13.98 (*1-56239-220-4*) Abdo & Dghtrs.

T

Tipper Gore: A Voice for the Voiceless. JoAnn B. Guernsey. LC 93-8165. (Achievers Ser.). (J). (gr. 4-9). 1993. pap. 6.95 (*0-8225-9651-2*, Lerner Publctns); lib. bdg. 19.95 (*0-8225-2876-2*, Lerner Publctns) Lerner Group.

Tipperary. Mairtin O. Corrbui. (Illus.). 219p. (Orig.). 1991. pap. 13.95 (*0-86322-131-9*, Pub. by Brandon Bk Pubs IE) Irish Bks Media.

Tipperary. Desmond O'Grady. 124p. 1991. pap. 13.95 (*0-948339-79-9*, Pub. by Salmon Pubng IE) Dufour.

Tipperary: A Treasure Chest. Elaine B. Houlihan. Ed. by Donal A. Murphy. 204p. (Orig.). 1995. pap. 13.95 (*0-946327-15-7*, Pub. by Relay Pubns IE) Irish Bks Media.

Tippett on Music. Michael Tippett. Ed. by Meirion Bowen. 240p. 1995. pap. 18.95 (*0-19-816542-0*) OUP.

Tipping Point. Fred Marchant. LC 93-61079. 80p. (Orig.). 1994. per. 10.00 (*0-915380-30-7*) Word Works.

Tipping the Balance Towards Primary Health Care: A Pan-European Analysis. Ed. by Tom Rathwell et al. 200p. 1995. 59.95 (*1-85628-941-9*, Pub. by Avebury Pub UK) Ashgate Pub Co.

Tipping the Scales see Henry Cecil Reprint Series

Tippoo Sultan: A Tale of Mysore War. Taylor Meadows. 460p. 1986. reprint ed. 22.00 (*0-8364-1734-8*, Pub. by Usha II) S Asia.

Tippu. Abigail Pizer & David Day. LC 94-28923. (J). 1995. 11.95 (*0-8120-6498-4*); pap. 4.95 (*0-8120-9183-3*) Barron.

Tippy Tail the Gentle Gray Whale. Wynne Gibson, pseud. LC 87-91041. (Illus.). 24p. (Orig.). (J). (gr. 2-5). 1994. 4.95 (*0-915715-22-8*); pap. write for info. (*0-915715-23-6*) Wynne Pub Co.

Tippy Toe Murder. Leslie Meier. 256p. 1996. mass mkt. 4.99 (*1-57566-099-7*, Knsington) Kensgtn Pub Corp.

***TIPS: Discipline in the Music Classroom.** Music Educators National Conference Staff. (TIPS Booklet Ser.). 32p. (Orig.). (C). 1989. pap. 7.75 (*0-940796-60-0*, 1095) Music Ed Natl.

***TIPS: Establishing a String & Orchestra Program.** Jacquelyn Dillon-Krass & Dorothy A. Straub. 32p. (Orig.). (C). 1991. pap. 7.75 (*0-940796-66-X*, 1098) Music Ed Natl.

***TIPS: Getting Started with Elementary School Music.** Music Educators National Conference Staff. (TIPS Booklet Ser.). 40p. (Orig.). (C). 1988. pap. 7.75 (*0-940796-44-9*, 1091) Music Ed Natl.

***TIPS: Music Activities in Early Childhood.** Music Educators National Conference Staff. (TIPS Booklet Ser.). 32p. (Orig.). (C). 1990. pap. 7.75 (*0-940796-76-7*, 1097) Music Ed Natl.

***TIPS: Retirement for Music Educators.** Music Educators National Conference Staff. Ed. by A. Verne Wilson. (TIPS Booklet Ser.). 24p. (Orig.). (C). 1989. pap. 5.50 (*0-940796-59-7*, 1094) Music Ed Natl.

***TIPS: Teaching Music to Special Learners.** Music Educators National Conference Staff. (TIPS Booklet Ser.). 48p. (Orig.). (C). 1988. pap. 7.75 (*0-940796-56-2*, 1092) Music Ed Natl.

TIPS: Technical Insert Production Specifications. Ed. by Peter Brehm. 62p. 1989. 31.75 (*0-933505-08-6*) Graph Comm Assn.

***TIPS: Technology for Music Educators.** Music Educators National Conference Staff. Ed. by Charles G. Boody. (TIPS Booklet Ser.). 48p. (Orig.). (C). 1990. pap. 7.75 (*0-940796-72-4*, 1096) Music Ed Natl.

Tips: The Imaginative Parent Succeeds. Verneta J. Milton & Robert G. Milton. (Illus.). 202p. (Orig.). 1985. pap. 6.95 (*0-9614763-9-7*) Ink Illusions.

TIPS: To Insure Perfect Spanish. Nancy L. Martin. (Illus.). 75p. pap. 19.95 (*0-9643508-0-7*) MCL Pubs.

***TIPS - Thinking Skills in the Music Classroom.** Jennifer Davidson. (TIPS Ser.). 24p. (C). 1994. pap. text ed. 5.50 (*1-56545-027-2*, 1100) Music Ed Natl.

Tips Against Crime Written from Prison: A Survival Guide for the 90's. Renee M. Rolle-Whatley. LC 93-84435. 176p. (Orig.). 1993. pap. 13.95 (*0-9627756-7-3*) Sandcastle Pub.

Tips & Ideas on Self-Publishing: How to Write Your Book & Make It Pay Off. rev. ed. Bernard Klein. LC 92-90298. (Illus.). 416p. 1993. pap. 24.95 (*0-9620859-2-8*) Campion Pub Co.

Tips & Other Bright Ideas for School Librarians. Linworth Publishing, Inc. Staff. (Professional Growth Ser.). (Illus.). 202p. 1993. reprint ed. pap. text ed. 26.95 (*0-87436-605-4*) Linworth Pub.

Tips & Programs for the HP-32S. Wlodek Mier-Jedrzejowicz. (Illus.). 81p. (Orig.). (C). 1988. pap. text ed. 7.95 (*0-937637-05-X*, 2014) EduCALC Pubns.

Tips & Tales of the Tennis Court. Paige J. O'Neill. (Illus.). 180p. (Orig.). 1995. pap. write for info. (*0-9649392-0-7*) P ONeill.

Tips & Techniques for Electronics Experimenters. 2nd ed. Don Tuite & Delton T. Horn. (Illus.). 144p. 1989. 19.95 (*0-8306-9145-6*); pap. 12.95 (*0-8306-3145-3*) McGraw-Hill Prof.

Tips & Techniques for Electronics Experiments. 2nd ed. Don Tuite & Delton T. Horn. 1989. pap. 12.95 (*0-07-156051-3*); text ed. 19.95 (*0-07-156039-4*) McGraw.

Tips & Techniques, Secrets from a Lifetime in Dentistry, 1. Tr. by Jerald L. Weitzel. (Illus.). 51p. (C). 1987. pap. 39.95 (*0-944375-00-6*) United Prof Pubns.

Tips & Techniques, Secrets from a Lifetime in Dentistry, No. 1. Tr. by Jerald L. Weitzel. (Illus.). 51p. (C). 1987. Cassette 1. audio 10.00 (*0-944375-02-2*) United Prof Pubns.

Tips & Techniques, Secrets from a Lifetime in Dentistry, No. 2. Tr. by Jerald L. Weitzel. (Illus.). 51p. (C). 1987. Cassette 2. audio write for info. (*0-944375-03-0*) United Prof Pubns.

Tips & Techniques, Secrets from a Lifetime in Dentistry, Set 1. Tr. by Jerald L. Weitzel. (Illus.). 51p. (C). 1987. write for info. (*0-944375-01-4*) United Prof Pubns.

Tips & Tidbits: A Book for Family Day Care Providers. Janet Gonzalez-Mena. LC 91-67248. (Illus.). 66p. 1991. pap. text ed. 5.00 (*0-935989-47-1*, NAEYC #303) Natl Assn Child Ed.

***Tips & Timesavers for Home Health Nurses.** SPC Staff. (Illus.). 192p. (Orig.). 1997. 19.95 (*0-87434-917-6*) Springhouse Pub.

Tips & Traps for Making Money in Real Estate. Robert Irwin. 1993. pap. text ed. 14.95 (*0-07-032384-4*) McGraw.

Tips & Traps for Negotiating Better Real Estate Deals. Robert Irwin. 1996. pap. text ed. 12.95 (*0-07-032747-5*) McGraw.

Tips & Traps for Saving on All Your Real Estate Taxes. Robert Irwin & Norman Lane. 240p. 1994. text ed. 24.95 (*0-07-032395-X*); pap. text ed. 12.95 (*0-07-032396-8*) McGraw.

Tips & Traps When Buying a Franchise. Mary E. Tomzack. 1994. pap. text ed. 14.95 (*0-07-065101-9*) McGraw.

Tips & Traps When Buying a Home. Robert Irwin. 192p. 1991. audio 9.95 (*0-07-032169-8*) McGraw.

Tips & Traps When Buying a Home. 2nd ed. Robert Irwin. (Illus.). 256p. 1996. pap. text ed. 14.95 (*0-07-032884-6*) McGraw.

Tips & Traps When Mortgage Hunting. Robert Irwin. 1992. pap. text ed. 12.95 (*0-07-032249-X*) McGraw.

Tips & Traps When Selling a Home. 2nd ed. Robert Irwin. (Illus.). 256p. 1996. pap. text ed. 14.95 (*0-07-032885-4*) McGraw.

***Tips & Tricks for Cat Owners.** Herta Puttner & Eva Rohrer. (Illus.). 160p. 1997. pap. 6.95 (*0-7938-0469-8*, TS-277) TFH Pubns.

***Tips & Tricks for Dog Owners.** Herta Puttner & Eva Rohrer. (Illus.). 160p. 1997. pap. 6.95 (*0-7938-0468-X*, TS-276) TFH Pubns.

Tips & Tricks for Toy Train Operators. Peter H. Riddle. 80p. 1994. 11.95 (*0-89778-395-6*, 10-7935, Greenberg Books) Kalmbach.

Tips & Tricks in Outdoor Education. 5th ed. Malcolm D. Swan. 260p. 1994. pap. text ed. 24.95 (*0-8134-2954-4*) Interstate.

Tips at Your Fingertips: Teaching Strategies for Adult Literacy Tutors. Ed. by Ola M. Brown. LC 95-43785. 140p. (Orig.). 1996. pap. 21.95 (*0-87207-141-3*, 141-3) Intl Reading.

Tips for Carefree Landscapes: Over Five Hundred Sure-Fire Ways to Beautify Your Yard & Garden. Marianne Binetti. Ed. by Ben Watson. LC 89-45739. (Illus.). 168p. (Orig.). 1990. pap. 9.95 (*0-88266-572-3*, Garden Way Pub) Storey Comm Inc.

Tips for Creating a Manageable Classroom: Understanding Your Students' Basic Needs. Julie Landsman. LC 94-31920. 16p. 1994. pap. 3.50 (*1-57131-200-5*) Milkweed Ed.

***Tips for Dirt Cheap Gardening.** Rhonda M. Hart. LC 96-43825. (Storey Publishing Bulletin Ser.). 1996. pap. 2.95 (*0-88266-574-X*) Storey Comm Inc.

Tips for Doing Library Research. Norman D. Anderson. 1993. write for info. (*0-935577-61-0*) Acid Rain Found.

Tips for Finding the Right Job. 1992. lib. bdg. 88.00 (*0-8490-5526-1*) Gordon Pr.

Tips for Improving School Climate. Jim Sweeney. 24p. (Orig.). 1988. pap. text ed. 1.50 (*0-87652-122-7*, 02100212) Am Assn Sch Admin.

Tips for Quilters: A Handbook of Hints, Shortcuts, & Practical Suggestions from Experienced Quilters. Rachel T. Pellman. LC 93-24758. 160p. (Orig.). 1993. pap. 9.95 (*1-56148-080-0*) Good Bks PA.

Tips for Recording Musicians. John Harris. (Illus.). 100p. 1996. pap. 13.95 (*1-870775-40-6*) Cimino Pub Grp.

Tips for Successful Freelancing. 1992. pap. 3.50 (*1-880407-04-3*) Edit Freelancers.

Tips for TAAS Grade 4 Science. Barbara A. Cobaugh & Margie L. Capron. (Illus.). 108p. (Orig.). 1994. pap. 16.00 (*0-9640524-0-7*) C & C Educ.

Tips for TAAS Grades 1-6 Mathematics: Critical Reading, Vocabulary, & Problem Solving. Barbara A. Cobaugh. 122p. (Orig.). (J). (gr. 1-6). 1995. pap. 23.00 (*0-9640524-1-5*) C & C Educ.

Tips for Teams: A Ready Reference for Solving Common Team Problems. Kimball Fisher et al. 1994. text ed. 29.95 (*0-07-021224-4*); pap. text ed. 14.95 (*0-07-021167-1*, 94-21376) McGraw.

Tips for Teens: Telephone Tactics, Petting Practices, & Other Milestones on the Road to Popularity. Benjamin Darling. LC 93-35815. 60p. (YA). (gr. 7-12). 1994. 9.95 (*0-8118-0520-4*) Chronicle Bks.

Tips for the Lazy Gardener. Linda Tilgner. LC 93-42253. 1994. 6.99 (*0-517-10109-2*) Random Hse Value.

Tips for the Lazy Gardener. Linda Tilgner. LC 85-70196. (Illus.). 128p. 1985. pap. 8.95 (*0-88266-390-9*, Garden Way Pub) Storey Comm Inc.

Tips for the Litigator: A Handbook of Oregon Trial Procedure. Robert P. Jones. 155p. ring bd. 29.50 (*0-614-04693-9*) Oregon Law Inst.

***Tips for the Savvy Traveler: The Book to Read Before Taking Any Trip.** Deborah Burns. LC 96-53199. 224p. (Orig.). 1997. pap. 12.95 (*0-88266-971-0*) Storey Comm Inc.

***Tips for Tired Dads.** Barbour Bargain Books Staff. (Little Library). 1997. pap. text ed. 0.99 (*1-55748-988-2*) Barbour & Co.

Tips for Toddlers. Brooke M. Beebe. 240p. (Orig.). 1987. pap. 9.95 (*0-440-50680-8*) Dell.

Tips for Traders & Investors: Trading U. S. Bonds & Stocks. Joseph B. Stowell. (Illus.). 155p. 1995. 54.00 (*1-886977-00-3*) Money Mgmt Inst.

***Tips for Travelers.** 1997. lib. bdg. 258.95 (*0-8490-6200-4*) Gordon Pr.

Tips for Working Parents: Creative Solutions to Everyday Problems. Kathleen McBride. Ed. by Deborah Burns. LC 88-62787. (Illus.). 144p. 1989. pap. 7.95 (*0-88266-546-4*, Storey Pub) Storey Comm Inc.

Tips for Writing on the Computer. N. D. Anderson. (Orig.). 1993. write for info. (*0-935577-66-1*) Acid Rain Found.

Tips from the Trenches: America's Best Teachers Describe Effective Classroom Methods. Charles M. Chase & Jacqueline E. Chase. LC 93-60578. 180p. 1993. pap. text ed. 24.95 (*1-56676-054-2*) Technomic.

Tips from Tina: Help Around the House. Tina Koch & Mary-Lane Kamberg. LC 95-10135. 107p. (Orig.). 1995. pap. 11.95 (*1-884834-01-9*, 1035) Redleaf Pr.

Tips from Top Cartoonists. Christensen. 1990. pap. 9.95 (*0-913035-40-8*) Eclipse Bks.

TIPS Index of Papers: An Index of Papers Prepared for the ABA Tort & Insurance Practice Section & Presented at Its Meetings & Through Its Publications. American Bar Association Staff. LC 85-243283. (Book about ... Ser.). 176p. 1985. pap. 5.00 (*0-89707-178-6*, 519-0041) Amer Bar Assn.

Tips on Evaluating & Re-Engineering the Help Desk. Candy F. Drew. (Illus.). 138p. (Orig.). 1993. pap. 30.00 (*1-883355-01-X*) Odelle Pubns.

Tips on Greeting Card Design. Bill Gray & Jane Van Milligen. 1991. pap. text ed. 15.95 (*0-07-157749-1*) McGraw.

Tips on Handling & Tensioning Strand. (PCI Journal Reprints Ser.). 16p. 1977. pap. 8.00 (*0-686-40104-2*, JR186) P-PCI.

Tips on How to Stay Safe & Survive Almost Anything! A Watchdog Resource for Students in Grades K Through 12 & Their Parents. William Lonberger. 1994. 14.00 (*0-910609-28-4*) Gifted Educ Pr.

Tips on Identifying & Appraising Clocks. Martha L. Tips. LC 89-90724. (Illus.). 312p. 1991. write for info. (*0-9628627-0-3*) Clock Bks All Time TX.

Tips on Landing a Federal Government Job: A Do-It-Yourself Guide to Effective SF-One Seventy-One Writing & Government Job Hunting. Ed. by I. Norman Johansen. 1976. 3.95 (*0-918350-01-8*) Job Hunters Forum.

Tips on Layout & Design. Jane Van Milligen & Bill Gray. (Illus.). 128p. 1992. pap. 12.95 (*0-8306-3976-4*, 4158, Design Pr) TAB Bks.

Tips on Lettering: For Artists, Graphic Designers, & Calligraphers. Bill Gray. LC 96-21654. (Illus.). 128p. 1996. pap. 14.95 (*0-393-73005-0*, Norton Paperbks) Norton.

Tips on Making Greeting Cards. Bill Gray & M. Jane Van Milligen. (Illus.). 128p. 1991. pap. 13.95 (*0-8306-0595-9*, 3788, Design Pr) TAB Bks.

***Tips on New York.** Jack Finkelstein. 1997. mass mkt. 6.95 (*1-56171-954-4*, S P I Bks) Sure Seller.

Tips on Succeeding in College. Stanley Fitch. 1991. pap. 1.39 (*1-56226-042-1*) CT Pub.

Tips on Taping: Language Recording in Social Sciences. Wayne B. Dickerson & Lonna J. Dickerson. LC 76-50023. (Applied Cultural Anthropology Ser.). 198p. 1977. pap. 5.95 (*0-87808-147-X*) William Carey Lib.

Tips on Tipping: The Ultimate Guide to Who, When, & How Much to Tip. Irene Frankel. 80p. (Orig.). 1990. pap. 5.00 (*0-9621395-0-5*) Martin Unltd.

Tips on Type. Bill Gray. LC 97-8338. (Illus.). 128p. 1996. pap. 14.95 (*0-393-73006-9*) Norton.

TIPS Standard Binder. 1982. 12.00 (*0-685-42975-X*, 519-0028) Amer Bar Assn.

TIPS (the Incidental & Pertinent Stuff) for Beginning Fiction Writers. Lynn Bradley. Ed. by Dot Fowler. (Illus.). 72p. (Orig.). 1993. pap. 10.00 (*0-9637150-0-3*, T-93) Talent By Lb.

Tips to Fly By. Richard L. Collins. Ed. by Eleanor Friede. LC 92-34460. 304p. 1993. 24.95 (*1-56566-035-8*) Thomasson-Grant.

Tips-to-Top Dollar: A Better Way to Sell Your Car, Truck, Or Van. Richard L. Miskowski. (Illus.). 32p. (Orig.). student ed. write for info. (*0-9640051-0-7*) RJC Enter.

Tips to Travelers: Central & South America. 1994. lib. bdg. 250.00 (*0-8490-6478-3*) Gordon Pr.

Tips to Travelers: Eastern Europe. 1994. lib. bdg. 250.00 (*0-8490-6479-1*) Gordon Pr.

Tips to Travelers: Mexico. 1994. lib. bdg. 250.00 (*0-8490-6480-5*) Gordon Pr.

Tips to Travelers: People's Republic of China. 1994. lib. bdg. 250.00 (*0-8490-6482-1*) Gordon Pr.

Tips to Travelers: Russia. 1994. lib. bdg. 250.00 (*0-8490-6483-X*) Gordon Pr.

Tips to Travelers: South Asia. 1994. lib. bdg. 250.00 (*0-8490-6484-8*) Gordon Pr.

Tips to Travelers: The Caribbean. 1994. lib. bdg. 250.00 (*0-8490-6477-5*) Gordon Pr.

Tips to Travelers: The Middle East & North Africa. 1994. lib. bdg. 250.00 (*0-8490-6481-3*) Gordon Pr.

***Tips, Tools, & Timesavers for Reading Success.** Imogene Forte. Ed. by Jan Keeling. (Tips, Tools, & Timesavers for Success Ser.). (Illus.). 96p. 1997. pap. text ed. 10.95 (*0-86530-349-5*) Incentive Pubns.

***Tips, Tools, & Timesavers for Science Success.** Imogene Forte. Ed. by Jan Keeling. (Tips, Tools, & Timesavers for Success Ser.). (Illus.). 96p. 1997. pap. text ed. 10.95 (*0-86530-350-9*) Incentive Pubns.

***Tips, Tools, & Timesavers for Thinking Success.** Imogene Forte. Ed. by Jan Keeling. (Tips, Tools, & Timesavers for Success Ser.). (Illus.). 96p. 1997. pap. text ed. 10.95 (*0-86530-351-7*) Incentive Pubns.

Tipster: Proceedings of the First Workshop. 300p. 1994. pap. 40.00 (*1-55860-337-9*) Morgan Kaufmann.

Tipster Text Program. Ed. by ARPA Staff. (Orig.). 1996. pap. 55.00 (*1-55860-426-X*) Morgan Kaufmann.

***Tiptionary.** Mary Hunt. 1997. pap. text ed. 8.99 (*0-8054-0147-4*) Broadman.

Tiptoe Round the Corner. Virginia Ferguson & Peter Durkin. LC 93-168. (J). 1994. write for info. (*0-383-03720-4*) SRA McGraw.

Tiptoes. (Ladybird Stories Ser.). (Illus.). (ARA.). (J). (gr. 1-3). 1987. 4.50 (*0-86685-240-9*) Intl Bk Ctr.

Tipton County, Tennessee: A Place of Memories: People Moving Forward. Mildred O. Wortham. LC 94-33416. 1994. write for info. (*0-89865-919-1*) Donning Co.

Tipton's Crew. P. La Ferriere & Vernon L. Burda. LC 94-37481. 1994. pap. 9.95 (*0-89802-492-7*) Beautiful Am.

***Tiptree Collection.** Tiptree Staff. Date not set. 23.95 (*0-312-85874-4*) St Martin.

***TIR Handbook: Including Customs Convention on the International Transport of Goods under Cover of TIR Carnets.** United Nations Economics Commission for Europe Staff. 205p. 1996. pap. 60.00 (*92-1-100710-0*, 68732) UN.

Tir Na Nog: A Shadowrun Sourcebook. FASA Staff. (Shadowrun Ser.). (Illus.). 128p. 1993. pap. 18.00 (*1-55560-209-6*, 7211) FASA Corp.

Tir Tairngire. FASA Staff. (Shadowrun Ser.). (Illus.). 128p. 1993. pap. 18.00 (*1-55560-197-9*) FASA Corp.

TIR Transit System. 19p. 1991. 9.00 (*92-1-139034-6*) UN.

Tira Tells Everything There Is to Know about Herself & the Bodybuilders: Two Plays. Michael Weller. 1972. pap. 5.25 (*0-8222-0132-1*) Dramatists Play.

Tirades & Evidence of Grace. Susan Bright. 164p. 1992. pap. 13.95 (*0-911051-58-9*) Plain View.

Tiranosaurio. Janet Riehecky. LC 88-1692. (Libros Sobre Dinosaurios! Ser.). (Illus.). 32p. (SPA.). (J). (gr. k-4). 1988. lib. bdg. 21.36 (*1-56766-123-8*) Childs World.

Tirant Lo Blanc. Joanot Martorell & Marti J. De Galba. Tr. by David H. Rosenthal. 688p. (C). 1996. pap. 19.95 (*0-8018-5421-0*) Johns Hopkins.

Tirant Lo Blanc: The Complete Translation. Joanot Martorell. Tr. by Ray La Fontaine from CAT. LC 93-20108. (Catalan Studies: Vol. 1). 820p. (Orig.). (C). 1994. pap. text ed. 39.95 (*0-8204-1688-6*) P Lang Pubng.

Tirant lo Blanc Revisited: A Critical Study. Kathleen McNerney. LC 83-62143. (Medieval & Renaissance Monograph Ser.: Vol. 4). 139p. reprint ed. pap. 39.70 (*0-685-17117-5*, 2027025) Bks Demand.

Tire House. Ed Paschich & Paula Hendricks. LC 95-1012. (Illus.). 96p. (Orig.). 1995. pap. 14.95 (*0-86534-215-6*) Sunstone Pr.

Tire Imprint Evidence. Peter McDonald. (Practical Aspects of Criminal & Forensic Investigations Ser.). 248p. 1992. 54.95 (*0-8493-9515-1*, HV8097) CRC Pr.

Tire Imprint Identification: Practical Aspects of Criminal Forensic Investigation Ser. P. McDonald. 448p. 1989. 45.00 (*0-444-01456-X*, CRC Reprint) Franklin.

Tire, Parachute Activities. rev. ed. Jack Capon. Ed. by Frank Alexander. (Perceptual-Motor Development Ser.: Bk. 5). (Illus.). 31p. 1994. reprint ed. teacher ed., pap. 8.00 (*0-915256-40-1*, 125) Front Row.

Tire Pavement Interface, STP 929. Ed. by Marion G. Pottinger & Thomas J. Yager. LC 86-20565. (Special Technical Publication (STP) Ser.). (Illus.). 330p. 1986. text ed. 54.00 (*0-8031-0497-9*, 04-929000-27) ASTM.

Tire Reinforcement & Tire Performance-STP-694. Ed. by R. A. Fleming & D. I. Livingston. 337p. 1980. 34.50 (*0-8031-0780-3*, 04-694000-37) ASTM.

Tire Rolling Resistance. Ed. by Dieterich J. Schuring. (Rubber Division Symposia Ser.: Vol. 1). (Illus.). viii, 398p. 1983. 29.00 (*0-912415-01-0*) Rubber Division.

Tire Shrinker to Dragster, Vol. 34. Ed. by Wilson M. Hudson. (Texas Folklore Society Publications). 1968. 15.00 (*0-88426-025-9*) Encino Pr.

Tire Tracks Back. Thomas D. Murray. LC 89-81149. 266p. (Orig.). 1990. pap. 14.95 (*0-916383-96-2*) Aegina Pr.

Tire Wars: Racing with Goodyear. William Neely. LC 93-72137. (Illus.). 192p. 1993. 34.95 (*0-89404-091-X*) Aztex.

Tired All the Time: How to Regain Your Lost Energy. Ronald L. Hoffman. Ed. by Julie Rubenstein. 256p. 1996. reprint ed. pap. 12.00 (*0-671-86812-8*, PB Trade Paper) PB.

Tired Apple Tree. Ruth Moore. 160p. (Orig.). 1990. pap. 8.50 (*0-942396-59-6*) Blackberry ME.

Tired Country Smiles. Nola P. Vandermeer. LC 83-81475. 242p. 1983. 10.00 (*0-8187-0053-X*) Harlo Press.

Tired of Being Tired: Overcoming Chronic Fatigue & Low Vitality. Michael A. Schmidt. LC 93-48676. (Illus.). 250p. (Orig.). (C). 1995. pap. 14.95 (*1-883319-16-1*) Frog Ltd CA.

Tired of Trying to Measure Up. Jeff JanVonderen. 176p. (Orig.). 1989. pap. 9.99 (*1-55661-030-0*) Bethany Hse.

Tired or Toxic. Sherry A. Rogers. 438p. 1990. pap. 17.95 (*0-9618821-2-3*) Prestige NY.

Tired Tourist's Concise Guide to Florence. rev. ed. Richard C. Alter. (Illus.). 1978. pap. 3.00 (*0-89726-000-7*) Foldabook Pub.

Tired Tourist's Concise Guide to London. Richard C. Alter. LC 78-55944. (Illus.). 1978. pap. 3.00 (*0-89726-002-3*) Foldabook Pub.

Tired Tourist's Concise Guide to Paris. Richard C. Alter. LC 78-75278. (Illus.). 1979. pap. 3.00 (*0-89726-005-8*) Foldabook Pub.

Tired Tourist's Concise Guide to Rome. Richard C. Alter. LC 79-57049. (Illus.). 1980. pap. 3.00 (*0-89726-031-7*) Foldabook Pub.

Tired Tubes & Ten-Speed Turkeys. Richard Wiman. 1991. 17.95 (*1-879034-05-0*) Greasy Bayou.

Tireless Traveler: Twenty Letters to the Liverpool Mercury. Anthony Trollope. 1978. pap. 12.00 (*0-520-03723-5*) U CA Pr.

T

Tires & Tracks. 7th rev. ed. Ed. by Deere & Company Staff. (Fundamentals of Service Ser.). (Illus.). 92p. 1992. pap. text ed. 12.95 (*0-86691-142-1*, FOS5507NC) Deere & Co.

***Tires & Tracks.** 7th rev. ed. Ed. by Deere & Company Staff. (Fundamentals of Service Ser.). 79p. 1992. sl. 79.95 (*0-614-24208-8*, FOS5507S) Deere & Co.

Tires, Suspension & Handling. 2nd ed. John C. Dixon. LC 96-27115. 435p. 1996. 69.00 (*1-56091-831-4*, R-168) Soc Auto Engineers.

Tiresias. Thomas Woolner. LC 73-148338. reprint ed. 32.50 (*0-404-07034-5*) AMS Pr.

Tiresias Strung Out on a Half Can of Pepsi. Rustin Larson. 25p. (Orig.). 1993. pap. 5.00 (*0-9619744-6-X*) Blue Light Pr.

Tirofijo va a Malaga y Otras Selecciones. Eduardo Zayas-Bazan. (Illus.). 48p. (C). 1994. pap. text ed. 14.80 (*0-13-185232-9*) P-H.

Tiroirs De L'inconnu. Marcel Ayme. (FRE.). 1960. pap. 19.95 (*0-8288-9056-0*) Fr & Eur.

Tiroirs De l'Inconnu. Marcel Ayme. 279p. (FRE.). 1986. pap. 12.95 (*0-7859-2030-7*, 2070377245) Fr & Eur.

Tirra Lirra by the River. Jessica Anderson. 160p. 1991. mass mkt. 6.95 (*0-14-099705-9*, Penguin Bks) Viking Penguin.

Tirso De Molina. Ivy L. McClelland. LC 76-28272. (Liverpool Studies in Spanish Literature 3rd Ser.). reprint ed. 50.00 (*0-404-15033-0*) AMS Pr.

Tirso de Molina: El Burlador de Sevilla. Tirso De Molina. Ed. by James A. Parr. (Spanish Classical Texts Ser.). 152p. 1994. pap. 8.95 (*0-86698-162-4*, P20) Pegasus Pr.

Tirso's Art in "La Venganza de Tamar" Tragedy of Sex & Violence. Everett W. Hesse. LC 90-61991. 95p. 1991. 16.00 (*0-938972-17-0*) Spanish Lit Pubns.

Tirso's Don Juan: The Metamorphosis of a Theme. Josep M. Sola-Sole. LC 87-23844. 189p. 1988. reprint ed. pap. 53.90 (*0-7837-9120-8*, 2049921) Bks Demand.

Tirumantiram. Tirumular. Ed. by N. Mahalinjam. Tr. by B. Natarajan. 465p. 1993. 18.95 (*81-7120-383-3*, Pub. by Ramakrishna Math II) Vedanta Pr.

Tiruvengadu Bronzes. Job Thomas. 139p. 1986. 34.00 (*0-8364-2082-9*, Pub. by Usha II) S Asia.

Tiryns: The Prehistoric Palace of the Kings of Tiryns. Heinrich Schliemann. LC 67-14967. (Illus.). 1972. reprint ed. 36.95 (*0-405-08932-5*, Pub. by Blom Pubns UK) Ayer.

Tirzah. Lucille Travis. Ed. by S. David Garber. LC 90-23580. 160p. (Orig.). (J). (gr. 3-7). 1991. pap. 5.99 (*0-8361-3546-6*) Herald Pr.

Tirzah Ann's Summer Trip & Other Sketches. Marietta Holley. 1981. reprint ed. lib. bdg. 19.00 (*0-403-01437-9*) Scholarly.

'Tis a Gift to Be Simple: Embracing the Freedom of Living with Less. Barbara Sorensen. LC 92-4181. 128p. 1992. pap. 9.99 (*0-8066-2573-2*, 9-2573) Augsburg Fortress.

'Tis Christmas Once Again. (Little Treasures Ser.). (Illus.). 1995. 4.99 (*1-57051-070-9*) Brownlow Pub Co.

'Tis Nature's Fault: Unauthorized Sexuality During the Enlightenment. Ed. by Robert P. Maccubbin. 270p. 1988. pap. text ed. 19.95 (*0-521-34768-8*) Cambridge U Pr.

***'Tis Pity She's a Whore.** Simon Barker. (Routledge English Texts Ser.). 240p. (C). 1997. pap. 17.95 (*0-415-04947-4*) Routledge.

'Tis Pity She's a Whore. John Ford. Ed. by Mark Stavig. (Crofts Classics Ser.). 128p. 1966. pap. text ed. write for info. (*0-88295-036-3*) Harlan Davidson.

***'Tis Pity She's a Whore.** John Ford. 1997. text ed. 12.95 (*0-7190-4359-X*) St Martin.

'Tis Pity She's a Whore. John Ford. Ed. by N. W. Bawcutt. LC 65-15339. xxii, 110p. 1966. pap. text ed. 6.95 (*0-8032-5261-7*, Bison Books) U of Nebr Pr.

'Tis Pity She's a Whore. John Ford. Ed. by Brian Morris. (New Mermaid Ser.). (C). 1978. pap. text ed. 4.95 (*0-393-90011-8*) Norton.

'Tis Pity She's a Whore & Other Plays: The Lover's Melancholy & The Broken Heart. John Ford. Ed. & Intro. by Marion Lomax. (World's Classics Ser.). 416p. 1995. pap. 10.95 (*0-19-282253-5*) OUP.

'Tis Pity She's a Whore & Other Plays: The Lover's Melancholy, The Broken Heart. John Ford. Ed. & Intro. by Marion Lomax. (World's Classics Ser.). 464p. 1995. 65.00 (*0-19-812151-2*) OUP.

'Tis So: Negro Folk Tales of South. Sam Short. 1972. 6.95 (*0-87511-105-X*) Claitors.

'Tis Sweet & Sad in an Irish Cottage. Patrick Tarrant. 152p. 1982. pap. 4.00 (*0-9608850-0-5*) Tarrant.

'Tis the Day after Christmas: The Christmas Curmudgeon. LC 91-61929. (Illus.). 32p. 1991. pap. 2.95 (*1-56352-010-9*) Longstreet Pr Inc.

'Tis the Season. 1990. pap. 5.95 (*0-7935-0158-X*, 00001310) H Leonard.

'Tis the Season. 1990. 4.95 (*0-7935-0198-9*, 00001476) H Leonard.

'Tis the Season. Mary Engelbreit. 1994. 4.95 (*0-8362-4624-1*) Andrews & McMeel.

***'Tis the Season.** Various. 1997. pap. 5.99 (*0-8217-5781-4*) Kensgtn Pub Corp.

'Tis the Season: A Vegetarian Christmas Cookbook. Nanette Blanchard. LC 95-34166. (Illus.). 256p. 1995. 30.00 (*0-684-81155-3*, S&S) S&S Trade.

'Tis the Season: Holiday Stories from Highlights. Highlights for Children Editors. LC 92-75842. (Illus.). 96p. (Orig.). (J). (gr. 2-5). 1993. pap. 2.95 (*1-56397-279-4*) Boyds Mills Pr.

'Tis the Season to Be Crabby. Charles M. Schulz. LC 96-17657. (Festive Peanuts Bks.). (Illus.). 32p. 1996. 7.95 (*0-00-225218-X*) Collins SF.

'Tis the Season to Be Murdered. Valerie Wolzien. (Holiday Mysteries Ser.). (Orig.). 1994. mass mkt. 4.99 (*0-449-14920-X*, GM) Fawcett.

***'Tis the Season...to Go Crazy!** Toni S. Brown. LC 96-71674. 110p. 1996. pap. text ed. 6.95 (*1-57636-030-X*) SunRise Pbl.

Tisa. large type ed. Helga Moray. 496p. 1985. 25.99 (*0-7089-1314-8*) Ulverscroft.

Tischler Alexander: Drawings. F. Sirkina. (C). 1987. 750.00 (*0-685-34417-7*, Pub. by Collets) St Mut.

Tischreden see Luthers Werke in Auswahl

Tish. Mary R. Rinehart. reprint ed. lib. bdg. 26.95 (*0-89190-329-1*, Rivercity Pr) Amereon Ltd.

***Tish Hinojosa - Culture Swing - Destiny's Gate.** Ed. by Carol Cuellar. 100p. (Orig.). (C). 1994. pap. text ed. 19.95 (*0-7692-0753-7*, VF2125) Warner Brothers.

***Tish No. 1-19.** Frank Davey. 24.95 (*0-88922-077-8*, Pub. by Talonbooks CN) Genl Dist Srvs.

Tish Returns. Mary R. Rinehart. 24.95 (*0-8488-0713-8*) Amereon Ltd.

Tish Sommers, Activist, & the Founding of the Older Women's League. Patricia Huckle. LC 90-46851. (Illus.). 304p. 1991. 32.00 (*0-87049-691-3*) U of Tenn Pr.

Tisha: The Story of a Young Teacher in the Alaska Wilderness. Robert Specht. 352p. (YA). (gr. 4-8). 1984. mass mkt. 5.99 (*0-553-26596-2*) Bantam.

Tisha B'Av. A. C. Feuer. (Holiday Ser.). 1992. 17.99 (*0-89906-609-7*); pap. 14.99 (*0-89906-610-0*) Mesorah Pubns.

Tisha B'Av. Y. Ganz. (ArtScroll Youth Holiday Ser.). (YA). 1992. 8.99 (*0-89906-983-5*) Mesorah Pubns.

Tisha B'av Service. Morris Silverman & Hillel. pap. 3.75 (*0-87677-068-5*) Prayer Bk.

Tissot: Physician of the Enlightenment. Antoinette S. Emch-Deriaz. LC 91-46129. (American University Studies: History: Ser. IX, Vol. 126). 238p. (C). 1992. text ed. 49.95 (*0-8204-1819-6*) P Lang Pubng.

Tissue Characterization with Ultrasound, Vol. I: Methods. Ed. by James F. Greenleaf. 272p. 1986. 136.00 (*0-8493-6221-0*, RC78, CRC Reprint) Franklin.

Tissue Characterization with Ultrasound, Vol. II: Results & Applications. Ed. by James F. Greenleaf. 304p. 1986. Vol. II: Results & Applicatios, 304p. 155.00 (*0-8493-6222-9*, CRC Reprint) Franklin.

Tissue Cleansing Through Bowel Management. Bernard Jensen. 1981. pap. 6.95 (*0-9608360-7-1*) B Jensen.

Tissue Culture: Plants: A Bibliography, January 1991-April 1993. Henry Gilbert. 72p. (Orig.). (C). 1994. pap. text ed. 30.00 (*0-7881-0731-3*) DIANE Pub.

Tissue Culture: Plants: A Bibliography, January 1992-March 1994. Henry Gilbert. 57p. (Orig.). (C). 1995. pap. text ed. 30.00 (*0-7881-2180-4*) DIANE Pub.

Tissue Culture & Reticuloendothelial System. Ed. by P. Rohlich & E. Bacsy. 569p. 1984. lib. bdg. 193.00 (*0-317-65951-0*, Pub. by VSP NE) Coronet Bks.

Tissue Culture Business. Business Communications Co., Inc. Staff. 200p. 1985. pap. 1,750.00 (*0-89336-415-0*, C-041) BCC.

Tissue Culture in Forestry & Agriculture. Randolph Henke et al. LC 85-585. (Basic Life Sciences Ser.: Vol. 32). 408p. 1985. 95.00 (*0-306-41919-X*, Plenum Pr) Plenum.

Tissue Culture in Neurobiology. fac. ed. Ed. by Ezio Giacobini et al. LC 79-66516. (Illus.). 530p. pap. 151.10 (*0-7837-7244-0*, 2047061) Bks Demand.

Tissue Culture Investigations. Ed. by Universities Federation for Animal Welfare Staff. 1982. 20.00 (*0-317-43845-X*) St Mut.

Tissue Culture Media Laboratory Disposables. (Market Research Reports: No. 162). (Illus.). 1991. 295.00 (*0-318-41195-4*) Theta Corp.

Tissue Culture of Epithelial Cells. Ed. by Mary Taub. LC 84-13470. 310p. 1985. 89.50 (*0-306-41740-5*, Plenum Pr) Plenum.

Tissue Culture Techniques. Luccio Nuzzolo & Augusto Vellucci. LC 67-26015. (Illus.). 256p. 1983. 37.50 (*0-87527-117-0*) Green.

Tissue Culture Techniques: An Introduction. B. Martin. LC 94-6357. xi, 247p. 1997. 45.00 (*0-8176-3643-9*) Birkhauser.

Tissue Culture Techniques: An Introduction. Bernice M. Martin. LC 94-6357. xi, 247p. 1994. 93.50 (*0-8176-3718-4*) Birkhauser.

Tissue Culture Techniques for Horticultural Crops. Kenneth C. Torres. (Illus.). 1987. text ed. write for info. (*0-87055-536-7*) AVI.

Tissue Culture Techniques for Horticultural Crops. Kenneth C. Torres. (Illus.). 224p. (C). (gr. 13). 1988. text ed. 78.95 (*0-442-28465-9*) Chapman & Hall.

Tissue Donations in Health, Disease & Post-Mortem Gifts: Index of Authors & Subjects. American Health Research Institute Staff. 180p. 1993. 47.50 (*1-55914-932-9*); pap. 44.50 (*1-55914-933-7*) ABBE Pubs Assn.

Tissue Engineering. E. Bell. 241p. 1993. 75.00 (*0-8176-3687-0*) Spr-Verlag.

Tissue Expansion. Rolf E. Nordstrom. (Illus.). 288p. 1995. 150.00 (*0-7506-9711-3*) Buttrwrth-Heinemann.

Tissue Growth Factors. Ed. by Renato Baserga. (Handbook of Experimental Pharmacology Ser.: Vol. 57). (Illus.). 500p. 1981. 272.00 (*0-387-10623-5*) Spr-Verlag.

***Tissue in Situ Hybridization: Methods in Animal Development.** Trevor Jowett. LC 96-35310. 128p. 1996. pap. text ed. 54.95 (*0-471-16403-8*) Wiley.

Tissue-Integrated Prostheses. Per-Ingvar Branemark et al. (Illus.). 352p. 1985. text ed. 96.00 (*0-86715-129-3*) Quint Pub Co.

Tissue Integration in Oral, Orthopedic, & Maxillofacial Reconstruction. Ed. by William R. Laney & Dan E. Tolman. (Illus.). 396p. 1992. text ed. 72.00 (*0-86715-251-6*) Quint Pub Co.

Tissue of Lies: Eudora Welty & the Southern Romance. Jennifer L. Randisi. LC 82-45042. 198p. (Orig.). (C). 1982. pap. text ed. 24.00 (*0-8191-2452-4*); lib. bdg. 55.00 (*0-8191-2451-6*) U Pr of Amer.

Tissue Oxygen Deprivation. Ed. by Haddad & Lister. LC 96-19881. (Lung Biology in Health & Disease Ser.: Vol. 95). 1120p. 1996. 225.00 (*0-8247-9493-1*) Dekker.

Tissue Perfusion & Organ Function. T. Kamada et al. 276p. 1996. 231.50 (*0-444-81967-3*) Elsevier.

Tissue Plasminogen Activator in Thrombolytic Therapy. Ed. by Burton E. Sobel et al. LC 87-501. (Illus.). 262p. reprint ed. pap. 74.70 (*0-7837-4316-5*, 2044002) Bks Demand.

Tissue Printing: Tools for the Study of Anatomy, Histochemistry, & Gene Expression. Ed. by Philip D. Reid et al. (Illus.). 188p. 1992. student ed., spiral bd. 29.95 (*0-12-585970-8*) Acad Pr.

Tissue Renin-Angiotensin System: Physiologic & Pharmacologic Implications. Ed. by Victor J. Dzau. LC 73-3001. (Circulation Monographs: No. 12). 78p. 1988. 9.60 (*0-87493-261-0*) Am Heart.

Tissue Renin-Angiotensin Systems: Current Concepts of Local Regulators in Reproductive & Endocrine Organs. Ed. by Amal K. Mukhopadhyay & Mohan K. Raizada. (Advances in Experimental Medicine & Biology Ser.: Vol. 377). 440p. 1995. 120.00 (*0-306-45077-1*) Plenum.

Tissue Runnability Seminar, 1991: Westin Seattle, Seattle, WA, April 10-12. Technical Association of the Pulp & Paper Industry Staff. (TAPPI Notes Ser.). 239p. 1991. reprint ed. pap. 68.20 (*0-7837-0258-2*, 2040567) Bks Demand.

Tissue Runnability Seminar, 1992: Opryland Hotel, Nashville, TN, April 8-10. Technical Association of the Pulp & Paper Industry Staff. (TAPPI Notes Ser.). reprint ed. pap. 82.40 (*0-7837-2446-2*, 2042595) Bks Demand.

Tissue Seminar, 1990: Westin Peachtree Plaza, Atlanta, GA, April 25-27. Technical Association of the Pulp & Paper Industry Staff. (TAPPI Notes Ser.). (Illus.). 151p. reprint ed. pap. 43.10 (*0-8357-4217-2*, 2036999) Bks Demand.

Tissue Specific Gene Expression. Ed. by R. Renkawitz. LC 89-16997. 221p. 1989. 160.00 (*3-527-27875-3*, VCH) Wiley.

Tissue-Specific Metabolic Alterations in Diabetes. Ed. by F. Belfiore & S. Gregorio. (Frontiers in Diabetes Ser.: Vol. 10). viii, 192p. 1990. 168.00 (*3-8055-5171-1*) S Karger.

Tissue Specific Toxicity: Biochemical Mechanisms. Ed. by Wolfgang Dekant & H. G. Neumann. (Illus.). 263p. 1992. text ed. 104.00 (*0-12-208860-3*) Acad Pr.

Tissue-Type Plasminogen Activator (t-PA) Physiological & Clinical Aspects, Vol. I. Cornelis Kluft. 256p. 1988. 140.00 (*0-8493-4608-8*, QP93, CRC Reprint) Franklin.

Tissue-Type Plasminogen Activator (t-PA) Physiological & Clinical Aspects, Vol. II. Cornelis Kluft. 192p. 1988. 111.00 (*0-8493-4609-6*, QP93, CRC Reprint) Franklin.

Tissue Type Plasminogen Activator T-PA Physiology & Clin, 2 vols., Set. Cornelis Kluft. 1988. reprint ed. 251.00 (*0-8493-4607-X*, CRC Reprint) Franklin.

Tissues & Plants see Transport in Plants Two

Tiszaszolos Treasure: In Search of a Copper Age Prince. Janos Makkay. (Studia Archaeologica Ser.: Vol. 10). (Illus.). 186p. (C). 1989. pap. 102.00 (*963-05-4726-0*, Pub. by Akad Kiado HU) St Mut.

Tit for Tat. M. Estes. LC 72-38649. (Black Heritage Library Collection). 1977. reprint ed. 28.95 (*0-8369-9007-2*) Ayer.

Tit. 17 Narradoras Latinoamericanas. Coedicion Latinoamericana Staff. 223p. 1996. pap. 14.95 (*0-929157-32-X*) Ediciones Huracan.

Titan. 1971. 435.00 (*0-387-93228-3*) Spr-Verlag.

***Titan.** Stephen Baxter. mass mkt. write for info. (*0-06-105713-4*, HarperPrism) HarpC.

***Titan.** Stephen Baxter. 1997. write for info. (*0-06-105259-0*, HarperPrism) HarpC.

Titan. John Varley. 320p. 1987. mass mkt. 5.99 (*0-441-81304-6*) Ace Bks.

Titan. Theodore Dreiser. LC 83-45747. reprint ed. 27.50 (*0-404-20084-2*) AMS Pr.

Titan & the Titanic: The Life, Works & Incredible Foresight of Morgan Robertson. John Vess. (Illus.). 175p. (Orig.). 1990. pap. write for info. (*0-318-65946-8*) Pleasant TN.

Titan of Twilight. Troy Denning. (Twilight Giants Ser.). (Orig.). 1995. pap. 5.99 (*0-7869-0172-1*) TSR Inc.

***Titan Tales: Diary of a Missle Crew Commander.** John Womack. LC 96-92994. 224p. (Orig.). 1997. per., pap. 15.95 (*0-9655546-0-0*) Soliloquy Pr.

Titan U. Lydia Andersen. LC 89-80152. 135p. (C). 1989. pap. 8.50 (*0-9622399-1-7*); lib. bdg. 9.00 (*0-9622399-0-9*); lib. bdg. 11.95 (*0-9622399-2-5*) Inniea Pub Co.

Titanic. Christopher Durang. 1983. pap. 5.25 (*0-8222-1155-6*) Dramatists Play.

Titanic. Deborah Kent. LC 93-12688. (Cornerstones of Freedom Ser.). (Illus.). 32p. (J). (gr. 3-6). 1993. pap. 4.95 (*0-516-46672-0*); lib. bdg. 18.00 (*0-516-06672-2*) Childrens.

Titanic. J. Rawlinson. (Great Adventure Ser.). (Illus.). 32p. (J). (gr. 4 up). 1988. lib. bdg. 17.27 (*0-86592-873-8*); lib. bdg. 12.95 (*0-685-58290-6*) Rourke Corp.

Titanic. Tom Stacey. LC 89-33553. (World Disasters Ser.). (Illus.). 64p. (J). (gr. 5-8). 1989. lib. bdg. 15.96 (*1-56006-006-9*) Lucent Bks.

***Titanic.** Geoff Tibballs. 1997. pap. 19.95 (*0-614-27389-7*) Readrs Digest Pr.

Titanic: A Survivor's Story. Archibald Gracie. Orig. Title: The Truth about the Titanic. (Illus.). 323p. 1996. reprint ed. pap. 12.95 (*0-89733-207-5*) Academy Chi Pubs.

***Titanic: Adventure Out of Time.** BradyGAMES Staff et al. 192p. 1996. 19.99 (*1-56686-657-X*) Mac Comp Pub.

Titanic: An Illustrated History. Illus. by Ken Marschall. LC 92-11587. 228p. 1992. 60.00 (*1-56282-918-1*) Hyperion.

Titanic: An Illustrated History. Illus. by Ken Marschall. 224p. 1995. pap. 29.95 (*0-7868-8147-X*) Hyperion.

Titanic: Destination Disaster. J. Eaton. Date not set. pap. 15.95 (*0-393-31513-4*) Norton.

Titanic: End of a Dream. Wyn C. Wade. 490p. 1992. pap. 13.95 (*0-14-016691-2*, Penguin Bks) Viking Penguin.

Titanic: In a New Light. Joseph B. MacInnis. LC 92-22682. (In a New Light Ser.). 96p. 1992. 29.95 (*1-56566-025-0*); pap. 16.95 (*1-56566-021-8*) Lickle Pubng.

***Titanic: Legacy of the World's Greatest Steamliner.** Ed. by Time-Life Books Editors. LC 97-16404. (Illus.). 228p. 1997. write for info. (*0-7835-5261-0*) Time-Life.

Titanic: Lost...& Found. Judy Donnelly. LC 86-20402. (Step into Reading Bks.). (Illus.). 48p. (J). (gr. 1-3). 1987. pap. 3.99 (*0-394-88669-0*); lib. bdg. 11.99 (*0-394-98669-5*) Random Bks Yng Read.

***Titanic: Safety, Speed & Sacrifice.** George Behe. LC 97-6521. 1997. write for info. (*0-933449-31-3*) Transport Trails.

Titanic: Sinking the Myths. Diana E. Bristow. (Illus.). 530p. (Orig.). (C). 1995. pap. text ed. 36.95 (*0-9646484-0-7*) KatCo Lit Grp.

Titanic: The Death & Life of a Legend. Michael Davie. LC 86-46021. 272p. 1987. 19.95 (*0-317-58565-7*) Knopf.

***Titanic: The Extraordinary Story of the Unsinkable Ship.** Geoff Tibballs. LC 97-14175. 1997. pap. text ed. 19.95 (*0-89577-953-6*) RD Assn.

***Titanic: The Extraordinary Story of the "Unsinkable" Ship.** Geoff Tibballs. LC 97-14175. 1997. write for info. (*0-89577-990-0*) RD Assn.

Titanic: Triumph & Tragedy. 2nd ed. John P. Eaton & Charles A. Haas. (Illus.). 352p. 1995. 50.00 (*0-393-03697-9*) Norton.

Titanic & Her Era. John M. Groff & Jane E. Allen. (Illus.). 32p. 1982. pap. 2.00 (*0-913346-07-1*) Indep Seaport.

***Titanic At Two A. M. An Illustrated Narrative with Survivor Accounts.** Paul J. Quinn. LC 96-61655. (Illus.). 128p. 1997. 39.95 (*0-9655209-3-5*) Fantail.

Titanic Conspiracy: Cover-ups & Mysteries of the World's Most Famous Sea Disaster. Robin Gardiner. 336p. 1996. 24.95 (*1-55972-347-5*, Birch Ln Pr) Carol Pub Group.

***Titanic Conspiracy: Cover-ups & Mysteries of the World's Most Famous Sea Disaster.** Robin Gardiner & Dan Van der Vat. 336p. 1997. pap. 18.95 (*0-8065-1890-1*, Citadel Pr) Carol Pub Group.

Titanic Crossing. Barbara Williams. LC 94-13066. (J). 1995. pap. 14.99 (*0-8037-1790-3*); pap. 14.89 (*0-8037-1791-1*) Dial Bks Young.

Titanic Crossing. Barbara Williams. Date not set. pap. write for info. (*0-14-037977-0*) Viking Penguin.

***Titanic Disaster: As Reported in the British National Press April-July 1912.** Compiled by David Bryceson. (Illus.). 320p. (C). 1997. 35.00 (*0-393-04108-5*) Norton.

Titanic Effect: Planning. K. F. Watt. 268p. 1974. 11.95 (*0-8159-6925-2*) Devin.

Titanic Hero. Shan F. Bullock. 22.95 (*0-8488-0928-9*) Amereon Ltd.

Titanic Interlude. Charles E. Ziavras. LC 83-80832. (Illus.). 359p. 1983. 14.95 (*0-915940-03-5*); pap. 6.95 (*0-915940-04-3*) Ithaca Pr MA.

Titanic Legacy: Disaster As Media Event & Myth. Paul Heyer. LC 95-22016. 200p. 1995. text ed. 39.95 (*0-275-95352-1*, Praeger Pubs) Greenwood.

Titanic Light: Paul de Man's Post-Romanticism, 1960-1969. Ortwin de Graef. LC 94-29809. (Texts & Contexts Ser.). xxiii, 289p. 1995. text ed. 35.00 (*0-8032-1695-5*) U of Nebr Pr.

Titanic R. I. P. Diana E. Bristow. 216p. 1989. per. 7.95 (*0-8187-0113-7*) Harlo Press.

Titanic Revisited. Leo Cohen. LC 84-60508. (Illus.). 78p. 1984. pap. 4.95 (*0-9613366-0-9*) L Cohen.

***Titanic Sinks!** Thomas Conklin. LC 97-4060. 1997. pap. 4.99 (*0-679-88606-0*) Random.

***Titanic Survivor.** Violet Jessop. Ed. & Anno. by John Maxtone-Graham. (Illus.). 272p. 1997. 23.95 (*1-57409-035-6*) Sheridan.

Titanic, the Psychic & the Sea. Rustie Brown. LC 80-70551. (Illus.). 176p. 1981. 14.95 (*0-9605278-0-X*) Blue Harbor.

***Titanic Voices.** Hyslop. LC 97-2253. 1997. 29.95 (*0-312-17428-4*) St Martin.

Titanic "Warning" Hearing the Voice of God in the Modern Age. Casey M. Sabella & Jim Fletcher. LC 94-68851. 160p. (Orig.). 1994. pap. 9.95 (*0-89221-271-3*) New Leaf.

Titanium. (Metals & Minerals Ser.). 1993. lib. bdg. 250.95 (*0-8490-8940-9*) Gordon Pr.

***Titanium.** (Environmental Health Criteria Ser.: No. 24). 68p. 1982. pap. text ed. 19.00 (*92-4-154084-2*, 1160024) World Health.

Titanium. Alan D. McQuillan & M. K. McQuillan. LC 56-4724. (Metallurgy of the Rarer Metals Ser.: No. 4). 486p. reprint ed. pap. 138.60 (*0-317-42137-9*, 2025759) Bks Demand.

***Titanium: A Technical Guide.** Ed. by M. J. Donachie. Date not set. 83.00 (*0-614-23290-2*, 9606) Intl Titanium.

Titanium: A Technical Guide. Ed. by Matthew J Donachie, Jr. (Illus.). 469p. 1988. 108.00 (*0-87170-309-2*, 6172U) ASM.

***Titanium: Everything You Wanted to Know.** unabridged ed. (NGF Info Pacs Ser.). (Illus.). 131p. (Orig.). 1996. pap. 45.00 (*1-57701-031-0*) Natl Golf.

Titanium Alloys in Surgical Implants - STP 796. Ed. by Hugh A. Luckey & Fred Kubli, Jr. LC 84-72888. 295p. 1983. text ed. 37.50 (*0-8031-0241-0*, 04-796000-54) ASTM.

An Asterisk (*) at the beginning of an entry indicates that the title is appearing in BIP for the first time.

***Titanium & Its Alloys: ASM Independent Study Course.** Date not set. 325.00 (*0-614-23291-0*, 9617) Intl Titanium.

Titanium & Superalloys II: Battling the Economics Elements. Ed. by Brian Nolk. 188p. 1984. pap. text ed. write for info. (*0-913333-04-2*) Metal Bulletin.

Titanium for Energy & Industrial Applications. Ed. by Daniel Eylon. LC 81-86049. (Technology of Metallurgy Ser.). (Illus.). 411p. reprint ed. pap. 117.20 (*0-8357-7508-9*, 2036000) Bks Demand.

Titanium Production, Processing, Handling & Storage of. (Forty Ser.). 1987. pap. 16.75 (*0-685-58154-3*, 481-87) Natl Fire Prot.

Titanium Rapid Solidifaction Technology: Proceedings for the Four Session Symposium on "Titanium, Rapid Solidification Technology," Sponsored by the Titanium Committee of the Metallurgical Society Held at the 1986 TMS-AIME Annual Meeting, New Orleans, Louisiana, March 2-6, 1986. Metallurgical Society of AIME Staff. Ed. by F. H. Froes & D. Eylon. LC 86-19176. (Illus.). 339p. reprint ed. pap. 96.70 (*0-7837-1969-8*, 2052447) Bks Demand.

Titanium Technology: Present Status & Future Trends. F. H. Froes et al. (Orig.). 1985. pap. 19.95 (*0-935297-00-6*, 9605) Intl Titanium.

Titanium the Choice... B. Bannon et al. 13p. (Orig.). 1987. pap. 5.00 (*0-935297-07-3*, 968) Intl Titanium.

Titanium 1980, Science & Technology: Proceedings of the Fourth International Conference on Titanium, Kyoto, Japan, May 19-22, 1980, 4 vols., Vol. 1. International Conference on Titanium Staff. Ed. by H. Kimura & O. Izumi. LC 80-84610. 806p. reprint ed. pap. 180.00 (*0-8357-2523-5*, 2052403) Bks Demand.

Titanium 1980, Science & Technology: Proceedings of the Fourth International Conference on Titanium, Kyoto, Japan, May 19-22, 1980, 4 vols., Vol. 2. International Conference on Titanium Staff. Ed. by H. Kimura & O. Izumi. LC 80-84610. 827p. reprint ed. pap. 180.00 (*0-8357-2524-3*) Bks Demand.

Titanium 1980, Science & Technology: Proceedings of the Fourth International Conference on Titanium, Kyoto, Japan, May 19-22, 1980, 4 vols., Vol. 3. International Conference on Titanium Staff. Ed. by H. Kimura & O. Izumi. LC 80-84610. 737p. reprint ed. pap. 180.00 (*0-8357-2525-1*) Bks Demand.

Titanium 1980, Science & Technology: Proceedings of the Fourth International Conference on Titanium, Kyoto, Japan, May 19-22, 1980, 4 vols., Vol. 4. International Conference on Titanium Staff. Ed. by H. Kimura & O. Izumi. LC 80-84610. 822p. reprint ed. pap. 180.00 (*0-8357-2526-X*) Bks Demand.

Titanium 1986: Products & Applications Proceedings of the Technical Program from the 1986 International Conference, 2 vols. Intro. by Titanium Development Association Staff. (Orig.). 1987. pap. 75.00 (*0-935297-04-9*) Intl Titanium.

Titanium 1994: A Statistical Review. Ed. by Titanium Development Association Staff. (Orig.). 1994. pap. 100.00 (*0-935297-20-0*) Intl Titanium.

***Titanium 92, Science & Technology Vol. 1: Proceedings of a Symposium/Sponsored by the Titanium Committee of the Minerals, Metals & Materials, Structural Metals Division, Held at the Seventh World Titanium Conference, June 29-July 2, 1992 in San Diego, CA.** World Titanium Conference Staff. Ed. by F. H. Froes & I. L. Caplan. LC 93-78482. (Illus.). 990p. pap. 180.00 (*0-608-04999-9*, 2065597) Bks Demand.

***Titanium 92, Science & Technology Vol. 2: Proceedings of a Symposium/Sponsored by the Titanium Committee of the Minerals, Metals & Materials, Structural Metals Division, Held at the Seventh World Titanium Conference, June 29-July 2, 1992 in San Diego, CA.** World Titanium Conference Staff. Ed. by F. H. Froes & I. L. Caplan. LC 93-78482. (Illus.). 1024p. pap. 180.00 (*0-608-05000-8*, 2065597) Bks Demand.

***Titanium 92, Science & Technology Vol. 3: Proceedings of a Symposium/Sponsored by the Titanium Committee of the Minerals, Metals & Materials, Structural Metals Division, Held at the Seventh World Titanium Conference, June 29-July 2, 1992 in San Diego, CA.** World Titanium Conference Staff. Ed. by F. H. Froes & I. L. Caplan. LC 93-78482. (Illus.). 1026p. pap. 180.00 (*0-608-05001-6*, 2065597) Bks Demand.

***Titanium '95: Proceedings of the 8th World Conference Birmingham 22-26 October 1995.** 1910p. 1996. 300.00 (*1-86125-005-3*, Pub. by Inst Materials UK) Ashgate Pub Co.

Titanotheres of Ancient Wyoming, Dakota, & Nebraska. Department of the Interior, U. S. Geological Survey, Monograph & Henry F. Osborn. Ed. by Stephen J. Gould. LC 79-83341. (History of Paleontology Ser.: 2 vols.). (Illus.). 1980. reprint ed. Set. lib. bdg. 246.95 (*0-405-12729-4*) Ayer.

Titanotheres of Ancient Wyoming, Dakota, & Nebraska, 1. Department of the Interior, U. S. Geological Survey, Monograph & Henry F. Osborn. Ed. by Stephen J. Gould. LC 79-83341. (History of Paleontology Ser.: 2 vols.). (Illus.). 1980. reprint ed. lib. bdg. 123.95 (*0-405-12730-8*) Ayer.

Titanotheres of Ancient Wyoming, Dakota, & Nebraska, Vol. 2. Department of the Interior, U. S. Geological Survey, Monograph & Henry F. Osborn. Ed. by Stephen J. Gould. LC 79-83341. (History of Paleontology Ser.: 2 vols.). (Illus.). 1980. reprint ed. lib. bdg. 123.95 (*0-405-12731-6*) Ayer.

Titans. Tim Green. LC 94-25574. 1994. 21.95 (*1-57036-057-X*) Turner Pub GA.

Titans. Tim Green. 1995. mass mkt. 5.99 (*0-312-95678-9*) St Martin.

Titans. Christopher Nicole. 352p. 1992. 20.00 (*0-7278-4319-2*) Severn Hse.

***Titans: Scissors, Paper, Stone.** Adam Warren. (Illus.). 48p. 1997. pap. 4.95 (*1-56389-363-0*) DC Comics.

Titans & Prometheans, 2 vols. Burton Rascoe. 1972. Set. 100.00 (*0-8490-1216-3*) Gordon Pr.

Titans of Literature from Homer to the Present. Burton Rascoe. LC 76-121502. (Essay Index Reprint Ser.). 1977. 23.95 (*0-8369-1775-8*) Ayer.

Titans of Takeover. Robert O. Slater. (Illus.). 240p. 1986. 29.95 (*0-13-922055-0*) P-H.

Titans of the Soil: Great Builders of Agriculture. Edward J. Dies. LC 76-49613. (Illus.). 216p. 1977. reprint ed. text ed. 65.00 (*0-8371-9329-X*, DITS, Greenwood Pr) Greenwood.

Titans ou les Trois Dumas. Andre Maurois. pap. 12.50 (*0-685-36963-3*) Fr & Eur.

Titan's Portraits Through Aretino's Lens. Luba Freedman. LC 94-33450. (Illus.). 240p. 1995. 55.00 (*0-271-01339-7*) Pa St U Pr.

***Titantic Is Sinking.** Cripwell. Date not set. pap. text ed. write for info. (*0-17-556580-5*) Addison-Wesley.

Titch. Mark Dunster. 24p. 1983. pap. 4.00 (*0-89642-103-1*) Linden Pubs.

Titch. Pat Hutchins. LC 92-1642. (Illus.). 40p. (J). (ps-1). 1993. reprint ed. pap. 5.95 (*0-689-71688-5*, Aladdin Paperbacks) S&S Childrens.

Titch & Daisy. Pat Hutchins. LC 95-2264. (Illus.). 32p. (J). 1996. 15.00 (*0-688-13959-0*); lib. bdg. 14.93 (*0-688-13960-4*) Greenwillow.

Titchfield: A Place in History. Ed. by George Watts. (C). 1989. 59.00 (*1-85455-029-2*, Pub. by Ensign Pubns & Print UK); pap. 39.00 (*1-85455-030-6*, Pub. by Ensign Pubns & Print UK) St Mut.

Titeleinfassungen der Reformationszeit, 3 pts. in 1. Johannes Luther. 20p. 1973. reprint ed. write for info. (*3-487-04662-8*) G Olms Pubs.

Titeres Sencillos: Easy Puppet Scripts. Compiled by Josie H. Smith. (Illus.). 96p. (SPA.). 1992. pap. 4.50 (*0-311-11073-8*) Casa Bautista.

Titeres y Otras Diversiones Populares de Madrid 1758-1840: Estudio y Documentos. J. E. Varey. (Fuentes Ser.: No. 7). (Illus.). 292p. (Orig.). (SPA.). (C). 1972. pap. 35.00 (*0-900411-34-1*, Pub. by Tamesis Bks Ltd UK) Boydell & Brewer.

Tithe: Challenge or Legalism. Douglas W. Johnson. LC 83-15890. (Creative Leadership Ser.). 128p. 1984. pap. 8.95 (*0-687-42127-6*) Abingdon.

Tithe as Gift: The Institution in the Pentateuch & in Light of Mauss's Prestation Theory. Menahem Herman. LC 91-33318. 208p. 1992. lib. bdg. 89.95 (*0-7734-9959-8*) E Mellen.

Tithe Maps of England & Wales: A Cartographic Analysis & County-by-County Catalogue. Roger J. Kain & Richard R. Oliver. LC 93-44929. (Illus.). 900p. (C). 1995. text ed. 200.00 (*0-521-44191-9*) Cambridge U Pr.

Tithe Proctor: Being a Tale of the Tithe Rebellion in Ireland. William Carleton. LC 79-8246. reprint ed. 44.50 (*0-404-61806-5*) AMS Pr.

Tithes - Offerings - Alms. Marilyn Hickey. 36p. (Orig.). pap. 1.00 (*1-56441-170-2*) M Hickey Min.

***Tithes of Blood: A Confederate Soldiers Story.** Billy Ellis. Ed. by John McGlone. (Journal of Confederate History Book Ser.: Vol. 18). (Illus.). 220p. 1997. 26.95 (*1-889332-11-9*) So Herit Pr.

Tithing. Arthur W. Pink. pap. 0.99 (*0-87377-077-3*) GAM Pubns.

Tithing: A Call to Serious, Biblical Giving. Doug Beacham & R. T. Kendall. 1991. teacher ed., pap. 12.95 (*0-911866-16-7*) LifeSprings Res.

Tithing: A Call to Serious, Biblical Giving. R. T. Kendall. 128p. 1983. pap. 9.99 (*0-310-38331-5*, 9279P) Zondervan.

Tithing: A Sixty Day Challenge to Financial Success. Walter E. Adams. 56p. (Orig.). 1992. pap. 7.95 (*0-685-62270-3*) GMI Pubns Inc.

Tithing: And Other Gifts. Glen Burch. 20p. (Orig.). 1994. pap. 2.00 (*1-880573-13-X*) Grace WI.

Tithing & the Church. Gary North. LC 93-47685. 1994. 25.00 (*0-930464-69-9*); pap. 9.95 (*0-930464-70-2*) Inst Christian.

***Tithing Is a Matter of Love...Not Law.** T. D. Jakes, Sr. (Orig.). 1997. pap. write for info. (*1-890521-03-5*) Jakes Ent.

Tithing Is Christian. Elmer L. Towns. 80p. 1984. pap. 2.79 (*0-941005-09-7*); ring bd. 29.98 incl. audio (*0-941005-10-0*) Chrch Grwth VA.

***Titian.** Bruce Cole. 1997. write for info. (*0-06-430905-3*, Icon Edns) HarpC.

***Titian.** Bruce Cole. 1998. pap. write for info. (*0-06-430193-1*, Icon Edns) HarpC.

Titian. Filippo Pedrocco. Tr. by Susan Madocks from ITA. (Library of Great Masters). (Illus.). 80p. (Orig.). 1993. pap. 12.99 (*1-878351-14-1*) Riverside NY.

Titian. Dario Cecchi. Tr. by Nora Wydenbruck from ITA. LC 72-13188. (Biography Index Reprint Ser.). 1977. reprint ed. 22.95 (*0-8369-8143-X*) Ayer.

Titian: Nymph & Shepherd. John Berger & Katya B. Andreadakis. (Illus.). 128p. 1996. 25.00 (*3-7913-1672-9*, Pub. by Prestel GW) te Neues.

Titian: Prince of Painters. Ed. by Susanna Biadene et al. (Illus.). 452p. 1995. 85.00 (*3-7913-1102-6*, Pub. by Prestel GW) te Neues.

Titian & His Drawings: With Reference to Giorgione & Some Close Contemporaries. Harold E. Wethey. (Kress Foundation Studies in the History of European Art: No. 8). (Illus.). 296p. 1988. text ed. 150.00 (*0-691-04040-0*) Princeton U Pr.

Titian Beresford Reader. Titian Beresford. (Orig.). 1993. mass mkt. 4.95 (*1-56333-114-4*) Masquerade.

Titian Committee. large type ed. Iain Pears. LC 93-48428. 1994. lib. bdg. 18.95 (*0-7862-0170-3*) Thorndike Pr.

Titian Five Hundred. Joseph Manca. 1993. 0.70 (*0-89468-194-X*) Natl Gallery Art.

***Titian's "Venus of Urbino"** Ed. by Rona Goffen. (Masterpieces in Western Painting Ser.). (Illus.). 192p. (C). 1997. pap. text ed. 14.95 (*0-521-44900-6*) Cambridge U Pr.

***Titian's "Venus of Urbino"** Ed. by Rona Goffen. (Masterpieces in Western Painting Ser.). (Illus.). 192p. (C). 1997. text ed. 49.95 (*0-521-44448-9*) Cambridge U Pr.

***Titian's Women.** Rona Goffen. LC 97-7650. 1997. write for info. (*0-300-06846-8*) Yale U Pr.

Titkos Tortenelmi Adatok Az 1944 Oktober 15.-I Esemenyek Sopronkohidai Kihallhatasok see Secret Historical Facts: Events of October 15, 1944; Record of Evidence of Interrogations at Sopronkohida, Hungary

Title. Arnold Bennett. LC 74-17056. (Collected Works of Arnold Bennett: Vol. 83). 1977. reprint ed. 19.95 (*0-518-19164-8*) Ayer.

Title: 1995 Supplement. Burke. 1995. 70.00 (*0-316-11635-1*) Little.

Title Bibliography of English Language Fiction in the Library of Congress Through 1950., 9 vols., Set. 1976. 875.00 (*0-8161-0020-9*, Hall Library) G K Hall.

***Title Deleted for Security Reasons.** (Paranoia Ser.). 4.95 (*0-87431-165-9*, 12303) West End Games.

Title Derivative Indexing Techniques: A Comparative Study. Hilda Feinberg. LC 73-2671. 307p. 1973. 49.50 (*0-8108-0602-9*) Scarecrow.

Title Examination in Virginia. Sydney F. Parham, Jr. 207p. 1965. 17.50 (*0-614-05983-6*) MICHIE.

Title Examiner. Jack Rudman. (Career Examination Ser.: C-809). 1994. pap. 23.95 (*0-8373-0809-7*) Nat Learn.

Title Fifty-Nine: Tort Claims Against Public Entities, Amendments to May 1, 1984: Comments & Annotations. Harry A. Margolis. LC 84-208513. (Illus.). vii, 352p. 1984. pap. 28.00 (*0-933902-10-7*) Gann Law Bks.

Title Guide to the Talkies, Nineteen Seventy-Five Through Nineteen Eighty-Four. Andrew A. Aros. LC 85-27682. 355p. 1986. 35.00 (*0-8108-1868-X*) Scarecrow.

Title Guide to the Talkies, Nineteen Sixty-Four to Nineteen Seventy-Four. Andrew A. Aros. LC 76-40451. 344p. 1977. 35.00 (*0-8108-0976-1*) Scarecrow.

***Title I Handbook, 2 vols.** Charles J. Edwards. 1400p. 1996. ring bd. 247.95 (*0-933538-62-6*) Ed Funding Res.

Title Index to the Nineteenth Century Short Title Catalogue: Series I: 1801-1815. Ed. by Gwen Averley. 850p. 1986. lib. bdg. 355.00 (*0-907977-82-0*) Chadwyck-Healey.

Title Insurance. 2nd ed. Burke. 1993. 145.00 (*0-316-11737-4*) Little.

Title Insurance: The Lawyer's Expanding Role. LC 85-73157. 564p. 1985. pap. 49.95 (*0-89707-205-7*, 543-0072-01) Amer Bar Assn.

Title Insurance & Real Estate Securities Terminology. Intro. by John R. Johnsich. (Orig.). 1980. pap. 6.95 (*0-914256-11-4*) Real Estate Pub.

Title Insurance in Troubled Times: What You Need to Know. (Real Estate Law & Practice Ser.). 345p. 1991. 70.00 (*0-685-51874-4*, N4-4557) PLI.

Title Insurance Law. Joyce D. Palomar. LC 93-50657. (Real Property-Zoning Ser.). 1994. ring bd. 135.00 (*0-87632-989-X*) Clark Boardman Callaghan.

Title Insurance Policy Coverage. James L. Gosdin. LC 96-5573. (Illus.). 1996. pap. write for info. (*1-57073-297-3*) Amer Bar Assn.

Title Insurance, 1990: The Basics & Beyond. James M. Pedowitz. 633p. 1990. pap. 17.50 (*0-685-69506-9*) PLI.

Title Insurance, 1994. (Real Estate Law & Practice Course Handbook Ser.). 1994p. 1994. pap. 90.00 (*0-685-69505-0*, N4-4587) PLI.

Title Insurance 1994. (Real Estate Law & Practice Course Handbook Ser.). 840p. 1994. pap. 99.00 (*0-614-17221-7*, N4-4587) PLI.

Title Insurance 1995. (Real Estate Law & Practice Course Handbook Ser.). Date not set. pap. 99.00 (*0-614-17226-8*, N4-4595) PLI.

Title IX: Evaluating Equity in Education. rev. ed. Kaye L. Willhite. LC 86-50437. 75p. 1986. ring bd. 39.00 (*0-937579-49-1*) Willco Pub.

Title Key Word & Author Index to Psychoanalytic Journals. Ed. by Paul W. Mosher. 1988. 38.00 (*0-318-32967-0*) Am Psychoanalytic.

Title Leaves of a Book. (National Information Standards Ser.). 1980. 10.00 (*0-88738-986-4*, Z39.15) Transaction Pubs.

Title Management Assertions & Aversions. Samuel Eilon. (Illus.). 208p. 16.25 (*0-317-66839-0*, Pergamon Pr); 33.00 (*0-317-66840-4*, Pergamon Pr) Elsevier.

***Title of Liberty.** Charles W. Whitman & Pat Dacis. 1992. pap. 5.00 (*1-57514-194-9*) Encore Perform Pub.

Title of the Letter: A Reading of Lacan. Jean-Luc Nancy & Philippe Lacoue-Labarthe. Tr. by David Pettigrew & Francois Raffoul from FRE. LC 91-15114. (SUNY Series in Contemporary Continental Philosophy). 151p. 1992. text ed. 49.50 (*0-7914-0961-9*); pap. text ed. 16.95 (*0-7914-0962-7*) State U NY Pr.

Title Page of the First Folio of Shakespeare's Plays: A Comparative Study of the Droeshout Potrait & the Stratford Monument. Marion H. Spielmann. LC 75-176001. reprint ed. 29.50 (*0-404-07869-9*) AMS Pr.

***Title Role.** large type ed. Cynthia Harrod-Eagles. (Dales Large Print Ser.). 288p. 1997. pap. 18.99 (*1-85389-444-3*) Ulverscroft.

Title Searcher. Jack Rudman. (Career Examination Ser.: C-1516). 1994. pap. 23.95 (*0-8373-1516-6*) Nat Learn.

Title Searching in Ontario: A Procedural Guide. 3rd ed. Janet M. Globe. 176p. 1991. text ed. 39.00 (*0-409-89382-X*) MICHIE.

Title to the Poem. Anne Ferry. LC 95-30608. 330p. (C). 1996. 39.50 (*0-8047-2610-8*) Stanford U Pr.

Title Variations on Nuclear Themes: In Honor of Stanley Hanna. C. M. Class & L. Cohen. 500p. 1994. text ed. 121.00 (*981-02-1480-4*) World Scientific Pub.

Title VII-Employment Discrimination. Charles Grimm. 26p. pap. 2.75 (*0-685-23162-3*, 41,575ED) NCLS Inc.

***Title VII Liability for Sexual Harassment in the Workplace.** 3rd ed. Joseph M. Pelliccioti. (Public Employee Relations Library: Vol. 77). (Orig.). 1997. pap. 18.00 (*0-614-23974-5*) Intl Personnel Mgmt.

Title VII Litigation (1994) 78p. 1994. 12.00 (*1-56986-256-7*) Federal Bar.

Titles & Symbols of Christ: 280 Titles & Symbols. James Large. (World Classic Reference Library). 578p. 1995. reprint ed. 19.99 (*0-529-10335-4*, TSC) World Pubing.

Titles of Addresses in Christian Greek Epistolography. L. Dinneen. 114p. 1980. 15.00 (*0-89005-376-6*) Ares.

Titles of Ebtun. Ralph L. Roys. LC 76-44711. (Carnegie Institution of Washington. Publications: No. 505). (Illus.). 512p. reprint ed. 110.00 (*0-404-15918-4*) AMS Pr.

Titles of Jesus. Michael Scanlan. (Illus.). 64p. (Orig.). 1989. pap. 3.95 (*0-940535-02-5*, UP100) Franciscan U Pr.

Titles of Mary. Maria J. Walsh. 52p. 1991. pap. 3.95 (*0-940535-45-9*, UP 145) Franciscan U Pr.

Titles of the Holy Spirit. Keith A. Fournier. 95p. 1989. pap. 4.50 (*0-940535-21-1*, UP119) Franciscan U Pr.

Titles VII & XI of Civil Rights Act of 1964 & the Equal Employment Opportunity Act of 1972, 2 vols. in 3, Set. U. S. National Labor Relations Board Staff. LC 68-62391. 1979. reprint ed. 95.00 incl. fiche (*0-89941-196-7*, 201350) W S Hein.

***Titletown Again: The Super Bowl Season of the 1996 Green Bay Packers.** Chuck Carlson. Ed. by Steve Cameron. LC 97-70764. Orig. Title: Official Story of the 1996 Green Bay Packers. (Illus.). 144p. 1997. 26.95 (*1-886110-21-2*); pap. 16.95 (*1-886110-22-0*) Addax Pubng.

Titlex at 25: Balancing National Family Planning Needs with State Flexibility. Lisa Kaeser et al. 28p. 1996. pap. 10.00 (*0-939253-40-2*) Guttmacher Inst.

Titmuss Regained: Movie-TV Tie-in. John Mortimer. 1992. pap. 10.00 (*0-14-017185-1*, Penguin Bks) Viking Penguin.

Tito. Lynne Ewing. LC 95-40463. 96p. (YA). (gr. 5 up). 1996. 13.95 (*0-06-027125-6*); lib. bdg. 13.89 (*0-06-027126-4*) HarpC Child Bks.

Tito. Vladimir Dedijer. LC 72-4269. (World Affairs Ser.: National & International Viewpoints). 450p. 1980. reprint ed. 35.95 (*0-405-04565-4*) Ayer.

Tito: A Biography. Jasper Ridley. 496p. 1996. pap. 37.50 (*0-09-475610-4*, Pub. by Constable Pubs UK) Trans-Atl Phila.

Tito: And the Rise & Fall of Yugoslavia. Richard West. (Illus.). 448p. 1995. 27.50 (*0-7867-0191-9*) Carroll & Graf.

TITO: Architect of Yugoslav Disintegration. Bosko S. Vukcevich. LC 94-25626. (Illus.). 512p. 1994. 29.95 (*0-944957-46-3*) Rivercross Pub.

Tito: Modern Leader of Yugoslavia. Joseph S. Roucek. Ed. by D. Steve Rahmas. LC 73-87625. (Outstanding Personalities Ser.: No. 62). 32p. (Orig.). (YA). (gr. 7-12). 1973. lib. bdg. 7.25 (*0-87157-562-0*) SamHar Pr.

Tito - Yugoslavia's Great Dictator: A Reassessment. Stevan K. Pavlowitch. LC 92-23760. 128p. 1992. 37.50 (*0-8142-0600-X*); pap. 14.95 (*0-8142-0601-8*) Ohio St U Pr.

Tito & the Rise & Fall of Yugoslavia. Richard West. (Illus.). 448p. 1996. pap. 15.95 (*0-7867-0332-6*) Carroll & Graf.

Tito, Mihailovic, & the Allies. Walter R. Roberts. LC 87-5357. (Illus.). xxi, 406p. 1987. pap. text ed. 23.95 (*0-8223-0773-1*) Duke.

***Tito Rodriguez - Inolvidable.** Ed. by Carol Cuellar. 52p. (Orig.). (C). 1995. pap. text ed. 10.95 (*0-7692-0835-5*, A0062OPX) Warner Brothers.

Tito Schipa: A Biography by Tito Schipa, Jr. Tito Schipa, Jr. Tr. by Brian Williams from ITA. LC 96-43574. (Great Voices Ser.: Vol. III). (Illus.). 330p. 1996. 36.00 (*1-880909-48-0*) Baskerville.

Tito, Tito: Rimas, Adivinaanzas y Juegos Infantiles - Tito, Tito: Rhymes, Riddles & Childrens... Isabel Schon. 1996. pap. text ed. 5.95 (*84-241-3336-6*) Lectorum Pubns.

Tito y Filemon. D. Edmond Hiebert. (Comentario Biblico Portavoz Ser.). Orig. Title: Titus & Philemon (Everyman's Bible Commentary). 136p. (SPA.). 1981. pap. 6.99 (*0-8254-1317-6*, Edit Portavoz) Kregel.

Titoist Artrocities in Vojvodina, 1944: Serbian Vendetta in Balska. Tibor Cseres. Ed. & Tr. by Jozsef Venerdy from HUN. 160p. (C). 1993. 25.00 (*1-882785-01-0*, HTA) Matthias Corvinus.

Tito's Yugoslavia. Duncan Wilson. LC 79-11009. 287p. reprint ed. pap. 81.80 (*0-685-16120-X*, 2027250) Bks Demand.

Titrating a Hydrochloric Acid Solution with a Standard Sodium Hydroxide Solution. Norman E. Griswold. Ed. by H. Anthony Neidig. (Modular Laboratory Program in Chemistry Ser.). 12p. (C). 1993. pap. text ed. 1.35 (*0-87540-425-1*, ANAL 425-1) Chem Educ Res.

Titrating Vinegar. H. Anthony Neidig & J. N. Spencer. (Modular Laboratory Program in Chemistry Ser.). 11p. (C). 1992. pap. text ed. 1.35 (*0-87540-395-6*, ANAL 395-6) Chem Educ Res.

Tits & Clits, No. 2. Farmer & Lyvely. (Women's Humor Ser.). (Illus.). 1976. 1.25 (*0-918440-03-3*) Nanny Goat.

Tits & Clits, No. 3. Chevli & Farmer. (Women's Humor Ser.). (Illus.). 1977. 1.25 (*0-918440-04-1*) Nanny Goat.

Tits & Clits, No. 4. Lyvely & Farmer. (Women's Humor Ser.). (Illus.). 1977. 1.25 (*0-918440-05-X*) Nanny Goat.

Tits & Clits, No. 5. Farmer & Chevli. (Women's Humor Ser.). (Illus.). 1979. 2.50 (*0-918440-06-8*) Nanny Goat.
Tits & Clits, No. 6. Farmer. (Women's Humor Ser.). (Illus.). 1980. 2.50 (*0-918440-07-6*) Nanny Goat.
Tits & Clits, No. 7. Farmer & Mary Fleener. (Women's Humor Ser.). 1987. 2.50 (*0-86719-204-6*) Nanny Goat.
Tits & Clits, No. 1. Chevli & Farmer. (Women's Humor Ser.). (Illus.). 1972. 1.25 (*0-918440-00-9*) Nanny Goat.
Titta Ruffo: An Anthology. Ed. by Andrew Farkas. LC 83-10681. (Contributions to the Study of Music & Dance Ser.: No. 4; Opera Biographies). (Illus.). xii, 289p. 1984. text ed. 55.00 (*0-313-23783-2*, FRU/, Greenwood Pr) Greenwood.
Tituba of Salem Village. Ann Petry. LC 64-20691. 254p. (YA). (gr. 7 up). 1988. lib. bdg. 14.89 (*0-690-04766-5*, Crowell Jr Bks) HarpC Child Bks.
Tituba of Salem Village. Ann Petry. LC 64-20691. (Trophy Bk.). 272p. (J). (gr. 5 up). 1991. pap. 4.50 (*0-06-440403-X*, Trophy) HarpC Child Bks.
***Tituba, Reluctant Witch of Salem.** Breslaw. 1997. pap. 17.95 (*0-8147-1307-6*) NYU Pr.
Tituba, Reluctant Witch of Salem: Devilish Indians & Puritan Fantasies. Elaine G. Breslaw. (American Social Experience Ser.). (Illus.). 296p. (C). 1995. 24.95 (*0-8147-1227-4*) NYU Pr.
Titus. (LifeChange Ser.). 1995. pap. 7.00 (*0-89109-911-5*) NavPress.
Titus. John J. MacArthur, Jr. (MacArthur New Testament Commentary Ser.). 1996. 19.99 (*0-8024-0758-7*) Moody.
***Titus.** Elon Salmon. 296p. 1997. 24.95 (*0-233-99008-9*, Pub. by A Deutsch UK) Trafalgar.
Titus: Living as God's Very Own People. Stuart Briscoe. LC 94-2437. (Understanding the Bk.). 136p. 1994. pap. 8.99 (*0-87788-813-2*) Shaw Pubs.
Titus Alone. Mervyn Peake. LC 81-18908. (Gormenghast Trilogy: Vol. III). (Illus.). 264p. 1982. 25.00 (*0-87951-145-1*) Overlook Pr.
Titus & Philemon. D. Edmond Hiebert. (Everyman's Bible Commentary Ser.). (C). 1957. pap. 9.99 (*0-8024-2056-7*) Moody.
Titus & Philemon. W. Kelly. 6.95 (*0-88172-110-7*) Believers Bkshelf.
Titus & Philemon (Everyman's Bible Commentary) see Tito y Filemon
Titus Andronicus. Maurice Charney. Ed. by Sylvan Barnet & Charney. Bd. with Timon of Athens. Ed. by Maurice Charney et al. 1986. Set pap. 3.95 (*0-451-52034-3*, Sig Classics) NAL-Dutton.
Titus Andronicus. Alan C. Dessen. LC 89-12594. (Shakespeare in Performance Ser.). 144p. 1990. text ed. 39.95 (*0-7190-2743-8*, Pub. by Manchester Univ Pr UK) St Martin.
Titus Andronicus. Alan C. Dessen. Ed. by J. R. Mulryne & James C. Bulman. LC 89-12594. (Shakespeare in Performance Ser.). 131p. 1992. text ed. 14.95 (*0-7190-2744-6*, Pub. by Manchester Univ Pr UK) St Martin.
Titus Andronicus. Hardis. 1997. text ed. 33.00 (*0-8240-9074-8*) Garland.
Titus Andronicus. Ed. by A. L. Rowse. LC 87-14757. (Modern Text with Introduction Ser.). 108p. (Orig.). (C). 1987. pap. text ed. 3.45 (*0-8191-3944-0*) U Pr of Amer.
Titus Andronicus. William Shakespeare. Ed. by Alan Hughes. LC 93-33992. (New Cambridge Shakespeare Ser.). (Illus.). 168p. (C). 1994. text ed. 39.95 (*0-521-22157-9*); pap. text ed. 10.95 (*0-521-29372-3*) Cambridge U Pr.
Titus Andronicus. William Shakespeare. Ed. by Eugene M. Waith. (Oxford English Texts Ser.). 232p. 1984. pap. 6.95 (*0-19-281442-7*) OUP.
Titus Andronicus. William Shakespeare. Ed. by Eugene M. Waith. (Oxford English Texts Ser.). 232p. 1984. 55.00 (*0-19-812902-5*) OUP.
Titus Andronicus. William Shakespeare. (BBC Television Plays Ser.). 1986. pap. 7.95 (*0-563-20279-3*, Pub. by BBC UK) Parkwest Pubns.
Titus Andronicus. William Shakespeare. Ed. by Louis B. Wright & Virginia A. La Mar. (Folger Library). 336p. 1988. pap. 2.95 (*0-685-05668-6*, WSP) PB.
Titus Andronicus. braille ed. William Shakespeare. 316p. 1993. text ed. 25.28 (*1-56956-486-8*, BR9150, Pub. by BBC UK) Parkwest Pubns.
Titus Andronicus. large type ed. William Shakespeare. 1992. pap. 24.95 (*0-7089-4515-5*) Ulverscroft.
Titus Andronicus. 3rd ed. Jonathan Bate. (Arden Shakespeare Ser.). (Illus.). 320p. (C). (gr. 13). 1995. text ed. 45.00 (*0-415-04867-2*, B4869) Routledge.
Titus Andronicus. 3rd ed. Jonathan Bate. (Arden Shakespeare Ser.). (Illus.). 320p. (C). (gr. 13). 1995. pap. 9.95 (*0-415-04868-0*, B4873) Routledge.
Titus Andronicus. 3rd ed. William Shakespeare. Ed. by J. C. Maxwell. (Arden Shakespeare Ser.). 1961. reprint ed. 49.95 (*0-416-47280-X*, NO. 2494, Pub. by BBC UK) Parkwest Pubns.
Titus Andronicus. 3rd ed. William Shakespeare. Ed. by J. C. Maxwell. (Arden Shakespeare Ser.). 1961. reprint ed. pap. 8.95 (*0-416-10430-4*, NO. 2495) Routledge Chapman & Hall.
Titus Andronicus: Critical Essays. Ed. by Philip C. Kolin. LC 95-10367. (Shakespeare Criticism Ser.: Vol. 12). (Illus.). 536p. 1995. text ed. 90.00 (*0-8153-1159-1*, H1670) Garland.
Titus Andronicus: With Twelve Signed Etchings. deluxe limited ed. William Shakespeare. (Illus.). 112p. 1969. boxed 1,650.00 (*1-55660-238-3*) A Wofsy Fine Arts.
Titus Andronicus & Timon of Athens. rev. ed. William Shakespeare. 1986. pap. 5.95 (*0-451-52269-9*, Sig Classics) NAL-Dutton.
Titus Canyon Road Guide: A Tour Through Time. Roger G. Brandt. (Illus.). 32p. (Orig.). (C). 1991. pap. 2.00 (*1-878900-21-8*) DVNH Assn.
***Titus Crow.** Brian Lumley. LC 96-33984. 1996. 24.95 (*0-312-86299-7*) St Martin.
***Titus Crow, Vol. 2.** Lumley. Date not set. 24.95 (*0-312-86347-0*) St Martin.
***Titus Crow, Vol. 3.** Lumley. Date not set. 24.95 (*0-312-86365-9*) St Martin.
Titus from Bla-Kaye. Elmer Hamilton, Jr. 80p. (Orig.). 1994. pap. 11.95 (*1-879260-26-3*) Evanston Pub.
Titus Groan. Mervyn Peake. LC 81-18909. (Gormenghast Trilogy: Vol. I). (Illus.). 512p. 1982. 25.00 (*0-87951-143-5*) Overlook Pr.
Titus Groan. Mervyn Peake. (Gormenghast Trilogy: Vol. I). (Illus.). 408p. 1991. pap. 13.95 (*0-87951-425-6*) Overlook Pr.
Titus of Andronicus. William Shakespeare. (New Folger Library). pap. 3.50 (*0-671-66915-X*) S&S Trade.
Titus, Philemon, & 1st & 2nd Peter Thru Jude see Bible Class Commentaries
Titus Risk Chart. Timothy Titus. 3p. 1989. pap. 1.50 (*0-925190-01-2*) Fairview Press.
Titus Tidewater. Suzy Verrier. LC 70-112636. (Illus.). 48p. (J). (gr. 2-4). 1990. reprint ed. 12.95 (*0-89272-289-4*) Down East.
Titusville Country. large type ed. George Flynn. (Linford Western Library). 240p. 1993. pap. 15.99 (*0-7089-7311-6*, Linford) Ulverscroft.
Titusvillidae, Paleozoic & Recent Branching Hexactinellida, No. 12 see Palaeontographica Americana: Vol. 2
Tiv Economy. Paul Bohannan & Laura Bohannan. LC 66-17013. (Northwestern University African Studies Ser.: No. 20). 279p. reprint ed. pap. 79.60 (*0-317-27800-2*, 2015288) Bks Demand.
Tiv of Central Nigeria. Laura Bohannan & Paul Bohannan. (Ethnographic Survey of Africa Ser.; Western Africa). 103p. reprint ed. pap. 29.40 (*0-317-11266-X*, 2055382) Bks Demand.
TIV Song: The Sociology of Art in a Classless Society. Charles Keil. LC 78-3178. 316p. 1979. lib. bdg. 36.00 (*0-226-42962-8*) U Ch Pr.
***Tiverton & Little Compton, RI.** Simpson & Devin. (Images of America Ser.). 1997. pap. 16.99 (*0-7524-0577-2*, Arcdia) Chalford.
Tiverton Tales. Alice Brown. LC 67-29259. (Americans in Fiction Ser.). 339p. 1968. reprint ed. lib. bdg. 29.50 (*0-8398-0173-4*) Irvington.
Tiverton Tales. Alice Brown. (Americans in Fiction Ser.). 339p. (C). 1986. reprint ed. pap. text ed. 6.95 (*0-8290-2042-X*) Irvington.
Tivoli Hadrian's Villa & Villa d'Este. Old Vicarage Publications Staff. 70p. (C). 1982. pap. text ed. 65.00 (*0-685-22054-0*, Pub. by Old Vicarage UK) St Mut.
Tiwanaku: Portrait of an Andean Civilization. Alan L. Kolata. LC 92-39248. (Peoples of America Ser.). (Illus.). 288p. 1993. 37.95 (*1-55786-183-8*) Blackwell Pubs.
Tiwanaku & Its Hinterland Vol. 1: Agroecology: Archaeology & Paleoecology of an Andean Civilization. Ed. by Alan L. Kolata. LC 95-5837. (Series in Archaeological Inquiry). (Illus.). 384p. 1996. text ed. 95.00 (*1-56098-600-X*) Smithsonian.
Tiwi of North Australia. 3rd ed. C. W. Hart et al. LC 87-7510. (Case Studies in Cultural Anthropology). (Illus.). 200p. (C). 1988. pap. text ed. 13.50 (*0-03-012019-5*) HB Coll Pubs.
Tiwi Wives: A Study of the Women of Melville Island, North Australia. Jane C. Goodale. (Illus.). 368p. (C). 1994. reprint ed. pap. text ed. 14.95 (*0-88133-784-6*) Waveland Pr.
Tizzy. Stephen Cosgrove. (Treasure Trolls Ser.). (Illus.). 32p. (J). (gr. k-5). 1993. lib. bdg. 12.95 (*1-56674-046-0*, HTS Bks) Forest Hse.
Tizzy. Stephen Cosgrove. (J). (ps-3). 1992. pap. 3.95 (*0-307-13453-9*) Western Pub.
Tizzy Boost. Bruce Andrews. 1993. pap. 10.00 (*0-935724-62-1*) Figures.
Tjanting. Ron Silliman. 1981. pap. 10.00 (*0-935724-06-0*) Figures.
Tjatjakiymatchan (Coyote) A Legend from Carmel Valley. Alex O. Ramirez. (Illus.). 16p. (Orig.). (J). 1995. pap. 6.00 (*0-9625175-3-4*) Oyate.
TJ's Secret Pitch. Fred Bowen. LC 95-44474. (AllStar Sport Story Ser.). (Illus.). 96p. (J). (gr. 3-7). 1996. pap. 4.95 (*1-56145-119-3*) Peachtree Pubs.
***TK (Indian Cooking)** Neelam Batra. Ed. by Pam Hoenig. 320p. 1998. write for info. (*0-614-30564-0*) Morrow.
TK Solver: A Tutorial. Gessler. 1994. pap. text ed. write for info. (*0-07-024084-1*) McGraw.
TK Solver for Engineers. Bob Ferguson. 1996. pap. text ed. write for info. (*0-8053-6447-1*) Addison-Wesley.
TK! Solver for Engineers. Victor Wright. (C). 1986. 22.50 (*0-8359-7711-0*, Reston) P-H.
TK Solver Plus. Universal Technical Systems, Inc. Staff. (C). 1988. write for info. (*0-07-834623-1*) McGraw.
Tkanyna: An Exhibit of Ukrainian Weaving. Ed. by Radomir Bilash & Barbara Wilberg. 63p. pap. 9.95 (*0-920862-58-6*) Ukrainian Acad.
TKFGRS Test of Kindergarten-First Grade Readiness Skills. Karen G. Codding. 1987. pap. 15.00 (*0-931421-14-4*); 5.95 (*0-685-30467-1*); lp 19.50 (*0-931421-15-2*) Psychol Educ Pubns.
TLA Film & Video GD. Wax. 1994. pap. 5.95 (*1-880707-00-4*) TLA Vid Mgt.
TLA Film & Video Guide 1996-1997. TLA Publication Staff. Ed. by David Bleiler. 704p. (Orig.). 1996. pap. 14.95 (*1-880707-02-0*) TLA Vid Mgt.
***TLA Film & Video Guide, 1998-1999: The Discerning Movie Lover's Guide.** David Bleiler. 1997. pap. text ed. 17.95 (*0-312-17053-X*) St Martin.
Tlaloc Weeps for Mexico. Laszlo Passuth. Tr. by Harry Hattyar from HUN. 487p. 1987. 19.95 (*0-918872-02-2*) Pac Pub Hse.
Tlar-Codpol. Robert Fox. LC 87-70597. 260p. 1987. pap. 12.50 (*0-913204-20-X*) December Pr.
Tlaxcala in the Sixteenth Century. Charles Gibson. (Illus.). xvi, 300p. 1952. 42.50 (*0-8047-0615-8*) Stanford U Pr.
Tlaxcalan Actas: A Compendium of the Records of the Cabildo of Tlaxcala (1545-1627) James Lockhart et al. LC 85-31510. (Illus.). 160p. 1986. 30.00 (*0-87480-253-9*) U of Utah Pr.
TLC: Tender Loving Covers. Junanita Simonich & Toni Phillips. Ed. & Illus. by Sharon Holmes. 136p. 1993. pap. 19.95 (*1-880972-06-9*, DreamSpinners) Pssblts Denver.
TLC for Aging Parents: A Practical Guide. Betty B. Robertson. 104p. (Orig.). 1992. pap. 9.99 (*0-8341-1456-9*, 85018) Beacon Hill.
TLC for Your PC. Thomas J. Zarecki. (Illus.). 68p. 1986. 9.95 (*0-936503-00-9*) TJ Enter IL.
TLC Prayer Network Training Manual. Iverna M. Tompkins. Ed. by Shirlee Green & Roberta Stultz. teacher ed. write for info. (*0-9611260-3-5*) I Tompkins.
Tlemcen Ou les Lieux de l'Ecriture. Mohammed Dib & Philippe Bordas. (Illus.). 160p. 1996. 29.95 (*2-909571-05-X*, 610601, Pub. by Revue Noire FR) Dist Art Pubs.
***Tlezalteotl: The Search for Filth Eater.** Stan Struble. 303p. (Orig.). 1997. mass mkt. 4.99 (*1-55237-118-2*, Pub. by Comnwlth Pub CN) Partners Pubs Grp.
Tlingit. Alice Osinski. LC 89-25345. (New True Bks.). (Illus.). 48p. (J). (gr. k-4). 1990. pap. 5.50 (*0-516-41189-6*); lib. bdg. 19.00 (*0-516-01189-8*) Childrens.
Tlingit, Beginning. 208p. (YA). 1991. pap. 55.00 incl. audio (*1-57970-018-7*, AFTL50) Audio-Forum.
Tlingit Indians. George T. Emmons. Ed. by Frederica De Laguna. LC 90-46274. (Anthropological Papers of the American Museum of Natural History: No. 70). (Illus.). 530p. 1991. 65.00 (*0-295-97008-1*) U of Wash Pr.
Tlingit Indians of Alaska. Anatolii Kamenskii. Ed. by Marvin Falk. Tr. by Sergei Kan from RUS. LC 85-51786. (Rasmuson Library Historical Translation Ser.: Vol. II). (Illus.). 166p. (Orig.). 1985. pap. 15.00 (*0-912006-18-8*) U of Alaska Pr.
Tlingit Myths & Texts. John R. Swanton. viii, 451p. 1990. reprint ed. pap. 49.00 (*1-878592-02-5*); reprint ed. lib. bdg. 69.00 (*1-878592-03-3*) Native Amer Bk Pubs.
Tlingit Tales: Potlach & Totem Pole. Lorie K. Harris. LC 85-8853. (Illus.). 48p. (J). (gr. 4 up). 1985. pap. 6.95 (*0-87961-153-7*) Naturegraph.
Tlingit, the Alaska Indian: Their Art, Culture & Legend. Dan Kaiper & Nan Kaiper. (Illus.). 96p. 1997. reprint ed. pap. 7.95 (*0-88839-010-6*) Hancock House.
Tlingit Totem Poles. Stephen Brown. (J). (gr. 1-9). 1992. pap. 5.95 (*0-88388-150-0*) Bellerophon Bks.
Tlingit Verb Dictionary. Illus. by Constance V. Youngkin. 392p. (C). 1973. pap. 7.00 (*0-933769-25-3*) Alaska Native.
Tlingit Woman's Root Basket. Louis Shotridge. 16p. 1984. pap. text ed. 3.00 (*1-880475-00-6*) Friends of SJM.
Tlinglt Myths & Texts. John R. Swanton. (Bureau of American Ethnology Bulletins Ser.). 451p. 1995. lib. bdg. 109.00 (*0-7812-4039-5*) Rprt Serv.
TM an Aid to Christian Growth. Ed. by Adrian B. Smith. 144p. (C). 1988. 30.00 (*0-85597-349-8*, Pub. by McCrimmon Pub) St Mut.
TM & Cult Mania. Michael A. Persinger et al. 208p. 1980. 12.95 (*0-8158-0392-3*) Chris Mass.
TM Technique: An Introduction to Transcendental Meditation & the Teachings of Maharishi Mahesh Yogi. Peter Russell. 208p. 1989. 12.95 (*0-14-019137-2*, Penguin Bks) Viking Penguin.
TMA Service Codes: A Standard for Reporting & Analyzing Bank Compensation. Ed. by Treasury Management Association Staff. 354p. 1993. pap. 152.50 (*0-9614799-4-9*) Treasry Mgmt.
TMEH Desk Edition. Ed. by R. Bakerjian & W. Cubberly. LC 88-63758. 1250p. 1988. 126.00 (*0-87263-351-9*) SME.
TMG to Choosing the Right College. Joseph Allen & Bart Astor. 144p. 1996. 10.95 (*0-02-860615-9*) Macmillan.
TMG to the Stock Market. Dian Vujovich. 1997. 10.95 (*0-02-861182-9*) Macmillan.
TMG to Windows NT. Dan Bobola. 1996. 14.99 (*0-7897-0683-0*) Que.
TMJ: Clinical & Practice Managememt. Errol Lader. 116p. ring bd. 85.00 (*0-9610782-0-0*) Vadare.
TMJ: Systems Manual of Insurance & Practice Management. Errol Lader. 97p. spiral bd. 65.00 (*0-9610782-1-9*) Vadare.
TMJ: The Self Help Program. rev. ed. John J. Taddey et al. LC 90-90095. (Illus.). 240p. 1991. 21.95 (*0-9625540-9-X*); pap. 13.95 (*0-9625540-3-0*) Surrey Park Pr.
TMJ - It's Many Faces. Wesley E. Shankland, II. (Illus.). 140p. (Orig.). 1996. pap. 19.50 (*0-9646891-6-2*) Anadem Pubng.
TMJ - The Jaw Connection, the Overlooked Diagnosis: A Self-Care Guide to Diagnosing & Managing this Hidden Ailment. Greg Goddard. LC 91-75870. (Illus.). 200p. (Orig.). 1991. pap. 12.50 (*0-943358-35-3*) Aurora Press.
TMJ & Craniofacial Pain: Diagnosis & Management. James R. Fricton et al. 185p. 1988. 45.00 (*0-912791-23-3*) Ishiyaku Euro.
TMJ Disorders: Management of the Craniomandibular Complex. Ed. by Steven L. Kraus. (Clinics in Physical Therapy Ser.: Vol. 18). (Illus.). 422p. 1987. pap. 45.95 (*0-443-08484-X*) Churchill.
TMJ Pain Control: A Self-Help Program. Sharon L. Carr & Terry L. Daugherty. (Illus.). 40p. 1989. 29.95 incl. audio (*0-924728-00-0*) S Carr.
TMJ Therapy Balances Body Chemistry. Robert J. Peshef. 1983. 65.00 (*0-9605902-6-9*) Color Coded Charting.
TMNT RPG Accessory Pack: Adventures in the Yucatan. Erick Wujcik & Kevin Siembieda. Ed. by Alex Marciniszyn. (Teenage Mutant Ninja Turtles RPG Adventures Ser.). (Illus.). 24p. (Orig.). (YA). (gr. 8 up). 1990. pap. 11.95 (*0-916211-45-2*, 512) Palladium Bks.
TMS320 Family Support Reference Guide. Texas Instruments Engineering Staff. 185p. 1990. 16.00 (*0-685-62509-5*, SPRU011C) Tex Instr Inc.
TMS320 First Generation User's Guide. Texas Instruments, Inc. Staff. 1987. pap. 18.95 (*0-13-922188-3*) P-H.
TMS320C1X First Generation User's Guide. Texas Instruments Engineering Staff. 400p. 1989. 14.95 (*0-685-62504-4*, SPRU013C) Tex Instr Inc.
TMS320C2X Second Generation User's Guide. Texas Instruments Engineering Staff. 400p. 1991. 19.95 (*0-685-62505-2*, SPRU014B) Tex Instr Inc.
TMS320C3X Third Generation User's Guide. Texas Instruments Engineering Staff. 900p. 1991. 24.95 (*0-685-62506-0*, SPRU031B) Tex Instr Inc.
TMS320C4X User's Guide. Texas Instruments Engineering Staff. 850p. 1991. 34.95 (*0-685-62507-9*, SPRU063) Tex Instr Inc.
TMS320C5X User's Guide. Texas Instruments Engineering Staff. 600p. 1991. 29.95 (*0-685-62508-7*, SPRU056A) Tex Instr Inc.
TMS340 Graphics Library User's Guide. Texas Instruments Engineering Staff. 360p. 1991. 14.95 (*0-685-62513-3*, SPVU027) Tex Instr Inc.
TMS34010 Applications Guide. Texas Instruments Engineering Staff. 170p. 1988. 14.95 (*0-685-62511-7*, SPVA007A) Tex Instr Inc.
TMS34010 User's Guide. Texas Instruments Engineering Staff. 600p. 1989. 24.95 (*0-685-62510-9*, SPVU001B) Tex Instr Inc.
TMS34020 User's Guide. Texas Instruments Engineering Staff. 1000p. 1991. 29.95 (*0-685-62512-5*, SPVU019) Tex Instr Inc.
TMS34082 Designer's Handbook. Texas Instruments Engineering Staff. 686p. 1991. 19.95 (*0-685-62516-8*, SCGU004) Tex Instr Inc.
TMS34082 Software Tool Kit Demo. Texas Instruments Engineering Staff. 286p. 1991. 34.95 (*0-685-62515-X*, SCGP001) Tex Instr Inc.
TMS370 Family Data Manual. Texas Instruments Engineering Staff. 480p. 1988. 19.95 (*0-685-62517-6*, SPNS014A) Tex Instr Inc.
TMS380 Second Generation Token-Ring User's Guide. Texas Instruments Engineering Staff. 538p. 1990. 24.95 (*0-685-62518-4*, SPWU005) Tex Instr Inc.
TND Online. 1991. write for info. (*0-8103-7917-1*) Gale.
TNM Atlas. 2nd ed. Ed. by B. Spiessl et al. (Illus.). 280p. 1985. pap. 19.00 (*0-387-13443-3*) Spr-Verlag.
TNM Atlas: Illustrated Guide to the TNM-PTNM Classification of Malignant Tumours. Leslie H. Sobin. (UICC International Union Against Cancer Ser.). (Illus.). xix, 343p. 1995. reprint ed. Incl. insert with the T & N definitions by sets. 29.00 (*0-387-17721-3*) Spr-Verlag.
***TNM Atlas: Illustrated Guide to the TNM/pTNM-Classification of Malignant Tumors.** 3rd rev. ed. B. Spiessl et al. 359p. 1992. pap. 29.00 (*3-540-17721-3*) Spr-Verlag.
***TNM Classification of Malignant Tumours.** Leslie H. Sobin & Christian Wittekind. LC 97-9162. 250p. 1997. pap. 29.95 (*0-471-18486-1*) Wiley.
***TNM Classification of Malignant Tumours.** 4th rev. ed. P. Hermanek & L. H. Sobin. 217p. 1992. 29.00 (*3-540-17366-8*) Spr-Verlag.
TNM Classification of Malignant Tumours. 4th rev. ed. Leslie H. Sobin. (International Union Against Cancer Ser.). 170p. 1996. 29.00 (*0-387-17366-8*) Spr-Verlag.
TNM Supplement 1993: A Commentary on Uniform Use. Ed. by E. Hermanek et al. LC 93-10973. 1994. 45.00 (*0-387-56556-6*) Spr-Verlag.
TNT: The Power Within You. Claude M. Bristol & Harold Sherman. 238p. 1974. pap. 10.00 (*0-671-76546-9*, Fireside) S&S Trade.
T.N.T. Total Neck & Traps. Health for Life Staff. (Illus.). 56p. 1988. pap. 14.95 (*0-944831-18-4*) Health Life.
TNT: Two Hundred Ninety-Two Activities for Literature & Language Arts. Eve Geiger. (J). (gr. 1-6). 1990. pap. 9.99 (*0-8224-6746-1*) Fearon Teach Aids.
TNT Hollywood Birthday Book. John Lynch. 1993. 10.95 (*1-878685-39-2*) Turner Pub GA.
TNT Teaching: Over 200 Dynamite Ways to Make Your Classroom Come Alive. Randy Moberg. Ed. by Pamela Espeland. LC 93-37991. (Free Spirited Classroom Ser.). (Illus.). 160p. (Orig.). 1994. pap. 19.95 (*0-915793-64-4*) Free Spirit Pub.
TNT Two: Two Ninety Two Activities for Across-the-Curriculum. Eve D. Geiger. 1991. 9.99 (*0-86653-995-6*) Fearon Teach Aids.
***Tnuyen Thuyet Moc Lan: Anh Thu eva Co Dai Trung Quoc.** rev. ed. Wei Jiang & Cheng A. Jiang. Tr. by Eileen Hu from CHI. Orig. Title: Hoa Moc Lan: Truyen ve nu Anh Hung Co Dai Trung Quoc. (Illus.). 32p. (ENG & VIE.). (J). (gr. 3-6). 1997. 14.95 (*1-878217-16-X*) Victory Press.
To. Jim Cartwright. (Methuen Modern Plays Ser.). 49p. (Orig.). (C). 1991. pap. 9.95 (*0-413-63570-8*, A0488, Pub. by Methuen UK) Heinemann.
To a Chinese Girl, Singing. Karla Andersdatter. 36p. 1984. 6.00 (*0-935430-08-3*) In Between.
To a Dancing God: Notes of a Spiritual Traveler. Sam Keen. LC 79-109061. 192p. 1990. reprint ed. pap. 12.00 (*0-06-250496-7*) Harper SF.
To a Different Drumbeat: A Practical Guide to Parenting Children with Special Needs. Patricia Clarke et al. (Lifeways Ser.). (Illus.). 240p. 1989. pap. 16.95 (*1-869890-09-4*, 1264, Pub. by Hawthorn Press UK) Anthroposophic.

An Asterisk (*) at the beginning of an entry indicates that the title is appearing in BIP for the first time.

***To a Far Country.** Melvin Cannon. 212p. (Orig.). 1997. mass mkt. 4.99 (1-55197-973-X, Pub. by Comnwlth Pub CN) Partners Pubs Grp.

To a Far Province with Basho. Liberty Campbell. 64p. (Orig.). 1983. pap. 3.95 (0-939332-04-3) J Pohl Assocs.

To a Friend. Laurence Craig-Green. (Illus.). 16p. 1985. pap. 6.50 (0-916922-10-3) Poet Tree Pr.

To a Friend: Sunny Thoughts for Monday Moods. Jim Beggs. LC 88-63460. (Illus.). 64p. 1989. 7.99 (0-88088-538-6) Peter Pauper.

To a God Unknown. John Steinbeck. (Fiction Ser.). 272p. 1976. mass mkt. 6.95 (0-14-004233-4, Penguin Bks) Viking Penguin.

To a God Unknown. John Steinbeck. 288p. 1995. pap. 10.95 (0-14-018751-0, Penguin Classics) Viking Penguin.

To a God Unknown. large type ed. John Steinbeck. 1974. 25.99 (0-85456-304-0) Ulverscroft.

To a Good Home Only. Jennifer Melrose. 230p. 1987. 70. 00 (1-85200-009-0, Pub. by United Writers Pubns UK) St Mut.

To a High Place. Teo Savory. LC 78-134748. 98p. 1973. 15.00 (0-87775-023-8) Unicorn Pr.

To a Land He Showed Us. Stanley W. Hoffman. 1993. pap. 11.95 (0-533-10309-6) Vantage.

To a Patient Named Nick: A Different Kind of Story of a Nurse & an AIDS Patient. Eva L. Altarejos-Espinosa. LC 95-71609. 152p. 1996. 14.95 (0-9648529-0-X) Carelife Pubng.

To a Rocky Moon: A Geologist's History of Lunar Exploration. Don E. Wilhelms. LC 92-33228. (Illus.). 477p. 1994. reprint ed. pap. 21.50 (0-8165-1443-7) U of Ariz Pr.

To a Sailor: Poems. Mary McGreevy & Dora Rosenbaum. (Illus.). 58p. (Orig.). 1989. pap. 10.00 (0-685-28888-9) M McGreevy.

To a Special Couple on Your Wedding Day. Pam Brown. Ed. by Helen Exley. (To Give & to Keep Ser.). (Illus.). 28p. 1996. 6.99 (1-85015-708-1) Exley Giftbooks.

To a Vanished World. Lee Sharkey. Ed. by Constance Hunting. 75p. (Orig.). 1995. pap. 10.95 (0-913006-58-0) Puckerbrush.

To a Very Special Dad. Pam Brown. Ed. by Helen Exley. (To Give & to Keep Ser.). (Illus.). 28p. 1993. 6.99 (1-85015-396-5) Exley Giftbooks.

To a Very Special Daughter. Susanne Starck. 78p. (Orig.). 1994. pap. 7.95 (1-56245-093-X) Great Quotations.

To a Very Special Daughter. Pam Brown. Ed. by Helen Exley. (To Give & to Keep Ser.). (Illus.). 28p. 1992. reprint ed. 6.99 (1-85015-278-0) Exley Giftbooks.

To a Very Special Friend. Helen Exley. (To Give & to Keep Ser.). (Illus.). 28p. 1992. 6.99 (1-85015-262-4) Exley Giftbooks.

To a Very Special Friend on Your Birthday. Ed. by Susan P. Schutz. LC 90-83141. (Illus.). 64p. 1990. pap. 7.95 (0-88396-285-3) Blue Mtn Pr CO.

To a Very Special Granddaughter. Pam Brown. Ed. by Helen Exley. (To Give & to Keep Ser.). (Illus.). 28p. 1993. 6.99 (1-85015-437-6) Exley Giftbooks.

To a Very Special Grandmother. Pam Brown. Ed. by Helen Exley. (To Give & to Keep Ser.). (Illus.). 28p. 1992. 6.99 (1-85015-265-9) Exley Giftbooks.

To a Very Special Grandpa. Ed. by Helen Exley. (To Give & to Keep Ser.). (Illus.). 28p. 1994. 6.99 (1-85015-497-X) Exley Giftbooks.

To a Very Special Grandparent. Susanne Starck. 78p. (Orig.). 1994. pap. 7.95 (1-56245-094-8) Great Quotations.

To a Very Special Grandson. Pam Brown. Ed. by Helen Exley. (To Give & to Keep Ser.). (Illus.). 28p. 1996. 6.99 (1-85015-694-8) Exley Giftbooks.

To a Very Special Husband. Ed. by Helen Exley. (To Give & to Keep Ser.). (Illus.). 28p. 6.99 (1-85015-264-0) Exley Giftbooks.

To a Very Special Love. Susanne Starck. 78p. (Orig.). 1994. pap. 7.95 (1-56245-095-6) Great Quotations.

To a Very Special Mother. Ed. by Helen Exley. (To Give & to Keep Ser.). (Illus.). 28p. 1992. 6.99 (1-85015-256-X) Exley Giftbooks.

To a Very Special Sister. Ed. by Helen Exley. (To Give & to Keep Ser.). (Illus.). 28p. 1994. 6.99 (1-85015-498-8) Exley Giftbooks.

***To a Very Special Son.** Ed. by Patrick Caton. 80p. 1997. spiral bd. 7.95 (1-56245-290-8) Great Quotations.

To a Very Special Son. Ed. by Helen Exley. (To Give & to Keep Ser.). (Illus.). 28p. 1993. 6.99 (1-85015-424-4) Exley Giftbooks.

To a Very Special Teacher. Ed. by Helen Exley. (To Give & to Keep Ser.). (Illus.). 28p. 1995. 6.99 (1-85015-648-4) Exley Giftbooks.

To a Very Special Wife. Ed. by Helen Exley. (To Give & to Keep Ser.). (Illus.). 28p. 1993. 6.99 (1-85015-325-6) Exley Giftbooks.

To a Violent Grave: An Oral Biography of Jackson Pollock. Jeffrey Potter. (Illus.). 1987. pap. 15.00 (0-916366-47-2) Pushcart Pr.

To a Widow with Children. Lionel G. Garcia. LC 93-36397. 1994. 19.95 (1-55885-069-4) Arte Publico.

To a Young Bird Artist: Selected Letters from Louis Agassiz Fuertes to George Miksch Sutton. George M. Sutton. LC 79-4754. (Illus.). 158p. 1979. 24.95 (0-8061-1589-0) U of Okla Pr.

To Abolish the Death Penalty. U. S. Congress Senate Committee on the Judiciary. LC 82-45650. (Capital Punishment Ser.). reprint ed. 44.00 (0-404-62433-2) AMS Pr.

To Abyssinia Through an Unknown Land. Chauncey H. Stigand. LC 75-81377. (Illus.). 352p. 1969. reprint ed. text ed. 35.00 (0-8371-1619-8, STA&, Greenwood Pr) Greenwood.

***To Accompany State & Local Politics.** 8th ed. David R. Berman. 72p. (C). (gr. 13). 1996. teacher ed., pap. text ed. write for info. (0-7656-0007-2) M E Sharpe.

To Achieve Security & Wealth: The Qing Imperial State & the Economy, 1644-1911. Ed. by Jane K. Leonard & John R. Watt. (Cornell East Asia Ser.: No. 56). (Illus.). 206p. (Orig.). (C). 1993. pap. 12.00 (0-939657-56-2) Cornell East Asia Pgm.

To Acknowledge the Wonder: The Story of Fundamental Physics. E. J. Squires. (Illus.). 208p. 1985. pap. 28.00 (0-85274-798-5) IOP Pub.

To Act Justly, Love Tenderly, Walk Humbly: An Agenda for Ministers. Walter Brueggemann et al. 88p. 1986. pap. 4.95 (0-8091-2760-1) Paulist Pr.

To Act, to Do, to Perform: Drama & the Phenomenology of Action. Alice Rayner. LC 94-3828. (Theater: Theory - Text - Performance Ser.). 168p. 1994. text ed. 37.50 (0-472-10537-X) U of Mich Pr.

To Advance Knowledge: The Growth of American Research Universities, 1900-1940. Roger L. Geiger. 352p. 1986. 35.00 (0-19-503803-7) OUP.

To Advance Learning: A Handbook on Developing K-12 - Postsecondary Partnerships. Manuel N. Gomez et al. (Illus.). 232p. (Orig.). (C). 1990. pap. text ed. 22.00 (0-8191-7943-4, Proj STEP U CA Irvine) U Pr of Amer.

To AIDS & Back: 3 Stories of Unconditional Love & Hope. Grady L. Etheridge et al. (Illus.). 35p. (Orig.). 1994. pap. 4.00 (0-937417-04-1) Etheridge Minist.

To Air Is Human: A Manual for People with Chronic Lung Disease (COPD) rev. ed. Madeline H. Barrow & Nancy R. Hull. Ed. by Faye Hoffman. LC 88-39495. (Illus.). 80p. 1995. pap. text ed. 7.95 (0-939838-26-5) Pritchett & Hull.

***To Air Is Human: Aviation Adventures & Anecdotes.** Ray Thiele. Ed. by R. Jensen & Patrick A. Thiele. (Illus.). 192p. (Orig.). 1996. pap. 9.95 (0-9643365-1-0) Olomana Pubs.

To All Appearances. Marilyn Bowering. Date not set. pap. 8.95 (0-14-013313-5) Viking Penguin.

To All Appearances: Ideology & Performance. Herbert Blau. LC 91-46688. 240p. (C). 1992. text ed. 69.95 (0-415-01364-X, Routledge NY) Routledge.

To All Appearances: The Ideology of Performance. Herbert Blau. LC 91-46688. 240p. (C). 1992. pap. 17.95 (0-415-01365-8, Pub. by Tavistock UK) Routledge Chapman & Hall.

***To All Grandmas & Grandpas with Love.** Ann Tuites. 159p. (Orig.). 1997. mass mkt. 4.99 (1-55197-843-1, Pub. by Comnwlth Pub CN) Partners Pubs Grp.

To All My Children As the World Turns. Gyeorgos C. Hatonn. (Phoenix Journals). 243p. 1993. pap. 7.95 (1-56935-003-5) Phoenix Source.

To All My Friends. Morris A. Mercer, Jr. (Illus.). 64p. (Orig.). 1986. pap. write for info. (0-9617362-0-8) M A Mercer.

To All My Grandchildren: Lessons in Indonesian Cooking. Leonie Samuel-Hool. Ed. by Sherman Hool. LC 80-84766. (Illus.). 120p. 1981. 12.95 (0-936016-50-7); pap. 7.95 (0-936016-75-2) Goodfellow.

To All Peoples: Missions World Book of the Christian & Missionary Alliance. Robert L. Niklaus. LC 90-81150. (Illus.). 412p. 1990. 29.99 (0-87509-432-5) Chr Pubns.

To All the Brethren: A Text-Linguistic & Rhetorical Approach to I Thessalonians. Bruce C. Johanson. (Coniectanea Biblica. New Testament Ser.: No. 16). xiv, 230p. (Orig.). 1987. pap. text ed. 44.00 (91-22-00865-9) Coronet Bks.

To All the Islands Now. Edgar Wolfe. 105p. 1986. pap. 5.00 (0-939391-05-8) B Woodley Pr.

***To All Things a Season: Twelve Months Afield with Fly Rod, Shotgun, & Longbow.** E. Donnall Thomas. (Illus.). 208p. 1997. 29.95 (1-885106-54-8) Wild Adven Pr.

***To All Things a Season: Twelve Months Afield with Fly Rod, Shotgun, & Longbow.** limited ed. E. Donnall Thomas. LC 97-60292. (Illus.). 208p. 1997. lthr. 95.00 (1-885106-55-6) Wild Adven Pr.

To America & Around the World: The First Logs of Columbus & Magellan. Christopher Columbus & Antonio Pigafetta. (Illus.). 340p. 1990. 25.95 (0-8283-1992-8) Branden Pub Co.

***To Amuse a Shrinking Sun.** John Digby. 70p. 1985. 21.95 (0-85646-138-5, Pub. by Anvil Press UK); pap. 14.95 (0-85646-139-3, Pub. by Anvil Press UK) Dufour.

To an Aging Nation (with Occult Overtones) see Gallery Series: Poets

To an Alien: To the Everlasting Eyes of Love. Alireza Zarrin. 32p. (Orig.). (gr. 8 up). 1991. pap. 6.00 (0-9622190-0-2) Alien Bks.

To an Ancient People: The Autobiography of Rabbi Leopold Cohn. Chosen People Ministries Staff. 83p. (Orig.). 1996. pap. 6.95 (1-882675-06-1) Chosen People.

To an Early Grave. Wallace Markfield. 1994. lib. bdg. 24.95 (1-56849-402-5) Buccaneer Bks.

To an Idea: A Book of Poems. David Shapiro. LC 82-22328. 96p. 1983. 14.95 (0-87951-176-1); 50.00 (0-87951-181-8) Overlook Pr.

To an Idea: A Book of Poems. David Shapiro. LC 82-22328. 96p. 1986. pap. 8.95 (0-87951-255-5) Overlook Pr.

To Analyze Data. 2nd ed. Carol T. Fitz-Gibbon & Lynn L. Morris. (Program Evaluation Kit Ser.: Vol. 8). 152p. (C). 1987. pap. text ed. 17.50 (0-8039-3133-6) Sage.

To Analyze Delight: A Hedonist Criticism of Shakespeare. Gary Taylor. LC 84-40617. 238p. 1985. 35.00 (0-87413-269-X) U Delaware Pr.

To Anchor a Cloud. Dilip Hiro. (Writers Workshop Bluebird Ser.). 96p. 1975. 15.00 (0-88253-662-1); pap. text ed. 6.75 (0-88253-661-3) Ind-US Inc.

To & For. Steve Levine. LC 92-3245. (Orig.). 1992. pap. 10. 95 (0-918273-71-4) Coffee Hse.

To & Fro in Southern California: With Sketches in Arizona & New Mexico. Emma H. Adams. Ed. by Carlos E. Cortes. LC 76-1220. (Chicano Heritage Ser.). 1977. reprint ed. 24.95 (0-405-09481-7) Ayer.

To & Through the Houston Texas Medical Center. William S. Fields. LC 95-31786. 1995. 24.95 (1-57168-052-7) Sunbelt Media.

To Anger the Devil. Alexander. 174p. 1978. 8.50 (0-85978-034-1, Pub. by C W Daniel UK) Natl Bk Netwk.

To Anger the Devil. Marc Alexander. (Illus.). 210p. 12.95 (0-8464-4301-5) Beekman Pubs.

To Annabella Pelican from Thomas Hippopotamus. Nancy Patz. LC 90-30038. (Illus.). 32p. (J). (ps-3). 1991. lib. bdg. 13.95 (0-02-770280-4, Four Winds Pr) S&S Childrens.

To Appomattox: Nine April Days, 1865. Burke Davis. 444p. 1989. reprint ed. pap. 4.25 (0-915992-17-5) Eastern Acorn.

To Appomattox & Beyond: The Civil War Soldier in War & Peace. Larry M. Logue. (American Ways Ser.). 170p. 1995. 22.50 (1-56663-093-2) I R Dee.

To Appomattox & Beyond: The Civil War Soldier in War & Peace. Larry M. Logue. LC 95-30217. (American Ways Ser.). 1996. pap. text ed. 9.95 (1-56663-094-0) I R Dee.

To Argentina with Love. Frederick S. Williams. LC 91-71706. 90p. (Orig.). (C). 1991. pap. 9.95 (0-944329-03-9) KOBO Ent.

To Asmara. Thomas Keneally. 1990. pap. 11.99 (0-446-39171-9) Warner Bks.

To Asmara: A Novel of Africa. large type ed. Thomas Keneally. 392p. 1991. 24.95 (1-85089-409-4, Pub. by ISIS UK) Transaction Pubs.

To Avoid Catastrophe: A Study in Future Nuclear Weapons Policy. Ed. by Michael P. Hamilton. LC 77-24983. 240p. reprint ed. pap. 68.40 (0-317-08052-0, 2012810) Bks Demand.

To Avoid Isolation: An Ambassador's View of the U. S. - Japanese Relations. Yoshio Okawara. 192p. 1990. text ed. 34.95 (0-87249-646-5) U of SC Pr.

To Awaken a Sleeping Giant. J. Spencer Lang. Ed. by Sharon L. Goodman. (Orig.). 1986. pap. 4.00 (0-935369-07-4) In Tradition Pub.

To Awaken My Afflicted Brethren: David Walker & the Problem of American Slave Resistance. Peter Hinks. 288p. 1996. 45.00 (0-271-01578-0); pap. 17.95 (0-271-01579-9) Pa St U Pr.

To Banbury Cross & Back: A Collection of Modern Poetry. Ed. by Louisa Persing. (Illus.). 1976. 5.95 (0-686-17956-0) Palomar.

To Bathe a Boa. C. Imbior Kudrna. (Carolrhoda Picture Bks.). (Illus.). 32p. (J). (ps-3). 1986. pap. 5.95 (0-87614-490-3, Carolrhoda); lib. bdg. 14.96 (0-87614-306-0, Carolrhoda) Lerner Group.

To Be a Catholic. Joseph V. Gallagher. LC 73-137884. 96p. 1970. pap. 2.95 (0-8091-5143-X) Paulist Pr.

To Be a Christian. Paul Smith. 68p. 1992. pap. 3.95 (0-940999-81-1, C2187) Star Bible.

To Be a Clown. Elizabeth Ballinger. 96p. (J). (gr. 5-8). 1994. pap. 7.95 (1-879331-44-6, Classc Pub) Marciel Pub & Print.

To Be a Doctor. Felix Marti-Ibanez. Bd. with The Young Princes. LC 68-27688.; Race & the Runner. LC 68-27688. LC 68-27688. 1968. 4.95 (0-910922-18-7) MD Pubns.

To Be a Doctor: A Health Education Workbook. Georgette B. Skolnick. (Illus.). 215p. (Orig.). (J). (gr. 6-9). 1982. student ed. 8.00 (0-913855-00-6) GBS CA.

***To Be a Drum.** Evelyn Coleman. LC 96-54068. (Illus.). (J). Date not set. write for info. (0-8075-8006-6) A Whitman.

To Be a Farmer's Boy. G. K. Nelson. (J). (gr. 5-12). 1991. 30.00 (0-86299-872-7, Pub. by Sutton Pubng UK); pap. 18.00 (0-7509-0182-9, Pub. by Sutton Pubng UK) Bks Intl VA.

To Be a Father Like the Father: Modeling the Fatherly Attributes of God. Michael Phillips. LC 91-76511. 309p. 1996. pap. 9.99 (0-87509-475-9) Chr Pubns.

To Be a Fine Lady. large type ed. Delia Ellis. 512p. 1992. 25.99 (0-7089-2570-7) Ulverscroft.

To Be a Jew: A Guide to Jewish Observance in Contemporary Life. Hayim H. Donin. LC 72-89175. 368p. 1991. pap. 13.00 (0-465-08632-2) Basic.

To Be a Jewish Woman. Lisa Aiken. LC 91-31680. 312p. 1997. reprint ed. pap. 19.95 (1-56821-153-8) Aronson.

***To Be a Man.** Heston. 1997. 17.95 (0-684-84116-9) S&S Trade.

To Be a Man. Ed. by Keith Thompson. (New Consciousness Reader Ser.). 320p. (Orig.). 1991. pap. 13. 95 (0-87477-637-6, Tarcher Putnam) Putnam Pub Group.

To Be a Man: Visions of Self, Views from Within. Daniel Kaufman. 192p. 1994. 20.00 (0-671-88107-8) S&S Trade.

To Be a Mother: The Agonies & the Ecstasies. Darla H. Isackson & Emma L. Thayne. 16p. (Orig.). 1996. pap. 3.95 (1-56236-161-9) Aspen Bks.

To Be a Muslim. Fathi Yakun. 103p. 1990. pap. 6.50 (0-89259-106-4) Am Trust Pubns.

To Be a Nurse. Linda Strangio et al. Ed. by Lisa Ruggerio & Carolyn S. Zagury. LC 94-61761. 216p. (Orig.). 1995. pap. 12.95 (1-880254-22-0) Vista.

***To Be a Nurse.** 2nd ed. Evelyn Adam. (Illus.). 167p. 1991. pap. write for info. (0-920513-06-9, Pub. by Saunders CN) Saunders.

To Be a Pilgrim. Basil Hume. (C). 1988. 60.00 (0-85439-232-7, Pub. by St Paul Pubns UK); pap. 30.00 (0-85439-231-9, Pub. by St Paul Pubns UK) St Mut.

To Be a Politician. Stimson Bullitt. 448p. 1994. pap. 15.95 (0-9631630-3-5) Willows WA.

To Be a Politician. rev. ed. Stimson Bullitt. LC 75-43310. 312p. reprint ed. pap. 89.00 (0-8357-8767-2, 2033685) Bks Demand.

To Be a Presbyterian. Louis B. Weeks. 96p. (Orig.). 1987. pap. 10.00 (0-8042-1880-3, John Knox) Westminster John Knox.

To Be a Redemptorist Today: Reflections on the Redemptorist Charism. Ed. by Noel Londono. LC 96-26511. 432p. (Orig.). 1996. pap. 20.00 (0-7648-0052-3) Liguori Pubns.

To Be a Slave. Julius Lester. LC 68-28738. (Illus.). (J). (gr. 7-12). 1968. pap. 16.99 (0-8037-8955-6) Dial Bks Young.

To Be a Slave. Julius Lester. 160p. (YA). (gr. 7-9). 1986. pap. 3.99 (0-590-42460-2) Scholastic Inc.

To Be a Slave in Brazil: 1550-1888. Katia M. De Queiros Mattoso. Tr. by Arthur Goldhammer. 35p. (C). 1986. text ed. 45.00 (0-8135-1154-2) Rutgers U Pr.

To Be a Slave in Brazil: 1550-1888. Katia M. De Queiros Mattoso. Tr. by Arthur Goldhammer. 35p. (C). 1986. pap. 16.95 (0-8135-1155-0) Rutgers U Pr.

To Be a Teacher: Voices from the Classroom. Eric Henry et al. LC 95-7734. 160p. 1995. 40.00 (0-8039-6323-8); pap. 18.00 (0-8039-6324-6) Corwin Pr.

To Be a Trial Lawyer. 2nd ed. F. Lee Bailey. 256p. 1994. pap. text ed. 17.95 (0-471-07256-7) Wiley.

To Be a Victim: Encounters with Crime & Injustice. Ed. by Diane Sank & David N. Caplan. (Illus.). 500p. 1991. 28. 50 (0-306-43962-X, Plenum Insight) Plenum.

To Be a Warrior. Robert B. Fox. LC 96-35851. 160p. (Orig.). 1997. pap. 12.95 (0-86534-253-9) Sunstone Pr.

To Be a Wolf. Carol A. Amato. LC 95-17155. (Young Readers' Ser.). (Illus.). 48p. (J). (gr. 2-4). 1995. pap. 4.95 (0-8120-9287-2) Barron.

***To Be a Wolf.** Carol A. Amato. (Young Reader Ser.). (Illus.). 48p. (J). (gr. 3-6). 1996. lib. bdg. 12.95 (1-56674-189-0) Forest Hse.

To Be a Woman. Ed. by Connie Zweig. (New Consciousness Reader Ser.). 288p. (Orig.). 1990. pap. 14. 95 (0-87477-561-2, Tarcher Putnam) Putnam Pub Group.

To Be Alive: A Woman's Guide to a Full Life After Cancer. C. D. Runowicz. 272p. 1996. pap. 14.95 (0-8050-2959-1, Owl) H Holt & Co.

To Be An American: Cultural Pluralism & the Rhetoric of Assimilation. Bill O. Hing. LC 96-35678. 336p. (C). 1996. text ed. 23.96 (0-8147-3523-1) NYU Pr.

***To Be an Anchor in the Storm Trade Guide for Families & Friends of Abused Women.** James A. Thom. LC 97-18577. 1997. pap. 12.95 (0-345-41719-4) Ballantine.

***To Be an Author: Letters of Charles W. Chestnut, 1889-1905.** Charles W. Chestnut. Ed. by Joseph R. McElrath, Jr. & Robert C. Lietz, 3rd. 1997. 24.95 (0-614-27817-1) Princeton U Pr.

To Be an Indian: An Oral History. Ed. by Joseph H. Cash & Herbert T. Hoover. LC 94-39879. (Illus.). xxiv, 239p. 1995. pap. 11.95 (0-87351-306-1, Borealis Book) Minn Hist.

To Be & Do unto Eternity: Spiritual & Sexual Journeys & Journal Keeping Processes. Marc G. Vohemian. (Illus.). 115p. (Orig.). (C). 1995. student ed., pap. text ed. 34.95 (1-884090-22-2) Ecumenics Intl.

To Be & Not to Be: An Analysis of Jean-Paul Sartre's Ontology. LC 61-12269. 198p. reprint ed. pap. 56.50 (0-317-09002-X, 2001334) Bks Demand.

To Be Chasidic: A Contemporary Guide. Chaim Dalfin. LC 96-13673. 280p. 1997. 30.00 (1-56821-905-9) Aronson.

***To Be Confirmed.** Reid. 8.99 (0-340-62132-X, Pub. by H & S UK) Trafalgar.

***To Be Confirmed.** Reid. 6.95 (0-340-21357-4, Pub. by H & S UK) Trafalgar.

To Be Continued. William Marchant. 1952. pap. 3.25 (0-8222-1156-4) Dramatists Play.

To Be Continued: An Annotated Guide to Sequels. Merle L. Jacob & Hope Apple. LC 95-3283. 376p. 1995. 45.50 (0-89774-842-5) Oryx Pr.

To Be Continued: Four Stories & Their Survival. Peter Conrad. 216p. 1995. 26.00 (0-19-818291-0) OUP.

To Be Continued: Soap Operas & Global Media Cultures. Ed. by Robert C. Allen. LC 94-11394. (Comedia Ser.). 416p. (C). 1995. pap. 19.95 (0-415-11007-6, C0004) Routledge.

To Be Continued: Soap Operas & Global Media Cultures. Ed. by Robert C. Allen. LC 94-11394. (Comedia Ser.). 416p. (C). (gr. 13). 1995. text ed. 69.95 (0-415-11006-8, C0001) Routledge.

To Be Continued: The Alcoholics Anonymous World Bibliography 1935-1994. 2nd ed. Charlie Bishop, Jr. & Bill Pittman. 528p. (Orig.). 1994. mass mkt., pap. 25.00 (1-877686-07-7) Bishop Bks.

To Be Damned. Kenneth Miller. 480p. 1995. mass mkt. 6.99 (1-896329-29-2, Pub. by Comnwlth Pub CN) Partners Pubs Grp.

To Be Free: Studies in American Negro History. Herbert Aptheker. 256p. 1992. pap. 9.95 (0-8065-1257-1, Citadel Pr) Carol Pub Group.

To Be Free: Studies in American Negro History. Herbert Aptheker. LC 48-5693. 256p. reprint ed. pap. 73.00 (0-317-28070-8, 2025544) Bks Demand.

To Be Gifted & Learning Disabled: From Definitions to Practical Intervention Strategies. Susan M. Baum et al. 149p. (Orig.). 1991. pap. write for info. (0-936386-59-2) Creative Learning.

To Be Holy: Principles for Living the Spirit-Filled Life. C. Neil Strait. 64p. 1984. pap. 4.99 (0-8341-0896-8) Beacon Hill.

To Be Human Against All Odds. Frederick Franck. (Illus.). 188p. (Orig.). (C). 1996. reprint ed. pap. 9.99 (0-88092-221-4) Royal Fireworks.

To Be Human Against All Odds: Illustrated with Drawings & Icons by the Author. LC 91-70002. (Nanzan Studies in Religion & Culture). (Illus.). 195p. 1991. reprint ed. pap. 55.60 (*0-608-01775-2*, 2062433) Bks Demand.

To Be Human Before God: Insights in Biblical Spirituality. Michael D. Guinan. 104p. (Orig.). 1994. pap. 7.95 (*0-8146-2207-0*) Liturgical Pr.

To Be in This Country: The Paintings of V. Douglas Snow. Allen Dodworth. (C). 1995. pap. text ed. 9.95 (*0-87480-475-2*) U of Utah Pr.

To Be Like Jesus. Rob Burkhart. LC 89-82758. (Sunday School Staff Training Book of the Year Ser.). 110p. 1990. pap. 2.95 (*0-88243-658-9*, 02-0658) Gospel Pub.

To Be Loved. large type ed. Lynne Collins. 1990. 25.99 (*0-7089-2292-9*) Ulverscroft.

To Be Loved: The Music, the Magic, the Memories of Motown: An Autobiography. Berry Gordy. 480p. 1995. mass mkt. 6.99 (*0-446-60236-1*) Warner Bks.

To Be Mature. H. L. Rutledge. LC 74-76988. 250p. 1974. reprint ed. pap. 5.00 (*0-914520-03-2*) Insight Pr.

To Be Mayor of New York: Ethnic Politics in the City. Chris McNickle. Ed. by Kenneth T. Jackson. LC 92-32583. (Columbia History of Urban Life Ser.). (Illus.). 300p. (C). 1993. 37.50 (*0-231-07636-3*) Col U Pr.

To Be Mayor of New York: Ethnic Politics in the City. Chris McNickle. 403p. 1995. pap. text ed. 17.50 (*0-231-07637-1*) Col U Pr.

To Be Modern: American Encounters with Cezanne & Company. Sylvia Yount & Elizabeth Johns. LC 96-15561. (Illus.). 80p. 1996. pap. 24.95 (*0-943836-18-2*) Penn Acad Art.

To Be Old & Sad: Understanding Depression in the Elderly. Nathan Billig. LC 85-45736. 114p. pap. 11.95 (*0-669-12279-3*, Lexington) Jossey-Bass.

To Be Once in Doubt: Certainty & the Marriage of Minds in Othello. Danny L. Smith. (American University Studies: English Language & Literature: Ser. IV, Vol. 90). 199p. (C). 1989. text ed. 36.50 (*0-8204-0882-4*) P Lang Pubng.

To Be One of Us: Cultural Conflict, Creative Democracy, & Education. Nancy Bevin Warehime. LC 92-3098. (SUNY Series, The Philosophy of Education). 190p. 1993. text ed. 57.50 (*0-7914-1321-7*) State U NY Pr.

To Be One of Us: Cultural Conflict, Creative Democracy, & Education. Nancy B. Warehime. LC 92-3098. (SUNY Series, The Philosophy of Education). 190p. 1993. pap. 18.95 (*0-7914-1322-5*) State U NY Pr.

To Be One Thing: Personal Unity in Kierkegaard's Thought. George Connell. LC 85-4812. xx, 198p. 1985. 17.95 (*0-86554-156-6*, MUP/H146) Mercer Univ Pr.

To Be or Not: An E-Prime Anthology. Ed. by Paul D. Johnston. 206p. (Orig.). 1991. pap. text ed. 14.00 (*0-918970-38-5*) Intl Gen Semantics.

To Be or Not to Be: An Artist's Guide to Not-for-Profit Incorporation. Volunteer Lawyers for the Arts Staff. 12p. 1986. 5.00 (*0-917103-03-3*) Vol Lawyers Arts.

To Be or Not To Be: Existential-Psychological Perspectives on the Self. Sidney M. Jourard. LC 67-65494. (University of Florida Monographs, Social Sciences: No. 34). 75p. reprint ed. pap. 25.00 (*0-8357-6732-9*, 2035374) Bks Demand.

To Be or Not to Be a Christian: Meditations & Essays on Authentic Christian Community. Gene W. Marshall. LC 94-65447. (Illus.). 336p. (Orig.). 1994. pap. 15.00 (*0-9611552-3-X*) Realistic Living.

To Be or Not to Be an SOB: A Reaffirmation of Business Ethics. 2nd ed. Ben B. Boothe. Ed. by Paulette H. Boothe. 81p. 1991. reprint ed. 10.00 (*0-89015-737-5*) Unicorn Pr USA.

To Be or Not To Be Human: The Nature of Human Nature. Ben Freedman. 1987. 20.00 (*0-533-06964-5*) Vantage.

To Be or Not to Be in the Party. Yuri Glazov. (C). 1988. lib. bdg. 102.50 (*90-277-2716-3*) Kluwer Ac.

To Be or Not to Be...Quiet. Elaine Weimann & Rita Friedman. (Read to Me Bks.). (Illus.). 30p. (J). (ps-1). 1986. lib. bdg. 12.50 (*0-89796-997-9*) New Dimens Educ.

***To Be or Not to Bop: Dizzy Gillespie Autobiography.** Dizzy Gillespie & Fraser. 1998. 30.00 (*0-02-864777-7*) S&S Trade.

To Be or Not to Bop: Memoirs of Dizzy Gillespie. Dizzy Gillespie & Al Fraser. (Quality Paperbacks Ser.). (Illus.). 574p. 1985. reprint ed. pap. 15.95 (*0-306-80236-8*) Da Capo.

To Be Popular or Smart: The Black Peer Group. Jawanza Kunjufu. 100p. 1988. pap. 7.95 (*0-913543-10-1*) African Am Imag.

***To Be Read Later: Pregnancy.** Sheila Cole. Date not set. lib. bdg. write for info. (*0-688-12849-1*) Lothrop.

To Be Real: Telling the Truth & Changing the Face of Feminism. Ed. by Rebecca Walker. LC 95-14412. 336p. pap. 12.95 (*0-385-47262-5*, Anchor NY) Doubleday.

To Be Recorded. Gabriel Preil. Ed. by Stanley H. Barkan. Tr. by Estelle Gilson. (Review Jewish Writers Chapbook Ser.: No. 6). 48p. 1991. 15.00 (*0-89304-306-0*); pap. 5.00 (*0-89304-307-9*); audio 10.00 (*0-89304-310-9*); vhs 50.00 (*0-89304-311-7*) Cross-Cultrl NY.

To Be Recorded: Mini Book. Gabriel Preil. Ed. by Stanley H. Barkan. Tr. by Estelle Gilson. (Review Jewish Writers Chapbook Ser.: No. 6). 48p. 1991. 15.00 (*0-89304-308-7*); pap. 5.00 (*0-89304-309-5*) Cross-Cultrl NY.

To Be Saved In The Life Of Christ As Revealed In Romans. Witness Lee. 45p. 1.75 (*0-87083-528-9*, 07024001) Living Stream Ministry.

To Be So Loved. large type ed. Judy Chard. (Linford Romance Library). 1991. pap. 15.99 (*0-7089-7047-8*) Ulverscroft.

To Be the Best. Barbara Taylor Bradford. 496p. 1994. mass mkt. 6.50 (*0-06-100809-5*, Harp PBks) HarpC.

To Be the Neighbor of Saint Peter: The Social Meaning of Cluny's Property, 909-1049. Barbara Rosenwein. LC 88-47912. 264p. 1989. 39.95 (*0-8014-2206-X*) Cornell U Pr.

To Be Trustworthy. Slightly Off Center Writers Group Staff. (YA). (gr. 6-11). 1995. 7.95 (*1-56721-092-9*) Twenty-Fifth Cent Pr.

To Be Useful to the World: Women in Revolutionary America. Joan R. Gundersen. LC 96-36313. 1996. 28.95 (*0-8057-9916-8*, Twayne) Scribnrs Ref.

To Be Wanted at Christmastime & Other Yuletide Yarns. Gerald D. Sullivan. LC 91-61753. (Illus.). 104p. (Orig.). 1991. pap. 9.95 (*0-9644573-3-4*) Shamrock Sky Bks.

To Be Worthy. Donna F. Crow. LC 94-32231. (Cambridge Chronicles Ser.: No. 4). 256p. 1995. reprint ed. pap. 9.99 (*0-89107-809-6*) Crossway Bks.

To Be Young & Gifted. Ed. by Pnina Klein & Abraham J. Tannenbaum. LC 92-19814. 408p. 1992. pap. 42.50 (*0-89391-956-X*); text ed. 78.50 (*0-89391-839-3*) Ablex Pub.

To Be Young, Gifted & Black. Lorraine Hansberry. 272p. (J). (gr. 7). 1970. pap. 5.99 (*0-451-15952-7*, Sig) NAL-Dutton.

To Be Young, Gifted & Black. Lorraine Hansberry. 1989. pap. 4.95 (*0-317-02801-4*) NAL-Dutton.

To Be Young, Gifted & Black. Lorraine Hansberry. 1996. pap. 12.00 (*0-679-76415-1*) Random.

To Be Young Was Very Heavenly. Adickes. Date not set. text ed. 35.00 (*0-312-16249-9*) St Martin.

To Become a Fine Actor. Norman Sturgis. 93p. (Orig.). 1986. student ed., pap. text ed. 20.00 (*0-911455-03-5*) Quartz Pr.

To Become a Sage: The Ten Diagrams on Sage Learning by Yi Toegye. Tr. & Comment by Michael C. Kalton. (Neo-Confucian Studies). (Illus.). 256p. 1988. text ed. 49.50 (*0-231-06410-1*) Col U Pr.

To Become a Teacher: Making a Difference in Children's Lives. William Ayers. 264p. (C). 1995. text ed. 42.00 (*0-8077-3456-X*); pap. text ed. 17.95 (*0-8077-3455-1*) Tchrs Coll.

To Become As Little Children: Fairytales for Adults - for the Child in You. Gloria D. Benish. LC 94-91358. (Illus.). 210p. (Orig.). 1994. pap. 16.95 (*0-9636100-1-5*) Miracle MT.

To Become One: The Torah Outlook on Marriage. Ezriel Tauber. Ed. by Yaakov Astor. (Hashkafa Dialogue Ser.). 196p. (Orig.). 1990. pap. 10.00 (*1-878999-01-X*) Shelheves.

To Bed...or Else! Ewa Lipniacka. LC 91-22118. (Illus.). 32p. (J). (ps-3). 1992. 13.95 (*0-940793-85-7*, Crocodile Bks) Interlink Pub.

To Bed...or Else! Ewa Lipniacka. LC 91-22118. (Illus.). 32p. (J). (ps-3). 1996. pap. 7.95 (*1-56656-214-7*, Crocodile Bks) Interlink Pub.

To Bed...or Else! Ewa Lipniacka. (Illus.). 32p. (ARA.). (J). (ps-2). 1996. 16.95 (*1-85430-388-0*); 16.95 (*1-85430-389-9*); 16.95 (*1-85430-390-2*); 16.95 (*1-85430-391-0*); 16.95 (*1-85430-392-9*); 16.95 (*1-85430-393-7*) Talman.

To Bee or Not to Bee. John Penberthy. 119p. 1987. pap. 7.95 (*0-945153-13-9*) Sound Pub CO.

To Begin Again: Stories & Memoirs, 1908-1929(nf) M. F. K. Fisher. 192p. 1993. reprint ed. pap. 12.00 (*0-679-75082-7*) Pantheon.

To Begin at the Beginning: An Introduction to the Christian Faith. Martin B. Copenhaver. LC 94-3891. 312p. (Orig.). 1994. pap. 12.95 (*0-8298-0992-9*) Pilgrim OH.

To Begin With: A Friendly Book for Serious New Cooks. Madge Griswold. 400p. 1994. 49.95 (*1-883531-01-2*) Brght Forest.

To Believe in Jesus. Ruth Burrows. 1983. pap. 11.95 (*0-87193-154-0*) Dimension Bks.

To Believe Is to Exist. John R. Sheets. 1986. pap. 14.95 (*0-87193-247-4*) Dimension Bks.

To Believe Is to Pray: Readings from Michael Ramsey. Ed. by James E. Griffiss. LC 96-35831. 200p. 1996. pap. 11.95 (*1-56101-128-2*) Cowley Pubns.

To Believe or Not to Believe: Readings in the Philosophy of Religion. E. D. Klemke. 800p. (C). 1992. pap. text ed. 32.00 (*0-15-592149-5*) HB Coll Pubs.

To Benji with Love. Mary Wilson & Lee Blackwell. 140p. 1987. 14.95 (*0-910671-07-9*); pap. 7.95 (*0-910671-08-7*) Path Pr Chicago.

To Bethlehem with the Shepherds. Rolf Krenzer & Eleonore Schmid. 100p. (J). (gr. 1-7). 1989. 35.00 (*0-85439-300-5*, Pub. by St Paul Pubns UK) St Mut.

To Bid or Not to Bid: The Law of Total Tricks. 2nd ed. Larry Cohen. Ed. by Karen T. McCallum. 272p. reprint ed. pap. 12.95 (*0-9634715-0-3*) L Cohen NJ.

To Bind the Nation: Solomon kaDinuzulu & Zulu Nationalism, 1913-1933. Nicholas Cope. (Illus.). 328p. 1993. pap. 31.95 (*0-86980-888-5*, Pub. by Univ Natal Pr SA) Intl Spec Bk.

To Bind up the Wounds: Catholic Sister Nurses in the U. S. Civil War. Mary D. Maher. LC 89-2217. (Contributions in Women's Studies: No. 107). 188p. 1989. text ed. 45.00 (*0-313-26458-9*, MRM/, Greenwood Pr) Greenwood.

To Bizerte with the Two Corps, 23 Apr.-May 1943. (Armed Forces in Action Ser.). (Illus.). 90p. 1990. per. 6.50 (*0-16-019219-6*, 008-029-00207-8) USGPO.

To Blanche from Elmer with Love. Elmer Riggins & David Rathgeber. 46p. 1995. pap. 9.95 (*0-9635337-5-4*) Realty Res.

To Bless All Peoples: Serving with Abraham & Jesus. Gerald W. Schlabach. LC 91-15133. (Peace & Justice Ser.: Vol. 12). 104p. (Orig.). 1991. pap. 6.99 (*0-8361-3553-9*) Herald Pr.

To Blight with Plague: Studies in a Literary Theme. Barbara F. Leavy. 300p. (C). 1992. text ed. 40.00 (*0-8147-5059-1*) NYU Pr.

To Blight with Plague: Studies in a Literary Theme. Barbara F. Leavy. 300p. (C). 1993. pap. 18.50 (*0-8147-5083-4*) NYU Pr.

To Boldly Go: A Practical Career Guide for Scientists. Peter S. Fiske. LC 96-16850. 1996. write for info. (*0-87590-889-6*) Am Geophysical.

To Bounce or Not to Bounce. Naif Al-Mutawa. (Illus.). 32p. (J). 1996. 9.00 (*0-9651807-0-0*); pap. 15.00 (*0-9651807-1-9*) N AL-Mutawa.

To Boys Unknown. Bradford. 1995. per. 7.95 (*0-85449-092-2*, Pub. by Gay Mens Pr UK) LPC InBook.

To Break a Tyrant's Chains: Neo-Guerrilla Techniques for Combat. Duncan Long. LC 91-70479. (Illus.). 152p. (Orig.). 1991. pap. 15.00 (*0-939427-91-5*, 09053) Alpha Pubns OH.

To Breathe Free: Eastern Europe's Environmental Crisis. Ed. by Joan DeBardeleben. 266p. 1991. text ed. 34.50 (*0-943875-26-9*); pap. text ed. 12.95 (*0-943875-23-4*) Johns Hopkins.

To Breathe Freely: Risk, Consent, & Air. Ed. by Mary Gibson. 1985. 51.50 (*0-317-05232-2*) IPPP.

To Breathe Freely: Risk, Consent, & Air. Ed. by Mary Gibson. LC 84-22278. (Maryland Studies in Public Philosophy). 312p. (C). 1985. 56.50 (*0-8476-7416-9*) Rowman.

To Brecht & Beyond: Soundings in Modern Dramaturgy. Darko Suvin. LC 84-252. (Studies in Contemporary Literature & Culture). 296p. 1984. 44.00 (*0-389-20463-3*, N8024) B&N Imports.

To Brighten All Our Future Days: The Life of F. M. Petree & the Story of Oklahoma City University's Miracle on 23rd Street. Pamela Byrd-Mauldin. (Oklahoma Commerce & Industry Hall of Honor Ser.). (Illus.). 100p. (Orig.). (C). 1992. pap. text ed. 12.95 (*0-9623357-1-1*) Okla City Univ Pr.

To Brighten Your Day. Velma S. Daniels. LC 96-14346. (Illus.). 72p. (Orig.). 1996. pap. 5.95 (*1-56554-181-2*) Pelican.

To Bring Spring. George Keithley. (Kestrel Chapbks.). 36p. (Orig.). 1987. pap. 4.00 (*0-914974-46-7*) Holmgangers.

To Bring You Joy. large type ed. Essie Summers. (Romance Ser.). 368p. 1992. 25.99 (*0-7089-2722-X*) Ulverscroft.

To Build a Canal: Sault Ste. Marie, 1853-1854 & After. John N. Dickinson. LC 80-27693. (Illus.). 221p. 1981. 42.50 (*0-8142-0309-4*) Ohio St U Pr.

To Build a Fire. Jack London. (Creative's Classic Short Stories Ser.). (Illus.). 48p. (J). (gr. 6 up). 1980. lib. bdg. 13.95 (*0-87191-769-6*) Creative Ed.

To Build A Fire. Jack London. 1996. pap. 1.99 (*0-679-77202-2*) Random.

To Build a Fire & Other Stories. Jack London. (Bantam Classics Ser.). 400p. 1986. mass mkt. 5.50 (*0-553-21335-0*) Bantam.

To Build a Fire & The Mexican. Jack London. (Canto Bello Ser.: No. 4). 58p. 1989. reprint ed. 45.00 (*0-939489-06-6*) Engdahl Typo.

To Build a House: GEMS & the Thematic Approach to Teaching Science. Jacqueline Barber et al. Ed. by Lincoln Bergman & Carl Babcock. (Great Explorations in Math & Science (GEMS) Ser.). (Illus.). 72p. (Orig.). 1991. teacher ed., pap. 9.00 (*0-912511-77-X*) Lawrence Science.

To Build a Nigerian Nation. Noser Igiehon. 352p. 1985. 30.00 (*0-317-39408-8*, Pub. by A H S Ltd UK) St Mut.

To Build a Nigerian Nation. Noser Igiehon. 352p. 1987. 35.00 (*0-7223-0714-4*, Pub. by A H S Ltd UK) St Mut.

To Build a Ship. Don Berry. LC 60-5835. 1977. reprint ed. pap. 3.95 (*0-89174-029-5*) Comstock Edns.

To Build a Wall: American Jews & the Separation of Church & State. Gregg Ivers. 304p. (C). 1995. text ed. 37.50 (*0-8139-1554-6*) U Pr of Va.

To Build in a New Land: Ethnic Landscapes in North America. Ed. by Allen G. Noble. (Creating the North American Landscape Ser.). (Illus.). 512p. 1992. text ed. 68.00 (*0-8018-4188-7*); pap. text ed. 29.95 (*0-8018-4189-5*) Johns Hopkins.

To Build Peace, Respect Minorities. Veritas Publications Staff. 1989. pap. 21.00 (*1-85390-083-4*, Pub. by Veritas IE) St Mut.

To Build the Life You Want, Create the Work You Love: The Spiritual Dimension of Entrepreneuring. Marsha Sinetar. LC 94-40050. 1994. 18.95 (*0-312-11905-4*) St Martin.

To Build the Life You Want, Create the Work You Love: The Spiritual Dimension of Entrepreneuring. Marsha Sinetar. 224p. 1995. pap. 10.95 (*0-312-14141-6*, Griffin) St Martin.

***To Build, to Create, to Produce: Ephraim P. Ellison's Life & Enterprises, 1850-1939.** William G. Hartley. LC 96-47333. 1996. write for info. (*0-87905-750-5*) Gibbs Smith Pub.

To Burn a Witch. James L. Bray. 1963. 3.00 (*0-87129-419-2*, T32) Dramatic Pub.

To Bury a Cousin. Gus Weill. 1968. pap. 5.25 (*0-8222-1157-2*) Dramatists Play.

To Bury Our Fathers: A Novel of Nicaragua. Sergio Ramirez. Tr. by Nick Caistor from SPA. LC 84-61849. (Illus.). 250p. (Orig.). (C). 1985. pap. 11.95 (*0-930523-03-2*) Readers Intl.

***To Bury the Dead.** Brian A. Laird. 1997. 20.95 (*0-312-15224-8*) Thomas Dunne Bks.

To Buy a Groom. Rita C. Estrada. (Temptation Ser.: No. 413). 1990. pap. 2.65 (*0-373-25413-X*) Harlequin Bks.

To Byzantium. Stories. Andrew Fetler. LC 76-13854. (Illinois Short Fiction Ser.). 115p. 1976. 9.95 (*0-252-00584-8*) U of Ill Pr.

To California by Sea: A Maritime History of the California Gold Rush. James P. Delgado. (Illus.). 251p. 1996. pap. 14.95 (*1-57003-153-3*) U of SC Pr.

***To Call It Home: The New Immigrants of Southwestern Minnesota.** Joseph Amato et al. (Illus.). 120p. (Orig.). 1997. pap. 10.95 (*0-9614119-7-X*) Crossings Pr.

To Care Enough: Intervention with Chemically Dependent Colleagues; a Guide for Healthcare & Other Professionals. Linda R. Crosby & LeClair Bissell. 312p. 1989. text ed. 24.95 (*0-935908-49-8*, P036) Johnsn Inst.

To Care for Him Who Has Borne the Battle: Research Guide to Civil War Material in the National Tribune, Vol. 1. Richard A. Sauers. 130p. 1995. pap. 16.95 (*1-887561-00-5*) Sauers Hist Shop.

To Cariboo & Back in 1862. W. Champness. 106p. 1972. 18.95 (*0-87770-109-1*) Ye Galleon.

To Carol with Love. C. Bewes. 11.99 (*1-85792-112-7*, Pub. by Christian Focus UK) Spring Arbor Dist.

To Cartooning... Sixty Years of Magic. Jud Hurd. (Illus.). 300p. 1993. 39.00 (*0-9637218-0-1*) Profiles Pr.

To Cassandra - Early Years. rev. ed. Christopher A. Anderson. LC 93-74326. 157p. 1994. pap. 12.50 (*0-931353-37-8*) Andersons Pubns.

To Catch a Bass. Tim Coleman. (Illus.). 160p. (Orig.). 1992. pap. text ed. write for info. (*0-929775-04-X*) MT Pubns.

To Catch a Dream: Explorations of Dreaming. David Koulack. LC 90-31667. (SUNY Series in Dream Studies). 192p. 1991. text ed. 59.50 (*0-7914-0501-X*); pap. text ed. 19.95 (*0-7914-0502-8*) State U NY Pr.

To Catch a Flame. Kimberly Cates. Ed. by Linda Marrow. 320p. (Orig.). 1991. mass mkt. 5.99 (*0-671-68494-9*) PB.

To Catch a Flying Star: A Scientific Theory of UFO's. John Ackerman. (Illus.). 150p. 1989. pap. 15.00 (*0-912183-03-9*) Univelt Inc.

To Catch a Ghost. Day Leclaire. (Romance Ser.). 1993. mass mkt. 2.99 (*0-373-03285-4*, 1-03285-3) Harlequin Bks.

To Catch a King. Jack Higgins. 256p. 1990. mass mkt. 5.50 (*0-671-67616-4*) PB.

To Catch A King. Jack Higgins. 1995. pap. 16.95 (*0-7871-0031-5*, Dove Bks) Dove Audio.

To Catch a King. large type ed. Harry Patterson. 1981. 25.99 (*0-7089-0612-5*) Ulverscroft.

To Catch a Largemouth. Rod Teehan. LC 93-40074. 1993. 9.95 (*0-929775-05-8*) MT Pubns.

To Catch a Little Fish. Erica Farber & J. R. Sansevere. (Mercer Mayer's Creepy Critters Picturebacks Shape Bks.). (J). (ps-1). 1996. pap. 3.25 (*0-614-15724-2*) Random.

To Catch a Man: The Art of Finding Romance. Barbara Schrodt. LC 94-90838. (Illus.). 104p. (Orig.). 1994. pap. 7.99 (*0-9644814-0-5*) Freedm Hse.

To Catch a Mouse Make a Noise Like a Cheese. 3rd rev. ed. Lewis Kornfeld. (Illus.). 320p. (C). 1992. reprint ed. pap. 14.95 (*1-56530-004-1*) Summit TX.

To Catch a Playboy. large type ed. Elizabeth Duke. (Silhouette Ser.). 1996. 19.95 (*0-263-14417-8*, Pub. by Mills & Boon UK) Thorndike Pr.

To Catch a Rainbow. large type ed. Estelle Thompson. (Dales Large Print Ser.). 266p. 1995. pap. 17.99 (*1-85389-503-2*, Dales) Ulverscroft.

***To Catch a Star.** Florence McCarty. (Illus.). iv, 220p. (Orig.). 1996. pap. 15.95 (*0-943640-03-2*) High Valley Pr.

To Catch a Tartar: A Dissident in Lee Kuan Yew's Prison. Francis Seow. LC 94-60647. (Monograph Ser.: No. 42). 293p. (Orig.). 1994. pap. 22.00 (*0-938692-56-9*) Yale U SE Asia.

To Catch a Thief! Carin G. Baker. LC 92-39517. (Karate Club Ser.: No. 6). 144p. (J). (gr. 3-7). 1993. pap. 3.99 (*0-14-036291-6*) Puffin Bks.

To Catch a Thief. Debra Carroll. (Temptation Ser.). 1996. 3.50 (*0-373-25678-7*, 1-25678-3) Harlequin Bks.

***To Catch a Thief.** Musman. 1970. pap. text ed. write for info. (*0-582-52738-4*, Pub. by Longman UK) Longman.

***To Catch a Thief.** Francine Pascal. (Sweet Valley High Ser.: No. 133). (YA). 1997. mass mkt. 3.99 (*0-553-57067-6*, Sweet Valley) BDD Bks Young Read.

To Catch a Thief! Barbara Sobel. LC 87-81234. (J). (gr. 3-6). 1987. 7.59 (*0-87386-047-0*); 16.99 incl. audio (*0-317-55326-7*); pap. 1.95 (*0-87386-046-2*) Jan Prods.

To Catch a Tuna. Al Anderson. (Illus.). 160p. (Orig.). 1990. pap. 9.95 (*0-929775-03-1*) MT Pubns.

To Catch the Moon. Dinie Akkerman & Paul J. Van Loon. (Illus.). 24p. (J). (ps-1). 1993. 12.95 (*0-8120-6341-4*); pap. 5.95 (*0-8120-1559-2*) Barron.

***To Catch the Spirit: The Memoir of A. C. Aitken.** A. C. Aitken. 124p. 1996. pap. 29.95 (*0-908569-99-8*, Pub. by Drake Intl Serv UK) Intl Spec Bk.

To Catch the Summer Wind. Doris E. Fell. LC 96-26675. (Seasons of Intrigue Ser.: Bk. 5). 368p. (Orig.). 1996. pap. 9.99 (*0-89107-914-9*) Crossway Bks.

***To Catch the Wind: A Photographers Journey.** Stephen Kirkpatrick. Ed. by Marlo Sibley. LC 97-90236. (Illus.). 128p. 1997. 38.00 (*0-9619353-9-1*) Thy Marvelous Works.

To Celebrate: Reshaping Holidays & Rites of Passage. 6th ed. Eugenia Smith-Durland. (Celebration Catalogues Ser.). 224p. 1990. pap. 5.00 (*0-914966-05-7*) Alternatives.

To Celebrate & to Mourn: Liturgical Resources for Worshiping Communities Living with AIDS. Louis F. Kavar. 48p. 1989. pap. 3.95 (*1-888493-06-2*) Chi Rho Pr.

To Celebrate the Burning of Greenesborough. Thomas Campbell. Ed. by John A. Ishee. 136p. (Orig.). (YA). (gr. 9 up). 1994. pap. 10.00 (*0-9640625-0-X*) J M Emory.

To Chain the Dog of War: The War Power of Congress in History & Law. 2nd ed. Francis D. Wormuth & Edwin B. Firmage. LC 88-20808. 376p. 1989. text ed. 39.95 (*0-252-01622-X*); pap. text ed. 14.95 (*0-252-06068-7*) U of Ill Pr.

An Asterisk (*) at the beginning of an entry indicates that the title is appearing in BIP for the first time.

To Change Place: Aztec Ceremonial Landscapes. Ed. by David Carrasco. (Illus.). 272p. (C). 1991. text ed. 35.00 (*0-87081-194-0*) Univ Pr Colo.

To Change Places. Ron Wray. (Chapbook Series II: No. 3). 24p. 1980. pap. 2.50 (*1-880649-09-8*) Writ Ctr Pr.

To Change Them Forever: Indian Education at the Rainy Mountain Boarding School, 1893-1920. Clyde Ellis. LC 95-45423. (Illus.). 288p. 1996. 24.95 (*0-8061-2825-9*) U of Okla Pr.

To Chase a Dream. Margie North. 418p. (YA). (gr. 8-12). 1989. 14.95 (*0-934188-26-2*) Evans Pubns.

To Cherish All Life: A Buddhist Case for Becoming Vegetarian. Roshi P. Kapleau. LC 81-51149. (Illus.). (Orig.). 1981. pap. text ed. 5.00 (*0-940306-00-X*) Rochester Zen Ctr.

To China & Back. Anthony Bollback. LC 90-86214. (Jaffray Collection of Missionary Portraits: Bk. 4). (Illus.). 130p. 1991. pap. 8.99 (*0-87509-444-9*) Chr Pubns.

To China & Back. Grace Cutts. (Junior Jaffray Collection: Bk. 4). 27p. (J). (ps-2). 1991. pap. 3.99 (*0-87509-453-8*) Chr Pubns.

To China & Back: Being a Diary Kept Out & Home. Albert Smith. LC 73-94227. 101p. 1974. reprint ed. pap. 28.80 (*0-608-01394-3*, 2062155) Bks Demand.

To Choose a Future. Ronald G. Ridker & William D. Watson, Jr. LC 79-3643. (Resources for the Future Ser.). 1980. 37.00 (*0-8018-2354-4*) Johns Hopkins.

To Choose Freedom. Vladimir Bukovsky. (Publication Ser.: No. 344). 188p. (C). 1987. pap. 11.95 (*0-8179-8442-9*) Hoover Inst Pr.

***To Christmas with Love.** 2nd ed. Susie Whiting. 63p. (Orig.). 1996. pap. 3.95 (*0-9653276-0-4*) Whiting Family.

To Circumjack MacDiarmid: The Poetry & Prose of Hugh MacDiarmid. W. N. Herbert. LC 92-11695. (OxfordEnglish Monographs). 256p. 1993. 65.00 (*0-19-811266-1*, Clarendon Pr) OUP.

To Climb a Purple Mountain. Dianne M. Henderson. Ed. by William P. Lane & Lana Wegeng. (Illus.). 85p. 1996. 6.95 (*1-889463-04-3*) Golden Apple.

To Cling with All Her Heart to Him: The Spirituality of St. Clare of Assisi. Benet A. Fonck. LC 96-16339. 1996. pap. 10.95 (*0-8199-0973-4*) Franciscan Pr.

To Cock a Cannon: A Pilots View of World War II Through the Eyes of a Naval Aviator. D. A. Pattie. LC 82-91126. (Illus.). 164p. 1983. 7.95 (*0-911789-01-4*); pap. 4.95 (*0-911789-00-6*) Pattie Prop Inc.

To Collect the Flesh: Poems. Greg Hewett. Ed. by C. W. Truesdale. LC 96-67817. (Minnesota Voices Project Ser.: No. 73). 88p. 1996. pap. 12.95 (*0-89823-167-1*) New Rivers Pr.

To Come & See. Roland Faley. 158p. 1985. 5.95 (*0-8199-0867-3*, Frncscn Herld) Franciscan Pr.

To Come Home (To) Theodore Enslin. 4.00 (*0-318-11913-7*) Great Raven Pr.

To Come to Have Become. Theodore Enslin. 1966. pap. 8.00 (*0-685-00998-X*) Elizabeth Pr.

To Come to Life More Fully: An East-West Journey. 2nd ed. John G. Sullivan. (Illus.). 231p. 1991. pap. 16.00 (*0-912381-01-9*) Trad Acupuncture.

To Comfort the Bereaved: A Guide for Mourners & Those Who Visit Them. Aaron Levine. LC 93-39381. 288p. 1994. 30.00 (*1-56821-109-0*) Aronson.

To Comfort the Bereaved: A Guide for Mourners & Those Who Visit Them. Aaron Levine. LC 93-39381. 288p. 1996. pap. 27.50 (*1-56821-966-0*) Aronson.

***To Comfort the Dying: Pain Control in Advanced Cancer.** Charles O. O'Shaughnessy. Ed. by John R. Kirschner. (Illus.). 250p. (Orig.). 1996. pap. 21.95 (*0-9654910-0-5*) Lovejoy Hospice.

To Comfort the Heart: Women in the 17th Century America. Treckel. 1996. 15.95 (*0-8057-9923-0*, Hall Reference) Macmillan.

To Command the Sky: The Battle for Air Superiority over Germany, 1942-1944. Stephen L. McFarland & Wesley P. Newton. LC 91-9712. (History of Aviation Ser.). (Illus.). 344p. (C). 1991. 37.50 (*1-56098-069-9*) Smithsonian.

To Compose: Teaching Writing in High School & College. 2nd ed. Thomas Newkirk. LC 89-31484. 312p. 1989. pap. text ed. 25.00 (*0-435-08496-8*, 08496) Heinemann.

To Confess the Faith Today. Ed. by Jack L Stotts & Jane D. Douglass. 120p. (Orig.). 1990. pap. 10.00 (*0-664-25098-X*) Westminster John Knox.

To Conquer a Peace: The War Between the United States & Mexico. John E. Weems. LC 87-33510. (Military History Ser.: No. 7). (Illus.). 528p. 1988. 34.95 (*0-89096-330-4*) Tex A&M Univ Pr.

***To Constitute a Nation: A Cultural History of Australia's Constitution.** Helen Irving. (Studies in Australian History). 288p. (C). 1997. text ed. 64.95 (*0-521-58417-5*) Cambridge U Pr.

To Construct a Clock. John Taggart. 1971. 10.00 (*0-685-56658-7*) Elizabeth Pr.

To Construct Peace: Thirty More Justice Seekers, Peace Makers. Michael True. LC 91-65199. 208p. (Orig.). 1992. pap. 9.95 (*0-89622-487-2*) Twenty-Third.

To Continue. Randy Blasing. 75p. (Orig.). (C). 1983. pap. 5.95 (*0-89255-071-6*) Persea Bks.

To Count a People: American Jewish Population Data, 1585-1984. Jacob R. Marcus. LC 89-22458. (Illus.). 274p. (C). 1990. lib. bdg. 52.50 (*0-8191-7583-8*) U Pr of Amer.

To Count a Sheep. James A. Cook. LC 88-51777. 58p. (Orig.). 1990. pap. 6.00 (*0-916383-83-0*) Aegina Pr.

To Craft Democracies: An Essay on Democratic Transitions. Giuseppe Di Palma. 214p. 1990. 40.00 (*0-520-07213-8*); pap. 16.95 (*0-520-07214-6*) U CA Pr.

To Creature. Merrill Gilfillan. LC 75-9973. 40p. 1975. pap. 6.95 (*0-912652-12-8*) Blue Wind.

To Criticize the Critic & Other Writings. T. S. Eliot. LC 91-41601. 189p. 1992. reprint ed. pap. 8.95 (*0-8032-6721-5*, Bison Books) U of Nebr Pr.

To Cross a Line. Karen Ray. LC 93-11813. 160p. (YA). (gr. 7 up). 1994. 15.95 (*0-531-06831-5*); lib. bdg. 16.99 (*0-531-08681-X*) Orchard Bks Watts.

To Cross a Line. Karen Ray. 160p. (YA). (gr. 7 up). 1995. pap. 3.99 (*0-14-037587-2*) Puffin Bks.

To Cross the River Barriers. Brooks Ranney. (Illus.). 450p. 1987. 15.00 (*0-9618939-0-7*) B Ranney.

To Crown the Year: Decorating the Church Through the Seasons. Peter Mazar. LC 95-6923. 220p. (Orig.). 1995. pap. 19.00 (*1-56854-041-8*, CROWN) Liturgy Tr Pubns.

To Cuba & Back. Richard H. Dana, Jr. (Notable American Authors Ser.). 1992. reprint ed. lib. bdg. 75.00 (*0-7812-2615-5*) Rprt Serv.

To Dad. Helen Exley & Richard. (Things Kids Say Ser.). (Illus.). 62p. 1992. reprint ed. 8.99 (*1-85015-222-5*) Exley Giftbooks.

To Dance: Paintings & Drawings with Performance in Mind. Mary B. Edelson. (Illus.). 28p. (Orig.). 1984. pap. 5.00 (*0-9604650-1-4*) Edelson.

To Dance a Tango. Katrina Conway. (Rainbow Romances Ser.). 160p. 1993. 14.95 (*0-7090-4912-9*, Hale-Parkwest) Parkwest Pubns.

To Dance Is Human: A Theory of Nonverbal Communication. Judith L. Hanna. LC 87-13875. (Illus.). 351p. (C). 1987. pap. text ed. 18.95 (*0-226-31549-5*) U Ch Pr.

To Dance with Angels. Don Pendleton & Linda Pendleton. 1992. pap. 10.00 (*0-8217-3755-4*, Zebra Kensgtn) Kensgtn Pub Corp.

To Dance with Angels. Don Pendleton & Linda Pendleton. 400p. 1995. mass mkt. 5.99 (*0-8217-0095-2*, Zebra Kensgtn) Kensgtn Pub Corp.

To Dance with Angels. Don Pendleton & Linda Pendleton. 288p. 1996. pap. 12.00 (*1-57566-105-5*, Knsington) Kensgtn Pub Corp.

To Dance with Angels: An Amazing Journey to the Heart with the Phenomenal Thomas Jacobson. Don Pendleton. 400p. 1995. mass mkt. 5.99 (*0-7860-0095-3*, Pinncle Kensgtn) Kensgtn Pub Corp.

To Dance with God: Family Ritual & Community Celebration. Gertrud M. Nelson. 256p. 1986. pap. 12.95 (*0-8091-2812-8*) Paulist Pr.

***To Dance with the Devil: The New War on Breast Cancer.** Karen Stabiner. LC 96-36187. 512p. 1997. 25.95 (*0-385-31284-9*) Doubleday.

To Dance with the White Dog. Terry Kay. LC 90-41752. 192p. 1990. 18.95 (*1-56145-002-2*) Peachtree Pubs.

To Dance with the White Dog. Terry Kay. 192p. 1997. pap. 9.00 (*0-671-72673-0*, WSP) PB.

To Dance with the White Dog. large type ed. Terry Kay. LC 94-42281. 1995. 20.95 (*0-7862-0376-5*) Thorndike Pr.

To Dance with the White Dog. Terry Kay. Ed. by Jane Rosenman. 1993. reprint ed. mass mkt. 5.50 (*0-671-88365-8*) PB.

***To Date & Not to Date: On the Date & Status of Byzantine Law Books.** Thomas E. Van Bochove. xxx, 252p. 1996. pap. 57.00 (*90-6980-096-9*) Benjamins North Am.

To Declare God's Forgiveness: Toward a Pastoral Theology of Reconciliation. Clark Hyde. LC 84-60626. 188p. (Orig.). 1984. pap. 8.95 (*0-8192-1348-9*) Morehouse Pub.

To Defend Ourselves: Ecology & Ritual in an Andean Village. Billie J. Isbell. (Illus.). 289p. (C). 1985. reprint ed. pap. text ed. 11.95 (*0-88133-173-2*) Waveland Pr.

To Deliver Their Souls: The Struggle of a Young Rabbi During the Holocaust. Emanuel Frieder. Tr. by Rachel Rowen from HEB. LC 90-45727. (Illus.). 342p. 1991. 24.95 (*0-89604-144-1*, Holocaust Library); pap. 14.95 (*0-89604-145-X*, Holocaust Library) US Holocaust.

To Denmark, with Love. Judy Falck-Madsen. (Illus.). 212p. 1995. pap. 10.95 (*0-9647835-0-9*) Lola Pr.

To Desire Differently: Feminism & the French Cinema. Sandy Flitterman-Lewis. LC 95-26029. (Illus.). 384p. 1996. pap. 19.50 (*0-231-10497-9*) Col U Pr.

To Destroy Painting. Louis Marin. Tr. by Mette Hjort. (Illus.). 196p. 1994. pap. text ed. 15.95 (*0-226-50535-9*); lib. bdg. 39.95 (*0-226-50534-0*) U Ch Pr.

To Destroy You Is No Loss. Dorothea H. Bonneau. 37p. 1992. pap. 3.00 (*0-87129-150-9*, T86) Dramatic Pub.

To Destroy You Is No Loss: The Odyssey of a Cambodian Family. JoAn D. Criddle. 294p. 1996. pap. 16.95 (*0-9632205-1-9*) East West Bdg.

To Die a Little. large type ed. Catherine Carfax. 432p. 1986. 25.99 (*0-7089-1499-3*) Ulverscroft.

To Die Before Death: The Sufi Way of Life. M. R. Muhaiyaddeen. 260p. 1997. text ed. 23.00 (*0-914390-37-6*) Fellowship Pr PA.

To Die Before Death: The Sufi Way of Life. M. R. Muhaiyaddeen. 260p. 1997. pap. 17.00 (*0-914390-39-2*) Fellowship Pr PA.

To Die For. 1993. pap. write for info. (*0-451-18373-8*) NAL-Dutton.

***To Die For.** Peter Birch. (Crime & Passion Ser.). (Orig.). 1997. mass mkt. 5.95 (*0-7535-0034-5*, Pub. by Virgin Pub UK) London Brdge.

To Die For. Joyce Maynard. 368p. 1993. pap. 5.99 (*0-451-17327-9*, Sig) NAL-Dutton.

To Die For. Joyce Maynard. 1995. mass mkt. 5.99 (*0-451-18607-9*) NAL-Dutton.

To Die For. M. J. Rodgers. (Intrigue Ser.). 1993. pap. 2.89 (*0-373-22214-9*, 1-22214-0) Harlequin Bks.

***To Die For.** M. J. Rodgers. 1998. mass mkt. 4.50 (*0-373-81055-5*, 1-81055-5) Harlequin Bks.

To Die for Germany: Heroes in the Nazi Pantheon. Jay W. Baird. LC 89-45189. (Illus.). 350p. 1990. reprint ed. 35.00 (*0-253-31125-X*, MB757); reprint ed. pap. 15.95 (*0-253-20757-6*) Ind U Pr.

To Die for the People. Huey P. Newton. Ed. by Toni Morrison. (Illus.). 250p. 1995. pap. 14.95 (*0-86316-327-0*) Writers & Readers.

To Die Gallantly: The Battle of the Atlantic. Ed. by Timothy Runyan & Jan Copes. LC 94-10715. (C). 1994. pap. text ed. 24.00 (*0-8133-2332-0*) Westview.

To Die Game: The Story of the Lowry Band, Indian Guerillas of Reconstruction. W. McKee Evans. (Illus.). 296p. 1995. pap. 14.95 (*0-8156-0359-2*) Syracuse U Pr.

To Die in Babylon. Harold Livingston. 1995. mass mkt. 5.99 (*0-312-95315-1*) Tor Bks.

To Die in Chicago: Confederate Prisons at Camp Douglas, 1862-1865. George Levy. (Illus.). 325p. 1994. boxed 25.00 (*1-879260-20-4*) Evanston Pub.

To Die in Dinetah. John H. Truett. LC 94-12376. 256p. (Orig.). 1994. pap. 14.95 (*0-86534-225-3*) Sunstone Pr.

To Die in Latin. William Ryan. LC 94-10673. 1994. 19.95 (*0-89924-089-5*); pap. 9.95 (*0-89924-088-7*) Lynx Hse.

To Die Is to Live. John M. Scott. (Illus.). 119p. (Orig.). 1989. pap. 3.95 (*0-8199-0956-4*, Frncscn Herld) Franciscan Pr.

To Die Like a Gentleman. large type ed. Bernard Bastable. LC 93-45725. 1994. lib. bdg. 18.95 (*0-7862-0165-7*) Thorndike Pr.

To Die on Your Feet: The Life, Times & Writing of Praxedis Guerrero. Ward S. Albro. LC 96-20198. (Illus.). 224p. 1996. 25.00 (*0-87565-163-1*) Tex Christian.

To Die or Not To Die. Nathan Breslau. (Orig.). 1982. pap. 2.95 (*0-9610716-0-5*) N Breslau.

To Die Or Not to Die? Cross-disciplinary, Cultural & Legal Perspectives on the Right to Choose Death. Ed. by Arthur S. Berger & Joyce Berger. LC 90-34370. 208p. 1990. text ed. 49.95 (*0-275-93585-X*, C3585, Praeger Pubs) Greenwood.

***To Die Well: A Holistic Approach for the Dying & Their Caregivers.** Richard Roech. LC 97-1340. 1997. pap. text ed. 15.00 (*0-06-273511-X*, Harper Ref) HarpC.

To Dine Here. Kate Ellis. (C). 1990. 50.00 (*0-906887-52-6*, Pub. by Greville Pr UK) St Mut.

To Dine with Duke Humphrey. Leonard Walker. 1993. pap. 3.00 (*0-86025-409-7*, Pub. by Ian Henry Pubns UK) Empire Pub Srvs.

To Dine with the Blameless Ethiopians. Kemba S. Mazloomian. 112p. 1995. pap. 10.95 (*1-870989-67-8*) Bahai.

To Discover, to Delight: A Book on Creative Activities for Young Children. Joyce Bolton & Yvonne Wilson. 1977. 6.95 (*0-9602368-1-3*) D J Bolton.

To Disembark. Gwendolyn Brooks. 63p. 1981. pap. 6.95 (*0-685-04902-7*) Third World.

To Disembark. Gwendolyn Brooks. 1992. pap. 6.95 (*0-88378-102-6*) Third World.

***To Do & To Be: Portraits of Four Women Activists, 1893-1986.** Ann Schofield. LC 96-32143. (Illus.). 200p. 1997. text ed. 42.50 (*1-55553-294-2*); pap. text ed. 15.95 (*1-55553-293-4*) NE U Pr.

***To Do Doing Done.** Snead et al. LC 96-49403. 1997. pap. 11.00 (*0-684-81887-6*, Fireside) S&S Trade.

***To Do Good to My Indian Brethren: The Writings of Joseph Johnson, 1751-1776.** Ed. by Laura J. Murray. (Native Americans of the Northeast). 360p. 1998. 60.00 (*1-55849-126-0*) U of Mass Pr.

***To Do Good to My Indian Brethren: The Writings of Joseph Johnson, 1751-1776.** Ed. by Laura J. Murray. (Native Americans of the Northeast). 360p. 1998. pap. 19.95 (*1-55849-127-9*) U of Mass Pr.

To Do Justice & Right upon the Earth: Papers from the Virgil Michel Symposium on Liturgy & Social Justice. Ed. by Mary E. Stamps. 128p. (Orig.). 1994. pap. text ed. 9.95 (*0-8146-2167-8*) Liturgical Pr.

To Do No Harm: A Journey Through Medical School. Philip R. Reilly. LC 86-26576. 309p. 1987. text ed. 49.95 (*0-86569-162-2*, Auburn Hse); pap. text ed. 16.95 (*0-86569-163-0*, Auburn Hse) Greenwood.

To Do No Harm: DES & the Dilemmas of Modern Medicine. Roberta J. Apfel & Susan M. Fisher. LC 83-16803. (Illus.). 204p. 1984. 32.50 (*0-300-03192-0*) Yale U Pr.

To Do No Harm: DES & the Dilemmas of Modern Medicine. Roberta J. Apfel & Susan M. Fisher. LC 83-16803. (Illus.). 204p. 1986. pap. 14.00 (*0-300-03619-1*, Y-560) Yale U Pr.

To Do or Not to Do. Cobus Van der Merwe. 263p. (Orig.). 1995. pap. 14.99 (*0-9649944-0-2*) C van der Merwe.

To Double Business Bound: Essays on Literature, Mimesis, & Anthropology. Rene Girard. LC 78-8418. 249p. reprint ed. pap. 71.00 (*0-317-20488-2*, 2022995) Bks Demand.

To Double Business Bound: Essays on Literature, Mimesis, & Anthropology. Rene Girard. LC 78-8418. 256p. 1988. reprint ed. pap. text ed. 14.95 (*0-8018-3655-7*) Johns Hopkins.

***To Draw Closer to God: A Collection of Discourses.** Henry B. Eyring. LC 97-19434. 1997. write for info. (*1-57345-267-X*) Deseret Bk.

To Dream Again. Robert D. Dale. LC 81-65386. 1981. pap. 7.99 (*0-8054-2541-1*, 4225-41) Broadman.

To Dream Again. Laura L. Gehrke. 464p. 1995. mass mkt. 4.99 (*0-06-108167-1*, Harp PBks) HarpC.

To Dream of Dreams: Religious Freedom & Constitutional Politics in Postwar Japan. David M. O'Brien & Yasuo Ohkoshi. LC 95-45936. (Illus.). 312p. 1996. pap. text ed. 30.00 (*0-8248-1166-6*) UH Pr.

To Dream of Freedom. Roy Clews. 1988. 20.00 (*0-904864-95-2*, Pub. by Y Lolfa UK) St Mut.

To Dream of Gold Apples. large type ed. Jean M. Long. (Linford Romance Library). 320p. 1989. pap. 15.99 (*0-7089-6664-0*, Linford) Ulverscroft.

To Dream of Love. Marion Chesney. (Orig.). 1993. 19.00 (*0-7278-4429-6*) Severn Hse.

To Dream of Pigs: Travels in South & North Korea. Clive Leatherdale. 256p. 1995. 24.50 (*1-874287-02-3*, Pub. by Desert Island Bks UK) Hollym Intl.

To Dream the Perfect Organization. Joel Fort & Lothar Salin. LC 80-53829. (Illus.). 144p. (C). 1981. pap. text ed. 9.95 (*0-89914-005-X*) Third Party Pub.

To Dress & Keep the Earth: The Nurseries & Nurserymen of Geneva, New York. Paul F. Grebinger & Ellen Grebinger. LC 93-77814. (Illus.). (Orig.). 1993. pap. 10.00 (*0-9613821-5-5*) Geneva Hist Soc Mus.

To Drink of Death: The Narrative of a Shuar Warrior. Janet W. Hendricks. LC 93-13838. 316p. 1993. 46.00 (*0-8165-1353-8*) U of Ariz Pr.

To Drink or Not to Drink. Phillip G. Goudeaux. 159p. 1992. pap. text ed. 10.95 (*1-56550-004-0*) Vis Bks Intl.

To Drop a Dime. Paul Hoffman & Ira Pecznick. 1994. reprint ed. lib. bdg. 29.95 (*1-56849-529-3*) Buccaneer Bks.

To Duet or Not to Duet. (Babar Story Bks.). (Illus.). 48p. (J). 1990. 6.99 (*0-517-05195-8*) Random Hse Value.

To Dust Returneth. Scribner S. Kirk. LC 85-90458. (Illus.). 112p. (Orig.). (C). 1986. 27.95 (*0-9615668-1-7*); pap. 18.75 (*0-9615668-0-9*) Road Runner Pr.

To Dwell Among Friends: Personal Networks in Town & City. Claude S. Fischer. LC 81-11505. 464p. 1982. pap. text ed. 22.00 (*0-226-25138-1*) U Ch Pr.

To Dwell in the Palace: Perspectives on Eretz Yisroel. Tzvia Ehrlich-Klein. 1991. 18.95 (*0-87306-563-8*) Feldheim.

To Dwell Is to Garden: A History of Boston's Community Gardens. Sam B. Warner, Jr. (Illus.). 144p. 1987. text ed. 24.95 (*1-55553-007-9*) NE U Pr.

***To Dye For: The Rit Book of Creative Dyeing Projects.** Juliet Bawden. LC 96-39666. (Illus.). 112p. (Orig.). 1997. pap. 15.95 (*0-87951-785-9*) Overlook Pr.

To Each His Own. Kathleen Eagle. (Intimate Moments Ser.: No. 428). 1992. mass mkt. 3.39 (*0-373-07428-X*, 5-07428-1) Harlequin Bks.

To Each His Own. Bernadine King. (Orig.). 1996. pap. write for info. (*1-57553-290-5*) Watermrk Pr.

To Each Its Own Meaning: An Introduction to Biblical Criticisms & Their Applications. Ed. by Steven L. McKenzie & Stephen R. Haynes. LC 92-26563. 256p. (Orig.). 1993. pap. 16.00 (*0-664-25236-2*) Westminster John Knox.

***To Eat Flesh They Are Willing Are Their Spirits Weak? Vegetarians Who Return to Meat.** Kristin Aronson. LC 96-92415. 352p. (Orig.). 1996. 18.95 (*0-9626169-3-1*) Pythago Bks.

T

To Educate the Human Potential. 1990. write for info. (*81-900106-1-1*, Pub. by Kalakshetra Pubns II) N Montessori.

To Eliminate the Opiate: An In-Depth Study of Communist & Conspiratorial Group Efforts to Destroy Jews & Judaism. Marvin S. Antelman. (Judaica Ser.). 1992. lib. bdg. 79.95 (*0-8490-5346-3*) Gordon Pr.

To Embrace the Universe: Drawings by Frederic Edwin Church. Elaine E. Dee. LC 88-120547. (Illus.). 125p. (Orig.). 1984. pap. 5.00 (*0-943651-09-3*) Hudson Riv.

To Emma. Veda Magee. 250p. 1995. text ed. write for info. (*1-882194-14-4*) TN Valley Pub.

To Empower As Jesus Did: Acquiring Spiritual Power through Apprenticeship. Aaron Milavec. LC 82-6466. (Toronto Studies in Theology: Vol. 9). 345p. (C). 1982. lib. bdg. 99.95 (*0-88946-966-0*) E Mellen.

To Empower People: From State to Civil Society. 20th anniversary ed. Peter L. Berger & Richard J. Neuhaus. Ed. by Michael Novak. 230p. 1996. 24.95 (*0-8447-3944-8*) Am Enterprise.

To End All Segregation: The Politics of the Passage of the Civil Rights Act of 1964. Robert D. Loevy. 382p. (Orig.). (C). 1990. pap. text ed. 28.50 (*0-8191-7689-3*); lib. bdg. 58.00 (*0-8191-7688-5*) U Pr of Amer.

To End All War. Jerry Ahern. (Survivalist Ser.: No. 21). 1990. mass mkt. 2.95 (*0-8217-3144-0*, Zebra Kensgtn) Kensgtn Pub Corp.

To End All Wars: Woodrow Wilson & the Quest for a New World Order. Thomas J. Knock. (Illus.). 416p. 1992. 30.00 (*0-19-507501-3*) OUP.

To End All Wars: Woodrow Wilson & the Quest for a New World Order. Thomas J. Knock. LC 95-5425. 400p. 1995. pap. text ed. 16.95 (*0-691-00150-2*) Princeton U Pr.

To End the Arms Race: Seeking a Safer Future. David R. Inglis. LC 85-13938. 279p. reprint ed. pap. 79.60 (*0-7837-4717-9*, 2059069) Bks Demand.

To Enforce Education: A History of the Founding Years of the United States Office of Education. Donald R. Warren. LC 73-8209. 240p. reprint ed. pap. 68.40 (*0-7837-3784-X*, 2043603) Bks Demand.

To Enforce Education: A History of the Founding Years of the United States Office of Education. Donald R. Warren. LC 73-8209. 239p. 1985. reprint ed. text ed. 59.75 (*0-313-25213-0*, WAEE, Greenwood Pr) Greenwood.

To Engineer Is Human: The Role of Failure in Successful Design. Henry Petroski. 1992. pap. 13.00 (*0-679-73416-3*, Vin) Random.

To Enjoy Him Forever. rev. ed. Malcolm Webber. 160p. 1991. pap. 5.95 (*0-9626908-0-5*) Pioneer Goshen.

To Enlighten, Not to Frighten: A Comparative Study of the Welfare Movement in Liverpool & Philadelphia, 1890-1918. Susan T. Shoemaker. LC 91-24635. (Modern European History Ser.). 350p. 1991. text ed. 72.00 (*0-8153-0477-3*) Garland.

An Asterisk (*) at the beginning of an entry indicates that the title is appearing in BIP for the first time.

To Enrich & to Serve: The Centennial History of the University of Massachusetts. Mary H. Blewett & Christine McKenna. Ed. by Mary McGauvran & Gordon Osborne. LC 94-42358. 1995. write for info. (0-89865-925-6) Donning Co.

To Ensure Individual & Family Security Through Health Care Coverage for All Americans, 4 vols., Set. 1994. lib. bdg. 2,555.95 (0-8490-5818-X) Gordon Pr.

To Establish Constitutional Procedures for the Imposition of Capital Punishment. U. S. Congress Senate Committee on the Judiciary. LC 82-45653. (Capital Punishment Ser.). reprint ed. 40.00 (0-404-62434-0) AMS Pr.

***To Establish Peace: Being the Chronicle of Later Han for the Years 189 to 220 A.D.** Tr. & Anno. by Rafe De Crespigny. (Faculty of Asian Studies Monographs: Vol. 21). (Illus.). 690p. 1997. pap. text ed. 60.00 (0-7315-2537-X, Pub. by Aust Nat Univ AT) UH Pr.

To Establish Rational Criteria for the Imposition of Capital Punishment. U. S. Congress Senate Committee on the Judiciary. LC 82-45677. (Capital Punishment Ser.). reprint ed. 47.50 (0-404-62435-9) AMS Pr.

To Even the Score. LaJoyce Martin. LC 93-44338. 200p. (Orig.). 1994. pap. 7.99 (1-56722-016-9) Word Aflame.

To Everest Via Antarctica: Climbing Solo on the Highest Peak on Each of the World's Seven Continents. Robert M. Anderson. (Illus.). 224p. 1996. 29.95 (0-8117-1598-1) Stackpole.

To Every Birth Its Blood. Mongane Serote. (African Writers Ser.). 206p. (Orig.). (C). 1984. pap. 10.95 (0-435-90263-6, 90263) Heinemann.

To Every Birth Its Blood: A Novel. Mongane Serote. 368p. (Orig.). 1997. pap. text ed. 14.95 (0-86975-216-2, Pub. by Ravan Pr ZA) Ohio U Pr.

To Every Birth Its Blood: A Novel of South Africa. Mongane Serote. 208p. 1989. pap. 10.95 (0-938410-70-9) Thunders Mouth.

To Every Nation, Tribe, Language & People. Ernst H. Wendland. LC 91-68507. (Orig.). 1992. pap. 12.99 (0-8100-0424-0, 15N0542) Northwest Pub.

***To Every Nation under Heaven: The Acts of the Apostles.** Howard C. Kee. (New Testament in Context Ser.). 304p. (Orig.). 1997. pap. 24.00 (1-56338-221-0) TPI PA.

***To Every Season: Holiday Family Cookbook.** Zalben. (J). Date not set. pap. 19.95 (0-689-81797-5) S&S Childrens.

To Every Thing a Season: Shibe Park & Urban Philadelphia, 1909-1976. Bruce Kuklick. (Illus.). 249p. 1991. pap. text ed. 10.95 (0-691-02104-X) Princeton U Pr.

To Everything a Season. Marilyn Halvorson. 1994. 10.95 (0-7737-5539-X) Genl Dist Srvs.

To Everything a Season: Shibe Park & Urban Philadelphia, 1909-1976. Bruce Kuklick. (Illus.). 248p. 1991. text ed. 39.50 (0-691-04788-X) Princeton U Pr.

***To Everything a Season: Words That Touch the Heart.** Gaye Hughes. (Illus.). v, 64p. 1984. reprint ed. pap. 7.00 (0-614-29823-7) G Hughes.

To Everything There Is a Season. Jeneanne Sieck & Mary Bevis. (Illus.). 14p. (Orig.). 1987. pap. 3.95 (0-944884-02-4) Heartland Samplers.

To Everything There Is a Season. Margaret Tucker. 222p. 1988. per. 9.95 (0-89697-351-4) Intl Univ Pr.

To Everything There Is a Season: Development in the Context of the Lifespan. Jean Mercer. 584p. (Orig.). (C). 1991. lib. bdg. 71.00 (0-8191-8391-1) U Pr of Amer.

***To Everything There Is a Season: Haiku & Senryu.** Nancy H. Kline. 44p. (Orig.). 1997. pap. 3.00 (1-884257-18-6) AGEE Keyboard.

To Everything There Is a Season: The Adventures in Roberts Junction. Mary A. Jansen. 450p. (Orig.). 1996. pap. 8.00 (1-57502-152-8) Morris Pubng.

To Expand, We Divide: The Practices & Principles of Bunsha Management. Kunlyasu Sakai & David Russell. LC 93-10759. (ICG Pocketbusiness Bks.). 160p. 1993. 11.95 (1-881267-06-7) Intercultural.

To Face the Inscription. Natalie Safir. Ed. by Kathleen Iddings. LC 86-82506. 73p. (Orig.). 1987. per. 5.95 (0-931721-02-4) La Jolla Poets.

To Fall from Athletics Gracefully. Robert Pankey. 156p. 1993. per. 12.54 (0-8403-8962-0) Kendall-Hunt.

To Fall Like Stars. Nancy Asire. 384p. 1996. mass mkt. 5.99 (0-671-87727-5) Baen Bks.

To Father, with Love. Norman Vincent Peale et al. LC 94-35286. 128p. 1995. 10.00 (0-687-00833-6) Dimen for Liv.

To Fathom More: African American Scientists & Inventors. Edward S. Jenkins. LC 95-45159. (C). 1996. pap. text ed. 49.00 (0-7618-0215-0); lib. bdg. 69.00 (0-7618-0214-2) U Pr of Amer.

To Fear a Painted Devil. Ruth Rendell. 208p. 1987. mass mkt. 5.99 (0-345-34951-2) Ballantine.

To Fear the Light. Ben Bova & A. J. Austin. 448p. mass mkt. 6.99 (0-8125-2382-2) Tor Bks.

To Fear the Light. Ben Bova & A. J. Austin. 1996. pap. write for info. (0-614-05521-0) Tor Bks.

To Feed Their Hopes: A Book of American Women. John Sanford. LC 80-16505. 220p. 1980. 24.95 (0-252-00804-9) U of Ill Pr.

To Feed this World: The Challenge & the Strategy. Sterling Wortman & Ralph W. Cummings, Jr. LC 78-8478. 480p. 1978. pap. text ed. 19.95 (0-8018-2137-1) Johns Hopkins.

To Feed Thy Soul. Edith A. Mitchell. Ed. by Romaine Blakely & Virginia Whitman. LC 85-63084. (Illus.). 50p. (Orig.). 1985. pap. 9.95 (0-88100-051-5) Natl Writ Pr.

To Feel These Things. Leonard Michaels. LC 92-45611. 160p. (Orig.). 1993. pap. 12.00 (1-56279-040-4) Mercury Hse Inc.

To Fight Better. R. Roberts & G. Roberts. 1989. pap. 6.95 (0-946616-58-2) OMF Bks.

To Fight Hell. Nathaniel K. Haney. (Spiritual Warfare Ser.). 1992. pap. 6.00 (1-880969-00-9) Schl Prophet.

To Fight or Not to Fight. J. Paul Reno. 1984. pap. 1.99 (1-56632-012-7) Revival Lit.

To Fill the Skies with Pilots: The Civilian Pilot Training Program, 1939-46. Dominick A. Pisano. LC 92-29061. (Illus.). 224p. 1993. text ed. 34.95 (0-252-01994-6) U of Ill Pr.

***To Find a Friend.** Brian Jones. LC 96-86543. (Illus.). 64p. (Orig.). (J). (ps-4). 1996. pap. 4.95 (1-57733-006-4) B Dolphin Pub.

To Find a Way Home. P. M. Malone. (Deep Woods Trilogy Ser.: Bk. III). (Illus.). 200p. (Orig.). (J). (gr. 1-8). 1993. pap. text ed. 11.95 (0-9631957-2-7) Raspberry Hill.

***To Find Hope: Simple Wisdom for Those Who Grieve.** Karlene K. Ryan. LC 97-15027. 1997. write for info. (0-8091-3735-6) Paulist Pr.

To Find Something New: Studies in Contemporary Literature. Ed. by Henry Grosshans. LC 71-6605. (Illus.). 166p. reprint ed. pap. 47.40 (0-8357-8353-7, 2034101) Bks Demand.

To Find the Biggest Tree. Wendell D. Flint. (Illus.). 116p. (Orig.). 1987. pap. 4.95 (0-685-30049-8) Sequoia Nat Hist Assn.

To Find the Gold. Susan Ludvigson. LC 89-28159. 80p. 1990. pap. 7.95 (0-8071-1600-9); text ed. 14.95 (0-8071-1599-1) La State U Pr.

To Find the Way. Susan Nunes. LC 91-31334. (Illus.). 48p. (J). (gr. 4-8). 1992. 12.95 (0-8248-1376-6, Kolowalu Bk) UH Pr.

***To Fish in Common: the Ethnohistory of Lummi Indian Salmon Fishing.** Daniel L. Boxberger. LC 88-20705. 227p. 1989. reprint ed. pap. 64.70 (0-608-02681-6, 2063334) Bks Demand.

To Fly & Flight. Clarence E. Anderson. (Illus.). 384p. 1990. 19.95 (0-312-05171-9) St Martin.

To Fly Once More. Alice G. Hart. (Illus.). 128p. 1988. 15. 00 (0-87421-136-0) Utah St U Pr.

To Fly Through the Air: The Experience of Learning to Fly. Tom Morrison. LC 91-8191. 200p. 1991. 24.95 (0-8138-0348-9) Iowa St U Pr.

To Fly with the Swallows: A Story of Old California. Dana C. De Ruiz. LC 92-14416. (Stories of America Ser.). (Illus.). 53p. (J). (gr. 2-5). 1992. lib. bdg. 25.68 (0-8114-7234-5) Raintree Steck-V.

***To Follow Him: 7 MDarks of a Disciple.** Mark Bailey. LC 96-30049. 192p. (Orig.). 1997. pap. 11.99 (1-57673-035-2, Multnomah Bks) Multnomah Pubs.

To Follow in Jesus' Steps. C. Wayne Zunkel. 106p. 1991. pap. 5.00 (0-87178-847-0) Brethren.

To Follow the Goddess. Linda Cargill. LC 90-83559. 288p. (Orig.). 1991. pap. 9.95 (0-9627258-7-0) Cheops Bks.

To, for & about a Girl Named Reilly-Shea. Patricia Quill. (Orig.). 1996. pap. write for info. (1-57553-237-9) Watermrk Pr.

To Foreign Shores: U. S. Amphibious Operations in World War II. John Lorelli. LC 94-32014. (Illus.). 416p. 1995. 42.95 (1-55750-520-9) Naval Inst Pr.

To Forgive, Divine. Jack Neary. 1990. pap. 5.25 (0-8222-1159-9) Dramatists Play.

***To Forgive Is Human: How to Put Your Past in the Past.** Michael G. McCullough et al. LC 96-46371. 324p. (Orig.). 1997. pap. 12.99 (0-8308-1683-6, 1683) InterVarsity.

To Form a More Perfect Union: The Critical Ideas of the Constitution. Ed. by Herman Belz et al. (U. S. Capitol Historical Society, Perspectives on the American Revolution Ser.). xvi, 371p. (C). 1992. text ed. 35.00 (0-8139-1343-8) U Pr of Va.

To Form a More Perfect Union: The Federal Constitution & Pennsylvania. Paul E. Doutrich. (Illus.). 20p. 1986. pap. 1.95 (0-89271-039-X) Pa Hist & Mus.

To Form a More Perfect Union: The Ratification of the Constitution & the Bill of Rights, 1787-1791. Craig R. Smith. 242p. (Orig.). (C). 1993. pap. text ed. 24.00 (0-8191-9153-1); lib. bdg. 54.00 (0-8191-9152-3) U Pr of Amer.

To Form or Preserve a Government: The Presidency, Congress & Political Discourse. Ed. by Kenneth W. Thompson. LC 87-10426. (Exxon Education Foundation Series on Rhetoric & Political Discourse: Vol. 9). 104p. 1987. lib. bdg. 35.50 (0-8191-6340-6, Pub. by White Miller Center) U Pr of Amer.

To Fortune Born. Elizabeth E. Allen. 352p. 1988. mass mkt. 4.50 (0-446-35174-1) Warner Bks.

To Foster & Enrich: The First Fifty Years of the Saltire Society. George Bruce. 84p. 1986. 30.00 (0-85411-006-2, Pub. by Saltire Soc) St Mut.

To Foster Knowledge: A History of the University of Tennessee, 1794-1970. James R. Montgomery et al. LC 83-1050. (Illus.). 506p. 1983. text ed. 40.00 (0-87049-391-4) U of Tenn Pr.

To Foster the Spirit of Professionalism: Southern Scientists & State Academies of Science. Nancy S. Midgette. LC 91-7765. (History of American Science & Technology Ser.). 248p. (C). 1991. text ed. 32.50 (0-8173-0549-1) U of Ala Pr.

To Free a People: American Jewish Leaders & the Jewish Problem in Eastern Europe, 1890 to 1914. Gary D. Best. LC 81-4265. (Contributions in American History Ser.: No. 98). xi, 240p. 1982. text ed. 38.50 (0-313-22532-X, BTO/, Greenwood Pr) Greenwood.

To Free or Freeze. Leonard E. Read. 224p. 1972. 12.95 (0-910614-44-X) Foun Econ Ed.

To Free the Cinema: Jonas Mekas & the New York Underground. Ed. by David E. James. (Illus.). 352p. 1992. text ed. 59.50 (0-691-07894-7); pap. text ed. 21.95 (0-691-02345-X) Princeton U Pr.

To Freedom Condemned: A Guide to the Philosophy of Jean-Paul Sartre. Justus Streller. 128p. 1973. reprint ed. pap. 1.95 (0-8065-0363-7, Citadel Pr) Carol Pub Group.

To Generations Yet Unborn: Predicting the Future Today - Mutational Madness. Ricardo A. Scott. (Ras Cardo Speaks on Reggae Truths Ser.: Vol. GRTS7391). (Illus.). 65p. (Orig.). (YA). Date not set. pap. write for info. (1-883427-80-0) Crnerstone GA.

To Get a New Life. Christin Vaughn. 1994. 16.95 (0-533-11083-1) Vantage.

To Get & Beget. rev. ed. Neil B. Kimerer. 153p. 1996. pap. 19.95 (0-9648589-3-2) Sagacity Pr. This book discusses the physiological differences & similarities between men & women which came about because those differences complemented each other & had survival value. Those differences also form the patterns & fabric of society & culture regardless of the nature of the culture from primitive to "civilized," in any part of the world. Thus, the division of labor has survival value for the individual as well as species & societies & brings order out of chaos. We, the living are not able to distinguish which of the various attributes we possess are the ones which have survival value & which do not. Each of us is an experiment of nature, or of GOD, depending on your concepts. Social organizations, culture, politics, form of government, economic structure, family life, all reflect the division of labor between the genders. There is no such thing as "superiority" of one sex over another. It is a division of labor based on what each gender is best, or at least, able to accomplish. Both sexes have assets & limitations in reference to the other. Sagacity Press, 2800 N.W. 25th Street, Oklahoma City, OK 73107. $19.95 S&H $5.00 Wholesale prices comparable. ***Publisher Provided Annotation.***

To Get Clear. J. P. Ward. 59p. 8100. pap. 8.95 (0-907476-04-X) Dufour.

To Get Full, Get Empty. George L. Eisberg et al. (To Be Your Own Ser.). (Illus.). 60p. (J). (gr. 4-6). 1994. pap. 6.95 (1-56721-042-2) Twnty-Fifth Cent Pr.

To Gettysburg & Beyond: The Parallel Lives of Joshua Lawrence Chamberlain & Edward Porter. Michael Golay. 1994. 27.50 (0-517-59285-1, Crown) Crown Pub Group.

To Gettysburg & Beyond: The Twelfth New Jersey Volunteer Infantry, II Corps, Army of the Potomac, 1862-1865. Edward G. Longacre. LC 87-82809. (Illus.). 467p. (C). 1988. 36.00 (0-944413-06-4) Longstreet Hse.

To Gettysburg by Train: The Gettysburg & Harrisburg Railroad Co. Intro. by Walter L. Powell. (Illus.). 68p. (C). 1989. pap. text ed. 4.95 (0-939631-17-2) Thomas Publications.

To Gillian on Her 37th Birthday. 1984. pap. 5.95 (0-88145-022-7) Broadway Play.

To Give, & Give Again: A Christian Imperative for Generosity. Donald Hinze. LC 89-78180. 144p. (Orig.). 1990. pap. 10.95 (0-8298-0830-2) Pilgrim OH.

To Give & Take All. large type ed. Elizabeth Murphy. 754p. 1992. 25.99 (0-7505-0099-9) Ulverscroft.

To Give & to Hold. large type ed. Sarah West. (Linford Romance Library). 208p. 1996. pap. 15.99 (0-7089-7893-2, Linford) Ulverscroft.

To Give It Up. Pam Rehm. LC 95-15850. (New American Poetry Ser.: No. 16). 80p. 1995. pap. 9.95 (1-55713-212-7) Sun & Moon CA.

To Give Thanks & Praise: General Instruction of the Roman Missal with Commentary for Musicians & Priests. Ralph Keifer. 184p. reprint ed. pap. 7.95 (1-56929-005-9) Pastoral Pr.

To Give Them Light. Roman Vishniac. 1995. pap. 20.00 (0-684-80039-X, Touchstone Bks) S&S Trade.

To Give Them Light: The Legacy of Roman Vishniac. Roman Vishniac. (Illus.). 160p. 1993. 45.00 (0-671-63872-6) S&S Trade.

To Glorify & Enjoy God: A Commemoration of the Westminster Assembly. Ed. by John L. Carson & David W. Hall. 338p. 1994. 32.99 (0-85151-668-8) Banner of Truth.

To Glory We Steer. Alexander Kent. 1976. 23.95 (0-8488-0551-8) Amereon Ltd.

To Glory We Steer. Alexander Kent. 1993. reprint ed. lib. bdg. 25.95 (1-56849-026-7) Buccaneer Bks.

To Go Free: Iowa's Legal Heritage. Richard L. Acton & Patricia N. Acton. LC 95-19307. 382p. 1995. text ed. 39.95 (0-8138-2178-9) Iowa St U Pr.

To God Be All Glory. Agnes M. Palmer. (Illus.). (Orig.). 1988. write for info. (0-318-68750-X) Forest Hills.

To God Be All Glory: Mini-Biography (Authentic Excerpts) Agnes M. Palmer. (Illus.). 149p. (Orig.). 1987. 12.00 (0-9617983-1-9) Forest Hills.

To God Be All Glory: Totally Authentic Excerpts from the Life of Agnes Mae High Palmer. (Illus.). 124p. (Orig.). 1987. 12.00 (0-614-14362-4) Forest Hills.

To God Be the Glory. Lucile M. Campbell. (Orig.). 1981. pap. 1.95 (0-9607114-0-6) L M Campbell.

To God Be the Glory. Sharyn Harms. (Orig.). 1996. pap. write for info. (1-57553-258-1) Watermrk Pr.

To God Be the Glory. large type ed. Billy Graham & Corrie Ten Boom. 62p. 1985. reprint ed. pap. text ed. 4.95 (0-8027-2473-6) Walker & Co.

***To God Be the Glory: A Celebration of the Life of Bishop Frederick Calhoun James.** Mankekolo Mahlangu-Ngcobo. LC 96-75560. 82p. 1996. 15.95 (0-9652001-1-6) Mahlangu-Ngcobo.

***To God Be the Glory: A Composer's Journey into Grace.** J. A. Redford. LC 97-19487. 288p. (YA). (gr. 10). 1997. 18.99 (0-8010-1120-5) Baker Bks.

To God Be the Glory for the Miraculous Power of God Through the Singing Prophet. Lawrence Rolle. LC 95-62092. 87p. 1996. 7.95 (1-55523-777-0) Winston-Derek.

To God the Glory. Annalee Skarin. 196p. 1980. pap. 6.95 (0-87516-094-8) DeVorss.

To God Through Faith: From Christ to Sri Ramakrishna. Sri Surath. 1978. pap. 3.00 (0-685-58452-6) Ranney Pubns.

To God with Love. Ed. by Barbara B. Bartlett & Willaim S. Haynie. 140p. (J). (ps-7). 1995. spiral bd. 12.00 (0-9622553-6-X, 125-110) Selah Pub Co.

To God with Love. B. Bres. (C). 1988. 35.00 (0-85439-112-6, Pub. by St Paul Pubns UK) St Mut.

To God with Love & Sorrow. B. Bres. (C). 1988. 45.00 (0-85439-117-7, Pub. by St Paul Pubns UK) St Mut.

To Govern a Changing Society: Constitutionalism & the Challenge of New Technology. Ed. by Robert S. Peck. LC 89-39868. 228p. (Orig.). 1990. pap. text ed. 17.95 (0-87474-783-X) Smithsonian.

***To Govern a Nation, Vol. 1.** Daynes. Date not set. pap. text ed. write for info. (0-312-15413-5) St Martin.

To Govern America. Roger Hilsman. LC 78-19177. 610p. reprint ed. 173.90 (0-685-16292-3, 2027613) Bks Demand.

***To Grandma: With Love.** Claudine Gandolfi. (Deluxe Gift Editions Ser.). (Illus.). 61p. 1997. 8.99 (0-88088-115-1) Peter Pauper.

To Grandmother with Love: A Special Tribute. Margaret Mead. (Illus.). 96p. 1992. 15.00 (0-8362-8001-6) Andrews & McMeel.

To Grandmother's House We Go. Willo D. Roberts. LC 89-34972. 192p. (J). (gr. 3-7). 1990. lib. bdg. 16.00 (0-689-31594-5, Atheneum Bks Young) S&S Childrens.

To Grandmother's House We Go. Willo D. Roberts. LC 94-466. (J). 1994. pap. 3.95 (0-689-71838-1, Aladdin Paperbacks) S&S Childrens.

To Green Angel Tower. Tad Williams. (Memory, Sorrow & Thorn Ser.: Bk. 3). 1040p. 1993. 25.00 (0-88677-521-3) DAW Bks.

To Green Angel Tower, Pt. 1. Tad Williams. (Memory, Sorrow & Thorn Ser.: Bk. 3). 816p. 1994. mass mkt. 5.99 (0-88677-598-1) DAW Bks.

To Grow by Storybook Phonics Readers, Set. Janet Friend. (Illus.). (J). (gr. k-3). 1990. pap. text ed. 44.95 (0-910311-69-2) Huntington Hse.

To Grow in Spirit. Joe J. Christensen. viii, 81p. 1989. reprint ed. pap. 4.95 (0-87579-207-3) Deseret Bk.

To Grow in Wisdom: An Anthology of Abraham Joshua Heschel. Ed. by Noam M. Neusner & Jacob Neusner. 234p. 1990. 19.95 (0-8191-7464-5) Madison Bks UPA.

To Grow Spiritually. Charles A. Phillips. 312p. 1989. 9.95 (0-685-26989-2) C A Phillips.

To Gwen with Love: A Tribute to Gwendolyn Brooks. Ed. by Patricia L. Brown et al. LC 76-128546. (Illus.). 149p. (Orig.). 1971. pap. 1.95 (0-87485-044-4) Johnson Chi.

To Handmake a Saddle. J. H. Sheilds. (Illus.). 15.00 (0-87556-618-9) Saifer.

To Handmake a Saddle. J. H. Shields. 79p. (C). 1990. pap. 25.00 (0-85131-222-5, Pub. by J A Allen & Co UK) St Mut.

To Hasten the Homecoming: How Americans Fought World War II Through the Media. Jordan Baverman. 1995. 22.95 (1-56833-047-2) Madison Bks UPA.

To Hatred Turned. Ken Englade. 1994. mass mkt. 4.99 (0-312-95132-9) St Martin.

***To Have a Center.** Frithjof Schuon. 184p. (Orig.). 1996. pap. 12.95 (0-614-21245-6, 1239) Kazi Pubns.

To Have a Center. Frithjof Schuon. LC 90-388811. (Library of Traditional Wisdom). 110p. (Orig.). (C). 1990. pap. 12.00 (0-941532-09-7) Wrld Wisdom Bks.

To Have & Have Not. Ernest Hemingway. (Hudson River Editions Ver.). 272p. 1977. 40.00 (0-684-15328-9) S&S Trade.

To Have & Have Not. Ernest Hemingway. 272p. 1996. pap. 11.00 (0-684-81898-1) S&S Trade.

To Have & Have Not. Jules Furthman. Ed. & Intro. by Bruce F. Kawin. LC 79-5403. (Wisconsin-Warner Bros. Screenplay Ser.). 231p. reprint ed. pap. 65.90 (0-7837-4384-X, 2044124) Bks Demand.

To Have & Have Not: Southeast Asia Raw Materials & the Origins of the Pacific War. Jonathan Marshall. LC 94-13367. 1994. 28.00 (0-520-08823-9) U CA Pr.

To Have & to Hold. (Words of Comfort Ser.). (Illus.). 64p. 1993. 6.95 (0-7117-0525-9, Pub. by Jarrold Pub UK) Seven Hills Bk.

To Have & To Hold. Patricia Gaffney. 384p. 1995. pap. 5.99 (0-451-40535-8, Topaz) NAL-Dutton.

***To Have & to Hold.** Garborg's Publishing Staff. (Precious Moments Ser.). 1997. 7.99 (1-881830-58-6) Garborgs.

To Have & to Hold. Mary Johnston. (Airmont Classics Ser.). (J). (gr. 8 up). 1968. mass mkt. 1.95 (0-8049-0160-0, CL-160) Airmont.

To Have & to Hold. Mary Johnston. 1976. lib. bdg. 18.95 (0-89968-149-2, Lghtyr Pr) Buccaneer Bks.

To Have & to Hold. William Keyes, Jr. 46p. 1996. pap. 5.00 (1-885778-07-4) Seaburn.

To Have & to Hold. Fern Michaels. 1995. mass mkt. 6.99 (0-345-37329-4) Ballantine.

***To Have & to Hold.** Charlene Raddon. 448p. 1997. mass mkt. 4.99 (0-8217-5643-5, Zebra Kensgtn) Kensgtn Pub Corp.

To Have & to Hold. Sally Wentworth. (Presents Ser.). 1996. mass mkt. 3.25 (0-373-11787-6, 1-11787-8) Harlequin Bks.

An Asterisk (*) at the beginning of an entry indicates that the title is appearing in BIP for the first time.

To Have & to Hold. large type ed. Fern Michaels. LC 94-34296. 529p. 1994. lib. bdg. 25.95 (*0-7862-0336-6*) Thorndike Pr.

To Have & to Hold. large type ed. Sally Wentworth. (Harlequin Romance Ser.). 1995. lib. bdg. 18.95 (*0-263-14131-4*, Pub. by Mills & Boon UK) Thorndike Pr.

To Have & to Hold. Mary Johnston. 403p. 1977. reprint ed. lib. bdg. 16.95 (*0-89966-252-8*) Buccaneer Bks.

To Have & to Hold: A Celebration of Marriage. Ed. by Lois L. Kaufman. (Keepsakes Ser.). (Illus.). 56p. 1995. 13.99 incl. audio compact disk (*0-88088-884-9*) Peter Pauper.

To Have & to Hold: Achieving Lifelong Sexual Intimacy & Satisfaction. Robert Moeller. 256p. 1995. pap. 9.99 (*0-88070-679-1*) Multnomah Pubs.

To Have & to Hold: Love Triumphs in War. John Hendrix. 274p. (Orig.). 1996. pap. 14.95 (*0-614-17683-2*) Emrld City.

To Have & to Hold: Marriage, the First Baby, & Preparing Couples for Parenthood. C. F. Clulow. 168p. 1982. text ed. 21.00 (*0-08-028470-1*, Pergamon Pr); pap. text ed. 12.00 (*0-08-028471-X*, Pergamon Pr) Elsevier.

***To Have & to Hold: Organizing for Our Right to Marry.** Robert Bray. 1997. pap. 10.00 (*0-9652779-1-7*) Natl Gay & Lesbian.

To Have & to Hold: Slave Work & Family Life in Antebellum South Carolina. Larry E. Hudson, Jr. LC 96-13711. (C). 1997. 35.00 (*0-8203-1830-2*) U of Ga Pr.

To Have & To Hold: The Meaning of Ownership in the United States. Neala J. Schleuning. LC 96-24359. 256p. 1997. text ed. 59.95 (*0-275-95723-3*, Praeger Pubs) Greenwood.

***To Have & to Hold Vol. 1: A Wedding Keepsake.** Daphne R. Kingma. (Illus.). 96p. 1997. 27.95 (*1-57324-098-2*) Conari Press.

To Have & to Hold - the Cowboy & the Lady. Diana Palmer. (Diana Palmer Duets Ser.: No. 6). 1990. mass mkt. 3.25 (*0-373-48227-2*) Harlequin Bks.

To Have Or to Be? Erich Fromm. 240p. 1996. pap. text ed. 16.95 (*0-8264-0912-1*) Continuum.

To Have or To Harm: True Stories of Stalkers & Their Victims. Linden Gross. 224p. (Orig.). 1994. mass mkt. 5.99 (*0-446-36543-2*) Warner Bks.

To Have vs. to Hold. M. J. Rodgers. (Intrigue Ser.). 1996. mass mkt. 3.75 (*0-373-22392-7*, 1-22392-4) Harlequin Bks.

***To Have...to Hold: A Parents' Guide to Childbirth & Early Parenting.** 6th ed. Joyce L. Kieffer. LC 84-51100. (Illus.). 152p. 1996. pap. write for info. (*0-933794-08-8*) Train Res Corp.

***To Heal a People: Afrikan Scholars Defining a New Reality.** Ed. by Erriel K. Addae, pseud. LC 96-77308. 300p. (Orig.). 1996. pap. write for info. (*0-9644932-2-5*) Kujichagulia Pr.

To Heal Again: Toward Serenity & the Resolution of Grief. Rusty Berkus. (Illus.). 64p. (Orig.). 1996. pap. 19.95 (*0-9609888-2-3*) Red Rose Pr.

***To Heal As Jesus Healed.** rev. ed. Barbara S. Ryan et al. 112p. 1997. pap. 7.95 (*1-878718-36-3*) Resurrection.

To Heal Kent State: A Memorial Meditation. Kim Sorvig. LC 90-70127. (Illus.). 178p. 1990. pap. 14.95 (*0-9625938-0-X*) Worldview Pr.

To Heal the Earth. Robert F. Harrington. (Illus.). 352p. (Orig.). 1990. pap. 16.95 (*0-88839-242-7*) Hancock House.

***To Heal the Earth.** Norman. teacher ed., pap. 1.95 (*0-8358-0719-3*) Upper Room Bks.

***To Heal the Earth.** Quinn. 14.80 (*0-687-61154-7*) Abingdon.

To Heal the Earth. Frederick Quinn. 160p. 1994. pap. 9.95 (*0-8358-0702-9*) Upper Room Bks.

To Heal the Heart of a Child: Helen Taussig, M.D. Joyce Baldwin. 128p. (J). 1992. 14.95 (*0-8027-8166-7*); lib. bdg. 15.85 (*0-8027-8167-5*) Walker & Co.

***To Heal the Heart's Eye.** Patricia H. Easton. LC 97-8755. (Stafford Chronicles Ser.: Vol. 2). 220p. 1997. pap. 10.99 (*0-89283-951-1*, Vine Bks) Servant.

To Heal the Soul: The Spiritual Journal of a Chasidic Rebbe. Kalonymus K. Shapira. Ed. & Tr. by Yehoshua Starrett. LC 94-24519. 232p. 1995. 25.00 (*1-56821-306-9*) Aronson.

To Hear & Proclaim: Introduction to the Lectionary for Mass with Commentary for Musicians & Priests. Ralph Keifer. 184p. reprint ed. pap. text ed. 7.95 (*1-56929-004-0*) Pastoral Pr.

To Hear Gods Word Listed to the World. William E. Reiser. 144p. (Orig.). 1997. pap. 14.95 (*0-8091-3696-1*) Paulist Pr.

***To Hear Ourselves As Others Hear Us: Tape Recording As a Tool in Music Practicing & Teaching.** James Boyk. 88p. (Orig.). (C). 1996. pap. text ed. 9.95 (*0-918812-87-9*, SE0205) MMB Music.

To Hear Such Tunes. H. J. Adams. LC 93-71551. 64p. 1993. lib. bdg. 14.50 (*0-923687-27-0*) Celo Valley Bks.

To Hear the Angels Sing: An Odyssey of Co-creation with the Devic Kingdom. Dorothy Maclean. 230p. 1990. reprint ed. pap. 10.95 (*0-940262-37-1*) Lindisfarne Bks.

To Hear the Faint Bells: Short Poems. Milton Acorn. LC 96-25934. 1996. pap. 6.00 (*1-884206-01-8*) Unfinish Monumnt.

To Hear the Word: Invitation to Serious Study of the Bible. Milton P. Brown. LC 86-31082. 256p. 1987. 29.95 (*0-86554-251-1*, MUP H-216); pap. 14.95 (*0-86554-252-X*, MUP/P040) Mercer Univ Pr.

To Heaven & Back: (Heartbeat) Tracy Hughes. (American Romance Ser.). 1995. mass mkt. 3.50 (*0-373-16578-1*, 1-16578-6) Harlequin Bks.

***To Heaven & Back: True Stories of Those Who Have Made the Journey.** Rita Bennett. LC 97-14381. 192p. 1997. pap. 10.99 (*0-310-21078-X*) Zondervan.

To Heaven Via Walthamstow. Les J. Milchard. (C). 1989. pap. 35.00 (*0-7223-2268-2*, Pub. by A H S Ltd UK) St Mut.

To Heck with Deer Hunting. Jim Zumbo. (Illus.). 188p. 1992. 17.95 (*0-9624025-3-2*) Wapiti Valley Pub Co.

To Heck with Elk Hunting. Jim Zumbo. (Illus.). 184p. 1990. 17.95 (*0-9624025-2-4*) Wapiti Valley Pub Co.

To Heck with Gravy. Glenn Helgeland & Judy Helgeland. (On Target Ser.). 120p. (Orig.). 1984. pap. 12.95 (*0-913305-05-7*) Target Comm.

To Heck with Moose Hunting. Jim Zumbo. (Illus.). 208p. Date not set. 17.95 (*0-9624025-5-9*) Wapiti Valley Pub Co.

To Hell & Back. Audie Murphy. (Military Classics Ser.). (Illus.). 304p. 1988. 21.95 (*0-8306-4002-9*, 40002) McGraw-Hill Prof.

To Hell & Back. Maurice S. Rawlings. 288p. 1996. mass mkt. 5.99 (*0-7852-7534-7*) Nelson.

To Hell & Back. A. Murphy. 288p. 1996. reprint ed. 7.98 (*1-56731-116-4*, MJF Bks) Fine Comms.

To Hell & Back. Audie Murphy. 284p. 1995. reprint ed. lib. bdg. 24.95 (*1-56849-579-X*) Buccaneer Bks.

***To Hell & Back: Further Experiences of Bomber Command's War.** Mel Rolfe. (Illus.). 192p. 1997. 29.95 (*1-898697-70-1*, Pub. by Grub St Pubns UK) Seven Hills Bk.

To Hell & Back: Life after Death-Startling New Evidence. Maurice S. Rawlings. 1993. pap. 12.99 (*0-8407-6758-7*) Nelson.

To Hell & Back: Over the Brink. Eric Duncan. LC 95-83404. (Illus.). 103p. (Orig.). 1995. pap. text ed. 9.95 (*1-888347-00-7*) Donnchad.

***To Hell & Back Again.** Mayfair Games Staff. 1993. 20.00 (*0-923763-62-7*) Mayfair Games.

To Hell & Back with Dante: A Modern Reader's Guide to the Divine Comedy. Joseph Gallagher. LC 95-45527. 256p. (Orig.). 1996. pap. 14.95 (*0-89243-817-7*, Triumph Books) Liguori Pubns.

To Hell Or to Hobart: A New Insight into Irish Convict History. Patrick Howard. (Illus.). 196p. (Orig.). 1995. pap. 16.95 (*0-86417-668-6*, Pub. by Kangaroo Pr AT) Seven Hills Bk.

To Hell with Culture: And Other Essays on Art & Society. Herbert E. Read. LC 72-3370. (Essay Index Reprint Ser.). 1977. reprint ed. 18.95 (*0-8369-2918-7*) Ayer.

To Hell with Dying. Alice Walker. LC 86-27122. (Illus.). 32p. (J). (ps up). 1993. pap. 6.00 (*0-15-289074-2*) HarBrace.

To Hell with Optimism!! A Slash & Burn Satire. Stanley Berne. (Illus.). 197p. (Orig.). 1997. pap. 12.95 (*0-913844-22-5*) Risng Tide NM.

To Hell with Paradise: A History of the Jamaican Tourist Industry. Frank F. Taylor. LC 93-1004. (Latin American Ser.). (Illus.). 264p. (C). 1993. text ed. 39.95 (*0-8229-3754-9*) U of Pittsburgh Pr.

To Hell-with Unity. C. C. Jobe. Ed. by Susan Coman. (Illus.). 237p. 1993. pap. 12.95 (*0-9625495-2-5*) Magen-J Enterprises.

To Hellenikon, Studies in Honor of Speros Vryonis, Jr., 2 vols., Set. Ed. by John S. Langdon et al. 1018p. 1993. lib. bdg. 140.00 (*0-89241-504-5*) Caratzas.

To Hellenikon, Studies in Honor of Speros Vryonis, Jr., Vol. I: Hellenic Antiquity & Byzantium. Ed. by John S. Langdon et al. 474p. 1993. lib. bdg. 75.00 (*0-89241-512-6*) Caratzas.

To Hellenikon, Studies in Honor of Speros Vryonis, Jr., Vol. II: Byzantinoslavica, Armeniaca, Islamica, the Balkans, & Modern Greece. Ed. by Jelisaveta S. Allen et al. 479p. 1993. lib. bdg. 75.00 (*0-89241-513-4*) Caratzas.

To Help You Through the Hurting. large type ed. Marjorie Holmes. (Large Print Inspirational Ser.). 116p. 1985. pap. 12.95 (*0-8027-2508-2*) Walker & Co.

To Helsinki: The Conference on Security & Cooperation in Europe, 1973-75. 2nd ed. John J. Maresca. LC 87-22261. xv, 315p. (C). 1987. pap. text ed. 22.95 (*0-8223-0791-X*) Duke.

To Her Dark Skin. Percival Everett. 1990. 16.00 (*0-937669-45-8*) Owl Creek Pr.

***To Herland & Beyond: The Life & Work of Charlotte Perkins Gilman.** Ann J. Lane. LC 96-37487. 432p. 1997. reprint ed. pap. text ed. 17.50 (*0-8139-1742-5*) U Pr of Va.

To Him Be Praise. C. Berselli. (C). 1988. 39.00 (*0-85439-211-4*, Pub. by St Paul Pubns UK) St Mut.

To Him Who Conquers. Stephen Sanders. LC 73-111183. 210p. 1970. 24.95 (*0-385-06306-7*) Fellowship Crown.

***To Hire Or Not to Hire.** Emil R. Dragan. (Illus.). (Orig.). 1997. pap. 8.95 (*0-9632744-1-4*) Interview Cnslts.

***"To His Coy Mistress" & Other Poems.** Andrew Marvell. LC 96-45478. (Dover Thrift Editions Ser.). 64p. (Orig.). 1997. pap. text ed. 1.00 (*0-486-29544-3*) Dover.

To His Excellency Thomas Jefferson: Letters to a President. Jack McLaughlin. (Illus.). 384p. 1993. reprint ed. pap. 12.00 (*0-380-71964-9*) Avon.

To Hold a Mirror to Nature: Dramatic Images & Reflections. Ed. by Karelisa V. Hartigan. LC 81-40310. (Comparative Drama Conference Papers: Vol. 1). 176p. (Orig.). (C). 1982. pap. text ed. 26.00 (*0-8191-2276-9*) U Pr of Amer.

To Hold an Eagle. Justine David. (Intimate Moments Ser.). 1993. mass mkt. 3.39 (*0-373-07497-2*, 5-07497-6) Silhouette.

To Hold in My Hand: Selected Poems, 1955-1983. Hilda Morley. LC 83-40199. 213p. 1983. 16.95 (*0-935296-46-8*) Sheep Meadow.

To Hold This Ground: A Desperate Battle at Gettsburg. Susan P. Beller. LC 94-12775. (Illus.). 95p. (YA). (gr. 5 up). 1995. 15.00 (*0-689-50621-X*, McElderry) S&S Childrens.

To Hold This Soil. Russell Lord. LC 78-171385. (FDR & the Era of the New Deal Ser.). (Illus.). 124p. 1972. reprint ed. lib. bdg. 22.50 (*0-306-70384-X*) Da Capo.

To Hold Us Together: Seven Conversations for Multicultural Understanding. Linda Crawford et al. (Illus.). 133p. (Orig.). 1990. pap. 8.95 (*0-938541-07-2*) Origins Program.

***To Honor & Comfort: Native Quilting Traditions.** Ed. by C. Kurt Dewhurst & Marsha McDowell. (Illus.). 160p. 1997. 50.00 (*0-89013-316-6*) Museum NM Pr.

***To Honor & Comfort: Native Quilting Traditions.** Ed. by C. Kurt Dewhurst & Marsha McDowell. (Illus.). 160p. 1997. pap. 35.00 (*0-89013-317-4*) Museum NM Pr.

To Honor Jernej Kopitar: Paper in Slavic Philology, No. 2. Ed. by Rado L. Lencek & Henry R. Cooper, Jr. 1982. pap. 10.00 (*0-930042-46-8*) Mich Slavic Pubns.

To Honor Rene Girard: On the Occasion of His Sixtieth Birthday. (Stanford French & Italian Studies: Vol. 34). 380p. 1986. pap. 46.50 (*0-915838-03-6*) Anma Libri.

To Honor the Sacred Trust of Civilization. Dickson A. Mungazi. 320p. 1983. 24.95 (*0-87073-454-7*); pap. 18.95 (*0-87073-455-5*) Schenkman Bks Inc.

***To Honor the Sacred Trust of Civilization: History, Politics, & Education in Southern Africa.** Dickson A. Mungazi. LC 83-20084. (Illus.). 333p. reprint ed. pap. 95.00 (*0-608-05328-7*, 2065055) Bks Demand.

To Hope Again. Mark Finley & Steven R. Mosley. LC 93-40868. 1993. pap. 1.49 (*0-8163-1204-4*) Pacific Pr Pub Assn.

To Humanity with Love. 2nd ed. J. Sig Paulson. LC 74-33594. (Illus.). 124p. 1982. reprint ed. pap. 6.95 (*0-87516-484-6*) DeVorss.

To Hunt in the Morning. Janet Siskind. LC 73-82674. (Illus.). 224p. 1975. pap. 16.95 (*0-19-501891-5*) OUP.

To Hunt, to Shoot, to Entertain: Clericalism & the Catholic Laity. Russell B. Shaw. LC 93-78201. 201p. 1993. 12.95 (*0-89870-455-3*) Ignatius Pr.

To Hyphenate or Not to Hyphenate: The Italian - American Writer. Anthony J. Tamburri. 1991. pap. 10.00 (*0-920717-57-8*) SPD-Small Pr Dist.

To Illuminate Our Time: The Blacklisted Teleplays of Abraham Polonsky. Abraham Polonsky. Ed. by Mark Schaubert. LC 92-84081. 352p. (Orig.). 1993. pap. text ed. 20.00 (*0-9635823-0-5*) Sadanlaur Pubns.

To Illustrate That. A. Brown. 1995. 8.50 (*0-906731-85-2*, Pub. by Christian Focus UK) Spring Arbor Dist.

To Image & to See: Crow Indian Photographs by Edward S. Curtis & Richard Throssel, 1905-1910. Tamara Northern & Wendi-Starr Brown. LC 93-8625. (Illus.). 1993. 6.00 (*0-944722-14-8*) Hood Mus Art.

***To Improve Health & Health Care: Lessons from the Program of the Robert Wood Johnson Foundation.** Stephen L. Isaacs. LC 97-16892. 1997. pap. text ed. 18.95 (*0-7879-0909-2*) Jossey-Bass.

To Improve the Administration of Justice: A History of the American Judicature Society. Michal R. Belknap. LC 92-72983. 320p. (C). 1992. 14.95 (*0-938870-57-2*) Am Judicature.

To Independence & Beyond: Memoirs of a Colonial Commonwealth Civil Servant. Peter Snelson. (Illus.). 200p. (C). 1993. text ed. 39.50 (*1-85043-572-3*, Pub. by I B Tauris UK) St Martin.

To Infinity & Beyond: A Cultural History of the Infinite. Eli Maor. (Illus.). 1991. 49.50 (*0-8176-3325-1*) Birkhauser.

To Infinity & Beyond: A Cultural History of the Institute. Eli Maor. (Illus.). 294p. 1991. pap. text ed. 17.95 (*0-691-02511-8*) Princeton U Pr.

To Inform or to Control? The New Communications Networks. 2nd rev. ed. Oswald H. Ganley & Gladys Ganley. Ed. by Brenda Dervin. LC 88-7567. (Communication & Information Science Ser.). 280p. (C). 1989. text ed. 73.25 (*0-89391-510-6*) Ablex Pub.

To Interpret the Earth: Ten Ways to Be Wrong. Stanley A. Schumm. (Illus.). 180p. (C). 1991. text ed. 30.95 (*0-521-39507-0*) Cambridge U Pr.

To James Bond with Love. Mary W. Bond. LC 80-17134. (Illus.). 224p. 1980. 17.95 (*0-915010-28-3*) Sutter House.

To Jerusalem: Devotional Studies in Mystical Religion. R. Somerset Ward. Ed. by Susan Howatch. (Library of Anglican Spirituality Ser.). 200p. 1994. reprint ed. pap. 9.95 (*0-8192-1627-5*) Morehouse Pub.

***To Jesus, with Love.** Melinda Hardiman. 80p. (Orig.). 1996. pap. 6.95 (*1-57502-285-0*, PO989) Morris Pubng.

To Join Together: The Rite of Marriage. Kenneth W. Stevenson. 281p. 1992. pap. 14.95 (*0-8146-6084-3*, Pueblo Bks) Liturgical Pr.

To Journey with Christ: 1996 Adult Reunion Text. Laurie Gordon & Robert O. Slasor. LC 95-47258. (Illus.). 72p. 1996. reprint ed. pap. text ed. 8.50 (*0-8309-0727-0*) Herald Hse.

***To Joy My Freedom: Southern Black Women's Lives & Labors after the Civil War.** LC 96-51473. 1997. write for info. (*0-674-89309-3*) HUP.

To Kairwan the Holy. Alexander A. Boddy. 320p. 1985. 250.00 (*1-85077-069-7*, Pub. by Darf Pubs Ltd UK) St Mut.

To Keep & Bear Arms: The Origins of an Anglo-American Right. Joyce L. Malcolm. LC 93-26710. 246p. 1994. 32.50 (*0-674-89306-9*) HUP.

To Keep & Bear Arms: The Origins of an Anglo-American Right. Joyce L. Malcolm. 256p. 1996. pap. 16.95 (*0-674-89307-7*) HUP.

To Keep Art Alive: The Effort of Kenneth Hayes Miller, American Painter (1876-1952) Lincoln Rothschild. (Illus.). 208p. 1974. 40.00 (*0-87982-012-8*) Art Alliance.

To Keep from Singing. Edward Ingebretsen. LC 85-60238. (Orig.). 1985. pap. 7.95 (*0-89390-061-3*) Resource Pubns.

***To Keep Him.** Beth D. Nordby. LC 96-90880. 1997. 16.95 (*0-533-12209-0*) Vantage.

To Keep Moving: Essays Nineteen Fifty-Nine to Nineteen Sixty-Nine. Donald Hall. 1979. pap. 5.95 (*0-934888-02-7*) Hobart & Wm Smith.

To Keep the House from Falling In. Richard D'Abate. 39p. 1973. 2.95 (*0-87886-028-2*, Greenfld Rev Pr) Greenfld Rev Lit.

To Keep the Peace: The United Nations Condemnatory Resolution. William W. Orbach. LC 75-41989. 165p. reprint ed. pap. 47.10 (*0-7837-5793-X*, 2045459) Bks Demand.

To Keep You Company. John M. Wetterau. 48p. (Orig.). 1990. pap. 9.50 (*0-9626935-0-2*) Turtle Gal Edit.

To Keera with Love: Abortion, Adoption, or Keeping the Baby, The Story of One Teen's Choice. Connie K. Heckert. LC 87-62400. (Illus.). 190p. (Orig.). (YA). 1989. pap. 9.95 (*1-55612-072-9*) Sheed & Ward MO.

To Kill a Black Man. Louis Lomax. 256p. (Orig.). (J). 1989. mass mkt. 3.25 (*0-87067-731-4*) Holloway.

To Kill a Boss: A Mystery Jigsaw Puzzle Thriller. Alan Robbins. (BePuzzled Ser.). (Orig.). (YA). (gr. 7 up). 1994. 20.00 (*0-922242-60-7*) Bepuzzled.

To Kill a Cardinal. Michael Rumaker. 160p. 1992. text ed. 11.95 (*0-9632962-2-1*) A Mann Kaye.

To Kill a Coconut. large type ed. Patricia Moyes. 336p. 1981. 25.99 (*0-7089-0632-X*) Ulverscroft.

To Kill a Cop. Robert Daley. 400p. 1996. mass mkt. 6.50 (*0-446-36571-8*) Warner Bks.

To Kill a Husband: A Mystery Jigsaw Puzzle Thriller. Joan Hess. (Bepuzzled Ser.). (Orig.). (YA). (gr. 7 up). 1995. 20.00 (*0-922242-75-5*) Bepuzzled.

To Kill a Lawyer: A Mystery Jigsaw Puzzle. Alan Robbins. (BePuzzled Ser.). (YA). (gr. 7 up). 1993. 20.00 (*0-922242-54-2*) Bepuzzled.

To Kill a Man's Pride: And Other Stories from South Africa. 2nd rev. ed. Ed. by Marcus Ramogale. 272p. 1996. pap. text ed. 14.95 (*0-86975-460-2*, Pub. by Ravan Pr ZA) Ohio U Pr.

To Kill a Man's Pride & Other Stories from Southern Africa. Ed. by Norman Hodge. 226p. (C). 1984. pap. text ed. 14.95 (*0-86975-146-8*, Pub. by Ravan Pr ZA) Ohio U Pr.

***To Kill a Mockingbird.** Ed. by Harold Bloom. (Modern Critical Interpretations Ser.). 150p. (YA). 1997. text ed. 34.95 (*0-7910-4779-2*) Chelsea Hse.

To Kill a Mockingbird. Holt. 1989. student ed., pap. 10.00 (*0-03-023447-6*) HR&W Schl Div.

To Kill a Mockingbird. Harper Lee. 288p. 1988. mass mkt. 4.99 (*0-446-31078-6*) Warner Bks.

To Kill a Mockingbird. Harper Lee. Date not set. pap. 2.50 (*0-590-03001-9*) Scholastic Inc.

To Kill a Mockingbird. anniversary ed. Harper Lee. 323p. 1995. 17.00 (*0-06-017322-X*, HarpT) HarpC.

To Kill a Mockingbird. rev. ed. Christopher Sergel. 1970. pap. 5.95 (*0-87129-086-3*, T34) Dramatic Pub.

To Kill a Mockingbird. Harper Lee. 300p. 1991. reprint ed. lib. bdg. 22.95 (*0-89966-858-5*) Buccaneer Bks.

To Kill a Mockingbird: A Study Guide. Joyce Friedland & Rikki Kessler. (Novel-Ties Ser.). 1983. student ed., teacher ed., pap. text ed. 15.95 (*0-88122-033-7*) Lrn Links.

To Kill a Mockingbird (Lee) Milton. (Book Notes Ser.). (C). 1984. pap. 3.50 (*0-8120-3446-5*) Barron.

To Kill a Mockingbird Literature Guide. Patricia Watson. 96p. 1992. pap. text ed. 10.95 (*0-944459-53-6*) ECS Lrn Systs.

To Kill a Mockingbird Notes. Eva Fitzwater. 1984. pap. 4.25 (*0-8220-1282-0*) Cliffs.

To Kill a Mockingbird, Tender Mercies, & The Trip to Bountiful: Three Screenplays. Horton Foote. 240p. 1989. pap. 11.95 (*0-8021-3125-5*, Grove) Grove-Atltic.

To Kill a Mother-in-Law. (YA). (gr. 7 up). 1995. 20.00 (*0-922242-93-3*) Bepuzzled.

To Kill A Text: The Dialogic Fiction to Hugo, Dickens, & Zola. Ilinca Zarifopol-Johnston. LC 94-17242. 264p. 1995. 39.50 (*0-87413-539-7*) U Delaware Pr.

To Kill Again: The Motivation & Development of Serial Murder. Donald J. Sears. LC 90-19292. 175p. 1991. 24.95 (*0-8420-2378-X*) Scholarly Res Inc.

To Kill an Eagle: Indian Views on the Last Days of Crazy Horse. Edward Kadlecek & Mabell Kadlecek. LC 81-81580. (Illus.). 174p. 1991. reprint ed. pap. 9.95 (*0-933472-54-4*) Johnson Bks.

To Kill & Be Killed - Case Studies from Florida's Death Row. Kent Miller & Betty D. Miller. LC 88-32360. 118p. 1989. pap. 9.95 (*0-932727-23-9*); lib. bdg. 16.95 (*0-932727-24-7*) Hope Pub Hse.

To Kill & Kill Again. John Coston. (Illus.). 352p. (Orig.). 1992. pap. 5.99 (*0-451-40323-1*, Onyx) NAL-Dutton.

***To Kill for a Fortune.** Lewis P. Gravis. 260p. (Orig.). 1997. mass mkt. 4.99 (*1-55237-220-0*, Pub. by Comnwlth Pub CN) Partners Pubs Grp.

To Kill Hitler: The Officers' Plot, July 1944. Constantine FitzGibbon. (Illus.). 288p. 1994. 35.00 (*0-907590-48-9*, Pub. by SPA Bks Ltd UK) Seven Hills Bk.

To Kill or Not to Kill: Thoughts on Capital Punishment. William L. Clay, Sr. Ed. by Michael Burgess & Mary A. Burgess. LC 87-812. (Great Issues of the Day Ser.: No. 4). 208p. 1990. pap. 23.00 (*0-89370-431-8*); lib. bdg. 33.00 (*0-89370-331-1*) Borgo Pr.

To Kill the Leopard. Theodore Taylor. LC 92-36464. 1993. 21.95 (*0-15-124097-3*) HarBrace.

To Kill the Leopard. Theodore Taylor. 1995. mass mkt. 5.99 (*0-671-89025-5*) PB.

To Kill the Leopard. large type ed. Theodore Taylor. LC 93-40529. 1994. 22.95 (*0-7862-0149-5*) Thorndike Pr.

To Kill the Past. large type ed. Janet Laurence. 413p. 1996. 25.99 (*0-7505-0877-9*, Pub. by Magna Print Bks UK) Ulverscroft.

To Kill the Potemkin. large type ed. Mark Joseph. 528p. 1989. 25.99 (*0-7089-2039-X*) Ulverscroft.

To Kill the Shepherd. E. Paul Braxton. 256p. (Orig.). 1996. pap. 9.95 (*0-939017-03-2*) Hermit Pr FL.

To Kiss a Thief. Kate Moore. (Regency Romance Ser.). 224p. (Orig.). 1992. mass mkt. 3.99 (*0-380-76473-3*) Avon.

To Kiss, or Kill. large type ed. Day Keene. 1990. pap. 15.99 (*0-7089-6995-X*, Trailtree Bookshop) Ulverscroft.

To Kiss the Chastening Rod: Domestic Fiction & Sexual Ideology in the American Renaissance. G. M. Goshgarian. LC 91-55560. 256p. 1992. 32.50 (*0-8014-2559-X*) Cornell U Pr.

To Know a Fly. Vincent G. Dethier. 1962. pap. text ed. write for info. (*0-07-016574-2*) McGraw.

To Know a Library: Essays & Annual Reports, 1970-1976. Daniel Gore. LC 77-84769. (New Directions in Librarianship Ser.: No. 1). 379p. 1978. text ed. 55.00 (*0-8371-9881-X*, GTK/, Greenwood Pr) Greenwood.

To Know a River: A Haig-Brown Reader. Roderick L. Haig-Brown. Ed. by Valerie Haig-Brown. LC 96-8736. (Illus.). 352p. 1996. 29.95 (*1-55821-499-2*) Lyons & Burford.

To Know a Woman. Amos Oz. 1991. 19.95 (*0-15-190499-5*) HarBrace.

To Know a Woman. Amos Oz. 1992. pap. 8.95 (*0-15-690680-5*, Harvest Bks) HarBrace.

*__To Know a Woman.__ Amos Oz. 262p. 4.98 (*0-8317-7448-7*) Smithmark.

To Know As We Are Known: A Spirituality of Education. Parker J. Palmer. LC 92-54712. 144p. 1993. reprint ed. pap. 11.00 (*0-06-066451-7*) Harper SF.

*__To Know Christ.__ Eugene Torpey. (YA). 1987. pap. 2.75 (*0-89942-248-9*, 248/04) Catholic Bk Pub.

To Know Christ Jesus. Francis J. Sheed. LC 92-71935. 402p. 1992. reprint ed. pap. 14.95 (*0-89870-419-7*) Ignatius Pr.

To Know Each Other & Be Known: Women's Writing Workshops. Beverly Tanenhaus. 70p. 1982. pap. 5.00 (*0-934238-06-5*) Motheroot.

To Know for Real: Royce S. Pitkin & Goddard College. Ann G. Benson & Frank Adams. LC 87-19562. (Illus.). 250p. 1987. 20.00 (*0-912362-06-5*) Adamant Pr.

To Know G-D - Ye Yadaata. Shalom Dovbaer Schneersohn Obm. Tr. by Eliyahu Touger. 80p. 1993. 9.00 (*0-8266-0534-6*) Kehot Pubn Soc.

To Know God: A Five-Day Plan. Morris L. Venden. Ed. by Raymond H. Woolsey. 125p. pap. 2.99 (*0-8280-0220-7*) Review & Herald.

*__To Know God: Understanding the Nature of God.__ Steve Atwater. 1997. pap. text ed. 4.97 (*1-55748-977-7*) Barbour & Co.

*__To Know Her by Name: A Novel.__ Lori Wick. LC 96-51683. (Rocky Mountain Memories Ser.). 300p. (Orig.). 1997. pap. 9.99 (*1-56507-574-9*) Harvest Hse.

To Know Him by Name. Kay Arthur. 144p. 1995. 21.99 (*0-88070-733-X*, Multnomah Bks) Multnomah Pubs.

To Know Him...Is to Love & Praise Him! A Bible Study of God's Attributes. Beverly J. Doswald. LC 92-70785. 327p. (Orig.). 1992. pap. 14.85 (*0-938783-02-5*) Helpful Beginnings.

To Know, Love & Serve God. Thomas C. Reinecke. (Illus.). 200p. (Orig.). 1994. pap. write for info. (*0-9643291-0-7*) Faith Hope & Love.

To Know or Not to Know: Beyond Realism & Anti-Realism. Jan T. Srzednicki. LC 94-20319. (Synthese Library: Vol. 244). 240p. (C). 1995. lib. bdg. 116.00 (*0-7923-2909-0*, Pub. by Klwr Acad Pubs NE) Kluwer Ac.

To Know the Knower. Swami Muktananda. 44p. (Orig.). 1979. pap. 4.75 (*0-914602-91-8*) SYDA Found.

To Know the Moon. Ines Martinez. LC 93-84222. 238p. (Orig.). 1993. pap. 14.95 (*0-9636433-0-4*) Sandia Pr.

To Know the Place: Teaching Local History. rev. ed. Ed. by Joann P. Krieg & Natalie A. Naylor. LC 94-27055. 160p. (Orig.). 1995. pap. 10.00 (*1-55787-128-0*, NY71049) Hrt of the Lakes.

To Know the Stars. Guy Ottewell. (Illus.). 41p. (J). (gr. 3 up). 1983. pap. 8.00 (*0-934546-12-6*) Univ Wrkshop.

To Know Your Self: The Essential Teachings of Swami Satchidananda. Ed. by Philip Mandelkorn. LC 77-80901. 264p. 1988. pap. 9.95 (*0-932040-34-9*) Integral Yoga Pubns.

*__To Know Yourself: To Know Zen.__ Albert Low. 1997. pap. text ed. 16.95 (*0-8048-3119-X*) C E Tuttle.

To Lasso a Lady. Renee Roszel. (Romance Ser.). 1996. mass mkt. 3.25 (*0-373-03397-4*, 1-03397-6) Harlequin Bks.

To Lay down One's Life for You, Brother. M. J. McCarthy. 450p. (Orig.). 1994. pap. 12.95 (*1-885689-00-4*) Spread the Wrd.

To Lead & Manage. Jules Bellaschi. LC 80-83869. 70p. (Orig.). (C). 1980. pap. 4.95 (*0-9605144-0-6*) MJ Pubns.

To Lead As Equals: Rural Protest & Political Consciousness in Chinandega, Nicaragua, 1912-1979. Jeffrey L. Gould. LC 89-29790. (Illus.). xi, 377p. (C). 1990. 55.00 (*0-8078-1904-2*); pap. 17.95 (*0-8078-4275-3*) U of NC Pr.

To Lead Is to Serve: How to Attract Volunteers & Keep Them. Shar McBee. 208p. 1994. pap. 14.95 (*0-9638560-0-6*) S McBee.

To Learn & to Teach Your Life as a Rabbi. Alfred Gottschalk. (Illus.). (YA). (gr. 7-12). 1988. lib. bdg. 12.95 (*0-8239-0700-7*) Rosen Group.

To Learn with Love. William Starr & Constance Starr. 242p. 1976. pap. text ed. 11.95 (*0-87487-606-0*) Summy-Birchard.

To Leave This Port. Francis J. Enright. LC 88-81198. (Illus.). 300p. 1989. text ed. 19.95 (*0-9620291-0-6*) Enright Pub Co.

To Leeward. Francis M. Crawford. (Works of Francis Marion Crawford Ser.). 1990. reprint ed. lib. bdg. 79.00 (*0-7812-2527-2*) Rprt Serv.

To Lhasa & Beyond. Guiseppe Tucci. LC 87-16441. 193p. 1988. reprint ed. pap. 14.95 (*0-937938-57-2*) Snow Lion Pubns.

*__To Liberate & Redeem: Moral Reflections on the Biblical Narrative.__ Edward L. Long, Jr. LC 97-5601. 256p. (Orig.). 1997. pap. 18.95 (*0-8298-1176-1*) Pilgrim OH.

To License a Journalist? A Landmark Decision in the Schmidt Case. R. Bruce McColm. LC 86-18407. 1986. 13.50 (*0-932088-09-0*) Freedom Hse.

To Lie with Lions. Dorothy Dunnett. 640p. 1996. 27.00 (*0-394-58629-8*) Random.

To Life. Roe Halper. (Illus.). 104p. (Orig.). 1972. 18.00 (*0-916326-00-4*) Bayberry Pr.

To Life. Ruth M. Sender. LC 88-9312. 192p. (YA). (gr. 7 up). 1988. lib. bdg. 14.95 (*0-02-781831-4*, Mac Bks Young Read) S&S Childrens.

To Life! A Celebration of Jewish Being & Thinking. Harold S. Kushner. LC 92-36310. 320p. 1994. pap. 13.99 (*0-446-67002-2*) Warner Bks.

To Life: A Celebration of Jewish Being & Thinking. Harold S. Kushner. 1994. pap. write for info. (*0-446-36422-3*) Warner Bks.

*__To Life! A Celebration of Jewish Being & Thinking.__ Harold S. Kushner. 304p. 4.98 (*0-8317-6669-7*) Smithmark.

To Life! A Celebration of Jewish Being & Thinking. large type ed. Harold S. Kushner. 320p. 1994. pap. 14.95 (*0-8027-2680-1*) Walker & Co.

*__To Life! A Collection of Prayers from Ramtha.__ Compiled by Diane Munoz-Smith. (Illus.). 156p. (Orig.). 1997. pap. 15.95 (*0-9652621-4-6*) Horus Pubng.

To Life: The Story of a Chicago Lawyer. 2nd ed. Elmer Gertz. LC 89-19726. 320p. (C). 1990. pap. 16.95 (*0-8093-1608-0*) S Ill U Pr.

To Life! Yoga with Priscilla Patrick. Priscilla Patrick. LC 82-71187. (Illus.). 76p. (Orig.). 1982. pap. 9.95 (*0-943274-00-1*) SC Ed Comm Inc.

*__To Listen & Tell: Commentary on the Introduction to the Lectionary for Masses with Children.__ Kate Dooley. 83p. 1993. pap. 9.95 (*1-56929-014-8*) Pastoral Pr.

To Listen Is to Heal. Albert J. Nimeth. 126p. 1984. pap. 5.00 (*0-8199-0950-5*, Frncscn Herld) Franciscan Pr.

To Listen to a Child. T. Berry Brazelton. 1986. pap. 9.57 (*0-201-10554-3*) Addison-Wesley.

To Listen to a Child: Understanding the Normal Problems of Growing Up. T. Berry Brazelton. (Illus.). 192p. 1992. pap. 13.00 (*0-201-63270-5*) Addison-Wesley.

To Listen to a Child: Understanding the Normal Problems of Growing Up. T. Berry Brazelton. 1984. 15.95 (*0-201-10617-5*) Addison-Wesley.

To Listen, to Comfort, to Care: Reflections on Death & Dying. Barbara Backer et al. LC 93-26362. (Real Nursing Ser.). 187p. 1994. pap. 20.95 (*0-8273-6178-5*) Delmar.

To Live Again. Catherine Marshall. (Orig.). 1976. mass mkt. 4.95 (*0-380-01586-2*) Avon.

To Live Again. Catherine Marshall. 336p. (Orig.). 1994. pap. 8.00 (*0-380-72236-4*) Avon.

To Live Again. Catherine Marshall. LC 57-13338. (Catherine Marshall Library). 348p. (Orig.). (gr. 10). 1996. pap. 10.99 (*0-8007-9243-2*) Chosen Bks.

To Live Again. Noreen Riols. LC 95-7540. (House of Annanbrae Ser.: Bk. 2). 320p. (Orig.). 1995. pap. 10.99 (*0-89107-844-4*) Crossway Bks.

To Live Ancient Lives: The Primitivist Dimension in Puritanism. Theodore D. Bozeman. LC 87-27803. (Institute of Early American History & Culture Ser.). xi, 413p. (C). 1988. 45.00 (*0-8078-1785-6*) U of NC Pr.

To Live & Die in Dixie. (*0-8317-5441-9*) Smithmark.

To Live & Die in Dixie. Kathy H. Trocheck. 320p. 1994. mass mkt. 4.99 (*0-06-109171-5*, Harp PBks) HarpC.

To Live & Die in Dixie: A Regimental History of the Third Mississippi Infantry, C. S. A. Ed. by H. Grady Howell, Jr. LC 91-71649. (Illus.). 660p. 1995. 42.50 (*0-9606372-1-4*) Chickasaw Bayou.

To Live & Die in Dixie, & Other Poems. John Beecher. LC 66-28695. (Illus.). 1966. 5.00 (*0-911234-00-4*) Red Mtn.

To Live & Die with Dignity: A Guide to Living Wills. Samuel L. Peluso. Ed. by Mary L. Diecker. LC 91-75021. 160p. 1991. pap. 19.95 (*1-880254-01-8*) Vista.

*__To Live & Dream: The Incredible Story of George Foreman.__ unabridged ed. Ed McCoyd. (Illus.). 96p. (Orig.). (J). (gr. 5-9). 1997. pap. 6.99 (*0-9654118-0-X*) New Street.

To Live & to Write: Selections by Japanese Women Writers, 1913-1938. Ed. & Tr. by Yukiko Tanaka from JPN. Tr. by Elizabeth Hanson et al. from JPN. LC 87-4595. (Women in Translation Ser.). (Illus.). 225p. (Orig.). 1987. pap. 12.95 (*0-931188-43-1*) Seal Pr WA.

To Live As Brothers: Southeast Sumatra in the Seventeenth & Eighteenth Centuries. Barbara W. Andaya. LC 93-1347. 336p. (C). 1993. text ed. 38.00 (*0-8248-1489-4*) UH Pr.

To Live Each Day: Stories by People with Cancer. Walter Stratford. 80p. (Orig.). 1995. pap. 11.95 (*1-86407-068-4*, Pub. by JBCE AT) Morehouse Pub.

To Live Forever. Jack Vance. 256p. 1993. mass mkt. 3.99 (*0-8125-1142-5*) Tor Bks.

To Live Heroically: Institutional Racism & American Indian Education. Delores J. Huff. LC 96-12965. (SUNY Series, the Social Context of Education). 211p. (C). 1997. text ed. 54.50 (*0-7914-3237-8*); pap. text ed. 17.95 (*0-7914-3238-6*) State U NY Pr.

To Live in Dignity: Pierce County Labor, 1883-1989. Ed. by Ottilie Markholt. (Illus.). (Orig.). 1989. pap. 10.00 (*0-9624071-0-0*) Pierce Cty Labor.

*__To Live in France.__ James Bentley. LC 97-60323. (Illus.). 224p. 1997. 45.00 (*0-500-01796-4*) Thames Hudson.

*__To Live in Paradise.__ Renee R. Denis. LC 96-42545. 368p. 1996. pap. 15.95 (*1-882897-07-2*) Lost Coast.

To Live in Peace. large type ed. Rosemary Friedman. 1990. 25.99 (*0-7089-2315-1*) Ulverscroft.

*__To Live in the Center of the Moment: Literary Autobiographies of Aging.__ Barbara F. Waxman. LC 97-25380. (Age Studies). 224p. 1997. text ed. 36.50 (*0-8139-1757-3*) U Pr of Va.

*__To Live in the New World: A. J. Downing & American Landscape Gardening.__ Judith K. Major. (Illus.). 304p. 1997. 35.00 (*0-262-13331-8*) MIT Pr.

To Live in Time: The Sesquicentennial History of Mary Baldwin College. Patricia H. Menk. 500p. 1992. write for info. (*0-9633486-0-4*) M Baldwin Coll.

To Live Is Christ: An Interactive Study of Philippians. Thomas Jones & Sheila Jones. (Daily Power Ser.). 131p. 1995. pap. 6.99 (*1-884553-60-5*) Discipleshp.

To Live Is to Think: The Thought of Twentieth-Century German Philosopher Constantin Brunner. Hans Goetz. Tr. by Graham Harrison. 260p. (C). 1996. text ed. 45.00 (*0-391-03946-6*) Humanities.

To Live Like Princes: A Short Treatise from the Young Collection of Early Maryland Manuscripts. John D. Krugler. 1976. pap. 6.00 (*0-910556-12-1*) Enoch Pratt.

To Live Long Enough: The Memoirs of Naum Jasny, Scientific Analyst. Ed. by Betty A. Laird & Roy D. Laird. LC 75-33900. x, 190p. 1976. 19.95 (*0-7006-0140-6*) U Pr of KS.

To Live on Earth: Man & His Environment in Perspective. Sterling Brubaker. LC 75-185514. 202p. 1972. pap. 16.50 (*0-8018-1378-6*) Resources Future.

To Live or Not to Live. Nirad C. Chaudhuri. 197p. 1970. 6.50 (*0-317-42522-6*) Ind-US Inc.

To Live, to Teach, to Learn, to Love. Mark M. Porter. LC 91-90404. 113p. 1991. pap. 12.95 (*0-9629790-0-7*) Kenmark Ent.

*__To Live until We Say Goodbye.__ Kbler-Ross. 1997. pap. 15.00 (*0-684-83948-2*, Touchstone Bks) S&S Trade.

To Live with Grace & Dignity. Lydia Gans. LC 94-75105. 72p. 1994. pap. 34.50 (*0-614-02645-8*) LRP Pubns.

To Live with Honor & Die with Honor: The Warsaw Ghetto Underground Archives. Ed. by Joseph Kermish. 1989. 49.50 (*0-89604-094-1*, Holocaust Library) US Holocaust.

To Live with Hope, to Die with Dignity: Spiritual Resistance in the Ghettos & Camps. Joseph Rudavsky. LC 96-340. 1997. pap. write for info. (*1-56821-940-7*) Aronson.

To Live Within: A Woman's Spiritual Pilgrimmage in a Himalayan Hermitage. Lizelle Reymond. 271p. (Orig.). 1995. pap. 14.95 (*0-915801-54-X*) Rudra Pr.

To Long Tan: The Second in the Official History Series of Australia's Operations in Vietnam. Ian McNeill. (Illus.). 552p. 1993. 49.00 (*1-86373-282-9*, Pub. by Allen Unwin AT) Paul & Co Pubs.

To Look on Christ. Joseph C. Ratzinger. 120p. (C). 1990. 35.00 (*0-85439-330-7*, Pub. by St Paul Pubns UK) St Mut.

To Loose the Bands of Wickedness: International Intervention in Defense of Human Rights. Ed. by Nigel S. Rodley. 287p. 1992. 40.00 (*1-85753-047-0*, Pub. by Brasseys UK) Brasseys Inc.

To Lose a Battle: France Nineteen Forty. Alistair Horne. (Illus.). 1979. pap. 7.95 (*0-14-005042-6*, Penguin Bks) Viking Penguin.

To Lose a War: Memories of a German Girl. Regina M. Shelton. LC 82-5916. (Illus.). 228p. 1982. 19.95 (*0-8093-1074-0*) S Ill U Pr.

To Love. Jane Hwahu. Ed. by Joseph D. Adams. LC 94-67990. 96p. (Orig.). 1995. pap. text ed. 10.95 (*1-880016-18-4*) Road Pubs.

To Love a Bent Winged Angel. LaJoyce Martin. LC 86-7820. (Pioneer Trilogy Ser.: Bk. 1). (Illus.). 288p. (Orig.). 1986. pap. 7.99 (*0-912315-99-7*) Word Aflame.

To Love a Child: A Reluctant Father Adopts a "Forgotten" Child. Ted Schwarz. 256p. 1995. 21.95 (*0-88282-136-9*) New Horizon NJ.

To Love a Dark Lord. Anne Stuart. 416p. (Orig.). 1994. mass mkt. 4.99 (*0-380-77604-9*) Avon.

*__To Love a Dark Stranger.__ Colleen Faulkner. 384p. 1997. mass mkt. 5.50 (*0-8217-5626-5*, Zebra Kensgtn) Kensgtn Pub Corp.

To Love a Dreamer. Ruth R. Langan. (Men Made in America Ser.). 1994. pap. 3.99 (*0-373-45192-X*, 1-45192-1) Harlequin Bks.

To Love a Man. Karen Robards. 384p. 1988. mass mkt. 5.99 (*0-446-35350-7*) Warner Bks.

To Love a Muslim. Ed Challen. 1988. pap. 3.99 (*0-946462-15-1*, Pub. by Evangelical Pr) Presby & Reformed.

To Love a Pirate. Virginia Nielsen. (Historical Ser.). 1993. mass mkt. 3.99 (*0-373-28761-5*, 1-28761-4) Harlequin Bks.

To Love a Runaway. LaJoyce Martin. LC 88-31620. 240p. (Orig.). 1989. pap. 7.99 (*0-932581-42-0*) Word Aflame.

To Love a Stranger. Elaine Barbieri. 1995. pap. 17.95 (*0-8217-5301-0*) NAL-Dutton.

*__To Love a Stranger.__ Connie Mason. 1997. mass mkt. 5.99 (*0-380-79340-7*) Avon.

To Love a Stranger. Marjorie Shoebridge. 352p. (Orig.). 1990. mass mkt. 3.95 (*0-445-21006-0*, Mysterious Paperbk) Warner Bks.

To Love a Thief. Margaret St. George. (Weddings by DeWilde Ser.). 1996. mass mkt. 4.50 (*0-373-82542-0*) Harlequin Bks.

To Love a Virginian. Mary W. Buxton. 200p. 1991. pap. 9.95 (*1-880902-03-6*) Rappahannock Pr.

To Love a Whale: Learning about Endangered Animals from the Young & Young-at-Heart. Ed. by Frances B. Cowden. LC 95-76847. (Illus.). 116p. (Orig.). (J). (gr. 3-9). 1995. per., pap. 11.95 (*1-884289-06-1*) Grandmother Erth.

To Love Again. Evelyn Kennedy. 288p. (Orig.). 1991. pap. 9.95 (*0-941483-85-1*) Naiad Pr.

To Love Again. Marian Oaks. 1992. mass mkt. 4.50 (*0-8217-3668-X*, Zebra Kensgtn) Kensgtn Pub Corp.

To Love Again. Danielle Steel. 304p. (Orig.). 1981. mass mkt. 6.50 (*0-440-18656-0*) Dell.

To Love Again. large type ed. Marian Oaks. LC 93-26491. 1993. lib. bdg. 17.95 (*0-7862-0019-7*) Thorndike Pr.

To Love Again: Intimate Relationships After 60. Florence B. Mason. LC 89-1463. 132p. 1989. pap. 7.95 (*0-933469-05-5*) Gateway Bks.

To Love Again: Lovers & Friends. Claire Bocardo. 512p. 1995. mass mkt. 4.99 (*0-8217-4839-4*, Zebra Kensgtn) Kensgtn Pub Corp.

*__To Love & Be Loved.__ Sam Keen. LC 96-52610. 256p. 1997. 21.95 (*0-553-08904-8*) Bantam.

To Love & Be Loved by Jesus: Mark see Our Sunday Visitor's Popular Bible Study Series

To Love & Be Wise. Josephine Tey. (Josephine Tey Mysteries Ser.). 208p. 1988. pap. 6.00 (*0-02-078060-5*) Macmillan.

To Love & Be Wise. Josephine Tey. 1987. pap. 3.95 (*0-671-64547-1*) PB.

To Love & Cherish & Storm Clouds over Chantel, 2 bks. in 1. Colleen L. Reece. (Romance Reader Ser.: No. 4). 7.95 (*1-55748-132-6*) Barbour & Co.

To Love & Honour. Jean Saunders. 400p. 1993. lib. bdg. 22.00 (*0-7278-4408-3*) Severn Hse.

To Love & Honour. large type ed. Jean A. Saunders. 781p. 1993. 25.99 (*0-7505-0508-7*, Pub. by Magna Print Bks UK) Ulverscroft.

To Love & Serve: Lectionary-Based Meditations, Year C. Gerald Darring. 84p. (Orig.). 1994. pap. 6.95 (*1-55612-700-6*) Sheed & Ward MO.

To Love & Serve: Lectionary-Based Meditations, Year A. Gerald Darring. 84p. (Orig.). 1994. pap. 6.95 (*1-55612-701-4*) Sheed & Ward MO.

To Love & Serve: Lectionary-Based Meditations Year B. Gerald Darring. 88p. (Orig.). 1993. pap. 6.95 (*1-55612-672-7*) Sheed & Ward MO.

To Love & to Cherish. Patricia Gaffney. 400p. (Orig.). 1995. pap. 5.50 (*0-451-40533-1*, Topaz) NAL-Dutton.

To Love & to Cherish. Leah Laiman. 1994. mass mkt. 5.50 (*0-671-86484-X*) PB.

*__To Love & to Cherish: Brides Remembered.__ Linda O. Lipsett. LC 96-33616. 1997. 24.95 (*0-8442-2651-3*) Quilt Digest Pr.

To Love & to Cherish: The Great American Wedding. Amy McKune. (Illus.). 21p. 1991. pap. 4.65 (*0-943924-16-2*) Mus Stony Brook.

To Love & to Honor: A Pre-Marriage Ministry Resource Manual. Liturgical Commission Publishings Diocese of Lansing Staff. Ed. by Myron Hawkins. 235p. (Orig.). (C). 1983. ring bd. 25.00 (*0-685-28963-X*) Lit Comm Pubs.

To Love As God Loves: Conversations with the Early Church. Roberta C. Bondi. LC 86-46421. 112p. 1987. pap. 11.00 (*0-8006-2041-0*, 1-2041, Fortress Pr) Augsburg Fortress.

To Love As We Are Loved: The Bible & Relationships. Bruce C. Birch. 128p. (Orig.). 1992. pap. 8.95 (*0-687-42188-8*) Abingdon.

To Love As You Are Loved: The Christian Education for Adults. Janet C. Irwin & John M. Hines. 104p. (Orig.). 1993. pap. 3.95 (*0-88028-138-3*, 1197) Forward Movement.

To Love Delilah: Claiming the Women of the Bible. Mary Cartledge-Hayes. LC 90-35856. (Illus.). 96p. (Orig.). 1990. pap. 10.95 (*0-931055-68-7*) Innisfree Pr.

To Love Fasting: The Monastic Experience. Adalbert De Vogue. Tr. by John B. Houde from FRE. 186p. (Orig.). 1993. pap. 10.95 (*0-932506-87-9*) St Bedes Pubns.

To Love, Honor, & Obey in Colonial Mexico: Conflicts over Marriage Choice, 1574-1821. Patricia Seed. xii, 320p. (C). pap. 16.95 (*0-8047-2159-9*) Stanford U Pr.

To Love, Honor, & Obey in Colonial Mexico: Conflicts over Marriage Choice, 1574-1821. Patricia Seed. LC 88-2374. 333p. 1988. 47.50 (*0-8047-1457-6*) Stanford U Pr.

To Love Is to Be Happy. Barry N. Kaufman. 1985. mass mkt. 5.99 (*0-449-21119-3*) Fawcett.

To Love Is to Give. Perry Tanksley. 4.50 (*0-686-15527-0*) Allgood Bks.

To Love Is to Live. Spiros Zodhiates. 369p. 1967. pap. 8.99 (*0-89957-503-X*) AMG Pubs.

To Love Is to Live: Building Bridges of Understanding. 264p. 1994. text ed. 50.00 (*0-89716-506-3*); pap. text ed. 25.00 (*0-89716-504-7*) P B Pubng.

To Love is to Live: First Corinthians 13. (First Corinthians Commentary Ser.). 10.99 (*0-89957-580-3*) AMG Pubs.

To Love or to Be Loved. 2nd ed. Tom Johnson. 48p. 1985. reprint ed. pap. 3.25 (*0-941992-14-4*) Los Arboles Pub.

To Love So Well the World: Essays on Robert Penn Warren: A Feschrift in Honor of Albert J. Montesi. Dennis L. Weeks. LC 91-45436. 332p. (C). 1993. text ed. 54.95 (*0-8204-1712-2*) P Lang Pubng.

To Love the Good: The Moral Philosophy of Iris Murdoch. Patricia J. O'Connor. LC 92-21786. (American University Studies Series V: Vol. 136). 312p. (C). 1996. pap. text ed. 32.95 (*0-8204-1805-6*) P Lang Pubng.

To Love the Sky. Mary A. Beatty. LC 86-70480. (Illus.). 299p. 1986. 17.95 (*0-932919-02-2*) Albright & Co.

*__To Love Thee More Dearly.__ Richard Huelsman. Ed. by Carl Koch. (Illus.). 112p. (Orig.). 1997. pap. 7.95 (*0-88489-498-3*) St Marys.

*__To Love Thee More Dearly.__ Richard Huelsman. Ed. by Carl Koch. (Illus.). 112p. (Orig.). 1997. spiral bd. 9.95 (*0-88489-507-6*) St Marys.

To Love, to Betray: Life As Betrayal. Aldo Carotenuto. LC 95-51849. 200p. (Orig.). 1996. pap. 14.95 (*0-933029-97-7*, 977) Chiron Pubns.

To Make a Double Bass with Plans. rev. ed. Harry S. Wake. (Illus.). 100p. 1995. pap. 35.00 (*0-9607048-6-8*) H S Wake.

An Asterisk (*) at the beginning of an entry indicates that the title is appearing in BIP for the first time.

To Make a Dream Come True. Fern B. Perrin. 198p. (Orig.). pap. 8.95 (*0-927022-04-4*) CHJ Pub.

To Make a Life. Dan Stryke. 1980. pap. 3.50 (*0-917652-21-5*) Confluence Pr.

To Make a Light. large type ed. Helga Moray. 393p. 1989. 25.99 (*0-7089-1947-2*) Ulverscroft.

To Make a Long Story Short. (Review Ser.: No. 4). 136p. 1994. pap. 6.00 (*0-9641292-6-4*) Global Cty Pr.

To Make a Mayor. Deborah L. Tucker. LC 95-7952. 184p. (C). 1995. pap. text ed. 27.50 (*0-8191-9918-4*); lib. bdg. 51.00 (*0-8191-9917-6*) U Pr of Amer.

To Make a Nation: The Rediscovery of American Federalism. Samuel H. Beer. 496p. 1994. pap. text ed. 17.95 (*0-674-89318-2*, BEEMAX) Belknap Pr.

To Make a Nation: The Rediscovery of American Federalism. Samuel H. Beer. 496p. (C). 1993. text ed. 29.95 (*0-674-89317-4*) HUP.

To Make a Poem. 2nd ed. Alberta Turner. (Illus.). 200p. (Orig.). (C). 1992. pap. text ed. 17.75 (*0-939693-22-4*) Collegiate Pr.

To Make a Poet Black. J. Saunders Redding. LC 86-47630. 184p. 1987. 32.50 (*0-8014-1982-4*); pap. 10.95 (*0-8014-9438-9*) Cornell U Pr.

To Make a Poet Black. Jay S. Redding. 8.00 (*0-405-18495-6*) Ayer.

To Make a Poet Black. Jay S. Redding. (BCL1-PS American Literature Ser.). 142p. 1993. reprint ed. lib. bdg. 69.00 (*0-7812-6567-3*) Rprt Serv.

To Make a Prairie: Essays on Poets, Poetry, & Country Living. Maxine Kumin. LC 79-13289. (Poets on Poetry Ser.). 1979. pap. 13.95 (*0-472-06306-5*) U of Mich Pr.

To Make a Spotless Orange: Biological Control in California. Richard C. Sawyer. LC 96-20194. (The Henry A. Wallace Series on Agricultural History & Rural Life). (Illus.). 316p. 1996. text ed. 42.95 (*0-8138-2755-8*) Iowa St U Pr.

To Make a World Safe for Revolution: Cuba's Foreign Policy. Jorge I. Dominguez. LC 88-16556. (Center for International Affairs Ser.). (Illus.). 365p. 1989. 45.00 (*0-674-89325-5*) HUP.

To Make All Laws: The Congress of the United States, 1789-1989. 1996. lib. bdg. 250.99 (*0-8490-6012-5*) Gordon Pr.

To Make All Laws: The Congress of the United States, 1789-1989. James H. Hutson. LC 89-600098. 120p. 1989. 9.50 (*0-8444-0646-5*, 030-000-00215-6) Lib Congress.

To Make Another World. Ed. by Colin Barker & Paul Kennedy. 256p. 1996. 59.95 (*1-85972-326-8*, Pub. by Avebury Pub UK) Ashgate Pub Co.

To Make Democracy Safe for America: Patricians & Preparedness in the Progressive Era. Michael D. Pearlman. LC 83-1107. (Illus.). 294p. 1984. text ed. 24.95 (*0-252-01019-1*) U of Ill Pr.

To Make It Home: Photographs of the American West, 1965-1986. Robert Adams. (Illus.). 176p. 1989. 75.00 (*0-89381-351-6*); pap. 29.95 (*0-89381-384-2*) Aperture.

To Make My Bread. Grace Lumpkin. LC 95-3561. (Radical Novel Reconsidered Ser.). 424p. 1995. 15.95 (*0-252-06501-8*) U of Ill Pr.

To Make the Wounded Whole: The Cultural Legacy of Martin Luther King, Jr. Lewis V. Baldwin. LC 91-34739. 344p. 1992. pap. 18.00 (*0-8006-2543-9*, 1-2543) Augsburg Fortress.

To Make Us Wise: How to Make Bible Study Relevant to Your Life Today. V. Bailey Gillespie. LC 95-38599. 1995. pap. 8.99 (*0-8163-1302-4*) Pacific Pr Pub Assn.

To Marcy with Love: A Novel. Henry Denker. LC 95-37577. 320p. 1996. 24.00 (*0-688-14612-0*) Morrow.

To Mark Our Place: A History of Canadian War Memorials. Robert Shipley. (Illus.). 200p. 1987. 24.95 (*1-55021-014-9*, Pub. by NC Press CN) U of Toronto Pr.

To Market. Anne Miranda. LC 95-26326. (Illus.). (J). 1997. write for info. (*0-15-200035-6*) HarBrace.

To Market to Market. Corinne Ross. (Illus.). 1980. pap. 4.50 (*0-89182-022-1*) Charles River Bks.

To Market, to Market...Home Again, Home Again. Ed. by Hadley Harrington et al. LC 84-81147. (Illus.). 350p. 1984. 15.00 (*0-9611770-0-4*) Jr League Owensboro.

***To Marry a British Lord.** O'Brien. 1997. mass mkt. 5.99 (*0-671-00039-X*) PB.

***To Marry a Stranger.** Renee Roszel. 1997. pap. 3.25 (*0-373-15716-9*, 1-15716-3) Harlequin Bks.

***To Marry a Stranger.** Renee Roszel. 1997. pap. 3.25 (*0-373-03470-9*, 1-03470-1) Harlequin Bks.

To Marry an English Lord: Or, How Anglomania Really Got Started. Carol M. Wallace. LC 85-40529. (Illus.). 416p. 1986. pap. 14.95 (*0-89480-939-3*, 939) Workman Pub.

To Marry at Christmas. Kasey Michaels. 1996. pap. 4.99 (*0-614-16982-8*) Harlequin Bks.

To Mars & Back. Decatur Celebration Writers. (Wee Write Bks.: No. 28). (Illus.). 45p. (J). (ps-3). 1995. pap. 8.95 (*1-884987-94-X*) WeWrite.

To Mars via the Moon: An Astronomical Story. Mark Wicks. LC 74-16526. (Science Fiction Ser.). (Illus.). 352p. 1975. reprint ed. 28.95 (*0-405-06318-0*) Ayer.

To Martin Luther King, with Love: A Southern Quaker's Tribute. David W. Pitre. LC 84-60119. 1984. pap. 3.00 (*0-87574-254-8*) Pendle Hill.

***To Master Self Is to Master Life.** Saint Germaine. 250p. (Orig.). 1997. pap. 1.88 (*1-883389-53-4*) Asn Int Mastery.

To Mean-to Understand Problems of Psychological Semantics. H. Hoermann. (Illus.). 350p. 1981. 70.95 (*0-387-10448-8*) Spr-Verlag.

To Meet at the Source: Hindus & Quakers. Martha Dart. LC 89-64310. (Orig.). 1990. pap. 3.00 (*0-87574-289-0*) Pendle Hill.

To Meet the First March Brown. Illus. by Aideen Canning. 176p. 1994. 29.95 (*1-85310-474-4*, Pub. by Swan Hill UK) Voyageur Pr.

To Meet the Real Dragon. 2nd ed. Gudo Nishijima & Jeffrey Bailey. 215p. 1992. pap. 10.95 (*0-9523002-0-6*) Windbell Pubns.

To Meet Will Shakespeare. Frank E. Hill. LC 77-109650. (Select Bibliographies Reprint Ser.). 1977. 36.95 (*0-8369-5259-6*) Ayer.

***To Mend a Broken Heart.** large type ed. Helena Bell. (Linford Romance Large Print Ser.). 272p. 1997. pap. 16.99 (*0-7089-5123-6*, Linford) Ulverscroft.

To Mend the World: Foundations of Post-Holocaust Jewish Thought. Emil L. Fackenheim. 408p. (C). 1993. 39.95 (*0-253-32113-1*); pap. 18.95 (*0-253-32114-X*) Ind U Pr.

To Middle River: Minnesota North Country New & Selected Poems. William D. Elliott. LC 84-60990. 70p. (Orig.). 1984. pap. 4.95 (*0-9613489-1-7*) MN North.

To Mock a Mockingbird. Raymond Smullyan. LC 84-737. 1985. 14.95 (*0-394-53491-3*) Knopf.

To Mock Doctor's Rules: A History of Education in Public Health. Elizabeth Fee & Roy M. Acheson. (Illus.). 384p. 1991. 49.95 (*0-19-261757-5*) OUP.

To Mom. Helen Exley & Richard. (Things Kids Say Ser.). (Illus.). 62p. 1992. reprint ed. 8.99 (*1-85015-215-2*) Exley Giftbooks.

To Mom, Keeper of the Zoo, Vol. 1. Maureen Wright. 160p. 1995. pap. 8.95 (*0-89221-303-5*) New Leaf.

To Mom, with Love. LC 92-41938. (Itty Bitty Bk.). 1993. 4.99 (*0-8407-6860-5*) Nelson.

To Moroni with Love. Ed Decker. LC 91-78415. (Salt Ser.). 48p. 1992. pap. 2.99 (*1-56384-021-9*) Huntington Hse.

To Mother: An Anthology of Motor Verse. 1994. 7.98 (*1-879582-43-0*) Platinum Pr.

To Mother: With Love. Compiled by Esther L. Beilenson. (Deluxe Gift Editions Ser.). (Illus.). 64p. 1996. 8.99 (*0-88088-113-5*) Peter Pauper.

To Mother with Love. 1991. mass mkt. 4.95 (*0-373-48235-3*) Harlequin Bks.

To Mother with Love. Andrews & McMeel Staff. (Illus.). 40p. 1994. 6.95 (*0-8362-4720-5*) Andrews & McMeel.

To Mother with Love. Ed. by Ann LaFarge. 480p. 1993. mass mkt. 4.50 (*0-8217-4138-1*, Zebra Kensgtn) Kensgtn Pub Corp.

To Mother with Love. Helen Steiner Rice. 96p. (gr. 10). 1992. 13.99 (*0-8007-1649-3*) Revell.

To Mother with Love. large type ed. Helen Steiner Rice. 96p. 1995. pap. 12.95 (*0-8027-2690-9*) Walker & Co.

To Mothers from the Book of Mormon. Blaine M. Yorgason & Brenton Yorgason. (Gospel Power Ser.). 41p. (Orig.). 1989. pap. 3.50 (*0-929985-22-2*) Jackman Pubng.

***To Move into the House.** unabridged ed. Richard Fein. 80p. (Orig.). 1996. pap. 10.00 (*0-932616-56-9*) Brick Hse Bks.

To Move with the Times: The Story of Transport & Travel in Scotland. Anne Gordon. (Illus.). 224p. 1988. 29.95 (*0-08-035080-1*, Pergamon Pr) Elsevier.

To Music & Children with Love! Reflections for Parents & Teachers. A. Ramon Rivera & Thelma Gruenbaum. 133p. (C). 1979. pap. 6.95 (*0-936190-03-5*) ExPressAll.

To My Beloved Wife & Boy at Home: The Letters & Diaries of Orderly Sergeant John F. L. Hartwell. Ed. by Ann H. Britton & Thomas J. Reed. LC 95-31189. (Illus.). 416p. 1997. 55.00 (*0-8386-3675-6*) Fairleigh Dickinson.

To My Best Friend: Correspondence Between Tchaikovsky & Nadezhda von Meck, 1876-1878. Ed. by Nigel Gotteri. Tr. by Galina Von Meck. LC 92-422. 522p. (C). 1993. 58.00 (*0-19-816158-1*) OUP.

***To My Child: A Mother's Journal.** Illus. by Sandra Kuck. 80p. 1997. 19.99 (*1-56507-607-9*) Harvest Hse.

***To My Child: We May No Longer Live in the Same House, but You're Always in My Heart: A Collection of Poems from Blue Mountain Arts.** Ed. by Gary Morris. LC 97-9936. 48p. 1997. 7.95 (*0-88396-447-3*) Blue Mtn Pr CO.

To My Children's Children. Sindiwe Magona. LC 94-4358. (Orig.). 1994. 24.95 (*1-56656-163-9*); pap. 11.95 (*1-56656-152-3*) Interlink Pub.

To My Comrades of Life. Michael T. Bell. Ed. by Elissa Gordon. (Illus.). 176p. (Orig.). 1995. pap. 10.00 (*0-9643047-9-1*) Cant Miss Pubng.

To My Daughter. Ed. by Lois L. Kaufman. LC 90-61139. (Illus.). 64p. 1990. 7.99 (*0-88088-541-6*) Peter Pauper.

To My Daughter. Schutz. 1992. 5.95 (*0-446-77633-5*) Warner Bks.

To My Daughter, with Love. Ed. by Helen Exley. (Suedel Giftbooks Ser.). (Illus.). 60p. 1994. 9.99 (*1-85015-501-1*) Exley Giftbooks.

To My Daughter with Love. Susan P. Schutz. 64p. 1988. pap. 6.99 (*0-446-38843-2*) Warner Bks.

To My Daughter with Love: A Mother Remembers. Donna Green. (Illus.). 80p. 1995. 10.98 (*0-8317-8778-3*) Smithmark.

To My Daughter, with Love: A Mother's Memory Book. Donna Green. (Illus.). 80p. 1993. 14.95 (*1-883746-08-6*) Vermilion.

To My Daughter, with Love: A Mother's Memory Book. deluxe ed. Donna Green. (Illus.). 80p. 1993. 18.95 (*1-883746-01-9*) Vermilion.

To My Daughter, with Love, on the Important Things in Life. Susan P. Schutz. LC 86-70638. (Illus.). 64p. 1986. 16.95 (*0-88396-246-2*) Blue Mtn Pr CO.

To My Daughters, with Love. Pearl S. Buck. 1992. reprint ed. lib. bdg. 23.95 (*0-89966-989-1*) Buccaneer Bks.

***To My Dear Friend: Oh, the Memories We've Made.** Kathleen Lashier. (Memory-a-Day Ser.). 366p. (Orig.). 1996. spiral bd., pap. 8.95 (*1-56383-061-2*, 5059) G & R Pub.

To My Dear Slimeball: Secret Letters from a Senior Demon to His Slippery Sidekick. Richard Miller. (Orig.). (YA). 1995. pap. 8.99 (*1-56507-187-5*) Harvest Hse.

To My Father. Schultz. 1993. pap. 7.99 (*0-446-77810-9*) Warner Bks.

To My Father's Village. William Kurelek. 1996. reprint ed. 19.95 (*0-88776-220-4*) Tundra Bks.

To My Grandmother, with Love. Ed. by Helen Exley. (Suedel Giftbooks Ser.). (Illus.). 60p. 1994. 9.99 (*1-85015-452-X*) Exley Giftbooks.

To My Husband with Love. Ed. by Helen Exley. (Miniature Square Bks.). (Illus.). 64p. 1996. 6.00 (*1-85015-709-X*) Exley Giftbooks.

***To My Memory Sing: A Memoir Based on Letters & Poems from Sol Chick Chaikin, an American Soldier in China, India, Burma During World War II.** Rosalind B. Chaikin. LC 96-29627. (Illus.). 300p. 1997. 25.00 (*0-912526-77-7*) Lib Res.

To My Mother with Love. Ed. by Helen Exley. (Heart Shaped Bks.). (Illus.). 32p. 1992. pap. 3.99 (*1-85015-298-5*) Exley Giftbooks.

To My People with Love: The Ten Commandments for Today. John Killinger. LC 88-10518. 144p. 1988. pap. 7.95 (*0-687-42200-0*) Abingdon.

To My Pocket. S. F. Lockhart. 1984. 39.00 (*0-946270-09-0*, Pub. by Pentland Pr UK) St Mut.

***To My Sister.** Kim Anderson. 1997. 6.95 (*0-7667-0953-1*) Gibson.

To My Son, with Love. Susan P. Schutz. LC 88-70960. (Illus.). 64p. 1988. 16.95 (*0-88396-268-3*) Blue Mtn Pr CO.

To My Sons. Harold B. Wright. 90.95 (*1-56723-111-X*) Yestermorrow.

To My Sons. Harold B. Wright. 261p. 1977. reprint ed. lib. bdg. 17.65 (*0-89966-267-6*) Buccaneer Bks.

To My Very Special Love. Ed. by Helen Exley. (To Give & to Keep Ser.). (Illus.). 28p. 1992. 6.99 (*1-85015-282-9*) Exley Giftbooks.

To Myself: Notes on Life, Art, & Artists. Odilon Redon. Tr. by Mira Jacob & Jeanne L. Wasserman from FRE. 144p. 1996. pap. 14.95 (*0-8076-1146-8*) Braziller.

To Myself a Stranger: A Biography of Rose Hawthorne Lathrop. Patricia D. Valenti. LC 90-23670. (Illus.). 248p. 1991. text ed. 32.50 (*0-8071-1612-2*) La State U Pr.

To Newfoundland: Poems. Caroline Knox. LC 88-26082. (Contemporary Poetry Ser.). 72p. 1989. pap. 14.95 (*0-8203-1115-4*) U of Ga Pr.

To Nietzsche: Dionysus, I Love You! Ariadne. Claudia Crawford. LC 93-50892. 308p. (C). 1994. text ed. 59.50 (*0-7914-2149-X*); pap. text ed. 19.95 (*0-7914-2150-3*) State U NY Pr.

To Nonviolent Political Science: From Seasons of Violence. Glenn D. Paige. LC 93-31768. 1993. 5.00 (*1-880309-07-6*) S M Matsunaga.

To Nourish Any Flower. Tom Hegg. (Illus.). 48p. 1994. 10.95 (*0-931674-25-5*) Waldman Hse Pr.

To Open Minds: Chinese Clues to the Dilemma of Contemporary Education. Howard Gardner. LC 89-42523. (Illus.). 352p. 1991. pap. 18.50 (*0-465-08629-2*) Basic.

To Oregon by Ox-Team in 1847. Fred Lockley. 16p. 1971. pap. 3.50 (*0-87770-061-3*) Ye Galleon.

To Organise the Air: The Evolution of Civil Aviation & the Role of Sir Frederick Tymm the Flying Civil Servant. E. A. Johnson. 407p. (C). 1995. text ed. 51.95 (*1-85628-952-4*, Pub. by Arena UK) Ashgate Pub Co.

To Other Beings. James Grabill. LC 80-15062. (Illus.). 72p. (Orig.). 1981. 12.00 (*0-89924-034-8*); pap. 7.00 (*0-89924-028-3*) Lynx Hse.

To Our Children's Children: Preserving Family Histories for Generations to Come. Bob Greene & D. G. Fulford. LC 92-29082. 224p. 1993. 15.95 (*0-385-46797-4*) Doubleday.

***To Our Health: Using the Inner Art of Dolosing in Search for Health - Happiness - Harmony.** rev. ed. Anneliese G. Hagemann & Doris K. Hagemann. (Illus.). 106p. 1997. pap. 21.95 (*0-9656653-0-5*) Hlth-Happiness-Harmony.

***To Our Heart's Content: Meditations for Women Turning 50.** Suzanne Cole. LC 96-44117. 1997. pap. 12.95 (*0-8092-3144-1*) Contemp Bks.

To Pace or Not to Pace, Controversial Subjects on Cardiac Pacing: Proceedings of the European Pacemaker Colloquium, 2nd, Brussels, April 1977. European Pacemaker Colloquium Staff. Ed. by Hilbert J. Thalen & J. Warren Hawthorne. 1978. lib. bdg. 165.00 (*90-247-2070-2*) Kluwer Ac.

***To Paint Her Life: Charlotte Salomon in the Nazi Era.** Mary L. Felstiner. LC 97-10636. 1997. pap. write for info. (*0-520-21066-2*) U CA Pr.

To Paris. Samuel Hazo. LC 80-22685. 96p. 1981. 11.95 (*0-8112-0787-0*); pap. 4.95 (*0-8112-0788-9*, NDP512) New Directions.

To Perceive & to Represent: A Comparative Study of Chinese & English Poetics of Nature Imagery, Vol. 24. Xiaoshan Yang. (Asian Thought & Culture Ser.). 176p. (C). 1995. 42.95 (*0-8204-2753-5*) P Lang Pubng.

To Perceive & to Write. Mary L. Murphy. 144p. 1970. pap. 4.35 (*0-85225-536-5*) Ed Solutions.

***To Perfect the World: Conversations with Rabbi Irving Greenberg As Interviewed by Dr. Shalom Freedman.** Shalom Freedman & Irving Greenberg. 1998. write for info. (*0-7657-9980-4*) Aronson.

To Peter with Love. Carol A. Vercz. 1985. 4.75 (*0-910119-18-X*) SOCO Pubns.

***To Phen or Not to Fen: That's the Question! Miraculous Pills, Diets, & Weight Loss That Lasts Forever...** Maher A. Abbas. (Illus.). 125p. (Orig.). 1997. pap. 14.95 (*0-9656065-2-X*) SYTAC Health.

To Place Bluff Life. limited ed. Illus. by Roni Horn. 34p. 1990. 35.00 (*0-935875-09-3*) P Blum Edit.

To Plan Is to Choose. Wilfred H. Whitely. LC 72-97699. (Hans Wolff Memorial Lecture Ser.). 50p. 1973. pap. text ed. 3.00 (*0-941934-04-7*) Indiana Africa.

To Plan Or Not to Plan Is the Question - The Answer Is Found in Your Desire to Succeed: How to Create a Winning Plan for Business Growth & Goal Setting for Small Business. Business Development Systems, Inc. Staff. (Self-Improvement Business Ser.). 40p. 1994. pap. text ed. 8.95 (*1-884392-09-1*) Busn Develop.

To Plant a Tree. Priscilla Klepser. LC 85-91312. 69p. 1986. 6.95 (*0-533-06832-0*) Vantage.

To Play the Fool. Laurie R. King. 320p. 1996. mass mkt. 5.99 (*0-553-57455-8*, Crimeline) Bantam.

To Play the Fool. Laurie R. King. 1995. 21.00 (*0-312-11907-0*) St Martin.

To Play the Game: A Travel Guide to the North America of Sherlock Holmes. David L. Hammer. (Illus.). 397p. (Orig.). 1991. 39.95 (*0-938501-11-9*); pap. text ed. 19.95 (*0-938501-12-7*) Wessex.

To Play the Game: An Analysis of Sports. J. Bowyer Bell. 205p. 1986. 39.95 (*0-88738-102-2*) Transaction Pubs.

To Please My Lady. large type ed. Jean Stewart. (Linford Romance Library). 304p. 1996. pap. 15.99 (*0-7089-7851-7*, Linford) Ulverscroft.

To Please the Caribou. Dorothy K. Burnham. (Illus.). 328p. 1996. 60.00 (*0-88854-399-9*, Pub. by Royal Ont Mus CN); pap. 35.00 (*0-88543-964-3*, Pub. by Royal Ont Mus CN) U of Toronto Pr.

To Please the Caribou: Painted Caribou-Skin Coats Worn by the Naskapi, Montagnais, & Cree Hunters of the Quebec-Labrador Peninsula. Dorothy K. Burnham. LC 91-50994. (Illus.). 328p. 1992. 60.00 (*0-295-97177-0*) U of Wash Pr.

To Pluto & Back: A Voyage in the Milky Way. Gunilla Ingves. (J). 1992. 15.00 (*91-29-62058-9*, Pub. by R & S Bks) FS&G.

***To Pomerania in Search of Dietrich Bonhoeffer: A Traveler's Companion & Guide.** 2nd expanded ed. Jane Pejsa. (Illus.). 70p. (Orig.). 1996. pap. 7.50 (*0-9612776-7-X*) Kenwood Pub.

To Possess the Land: A Biography of Arthur Rochford Manby. Frank Waters. LC 93-36914. (Illus.). 295p. 1993. reprint ed. pap. 16.95 (*0-8040-0980-5*) Swallow.

To Poughkeepsie & Back: The Story of the Poughkeepsie-Highland Ferry. Glendon L. Moffett. LC 94-37041. (Illus.). 1994. pap. 10.00 (*0-935796-56-8*) Purple Mnt Pr.

To Praise the Music. William Bronk. 1972. 16.00 (*0-685-27707-0*); pap. 8.00 (*0-686-66726-3*) Elizabeth Pr.

To Pray & to Love: Conversations on Prayer with the Early Church. Roberta C. Bondi. LC 91-3026. 128p. 1991. pap. 11.00 (*0-8006-2511-0*, 1-2511, Fortress Pr) Augsburg Fortress.

To Pray & to Love: Conversations with the Deserts Fathers. Roberta Bondi. 160p. 1994. pap. 21.00 (*0-86012-195-X*, Pub. by Srch Pr UK) St Mut.

To Pray As a Jew: A Guide to the Prayer Book & the Synagogue Service. Hayim H. Donin. LC 80-50554. 416p. 1991. pap. 15.00 (*0-465-08633-0*) Basic.

To Pray God's Will: Continuing the Journey. Ben C. Johnson. LC 87-14272. 134p. (Orig.). 1984. pap. 9.00 (*0-664-24085-2*, Westminster) Westminster John Knox.

To Pray or Not to Pray: A Handbook for Study of Recent Supreme Court Decisions & American Church-State Doctrine. enl. ed. Charles W. Lowry. LC 68-8899. 260p. 1969. 24.95 (*0-87419-013-4*) Cherokee.

To Preserve & Protect. D. Kears. 512p. 1997. 30.00 (*0-06-017055-7*, HarpT) HarpC.

To Preserve Biodiversity: An Overview. Ed. by David Ehrenfeld. LC 94-46717. (Readings from Conservation Biology Ser.). 249p. 1995. 24.95 (*0-86542-451-9*) Blackwell Sci.

To Preserve the Faith: Catholic Charities in Boston, 1870-1930. Susan S. Walton. LC 92-32635. (Non-profit Institutions in America Ser.). 208p. 1993. text ed. 15.00 (*0-8153-0902-3*) Garland.

To Preserve the Republic. Frederick H. Hartmann & Robert N. Wendzel. 596p. (C). 1985. pap. write for info. (*0-02-351300-4*, Macmillan Coll) P-H.

To Prevent War. Walter F. Zeltmann. LC 89-127754. 84p. 1989. 24.90 (*0-9622705-0-4*) Yellow Hook Pr.

To Prison with Love: The True Story of Sandy Musser's Indecent Indictment & America's Adoption Travesty. Sandra K. Musser. Ed. by Terri Pesatrice. (Illus.). 276p. (Orig.). 1995. pap. 14.95 (*0-934896-37-2*) Adopt Aware Pr.

To Promote, Defend & Redeem: The Catholic Literary Revival & the Cultural Transformation of American Catholicism, 1920 Through 1960. Arnold Sparr. LC 89-25853. (Contributions to the Study of Religion Ser.: No. 25). 240p. 1990. text ed. 59.95 (*0-313-26391-4*, SCX/) Greenwood.

To Promote Peace: U. S. Foreign Policy in the Mid-1980's. Ed. by Dennis L. Bark. (Publication Ser.: No. 294). 298p. 1984. 7.98 (*0-8179-7941-7*) Hoover Inst Pr.

To Promote Prosperity: U. S. Domestic Policy in the Mid-1980's. Ed. by John H. Moore. (Publication Ser.: No. 295). 464p. 1984. 7.98 (*0-8179-7951-4*) Hoover Inst Pr.

To Promote the General Welfare: Market Processes vs. Political Transfers. Richard E. Wagner. LC 88-64203. 238p. (Orig.). (C). 1989. 29.95 (*0-936488-25-5*); pap. 14.95 (*0-936488-26-3*) PRIPP.

To Protect & Serve: A History of the San Diego Police Department & Its Chiefs, 1889-1989. Pliny Castanien. LC 92-47133. (Illus.). 130p. (Orig.). 1993. pap. 14.95 (*0-918740-14-2*) San Diego Hist.

To Protect & Serve: The L. A. P. D. at War. Joe Domanick. 1994. 23.00 (*0-671-75111-5*) PB.

T

To Protect & to Serve: The LAPD's Century of War in the City of Dreams. Joe A. Domanick. 1995. mass mkt., pap. 6.99 (0-671-75113-1) PB.

To Protect the Guilty. large type ed. Jeffrey Ashford. (Linford Mystery Library). 352p. 1992. pap. 15.99 (0-7089-7223-3, Trailtree Bookshop) Ulverscroft.

To Prove a Villain. Guy M. Townsend. LC 89-7388. 190p. (Orig.). 1988. pap. 19.00 (0-8095-4213-7) Borgo Pr.

To Prove a Villain. Guy M. Townsend. LC 84-63065. 190p. (Orig.). 1985. pap. 8.95 (0-9602676-2-X) Persevrnce Pr.

To Prove a Villain. Guy M. Townsend. LC 89-7388. 190p. (Orig.). (C). 1988. reprint ed. lib. bdg. 29.00 (0-8095-4205-6) Borgo Pr.

To Prove I'm Not Forgot: Living & Dying in a Victorian City. S. M. Barnard. 1990. text ed. 39.95 (0-7190-2522-2, Pub. by Manchester Univ Pr UK) St Martin.

To Puedes Ser una Paleontologa. Diane Gabriel & Judith Cohen. Tr. by Juan Yanez from ENG. (Illus.). 40p. (SPA.). (J). (gr. 3-7). 1993. pap. text ed. 7.00 (1-880599-13-9) Cascade Pass.

To Purge This Land with Blood: A Biography of John Brown. 2nd ed. Stephen B. Oates. LC 84-2635. (Illus.). 448p. 1984. pap. 20.95 (0-87023-458-7) U of Mass Pr.

To Quench Our Thirst. David A. Franko & Robert G. Wetzel. (Illus.). 176p. 1983. pap. text ed. 19.95 (0-472-08037-7) U of Mich Pr.

To Quiet a Foreign Pain. Susan Schwartzenberg. (Illus.). 16p. (Orig.). 1990. pap. 9.00 (0-685-72902-8) Visual Studies.

To Rabbittown. April H. Wayland. (Illus.). 32p. (J). 1992. pap. 3.95 (0-590-44777-7, Blue Ribbon Bks) Scholastic Inc.

To Race a Dream. Deborah Savage. LC 93-32654. (Trophy Bk.). 256p. (YA). (gr. 7 up). 1996. pap. 4.95 (0-06-440611-3, Trophy) HarpC Child Bks.

To Race a Dream. Deborah Savage. (YA). 1994. 15.95 (0-395-69252-0) HM.

To Raise a Jewish Child: A Guide for Parents. Hayim H. Donin. LC 76-7679. 256p. 1991. pap. 13.00 (0-465-08635-7) Basic.

To Raise a Rainbow. Teo Savory. 226p. 1980. 19.95 (0-87775-130-7); pap. 10.00 (0-87775-131-5) Unicorn Pr.

To Raise an Army: The Draft Comes to Modern America. John W. Chambers, II. LC 87-15150. 448p. 1987. 40.00 (0-02-905820-1, Free Press) Free Pr.

To Raise, Destroy, & Create: The Poetry, Drama, and Fiction of Imamu Amiri Baraka (Le Roi Jones) Henry C. Lacey. LC 80-50078. 220p. 1981. 15.00 (0-87875-185-8) Whitston Pub.

To Reach Eternity: The Letters of James Jones. Ed. by George Hendrick. 1989. 22.50 (0-394-57538-5) Random.

To Reach This Season: A Russians Odyssey to the West. Grigory I. Pasternak & Eugene Raleigh. LC 84-82476. 241p. 1985. pap. 12.95 (0-943376-23-8) Magnes Mus.

To Read a Poem. 2nd ed. Donald Hall. 432p. (C). 1992. pap. text ed. 21.50 (0-03-055539-6); pap. text ed. 34.00 (0-03-073424-X) HB Coll Pubs.

To Read Fiction. Donald Hall. 608p. (C). 1987. pap. text ed. 18.00 (0-03-012218-X) HB Coll Pubs.

To Read Literature. 2nd ed. Donald Hall. 1280p. 1987. text ed. 28.75 (0-03-006207-1) HB Coll Pubs.

To Read Literature. 3rd ed. Donald Hall. 1380p. (C). 1992. pap. text ed. 29.50 (0-03-055542-6); pap. text ed. 34.00 (0-03-073427-4) HB Coll Pubs.

To Read Poetry. Ed. by Donald Hall. 402p. (C). 1982. pap. text ed. 19.50 (0-03-060549-0) HB Coll Pubs.

To Realize Enlightenment: Practice of the Cultivation Path. Nan Huai-Chin. Tr. by J. C. Cleary from CHI. LC 94-12741. 188p. (Orig.). 1994. pap. 14.95 (0-87728-802-X) Weiser.

To Reap a Bountiful Harvest: Czech Immigration Beyond the Mississippi, 1850-1900. Stepanka Korytova-Magstadt. LC 93-3364. 1993. 24.95 (0-945213-09-3); pap. 14.95 (0-945213-07-7) Rudi Pub.

To Reason Why. Denis Forman. (Illus.). 220p. 1992. 34.95 (0-233-98731-2, Pub. by A Deutsch UK) Trafalgar.

To Reason Why. Rose B. Green. 4.95 (0-8453-1042-9, Cornwall Bks) Assoc Univ Prs.

To Reason Why: The Debate About the Causes of U. S. Involvement in the Vietnam War. Jeffrey P. Kimball. 448p. (C). 1990. pap. text ed. write for info. (0-07-557132-3) McGraw.

To Reason Why: The Debate about the Causes of U. S. Involvement in the Vietnam War. Ed. by Jeffrey P. Kimball. (Illus.). 216p. 1990. 39.95 (0-87722-709-8) Temple U Pr.

To Rebel Is Justified: A Rhetorical Study of China's Cultural Revolution Movement 1966-1969. Shaorong Huang. LC 96-8854. 238p. 1996. lib. bdg. 39.50 (0-7618-0418-8) U Pr of Amer.

*__To Receive a Text: Literary Reception Theory As a Key to Ecumenical Reception.__ Linda L. Gaither. (American University Studies, VII: Vol. 192). 336p. (C). 1997. 51.95 (0-8204-3302-0) P Lang Pubng.

To Reclaim a Legacy of Diversity: Analyzing the Political Correctness Debates in Higher Education. Debra Schultz. (Orig.). pap. text ed. write for info. (1-880547-13-9) Nat Coun Res Wom.

To Recognize This Dying. Joe Napora. Ed. by John M. Gogol & Robert A. Davies. (Poetry Chapbook Ser.). 48p. (Orig.). 1987. pap. 10.00 (0-932191-09-6) Mr Cogito Pr.

To Redeem a Nation: A History & Anthology of the Civil Rights Movement. Ed. by Thomas R. West & James W. Mooney. (Illus.). 312p. (Orig.). (C). 1993. pap. text ed. 14.50 (1-881089-20-7) Brandywine Press.

To Redeem the Soul of America: The Southern Christian Leadership Conference & Martin Luther King, Jr. Adam Fairclough. LC 86-11352. (Illus.). 514p. 1987. pap. 20.00 (0-8203-0938-9) U of Ga Pr.

To Rejoice As Women: Talks from the 1994 Women's Conference. Ed. by Susette F. Green & Dawn H. Anderson. 320p. 1995. 15.95 (0-87579-894-2) Deseret Bk.

*__To Relieve the Human Condition: Bioethics, Technology, & the Body.__ Gerald P. McKenny. LC 96-45998. 288p. (C). 1997. pap. text ed. 19.95 (0-7914-3474-5) State U NY Pr.

*__To Relieve the Human Condition: Bioethics, Technology, & the Body.__ Gerald P. McKenny. LC 96-45998. 288p. (C). 1997. text ed. 59.50 (0-7914-3473-7) State U NY Pr.

To Remain. Edward Kleinschmidt. (Flowering Quince Poetry Ser.: No. 6). 24p. (Orig.). 1990. pap. 7.50 (0-940592-24-X) Heyeck Pr.

To Remember & Celebrate: Worship Resources for Heritage Events. Ed. by Kenneth E. Rowe et al. 65p. (Orig.). Date not set. pap. 7.00 (1-880927-19-5) Gen Comm Arch.

*__To Remember & Heal: Theological & Psychological Reflections on Truth & Reconciliation.__ H. Russel. 1997. pap. text ed. 19.95 (0-7981-3644-8) Human & Rousseau.

To Remember Spain: The Anarchist & Syndicalist Revolution of 1936. Ed. by Murray Bookchin. LC 94-1376. 1994. 6.00 (1-873176-87-2, AK Pr San Fran) AK Pr Dist.

To Remember the Faces of the Dead: The Plenitude of Memory in Southwestern New Britain. Thomas Maschio. LC 93-32388. 256p. 1994. 48.50 (0-299-14090-3); pap. 22.75 (0-299-14094-6) U of Wis Pr.

To Remember What Is Lost. Kenneth Brewer. LC 82-13530. (Illus.). 65p. reprint ed. pap. 25.00 (0-8357-3570-2, 2034608) Bks Demand.

To Renew America. Newt Gingrich. 320p. 1996. mass mkt. 6.99 (0-06-109539-7, Harp PBks) HarpC.

*__To Repair the Shattered American Dream.__ Philip R. Hancock. 160p. 1996. pap. 9.95 (1-878853-58-9) Venture Pr FL.

To Ride a Silver Broomstick: New Generation Witchcraft. Silver RavenWolf. LC 92-38151. (Illus.). 316p. 1993. pap. 14.95 (0-87542-791-X) Llewellyn Pubns.

To Ride Pegasus. Anne McCaffrey. 256p. 1986. mass mkt. 5.99 (0-345-33603-8, Del Rey) Ballantine.

To Ride, Shoot Straight & Speak the Truth. Jeff Cooper. LC 88-82323. (Illus.). 400p. 1988. 26.00 (0-9621342-0-1) Gunsite Trng Ctr.

To Rise a Trout. John Roberts. (Illus.). 224p. (Orig.). 1989. pap. 24.95 (0-88317-151-1) Stoeger Pub Co.

To Rise from Earth: An Easy-to-Understand Guide to Space Flight. Wayne Lee. LC 95-38941. (Illus.). 352p. 1996. 35.00 (0-8160-3353-6) Facts on File.

To Rouse the Slumbering Land, 1868-1879 see Letters of William Lloyd Garrison

To Rule & Reign. E. L. Coghlan. 250p. 1992. 8.95 (1-880495-02-3) Rhenaria.

*__To Rule in Hell.__ Michael P. Murphy. 272p. (Orig.). 1998. mass mkt. 7.99 (1-889501-36-0, Stargate Pr) Sovereign.

To Rule Jerusalem. Roger Friedland & Richard Hecht. (Cultural Social Studies). (Illus.). 600p. (C). 1996. text ed. 39.95 (0-521-44046-7) Cambridge U Pr.

To Run a Constitution: The Legitimacy of the Administrative State. John A. Rohr. LC 85-28867. xvi, 272p. 1986. 35.00 (0-7006-0291-7); pap. 12.95 (0-7006-0301-8) U Pr of KS.

*__To Run after Them: Cultural & Social Bases of Cooperation in a Navajo Community.__ Louise Lamphere. 230p. 1977. write for info. (0-8165-1744-4) U of Ariz Pr.

To Run & Not Grow Tired: Restoring Your Soul in Times of Trauma, Hurt or Depression - Twelve Bible Studies of God's People under Pressure. Fran Sciacca. 96p. 1991. student ed., pap. 7.00 (0-89109-393-1) NavPress.

To Run Like the Wind: or The Wisdom of the Cheetah. Nelson A. Ossorio et al. (To Be Your Own Ser.). (Illus.). 48p. (J). (gr. 4-6). 1994. pap. 6.95 (1-56721-047-3) Twenty-Fifth Cent Pr.

*__To Run the Race with Joy.__ Sandra R. Rice. LC 96-51817. (Orig.). 1997. pap. 12.75 (0-7880-1064-6) CSS OH.

To Sail Beyond the Sunset. Robert A. Heinlein. 1988. mass mkt. 6.99 (0-441-74860-0) Ace Bks.

To Sandakan: The Diaries of Charlie Johnstone, Prisoner of War 1942-1945. Christopher Dawson. 136p. 1995. pap. 19.95 (1-86373-818-5, Pub. by Allen & Unwin Aust Pty AT) IPG Chicago.

To Sappho, My Sister: Lesbian Sisters Write about Their Lives. Ed. by Lee Fleming. (Illus.). 256p. 1995. pap. 16.95 (0-921881-36-3, Pub. by Gynergy-Ragweed CN) LPC InBook.

To Sara - With Love. large type ed. Lorna McKenzie. (Romance Ser.). 1994. pap. 15.99 (0-7089-7616-6, Linford) Ulverscroft.

To Satisfy & Delight Your Customer: How to Manage for Customer Value. William J. Pardee. LC 96-22181. (Illus.). 340p. 1996. 40.00 (0-932633-35-8) Dorset Hse Pub Co.

To Save a Child: Things You Can Do to Protect, Nurture, & Teach Our Children. Audrey E. Talkington & Barbara A. Hill. LC 93-10473. 352p. pap. 9.95 (0-89529-533-4) Avery Pub.

To Save a Nation: American Extremism, the New Deal, & the Coming of World War II. rev. ed. Geoffrey S. Smith. 252p. 1992. reprint ed. pap. text ed. 12.95 (0-929587-97-9, Elephant Paperbacks) I R Dee.

To Save a World. David Kranzler & Eliezer Gewirtz. 256p. (C). 1991. 14.95 (1-56062-060-9); pap. 11.95 (1-56062-061-7) CIS Comm.

To Save a World, No. 2. David Kranzler & Eliezer Gevirtz. 250p. (C). 1991. 14.95 (1-56062-088-9); pap. 11.95 (1-56062-089-7) CIS Comm.

*__To Save Bastogne.__ rev. unabridged ed. Robert F. Phillips. LC 96-84715. (Illus.). 280p. 1996. pap. 14.00 (0-9653229-0-4) Borodino Bks.

To Save China, To Save Ourselves: The Chinese Hand Laundry Alliance of New York. Renqiu Yu. LC 92-9205. (C). 1995. pap. text ed. 19.95 (1-56639-395-7) Temple U Pr.

To Save His Child. Margaret Watson. 1996. mass mkt. 3.99 (0-373-07750-5, 1-07750-2) Silhouette.

*__To Save My Child.__ Elizabeth Morgan. mass mkt. write for info. (0-06-109599-0, Harp PBks) HarpC.

To Save My Child: The Elizabeth Morgan Story. Elizabeth Morgan. 288p. 1996. 25.00 (0-06-017503-6) HarpC.

To Save Our Schools, to Save Our Children. ABC News Staff & Marshall Frady. LC 85-18798. (Illus.). 220p. 1986. 16.95 (0-88282-013-3) New Horizon NJ.

To Save Our World. Donald C. Kipfer, Sr. (Illus.). 130p. Date not set. write for info. (0-614-13802-7) Maedon.

*__To Save Our World.__ Donald C. Kipfer. LC 96-90432. 128p. (Orig.). 1997. pap. 7.50 (1-56002-683-9, Univ Edtns) Aegina Pr.

*__To Save Russia.__ Donald Norsic. 1997. 22.95 (1-887472-35-5) Sunstar Pubng.

*__To Save Russia.__ Donald Norsic. Ed. by Rodney Charles. LC 97-65714. (Illus.). 440p. (Orig.). (YA). 1998. pap. 16.95 (1-887472-33-9) Sunstar Pubng.

To Save the Blood of Black Babies. Kiarri T-H. Cheatwood. LC 94-68864. 184p. (Orig.). 1995. pap. 15.50 (1-879289-05-9) Native Sun Pubs.

To Save the Planet: A Musical Fable about the Global Environment & What We Can Do to Help. Tobin J. Mueller. 54p. (J). (gr. 4-9). 1991. Inc. audio cass. 14.95 incl. audio (1-56213-078-1) Ctr Stage Prodns.

To Save the Sun. Ben Bova. 384p. 1993. mass mkt. 4.99 (0-8125-1448-3) Tor Bks.

To Save Their Heathen Souls: Voyage to & Life in Foochow, China, Based on Wentworth Diaries & Letters, 1854-1858. Ed. by Polly Park. LC 84-4247. (Pittsburgh Theological Monographs, New Ser.: No. 9). (Illus.). (Orig.). 1984. pap. 6.00 (0-915138-66-2) Pickwick.

To Save Us From Ourselves: The Vision of a Future President. Richard D. MacCann. 226p. (Orig.). 1994. pap. 19.95 (0-934570-02-7) Image & Idea.

*__To Say Nothing of the Dog: How We Found the Bishop's Bird.__ Connie Willis. LC 97-16002. 544p. 1997. 23.95 (0-553-09995-7) Bantam.

*__To Scare a Tiger.__ John Costello. Date not set. write for info. (0-688-04484-0) Morrow.

*__To Scatter Stones.__ M. T. Dohaney. 192p. 1992. pap. 10.95 (0-921556-23-3, Pub. by Gynergy-Ragweed CN) LPC InBook.

To School Through the Fields. Alice Taylor. 160p. 1994. pap. 9.95 (0-312-10560-6) St Martin.

To Scorch or Freeze: Poems About the Sacred. Donald Davie. (Phoenix Poets Ser.). 62p. 1988. pap. 9.95 (0-226-13755-4); lib. bdg. 29.00 (0-226-13754-6) U Ch Pr.

To Sea, What Would I See? Steven W. Kendrick. LC 93-94213. 272p. (Orig.). 1994. pap. 9.00 (1-56002-394-5, Univ Edtns) Aegina Pr.

To Sea with a Lyre. Marion Maguire. 98p. (C). 1990. 38.00 (0-9598076-8-3, Pub. by Pascoe Pub AT) St Mut.

To Seattle by Trolley. Warren W. Wing. Ed. by Pacific Fast Mail Staff. 160p. 1995. reprint ed. 39.50 (0-915713-16-0) Pac Fast Mail.

To Secure the Blessings of Liberty: American Constitutional Law & the New Religious Movements. William C. Shepherd. LC 84-1347. (American Academy of Religion, Studies in Religion: No. 35). 155p. 1985. 24.95 (0-89130-733-8, 01-00-35); pap. 15.95 (0-89130-824-5) Scholars Pr GA.

To Secure the Blessings of Liberty: Pennsylvania & the Changing U. S. Constitution. Louis M. Waddell. (Illus.). 69p. 1986. pap. 3.95 (0-89271-035-7) Pa Hist & Mus.

To Secure the Blessings of Liberty: Report of the National Commission on the Role & Future of State Colleges & Universities. 1986. pap. text ed. 19.50 (0-88044-080-5) AASCU Press.

To Secure These Rights: The Declaration of Independence & Constitutional Interpretation. Scott D. Gerber. 315p. (C). 1995. 45.00 (0-8147-3066-3) NYU Pr.

To Secure These Rights: The Declaration of Independence & Constitutional Interpretation. Scott D. Gerber. 315p. (C). 1996. pap. 20.00 (0-8147-3089-2) NYU Pr.

To See. Elizabeth Matheson & Michael McFee. LC 91-62756. 80p. 1991. 24.95 (0-933598-34-3) NC Wesleyan Pr.

To See. limited ed. Elizabeth Matheson & Michael McFee. LC 91-62756. 80p. 1991. 150.00 (0-933598-35-1) NC Wesleyan Pr.

*__To See a Miracle.__ 40p. 1983. 5.25 (0-8341-9350-7) Lillenas.

To See a Miracle. Linda Rebuck & Tom Fettke. 1983. 5.50 (0-685-68647-7, MB-522); 86.00 (0-685-68650-7, OR-9049); audio 10.99 (0-685-68648-5, TA-9049C); audio 65.00 (0-685-68649-3, MU-9049C) Lillenas.

*__To See a Pimp in School.__ Chris Weaver. LC 96-90438. (Orig.). 1996. pap. 10.95 (0-533-12003-9) Vantage.

To See a Promised Land: Americans & the Holy Land in the Nineteenth Century. Lester I. Vogel. LC 92-32742. (Illus.). 368p. (C). 1993. 35.00 (0-271-00884-9) Pa St U Pr.

To See a Stranger. Margaret Lynn. (Black Dagger Crime Ser.). 1990. 18.50 (0-86220-787-8, C1027, Black Dagger) Chivers N Amer.

To See a Thing. Keith Gunderson. (Poetry Ser.). (Illus.). 1975. reprint ed. pap. 1.00 (5-555-50074-2) Nodin Pr.

To See a World. John Harrington. 155p. (Orig.). 1995. pap. 15.00 (0-9638731-0-5) Holocene Pr.

To See a World in a Grain of Sand. Illus. by Edward Richardson. 96p. 1972. 8.95 (0-8378-1789-7) Gibson.

To See Differently: Personal Growth & Being of Service Through Attitudinal Healing. Susan S. Trout. LC 89-52112. 264p. (Orig.). 1990. pap. 12.95 (0-9625386-0-4) Three Roses Pr.

*__To See Each Other's Good.__ Dorothy Y. Nyce. (Illus.). 148p. (Orig.). 1996. pap. write for info. (1-57579-016-5) Pine Hill Pr.

To See Ourselves: Level 16. Evertts. 1983. 59.95 (0-03-061399-X) HB Schl Dept.

To See Ourselves: Level 16. Evertts. 1986. 50.50 (0-03-002403-X) HB Schl Dept.

To See Ourselves: Level 16. E. Evertts. (J). 1983. wbk. ed., pap. 17.50 (0-03-061442-2) HB Schl Dept.

To See Ourselves As Others See Us: Christians, Jews, "Others" in Late Antiquity. Ed. by Jacob Neusner & Ernest S. Frerichs. (Studies in Humanities). 512p. (Orig.). 1985. pap. 29.95 (0-89130-820-2, 00 01 09) Scholars Pr GA.

To See Ourselves 1986: Level 16. Evertts. (J). 1986. wbk. ed., pap. 14.50 (0-03-002407-2) HB Schl Dept.

To See the Buddha: A Philosopher's Quest for the Meaning of Emptiness. Malcolm D. Eckel. LC 94-26082. 232p. 1995. pap. text ed. 18.95 (0-691-03773-6) Princeton U Pr.

To See the Dawn: Baku, Nineteen Twenty - First Congress of the Peoples of the East. Ed. & Intro. by John Riddell. LC 93-85321. (Communist International in Lenin's Time Ser.). (Illus.). 344p. (Orig.). 1993. pap. 19.95 (0-87348-769-9); lib. bdg. 55.00 (0-87348-768-0) Pathfinder NY.

To See the Light. 72p. 25.00 (0-685-65464-8, PUB 119) Laser Inst.

To See the Matter Clearly & Other Poems. Ruth Fainlight. LC 68-8308. 6900. 15.95 (0-8023-1181-4) Dufour.

To See the Moon. Ethel Bacon. LC 95-8070. (Illus.). 32p. (J). (gr. k-3). 1996. pap. 14.95 (0-8167-3822-X) BrdgeWater.

To See the Obvious. Arthur J. Birch. Ed. by Jeffrey I. Seeman. LC 95-18601. (Profiles, Pathways, & Dreams Ser.). (Illus.). xxviii, 269p. 1995. 34.95 (0-8412-1840-4) Am Chemical.

To See the Promised Land. Fred L. Downing. LC 86-16459. 288p. 1986. 27.50 (0-86554-207-4, MUP-H189) Mercer Univ Pr.

*__To See the Unseen: A History of Planetary Radar Astronomy.__ 1997. lib. bdg. 259.95 (0-8490-6263-2) Gordon Pr.

*__To See the Unseen: A History of Planetary Radar Astronomy.__ Andrew J. Butrica. (Illus.). 301p. (Orig.). (C). 1997. pap. text ed. 50.00 (0-7881-4005-1) DIANE Pub.

To See the World. M. LeSueur Stewart. (C). 1991. lib. bdg. 192.00 (90-247-3744-3) Kluwer Ac.

*__To See with a Better Eye: A Life of R. T. H. Laennec.__ Jacalyn Duffin. LC 97-19779. 1998. write for info. (0-691-03708-6) Princeton U Pr.

To See with the Heart: The Life of Sitting Bull. Judith S. St. George. 192p. (J). (gr. 5-9). 1996. 17.95 (0-399-22930-2, Putnam) Putnam Pub Group.

*__To See Your Face Again.__ Eugenia Price. 1997. mass mkt. 6.99 (0-312-96233-9) St Martin.

To See Your Face Again. Eugenia Price. 1995. reprint ed. lib. bdg. 29.95 (1-56849-597-8) Buccaneer Bks.

To Seed the New Planet: A Story of Self-Realization & Divine Union Through Psychodelic Transformation. John Walker & Phil Rowe. 243p. (Orig.). 1995. pap. 12.95 (0-9645262-9-8) Beyond All.

To Seek a Better World: The Haitian Minority in America. Brent Ashabranner. LC 96-42967. 1997. pap. 16.99 (0-525-65219-1) NAL-Dutton.

To Seek America: A History of Ethnic Life in the United States. enl. rev. ed. Maxine S. Seller. LC 88-22486. 388p. 1988. pap. text ed. 24.95 (0-89198-137-3) Ozer.

To Seek & To Serve: Congregations in Mission. Anne Rowthorn. 406p. 1991. pap. 6.70 (0-88028-122-7, 1134) Forward Movement.

To Seek His Fortune. Mona McElderry. LC 96-66997. (Illus.). 64p. 1994. 10.00 (0-9641573-0-6) Sisu Pr.

*__To Seek My Fortune: Myth.__ Diane M. Meehan. Date not set. write for info. (0-688-12123-3) Morrow.

To Self Be True: The Search Within. Compiled by Evarts G. Loomis. 144p. (Orig.). 1991. pap. 8.00 (0-9630266-0-7) Friendly Hills.

To Serve & Collect: Chicago Politics & Police Corruption from the Lager Beer Riot to the Summerdale Scandal. Richard C. Lindberg. LC 90-38713. 384p. 1991. text ed. 49.95 (0-275-93415-2, C3415, Praeger Pubs) Greenwood.

To Serve & Protect: The Spirituality of Law Enforcement Officers. Judith Kowalski & Dean Collins. 128p. 1992. pap. 8.95 (0-87946-065-2, 143) ACTA Pubns.

To Serve & Protect: The True Story. Kelly E. Riddle. 122p. (Orig.). 1996. pap. 12.95 (0-9653096-0-6) Kelmar & Assocs.

To Serve As Cantor, Set. (Illus.). 1985. write for info. incl. audio (1-56125-002-3) Educ Services.

To Serve As Cantor, I: Basics of Church Singing. (Illus.). 44p. 1985. student ed. 20.00 incl. audio (1-56125-003-1) Educ Services.

To Serve As Cantor, II: The Divine Liturgy. (Illus.). 79p. 1987. student ed. 40.00 incl. audio (1-56125-012-0) Educ Services.

To Serve As Cantor, III: The Daily Offices. (Illus.). 76p. 1988. student ed. 30.00 incl. audio (1-56125-013-9) Educ Services.

To Serve As Jesus Served. Clem J. Walters. LC 83-70964. 132p. 1983. pap. 5.95 (0-943780-04-7, 8047) Greenlawn Pr.

To Serve As Jesus Served. Clem J. Walters. LC 83-70964. 132p. 1983. reprint ed. pap. 5.95 (0-937779-12-1) Greenlawn Pr.

To Serve Canada: A History of the Royal Military College Since the Second World War. Richard A. Preston. 250p. 1991. 34.95 (0-7766-0327-2, Pub. by Univ Ottawa Pr CN) Paul & Co Pubs.

To Serve In The Human Spirit. Witness Lee. 112p. per. 4.25 (0-87083-102-X, 14008001) Living Stream Ministry.

To Serve Man: A Cookbook for People. Karl Wurf. (Illus.). 1976. 10.00 (0-913896-05-5) Owlswick Pr.

***To Serve My Country ... Race.** Moore. 1998. pap. 17.95 (0-8147-5587-9) NYU Pr.

To Serve My Country, to Serve My Race: The Story of the Only African-American WACs Stationed Overseas During World War II. Brenda L. Moore. (Illus.). 272p. (C). 1996. 24.95 (0-8147-5522-4) NYU Pr.

To Serve One Another. W. B. Spillman. LC 92-28786. 1993. pap. 7.50 (0-8309-0627-4) Herald Hse.

***To Serve the Community Best: The Collected Papers on Communal Services of Martha K. Selig, M. S. W.** Martha K. Selig. LC 96-80343. 500p. (C). 1997. text ed. 99.95 (0-9638886-3-3) Granite Hills Pr.

***To Serve the Devil.** Walton Mendelson. 205p. (Orig.). 1998. mass mkt. 4.99 (1-55237-371-1, Pub. by Comnwlth Pub CN) Partners Pubs Grp.

***To Serve the Greatest Number: A History of Group Health Cooperative of Puget Sound.** Walt Crowley & Group Health Cooperative of Puget Sound Staff. LC 96-38972. (Illus.). 312p. 1997. 19.95 (0-295-97587-3) U of Wash Pr.

To Serve the People: Congress & Constituency Service. John R. Johannes. LC 83-17050. 310p. 1984. reprint ed. pap. 88.40 (0-608-02049-4, 2062702) Bks Demand.

To Serve the Present Age: The Brethren Service Story. M. R. Zigler. Ed. by Donald F. Durnbaugh. LC 75-6633. reprint ed. pap. 64.50 (0-608-02173-3, 2062842) Bks Demand.

To Serve the Present Age: The Gifts & Promise of United Methodism. Philip J. Wogaman. 128p. (Orig.). 1995. pap. 9.95 (0-687-01711-4) Abingdon.

To Serve the Public Interest: Educational Broadcasting in the United States. Robert J. Blakely. (C). 1979. 39.95 (0-8156-2198-1); pap. 14.95 (0-8156-0153-0) Syracuse U Pr.

To Serve Well & Faithfully: Labor & Indentured Servants in Pennsylvania, 1682-1800. Sharon V. Salinger. (Illus.). 224p. 1987. text ed. 54.95 (0-521-33442-X) Cambridge U Pr.

To Serve with Honor: A Treatise on Military Ethics & the Way of the Soldier. Richard A. Gabriel. LC 81-6254. xviii, 243p. 1982. text ed. 59.95 (0-313-22545-1, GME/, Greenwood Pr) Greenwood.

To Serve with Honor: A Treatise on Military Ethics & the Way of the Soldier. Richard A. Gabriel. LC 81-6254. 234p. 1987. pap. text ed. 14.95 (0-275-92711-3, B2711, Praeger Pubs) Greenwood.

To Serve with Love. Assistance League of Atlanta Staff. (Illus.). Date not set. text ed. write for info. (0-9648357-0-3) Assistance League of Corvallis.

To Set Before the King: Katharina Schratt's Festive Recipes. Ed. by Gertrud G. Champe. Tr. by Paula V. Arno & Louis Szathmary. LC 95-45507. (Iowa Szathmary Culinary Arts Ser.). (Illus.). 236p. (C). 1996. 24.95 (0-87745-535-X) U of Iowa Pr.

To Set One's Heart: Belief & Teaching in the Church. Sara P. Little. LC 82-49020. 160p. 1986. pap. 11.00 (0-8042-1442-5, John Knox) Westminster John Knox.

To Set the Captives Free: Reverend Jermain Wesley Loguen & the Struggle for Freedom in Central New York, 1835-1872. Carol Hunter. LC 92-36025. (Studies in African American History & Culture). (Illus.). 304p. 1993. text ed. 74.00 (0-8153-1014-5) Garland.

To Settle the Succession of the State: Literature & Politics, 1678-1750. J. A. Downie. LC 93-44269. 1994. text ed. 49.95 (0-312-12117-2) St Martin.

To Share a Dream. Willo D. Roberts. (Orig.). 1986. pap. 4.50 (0-373-97028-5) Harlequin Bks.

To Share a Dream. Willo D. Roberts. (Historical Ser.). (Orig.). 1994. mass mkt. 3.99 (0-373-28831-X, 1-28831-5) Harlequin Bks.

To Share a Moment. Monroe County Library System Staff. (Community Anthology Ser.). 144p. (Orig.). 1987. pap. 4.00 (0-940696-15-0) Monroe County Lib.

To Sheathe the Sword: Civil-Military Relations in the Quest for Democracy. John P. Lovell & David E. Albright. LC 96-28068. (Contributions in Political Science Ser.). 248p. 1997. text ed. 59.95 (0-313-30037-2) Greenwood.

***To Shield the Queen: A Mystery at Queen Elizabeth I's Court.** Fiona Buckley. LC 97-15684. (A Mystery at Queen Elizabeth I's Court Ser.). 1997. 21.00 (0-684-83841-9, S&S) S&S Trade.

To Shoot, Burn & Hang: Folk History from a Kentucky Mountain Family & Community. Daniel N. Rolph. LC 93-48781. (Illus.). 192p. (C). 1994. text ed. 25.00 (0-87049-844-4) U of Tenn Pr.

***To Sift Through Bitter Ashes, Vol. 1.** David N. Wilson. (Grails Covenant Ser.). (Orig.). 1997. mass mkt. 5.99 (1-56504-995-0, 11031, Wrld of Darkness) White Wolf.

To Sing in English: A Guide to Improved Diction. Dorothy Uris. LC 79-17264. 317p. (Orig.). (C). 1971. pap. text ed. 26.00 (0-913932-00-0) Boosey & Hawkes.

To Sing Our Own Songs: Cognition & Culture in Indian Education. 1985. pap. 2.50 (0-318-19173-3) Assn Am Indian.

To Sing with Pigs Is Human: The Concept of Person in Papua New Guinea. Jane C. Goodale. LC 94-40671. 252p. 1995. text ed. 50.00 (0-295-97454-0); pap. text ed. 25.00 (0-295-97436-2) U of Wash Pr.

To Singles with Love: Quotations of Inspiration for You Alone. Gayle T. Watts. 385p. (Orig.). 1992. pap. 14.95 (0-945772-11-4) Clarkston Pub.

To Sir, with Love. E. R. Braithwaite. (J). (gr. 9-12). 1990. mass mkt. 4.50 (0-515-10519-8) Jove Pubns.

***To Skim the Smoke: Poems.** Jay Liveson. LC 96-53097. 92p. 1997. pap. 14.95 (0-7734-2707-4, Mellen Poetry Pr) E Mellen.

To Skin a Cat. Thomas McGuane. LC 87-40093. (Vintage Contemporaries Ser.). 224p. 1987. pap. 10.00 (0-394-75521-9, Vin) Random.

To Skin a Cat. Thomas McGuane. 1994. pap. 10.00 (0-394-25888-6) Random.

To Skin a Cat. Stan Smith. LC 92-60525. 240p. 1992. pap. 5.95 (0-9632824-0-9) Sundance Pr.

To Slay the Dragon. Jay Liveson. LC 95-51017. 92p. 1996. pap. 14.95 (0-7734-2676-0, Mellen Poetry Pr) E Mellen.

To Slay the Dreamer. large type ed. Alexander Cordell. 511p. 1982. 25.99 (0-7089-0766-0) Ulverscroft.

To Sleep With Evil. Andria Cardarelle. 1996. pap. 5.99 (0-7869-0515-8) TSR Inc.

To Sleep with the Angels: The Story of a Fire. David Cowan & John Kuenster. LC 95-46795. (Illus.). 320p. 1996. 25.00 (1-56663-102-5) I R Dee.

To Snag a Sparrow. Donald A. Bowes. LC 88-70444. 92p. (Orig.). 1989. pap. 6.00 (0-916383-52-0) Aegina Pr.

To Soar with the Eagle. Blaine M. Yorgason. LC 93-5325. 280p. 1993. 13.95 (0-87579-745-8) Deseret Bk.

To Sow a Seed. Robert Albert. (C). 1990. text ed. 31.00 (0-7223-2553-3, Pub. by A H S Ltd UK) St Mut.

To Sow One Acre More: Childbearing & Farm Productivity in the Antebellum North. Lee A. Craig. LC 92-40483. (Studies in Historical & Political Science). 168p. (C). 1993. text ed. 30.00 (0-8018-4529-7) Johns Hopkins.

***To Space & Back.** HarBrace Staff. 1995. pap. 11.00 (0-15-305606-1) HarBrace.

To Space & Back. Susan Okie & Sally K. Ride. LC 85-23757. (Illus.). 96p. (J). (gr. 1 up). 1989. pap. 12.95 (0-688-09112-1) Morrow.

To Space & Back. Susan Okie & Sally K. Ride. LC 85-23757. (Illus.). 96p. (J). (gr. 1 up). 1986. reprint ed. 19.00 (0-688-06159-1) Lothrop.

To Space & Back: The Story of the Shuttle. Susan D. Gold. LC 91-42565. (Adventures in Space Ser.). (Illus.). 48p. (J). (gr. 5-6). 1992. lib. bdg. 12.95 (0-89686-688-2, Crstwood Hse) Silver Burdett Pr.

To Spank or Not to Spank: A Parent's Handbook. John K. Rosemond. LC 94-30050. (Illus.). 128p. 1994. pap. 8.95 (0-8362-2813-8) Andrews & McMeel.

To Speak Again. Raymond A. Berte. 196p. 1987. 19.95 (0-941219-50-X) Phillips Pub MA.

To Speak Again: My Victory over Throat Cancer. Raymond Berte. 192p. 1988. 14.95 (0-8159-6923-6) Devin.

To Speak in Pairs: Essays on the Ritual Languages of Eastern Indonesia. Ed. by James J. Fox. (Cambridge Studies in Oral & Literate Culture: No. 15). (Illus.). 300p. 1988. text ed. 89.95 (0-521-34332-1) Cambridge U Pr.

To Speak of Love. large type ed. Claudia Jameson. 306p. 1993. 25.99 (0-7505-0476-5) Ulverscroft.

To Speak of Love. large type ed. Ann Redmayne. (Linford Romance Library). 1991. pap. 15.99 (0-7089-6988-7, Trailtree Bookshop) Ulverscroft.

To Speak or Be Silent: The Paradox of Disobedience in the Lives of Women. Ed. by Lena B. Ross. LC 92-45106. 304p. (Orig.). 1993. pap. 5.95 (0-933029-68-3) Chiron Pubns.

To Speak the Truth: Why Washington's 'Cold War' against Cuba Doesn't End. Fidel Castro & Che Guevara. LC 91-75347. (Illus.). 232p. (Orig.). (C). 1992. pap. 16.95 (0-87348-633-1); lib. bdg. 50.00 (0-87348-634-X) Pathfinder NY.

To Speak While Dreaming. Eleni Sikelianos. Ed. by Joseph Richey. (Illus.). 64p. (Orig.). 1993. pap. 8.00 (1-882775-03-1) Selva Edit.

To Speak with Cloth: Studies in Indonesian Textiles. Ed. by Mattiebelle Gittinger. LC 89-50052. (Illus.). 256p. 1989. 40.00 (0-930741-18-8); pap. 27.00 (0-930741-17-X) UCLA Fowler Mus.

To Split a Human. Carmen Tafoya. (Illus.). 115p. 1985. write for info. (0-614-04876-1) Mex Am Cult.

To Split a Human: Mitos, Machos y la Mujer Chicana. Carmen Tafolla. (Illus.). 117p. (Orig.). (ENG & SPA.). 1985. pap. 9.95 (0-932545-00-9) Mex Am Cult.

To Spoil the Sun. Joyce Rockwood. (YA). (gr. 7 up). 1994. pap. 7.95 (0-8050-3465-X, Bks Young Read) H Holt & Co.

To Spread the Power. George G. Hunter, III. LC 86-26507. 224p. 1987. pap. 14.95 (0-687-42259-0) Abingdon.

To Square with Genesis: Causal Statements & Shamanic Ideas in Wayapi. Alan T. Campbell. LC 88-51972. (Illus.). 214p. 1989. text ed. 29.95 (0-87745-248-2) U of Iowa Pr.

To Squat or Not to Squat...That Is the Question? Rickey D. Crain. (Illus.). 140p. (Orig.). 1994. pap. text ed. 16.95 (0-929994-06-X) Crains Muscle.

To Squat or Not to Squat...That Is the Question? Rickey D. Crain. (Illus.). 140p. (C). 1994. text ed. 29.95 (0-929994-07-8) Crains Muscle.

To Stalk the Oomingmak...An Artist's Arctic Journal. Chris Czajowski. LC 89-85389. (Illus.). 112p. 1989. 19.95 (0-9616679-1-5) Aquarelle Pr.

To Stand Alone: Inside the KKK for the FBI. Delmar D. Dennis. 208p. (Orig.). 1991. pap. 14.95 (0-925591-05-X) Covenant Hse Bks.

***To Stand & Not Be Moved: Strenghtening Your Faith to Face Life's Challenges.** Fran Sciacca. 1997. pap. text ed. 6.00 (0-89109-989-1) NavPress.

To Starve the Army at Pleasure: Continental Army Administration & American Political Culture, 1775-1783. E. Wayne Carp. LC 83-19697. (Illus.). xv, 305p. 1984. 39.95 (0-8078-1587-X); pap. 13.95 (0-8078-4269-9) U of NC Pr.

To Steal a Book Is an Elegant Offense: Intellectual Property Law in Chinese Civilization. William P. Alford. LC 94-15742. (Studies in East Asian Law). xiii ,p. 1994. 39.50 (0-8047-2270-6) Stanford U Pr.

To Steal a Kingdom: Probing Hawaiian History. Michael Dougherty. 245p. (Orig.). 1995. pap. 12.95 (0-9633484-0-X) Island Style.

To Steal a March on God. Hanna Krall. (Polish Theatre Archive Ser,). 1996. text ed. 46.00 (3-7186-5776-7); pap. text ed. 23.00 (3-7186-5777-5) Gordon & Breach.

To Stem This Tide, a Survey of Racial Tension Areas in the United States. Charles S. Johnson. LC 74-99890. reprint ed. 29.50 (0-404-00175-0) AMS Pr.

To Step among Wrack. Fiona MacInnes. LC 86. 40.00 (0-907618-17-0, Pub. by Orkney Pr UK) St Mut.

To Stir a Magick Cauldron: A Witch's Guide to Casting & Conjuring. Silver RavenWolf. LC 95-45595. (Illus.). 312p. 1996. pap. 16.95 (1-56718-424-3) Llewellyn Pubns.

To Stop a Rising Sun: Reminiscences of Wartime in India & Burma. Roy Humphreys. (Illus.). 224p. 1996. 30.95 (0-7509-1181-6, Pub. by Sutton Pubng UK) Bks Intl VA.

To Stop a War. Roderick Glaswich. (C). 1989. text ed. 59.00 (1-85821-019-4, Pub. by Pentland Pr UK) St Mut.

To Stretch a Plank: A Survey of Psychokinesis. Diana M. Robinson. LC 80-12335. 282p. 1981. 29.95 (0-88229-404-0) Nelson-Hall.

***To Strike a Match.** LaJoyce Martin. LC 97-25227. 250p. 1997. pap. 7.99 (1-56722-206-4) Word Aflame.

To Strike at a King: The Turning Point in the McCarthy Witch Hunts. Michael Ranville. (Illus.). 292p. 1996. 29.95 (1-879094-53-3) Momentum Bks.

To Strive, to Search, to Find. (Illus.). 144p. 1976. 5.95 (0-685-19260-1) Shepherd-Moore Ed Foun.

To Strive, to Search, to Find. Marie Shepherd-Moore. LC 80-2367. 1979. pap. 5.95 (0-9603948-1-8) Shepherd-Moore Ed Foun.

To Struga with Love. Ed. by Stanley H. Barkan. LC 78-67775. (Illus.). (Orig.). 1978. 25.00 (0-89304-098-3, CCC115); 15.00 (0-685-01276-X); boxed 30.00 (0-89304-050-9) Cross-Cultrl NY.

To Supplement or Not to Supplement. Bader. 1995. pap. 17.95 (0-9632899-5-0) Mylin Pub.

To Surf & Detect: Crime & Punishment on the Internet. Dennis Bolen. (Go! Guides Ser.). (Illus.). 64p. (Orig.). 1996. pap. 10.95 (1-57712-004-3) Motion Works.

To Tacoma by Trolley. Warren W. Wing. LC 94-73942. (Illus.). 144p. 1996. 39.50 (0-915713-29-2) Pac Fast Mail.

***To Take a Queen.** Jan Smith. (Black Lace Ser.). 300p. 1996. mass mkt. 5.95 (0-352-33098-8, Pub. by Virgin Pub UK) London Brdge.

To Take Charleston: The Civil War on Folly Island. James W. Hagy. LC 93-83754. (Illus.). 100p. (Orig.). 1993. pap. 9.95 (0-929521-73-0) Pictorial Hist.

To Take Place: Toward Theory in Ritual. Jonathan Z. Smith. LC 86-30869. (Chicago Studies in the History of Judaism). xviii, 202p. 1992. pap. text ed. 15.50 (0-226-76361-7) U Ch Pr.

To Tame a Land. Louis L'Amour, pseud. 22.95 (0-89190-159-0) Amereon Ltd.

To Tame a Land. Louis L'Amour. 160p. 1991. 3.99 (0-553-28031-7) Bantam.

To Tame a Texan's Heart. Jodi Thomas. 320p. 1994. mass mkt. 4.99 (0-7865-0059-X) Diamond.

***To Tame a Texan's Heart.** large type ed. Jodi Thomas. (Niagara Large Print Ser.). 384p. 1996. 27.99 (0-7089-5845-1) Ulverscroft.

***To Tame a Warrior's Heart.** Sharon Schulze. 1997. mass mkt. 4.99 (0-373-28986-3, 1-28986-7) Harlequin Bks.

To Tame a Wild Heart. Emma Darcy. (Presents Ser.: No. 455). 1992. pap. 2.89 (0-373-11455-9, 1-11455-2) Harlequin Bks.

To Tame a Wild Heart. large type ed. Emma Darcy. 261p. 1992. reprint ed. lib. bdg. 16.95 (1-56054-496-1) Thorndike Pr.

To Tame a Wolfe. Anne McAllister. 1994. 3.59 (0-373-45172-5) Harlequin Bks.

To Tame the Hunter. Stephanie James. (Men Made in America Ser.). 1995. pap. 3.59 (0-373-45194-6, 1-45194-7) Harlequin Bks.

To Tangle with Tarzan: Seven Short Stories & an Epic. P. Chudi Uwazurike. LC 91-71025. 160p. 1992. 29.95 (0-86543-246-5); pap. 9.95 (0-86543-247-3) Africa World.

To Taste the Wine. Fern Michaels. (Orig.). 1987. mass mkt. 5.95 (0-345-30360-1) Ballantine.

To Teach: The Journey of a Teacher. William Ayers. LC 92-43749. 160p. (C). 1993. Alk. paper. 14.95 (0-8077-3262-1) Tchrs Coll.

To Teach a Dyslexic. unabridged ed. Don McCabe. 288p. (Orig.). 1996. pap. 14.95 (1-56400-004-4, 663) AVKO Educ Res.

To Teach, To Love. Jesse H. Stuart. LC 92-808. 317p. (YA). (gr. 10 up). 1987. reprint ed. 22.00 (0-945084-02-1) J Stuart Found.

To Teachers with Love. Ingeborg S. MacHaffie. Ed. by Margaret Nielsen. (Illus.). 90p. (Orig.). 1986. per. 5.95 (0-9609374-2-0) Skribent.

To Tell a Free Story: The First Century of Afro-American Autobiography, 1760-1865. William L. Andrews. 368p. 1986. text ed. 29.95 (0-252-01222-4); pap. text ed. 19.95 (0-252-06033-4) U of Ill Pr.

To Tell at Last: Survival under False Identity, 1941-45. Blanca Rosenberg. LC 92-32695. (Illus.). 206p. (C). 1993. 19.95 (0-252-01998-9) U of Ill Pr.

To Tell at Last: Survival under False Identity, 1941-45. Blanca Rosenberg. (C). 1995. 12.95 (0-252-06520-4) U of Ill Pr.

To Tell Me Terrible Lies: First of the Wainwright Chronicles, 1778-1783. Katherine St. Clare. LC 92-64334. (Wainwright Chronicles Ser.). 348p. 1993. 24.95 (0-9632830-1-4) Wainwright PA.

To Tell the Mystery. T. E. Schmidt & M. Silva. (Journal for the Study of the New Testament Supplement Ser.: No. 100). 266p. 56.00 (1-85075-486-1, Pub. by Sheffield Acad UK) CUP Services.

To Tell the Story. Yala Korwin. LC 87-80791. (Illus.). 130p. 1987. 13.95 (0-89604-090-9, Holocaust Library); pap. 8.95 (0-89604-091-7, Holocaust Library) US Holocaust.

To Tell the Truth. Janet Dailey. (Americana Ser.: No. 887). 1992. mass mkt. 3.59 (0-373-89887-8) Harlequin Bks.

To Tell the Truth. Brian K. Ogawa et al. LC 88-51256. (Illus.). 40p. (J). (gr. 4-6). 1988. text ed. write for info. (0-9621260-0-4) VWAD.

***To Tell the Truth.** Brian K. Ogawa. LC 97-576. (Illus.). (J). 1997. 9.95 (1-884244-15-7) Volcano Pr.

To Tell the Truth. Linda Rebuck & Tom Fettke. (J). 1985. 5.50 (0-685-68203-X, MB-546) Lillenas.

To Tell the Truth. Linda Rebuck & Tom Fettke. (J). 1985. audio 10.99 (0-685-68204-8, TA-9065C) Lillenas.

***To Tell the Truth.** unabridged ed. Patri Farmer. (Illus.). 32p. (J). (gr. k up). 1997. 13.95 (0-7737-3005-2, Pub. by Stoddart Kids CN) Genl Dist Srvs.

***To Tell the Truth.** 3rd rev. ed. Brian Ogawa. LC 97-576. (Illus.). 32p. (J). (gr. 2-6). 1997. pap. 9.95 (0-614-30182-3) Volcano Pr.

To Tempt a Man. Joanna McGrauran. 352p. 1995. mass mkt. 4.99 (0-440-21875-6) Dell.

***To Thank a River.** Jean Clausen. 1996. pap. 9.95 (1-878569-37-6) Badger Bks Inc.

To That Solitary Individual: An Octogenarian's Counsel on Living & Dying. John R. Yungblut. LC 94-6758. 32p. 1994. pap. 3.00 (0-87574-316-1) Pendle Hill.

To the American Indian: Reminiscences of a Yurok Woman. rev. ed. Lucy Thompson. LC 91-70671. (Illus.). 322p. 1991. reprint ed. pap. 13.95 (0-930588-47-9) Heyday Bks.

To the American Indian: Reminiscences of a Yurok Woman. Lucy Thompson. 322p. 1991. reprint ed. lib. bdg. 37.00 (0-8095-4952-2) Borgo Pr.

To the Angel of the Church in Philadelphia. Vincent M. Walsh. 90p. 1989. pap. 4.00 (0-943374-19-7) Key of David.

To the Arctic: An Introduction to the Far Northern World. Steven B. Young. 354p. 1994. pap. text ed. 16.95 (0-471-07889-1) Wiley.

To the Arctic by Canoe: The Journal & Paintings of Robert Hood, Midshipman with Franklin. Ed. by C. Stuart Houston. (Illus.). 280p. 1994. pap. 22.95 (0-7735-1222-5, Pub. by McGill CN) U of Toronto Pr.

To the Beach see Set 2

To the Best of My Ability. (C). 1988. pap. text ed. 8.95 (0-393-95781-0) Norton.

To the Best of My Knowledge & Belief. Michael Allamby. 156p. (Orig.). 1996. pap. 19.95 (0-9651029-0-4) Lemcas Bks.

***To the Best of My Recollection: A Childhood Memory Journal for Adults.** Kathleen Lashier. (Memory-a-Day Ser.). 366p. (Orig.). 1996. spiral bd., pap. 8.95 (1-56383-060-4, 5058) G & R Pub.

To the Birdhouse. Cathleen Schine. 1990. 10.95 (0-374-27828-8) FS&G.

To the Birdhouse. Cathleen Schine. 288p. 1996. pap. 10.95 (0-452-27662-4, Plume) NAL-Dutton.

To the Bone: New & Selected Poems. Sydney Lea. LC 95-50189. 232p. (C). 1996. 17.95 (0-252-06519-0); text ed. 29.95 (0-252-02223-8) U of Ill Pr.

To the Bottom of the Sea: True Accounts of Major Ship Disasters. John Protasio. 1990. 18.95 (0-8184-0530-9) Carol Pub Group.

***To the Bright & Shining Sun.** James L. Burke. Date not set. lib. bdg. 24.95 (0-8488-1776-1) Amereon Ltd.

To the Bright & Shining Sun. James Lee Burke. LC 94-35202. 224p. 1995. pap. 10.95 (0-7868-8012-0) Hyperion.

To the Center of the Earth: Poems. Michael Fried. LC 94-7552. 1994. 18.00 (0-374-27829-6) FS&G.

To the Center of the Earth: Poems. Michael Fried. 68p. 1996. pap. text ed. 9.00 (0-374-52471-8, Noonday) FS&G.

To the Central African Lakes & Back, 2 vols., Set. 2nd rev. ed. Joseph Thomson. 1968. reprint ed. 95.00 (0-7146-1857-8, Pub. by F Cass Pubs UK) Intl Spec Bk.

To the Chukchi Peninsula & to the Tlingit Indians, 1881-1882: Journals & Letters by Aurel & Arthur Krause. Tr. by Margot K. McCaffrey. LC 92-47100. (Rasmuson Library Historical Translation Ser.: Vol. VIII). (Illus.). xiii, 230p. (ENG & GER.). 1993. pap. 17.50 (0-912006-66-8) U of Alaska Pr.

To the Circus. Fred Church. 216p. 1991. write for info. (0-9630027-0-8) R Church Co.

To the Columbia Gateway: The Oregon Railway & the Northern Pacific, 1879-1884. Peter J. Lewty. LC 87-21041. (Illus.). 202p. 1987. 30.00 (0-87422-030-0); pap. 20.00 (0-87422-029-7) Wash St U Pr.

To the Credit of the Sea. Lawrence Mott. LC 78-150555. (Short Story Index Reprint Ser.). 1977. reprint ed. 21.95 (0-8369-3852-6) Ayer.

To the Deacon. Rodney Ryce. 90p. 1995. write for info. (0-9648514-0-7); write for info. (0-9648514-1-5) PRO-FAN.

To the Death. Robert Merritt. 320p. 1990. mass mkt. 4.50 (0-380-70904-X) Avon.

To the Death. Robert Merritt. 276p. 1988. 17.95 (0-945167-04-0) British Amer Pub.

T

To the Desert with Stuart - Eighteen Forty-Four. Daniel G. Brock. 240p. (C). 1989. pap. text ed. 40.00 (0-89771-021-5, Pub. by Bob Mossel AT) St Mut.
To the Desert with Sturt: A Diary of the 1844 Expedition SA Government Printer & RGSA (SA) Daniel G. Brock. 222p. (C). 1989. 39.00 (0-7855-0328-5, Pub. by Royal Geograp Soc AT) St Mut.
To the Devil. William Jack. 144p. (Orig.). 1990. pap. 9.95 (0-86072-132-9, Pub. by Quartet UK) Interlink Pub.
To the Director & Playwright. Michael Chekhov. LC 77-8158. (Illus.). 329p. 1977. reprint ed. text ed. 35.00 (0-8371-9615-9, CHTD, Greenwood Pr) Greenwood.
To the Distant Observer: Form & Meaning in Japanese Cinema. Noel Burch. LC 77-20316. 1979. 48.00 (0-520-03605-0) U CA Pr.
To the Dogs. Elliot Erwitt. (Illus.). 144p. 1992. 49.95 (1-881616-01-0) Dist Art Pubs.
To the Dreams of Youth: Winchester .22 Caliber Single Shot Rifle. Herbert Houze. LC 92-74799. (Illus.). 192p. 1993. 34.95 (0-87341-237-0, WD01) Krause Pubns.
To the Earthmen. Solomon Simonson. LC 89-42582. 104p. 1989. 11.95 (0-88400-134-2) Shengold.
*__To the East from Istanbul to Indonesia Travellers Survival Kit.__ Emily Hatchwell. 448p. (Orig.). 1997. pap. 14.95 (1-85458-031-0, Pub. by Vac Wrk Pubns UK) Seven Hills Bk.
To the Edge of the Universe. Bill Yenne. 1986. 12.98 (0-671-08196-9) S&S Trade.
To the End of the Trail. Richard Hovey. (Notable American Authors Ser.). 1992. reprint ed. lib. bdg. 75.00 (0-7812-3195-7) Rprt Serv.
To the End of the World. Blaise Cendrars. 251p. 9100. reprint ed. 30.00 (0-7206-0819-8, Pub. by P Owen Ltd UK) Dufour.
To the End of West. Henry Chapin. 1970. pap. 6.95 (0-87233-017-6) Bauhan.
*__To the Ends of the Earth.__ Lucille C. Outhwaite. (Illus.). 132p. (Orig.). 1997. pap. 19.95 (0-9631722-7-1) Hamilton Print.
To the Ends of the Earth. Paul Theroux. 1994. mass mkt. 6.99 (0-8041-1122-7) Ivy Books.
*__To the Ends of the Earth, Pts. I & II.__ 324p. (Orig.). 1996. pap. 14.95 (0-9655658-1-5) SS Pub Co.
*__To the Ends of the Earth: A Journey Through Acts.__ A. L. Barry. LC 97-6400. 1997. 12.99 (0-570-04985-7) Concordia.
To the Ends of the Earth: A Novel of the Byzantine Empire. T. Davis Bunn. LC 95-34248. 400p. 1995. 22.99 (0-7852-7898-2) Nelson.
To the Ends of the Earth: A Novel of the Byzantine Empire. T. Davis Bunn. LC 95-34248. 352p. 1997. pap. 12.99 (0-7852-7214-3) Nelson.
*__To the Ends of the Earth: Aspects of Eastern Catholic Church History.__ 100p. (Orig.). 1997. pap. 7.00 (1-887158-10-3) God With Us.
To the Ends of the Earth: Women's Search for Education in Medicine. Thomas N. Bonner. (Illus.). 232p. (C). 1992. 39.00 (0-674-89303-4) HUP.
To the Ends of the Earth: Women's Search for Education in Medicine. Thomas N. Bonner. (Illus.). 232p. 1995. pap. text ed. 16.95 (0-674-89304-2, BONENX) HUP.
*__To the Ends of the Earth Pt. I: A Spiritual Journey to God's Holy Mountain.__ Bob Cerami. LC 96-92900. 176p. (Orig.). 1997. pap. 9.95 (0-9655658-0-7) SS Pub Co.
*__To the Ends of the Earth Pt. II: Ascending the Mountain.__ Bob Cerami. LC 96-93119. 148p. (Orig.). 1997. pap. 9.95 (0-9655658-3-1) SS Pub Co.
*__To the Euphrates & Beyond.__ Ed. by O. M. Haex et al. 352p. 1989. 95.00 (90-6191-866-9, Pub. by A A Balkema NE) Ashgate Pub Co.
To the Fallen Angels: Man's Spiritual Heritage, Earthly Missing, & Evolutionary Destiny. Richard D. Murad. LC 94-92105. 104p. 1994. pap. 11.45 (1-885384-00-9) Soldier Mystic.
To the Far Blue Mountains. Louis L'Amour. 288p. 1984. mass mkt. 3.99 (0-553-27688-3) Bantam.
To the Farewell Address: Ideas of Early American Foreign Policy. Felix Gilbert. 181p. 1961. pap. text ed. 12.95 (0-691-00574-5) Princeton U Pr.
To the Farthest Gulf: The Story of the American China Trade. Dorothy S. Hawes. Ed. by John Q. Feller. (Illus.). 120p. (Orig.). 1990. pap. 10.95 (0-938864-13-0) Ipswich Pr.
To the Fierce Guard in the Assyrian Saloon. Howard W. Robertson. Ed. by Tom Trusky. LC 86-71904. (Ahsahta Press Modern & Contemporary Poets of the West Ser.). 65p. (Orig.). 1987. pap. 6.95 (0-916272-33-8) Ahsahta Pr.
To the Finland Station. Edmund Wilson. 1994. reprint ed. lib. bdg. 27.95 (1-56849-574-9) Buccaneer Bks.
To the Forbidden Land: Discoveries & Adventures in Tibet Selected & Adapted from Sven Hedin's Trans-Himalaya. Sven A. Hedin. (C). 1988. reprint ed. 17.50 (81-206-0390-7, Pub. by Asian Educ Servs II) S Asia.
To the Four Corners: A Festschrift in Honor of Rose Brandel. Rose Brandel & Ellen C. Leichtman. LC 94-23360. (Detroit Monographs in Musicology, Studies In Music: No. 14). 1995. 45.00 (0-89990-070-4) Info Coord.
To the Friend Who Did Not Save My Life. Herve Guibert. Tr. by Linda Coverdale from FRE. 272p. 1991. text ed. 18.95 (0-689-12120-2, Pub. by Ctrl Bur voor Schimmel NE) Macmillan.
To the Friend Who Did Not Save My Life. Herve Guibert. Tr. by Linda Coverdale from FRE. (High Risk Bks.). 240p. 1994. reprint ed. pap. 11.95 (1-85242-328-5) Serpents Tail.
*__To the Garden Alone.__ large type ed. Eve Ebbett. (Large Print Ser.). 304p. 1997. 27.50 (0-7089-3683-0) Ulverscroft.
To the Gates of Richmond: The Peninsula Campainge. Stephen W. Sears. 1994. pap. 14.95 (0-395-70101-5) Ticknor & Fields.
*__To the Glory of Her Sex: Women's Roles in the Composition of Medieval Texts.__ Joan M. Ferrante. LC 96-43546. (Women of Letters Ser.). 1997. write for info. (0-253-33254-0); pap. write for info. (0-253-21108-5) Ind U Pr.
To the Golden Cities: Pursuing the American Jewish Dream in Miami & L. A. Deborah D. Moore. 300p. 1994. 24.95 (0-02-922111-0, Free Press) Free Pr.
To the Golden Cities: Pursuing the American Jewish Dream in Miami & L. A. Deborah D. Moore. (Illus.). 384p. 1996. pap. 15.95 (0-674-89305-0) HUP.
To the Golden Door. George Potter. LC 73-3928. (Illus.). 631p. 1973. reprint ed. text ed. 35.00 (0-8371-6862-7, POGD, Greenwood Pr) Greenwood.
To the Golden Shore. Peter Browning. LC 95-35819. (Illus.). 432p. (Orig.). (C). 1995. pap. 22.95 (0-944220-07-X) Great West Bks.
To The Golden Shore: The Life of Adoniram Judson. Courtney Anderson. 544p. (Orig.). 1987. pap. 13.50 (0-8170-1121-8) Judson.
To the Graduate - Keys to Success. Ed. by Mac Anderson. 78p. (Orig.). 1985. pap. 7.95 (0-931089-15-8) Great Quotations.
To the Gutter & Back. Len Bromby. (C). 1989. text ed. 35.00 (0-948929-36-7) St Mut.
To the Halls of the Montezumas: The Mexican War in the American Imagination. Robert W. Johannsen. (Illus.). 384p. 1988. pap. 18.95 (0-19-504981-0) OUP.
To the Hands of the Poor, Water & Trees. B. Chambers et al. (C). 1989. 24.00 (81-204-0428-9, Pub. by Oxford IBH II) S Asia.
To the Happy Few: Selected Letters. Stendhal, pseud. Ed. by E. Boudot-Lamotte. Tr. by Norman Cameron from FRE. 384p. 8600. reprint ed. pap. 16.95 (0-948166-09-6, Pub. by Soho Bk Co UK) Dufour.
*__To the Heart of Spain: Food & Wine Adventures Beyond the Pyrenees.__ Ann Walker & Larry Walker. LC 96-86239. 320p. 1997. pap. 14.95 (0-9653774-0-7) Berkeley Hills.
To the Heart of the Storm. Will Eisner. Ed. by Dave Schreiner. LC 91-6607. (Illus.). 208p. (Orig.). 1991. 24.95 (0-87816-132-5); pap. 14.95 (0-87816-133-3) Kitchen Sink.
To the Heart of the Storm. deluxe ed. Will Eisner. Ed. by Dave Schreiner. LC 91-6607. (Illus.). 208p. (Orig.). 1991. 39.95 (0-87816-142-2) Kitchen Sink.
To the Hebrews. Tr. by George W. Buchanan. LC 72-76127. (Anchor Bible Ser.: Vol. 36). 312p. 1972. 29.00 (0-385-02995-0, Anchor NY) Doubleday.
To the Hilt. Dick Francis. 320p. 1996. 24.95 (0-399-14185-5, Putnam) Putnam Pub Group.
*__To the Hilt.__ Dick Francis. 352p. 1997. mass mkt. 6.99 (0-515-12148-7) Jove Pubns.
*__To the Hilt.__ large type ed. Dick Francis. LC 96-41323. (Basic Ser.). 447p. 1996. 26.95 (0-7862-0892-9, Thorndike Lrg Prnt); 24.95 (0-7862-0893-7, Thorndike Lrg Prnt) Thorndike Pr.
*__To the Hoop: The Seasons of a Basketball Life.__ Ira Berkow. LC 97-2009. 295p. 1997. 23.00 (0-465-08495-8) Basic.
To the House Ghost. Paula Rankin. LC 84-72993. (Poetry Ser.). 56p. 1985. 20.95 (0-88748-013-6); pap. 11.95 (0-88748-014-4) Carnegie-Mellon.
To the Ladies: How to Enjoy a Day's Fishing on the Pacific Ocean. Norma Engel. LC 87-51191. (Illus.). 45p. (Orig.). 1987. pap. 3.95 (0-938711-03-2) Tecolote Pubns.
To the Lake of the Skies: The Benedicts in the Adirondacks. Barbara McMartin. (Illus.). 192p. 1996. pap. text ed. 20.00 (1-888374-02-0) Lake View NY.
To the Land of Gold & Wickedness: The 1848-59 Diary of Lorena L. Hays. Ed. by Jeanne H. Watson. LC 88-19590. xvi, 488p. (Orig.). 1988. pap. 14.95 (0-935284-87-7) Patrice Pr.
To the Land of the Cattails. Aharon Appelfeld. 148p. 1994. pap. 11.00 (0-8021-3359-2, Grove) Grove-Atltic.
To the Land of the Living. Robert Silverberg. 1990. mass mkt. 4.95 (0-445-20844-9) Warner Bks.
To the Land Where the Sun Might Never Set: The Story of Newgrange. Paul Francis. LC 95-72792. (Illus.). 30p. (Orig.). (J). (gr. 1-5). 1996. pap. 6.95 (1-57098-065-9) R Rinehart.
To the Last Bird: The Story of a Wisconsin Pioneer Family. Evalyn A. Blumer & Jerry W. Carlton. LC 85-72500. (Illus.). 397p. 1985. 27.95 (0-318-22234-5); pap. 23.95 (0-318-22235-3) Carlton & Blumer.
To the Last Cartridge. Robert Barr-Smith. 400p. (Orig.). 1994. pap. 12.50 (0-380-77212-4) Avon.
To the Last Man. Zane Grey. 1976. 24.95 (0-8488-1023-6) Amereon Ltd.
To the Last Man. Zane Grey. 352p. 1991. mass mkt. 3.99 (0-06-100218-6, Harp PBks) HarpC.
*__To the Last Round: The South Nottinghamshire Hussars, 1939-1942.__ Peter Hart. 1996. 26.95 (0-85052-514-4, Pub. by L Cooper Bks UK) Trans-Atl Phila.
To the Left of the Worshiper. Jeffrey Greene. LC 91-17407. 72p. (Orig.). 1991. pap. 9.95 (0-914086-93-6) Alicejamesbooks.
To the Letter. Diana D. Booher. 524p. pap. 24.95 (0-669-16818-1, Lexington) Jossey-Bass.
To the Lighthouse. Virginia Woolf. LC 92-52912. 272p. 1992. 17.00 (0-679-40537-2) Knopf.
To the Lighthouse. Virginia Woolf. 1989. pap. 9.00 (0-15-690739-9) HarBrace.
To the Lighthouse. Virginia Woolf. 1990. 17.00 (0-15-190737-4) HarBrace.
*__To the Lighthouse.__ Virginia Woolf. LC 97-7313. (Perennial Ser.). 278p. 1997. 24.95 (0-7838-8137-1, GK Hall) Thorndike Pr.
*__To the Lighthouse: New York Public Library Collector's Edition.__ Virginia Woolf. 1997. 18.50 (0-385-48720-7) Doubleday.
To the Lighthouse: Virginia Woolf. Virginia Woolf. Ed. by Sandra Kemp. LC 93-38757. (English Text Ser.). 224p. (Orig.). (C). 1995. pap. 16.95 (0-415-01663-0, A7125) Routledge.
To the Lighthouse & Back: Writings on Teaching & Living, Vol. 19. Mary A. Doll. (Counterpoints Ser.). 184p. (C). 1995. pap. 29.95 (0-8204-2777-2) P Lang Pubng.
To the Lighthouse & Beyond: Transformations in the Narratives of Virginia Woolf. Virginia Hyman. (American University Studies: English Language & Literature: Ser. IV, Vol. 66). 288p. (C). 1989. text ed. 39.10 (0-8204-0620-1) P Lang Pubng.
To the Lightning. Catherine Ennis. 208p. 1988. pap. 8.95 (0-941483-06-1) Naiad Pr.
To the Limit. J. Crelinsten. (Illus.). 64p. (J). (gr. 3 up). 1993. 18.00 (0-15-200616-8, Gulliver Bks) HarBrace.
*__To the Limit: The Untold Story of the Eagles.__ Marc Eliot. 1997. 23.95 (0-316-23370-6) Little.
To the Limit of Their Endurance: A Family Story of the VII Fighter Command. Lynn Farnol. 100p. (Orig.). 1986. pap. 13.95 (0-89745-076-0) Sunflower U Pr.
To the Linksland. Michael Bamberger. 208p. 1993. pap. 12.95 (0-14-015941-X, Penguin Bks) Viking Penguin.
To the Lion Throne. Whitney Stewart. (Illus.). 165p. (Orig.). (J). (gr. 3 up). 1990. pap. 8.95 (0-937938-75-0) Snow Lion Pubns.
To the Mafia with Love. Marta Estrada. 322p. 1994. pap. 9.95 (1-883928-04-4) Longwood.
To the Majestie of King James, a Gratulatorie Poem. Michael Drayton. LC 71-25832. (English Experience Ser.: No. 169). 16p. 1969. reprint ed. 15.00 (90-221-0169-X) Walter J Johnson.
To the Man I Love, Thank You for Being Mine. Tamara Nikuradse & Scott Matthews. 160p. (Orig.). 1994. pap. 5.99 (0-449-90914-X, Columbine) Fawcett.
To the Man Reporter from the Denver Post. rev. ed. Chocolate Waters. 1980. pap. 5.00 (0-935060-05-7) Eggplant Pr.
To the Manner Born: The Life of General William H. T. Walker. Russell K. Brown. LC 93-9954. (Illus.). 392p. (C). 1994. 50.00 (0-8203-1569-9) U of Ga Pr.
To the Marianas: War in the Central Pacific - 1944. Edwin P. Hoyt. 320p. 1983. pap. 3.95 (0-380-65839-9) Avon.
To the Market Place. Berry Fleming. LC 88-92464. 528p. 1989. reprint ed. 24.95 (0-933256-72-8) Second Chance.
To the Memory of Childhood. Lydia Chukovskaya. Tr. by Eliza K. Klose from RUS. (Illus.). 168p. 1988. pap. 11.95 (0-8101-0790-2) Northwestern U Pr.
To the Most Excellente Kyng, Kyng Edward 4th Cohan Kay Hys Humble Poete Lawreate, etc. Gulielmus Caorsin. LC 72-179. (English Experience Ser.: No. 236). 48p. 1970. reprint ed. 21.00 (90-221-0236-X) Walter J Johnson.
To the Mountain & Back: The Mysteries of Guatemalan Highland Family Life. Jody Glittenberg. (Illus.). 203p. (Orig.). (C). 1994. pap. text ed. 10.95 (0-88133-792-7) Waveland Pr.
*__To the Mountain of Fire & Beyond: The Fifty-Third Indiana Regiment from Shiloh to Glory.__ Garland Haas. LC 96-78248. 210p. (Orig.). 1997. 29.95 (1-878208-98-5); pap. 19.95 (1-878208-99-3) Guild Pr IN.
To the Mountains by Morning Independent Reader 5-Pack, Unit 10. (Networks Ser.). 1991. 15.00 (0-88106-783-0, N328) Charlesbridge Pub.
To the Natural World. Genevieve Taggard. Ed. by Dale Boyer & Marcia T. Liles. LC 79-52709. (Ahsahta Press Modern & Contemporary Poets of the West Ser.). 84p. (Orig.). 1980. pap. 6.95 (0-916272-13-3) Ahsahta Pr.
To the New Mother. Helen Brenneman. 1969. pap. 1.99 (0-8361-1600-3) Herald Pr.
To the Newly-Baptized. Gregory Williams. 8p. (Orig.). 1990. pap. 0.50 (0-912927-43-7, X043) St John Kronstadt.
To the North. Elizabeth Bowen. 1997. pap. 11.95 (0-14-018306-X) Viking Penguin.
To the One I Love. Devereaux Macy Staff. pap. write for info. (1-886716-09-9) Devereaux.
To the One I Love. Christopher Hills. Ed. by Ann Ray & Norah Hills. LC 84-11814. (Illus.). 256p. 1984. text ed. 17.95 (0-916438-51-1) Dr Hills Technol.
To the Orthodox Christians of the U. S. A. Chrysostemos H. Stratman. 6p. 1949. pap. 1.00 (0-317-30430-5) Holy Trinity.
To the Other: An Introduction to the Philosophy of Emmanuel Levinas. Adriaan Peperzak. LC 91-44845. (Series in the History of Philosophy). 240p. 1992. 30.00 (1-55753-023-8); pap. 14.95 (1-55753-024-6) Purdue U Pr.
*__To the Other Shore: The Russian Jewish Intellectuals Who Came to America.__ Steven Cassedy. 320p. 1997. text ed. 29.95 (0-691-02975-X) Princeton U Pr.
To the People: The Russian Government & the Newspaper "Sel'skii Vestnick" (Village Herald), 1881-1917. James H. Krukones. Ed. by William H. McNeill & Barbara Jelavich. (Modern European History Ser.). 871230p. 1987. text ed. 15.00 (0-8240-8057-2) Garland.
To the People: Y. C. James Yen & Rural Reconstruction in China. Charles W. Hayford. (United States & Pacific Asia: Studies in Social, Economic & Political Interaction). 320p. 1990. text ed. 49.50 (0-231-07204-X) Col U Pr.
To the Perplexed. M. K. Gandhi. Ed. by A. T. Hingorani. 236p. 1981. 12.00 (0-934676-27-5) Greenlf Bks.
To the Point. 1989. write for info. (0-9627652-0-1, TXU 380-459) A A Wenger.
To the Point: A Story about E. B. White. David R. Collins. (Illus.). 56p. (J). (gr. 3-6). 1989. pap. 5.95 (0-87614-508-X, Carolrhoda); lib. bdg. 14.21 (0-87614-345-1, Carolrhoda) Lerner Group.
To the Point: Efficient & Attractive Writing for Almost Any Audience. Arnold M. Tibbetts. (C). 1983. pap. text ed. 17.00 (0-673-15491-2) Addson-Wesley Educ.
To the Point: The United States Military Academy, 1802-1902. George S. Pappas. LC 92-36632. 528p. 1993. text ed. 59.95 (0-275-94329-1, C4329, Praeger Pubs) Greenwood.
To the Point, Effective Business Communication. Barrie A. Wilson. LC 87-71925. 1988. pap. 7.95 (0-8158-0444-X) Chris Mass.
To the Point, Ingles Para Hispanohablantes: English for Spanish Speakers. 2nd ed. Priscilla Gac-Artigas & Gustavo Gac-Artigas. LC 96-90412. (Innovative, Non-Traditional Grammars Ser.). (Illus.). 107p. (Orig.). (ENG & SPA.). 1997. pap. 8.95 (0-9653060-2-X) To the Pt Bks.
To the Poles by Ski & Dogsled, 2 vols. in 1. Joseph E. Murphy. (Illus.). 348p. 1996. pap. 9.95 (0-9646292-1-6) Crossgar Pr.
To the Post Office with Mama. Sue Farrell. (Illus.). 24p. (J). (ps-1). 1994. 15.95 (1-55037-359-5, Pub. by Annick CN); pap. 4.95 (1-55037-358-7, Pub. by Annick CN) Firefly Bks Ltd.
To the Power of One. Philip S. Berg. 256p. 1991. 14.95 (0-924457-02-3); pap. 14.95 (0-924457-03-1) Res Ctr Kabbalah.
To the Power of One. Philip S. Berg. 13p. (SPA.). 1992. pap. 14.95 (0-924457-64-3) Res Ctr Kabbalah.
To the Power of One. Philip S. Berg. 13p. (FRE.). 1994. pap. 14.95 (0-924457-63-5); pap. 12.95 (0-924457-71-6) Res Ctr Kabbalah.
To the President: Folk Portraits by the People. James G. Barber. Ed. by Smithsonian Institution, National Portrait Gallery Staff. (Illus.). 96p. (Orig.). 1993. pap. 19.95 (1-56833-023-5) Madison Bks UPA.
*__To the Promised Land.__ David Goldberg. 1997. pap. 12.95 (0-14-012512-4) Viking Penguin.
To the Promised Land. Ken Light et al. (Illus.). 90p. 1988. 25.00 (0-89381-324-9) Aperture.
To the Quick. Heather McHugh. LC 85-29504. (Wesleyan Poetry Ser.). 69p. 1987. pap. 11.95 (0-8195-6162-2, Wesleyan Univ Pr) U Pr of New Eng.
To the Red Planet. Eric Burgess. LC 78-6911. (Illus.). 181p. 1978. text ed. 49.00 (0-231-04392-9) Col U Pr.
To the Refreshing of the Children of Light. Geoffrey F. Nuttall. (C). 1959. pap. 3.00 (0-87574-101-0) Pendle Hill.
To the Rescue! Leah Klein. (Operation Firestorm Ser.: Pt. 2). 171p. (J). (gr. 6-8). 1994. 9.95 (1-56871-042-9) Targum Pr.
To the Rescue. Kristina Logan. (Romance Ser.). 1993. mass mkt. 2.69 (0-373-08918-X, 5-08918-0) Silhouette.
To the Rescue! Stephanie St. Pierre. (Talking Toy Tales Ser.). (Illus.). 18p. (J). (ps-1). 1995. 15.99 (0-88705-824-8, Wshng Well Bks) Joshua Morris.
To the Rescue. large type ed. Kristina Logan. LC 93-20049. 226p. 1993. reprint ed. Alk. paper. 13.95 (1-56054-682-4) Thorndike Pr.
To the Rescue: Fire Trucks Then & Now. Steven Otfinoski. LC 96-18480. (Here We Go! Ser.). (J). 1997. lib. bdg. 14.95 (0-7614-0406-6, Benchmark NY) Marshall Cavendish.
To the Rescue: Helping Students Take Control. Nancy Baker & Dayna Fenker. (Illus.). 64p. (Orig.). 1991. pap. text ed. 11.95 (0-940352-07-9) Mesa Hse.
To the Rescue: How Immigrants Saved the American Film Industry, 1896-1912. Ken Weiss. LC 96-46971. (Illus.). 312p. 1997. 69.95 (1-57292-051-3); pap. 49.95 (1-57292-050-5) Austin & Winfield.
To the Rescue of Art: Twenty-Six Essays. Rudolf Arnheim. LC 91-9038. (Illus.). 243p. 1992. 45.00 (0-520-07458-0); pap. 17.95 (0-520-07459-9) U CA Pr.
To the Right: The Transformation of American Conservatism. Jerome L. Himmelstein. 300p. 1989. 27.50 (0-520-06649-9) U CA Pr.
To the Right: The Transformation of American Conservatism. Jerome L. Himmelstein. (C). 1992. pap. 14.95 (0-520-08042-4) U CA Pr.
To the Right High & Mightie Prince James...An Humble Supplication for Toleration & Libertie. Henry Jacob. LC 74-28869. (English Experience Ser.: No. 748). 1975. reprint ed. 15.00 (90-221-0748-5) Walter J Johnson.
To the Royal Crown Restored: The Journals of Don Diego de Vargas, New Mexico, 1692-94. Ed. by John L. Kessell et al. LC 94-36599. (Journals of Don Diego de Vargas). 627p. 1995. 18.95 (0-8263-1559-3) U of NM Pr.
To the Sacred Ruins. K. J. Stavrinides. LC 92-17377. 80p. (Orig.). (ENG & GRE.). 1992. pap. 8.95 (1-56474-032-3) Fithian Pr.
*__To the Sea.__ Robert Kunzig. Date not set. write for info. (0-393-04562-5) Norton.
To the Sea: A History & Tour Guide of Sherman's March. Jim Miles. LC 89-24232. (Illus.). 224p. (Orig.). 1989. pap. 18.95 (1-55853-047-9) Rutledge Hill Pr.
To the Seventh Continent: The German Antarctic Expedition 1911 - 1912. Wilhelm Filchner. Tr. & Intro. by William Barr. 1994. 255.00 (1-85297-038-3, Pub. by Archival Facs UK) St Mut.
To the Seventh Power. Felice Picano. 320p. 1990. mass mkt. 4.50 (0-380-70276-2) Avon.
*__To the Shelter: Journeys of Faith in the Middle East.__ 1996. 6.50 (0-8341-1641-3) Nazarene.
To the Slaughterhouse. Jean Giono. 1969. 28.00 (0-7206-3602-7) Dufour.

An Asterisk (*) at the beginning of an entry indicates that the title is appearing in BIP for the first time.

To the Sound of Musketry & Tap of the Drum. 2nd ed. James G. Genco. LC 89-83405. (Illus.). 195p. 1990. 20.00 (0-914905-49-X) Detroit Bk Pr.

To the Sound of the Guns. John Hill & Dean West. (Johnny Reb Ser.). (Illus.). 49p. (Orig.). 1988. pap. 8.00 (0-943580-64-1) Game Designers.

To the South Polar Regions. Ed. by Louis Bernacchi. 346p. 1989. 230.00 (1-85297-035-9, Pub. by Archival Facs UK) St Mut.

To the Stars: The Autobiography of George Takei, Star Trek's Mr. Sulu. abr. ed. George Takei. (J). (gr. 6 up). 1995. mass mkt. 3.99 (0-671-53623-0) PB.

To the Stars: The Autobiography of Star Trek's Mr. Sulu. George Takei. Ed. by Kevin Ryan. 416p. (gr. 6 up). 1995. reprint ed. pap. 12.00 (0-671-89009-3, PB Trade Paper) PB.

To the Storm: The Odyssey of a Revolutionary Chinese Woman. Daiyun Yue & Carolyn Wakeman. LC 85-8482. 300p. 1985. pap. 13.95 (0-520-06029-6) U CA Pr.

To the Stutterer, No. 9. Intro. by Malcolm Fraser. LC 76-376781. 116p. 1972. pap. 2.00 (0-933388-07-1) Stuttering Fnd Am.

To the Summit. Rod Gonzales & Chip Faurot. Ed. by Mike McDonald. (Max North's AK Comics Ser.: No. 2). (Illus.). 32p. (Orig.). (YA). (gr. 5-10). 1993. pap. 3.95 (1-882724-00-3) Alaska Comics.

***To the Summit: A Woman's Journey into the Mountains to Find Her Soul.** Margo Chisholm & Ray Bruce. LC 96-45210. 336p. 1997. 24.00 (0-380-97359-6) Avon.

To the Sundown Side. rev. ed. Roland O. Byers. LC 86-90569. (Illus.). 216p. 1986. reprint ed. pap. 7.95 (0-9614563-1-0) Pawpaw Pr.

To the Tally of My Soul: Whitman's Image of Voice. Harold Bloom. (Chapbooks in Literature Ser.). 36p. (Orig.). 1980. pap. text ed. 5.00 (0-9614940-4-2) Bennington Coll.

To the Third Empire: Ibsen's Early Drama. Brian Johnston. LC 79-28329. (Nordic Ser.: No. 4). 350p. 1980. reprint ed. pap. 99.80 (0-7837-2944-8, 2057510) Bks Demand.

To the Third Power: The Inside Story of Bill Koch's Winning Strategies for the America's Cup. Paul C. Larsen. (Illus.). 256p. 1995. 24.95 (0-88448-147-6) Tilbury Hse.

To the Toilers & Other Verses. Basil Dahl. 1972. 59.95 (0-8490-1217-1) Gordon Pr.

To the Top! Climbing the World's Highest Mountain. S. A. Kramer. LC 92-22164. (Step into Reading Bks.: Step 4). (Illus.). 48p. (Orig.). (J). (gr. 2-4). 1993. pap. 3.99 (0-679-83885-6) Random Bks Yng Read.

To the Top of Denali: Climbing Adventures on North America's Highest Peak. Bill Sherwonit. LC 90-35950. (Illus.). 368p. (Orig.). 1990. pap. 14.95 (0-88240-402-4) Alaska Northwest.

***To the Top of the Continent: The First Ascent of Mt. McKinley, 1903-1906.** Frederick A. Cook. Ed. by Russell W. Gibbons. (Illus.). 368p. 1996. reprint ed. 49.95 (0-9653995-0-8); reprint ed. pap. 19.95 (0-9653995-1-6) F A Cook.

To the Top of the World: Adventures with Arctic Wolves. Jim Brandenburg. Ed. by JoAnn B. Guernsey. LC 93-12105. (Illus.). 48p. (Orig.). (J). (gr. 4 up). 1993. 16.95 (0-8027-8219-1); lib. bdg. 17.85 (0-8027-8220-5) Walker & Co.

To the Top of the World: Adventures with Arctic Wolves. Jim Brandenburg. (Illus.). 48p. (Orig.). (YA). (gr. 3 up). 1995. pap. 6.95 (0-8027-7462-8) Walker & Co.

To the Top of the World: Climbing Mount Everest with Brian Blessed. Brian Blessed. 1995. 17.98 (0-8317-3298-9) Smithmark.

To the Top Without a Glass. Ted Leszkiewicz. LC 86-50264. 180p. (Orig.). 1986. pap. 7.95 (0-938287-00-1) Warren Bk Pub.

To the Tub. Peggy P. Anderson. LC 95-53267. (Illus.). 32p. (J). (ps-2). 1996. 13.95 (0-395-77614-7) HM.

To the Tune of Hope. Hope Taylor-McGriff. LC 95-77169. 210p. (Orig.). 1995. pap. 11.95 (0-9638672-5-3) Bryant & Dillon.

To the Tyrants Never Yield: A Texas Civil War Sampler. Kevin R. Young. LC 91-20143. (Illus.). 280p. (Orig.). 1991. pap. 12.95 (1-55622-146-6, Rep of TX Pr) Wordware Pub.

To the Undiscovered Ends. Kathleen Upton. 141p. (C). 1989. text ed. 50.00 (1-85821-001-1, Pub. by Pentland Pr UK) St Mut.

***To the Unknown God: The God of Science & the Bible.** Emerson A. Cooper. LC 97-90079. (Orig.). 1997. pap. 12.95 (0-533-12278-3) Vantage.

***To the Victor: Louisiana Politics.** Jock Scott. 1986. pap. 15.95 (0-87511-814-3, STOTHP) Claitors.

To the Victor the Spoils. large type ed. Jock Gallagher. 236p. 1991. 19.95 (1-85089-384-5, Pub. by ISIS UK) Transaction Pubs.

To The Waters & the Wild: Petroleum Geology, 1918 to 1941. Ellen S. Blake. (Illus.). 207p. 1991. 15.00 (0-89181-804-9, 713) AAPG.

To the Webster-Ashburton Treaty: A Study in Anglo-American Relations, 1783-1843. Howard Jones. LC 76-58341. (Illus.). 272p. reprint ed. pap. 77.60 (0-8357-3886-8, 2036618) Bks Demand.

To the Wedding. John Berger. 1996. pap. 11.00 (0-679-76777-0) Random.

To the Wedding: A Novel. John Berger. 192p. 1995. 22.00 (0-679-43981-1) Pantheon.

To the White Sea. James Dickey. 288p. 1994. pap. 11.95 (0-385-31309-8, Delta) Dell.

To the White Sea. large type ed. James Dickey. LC 93-47354. 1994. 24.95 (1-56895-046-2) Wheeler Pub.

To the Winds: A Novel. Madison Jones. 320p. 1996. 21.95 (1-56352-278-0) Longstreet Pr Inc.

To the Woman: Three Essays. Prince Cuba. (Illus.). 17p. (Orig.). 1984. pap. 2.95 (1-56411-112-1) Untd Bros & Sis.

To the Woman I Love, Thank You for Being Mine. Scott Matthews & Tamara Nikuradse. 160p. (Orig.). 1994. pap. 5.99 (0-449-90915-8, Columbine) Fawcett.

To the Woods & Waters Wild: A Collection of Irish Writings. Ross Brinn. Ed. by Kieran O'Mahony. LC 90-80516. 150p. (Orig.). (YA). 1990. pap. 9.95 (0-944638-02-3) EduCare Pr.

To the World's Best Dad. Helen Exley. (To the World's Best Ser.). (Illus.). 28p. 1992. 6.99 (1-85015-330-2) Exley Giftbooks.

To the World's Best Grandma. Helen Exley. (To the World's Best Ser.). (Illus.). 28p. 1992. 6.99 (1-85015-331-0) Exley Giftbooks.

To the World's Best Grandpa. Helen Exley. (To the World's Best Ser.). (Illus.). 28p. 1992. 6.99 (1-85015-349-3) Exley Giftbooks.

To the World's Best Mother. Helen Exley. (To the World's Best Ser.). (Illus.). 28p. 1992. 6.99 (1-85015-296-9) Exley Giftbooks.

***To the Young Environmentalist: Lives Dedicated to Preserving the Natural World.** Linda Leuzzi. LC 97-1042. (J). 1997. write for info. (0-531-11359-0) Watts.

To the Young Scientist: Reflections on Doing & Living Science. Alfred B. Bortz. LC 96-25864. (Venture Bks.). (J). 1997. lib. bdg. 22.00 (0-531-11325-6) Watts.

To the Youth of the World. 64p. 1985. pap. 3.95 (1-55586-962-9) US Catholic.

To Thee I Come. Mildred E. Reeves. 220p. 1975. 7.50 (0-686-12109-0) Prairie Pub.

To Their Own Soil: Agriculture in the Antebellum North. Jeremy Atack & Fred Bateman. LC 86-21349. (Henry A. Wallace Series on Agricultural History & Rural Studies: Vol. 5). 334p. 1987. text ed. 34.95 (0-8138-0086-2) Iowa St U Pr.

To Thine Own Self Be Good. Slightly Off Center Writers Group Staff. (Orig.). 1995. pap. 9.95 (1-56721-125-9) Twenty-Fifth Cent Pr.

To Thine Own Self Be True. Lewis M. Andrews. 240p. 1989. pap. 12.95 (0-385-23737-5) Doubleday.

To Think. Frank Smith. 192p. (C). 1990. pap. text ed. 17.95 (0-8077-3057-2) Tchrs Coll.

To Think Differently. Stephen Wynacht. 44p. (Orig.). 1994. pap. 2.95 (0-9633111-1-5) S Wynacht Minist.

To This Cedar Fountain. K. Linda Kivi & Kate Braid. (Illus.). 108p. 1995. pap. 13.95 (1-896095-08-9, Pub. by Polestar Bk Pubs CN) Orca Bk Pubs.

To Those Far Away Places with Their Strange Sounding Names. Harold Rowley. LC 86-60808. (Illus.). 128p. (Orig.). 1986. pap. 5.95 (0-9616729-0-0) Rapport Unltd Pubns.

To Those Who Need It Most, Hospice Means Hope. Kenneth B. Wentzel. 1980. 20.00 (0-89182-020-5); pap. text ed. 9.95 (0-89182-030-2) Charles River Bks.

***To Three Mile Creek.** Vera J. Larsen. (Illus.). 314p. 22.95 (1-888106-12-3, CFP Books) Custom Fmly.

To Tilt at Windmills: A Memoir of the Spanish Civil War. Fred A. Thomas. (Illus.). 175p. 1996. 28.95 (0-87013-421-3) Mich St U Pr.

***To Timbuktu: A Journey Down the Niger.** Mark Jenkins. LC 96-38092. 1997. 25.00 (0-688-11585-3) Morrow.

To Toil the Livelong Day: America's Women at Work, 1780-1980. Ed. by Carol Groneman & Mary B. Norton. LC 86-47975. 320p. 1987. pap. 16.95 (0-8014-9452-4) Cornell U Pr.

***To Touch a Dream.** Eutice E. Green. 1997. mass mkt. 4.99 (1-55197-365-0, Pub. by Comnwlth Pub CN) Partners Pubs Grp.

***To Touch a Heart.** A. Daniels. 1997. pap. 12.95 (1-887650-06-7) Factor Pr.

To "Touch" God. Jerome Nahas. LC 95-91057. 1996. 10.00 (0-533-11844-1) Vantage.

To Touch the Divine: A Jewish Mysticism Primer. Pref. by Benzion Rader. 144p. 1989. reprint ed. 17.00 (0-8266-0494-3) Kehot Pubn Soc.

To Touch the Face of God: One Soul's Journey. Karen Geurin. Ed. by Dean Guest. (Illus.). 80p. (Orig.). 1992. pap. 7.00 (1-879667-10-X) Dove Pr TX.

To Touch the Future: The Educators' Book of Quotations. Ed. & Pref. by Alice McDonald. LC 86-82570. 179p. (Orig.). 1986. pap. 8.95 (0-935680-31-4) Kentucke Imprints.

To Touch the Light. Kevin D. Randle. 320p. 1994. mass mkt. 4.99 (0-7860-0047-3, Pinncle Kensgtn) Kensgtn Pub Corp.

To Touch the Moon. Mark A. Young. Ed. by Earl R. Bostic, Jr. (Illus.). 32p. (Orig.). (J). (gr. k-7). 1996. pap. write for info. (0-9644710-3-5) B-Bye Pub.

To Touch the Past: The Painted Pottery of the Mimbres People. J. J. Brody et al. LC 95-44485. (Illus.). 120p. (Orig.). 1996. pap. 29.95 (1-55595-128-7) Hudson Hills.

To Touch the Sky. Anne L. Squire-Buresh. LC 89-50050. 44p. (J). (gr. k-3). 1989. 5.95 (1-55523-224-8) Winston-Derek.

To Touch the Stars. large type ed. Judith Hagar. (Linford Romance Library). 240p. 1996. pap. 15.99 (0-7089-7889-4, Linford) Ulverscroft.

To Touch the Sun: A Portrait of Muhammed Ali. Jack McGonagle. LC 93-85308. 94p. 1995. 10.95 (1-55523-639-1) Winston-Derek.

To Touch the Water. 2nd ed. Gretel Ehrlich. Ed. by Tom Trusky. LC 80-69276. (Ahsahta Press Modern & Contemporary Poets of the West Ser.). 60p. (C). 1981. pap. 6.95 (0-916272-16-8) Ahsahta Pr.

To Touch the World: The Peace Corps Experience. 192p. (YA). 1995. pap. write for info. (0-9644472-0-7) Peace Crps DC.

To Touch Your Heart. Ronald K. Grooters. 1993. 16.95 (0-533-10242-1) Vantage.

To Track a Copycat. Marian Weston & Esther Lakritz. Ed. by M. L. Jones. LC 95-68519. 205p. (Orig.). 1996. pap. 8.95 (1-882270-34-7) Old Rugged Cross.

To Tread Gently. Nelson A. Ossorio & George L. Eisberg. (Orig.). 1995. pap. 8.95 (1-56721-098-8) Twnty-Fifth Cent Pr.

To Treat or Not to Treat: Bioethics & the Handicapped Newborn. Richard Sparks. 352p. 1988. pap. 9.95 (0-8091-2993-0) Paulist Pr.

To Trust a Stranger. large type ed. Rosemary A. Gibson. 295p. 1993. 25.99 (0-7505-0571-0, Pub. by Magna Print Bks UK) Ulverscroft.

To Trust Again: A Remarriage Preparation Program - Couple's Workbook. William Urbine. 48p. 1990. student ed. 4.95 (0-915388-42-1, 158) ACTA Pubns.

To Trust Again: A Remarriage Preparation Program - Leader's Guide. William Urbine. 48p. 1990. teacher ed. 9.95 (0-915388-43-X, 159) ACTA Pubns.

To Trust Again: A Remarriage Preparation Program - Remarriage Inventory. William Urbine. 32p. 1990. student ed. 4.95 (0-915388-44-8, 160) ACTA Pubns.

To Try Men's Souls: Loyalty Tests in American History. Harold M. Hyman. LC 81-13422. (Illus.). ix, 414p. 1982. reprint ed. text ed. 75.00 (0-313-23343-8, HYTM, Greenwood Pr) Greenwood.

To Understand & Be Understood. Erik Blumenthal. 160p. (Orig.). 1994. pap. 7.50 (1-85168-004-7) Onewrld Pubns.

To Understand & to Help: The Life Work of Susan Isaacs (1885-1948) Lydia A. Smith. LC 83-48187. (Illus.). 352p. 1985. 45.00 (0-8386-3211-4) Fairleigh Dickinson.

To Understand Each Other. Paul Tournier. 1966. 10.00 (0-8042-2235-5, John Knox) Westminster John Knox.

To Understand God Truly: What's Theological about a Theological School. David H. Kelsey. 208p. (Orig.). 1992. pap. 17.00 (0-664-25397-0) Westminster John Knox.

To Understand Your Child. rev. ed. Kay Kuzma. 128p. 1985. pap. 5.95 (0-910529-00-0) Family Mtrs.

To Unite Our Strength: Enhancing United Nations Peace & Security. John M. Lee et al. LC 92-26899. 180p. (Orig.). (C). 1992. pap. text ed. 22.50 (0-8191-8866-2) U Pr of Amer.

To up from Down. D. G. Cox. 48p. 1994. pap. 7.00 (0-8059-3602-5) Dorrance.

To Urania. Joseph Brodsky. LC 87-24589. 160p. 1988. 14.95 (0-374-17253-6) FS&G.

To Urania. Joseph Brodsky. 174p. 1992. pap. 11.00 (0-374-52333-9, Noonday) FS&G.

To Us, All Flowers Are Roses: Poems. Lorna Goodison. LC 94-31978. 96p. 1995. 11.95 (0-252-06459-3) U of Ill Pr.

To Vanquish the Dragon. Pearl Benisch. 1991. 20.95 (0-87306-570-0); pap. 16.95 (0-87306-571-9) Feldheim.

To Veronica 's New Lover. Marc M. Dion. (Target Midwest Poetry Ser.). 64p. 1987. 7.95 (0-933532-60-1) BkMk.

To Vietnam with Love. Hope Marston. (Junior Jaffray Collection: Bk. 12). (Illus.). 32p. (J). (ps-2). 1995. pap. 3.99 (0-87509-583-6) Chr Pubns.

To Vietnam with Love: The Story of Charlie & E. G. Long. Charlie Long. (Jaffray Collection of Missionary Portraits: Bk. 12). 204p. 1995. pap. 8.99 (0-87509-582-8) Chr Pubns.

***To Wait for an Angel: A Father's Story.** William T. Sette. iv, 180p. 1997. 16.99 (0-9654650-6-3) Harpus Pr Intl.

To Wake the King: A Dramatic Legend. 108p. 4.00 (0-318-13640-6) Board Jewish Educ.

To Wake the Nations: Race in the Making of American Literature. Eric J. Sundquist. LC 92-34164. 705p. 1993. text ed. 29.95 (0-674-89330-1) Belknap Pr.

To Wake the Nations: Race in the Making of American Literature. Eric J. Sundquist. 705p. 1994. pap. text ed. 16.95 (0-674-89331-X, SUNWAX) Belknap Pr.

***To Wake the Sleeping Dogs.** Russell Harris. 1997. pap. text ed. 12.00 (1-887369-06-6) Global Cty Pr.

To Walk Alone. Anita M. Fowler. LC 96-92087. 272p. (Orig.). (YA). (gr. 7-12). 1996. pap. 10.95 (0-9651724-1-4) SonShine Pubns.

***To Walk & Not Faint: A Month of Meditations on Isaiah 40.** 2nd ed. Marva J. Dawn. 202p. 1997. pap. 14.00 (0-8028-4290-9) Eerdmans.

To Walk & Not Grow Weary. Fran Sciacca. 84p. 1985. pap. 5.00 (0-89109-034-7) NavPress.

To Walk in God's Ways: Jewish Pastoral Perspectives on Illness & Bereavement. Joseph S. Ozarowski. LC 94-40782. 232p. 1995. 30.00 (1-56821-388-3) Aronson.

To Walk in Heaven. Joe Powlas. 176p. 1991. 15.00 (0-8187-0144-7) Harlo Press.

To Walk in Rivers of Fire: A Cornerstone Press Poetry Chapbook. Tammy Boyd. Ed. by Patrick Peterson. 32p. 1996. pap. 5.00 (0-940895-29-3) Cornerstone IL.

To Walk in Silence. Nelson A. Ossorio & George L. Eisberg. (Orig.). 1995. pap. 9.95 (1-56721-131-3) Twnty-Fifth Cent Pr.

To Walk in Stardust: A Selection of Writings for Those Who Dream. Flavia M. Weedn. (Illus.). 90p. reprint ed. 10.00 (0-929632-03-6) Applause Inc.

To Walk in Wilderness. John Fielder & T. A. Barron. 190p. 1993. 39.95 (1-56579-038-3) Westcliffe Pubs.

To Walk the Skypath. Phyllis R. Naylor. 144p. (J). (gr. 4-7). 1992. pap. 3.99 (0-440-40636-6, YB BDD) BDD Bks Young Read.

To Walk with a Quiet Mind: Hikes in the Woodlands, Parks & Beaches of the San Francisco Bay Area. Nancy Olmsted. LC 75-1053. (Totebook Ser.). (Illus.). 256p. 1982. pap. 9.95 (0-87156-125-5) Sierra.

To Walk with Jesus: A Guide Through Lent. Roberta P. Martin. LC 93-74039. 144p. (Orig.). 1994. pap. 6.95 (0-87793-520-3) Ave Maria.

To Walk with Nature: The Drawings of Thomas Cole. Howard S. Merritt. LC 81-84873. (Illus.). 64p. (Orig.). 1981. pap. 5.00 (0-943651-11-5) Hudson Riv.

***To Watch the River.** Thomas W. Oliver. LC 96-90515. (Orig.). 1997. pap. 10.95 (0-533-12089-6) Vantage.

To Wear a City's Crown: The Beginnings of Urban Growth in Texas, 1836-1865. Kenneth W. Wheeler. LC 68-28698. (Illus.). 222p. reprint ed. pap. 63.30 (0-7837-4199-5, 2059049) Bks Demand.

To Weave & Sing: Art, Symbol & Narrative in the South American Rain Forest. David M. Guss. (Illus.). 288p. 1989. pap. 17.00 (0-520-07185-9) U CA Pr.

To Weave & Sing: Art, Symbol, & Narrative in the South American Rainforest. David M. Guss. LC 88-20734. (Illus.). 288p. reprint ed. pap. 82.10 (0-7837-4826-4, 2044473) Bks Demand.

To Weave for the Sun: Ancient Andean Textiles. Rebecca Stone-Miller. LC 94-60350. (Illus.). 272p. (Orig.). 1994. pap. 34.95 (0-500-27793-1) Thames Hudson.

***To Wed Again?** Deanna Talcott. (Romance Ser.). 1997. 3.25 (0-373-19206-1, 1-19206-1) Silhouette.

To Wed at Christmas: (Under the Mistletoe) Helen R. Myers. (Romance Ser.). 1994. pap. 2.75 (0-373-19049-2, 1-19049-5) Silhouette.

To Wee Or Not to Wee. Pat Pollari. (Barf-O-Rama Ser.: No. 6). 128p. (YA). 1996. mass mkt. 3.50 (0-553-48412-5, Skylark BDD) BDD Bks Young Read.

To Western Woods: The Breckinridge Family Moves to Kentucky in 1793. Hazel Dicken-Garcia. LC 89-46408. 1991. 39.50 (0-8386-3342-0) Fairleigh Dickinson.

To What Should We Be Loyal. William MacDonald. 1981. pap. 3.00 (0-937396-47-8) Walterick Pubs.

To Where the Birds Migrate. Saud Al-Harkan. 250p. (Orig.). 1994. pap. 5.99 (0-9642938-3-8) Ravenala Pubns.

To Wherever Oceans Go. Beverley A. Bryant. 300p. (Orig.). 1996. pap. 15.00 (1-882332-01-6) Wings Pub.

To Whom It May Concern. Nicole R. Bartok. (Orig.). 1996. pap. write for info. (1-57553-257-3) Watermrk Pr.

To Whom It May Concern. Raymond Federman. 186p. 1990. text ed. 18.95 (0-932511-31-7); pap. text ed. 8.95 (0-932511-32-5) Fiction Coll.

To Whom It May Concern. Ruth Feldman. LC 86-17238. 93p. (Orig.). 1986. pap. 8.95 (0-87233-086-9) Bauhan.

To Whom Shall We Go: Christ & the Mystery of Man. Zachary Hayes. (Synthesis Ser.). 96p. 1975. pap. 1.00 (0-8199-0702-2, Frncscn Herld) Franciscan Pr.

To Whom the Angel Spoke. Terry Kay. (Illus.). 32p. 1991. 12.95 (1-56145-034-0) Peachtree Pubs.

To Whom This May Concern. Thaddeus W. Johnson. LC 90-90458. (Illus.). 52p. (Orig.). 1991. pap. 5.95 (0-9628219-0-X) T W Johnson.

To Will God's Will: Beginning the Journey. Ben C. Johnson. LC 87-14271. 126p. (Orig.). 1987. pap. 11.00 (0-664-24086-0, Westminster) Westminster John Knox.

To Will One Thing. rev. ed. Ed. by William Scarlett. 64p. 1994. pap. 2.95 (0-88028-151-0, 1268) Forward Movement.

To Will One Thing: Reflections on Kierkegaard's Purity of Heart. Jeremy D. Walker. LC 72-81506. 175p. reprint ed. pap. 49.90 (0-317-26052-9, 2023841) Bks Demand.

To Will One Thing: Solar Action at the Local Level. International Solar Energy Society, American Section Staff. Ed. by Alec F. Jenkins. 1979. pap. text ed. 30.00 (0-89553-022-8) Am Solar Energy.

To Will or Not to Will. Joseph E. Bright. xii, 72p. 1939. lib. bdg. 27.50 (0-89941-597-0, 500260) W S Hein.

To Will? Or To Trust? That Is the Question. Mario Risso & J. David Grathwohl. (Illus.). 160p. (Orig.). 1992. pap. text ed. 19.95 (0-917035-01-1) Chicken Little.

***To Win a Nuclear War: The Pentagon's Secret War Plans.** Michio Kaku & Daniel Axelrod. (Orig.). 48.99 (0-921689-07-1, Pub. by Black Rose Bks CN); pap. 19.99 (0-921689-06-3, Pub. by Black Rose Bks CN) Consort Bk Sales.

To Win a Nuclear War: The Pentagon's Secret War Plans. Michio Kaku & Daniel Axelrod. LC 86-2794. 357p. (Orig.). 1987. 35.00 (0-89608-322-5); pap. 14.00 (0-89608-321-7) South End Pr.

To Win the Hearts. James V. Hall. 504p. 1996. 22.00 (0-8059-3842-7) Dorrance.

To Win the Lady. large type ed. Mary Nichols. 350p. 1996. 21.50 (0-263-14524-7, Pub. by M & B UK) Ulverscroft.

***To Win the Peace: British Propaganda in the United States During World War II.** Susan A. Brewer. LC 97-15057. 240p. 1997. 35.00 (0-8014-3367-3) Cornell U Pr.

To Win the War: Home Front Memorabilia of World War II. Gary N. Skoloff. LC 95-69532. (Illus.). 200p. 1995. pap. 29.95 (1-57510-000-2) Pictorial Hist.

To Win the West: Missionary Reports, 1814-1815. LC 73-38467. (Religion in America, Ser. 2). 167p. 1979. reprint ed. 23.95 (0-405-04091-1) Ayer.

To Win the Winter Sky: Air War over the Ardennes, 1944-1945. Danny S. Parker. (Illus.). 528p. 1994. 29.95 (0-938289-35-7, 7344) Combined Pub.

To Work & to Love: A Theology of Creation. Dorothee Soelle & Shirley A. Cloyes. LC 84-47936. 160p. 1984. pap. 14.00 (0-8006-1782-7, 1-1782, Fortress Pr) Augsburg Fortress.

To Work & to Wed: Female Employment, Feminism, & the Great Depression. Lois Scharf. LC 79-52325. (Contributions in Women's Studies: No. 15). 240p. 1980. text ed. 45.00 (0-313-21445-X, STW/) Greenwood.

To Work & to Wed: Female Employment, Feminism, & the Great Depression. Lois Scharf. LC 79-52325. (Contributions in Women's Studies: No. 15). 240p. 1985. pap. text ed. 12.95 (0-313-25059-6, STWPB) Greenwood.

***To Work at the Foundations: Essays in Memory of Aron Gurwitsch.** Ed. by J. Claude Evans. LC 96-39539. (Contributions to Phenomenology Ser.). 292p. (C). 1996. lib. bdg. 140.00 (0-7923-4317-4) Kluwer Ac.

T

***To Work Is Human, but Retirement Divine.** Yvette J. Silver. 96p. 1997. mass mkt. 5.99 (0-7860-0401-0, Pinncle Kensgtn) Kensgtn Pub Corp.

To Wrestle with Demons: A Psychiatrist Struggles to Understand His Patients & Himself. Keith R. Ablow. LC 92-10468. 158p. 1992. 19.95 (0-88048-546-9, 8546) Am Psychiatric.

To Wrestle with Demons: A Psychiatrist Struggles to Understand His Patients & Himself. Keith R. Ablow. 158p. 1994. pap. 9.95 (0-7867-0166-8) Carroll & Graf.

To Write a Wrong: The Revocation of the U. N. General Assembly Resolution 3379 Defaming. Yohanan Manor. (Illus.). 304p. 1996. 25.00 (0-88400-189-X) Shengold.

To Write Like a Woman: Essays in Feminism & Science Fiction. Joanna Russ. LC 95-3576. 200p. 1995. 27.95 (0-253-32914-0); pap. 12.95 (0-253-20983-8) Ind U Pr.

To Write Paradise: Style & Error in Pound's Cantos. Christine Froula. LC 84-3649. 219p. 1984. reprint ed. pap. 62.50 (0-7837-3279-1, 2057677) Bks Demand.

To Write the Lips of Sleepers: The Poetry of Amir Gilboa. Warren Bargad. LC 93-49756. (Monographs of the Hebrew Union College: No. 17). 300p. 1994. 44.95 (0-87820-416-4) Hebrew Union Coll Pr.

To Write, Write: Writing. James C. Durham. 240p. (gr. 9-12). 1981. pap. 8.95 (0-88334-144-1) Longman.

To Writers with Love. Mary Wibberly. 1988. 15.95 (0-911403-26-4); pap. 8.95 (0-911403-34-5) Seven Hills Bk.

To Writing Sociology Paper. Sociology Writing Group Staff. Date not set. student ed., pap. text ed. write for info. (0-312-13762-1) St Martin.

***To You with Love.** Jayne Casciato. (Orig.). 1997. pap. write for info. (1-57553-487-8) Watermrk Pr.

To Your Body: The Health Effects of Illicit Drugs & Alcohol. L. A. Chotkowski. 1989. pap. 12.95 (1-55691-043-6, 436) Learning Pubns.

To Your Health. A. M. Behnam. 75p. 1993. pap. 3.95 (0-88172-181-6) Believers Bkshelf.

***To Your Health.** Dorie Erickson. 23p. 1987. spiral bd., pap. 3.95 (0-937242-10-1) Scandia Pubs.

***To Your Health: Exploring the Healing Properties of Alcohol.** Barry Fox. LC 96-37425. 1997. 18.95 (0-312-15226-4) St Martin.

To Your Success: Thoughts to Give Wings to Your Work & Your Dreams. Daniel Zadra. (Gift of Inspiration Ser.). (Illus.). 172p. 1994. 12.95 (0-9640178-1-4) Compendium Inc.

To Your Wealth: How to Trade in Your Salaried Job for Your Own Small Business. 1987. lib. bdg. 76.00 (0-8490-3893-6) Gordon Pr.

T.O. 1F-86D-1 Flight Handbook: F-86D & TF-86D Aircraft. LC 95-67633. (U. S. A. F. Ser.). (Illus.). 304p. 1995. pap. 24.95 (0-88740-822-2) Schiffer.

To 1650, Vol. 1 see Societies & Cultures in World History

To 1650: World History Map see Societies & Cultures in World History

To 1715, 2 vol., Vol. 2. 5th ed. Mortimer Chambers & Raymond Crew. 1991. student ed., pap. text ed. write for info. (0-07-010622-3) McGraw.

***Toad.** Ruth Brown. (J). 1997. pap. 14.99 (0-525-45757-7) Dutton Child Bks.

Toad. Contrib. by Andrienne Soutler-Perrot. LC 92-14165. (My First Nature Bks.). (J). (gr. 5 up). 1992. lib. bdg. 10.95 (0-88682-568-7) Creative Ed.

Toad & the Green Princess. David Kherdian. LC 92-39314. (Illus.). (J). 1994. 15.95 (0-399-22539-0, Philomel Bks) Putnam Pub Group.

Toad at Harrow: P. G. Wodehouse in Perspective. Charles E. Gould, Jr. (Wodehouse Monograph: No. 3). 10p. (Orig.). 1995. 10.50 (0-87008-102-0) JAS Heineman.

Toad Eats Out. Susan Schade. LC 94-5285. (Step into Reading: Step 1 Bks.). (Illus.). (J). (gr. k-4). 1995. pap. 3.99 (0-679-85009-0) Random.

Toad Eats Out. Susan Schade. LC 94-5285. (Step into Reading: Step 1 Bks.). (Illus.). (J). 1995. lib. bdg. 11.99 (0-679-95009-5) Random.

Toad for Tuesday. Russell Erickson. LC 73-19900. (Illus.). 64p. (J). (gr. k-4). 1974. lib. bdg. 12.93 (0-688-51569-X) Lothrop.

Toad for Tuesday. Russell E. Erickson. LC 92-24595. (Illus.). 64p. (J). (gr. 3 up). 1993. reprint ed. pap. 3.95 (0-688-12276-0) Morrow.

Toad Is the Uncle of Heaven. Illus. & Retold by Jeanne M. Lee. LC 85-5639. 32p. (J). (ps-2). 1985. 13.95 (0-8050-1146-3, Bks Young Read) H Holt & Co.

Toad Is the Uncle of Heaven: A Vietnamese Folk Tale. Illus. & Retold by Jeanne M. Lee. LC 85-5639. 32p. (J). (ps-2). 1989. pap. 5.95 (0-8050-1147-1, Owlet BYR) H Holt & Co.

Toad on the Road. Jon Buller & Susan Schade. LC 91-4246. (Step into Reading Bks.). (Illus.). 32p. (Orig.). (J). (ps-1). 1992. pap. 3.99 (0-679-82689-0); lib. bdg. 7.99 (0-679-92689-5) Random Bks Yng Read.

Toad or Frog, Swamp or Bog? A Big Book of Nature's Confusables. Lynda Graham-Barber. LC 92-35398. (Illus.). 48p. (J). (gr. k-5). 1994. lib. bdg. 16.00 (0-02-736931-5, Four Winds Pr) S&S Childrens.

Toad Overload: A True Tale of Nature Knocked Off Balance in Australia. Patricia Seibert. LC 95-14179. (Illus.). 32p. (J). (gr. k-3). 1996. lib. bdg. 16.40 (1-56294-613-7) Millbrook Pr.

Toad Sleeps Over. John Bianchi. (Illus.). 24p. (J). (ps-2). 1995. pap. 4.95 (0-921285-40-X, Pub. by Bungalo Bks CN); lib. bdg. 14.95 (0-921285-41-8, Pub. by Bungalo Bks CN) Firefly Bks Ltd.

Toad Takes Off. Susan Schade. 1997. pap. 3.99 (0-679-86935-2); lib. bdg. 11.99 (0-679-96935-7) Random.

Toad That Taught Flying. Malia Maness. LC 93-86144. (Illus.). 32p. (J). (ps-3). 1993. 9.95 (0-9633493-1-7) Pacific Greetings.

Toad the Wet Sprocket Collection. 104p. otabind 19.95 (0-7935-5033-5, 00690030) H Leonard.

Toad Triumphant. William Horwood. LC 96-8700. 288p. 1996. 19.95 (0-312-14821-6) St Martin.

Toad Turns Fifty: Selected Poems by Gerald Locklin. Gerald Locklin. Ed. by D. H. Lloyd. 128p. 1993. 23.95 (0-930090-60-8); pap. 10.95 (0-930090-62-4) Applezaba.

Toad Turns Fifty: Selected Poems by Gerald Locklin. deluxe ed. Gerald Locklin. Ed. by D. H. Lloyd. 128p. 1993. 30.00 (0-930090-61-6) Applezaba.

Toad Within: How to Control Eating Choices. James W. Worth. (Illus.). 92p. 1995. pap. 12.95 (0-9641919-2-X) Islewest Pub.

***Toad-1.** Beverly Warner. 43p. (Orig.). (J). (gr. 4-12). 1994. pap. 3.50 (1-57514-189-2, 0012) Encore Perform Pub.

Toads. James E. Gerholdt. LC 94-19202. (Amazing Amphibians Ser.). (J). 1994. lib. bdg. 14.98 (1-56239-312-X) Abdo & Dghtrs.

Toads. Lynn M. Stone. LC 93-15696. (Nighttime Animals Ser.). (J). (gr. 4 up). 1993. write for info. (0-86593-294-8) Rourke Corp.

Toads & Diamonds. Illus. & Retold by Robert Bender. LC 93-46602. 32p. (J). 1995. pap. 13.99 (0-525-67509-4, Lodestar Bks) Dutton Child Bks.

Toads & Diamonds. Ed. & Retold by Charlotte S. Huck. LC 94-27292. (Illus.). (J). 1996. 16.00 (0-688-13680-X); lib. bdg. 15.93 (0-688-13681-8) Greenwillow.

Toads & Toadstools: The Natural History, Mythology, & Cultural Oddities of This Strange Association. Adrian Morgan. (Illus.). 224p. 1995. pap. 24.95 (0-89087-777-7) Ten Speed Pr.

Toads of War. Eddie Iroh. LC 79-670372. (African Writers Ser.). 144p. (C). 1979. pap. 8.95 (0-435-90213-X, 90213) Heinemann.

***Toad's Song.** Lynette D. Vuong. (J). Date not set. write for info. (0-688-13782-2) Lothrop.

Toadswart D'Amplestone. Conrad. (Illus.). 1990. 35.00 (1-56060-012-8); pap. 12.95 (1-56060-013-6) Eclipse Bks.

Toady & Dr. Miracle. Christian. LC 96-19214. 1997. pap. 3.99 (0-689-80891-7, S&S Bks Young Read) S&S Childrens.

Toady & Dr. Miracle. Christian. LC 96-19214. (J). 1997. 15.00 (0-689-80890-9, S&S Bks Young Read) S&S Childrens.

Toady Jewels. Carolyn W. Greenlee. (Illus.). 61p. (Orig.). 1992. pap. 8.50 (1-887400-00-1) Earthen Vessel Prodns.

Toady Jewels Too. Carolyn W. Greenlee. 57p. 1993. pap. 8.50 (1-887400-01-X) Earthen Vessel Prodns.

Toady Tales. 2nd ed. Anna L. Carlson. LC 80-83018. 24p. (J). (gr. k-4). 1980. pap. 1.95 (0-939938-02-2) Karwyn Ent.

To'aga Site: Three Millennia of Polynesian Occupation in the Manu'a Islands, American Samoa. W. R. Dickinson et al. (Contributions of the University of California Archaeological Research Facility Ser.: No. 51). 249p. 1993. pap. text ed. 24.00 (1-882744-01-2) U CA Arch Res Fac.

Toast for You & Me: America's Participation, Sacrifice & Victory. Robert C. Valentine. Ed. by Darlene Hoffa. (Illus.). 264p. 1993. 39.95 (1-880633-88-4) AMDG Pict.

Toast for You & Me, a Visual History, Vol. 1. Robert C. Valentine. 192p. 1991. 39.99 (0-685-50359-3) AMDG Pict.

Toast of the Town. write for info. (0-9615622-5-0) McElyea Pubns.

***Toast of the Town: The Life & Times of Sunnie Wilson.** Sunnie Wilson & John Cohassey. (Great Lakes Books Ser.). (Illus.). 224p. 1998. 24.95 (0-8143-2695-1) Wayne St U Pr.

Toast the Host. Cy DeCosse Incorporated Staff. LC 96-15851. (Great Gifts Ser.). (Illus.). 95p. 1996. 14.95 (0-86573-988-9) Cowles Creative.

Toast to Cousin Julian. Estelle Thompson. 192p. 1987. 15.95 (0-8027-5665-4) Walker & Co.

Toast To Cousin Julian. large type ed. Estelle Thompson. 320p. 1987. 25.99 (0-7089-1634-1) Ulverscroft.

Toast to Ireland: A Celebration of Irish Traditional Drinks. John Booth. (Illus.). 128p. 1995. pap. text ed. 19.95 (0-85640-536-1, Pub. by Blackstaff Pr IE) Dufour.

Toast to Ireland: A Celebration of Irish Traditional Drinks. John Booth. LC 95-72791. 128p. 1996. reprint ed. pap. 18.95 (1-57098-062-4) R Rinehart.

Toast to Tomorrow. Manning Coles. (Spies & Intrigues Ser.: No. 3). 320p. 1984. pap. 5.95 (0-918172-15-2) Leetes Isl.

Toast to You. write for info. (0-9615622-2-6) McElyea Pubns.

***Toasted Bagels.** Joyce A. Zarins. Date not set. 10.99 (0-698-20634-7) Putnam Pub Group.

Toasted Onions: Reading Level 3-4. (Stormy Night Stories Ser.). 16p. 1993. 2.50 (0-88336-076-4) New Readers.

Toaster Oven Cookbook. David DiResta & Joanne Foran. (Illus.). 160p. (Orig.). 1995. pap. 8.95 (1-55867-124-2, Nitty Gritty Ckbks) Bristol Pub Ent CA.

Toasters: 1909-1960. E Townsend Artman. (Illus.). 112p. 1996. pap. 29.95 (0-88740-956-3) Schiffer.

***Toasters & Small Kitchen Appliances.** (Illus.). 144p. (Orig.). 1995. pap. 19.95 (0-89538-039-0) L-W Inc.

***Toaster's Handbook: Jokes, Stories, & Quotations.** 3rd ed. Peggy Edmund & Harold W. Williams. LC 97-14599. 483p. 1997. reprint ed. lib. bdg. 46.00 (0-7808-0270-5) Omnigraphics Inc.

Toastin' the Dogs: Recipes of the Famous & Distinguished. Celebrity Collection of Recipes Staff. Ed. by Lane Bresticker et al. (Illus.). (Orig.). 1994. pap. text ed. 16.95 (0-9643198-0-2) Paws With A Cause.

Toasting Cheers: An Episode Guide to the 1982-1993 Comedy Series, with Cast Biographies & Character Profiles. Dennis J. Bjorklund. LC 96-31359. (Illus.). 419p. 1997. lib. bdg. 55.00 (0-89950-962-2) McFarland & Co.

***Toasting Temecula Wines: A Guide to Southern California's Temecula Wine Country.** Vick Knight, Jr. LC 96-86420. (Illus.). 115p. (Orig.). 1996. pap. 12.95 (0-931407-05-2) Aristan Pr.

***Toastmasters International Guide to Audiovisual Presentations.** 2nd rev. ed. Peter H. Putman. (Illus.). 106p. 1997. pap. 9.95 (0-9658991-0-1) Toastmasters.

Toastmasters International Guide to Successful Speaking. Jeff Slutsky & Michael Aun. 224p. (Orig.). 1996. pap. 17.95 (0-7931-2352-6, 5614-5301) Dearborn Finan.

Toasts: Over Fifteen Hundred of the Best Toasts, Blessings, Sentiments, & Graces. Paul Dickson. (Illus.). 256p. 1991. 19.00 (0-517-58412-3, Crown) Crown Pub Group.

Toasts: The Illustrated Book of Drinking Poems, Salty Salutations, Eloquent Epithets, & Vivid Verbosity. (Illus.). 144p. (Orig.). 1994. pap. 9.95 (1-57223-012-6) Idyll Arbor.

Toat Yeu Sach Giao Ly Hoi Thanh Cong-Giao. Dong D. Viet. Ed. by Dong D. Vietnam. 205p. pap. text ed. 7.00 (1-885550-05-7) Du-Sinh St Joseph.

***Toba Khedoori.** Elizabeth A. Smith & Anthony Vidler. (Focus Ser.). (Illus.). 48p. (Orig.). 1997. pap. 25.00 (0-914357-39-5) Los Angeles Mus Contemp.

Tobacciana Price Guide. Tony Hyman. (Illus.). 144p. (Orig.). 1997. pap. 29.95 (0-937111-07-4) Treasure Hunt Pubns.

Tobacco. Philip Cohen. LC 91-32583. (Drugs: the Complete Story Ser.). (Illus.). 64p. (YA). (gr. 6-12). 1991. lib. bdg. 25.68 (0-8114-3202-5) Raintree Steck-V.

Tobacco. Mark S. Gold. (Drugs of Abuse: A Comprehensive Series for Clinicians: Vol. 4). 211p. 1995. 37.50 (0-306-44933-1) Plenum.

Tobacco. Sue Rusche & Paula Kemp. (You Have the Right to Know Ser.: No. 3). 130p. 1992. pap. write for info. (1-880958-02-3) Natl Fam Act.

Tobacco. Judith K. Scheer. (Comprehensive Health for Middle Grades Ser.). (J). (gr. 6-9). 1996. 24.00 (1-56071-469-7, H571) ETR Assocs.

Tobacco: A Major International Health Hazard. Ed. by D. Zaridze & Richard Peto. (IARC Scientific Publications: No. 74). (Illus.). 350p. 1987. 46.00 (92-832-1174-X) OUP.

Tobacco: An International Perspective. David Tucker. 224p. 1990. 310.00 (0-903706-86-5, Pub. by Euromonitor Pubns UK) St Mut.

Tobacco: Health Facts. Nora J. Krantzler & Kathleen R. Miner. LC 94-42445. 1995. 12.95 (1-56071-477-8, H414) ETR Assocs.

Tobacco: Index of Modern Information with Bibliography. Scott T. Dowling. LC 90-32063. 160p. 1990. 44.50 (1-55914-154-9); pap. 39.50 (1-55914-155-7) ABBE Pubs Assn.

Tobacco: Peer Puppet Program. (Peer Leadership Training). (Illus.). (J). (gr. k-4). ring bd. 195.00 incl. audio (0-614-96205-6, 252400-SG) Sunburst Comm.

Tobacco: Peer Puppet Program, Set, incl. puppets. (Peer Leadership Training). (Illus.). (J). (gr. k-4). ring bd. 295.00 incl. audio, vhs (0-614-96204-8, 2524-SG) Sunburst Comm.

***Tobacco: People, Profits & Public Health.** Ed. by Gary E. McCuen. (Ideas in Conflict Ser.). (Illus.). 188p. 1996. lib. bdg. 13.95 (0-86596-142-5) G E M.

Tobacco: What It Is, What It Does. Judith S. Seixas. LC 81-837. (Greenwillow Read-Alone Bks.). (Illus.). 56p. (J). (gr. 1 up). 1981. 12.95 (0-685-42145-7, Mulberry) Morrow.

Tobacco Advertising: The Great Seduction. Gerard S. Petrone. LC 96-6405. (Illus.). 264p. (YA). (gr. 10-13). 1996. 49.95 (0-88740-972-5) Schiffer.

Tobacco Advertising Bans & Consumption in 16 Countries. Ed. by J. J. Boddewyn. 31p. 1986. 15.00 (0-317-01314-9) Intl Advertising Assn.

Tobacco, Alcohol & Cancer Prevention. Ernest H. Rosenbaum et al. Ed. by Sheila Mahoney & Nancy Wiltsek. (Illus.). 29p. 1984. pap. 2.50 (0-933161-02-6) Better H Prog.

Tobacco among the Karuk Indians of California. John P. Harrington. (Bureau of American Ethnology Bulletins Ser.). 284p. 1995. lib. bdg. 89.00 (0-7812-4094-8) Rprt Serv.

Tobacco & Health: Proceedings of the 9th World Conference Held in Paris, France, October 10-14, 1994. Ed. by Karen Slama. (Illus.). 1030p. (C). 1995. 175.00 (0-306-45111-5, Plenum Pr) Plenum.

Tobacco & Marijuana. Ochsner et al. 1976. per. 16.00 (0-88252-048-2) Paladin Hse.

Tobacco & Shamanism in South America. Johannes Wilbert. (Latin American Studies). (Illus.). 288p. (C). 1993. pap. 18.00 (0-300-05790-3) Yale U Pr.

Tobacco & Slaves: The Development of Southern Cultures in the Chesapeake, 1680-1800. Allan Kulikoff. LC 85-8452. xviii, 449p. (C). 1986. 39.95 (0-8078-1671-X); pap. 16.95 (0-8078-4224-9) U of NC Pr.

Tobacco & the Clinician: Interventions for Medical & Dental Practice. (Illus.). 389p. (Orig.). (C). 1994. pap. text ed. 50.00 (0-7881-1142-6) DIANE Pub.

***Tobacco & Your Oral Health.** Arden Christen & Jennifer Klein. (Illus.). 52p. write for info. (0-86715-326-1) Quint Pub Co.

Tobacco Coast. Arthur P. Middleton. LC 84-47962. (Maryland Paperback Bookshelf Ser.). 528p. (C). 1984. reprint ed. pap. 16.95 (0-8018-2534-2) Johns Hopkins.

***Tobacco Control Laws: Implementation & Enforcement.** Peter D. Jacobson & Jeffrey Wasserman. LC 97-5328. 180p. 1997. pap. 15.00 (0-8330-2486-8, MR-841-RWJ) Rand Corp.

Tobacco Culture: The Mentality of the Great Tidewater Planters on the Eve of Revolution. T. H. Breen. LC 85-42676. (Illus.). 210p. 1985. text ed. 49.50 (0-691-04729-4); pap. text ed. 12.95 (0-691-00596-6) Princeton U Pr.

Tobacco Diseases & Decays. Frederick A. Wolf. LC 57-6286. 412p. reprint ed. pap. 117.50 (0-317-26801-5, 2023473) Bks Demand.

Tobacco Economics Today. CABI Staff. 78p. (Orig.). 1985. pap. text ed. 63.00 (0-85198-551-3) CAB Intl.

Tobacco Effects in the Mouth. R. E. Mecklenburg et al. (Illus.). 28p. (Orig.). (C). 1995. pap. text ed. 25.00 (0-7881-2182-0) DIANE Pub.

Tobacco Free Youth: How to Reduce Sales to Minors in Your Community. Ellen Feighery et al. Ed. by Prudence Breitrose. 128p. (Orig.). 1992. pap. 22.50 (1-879552-11-6) Stanford CRDP.

***Tobacco Habit.** P. B. Randolph. 16p. 1972. pap. 2.00 (0-916285-57-X) Humanitarian.

Tobacco Habits Other Than Smoking: Betel-Quid & Areca-Nut Chewing; & Some Related Nitrosamines. (IARC Monographs on the Evaluation of the Carcinogenic Risk of Chemicals to Humans: Vol. 37). 291p. 1985. pap. text ed. 77.00 (92-832-1537-0, 1720037) World Health.

***Tobacco Habits Other Than Smoking - Betel-Quid & Areca-Nut Chewing & Some Related Nitrosamines: The Evaluation of Carcinogenic Risks to Humans.** (IARC Monographs: No. 37). 291p. 1985. text ed. 77.00 (92-832-1237-1) World Health.

Tobacco in Atlantic Trade: The Chesapeake, London & Glasgow, 1675-1775. Jacob M. Price. LC 95-30952. (Collected Studies: Vol. CS513). 336p. 1995. 82.50 (0-86078-548-3, Pub. by Variorum UK) Ashgate Pub Co.

Tobacco in History. Jordan Goodman. 288p. (C). (gr. 13). 1994. pap. 17.95 (0-415-11669-4, B4700) Routledge.

***Tobacco Industry Report 1996 Edition: Profiles of Domestic & International Tobacco Industry Manufacturers & Suppliers.** rev. ed. Catherine Sheehy. Ed. by Doug Cogan. 75p. 1996. 395.00 (1-879775-43-3) IRRC Inc DC.

Tobacco Kingdom. Joseph C. Robert. 1938. 14.50 (0-8446-1386-X) Peter Smith.

Tobacco Lords: A Study of the Tobacco Merchants of Glasgow & Their Trading Activities, 1740-1790. Thomas M. Devine. (Illus.). 222p. 1990. pap. 20.00 (0-7486-0172-4, Pub. by Edinburgh U Pr UK) Col U Pr.

Tobacco Merchant: The Story of Universal Leaf Tobacco Company. Ed. by Maurice Duke & Daniel P. Jordan. LC 94-26776. 248p. 1995. lib. bdg. 25.00 (0-8131-1892-1) U Pr of Ky.

Tobacco or Health: Status in the Americas: A Report of the Pan American Health Organization. (PAHO Scientific Publication Ser.: No. 536). xiv, 387p. (ENG & SPA.). 1992. pap. text ed. 40.00 (92-75-11536-2, 1610536) World Health.

Tobacco, Peacepipes & Indians. Louis Seig. LC 73-90817. (Wild & Woolly West Ser., No. 15). (Illus.). (Orig.). 1971. pap. 4.00 (0-910584-91-5) Filter.

Tobacco Product Liability: Affirmative & Defensive Tools, Asbestos Property Damage Litigation: Fourth Annual Toxic Tort Advocacy Institute. iv, 192p. write for info. (0-318-61621-1) HarBrace.

***Tobacco-Related Litigation & Insurance.** David L. Leitner & American Bar Association Staff. LC 97-4246. 1997. pap. write for info. (1-57073-398-8) Amer Bar Assn.

Tobacco Road. Erskine Caldwell. LC 78-55752. 1970. pap. 2.95 (0-451-12156-2, AE2156, Sig) NAL-Dutton.

Tobacco Road. large type ed. Erskine Caldwell. LC 95-14356. 236p. 1995. lib. bdg. 20.95 (0-7838-1365-1, GK Hall) Thorndike Pr.

Tobacco Road. Erskine Caldwell. LC 78-55752. 1993. reprint ed. lib. bdg. 27.95 (0-89966-304-4) Buccaneer Bks.

Tobacco Road. Erskine Caldwell. LC 78-55752. 1978. reprint ed. lib. bdg. 14.00 (0-8376-0422-2) Bentley.

Tobacco Road. Erskine Caldwell. LC 78-55752. (Brown Thrasher Bks.). 200p. 1995. reprint ed. pap. 9.95 (0-8203-1661-X) U of Ga Pr.

Tobacco Scare Found Faked: Revealing the Biggest Science Scandal in History. Paul A. Murtaugh. 200p. 1992. 16.95 (0-9633367-0-3) Am Rights Coun.

Tobacco Smoke in Active & Passive Pollution: Reports of Harmful Conditions & Effects: Index of Authors & Subjects. Wayne W. Weiss. LC 94-31240. 1994. 47.50 (0-7883-0362-7); pap. 44.50 (0-7883-0363-5) ABBE Pubs Assn.

Tobacco Smoking. (IARC Monographs on the Evaluation of the Carcinogenic Risk of Chemicals to Humans: Vol. 38). 421p. 1986. pap. text ed. 74.70 (92-832-1538-9, 1720038) World Health.

***Tobacco Smoking: The Evaluation of Carcinogenic Risks to Humans.** (IARC Monographs: No. 38). 421p. 1986. text ed. 83.00 (92-832-1238-X) World Health.

Tobacco Smoking & Atherosclerosis: Pathogenesis & Cellular Mechanisms. Ed. by J. N. Diana. LC 90-7922. (Advances in Experimental Medicine & Biology Ser.: Vol. 273). (Illus.). 390p. 1990. 120.00 (0-306-43668-X, Plenum Pr) Plenum.

Tobacco Smoking & Nicotine: A Neurobiological Approach. Ed. by W. R. Martin et al. LC 87-18513. (Advances in Behavioral Biology Ser.: Vol. 31). (Illus.). 534p. 1987. 120.00 (0-306-42611-0, Plenum Pr) Plenum.

Tobacco Smoking & Nutrition: Influence of Nutrition on Tobacco-Associated Health Risks. Ed. by John N. Diana & William A. Pryor. LC 93-10409. (Annals Ser.: Vol. 686). 366p. 1993. write for info. (0-89766-807-3); pap. 90.00 (0-89766-808-1) NY Acad Sci.

Tobacco Smoking & the Law in Canada. Grossman & Price. 258p. 1992. boxed 51.00 (0-409-89370-6) MICHIE.

Tobacco Society of the Crow Indians. Robert H. Lowie. LC 74-7988. reprint ed. 35.00 (0-404-11878-X) AMS Pr.

An Asterisk (*) at the beginning of an entry indicates that the title is appearing in BIP for the first time.

Tobacco-Specific N-Nitrosomes: Recent Advances. Roger O. McClellan. 1996. lib. bdg. 59.95 (*0-8493-1156-X*) CRC Pr.

***Tobacco Sticks.** William E. Hazelgrove. 1997. mass mkt. 5.99 (*0-553-57559-7*) Bantam.

Tobacco Sticks. William E. Hazelgrove. LC 94-61347. 308p. 1995. 18.95 (*0-9630052-8-6*) Pantonne Pr.

***Tobacco Times.** William J. Strong & Reed R. Callister. (Illus.). 200p. (Orig.). 1996. pap. 10.00 (*0-9611938-3-2*) Soundprint.

Tobacco Tins: A Collector's Guide. Douglas Congdon-Martin. LC 92-60632. (Illus.). 160p. 1992. pap. 29.95 (*0-88740-429-4*) Schiffer.

Tobago. Wilson Ltd. Staff & Imray L. Norie. (C). 1987. 65.00 (*0-685-40382-3*, Pub. by Imray Laurie Norie & Wilson UK) St Mut.

***Tobal No. 1: The Official Strategy Guide, No. 1.** PCS Staff. 96p. 1996. pap. 12.99 (*0-7615-0984-4*) Prima Pub.

Tobe. Frank R. Nichols. LC 94-68961. 160p. 1994. lib. bdg. 22.95 (*0-923687-33-5*) Celo Valley Bks.

Tobermory. Saki. (Classic Short Stories Ser.). 32p. (J). (gr. 6). 1990. lib. bdg. 13.95 (*0-88682-305-6*) Creative Ed.

Tobey: A Tale of Transition. Toni Acker. (Illus.). 40p. (YA). (gr. 7-12). 1987. pap. 5.95 (*0-942953-00-2*) Wonder Works Studio.

Tobey (Tobie, Toby) Genealogy: Thomas of Sandwich & James of Kittery & Their Descendants. Charles H. Pope & R. Tobey. (Illus.). 350p. 1989. reprint ed. pap. 52.50 (*0-8328-1171-8*); reprint ed. lib. bdg. 60.50 (*0-8328-1170-X*) Higginson Bk Co.

***Tobi Kahn: Metamorphoses.** Peter Selz et al. LC 97-66919. (Illus.). 80p. (Orig.). 1997. pap. write for info. (*1-890789-05-4*) Coun for Creat Proj.

Tobiaden und die Oniaden. Adolf Buchler. 398p. 1975. reprint ed. write for info. (*3-487-05582-1*) G Olms Pubs.

Tobias & the Angel. Rabbit. 1997. pap. 19.95 (*0-689-80237-4*) Macmillan.

Tobias George Smollett. Robert D. Spector. LC 68-24286. (Twayne's English Authors Ser.). 1968. lib. bdg. 17.95 (*0-89197-968-9*) Irvington.

Tobias George Smollett: A Bibliographical Guide. Francesco Cordasco. LC 77-83136. (Studies in the Eighteenth Century: No. 2). lib. bdg. 32.50 (*0-404-16018-2*) AMS Pr.

Tobias Smollett. Ed. by Lionel Kelly. 400p. 1987. 69.50 (*0-7102-0905-3*, 09053, RKP) Routledge.

Tobias Smollett. George S. Rousseau. 210p. 1982. 24.95 (*0-567-09330-1*, Pub. by T & T Clark UK) Bks Intl VA.

Tobias Smollett see Early English Novelist: Critical Heritage

Tobias Turkey: A Thanksgiving Tale. Sandra Robbins. (See-More's Stories Ser.). (Illus.). 32p. (Orig.). (J). (ps-3). 1993. pap. 4.95 (*1-882601-07-6*); pap. 9.98 incl. audio (*1-882601-06-8*) See-Mores Wrkshop.

Tobias Wolff: A Study of the Short Fiction. Hannah. 1996. 24.95 (*0-8057-0864-2*, Twayne) Scribnrs Ref.

***Tobin Tax: Coping with Financial Volatility.** Ed. by Mahbub Ul Haq et al. (Illus.). 336p. 1996. pap. 21.00 (*0-19-511181-8*) OUP.

***Tobin Tax: Coping with Financial Volatility.** Ed. by Mahbub Ul Haq et al. (Illus.). 336p. 1996. 35.00 (*0-19-511180-X*) OUP.

Tobin's English Usage. Richard L. Tobin. LC 84-72354. 114p. (Orig.). 1985. pap. 4.75 (*0-89730-149-8*) R J Berg.

Tobin's English Usage. 2nd ed. Richard L. Tobin. 128p. (Orig.). 1988. pap. 5.95 (*0-89730-178-1*) R J Berg.

Tobit: A New Translation with Introduction & Commentary. Carey A. Moore. (Anchor Bible Ser.: Vol. 40A). (Illus.). 352p. 1996. 34.95 (*0-385-18913-3*) Doubleday.

Tobramycin Profile. Ed. by Michael Oellerich. 30p. 1988. pap. text ed. 20.00 (*3-527-27370-0*, Pub. by Deutsche Fors GW) Wiley.

Tobruk: The Great Siege Reassessed. Frank Harrison. (Illus.). 360p. 1996. 29.95 (*1-85409-361-4*, Pub. by Arms & Armour UK) Sterling.

Tobruk Rescue. Duncan Harding. 224p. 1995. 20.00 (*0-7278-4800-3*) Severn Hse.

Toby see Toby & the Phantoms of the Fourth Grade

Toby & the Phantoms of the Fourth Grade. Art Wallace. LC 93-760. Orig. Title: Toby. (Illus.). (J). (gr. 4-7). 1994. reprint ed. 11.95 (*0-89015-917-3*) Sunbelt Media.

Toby Belfer Never Had a Christmas Tree. Gloria T. Pushker. LC 91-14514. (Illus.). 32p. (J). 1991. reprint ed. 14.95 (*0-88289-855-8*) Pelican.

Toby Belfer's Seder: A Passover Story Retold. Gloria T. Pushker. LC 93-5585. (Illus.). 32p. (J). 1994. 14.95 (*0-88289-987-2*) Pelican.

Toby Lived Here. Hilma Wolitzer. (J). (gr. 5-11). 1986. pap. 3.45 (*0-374-47924-0*, Sunburst Bks) FS&G.

Toby Scudder, Ultimate Warrior. David Gifaldi. LC 92-39532. (J). 1993. 13.95 (*0-395-66400-4*, Clarion Bks) HM.

Toby Show. Aurand Harris. (J). (gr. k up). 1978. 5.00 (*0-87602-210-7*) Anchorage.

Toby Takes the Cake. Fran Manushkin. 96p. (J). 1995. pap. 3.99 (*0-14-037199-0*) Puffin Bks.

Toby the Splendid. Isabelle Holland. LC 86-24681. 160p. (J). (gr. 5 up). 1987. 13.95 (*0-8027-6674-9*); lib. bdg. 14.85 (*0-8027-6675-7*) Walker & Co.

Toby the Tabby Kitten. Photos & Text by Colleen S. Bare. LC 94-42912. (Illus.). (J). 1995. pap. 13.99 (*0-525-65211-6*, Cobblehill Bks) Dutton Child Bks.

***Toby the Tortoise.** Gerald Durrell. (Illus.). 32p. (J). 1992. pap. write for info. (*1-85479-069-2*, Pub. by M OMara UK) Assoc Pubs Grp.

***Toby Toucan & His Noisy Beak, Incl. toy.** Paul Flemming. (Snappy Fun Bks.: Vol. 2). (Illus.). 13p. (J). (gr. k-2). 1997. bds. 4.99 (*1-57584-172-X*) Rdrs Dgst Yng Fam.

Toby Turtle Takes a Tumble. Ed. by Tim Peters. (Illus.). (J). (ps-2). pap. 4.95 (*1-879874-29-6*) T Peters & Co.

Toby Tyler. James Otis. 152p. (J). 1981. reprint ed. lib. bdg. 25.95 (*0-89966-363-X*) Buccaneer Bks.

Toby Tyler. James Otis. 188p. (J). 1981. reprint ed. lib. bdg. 19.95 (*0-89967-037-7*) Harmony Raine.

***Toby Tyler: Or Ten Weeks with a Circus.** unabridged ed. James Otis. LC 97-2078. (Illus.). 135p. (J). 1996. reprint ed. pap. text ed. 2.00 (*0-486-29349-1*) Dover.

***Toby, Where Are You?** William Steig. LC 96-85448. (Michael di Capua Bks.). (Illus.). 32p. (J). (ps up). 1997. 13.95 (*0-06-205082-6*); lib. bdg. 13.89 (*0-06-205083-4*) HarpC Child Bks.

***Toby/Charlie's Game: A 2-in-1 Read & Color Book.** Peggy Conffin. (Illus.). 70p. (Orig.). (J). 1997. pap. write for info. (*1-57502-521-3*, P01547) Morris Pubng.

Toby's Big Truck Adventure. Reta Spears-Stewart. LC 92-35750. (J). 1993. pap. 0.97 (*0-8163-1141-2*) Pacific Pr Pub Assn.

Toby's Folly. Margot Arnold. (Penny Spring & Sir Toby Glendower Mystery Ser.). 256p. pap. 6.50 (*0-88150-228-6*) Countryman.

Toby's Lie: A Novel. Daniel Vilmure. LC 96-2122. 1996. write for info. (*0-614-97954-4*, PL) HarpC.

Toby's Lie: A Novel. Daniel Vilmure. 1995. 21.00 (*0-684-80204-X*) S&S Trade.

Tocante a los Dones Espirituales. Kenneth E. Hagin. (SPA.). 1990. pap. 3.95 (*0-89276-187-3*) Hagin Ministries.

Tocca a Te. Carmela Taliercio & Christine Acocella. (Aiming for Proficiency Ser.). (Illus.). 160p. (Orig.). (ITA.). 1990. student ed. 14.95 (*1-879279-03-7*, TX 3-018-189) Proficiency Pr.

Toccata. Khachaturian. 12p. 1985. pap. 4.95 (*0-7935-0439-2*, 00121161) H Leonard.

***Toccatas: Poems from Hollywood.** 12p. (Orig.). (YA). (gr. 9-12). 1997. pap. 5.00 (*0-89642-381-6*) Linden Pubs.

Tocharian Historical Phonology & Morphology. Douglas Q. Adams. (Amer. Oriental Ser.: Vol. 71). xii, 199p. 1988. 35.00 (*0-940490-71-4*) Am Orient Soc.

Tocqueville. Larry A. Siedentop. LC 93-36218. (Past Masters Ser.). 128p. 1994. pap. 8.95 (*0-19-287690-2*) OUP.

Tocqueville: A Biography. Andre Jardin. Tr. by Andre Davis from FRE. 544p. 1988. 35.00 (*0-374-27836-9*) FS&G.

Tocqueville: Centralization & Liberty. Henry S. Commager. 16p. (Orig.). 1977. pap. text ed. 11.00 (*0-8191-5828-3*, Aspen Inst for Humanistic Studies) U Pr of Amer.

Tocqueville & American Civilization. Max Lerner. 136p. (C). 1993. reprint ed. pap. text ed. 21.95 (*1-56000-703-6*) Transaction Pubs.

Tocqueville & England. Seymour I. Drescher. LC 63-20764. (Historical Monographs: No. 55). 271p. 1964. 20.00 (*0-674-89430-8*) HUP.

Tocqueville & the Nature of Democracy. Pierre Manent. Tr. by John Waggoner. LC 95-38604. 144p. (C). 1995. pap. text ed. 18.95 (*0-8476-8116-5*); lib. bdg. 40.00 (*0-8476-8115-7*) Rowman.

Tocqueville & the Problem of Democracy. Marvin Zetterbaum. LC 67-13664. 120p. reprint ed. pap. 34.20 (*0-318-35031-9*, 2030977) Bks Demand.

Tocqueville & the Two Democracies. Jean-Claude Lamberti. Tr. by Arthur Goldhammer from FRE. LC 88-18758. 323p. 1989. 50.00 (*0-674-89435-9*) HUP.

Tocqueville in America. George W. Pierson. 852p. 1996. reprint ed. pap. text ed. 24.95 (*0-8018-5506-3*) Johns Hopkins.

Tocqueville's America: The Great Quotations. Alexis De Tocqueville. LC 83-60625. 120p. 1983. pap. 7.95 (*0-8214-0753-8*) Ohio U Pr.

Tocqueville's Civil Religion: American Christianity & the Prospects for Freedom. Sanford Kessler. LC 93-26778. (SUNY Series in Religion, Culture, & Society). 238p. (C). 1994. text ed. 59.50 (*0-7914-1929-0*); pap. text ed. 19.95 (*0-7914-1930-4*) State U NY Pr.

Tocqueville's Defense of Human Liberty: Current Essays. Ed. by Peter A. Lawler & Joseph Alulis. LC 92-22994. 384p. 1992. text ed. 62.00 (*0-8153-0051-4*, 1492) Garland.

Tocqueville's Political Science, Vol. 1: Classic Essays. Ed. by Peter A. Lawler. LC 91-35663. 422p. 1992. text ed. 66.00 (*0-8153-0050-6*, H1491) Garland.

Tod in Venedig und Andere Erzaehlungen. Thomas Mann. 330p. (GER.). 1995. pap. 13.50 (*3-596-20054-7*, Pub. by Fischer Taschbch Verlag GW) Intl Bk Import.

Tod Sloan, by Himself. Tod S. Sloan. Ed. by A. Dick Luckman. (Illus.). 232p. 1988. reprint ed. pap. 14.50 (*0-916304-78-7*, SF 336.S 553 A3) SDSU Press.

***Tod und Jenseits in der Vorstellungswelt der Prakolumbischen Maya.** Karin Vincke. (Grazer Altertumskundliche Studien Ser.: Bd. 3). (Illus.). 252p. (GER.). 1997. 51.95 (*3-631-49642-7*) P Lang Pubng.

Tod und Leben nach den Vorstellungen der Babylonier. Erich Ebeling. LC 78-72732. (Ancient Mesopotamian Texts & Studies). reprint ed. 32.50 (*0-404-18169-4*) AMS Pr.

Tod Williams, Billie Tsien & Associates. Douglas Heller. LC 92-43467. (CPL Bibliographies Ser.: No. 288). 20p. 1993. pap. 10.00 (*0-86602-288-0*, Sage Prdcls Pr) Sage.

Toda Grammar & Texts. Murray B. Emeneau. LC 82-72155. (Memoirs Ser.: Vol. 155). 1984. pap. 29.00 (*0-87169-155-8*, M155-EMM) Am Philos.

Toda Lattices Cosymplectic Manifolds. (Interdisciplinary Mathematics Ser.: Vol. 15, Pt. A). 225p. 1977. 40.00 (*0-915692-20-1*) Math Sci Pr.

Toda Lattices, Cosymplectic Manifolds, Baecklund Transformations & Kinks, Pt. B. Robert Hermann. (Interdisciplinary Mathematics Ser.: No. 18). 145p. 1977. 32.00 (*0-915692-24-4*, 991600312) Math Sci Pr.

Todai-Ji No Daibutsu see Nara Buddhist Art: Todai-Ji

Todas, 2 vols., Set. W. H. Rivers. 1990. reprint ed. 78.00 (*81-7033-014-9*, Pub. by Rawat II) S Asia.

Todas of South India. Anthony R. Walker. 1986. 48.00 (*0-8364-2156-6*, Pub. by Hindustan IA) S Asia.

Today. Emotions Anonymous Members. LC 87-81559. 400p. 1987. pap. 8.00 (*0-9607356-2-3*) Emotions Anony Intl.

Today: A Primer on the Philosophic Path. 4th ed. Sara Robbins. 1979. pap. 5.00 (*0-87516-283-5*) DeVorss.

Today: A Text-Workbook for English Language & Composition. 3rd ed. Hans P. Guth & Paul H. Wilson. (gr. 7). 1980. text ed. 8.56 (*0-07-025037-5*) McGraw.

Today: A Text-Workbook for English Language & Composition. 3rd ed. Hans P. Guth & Paul H. Wilson. (gr. 8). 1980. text ed. 8.56 (*0-07-025038-3*) McGraw.

Today & Forever: Daily Strength for a Brighter Tomorrow. deluxe ed. Leroy Brownlow. (Devotions for Today Ser.). 1989. 14.99 (*0-915720-94-9*); 14.99 (*0-915720-93-0*); lthr. 16.99 (*0-915720-95-7*) Brownlow Pub Co.

Today & Tommorrow's Woman - Menopause: Before & After (Girls of 16 to Women of 99) Virginia L. Millonig. LC 95-48849. 300p. (Orig.). 1996. pap. text ed. 19.95 (*1-878028-23-5*) Hlth Lead Assoc.

Today & Tomorrow. Alvin N. Rogness. LC 77-84095. 96p. 1978. pap. 9.99 (*0-8066-1621-0*, 10-6660, Augsburg) Augsburg Fortress.

Today & Tomorrow. 2nd ed. A. K. Mozumdar. 1979. pap. 9.00 (*0-87516-066-2*) DeVorss.

Today & Tomorrow. Henry Ford. LC 88-42628. (Illus.). 300p. 1988. reprint ed. 30.00 (*0-915299-36-4*) Prod Press.

Today & Yesterday Big Book, Unit 5. (Networks Ser.). 1991. 19.50 (*0-88106-738-5*, N210) Charlesbridge Pub.

Today I Am a Fountain Pen. rev. ed. Morley Torgov. 1996. pap. 5.25 (*0-8222-1529-2*) Dramatists Play.

Today I Am Lovable: 365 Positive Activities for Kids. Diane Loomans. Ed. by Nancy Carleton. (Illus.). 372p. (Orig.). (J). (gr. 2-6). 1996. pap. 14.00 (*0-915811-68-5*) H J Kramer Inc.

Today I Baled Some Hay to Feed the Sheep the Coyotes Eat. 2nd ed. Bill Stockton. LC 83-81970. (Illus.). 111p. 1991. reprint ed. pap. 7.95 (*0-934318-26-3*) Falcon Pr MT.

Today I Commanded the Wind: Heute Befahl Ich Dem Eind. Lisa Kahn. LC 94-14760. (Illus.). 72p. (ENG & GER.). 1994. pap. 12.95 (*0-7734-0019-2*, Mellen Poetry Pr) E Mellen.

Today I Feel Shy. William L. Coleman. LC 83-9216. (Illus.). 128p. (Orig.). (J). (gr. 3-4). 1983. pap. 6.99 (*0-87123-588-9*) Bethany Hse.

Today, I Have Cancer... ...A Daily Journal of Life with Cancer. Debi Estabrook. 376p. (Orig.). 1995. pap. 9.95 (*1-56383-049-3*, 9250) G & R Pub.

Today I Took My Diaper Off (Baby Songs) (Golden Story Book 'n' Tape Ser.). (Illus.). 24p. (J). (ps-3). 5.95 incl. audio (*0-307-14186-1*, 14186-01) Western Pub.

***Today I Went to Sea: The Ultimate Nursery Rhyme Activity Book.** Kate Burns & Sally Chambers. (J). 1997. 14.95 (*0-7641-5006-5*) Barron.

Today I Will Do One Thing: Daily Readings for Awareness & Hope. Tim Mc. LC 95-1887. 400p. 1995. pap. 9.95 (*1-56838-083-6*) Hazelden.

***Today I'm a Basket Case.** Davis. Date not set. pap. write for info. (*0-312-18197-3*) St Martin.

Today I'm Going Fishing with My Dad. N. L. Sharp. LC 92-73994. (Illus.). 32p. (J). (ps-3). 1993. 14.95 (*1-56397-107-0*) Boyds Mills Pr.

***Today I'm Going Fishing with My Dad.** N. L. Sharp. LC 92-73994. (Illus.). 32p. (J). (ps-3). 1997. pap. 7.95 (*1-56397-613-7*) Boyds Mills Pr.

Today in American Drama. Frank O'Hara. (BCL1-PS American Literature Ser.). 277p. 1993. reprint ed. lib. bdg. 79.00 (*0-7812-6588-6*) Rprt Serv.

Today in American Drama. Frank H. O'Hara. LC 40-666. (Illus.). 277p. 1969. reprint ed. text ed. 35.00 (*0-8371-0600-1*, OHAD, Greenwood Pr) Greenwood.

***Today in the Cafe Trieste.** Richard Tillinghast. 88p. 1997. pap. 12.95 (*1-897648-84-7*, Pub. by Salmon Poetry IE) Dufour.

Today in the Republic of Texas. Hal Kopel. 1987. 14.95 (*0-87244-071-0*) Texian.

Today in Western New York, 1995. Retention Marketing Staff. 112p. 1994. pap. 9.95 (*0-9644538-0-0*) RMI Pub.

Today Is: An Ecumenical Prayer Journal for Young Teens. rev. ed. Center for Learning Network Staff. 80p. (J). (gr. 6-9). 1992. pap. text ed. 3.95 (*1-56077-217-4*) Ctr Learning.

Today Is Christmas. P. K. Hallinan. (P. K. Hallinan Holiday Bks.). (Illus.). 24p. (J). (ps-3). 1993. lib. bdg. 11.95 (*1-878363-93-X*) Forest Hse.

Today Is Christmas! P. K. Hallinan. (Illus.). 24p. (J). (ps-3). 1993. per., pap. 4.95 (*0-8249-8643-1*, Ideals Child) Hambleton-Hill.

Today Is Easter! P. K. Hallinan. (Illus.). 24p. (Orig.). (J). (ps-3). 1993. per., pap. 4.95 (*0-8249-8604-0*, Ideals Child) Hambleton-Hill.

Today Is Easter. P. K. Hallinan. (P. K. Hallinan Holiday Bks.). (Illus.). 24p. (J). (ps-3). 1993. lib. bdg. 11.95 (*1-878363-94-8*) Forest Hse.

Today Is Halloween! P. K. Hallinan. (Illus.). 24p. (J). (ps-3). 1992. per., pap. 4.95 (*0-8249-8557-5*, Ideals Child) Hambleton-Hill.

Today Is Halloween. P. K. Hallinan. (P. K. Hallinan Holiday Bks.). (Illus.). 24p. (J). (ps-3). 1992. lib. bdg. 11.95 (*1-878363-95-6*) Forest Hse.

Today Is Independence Day: Manuscript Edition. William Hanley. 1967. pap. 13.00 (*0-8222-0070-8*) Dramatists Play.

Today Is Mine. deluxe ed. Leroy Brownlow. (Devotions for Today Ser.). 1972. 14.99 (*0-915720-90-6*); 14.99 (*0-915720-14-0*); 14.99 (*0-915720-98-1*); lthr. 16.99 (*0-915720-57-4*) Brownlow Pub Co.

Today Is Monday. Eric Carle. LC 91-45866. (Illus.). 32p. (J). (ps-1). 1993. 15.95 (*0-399-21966-8*, Philomel Bks) Putnam Pub Group.

***Today Is Monday.** Eric Carle. (Illus.). 32p. (Orig.). (J). (ps-1). 1997. pap. 6.95 (*0-698-11563-5*, Paperstar) Putnam Pub Group.

Today Is Not Like Yesterday: A Chilean Journey. Ted Polumbaum & Nyna B. Polumbaum. (Illus.). 132p. (Orig.). 1992. pap. 22.95 (*0-9633526-0-1*) Light & Shadow.

Today Is Thanksgiving. P. K. Hallinan. (P. K. Hallinan Holiday Bks.). (Illus.). 24p. (J). (ps-3). 1993. lib. bdg. 11.95 (*1-878363-96-4*) Forest Hse.

Today Is Thanksgiving! P. K. Hallinan. (Illus.). 24p. (J). (ps-3). 1993. per., pap. 4.95 (*0-8249-8637-7*, Ideals Child) Hambleton-Hill.

Today Is the Day. Nancy Riecken. LC 95-23927. (Illus.). 32p. (J). (ps-3). 1996. 14.95 (*0-395-73917-9*) HM.

***Today Is the Day, Vol. 152.** Andre Du Bouchet. (Sun & Moon Classics Ser.). 1998. pap. text ed. 11.95 (*1-55713-321-2*) Sun & Moon CA.

***Today Is the First Day of the Rest of Your Layout.** Dwain Meyer. 80p. (Orig.). 1997. pap. 9.95 (*0-89024-321-2*, 12193, Kalmbach Books) Kalmbach.

Today Is Tomorrow. Betty S. Herman. 1995. pap. 10.95 (*0-533-11258-3*) Vantage.

Today Is Valentine's Day! P. K. Hallinan. (Illus.). 24p. (Orig.). (J). (ps-3). 1995. per., pap. 4.95 (*1-57102-014-4*, Ideals Child) Hambleton-Hill.

Today Is Valentine's Day. P. K. Hallinan. LC 94-29733. (P. K. Hallinan Holiday Books Ser.). (Illus.). 24p. (J). (ps-3). 1995. lib. bdg. 11.95 (*1-878363-78-6*) Forest Hse.

***Today Is Very Windy.** Gill Davies. (Illus.). 14p. (J). (ps). Date not set. bds. 4.98 (*1-85854-595-1*) Brimax Bks.

Today Is Your Birthday! P. K. Hallinan. (Illus.). 24p. (Orig.). (J). (ps-3). 1991. per., pap. 4.95 (*0-8249-8493-5*, Ideals Child) Hambleton-Hill.

Today Is Your Birthday. Illus. by P. K. Hallinan. (P. K. Hallinan Personal Values Ser.). 24p. (J). (ps-4). 1991. lib. bdg. 11.95 (*1-878363-29-8*) Forest Hse.

Today Pop Goes Home: A Play. Merle Good. LC 93-24453. 80p. (Orig.). 1993. pap. 6.95 (*1-56148-098-3*) Good Bks PA.

Today the Struggle: Literature & Politics in England During the Spanish Civil War. Katharine B. Hoskins. LC 78-83763. 312p. reprint ed. pap. 89.00 (*0-8357-7746-4*, 2036103) Bks Demand.

Today There is No Misery: The Ethnography of Farming in Northwest Portugal. Jeffery W. Bentley. LC 91-24390. (Arizona Studies in Human Ecology). (Illus.). 177p. 1992. 33.50 (*0-8165-1244-2*) U of Ariz Pr.

Today, Tomorrow & Always. Tim Kincaid. 432p. 1996. 22.00 (*1-57566-077-6*, Knsington) Kensgtn Pub Corp.

***Today, Tomorrow & Always.** Tim Kincaid. 480p. 1997. mass mkt. 5.99 (*1-57566-187-X*, Knsington) Kensgtn Pub Corp.

Today Was a Terrible Day. (Story Tapes Ser.). (Illus.). (J). (ps-3). 1988. pap. 6.95 (*0-14-095073-7*, Puffin) Puffin Bks.

Today Was a Terrible Day. Patricia R. Giff. (Illus.). (J). (gr. k-3). 1984. 22.95 incl. audio (*0-941078-50-7*); pap. 15.95 incl. audio (*0-941078-48-5*); pap. 31.95 incl. audio (*0-941078-49-3*); flmstrp 32.95 (*0-941078-47-7*) Live Oak Media.

Today Was a Terrible Day. Patricia R. Giff. (Illus.). (J). 1993. pap. 7.99 incl. audio (*0-14-095119-9*, Puffin) Puffin Bks.

Today Was a Terrible Day. Patricia R. Giff. (Illus.). (J). 1980. pap. 14.99 (*0-670-71830-0*) Viking Child Bks.

Today Was a Terrible Day. Patricia R. Giff. (Illus.). 32p. (J). (ps). 1984. pap. 4.99 (*0-14-050453-2*) Viking Child Bks.

Today Was a Terrible Day. Patricia R. Giff. (Picture Puffins Ser.). (Illus.). 32p. (J). (ps). 1984. pap. 3.95 incl. audio (*0-685-54175-4*, Penguin Bks) Viking Penguin.

Today 1994: A Personal Record & Reference Book. Ed. by World Book Editors. LC 76-27228. (Illus.). 192p. (YA). (gr. 9 up). 1993. lib. bdg. write for info. (*0-7166-0794-8*) World Bk.

Today 1995: A Personal Record & Reference Book. World Book Editors. LC 76-27228. (Illus.). 192p. 1994. text ed. write for info. (*0-7166-0795-6*) World Bk.

Today's American: How Free? James Finn & Leonard R. Sussman. LC 86-25663. (Studies in Freedom: No. 4). 1986. 34.50 (*0-932088-10-4*) Freedom Hse.

***Today's & Yesterday's Haiku.** Albert Krassner. 536p. (Orig.). 1997. mass mkt. 5.99 (*1-55197-903-9*, Pub. by Comnwlth Pub CN) Partners Pubs Grp.

Today's Art of Peritoneal Dialysis: Proceedings of the International Symposium, 1st Chapala, Jalisco, Mexico, June 25-28, 1978. International Symposium on Peritoneal Dialysis Staff. Ed. by A. T. Becerra & F. S. Boen. (Contributions to Nephrology Ser.: Vol. 17). (Illus.). 1979. pap. 60.00 (*3-8055-3006-4*) S Karger.

Today's Best Poems. Ed. by Eddie-Lou Cole. 39.95 (*0-317-29091-6*) World Poetry Pr.

Today's Black Hollywood. James R. Parish. 1995. mass mkt. 4.99 (*0-7860-0104-6*, Pinncle Kensgtn) Kensgtn Pub Corp.

Today's Black Hollywood. James R. Parrish. 480p. 1995. mass mkt. 4.99 (*0-8217-0104-5*, Zebra Kensgtn) Kensgtn Pub Corp.

Today's Business Math: A Text-Workbook. 2nd ed. Burton S. Kaliski. 424p. (C). 1985. pap. text ed. 39.00 (*0-15-592162-2*) SCP.

Today's Challenge: Content of the Health Record. Barbara Glondys. 257p. 1988. write for info. (*0-318-21462-8*); 35.00 (*0-317-05441-4*) Am Hlth Info.

Today's Challenge to Tomorrow's Vision: A Study of Facilities Conditions at Schools of Theology. APPA Staff & Lilly Endowment, Inc. Staff. (Illus.). 97p. 1991. pap. 35.00 (*0-913359-65-3*) APPA VA.

Today's Children, Tomorrow's Survival: Restructuring Schools. 34p. 1989. 6.00 (*0-317-05341-8*) NASBE.

Today's Country Hits. Ed. by Milton Okun. 1994. pap. 12.95 (*0-89524-789-5*) Cherry Lane.

Today's Country Hits: Easy Piano. Ed. by Milton Okun. pap. 14.95 (*0-89524-801-8*) Cherry Lane.

Today's Custom Tailoring. Ethel K. Wyllie. 1979. teacher ed. 5.32 (*0-02-665990-5*); text ed. 26.00 (*0-02-665980-8*) Glencoe.

Today's Delinquent, Vol. 4: On Family. Ed. by Hunter Hurst. 97p. 1985. 10.00 (*0-318-36236-8*) Natl Juv & Family Ct Judges.

Today's Destructive Cults & Religious Movements. Lawrence J. Gesy. LC 92-83995. (Orig.). 1993. pap. 11.95 (*0-87973-498-1*, 498) Our Sunday Visitor.

***Today's Disciple.** 224p. 1996. 14.99 (*0-8341-1653-7*) Nazarene.

Today's Economic Issues. Reuben Schlesinger & Marty Wolfson. (Illus.). 1974. pap. 5.95 (*0-916114-04-X*) Wolfson.

Today's Electronics. Joseph G. Sloop. Ed. by Larry Ryan. (Illus.). 260p. 1990. ring bd. write for info. (*0-89704-051-1*) E&L Instru.

Today's Elementary Social Studies. 2nd ed. Dorothy G. Hennings et al. (Illus.). 555p. (C). 1993. reprint ed. text ed. 42.95 (*0-88133-755-2*) Waveland Pr.

Today's Evangelism: Counterfeit or Genuine? Gordon H. Clark. Ed. & Intro. by John W. Robbins. 136p. (Orig.). 1990. pap. 6.95 (*0-940931-28-1*) Trinity Found.

Today's Evangelism: It's Message & Methods. Ernest C. Reisinger. 1982. pap. 6.99 (*0-87552-417-6*, Pub. by Evangelical Pr) Presby & Reformed.

Today's Family Guide to Austin. rev. ed. Lynda Crowell. 300p. (Orig.). 1993. pap. 12.95 (*0-938934-29-5*) LCN.

Today's Family Guide to Dallas. 1995. 12.95 (*0-938934-27-9*) LCN.

Today's Family Guide to Houston. Lynda Crowell. 400p. (Orig.). 1992. pap. text ed. 12.95 (*0-938934-26-0*) LCN.

Today's Family Guide to San Antonio. Lynda Crowell. 150p. (Orig.). 1993. pap. 8.95 (*0-938934-28-7*) LCN.

Today's Forty Most Frequently Used Fittings, Vol. 1. 6th ed. Richard S. Budzik. 346p. 1988. 39.95 (*0-912914-41-6*) Practical Pubns.

Today's Forty Most Frequently-Used Fittings, Vol. 2. 5th ed. Richard S. Budzik. LC 73-188876. (Illus.). 402p. 1989. 39.95 (*0-912914-42-4*) Practical Pubns.

T

Today's French Theatre. Motley. (Yale French Studies). 1954. 25.00 (*0-527-01722-1*) Periodicals Srv.

Today's Gift. Illus. by David Spohn. (Meditation Ser.). 400p. (Orig.). 1985. pap. 11.00 (*0-89486-302-9*, 1031A) Hazelden.

Today's Girl in Today's Society. Ruth H. Smith. 1980. pap. 2.95 (*0-89137-812-X*) Quality Pubns.

Today's Gospel. Walter J. Chantry. 1980. pap. 5.99 (*0-85151-027-2*) Banner of Truth.

Today's Gourmet: Light & Healthy Cooking for the '90s. Jacques Pepin. LC 90-92204. (Illus.). 176p. (Orig.). 1991. pap. 15.95 (*0-912333-08-1*) BB&T Inc.

Today's Gourmet II see Good Life Cooking: Light Classics from Today's Gourmet

Today's Greatest Poems. John T. Campbell. 665p. 1983. 59.95 (*0-910147-01-9*) World Poetry Pr.

Today's Handbook for Solving Bible Difficulties. David E. O'Brien. 498p. 1990. 19.99 (*0-87123-814-4*) Bethany Hse.

Today's Handbook of Bible Characters. Edward M. Blaiklock. LC 87-8066. 640p. 1987. 19.99 (*0-87123-948-5*) Bethany Hse.

Today's Health Alternative. Raquel Martin. (Illus.). 456p. (Orig.). (C). 1992. pap. text ed. 16.95 (*0-922356-45-9*) Amer West Pubs.

Today's Health Movement & the Future of America. Harold E. Buttram. 72p. 1982. pap. 3.00 (*0-916285-31-6*) Humanitarian.

Todays Healthy Eating. Louise Tenney. 249p. pap. 12.95 (*0-913923-09-5*) Woodland UT.

Today's Healthy Eating. Louise Tenney. 249p. spiral bd. 14.95 (*0-913923-76-1*) Woodland UT.

Today's Hearing Impaired Child: Into the Mainstream of Education. Ed. by Vira J. Froehlinger. 240p. (Orig.). (C). 1981. pap. 9.95 (*0-88200-143-4*, N6184) Alexander Graham.

Today's Herbal Health. 3rd ed. Louise Tenney. 375p. 1993. pap. 12.95 (*0-913923-91-5*); spiral bd. 14.95 (*0-913923-84-2*) Woodland UT.

Today's Herbal Health. 3rd ed. Louise Tenney. 377p. 1992. pap. text ed. 16.95 (*0-913923-83-4*) Woodland UT.

***Today's Herbal Health: The Essential Guide to Understanding Herbs Used for Medicinal Purposes.** Louise Tenney. 1997. pap. text ed. 16.95 (*1-885670-76-1*) Woodland UT.

***Today's Herbal Health: The Essential Reference Guide.** 4th rev. ed. Louise Tenney. 381p. (Orig.). 1997. pap. 14.95 (*1-885670-06-0*) Woodland UT.

Today's Herbal Health for Children. Louise Tenney. 1996. pap. text ed. 11.95 (*1-885670-04-4*) Woodland UT.

***Today's Herbal Health for Women.** Louise Tenney. 1996. pap. text ed. 12.95 (*1-885670-35-4*) Woodland UT.

Today's Herbal Kitchen: How to Cook & Design with Herbs Through the Seasons. Memphis Herb Society Staff. Ed. by Carol Boker. (Illus.). 256p. 1996. 19.95 (*1-879958-28-7*) Tradery Hse.

Today's Heroes: For Men. (Today's Heroes Ser.). (J). 1995. boxed, pap. 19.96 (*0-310-20925-0*) Zondervan.

Today's Heroes: For Women. (Today's Heroes Ser.). (J). 1995. boxed, pap. 14.97 (*0-310-20924-2*) Zondervan.

Today's Highways: A Comprehensive History, Study & Guide on Motor Carriers of Property in the United States. John P. Martell. LC 88-51766. 200p. (Orig.). (C). 1989. pap. text ed. 24.95 (*0-9621540-1-6*) Transmart.

Today's Immigrants, Their Stories: A New Look at the Newest Americans. Thomas Kessner & Betty B. Caroli. (Illus.). 330p. (C). 1983. pap. 11.95 (*0-19-503270-5*) OUP.

Today's Isms: Socialism, Capitalism, Fascism, Communism. 10th rev. ed. Alan O. Ebenstein et al. LC 93-948. 212p. (C). 1993. pap. text ed. 34.60 (*0-13-138595-X*) P-H.

Today's Italian Touch from Progresso. (Favorite All Time Recipes Ser.). (Illus.). 96p. 1993. spiral bd. 3.50 (*1-56173-556-6*, 2015000) Pubns Intl Ltd.

Today's Kindergarten: Exploring the Knowledge Base, Expanding the Curriculum. Bernard Spodek. (Early Childhood Education Ser.). 160p. 1986. pap. text ed. 17.95 (*0-8077-2808-X*) Tchrs Coll.

Today's Kings of Country Music, Vol. 2. Ed. by Carol Cuellar. 172p. (Orig.). (YA). 1994. pap. text ed. 12.95 (*0-89898-780-6*, F3306SMA) Warner Brothers.

Todays' Ladies of Country Music. Ed. by Carol Cuellar. 148p. (Orig.). (YA). 1991. pap. 12.95 (*0-89898-591-9*, F3191SMX) Warner Brothers.

Today's Law Teachers: Lawyers or Academics?: A Research Report on Law Teachers in U. K. Higher Education, 1994. Patricia Leighton et al. 81p. 1995. pap. 50.00 (*1-85941-009-X*, Pub. by Cavendish UK) Gaunt.

Today's Love Songs. 144p. 1992. per. 14.95 (*0-7935-1177-1*, 00222541) H Leonard.

Today's Love Songs: Thirty-One Contemporary Romantic Favorites. (Piano-Vocal-Guitar Ser.). 160p. 1991. pap. 14.95 (*0-7935-1178-X*, 00311550) H Leonard.

Today's Management: The Good, the Bad & the Useless. Sandy Klemash. 96p. (Orig.). 1996. pap. 12.00 (*1-884570-44-5*) Research Triangle.

Today's Management Methods: A Guide for the Health Care Executive. Ed. by Robert G. Gift & Catherine F. Kinney. LC 96-5097. (Illus.). 328p. (Orig.). 1996. pap. 69.00 (*1-55648-153-5*, 001117) AHPI.

***Today's Mathematics.** 9th ed. James W. Heddens & William R. Speer. LC 96-28398. 1997. 60.00 (*0-13-493362-1*) P-H.

***Today's Mathematics.** 9th ed. James W. Heddens & William R. Speer. LC 96-28398. 1996. text ed. write for info. (*0-13-589011-X*); pap. text ed. write for info. (*0-13-589003-9*) P-H.

Today's Media. (Cross Training Ser.: Vol. 1). 64p. (J). (gr. 7-9). 1994. pap. 29.95 (*1-57405-006-0*) CharismaLife Pub.

Today's Military Wife. 3rd ed. Lydia S. Cline. (Illus.). 240p. 1995. pap. 14.95 (*0-8117-2580-4*) Stackpole.

Today's Moral Issues: Classical & Contemporary Perspectives. 2nd ed. Daniel Bonevac. LC 95-33959. 584p. (C). 1996. pap. text ed. 38.95 (*1-55934-513-6*, 1513) Mayfield Pub.

Today's Myths & Tomorrow's Realities: Overcoming Obstacles to Academic Leadership in the Twenty-First Century. Richard M. Millard. LC 91-11251. (Higher & Adult Education Ser.). 340p. text ed. 34.95 (*1-55542-361-2*) Jossey-Bass.

Today's Pawnbroker Digest. Jerry Stokes. 54p. 1993. 39.95 (*1-883103-00-2*) United NC.

Today's Pop Hits. 64p. 1994. pap. 8.95 (*0-7935-3336-8*, 00221817) H Leonard.

Today's Practical Guide to Increasing Profits for Contractors with Easy-to-Use Suggestions & Aids. Richard S. Budzik & Janet K. Budzik. LC 74-79535. (Illus.). (C). 1974. 59.95 (*0-912914-03-3*) Practical Pubns.

Today's Problems, Tomorrow's Solutions: The Future Structure of Muslim Societies. Ed. by A. Naseef. 190p. 1988. text ed. 80.00 (*0-7201-1991-X*, Mansell Pub) Cassell.

Today's Reform Response. Solomon B. Freehof. (Alumni Series of the Hebrew Union College Press). 175p. reprint ed. pap. 49.90 (*0-7837-7051-0*, 2046863) Bks Demand.

***Today's Refugees & the World of Communications.** Silvano M. Tomasi. (Pastoral Ser.). 12p. 1995. pap. 5.00 (*0-934733-92-9*) CMS.

***Today's S. O. S. (Secrets of Survival)** Anolia O. Facun. Ed. by William Cohen. LC 97-60128. 202p. (Orig.). 1997. pap. 15.95 (*0-9656671-0-3*) What A Wnderful Wrld.

Today's Science, Tomorrow's Technology. Ed. by M. H. Brennan & D. D. Millar. (Illus.). 161p. 1989. pap. text ed. 21.95 (*0-08-040067-1*, PPA) Elsevier.

Today's Specials. Holli Rovenger & Alexa Bosshardt. 328p. 1991. pap. 14.95 (*0-9630382-0-6*) Nutrit Mktg.

Today's Spirituality. Thomas R. Haney. 1990. pap. 12.95 (*0-88347-245-7*) Res Christian Liv.

Today's Swingers: The Complete Guide to Successful Swinging. Steve Marks & Cathy Marks. LC 95-78394. 160p. (Orig.). 1995. pap. 16.95 (*0-9640903-1-7*) M S W Pubng.

Today's Tech: Auto Computer System Classroom Manager. Knowles. (C). 1996. text ed. 270.00 (*0-8273-7585-9*) Delmar.

Today's Tech: Auto Electric/Classroom Manager. Erjavec. (Automotive Technology Ser.). 1994. 150.00 (*0-8273-6493-8*) Delmar.

Today's Tech: Auto Heating & Air Conditioning. Dwiggins. 640p. (C). 1996. text ed. 232.95 (*0-8273-7584-0*) Delmar.

Today's Tech: Classroom Manager. Erjavec. (Automotive Technology Ser.). 1994. 236.50 incl. trans. (*0-8273-6492-X*) Delmar.

Today's Tech: Engine Repair Classroom Manager. Barry Hollembeak. (C). 1997. text ed. 270.00 (*0-8273-7586-7*) Delmar.

Today's Technician: Auto Fuel & Emmission. Al Santini. (Automotive Technology Ser.). 1997. 53.50 (*0-8273-6183-1*) Delmar.

Today's Technician: Auto Heating & Air Conditioning. Erjavec. (Automotive Technology Ser.). 176p. 1996. teacher ed. 19.50 (*0-8273-6888-7*) Delmar.

Todays Technician: Automotive Brakes Systems. 2nd ed. Eichhorn. (Automotive Technology Ser.). 464p. 1996. text ed. 270.00 (*0-8273-7583-2*) Delmar.

Today's Technician: Automotive Computer Systems. Knowles. (Automotive Technology Ser.). 224p. 1996. teacher ed., text ed. 21.95 (*0-8273-6885-2*) Delmar.

Today's Technician: Automotive Computer Systems. Don Knowles & Jack Erjavec. (Automotive Technology Ser.). (Illus.). 976p. 1996. spiral bd., pap. 53.50 (*0-8273-6884-4*) Delmar.

***Today's Technician: Automotive Electricity & Electronics.** 2nd ed. Hollembeak & Erjavec. 672p. 1997. text ed. 242.95 (*0-8273-7636-7*) Delmar.

Today's Technician: Automotive Electricity & Electronics Class & Shop Manual. 2nd ed. Barry Hollembeak & Erjavec. LC 96-42050. (C). 1996. 60.95 (*0-8273-7635-9*) Delmar.

Today's Technician: Brake Systems. Eichhorn. (Automotive Technology Ser.). 1996. teacher ed. 17.50 (*0-8273-6892-5*) Delmar.

Today's Technician: Electricity & Electronics Class Manager. 2nd ed. Barry Hollembeak. (C). 1997. teacher ed. 22.95 (*0-8273-7648-3*) Delmar.

Today's Technician: Emission Control/Fuel System. Al Santini. (Automotive Technology Ser.). 1997. teacher ed. 16.80 (*0-8273-6887-9*) Delmar.

Today's Technician: Engine Repair. Barry Hollembeak. (Automotive Technology Ser.). 768p. 1996. text ed. 48.95 (*0-8273-6187-4*) Delmar.

Today's Technician: Engine Repair. Barry Hollembeak. (Automotive Technology Ser.). 1997. teacher ed. 19.50 (*0-8273-6893-3*) Delmar.

Today's Technician: Heavy Duty Truck Electric. Ralbovsky. (Automotive Technology Ser.). 1997. 56.00 (*0-8273-7006-7*); teacher ed. 16.00 (*0-8273-7007-5*) Van Nos Reinhold.

Today's Technician: Manual Transmissions. 2nd ed. Erjavec. (Automotive Technology Ser.). 704p. 1997. 54.95 (*0-8273-7676-6*) Delmar.

Today's Technician: Manual Transmissions. 2nd ed. Erjavec. (Automotive Technology Ser.). 1997. 242.95 (*0-8273-7677-4*) Delmar.

Today's Technician: Manual Transmissions. 2nd ed. Erjavec Staff. (Automotive Technology Ser.). 176p. 1997. teacher ed. 20.00 (*0-8273-7678-2*) Delmar.

Today's Technician: Manual Transmissions & Transaxles. Jack Erjavec. 154p. 1995. teacher ed. 19.50 (*0-8273-6530-6*) Delmar.

Today's Technician: Medium/Heavy Engine Repair. Myshanick. (Automotive Technology Ser.). 1998. pap. 56.00 (*0-8273-7221-3*) Delmar.

Today's Technician: Medium/Heavy Engine Repair. Myshanick. (Automotive Technology Ser.). 1998. teacher ed., pap. 16.50 (*0-8273-7222-1*) Delmar.

Today's Technician: Medium/Heavy Engine Repair IRK. Myshanick. (Automotive Technology Ser.). 1998. 99.99 (*0-8273-7223-X*) Delmar.

Today's Technician: Medium/Heavy Truck AC & Refrigeration. Myshaniuk. (Automotive Technology Ser.). Date not set. teacher ed. 16.00 (*0-8273-7255-8*) Delmar.

Today's Technician: Medium/Heavy Truck Air Conditioning & Refrigeration. Myshaniuk. (Automotive Technology Ser.). Date not set. pap. 56.00 (*0-8273-7254-X*) Delmar.

Today's Technician: Medium/Heavy Truck Air Conditioning & Refrigeration IRK. Myshaniuk. (Automotive Technology Ser.). Date not set. 99.99 (*0-8273-7256-6*) Delmar.

Today's Technician: Medium/Heavy Truck ASE Preptest. Knowles. (Automotive Technology Ser.). 1998. teacher ed. 16.95 (*0-8273-7259-0*); pap. 32.95 (*0-8273-7258-2*) Delmar.

Today's Technician: Medium/Heavy Truck Brakes. Knowles. (Automotive Technology Ser.). 1998. pap. 56.00 (*0-8273-7287-6*) Delmar.

Today's Technician: Medium/Heavy Truck Brakes. Knowles. (Automotive Technology Ser.). 1998. teacher ed. 16.95 (*0-8273-7288-4*) Delmar.

Today's Technician: Medium/Heavy Truck Brakes IRK. Knowles. (Automotive Technology Ser.). 1998. 134.95 (*0-8273-7289-2*) Delmar.

Today's Technician: Medium/Heavy Truck Steering & Suspension. Knowles. (Automotive Technology Ser.). Date not set. pap. 56.00 (*0-8273-7284-1*) Delmar.

Today's Technician: Medium/Heavy Truck Steering & Suspension. Knowles. (Automotive Technology Ser.). Date not set. teacher ed. 16.95 (*0-8273-7285-X*) Delmar.

Today's Technician: Medium/Heavy Truck Steering & Suspension IRK. Knowles. (Automotive Technology Ser.). Date not set. 133.99 (*0-8273-7286-8*) Delmar.

Today's Technology: Automotive Electronics. Erjavec. (Automotive Technology Ser.: I). (C). 1995. 19.50 (*0-8273-6531-4*) Delmar.

Today's Technology: Heavy Duty Truck Electronics. Ralbovsky. (Automotive Technology Ser.). 1997. teacher ed. 134.95 (*0-8273-7008-3*) Delmar.

Today's Technology in Bible Prophecy. Charles W. Miller. (Illus.). 512p. (Orig.). 1990. pap. 10.00 (*0-9627032-0-6*) TIP MI.

Today's Teen. rev. ed. Kelly & Landers. (gr. 7-9). 1981. text ed. 23.04 (*0-02-666030-X*) Glencoe.

Today's Teen. rev. ed. Kelly & Landers. (J). (gr. 7-9). 1981. teacher ed. 12.32 (*0-02-666040-7*); student ed. 6.00 (*0-02-666010-5*) Glencoe.

Today's Tips for Easy Living: Dian Thomas Featured on the Today Show. 3rd ed. Dian Thomas. (Illus.). 160p. (C). 1988. reprint ed. pap. 12.95 (*0-9621257-0-9*) D Thomas Co.

Today's Traditional: Jewish Cooking with a Lighter Touch. Ed. by Bettie G. Roth & Harriette Schneider. LC 93-70841. (Illus.). 208p. (Orig.). 1993. pap. 11.95 (*0-9636626-0-0*) Congreg Beth Shalom.

Today's Victorious Woman, Vol. I. J. B. Livingston. 1983. pap. 5.25 (*0-89137-426-4*) Quality Pubns.

Today's Victorious Woman, Vol. 2. J. B. Livingston. 1983. pap. 5.25 (*0-89137-427-2*) Quality Pubns.

Today's Video: Equipment, Setup, & Production. 2nd ed. Peter Utz. 624p. 1992. text ed. 66.00 (*0-13-925033-6*) P-H.

Today's Wedding - San Antonio. Kay Puryear & Tracy Corry. Ed. by Lynda Crowell. 260p. (Orig.). pap. 21.95 (*0-938934-34-1*) LCN.

Today's Wedding - San Antonio. Kay Puryear & Tracy Corry. Ed. by Lynda Crowell. 225p. (Orig.). 1993. pap. 18.95 (*0-938934-31-7*) LCN.

Today's Wedding-Austin. Kay Puryear & Tracy Corry. Ed. by Lynda Crowell. 250p. 1995. pap. 21.95 (*0-938934-30-9*) LCN.

Today's Wedding Dallas-Ft. Worth-Metroplex. Kay Puryear & Tracy Corry. Ed. by Lynda Crowell. 260p. (Orig.). pap. 21.95 (*0-938934-33-3*) LCN.

Today's Wedding Houston. Kay Puryear & Tracy Corry. Ed. by Lynda Crowell. 260p. (Orig.). pap. 21.95 (*0-938934-32-5*) LCN.

Today's Woman in World Religions. Ed. by Arvind Sharma. LC 92-40319. (McGill Studies in the History of Religions). 459p. 1993. text ed. 71.50 (*0-7914-1687-9*); pap. text ed. 23.95 (*0-7914-1688-7*) State U NY Pr.

Today's World. Linda R. Fellag. (College ESL Ser.). 1996. pap. 26.95 (*0-8384-5858-0*) Heinle & Heinle.

Today's World. Linda R. Fellag. (College ESL Ser.). 1996. teacher ed., pap. 7.95 (*0-8384-5859-9*) Heinle & Heinle.

Today's World: A New World Atlas from the Cartographers of Rand McNally. LC 92-16250. 1995. 29.95 (*0-528-83778-8*) Rand McNally.

Today's World in a Mess. Fred J. Wall. 125p. (Orig.). 1989. pap. 6.95 (*1-882021-03-7*) Salt River Pr.

Today's World in Space, 6 bks., Set I, Reading Level 5. D. Baker. (Illus.). 288p. (J). (gr. 3-8). 1988. Set. lib. bdg. 111.60 (*0-86592-403-1*); lib. bdg. 83.70 (*0-685-58830-0*) Rourke Corp.

Today's World in Space, 6 bks., Set II, Reading Level 5. David Baker. (Illus.). 288p. (J). (gr. 3-8). 1989. Set. lib. bdg. 111.60 (*0-86592-370-1*); lib. bdg. 83.70 (*0-685-58762-2*) Rourke Corp.

Todd. James Colton. 1995. mass mkt. 6.95 (*1-56333-312-0*, Hard Candy) Masquerade.

Todd. David Melton. (Gentle Revolution Ser.). (Illus.). 266p. 1985. 12.95 (*0-936676-52-3*) Better Baby.

Todd County, Ky. Turner Publishing Company Staff. LC 92-61842. 96p. 1992. 48.00 (*1-56311-096-2*) Turner Pub KY.

Todd Genealogy: Or, Register of the Descendants of Adam Todd. R. H. Greene. 150p. 1990. reprint ed. pap. 23.00 (*0-8328-1553-5*); reprint ed. lib. bdg. 31.00 (*0-8328-1552-7*) Higginson Bk Co.

Todd Lecture Series, Set, Vols. 1-17. Royal Irish Academy Staff. reprint ed. Set. 388.00 (*0-404-60560-5*) AMS Pr.

Todd Memorial Volumes: Philological Studies, 2 Vols. Ed. by J. D. Fitz-Gerald & P. Taylor. LC 68-22950. (Essay Index Reprint Ser.). 1977. reprint ed. 34.95 (*0-8369-0948-8*) Ayer.

***Todd Oldham: Without Boundarie.** Oldham. 1997. 45.00 (*0-7893-0043-5*) St Martin.

***Todd Oldham Without Boundaries.** Oldham. 1997. pap. 27.50 (*0-7893-0044-3*) St Martin.

Todd Road Incident. Willie W. Payne. 89p. 1992. pap. 10.00 (*0-9637462-0-0*) Alcus Pub.

Todd Runs Away. Francine Pascal. (Sweet Valley Twins Ser.: No. 77). 144p. (J). 1994. pap. 3.50 (*0-553-48100-2*) Bantam.

Todd Strasser Biography. (J). 1995. pap. write for info. (*0-590-39193-3*) Scholastic Inc.

***Todd. The Todds, the Wheelers, "Et Id Genus Omne" (Including Also Staniford, brocklebank, Springer, Toppan Kent Saunders, Lord Kimball, Adams, Morse, Kendall Et Al)** Thomas Todd. 62p. 1996. reprint ed. pap. 12.50 (*0-8328-5288-0*) Higginson Bk Co.

***Todd. The Todds, the Wheelers, "Et Id Genus Omne" (Including Also Staniford, Brocklebank, Springer, Toppan Kent Saunders, Lord Kimball, Adams, Morse, Kendall Et Al)** Thomas Todd. 62p. 1996. reprint ed. lib. bdg. 22.50 (*0-8328-5287-2*) Higginson Bk Co.

Todd Walker, Photographs. Illus. by Todd Walker. LC 85-70352. (Untitled Ser.: No. 38). 48p. (Orig.). 1985. pap. 9.98 (*0-933286-42-2*) Frnds Photography.

Todd Watts: New Lamps for Old. Thomas Sokdowski & F. David Peat. LC 94-75852. (Illus.). 48p. 1994. pap. 20.00 (*0-934349-13-4*) Grey Art Gallery Study Ctr.

Todd Webb: Photographs of New York & Paris, 1945-1960. Keith F. Davis. 116p. 1986. pap. 16.95 (*0-87529-620-3*) Hallmark.

Toddlecreek Post Office. Uri Shulevitz. (Illus.). 32p. (J). 1990. 14.95 (*0-374-37635-2*) FS&G.

***Toddler Adoption: The Weaver's Craft.** Mary Hopkins-Best. LC 97-5617. 272p. 1997. 23.95 (*0-944934-17-X*) Perspect Indiana.

Toddler-Hunting & Other Stories. Taeko Kono. Tr. by Lucy North & Lucy Lower from JPN. LC 95-47600. 256p. 1996. 21.95 (*0-8112-1305-6*) New Directions.

An Asterisk (*) at the beginning of an entry indicates that the title is appearing in BIP for the first time.

Toddler SingAlong Time. V. Gilbert Beers & Elwell. (J). 1995. 14.99 (89-00-88168-X, 3-1230, Victor Bks) Chariot Victor.

Toddler Storytime Programs. Diane Briggs. (School Library Media Programs Ser.: No. 2). (Illus.). 198p. 1993. pap. 29.50 (0-8108-2777-8) Scarecrow.

Toddler Talk: The First Signs of Intelligent Life. Joseph Garcia. LC 93-84098. 107p. 1993. pap. 12.95 (0-9636229-4-3) Stratton Kehl.

Toddler Taming. Green. Date not set. 6.99 (0-09-177258-3) Random.

Toddler Taming. Christopher Green. 256p. 1985. pap. 10.00 (0-449-90155-6, Columbine) Fawcett.

Toddler Theme-a-Saurus: The Great Big Book of Toddler Teaching Themes. Jean Warren. Ed. by Gayle Bittinger & Elizabeth S. McKinnon. LC 90-71273. (Theme-A-Saurus Ser.). (Illus.). 280p. (Orig.). (J). (ps). 1991. pap. 21.95 (0-911019-37-5, WPH 1003) Warren Pub Hse.

Toddler Totes: Animals. (Illus.). 12p. (J). (ps). 1993. pap. 4.99 (0-525-45129-3) Dutton Child Bks.

Toddler Totes: Clothes. (Illus.). 12p. (J). (ps). 1993. pap. 4.99 (0-525-45130-7) Dutton Child Bks.

Toddler Totes: Food. (Illus.). 12p. (J). (ps). 1993. pap. 4.99 (0-525-45131-5) Dutton Child Bks.

Toddler Totes: Toys. (Illus.). 12p. (J). (ps). 1993. pap. 4.99 (0-525-45132-3) Dutton Child Bks.

Toddlerobics. Zita Newcome. LC 95-21062. (Illus.). 32p. (J). (ps-k). 1996. 14.99 (1-56402-809-7) Candlewick Pr.

Toddlerobics. Zita Newcome. (Illus.). 32p. (J). (ps up). 1997. reprint ed. pap. 5.99 (0-7636-0113-6) Candlewick Pr.

Toddlers. Catherine Anholt & Laurence Anholt. LC 92-54588. (Illus.). 24p. (J). (ps). 1993. 5.95 (1-56402-242-0) Candlewick Pr.

Toddler's ABC Book: Big Lessons for Little Ones. Andy Stanley & Sandra Stanley. (Illus.). 24p. (J). 1995. 9.99 (0-7852-7990-3) Nelson.

Toddlers & Parents. rev. ed. T. Berry Brazelton. 272p. 1989. pap. 16.95 (0-440-50643-3) Dell.

Toddlers & Preschoolers: A Practical & Effective Guide to Understanding & Caring for Your Preschool Child. Lawrence Kutner. (Parent & Child Ser.). 208p. 1995. pap. 11.00 (0-380-71353-5) Avon.

Toddlers & Their Mothers: A Study in Early Personality Development. Erna Furman. LC 91-35415. 420p. (C). 1992. 49.50 (0-8236-6555-0) Intl Univs Pr.

Toddlers & Their Mothers: Abridged Version for Parents & Educators. Erna Furman. LC 93-1871. 243p. 1993. pap. 24.95 (0-8236-8318-4) Intl Univs Pr.

Toddlers Bedtime Storybook. V. Gilbert Beers. (Toddlers Ser.). (Illus.). 352p. (J). (ps). 1993. 15.99 (1-56476-181-9, 6-3181, Victor Bks) Chariot Victor.

Toddler's Behavior with Agemates: Issues of Interaction, Cognition & Affect. Wanda C. Bronson. LC 81-12896. (Monographs on Infancy: Vol. 1). 128p. (C). 1981. text ed. 73.25 (0-89391-080-5) Ablex Pub.

***Toddlers Bible.** (J). 1994. write for info. (1-56476-441-9, Chariot Bks) Chariot Victor.

***Toddlers Bible.** (J). 1993. write for info. (1-56476-294-7) SP Pubns.

Toddler's Bible Coloring Book: New Testament. V. Gilbert Beers. (Toddlers Ser.). (Illus.). 48p. (Orig.). (J). 1994. pap. 2.50 (1-56476-302-1, 6-3302, Victor Bks) Chariot Victor.

Toddler's Bible Coloring Book: Old Testament. V. Gilbert Beers. (Toddlers Ser.). (Illus.). 48p. (Orig.). (J). 1994. pap. 2.50 (1-56476-301-3, 6-3301, Victor Bks) Chariot Victor.

Toddlers Bible Easter Book. V. Gilbert Beers. 32p. (J). 1995. 5.99 (1-56476-526-1, 6-3526, Victor Bks) Chariot Victor.

Toddlers Bible Library. V. Gilbert Beers. (Toddlers Ser.). (J). (ps). 1993. 10.99 (1-56476-150-9, 6-3150, Victor Bks) Chariot Victor.

Toddler's Bible Paint with Water. V. Gilbert Beers. (Illus.). (J). 1995. 2.99 (1-56476-529-6, 6-3529, Victor Bks) Chariot Victor.

Toddlers Bible Sticker Book. V. Gilbert Beers. (Illus.). (J). (ps). 1995. 2.99 (1-56476-528-8, 6-3528, Victor Bks) Chariot Victor.

Toddlers Book of Prayers. V. Gilbert Beers. 96p. (J). 1996. 6.99 (1-56476-557-1, 6-3557, Victor Bks) Chariot Victor.

Toddlers Christmas Book. V. Gilbert Beers. (Toddlers Ser.). (Illus.). 32p. (J). (ps). 1995. 5.99 (1-56476-527-X, 6-3527, Victor Bks) Chariot Victor.

Toddler's First Songbook. V. Gilbert Beers. (Toddlers Bible Video Ser.). 168p. (J). 1994. 16.99 incl. audio (1-56476-300-5, 6-3300, Victor Bks) Chariot Victor.

Toddler's Home Learning Kit. V. Gilbert Beers. (Toddlers Bible Video Ser.). 1995. 79.99 (0-614-21955-8, 3-1226, Victor Bks) Chariot Victor.

Toddlers Learn by Doing: Toddler Activities & Activity Log for Parents & Teachers. Rita Schrank. 144p. (Orig.). 1985. pap. 15.95 (0-89334-085-5) Humanics Ltd.

Toddlers Learn by Doing: Toddler Activities & Parent-Teacher Activity Log. Rita Schrank. (Illus.). 144p. 1985. lib. bdg. 25.95 (0-89334-210-6, 210-6) Humanics Ltd.

Toddler's Life: Becoming a Person. Marilyn Shatz. (Illus.). 240p. (C). 1995. reprint ed. pap. 16.95 (0-19-509923-0) OUP.

Toddlers Moving & Learning. 2nd ed. Rae Pica. LC 89-24588. (Illus.). 88p. 1990. ring bd. 39.00 incl. audio (0-87322-275-X, BPIC0275) Human Kinetics.

Toddler's Potty Book. Alida Allison. (Illus.). 32p. (Orig.). (J). (ps). 1978. pap. 5.95 (0-8431-0673-5) Price Stern Sloan.

Toddlers Tiny Bible. V. Gilbert Beers. 96p. (J). 1996. 6.99 (1-56476-556-3, 6-3556, Victor Bks) Chariot Victor.

Toddlers Together: The Complete Planning Guide to a Toddler Curriculum. Cynthia Catlin. (Illus.). 319p. (Orig.). 1994. pap. text ed. 24.95 (0-87659-171-3) Gryphon Hse.

Todd's Story. Francine Pascal. (Sweet Valley High Super Star Ser.: No. 4). 224p. (YA). 1992. pap. 3.50 (0-553-29207-2) Bantam.

Toddy Bear's Good Food Book. V. Gilbert Beers. (Toddy Bear Bks.). (Illus.). 24p. (J). 1994. 5.99 (1-56476-165-7, 6-3165, Victor Bks) Chariot Victor.

Toddy Bear's Good Morning Book. V. Gilbert Beers. (Toddy Bear Bks.). (Illus.). 24p. (J). 1994. 5.99 (1-56476-166-5, 6-3166, Victor Bks) Chariot Victor.

Toddy Bear's One-Two-Three Counting Book. V. Gilbert Beers. (Toddy Bear Bks.). (Illus.). 24p. (J). 1994. 5.99 (1-56476-167-3, 6-3167, Victor Bks) Chariot Victor.

Toddy Bear's Tall & Short Book. V. Gilbert Beers. (Toddy Bear Bks.). (Illus.). 24p. (J). 1994. 5.99 (1-56476-168-1, 6-3168, Victor Bks) Chariot Victor.

Todeserlebnis Des Manes see Death Experience of Manes

Todesverstaendnis bei Simone de Beauvoir: Eine Theologische Untersuchung. Erich Schmalenberg. LC 72-77421. (Theologische Bibliothek Toepelmann Ser.: Vol. 25). (C). 1972. 60.00 (3-11-004036-0) De Gruyter.

Todlicher Schnee. (Easy Reader Ser.: Level 1). 48p. 1991. 5.95 (3-468-49680-X) Langenscheidt.

Todo Lo Dieron Por Cuba: A Shocking Testimony by 30 Women Political Prisoners. Mignon Medrano. 220p. 1995. pap. text ed. 25.00 (1-884619-04-5) Endowment CAS.

Todo Lo Que Debe Saber el Inmigrante. Maria C. Urrutia. LC 90-80201. (SPA.). 1991. pap. 6.99 (0-9625664-0-3) Editorial FL.

Todo Lo Que Han Oido es Erroneo. Tony Campolo. 192p. (SPA.). 1992. pap. 6.99 (1-56063-380-8, 490277) Editorial Unilit.

Todo Lo Que Necesitas Saber Cuando Termina Tu Noviazgo. Alicia Thomas. (Helping Books in Spanish Ser.). (Illus.). 64p. (SPA.). (YA). (gr. 7-12). 1993. pap. 8.95 (0-8239-1793-2, D1793-2) Rosen Group.

Todo Lo Que Necesitas Saber Cuando Tus Padres Se Divorcian. Linda C. Johnson. (Helping Books in Spanish Ser.). (Illus.). 64p. (SPA.). (YA). (gr. 7-12). 1994. pap. 8.95 (0-8239-1797-5, D1797-5) Rosen Group.

Todo Lo Que Necesitas Saber Sobre el SIDA. Barbara Taylor. (Helping Books in Spanish Ser.). (Illus.). 64p. (SPA.). (YA). (gr. 7-12). 1995. pap. 8.95 (0-8239-2238-3, D2238-3) Rosen Group.

Todo Lo Que Necesitas Saber Sobre Esos Dias. Ellen V. Mahoney. (Helping Books in Spanish Ser.). (Illus.). 64p. (SPA.). (YA). (gr. 7-12). 1993. pap. 13.95 (0-8239-1794-0, D1794-0) Rosen Group.

Todo Lo Que Necesitas Saber Sobre la Adolescente y la Ginecologia. Luis A. Balbas & Luis A. Topete. (Helping Books in Spanish Ser.). (Illus.). 64p. (SPA.). (YA). (gr. 7-12). 1993. pap. 13.95 (0-8239-2028-3, D2028-3) Rosen Group.

Todo Lo Que Necesitas Saber Sobre Sexo Seguro. Ellen V. Mahoney. (Helping Books in Spanish Ser.). (Illus.). 64p. (SPA.). (YA). (gr. 7-12). 1993. pap. 13.95 (0-8239-1792-4, D1792-4) Rosen Group.

Todo Lo Que Usted Debe Saber Sobre Arte y Literatura, Tomo 1. Editorial America, S. A. Staff. Ed. by Maria E. Del Real. (Illus.). 240p. (Orig.). (SPA.). 1990. pap. write for info. (0-944499-67-8) Editorial Amer.

Todo Mexico 1995. Sabeca International Investment Corp. Staff. 448p. (SPA.). 1995. write for info. (1-56409-013-2) Ency Brit Inc.

Todo Mexico 1996. Sabeca International Investment Corp. Staff. (Illus.). 448p. (YA). (gr. 8 up). 1996. write for info. (1-56409-018-3) EBP Latin Am.

***Todo Mexico 1997.** Sebeca International Investment Corp. Staff. (Illus.). 448p. (SPA.). (YA). 1997. write for info. (1-56409-020-5) EBP Latin Am.

***Todo Tiene su Tiempo.** Luis Aguilar Leon. (SPA.). Date not set. pap. write for info. (0-89729-832-2) Ediciones.

Todos Estamos Encarcelados. Bo Lozoff. Ed. by Dialogos International Staff. Tr. by Ricardo Beas from ENG. (Illus.). 336p. (Orig.). (SPA.). 1989. pap. 10.00 (0-9614444-3-6) Human Kind Found.

***Todos Hacemos Caca.** Taro Gomi. LC 97-72907. (Illus.). 28p. (Orig.). (SPA.). (J). (ps-k). 1997. pap. 6.95 (0-916291-77-4, Curious Nell Bks) Kane-Miller Bk.

Todos, Listos, CANTEN! Canciones para Ninos y para Aprender el Espanol. Sarah Barchas. Tr. by Marilyn McClure et al. (Illus.). 40p. (Orig.). (SPA.). (J). (ps-3). 1995. pap. 12.95 incl. audio (0-9632621-3-0); pap. 15.98 incl. audio compact disk (0-9632621-4-9) High Haven Mus.

Todos Santos in Rural Tlaxcala: A Syncretic, Expressive, & Symbolic Analysis of the Cult of the Dead. Hugo G. Nutini. LC 87-15173. 492p. 1988. reprint ed. pap. 140.30 (0-7837-9404-5, 2060149) Bks Demand.

Todos Somos Culpables. Guillermo De Zendegui. LC 91-75691. 155p. 1991. 12.00 (0-89729-620-6) Ediciones.

Toe: The Lou Groza Story. Lou Groza & Mark Hodermarsky. 128p. 1996. per., pap. text ed. 16.95 (0-7872-1844-8) Kendall-Hunt.

Toe, & Other Tales. Alexander Harvey. LC 73-125215. (Short Story Index Reprint Ser.). 1977. 18.95 (0-8369-3582-9) Ayer.

Toe Shoe Trouble. Quin Harkin. (TGIF Ser.: No. 5). (J). (gr. 3-6). 1996. pap. 3.50 (0-671-51021-5, Pocket Books) PB.

***TOEFL.** Kaplan Staff. 1997. pap. 39.95 incl. audio (0-684-83753-6) S&S Trade.

TOEFL: Test of English as a Foreign Language. Edith H. Babin et al. 1992. pap. 32.00 incl. audio (0-13-923368-7, Arco) Macmillan Gen Ref.

TOEFL Assistant Test of Written English. Milada Broukal & Kathleen Flynn. LC 93-47011. 1994. pap. 21.95 (0-8384-4281-1) Heinle & Heinle.

TOEFL Grammar Workbook. 2nd ed. Phyllis L. Lim & Mary Kurtin. Ed. by Laurie Wellman. 256p. 1992. pap. 11.95 (0-13-921917-X, Arco) Macmillan Gen Ref.

TOEFL Manual with 3 Listening Comprehension Cassettes. 8th ed. Pamela J. Sharpe. 656p. 1996. pap. 35.00 incl. audio (0-8120-8420-9) Barron.

TOEFL Practice Exercises. 3rd ed. Pamela J. Sharpe. 1995. student ed., pap. text ed. 12.95 (0-8120-3398-1) Barron.

Toefl Practice Exercises. 3rd ed. Pamela J. Sharpe. 1995. pap. text ed. 29.95 incl. audio (0-8120-8272-9) Barron.

TOEFL Preparation: Teacher's Handbook. David Daum & Carol Morey. 83p. (Orig.). 1985. pap. 8.95 (0-920490-46-8) Temeron Bks.

TOEFL Preparation Guide with 2 Cassettes: Test of English As a Foreign Language. 5th rev. ed. Michael A. Pyle & Mary E. Munoz. (Cliffs Test Preparation Ser.). 482p. (C). 1995. pap. text ed. 29.95 incl. audio (0-8220-2079-3) Cliffs.

TOEFL Reading & Vocabulary Workbook. 2nd ed. Elizabeth Davy & Karen Davy. 256p. 1992. pap. 11.00 (0-13-926965-7, Arco) Macmillan Gen Ref.

TOEFL Strategies: With Practice Tests for Learning Progress. Eli Hinkel. LC 93-2835. 1993. Incl. cass. 35.00 incl. audio (0-8120-8111-0); pap. 12.95 (0-8120-4923-3); Cass. audio 26.95 (0-8120-1804-4) Barron.

TOEFL Success. LC 96-50206. (Test Success Ser.). 512p. (Orig.). 1996. pap. 12.95 (1-56079-687-1); pap. 29.95 incl. audio (1-56079-690-1) Petersons.

***TOEFL Success.** Petersons Staff. 1997. pap. text ed. 14.95 (1-56079-928-5) Petersons.

***TOEFL Success Practice Tests.** Peterson's Staff. (Peterson's Guides Ser.). 1997. pap. text ed. 14.95 (1-56079-692-8) Petersons.

TOEFL Supercourse. 3rd ed. Grace Y. Qiu Zhong & Patricia Noble Sullivan. LC 95-2445. 1995. 18.95 (0-02-860338-9) Macmillan.

TOEFL Test Preparation Kit, 2 cassettes & exercise bk. 1995. student ed., pap. text ed. 20.00 incl. audio (0-446-39580-3) Warner Bks.

TOEFL Vocabulary Builder. rev. ed. Ewald Neumann. (Vocabulary Builder Ser.). 80p. (C). 1994. pap. text ed. 24.95 incl. audio (0-9625001-4-3) Spargo Comns.

***TOEIC.** Kaplan Staff. 1997. pap. 39.95 incl. audio (0-684-83755-2) S&S Trade.

***TOEIC Preparation Workbook.** Lin Lougheed. 1991. pap. text ed. 14.19 (0-201-56236-7) Addison-Wesley.

Toeing the Lines: Women & Party Politics in English Canada. Sylvia B. Bashevkin. LC 83-145327. (Illus.). 240p. reprint ed. pap. 68.40 (0-7837-0534-4, 2040862) Bks Demand.

Toenails. David Drew. LC 92-31135. (Voyages Ser.). (Illus.). (J). 1993. 2.50 (0-383-03661-5) SRA McGraw.

***Toenails, Tonsils, & Tornadoes.** Bonnie Pryor. LC 96-30637. (Illus.). (J). 1997. 15.00 (0-688-14885-9, Morrow Junior) Morrow.

Toeplitz Forms & Their Applications. 2nd ed. Ulf Grenander & Gabor Szego. LC 83-62686. ix, 245p. text ed. 19.95 (0-8284-0321-X) Chelsea Pub.

Toeplitz Operators & Index Theory in Several Complex Variables. Harald Upmeier. (Operator Theory, Advances & Applications Ser.: Vol. 81). 1996. write for info. (0-8176-5282-5) Birkhauser.

Toeplitz Operators & Index Theory in Several Complex Variables. Harald Upmeier. (Operator Theory, Advances & Applications Ser.: Vol. 81). 496p. 1996. 161.00 (3-7643-5282-5) Birkhauser.

Toeplitz Operators & Related Topics: The Harold Widom Anniversary Volume. Ed. by E. I. Basor & I. Gohberg. LC 94-13097. (Operator Theory, Advances & Applications Ser.: Vol. 71). 208p. 1994. 77.00 (0-8176-5068-7) Birkhauser.

***Toes Are to Tickle.** Shen Roddie. LC 96-31428. (Illus.). 24p. (J). (ps-k). 1997. 13.95 (1-883672-49-X) Tricycle Pr.

Toes in My Nose. Sheree Fitch. 48p. 1991. pap. 6.95 (0-385-25325-7) Doubleday.

Toes in My Nose. Sheree Fitch. 48p. 1995. pap. 12.95 (0-385-25521-7) Doubleday.

Toes in My Nose: And Other Poems. Sheree Fitch. LC 92-62543. (Illus.). 48p. (J). (gr. 1-5). 1993. pap. 6.95 (1-56397-127-5, Wordsong) Boyds Mills Pr.

Tofaha's Basket see Aruba Stories Series

***Toff Goes to Market.** large type ed. John Creasey. LC 96-43100. (Nightingale Ser.). 245p. 1997. pap. 17.95 (0-7838-1991-9, GK Hall) Thorndike Pr.

Tofu & Soymilk Production. William Shurtleff & Akiko Aoyagi. LC 74-31629. (Soyfoods Production Ser.). (Illus.). 336p. 1990. 59.95 (0-933332-73-4) Soyfoods Center.

Tofu & Soymilk Production. William Shurtleff & Akiko Aoyagi. LC 74-31629. (Soyfoods Production Ser.: No. 2). (Illus.). 336p. 1990. pap. 49.95 (0-933332-72-6) Soyfoods Center.

Tofu As a Potentially Hazardous Food: Crisis or Opportunity? 67p. (Orig.). 1989. spiral bd. 90.00 (0-933332-65-3) Soyfoods Center.

Tofu Book: The New American Cuisine. John Paino & Lisa Messinger. LC 91-46079. (Illus.). 184p. (Orig.). pap. 10.95 (0-89529-409-5) Avery Pub.

Tofu Consumer Awareness & Purchasing Patterns. Ed. by Peter Allen. 87p. (Orig.). 1981. pap. 750.00 (0-931634-20-2) FIND-SVP.

Tofu Cookbook. Leah Leneman. 1992. pap. 11.00 (0-7225-2587-7) Thorsons SF.

Tofu Cookbook: Recipes for Traditional & Modern Cooking. Junko Lampert. LC 85-25546. (Illus.). 102p. (Orig.). 1986. pap. 12.95 (0-87701-383-7) Chronicle Bks.

Tofu Cookery. rev. ed. Louise Hagler. LC 90-20943. (Illus.). 160p. (Orig.). 1991. pap. 15.95 (0-913990-76-0) Book Pub Co.

***Tofu Gourmet.** Barber & Junko Lampert. 1996. 39.95 (4-07-975109-5) Shufu no Tomo-Sha.

Tofu Magic: Zero to Low Cholesterol & Low Sodium Recipes. Julia B. Weinberg. Ed. by Terry Stewart. (Illus.). 64p. (Orig.). 1988. pap. 6.95 (0-922446-00-8) Cookwrite Pub.

Tofu Quick & Easy. Louise Hagler. LC 86-72222. (Illus.). 96p. (Orig.). 1986. pap. 7.95 (0-913990-50-7) Book Pub Co.

Tofu, Tempeh, Miso & Other Soyfoods. Richard Leviton. Ed. by Richard A. Passwater & Earl R. Mindell. (Good Health Guide Ser.). 32p. 1982. pap. 2.50 (0-87983-284-3) Keats.

Tofu Tollbooth: A Directory of Great Natural & Organic Food Stores. Dar Williams. (Illus.). 176p. (Orig.). 1994. pap. 8.95 (0-9639926-1-9) Ardwork Pr.

Tofutti & Other Soy Ice Creams: Non-Dairy Frozen Dessert Industry & Market, 2 vols., Set. William Shurtleff & Akiko Aoyagi. (Soyfoods Market Studies). (Orig.). 1985. spiral bd. 135.00 (0-933332-19-X) Soyfoods Center.

Tog. (Hawkins Scribble Bks.). (Illus.). 16p. (J). 1996. 6.95 (0-7894-1169-5) DK Pub Inc.

Tog Docs: Managing the Search for Physician Leaders. George F. Longshore. LC 92-75187. 129p. (Orig.). (C). 1993. pap. text ed. 32.00 (0-924674-20-2) Am Coll Phys Execs.

Tog on Interface. Bruce Tognazzini. LC 91-60590. 352p. 1992. pap. 29.95 (0-201-60842-1) Addison-Wesley.

Tog on Software Design. Bruce Tognazzini. LC 95-38790. 496p. (C). 1996. pap. text ed. 29.95 (0-201-48917-1) Addison-Wesley.

Tog the Dog. (Hawkins Reading Ser.). (J). write for info. (0-7894-0176-2, 5-70604) DK Pub Inc.

Tog the Ribber: Or Granny's Tales. Paul Coltman. LC 84-82555. (Illus.). 32p. (J). (ps-5). 1985. 15.00 (0-374-37630-1) FS&G.

Toga & the Kingdom of Croone: Frogs, Turtles, Dragon Snakes, Whales, & Magic Mushrooms. John P. Feltman. LC 93-87067. (Illus.). 120p. (J). (gr. k-8). 1994. 17.95 (0-9639277-0-1) Samantha Bks.

Toga Therapy: Safe, Natural Methods to Promote Healing & Restore Health & Well-Being. Stella Weller. (Illus.). 154p. 1995. pap. 17.00 (0-7225-2998-8) Harper SF.

Togail Tir Marking Time. Ed. by Finlay Macleod. 160p. (C). 1992. text ed. 75.00 (0-86152-842-5, Pub. by Acair Ltd UK) St Mut.

Togakushi Legend Murders. Yasuo Uchida. 1994. pap. 12.95 (0-8048-1928-9) C E Tuttle.

Togaviridae & Flaviviridae. Milton J. Schlesinger. LC 86-4914. (Viruses Ser.). 470p. 1986. 105.00 (0-306-42176-3, Plenum Pr) Plenum.

Together. George E. Lyon. LC 89-2892. (Illus.). 32p. (J). (ps-1). 1989. 15.95 (0-531-05831-X) Orchard Bks Watts.

Together. George E. Lyon. LC 89-2892. (Illus.). 32p. (J). (ps-1). 1994. pap. 6.95 (0-531-07047-6) Orchard Bks Watts.

Together. Linda L. Miller. 384p. (Orig.). 1996. mass mkt. 5.99 (0-380-78405-X) Avon.

Together. Robert Herrick. (Collected Works of Robert Herrick). 1988. reprint ed. lib. bdg. 59.00 (0-7812-1270-7) Rprt Serv.

***Together: Breaking down the Walls That Divide Us.** Bonny Wynia. (Life Wise Ser.). 40p. (Orig.). 1997. teacher ed., pap. 7.35 (1-56212-230-4, 1210-4010) CRC Pubns.

Together: Communicating Interpersonally. 4th ed. John Stewart & Carole Logan. LC 92-27874. 1993. pap. text ed. write for info. (0-07-061539-X) McGraw.

***Together: Communicating Interpersonally.** 5th ed. John R. Stewart & Carole Logan. LC 97-11604. 1997. write for info. (0-07-061491-1) McGraw.

***Together: How We Belong.** Dave Barry et al. (Target Ser.). 160p. (Orig.). (J). (gr. 2-4). 1997. pap. text ed. 11.95 (0-8167-4277-4) Troll Communs.

Together see Collected Works of Robert Herrick

Together, a New People: Pastoral Statement on Migrants & Refugees. National Conference of Catholic Bishops Staff. 32p. (Orig.). 1987. pap. 3.95 (1-55586-147-4) US Catholic.

Together Again. Laura Parker. 1995. mass mkt. 3.75 (0-373-07682-7, 1-07682-7) Silhouette.

Together Again: Family Reunification in Foster Care. Anthony N. Maluccio et al. 1993. 21.95 (0-87868-525-1) Child Welfare.

Together Alone. Barbara Delinsky. 512p. 1996. mass mkt. 6.99 (0-06-109281-9) HarpC.

Together Alone: The Diary of an Addict's Addict. Barbara M. Youngert. (Illus.). 84p. 1985. pap. 5.00 (0-944642-00-4, TX1741844) Hector Marie.

Together Alone: The Text of the Internationally Acclaimed Film. P. J. Castellaneta. (Illus.). 100p. (Orig.). pap. 9.95 (0-9646504-0-1) PJ Party Prodns.

Together Always. Dallas Schulze. (Winner's Circle Ser.). 1996. mass mkt. 3.99 (0-373-60076-3, 1-60076-6) Harlequin Bks.

Together As a Companionship: A History of the Thirty-First, Thirty-Second, & Thirty-Third General Congregations of the Society of Jesus. John W. Padberg. (Series IV: No. 15). viii, 145p. (Orig.). 1994. 14.95 (1-880810-08-5) Inst Jesuit.

Together As a Family. Claudia L. Boysen. (Illus.). 366p. 1993. spiral bd. 6.50 (1-879127-27-X) Lighten Up Enter.

Together As Parish: An Innovative Strategy to Nourish Family & Parish. Dolores A. Mortimer. LC 91-76777. (Illus.). 56p. (Orig.). 1992. pap. 2.95 (0-87793-476-2); spiral bd. 12.95 (0-87793-475-4) Ave Maria.

Together at Baptism: Preparing for the Celebration of Your Child's Baptism. Robert M. Hamma. LC 93-74197. 112p. 1994. pap. 2.95 (*0-87793-523-8*) Ave Maria.

Together at Home: A Proven Plan to Nurture Your Child's Faith & Spend Family Time. Dean Merrill & Grace Merrill. 272p. 1996. reprint ed. pap. 10.99 (*0-8423-7175-3*) Tyndale.

Together at Mass. Gaynell B. Cronin & Joan Bellina. LC 87-70417. (Illus.). 32p. (Orig.). (J). (ps-2). 1987. pap. 2.95 (*0-87793-357-X*) Ave Maria.

Together Black Women. 2nd ed. Inez S. Reid. LC 73-83156. 348p. 1974. reprint ed. 29.95 (*0-89388-114-7*); reprint ed. pap. 19.95 (*0-89388-115-5*) Okpaku Communications.

Together Bound: God, History, & the Religious Community. Frank G. Kirkpatrick. LC 93-18204. 216p. 1994. 42.00 (*0-19-508342-3*) OUP.

Together But Apart: The Jewish Experience in the Hamptons. Abe Frank. (Illus.). 161p. 1996. 20.00 (*0-88400-188-1*) Shengold.

Together Day by Day. Marilyn Phillipps. 1995. pap. text ed. write for info. (*1-884794-16-5*) Eden Pubng.

***Together Everyone Accomplishes More: A Stewardship Plan for Multiplying Your Ministry.** David B. Earley. Ed. by Cindy G. Spear. 84p. 1996. ring bd. 89.95 (*1-57052-055-0*) Chrch Grwth VA.

***Together for Life.** alternate rev. ed. Joseph M. Champlin. (Illus.). 96p. 1996. pap. 2.95 (*0-87793-616-1*) Ave Maria.

Together for Life: A Couple's Guide to a Happy Marriage. James F. Skoney. 240p. 1993. pap. 9.95 (*0-9638740-0-4*) DDS Pubng.

Together for Life: Outside Mass. Joseph M. Champlin. (Illus.). 96p. 1972. pap. 2.25 (*0-87793-118-6*) Ave Maria.

Together for Life: Regular Edition. Joseph M. Champlin. (Illus.). 96p. 1977. pap. 2.25 (*0-87793-018-X*) Ave Maria.

***Together for Life: Special Edition for Marriage Outside Mass.** alternate rev. ed. Joseph M. Champlin. (Illus.). 96p. 1996. pap. 2.95 (*0-87793-617-X*) Ave Maria.

***Together Forever.** Cameron Dokey. (Love Stories Ser.: No. 16). 192p. 1997. mass mkt. 3.99 (*0-553-57046-3*) BDD Bks Young Read.

Together Forever: A Handbook for Creating a Successful Marriage. Khalil Khavari. 224p. 1994. pap. 14.95 (*1-85168-061-6*) Onewrld Pubns.

Together Forever: An Adoption Story Coloring Book. Sara L. Barris & Doryle P. Seltzer. (Illus.). 32p. (J). 1992. pap. 3.95 (*0-9632023-0-8*) Shoot Star Pr.

Together Forever: An Invitation to Physical Immortality. Charles P. Brown et al. LC 89-82414. (Illus.). 176p. (Orig.). 1990. pap. 9.95 (*0-9625346-0-9*) People Forever Intl.

Together Forever: How to Overcome Problems and Rekindle the Love in Your Marriage. Anne K. Carroll. 384p. 1995. mass mkt. 5.99 (*0-06-104338-9*) Zondervan.

Together Forever: One Hundred & Twenty-Five Ways to Have a Vital & Romantic Marriage. Lew Richfield & Gloria Richfield. LC 94-43296. 192p. 1995. 18.95 (*0-385-31411-6*) Delacorte.

Together Forever: Reflections on the Joys of Marriage. Compiled by Mary Hollingsworth. LC 93-1134. 1993. 4.99 (*0-8499-5029-5*) Word Pub.

Together Forever! 125 Living Ways to Have a Vital & Romantic Marriage. Lew Richfield & Gloria Richfield. 192p. 1997. pap. 10.95 (*0-440-50780-4*, Dell Trade Pbks) Dell.

Together I Can: Increasing Personal Growth & Creating Lifelong Learners Through Cooperative Learning. Susan Finney. 193p. (J). (gr. k-8). 1991. student ed. 19.95 (*1-56499-002-8*) Innerchoice Pub.

Together in Hope: Fifty Years of Lutheran World Relief. John W. Bachman. LC 95-3114. 192p. 1995. pap. 11.95 (*1-886513-01-5*) Kirk Hse Pubs.

Together in Ministry: With Hearts Set on Pilgrimage. Phyllis H. Perkins. 100p. 1992. pap. 6.99 (*0-8341-1444-5*) Beacon Hill.

Together in Mission. Ed. by Theodore Williams. 90p. (Orig.). 1983. pap. 2.00 (*0-685-08189-3*) World Evang Fellow.

Together in My Name. John N. Wijngaards. LC 94-32874. (Walking on Water Ser.). 1995. pap. 9.95 (*0-8091-3546-9*) Paulist Pr.

***Together in Our Differences: How Newcomers & Established Residents Are Rebuilding American Communities.** Julia T. Quiroz. 100p. 1995. pap. text ed. 12.95 (*0-9645220-0-4*) Nat Immig Forum.

***Together in Pinecone Patch.** Thomas Yezerski. LC 97-10874. (J). 1998. write for info. (*0-374-37647-6*) FS&G.

Together in Prayer: Learning to Love the Liturgy of the Hours. Ed. by Charles E. Miller. LC 94-23025. 124p. (Orig.). 1994. pap. 9.95 (*0-8189-0712-6*) Alba.

Together in the Kitchen. Colleen Miner & Victoria L. Estrem. (Illus.). 366p. 1993. spiral bd. 7.50 (*1-879127-25-3*) Lighten Up Enter.

Together in the Land: A Reading of the Book of Joshua. Gordon Mitchell. (Journal for the Study of the Old Testament Supplement Ser.: Vol. 134). 224p. 45.00 (*1-85075-409-8*, Pub. by Sheffield Acad UK) CUP Services.

***Together in Time: A Book of Friendship.** Flavia Weedn. (Flavia Main Street Gift Bks.). 1997. 6.95 (*0-8362-5105-9*) Andrews & McMeel.

Together in Trust. Horace B. King. (Orig.). 1989. pap. 6.95 (*1-55673-108-6*, 9819) CSS OH.

Together Is Forever. Edward H. Pauley & Robert C. Larson. LC 95-18138. 144p. 1995. 7.99 (*0-8499-5160-7*) Word Pub.

Together It Works AIT Preceptor. Robert W. Haacker. 336p. 1994. student ed. 49.95 (*0-929442-22-9*) Publicare Pr.

Together Met, Together Bound: Hymn Settings by William Rowan. William Rowan. 80p. 1994. pap. 9.95 (*0-9622553-5-1*, 125-030) Selah Pub Co.

Together They Built a Mountain. Patricia T. Davis. LC 74-14727. (Illus.). 196p. 1974. 14.95 (*0-915010-00-3*) Sutter House.

Together... Till Death Us Do Part. John Braaten. Ed. by Michael L. Sherer. LC 86-28386. (Orig.). 1987. pap. 6.85 (*0-89536-852-8*, 7811) CSS OH.

Together Toward Hope: A Journey to Moral Theology. Philip Rossi. LC 83-1279. 224p. 1983. 26.50 (*0-268-01844-8*) U of Notre Dame Pr.

Together We Can: A Guide for Crafting a Profamily System of Education & Human Services. 1995. lib. bdg. 251.95 (*0-8490-6685-9*) Gordon Pr.

Together We Can: A Guide for Crafting a Profamily System of Education & Human Services. Atelia I. Melaville et al. Ed. by Bruce A. Thompson. 157p. (Orig.). (C). 1993. pap. text ed. 25.00 (*0-7881-0098-X*) DIANE Pub.

***Together We Can! Classwide Peer Tutoring to Improve Basic Academic Skills.** Charles R. Greenwood et al. (Illus.). 94p. (Orig.). 1997. pap. text ed. 29.50 (*1-57035-125-2*, C95CWPT) Sopris.

Together We Can Make It Work: A National Agenda To Provide Quality Education for Minorities in Mathematics, Science, & Engineering. 52p. (Orig.). (C). 1994. pap. text ed. 20.00 (*0-7881-0678-3*) DIANE Pub.

Together We Can Meet the Challenge: Law Enforcement Strategies & Practices to Eliminate Drugs in Public Housing. (Illus.). 103p. (Orig.). (C). 1995. pap. text ed. 25.00 (*0-7881-2066-2*) DIANE Pub.

***Together We Dance: A Teacher's Collection of Miracles & Memories.** Ann Carroll. 64p. (Orig.). pap. 9.95 (*1-57736-010-9*) Providence Hse.

Together We Go, Level 5. Early. 1983. 28.95 incl. 5.25 hd (*0-15-331255-6*) HB Schl Dept.

Together We Pray: General Intercessions for Sundays, Solemnities, Feasts, & Other Celebrations. Ed. by Robert Borg. 260p. (Orig.). 1993. pap. text ed. 39.95 (*0-8146-2266-6*) Liturgical Pr.

Together We Stand: The Commissioning, Role & Management of Child & Adolescent. 212p. 1995. pap. 25.00 (*0-11-321904-0*, HM19040, Pub. by Stationery Ofc UK) Bernan Associates.

Together We Were Eleven Foot Nine: The Twenty-Year Friendship of Hall of Fame Pitcher Jim Palmer & Orioles Manager Earl Weaver. Jim Palmer & Jim Dale. (Illus.). 192p. 1996. 21.95 (*0-8362-0781-5*) Andrews & McMeel.

Together We're Better: Establishing a Coactive Learning Environment. Bev Bos. Ed. by Kay Glowes. LC 90-71653. (Illus.). 175p. (C). 1990. pap. 17.95 (*0-931793-01-7*) Turn-the-Page.

Together with God. George Douma. 1959. pap. 0.70 (*0-686-23478-2*) Rose Pub MI.

Together with the Ainu: A Vanishing People. M. Inez Hilger. LC 70-145504. (Illus.). 252p. reprint ed. 71.90 (*0-8357-9743-0*, 2016223) Bks Demand.

***Togetherness Routines & I Love You Danny Rocc.** Pearce & Bentley. (Clipper Fiction Ser.). 1991. pap. text ed. write for info. (*0-582-87552-8*, Pub. by Longman UK) Longman.

Togo. Maxine McCarty. LC 95-22468. (Country Guide Series Report from the AACRAO-AID Project). 1996. 24.00 (*0-929851-67-6*) Am Assn Coll Registrars.

Togo. Frank Parker. (World Bibliographical Ser.). 1995. lib. bdg. 57.00 (*1-85109-160-2*) ABC-CLIO.

Togo: Portrait of a West African Francophone Republic in the 1980s. A. A. Curkeet. LC 92-50377. (Illus.). 228p. 1993. pap. 27.50 (*0-89950-759-X*) McFarland & Co.

Togo: Reflections of an African American in Togo, West Africa. James L. Canada. 250p. (Orig.). 1996. mass mkt. 4.99 (*1-55197-294-8*, Pub. by Comnwlth Pub CN) Partners Pubs Grp.

Togo Murano: Master Architect of Japan. Botond Bognar & Fumihiko Maki. LC 95-46479. (Illus.). 160p. 1996. 40.00 (*0-8478-1887-X*) Rizzoli Intl.

Togodoo - A Pathwalk with the African Thirteen Moon Cycles. Moses Yao. 220p. 1994. 75.00 (*1-880047-14-4*) Creative Des.

Toh Shin Den Fighters Companion. Anthony Lynch. 1995. pap. text ed. 9.99 (*1-56686-341-4*) Brady Pub.

***Tohi Vagahau Niue: Niue Language Dictionary.** Ed. by Wolfgang B. Sperlich. LC 96-47328. 608p. 1997. text ed. 45.00 (*0-8248-1933-0*) UH Pr.

***Tohono O'Odham.** Jacqueline D. Greene. LC 97-11688. (First Book Ser.). (J). 1998. write for info. (*0-531-20326-3*) Watts.

Tohono O'odham (Papago) Indian Coloring Book. rev. ed. Connie Asch. (Illus.). 32p. (Orig.). (J). (gr. 1-6). 1983. reprint ed. pap. 2.95 (*0-918080-60-6*) Treas Chest Bks.

Toi, Qui Es-Tu? Paul Claudel. 126p. (FRE.). 1936. 10.95 (*0-7859-1112-X*, 2070214990) Fr & Eur.

Toil & Plenty: Images of the Agricultural Landscape in England, 1780-1890. Christiana Payne. LC 93-13885. (Agrarian Studies Ser.). (Illus.). 272p. 1993. 50.00 (*0-300-05773-3*) Yale U Pr.

***Toil & Struggle.** Maajid Al-Kush. 40p. 1996. write for info. (*0-9627663-3-X*) Designer Comns.

Toil & Toxics: Workplace Struggles & Political Strategies for Occupational Health. James C. Robinson. LC 90-20986. 253p. 1991. 37.50 (*0-520-07164-6*); pap. 13.00 (*0-520-08448-9*) U CA Pr.

Toil & Trouble: Good Work, Smart Workers, & the Integration of Academic & Vocational Education. Joe L. Kincheloe. LC 94-40615. (Counterpoints Ser.: Vol. 7). 376p. (C). 1995. pap. text ed. 29.95 (*0-8204-1787-4*) P Lang Pubng.

Toil of the Brave. Inglis Fletcher. (Carolina Ser.). 548p. reprint ed. lib. bdg. 32.95 (*0-89244-010-4*, Queens House) Amereon Ltd.

Toil, Tears & Sweat. S. Jacoby. 1998. 19.95 (*0-06-019015-9*, HarpT) HarpC.

Toil, Turmoil, & Triumph: A Portrait of the Tennessee Labor Movement. Perry C. Cotham. LC 95-71978. 352p. (C). 1995. 29.95 (*1-881576-64-7*, Hillsboro Pr) Providence Hse.

Toiler's Life. Edward N. Harleston. LC 79-37596. (Black Heritage Library Collection). 1977. reprint ed. 20.95 (*0-8369-8972-4*) Ayer.

Toilers of the Sea. Victor Hugo. Ed. by Patricia LeChevalier. Tr. by W. May Thomas from FRE. (Illus.). 384p. 1993. 26.00 (*0-9626854-8-8*) Atlantean Pr.

Toilet Learning: The Picture Book Technique for Children & Parents. Alison Mack. 1983. pap. 11.95 (*0-316-54237-7*) Little.

Toilet Paper Tigers. Gordon Korman. 176p. (J). 1995. pap. 3.50 (*0-590-46231-8*) Scholastic Inc.

Toilet Papers: Recycling Waste & Conserving Water. Sim Van der Ryn. (Illus.). 128p. 1995. pap. 10.95 (*0-9644718-0-9*) Ecol Design Pr.

Toilet Tales. A. Wayne Von Konigslow. (Illus.). 24p. (J). (ps-8). 1985. pap. 4.95 (*0-920303-13-7*, Pub. by Annick CN); lib. bdg. 15.95 (*0-920303-14-5*, Pub. by Annick CN) Firefly Bks Ltd.

Toilet Tales. Andrea W. Von Konigslow. (Annikins Ser.: No. 6). (Illus.). 24p. (J). (ps-1). 1986. pap. 0.99 (*0-920303-81-1*, Pub. by Annick CN) Firefly Bks Ltd.

***Toilet Tips.** Herbert I. Kavet. (Illus.). 96p. 1996. pap. 5.95 (*1-889647-03-9*) Boston Am.

Toilet Training: A Practical Guide to Daytime & Nighttime Training. rev. ed. Vicki Lansky. LC 92-35022. 80p. 1984. pap. 5.99 (*0-553-37140-1*) Bantam.

Toilet Training in Less Than a Day. Nathan H. Azrin. 1989. mass mkt. 5.50 (*0-671-69380-8*) PB.

Toilet Training Persons with Developmental Disabilities: A Rapid Program for Day & Nighttime Independent Toileting. Richard M. Foxx & Nathan H. Azrin. 156p. 1973. pap. 9.95 (*0-87822-025-9*, 0260) Res Press.

Toilet Training to Independence for the Handicapped: A Manual for Trainers. Sue Bettison. (Illus.). 144p. (C). 1982. spiral bd., pap. 26.95 (*0-398-04678-6*) C C Thomas.

Toilet Training Without Tears. Charles E. Schaefer & Theresa F. DiGeronimo. 192p. 1989. 4.99 (*0-451-16273-0*, Sig) NAL-Dutton.

Toilets, Bathtubs, Sinks, & Sewers: A History of the Bathroom. Photos by Penny Colman. LC 93-48413. (Illus.). 96p. (J). (gr. 5-9). 1994. text ed. 16.00 (*0-689-31894-4*, Atheneum Bks Young) S&S Childrens.

Toilets of New York. Ken Eichenbaum. (Illus.). 160p. (Orig.). 1990. pap. text ed. 8.95 (*0-9620271-2-X*) Litterati Bks.

Toiling in Soil: A Guide to Southern Gardening. Elizabeth DesChamps. (Illus.). 173p. (Orig.). 1990. pap. 8.95 (*0-941711-06-4*) Wyrick & Co.

Toils of Language. Noah J. Jacobs. 128p. (C). 1990. 18.95 (*0-941533-47-6*) New Amsterdam Bks.

Toils of Scepticism. Jonathan Barnes. (Illus.). 192p. (C). 1990. text ed. 44.95 (*0-521-38339-0*) Cambridge U Pr.

Toine. Guy De Maupassant. 1991. pap. 12.95 (*0-7859-2926-6*) Fr & Eur.

Toine. Guy De Maupassant. (Folio Ser.: No. 2278). (FRE.). pap. 10.95 (*2-07-038380-6*) Schoenhof.

Toit. Lewis A. Kelly. (Illus.). 80p. (Orig.). 1994. pap. 6.95 (*0-9637778-0-7*) Ertia Unltd.

Toit: A Treasury of Touchstones for Personal Achievement. Lewis A. Kelly. (Illus.). 96p. 1994. reprint ed. 8.95 (*0-9637778-1-5*) Ertia Unltd.

Toiyabe Patrol: Five U. S. Forest Service Summers. Les Joslin. LC 92-84079. (Illus.). 90p. (Orig.). 1993. pap. 7.95 (*0-9647167-0-4*) Wilderness Assocs.

Tojo & the Coming of the War. R. J. C. Butow. (Illus.). xii, 584p. 1961. 65.00 (*0-8047-0690-5*) Stanford U Pr.

Tojolabal Maya: Ethnographic & Linguistic Approaches. Ed. by M. Jill Brody & John S. Thomas. LC 88-81803. (Geoscience & Man Ser.: Vol. 26). (Illus.). 84p. (Orig.). (C). 1988. pap. text ed. 18.00 (*0-938909-61-4*) Geosci Pubns LSU.

Tojolabal Maya-English Dictionary. L. Furbee. 1981. 2.00 incl. mic. film (*0-913134-77-5*) Mus Anthro MO.

Tojolabal Maya Texts Concordance. L. Furbee. 1981. 5.00 incl. mic. film (*0-913134-76-7*) Mus Anthro MO.

Tokaido Road. Lucia St. Clair Robson. 1992. mass mkt. 5.99 (*0-345-35639-X*) Ballantine.

Tokaidoi I: Adventures on the Road in Old Japan. Ed. by Stephen Addiss. LC 80-53851. (Illus.). 120p. 1980. pap. 8.50 (*0-913689-06-8*) Spencer Muse Art.

Tokali Kilise: Tenth-Century Metropolitan Art in Byzantine Cappadocia. Ann W. Epstein. LC 85-27536. (Dumbarton Oaks Studies: Vol. 22). (Illus.). 228p. 1986. 45.00 (*0-88402-145-9*, EPTO) Dumbarton Oaks.

Tokamak Plasma: A Complex Physical System. B. B. Kadomtsev. (Illus.). 232p. 1993. 134.00 (*0-7503-0234-8*) IOP Pub.

Tokamak Start-Up: Problems & Scenarios Related to the Transient Phase of a Thermonuclear Fusion Reactor. Ed. by Heinz Knoepfel. (Ettore Majorana International Science Series, Life Sciences: Vol. 26). 442p. 1986. 110.00 (*0-306-42236-0*, Plenum Pr) Plenum.

***Tokamaks.** 2nd ed. John Wesson. (Oxford Engineering Science Ser.: No. 48). (Illus.). 608p. 1997. 185.00 (*0-19-856293-4*) OUP.

Tokarev Report. Salvatore Puledda. 140p. (Orig.). 1992. 15.00 (*1-878977-17-2*) Latitude Pr.

Tokefield Papers, Old & New. Frank A. Swinnerton. LC 73-134141. (Essay Index Reprint Ser.). 1977. reprint ed. 20.95 (*0-8369-2374-X*) Ayer.

***Tokelau: A Historical Ethnography.** Judith Huntsman & Antony Hooper. LC 96-27748. 1997. text ed. 39.00 (*0-8248-1912-8*) UH Pr.

***Token.** Elaine Sishton. LC 94-79400. (Ten-Minute Mysteries Ser.). 32p. 1994. pap. 2.95 (*0-7854-0848-7*, 40775) Am Guidance.

Token: America's Other Money, Vol. 3. Ed. by Richard G. Doty. (Coinage of the Americas Conference Ser.). (Illus.). 224p. 1995. 25.00 (*0-89722-260-1*) Am Numismatic.

Token Economy System. David Lauridsen. Ed. by Danny G. Langdon. LC 77-25897. (Instructional Design Library). (Illus.). 96p. 1978. 27.95 (*0-87778-123-0*) Educ Tech Pubns.

Token for Children: A Token for the Children of New England. James Janeway & Cotton Mather. Ed. by Don Kistler. 176p. 1994. 18.95 (*1-877611-76-X*) Soli Deo Gloria.

Token Gift. Hugh W. McKibbon. (Illus.). 32p. (Orig.). (J). (gr. 1-6). 1996. 16.95 (*1-55037-499-0*, Pub. by Annick CN); pap. 6.95 (*1-55037-498-2*, Pub. by Annick CN) Firefly Bks Ltd.

Token of Friendship: A Collection of Sentiments, Thoughts, Gift Ideas, & Recipes for Special Friends. deluxe ed. Barbara M. Ohrbach. (Illus.). 64p. 1987. 10.00 (*0-517-56657-5*, C P Pubs) Crown Pub Group.

***Token of Love.** Ed. by Helen Exley. (Illus.). 60p. 1995. 8.00 (*1-85015-644-1*) Exley Giftbooks.

Token of Love. Compiled by Evelyn Loeb. (Keepsakes Ser.). (Illus.). 56p. 1994. 13.99 incl. audio compact disk (*0-88088-877-6*) Peter Pauper.

***Token of Remorse.** Michael Stone. LC 97-22193. 1998. pap. 20.95 (*0-670-87774-3*) Viking Penguin.

Token Professionals & Master Critics: A Critique of Orthodoxy in Literary Studies. James J. Sosnoski. LC 93-749. 272p. 1994. pap. text ed. 64.50 (*0-7914-1809-X*); pap. text ed. 21.95 (*0-7914-1810-3*) State U NY Pr.

***Token Readalong.** Elaine Sishton. LC 94-79400. (Ten-Minute Mysteries Ser.). 32p. 1994. pap. 12.95 incl. audio (*0-7854-1057-0*, 40777) Am Guidance.

Token Ring. Hans-George Gohring & Franz-Joachim Kauffels. (Illus.). 356p. (C). 1992. text ed. 46.95 (*0-201-56895-0*) Addison-Wesley.

Token-Ring Management Guide. Martin A. Nemzow. (Computer Communications Ser.). 450p. 1993. text ed. 48.00i (*0-07-046321-2*) McGraw.

Token Ring Network Design. David Bird. (C). 1994. text ed. 30.95 (*0-201-62760-4*) Addison-Wesley.

Token-Ring Networks: Characteristics, Operation, Construction, & Management. Gilbert Held. LC 93-13740. 309p. 1993. text ed. 62.95 (*0-471-94041-0*) Wiley.

Token Shipment (Oswego Camp) War Refugee Board "Final Summary Report" Intro. by David S. Wyman. (America & the Holocaust Ser.: Vol. 10). 900930p. 1990. reprint ed. text ed. 30.00 (*0-8240-4542-4*) Garland.

Token Shipment: The Story of America's War Refugee Shelter see U. S. War Relocation Authority

Tokens: A Poem. Judy Ray. Ed. by Gloria V. Hickok. 8p. (Orig.). 1995. pap. 3.00 (*1-884235-15-8*) Helicon Nine Eds.

Tokens & Treasures: Gifts to Twelve Presidents: Catalog of an Exhibition at the National Archives, Washington, D. C., February 16, 1995-February 2, 1996. Lisa B. Auel. (Illus.). 144p. 1996. pap. 24.95 (*1-880875-10-1*, 200052) National Archives & Recs.

Tokens, Checks, Metallic Tickets, Passes, & Tallies of the British Caribbean & Bermuda. Bob Lyall. Ed. by David E. Schenkman. (Illus.). 210p. 1989. text ed. 35.00 (*0-918492-08-4*) TAMS.

***Tokens of Affection.** Alda Ellis. (Remembrance of Times Past Ser.). (Illus.). 16p. (Orig.). 1997. 6.99 (*1-56507-681-8*) Harvest Hse.

Tokens of Affection: The Letters of a Planter's Daughter in the Old South. Ed. by Carol Bleser. LC 94-40961. (Southern Voices from the Past Ser.). 1995. 45.00 (*0-8203-1727-6*) U of Ga Pr.

Tokens of Grace: A Novella in Stories. Sheila O'Connor. LC 90-5438. 128p. 1990. pap. 9.95 (*0-915943-47-6*) Milkweed Ed.

Tokens of Love. Roberta B. Etter. (Illus.). 132p. 1990. 14.95 (*1-55859-100-1*) Abbeville Pr.

Tokens of Love: Five Regency Love Stories. Mary Balogh et al. 352p. (Orig.). 1993. pap. 4.99 (*0-451-17342-2*, Sig) NAL-Dutton.

Tokens of the Eighteenth Century, Connected with Booksellers & Bookmaker: Authors, Printers, Publishers, Engravers & Paper Makers. W. Longman. (Illus.). 1970. reprint ed. 35.00 (*1-55888-237-5*) Omnigraphics Inc.

Tokens of the Gay Nineties. Ed. by Russell Rulau. LC 87-80401. (Illus.). 160p. 1987. pap. 12.95 (*0-87341-097-1*, GN01) Krause Pubns.

Toko Shinoda: A New Appreciation. Mary Tolman & Norman Tolman. (Illus.). 212p. 1993. pap. 49.95 (*0-8048-1904-1*) C E Tuttle.

***Tokoloshe: An African Zulu Folktale.** Pieter Scholtz. (Orig.). (J). 1998. pap. 5.00 (*0-87602-364-2*) Anchorage.

Tokoloshe! I Married Eleven Dachshunds! William Sears & Marguerite Sears. LC 89-62159. (Illus.). 279p. (Orig.). 1991. pap. 12.50 (*0-9623596-0-2*) Natl Spir Assy HI.

Tokoloshi: African Folktales Retold. Diana Pitcher. LC 93-26253. (Illus.). 64p. (J). (gr. 4 up). 1993. reprint ed. pap. 8.95 (*1-883672-03-1*) Tricycle Pr.

Tokugawa Confucian Education: The Kangien Academy of Hirose Tanso (1782-1856) Marleen Kassel. LC 95-17244. 250p. (C). 1996. pap. text ed. 21.95 (*0-7914-2808-7*) State U NY Pr.

Tokugawa Confucian Education: The Kangien Academy of Hirose Tanso (1782-1856) Marleen Kassel. LC 95-17244. 250p. (C). 1996. text ed. 64.50 (*0-7914-2807-9*) State U NY Pr.

An Asterisk (*) at the beginning of an entry indicates that the title is appearing in BIP for the first time.

***Tokugawa Ideology: Early Constructs, 1570-1680.** Herman Ooms. LC 84-42897. 366p. reprint ed. pap. 104.40 (*0-608-04530-6*, 2065273) Bks Demand.

Tokugawa Ieyasu: Shogun. Conrad Totman. (Illus.). 205p. (Orig.). (C). 1983. pap. 12.95 (*0-89346-210-1*) Heian Intl.

Tokugawa Japan: The Great Peace & the Development of Urban Culture. Lynn S. Parisi et al. (Humanities Approach to Japanese History Ser.). (Illus.). 146p. (Orig.). (YA). (gr. 9-12). 1995. pap. 37.95 (*0-89994-380-2*) Soc Sci Ed.

Tokugawa Japan: The Social & Economic Antecedents of Modern Japan. Chie Nakane & Shinsaburo Oishi. Tr. by Conrad Totman. 248p. 1992. pap. 19.50 (*0-86008-490-6*, Pub. by U of Tokyo JA) Col U Pr.

Tokugawa Religion: The Cultural Roots of Modern Japan. 2nd ed. Robert N. Bellah. 272p. 1985. pap. 14.95 (*0-02-902460-9*, Free Press) Free Pr.

Tokugawa Village Practice: Class, Status, Power, Law. Herman Ooms. LC 95-41444. (Philip E. Lilienthal Bk.). (Illus.). 424p. (C). 1996. 45.00 (*0-520-20209-0*) U CA Pr.

Tokutomi Soho, 1863-1957: A Journalist for Modern Japan. John D. Pierson. LC 79-3226. 464p. 1980. reprint ed. pap. 131.70 (*0-7837-9421-5*, 2060162) Bks Demand.

Tokuwa Batholith, Central Japan: An Example of Occurences of Ilmenite-Series & Magnetite-Series Granitoids in a Batholith. Masaaki Shimizu. (Illus.). 156p. 1987. 62.50 (*0-86008-401-9*, Pub. by U of Tokyo JA) Col U Pr.

Tokyo. Karl Baedeker. (Baedeker's City Guides Ser.). 1987. pap. 10.95 (*0-317-51985-9*) P-H.

***Tokyo.** Botond Bognar. (World Cities Ser.: Vol. IV). (Illus.). 368p. 1997. 95.00 (*1-85490-485-X*) Academy Ed UK.

Tokyo. Fodor's Travel Staff. (Fodor's AAA City Pocket Guide Ser.). 1997. pap. 11.00 (*0-679-03169-3*) Fodors Travel.

Tokyo. Deborah Kent. LC 95-39242. (Cities of the World Ser.). (Illus.). 64p. (J). (gr. 4-6). 1996. lib. bdg. 24.00 (*0-516-00354-2*) Childrens.

***Tokyo.** Deborah Kent. (Cities of the World Ser.). 64p. (J). 1997. pap. 8.95 (*0-516-26123-1*) Childrens.

Tokyo. Robert Newton. LC 92-2498. (Cities at War Ser.). (Illus.). 96p. (YA). (gr. 6 up). 1992. lib. bdg. 14.95 (*0-02-768235-8*, Mac Bks Young Read) S&S Childrens.

Tokyo: A Bilingual Atlas. Ed. by Umeda Atsushi. LC 87-81687. (Illus.). 132p. 1988. pap. 18.00 (*0-87011-845-5*) Kodansha.

Tokyo: A Bilingual Map. 1990. pap. 7.00 (*0-87011-978-8*) Kodansha.

Tokyo: A Cultural Guide to Japan's Capital City. John H. Martin & Phyllis G. Martin. (Illus.). 312p. (Orig.). 1996. pap. 14.95 (*0-8048-2057-0*) C E Tuttle.

Tokyo: A Spatial Anthropology. Hidenobu Jinnai. Tr. by Kimiko Nishimura from JPN. (Illus.). 312p. 1995. 40.00 (*0-520-07135-2*) U CA Pr.

Tokyo: City Guide. 2nd ed. Chris Taylor. (Illus.). 366p. (Orig.). 1995. pap. 10.95 (*0-86442-301-2*) Lonely Planet.

Tokyo: City of Stories. Paul Waley. (Illus.). 288p. (Orig.). 1991. pap. 17.50 (*0-8348-0227-9*) Weatherhill.

Tokyo: Sights & Insights. Ryosake Kami. (Illus.). 192p. (Orig.). 1992. pap. 10.95 (*0-8048-1717-0*) C E Tuttle.

Tokyo Adventures: Glimpses of the City in Bygone Eras. Tae Moriyama. Tr. by Bob Garvey & Reiko Garvey. (Illus.). 376p. 1993. 19.95 (*4-07-975842-1*, Pub. by Shufunomoto Co Ltd JA) C E Tuttle.

Tokyo Chronicles: A Guigin's Reflections on Japanese Life & Business. Albert L. Sieg. 256p. (C). 1994. 66.00 (*0-939246-70-8*) Wiley.

Tokyo Chronicles: An American Gaijin Reveals the Hidden Truths of Japanese Life & Business. Albert L. Sieg & J. Bennett Steven. 256p. 1995. text ed. 24.95 (*0-471-13174-1*) Wiley.

Tokyo City Guide. rev. ed. Mayumi Barakan & Judith C. Greer. (Illus.). 364p. 1995. pap. 14.95 (*0-8048-1964-5*) C E Tuttle.

***Tokyo Citybook.** (Torg Ser.). 18.00 (*0-87431-349-X*, 20523) West End Games.

***Tokyo Comedy.** Elfried Jelinek & Toshihara Ito. 272p. 1997. pap. 32.00 (*4-7713-0250-2*) Dist Art Pubs.

Tokyo International Forum: A Work in Progress. Rafael Vinoly. Ed. by Jay Bargmann & Jonathan Schloss. LC 93-92715. (Illus.). 1993. 24.95 (*0-9637436-0-0*) R Vinoly Architects.

Tokyo Life, New York Dreams: Urban Japanese Visions of America, 1890-1924. Mitziko Sawada. LC 96-19699. (Illus.). 300p. (C). 1996. 40.00 (*0-520-07379-7*) U CA Pr.

Tokyo Love. Nan Goldin & Nobuyoshi Araki. 212p. 1995. pap. 45.00 (*1-881616-57-6*, Pub. by Scalo Pubs) Dist Art Pubs.

Tokyo Metropolitan Area: A Bilingual Map. (Guide Ser.). 16p. 1990. pap. 6.95 (*4-7700-1522-4*) Kodansha.

Tokyo National Museum see Oriental Ceramics: The World's Great Collections

Tokyo Night City: Where to Drink & Party. Jude Brand. 172p. 1993. pap. 9.95 (*0-8048-1896-7*) C E Tuttle.

Tokyo Nights. Donald Richie. 118p. 1994. pap. 9.95 (*0-8048-1923-8*) C E Tuttle.

***Tokyo Novelle.** Nobuyoshi Araki. 1997. 35.00 (*3-89322-853-5*, Pub. by Edition Cantz GW) Dist Art Pubs.

Tokyo Observer. Leighton Willgerodt. 142p. (Orig.). 1988. pap. 8.75 (*0-930693-04-3*) Cross Cult Pr.

Tokyo Pink Guide. Susan L. Clemens. 200p. 1993. pap. 12.95 (*0-8048-1915-7*) C E Tuttle.

Tokyo Plenary Meeting of the Trilateral Commission, 1988. Ed. by Andrew V. Frankel & Charles B. Heck. (Trialogue Ser.: No. T40). (Illus.). 72p. (Orig.). pap. 6.00 (*0-930503-09-0*) Trilateral Comm.

***Tokyo Portraits: An Enigmatic View of the City.** Akihiro Matsumura. (Illus.). 144p. 1997. write for info. (*4-07-976534-7*, Pub. by Shufunotomo JA) Weatherhill.

Tokyo Rail & Road Atlas: A Bilingual Guide. Kodansha International Staff. Ed. by Tetsuo Kuramochi. 80p. 1993. 20.00 (*4-7700-1781-2*) Kodansha.

Tokyo Restaurant Guide. John Kennerdell. (Illus.). 264p. 1995. pap. 12.95 (*4-89684-246-4*, Pub. by Yohan Pubns JA) Weatherhill.

Tokyo Rising: The City since the Great Earthquake. Edward G. Seidensticker. 362p. (C). 1991. pap. text ed. 14.95 (*0-674-89461-8*) HUP.

Tokyo Sketches. Pete Hamill. Ed. by Pockell & Tetsuo Kuramochi. 224p. 1993. 20.00 (*4-7700-1697-2*) Kodansha.

Tokyo Sketches. Pete Hamill. Ed. by S. Shaw. 168p. 1995. pap. 10.00 (*4-7700-1950-5*) Kodansha.

Tokyo Spirit in Architecture No. 123: Tokyo Spirit in Architecture: Works by Takenaka Corporation. Takenaka Corp. Staff. (Process Architecture Ser.: No. 123). (Illus.). 201p. 1995. pap. 44.95 (*4-89331-123-9*, Pub. by Process Archit JA) Bks Nippan.

Tokyo Story. Robert Whiting. Date not set. pap. write for info. (*0-679-41976-4*) Random.

Tokyo Style. Kyoichi Tsuzuki. (Illus.). 375p. 1995. 150.00 (*4-7636-3218-3*) RAM Publications.

Tokyo Symposium '77 (International) on Photo-&-Electro-Imaging: Extended Abstracts of Papers: Tokyo, Japan, September 26-30, 1977. Society of Photographic Scientists & Engineers Staff. 376p. reprint ed. pap. 107.20 (*0-317-42079-8*, 2025706) Bks Demand.

Tokyo Trial & Beyond. B. V. Roling. 152p. 1994. pap. 17.95 (*0-7456-1485-X*, Pub. by Polity Pr UK) Blackwell Pubs.

***Tokyo Typedirectors Club Annual 96-97.** Ed. by Tokyo Typedirectors Club Staff. (Illus.). 248p. 1997. pap. 89.95 (*4-89444-057-1*, Pub. by PIE Bks JA) Bks Nippan.

Tokyo Typodirecturs Club Annual 95/96, Vol. 7. Tokyo Typodirecturs Club Staff. (Illus.). 250p. 1996. pap. 69.95 (*4-89444-018-0*, Pub. by PIE Bks JA) Bks Nippan.

Tokyo, 1970 see General Assembly Proceedings

Tokyo, 1992-1993. Beth Reiber. (Frommer's Comprehensive Travel Guide Ser.). (Illus.). 288p. 1992. pap. 13.00 (*0-13-333477-5*, P-H Travel) P-H Gen Ref & Trav.

Tolbert of Texas: The Man & His Work. Frank Tolbert. Ed. by Evelyn Oppenheimer. LC 86-1472. 356p. (Orig.). 1986. pap. 13.95 (*0-87565-068-6*) Tex Christian.

Told by the Colonel. William L. Alden. (Illus.). 1971. reprint ed. 19.00 (*0-403-01435-2*) Scholarly.

Told by the Weather. Ernest Tedlock. (Kestrel Chapbks.: No. 9). 1983. pap. 3.00 (*0-914974-41-6*) Holmgangers.

Told by Uncle Remus. Joel C. Harris. LC 76-39087. (Black Heritage Library Collection). (Illus.). 1977. reprint ed. 27.95 (*0-8369-9025-0*) Ayer.

Told in a French Garden, August, 1914. Mildred Aldrich. (Short Story Index Reprint Ser.). 1977. 20.95 (*0-8369-3327-3*) Ayer.

Told in Gath. Max Wright. 177p. (Orig.). 1990. pap. 14.95 (*0-85640-439-X*, Pub. by Blackstaff Pr IE) Dufour.

Told in Gath. Max Wright. 177p. (Orig.). 9000. 30.00 (*0-85640-449-7*, Pub. by Blackstaff Pr IE) Dufour.

Told in Norway: An Introduction to Modern Norwegian Fiction. Ed. by Hanna A. Larsen. Tr. by Anders Orbeck. LC 72-3366. (Short Story Index Reprint Ser.). 1977. reprint ed. 23.95 (*0-8369-4152-7*) Ayer.

Told Round a Brushwood Fire: The Autobiography of Arai Hakuseki. Arai Hakuseki. Tr. by Joyce Ackroyd. 360p. 1995. 40.00 (*0-86008-248-2*, Pub. by U of Tokyo JA) Col U Pr.

Told Round a Bushwood Fire: The Autobiography of Arai Hakuseki. Hakuseki Arai. (Princeton Library of Asian Translations). (Illus.). 359p. reprint ed. pap. 102.40 (*0-8357-4046-3*, 2036736) Bks Demand.

Told Tales: Nine Folktales from Around the World. Josepha Sherman. (Illus.). 64p. (J). (gr. 3 up). 1995. lib. bdg. 13.95 (*1-881889-64-5*) Silver Moon.

Told Through the Ages: A Series of Masonic Stories. J. S. Ward. 240p. 1993. pap. 17.95 (*1-56459-386-X*) Kessinger Pub.

Toldos Chabad Bartzos Habris. 414p. (HEB.). 1988. 20.00 (*0-8266-5333-2*) Kehot Pubn Soc.

Toldos Chabad Benetz Hakoidesh. 334p. (HEB.). 1988. 20.00 (*0-8266-5332-4*) Kehot Pubn Soc.

Toldos Chabad Birussah Ha'sovyeties. 476p. (HEB.). 1989. 20.00 (*0-8266-5331-6*) Kehot Pubn Soc.

***Tole Fairytales.** Gerry Wright. Date not set. pap. text ed. 9.95 (*1-57377-003-5*) Easl Pubns.

Tole Painting Made Easy. Ondori Publishing Company Staff. (Illus.). 96p. (Orig.). 1996. pap. 17.00 (*0-87040-985-9*) Kodansha.

Toledo. Tom Burns. (Everything under the Sun Ser.). (Illus.). 176p. 1995. pap. 6.95 (*0-8442-9204-4*, Passport Bks) NTC Pub Grp.

Toledo. A. Calvert. 1976. lib. bdg. 59.95 (*0-8490-2752-7*) Gordon Pr.

Toledo: The Story of an Old Spanish Capital. H. Lynch. (Mediaeval Towns Ser.: Vol. 5). 1974. reprint ed. pap. 35.00 (*0-8115-0847-1*) Periodicals Srv.

Toledo & Lucas County, Ohio, Vol. I. John M. Killits. (Illus.). 762p. 1993. reprint ed. lib. bdg. write for info. (*0-8328-2962-5*) Higginson Bk Co.

Toledo & Lucas County, Ohio, Vol. II. John M. Killits. (Illus.). 686p. 1993. reprint ed. lib. bdg. write for info. (*0-8328-2963-3*) Higginson Bk Co.

Toledo & Lucas County, Ohio, Vol. III. John M. Killits. (Illus.). 697p. 1993. reprint ed. lib. bdg. write for info. (*0-8328-2964-1*) Higginson Bk Co.

Toledo & Madrid. L. Williams. 1976. lib. bdg. 59.95 (*0-8490-2753-5*) Gordon Pr.

Toledo Bend. Sam Mims. LC 74-186988. 1972. 12.95 (*0-911116-57-5*); pap. 9.95 (*0-911116-70-2*) Pelican.

Toledo Museum of Art, American Paintings. Susan E. Strickler & William Hutton. LC 79-66974. (Illus.). 228p. 1980. pap. 14.50 (*0-685-04910-8*); lib. bdg. 24.50 (*0-685-04909-4*) Toledo Mus Art.

Toledo Museum of Art, European Paintings. Toledo Museum of Art Staff. LC 76-24500. (Illus.). 396p. 1976. pap. 12.95 (*0-685-04912-4*); lib. bdg. 22.50 (*0-685-04911-6*) Toledo Mus Art.

Toledo, Peoria & Western: Tried, Proven & Willing. Paul H. Stringham. LC 93-90979. (Illus.). 158p. (Orig.). 1993. pap. 27.95 (*0-9638676-0-1*) Deller Archive.

***Toledo, Port Clinton & Lakeside Railway.** George W. Hilton. (Illus.). 58p. 1997. reprint ed. pap. 11.95 (*0-9658624-0-2*) Montevallo Hist.

Toledo Treasures: Selections from the Toledo Museum of Art. Lawrence W. Nichols et al. LC 95-21385. (Illus.). 192p. 1995. 50.00 (*1-55595-118-X*) Hudson Hills.

Tolerance. John K. Carmack. 1993. 10.95 (*0-88494-890-0*) Bookcraft Inc.

Tolerance. rev. ed. Kevin Osborn. (Values Library). (Illus.). 64p. (YA). (gr. 7-12). 1993. lib. bdg. 15.95 (*0-8239-1508-5*) Rosen Group.

Tolerance: Towards an Ethic of Solidarity & Peace. Bernard Haring & Valentin Salvoldi. Tr. by Edmund C. Lane from ITA. LC 95-13193. (Towards an Ethic of Solidarity & Peace). 105p. (Orig.). 1995. pap. 5.95 (*0-8189-0738-X*) Alba.

Tolerance & Community. rev. ed. Glenn Tinder. LC 95-34437. 256p. (C). 1995. 39.95 (*0-8262-1022-8*) U of Mo Pr.

***Tolerance & Education: Learning to Live with Diversity & Difference.** W. Paul Vogt. LC 97-4675. 1997. write for info. (*0-7619-0216-3*); pap. write for info. (*0-7619-0217-1*) Sage.

***Tolerance & Intolerance in Early Judaism & Christianity.** Ed. by Graham N. Stanton & Guy G. Stroumsa. 320p. (C). 1998. text ed. 59.95 (*0-521-59037-X*) Cambridge U Pr.

Tolerance & Intolerance in the European Reformation. Ed. by Ole P. Grell & Bob Scribner. 320p. (C). 1996. text ed. 59.95 (*0-521-49694-2*) Cambridge U Pr.

Tolerance & Movements of Religious Dissent in Eastern Europe. Ed. by Bela K. Kiraly. (East European Monographs: No. 13). 227p. 1976. text ed. 52.50 (*0-914710-06-0*) East Eur Monographs.

Tolerance & Transformation: Jewish Approaches to Religious Pluralism. Sandra B. Lubarsky. LC 90-4206. (Jewish Perspectives Ser.: Vol. 4). 159p. 1990. reprint ed. pap. 45.40 (*0-608-00734-X*, 2061510) Bks Demand.

Tolerance Control. 60p. 1988. pap. text ed. 14.50 (*0-87263-309-8*) SME.

***Tolerance Design: A Handbook for Developing Optimal Specifications.** C. M. Creveling. LC 96-37196. 576p. 1996. 32.23 (*0-201-63473-2*) Addison-Wesley.

***Tolerance Design of Electronic Circuits.** 232p. 1997. 26.00 (*1-86094-040-4*) World Scientific Pub.

Tolerance for Diversity of Beliefs: A Secondary Curriculum Unit. Patricia Avery et al. (Illus.). 113p. (Orig.). 1993. pap. 17.95 (*0-89994-374-8*) Soc Sci Ed.

Tolerance for Nonconformity. Clyde Z. Nunn et al. LC 77-82920. (Jossey-Bass Social & Behavioral Science Ser.). 230p. reprint ed. pap. 65.60 (*0-685-23667-6*, 2052201) Bks Demand.

Tolerance to Beneficial & Adverse Effects of Antiepileptic Drugs. Ed. by Hand-Hasso Frey et al. LC 86-20431. 192p. 1986. reprint ed. pap. 54.80 (*0-608-00406-5*, 2061120) Bks Demand.

Tolerances: Geometric & Position Reference & Workbook. 2nd ed. Aubrey Yuen. Ed. by Marian Coombs. (Illus.). 258p. 1986. write for info. (*0-318-59174-X*); pap. text ed. 39.95 (*0-9614079-2-1*) TVR Pub Co.

Tolerances see Steel Casting Handbook Supplements

Tolerances for Precast & Prestressed Concrete. (PCI Journal Reprints Ser.). 87p. 1985. pap. 20.00 (*0-318-19820-7*, JR307) P-PCI.

Tolerant Personality. James G. Martin. LC 64-15881. (Wayne State University Studies - Sociology: No. 15). (Illus.). 182p. reprint ed. pap. 51.90 (*0-7837-3599-5*, 2043464) Bks Demand.

Tolerant Populists: Kansas Populism & Nativism. Walter T. Nugent. LC 63-13069. 268p. reprint ed. 76.40 (*0-8357-9659-0*, 2015761) Bks Demand.

Tolerant Society. Lee C. Bollinger. 320p. 1988. pap. 18.95 (*0-19-505430-X*) OUP.

Tolerant Society: Freedom of Speech & Extremist Speech in America. Lee C. Bollinger. LC 85-21410. 320p. 1986. 30.00 (*0-19-504000-7*) OUP.

Tolerating Terrorism in the West: An International Survey. Ed. by Noemi Gal-Or. 176p. (C). (gr. 13). 1991. text ed. 89.95 (*0-415-02441-2*, A6150) Routledge.

Tolerating the Private Sector: Grain Trade in Tanzania after Adjustment. CFNPP Staff et al. (Working Papers). (C). 1992. pap. 7.00 (*1-56401-132-1*) Cornell Food.

Toleration. Nick Fotion & Gerard Elfstrom. 216p. (C). 1992. text ed. 29.95 (*0-8173-0581-5*) U of Ala Pr.

Toleration. Preston King. LC 96-13013. 1996. write for info. (*0-7146-4652-0*, Pub. by F Cass Pubs UK) Intl Spec Bk.

Toleration: An Elusive Virtue. Ed. by David Heyd. LC 95-34037. 252p. 1996. text ed. 39.50 (*0-691-04371-X*) Princeton U Pr.

Toleration: Philosophy & Practice. Ed. by John Horton & Peter Nicholoson. 197p. 1992. 68.95 (*1-85628-314-3*, Pub. by Avebury Pub UK) Ashgate Pub Co.

Toleration, & Other Essays & Studies. John Bigelow. LC 78-84298. (Essay Index Reprint Ser.). 1977. 17.95 (*0-8369-1075-3*) Ayer.

Toleration & the Constitution. David A. Richards. 368p. 1989. reprint ed. pap. 22.00 (*0-19-505947-6*) OUP.

Toleration in Religion & Politics. Adam Watson. LC 80-65746. (Second Distinguished CRIA Lecture on Morality & Foreign Policy). 1980. pap. 4.00 (*0-87641-218-5*) Carnegie Ethics & Intl Affairs.

Toliver's Secret. Esther W. Brady. LC 76-15997. (Illus.). 176p. (J). (gr. 3-7). 1993. pap. 3.99 (*0-679-84804-5*) Random Bks Yng Read.

Tolkein: A Critical Assessment. Brian Rosebury. LC 91-33345. 176p. 1992. text ed. 49.95 (*0-312-07583-9*) St Martin.

Tolkien, 4 vols. J. R. R. Tolkien. 1986. boxed 23.96 (*0-345-34042-6*) Ballantine.

Tolkien: New Critical Perspectives. Ed. by Neil D. Isaacs & Rose A. Zimbardo. LC 80-51015. 184p. 1981. 20.00 (*0-8131-1408-X*) U Pr of Ky.

Tolkien: The Illustrated Encyclopaedia. Ed. by David Day. (Illus.). 288p. 1991. text ed. 29.95 (*0-02-533431-X*) Macmillan.

Tolkien: The Illustrated Encyclopedia. David Day. (Illus.). 288p. 1992. pap. 18.00 (*0-02-031275-X*) Macmillan.

***Tolkien: The Illustrated Encylopedia.** David Day. 1997. pap. text ed. 20.00 (*0-684-83979-2*) S&S Trade.

Tolkien & the Critics: Essays on J. R. R. Tolkien's "The Lord of the Rings" Ed. by Neil D. Isaacs & Rose A. Zimbardo. LC 68-20436. (Illus.). 306p. 1968. reprint ed. pap. 87.30 (*0-608-00890-7*, 2061684) Bks Demand.

Tolkien Beastiary. David Day. 1995. 19.99 (*0-517-12077-1*) Random Hse Value.

Tolkien Bestiary. David Day. 1990. 14.99 (*0-517-47325-9*) Random Hse Value.

Tolkien Companion. J. E. Tyler. 1995. 12.99 (*0-517-14648-7*) Random Hse Value.

Tolkien Criticism: An Annotated Checklist. rev. ed. Richard C. West. LC 81-8135. (Serif Series: Bibliographies & Checklists: No. 39). 193p. 1981. reprint ed. pap. 55.10 (*0-7837-0572-7*, 2040916) Bks Demand.

Tolkien Family Album. John Tolkien & Priscilla Tolkien. (Illus.). 128p. 1992. 24.95 (*0-395-59938-5*) HM.

Tolkien Reader. J. R. R. Tolkien. 272p. 1986. mass mkt. 5.99 (*0-345-34506-1*) Ballantine.

Tolkien Thesaurus. Richard E. Blackwelder. LC 89-25949. 286p. 1990. text ed. 44.00 (*0-8240-5296-X*, H1326) Garland.

Tolkien's Dragons & Monsters: A Book of Twenty Postcards. Alan Lee et al. 44p. 1994. pap. 8.00 (*0-261-10301-6*, Haas Ent NH) HarpC.

Tolkien's Peaceful War: A History & Explanation of Tolkien Fandom & War. Philip W. Helms. Ed. & Intro. by Paul S. Ritz. 38p. (Orig.). 1994. pap. 7.50 (*1-881799-09-3*) Am Tolkien Soc.

Tolkien's World. J. R. R. Tolkien. 144p. 1995. pap. 19.00 (*0-261-10307-5*) HarpC.

Toll Bridge. Aiden Chambers. LC 94-36602. (Laura Geringer Bk.). 208p. (YA). (gr. 8 up). 1995. 14.95 (*0-06-023598-5*); lib. bdg. 14.89 (*0-06-023599-3*) HarpC Child Bks.

Toll-Bridge Troll. Patricia R. Wolff & Kimberly B. Root. LC 93-32298. (Illus.). 24p. (J). (ps-2). 1995. 14.00 (*0-15-277665-6*, Browndeer Pr) HarBrace.

Toll Call. Stephen Greenleaf. 1988. mass mkt. 4.99 (*0-345-35349-8*) Ballantine.

Toll Collector. Jack Rudman. (Career Examination Ser.: C-810). 1994. pap. 23.95 (*0-8373-0810-0*) Nat Learn.

Toll Equipment Maintenance Supervisor. Jack Rudman. (Career Examination Ser.: C-2547). 1994. pap. 29.95 (*0-8373-2547-1*) Nat Learn.

Toll Equipment Mechanic. Jack Rudman. (Career Examination Ser.: C-2546). 1994. pap. 27.95 (*0-8373-2546-3*) Nat Learn.

Toll for the Brave. Jack Higgins. 1995. pap. 16.95 (*0-7871-0033-1*, Dove Bks) Dove Audio.

***Toll Fraud & Telabuse: A Multibillion Dollar National Problem.** 2nd rev. ed. John J. Haugh. 434p. 1996. pap. 149.00 (*0-935453-77-6*) Pasha Pubns.

***Toll-Free Phone Book U. S. A. 1998: A Directory of Toll-Free Telephone Numbers for Businesses & Organizations Nationwide.** 2nd ed. 1150p. 1997. pap. 95.00 (*0-7808-0281-0*, B705-1998) Omnigraphics Inc.

Toll-Free Services: A Complete Guide to Design, Implementation, & Management. Robert A. Gable. LC 95-6094. 186p. 1995. 69.00 (*0-89006-787-2*) Artech Hse.

Toll-Free Travel & Vacation Information Directory. LC 87-32774. 40p. 1995. pap. 5.95 (*0-87576-169-0*) Pilot Bks.

***Toll-Free Traveler: The Complete (800) & (888) Directory for Pleasure & Business Travel.** Don W. Martin & Betty W. Martin. (Illus.). 160p. (Orig.). 1997. pap. 8.95 (*0-942053-22-2*) Pine Cone Pr CA.

Toll-Free U. S. A. 1997: A Directory of Toll-Free Telephone Numbers for Businesses & Organizations Nationwide. Ed. by Kay Gill. 1996. pap. 75.00 (*0-7808-0173-3*) Omnigraphics Inc.

Toll House Tried & True Recipes. Ruth G. Wakefeld. LC 77-23560. (Cookbook Ser.). 1977. reprint ed. pap. 6.95 (*0-486-23560-2*) Dover.

Toll of Victory. Annette Reid. LC 79-144169. (Short Story Index Reprint Ser.). 1977. reprint ed. 19.95 (*0-8369-3784-8*) Ayer.

Toll Section Supervisor. Jack Rudman. (Career Examination Ser.: C-1947). 1994. pap. 29.95 (*0-8373-1947-1*) Nat Learn.

***Tollbooths & Townhouses: Civic Architecture in Scotland to 1833.** Royal Commission. (Illus.). 192p. 1997. pap. 70.00 (*0-11-495799-1*, Pub. by Statnry Ofc UK) Seven Hills Bk.

Tollbridge. Wilma E. McDaniel. 32p. 1980. 3.00 (*0-936556-01-3*) Contact Two.

Tolley's Accounting for Pension Costs. Teresa Sienkiewicz & David Campbell. 272p. 1991. 75.00 (*0-85459-513-9*, Pub. by Tolley Pubng UK) St Mut.

T

Tolley's Accounting Principles for Tax Purposes. F. Michael Cochrane. 250p. (C). 1994. 105.00 (*0-85459-913-4*, Pub. by Tolley Pubng UK) St Mut.

Tolley's Administration of Small Self-Administered Pension Schemes: A Practical Guide to Director Plans. John Hayward. 280p. 1991. 100.00 (*0-85459-543-0*, Pub. by Tolley Pubng UK) St Mut.

Tolley's Administration of Small Self-Administered Pension Schemes: A Practical Guide to Director Plans. John Hayward. 300p. (C). 1994. 105.00 (*0-85459-879-0*, Pub. by Tolley Pubng UK) St Mut.

Tolley's Adviser's Guide to Investment Planning 1994-95. Richard Stevenson & Cherrill Braithwaite. 300p. (C). 1994. 100.00 (*0-85459-924-X*, Pub. by Tolley Pubng UK) St Mut.

Tolley's Anti-Avoidance Provisions. Robert W. Maas. 632p. 1992. 150.00 (*0-85459-519-8*, Pub. by Tolley Pubng UK) St Mut.

Tolley's Auditing Charities. Clark Whitehill. 150p. (C). 1994. 105.00 (*0-85459-884-7*, Pub. by Tolley Pubng UK) St Mut.

Tolley's Auditing Housing Associations. Touche Ross Intl. Staff & Trowers & Hamlins Staff. 150p. (C). 1994. 105.00 (*0-85459-961-4*, Pub. by Tolley Pubng UK) St Mut.

Tolley's Capital Allowances 1993-94. Patrick Noakes et al. 440p. 1993. 140.00 (*0-85459-783-2*, Pub. by Tolley Pubng UK) St Mut.

Tolley's Capital Allowances 1995-96. Patrick Noakes & Gary B. Mackley-Smith. 550p. 1995. 250.00 (*0-614-07525-4*, Pub. by Tolley Pubng UK) St Mut.

Tolley's Capital Gains Tax 1993-94. Patrick Noakes & Stephen Savory. 470p. 1993. 81.00 (*0-85459-772-7*, Pub. by Tolley Pubng UK) St Mut.

Tolley's Capital Gains Tax 1995-96. Patrick Noakes & Gary B. Mackley-Smith. 650p. 1995. 195.00 (*1-86012-010-5*, Pub. by Tolley Pubng UK) St Mut.

Tolley's Charities Handbook. Allan Hargreaves. 450p. (C). 1994. 200.00 (*0-85459-952-5*) St Mut.

Tolley's Child Care Law. Leo Goodman & Maggie Rae. 176p. (C). 1992. 135.00 (*0-85459-660-7*, Pub. by Tolley Pubng UK) St Mut.

Tolley's Commercial Loan Agreements. James R. Lingard. 136p. 1990. 105.00 (*0-85459-453-1*, Pub. by Tolley Pubng UK) St Mut.

Tolley's Companies Accounts Checklist 1993. Kpmg Peat Marwick Staff. 79p. 1993. 65.00 (*0-85459-701-8*, Pub. by Tolley Pubng UK) St Mut.

Tolley's Companies Accounts Checklist 1993 for Modified & Abbreviated Accounts of Small Companies. Kpmg Peat Marwick Staff. 1993. 39.00 (*0-85459-769-7*, Pub. by Tolley Pubng UK) St Mut.

Tolley's Companies Handbook. 2nd ed. Tolley Publ. Co. Ltd. Staff. 600p. 1993. 96.00 (*0-85459-702-6*, Pub. by Tolley Pubng UK) St Mut.

***Tolley's Company Law Handbook.** 3rd ed. Robert Wareham & David Smailes. 768p. 1996. pap. 175.00 (*1-86012-261-2*, Pub. by Tolley Pubng UK) St Mut.

Tolley's Company Secretary's Handbook. 3rd ed. Kpmg Peat Marwick Staff. 430p. 1993. 87.00 (*0-85459-742-5*, Pub. by Tolley Pubng UK) St Mut.

Tolley's Control of Chemicals at Work: A Manager's Guide. M. Hayes & N. J. Lungies. 110p. 1993. 60.00 (*0-85459-685-2*, Pub. by Tolley Pubng UK) St Mut.

Tolley's Corporate Insolvency Handbook. 2nd ed. Shashi Rajani et al. 795p. 1994. 195.00 (*0-85459-748-4*, Pub. by Tolley Pubng UK) St Mut.

Tolley's Corporation Tax 1995-96. Glyn Saunders & Alan Dolton. 550p. 1995. 195.00 (*1-86012-011-3*, Pub. by Tolley Pubng UK) St Mut.

Tolley's Director's Handbook. 2nd ed. Tolley Publ. Co. Ltd. Staff. 300p. 1993. 96.00 (*0-85459-746-8*, Pub. by Tolley Pubng UK) St Mut.

Tolley's Discrimination Law Handbook. Paul Nicholls. 304p. 1991. 66.00 (*0-85459-425-6*, Pub. by Tolley Pubng UK) St Mut.

Tolley's Double Taxation Agreement. Malcolm J. Finney. 250p. (C). 1994. 175.00 (*0-85459-914-2*, Pub. by Tolley Pubng UK) St Mut.

Tolley's Drafting Contracts of Employment. 2nd ed. Gillian Howard. 300p. 1993. 200.00 (*0-85459-687-9*, Pub. by Tolley Pubng UK) St Mut.

Tolley's Employment & Maternity Benefits. 3rd ed. Roger Self & Tolley Publ. Co. Ltd Staff. 300p. (C). 1994. 105.00 (*0-85459-632-1*, Pub. by Tolley Pubng UK) St Mut.

Tolley's Employment & Pension Rights in Corporate Insolvency. David Pollard. 364p. 1994. 300.00 (*0-85459-737-9*, Pub. by Tolley Pubng UK) St Mut.

Tolley's Employment Handbook. 8th ed. Elizabeth Slade & Nigel Giffin. 450p. 1993. 300.00 (*0-85459-528-7*, Pub. by Tolley Pubng UK) St Mut.

Tolley's Environmental Handbook. 1994. 175.00 (*0-85459-868-5*, Pub. by Tolley Pubng UK) St Mut.

Tolley's Environmental Handbook. Freshfield's Environmental Group Staff. 485p. 1993. pap. 210.00 (*0-85459-686-0*, Pub. by Tolley Pubng UK) St Mut.

Tolley's Estate Planning 1993-94. Price Waterhouse Staff. 450p. 1993. 90.00 (*0-85459-785-9*, Pub. by Tolley Pubng UK) St Mut.

Tolley's Estate Planning 1995-96. Price Waterhouse. 500p. 1995. 195.00 (*1-86012-031-8*, Pub. by Tolley Pubng UK) St Mut.

Tolley's Form & Content of Financial Statements. Neville Russell. 270p. (C). 1994. 90.00 (*0-85459-883-9*, Pub. by Tolley Pubng UK) St Mut.

Tolley's Guide to Self-Assessment for Employers & Employees. Peter Gravestock. 100p. 1995. 195.00 (*1-86012-033-4*, Pub. by Tolley Pubng UK) St Mut.

Tolley's Guide to Self-Assessment for the Self Employed. Peter Gravestock. 120p. (C). 1994. pap. 55.00 (*0-85459-915-0*, Pub. by Tolley Pubng UK) St Mut.

Tolley's Guide to Self-Assessment for the Self-Employed. Peter Gravestock. 120p. 1995. 195.00 (*1-86012-032-6*, Pub. by Tolley Pubng UK) St Mut.

Tolley's Guide to Statutory SickPay & Statutory Maternity Pay. 2nd ed. Roger Self. 216p. 1991. 84.00 (*0-85459-590-2*, Pub. by Tolley Pubng UK) St Mut.

Tolley's Health & Safety at Work Handbook 1994. Malcolm Dewis. 730p. 1993. 150.00 (*0-85459-745-X*, Pub. by Tolley Pubng UK) St Mut.

Tolley's Health & Safety at Work Handbook 1995. Malcolm. 900p. (C). 1994. 175.00 (*0-85459-945-2*, Pub. by Tolley Pubng UK) St Mut.

Tolley's Income Tax 1993-94. Glyn Sanders & David Smailes. 720p. 1993. 90.00 (*0-85459-770-0*, Pub. by Tolley Pubng UK) St Mut.

Tolley's Income Tax 1995-96. Glyn Saunders & David Smailes. 950p. 1995. 195.00 (*1-86012-008-3*, Pub. by Tolley Pubng UK) St Mut.

Tolley's Indemnities & Warranties. Tim Sanders & Philip Ridgway. 280p. 1992. 120.00 (*0-85459-557-0*, Pub. by Tolley Pubng UK) St Mut.

Tolley's Index to Companies Legislation. Josephine Joyce. 160p. 1990. 39.00 (*0-85459-438-8*, Pub. by Tolley Pubng UK) St Mut.

Tolley's Inheritance Tax 1993-94. Patrick Noakes & Stephen Savory. 260p. 1993. 72.00 (*0-85459-773-5*, Pub. by Tolley Pubng UK) St Mut.

Tolley's Inheritance Tax 1995-96. Patrick Noakes & Jon Golding. 270p. 1995. 195.00 (*1-86012-009-1*, Pub. by Tolley Pubng UK) St Mut.

Tolley's Insurance Handbook. Robert Merkin. 350p. (C). 1994. 105.00 (*0-85459-806-5*, Pub. by Tolley Pubng UK) St Mut.

Tolley's Interest & Penalty Provisions. John T. Newth. 350p. 1993. 105.00 (*0-85459-580-5*, Pub. by Tolley Pubng UK) St Mut.

Tolley's Intl. Tax Planning, 2 vols. Malcolm J. Finney. 1400p. 1993. pap. 255.00 (*0-85459-676-3*, Pub. by Tolley Pubng UK) St Mut.

Tolley's Manual of Accounting, Vol. I: Primarily Individual Companies. Coopers & Lybrand Staff. 1160p. 1990. 110.00 (*0-85459-473-6*, Pub. by Tolley Pubng UK) St Mut.

Tolley's Manual of Accounting, Vol. II: Groups of Companies. Coopers & Lybrand Staff. 576p. 1990. 60.00 (*0-85459-467-1*, Pub. by Tolley Pubng UK) St Mut.

Tolley's Manual of Accounting, Vol. III: Specialised Businesses. Coopers & Lybrand Staff. 1180p. 1991. 90.00 (*0-85459-474-4*, Pub. by Tolley Pubng UK) St Mut.

Tolley's National Insurance Contributions Legislation 1993-94. Robert Wareham. 600p. 1993. 66.00 (*0-85459-779-4*, Pub. by Tolley Pubng UK) St Mut.

Tolley's National Insurance Contributions 1993-94. Neil Booth. 500p. 1993. 96.00 (*0-85459-775-1*, Pub. by Tolley Pubng UK) St Mut.

Tolley's National Insurance Contributions 1995. Neil D. Booth. 500p. 1994. pap. 150.00 (*0-85459-894-4*, Pub. by Tolley Pubng UK) St Mut.

Tolley's National Insurance Contributions 1995-96. Neil D. Booth. Ed. by Jon Golding. 510p. 1995. 195.00 (*1-86012-013-X*, Pub. by Tolley Pubng UK) St Mut.

Tolley's Official Tax Statements 1995-96. Jacqueline Scott. 900p. 1995. 195.00 (*1-86012-035-0*, Pub. by Tolley Pubng UK) St Mut.

Tolley's Partnership Taxation. Arnold Homer & Rita Burrows. 272p. 1992. 90.00 (*0-85459-579-1*, Pub. by Tolley Pubng UK) St Mut.

Tolley's Partnership Taxation. Arnold Homer & Rita Burrows. 272p. (C). 1994. 110.00 (*0-85459-896-0*, Pub. by Tolley Pubng UK) St Mut.

Tolley's Pay & Benefits Handbook. Ed. by Brian Friedman & Martin Kaye. 230p. (C). 1994. 175.00 (*0-85459-927-4*, Pub. by Tolley Pubng UK) St Mut.

Tolley's Payroll Handbook 1994. Tolley Publ. Co. Ltd Staff. 500p. 1993. 96.00 (*0-85459-804-9*, Pub. by Tolley Pubng UK) St Mut.

***Tolley's Pension Fund Trustee Handbook.** Roger Self. 150p. 1995. pap. 125.00 (*0-614-19441-5*, Pub. by Tolley Pubng UK) St Mut.

***Tolley's Pensions Administration.** Roger Self et al. Ed. by Margaret Snowdon. 1996. write for info. (*0-614-19442-3*, Pub. by Tolley Pubng UK) St Mut.

Tolley's Pensions Handbook. 500p. 1993. 120.00 (*0-85459-585-6*, Pub. by Tolley Pubng UK) St Mut.

Tolley's Pensions Handbook. 2nd ed. Jonathan Fenton et al. 500p. (Orig.). (C). 1994. 210.00 (*0-85459-916-9*, Pub. by Tolley Pubng UK) St Mut.

Tolley's Personal Tax & Investment Planning 1993-94. Arthur Andersen. 220p. 1993. 90.00 (*0-85459-786-7*, Pub. by Tolley Pubng UK) St Mut.

Tolley's Practical Guide to Company Acquisitions. 3rd ed. Tolley Publ. Co. Ltd Staff. 300p. (C). 1994. 105.00 (*0-85459-793-X*, Pub. by Tolley Pubng UK) St Mut.

Tolley's Practical Guide to Employees Share Schemes. Colin E. Chamberlain. 250p. (C). 1994. 105.00 (*0-85459-818-9*, Pub. by Tolley Pubng UK) St Mut.

Tolley's Practical VAT Guide to VAT in 1993. Brian D. Toll. 1993. pap. 30.00 (*0-85459-736-0*, Pub. by Tolley Pubng UK) St Mut.

Tolley's Practice Development Handbook. Gavon I. Brookes. 70p. (C). 1994. 175.00 (*0-85459-857-X*, Pub. by Tolley Pubng UK) St Mut.

Tolley's Property Taxes 1993-94. Robert W. Maas. 460p. 1993. 80.00 (*0-85459-788-3*, Pub. by Tolley Pubng UK) St Mut.

Tolley's Property Taxes 1995-96. Robert W. Maas. 450p. 1995. 195.00 (*1-86012-036-9*, Pub. by Tolley Pubng UK) St Mut.

Tolley's Purchase & Sale of a Private Company's Share. Tony Foreman et al. 248p. (C). 1994. 105.00 (*0-614-00326-1*) St Mut.

Tolley's Purchase & Sale of a Private Company's Shares. Tony Foreman & David Adams. 248p. 1990. 110.00 (*0-85459-481-7*, Pub. by Tolley Pubng UK) St Mut.

Tolley's Purchase & Sale of a Private Company's Shares. 5th ed. Tony Foreman et al. 248p. (C). 1994. 105.00 (*0-85459-792-1*, Pub. by Tolley Pubng UK) St Mut.

Tolley's Roll-Over Hold-Over & Retirement Reliefs. K. R. Tingley. 400p. (C). 1994. 114.00 (*0-614-00329-6*) St Mut.

Tolley's Roll-Over, Hold-Over & Retirement Reliefs. 3rd ed. K. R. Tingley. 400p. 1993. 100.00 (*0-85459-794-8*, Pub. by Tolley Pubng UK) St Mut.

Tolley's Roll-Over, Hold-Over & Retirement Reliefs. 4th ed. K. R. Tingley. 400p. (C). 1994. 114.00 (*0-85459-898-7*, Pub. by Tolley Pubng UK) St Mut.

Tolley's Roll-Over, Hold-Over & Retirement Reliefs. K. R. Tingley. 540p. 1995. 195.00 (*1-86012-037-7*, Pub. by Tolley Pubng UK) St Mut.

Tolley's Schedule D. 2nd ed. David Smailes et al. 600p. (C). 1994. 120.00 (*0-85459-912-6*, Pub. by Tolley Pubng UK) St Mut.

Tolley's Self-Assessment. Jan Matthews & Nigel Eastaway. 280p. 1995. 195.00 (*1-86012-038-5*, Pub. by Tolley Pubng UK) St Mut.

Tolley's Simplified Assessing. Jan Mathews & Nigel Eastaway. 250p. (C). 1994. 105.00 (*0-614-00322-9*) St Mut.

Tolley's Simplified Assessing. Jim Matthews & Nigel Eastaway. 250p. (C). 1994. 105.00 (*0-85459-925-8*, Pub. by Tolley Pubng UK) St Mut.

Tolley's Social Security & State Benefits Handbook 1995-96. Jim Matthewman et al. 580p. 1995. pap. 310.00 (*1-86012-072-5*, Pub. by Tolley Pubng UK) St Mut.

Tolley's Social Security & State Benefits 1993-94. Jim Matthewman et al. 580p. 1993. 105.00 (*0-85459-744-1*, Pub. by Tolley Pubng UK) St Mut.

Tolley's Stamp Duties & Stamp Duty Reserve Tax. Patrick Cannon. 150p. 1993. 115.00 (*0-85459-796-4*, Pub. by Tolley Pubng UK) St Mut.

Tolley's Stamp Duties & Stamp Duty Reserve Tax. Patrick Cannon. 150p. 1995. 195.00 (*1-86012-071-7*, Pub. by Tolley Pubng UK) St Mut.

Tolley's Tax Appeals to the Commissioners. Eric Harvey. 136p. 1990. 48.00 (*0-85459-370-5*, Pub. by Tolley Pubng UK) St Mut.

Tolley's Tax Cases 1993. Alan Dolton & Glyn Saunders. 760p. 1993. 93.00 (*0-85459-696-8*, Pub. by Tolley Pubng UK) St Mut.

Tolley's Tax Cases 1995. Alan Dolton & Glyn Saunders. 750p. 1995. 195.00 (*0-85459-972-X*, Pub. by Tolley Pubng UK) St Mut.

Tolley's Tax Compliance & Investigations. David Jeffery et al. Ed. by Williams J. Barber. 424p. 1992. 105.00 (*0-85459-681-X*, Pub. by Tolley Pubng UK) St Mut.

Tolley's Tax Computations 1993-94. David Smailes et al. 580p. 1993. 102.00 (*0-85459-780-8*, Pub. by Tolley Pubng UK) St Mut.

Tolley's Tax Computations 1995-96. Robert Wareham et al. 620p. 1995. 195.00 (*1-86012-040-7*, Pub. by Tolley Pubng UK) St Mut.

Tolley's Tax Data 1993-94. Nicholas Bowen & Alan Dolton. 80p. 1993. 69.00 (*0-85459-699-2*, Pub. by Tolley Pubng UK) St Mut.

Tolley's Tax Guide 1993-94. Arnold Homer & Rita Burrows. 560p. 1993. 85.00 (*0-85459-726-3*, Pub. by Tolley Pubng UK) St Mut.

Tolley's Tax Guide 1994-95. Arnold Homer & Rita Burrows. 600p. 1994. 150.00 (*0-85459-877-4*, Pub. by Tolley Pubng UK) St Mut.

Tolley's Tax Guide 1995-96. Arnold Homer & Rita Burrows. 600p. 1995. 150.00 (*1-86012-014-8*, Pub. by Tolley Pubng UK) St Mut.

***Tolley's Tax Guide 1996-97.** Arnold Homer & Rita Burrows. 670p. 1996. 195.00 (*1-86012-284-1*, Pub. by Tolley Pubng UK) St Mut.

Tolley's Tax Havens. Tolley Publ. Co. Ltd. Staff. 600p. 1993. 150.00 (*0-85459-797-2*, Pub. by Tolley Pubng UK) St Mut.

Tolley's Tax Legislation 1993-94: Income Tax, Corporation Tax & Capital Gains Tax. Nicholas Bowen & Robert Wareham. 4000p. 1993. 96.00 (*0-85459-776-X*, Pub. by Tolley Pubng UK) St Mut.

Tolley's Tax Legislation 1993-94: Inheritance Tax. Nicholas Bowen. 320p. 1993. 75.00 (*0-85459-777-8*, Pub. by Tolley Pubng UK) St Mut.

Tolley's Tax Legislation 1993-94: Value Added Tax. Robert Wareham. 1000p. 1993. 66.00 (*0-85459-778-6*, Pub. by Tolley Pubng UK) St Mut.

***Tolley's Tax Office Directory 1996.** Ian Dodds. 100p. 1995. pap. 95.00 (*1-86012-055-5*, Pub. by Tolley Pubng UK) St Mut.

Tolley's Tax Planning for Family Companies. Gerry Hart & Peter Rayney. 300p. (C). 1994. 175.00 (*0-85459-675-5*, Pub. by Tolley Pubng UK) St Mut.

Tolley's Tax Planning for New Businesses. W. E. Pritchard. 150p. 1993. 90.00 (*0-85459-565-1*, Pub. by Tolley Pubng UK) St Mut.

Tolley's Tax Planning for Post Death Variations. Philip Laidlow. 150p. 1993. 90.00 (*0-85459-684-4*, Pub. by Tolley Pubng UK) St Mut.

Tolley's Tax Planning for Private Residences. Matthew Hutton. 248p. 1992. 98.00 (*0-85459-584-8*, Pub. by Tolley Pubng UK) St Mut.

Tolley's Tax Planning for Private Residences. 2nd ed. Matthew Hutton. 248p. (C). 1994. 115.00 (*0-85459-901-0*, Pub. by Tolley Pubng UK) St Mut.

Tolley's Tax Planning 1993-94. Tolley Publ. Co. Ltd. Staff. 1700p. 1993. 200.00 (*0-85459-784-0*, Pub. by Tolley Pubng UK) St Mut.

Tolley's Tax Planning 1994-95, 2 vols., Set. Tolley Publ. Co. Ltd. Staff. 1968p. 1994. pap. text ed. 300.00 (*0-85459-900-2*, Pub. by Tolley Pubng UK) St Mut.

Tolley's Tax Planning 1995-96. 968p. 1995. 195.00 (*1-86012-021-0*, Pub. by Tolley Pubng UK) St Mut.

Tolley's Tax Tables 1993-94. Peter Diggles & Jill Howis. 1993. 40.00 (*0-85459-695-X*, Pub. by Tolley Pubng UK) St Mut.

Tolley's Taxation in Corporate Insolvency. Anthony C. Davis. 288p. 1991. 105.00 (*0-85459-536-8*, Pub. by Tolley Pubng UK) St Mut.

Tolley's Taxation in Corporate Insolvency. Anthony C. Davis. 290p. (C). 1995. 195.00 (*0-85459-573-2*, Pub. by Tolley Pubng UK) St Mut.

Tolley's Taxation in the Channel Islands & Isle of Man 1995-96. Martin Shires & Guernsey K. Jones. 280p. 1995. 195.00 (*1-86012-020-2*, Pub. by Tolley Pubng UK) St Mut.

Tolley's Taxation in the Republic of Ireland 1995-96. Glyn Saunders. 380p. 1995. 195.00 (*1-86012-019-9*, Pub. by Tolley Pubng UK) St Mut.

Tolley's Taxation of Employments. Robert W. Maas. 352p. 1991. 90.00 (*0-85459-578-3*, Pub. by Tolley Pubng UK) St Mut.

Tolley's Taxation of Employments. Robert W. Maas. 420p. 1995. 195.00 (*1-86012-044-X*, Pub. by Tolley Pubng UK) St Mut.

Tolley's Taxation of Employments. 3rd ed. Robert W. Maas. 352p. (C). 1994. 105.00 (*0-85459-904-5*, Pub. by Tolley Pubng UK) St Mut.

Tolley's Taxation of Foreign Exchange Gains & Losses. Coopers & Lybrand Foreign Exchange Tax Team Staff. 432p. (C). 1995. 195.00 (*0-85459-851-0*, Pub. by Tolley Pubng UK) St Mut.

Tolley's Taxation of Intellectual Property. John Dixon & Kevin Thorne. 500p. (C). 1994. 175.00 (*0-85459-926-6*, Pub. by Tolley Pubng UK) St Mut.

Tolley's Taxation of Lloyd's Underwriters. David Harris. Ed. by Pannell K. Forster. 280p. 1994. 195.00 (*0-85459-791-3*, Pub. by Tolley Pubng UK) St Mut.

Tolley's Taxation of Losses. Paul Yerbury. 250p. (C). 1994. 175.00 (*0-85459-853-7*, Pub. by Tolley Pubng UK) St Mut.

Tolley's Taxation of Offshore Trusts & Funds. R. D. Fraser & J. R. Wood. 216p. 1992. 128.00 (*0-85459-566-X*, Pub. by Tolley Pubng UK) St Mut.

Tolley's Taxation of Trades & Professions. David Smailes et al. 544p. 1992. 108.00 (*0-85459-683-6*, Pub. by Tolley Pubng UK) St Mut.

Tolley's Taxes Management Provisions. Basil Sabines. 174p. 1991. 81.00 (*0-85459-583-X*, Pub. by Tolley Pubng UK) St Mut.

Tolley's Taxwise 1 1995-96. Arnold Homer & Rita Burrows. 705p. 1995. 195.00 (*1-86012-015-6*, Pub. by Tolley Pubng UK) St Mut.

Tolley's Taxwise 11 1995-96. Arnold Homer et al. 560p. 1995. 195.00 (*1-86012-016-4*, Pub. by Tolley Pubng UK) St Mut.

Tolley's Taxwise 1993-94: Taxwise I. Arnold Homer et al. 670p. 1993. 75.00 (*0-85459-781-6*, Pub. by Tolley Pubng UK) St Mut.

Tolley's Taxwise 1993-94: Taxwise II. Arnold Homer et al. 500p. 1993. 72.00 (*0-85459-782-4*, Pub. by Tolley Pubng UK) St Mut.

Tolley's Trading in Europe: A Guide to Business & Taxation. John C. Dixon. 448p. 1992. 140.00 (*0-85459-569-4*, Pub. by Tolley Pubng UK) St Mut.

Tolley's U. K. Taxation of Trusts. Tony Sherring & Ian Ferrier. 230p. 1995. 195.00 (*1-86012-054-7*, Pub. by Tolley Pubng UK) St Mut.

Tolley's U. K. Taxation of Trusts. 4th ed. Tony Sherring & Ian Ferrier. 220p. (C). 1994. 111.00 (*0-85459-907-X*, Pub. by Tolley Pubng UK) St Mut.

Tolley's UK Taxation of Trusts. Tony Sherring & Ian Ferrier. 220p. 1993. 108.00 (*0-85459-812-X*, Pub. by Tolley Pubng UK) St Mut.

Tolley's Understanding Occupational Pension Schemes. 5th ed. Maurice Oldfield. Orig. Title: Tolley's Understanding Pension Schemes. 150p. (C). 1994. 60.00 (*1-85190-878-1*, Pub. by Tolley Pubng UK) St Mut.

Tolley's Understanding Occupational Pension Schemes. 5th ed. Ed. by Maurice Oldfield. Orig. Title: Tolley's Understanding Pension Schemes. 150p. 1994. 60.00 (*0-614-07526-2*, Pub. by Tolley Pubng UK) St Mut.

Tolley's Understanding Pension Schemes see Tolley's Understanding Occupational Pension Schemes

Tolley's Value Added Tax 1993-94. Robert Wareham & Nicholas Bowen. 700p. 1993. 81.00 (*0-85459-774-3*, Pub. by Tolley Pubng UK) St Mut.

Tolley's Value Added Tax 1995-96. Robert Wareham. 800p. 1995. 195.00 (*1-86012-012-1*, Pub. by Tolley Pubng UK) St Mut.

***Tolley's Value Added Tax 1996-97.** Robert Wareham & Alan Dotton. 760p. 1996. pap. 195.00 (*1-86012-277-9*, Pub. by Tolley Pubng UK) St Mut.

Tolley's VAT & Duties Appeals. Penny Hamilton. Ed. by Allan Dolton. 250p. 1996. pap. 195.00 (*1-86012-174-8*, Pub. by Tolley Pubng UK) St Mut.

Tolley's VAT & Retailers. Ian Somerville. 200p. (C). 1994. 175.00 (*0-85459-928-2*, Pub. by Tolley Pubng UK) St Mut.

Tolley's Vat & the Partial Exemption Rules. Peter Sheppard. 120p. (C). 1995. 195.00 (*0-85459-930-4*, Pub. by Tolley Pubng UK) St Mut.

Tolley's Vat & the Partial Exemption Rules. 2nd ed. Peter Sheppard. 100p. 1994. 195.00 (*0-85458-930-9*, Pub. by Tolley Pubng UK) St Mut.

Tolley's VAT Cases 1993. Alan Dolton & Robert Wareham. 850p. 1993. 195.00 (*0-85459-697-6*, Pub. by Tolley Pubng UK) St Mut.

An Asterisk (*) at the beginning of an entry indicates that the title is appearing in BIP for the first time.

Tolley's VAT Cases 1995. Alan Dolton & Robert Wareham. 990p. 1995. 195.00 (*0-85459-975-4*, Pub. by Tolley Pubng UK) St Mut.

Tolley's VAT in Europe. Nexia International Staff. 200p. (C). 1994. 105.00 (*0-85459-849-9*, Pub. by Tolley Pubng UK) St Mut.

Tolley's Vat in Europe. Nexia International Staff. 200p. (C). 1994. 105.00 (*0-614-00331-8*) St Mut.

Tolley's VAT on Construction, Land & Property. Alan Buckett. 216p. 1991. 72.00 (*0-85459-537-6*, Pub. by Tolley Pubng UK) St Mut.

Tolley's VAT on Construction, Land & Property. Robert Crooks. 220p. 1995. 195.00 (*1-86012-045-8*, Pub. by Tolley Pubng UK) St Mut.

Tolley's VAT on Construction Land & Property. 3rd ed. Robert Crooks. 220p. (C). 1994. 175.00 (*0-85459-700-X*, Pub. by Tolley Pubng UK) St Mut.

Tolley's VAT Penalty & Compliance Provisions. 3rd ed. Lesley Lloyd-Eley. 200p. 1994. 175.00 (*0-85459-805-7*, Pub. by Tolley Pubng UK) St Mut.

Tolley's VAT Planning 1993-94. Tolley Publ. Co. Ltd. Staff. 600p. 1993. 110.00 (*0-85459-790-5*, Pub. by Tolley Pubng UK) St Mut.

Tolley's VAT Planning 1995-96. 770p. 1995. 195.00 (*1-86012-046-6*, Pub. by Tolley Pubng UK) St Mut.

Tolliver. Paul A. Hawkins. 352p. (Orig.). 1994. pap. 4.50 (*0-451-17881-5*, Sig) NAL-Dutton.

Tolly in the Loblolly. Helen D. Turley. 40p. (J). 1993. text ed. 9.95 (*1-882194-02-0*) TN Valley Pub.

Tolmar Trust. large type ed. Hilary Grenville. (Linford Mystery Library). 416p. 1996. pap. 15.99 (*0-7089-7874-6*, Linford) Ulverscroft.

Tolowa & Their Southwest Oregon Kin. fac. ed. Philip Drucker. (University of California Publications in American Archaeology & Ethnology: Vol. 36: 4). (Illus.). 86p. (C). 1937. reprint ed. pap. text ed. 7.75 (*1-55567-305-8*) Coyote Press.

Tolpuddle Woman. large type ed. E. V. Thompson. 784p. 1996. 27.99 (*0-7089-8858-X*, Charnwood) Ulverscroft.

Tolstaia: Three Stories - Tri Rasskasa. Ed. by S. Dalton-Brown. (Russian Texts Ser.). 88p. (RUS.). 1996. pap. 14. 95 (*1-85399-475-8*, Pub. by Brstl Class Pr UK) Focus Pub-R Pullins.

Tolstoi. Edward Garnett. LC 74-7035. (Studies in Tolstoy: No. 62). 1974. lib. bdg. 49.95 (*0-8383-1970-X*) M S G Haskell Hse.

Tolstoi & Britain. Ed. by W. Gareth Jones & Anthony Cross. (Anglo-Russian Affinities Ser.). (Illus.). 320p. 1995. 45.95 (*1-85973-028-0*) Berg Pubs.

Tolstoi As Man & Artist. Dmitri S. Merezhkovsky. LC 69-13996. 310p. 1970. reprint ed. text ed. 59.75 (*0-8371-4098-6*, METO, Greenwood Pr) Greenwood.

Tolstoi the Man. Edward A. Steiner. LC 70-92986. (Studies in Philosophy: No. 40). 1969. reprint ed. lib. bdg. 64.95 (*0-8383-1006-0*) M S G Haskell Hse.

Tolstoi the Teacher. C. Baudouin. 1973. 59.95 (*0-8490-1218-X*) Gordon Pr.

Tolstoi's Death of Ivan Ilych: And Commentary. Ed. by Arthur C. Carr. Tr. by Aylmer Maud. LC 73-9700. 94p. 1973. pap. 4.95 (*0-930194-75-6*) Ctr Thanatology.

Tolstoy. Gerald Abraham. LC 74-7018. (Studies in Tolstoy: No. 62). 1974. lib. bdg. 49.95 (*0-8383-1965-3*) M S G Haskell Hse.

Tolstoy. Henry B. Stevens. 1973. 59.95 (*0-8490-1219-8*) Gordon Pr.

Tolstoy: "Anna Karenina" Anthony Thorlby. (Landmarks of World Literature Ser.). 128p. 1987. text ed. 29.95 (*0-521-32819-5*); pap. text ed. 11.95 (*0-521-31325-2*) Cambridge U Pr.

Tolstoy: Art Time. 226p. 1981. 110.00 (*0-317-40658-2*) St Mut.

Tolstoy: Childhood (Detstvo) Ed. by M. Pursglove. (Bristol Russian Texts Ser.). 152p. (RUS.). 1993. pap. 15.95 (*1-85399-294-1*, Pub. by Brstl Class Pr UK) Focus Pub-R Pullins.

Tolstoy: His Life & Works. John C. Kenworthy. LC 70-155115. (Studies in European Literature: No. 56). 1971. reprint ed. lib. bdg. 62.95 (*0-8383-1287-X*) M S G Haskell Hse.

Tolstoy: Literary Fragments, Letters & Reminiscences. Leo Tolstoy. Ed. by Rene Fullop-Miller. LC 68-57229. reprint ed. 57.50 (*0-404-06479-5*) AMS Pr.

Tolstoy: Plays, 1886-1889. Leo Tolstoy. Tr. by Marvin Kantor. (European Drama Classics Ser.: Vol. 2). 176p. 1996. text ed. 59.95 (*0-8101-1394-5*) Northwestern U Pr.

Tolstoy: Plays, 1886-1889. Leo Tolstoy. Tr. by Marvin Kantor. (European Drama Classics Ser.: Vol. 2). 176p. 1996. pap. text ed. 15.95 (*0-8101-1395-3*) Northwestern U Pr.

Tolstoy: Principles for a New World Order. David Redfearn. 196p. 1994. pap. text ed. 18.95 (*0-85683-134-4*, Pub. by Shepheard-Walwyn Pubs UK) Paul & Co Pubs.

Tolstoy: Principles for a New World Order. David Redfearn. 196p. 1992. pap. 18.95 (*0-685-70315-0*) Schalkenbach.

Tolstoy: Sebastopol in December (Sevastopol' V Dekabre Mesyatse) Ed. by M. Pursglove. (Bristol Russian Texts Ser.). (RUS.). 1994. pap. 15.95 (*1-85399-353-0*, Pub. by Brstl Class Pr UK) Focus Pub-R Pullins.

Tolstoy: Tales of Courage & Conflict. Ed. by Charles Neider. 578p. 1985. pap. 11.95 (*0-88184-165-X*) Carroll & Graf.

Tolstoy: The Critical Heritage. Ed. by A. V. Knowles. 1978. 69.50 (*0-7100-8947-3*, RKP) Routledge.

Tolstoy: The Death of Ivan Ilyich (Smert' Ivana Il'icha) Ed. by M. Beresford. (Bristol Russian Texts Ser.). (RUS.). 1992. pap. 17.95 (*1-85399-359-X*, Pub. by Brstl Class Pr UK) Focus Pub-R Pullins.

Tolstoy: What Is Art? L. Tolstoy. Tr. by W. Gareth Jones. (Bristol Russian Texts Ser.). 246p. (ENG & RUS.). 1994. pap. 19.95 (*1-85399-381-6*, Pub. by Brstl Class Pr UK) Focus Pub-R Pullins.

Tolstoy & Chekhov. Logan Speirs. LC 79-120195. 245p. reprint ed. pap. 69.90 (*0-317-20629-X*, 2024583) Bks Demand.

Tolstoy & Education. Daniel Murphy. 304p. 1992. 45.00 (*0-7165-2484-8*, Pub. by Irish Acad Pr IE) Intl Spec Bk.

Tolstoy & His Problems. Aylmer Maude. 1973. 250.00 (*0-8490-1220-1*) Gordon Pr.

Tolstoy & His Problems. Aylmer Maude. LC 74-7137. (Studies in Tolstoy: No. 62). 1974. lib. bdg. 75.00 (*0-8383-1999-8*) M S G Haskell Hse.

Tolstoy & India. 2nd ed. Alexander Shifman. 1978. 6.00 (*0-8364-1586-8*, Pub. by National Sahitya Akademi II) S Asia.

Tolstoy & Nietzsche. Helen E. Davis. LC 72-119083. (Studies in Comparative Literature: No. 35). 1970. reprint ed. lib. bdg. 59.95 (*0-8383-1079-6*) M S G Haskell Hse.

Tolstoy & the Genesis of "War & Peace" Katherine B. Feuer. Ed. by Robin F. Miller & Donna T. Orwin. LC 96-24057. 304p. 1996. 29.95 (*0-8014-1902-6*) Cornell U Pr.

Tolstoy & the Novel. John O. Bayley. iv, 320p. 1988. pap. 16.95 (*0-226-03960-9*) U Ch Pr.

***Tolstoy at Yasnaya Polyanna.** George Woodcock. 120p. 1991. pap. 12.95 (*1-55082-005-2*, Pub. by Quarry Pr CN) LPC InBook.

Tolstoy Foundation, Inc: History, Aims & Achievements. Tolstoy Foundation, Inc. Staff. (Illus.). 48p. 1976. 3.00 (*0-686-16259-5*) Tolstoy Found.

Tolstoy in Prerevolutionary Russian Criticism. Boris Sorokin. LC 78-31289. 339p. 1979. 39.00 (*0-8142-0295-0*) Ohio St U Pr.

Tolstoy on Art. Aylmer Maude. LC 72-2134. (Studies in European Literature: No. 56). 1972. reprint ed. lib. bdg. 75.00 (*0-8383-1459-7*) M S G Haskell Hse.

Tolstoy on Education: Tolstoy's Educational Writings, 1861-62. Ed. by Alan Pinch & Michael Armstrong. LC 81-65867. 336p. 1982. 44.50 (*0-8386-3121-5*) Fairleigh Dickinson.

***Tolstoy or Dostoevsky: An Essay in the Old Criticism.** George Steiner. 384p. 1996. pap. 17.00 (*0-300-06917-0*) Yale U Pr.

Tolstoy Plays, Vol. One: 1856-1886. Leo Tolstoy. Tr. by Marvin Kantor & Tanya Tulchinsky from RUS. (European Drama Classics Ser.). 150p. 1994. 49.95 (*0-8101-1109-8*); pap. 14.95 (*0-8101-1110-1*) Northwestern U Pr.

Tolstoy Story Play. V. Glasgow Koste. 37p. 1991. pap. 3.45 (*0-87129-043-X*, T84) Dramatic Pub.

***Tolstoy, the Inconstant Genius: A Biography.** Alexandra I. Nazaroff. 351p. Date not set. 27.95 (*0-8369-6619-8*) Ayer.

Tolstoy the Rebel. Leo Hecht. (Illus.). 400p. 1975. lib. bdg. 250.00 (*0-87700-222-3*) Revisionist Pr.

***Tolstoy, Woman, & Death: A Study of War & Peace & Anna Karenina.** David Holbrook. LC 96-38804. 272p. 1997. 41.50 (*0-8386-3701-9*) Fairleigh Dickinson.

Tolstoy's Aesthetics & His Art. Rimvydas Silbajoris. 319p. 1991. 24.95 (*0-89357-216-0*) Slavica.

Tolstoy's Art & Thought, 1847-1880. Donna T. Orwin. LC 92-37860. 296p. (C). 1993. text ed. 39.50 (*0-691-06991-3*) Princeton U Pr.

Tolstoy's Childhood: Critical Study. G. Williams. (Critical Studies in Russian Literature Ser.). 128p. 1995. pap. 13. 95 (*1-85399-383-2*, Pub. by Brstl Class Pr UK) Focus Pub-R Pullins.

***Tolstoy's Diaries.** Leo Tolstoy. Ed. & Tr. by R. F. Christian. 606p. 1996. 41.00 (*0-614-22050-5*) Borgo Pr.

Tolstoy's Message for Our Times. Francis Neilson. 1979. lib. bdg. 39.00 (*0-685-96643-7*) Revisionist Pr.

Tolstoy's Pierre Bezukhov: A Psychoanalytic Study. Daniel Rancour-Laferriere. 257p. 1993. 65.95 (*1-85399-362-X*, Pub. by Brstl Class Pr UK) Focus Pub-R Pullins.

Tolstoy's Short Stories. Leo Tolstoy. Ed. by Michael R. Katz. (Critical Editions Ser.). (Orig.). (C). 1990. pap. text ed. 11.95 (*0-393-96016-1*) Norton.

Tolstoy's Translation of the Gospels: A Critical Study. David Matual. LC 92-6906. 212p. 1992. lib. bdg. 89.95 (*0-7734-9502-9*) E Mellen.

Tolstoy's "What Is Art?" An Essay in the Philosophy of Art. T. J. Diffey. LC 85-16667. 240p. 1986. 39.50 (*0-7099-0891-1*, Pub. by Croom Helm UK) Routledge Chapman & Hall.

Toltec Heritage: From the Fall of Tula to the Rise of Tenochtitlan. Nigel Davies. LC 78-21384. (Civilization of the American Indian Ser.: Vol. 153). (Illus.). 1980. 29. 95 (*0-8061-1505-X*) U of Okla Pr.

Toltec Path: A User's Guide to the Teachings of Don Juan Matus, Carlos Castaneda & Other Toltec Seers. Ken Eagle Feather. 274p. (Orig.). 1995. pap. 12.95 (*1-57174-023-6*) Hampton Roads Pub Co.

Toltecs of the New Millennium. Victor Sanchez. Tr. by Robert Nelson from SPA. 228p. (Orig.). 1996. reprint ed. pap. 14.00 (*1-879181-35-5*) Bear & Co.

Toluca Street. Maxine Scates. LC 89-4859. (Poetry Ser.). 104p. 1989. 19.95 (*0-8229-3623-2*); pap. 10.95 (*0-8229-5420-6*) U of Pittsburgh Pr.

Toluene. (Environmental Health Criteria Ser.: No. 52). 146p. 1985. pap. text ed. 23.00 (*92-4-154192-X*, 1160052) World Health.

***Toluene Diisocyanates.** WHO Staff. (Environmental Health Criteria Ser.: No. 75). 72p. 1987. 15.00 (*92-4-154275-6*) World Health.

***Tom.** Tomie De Paola. (Illus.). 32p. (Orig.). (J). (ps-3). 1997. pap. 5.95 (*0-698-11448-5*, Paperstar) Putnam Pub Group.

Tom. Tomie Depaola. (Illus.). 32p. (J). (ps-3). 1993. lib. bdg. 15.95 (*0-399-22417-3*, Putnam) Putnam Pub Group.

Tom. Lyle Leverich. LC 95-6038. (Illus.). 644p. 1995. 35.00 (*0-517-70225-8*, Crown); 30.00 (*0-614-15414-6*, Crown) Crown Pub Group.

***Tom.** Daniel Torres. 1997. 19.95 (*84-7904-244-3*) Lectorum Pubns.

Tom. Daniel Torres. (Illus.). 64p. (J). (PS-3). 1996. pap. 15. 99 (*0-670-86665-2*) Viking Child Bks.

***Tom: The Unknown Tennessee Williams.** Lyle Leverich. (Illus.). 644p. (C). 1997. pap. 18.00 (*0-393-31663-7*) Norton.

Tom a Lincoln. Ed. by G. R. Proudfoot. (Malone Society Reprints Ser.: No. 153). 120p. 1992. 45.00 (*0-19-729030-2*) OUP.

Tom & Huck. Liz Fox. LC 95-74736. 64p. (J). (gr. 2-6). 1995. pap. 4.95 (*0-7868-4064-1*) Disney Pr.

***Tom & Huck.** Michael Lancy & Chuck Lakin. 64p. 1983. pap. 5.00 (*1-890298-06-9*) Centerstage Pr.

Tom & I on the Old Plantation. Archibald Rutledge. LC 72-4643. (Black Heritage Library Collection). (Illus.). 1977. reprint ed. 18.95 (*0-8369-9124-9*) Ayer.

Tom & Jerry: Skate, Rattle & Roll. Bedrock Staff. 1995. 4.98 (*1-57036-246-7*, Bedrock Press) Turner Pub GA.

Tom & Jerry: The Midnight Snack. Bedrock Staff. 1995. 4.98 (*1-57036-248-3*, Bedrock Press) Turner Pub GA.

***Tom & Jerry, Friends to the End.** Adapted by Wendy Wax. (Illus.). 96p. (J). 4.98 (*0-8317-6677-8*) Smithmark.

Tom & Kate & the Mysterious Cave. Sarah Wong. (J). (gr. 2-7). 1995. 7.95 (*0-533-11203-6*) Vantage.

Tom & Patti Mount's Dive & Travel Florida's Gold Coast. Tom Mount et al. (Illus.). 86p. pap. 9.95 (*0-915539-02-0*) Sea-Mount Pub Co.

Tom & Patti Mount's Dive & Travel Haiti. Tom Mount & Patti Mount. (Illus.). 86p. pap. 9.95 (*0-915539-03-9*) Sea-Mount Pub Co.

Tom & Pippo & the Bicycle. Helen Oxenbury. LC 92-42379. (Illus.). 24p. (J). (ps). 1997. reprint ed. pap. 3.99 (*0-7636-0162-4*) Candlewick Pr.

Tom & Pippo at the Beach. Helen Oxenbury. LC 92-53130. (Illus.). 24p. (J). (ps). 1997. reprint ed. pap. 3.99 (*0-7636-0163-2*) Candlewick Pr.

Tom & Pippo Go Shopping. Helen Oxenbury. LC 88-10497. (Tom & Pippo Bks.). (Illus.). 14p. (J). (ps-1). 1989. reprint ed. pap. 5.95 (*0-689-71278-2*, Aladdin Paperbacks) S&S Childrens.

Tom & Pippo in the Garden. Helen Oxenbury. LC 88-9145. (Tom & Pippo Bks.). (Illus.). 14p. (J). (ps-1). 1989. reprint ed. pap. 5.95 (*0-689-71275-8*, Aladdin Paperbacks) S&S Childrens.

Tom & Pippo on the Beach. Helen Oxenbury. LC 92-53130. (Illus.). 24p. (J). (ps). 1993. 5.95 (*1-56402-181-5*) Candlewick Pr.

Tom & Pippo See the Moon. Helen Oxenbury. (Tom & Pippo Bks.). (Illus.). 14p. (J). (ps-1). 1989. reprint ed. pap. 5.95 (*0-689-71277-4*, Aladdin Paperbacks) S&S Childrens.

Tom & Ricky Mystery Series, 9 sets, 5 different novels per set. Bob Wright. (Illus.). (J). (gr. 1-5). 1983. Set 1. pap. 17.00 (*0-87879-326-7*) High Noon Bks.

Tom & Ricky Mystery Series, 9 sets, 5 different novels per set. Bob Wright. (Illus.). (J). (gr. 1-5). 1983. Set 2. pap. 17.00 (*0-87879-336-4*) High Noon Bks.

Tom & Ricky Mystery Series, 9 sets, 5 different novels per set. Bob Wright. (Illus.). (J). (gr. 1-5). 1983. Set 3. pap. 17.00 (*0-87879-357-7*); Set 4. pap. 17.00 (*0-87879-363-1*) High Noon Bks.

Tom & Ricky Mystery Series, 9 sets, 5 different novels per set. Bob Wright. (Illus.). (J). (gr. 1-5). 1984. Set 5. pap. 17.00 (*0-87879-390-9*); Set 6. pap. 17.00 (*0-87879-396-8*) High Noon Bks.

Tom & Ricky Mystery Series, 9 sets, 5 different novels per set. Bob Wright. (Illus.). (J). (gr. 1-5). 1984. Set 7. pap. 17.00 (*0-87879-419-0*); Set 8. pap. 17.00 (*0-87879-425-5*) High Noon Bks.

Tom & the Boys. Dave Klein. 1990. 18.95 (*0-8217-3184-X*, Zebra Kensgtn) Kensgtn Pub Corp.

Tom & the Boys. Dave Klein. 1991. mass mkt. 4.95 (*0-8217-3511-X*, Zebra Kensgtn) Kensgtn Pub Corp.

Tom Ashley, Sam McGee, Bukka White: Tennessee Traditional Singers. Ed. by Thomas G. Burton. LC 79-19655. (Illus.). 251p. reprint ed. pap. 71.60 (*0-8357-6539-3*, 2035901) Bks Demand.

***Tom, Babette, & Simon: Three Tales of Transformation.** Avi. 112p. (J). 1997. mass mkt. 4.50 (*0-380-72770-6*, Camelot) Avon.

Tom, Babette, & Simon: Three Tales of Transformation. Avi. (Illus.). 43p. (J). 1995. 15.00 (*0-02-707765-9*, Mac Bks Young Read) S&S Childrens.

***Tom Baril "Photographs"** Photos by Tom Baril. (Illus.). 178p. 1997. 65.00 (*0-9657450-0-7*) Four AD US.

Tom-Based Project Planning. D. Kimbler & W. Ferrell. (Illus.). 320p. 1996. 59.95 (*0-412-58860-9*) Chapman & Hall.

Tom Benton & His Drawings: A Biographical Essay & Collection of His Sketches, Studies & Mural Cartoons. Karal A. Marling. LC 85-992. (Illus.). 232p. 1985. text ed. 37.50 (*0-8262-0480-5*) U of Mo Pr.

Tom Bethany, No. 2. 1994. pap. 4.99 (*0-671-74570-0*) S&S Trade.

Tom Brace Who He Was & How He Fared. Horatio Alger, Jr. (Works of Horatio Alger Jr.). 1989. reprint ed. lib. bdg. 79.00 (*0-685-27549-3*) Rprt Serv.

Tom Bradley: The Impossible Dream. J. Gregory Payne & Scott C. Ratzan. LC 85-52373. (Illus.). 384p. 1986. pap. 24.95 (*0-915677-29-6*) Roundtable Pub.

Tom Bradley's Campaign for Governor: The Dilemma of Race & Political Strategies. Thomas F. Pettigrew & Denise A. Alston. 96p. 1988. pap. 16.25 (*0-941410-63-3*) Jt Ctr Pol Studies.

Tom Brown's Field Guide to City & Suburban Survival, Vol. 3. Tom Brown, Jr. & Brandt Morgan. 288p. (Orig.). 1986. pap. 12.00 (*0-425-09172-4*) Berkley Pub.

Tom Brown's Field Guide to Living with the Earth. Tom Brown, Jr. & Brandt Morgan. (Illus.). 288p. 1986. pap. 12.00 (*0-425-09147-3*, Berkley Trade) Berkley Pub.

Tom Brown's Field Guide to Nature & Survival for Children. Tom Brown, Jr. (Tom Brown's Field Guide Ser.: No. 7). (J). 1989. pap. 12.00 (*0-425-11106-7*, Berkley Trade) Berkley Pub.

Tom Brown's Field Guide to Nature Observation & Tracking. Tom Brown, Jr. & Brandt Morgan. 256p. 1986. pap. 12.00 (*0-425-09966-0*, Berkley Trade) Berkley Pub.

Tom Brown's Guide to Wild Edible & Medicinal Plants. Tom Brown, Jr. 288p. 1986. pap. 12.00 (*0-425-10063-4*, Berkley Trade) Berkley Pub.

Tom Brown's Guide to Wilderness Survival. Tom Brown, Jr. & Brandt Morgan. (Illus.). 240p. (Orig.). 1987. pap. 12.00 (*0-425-10572-5*, Berkley Trade) Berkley Pub.

Tom Brown's School Days. Thomas Hughes. (Airmont Classics Ser.). (J). (gr. 7 up). 1968. mass mkt. 1.95 (*0-8049-0174-0*, CL-174) Airmont.

Tom Brown's School Days. Thomas Hughes. (J). 1997. pap. 2.95 (*0-8167-1461-4*) Troll Communs.

Tom Brown's School Days. Thomas Hughes. (J). 1987. reprint ed. lib. bdg. 21.95 (*0-89966-554-3*) Buccaneer Bks.

Tom Brown's Schooldays. Thomas P. Hughes. Ed. by Andrew Sanders. (World's Classics Ser.). (Illus.). 456p. (YA). 1989. pap. 4.95 (*0-19-282198-9*) OUP.

Tom Brown's Schooldays. large type ed. Thomas Hughes. 1988. 27.99 (*0-7089-8506-8*) Ulverscroft.

Tom Chapin: Zig Zag. (Illus.). 112p. (Orig.). (J). (gr. 3 up). pap. 14.95 (*0-89524-896-4*, HL02502144) H Leonard.

Tom Chaton. Beatrix Potter. (Illus.). 58p. (FRE.). (J). 1980. 9.95 (*0-7859-3626-2*, 2070560715) Fr & Eur.

Tom Chaton. Beatrix Potter. (Gallimard Ser.). 58p. (FRE.). (J). 1980. 10.95 (*2-07-056071-6*) Schoenhof.

Tom Clancy: A Critical Companion. Helen S. Garson. LC 95-50454. (Critical Companions to Popular Contemporary Writers Ser.). 192p. 1996. text ed. 29.95 (*0-313-29505-0*, Greenwood Pr) Greenwood.

Tom Clancy Companion. Ed. by Martin H. Greenberg. 368p. (Orig.). 1992. pap. 12.95 (*0-425-13407-5*) Berkley Pub.

***Tom Clancy's Net Force: Young Adult No. 1.** 1998. mass mkt. write for info. (*0-425-16173-0*) Berkley Pub.

***Tom Clancy's Net Force: Young Adult No. 2.** 1998. mass mkt. write for info. (*0-425-16174-9*) Berkley Pub.

***Tom Clancy's Op-Center: Acts of War.** Tom Clancy & Steve Pieczenik. 1997. mass mkt. 6.99 (*0-425-15601-X*) Berkley Pub.

***Tom Clancy's Op-Center: Games of State.** large type ed. Tom Clancy & Steve R. Pieczenik. LC 96-41769. (Basic Ser.). 632p. 1997. lib. bdg. 26.95 (*0-7862-0912-7*) Thorndike Pr.

***Tom Clancy's Op-Center: Games of State.** large type ed. Tom Clancy & Steve R. Pieczenik. LC 96-41769. 1997. pap. 20.00 (*0-7862-0913-5*) Thorndike Pr.

Tom Clancy's Op-Center: Mirror Image, Vol. II. Tom Clancy & Steve Pieczenik. (Op-Center Ser.). 448p. 1995. mass mkt. 6.99 (*0-425-15014-3*) Berkley Pub.

Tom Clancy's Op-Center I. Created by Tom Clancy & Steve Pieczenik. (Op-Center Ser.). 387p. 1995. mass mkt. 6.99 (*0-425-14736-3*) Berkley Pub.

Tom Clancy's Op-Center I. large type ed. Created by Tom Clancy & Steve Pieczenik. LC 95-17609. (Op-Center Ser.). 1996. lib. bdg. 22.95 (*0-7862-0492-3*) Thorndike Pr.

Tom Clancy's Op-Center I. large type ed. Created by Tom Clancy & Steve Pieczenik. (Op-Center Ser.). 1995. 25.95 (*0-7862-0491-5*) Thorndike Pr.

Tom Clancy's Op-Center II: Mirror Image. large type ed. Tom Clancy & Steve Pieczenik. (Thorndike Basic Ser.). 1996. text ed. 25.95 (*0-7862-0617-9*, Thorndike Lrg Prnt) Thorndike Pr.

Tom Clancy's Op-Center II: Mirror Image. large type ed. Tom Clancy & Steve Pieczenik. (Thorndike Basic Ser.). 1996. pap. 23.95 (*0-7862-0618-7*, Thorndike Lrg Prnt) Thorndike Pr.

Tom Corkery's Dublin. Tom Corkery. (Illus.). 128p. 1989. reprint ed. pap. 15.95 (*0-900068-75-2*, Pub. by Anvil Bks Ltd IE) Irish Bks Media.

Tom Cruise. Julie S. Bach. LC 93-1981. (Reaching for the Stars Ser.). (J). (gr. 4 up). 1993. lib. bdg. 13.98 (*1-56239-228-X*) Abdo & Dghtrs.

Tom Cruise: Unauthorised. Wensley Clarkson. 1996. 24.95 (*1-85782-086-X*, Pub. by Blake Publng UK) Seven Hills Bk.

Tom Disch Checklist. Compiled by Chris Drumm. (Booklet Ser.: No. 4). 24p. 1983. pap. 1.00 (*0-936055-02-2*) C Drumm Bks.

***Tom Doesn't Visit Us Anymore.** Maryleah Otto. (Illus.). 24p. (J). reprint ed. pap. 4.95 (*0-88961-117-3*, Pub. by Wmns Pr CN) LPC InBook.

Tom Edison's Bright Idea. Jack Keller. (Real Readers Ser.: Level Green). (Illus.). 32p. (J). (gr. 1-4). 1989. lib. bdg. 19.97 (*0-8172-3532-9*) Raintree Steck-V.

Tom Edison's Bright Idea. Jack Keller. (Real Readers Ser.: Level Green). (Illus.). 32p. (J). (gr. 1-4). 1989. pap. 4.95 (*0-8114-6733-3*) Raintree Steck-V.

Tom Foolery. Curtis Parkinson. LC 92-7852. (Illus.). 32p. (J). (ps-2). 1993. lib. bdg. 13.95 (*0-02-770025-9*, Bradbury S&S) S&S Childrens.

Tom Gibson: False Evidence Appearing Real. Martha Langford. 115p. 1994. text ed. 25.00 (*0-88884-567-7*) U Ch Pr.

Tom Glazer's Treasury of Songs for Children. Ed. by Tom Glazer. (Illus.). (J). (gr. 1-6). 1988. 12.95 (*0-686-74302-4*) J R Pubns.

Tom Grant Piano Collection. 80p. 1994. otabind 18.95 (*0-7935-3128-4*, 00673243) H Leonard.

Tom Hanks: Journey to Stardom. Roy Trakin. 1995. mass mkt. 4.99 (*0-312-95596-0*) St Martin.

Tom Hanks: Journey to Stardom. Roy Trakin. 1995. mass mkt. 4.99 (*0-312-95569-3*) St Martin.

***Tom Hayden: An Activist Life.** Tom Hayden. (Illus.). 560p. 1997. pap. 18.95 (*1-57098-155-8*) R Rinehart.

Tom Henry's Key Word Index. rev. ed. Tom Henry. 49p. (Orig.). (C). 1993. pap. text ed. 12.00 (*0-945495-21-8*) T Henrys CECB.

Tom Hopkins' Guide to Greatness in Sales: How to Become a Complete Salesperson. Tom Hopkins. 320p. 1993. pap. 14.99 (*0-446-39370-3*) Warner Bks.

Tom Horn: Killing Men Is My Specialty...: The Definitive History of the Notorious Wyoming Stock Detective. Chip Carlson. (Illus.). 261p. (Orig.). 1991. pap. 16.95 (*0-9630248-0-9*) Beartooth.

***Tom Horn: Last of the Bad Men.** Jay Monaghan. LC 97-1508. (Illus.). xix, 290p. 1997. pap. 14.95 (*0-8032-8234-6*, Bison Books) U of Nebr Pr.

Tom Jackson's Interview Express: The Fastest Way to Your Best Job Offer. Tom Jackson & Bill Buckingham. LC 92-56822. (Job Express Ser.). 96p. 1993. pap. 8.00 (*0-8129-2129-1*, Times Bks) Random.

Tom Jackson's Resume Express: The Fastest Way to Write a Winning Resume. Tom Jackson & Bill Buckingham. LC 92-56821. (Job Express Ser.). 96p. 1993. pap. 8.00 (*0-8129-2128-3*, Times Bks) Random.

Tom Jefferson: The Third President of the United States. Helen A. Monsell. LC 89-37841. (Childhood of Famous Americans Ser.). (Illus.). 192p. (J). (gr. 2-6). 1989. reprint ed. pap. 4.95 (*0-689-71347-9*, Aladdin Paperbacks) S&S Childrens.

Tom Jerome Roma's 1996 Weekly Astrological Forecasts. unabridged ed. Tom J. Roma. Ed. by John D. Ball. 124p. 1995. spiral bd. 12.95 (*0-9650599-0-1*) Amass Pubng.

***Tom Jerome Roma's 1997 Weekly Astrological Forecasts & Guide.** Tom J. Roma. Ed. by John D. Ball. (Illus.). 124p. 1996. spiral bd. 14.50 (*0-9650599-1-X*) Amass Pubng.

Tom Johnson of Cleveland. Eugene C. Murdock. 379p. (C). 1992. lib. bdg. 56.00 (*1-882090-05-5*) Wright State Univ Pr.

Tom Jones. Henry Fielding. (Airmont Classics Ser.). (YA). (gr. 11 up). 1967. mass mkt. 2.50 (*0-8049-0135-X*, CL-135) Airmont.

Tom Jones. Henry Fielding. 1200p. 1991. 20.00 (*0-679-40569-0*, Everymans Lib) Knopf.

***Tom Jones.** Henry Fielding. 1997. mass mkt. 5.95 (*0-553-21457-8*, Bantam Classics) Bantam.

Tom Jones. Henry Fielding. (Book Notes Ser.). (C). 1986. pap. 2.50 (*0-8120-3546-1*) Barron.

Tom Jones. Henry Fielding. 848p. 1992. pap. 6.95 (*0-460-87168-4*, Everyman's Classic Lib) C E Tuttle.

Tom Jones. Henry Fielding. 1963. pap. 5.95 (*0-451-52334-2*, CE1827, Sig Classics) NAL-Dutton.

***Tom Jones.** Henry Fielding. Ed. by John Bender & Simon Stern. (The World's Classics Ser.). (Illus.). 968p. 1996. pap. 5.95 (*0-19-283110-0*) OUP.

Tom Jones. Henry Fielding. LC 84-25513. 1003p. 1985. pap. 10.95 (*0-394-60519-5*, Modern Lib) Random.

Tom Jones. Henry Fielding. 1994. 20.00 (*0-679-60126-0*, Modern Lib) Random.

Tom Jones. Henry Fielding. Ed. by Reg Mutter. (English Library). 1989. mass mkt. 6.95 (*0-14-031117-5*, Penguin Classics) Viking Penguin.

Tom Jones. Henry Fielding. Ed. by Sheridan Baker. (Critical Editions Ser.). (C). 1973. pap. text ed. 12.95 (*0-393-09394-8*) Norton.

Tom Jones. Henry Fielding. Ed. by R. P. Mutter. 912p. 1966. pap. 8.95 (*0-14-043009-1*, Penguin Classics) Viking Penguin.

Tom Jones. 2nd ed. Henry Fielding. (C). 1995. pap. text ed. 12.95 (*0-393-96594-5*, Norton Paperbks) Norton.

Tom Jones. Henry Fielding. 1982. reprint ed. lib. bdg. 39.95 (*0-89966-398-2*) Buccaneer Bks.

Tom Jones: A Biography. large type ed. Stafford Hildred & David Gritten. 300p. 1991. 21.95 (*1-85089-486-8*, Pub. by ISIS UK) Transaction Pubs.

***Tom Jones: 1-Act.** David Rogers & Henry Fielding. 48p. 1964. pap. 3.95 (*0-87129-763-9*, T54) Dramatic Pub.

Tom Jones - Full. Henry Fielding. 1964. pap. 5.00 (*0-87129-326-9*, T36) Dramatic Pub.

Tom Jones Notes. James C. Evans. 1972. pap. 4.25 (*0-8220-1293-6*) Cliffs.

Tom Jones Slept Here. John L. Hughes. 157p. (C). 1971. text ed. 49.00 (*0-85088-126-9*, Pub. by Gomer Pr UK) St Mut.

Tom-Kav: A Late San Luis Rey Site in Northern San Diego County, California, & Its Place in the San Luis Rey Complex. D. L. True et al. (UC Publications in Anthropological Records: Vol. 30). (C). 1991. pap. 40.00 (*0-520-09759-9*) U CA Pr.

Tom Kid Sketchbook. Tom Kidd. (Sketchbook Ser.: Vol. 11). (Illus.). 48p. 1992. 4.95 (*1-56862-006-3*) Tundra MA.

Tom Kitten. (Beatrix Potter Coloring Bks.: No. S884-4). (Illus.). (J). (ps-2). 1.95 (*0-7214-5219-1*, Ladybrd) Penguin.

Tom Kitten. (Classic Tales Ser.). (Illus.). 24p. (J). 1993. 4.98 (*1-56173-475-6*) Pubns Intl Ltd.

Tom Kitten. Illus. by T. F. Marsh et al. (Classic Tales Ser.). 24p. (J). (gr. 2-4). 1992. lib. bdg. 10.95 (*1-56674-010-X*, HTS Bks) Forest Hse.

Tom Kitten. Beatrix Potter. (Little Hide-&-Seek Bks.). (Illus.). 12p. (J). (ps-1). 1994. pap. 3.50 (*0-7232-4106-6*) Warne.

Tom Kitten. deluxe ed. (Beatrix Potter Collector Ser.). 224p. Date not set. text ed. 5.95 (*1-56987-342-9*) Landoll.

Tom Kitten: Bath Book. Beatrix Potter. (J). 1989. pap. 3.50 (*0-7232-3585-6*) Warne.

Tom Kitten Puzzle Play Book. Seafarer Staff. 5.98 (*0-8289-0842-7*) Seafarer Bks.

Tom Kitten's Playtime Mini Board Book. Beatrix Potter. (Illus.). 24p. (J). (ps). 1994. pap. 2.99 (*0-7232-4092-2*) Warne.

***Tom Kovac.** Ed. by Charles Jencks et al. (Architectural Monographs: Vol. 50). (Illus.). 128p. 1997. pap. 38.00 (*1-85490-458-2*) Academy Ed UK.

Tom Landry. large type ed. Tom Landry & Gregg Lewis. (Illus.). 336p. 1991. reprint ed. pap. 15.95 (*0-8027-2659-3*) Walker & Co.

Tom Lea: An/Oral History. Ed. by Rebecca Craver & Adair Margo. LC 94-61797. (Illus.). 185p. 1995. 50.00 (*0-87404-234-8*) Tex Western.

Tom Lehrer's Song Book. Tom Lehrer. Date not set. reprint ed. lib. bdg. 16.95 (*0-89190-092-6*, Am Repr) Amereon Ltd.

Tom Little's Great Halloween Scare. John Peterson. 80p. (J). 1994. pap. 2.99 (*0-590-42235-9*) Scholastic Inc.

Tom Loeser - Sixty Five Drawers, Eleven Doors & Four Lids: Peter Joseph Gallery, New York. Photos by Michael Galatis. LC 92-85202. (Illus.). 1992. write for info. (*1-881658-03-1*) P J Gallery.

Tom Loves Anna Loves Tom. Bruce Clements. 1990. 15.00 (*0-374-37673-5*) FS&G.

Tom Loves Anna Loves Tom. Bruce Clements. (YA). (gr. 7 up). 1992. reprint ed. pap. 3.95 (*0-374-47939-9*) FS&G.

Tom Mann, 1856-1941: The Challenges of Labour. Chushichi Tsuzuki. (Illus.). 308p. 1991. 75.00 (*0-19-820217-2*) OUP.

Tom Mann's Social & Economic Writings. Ed. by John Laurent. 148p. 1988. 42.50 (*0-85124-458-0*, Pub. by Spokesman Bks UK) Coronet Bks.

***Tom Marshall's Tucson.** Patricia Stephenson & Alex J. Kimmelman. (Illus.). 86p. (Orig.). 1996. pap. 16.95 (*0-9656337-0-5*) P Stephenson.

Tom MBoya: The Man Who Kenya Wanted to Forget. David Goldsworthy. LC 81-22870. 308p. 1982. 42.00 (*0-8419-0787-0*, Africana) Holmes & Meier.

Tom McDonald's PC Games Extravaganza! T. Liam McDonald. LC 94-74084. 202p. 1995. 19.99 (*0-7821-1654-X*) Sybex.

Tom Mix: A Heavily-Illustrated Biography of the Western Star, with a Filmography. Paul E. Mix. LC 94-35404. (Illus.). 336p. 1995. lib. bdg. 35.00 (*0-89950-964-9*) McFarland & Co.

Tom Mix Highlights. Andy Woytowich. Ed. by Rhonda K. Lemons. LC 89-80285. (Illus.). 52p. (Orig.). 1989. pap. text ed. 5.00 (*0-944019-08-0*) Empire NC.

Tom Moore's Diary. Thomas Moore. Ed. by J. B. Priestley. LC 76-131783. 1971. reprint ed. 49.00 (*0-403-00670-8*) Scholarly.

Tom Moore's Diary. J. B. Priestly. 1988. reprint ed. lib. bdg. 75.00 (*0-7812-0039-3*) Rprt Serv.

Tom Moore's Diary: A Selection. Thomas Moore. (BCL1-PR English Literature Ser.). 218p. 1992. reprint ed. lib. bdg. 79.00 (*0-7812-7607-1*) Rprt Serv.

Tom Northway. Marshall Terry. 192p. 1991. reprint ed. 16.00 (*0-89672-257-0*) Tex Tech Univ Pr.

Tom O'Bedlam's Night Out & Other Strange Excursions. Darrell Schweitzer. LC 85-80505. (Illus.). 192p. 1985. pap. 7.50 (*0-932445-14-4*) Ganley Pub.

Tom O'Bedlam's Night Out & Other Strange Excursions. Darrell Schweitzer. LC 85-80505. (Illus.). vii, 191p. 1985. lib. bdg. 20.00 (*0-932445-15-2*) Ganley Pub.

***Tom of Finland.** Benedikt Taschen GW Staff. 1995. pap. text ed. 12.99 (*3-8228-9342-0*) Taschen Amer.

Tom of Finland: His Life & Times. F. Valentine Hooven, III. 208p. 1994. pap. 12.95 (*0-312-11365-X*, Stonewall Inn) St Martin.

Tom of Finland: Retrospective II. Tom of Finland. (Series on Artist: No. 2). (Illus.). 192p. (Orig.). 1991. 48.00 (*1-879055-29-5*); pap. 27.50 (*1-879055-28-7*) Tom Finland.

Tom Otterness. (Contemporary Art Ser.: No. 1). (Illus.). 19p. 1994. pap. write for info. (*1-883015-07-3*) Krannert Art.

Tom Pain & William Cobbett: The Trans-Atlantic Connection. David A. Wilson. (Studies in the History of Ideas). 248p. (C). 1988. text ed. 55.00 (*0-7735-1013-3*, Pub. by McGill CN) U of Toronto Pr.

Tom Paine. J. W. Skelton. 208p. 1993. pap. 9.95 (*0-685-70276-6*) Prof Pr NC.

Tom Paine: A Political Life, Vol. 1. John Keane. 1995. 27.95 (*0-316-48419-9*) Little.

Tom Paine: Voice of Revolution. Milton Meltzer. LC 96-11956. (Milton Meltzer Biographies Ser.). 192p. (J). 1996. lib. bdg. 25.80 (*0-531-11291-8*) Watts.

Tom Paine & the American Revolution. Eric Foner. LC 75-25456. (Illus.). 348p. 1977. pap. 18.95 (*0-19-502182-7*) OUP.

Tom Patterson: Colorado Crusader for Change. Sybil Downing & Robert E. Smith. LC 95-2671. (Illus.). 288p. 1995. 29.95 (*0-87081-364-1*) Univ Pr Colo.

Tom Patti: Glass. (Illus.). 32p. 1980. 4.00 (*0-916746-55-0*) Springfield Lib & Mus.

Tom Paxton - Anthology (Piano - Vocal) Ed. by Mark Phillips. (Illus.). 63p. 1990. pap. text ed. 12.95 (*0-89524-390-3*) Cherry Lane.

Tom Paxton - Authentic Guitar Style: Guitar Transcriptions. Ed. by Milton Okun. pap. 14.95 (*0-89524-448-9*) Cherry Lane.

Tom Paxton - Politics: Guitar/Vocal Arrangements. Ed. by Milton Okun. pap. 9.95 (*0-89524-435-7*) Cherry Lane.

Tom Paxton Ramblin' Boy & Other Songs. Tom Paxton. (Illus.). pap. 11.95 (*0-8256-0007-3*, OK61069, Oak) Music Sales.

Tom Paxton-Wearing the Time. Ed. by Milton Okun. 63p. (YA). 1994. pap. 14.95 (*0-89524-881-6*, 02502157) Cherry Lane.

Tom Peters. Random House Value Publishing Staff. Date not set. 6.25 (*0-517-14817-X*) Random Hse Value.

***Tom Peters Business School.** Eric Goldberg. (RHVP-Remainder Ser.). 1996. 14.99 (*0-517-17001-9*) Random Hse Value.

Tom Peters Business School in a Box. Debbie Notkin & Richard F. Dutcher. LC 93-43001. 1995. 50.00 (*0-394-58159-8*) Knopf.

Tom Petrie's Reminiscences of Early Queensland. Constance C. Petrie. (Orig.). pap. 18.95 (*0-7022-2383-2*, Pub. by Univ Queensland Pr AT) Intl Spec Bk.

Tom Petty: Wildflowers. Ed. by Tom Roed. 104p. (Orig.). (YA). 1995. pap. text ed. 19.95 (*0-89724-702-7*, PG9507); pap. text ed. 16.95 (*0-89724-703-5*, PF9508) Warner Brothers.

Tom Petty & the Heartbreakers: Greatest Hits (Guitar) Tom Petty. Ed. by Tom Roed. (Illus.). 100p. (Orig.). 1994. pap. text ed. 19.95 (*0-89898-766-0*, P1061GTX) Warner Brothers.

Tom Petty & the Heartbreakers: Greatest Hits (Piano) Tom Petty. Ed. by Tom Roed. (Illus.). 80p. (Orig.). 1994. pap. text ed. 16.95 (*0-89898-765-2*, P1061SMX) Warner Brothers.

Tom Philbin's Do-It-Yourself Bargain Book. Tom Philbin. 256p. (Orig.). 1992. pap. 9.99 (*0-446-39339-8*) Warner Bks.

Tom Phillips: Selections from the Ruth & Marvin Sackner Archive of Concrete & Visual Poetry. Frwd. by Tom Phillips. LC 90-63612. (Illus.). 28p. (Orig.). 1990. pap. 4.95 (*0-88259-961-5*) NCMA.

Tom Phillips: The Portrait Works. (Illus.). 104p. 1989. pap. 35.00 (*1-85514-021-7*, Pub. by Natl Port Gall UK) Antique Collect.

Tom Phillips: Words & Texts. Intro. by Huston Paschal. (Illus.). 1993. pap. 34.95 (*0-500-97402-0*) Thames Hudson.

Tom Pilgrim's Progress among the Consequences of Christianity. Dubsky. 1994. per. 17.50 (*0-907040-09-8*, Pub. by Gay Mens Pr UK) LPC InBook.

Tom Plant: The Making of a Franco-American Entrepreneur, 1859-1941. Barry H. Rodrigue. LC 93-42755. (Studies in Entrepreneurship). 304p. 1994. text ed. 70.00 (*0-8153-0988-0*) Garland.

Tom Reber's Last Retreat. Oystein Lonn. Tr. by David McDuff. 176p. (NOR.). 1992. 19.95 (*0-7145-2933-8*) M Boyars Pubs.

Tom Robbins. Catherine Hoyser. LC 96-53851. (Critical Companions to Popular Contemporary Writers Ser.). 1997. text ed. 29.95 (*0-313-29418-6*, Greenwood Pr) Greenwood.

Tom Robbins. Mark Siegel. LC 80-69013. (Western Writers Ser.: No. 42). (Illus.). 52p. (Orig.). 1980. pap. 4.95 (*0-88430-066-8*) Boise St U W Writ Ser.

***Tom Roed's Original Plus 12.** Ed. by Tony Esposito. 52p. (Orig.). (YA). 1997. pap. text ed. 10.95 (*0-7692-0061-3*) Warner Brothers.

Tom Rolt & the Cressy Years. Ian Mackersey. 106p. (C). 1989. 45.00 (*0-947712-01-1*, Pub. by S A Baldwin UK) St Mut.

Tom Sawyer. (Book Notes Ser.). 1985. pap. 3.95 (*0-8120-3547-X*) Barron.

Tom Sawyer. (Spanish Children's Classics Ser.: No. 800-1). (SPA.). (J). 1990. boxed 3.50 (*0-7214-1395-1*, Ladybrd) Penguin.

***Tom Sawyer.** (Classic Illustrated Study Guides Ser.). (Illus.). 64p. (Orig.). (YA). (gr. 7 up). 1997. student ed., mass mkt. 4.99 (*1-57840-001-5*) Acclaim Bks.

Tom Sawyer. Sara Spencer. (J). (gr. 1-9). 1935. 5.00 (*0-87602-211-5*) Anchorage.

Tom Sawyer. Mark Twain. (Airmont Classics Ser.). (Orig.). (YA). (gr. 5 up). 1962. mass mkt. 3.95 (*0-8049-0006-X*, CL-6) Airmont.

***Tom Sawyer.** Mark Twain, pseud. (Illustrated Classics Collection: Vol. 1). 64p. (Orig.). 1994. pap. 4.95 (*0-7854-0671-9*, 40358) Am Guidance.

Tom Sawyer. Mark Twain, pseud. 36p. (Orig.). (YA). (gr. 7-12). 1988. pap. 3.50 (*1-57514-236-8*, 1007) Encore Perform Pub.

Tom Sawyer. Mark Twain, pseud. (Illustrated Classics Ser.). (Illus.). 240p. (Orig.). (J). (ps-6). Date not set. text ed. 9.95 (*1-56987-395-X*); pap. text ed. 2.95 (*1-56987-403-4*); pap. text ed. 3.95 (*1-56987-412-3*) Landoll.

Tom Sawyer. Mark Twain, pseud. Ed. by Irwin Shapiro. LC 73-75465. (Now Age Illustrated Ser.). (Illus.). 64p. (Orig.). (J). (gr. 5-10). 1973. student ed. 1.25 (*0-88301-179-4*); pap. 2.95 (*0-88301-103-4*) Pendulum Pr.

Tom Sawyer. Mark Twain, pseud. LC 80-22095. (Short Classics Ser.). (Illus.). 48p. (Orig.). (J). (gr. 4 up). 1983. lib. bdg. 24.26 (*0-8172-1665-0*) Raintree Steck-V.

Tom Sawyer. Mark Twain, pseud. (Classic Story Bks.). (Orig.). (J). 1994. 4.98 (*0-8317-1646-0*) Smithmark.

Tom Sawyer. Mark Twain, pseud. (Orig.). (YA). (gr. 5 up). 1996. pap. 2.50 (*0-614-15791-9*) Tor Bks.

Tom Sawyer. Mark Twain, pseud. (Children's Classics Ser.). (Illus.). (Orig.). (J). 1992. write for info. (*0-89434-127-8*) Ferguson.

Tom Sawyer. Mark Twain, pseud. (American Short Classics Ser.). (Orig.). (J). (gr. 4-7). 1993. pap. 4.95 (*0-8114-6843-7*) Raintree Steck-V.

Tom Sawyer. adapted ed. Mark Twain, pseud. (Children's Thrift Classics Ser.). (Illus.). 96p. (Orig.). (J). (gr. 1). pap. 1.00 (*0-486-29156-1*) Dover.

***Tom Sawyer, Vol. 1.** Mark Twain. Date not set. pap. 14.95 (*0-8050-3394-7*) St Martin.

Tom Sawyer: A Comedy in Two Acts. Tim Kelly. 56p. (J). (gr. 2 up). 1983. pap. 4.50 (*0-88680-191-5*) I E Clark.

Tom Sawyer: Detective. Mark Twain, pseud. (Works of Samuel Clemens). 1989. reprint ed. lib. bdg. 79.00 (*0-685-28368-2*) Rprt Serv.

Tom Sawyer Abroad. Mark Twain. Date not set. pap. write for info. (*0-14-043383-X*) Viking Penguin.

Tom Sawyer Abroad. Mark Twain. 128p. 1993. pap. 2.50 (*0-8125-2334-2*) Tor Bks.

***Tom Sawyer Abroad.** Created by Mark Twain. (J). Date not set. pap. 2.95 (*0-8167-3242-6*) Troll Communs.

Tom Sawyer Abroad. Samuel L. Clemens. (Works of Mark Twain). 1988. reprint ed. lib. bdg. 59.00 (*0-7812-1125-5*) Rprt Serv.

***Tom Sawyer Abroad & Tom Sawyer Detective.** Mark Twain. (Classics Ser.). (YA). (gr. 5 up). 1966. mass mkt. 1.50 (*0-8049-0126-0*, Cl-126) Airmont.

Tom Sawyer Abroad & Tom Sawyer Detective. Mark Twain. LC 81-40325. (Mark Twain Library: No. 2). (Illus.). 160p. 1981. 35.00 (*0-520-04560-2*); pap. 11.95 (*0-520-04561-0*) U CA Pr.

***Tom Sawyer Abroad (1894)** Mark Twain. Ed. by Shelley F. Fishkin. (Oxford Mark Twain Ser.). 304p. 1997. lib. bdg. 25.00 (*0-19-511414-0*) OUP.

Tom Sawyer & Huckleberry Finn. Mark Twain. 464p. 1991. 20.00 (*0-679-40584-4*, Everymans Lib) Knopf.

Tom Sawyer Companion: An Autobiographical Guided Tour with Mark Twain. John D. Evans. 128p. (Orig.). (C). 1993. pap. text ed. 14.95 (*0-8191-9060-8*); lib. bdg. 37.50 (*0-8191-9059-4*) U Pr of Amer.

Tom Sawyer Detective. Mark Twain. (J). Date not set. pap. 2.95 (*0-8167-3240-X*) Troll Communs.

Tom Sawyer, Detective. Mark Twain. 96p. 1993. pap. 2.50 (*0-8125-3035-7*) Tor Bks.

***Tom Sawyer Readalong.** Mark Twain, pseud. (Illustrated Classics Collection: No. 1). 64p. 1994. pap. 14.95 incl. audio (*0-7854-0712-X*, 40360) Am Guidance.

***Tom Sawyer, Romeo & Juliet & Tale of Two Cities, Jane Eyre.** Acclaim Books Staff. (Classics Illustrated Ser.). 1997. pap. text ed. 179.64 (*1-57840-000-7*) Acclaim Bks.

Tom Seaver. Norman L. Macht. (Baseball Legends Ser.). (Illus.). 64p. (J). (gr. 3 up). 1994. lib. bdg. 15.95 (*0-7910-1951-9*) Chelsea Hse.

Tom Sexton Fish Finishing System. Tom Sexton. Ed. by Bob Williamson & Ken Edwards. (Illus.). 116p. (C). 1987. pap. text ed. 24.95 (*0-925245-04-6*) WASCO Manufact.

Tom Sheppard: Hull's Great Collector. Tim Schadla-Hall. (C). 1989. text ed. 35.00 (*0-948929-22-7*) St Mut.

***Tom Shields, Free at Last.** Tom Shields. (Illus.). 176p. 1997. pap. 17.95 (*1-85158-880-9*, Pub. by Mnstream UK) Trafalgar.

Tom Short Photographs 1971-1994. Isaac B. Singer. LC 94-96334. (Illus.). 96p. (Orig.). 1994. pap. 29.00 (*0-9642834-0-9*) Artsquad Bks.

Tom Spoon. Frederic Bean. 192p. 1990. 18.95 (*0-8027-4103-7*) Walker & Co.

Tom Spoon. large type ed. Frederic Bean. LC 90-46132. 236p. 1990. reprint ed. lib. bdg. 15.95 (*1-56054-075-3*) Thorndike Pr.

Tom Stone's Greek Food & Drink Book. Tom Stone. 166p. 1988. pap. 7.95 (*960-7269-19-5*, Pub. by Lycabettus Pr GR) Bosphorus Bks.

Tom Stoppard. Ed. by Anthony Jenkins. (Critical Essays on British Literature Ser.). 1990. 47.00 (*0-8161-8854-8*) G K Hall.

Tom Stoppard: An Analytical Study of His Plays. Richard A. Andretta. (C). 1991. 40.00 (*0-7069-5827-6*) Advent Bks Div.

Tom Stoppard: An Assessment. Tim Brassell. LC 83-40126. 220p. 1985. text ed. 35.00 (*0-312-80888-7*) St Martin.

Tom Stoppard: Comedy As a Moral Matrix. Joan F. Dean. LC 80-26400. (Literary Frontiers Editions Ser.). 128p. 1981. text ed. 12.95 (*0-8262-0332-9*) U of Mo Pr.

***Tom Stoppard: Plays 2.** Tom Stoppard. 1997. pap. 14.95 (*0-571-17977-0*); pap. text ed. 14.95 (*0-571-19008-1*) Faber & Faber.

Tom Stoppard & the Craft of Comedy: Medium & Genre at Play. Katherine E. Kelly. 180p. 1990. 37.50 (*0-472-10188-9*) U of Mich Pr.

Tom Stoppard in Conversation. Tom Stoppard. Ed. by Paul Delaney. LC 94-10262. (Theater: Theory - Text - Performance Ser.). 328p. (C). 1994. pap. 17.95 (*0-472-06561-0*); text ed. 44.50 (*0-472-09561-7*) U of Mich Pr.

Tom Stoppard Plays 1 Plays 1: The Real Inspector Hound; Dirty Linen; Dogg's Hamlet; Cahoot's MacBeth... Tom Stoppard. 224p. (Orig.). 1996. pap. text ed. 15.95 (*0-571-17765-4*) Faber & Faber.

Tom Stoppard's Stagecraft. Stephen Hu. (American University Studies: English Language & Literature: Ser. IV, Vol. 78). 274p. 1989. 37.00 (*0-8204-0709-7*) P Lang Pubng.

Tom Sullivan, Forty-Ninth Regiment of Foot: Redcoat to Yankee, 1775-1778. rev. ed. Sydney Bradford. (Illus.). 168p. 1994. pap. 19.95 (*1-879663-00-7*) Audacious PA.

Tom Swan's Mastering Borland C++ 5. 3rd ed. Tom Swan. 1088p. 1996. pap. text ed. 59.99 incl. cd-rom (*0-672-30802-9*) Sams.

***Tom Swan's Mastering Visual J++** Tom Swan. 750p. 1997. pap. text ed. 39.99 incl. cd-rom (*1-57521-210-2*, SamsNet Bks) Sams.

Tom Swayer: A Musical. Mark Twain. 54p. (Orig.). (J). (gr. 3-12). 1992. pap. 4.50 (*1-57514-235-X*, 0053) Encore Perform Pub.

Tom Swift & His Airship. Victor Appleton. LC 92-29496. (Tom Swift Ser.). 216p. (J). (gr. 2-6). 1992. 12.95 (*1-55709-177-3*) Applewood.

Tom Swift & His Motor Boat. Victor Appleton. LC 92-29497. (Tom Swift Ser.). 212p. (J). (gr. 2-6). 1992. 12.95 (*1-55709-176-5*) Applewood.

An Asterisk (*) at the beginning of an entry indicates that the title is appearing in BIP for the first time.

Tom Swift & His Motor Cycle. Victor Appleton. LC 92-28649. (Tom Swift Ser.). 206p. (J). (gr. 2-6). 1992. 12.95 (*1-55709-175-7*) Applewood.

Tom Swift Gift Set, 3 vols., Set. Victor Appleton. (J). boxed 7.95 (*0-317-12430-7*) S&S Trade.

***Tom Swift, the Bobbsey Twins, & Other Heroes of American Juvenile Literature.** John T. Dizer. LC 97-4374. (Studies in American Literature). 1997. write for info. (*0-7734-8641-0*) E Mellen.

***Tom T. Hall's Country Songs for Children.** Ed. by Carol Cuellar. 68p. (Orig.). (C). 1996. pap. text ed. 12.95 (*1-57623-460-6*, PF9620) Warner Brothers.

Tom Taylor & the Victorian Drama. Winton Tolles. LC 41-3081. reprint ed. 31.50 (*0-404-06474-4*) AMS Pr.

Tom Temple's Career. Horatio Alger, Jr. (Works of Horatio Alger Jr.). 1989. reprint ed. lib. bdg. 79.00 (*0-685-27548-5*) Rprt Serv.

Tom Thatcher's Fortune. Horatio Alger, Jr. (Works of Horatio Alger Jr.). 1989. reprint ed. lib. bdg. 79.00 (*0-685-27545-0*) Rprt Serv.

***Tom the Dancing Bug: Everything I Ever Needed to Know I Learned from My Golf-Playing Cats.** Ruben Bolling. (Illus.). 80p. 1997. pap. 8.95 (*1-56163-183-3*) NBM.

Tom, the Orphan Cat. James C. Russell. (Illus.). (J). (gr. 3-5). 1996. 7.95 (*0-533-11445-4*) Vantage.

Tom the TV Cat: A Step Two Book. Joan Heilbroner. LC 83-24600. (Step into Reading Bks.). (Illus.). 48p. (J). (ps-2). 1984. lib. bdg. 7.99 (*0-394-96708-9*) Random Bks Yng Read.

Tom the TV Cat: A Step Two Book. Joan Heilbroner. LC 83-24600. (Step into Reading Bks.). (Illus.). 48p. (J). (ps-2). 1984. pap. 3.99 (*0-394-86708-4*) Random Bks Yng Read.

***Tom Thomson.** Joan Murray. Ed. by Douglas Fetherling. (New Views on Canadian Artists Ser.). (Illus.). 96p. 1996. pap. 18.95 (*1-55082-155-5*, Pub. by Quarry Pr CN) LPC InBook.

Tom Thumb. (FRE.). (J). (gr. k-3). 3.50 (*0-685-28452-2*) Fr & Eur.

Tom Thumb. (Favorite Tale Pop-Up Bks.). (Illus.). (J). (ps-1). 1.79 (*0-517-46236-2*) Random Hse Value.

Tom Thumb. 32p. (J). (ps-2). 1996. pap. 2.50 (*0-7214-5645-6*, Ladybrd) Penguin.

Tom Thumb. Audrey Daly. (Favorite Tales Ser.). (Illus.). 28p. (J). 1994. 2.99 (*0-7214-5446-1*, Ladybrd) Penguin.

Tom Thumb. Margaret Hillert. (Illus.). (J). (ps). 1982. pap. 28.60 (*0-8136-5591-9*, TK2175); lib. bdg. 44.95 (*0-8136-5091-7*, TK2174) Modern Curr.

Tom Thumb. Ed. by Margaret R. MacDonald. LC 93-21. (Multicultural Folktale Ser.). 184p. 1993. pap. 24.95 (*0-89774-728-3*) Oryx Pr.

***Tom Thumb.** Marianna Meyer. Date not set. lib. bdg. write for info. (*0-688-06601-1*, Morrow Junior) Morrow.

***Tom Thumb.** Marianna Meyer. (J). Date not set. write for info. (*0-688-06600-3*, Morrow Junior) Morrow.

Tom Thumb. Rabbit. 1997. pap. 19.95 (*0-689-80219-6*, Aladdin Paperbacks) S&S Childrens.

Tom Thumb. Richard J. Watson. (Illus.). 32p. (J). (ps-3). 1989. 13.00 (*0-15-289280-X*) HarBrace.

Tom Thumb. Richard J. Watson. LC 87-12045. (Illus.). 32p. (J). (ps-3). 1993. pap. 6.00 (*0-15-289281-8*, HB Juv Bks) HarBrace.

Tom Thumb & Other Stories. Charles Perrault. 1996. 13.95 (*0-679-45103-X*) McKay.

Tom-Toms: Indian Poetry. Bret Wooldridge. 40p. 1995. pap. 7.50 (*1-887963-03-0*) Pota Pr.

Tom Tracey. Horatio Alger, Jr. (Works of Horatio Alger Jr.). 1989. reprint ed. lib. bdg. 79.00 (*0-685-27544-2*) Rprt Serv.

Tom Tracy: The Trials of a New York Newsboy. Horatio Alger, Jr. (Illus.). 208p. 1978. reprint ed. 24.00 (*0-686-35749-3*) G K Westgard.

Tom Turner's Legacy. Horatio Alger, Jr. (Works of Horatio Alger Jr.). 1989. reprint ed. lib. bdg. 79.00 (*0-685-27543-4*) Rprt Serv.

Tom Tyler & His Wife. LC 70-133746. (Tudor Facsimile Texts. Old English Plays Ser.: No. 144). reprint ed. 49.50 (*0-404-53444-9*) AMS Pr.

***Tom Waits: Beautiful Maladies.** 256p. pap. 29.95 (*0-8256-1581-X*, AM 940291) Omnibus NY.

Tom Waits: Big Time. (Illus.). 60p. 1988. pap. 15.95 (*0-8256-1207-1*, AM72463) Music Sales.

***Tom Waits: Big Time.** 60p. 1997. 15.95 (*0-8256-2518-1*, AM 72463) Music Sales.

Tom Waits Anthology. (Illus.). 144p. 1988. pap. 21.95 (*0-8256-2503-3*, AM71168) Music Sales.

Tom-Walker. Mari Sandoz. LC 84-5221. viii, 372p. 1984. reprint ed. text ed. 32.00 (*0-8032-4150-X*) U of Nebr Pr.

Tom-Walker. Mari Sandoz. LC 84-5221. viii, 372p. 1984. reprint ed. pap. 8.95 (*0-8032-9147-7*, Bison Books) U of Nebr Pr.

Tom Watson: Agrarian Rebel. C. Vann Woodward. 528p. 1963. pap. 19.95 (*0-19-500707-7*) OUP.

Tom Watson: Agrarian Rebel. Comer V. Woodward. (History - United States Ser.). 518p. 1993. reprint ed. lib. bdg. 99.00 (*0-7812-4909-0*) Rprt Serv.

Tom Watson, Agrarian Rebel. C. Vann Woodward. LC 73-77845. 430p. 1982. reprint ed. text ed. 35.00 (*0-8139-0952-X*) U Pr of Va.

Tom Watson's Getting Back to Basics. Tom Watson & Nick Seitz. Ed. by Sally Peters. 96p. 1992. 18.00 (*0-671-74293-0*) PB.

Tom Watson's Getting Back to Basics. Tom Watson & Nick Seitz. 128p. 1993. reprint ed. pap. 13.00 (*0-671-88056-X*) PB.

Tom Watson's Strategic Golf. Tom Watson & Nick Seitz. Ed. by Donna Ruvituso. (Illus.). 144p. 1995. reprint ed. pap. 14.00 (*0-671-53711-3*, PB Trade Paper) PB.

Tom Wedgwood, the First Photographer. R. B. Litchfield. LC 72-9217. (Literature of Photography Ser.). 1979. reprint ed. 21.95 (*0-405-04924-2*) Ayer.

Tom Wesselmann. Sam Hunter. LC 94-7385. 128p. 1994. 27.50 (*0-8478-1831-4*) Rizzoli Intl.

Tom Wolfe. William McKeen. (Twayne's United States Authors Ser.). 1995. 22.95 (*0-8057-4004-X*, Twayne) Scribnrs Ref.

Tom Wolfe Carves Dragons. Tom Wolfe & Douglas C. Martin. LC 93-87046. (Illus.). 80p. (Orig.). 1994. pap. 12.95 (*0-88740-576-2*) Schiffer.

Tom Wolfe Carves Jointed Santas. Tom Wolfe & Douglas Congdon-Martin. LC 93-85230. (Illus.). 64p. 1993. pap. 12.95 (*0-88740-539-8*) Schiffer.

Tom Wolfe Carves Wood Spirits & Walking Sticks. Tom Wolfe. LC 92-60642. (Illus.). 64p. 1992. pap. 12.95 (*0-88740-441-3*) Schiffer.

Tom Wolfe Carves...A Horse of a Different Color. Photos & Text by Douglas Congdon-Martin. LC 95-5962. (Illus.). 64p. (Orig.). 1995. pap. 12.95 (*0-88740-787-0*) Schiffer.

Tom Wolfe Goes to the Dogs: Dog Carving. Tom Wolfe & Douglas Congdon-Martin. LC 91-61157. (Illus.). 64p. 1991. pap. 12.95 (*0-88740-367-0*) Schiffer.

***Toma de Decisiones para Lideres: El Proceso Analitico Jerarquico la Toma de Decisiones en un Mundo Complejo.** Thomas L. Saaty. Tr. by Mauricio Escudey et al. (Analytic Hierarchy Ser.: Vol. II). (Illus.). 414p. (Orig.). (SPA.). 1997. pap. text ed. write for info. (*1-888603-01-1*) RWS Pubns.

***Tomahawk.** Poyer. Date not set. write for info. (*0-312-17975-8*) St Martin.

Tomahawk & Cross: Lutheran Missionaries among Northern Prairie Indians, 1858-1866. Gerhard M. Schmutterer. LC 89-23879. xvi, 219p. (Orig.). 1989. pap. 12.95 (*0-931170-43-5*) Ctr Western Studies.

Tomahawk Cruise Missile. Nigel Macknight. (Mil-Tech Ser.). (Illus.). 96p. 1995. pap. 9.95 (*0-87938-717-3*) Motorbooks Intl.

Tomahawk Revenge. David Thompson. (Wilderness Ser.: No. 5). 1995. mass mkt. 3.99 (*0-8439-3926-5*) Dorchester Pub Co.

***Tomahawk Revenge/Black Powder Justice, 2 vols. in 1.** David Thompson. (Wilderness Ser.: Vols. 5 & 6). 352p. 1997. mass mkt. 4.99 (*0-8439-4259-2*, Leisure Bks) Dorchester Pub Co.

Tomahawked! The Inside Story of the Atlanta Braves' Tumultuous Season. Bill Zack. (Illus.). 224p. 1993. 20.00 (*0-671-86878-0*) S&S Trade.

***Tomahawks - Pipe Axes - of the American Frontier.** (Illus.). 128p. 1997. 75.00 (*0-9651146-0-0*) Early Am Artistry.

***Tomale Guigos I.** Hans J. Becker. xxvi, 283p. (GER.). 1975. 44.80 (*3-615-00156-7*, Pub. by Weidmann GW) Lubrecht & Cramer.

***Tomart's Encyclopedia & Price Guide to Action Figures, A-Team & G. I. Joe Collectibles.** Bill Sikora. 1996. pap. 26.95 (*0-914293-27-3*) Tomart Pubns.

***Tomart's Encyclopedia & Price Guide to Action Figures, G. I. Joe & Star Trek Collectibles.** Bill Sikora. 1996. pap. 26.95 (*0-914293-31-1*) Tomart Pubns.

***Tomart's Encyclopedia & Price Guide to Action Figures, Star Wars & Zybots Collectibles.** Bill Sikora. 1996. pap. 26.95 (*0-914293-32-X*) Tomart Pubns.

Tomart's Price Guide to American Paper Dolls: Lowe & Whitman. Mary Young. LC 92-60232. (Illus.). 168p. 1993. pap. 24.95 (*0-914293-19-2*) Tomart Pubns.

***Tomart's Price Guide to Character to Promotional Glasses.** Carol Markowski & Tom Hoder. (Illus.). 176p. 1997. pap. write for info. (*0-914293-35-4*) Tomart Pubns.

***Tomart's Price Guide to Golden Book Collectibles.** 2nd rev. ed. Rebecca Greason. (Illus.). 240p. 1997. pap. write for info. (*0-914293-36-2*) Tomart Pubns.

***Tomart's Price Guide to Hot Wheels Collectibles.** 2nd ed. Michael T. Strauss. LC 92-82853. 184p. 1997. pap. text ed. 29.95 (*0-914293-33-8*) Tomart Pubns.

Tomart's Price Guide to Kid's Meal Collectibles. Suzan Hufferd & Ken Clee. LC 93-60871. (Illus.). 176p. (Orig.). 1994. pap. 25.95 (*0-914293-24-9*) Tomart Pubns.

Tomart's Price Guide to McDonald's Happy Meal Collectibles. 2nd enl. ed. T. E. Tumbusch. (Illus.). 176p. (Orig.). 1995. pap. 27.95 (*0-914293-29-X*) Tomart Pubns.

Tomart's Price Guide to Radio Premium & Cereal Box Collectibles. Tom N. Tumbusch. (Illus.). 192p. 1991. pap. 22.95 (*0-87069-635-1*) Chilton.

***Tomart's Price Guide to Tin Lithodoll Houses & Plastic Doll House Furniture.** Mary Brett. Ed. by Rebecca S. Trissel. LC 97-60705. (Illus.). 72p. 1997. pap. 17.95 (*0-914293-34-6*) Tomart Pubns.

Tomart's Price Guide to Twentieth Century Books. John Wade. LC 93-60872. (Illus.). 192p. (Orig.). 1994. pap. 24.95 (*0-914293-25-7*) Tomart Pubns.

***Tomart's Price Guide to Worldwide Star Wars Collectibles.** 2nd ed. Stephen J. Sansweet & T. N. Tumbusch. (Illus.). 224p. 1997. pap. write for info. (*0-914293-37-0*) Tomart Pubns.

Tomas & the Library Lady. Mora. LC 89-37490. 1997. 17.00 (*0-679-80401-3*) Random.

Tomas & the Library Lady. Pat Mora. LC 89-37490. 1997. lib. bdg. 18.99 (*0-679-90401-8*) Random.

Tomas de Iriarte. R. Merritt Cox. LC 79-169629. (Twayne's World Authors Ser.). 161p. (C). 1972. lib. bdg. 17.95 (*0-8290-1736-4*) Irvington.

Tomas de Suria & His Voyage with Malaspina, 1791. Tomas De Suria. 91p. 1980. 14.95 (*0-87770-239-X*) Ye Galleon.

Tomas Godoy Cruz: Su Tiempo, Su Vida, Su Drama. Cristian Garcia-Godoy. 872p. 1991. pap. 23.00 (*0-9631307-0-6*) F L-Vida Plena.

Tomas Gonda: A Life in Design. Philip B. Meggs. LC 93-74787. 92p. (Orig.). 1994. 15.00 (*0-935519-17-3*) Anderson Gal.

***Tomas Luis De Victoria: A Research Guide.** Eugene C. Cramer. Ed. by Guy A. Marco. (Composer Resource Manuals Ser.). 300p. Date not set. text ed. 45.00 (*0-8153-2096-5*) Garland.

Tomas Rivera Complete Works. Julian Olivares. 1995. 38.95 (*1-55885-153-4*) Arte Publico.

Tomas Rivera, 1935-1984: The Man & His Work. Ed. by Vernon E. Lattin et al. LC 88-71440. (Illus.). xviii, 158p. 1988. pap. 20.00 (*0-916950-89-1*) Biling Rev-Pr.

Tomas Schmit: Fishing for Nets. 1994. 25.00 (*1-885013-02-7*) M Werner.

Tomas Taveira: Architectural Works & Designs. 1991. 79.50 (*0-312-05564-1*) St Martin.

Tomas Taviera. (Art & Design Monographs). (Illus.). 144p. 1994. 50.00 (*1-85490-335-7*) Academy Ed UK.

Tomas Taviera. (Art & Design Monographs). (Illus.). 144p. 1994. pap. 38.00 (*1-85490-336-5*) Academy Ed UK.

Tomas' Tequila Book: Eats, Drinks, Info, Etc. Don Hutson et al. (Illus.). 151p. 1993. pap. 14.95 (*0-9638135-0-1*) Pasquale Pub.

***Tomas y la Senora de la Biblioteca/Tomas & the Library Lady.** Pat Mora. 1997. pap. 7.99 (*0-679-84173-3*) Random.

***Tomaso Albinoni: Pimpinone - Intermezzi Comici Musicali.** Tomaso Albinoni. Ed. by Michael Talbot. (Recent Researches in Music of the Baroque Era Ser.: Vol. RRB43). (Illus.). xxx, 77p. 1983. pap. 33.60 (*0-89579-169-2*) A-R Eds.

Tomaso Albinoni: The Venetian Composer & His World. Michael Talbot. (Illus.). 320p. 1994. reprint ed. pap. 22.00 (*0-19-816420-3*) OUP.

***Tomasol, el Mago del Color - Balderdash the Brilliant.** (Early Learning Program Ser.). (Illus.). 64p. (SPA.). (J). (gr. k-2). 16.95 (*0-7835-3529-5*) Time-Life.

Tomaszewski's Mime Theatre. Andrzej Hausbrandt. (Theatre, Film & Literature Ser.). (Illus.). 176p. 1977. 22.50 (*0-306-77436-4*) Da Capo.

Tomato. (Magnet Gourmet Ser.). 10p. 1996. pap. 5.95 (*0-8069-4205-3*) Sterling.

Tomato. Barrie Watts. (Stopwatch Ser.). (Illus.). 25p. (J). (ps-4). 1990. pap. 3.95 (*0-382-24344-7*); lib. bdg. 9.95 (*0-382-24008-1*) Silver Burdett Pr.

Tomato & Other Colors. Ivan Chermayeff. (J). (ps-3). 1981. 13.55 (*0-13-924753-X*) P-H.

***Tomato Blessings & Radish Teachings: Recipes & Reflections.** Edward E. Brown. LC 96-43994. 336p. 1997. 24.95 (*1-57322-038-8*, Riverhead Books) Putnam Pub Group.

Tomato Book. Yvonne Y. Tarr. 1995. 5.99 (*0-517-12267-7*, Wings Books) Random.

Tomato Can. Ron Ross. LC 93-86844. 192p. 1994. pap. 11.95 (*0-9638230-5-1*) Oyster Bay Bks.

Tomato Cookbook. Roy F. Guste, Jr. LC 94-1488. 192p. (Orig.). 1995. pap. 14.95 (*1-56554-045-X*) Pelican.

Tomato Cookbook. Victoria Lloyd-Davies. LC 94-30358. 96p. 1994. 9.98 (*0-8317-8661-2*) Smithmark.

Tomato Cookbook: More than Sixty Easy, Imaginative Recipes. Ed. by Nicola Hill. (Basic Ingredients Ser.). (Illus.). 64p. 1995. 8.98 (*1-56138-493-3*) Courage Bks.

Tomato Crop: A Scientific Basis for Improvement. J. G. Atherton & J. Rudich. 500p. (gr. 13). 1987. text ed. 166.95 (*0-412-25120-5*) Chapman & Hall.

***Tomato Handbook: Tips & Tricks of Gardener's Guide.** Jennifer Bennett. (Gardener's Guide Ser.: Vol. 6). (Illus.). 96p. (Orig.). 1997. pap. 10.95 (*1-55209-107-4*) Firefly Bks Ltd.

Tomato Imperative! Fried Green Tomatoes to Summer's Ripe Bounty, More Than 130 Recipes for Tomatoes, Fresh & Preserved. Sharon Nimtz & Ruth Cousineau. LC 93-35618. 1994. 14.95 (*0-316-60794-0*) Little.

Tomato in America: Early History, Culture & Cookery. Andrew F. Smith. LC 94-3208. (Illus.). 220p. 1994. 24.95 (*1-57003-000-6*) U of SC Pr.

Tomato Production, Processing & Technology. Wilbur A. Gould. (Illus.). 550p. 1992. 93.00 (*0-930027-18-3*) CTI Pubns.

Tomato Products. (Food Markets in Review Ser.). 1996. pap. 210.00 (*0-614-10656-7*) Food Inst.

Tomato Soup. Hurd. 1994. 4.99 (*0-517-13538-8*) Random Hse Value.

Tomato Ties "n" Growers. Kathryn V. Kermode. 101p. 1995. pap. text ed. write for info. (*0-9646857-0-1*) K Kermode.

Tomatoes. (Burpee American Gardening Ser.). 1997. pap. 9.00 (*0-671-89943-0*, P-H Gardening) P-H Gen Ref & Trav.

***Tomatoes.** 65p. (J). 1996. pap. 3.95 (*0-614-21042-9*, 1513) Kazi Pubns.

***Tomatoes.** Robert Hendrickson. 1997. pap. 16.95 (*0-02-861607-3*) Macmillan.

***Tomatoes.** Uthman Hutchinson. LC 95-80040. (Children Stories Project Ser.). (Illus.). (Orig.). (J). (gr. 2 up). 1995. pap. 3.95 (*0-915957-36-1*) amana pubns.

Tomatoes. National Gardening Association Staff. 1987. pap. 4.95 (*0-317-56624-5*, Villard Bks) Random.

***Tomatoes.** Ed. by Smallwood & Stewart Staff. LC 96-86644. (Little Books for Cook). (Illus.). 80p. 1997. 4.95 (*0-8362-2781-6*) Andrews & McMeel.

Tomatoes! Three Hundred Sixty-Five Healthy Recipes for Year-Round Enjoyment. Garden Way Publishing Editors. Ed. by Constance Oxley. LC 90-55864. 288p. 1991. pap. 14.95 (*0-88266-672-X*, Garden Way Pub) Storey Comm Inc.

Tomatoes see **NGA Garden Library**

Tomatoes & Other Killer Vegetable Jokes & Riddles. Stephanie Johnson. 1992. mass mkt. 3.99 (*0-8125-1995-7*) Tor Bks.

Tomatoes Book Club Version. 19.95 (*0-00-255460-7*, Pub. by HarpC UK) HarpC.

Tomatoes from Mars. Arthur Yorinks. LC 96-86483. (Michael di Capua Bks.). (Illus.). 32p. (J). (ps up). 1997. 14.95 (*0-06-205070-2*); lib. bdg. 14.89 (*0-06-205071-0*) HarpC Child Bks.

Tomatoes in the Treetops: Collected Tales of Harry Rhine. Ben E. Kitchens. LC 82-16980. 73p. (C). 1982. pap. 5.95 (*0-943054-39-7*) Thornwood Bk.

Tomatoes Love Herbs. Ruth Bass. LC 96-10636. (Illus.). 64p. 1996. 9.95 (*0-88266-931-1*) Storey Comm Inc.

***Tomatoes, Potatoes, Corn, & Beans: How the Foods of the Americas Changed Eating Around the World.** Sylvia Johnson. (J). (gr. 5-9). 1997. 16.00 (*0-614-29090-2*, Atheneum Bks Young) S&S Childrens.

Tomatoes Were Cheaper: Tales of the Thirties. Charles A. Jellison. 1977. 34.95 (*0-8156-0130-1*) Syracuse U Pr.

Tomb & Other Tales. H. P. Lovecraft. 192p. 1986. mass mkt. 5.99 (*0-345-33661-5*) Ballantine.

***Tomb & Other Tales.** H. P. Lovecraft. 1997. pap. write for info. (*0-345-41955-3*, Del Rey) Ballantine.

Tomb & the Tiara: Curial Tomb Sculpture in Rome & Avignon in the Later Middle Ages. Julian Gardner. (Clarendon Studies in the History of Art). (Illus.). 292p. 1992. 155.00 (*0-19-817510-8*) OUP.

Tomb-Builders of the Pharaohs. Morris L. Bierbrier. (Illus.). 160p. 1975. pap. 15.00 (*977-424-210-6*, Pub. by Am Univ Cairo Pr UA) Col U Pr.

Tomb Chamber of HSW the Elder Pt. 1: The Inscribed Material at Kom el-Hisn: The Plates. D. P. Silverman. (American Research Center in Egypt, Reports Ser.). ix, 146p. 1989. text ed. 31.50 (*0-936770-17-1*, Pub. by Amer Res Ctr Egypt UA) Eisenbrauns.

***Tomb of Amenemhab No. 44 at Qurnah: The Tomb Chapel of a Priest Carrying the Shrine of Amun.** Hassan El-Saady. (Illus.). 136p. (Orig.). 1997. pap. 42.00 (*0-85668-679-4*, Pub. by Aris & Phillips UK) David Brown.

Tomb of Beowulf & Other Essays. Fred C. Robinson. LC 92-27331. 1993. 61.95 (*0-631-17328-5*) Blackwell Pubs.

Tomb of Dracula, No. 1. Al Williamson et al. 48p. 1991. 4.95 (*0-87135-837-9*) Marvel Entmnt.

Tomb of Dracula, No. 3. Al Williamson et al. 48p. 1991. 4.95 (*0-87135-839-5*) Marvel Entmnt.

Tomb of Dracula, No. 4. Al Williamson et al. 48p. 1991. 4.95 (*0-87135-840-9*) Marvel Entmnt.

Tomb of Dracula, No.2. Al Williamson et al. 48p. 1991. 4.95 (*0-87135-838-7*) Marvel Entmnt.

***Tomb of God: The Body of Jesus & the Solution to a 2,000-Year-Old Mystery.** Richard Andrews & Paul Schellenberger. write for info. (*0-614-22235-4*) Little.

Tomb of Horrors. Gary Gygax. 1980. 5.50 (*0-394-51183-2*) Random.

Tomb of Ice: Percevan. Jean Leturgie & Xavier Fauche. (Illus.). 48p. (ENG & FRE.). (YA). (gr. 6 up). 1996. pap. 8.95 (*1-887911-57-X*) Fantasy Flight.

Tomb of Ip at El Saff. Henry G. Fischer. (Illus.). xiv, 44p. 1996. 25.00 (*0-87099-756-4*) Metro Mus Art.

Tomb of Julius II & Other Works in Rome. William E. Wallace. LC 95-4441. (Michelangelo, Selected Scholarship in English Ser.: Vol. 4). (Illus.). 488p. 1995. reprint ed. text ed. 99.00 (*0-8153-1827-8*) Garland.

Tomb of Ken-Amun at Thebes: Metropolitan Museum of Art Egyptian Expedition Publications, 2 Vols., Vol. 5. Norman De Garis Davies. LC 78-168401. (Metropolitan Museum of Art Publications in Reprint). (Illus.). 208p. 1972. reprint ed. 39.00 (*0-685-00518-6*) Ayer.

Tomb of Kheruef: Theban Tomb No. 192. Epigraphic Survey Staff. LC 79-88739. (Oriental Institute Publications: No. 102). (Illus.). 1980. 110.00 (*0-918986-23-0*) Orient Inst.

Tomb of Lizard King. Mark Acres. 1983. 5.50 (*0-394-53152-3*) Random.

Tomb of Martek. Tracy Hickman. 1983. 6.00 (*0-394-53160-4*) Random.

Tomb of Nefer-Hotep at Thebes: Metropolitan Museum of Art Egyptian Expedition Publications, 2 vols in 1, Vol. 9. Norman De Garis Davies. LC 71-168402. (Metropolitan Museum of Art Publications in Reprint). (Illus.). 192p. 1972. reprint ed. 39.00 (*0-685-00519-4*) Ayer.

Tomb of Nyhetep-Ptah at Giza & the Tomb of Ankhmahor at Saqqara. Alexander Badawy. LC 77-7350. (University of California Publications: No. 11, Archaeology). 208p. 1978. pap. 59.30 (*0-7837-7469-9*, 2049191) Bks Demand.

Tomb of Queen Meryet-Amun at Thebes: Metropolitan Museum of Art Egyptian Expedition Publication, Vol. 6. Herbert E. Winlock. LC 70-168415. (Metropolitan Museum of Art Publications in Reprint). (Illus.). 204p. 1973. reprint ed. 35.95 (*0-405-02253-0*) Ayer.

Tomb of Queen Tiyi. Ed. by Dennis C. Forbes. (Illus.). 129p. 1990. reprint ed. 59.95 (*1-879388-01-4*); reprint ed. pap. 39.95 (*1-879388-00-6*) KMT Commns.

Tomb of Ramesses VI, 2 vols., Vol. 1 - Texts. Ed. by A. Piankoff & N. Rambova. LC 54-5646. (Bollingen Ser.: No. 40). reprint ed. Vol. 1- Texts. pap. 145.80 (*0-317-28638-2*, 2051348) Bks Demand.

Tomb of Ramesses VI, 2 vols., Vol. 2 - Plates. Ed. by A. Piankoff & N. Rambova. LC 54-5646. (Bollingen Ser.: No. 40). reprint ed. Vol. 2- Plates. pap. 53.00 (*0-317-28639-0*) Bks Demand.

Tomb of Rekh-Mi-Re at Thebes: Metropolitan Museum of Art Egyptian Expedition Publications, 2 Vols., Vol. 11. Norman Davies. LC 75-168403. (Metropolitan Museum of Art Publications in Reprint). (Illus.). 374p. 1980. reprint ed. 52.95 (*0-405-02267-0*) Ayer.

Tomb of Senebtisi at Lisht: Metropolitan Museum of Art Egyptian Expedition Publications, Vol. 1. Arthur C. Mace & Herbert E. Winlock. LC 73-168408. (Metropolitan Museum of Art Publications in Reprint). (Illus.). 228p. 1973. reprint ed. 35.95 (*0-405-02241-7*) Ayer.

Tomb of the Eagles: Death & Life in a Stone Age Tribe. John W. Hedges. LC 87-20316. (Illus.). 256p. (Orig.). 1987. pap. 11.95 (*0-941533-05-0*) New Amsterdam Bks.
Tomb of the Kalhora Chiefs at Hyderabad. Siddique G. Memon. (Illus.). 100p. 1995. 55.00 (*0-19-577502-3*) OUP.
***Tomb of the Kings.** Anne Hebert. 9600. pap. 19.95 (*1-85224-185-3*, Pub. by Bloodaxe Bks UK) Dufour.
Tomb of the Vizier Re-Wer at Saqqara, Vol. 4: Egyptology Today. El Fikey. 1980. pap. 32.50 (*0-85668-158-X*, Pub. by Aris & Phillips UK) David Brown.
Tomb of Tutan Khamen. (Sense of History Ser.). 1991. pap. text ed. 7.99 (*0-582-06816-9*) Longman.
***Tomb Raider Game Secrets.** PCS Staff. 96p. 1996. per., pap. 14.99 (*0-7615-0931-3*) Prima Pub.
***Tomb Raider 2 Official Game Secrets.** Ed. by Judie Svabik. 112p. 1997. per. 12.99 (*0-7615-1106-7*) Prima Pub.
Tomb Sculpture: Its Changing Aspects from Ancient Egypt to Bernini. Erwin Panofsky. (Illus.). 320p. 1992. 75.00 (*0-8109-3870-7*) Abrams.
***Tomb Sculptures of Ancient West Mexico: Nayarit-Jalisco-Colima (Objects from The Mexican Museum's Permanent Collection)** Bea C. Hocker. 8p. 1995. write for info. (*0-614-24037-9*) Mexican Museum.
Tomb Treasures from China: The Burried Art of Ancient Xi'an. Patricia Berger & Jennifer R. Casler. LC 94-27657. 80p. 1994. pap. 15.00 (*0-912804-30-0*) Kimbell Art.
Tombeau de Charles Baudelaire. Stephane Mallarme et al. LC 77-11490. reprint ed. 64.50 (*0-404-16350-5*) AMS Pr.
***Tombeau Mysterieux.** Louise Leblanc. (Novels in the Premier Roman Ser.). 64p. (FRE.). (J). (gr. 2-5). 1996. pap. 7.95 (*2-89021-222-X*, Pub. by Les Editions CN) Firefly Bks Ltd.
Tombeaux Ferment Mal. Jacques Audiberti. 240p. (FRE.). 1963. pap. 24.95 (*0-7859-1101-4*, 2070203522) Fr & Eur.
Tombigbee & Other Stories. Wayne Greenhaw. 160p. (Orig.). 1991. pap. 9.95 (*0-944404-02-2*) Sycamore AL.
Tombigbee Watershed in Southeastern Prehistory. Ned J. Jenkins & Richard A. Krause. LC 85-20879. (Illus.). 171p. 1986. reprint ed. pap. 48.80 (*0-608-01670-5*, 2062326) Bks Demand.
Tombleson's Thames & the Medway. Ed. by Bishopsgate Press Ltd. Staff. 254p. 1985. 45.00 (*0-900873-30-2*, Pub. by Bishopsgate Pr Ltd UK) St Mut.
Tombley's Walk. Crosland Brown. 416p. 1991. mass mkt. 4.50 (*0-380-76097-5*) Avon.
***Tombola: Communication Activities for Teenagers.** Palim et al. (YA). 1992. pap. text ed. write for info. (*0-17-555967-8*) Addison-Wesley.
Tomboy. Mary L. Rich. 304p. (Orig.). 1996. mass mkt. 4.99 (*0-515-11810-9*) Jove Pubns.
Tomboy Bride: A Woman's Personal Account of Life in Mining Camps of the West. Harriet F. Backus. LC 79-80764. (Illus.). 273p. 1969. pap. 14.95 (*0-87108-512-7*) Pruett.
Tomboy Trouble. Sharon D. Wyeth. LC 96-41723. (J). 1998. pap. 3.99 (*0-679-88127-1*); lib. bdg. 11.99 (*0-679-98127-6*) Random Bks Yng Read.
Tomboys! Tales of Dyke Derring-Do. Ed. by Lynne Yamaguchi & Karen Barber. (Illus.). 304p. (Orig.). 1995. pap. 9.95 (*1-55583-285-7*) Alyson Pubns.
Tombs. Edward E. Kramer. 1995. 19.99 (*1-56504-905-5*, 04905/13005) White Wolf.
Tombs. Lisa Tuttle et al. Ed. by Edward E. Kramer. 1996. pap. 5.99 (*1-56504-906-3*, 13006, Borealis) White Wolf.
***Tombs & Moon Temple of Hureidha (Hadhramaut)** G. Thompson. (Illus.). 192p. 1944. 15.00 (*0-85431-201-3*, Pub. by Soc Antiquaries UK) David Brown.
Tombs & Treasures. Catherine Charley. (See Through History Ser.). (Illus.). 48p. (J). (gr. 5-7). 1995. pap. 15.99 (*0-670-85899-4*) Viking Child Bks.
Tombs, Despoiled & Haunted: Under-Textures & 'After-Thoughts' in Walter Pater. Jay Fellows. LC 90-29333. 216p. 1991. 37.50 (*0-8047-1578-5*) Stanford U Pr.
Tombs for the Living: Andean Mortuary Practices: a Symposium at Dumbarton Oaks, 12th & 13th October, 1991. Ed. by Tom D. Dillehay. LC 93-29342. 1995. 28.00 (*0-88402-220-X*) Dumbarton Oaks.
***Tombs of Amenhotep, Khnummose & Amenmose at Thebes: (Nos. 294, 253, & 254) with Contributions by Jeffrey Burden, Gunter Heindl, Carol Meyer, Pamela Rose, Stuart T. Smith, & Tony Waldron, 2 vols.** Nigel Strudwick & Helen M. Strudwick. (Illus.). 304p. 1996. 240.00 (*0-900416-58-0*, Pub. by Aris & Phillips UK) David Brown.
Tombs of Anak. Frank E. Peretti. LC 86-73183. (Cooper Kids Adventure Ser.: No. 3). 144p. (Orig.). (J). (gr. 4-7). 1990. pap. 5.99 (*0-89107-593-3*) Crossway Bks.
Tombs of Atuan. Ursula K. Le Guin. 160p. 1984. mass mkt. 6.50 (*0-553-27331-0*, Bantam Classics) Bantam.
Tombs of Atuan. Ursula K. Le Guin. LC 70-154753. (Illus.). 176p. (J). (gr. 6-9). 1990. lib. bdg. 18.00 (*0-689-31684-4*, Atheneum Bks Young) S&S Childrens.
Tombs of Iteti, Sekhem ankh-Ptah, & Kaemnofert at Giza. Alexander Badawy. (University of California Publications, Occasional Papers: No. 9). 105p. pap. 30.00 (*0-317-29106-8*, 2021386) Bks Demand.
Tombs of the Ancient Americas. Jeanne Bendick. LC 92-24546. (First Bks.). (Illus.). 64p. (J). (gr. 5-8). 1993. lib. bdg. 21.00 (*0-531-20148-1*) Watts.
Tombs of the Pharaohs: A Three-Dimensional Discovery. Illus. by Sue Clarke. 10p. (J). (gr. 3 up). 1994. 16.95 (*1-56282-485-6*) Hyprn Child.
Tombs, Travel & Trouble. Lawrence Griswold. pap. text ed. 16.95 (*1-57090-043-4*) Alexander Bks.
***Tombstone.** Shane L. Hensley. (Illus.). 186p. (Orig.). 1997. boxed, pap. 30.00 (*1-889546-07-0*) Pinnacle Ent.
***Tombstone Adventures for Kids.** unabridged ed. Silvia A. Sheafer. (Illus.). 64p. (Orig.). (J). (gr. 4-12). 1996. pap. text ed. 8.95 (*1-889971-01-4*) Journal Pubns.
Tombstone, Arizona, 1880 Business & Professional Directory. Ed. by Lonnie E. Underhill. LC 82-551. (Illus.). vi, 38p. pap. 35.00 (*0-933234-04-X*, AACR2) Roan Horse.
Tombstone, Arizona, 1880 Business & Professional Directory. deluxe ed. Ed. by Lonnie E. Underhill. LC 82-551. (Illus.). vi, 38p. 50.00 (*0-933234-05-8*) Roan Horse.
Tombstone Courage. J. A. Jance. (Joanna Brady Ser.). 416p. 1995. mass mkt. 5.99 (*0-380-76546-2*) Avon.
Tombstone Inscriptions, Luzerne County, PA, Pt. 2. Norm Drasher & Peggy Drasher. 157p. 1994. pap. text ed. 14.95 (*1-55856-169-2*) Closson Pr.
Tombstone Inscriptions Luzerne County, Pt. 1. Norm Drasher & Peggy Drasher. 128p. 1993. pap. text ed. 14.95 (*1-55856-160-9*) Closson Pr.
Tombstone Inscriptions of King George County, Virginia. Margaret C. Klein. 84p. 1994. reprint ed. pap. 10.00 (*0-614-16571-7*, 3230) Clearfield Co.
***Tombstone Inscriptions of Snyder County: All Epitaphs Taken from the Markers in Every Burying Ground of Snyder County, Complete Record from the Time of Settlement of This Territory by the Pioneers Before the Revolutionary War Down to the Year 1904.** George W. Wagenseller. (Illus.). 279p. 1997. reprint ed. lib. bdg. 35.00 (*0-8328-6452-8*) Higginson Bk Co.
Tombstone Inscriptions of Upper Accomack Co., VA. Barry W. Miles et al. (Illus.). 372p. (Orig.). 1995. 27.50 (*0-7884-0223-4*) Heritage Bk.
Tombstone Inscriptions St. John's Lutheran & Reformed CEM St. Johns: Formerly Hughesville, Luzerne County, PA. Norm Drasher & Peggy Drasher. 202p. 1993. pap. 19.95 (*1-55856-116-1*) Closson Pr.
Tombstone Lettering on Slate. Frederick Burgess. 1989. reprint ed. pap. 6.50 (*0-930194-20-9*) Ctr Thanatology.
Tombstone Records of Eighteen Cemeteries in Pound Ridge, Westchester Co., N. Y. Mable L. Jordan & Natalie M. Seth. LC 83-12997. 1983. reprint ed. pap. 9.50 (*0-916346-49-8*, 1349) Picton Pr.
Tombstone Showdown. Walt Denver. 1990. mass mkt. 2.95 (*0-8217-2873-3*, Zebra Kensgtn) Kensgtn Pub Corp.
Tombstone Ten Gauge - Death Draw. Kit Dalton. (Buckskin Double Edition Ser.). 352p. 1996. mass mkt., pap. text ed. 5.99 (*0-8439-3901-X*) Dorchester Pub Co.
Tombstones. Dan Mckinnon. 106p. 1995. pap. 14.95 (*0-941437-03-5*) House Hits.
Tombstones: A Lawyer's Tales from the Takeover Decades. Lawrence Lederman. 342p. 1992. 24.00 (*0-374-27845-8*) FS&G.
Tombstones: Dances with Werewolves. John Peel. (J). (gr. 7 up). 1995. pap. 3.99 (*0-671-53529-3*, Archway) PB.
Tombstones: 80 Famous People & Their Final Resting Places. Gregg Felsen. (Illus.). 160p. (Orig.). 1996. 19.95 (*0-89815-860-5*) Ten Speed Pr.
Tombstones & Tumbleweed. Edna Van Leuven. 1994. 17.95 (*0-8034-9090-9*, 094542) Bouregy.
Tombstone's Early Years. John M. Myers. LC 94-41319. (Illus.). 266p. 1995. pap. 12.00 (*0-8032-8215-X*, Bison Books) U of Nebr Pr.
***Tombstone's "Epitaph"** Douglas D. Martin. LC 97-16089. (Illus.). 304p. 1997. pap. 16.95 (*0-8061-2982-4*) U of Okla Pr.
Tombstones of the Irish Born: Cemetery of the Holy Cross Flatbush, Brooklyn. Joseph M. Silinonte. (Illus.). 112p. (Orig.). 1994. pap. text ed. 20.00 (*0-7884-0077-0*) Heritage Bk.
Tombstones of Your Ancestors. Louis S. Schafer. viii, 156p. (Orig.). 1991. pap. 15.00 (*1-55613-436-3*) Heritage Bk.
Tomcat's Big CB Handbook: Everything They Never Told You. Tom Kneitel. (Illus.). 221p. (Orig.). 1988. pap. text ed. 15.95 (*0-939780-07-0*) CRB Res.
Tome I, Livre I-VI see Fables
Tome II, Livres VII-XII see Fables
Tome of Forgotten Magical Items: Weapons & Armor, Vol. I. Jon Volden. Ed. by Nancy McDonald. (Illus.). 120p. (Orig.). (J). (gr. 2 up). 1994. pap. text ed. 15.00 (*0-9643929-4-1*) Stainless Steel.
Tome of Magic. David Cook. (Advanced Dungeons & Dragons Ser.). 1991. 20.00 (*1-56076-107-5*) TSR Inc.
Tome Premier. Francis Ponge. 620p. 1965. pap. 45.00 (*0-7859-1300-9*, 2070251675) Fr & Eur.
Tome Recapitulatif (1910-1965) see Oeuvres Completes
Tome 1-Exercises Corriges sur des Structures Elementaires see Cahiers Mathematiques
Tome 2-Exercises Corriges sur des Structures Elementaires see Cahiers Mathematiques
Tome 3-Morceaux Choisis D'algebre et de Combinatiore pour les Sciences Humaines see Cahiers Mathematiques
Tome 4-Distributions Statistiques et Lois de Probabilite see Cahiers Mathematiques
***Tomen Assesses Chemical Export Opportunities in Latin America.** Michael P. Ryan. (Pew Case Studies in International Affairs). 50p. (C). 1996. text ed. 3.50 (*1-56927-723-0*) Geo U Inst Dplmcy.
Tomentelloid Fungi of North America, No. 93. 1968. 2.00 (*0-686-20703-3*) SUNY Environ.
Tomer Devorah . Moshe Cordevero. Tr. by Moshe Miller. (ENG & HEB.). 1994. 16.95 (*1-56871-027-5*) Feldheim.
Tomer Devorah. Tr. by Moshe Miller. 1994. 14.95 (*0-944070-99-X*) Targum Pr.
***Tomi Ungerer's "Heidi"** Johanna Spyri. (Illus.). 320p. 1997. pap. 14.95 (*1-57098-162-0*) R Rinehart.
***Tomie de Folk Mobile.** Tomie Depaola. (J). Date not set. write for info. (*0-399-23064-5*) Putnam Pub Group.
***Tomie de Lit Miracle.** Tomie Depaola. (J). Date not set. 8.95 (*0-399-21343-0*) Putnam Pub Group.
Tomie de Paola. Julie Berg. LC 93-12960. (Young at Heart Ser.). (Illus.). (J). 1993. pap. 4.95 (*1-56239-363-4*); lib. bdg. 14.98 (*1-56239-223-9*) Abdo & Dghtrs.
Tomie De Paola's Book of Bible Stories. Tomie De Paola. 128p. (J). 1990. 24.95 (*0-399-21690-1*, Putnam) Putnam Pub Group.
Tomie De Paola's Book of Poems. Tomie De Paola. (Illus.). 80p. (J). (ps-3). 1988. 22.95 (*0-399-21540-9*, Putnam) Putnam Pub Group.
Tomie de Paola's Book of the Old Testament. Illus. by Tomie De Paola. LC 94-22219. 80p. 1995. 18.95 (*0-399-22830-6*, Putnam) Putnam Pub Group.
Tomie de Paola's Favorite Nursery Tales. Illus. & Selected by Tomie De Paola. 128p. (J). (gr. 1 up). 1986. 24.95 (*0-399-21319-8*, Putnam) Putnam Pub Group.
Tomie dePaola's Mother Goose. Illus. by Tomie DePaola. LC 84-26314. 127p. (J). (ps-2). 1985. 24.95 (*0-399-21258-2*, Putnam) Putnam Pub Group.
***Tomie's Little Mother Goose.** Tomie De Paola. LC 96-44947. (Illus.). 32p. (J). (ps). 1997. 7.95 (*0-399-23154-4*, Putnam) Putnam Pub Group.
***Tomiki Aikido: Randori & Koryu No Kata.** Lee A. Loi. 1996. pap. 24.95 (*1-874250-20-0*, Pub. by P H Crompton UK) Talman.
Tomkins - Tomkins Genealogy. R. A. Tompkins & C. F. Tompkins. (Illus.). 720p. 1991. reprint ed. pap. 99.50 (*0-8328-1948-4*); reprint ed. lib. bdg. 109.50 (*0-8328-1947-6*) Higginson Bk Co.
Tomkins Pavan (a Five) & Simpson Galliard (a Five) Ed. by William Hettrick. (Renaissance Recorder Ser.: No. 5). 1976. 2.75 (*0-913334-22-7*, CM1026) Consort Music.
Tomlin's Crew. J. William Smallwood, Jr. (Illus.). 296p. 1992. pap. 21.95 (*0-89745-154-6*) Sunflower U Pr.
***Tommaso Campanella & the Transformation of the World.** John M. Headley. LC 96-37931. 1997. write for info. (*0-691-02679-3*) Princeton U Pr.
Tommaso Campanella in America: A Critical Bibliography & a Profile. Francesco Grillo. 109p. (C). 1954. 10.00 (*0-913298-43-3*) S F Vanni.
Tommaso Campanella in America: A Supplement to the Critical Bibliography. Francesco Grillo. 48p. 1957. pap. 5.00 (*0-913298-49-2*) S F Vanni.
***Tommaso Giordani: Three Quintets for Keyboard & Strings.** Tommas Giordani. Ed. by Nicholas Temperley. (Recent Researches in Music of the Classic Era Ser.: Vol. RRC25). (Illus.). xv, 128p. 1987. pap. 43.20 (*0-89579-214-1*) A-R Eds.
Tommaso Landolfi's Grotesque Images. Romana Capek-Habekovic. (Studies in the Humanities: Literature-Politics-Society: Vol. 3). 161p. 1987. text ed. 33.00 (*0-8204-0263-X*) P Lang Pubng.
Tomorrow's Alphabet. George Shannon. LC 94-19484. (Illus.). 56p. (J). (gr. k up). 1996. 16.00 (*0-688-13504-8*); lib. bdg. 15.93 (*0-688-13505-6*) Greenwillow.
Tommy. Betsy Brown. 16p. (J). (gr. 1-3). 1995. write for info. (*1-888479-02-7*) Tarpley Pubng.
***Tommy & Chuckie on the Go: Rugrats.** Sarah Willson. (J). 1997. pap. 5.99 (*0-689-81642-1*, Aladdin Paperbacks) S&S Childrens.
Tommy & Grizel see Works of J. M. Barrie. Peter Pan Edition
Tommy & James Cell. Neva Howard. 32p. (J). 1989. write for info. (*0-318-65131-9*) N Howard.
Tommy & Jimmy: The Dorsey Years. Herb Sanford. LC 79-27093. (Quality Paperbacks Ser.). (Illus.). 1980. reprint ed. pap. 6.95 (*0-306-80117-5*) Da Capo.
Tommy & Neil. Sheila E. Murphy. LC 93-14485. (Illus.). 96p. (Orig.). 1993. 20.00 (*0-933313-17-9*); pap. 12.95 (*0-933313-18-7*) SUN Gemini Pr.
Tommy & Neil. limited ed. Sheila E. Murphy. LC 93-14485. (Illus.). 96p. (Orig.). 1993. 30.00 (*0-933313-16-0*) SUN Gemini Pr.
Tommy & the Trash Monster. Cissy R. Metcalf. (Illus.). 1995. pap. 7.95 (*0-533-11308-3*) Vantage.
Tommy & the Wishing Stone. Thornton W. Burgess. (J). 19.95 (*0-8488-0932-7*) Amereon Ltd.
Tommy at the Grocery Store. Bill Grossman. LC 88-35756. (Trophy Picture Bk.). (Illus.). 32p. (J). (ps-2). 1991. pap. 4.95 (*0-06-443266-1*, Trophy) HarpC Child Bks.
Tommy Bent: Bent by Name, Bent by Nature. Margaret Glass. 236p. (Orig.). 1993. pap. 24.95 (*0-522-84521-5*, Pub. by Melbourne Univ Pr AT) Paul & Co Pubs.
Tommy Dorsey: On the Side. Robert L. Stockdale. LC 94-33911. (Studies in Jazz: No. 19). (Illus.). 474p. 1995. 52.50 (*0-8108-2951-7*) Scarecrow.
***Tommy Makems Secret Ireland.** Makem. Date not set. 21.95 (*0-312-15675-8*) St Martin.
***Tommy Nunez.** Barbara Marvis. LC 97-21986. (Real Life Reader Biographies Ser.). (Illus.). 32p. (J). (gr. k-4). 1997. lib. bdg. 15.95 (*1-883845-52-1*) M Lane Pubs.
Tommy Nunez - NBA Referee: Taking My Best Shot. Barbara J. Marvis. Ed. by Susan R. Scarfe. (Illus.). 80p. (Orig.). (J). (gr. 6-8). 1996. pap. 10.95 (*1-883845-28-9*) M Lane Pubs.
Tommy Seven Years. unabridged ed. James D. Hall. LC 97-93622. (Illus.). viii, 171p. (Orig.). 1997. pap. 11.25 (*0-9658317-0-1*, 001) Grindall St Pr.
Tommy Snake. Marsha Marquardt. 8p. (J). (gr. 1). 1989. pap. text ed. 3.00 (*1-882225-02-3*) Tott Pubns.
Tommy Stands Alone. Gloria Velasquez. LC 95-13551. 135p. (YA). (gr. 6 up). 1995. 14.95 (*1-55885-146-1*, Pinata Bks); pap. 7.95 (*1-55885-147-X*, Pinata Bks) Arte Publico.
***Tommy Stays up Late.** (Ready Readers Stage I Ser.). (Illus.). 32p. (J). (gr. k-2). 1995. pap. write for info. (*1-56144-741-2*, Honey Bear Bks) Modern Pub NYC.
Tommy Tang's Modern Thai Cuisine. Tommy Tang. 160p. 1991. 25.00 (*0-385-41943-0*) Doubleday.
Tommy Tedesco: Confessions of a Guitar Player. Tommy Tedesco. LC 93-71095. (Illus.). 104p. (Orig.). 1993. pap. 24.95 (*0-931759-71-4*) Centerstream Pub.
Tommy the Toothbrush. Robert D. Miller. (Illus.). 16p. (J). (gr. 2-4). 1982. write for info. (*0-318-56644-3*) Miller OH.
Tommy Traveller in the World of Black History. Tom Feelings. (Illus.). 48p. (J). (gr. 3-6). 1991. 13.95 (*0-86316-202-9*) Writers & Readers.
Tommy Traveller in the World of Black History. Tom Feelings. (J). (gr. 4-7). 1993. pap. 6.95 (*0-86316-211-8*) Writers & Readers.
Tommyknockers. Stephen King. 1993. pap. 6.99 (*0-451-17842-4*, Sig) NAL-Dutton.
Tommyknockers. Stephen King. 1988. reprint ed. pap. 6.99 (*0-451-15660-9*) NAL-Dutton.
Tommy's Change of Heart. Thornton W. Burgess. (J). 19.95 (*0-8488-1418-5*) Amereon Ltd.
Tommy's First Speaker. Ed. by Thomas W. Handford. LC 71-149104. (Granger Index Reprint Ser.). 1977. 18.95 (*0-8369-6229-X*) Ayer.
Tommy's Long Yard. Matthew V. Smith. (Illus.). 17p. (J). (gr. k-3). 1994. pap. 9.95 (*1-56606-024-9*) Bradley Mann.
Tommy's Mommy's Fish. Nancy D. Watson. (Illus.). 32p. (J). (ps-3). 1996. pap. 14.99 (*0-670-85681-9*, Viking) Viking Child Bks.
***Tommy's Tattered Teddy Bear.** Virginia H. Wark. (Illus.). 22p. (Orig.). (J). (gr. 1-4). 1997. pap. 8.99 (*1-55237-063-1*, Pub. by Comnwlth Pub CN) Partners Pubs Grp.
***Tommy's Treehouse.** Tom Toombs. Date not set. write for info. (*0-7601-1385-8*, VH0006, Brentwood Kids) Brentwood Music Inc.
Tommy's Wishes Come True. Thornton W. Burgess. (J). 19.95 (*0-8488-1419-3*) Amereon Ltd.
Tomographic Methods in Nuclear Medicine: Physical Principles, Instruments, & Clinical Applications. Ed. by Bhagwat D. Ahluwalia. 288p. 1989. 190.00 (*0-8493-6198-2*, RC78) CRC Pr.
Tomographic Techniques for Process Design & Operation. Ed. by M. S. Beck et al. LC 93-70678. 504p. 1993. 172.00 (*1-56252-170-5*, 2467) Computational Mech MA.
Tomography, Impedence Imaging & Integral Geometry: Proceedings of the 1993 AMS-SIAM Seminar in Applied Mathematics on Tomography, Impedance Imaging & Integral Geometry, June 7-18, 1993, Mt. Holyoke College, Massachusetts. Ed. by Eric T. Quint et al. LC 94-28800. (Lectures in Applied Mathematics: Vol. 30). 1994. 57.00 (*0-8218-0337-9*, LAM/30) Am Math.
Tomography of Soil - Water - Root Processes: Proceedings of a Symposium Sponsored by Division S-1 & S-6 of the Soil Science Society of America in Minneapolis, Minnesota, 4 Nov. 1992. Ed. by S. H. Abnderson & J. W. Hopmans. LC 94-20002. (Publications: No. 36). 1994. pap. 21.00 (*0-89118-808-8*) Soil Sci Soc Am.
Tomorrow. Lou Berry. LC 94-60123. 170p. 1994. pap. 9.95 (*1-55523-681-2*) Winston-Derek.
Tomorrow. Elisabeth R. Taylor. 136p. 9100. 30.00 (*0-7206-0806-6*, Pub. by P Owen Ltd UK) Dufour.
Tomorrow??? D. O. Van Buren. LC 88-51338. (Illus.). 252p. (Orig.). 1988. pap. 11.95 (*0-945383-01-0*, 940-5701) Teach Servs.
Tomorrow: A Personal Journal with Quotations. Running Press Staff. (Illus.). 96p. 1995. pap. text ed. 5.95 (*1-56138-728-2*) Running Pr.
Tomorrow: Adapted from a Story by William Faulkner. rev. ed. William Faulkner. 1996. pap. 5.25 (*0-8222-1519-5*) Dramatists Play.
Tomorrow a New World. Paul Conklin. (FDR & the Era of the New Deal Ser.). 1976. reprint ed. lib. bdg. 39.50 (*0-306-70805-1*) Da Capo.
Tomorrow about This Time. Grace L. Hill. (Grace Livingston Hill Ser.: Vol. 52). 1993. pap. 4.99 (*0-8423-7186-9*) Tyndale.
Tomorrow about This Time. Grace L. Hill. reprint ed. lib. bdg. 25.95 (*0-89190-049-7*, Rivercity Pr) Amereon Ltd.
Tomorrow & Always. Barbara Bretton. (Promo Ser.). 1994. 15.95 (*0-373-15236-1*, 1-15236-2) Harlequin Bks.
Tomorrow & Always. Barbara Bretton. 1994. pap. 4.99 (*1-55166-004-0*, 1-66004-2, Mira Bks) Harlequin Bks.
Tomorrow & Forever. Bernard Palmer & Marjorie Palmer. 280p. (Orig.). Date not set. pap. 10.95 (*1-57532-012-6*) Press-Tige Pub.
Tomorrow & Tomorrow. Charles Sheffield. LC 96-15643. 368p. 1997. pap. 13.95 (*0-553-37808-2*, Spectra) Bantam.
Tomorrow & Tomorrow & Tomorrow: Book of Days. (ASF Engagement Book). 120p. 1992. 15.00 (*0-9633854-0-2*) AL Shakespeare.
Tomorrow & Yesterday. Heinrich Boll. LC 95-54204. 250p. (C). 1996. 16.95 (*0-8101-1206-X*) Northwestern U Pr.
Tomorrow Bites. Greg Cox & T. K. Weisskopf. 1995. mass mkt. 5.99 (*0-671-87691-0*) Baen Bks.
***Tomorrow Box.** Anne Chislett. LC 81-1372. 1997. pap. text ed. 10.95 (*0-88754-198-4*, Pub. by Playwrights CN Pr CN) Theatre Comm.
Tomorrow by Design: A Regional Design Process for Sustainability. Philip H. Lewis. LC 95-43871. (Series in Sustainable Design). (Illus.). 300p. 1996. text ed. 54.95 (*0-471-10935-5*) Wiley.
Tomorrow File. Lawrence Sanders. 560p. 1985. mass mkt. 6.99 (*0-425-08179-6*) Berkley Pub.
***Tomorrow Forever.** Barbara Wigent. 367p. (Orig.). 1997. mass mkt. 5.99 (*1-55197-790-7*, Pub. by Comnwlth Pub CN) Partners Pubs Grp.
Tomorrow, God Willing: Self-Made Destinies in Cairo. Unni Wikan. (Illus.). 352p. 1996. pap. 18.95 (*0-226-89835-0*); lib. bdg. 55.00 (*0-226-89834-2*) U Ch Pr.
Tomorrow I'll Be Different. Beauchamp Colclough. 240p. 1995. pap. 11.95 (*0-87951-629-1*) Overlook Pr.

An Asterisk (*) at the beginning of an entry indicates that the title is appearing in BIP for the first time.

Tomorrow I'll Be Different: The Effective Way to Stop Drinking. Beauchamp Colclough. 242p. 1994. 21.95 (*0-87951-565-1*) Overlook Pr.

Tomorrow I'll Say, Enough. Silvina Bullrich. Ed. by Yvette E. Miller et al. Tr. by Julia S. Smith from SPA. LC 95-21098. (Discoveries Ser.). 192p. (Orig.). (C). 1996. pap. 15.95 (*0-935480-70-6*) Lat Am Lit Rev Pr.

***Tomorrow in the Battle Think on Me.** Javier Marias & Margaret J. Costa. LC 97-5841. 1997. write for info. (*0-15-100276-2*) HarBrace.

Tomorrow in the Making. Ed. by John N. Andrews & Carl A. Marsden. LC 72-546. (Essay Index Reprint Ser.). 1977. reprint ed. 30.95 (*0-8369-2782-6*) Ayer.

Tomorrow Is a Promise. Fritzi Francis. 1995. pap. 12.95 (*0-533-11225-7*) Vantage.

Tomorrow Is a River. Peggy H. Dopp & Barbara F. Vroman. LC 76-52054. 390p. (Orig.). 1977. 15.95 (*0-931762-00-6*) Phunn Pubs.

Tomorrow Is Another Country. Allister Sparks. 1995. 22.00 (*0-8090-9405-3*) Hill & Wang.

Tomorrow Is Another Country: The Inside Story of South Africa's Road to Change. Allister Sparks. 266p. 1996. pap. 14.95 (*0-226-76855-4*) U Ch Pr.

Tomorrow Is Another Day. Stuart M. Kaminsky. 224p. 1996. mass mkt. 5.99 (*0-446-40336-9*, Mysterious Paperbk) Warner Bks.

Tomorrow Is Another Day: Hope of a Better Future for Black Americans. Eliza Washington. 4.00 (*0-939354-00-4*) E Washington.

Tomorrow Is Another Day: The Woman Writer in the South, 1859-1936. Anne G. Jones. LC 80-29123. (Illus.). 413p. (C). 1994. pap. text ed. 17.95 (*0-8071-0866-9*) La State U Pr.

Tomorrow Is Beautiful. Lucy Lang. (American Autobiography Ser.). 303p. 1995. reprint ed. lib. bdg. 99.00 (*0-7812-8573-9*) Rprt Serv.

Tomorrow Is Daddy's Birthday. Ginger Wadsworth. LC 92-71870. (Illus.). 32p. (J). (ps-1). 1994. 14.95 (*1-56397-042-2*) Boyds Mills Pr.

Tomorrow Is for Weeping. Judith MacEachron. LC 79-63106. 1979. 8.95 (*0-914338-04-8*) Regmar Pub.

Tomorrow Is Forever. Gwen Bristow. 320p. 1976. lib. bdg. 25.95 (*0-89966-027-4*) Buccaneer Bks.

Tomorrow Is Forever. Mary J. Springer. LC 95-71981. 1997. 13.95 (*0-8158-0520-9*) Chris Mass.

***Tomorrow Is Forever.** Ree Ree Thurman. 448p. (Orig.). 1997. mass mkt. 5.99 (*1-55197-817-2*, Pub. by Comnwlth Pub CN) Partners Pubs Grp.

Tomorrow Is Mom's Birthday. Carolyn Dorflinger. LC 93-19607. (Illus.). 32p. (J). 1994. lib. bdg. 14.95 (*1-879085-84-4*) Whsprng Coyote Pr.

Tomorrow Is Mom's Birthday. Carolyn Dorflinger. (Illus.). 32p. (J). (ps-2). 1996. pap. 5.95 (*1-879085-67-4*) Whsprng Coyote Pr.

Tomorrow Is Ours. Rosa Wake. (C). 1989. text ed. 50.00 (*1-85821-017-8*, Pub. by Pentland Pr UK) St Mut.

***Tomorrow Is Ours.** large type ed. Barbara Best. (Linford Romance Large Print Ser.). 288p. 1997. pap. 16.99 (*0-7089-5112-0*, Linford) Ulverscroft.

Tomorrow Is Sunday. Jean Daniel. (C). 1988. 39.00 (*0-85439-141-X*, Pub. by St Paul Pubns UK) St Mut.

Tomorrow Is Today. Shelley Bruce. 1983. 15.95 (*0-02-517800-8*) Macmillan.

Tomorrow Is Today. Shelley Bruce. LC 83-3797. (Illus.). 224p. 1983. write for info. (*0-672-52756-1*) Macmillan.

Tomorrow Is Too Late: Development & the Environmental Crisis in the Third World. Fidel Castro. 54p. 1993. pap. 6.95 (*1-875284-73-7*) Ocean Pr NY.

Tomorrow Leaves. Carlus B. Harris. 166p. (Orig.). 1993. pap. 9.95 (*0-9637950-0-7*) Harris Hse.

Tomorrow May Be Even Worse. limited ed. John Brunner. (Illus.). 64p. 1978. pap. 4.00 (*0-915368-15-3*) New Eng SF Assoc.

***Tomorrow May Be Too Late: An Assimilated Journalist's Involvement in the Notorious Dreyfus Trial Reunites Him with His Jewish Heritage.** Chana S. Rubin. 15.99 (*0-89906-619-4*, TOMH); pap. 12.99 (*0-89906-620-8*, TOMP) Mesorah Pubns.

***Tomorrow Never Dies.** Raymond Benson. (James Bond Ser.). 1997. mass mkt. 5.99 (*1-57297-345-5*) Blvd Books.

Tomorrow Never Knows. Ed. by Diana Zeiger. 1995. 69.95 (*1-56167-267-X*) Nat Lib Poetry.

Tomorrow Never Knows: The Beatles' Last Concert. Eric Lefcowitz. Ed. by Anita Sethi. LC 87-80730. (Illus.). 104p. (Orig.). 1987. pap. 12.95 (*0-943249-02-3*) Terra Firma Bks.

Tomorrow Never Knows: The Beatles' Last Concert. 2nd ed. Eric Lefcowitz. (Illus.). 104p. (Orig.). 1991. 24.95 (*0-943249-04-X*) Terra Firma Bks.

Tomorrow on Rocky Pond. Lynn W. Reiser. LC 91-45801. (Illus.). 32p. (J). (ps up). 1993. 14.00 (*0-688-10672-2*); lib. bdg. 13.93 (*0-688-10673-0*) Greenwillow.

***Tomorrow or the Next Day.** Tom Clapp. 55p. (Orig.). 1996. pap. 6.00 (*0-88734-279-5*) Players Pr.

Tomorrow People Archives. T. C. Kirkham. (Archives Ser.). 1988. 10.00 (*0-317-91288-7*) Jaunt Pr.

Tomorrow Sucks: SF Vampire Stories. Greg Cox & T. K. Weisskopf. 304p. (Orig.). 1994. mass mkt. 4.99 (*0-671-87626-0*) Baen Bks.

Tomorrow Today: Geelong Alive with Ideas. Ed. by Kathleen Walsh. 1992. pap. 36.00 (*0-949823-28-7*, Pub. by Deakin Univ AT) St Mut.

Tomorrow Trap: Unlocking the Secrets of the Procrastination-Protection Syndrome. Karen E. Peterson. 356p. (Orig.). 1996. pap. 12.95 (*1-55874-417-7*, 4177) Health Comm.

Tomorrow Triumphant: Selected Poems of Otto Rene Castillo. Roque Dalton Cultural Brigade Staff. (Literature Ser.: No. 3). 144p. (Orig.). (ENG & SPA.). 1984. pap. 6.95 (*0-941842-02-9*) Night Horn Books.

Tomorrow We Die. Elisaveta Fen. 245p. 1989. 85.00 (*0-7223-1575-9*, Pub. by A H S Ltd UK) St Mut.

Tomorrow We Go to Bethlehem. John McTavish. 1986. pap. 5.25 (*0-687-42330-9*) Abingdon.

Tomorrow We Live. O. Mosley. 1973. 59.95 (*0-8490-1221-X*) Gordon Pr.

Tomorrow Wears a Veil. large type ed. Kathleen Treves. 400p. 1987. 25.99 (*0-7089-1635-X*) Ulverscroft.

Tomorrow, We're Taking a Test. Donna Roppelt & Mary Mowl. 1982. Set. pap. 1.95 (*0-932666-16-7*) T J Pubs.

Tomorrow, When the War Began. John Marsden. LC 94-29299. 288p. (J). (gr. 7 up). 1995. 15.00 (*0-395-70673-4*) HM.

Tomorrow, When the War Began. John Marsden. 288p. (J). 1996. mass mkt. 3.99 (*0-440-21985-X*) Dell.

Tomorrow Will Always Come. Clara R. DeLima. 1965. 12.95 (*0-8392-1141-4*) Astor-Honor.

Tomorrow Will Be a Nice Day. Christiane Renauld. (Child's World Library). (Illus.). 32p. (J). (gr. k-5). 1991. lib. bdg. 18.50 (*0-89565-763-5*) Childs World.

Tomorrow Will Be Better. Betty Smith. 1942. pap. 2.50 (*0-06-080049-6*, P49, PL) HarpC.

Tomorrow Will Be Later. Betty Smith. 23.95 (*0-8488-1171-2*) Amereon Ltd.

Tomorrow Will Be Too Late: East Meets West on Global Ecology. Rolf Edberg & Alexei Yablokov. Tr. by Sergei Chulaki from RUS. LC 90-44528. 210p. (Orig.). 1991. 33.50 (*0-8165-1217-5*); pap. 7.50 (*0-8165-1228-0*) U of Ariz Pr.

***Tomorrow You Die.** rev. ed. Reona P. Joly. (International Adventures Ser.). 150p. 1997. pap. 8.99 (*0-927545-92-6*) YWAM Pub.

Tomorrow's Architectural Heritage: Landscape & Buildings in the Countryside. J. M. Fladmark et al. (Illus.). 192p. 1992. 34.95 (*1-85158-378-5*, Pub. by Mnstream UK) Trafalgar.

Tomorrow's Banks: Developments Shaping the 1990's. Warren F. Cooke. 1989. pap. 59.95 (*1-55840-279-9*) Exec Ent Pubns.

Tomorrow's Blossoms. large type ed. Barbara Taylor. (Linford Romance Library). 304p. 1992. pap. 15.99 (*0-7089-7277-2*, Trailtree Bookshop) Ulverscroft.

Tomorrow's Bride. Alexandra Scott. (Romance Ser.). 1996. mass mkt. 2.99 (*0-373-03393-1*, 1-03393-5) Harlequin Bks.

Tomorrow's Capitalism: Search for a New Paradigm Beyond the Competing National Models. Ed. by Jai-Hoon Yang. 208p. (Orig.). 1995. pap. 19.50 (*1-883223-06-7*) Pacific NY.

***Tomorrow's Catholic: Understanding God & Jesus in a New Millennium.** Michael Morwood. LC 97-60030. 160p. (Orig.). 1997. pap. 9.95 (*0-89622-724-3*) Twenty-Third.

Tomorrow's Catholics, Yesterday's Church. Eugene Kennedy. LC 88-45037. 1990. pap. 9.95 (*0-06-064578-4*) Harper SF.

Tomorrow's Catholics, Yesterday's Church: The Two Cultures of American Catholicism. Eugene Kennedy. LC 94-41663. 224p. 1995. pap. 12.95 (*0-89243-580-1*, Triumph Books) Liguori Pubns.

Tomorrow's Classroom Today: Strategies for Creating Active Readers, Writers, & Thinkers. Faye Brownlie et al. Ed. by Art Hughes. LC 90-43250. (Illus.). 160p. (Orig.). (C). 1990. pap. text ed. 21.00 (*0-435-08550-6*, 08550) Heinemann.

Tomorrow's Community College. Roy W. Smith. LC 95-79403. 100p. (Orig.). 1995. pap. 14.95 (*0-9648119-8-7*) Life Pr NJ.

Tomorrow's Competition: The Next Generation of Growth Strategies. Mack Hanan. 192p. 1993. pap. 15.95 (*0-8144-7862-X*) AMACOM.

Tomorrow's Doctors: The Path to Successful Practice in the 1990's. B. H. Natelson. LC 89-26563. (Illus.). 302p. 1990. 19.95 (*0-306-43195-5*, Plenum Insight) Plenum.

Tomorrow's Dream. Ed. by Joy Esterby. 1996. 69.95 (*1-57553-007-4*) Watermrk Pr.

Tomorrow's Dream, Today's Courage. Max Lucado. 32p. 1995. pap. 2.99 (*0-8499-5212-3*) Word Pub.

Tomorrow's Dreams. Heather Cullman. 384p. 1996. pap. 5.50 (*0-451-40684-2*, Onyx) NAL-Dutton.

Tomorrow's Food. James Rorty & Philip Norman. 9.95 (*0-8159-6906-6*) Devin.

Tomorrow's Food. enl. rev. ed. James Rorty & N. Philip Norman. LC 56-8132. 309p. reprint ed. pap. 88.10 (*0-317-28232-8*, 2022712) Bks Demand.

Tomorrow's God: How We Create Our Worlds. Lloyd Geering. 249p. 1996. pap. 19.95 (*0-908912-66-8*) Paul & Co Pubs.

Tomorrow's Harvest. Hiram M. Drache. LC 78-57250. 315p. 1978. 20.95 (*0-8134-2032-6*, 2032) Interstate.

***Tomorrow's Harvest.** large type ed. Alison York. (Magna Large Print Ser.). 292p. 1997. 27.50 (*0-7505-1131-1*) Ulverscroft.

***Tomorrow's Heirlooms: Fashions of the '60's & '70's.** Trina Robbins. LC 97-20315. 1997. pap. write for info. (*0-7643-0354-6*) Schiffer.

Tomorrow's Hospital: A Look to the Twenty-First Century. Eli Ginzberg. 1996. write for info. (*0-300-06574-4*) Yale U Pr.

***Tomorrow's HR Management: 48 Thought Leaders Call for Change.** Ed. by David Ulrich et al. 256p. 1997. 35.95 (*0-471-19714-9*) Wiley.

Tomorrow's Jobs: Employment, Changes in Population & the Labor Force, Job Opportunities, Careers, Training & Financial Aid. 1991. lib. bdg. 75.00 (*0-8490-5157-6*) Gordon Pr.

Tomorrow's Joy. Kenneth L. Hardin. (Illus.). 187p. (Orig.). 1987. pap. 4.00 (*0-9619153-1-5*) K L Hardin.

Tomorrow's Law. Ed. by Hugh Selby. 316p. 1995. pap. 25.00 (*1-86287-196-5*, Pub. by Federation Pr AU) Gaunt.

Tomorrow's Lawyers. Ed. by Philip A. Thomas. LC 92-19238. 1992. pap. 24.95 (*0-631-18267-5*) Blackwell Pubs.

Tomorrow's Learning Environment: Planning for Technology: the Basics. Franklin Hill. Ed. by Anne Ward. (Illus.). 154p. (Orig.). 1988. pap. text ed. 35.00 (*0-88364-165-8*) Natl Sch Boards.

Tomorrow's Managers Today: The Identification & Development of Management Potential. Andrew Stewart & Valerie Stewart. 270p. (C). 1981. 72.00 (*0-85292-300-7*, Pub. by IPM Hse UK) St Mut.

Tomorrow's Materials. 2nd ed. Ken Easterling. 183p. 1990. pap. text ed. 29.00 (*0-901462-83-7*, Pub. by Inst Materials UK) Ashgate Pub Co.

Tomorrow's Materials Today: Alloys, Blends, & Modified Polymers, a Unique Technical Conference, October 5 & 6, 1993, Quaker Square Hilton Inn & Conference Center, Akron, OH. Society of Plastics Engineers Staff. (Illus.). 380p. 1993. reprint ed. pap. 108.30 (*0-7837-9705-2*, 2060436) Bks Demand.

Tomorrow's Materials: Today: 34th International SAMPE Symposium & Exhibition, Reno Conventionk Center, Reno, NV, May 8-11, 1989. International SAMPE Symposium & Exhibition Staff. Ed. by G. A. Zakrzewski et al. (Science of Advanced Materials & Process Enginnering Ser.: No. 34). (Illus.). 1350p. 1989. reprint ed. pap. 180.00 (*0-7837-9633-1*, 2060387); reprint ed. pap. 180.00 (*0-7837-9634-X*, 2060387) Bks Demand.

Tomorrow's Medicine. Richard Grossman. 1996. write for info. (*0-201-62689-6*) Addison-Wesley.

Tomorrow's Miracle. large type ed. Frank G. Slaughter. 1978. 12.00 (*0-7089-0091-7*) Ulverscroft.

Tomorrow's Mission: World War II Diary of a Combat Aircrewman Aboard the U. S. S. Yorktown (CV-10), the Fighting Lady, During the Pacific War 1943-1945. Raymond J. Dausereau. LC 92-74143. (Illus.). 396p. (Orig.). (YA). (gr. 11-12). Date not set. pap. 18.95 (*0-923687-24-6*) Celo Valley Bks.

Tomorrow's Office: Creating Effective & Humane Interiors. S. Raymond & R. Cunliffe. (Illus.). 312p. 1996. 64.95 (*0-419-21240-X*, E & FN Spon) Routledge Chapman & Hall.

***Tomorrow's Professor: Preparing for Academic Career's in Science & Engineering.** Rick Reis. LC 96-37355. 424p. 1997. pap. 39.95 (*0-7803-1136-1*, PC5602) Inst Electrical.

Tomorrow's Promise. Judy Baer. (Cedar River Daydreams Ser.: Vol. 10). 128p. (Orig.). (YA). (gr. 7-10). 1990. mass mkt. 4.99 (*1-55661-143-9*) Bethany Hse.

Tomorrow's Promise. Sandra Brown. (American Romance Ser.). 192p. 1993. mass mkt. 4.99 (*0-373-83282-6*) Harlequin Bks.

Tomorrow's Promise. Sandra Brown. 1994. pap. 4.99 (*1-55166-034-2*, 1-66034-9, Mira Bks) Harlequin Bks.

Tomorrow's Promise. large type ed. Kate Ward. (Linford Romance Library). 272p. 1992. pap. 15.99 (*0-7089-7213-6*, Trailtree Bookshop) Ulverscroft.

***Tomorrow's Promise & Other Poems: Pieces of One Man's Heart.** 2nd rev. ed. William G. Carrington. Ed. by Sue McKee. LC 95-95350. 84p. (Orig.). 1995. pap. 9.95 (*1-888701-00-5*) Jarrett Pr.

Tomorrow's Retiree: A National Publication of Local Resources. Ed. by Bryna Lansky. (Midwest Edition - 1993-1994 Ser.). 144p. 1993. pap. 14.95 (*0-9618885-2-0*) Tomorrows Retiree.

Tomorrow's Retiree: A National Publication of Local Resources. Ed. by Bryna Lansky. (West Edition - 1993-1994 Ser.). 1993. pap. 14.95 (*0-9618885-4-7*) Tomorrows Retiree.

Tomorrow's Retiree: A National Publication of Local Resources. Ed. by Bryna Lansky. (South Edition - 1993-1994 Ser.). 1993. pap. 14.95 (*0-9618885-3-9*) Tomorrows Retiree.

Tomorrow's Retiree: A National Publication of Local Resources. rev. ed. Ed. by Bryna Lansky. (Northeast Edition - 1993-1994 Ser.). 144p. 1993. pap. 14.95 (*0-9618885-1-2*) Tomorrows Retiree.

Tomorrow's Retiree: A Planning & Resource Publication. Bryna Lansky. (Northeast Edition - 1990-1992 Ser.). 1990. pap. 12.95 (*0-9618885-0-4*) Tomorrows Retiree.

Tomorrow's Surprises: What a Difference a Day Makes. Pamela Y. Hafner. 131p. (Orig.). 1995. pap. 10.00 (*0-9644370-3-1*) Dryden Publ.

Tomorrow's Technology: Experimenting with the Science of the Future. Irwin Math. LC 91-32341. (Illus.). 80p. (YA). (gr. 7 up). 1992. lib. bdg. 13.95 (*0-684-19294-2*, C Scribner Sons Young) S&S Childrens.

Tomorrow's Television. Frwd. by Frederick M. Remley. (Illus.). 256p. 1982. pap. text ed. 30.00 (*0-940690-06-3*) Soc Motion Pic & TV Engrs.

***Tomorrows Tide.** MacDonald. LC 97-8189. 1997. 23.95 (*0-312-15676-6*) St Martin.

***Tomorrow's Tide.** Malcolm Ross. 579p. write for info. (*0-7505-1066-8*, Pub. by Magna Print Bks UK) Ulverscroft.

Tomorrows to Come. Joseph Berry. LC 87-72433. 85p. (Orig.). 1988. pap. text ed. 3.95 (*0-87029-212-9*, 20258-0) Abbey.

Tomorrow's Tomorrow: The Black Woman. Joyce A. Ladner. LC 95-22989. xxxiv, 306p. (C). 1995. pap. text ed. 12.00 (*0-8032-7956-6*, Bison Books) U of Nebr Pr.

Tomorrow's Treason. large type ed. Palma Harcourt. 344p. 1981. 25.99 (*0-7089-0619-2*) Ulverscroft.

Tomorrow's Treasures. Pat Andreatta. (Illus.). 28p. 1987. student ed. 14.95 (*0-9616848-1-X*) Heirloom Stitches.

***Tomorrow's Troubles.** Betty B. Robison. LC 97-60733. 240p. (Orig.). 1997. pap. 11.99 (*1-57921-024-4*) WinePress Pub.

Tomorrow's Tyrants: The Radical Right & the Politics of Hate. Arthur F. Ide. LC 85-277. (Woman in History Ser.: Vol. 109). (Illus.). 340p. (Orig.). 1985. pap. 25.00 (*0-930383-05-2*) Monument Pr.

Tomorrow's War: The Threat of High-Technology Weapons. David Shukman. LC 95-47575. 272p. 1996. 26.00 (*0-15-100198-7*) HarBrace.

Tomorrow's War, Today's Decisions: Iraqi Weapons of Mass Destruction & the Implications of WMD-Armed Adversaries for Future U. S. Military Strategy. Robert W. Chandler. 243p. 1996. pap. 17.95 (*0-9650770-0-4*) AMCODA Pr.

Tomorrow's Wishes. Diana Fox. 1994. 17.95 (*0-8034-9034-8*) Bouregy.

Tomorrow's Wizard. Patricia MacLachlan. LC 81-47733. (Charlotte Zolotow Bk.). (Illus.). 96p. (J). (gr. 3-6). 1982. lib. bdg. 13.89 (*0-06-024074-1*) HarpC Child Bks.

Tomorrow's Wizard. Patricia MacLachlan. LC 95-33453. 80p. (J). (gr. 3 up). 1996. pap. 6.00 (*0-15-201276-1*) HarBrace.

Tomorrrow Book of Verse. Elsbeth Liebowitz. (Illus.). 1995. pap. 6.95 (*0-9636373-0-4*) OverBoard Pr.

***Tomo's Lot.** Mike P. Ireland. 226p. (Orig.). 1997. mass mkt. 4.99 (*1-55237-377-0*, Pub. by Comnwlth Pub CN) Partners Pubs Grp.

Tomoshibi - Light: Collected Poetry. Emperor Akihito & Empress Michiko. Ed. by Marie Philomene & Masako Saito. 200p. 1991. 29.95 (*0-8348-0237-6*) Weatherhill.

Tompets: The Absolutely True, More or Less, Story. A. T. Traver. Ed. by Thomas Traver. (Tompets Ser.). 96p. 1995. pap. 3.95 (*0-9645028-0-1*) Tompet Prods.

Tompkins: World Journal Surgery. 1996. 195.00 (*0-387-14226-6*) Spr-Verlag.

Tompkins & Other Folks: Stories of the Hudson & the Adirondacks. Philander Deming. 1972. reprint ed. lib. bdg. 26.50 (*0-8422-8039-1*) Irvington.

Tompkins School 1925-1953: A Community Institution. T. Felder Dorn. 114p. (Orig.). 1994. pap. 15.00 (*0-87921-085-0*) Attic Pr.

Tompkins Square & Other Illfated Riots. Arthur Nersesian. (Illus.). 48p. 1990. pap. 2.95 (*0-685-56991-8*) SPD-Small Pr Dist.

Tom's Amazing Machine Zaps Back! Gordon Snell. (Illus.). 144p. (J). (gr. 4-6). 1992. 15.95 (*0-09-173888-1*, Pub. by Hutchinson UK) Trafalgar.

Toms, Coons, Mulattoes, Mammies, & Bucks: A History of Blacks in American Films from Birth of a Nation to Malcolm X. 3rd ed. Donald Bogle. (Illus.). 412p. 1994. reprint ed. pap. text ed. 19.95 (*0-8264-0578-9*) Continuum.

Tom's Fish. Nancy Coffelt. LC 92-44114. (Illus.). 32p. (J). (ps-3). 1994. 14.00 (*0-15-200587-0*, Gulliver Bks) HarBrace.

Tom's Friend. Pat Reynolds. LC 93-170. (J). 1994. write for info. (*0-383-03797-2*) SRA McGraw.

Tom's Girl. large type ed. Marjorie Warby. 352p. 1987. 25.99 (*0-7089-1593-0*) Ulverscroft.

Tom's Lucky Quarter. Morrell Gipson & Herta Frank. Ed. by Rebecca Stefoff. LC 90-13796. (Magic Mountain Fables Ser.). (Illus.). 24p. (J). (gr. k-3). 1990. lib. bdg. 14.60 (*0-944483-89-5*) Garrett Ed Corp.

Tom's Midnight Garden. Philippa Pearce. LC 69-12008. 240p. (J). (gr. 5-9). 1992. lib. bdg. 13.89 (*0-397-30477-3*, Lipp Jr Bks) HarpC Child Bks.

Tom's Midnight Garden. Philippa Pearce. LC 69-12008. (Trophy Bk.). (Illus.). 240p. (J). (gr. 3-7). 1992. pap. 4.95 (*0-06-440445-5*, Trophy) HarpC Child Bks.

Tom's Storybook. (Read with Me Key Words to Reading Ser.: No. 9010-8). (Illus.). (J). (ps-2). 1990. 3.50 (*0-7214-1321-8*, Ladybrd); teacher ed. 3.95 (*0-317-04636-5*, Ladybrd) Penguin.

Tom's Tail. Arlene Dubanevich. LC 92-8615. (J). (gr. 4 up). 1992. pap. 4.50 (*0-14-054177-2*) Puffin Bks.

Tom's Tail. Linda Jennings. (Illus.). (J). (ps-3). 1995. 14.95 (*0-316-13341-8*) Little.

Tom's Terps. Oren J. Hill. Ed. by M. L. Jones. LC 94-74081. 200p. (Orig.). 1995. pap. 12.95 (*1-882270-31-2*) Old Rugged Cross.

Tom's Town: Kansas City & the Pendergast Legend. William M. Reddig. LC 85-20888. 400p. (C). 1986. pap. 22.50 (*0-8262-0498-8*) U of Mo Pr.

Tom's Train. Debbie Mackinnon. 1997. pap. 4.99 (*0-8037-2105-6*) Dial Bks Young.

***Tom's Train.** Debbie MacKinnon. (Illus.). (J). (ps-k). 1997. bds. 4.99 (*0-614-28688-3*) Dial Bks Young.

TOMSK: Texture in Wood. W. Blaser. (Illus.). 112p. (ENG, FRE & GER.). 1994. 49.00 (*0-8176-2849-5*) Spr-Verlag.

***Tomsk: Texture in Wood.** Werner Blaser. 1996. pap. text ed. 62.00 (*3-7643-2849-5*) Birkhauser.

***Tomsk Oblast: Economy, Industry, Government, Business.** 2nd rev. ed. Russian Information & Business Center, Inc. Staff. (Russian Regional Business Directories Ser.). (Illus.). 200p. 1997. pap. 99.00 (*1-57751-417-3*) Russ Info & Busn Ctr.

Tomten. Astrid Lindgren. (Sandcastle Ser.). (Illus.). 32p. (J). (ps-3). 1990. pap. 6.95 (*0-698-20680-0*, Sandcastle Bks) Putnam Pub Group.

***Tomten.** Astrid Lindgren. (Illus.). 32p. (J). (ps-3). 1997. pap. 4.95 (*0-698-11591-0*, Paperstar) Putnam Pub Group.

Tomten & the Fox. Astrid Lindgren. (Illus.). 32p. (J). (ps-3). 1989. pap. 5.95 (*0-698-20644-4*, Sandcastle Bks) Putnam Pub Group.

***Tomten & the Fox.** Astrid Lindgren. (Illus.). 32p. (J). (ps-3). 1997. pap. 4.95 (*0-698-11592-9*, Paperstar) Putnam Pub Group.

Tomten's Christmas Porridge. Sven Nordqvist. Tr. by Arden Haug from SWE. (Illus.). 28p. (J). (gr. 1-6). 1991. 14.95 (*0-9615394-2-9*) Skandisk.

Tomtit Poems, Vol. 1: Poems of Nature & Life. Carol E. Custer. 55p. 1991. pap. 10.00 (*0-9631565-0-0*, 3-141-875) Tomtit Ent.

Tomy AF-X. Rob Budano & Richard Kerr. Ed. by Timothy Kevin. (Collector's Quick Reference Ser.: Vol. 4). 100p. (Orig.). pap. text ed. 14.95 (*0-88379-608-2*) What It Is.

Ton Albert Qui T'adore: Courtship Letters of Albert Spalding to Mary V. Pyle. Ed. by Suzanne S. Winston. LC 88-19527. (Illus.). 120p. 1988. 22.50 (*0-914659-36-7*) Phoenix Pub.

*__Ton Beau de Marot: In Praise of the music of Langauge.__ Douglas R. Hofstadter. LC 97-3999. 816p. 1997. 30.00 (*0-465-08643-8*) Basic.

Ton De Leeuw. Ed. by Jurrien Sligter. (Netherlands Music Archive Ser.: Vol. 1). 257p. 1996. text ed. 87.00 (*3-7186-5695-7*, ECU69, Harwood Acad Pubs); pap. text ed. 36.00 (*3-7186-5696-5*, ECU29, Harwood Acad Pubs) Gordon & Breach.

Ton-Ton el Giganton: Big Book. Ina Cumpiano. (Que Maravilla! Ser.). (Illus.). 24p. (Orig.). (SPA.). (J). (gr. 1-3). 1992. pap. text ed. 29.95 (*1-56334-025-9*) Hampton-Brown.

Ton-Ton el Giganton: Small Book. Ina Cumpiano. (Que Maravilla! Ser.). (Illus.). 24p. (Orig.). (SPA.). (J). (gr. 1-3). 1992. pap. text ed. 6.00 (*1-56334-039-9*) Hampton-Brown.

Tonal Allegory in the Vocal Music of J. S. Bach. Eric Chafe. LC 90-40050. (Illus.). 460p. 1991. 79.95 (*0-520-05856-9*) U CA Pr.

Tonal & Rhythmic Principles see Jazz Improvisation

Tonal Application of Finger Patterns to Viola Technique. Heidi Castleman, II & Joseph E. Koob. 50p. 1990. lib. bdg. write for info. (*0-929918-04-5*) Midstates Pub.

Tonal Coherence in Mahler's Ninth Symphony. Christopher O. Lewis. LC 84-2754. (Studies in Musicology: No. 79). 148p. reprint ed. pap. 42.20 (*0-8357-1585-X*, 2070558) Bks Demand.

Tonal Counterpoint in the Style of the Eighteenth Century. Ernst Krenek. LC 59-17691. 44p. (C). 1958. pap. 10.00 (*0-913932-12-4*) Boosey & Hawkes.

Tonal Grammar of Etsakro. Baruch Elimelech. LC 77-76178. (University of California Publications in Social Welfare: No. 87). (Illus.). 155p. reprint ed. pap. 44.20 (*0-685-23802-4*, 2032902) Bks Demand.

Tonal Harmonic Dictation: A Workbook. Thomas L. Durham. (Illus.). 134p. (C). 1987. 28.00 (*0-8191-6283-3*) U Pr of Amer.

Tonal Harmony: Introduction to Twentieth Century Music. 2nd ed. Stefan Kostka & Dorothy Payne. 1989. wbk. ed., pap. text ed. write for info. (*0-07-557017-3*) McGraw.

*__Tonal Harmony: Theory & Practice.__ 3rd ed. Forte. (C). 1979. spiral bd. write for info. (*0-15-504218-1*) HB Coll Pubs.

*__Tonal Harmony: With an Introduction to Twentieth-Century Music.__ 3rd ed. Stefan Kostka & Dorothy Payne. 1994. pap. text ed. write for info. incl. audio (*0-07-911863-1*) McGraw.

Tonal Harmony, with an Introduction to Twentieth-Century Music. Stefan Kostka & Dorothy Payne. 656p. (C). 1994. teacher ed. write for info. (*0-318-72111-2*) McGraw.

Tonal Harmony, with an Introduction to Twentieth-Century Music. 2nd ed. Stefan Kostka & Dorothy Payne. LC 93-39224. 1989. pap. text ed. write for info. (*0-07-557016-5*) McGraw.

Tonal Harmony, with an Introduction to Twentieth-Century Music. 3rd ed. Stefan Kostka & Dorothy Payne. 656p. (C). 1994. Wkbk. student ed., pap. text ed. write for info. (*0-07-035882-6*) McGraw.

Tonal Harmony, with an Introduction to Twentieth-Century Music. 3rd ed. Stefan Kostka & Dorothy Payne. 656p. (C). 1994. text ed. write for info. (*0-07-035874-5*) McGraw.

Tonal Harmony, with an Introduction to Twentieth-Century Music. 3rd ed. Stefan Kostka & Dorothy Payne. 656p. (C). 1994. audio write for info. (*0-318-72112-0*) McGraw.

Tonal Structures in Early Music. Christie C. Judd. Ed. by Jessie A. Owens. (Criticism & Analysis of Early Music Ser.). 250p. 1997. text ed. 37.00 (*0-8153-2388-3*) Garland.

Tonal System of Igbo. Mary M. Clark. (Publications in African Languages & Linguistics). 324p. 1990. pap. 106.15 (*3-11-013041-6*) Mouton.

Tonal Values: How to See Them, How to Paint Them. Angela Gair. (Illus.). 144p. 1992. pap. 19.95 (*0-89134-399-7*, 30401, North Lght Bks) F & W Pubns Inc.

Tonality & Atonality in Sixteenth-Century Music. Edward E. Lowinsky. (Music Reprint Ser.). 1989. 25.00 (*0-306-76299-4*) Da Capo.

Tonality, Atonality, Pantonality: A Study of Some Trends in Twentieth Century Music. Rudolph R. Reti. LC 78-6162. (Illus.). 166p. 1978. reprint ed. text ed. 38.50 (*0-313-20478-0*, RETO, Greenwood Pr) Greenwood.

Tonality in Austronesian Languages. Ed. by Jerold A. Edmondson & Kenneth J. Gregerson. (Oceanic Linguistics Special Publications: No. 24). 192p. (Orig.). (C). 1993. pap. text ed. 22.00 (*0-8248-1530-0*) UH Pr.

Tonality in Western Culture: A Critical & Historical Perspective. Richard Norton. LC 83-43030. (Illus.). 336p. 1984. 35.00 (*0-271-00359-6*) Pa St U Pr.

Tonalization. Shinichi Suzuki. (Suzuki Method Ser.). (Illus.). 64p. (Orig.). 1985. pap. text ed. 9.95 (*0-87487-214-6*, Suzuki Method) Summy-Birchard.

Tonawanda, NY. J. Percy. (Images of America Ser.). 1997. pap. 16.99 (*0-7524-0423-7*, Arcdia) Chalford.

Tondaecher von Olympia. Joachim Heiden. (Olympische Forschungen Ser.: Bd XXIV). xvi, 242p. (GER.). (C). 1995. lib. bdg. 261.55 (*3-11-014374-7*) De Gruyter.

Tondrakian Movement: Religious Movements in the Armenian Church from the Fourth to the Tenth Centuries. Vrej Nersessian. LC 88-4066. (Princeton Theological Monographs: No. 15). 156p. 1988. reprint ed. pap. 10.00 (*0-915138-99-9*) Pickwick.

Tone: A Study in Musical Acoustics. rev. ed. Siegmund Levarie & Ernst Levy. LC 80-16794. 273p. 1980. pap. 8.50 (*0-87338-250-1*) Kent St U Pr.

Tone: A Study in Musical Acoustics. 2nd ed. Siegmund Levarie & Ernst Levy. LC 80-29383. (Illus.). xvii, 256p. 1981. reprint ed. text ed. 59.75 (*0-313-22499-4*, LETO, Greenwood Pr) Greenwood.

Tone-A-Metrics: Bedroom Shapeup. Brian Heir. 1994. pap. 12.00 (*0-671-79654-2*) PB.

Tone & Color Correction. Gary G. Field. Ed. by Thomas M. Destree. LC 90-84339. (Illus.). 150p. (C). 1991. text ed. 80.00 (*0-88362-125-8*) Graphic Arts Tech Found.

Tone & Intonation on the Recorder. Edward L. Kottick. 1974. 8.00 (*0-941084-04-3*) McGinnis & Marx.

Tone Clock. Peter Schat. Tr. & Intro. by Jenny McLeod. LC 93-20273. 432p. 1993. text ed. 112.00 (*3-7186-5369-9*); pap. text ed. 36.00 (*3-7186-5370-2*) Gordon & Breach.

Tone Deaf & All Thumbs? Frank R. Wilson. LC 87-40086. 224p. 1988. pap. 12.00 (*0-394-75354-2*, Vin) Random.

Tone Development for Flute: Through the Works of J. S. Bach, Level 1. Dona Gilliam & Mizzy McCaskill. 1993. 4.95 (*1-56222-227-9*, 94543) Mel Bay.

Tone Development Through Extented Techniques. rev. ed. Robert Dick. LC 86-61675. 60p. (Orig.). 1986. pap. 19.95 (*0-939407-00-0*) Multiple Breath Music.

Tone in Five Languages of Cameroon. Ed. by Stephen C. Anderson. LC 91-66073. (Publications in Linguistics: No. 102). x, 144p. (Orig.). 1991. fiche 12.00 (*0-88312-496-3*) Summer Instit Ling.

Tone Lexical Phonology. Douglas Pulleyblank. 1986. lib. bdg. 120.00 (*90-277-2123-8*, Pub. by Klwr Acad Pubs NE) Kluwer Ac.

*__Tone of Teaching.__ Max Van Manen. pap. 12.50 (*0-590-71631-X*) Scholastic Inc.

Tone of Teaching: A Parent/Teacher Guide to Children's Learning. Max Van Manen. 55p. 1986. pap. text ed. 10.00 (*0-435-08255-8*, 08255) Heinemann.

Tone Poems in Full Score. Jean Sibelius. 1990. pap. 16.95 (*0-486-26483-1*) Dover.

Tone Poems, Series I: Don Juan, Tod und Verklarung & Don Quixote in Full Score from the Original Editions. Richard Strauss. LC 78-67060. 1979. reprint ed. pap. 12.95 (*0-486-23754-0*) Dover.

Tone Poems, Series II: Till Eulenspiegels Lustige Streiche, Also Sprach Zarathustra, & ein Heldenleben in Full Score from the Original Editions. Richard Strauss. LC 78-68041. 1979. reprint ed. pap. 12.95 (*0-486-23755-9*) Dover.

Tone, Segment, & Syllable in Chinese: A Polydimensional Approach to Surface Phonetic Structure. A. Ronald Walton. LC 83-126802. (Cornell East Asia Ser.: No. 32). 372p. 1983. pap. 12.00 (*0-939657-32-5*) Cornell East Asia Pgm.

Tone the Bell Easy. Ed. by J. Frank Dobie. LC 33-1135. (Texas Folklore Society Publications: No. 10). (Illus.). 200p. 1965. reprint ed. 12.95 (*0-87074-045-8*) UNTX Pr.

Toner. Ron Silliman. 67p. (Orig.). 1993. pap. 9.50 (*0-937013-43-9*) Potes Poets.

Tonette a Method for Beginners Also for Song Flute & Flutophone. D. Bennett. 32p. 1986. pap. 3.50 (*0-7935-5419-5*, 50502360) H Leonard.

Tonetti Years at Snedens Landing. 2nd ed. Isabelle K. Savelle. LC 77-77802. (Illus.). 1977. reprint ed. pap. 9.95 (*0-911183-05-1*) Rockland County Hist.

Toney Family History. Elma Henning & Merle Rummel. 535p. 1994. pap. 69.50 (*0-8328-4486-1*); lib. bdg. 79.50 (*0-8328-4485-3*) Higginson Bk Co.

Tonfa: Karate Weapon of Self-Defense. Fumio Demura. Ed. by Greglon Lee. LC 82-81557. (Weapons Ser.). (Illus.). 144p. (Orig.). 1982. pap. 10.95 (*0-89750-080-6*, 417) Ohara Pubns.

Tonfa Police Baton Academy Manual. Sid Campbell. 85p. 1987. pap. 45.00 (*0-318-21812-7*) Gong Prods.

Tonfa Police Baton Master Instructor Handbook. Sid Campbell. 225p. 1987. pap. 45.00 (*0-318-21811-9*) Gong Prods.

Tonga: Travel Survival Kit. 2nd ed. Deanna Swaney. (Illus.). 206p. 1994. pap. 11.95 (*0-86442-242-3*) Lonely Planet.

*__Tonga Tales: Folk Narratives from Zambia.__ Ed. by Clement A. Okafor. (Three Continents Ser.). 150p. 1997. 25.00 (*0-89410-570-1*) Lynne Rienner.

Tongan Herbal Medicine. W. Arthur Whistler. (Illus.). 120p. 1992. pap. text ed. 13.00 (*0-8248-1527-0*) UH Pr.

Tongan Place Names. E. W. Gifford. (BMB Ser.). 1974. reprint ed. 35.00 (*0-527-02109-1*, BMB, NO. 6) Periodicals Srv.

Tongan Saints: Legacy of Faith. Eric B. Shumway. LC 91-7947. (Illus.). 376p. 1991. 19.95 (*0-939154-52-8*) Inst Polynesian.

Tongan Society. E. W. Gifford. (BMB Ser.). 1974. reprint ed. 65.00 (*0-527-02167-9*, BMB, NO. 61) Periodicals Srv.

Tongass: Alaska's Vanishing Rain Forest. Robert G. Ketchum. (Illus.). 120p. 1994. pap. 29.95 (*0-89381-600-0*) Aperture.

Tongefaesse aus dem Brunnen Unterm Stadion-Nordwall und im Suedost-Gebiet. Werner Gauer. (Olympische Forschungen Ser.: Vol. 8). (Illus.). 254p. 1975. pap. 90.80 (*3-11-004602-4*) De Gruyter.

Tongs, Gangs, & Triads: Chinese Crime Groups in North America. Peter Huston. (Illus.). 280p. 1995. pap. 30.00 (*0-87364-835-8*) Paladin Pr.

Tongue: A Creative Force. Charles Capps. 159p. (Orig.). 1976. pap. 5.99 (*0-89274-061-2*) Harrison Hse.

Tongue - Our Measure. Simo Ralevic. 62p. 1987. pap. 4.99 (*0-85151-507-X*) Banner of Truth.

*__Tongue & the Tiger.__ 200p. 1998. 20.00 (*981-02-3004-4*) World Scientific Pub.

Tongue Diagnosis in Chinese Medicine. rev. ed. Giovanni Maciocia. LC 94-61961. (Illus.). 210p. (C). 1995. text ed. 45.00 (*0-939616-19-X*) Eastland.

*__Tongue Fu.__ Horn. 1997. pap. 12.95 (*0-312-15227-2*) St Martin.

Tongue Fu! Deflect, Disarm, & Diffuse Any Verbal Conflict. Sam Horn. 256p. 1996. 22.95 (*0-312-14054-1*) St Martin.

*__Tongue-in-Cheek Guide to Pittsburgh.__ Ken Abel & Jackie Abel. (Illus.). 128p. 1997. reprint ed. pap. 4.95 (*0-944214-14-2*) ABELexpress.

Tongue Is Fire: South African Storytellers & Apartheid. Harold Scheub. LC 96-17774. (Illus.). 476p. 1996. pap. 24.95 (*0-299-15094-1*) U of Wis Pr.

Tongue Is Fire: South African Storytellers & Apartheid. Harold Scheub. LC 96-17774. (Illus.). 476p. 1996. 55.00 (*0-299-15090-9*) U of Wis Pr.

*__Tongue Moves Talk.__ Karen Mac Cormack. LC 97-278. 1997. pap. write for info. (*0-925904-12-0*) Chax Pr.

Tongue of Angels: The Mary Marcy Reader. Ed. by Frederick C. Giffin. LC 87-42930. 192p. 1988. 29.50 (*0-941664-91-0*) Susquehanna U Pr.

Tongue of the Prophets. Robert St. John. 1979. pap. 10.00 (*0-87980-166-2*) Wilshire.

Tongue of the Prophets: The Life Story of Eliezer Ben Yehuda. Robert St. John. LC 77-97303. 377p. 1972. reprint ed. text ed. 65.00 (*0-8371-2631-2*, STTP, Greenwood Pr) Greenwood.

Tongue Snatchers. Claudine Herrmann. Tr. & Intro. by Nancy Kline. LC 89-31136. (European Women Writers Ser.). xxx, 145p. 1989. pap. 9.95 (*0-8032-7252-9*, Bison Books) U of Nebr Pr.

Tongue Twisters. Gary Chmielewski. LC 86-17701. (Smile-a-While Ser.). (Illus.). (J). (gr. 2-3). 1986. 13.27 (*0-86592-685-9*); 9.95 (*0-685-58366-X*) Rourke Corp.

Tongue Twisters Coloring book. Victoria Fremont. (Illus.). (J). (gr. k-3). 1993. pap. 1.00 (*0-486-27736-4*) Dover.

Tongue Twisting Teasers from A to Z. Brad A. Steventon. (Illus.). 32p. (Orig.). (J). (gr. 2-6). 1996. pap. 5.95 (*1-885744-05-6*) Otter Creek.

Tongues. Charles R. Swindoll. (Swindoll Booklets Ser.). 32p. 1995. pap. 3.99 (*0-310-20093-8*) Zondervan.

Tongues. J. D. Whitney. 1976. 10.00 (*0-685-79200-5*); pap. 5.00 (*0-685-79201-3*) Elizabeth Pr.

Tongues? Spiros Zodhiates. 188p. 1991. pap. 6.99 (*0-89957-512-9*) AMG Pubs.

Tongues: Interpretation & Prophecy. Don Basham. Orig. Title: Handbook on Tongues: Interpretation. 128p. 1971. mass mkt. 4.99 (*0-88368-395-4*) Whitaker Hse.

Tongues: The Answer to the Debate. Donald L. Barnett & Jeffrey P. McGregor. 299p. (Orig.). 1988. pap. 9.95 (*0-934287-24-4*) Comm Chapel Pubns.

Tongues & Tails. Theresa Greenaway. LC 94-16739. (Head to Tail Ser.). (J). 1995. lib. bdg. 24.26 (*0-8114-8271-5*) Raintree Steck-V.

Tongues in Biblical Perspective. Charles R. Smith. pap. 7.99 (*0-88469-005-9*) BMH Bks.

Tongues in Trees: Studies in Literature & Ecology. Kim Taplin. (Illus.). 224p. (Orig.). 1996. pap. 18.95 (*1-870098-22-6*, Pub. by Green Bks UK) Coun Oak Bks.

Tongues Movement. Lewis Bauman. 1979. pap. 1.00 (*0-88469-047-4*) BMH Bks.

Tongues of Angels. Reynolds Price. 244p. 1991. mass mkt. 5.99 (*0-345-37102-X*) Ballantine.

Tongues of Angels. Reynolds Price. 176p. 1990. 17.95 (*0-689-12093-1*, Atheneum S&S) S&S Trade.

Tongues of Angels. Alan Robinson. 190p. 1994. pap. 39.00 (*0-85439-471-0*, Pub. by St Paul Pubns UK) St Mut.

Tongues of Conscience. Robert S. Hichens. LC 75-178440. (Short Story Index Reprint Ser.). 1977. reprint ed. 21.95 (*0-8369-4041-5*) Ayer.

Tongues of Fallen Angels. Selden Rodman. LC 73-89485. (Illus.). 288p. 1974. 12.00 (*0-8112-0528-2*); pap. 3.75 (*0-8112-0529-0*, NDP373) New Directions.

Tongues of Fire: A Bible of Sacred Scripyures of the Pagan World. Grace H. Turnbull. 1979. 35.95 (*0-405-10634-3*) Ayer.

Tongues of Fire: New Life in the Spirit. John A. Stroman. LC 94-36867. 164p. (Orig.). 1995. pap. 12.75 (*0-7880-0349-6*) CSS OH.

*__Tongues of Fire, Today.__ Dennis B. Harris. Ed. by Kay Harris. (Illus.). 44p. 1997. 19.95 (*1-890022-48-9*) Lfestyle Min.

Tongues of Flame. Mary W. Brown. LC 93-8608. (Library of Alabama Classics). 184p. (C). 1993. pap. 14.95 (*0-8173-0722-2*) U of Ala Pr.

Tongues of Men. Stephen N. Dunning. LC 79-10729. (American Academy of Religion. Dissertation Ser.: No. 27). 272p. reprint ed. pap. 77.60 (*0-7837-5410-8*, 2045174) Bks Demand.

Tongues of Men & of Angels. Robert A. Fink. 80p. 1995. 16.50 (*0-89672-341-0*) Tex Tech Univ Pr.

Tongues of Men & of Angels: Inspirational Poetry & Prose from the Renaissance to the..., Vol. 1. James Bentley. 1996. 19.95 (*0-8212-2336-4*) Bulfinch Pr.

Tongues of Men & Speech. J. R. Firth. LC 86-22837. (Languages & Language Learning Ser.). 223p. 1987. reprint ed. text ed. 59.75 (*0-313-25275-0*, FITO, Greenwood Pr) Greenwood.

Tongues, the Greatest Gift? Charismatics, Are We Missing Something? R. L. Brandt. LC 92-70134. 138p. (Orig.). 1992. pap. 6.95 (*0-88270-654-3*) Bridge-Logos.

Tongues We Speak: New & Selected Poems. Patricia Goedicke. LC 89-3105. 168p. (Orig.). 1989. pap. 9.95 (*0-915943-34-4*) Milkweed Ed.

Tonguing the Zeitgeist. Lance Olsen. 192p. (Orig.). 1994. pap. 11.95 (*1-882633-04-0*) Permeable.

Toni. Fiorella D. Calce. 1990. pap. 8.00 (*0-920717-42-X*) Guernica Editions.

Toni Cade Bambara. Vertreace. 1998. 22.95 (*0-8057-7822-5*, Twayne) Scribnrs Ref.

Toni Francis, Princess for a Day. Mallory Tarcher. (Adventurers, Inc. Ser.: No. 9). 144p. 1995. mass mkt. 3.50 (*0-8217-4916-1*, Zebra Kensgtn) Kensgtn Pub Corp.

*__Toni Morrison.__ LC 96-45136. (Contemporary African Americans Ser.). 1997. lib. bdg. 24.26 (*0-8172-3987-1*) Raintree Steck-V.

Toni Morrison. Donald J. Gibson. 150p. 1995. pap. text ed. 36.00 (*2-88449-201-1*) Gordon & Breach.

Toni Morrison. Linden Peach. LC 94-46867. (Modern Novelists Ser.). 1995. text ed. 35.00 (*0-312-12595-X*) St Martin.

Toni Morrison. Wilfred D. Samuels & Clenora Hudson. (United States Authors Ser.: No. 559). 184p. 1990. 24.95 (*0-8057-7601-X*) Macmillan.

Toni Morrison: A Guide to Her Novels. Barbara Parke. 32p. 1994. pap. text ed. 4.50 (*0-9644061-0-1*) Angell Pubns.

Toni Morrison: Author. Douglas Century. Ed. by Nathan I. Huggins. LC 93-31166. (Black Americans of Achievement Ser.). (Illus.). (YA). (gr. 5 up). 1994. pap. 8.95 (*0-7910-1906-3*); lib. bdg. 19.95 (*0-7910-1877-6*) Chelsea Hse.

*__Toni Morrison: Critical & Theoretical Approaches.__ Nancy J. Peterson. LC 97-13838. (Modern Fiction Studies). 1998. write for info. (*0-8018-5701-5*); pap. write for info. (*0-8018-5702-3*) Johns Hopkins.

Toni Morrison: Critical Perspectives Past & Present. Henry Louis Gates, Jr. & K. A. Appiah. LC 92-45755. (Literary Ser.). 448p. 1993. 14.95 (*1-56743-012-0*); pap. 14.95 (*1-56743-025-2*) Amistad Pr.

Toni Morrison: Nobel Prize-Winning Author. Barbara Kramer. LC 96-752. (African-American Biographies Ser.). 112p. (YA). (gr. 6 up). 1996. lib. bdg. 18.95 (*0-89490-688-7*) Enslow Pubs.

Toni Morrison see Modern Critical Views Series

Toni Morrison & the American Tradition: A Rhetorical Reading. H. William Rice. LC 94-34714. (American University Studies: Vol. 60). 168p. (C). 1996. text ed. 35.95 (*0-8204-2679-2*) P Lang Pubng.

Toni Morrison, Author. Garnet N. Jackson. (Illus.). (J). (gr. 1-4). 1995. pap. 4.95 (*0-8136-5739-3*); lib. bdg. 10.60 (*0-8136-5733-4*) Modern Curr.

*__Toni Morrison for Beginners.__ Ron David. (Illus.). 176p. 1997. pap. 11.00 (*0-86316-226-6*) Readers & Writers.

Toni Morrison's Developing Class Consciousness. Doreatha D. Mbalia. LC 90-50402. 144p. 1991. 32.50 (*0-945636-17-2*) Susquehanna U Pr.

Toni Morrison's Fiction. Jan Furman. Ed. by Matthew J. Bruccoli. LC 95-4423. (Understanding Contemporary American Literature Ser.). 190p. 1995. 19.95 (*1-57003-067-7*) U of SC Pr.

*__Toni Morrison's Fiction: Contemporary Criticism.__ Ed. by David L. Middleton & C. James Trotman. LC 96-43555. (Critical Studies in Black Life & Culture: Vol. 30). 344p. 1996. text ed. 46.00 (*0-8153-0869-8*) Garland.

Toni Morrison's World of Fiction. Karen Carmean. 133p. 1993. 12.50 (*0-87875-432-6*) Whitston Pub.

Tonia the Tree. Sandy Stryker. LC 88-16769. (Illus.). 32p. (J). (ps up). 1988. 14.95 (*0-911655-16-6*) Advocacy Pr.

Tonibah & the Rainbow. Jack L. Crowder & Faith Hill. Tr. by Clara Tohtsonie & Joe Wilson. (Illus.). 32p. (Orig.). (ENG & NAV.). (J). (gr. 7 up). 1986. pap. 6.95 (*0-9616589-1-6*) Upper Strata.

Tonic Functions of Sensory Systems. Ed. by Bernice M. Wenzel & H. Philip Zeigler. (Annals Ser.: Vol. 290). 435p. 1977. 52.00 (*0-89072-036-3*) NY Acad Sci.

*__Tonics: 200 Recipes that Improve the Body & the Mind.__ Robert A. Barnett. 256p. (Orig.). 1997. pap. 12.50 (*0-06-095111-7*, PL) HarpC.

Tonight & Always. Linda L. Miller. 352p. (Orig.). 1996. mass mkt. 6.50 (*0-425-15541-2*) Berkley Pub.

Tonight & Forever. Brenda Jackson. 288p. 1995. mass mkt. 4.99 (*0-7860-0172-0*, Pinncle Kensgtn) Kensgtn Pub Corp.

Tonight & Forever. Caryl Wilson. Ed. by Carolyn Tolley. 352p. (Orig.). 1993. mass mkt. 4.99 (*0-671-79905-3*) PB.

*__Tonight, by Sea.__ Frances Temple. LC 94-32167. 160p. (J). (gr. 3-7). 1997. pap. 4.50 (*0-06-440670-9*, Trophy) HarpC Child Bks.

Tonight, by Sea. Frances Temple. LC 94-32167. 160p. (J). (gr. 5 up). 1995. 15.95 (*0-531-06899-4*); lib. bdg. 16.99 (*0-531-08749-2*) Orchard Bks Watts.

Tonight Is Carnaval. Arthur Dorros. LC 90-32391. (Illus.). 32p. (Orig.). (J). (gr. k-3). 1991. pap. 14.99 (*0-525-44641-9*) Dutton Child Bks.

Tonight Is Carnaval. Arthur Dorros. (Illus.). 32p. (Orig.). (J). 1995. pap. 4.99 (*0-14-055467-X*) Puffin Bks.

*__Tonight or Never.__ Dara Joy. 400p. (Orig.). 1997. mass mkt. 5.99 (*0-505-52216-0*, Love Spell) Dorchester Pub Co.

Tonight the Ballet & Russian Ballets. Adrian Stokes. LC 82-1477. (Series in Dance). 213p. 1982. reprint ed. lib. bdg. 39.50 (*0-306-76152-1*) Da Capo.

Tonight We Improvise & "Leonora, Addio!" Luigi Pirandello. Tr. by Leonard G. Sbrocchi & J. Douglas Campbell from ITA. (Biblioteca di Quaderni d'Italianistica Ser.: Vol. 3). (Illus.). 122p. (Orig.). 1987. pap. 10.00 (*0-9691979-2-6*, Pub. by Can Soc Ital Stu CN) Speedimpex.

Tonight, We Wrestle. Donald Wright. 168p. (Orig.). 1994. pap. 14.99 (*1-56043-816-9*) Destiny Image.

Toning: The Creative Power of the Voice. rev. ed. Laurel E. Keyes. LC 73-86021. 128p. 1973. pap. 6.95 (*0-87516-176-6*) DeVorss.

T

An Asterisk (*) at the beginning of an entry indicates that the title is appearing in BIP for the first time.

***Toning & Tinting Made Easy.** Melvin C. Davis. (Illus.). 76p. 1996. pap. text ed. 35.00 (*1-874031-24-X*, Pub. by Hove Photo UK) Watsn-Guptill.

Toning the Sweep. Angela Johnson. LC 92-34062. 112p. (YA). (gr. 6 up). 1993. 15.95 (*0-531-05476-4*) Orchard Bks Watts.

Toning the Sweep. Angela Johnson. 112p. (J). (gr. 7-9). 1994. pap. 3.95 (*0-590-48142-8*) Scholastic Inc.

Tonio Kroeger/Mario und der Zauberer. Thomas Mann. 128p. (GER.). 1996. pap. 10.00 (*3-596-21381-9*, Pub. by Fischer Taschbch Verlag GW) Intl Bk Import.

Tonio Kroger. Thomas Mann. 126p. (GER.). (C). 1992. reprint ed. pap. text ed. 7.95 (*0-88133-655-6*) Waveland Pr.

Tonio's Cat. Mary Calhoun. LC 95-35386. (Illus.). (J). 1996. lib. bdg. 15.93 (*0-688-13315-0*, Morrow Junior) Morrow.

Tonio's Cat. Mary Calhoun. LC 95-35386. (Illus.). (J). (gr. k up). 1996. 16.00 (*0-688-13314-2*, Morrow Junior) Morrow.

Tonka Big Book of Trucks. Patricia Relf. (Illus.). 48p. (J). (ps-2). 1996. 11.95 (*0-590-84572-1*, Cartwheel) Scholastic Inc.

***Tonka Busy Builders.** Illus. by Thomas LaPadula. (Tonka Wheel Bks.). 12p. (J). (ps-1). 1997. bds. 5.95 (*0-590-97303-7*) Scholastic Inc.

Tonka Fire Truck to the Rescue. Ann M. Martin. (Tonka Trucks Storybook Ser.). 32p. (J). (ps-3). 1994. pap. 2.50 (*0-590-48854-6*) Scholastic Inc.

***Tonka Trucks Around Town.** Illus. by Thomas LaPadula. (Tonka Wheel Bks.). 12p. (J). (ps-1). 1997. bds. 5.95 (*0-590-97304-5*) Scholastic Inc.

***Tonka Working Hard with the Mighty Tractor Trailer & Bulldozer.** Justine Korman. (Illus.). (J). (ps-2). 1997. pap. 2.99 (*0-614-29037-6*, Cartwheel) Scholastic Inc.

***Tonka Working Hard with the Rescue Helicopter.** Cynthia Benjamin. (Tonka Ser.). (Illus.). (J). (ps-2). 1997. pap. 2.99 (*0-614-29036-8*, Cartwheel) Scholastic Inc.

Tonkawa, an Indian Language of Texas. Harry Hoijer. pap. 15.00 (*0-685-71708-9*) J J Augustin.

Tonkawa People: A Tribal History From Earliest Times to 1893. Deborah L. Newlin. Ed. by Gale Richardson. (Museum Journals). (Illus.). 119p. 1982. pap. 5.00 (*0-911618-07-4*) West Tex Mus.

Tonkin Gulf & the Escalation of the Vietnam War. Edwin E. Moise. LC 96-12159. 400p. (C). 1996. 39.95 (*0-8078-2300-7*) U of NC Pr.

Tonmeister Technology: Recording Environments, Sound Sources, & Microphone Techniques. Michael Dickretter. Tr. by Stephen F. Temmer. 142p. (GER.). 1989. 34.95 (*0-9617200-0-X*); pap. 19.95 (*0-9617200-1-8*) Temmer Enterps.

Tonnage Measurement: Treatment of Shelter-Deck & Other "Open" Spaces. International Maritime Organization Staff. 1964. text ed. 65.00 (*0-685-61558-8*, Pub. by Intl Maritime Org UK) St Mut.

Tonnancour, Vol. 1. large type ed. Ed. by Arthur M. Woodford. (Illus.). 1994. lib. bdg. 40.00 (*0-7808-0035-4*) Omnigraphics Inc.

Tonnancour Vol. 2: Life in Grosse Pointe & along the Shores of Lake St. Clair. large type ed. Ed. by Arthur M. Woodford. (Philosophy & Lifestyle Ser.). (Illus.). 250p. 1996. lib. bdg. 40.00 (*0-7808-0099-0*, B-258-2) Omnigraphics Inc.

Tono-Bungay. H. G. Wells. Ed. by John Hammond. 416p. 1994. pap. text ed. 7.95 (*0-460-87421-7*, Everyman's Classic Lib) C E Tuttle.

***Tono-Bungay.** H. G. Wells. Ed. by Bryan Cheyette. (The World's Classics Ser.). (Illus.). 432p. 1997. pap. 11.95 (*0-19-282829-0*) OUP.

Tono-Bungay. H. G. Wells. LC 77-28027. 317p. 1978. pap. text ed. 9.95 (*0-8032-9701-7*, Bison Books) U of Nebr Pr.

Tono-Bungay. H. G. Wells. 1990. reprint ed. lib. bdg. 19.95 (*0-89966-691-4*) Buccaneer Bks.

Tonopah: The Greatest, the Richest, & the Best Mining Camp in the World. Robert D. McCracken. (Illus.). 96p. (Orig.). 1996. pap. 12.95 (*1-878138-50-2*) Nye Cty Pr.

Tonopah Nevada Silver Camp. Stanley W. Paher. (Illus.). 17p. 1978. pap. 3.95 (*0-913814-18-0*) Nevada Pubns.

Tonos a lo Divino y a lo Humano. Ed. by Rita Goldberg. (Textos B Ser.: No. 24). 202p. (SPA.). (C). 1981. 45.00 (*0-7293-0075-7*, Pub. by Tamesis Bks Ltd UK) Boydell & Brewer.

Tonquish Tales: A Story of Early d'Etroit, Pioneers & Michigan Indians. 2nd ed. Helen F. Gilbert. (Illus.). 180p. 1984. pap. 5.00 (*0-9622346-0-5*) Plymouth Heritage.

***Tons of Fun.** Joanna Cole. (J). Date not set. pap. 15.00 (*0-688-15210-4*, Beech Tree Bks) Morrow.

Tons of Trash: Why You Should Recycle & What Happens When You Do. Joan R. Heilman. 80p. (J). (gr. 2-4). 1992. pap. 3.50 (*0-380-76379-6*, Camelot) Avon.

Tonsils: A Clinical-Oriented Update. Ed. by G. B. Galioto. LC 92-49677. (Advances in Oto-Rhino-Laryngology Ser.: Vol. 47). (Illus.). x, 350p. 1992. 195.75 (*3-8055-5604-7*) S Karger.

Tonsils & Adenoids: A Guide for Parents. Jack Paradise. Ed. by Frank A. Oski. (Pediatrics Ser.). (Illus.). 16p. 1995. pap. 2.95 (*1-885274-11-4*) HIN.

Tonsteins: Altered Volcanic Ash Layers in Coal-Bearing Sequences. Bruce F. Bohor & Don M. Triplehorn. LC 93-17797. (Special Papers: No. 285). 1993. pap. 12.00 (*0-8137-2285-3*) Geol Soc.

Tontimundo y el Barco Volador. Arthur Ransome. Tr. by Maria Negroni. (Mirasol Ser.). (Illus.). 48p. (SPA.). (J). (ps-3). 1991. 15.95 (*0-374-32443-3*) FS&G.

***Tontine.** H. C. Wolford. 256p. 1997. 19.95 (*0-9654563-2-3*) Easy Money.

Tontine: From the Reign of Louis XIV to the French Revolutionary Era. Robert M. Jennings & Andrew P. Trout. LC 82-81028. (S. S. Huebner Foundation Monographs: No. 12). 91p. (Orig.). 1982. pap. 17.95 (*0-918930-12-X*) Huebner Foun Insur.

Tonto National Monument. Kay Threlkeld. Ed. by T. J. Priehs. LC 88-60173. 16p. 1988. pap. 3.95 (*0-911408-76-2*) SW Pks Mnmts.

***Tonto's Revenge: Reflections on American Indian Law, Life, Culture, & Art.** Rennard Strickland. LC 97-4874. (Calvin P. Horn Lectures in Western History & Culture). 1997. write for info. (*0-8263-1821-5*); pap. write for info. (*0-8263-1822-3*) U of NM Pr.

Tonwerke des XVI. und XVII. Jahrhunderts. Carl F. Becker. 1969. reprint ed. 70.00 (*0-318-71735-2*) G Olms Pubs.

Tony. Vivienne Wood. (Illus.). pap. 7.99 (*0-907821-05-7*) Revival Lit.

Tony & Susan. Austin Wright. LC 92-74825. 334p. 1993. 20.00 (*1-880909-01-4*) Baskerville.

Tony & Susan. Austin Wright. 384p. 1994. mass mkt. 5.99 (*0-446-60105-5*) Warner Bks.

Tony & Susan. large type ed. Austin Wright. LC 93-17001. 1993. lib. bdg. 18.95 (*1-56054-739-1*) Thorndike Pr.

Tony Award. Ed. by Isabelle Stevenson. LC 74-28337. 1975. 12.95 (*0-405-06485-3*) Ayer.

Tony Award: A Complete Listing of Winners & Nominees with a History of the American Theatre Wing. American Theatre Wing Staff. LC 94-36644. 176p. 1994. pap. 14.95 (*0-435-08658-8*, 08658) Heinemann.

Tony Benn: A Political Biography. Robert Jenkins. (Illus.). 300p. 1981. 12.95 (*0-906495-35-0*) Writers & Readers.

***Tony Bennett: The Best Is Yet to Come.** Matthew Hoffman. LC 96-50281. 1997. write for info. (*1-56799-426-1*, MetroBooks) M Friedman Pub Grp Inc.

Tony Bennett: What My Heart Has Seen. Tony Bennett. (Illus.). 151p. 1996. 40.00 (*0-8478-1972-8*) Rizzoli Intl.

***Tony Bennett - On Holiday: A Tribute to Billie Holiday.** Ed. by Sy Feldman. 76p. (Orig.). (J). Date not set. pap. text ed. 19.95 (*1-57623-937-3*) Warner Brothers.

***Tony Bennett Songbook.** Ed. by Carol Cuellar. 156p. (Orig.). (C). 1996. pap. text ed. 22.95 (*1-57623-468-1*, PF9619) Warner Brothers.

***Tony Bennett Unplugged.** Ed. by Carol Cuellar. 80p. (Orig.). (C). 1994. pap. text ed. 19.95 (*0-89724-393-5*, VF2155) Warner Brothers.

***Tony Bennett/Here's to the Ladies.** Ed. by Carol Cuellar. 64p. (Orig.). (C). 1995. pap. text ed. 19.95 (*1-57623-274-3*, PF9548) Warner Brothers.

Tony Bennett/Steppin' Out: Steppin' Out. Ed. by Carol Cuellar. (Illus.). 88p. (Orig.). (C). 1993. pap. text ed. 19.95 (*0-89724-095-2*, VF2078) Warner Brothers.

Tony Berlant. (Illus.). (Orig.). 1990. write for info. (*0-9624271-1-X*) Louver Gallery.

Tony Berlant's Recent Work. Tony Berlant. 1991. pap. 14.00 (*0-932499-29-5*) Lapis Pr.

Tony Bevan. Louver Gallery New York Staff & Dan Cameron. (Illus.). 80p. 1991. pap. write for info. (*0-9624271-4-4*) Louver Gallery.

Tony Bingelis on Engines, Vol. 4. Tony Bingelis. 240p. 1995. pap. 21.95 (*0-940000-54-7*) EAA Aviation.

***Tony C: The Triumph & Tragedy of Tony Conigliaro.** David Cataneo & Linda Householder. (Illus.). 288p. 1997. 19.95 (*1-55853-532-2*) Rutledge Hill Pr.

Tony Chachere's Cajun Country Cookbook. Tony Chachere. Ed. by Griffin L. Gomez. (Illus.). 196p. 1972. pap. 9.95 (*0-9604580-1-8*) T Chacheres.

Tony Chachere's Second Helping: A Lifetime Collection of the Ole Master's Favorite Cajun & Creole Recipes. Tony Chachere. (Illus.). 240p. 1995. 22.95 (*0-9604580-3-4*) T Chacheres.

Tony Clark's New Blueberry Hill Cookbook. Arlyn Hertz. LC 90-61409. 176p. 1990. spiral bd. 12.95 (*0-89272-286-X*) Down East.

Tony Couch Watercolor Techniques. Tony Couch. (Illus.). 96p. 1990. pap. 14.99 (*0-89134-389-X*, 30309, North Lght Bks) F & W Pubns Inc.

Tony Couch's Keys to Successful Painting. Tony Couch. (Illus.) 144p. 1992. 27.95 (*0-89134-427-6*, 30413, North Lght Bks) F & W Pubns Inc.

Tony Cragg. Germano Celant. LC 96-60053. (Illus.). 352p. 1996. 65.00 (*0-500-23723-9*) Thames Hudson.

Tony Cragg: Sculpture, 1975-1990. Lucinda Barnes et al. Ed. & Intro. by Paul Schimmel. LC 90-6394. (Illus.). 178p. (Orig.). 1990. pap. 29.95 (*0-917493-17-6*) Newport Harbor.

Tony Cragg: Sculpture, 1975-1990. Lucinda Barnes et al. Ed. by Paul Schimmel. (Illus.). 178p. (Orig.). 1991. 45.00 (*0-500-09218-4*) Thames Hudson.

Tony Cragg: Writings (1981-1992) Tony Cragg. (Illus.). 25p. 1992. pap. 17.50 (*2-903004-24-2*, Pub. by Galerie Isy Brachot FR) Dist Art Pubs.

Tony Geary. (YA). pap. 1.25 (*0-590-32211-7*) Scholastic Inc.

***Tony Greenland's Panzer Modelling Masterclass.** Tony Greenland. 1996. 29.95 (*1-85915-067-5*, Pub. by Windrow & Green UK) Motorbooks Intl.

Tony Gwynn's Total Baseball Player. Tony Gwynn & Jim Rosenthal. (Illus.). 176p. (Orig.). 1992. pap. 12.95 (*0-312-07098-5*) St Martin.

Tony Harrison. Ed. by Neil Astley. 9100. pap. 27.00 (*1-85224-080-6*) Dufour.

Tony Harrison. Joe Kelleher. (Writers & Their Work Ser.). 95p. (Orig.). 1996. pap. text ed. 17.00 (*0-7463-0789-6*, Pub. by Nrthcote House UK) U Pr of Miss.

Tony Harrison: A Bibliography. J. R. Kaiser. 118p. 1989. text ed. 65.00 (*0-7201-2024-1*, Mansell Pub) Cassell.

Tony Harrison: Bloodaxe Critical Anthologies, No. 1. Ed. by Neil Astley. 510p. 1991. pap. 27.50 (*0-685-50820-X*, Pub. by Bloodaxe Bks UK) Dufour.

Tony Harrison: Bloodaxe Critical Anthologies, No. 1. Ed. by Neil Astley. 510p. 9100. 60.00 (*1-85224-079-2*, Pub. by Bloodaxe Bks UK) Dufour.

***Tony Harrison: Loiner.** Ed. by Sandie Byrne. 240p. 1997. 49.95 (*0-19-818430-1*) OUP.

Tony Harrison: Plays Three: Poetry or Bust, The Kaisers of Carnuntum, The Labourers of Herakles. Tony Harrison. 160p. (Orig.). 1996. pap. 13.95 (*0-571-17966-5*) Faber & Faber.

Tony Hillerman. Fred Erisman. LC 89-60055. (Western Writers Ser.: No. 87). (Illus.). 51p. (Orig.). 1989. pap. 4.95 (*0-88430-086-2*) Boise St U W Writ Ser.

Tony Hillerman. Tony Hillerman. (Joe Leaphorn Mysteries Ser.). 512p. 1992. reprint ed. Omnibus incl. The Blessing Way, Dance Hall of the Dead, & Listening Woman. 13.99 (*0-517-07771-X*) Random Hse Value.

Tony Hillerman: A Critical Companion. John M. Reilly. LC 95-50459. (Critical Companions to Popular Contemporary Writers Ser.). 208p. 1996. text ed. 29.95 (*0-313-29416-X*, Greenwood Pr) Greenwood.

Tony Hillerman: A Public Life. John Sobol. 1994. pap. 9.95 (*1-55022-214-7*, Pub. by ECW Pr CN) LPC InBook.

Tony Hillerman: Jim Chee Mysteries. Tony Hillerman. 1993. 13.99 (*0-517-09281-6*) Random Hse Value.

Tony Hillerman Companion. Martin Greenberg. 496p. 1995. mass mkt. 6.99 (*0-06-109215-0*, Harp PBks) HarpC.

Tony Hillerman's Frontier: People of the Plains. Ken Englade. 320p. 1996. mass mkt. 5.50 (*0-06-100947-4*) HarpC.

Tony Hillerman's Frontier: People of the Plains: Battle Cry. Ken Englade. (Orig.). 1997. mass mkt. 5.99 (*0-06-100944-X*, Harp PBks) HarpC.

Tony Hillerman's Frontier: Soldiers: People of the Plains. Ken Englade. 320p. 1996. mass mkt. 5.99 (*0-06-100945-8*, Harp PBks) HarpC.

Tony Hillerman's Frontier Tribes. Ken Englade. 320p. 1996. mass mkt. 5.99 (*0-06-100946-6*, Harp PBks) HarpC.

Tony Hinkle: Coach for All Seasons. Howard Caldwell. LC 90-49194. (Illus.). 208p. 1991. 19.95 (*0-253-31298-1*) Ind U Pr.

***Tony Kushner in Conversation.** Ed. by Robert Vorlicky. (C). 1997. pap. 16.95 (*0-472-06661-7*) U of Mich Pr.

***Tony Kushner in Conversation.** Ed. by Robert Vorlicky. (C). 1997. text ed. 42.50 (*0-472-09661-3*) U of Mich Pr.

Tony Meola. Mark Stewart. LC 96-17503. (Grolier All-Pro Biographies Ser.). (J). 1996. pap. 3.95 (*0-516-26029-4*); lib. bdg. 20.00 (*0-516-20181-6*) Childrens.

Tony O'Malley. Ed. by Brian Lynch. (Illus.). 324p. 1996. 59.95 (*1-85928-235-0*, Pub. by Scolar Pr UK) Ashgate Pub Co.

Tony Ray-Jones. Intro. by Richard Ehrlich. (Illus.). 108p. 1991. 39.95 (*0-89381-484-9*) Aperture.

Tony Richardson: A Bio-Bibliography. Don Radovich. LC 95-32990. (Bio-Bibliographies in the Performing Arts Ser.: No. 69). 304p. 1995. text ed. 59.95 (*0-313-28981-6*, Greenwood Pr) Greenwood.

Tony Salerno's Good News Express. Tony Salerno et al. (Illus.). 64p. (Orig.). (J). (gr. k-6). pap. write for info. (*1-881597-00-8*) Magination CA.

***Tony Smith: A Drawing Retrospective.** Text by Klaus Kertess & Joan Pachner. (Illus.). 127p. 1996. pap. 20.00 (*1-880146-13-4*, 620773) M Marks.

Tony the Hero. Horatio Alger, Jr. (Works of Horatio Alger Jr.). 1989. reprint ed. lib. bdg. 79.00 (*0-685-27552-3*) Rprt Serv.

Tony the Tokay Gecko. Illus. by Bob Storms. (World of Animals Ser.). 24p. (Orig.). (J). (gr. k-4). 1993. pap. 4.95 (*0-89346-531-3*) Heian Intl.

Tony the Tramp. Horatio Alger, Jr. (Works of Horatio Alger Jr.). 1989. reprint ed. lib. bdg. 79.00 (*0-685-27542-6*) Rprt Serv.

Tonya. Pappy Boyington. 16.00 (*0-933458-01-0*) Wilson Pr.

Tony's: A Cookbook. George Fuermann. (Illus.). 276p. 1986. 21.95 (*0-940672-38-3*) Shearer Pub.

Tony's Book. Hugh Hood. 256p. 1988. pap. 14.95 (*0-7737-5208-0*) Genl Dist Srvs.

Tony's Bread. Tomie De Paola. (Whitebird Bks.). (Illus.). 32p. (J). (ps-3). 1989. 15.95 (*0-399-21693-6*, Whitebird Bks) Putnam Pub Group.

Tony's Bread. Tomie DePaola. (Illus.). 32p. (J). (ps-3). 1996. pap. 5.95 (*0-698-11371-3*, Paperstar) Putnam Pub Group.

Tony's Tummy. Lucile Jones. Ed. by Bobbie J. Van Dolson. 32p. (J). (gr. k up). 1981. pap. 3.99 (*0-8280-0039-5*) Review & Herald.

Too. Vinnie Robinson. 64p. 1985. 5.95 (*0-9610404-1-6*) Mogul Bk.

Too Bad, Ahab! Naboth's Vineyard. Marilyn Lashbrook. LC 90-60457. (Me Too! Readers Ser.). (Illus.). 32p. (J). (gr. k-3). 1990. 5.95 (*0-86606-441-9*, 872) Treasure Pub.

***Too Bad It Wasn't a Dream.** Sandra Murphy. 180p. 1997. pap. 14.95 (*0-89896-181-5*) Larksdale.

Too Bad, That Common Sense Has Died. Eberhard W. Gress. (Orig.). 1996. pap. write for info. (*1-57553-266-2*) Watermrk Pr.

Too Beautiful a Day to Die. Joyce Egginton. 368p. (Orig.). 1992. mass mkt. 5.50 (*0-425-13420-2*) Berkley Pub.

Too Beautiful to Die. large type ed. Martin Carroll. (Linford Mystery Library). 1988. pap. 15.99 (*0-7089-6509-1*) Ulverscroft.

Too Big Bear. Marsha Kideckel. (Annikins Ser.: No. 13). (Illus.). 24p. (Orig.). (J). (ps-1). 1994. pap. 0.99 (*1-55037-347-1*, Pub. by Annick CN) Firefly Bks Ltd.

Too Big for the Bag. Beverly Amstutz. (Illus.). (J). (gr. k-7). 1981. pap. 2.50 (*0-937836-05-2*) Precious Res.

Too Big for the Bag: A Christmas Play for Children. rev. ed. Beverly Amstutz. (Illus.). 25p. (Orig.). (J). (ps-8). 1996. pap. 7.00 (*0-937836-10-9*) Precious Res.

Too Big to Fail. Stewart. Date not set. 4.98 (*0-8317-4644-0*) Smithmark.

Too Big to Fail: Olympia & York - The Story Behind the Headlines. Walter Stewart. (Illus.). 368p. 1993. 23.95 (*0-7710-0177-0*) McCland & Stewart.

Too Bizarro. Dan Piraro. (Illus.). 104p. 1988. pap. 5.95 (*0-87701-536-8*) Chronicle Bks.

***Too Blessed to Be Stressed.** Suzan J. Cook. 224p. Date not set. 23.00 (*0-06-039192-8*, ReganBooks) HarpC.

***Too Blue to Fly.** Judith Richards. 1997. 20.00 (*1-56352-383-3*) Longstreet Pr Inc.

Too Busy: A Days of the Week Story. Marianne M. Miller. Ed. by Rhonda Wray. LC 93-11657. (Illus.). 36p. (Orig.). (J). (gr. k-3). 1993. pap. 9.95 (*0-916260-96-8*, B114) Meriwether Pub.

Too Busy for God? Think Again! Louise D'Angelo. LC 81-52423. 120p. 1992. reprint ed. pap. 5.00 (*0-89555-166-7*) TAN Bks Pubs.

Too Busy for God? Think Again: A Spiritual Guide for Working Women & Housewives. Louise D'Angelo. 119p. reprint ed. pap. 4.50 (*1-878886-16-9*) Maryheart Crusaders.

Too Busy Not to Pray. Bill Hybels. LC 88-23405. 156p. (Orig.). 1988. pap. 9.99 (*0-8308-1256-3*, 1256) InterVarsity.

Too Busy to Clean? Over 500 Tips & Techniques to Make Housecleaning Easier. Patti Barrett. Ed. by Ben Watson. LC 89-46015. (Illus.). 128p. (Orig.). 1990. pap. 9.95 (*0-88266-598-7*, Storey Pub) Storey Comm Inc.

Too Busy to Cook. Chriscilla M. Thornock & Lori Rogers. (Illus.). 108p. 1994. pap. text ed. 9.95 (*0-9629060-7-7*) Thornock Intl.

Too Busy to Exercise. Porter Shimer. LC 96-35038. 160p. (Orig.). 1996. pap. 12.95 (*0-88266-936-2*) Storey Comm Inc.

***Too Cheap to Meter: An Economic & Philosophical Analysis of the Nuclear Dream.** Steven M. Cohn. LC 96-41499. (SUNY Series in Radical, Social & Political Theory). 384p. (C). 1997. text ed. 65.50 (*0-7914-3389-7*); pap. text ed. 21.95 (*0-7914-3390-0*) State U NY Pr.

Too Clever by Half or The Diary of a Scoundrel. Alexander Ostrovsky. Tr. by Rodney Ackland & Daniel Gerould from RUS. (Old Vic Theatre Collection Ser.: Vol. 3). 120p. (Orig.). 1988. pap. 7.95 (*1-55783-023-1*) Applause Theatre Bk Pubs.

Too Close Apart. deluxe ed. Jean G. Howard. LC 77-92190. (Illus.). 1977. boxed 75.00 (*0-930954-02-5*) Tidal Pr.

Too Close Apart. limited ed. Jean G. Howard. LC 77-92190. (Illus.). 1977. 7.50 (*0-930954-01-7*) Tidal Pr.

Too Close for Comfort. Ellen Feldman. 400p. 1995. mass mkt. 5.99 (*0-440-21513-7*) Dell.

***Too Close for Comfort.** Eve Gaddy. (Loveswept Ser.: No. 820). 240p. 1997. mass mkt. 3.50 (*0-553-44573-1*, Loveswept) Bantam.

***Too Close for Comfort.** Ashley McConnell. (Quantum Leap Ser.: No. 2). 1994. mass mkt. 5.99 (*1-57297-157-6*) Blvd Books.

Too Close for Comfort. Francine Pascal. (The Unicorn Club Ser.: Vol. 7). 144p. (Orig.). (J). (gr. 3-7). 1995. pap. 3.50 (*0-553-48351-X*, Sweet Valley) BDD Bks Young Read.

Too Close for Comfort. large type ed. Margaret A. Carr. (Linford Mystery Library). 276p. 1988. pap. 15.99 (*0-7089-6624-1*, Linford) Ulverscroft.

Too Close for Comfort: Exploring the Risks of Intimacy. G. K. Piorkowski. (Illus.). 334p. 1994. 25.95 (*0-306-44641-3*, Plenum Insight) Plenum.

Too Close for Comfort: Rightwing Populism, Scapegoating, & Fascist Potentials in U. S. Political Traditions. Chip Berlet & Matthew N. Lyons. 400p. 1997. 40.00 (*0-89608-510-4*); pap. 21.00 (*0-89608-509-0*) South End Pr.

Too Close for Comfort: Understanding & Responding to the Reality of Abuse. Beth Swagman. LC 93-46973. (Issues in Christian Living Ser.). 1994. 7.15 (*1-56212-053-0*) CRC Pubns.

***Too Close Friends.** Shen Roddie. LC 96-48566. (Illus.). (J). 1998. pap. 13.99 (*0-8037-2188-9*) Dial Bks Young.

Too Close to the Edge. Susan Dunlap. 224p. 1989. reprint ed. mass mkt. 5.50 (*0-440-20356-2*) Dell.

Too Close Too Soon. expanded ed. Jim Talley. 170p. 1989. pap. 9.99 (*0-8407-3045-4*) Nelson.

Too Cool. Ed. by Gene Sculatti. LC 92-36037. 1993. pap. 12.95 (*0-312-08915-5*) St Martin.

Too Cool for Drugs. Sharon Scott. 1993. pap. 8.95 (*0-87425-236-9*) HRD Press.

***Too Cool for School.** Debra M. Zakarin. (Party of Five: Claudia Ser.: No. 2). (Orig.). (J). (gr. 3-6). 1997. pap. 3.99 (*0-671-00677-0*, Minstrel Bks) PB.

Too Cool for the Unicorns. Francine Pascal. (Unicorn Club Ser.: No. 15). 144p. (J). 1997. pap. 3.50 (*0-553-48401-X*) BDD Bks Young Read.

Too Cool Jokes for School. Victoria G. Hartman. (Illus.). 32p. (Orig.). (J). (ps-3). 1996. pap. 2.95 (*0-8167-3969-2*, Whistlstop) Troll Communs.

Too Damn Rich. Judith Gould. 624p. 1996. pap. 6.99 (*0-451-40623-0*, Onyx) NAL-Dutton.

Too Dangerous to Love. large type ed. Sandra Clark. 306p. 1993. 25.99 (*0-7505-0477-3*) Ulverscroft.

Too Dark for the Hall. James A. Riley. (Illus.). 175p. (Orig.). 1991. pap. 15.95 (*0-9614023-6-9*) TK Pubs.

Too Deep for Tears. Kathryn L. Davis. (Illus.) (J). 1990. mass mkt. 6.99 (*0-671-72532-7*) PB.

Too Deep for Words: Rediscovering Lectio Divina. Thelma Hall. 128p. 1988. pap. 6.95 (*0-8091-2959-0*) Paulist Pr.

Too Easy. Bruce D. Price. 1994. 21.00 (*0-671-88673-8*) S&S Trade.

Too Easy Gourmet: The World's First Non-Fiction Cookbook. Ben Levitan. LC 94-90329. (Orig.). 1995. pap. 6.95 (*0-9640023-0-2*) Too Easy Gourmet.

T

Too Familiar. Caroline Burnes. (Intrigue Ser.). 1993. pap. 2.89 (0-373-22215-7, 1-22215-7) Harlequin Bks.

Too Far Away to Touch. Leslea Newman. LC 93-30327. (Illus.). 32p. (J). (ps-4). 1995. 14.95 (0-395-68968-6, Clarion Bks) HM.

Too Far from Home: The Selected Writings of Paul Bowles. Paul Bowles. 1992. 29.95 (0-88001-295-1) Ecco Pr.

Too Far from Home: The Selected Writings of Paul Bowles. Paul Bowles. 1995. pap. 17.00 (0-88001-391-5) Ecco Pr.

Too Far from Home & Other Stories. T. N. Rogers. LC 87-25514. 128p. (Orig.). 1988. pap. 12.95 (0-8262-0671-9) U of Mo Pr.

Too Far to Go. John Updike. 256p. 1982. mass mkt. 5.99 (0-449-20016-7, Crest) Fawcett.

Too Few for Drums. large type ed. Ronald F. Delderfield. 368p. 1988. 25.99 (0-7089-1756-9) Ulverscroft.

Too Few Tomorrows: Urban Appalachians in the 1980's. Ed. by William W. Philliber & Phillip J. Obermiller. LC 86-28816. 170p. (Orig.). 1987. pap. 8.95 (0-913239-47-X) Appalach Consortium.

Too Good for Her Own Good: Searching for Self & Intimacy in Important Relationships. Claudia Bepko & Jo-Ann Krestan. LC 89-46071. 256p. 1991. pap. 12.00 (0-06-092081-5, PL) HarpC.

Too Good to Be Entirely True. Donna Wyszomierski. 16p. (Orig.). 1979. pap. 3.00 (0-917061-01-2) Top Stories.

Too Good to Be Through: A Resale & Vintage Goods Guide to Austin. Carol Siler. Ed. by Allison Faust. (Illus.). vi, 50p. (Orig.). 1996. pap. 6.95 (0-9650919-0-2) Cat Paw Pr.

Too Good to Be True. Janet P. Beck. 384p. (Orig.). 1992. pap. 4.99 (0-451-40284-7, Onyx) NAL-Dutton.

Too Good to Be True. Francine Pascal. (SVH Ser.: No. 11). 160p. (Orig.). (YA). 1985. 3.99 (0-553-27941-6) Bantam.

Too Good to Be True: Alcan's Kemano Completion Project. Bev Christensen. 1995. pap. 16.95 (0-88922-354-8) Genl Dist Srvs.

Too Good to Be True: The Perils & Pitfalls of Work-at-Home Programs. Pierre-George O'Neill. 128p. (Orig.). 1990. pap. 12.95 (0-9693942-0-9, Pub. by Factfinder CN) Quality Bks IL.

Too Good to Be True: The Story of Denise Redlick's Murder. Janet P. Beck. LC 90-53558. 360p. 1990. 21.95 (0-88282-066-4) New Horizon NJ.

***Too Good to Leave, Too Bad to Stay: A Step-by-Step Guide to Help You Decide Whether to Stay in or Get Out of Your Relationship.** Mira Kirshebaum. 1997. pap. 11.95 (0-452-27535-0, Plume) NAL-Dutton.

Too Good to Leave, Too Bad to Stay: A Step-by-Step Guide to Helping You Decide Whether to Stay in or Get Out of Your Relationship. Mira Kirshenbaum. 256p. 1996. pap. 22.95 (0-525-94069-3, Dutton) NAL-Dutton.

Too Great a Temptation: The Seductive Power of America's Super Church. Joel Gregory. Ed. by Mike Towle & Chris Tucker. (Illus.). 332p. 1994. 24.95 (1-56530-141-2) Summit TX.

***Too Great Expectations: The Academic Outlook of Young Children.** Doris R. Entwisle & Leslie A. Hayduk. LC 77-23344. (Illus.). 208p. 1978. reprint ed. pap. 59.30 (0-608-04072-X, 2064804) Bks Demand.

Too Grown up to Remember Being a Child. Joy C. Cagle. 144p. (Orig.). 1996. mass mkt. 4.99 (1-55197-429-0, Pub. by Comnwlth Pub CN) Partners Pubs Grp.

Too Hot to Cool Down. Illus. by Terrance Cummings. 64p. 1996. 22.50 (1-55670-510-7) Stewart Tabori & Chang.

Too Hot to Handle. (Silhouette Romance Ser.). 1995. mass mkt. 4.99 (0-373-48287-6, 1-48287-6) Harlequin Bks.

Too Hot to Handle. Matt Christopher. (J). (gr. 4-7). 1991. mass mkt. 3.95 (0-316-14074-0) Little.

Too Hot to Handle. Elizabeth Lowell. 1992. mass mkt. 3.99 (0-373-48249-3, 5-48249-2) Harlequin Bks.

***Too Hot to Handle.** Elizabeth Lowell. 1997. mass mkt. 5.50 (1-55166-267-1, 1-66267-5, Mira Bks) Harlequin Bks.

***Too Hot to Handle.** Created by Francine Pascal. (Sweet Valley High Ser.: No. 136). 208p. (Orig.). (YA). (gr. 7 up). 1997. mass mkt. 3.99 (0-553-57070-6) BDD Bks Young Read.

***Too Hot to Handle.** Fiona Pitt-Kethley. 136p. 9200. 32.00 (0-7206-0875-9, Pub. by P Owen Ltd UK) Dufour.

Too Hot to Handle: Recipes from the Greater Omaha Barbeque Society. Greater Omaha Barbeque Society Staff. (Illus.). 144p. (Orig.). 1994. pap. 10.95 (1-882907-00-0) Old Market.

Too Hot to Handle? Social & Policy Issues in the Management of Radioactive Wastes. Ed. by Charles A. Walker et al. LC 82-20000. (Illus.). 223p. reprint ed. pap. 63.60 (0-7837-5310-1, 2080340) Bks Demand.

Too Hot to Handle: The Kids' Book about Fire Safety. Gino Desalvatore et al. (Illus.). (Orig.). (J). (ps-6). 1995. pap. 9.95 (0-914525-29-8) Waterfront Bks.

Too Hot to Handle: The Race for Cold Fusion. Frank Close. (Illus.). 392p. 1991. text ed. 39.50 (0-691-08591-9) Princeton U Pr.

Too Hot to Hoot: Funny Palindrome Riddles. Marvin Terban. LC 84-14942. (Illus.). 64p. (J). (gr. 2-5). 1985. pap. 6.95 (0-89919-320-X, Clarion Bks) HM.

Too Hot Tofer. Koehler. (J). 1997. 11.95 (0-02-750907-9, S&S Bks Young Read) S&S Childrens.

Too Hot Tofer. Elizabeth Koehler-Pentacoff. (J). 1997. 12.00 (0-689-80542-X) S&S Childrens.

Too Hot Too Cold Just Right. Ann L. Williamson. 81p. (Orig.). 1994. pap. text ed. 13.95 (0-911051-80-5) Plain View.

Too Hot, Went to Lake: Seasonal Photos from Minnesota's Past. Peg Meier. (Illus.). (Orig.). 1993. pap. 24.95 (0-933387-03-2) Neighbors Pub.

***Too Hottie to Handle.** Randi Reisfeld. (Clueless Ser.). (J). 1997. mass mkt. 3.99 (0-671-01160-X, Archway) PB.

Too Jewish? Challenging Traditional Identities. Norman L. Kleeblatt. LC 95-50861. (Illus.). 230p. (C). 1996. pap. text ed. 29.95 (0-8135-2327-3) Rutgers U Pr.

Too Jewish? Challenging Traditional Identities. Ed. by Norman L. Kleeblatt. LC 95-50861. (Illus.). 230p. (C). 1996. text ed. 49.95 (0-8135-2326-5) Rutgers U Pr.

Too Late after a University Degree. James N. Rugiireheh-Runaku. xxiii, 169p. 1995. 17.00 (81-7024-664-4, Pub. by Ashish Pub Hse II) Nataraj Bks.

Too Late for Goya: Works by Francesc Torres. Marilyn A. Zeitlin et al. (Illus.). 124p. (Orig.). (ENG & SPA.). 1993. pap. 40.00 (1-879286-07-6) Ariz St U Art Mus.

Too Late for Goya: Works by Francesc Torres. limited ed. Marilyn A. Zeitlin. 124p. (ENG & SPA.). 1993. 125.00 (0-614-14077-3) Ariz St U Art Mus.

Too Late for Logic. Tom Murphy. (Methuen Modern Plays Ser.). 54p. (C). 1990. pap. 9.95 (0-413-63220-2, A0484, Pub. by Methuen UK) Heinemann.

Too Late for Man: Essays. William Ospina. Tr. by Nathan Budoff from SPA. (New Voices from Latin America Ser.). 108p. 1995. pap. 13.95 (1-57129-018-4) Brookline Bks.

Too Late for Tears. Evelyn C. Rosser. 52p. 1994. 7.95 (0-8059-3508-8) Dorrance.

***Too Late for the Funeral.** large type ed. Roger Ormerod. (Linford Mystery Library). 304p. 1997. pap. 16.99 (0-7089-7991-2, Linford) Ulverscroft.

***Too Late the Hunter.** Barry Grills. 240p. 1996. pap. 16.95 (1-55082-174-1, Pub. by Quarry Pr CN) LPC InBook.

Too Late the Phalarope. Alan Paton. 23.95 (0-89190-392-5) Amereon Ltd.

Too Late the Phalarope. Alan Paton. 1983. pap. 7.95 (0-684-10455-5) S&S Trade.

Too Late the Phalarope. Alan Paton. 1996. pap. 11.00 (0-684-81895-7) S&S Trade.

Too Late to Die. Bill Crider. 192p. 1986. 14.95 (0-8027-5650-6) Walker & Co.

Too Late to Say Good-Bye: My Experience with Aging Parents. Ethel McIndoo. 64p. (Orig.). 1988. pap. 2.95 (0-936625-28-7, New Hope AL) Womans Mission Union.

***Too Late Toby.** (Little Monsters Ser.). (J). 1997. write for info. (0-614-21793-8, Pub. by Splash UK) Assoc Pubs Grp.

Too Little. Mary Rogers. (Cityscapes Ser.). 30p. (J). (ps). 1992. pap. text ed. 4.50 (1-56843-052-3) BGR Pub.

Too Little: Big Book. Mary Rogers. (Cityscapes Ser.). 30p. (J). (ps). 1992. pap. text ed. 23.00 (1-56843-002-7) BGR Pub.

***Too Little or to Big?** Sandra C. Billieu. (Illus.). 40p. (Orig.). (J). (gr. 1-3). 1997. pap. 8.99 (1-55237-350-9, Pub. by Comnwlth Pub CN) Partners Pubs Grp.

Too Little, Too Big. Colette Hellings. 40p. (J). (ps-3). 1993. 10.95 (0-8118-0530-1) Chronicle Bks.

Too Little, Too Big, Just Right. Beverley B. Ashwill. LC 90-83314. (Illus.). 18p. (J). (ps-3). 1990. pap. 3.98 (0-941381-04-8) BJO Enterprises.

Too Little, Too Late: Dealing with the Health Needs of Women in Poverty. Ed. by Cesar A. Perales & Lauren S. Young. LC 88-908. (Women & Health Ser.: Vol. 12, Nos. 3-4). 259p. 1988. text ed. 17.95 (0-918393-50-7) Harrington Pk.

Too Long a Stranger. Janette Oke. (Women of the West Ser.: Bk. 9). 1994. pap. 9.99 (1-55661-456-X) Bethany Hse.

Too Long a Stranger. large type ed. Janette Oke. (Women of the West Ser.: Bk. 9). 1994. pap. 13.99 (1-55661-457-8) Bethany Hse.

Too Long at the Dance. Mike Blakely. LC 95-33673. 352p. 1996. 23.95 (0-312-86093-5) Forge NYC.

Too Long in the West. Balachandra Rajan. 1961. pap. 2.00 (0-88253-175-1) Ind-US Inc.

Too Loud a Solitude. Bohumil Hrabal. Tr. by Michael H. Heim. 112p. 1990. 16.95 (0-15-190491-X) HarBrace.

Too Loud a Solitude. Bohumil Hrabal. Tr. by Michael H. Heim. 1992. pap. 9.00 (0-15-690458-6, Harvest Bks) HarBrace.

Too Many Angels to Count. 31p. (J). 1996. 5.95 (0-87510-308-1) Christian Sci.

Too Many Animals Sleep in My Bed. Judith Clark. (Illus.). (J). (ps). 1993. write for info. (1-56156-264-5) Kidsbks.

Too Many Apples. Dorothy H. Moffat. LC 95-17836. 1995. pap. 9.95 (0-87233-141-5) Bauhan.

Too Many Are Hungry: What Can I Do? Bonnie Jorgenson & Arthur Simon. (Illus.). 32p. 1985. pap. text ed. 2.95 (0-934134-17-0) Sheed & Ward MO.

Too Many Babas. Carolyn Croll. LC 92-18779. (I Can Read Bk.). (Illus.). 64p. (J). (gr. k-3). 1994. lib. bdg. 14.89 (0-06-021384-1) HarpC Child Bks.

Too Many Babas. Carolyn Croll. LC 92-18779. (Trophy I Can Read Bk.). (Illus.). 64p. (J). (gr. k-4). 1994. pap. 3.50 (0-06-444168-7, Trophy) HarpC Child Bks.

Too Many Babies? The Myth of the Population Explosion. 3rd ed. Joseph Hansen. 43p. 1987. pap. 3.50 (0-87348-491-6) Pathfinder NY.

Too Many Balloons. Catherine Matthias. LC 81-15520. (Rookie Readers Ser.). (Illus.). 32p. (J). (ps-2). 1982. pap. 3.50 (0-516-43633-3); lib. bdg. 15.00 (0-516-03633-5) Childrens.

Too Many Bosses. Jan Freed. (Superromance Ser.). 1995. mass mkt. 3.75 (0-373-70645-6, 1-70645-6) Harlequin Bks.

Too Many Boys!, No. 1. Cherie Bennett. (Club Sunset Ser.). 128p. (Orig.). (J). 1994. pap. 3.50 (0-425-14252-3) Berkley Pub.

Too Many Boys: International Edition. (YA). 1994. pap. 3.50 (0-553-24355-1) Bantam.

***Too Many Bunnies.** Tomie Depaola. 1997. pap. 2.95 (0-8167-4064-X) Troll Communs.

***Too Many Chickens.** Paulette Bourgeois. (Illus.). 32p. (J). (gr. k-2). 1990. pap. 4.95 (1-55074-067-9, Pub. by Kids Can Pr CN) Genl Dist Srvs.

Too Many Cooks. Nellie McCaslin. LC 93-5250. 20p. (J). 1993. pap. 5.00 (0-88734-434-8) Players Pr.

Too Many Cooks. Joanne Pence. 352p. 1994. mass mkt. 4.50 (0-06-108199-X, Harp PBks) HarpC.

Too Many Cooks: And Other Proverbs. Maggie Kneen. LC 91-4455. (J). (ps-3). 1992. 13.00 (0-671-78120-0, Green Tiger S&S) S&S Childrens.

Too Many Counselors. Marilyn Kaye. (Camp Sunnyside Friends Ser.: No. 8). 128p. (J). 1990. pap. 2.95 (0-380-75913-6, Camelot) Avon.

Too Many Cousins. Douglas G. Browne. (Detective Stories Ser.). 192p. 1985. reprint ed. pap. 3.95 (0-486-24774-0) Dover.

Too Many Crooks Spoil the Broth. Tamar Myers. 256p. 1995. mass mkt. 5.99 (0-451-18296-0, Sig) NAL-Dutton.

Too Many Curls. Marilyn Kahalewai & Karen Poepoe. LC 89-82131. (Illus.). 16p. (J). (ps-2). 1992. 12.95 (0-935848-83-5); pap. 4.95 (1-880188-20-1) Bess Pr.

Too Many Dogs! Hannah Jordan. LC 95-7899. (Early Step into Reading Ser.). (Illus.). (J). 1998. pap. 3.99 (0-679-86443-1); lib. bdg. 11.99 (0-679-96443-6) Random.

***Too Many Dragons: Great Adventures.** Roger Befelar. (Great Adventures Ser.). (Illus.). 24p. (Orig.). (J). (ps up). 1997. pap. 2.99 (0-88743-451-7, 06781) Sch Zone Pub Co.

Too Many Eggs. M. Christina Butler. LC 83-49007. (Illus.). 25p. (J). (gr. k-12). 1988. 15.95 (0-87923-741-4) Godine.

Too Many Enemies: The Palestinian Experience in Lebanon. Rosemary Sayigh. LC 93-36792. 256p. (C). 1994. pap. 25.00 (1-85649-056-4, Pub. by Zed Bks Ltd UK); text ed. 69.95 (1-85649-055-6, Pub. by Zed Bks Ltd UK) Humanities.

Too Many for Whom? Ecologist Staff. 1995. 17.95 (1-85383-197-2, Pub. by Erthscan Pubns UK) Island Pr.

Too Many Ghosts. Paul Gallico. 286p. 1988. pap. 5.95 (0-930330-80-3) Intl Polygonics.

Too Many Grooms. Kay Wilding. (American Romance Ser.). 1995. mass mkt. 3.50 (0-373-16595-1, 1-16595-0) Harlequin Bks.

Too Many Jellybeans! Mary J. Fulton. (Little Look-Look Bks.). (Illus.). 24p. (J). (ps). 1993. pap. 1.49 (0-307-11539-9, 11539, Golden Pr) Western Pub.

Too Many Kangaroo Things to Do! Stuart J. Murphy. LC 95-20879. (MathStart Ser.). (Illus.). 40p. (J). (gr. 2 up). 1996. 14.95 (0-06-025883-7); lib. bdg. 14.89 (0-06-025884-5) HarpC Child Bks.

Too Many Kangaroo Things to Do! Stuart J. Murphy. LC 95-20879. (MathStart Ser.: Level 3). (Illus.). 40p. (J). (gr. 2 up). 1996. pap. 4.95 (0-06-446712-0, Trophy) HarpC Child Bks.

Too Many Kangaroo Things to Do! Stuart J. Murphy. LC 95-20879. (MathStart Ser.). (Illus.). (J). 1996. pap. write for info. (0-06-446185-8) HarpC Child Bks.

***Too Many Kittens.** Olivia Long. (Pets & Their People Ser.). (Illus.). 32p. (J). (ps-4). Date not set. write for info. (1-880042-09-6) Shelf-Life Bks.

Too Many Mice. (Bank Street Ready-to-Read Ser.: No. 33). 32p. (J). 1992. pap. 3.99 (0-553-35160-5) Bantam.

Too Many Moms. Cathy G. Thacker. (American Romance Ser.). 1994. mass mkt. 3.50 (0-373-16529-3, 1-16529-9) Harlequin Bks.

***Too Many Neurons.** Ken A. Sifr. LC 96-90874. (Orig.). 1997. pap. 9.95 (0-533-12188-4) Vantage.

Too Many Notes, Mr. Mozart. Bernard Bastable, pseud. 192p. 1996. 21.00 (0-7867-0315-6) Carroll & Graf.

Too Many Nuts. (Little Landoll Julie's Journey Ser.). 24p. (J). (ps-6). Date not set. text ed. 1.99 (1-56987-325-9) Landoll.

Too Many People? Jean F. Blashfield & Wallace B. Black. LC 91-34603. (Saving Planet Earth Ser.). 128p. (J). (gr. 4-8). 1992. lib. bdg. 29.30 (0-516-05513-5) Childrens.

Too Many People: A Radical Solution to the Population Explosion & a Survey of What Has Led to It. Roy Caine. 150p. 1995. lib. bdg. 41.00 (0-8095-4887-9) Borgo Pr.

Too Many People: A Radical Solution to the Population Explosion & a Survey of What Has Led to It. Roy Calne. LC 94-16384. (World in Crisis Ser.: No. 1). (Illus.). 150p. pap. 15.95 (0-7145-4269-5) Riverrun NY.

Too Many People & Other Reflections. J. B. Priestley. LC 71-128289. (Essay Index Reprint Ser.). 1977. 21.95 (0-8369-2016-3) Ayer.

Too Many People, Too Little Land: The Human Ecology of a Wet Rice-Growing Village in the Red River Delta of Vietnam. Ed. by Trong Cuc Le & A. Terry Rambo. LC 93-23834. (Occasional Paper: Vol. 15). 1993. write for info. (0-86638-157-0) EW Ctr HI.

***Too Many People, Too Little Land: The Human Ecology of a Wet Rice-Growing Village in the Red River Delta of Vietnam: Report of the SUAN-EWC-CRES Workshop on Sustainable Rural Resources Management & Biological Diversity Conservation, Held in Hanoi & Thai Binh Province from 15-26 July 1991.** Ed. by Trong Cuc Le et al. LC 93-23834. (Occasional Paper Ser.: Vol. 15). 234p. 1993. reprint ed. pap. 66.70 (0-608-03576-9, 2064399) Bks Demand.

Too Many Ponies. Jeanne Betancourt. (Pony Pals Ser.: Vol. 6). 96p. (J). 1995. pap. 2.99 (0-590-25245-3) Scholastic Inc.

Too Many Promises. C. C. Post. 456p. 1996. 21.95 (0-9652168-0-2) C C Pondbank.

Too Many Pumpkins. Linda White. LC 95-45376. (Illus.). 32p. (J). (ps-3). 1996. lib. bdg. 15.95 (0-8234-1245-8) Holiday.

***Too Many Pumpkins.** Linda White. (Illus.). 1997. pap. 6.95 (0-8234-1339-X) Holiday.

Too Many Puppies. Patience Brewster. (Hello Reader! Ser.). 1997. 3.50 (0-590-60276-4) Scholastic Inc.

Too Many Puppies: Dear Barbie. Lisa T. Parker. (J). (ps-3). 1996. pap. text ed. 3.95 (0-307-12840-7, Golden Pr) Western Pub.

Too Many Rabbits. Peggy Parish. 48p. (J). (ps-3). 1992. mass mkt. 3.99 (0-440-40591-2) Dell.

Too Many Rabbits. Peggy Porish. (J). pap. 1.50 (0-590-10157-9) Scholastic Inc.

Too Many Rabbits & Other Fingerplays: About Animals, Nature, Weather, & the Universe. Kay Cooper. LC 94-39720. (Illus.). 48p. (J). (ps-1). 1995. 12.95 (0-590-45564-8, Cartwheel) Scholastic Inc.

Too Many Schools of Education? Too Little Scholarship? Richard Wisniewski. (SPE Monographs). 1983. 3.00 (0-933669-19-4) Soc Profs Ed.

Too Many Secrets. Patricia H. Rushford. (Jennie McGrady Mystery Ser.: No. 1). (YA). (gr. 7-10). 1993. mass mkt. 4.99 (1-55661-331-8) Bethany Hse.

***Too Many Secrets.** Betty R. Wright. LC 96-35254. (J). 1997. 14.95 (0-590-25235-6) Scholastic Inc.

Too Many Songs by Tom Lehrer with Not Enough Pictures by Ronald Searle. Tom Lehrer. (Illus.). 1981. pap. 17.00 (0-394-74930-8) Pantheon.

Too Many Spies. Debra Hess. LC 95-529. (Spy from Outer Space Ser.). (Illus.). 128p. (J). (gr. 3-6). 1993. pap. 3.50 (1-56282-569-0) Hyprn Child.

***Too Many Suns.** unabridged ed. Julie Lawson. (Illus.). 32p. (J). (gr. 1 up). 1996. 14.95 (0-7737-2897-X, Pub. by Stoddart Kids CN) Genl Dist Srvs.

Too Many Tamales. Gary Soto. (Illus.). 32p. (J). (ps-3). 1993. 15.95 (0-399-22146-8, Putnam) Putnam Pub Group.

Too Many Tamales. Gary Soto. (Illus.). 32p. (J). (ps-3). 1996. pap. 5.95 (0-698-11412-4, Paperstar) Putnam Pub Group.

Too Many Teddies. Gus Clarke. (Illus.). 32p. (J). (ps-1). 1996. 12.95 (0-86264-573-5, Pub. by Anderson Pr UK) London Brdge.

***Too Many Tomatoes, Squash, Beans & Other G Things: A Cookbook for When Your Garden Explodes.** large type ed. Lois M. Landau & Laura G. Myers. LC 97-8469. (Spec-Hall Ser.). 412p. 1997. lib. bdg. 25.95 (0-7838-8210-6, GK Hall) Thorndike Pr.

Too Many Tomatoes, Squash, Beans, & Other Good Things: A Cookbook for When Your Garden Explodes. Lois Landau & Laura G. Myers. LC 75-34581. (Illus.). 288p. 1991. reprint ed. pap. 16.00 (0-06-096857-5, PL) HarpC.

Too Many, Too Long: Sudan's Twenty-Year Refugee Dilemma. John R. Rogge. LC 85-2058. (Illus.). 214p. (C). 1985. 56.50 (0-8476-7412-6, R7412) Rowman.

Too Many Toys. Betty Clark. LC 96-75798. (Illus.). 32p. (J). (ps-3). 1996. 14.95 (0-9641285-5-1) Little Frnd.

***Too Many Toys.** Arnold Fine & Howard Spielman. (J). 9.99 (0-89906-422-1, TOYH) Mesorah Pubns.

***Too Many Toys.** Arnold Fine & Howard Spielman. (J). pap. 6.99 (0-89906-423-X, TOYP) Mesorah Pubns.

Too Many Traitors. Franklin W. Dixon. (Hardy Boys Casefiles Ser.: No. 14). 160p. (Orig.). (J). (gr. 6 up). 1991. pap. 3.50 (0-671-73677-9, Archway) PB.

Too Many Treasures. Mary C. Reid. (Backpack Mysteries Ser.: No. 1). (Illus.). 80p. (J). (gr. 2-5). 1996. pap. 3.99 (1-55661-715-1) Bethany Hse.

Too Many Women? The Sex Ratio Question. Marcia Guttentag & Paul F. Secord. 336p. 1983. 32.50 (0-8039-1918-2); pap. 24.00 (0-8039-1919-0) Sage.

Too Marvelous for Words: The Life & Genius of Art Tatum. James Lester. (Illus.). 304p. 1994. 30.00 (0-19-508365-2) OUP.

Too Marvelous for Words: The Life & Genius of Art Tatum. James Lester. (Illus.). 264p. 1995. pap. 10.95 (0-19-509640-1) OUP.

Too Much. Dorothy Stott. Date not set. pap. 18.99 (0-14-055295-2) NAL-Dutton.

***Too Much a Gentleman.** 350p. (Orig.). 1997. pap. 12.95 (0-9653700-1-1) B L Pubng.

Too Much Bliss. limited ed. Henrik Drescher. (Illus.). 46p. 1992. 3,500.00 (1-887123-05-9) Granary Bks.

Too Much Christmas Pudding: In the Style of a Celtic Folktale. 20p. (Orig.). 1996. pap. 3.50 (1-889238-05-8) Papa Joes.

Too Much Flesh & Jabez. Coleman Dowell. LC 86-73236. 160p. 1987. pap. 9.95 (0-916583-21-X) Dalkey Arch.

Too Much Government. Charles E. Wood. 1972. 75.00 (0-8490-1222-8) Gordon Pr.

Too Much In Love. Francine Pascal. (SVH Ser.: No. 22). 160p. (YA). 1985. mass mkt. 3.99 (0-553-27952-1) Bantam.

Too Much Is Never Enough. William Evans. Ed. by James Jenkins. (Illus.). 153p. (Orig.). 1988. pap. 22.50 (0-9619258-0-9) Clearwtr Pools Pub Co.

Too Much Is Never Enough: Behaviors You Never Thought Were Addictions: How to Recognize & Overcome Them: A Christian's Guide. Gaylen Larson & Marita Littauer. LC 92-5729. (Lifeline Ser.). 125p. 1992. pap. 0.97 (0-8163-1109-9) Pacific Pr Pub Assn.

Too Much Is Never Enough: The Autobiography of Morris Lapidus, Architect. Morris Lapidus. LC 96-13259. (Illus.). 304p. 1996. 45.00 (0-8478-1978-7) Rizzoli Intl.

Too Much Is Not Enough. 1985. 40.00 (0-932455-04-2) Henderikse.

Too Much Is Not Enough. Orson Bean. 192p. 1988. 14.95 (0-8184-0465-5) Carol Pub Group.

Too Much Liberty? Perspectives on Freedom & the American Dream. David J. Saari. LC 94-22649. 192p. 1995. text ed. 57.95 (0-275-94879-X, Praeger Pubs); pap. text ed. 17.95 (0-275-94880-3, Praeger Pubs) Greenwood.

Too Much Might in Stupid Hands. Alexander H. Cerny. 231p. 1994. 45.00 (0-86332-887-3, Pub. by Bk Guild Ltd UK) St Mut.

An Asterisk (*) at the beginning of an entry indicates that the title is appearing in BIP for the first time.

Too Much Mush! Abby Levine. Ed. by Kathy Tucker. LC 88-33906. (Illus.). 32p. (J). (ps-2). 1989. lib. bdg. 14.95 (*0-8075-8025-2*) A Whitman.
Too Much Noise. Ann McGovern. (J). (gr. k-3). 1967. 16.00 (*0-395-18110-0*) HM.
Too Much Noise. Ann McGovern. (Illus.). 48p. (J). (gr. k-3). 1992. pap. 6.95 (*0-395-62985-3*, Sandpiper) HM.
Too Much Noise. Ann McGovern. (Illus.). 48p. (J). (gr. k-3). pap. 1.95 (*0-590-02435-3*) Scholastic Inc.
Too Much of a Good Thing. John Sparrow. LC 77-6389. 102p. 1977. lib. bdg. 11.50 (*0-226-76848-1*) U Ch Pr.
Too Much of a Good Thing: Mae West As Cultural Icon. Ramona Curry. LC 95-25838. 288p. 1996. pap. 19.95 (*0-8166-2791-6*); text ed. 49.95 (*0-8166-2790-8*) U of Minn Pr.
Too Much Schooling, Too Little Education: A Paradox of Black Life in White Societies. Ed. by Mwalimu J. Shujaa. LC 93-45417. 350p. 1994. 49.95 (*0-685-70589-7*); pap. 16.95 (*0-685-70590-0*) Africa World.
Too Much Schooling, Too Little Education: A Paradox of Black Life in White Societies. Ed. by Mwalimu J. Shujaa. LC 91-78393. 412p. 1994. 16.95 (*0-86543-386-0*) Africa World.
Too Much Talk. Angela S. Medearis. LC 95-16184. (Illus.). 32p. (J). (ps up). 1995. 15.95 (*1-56402-323-0*) Candlewick Pr.
***Too Much Talk.** Angela S. Medearis. LC 95-16184. (Illus.). 32p. (J). (ps-2). 1997. reprint ed. pap. 5.99 (*0-7636-0398-8*) Candlewick Pr.
Too Much Talking. Barbara L. McCombs & Linda Brannan. (Skills for Job Success Ser.). (Illus.). 32p. (Orig.). 1990. student ed., pap. 4.95 (*1-56119-011-X*) Educ Pr MD.
Too Much Talking. Barbara L. McCombs & Linda Brannan. (Skills for Job Success Ser.). (Illus.). 32p. (Orig.). (YA). (gr. 7-12). 1990. Set. student ed., teacher ed. 44.95 (*1-56119-064-0*); teacher ed. 1.95 (*1-56119-012-8*); disk 39.95 (*1-56119-106-X*) Educ Pr MD.
***Too Much Tattling at Pickle Mountain School.** Patricia T. Kienzle. (Illus.). 28p. (J). (gr. 2 up). 1996. teacher ed. 7.95 (*1-890798-06-1*) P T Kienzle.
Too Much, Too Soon. Frank Barrymore & D. Barrymore. 1981. reprint ed. lib. bdg. 21.95 (*0-89966-425-3*) Buccaneer Bks.
Too Much Trash! Fay Robinson. LC 95-5560. (Rookie Read-About Science Ser.). 32p. (J). (ps-2). 1995. lib. bdg. 17.30 (*0-516-06042-2*) Childrens.
Too Much Trash. Fay Robinson. (Rookie Read-About Science Ser.). (Illus.). 32p. (J). (ps-2). 1996. reprint ed. pap. 3.95 (*0-516-46042-0*) Childrens.
Too Much Trick or Treat. Jayne Miller. Ed. by Nancy R. Thatch. LC 91-14930. (Books for Students by Students). (Illus.). 26p. (J). (gr. k-4). 1991. lib. bdg. 14.95 (*0-933849-37-0*) Landmark Edns.
***Too Much Trouble for Grandpa.** Rob Lewis. LC 97-14197. (J). 1998. pap. write for info. (*1-57255-551-3*) Mondo Pubng.
Too Near the Fire. Lindsay McKenna. (Men Made in America Ser.). 1995. mass mkt. 3.99 (*0-373-45185-7*, 1-45185-5) Harlequin Bks.
Too Nice a Girl to Forget. Myron Farber. 1997. 25.00 (*0-679-42515-2*) Fodors Travel.
Too Noisy! Sonja Lamut. (All Aboard Reading Picture Readers Ser.). 32p. (J). (ps-1). 1996. pap. text ed. 3.95 (*0-448-41306-X*, G&D) Putnam Pub Group.
Too Old for Health Care? Controversies in Medicine, Law, Economics, & Ethics. Ed. by Robert H. Binstock & Stephen G. Post. LC 90-23237. (Series in Contemporary Medicine & Public Health). 232p. 1991. pap. text ed. 18.95 (*0-8018-4248-4*) Johns Hopkins.
Too Old for Summer Camp & Too Young to Retire. Jeff Macnelly. (New Shoe Book Ser.). 128p. 1988. pap. 5.95 (*0-312-01822-3*) St Martin.
Too Old to Cry, Too Hurt to Laugh: Abused Teens in Today's America. Robert J. Ackerman & Lee M. Joiner. 140p. 1989. pap. 9.95 (*0-8306-3407-X*) McGraw-Hill Prof.
Too Perfect. Allan Mallinger & Jeannette Dewyze. 224p. 1993. pap. 10.00 (*0-449-90800-3*, Columbine) Fawcett.
Too Poor to Be Sick: Access to Medical Care for the Uninsured. Patricia A. Butler. 128p. 1988. 17.50 (*0-87553-151-2*) Am Pub Health.
Too Precious Child. Lynne H. Williams et al. 336p. 1989. pap. 12.95 (*0-446-38935-8*) Warner Bks.
***Too Proud to Beg: Self-Empowerment for Today's Dog.** John Olson. (Illus.). 96p. (Orig.). 1997. pap. 10.95 (*0-8362-2772-7*) Andrews & McMeel.
Too Queer: Essays from a Radical Life. Victoria A. Brownworth. LC 96-2701. 256p. (Orig.). 1996. pap. 13.95 (*1-56341-074-5*); lib. bdg. 26.95 (*1-56341-075-3*) Firebrand Bks.
***Too Quiet for These Old Bones.** Tres Seymour. LC 96-53301. (Illus.). 32p. (J). (ps-2). 1997. 15.95 (*0-531-30052-8*); lib. bdg. 16.99 (*0-531-33052-4*) Orchard Bks Watts.
Too Rich. Melissa Chan. 108p. 1993. pap. 10.95 (*1-875559-02-7*, Pub. by SpiniFex Pr AT) LPC InBook.
Too Rich: The Family Secrets of Doris Duke. Duke. 1996. 25.00 (*0-06-172185-9*) Harper SF.
Too Rich: The Family Secrets of Doris Duke. Pony Duke & Jason Thomas. LC 95-42526. 288p. 1996. 25.00 (*0-06-017218-5*) HarpC.
Too Rich for Her Pride. large type ed. Jacqueline Hacsi. (Linford Romance Library). 320p. 1995. pap. 15.99 (*0-7089-7746-4*, Linford) Ulverscroft.
Too Rich to Live. Stanley Morgan. (Orig.). 1979. pap. 2.25 (*0-449-14269-8*, GM) Fawcett.
Too Sad to Sing: A Memoir with Postcards. Kenneth S. Brecher. 144p. 1988. 22.95 (*0-318-32726-0*); pap. 11.95 (*0-318-32727-9*) HarBrace.
Too Scared to Cry: Psychic Trauma in Childhood. Lenore Terr. LC 89-46121. 372p. 1992. reprint ed. pap. 15.00 (*0-465-08644-6*) Basic.
Too Scared to Sleep. Francine Pascal. (Sweet Valley Twins Ser.: No. 97). 144p. (J). (gr. 4-7). 1996. mass mkt. 3.50 (*0-553-48201-7*, Sweet Valley) BDD Bks Young Read.
Too See Ourselves: Rural Scotland in Old Photographs. Dorothy I. Kidd. (Photography Ser.). (Illus.). 160p. (Orig.). Date not set. pap. 19.95 (*0-948636-79-3*, 8636, Pub. by Natl Mus Scotland UK) A Schwartz & Co.
Too Shy to Surrender. Manya C. Bean. 54p. (Orig.). 1993. pap. 8.95 (*0-9639821-0-9*) Osage.
Too Small a World. 1989. pap. 7.00 (*0-9619397-3-7*) MSSH.
Too Smart for Trouble. Sharon Scott. (Illus.). 112p. (Orig.). (J). (gr. k-5). 1990. pap. 7.95 (*0-87425-121-4*) HRD Press.
Too Smart to be Rich: A Satiric Look at Being a "Yuffie" Patty Friedmann. (Illus.). 160p. (Orig.). 1987. pap. 8.95 (*0-944681-01-8*) Celestial Pub.
***Too Soar Without Leaving the Ground: Poems & Narratives.** Brook S. Parker. (Illus.). 103p. (Orig.). 1996. pap. 9.95 (*0-9654415-0-4*) To Soar Pub.
***Too Soon Dead.** Michael Kurland. LC 96-44226. 1997. 22.95 (*0-312-15228-0*) St Martin.
Too Soon for Jeff. Marilyn Reynolds. 224p. (Orig.). (YA). (gr. 7 up). 1994. 15.95 (*0-930934-90-3*); pap. 8.95 (*0-930934-91-1*) Morning Glory.
***Too Soon Forgotten: Legend of the Old South.** 246p. 1997. pap. 6.95 (*0-9644574-9-0*) Shoeless Pub.
Too Soon Old, Too Late Smart: How to Get Control of Your Money (Before Your Money Gets Control of You) Robert G. Moscatelli. LC 94-96692. (Illus.). 294p. (Orig.). 1995. pap. 14.95 (*0-9643601-0-1*) Blck Knight.
Too Soon to Die. David Potter. 1982. pap. 3.99 (*0-85234-169-5*, Pub. by Evangelical Pr) Presby & Reformed.
***Too Soon to Leave.** Steven Schreiner. vii, 72p. (Orig.). 1997. pap. text ed. 12.00 (*1-56439-063-2*) Ridgeway.
***Too Soon to Panic.** Gordon Forbes. LC 96-52805. 396p. 1997. 24.95 (*1-55821-566-2*) Lyons & Burford.
Too Soon to Quit: Patterns to Clear Life's Hurdles. rev. ed. Harry M. Tippett. LC 94-62053. 136p. 1995. pap. 8.95 (*0-9643772-0-9*) VIA Pr CA.
Too Soon To Quit: The Daily Encouragement Factor. Lareau Lindquist. 192p. 1994. 17.95 (*1-885481-00-4*) Quadrus Media.
Too Soon To Quit: The Daily Encouragement Factor. Lareau Lindquist. 192p. 1994. pap. 9.95 (*1-885481-01-2*) Quadrus Media.
Too Soon to Say Good-Bye. Deborah Kent. (J). 1996. pap. 3.50 (*0-590-47798-6*) Scholastic Inc.
Too Soon to Tell. Calvin Trillin. LC 94-24629. 1995. 18.00 (*0-374-27846-6*) FS&G.
Too Soon to Tell. Calvin Trillin. 304p. 1996. pap. 11.99 (*0-446-67230-0*) Warner Bks.
Too Soon to Tell. large type ed. Calvin Trillin. (Niagara Large Print Ser.). 313p. 1996. 27.99 (*0-7089-5821-4*) Ulverscroft.
Too Strong for Fantasy. Marcia Davenport. LC 92-53723. (Illus.). 504p. (C). 1992. reprint ed. text ed. 49.95 (*0-8229-3834-0*); reprint ed. pap. text ed. 15.95 (*0-8229-5909-7*) U of Pittsburgh Pr.
Too Strong to Deny. Emma Darcy. (Presents Ser.: No. 1335). 1991. pap. 2.50 (*0-373-11335-8*) Harlequin Bks.
Too Strong to Deny. large type ed. Emma Darcy. 1990. reprint ed. lib. bdg. 18.95 (*0-263-12267-0*, Pub. by Mills & Boon UK) Thorndike Pr.
Too Stubborn to Die. Cato Jaramillo. LC 95-35913. 250p. 1995. 16.95 (*1-882723-18-X*) Gold Leaf Pr.
Too Tall, Too Small: Zacchaeus. Mary M. Simon. (Hear Me Read Ser.). (Illus.). 24p. (J). (ps-1). 1990. pap. 2.49 (*0-570-04185-6*, 56-1644) Concordia.
Too Tired Tofer. Elizabeth Koehler-Pentacoff. (J). 1997. 12.00 (*0-689-80586-1*) S&S Childrens.
Too-Too Justin. Lynea Bowdish. (Illus.). 24p. (J). (gr. 1-2). 1995. pap. 2.50 (*0-87406-731-6*) Willowisp Pr.
Too Tough to Care. Malka Millman. 150p. (J). (gr. 6). 8.95 (*1-56062-237-7*) CIS Comm.
Too Tough to Die. Gordon D. Shirreffs. 128p. 1989. mass mkt. 2.75 (*0-380-70638-5*) Avon.
Too Tough to Tame. Deborah Camp. 1996. mass mkt. 5.50 (*0-380-78251-0*) Avon.
Too Wet to Plow. Jeanne Simonelli. LC 89-18009. (Illus.). 128p. (C). 1990. 25.00 (*0-941533-64-6*) New Amsterdam Bks.
Too Wet to Plow. rev. ed. Frank Fuis, Jr. 1977. 14.95 (*0-682-48844-5*, Exposition Pr) Norris World.
Too Wise to Want to Be Young Again: A Witty View of How to Stop Counting the Years & Start Living Them. Natasha Josefowitz. LC 95-25077. 1995. pap. text ed. 7.95 (*0-88396-422-8*) Blue Mtn Pr CO.
Too Wise to Want to Be Young Again: A Witty View of How to Stop Counting the Years & Start Living Them. Natasha Josefowitz. (Illus.). 63p. (Orig.). 1995. pap. 7.95 (*0-614-13536-2*) Prestwick Pub.
***Too Wise to Wed?** Penny Jordan. (Presents Ser.: No. 1895). 1997. mass mkt. 3.50 (*0-373-11895-3*, 1-11895-9) Harlequin Bks.
***Too Wise to Wed?** Penny Jordan. (Harlequin Ser.). 1997. 20.95 (*0-263-15043-7*, Pub. by Mills & Boon UK) Thorndike Pr.
Too Young Americans. J. R. Shelton. LC 92-67756. 142p. (Orig.). 1992. pap. 9.00 (*1-56002-170-5*, Univ Edtns) Aegina Pr.
***Too Young the Heroes: A World War II Marine's Account of Facing a Veteran Enemy at Guadalcanal, the Solomons & Okinawa.** George Lince. LC 97-273. (Illus.). 207p. 1997. pap. 26.50 (*0-7864-0330-6*) McFarland & Co.
Too Young to Be Old: Secrets from Bible Seniors. John Gilmore. 190p. 1992. pap. 8.99 (*0-87788-839-6*) Shaw Pubs.
Too Young To Die. (Consumer Guide Ser.). 320p. 1994. pap. 4.99 (*0-451-17901-3*, Sig) NAL-Dutton.
Too Young to Die. Lurlene McDaniel. 176p. (YA). (gr. 7 up). 1989. pap. 3.99 (*0-553-28008-2*, Starfire BDD) BDD Bks Young Read.
Too Young to Die (Testicular Cancer) Rick Hill. 5.00 (*0-685-42037-X*) Cancer Control Soc.
Too Young to Drive, Too Old to Ride: Surviving Your Child's Middle School Years. rev. ed. Gary Hunt & Angela E. Hunt. Orig. Title: Surviving the Tweenage Years. 1992. reprint ed. pap. 8.99 (*0-8407-4599-0*) Nelson.
Too Young to Remember. Julie Heifitz. LC 88-20896. 128p. (C). 1989. pap. 29.95 (*0-8143-2026-0*) Wayne St U Pr.
Too Young to Travel Abroad: Journal of a Year of European Travel in 1856-7. Agnes Woolsey. Ed. by Louise H. Tallman. (Illus.). 192p. (Orig.). (J). (gr. 5-12). 1995. 25.00 (*0-914339-53-2*) P E Randall Pub.
Too Young to Understand. Marilyn C. Gatewood. 24p. 1995. pap. 6.00 (*0-8059-3645-9*) Dorrance.
Toobers & Zots Home Companion: An Infinite Idea Book. 1995. pap. 14.99 (*0-201-87045-2*) Addison-Wesley.
Toobers & Zots Travel Companion. Planet Dexter Editors. 1996. pap. 14.99 (*0-201-48365-3*) Addison-Wesley.
Toodle D. Poodle. Katherine Dana. Ed. by Albert H. Shuster. (Fables for Today Ser.: Vol. VI). (Illus.). 22p. (Orig.). (J). 1992. pap. 5.52 (*0-914127-14-4*) Univ Class.
Toodle-oo Taxahaw: One Hundred One Tales or a Small History of the World. J. Donald McManus. (Illus.). 228p. (Orig.). 1991. pap. 10.00 (*0-939710-15-3*) Meridional Pubns.
Toohey's Medicine: A Textbook for Students in the Health Care Professions. 15th ed. Ed. by Stephen R. Bloom. 377p. 1995. pap. 31.95 (*0-443-04704-9*) Churchill.
Toohey's Medicine for Nurses. 14th ed. Arnold Bloom & Stephen Bloom. (Illus.). 335p. 1986. text ed. 34.00 (*0-443-03076-6*) Churchill.
Toohy & Wood. Mary E. Monsell. LC 91-38217. (Illus.). 80p. (J). (gr. 2-5). 1992. lib. bdg. 12.95 (*0-689-31721-2*, Atheneum Bks Young) S&S Childrens.
***Tookie Speaks Out - Gangs & Drugs.** Stanley T. Williams. (J). (gr. k-4). 1997. pap. text ed. 6.95 (*1-56838-135-2*) Hazelden.
***Tookie Speaks Out - Gangs & Self Esteem.** Stanley T. Williams. (J). (gr. k-4). 1997. pap. text ed. 6.95 (*1-56838-133-6*) Hazelden.
***Tookie Speaks Out - Gangs & Violence.** Stanley T. Williams. (J). (gr. k-4). 1997. pap. text ed. 6.95 (*1-56838-134-4*) Hazelden.
***Tookie Speaks Out - Gangs & Your Friends.** Stanley T. Williams. (J). (gr. k-4). 1997. pap. text ed. 6.95 (*1-56838-136-0*) Hazelden.
***Tookie Speaks Out - Gangs & Your Neighborhood.** Stanley T. Williams. (J). (gr. k-4). 1997. pap. text ed. 6.95 (*1-56838-137-9*) Hazelden.
***Tookie Speaks Out Gangs & the Abuse of Power.** Stanley T. Williams. (J). (gr. k-4). 1997. pap. text ed. 6.95 (*1-56838-130-1*) Hazelden.
***Tookie Speaks Out Gangs & Wanting to Belong.** Stanley T. Williams. (J). (gr. k-4). 1997. pap. text ed. 6.95 (*1-56838-131-X*) Hazelden.
***Tookie Speaks Out Gangs & Weapons.** Stanley T. Williams. (J). (gr. k-4). 1997. pap. text ed. 6.95 (*1-56838-132-8*) Hazelden.
Tool: An Inner-Active Communication Technique to Add Balance & Focus to Your Life. Larry Hawes. (Illus.). 104p. (Orig.). 1994. pap. text ed. 14.95 (*1-878803-03-4*) Balance Prodns.
Tool & Die Failures. Ed. by Serope Kalpakjian. LC 82-73088. (American Society for Metals - Source Book Ser.). (Illus.). 440p. reprint ed. pap. 125.40 (*0-8357-4101-X*, 2036867) Bks Demand.
Tool & Manufacturing Engineers Handbook: Design for Manufacturability, Vol. 6. Ed. by Philip Mitchell. LC 91-60347. (Illus.). 675p. 1992. 126.00 (*0-87263-402-7*) SME.
Tool & Manufacturing Engineers Handbook Vol. VIII: Plastic Part Manufacturing. Ed. by Philip Mitchell. LC 82-60312. 650p. 1996. 126.00 (*0-87263-456-6*) SME.
Tool & Manufacturing Engineers Handbook, Vol. 1: Machining. 4th ed. Society of Manufacturing Engineers Staff. Ed. by C. Wick & T. Drozda. LC 82-60312. 1494p. 1983. 126.00 (*0-87263-085-4*) SME.
Tool & Manufacturing Engineers Handbook, Vol. 2: Forming. 4th ed. Society of Manufacturing Engineers Staff. Ed. by C. Wick et al. LC 82-60312. 936p. 1984. 126.00 (*0-87263-135-4*) SME.
Tool & Manufacturing Engineers Handbook, Vol. 3: Materials, Finishing & Coating. 4th ed. Ed. by C. Wick & R. Veilleux. LC 82-60312. 864p. 1985. 126.00 (*0-87263-176-1*) SME.
Tool & Manufacturing Engineers Handbook, Vol. 4: Quality Control & Assembly. Society of Manufacturing Engineers Staff. Ed. by C. Wick & R. Veilleux. LC 82-60312. 840p. 1987. 126.00 (*0-87263-177-X*) SME.
Tool & Manufacturing Engineers Handbook, Vol. 5: Manufacturing Management. Ed. by R. Veilleux & L. Petro. LC 82-60312. 600p. 1988. 126.00 (*0-87263-306-3*) SME.
Tool & Manufacturing Engineers Handbook, Vol. 7: Continuous Improvement. Ed. by R. Bakerjian. LC 92-81156. 400p. 1993. 126.00 (*0-87263-420-5*) SME.
Tool & Parts Clerk (USPS) Jack Rudman. (Career Examination Ser.: C-1610). 1994. pap. 27.95 (*0-8373-1610-3*) Nat Learn.
Tool Book. Gail Gibbons. LC 81-13386. (Illus.). 32p. (J). (ps-3). 1982. lib. bdg. 15.95 (*0-8234-0444-7*) Holiday.
Tool Book. Gail Gibbons. LC 81-13386. (Illus.). 32p. (J). (ps-3). 1988. pap. 6.95 (*0-8234-0694-6*) Holiday.
Tool Box. Norma N. Bracy. (Illus.). 35p. (J). (gr. 5-12). 1987. pap. text ed. 2.50 (*0-915783-04-5*) Book Binder.
Tool Design. 3rd ed. Cyril Donaldson & George Le Cain. (Illus.). 840p. 1973. text ed. 48.95 (*0-07-017531-4*) McGraw.
Tool Design: Fundamental Principles of Design as Applied to Tooling for Production. Charles B. Cole. LC 41-19998. (Illus.). 595p. reprint ed. pap. 169.60 (*0-317-11004-7*, 2004574) Bks Demand.
Tool Encapsulation Specification, Vol. 3. Domain Independent Services Technical Committee Staff. 140p. 1993. pap. text ed. 100.00 (*1-882750-03-9*) CAD Framewk.
Tool Engineering. Samuel E. Rusinoff. LC 59-13786. (Illus.). 335p. reprint ed. pap. 95.50 (*0-317-11000-4*, 2004566) Bks Demand.
Tool Integration: Environments & Frameworks. Ed. by D. Schefstrom. 447p. 1993. text ed. 85.00 (*0-471-93554-9*) Wiley.
Tool Integration & Design Environments: Proceeding of the IFIP WG10.2 Workshop on Tool Integration & Design Environments, Paderborn, FRG, 26-27 Nov., 1987. Ed. by F. J. Rammig. 334p. 1988. 125.00 (*0-444-70446-9*, North Holland) Elsevier.
Tool Kit: dBASE III Plus. Tim Duffy. 161p. (C). 1993. pap. 17.95 (*0-534-30269-6*) Course Tech.
Tool Kit: dBASE IV. Tim Duffy. 178p. (C). 1993. pap. 17.95 (*0-534-30273-4*) Course Tech.
Tool Kit: dBASE IV (Release 2) Tim Duffy. 1995. pap. text ed., spiral bd., pap. 17.95 (*0-534-30838-4*) Course Tech.
Tool Kit: DOS 3.3. Tim Duffy. 120p. (C). 1993. pap. 17.95 (*0-534-30240-8*) Course Tech.
Tool Kit: DOS 5.0. Tim Duffy. 169p. (C). 1993. pap. 17.95 (*0-534-30244-0*) Course Tech.
Tool Kit: DOS 6.0. Tim Duffy. 146p. 1994. pap. 17.95 (*0-534-30279-3*) Course Tech.
Tool Kit: DOS 6.2. Tim Duffy. 154p. 1995. pap. 17.95 (*0-534-30829-5*) Course Tech.
Tool Kit: Lotus 1-2-3 (Release 2.2) Tim Duffy. 296p. (C). 1993. pap. 17.95 (*0-534-30260-2*) Course Tech.
Tool Kit: Lotus 1-2-3 (Release 2.3) Tim Duffy. 283p. (C). 1993. pap. 17.95 (*0-534-30264-5*) Course Tech.
Tool Kit: Lotus 1-2-3 (Release 3.4) Tim Duffy. 354p. 1994. pap. 17.95 (*0-534-30246-7*) Course Tech.
Tool Kit: Microsoft Office. Duffy. (Management Information Systems Ser.). 1996. pap. 52.95 (*0-7895-0672-6*) S-W Pub.
Tool Kit: Paradox 3.5. Tim Duffy. 178p. (C). 1993. pap. 17.95 (*0-534-30256-4*) Course Tech.
Tool Kit: Quattro Pro 4.0. Tim Duffy. 338p. (C). 1993. pap. 17.95 (*0-534-30252-1*) Course Tech.
Tool Kit: Windows 3.1. Tim Duffy. 144p. (C). 1993. pap. 17.95 (*0-534-30277-7*) Course Tech.
Tool Kit: WordPerfect for Windows. Tim Duffy. 246p. 1994. pap. 17.95 (*0-534-30242-4*) Course Tech.
Tool Kit: WordPerfect 5.1. Tim Duffy. 213p. (C). 1993. pap. 17.95 (*0-534-30248-3*) Course Tech.
Tool Kit: WordPerfect 6.0 & 6.0a for Windows. Tim Duffy. 258p. 1995. pap. 17.95 (*0-534-30835-X*) Course Tech.
Tool Kit: WordPerfect 6.0 for DOS. Tim Duffy. 259p. 1994. pap. 17.95 (*0-534-30812-0*) Course Tech.
***Tool Kit for Buying or Selling a Law Practice.** 38p. 1996. wbk. ed., pap. 249.00 (*0-9654948-0-2*) E Poll & Assocs.
Tool Kit for Re-Energizing Your Organizations TQM Program. Charles T. Bargerstock. 114p. 1996. ring bd. 29.00 (*0-9639557-7-2*, Jacob-Cameron) A R K Co.
Tool Kit for Trainers: A Compendium of Techniques for Trainers & Group Workers. Tim Pickles. LC 96-26045. 214p. (Orig.). 1996. pap. 27.95 (*1-55561-112-5*) Fisher Bks.
Tool Materials: Tool Materials. Ed. by J. R. Davis. (Specialty Handbook Ser.). (Illus.). 501p. 1995. 173.00 (*0-87170-545-1*, 6506) ASM.
***Tool Materials for High-Speed Machining: Proceedings of a Conference on Advances in Tool Materials for Use in High Speed Machining, Held February 25-27, 1987, Scottsdale, AZ.** Ed. by J. A. Swartley-Loush. LC 87-70938. (Illus.). 145p. 1987. reprint ed. pap. 41.40 (*0-608-02624-7*, 2063282) Bks Demand.
Tool Materials for Molds & Dies: Application & Performance. Ed. by G. Krauss & H. Nordberg. LC 87-18407. (Illus.). 448p. 1987. text ed. 64.95 (*0-918062-74-8*) Colo Sch Mines.
Tool of the Trade. Joe W. Haldeman. 256p. 1988. mass mkt. 3.95 (*0-380-70438-2*) Avon.
***Tool Shed Treasury: The Best Articles on Antique Tool Collecting from Crafts.** Ed. by Hank Allen. (Illus.). 176p. (Orig.). 1996. pap. 18.50 (*1-879335-71-9*) Astragal Pr.
Tool Steel Simplified. 4th ed. Frank R. Palmer et al. LC 78-7181. 555p. reprint ed. pap. 158.20 (*0-317-55805-6*, 2029387) Bks Demand.
Tool Steels. LC 88-80176. 88p. 1988. 27.00 (*0-932897-31-2*) Iron & Steel.
***Tool Steels.** George Roberts et al. 400p. 1997. 190.00 (*0-87170-599-0*, 6590) ASM.
Tool Steels. 4th ed. G. Roberts & R. Cary. 820p. 1980. 120.00 (*0-87170-096-4*, 6280) ASM.
***Tool Steels.** 5th ed. G. Krauss. (C). 1997. write for info. (*0-614-20002-4*) ASM.
Tool That Built Niagara. Mark H. Beecher. (Illus.). 62p. (Orig.). 1976. pap. 4.00 (*0-685-29129-4*) Niagara Cnty Hist Soc.
Toolbook: Decision Making & Planning for Optimum Results. Glen D. Hoffherr. 51p. (Orig.). 1993. pap. text ed. 3.95 (*0-9638223-0-6*) Markon.

T

Toolbook for Quality Improvement & Problem Solving. David Straker. LC 95-18127. 1995. pap. text ed. 37.00 (0-13-746892-X) P-H Gen Ref & Trav.

***Toolbook for Successful Redesign.** Ruth Hansten & Marilynn Washburn. LC 97-21698. 250p. 1997. 55.00 (0-8342-0907-1, 20907) Aspen Pub.

Toolbox. Fabio Morabito & Geoff Hargreaves. LC 96-24823. (Xenos Dual-Language Book Ser.). 1996. pap. 10.00 (1-879378-19-1) Xenos Riverside.

Toolbox. Fabio Morabito & Jaime M. Villarreal. Tr. by Geoff Hargreaves. LC 96-24823. (Xenos Dual-Language Book Ser.). (Illus.). x, 104p. 1996. 20.00 (1-879378-20-5) Xenos Riverside.

***Toolbox.** Fabio Morabito. Tr. by Geoff Hargreaves from SPA. 1996. write for info. (0-614-24574-5) Xenos Riverside.

Toolbox. Anne Rockwell. LC 89-34818. (Illus.). 24p. (J). (ps-1). 1990. pap. 3.95 (0-689-71382-7, Aladdin Paperbacks) S&S Childrens.

Toolbox Book. Jim Tolpin. LC 95-15048. (Illus.). 224p. 1995. 34.95 (1-56158-092-9) Taunton.

***Toolbox Box: A Craftsman's Guide to Tool Chests, Cabinets & Storage Systems.** Jim Tolpin. 1996. text ed. 34.95 (0-07-064839-5) McGraw.

***Toolbox for Solving Behavior Problem.** Terry Ryan. 1997. 19.95 (0-87605-049-6) Howell Bk.

***Toolbox Organic Chemistry.** 6th ed. Fessenden. 1998. 32.95 (0-534-35207-3) Brooks-Cole.

Toolbox Reprint Series: Diagnosing Systemic Issues & Designing High Leverage Interventions. rev. ed. Daniel H. Kim. (Illus.). 26p. 1993. pap. text ed. 15.00 (1-883823-00-5) Pegasus Comm.

Toolchest: A Primer of Woodcraft. Jan Adkins. Ed. by Margery Cuyler. LC 72-81374. (Illus.). 48p. 1973. pap. 4.95 (0-8027-7218-8) Walker & Co.

Tooley's Handbook for Map Collectors. Ronald V. Tooley. 1985. text ed. 17.00 (0-932757-00-6) Speculum Orbis.

Toolik Lake: Ecology of an Aquatic Ecosystem in Arctic Alaska. Ed. by W. J. O'Brien. LC 92-26746. (Developments in Hydrobiology Ser.: Vol. 78). (C). 1992. lib. bdg. 216.00 (0-7923-1952-4) Kluwer Ac.

Tooling Challenges for the 80's: Injection Molding Tooling: Design, Materials, Methods: Regional Technical Conference, the Erie Hilton Hotel, Erie, Pennsylvania, April 2-3, 1985, Pts. 1 & 2. Society of Plastics Engineers Staff. (Illus.). 228p. reprint ed. pap. 65.00 (0-317-42304-5, 2025804) Bks Demand.

Tooling Design for Powder Metallurgy Parts: Prepared Courses of Instruction. Robert N. Kunkel. 168p. reprint ed. pap. 47.90 (0-317-27675-1, 2024168) Bks Demand.

Toolkit: Tools & Techniques to Unlock the Potential of Your Team. Rosaria Taraschi & Diane Robinette. 94p. 1994. 39.95 (0-9641834-0-4) Take Charge Cnslts.

Toolkit for College Success. Daniel R. Walther. 241p. 1994. pap. 22.95 (0-534-23052-0) Wadsworth Pub.

Toolmaker. Jack Rudman. (Career Examination Ser.: C-1517). 1994. pap. 29.95 (0-8373-1517-4) Nat Learn.

Toolmaking. 1994. lib. bdg. 250.95 (0-8490-5680-2) Gordon Pr.

Toolmaking. 1996. lib. bdg. 250.95 (0-8490-8312-5) Gordon Pr.

***Toolmaking for Woodworkers.** Ray Larsen. (Illus.). 160p. (Orig.). 1997. pap. 19.95 (0-9643999-4-6) Cambium Pr.

Toolpack 1: Introductory Guide. W. R. Cowell et al. (Orig.). 1985. pap. 4.20 (0-317-52233-7, Pub. by Numer Algo UK) Numer Algorithms.

Tools. Byron Barton. (Illus.). 12p. (J). (ps). 1996. bds. 3.95 (0-694-00623-8, Festival) HarpC Child Bks.

Tools. Karen Bryant-Mole. LC 95-51187. (J). 1996. lib. bdg. 10.95 (0-382-39584-0) Silver Burdett Pr.

Tools. Karen Bryant-Mole. LC 95-51187. (J). 1996. pap. 4.95 (0-382-39620-0, Silver Pr NJ) Silver Burdett Pr.

Tools. Robert D. Hoeft. (Illus.). 48p. 1982. 20.00 (0-88014-043-7) Mosaic Pr OH.

Tools. Ann Morris. (ESL Theme Links Ser.). (Illus.). 24p. 1993. teacher ed. 15.00 (1-56334-302-9); student ed., teacher ed. 10.50 incl. audio (1-56334-303-7); student ed., teacher ed. 35.00 (1-56334-304-5); student ed., teacher ed. 99.50 (1-56334-305-3) Hampton-Brown.

Tools. Ann Morris. LC 92-3871. (Illus.). 32p. (J). (ps-2). 1992. 16.00 (0-688-10170-4); lib. bdg. 15.93 (0-688-10171-2) Lothrop.

***Tools.** Brenda Parkes. Ed. by Jennifer Mooney. (Newbridge Links Ser.). 8p. (J). (gr. k up). 1997. pap. 2.75 (1-56784-907-5) Newbridge Comms.

Tools. Ed. by George W. Zobrist. (Progress in Computer Aided VLSI Design Ser.: Vol. 1). 416p. (C). 1989. text ed. 82.50 (0-89391-538-6) Ablex Pub.

Tools: Big Book. Ann Morris. (ESL Theme Links Ser.). (Illus.). 24p. 1993. Big Book. pap. text ed. 29.95 (1-56334-300-2) Hampton-Brown.

Tools: Readiness Activities for Preschool & Kindergarten. Kenn Goin & Gloria Harbin. (Topics for Preschool Ser.). (Illus.). 64p. 1987. pap. text ed. 8.95 (0-943129-00-1) Chatterbox Pr.

Tools: Small Book. Ann Morris. (ESL Theme Links Ser.). (Illus.). 24p. 1993. Small Book. pap. text ed. 6.00 (1-56334-301-0) Hampton-Brown.

Tools: Working Wood in Eighteenth-Century America. James M. Gaynor & Nancy L. Hagedorn. LC 93-31754. (Wallace Gallery Decorative Arts Publication Ser.). (Illus.). 126p. (Orig.). (C). 1994. pap. text ed. 19.95 (0-87935-098-9, Pub. by Williamsburg) U Pr of Va.

Tools & Activities for a Diverse Work Force. Anthony P. Carnevale. 1996. text ed. 149.95 (0-07-011375-0) McGraw.

***Tools & Activities for Strategic Planning: Creative Techniques for Facilitating Your Organization's Planning Process.** Rod Napier & Clint Sidle. 1997. text ed. 149.95 (0-07-046067-1) McGraw.

Tools & Algorithms for the Construction & Analysis of Systems: First International Workshop, TACAS '95, Aarhus, Denmark, May 19-20, 1995, Selected Papers. Ed. by E. Brinksma et al. LC 95-47444. (Lecture Notes in Computer Science Ser.: No. 1019). 291p. 1995. 49.00 (3-540-60630-0) Spr-Verlag.

Tools & Algorithms for the Construction & Analysis of Systems: Proceedings, Second International Workshop, TACAS '96, Passau, Germany, March 1996. Ed. by Tiziana Margaria & Bernhard Steffen. LC 96-4088. (Lecture Notes in Computer Science Ser.: Vol. 1055). 435p. 1996. pap. 68.00 (3-540-61042-1) Spr-Verlag.

***Tools & Algorithms for the Construction & Analysis of Systems: Third International Workshop, Tacas 97, Enschede, The Netherlands, April 2-4, 1997: Proceedings, Vol. 121.** Ed Brinksma. LC 97-11043. (Lecture Notes in Computer Science Ser.). 1997. pap. write for info. (3-540-62790-1) Spr-Verlag.

Tools & Environments for Parallel & Distributed Systems. Ed. by Amr Zaky & Ted Lewis. (International Series in Software Engineering). 320p. (C). 1996. lib. bdg. 115.00 (0-7923-9675-8) Kluwer Ac.

Tools & Gadgets. Bobbie Kalman. (Historic Communities Ser.). (Illus.). 32p. (J). (gr. k-9). 1992. pap. 7.95 (0-86505-508-4); lib. bdg. 19.16 (0-86505-488-6) Crabtree Pub Co.

Tools & Methods for the Improvement of Quality. Howard Gitlow et al. 624p. (C). 1989. 61.00 (0-256-05680-3) Irwin.

Tools & Techniques for Strategic Management. Patrick B. McNamee. (Illus.). 350p. 1985. text ed. 74.00 (0-08-031810-X, Prgamon Press); pap. text ed. 29.00 (0-08-031809-6, Prgamon Press) Buttrwrth-Heinemann.

Tools & Techniques for Structured Systems Analysis & Design. William S. Davis. LC 83-4629. 208p. 1983. pap. text ed. 15.96 (0-201-10274-9) Addison-Wesley.

Tools & Techniques for Transputer Applications. Ed. by Stephen J. Turner. (Transputer & Occam Engineering Ser.). 244p. (gr. 12). 1990. pap. 69.00 (90-5199-029-4, Pub. by IOS Pr NE) IOS Press.

Tools & Techniques in Physical Metallurgy, Vol. 1. Ed. by Fred Weinberg. LC 76-107759. (Illus.). 414p. reprint ed. pap. 118.00 (0-7837-0983-8, 2041290) Bks Demand.

Tools & Techniques in Physical Metallurgy, Vol. 2. Ed. by Fred Weinberg. LC 76-107759. (Illus.). 372p. reprint ed. pap. 106.10 (0-7837-0984-6, 2041290) Bks Demand.

Tools & Techniques of Executions. 1991. lib. bdg. 75.00 (0-8490-4691-2) Gordon Pr.

Tools & Techniques of Financial Planning. 4th rev. ed. Stephan R. Leimberg et al. LC 88-62296. 545p. 1993. pap. 37.50 (0-87218-114-6) Natl Underwriter.

***Tools & Techniques to Inspire Classroom Learning.** Barbara A. Cleary & Sally J. Duncan. LC 96-44602. (Illus.). 161p. 1996. 20.00 (0-87389-411-1, H0952) ASQC Qual Pr.

Tools & the Man. Helen D. Lockwood. LC 21-12534. reprint ed. 27.50 (0-404-03999-5) AMS Pr.

Tools & Their Uses. 1991. lib. bdg. 250.00 (0-8490-4938-5) Gordon Pr.

Tools & Their Uses. Bureau of Naval Personnel. (Illus.). 1990. 12.75 (0-8446-4718-7) Peter Smith.

Tools & Their Uses. U. S. Navy, Bureau of Naval Personnel Staff. LC 72-93611. (Illus.). 180p. 1973. reprint ed. pap. 4.95 (0-486-22022-2) Dover.

Tools & Their Uses: The Proper Use & Maintenance of Power Tools. 1984. lib. bdg. 250.00 (0-87700-552-4) Revisionist Pr.

Tools & Tomorrow see Macmillan Encyclopedia of Science

Tools & Toys: Fifty Fun Ways to Love Your Class. (Illus.). xiv, 114p. 1996. teacher ed., pap. 10.00 (1-889236-01-2) New Mgmt CA.

Tools & Traditions: Studies in European Ethnology Presented to Alexander Fenton. Ed. by Hugh Cheape. (Illus.). 256p. 1995. 45.00 (0-948636-53-X, 653-X, Woodstocker Bks) A Schwartz & Co.

Tools as Art: The Hechinger Collection. Pete Hamill. LC 95-890. (Illus.). 208p. 1995. 39.95 (0-8109-3873-1) Abrams.

Tools Every (Handy) Woman Should Have: And Annual Home Maintenance Schedule for the Novice. Sharon L. Turman. 84p. 1994. pap. 3.26 (0-9643796-0-0) Amer Mantels.

Tools for a Learning Organisation. Pearn Kandola et al. 1995. 1,200.00 (0-85292-593-X, Pub. by IPM UK) St Mut.

Tools for Achieving TQE. Raymond F. Latta & Carolyn J. Downey. LC 94-9174. (Total Quality Education for the World's Best Schools Ser.: Vol. 10). 160p. 1994. pap. 18.95 (0-8039-6178-2) Corwin Pr.

Tools for Active Christians. Herbert Miller. LC 79-14795. (P.A.C.E. Ser.). (Orig.). 1979. pap. 9.99 (0-8272-3624-7) Chalice Pr.

Tools for Analyzing & Constructing Agile Capabilities. Rick Dove. (Perspectives on Agility Ser.). (Illus.). 15p. (Orig.). 1996. pap. 10.00 (1-885166-08-7, PA96-01) Agility Forum.

Tools for Building. Ed. by Fine Homebuilding Magazine Staff. LC 88-50565. (Fine Homebuilding Builder's Library). (Illus.). 176p. 1988. 23.95 (0-942391-10-1) Taunton.

Tools for Building Your Volunteer Ministries. Margie Morris. 148p. (Orig.). 1991. pap. 17.95 (0-9620898-6-9) Newton-Cline.

Tools for Code Management: Using Make, Revision Control, Debuggers, Profilers. Lawrence Reznick. 1994. pap. text ed. 30.00 (0-13-100207-4) P-H.

***Tools for Code Management: Using Make, Revision Control, Depluggers, Profilers & Lint.** Larry Reznick. 280p. 1996. pap. 29.95 (0-87930-435-9) R & D Books.

Tools for Creating & Sustaining Drug-Free Communities: Prevention Plus, 2 vols. 1993. lib. bdg. 589.95 (0-8490-8920-4) Gordon Pr.

Tools for Dreamers: Strategies for Creativity. Robert Dilts. LC 91-61373. 1991. 29.95 (0-916990-26-5) META Pubns.

Tools for Evaluating Health Technologies. 1996. lib. bdg. 250.99 (0-8490-6892-4) Gordon Pr.

***Tools for Evaluating Health Technologies.** 1997. lib. bdg. 250.95 (0-8490-6232-2) Gordon Pr.

Tools for Evaluating Health Technologies: Five Background Papers. (Illus.). 149p. (Orig.). (C). 1995. pap. text ed. 40.00 (0-7881-1832-3) DIANE Pub.

Tools for Exploring Math. Nina Kowalczyk. (Mathematics Ser.). 1991. pap. 16.95 (0-534-15530-8) Brooks-Cole.

Tools for Facilitating Team Meetings: Easy Tools That Help Plan, Organize, Conduct, & Evaluate Team Meetings. Johnna L. Howell. LC 94-96899. (Illus.). 300p. 1995. pap. 29.95 (1-886671-00-1) Integrty Pub.

Tools for Healing: Working Toward Harmony & Balance. Kathy Mengle. LC 84-72359. (Illus.). 172p. (Orig.). 1985. pap. 10.95 (0-87516-548-6) DeVorss.

Tools for Learning. M. D. Gall et al. LC 90-36146. 209p. 1990. pap. 16.95 (0-87120-170-4, 611-90086) Assn Supervision.

Tools for Literacy & Communication. Tammy Simmons & Cindy Young. (Illus.). 172p. (J). 1994. spiral bd. 24.00 (1-884135-10-2) Mayer-Johnson.

Tools for Making Acute Risk Decisions with Chemical Process Safety Applications. Center for Chemical Process Safety Staff. LC 94-2462. 1994. 140.00 (0-8169-0552-5, G-21) Am Inst Chem Eng.

Tools for Mining. Michael Priester. 537p. 1993. pap. 70.00 (3-528-02077-6) Informatica.

Tools for Missionaries: Harvesting the Lord's Way. Grant Von Harrison. (Missionary Success Ser.: No. 1). 252p. (Orig.). 1991. pap. write for info. (0-910558-09-4) Ensign Pub.

Tools for Organic Farming: A Manual of Appropriate Equipment & Treatments. George McRobie. 80p. (Orig.). 1990. pap. 11.50 (0-942850-19-X) Bootstrap Pr.

Tools for Parents of Children with Developmental Disabilities. Pref. by James J. Messina. (Tools-for-Coping Ser.). 98p. (Orig.). 1987. pap. text ed. 11.00 (0-931975-07-7) Advanced Dev Sys.

Tools for Population Information: Indexing & Abstracting Services. Carann G. Turner. LC 79-11557. 24p. (Orig.). 1979. pap. 5.00 (0-933438-02-8, SP 3) APLIC Intl.

Tools for Preaching & Teaching the Bible. Stewart Custer. 240p. (Orig.). 1979. pap. 10.75 (0-89084-064-4, 013821) Bob Jones Univ Pr.

***Tools for Primary Care Research.** Ed. by Moira Stewart et al. LC 92-2706. (Research Methods for Primary Care Ser.: No. 2). (Illus.). 301p. pap. 85.80 (0-608-05073-3, 2065628) Bks Demand.

Tools for Primary Care Research. Ed. by Moira A. Stewart et al. (Research Methods for Primary Care Ser.: Vol. 2). (Illus.). 272p. (C). 1992. 54.00 (0-8039-4403-9); pap. 24.95 (0-8039-4404-7) Sage.

Tools for Schools: Applications Software for the Classroom. Sandra Turner & Michael Land. 316p. (C). 1988. Incl. disk. pap. text ed., pap. 48.95 incl. disk (0-534-09030-3) Wadsworth Pub.

Tools for Schools: Claris Works Edition. 2nd ed. Michael Land & Sandra Turner. LC 96-36362. (Education Ser.). (C). 1997. pap. text ed. 40.95 (0-534-21492-4) Wadsworth Pub.

Tools for Statistical Inference: Methods for the Exploration of Posteriors & Likelihoods. 2nd ed. Martin A. Tanner. (Series in Statistics). (Illus.). 170p. 1993. write for info. (3-540-94031-6) Spr-Verlag.

Tools for Statistical Inference: Observed Data & Data Augmentation Methods. Martin A. Tanner. Ed. by J. O. Berger et al. (Lecture Notes in Statistics Ser.: Vol. 67). (Illus.). vi, 110p. 1993. pap. 29.00 (0-387-97525-X) Spr-Verlag.

Tools for Statistical Inference: Observed Data & Data Augmentation Methods. 2nd ed. Martin A. Tanner. LC 93-3270. (Series in Statistics). 1994. 43.95 (0-387-94031-6) Spr-Verlag.

Tools for Statistical Inferface: Methods for the Exploration of Posterior Distributions & Likelihood Functions. 3rd ed. Martin A. Tanner. LC 96-10784. (Springer Series in Statistics). (Illus.). 248p. 1996. student ed., text ed. 52.95 (0-387-94688-8) Spr-Verlag.

***Tools for Structured Design.** 4th ed. Bohl & Rynn. 1997. pap. text ed. 60.00 (0-13-626466-2) P-H.

Tools for Structured Design: An Introduction to Programming Logic. Marilyn Bohl & Maria Rynn. (Illus.). 320p. (C). 1992. teacher ed. write for info. (0-318-69282-1) Macmillan.

Tools for Structured Design: An Introduction to Programming Logic. 3rd ed. Marilyn Bohl & Maria Rynn. LC 92-14572. (Illus.). 320p. (C). 1992. pap. text ed. 56.00 (0-02-311861-X, Macmillan Coll) P-H.

Tools for Success in Economics. Gottheil. (HB - Economics Ser.). 1996. student ed., pap. 17.00 (0-538-84045-5) S-W Pub.

Tools for Success in Macroeconomics. Gottheil. (HB - Economics Ser.). 1996. student ed., pap. 14.25 (0-538-84047-1) S-W Pub.

Tools for Success in Microeconomics. Gottheil. (HB - Economics Ser.). 1996. student ed., pap. 14.25 (0-538-84046-3) S-W Pub.

Tools for Tantra. Harish Johari. (Illus.). 146p. 1986. pap. 18.95 (0-89281-055-6) Inner Tradit.

Tools for Teachers. Frank J. Orlando & Lynne Levy. 256p. (C). 1996. pap. text ed., ring bd. 26.25 (0-7872-1230-X) Kendall-Hunt.

Tools for Teaching. Barbara G. Davis. LC 93-19500. (Higher Education-Adult & Continuing Education Ser.). 457p. text ed. 32.95 (1-55542-568-2) Jossey-Bass.

***Tools for Teaching Biotechnology: A Bibliography of Resources.** Janet Glaser. 52p. (C). 1996. reprint ed. pap. 25.00 (0-7881-3082-X) DIANE Pub.

Tools for Team Development. Ronald Dingwall. 44p. (C). 1986. 60.00 (0-86236-002-1, Pub. by Granary UK) St Mut.

Tools for Team Excellence: Getting Your Team into High Gear & Keeping It There. Gregory E. Huszczo. LC 95-44374. 230p. 1996. 25.95 (0-89106-081-2, 7356) Davies-Black.

***Tools for Teams.** Harrison Snow. 204p. (Orig.). 1997. mass mkt. 4.99 (1-55237-201-4, Pub. by Comnwlth Pub CN) Partners Pubs Grp.

Tools for Technical & Professional Communication. Arthur H. Bell. 448p. (Orig.). 1996. pap. 29.95 (0-8442-5815-6, NTC Busn Bks) NTC Pub Grp.

Tools for the Carpenter. Jacqueline Quern. 1994. pap. 8.95 (1-55673-897-8) CSS OH.

Tools for the Cooperative Classroom. Susan A. Marcus & Penny McDonald. (Illus.). 128p. (Orig.). 1990. pap. text ed. 22.95 (0-932935-27-3) IRI-SkyLght.

Tools for the Electrical Trade. Richard Hunter. LC 85-702734. (Orig.). 1985. student ed. 6.00 (0-8064-0327-6, 819); audio, vhs 289.00 (0-8064-0328-4) Bergwall.

Tools for the Field: Methodologies Handbook for Gender Analysis in Agriculture. Ed. by Hilary S. Feldstein & Janice Jiggins. LC 93-33664. (Library of Management for Development). (Illus.). 286p. 1994. pap. 24.95 (1-56549-028-2) Kumarian Pr.

Tools for the Mac. Jerry P. Galloway. 288p. 1995. pap. text ed., spiral bd. 47.19 (0-7872-1861-8) Kendall-Hunt.

Tools for the Soft Path. International Project for Soft Energy Paths Staff & Jim Harding. 1982. 25.00 (0-913890-52-9); pap. 11.95 (0-913890-53-7) Friends of Earth.

Tools for the Trades & Crafts. Kenneth D. Roberts. 1976. 25.00 (0-913602-18-3) K Roberts.

Tools for the Workplace. Concept by L. Ron Hubbard. 40p. 1994. pap. 4.00 (0-88404-922-1) Bridge Pubns Inc.

***Tools for Thinking: Modelling in Management Science.** Michael Pidd. LC 96-32158. 1996. text ed. 45.00 (0-471-96455-7) Wiley.

Tools for Thinking & Problem Solving. Moshe F. Rubinstein. (Illus.). 416p. (C). 1985. text ed. 72.00 (0-13-925140-5) P-H.

Tools for Today's Engineer: Strategy for Achieving Engineering Excellence. 100p. 1992. pap. 19.00 (1-56091-230-8, SP-913) Soc Auto Engineers.

***Tools for Tosafos.** Haim Perlmutter. 147p. 1996. 13.95 (1-56871-093-3) Targum Pr.

Tools for Transformation. Rita Milios. LC 94-60530. 128p. 1995. pap. 9.95 (0-9641657-1-6) Tools for Transform.

Tools for Transformation: A Personal Study. Adam Curle. (Conflict & Peacemaking Ser.). 204p. (Orig.). pap. text ed. 21.95 (1-869890-21-3, Pub. by Hawthorn Press UK) Anthroposophic.

Tools for Transition: Complete Program. Elizabeth Aune & Jean Ness. 1991. 129.95 (0-88671-413-3, 8250) Am Guidance.

Tools for Transition Manual. Elizabeth Aune & Jean Ness. (Tools for Transition Ser.). (Orig.). 1991. pap. 27.95 (0-88671-412-5, 8251) Am Guidance.

Tools for Transition Script Book. Elizabeth Aune & Jean Ness. (Tools for Transition Ser.). (Orig.). 1991. pap. 9.95 (0-88671-415-X, 8254) Am Guidance.

Tools for Transition Student Book. Elizabeth Aune & Jean Ness. (Tools for Transition Ser.). (Orig.). 1991. pap. 8.95 (0-88671-414-1, 8252) Am Guidance.

***Tools for Unix System Administrators.** Evi Nemeth. 1997. pap. text ed. 38.67 (0-13-665431-2) P-H.

Tools for Valuing Diversity: A Practical Guide to Techniques to Capitalize in Team Diversity. Selma G. Myers & Anthony W. Harris. (Workplace Diversity Ser.). (Illus.). 120p. 1995. pap. 12.95 (1-883553-70-9) R Chang Assocs.

***Tools for Virtual Teams: A Team Fitness Companion.** Jane Henry & Meg Hartzler. LC 97-14340. 100p. 1997. 20.00 (0-87389-381-6, H0970) ASQC Qual Pr.

Tools for Writing. Linda R. Fellag & Laura T. Le Drean. LC 94-28720. 192p. 1995. pap. 22.95 (0-8384-5294-9) Heinle & Heinle.

Tools for Writing: Creating Writer's Workshops for Grades 2-8. Barbara Z. Boone. LC 96-16600. (1-Off Ser.). 144p. 1996. 42.95 (0-8039-6456-0); pap. 18.95 (0-8039-6457-9) Corwin Pr.

Tools in the Learning Trade. Barbara C. Bell. LC 83-15105. 192p. 1984. pap. 12.50 (0-8108-1743-8) Scarecrow.

Tools in the Learning Trade: A Guide to Eight Indispensable Tools for College Students. Barbara C. Bell. LC 83-15105. 192p. 1984. text ed. 20.00 (0-8108-1655-5) Scarecrow.

Tools, Language & Cognition in Human Evolution. Ed. by Kathleen R. Gibson & Tim Ingold. (Illus.). 520p. (C). 1993. text ed. 85.00 (0-521-41474-1) Cambridge U Pr.

Tools, Language & Cognition in Human Evolution. Ed. by Kathleen R. Gibson & Tim Ingold. (Illus.). 495p. (C). 1995. pap. text ed. 30.95 (0-521-48541-X) Cambridge U Pr.

Tools of Biochemistry. Terrance C. Cooper. 448p. 1977. text ed. 79.95 (0-471-17116-6) Wiley.

Tools of Continuous Improvement. Robin E. McDermott et al. (Illus.). 40p. (C). 1993. teacher ed. 150.00 (1-882307-01-1); student ed. 20.00 (1-882307-13-5) Res Engineering.

Tools of Critical Thinking. Levy. LC 96-27649. 1996. pap. text ed. 24.00 (0-205-26083-7) Allyn.

Tools of Dominion: The Case Laws of Exodus. Gary North. LC 90-4054. 1296p. 1989. 29.95 (0-930464-10-9) Inst Christian.

Tools of Empire: Technology & European Imperialism in the Nineteenth Century. Daniel R. Headrick. 232p. (C). 1981. pap. text ed. 17.95 (0-19-502832-5) OUP.

Tools of Government. fac. ed. Christopher C. Hood. (Public Policy & Politics Ser.). (Illus.). 190p. (Orig.). 1986. pap. 54.20 (0-7837-7684-5, 2047437) Bks Demand.

Tools of My Trade: Annotated Books in Jack London's Library. David M. Hamilton. LC 84-40323. (Illus.). 350p. 1986. 25.00 (0-295-96157-0) U of Wash Pr.

Tools of Radio Astronomy. K. Rohlfs. (Astronomy & Astrophysics Library). (Illus.). xii, 319p. 1986. 79.00 (0-387-16188-0) Spr-Verlag.

Tools of Radio Astronomy. 2nd enl. rev. ed. K. Rohlfs & T. L. Wilson. LC 96-5678. (Astronomy & Astrophysics Library). (Illus.). 438p. 1996. 69.50 (3-540-60981-4) Spr-Verlag.

Tools of Radio Astronomy: Study Edition. 2nd ed. K. Rohlfs. Ed. by Martin D. Harwit et al. (Astronomy & Astrophysics Library). (Illus.). xv, 319p. 1990. reprint ed. pap. 45.00 (0-387-52744-3) Spr-Verlag.

Tools of Science: Ideas & Activities for Guiding Young Scientists. Jean Stangl. 1998. pap. 8.95 (0-07-156898-0) McGraw.

Tools of Science: Ideas & Activities for Guiding Young Scientists. rev. ed. Jean Stangl. (Illus.). 160p. (J). 1989. 16.95 (0-8306-9216-9); pap. 8.95 (0-8306-3216-6) McGraw-Hill Prof.

Tools of Screenwriting. David Howard & Edward Mabley. 272p. 1993. 22.95 (0-312-09405-1) St Martin.

Tools of Screenwriting: A Writer's Guide to the Craft & the Elements of a Screenplay. David Howard. 1995. pap. 13.95 (0-312-11908-9) St Martin.

Tools of the Bear: How Any Investor Can Make Money When Stocks Go Down. Charles J. Caes. 225p. 1992. text ed. 24.95 (1-55738-419-3) Irwin Prof Pubng.

Tools of the Bull: How to Make Money in Bull Markets. Charles J. Caes. 1994. text ed. 24.95 (1-55738-563-7) Irwin Prof Pubng.

Tools of the Cowboy Trade: Today's Crafters of Saddles, Bits, Spurs & Trappings. Casey Beard. LC 95-42171. (Illus.). 96p. (Orig.). 1997. pap. 19.95 (0-87905-732-7) Gibbs Smith Pub.

Tools of the Mind: The Vygotskian Approach to Early Childhood. Deborah J. Leong & Elena Bodrova. 1995. pap. text ed. 25.00 (0-02-369874-8, Macmillan Coll) P-H.

Tools of the Profession. 2nd ed. SLA Divisions Staff. 129p. (Orig.). 1991. pap. 14.00 (0-87111-378-3) SLA.

Tools of the Profession. Special Libraries Association Staff. LC 88-166908. 135p. reprint ed. pap. 38.50 (0-7837-1303-7, 2041444) Bks Demand.

Tools of the Trade. K. T. Butler. (Orig.). 1996. mass mkt. 5.95 (1-56333-420-8, Rosebud) Masquerade.

Tools of the Trade. Nathan Levy & Amy M. Burke. (J). (gr. 4-12). 1992. pap. 7.95 (1-878347-18-7) NL Assocs.

Tools of the Trade. Gordon Stokes & Daniel Whiteside. (Illus.). 101p. (Orig.). pap. 16.50 (0-918993-25-3) Thoth NV.

Tools of the Trade, Vol. 2. Amy M. Burke. 40p. 1993. pap. 7.95 (1-878347-33-0) NL Assocs.

***Tools of the Trade: Firefighting Hand Tools & Their Use.** Richard A. Fritz. LC 97-3661. 1997. write for info. (0-912212-62-4) Fire Eng.

***Tools of the Trade: Practical Legal Writing.** Jeffrey M. Ellinport. 1997. 49.95 (1-57292-077-7) Austin & Winfield.

***Tools of the Trade: Practical Legal Writing for the 21st Century.** Jeffrey M. Ellinport. 1997. pap. 29.95 (1-57292-076-9) Austin & Winfield.

Tools of the Trade: The Art & Craft of Carpentry. Jeff Taylor. LC 95-47428. (Illus.). 176p. 1996. 25.00 (0-8118-1273-1) Chronicle Bks.

Tools of Thought. Peter H. Barnett. 287p. 1981. 18.95 (0-87073-392-3) Schenkman Bks Inc.

Tools of Total Quality: An Introduction to Statistical Process Control. P. Lyonnet. (Illus.). 184p. 1991. 42.95 (0-412-37690-3) Chapman & Hall.

Tools of War: Instruments, Ideas, & Institutions of Warfare, 1445-1871. fac. ed. Ed. by John A. Lynn. LC 89-4887. 276p. 1990. reprint ed. pap. 78.70 (0-7837-8077-X, 2047830) Bks Demand.

Tools of War: Technology in Vietnam, 1965-1973. Ed. by Boston Publishing Company Editors & E. Doleman. (Illus.). 192p. 1985. 16.30 (0-201-11269-8) Addison-Wesley.

Tools Quattra Windows. Capron. (C). 1993. write for info. (0-201-44337-6) Addison-Wesley.

Tools, Targets, & Troopers: The History of the Frankford Arsenal. James Zupan. 28.95 (0-8488-0036-2, J M C & Co) Amereon Ltd.

Tools to Help Small Business Improve Their Operations. 1992. lib. bdg. 88.00 (0-8490-5372-2) Gordon Pr.

Tools, Treasures, & Measures: For Middle Grade Success. Imogene Forte & Sandra Schurr. Ed. by Jan Keeling & Leslie Britt. (Illus.). 304p. (Orig.). 1994. pap. text ed. 21.95 (0-86530-274-X) Incentive Pubns.

Tools U.S.A. 95. Bertrand Meyer. 500p. (C). 1995. pap. text ed. 65.00 (0-13-461484-4) P-H.

Tools with Artificial Intelligence, 6th International Conference. LC 10-636730. 872p. 1994. pap. 180.00 (0-8186-6785-0) IEEE Comp Soc.

Tools with Artificial Intelligence, 7th International Conference. LC 10-823409. 502p. 1995. pap. 100.00 (0-8186-7312-5, Q334) IEEE Comp Soc.

Tools 11: Technology of Object-Oriented Languages & Systems. Bertrand Meyer et al. 1993. pap. text ed. 60.00 (0-13-103979-2) P-H.

Tools 4: Technology of Object-Oriented Languages & Systems. Bertrand Meyer & Jean Beziven. 415p. 1991. pap. text ed. 92.00 (0-13-923160-9, 270609) P-H.

ToolTalk Messaging Overview. Common Desktop Environment Documentation Group Staff. LC 95-11115. (Common Desktop Environment 1.0 Ser.). 288p. 1995. pap. 23.95 (0-201-48956-2) Addison-Wesley.

Toon. deluxe ed. Illus. & Contrib. by Jackson, Steve, Games Staff. 208p. 1991. pap. 19.95 (1-55634-197-0) S Jackson Games.

Toon Ace Catalog. Jackson, Steve, Games Staff. (Illus.). 1994. pap. 19.95 (1-55634-278-0) S Jackson Games.

Toon Studio: The Easy to Learn, Fun to Use Animation Software for Children. Chuck Boyle. 1996. pap. text ed. 19.95 incl. cd-rom (1-57712-037-X) Motion Works.

Toon Tales. Jackson, Steve, Games Staff. (Illus.). 1993. pap. 19.95 (1-55634-268-3) S Jackson Games.

***Toon Town Halloween.** Golden Books Staff. 1997. pap. text ed. 1.09 (0-307-08748-4, Golden Books) Western Pub.

Tooniversal Tour Guide. Jackson, Steve, Games Staff. (Illus.). 1992. pap. 19.95 (1-55634-216-0) S Jackson Games.

Toons for Our Times: A Bloom County Book. Berkeley Breathed. (Orig.). 1984. pap. 10.95 (0-316-10709-3) Little.

Toonstruck Official Hints & Solutions. BradyGAMES Staff et al. (Illus.). 192p. (Orig.). 1996. 19.99 (1-56686-405-4) Mac Comp Pub.

***Toot & Puddle.** Holly Hobbie. (J). 1997. write for info. (0-614-29255-7) Little.

***Toot & Puddle: A Present for Toot.** Holly Hobbie. LC 97-15746. (J). 1998. write for info. (0-316-36556-4) Little.

Toot-in-Time Band: Introducing Children to the World of Music. Carmela Mercuri. (Illus.). (Orig.). (J). (gr. 1-6). 1993. pap. 10.95 (0-935474-21-8) Carousel Pubns Ltd.

Toot Suite for Trumpet & Jazz Piano. C. Bolling. 1990. 6.00 (0-685-32183-5, SIL55) Hansen Ed Mus.

Toot Suite for Trumpet & Jazz Piano. C. Bolling. 1991. pap. text ed. 40.00 (0-7935-0840-1, 00673217) H Leonard.

Toot the Train. (J). 1994. 3.99 (0-517-10279-X) Random Hse Value.

Toot Toot. Sian Tucker. (J). 1994. 4.50 (0-671-89117-0, Litl Simon S&S) S&S Childrens.

***Toot, Toot.** Brian Wildsmith. (Cat on the Mat Book). (Illus.). 16p. 1997. pap. 3.95 (0-19-849001-1) OUP.

Toot! Toot! The Fall of Jericho. Mary M. Simon. (Hear Me Read Ser.). (Illus.). 24p. (J). (ps-1). 1990. pap. 2.49 (0-570-04184-8, 56-1643) Concordia.

Tootenham Hotspur Greats. Harry Harris. 180p. (C). 1989. pap. text ed. 21.00 (0-85976-309-9, Pub. by J Donald UK) St Mut.

Tooter Pepperday. LC 94-25689. 1995. lib. bdg. 11.99 (0-679-94702-7) Random.

Tooter Pepperday. Jerry Spinelli. LC 94-25689. (J). 1995. pap. 3.99 (0-679-84702-2) Random.

***Tooter Pepperday: Blue Ribbon Blues, No. 2.** Jerry Spinelli. (Stepping Stone Bks.). (J). 1998. 3.99 (0-679-88753-9) Random Bks Yng Read.

***Tooth: A Tale of Love & Death in Paradox.** Nova K. Kruger. LC 95-90578. (Illus.). 136p. (Orig.). 1996. pap. 8.00 (1-56002-584-0, Univ Edtns) Aegina Pr.

Tooth & Claw. 1991. pap. 5.25 (0-19-422676-X) OUP.

Tooth & Claw. Frank Frazetta. (Death Dealer Ser.: No. 3). 1989. pap. 3.95 (0-8125-0330-9) Tor Bks.

Tooth & Claw. Don Pendleton. (Super Bolan Ser.: No. 49). 1996. mass mkt. 5.50 (0-373-61449-7, 1-61449-4, Wrldwide Lib) Harlequin Bks.

Tooth & Nail. Ian Rankin. 1996. pap. 5.99 (0-312-95878-1) St Martin.

Tooth & Nail: A Novel Approach to the new SAT. Charles H. Elster. 360p. 1994. pap. 11.00 (0-15-601382-7, Harvest Bks) HarBrace.

***Tooth Bearings in Bevel Gears.** A. H. Candee. (Technical Papers). 1940. pap. text ed. 30.00 (1-55589-418-6) AGMA.

Tooth Book. Theodore Le Sieg. LC 80-28320. (Bright & Early Bks.: No. 25). (Illus.). 48p. (J). (ps-1). 1981. 7.99 (0-394-84825-X, XBYR); lib. bdg. 11.99 (0-394-94825-4) Random Bks Yng Read.

Tooth Book. Alan E. Nourse. (J). (gr. 6-p). 1977. 6.95 (0-679-20376-1) McKay.

***Tooth by Tooth Induction Hardening Vehicle Gearing.** W. F. Hall. (Technical Papers). 1973. pap. text ed. 30.00 (1-55589-325-2) AGMA.

Tooth Chicken. 8.40 (0-934510-24-5, W013) Am Dental.

Tooth Development & Caries, 2 vols. F. C. Driessens & J. H. Woltgens. 1986. Set. 239.95 (0-8493-6500-7, RK331) CRC Pr.

Tooth Development & Caries, Vol. 1. F. Driessens & J. H. Woltgens. LC 85-27002. 108p. 1986. 99.00 (0-8493-6503-1, CRC Reprint) Franklin.

Tooth Development & Caries, Vol. 2. F. Driessens & J. H. Woltgens. LC 85-27002. 208p. 1986. 122.00 (0-8493-6504-X, CRC Reprint) Franklin.

Tooth Development & Caries, Vols. I & II. F. C. Driessens & J. H. Woltgens. 1986. Vol. I, 192 pgs. write for info. (0-318-61547-9); Vol. 2, 224 pgs. write for info. (0-318-61548-7) CRC Pr.

***Tooth Enamel Microstructure.** Ed. by W. Von Koenigswald & P. M. Sander. (Illus.). 288p. (C). 1997. text ed. 95.00 (90-5410-667-0, Pub. by A A Balkema NE) Ashgate Pub Co.

***Tooth Faerie.** Joyce. Date not set. 22.95 (0-312-86261-X) St Martin.

Tooth Fairy. Julie Brinckloe. LC 88-22038. 1999. write for info. (0-688-07936-9, Morrow Junior); lib. bdg. write for info. (0-688-07937-7, Morrow Junior) Morrow.

Tooth Fairy. Peter Collington. (Illus.). 32p. (J). 1995. 17.00 (0-679-87168-3); lib. bdg. 18.99 (0-679-97168-8) Knopf.

Tooth Fairy. Kirsten Hall. (My First Reader Ser.). (Illus.). 28p. (J). (ps-2). 1994. lib. bdg. 15.50 (0-516-05368-X) Childrens.

Tooth Fairy. Kirsten Hall. (My First Reader Ser.). (J). (ps-2). 1994. pap. 3.95 (0-516-45368-8) Childrens.

Tooth Fairy. Ewa Lipniacka. LC 92-33328. (Jamie & Luke Ser.). (Illus.). (J). 1993. 6.95 (1-56656-120-5, Crocodile Bks) Interlink Pub.

Tooth Fairy. James Magorian. LC 93-73338. (Illus.). 22p. (Orig.). (J). (gr. 1-3). 1993. pap. 3.00 (0-930674-38-3) Black Oak.

Tooth Fairy. Sharon Peters. LC 81-5100. (Illus.). 32p. (J). (gr. k-2). 1997. pap. 3.95 (0-89375-520-6) Troll Communs.

Tooth Fairy. Audrey Wood. LC 90-46911. (J). 1989. 7.99 (0-85953-237-2); pap. 3.99 (0-85953-238-0) Childs Play.

***Tooth Fairy.** Audrey Wood. (FRE.). (J). 1989. pap. 3.99 (0-85953-463-4); pap. 3.99 (0-85953-818-4); pap. 3.99 (0-85953-574-6) Childs Play.

***Tooth Fairy.** Audrey Wood. (J). 1996. lib. bdg. 11.95 (0-85953-833-8) Childs Play.

Tooth Fairy. Anita Feagles. (Illus.). 32p. (J). (gr. k-2). reprint ed. lib. bdg. write for info. (0-208-02323-2, Linnet Bks) Shoe String.

Tooth Fairy Book. Deborah Kovacs. LC 92-53679. (Illus.). 32p. (J). 1992. 9.95 (1-56138-147-0) Running Pr.

Tooth Fairy Legend. Frank McAllister & Fran McAllister. LC 76-9595. (J). (gr. k-4). 1976. 9.95 (0-916864-01-4) Block.

Tooth Fairy Legend. Frank McAllister. LC 90-28136. (Illus.). 40p. (J). (gr. k-6). 1992. 12.95 (0-915677-54-7) Roundtable Pub.

Tooth Fairy Legend: How the Custom Came to Be. Dr. Mac. (Illus.). 40p. (J). (gr. k-5). 1994. 12.95 (0-9638033-8-7) Storybk Pub.

Tooth Fairy Magic. Joanne Barkan. (Sparkle & Glow Bks.). (Illus.). 24p. (J). (ps-3). 1995. 3.95 (0-590-48933-X, Cartwheel) Scholastic Inc.

Tooth Fairy Tale. Stephen S. Berger & Jeanette K. Berger. (Illus.). 30p. (Orig.). (J). (ps-3). 1996. pap. 12.95 (0-9651089-9-6) Dragon Breath.

Tooth Fairy's Tale. David Christiana. (J). (ps-3). 1994. 16.00 (0-374-37677-8) FS&G.

Tooth Fairy's Tale. David Christiana. 32p. (J). (gr. k-3). 1996. pap. 6.95 (0-374-47942-9, Sunburst Bks) FS&G.

Tooth Fairy's Wish. P. Z. Mann. (J). (ps-3). 1996. pap. text ed. 4.95 (0-307-13040-1, Golden Pr) Western Pub.

Tooth Fitness: Your Guide to Healthy Teeth. Thomas McGuire. Ed. by Alice Klein. LC 93-86744. (Illus.). 336p. (J). (ps up). 1993. 24.95 (0-9638321-3-1) Saint Michaels.

Tooth for a Tooth: Selected Poems of Juan Larrea (1925-1932) Tr. & Intro. by David Bary. LC 86-28093. 142p. 1987. lib. bdg. 34.50 (0-8191-5753-8) U Pr of Amer.

Tooth-Gnasher Superflash. Daniel M. Pinkwater. LC 89-18207. (Illus.). 32p. (J). (gr. k-3). 1990. pap. 3.95 (0-689-71407-6, Aladdin Paperbacks) S&S Childrens.

Tooth-Gnasher Superflash. 2nd ed. Daniel M. Pinkwater. LC 89-18207. (Illus.). 32p. (J). (gr. k-3). 1990. reprint ed. lib. bdg. 15.00 (0-02-774655-0, Mac Bks Young Read) S&S Childrens.

Tooth Imprints on a Corn Dog. Mark Leyner. 1995. 19.00 (0-517-59384-X, Crown) Crown Pub Group.

Tooth Imprints on a Corn Dog. Mark Leyner. 1996. 3.99 (0-517-16900-2) Random Hse Value.

Tooth Imprints on a Corn Dog. Leyner Mark. 240p. 1996. pap. 11.00 (0-679-74521-1) Random.

Tooth Imprints on a Corndog. Mark Leyner. 1996. pap. write for info. (0-614-12877-3, Vin) Random.

***Tooth Mutilations & Dentistry in Pre-Columbian Mexico.** Samuel Fastlicht. (Illus.). 164p. 1976. text ed. 82.00 (3-87652-611-6) Quint Pub Co.

***Tooth Proportions for Fine-Pitch Involute Spur & Helical Gears.** 7th rev. ed. AGMA Technical Committee. (ANSI/AGMA Standard Ser.: ANSI/AGMA 1003-G93). Date not set. pap. text ed. 60.00 (1-55589-015-6) AGMA.

***Tooth Proportions for Plastic Gears.** AGMA Technical Committee. (ANSI/AGMA Standard Ser.: Vol. 1006-A97). Date not set. pap. text ed. write for info. (1-55589-684-7) AGMA.

***Tooth Proportions for Plastic Gears.** AGMA Technical Committee. (ANSI/AGMA Standard Ser.: Vol. 1106-A97). Date not set. pap. text ed. write for info. (1-55589-685-5) AGMA.

***Tooth Race: Level 2.** Catherine Peters. (Special Times, Little Readers Ser.). (J). 1997. pap. text ed. 2.50 (0-395-88306-7) HM.

Tooth Survival Book. (Illus.). 1977. 5.00 (0-685-57765-1) Am Dental.

Tooth Thickness Specification & Measurement. 2nd ed. (AGMA Ser.: No. 2002-B88). (Illus.). 80p. 1989. pap. 75.00 (1-55589-503-4) AGMA.

Tooth Truth: Fun Facts & Projects. Jennifer S. Gillis. LC 96-11024. (Illus.). 64p. (Orig.). (J). (gr. 1-5). 1996. pap. 9.95 (0-88266-937-0) Storey Comm Inc.

Toothed Whales. Jason Cooper. LC 96-19190. (Read All About Whales Ser.). (J). 1996. write for info. (0-86593-448-7) Rourke Corp.

Toothed World: Poems by Cori Adler. Cori Adler. Ed. & Intro. by Eliza M. Young. 30p. (Orig.). 1988. pap. 6.95 (0-933865-15-5, 70968) Doris Pubns.

Toothless Albert. Carol Taylor. LC 93-28937. (Voyages Ser.). (Illus.). (J). 1994. 4.25 (0-383-03780-8) SRA McGraw.

Toothpaste & Peanut Butter. Terry Moore. Ed. by Herb Bryce. (Illus.). 140p. (Orig.). 1987. pap. 9.95 (0-88839-207-9) Hancock House.

Toothpaste & Railroad Tracks. Ed. & Intro. by Kenneth Jernigan. (Kernel Bk.: No. 8). (Illus.). 76p. (Orig.). 1995. pap. text ed. 3.00 (1-885218-02-8) Natl Fed Blind.

***Toothpaste Genie.** Sandy F. Duncan. (J). pap. 3.99 (0-590-73628-0) Scholastic Inc.

Toothpaste Millionaire. Jean Merrill. LC 73-22055. (Illus.). 96p. (J). (gr. 2-5). 1974. 15.95 (0-395-18511-4) HM.

Toothpaste Millionaire. Jean Merrill. (J). (gr. 4-7). 1993. pap. 4.95 (0-395-66954-5) HM.

Toothpaste with Chlorophyll & Maritime Hot Baths. Elias Papadimitrakopoulos. Tr. & Intro. by John Taylor. LC 91-76941. (Illus.). 104p. (Orig.). 1992. 17.95 (1-878580-42-6); pap. 8.95 (1-878580-43-4) Asylum Arts.

Toothpick. Kenneth Ethridge. 128p. (YA). (gr. 7 up). 1988. reprint ed. pap. 2.50 (0-8167-1316-2) Troll Communs.

Toothpick Airforce: Real Glider Replicas, Vol. I. Robert B. Elliott. (Illus.). 36p. (Orig.). (J). (gr. 4 up). 1995. pap. 9.95 (0-9650751-1-7) Booger Reds.

Toothpick Building Illustrated. Katrina Davis. (Illus.). 48p. (Orig.). 1980. spiral bd., pap. 4.95 (0-937242-04-7) Scandia Pubs.

Toothpick Holders: China, Glass, & Metal. National Toothpick Holder Collector's Society Staff. (Illus.). 152p. 1993. 44.95 (0-915410-89-3, 4048) Antique Pubns.

Toothpick Holders: Glass, China, & Metal. National Toothpick Holder Collector's Society Staff. (Illus.). 152p. 1993. pap. 29.95 (0-915410-88-5, 4047) Antique Pubns.

Toothpick House. Lee Lynch. LC 83-4093. 272p. (Orig.). 1983. pap. 7.95 (0-930044-45-2) Naiad Pr.

Toothy Tongue & One Long Foot: Nature Activities for Kids. Diane Swanson. (J). (gr. 2 up). 1994. pap. 6.95 (1-55850-379-X) Adams Media.

Tootle. Golden Books Staff. (Little Golden Bks.). (Illus.). 24p. (J). (ps-2). 1995. 1.49 (0-307-02097-5, Golden Pr) Western Pub.

Tootle the Train. (Little Golden Sound Story Bks.). (Illus.). 24p. (J). (ps up). 1992. 6.95 (0-307-74806-5, 64806, Golden Pr) Western Pub.

***Toots & the Upside down House.** Carol Hughes. LC 96-51003. (J). 1997. 17.00 (0-679-88653-2); lib. bdg. 18.99 (0-679-98653-7) Random Bks Yng Read.

***Toots & the Upside down House.** Carol Hughes. (J). 1998. pap. write for info. (0-679-88654-0) Random Bks Yng Read.

Toots in Solitude. John Yount. LC 92-53616. 200p. 1995. pap. 10.95 (0-87074-384-8) SMU Press.

Tootsie Tanner, Why Don't You Talk. Patricia R. Giff. 192p. (J). (gr. k-6). 1990. pap. 2.95 (0-440-40239-5, YB BDD) BDD Bks Young Read.

Top Adult Contemporary: 1961-1993. Joel Whitburn. 368p. 1995. 24.95 (0-7935-5044-0, 00330162) H Leonard.

Top Adult Contemporary: 1961-1993. Joel Whitburn. (Record Research Ser.). 368p. 1993. 39.95 (0-89820-099-7, ACN101H) Record Research.

***Top & Bottom of the World.** Allan Fowler. LC 96-28767. (Rookie Read-About Science Ser.). (J). 1997. lib. bdg. 17.50 (0-516-20321-5) Childrens.

Top & the Ball. Hans Christian Andersen. LC 92-83. (Illus.). 32p. (J). (gr. k-3). 1992. 14.95 (0-8249-8547-8, Ideals Child); lib. bdg. 15.00 (0-8249-8583-4, Ideals Child) Hambleton-Hill.

***Top & the Bottom of the World.** Allan Fowler. (Rookie Read-About Science Ser.). 1997. pap. 4.95 (0-516-26160-6) Childrens.

***Top Banana.** Cari Best. LC 96-42286. (Illus.). 32p. (J). (ps-3). 1997. 15.95 (0-531-30009-9); lib. bdg. 16.99 (0-531-33009-5) Orchard Bks Watts.

***Top Bass Fishing Guides.** Maurice Valerio. Ed. by Allison C. Mickens. (Picked-by-You Guides). (Illus.). 200p. (Orig.). 1997. pap. 19.95 (1-889807-05-2) Valerio Pub.

Top Careers for the Next 30 Years. Margie Sherman. (Illus.). 8p. 1994. pap. 2.50 (1-884241-45-X, SPSO309) Energeia Pub.

***Top Cat.** Ehlert. 1998. write for info. (0-15-201739-9) HarBrace.

Top Chefs in New Orleans. Sarah J. English. (Illus.). 176p. 1992. 16.95 (0-89015-827-4) Sunbelt Media.

Top Chefs in Texas: Recipes from Celebrated "Tocques" with a Touch of Texas. Sarah J. English. 1990. 15.95 (0-89015-756-1) Sunbelt Media.

Top Class Management: Lessons for Effectiveness. Richard Graham & Edwin J. Singer. 208p. (C). 1993. pap. 20.00 (0-614-03378-0, Pub. by IPM Hse UK) St Mut.

Top Class Management: Lessons for Effectiveness. Richard Graham & Edwin J. Singer. 288p. 1993. 60.00 (0-85292-530-1, Pub. by IPM Hse UK) St Mut.

Top Colleges for Science: A Guide to Leading Four-Year Programs in the Biological, Chemical... Petersons. 650p. 1995. pap. text ed. 24.95 (1-56079-390-2) Petersons.

***Top Consultant.** Calvert Markham. (Business & Management Ser.). 1994. pap. 24.95 (0-7494-1439-1) Kogan Page Ltd.

Top Country Hits. Astor. 1995. pap. 14.95 (1-57007-015-6) Astor Bks.

Top Country Hits of 1993 & 1994. 112p. 1994. otabind 9.95 (0-7935-3677-4, 00311685) H Leonard.

***Top Country Hits of 1996.** Ed. by Carol Cuellar. 308p. (Orig.). (YA). 1996. pap. text ed. 18.95 (1-57623-700-1, MF9650) Warner Brothers.

Top Country Hits of 94-95. 128p. 1995. per. 9.95 (0-7935-4734-2, 00310060) H Leonard.

Top Country Singles: 1944-1993. Joel Whitburn. 624p. 1995. pap. 39.95 (0-7935-5013-0, 00330054) H Leonard.

Top Country Singles 1944-1993. Joel Whitburn. (Record Research Ser.). 624p. 1994. 59.95 (0-89820-100-4, TCS401H) Record Research.

Top Courtroom Performance. James S. Bell. LC 88-70834. 80p. (Orig.). 1994. text ed. 85.00 (0-910355-02-9) Courtroom Comp.

Top Decisions: Strategic Decision Making in Organizations. David J. Hickson et al. LC 85-10071. (Management Ser.). 313p. 1986. 45.95 (0-87589-653-7) Jossey-Bass.

T

An Asterisk (*) at the beginning of an entry indicates that the title is appearing in BIP for the first time.

Top Decisions: Strategic Decision-Making in Organizations. David J. Hickson et al. LC 85-10071. (Jossey-Bass Management Ser.). (Illus.). 314p. reprint ed. pap. 89.50 (0-7837-6515-0, 2045627) Bks Demand.

Top Deck Twenty! Best West Coast Sea Stories! Stan Allyn. LC 89-60951. (Illus.). 160p. (Orig.). 1989. pap. 10.00 (0-8323-0469-7) Binford Mort.

Top Dog. Mercer Mayer. (LC & the Critter Kids Mini-Novels Ser.). (Illus.). 72p. (J). 1994. 3.50 (0-307-15981-7, Golden Pr) Western Pub.

Top Dog: A Different Kind of Book about Becoming an Excellent Leader. J. David Pincus. 1994. text ed. 24.95 (0-07-050129-7) McGraw.

Top Dog: A Different Kind of Book about Becoming an Excellent Leader. J. David Pincus & J. Nicholas DeBonis. 350p. 1996. pap. text ed. 14.95 (0-07-050188-2) McGraw.

Top Dog: A Novel. Jerry J. Carroll. 320p. 1996. pap. text ed. 12.00 (0-441-00368-0) Ace Bks.

Top Dollar Paid: The Complete Guide to Selling Your Stamps. Stephen R. Datz. (Illus.). 176p. (Orig.). 1989. pap. 14.95 (0-88219-022-9) General Trade.

*Top-Down Constraint-Driven Design Methodology for Analog Integrated Circuits. Henry Chang. LC 96-41792. 384p. (C). 1996. lib. bdg. 115.00 (0-7923-9794-0) Kluwer Ac.

*Top down Programming Using Turbo Pascal. Clark. (De-Computer Science Ser.). 1997. pap. 27.95 (0-340-66287-5) Van Nos Reinhold.

Top Eighteen Business Guides for the Twentieth Century: Step-by-Step Guides to Business Success. Jerre G. Lewis & Leslie D. Renn. 300p. (Orig.). 1994. pap. 269.10 (0-9628759-2-9) Lewis Renn.

Top End. Steven L. Thompson. 384p. (Orig.). 1989. mass mkt. 4.50 (0-373-97091-9) Harlequin Bks.

Top Entrepreneurs & Their Businesses. Robert B. Pile. LC 92-38267. (Profiles Ser.). (Illus.). 160p. (YA). (gr. 5-12). 1993. lib. bdg. 16.95 (1-881508-04-8) Oliver Pr MN.

*Top Executive Compensation: United States, United Kingdom, & Canada. Marc-Andreas Klein. (Report: No. 1155-96-RR). (Illus.). 76p. (Orig.). 1996. pap. text ed. 160.00 (0-8237-0604-4) Conference Bd.

Top Executive Compensation: 1993 Edition. Elizabeth R. Arreglado. (Report: No. 1053). (Illus.). 74p. 1993. pap. text ed. 120.00 (0-8237-0475-0) Conference Bd.

Top Executive Compensation: 1994 Edition. Charles A. Peck. (Report: No. 1099-94-RR). (Illus.). 80p. (Orig.). 1994. pap. text ed. 120.00 (0-8237-0546-3) Conference Bd.

Top Executive Compensation: 1995 Edition. Marc-Andreas Klein. (Report: No. 1138-95-RR). (Illus.). 95p. (Orig.). 1995. pap. text ed. 120.00 (0-8237-0586-2) Conference Bd.

*Top Executive Compensation in 1995. Jonathan Drum et al. (Report Ser.: No. 1170-96-RR). (Illus.). 94p. (Orig.). 1996. pap. text ed. 120.00 (0-8237-0619-2) Conference Bd.

Top Executive Pay Package. Leonard R. Burgess. LC 63-8414. 1963. 19.95 (0-02-904990-3, Free Press) Free Pr.

Top Farmer Guide to Using Options for Profitable Marketing of Farm Commodities. Top Farmers of America Staff. 76p. 1986. pap. 24.95 (0-910939-11-X) AgriData.

Top Fiddle Solos. Craig Duncan. 1993. 9.95 (0-87166-520-4, 94095) Mel Bay.

*Top Fiddle Solos. Craig Duncan. 1993. 24.95 incl. audio compact disk (0-7866-1740-3, 94095CDP) Mel Bay.

Top Firm Strategies for Profitability. 96th ed. Harcourt. 1996. pap. text ed. 49.00 (0-15-606433-2) HarBrace.

Top Five Percent: How to Save & Invest While Minimizing Taxes. Gordon G. Ryan. 140p. (Orig.). 1988. pap. 12.95 (0-9621442-0-7) Mntnview Pub WA.

Top-Floor Killer. Walter A. Roberts. LC 73-18604. reprint ed. 42.50 (0-404-11414-8) AMS Pr.

*Top Fly Fishing Guides. Maurice Valerio. Ed. by Allison C. Mickens. (Picked-by-You Guides). (Illus.). 200p. (Orig.). 1997. pap. 19.95 (1-889807-01-X) Valerio Pub.

Top Forty Music on Compact Disc, 1955-1981. Pat Downey. xii, 658p. 1994. lib. bdg. 49.50 (1-56308-307-8) Libs Unl.

Top Forty Real Alto Saxophone Solos. 1990. 8.95 (0-685-32219-X, HH060) Hansen Ed Mus.

Top Forty Real Clarinet Solos. Edomondson. 1990. 8.95 (0-685-32205-X, HH019) Hansen Ed Mus.

Top Forty Real Flute Solos. Edmondson. 1990. 8.95 (0-685-32131-2, HH053) Hansen Ed Mus.

Top Forty Real Trumpet Solos. 1990. 8.95 (0-685-32188-6, H018) Hansen Ed Mus.

Top Forty Things Considerate Golfers Do. Ryan Lancaster. Ed. by Mary Westheimer. (Illus.). 44p. (Orig.). 1994. pap. 10.00 (1-885001-04-5) Via Press.

*Top Freshwater Fishing Guides. Maurice Valerio. Ed. by Allison C. Mickens. (Picked-by-You Books). (Illus.). 200p. (Orig.). 1997. pap. 19.95 (1-889807-10-9) Valerio Pub.

Top Fuel Drag Racing. Martin Hintz & Kate Hintz. LC 96-22345. (Drag Racing Ser.). 1996. write for info. (1-56065-389-2) Capstone Pr.

*Top Fuel Drag Racing. Martin Hintz & Kate Hintz. (Drag Racing Ser.). (Illus.). 48p. (J). (gr. 3-7). 1996. 18.40 (0-516-20241-3) Childrens.

Top Fuel Dragster: The Anatomy & Development. Tony Sakkis. 1993. pap. 21.95 (0-87938-770-X) Motorbooks Intl.

Top Girls. rev. ed. Caryl Churchill. 87p. (C). 1988. pap. 9.95 (0-413-55480-5, A0298, Pub. by Methuen UK) Heinemann.

Top Golf: Peak Performance Through Brain - Body Integration. Clyde Porter. (Illus.). 150p. (Orig.). 1993. pap. 14.95 (0-9637669-4-5) Life Enhance.

Top Gun. Christopher Chant. 1992. 19.98 (1-55521-814-8) Bk Sales Inc.

Top Gun Dreams. Ruth Snyder. (Illus.). 21p. (J). (gr. 3-6). 1992. pap. 3.95 (0-939566-07-9) Pensacola Hist.

Top Gun Official Strategy Guide. Scott Wolf. (Illus.). 300p. (Orig.). 1996. 19.99 (1-56686-314-7) Brady Pub.

Top Guns. Joe Foss & Matthew Brennan. Ed. by Paul McCarthy. 480p. 1992. mass mkt. 5.99 (0-671-68318-7) PB.

*Top Guns. Hugh McManners. 1996. 29.95 (0-563-38707-6) BBC Pubns.

Top Guns: A Common Cause Guide to Defense Contractor Lobbying. Philip Simon et al. 112p. (Orig.). 1987. pap. 4.00 (0-914389-38-6) Common Cause.

*Top Hat, the Grey Wolf, & the Crescent: Turkish Nationalism & the Turkish Republic. Hugh Poulton. LC 96-41941. 1997. 35.00 (0-8147-6648-X) NYU Pr.

Top Heavy: A Study of the Increasing Inequality of Wealth in America. Edward N. Wolff. LC 94-23555. (Twentieth Century Fund Papers). 93p. (C). 1995. pap. 9.95 (0-87078-360-2) TCFP-PPP.

Top Heavy: The Increasing Inequality of Wealth in America & What Can Be Done about It. Edward N. Wolff. 1996. pap. text ed. 7.95 (1-56584-347-9) New Press NY.

Top Hits Featuring Lost in Your Eyes & Vision of Love: Easy Piano Solos. 48p. 1991. pap. 8.95 (0-7935-0786-3, 00290346) H Leonard.

Top Hits for Alto Saxophone. 48p. 1989. pap. 5.95 (0-7935-3407-0, 00660005) H Leonard.

Top Hits for Clarinet. 48p. 1989. pap. 5.95 (0-7935-4839-X, 00660003) H Leonard.

Top Hits in Big Notes, Issue No. 2. Ed. by Tony Esposito & Richard Bradley. 64p. (YA). 1995. pap. text ed. 7.95 (0-89724-718-3, BP3306C) Warner Brothers.

Top Hits of 1992. 192p. 1992. otabind 14.95 (0-7935-1799-0, 00311595) H Leonard.

Top Hits of 1994. 112p. 1994. per. 10.95 (0-7935-3760-6, 00311697) H Leonard.

*Top Italian Wines 1997. Daniele Cernilli. (Illus.). 64p. (Orig.). 1996. pap. 5.99 (1-890142-00-X) Gambero Pr.

Top Lawyers & Their Famous Cases. Phyllis R. Emert. LC 95-42908. (Profiles Ser.). (Illus.). 160p. (YA). (gr. 5-12). 1996. lib. bdg. 16.95 (1-881508-31-5) Oliver Pr MN.

Top Management & Quality. Hans D. Seghezzi. 170p. (C). 1992. text ed. 39.95 (1-56990-094-9) Hanser-Gardner.

Top Management Control in Europe. Jacques H. Horovitz. 210p. 1980. text ed. 18.95 (0-312-80908-5) St Martin.

Top Management Strategy. Benjamin B. Tregoe & John W. Zimmerman. 128p. 1983. pap. 10.00 (0-671-25402-2, Touchstone Bks) S&S Trade.

Top Notch Teacher, No. 1. 1991. pap. 12.95 (0-590-49098-2) Scholastic Inc.

Top Notch Teacher, No. 2. 1991. pap. 12.95 (0-590-49122-9) Scholastic Inc.

*Top Ocean Fishing Guides & Captains. Maurice Valerio. Ed. by Allison C. Mickens. (Picked-by-You Guides). (Illus.). 200p. (Orig.). 1997. pap. 19.95 (1-889807-04-4) Valerio Pub.

Top of the Charts, Vol. 1: Five of the Best - Play-It-Like-It-Is-Guitar. pap. 9.95 (0-89524-567-1) Cherry Lane.

Top of the Charts 5 of the Best for Guitar Vol. 1: With Tablature. 1990. 9.95 (0-89524-568-X, 02506213) Cherry Lane.

Top of the Class: Guiding Children along the Smart Path to Happiness. Arline L. Bronzaft. (Creative Research Monographs). (Illus.). 206p. 1996. pap. 39.50 (1-56750-185-0); text ed. 73.25 (1-56750-184-2) Ablex Pub.

Top of the Hill. Morris Taylor. 64p. (J). (gr. 4 up). 1988. pap. 5.95 (0-87961-183-9) Naturegraph.

Top of the House. Burgundy Group, Inc. Staff. 112p. 1995. pap. text ed., spiral bd. 39.95 (0-7872-0815-9) Kendall-Hunt.

*Top of the Line Fishing Collectibles. Donna Tonelli. LC 96-49087. (Illus.). 176p. 1997. 39.95 (0-7643-0209-4) Schiffer.

*Top of the World. Hans Ruesch. Date not set. mass mkt. 4.50 (0-671-73928-X) PB.

Top Office Supply Companies. Al Toth. 256p. 1993. 29.95 (1-881624-11-0) PBM Pub.

Top One Hundred: The Best Baseball Cards to Own, Ranked & Rated for the Collector & Investor. Paul Green & Kit Kiefer. LC 89-82208. (Illus.). 303p. (Orig.). 1990. pap. 8.95 (0-933893-88-4) Bonus Books.

Top One-Hundred Cajun Recipes of All Time. Ed. & Pref. by Trent Angers. 48p. (Orig.). 1995. pap. 6.95 (0-925417-20-3) Acadian Hse Pub.

Top One Hundred Chinese Dishes. Kenneth H. Lo. LC 92-12158. 128p. 1992. pap. 15.95 (0-89815-497-9) Ten Speed Pr.

Top 100 Coffee Recipes. Mary Ward. (Illus.). 192p. 1995. 9.99 (0-517-14713-0) Random Hse Value.

Top One Hundred Credit Card Crimes & How to Stop Them. 8th ed. Larry Schwartz & Pearl Sax. 96p. 1997. 49.95 (0-914801-02-3) Nat Assn Credit.

Top One Hundred DP Almanac, 1984. Gartner Group, Inc. Staff. Ed. by William S. Cappelli & Thomas A. Ryan. (Illus.). 497p. 1984. 295.00 (0-317-15127-4); 85.00 (0-317-15128-2) Gartner Group.

Top One Hundred Guide. MZ Media Group, Inc. Staff. 1994. 14.95 (1-885313-00-4) MZ Group.

Top One Hundred Italian Dishes. Diane Seed. (Illus.). 144p. (Orig.). 1991. pap. 15.95 (0-89815-434-0) Ten Speed Pr.

Top One Hundred Pasta Sauces: A Rosendale Press Book. Diane Seed. (Illus.). 128p. (Orig.). 1987. pap. 12.95 (0-89815-232-1); text ed. 19.95 (0-89815-257-7) Ten Speed Pr.

*Top Outdoor Family Adventures: Vacationing in the Outdoors with Your Children. Maurice Valerio. Ed. by Allison C. Mickens. (Picked-by-You Books). (Illus.). 200p. (Orig.). 1997. pap. write for info. (1-889807-09-5) Valerio Pub.

*Top Outfitters of Big Game Hunting. Maurice Valerio. Ed. by Allison C. Mickens. LC 96-90660. (Picked-by-You Guides). (Illus.). 152p. (Orig.). 1996. pap. 19.95 (1-889807-00-1) Valerio Pub.

Top People in Peru. Ed. by Jonathan Cavanagh. 898p. (ENG & SPA.). 1992. pap. 50.00 (1-886617-06-6) Peru Rept.

Top Performance: How to Develop Excellence in Yourself & Others. Zig Ziglar. 288p. 1987. pap. 12.00 (0-425-09973-3, Berkley Trade) Berkley Pub.

Top Performance: How to Develop Excellence in Yourself & Others. Zig Ziglar & Jim Savage. 288p. 1986. 19.99 (0-8007-1475-X) Revell.

Top Pop Album Tracks, 1955-1992. Joel Whitburn. 544p. 1993. 34.95 (0-89820-094-6) Record Research.

*Top Pop Album Tracks 1993-1996. Joel Whitburn. (Record Research Ser.). 70p. (Orig.). 1996. pap. 14.95 (0-89820-118-7) Record Research.

Top Pop Albums: 1955-1992. Joel Whitburn. 978p. 1995. 59.95 (0-7935-5015-7, 00330056) H Leonard.

Top Pop Albums, 1955-1992. Joel Whitburn. (Illus.). 976p. 1993. 54.95 (0-89820-093-8) Record Research.

*Top Pop Albums, 1955-1996. Joel Whitburn. 1000p. 1996. 69.95 (0-7935-6677-0, 00330234) H Leonard.

*Top Pop Albums 1955-1996. 4th rev. ed. Joel Whitburn. (Record Research Ser.). 1000p. 1996. 89.95 (0-89820-117-9) Record Research.

Top Pop Duets. 88p. 1994. otabind 12.95 (0-7935-3414-3, 00311677) H Leonard.

Top Pop Hits of the 90's. 5th ed. Ed. by Carol Cuellar. 176p. (Orig.). (YA). 1995. pap. text ed. 12.95 (0-89724-539-3, F3471P2X) Warner Brothers.

Top Pop Hits of the 90's. 6th ed. Ed. by Carol Cuellar. 188p. (Orig.). (YA). 1996. pap. text ed. 14.95 (1-57623-268-9, AF9563) Warner Brothers.

*Top Pop Hits of the 90's. 6th ed. Ed. by Carol Cuellar. 390p. 1995. pap. text ed. 19.95 (0-89724-828-7, MF9568) Warner Brothers.

*Top Pop Hits of 1996. Ed. by Carol Cuellar. 328p. (Orig.). (YA). 1996. pap. text ed. 18.95 (1-57623-697-8) Warner Brothers.

*Top Pop Hits of 1996: Easy Piano Edition. Ed. by Carol Cuellar. 160p. (Orig.). (YA). 1996. pap. text ed. 16.95 (1-57623-701-X, AF9694) Warner Brothers.

Top Pop Singles: 1955-1993. Joel Whitburn. 912p. 1995. pap. 49.95 (0-7935-5011-4, 00330042) H Leonard.

Top Pop Singles CD Guide: 1955-1979. Joel Whitburn. 276p. 1995. pap. 19.95 (0-7935-5012-2, 00330052) H Leonard.

Top Pop Singles CD Guide, 1955-1979. Joel Whitburn & Jerry Reuss. (Record Research Ser.). 270p. 1995. pap. 24.95 (0-89820-107-1) Record Research.

Top Pop Singles 1955-1993. Joel Whitburn. (Illus.). 850p. 1994. 74.95 (0-89820-104-7); pap. 64.95 (0-89820-105-5) Record Research.

Top Priority: Building an Evangelistic Church. John Caldwell. LC 95-17518. 1995. pap. 8.99 (0-89900-739-2) College Pr Pub.

Top Professions: The 100 Most Popular, Dynamic, & Profitable Careers in America Today. Nicholas Basta. LC 89-22898. 228p. (Orig.). 1989. pap. 10.95 (0-87866-866-7) Petersons.

Top Ramen Noodle Cookbook: Over 175 Delicious, Inexpensive, Quick, & Easy Recipes Using America's Favorite Noodle. Elizabeth Prungel & Heather Spyer. LC 94-21450. 1994. pap. 10.95 (1-55958-565-X) Prima Pub.

*Top R&B Singles: 1942-1995. Joel Whitburn. 704p. 1996. 49.95 (0-7935-6675-4, 00330232) H Leonard.

Top R&B Singles, 1942-1988. 1995. 29.95 (0-7935-5611-2, 00330177) H Leonard.

*Top R&B Singles, 1942-1995. Compiled by Joel Whitburn. 700p. 1996. 64.95 (0-89820-115-2, RBS301H) Record Research.

Top Retirement Havens of the World. 1991. lib. bdg. 79.95 (0-8490-4684-X) Gordon Pr.

*Top River Guides & Outfitters. Maurice Valerio. Ed. by Allison C. Mickens. (Picked-by-You Guides). (Illus.). 200p. (Orig.). 1997. pap. 19.95 (1-889807-03-6) Valerio Pub.

*Top Roping. Peter Lewis. (How to Rock Climb Ser.). (Illus.). (Orig.). 1997. pap. 12.95 (1-57540-082-0) Chockstone Pr.

Top Score Solo Songbook. Lee & Progris. 1990. 1.95 (0-685-32120-7, N245); 1.95 (0-685-32198-3, N258); 1.95 (0-685-47133-0, N250); 1.95 (0-685-47134-9, N247) Hansen Ed Mus.

Top Score Solo Songbook: Alto Saxophone. Lee & Progris. 1990. 1.95 (0-685-32212-2, N248) Hansen Ed Mus.

Top Score Solo Songbook: Tenor Saxophone. 1990. 1.95 (0-685-32213-0, N249) Hansen Ed Mus.

Top Secret. Ted Dewan. LC 96-23323. 32p. (J). 1997. 15.95 (0-385-32324-7, DD Bks Yng Read) BDD Bks Young Read.

Top Secret. John R. Gardiner. (J). (gr. 3-7). 1995. pap. 3.95 (0-316-30363-1) Little.

*Top Secret. Dennis Rodman. 1997. 15.00 (0-385-31898-7) Delacorte.

Top Secret: A Graphic Novel. Bill Barry. Ed. by Joan Harryman. (Illus.). 80p. (Orig.). 1988. pap. 9.95 (0-944099-04-1) Comic Art.

Top Secret: A Shraga Morgenstern-Pinny Katz Mystery Trilogy. Libby Lazewnik. (Little Black Box Ser.: Pt. 1). 165p. (J). (gr. 5-9). 1995. 11.95 (1-56871-078-X) Targum Pr.

*Top Secret: MIS-X China - Escape & Evasion. A. R. Wichtrich. LC 97-65969. (Illus.). 160p. 1997. 21.95 (1-57197-067-3) Pentland Pr.

Top Secret: Sexual Assault Information for Teenagers Only. Jennifer Fay & Billie J. Flerchinger. (Illus.). 32p. (Orig.). 1982. pap. 4.50 (0-941953-03-3) KCSA Res Ctr.

Top Secret: The Details of the Planned World War II Invasion of Japan & How the Japanese Would Have Met It (the Japanese Atomic Bomb)(Documentary) James M. Davis & Bert Webber. LC 94-44934. (Illus.). 88p. (Orig.). 1994. pap. 9.95 (0-936738-85-5) Webb Research.

Top Secret Bird: The Luftwaffe's ME-163 Comet. Wolfgang Spate. LC 88-90967. (Illus.). 270p. (Orig.). (YA). (gr. 8-12). 1989. pap. text ed. 11.95 (0-929521-08-0) Pictorial Hist.

Top Secret Exchange: The Tizard Mission & the Scientific War. David Zimmerman. (Illus.). 224p. Date not set. 33.95 (0-7509-1242-1, Pub. by Sutton Pubng UK) Bks Intl VA.

*Top Secret Exchange: The Tizard Mission & the Scientific War. David Zimmerman. 252p. (C). 1996. 29.95 (0-7735-1401-5, 71184, Pub. by McGill CN) U of Toronto Pr.

*Top Secret File. (Activity Fun Packs Ser.). (Illus.). (YA). (gr. 6 up). 1996. pap. 5.95 (0-7894-0761-2) DK Pub Inc.

Top Secret Majic. Stanton T. Friedman. (Illus.). 250p. 1996. 22.95 (1-56924-830-3) Marlowe & Co.

*Top Secret-Majic. Stanton T. Friedman. 1997. pap. text ed. 13.95 (1-56924-741-2) Marlowe & Co.

Top Secret Recipes: Creating Kitchen Clones of America's Favorite Foods. Todd Wilbur. LC 92-38670. 1993. pap. 10.00 (0-452-26995-4, Plume) NAL-Dutton.

Top Secret Registry of U. S. Government Radio Stations. 8th ed. Tom Kneitel. (Illus.). 268p. 1993. pap. 22.95 (0-939780-20-8) CRB Res.

*Top Secret Restaurant Recipes: Creating Kitchen Clones from America's Favorite Restaurant Chains. Todd Wilbur. LC 96-49396. 1997. pap. 12.95 (0-452-27587-3, Plume) NAL-Dutton.

Top Secret Resumes & Cover Letters. Steven A. Provenzano. 218p. (Orig.). 1995. pap. text ed. 12.95 (0-7931-1359-8, 5614-3401) Dearborn Finan.

Top Secret Resumes & Cover Letters. Steven A. Provenzano. (Orig.). 1995. pap. text ed. 34.95 incl. cd-rom (0-7931-1705-4, 1800-4001) Dearborn Trade.

TOP SECRET Resumes for the '90s: Discover What Really Works, & the Secrets "Professional" Resume Writers Won't Tell You. rev. ed. Steven A. Provenzano. Ed. by Desktop Publishing Inc. Staff. LC 93-70858. (Careers-Resume Writing Ser.). 214p. (Orig.). 1994. reprint ed. pap. 10.95 (0-9633558-1-3) DeskTop IL.

Top Secret Screen & Minimum. Corey Koebernick. 1982. 5.50 (0-394-52702-X) Random.

Top Secret-Trade Secret: Accessing & Safeguarding Restricted Information. Ellis Mount & Wilda B. Newman. LC 85-19864. 214p. 1985. pap. text ed. 39.95 (0-918212-90-1) Neal-Schuman.

Top Secrets: Screenwriting. Jurgen Wolff & Kerry Cox. 352p. 1993. pap. 21.95 (0-943728-50-9) Lone Eagle Pub.

Top Sergeant: The Life & Times of Sergeant Major of the Army William G. Bainbridge. William G. Bainbridge & Dan Cragg. LC 94-20465. 368p. 1995. 23.00 (0-449-90892-5, Columbine) Fawcett.

Top Sergeant: The Life & Times of Sergeant Major of the Army William G. Bainbridge. William G. Bainbridge & Dan Cragg. 1996. mass mkt. 5.99 (0-8041-0758-0) Ivy Books.

Top Shape: Two Hours a Week to the Body of Your Dreams. Joyce L. Vedral. 272p. (Orig.). 1995. pap. 13.99 (0-446-39533-1) Warner Bks.

Top Shopping in Japan. Tetsuya Ogaki. Ed. by Yutaka Iwakiri. Tr. by Ayako Maene & Hiroko Motoyoshi from JPN. (Illus.). 304p. (Orig.). 1984. pap. 19.95 (0-8048-1477-5) C E Tuttle.

*Top Shops! A Beginner's Guide to Team Building & Shop Management. Robert G. Wilson & John D. Linscott. LC 96-9704. 1996. write for info. (1-56990-213-5) Hanser-Gardner.

*Top Spy. Jon Lake. LC 95-76744. (Ten-Minute Thrillers Ser.). 32p. (YA). (gr. 6-12). 1995. pap. 2.95 (0-7854-1071-6, 40823) Am Guidance.

*Top Spy Readalong. Jon Lake. (Ten-Minute Thrillers Ser.). 32p. (YA). (gr. 6-12). 1995. pap. 12.95 incl. audio (0-7854-1082-1, 40825) Am Guidance.

Top Stories Set, Vol. I, Nos. 1-10. Ed. by Anne Turyn. 1982. pap. text ed. 59.00 (0-917061-00-4) Top Stories.

Top Stories Set, Vol. II, Nos. 11-20. Ed. by Anne Turyn. 1984. pap. 30.00 (0-917061-20-9) Top Stories.

Top Tax Saving Ideas for Today's Small Business. 3rd ed. Thomas J. Stemmy. Ed. by Camille Akin. LC 96-30483. (Successful Business Library). 336p. (Orig.). 1996. pap. 16.95 (1-55571-379-3) Oasis Pr OR.

Top Team Audit. Dave Francis & Don Young. 250p. 1993. text ed. 262.95 (0-566-02680-5, Pub. by Gower UK) Ashgate Pub Co.

*Top 10 Baseball Home Run Hitters. Bill Deane. LC 96-39057. (Sports Top Ten Ser.). (Illus.). 48p. (J). (gr. 4-10). 1997. lib. bdg. 17.95 (0-89490-804-9) Enslow Pubs.

Top 10 Basketball Point Guards. Jeff Savage. LC 96-9132. (Sports Top 10 Ser.). (Illus.). 48p. (J). (gr. 4-10). 1997. lib. bdg. 17.95 (0-89490-807-3) Enslow Pubs.

Top 10 Basketball Power Forwards. Jeff Savage. LC 96-9131. (Sports Top 10 Ser.). (Illus.). 48p. (J). (gr. 4-10). 1997. lib. bdg. 17.95 (0-89490-808-1) Enslow Pubs.

Top Ten Estate Planning Techniques for the 1990's. Keith V. Abramson. 160p. 1992. pap. 29.95 (0-9635266-0-X) Am Legal Pub.

Top 10 Football Sackers. Jeff Savage. LC 96-25399. (Sports Top 10 Ser.). (Illus.). 48p. (J). (gr. 4-10). 1997. lib. bdg. 17.95 (0-89490-805-7) Enslow Pubs.

An Asterisk (*) at the beginning of an entry indicates that the title is appearing in BIP for the first time.

*Top 10 Heavyweight Boxers. Ron Knapp. LC 96-52841. (Sports Top Ten Ser.). 48p. (J). 1997. lib. bdg. 17.95 (0-89490-806-5) Enslow Pubs.

*Top Ten List for Graduates: Priorities for Faithful Living. James W. Moore. (Illus.). 112p. 1997. pap. 12.00 (0-687-00700-3) Abingdon.

Top Ten Mistakes Leaders Make. Hans Finzel. 168p. 1994. 12.99 (1-56476-246-7, 6-3246, Victor Bks) Chariot Victor.

Top Ten Money Myths of the Century. Margaret Thoren. 200p. pap. 10.00 (0-9606938-3-1) Truth in Money.

Top Ten of Everything 1996. Russell Ash. LC 95-11541. (Illus.). 288p. 1995. 24.95 (0-7894-0196-7, 6-70510) DK Pub Inc.

Top Ten of Everything 1996. Russell Ash. (Illus.). 288p. 1995. pap. 16.95 (0-7894-0338-2, 6-70524) DK Pub Inc.

Top Ten of Everything, 1997. Russell Ash. LC 96-14203. 1996. 24.95 (0-7894-1083-4); pap. 16.95 (0-7894-1264-0) DK Pub Inc.

*Top Ten of Everything 1998. Russell Ash. LC 97-15018. 256p. 1997. pap. 17.95 (0-7894-2082-1) DK Pub Inc.

*Top Ten of Everything 1998. Russell Ash. LC 97-15018. 256p. 1997. 24.95 (0-7894-2199-2) DK Pub Inc.

*Top Ten Scientifically Proven Natural Products. Richard Ogletree & Richard Fischer. 64p. (Orig.). 1997. pap. 11.95 (0-944351-13-1) N S D Products.

*Top Ten Technologies & Their Impact on CPAs. Sandi Smith. 250p. (Orig.). 1997. pap. 29.00 (0-87051-184-X, 043009) Am Inst CPA.

Top the TOEFL Test: Ten Days to a Higher Score. Carla B. Hughes. 1994. pap. 29.25 incl. audio (0-13-123571-0) P-H.

Top the TOEFL Test: Ten Days to Higher Score. LC 94-7682. 192p. 1994. pap. text ed. 12.00 (0-13-064973-2) P-H.

Top Three Thousand Plus, 1955-1990. Joel Whitburn. (Record Research Ser.). 178p. 1990. pap. 14.95 (0-89820-077-6) Record Research.

*Top Tips in Primary Care Management. Derek Gallen & Glynis Buckle. LC 97-3775. 1997. write for info. (0-86542-976-6) Blackwell Sci.

Top Tips in Urology. Ed. by J. McLoughlin et al. LC 95-11624. 117p. 1995. pap. 14.95 (0-86542-610-4) Blackwell Sci.

Top Top Stories. Ed. by Anne Turyn. 200p. (Orig.). 1991. pap. 9.95 (0-87286-258-5) City Lights.

Top Trader's Guide to Technical Analysis. Nathan Sambul. 256p. 1995. 39.95 (0-7931-1415-2, 5680-1901) Dearborn Finan.

*Top Turkey Hunting Guides. Maurice Valerie. Ed. by Allison C. Mickes. (Picked by You Books). (Illus.). 200p. (Orig.). 1997. pap. 19.95 (1-889807-06-0) Valerio Pub.

Top Twenty ESL Word Games. Marjorie Fuchs et al. 1991. pap. text ed. 37.27 (0-8013-0365-6, 78138) Longman.

Top Twenty-Five Book of Lists. Ed. by Beth Ewen. 100p. pap. 16.95 (0-9634146-0-7) MN St Paul CityBusn.

Top Twenty-Four French Word Game Hits. B. Pliskin & Sargent. 1987. pap. text ed. 18.00 (0-582-99858-1, 75283) Longman.

Top Twenty-Four Spanish Word Game Hits. Berenice Plisken & Claudia K. Sargent. 1987. pap. text ed. 18.00 (0-582-99852-2, 75277) Longman.

Top Two Hundred Corporations in the U. S. 1978. 35.95 (0-916210-02-2) J R Albin.

Top Two Hundred Drugs. 9th ed. Jeffrey D. Sigler. Ed. by Brent E. Flanders. 216p. (C). 1993. student ed., ring bd. 39.95 (1-880579-08-1); student ed., ring bd. 35.95 (1-880579-11-1) Sigler & Flanders.

Top 200 Reasons Not to Vote for Bill Clinton. Bradley S. O'Leary. LC 96-85055. 128p. 1996. pap. 5.95 (1-887161-11-2) Boru Pubng.

*Top Upland Bird Hunting Guides. Maurice Valerio. Ed. by Allison C. Mickens. (Picked-by-You Guides). (Illus.). 200p. (Orig.). 1997. pap. 19.95 (1-889807-02-8) Valerio Pub.

*Top Waterfowl Hunting Guides. Maurice Valerio. Ed. by Allison C. Mickens. (Picked by You Books). (Illus.). 200p. (Orig.). 1997. pap. 19.95 (1-889807-07-9) Valerio Pub.

Top Ways to Get Tax-Free Income Under the Latest Tax Set-Up. 33p. 1982. 1.80 (0-686-89049-3, 95584-9) P-H.

*Top Western Adventures: Guest Ranches, Pack Trips & Cattle Drives. Maurice Valerio. Ed. by Allison C. Mickens. (Picked-by-You Books). (Illus.). 200p. (Orig.). 1997. pap. 19.95 (1-889807-08-7) Valerio Pub.

Top Wing. Matt Christopher. (Illus.). (YA). (gr. 8-12). 1994. 15.95 (0-316-14099-6) Little.

Top Wing. Matt Christopher. (J). (gr. 3-7). 1995. pap. 3.95 (0-316-14126-7) Little.

Top Working Dogs: A Training Manual. 3rd exp. rev. ed. Dietmar Schellenberg. LC 82-90110. (Illus.). 208p. (Orig.). 1995. pap. 24.90 (0-9608798-0-3) DBC.

*Top 10 American Women Sprinters. Arlene B. Molzahn. LC 97-19993. (Sports Top 10 Ser.). (J). 1998. write for info. (0-7660-1011-2) Enslow Pubs.

Top 10 Baseball Base Stealers. Peter C. Bjarkman. LC 94-45890. (Sports Top 10 Ser.). (Illus.). 48p. (J). (gr. 4-10). 1995. lib. bdg. 17.95 (0-89490-609-7) Enslow Pubs.

*Top 10 Baseball Hitters. Bill Deane. LC 97-21633. (Sports Top Ten Ser.). (J). 1998. write for info. (0-7660-1007-4) Enslow Pubs.

Top 10 Baseball Pitchers. Michael J. Sullivan. LC 94-2157. (Sports Top 10 Ser.). (Illus.). 48p. (J). (gr. 4-10). 1994. lib. bdg. 17.95 (0-89490-520-1) Enslow Pubs.

Top 10 Basketball Centers. Ron Knapp. LC 94-15808. (Sports Top 10 Ser.). (Illus.). 48p. (J). (gr. 4-10). 1994. lib. bdg. 17.95 (0-89490-515-5) Enslow Pubs.

Top 10 Basketball Legends. Ken Rappoport. LC 94-32060. (Sports Top 10 Ser.). (Illus.). 48p. (J). (gr. 4-10). 1995. lib. bdg. 17.95 (0-89490-610-0) Enslow Pubs.

Top 10 Basketball Scorers. Ron Knapp. LC 94-15809. (Sports Top 10 Ser.). (Illus.). 48p. (J). (gr. 4-10). 1994. lib. bdg. 17.95 (0-89490-516-3) Enslow Pubs.

Top 10 Basketball Slam Dunkers. Peter C. Bjarkman. LC 94-45889. (Sports Top 10 Ser.). (Illus.). 48p. (J). (gr. 4-10). 1995. lib. bdg. 17.95 (0-89490-608-9) Enslow Pubs.

*Top 10 Big Men. Chris W. Sehnert. LC 97-2106. (Top 10 Champions Ser.). (J). 1997. write for info. (1-56239-794-X) Abdo & Dghtrs.

Top 10 Fears of Job Seekers: Your Guide to an Effective, Stress-Free Job Search. Gary J. Grappo. 128p. 1997. pap. text ed. 12.00 (0-425-15449-1) Berkley Pub.

Top 10 Football Quarterbacks. William W. Lace. LC 93-40469. (Sports Top 10 Ser.). (Illus.). 48p. (J). (gr. 4-10). 1994. lib. bdg. 17.95 (0-89490-518-X) Enslow Pubs.

Top 10 Football Receivers. Stew Thornley. LC 94-32062. (Sports Top 10 Ser.). (Illus.). 48p. (J). (gr. 4-10). 1995. lib. bdg. 17.95 (0-89490-607-0) Enslow Pubs.

Top 10 Football Rushers. William W. Lace. LC 93-40470. (Sports Top 10 Ser.). (Illus.). 48p. (J). (gr. 4-10). 1994. lib. bdg. 17.95 (0-89490-519-8) Enslow Pubs.

*Top 10 Hockey Goalies. Dean Spiros. (Sports Top Ten Ser.). (J). 1998. write for info. (0-7660-1010-4) Enslow Pubs.

Top 10 Hockey Scorers. Ron Knapp. LC 94-1317. (Sports Top 10 Ser.). (Illus.). 48p. (J). (gr. 4-10). 1994. lib. bdg. 17.95 (0-89490-517-1) Enslow Pubs.

Top 10 Keys to Personal Excellence, Vol. 1. Fordson Wilder. 22.95 (0-911505-10-5) Lifecraft.

*Top 10 Men's Tennis Players. Andre Christopher. LC 97-19979. (Sports Top Ten Ser.). 1998. write for info. (0-7660-1009-0) Enslow Pubs.

Top 10 NASCAR Drivers. Gail B. Riley. LC 94-32061. (Sports Top 10 Ser.). (Illus.). 48p. (J). (gr. 4-10). 1995. lib. bdg. 17.95 (0-89490-611-9) Enslow Pubs.

*Top 10 of Everything 1997. Russell Ash. 1996. 24.95 (0-614-20408-9); pap. 16.95 (0-614-20409-7) DK Pub Inc.

*Top 10 Pitchers. Chris W. Sehnert. LC 97-15846. (Top 10 Champions Ser.). (J). 1997. write for info. (1-56239-798-2) Abdo & Dghtrs.

*Top 10 Playmakers. Chris W. Sehnert. LC 97-20093. 1997. write for info. (1-56239-796-6) Abdo & Dghtrs.

*Top 10 Professional Basketball Coaches. Ron Knapp. LC 97-21634. (Sports Top Ten Ser.). 1998. write for info. (0-7660-1008-2) Enslow Pubs.

*Top 10 Professional Football Coaches. Jeff Savage. LC 97-20381. (Sports Top 10 Ser.). 1998. write for info. (0-7660-1006-6) Enslow Pubs.

*Top 10 Quarterbacks. LC 96-52410. (Top 10 Champions Ser.). (J). 1997. write for info. (1-56239-791-5) Abdo & Dghtrs.

Top 10 Quiz Book. (Illus.). 64p. (J). 1996. 9.95 (0-7894-1022-2) DK Pub Inc.

*Top 10 Running Backs. LC 96-52409. (Top 10 Champions Ser.). (J). 1997. write for info. (1-56239-792-3) Abdo & Dghtrs.

*Top 10 Sluggers. Chris W. Sehnert. LC 97-14481. (Top 10 Champions Ser.). 1997. write for info. (1-56239-797-4) Abdo & Dghtrs.

Top 10 Ways to Make Your Wife Crazy. Hans Finz & Donna Finz. LC 96-21994. 200p. 1996. 12.99 (1-56476-578-4, 6-3578, Victor Bks) Chariot Victor.

Top 10 Women Tennis Players. Denis J. Harrington. LC 94-31888. (Sports Top 10 Ser.). (Illus.). 48p. (J). (gr. 4-10). 1995. lib. bdg. 17.95 (0-89490-612-7) Enslow Pubs.

Top 100 Business Schools Directory. Research & Education Association Staff. 352p. 1996. pap. text ed. 19.95 (0-87891-747-0) Res & Educ.

Top 100 International Coffee Recipes: How to Prepare, Serve & Experience Great Cups of Tasty & Healthy Coffee for All Occasions. Mary Ward. (Illus.). 144p. 1996. pap. 14.95 (0-8119-0818-6) LIFETIME.

Top 100 International Low-Fat Recipes: Cook Your Weight off with Tasty & Easy-to-Prepare Dishes. Virginia Aronson. Ed. by Donald A. Kullman. (Illus.). 144p. 1996. pap. 14.95 (0-8119-0672-8) LIFETIME.

Top 100 International Tea Recipes: How to Prepare, Serve & Experience Great Cups of Tasty & Healthy Tea & Tea Desserts. Mary Ward. (Illus.). 144p. 1996. pap. 14.95 (0-8119-0817-8) LIFETIME.

*Top 100 Morgan Dollar Varieties: The VAM Keys. Michael S. Fey & Jeff Osman. (Illus.). vii, 137p. (Orig.). 1996. pap. 24.95 (0-9653645-0-X) Rare Coin Invstmnts.

*Top 100 Morgan Dollar Varieties: The VAM Keys. 2nd ed. Michael S. Fey & Jeff Osman. (Illus.). vii, 137p. (Orig.). 1997. pap. 49.95 (0-9653645-1-8) Rare Coin Invstmnts.

*Top 100 Morgan Dollar Varieties: The VAM Keys. 2nd ed. Michael S. Fey & Jeff Oxman. (Illus.). 137p. 1997. reprint ed. pap. 24.95 (0-9653645-2-6) Rare Coin Invstmnts.

Top 100 Recipes for Diabetics: The Comprehensive Diabetic Cookbook. 3rd ed. Dorothy Kaplan. (Illus.). 144p. 1996. pap. 14.95 (0-8119-0819-4) LIFETIME.

*Top 1000 X 5. 2nd rev. ed. Joel Whitburn. 288p. 1996. pap. 29.95 (0-89820-121-7) Record Research.

*Top 102 7:20 Lists & Other Morning Show Stuff. David Stein. Ed. by Wanda N. Colon. 144p. (Orig.). 1996. pap. text ed. 12.95 (0-9655567-0-0) Stein Prods.

Top 200 "Meds" for the Surgical Patient. Robert L. McEntyre. 263p. 1991. pap. 19.95 (0-942219-23-6) Quality Med Pub.

Top 30 Business Schools. Martinson. 1994. pap. 18.00 (0-671-86594-3) S&S Trade.

*Top 40 Music on Compact Disc 1955-1996. Pat Downey. 620p. 1997. 49.95 (0-9633718-5-1) P Downey Ent.

Top 4000 Private Companies. Britians. 1900. pap. text ed. 97.00 (0-00-033504-5) Kluwer Ac.

Top 4000 Private Companies. 2nd ed. Britians. 1900. pap. text ed. 97.00 (0-00-033503-7) Kluwer Ac.

Top 50 BMI Motion Picture Songs & Themes. CPP Belwin Staff. 1994. pap. 14.95 (0-89898-757-1, F3406SMX) Warner Brothers.

*Top 50 Country Classics: BMI 50th Anniversary Songbook. Ed. by Carol Cuellar & David C. Olson. 160p. (Orig.). (YA). 1997. pap. text ed. 16.95 (1-57623-930-6) Warner Brothers.

Top 500 Foreign Joint Venture Industrial Enterprises in China. annuals 501p. (CHI & ENG.). 1994. 135.00 (7-80036-797-5, Pub. by HUWEI Cnslts CH) Am Overseas Bk Co.

Top 500 Foreign Trade Companies in China. annuals 600p. (CHI & ENG.). 1995. 205.00 (0-614-11841-7, Pub. by HUWEI Cnslts CH) Am Overseas Bk Co.

Topanga Culture, Final Report on Excavations, 1948. Clement W. Merghan. (University of California Publications: No. 20:2). (Illus.). 46p. (C). 1958. reprint ed. pap. 4.35 (1-55567-154-3) Coyote Press.

Topanga Culture First Season's Excavation of the Tank Site, 1947. fac. ed. Ronald L. Olson & Adam E. Treganza. (University of California Publications: No. 12:4). 56p. (C). 1950. reprint ed. pap. 5.30 (1-55567-129-2) Coyote Press.

Topanga Story. Ed. by Louise A. York. LC 92-34648. 1992. pap. write for info. (0-89865-852-7) Donning Co.

Topaz. Donald B. Hoover. (Gem Bks.). (Illus.). 196p. 1993. 49.95 (0-7506-1087-5) Buttrwrth-Heinemann.

*Topaz. Beverly Jenkins. 1997. mass mkt. 5.99 (0-380-78660-5) Avon.

*Topaz Dreams. Marilyn Campbell. 368p. 1997. mass mkt. 5.50 (0-505-52181-4) Dorchester Pub Co.

Topaz Island. large type ed. Patricia Robins. (Dales Large Print Ser.). 1994. pap. 17.99 (1-85389-462-1, Pub. by Magna Print Bks UK) Ulverscroft.

Topaz Man Presents: A Dream Come True. Jennifer Blake et al. 384p. (Orig.). 1994. pap. 4.99 (0-451-40451-3, Topaz) NAL-Dutton.

Topaze. Marcel Pagnol. (FRE.). 1988. pap. 13.95 (0-7859-3328-X, 2877060594) Fr & Eur.

Topaze: Comedie en 4 Actes. Marcel Pagnol. pap. 9.95 (0-685-37013-5) Fr & Eur.

Topcoats for Zinc Coatings (Five Year Report) John D. Keane et al. 58p. 1981. 40.00 (0-938477-10-2) SSPC.

Topeka: An Illustrated History of the Kansas Capital. Roy Bird. 152p. 1985. 19.95 (0-941974-06-5) Baranski Pub Co.

TopFit 2.0: Pharmacokinetic & Pharmacodynamic Data Analysis for the PC. Gunther Heinzel et al. 667p. (Orig.). 1993. pap. 130.00 incl. disk (1-56081-368-7, Pub. by G Fischer Verlag GW) Lubrecht & Cramer.

*Topgun. Chelsea House Publishing Staff. (Concise Collection). 1997. 15.95 (1-85627-787-9) Chelsea Hse.

Topi Dictionary of Architecture, Urbanism and Construction, English-Spanish/Spanish-English: English-Spanish, Spanish-English. 488p. (ENG & SPA.). 1995. 95.00 (0-7859-9873-X) Fr & Eur.

*Topiaries & Pomanders: Gifts from Nature. Beverly Jollands. (Illus.). 64p. 1997. 12.95 (1-85967-500-X, Lorenz Bks) Anness Pub.

Topiary & Plant Sculpture: A Beginner's Step-by-Step Guide. David Carr. (Illus.). 144p. 1995. pap. 22.95 (1-85223-881-X, Pub. by Crowood Pr UK) Trafalgar.

Topiary Garden. Janni Howker. LC 94-27867. (Illus.). 64p. (J). (gr. 2 up). 1995. 14.95 (0-531-06891-9) Orchard Bks Watts.

Topias & Utopias in Health: Policy Studies. Ed. by Stanley R. Ingman & Anthony E. Thomas. (World Anthropology Ser.). (Illus.). xiv, 548p. 1975. 51.55 (90-279-7559-0) Mouton.

Topic, Antitopic & Verb Agreement in Non-Standard French. Knud Lambrecht. (Pragmatics & Beyond Ser.: II: 6). vii, 113p. (Orig.). 1981. pap. 29.00 (90-272-2526-5) Benjamins North Am.

Topic Coded Titles on Public Employees Collective Bargaining with Emphasis on State & Local Levels. 8th ed. Helene S. Tanimoto. (Occasional Publications: No. 158). 170p. 1986. 3.00 (0-318-23503-X) U Hawaii.

Topic Continuity in Discourse: A Quantitative Cross-Language Study. Ed. by T. Givon. (Typological Studies in Language: 3). vi, 492p. 1983. 83.00 (90-272-2867-1) Benjamins North Am.

Topic Focus & Configurationality: Papers from the 6th Groningen Grammar Talks. Groningen, 1984. Werner Abraham & Sjaak DeMeii. LC 85-17515. (Linguistik Aktuell Ser.: No. 4). v, 349p. 1986. 97.00 (90-272-2724-1) Benjamins North Am.

Topic Talk: An Interactive Communication Program for Adults. Linda Carey et al. Ed. by Cindy Drolet & C. Gilles-Brown. (Illus.). 239p. (Orig.). 1991. pap. text ed. 102.00 (0-9609464-5-4) Imaginart Pr.

Topic Teaching in the Primary School: Teaching about Society Through Topic Work. Stella Gunning et al. 220p. (C). 1981. 23.00 (0-7099-0437-1, Pub. by Croom Helm UK); pap. 9.00 (0-7099-1118-1, Pub. by Croom Helm UK) Routledge Chapman & Hall.

Topic Work in the Early Years: Organising the Curriculum for Four to Eight-Year-Olds. Joy A. Palmer & Deirdre Pettitt. LC 92-47344. 192p. (C). 1993. pap. text ed. 18.95 (0-415-08041-X, B2550) Routledge.

Topica see De Inventione

Topica et Sophistici Elenchi. Aristotle. Ed. by W. David Ross. (Oxford Classical Texts Ser.). 270p. 1958. 29.95 (0-19-814516-0) OUP.

Topical Analysis of the Bible: Using the New International Version. Ed. by Walter A. Elwell. LC 91-11543. (Baker Reference Library). 912p. (Orig.). (C). 1991. 44.99 (0-8010-3205-9) Baker Bks.

*Topical Application of Antibiotics: Recent Advances in Ophthalmology. Ed. by Yoshihito Honda & Wolfgang Behrens-Baumann. (Ophthalmologica Ser.: Vol. 211, Suppl. 1, 1997). (Illus.). vi, 82p. 1997. pap. 38.25 (3-8055-6479-1) S Karger.

*Topical Bible: Bible Answers to Modern Questions. Naomi Pasachoff. Ed. by Sarah Feldman & William Cutter. LC 96-48039. (Illus.). 96p. (Orig.). (J). (gr. 4-6). 1996. pap. text ed. 5.95 (0-87441-618-3) Behrman.

Topical Budget: The Great British Newsfilm. Luke McKernan. (Illus.). 128p. 1992. 39.95 (0-253-33615-5, Pub. by British Film Inst UK); pap. 16.95 (0-85170-305-4, Pub. by British Film Inst UK) Ind U Pr.

Topical Child Development. Roberta M. Berns. LC 90-20927. 1994. text ed. 53.95 (0-8273-5727-3) Delmar.

Topical Child Development. James Cantrell. 186p. 1994. student ed. 25.50 (0-8273-6092-4) Delmar.

Topical Child Development. Hilda Jackson. 129p. 1994. teacher ed. 25.50 (0-8273-5728-1) Delmar.

Topical Concordance of the Old Testament: Using the Hebrew & Aramaic Text. Ed. by Eliezer Katz. 1200p. 1992. text ed. 125.00 (0-8010-5251-3) Baker Bks.

Topical Conference on Ferritic Alloys for Use in Nuclear Energy Technologies: Proceedings of Conference, Snowbird, Utah, June 19-23, 1983. Topical Conference on Ferritic Alloys for Use in Nuclear Energy Technologies Staff. Ed. by D. J. Michael & J. W. Davis. LC 84-61008. (Technology of Metallurgy Ser.: No. 6). 668p. reprint ed. pap. 180.00 (0-8357-2504-9, 2052384) Bks Demand.

Topical Conference Paper Summaries of the 1995 International Chemical & Petroleum Industry Inspection Technology (ICPITT) IV. (Illus.). 260p. (C). 1995. pap. 19.00 (1-57117-011-1, 1348) Am Soc Nondestructive.

Topical Corticosteroid Therapy: A Novel Approach to Safer Drugs. Ed. by Enno Christophers et al. 214p. 1988. text ed. 55.50 (0-88167-447-8) Lppncott-Raven.

Topical Corticosteroids. Ed. by Howard I. Maibach & C. Surber. (Illus.). viii, 518p. 1991. 275.75 (3-8055-5332-3) S Karger.

Topical Diagnosis in Neurology. 2nd ed. Peter Duus. (Flexibook Ser.). (Illus.). 516p. 1989. text ed. 33.00 (0-86577-305-X) Thieme Med Pubs.

*Topical Diagnosis in Neurology: Anatomy, Physiology, Sight, Symptoms. Peter Daus. (Illus.). 348p. 1997. pap. 35.00 (0-86577-711-X) Thieme Med Pubs.

*Topical Dictionary of Specialized Terminology English-Spanish. M. Antonieta Gallegos-Ruiz & H. Rafael Ruiz. 120p. (C). 1996. per., pap. text ed. 37.74 (0-7872-2677-7) Kendall-Hunt.

Topical Dictionary of Statistics: Advanced Industrial Technology Ser. Gary L. Tietjen. 200p. (C). 1985. text ed. 24.50 (0-412-01201-4, 9853, Chap & Hall NY) Chapman & Hall.

Topical Drug Bioavailability, Bioequivalence, & Penetration. Ed. by V. P. Shah & Howard I. Maibach. (Illus.). 476p. (C). 1994. 105.00 (0-306-44367-8, Plenum Pr) Plenum.

Topical Drug Delivery Formulations. Osborne & Amann. (Drugs & the Pharmaceutical Sciences Ser.: Vol. 42). 448p. 1989. 190.00 (0-8247-8183-X) Dekker.

Topical Family Bible Companion. Janice Y. Cook. LC 94-27013. 204p. (Orig.). 1994. pap. 8.99 (0-8308-1172-9, 1172) InterVarsity.

Topical Fluid Mechanics: Proceedings of the IUTAM Symposium. Ed. by H. K. Moffatt & A. Tsinober. 800p. (C). 1990. text ed. 140.00 (0-521-38145-2) Cambridge U Pr.

Topical French. Ed. by P. Rosenberg. 10p. 1979. pap. 14.95 (0-8288-4838-6, M9205) Fr & Eur.

Topical Glucocorticoids with Increased Benefit- Risk Ratio. Ed. by H. C. Korting & Howard I. Maibach. (Current Problems in Dermatology Ser.: Vol. 21). (Illus.). viii, 208p. 1993. 182.75 (3-8055-5712-4) S Karger.

Topical Guide to "Folia Primatologica", Volumes 1-30 (1963-1978) Ed. by E. Biegert. 160p. 1980. pap. 31.25 (3-8055-0781-X) S Karger.

Topical History of the United States. Gerald R. Baydo. LC 86-26949. (Illus.). 1978. reprint ed. pap. text ed. 16.95 (0-88273-008-8) Forum Pr IL.

Topical History of U. S. Jerry R. Baydo. 585p. 1993. 24.00 (0-911541-25-X) Gregory Pub.

*Topical Index of Early U. S. Almanacs, 1776-1800. Robert K. Dodge. LC 97-9374. (Bibliographies & Indexes in American Literature: Vol. 26). 424p. 1997. text ed. 89.50 (0-313-26049-4, Greenwood Pr) Greenwood.

*Topical Index of the Bible. Doyle Gilliam. (Orig.). 1976. pap. 3.00 (0-933672-05-5, C-1243) Star Bible.

Topical Memory System. 12.00 (0-615-00513-6) NavPress.

Topical Minoxidil: Experimental & Clinical Results. Ed. by J. J. Voorhees. (Journal: Dermatologica: Vol. 175, Suppl. 2, 1987). (Illus.). iv, 60p. 1987. pap. 18.50 (3-8055-4723-4) S Karger.

Topical Notebooks of Ralph Waldo Emerson, Vol. I. Ed. by Susan S. Smith & Ralph H. Orth. (Illus.). 360p. 1990. text ed. 37.50 (0-8262-0730-8) U of Mo Pr.

Topical Notebooks of Ralph Waldo Emerson, Vol. 2. Ed. by Ronald A. Bosco & Ralph H. Orth. (Illus.). 432p. 1992. text ed. 44.95 (0-8262-0858-4) U of Mo Pr.

Topical Notebooks of Ralph Waldo Emerson, Vol. 3. Ed. by Ralph H. Orth & Glen M. Johnson. (Illus.). 392p. 1994. text ed. 44.95 (0-8262-0951-3) U of Mo Pr.

Topical Readings in U. S. History. 2nd ed. Jerry R. Baydo. 400p. 1991. 17.95 (0-911541-23-3) Gregory Pub.

Topical Reference Books: Authoritative Evaluations of Recommended Resources in Specialized Subject Areas. Ed. by Marion Sader. (Buying Guide Ser.). 892p. 1991. 109.00 (0-8352-3087-2) Bowker.

Topical Relevance in Argumentation. Douglas Walton. (Pragmatics & Beyond Ser.: Vol. III, No. 8). vii, 81p. 1982. pap. 33.00 (*90-272-2524-9*) Benjamins North Am.

Topical Reviews in Neurosurgery, Vol. 1. J. Rice Edwards. 192p. 1982. 69.95 (*0-7236-0576-9*, Pub. by John Wright UK) Buttrwrth-Heinemann.

Topical Reviews in Rheumatic Disorders, Vol. 1. Ed. by A. G. Hill. (Topical Reviews Ser.). (Illus.). 196p. 1980. 69. 95 (*0-7236-0554-8*, Pub. by John Wright UK) Buttrwrth-Heinemann.

Topical Reviews in Rheumatic Disorders, Vol. 2. V. Wright. (Illus.). 235p. 1982. pap. 69.95 (*0-7236-0642-0*, Pub. by John Wright UK) Buttrwrth-Heinemann.

Topical Reviews in Vascular Surgery, Vol. 1. J. G. Pollock. (Illus.). 229p. 1982. 69.95 (*0-7236-0575-0*, Pub. by John Wright UK) Buttrwrth-Heinemann.

Topical Study Outlines. Gleason H. Ledyard. 160p. 1970. pap. text ed. 5.00 (*0-913201-34-0*) Christian Lit.

Topical Study Outlines Workbook. Gleason H. Ledyard. 112p. 1988. 3.00 (*0-913201-35-9*) Christian Lit.

Topical Time, Vol. 12-13. 2nd ed. Ed. by John H. Richter. (Illus.). 44p. 1970. reprint ed. pap. text ed. 7.00 (*0-935991-26-3*) Am Topical Assn.

Topics & Language Competencies, Bk. 3. Michael Kerwin. 112p. 1995. pap. text ed. 6.95 (*0-13-435884-8*) P-H.

Topics & Language Competencies, Bk. 5. Michael Kerwin. 112p. 1996. pap. 6.95 (*0-13-435900-3*) P-H.

Topics & Language Competencies, Bk. 6. Michael Kerwin. 144p. 1996. pap. text ed. 6.95 (*0-13-435918-6*) P-H.

Topics & Language Competencies Book. Michael Kerwin. 144p. 1996. pap. 6.95 (*0-13-460320-6*) P-H.

Topics & Language Competencies Book, Bk. 4. Michael Kerwin. 112p. 1995. pap. 6.95 (*0-13-435892-9*) P-H.

Topics & Language Competencies Book, No. 1. Michael Kerwin. 1995. pap. text ed. 6.95 (*0-13-435868-6*) P-H.

Topics & Language Competencies Book, No. 2. Michael Kerwin. 1995. pap. text ed. 6.95 (*0-13-435876-7*) P-H.

Topics & Perspectives in Adenosine Research. Ed. by E. Gerlach & B. F. Becker. (Illus.). 650p. 1987. 146.00 (*0-387-17364-1*) Spr-Verlag.

***Topics & Skills in English.** Barr & Fletcher. 1991. pap. text ed. write for info. (*0-17-556231-8*) Addison-Wesley.

Topics & Trends: First Authentic Readings for ESL Writers. Elena Gorokhova & Jose Carmona. 200p. (C). 1996. per. 31.43 (*0-8403-9158-7*) Kendall-Hunt.

Topics Books I & VIII: With Excerpts from Related Texts. Aristotle. Tr. by Robin Smith. (Clarendon Aristotle Ser.). 246p. 1997. pap. 29.95 (*0-19-823942-4*) OUP.

Topics Books I & VIII: With Excerpts from Related Texts. Aristotle. Tr. by Robin Smith. (Clarendon Aristotle Ser.: Bks. 1 & 8). 246p. 1997. text ed. 68.00 (*0-19-823945-9*) OUP.

Topics for a Statistical Description of Radar Cross Section. Andrew L. Maffett. LC 88-20698. (Remote Sensing & Image Processing Ser.). 373p. 1989. text ed. 125.00 (*0-471-61357-6*) Wiley.

Topics for Discussion & Language Practice, Bk. 1. Philip Sauvain & Michael Carrier. 64p. (C). 1988. 40.00 (*0-7175-0855-2*, Pub. by S Thornes Pubs UK) St Mut.

Topics for Discussion & Language Practice, Bk. 2. Philip Sauvain & Michael Carrier. 64p. (C). 1988. pap. 29.00 (*0-7175-0856-0*, Pub. by S Thornes Pubs UK) St Mut.

Topics for Getting in Touch: A Poetry Therapy Sourcebook. 10th ed. Jennifer Bosveld. 1995. pap. 18.95 (*0-685-53841-9*) Pudding Hse Pubns.

Topics for Mathematics Clubs. 2nd ed. LeRoy C. Dalton & Henry D. Snyder. LC 83-8296. 106p. (YA). (gr. 8-12). 1983. pap. 7.00 (*0-87353-208-2*) NCTM.

Topics for the Restless Book Bk. 1, 4 Bks., Bk. 1. rev. ed. (C). 1989. pap. text ed. 14.56 (*0-89061-527-6*) Jamestown Pubs.

Topics for the Restless Book Bk. 2, 4 Bks., Bk. 2. rev. ed. (C). 1989. Bk. 1. pap. text ed. 14.56 (*0-89061-528-4*) Jamestown Pubs.

Topics for the Restless Book Bk. 3, 4 Bks., Bk. 3. rev. ed. (C). 1989. Bk. 2. pap. text ed. 14.56 (*0-89061-529-2*) Jamestown Pubs.

Topics for the Restless Book Bk. 4, 4 Bks., Bk. 4. rev. ed. (C). 1989. Bk. 3. pap. text ed. 14.56 (*0-89061-530-6*) Jamestown Pubs.

Topics for Today. Smith & Nancy N. Mare. 1991. pap. 25. 95 (*0-8384-3099-6*) Heinle & Heinle.

***Topics for Today International Edition.** 2nd ed. Smith. (College Esl Ser.). (C). 1997. pap. 25.95 (*0-8384-7640-6*) Heinle & Heinle.

***Topics in Abstract Differential Equations.** S. Zaidman. 1994. pap. 46.95 (*0-582-23744-0*, Pub. by Longman UK) Longman.

Topics in Adolescent Medicine. Ed. by Robert B. Shearin. LC 83-60526. (Year Book Ser.). (Illus.). 308p. reprint ed. pap. 87.80 (*0-8357-7603-4*, 2056925) Bks Demand.

Topics in Advance Econometrics: Linear & Nonlinear Simultaneous Equations, Vol. 2. P. J. Dhrymes. 408p. 1994. 59.95 (*0-387-94156-8*) Spr-Verlag.

Topics in Advanced Clinical Coding. Launa L. Graham. 130p. 1993. 42.00 (*0-317-05442-2*) Am Hlth Info.

Topics in Advanced Econometrics. D. J. Dhrymes. xii, 379p. 1989. 49.95 (*0-387-97178-5*) Spr-Verlag.

Topics in Advanced Econometrics: Estimation, Testing & Specification of Cross-Section & Time Series Models. Herman J. Bierens. LC 92-47068. 280p. (C). 1994. text ed. 59.95 (*0-521-41900-X*) Cambridge U Pr.

Topics in Advanced Econometrics: Estimation, Testing & Specification of Cross-Section & Time Series Models. Herman J. Bierens. 270p. 1996. pap. text ed. 19.95 (*0-521-56511-1*) Cambridge U Pr.

***Topics in Advanced Emission Control & Diagnostic Sensors.** 1996. 36.00 (*1-56091-823-3*, SP-1180) Soc Auto Engineers.

Topics in Advanced Language Implementation. Peter Lee. 350p. 1990. 42.00 (*0-262-12151-4*) MIT Pr.

Topics in Advanced Scientific Computation. Richard E. Crandall. (Electronic Library of Science). 340p. 1995. 53.95 (*0-387-94473-7*) Spr-Verlag.

Topics in African Linguistics. Ed. by Salikoko Mufwene & Lioba Moshi. LC 93-5761. (Current Issues in Linguistic Theory Ser.: No. 100). x, 304p. 1993. 76.00 (*1-55619-553-2*) Benjamins North Am.

Topics in Algebra. 2nd ed. Israel N. Herstein. 432p. (C). 1975. Net. text ed. 61.00 (*0-471-01090-1*) Wiley.

Topics in Algebraic & Analytic Geometry. Phillip Griffiths. LC 74-2968. (Mathematical Notes Ser.: No. 13). 227p. 1974. pap. text ed. 35.00 (*0-691-08151-4*) Princeton U Pr.

Topics in Almost Everywhere Convergence. Adriano M. Garsia. (Wadsworth & Brooks-Cole Mathematics Ser.). 154p. (C). 1970. pap. text ed. 22.95 (*0-534-98045-7*) Chapman & Hall.

***Topics in Alternative Fuels & Their Emissions.** 1996. 99. 00 (*1-56091-865-9*, SP-1208) Soc Auto Engineers.

Topics in Applied Mechanics: Integration of Theory & Applications in Applied Mechanics. Ed. by J. F. Dijksman. LC 93-24466. 392p. (C). 1993. lib. bdg. 185. 00 (*0-7923-2442-0*) Kluwer Ac.

Topics in Artificial Intelligence: Proceedings Fourth Conference of the Italian Association for Artificial Intelligence, AI-IA '95, Florence, Italy, October 11-13, 1995. Ed. by Marco Gori & Giovanni Soda. (Lecture Notes in Computer Science Ser.: Vol. 992). 451p. 1995. 75.00 (*3-540-60437-5*) Spr-Verlag.

Topics in Atomic & Nuclear Collisions. Ed. by B. Remaud et al. (NATO ASI Series B, Physics: Vol. 321). (Illus.). 456p. (C). 1994. 125.00 (*0-306-44662-6*, Plenum Pr) Plenum.

***Topics in Atomic Collision Theory.** Sydney Geltman. LC 96-50398. (Illus.). 256p. 1997. reprint ed. 30.50 (*1-57524-033-5*) Krieger.

***Topics in Automotive Filtration Design.** 1997. 49.00 (*1-56091-964-7*) Soc Auto Engineers.

Topics in Behavioral Medicine: Annual Series of European Research in Behavior Therapy, Vol. 1. Ed. by J. Vinck. vii, 348p. 1986. pap. 52.00 (*90-265-0762-3*) Swets.

Topics in Bifurcation Theory & Applications. Gerard Iooss & Moritz Adelmeyer. LC 92-10267. (Advanced Series in Nonlinear Dynamics: Vol. 3). 130p. 1992. text ed. 32.00 (*981-02-1009-4*) World Scientific Pub.

Topics in Bioelectrochemistry & Bioenergetics, 2 vols., 4. Ed. by Giulio Milazzo. LC 76-18231. 356p. reprint ed. pap. 101.50 (*0-685-20645-9*, 2030431) Bks Demand.

Topics in Bioelectrochemistry & Bioenergetics, 2 vols., 5. Ed. by Giulio Milazzo. LC 76-18231. 356p. reprint ed. pap. 91.00 (*0-685-44058-3*, 2030431) Bks Demand.

Topics in Biological Monitoring. 123p. 1995. pap. 36.00 (*1-882417-10-0*, 9536) Am Conf Govt Indus Hygienist.

Topics in Blood Banking. Neva M. Abelson. LC 74-8253. 171p. reprint ed. pap. 48.80 (*0-317-26672-1*, 2055994) Bks Demand.

Topics in Boundary Elements Research--Complete Series, 7 vols., Set. Ed. by C. A. Brebbia. (Topics in BE Research Ser.). 1990. 239.00 (*1-56252-292-2*) Computational Mech MA.

Topics in Boundary Elements Research Plus BE Techniques, 8 vols., Set. Ed. by C. A. Brebbia. (Topics in BE Research Ser.). 1990. 284.00 (*1-56252-293-0*) Computational Mech MA.

Topics in C Programming, Revised. Stephen G. Kochan. LC 91-3727. 528p. 1991. pap. text ed. 29.95 (*0-471-53404-8*) Wiley.

Topics in Calculus of Variations. Ed. by Mariano Giaquinta. (Lecture Notes in Mathematics Ser.: Vol. 1365). x, 196p. 1989. 37.95 (*0-387-50727-2*) Spr-Verlag.

Topics in Carbocyclic Chemistry, Vol. 1. Ed. by Douglas R. Lloyd. LC 74-80937. 383p. reprint ed. pap. 109.20 (*0-685-15923-X*, 2026310) Bks Demand.

Topics in Carbon-13 NMR Spectroscopy, Vol. 4. Ed. by George C. Levy. (Topics in Carbon-13 NMR Spectroscopy Ser.: 1-683). 282p. 1984. text ed. 155.00 (*0-471-09857-4*) Wiley.

Topics in Case-Based Reasoning, Vol. 837. Joerg H. Siekmann. (Lecture Notes in Artificial Intelligence Ser.). 471p. 1994. 65.95 (*0-387-58330-0*) Spr-Verlag.

Topics in Chemistry. 2nd ed. Hageman. 1994. pap. text ed. write for info. (*0-07-025455-9*) McGraw.

Topics in Child Neurology, Vol. 2. Ed. by G. Wise et al. (Illus.). 280p. 1983. text ed. 42.50 (*0-88331-207-7*) Luce.

***Topics in Classical Automorphic Forms.** Henryk Iwaniec. LC 97-24332. (Graduate Studies in Mathematics). 1997. write for info. (*0-8218-0777-3*) Am Math.

***Topics in Clinical Cardiology: Indications for Diagnostic Procedures.** Ed. by Albert E. Raizner. LC 96-30883. (Topics in Clinical Cardiology Ser.). (Illus.). 216p. 1996. 69.50 (*0-89640-318-1*) Igaku-Shoin.

***Topics in Clinical Cardiology: Indications for Diagnostic Procedures.** Albert E. Raizner. LC 96-30883. (Topics in Clinical Cardiology Ser.). 1996. write for info. (*4-260-14318-2*) Igaku-Shoin.

Topics in Clinical Pharmacology & Therapeutics. Ed. by R. F. Maronde. (Illus.). 530p. 1986. 138.00 (*0-387-96196-8*) Spr-Verlag.

Topics in Coding Theory. G. H. Einarsson et al. (Lecture Notes in Control & Information Sciences Ser.: Vol. 128). vii, 176p. 1989. pap. 31.00 (*0-387-51405-8*) Spr-Verlag.

Topics in Cohomology of Groups, Vol. 162. S. Lang. LC 96-26607. (Lecture Notes in Mathematics Ser.). 226p. 1996. 43.00 (*3-540-61181-9*) Spr-Verlag.

Topics in Colloquial Russian. Ed. by Margaret H. Mills. LC 90-20776. (American University Studies: Slavic Languages & Literature: Ser. XII, Vol. 11). 203p. (C). 1991. text ed. 36.95 (*0-8204-1251-1*) P Lang Pubng.

Topics in Combinatorial Group Theory. Gilbert Baumslag. LC 93-8950. (Lectures in Mathematics ETH Zurich). 164p. 1993. 34.50 (*0-8176-2921-1*) Birkhauser.

Topics in Combinatorics & Graph Theory: Essays in Honour of Gerhard Ringel. Ed. by R. Bodendiek & R. Henn. (Illus.). xx, 792p. 1992. 140.95 (*0-387-91373-4*) Spr-Verlag.

Topics in Communication. W. J. Haynie. (Tech & Industrial Education Ser.). 1995. teacher ed. 14.00 (*0-8273-6715-5*) Delmar.

Topics in Communications Theory. David Middleton. LC 64-25001. 126p. 1987. reprint ed. 19.95 (*0-932146-14-7*) Peninsula CA.

Topics in Complex Analysis. Mats Andersson. LC 96-11793. (Universitext Ser.). 168p. 1996. pap. 32.50 (*0-387-94754-X*) Spr-Verlag.

Topics in Complex Analysis. Ed. by D. Shaffer. LC 84-24550. (Contemporary Mathematics Ser.: Vol. 38). 141p. 1985. pap. 26.00 (*0-8218-5037-7*, CONM/38) Am Math.

Topics in Complex Function Theory, Vol. 3: Abelian Functions & Modular Functions of Several Variables, Vol. 3. Carl L. Siegel. 244p. 1989. pap. text ed. 62.95 (*0-471-50401-7*) Wiley.

Topics in Complex Functions, 2 vols., Vol. 1: Elliptic Functions & Uniformization Theory. Carl L. Siegel. (Classics Library). 186p. 1988. pap. text ed. 64.95 (*0-471-60844-0*) Wiley.

Topics in Complex Functions, 2 vols., Vol. 2. Carl L. Siegel. (Classics Library). 193p. 1988. pap. text ed. 62.95 (*0-471-60843-2*) Wiley.

***Topics in Computational Group Theory.** Robertson. (C). (gr. 13 up). 1997. text ed. write for info. (*0-412-31000-7*) Chapman & Hall.

Topics in Condensed Matter Physics. Ed. by M. P. Das. (Illus.). 297p. (C). 1994. lib. bdg. 89.00 (*1-56072-180-4*) Nova Sci Pubs.

Topics in Conditional Logic. Donald Nute. (Philosophical Studies in Philosophy: No. 20). 168p. 1980. lib. bdg. 82. 50 (*90-277-1049-X*, D Reidel) Kluwer Ac.

Topics in Contemporary Mathematics. 4th ed. Britton. 1989. text ed. 73.00 (*0-02-308061-2*, Macmillan Coll) P-H.

Topics in Contemporary Mathematics. 5th ed. Ignacio Bello & Jack R. Britton. 896p. (C). 1993. text ed. 57.16 (*0-669-28957-4*); Instr.'s guide. teacher ed. 2.66 (*0-669-28958-2*); Student solution guide. student ed. 21. 96 (*0-669-28959-0*); CLAST study guide. student ed. write for info. (*0-669-28960-4*) HM College Div.

***Topics in Contemporary Mathematics.** 6th ed. Ignacio Bello & Jack R. Britton. 800p. (C). 1997. text ed. 57.16 (*0-669-41784-X*) HM College Div.

***Topics in Contemporary Mathematics.** 6th ed. Ignacio Bello & Jack R. Britton. (C). 1997. student ed., text ed. 21.96 (*0-669-41786-6*) HM College Div.

Topics in Contemporary Probability and Its Applications. Compiled by J. Laurie Snell. LC 94-23472. (Probability & Stochastics Ser.). 400p. 1995. 69.95 (*0-8493-8073-1*) CRC Pr.

Topics in Control Theory. Hans W. Knobloch et al. LC 93-39836. (DMV Seminar Ser.). 1993. 39.50 (*0-8176-2953-X*) Birkhauser.

***Topics in Controlled Markov Chains.** Borkar. (C). 1996. text ed. 57.50 (*0-582-06821-5*, Pub. by Longman UK) Longman.

***Topics in Controlled Markov Chains.** Vivek S. Borkar. LC 90-42154. (Pitman Research Notes in Mathematics Ser.: Vol. 240). 191p. 1991. reprint ed. pap. 54.50 (*0-608-03595-5*, 2064418) Bks Demand.

Topics in Current Aerosol Research, Pt. 1 see International Reviews in Aerosol Physics & Chemistry

Topics in Current Chemistry: Cyclophanes, Vol. 172. Ed. by E. Weber. 205p. 1994. 157.95 (*0-387-58257-6*) Spr-Verlag.

***Topics in Current Chemistry: Electrochemistry VI, Vol. 185.** Ed. by E. Steckhan. (Illus.). 215p. 1996. 139.50 (*3-540-61454-0*) Spr-Verlag.

Topics in Current Chemistry: Electronic & Vibronic Spectra of Transition Metal Complexes, Vol. 171. H. Yersin. 206p. 1994. 157.95 (*0-387-58155-3*) Spr-Verlag.

***Topics in Current Chemistry: Organolanthoid Chemistry-Synthesis, Structure, Catalysis, Vol. 179.** Ed. by W. A. Hermann. (Illus.). viii, 225p. 1996. 170.00 (*3-540-61009-X*) Spr-Verlag.

Topics in Current Chemistry Vol. 176: Technetium & Rhenium, Their Chemistry & Its Applications. Ed. by K. Yoshibara & T. Omori. (Illus.). 379p. 1995. 240.95 (*3-540-59469-8*) Spr-Verlag.

Topics in Current Chemistry Vol. 177: Electron Transfer II. Ed. by J. Mattay et al. (Illus.). viii, 268p. 1995. 207.95 (*3-540-60110-4*) Spr-Verlag.

***Topics in Current Chemistry Vol. 180: Density Functional Theory I.** Ed. by R. F. Nalewajski. XIV, 252p. 1996. 149.50 (*3-540-61091-X*) Spr-Verlag.

***Topics in Current Chemistry Vol. 181: Density Functional Theory II.** Ed. by R. F. Nalewajski. XIV, 206p. 1996. 146.00 (*3-540-61092-8*) Spr-Verlag.

***Topics in Current Chemistry Vol. 182: Density Functional Theory III.** Ed. by R. F. Nalewajski. XIV, 175p. 1996. 125.00 (*3-540-61132-0*) Spr-Verlag.

***Topics in Current Chemistry Vol. 183: Density Functional Theory IV.** Ed. by R. F. Nalewajski. XIV, 205p. 1996. 139.50 (*3-540-61131-2*) Spr-Verlag.

***Topics in Current Chemistry Vol. 184: Bioorganic Chemistry.** Ed. by F. P. Schmidtchen. X, 195p. 1996. 139.50 (*3-540-61388-9*) Spr-Verlag.

***Topics in Current Chemistry Vol. 190: Stereoselective Heterocyclic Synthesis II.** Ed. by P. Metz. (Illus.). 180p. 1997. 109.00 (*3-540-62700-6*) Spr-Verlag.

Topics in Differential & Integral Equations & Operator Theory. M. G. Krein. (Operator Theory, Advances & Applications Ser.: Vol. 7). 312p. (C). 1983. 71.00 (*0-8176-1517-2*) Birkhauser.

Topics in Distributed Algorithms. Gerard Tel. (International Series on Parallel Computation: No. 1). 250p. (C). 1991. text ed. 52.95 (*0-521-40376-6*) Cambridge U Pr.

Topics in Dynamic Bifurcation Theory. Jack K. Hale. LC 81-3445. (CBMS Regional Conference Series in Mathematics: No. 47). 84p. 1981. reprint ed. pap. 11.00 (*0-8218-1698-5*, CBMS/47) Am Math.

***Topics in Early Childhood Education: Playing for Keeps, Vol. 2.** Ed. by Amy L. Phillips. LC 96-35870. (Topics for Early Childhood Education). 192p. (Orig.). (C). 1996. pap. 14.95 (*1-884834-29-9*) Redleaf Pr.

Topics in Education: Lectures on the Philosophy of Education. Bernard Lonergan. Ed. by Robert M. Doran & Frederick E. Crowe. (Collected Works of Bernard Lonergan: No. 10). 304p. 1993. 60.00 (*0-8020-3440-3*); pap. 24.95 (*0-8020-3441-1*) U of Toronto Pr.

***Topics in Electroweak Physics.** 550p. 1997. 65.00 (*981-02-3040-0*) World Scientific Pub.

Topics in Engineering Mathematics: Modeling & Methods. Ed. by Adriaan Van der Burgh & Juriaan Simonis. LC 92-33608. (Mathematics & Its Applications Ser.: Vol. 81). 280p. (C). 1992. lib. bdg. 145.00 (*0-7923-2005-0*) Kluwer Ac.

Topics in Engineering Meteorology. J. M. Biggs et al. (Meteorological Monograph: Vol. 4, No. 22). (Illus.). 98p. 1960. pap. 17.00 (*0-933876-10-6*) Am Meteorological.

***Topics in Environmental Epidemiology.** David A. Savitz. (Illus.). 376p. 1997. text ed. 49.50 (*0-19-509564-2*) OUP.

Topics in Ergodic Theory. Ya G. Sinai. LC 93-16644. (Mathematical Ser.: No. 44). (Illus.). 120p. 1993. text ed. 45.00 (*0-691-03277-7*) Princeton U Pr.

Topics in Finance: A Guide for the Financially Perplexed. Katz & Friedman. 1992. pap. text ed. write for info. (*0-07-033756-X*) McGraw.

Topics in Finite Elasticity. M. E. Gurtin. LC 80-53711. (CBMS-NSF Regional Conference Series in Applied Mathematics: No. 35). v, 58p. 1981. pap. text ed. 16.00 (*0-89871-168-1*) Soc Indus-Appl Math.

Topics in Finite Mathematics. Samuel W. Spero. LC 92-39060. 1992. write for info. (*0-00-650030-7*) HarpC.

Topics in Fluid Film Bearing & Rotor Bearing Systems Design & Optimization: Presented at the Design Engineering Conference, Chicago, Ill., April 17-20, 1978. Fluid Film Bearing Committee of the Lubrication Division. Ed. by S. M. Rohde et al. LC 78-52526. 280p. reprint ed. pap. 79.80 (*0-317-11248-1*, 2017648) Bks Demand.

Topics in Fluid Mechanics. Rene Chevray & Jean Mathieu. LC 92-10886. (Illus.). 429p. (C). 1993. text ed. 150.00 (*0-521-41082-7*); pap. text ed. 52.95 (*0-521-42272-8*) Cambridge U Pr.

***Topics in Fluorescence Spectroscopy.** Ed. by J. R. Lakowicz. (Illus.). 460p. (C). 1997. write for info. (*0-306-45553-6*, Plenum Pr) Plenum.

Topics in Fluorescence Spectroscopy, 4. Ed. by J. R. Lakowicz. (Illus.). 530p. (C). 1994. 95.00 (*0-306-44784-3*, Plenum Pr) Plenum.

Topics in Fluorescence Spectroscopy, Vol. 1: Techniques. Ed. by Joseph R. Lakowicz. (Illus.). 460p. 1991. 95.00 (*0-306-43874-7*, Plenum Pr) Plenum.

Topics in Fluorescence Spectroscopy, Vol. 2: Principles. Ed. by Joseph R. Lakowicz. (Illus.). 466p. 1991. 95.00 (*0-306-43875-5*, Plenum Pr) Plenum.

Topics in Fluorescence Spectroscopy, Vol. 3: Biochemical Applications. Ed. by Joseph R. Lakowicz. (Illus.). 406p. 1991. 95.00 (*0-306-43954-9*, Plenum Pr) Plenum.

Topics in Fourier Analysis & Function Spaces. Hans-Jurgen Schmeisser & Hans Triebel. 300p. 1987. text ed. 125.00 (*0-471-90895-9*) Wiley.

Topics in Fourier & Geometric Analysis. Victor L. Shapiro. LC 52-42839. (Memoirs Ser.: No. 1/39). 100p. 1988. reprint ed. pap. 17.00 (*0-8218-1239-4*, MEMO/1/39) Am Math.

Topics in Fracture & Fatigue. Ed. by A. S. Argon. (Illus.). 346p. 1992. 109.95 (*0-387-97833-X*) Spr-Verlag.

Topics in French Syntax. rev. ed. Geraldine Legendre. Ed. by Jorge Hankamer. LC 93-46502. (Outstanding Dissertations in Linguistics Ser.). (Illus.). 346p. 1994. text ed. 20.00 (*0-8153-1689-5*) Garland.

Topics in Galois Theory. Jean-Pierre Serre. LC 91-42857. (Research Notes in Mathematics Ser.). 144p. 1992. pap. text ed. 29.95 (*0-86720-210-6*) AK Peters.

Topics in General Relativity. Robert Hermann. (Interdisciplinary Mathematics Ser.: No. 5). 161p. 1973. 25.00 (*0-915692-04-X*, 991600223) Math Sci Pr.

Topics in General Topology. Ed. by K. Morita & J. Nagata. (Mathematical Library: No. 41). 748p. 1989. 320.50 (*0-444-70455-8*, North Holland) Elsevier.

Topics in Geometry. Robert Bix. (Illus.). 538p. 1993. text ed. 67.00 (*0-12-102740-6*) Acad Pr.

Topics in Geometry. Howard Levi. LC 75-19477. 112p. 1976. reprint ed. 13.50 (*0-88275-280-4*) Krieger.

Topics in Geometry: In Memory of Joseph D'Atri. S. Gindikin. LC 96-1703. (Progress in Nonlinear Differential Equations & Their Applications Ser.: Vol. 20). 368p. 1996. 79.50 (*0-8176-3828-8*) Spr-Verlag.

Topics in Geophysical Fluid Dynamics: Atmospheric Dynamics, Dynamo Theory & Climate Dynamics. M. Ghil & S. Childress. (Applied Mathematical Sciences Ser.: Vol. 60). (Illus.). 500p. 1987. 59.95 (*0-387-96475-4*) Spr-Verlag.

Topics in Gerontology: Selected Annotated Bibliographies. Ed. by Thomas O. Blank. LC 93-9311. (Bibliographies & Indexes in Gerontology Ser.: No. 22). 256p. 1993. text ed. 65.00 (*0-313-28337-0*, BTY/, Greenwood Pr) Greenwood.

An Asterisk (*) at the beginning of an entry indicates that the title is appearing in BIP for the first time.

Topics in Graph Theory. Ed. by Frank Harary et al. (Annals Ser.: Vol. 328). 206p. (Orig.). 1979. write for info. (*0-89766-028-5*); pap. 42.00 (*0-89766-029-3*) NY Acad Sci.

Topics in Group Rings. Sehgal. (Pure & Applied Mathematics Ser.: Vol. 50). (Illus.). 264p. 1978. 125.00 (*0-8247-6755-1*) Dekker.

Topics in Growth & Device Processing of III-V Semiconductor. S. J. Pearton et al. 400p. 1996. text ed. 81.00 (*981-02-1884-2*) World Scientific Pub.

Topics in Hadron Spectroscopy. Ed. by David C. Peaslee. 285p. (C). 1992. lib. bdg. 115.00 (*1-56072-036-0*) Nova Sci Pubs.

Topics in Hadron Spectroscopy, Vol. 3. Ed. by David C. Peaslee. 202p. (C). 1995. lib. bdg. 95.00 (*1-56072-225-8*) Nova Sci Pubs.

Topics in Hadron Spectroscopy Vol. 2. Ed. by David C. Peaselee. 247p. (C). 1995. lib. bdg. 95.00 (*1-56072-224-X*) Nova Sci Pubs.

Topics in Hardy Classes & Univalent Functions. Marvin Rosenblum & James Rovnyak. LC 94-23454. (Baser Lehrb Ucher). 1994. write for info. (*3-7643-5111-X*) Birkhauser.

Topics in Hardy Classes & Univalent Functions. Marvin Rosenblum & James Rovnyak. LC 94-23454. (Baser Lehrb Ucher). xii, 250p. 1994. 49.50 (*0-8176-5111-X*) Birkhauser.

Topics in Harmonic Analysis. Charles F. Dunkl & Donald E. Ramirez. LC 73-153387. (Century Mathematics Ser.). (C). 1971. 34.50 (*0-89197-454-7*) Irvington.

Topics in Harmonic Analysis on Homogeneous Spaces. Sigurdur Helgason. (Progress in Mathematics Ser.: No. 13). 160p. 1990. 45.00 (*0-8176-3051-1*) Birkhauser.

***Topics in Health Psychology.** Ed. by Stan Maes et al. LC 88-5646. (Illus.). 330p. reprint ed. pap. 94.10 (*0-608-05264-7*, 2065802) Bks Demand.

Topics in Heterocyclic Chemistry. Ed. by Raymond N. Castle. LC 71-78478. 276p. reprint ed. pap. 78.70 (*0-317-08776-2*, 2011959) Bks Demand.

Topics in Human Factors Research. John Schmid et al. 418p. (C). 1972. pap. text ed. 12.95 (*0-8422-0186-6*) Irvington.

Topics in Imaging Processing Techniques in Cardiac Dynamics: Special Issue Journal Automedica, Vol. 10, No. 1. Ed. by Michiyoshi Kuwahara & Barry W. Hyndman. 92p. 1988. text ed. 240.00 (*0-677-25710-4*) Gordon & Breach.

Topics in Integral Geometry. D. L. Ren. 256p. 1994. text ed. 55.00 (*981-02-1101-5*); pap. text ed. 32.00 (*981-02-1107-4*) World Scientific Pub.

Topics in Intermediate Statistical Methods. Theodore A. Bancroft. LC 68-17487. 143p. 1968. reprint ed. pap. 40.80 (*0-608-00156-2*, 2060937) Bks Demand.

***Topics in Interpolation Theory.** H. Dym. LC 97-8157. (Operator Theory, Advances & Applications Ser.). 1997. write for info. (*0-8176-5723-1*); write for info. (*3-7643-5723-1*) Birkhauser.

Topics in Interpolation Theory of Rational Matrix Valued Functions. I. Gohberg. (Operator Theory Ser.: No. 33). 256p. 1988. 110.00 (*0-8176-2233-0*) Birkhauser.

Topics in Interstellar Matter. Ed. by Hugo Van Woerden. (Astrophysics & Space Science Library: No. 70). 1977. lib. bdg. 104.50 (*90-277-0835-5*) Kluwer Ac.

Topics in Language Disorders Series, 8 vols., Set. Ed. by Katharine G. Butler. 1900p. 1994. 198.00 (*0-8342-0590-4*) Aspen Pub.

Topics in Management Science. 3rd ed. Robert D. Markland. LC 88-33751. 847p. 1989. Net. text ed. 49.50 (*0-471-61786-5*) Wiley.

Topics in Math. Betty Cornelius & Edith Silver. 1988. spiral bd. 53.00 (*0-88252-156-X*) Paladin Hse.

Topics in Mathematical Analysis. Themistocles M. Rassias. 992p. (C). 1989. pap. 55.00 (*9971-5-0801-X*); text ed. 147.00 (*9971-5-0666-1*) World Scientific Pub.

***Topics in Mathematical Analysis & Differential Geometry.** N. K. Laos. 600p. 1997. text ed. 60.00 (*981-02-3180-6*) World Scientific Pub.

Topics in Mathematical Physics: Papers Presented at an International Symposium held July 28-August 2, 1975 at Bogazici University, Istanbul, Turkey. Ed. by Halis Odabasi & O. Akyuz. LC 77-84853. (Illus.). 291p. reprint ed. pap. 83.00 (*0-8357-5511-8*, 2035126) Bks Demand.

Topics in Mathematics. Steven Roman. (Illus.). 54p. (Orig.). (C). 1992. pap. text ed. write for info. (*1-878015-12-5*) Innov Textbooks.

Topics in Matrix Analysis. Roger A. Horn & Charles R. Johnson. (Illus.). 250p. 1991. text ed. 90.00 (*0-521-30587-X*) Cambridge U Pr.

Topics in Matrix Analysis. Roger A. Horn & Charles R. Johnson. 615p. 1994. pap. text ed. 35.95 (*0-521-46713-6*) Cambridge U Pr.

Topics in Matrix & Operator Theory: Workshop on, Rotterdam, Netherlands, June 26-29, 1989. Ed. by H. Bart et al. (Operator Theory Ser.: Vol. 50). 388p. 1991. 129.00 (*0-8176-2570-4*) Birkhauser.

Topics in Medicinal Chemistry, No. 65. Leeming. 1988. 143.00 (*0-85186-726-X*) CRC Pr.

Topics in Metallurgical Thermodynamics. Owen F. Devereux. LC 88-13172. 508p. (C). 1989. reprint ed. lib. bdg. 57.50 (*0-89464-329-0*) Krieger.

Topics in Metric Fixed Point Theory. K. Goebel & W. A. Kirk. (Cambridge Studies in Advanced Mathematics: No. 28). 365p. (C). 1990. text ed. 59.95 (*0-521-38289-0*) Cambridge U Pr.

Topics in Micrometerology: A Festschrift for Arch Dyer. Ed. by B. B. Hicks. (C). 1988. lib. bdg. 113.50 (*90-277-2694-9*) Kluwer Ac.

Topics in Modern Mathematics: Petrovskii Seminar, No. 5. Ed. by O. A. Oleinik. LC 84-14291. (Contemporary Soviet Mathematics Ser.). 346p. 1985. 110.00 (*0-306-10980-8*, Consultants) Plenum.

Topics in Modern Physics: A Tribute to Edward U. Condon. Ed. by Wesley E. Brittin & Halis Odabasi. LC 70-135286. (Illus.). 392p. reprint ed. pap. 111.80 (*0-8357-5524-X*, 2035140) Bks Demand.

Topics in Nevanlinna Theory. Serge A. Lang & W. Cherry. Ed. by A. Dold et al. (Lecture Notes in Mathematics Ser.: Vol. 1433). (Illus.). ii, 174p. 1990. 34.95 (*0-387-52785-0*) Spr-Verlag.

Topics in Nevome Syntax. David L. Shaul. LC 86-16095. (University of California Publications in Entomology: No. 109). 152p. 1986. pap. 43.40 (*0-7837-8426-0*, 2049228) Bks Demand.

Topics in Non-Gaussian Signal Processing. Ed. by E. J. Wegman et al. (Illus.). xii, 235p. 1988. 58.00 (*0-387-96927-6*) Spr-Verlag.

Topics in Noncommutative Geometry. Yuri I. Manin. 163p. 1991. text ed. 39.50 (*0-691-08588-9*) Princeton U Pr.

***Topics in Nonlinear Analysis & Applications.** 700p. 1997. 81.00 (*981-02-2534-2*) World Scientific Pub.

***Topics in Nonlinear Dynamics: Applications to Physics, Biology & Economic Systems.** 300p. 1997. lib. bdg. 34.00 (*981-02-2764-7*) World Scientific Pub.

Topics in Nonlinear Dynamics with Computer Algebra. Richard Rand. LC 94-2869. (Computers in Education Ser.: Vol. 1). xi, 229p. 1994. text ed. 48.00 (*2-88449-113-9*); pap. text ed. 22.00 (*2-88449-114-7*) Gordon & Breach.

Topics in Nonparametric Estimation. Ed. by R. Z. Khasminskii. LC 91-640741. (Advances in Soviet Mathematics Ser.: Vol. 12). 150p. 1992. 99.00 (*0-8218-4111-4*, ADVSOV/12C) Am Math.

Topics in Nonsmooth Mechanics. J. J. Moreau et al. 320p. 1988. 267.00 (*0-8176-1907-0*) Birkhauser.

Topics in Northern Pomo Grammar. Mary C. O'Connor. LC 92-13239. (Outstanding Dissertations in Linguistics Ser.). 360p. 1992. text ed. 28.00 (*0-8153-0700-4*) Garland.

Topics in Number Theory. J. S. Chahal. (University Series in Mathematics). (Illus.). 183p. 1988. 65.00 (*0-306-42866-0*, Plenum Pr) Plenum.

Topics in Ocean Engineering, 3 vols., 1. Charles L. Bretschneider. LC 78-87230. (Illus.). 231p. reprint ed. pap. 122.60 (*0-685-23777-X*, 2032860) Bks Demand.

Topics in Ocean Engineering, 3 vols., 2. Charles L. Bretschneider. LC 78-87230. (Illus.). 231p. reprint ed. pap. 106.10 (*0-685-23778-8*, 2032860) Bks Demand.

Topics in Ocean Engineering, 3 vols., 3. Charles L. Bretschneider. LC 78-87230. (Illus.). 231p. reprint ed. pap. 65.90 (*0-685-23779-6*, 2032860) Bks Demand.

Topics in One-Parameter Bifurcation Problems. P. J. Rabier. (Tata Institute Lectures on Mathematics). vi, 290p. 1985. 42.95 (*0-387-13907-9*) Spr-Verlag.

Topics in Operator Theory. Ed. by L. De Branges et al. (Operator Theory Ser.: Vol. 48). 464p. 1990. 139.00 (*0-8176-2532-1*) Birkhauser.

Topics in Operator Theory. I. Gohberg. (Operator Theory Ser.: No. 32). 288p. 1988. 122.00 (*0-8176-2232-2*) Birkhauser.

Topics in Operator Theory. Ed. by Carl M. Pearcy. LC 74-8254. (Mathematical Surveys & Monographs: No. 13). 235p. 1974. reprint ed. pap. 44.00 (*0-8218-1513-X*, SURV/13) Am Math.

Topics in Operator Theory & Interpolation. Ed. by I. Gohberg. (Operator Theory Ser.: No. 29). 243p. 1988. 105.00 (*0-8176-1960-7*) Birkhauser.

Topics in Operator Theory Systems & Networks, Vol. 12. Ed. by Harry Dym et al. (Operator Theory Ser.). 300p. 1984. 75.00 (*3-7643-1550-4*) Birkhauser.

Topics in Ophthalmolgy. Jack J. Kanski. 1985. write for info. (*0-7020-1103-7*) Saunders.

Topics in Ordinary Differential Equations. William D. Laken & David A. Sanchez. 160p. 1982. reprint ed. pap. 5.95 (*0-486-61606-1*) Dover.

Topics in Organic Electrochemistry. Ed. by Albert J. Fry & Wayne E. Britton. 310p. 1986. 85.00 (*0-306-42058-9*, Plenum Pr) Plenum.

***Topics in Palliative Care, Vol. 1.** Ed. by Russell K. Portenoy & Eduardo Bruera. (Illus.). 328p. 1997. 46.95 (*0-19-510244-4*) OUP.

Topics in Parallel Computation: A Guide to the Theory of P-Completeness. Raymond Greenlaw et al. (Illus.). 320p. 1995. text ed. 59.00 (*0-19-508591-4*) OUP.

Topics in Parallel Computing in Mathematical Programming. J. B. Rosen et al. Ed. by Du Dingzhu. (Applied Discrete Mathematics & Theoretical Computer Science Ser.: Vol. 2). 124p. 1993. 32.95 (*1-880132-11-7*) Sci Pr NY.

Topics in Pathology for Hong Kong. Ed. by C. S. Ho & P. C. Wu. (Illus.). 170p. (Orig.). 1995. pap. 42.50 (*0-614-96354-0*) Coronet Bks.

Topics in Pathology for Hong Kong. Ed. by Faith Ho & P. C. Wu. 176p. (Orig.). 1995. pap. 37.00 (*962-209-336-1*, Pub. by Hong Kong U Pr HK) St Mut.

Topics in Pathophysiology of Hypertension. Ed. by Herman Villarreal & Mohinder P. Sambhi. 1983. lib. bdg. 281.50 (*0-89838-595-4*) Kluwer Ac.

Topics in Pediatrics: A Festschrift for Lewis A. Barness. Ed. by H. H. Pomerance & B. B. Bercu. xxvi, 307p. 1990. 162.00 (*0-387-96964-0*) Spr-Verlag.

Topics in Pharmaceutical Science, 1991. Crommelin. 1992. 143.00 (*3-88763-016-5*) CRC Pr.

***Topics in Phosphate Chemistry.** M. Averbuch-Pouchot & A. Durif. LC 96-28448. 420p. 1996. write for info. (*981-02-2634-9*) World Scientific Pub.

Topics in Photomedicine. Ed. by Kendric C. Smith. LC 83-24509. 412p. 1984. 110.00 (*0-306-41510-0*, Plenum Pr) Plenum.

Topics in Physical Geometry. Robert Hermann. (Interdisciplinary Mathematics Ser.: Vol. XXIV). 595p. (C). 1988. text ed. 85.00 (*0-915692-40-6*) Math Sci Pr.

Topics in Plant Population Biology. Ed. by Otto T. Solbrig et al. LC 78-27630. (Illus.). 607p. reprint ed. pap. 173.00 (*0-8357-4577-5*, 2037486) Bks Demand.

Topics in Policy Appraisal. Ed. by V. N. Balasubramanyam & John M. Bates. (Case Studies in Economic Development: Vol. 2). 192p. (C). 1993. text ed. 75.00 (*0-312-08546-X*) St Martin.

Topics in Polynomials: Extremal Problems, Inequalities, Zeros. G. V. Milovanovic et al. 300p. 1994. text ed. 146.00 (*981-02-0499-X*) World Scientific Pub.

Topics in Polynomials of One & Several Variables & Their Applications. Themistocles M. Rassias et al. 500p. (C). 1993. text ed. 127.00 (*981-02-0614-3*) World Scientific Pub.

Topics in Population Genetics. Bruce Wallace. (C). 1968. text ed. 24.95 (*0-393-09813-3*) Norton.

Topics in Preventive Psychiatry. Ed. by G. N. Christodoulou & V. Kontaxakis. (Bibliotheca Psychiatrica Ser.: No. 165). (Illus.). viii, 152p. 1994. 121.75 (*3-8055-5877-5*) S Karger.

Topics in Production Theory. Ed. by Finn R. Forsund. LC 83-40610. 220p. 1984. text ed. 32.50 (*0-312-80914-X*) St Martin.

***Topics in Pseudo-Differential Operators.** LC 96-31181. (Pitman Research Notes in Mathematics Ser.). 1997. pap. 37.48 (*0-582-27782-5*) Longman.

Topics in Psychology. 4th ed. Anthony Fazio. 76p. (C). 1996. per., pap. text ed. 14.51 (*0-7872-0431-5*) Kendall-Hunt.

***Topics in Public Economics: Theoretical & Applied Analysis.** Ed. by David Pines et al. (Illus.). 384p. (C). 1997. text ed. 59.95 (*0-521-56136-1*) Cambridge U Pr.

Topics in Quantum Field Theory: Modern Methods in Fundamental Physics. D. H. Tchrakian. 200p. 1995. text ed. 56.00 (*981-02-2350-1*) World Scientific Pub.

Topics in Radioelectronic & Laser System Design. Ed. by I. Fedorov. Tr. by M. Edelev from RUS. (Advances in Science & Technology in the U. S. S. R. Ser.). 256p. 1992. 83.00 (*0-8493-7544-4*, TA1750) CRC Pr.

Topics in Representation Theory. A. A. Kirillov. LC 90-26017. (Advances in Soviet Mathematics Ser.: Vol. 2). 247p. 1991. 86.00 (*0-8218-4101-7*, ADVSOV/2) Am Math.

Topics in Respiratory & Comparative Physiology. Michael Meyer & Heisler. 1996. text ed. 60.00 (*0-89574-236-5*, Pub. by G Fischer Verlag GW) Lubrecht & Cramer.

Topics in Ring Theory. I. N. Herstein. LC 69-17035. (Chicago Lectures in Mathematics). 143p. reprint ed. pap. 40.80 (*0-685-23857-1*, 2056642) Bks Demand.

Topics in Rolling Bearing Technology. Tedric A. Harris. LC 87-4987. 1988. write for info. (*0-471-83039-9*) Wiley.

Topics in Scandinavian Syntax. Ed. by Lars Hellan & Kirsti K. Christiansen. 1986. lib. bdg. 136.00 (*90-277-2166-1*) Kluwer Ac.

Topics in Semiconductor Physics: Selected Papers from the First Regional Workshop, Bangkok, Thailand. Ed. by W. Sritrakool & V. Sa-Yakanit. 224p. 1988. text ed. 70.00 (*9971-5-0670-X*) World Scientific Pub.

Topics in Set Theory: Lebesgue Measurability, Large Cardinals, Forcing Axioms, Rho-Functions. M. Bekkali. (Lecture Notes in Mathematics Ser.: Vol. 1476). vii, 120p. 1991. pap. 24.00 (*0-387-54121-7*) Spr-Verlag.

Topics in Slavic Phonology. Ed. by Demetrius J. Koubourlis. viii, 270p. 1974. 24.95 (*0-89357-017-6*) Slavica.

Topics in Social Choice: Sophisticated Voting, Efficacy & Proportional Representation. Dan S. Felsenthal. LC 89-23006. 240p. 1990. text ed. 55.00 (*0-275-93430-6*, C3430, Praeger Pubs) Greenwood.

***Topics in Soliton Theory.** R. W. Carroll. (North-Holland Mathematics Studies: Vol. 167). 428p. 1991. 144.00 (*0-444-88869-1*, North Holland) Elsevier.

Topics in Soliton Theory & Exactly Solvable Nonlinear Equations: Proceedings of the Conference, Oberwolfach, F R Germany, July 27-August 2, 1986. Ed. by M. D. Kruskal et al. 352p. (C). 1987. text ed. 89.00 (*9971-5-0253-4*) World Scientific Pub.

Topics in Sports Physical Therapy. Compiled by Sara Brown. 136p. (Orig.). (C). 1996. pap. text ed. write for info. (*1-57790-002-2*) Book Tech.

***Topics in Statistical & Theoretical Physics: F. A. Berezin Memorial Volume.** Ed. by R. L. Dobrushin et al. (Translations Ser. II: Vol. 177). 223p. 1996. 99.00 (*0-8218-0425-1*) Am Math.

Topics in Statistical Dependence. Ed. by H. W. Block et al. LC 91-71759. (IMS Lecture Notes - Monograph Ser.: Vol. 16). x, 522p. 1990. pap. 45.00 (*0-940600-23-4*) Inst Math.

Topics in Statistical Mechanics & Biophysics-A Memorial to Julius L. Jackson, No. 27. American Institute of Physics. Ed. by R. A. Piccirelli. LC 75-36309. (AIP Conference Proceedings Ser.). 209p. 1976. 17.00 (*0-88318-126-6*) Am Inst Physics.

Topics in Stereochemistry, Vol. 10. Ed. by Ernest L. Eliel & Norman L. Allinger. LC 67-13943. 365p. reprint ed. pap. 104.10 (*0-317-30020-2*, 2025020) Bks Demand.

Topics in Stereochemistry, Vol. 14. Ed. by Norman L. Allinger et al. 328p. 1983. 113.00 (*0-471-89858-9*) Krieger.

Topics in Stereochemistry, Vol. 18. Ed. by Ernest L. Eliel & Samuel H. Wilen. 346p. 1988. text ed. 205.00 (*0-471-60026-1*) Wiley.

Topics in Stereochemistry, Vol. 19. Ed. by Ernest L. Eliel & Norman L. Allinger. 424p. 1989. text ed. 190.00 (*0-471-50752-0*) Wiley.

Topics in Stereochemistry, Vol. 20. Ed. by Ernest L. Eliel et al. 344p. 1991. text ed. 196.00 (*0-471-50801-2*) Wiley.

Topics in Stereochemistry, Vol. 21. Ed. by Ernest L. Eliel & Samuel H. Wilen. 533p. 1994. text ed. 150.00 (*0-471-52120-5*) Wiley.

Topics in Stereochemistry, Vol. 11: 1979. Ernest L. Eliel. LC 67-13943. 356p. pap. 101.50 (*0-685-20437-5*, 2056446) Bks Demand.

Topics in Sterochemistry, Vol. 3. Ed. by Norman L. Eliel. LC 67-13943. 389p. reprint ed. pap. 110.90 (*0-317-08878-5*, 2055275) Bks Demand.

Topics in Stochastic Differential Equations. Daniel W. Stroock. (Tata Institute Lectures on Mathematics). 91p. 1983. 36.95 (*0-387-11549-8*) Spr-Verlag.

Topics in Stochastic Systems: Modelling, Estimation & Adaptive Control. Ed. by L. Gerencser et al. (Lecture Notes in Control & Information Sciences Ser.: Vol. 161). 465p. 1991. 80.95 (*0-387-54133-0*) Spr-Verlag.

Topics in Strong Interactions. Ed. by Asim O. Barut & Wesley E. Brittin. LC 72-197924. (Lectures in Theoretical Physics: No. 14A). (Illus.). 479p. reprint ed. pap. 136.60 (*0-8357-5512-6*, 2035127) Bks Demand.

Topics in Structural Mechanics. Wan. (International Journal of Solids & Structure). 1985. pap. 35.00 (*0-08-032788-5*, Pergamon Pr) Elsevier.

***Topics in Structural VAR Econometrics, Vol. XIII.** 2nd enl. rev. ed. Gianni Amisano & Carlo Giannini. LC 96-53414. (Illus.). 181p. 1997. 69.95 (*3-540-61942-9*) Spr-Verlag.

Topics in Surface Modeling. H. Hagen. LC 92-12065. (Miscellaneous Bks.: No. 30). ix, 219p. 1992. pap. 53.00 (*0-89871-282-3*) Soc Indus-Appl Math.

Topics in the Basic & Clinic. 1987. 108.00 (*0-387-81996-7*) Spr-Verlag.

Topics in the Calculus of Variation. Martin Fuchs. (Advanced Lectures in Mathematics Ser.). 145p. 1994. pap. 28.00 (*3-528-06623-7*) Informatica.

Topics in the Constructive Theory of Markov Chains. G. Fayolle et al. (Illus.). 175p. (C). 1995. text ed. 47.95 (*0-521-46197-9*) Cambridge U Pr.

Topics in the Economics of Aging. Ed. by David A. Wise. 326p. 1992. 63.50 (*0-226-90298-6*) U Ch Pr.

Topics in the Formal Methodology of Empirical Sciences. Ryszard Wojcicki. Tr. by Ewa Jansen from POL. (Synthese Library: No. 135). 290p. 1980. lib. bdg. 129.50 (*90-277-1004-X*, D Reidel) Kluwer Ac.

***Topics in the Foundation of Statistics.** Ed. by Bas C. Van Fraassen. LC 96-53321. (Spinoff FODA Ser.). 168p. (C). 1997. lib. bdg. 62.00 (*0-7923-4405-7*) Kluwer Ac.

Topics in the Geometric Theory of Integrable Systems. R. Hermann. (Interdisciplinary Mathematics Ser.: Vol. XXIII). 347p. 1984. 75.00 (*0-915692-36-8*, 991600169) Math Sci Pr.

Topics in the Geometric Theory of Linear Systems. R Hermann. (Interdisciplinary Mathematics Ser.: Vol. XXII). 281p. 1984. 65.00 (*0-915692-35-X*, 991600177) Math Sci Pr.

Topics in the Geometry of Projective Space: Recent Work of F. L. Zak. Ed. by P. F. Lazarsfeld & Van de Ven. (DMV Seminar Ser.: No. 4). 52p. 1985. 29.00 (*0-8176-1660-8*) Birkhauser.

Topics in the History of Psychology, Vol. I. Ed. by Gregory A. Kimble & Kurt Schlesinger. 424p. (C). 1985. text ed. 49.95 (*0-89859-311-5*) L Erlbaum Assocs.

Topics in the History of Psychology, Vol. II. Gregory A. Kimble & Kurt Schlesinger. 448p. (C). 1985. 49.95 (*0-89859-312-3*) L Erlbaum Assocs.

Topics in the Homological Theory of Modules over Commutative Rings. Melvin Hochster. LC 75-1325. (CBMS Regional Conference Series in Mathematics: No. 24). 75p. 1985. reprint ed. pap. 17.00 (*0-8218-1674-8*, CBMS/24) Am Math.

Topics in the Homology Theory of Fibre Bundles. Armand Borel. (Lecture Notes in Mathematics Ser.: Vol. 36). 1967. pap. 19.90 (*0-387-03907-4*) Spr-Verlag.

Topics in the Logic of Relevance. M. Richard Diaz. (Analytica Ser.). 144p. 1981. lib. bdg. 52.00 (*3-88405-003-6*) Philosophia Pr.

***Topics in the Mathematical Modelling of Composite Materials.** Ed. by Andrej Cherkaev & Robert V. Kohn. LC 97-180. (Progress in Nonlinear Differential Equations & Their Applications Ser.). 300p. 120.00 (*0-8176-3662-5*) Birkhauser.

Topics in the Mathematics of Quantum Mechanics. Robert Hermann. (Interdisciplinary Mathematics Ser.: No. 6). 250p. 1973. 32.00 (*0-915692-05-8*, 991600231) Math Sci Pr.

***Topics in the Structure of Russian: An Introduction to Russian Linguistics.** David K. Hart. (Illus.). x, 294p. (Orig.). (C). 1996. pap. text ed. 22.95 (*0-89357-268-3*) Slavica.

Topics in the Theoretical Bases & Applications of Computer Science: Proceedings of the 4th Hungarian Computer Science Conference, Gyor, Hungary, July 8-10, 1985. M. Arato et al. 513p. (C). 1986. 162.00 (*963-05-4242-0*, Pub. by Akad Kiado HU) St Mut.

Topics in the Theory of Generative Grammar. Noam Chomsky. (Janua Linguarum, Ser. Minor: No. 56). (Orig.). 1978. pap. text ed. 15.40 (*90-279-3122-4*) Mouton.

Topics in the Theory of Random Noise, 2 vols, Vol. 2. R. L. Stratonovich. (Mathematics & Its Applications Ser.). 1967. Set. text ed. 440.00 (*0-677-00800-7*); text ed. 257.00 (*0-677-00790-6*) Gordon & Breach.

Topics in the Theory of Riemann Surfaces. Robert D. Accola. LC 94-41550. (Lecture Notes in Mathematics Ser.: Vol. 1595). 1994. write for info. (*0-387-58721-7*) Spr-Verlag.

Topics in the Theory of Riemann Surfaces. Ed. by A. Dold et al. (Lecture Notes in Mathematics Ser.: Vol. 1595). 105p. 1994. 29.95 (*3-540-58721-7*) Spr-Verlag.

***Topics in Theoretical Physics.** 300p. 1997. text ed. 53.00 (*981-02-3083-4*) World Scientific Pub.

Topics in Therapeutics. Royal College of Physicians Staff. Ed. by A. M. Breckenridge. 1974. pap. text ed. 45.00 (*0-685-83077-2*) St Mut.

Topics in Therapeutics. Ed. by D. W. Vere. 224p. 1978. 32.00 (*0-8464-1144-X*) Beekman Pubs.

Topics in Therapeutics, 1976. Royal College of Physicians Staff. Ed. by R. G. Shanks. 1976. pap. text ed. 65.00 (*0-685-83078-0*) St Mut.

Topics in Topicals. Ed. by R. M. Marks. 1985. lib. bdg. 103.50 (*0-85200-891-0*) Kluwer Ac.

***Topics in Topology, Vol. 165.** Stevo Todorcevic. LC 97-7252. (Lecture Notes in Mathematics Ser.). 1997. pap. 33.00 (*3-540-62611-5*) Spr-Verlag.

Topics in Topology & Mathematical Physics. Ed. by S. P. Novikov. LC 91-640741. (American Mathematical Society Translations Ser.: Series 2, Vol. 170). 206p. 1995. 89.00 (*0-8218-0455-3*, TRANS2/170) Am Math.

Topics in Two-Phase Heat Transfer & Flow: Presented at the Winter Annual Meeting of ASME, San Francisco, CA, Dec. 10-15, 1978. Ed. by S. G. Bankoff. LC 78-68087. 239p. reprint ed. pap. 68.20 (*0-317-08175-6*, 2013876) Bks Demand.

Topics in Urology: New Diagnostic Tests. Ed. by Martin I. Resnick & J. Patrick Spirnak. LC 95-32007. (Topics in Clinical Urology Ser.). (Illus.). 216p. 1995. 69.50 (*0-89640-290-8*) Igaku-Shoin.

Topics in Vaccine Adjuvant Research. Spriggs & Koff. 168p. 1990. 129.95 (*0-8493-5719-5*, RC919) CRC Pr.

Topics in Validated Computations: Proceedings of IMACS-GAMM International Workshop on Validated Computations, Oldenburg, Germany, 30 August - 3 September, 1993. Ed. by Jurgen Herzberger. LC 94-36669. (Studies in Computational Mathematics: Vol. 5). 506p. 1994. 188.50 (*0-444-81685-2*) Elsevier.

Topics in Varieties of Group Representations. Samuel M. Vovsi. (London Mathematical Society Lecture Note Ser.: No. 163). (Illus.). 200p. (C). 1992. pap. text ed. 39.95 (*0-521-42410-0*) Cambridge U Pr.

***Topics in Vehicle Aerodynamics.** 1997. 74.00 (*1-56091-944-2*) Soc Auto Engineers.

Topics in Vehicle Safety Technology: 1996 International Congress & Exposition. (Special Publications). 21p. 1996. pap. 55.00 (*1-56091-769-5*, SP-1139) Soc Auto Engineers.

T

Topics in West African History. 2nd ed. A. Adu Boahen et al. 202p. (C). 1986. pap. text ed. 29.50 (*0-582-58504-X*, 74457) Longman.

***Topics of Complex Analysis, Differential Geometry & Methematical Physics.** 230p. 1997. text ed. 40.00 (*981-02-3194-6*) World Scientific Pub.

Topics of Our Time: Comments on Twentieth-Century Issues in Learning & in Art. Ernest H. Gombrich. (Illus.). 224p. 1991. 45.00 (*0-520-07516-1*) U CA Pr.

Topics of Our Times Series, 11 vols. Set. lib. bdg. 71.72 (*0-87157-800-X*) SamHar Pr.

Topics of Psychosomatic Research: Proceedings of the European Conference on Psychomatic Research, 9th, Vienna, April 1972. European Conference on Psychosomatic Research Staff. Ed. by H. Freyberger. (Journal: Psychotherapy & Psychosomatics: Vol. 22, Nos. 2-6). 305p. 1973. reprint ed. 72.00 (*3-8055-1616-9*) S Karger.

Topics on Biomathematics: Proceedings of the Second International Conference. I. Barbieri et al. 352p. 1993. text ed. 105.00 (*981-02-1490-1*) World Scientific Pub.

Topics on Biomedical Physics: Proceedings of the 6th National Congress of the Italian Association of Medical Physicians. L. Andreucci & A. Schenone. 700p. 1992. text ed. 121.00 (*981-02-1037-X*) World Scientific Pub.

Topics on Diffusion in Emulsions. M. Nichelatti. 152p. 1995. text ed. 48.00 (*981-02-1789-7*) World Scientific Pub.

Topics on Image Restoration/Filtering of Image Sequences. A. K. Katsaggelos & N.P. Galatsanos. 1996. write for info. (*0-614-17888-6*) Elsevier.

Topics on Nonlinear Wave Plasma Interaction. K. Baumgartel & Kenneth H. Sauer. 224p. 1988. 58.00 (*0-8176-1864-3*) Birkhauser.

Topics on Physics at High Energy Colliders: Proceedings of the Nineteenth International Winter Meeting. E. Fernandez & R. Pascual. 248p. 1992. text ed. 95.00 (*981-02-1144-9*) World Scientific Pub.

Topics on Real Analytic Spaces. Francesco Guaraldo et al. (Advanced Lectures in Mathematics). x, 164p. 1986. pap. 30.00 (*3-528-08963-6*, Pub. by Vieweg & Sohn GW) Informatica.

Topics on Regenerative Process. Kalashnikov. 240p. 1994. 71.95 (*0-8493-8641-1*) CRC Pr.

Topics on Toeplitz Operators & Spectral Function Theory. N. K. Nikolskii. (Operator Theory Ser.: No. 42). 300p. 1989. 156.00 (*0-8176-2344-2*) Birkhauser.

***Topics 1: Transformational Leadership.** Elizabeth Jones. 1996. pap. text ed. 6.95 (*1-884834-37-X*) Redleaf Pr.

***Topkapa Scroll-Geometry & Ornament in Islamic Architecture.** Gulru Necipoglu. 384p. 1996. 160.00 (*0-614-21592-7*, 1432) Kazi Pubns.

***Topkapi Architecture.** Tr. by J. M. Rogers. 215p. 1996. 150.00 (*0-614-21593-5*, 1240) Kazi Pubns.

Topkapi Scroll: Geometry & Ornament in Islamic Architecture. Gulru Necipoglu. LC 95-14621. (Sketches & Albums Ser.). (Illus.). 412p. 1995. 160.00 (*0-89236-335-5*, Getty Res Inst) J P Getty Trust.

***Topley & Wilson's Microbiology & Microbial Infections, 6 vols.** 9th ed. Ed. by Leslie Collier & Albert Balows. (Arnold Publication). 4500p. 1997. text ed. 1,295.00 (*0-340-61470-6*, Pub. by Ed Arnold UK) OUP.

***Topley & Wilson's Microbiology & Microbial Infections, 6 vols.** 9th ed. Ed. by Leslie Collier et al. (Arnold Publication). 1997. text ed. 1,595.00 incl. cd-rom (*0-340-70069-6*, Pub. by Ed Arnold UK) OUP.

***Topley & Wilson's Principles of Bacteriology, Virology & Immunity.** 8th ed. write for info. (*0-7131-4589-7*, Pub. by E Arnold UK) Routledge Chapman & Hall.

***Topley & Wilson's Principles of Bacteriology, Virology & Immunity.** 8th ed. write for info. (*0-7131-4590-0*, Pub. by E Arnold UK) Routledge Chapman & Hall.

***Topley & Wilson's Principles of Bacteriology, Virology & Immunity.** 8th ed. write for info. (*0-7131-4591-9*, Pub. by E Arnold UK) Routledge Chapman & Hall.

***Topley & Wilson's Principles of Bacteriology, Virology & Immunity.** 8th ed. write for info. (*0-7131-4592-7*, Pub. by E Arnold UK) Routledge Chapman & Hall.

***Topley & Wilson's Principles of Bacteriology, Virology & Immunity.** 8th ed. write for info. (*0-7131-4593-5*, Pub. by E Arnold UK) Routledge Chapman & Hall.

***Topley & Wilson's Principles of Bacteriology, Virology & Immunity.** 8th ed. write for info. (*0-7131-4594-3*, Pub. by E Arnold UK) Routledge Chapman & Hall.

Topley & Wilson's Principles of Bacteriology, Virology & Immunity, 5 vols., Set. Parker. 2456p. (gr. 13). 1990. 415.00 (*1-55664-288-1*) Mosby Yr Bk.

Topliff's Travels: Letters from Abroad in the Years 1828 & 1829. Samuel Topliff. Ed. by Ethel S. Bolton. LC 78-173189. 1972. reprint ed. 24.95 (*0-405-09030-7*) Ayer.

Toplin. Michael McDowell. (Illus.). 186p. 1985. lib. bdg. 22.50 (*0-910489-11-4*) Scream Pr.

Topmost Yoga. Srila Prabhupada. 112p. 1991. pap. 2.95 (*0-912776-11-0*) Bhaktivedanta.

Topo Gigio e il Pirata - Topo Gigio & the Pirate with the Beard. Maria Perego. Tr. by Giochi Preziosi from ENG. (Comes to Life Bks.). 16p. (ITA.). (J). (ps-2). 1994. write for info. (*1-57234-005-3*) YES Ent.

Topobiology: An Introduction to Molecular Embryology. Gerald M. Edelman. LC 88-47678. 256p. 1993. reprint ed. pap. 17.00 (*0-465-08653-5*) Basic.

Topographia Hibernica see Giraldi Cambrensis Opera

Topographic Anatomy - Athletic Injury Assessment. Russell. 1992. write for info. (*0-8493-4978-8*) CRC Pr.

***Topographic Effects in Stratified Flows.** 498p. 1998. pap. text ed. 27.95 (*0-521-62923-3*) Cambridge U Pr.

Topographic Effects in Stratified Flows. Peter G. Baines. (Monographs on Mechanics). (Illus.). 500p. (C). 1995. text ed. 80.00 (*0-521-43501-3*) Cambridge U Pr.

Topographic Histochemistry of the Cerebellum. Enrico Marani. LC 86-12132. (Progress in Histochemistry & Cytochemistry Ser.: Vol. 16, No. 4). (Illus.). 169p. 1986. pap. 105.00 (*0-89574-221-7*) G F Verlag.

Topographic, Hydrographic & Sedimentologic Setting of Little Lake, San Salvador Island, Bahamas. J. W. Teeter. (Occasional Papers - 1983: No. 1). 10p. 1983. pap. text ed. 1.00 (*0-935909-09-5*) Bahamian.

Topographic Map--Golden Grizzly Project: Gold Exploration in Montana. limited ed. (Illus.). 1981. 75.00 (*0-943435-02-1*) Cartographer Ink.

Topographic Mapping of Africa, Antarctica, & Eurasia. Mary L. Larsgaard. LC 92-39327. (Occasional Papers: No. 14). (Illus.). 1992. 45.00 (*0-939112-29-9*) Western Assn Map.

Topographic Positions of the Measurement Points in Electro-Acupuncture: Illustrated (Anatomic Atlas), Vol. I. Reinhold Voll. Tr. by Hartwig Schuldt from GER. (Electro-Acupuncture According to Voll Ser.). (Illus.). 160p. 1977. text ed. 65.00 (*3-88136-042-5*, Pub. by ML-Verlag GW) Medicina Bio.

Topographic Positions of the Measurement Points in Electro-Acupuncture: Illustrated (Anatomic Atlas), Vol. II. Reinhold Voll. Tr. by Hartwig Schuldt from GER. (Electro-Acupuncture According to Voll Ser.). (Illus.). 156p. 1977. text ed. 65.00 (*3-88136-049-2*, Pub. by ML-Verlag GW) Medicina Bio.

Topographic Positions of the Measurement Points in Electro-Acupuncture Vol. 1: Textual, Vol. I. Reinhold Voll. Tr. by Hartwig Schuldt from GER. (Electro-Acupuncture According to Voll Ser.). (Illus.). 168p. 1977. text ed. 65.00 (*3-88136-053-0*, Pub. by ML-Verlag GW) Medicina Bio.

Topographic Positions of the Measurement Points in Electro-Acupuncture Vol. 3: Textual & Illustrated, Vol. III. Reinhold Voll. Tr. by Hartwig Schuldt from GER. (Electro-Acupuncture According to Voll Ser.). (Illus.). 152p. 1978. text ed. 65.00 (*3-88136-060-3*, Pub. by ML-Verlag GW) Medicina Bio.

Topographic Terms in the Ohio Valley 1748-1800. W. Bruce Finnie. (Publications of the American Dialect Society: No. 53). 119p. 1970. pap. text ed. 11.90 (*0-8173-0653-6*) U of Ala Pr.

Topographic Waves in Channels & Lakes on the f-Plane. T. Stocker & Kolumban Hutter. (Lecture Notes on Coastal & Estuarine Studies: Vol. 21). x, 176p. 1987. pap. 26.00 (*0-387-17623-3*) Spr-Verlag.

Topographical Account of the District of Cunningham, Ayrshire. Timothy Pont. LC 74-174280. (Maitland Club, Glasgow. Publications: No. 74). reprint ed. 37.50 (*0-404-53112-1*) AMS Pr.

Topographical Anatomy of Neuropeptides in the Rat Brain. M. Palkovits. 1992. write for info. (*0-8493-6270-9*, CRC Reprint) Franklin.

Topographical & Motion Palpation of the Appendicular Skeleton. Kent L. Boyer. LC 95-9283. (Illus.). 184p. 1995. pap. text ed. 29.95 (*0-7734-9919-9*) E Mellen.

Topographical & Motion Palpation of the Axial Skeleton. Kent L. Boyer. LC 91-19648. (Illus.). 128p. 1991. pap. 39.95 (*0-7734-9904-0*) E Mellen.

Topographical Bibliography (Gr) No. 8i: Objects of Unknown Provenance, Statues. Malek. write for info. (*0-900416-29-7*, Pub. by Aris & Phillips UK) David Brown.

Topographical Description of Pensacola & Vicinity in 1821. Henry M. Brackenridge. Ed. by Brian R. Rucker. (Illus.). 69p. (Orig.). 1991. mass mkt. 7.95 (*1-882695-02-X*) Patagonia Pr.

Topographical Description of the Dominions of the United States of America. Thomas Pownall. Ed. by Lois Mulkearn. LC 75-22835. (America in Two Centuries Ser.). 1976. reprint ed. 23.95 (*0-405-07706-8*) Ayer.

Topographical Description of the State of Ohio, Indiana Territory, & Louisiana. Jervis Cutler. LC 78-146388. (First American Frontier Ser.). (Illus.). 1977. reprint ed. 27.95 (*0-405-02839-3*) Ayer.

Topographical Description of the Western Territory of North America. 3rd ed. Gilbert Imlay. LC 68-55739. (Illus.). xii, 598p. 1969. reprint ed. 65.00 (*0-678-00541-9*) Kelley.

Topographical Dictionary of England, 4 vols. in 2, Set. Samuel Lewis. (Illus.). 2464p. 1996. reprint ed. text ed. 150.00 (*0-8063-1508-3*, 3360) Genealog Pub.

Topographical Dictionary of Ireland, 2 Vols., Set. Samuel Lewis. LC 83-82827. 1480p. 1995. reprint ed. 85.00 (*0-8063-1063-4*) Genealog Pub.

Topographical Dictionary of Scotland, 2 vols. Samuel Lewis. LC 89-83729. 1233p. 1989. 75.00 (*0-8063-1255-6*) Genealog Pub.

Topographical Dictionary of 2885 English Emigrants to New England, 1620-1650. Charles E. Banks. LC 63-4154. (Illus.). 333p. 1992. reprint ed. 25.00 (*0-8063-0019-1*, 305) Genealog Pub.

Topographical Dictionary to the Works of Shakespeare & His Fellow Dramatists. Edward H. Sugden. (Anglistica & Americana Ser.: No. 17). xix, 580p. 1970. reprint ed. 96.20 (*0-685-66522-4*, 05102702) G Olms Pubs.

Topographical Memoir. Thomas J. Cram. 126p. 1978. 16.95 (*0-87770-193-8*) Ye Galleon.

Topographie Ideale pour une Agression Caracterisee. Rachid Boudjedra. 250p. (FRE.). 1986. pap. 11.95 (*0-7859-2046-3*, 2070377660) Fr & Eur.

Topographie von Athen. 3rd ed. W. Judeich. (Illus.). 485p. (GER.). 1994. reprint ed. text ed. 50.00 (*0-89005-511-4*) Ares.

Topographies. J. Hillis Miller. LC 94-25351. (Meridian: Crossing Aesthetics Ser.). xv ,p. 1995. 49.50 (*0-8047-2378-8*); pap. 16.95 (*0-8047-2379-6*) Stanford U Pr.

Topographies of Hellenism: Mapping the Homeland. Artemis Leontis. (Myth & Poetics Ser.). 240p. 1995. 29.95 (*0-8014-3057-7*) Cornell U Pr.

Topographische Anatomie des Plexus Brachialis und Thoracic-Outlet-Syndrom. J. Lang. (Illus.). 74p. (GER.). 1985. pap. 43.85 (*3-11-010160-2*) De Gruyter.

Topography & Architecture. Oscar Broneer. LC 75-27618. (Isthmia Ser.: Vol. 2). (Illus.). xiv, 148p. 1973. 40.00 (*0-87661-932-4*) Am Sch Athens.

Topography & History of Beth-shan: With Details of the Egyptian & Other Inscriptions Found on the Site. Alan Rowe. LC 31-13812. (Publications of the Palestine Section of the Museum of the University of Pennsylvania: Vol. 1). 144p. reprint ed. pap. 41.10 (*0-317-28548-3*, 2052030) Bks Demand.

Topography & Population of Ancient Boiotia, 2 vols. in 1. 552p. pap. 50.00 (*0-89005-482-7*) Ares.

Topography & Systems in Psychoanalytic Theory. Merton M. Gill. LC 59-9821. (Psychological Issues Monograph: No. 10, Vol. 3, No. 2). 179p. (Orig.). 1963. 27.50 (*0-8236-6560-7*); pap. 22.50 (*0-8236-6580-1*) Intl Univs Pr.

Topography of Baghdad in the Early Middle Ages: Text & Studies. Jacob Lassner. LC 69-11339. 325p. reprint ed. pap. 92.70 (*0-7837-3580-4*, 2043439) Bks Demand.

Topography of Remembrance: The Dead, Tradition & Collective Memory in Mesopotamia. Gerdien Jonker. (Numen Bookseries: No. 68). 250p. 1995. 103.50 (*90-04-10162-4*) E J Brill.

***Topography of Thebes from the Bronze Age to Modern Times.** Sarantis Symeonoglou. LC 84-24890. (Illus.). 404p. 1985. reprint ed. pap. 115.20 (*0-608-02586-0*, 2063243) Bks Demand.

Topoi: The Categorical Analysis of Logic. 2nd rev. ed. (Studies in Logic & the Foundations of Mathematics: Vol. 98). 552p. 1984. 179.75 (*0-444-86711-2*, I-499-83, North Holland) Elsevier.

Topological, Algebraical, & Combinatorial Structures: Frolik's Memorial Volume. Ed. by J. Nesetril. LC 93-275. (Topics in Discrete Mathematics Ser.: No. 8). 1993. 181.25 (*0-444-89236-2*, North Holland) Elsevier.

Topological Algorithms for Digital Image Processing. Ed. by T. Yung Kong & Azriel Rosenfeld. LC 96-23355. (Machine Intelligence & Pattern Recognition Ser.: Vol. 19). 300p. 1996. text ed. 179.25 (*0-444-89754-2*, North Holland) Elsevier.

Topological Analysis. Gordon T. Whyburn. LC 64-12193. (Princeton Mathematical Ser.: Vol. 23). 137p. reprint ed. 39.10 (*0-8357-9515-2*, 2015485) Bks Demand.

Topological Analysis & Synthesis of Communication Networks. Wan-hui Kim & Robert T. Chien. LC 62-14636. (Illus.). 322p. reprint ed. pap. 91.80 (*0-317-08767-3*, 2010965) Bks Demand.

Topological & Geometrical Methods in Field Theory: Proceedings of the Symposium, Espoo, Finland, June 8-14, 1986. Ed. by J. Hietarinta. 460p. 1987. pap. 47.00 (*9971-5-0230-5*); text ed. 131.00 (*9971-5-0229-1*) World Scientific Pub.

Topological & Geometrical Methods in Field Theory: Proceedings of the 2nd International Symposium, Turku, Finland, 26 May-1 June 1991. Ed. by J. Mickelsson & O. Pekonen. 448p. 1992. text ed. 109.00 (*981-02-0961-4*) World Scientific Pub.

Topological & Uniform Spaces. I. M. James. (Undergraduate Texts in Mathematics Ser.). (Illus.). 175p. 1987. 42.95 (*0-387-96466-5*) Spr-Verlag.

***Topological & Variational Methods for Nonlinear Boundary Value Problems.** Pavel Drabek. 1997. pap. 38.98 (*0-582-30921-2*, Pub. by Longman UK) Longman.

Topological Aspects of the Dynamics of Fluids & Plasmas. Ed. by H. K. Moffatt. (NATO Advanced Science Institutes Series C: Mathematical & Physical Sciences). 624p. (C). 1992. lib. bdg. 251.00 (*0-7923-1900-1*) Kluwer Ac.

Topological Chern-Weil Theory. Anthony V. Phillips & David A. Stone. LC 93-25081. (Memoirs of the American Mathematical Society Ser.: No. 504). 79p. 1993. pap. 28.00 (*0-8218-2566-6*, MEMO/105/504) Am Math.

Topological Circle Planes & Topological Quadrangles. A. Schroth. LC 95-22088. (Pitman Research Notes in Mathematics Ser.). 1995. write for info. (*0-614-08559-4*) Longman.

***Topological Circle Planes & Topological Quadrangles.** Andreas E. Schroth. 1996. pap. 51.06 (*0-582-28811-8*, Pub. by Longman UK) Longman.

Topological Classification of Integrable Systems. A. Fomenko. LC 91-640741. (Advances in Soviet Mathematics Ser.: Vol. 6). 345p. 1991. 180.00 (*0-8218-4105-X*, ADVSOV/6) Am Math.

Topological Classification of Stratified Spaces. Shmuel Weinberger. (Chicago Lectures in Mathematics). 298p. 1994. pap. text ed. 18.95 (*0-226-88567-4*); lib. bdg. 47.50 (*0-226-88566-6*) U Ch Pr.

***Topological Defects in Cosmology.** 400p. 1997. text ed. 47.00 (*981-02-3145-8*) World Scientific Pub.

Topological Degree Methods in Non-Linear Boundary Value Problems. Jean Mawhin. LC 78-31906. (CBMS Regional Conference Series in Mathematics: No. 40). 122p. 1979. reprint ed. pap. 18.00 (*0-8218-1690-X*, CBMS/40) Am Math.

Topological Disorder in Condensed Matter. Ed. by F. Yonezawa & T. Ninomiya. (Solid-State Sciences Ser.: Vol. 46). (Illus.). 270p. 1983. 63.95 (*0-387-12663-5*) Spr-Verlag.

Topological Dynamics. W. H. Gottschalk & G. A. Hedlund. LC 55-12710. (Colloquium Publications: Vol. 36). 167p. 1955. reprint ed. pap. 41.00 (*0-8218-1036-7*, COLL/36) Am Math.

***Topological Dynamics of Random Dynamical Systems.** Nguyen D. Cong. LC 97-19731. (Oxford Mathematical Monographs). 224p. 1997. 85.00 (*0-19-850157-9*) OUP.

Topological Entropy & Equivalence of Dynamical Systems. R. L. Adler & B. Marcus. LC 79-15040. (Memoirs Ser.: No. 20/219). 84p. 1981. reprint ed. pap. 21.00 (*0-8218-2219-5*, MEMO/20/219) Am Math.

Topological Fields. S. Warner. (Mathematical Studies: No. 157). 564p. 1989. 179.75 (*0-444-87429-1*, North Holland) Elsevier.

Topological Fields. Wieslaw. (Pure & Applied Mathematics Ser.: Vol. 119). 328p. 1988. 160.00 (*0-8247-7731-X*) Dekker.

Topological Fields & Near Valuations. Shell. (Pure & Applied Mathematics Ser.: Vol. 135). 248p. 1990. 125.00 (*0-8247-8412-X*) Dekker.

Topological Fixed Point Theory & Applications. Ed. by B. J. Jiang. (Lecture Notes in Mathematics Ser.: Vol. 1411). vi, 203p. 1989. 33.00 (*0-387-51932-7*) Spr-Verlag.

Topological Function Spaces. A. V. Arkhangel'skii. (C). 1991. lib. bdg. 113.50 (*0-7923-1531-6*) Kluwer Ac.

Topological Groups: Characters, Dualities & Minimal Group Topologies. Dikranjan et al. (Pure & Applied Mathematics Ser.: Vol. 130). 312p. 1989. 160.00 (*0-8247-8047-7*) Dekker.

Topological Imbeddings in Euclidean Space: Proceedings. Ed. by L. V. Keldys. (Proceedings of the Steklov Institute of Mathematics Ser.: No. 81). 203p. 1968. pap. 79.00 (*0-8218-1881-3*, STEKLO/81) Am Math.

Topological Introduction to Nonlinear Analysis. 2nd ed. R. F. Brown. LC 93-3192. 146p. 1996. pap. 26.50 (*0-8176-3706-0*) Spr-Verlag.

Topological Invariants of Plane Curves & Caustics. V. I. Arnold. LC 94-16254. (University Lectures: Vol. 5). 1994. 15.00 (*0-8218-0308-5*, ULECT/5) Am Math.

Topological Invariants of Quasi-Ordinary Singularities & Embedded Topological Classification of Quasi-Ordinary Singularities. J. Lipman & Y. Gau. LC 88-10559. (Memoirs Ser.: No. 74/388). 129p. 1989. reprint ed. pap. 22.00 (*0-8218-2451-1*, MEMO/74/388) Am Math.

Topological Methds for Variational Problems with Symmetries. Thomas Bartsch. LC 93-41151. (Lecture Notes in Mathematics Ser.: Vol. 1560). 1993. write for info. (*3-540-57378-X*) Spr-Verlag.

Topological Methods for Ordinary Differential Equations: Lectures Given at the First Session of the Centro Internazionale Matematico Estivo, Montecatini Terme, Italy, 1991. C. Fitzpatrick et al. Ed. by M. Furi & P. Zecca. LC 93-9406. (Lecture Notes in Mathematics Ser.: Vol. 1537). 1993. 45.95 (*0-387-56461-6*) Spr-Verlag.

Topological Methods for Variational Problems with Symmetries. Ed. by A. Dold et al. (Lecture Notes in Mathematics Ser.: Vol. 1560). 1993. 35.95 (*0-387-57378-X*) Spr-Verlag.

Topological Methods in Algebraic Geometry. F. Hirzebruch. Tr. by R. L. Schwarzberger from GER. (Grundlehren der Mathematischen Wissenschaften Ser.: Vol. 131). 1982. 59.00 (*0-387-03525-7*) Spr-Verlag.

Topological Methods in Algebraic Geometry. 4th ed. F. Hirzebruch. LC 94-39728. (ENG & GER.). 1995. 35.00 (*3-540-58663-6*) Spr-Verlag.

Topological Methods in Algebraic Transformation Groups. H. Kraft et al. (Progress in Mathematics Ser.: No. 80). 216p. 1989. 46.00 (*0-8176-3436-3*) Birkhauser.

Topological Methods in Chemistry. Howard Simmons & Richard E. Merrifield. LC 87-30530. 256p. 1989. text ed. 99.95 (*0-471-83817-9*) Wiley.

An Asterisk (*) at the beginning of an entry indicates that the title is appearing in BIP for the first time.

Topological Methods in Differential Equations & Inclusions: Proceedings of the NATO ASI & Seminaire de Mathematiques Superieures, Montreal, Canada, July 11-22, 1994, Vol. 472. Ed. by Andrzej Granas et al. LC 95-34346. (NATO ASI Series C: Series C). 540p. (C). 1995. lib. bdg. 245.00 (*0-7923-3678-X*) Kluwer Ac.

*__Topological Methods in Hydrodynamics.__ Vladimir I. Arnold. LC 97-10079. 1997. 59.95 (*0-387-94947-X*) Spr-Verlag.

Topological Methods in Modern Mathematics: A Symposium in Honor of John Milnor's Sixtieth Birthday. Ed. by Lisa R. Goldberg & Anthony V. Phillips. (Illus.). xxii, 566p. 1993. 70.00 (*0-914098-26-8*) Publish or Perish.

Topological Methods in Nonlinear Functional Analysis. Ed. by S. P. Singh et al. LC 83-11824. (Contemporary Mathematics Ser.: Vol. 21). 218p. 1983. pap. text ed. 30.00 (*0-8218-5023-7*, CONM/21) Am Math.

Topological Methods in Quantum Field Theories. W. Nahm et al. 184p. 1991. pap. 28.00 (*981-02-0497-3*); text ed. 68.00 (*981-02-0496-5*) World Scientific Pub.

Topological Methods in the Theory of Functions of a Complex Variable. Marston Morse. (Annals of Mathematics Studies). 1947. 25.00 (*0-527-02731-6*) Periodicals Srv.

Topological Methods Theory of Nonlinear Integral Equations. M. M. Krasnosel'Skii & A. Armstrong. LC 63-10052. (International Series of Monographs on Pure & Applied Mathematics: Vol. 45). 1964. 181.00 (*0-08-010114-3*, Pub. by Pergamon Repr UK) Franklin.

Topological Model Theory. 1980. 33.95 (*0-387-09732-5*) Spr-Verlag.

Topological Model Theory. J. Flum & M. Ziegler. (Lecture Notes in Mathematics Ser.: Vol. 769). 151p. 1980. pap. 15.00 (*3-540-09732-5*) Spr-Verlag.

Topological Nonlinear Analysis: Degree, Singularity, & Variations. Ed. by Michele Matzeu & Alfonso Vignoli. LC 94-5251. (Progress in Nonlinear Differential Equations & Their Applications Ser.: Vol. 15). ix, 531p. 1994. 104.50 (*0-8176-3742-7*) Birkhauser.

*__Topological Nonlinear Analysis II.__ Ed. by M. Matzeu & A. Vignoli. (Progress in Nonlinear Differential Equations & Their Applications Ser.). 325p. 1997. 120.00 (*0-8176-3886-5*) Birkhauser.

Topological Phases in Quantum Theory: International Seminar on Geometrical Aspects of Quantum Theory. Ed. by S. I. Vinitsky et al. 464p. (C). 1989. text ed. 130.00 (*9971-5-0877-X*) World Scientific Pub.

Topological Picturebook. G. K. Francis. (Illus.). 210p. 1988. 46.95 (*0-387-96426-6*) Spr-Verlag.

Topological Projective & Combinatorial Properties of Space. Ed. by G. S. Chogoshvili. 192p. 1992. text ed. 115.00 (*1-56072-058-1*) Nova Sci Pubs.

Topological Properties & Global Structure of Space Time. Ed. by Peter Bergmann & Venzo De Sabbata. (NATO ASI Series B, Physics: Vol. 138). 280p. 1986. 69.50 (*0-306-42367-7*, Plenum Pr) Plenum.

Topological Properties of Spaces of Continuous Functions. R. A. McCoy & I. Ntantu. (Lecture Notes in Mathematics Ser.: Vol. 1315). 124p. 1988. 30.95 (*0-387-19302-2*) Spr-Verlag.

Topological Quantum Field Theories & Geometry of Loop Spaces. L. Feher & A. Stipsicz. 124p. 1992. text ed. 59.00 (*981-02-1173-2*) World Scientific Pub.

*__Topological Quantum Numbers in Nonrelativistic Physics.__ 450p. 1997. 54.00 (*981-02-2900-3*); 26.00 (*981-02-3025-7*) World Scientific Pub.

Topological Rings. Seth Warner. LC 93-15938. (North-Holland Mathematics Studies: Vol. 178). 508p. 1993. 170.50 (*0-444-89446-2*, North Holland) Elsevier.

Topological Semifields & Their Applications to General Topology. M. Ja Antonovskii et al. LC 77-11046. (Translations Ser.: Series 2, Vol. 106). 142p. 1977. reprint ed. pap. 34.00 (*0-8218-3056-2*, TRANS2/106) Am Math.

*__Topological Spaces: From Distance to Neighborhood.__ Gerard Buskes & A. C. Van Rooij. LC 97-3756. (Undergraduate Texts in Mathematics Ser.). 1997. write for info. (*0-387-94994-1*) Spr-Verlag.

*__Topological Spaces: Including a Treatment of Mutli-Valued Functions, Vector Spaces & Convexity.__ Claude Berge. (Illus.). 284p. 1997. reprint ed. pap. text ed. 9.95 (*0-486-69653-7*) Dover.

Topological Theory of Dynamical Systems: Recent Advances. N. Aoki & K. Hiraide. LC 94-11678. (North-Holland Mathematical Library: No. 52). 424p. 1994. 145.75 (*0-444-89917-0*, North Holland) Elsevier.

*__Topological Tolerancing of Worm-Gear Tooth Surfaces.__ Vadim Kin. (1993 Fall Technical Meeting). 1993. pap. text ed. 30.00 (*1-55589-595-6*) AGMA.

*__Topological Tooth Modifications & Contact Patterns of Spur & Helical Gears.__ Hans Winte & K. Stolzle. (1989 Fall Technical Meeting). 1989. pap. text ed. 30.00 (*1-55589-532-8*) AGMA.

Topological Topics: Articles on Algebra & Topology. Ed. by I. M. James. LC 83-7745. (London Mathematical Society Lecture Note Ser.: No. 86). 192p. 1983. pap. text ed. 42.95 (*0-521-27581-4*) Cambridge U Pr.

Topological Tribute. Ed. by I. M. James et al. (London Mathematical Society Lecture Note Ser.: No. 94). 250p. 1985. pap. text ed. 49.95 (*0-521-27815-5*) Cambridge U Pr.

Topological Triviality & Versality for Subgroups A & K. J. Damon. LC 88-15554. (Memoirs Ser.: No. 75/389). 106p. 1988. pap. text ed. 18.00 (*0-8218-2452-X*, MEMO/75/389) Am Math.

*__Topological Uniform Structures.__ Warren Page. pap. 9.95 (*0-486-65808-2*) Dover.

Topological Vector Spaces. A. Grothendieck. (Notes on Mathematics & Its Applications Ser.). x, 264p. 1973. text ed. 205.00 (*0-677-30020-4*) Gordon & Breach.

Topological Vector Spaces. Narici & Beckenstein. (Pure & Applied Mathematics Ser.: Vol. 95). 432p. 1985. 160.00 (*0-8247-7315-2*) Dekker.

Topological Vector Spaces. H. H. Schaefer. LC 65-24692. (Graduate Texts in Mathematics Ser.: Vol. 3). (C). 1986. reprint ed. 43.95 (*0-387-90026-8*) Spr-Verlag.

*__Topological Vector Spaces, Algebras & Related Areas.__ Lau A To-Ming. 1994. pap. 74.95 (*0-582-25777-8*) Addison-Wesley.

Topological Vector Spaces One. G. Koethe. Tr. by D. J. Garling. (Grundlehren der Mathematischen Wissenschaften Ser.: Vol. 159). 456p. 1983. 118.95 (*0-387-04509-0*) Spr-Verlag.

Topologie. Paul S. Alexandroff & H. Hopf. LC 65-21833. (GER.). 25.00 (*0-8284-0197-7*) Chelsea Pub.

Topologie d'une Cite Fantome. Alain Robbe-Grillet. 204p. (FRE.). 1976. pap. 20.95 (*0-7859-1506-0*, 2707300713) Fr & Eur.

Topologies on Closed & Closed Convex Sets. Gerald Beer. LC 93-31538. (Mathematics & Its Applications Ser.: Vol. 268). 352p. 1993. lib. bdg. 177.50 (*0-7923-2531-1*) Kluwer Ac.

Topologies on Pseudo-Trees & Applications. J. Nikiel. LC 89-17764. (Memoirs Ser.: Vol. 82/416). 116p. 1989. pap. 21.00 (*0-8218-2479-1*, MEMO/82/416) Am Math.

Topology. James Dungundji. 447p. (C). 1988. per. write for info. (*0-697-06889-7*) Wm C Brown Pubs.

Topology. K. Janich. Tr. by S. Levy. (Undergraduate Texts in Mathematics Ser.). (Illus.). x, 198p. 1994. 43.95 (*0-387-90892-7*) Spr-Verlag.

Topology. 2nd rev. ed. Solomon Lefschetz. LC 56-11513. (Illus.). 410p. (C). 1990. text ed. 23.95 (*0-8284-0116-0*, 116) Chelsea Pub.

Topology. John G. Hocking & Gail S. Young. (Illus.). 384p. 1988. reprint ed. pap. 9.95 (*0-486-65676-4*) Dover.

*__Topology, Vol. 1.__ 1996. text ed. 115.00 (*3-540-17007-3*) Spr-Verlag.

Topology: A Collection of Papers. Ed. by P. Aleksandrov. LC 85-7326. (Proceedings of the Steklov Institute of Mathematics Ser.: Vol. 154). 333p. 1985. pap. text ed. 111.00 (*0-8218-3086-4*, STEKLO/154) Am Math.

Topology: A First Course. James Munkres. (Illus.). 448p. 1974. text ed. 77.00 (*0-13-925495-1*) P-H.

Topology: An Introduction to the Point-Set & Algebraic Areas. Donald W. Kahn. LC 95-1157. (Illus.). 240p. 1995. pap. text ed. 7.95 (*0-486-68609-4*) Dover.

Topology: An Introduction with Application to Topological Groups. George McCarty. (Illus.). 288p. 1988. reprint ed. pap. text ed. 8.95 (*0-486-65633-0*) Dover.

Topology: An Outline for a First Course. Lewis E. Ward. LC 72-76065. (Pure & Applied Mathematics Ser.: Vol. 10). 123p. reprint ed. pap. 35.10 (*0-685-16361-X*, 2027126) Bks Demand.

Topology: General & Algebraic Topology & Applications, Proceedings of the International Topological Conference Held in Leningrad, August 23-27, 1982. Ed. by L. D. Fadeev & A. A. Mal'Cev. (Lecture Notes in Mathematics Ser.: Vol. 1060). vi, 389p. 1984. 49.95 (*0-387-13337-2*) Spr-Verlag.

Topology: Proceedings of the Memphis State University Conference. Ed. by Stanley P. Franklin & Barbara V. Thomas. LC 76-9462. (Lecture Notes in Pure & Applied Mathematics Ser.: No. 24). 312p. 1976. reprint ed. pap. 89.00 (*0-608-00257-7*, 2060770) Bks Demand.

Topology: Theory & Applications 2. Ed. by A. Csaszar. (Colloquia Mathematica Societatis Janos Bolyai Ser.: Vol. 55). 528p. 1993. 269.25 (*0-444-98760-6*, North Holland) Elsevier.

Topology - Hawaii. Ed. by K. H. Dovermann. 500p. (C). 1992. text ed. 81.00 (*981-02-0683-6*) World Scientific Pub.

Topology & Analysis. B. Booss & D. D. Bleecker. Tr. by A. Mader from GER. (Universitext Ser.). (Illus.). xvi, 451p. 1989. 64.95 (*0-387-96112-7*) Spr-Verlag.

Topology & Category Theory in Computer Science. Ed. by G. M. Reed et al. 408p. (C). 1991. 79.00 (*0-19-853760-3*) OUP.

Topology & Combinatorial Group Theory: Proceedings of the Fall Foliage Topology Seminars Held in New Hampshire, 1985-1988. Ed. by P. Latiolais et al. (Lecture Notes in Mathematics Ser.: Vol. 1440). vi, 207p. 1990. 38.95 (*0-387-52990-X*) Spr-Verlag.

Topology & Combinatorics of 3-Manifolds. Klaus Johannson. LC 95-4082. (Lecture Notes in Mathematics Ser.: Vol. 1599). 1995. write for info. (*0-387-59063-3*) Spr-Verlag.

Topology & Geometry, Vol. XIV. rev. ed. Glen E. Bredon. Ed. by J. H. Ewing et al. LC 92-31618. (Graduate Texts in Mathematics Ser.: Vol. 139). (Illus.). 557p. (C). 1995. 75.95 (*0-387-97926-3*) Spr-Verlag.

Topology & Geometry: Rohlin Seminar. Ed. by O. Y. Viro. (Lecture Notes in Mathematics Ser.: Vol. 1346). xi, 581p. 1988. 74.95 (*0-387-50237-8*) Spr-Verlag.

Topology & Geometry for Physicists. Charles Nash & Siddartha Sen. 1983. text ed. 108.00 (*0-12-514080-0*) Acad Pr.

Topology & Geometry for Physicists. Charles Nash & Siddharta Sen. 311p. 1988. reprint ed. pap. text ed. 55.00 (*0-12-514081-9*) Acad Pr.

Topology & Its Applications. Ed. by S. Thomeier. (Lecture Notes in Pure & Applied Mathematics Ser.: Vol. 12). 216p. 1975. 110.00 (*0-8247-6212-6*) Dekker.

Topology & Its Applications: Proceedings of the International Topology Conference, Baku, October 3-8, 1987. Ed. by S. P. Novikov. LC 93-6106. (Proceedings of the Steklov Institute of Mathematics Ser.: Vol. 193). 1993. pap. 180.00 (*0-8218-3151-8*, STEKLO/193) Am Math.

Topology & Order. Leopoldo Nachbin. Tr. by Lulu Bechtolsheim from POR. LC 76-59. (Illus.). 128p. reprint ed. pap. 36.50 (*0-8357-7057-5*, AU00369) Bks Demand.

Topology & Order. Leopoldo Nachbin. LC 76-59. 128p. 1976. reprint ed. 15.00 (*0-88275-387-8*) Krieger.

Topology & Physics of Circular DNA. Vologodskii. 192p. 1992. 110.00 (*0-8493-4228-7*, QP624) CRC Pr.

Topology & Representation Theory: Proceedings of a Conference Held on Connections Between Algebraic Topology & Representation Theory, May 1-5, 1992, Northwestern University, Evanston, Illinois. Ed. by Eric M. Friedlander & Mark E. Mahowald. LC 93-39673. (Contemporary Mathematics Ser.: Vol. 158). 332p. 1994. pap. 34.00 (*0-8218-5165-9*, CONM/158) Am Math.

*__Topology & Teichmuller Spaces: Proceedings of the 37th Taniguchi Symposium.__ 400p. 1996. lib. bdg. 60.00 (*981-02-2686-1*) World Scientific Pub.

*__Topology & Topological Algebra.__ American Mathematical Society Staff. (American Mathematical Society Ser.: Series 1, 8). 467p. pap. 133.10 (*0-608-05172-1*, 2052593) Bks Demand.

Topology & Topological Algebra. V. G. Boltyanskii et al. (Translations Ser.: Series 1, Vol. 8). 455p. 1962. 35.00 (*0-8218-1608-X*, TRANS1/8) Am Math.

Topology Design of Structures. Ed. by Martin P. Bendse & Carlos A. Mota Soares. (C). 1992. lib. bdg. 243.00 (*0-7923-2055-7*) Kluwer Ac.

Topology for Analysis. Albert Wilansky. LC 81-1616. 400p. 1983. reprint ed. 42.50 (*0-89874-343-5*) Krieger.

Topology for Physicists. Albert S. Schwarz. Tr. by Silvio Levy. LC 96-15840. (Grundlehren der Mathematischen Wissenschaften Ser.: Vol. 308). 1996. write for info. (*3-540-54754-1*) Spr-Verlag.

Topology for Physicists. Albert S. Schwarz. Tr. by Silvio Levy. LC 94-13317. (Grundlehren der Mathematischen Wissenschaften Ser.). 1996. 129.95 (*0-387-54754-1*) Spr-Verlag.

*__Topology from the Differentiable Viewpoint.__ John Milnor. (Princeton Landmarks in Mathematics & Physics Ser.). 1997. pap. text ed. 9.95 (*0-691-04833-9*) Princeton U Pr.

Topology from the Differentiable Viewpoint. John W. Milnor. LC 65-26874. (Illus.). 64p. 1965. pap. text ed. 6.95 (*0-8139-0181-2*) U Pr of Va.

Topology from the Differentiable Viewpoint. John W. Milnor. LC 65-26874. (Illus.). 76p. 1969. reprint ed. pap. 25.00 (*0-608-03186-0*, 2063639) Bks Demand.

*__Topology, Geometry & Gauge Fields: Foundations.__ Gregory L. Naber. LC 96-49166. (Texts in Applied Mathematics Ser.: Vol. 25). (Illus.). 400p. 1997. 49.95 (*0-387-94946-1*) Spr-Verlag.

Topology I, Vol. 12. Ed. by S. P. Novikov. Tr. by B. Botvinnik & R. Burns. (Encyclopedia of Mathematical Sciences Ser.). (Illus.). 344p. 1996. 115.00 (*0-387-17007-3*) Spr-Verlag.

*__Topology II: Homotopies & Homologies, Classical Manifolds.__ D. B. Fuks. (Encyclopedia of Mathematical Sciences Ser.: Vol. 24). 250p. 1997. 98.00 (*3-540-51996-3*) Spr-Verlag.

Topology in Spaces of Holomorphic Mappings. Leopoldo Nachbin. LC 68-29710. (Ergebnisse der Mathematik und Ihrer Grenzgebiete Ser.: Vol. 47). 1969. 64.95 (*0-387-04470-1*) Spr-Verlag.

*__Topology, Measures & Fractals.__ Ed. by Christon Bandt et al. 1992. pap. text ed. 55.00 (*3-05-501554-1*) Wiley.

Topology of Being: The Poetics of Charles Olson. Judith Halden-Sullivan. LC 89-37366. (American University Studies: American Literature: Ser. XXIV, Vol. 18). 151p. (C). 1990. text ed. 33.95 (*0-8204-1148-5*) P Lang Pubng.

Topology of Classical Groups & Related Topics. S. Y. Husseini. (Notes on Mathematics & Its Applications Ser.). viii, 128p. 1969. text ed. 132.00 (*0-677-02160-7*) Gordon & Breach.

Topology of Fibre Bundles. N. E. Steenrod. (Mathematical Ser.: Vol. 14). 240p. 1951. text ed. 49.50 (*0-691-08055-0*) Princeton U Pr.

Topology of Foliations: An Introduction. Itiro Tamura. LC 91-37135. (Translations of Mathematical Monographs: Vol. 97). 193p. 1992. 39.00 (*0-8218-4543-8*, MMONO/97C) Am Math.

Topology of Function Spaces & the Calculus of Variations in the Large. L. A. Ljusternik. LC 66-25298. (Translations of Mathematical Monographs: Vol. 16). 96p. 1967. reprint ed. pap. 31.00 (*0-8218-1566-0*, MMONO/16) Am Math.

Topology of Gauge Fields & Condensed Matter. M. Monastyrsky. LC 92-43571. (Illus.). 372p. (C). 1993. 95.00 (*0-306-44336-8*, Plenum Pr) Plenum.

Topology of Lagrangian Manifolds. A. S. Mishchenko et al. (Illus.). 320p. 1990. 136.95 (*0-387-13613-4*) Spr-Verlag.

Topology of Lie Groups, I & II. M. Mimura & H. Toda. LC 91-9459. (Translations of Mathematical Monographs: Vol. 91). 451p. 1991. 49.00 (*0-8218-4541-1*, MMONO/91) Am Math.

Topology of Manifolds. Raymond L. Wilder. LC 49-6722. (Colloquium Publications: Vol. 32). 403p. 1949. reprint ed. pap. 61.00 (*0-8218-1032-4*, COLL/32) Am Math.

Topology of Real Algebraic Sets. S. Akbulut & H. King. (Mathematical Sciences Research Institute Publications: Vol. 25). x, 249p. 1991. 57.95 (*0-387-97744-9*) Spr-Verlag.

Topology of Real Algebraic Varieties & Related Topics. Ed. by V. Kharlamov et al. (American Mathematical Society Translations Ser.: Series 2, Vol. 173). 264p. 1996. 99.00 (*0-8218-0555-X*, TRANS2/173) Am Math.

Topology of Surfaces. Andre Gramain. Tr. by Leo F. Boron et al. from FRE. LC 84-70461. (Illus.). 120p. 1984. pap. text ed. 24.00 (*0-914351-01-X*) BCS Assocs.

Topology of Surfaces. L. Christine Kinsey. LC 93-2605. (Undergraduate Texts in Mathematics Ser.). 262p. 1993. 42.95 (*0-387-94102-9*); write for info. (*3-540-94102-9*) Spr-Verlag.

Topology of Torus Actions on Symplectic Manifolds. M. Audin. 181p. 1991. 73.00 (*0-8176-2602-6*) Spr-Verlag.

Topology of 4-Manifolds. 1995. 29.00 (*0-387-51148-2*) Spr-Verlag.

Topology of 4-Manifolds. Michael Freedman & Frank Quinn. 292p. 1990. text ed. 62.50 (*0-691-08577-3*) Princeton U Pr.

Topology, Ordinary Differential Equations, Dynamical Systems: A Collection of Survey Articles. Ed. by E. F. Mishchenko. LC 87-959. (Proceedings of the Steklov Institute of Mathematics Ser.: Vol. 169). 260p. 1987. pap. text ed. 129.00 (*0-8218-3100-3*, STEKLO/169) Am Math.

Topology Problem Solver. Research & Education Association Staff. (Illus.). 1008p. 1994. pap. text ed. 29.95 (*0-87891-925-2*) Res & Educ.

Topology via Logic. Steven Vickers. (Cambridge Tracts in Theoretical Computer Science Ser.). (Illus.). 120p. 1989. 52.95 (*0-521-36062-5*) Cambridge U Pr.

*__Topology via Logic.__ Steven Vickers. (Cambridge Tracts in Theoretical Computer Science Ser.: No. 5). 215p. (C). 1996. pap. text ed. 24.95 (*0-521-57651-2*) Cambridge U Pr.

Topology '90: Proceedings of the Research Semester in Low Dimensional Topology at Ohio State University. Ed. by Boris Apanasov et al. LC 92-16406. (Ohio State Mathematical Research Institute Publications: Vol. 1). xii, 457p. (C). 1992. lib. bdg. 69.95 (*3-11-012598-6*) De Gruyter.

Topol's Treasury of Jewish Wit & Wisdom. Compiled by Topol. LC 94-46453. 256p. 1995. pap. 12.00 (*1-56980-032-4*) Barricade Bks.

Toponymie Ecossaise. J. Berton. 29p. (ENG & GAE.). 1990. pap. 11.95 (*0-8288-3377-X*, F119710) Fr & Eur.

Topophilia: A Study of Environmental Perceptions, Attitudes, & Values. Yi-Fu Tuan. 296p. 1990. text ed. 49.50 (*0-231-07394-1*); pap. text ed. 16.50 (*0-231-07395-X*) Col U Pr.

Toposes, Triples & Theories. M. Barr & C. H. Wells. (Grundlehren der Mathematischen Wissenschaften Ser.: Vol. 278). (Illus.). xiii, 345p. 1984. 82.95 (*0-387-96115-1*) Spr-Verlag.

Topper. Thorne Smith. 208p. 1980. pap. 2.25 (*0-345-28722-3*, Del Rey) Ballantine.

Topper. Thorne Smith. reprint ed. lib. bdg. 23.95 (*0-89190-448-4*, Rivercity Pr) Amereon Ltd.

Topper. Thorne Smith. 1990. reprint ed. lib. bdg. 25.95 (*0-89968-550-1*) Buccaneer Bks.

Topper Debate. Pictureback Books Staff. 1989. write for info. (*0-679-80319-X*) Random.

Topper Sailing. John Caig. (C). 1990. text ed. 59.00 (*0-906754-04-6*, Pub. by Fernhurst Bks UK) St Mut.

Topper Takes a Trip. Thorne Smith et al. 240p. 1980. pap. 2.25 (*0-345-28723-1*, Del Rey) Ballantine.

Topper Takes a Trip. Thorne Smith. reprint ed. lib. bdg. 25.95 (*0-89190-437-9*, Rivercity Pr) Amereon Ltd.

Topper Takes a Trip. Thorne Smith. 1990. reprint ed. lib. bdg. 21.95 (*0-89968-551-X*) Buccaneer Bks.

*__Topping Book: Or, Getting Good at Being Bad.__ Dossie Easton & Catherine A. Liszt. (Illus.). 176p. (Orig.). 1996. pap. 11.95 (*0-9639763-5-4*) Greenery Pr.

Topping from Below. Laura Reese. 368p. 1995. 22.95 (*0-312-12000-1*) St Martin.

Topping from Below. Laura Reese. 384p. 1996. pap. 12.95 (*0-312-14435-0*) St Martin.

Topping Out. Sullivan. Date not set. write for info. (*0-395-34426-3*) HM.

*__Toppling the Pyramids.__ Gerald Ross & M. Kay. Date not set. 4.99 (*0-517-17814-1*) Random Hse Value.

Toppling the Pyramids: Redefining the Way Companies Are Run. Gerald Ross. 1994. 25.00 (*0-8129-2341-3*, Times Bks) Random.

*__Topps Baseball Update.__ Slocum. 1986. 3.95 (*0-446-38515-8*) Warner Bks.

TOPS: Tested Overhead Projection Series. 3rd ed. Journal of Chemical Education Staff. LC 67-25495. 138p. 1967. reprint ed. pap. 39.40 (*0-317-41843-2*, 2025632) Bks Demand.

TOPS: The IBM-Macintosh Connection. Stephen Cobb & Marty Jost. (Illus.). 352p. (Orig.). 1989. pap. 24.95 (*0-685-25403-8*, TAB-Aero) TAB Bks.

Tops: The IBM-Macintosh Connection. Stephen Cobb. 1989. pap. 24.95 (*0-8306-3210-7*, Windcrest) TAB Bks.

TOPS Adolescent Test Kit: Test of Problem Solving - Adolescent. Rosemary Huisingh et al. (YA). (gr. 7-12). 1991. 64.95 (*1-55999-208-5*) LinguiSystems.

Tops & Bottoms. 2nd ed. Pamela Granovetter & Matthew Granovetter. 182p. 1987. pap. 11.95 (*0-940257-00-9*) Granovetter Bks.

Tops & Yo-Yos. Bernie Zubrowski. (Illus.). 80p. (J). (gr. 5-8). 1994. pap. text ed. 12.50 (*0-938587-37-4*) Cuisenaire.

*__Tops & Yo-Yos & Other Spinning Toys.__ (Illus.). 112p. (Orig.). 1995. pap. 12.00 (*0-89538-037-4*) L-W Inc.

TOPS Kit - Adolescent (Tasks of Problem Solving) A Real-Life Approach to Thinking & Reasoning. Linda Zachman et al. 1992. Complete kit incls. newspapers, tchr's. manual, cards. 59.95 (*1-55999-234-4*) LinguiSystems.

TOPS Kit - Elementary (Tasks of Problem Solving) A Program to Build Thinking & Reasoning Skills. Linda Zachman et al. (Illus.). 215p. (Orig.). (J). (gr. k-6). 1990. student ed., spiral bd. 109.95 (*1-55999-117-8*) LinguiSystems.

Topsides Capacities for Tentech 850C. Leif Haukom. 1989. 125.00 (*90-6314-863-1*, Pub. by Lorne & MacLean Marine) St Mut.

Topspin: The Ups & Downs in Big-Time Tennis. Eliot Berry. LC 95-37235. 320p. 1996. 27.50 (*0-8050-3543-5*, J Macrae Bks) H Holt & Co.

Topsy: The Story of a Golden-Haired Chow. Marie Bonaparte. (Illus.). 193p. (C). 1993. text ed. 29.95 (*1-56000-127-5*) Transaction Pubs.

Topsy Dingo Wild Dog. Camilla Carr. Ed. by Stewart Richardson. 410p. 1989. 16.95 (*1-55972-013-1*, Birch Ln Pr) Carol Pub Group.

Topsy Tail Book. Tomima L. Edmark. (Illus.). 112p. (Orig.). 1994. pap. 8.99 (*0-446-67061-8*) Warner Bks.

Topsy-Turvies. Francesca Simon. LC 95-17685. (Illus.). 32p. (J). (ps-3). 1996. pap. 14.99 (*0-8037-1969-8*) Dial Bks Young.

Topsy-Turvy. Vernon Bartlett. LC 77-110179. (Short Story Index Reprint Ser.). 1977. 20.95 (*0-8369-3330-3*) Ayer.

Topsy Turvy. Monika Beisner. LC 87-45751. (Illus.). 32p. (J). (ps up). 1988. 15.00 (*0-374-37679-4*) FS&G.

***Topsy-Turvy Day.** Kari James. (Allegra's Window 8 by 8s Ser.). (Illus.). (J). (ps-1). 1997. pap. 3.25 (*0-614-29074-0*, Aladdin Paperbacks) S&S Childrens.

Topsy Turvy Day, Pop-Up Book. Mouse Works Staff. (Illus.). (J). 1996. 6.98 (*1-57082-294-8*) Mouse Works.

Topsy-Turvy Emperor of China. Isaac B. Singer. Tr. by Elizabeth Shub from YID. LC 95-44127. (Illus.). 32p. (J). 1996. 16.00 (*0-374-37681-6*) FS&G.

Topsy-Turvy Emperor of China. Isaac B. Singer. Tr. by Elizabeth Shub. 32p. (J). 1996. pap. 5.95 (*0-374-47588-1*, Sunburst Bks) FS&G.

Topsy-Turvy Kingdom. Josh McDowell et al. LC 96-18987. 48p. (J). 1996. 12.99 (*0-8423-7218-0*) Tyndale.

***Topsy-Turvy Magic.** Illus. by Rebecca Thornburgh. (Jewel Sticker Stories Ser.). 24p. (Orig.). (J). (gr. k-2). 1997. pap. 3.95 (*0-448-41597-6*, G&D) Putnam Pub Group.

Topsys & Turvys. Peter S. Newell. LC 87-51208. 72p. (J). (gr. k-4). 1988. 12.95 (*0-8048-1551-8*) C E Tuttle.

Topsys & Turvys. Peter S. Newell. (Illus.). 76p. (J). (gr. 3-7). pap. 3.50 (*0-486-21231-9*) Dover.

Topsys & Turvys, No. 2. Peter S. Newell. LC 87-51208. 72p. (J). (gr. k-4). 1988. 12.95 (*0-8048-1552-6*) C E Tuttle.

Toque de Diana. Rafael H. Moreno-Duran. 269p. (SPA.). 1981. pap. 8.50 (*84-85859-06-5*, 2009) Ediciones Norte.

***Toque de Trompeta en Sion, Pt. 1.** D. Wilkerson. (SPA.). 1.50 (*0-8297-0314-4*) Life Pubs Intl.

Tora Tora, Pearl Harbor: The Aircraft & Airmen, Dec. 7, 1941. Edward Maloney & Donald Thorpe. (Illus.). 175p. 1991. pap. 24.95 (*0-614-03027-7*, WW II Pubns) Aviation.

Torah. Rodney Mariner. (Illus.). 400p. 1997. 30.00 (*0-8050-4820-0*) H Holt & Co.

***Torah.** Rodney Mariner. 1997. pap. 14.95 (*0-614-19807-0*) H Holt & Co.

Torah: A Modern Commentary (Deluxe Edition) W. Gunther Plaut et al. 1824p. 1981. 55.00 (*0-8074-0333-4*, 381630) UAHC.

Torah: A Modern Commentary (English Opening) W. Gunther Plaut & Bernard J. Bamberger. 1824p. 1981. 40.00 (*0-8074-0055-6*, 381600) UAHC.

Torah: A Modern Commentary (Pulpit Edition) W. Gunther Plaut & Bernard J. Bamberger. 1824p. 1981. 100.00 (*0-8074-0286-9*, 381597) UAHC.

Torah: A Modern Commentary (Pulpit Edition) W. Gunther Plaut et al. 1824p. 1981. 40.00 (*0-8074-0165-X*, 381590) UAHC.

Torah: The Five Books of Moses, 5 vols. large type ed. (HEB.). 1987. (*0-318-65997-2*); (*0-318-65998-0*) Jewish Braille Inst.

Torah: The Growing Gift. Steven E. Steinbock. (Illus.). (Orig.). (J). (gr. 4-6). 1994. teacher ed., pap. 12.00 (*0-8074-0503-5*, 208035) UAHC.

Torah: The Growing Gift. Steven E. Steinbock. (Illus.). (Orig.). (J). (gr. 4-6). 1994. pap. 8.00 (*0-8074-0502-7*, 123939) UAHC.

Torah: Theology & Social History of Old Testament Law. Frank Crusemann. 480p. 1996. 44.00 (*0-8006-2856-X*, Fortress Pr) Augsburg Fortress.

Torah & Canon. James A. Sanders. LC 72-171504. 144p. (Orig.). 1972. pap. 11.00 (*0-8006-0105-X*, 1-105) Augsburg Fortress.

***Torah & Constitution: Essays in American Jewish Thought.** Milton R. Konvitz. 256p. 1997. 44.95 (*0-8156-2755-6*) Syracuse U Pr.

***Torah & Constitution: Essays in American Jewish Thought.** Milton R. Konvitz. 256p. 1997. pap. 18.95 (*0-8156-2762-9*) Syracuse U Pr.

Torah & Dharma: Jewish Seekers in Eastern Religions. Judith Linzer. LC 96-13676. 360p. 1996. 30.00 (*1-56821-916-4*) Aronson.

Torah & Law in Paradise Lost. Jason P. Rosenblatt. LC 93-37043. 288p. 1994. text ed. 39.50 (*0-691-03340-4*) Princeton U Pr.

Torah & Revelation. Ed. by Dan Cohn-Sherbok. LC 92-34722. 256p. 1992. text ed. 89.95 (*0-7734-9165-1*) E Mellen.

Torah & Science. Judah Landa. 1990. 39.50 (*0-88125-320-0*) Ktav.

Torah & Sophia: The Life & Thought of Shem Tov Ibn Falaquera. Raphael Jospe. LC 86-29484. (Monographs of the Hebrew Union College: Vol. 11). 519p. (ENG & HEB.). 1988. reprint ed. pap. 148.00 (*0-608-02083-4*, 2062736) Bks Demand.

***Torah & the Chronicler's History Work: An Inquiry into the Chronicler's References to Laws, Festivals & Cultic Institutions in Relationship to Pentateuchal Legislation.** Judson R. Shaver. 178p. 1990. 46.95 (*1-55540-417-0*, 140196) Scholars Pr GA.

Torah & Wisdom: Studies in Jewish Philosophy. Halakah & Kabbala. Ed. by Ruth Link-Salinger. LC 92-80955. 264p. 1992. 25.00 (*0-88400-157-1*) Shengold.

Torah Anthology: Book of Judges Shoftim. Shmuel Yerushalmi. Tr. & Adapted by Nathan Bushwick. (Torah Anthology - Meam Loez Ser.). (Illus.). 453p. 1991. 22.00 (*0-940118-52-1*) Moznaim.

Torah Anthology: Book of Yermiyahu I. Shmuel Yerushalmi. Tr. by Shlomo Carmel from HEB. (Torah Anthology - Meam Loez Ser.: 1). 306p. 1994. 14.00 (*0-940118-96-3*) Moznaim.

Torah Anthology: Meam Lo'ez, 41 vols. Incl. Vol. 1. Beginnings: From Creation Until Abraham. Yaakov Culi. Tr. by Aryeh Kaplan. 540p. 1977. 19.95 (*0-940118-01-7*); Vol. 2. Patriarchs: From Abraham Until Jacob. Yaakov Culi. Tr. by Aryeh Kaplan. 600p. 1977. 19.95 (*0-940118-02-5*); Vol. 3A. Twelve Tribes: From Jacob Until Joseph. Yaakov Culi. 358p. 1977. 19.95 (*0-940118-88-2*); Vol. 4. Israel in Egypt: Subjugation & Prelude to the Exodus. Yaakov Culi. Tr. by Arteh Kaplan. 280p. 1977. 19.95 (*0-940118-04-1*); Vol. 5. Redemption: The Exodus from Egypt. Yaakov Culi. Tr. by Aryeh Kaplan. 436p. 1977. 19.95 (*0-940118-05-X*); Vol. 6. Ten Commandments: Revelation at Sinai. Yaakov Culi. Tr. by Aryeh Kaplan. 534p. 1977. 19.95 (*0-940118-06-8*); Vol. 7. Laws: The First Codification. Yaakov Culi. Tr. by Aryeh Kaplan. 363p. 1977. 19.95 (*0-940118-07-6*); Vol. 8. Acceptance: Establishing the Covenant. Yaakov Culi. Tr. by Aryeh Kaplan. 250p. 1977. 19.95 (*0-940118-08-4*); Vol. 9. Tabernacle: Plans for the Sanctuary. Yaakov Culi. Tr. by Aryeh Kaplan. 413p. 1977. 19.95 (*0-940118-09-2*); Vol. 10. Sin & Reconciliation. Yitzchok Magriso. 358p. 1981. 19.95 (*0-940118-00-9*); Divine Service. Yitzchok Magriso. 459p. 1982. 19.95 (*0-940118-84-X*); Holiness. Yitzchok Magriso. 360p. 1982. 19.950-*940118-37-8*); First Journeys. Yitzchok Magriso. 448p. 1982. 19.95 (*0-940118-03-3*); Final Wanderings. Yitzchok Magriso. 478p. 1983. 19.95 (*0-940118-43-2*); Admonotion. Yitzchok Arguiti. 253p. 1984. 19.95 (*0-940118-44-0*); Faith & Optimism: Meam Lo'ez. Yitzchok Argueti. Ed. by Alexader Tobais. 318p. 1984. 19.95 (*0-940118-45-9*); Gratitude & Discipline Deut. No. 3. Yitzchok Argueti. Ed. by M. Sprecher & S. Sprecher. 288p. 1985. 19.95 (*0-940118-46-7*); Laws & Warning Deut. No. 4. Shmuel Yerushalmi. Tr. by Eli Touger from HEB. 203p. 1987. 19.95 (*0-940118-54-8*); Repentance & Blessings Deut. No. 5. Shmuel Yerushalmi. Tr. by Eli Touger. 212p. 1987. 19.95 (*0-940118-55-6*); Joseph in Egypt. Yaakov Culi. Tr. by Aryeh Kaplan. 1982. 19.95 (*0-940118-89-0*); (Torah Anthology - Meam Loez Ser.). (Illus.). 1977. 705.00 (*1-885220-03-0*) Moznaim.

Torah Anthology: The Book of Melakhim I, the Book of Kings. Shmuel Yerushalmi. Tr. by N. Bushwick from HEB. (Torah Anthology - Meam Loez Ser.: 1). 517p. 1994. 22.00 (*0-940118-99-8*) Moznaim.

Torah Anthology: The Book of Tehilim, Vol. 1. Shmuel Yerushalm. Tr. & Intro. by Zvi Faier. (Torah Anthology - Meam Loez Tehilim Ser.: 1). 379p. 1989. 18.00 (*0-940118-39-4*) Moznaim.

Torah Anthology: The Book of Tehilim, Vol. 2. Shmuel Yerushalmi. Tr. by Tzvi Faier. (Torah Anthology - Meam Loez Tehilim Ser.: 2). 404p. 1990. 18.00 (*0-940118-74-2*) Moznaim.

Torah Anthology: The Book of Tehilim, Vol. 3. Shmuel Yerushalmi. Tr. by Tzvi Faier. (Torah Anthology - Meam Loez Tehilim Ser.: 3). 494p. 1990. 18.00 (*0-940118-75-0*) Moznaim.

Torah Anthology: The Book of Tehilim, Vol. 4. Shmuel Yerushalmi. Tr. by Zvi Faier. (Torah Anthology - Meam Loez Tehilim Ser.: 4). 399p. 1991. 18.00 (*0-940118-76-9*) Moznaim.

Torah Anthology: The Book of Tehilim, Vol. 5. Shmuel Yerushalm. Tr. by Zvi Faier. (Torah Anthology - Meam Loez Tehilim Ser.: 5). 446p. 1991. 18.00 (*0-940118-77-7*) Moznaim.

Torah Anthology: The Book of Yermiyahu II. Shmuel Yerushalmi. Tr. by Shlomo Carmel from HEB. (Torah Anthology - Meam Loez Ser.: 2). 621p. 1994. 14.00 (*0-940118-97-1*) Moznaim.

torah Anthology - Book of Ruth. Shmuel Yerushalmi. Ed. by Zvi Faier. Tr. by E. Van Handel. (Torah Anthology - Meam Loez Ser.). 147p. (C). 1985. 13.00 (*0-940118-14-9*) Moznaim.

Torah Anthology - The Book of Kohelet (Ecclesiastes) Shmuel Yerushalmi. Tr. by Zvi Faier. (Torah Anthology - Meam Loez Ser.). 297p. 1988. 18.00 (*0-940118-16-5*) Moznaim.

Torah Anthology Book of Eicha: Lamentations, with Evening Service. Shmuel Yerushalmi. Tr. by Eliyahu Touger. (Torah Anthology - Meam Loez Ser.). 252p. 1990. 15.00 (*0-940118-78-5*) Moznaim.

Torah Anthology Book of Esther. Yaacov Culi. Tr. by Aryeh Kaplan. (Torah Anthology - Meam Loez Ser.). 252p. 1978. 15.00 (*0-940118-13-0*) Moznaim.

Torah Anthology, Book of Joshua. Shmuel Yerushalmi. Tr. & Intro. by Nathan Bushwich. (Torah Anthology - Meam Loez Ser.). (Illus.). 518p. 1991. 22.00 (*0-940118-51-3*) Moznaim.

Torah Anthology Book of Mishlei I, Pt. 1, Chapters 1-15: Proverbs. Shmuel Yerushalmi. Tr. by Tzvi Faler from HEB. (Torah Anthology - Meam Loez Tehilim Ser.: 1). 426p. 1993. 22.00 (*0-940118-94-7*) Moznaim.

Torah Anthology Book of Mishlie II: Book of Proverbs II. Shmuel Yerushalmi. Tr. by Tzvi Faier from HEB. (Torah Anthology - Meam Loez Ser.: 2). 381p. 1994. 22.00 (*0-940118-95-5*) Moznaim.

Torah Anthology, Book of Samuel, No. 1. Shmuel Yerushalmi. Ed. by Yaakov Weiss. Tr. by Moshe Mykoff & Yaakov Weiss from HEB. (Torah Anthology - Meam Loez Ser.: 1). (Illus.). 509p. 1991. 22.00 (*0-940118-53-X*) Moznaim.

Torah Anthology Shir Hashirim (Song of Songs) Shmuel Yerushalmi. Tr. by Zvi Faier. (Torah Anthology - Meam Loez Ser.). 352p. 1988. 18.00 (*0-940118-15-7*) Moznaim.

Torah Anthology Shmuel II: The Book of Samuel II. Shmuel Yerushalmi. Tr. by Moshe Mykoff from HEB. (Torah Anthology - Meam Loez Ser.: 2). (Illus.). 537p. 1993. 22.00 (*0-940118-85-8*) Moznaim.

Torah Anthology Spanish Edition Book of Ruth: El Ubro de Rut. Shmuel Yerodhalmi. Tr. by Anita B. Lusry. (Torah Anthology - Meam Loez Ser.). 254p. (ENG & SPA.). 1993. 13.00 (*1-885220-11-1*) Moznaim.

Torah Anthology Spanish Edition Genesis 1. Yaakov Culi. Tr. by Israel Jabif from HEB. (Torah Anthology - Meam Loez Ser.: No. 1). 362p. (SPA.). 1992. 20.00 (*1-885220-08-1*) Moznaim.

Torah Anthology Spanish Edition Genesis 2. Yaacov Culi. Tr. by Israel Jabif from HEB. (Torah Anthology - Meam Loez Ser.: No. 2). 479p. (SPA.). 1993. 20.00 (*1-885220-09-X*) Moznaim.

Torah Anthology Spanish Edition Genesis 3. Yaacov Culi. Tr. by Israel Jabif from HEB. (Torah Anthology - Meam Loez Ser.: No. 3). 483p. (SPA.). 1994. 20.00 (*1-885220-10-3*) Moznaim.

Torah Binders of the Judah L. Magnes Museum. Ruth Eis. LC 79-83877. 80p. 1979. pap. 18.00 (*0-943376-15-7*) Magnes Mus.

***Torah Codes & Israel Today.** Robert M. Haralick & Matityahu Glazerson. 207p. (Orig.). 1996. pap. 16.99 (*1-880880-19-9*, Pub. by Raz Ot Insti IS) Israeli Trad.

Torah Commentary for Our Times, 3 vols. Harvey J. Fields. (Illus.). (Orig.). (J). (gr. 7-9). 1994. boxed 35.00 (*0-8074-0530-2*, 164054) UAHC.

Torah Commentary for Our Times: Genesis, Vol. I. Ed. by Harvey J. Fields. LC 89-28478. (Illus.). (YA). (gr. 7 up). 1990. pap. text ed. 12.00 (*0-8074-0308-3*, 164000) UAHC.

Torah Commentary for Our Times, Vol. 2: Exodus & Leviticus. Harvey J. Fields. LC 89-28478. (Illus.). (YA). (gr. 7-9). 1991. pap. text ed. 12.00 (*0-8074-0334-2*, 164010) UAHC.

Torah Commentary for Our Times, Vol. 3: Numbers & Deuteronomy. Harvey J. Fields. LC 89-28478. (Illus.). (Orig.). (YA). (gr. 7-9). 1993. pap. text ed. 12.00 (*0-8074-0511-6*, 164020) UAHC.

Torah Discourses of the Holy Tzaddik Reb Menachem Mendel of Rimanov, 1745-1815. Tr. by Dov Levine. LC 96-248. (ENG, HEB & YID.). 1996. write for info. (*0-88125-540-8*) Ktav.

Torah Dynamics: Pirkei Avos Looks at Life. 1991. 21.95 (*0-87306-541-7*) Feldheim.

Torah for Children. Aaron Falk. LC 92-28623. (Illus.). 32p. (J). (gr. k-4). 1993. 12.95 (*1-880582-06-6*); pap. 9.95 (*1-880582-07-4*) Judaica Pr.

Torah for Family Reading. Ed. by Joseph Gaer. LC 86-70620. 576p. 1992. 40.00 (*0-87668-915-2*) Aronson.

Torah for Family Reading. Joseph Gaer. LC 86-70620. 576p. 1996. pap. 30.00 (*1-56821-982-2*) Aronson.

Torah from Heaven Vol. 2: The Theology of Classical Judaism. Abraham J. Heschel. 912p. 1998. 79.50 (*0-8264-0802-8*) Continuum.

Torah from Our Sages: Pirke Avot. Jacob Neusner. 214p. 1986. pap. 9.95 (*0-685-43435-4*) Rossel Bks.

Torah from Our Sages: Pirke Avot. Jacob Neusner. 1997. reprint ed. pap. 9.95 (*0-940646-36-6*) Behrman.

Torah from Scroll to Symbol in Formative Judaism. Jacob Neusner. (Brown Judaic Studies). 204p. 1988. 34.95 (*1-55540-219-4*, 14 01 36) Scholars Pr GA.

Torah Guide for the Businessman. S. Wasschal. 1990. 19.95 (*0-685-38892-1*) Feldheim.

***Torah Guide to Money Matters.** Shaul Wagshal. 1996. 19.95 (*0-614-19801-1*) Feldheim.

Torah in Gematria: Word for Word. Leon L. Solonche. 136p. (Orig.). (HEB.). 1982. pap. 12.50 (*0-911001-00-X*) NY Stets.

Torah in Motion: Creating Dance Midrash. JoAnne Tucker & Susan Freeman. LC 90-80913. (Illus.). 273p. (Orig.). 1990. 20.50 (*0-86705-024-1*) A R E Pub.

Torah in the Talmud: A Taxonomy of the Uses of Scripture in the Talmud: Tractate Qiddushin in the Talmud of Babylonia & the Talmud of the Land of Israel, 2 vols., Vol. 1. Jacob Neusner. LC 92-46278. (USF Studies in the History of Judaism: Nos. 69 & 70). 197p. 1993. 59.95 (*1-55540-828-1*, 24 00 69) Scholars Pr GA.

Torah in the Talmud: A Taxonomy of the Uses of Scripture in the Talmud: Tractate Qiddushin in the Talmud of Babylonia & the Talmud of the Land of Israel, 2 vols., Vol. 2. Jacob Neusner. LC 92-46278. (USF Studies in the History of Judaism: Nos. 69 & 70). 194p. 1993. 59.95 (*1-55540-829-X*, 24 00 70) Scholars Pr GA.

Torah Is Written. Paul Cowan & Rachel Cowan. (Illus.). 32p. (gr. 3 up). 1986. 14.95 (*0-8276-0270-7*) JPS Phila.

Torah, Light & Healing: Mystical Insights into Healing Based on the Hebrew Language. Matityahu Glazerson. LC 95-50733. 232p. 1996. pap. 22.50 (*1-56821-934-2*) Aronson.

Torah Lishmah: The Study of Torah for Torah's Sake in the Work of Rabbi Hayyim of Volozhin & His Contemporaries. Norman Lamm. (Studies & Sources in Kabbalah, Hasidism & Jewish Thought Ser.: Vol. I). 1988. 25.00 (*0-88125-117-8*); pap. 16.95 (*0-88125-133-X*) Ktav.

***Torah Lives.** Ed. by Nisson Wolpin. (Judaiscope Ser.). 19.99 (*0-89906-319-5*, TL1H); pap. 15.99 (*0-89906-320-9*, TL1P) Mesorah Pubns.

***Torah Luminaries.** Ed. by Nisson Wolpin. 19.99 (*0-89906-439-6*, TOLH); pap. 16.99 (*0-89906-440-X*, TOLP) Mesorah Pubns.

Torah Nebiim u Ketubim. Norman H. Snaith. 1362p. 1986. 13.00 (*0-564-00029-9*, 104072, Pub. by British & Foreign Bible Society UK) Am Bible.

Torah (New Translation) 394p. 1962. 15.95 (*0-8276-0015-1*) JPS Phila.

Torah Or. 400p. (HEB.). 25.00 (*0-8266-5550-5*) Kehot Pubn Soc.

Torah Personality: A Treasury of Biographical Sketches. Nisson Wolpin. (ArtScroll Judaicascope Ser.). (Illus.). 288p. 1981. 19.99 (*0-89906-850-2*) Mesorah Pubns.

Torah Perspectives: An Eminent Torah Leader Expounds on Timely Subjects. Mordechai Gifter. (ArtScroll Ser.). (Illus.). 112p. 1986. 16.99 (*0-89906-228-8*); pap. 13.99 (*0-89906-229-6*) Mesorah Pubns.

Torah Profile: A Treasury of Biographical Sketches. Nisson Wolpin. (ArtScroll Judaiscope Ser.). 328p. 1988. 19.99 (*0-89906-860-X*); pap. 16.99 (*0-89906-861-8*) Mesorah Pubns.

Torah Readings for Festivals. 6.95 (*0-87677-069-3*) Prayer Bk.

Torah Rhymes & Riddles. S. Lepon. 1992. 13.99 (*0-89906-995-9*); pap. 10.99 (*0-89906-996-7*) Mesorah Pubns.

Torah Shapes. R. Sebarg & Adina Zakutinsky. (Illus.). 12p. (J). (ps). 1987. 4.95 (*0-911643-08-7*) Aura Bklyn.

***Torah Studies.** 4th ed. Menachem M. Schneerson. Tr. by Jonathan Sacks from HEB. 400p. 1996. reprint ed. 25.00 (*0-8266-0493-5*) Kehot Pubn Soc.

Torah Study: A Survey of Classic Sources on Timely Issues. Yehuda Levi. 20.95 (*0-87306-555-7*) Feldheim.

Torah Talk: An Early Childhood Teaching Guide. Yona Chubara et al. LC 89-80336. 308p. (Orig.). 1989. pap. text ed. 22.50 (*0-86705-023-3*) A R E Pub.

Torah, Tarot & Tantra: A Guide to Jewish Spiritual Growth. William Blank. 1991. 29.95 (*0-904575-52-7*); pap. 16.95 (*0-904575-51-9*) Sigo Pr.

Torah Teddy Learns Colors. Shaindy Shulman. (gr. k-2). 1985. 6.95 (*0-87306-942-0*) Feldheim.

Torah Through the Ages: A Short History of Judaism. Jacob Neusner. LC 89-20646. 192p. (C). 1990. text ed. 21.95 (*0-334-02456-0*) TPI PA.

Torah Toons I. Joel L. Grishaver. (Illus.). 115p. (Orig.). (J). (gr. 4 up). 1985. pap. text ed. 5.95 (*0-933873-01-8*) Torah Aura.

Torah Toons II. Joel L. Grishaver. (Illus.). 114p. (Orig.). (J). (gr. 6 up). 1985. pap. text ed. 5.95 (*0-933873-02-6*) Torah Aura.

Torah Treasures. Dov Furer. 300p. (C). 1990. 15.95 (*1-56062-048-X*); pap. 12.95 (*1-56062-049-8*) CIS Comm.

Torah Umadda: The Encounter of Religious Learning & Worldly Knowledge in the Jewish Tradition. Norman Lamm. LC 89-18519. 264p. 1994. pap. 20.00 (*1-56821-231-3*) Aronson.

Torah World: A Treasury of Biographical Sketches. Nisson Wolpin. (ArtScroll Judaicascope Ser.). (Illus.). 320p. 1982. 19.99 (*0-89906-854-5*); pap. 16.99 (*0-89906-855-3*) Mesorah Pubns.

Torani Cookbook: Cooking with Italian Flavoring Syrups. Lisa Lucheta. LC 95-39486. 128p. (Orig.). 1996. pap. 16.95 (*0-89815-803-6*) Ten Speed Pr.

Torant lo Blanc: Text & Context: (Proceedings of the Second Catalan Symposium), Vol. 11. Josep M. Sola-Sole. LC 92-41846. (Catalan Studies). 224p. (C). 1993. text ed. 41.95 (*0-8204-2158-8*) P Lang Pubng.

***Toras Chaim Vol. 2: Schemois.** 3rd ed. Dov B. Schneersohn. 1344p. (HEB.). 1947. reprint ed. 30.00 (*0-8266-5589-0*) Kehot Pubn Soc.

Toras Chaim Beneishes. Dov B. Schneuri. 712p. (HEB.). reprint ed. 35.00 (*0-8266-5588-2*) Kehot Pubn Soc.

***Toras Shalom: Sefer Hasichos.** 4th ed. Shalom D. Schneersohn. 342p. (HEB.). 1946. reprint ed. 17.00 (*0-8266-5644-7*) Kehot Pubn Soc.

Torasemide - Clinical Pharmacology & Therapeutic Applications: Proceedings of the International Symposium on Torasemide, Munich, October 21-23, 1988. Ed. by F. Kruck et al. (Progress in Pharmacology & Clinical Pharmacology Ser.: Vol. 8, No. 1). 273p. (Orig.). 1991. pap. text ed. 75.00 (*0-89574-321-3*) G F Verlag.

Torbern Bergman, a Man Before His Time. J. A. Schufle. (Illus.). 509p. 1985. 35.00 (*0-87291-169-1*) Coronado Pr.

Torch. Jill Paton Walsh. LC 87-45995. 176p. (YA). 1988. 15.00 (*0-374-37684-0*) FS&G.

Torch. George E. Woodberry. LC 73-84349. (Essay Index Reprint Ser.). 1977. 18.95 (*0-8369-1115-6*) Ayer.

Torch, & Other Tales. Eden Phillpotts. LC 71-144167. (Short Story Index Reprint Ser.). 1977. reprint ed. 19.95 (*0-8369-3782-1*) Ayer.

Torch & the Spear. Patrick Regan. (Illus.). (Orig.). 1996. pap. 19.95 (*1-898307-72-5*, Pub. by Capall Bann Pubng UK) Holmes Pub.

***Torch-Bearer to Light the Way: The Life of Myrtle Fillmore.** Neal Vahle. (Illus.). 304p. 1996. pap. 14.95 (*0-9655906-0-7*) Open View Pr.

Torch Bearers. Archer M. Huntington. 1955. 5.00 (*0-87535-084-4*) Hispanic Soc.

***Torch for Meg.** Evan Skolnick. (Disney's Enchanting Stories Ser.). 1997. pap. text ed. 4.50 (*1-57840-075-9*) Acclaim Bks.

***Torch Hardening Method for Gears.** W. E. Sykes. (Technical Papers). 1937. pap. text ed. 30.00 (*1-55589-332-5*) AGMA.

Torch in My Ear. Elias Canetti. Tr. by Joachim Neugroschel from GER. 384p. 1982. 16.50 (*0-374-27847-4*) FS&G.

Torch in My Ear. Elias Canetti. Tr. by Joachim Neugroschel from GER. 384p. 1983. pap. 9.95 (*0-374-51804-1*) FS&G.

Torch in the Night: Worship Resources from South Africa. Anne Hope. 144p. 1988. pap. 5.95 (*0-377-00182-1*) Friendship Pr.

An Asterisk (*) at the beginning of an entry indicates that the title is appearing in BIP for the first time.

Torch Is Passed: The Kennedy Brothers & American Liberalism. 2nd ed. David Burner & Thomas R. West. (Series in American History: No. 4). 321p. (C). 1992. reprint ed. pap. 12.50 (*1-881089-03-7*) Brandywine Press.

Torch Job. Patricia Rosemoor. (Intrigue Ser.). 1993. pap. 2.89 (*0-373-22219-X*, 1-22219-9) Harlequin Bks.

Torch of Certainty. Jamgon Kongtrul. Tr. by Judith Hanson. 184p. 1994. pap. 12.00 (*0-87773-786-X*) Shambhala Pubns.

Torch of Certainty. Jamgon Kongtrul. Tr. by Judith Hanson from TIB. LC 86-11837. 161p. 1994. reprint ed. pap. 12.00 (*1-57062-051-2*) Shambhala Pubns.

Torch of the Testimony. John W. Kennedy. (Orig.). 1983. pap. 9.95 (*0-940232-12-X*) Seedsowers.

***Torch of Triumph.** Sally Laity & Dianna Crawford. LC 96-47576. (Freedom's Holy Light Ser.: Bk. 6). 1997. pap. 10.99 (*0-8423-1417-2*) Tyndale.

Torch Song. Valerie Kirkwood. 384p. 1996. mass mkt. 4.99 (*0-8217-5459-9*, Zebra Kensgtn) Kensgtn Pub Corp.

Torch Song Trilogy. Harvey Fierstein. 1983. 12.95 (*0-394-53428-X*, Villard Bks) Random.

Torch Songs. Jesse Rider. 48p. 1995. pap. 5.00 (*1-888431-05-9*) Small Garlic.

Torch Songs, No. 66. 152p. 1994. otabind 14.95 (*0-7935-3283-3*, 00102312) H Leonard.

Torch Syndrome: Infections of the Human Fetus. Gilles R. Monif. (Illus.). 171p. (C). 1993. text ed. 34.95 (*1-880906-02-3*) IDI Pubns.

Torch to the Heart: Anthology of Lesbian Art & Drama. Ed. by Sue McConnell-Celi. (Illus.). 250p. (Orig.). 1994. pap. 18.25 (*1-884541-00-3*) Lavender Crystal.

Torch Town Boogie. Steven Womack. (Southern Mysteries Ser.). 1993. mass mkt. 4.99 (*0-345-38010-X*) Ballantine.

Torch Use of Flammable Gases License. (Career Examination Ser.: C-3770). pap. 23.95 (*0-8373-3770-4*) Nat Learn.

Torchbearers. Torkom Saraydarian. 1981. pap. 2.50 (*0-911794-49-2*) Aqua Educ.

Torchbearers: Women & Their Amateur Arts Associations in America, 1890-1930. Karen J. Blair. LC 93-485. (Philanthropic Studies). 276p. 1994. 31.50 (*0-253-31192-6*) Ind U Pr.

Torchbearers in Honan. Annie J. Sallee. LC 72-5437. (Biography Index Reprint Ser.). 1977. reprint ed. 23.95 (*0-8369-8138-3*) Ayer.

Torchbearers of the Middle Ages. Alvin S. Luchs. LC 77-160924. (Biography Index Reprint Ser.). (Illus.). 1977. reprint ed. 18.95 (*0-8369-8087-5*) Ayer.

***Torches: Poems from Hollywood.** Mark Dunster. 23p. (Orig.). (YA). (gr. 9-12). 1997. pap. 5.00 (*0-89642-361-1*) Linden Pubs.

Torches Extinguished: Memories of a Communal Bruderhof Childhood in Paraguay, Europe & the U. S. A. Elizabeth Bohlken-Zumpe. Ed. by Gertrude E. Huntington. LC 93-72237. (Women from Utopia Ser.). (Illus.). 330p. (Orig.). 1993. pap. 17.00 (*1-882260-01-5*) Carrier Pigeon.

Torches of Joy: The Dynamic Story of a Stone Age Tribe's Encounter with the Gospel of Jesus Christ. John Dekker. 1993. pap. 7.99 (*0-927545-43-8*) YWAM Pub.

Torches Rekindled: The Bruderhof's Struggle for Renewal. 3rd rev. ed. Merrill Mow. Ed. by Hutterian Brethren Staff. LC 90-49626. (Illus.). 354p. (Orig.). (C). 1991. pap. 8.00 (*0-87486-032-6*) Plough.

Torches Together: The Beginning & Early Years of the Bruderhof Communities. Society Of Brothers Staff. LC 77-166341. (Illus.). 1976. pap. 8.00 (*0-87486-171-3*) Plough.

Torching. Marcy Heidish. 272p. 1993. reprint ed. mass mkt. 4.99 (*0-380-72054-X*) Avon.

Torchlight. Lisa Bergren. 249p. 1994. pap. 8.99 (*0-88070-806-9*, Multnomah Bks) Multnomah Pubs.

***Torchlight.** Robert Louis Stevenson. LC 97-12395. 352p. 1997. 23.95 (*0-399-14315-7*) Putnam Pub Group.

Torchlight for America. Louis Farrakhan. LC 93-79288. 171p. (Orig.). 1993. pap. 12.00 (*0-9637642-4-1*) FCN Pub.

Torchlight Parade. Sherwin L. Cook. LC 70-128227. (Essay Index Reprint Ser.). 1977. 23.95 (*0-8369-1911-4*) Ayer.

Torchlight to Valhalla. Gale Wilhelm. 128p. 1985. pap. 7.95 (*0-930044-68-1*) Naiad Pr.

Torchlight to Valhalla. Gale Wilhelm. LC 75-12358. (Homosexuality Ser.). 1975. reprint ed. 17.95 (*0-405-07381-X*) Ayer.

Torchlights to the Cherokees. Robert S. Walker. 352p. 1993. reprint ed. 19.95 (*0-932807-95-X*) Overmountain Pr.

Torchon Lace for Today. Jennifer Fisher. (Illus.). 1985. 19.95 (*0-949924-45-8*) Branford.

Torchon Lace Patterns. Henk Hardeman. 1986. pap. 22.50 (*0-7134-4878-4*) Robin & Russ.

Torchon Lace Workbook. Bridget M. Cook. (Color Craft Workbooks Ser.). (Illus.). 96p. 1988. pap. 14.95 (*0-312-02119-4*) St Martin.

Torchon Lacemaking: Manual of Techniques. Elizabeth Wade. (Illus.). 176p. 1996. pap. 29.95 (*1-85223-979-4*, Pub. by Crowood Pr UK) Trafalgar.

***Tordus Debarquent!** Christiane Duchesne. (Novels in the Premier Roman Ser.). 64p. (FRE.). (J). (gr. 2-5). 1996. pap. 7.95 (*2-89021-161-4*, Pub. by Les Editions CN) Firefly Bks Ltd.

Toreadors from Carmen. William Starr & Constance Starr. (Sounds of Symphony Ser.). 1988. pap. text ed. 18.00 (*0-87487-616-8*) Summy-Birchard.

Torejazu Three: Nihon to Oregon No Jido Seito Ni Yoru Bungei Sa Kuhin-shu. Tr. by Ako Harada et al. (Illus.). 272p. (Orig.). (J). (gr. k-12). 1994. pap. 13.95 (*0-9616058-3-9*) OR Students Writing.

***Torero.** Adam Shaw. 1998. pap. 23.95 (*1-55611-521-0*) D I Fine.

Toreros: Poems. John Gawsworth. Ed. by Steve Eng. (Blue Meadow Poetry Ser.: No. 2). 68p. 1990. pap. 10.00 (*0-910151-01-6*) Nashville Hse.

Torg Replaying Game Box, Set. (Torg Ser.). Boxed set. boxed 30.00 (*0-87431-300-7*, 20501) West End Games.

Tori Amos. Jim Stapleton. (CD Bks.). (Illus.). 120p. 1995. pap. 7.99 (*1-886894-23-X*, MBS Paperbk) Mus Bk Servs.

***Tori Amos: Collectables.** Paul Campbell. (Illus.). 160p. pap. 29.95 (*0-8256-1578-X*, OP 47869) Omnibus NY.

Tori Amos: Cornflake Girl. Susan Wilson. (Illus.). 64p. 1996. pap. 16.99 (*1-886894-37-X*, MBS Paperbk) Mus Bk Servs.

***Tori Amos: Cornflake Girl.** Susan Wilson. 1996. pap. 16.99 (*1-873884-56-7*, Pub. by UFO Books UK) Music Sales.

***Tori Amos: Images & Insights.** (Illus.). 96p. (Orig.). (C). pap. 24.95 (*0-8256-1567-4*, OP 47856) Omnibus NY.

***Tori Amos: Interview CD Book.** (Interview CD Bks.). (Illus.). Date not set. 14.99 (*1-886894-87-6*) Mus Bk Servs.

Tori Amos: Little Earthquakes. (Illus.). 132p. 1992. pap. 21.95 (*0-8256-1345-0*, AM90041) Music Sales.

***Tori Amos: MTV Unplugged.** Tori Amos. pap. 17.95 (*0-8256-1565-8*) Omnibus NY.

Tori Amos: The Authorized Biography. 2nd rev. ed. Kalen Rogers. (Illus.). 132p. (Orig.). (C). pap. 19.95 (*0-8256-1448-1*, OP 47756) Omnibus NY.

***Tori Amos: The Bee Sides.** Tori Amos. 1996. pap. 19.95 (*0-8256-1494-5*, AM 931315) Music Sales.

Tori Amos: Under the Pink. 124p. 1996. pap. 24.95 (*0-8256-1405-8*, AM 92048) Music Sales.

Tori Amos Boys for Pele. Tori Amos. 1996. pap. text ed. 24.95 (*0-8256-1544-5*, AM937750) Omnibus NY.

Tori Amos Pink Earthquakes. (Illus.). 48p. (Orig.). 1995. pap. 19.99 (*1-886894-28-0*, MBS Paperbk) Mus Bk Servs.

Tori & Aaron Spelling. Skip Press. LC 95-11600. (Star Families Ser.). (J). (gr. 5-6). 1995. pap. 4.95 (*0-382-39179-9*, Crstwood Hse); lib. bdg. 15.95 (*0-89686-885-0*, Crstwood Hse) Silver Burdett Pr.

Tories & the Welfare State: A History of Conservative Social Policy since the Second World War. Timothy Raison. LC 89-37094. 236p. 1990. text ed. 55.00 (*0-312-04079-2*) St Martin.

Tories, Dons, & Rebels: The American Revolution in British West Florida. J. Barton Starr. LC 76-28953. 1976. 17.95 (*0-8130-0543-4*) U Press Fla.

***Torina's World: The Villages of Madagascar.** Joni Kabana. Ed. by Benjamin Opsahl. LC 97-71980. (Illus.). 48p. (Orig.). (J). (ps-3). 1997. pap. 12.95 (*1-888803-04-5*) Lenswrk.

Torment. Stephen R. George. 384p. 1994. mass mkt. 4.50 (*0-8217-4628-6*, Zebra Kensgtn) Kensgtn Pub Corp.

Torment. Todd McFarlane. (Spiderman Ser.). (Illus.). 128p. 1992. pap. 12.95 (*0-87135-805-0*) Marvel Entmnt.

Torment of Secrecy: The Background & Consequences of American Security Policies. Edward A. Shils. LC 95-50421. 266p. 1996. pap. 12.95 (*1-56663-105-X*) I R Dee.

Tormented? God's Key's to Life. rev. ed. Nancy Curtis & Ken Curtis. (Illus.). 1985. pap. 4.95 (*0-9615445-0-3*) MDI Inc.

Tormented Master: The Life & Spiritual Quest of Rabbi Nahman of Bratslav. Arthur Green. LC 92-1085. 408p. 1992. reprint ed. pap. 18.95 (*1-879045-11-7*) Jewish Lights.

Tormentil & Bleached Bones. Thomas A. Clark. 1994. pap. 10.95 (*0-7486-6168-9*, Pub. by Edinburgh U Pr UK) Col U Pr.

Tormentng Flame. John Sawyer. 1980. pap. 1.50 (*0-373-58054-1*) Harlequin Bks.

Tormentors. Lynn Hall. 319p. (J). (gr. 3-7). 1990. 14.95 (*0-15-289470-5*) HarBrace.

Tormentors. Lynn Hall. LC 90-4805. 128p. (J). (gr. 3-7). 1993. pap. 3.95 (*0-15-289471-3*) HarBrace.

Torments. Lisa W. Cantrell. 1990. mass mkt. 4.95 (*0-8125-0668-5*) Tor Bks.

***Torments Ancient & Modern: An Anglo-Welsh Experience.** Keith Nurse. 55p. 1997. pap. 8.95 (*1-85756-234-8*, Pub. by Janus Pubng UK) Paul & Co Pubs.

Torments of Love. Helisenne De Crenne. Ed. & Tr. by Lisa Neal. Tr. by Steven Rendall. LC 95-41011. (C). 1996. pap. 18.95 (*0-8166-2789-4*); text ed. 47.95 (*0-8166-2788-6*) U of Minn Pr.

Torn Allegiances: The Story of a Gay Cadet. Jim Holobaugh & Keith Hale. LC 92-56166. (Illus.). 220p. (Orig.). 1993. pap. 9.95 (*1-55583-216-4*) Alyson Pubns.

***Torn Apart.** Romen Basu. 198p. 1997. write for info. (*0-932377-67-X*) R Basu.

Torn Asunder: Recovering from Extramarital Affairs. expanded rev. ed. Dave Carder & Duncan Jaenicke. 1995. pap. 14.99 (*0-8024-7748-8*) Moody.

Torn Away. James Heneghan. (Illus.). 192p. (J). (gr. 7 up). 1994. pap. 14.99 (*0-670-85180-9*) Viking Child Bks.

Torn Away. James Heneghan. 192p. (J). (gr. 5-9). 1996. pap. 4.99 (*0-14-036646-6*, Puffin) Puffin Bks.

Torn Between Empires: Economy, Society, & Patterns of Political Thought in the Hispanic Caribbean, 1840-1878. Luis Martinez-Fernandez. LC 93-14972. 344p. (C). 1994. 50.00 (*0-8203-1568-0*) U of Ga Pr.

Torn Between Two Lands: Armenians in America, 1890 to World War I. Robert Mirak. (Armenian Texts & Studies: No. 7). (Illus.). 378p. 1984. reprint ed. pap. 12.95 (*0-674-89541-X*) HUP.

Torn by Light: Selected Poems. Joanne De Longchamps. Ed. by Shaun T. Griffin. LC 92-40531. (Western Literature Ser.). (Illus.). 176p. 1993. 24.95 (*0-87417-218-7*); pap. 13.95 (*0-87417-217-9*) U of Nev Pr.

Torn by the Issues: An Unbiased Review of the Watershed Issues in American Life - a Collaboration of Unlike Minds. Jennifer Maguire et al. Ed. by Fred Hoey et al. 400p. (Orig.). 1994. pap. 15.95 (*1-56474-093-5*) Fithian Pr.

Torn from My Heart: The True Story of a Mother's Desperate Search for Her Stolen Children. Patsy Heymans et al. 432p. 1996. 23.95 (*0-446-52006-3*) Warner Bks.

Torn from My Heart: The True Story of a Mother's Desperate Search for Her Stolen Children. Patsy Heymans et al. 1997. mass mkt. write for info. (*0-446-60412-7*) Warner Bks.

Torn Halves: Political Conflict in Literary & Cultural Theory. Robert J. Young. LC 95-30849. 256p. (C). 1996. text ed. 74.95 (*0-7190-4776-5*, Pub. by Manchester Univ Pr UK); text ed. 24.95 (*0-7190-4777-3*, Pub. by Manchester Univ Pr UK) St Martin.

Torn Illusions: Fully-Documented, Private & Public Expose of the Worldwide Medical Tragedy of Silicone Implants. 2nd rev. ed. Pamela Stott-Kendall. LC 96-96404. Orig. Title: Torn Illusions: One Woman's Basic Experience With the Silicone Conspiracy. 288p. 1996. 22.95 (*0-9652783-1-X*, 1323); pap. 22.95 (*0-9652783-0-1*, 1323) Debcar Pub.

Torn Illusions: One Woman's Basic Experience With the Silicone Conspiracy see Torn Illusions: Fully-Documented, Private & Public Expose of the Worldwide Medical Tragedy of Silicone Implants

Torn Jacket. Mary Rogers. (Cityscapes Ser.). 30p. (J). (gr. 1). 1992. pap. text ed. 4.50 (*1-56843-068-X*) BGR Pub.

Torn Jacket: Big Book. Mary Rogers. (Cityscapes Ser.). 30p. (J). (gr. 1). 1992. pap. text ed. 23.00 (*1-56843-018-3*) BGR Pub.

***Torn Lace: And Other Stories. Emilia Pardo Bazan. Tr. by Maria C. Urruela from SPA. LC 96-41223. (MLA Texts & Translations Ser.: Vol. 5b). xxxiv, 141p. (Orig.). 1996. pap. 7.95 (*0-87352-784-4*, Q005P) Modern Lang.**
Although written a century ago, the sixteen stories by Emilia Pardo Bazan collected in this volume are strikingly relevant to contemporary concerns. Noted for narrative complexity, stylistic variety & feminist themes, Pardo Bazan's stories explore many aspects of the relationships between men & women. Readers of these stories, most of which are here translated into English for the first time, will encounter memorable & affecting characters. A mysterious nun spends her days in a convent crying over something that happened to her many years ago, when she was a young woman. A young man tries to uncover the true reason a scheming woman married his uncle. An unwed pregnant woman finds unexpected help from a misogynist doctor. A bachelor wishing to marry develops a special test for prospective wives, only to see it backfire. And in the title story, a bride suddenly calls off her wedding at the last possible moment without an explanation. Both outspoken & witty, melancholy & humorous, these stories will interest general readers as well as students & scholars of Spanish literature. ***Publisher Provided Annotation.***

Torn Out by the Roots: The Recollections of a Former Communist. Hilda Vitzthum. Tr. & Intro. by Paul Schach. LC 92-23837. (Illus.). xviii, 273p. 1993. text ed. 27.50 (*0-8032-4660-9*) U of Nebr Pr.

Torn Pages of History. Gilbert W. Davies. LC 96-75247. 130p. (Orig.). (C). 1996. pap. 6.95 (*1-887200-02-9*) HiSt Ink Bks.

***Torn Shapes of Desire: Internet Erotica.** Mary A. Mohanraj. Ed. by Dale L. Larson. (Illus.). 128p. (Orig.). 1997. pap. 14.95 (*1-885876-03-3*) Intangible Assets.

Torn Sprockets: The Uncertain Projection of the Canadian Film. Gerald Pratley. LC 83-40110. (Illus.). 336p. 1987. 65.00 (*0-87413-194-4*) U Delaware Pr.

Torn Togas: The Dark Side of Campus Greek Life. Esther Wright. 224p. 1996. 19.95 (*0-925190-94-2*) Fairview Press.

Torn Veil. Gulshan Esther. 1989. pap. 5.95 (*0-87508-473-7*) Chr Lit.

Torn Wings & Faux Pas: A Flashbook of Style, a Beastly Guide Through the Writer's Labyrinth. Karen Gordon. LC 97-11232. 1997. 23.00 (*0-679-44242-1*) Random.

Tornado! Jules Archer. LC 90-45373. (Nature's Disasters Ser.). (Illus.). 48p. (J). (gr. 5-6). 1991. lib. bdg. 12.95 (*0-89686-594-0*, Crstwood Hse) Silver Burdett Pr.

Tornado. Betsy C. Byars. LC 95-41584. (Illus.). 64p. (J). (gr. 2-5). 1996. 13.95 (*0-06-026449-7*) HarpC Child Bks.

Tornado. Betsy C. Byars. LC 95-41584. (Illus.). 64p. (J). (gr. 2-5). 1996. lib. bdg. 13.89 (*0-06-026452-7*) HarpC Child Bks.

***Tornado.** Betsy C. Byars. LC 95-41584. (Chapter Bk.). 64p. (J). (gr. 2-6). 1997. pap. 3.95 (*0-06-442063-9*, Trophy) HarpC Child Bks.

Tornado. Stephen Kramer. (J). (gr. 1-4). 1992. lib. bdg. 14.96 (*0-87614-660-4*, Carolrhoda) Lerner Group.

Tornado. Christopher Lampton. (Disaster! Book). (Illus.). 64p. (J). (gr. 4-6). 1991. pap. 5.95 (*1-56294-785-0*) Millbrook Pr.

Tornado. John E. Weems. LC 90-38296. 200p. 1991. pap. 11.95 (*0-89096-460-2*) Tex A&M Univ Pr.

Tornado! Russell Wright. Ed. by Cathy Anderson et al. (Event-Based Science Ser.). (Illus.). (Orig.). (YA). (gr. 6-9). 1996. wbk. ed., pap. text ed. 7.95 (*0-201-49595-3*) Supplementary Div.

Tornado! Russell Wright. Ed. by Cathy Anderson et al. (Event-Based Science Ser.). (Illus.). (Orig.). (YA). (gr. 6-9). 1996. teacher ed., pap. text ed. 19.95 incl. vhs (*0-201-49598-8*) Supplementary Div.

Tornado!, Set. Russell Wright. Ed. by Cathy Anderson et al. (Event-Based Science Ser.). (Illus.). (Orig.). (YA). (gr. 6-9). 1996. teacher ed., wbk. ed., pap. text ed. 115.00 incl. vhs (*0-201-49604-6*) Supplementary Div.

Tornado: A Community Responds to Disaster. James B. Taylor et al. LC 73-129005. (Illus.). 205p. 1970. 25.00 (*0-295-95088-9*) U of Wash Pr.

Tornado: A Disaster Book. Christopher Lampton. (J). (gr. 4-7). 1992. pap. 6.56 (*0-395-63644-2*) HM.

Tornado! Eighty-Four Minutes Ninety-Four Lives. John O'Toole & Marvin Richmond. LC 93-70976. (Illus.). 320p. (Orig.). 1993. pap. 16.95 (*0-9636277-0-8*); vhs 19.95 (*0-9636277-1-6*) Databks.

Tornado! Eighty-Four Minutes Ninety-Four Lives, Set. John O'Toole & Marvin Richmond. LC 93-70976. (Illus.). 320p. (Orig.). 1993. pap. 34.95 incl. audio, vhs (*0-9636277-2-4*) Databks.

Tornado: Its Structure, Dynamics, Prediction, & Hazards. Ed. by Church et al. (Geophysical Monograph Ser.: Vol. 79). 1993. 85.00 (*0-87590-038-0*) Am Geophysical.

Tornado: Panavia Tornado GR Mk1. (Aeroguide Ser.: No. 4). 1984. pap. 6.00 (*0-918805-03-1*) Pac Aero Pr.

Tornado Alert. Franklyn M. Branley. LC 87-29379. (Let's-Read-&-Find-Out Science Bk.). (Illus.). 32p. (J). (ps-3). 1988. lib. bdg. 14.89 (*0-690-04688-X*, Crowell Jr Bks) HarpC Child Bks.

Tornado Alert. Franklyn M. Branley. LC 87-29379. (Trophy Let's-Read-&-Find-Out Bk.). (Illus.). 32p. (J). (gr. k-4). 1990. reprint ed. pap. 4.95 (*0-06-445094-5*, Trophy) HarpC Child Bks.

Tornado Alley. William S. Burroughs. (Illus.). 56p. (Orig.). 1989. pap. 9.00 (*0-916156-83-4*) Cherry Valley.

Tornado Alley. Yvonne Lehman. (White Dove Romance Ser.: Vol. 1). 176p. (Orig.). (YA). (gr. 7 up). 1995. mass mkt. 4.99 (*1-55661-705-4*, Hampshire MN) Bethany Hse.

Tornado & Sweep. Dave Sargent. Ed. by Debbie Bowen. Tr. by Migel Zapata from ENG. (Tornado & Sweep Ser.). (Illus.). 96p. (Orig.). (SPA.). (J). (gr. k-6). 1993. pap. text ed. 6.95 (*1-56763-107-X*); lib. bdg. 16.95 (*1-56763-106-1*) Ozark Pub.

Tornado & Sweep Bk. II. Dave Sargent. Ed. by Debbie Bowen. Tr. by Miguel Zapata from ENG. (Illus.). (SPA.). (J). (gr. k-6). pap. text ed. 6.95 (*1-56763-123-1*); lib. bdg. 16.95 (*1-56763-122-3*) Ozark Pub.

Tornado & Sweep Bk. III. Dave Sargent. Ed. by Debbie Bowen. Tr. by Miguel Zapata from ENG. (Illus.). (SPA.). (J). (gr. k-6). pap. text ed. 6.95 (*1-56763-126-6*); lib. bdg. 16.95 (*1-56763-125-8*) Ozark Pub.

Tornado Pilot. Ian Black. (Osprey Colour Library). (Illus.). 128p. 1994. pap. 15.95 (*1-85532-429-6*, Pub. by Osprey Pubng Ltd UK) Motorbooks Intl.

Tornado Pratt. Paul Ableman. LC 92-14922. 223p. 1992. 20.00 (*0-929701-25-9*); pap. 11.00 (*0-929701-26-7*) McPherson & Co.

Tornado Terror & Survival: The Andover Tornado. Howard Inglish. 1991. pap. 8.95 (*0-9631191-0-9*) Butler Cty Coun.

Tornado Trail. Jon Sharpe. (Trailsman Ser.: No. 160). 1995. mass mkt. 3.99 (*0-451-18217-0*, Sig) NAL-Dutton.

Tornado Treaty. Janie Geiser. 1985. 20.00 (*0-932526-23-3*) Nexus Pr.

***Tornado Warning: A Triangle Club Adventure.** Steven J. Givens. 100p. (Orig.). (J). (gr. 3-5). 1997. pap. 3.75 (*1-889658-08-1*) New Canaan Pub.

Tornado Watch. Gordon Grigsby. LC 77-8855. 71p. 1977. 22.50 (*0-8142-0281-0*) Ohio St U Pr.

Tornado Weather. Emile Luria. LC 93-13597. 64p. 1993. pap. 12.95 (*0-7734-2763-5*, Mellen Poetry Pr) E Mellen.

Tornado Wind & Hail Claims: Trade Secrets You Must Know. Travis Gunn. (Gunn Guides Ser.). 176p. 1995. pap. 19.99 (*1-885518-02-1*) Crossfire Pubng.

***Tornado Zone.** vii, 203p. (Orig.). 1997. pap. 14.95 (*0-9658320-0-7*) Jetma Pub.

Tornadoes. Ann Armbruster & Elizabeth A. Taylor. (First Bks.). (Illus.). 64p. (J). (gr. 5-8). 1993. pap. 6.95 (*0-531-15666-4*) Watts.

Tornadoes. Arlene Erlbach. LC 94-10472. (New True Bks.). (Illus.). 48p. (J). (gr. k-4). 1994. pap. 5.50 (*0-516-41071-7*); lib. bdg. 19.00 (*0-516-01071-9*) Childrens.

Tornadoes. Merrilee Hooker. LC 92-41101. (Discovery Library of Disasters). (J). 1993. 12.67 (*0-86593-248-4*); 9.50 (*0-685-66349-3*) Rourke Corp.

Tornadoes. Peter Murray. LC 95-5000. (Nature Bks.). (Illus.). 32p. (J). (gr. 2-6). 1995. lib. bdg. 22.79 (*1-56766-195-5*) Childs World.

Tornadoes. Charles Rotter. LC 93-46803. (Images Ser.). (Illus.). 32p. (J). (gr. 4 up). 1997. lib. bdg. 16.95 (*0-88682-712-4*) Creative Ed.

Tornadoes: Chaos from the Sky. Keay Davidson. 1996. pap. 14.00 (*0-614-97659-6*, Pocket Books) PB.

Tornadoes & Hurricanes. Ruth Deery. (Natural Disaster Ser.). (Illus.). 48p. (J). (gr. 4-8). 1985. student ed. 7.99 (*0-86653-318-4*, GA 631) Good Apple.

***Tornadoes Can Make It Rain Crabs: Weird Facts about Natural Disasters.** Melvin Berger. (Strange World Ser.). (J). 1997. pap. text ed. 2.99 (*0-590-93995-5*) Scholastic Inc.

Tornadoes, Dark Days, Anomalous Precipitation & Related Weather Phenomena. William R. Corliss. LC 82-63156. (Catalog of Geophysical Anomalies Ser.). (Illus.). 196p. 1983. 14.95 (*0-915554-10-0*) Sourcebook.

Torneiment Anticrist by Huon De Meri: A Critical Edition. Margaret O. Bender. LC 75-33765. (Romance Monographs: No. 17). 1976. 24.00 (*84-399-4702-X*) Romance.

Toro Pinto: And Other Songs in Spanish. Anne Rockwell. (J). 1995. pap. 5.95 (*0-689-71880-2*, Aladdin Paperbacks) S&S Childrens.

Toro y el Becerrito. Frances Sainz. (Cityscapes Ser.). 11p. (J). (ps-1). 1992. pap. text ed. 4.50 (*1-56843-095-7*) BGR Pub.

Toro y el Becerrito: Big Book. Frances Sainz. (Cityscapes Ser.). 11p. (J). (ps-1). 1992. pap. text ed. 23.00 (*1-56843-048-5*) BGR Pub.

Torokina: A Wartime Memoir, 1941-1945. Donald D. Jackson. LC 88-13464. (Illus.). 154p. 1989. reprint ed. pap. 43.90 (*0-608-00137-6*, 2060918) Bks Demand.

Toronto. (Best-Kept Secrets Ser.). 1995. pap. 9.95 (*0-8442-9639-2*, Passport Bks) NTC Pub Grp.

Toronto. (Bertinetti Ser.). 1992. 14.98 (*0-8317-8776-7*) Smithmark.

Toronto. Berlitz Editors. (Pocket Guides Ser.). 1992. pap. 7.95 (*2-8315-2362-1*) Berlitz.

*__Toronto.__ Penina Coopersmith. (Colour Guides Ser.). (Illus.). 200p. (Orig.). 1997. pap. 16.95 (*0-88780-394-6*, Pub. by Formac Pub CN) Seven Hills Bk.

Toronto: No Mean City. 3rd ed. Eric R. Arthur. 336p. 1986. 47.50 (*0-8020-5668-7*); pap. 22.95 (*0-8020-6587-2*) U of Toronto Pr.

Toronto: The Complete Guide with Walking Tours, Museums, Restaurants, Shopping & Nightlife. 10th ed. Fodor's Travel Staff. 1997. pap. 13.50 (*0-679-03291-6*) Fodors Travel.

Toronto Architect Edmund Burke: Redefining Canadian Architecture. Angela Carr. (Illus.). 248p. 1995. 44.95 (*0-7735-1217-9*, Pub. by McGill CN) U of Toronto Pr.

Toronto Blessing: What Would the Holy Spirit Say? Robert Kuglin. 200p. 1996. pap. 10.99 (*0-88965-131-0*, Pub. by Horizon Books CN) Chr Pubns.

Toronto Blue Jays. Paul Joseph. (America's Game Ser.). (J). 1997. lib. bdg. 15.95 (*1-56239-679-X*) Abdo & Dghtrs.

Toronto Blue Jays. Richard Rambeck. (Baseball: The Great American Game Ser.). 48p. (J). (gr. 4-10). 1992. lib. bdg. 14.95 (*0-88682-442-7*) Creative Ed.

*__Toronto Blue Jays.__ Richard Rambeck. LC 97-9229. (Baseball). (Illus.). 32p. (J). (gr. 4 up). 1998. lib. bdg. 15.95 (*0-88682-928-3*) Creative Ed.

Toronto Hydro Recollections. E. M. Ashworth. (Illus.). 246p. reprint ed. pap. 70.20 (*0-317-09137-9*, 2014116) Bks Demand.

Toronto Legal Directory. 71th ed. Ed. by Elizabeth Lumley. 890p. 1997. 48.00 (*0-8020-4985-0*) U of Toronto Pr.

Toronto Legal Directory 1995. annuals 70th ed. Ed. by Kieran Simpson. 844p. (C). 1995. 44.00 (*0-8020-4686-X*) U of Toronto Pr.

Toronto Map, 1991. 1990. pap. 4.95 (*0-13-924598-7*) P-H.

Toronto Maple Leafs. Chrys Goyens. LC 94-1361. (NHL Today Ser.). 32p. (J). 1995. lib. bdg. 15.95 (*0-88682-689-6*) Creative Ed.

*__Toronto, Mississippi & Jewel.__ Joan MacLeod. LC 90-175678. 1997. pap. text ed. 12.95 (*0-88754-474-6*, Pub. by Playwrights CN Pr CN) Theatre Comm.

*__Toronto, My City: A Photographic Memoir.__ Kim Ondaatje. (Illus.). 144p. 1993. 25.00 (*1-55082-062-1*, Pub. by Quarry Pr CN) LPC InBook.

Toronto Places: Elements of Urban Design. Ed. by Marc Baraness & Larry Richards. (Illus.). 108p. 1992. 50.00 (*0-8020-2834-9*) U of Toronto Pr.

*__Toronto Raptors.__ Michael E. Goodman. LC 97-6651. (NBA Today Ser.). (J). 1997. write for info. (*0-88682-894-5*) Creative Ed.

*__Toronto Raptors.__ Bob Italia. LC 96-39621. (Inside the NBA Ser.). (J). 1997. write for info. (*1-56239-775-3*) Abdo & Dghtrs.

Toronto Remembered: A Celebration of the City. William Kilbourn. (Illus.). 336p. 1984. 21.95 (*0-7737-2029-4*) Genl Dist Srvs.

Toronto Story. Claire MacKay. (Illus.). 112p. (Orig.). (J). (gr. 5 up). 1991. 34.95 (*1-55037-137-1*, Pub. by Annick CN); pap. 24.95 (*1-55037-135-5*, Pub. by Annick CN) Firefly Bks Ltd.

*__Toronto Tapestry.__ Robert Fulford & Lesley Byrne. (Urban Tapestry Ser.). (Illus.). 1997. write for info. (*1-881096-48-3*) Towery Pub.

Toronto the Wild: Filed Notes of an Urban Naturalist. Wayne Grady. 256p. 1996. 22.95 (*0-921912-90-0*, Pub. by Macfarlane Walter & Ross CN) Genl Dist Srvs.

Toronto with Kids: The Complete Family Travel Guide. Anne Holloway. (Illus.). 240p. (Orig.). 1995. pap. 11.95 (*0-921912-84-6*, Pub. by Macfarlane Walter & Ross CN) Genl Dist Srvs.

Toronto Workers Respond to Industrial Capitalism 1867-1892. Gregory S. Kealey. (Reprints in Canadian History Ser.). 448p. 1991. pap. 24.95 (*0-8020-6883-9*) U of Toronto Pr.

Toronto, 1957 see General Assembly Proceedings

Toronto 1995. Frommer Staff. 1995. pap. 12.95 (*0-614-00678-3*) Macmillan.

Toronto 1995-96. Frommer Staff. (Frommer's Travel Guides Ser.). 1995. 12.95 (*0-02-860066-5*) Macmillan.

Toronto's Chinatown: The Changing Social Organization of an Ethnic Community. Richard H. Thompson. LC 87-45794. (Immigrant Communities & Ethnic Minorities in the U. S. & Canada Ser.: No. 29). 1987. 64.50 (*0-404-19439-7*, F1059) AMS Pr.

Toronto's Girl Problem: The Perils & Pleasures of the City, 1880-1930. Carolyn Strange. (Studies in Gender & History). (Illus.). 344p. 1995. pap. 22.95 (*0-8020-7203-8*) U of Toronto Pr.

Toros: Tratado Tecnico e Historico, 11 vols., Set. Jose M. Cossio. 1989. 3,250.00 (*84-239-6008-0*) Elliots Bks.

Toros en el Arte. 2nd ed. Jose L. Morales y Marin. 310p. 1989. 295.00 (*84-239-5262-2*) Elliots Bks.

Torpedo Junction: U-Boat off America's East Coast, 1942. Homer H. Hickam, Jr. (Illus.). 392p. 1996. pap. 15.95 (*1-55750-362-1*) Naval Inst Pr.

Torpedo Leader. Patrick Gibbs. (Illus.). 216p. 1992. 29.95 (*0-948817-56-9*, Pub. by Grub St Pubns UK) Seven Hills Bk.

Torpedo 1936, Vol. 1. Sanchez Abuli. Ed. by Bernd Metz. Tr. by David Rosenthal from SPA. (Torpedo 1936 Ser.). (Illus.). 118p. (Orig.). 1984. pap. 9.95 (*0-87416-006-5*) Catalan Communs.

Torpedo 1936, Vol. 3. Sanchez Abuli. Ed. by Bernd Metz. Tr. by Jeff Lisle & Dale Luciano from SPA. (Illus.). 90p. (Orig.). 1986. pap. 8.95 (*0-87416-023-5*) Catalan Communs.

Torpedo 1936, Vol. 6. Sanchez Abuli. Ed. by Bernd Metz. Tr. by David Rosenthal & Elizabeth Bell from SPA. (Illus.). 64p. (Orig.). 1990. pap. 11.95 (*0-87416-078-2*) Catalan Communs.

Torpedo 1936, Vol. 7. Sanchez Abuli. Ed. by Bernd Metz. Tr. by David H. Rosenthal from SPA. (Illus.). 49p. (Orig.). 1991. pap. 9.95 (*0-87416-125-8*) Catalan Communs.

Torpedo Technology. Louis Gerken. LC 89-3. (History Highlights Ser.). (Illus.). 300p. (C). 1989. 40.00 (*0-9617163-2-0*) Amer Scientific.

*__Torpedo Tide.__ large type ed. Henry Chesham. (Dales Large Print Ser.). 304p. 1996. pap. 17.99 (*1-85389-676-4*, Dales) Ulverscroft.

Torpedo Town, U. S. A. A History of the Naval Undersea Warfare Engineering Station, 1914-1989. Lisa I. Poole & Dianne P. Robinson. LC 88-51503. (Illus.). 120p. (Orig.). 1989. pap. 8.00 (*0-9621829-0-7*) Diamond Anniversary.

Torpedoes in the Gulf: Galveston & the U-Boats, 1942-1943. Melanie Wiggins. LC 94-31861. (Military History Ser.: No. 40). (Illus.). 256p. 1995. pap. 15.95 (*0-89096-648-6*) Tex A&M Univ Pr.

Torpedoes in the Gulf: Galveston & the U-Boats, 1942-1943, 40. Melanie Wiggins. LC 94-31861. (Military History Ser.: No. 40). (Illus.). 256p. 1995. 29.50 (*0-89096-627-3*) Tex A&M Univ Pr.

Torpedoman. Ron Smith. 365p. 1993. per., pap. 14.95 (*0-9643390-0-5*) Ron Smith.

*__Torpedoman.__ Ron Smith. 330p. (Orig.). 1998. mass mkt. 8.99 (*1-58006-008-0*, Appaloosa) Sovereign.

Torquato Tasso. Johann Wolfgang Von Goethe. Tr. by Alan Brownjohn from GER. LC 85-73378. 160p. 8600. pap. 15.95 (*0-946162-19-0*, Pub. by Angel Bks UK) Dufour.

Torquato Tasso, Creation of the World. Tr. by Joseph Tusiani. LC 81-18970. (Medieval & Renaissance Texts & Studies: Vol. 12). 272p. 1982. 20.00 (*0-86698-019-9*, MR12) MRTS.

Torquato Tasso in Deutschland: Seine Wirkung in Literatur, Kunst und Musik Seit der Mitte des 18.Jahrhunderts. Ed. by Achim Aurnhammer. (Quellen und Forschungen Zur Literatur und Kulturgeschichte Ser.: Bd. 3(237)). xii, 742p. (GER.). (C). 1995. lib. bdg. 223.10 (*3-11-014546-4*) De Gruyter.

Torquato Tasso's Aminta Englisht: The Henry Reynolds Translation of 1628. Ed. by Clifford Davidson. LC 72-78233. (North American Mentor Texts & Studies: No. 1). (Illus.). 80p. 1972. pap. 20.00 (*0-87423-007-1*) Westburg.

Torque. David Rivard. LC 88-2167. (Poetry Ser.). 61p. (Orig.). 1988. 19.95 (*0-8229-3595-3*); pap. 10.95 (*0-8229-5410-9*) U of Pittsburgh Pr.

Torque & Torque Wrenches. W. Forrest Bear & Thomas A. Hoerner. (Illus.). 24p. 1971. pap. text ed. 5.20 (*0-913163-05-8*, 171) Hobar Pubns.

*__Torque Converter in Power Transmissions.__ P. L. Fosburg. (Technical Papers). 1955. pap. text ed. 30.00 (*1-55589-232-9*) AGMA.

Torquemada Killer. John Warren. (Orig.). 1995. mass mkt. 6.95 (*1-56333-367-8*, Badboy) Masquerade.

Torre. General de la Universidad de Puerto Rico Staff. 3.00 (*0-317-41477-1*) U of PR Pr.

Torre see Aguilas

Torreites Sanchezi (Douville) from Jamaica see Palaeontographica Americana: Vol. 7

*__Torrence & Allied Families.__ Robert M. Torrence. (Illus.). 559p. 1996. reprint ed. pap. 85.00 (*0-8328-5454-9*); reprint ed. lib. bdg. 95.00 (*0-8328-5453-0*) Higginson Bk Co.

Torrens System in Australia. Douglas J. Whalan. lxvii, 410p. 1982. pap. 49.00 (*0-455-20358-X*, Pub. by Law Bk Co AT) Gaunt.

Torrens Title. M. A. Stone. 512p. 1991. boxed 102.00 (*0-409-49497-6*, Austral) MICHIE.

Torrent: Novellas & Short Stories. Anne Hebert. LC 73-83340. (French Writers of Canada Ser.). 141p. reprint ed. pap. 40.20 (*0-317-28416-9*, 2022300) Bks Demand.

Torrent & the Night Before. 2nd ed. Edwin Arlington Robinson. LC 96-8320. 56p. 1996. reprint ed. 12.95 (*0-88448-183-2*) Tilbury Hse.

Torrent of Portyngale. Ed. by E. Adam. (EETS, ES Ser.: No. 51). 1974. reprint ed. 35.00 (*0-527-00257-7*) Periodicals Srv.

Torrents of Spring. Ernest Hemingway. (Hudson River Editions Ser.). 90p. 1987. 30.00 (*0-02-550750-8*) S&S Trade.

Torrents of Spring. Ivan S. Turgenev. LC 96-14697. (Illus.). 224p. 1996. 25.00 (*0-8021-1594-2*, Grove) Grove-Atltic.

Torrents of Spring: Soviet & Post-Soviet Politics. Jonathan R. Adelman. LC 94-16403. 1994. pap. text ed. write for info. (*0-07-000359-9*) McGraw.

Torrents of Spring, etc. Ivan S. Turgenev. Tr. by Constance Garnett from RUS. LC 76-150489. (Short Story Index Reprint Ser.). 1977. reprint ed. 21.95 (*0-8369-3830-5*) Ayer.

Torres Strait Islanders: Custom & Colonialism. Jeremy Beckett. (Illus.). 230p. 1988. text ed. 54.95 (*0-521-33361-X*) Cambridge U Pr.

Torres Strait Islanders: Custom & Colonialism. Jeremy Beckett. (Illus.). 272p. (C). 1990. pap. 19.95 (*0-521-37862-1*) Cambridge U Pr.

Torrey Pines: Landscape & Legacy. Bill Evarts. (Illus.). 96p. (Orig.). 1994. 27.95 (*0-9629917-1-6*); pap. 17.95 (*0-9629917-2-4*) Torrey Pines.

Torrey Pines State Reserve: A Scientific Reserve of the Department of Parks & Recreation, State of California. 3rd rev. ed. Ed. by Freda M. Reid. LC 91-65594. (Illus.). 108p. 1991. student ed., pap. 4.00 (*0-9629917-0-8*) Torrey Pines.

Torrey's Morphogenesis of the Vertebrates. 5th ed. Alan Feduccia & Edward McCrady. LC 90-24801. 517p. 1991. text ed. 69.95 (*0-471-62314-8*) Wiley.

Torrid Lands. William Braithwaite. 1993. 19.95 (*0-533-10472-6*) Vantage.

Torrid Lands. Keith Hallam. 480p. 1995. mass mkt. 4.99 (*1-896329-44-6*, Pub. by Comnwlth Pub CN) Partners Pubs Grp.

Torrid Piece of Murder: A Dr. Jean Montrose Mystery. C. F. Roe. 256p. (Orig.). 1994. pap. 5.50 (*0-451-18182-4*, Sig) NAL-Dutton.

*__Torrid Zone.__ Rebecca Beguin. LC 96-45121. 200p. (Orig.). 1997. pap. 10.95 (*0-934678-81-2*) New Victoria Pubs.

Torrid Zone: Seven Stories from the Gulf Coast. Jonathan E. Maslow. LC 95-3000. 304p. 1996. 25.00 (*0-679-40876-2*) Random.

Torrid Zones: Maternity, Sexuality & Empire in Eighteenth Century English Narratives. Felicity A. Nussbaum. LC 95-11801. (Parallax). (Illus.). 248p. 1995. text ed. 45.00 (*0-8018-5074-6*); pap. text ed. 14.95 (*0-8018-5075-4*) Johns Hopkins.

*__TORS Facilitator's Guide.__ Donald Shandler & Susan E. Kruppenbach. 24.95 (*1-56052-415-4*) Crisp Pubns.

Torsion. 1980. 11.50 (*0-8176-0608-4*) Spr-Verlag.

Torsion Design of Prestressed Concrete. (PCI Journal Reprints Ser.). 22p. 1974. pap. 12.00 (*0-686-40064-X*, JR142) P-PCI.

Torsion-Free Groups of Rank Two. Ross A. Beaumont & Richard S. Pierce. (Memoirs Ser.: No. 1/38). 41p. 1985. reprint ed. pap. 16.00 (*0-8218-1238-6*, MEMO/1/38) Am Math.

Torsion-Free Modules. Eben Matlis. (Chicago Lectures in Mathematics). 174p. (C). 1973. pap. text ed. 15.00 (*0-226-51074-3*) U Ch Pr.

Torsion in Concrete, 1784-1974: Annotated - Prepared by ACI Committee 438, Torsion; E. L. Kemp, Chairman. American Concrete Institute Staff. LC 78-103744. (ACI Bibliography Ser.: No. 12). 150p. reprint ed. pap. 42.80 (*0-7837-5213-X*, 2044944) Bks Demand.

Torsion in Structures: An Engineering Approach. C. F. Kollbrunner & K. Basler. Tr. by E. C. Glauser. 1970. 56.95 (*0-387-04582-1*) Spr-Verlag.

Torsion in SU-Bordism. Pierre E. Conner & E. E. Floyd. (Memoirs Ser.: No. 1/60). 72p. 1969. reprint ed. pap. 17.00 (*0-8218-1260-2*, MEMO/1/60) Am Math.

*__Torsion in SU-bordism.__ Pierre E. Connor & E. E. Floyd. LC 52-42839. (American Mathematical Society Ser.: No. 60). 76p. 1969. reprint ed. pap. 25.00 (*0-608-04437-7*, 2052573) Bks Demand.

*__Torsion Theories.__ Golan. 1986. text ed. write for info. (*0-582-99808-5*, Pub. by Longman UK) Longman.

*__Torsion Theories over Commutative Rings.__ Willy Brandal & Erol Barbut. (Illus.). vi, 120p. (Orig.). (C). 1996. pap. text ed. 28.00 (*0-914351-06-0*) BCS Assocs.

Torsional Analysis of Steel Members. 1997. 30.00 (*1-56424-021-5*, D809) Am Inst Steel Construct.

Torsional Strength of Reinforced & Prestressed Concrete Beams: CEB Approach. Bruno Thurlimann. (IBA Ser.: No. 92). 27p. 1980. 19.50 (*0-8176-1125-8*) Birkhauser.

Torso. Steven Nickel. 264p. 1990. mass mkt. 4.95 (*0-380-70987-2*) Avon.

Torso: The True Story of Eliot Ness & the Search for a Psychopathic Killer. Steven Nickel. LC 89-792. (Illus.). 232p. 1989. 18.95 (*0-89587-072-X*) Blair.

Torso Killer: Shocking True Crimes. Ron Leith. 1991. mass mkt. 4.50 (*1-55817-518-0*, Pinncle Kensgtn) Kensgtn Pub Corp.

Torsos. John P. Cooke. 352p. 1995. mass mkt. 5.99 (*0-446-40454-3*, Mysterious Paperbk) Warner Bks.

Tort. G. H. Fridman. (Civil Law Library). 608p. 1990. 170.00 (*0-08-033080-0*, Waterlow) Macmillan.

Tort. Ewan McKendrick. 270p. (C). 1991. 60.00 (*1-85352-799-8*, Pub. by HLT Pubns UK); 60.00 (*1-85352-378-X*, Pub. by HLT Pubns UK); pap. 60.00 (*1-85352-863-3*, Pub. by HLT Pubns UK) St Mut.

Tort. Ed. by E. D. Pitchfork. 248p. (C). 1990. pap. 60.00 (*1-85352-765-3*, Pub. by HLT Pubns UK) St Mut.

Tort - Cases & Materials. 4th ed. B. A. Hepple & M. H. Matthews. 1991. pap. 56.00 (*0-406-54001-2*, U.K.) MICHIE.

Tort Actions under the General Municipal Law in N. Y. C. Kirk M. Miller. 1997. ring bd. 24.95 (*0-930137-79-5*) Looseleaf Law.

Tort & Accident Law. 2nd ed. Page Keeton et al. (American Casebook Ser.). 1318p. 1991. reprint ed. text ed. 53.00 (*0-314-52813-X*) West Pub.

Tort & Insurance Litigation Reference, 5 vols., Set. Mark S. Rhodes. LC 92-71126. 1992. ring bd. 420.00 (*0-685-59871-3*) Clark Boardman Callaghan.

Tort Cases. 6th ed. Epstein. 1995. 57.00 (*0-316-24587-9*) Little.

Tort, Contract, & Other Common Law Problems in the Substansive Law of Parent & Subsidiary Corporations. Phillip I. Blumberg. (Law of Corporate Groups Ser.). 816p. 1988. suppl. ed. 30.00 (*0-685-27093-9*) Little.

Tort, Contract, & Other Common Law Problems in the Substansive Law of Parent & Subsidiary Corporations. Phillip I. Blumberg. (Law of Corporate Groups Ser.). 816p. 1988. 155.00 (*0-316-10055-2*) Little.

Tort, Crime & Police in Mediaeval Britain: A Review of Some Early Law & Custom. J. W. Jeudwine. xix, 292p. 1983. reprint ed. lib. bdg. 25.00 (*0-8377-0742-0*) Rothman.

Tort Law. Catherine Elliott & Frances Quinn. LC 96-10738. 1996. pap. write for info. (*0-582-29876-8*, Pub. by Longman UK) Longman.

Tort Law. Ed. by Ernest J. Weinrib. (International Library of Essays in Law & Legal Theory). 582p. (C). 1991. 150.00 (*0-8147-9243-X*) NYU Pr.

Tort Law. rev. ed. Basil S. Markesinis & Simon F. Deakin. LC 93-43258. 900p. 1994. write for info. (*0-19-876293-3*, Clarendon Pr) OUP.

Tort Law. 2nd ed. Baum. (LA - Business Law Ser.). 1988. wbk. ed., pap. 16.95 (*0-538-12550-0*) S-W Pub.

Tort Law. 4th ed. Robert L. Rabin. 1995. 19.95 (*0-316-73007-6*) Little.

Tort Law: Cases & Economic Analysis. Richard A. Posner. LC 81-82981. 792p. 1982. 40.00 (*0-316-71436-4*) Little.

Tort Law & Alternatives: Cases & Materials On. 6th ed. Marc A. Franklin & Robert L. Rabin. (University Casebook Ser.). 1155p. 1996. text ed. write for info. (*1-56662-342-1*) Foundation Pr.

Tort Law & Alternatives, Cases & Materials. 5th ed. Marc A. Franklin & Robert L. Rabin. (University Casebook Ser.). 1208p. 1992. text ed. 46.00 (*0-88277-970-2*) Foundation Pr.

Tort Law & Alternatives, Teacher's Manual for Use with Cases & Materials On. 5th ed. Marc A. Franklin & Robert L. Rabin. (University Casebook Ser.). 224p. (C). 1992. pap. text ed. write for info. (*1-56662-033-3*) Foundation Pr.

Tort Law & Economic Interests. 2nd ed. Peter Cane. LC 95-46834. 568p. (C). 1996. 98.00 (*0-19-876430-8*, Clarendon Pr); pap. 45.00 (*0-19-876429-4*, Clarendon Pr) OUP.

Tort Law & the Public Interest: Competition, Innovation, & Consumer Welfare. Ed. by Peter H. Schuck. 304p. (Orig.). (C). 1991. pap. text ed. 10.95 (*0-393-96109-5*) Norton.

Tort Law for Legal Assistants: A Practical Guide. Linda L. Edwards & J. Stanley Edwards. Ed. by Hannan. 445p. (C). 1992. text ed. 57.50 (*0-314-93447-2*) West Pub.

Tort Law in America: An Intellectual History. G. Edward White. 300p. 1985. pap. 17.95 (*0-19-503599-2*) OUP.

Tort Liability & Risk Management. (Transportation Research Circular Ser.: No. 361). 140p. 1990. 15.00 (*0-685-38589-2*) Transport Res Bd.

*__Tort Liability & the Music Educator.__ William R. Hazard. LC 80-109105. (Music Brief Ser.: No. 2). 32p. 1979. reprint ed. pap. 25.00 (*0-608-04243-9*, 2064999) Bks Demand.

Tort Liability for Psychiatric Damage. N. Mullany & P. Handford. 1993. write for info. (*0-455-21175-2*, Pub. by Law Bk Co AT) Gaunt.

Tort Liability of Government Officers & Employees. Chester J. Antieau. 120p. 1994. suppl. ed., pap. text ed. 57.00 (*0-471-02384-1*) Wiley.

*__Tort Liability of Government Officers & Employees: 1995 Cumulative Supplement.__ Milo R. Mecham. 1995. suppl. ed., pap. text ed. 70.00 (*0-471-11751-X*) Wiley.

Tort Liability Standards & the Firm's Response to Regulation. Robert W. Moreschi. LC 90-44983. (Environment: Problems & Solutions Ser.: Vol. 22). 207p. 1990. text ed. 25.00 (*0-8240-9299-6*) Garland.

Tort Liability Today. 66p. 1986. 25.00 (*0-318-36217-1*) Pub Risk Ins Mgmt.

Tort of Discovery Abuse. Warren Freedman. LC 88-32441. 172p. 1989. text ed. 69.50 (*0-89930-332-3*, FTT/, Quorum Bks) Greenwood.

Tort Reform & Related Proposals: Annotated Bibliographies on Product Liability & Medical Malpractice. Ed. by Bruce A. Levin & Robert Coyne. LC 79-54074. xiii, 249p. 1979. 36.00 (*0-910058-94-6*, 305050) W S Hein.

Tort Reform by Contract. Paul H. Rubin. LC 92-38918. 100p. (Orig.). 1993. 29.75 (*0-8447-3829-8*, AEI Pr); pap. 9.75 (*0-8447-3828-X*, AEI Pr) Am Enterprise.

*__Tort Remedies in Connecticut.__ Richard L. Newman & Jeffrey S. Wildstein. 1996. 95.00 (*1-55834-327-X*, 65203) MICHIE.

Torta de Cumpleanos Para Osito. Max Velthuijs. (Illus.). 32p. (J). Date not set. 15.95 (*1-55858-562-1*, Ediciones NY); pap. 6.95 (*1-55858-560-5*, Ediciones NY) North-South Bks NYC.

*__Torticollis: Differential Diagnosis, Assessment & Treatment, Surgical Management & Bracing.__ Ed. by Karen Karmel-Ross. LC 97-10982. (Physical & Occupational Therapy in Pediatrics Monographs: Vol. 17, No. 2). 131p. 1997. 39.95 (*0-7890-0316-3*) Haworth Pr.

*__Torticollis: Differential Diagnosis, Assessment & Treatment, Surgical Management & Bracing.__ Ed. by Karen Karmel-Ross. LC 97-10982. (Physical & Occupational Therapy in Pediatrics Monographs: Vol. 17, No. 2). 131p. 1997. pap. 19.95 (*0-7890-0317-1*) Haworth Pr.

Tortilla Cat. Nancy Willard. LC 95-45731. (J). 1997. write for info. (*0-15-289587-6*) HarBrace.

Tortilla Curtain. T. Coraghessan Boyle. 368p. 1996. pap. 11.95 (*0-14-023828-X*) Viking Penguin.

Tortilla Curtain. large type ed. T. Coraghessan Boyle. LC 95-50040. 1996. 24.95 (*1-56895-287-2*) Wheeler Pub.

*__Tortilla Factory.__ Paulsen. 1998. pap. write for info. (*0-15-201698-8*, HB Juv Bks) HarBrace.

Tortilla Factory. Gary Paulsen. LC 93-48590. (Illus.). 32p. (J). 1995. 14.00 (*0-15-292876-6*, HB Juv Bks) HarBrace.

An Asterisk (*) at the beginning of an entry indicates that the title is appearing in BIP for the first time.

*Tortilla Favorites: Fresh & Simple Mexican Recipes.** Marlena Spieler. 144p. 1997. 18.00 (*1-56565-796-9*, Global Gourmet) Lowell Hse.

Tortilla Flat. John Steinbeck. 1935. pap. 16.95 (*0-670-72109-3*) Viking Penguin.

Tortilla Flat. John Steinbeck. (Fiction Ser.). 224p. 1977. pap. 6.95 (*0-14-004240-7*, Penguin Bks) Viking Penguin.

Tortilla Flat. John Steinbeck. LC 96-47245. 1997. pap. 8.95 (*0-14-018740-5*, Viking) Viking Penguin.

Tortilla Flat. large type ed. John Steinbeck. LC 94-5439. 226p. 1994. reprint ed. lib. bdg. 20.95 (*0-8161-5901-7*, GK Hall) Thorndike Pr.

Tortilla International. Ed. by Cole Group Staff. LC 94-45540. (Cooking Companion Ser.). 96p. (Orig.). 1995. pap. 7.95 (*1-56426-803-9*) Cole Group.

Tortilla Lovers Cook Book. Bruce Fischer. LC 96-15425. 1996. pap. 6.95 (*1-885590-13-X*) Golden West Pub.

*Tortilla Quilt.** Jane Tenorio-Coscarelli. (Illus.). 52p. (Orig.). (J). (ps-6). 1996. pap. 9.95 (*0-9653422-1-2*) Quarter-Inch.

*Tortilla Quilt.** large type ed. Jane Tenorio-Coscarelli. (Illus.). 52p. (Orig.). (J). (ps-6). 1996. 13.95 (*0-9653422-0-4*) Quarter-Inch.

Tortillas. W. Park Kerr. LC 95-16924. 1996. 15.00 (*0-688-13252-9*) Morrow.

Tortillas. Sparks. Date not set. pap. 8.95 (*0-312-08325-4*) St Martin.

Tortillas! Pat Sparks & Barbara Swanson. LC 92-41316. 1993. pap. 10.95 (*0-312-08912-0*) St Martin.

*Tortillas & Lullabies.** Lynn W. Reiser. LC 97-7096. (Illus.). 40p. (J). (ps up). 1998. lib. bdg. 14.93 (*0-688-14629-5*) Greenwillow.

*Tortillas & Lullabies.** Lynn W. Reiser. LC 97-7096. 40p. (J). (ps up). 1998. write for info. (*0-688-14628-7*) Greenwillow.

Tortillas, Beans & M-16s: A Year with the Guerillas in El Salvador. Wendy Shaull. 123p. (C). 49.95 (*0-7453-0351-X*, Pub. by Pluto Pr UK); pap. 17.00 (*0-7453-0352-8*, Pub. by Pluto Pr UK) LPC InBook.

Tortillas for the Gods: A Symbolic Analysis of Zinacanteco Rituals. Evon Z. Vogt. LC 93-18821. 1993. pap. 18.95 (*0-8061-2559-4*) U of Okla Pr.

Tortillas for the Gods: A Symbolic Analysis of Zinacanteco Rituals. Evon Z. Vogt. LC 75-28470. (Illus.). 253p. reprint ed. pap. 72.20 (*0-7837-3859-5*, 2043681) Bks Demand.

*Tortilleria.** Paulsen. (J). 1998. pap. write for info. (*0-15-201714-3*, HB Juv Bks) HarBrace.

Tortilleria. Gary Paulsen. Tr. by Gloria De Aragon Andujar. LC 94-18543. (Illus.). 32p. (J). 1995. 15.00 (*0-15-200237-5*, Red Wagon Bks) HarBrace.

Tortillitas Para Mama: And Other Nursery Rhymes, Spanish & English. Margo C. Griego et al. LC 81-4823. (Illus.). 32p. (J). (ps-2). 1981. 14.95 (*0-8050-0285-5*, Bks Young Read) H Holt & Co.

Tortillitas Para Mama: And Other Nursery Rhymes, Spanish & English. Margo C. Griego et al. LC 81-4823. (Illus.). 32p. (J). (ps-2). 1988. pap. 5.95 (*0-8050-0317-7*, Owlet BYR) H Holt & Co.

Tortious Liability for Unintentional Harm in the Common Law & the Civil Law, 2 vols. Frederick H. Lawson & Basil S. Markesinis. LC 81-102302. (Cambridge Studies in International & Comparative Law). 1982. pap. 39.95 (*0-521-27210-6*); pap. text ed. 39.95 (*0-521-27209-2*) Cambridge U Pr.

Tortious Liability for Unintentional Harm in the Common Law & the Civil Law, 2 vols., Vol. 1: Texts. Frederick H. Lawson & Basil S. Markesinis. LC 81-102302. (Cambridge Studies in International & Comparative Law). 270p. 1982. text ed. 110.00 (*0-521-23585-5*) Cambridge U Pr.

Tortipelvis: The Slipped Disc Syndrome, Its Cause & Correction, Vol. I. 4th ed. Fredrick H. Barge. LC 94-72716. 164p. 1994. text ed. 37.50 (*1-885048-00-9*) Barge Chiropract.

Tortmann Diaries. Howard Barker. 88p. 1996. pap. 10.95 (*0-7145-4281-4*) Riverrun NY.

Tortoise & Hare. Aesop Staff. (J). (gr. 1 up). 1994. pap. 23.75 incl. cd-rom (*1-57135-057-8*) Living Bks.

Tortoise & Hare Little Play-a-Sound. (J). 1994. write for info. (*0-7853-1040-1*) Pubns Intl Ltd.

Tortoise & the Hare. Illus. by Darrell Baker. (Little Golden Sound Story Bks.). 24p. 1993. 6.95 (*0-307-74814-6*, 64814, Golden Pr) Western Pub.

*Tortoise & the Hare.** Carla Dijs. (My First Book of Fables Ser.: Vol. 3). (J). 1997. 5.99 (*0-689-81482-8*, Litl Simon S&S) S&S Childrens.

Tortoise & the Hare. Ken Forsse & Margaret A. Hughes. Ed. by Mary Becker. (Talking Mother Goose Ser.). (Illus.). 26p. (J). (ps). 1986. 9.95 incl. audio (*0-934323-21-6*) Alchemy Comms.

*Tortoise & the Hare.** Betty Miles & Aesop. LC 97-17355. (Ready-to-Read Ser.). 1998. write for info. (*0-689-81792-4*, S&S Bks Young Read) S&S Childrens.

Tortoise & the Hare. Jane P. Resnick. (Aesop's Fables Ser.). (Illus.). (J). 1992. bds. 3.25 (*0-8378-2524-5*) Gibson.

Tortoise & the Hare: An Aesop Fable. Janet Stevens. LC 83-18668. (Illus.). 32p. (J). (ps-3). 1984. lib. bdg. 15.95 (*0-8234-0510-9*) Holiday.

Tortoise & the Hare: An Aesop Fable. Janet Stevens. LC 83-18668. (Illus.). 32p. (J). (ps-3). 1985. pap. 6.95 (*0-8234-0564-8*) Holiday.

Tortoise & the Hare: Friends at the End. Alvin Granowsky. LC 95-9607. (Illus.). (J). 1995. pap. 5.95 (*0-8114-6637-X*) Raintree Steck-V.

Tortoise & the Hare: Friends at the End. Alvin Granowsky. LC 95-9607. (Another Point of View Ser.). (Illus.). 48p. (J). (gr. k-2). 1996. lib. bdg. 22.83 (*0-8114-7130-6*) Raintree Steck-V.

Tortoise & the Hare: Story Pak. Retold by K. Hollenbeck. (Graphic Learning Literature Program Series: Folk Tales). (Illus.). (ENG & SPA.). 1992. 43.00 (*0-87746-247-X*) Graphic Learning.

Tortoise & the Hare - La Tortue et le Lievre. Dorothy S. Bishop. (French-English Bilingual Fables Ser.). 15p. (ENG & FRE.). (J). (gr. 4 up). 1992. pap. 4.95 (*0-8442-1085-4*, Natl Textbk) NTC Pub Grp.

Tortoise & the Jackrabbit. Susan Lowell. LC 94-19461. (Illus.). 32p. (J). (ps up). 1994. lib. bdg. 14.95 (*0-87358-586-0*) Northland AZ.

Tortoise & the Lyre: Aesthetic Reconstructions. L. Santoro-Brienza. 1993. pap. 18.50 (*0-7165-2471-6*, Pub. by Irish Acad Pr IE) Intl Spec Bk.

*Tortoise Brings the Mail.** Dee Lillegard. LC 96-50151. (Illus.). (J). 1997. pap. 14.99 (*0-525-45156-0*) Dutton Child Bks.

Tortoise Fair. (Tales from Fern Hollow Ser.). (Illus.). 22p. (J). (ps-1). 1985. 1.98 (*0-517-45797-0*) Random Hse Value.

*Tortoise Shell.** Fanny Frewen. 384p. 1997. pap. 10.95 (*0-09-964951-9*, Pub. by Arrow Bks UK) Trafalgar.

Tortoise Wins Again: From Farm Boy to President, the True Story of the Race. Keith A. Grimaud. LC 94-92313. 144p. 1994. pap. 9.95 (*0-9642959-0-3*) Palmetto Prodns.

Tortoises & Terrapins. (Colorguide Ser.). 1982. pap. 6.95 (*0-940842-06-8*) South Group.

Tortoise's Flying Lesson: Animal Stories. Margaret Mayo. LC 94-19752. (Illus.). 72p. (J). (ps-5). 1995. 17.00 (*0-15-200332-0*) HarBrace.

Tortoises, Natural History, Care & Breeding in Captivity: Natural History, Care & Breeding in Captivity. Jerry G. Walls. (Illus.). 64p. 1996. pap. 9.95 (*0-7938-2070-7*, RE141) TFH Pubns.

Tortoises of the Mediterranean. A. C. Highfield. 1998. write for info. (*0-89464-951-5*) Krieger.

*Tortoises of the World Vol. 1: "The Eight Great"** Richard C. Paull. Date not set. write for info. (*1-888089-13-X*) Green Nature Bks.

*Tortoises of the World Vol. 2: "In the Small & Medium Sized"** Richard C. Paull. Date not set. write for info. (*1-888089-08-3*) Green Nature Bks.

Tortoises of the World Vol. 3: "The Sulcata" Richard C. Paull. (Illus.). 52p. 1996. ring bd. 28.95 (*1-888089-09-1*) Green Nature Bks.

Tortoises, Terrapins & Turtles. Sowerby & Lear. 1984. write for info. (*0-916984-14-1*) SSAR.

*Tortora Anatomy & Physiology with Marieb Anatomy & Physiology Fetal Pig.** 8th ed. Tortora. (C). 1996. lab manual ed., text ed. 115.50 (*0-201-30249-7*) Addison-Wesley.

Tortricid Pests: Their Biology, Natural Enemies & Control. Ed. by L. P. Van der Geest & H. H. Evenhuis. (World Crop Pests Ser.: No. 5). 808p. 1991. 353.25 (*0-444-88000-3*) Elsevier.

Torts. George C. Christie & Jerry J. Phillips. Ed. by Peter Tenen & Norman S. Goldenberg. (Law Outlines Ser.). 320p. (Orig.). 1996. pap. text ed. write for info. (*0-87457-177-4*, 5000) Casenotes Pub.

Torts. Steven Finz. (Smith's Review Ser.). 340p. 1991. pap. text ed. 13.95 (*1-56542-178-7*) E Pub Corp.

*Torts.** Larry Lavine. (Quick Review Ser.). 222p. (Orig.). (C). 1993. pap. text ed. 18.95 (*0-614-30137-8*) Sum & Substance.

Torts. Theodore Schussler. 171p. pap. 10.00 (*0-87526-166-3*) Gould.

*Torts.** Kate Squires. (LawPrep Essentials Ser.). 280p. (Orig.) (C). 1996. pap. 12.95 (*1-878844-04-0*) Lawprep.

Torts. 2nd ed. Mark Boulton. (LCB Nutshell Ser.). xii, 116p. 1988. pap. 11.95 (*0-455-20825-5*, Pub. by Law Bk Co AT) Gaunt.

Torts. 2nd ed. Edward J. Kionka. (Black Letter Ser.). 433p. 1993. pap. text ed. 24.50 (*0-314-02114-0*) West Pub.

Torts. 2nd ed. William P. Statsky. Date not set. teacher ed., pap. text ed. write for info. (*0-314-67015-7*) West Pub.

Torts. 3rd ed. Shulman et al. 1976. text ed. 36.75 (*0-88277-423-9*) Foundation Pr.

Torts: Adaptable to Courses Utilizing Dobbs' Casebook on Torts & Compensation. Casenotes Publishing Co., Inc. Staff. Ed. by Norman S. Goldenberg & Peter Tenen. (Legal Briefs Ser.). (Orig.). 1993. pap. text ed. write for info. (*0-87457-148-0*, 1006) Casenotes Pub.

Torts: Adaptable to Courses Utilizing Epstein's Casebook on Torts. Casenotes Publishing Co., Inc. Staff. Ed. by Peter Tenen et al. (Legal Briefs Ser.). 1995. pap. write for info. (*0-87457-134-0*, 1003) Casenotes Pub.

Torts: Adaptable to Courses Utilizing Franklin & Rabin's Casebook on Tort Law & Alternatives. Casenotes Publishing Co., Inc. Staff. Ed. by Peter Tenen et al. (Legal Briefs Ser.). 1996. pap. write for info. (*0-87457-135-9*, 1004) Casenotes Pub.

Torts: Adaptable to Courses Utilizing Henderson, Pearson & Siliciano's Casebook on the Torts Process. Casenotes Publishing Co., Inc. Staff. Ed. by Peter Tenen et al. (Legal Briefs Ser.). 1994. pap. write for info. (*0-87457-136-7*, 1001) Casenotes Pub.

Torts: Adaptable to Courses Utilizing Keeton, Keeton, Sargentich & Steiner's Casebook on Torts. Casenotes Publishing Co., Inc. Staff. Ed. by Peter Tenen et al. (Legal Briefs Ser.). 1989. pap. write for info. (*0-87457-137-5*, 1002) Casenotes Pub.

Torts: Adaptable to Courses Utilizing Materials by Franklin. Marc A. Franklin. LC 87-128751. (Legalines Ser.). 150p. 9.95 (*0-685-19024-2*) HarBrace.

Torts: Adaptable to Courses Utilizing Materials by Keeton. 2nd ed. Page Keeton. LC 87-114987. (Legalines Ser.). 298p. 12.95 (*0-685-18532-X*) HarBrace.

Torts: Adaptable to Courses Utilizing Materials by Prosser. 3rd ed. William L. Prosser. LC 87-116625. (Legalines Ser.). 362p. 13.95 (*0-685-18533-8*) HarBrace.

Torts: Adaptable to Courses Utilizing Prosser, Wade, Schwartz, Kelly & Partlett's Casebook on Torts. Casenotes Publishing Co., Inc. Staff. Ed. by Peter Tenen et al. (Legal Briefs Ser.). 1994. pap. write for info. (*0-87457-138-3*, 1000) Casenotes Pub.

Torts: Adaptable to Courses Utilizing Shulman, James & Grey's Casebook on Torts. Casenotes Publishing Co., Inc. Staff. Ed. by Peter Tenen et al. (Legal Briefs Ser.). 1979. pap. write for info. (*0-87457-139-1*, 1005) Casenotes Pub.

Torts: Analytical Briefs of Cases Suitable for Use with Dobbs, 1985 Edition. 169p. 1985. pap. text ed. 14.00 (*0-685-54304-8*, Chicago Law Bk) Cambridge Law.

Torts: Casebook Edition. Steven Emanuel. 378p. 1994. pap. text ed. 17.95 (*1-56542-080-2*) E Pub Corp.

Torts: Cases & Commentary. 3rd ed. 1076p. 1992. pap. 108.00 (*0-409-30255-4*, Austral) MICHIE.

Torts: Cases & Materials. 9th ed. Victor E. Schwartz et al. (University Casebook Ser.). 1234p. 1994. text ed. 49.00 (*1-56662-152-6*) Foundation Pr.

Torts: Cases & Materials On. 9th ed. Victor E. Schwartz et al. (University Casebook Ser.). 252p. 1994. teacher ed. write for info. (*1-56662-211-5*) Foundation Pr.

Torts: Commentary & Materials. 8th ed. W. Morison & C. M. Sappideen. 1993. 130.00 (*0-455-21172-8*, Pub. by Law Bk Co AT); pap. 94.00 (*0-455-21173-6*, Pub. by Law Bk Co AT) Gaunt.

Torts: General Edition. Steven Emanuel. 411p. 1994. pap. text ed. 17.95 (*1-56542-070-5*) E Pub Corp.

Torts: Michigan Law & Practice. Ed. by Linda M. Atkinson & Katharine B. Soper. 1300p. 1991. suppl. ed., ring bd. 155.00 (*0-685-51912-0*, 91-024) U MI Law CLE.

Torts: Michigan Law & Practice. Ed. by Linda M. Atkinson & Katharine B. Soper. 1300p. 1993. suppl. ed. 50.00 (*0-685-59117-4*, 93-001) U MI Law CLE.

Torts: Personal Injury Litigation. 2nd ed. William P. Statsky. Ed. by Tubb. 759p. (C). 1990. text ed. 62.50 (*0-314-54919-6*) West Pub.

Torts: Personal Injury Litigation. 3rd ed. William P. Statsky. LC 94-37746. 796p. (C). 1995. text ed. 64.25 (*0-314-04384-5*) West Pub.

Torts: Suitable for Use with Epstein. James R. Adams. (Cambridge Ser.). 289p. 1990. pap. text ed. 16.00 (*0-685-54302-1*, Chicago Law Bk) Cambridge Law.

Torts: Suitable for Use with Prosser. James R. Adams. (Cambridge Ser.). 167p. 1988. pap. text ed. 16.00 (*0-685-54300-5*, Chicago Law Bk) Cambridge Law.

Torts: The Civil Law of Reparation for Harm Done by Wrongful Act. Little. 1985. Incl. '88 Update. teacher ed. write for info. (*0-8205-0507-2*) Bender.

*Torts & Compensation: Personal Accountability & Social Responsibility for Injury.** 2nd ed. Dan B. Dobbs & Paul T. Hayden. (American Casebook Ser.). 1005p. 1997. text ed. write for info. (*0-314-21111-X*) West Pub.

Torts & Compensation-Personal Accountability & Social Responsibility for Injury. 2nd ed. Dan B. Dobbs. (American Casebook Ser.). 1082p. 1993. 50.50 (*0-314-02224-4*) West Pub.

*Torts & Compensation, Personal Accountability & Social Responsibility for Injury, Teacher's Manual to Accompany.** 3rd ed. Dan B. Dobbs & Paul T. Hayden. (American Casebook Ser.). 1030p. 1997. pap. text ed. write for info. (*0-314-22583-8*) West Pub.

Torts & Personal Injury. Charles P. Nemeth. (Paralegal Workbook Ser.). (Illus.). 124p. (C). 1995. pap. text ed. 9.95 (*0-87084-613-2*) Anderson Pub Co.

Torts & Personal Injury Law. William Buckley. LC 92-23761. 451p. 1993. text ed. 40.95 (*0-8273-5056-2*) Delmar.

Torts & Personal Injury Law. William R. Buckley. 92p. 1993. teacher ed., pap. 13.00 (*0-8273-5057-0*) Delmar.

Torts & Personal Injury Law. 2nd ed. Buckley & Okrent. LC 96-20067. (Paralegal Ser.). 1998. 40.95 (*0-8273-7572-7*) Delmar.

Torts & Personal Injury Law. 2nd ed. Buckley & Okrent. (Paralegal Ser.). 1998. teacher ed. 15.00 (*0-8273-7573-5*) Delmar.

*Torts & Retorts: The (In)Justice of Accident Law?** Peter A. Bell & Jeffrey P. O'Connell. LC 96-36656. (Contemporary Law Ser.). 1997. write for info. (*0-300-06257-5*) Yale U Pr.

Torts & Sports: Legal Liability in Professional & Amateur Athletics. Raymond L. Yasser. LC 84-24948. xiii, 163p. 1985. text ed. 49.95 (*0-89930-092-8*, YLL/, Quorum Bks) Greenwood.

Torts Anthology. Ed. by Lawrence C. Levine et al. LC 92-47129. 1993. 26.00 (*0-87084-849-6*) Anderson Pub Co.

Torts, Cases & Materials On. 8th ed. William L. Prosser et al. (University Casebook Ser.). 1266p. 1991. reprint ed. text ed. 39.75 (*0-88277-641-X*) Foundation Pr.

Torts Cases & Materials on, Teachers Manual to Accompany. David W. Robertson et al. (American Casebook Ser.). 201p. 1989. pap. text ed. write for info. (*0-314-55687-7*) West Pub.

Torts in a Nutshell. 2nd ed. Edward J. Kionka. (Nutshell Ser.). 449p. 1992. reprint ed. pap. 16.00 (*0-314-93049-3*) West Pub.

Torts, Problem Supplement to Cases & Materials On. Mark F. Grady. (American Casebook Ser.). 262p. 1996. suppl. ed., pap. text ed. write for info. (*0-314-09714-7*) West Pub.

Torts Procedure. 4th ed. Henderson. 1994. 54.00 (*0-316-35666-2*) Little.

Torts Process. 3rd ed. James A. Henderson, Jr. & Richard N. Pearson. 1400p. 1988. 48.00 (*0-316-35615-8*) Little.

Torts, Teacher's Manual to Accompany Cases & Materials On. Mark F. Grady. (American Casebook Ser.). 571p. 1996. teacher ed., pap. text ed. write for info. (*0-314-09716-3*) West Pub.

Torts, 1988. Ed. by Win Calkins & Art Johnson. write for info. (*0-318-61752-8*) OR Bar CLE.

Torts, 1996 Edition for Use with Cases & Materials On. 9th rev. ed. Kathryn Kelly et al. (University Casebook Ser.). 561p. 1996. teacher ed., pap. text ed. write for info. (*1-56662-390-1*) Foundation Pr.

Tortuga. Rudolfo Anaya. LC 87-35665. 202p. 1988. reprint ed. pap. 13.95 (*0-8263-1074-5*) U of NM Pr.

Tortuga Encantadora - Turtle Magic. Vachel Lindsay. LC 90-62625. (Illus.). 12p. (J). 1991. bds. 5.95 (*1-877779-22-9*) Schneider Educational.

Tortugas So Se Apuran - Turtles Take Their Time. Allan Fowler. LC 92-7403. (Rookie Read-about Science - Spanish Ser.). (Illus.). 32p. (SPA.). (J). (ps-2). 1993. pap. 3.95 (*0-516-56005-0*); lib. bdg. 15.30 (*0-516-36005-1*) Childrens.

*Tortugas Son Huerfanas Al Nacer.** Tr. by Angelita L. Aguilar. (SPA.). (J). (gr. k-3). 1995. write for info. (*1-57842-090-3*) Delmas Creat.

Tortugas (Turtles) Janet Craig. (J). 1996. pap. 3.50 (*0-8167-3039-3*) Troll Communs.

Tortula Hedw. Sect. Rurales de Not. Pottiaceae, Musci in der Oestlichen Holarktis. Wolfgang Kramer. (Bryophytorum Bibliotheca Ser.: Vol. 21). 250p. (GER.). 1980. lib. bdg. 50.00 (*3-7682-1266-1*) Lubrecht & Cramer.

*Tortuous Serpent: An Occult Adventure.** Donald Tyson. LC 97-16774. 464p. (Orig.). 1997. pap. 12.95 (*1-56718-743-9*) Llewellyn Pubns.

Torture. expanded ed. Edward Peters. 304p. 1996. pap. 16.95 (*0-8122-1599-0*) U of Pa Pr.

Torture: Human Rights & Medical Ethics & the Case of Israel. Ed. by Neve Gordon & Ruchama Marton. LC 95-13688. 224p. (C). 1995. pap. 29.95 (*1-85649-314-8*, Pub. by Zed Bks Ltd UK) Humanities.

Torture: Human Rights, Medical Ethics & the Case of Israel. Ed. by Neve Gordon & Ruchama Marton. LC 95-13688. 224p. (C). 1995. text ed. 69.95 (*1-85649-313-X*, Pub. by Zed Bks Ltd UK) Humanities.

Torture: The Role of Ideology in the French-Algerian War. Rita Maran. LC 88-37478. 230p. 1989. text ed. 55.00 (*0-275-93248-6*, C3248, Praeger Pubs) Greenwood.

Torture & English Law: An Administrative & Legal History from the Plantagenets to the Stuarts. James Heath. LC 80-24552. (Contributions in Legal Studies: No. 18). xviii, 324p. 1982. text ed. 65.00 (*0-313-22598-2*, HTE/, Greenwood Pr) Greenwood.

Torture & Its Consequences: Current Treatment Approaches. Ed. by Metin Basoglu. (Illus.). 500p. (C). 1992. text ed. 110.00 (*0-521-39299-3*) Cambridge U Pr.

Torture & Rape in Police Custody: An Analysis. S. K. Ghosh. x, 152p. 1993. 12.95 (*1-881338-09-6*) Nataraj Bks.

Torture & Rape in Police Custody: An Analysis. S. K. Ghosh. (C). 1993. 18.00 (*81-7024-585-0*, Pub. by Ashish II) S Asia.

Torture & Truth. Page Dubois. 270p. (C). 1991. pap. 17.95 (*0-415-90213-4*, Routledge NY) Routledge.

Torture by Governments. Compiled by Amnesty International USA Staff. 75p. 1984. 3.95 (*0-685-23311-1*) Amnesty Intl USA.

Torture Garden. Octave Mirbeau. 206p. 1996. pap. 16.95 (*1-873982-51-8*, Pub. by Dedalus Bks UK) Hippocrene Bks.

Torture Garden. Octave Mirbeau. 1996. pap. text ed. 13.99 (*0-9651042-6-5*) Juno Bks.

*Torture Garden.** rev. ed. Octave Mirbeau. Ed. by Brian Stableford. Tr. by Michael Richardson from FRE. (Empire of the Senses Ser.). 208p. 1997. pap. 11.99 (*1-873982-53-4*, Pub. by Dedalus UK) Subterranean Co.

Torture Garden: A Photographic Archive of the New Flesh. Ed. by David Wood. (Velvet Ser.). (Illus.). 160p. (Orig.). 1996. pap. 19.95 (*1-871592-33-X*) Creation Bks.

Torture in El Salvador: September 1986. Comite de Derechos Humanos de el Salvador Staff. (Illus.). 150p. (Orig.). 1988. pap. text ed. 25.00 (*0-929873-00-9*); 15.00 (*0-929873-01-7*) MITF Cent Am.

Torture in the Eighties. Amnesty International U. S. A. Staff. (Illus.). 263p. 1984. pap. 5.95 (*0-86210-066-6*) Amnesty Intl USA.

*Torture in Turkey & Its Unwilling Accomplices: The Scope of State Persecution & the Coercion of Physicians.** Physicians for Human Rights Staff. (Illus.). 288p. (Orig.). 1996. pap. text ed. 10.00 (*1-879707-21-7*) Phy Human Rights.

Torture Killers. Rose G. Mandelsberg. 1991. mass mkt. 4.95 (*1-55817-506-7*, Pinncle Kensgtn) Kensgtn Pub Corp.

Torture Trek, & Eleven Other Tales of the Wild West. Ryerson Johnson. Ed. by Martin H. Greenberg & Bill Pronzini. LC 94-45790. 226p. 1995. pap. 12.00 (*1-56980-033-2*) Barricade Bks.

Torture with Impunity. 1991. pap. 6.00 (*0-939994-68-2*) Amnesty Intl USA.

Tortured Boy. large type ed. Howard C. Davis. 384p. 1992. pap. 15.99 (*0-7089-7216-0*, Trailtree Bookshop) Ulverscroft.

Tortured Earth. Date not set. write for info. (*0-312-93038-0*) St Martin.

Tortured for Christ. Richard Wurmbrand. LC 93-4253. 1973. pap. 2.95 (*0-88264-001-1*) Living Sacrifice Bks.

Tortured People: The Politics of Colonization. Howard Adams. 208p. 1995. pap. 10.95 (*0-919441-77-7*, Pub. by Theytus Bks Ltd CN) Orca Bk Pubs.

*Tortured Soul.** Lawrence E. Mye. (Illus.). 24p. (Orig.). 1997. pap. 7.95 (*1-56167-371-4*) Am Literary Pr.

Tortures & Torments of the Christian Martyrs. Antonio Gallonio. 1989. pap. 25.00 (*0-922915-02-4*) Feral Hse.

Toru Dutt. A. N. Dwivedi. (Indian Writers Ser.: Vol. 15). 168p. 1977. 8.50 (*0-86578-002-1*) Ind-US Inc.

An Asterisk (*) at the beginning of an entry indicates that the title is appearing in BIP for the first time.

Torus Occipitus & Related Structures: Their Transformations in the Course of Human Evolution. Franz Weidenreich. LC 77-86451. (China Geological Survey. Bulletin of the Geological Survey of China Ser.). 1977. reprint ed. 18.00 (*0-404-16694-6*) AMS Pr.

***Torvill & Dean.** Jayne Torvill. 1996. 22.95 (*1-55972-390-4*, Birch Ln Pr) Carol Pub Group.

Torvill & Dean: Ice Dancing's Perfect Pair. Frances Shuker-Haines. LC 94-46684. (Partners II Ser.). 112p. (J). (gr. 5 up). 1995. lib. bdg. 16.95 (*1-56711-134-3*) Blackbirch.

***Tory & Whig: The Parlimentary Papers of Edward Harley, Third Earl of Oxford, & William Hay, MP for Seaford, 1716-1753.** Ed. by Stephen Taylor & Clyve Jones. LC 97-15604. (Parlimentary History Record Ser.). 576p. 1997. 89.00 (*0-85115-589-8*, Boydell Pr) Boydell & Brewer.

Tory Case. Chris Patten. LC 82-17085. (Jossey-Bass Higher Education Ser.). 208p. reprint ed. pap. 59.30 (*0-317-08605-7*, 2022524) Bks Demand.

Tory Criticism in the Quarterly Review, 1809 - 1853. Walter Graham. LC 77-110570. 1970. reprint ed. 20.00 (*0-404-02889-6*) AMS Pr.

Tory Hole. Louise H. Tharp. (Illus.). (J). (gr. 4-p). 1976. pap. 7.50 (*0-686-16261-7*) DCA.

Tory Islanders: A People of the Celtic Fringe. Robin Fox. LC 94-44404. (C). 1995. pap. text ed. 16.95 (*0-268-01890-1*) U of Notre Dame Pr.

***Tory Lover.** Sarah Orne Jewett. (Collected Works of Sarah O. Jewett). 1988. reprint ed. lib. bdg. 59.00 (*0-7812-1315-0*) Rprt Serv.

Tory Mind on Education. Denis Lawton. LC 94-28780. 168p. 1994. 75.00 (*0-7507-0350-4*, Falmer Pr); pap. 24.95 (*0-7507-0351-2*, Falmer Pr) Taylor & Francis.

***Tory Radicalism: Margaret Thatcher, John Major, & the Transformation of Modern Britain, 1979-1997.** Earl A. Reitan. LC 97-18649. 272p. 1997. 63.00 (*0-8476-8524-1*) Rowman.

***Tory Radicalism: Margaret Thatcher, John Major, & the Transformation of Modern Britain, 1979-1997.** Earl A. Reitan. LC 97-18649. 272p. (Orig.). 1997. pap. 23.95 (*0-8476-8525-X*) Rowman.

Tory Syndrome: Leadership Politics in the Progressive Conservative Party. George C. Perlin. LC 80-474879. 262p. reprint ed. pap. 74.70 (*0-7837-1025-9*, 2041336) Bks Demand.

Tory View of Landscape. Nigel Everett. LC 94-2734. (Illus.). 264p. 1994. 45.00 (*0-300-05904-3*) Yale U Pr.

Toryminae (Hymenoptera: Chalcidoidea: Torymidae) A Redefinition, Generic Classification, & Annotated World Catalog of Species, Vol. 2. E. E. Grissell. Ed. by Virendra K. Gupta. (Memoirs on Entomology, International Ser.). (Illus.). 480p. 1995. 60.00 (*1-56665-057-7*) Assoc Pubs FL.

***Tory's Tuesday.** Linda K. Silva. 184p. (Orig.). 1996. pap. 8.95 (*1-887237-06-2*) Bluestcking.

Tosafot Yeshanim Al Massekheth Yebamoth. Thirteenth Century Tosafist Staff. LC 92-80592. 375p. (HEB.). (C). 1992. 16.00 (*1-881255-07-7*) OFEQ Inst.

Tosca. Giacomo Puccini. Ed. & Tr. by Nicholas John from ITA. (English National Opera Guide Series: Bilingual Libretto, Articles: No. 16). (Illus.). 128p. (Orig.). 1982. pap. 9.95 (*0-7145-3772-1*) Riverrun NY.

Tosca: The Drama Behind the Opera. Victorien Sardou. Ed. & Tr. by Laird Kleine-Ahlbrandt. LC 89-13084. (Studies in the History & Interpretation of Music: Vol. 18). 169p. 1990. lib. bdg. 79.95 (*0-88946-444-8*) E Mellen.

Tosca: Vocal Score. Giacomo Puccini. 320p. (ENG & ITA.). 1986. pap. 28.95 (*0-7935-4708-3*, 50337970) H Leonard.

Tosca Liberetto. Giacomo Puccini. 88p. (ENG & ITA.). 1986. pap. 4.95 (*0-7935-2607-8*, 50340040) H Leonard.

Toscanelli & Columbus. Henry Vignaud. LC 73-150204. (Select Bibliographies Reprint Ser.). 1977. reprint ed. 35.95 (*0-8369-5717-2*) Ayer.

Toscanini. John W. Freeman. Ed. by Walfredo Toscanini. (Portraits of Greatness Ser.). (Illus.). 92p. (ENG & ITA.). 1986. pap. 12.50 (*0-918367-16-6*); pap. write for info. (*0-918367-17-4*) Elite.

Toscanini. Harvey Sachs. LC 78-17245. 1995. pap. 16.95 (*0-7615-0137-1*) Prima Pub.

Toscanini. Harvey Sachs. (Da Capo Quality Paperbacks Ser.). (Illus.). 380p. 1981. reprint ed. pap. 8.95 (*0-306-80137-X*) Da Capo.

Toscanini: An Intimate Portrait. Samuel Chotzinoff. LC 76-7576. (Music Reprint Ser.). 1976. reprint ed. lib. bdg. 27.50 (*0-306-70777-2*) Da Capo.

Toscanini & Great Music. Lawrence Gilman. 1977. 15.95 (*0-8369-7253-8*, 8052) Ayer.

Tosca's Christmas. Matthew Sturgis. (Illus.). 32p. (J). (ps-3). 1992. pap. 3.99 (*0-14-054840-8*, Puff Pied Piper) Puffin Bks.

Tosca's Surprise. Matthew Stufgis. (Illus.). 32p. (J). (ps-3). 1994. pap. 4.99 (*0-14-055270-7*, Puff Pied Piper) Puffin Bks.

Tosefta: An Introduction. Jacob Neusner. LC 92-10435. (USF Studies in the History of Judaism: No. 47). 367p. 1992. 89.95 (*1-55540-713-7*, 240047) Scholars Pr GA.

Tosefta: Structure & Sources. Jacob Neusner. LC 86-15638. (Brown Judaic Studies). 250p. (C). 1986. 41.95 (*1-55540-049-3*, 14-01-12) Scholars Pr GA.

Tosefta: Translated from the Hebrew Sixth Division Tororot, the Order of Purities. Jacob Neusner. 442p. 1991. 79.95 (*1-55540-477-4*, 24 00 10) Scholars Pr GA.

Tosefta, Translated from the Hebrew: Pt. II. Moed. The Order of Appointed Times. Jacob Neusner. 59.50 (*0-87068-691-7*) Ktav.

Tosefta, Translated from the Hebrew: Pt. III Nashim. The Order of Women. Jacob Neusner. 59.50 (*0-87068-684-4*) Ktav.

Tosefta Translated from the Hebrew I. Zeraim: The Order of Seeds. Jacob Neusner. 1986. 59.50 (*0-87068-693-3*) Ktav.

Tosefta Translated from the Hebrew IV. Neziqin: The Order of Damages. Jacob Neusner. 1981. 59.50 (*0-87068-692-5*) Ktav.

Toshiba Medium PLC Primer. Edwin Dropka. (Illus.). 192p. 1995. pap. 31.95 incl. disk (*0-7506-9694-X*) Buttrwrth-Heinemann.

***Toshio Shibata.** Toshiharu Ito. 96p. 1997. 29.95 (*4-7713-2835-8*) Dist Art Pubs.

Toshokan: Libraries in Japanese Society. Theodore F. Welch. LC 77-359611. 316p. reprint ed. pap. 90.10 (*0-317-26358-7*, 2024225) Bks Demand.

***Toss: A New Offensive Attack for High-Scoring Football.** Jerry Vallotton. LC 97-13589. 1997. write for info. (*0-13-632548-3*) P-H.

Toston: Reminiscences of a Mexican-American. Rafael Estupinian. 115p. 1973. 10.00 (*0-916304-09-4*) SDSU Press.

***Tot Shabbat.** Camille Kress. (Illus.). 6p. (J). (ps). 1997. bds. 5.95 (*0-8074-0607-4*, 102005) UAHC.

Tota Rosa. Jacqueline Dana. 256p. (FRE.). 1985. pap. 11.95 (*0-7859-2009-9*, 2070376370) Fr & Eur.

Total Abolition of Personal Restraint in the Treatment of the Insane. Robert G. Hill. LC 75-16725. (Classics in Psychiatry Ser.). 1976. reprint ed. 20.95 (*0-405-07433-6*) Ayer.

Total Abstinence: Is It Biblical? Henry E. Griffin, Jr. 64p. (Orig.). 1987. pap. 2.50 (*0-934942-69-2*) White Wing Pub.

Total Aikido: The Master Course. Gozo Shioda & Yasuhisa Shioda. Tr. by David Rubens. LC 97-1318. (Illus.). 208p. 1997. 30.00 (*4-7700-2058-9*) Kodansha.

Total Alpinism. Rene Desmaison. Tr. by Jane Taylor from FRE. 200p. 1982. 35.00 (*0-8464-1278-0*) Beekman Pubs.

Total & Diffuse Reflectance. (Lighting Measurements Ser.). (Illus.). 5p. 1991. pap. 15.00 (*0-87995-079-X*, LM-44-90) Illum Eng.

Total Area Networking. John Atkins & Norris. 1996. text ed. 44.95 (*0-471-95480-2*) Wiley.

Total Area of Computing: A Distributed Approach. Mark Norris. 352p. (C). 1996. pap. text ed. 31.95 (*0-201-87738-4*) Addison-Wesley.

Total Art of Stalinism: Avant-Garde, Aesthetic Dictatorship, & Beyond. Boris Groys. Tr. by Charles Rougle. 176p. 1992. text ed. 29.95 (*0-691-05596-3*) Princeton U Pr.

Total Auto Body Repair. L. C. Rhone. LC 75-2551. (Illus.). 1976. 23.95 (*0-672-97659-5*, Bobbs) Macmillan.

Total Auto Body Repair. L. C. Rhone. LC 75-2551. 1978. teacher ed. write for info. (*0-672-97137-2*, 2319); student ed. write for info. (*0-672-97200-X*) Macmillan.

Total Auto Body Repair. 2nd ed. L. C. Rhone & H. David Yates. 464p. (C). 1982. student ed., teacher ed. write for info. (*0-672-97969-1*); student ed. write for info. (*0-672-97968-3*); text ed. write for info. (*0-672-97967-5*) Macmillan.

Total Auto Body Repair. 2nd ed. Rohne. 1985. 34.64 (*0-02-682110-9*) Macmillan.

Total Auto Body Repair. 21th ed. L. C. Rhone. 1983. pap. 10.64 (*0-02-682130-3*) Macmillan.

Total Auto Body Repair, No. 3. L. C. Rhone. 1984. 39.96 (*0-02-682161-3*) Macmillan.

Total Baseball. John Thorn & Pete Palmer. 2294p. 1991. 24.99 (*0-517-05464-7*) Random Hse Value.

***Total Baseball.** John Thorn. 1999. pap. 64.95 (*0-670-78130-4*) Viking Penguin.

***Total Baseball.** 5th ed. John Thorn. 1997. pap. 64.95 (*0-670-87511-2*) Viking Penguin.

Total Baseball: The Official Encyclopedia of Major League Baseball. 4th ed. Ed. by John Thorn & Pete Palmer. 2650p. 1995. pap. 59.95 (*0-670-86099-9*, Viking) Viking Penguin.

***Total Bastard's Guide to Golf.** Jed Pascoe. Ed. by Cliff Carle. 1996. pap. 5.95 (*1-57644-028-1*) CCC Pubns.

***Total Bedroom: Easy-To-Make Quilts & Custom Fabric Furnishings.** Donna Babylon. Ed. by Melissa Lowe. LC 96-35589. 88p. (Orig.). 1997. pap. 19.95 (*1-56477-114-8*, B229) That Patchwork.

Total Biocombustion of Sewage Sludge by the Bicycle Process. S. John Pirt. (Pirtferm Papers). (C). 1993. 80.00 (*1-874685-05-3*, Pub. by Pirtferm Ltd UK) St Mut.

***Total Branding by Design.** rev. ed. Paul Southgate. (Marketing & Sales Ser.). 1996. pap. 24.95 (*0-7494-1864-8*) Kogan Page Ltd.

Total Braves. John Thorn & Pete Palmer. 224p. 1996. pap. 18.95 (*0-14-025729-2*, Penguin Bks) Viking Penguin.

Total Burn Care. Herndon. 1995. text ed. 150.00 (*0-7020-1827-9*) Saunders.

Total Business Design. Neil Farmer & Bob Lankester. LC 96-8146. 1996. text ed. 35.00 (*0-471-96479-4*) Wiley.

Total Business Plan: How to Write, Rewrite, & Revise. 2nd ed. Patrick D. O'Hara. 320p. 1994. pap. text ed. 49.95 (*0-471-07829-8*) Wiley.

Total Business Planning: A Step-by-Step Guide with Forms. E. James Burton & W. Blan McBride. 205p. 1991. pap. text ed. 22.95 (*0-471-52826-9*) Wiley.

Total Cartoonist. Kenneth Muse. (Illus.). 240p. (C). 1986. 21.00 (*0-13-925263-0*) P-H.

Total Cash Management: A Company-Wide System for Forecasting, Managing, & Improving Cash Flow. Alfred M. King. LC 93-49531. 352p. 1994. text ed. 29.95 (*0-07-034604-6*) McGraw.

Total Chargeback & Fraud Control Manual. 8th ed. Larry Schwartz & Pearl Sax. 330p. 1997. 199.95 (*0-914801-11-2*) Nat Assn Credit.

Total Christian Guy. Phil Callaway. 180p. (Orig.). 1996. pap. 9.99 (*1-56507-447-5*) Harvest Hse.

Total Church Life. Darrell W. Robinson. LC 85-7900. 176p. 1990. 8.99 (*0-8054-6250-3*, 4262-50) Broadman.

***Total Church Life.** rev. ed. Darrell W. Robinson. 224p. (Orig.). 1997. pap. 10.99 (*0-8054-6371-2*) Broadman.

Total Clubfitting. Jeff Jackson. (Illus.). 114p. 1993. pap. text ed. 14.95 (*0-9619413-6-7*) Dyna Golf Prods.

Total Colourings of Graphs. Hian Poh Yap. LC 95-52723. (Lecture Notes in Mathematics Ser.: Vol. 1623). 131p. 1996. pap. text ed. 29.00 (*3-540-60717-X*) Spr-Verlag.

Total Commitment. Yosef Almogi. LC 81-70146. (Illus.). 320p. 1982. 20.00 (*0-8453-4749-7*, Cornwall Bks) Assoc Univ Prs.

Total Commitment to Christ: What Is It? Aiden W. Tozer. (Heritage Ser.). pap. 1.49 (*0-87509-610-7*) Chr Pubns.

Total Communication: Structure & Strategy. Lionel Evans. LC 81-85672. (Illus.). 176p. 1982. 13.95 (*0-913580-75-9*) Gallaudet Univ Pr.

Total Community: The Monks of Caldey Island. Roscoe Howells. 228p. 1994. pap. 21.00 (*1-85902-106-9*, Pub. by Gomer Pr UK) St Mut.

Total Competitiveness: The 7 Key Questions for Re-Engineering--Where You Are, Where You Want to Be, & How to Get There. Maurice Hardaker. 1995. text ed. 27.95 (*0-07-707992-2*) McGraw.

Total Concentration: How to Understand Attention Deficit Disorder, Maximize Your Mental Energy, & Reach Your Full Potential. Harold N. Levinson. LC 90-48943. 1992. pap. 11.95 (*0-87131-708-7*) M Evans.

Total Conditioning for Football: The Syracuse Way. Mike Woicik. LC 81-85633. 128p. reprint ed. pap. 36.50 (*0-317-55503-0*, 2029535) Bks Demand.

Total-Condylar Knee Arthroplasty. Ed. by C. S. Ranawat. (Illus.). 250p. 1985. 147.00 (*0-387-96043-0*) Spr-Verlag.

Total Confidence: A Complete Guide to Self Assurance & Personal Success. Philippa Davies. 208p. 1995. pap. 14.95 (*0-7499-1434-3*, Pub. by Piatkus Bks UK) London Brdge.

Total Consecration to Mary, Spouse of the Holy Spirit. Anselm W. Romb. 64p. 1982. pap. 2.00 (*0-913382-13-2*, 105-37) Marytown Pr.

Total Construction Project Management. George J. Ritz. LC 93-27856. 1994. text ed. 52.95 (*0-07-052986-8*) McGraw.

Total Contingency Planning for Disasters. Kenneth N. Myers. LC 92-31676. 288p. 1996. pap. text ed. 24.95 (*0-471-15379-6*) Wiley.

***Total Control.** David Baldacci. 1997. 24.95 (*0-7862-0964-X*) Thorndike Pr.

Total Control. David Baldacci. LC 96-32869. 528p. 1997. 25.00 (*0-446-52095-0*) Warner Bks.

Total Control. David Baldacci. 720p. 1997. pap. 7.50 (*0-446-60484-4*, Warner Vision) Warner Bks.

***Total Control.** David Baldacci. 528p. 1997. pap. write for info. (*0-446-67374-9*) Warner Bks.

***Total Control.** large type ed. David Baldacci. LC 96-47710. 846p. 1997. 26.95 (*0-7862-0963-1*, Thorndike Lrg Prnt) Thorndike Pr.

***Total Cost Assessment for Environmental Engineers & Managers.** Mitchell L. Kennedy. 350p. 1997. text ed. 59.95 (*0-471-19098-5*) Wiley.

Total Cost Modeling in Purchasing. Lisa M. Ellram. Ed. by Carol L. Ketchum. LC 94-71406. 93p. (Orig.). (C). 1994. pap. text ed. 20.00 (*0-945968-17-5*) Ctr Advanced Purchasing.

Total Costs of Cleaning up Nonfederal Superfund Sites. (Illus.). 52p. (Orig.). (C). 1994. pap. text ed. 25.00 (*0-7881-0556-6*) DIANE Pub.

Total Current Spectroscopy of Surfaces. S. A. Komolov. LC 91-46340. 270p. 1992. text ed. 194.00 (*2-88124-813-6*) Gordon & Breach.

Total Customer Satisfaction: Lessons from 50 European Companies with Top Quality Service. Jacques Horovitz & Michele J. Panak. (Financial Times - Pitman Ser.). 320p. 1992. 87.50 (*0-273-03447-2*, Pub. by Pitman Pub Ltd UK) Trans-Atl Phila.

Total Customer Satisfaction: Putting the World's Best Programs to Work. Jacques Horovitz. LC 93-39281. 264p. 1994. text ed. 25.00 (*0-7863-0108-2*) Irwin Prof Pubng.

Total Customer Service: The Ultimate Weapon. William H. Davidow & Bro Uttal. LC 89-45033. 240p. 1990. reprint ed. pap. 12.00 (*0-06-092009-2*, PL) HarpC.

Total Data Quality for the Coding Manager. Vickie L. Rogers. 1993. 42.00 (*0-317-05443-0*) Am Hlth Info.

Total Design. Stuart Pugh. (C). 1991. pap. text ed. 31.25 (*0-201-41639-5*) Addison-Wesley.

Total Design: Managing the Design Process in the Service Sector. Gillian Hollins & Bill Hollins. (Orig.). 1991. pap. 55.00 (*0-273-03338-7*, Pub. by Pitman Pub Ltd UK) Trans-Atl Phila.

Total Design: Steps Along the Way. Stuart Pugh. 544p. (C). 1996. text ed. 54.95 (*0-201-63485-6*) Addison-Wesley.

Total Drill Team Dimension: A Textbook for Student & Adult Leaders. Marie Parkinson & Naoni Zervas. (Illus.). 541p. (C). 1985. pap. text ed. 29.95 (*0-89641-153-2*) American Pr.

Total Drumming Warm Ups for Feet & Hands. Joe Frisina. 1994. 9.50 (*0-918194-28-8*) Accura.

Total Eclipse. Christopher Hampton. (Illus.). 120p. 1996. pap. 10.95 (*0-571-17873-1*) Faber & Faber.

Total Eclipse. Liz A. Rigbey. Ed. by Bill Grose. 480p. 1995. 22.00 (*0-671-79579-1*) PB.

Total Eclipse. Liz A. Rigbey. 1996. mass mkt., pap. 5.99 (*0-671-79580-5*, PB Trade Paper) PB.

Total Eclipse. large type ed. Liz A. Rigbey. 876p. 1995. 26.95 (*0-7838-1503-4*, GK Hall) Thorndike Pr.

Total Eclipse: A Shadowrun Adventure. FASA Staff. (Shadowrun Ser.). (Illus.). 1991. pap. 8.00 (*1-55560-151-0*, 7308) FASA Corp.

Total Eclipses of the Sun. exp. ed. Jack B. Zirker. LC 94-47241. (Science Library). 248p. 1995. pap. text ed. 12.95 (*0-691-02952-0*) Princeton U Pr.

Total Education in Ethnic Dance. Russell M. Hughes. LC 76-58610. (Dance Program Ser.: No. 6). (Illus.). 159p. reprint ed. pap. 45.40 (*0-7837-0787-8*, 2041101) Bks Demand.

Total Energy. R. M. Diamant. 1970. 190.00 (*0-08-006918-5*, Pub. by Pergamon Repr UK) Franklin.

Total Energy Management Handbook. 2nd ed. 90p. 1979. 2.50 (*0-318-17067-1*); 2.00 (*0-318-17068-X*); 1.75 (*0-318-17069-8*) Natl Elec Mfrs.

Total Engineering Quality Management: The Care & Feeding of the Engineering Process. Ronald J. Cottmon. LC 92-25552. (Quality & Reliability Ser.: Vol. 37). 152p. 1992. 55.00 (*0-8247-8740-4*) Dekker.

Total Evangelism. Ed. by Clayton Pepper. 1982. pap. 3.95 (*0-89137-203-2*) Quality Pubns.

Total Executive. Herbert Knoll. 112p. 1986. pap. 9.95 (*0-940077-00-0*) Total Exec.

Total Exposure: The Movie Buff's Guide to Celebrity Nude Scenes. Jami Bernard. (Illus.). 288p. 1995. pap. 17.95 (*0-8065-1619-4*, Citadel Pr) Carol Pub Group.

Total Exposure & Assessment Methodology (TEAM) Pt. I: Toxic Substances & Chemicals, an International Symposium. Ed. by Steve Colome et al. (Journal of Exposure Analysis & Environmental Epidemiology Ser.: Vol. 1, No. 1). (Illus.). 1991. pap. text ed. 60.00 (*0-911131-30-2*) Princeton Sci Pubs.

Total Exposure & Assessment Methodology (TEAM) Pt. II: Toxic Substances & Chemicals, an International Symposium. Ed. by Michael Dellarco et al. (Journal of Exposure Analysis & Environmental Epidemiology Ser.: Vol. 1, No. 2). (Illus.). 1991. pap. text ed. 60.00 (*0-911131-73-6*) Princeton Sci Pubs.

Total Facility Control. Don T. Cherry. (Illus.). 432p. 1986. 54.95 (*0-409-95149-8*) Buttrwrth-Heinemann.

***Total Father.** Harris. 1997. 22.50 (*0-8050-4805-7*) St Martin.

Total Father. Stephen Harris. LC 97-6892. 1997. 25.00 (*0-8050-4815-4*) H Holt & Co.

Total Financial Planning: A Guide for Advisors & Serious Investors. Harold W. Gourgues & David E. Homrich. LC 87-27863. 1988. 64.95 (*0-13-925272-X*) NY Inst Finance.

Total Fitness: Exercise, Nutrition, & Wellness. Scott K. Powers & Stephen L. Dodd. 1995. pap. text ed. 30.00 (*0-13-095894-8*) Allyn.

Total Fitness for the Physical Educator: A Programmed Approach for Assessment. George Colfer & Emma Gibbons. 138p. (C). 1990. pap. text ed. 9.80 (*0-87563-412-5*) Stipes.

Total Fitness in 30 Minutes. Laurence E. Morehouse. 1990. pap. 5.99 (*0-671-72993-4*) S&S Trade.

Total Fitness Log: The Essential Training Tool for Optimal Fitness. Tony Svensson. 184p. (Orig.). 1995. pap. 9.95 (*0-9634568-6-5*) Trimarket.

***Total Football: The Official Encyclopedia of the National Football.** Bob Carroll. LC 97-16987. 1997. 55.00 (*0-06-270170-3*, Harper Ref) HarpC.

Total Force Pilot Requirements & Management: An Executive Summary. Harry J. Thie et al. (Illus.). xi, 35p. 1995. pap. text ed. 7.50 (*0-8330-2322-5*, MR-646-OSD) Rand Corp.

Total Forecast Japan: The Nineteen Nineties. Noboru Makino. 352p. 1993. text ed. 79.95 (*0-304-32717-4*) Cassell.

Total Freedom: The Essential Krishnamurti. Jiddu Krishnamurti. LC 96-20115. 1996. pap. 18.00 (*0-06-064880-5*) Harper SF.

Total Garden: A Complete Guide to Integrating Flowers, Herbs, Fruits, & Vegetables. A. M. Clevely. (Illus.). 192p. 1988. 14.99 (*0-517-05120-6*) Random Hse Value.

Total Geostrophic South Pacific: Flow Patterns, Tracers & Transports. J. L. Reid. 1985. pap. 50.00 (*0-08-034011-3*, Pub. by PPL UK) Elsevier.

Total Global Strategy: Managing for Worldwide Competitive Advantage. George S. Yip. 1992. 24.95 (*0-13-357658-2*, Busn) P-H.

Total Global Strategy: Managing for Worldwide Competitive Advantage. George S. Yip. LC 94-17656. 1994. pap. 25.95 (*0-13-124488-4*) P-H.

***Total Guide to College Life.** Alice Lawhead & Steve Lawhead. LC 97-486. 1997. write for info. (*0-87788-848-5*, North Wind Bks) Shaw Pubs.

Total Harvest Diet: A Complete Body Tune Up. Elaine B. Swanson. (Illus.). 178p. 1984. pap. 9.95 (*0-933379-00-5*) Fraser Prods Co.

***Total Health.** vi, 108p. (Orig.). 1996. pap. 10.00 (*1-890143-00-6*) Kinetic Aesthetics.

Total Health: Designed for the HIV Challenged Individual. Karen A. Masterson. LC 91-66084. 156p. 1991. spiral bd. 29.95 (*0-942259-04-1*) Westerfield Enter.

Total Health & Food Power. Rose B. Ludlow. LC 85-29594. (Illus.). 240p. (Orig.). 1986. pap. 7.95 (*0-88007-158-3*) Woodbridge Pr.

Total Health at the Computer: A How-To Guide to Saving Your Eyes & Body at the VDT Screen in 3 Minutes a Day. Martin A. Sussman et al. LC 93-1721. 1993. 13.95 (*0-88268-162-1*) Station Hill Pr.

***Total Health for Men.** Ed. by Neil Wertheimer. LC 95-15909. 600p. 1997. pap. 17.95 (*0-87596-459-1*) Rodale Pr Inc.

***Total Health for Men, Vol. 1.** Wertheimer. 1995. 31.95 (*0-87596-309-9*) St Martin.

Total Health for Men: How to Prevent & Treat the Health Problems That Trouble Men Most. Ed. by Neil Wertheimer. LC 95-15909. 600p. 1995. 31.95 (*0-87596-312-9*) Rodale Pr Inc.

Total Health for Women: From Allergies & Back Pain to Overweight & PMS, the Best Preventive & Curative Advice for Over 110 Women's Health Problems. Ellen Michaud et al. LC 95-9810. 1995. 31.95 (*0-87596-311-0*) Rodale Pr Inc.

***Total Health for Women: From Allergies & Back Pain to Overweight & PMS, the Best Preventive & Curative Advice for Over 110 Women's Health Problems.** Ellen Michaud et al. LC 97-8823. 1997. pap. 15.95 (*0-87596-463-X*) Rodale Pr Inc.

***Total Health: The Next Level: Exploding the Myths of America's Diet & Exercise Programs.** Peter Burwash. Ed. by Michael Klapper. LC 97-16674. 140p. (Orig.). 1997. pap. 11.95 (*1-887089-10-1*) Torchlght Pub.

Total Hip Arthroplasty. Robert E. Booth et al. (Illus.). 336p. 1988. text ed. 127.00 (*0-03-013328-9*) Saunders.

Total Hip Prostheses. Ed. by M. E. Muller & R. Ganz. 1976. 263.00 (*0-387-92103-6*) Spr-Verlag.

Total Hip Replacement. E. Eggers. (Orthopedic Ser.). 32p. 1994. pap. text ed. 3.95 (*1-885274-02-5*) HIN.

Total Hockey Player: Brawn Is Not Enough. Douglas Thom & Donald Ward. (Illus.). 123p. (Orig.). 1981. pap. 7.95 (*0-920490-63-8*, Pub. by Detselig CN) Temeron Bks.

Total Horoscope: Aquarius 1997. Jove Publications Staff. 1996. mass mkt. 5.50 (*0-515-11911-3*) Jove Pubns.

Total Horoscope: Aries 1997. Jove Publications Staff. 1996. mass mkt. 5.99 (*0-515-11901-6*) Jove Pubns.

Total Horoscope: Cancer 1997. Jove Publications Staff. 1996. mass mkt. 5.99 (*0-515-11904-0*) Jove Pubns.

Total Horoscope: Capricorn 1997. Jove Publications Staff. 1996. mass mkt. 5.50 (*0-515-11910-5*) Jove Pubns.

Total Horoscope: Gemini 1997. Jove Publications Staff. 1996. mass mkt. 5.99 (*0-515-11903-2*) Jove Pubns.

Total Horoscope: Leo 1997. Jove Publications Staff. 1996. mass mkt. 5.99 (*0-515-11905-9*) Jove Pubns.

Total Horoscope: Libra 1997. Jove Publications Staff. 1996. mass mkt. 5.99 (*0-515-11907-5*) Jove Pubns.

Total Horoscope: Pisces 1997. Jove Publications Staff. 1996. mass mkt. 5.50 (*0-515-11912-1*) Jove Pubns.

Total Horoscope: Sagittarius 1997. Jove Publications Staff. 1996. mass mkt. 5.99 (*0-515-11909-1*) Jove Pubns.

Total Horoscope: Scorpio 1997. Jove Publications Staff. 1996. mass mkt. 5.99 (*0-515-11908-3*) Jove Pubns.

Total Horoscope: Taurus 1997. Jove Publications Staff. 1996. mass mkt. 5.99 (*0-515-11902-4*) Jove Pubns.

Total Horoscope: Virgo 1997. Jove Publications Staff. 1996. mass mkt. 5.99 (*0-515-11906-7*) Jove Pubns.

Total Immersion: A Mikvah Anthology. Rivkah Slonim. LC 95-21766. 296p. 1996. 30.00 (*1-56821-534-7*) Aronson.

***Total Immersion: A Mikvah Anthology.** Rivkah Slonim. LC 95-21766. 296p. 1997. pap. 24.95 (*0-7657-9955-3*) Aronson.

Total Immersion: A Revolutionary Way to Swim Better & Faster. Terry Laughlin & John Delves. 320p. 1996. pap. 13.00 (*0-684-81885-X*, Fireside) S&S Trade.

Total Improvement Management: How to Coordinate Diverse Improvement Efforts for Maximum Gain. H. James Harrington. 320p. 1994. text ed. 32.95 (*0-07-026770-7*) McGraw.

***Total Income of Agricultural Households: 1996 Report.** Eurostat Staff. 217p. 1997. pap. 25.00 (*92-827-9614-0*, CA-99-96-4553AC, Pub. by Europ Com UK) Bernan Associates.

Total Incomes System of Accounts. Robert Eisner. (Illus.). 424p. 1989. 54.00 (*0-226-19638-0*) U Ch Pr.

Total Indians. John Thorn & Pete Palmer. 208p. 1996. pap. 18.95 (*0-14-025728-4*, Penguin Bks) Viking Penguin.

Total Information Systems Management: Guidelines & Examples on How to Get More Value Out of Your Information System. Hubert Osterle et al. LC 93-12283. (Series in Information Systems). 305p. 1993. text ed. 70.00 (*0-471-93932-3*) Wiley.

Total Institutions. Ed. by Samuel E. Wallace. 198p. 1971. reprint ed. 32.95 (*0-87855-057-7*); reprint ed. pap. 18.95 (*0-87855-550-1*) Transaction Pubs.

Total Intravenous Anaesthesia. B. Kay. (Monographs in Anaesthesiology: Vol. 21). 382p. 1991. 220.75 (*0-444-81198-2*, MIA 21) Elsevier.

Total Joint Replacement. Petty. (Illus.). 896p. 1991. text ed. 179.00 (*0-7216-3367-6*) Saunders.

Total Joplin. (Illus.). 600p. (Orig.). (J). (gr. 4-6). 1996. 44.95 (*0-9652955-0-8*) Sunhawk Corp.

Total Justice. Lawrence M. Friedman. LC 84-51638. (Russell Sage Foundation 75th Anniversary Ser.). 176p. 1985. text ed. 34.95 (*0-87154-297-8*) Russell Sage.

Total Justice. Lawrence M. Friedman. 166p. 1994. reprint ed. pap. 14.95 (*0-87154-268-4*) Russell Sage.

Total Karate. J. Allen Queen. LC 89-49313. (Illus.). 128p. (J). (gr. 4 up). 1991. pap. 8.95 (*0-8069-6715-3*) Sterling.

Total Knee Arthroplasty. Ed. by James A. Rand. LC 92-12132. 480p. 1992. text ed. 136.50 (*0-88167-930-5*) Lppncott-Raven.

Total Knee Replacement. 1988. 107.95 (*0-387-70031-5*) Spr-Verlag.

Total Knee Replacement. Ed. by R. S. Laskin. (Illus.). xvi, 268p. 1991. 192.00 (*0-387-19644-7*) Spr-Verlag.

Total Knee Replacement: A Guide for Patients. David S. Hungerford. Ed. by David Seligson. (Orthopedic Ser.). (Illus.). 32p. (Orig.). 1995. pap. 3.95 (*1-885274-06-8*) HIN.

***Total Learning.** 4th ed. Hendrick. 1997. pap. text ed. 63.00 (*0-13-686569-0*) P-H.

***Total Learning.** 5th ed. Hendrick. LC 97-12818. 1997. text ed. 60.00 (*0-13-652009-X*) P-H.

Total Learning: Developmental Curriculum for the Young Child. 4th ed. Joanne Hendrick. 512p. (C). 1993. text ed. 63.00 (*0-02-353160-6*, Macmillan Coll) P-H.

Total Least Squares Problem: Computational Aspects & Analysis. Sabine Van Huffel & J. Vandewalle. LC 91-18739. (Frontiers in Applied Mathematics Ser.: No. 9). xiii, 300p. 1991. pap. text ed. 33.75 (*0-89871-275-0*) Soc Indus-Appl Math.

Total Liberation: Zen Spirituality & the Social Dimension. Ruben Habito. LC 89-2863. 1989. pap. 15.00 (*0-88344-537-9*) Orbis Bks.

Total Life. Wayne Bristow. 104p. (Orig.). 1996. pap. 10.00 (*1-57087-216-3*) Prof Pr NC.

Total Living: A State of Well-Being. A. L. Knight. 96p. (Orig.). 1995. pap. 8.95 (*1-886622-02-7*) Bayrock.

Total Loss. Ed. by Jack Coote. (Illus.). 322p. 1992. pap. 19.95 (*0-924486-33-3*) Sheridan.

Total Love. 1983. 14.59 (*0-932814-32-8*); pap. 10.99 (*0-932814-33-6*) Kings Farspan.

Total Madness. George Marshall. (Illus.). (Orig.). 1993. pap. 19.95 (*0-9518497-4-3*, Pub. by S T Pubng UK) AK Pr Dist.

Total Man. Sonny Landham. LC 79-11128. 1981. 21.95 (*0-87949-157-4*) Ashley Bks.

Total Man. Lester Sumrall. 102p. (Orig.). (C). 1982. pap. text ed. 12.00 (*0-937580-57-0*) LeSEA Pub Co.

Total Man. Lester Sumrall. 64p. (Orig.). 1984. pap. text ed. 1.95 (*0-937580-34-1*) LeSEA Pub Co.

Total Management by Ratios: An Integrated Approach for the Control & Monitoring of Business Enterprises. Hrishikes Bhattacharya. 256p. 1995. 38.00 (*0-8039-9271-8*) Sage.

Total Management Thinking. Sultan Kermally. 384p. Date not set. 32.95 (*0-7506-2614-3*) Buttrwrth-Heinemann.

Total Manufacturing Assurance. Douglas C. Brauer & John Cesarone. (Quality & Reliability Ser.: Vol. 24). 248p. 1991. 75.00 (*0-8247-8441-3*) Dekker.

***Total Manufacturing Solutions.** Ron Basu. 269p. 1996. 59.95 (*0-7506-2587-2*) Buttrwrth-Heinemann.

***Total Materials Cycle: The Pathway for Technology Advancement.** (Illus.). 193p. (Orig.). (C). 1996. pap. 65.00 (*0-7881-3551-1*) DIANE Pub.

Total Materials Management: Achieving Maximum Profits Through Materials-Logistics Operations. Eugene L. Magad & John M. Amos. LC 94-47941. (Materials Management-Logistics Ser.). 1995. write for info. (*0-615-00452-0*, Chap & Hall NY) Chapman & Hall.

Total Materials Management: Achieving Maximum Profits Through Materials, Logistics Operations. 2nd ed. Eugene L. Magad. 600p. (gr. 13). 1995. text ed. 59.95 (*0-412-06501-0*) Chapman & Hall.

***Total Materials Management: The Frontier for Maximizing Profit in the 1990s.** Magad & Amos. (Illus.). 568p. 1994. text ed. 58.50 (*0-412-99051-2*, Chap & Hall NY) Chapman & Hall.

Total Mean Curvature & Submanifolds of Finite Type. Bang-Yen Chen. (Pure Mathematics Ser.: Vol. 1). 352p. 1984. text ed. 54.00 (*9971-966-02-6*); pap. text ed. 28.00 (*9971-966-03-4*) World Scientific Pub.

Total Mind Body Training: A Guide to Peak Athletic Performance. Jacob Jordan. (Illus.). 112p. 1995. pap. 9.95 (*1-880336-06-5*) Turtle CT.

Total Mind Power. Donald L. Wilson. (Illus.). 254p. (C). 1978. 14.95 (*0-930298-22-5*) Westwood Pub Co.

Total Ministry: Reclaiming the Ministry of All God's People. Stewart C. Zabriskie. pap. 13.95 (*1-56699-155-2*) Alban Inst.

Total Mixed Rations & Supercows. rev. ed. Marshall E. McCullough. (Illus.). 63p. (C). 1994. pap. text ed. 4.00 (*0-932147-22-4*, Hoards Dairyman) Hoard & Sons Co.

Total Needs Selling. 5th ed. Dearborn Staff. LC 92-12710. 155p. 1992. pap. text ed. 26.95 (*0-7931-0431-9*, 5410-0405, R & R Newkirk) Dearborn Finan.

Total Negotiator. Stephen M. Pollan & Mark Levine. 272p. 1994. pap. 10.00 (*0-380-77019-9*) Avon.

Total Nutrition: The Only Guide You'll Ever Need - From the Mount Sinai School of Medicine. Ed. by Victor Herbert & Genell J. Subak-Sharpe. 816p. 1995. pap. 16.95 (*0-312-11386-2*) St Martin.

Total Package: The Evolution & Secret Meanings of Boxes, Bottles, Cans, & Tubes. Thomas Hine. LC 94-36445. (Illus.). 289p. 1995. 25.95 (*0-316-36480-0*) Little.

***Total Package: The Secret History & Hidden Meanings of Boxes, Bottles, Cans & Other Persuasive Containers.** Thomas Hine. 1997. pap. 14.95 (*0-316-36546-7*) Little.

***Total Panic.** (Wild Side Ser.). (Illus.). (J). (gr. 1-7). 12.66 (*0-614-20170-5*) Contemp Bks.

Total Parenteral Nutrition. Josef E. Fischer. LC 75-30283. 1976. 45.00 (*0-316-28370-3*) Little.

Total Parenteral Nutrition. 2nd ed. Josef E. Fischer. 1991. 95.00 (*0-316-28379-7*) Little.

Total Parenteral Nutrition: Indications, Utilization, Complications, & Pathophysiological Considerations. Ed. by Emanuel Lebenthal. LC 85-23239. 528p. 1986. reprint ed. pap. 150.50 (*0-608-00412-X*, 8523239) Bks Demand.

Total Parenteral Nutrition: Premises & Promises. Hossein Ghadimi. LC 74-17152. (Wiley Clinical Pediatrics, Maternal & Child Health Ser.). 656p. reprint ed. 180.00 (*0-8357-9994-8*, 2015192) Bks Demand.

Total Parenteral Nutrition in the Hospital & at Home. Ed. by K. N. Jeejeebhoy. 255p. 1983. 152.00 (*0-8493-6120-6*, RM224, CRC Reprint) Franklin.

Total Parish Manual: Everything You Need to Empower Your Faith Community. William J. Bausch. LC 94-60340. 328p. (Orig.). 1994. pap. 29.95 (*0-89622-607-7*) Twenty-Third.

Total Pattern Fit Minott Method. Jan Minott. (Illus.). 221p. (C). 1991. ring bd. 17.00 (*0-9633880-4-5*) Minott Method.

Total Physical Fun: Strategies & Activities for Teaching & Learning Language Through Cooperative Play. Jo A. Olliphant. (Illus.). 168p. 1991. pap. text ed. 24.95 (*1-879725-00-2*) Sahmarsh Pub.

***Total Physical Response.** K. Lyn Savage. 1993. wbk. ed. pap. text ed. 8.75 (*0-8013-0997-2*) Addison-Wesley.

Total Physical Response in First Year French. Francisco Cabello et al. (Illus.). 156p. (Orig.). 1996. pap. text ed. 15.95 (*1-56018-493-0*) Sky Oaks Prodns.

Total Physical Response in First Year Spanish. 2nd ed. Francisco L. Cabello. (Illus.). 207p. (Orig.). 1995. pap. text ed. 15.95 (*1-56018-499-X*) Sky Oaks Prodns.

Total Positivity: Vol. 1. Samuel Karlin. xiv, 576p. 1968. 69.50 (*0-8047-0314-0*) Stanford U Pr.

Total Positivity & Its Applications. Ed. by Mariano Gasca & Charles A. Micchelli. LC 95-48405. (Mathematics & Its Applications Ser.: Vol. 359). 532p. (C). 1996. lib. bdg. 196.00 (*0-7923-3924-X*) Kluwer Ac.

***Total Potency Vol. 7: Advanced Techniques for Liberated Lovers.** (Sex Masters Collection). (Illus.). 78p. (Orig.). 1997. pap. write for info. (*1-890677-06-X*) Delphi Pr.

Total Power of One in America: Discover What You Need to Know, Why & How to Be a More Powerful Person & Citizen. Fred Holden. LC 88-92792. (Illus.). 586p. 1991. 21.95 (*0-9621767-0-2*) Phoenix Enterps.

Total Pressure Measurements in Vacuum Technology. Armand Berman. 1985. text ed. 115.00 (*0-12-092440-4*) Acad Pr.

***Total Production Maintenance.** Kenneth E. Rizzo. Ed. by Erika L. Kendra. LC 97-70433. (Illus.). 160p. (C). 1997. text ed. 60.00 (*0-88362-199-1*) Graphic Arts Tech Found.

Total Productive Maintenance. Multimedia Development Services Staff. (Plant Fundamentals Ser.: Vol. XI, Module I). (Illus.). 1995. teacher ed. 65.00 (*1-57431-074-7*); student ed. 30.00 (*1-57431-034-8*) Tech Trng Systs.

Total Productive Maintenance. Terry Wireman. 206p. 1992. 36.95 (*0-8311-3036-9*) Indus Pr.

***Total Productive Maintenance: A Collection of Applications & Thoughts.** 216p. (Orig.). 1994. pap. 16.50 (*0-614-24986-4*) Am Prod & Inventory.

Total Productive Maintenance in America. 128p. 1995. 25.00 (*0-87263-461-2*) SME.

Total Productivity & Quality Management for Construction. James J. Adrian & Douglas J. Adrian. 362p. (C). 1995. text ed. 39.80 (*0-87563-552-0*) Stipes.

Total Productivity Management: A Systemic & Quantitative Approach to Compete in Quality, Price & Time. David J. Sumanth. (Illus.). 375p. 1997. 44.95 (*1-57444-057-8*) St Lucie Pr.

Total Project Management: Strategies & Tactics for the Healthcare Industries. Roger Dabbah. (Illus.). 340p. 1993. 97.85 (*0-935184-45-7*) Interpharm.

***Total Propaganda: From Mass Culture to Popular Culture.** Alex S. Edelskin. LC 96-49160. (LEA's Communication Ser.). 376p. 1997. 79.95 (*0-8058-0891-4*); pap. 29.95 (*0-8058-0892-2*) L Erlbaum Assocs.

Total Proposal Building: An Expert System Dedicated to One Result: Winning Grants & Contracts from Government, Corporations & Foundations. Richard Steiner. LC 86-72350. (Illus.). 221p. (Orig.). 1987. pap. 17.95 (*0-939109-00-X*) Trestleetree Pubns.

Total Proposal Building: An Expert System Dedicated to One Result: Winning Grants & Contracts from Government, Corporations & Foundations. 2nd ed. Richard Steiner. LC 87-51591. (Illus.). 228p. (Orig.). 1988. pap. 17.95 (*0-685-45398-7*) Trestleetree Pubns.

Total Prosthetic Replacement of the Hip: A Biomechanical Concept & its Consequences. Robert Schneider & Biel. LC 86-4785. (Illus.). 335p. 1989. 170.00 (*0-920887-03-1*) Hogrefe & Huber Pubs.

Total Purchasing: A Model for Locality Commissioning. Ed. by Rod Smith et al. 1996. write for info. (*1-85775-146-9*, Radcliffe Med Pr) Scovill Paterson.

Total Quality. Dean. Date not set. teacher ed., pap. text ed. write for info. (*0-314-03336-X*) West Pub.

Total Quality: A Framework for Leadership. D. Otis Wolkins. (Management Master Ser.). 1995. 15.95 (*1-56327-154-0*) Prod Press.

Total Quality: A Framework for Leadership. D. Otis Wolkins. 92p. 1996. pap. 12.95 (*1-56327-102-8*) Prod Press.

Total Quality: A Textbook of Strategic Quality Leadership & Planning. K. D. Lam et al. 360p. (C). 1992. pap. 35.00 (*0-9622176-9-7*) Air Acad Pr.

Total Quality: A Users' Guide for Implementation. Dan Ciampa. (Organization Development Ser.). (Illus.). 300p. (C). 1992. pap. text ed. 26.95 (*0-201-54992-1*) Addison-Wesley.

Total Quality: An Executive's Guide for the 1990's. Ernst & Whinney Quality Improvement Consulting Group Staff. (APICS Series in Production Management). 185p. 1989. text ed. 50.00 (*1-55623-188-1*) Irwin Prof Pubng.

Total Quality: Key Terms & Concepts. Ed. by Luftig & Warren Associates International Staff & William L. Duncan. (Illus.). 192p. (Orig.). 1995. pap. 19.95 (*0-8144-7876-X*) AMACOM.

Total Quality: Management, Organization, & Strategy. James W. Dean, Jr. & James R. Evans. Ed. by Fenton. 300p. (C). pap. text ed. 23.25 (*0-314-02826-9*) West Pub.

Total Quality: Success Through People. Ron Collard. 224p. (C). 1989. 95.00 (*0-85292-423-2*, Pub. by IPM Hse UK) St Mut.

Total Quality: Success Through People. Ron Collard. 216p. (C). 1993. 51.00 (*0-85292-511-5*, Pub. by IPM Hse UK) St Mut.

Total Quality Accounting. Michael D. Woods. 240p. 1994. text ed. 65.00 (*0-471-31185-5*) Wiley.

Total Quality & Customer Satisfaction. Dawson. (C). 1996. pap. text ed. write for info. (*0-03-098225-1*) HB Coll Pubs.

Total Quality & Human Resources: An Executive Guide. Barrie Dale & Cary Cooper. 288p. 1992. pap. 40.95 (*0-631-18716-2*) Blackwell Pubs.

Total Quality & Organization Development. William Lindsay & Joseph A. Petrick. (Total Quality Ser.). 400p. 1996. 39.95 (*1-884015-22-0*) St Lucie Pr.

Total Quality Approach. Gordon Gatiss. (Management Skills-ISM Ser.). (Illus.). 160p. 1996. pap. 19.95 (*0-304-33795-1*) Cassell.

Total Quality Assurance for the Food Industries. 2nd ed. Wilbur A. Gould & Ronald W. Gould. LC 92-37494. 465p. 1993. 63.00 (*0-930027-20-5*) CTI Pubns.

Total Quality Control Essentials: Key Elements, Methodologies, & Managing for Success. Sarv S. Soin. 1992. text ed. 39.95 (*0-07-059548-8*) McGraw.

Total Quality Control for Management: Strategies & Techniques from Toyota & Toyoda Gosei. Maseo Nemoto. 270p. 1987. 24.95 (*0-13-925637-7*) P-H.

Total Quality Control for the Men's Clothing Industry. 16p. 1967. 7.00 (*0-318-19672-7*) Clothing Mfrs.

***Total Quality Corporation: How 10 Major Companies Added to Profits & Cleaned up the Environment in the 1990s.** Francis McInerney & Sean White. 1997. pap. 13.95 (*0-452-27347-1*, Plume-Truman Talley Bks) NAL-Dutton.

Total Quality Corporation: How 10 Major Companies Turned Quality & Environmental Challenges to Competitive Advantage in the 1990s. Francis McInerney & Sean White. 320p. 1995. pap. 24.95 (*0-525-93928-8*, Dutton-Truman Talley) NAL-Dutton.

***Total Quality Counseling: A Comprehensive Manual for Elementary & Middle School Counselors.** David Burgess. 151p. (Orig.). 1991. teacher ed., pap. 21.95 (*1-884063-44-6*) Mar Co Prods.

Total Quality Customer Service: How to Make It Your Way of Life. Jim Temme. LC 94-2719. vi, 142p. 1994. pap. 15.95 (*1-878542-44-3*, 13-0004) SkillPath Pubns.

Total Quality Development: Improved Total Development Process. Don P. Clausing. 350p. 1994. 49.95 (*0-7918-0035-0*, 800350) ASME Pr.

Total Quality Distribution. Walpert Smullian & Blumenthal Staff. 119p. 1993. pap. 79.95 (*0-614-02666-0*) Natl Assn Wholesale Dists.

Total Quality Education: Transforming Schools into Learning Places. Fenwick W. English & John C. Hill. LC 93-40953. (Total Quality Education for the World's Best Schools Ser.: Vol. 2). 136p. 1994. pap. 18.00 (*0-8039-6106-5*) Corwin Pr.

Total Quality Education - Teaching Techniques for Technical Educators. Mary A. Roe. 32p. (C). 1991. pap. text ed. 5.95 (*0-940017-16-4*) Info Tec OH.

Total Quality Education, Technology & Teaching. Eugene R. Hertzke & Warren E. Olson. LC 93-40543. (Total Quality Education for World-Class Schools Ser.: Vol. 9). 152p. 1994. pap. 18.95 (*0-8039-6122-7*) Corwin Pr.

***Total Quality Environmental Management: An ISO 14000 Approach.** Vasanthakumar N. Bhat. LC 97-19761. 1998. text ed. write for info. (*1-56720-097-4*, Quorum Bks) Greenwood.

Total Quality for Safety & Health Professionals. F. David Pierce. LC 95-8268. 1995. 59.00 (*0-86587-462-X*) Gov Insts.

Total Quality for Schools: A Guide for Implementation. Joseph C. Fields. LC 94-16402. 204p. 1994. 20.00 (*0-87389-273-9*, H0829) ASQC Qual Pr.

Total Quality for Schools: A Suggestion for American Education. Joseph C. Fields. LC 93-955. 127p. 1993. 20.00 (*0-87389-206-2*, H0753) ASQC Qual Pr.

Total Quality Handbook. 1990. 390.00 (*3-9520013-6-8*, Pub. by Strategic Direction SZ) St Mut.

***Total Quality Improvement & the Internal Auditing Function.** Praveen P. Gupta & Manash R. Ray. Ed. by Lee a. Campbell. 1995. pap. 50.00 (*0-89413-327-6*, A868) Inst Inter Aud.

Total Quality Improvement Guide for Institutions of Higher Education. Robert A. Cornesky & Samuel A. McCool. LC 92-15863. 162p. 1992. pap. 34.95 (*0-912150-21-1*) Magna Pubns.

Total Quality in Action. 1990. 270.00 (*3-9520013-7-6*, Pub. by Strategic Direction SZ) St Mut.

Total Quality in Construction Projects: Achieving Profitability with Customer Satisfaction. Ron B. Hellard. 200p. 1993. 62.00 (*0-685-75151-1*, 1951-3) Am Soc Civil Eng.

Total Quality in Health Care: From Theory to Practice. Ellen M. Gaucher & Richard J. Coffey. LC 92-37677. (Health Ser.). 651p. 1993. text ed. 47.95 (*1-55542-534-8*) Jossey-Bass.

Total Quality in Higher Education. Ralph Lewis & Douglas Smith. LC 93-23440. (Total Quality Ser.). (Illus.). 336p. 1994. 45.95 (*0-9634030-7-9*) St Lucie Pr.

Total Quality in Information Systems & Technology. Jack Woodall et al. (Total Quality Ser.). (Illus.). 300p. 1996. 42.95 (*1-884015-70-0*) St Lucie Pr.

Total Quality in Managing Human Resources. Joseph A. Petrick & Dianna Fur. LC 94-46630. (Total Quality Ser.). 370p. 1995. 44.95 (*1-884015-24-7*) St Lucie Pr.

Total Quality in Marketing. William C. Johnson & Richard J. Chvala. (Total Quality Ser.). 300p. 1995. 39.95 (*1-884015-13-1*) St Lucie Pr.

Total Quality in Purchasing & Supplier Management. Ricardo R. Fernandez. LC 94-9069. (Total Quality Ser.). (Illus.). 336p. 1994. 45.95 (*1-884015-00-X*) St Lucie Pr.

Total Quality in Radiology: A Guide to Implementation. Henry G. Adams & Sudhir Arora. LC 93-41954. 216p. 1994. text ed. 45.95 (*1-884015-07-7*) St Lucie Pr.

Total Quality in Research & Development. Gregory McLaughlin. (Total Quality Ser.). 256p. 1995. 45.95 (*1-884015-02-6*) St Lucie Pr.

***Total Quality Learning.** 1996. text ed. 44.00 (*3-540-61408-7*) Spr-Verlag.

Total Quality Learning. Ronnie Lessem. (Developmental Management Ser.). 300p. 1991. 44.95 (*0-631-16828-1*) Blackwell Pubs.

Total Quality Learning. Ronnie Lessem. 1994. pap. 22.95 (*0-631-19306-5*) Blackwell Pubs.

Total Quality Loan Management: Applying the Principles of TQM for Superior Lending Performance. S. Wayne Linder. 1992. per. 50.00 (*1-55738-371-5*) Irwin Prof Pubng.

T

An Asterisk (*) at the beginning of an entry indicates that the title is appearing in BIP for the first time.

Total Quality Management. 1993. pap. 11.95 (*0-7871-0145-1*, Dove Bks) Dove Audio.

Total Quality Management. Dale H. Besterfield. LC 94-37020. 445p. 1994. text ed. 78.00 (*0-13-030651-7*) P-H.

Total Quality Management. Peter Capezio & Debra L. Morehouse. (Leadership Ser.). (Illus.). 290p. (Orig.). 1992. pap. 19.95 (*1-55852-092-9*) Natl Pr Pubns.

Total Quality Management. Stephen George et al. 1996. pap. 19.95 (*0-7871-0729-8*, Dove Bks) Dove Audio.

Total Quality Management. Debra L. Morehouse. (Leadership Ser.). (Illus.). 105p. (Orig.). pap. 9.95 (*1-55852-079-1*) Natl Pr Pubns.

Total Quality Management. NCMA Staff. (National Contract Management Association Workshop Ser.). 36p. 1989. pap. 10.95 (*0-940343-61-4*, TQMPG) Natl Contract Mgmt.

Total Quality Management. Peratec. 1994. pap. 25.95 (*0-412-58640-1*) Chapman & Hall.

Total Quality Management. Richardson. LC 96-16564. (Mechanical Technology Ser.). 448p. 1996. text ed. 42.95 (*0-8273-7192-6*) Delmar.

Total Quality Management. Marshall Sashkin & Kenneth J. Kiser. LC 91-92982. (Illus.). vi, 182p. (Orig.). 1991. pap. 19.95 (*0-9630714-0-8*) Ducochon Pr.

Total Quality Management. 2nd ed. John Oakland. 316p. (C). 1993. text ed. 37.95 (*0-89397-386-6*) Nichols Pub.

Total Quality Management. 2nd ed. John S. Oakland. LC 92-40747. 1995. 59.95 (*0-7506-0993-1*) Buttrwrth-Heinemann.

Total Quality Management: A Continuous Process for Improvement. 52p. 1993. pap. text ed. 28.00 (*0-910329-76-1*, 0111761) Am Speech Lang Hearing.

Total Quality Management: A Cross Functional Approach. Ashok Rao et al. LC 95-46097. 630p. 1996. text ed. 72.95 (*0-471-10804-9*) Wiley.

Total Quality Management: A Survey of Its Important Aspects. LC 94-30860. 1995. pap. 21.25 (*0-87709-274-5*) Course Tech.

Total Quality Management: An Introductory Text. Paul T. James. 1996. 44.00 (*0-13-207119-3*) P-H.

Total Quality Management: Guiding Principles for Application. Jack P. Pekar. LC 95-12661. (Manual Ser.: MNL 22). 1995. 54.00 (*0-8031-2062-1*) ASTM.

Total Quality Management: Implications for Higher Education. Ed. by Allan Hoffman & Daniel Julius. 454p. 1995. 29.95 (*1-886626-00-6*) Prescott Pub.

Total Quality Management: Mastering Your Small Business. Jill Rossiter. 1996. pap. 22.95 (*1-57410-039-4*, 61010401, Upstart) Dearborn Finan.

Total Quality Management: Strategies & Techniques Proven at Today's Most Successful Companies. Arnold Weimerskirch & Stephen George. 304p. 1994. text ed. 32.95 (*0-471-59538-1*) Wiley.

Total Quality Management: Student Edition with Cases. John S. Oakland & Les Porter. 448p. 1995. pap. 32.95 (*0-7506-2124-9*, Focal) Buttrwrth-Heinemann.

Total Quality Management: Text, Cases & Readings. 2nd ed. Joel E. Ross. LC 94-9068. (Illus.). 464p. (C). 1994. pap. text ed. 42.95 (*1-884015-08-5*) St Lucie Pr.

Total Quality Management: The Health Care Pioneers. Mara M. Melum & Marie K. Sinioris. LC 92-11056. 404p. 1992. pap. 69.00 (*1-55648-089-X*, 169410) AHPI.

Total Quality Management: The Key to Business Improvement. Ed. by C. Hakes. 160p. 1991. 62.95 (*0-442-31181-8*) Chapman & Hall.

Total Quality Management: Three Steps to Continuous Improvement. Arthur Tenner & Irving De Toro. 266p. 1992. 34.95 (*0-201-56305-3*) Addison-Wesley.

***Total Quality Management Vol. XXIII: Komponenten und Organisatorische Umsetzung einer Unternehmensweiten Qualitatskonzeption.** Anette Von Ahsen. (Schriften zum Controlling Ser.: Bd. 16). (Illus.). 340p. (GER.). 1996. pap. 61.95 (*3-631-30309-2*) P Lang Pubng.

Total Quality Management & the School. Stephen Murgatroyd & Colin Morgan. LC 92-17386. 1992. 90.00 (*0-335-15723-8*, Open Univ Pr); pap. 29.00 (*0-335-15722-X*, Open Univ Pr) Taylor & Francis.

Total Quality Management Approach to IT Security. Mario Devargas. 224p. 1995. text ed. 52.95 (*1-85554-352-4*) Blackwell Pubs.

Total Quality Management for Custodial Operations. Stephen Gaudreau. 128p. (Orig.). 1994. pap. text ed. 49.95 (*1-884015-51-4*) St Lucie Pr.

Total Quality Management for Custodial Operations: A Guide to Understanding & Applying the Key Elements of T. Q. M. Stephen D. Gaudreau et al. 141p. 1994. pap. 59.95 (*0-9642640-0-5*) Power Inc.

Total Quality Management for Engineers. Mohamed Zairi. 1993. 45.00 (*0-88415-150-6*) Gulf Pub.

Total Quality Management for Home Care. Elaine R. Davis. 368p. 1994. 65.00 (*0-8342-0332-4*, 20332) Aspen Pub.

Total Quality Management for Hospital Nutrition Services. M. Rosita Schiller et al. LC 93-39360. 400p. 1994. 59.00 (*0-8342-0551-3*) Aspen Pub.

Total Quality Management for Law Firms. (Commercial Law & Practice Course Handbook Ser.: Vol. 636). 327p. 1992. 70.00 (*0-685-65480-X*, A4-4395) PLI.

Total Quality Management for Schools. LC 92-61824. 1994. vhs 149.95 (*1-56676-149-2*) Technomic.

Total Quality Management for Schools. Leo Bradley. LC 92-61824. 220p. 1992. text ed. 39.95 (*0-87762-972-2*) Technomic.

Total Quality Management for Software. Ed. by G. Gordon Schulmeyer & James I. McManus. LC 92-938. 550p. 1992. text ed. 69.95 (*0-442-00794-9*) Van Nos Reinhold.

Total Quality Management for Software. Gordon G. Schulmeyer. (C). 1992. text ed. 70.95 (*1-85032-836-6*) ITCP.

Total Quality Management for the Food Industries. Wilbur A. Gould. LC 92-11409. 165p. 1992. 52.00 (*0-930027-19-1*) CTI Pubns.

Total Quality Management Handbook. J. L. Hradesky. 1994. text ed. 74.50 (*0-07-030511-0*) McGraw.

Total Quality Management in Academic Libraries: Initial Implementation Efforts; Proceedings of the 1st International Conference on TQM & Academic Libraries. 348p. 1995. 60.00 (*0-918006-75-9*) ARL.

***Total Quality Management in Action.** Gopal K. Kanji. 304p. 1996. text ed. write for info. (*0-412-78220-0*, Chap & Hall NY) Chapman & Hall.

Total Quality Management in Geriatric Care. Douglas K. Miller et al. 176p. 1995. 31.95 (*0-8261-8840-0*) Springer Pub.

Total Quality Management in Golf & Country Clubs. Andrew R. Cornesky & Robert A. Cornesky. 320p. 1993. pap. 19.00 (*1-881807-04-5*) Cornesky & Assocs.

Total Quality Management in Government: A Practical Guide for the Real World. Steven Cohen & Ronald Brand. LC 92-42281. (Public Administration Ser.). 252p. 27.95 (*1-55542-539-9*) Jossey-Bass.

Total Quality Management in Healthcare: From Theory to Execution. Dean H. Stamatis. 336p. 1996. text ed. 45.00 (*0-7863-0980-6*) Irwin.

Total Quality Management in Higher Education. James B. Rieley. 52p. (Orig.). (C). 1994. pap. text ed. 25.00 (*0-7881-1293-7*) DIANE Pub.

Total Quality Management in Higher Education. Ed. by Lawrence A. Sherr & Deborah J. Teeter. LC 85-645339. (New Directions for Institutional Research Ser.: No. IR 71). 1991. 19.00 (*1-55542-773-1*) Jossey-Bass.

Total Quality Management in Higher Education: Is It Working? Why or Why Not? Ed. by Serbrenia J. Sims & Ronald R. Sims. LC 95-3340. 224p. 1995. text ed. 55.00 (*0-275-94946-X*, Praeger Pubs) Greenwood.

Total Quality Management in Human Service Organizations. Ed. by John Gunther & Frank Hawkins. LC 96-5017. (Social Work Ser.: Vol. 25). (Illus.). 264p. 1996. 42.95 (*0-8261-9340-4*) Springer Pub.

Total Quality Management in Human Service Organizations. Lawrence L. Martin. (Human Services Guides Ser.: Vol. 67). (Illus.). 112p. (C). 1993. text ed. 39.95 (*0-8039-4949-9*); pap. text ed. 17.95 (*0-8039-4950-2*) Sage.

Total Quality Management in Information Services. Ed. by John A. Buckland. 56p. 1993. pap. text ed. 54.95 (*0-471-56046-4*) Wiley.

Total Quality Management in Information Services. Guy St. Clair. LC 96-43536. (Information Services Management Ser.). 200p. 1996. 45.00 (*1-85739-039-3*) Bowker-Saur.

Total Quality Management in Libraries: A Sourcebook. Rosanna M. O'Neil. xvi, 194p. 1994. pap. text ed. 25.00 (*1-56308-247-0*) Libs Unl.

***Total Quality Management in Psychiatric Services.** Koch. 1994. text ed. write for info. (*0-582-23680-0*, Pub. by Longman UK) Longman.

Total Quality Management in the Chemical Industry: Strategies for Success. R. P. Hadfield. Ed. by G. R. Turner. 198p. 1994. 73.00 (*0-85186-624-7*, R6624) CRC Pr.

Total Quality Management in the Clinical Laboratory. Doug Hutchison. LC 93-42922. 270p. 1994. 10.75 (*0-87389-252-6*, H0807) ASQC Qual Pr.

Total Quality Management in the Electronics Industry: A User's & Supplier's Guide. Keith Beasley. (C). 1994. 150.00 (*0-946655-54-5*, Pub. by Stanley Thornes UK) Trans-Atl Phila.

Total Quality Management in the Printing & Publishing Industry. Ed. by Kristin K. Richardson. 48p. 1992. 28.50 (*0-933505-23-X*) Graph Comm Assn.

Total Quality Management in the Public Sector: An International Perspective. Colin Morgan & Stephen Murgatroyd. LC 93-24014. 208p. 1994. 85.00 (*0-335-19103-7*, Open Univ Pr); pap. 29.50 (*0-335-19102-9*, Open Univ Pr) Taylor & Francis.

***Total Quality Management Master Plan Research Report: An Implementation Strategy.** 63p. 1990. pap. write for info. (*1-879364-16-6*) GOAL-QPC.

Total Quality Management on Campus: Is It Worth Doing? Daniel T. Seymour. LC 85-644752. (New Directions for Higher Education Ser.: No. 86). 96p. (Orig.). 1994. pap. 19.00 (*0-7879-9962-8*) Jossey-Bass.

***Total Quality Management to Your Kitchen & Bathroom Business.** David Newton. (Illus.). 161p. (Orig.). 1996. pap. text ed. 30.00 (*1-887127-03-8*, 5304) Natl Kit Bath.

***Total Quality Management Using FOCUS-PDCA.** Marianne Dolson & Nancy E. Fritch. (Illus.). 55p. 1997. pap. text ed. 13.00 (*1-880610-77-9*) PRO-ACT Pub.

***Total Quality Management Using FOCUS-PDCA: A Self Study for: Leadership.** Marianne Dolson & Wade Curl. (Illus.). 88p. 1995. pap. text ed. 15.95 (*1-880610-75-2*) PRO-ACT Pub.

***Total Quality Management Using FOCUS-PDCA, Team Member Training Manual.** Marianne Dolson & Nancy E. Fritch. (Illus.). 38p. 1997. pap. text ed. 10.00 (*1-880610-78-7*) PRO-ACT Pub.

Total Quality Mangement & Beyond. Haavind. Date not set. write for info. (*0-7506-9263-4*) Buttrwrth-Heinemann.

Total Quality Marketing: The Key to Regaining Market Shares. Allan C. Reddy. LC 94-15885. 200p. 1994. text ed. 55.00 (*0-89930-893-7*, Quorum Bks) Greenwood.

Total Quality Measurement in the Oil Industry. J. D. Symonds. 1994. 120.00 (*0-7514-0040-8*, Pub. by Blackie Acad & Prof UK) Routledge Chapman & Hall.

Total Quality Ministry. Walt Kallestad & Steven Schey. LC 94-25107. 1994. pap. 10.99 (*0-8066-2778-6*, Augsburg) Augsburg Fortress.

***Total Quality Outcomes Management: A Guide to Integrating Outcomes Measurement & TQM to Improve Health.** Mara M. Melum. 333p. 1995. pap. write for info. (*1-879364-48-4*) GOAL-QPC.

Total Quality Process Control for Injection Molding. Joseph M. Gordon. 496p. (C). 1992. text ed. 145.00 (*1-56990-031-0*) Hanser-Gardner.

Total Quality Project Management for the Design Firm: How to Improve Quality, Increase Sales & Reduce Costs. Frank A. Stasiowski. LC 93-19850. 405p. 1993. text ed. 59.95 (*0-471-30787-4*) Wiley.

Total Quality Safety Management: An Introduction. Edward E. Adams. LC 95-13971. (Illus.). 203p. (Orig.). 1995. pap. text ed. 34.95 (*1-885581-03-3*, 4553) ASSE.

***Total Quality Safety Management & Auditing: Your Complete Guide to Developing & Auditing a Safety Management System.** Michael B. Weinstein. LC 97-21402. 1997. write for info. (*1-56670-283-6*) Lewis Pubs.

Total Quality Selling. Louis DeGeorge. (Business Skills Express Ser.). 1995. pap. 10.00 (*0-7863-0324-7*) Irwin Prof Pubng.

Total Quality Service. Stanley Brown. 1993. 21.95 (*0-13-923392-X*); 21.95 (*0-13-091034-1*) P-H.

Total Quality Service: A Simplified Approach to Using the Baldrige Award Criteria. Sheila Kessler. (Illus.). 161p. 1995. pap. 24.00 (*0-87389-336-0*, H0893) ASQC Qual Pr.

Total Quality Service: Principles, Practices, & Implementation. Dean H. Stamatis. LC 94-46634. 330p. 1995. 39.95 (*1-884015-83-2*) St Lucie Pr.

Total Quality Service in Radio. Sheila Kessler. (Illus.). 140p. 1995. pap. 29.00 (*1-879404-17-6*) Cmpetitive Edge.

Total Quality Simulation: Leader's Guide. Cresencio Torres. (Consensus Decision-Making Simulations Ser.). 1995. pap. write for info. (*0-87425-279-2*) HRD Press.

Total Quality Through Project Management. Jeffrey S. Leavitt. 1994. text ed. 49.00 (*0-07-036980-1*) McGraw.

Total Quality Transformation Improvement Tools. PQ Systems, Inc. Staff. 338p. 1991. spiral bd. 85.00 (*1-882683-00-5*) PQ Systs.

Total Quality Transformation Improvement Tools - Educational. Pq Systems, Inc. Staff. 300p. (Orig.). 1995. spiral bd., pap. 39.95 (*1-882683-01-3*) PQ Systs.

Total Quality Transformation Improvement Tools-Commercial. Pq Systems, Inc. Staff. 300p. (Orig.). 1995. spiral bd., pap. 39.95 (*1-882683-02-1*) PQ Systs.

Total Quality Transformations: A Resource Guide for Implementing Total Quality Training. Marlene Caroselli. 247p. 1991. ring bd. 49.95 (*0-87425-158-3*) HRD Press.

Total Recall. Piers Anthony. 1990. mass mkt. 4.50 (*0-380-70874-4*) Avon.

Total Recall. Joan Minninger. 1994. 7.98 (*1-56731-011-7*, MJF Bks) Fine Comms.

Total Recall. Joan Minninger. 1989. mass mkt. 5.99 (*0-671-69134-1*) PB.

Total Recall Murder. Bohn & Stowell. 400p. 1995. mass mkt. 5.99 (*0-440-21587-0*) Dell.

Total Recovery: Lifestyle Management in Recovery from Drugs & Alcohol. Jim Parker. (Orig.). 1995. pap. 2.00 (*0-89230-231-3*) Do It Now.

Total Reflection X-Ray Fluorescence Analysis. Reinhold Klockenkamper. LC 96-20190. (Chemical Analysis: A Series of Monographs on Analy). 1996. text ed. 74.95 (*0-471-30524-3*, Wiley-Interscience) Wiley.

Total Rider: Health & Fitness for the Equestrian. Tom Holmes. LC 95-45069. 1995. pap. 24.95 (*0-939481-44-8*) Half Halt Pr.

Total Risk: Nick Leeson and the Fall of Barings Bank. Judith H. Rawnsley. LC 95-44301. (Illus.). 224p. 1995. 24.00 (*0-88730-781-7*) Harper Busn.

Total Risk: Nick Leeson & the Fall of Barings Bank. Judith H. Rawnsley. 272p. 1996. mass mkt. 5.99 (*0-06-109535-4*, Harp PBks) HarpC.

Total Rugby: Fifteen-Man Rugby for Coach & Player. 3rd ed. Jim Greenwood. (Illus.). 320p. 1992. pap. 24.95 (*0-7136-3443-X*, Pub. by A&C Black UK) Talman.

Total Runner: A Complete Mind-Body Guide to Optimal Performance. Jerry Lynch. (Illus.). 224p. 1987. 21.95 (*0-13-925678-4*); pap. 10.95 (*0-13-925660-1*) P-H.

Total Runner's Almanac. Sharon Svensson. 184p. 1994. pap. 12.95 (*0-9634568-4-9*); spiral bd. 12.95 (*0-9634568-3-0*) Trimarket.

***Total Runner's Almanac: A Must Book for Every Runner.** 2nd rev. ed. Sharon Svensson. (Illus.). 144p. 1997. pap. 12.95 (*0-9634568-9-X*) Trimarket.

***Total Scheme of Things: Totalistic Science.** abr. ed. Harry S. Miller. (Illus.). 450p. (Orig.). 1996. pap. 45.00 (*0-9657604-0-5*) Uniscience Educ.

***Total Security Package.** Douglas A. Ross. 180p. (Orig.). 1997. pap. 12.95 (*1-55197-947-0*, Pub. by Comnwlth Pub CN) Partners Pubs Grp.

***Total Service Medical Practice: 17 Steps to Satisfying Your Internal & External Customers.** Vicky Bradford. LC 96-41980. 336p. (C). 1996. text ed. 45.00 (*1-55738-645-5*) Irwin.

Total Sex. Dan Abelow. 1988. mass mkt. 5.99 (*0-425-11205-5*) Berkley Pub.

***Total Shiba, Vol. 1.** Gretchen Haskett & Susan Houser. LC 96-39711. (Illus.). 164p. 1997. 29.95 (*0-931866-98-7*, Blue Rib Books) Alpine Pubns.

Total Shotmaking: The Golfer's Guide to Par Shooting. Fred Couples & John Andrisani. (Illus.). 192p. 1995. pap. 15.00 (*0-06-272060-0*, Harper Ref) HarpC.

***Total SNMP: Exploring the Simple Network Management Protocol.** 2nd ed. Harnedy. LC 97-14616. (C). 1997. pap. text ed. 55.00 (*0-13-646994-9*) P-H.

Total SNMP: Exploring the Simple Network Management Protocol. 2nd ed. Sean J. Harnedy. 1996. pap. 45.00 (*1-878956-67-1*) CBM Bks.

Total Speech: An Integrational Linguistic Approach to Language. Michael Toolan. LC 95-42485. (Post-Contemporary Interventions Ser.). 376p. 1996. text ed. 57.95 (*0-8223-1781-8*); pap. text ed. 19.95 (*0-8223-1790-7*) Duke.

***Total Sports Experience - For Kids: A Parent's Guide for Success in Youth Sports.** Aubrey H. Fine & Michael L. Sachs. LC 96-45052. 1997. pap. 12.95 (*1-888698-06-3*) Diamond Communications.

Total Strangers. Terence Winch. LC 82-19278. (Illus.). 13p. (Orig.). 1982. pap. 7.50 (*0-915124-77-7*, Toothpaste) Coffee Hse.

Total Strength: A Comprehensive Guide to Increasing Your Health Through Scientifically Founded Weightlifting. Robert G. Dennis & John B. Hahn. LC 95-69718. 160p. 1995. pap. 15.95 (*1-886783-02-0*) Prometheus OH.

Total Success Book: A Guide to Personal Fulfillment. Leonard Diamond. 192p. (C). 1994. pap. 14.95 (*0-87975-871-6*) Prometheus Bks.

Total Surrender. large type ed. Mother Teresa. Ed. by Angelo DeVananda. LC 93-8541. (EasyRead Type Ser.). 162p. (Orig.). 1993. reprint ed. pap. 8.95 (*0-8027-2676-3*) Walker & Co.

Total Surrender. rev. ed. Mother Teresa. Ed. by Bro. Angelo Devananda. 158p. (Orig.). (C). 1989. pap. 6.99 (*0-89283-651-2*, Charis) Servant.

Total Surrender to God. Arthur F. Hallam. 236p. (Orig.). 1985. pap. 19.95 (*0-938770-05-5*) Capitalist Pr OH.

Total Survey Error. Ronald M. Andersen et al. LC 79-88104. (Jossey-Bass Social & Behavioral Science Ser.). 336p. reprint ed. pap. 95.80 (*0-8357-4963-0*, 2037896) Bks Demand.

Total Survival: A Comprehensive Guide for the Physical, Psychological, Emotional, & Professional Survival of Law Enforcement Officers. Edward J. Nowicki. LC 92-85340. 1993. pap. 24.95 (*1-879411-18-0*) Perf Dimensions Pub.

Total Synthesis of Natural Products, 9 vols. Ed. by John W. Apsimon. 5106p. 1992. text ed. 1,107.00 (*0-471-58083-X*) Wiley.

Total Synthesis of Natural Products, Vol. 1. Ed. by John W. Apsimon. LC 72-4075. 603p. 1973. text ed. 137.00 (*0-471-03251-4*) Wiley.

Total Synthesis of Natural Products, Vol. 2. Ed. by John W. Apsimon. 754p. 1973. text ed. 148.00 (*0-471-03252-2*) Wiley.

Total Synthesis of Natural Products, Vol. 3. Ed. by John W. Apsimon. 566p. 1977. text ed. 148.00 (*0-471-02392-2*) Wiley.

Total Synthesis of Natural Products, Vol. 4. Ed. by John W. Apsimon. LC 72-4075. (Total Synthesis of Natural Products Ser.). 610p. 1981. text ed. 157.00 (*0-471-05460-7*) Wiley.

Total Synthesis of Natural Products, Vol. 5. Ed. by John W. Apsimon. (Total Synthesis of Natural Products Ser.). 550p. 1983. text ed. 148.00 (*0-471-09808-6*) Wiley.

Total Synthesis of Natural Products, Vol. 6. Ed. by John W. Apsimon. LC 72-4075. (Total Synthesis of Natural Products Ser.). 291p. 1984. text ed. 102.00 (*0-471-09900-7*) Wiley.

Total Synthesis of Natural Products, Vol. 7. Ed. by John W. Simon. 468p. 1988. text ed. 140.00 (*0-471-88076-0*) Wiley.

Total Synthesis of Natural Products, Vol. 8. Ed. by John W. Apsimon. 720p. 1992. text ed. 210.00 (*0-471-54507-4*) Wiley.

Total Synthesis of Natural Products, Vol. 9. John W. Apsimon. 544p. 1992. text ed. 174.00 (*0-471-55189-9*) Wiley.

***Total Synthesis of Natural Products, Vol. 10.** David Goldsmith. (Total Synthesis of Natural Products Ser.). 195p. 1997. 60.00 (*0-471-59679-5*) Wiley.

Total Synthesis of Natural Products: The 'Chiron' Approach. S. Hanessian. LC 83-19307. (Organic Chemistry Ser.: Vol. 3). 310p. 1983. 139.00 (*0-08-029247-X*, Pub. by Pergamon Repr UK) Franklin.

Total Tattoo Book. Amy Krakow. (Illus.). 240p. (Orig.). 1994. pap. 11.99 (*0-446-67001-4*) Warner Bks.

Total Teaching for Today's Church. rev. ed. Mary Wallace et al. Orig. Title: Centers of Interest. (Illus.). 200p. (Orig.). (C). 1985. pap. 6.99 (*0-912315-85-7*) Word Aflame.

Total Telemarketing: Complete Guide to Increasing Sales & Profits. Robert J. McHatton. LC 87-21547. 246p. 1988. text ed. 47.95 (*0-471-62754-2*); pap. text ed. 16.95 (*0-471-62755-0*) Wiley.

Total Telemarking. Brad English. LC 83-83417. (Illus.). (Orig.). 1984. pap. 15.95 (*0-915789-00-0*) East River Pub CO.

***Total Television.** Alex McNeil. 1997. pap. 29.95 incl. cd-rom (*0-14-026737-9*) Viking Penguin.

Total Television: The Comprehensive Guide to Programming from 1948 to the Present. 4th ed. Alex McNeil. 1264p. (Orig.). 1996. pap. 22.95 (*0-14-024916-8*, Penguin Bks) Viking Penguin.

Total Tennis: A Complete Guide for Today's Player. Peter Burwash & John Tullius. (Illus.). 256p. 1991. pap. 12.95 (*0-02-079261-1*) Macmillan.

Total Tennis Training see Coaching Tennis

Total Traveler by Ship. 12th ed. Ethel Blum. 476p. 1993. pap. 16.95 (*1-55868-158-2*) Gr Arts Ctr Pub.

Total Triathlon Almanac - 1993. Tony Svensson. 164p. 1992. spiral bd. 16.95 (*0-9634568-0-6*) Trimarket.

Total Triathlon Almanac - 1993. Tony Svensson. 184p. 1994. pap. 16.95 (*0-9634568-2-2*); spiral bd. 16.95 (*0-9634568-1-4*) Trimarket.

Total Triathlon Almanac-3: The Essential Training Tool & Information Source for the Triathlete & Duathlete. Tony Svensson. (Illus.). 164p. (Orig.). 1996. pap. 16.95 (*0-9634568-7-3*) Trimarket.

An Asterisk (*) at the beginning of an entry indicates that the title is appearing in BIP for the first time.

Total TV Book. 128p. 1993. pap. 39.00 (0-9637522-0-0) Homily Pr.

Total TV Book. 2nd ed. (Entertainment Directory Ser.). 1994. pap. 39.00 (0-9637522-4-3) Homily Pr.

Total Victory! The Complete Management Guide to a Successful NLRB Representation Election Campaign. Donald P. Wilson. 392p. 1994. 39.95 (0-9638554-0-9) Labor Relations.

Total Victory At the Track. William L. Scott. 1989. pap. 12.95 (0-89709-183-3) Liberty Pub.

Total Victory at the Track: The Promise & the Performance. William L. Scott. 300p. 1988. 24.00 (0-914861-02-6) Amicus Pr.

Total War. Jerry Ahern. (Survivalist Ser.: No. 1). (Orig.). 1982. mass mkt. 2.95 (0-8217-2445-2, Zebra Kensgtn) Kensgtn Pub Corp.

Total War: Causes & Courses of the Second World War, Vol. 2. 2nd rev. ed. Peter Calvocoressi et al. LC 90-52557. (Illus.). 736p. 1990. pap. 16.95 (0-679-73099-0) Pantheon.

Total War & the Constitution. Edward S. Corwin. LC 70-127590. (Essay Index Reprint Ser.). 1977. 20.95 (0-8369-1796-0) Ayer.

Total War & Twentieth-Century Higher Learning: Universities of the Western World in the First & Second World Wars. S. Willis Rudy. LC 90-55172. 136p. 1991. 30.00 (0-8386-3409-5) Fairleigh Dickinson.

Total Well Being. Jack E. Young. Ed. by Celia Straus. (Illus.). 256p. (Orig.). 1995. pap. 19.95 (0-9644716-0-4) Tri Health.

***Total Wellness: Improve Your Health by Understanding the Body's Healing System.** Joseph Pizzorno. 432p. 1997. per. 15.00 (0-7615-1094-X) Prima Pub.

Total Wellness: Improve Your Health by Understanding the Body's Healing Systems. Joseph E. Pizzorno. LC 96-224. 432p. 1996. boxed 22.95 (0-7615-0433-8) Prima Pub.

***Total Wellness Program for Women over 30: Comprehensive Manual with Medical Guidelines for Health Care Professionals. Barbara Kass-Annese. Ed. by Jerry Byrd. LC 97-70430. 350p. (Orig.). 1997. spiral bd. 35.95 (0-9655715-0-5) Health Choice.**

A TOTAL WELLNESS PROGRAM FOR WOMEN OVER THIRTY, A COMPREHENSIVE MANUAL FOR MEDICAL GUIDELINES FOR HEALTH CARE PROFESSIONALS, 1ST ED. "An A to Z comprehensive guide for health care professionals & a significant contribution for the treatment of women."--Marie Lugani, President & Founder of the American Menopause Foundation Inc. This manual is the best practical & user-friendly resource health care professionals can have for the care of their perimenopausal & postmenopausal patients. Many books have been written about menopause but none offer such a comprehensive approach to the prevention & treatment of symptoms & health care problems associated with menopause. This manual serves as a summary of key research in the areas of nutrition, exercise, stress reduction, psychosocial & sexual issues, & hormone replacement & drug therapies. Complementary (alternative) health care practices are discussed as well. It includes samples of several health assessments for use by health care professionals & their patients. It also includes a Guidelines section which can serve as a foundation for protocols of clinical practice. The Guidelines section summarizes basic recommendations for medical evaluation of women over 30 & outlines major nutritional, exercise & stress recommendations including nutritional supplementation. It also presents basic recommendations for hormonal & drug therapies & for herbal & homeopathic treatments & includes an extensive resource section. The manual can be purchased prepaid for $26.95 ($3. 95 S&H) by ordering from Health Choice Productions, 2554 Lincoln Blvd., Ste. 484, Marina Del Ray, CA 90291. Tel. (310) 840-5163. Please call for quantity discounts. ***Publisher Provided Annotation.***

Total Woman. Marabel Morgan. LC 73-11474. 192p. 1981. mass mkt. 4.99 (0-8007-8218-6, Spire) Revell.

Total Woman. Marabel Morgan. 1990. pap. 6.50 (0-671-73211-0) S&S Trade.

Total Woman Fitness Guide. Gail Shierman. 1979. pap. 4.95 (0-02-499820-6, Macmillan Coll) P-H.

Total Workout Book: For Men Only. A. Dugan. Ed. by Consumer Guide Staff. (Illus.). 1991. spiral bd. 4.99 (0-517-42466-5) Random Hse Value.

Total Zone. Martina Navratilova & Nickles. 1995. mass mkt. 6.99 (0-345-38867-4) Ballantine.

***Total Zone.** Martina Navratilova. Date not set. 4.99 (0-517-17831-1) Random Hse Value.

Total 1 2 3. Randall Bennett. 34.75 (0-13-925280-0) P-H.

Totalee Awesome. Lee Haney. LC 87-80978. (Illus.). 149p. 1987. pap. 14.95 (0-934601-34-8) Peachtree Pubs.

Totalitarian & Post-Totalitarian Law: A Sociolegal Analysis. Adam Podgorecki & Vittorio Olgiati. LC 95-46957. (Onati Series in Law & Society). (Illus.). 384p. 1996. 67.95 (1-85521-779-1, Pub. by Dartmth Pub UK); pap. 27.95 (1-85521-783-X, Pub. by Dartmth Pub UK) Ashgate Pub Co.

Totalitarian Claim of the Gospels. Dora Wilson. (C). 1935. pap. 3.00 (0-87574-004-9) Pendle Hill.

Totalitarian Enemy. Franz Borkenau. LC 78-63654. (Studies in Fascism: Ideology & Practice). reprint ed. 42.50 (0-404-16914-7) AMS Pr.

Totalitarian Language: Orwell's Newspeak & Its Nazi & Communist Antecedents. John W. Young. 1991. text ed. 45.00 (0-8139-1324-1) U Pr of Va.

Totalitarian Nightmare. Enrico Arrigoni. 280p. 1982. reprint ed. pap. 8.95 (0-88189-001-4) West World Pr.

Totalitarian Party: Party & People in Nazi Germany & Soviet Russia. Aryeh L. Unger. LC 73-92786. (International Studies). 296p. reprint ed. pap. 84.40 (0-685-16125-0, 2027252) Bks Demand.

Totalitarian Science & Technology. Paul R. Josepheson. (Control of Nature Ser.). 120p. (C). 1996. pap. 12.50 (0-391-03980-6) Humanities.

Totalitarian Science & Technology. Paul R. Josephson. (The Control of Nature). 120p. (C). 1996. text ed. 39.95 (0-391-03979-2) Humanities.

Totalitarianism. Ed. by Michael Curtis. LC 78-66238. (Issues in Contemporary Civilization Ser.). 128p. 1979. 29.95 (0-87855-288-X) Transaction Pubs.

Totalitarianism. Hannah Arendt. LC 66-22273. Orig. Title: Origins of Totalitarianism Pt. 3. 196p. 1968. reprint ed. pap. 9.95 (0-15-690650-3, Harvest Bks) HarBrace.

Totalitarianism: The Inner History of the Cold War. Abbott Gleason. 307p. 1995. 25.00 (0-615-00833-X) OUP.

***Totalitarianism: The Inner History of the Cold War.** Abbott Gleason. 320p. (C). 1997. reprint ed. pap. 19.95 (0-19-505018-5) OUP.

Totalitarianism at the Crossroads. Ed. by Ellen F. Paul. 196p. (C). 1990. 34.95 (0-88738-351-3); pap. 21.95 (0-88738-850-7) Transaction Pubs.

Totalite et Infini. Emmanuel Levinas. (Phaenomenologica Ser.: No. 8). 302p. 1981. lib. bdg. 112.00 (90-247-5105-5, Pub. by M Nijhoff NE) Kluwer Ac.

Totalite et Infini: Essai sur l'Exteriorite. 4th ed. Emmanuel Levinas. (Phaenomenologica Ser.: Vol. 8). 302p. (FRE.). 1984. pap. text ed. 49.50 (90-247-2971-8, Pub. by M Nijhoff NE) Kluwer Ac.

Totality. Edward Sapir. (LM Ser.: No. 6). 1930. pap. 25.00 (0-527-00810-9) Periodicals Srv.

Totality & Infinity. Emmanuel Levinas. Tr. by Alphonso Lingis. LC 69-14431. (Duquesne Studies: Philosophical). 307p. 1969. pap. text ed. 21.50 (0-8207-0245-5) Duquesne.

Totality & Infinity. Emmanuel Levinas. Tr. by Alphonso Lingis. (Martinus Nijhoff Philosophy: Vol. 1). 307p. 1980. lib. bdg. 78.00 (90-247-2288-8, Pub. by M Nijhoff NE) Kluwer Ac.

Totality in Essence. Vimala Thakar. 132p. 1986. reprint ed. 5.00 (81-208-0048-6, Pub. by Motilal Banarsidass II) S Asia.

Totalizing Act: Key to Husserl's Early Philosophy. Jonathan K. Cooper-Wiele. 160p. (C). 1989. lib. bdg. 92.00 (0-7923-0077-7, Pub. by Klwr Acad Pubs NE) Kluwer Ac.

Totalled Roadkill Cookbook. Buck Peterson. 96p. 1996. pap. 5.95 (0-89087-812-9) Celestial Arts.

Totally - FUNdamental Soccer. Karl Dewazien. Ed. by Terri Monson & Alan Maher. (Illus.). 64p. (Orig.). (J). (gr. k-6). 1996. 6.95 (0-9619139-4-0) Fun Soccer Ent.

***Totally Alien Life Form.** Sydney Lewis. Date not set. pap. 15.95 (1-56584-283-9) New Press NY.

Totally Alien Life Form" - Teenagers. Sydney Lewis. LC 96-5574. 320p. 1996. 25.00 (1-56584-282-0) New Press NY.

***Totally Amazing Games & Puzzles.** Rolf Heimann. 1997. pap. 3.95 (0-8167-4272-3) Troll Communs.

Totally Awesome Business Book for Kids (& Their Parents) With Twenty Super Businesses You Can Start Right Now. Adriane G. Berg & Arthur B. Bochner. (Illus.). 160p. (YA). 1995. pap. 10.95 (1-55704-226-8) Newmarket.

Totally Awesome Business Book for Kids (& Their Parents) With Twenty Super Businesses You Can Start Right Now. Adriane G. Berg & Arthur B. Bochner. (Illus.). 160p. (YA). 1996. 18.95 (1-55704-229-2) Newmarket.

***Totally Awesome Health.** Linda B. Meeks. (YA). (gr. 9-12). Date not set. text ed. write for info. (1-886693-15-3) Meeks Heit.

***Totally Awesome Health.** Linda B. Meeks. (Illus.). 424p. (J). (gr. 6). 1996. text ed. 27.00 (1-886693-18-8) Meeks Heit.

***Totally Awesome Health.** Linda B. Meeks. LC 96-97034. (Illus.). 679p. (J). (gr. 7-8). 1996. text ed. 35.00 (1-886693-12-9) Meeks Heit.

Totally Awesome Health: Grade K. Linda B. Meeks et al. (Illus.). 650p. 1996. teacher ed., ring bd. 125.00 (1-886693-00-5) Meeks Heit.

Totally Awesome Health: Grade 1. Linda B. Meeks et al. (Illus.). 650p. 1996. teacher ed., ring bd. 125.00 (1-886693-01-3) Meeks Heit.

Totally Awesome Health: Grade 2. Linda B. Meeks et al. (Illus.). 650p. 1996. teacher ed., ring bd. 125.00 (1-886693-02-1) Meeks Heit.

Totally Awesome Health: Grade 3. Linda B. Meeks et al. (Illus.). 650p. 1996. teacher ed., ring bd. 125.00 (1-886693-03-X) Meeks Heit.

Totally Awesome Health: Grade 4. Linda B. Meeks et al. (Illus.). 650p. 1996. teacher ed., ring bd. 125.00 (1-886693-04-8) Meeks Heit.

Totally Awesome Health: Grade 5. Linda B. Meeks et al. (Illus.). 650p. 1996. teacher ed., lib. bdg. 125.00 (1-886693-05-6) Meeks Heit.

Totally Awesome Health: Grade 6. Linda B. Meeks et al. (Illus.). 650p. 1996. teacher ed., ring bd. 125.00 (1-886693-06-4) Meeks Heit.

***Totally Awesome Health: Grade 6.** Linda B. Meeks et al. (Illus.). 650p. 1997. teacher ed., ring bd. 195.00 (1-886693-19-6) Meeks Heit.

Totally Awesome Health: Grade 7/8. Linda B. Meeks et al. (Illus.). 650p. 1997. teacher ed., ring bd. 195.00 (1-886693-07-2) Meeks Heit.

Totally Awesome Money Book for Kids (& Their Parents) Adriane G. Berg & Arthur B. Bochner. (Illus.). 160p. (J). (gr. 4-12). 1993. pap. 10.95 (1-55704-176-8) Newmarket.

Totally Awesome Money Book for Kids (& Their Parents) Adriane G. Berg & Arthur B. Bochner. (Illus.). 176p. (J). (gr. 4-12). 1993. 18.95 (1-55704-183-0) Newmarket.

Totally Awesome 80's: A Lexicon of the Music, Videos, Movies, TV Shows, Stars & Trends of That Awesome Decade. Matthew Rettenmund. 224p. 1996. pap. 15.95 (0-312-14436-9) St Martin.

***Totally Bagels.** Helene Siegel. LC 97-1075. (Totally Cookbooks Ser.). 96p. (Orig.). 1997. pap. 4.95 (0-89087-832-3) Celestial Arts.

Totally Burgers. Helene Siegel & Karen Gillingham. LC 96-11355. (Totally Cookbooks Ser.). 1996. pap. 4.95 (0-89087-806-4) Celestial Arts.

Totally Camping. Helene Siegel. (Totally Cookbooks Ser.). 96p. (Orig.). Date not set. pap. 4.95 (0-89087-807-2) Celestial Arts.

Totally Chile Peppers. Helene Siegel & Karen Gillingham. LC 94-1224. (Totally Cookbooks Ser.). 96p. 1995. pap. 4.95 (0-89087-724-6) Celestial Arts.

Totally Chocolate. Helene Siegel. (Totally Cookbooks Ser.). 1996. pap. 4.95 (0-89087-805-6) Celestial Arts.

Totally Coffee. Helene Siegel & Karen Gillingham. LC 95-10967. (Totally Cookbooks Ser.). 96p. 1995. pap. 4.95 (0-89087-754-8) Celestial Arts.

Totally Cookies. Helene Siegel & Karen Gillingham. LC 95-14013. (Totally Cookbooks Ser.). 96p. 1995. pap. 4.95 (0-89087-757-2) Celestial Arts.

***Totally Cool Clean Jokes for Kids.** Bob Phillips. 200p. (Orig.). (YA). (gr. 5-12). 1997. mass mkt. 3.99 (1-56507-571-4) Harvest Hse.

***Totally Cool Grandparents.** Linsley. LC 97-18978. 1997. pap. 11.95 (0-312-17047-5) St Martin.

Totally Corn. Helene Sigel & Karen Gillingham. LC 94-2127. (Totally Cookbooks Ser.). 96p. 1995. pap. 4.95 (0-89087-726-2) Celestial Arts.

***Totally Crab.** Helene Siegel. LC 96-39304. (Totally Cookbooks Ser.). 1997. pap. 4.95 (0-89087-821-8) Celestial Arts.

Totally Disgusting! Bill Wallace. LC 90-47561. (Illus.). 112p. (J). (gr. 3-7). 1991. 15.95 (0-8234-0873-6) Holiday.

Totally Disgusting. Bill Wallace. Ed. by Patricia MacDonald. 128p. (J). (gr. 3-6). reprint ed. pap. 3.50 (0-671-75416-5, Minstrel Bks) PB.

Totally Eggplant Cookbook. Helene Siegel & Karen Gillingham. LC 95-39671. 96p. 1996. 4.95 (0-89087-787-4) Celestial Arts.

***Totally Eggs.** Helene Siegel. LC 97-20154. (Totally Cookbooks Ser.). 96p. 1997. pap. 4.95 (0-89087-833-1) Celestial Arts.

Totally Fit Living: A 30-Day Program for Total Health & Happiness. Robert Kronemeyer. 300p. 1996. pap. 12.95 (1-55874-396-0) Health Comm.

Totally Free Lunch: Meals from the Fields. Peter A. Gail. (Illus.). 300p. 1996. pap. 15.95 (1-879863-52-9) Goosefoot Acres.

Totally Free Man: An Unauthorized Autobiography of Fidel Castro. John Krich. 192p. 1981. 15.00 (0-916870-38-3) Creat Arts Bk.

Totally Garlic. Helene Siegel & Karen Gillingham. LC 94-1217. (Totally Cookbooks Ser.). 96p. 1995. pap. 4.95 (0-89087-725-4) Celestial Arts.

Totally Gross Jokes. Julius Alvin. 1991. mass mkt. 3.50 (0-8217-3622-1, Zebra Kensgtn) Kensgtn Pub Corp.

Totally Haunted Kids: True Ghost Stories. Bruce Nash & Allan Zullo. LC 94-18862. 128p. (J). (gr. 3-5). 1996. pap. 3.95 (0-8167-3538-7) Troll Communs.

Totally JTT: Johnathan Taylor Thomas. Michael-Anne Johns. (YA). (gr. 7 up). 1996. pap. 3.99 (0-671-56272-X, Pocket Books) PB.

***Totally Lobster.** Helene Siegel. LC 96-39304. (Totally Cookbooks Ser.). 96p. (Orig.). 1997. pap. 4.95 (0-89087-822-6) Celestial Arts.

***Totally Loony Jokes & Riddles.** Michael Pellowski. (J). Date not set. write for info. (0-8069-9897-0) Sterling.

Totally Mary: The Complete Mary Tyler Moore Show Companion. Ron Newcomer & Nick Toth. (Illus.). 256p. 1995. pap. 14.95 (0-8065-1707-7, Citadel Pr) Carol Pub Group.

Totally Muffins. Helene Siegel & Karen Gillingham. LC 95-13579. (Totally Cookbooks Ser.). 96p. 1995. pap. 4.95 (0-89087-756-4) Celestial Arts.

Totally Mushrooms. Helene Siegel & Karen Gillingham. LC 94-2128. (Totally Cookbooks Ser.). 96p. 1995. pap. 4.95 (0-89087-727-0) Celestial Arts.

Totally Naked Investing: The Guide That Strips Away All the Confusion! Gordon Williamson. 1997. pap. text ed. 15.95 (1-55850-651-9) Adams Media.

***Totally Nuts.** Helene Siegel. LC 97-24699. (Totally Cookbooks Ser.). 96p. 1997. pap. 4.95 (0-89087-835-8) Celestial Arts.

Totally Orchids. Rod Cardilla. (Totally Flowers Ser.). 96p. 1996. pap. text ed. 5.95 (0-89087-782-3) Celestial Arts.

Totally Organized the Bonnie McCullough Way. Bonnie R. McCullough. (Illus.). 400p. 1986. pap. 12.95 (0-312-80747-3) St Martin.

Totally Outrageous Bumper-Snickers. Edgar Allen Poe et al. Ed. by Cliff Carle. (Illus.). 96p. (Orig.). (YA). 1988. pap. 2.95 (0-918259-13-4) CCC Pubns.

Totally Pancakes & Waffles. Helene Siegel. LC 96-33746. (Totally Cookbooks Ser.). 1996. pap. 4.95 (0-89087-804-8) Celestial Arts.

Totally Picnic. Helene Siegel. (Totally Cookbooks Ser.). (Illus.). 96p. 1996. pap. text ed. 4.95 (0-89087-785-8) Celestial Arts.

Totally Pizza. Helene Siegel. (Totally Cookbooks Ser.). 96p. 1996. pap. text ed. 4.95 (0-89087-786-6) Celestial Arts.

Totally Private & Personal: Journaling Ideas for Girls & Young Women. Jessica Wilber. Ed. by Elizabeth Verdick. LC 96-5834. 168p. (Orig.). (J). (gr. 5-11). 1996. pap. 8.95 (1-57542-005-8) Free Spirit Pub.

Totally Roses. Scott Meyer. (Totally Flowers Ser.). 96p. 1996. pap. text ed. 5.95 (0-89087-781-5) Celestial Arts.

***Totally Salmon.** Helene Siegel. LC 96-36393. (Totally Cookbooks Ser.). 1997. pap. 4.95 (0-89087-824-2) Celestial Arts.

***Totally Shrimp.** Helene Siegel. LC 96-45672. (Totally Cookbooks Ser.). 96p. (Orig.). 1997. pap. 4.95 (0-89087-823-4) Celestial Arts.

***Totally Steak.** Helene Siegel. LC 97-12653. (Totally Cookbooks Ser.). 96p. 1997. pap. 4.95 (0-89087-836-6) Celestial Arts.

***Totally Sufficient: Why the Bible Is All You Need.** Ed Hindson. LC 96-51722. 300p. (Orig.). 1997. pap. 11.99 (1-56507-630-3) Harvest Hse.

Totally Sunflowers. Joanna Poncavage. (Totally Flowers Ser.). 96p. 1996. pap. text ed. 5.95 (0-89087-783-1) Celestial Arts.

Totally Tasteless Tabloid Trivia Test. Christian Darby & Stacy Fields. 192p. (Orig.). 1993. pap. 6.95 (0-944007-66-X, S P I Bks) Sure Seller.

Totally Tasteless Tragic Jokes: Is Nothing Sacred. Hugh B. Shocked. (Orig.). 1993. pap. 7.99 (1-56171-042-3, S P I Bks) Sure Seller.

Totally Teabreads: Quick & Easy Recipes for More than 60 Delicious Quick Breads & Spreads. Barbara Albright & Leslie Weiner. LC 93-43659. (Illus.). 144p. (Orig.). 1994. pap. 6.95 (0-312-10561-4) St Martin.

Totally Teatime Cookbook. Helene Siegel. LC 95-21840. (Totally Cookbooks Ser.). 96p. 1995. pap. 4.95 (0-89087-755-6) Celestial Arts.

Totally Terrific Valentine Party Book. Judith B. Stamper. 64p. (J). 1990. pap. 1.95 (0-590-41713-4) Scholastic Inc.

Totally Tomatoes. Helene Siegel. (Totally Cookbooks Ser.). 96p. 1996. pap. 4.95 (0-89087-788-2) Celestial Arts.

Totally Trusting. Chas Lee. LC 92-61475. (Illus.). 222p. (YA). (gr. 6-12). 1992. 19.95 (1-878044-09-5) Mayhaven Pub.

Totally Tulips. Matt Damsker. (Totally Flowers Ser.). 96p. 1996. pap. text ed. 5.95 (0-89087-780-7) Celestial Arts.

Totally Unauthorized Donkey Kong Country 2. Joseph A. Cain. (Illus.). (Orig.). Date not set. pap. 9.99 (0-614-10338-X) Brady Pub.

Totally Unauthorized Donkey Kong Country 2 Secret Rooms Guide. BradyGAMES Staff. (Illus.). (Orig.). 1996. 7.99 (1-56686-437-2) Brady Pub.

Totally Unauthorized Guide to Doom 11. Robert Waring & Brady Games Staff. (Illus.). 256p. (Orig.). 1995. pap. 26.99 incl. cd-rom (1-56686-228-0) Brady Pub.

Totally Unauthorized Guide to Duke Nukem 3D. Bradygames Staff. 200p. 1996. 19.99 (1-56686-509-3) Brady Pub.

Totally Unauthorized Guide to Killer Instinct. Tristan Matthews & BradyGAMES Staff. (Illus.). 160p. (Orig.). 1995. 9.99 (1-56686-320-1) Brady Pub.

***Totally Unauthorized Guide to Killer Instinct 64.** David Cassidy. 112p. 1996. 9.99 (1-56686-605-7) Mac Comp Pub.

Totally Unauthorized Guide to Magic the Gathering Card Game. Joseph G. Bell & BradyGAMES Staff. (Illus.). 350p. (Orig.). 1996. 12.99 (1-56686-292-2) Brady Pub.

Totally Unauthorized Guide to Primal Rage. Jim Fink. (Illus.). 128p. (Orig.). 1995. 9.99 (1-56686-345-7) Brady Pub.

Totally Unauthorized Guide to Stonekeep. Bradygames Staff. 1996. 9.99 (1-56686-529-8) Brady Pub.

Totally Unauthorized Guide to Super Mario 64: Totally Unauthorized. Christine Watson. 112p. 1996. 9.99 (1-56686-561-1) Mac Comp Pub.

***Totally Unauthorized Magic: The Gathering Tournament Guide.** BradyGames Staff. 1996. pap. text ed. 19.99 (1-56686-642-1) Brady Pub.

Totally Unauthorized Myst. Ellen Cameron. (Illus.). 126p. (Orig.). 1995. pap. 7.99 (1-56686-313-9) Brady Pub.

***Totally Unauthorized Nintendo 64 Games Guide, Vol. 2.** C. Cain & J. Rich. (Nintendo 64 Games Guide Ser.). 112p. 1997. 11.99 (1-56686-693-6) Brady Pub.

***Totally Unauthorized Playstation Games Book, Vol. 3.** BradyGames Staff. 128p. 1996. pap. text ed. 9.99 (1-56686-623-5) Brady Pub.

Totally Unauthorized PlayStation Games Guide, Vol. 2. Bradygames Staff. 144p. 1996. 9.99 (1-56686-573-5) Mac Comp Pub.

Totally Unauthorized Resident Evil Pocket Guide. Christine Watson. 160p. 1996. 7.99 (1-56686-624-3) Mac Comp Pub.

Totally Unauthorized Sega Games Guide II. Anthony Lynch. (Illus.). 176p. (Orig.). 1995. pap. 9.99 (1-56686-342-2) Brady Pub.

***Totally Unauthorized Sports Game Playbook.** BradyGames Staff. 112p. 1996. 9.99 (1-56686-619-7) Mac Comp Pub.

Totally Unauthorized 11th Hour Pocket Guide. Gradygames Staff. 302p. 1996. pap. 11.99 (1-56686-300-7) Brady Pub.

An Asterisk (*) at the beginning of an entry indicates that the title is appearing in BIP for the first time.

Totally Useless Office Skills. Rick Davis. (Illus.). 128p. (Orig.). 1996. pap. 12.95 (*0-9636413-2-8*) Hobblebush Bks.

Totally Useless Skills. Rick Davis. 64p. (J). (gr. 3 up). 1994. pap. 2.99 (*0-87406-707-3*) Willowisp Pr.

***Totally Wired Web Toolkit.** Nathan J. Muller. LC 96-38027. (Illus.). 400p. 1997. pap. text ed. 24.95 (*0-07-044434-X*) McGraw.

Totally Yours. Dana Ransom. 320p. 1993. mass mkt. 3.99 (*0-8217-4053-9*, Zebra Kensgtn) Kensgtn Pub Corp.

Totch: A Life in the Everglades. Loren Totch G. Brown. LC 93-4529. (Illus.). 320p. 1993. 29.95 (*0-8130-1227-9*); pap. 17.95 (*0-8130-1228-7*) U Press Fla.

Totel's Miscellany, 1557-1587, 2 vols., Set. Richard Tottel. (BCL1-PR English Literature Ser.). 1992. reprint ed. lib. bdg. 150.00 (*0-7812-7137-1*) Rprt Serv.

Totem. Blyden Jackson. LC 74-82729. 1974. 25.00 (*0-89388-172-4*) Okpaku Communications.

Totem. David Morrell. 384p. 1995. mass mkt. 6.50 (*0-446-36446-0*) Warner Bks.

***Totem.** Mike Savage. (Illus.). 508p. 1996. 25.95 (*1-886028-18-4*) Savage Pr.

Totem & Taboo. Sigmund Freud. 1976. 27.95 (*0-8488-1331-6*) Amereon Ltd.

Totem & Taboo. Sigmund Freud. Tr. by Abraham A. Brill. 1960. pap. 8.00 (*0-394-70124-0*, Vin) Random.

Totem & Taboo. Sigmund Freud. 1989. reprint ed. lib. bdg. 26.95 (*0-89966-634-5*) Buccaneer Bks.

Totem Atlas of Island, Skagit, Whatcom & San Juan Counties. 5th ed. 1994. 24.95 (*1-881015-10-6*) Totem Pubns.

Totem Atlas of Jefferson & Clallam Counties. 1994. 12.95 (*1-881015-04-1*) Totem Pubns.

Totem Atlas of Jefferson Clallam & Mason Counties. 1994. 17.95 (*1-881015-05-X*) Totem Pubns.

Totem Atlas of Thurston & Mason County. 3rd ed. (Illus.). 1994. 22.95 (*1-881015-06-8*) Totem Pubns.

Totem Atlas of Thurston County. 3rd ed. 1994. 17.95 (*1-881015-07-6*) Totem Pubns.

Totem (Complete & Unaltered) David Morrell. (Illus.). 1994. boxed 100.00 (*1-880418-25-8*) D M Grant.

Totem (Complete & Unaltered) deluxe ed. David Morrell. (Illus.). 1994. 24.95 (*1-880418-26-6*) D M Grant.

Totem et Tabou: Interpretation par la Psychanalyse de la Vie Sociale. Sigmund Freud. (FRE.). 1989. pap. 19.95 (*0-7859-3038-8*) Fr & Eur.

Totem of the Depraved. abr. ed. Nick Zedd. (Illus.). 178p. (Orig.). 1997. pap. 12.00 (*1-880985-35-7*) Two Thirteen Sixty-one.

Totem Pole. Diane Hoyt-Goldsmith. LC 89-26720. (Illus.). 32p. (J). (gr. 3-7). 1990. lib. bdg. 16.95 (*0-8234-0809-4*) Holiday.

Totem Pole. Diane Hoyt-Goldsmith. LC 89-26720. (Illus.). 32p. (J). (gr. 3-7). 1994. pap. 6.95 (*0-8234-1135-4*) Holiday.

Totem Pole Indians of the Northwest. Don E. Beyer. (Illus.). 64p. (J). (gr. 3 up). 1991. pap. 6.95 (*0-531-15607-9*) Watts.

Totem Poles. Bellerophon Staff. (J). (gr. 1-9). 1992. pap. 5.95 (*0-88388-081-4*) Bellerophon Bks.

Totem Poles. Halpin. (C). 19.95 (*0-7748-0138-7*, Pub. by U BC Pr) U of Wash Pr.

Totem Poles: An Ancient Art. Carol Batdorf. (Illus.). 24p. (Orig.). (J). (gr. 1-6). 1990. pap. 6.95 (*0-88839-248-6*) Hancock House.

Totem Poles: An Illustrated Guide. Marjorie M. Halpin. (Illus.). 64p. 1981. pap. 14.95 (*0-7748-0141-7*, Pub. by U BC Pr) U of Wash Pr.

Totem Poles Vol. 1: According to Crests & Topics, Vol. I. Marius Barbeau. (Illus.). 460p. 1990. pap. 29.95 (*0-660-12902-7*, Pub. by Can Mus Civil CN) U of Wash Pr.

Totem Poles Vol. 2: According to Crests & Topics, Vol. II. Marius Barbeau. (Illus.). 470p. 1990. pap. 29.95 (*0-660-12903-5*, Pub. by Can Mus Civil CN) U of Wash Pr.

Totem Poles Vol. 3: Kwakiutl. Bellerophon Books Staff. (J). (gr. 4-7). 1995. pap. 5.95 (*0-88388-199-3*) Bellerophon Bks.

Totem Poles of the Northwest. D. Allen. (Illus.). 32p. pap. 4.95 (*0-919654-83-5*) Hancock House.

Totem Poles of the Pacific Northwest Coast. Edward Malin. (Illus.). 195p. 1994. pap. 19.95 (*0-88192-295-1*) Timber.

Totem Voices: Plays from the Black World Repertory. Ed. by Paul C. Harrison. LC 88-21420. 523p. 1989. pap. 15.95 (*0-8021-3126-3*, Grove) Grove-Atltic.

Totemic. deluxe ed. Deirdra Baldwin. (Burning Deck Poetry Chapbooks Ser.). 32p. 1983. pap. 15.00 (*0-930901-13-4*) Burning Deck.

Totemism. Alexander Goldenweiser. 1972. 59.95 (*0-8490-1223-6*) Gordon Pr.

Totemism. Claude Levi-Strauss. Tr. by Rodney Needham. (Orig.). 1963. pap. 13.00 (*0-8070-4671-X*) Beacon Pr.

Totemism, the TAO-TiEH & the Chinese Ritual Bronzes. enl. ed. Helen F. Snow. 100p. 1986. 35.00 (*0-686-64038-1*) H F Snow.

Totems. Stanley Diamond. 96p. 1981. pap. 13.00 (*0-940170-02-7*) Open Bk Pubns.

Totems. Stanley Diamond. 96p. 1983. pap. 6.50 (*0-317-17093-7*) Station Hill Pr.

***Totems: The Transformative Power of Your Personal Animal Totem.** Brad Steiger. 1997. pap. text ed. 16.00 (*0-06-251425-3*) Harper SF.

Totems of Seldovia. Michael Prince. 160p. (J). (gr. 5-6). 1994. pap. 8.95 (*0-9642662-1-0*) Sundog Pubng.

Totems of the Kisii. Okeragori. 1995. 14.95 (*9966-884-74-2*) Nocturnal Sun.

Totenkult der Skythen. Renate Rolle. (Vorgeschichtliche Forschungen Ser.). (Illus.). (C). 1979. 307.70 (*3-11-006620-3*) De Gruyter.

Toting the Lead Row: Ruby Pickens Tartt, Alabama Folklorist. fac. ed. Virginia P. Brown & Laurella Owens. LC 81-4902. (Illus.). 192p. 1981. pap. 54.80 (*0-7837-8106-7*, 2059175) Bks Demand.

***Toto - Fahrenheit.** Ed. by Carol Cuellar. 52p. (Orig.). (C). 1987. pap. text ed. 12.95 (*0-7692-0855-X*, VF1350) Warner Brothers.

Toto - Past to Present. Ed. by Carol Cuellar. 72p. (Orig.). 1994. pap. 16.95 (*0-89724-439-7*, VF1692) Warner Brothers.

***Toto - The Seventh One.** Ed. by Carol Cuellar. 68p. (Orig.). (C). 1988. pap. text ed. 12.95 (*0-7692-0862-2*, VF1463) Warner Brothers.

Toto in France. Biddy Strevens. (Toto in ... Ser.). 24p. (FRE.). (J). (gr. 4-7). 1994. 12.95 (*0-8442-9180-3*, Natl Textbk) NTC Pub Grp.

Toto in Italy. Biddy Strevens. (Toto in ... Ser.). 24p. (ITA.). (J). (gr. 4-7). 1994. 12.95 (*0-8442-9289-3*, Natl Textbk) NTC Pub Grp.

Toto in Spain. Biddy Stevens. (Toto in ... Ser.). (Illus.). 32p. (ENG & SPA.). (J). 1995. 12.95 (*0-8442-9170-6*, Natl Textbk) NTC Pub Grp.

Toto in Trouble. Jill Barnes & Ken Asuka. Ed. by Caroline Rubin. Tr. by Japan Foreign Rights Centre Staff from JPN. LC 90-37749. (Dragonfly Tales Ser.). (Illus.). 32p. (J). (gr. k-4). 1990. lib. bdg. 14.60 (*0-944483-86-0*) Garrett Ed Corp.

***Toto la Brute.** Dominique Demers. (Novels in the Premier Roman Ser.). 64p. (FRE.). (J). (gr. 2-5). 1996. pap. 7.95 (*2-89021-172-X*, Pub. by Les Editions CN) Firefly Bks Ltd.

Toto the Timid Turtle. Howard Goldsmith. LC 80-15096. (Illus.). 32p. (J). (ps-3). 1980. 16.95 (*0-87705-525-4*) Human Sci Pr.

Toto Visits Mystic Mountain. Ken Asuka. Ed. by Richard Y. Young. Tr. by Kaisei-sha. LC 89-11754. (Illus.). 32p. (J). (gr. 1-3). 1989. lib. bdg. 14.60 (*0-944483-46-1*) Garrett Ed Corp.

Tots Goes to Gbarnga. Mattiedna Johnson. Ed. by Bobby L. Kelley. 360p. 1992. 14.95 (*0-9631743-2-0*) Mattiedna J.

Tots in Tinseltown. 1984. pap. 5.95 (*0-88145-021-9*) Broadway Play.

Tot's 'n Tension. Rita T. Liberman & Hal Liberman. 100p. (Orig.). 1985. pap. 5.95 (*0-9614923-0-9*) Tranquil Pr.

Totschweigetaktiken. Oyvind Berg. Tr. by Anthony Barnett from GER. 64p. (Orig.). 1991. pap. 9.00 (*0-907954-14-6*, Pub. by Allardyce Barnett UK) SPD-Small Pr Dist.

Tottel's Miscellany, 1557-1587, 2 vols., Set. rev. ed. Richard Tottel. Ed. by Hyder E. Rollins. LC 64-22722. 772p. 1965. boxed 50.00 (*0-674-89610-6*) HUP.

Tottering in My Garden: A Gardener's Memoir. Midge E. Keeble. (Illus.). 224p. 1994. pap. 9.95 (*0-921820-90-9*, Pub. by Camden Hse CN) Firefly Bks Ltd.

Tottering Transcendance: Civil vs. Cultic Aspects of the Sacred. Nicholas J. Demerath, III. LC 73-10476. (Studies in Sociology). 39p. (C). 1973. pap. text ed. write for info. (*0-672-61175-9*, Bobbs) Macmillan.

Totto-Chan: The Little Girl at the Window. Tetsuko Kuroyanagi. Tr. by Dorothy Britton from JPN. (International Ser.). (Illus.). 232p. 1996. pap. 10.00 (*4-7700-2067-8*) Kodansha.

Totty - Young Eleanor Roosevelt (Playscript) Sharon Whitney. (Orig.). (YA). 1992. pap. 6.00 (*0-87602-306-5*) Anchorage.

Totus Tuus: John Paul II's Program of Marian Consecration & Entrustment. Arthur B. Calkins. LC 92-74257. (Studies & Texts: No. 1). 344p. (Orig.). 1992. pap. 15.00 (*0-9635345-0-5*) Acad Immaculate.

Toubleshooting with Your Triggered-Sweep Oscilloscope. Robert L. Goodman. 1992. pap. text ed. 21.95 (*0-07-157656-8*) McGraw.

Touch. Michael Brownstein. 122p. Date not set. 7.00 (*0-936756-80-2*) Autonomedia.

Touch. Field. Date not set. 22.95 (*0-02-910135-2*, Free Press) Free Pr.

***Touch.** Tiffany M. Field. 288p. Date not set. pap. 13.00 (*0-06-095221-0*, PL) HarpC.

***Touch.** Sue Hurwitz. LC 96-29960. (Library of the Five Senses (Plus the Sixth Sense)). (J). 1997. write for info. (*0-8239-5054-9*) Rosen Group.

Touch. Elmore Leonard. 240p. 1988. mass mkt. 6.50 (*0-380-70386-6*) Avon.

Touch. Andreu Llamas. LC 95-14781. (Five Senses of the Animal World Ser.). (Illus.). (J). 1996. lib. bdg. 15.95 (*0-7910-3494-1*) Chelsea Hse.

Touch. Julie Myerson. LC 95-43266. 320p. 1996. 21.95 (*0-385-47507-1*, N A Talese) Doubleday.

Touch. Photos by Stephen Oliver. LC 89-63095. (My First Look At Ser.). (Illus.). (J). (ps). 1990. 6.95 (*0-679-80623-7*) Random Bks Yng Read.

Touch. J. M. Parramon & J. J. Puig. (Five Senses Ser.). (Illus.). 32p. (Orig.). (J). (ps). 1985. pap. 6.95 (*0-8120-3567-4*); Span. ed. pap. 6.95 (*0-8120-3609-3*) Barron.

***Touch.** Maria Rius et al. (Five Senses Ser.). (J). 1985. 6.95 (*0-8120-5740-6*) Barron.

Touch. Mandy Suhr. LC 93-44192. (Illus.). (J). (ps-1). 1993. lib. bdg. 14.21 (*0-87614-837-2*, Carolrhoda) Lerner Group.

Touch. Brenda Walpole. LC 96-6173. (See for Yourself Ser.). (Illus.). (J). 1996. lib. bdg. 21.40 (*0-8172-4216-3*) Raintree Steck-V.

Touch. F. Paul Wilson. 336p. 1986. mass mkt. 5.99 (*0-515-08733-5*) Jove Pubns.

Touch: A Novel. Charlotte W. Sherman. 224p. 1996. pap. text ed. 12.00 (*0-06-092753-4*) HarpC.

Touch: An Exploration. Gabriel Josipovici. (Illus.). 224p. 1996. 27.50 (*0-300-06690-2*) Yale U Pr.

Touch: The Foundation of Experience. Ed. by Kathryn E. Barnard & T. Berry Brazelton. (Clinical Infant Reports: No. 4). 610p. 1990. 67.50 (*0-8236-6605-0*, BN 06605) Intl Univs Pr.

Touch & Expression in Piano Playing. Clarence G. Hamilton. LC 74-27348. reprint ed. 30.00 (*0-404-12950-1*) AMS Pr.

Touch & Go. M. R. Meek. 1994. mass mkt. 3.99 (*0-373-26146-2*, 1-26146-0) Harlequin Bks.

***Touch & Go.** Eugene Stein. LC 96-52569. 192p. 1997. 22.00 (*0-688-15042-X*, R Weisbach Bks) Morrow.

Touch & Go: A Novel. Sam McAughtry et al. 233p. 9400. pap. 13.95 (*0-85640-503-5*, Pub. by Blackstaff Pr IE) Dufour.

Touch & Go - The Nature of Intimacy: Relating in the Coming Times. Judy G. Borich. (Illus.). 250p. (Orig.). Date not set. write for info. (*0-614-07555-6*) Interact NM.

Touch & Read. Tiziano Sclavi. LC 93-72918. (Illus.). 10p. (J). (ps). 1994. bds. 4.95 (*1-56397-343-X*) Boyds Mills Pr.

Touch for Health: A New Approach to Restoring Our Natural Energies. John F. Thie. LC 73-86019. (Illus.). 132p. 1996. reprint ed. spiral bd., pap. 24.95 (*0-87516-180-4*) DeVorss.

***Touch from the Master's Hand.** Patricia A. Williams. (Orig.). 1996. pap. 10.95 (*0-9653812-0-X*) KelVic Pub.

Touch Holiness: Resources for Worship. Ed. by Ruth C. Duck & Maren C. Tirabassi. LC 89-39435. 272p. (Orig.). 1990. pap. 14.95 (*0-8298-0809-4*) Pilgrim OH.

Touch in Early Development. Ed. by Tiffany M. Field. 136p. 1995. text ed. 34.50 (*0-8058-1890-1*) L Erlbaum Assocs.

Touch Me Book. Eve Witte & Pat Witte. (Golden Touch & Feel Bks.). (Illus.). (J). (ps). 1961. spiral bd. 6.50 (*0-307-12146-1*, Golden Books) Western Pub.

Touch Me in the Dark. Patricia Rosemoor. (Intrigue Ser.). 1996. mass mkt. 3.75 (*0-373-22390-0*, 1-22390-8) Harlequin Bks.

Touch Me Inside. Henry Lauchland. LC 74-24548. 46p. (C). 1975. reprint ed. 9.95 (*0-931820-00-6*) High Q.

Touch Me Not! Beverly Amstutz. (Illus.). 20p. (J). (ps-7). 1983. pap. 2.50 (*0-937836-09-5*) Precious Res.

***Touch Me Not.** Julie Kistler. 1997. mass mkt. 3.75 (*0-373-16690-7*, 1-16690-9) Harlequin Bks.

Touch Me Who Dares. Lionel Shelley. 163p. (C). 1985. pap. 30.00 (*0-86383-225-3*, Pub. by Gomer Pr UK) St Mut.

Touch Me with Fire. Nicole Jordan. 400p. (Orig.). 1993. mass mkt. 4.50 (*0-380-77279-5*) Avon.

Touch Me with Fire. large type ed. Jeanne Montague. (Dales Large Print Ser.). 422p. 1995. pap. 17.99 (*1-85389-508-3*, Dales) Ulverscroft.

Touch Monkeys: Nonsense Strategies for Reading Twentieth-Century Poetry. Marnie Parsons. LC 93-94817. (Theory - Culture Ser.). 262p. 1993. 50.00 (*0-8020-2983-3*) U of Toronto Pr.

Touch My People - June. Dottie Henneberry. 44p. 1980. pap. 0.50 (*1-882825-11-X*) Hse of Prayer.

Touch 'n' Type: Twenty-Five Words to Success. Frank P. Donnelly. 95p. 1981. 10.00 (*0-936862-11-4*, TNT) DDC Pub.

Touch of Acceptance. Richard E. Stephens. 176p. (Orig.). 1988. pap. 5.00 (*0-9611220-3-X*) Crnrstn Cmns.

Touch of Aphrodite. Joanna Mansell. (Presents Ser.). 1994. mass mkt. 2.99 (*0-373-11684-5*, 1-11684-7) Harlequin Bks.

Touch of Atlanta. Ed. by Marist Parents' Club Staff. (Illus.). 256p. 1990. 16.95 (*0-9626204-0-8*) Marist Parents.

***Touch of Camelot.** Donna Grove. 400p. mass mkt. 3.99 (*0-06-108528-6*) HarpC.

Touch of Camelot. Donna Grove. 400p. 1994. mass mkt. 4.50 (*0-06-108272-4*, Harp PBks) HarpC.

Touch of Chill. Joan Aiken. 192p. (J). (gr. k up). 1989. pap. 3.50 (*0-440-20459-3*, LLL BDD) BDD Bks Young Read.

Touch of Christmas. Honor Books Staff. Date not set. pap. text ed. 10.99 (*1-56292-122-3*) Honor Bks OK.

***Touch of Class.** Phoebe Conn. 416p. 1997. mass mkt. 5.50 (*0-8217-5662-1*, Zebra Kensgtn) Kensgtn Pub Corp.

Touch of Class. JoAnn Stearns. 8p. 1995. pap. 3.95 (*1-888837-10-1*) Silver Shuttle.

***Touch of Class.** Lydia Trusz. 288p. 1997. mass mkt. 4.99 (*0-8217-5648-6*, Zebra Kensgtn) Kensgtn Pub Corp.

Touch of Classic Soul: Soul Singers of the Early 1970s. Marc Taylor. LC 96-84835. (Illus.). 368p. (Orig.). 1996. pap. 20.00 (*0-9652328-4-0*) Aloiv Pub.

Touch of Diabetes. expanded rev. ed. Lois Jovanovic-Peterson. 1995. pap. 10.95 (*1-56561-079-2*) Chronimed.

Touch of Divinity. Thaddeus M. Swirski. LC 91-65986. 101p. 1991. pap. 6.95 (*1-55523-452-6*) Winston-Derek.

Touch of Earth. large type ed. Margaret James. 1996. 25.99 (*0-7505-0862-0*, Pub. by Magna Print Bks UK) Ulverscroft.

***Touch of Enchantment.** Teresa Medeiros. 1997. mass mkt. 5.99 (*0-553-57500-7*, Fanfare) Bantam.

Touch of Europe Cookbook. Erika G. Cenci. (Illus.). 96p. (Orig.). 1992. pap. 19.95 (*1-880222-09-4*) Red Apple Pub.

***Touch of Evil.** Whit Masterson. 3.95 (*0-7867-0886-7*) Carroll & Graf.

Touch of Evil. Whit Masterson. (Mystery Scene Bk.). 176p. 1992. pap. 3.95 (*0-88184-886-7*) Carroll & Graf.

Touch of Evil: Orson Welles, Director. Ed. by Terry Comito. (Films in Print Ser.). (Illus.). 289p. (C). 1985. 35.00 (*0-8135-1096-1*); pap. 17.00 (*0-8135-1097-X*) Rutgers U Pr.

Touch of Fire. Linda Howard. Ed. by Claire Zion. 336p. (Orig.). 1992. mass mkt. 5.99 (*0-671-72858-X*, Pocket Star Bks) PB.

Touch of Forgiveness. Emma Goldrick. (Romance Ser.: No. 164). 1991. pap. 2.79 (*0-373-03164-5*) Harlequin Bks.

Touch of Frost. R. D. Wingfield. 368p. 1995. mass mkt. 5.99 (*0-553-57169-9*) Bantam.

Touch of Georgia: Where to Go & What to Do in the Peach State. 288p. 1996. pap. 14.99 (*0-7852-7500-2*) Nelson.

Touch of Ginger. Virginia M. Spivey. 64p. (Orig.). 1989. pap. write for info. (*0-318-65323-0*) Blue Pencil Pr.

Touch of Glass: Contempory Views of Glass Art & Its Origin. Ed. by Paul Hanna & Gale Richardson. 159p. 1984. pap. 6.00 (*0-911618-08-2*) West Tex Mus.

Touch of Glory. Elizabeth Farmer. 148p. 1996. text ed. 14.00 (*0-8059-3818-4*) Dorrance.

Touch of God: A Practical Handbook on the Anointing. Rodney M. Howard-Browne. 169p. 1992. text ed. 14.95 (*0-9583066-9-9*) Revival Minst Intl.

***Touch of Grace.** Maurine McGowan. 26p. (Orig.). 1997. mass mkt. 8.00 (*0-9657234-2-9*, 97-002) W & M Pub.

Touch of Grace. large type ed. (Rosary Pictorials Collection). (Illus.). 104p. pap. 5.95 (*0-9620994-8-1*) Cath Treas.

***Touch of Healing: Energizing the Body, Mind, & Spirit with the Art of Jin Shin Jyutsu.** Alice Burmeister & Tom Monte. 1997. pap. 14.95 (*0-614-27435-4*) Bantam.

Touch of Heaven: Eternal Stories for Jewish Living. Ed. by Annette Labovitz & Eugene Labovitz. LC 90-166. 304p. 1990. 30.00 (*0-87668-886-5*) Aronson.

Touch of His Freedom. Charles Stanley. 144p. 1991. 13.99 (*0-310-54620-6*) Zondervan.

***Touch of His Freedom: Meditations on Freedom in Christ, with Original Photos.** large type ed. Charles F. Stanley. LC 96-46015. 160p. 1997. pap. 12.95 (*0-8027-2713-1*) Walker & Co.

***Touch of His Hand.** Linda Hascall. 190p. (Orig.). 1997. mass mkt. 10.95 (*1-57532-111-4*) Press-Tige Pub.

Touch of His Love. Charles Stanley. (In Touch Ser.: No. 4). 144p. 1994. 13.99 (*0-310-54560-9*); audio 14.99 (*0-310-54569-2*) Zondervan.

Touch of His Peace: Meditations on Experiencing the Peace of God. Charles Stanley. LC 92-43289. 144p. 1993. 13.99 (*0-310-54550-1*) Zondervan.

***Touch of His Wisdom: Meditations on the Book of Proverbs with Original Photographs by Charles Stanley.** large type ed. Charles F. Stanley. LC 97-21626. (Illus.). 208p. 1997. pap. 12.95 (*0-8027-2720-4*) Walker & Co.

Touch of Honey. large type ed. Marjorie Everitt. 216p. 1992. reprint ed. lib. bdg. 13.95 (*1-56054-536-4*) Thorndike Pr.

Touch of Honey. large type ed. Lucy Gillen. (Linford Romance Library). 295p. 1984. pap. 15.99 (*0-7089-6025-1*) Ulverscroft.

Touch of Innocence. Katherine Dunham. LC 79-7760. (Dance Ser.). 1980. reprint ed. lib. bdg. 35.95 (*0-8369-9289-X*) Ayer.

Touch of Innocence: Memoirs of Childhood. Katherine Dunham. LC 93-46125. 320p. (C). 1994. pap. 12.95 (*0-226-17112-4*) U Ch Pr.

Touch of Jesus. Paul Eshleman. LC 95-4462. 224p. 1995. pap. 14.99 (*1-56399-067-9*) NewLife Pubns.

Touch of Jesus. Paul Eshleman. LC 95-4462. 1995. pap. 9.99 (*1-56399-071-7*) NewLife Pubns.

***Touch of Jesus: Stories of Faith from the Life of Christ.** H. S. Vigeveno. LC 97-14645. 1997. write for info. (*1-57293-024-1*) Discovery Hse Pubs.

Touch of Joy: Devotional Thoughts for Women by Women. Ed. by Rose Otis. 1995. 5.99 (*0-8280-1038-2*) Review & Herald.

***Touch of Kindness.** Deborah Hansen. Ed. by Patrick Caton. 365p. 1997. spiral bd., pap. 6.50 (*1-56245-313-0*) Great Quotations.

Touch of Lace. Margaret Brownley. (Historical Romance Ser.). 384p. 1996. mass mkt., pap. 5.50 (*0-451-40658-3*, Topaz) NAL-Dutton.

Touch of Lace. Betty S. Scearce. (Orig.). 1996. pap. write for info. (*1-57553-278-6*) Watermrk Pr.

Touch of Larceny: The Insurance Agent's Survival Guide. Kent P. Larsen. LC 84-60877. 120p. (Orig.). 1984. pap. 7.95 (*0-913581-01-1*) Publitec.

Touch of Lightening. Carin Rafferty. 384p. 1996. mass mkt., pap. 5.50 (*0-451-40613-3*, Topaz) NAL-Dutton.

Touch of Love. Minnie L. Griffith. 288p. 1996. 19.00 (*0-8059-3838-9*) Dorrance.

Touch of Love. large type ed. Jenny Boston. 1995. 25.99 (*0-7089-3401-3*) Ulverscroft.

Touch of Love. large type ed. Vanessa Grant. 1991. reprint ed. lib. bdg. 18.95 (*0-263-12676-5*) Thorndike Pr.

Touch of Love (from the 'Sixties) E. Martin De Larkin, Jr. Ed. by S. P. Owens. (Illus.). 57p. (Orig.). 1979. pap. text ed. write for info. (*0-9603844-0-5*) Hse of Larkin.

Touch of Magic. Carin Rafferty. 384p. (Orig.). 1995. pap. 4.99 (*0-451-40515-3*, Topaz) NAL-Dutton.

***Touch of Magic.** large type ed. Geoffrey Morgan. (Dales Large Print Ser.). (Illus.). 234p. 1996. pap. 17.99 (*1-85389-636-5*) Ulverscroft.

Touch of Merry. Loyd Black. 1995. pap. text ed. 4.50 (*0-8217-5175-1*) NAL-Dutton.

***Touch of Mortality.** Ann Granger. 1997. pap. text ed. 21.95 (*0-7862-0961-5*) Thorndike Pr.

***Touch of Mortality: A Mitchell & Markby Village Whodunit.** Ann Granger. LC 96-44503. 1997. 21.95 (*0-312-15231-0*) St Martin.

Touch of Music. Dorothy Clarke. LC 90-24052. 192p. (Orig.). 1991. pap. 8.95 (*0-934678-31-6*) New Victoria Pubs.

Touch of Nostalgia: A Glimpse of America's Past. John K. Gates. LC 80-84010. (Illus.). 192p. (Orig.). 1980. pap. 14.95 (*0-9605168-0-8*) Photographit.

Touch of Oregon. Ralph Friedman. LC 74-132470. 1976. reprint ed. pap. 3.95 (*0-89174-005-8*) Comstock Edns.

Touch of Panic. 288p. 1995. mass mkt. 7.99 (*0-7704-2620-4*) Bantam.

Touch of Panic. Laurali R. Wright. 288p. 1995. pap. 5.95 (0-14-023300-8, Penguin Bks) Viking Penguin.
Touch of Panic: A Karl Alberg Mystery. Eric Wright. LC 93-42386. 288p. 1994. 20.00 (0-684-19672-7) S&S Trade.
Touch of Paradise. Alexa Smart. 1996. mass mkt. 4.99 (0-7860-0271-9, Pinncle Kensgtn) Kensgtn Pub Corp.
Touch of Rhetoric: Ezra Pound's Malatesta Cantos. Peter D'Epiro. LC 83-5729. (Studies in Modern Literature: No. 2). (Illus.). 182p. reprint ed. pap. 51.90 (0-8357-1404-7, 2070529) Bks Demand.
***Touch of Romance.** large type ed. Julia Ashwell. 336p. 1996. 25.99 (0-7089-3623-7) Ulverscroft.
Touch of Sabotage. Jack Goyder. 143p. (C). 1990. 48.00 (0-685-67402-9, Pub. by Boolarong Pubns AT) St Mut.
Touch of Santa Fe. Shirley Phipps. LC 90-60514. 52p. (Orig.). 1990. pap. 9.95 (0-916809-41-2) Scott Pubns MI.
Touch of Sepia. Anne-Marie Althaus. LC 93-26299. (Illus.). (J). 1994. 4.25 (0-383-03781-6) SRA McGraw.
Touch of Smile. Helen L. Ross. (Illus.). 1978. pap. 5.00 (0-933992-01-7) Coffee Break.
Touch of Spring. Viola B. Smith. Ed. by Sandra S. Michel. (Illus.). (J). (gr. k-4). 1976. pap. 4.00 (0-917178-02-5) Lenape Pub.
Touch of Spring Fever. large type ed. Grace Goodwin. (Linford Romance Library). 304p. 1994. pap. 15.99 (0-7089-7533-X, Linford) Ulverscroft.
Touch of Spring: or Avanti! Samuel Taylor. 1975. pap. 5.25 (0-8222-1161-0) Dramatists Play.
Touch of Strange. Edward H. Waldo. LC 70-121565. (Short Story Index Reprint Ser.). 1977. 21.95 (0-8369-3522-5) Ayer.
Touch of Sun: And Other Stories. Mary H. Foote, pseud. LC 72-4422. (Short Story Index Reprint Ser.). 1977. reprint ed. 23.95 (0-8369-4175-6) Ayer.
Touch of Sun & Other Stories. Mary H. Foote. (C). 1972. reprint ed. lib. bdg. 17.00 (0-8422-8046-4) Irvington.
Touch of Sun & Other Stories. Mary H. Foote. 1986. reprint ed. pap. text ed. 6.95 (0-8290-2043-8) Irvington.
***Touch of Sunshine.** Ed. by Janice Braud & Claire Ottenstein. (Illus.). 46p. (Orig.). 1996. pap. 10.00 (1-878149-34-2) Counterpoint Pub.
***Touch of Tenderness.** large type ed. Juliet Gray. (Linford Romance Library). 272p. 1997. pap. 16.99 (0-7089-5079-5, Linford) Ulverscroft.
Touch of Terrell. Bob Terrell. 1976. 6.95 (0-686-17331-7) B Terrell.
Touch of Terror. Patricia Matthews. 256p. 1995. 20.00 (0-7278-4746-5) Severn Hse.
***Touch of Texas.** Kristine Rolofson. (Hometown Reunion Ser.). 1997. mass mkt. 4.50 (0-373-82555-2, 1-82555-3) Harlequin Bks.
Touch of the Artist: Master Drawings from the Woodner Family Collections. Noel Annesley. Ed. by Margaret M. Grasselli. LC 95-23191. (Illus.). 288p. 1995. 60.00 (0-8109-3882-0) Abrams.
Touch of the Artist: Master Drawings from the Woodner Family Collections. Ed. by Margaret M. Grasselli. LC 95-23191. 1995. pap. write for info. (0-89468-218-0) Natl Gallery Art.
Touch of the Earth. large type ed. Jean Hersey. 396p. 1985. reprint ed. pap. 10.95 (0-8027-2481-7) Walker & Co.
Touch of the Marvelous. Philip Lamantia. 1966. pap. 1.95 (0-685-04678-8) Oyez.
Touch of the Master's Hand. Myra B. Welch. LC 96-11711. (Illus.). 32p. (J). (gr. 2 up). 1996. 16.95 (1-885628-03-X) Buckaroo Bks.
***Touch of the Master's Hand: A Journey into Stolen Innocence.** Blondie Clayton. 227p. (Orig.). 1996. pap. 10.00 (0-9653700-0-3) B L Pubng.
Touch of the Orient. John Haylock. 199p. 9000. 30.00 (0-7206-0781-7, Pub. by P Owen Ltd UK) Dufour.
Touch of the Orient. John Haylock. 176p. 1990. 30.00 (0-685-38819-0, Pub. by P Owen Ltd UK) Dufour.
Touch of the Past. Jon L. Breen. 192p. 1988. 16.95 (0-8027-5704-9) Walker & Co.
Touch of the Poet. Eugene O'Neill. 1994. pap. 5.25 (0-8222-1393-1) Dramatists Play.
Touch of thee Shepherd: Reflections on the Life of Vernon S. Broyles, Jr. Celestine Sibley. (Illus.). 221p. 1994. 19.95 (0-89176-043-1, Mckingbird) R Bemis Pub.
Touch of Tiffany. Patrice Lampton. (Illus.). 40p. 1989. pap. 13.95 (0-935133-25-9) CKE Pubns.
Touch of Wisdom, Touch of Wit. S. Heinvulstein. 1991. pap. 16.99 (0-89906-865-0) Mesorah Pubns.
Touch of Wisdom, Touch of Wit. S. Himelstein. 1991. 19.99 (0-89906-864-2) Mesorah Pubns.
Touch of Wonder. Arthur Gordon. (Orig.). 1986. mass mkt. 4.99 (0-515-08987-7) Jove Pubns.
Touch of Wonder: Staying in Love with Life. Arthur Gordon. LC 74-23794. 256p. (Orig.). (gr. 10). 1996. pap. 9.99 (0-8007-5602-9) Revell.
Touch Operation of the Electronic Calculator. Jones. (KH - Office Machines Ser.). 1985. pap. 10.95 (0-538-13580-8) S-W Pub.
Touch Operation of the Electronic Calculator. 2nd ed. Jones. (KH - Office Machines Ser.). 1993. pap. 7.95 (0-538-61237-1) S-W Pub.
Touch Sensitivity see Teach Yourself Keyboard Playing & Improvisation
Touch Softly: Inspirational Poetry. Debby Mitchell, pseud. (Illus.). 60p. 1995. pap. 12.00 (0-9650828-0-6) All Things.
Touch Starvation in America: A Call to Arms. Denny Johnson. Ed. by Deborah Monroe. LC 85-60729. (Illus.). 170p. (Orig.). 1985. pap. 4.95 (0-917197-02-X) Rayid Pubns.
Touch Stones: Reconnecting After a Cult Experience. Carroll Stoner & Synthia Kisser. 80p. (Orig.). pap. 5.95 (0-9634572-0-9) Cult Awareness.
Touch, Taste & Smell. rev. ed. Steve Parker. LC 88-51607. (Human Body Ser.). (Illus.). 48p. (J). (gr. 5-6). 1989. lib. bdg. 20.60 (0-531-10655-1) Watts.
Touch, Temperature, & Pain in Health & Disease: Mechanisms & Assessments. Ed. by Jorgen Boivie et al. LC 94-36236. (Progress in Pain Research & Management Ser.: 3). (Illus.). 548p. 1994. 69.00 (0-931092-08-6, PPRM3) Intl Assn Study Pain.
Touch the Angel's Hand: A Family's Struggle With Depression. Pam Martin. LC 87-62874. 96p. (Orig.). 1988. pap. 6.95 (0-940989-21-2) Meyer Stone Bks.
Touch the Concrete, Feel the Abstract. Anthony Grenek, Jr. LC 94-84985. 64p. 1997. pap. 4.75 (0-943512-27-1) Linwood Pub.
Touch the Dawn. Chelley Kitzmiller. 384p. (Orig.). 1993. pap. 4.99 (0-451-40364-9, Topaz) NAL-Dutton.
Touch the Dawn. Karen Young. 1993. mass mkt. 3.39 (0-373-70532-8, 1-70532-6) Harlequin Bks.
Touch the Devil. Jack Higgins. 352p. 1983. pap. 5.99 (0-451-16677-9, Sig); pap. 4.50 (0-451-15688-9, Sig) NAL-Dutton.
Touch the Devil. Jack Higgins. Ed. by Bill Grose. 352p. 1993. mass mkt. 6.50 (0-671-67620-2) PB.
Touch the Dragon: A Thai Journal. Connelly. 1992. per. 10.95 (0-88801-162-8) LPC InBook.
***Touch the Earth.** 10.95 (1-56176-910-X) Mystic Fire.
***Touch the Earth.** Jane Baskwill. LC 97-3944. (J). 1998. write for info. (1-57255-429-0); pap. write for info. (1-57255-428-2) Mondo Pubng.
Touch the Earth. T. C. McLuhan. 1989. 7.98 (0-88394-000-0) Promntory Pr.
Touch the Earth: A Self Portrait of Indian Existence. T. C. McLuhan. 186p. 1976. pap. 14.00 (0-671-22275-9, Touchstone Bks) S&S Trade.
Touch the Future. Houston. Date not set. teacher ed., pap. text ed. write for info. (0-314-65747-9) West Pub.
Touch the Future: Teach! W. Robert Houston et al. 401p. (C). 1988. text ed. 45.25 (0-314-62759-6) West Pub.
Touch the Moon. Marion Dane Bauer. LC 87-663. 96p. (J). (gr. 4-7). 1987. 14.95 (0-89919-526-1, Clarion Bks) HM.
Touch the Past. Esther Kreek. LC 84-743256. 15p. 1984. pap. 10.00 incl. audio (1-884483-01-1) St Joseph Mus.
Touch the Poem. Arnold Adoff. LC 95-34473. (Illus.). 1996. write for info. (0-590-47970-9) Scholastic Inc.
Touch the Sea. Dee Scarr. (Illus.). 127p. 1988. pap. text ed. 19.95 (1-878663-05-X) PADI.
***Touch the Sky.** Robert Elmer. LC 97-4733. (Young Underground Ser.: No. 8). (J). Date not set. pap. text ed. 5.99 (1-55661-661-9) Bethany Hse.
***Touch the Sky: A Coloring Book for the Whole Family.** A. J. Wolff. (Illus.). 48p. (Orig.). (J). 1997. pap. 6.95 (0-931481-06-6) Rosebush Pub.
Touch the Sky: Meeting Your Inner Child Coloring Book. Tamara Kestrel & A. J. Wolff. (Illus.). 80p. (Orig.). 1996. pap. 9.95 (0-931481-02-3) Rosebush Pub.
Touch the Sky: The Needles in the Black Hills of South Dakota. Paul Piana. LC 82-71892. (Illus.). 301p. 1983. pap. 13.50 (0-930410-16-5) Amer Alpine Club.
***Touch the Sky Summer.** Jean Van Leeuwen. (Illus.). (J). (ps-3). 1997. 14.99 (0-614-28690-5) Dial Bks Young.
Touch the Sky Summer. Jean Van Leeuwen. LC 96-2380. (J). 1997. pap. 14.99 (0-8037-1819-5) Dial Bks Young.
***Touch the Water Touch the Wind.** Delange. (C). 1993. pap. write for info. (0-15-680722-X) HB Coll Pubs.
Touch the Water, Touch the Wind. Amos Oz. 1991. pap. 7.95 (0-15-690772-0, Harvest Bks) HarBrace.
***Touch the Wild Wind.** Cassie Edwards. 448p. (Orig.). 1997. mass mkt. 5.50 (0-505-52211-X, Love Spell) Dorchester Pub Co.
Touch the Wind. Janet Dailey. 1994. pap. 5.99 (0-671-87520-5) PB.
Touch the World Through Prayer: Leader's Guide. Wesley L. Duewel & Beverly Oxley. 1990. pap. 11.95 (0-911866-23-X) LifeSprings Res.
Touch Them with Love. Phil Edwardes. 1994. pap. 10.95 (1-85230-555-X) Element MA.
Touch Therapy. H. Colton. 1989. pap. 4.95 (0-8217-2774-5) NAL-Dutton.
Touch Therapy. Helen Colton. Orig. Title: The Gift of Touch. 320p. 1988. mass mkt. 4.95 (0-8217-2361-8, Zebra Kensgtn) Kensgtn Pub Corp.
Touch Training for Strength. Beth Rothenberg & Oscar Rothenberg. LC 94-1605. 152p. 1994. pap. 13.95 (0-87322-437-X, PROT0437) Human Kinetics.
Touch-Type the Computer in Four Hours. Frank Donnelly. 64p. 1989. spiral bd. 8.00 (0-936862-85-8, CKP-1) DDC Pub.
Touch Typing in Ten Lessons. rev. ed. Ruth Ben'Ary. 80p. (Orig.). 1989. pap. 8.95 (0-399-51529-1, Perigee Bks) Berkley Pub.
Touch Typing Made Simple. Lillian S. Marks. LC 85-4431. (Made Simple Ser.). (Illus.). 192p. 1985. pap. 12.95 (0-385-19426-9) Doubleday.
Touch Voltages in Electrical Installations. B. D. Jenkins. LC 93-18659. 1993. 59.95 (0-632-03485-8) Blackwell Sci.
Touch with Your Eyes! Mary K. Atherton et al. (Illus.). 48p. (Orig.). (J). (gr. k-8). 1982. pap. 4.50 (0-9613069-0-4) Orinda Art Coun.
Touch Wood. Ed. by Peter Crowther. 384p. 1996. mass mkt. 5.99 (0-446-60162-4, Aspect) Warner Bks.
Touch Wood: A Girlhood Occupied In France. Renee Roth-Hano. (ALA Notable Bk.). 304p. (J). (gr. 5 up). 1989. pap. 5.99 (0-14-034085-8, Puffin) Puffin Bks.
Touch Wood: A Play. C. L. Anthony. 128p. 1934. 8.95 (0-910278-67-9) Boulevard.
Touch Your Dream. Iris E. Hackett. (Illus.). 96p. (Orig.). (YA). (gr. 8-13). 1994. pap. 13.95 (0-9643422-0-0) H To H Pubs.
Touchable Lovables Book. (Looney Tunes Bks.). (Illus.). (J). 1996. 12.99 (0-8289-0978-4) Penguin.
Touchdown. Richard Steel. Ed. by Liz Parker. (Take Ten Bks.). (Illus.). 45p. (Orig.). (J). (gr. 6-12). 1992. pap. text ed. 3.95 (1-56254-054-8) Saddleback Pubns.
Touchdown: A Guide to Understanding & Enjoying Football. Donna P. Foehr. LC 92-72678. (Illus.). 237p. pap. 12.95 (0-9633797-0-4) Franklin MI.
Touchdown! Great Moments & Dubious Achievements in Football History. John Snyder. 208p. 1992. pap. 6.95 (0-8118-0280-9) Chronicle Bks.
Touchdown: Level 1 - Secondary. J. Harmer et al. (Illus.). (YA). 1993. teacher ed. 18.50 (0-582-04058-2, 79799); audio 24.95 (0-582-04056-6, 79801) Longman.
Touchdown: Level 1 - Secondary. J. Harmer et al. (Illus.). (YA). 1993. student ed., pap. text ed. 16.52 (0-582-04060-4, 79798); student ed., pap. text ed. 10.59 (0-582-06031-1, 79800) Longman.
Touchdown: Level 2 - Secondary. J. Harmer et al. (Illus.). (YA). 1993. audio 24.95 (0-582-04066-3, 79805) Longman.
Touchdown: Level 2 - Secondary. J. Harmer et al. (Illus.). (YA). 1993. student ed., pap. text ed. 16.52 (0-582-04059-0, 79802); teacher ed., pap. text ed. 22.44 (0-582-04057-4, 79803) Longman.
Touchdown: Level 3 - Secondary. J. Harmer et al. (Illus.). (YA). 1993. teacher ed. 18.95 (0-582-06027-3, 79806); audio 24.95 (0-582-06035-4, 79809) Longman.
Touchdown: Level 3 - Secondary. J. Harmer et al. (Illus.). (YA). 1993. student ed., pap. text ed. 16.52 (0-582-06033-8, 79806); student ed., pap. text ed. 10.59 (0-582-06029-X, 79808) Longman.
Touchdown: Level 4 - Secondary. J. Harmer et al. (Illus.). (YA). 1993. teacher ed. 18.95 (0-582-06026-5, 79811); student ed. 8.95 (0-582-06028-1, 79812); student ed., pap. text ed. 13.95 (0-582-06032-X, 79810); audio 24.95 (0-582-06034-6, 79813) Longman.
***Touchdown! The Favorite Football Stories of Great Coaches.** Larry S. Roseberry & Ted Royal. 240p. (Orig.). 1997. pap. 22.95 (1-57488-131-0) Brasseys Inc.
Touchdown for Tommy. Matt Christopher. (Illus.). 145p. (J). (gr. 4-6). 1985. mass mkt. 3.95 (0-316-13982-3) Little.
Touchdown Pass. Clair Bee. 1993. reprint ed. lib. bdg. 25.95 (1-56849-182-4) Buccaneer Bks.
Touchdown Riddles. Joanne E. Bernstein & Paul Cohen. Ed. by Abby Levine. LC 88-21761. (Illus.). 32p. (J). (gr. 1-5). 1989. lib. bdg. 8.95 (0-8075-8036-8) A Whitman.
Touchdown Wolfpack: An Illustrated History of North Carolina State Football. Douglas Herakovich. Ed. by Frank Weedon & Stuart Coman. (Illus.). 132p. 1995. 39.95 (0-9646026-1-X) Yesterdays Future.
Touche: Programming Tools for Shaping Solutions. Albert F. Rodriguez. 50p. (Orig.). (C). 1994. pap. text ed. 12.50 (0-9642829-4-1) AFR Software.
Touche Ross: Accounts & Audit of Pension Schemes. 2nd ed. Amyas Mascarenhas & Teresa Sienkiewics. 1991. pap. 84.00 (0-406-00348-3, U.K.) MICHIE.
Touche Ross: Rights & Duties of Directors. 2nd ed. Brian Creighton & D. Wright. 1991. pap. 56.00 (0-406-67846-4, U.K.) MICHIE.
Touche Ross: Summary & Simplified Financial Reporting. Roger Hussey & Haydn Everitt. 1991. pap. 77.00 (0-406-67841-3) MICHIE.
Touche-Ross: VAT: A Business by Business Guide 1994-95. Andrew Ball & Lakshmi Narain. 1994. pap. 32.95 (0-406-04477-5) MICHIE.
Touche Ross Financial Reporting & Accounting Manual: Getting Reports Right. 4th ed. Ken Wild & Clive Goodhead. (Orig.). 1994. pap. 32.95 (0-406-02883-4) MICHIE.
Touche Ross Government Executives' Guide to Selecting a Small Computer. Raymond W. Bolek et al. LC 84-4726. 244p. 1984. 49.95 (0-13-925611-3, Busn) P-H.
Touche Ross Guide to Granting Credit to Contractors. Denton Hammond. LC 83-19275. 122p. 1984. 39.95 (0-13-925652-0, Busn) P-H.
Touche Ross Guide to Personal Financial Management. rev. ed. John R. Connell et al. 336p. 1987. 39.95 (0-13-925413-7) P-H.
Touche Ross Guide to Selecting a Small Business Computer. Michael J. Berkery & Raymond W. Bolek. LC 84-26528. 337p. 1985. pap. 19.95 (0-13-925744-6) P-H.
Touche Ross Guide to Taxation for Cooperatives. 5th ed. Touche Ross & Co. Staff. 415p. 1984. 79.95 (0-13-925801-9, Busn) P-H.
Touche Ross Personal Financial Planning & Investment Workbook. 3rd ed. John R. Connell et al. 360p. 1989. 39.95 (0-13-925844-2); pap. 19.95 (0-13-925546-X) P-H.
Touched. Scott Campbell. LC 95-16172. 304p. 1996. 21.95 (0-553-09996-5, Bantam Trade Bks) Bantam.
Touched. Carolyn Haines. 384p. 1996. pap. 23.95 (0-525-94160-6, Dutton) NAL-Dutton.
***Touched.** Carolyn Haines. 1997. pap. 11.95 (0-452-27670-5, Plume) NAL-Dutton.
Touched. Robin Johnson. 1991. pap. text ed. 3.25 (0-9629297-0-0) R Johnson.
Touched. Stephen Lowe. (Methuen Modern Plays Ser.). 80p. (C). 1989. reprint ed. pap. 8.95 (0-413-61210-4, A0372, Pub. by Methuen UK) Heinemann.
***Touched: A Novel.** Scott Campbell. 304p. 1997. reprint ed. pap. 12.95 (0-553-37822-8, Bantam Trade Bks) Bantam.
Touched by Africa. Edwin S. Munger. 1983. 12.50 (0-934912-00-9) Munger Africana Lib.
Touched by AIDS. Margaret A. Cummings. Ed. by Cathy Butler. 22p. (Orig.). (YA). (gr. 7-12). 1992. pap. text ed. 1.95 (1-56309-024-4, Wrld Changers Res) Womans Mission Union.
***Touched by an Angel: Stories from the Hit Television Series.** rev. ed. Martha Williamson & Robin Sheets. LC 96-49116. (Illus.). 224p. 1997. pap. 12.99 (0-310-21397-5) Zondervan.
Touched by Angels. Eileen E. Freeman. 224p. 1993. 14.95 (0-446-51769-0) Warner Bks.
Touched by Angels. Eileen E. Freeman. 224p. 1994. pap. 9.99 (0-446-67033-2) Warner Bks.
Touched by Angels. Debbie Macomber. 320p. 1995. mass mkt. 5.99 (0-06-108344-5, Harp PBks) HarpC.
Touched by Desire. Lynsey Stevens. (Presents Ser.). 1994. mass mkt. 2.99 (0-373-11643-8, 1-11643-3) Harlequin Bks.
Touched by Desire. large type unabridged ed. (Harlequin Ser.). 1993. lib. bdg. 19.95 (0-263-13583-7, Pub. by Mills & Boon UK) Thorndike Pr.
***Touched by Fire.** Larry Yeagley. 123p. (Orig.). 1996. pap. 7.99 (0-8280-1035-8) Review & Herald.
Touched by Fire: A Bilingual Edition of Manuel de Pedrolo's "Tocats pel Foc" Manuel De Pedrolo. Tr. by Peter Griffin from CAT. LC 92-44185. (Catalan Studies: Vol. 10). 199p. (Orig.). (CAT & ENG.). (C). 1994. pap. text ed. 29.95 (0-8204-2133-2) P Lang Pubng.
***Touched by Fire: A National Historical Society Photographic Portrait of the Civil War.** William C. Davis. (Illus.). 1997. 29.98 (1-57912-001-6) Blck Dog & Leventhal.
Touched by Fire: The Land War in the South Pacific. Eric M. Bergerud. LC 95-34149. 576p. 1996. pap. 34.95 (0-670-86158-8, Viking) Viking Penguin.
Touched by Fire: The Life, Death & Mythic Afterlife of George Armstrong Custer. Louise Barnett. 320p. 1996. 30.00 (0-8050-3720-9) H Holt & Co.
***Touched by Fire: The Life, Death & Mythic Afterlife of George Armstrong Custer.** Louise Barnett. 1997. pap. 14.95 (0-8050-5359-X, Owl) H Holt & Co.
Touched by God: My Pilgrimage of Prayer. John Powell. (Illus.). (Orig.). 1996. pap. 6.95 (0-88347-328-3, 7328) Res Christian Liv.
***Touched by Gods.** Watt-Evans. LC 97-15569. 1997. 24.95 (0-312-86060-9) St Martin.
Touched by His Hand: The Reflections of Phillip Keller. Phillip W. Keller. 496p. 1996. 14.98 (0-88486-156-2, Inspirational Pr) Arrowood Pr.
***Touched by Light.** Ruth E. Norman. LC 97-60335. (Illus.). 150p. (Orig.). 1997. pap. 15.00 (0-935097-37-6) Unarius Acad Sci.
Touched by Love. Dorothy McManus. (Illus.). 191p. (Orig.). 1994. pap. 9.95 (0-929686-03-9) Temple Golden Pubns.
Touched by Magic. Doranna Durgin. 352p. 1996. mass mkt. 5.99 (0-671-87737-2) Baen Bks.
Touched by Magic. Laura Palmer & Marilyn Willison. 238p. (Orig.). 1992. pap. 19.95 (0-9631899-0-5) Angel Ink.
Touched by Magic. Patricia Rice. 384p. (Orig.). 1992. pap. 4.99 (0-451-40298-7, Onyx) NAL-Dutton.
Touched by Moonlight. Carole Howey. 448p. (Orig.). 1995. mass mkt., pap. text ed. 4.99 (0-8439-3824-2) Dorchester Pub Co.
Touched by the Father's Hand. Mark A. Rivera & Joanne Jacquart. 138p. (Orig.). 1991. pap. 9.95 (0-9625097-2-8) Stonecrest FL.
Touched by the Great Spirit. Paul Hurley. (Orig.). 1996. pap. write for info. (1-57553-190-9) Watermrk Pr.
Touched by the Master: Discover the Healing Power of a Face-to-Face Encounter with the Lord. Fred Littauer. 200p. (Orig.). 1996. pap. 10.99 (0-88419-440-X) Creation House.
Touched with Fire. Kay R. Jamison. 384p. 1996. pap. 15.00 (0-684-83183-X) S&S Trade.
Touched with Fire: An American Community in WWII. Allison M. Lockwood. (Illus.). 216p. (Orig.). 1993. pap. 19.95 (0-9618052-3-4) Daily Hampshire.
Touched with Fire: Manic-Depressive Illness & the Artistic Temperament. Kay R. Jamison. 370p. 1994. pap. 14.95 (0-02-916003-0, Free Press) Free Pr.
***Touched with Fire: The Land War in the South Pacific.** Eric Bergerud. (Illus.). 566p. 1996. 34.95 (0-614-19994-8) Viking Penguin.
***Touched with Fire: The Land War in the South Pacific.** Eric M. Bergerud. 1997. pap. 14.95 (0-14-024696-7) Penguin.
Touches of Sweet Harmony: Pythagorean Cosmology & Renaissance Poetics. S. K. Heninger. LC 73-78049. (Illus.). 464p. reprint ed. pap. 132.30 (0-8357-7535-6, 2036250) Bks Demand.
Touches the Stars. Lynn A. McKee. 352p. (Orig.). 1992. mass mkt. 5.50 (1-55773-752-5) Diamond.
Touching. Coalition for Child Advocacy Staff. (Illus.). 32p. (Orig.). (J). (ps). 1985. pap. 5.95 (0-934671-00-1) Whatcom Cty Opp.
Touching. Deldon A. McNeely. 1995. pap. 15.00 (0-919123-29-5, Pub. by Inner City CN) BookWorld Dist.
Touching. Kathie B. Smith & Victoria Crenson. LC 87-5885. (Question Bks.). (Illus.). 24p. (J). (gr. k-3). 1988. lib. bdg. 11.89 (0-8167-1012-0) Troll Communs.
Touching. Lillian Wright. (What about...? Ser.). (Illus.). 32p. (J). (gr. 2-4). 1994. lib. bdg. 21.40 (0-8114-5517-3) Raintree Steck-V.
Touching. Lillian Wright. (J). 1996. pap. text ed. 4.95 (0-8114-7993-5) Raintree Steck-V.
Touching: The Human Significance of the Skin. Ashley Montagu. LC 75-151290. (Illus.). 1971. text ed. 45.00 (0-231-03488-1) Col U Pr.
***Touching: The Human Significance of the Skin.** Ashley Montagu. 1986. pap. 15.50 (0-06-096028-0, PL) HarpC.
Touching All the Bases: Baseball for Kids of All Ages. Claire Mackay. (Illus.). 96p. (Orig.). (J). 1996. pap. 9.95 (1-55209-000-0) Firefly Bks Ltd.
Touching Base: Professional Baseball & American Culture in the Progressive Era. Steven A. Riess. LC 79-6570. (Contributions in American Studies: No. 48). (Illus.). xv, 268p. 1980. text ed. 38.50 (0-313-20671-6, RTB/, Greenwood Pr) Greenwood.

T

An Asterisk (*) at the beginning of an entry indicates that the title is appearing in BIP for the first time.

Touching Certain Things. deluxe ed. Beatrice Wood. Ed. by Michael G. Michaud. (Illus.). 24p. (Orig.). 1992. pap. 75.00 (*0-9620574-5-2*) MGM Pr.

Touching China: Close Encounters of the Christian Kind. Leona Choy. Ed. by W. Lee Troup. (Illus.). 224p. 1993. pap. 9.95 (*1-882324-00-5*) Ambssdrs Christ.

Touching Evil. Norma Rosen. LC 89-38145. 278p. (C). 1990. reprint ed. 32.50 (*0-8143-2298-0*); reprint ed. pap. 11.95 (*0-8143-2299-9*) Wayne St U Pr.

*__Touching Fire.__ Ed. by Louise Thornton et al. 9.95 (*0-7867-0649-X*) Carroll & Graf.

Touching Fire: Erotic Writings by Women. Ed. by Louise Thornton et al. 1989. 18.95 (*0-88184-527-2*) Carroll & Graf.

Touching Fire: Erotic Writings by Women. Ed. by Louise Thornton et al. 222p. 1990. pap. 9.95 (*0-88184-649-X*) Carroll & Graf.

Touching from a Distance: Deborah Curtis. Deborah Curtis. (Illus.). 212p. 1996. pap. text ed. 15.95 (*0-571-17445-0*) Faber & Faber.

Touching Hearts & Minds. Lisa Blau. 104p. 1992. teacher ed. 10.95 (*0-9640333-0-5*) One Heart Educ.

Touching Incidents & Remarkable Answers to Prayer. 135p. (J). (gr. k up). pap. 1.00 (*0-686-29172-7*) Faith Pub Hse.

Touching Liberty: Abolition, Feminism, & the Politics of the Body. Karen Sanchez-Eppler. LC 92-20377. 208p. 1993. 35.00 (*0-520-07959-0*) U CA Pr.

*__Touching Liberty: Abolition, Feminism & the Politics of the Body.__ Karen Sanchez-Eppler. 1997. pap. text ed. 15.95 (*0-520-21234-7*) U CA Pr.

Touching Our Strength: The Erotic As Power & the Love of God. Carter Heyward. LC 89-45244. 1989. pap. 13.00 (*0-06-250396-0*) Harper SF.

Touching Peace: Practicing the Art of Mindful Living. Thich Nhat Hanh. LC 92-33718. 128p. 1992. pap. 9.50 (*0-938077-57-0*) Parallax Pr.

Touching Place. 1987. 20.00 (*0-947988-09-2*, Pub. by Wild Goose Pubns UK); audio 10.00 (*0-317-89959-7*, Pub. by Wild Goose Pubns UK) St Mut.

Touching Place. Ed. by Wild Goose Publications Staff. (C). 1990. 25.00 (*0-685-36116-0*, Pub. by Wild Goose Pubns UK) St Mut.

Touching Places Foreign & Familiar: Vignettes. Joan Krieger. (Illus.). 80p. 1993. pap. 9.95 (*1-56474-066-8*) Fithian Pr.

Touching Rock: Selected Poems. Norman Kreitman. 56p. 1987. pap. text ed. 7.75 (*0-08-035072-0*, Pub. by Aberdeen U Pr) Macmillan.

Touching Second: Science of Baseball. Evers. 1976. 24.95 (*0-8488-1581-5*) Amereon Ltd.

Touching Spirit: A Journey of Healing & Personal Resurrection. Elizabeth K. Stratton. 288p. 1996. 22.00 (*0-684-83093-0*) S&S Trade.

*__Touching the Body, Reaching the Soul: How Touch Influences the Nature of Human Beings.__ Sandra Wooten. (Illus.). 64p. (Orig.). 1995. pap. 12.95 (*0-9654790-0-5*) Taos Mntn Pr.

Touching the Clouds: The General Claire Chennault Story. James Odiear. Date not set. pap. 19.95 (*1-57090-019-1*) Alexander Bks.

Touching the Earth. Roberta Bondar. (Illus.). 144p. (Orig.). 1994. pap. 19.95 (*1-55013-657-7*, Pub. by Key Porter Bks CN) Firefly Bks Ltd.

Touching the Face of God. Bob Russell. LC 91-77441. 224p. 1991. pap. 8.99 (*1-56384-010-3*) Huntington Hse.

Touching the Face of God: Intimacy & Celibacy in the Priesthood. Donna T. Mahoney. LC 91-76864. 233p. 1991. pap. 12.95 (*0-9631517-0-3*) Jeremiah Pr.

*__Touching the Fire: Buffalo Dancers, the Sky Bundle, & Other Tales.__ Roger Welsch. LC 97-17729. 304p. 1997. pap. 12.00 (*0-8032-9798-X*, Bison Books) U of Nebr Pr.

*__Touching the Future: The Foundation for Physical Therapy.__ Victoria Stuart. Ed. by Holtzman, Robert, & Assoc., Inc. Staff. (Illus.). 70p. (Orig.). 1997. pap. write for info. (*0-9628807-2-8*) FPT VA.

Touching the Heart: Stories by Melodye Webb. Melodye Webb. 1993. 12.95 (*0-533-10412-2*) Vantage.

Touching the Heart of God. Ernest J. Gruen. 288p. 1986. mass mkt. 4.99 (*0-88368-175-7*) Whitaker Hse.

Touching the Holy: Ordinariness, Self-Esteem, & Friendship. Robert J. Wicks. LC 92-72925. 160p. (Orig.). 1992. pap. 7.95 (*0-87793-490-8*) Ave Maria.

Touching the Invisible. Norman P. Grubb. 1979. pap. 2.95 (*0-87508-222-X*) Chr Lit.

Touching the Mountain: The Self Breema Handbook: Ancient Exercises for the Modern World. Jon Schreiber. LC 89-85099. (Illus.). 189p. (Orig.). 1989. pap. 24.95 (*0-9623581-2-6*) CA Health Pubns.

Touching the Rock: An Experience of Blindness. John M. Hull. 1992. pap. 10.00 (*0-679-73547-X*, Vin) Random.

Touching the Sky. Denise Low. 132p. 1994. pap. 16.50 (*0-9632475-8-1*) Penthe Pub.

Touching the Soul. Fay P. Claud. 51p. (Orig.). 1995. pap. 6.95 (*1-56411-120-2*) Untd Bros & Sis.

Touching the Stones. Oregon Nikkei Endowment Staff. 112p. 34.95 (*0-9644806-0-3*); pap. 19.95 (*0-9644806-1-1*) OR Nikkei Endow.

Touching the Truth: A Summary & Commentary on the Splendor of Truth. William F. Urbine et al. 64p. (Orig.). 1995. pap. 2.25 (*0-8198-7379-9*) Pauline Bks.

Touching the Unseen World. Betty Malz. LC 91-10142. 160p. 1990. 11.99 (*0-8007-9180-0*) Chosen Bks.

Touching the Void. large type ed. Joe Simpson. 1990. 25.99 (*0-7089-2247-3*) Ulverscroft.

Touching the Void: The Harrowing First-Person Account of One Man's Miraculous Survival. Joe Simpson. LC 88-45524. (Illus.). 176p. 1990. reprint ed. pap. 12.00 (*0-06-091654-0*, PL) HarpC.

Touching the World: Reference in Autobiography. Paul J. Eakin. 288p. 1992. text ed. 35.00 (*0-691-06820-8*) Princeton U Pr.

*__Touching Thomas.__ Thomas Crain. 130p. (Orig.). 1996. pap. 8.99 (*0-9627099-6-4*) Zephyr Pub Corp.

Touching You Touching Me. Jim Wortham. LC 74-28919. 64p. 1974. pap. 2.95 (*0-915216-00-0*) Marathon Intl Bk.

Touchline: Photographs. Williams. (Illus.). 1995. per. 29.95 (*0-85449-141-4*, Pub. by Gay Mens Pr UK) LPC InBook.

Touchlines of War. Peter Tennant. (Illus.). 270p. (Orig.). 1992. pap. 18.95 (*0-85958-603-0*, Pub. by Univ of Hull Pr UK) Paul & Co Pubs.

Touchpebbles, Vol. B. Geoffrey Comber et al. 82p. 1993. student ed., pap. text ed. 8.00 (*1-878461-14-1*) CZM Pr.

Touchpebbles: Texts for Discussions, Vol. B. Ed. by Howard Zeiderman & Nicholas Maistrellis. 219p. 1993. teacher ed. 24.00 (*1-878461-15-X*) CZM Pr.

Touchpebbles Vol. A. Geoffrey Comber et al. (Touchpebbles Ser.). 80p. (J). (gr. 2-3). 1994. student ed., pap. text ed. 8.00 (*1-878461-26-5*) CZM Pr.

Touchpebbles Vol. A. Geoffrey Comber et al. (Touchpebbles Ser.). 219p. 1994. teacher ed. 24.00 (*1-878461-27-3*) CZM Pr.

*__Touchpebbles Vol. A: Texts for Discussion.__ 2nd rev. ed. Ed. by Geoffrey Comber et al. (Illus.). 72p. (J). (gr. 2-5). 1997. pap. text ed. 8.00 (*1-878461-43-5*) CZM Pr.

*__TouchPoints.__ Date not set. mass mkt. write for info. (*0-8423-7094-3*) Tyndale.

Touchpoints: Your Child's Emotional & Behavioral Development, the Essential Reference. T. Berry Brazelton. (Illus.). 400p. 1992. 24.95 (*0-201-09380-4*) Addison-Wesley.

Touchpoints - the Essential Reference: Your Child's Emotional & Behavioral Development. T. Berry Brazelton. (Illus.). 512p. 1994. pap. 16.00 (*0-201-62690-X*) Addison-Wesley.

Touchstone. Linda Hilton. 1996. mass mkt. 5.99 (*0-671-89810-8*) PB.

Touchstone. Paul Horsfall. 300p. 1996. pap. text ed. 11.95 (*1-86373-871-1*, Pub. by Allen Unwin AT) Paul & Co Pubs.

Touchstone. Robyn Sarah. 139p. (Orig.). pap. 16.95 (*0-88784-528-2*, Pub. by Hse of Anansi Pr CN) Genl Dist Srvs.

*__Touchstone.__ Beatrice W. Sims. LC 96-44494. 48p. 1996. pap. 10.50 (*0-915010-40-2*) Sutter House.

*__Touchstone.__ large type ed. Aileen Armitage. (Magna Large Print Ser.). 384p. 1996. 25.99 (*0-7505-0950-3*, Pub. by Magna Print Bks UK) Ulverscroft.

Touchstone. Edith Wharton. LC 76-80628. reprint ed. 29.50 (*0-404-01968-4*) AMS Pr.

Touchstone. Edith Wharton. 1990. reprint ed. 49.00 (*0-403-00045-9*) Scholarly.

Touchstone: An Autobiography. K. R. Terry. LC 95-60835. 398p. 1996. pap. 15.95 (*1-55523-747-9*) Winston-Derek.

Touchstone & Me: Experiences of a Missionary Wife. Esther R. Cimino. 275p. (Orig.). 1993. write for info. (*0-9639059-0-2*) E R Cimino.

Touchstone Art Magic. Gary Layman. 153p. 1985. pap. 19.95 (*0-9616550-0-3*) Touch Art Magic.

Touchstone for Ethics, 1893-1943. Thomas H. Huxley & Julian S. Huxley. LC 74-156661. (Essay Index Reprint Ser.). 1977. reprint ed. 24.95 (*0-8369-2402-9*) Ayer.

Touchstone for Greatness: Essays, Addresses & Occasional Pieces about Abraham Lincoln. Roy P. Basler. LC 72-781. (Contributions in American Studies: No. 4). 257p. 1973. text ed. 49.95 (*0-8371-6135-5*, BTG/, Greenwood Pr) Greenwood.

Touchstone for Public Leadership: A Focus on City Government. Garland S. Novosad. (Illus.). 150p. 1988. 15.00 (*0-918464-77-3*) D Armstrong.

Touchstone for This Time Present. Edward Hake. LC 74-80182. (English Experience Ser.: No. 663). 96p. 1974. reprint ed. 15.00 (*90-221-0663-2*) Walter J Johnson.

Touchstone of Sincerity. J. D. Albert. 256p. 1986. pap. 7.50 (*0-85398-223-6*) G Ronald Pub.

Touchstone Study: Bringing the Arts to the Schools. Lillian Goldberg. 232p. (Orig.). 1984. pap. text ed. 15.00 (*0-89062-201-9*) Touchstone Ctr Child.

Touchstones. Sallie Phillips-McClenahan. LC 82-11454. (Illus.). 300p. (Orig.). 1982. pap. 8.95 (*0-87233-066-4*) Bauhan.

Touchstones. Illus. by David Spohn. (Meditation Ser.). 400p. (Orig.). 1986. pap. 10.00 (*0-89486-394-0*, 5029A) Hazelden.

Touchstones. Cherise Wyneken. LC 85-51973. 86p. 1986. pap. 3.95 (*1-55523-009-1*) Winston-Derek.

Touchstones: American Poets on a Favorite Poem. Ed. by Robert Pack & Jay Parini. LC 95-32557. (Bread Loaf Anthology Ser.). 346p. 1996. pap. 19.95 (*0-87451-723-0*) U Pr of New Eng.

Touchstones: American Poets on a Favorite Poem. Ed. by Robert Pack & Jay Parini. LC 95-32557. (Bread Loaf Anthology Ser.). 346p. (C). 1996. text ed. 45.00 (*0-87451-722-2*) U Pr of New Eng.

Touchstones: Classic Texts in the Humanities. Robert L. Platzner & Stephen L. Harris. 600p. (C). 1991. pap. text ed. 20.00 (*0-03-047504-X*) HB Coll Pubs.

Touchstones: Readings in Social Studies. Ed. by Geoffrey Comber et al. 163p. (Orig.). 1991. pap. text ed. 20.00 (*1-878461-07-9*) CZM Pr.

Touchstones: Reflections on the Best in Children's Literature, 3 vols., 1. Children's Literature Association Publications Staff. Ed. by Perry Nodelman. 445p. (C). 1986. 25.00 (*0-937263-01-X*) CHLA Pubns.

Touchstones: Reflections on the Best in Children's Literature, 3 vols., Set. Children's Literature Association Publications Staff. Ed. by Perry Nodelman. 445p. (C). 1986. 60.00 (*0-937263-00-1*) CHLA Pubns.

Touchstones: Ten New Ideas Revolutionizing Business. William Band. 306p. 1994. text ed. 24.95 (*0-471-31096-4*) Wiley.

Touchstones Vol. 1: Guide for Leading Discussions. Howard Zeiderman. 189p. 1989. teacher ed. 24.00 (*1-878461-00-1*) CZM Pr.

Touchstones Vol. I: Texts for Discussion. 3rd ed. Ed. by Geoffrey Comber & Howard Zeiderman. Tr. & Intro. by Nicholas Maistrellis. 160p. (YA). (gr. 9-12). 1995. pap. text ed. 11.00 (*1-878461-34-6*) CZM Pr.

Touchstones Vol. II: Texts for Discussion. Geoffrey Comber et al. (Touchstones Ser.: No. 2). 167p. (Orig.). 1988. pap. 12.00 (*1-878461-23-0*) CZM Pr.

Touchstones Vol. III: Texts for Discussion. Ed. by Geoffrey Comber et al. 182p. (Orig.). 1986. pap. text ed. 14.00 (*1-878461-24-9*) CZM Pr.

Touchstones Vol. IV: Texts for Discussion. Ed. by Geoffrey Comber et al. 178p. (Orig.). 1994. pap. text ed. 14.00 (*1-878461-25-7*) CZM Pr.

Touchstones & Wellsprings: The Survivor's Guide. Leo G. Frangipane, Jr. Ed. by Gretchen E. Hardy. (Illus.). 250p. 1995. pap. 11.00 (*0-9647313-4-7*); audio 11.00 (*0-9647313-5-5*); vhs 14.95 (*0-9647313-0-4*) L G Frangipane.

Touchstones en Espanol, Vol. I: Textos para la Discusion. Ed. by Howard Zeiderman & Nicholas Maistrellis. Tr. by Tommasina Hannum. 250p. (Orig.). 1990. pap. text ed. 11.00 (*1-878461-05-2*) CZM Pr.

Touchstones for Middle Schools, Vol. A. Geoffrey Comber et al. 230p. 1994. teacher ed., pap. 24.00 (*1-878461-08-7*) CZM Pr.

Touchstones for Middle Schools Vol. A: Texts for Discussion. Ed. by Geoffrey Comber et al. 94p. (Orig.). (J). (gr. 6-8). 1995. pap. text ed. 9.50 (*1-878461-33-8*) CZM Pr.

Touchstones for Middle Schools en Espanol, Vol. A. Geoffrey Comber et al. Tr. by Thomasina Hannum from ENG. 121p. (Orig.). (SPA.). 1993. pap. 9.50 (*1-878461-21-4*) CZM Pr.

Touchstones for Middle Schools, Vol. B: Teacher's Edition. Geoffrey Comber et al. 227p. (Orig.). 1992. pap. 24.00 (*1-878461-11-7*) CZM Pr.

Touchstones for Middle Schools, Vol. B: Texts for Discussion. Geoffrey Comber et al. (Touchstones for Middle Schools Ser.: No. 2). 116p. (Orig.). 1992. student ed., pap. text ed. 9.50 (*1-878461-10-9*) CZM Pr.

Touchstones of Matthew Arnold. John S. Eells, Jr. 1955. pap. 14.95 (*0-8084-0302-8*) NCUP.

Touchstones of Matthew Arnold. John S. Eells. LC 76-136388. reprint ed. 42.50 (*0-404-02263-4*) AMS Pr.

Touchstones, Reflections on the Best in Children's Literature Vol. 3: Picture Books. Children's Literature Association Staff. Ed. by Perry Nodelman. 191p. 1989. 25.00 (*0-8108-2563-5*) Scarecrow.

Touchstones, Reflections on the Best in Childrens's Literature Vol. 1: Children's Novels. Children's Literature Association Staff. Ed. by Perry Nodelman. 315p. 1985. 25.00 (*0-8108-2561-9*) Scarecrow.

Touchstones, Reflections on the Best of Children's Literature, 3 vols., Set. Children's Literature Association Staff. Ed. by Perry Nodelman. 1989. 60.00 (*0-8108-2564-3*) Scarecrow.

Touchstones, Reflections on the Best of Children's Literature Vol. 2: Fairy Tales, Fables, Myths, Legends, & Poetry. Children's Literature Association Staff. Ed. by Perry Nodelman. 236p. 1987. 25.00 (*0-8108-2562-7*) Scarecrow.

Touchstones, Vol. 2: Reflections on the Best in Children's Literature. Children's Literature Association Publications Staff. Ed. by Perry Nodelman. 1988. 25.00 (*0-318-41397-3*) CHLA Pubns.

Touchstones, Vol. 3: Reflections on the Best in Children's Literature. Children's Literature Association Publications Staff. Ed. by Perry Nodelman. 1989. 25.00 (*0-318-41398-1*) CHLA Pubns.

Touchtone Telephone - Voice Response Registration: A Guide for Successful Implementation. Ed. by Melanie M. Bell. LC 93-4306. 240p. 1993. 50.00 (*0-929851-15-3*) Am Assn Coll Registrars.

Touch...What Do You Feel? Nicholas Wood. LC 90-10925. (First Science Ser.). (Illus.). 32p. (J). (gr. k-3). 1991. lib. bdg. 12.95 (*0-8167-2126-2*) Troll Communs.

Touch...What Do You Feel? Nicholas Wood. LC 90-10925. (First Science Ser.). (Illus.). 32p. (J). (gr. k-3). 1997. pap. 3.95 (*0-8167-2127-0*) Troll Communs.

*__Touchwood.__ Dick Davis. 80p. 1996. pap. 15.95 (*0-85646-269-1*, Pub. by Anvil Press UK) Dufour.

Touchwood. Karin Kallmaker. 240p. (Orig.). 1991. pap. 9.95 (*0-941483-76-2*) Naiad Pr.

Touchwood: A Collection of Ojibway Prose. 2nd ed. Ed. by Gerald Vizenor. (Illus.). 1994. pap. 16.95 (*0-89823-091-8*) New Rivers Pr.

Touchy Situations: An Advanced Conversation Text for ESL Students. rev. ed. Glen A. Penrod. (Illus.). 160p. (C). 1993. pap. text ed. 16.75 (*0-9637742-0-4*) Dymon Pubns.

*__Toue Napa: An Insider's Guide to the Valley's Best.__ 2nd rev. ed. LC 96-68696. (Illus.). 96p. 1996. pap. 9.49 (*1-57087-257-0*, 961) Eureka Bks.

Tough Acts to Follow: One-Act Plays on the Gay-Lesbian Experience. Ed. by Noreen C. Barnes & Nicholas Deutsch. 160p. (Orig.). 1992. pap. 9.95 (*0-9624751-6-5*) Alamo Sq Pr.

Tough Baby. Jesse Sublett. Date not set. pap. 4.95 (*0-14-012397-0*, Viking) Viking Penguin.

Tough Boris. Mem Fox. LC 92-8015. (Illus.). 32p. (J). (ps-3). 1994. 15.00 (*0-15-289612-0*) HarBrace.

*__Tough Boris: Signed Copy.__ Fox. 1994. 15.00 (*0-15-201757-7*) HarBrace.

Tough Calls: Selling Strategies to Win over Your Most Difficult Customers. Josh Gordon. LC 96-35064. 176p. (Orig.). 1996. pap. 17.95 (*0-8144-7925-1*) AMACOM.

Tough Changes: Growing up on Your Own in America. Bernard Lefkowitz. 1987. text ed. 29.95 (*0-02-918490-8*, Free Press) Free Pr.

Tough Choices. Nancy Antle. 1998. pap. 3.99 (*0-14-036388-2*, Viking) Viking Penguin.

Tough Choices: A Book about Substance Abuse. John Langone. LC 94-17580. (J). 1995. 15.95 (*0-316-51407-1*) Little.

Tough Choices: Facing the Challenge of Food Scarcity. Lester Brown. 160p. 1996. pap. 11.00 (*0-393-31573-8*) Norton.

*__Tough Choices: Health Care Decisions & the Faith Community.__ Graydon F. Snyder. LC 87-35401. 143p. 1988. reprint ed. pap. 40.80 (*0-608-04181-5*, 2064916) Bks Demand.

Tough Choices: In Vitro Fertilization & the Reproductive Technologies. Ed. by Patricia Stephenson & Marsden G. Wagner. LC 92-48989. (Health, Society, & Policy Ser.). 192p. (C). 1993. 44.95 (*1-56639-060-5*) Temple U Pr.

Tough Choices: Jewish Perspectives on Social Justice. Albert Vorspan & David Saperstein. LC 92-31747. (J). 1992. pap. 11.00 (*0-8074-0482-9*, 167275) UAHC.

Tough Choices - Finding Ways to Balance Criminal Justice Policy & Criminal Justice Dollars: A Review of Management Controls at the Texas Department of Criminal Justice. Lawrence F. Alwin. (Illus.). 60p. (Orig.). (C). 1994. pap. text ed. 20.00 (*0-7881-0218-4*) DIANE Pub.

*__Tough Choices for Men.__ Len Woods. 1998. pap. 9.99 (*1-57673-255-X*) Multnomah Pubs.

Tough Choices for Roxie. Hilda Stahl. LC 92-37055. (Best Friends Ser.: Vol. 9). 160p. (J). (gr. 4 up). 1993. pap. 4.99 (*0-89107-711-1*) Crossway Bks.

*__Tough Cookie.__ David Wisniewski. (J). Date not set. write for info. (*0-688-15337-2*); lib. bdg. write for info. (*0-688-15338-0*) Lothrop.

Tough Customers: Counseling Unwilling Clients. Ed. by George A. Harris. 147p. 1991. 22.00 (*0-929310-57-8*, 134) Am Correctional.

Tough Customers: How to Keep Them Smiling...& Yourself Sane! Dartnell Corp Staff. (Customer Service Rep's Survival Guide Ser.). 230p. 1995. pap. 13.95 (*0-85013-210-X*) Dartnell Corp.

Tough Customers: True Adventures of Game Wardens & the Outlaws They Pursue. Terry Hodges. Ed. by Joe Sheehan. (Illus.). 301p. 1994. 17.95 (*0-9634092-1-2*) T&C Bks.

Tough Daisies: Kansas Humor from "The Lane County Bachelor" to Bob Dole. C. Robert Haywood. LC 95-20825. (Illus.). 302p. (C). 1995. 22.50 (*0-7006-0732-3*) U Pr of KS.

Tough Decisions: A Casebook in Medical Ethics. John M. Freeman & Kevin McDonnell. (Illus.). 202p. 1987. 35.00 (*0-19-504255-7*) OUP.

Tough Decisions: A Casebook in Medical Ethics. John M. Freeman & Kevin McDonnell. (Illus.). 202p. 1987. pap. 18.95 (*0-19-504256-5*) OUP.

Tough Enough: The Nineteen Ninety-Two - Ninety-Three Phoenix Suns - NBA Champions. Arizona Republic - Phoenix Gazette Staff. Ed. by David Gianelli. (Illus.). 120p. 1993. pap. 15.00 (*0-9636832-0-9*) Phoenix News.

Tough Fabric: The Domestic Apparel & Textile Chain Regain Market Share. John Covington. 63p. 1995. pap. text ed. 12.95 (*0-9647126-0-1*) Chesapke Cnslting.

Tough Gazoobies on That! Sherry S. Cohen. Ed. by Billie Young. LC 73-83476. 1974. 17.95 (*0-87949-016-0*) Ashley Bks.

Tough Guy. Eddie Maloney & William Hoffman. 384p. 1995. mass mkt. 4.99 (*0-7860-0168-2*, Pinncle Kensgtn) Kensgtn Pub Corp.

Tough Guy: The American Movie Macho. James L. Neibaur. LC 88-27309. (Illus.). 232p. 1989. lib. bdg. 32.50 (*0-89950-382-9*) McFarland & Co.

Tough Guy Writers of the Thirties. Ed. by David Madden. LC 68-10115. (Crosscurrents-Modern Critiques Ser.). 287p. 1968. 16.95 (*0-8093-0287-X*) S Ill U Pr.

Tough Guy Writers of the Thirties. Ed. by David Madden. LC 78-24304. (Arcturus Books Paperbacks). 287p. 1979. reprint ed. pap. 10.95 (*0-8093-0912-2*) S Ill U Pr.

Tough Guys. Andrew Demsky. LC 92-28036. 1992. 5.99 (*0-8280-0688-1*) Review & Herald.

Tough Guys Don't Dance. Norman Mailer. 288p. 1985. mass mkt. 5.95 (*0-345-32321-1*) Ballantine.

Tough Guys Don't Dance. Norman Mailer. LC 84-42514. 240p. 1984. 16.95 (*0-394-53786-6*) Random.

*__Tough Guys Don't Give Up: Storytellers.__ Asmundson et al. 200p. 1996. 16.95 (*0-9644683-3-6*) Sunporch Prods.

Tough Hand. large type ed. Wayne D. Overholser. (Nightingale Ser.). 1996. pap. 17.95 (*0-7838-1618-9*) G K Hall.

Tough Issues. (Cross Training Ser.: Vol. 3). 64p. (YA). (gr. 10-12). 1995. pap. 29.95 (*1-57405-026-5*) CharismaLife Pub.

Tough Kid Book: Practical Classroom Management Strategies. Ginger Rhode et al. (Tough Kid Ser.). (Illus.). 120p. 1992. teacher ed., pap. text ed. 19.50 (*0-944584-54-3*, 40TK) Sopris.

Tough Kid Social Skills Book. Susan M. Sheridan. (Tough Kid Ser.). (Illus.). 228p. 1995. pap. text ed. 19.50 (*1-57035-051-5*, 75SOCIAL) Sopris.

Tough Kid Tool Box. William R. Jenson et al. (Tough Kid Ser.). (Illus.). 214p. 1994. teacher ed., ring bd. 16.95 (*1-57035-000-0*, 58TB) Sopris.

Tough Kid Tool Box: Spanish Packet. William R. Jenson et al. Tr. by Sergio G. Waisman. (Illus.). 82p. (SPA.). 1995. ring bd. 16.95 (*1-57035-049-3*, 58SPAN) Sopris.

An Asterisk (*) at the beginning of an entry indicates that the title is appearing in BIP for the first time.

***Tough Kid Video Series, 6 bks., 6 videos.** Bob Algozzine et al. 132p. 1996. pap. text ed. 2,500.00 (1-57035-104-X, 76SERIES) Sopris.

***Tough Kids, Cool Counseling: User-Friendly Approaches with Challenging Youth.** John Sommeres-Flanagan & Rita Sommers-Flanagan. LC 97-5512. 279p. (Orig.). 1997. pap. text ed. 23.95 (1-55620-172-9, 72642) Am Coun Assn.

Tough Little Town on the Truckee: Reno to 1900. John M. Townley. (History of Reno Ser.: Vol. 1). (Illus.). 295p. 1983. pap. 19.95 (0-913381-00-4) Jamison Stn.

Tough Loser. Barthe DeClements. 128p. (J). (gr. 3-7). 1994. pap. 13.99 (0-670-85619-3) Viking Child Bks.

Tough Loser. Barthe DeClements. 128p. (J). 1996. pap. 3.99 (0-14-037075-7) Viking Penguin.

Tough Love: Cultural Criticism & Familial Observations on the Life & Death of Tupac Shakur. Ed. by Michael Datcher & Kwame Alexander. (Black Words Ser.). 200p. 1996. pap. 12.95 (1-888018-05-4) Alexndr Pub.

Tough Love: How Parents Can Deal With Drug Abuse. rev. ed. Pauline Neff. 160p. 1996. pap. text ed. 10.95 (0-687-01825-0) Abingdon.

Tough Love: How Parents Can Deal with Drug Abuse. Pauline Neff. 160p. 1984. reprint ed. pap. 10.95 (0-687-42407-0) Abingdon.

Tough-Luck Karen. Johanna Hurwitz. LC 82-6443. (Illus.). 160p. (J). (gr. 4-6). 1982. 16.00 (0-688-01485-2, Morrow Junior) Morrow.

Tough Luck Karen. Johanna Hurwitz. LC 82-6443. (Illus.). 160p. (J). (gr. 3 up). 1991. reprint ed. pap. 3.95 (0-688-10974-8) Morrow.

Tough-Luck Karen see Best-Selling Apples

***Tough Machines.** Snapshot Staff. (My First Board Bks.). (Illus.). 22p. (J). 1997. bds. 2.95 (0-7894-1540-2) DK Pub Inc.

***Tough Mazes: Maze Funbook.** Illus. by Scott Sullivan. (Troubador Ser.). 32p. (J). (ps up). 1997. reprint ed. pap. 3.50 (0-8431-8229-6) Price Stern Sloan.

***Tough Mazes 2: States of Confusion.** Illus. by Scott Sullivan. (Troubador Ser.). 32p. (J). (ps up). 1997. reprint ed. pap. 3.50 (0-8431-7961-9) Price Stern Sloan.

***Tough Mazes 3: Monuments & Landscapes.** Illus. by Scott Sullivan. (Troubador Ser.). 32p. (J). (ps up). 1997. reprint ed. pap. 3.50 (0-8431-7962-7) Price Stern Sloan.

Tough-Minded Faith for Tender Hearted People. Robert H. Schuller. 384p. 1985. mass mkt. 5.99 (0-553-24704-2) Bantam.

Tough-Minded Leadership. Joe D. Batten. 240p. 1991. pap. 15.95 (0-8144-7761-5) AMACOM.

Tough-Minded Management: A Guide for Managers Who Are Too Nice for Their Own Good. Gareth Gardiner. 208p. 1993. pap. 10.00 (0-449-90771-6, Columbine) Fawcett.

Tough Minded Management of Problem Employees. Gareth Gardiner. 1991. pap. 10.95 (0-9623414-0-1) Smith Collins.

Tough-Minded Management of Problem Employees: Don't Be a Gutless Nice Guy. Gareth S. Gardiner. Ed. by Gwyneth M. Vaughn. (Managerial Action Ser.). (Illus.). 175p. (Orig.). 1989. pap. 10.95 (0-685-26433-5) Smith Collins.

***Tough-Minded Optimist.** Norman Vincent Peale. 1996. pap. 10.00 (0-449-91202-7) Fawcett.

Tough Minded Optimist. Norman Vincent Peale. 1986. mass mkt. 5.99 (0-449-21171-1) Fawcett.

Tough-Minded Parenting. Joe D. Batten. 224p. 1991. 14.99 (0-8054-6048-9, 4260-48) Broadman.

Tough on Crime Myth: Real Solutions to Cut Crime. Peter T. Elikann. (Illus.). 310p. (C). 1996. 25.95 (0-306-45403-3, Plenum Insight) Plenum.

Tough Plants for Tough Places: How to Grow 101 Easy-Care Plants for Every Part of Your Yard. Peter H. Loewer. Date not set. pap. 15.95 (0-87596-730-2) Rodale Pr Inc.

Tough Plastics. 178p. 1992. 2,350.00 (0-89336-910-1, P-128) BCC.

Tough Questions: Talking Straight with Your Kids about the Real World. Sheila Kitzinger. Ed. by Celia Kitzinger. 336p. 1995. mass mkt. 5.99 (0-425-14730-4) Berkley Pub.

Tough Questions: Talking Straight with Your Kids about the Real World. Sheila Kitzinger & Celia Kitzinger. 320p. 1991. 19.95 (1-55832-033-4) Harvard Common Pr.

***Tough Questions, Great Answers: Responding to Patient Concerns about Today's Dentistry.** Robin Wright. LC 97-19573. (Illus.). 100p. 1997. write for info. (0-86715-320-2) Quint Pub Co.

Tough Romance. Pier G. Di Cicco. 1990. pap. 9.00 (0-920717-03-9) Guernica Editions.

Tough Roots. Jean McCallion. 78p. 1987. 9.95 (0-920806-94-5, Pub. by Penumbra Pr CN) U of Toronto Pr.

Tough Row to Hoe. Ray V. Pryor, Jr. LC 88-70099. 184p. (Orig.). 1988. pap. 5.95 (0-916383-49-0) Aegina Pr.

Tough Stuff. Sam Huff. 1989. pap. 3.95 (0-312-91700-7) St Martin.

***Tough Talk & Tender Kisses.** Deborah Camp. 384p. (Orig.). 1997. mass mkt. 5.99 (0-380-78250-2) Avon.

Tough Talk to a Stubborn Spouse. Stephen Schwambach. (Orig.). 1990. pap. 9.99 (0-89081-783-9) Harvest Hse.

Tough Talking: How to Handle Awkward Situations. David Martin. (Institute of Management Ser.). 192p. (Orig.). 1993. pap. 42.50 (0-273-60163-6, Pub. by Pitman Pub Ltd UK) Trans-Atl Phila.

***Tough Target: A Street-Smart Guide to Staying Safe.** J. J. Bettenbinder. 1997. 18.95 (0-7624-0090-0) Running Pr.

***Tough Tender.** Max A. Collins. 4.95 (0-7867-0774-7) Carroll & Graf.

Tough Tender. Max A. Collins. 368p. 1991. pap. 4.95 (0-88184-774-7) Carroll & Graf.

Tough Terminators. Sneed Collard. LC 93-19627. (J). (gr. 1-5). 1994. 9.95 (1-55971-223-6) NorthWord.

Tough Times. Jim Boulden & Joan Boulden. (Illus.). 32p. (Orig.). (J). (gr. 1-6). 1993. pap. 5.95 (1-878076-29-9) Boulden Pub.

Tough Times. Robert H. Schuller. LC 93-12207. (Itty Bitty Bk.). 1993. 4.99 (0-8407-6309-3) Nelson.

Tough Times for Father Bear. Christa Wisskirchen. (Illus.). 32p. (J). 1995. 12.95 (0-7892-0070-8, Abbeville Kids) Abbeville Pr.

Tough Times in Rough Places: Personal Narratives of Adventure, Death & Survival on the Western Frontier. Ed. by Neil B. Carmony & David E. Brown. LC 92-71023. (Illus.). 296p. 1995. reprint ed. pap. 14.95 (0-944383-26-2) High-Lonesome.

***Tough Times Never Last but Tough People Do!** Robert Schuller. 1996. 16.99 (0-7852-7167-8) Nelson.

Tough Times Never Last but Tough People Do! Robert H. Schuller. 256p. 1984. 5.99 (0-553-27332-9) Bantam.

***Tough Times, Strong Women.** Taste of Home Staff. 1997. 14.95 (0-89821-203-0) Reiman Pubns.

Tough Times, Tough People, & a Good God. David T. Demola. 230p. (Orig.). 1994. pap. 8.95 (0-88270-716-7) Bridge-Logos.

Tough to Reach, Tough to Teach: Students with Behavior Problems. Sylvia Rockwell. LC 92-43363. 106p. 1993. pap. text ed. 24.00 (0-86586-235-4, P387) Coun Exc Child.

Tough to Tackle. Matt Christopher. (Illus.). 152p. (YA). (gr. 4-6). 1987. mass mkt. 3.95 (0-316-14058-9) Little.

Tough Trip Through Paradise. Andrew Garcia. LC 66-14758. (Illus.). 1976. pap. 7.95 (0-89174-008-2) Comstock Edns.

Toughboy & Sister. Kirkpatrick Hill. 128p. (J). (gr. 3-7). 1992. pap. 3.99 (0-14-034866-2) Puffin Bks.

Toughboy & Sister. Kirkpatrick Hill. LC 90-31297. 128p. (J). (gr. 3-7). 1990. lib. bdg. 15.00 (0-689-50506-X, McElderry) S&S Childrens.

Toughened Composites. Ed. by Norman J. Johnson. LC 87-1387. (Special Technical Publication Ser.: No. 937). (Illus.). 478p. 1987. text ed. 69.00 (0-8031-0934-2, 04-937000-33) ASTM.

***Toughened Plastics II: Novel Approaches in Science & Engineering.** American Chemical Society Staff et al. Ed. by C. Keith Riew & Anthony J. Kinloch. LC 96-38478. (Advances in Chemistry Ser.: Vol. 252). 384p. 1996. 149.95 (0-8412-3151-6) Am Chem Soc.

Toughened Plastics, No. 1: Science & Engineering. Ed. by C. Keith Riew & Anthony J. Kinloch. LC 92-34578. (Advances in Chemistry Ser.: Vol. 233). (Illus.). 589p. 1992. 139.95 (0-8412-2500-1) Am Chemical.

Toughening Mechanisms in Quasi-Brittle Materials. Ed. by Surendra P. Shah. (C). 1991. lib. bdg. 225.50 (0-7923-1198-1) Kluwer Ac.

Toughest Days of Grief. Meg Woodson. 192p. 1994. pap. 9.99 (0-310-40001-5) Zondervan.

Toughest Days of Grief. Meg Woodson. 240p. 1995. mass mkt. 5.99 (0-06-104364-8, Harp PBks) HarpC.

Toughest Job in Baseball: What Managers Do, How They Do It & Why It Gives Them Ulcers. Peter Pascarelli. LC 93-16572. 288p. 1993. 21.00 (0-671-79331-4) S&S Trade.

Toughing It. Nancy Springer. LC 93-42231. 144p. (YA). (gr. 7 up). 1994. 11.00 (0-15-200008-9); pap. 4.95 (0-15-200011-9) HarBrace.

Toughing out Tourette's & ADHD-ADD. Intro. by Joan E. Murphy. 240p. (Orig.). 1989. pap. text ed. 12.00 (0-9625194-0-5) Baton Rouge Tourette Grp.

Toughlove. Yorks & Ted Wachtel. 256p. 1985. mass mkt. 5.99 (0-553-26783-3) Bantam.

Toughlove: Beyond the Last Straw. David York & Phyllis York. Ed. by Margaret Bynum & Nate Rosenblatt. 48p. (Orig.). 1989. student ed. 20.00 (0-685-29991-0) Natl Ctr Personal Dev.

Toughlove for Education: How Accreditation Has Hurt Our Schools & What to Do about It. Charles A. Manning. 120p. 1997. pap. 16.95 (1-880153-88-2) AmericaWORKS.

Toughlove Solutions. Phyllis York & Wachtel. 208p. 1985. mass mkt. 5.99 (0-553-27439-2) Bantam.

Toughness & Brittleness of Plastics. Ed. by Rudolph D. Deanin & Aldo M. Crugnola. LC 76-41267. (Advances in Chemistry Ser.: No. 154). 1976. 54.95 (0-8412-0221-4) Am Chemical.

***Toughness & Brittleness of Plastics.** Ed. by Rudolph D. Deanin & Aldo M. Crugnola. LC 76-41267. (Advances in Chemistry Ser.: Vol. 154). 423p. 1976. pap. 120.60 (0-608-03861-X, 2064308) Bks Demand.

Toughness & Fracture Behavior of Titanium - STP 651. Ed. by R. G. Broadwell & C. F. Hickey. 294p. 1978. 28.50 (0-8031-0591-6, 04-651000-30) ASTM.

Toughness Characterization & Specifications for HSLA & Structural Steels: Proceedings of a Symposium. Metallurgical Society of AIME Staff. Ed. by P. L. Mangonon. LC 79-52169. 394p. reprint ed. pap. 112.30 (0-317-42102-6, 2026227) Bks Demand.

Toughness of Ferritic Stainless Steels, Vol. STP 706. Ed. by R. Lula. 348p. 1980. 32.50 (0-8031-0792-7, 04-706000-02) ASTM.

Toughness Requirements for Steels: An International Compendium. C. S. Wiesner. (Illus.). 178p. 1993. pap. 185.00 (1-85573-132-0, Pub. by Woodhead Pubng UK) Am Educ Systs.

Toughness Training for Life: A Revolutionary Program for Maximizing Health, Happiness, & Productivity. James E. Loehr. 320p. 1994. pap. 12.95 (0-452-27243-2, Plume) NAL-Dutton.

Toughy. Alberta R. Metz. (Illus.). 94p. (Orig.). (J). (gr. 4-7). Date not set. pap. 4.99 (0-89827-009-X, BKF63) Wesleyan Pub Hse.

"Toughy" Learns to Fight. Alberta R. Metz. (Illus.). 101p. (Orig.). (J). (gr. 4-7). Date not set. pap. 3.95 (0-89827-056-1, BKF64) Wesleyan Pub Hse.

***Touhami Ennadre: Black Light Lumiere Noire Shwarzes Licht.** Photos by Touhami Ennadre. (Illus.). 128p. 1997. 55.00 (3-7913-1735-0, Pub. by Prestel GW) te Neues.

Toujours Cricklewood? Alan Coren. 1995. pap. 10.95 (0-86051-941-4, Robson-Parkwest) Parkwest Pubns.

Toujours Provence. Peter Mayle. 1991. 23.00 (0-679-40253-5) Knopf.

***Toujours Provence.** Peter Mayle. 1997. 3.99 (0-517-18011-1) Random Hse Value.

Toujours Provence. Peter Mayle. 1992. pap. 11.00 (0-679-73604-2, Vin) Random.

***Toujours Provence.** Peter Mayle. 1991. pap. 15.95 (1-55927-183-3) St Martin.

Toujours Provence. large type ed. Peter Mayle. 336p. 1991. reprint ed. lib. bdg. 22.95 (1-56054-262-4) Thorndike Pr.

***Toulon City Plan.** (Grafocarte Maps Ser.). 1995. 8.95 (2-7416-0039-2, 80039) Michelin.

Toulouse: The Story of a Canada Goose. Priscilla Cummings. (Chadwick the Crab Ser.). (Illus.). 28p. (J). (gr. 1-3). 1996. bds. 9.95 (0-87033-460-3, Tidewtr Pubs) Cornell Maritime.

***Toulouse City Plan.** (Grafocarte Maps Ser.). 1995. 8.95 (2-7416-0040-6, 80040) Michelin.

***Toulouse-Lautrec.** Matthias Arnold. 1994. pap. text ed. 9.99 (3-8228-9641-1) Taschen Amer.

Toulouse-Lautrec. Douglas Cooper. (Masters of Art Ser.). 1983. 22.95 (0-8109-1678-9) Abrams.

Toulouse-Lautrec. Bernard Denvir. LC 90-71451. (World of Art Ser.). (Illus.). 216p. (Orig.). 1991. pap. 14.95 (0-500-20250-8) Thames Hudson.

Toulouse-Lautrec. Julia Frey. 680p. 1994. pap. 34.95 (0-670-80844-X, Viking) Viking Penguin.

Toulouse Lautrec. Julia Frey. 1999. pap. 14.95 (0-14-024750-5) Viking Penguin.

Toulouse-Lautrec. Tony Hart. LC 93-22146. (Famous Children Ser.). (Illus.). 24p. (J). (ps-3). 1994. pap. 5.95 (0-8120-1825-7) Barron.

Toulouse-Lautrec. Francois Le Target. (Grandes Monografias). (Illus.). 200p. (SPA.). 1993. 200.00 (84-343-0541-0) Elliots Bks.

Toulouse-Lautrec. Jesse McDonald. 1994. 5.98 (0-7858-0209-6) Bk Sales Inc.

Toulouse-Lautrec. Frank Milner. (Gallery of Art Ser.). (Illus.). 176p. 1992. 19.98 (0-8317-5449-4) Smithmark.

Toulouse-Lautrec. Richard Thomson et al. 557p. 1992. 70.00 (0-300-05190-5); pap. 50.00 (0-300-05196-4) Yale U Pr.

Toulouse-Lautrec. Edward Lucie-Smith. (Color Library). (Illus.). 128p. (C). 1994. reprint ed. pap. 14.95 (0-7148-2761-4, Pub. by Phaidon Press UK) Chronicle Bks.

Toulouse-Lautrec. Henri Perruchot. (Illus.). 320p. 1994. reprint ed. pap. 33.50 (0-09-473720-7, Pub. by Constable Pubs UK) Trans-Atl Phila.

Toulouse-Lautrec: A Retrospective. Gale B. Murray. (Illus.). 384p. 1992. 75.00 (0-88363-492-9) H L Levin.

Toulouse-Lautrec: Catlogue Complet des Estampes. Wittrock. 832p. (FRE.). 1991. 895.00 (0-8288-7316-X, 2867700140) Fr & Eur.

Toulouse-Lautrec: Scenes of the Night. Claire Freches. (Discoveries Ser.). (Illus.). 1994. pap. 12.95 (0-8109-2863-9) Abrams.

Toulouse-Lautrec: The Baldwin M. Baldwin Collection, San Diego Museum of Art. Nora Desloge. 1989. pap. 29.95 (0-937108-07-3) San Diego Museum of Art.

Toulouse-Lautrec: The Complete Prints, 2 vols. Wolfgang Wittrock. LC 85-50981. (Illus.). 830p. 1985. Set. 395.00 (0-85667-192-4) Sothebys Pubns.

Toulouse-Lautrec: The Formative Years, 1878-1891. Gale B. Murray. (Clarendon Studies in the History of Art). (Illus.). 289p. 1991. 130.00 (0-19-817505-1) OUP.

***Toulouse-Lautrec: The Soul of Montmarte.** Reinhold Heller. LC 97-3739. (Pegasus Library). (Illus.). 128p. 1997. 25.00 (3-7913-1739-3, Pub. by Prestel GW) te Neues.

***Toulouse-Lautrec: The Soul of Montmartre.** Reinhold Heller. LC 97-3739. (Pegasus Library). 1997. write for info. (3-7913-1792-X, Pub. by Prestel GW) te Neues.

Toulouse-Lautrec & His Contemporaries: Posters of the Belle Epoque. Ebria Feinblatt & Bruce Davis. (Illus.). 264p. 1986. 35.00 (0-685-12115-1) Abrams.

Toulouse-Lautrec in the Metropolitan Museum of Art. Colta Ives. LC 96-17722. (Illus.). 96p. 1996. pap. 14.95 (0-87099-804-8) Metro Mus Art.

Toulouse the Goose & Other Ridiculous Stories. Robert F. Karolevitz. LC 85-62753. (Illus.). 140p. (Orig.). 1985. pap. 7.95 (0-940161-00-1) Dakota Homestead Pub.

Toulouse the Mouse. Gale Brennan. (Illus.). 16p. (Orig.). (J). (gr. k-6). 1981. pap. 1.25 (0-685-02458-X) Brennan Bks.

Toumba Tou Skourou: A Bronze Age Potter's Quarter on Morphou Bay in Cyprus. Emily D. Vermeule & Florence Z. Wolsky. LC 90-5127. (Illus.). 522p. 1991. 100.00 (0-674-89635-1, VERTOU) HUP.

Tour: New & Selected Poems. Peter Sears. LC 87-5196. 125p. 1987. pap. 8.95 (0-932576-49-4) Breitenbush Bks.

Tour Book for Antique Car Buffs. 2nd ed. Richard E. Osborne. LC 94-67962. (Illus.). 304p. (Orig.). 1994. per. 12.00 (0-9628324-2-1) Riebel Roque.

Tour de Babel, Vol. 11. Fernando Arrabal. 120p. (FRE.). 1976. pap. 13.95 (0-8288-9024-2) Fr & Eur.

Tour de Force. Christianna Brand. 272p. 1988. pap. 3.95 (0-88184-439-X) Carroll & Graf.

Tour de Force. Christianna Brand. 272p. 1996. mass mkt. 4.95 (0-7867-0340-7) Carroll & Graf.

Tour de France. (Illus.). 64p. (Orig.). 1992. pap. 9.95 (1-880682-03-6) Winning Intl.

Tour de France. Skip Berry. (Great Moments in Sports Ser.). (YA). (gr. 5 up). 1992. lib. bdg. 14.95 (0-88682-539-3) Creative Ed.

Tour de France. Rene De Goscinny & M. Uderzo. (Illus.). (GER.). (J). 1990. 19.95 (0-8288-4907-2) Fr & Eur.

Tour De France: The 75th Anniversary Bicycle Race. Robin Magowan. (Illus.). 208p. 1996. pap. 14.95 (1-884737-13-7) VeloPress.

Tour de France: Three Weeks to Glory. Samuel Abt. LC 91-70410. (Illus.). 192p. 1991. 22.95 (0-933201-40-0) Motorbooks Intl.

Tour de France Complete Book of Cycling. David Chauner & Michael Halstead. (Illus.). 256p. 1990. pap. 15.95 (0-679-72936-4, Villard Bks) Random.

Tour de France D'Un Chasseur de Champignons. Jean-Jack Martin. (Livres Gourmands et Beaux Livres Collection). (Illus.). 160p. (FRE.). 1995. 79.95 (2-86808-093-6) Intl Scholars.

Tour de France '86: The American Invasion. Don Alexander & Jim Ochowicz. (Illus.). 192p. (Orig.). 1986. pap. 19.95 (0-939353-01-6) Alexander & Alexander.

Tour de Gaulle. Rene De Goscinny & M. Uderzo. (Illus.). (FRE.). (J). 19.95 (0-8288-4908-0) Fr & Eur.

Tour de Gaulle. Rene De Goscinny. (FRE.). (J). (gr. 3-8). 1990. 19.95 (0-8288-4909-9) Fr & Eur.

Tour de Grammaire: A Study Guide for French Grammar. 2nd ed. Karen W. Sandler & Susan Whitebook. 318p. (ENG & FRE.). (C). 1985. pap. text ed. 32.36 (0-669-07637-6) HM College Div.

Tour de la Prison. Marguerite Yourcenar. 187p. (FRE.). 1991. 34.95 (0-7859-0553-7, 207072204X) Fr & Eur.

Tour de Monde en Quatre-Vingts Jours, Verne: Critical Monographs in English. Timothy Unwin. 88p. 1993. pap. 32.00 (0-85261-292-3, Pub. by Univ of Glasgow UK) St Mut.

Tour de Taste. Ed. by Manya Winsted. 80p. (Orig.). 1991. pap. 5.95 (0-9625961-0-8) PHG AZ.

Tour des Miracles. Georges Brassens. (FRE.). 1973. pap. 15.95 (0-7859-3426-X, 226400486X) Fr & Eur.

Tour Design, Marketing, & Management. James M. Poynter. LC 92-15906. 400p. 1992. text ed. 63.00 (0-13-205345-4) P-H.

Tour du Calendrier. G. Bishop. (C). 1988. 45.00 (0-85950-831-5, Pub. by S Thornes Pubs UK) St Mut.

Tour du Monde en Quatre-Vingts Jours. Jules Verne. (Folio - Junior Ser.: No. 521). (Illus.). 333p. (FRE.). (J). (gr. 5-10). 1988. pap. 10.95 (2-07-033521-6) Schoenhof.

Tour du Monde en 80 Jours. Jules Verne. pap. 8.95 (0-685-37136-0) Fr & Eur.

Tour du Monde en 80 Jours. Jules Verne. (Illus.). 442p. (FRE.). 1990. pap. 10.95 (0-7859-1483-8, 2266033522) Fr & Eur.

Tour du Monde en 80 Jours. Jules Verne. (FRE.). 1984. pap. 10.95 (0-7859-2854-5) Fr & Eur.

Tour du Monde en 80 Jours. unabridged ed. Verne. (FRE.). pap. 7.95 (2-87714-213-2, Pub. by Bookking Intl FR) Distribks Inc.

Tour from the City of New York to Detroit in the Michigan Territory. William Darby. 1988. reprint ed. lib. bdg. 49.00 (0-317-90011-0) Rprt Serv.

Tour from the City of New York to Detroit in the Michigan Territory, Made Between the Second of May & the 22nd of September, 1818, Etc. William Darby. 1977. reprint ed. 49.00 (0-403-07894-6) Scholarly.

Tour Guide of Computing at Northeast Iowa Community College. 7th ed. Joyce M. Dick et al. (C). 1995. 22.50 (0-256-21256-2) Irwin.

Tour Guide to Historic Sites of the Texas-Mexico Border. Ed. by Art Gomez. (Illus.). 27p. (Orig.). 1992. pap. 1.25 (0-912001-18-6) Big Bend.

Tour Guide to the Civil War. 4th rev. ed. Alice Cromie. LC 92-22746. (Illus.). 336p. (Orig.). 1992. pap. 12.95 (1-55853-200-5) Rutledge Hill Pr.

Tour in America in Seventeen Ninety-Eight, Seventeen Ninety-Nine, & 1800..., 2 vols. Richard Parkinson. (BCL1 - U. S. History Ser.). 1991. reprint ed. Set. lib. bdg. 150.00 (0-7812-6014-0) Rprt Serv.

***Tour in Lapland.** Carl Linnaeus. Date not set. 45.95 (0-405-01717-0) Arno Press.

Tour in Scotland in Eighteen Hundred Three. Dorothy Wordsworth. 260p. (C). 1986. 60.00 (0-901824-29-1, Pub. by Mercat Pr Bks UK) St Mut.

Tour in Scotland, 1817: And Other Manuscript Notes. Washington Irving. (BCL1-PS American Literature Ser.). 1992. reprint ed. lib. bdg. 79.00 (0-7812-6756-0) Rprt Serv.

Tour of Danger. Carolyn Keene. Ed. by Anne Greenberg. (Nancy Drew & Hardy Boys Supermystery Ser.). 224p. (Orig.). (J). 1992. mass mkt. 3.99 (0-671-67468-4) PB.

Tour of Four Great Rivers: Hudson, Mohawk, Susquehanna, & Delaware. Richard Smith. 102p. 1993. reprint ed. lib. bdg. 69.00 (0-7812-5135-4) Rprt Serv.

Tour of Mendocino: Thirty-Two Historic Buildings along the Streets of Mendocino. 4th rev. ed. Dorothy Bear & Beth Stebbins. (Illus.). 32p. 1991. reprint ed. pap. 6.00 (0-939431-06-8) Bored Feet Pubns.

Tour of Modern Geometry. Herbert Holden. (C). 1997. text ed. write for info. (0-201-87997-2) Addison-Wesley.

Tour of Pendleton's Historic Homes. Keith F. May. (Illus.). 72p. (Orig.). 1995. pap. 9.95 (1-57502-090-4) Morris Pubng.

Tour of Scotland (Seventeen Ninety-Six) Thomas Pennant. 496p. (C). 1986. 42.00 (0-685-30236-9, Pub. by Mercat Pr Bks UK) St Mut.

Tour of the Calculus. David Berlinski. LC 95-4042. 352p. 1996. 27.50 (0-679-42645-0) Pantheon.

***Tour of the Calculus.** David Berlinski. 1997. pap. 14.00 (0-679-74788-5, Vin) Random.

***Tour of the Calculus.** David Berlinski. 1997. pap. 14.00 (0-676-52041-3, Vin) Random.

T

Tour of the Highlands in Eighteen Hundred Three. James Hogg. 118p. (C). 1986. 45.00 (*0-901824-80-1*, Pub. by Mercat Pr Bks UK) St Mut.

Tour of the Planets. Melvin Berger. Ed. by Natalie Lunis. (Ranger Rick Science Spectacular Ser.). 16p. (J). (gr. 2-4). 1994. pap. 14.95 (*1-56784-207-0*) Newbridge Comms.

Tour of the Planets: Student Book. Melvin Berger. Ed. by Natalie Lunis. (Ranger Rick Science Spectacular Ser.). (Illus.). 16p. (Orig.). (J). (gr. 2-4). 1996. pap. write for info. (*1-56784-232-1*) Newbridge Comms.

***Tour of the Planets: Theme Pack.** Melvin Berger. Ed. by Natalie Lunis. (Ranger Rick Science Spectacular Ser.). (Illus.). (Orig.). (J). (gr. 2-4). 1996. pap. write for info. (*1-56784-279-8*) Newbridge Comms.

Tour of the Subatomic Zoo: A Guide to Particle Physics. 2nd ed. Cindy Schwarz. (Illus.). 150p. (Orig.). (C). 1996. pap. text ed. 29.95 (*1-56396-617-4*) Spr-Verlag.

Tour of the Subatomic Zoo: An Introduction to Particle Physics. Cindy Schwarz. LC 92-12366. 128p. 1992. 25.00 (*0-88318-954-2*) Spr-Verlag.

Tour of the Summa. Paul J. Glenn. LC 78-66307. 1992. reprint ed. pap. 18.00 (*0-89555-081-4*) TAN Bks Pubs.

Tour of the United States of America Containing an Account of the Present Situation in That Country, 2 Vols. John F. Smyth. LC 67-29020. (Eyewitness Accounts of the American Revolution Ser., No. 1). 1968. reprint ed. Set. 36.95 (*0-405-01134-2*) Ayer.

Tour of the United States of America Containing an Account of the Present Situation in That Country, 2 Vols., Vol. 1. John F. Smyth. LC 67-29020. (Eyewitness Accounts of the American Revolution Ser., No. 1). 1968. reprint ed. 19.95 (*0-405-01122-9*) Ayer.

Tour of the United States of America Containing an Account of the Present Situation in That Country, 2 Vols., Vol. 2. John F. Smyth. LC 67-29020. (Eyewitness Accounts of the American Revolution Ser., No. 1). 1968. reprint ed. 19.95 (*0-405-01129-6*) Ayer.

Tour on the Prairies. Washington Irving. LC 56-11232. (Illus.). 256p. (Orig.). 1985. pap. 10.95 (*0-8061-1958-6*) U of Okla Pr.

Tour the San Juans Vol. II: E Z Guide. (Illus.). 248p. (Orig.). 1995. pap. 12.95 (*0-9643172-1-4*) Tour San Juans.

Tour Thro' London about the Year 1725. Daniel Defoe. Ed. by Mayson M. Beeton & E. Beresford Chancellor. LC 68-56542. (Illus.). 144p. 1972. reprint ed. 33.95 (*0-405-08441-2*, Pub. by Blom Pubns UK) Ayer.

Tour Through North America: Together with a Comprehensive View of the Canada & United States, As Adapted for Agricultural Emigration. Patrick Shirreff. LC 75-173121. 1972. reprint ed. 30.95 (*0-405-08970-8*) Ayer.

Tour Through Part of the North Provinces of America. P. M'Robert. LC 67-29039. (Eyewitness Accounts of the American Revolution Ser., No. 1). 1979. reprint ed. 17.95 (*0-405-01136-9*) Ayer.

Tour Through the Exhibition. Gunther Behnisch. 1994. pap. 35.00 (*3-7757-0480-9*, Pub. by Gerd Hatje GW) Dist Art Pubs.

Tour Through the Famine Districts of India. F. H. Merewether. 1986. reprint ed. 34.00 (*0-8364-1615-5*, Pub. by Usha II) S Asia.

Tour Through the Southern & Western Territories of the United States of North-America: The Spanish Dominions on the River Mississippi, & the Floridas; the Countries of the Creek Nations; & Many Uninhabited Parts. John Pope. Ed. by J. Barton Starr. LC 78-26408. (Floridiana Facsimile & Reprint Ser.). 1979. reprint ed. 19.95 (*0-8130-0418-7*) U Press Fla.

Tour Through the Southern & Western Territories of the United States of North America, the Spanish Dominions on the River Mississippi & the Floridas, the Countries of the Creek Nations, & Many Uninhabited Parts. John Pope. LC 70-146411. (First American Frontier Ser.). 1971. reprint ed. 13.95 (*0-405-02875-X*) Ayer.

Tour Through the Whole Island of Great Britain. Daniel Defoe. Ed. & Abr. by Pat Rogers. 736p. 1978. pap. 13.95 (*0-14-043066-0*, Penguin Classics) Viking Penguin.

Tour Through the Whole Island of Great Britain. abr. ed. Daniel Defoe. Ed. by P. N. Furbank et al. (Illus.). 432p. (C). 1991. text ed. 47.50 (*0-300-04980-3*) Yale U Pr.

Tour to New Connecticut in 1811: The Narrative of Henry Leavitt Ellsworth. Ed. by Phillip R. Shriver. 141p. 1985. 11.95 (*0-911704-32-9*) Western Res.

Tour to Sheeraz by the Route of Kazroon & Feerozabad. Edward S. Waring. LC 73-6309. (Middle East Ser.). 1973. reprint ed. 25.95 (*0-405-05370-3*) Ayer.

Tourer & GT Drive Handbk. 68. Robert Bentley. 1994. pap. 16.00 (*0-8376-0585-7*) Bentley.

Tourette Syndrome & Human Behavior. David E. Comings. LC 89-83294. (Illus.). 828p. 1990. 49.95 (*1-878267-27-2*); pap. 39.95 (*1-878267-28-0*) Hope Pr CA.

Tourette's & Attention Deficit Hyperactivity Disorder: Toughing It out at Home & at School. Ed. & Intro. by Joan E. Murphy. 218p. (Orig.). 1995. pap. 18.00 (*0-9625194-1-3*) Baton Rouge Tourette Grp.

Tourette's Syndrome: Index of Modern Authors & Subjects with Guide for Rapid Research. rev. ed. Jesse S. Winograd. LC 92-27855. 180p. 1992. 47.50 (*1-55914-752-0*); pap. 44.50 (*1-55914-753-9*) ABBE Pubs Assn.

Tourette's Syndrome & Tic Disorders: Clinical Understanding & Treatment. Donald J. Cohen. LC 87-29449. (Child & Adolescent Mental Health Ser.). 380p. 1988. text ed. 80.00 (*0-471-62924-3*) Wiley.

Tourgueniev. Andre Maurois. (Coll. Grandes Figures Litteraires). pap. 16.50 (*0-685-36964-1*) Fr & Eur.

Touring Bikes: A Practical Guide. Tony Oliver. (Illus.). 176p. 1991. 39.95 (*1-85223-339-7*, Pub. by Crowood Pr UK) Trafalgar.

Touring British Antique Shops. Carol Fisher. 1996. pap. text ed. 19.95 (*0-9519653-2-8*, Pub. by C Fisher Adver UK) Seven Hills Bk.

***Touring California & Nevada Hot Springs.** Matt C. Bischoff. (Illus.). 168p. (Orig.). 1997. pap. 16.95 (*1-56044-578-5*) Falcon Pr MT.

Touring California's Wine Country by Bicycle: Cycling in the Wine Growing Regions of North & Central California. Peter Powers. 174p. 1990. pap. 10.95 (*0-944376-06-1*) Terragraphics.

Touring Caravans. Jon Pressnell. 1989. pap. 25.00 (*0-7478-0119-3*, Pub. by Shire UK) St Mut.

Touring Club: Italy. Ed. by Dunbar. (Illus.). 448p. 1997. pap. 25.00 (*1-885254-26-1*) Monacelli Pr.

Touring Club of Italy - Florence: The Surrounding Countryside & the Chianti Region. Touring Club of Italy Staff. (Illus.). 200p. 1997. pap. 16.95 (*1-885254-30-X*) Monacelli Pr.

***Touring Club of Italy - Rome & the Vatican: The Eternal City, with Its Museums, Churches, Landmarks & Archeological Sites.** Touring Club of Italy Staff. 1997. pap. 16.95 (*1-885254-61-X*) Monacelli Pr.

Touring Club of Italy - Venice: The Islands of Murano, Burano & Trcello, & the Villas of the Riviera del Brenta. Touring Club of Italy Staff. (Illus.). 200p. 1997. pap. 16.95 (*1-885254-31-8*) Monacelli Pr.

***Touring Cultures: Transformations of Travel & Theory.** Ed. by John Urry & Lancaster. 240p. (C). 1997. pap. 18.95 (*0-415-11125-0*); text ed. 65.00 (*0-415-11124-2*) Routledge.

Touring Exhibitions: The Touring Exhibitions Group's Manual of Good Practice. Ed. by Mike Sixsmith. LC 95-24198. (Illus.). 288p. 1995. pap. 69.95 (*0-7506-2518-X*) Buttrwrth-Heinemann.

Touring in Wine Country: Alsace. Ed. by Hugh Johnson. 1996. 21.95 (*1-85732-581-8*, Pub. by Reed Illust Books UK) Antique Collect.

***Touring in Wine Country: Bavaria.** Hugh Johnson & Stuart Pigott. (Touring in Wine Country Ser.). (Illus.). 144p. 21.95 (*1-85732-874-4*, Pub. by M Beazley Pubs Ltd UK) Antique Collect.

Touring in Wine Country: Bordeaux. Ed. by Hugh Johnson. 1996. 21.95 (*1-85732-558-3*, Pub. by Reed Illust Books UK) Antique Collect.

Touring in Wine Country: Burgundy. Ed. by Hugh Johnson. 1996. 21.95 (*1-85732-580-X*, Pub. by Reed Illust Books UK) Antique Collect.

***Touring in Wine Country: Northwest Italy.** Maureen Ashley. Ed. by Hugh Johnson. (Touring in Wine Country Ser.). (Illus.). 144p. 21.95 (*1-85732-864-7*, Pub. by M Beazley Pubs Ltd UK) Antique Collect.

***Touring in Wine Country: The Loire.** Hubrecht Duijker. Ed. by Hugh Johnson. (Touring in Wine Country Ser.). (Illus.). 144p. 21.95 (*1-85732-876-0*, Pub. by M Beazley Pubs Ltd UK) Antique Collect.

***Touring in Wine Country: The Mosel & Rheingau.** Hugh Johnson. (Touring in Wine Country Ser.). (Illus.). 144p. 21.95 (*1-85732-875-2*, Pub. by M Beazley Pubs Ltd UK) Antique Collect.

Touring in Wine Country: Tuscany. Ed. by Hugh Johnson. 1996. 21.95 (*1-85732-582-6*, Pub. by Reed Illust Books UK) Antique Collect.

Touring Jacob's Ladder Trail by Bicycle or Car. Bonnie Parsons & James M. Mazik. 126p. 1994. pap. 10.00 (*0-9643910-0-7*) Pioneer Valley.

***Touring Nam: Vietnam.** Martin Greenberg. 1997. pap. write for info. (*0-688-15388-7*, Quill) Morrow.

Touring New England by Bicycle: Cycling in Vermont, Maine & the Cape Islands. Peter Powers. 174p. (Orig.). 1991. pap. 10.95 (*0-944376-08-8*) Terragraphics.

Touring New Mexico. Polly Arango et al. LC 94-16724. 432p. (C). 1995. pap. 19.95 (*0-8263-1622-0*) U of NM Pr.

Touring North America, 13 vols. Ed. by Anthony R. De Souza. (Illus.). 1992. Set. pap. 129.95 (*0-8135-1907-1*) Rutgers U Pr.

Touring Pittsburgh by Trolley. Harold Smith. 1992. pap. 14.95 (*0-915276-48-8*) Quadrant Pr.

Touring Prose. L. Rubenstein. pap. 13.00 (*0-394-22331-4*) Random.

Touring Pullman. 2nd ed. William Adelman. LC 72-80226. 46p. 1977. pap. 3.95 (*0-685-02464-4*) Ill Labor Hist Soc.

Touring Seattle by Bicycle: Cycling in Seattle & the Lower Puget Sound Area. Peter Powers. 174p. (Orig.). 1994. pap. 10.95 (*0-944376-02-9*) Terragraphics.

Touring Southern Africa. Maxwell Leigh. (Illus.). 1990. pap. 20.00 (*0-87556-731-2*) Saifer.

Touring Tennessee: A Postcard Panorama, 1898-1995. Ridley Wills, II. LC 96-78433. 224p. 1996. 29.95 (*1-881576-98-1*, Hillsboro Pr) Providence Hse.

***Touring the Backroads of North & South Georgia.** Victoria Logue & Frank Logue. LC 97-19095. (Touring the Backroads Ser.). (Illus.). (Orig.). 1997. pap. 19.95 (*0-89587-171-8*) Blair.

Touring the Backroads of North Carolina's Lower Coast. Daniel Barefoot. LC 94-47828. (Touring the Backroads Ser.). (Illus.). 363p. (Orig.). 1996. pap. 15.95 (*0-89587-126-2*) Blair.

Touring the Backroads of North Carolina's Upper Coast. Daniel Barefoot. LC 94-40668. (Touring the Backroads Ser.). (Illus.). 365p. (Orig.). 1996. pap. 15.95 (*0-89587-125-4*) Blair.

***Touring the California Wine Country.** Dennis Schaefer. LC 97-17680. 250p. 1997. pap. 16.95 (*0-88415-159-X*, 5159) Gulf Pub.

Touring the Carolinas' Civil War Sites. Clint Johnson. LC 96-6236. (Orig.). 1996. pap. 19.95 (*0-89587-146-7*) Blair.

Touring the Coastal Georgia Backroads. Nancy Rhyne. LC 93-47130. (Touring the Backroads Ser.). (Illus.). 188p. (Orig.). 1994. pap. 14.95 (*0-89587-111-4*) Blair.

Touring the Coastal South Carolina Backroads. Nancy Rhyne. LC 91-41378. (Touring the Backroads Ser.). (Illus.). 276p. (Orig.). 1992. pap. 14.95 (*0-89587-090-8*) Blair.

Touring the East Tennessee Backroads. Carolyn Sakowski. LC 93-1078. (Touring the Backroads Ser.). (Illus.). 385p. (Orig.). 1993. pap. 14.95 (*0-89587-103-3*) Blair.

Touring the Giant's Rib: A Guide to the Niagara Escarpment. Lorina Stephens & Gary Stephens. (Illus.). 80p. (Orig.). pap. 18.95 (*1-55046-084-6*, Pub. by Boston Mills Pr CN) Genl Dist Srvs.

Touring the Islands: Bicycling in the San Juan, Gulf, & Vancouver Islands. Peter Powers & Renee Travis. 174p. (Orig.). 1994. pap. 12.95 (*0-944376-01-0*) Terragraphics.

Touring the Los Angeles Area by Bicycle: Cycling in Santa Barbara, Ventura, Los Angeles, Riverside & Orange Counties. Peter Powers. 174p. (Orig.). 1992. pap. 12.95 (*0-944376-09-6*) Terragraphics.

Touring the Middle Tennessee Backroads. Robert Brandt. LC 95-15101. (Touring the Backroads Ser.). (Illus.). 412p. (Orig.). 1995. pap. 16.95 (*0-89587-129-7*) Blair.

Touring the Newsroom: An Inside Look at Newspapers. Dick Haws. LC 93-12934. 106p. 1993. pap. text ed. 16.95 (*0-8138-2292-0*) Iowa St U Pr.

Touring the Old West. Kent Ruth. LC 86-19305. (Illus.). x, 218p. 1987. text ed. 26.00 (*0-8032-3881-9*) U of Nebr Pr.

Touring the Peak District & Derbyshire by Car. John Merrill. 60p. 1989. 50.00 (*0-907496-22-9*, Pub. by JNM Pubns UK) St Mut.

Touring the Pennsylvania Countryside by Bicycle: Cycling in Southeastern Pennsylvania & Western New Jersey. Peter Powers. 174p. (Orig.). 1992. pap. 12.95 (*0-944376-12-6*) Terragraphics.

Touring the Pueblos. Ron Swartley. (Illus.). 162p. (Orig.). 1993. pap. 10.95 (*0-9634309-1-2*) Frontier Image.

Touring the Pueblos. 2nd ed. Ron Swartley. (Illus.). 172p. (Orig.). 1994. pap. 10.95 (*0-9634309-3-9*) Frontier Image.

Touring the San Francisco Bay Area by Bicycle: Cycling in Marin, Contra Costa, San Mateo, Alameda, Santa Clara & Santa Cruz Counties. Peter Powers. 174p. (Orig.). 1994. pap. 11.95 (*0-944376-05-3*) Terragraphics.

Touring the Universe Through Binoculars: A Complete Astronomer's Guidebook. Phillip S. Harrington. LC 90-35740. (Science Editions Ser.). 294p. 1990. pap. text ed. 32.95 (*0-471-51337-7*) Wiley.

Touring the Washington D.C. Area by Bicycle: Cycling in Maryland, Virginia & D.C. Peter Powers. 1991. pap. 12.95 (*0-944376-07-X*) Terragraphics.

Touring the Western North Carolina Backroads. 2nd ed. Carolyn Sakowski. LC 95-35905. (Touring the Backroads Ser.). (Illus.). 285p. 1995. pap. 16.95 (*0-89587-134-3*) Blair.

Touring U. S. A. Eastern Edition: Flexible Day-by-Day Itineraries for Independent Travelers. 1992. pap. 16.00 (*0-679-02240-6*) Fodors Travel.

***Tourism.** Mathieson. 1997. pap. write for info. (*0-582-49475-3*, Pub. by Longman UK) Longman.

Tourism. Neil McBurney. LC 95-40082. (Professional Reading Skills Ser.). 1996. pap. write for info. (*0-13-186370-3*) P-H.

Tourism: A Community Approach. Peter E. Murphy. 260p. 1986. 42.50 (*0-416-39790-5*, 9612) Routledge Chapman & Hall.

Tourism: A Gender Analysis. Ed. by Vivian Kinnaird & Derek Hall. text ed. 49.95 (*0-470-22007-4*) Wiley.

Tourism: A Gender Analysis. Ed. by Vivian Kinnaird & Derek Hall. 218p. 1994. text ed. 58.00 (*0-471-94833-0*) Wiley.

Tourism: A New Perspective. Burns. 1995. pap. text ed. 32.00 (*0-13-191552-5*) P-H.

Tourism: An Exploration. 2nd ed. Jan Van Harssel. (Illus.). 348p. (C). 1986. text ed. 29.50 (*0-317-59111-8*, Ntl Pubs Blck); pap. text ed. 23.95 (*0-935920-33-1*, Ntl Pubs Blck) P-H.

Tourism: An Exploration. 3rd ed. Jan Van Harssel. LC 93-6381. 384p. (C). 1993. pap. text ed. 57.00 (*0-13-923343-1*) P-H Gen Ref & Trav.

***Tourism: An Introductory Framework.** Ray Youell. 304p. 1997. pap. 22.95 (*0-415-13185-5*, Pub. by Intl Thomson Busn UK) Inter Thomson.

***Tourism: An Introductory Framework.** Ray Youell. 256p. 1996. 59.00 (*0-415-13184-7*) Routledge.

***Tourism: Annual Statistics 1994.** European Communities Staff. 289p. 1997. pap. 50.00 (*92-827-9310-9*, CA-98-96-833-3A, Pub. by Europ Com UK) Bernan Associates.

Tourism: How Effective Management Makes the Difference. Roger Doswell. 240p. 1996. pap. 32.95 (*0-7506-2272-5*) Buttrwrth-Heinemann.

Tourism: Management of Facilities. Judy Slinn. 364p. (Orig.). 1992. pap. 33.50 (*0-7121-2043-2*, Pub. by Pitman Pub Ltd UK) Trans-Atl Phila.

Tourism: Principles & Practice. Chris Cooper et al. 384p. (Orig.). 1993. pap. 47.50 (*0-273-60118-0*, Pub. by Pitman Pub Ltd UK) Trans-Atl Phila.

Tourism: Principles, Practices, Philosophies. 7th ed. Robert W. McIntosh et al. 608p. 1994. text ed. 28.50 (*0-471-01557-1*) Wiley.

Tourism: The State of the Art. Ed. by A. V. Seaton. LC 94-9552. 1400p. 1994. text ed. 115.00 (*0-471-95092-0*) Wiley.

***Tourism: Towards a Behavioural Approach.** Y. Mansfeld. (Progress in Planning Ser.: Vol. 38). 1992. 66.00 (*0-08-042039-7*, Pergamon Pr) Elsevier.

Tourism Alternatives: Potential Problems in the Development of Tourism. Ed. by Valene L. Smith & William R. Eadington. 288p. 1997. pap. text ed. write for info. (*0-471-94881-0*) Wiley.

Tourism Alternatives: Potentials & Problems in the Development of Tourism. Ed. by Valene L. Smith & William R. Eadington. (International Academy for the Study of Tourism Ser.). 274p. (Orig.). (C). 1992. text ed. 39.95 (*0-8122-3148-1*); pap. text ed. 16.95 (*0-8122-1391-2*) U of Pa Pr.

***Tourism Analysis.** Smith. 1996. pap. 53.95 (*0-582-30150-5*, Pub. by Longman UK) Longman.

Tourism Analysis: A Handbook. 2nd ed. Stephen L. Smith. 336p. (C). 1995. text ed. 30.50 (*0-582-25160-5*) Longman.

Tourism & Communities: Process, Problems, & Solutions, Vol. 1. Ed. by Carole Rifkind. (Livability Digest Ser.: No. 1). 46p. 1981. pap. 6.00 (*0-317-44277-5*) Partners Livable.

***Tourism & Culture: An Applied Perspective.** Ed. by Erve Chambers. LC 96-41497. (SUNY Series in Advances in Applied Anthropology). 288p. (C). 1997. pap. text ed. 19.95 (*0-7914-3428-1*) State U NY Pr.

***Tourism & Culture: An Applied Perspective.** Ed. by Erve Chambers. LC 96-41497. (SUNY Series in Advances in Applied Anthropology). 288p. (C). 1997. text ed. 59.50 (*0-7914-3427-3*) State U NY Pr.

Tourism & Development: A Case Study of the Commonwealth Caribbean. John M. Bryden. LC 73-77260. 248p. reprint ed. pap. 70.70 (*0-317-26084-7*, 2024415) Bks Demand.

Tourism & Development in India. Suhita Chopra. (C). 1991. 27.00 (*81-7024-363-7*, Pub. by Ashish II) S Asia.

Tourism & Development in the Third World. John P. Lea. (Introductions to Development Ser.). 80p. (C). 1988. pap. 9.95 (*0-415-00671-6*) Routledge.

Tourism & Economic Development: Western European Experiences. 2nd ed. Ed. by Allan M. Williams & Gareth Shaw. 291p. 1992. pap. text ed. 37.95 (*0-470-21902-5*) Halsted Pr.

Tourism & Economic Development in Asia & Australasia. Carson L. Jenkins & Frank M. Go. LC 96-23789. (Tourism, Leisure & Recreation Ser.). 1997. write for info. (*1-85567-417-3*, Pub. by Pntr Pubs UK) Bks Intl VA.

Tourism & Economic Development in Eastern Europe & the Soviet Union. Ed. by Derek R. Hall. LC 00-91. 1991. text ed. 69.95 (*0-470-21758-8*) Halsted Pr.

Tourism & Economic Development in Eastern Europe & the Soviet Union. Derek R. Hall. LC 91-9122. 321p. 1993. text ed. 88.00 (*0-471-94616-8*) Wiley.

Tourism & Economic Development: Western European Experience. 2nd ed. Ed. by Allan William & Gareth Shaw. 291p. 1993. pap. text ed. 51.95 (*0-471-94794-6*) Wiley.

***Tourism & Health: Risks, Research & Responses.** Stephen Clift & Peter Grabowski. LC 96-39581. (Cutting Edge of Tourism Ser.). (Illus.). 256p. 1997. 90.00 (*1-85567-474-2*, Pub. by Pntr Pubs UK) Bks Intl VA.

***Tourism & Indigenous Peoples.** Ed. by Richard J. Butler & Tom Hinch. (Tourism & Hospitality Management Ser.). 352p. 1996. 59.00 (*0-415-12529-4*) Routledge.

***Tourism & Politics: Policy, Power & Place.** Colin M. Hall. 1996. pap. text ed. 30.00 (*0-471-96547-2*) Wiley.

***Tourism & Recreation in Rural Areas.** Richard Butler et al. LC 97-25520. 1997. write for info. (*0-471-97680-6*); pap. write for info. (*0-471-97825-6*) Wiley.

Tourism & Regional Growth. Ed. by Moheb A. Ghali. (Studies in Applied Regional Science: No. 11). 1977. pap. text ed. 60.00 (*90-207-0716-7*) Kluwer Ac.

Tourism & Religion. Boris Vukonic. (Tourism Social Science Ser.). 200p. 1996. text ed. 68.00 (*0-08-042561-5*, Pergamon Pr) Elsevier.

Tourism & Society. Selwyn. 1995. pap. text ed. 21.00 (*0-13-433426-4*) P-H.

Tourism & Spatial Transformation: Implications for Policy & Planning. Ed. by Ashworth & Dietvorst. 360p. 1996. 85.00 (*0-85198-981-0*) OUP.

***Tourism & Sustainability.** Ed. by M. J. Stabler. 416p. 1997. 90.00 (*0-85199-184-X*) OUP.

***Tourism & Sustainability: Critical Perspectives on the Developing World.** Martin Mowforth & Ian Munt. 288p. (C). 1998. text ed. 59.95 (*0-415-13763-2*, Routledge NY) Routledge.

***Tourism & Sustainability: Critical Perspectives on the Developing World.** Munt & Mowforth. 288p. (C). 1998. pap. 18.95 (*0-415-13764-0*, Routledge NY) Routledge.

***Tourism & the Hospitality Industry.** Joseph D. Fridgen. (Illus.). 368p. 1996. pap. write for info. (*0-86612-123-4*) Educ Inst Am Hotel.

Tourism & the Hotel & Catering Industries in the EC. Frans Van Kraay. LC 93-7263. (European Community Law Ser.). 208p. (C). 1993. text ed. 90.00 (*0-485-70011-5*, Pub. by Athlone Pr UK) Humanities.

Tourism & the Travel Industry: An Information Sourcebook. Peter M. Enggass. LC 87-37196. (Sourcebook Series in Business & Management). 160p. 1988. 35.00 (*0-89774-267-2*) Oryx Pr.

Tourism Community Relationships. Pearce et al. 330p. 1996. 67.00 (*0-08-042395-7*, Pergamon Pr) Elsevier.

Tourism, Crime & International Security Issues. Abraham Pizam & Yoel Mansfeld. LC 95-20449. 300p. 1996. text ed. 55.00 (*0-471-96107-8*) Wiley.

Tourism Destination Geography. Jackson. (Hospitality, Travel & Tourism Ser.). 1990. teacher ed., pap. 15.00 (*0-8273-3305-6*) Delmar.

Tourism Development. W. Gartner. (Hospitality, Travel & Tourism Ser.). 544p. 1996. text ed. 44.95 (*0-442-00893-7*) Van Nos Reinhold.

An Asterisk (*) at the beginning of an entry indicates that the title is appearing in BIP for the first time.

***Tourism Development: Environmental & Community Issues.** S. R. Wanhill. pap. text ed. 35.95 (*0-471-97116-2*) Wiley.

Tourism Development: Principles & Practices. 3rd rev. ed. A. K. Bhatia. (Illus.). 354p. 1985. text ed. 40.00 (*0-86590-543-6*, Pub. by Sterling Pubs II) Apt Bks.

Tourism Economics. Donald E. Lundberg et al. 256p. 1995. text ed. 42.95 (*0-471-57884-3*) Wiley.

Tourism, Ecotourism & Protected Areas. Hector Ceballos-Lascurain. 301p. (Orig.). 1996. pap. 35.00 (*2-8317-0124-4*, Pub. by IUCN SZ) Ecotourism Soc.

***Tourism, Ethnicity, & the State in Asian & Pacific Societies.** Ed. by Michel Picard & Robert E. Wood. LC 96-53034. (Illus.). 1997. text ed. 47.00 (*0-8248-1863-6*) UH Pr.

***Tourism, Ethnicity & the State in Asian & Pacific Societies.** Ed. by Michel Picard & Robert E. Wood. LC 96-53034. (Illus.). 1997. pap. text ed. 22.95 (*0-8248-1911-X*) UH Pr.

Tourism Geography. Davidoff. 1999. pap. text ed. 54.00 (*0-13-925397-1*) P-H.

Tourism Geography. Philip G. Davidoff et al. (Illus.). 650p. (Orig.). 1988. pap. text ed. 27.50 (*0-935920-48-X*, Ntl Pubs Blck) P-H.

Tourism Geography. 2nd ed. Phillip G. Davidoff et al. LC 94-47027. (C). 1995. pap. text ed. 61.00 (*0-13-148735-3*) P-H.

Tourism Geography Workbook. Philip G. Davidoff et al. 144p. 1992. pap. text ed. 37.40 (*0-13-923152-8*) P-H.

Tourism in Action. John Ward. 192p. 1991. pap. 45.00 (*0-7487-1180-5*, Pub. by Stanley Thornes UK) Trans-Atl Phila.

Tourism in Action. John Ward. 224p. (C). 1991. pap. 49.00 (*0-7478-1180-6*, Pub. by Stanley Thornes UK) Trans-Atl Phila.

***Tourism in Balance.** Sally Morgan. LC 97-6479. (Living for the Future Ser.). (J). 1998. write for info. (*0-531-14476-3*) Watts.

Tourism in Contemporary Society: An Introductory Text. Lloyd E. Hudman & Donald E. Hawkins. 304p. 1989. pap. text ed. 49.00 (*0-13-925447-1*) P-H.

***Tourism in Developing Countries.** Martin Opperman & Kye-Sung Chon. 180p. 1997. pap. 19.95 (*0-415-13939-2*) Inter Thomson.

Tourism in Europe. Rob Davidson. 224p. (Orig.). 1992. pap. 33.50 (*0-273-03829-X*, Pub. by Pitman Pub Ltd UK) Trans-Atl Phila.

Tourism in Europe: Structures & Developments. Ed. by W. Pompl & P. Lavery. 384p. (Orig.). 1993. pap. 50.00 (*0-85198-852-0*) CAB Intl.

Tourism in Garhwal Himalaya: With Special Reference to Mountaineering & Trekking in Uttarkashi & Chamoli Districts. Harshwanti Bisht. (C). 1995. 32.00 (*81-7387-006-3*, Pub. by Indus Pub II) S Asia.

Tourism in India. V. K. Gupta. 1987. 16.95 (*0-8121-2012-4*) Asia Bk Corp.

***Tourism in Major Cities.** Christopher M. Law. (Tourism & Hospitality Management Ser.). 256p. 1996. 59.00 (*0-415-08986-7*) Routledge.

Tourism in Spain. Ed. by M. T. Newton et al. (A CAB International Publication). 448p. 1996. 90.00 (*0-85198-929-2*, Pub. by CAB Intntl UK) OUP.

***Tourism in the Pacific.** Ed. by C. Michael Hall & Stephen J. Page. LC 96-44668. (Tourism & Hospitality Management Ser.). 304p. 1996. 59.00 (*0-415-12499-9*); pap. 22.95 (*0-415-12500-6*) Routledge.

***Tourism in the Pacific Rim.** Hall. 1995. pap. text ed. write for info. (*0-582-91343-8*, Pub. by Longman UK) Longman.

Tourism in the Third World: Christian Reflections. Ron O'Grady. LC 82-8227. 91p. (Orig.). reprint ed. pap. 26.00 (*0-8357-4076-5*, 2036766) Bks Demand.

Tourism Industry: An International Analysis. Ed. by M. T. Sinclair & M. J. Stabler. 256p. 1991. 70.00 (*0-85198-718-4*, Pub. by CAB Intntl UK) OUP.

Tourism Law. J. Corke. (C). 1989. 90.00 (*0-946139-96-2*, Pub. by Elm Pubns UK) St Mut.

Tourism Marketing: Service & Quality Management Perspectives. Eric Laws. 288p. (Orig.). 1991. pap. 47.50 (*0-7487-0428-0*, Pub. by Stanley Thornes UK) Trans-Atl Phila.

Tourism Marketing & Management Handbook. Stephen F. Witt & Luiz Moutinho. 672p. 1989. text ed. 65.00 (*0-13-925885-X*) P-H.

Tourism Marketing Service & Quality Management Perspectives. Eric Laws. 288p. (C). 1991. 75.00 (*0-7478-0428-1*, Pub. by Stanley Thornes UK) Trans-Atl Phila.

Tourism, Museums & the Local Economy: The Economic Impact of the North of England Open Air. Peter Johnson & Barry Thomas. 160p. 1992. 75.00 (*1-85278-617-5*) E Elgar.

Tourism Planning. David W. Marcouiller. LC 95-8753. (CPL Bibliographies Ser.: No. 316). 37p. 1995. pap. 10.00 (*0-86602-316-X*, Sage Prdcls Pr) Sage.

Tourism Planning: An Integrated & Sustainable Development Approach. Edward Inskeep. (Illus.). 576p. 1991. text ed. 57.95 (*0-442-00122-3*) Van Nos Reinhold.

Tourism Planning: Basics, Concepts, Cases. 3rd ed. Clare A. Gunn. 300p. 1993. 59.50 (*0-8448-1742-2*, Crane Russak); pap. 24.50 (*0-8448-1743-0*, Crane Russak) Taylor & Francis.

Tourism Policy & International Tourism in OECD Countries 1992-1993: Special Feature "Tourism & Employment" 203p. (Orig.). (ENG & FRE.). 1995. pap. 50.00 (*92-64-14571-0*, Pub. by Org for Econ FR) OECD.

***Tourism Policy & International Tourism in OECD Countries 1993-1994 (1996 Edition)** OECD Staff. 272p. (Orig.). 1996. pap. 50.00 (*92-64-14896-5*, 78-96-01-1, Pub. by Org for Econ FR) OECD.

***Tourism Policy & Performance.** James Deegan & Donal Dineen. (Tourism & Hospitality Management Ser.). 256p. 1996. 59.00 (*0-415-09315-5*) Routledge.

***Tourism Policy & Planning: Case Studies from the Commonwealth Caribbean.** Paul F. Wilkinson. LC 97-18753. (Tourism Dynamics Ser.). 1997. write for info. (*1-882345-12-6*); pap. write for info. (*1-882345-13-4*) Cognizant Comm.

***Tourism Principles & Practice.** Cooper. 1995. pap. 37.92 (*0-582-28694-8*, Pub. by Longman UK) Longman.

Tourism Resources Planning: The Proceedings of the 1992 World Congress on Adventure Travel & Eco-Tourism. World Congress on Adventure Travel & Eco-Tourism Staff. Ed. by Adventure Travel Society Staff. (Illus.). 252p. (Orig.). 1992. pap. 40.00 (*1-885789-01-7*) Advent Trvl Soc.

***Tourism, Sustainability & Growth.** Salah Wahab & J. J. Pigram. LC 97-8840. 272p. (C). 1997. pap. write for info. (*0-415-16002-2*); text ed. write for info. (*0-415-16001-4*) Routledge.

Tourism, Technology & Competitive Strategies. Auliana Poon. 384p. 1993. 50.00 (*0-85198-950-0*) CAB Intl.

Tourism Today: A Geographical Analysis. 2nd ed. Douglas Pearce. 352p. (C). 1995. pap. text ed. 38.50 (*0-582-22822-0*) Longman.

Tourism Training in Hawaii, 1992. 74p. (Orig.). (C). 1993. pap. text ed. 20.00 (*1-56806-303-2*) DIANE Pub.

Tourism Training in Hawaii, 1993. 44p. (Orig.). (C). 1993. pap. text ed. 20.00 (*1-56806-304-0*) DIANE Pub.

Tourism vs. Environment: The Case for Coastal Areas; A Research Project of the Commission on the Coastal Environment, International Geographical Union. Ed. by P. P. Wong. LC 93-25457. (GeoJournal Library). 244p. (C). 1993. lib. bdg. 126.00 (*0-7923-2404-8*) Kluwer Ac.

Tourisme & Hotellerie: Tourism & Hotel Management, Lectures & Vocabulary. Katia B. Lutz & Conrad J. Schmitt. (FRE.). 1993. pap. text ed. 10.95 (*0-07-056820-0*) McGraw.

Tourismus - Management. Gunther Haedrich et al. 592p. (GER.). 1983. 129.25 (*3-11-008470-8*) De Gruyter.

Tourist: A New Theory of the Leisure Class. Dean Maccannell. 1989. pap. 9.56 (*0-8052-0895-X*) Schocken.

Tourist: Travel in Twentieth-Century North America. John A. Jakle. LC 84-3698. 396p. reprint ed. pap. 112.90 (*0-7837-1835-7*, 2042035) Bks Demand.

Tourist & Camping Information. Amoco Pathfinder Staff. 1992. pap. 2.25 (*0-671-84033-9*) S&S Trade.

Tourist Atlas of China. (Illus.). 102p. 1995. lib. bdg. 35.00 (*0-8095-4902-6*) Borgo Pr.

Tourist Atlas of China. Ed. by Zhao Xilin et al. (Illus.). 99p. (Orig.). 1985. pap. 9.95 (*0-8351-2176-3*) China Bks.

Tourist Attractions. Constance DeJong et al. Ed. by Anne Turyn & Brian Wallis. 80p. (Orig.). 1987. pap. 6.00 (*0-917061-25-X*) Top Stories.

Tourist Development. 2nd ed. Pearce Doublas. (C). 1996. pap. text ed. 29.50 (*0-582-01435-2*) Addison-Wesley.

Tourist Events, 1991: Beam's Directory of International Tourist Events. Amy L. Beam. 448p. 1990. pap. 19.95 (*1-879177-27-7*) TTA Pr.

***Tourist Experience: A New Introduction.** Ed. by Chris Ryan. (Studies in Tourism). (Illus.). 192p. 1996. pap. 32.00 (*0-304-33806-0*); text ed. 75.00 (*0-304-33807-9*) Cassell.

Tourist Gaze: Leisure & Travel in Contemporary Societies. John Urry. (Theory, Culture & Society Ser.). 192p. (C). 1990. text ed. 55.00 (*0-8039-8182-1*); pap. text ed. 21.95 (*0-8039-8183-X*) Sage.

Tourist Guides. Cohen. (Annals of Tourism Research Ser.). 1985. pap. 19.75 (*0-08-032397-9*, Pergamon Pr) Elsevier.

Tourist Heart. Paul Agostino. 32p. 1994. pap. 4.00 (*0-940895-32-3*) Cornerstone IL.

Tourist Historic City. Ashworth. 1989. 46.25 (*1-85293-022-5*, Belhaven) Halsted Pr.

Tourist-Historic City. G. J. Ashworth & J. E. Turnbridge. LC 90-37103. 283p. 1993. text ed. 88.00 (*0-471-94471-8*) Wiley.

Tourist Historic City. John E. Tunbridge. LC 00-90. 283p. 1992. text ed. 64.95 (*0-470-21960-2*, Pub. by Pinter Publishers UK) Wiley.

Tourist Image. Ed. by Tom Selwyn. LC 95-42632. (Myths & Myth Making in Tourism Ser.). 1996. text ed. 65.00 (*0-471-96309-7*) Wiley.

Tourist in Africa. Evelyn Waugh. LC 76-30533. (Illus.). 201p. 1977. reprint ed. text ed. 35.00 (*0-8371-9358-3*, WATAF, Greenwood Pr) Greenwood.

Tourist in Ludlow. Charles E. Wadsworth. LC 83-72233. (Illus.). 83p. 1984. 10.00 (*0-930954-19-X*) Tidal Pr.

Tourist Map of China. 1986. 5.95 (*0-8351-1810-X*) China Bks.

Tourist Map of Korea. 32p. 1987. pap. 3.50 (*0-941009-06-8*) Hollym Corp Pubs.

Tourist Organizations. Douglas Pearce. 240p. (Orig.). 1992. pap. 47.50 (*0-582-07010-4*, Pub. by Longman Group UK) Trans-Atl Phila.

Tourist Season. Carl Hiaasen. 384p. 1987. mass mkt. 6.99 (*0-446-34345-5*) Warner Bks.

Tourist Season. large type ed. Carl Hiaasen. LC 96-15115. 524p. 1996. lib. bdg. 23.95 (*0-7838-1647-2*, GK Hall) Thorndike Pr.

Tourist Trap. Julie Smith. 1992. mass mkt. 4.99 (*0-8041-0930-3*) Ivy Books.

Touristocrates. Pierre Daninos. 208p. (FRE.). 1974. 10.95 (*0-8288-9177-X*, M3363); pap. 8.95 (*0-686-55579-1*) Fr & Eur.

Tourists. Lisa Goldstein. 288p. 1994. pap. 11.95 (*0-312-89011-7*) Orb NYC.

Tourists: How the Fastest Growing Industry Is Changing the World. Larry Krotz. LC 96-14821. 264p. 1996. 23.95 (*0-571-19893-7*) Faber & Faber.

Tourists & the Economy. Virender Kaul. (C). 1994. 14.00 (*81-241-0190-6*, Pub. by Har-Anand Pubns II) S Asia.

***Tourists & Tourism.** Abram. 1997. 45.00 (*1-85973-900-8*, Pub. by Berg Pubs UK); pap. 19.50 (*1-85973-905-9*, Pub. by Berg Pubs UK) NYU Pr.

Tourists in Our Own Land: Cultural Literacies & the College Curriculum. (Illus.). 74p. (Orig.). (C). 1993. pap. text ed. 20.00 (*1-56806-193-5*) DIANE Pub.

Tourists in Our Own Land: Cultural Literacies & the College Curriculum. 1994. lib. bdg. 250.95 (*0-8490-6426-0*) Gordon Pr.

Tourmaline. Jon Henderson. 476p. 1992. pap. 10.99 (*0-8423-7287-3*) Tyndale.

Tourmaline Group. Richard V. Dietrich. (Illus.). 228p. (gr. 13). 1985. text ed. 60.95 (*0-442-21857-5*) Chapman & Hall.

Tournament. Heather Amery. (Castle Tales Ser.). (Illus.). 16p. (J). (ps up). 1996. pap. 4.50 (*0-7460-2514-9*, Usborne) EDC.

Tournament. Heather Amery. (Castle Tales Ser.). (Illus.). 16p. (J). (ps up). 1996. lib. bdg. 12.95 (*0-88110-866-9*, Usborne) EDC.

Tournament. Bellerophon Books Staff. (J). (gr. 4-7). 1994. pap. 3.95 (*0-88388-181-0*) Bellerophon Bks.

***Tournament.** Ron Hamlin & Herbert B. Livesey. (Illus.). 376p. 1997. pap. 19.95 (*0-9658195-3-1*) Pro Slot.

Tournament. Kenneth Kirkeby. (Orig.). 1996. pap. 11.95 (*0-9651410-0-4*) Bick Riv Bks.

Tournament. Peter Vansittart. 224p. 8400. 32.00 (*0-7206-0616-0*) Dufour.

Tournament. 2nd rev. ed. Shelby Foote. 270p. 1987. reprint ed. pap. 19.95 (*0-917786-56-4*) Summa Pubns.

Tournament Acol: A System for Winners. David Bird & Tim Bourke. 160p. 1996. pap. 17.95 (*0-575-06113-8*, Pub. by V Gollancz UK) Trafalgar.

Tournament & Tower. Debra Doyle & James Macdonald. LC 89-33881. (Circle of Magic Ser.). (Illus.). 144p. (J). (gr. 5-9). 1990. pap. 2.95 (*0-8167-1829-6*) Troll Communs.

Tournament Bridge: An Uncensored Memoir. Jerome S. Machlin. LC 84-223705. 121p. 1980. pap. 5.95 (*0-939460-06-8*) Devyn Pr.

Tournament Chess. Ed. by M. Chandler & A. J. Miles. (Tournament Chess Ser.: Vol. 5). 176p. 1982. pap. 21.95 (*0-08-029720-X*) Elsevier.

Tournament Chess, Vol. 1. M. Chandler. Ed. by A. J. Miles. 128p. 1981. pap. 21.95 (*0-08-026888-9*, Pergamon Pr) Elsevier.

Tournament Chess, Vol. 2. Ed. by M. Chandler. (Illus.). 128p. 1982. pap. 21.95 (*0-08-026891-9*, Pergamon Pr) Elsevier.

Tournament Chess, Vol. 3. Ed. by M. Chandler & A. J. Miles. (Illus.). 170p. 1982. pap. 21.95 (*0-08-026892-7*, Pergamon Pr) Elsevier.

Tournament Chess, Vol. 4. Ed. by M. Chandler & A. J. Miles. 150p. 1982. pap. 21.95 (*0-08-026893-5*, Pergamon Pr) Elsevier.

Tournament Chess, Vol. 6. A. J. Miles. 176p. 1983. pap. 21.95 (*0-08-029721-8*, Pergamon Pr) Elsevier.

Tournament Chess, Vol. 7. Ed. by M. Chandler & A. J. Miles. (Illus.). 143p. 1983. pap. 21.95 (*0-08-029736-6*, Pergamon Pr) Elsevier.

Tournament Chess, Vol. 8. Ed. by M. Chandler & A. J. Miles. (Illus.). 200p. 1983. pap. 21.95 (*0-08-029737-4*, Pergamon Pr) Elsevier.

Tournament Chess, Vol. 9. Ed. by M. Chandler & A. J. Miles. (Illus.). 176p. 1983. pap. 21.95 (*0-08-029742-0*, 62, Pergamon Pr) Elsevier.

Tournament Chess, Vol. 10. Ed. by M. Chandler & A. J. Miles. 166p. 1983. pap. 21.95 (*0-08-029743-9*, Pergamon Pr) Elsevier.

Tournament Chess, Vol. 12. Ed. by M. Chandler. 215p. 1984. pap. 21.95 (*0-08-029758-7*, Pergamon Pr) Elsevier.

Tournament Chess, Vol. 14. Ed. by M. Chandler. 178p. 1984. pap. 32.00 (*0-08-029760-9*, Pergamon Pr) Elsevier.

Tournament Chess, Vol. 15. Ed. by M. Chandler. 188p. 1985. pap. 32.00 (*0-08-029761-7*, Pergamon Pr) Elsevier.

Tournament Chess, Vol. 16. Ed. by M. Chandler. (Illus.). 176p. 1985. pap. 32.00 (*0-08-029762-5*, Pub. by PPL UK) Elsevier.

Tournament Days Independent Reader 5-Pack, Unit 9. (Networks Ser.). 1991. 15.00 (*0-88106-776-8*, N318) Charlesbridge Pub.

Tournament of Hearts. Cathleen Clare. 256p. (Orig.). 1994. mass mkt. 3.99 (*0-380-77432-1*) Avon.

Tournament of Knights. Joe Lasker. LC 85-48075. (Trophy Picture Bk.). (Illus.). 32p. (J). (gr. 3 up). 1989. reprint ed. pap. 5.95 (*0-06-443192-4*, Trophy) HarpC Child Bks.

Tournament of Lawyers: The Transformation of the Big Law Firm. Marc Galanter & Thomas Palay. LC 90-45088. (Illus.). 208p. 1991. 32.50 (*0-226-27877-8*) U Ch Pr.

Tournament of Lawyers: The Transformation of the Big Law Firm. Marc Galanter & Thomas Palay. LC 90-45088. (Illus.). xii, 210p. 1993. pap. text ed. 12.95 (*0-226-27878-6*) U Ch Pr.

***Tournament of Murders: The Franklin's Tale of Mystery & Murder As He Goes on Pilgrimage from London to Canterbury.** P. C. Doherty. LC 97-16501. 1997. write for info. (*0-312-17048-3*) St Martin.

***Tournament of Shadows: Britain, Russia & the Great Game.** Karl Meyer & Shareen Brysac. 384p. 1997. 27.50 (*0-06-017382-3*) HarpC.

Tournament of Time. Elaine M. Alphin. LC 94-96624. 125p. (Orig.). (J). (gr. 4-6). 1994. per., pap. 3.95 (*0-9643683-0-7*) Bluegrass Bks.

Tournament Poker. Tom McEvoy. 312p. (Orig.). 1995. 59.95 (*1-884466-06-0*); pap. 39.95 (*1-884466-05-2*) Poker Plus.

***Tournament Reports for Magic: The Gathering.** Jamie C. Wakefield. 1997. pap. text ed. 14.95 (*1-55622-579-2*) Wordware Pub.

Tournament Scheduling: The Easy Way. Gunsten. 84p. 1978. pap. text ed. 10.95 (*0-88725-944-8*) Hunter Textbks.

***Tournament Solutions & Majority Voting.** Jean-Francois Laslier. LC 97-21690. (Studies in Economic Theory). 1997. write for info. (*3-540-62897-5*) Spr-Verlag.

Tournament Tradition & Staging the Castle of Perseverance. Steven I. Pederson. LC 86-25050. (Theater & Dramatic Studies: No. 38). (Illus.). 148p. reprint ed. pap. 42.20 (*0-8357-1768-2*, 2070568) Bks Demand.

Tournament Upstart. Thomas J. Dygard. 208p. (J). (gr. 5-9). 1989. pap. 4.99 (*0-14-034114-5*, Puffin) Puffin Bks.

Tournaments & Events: Organization & Management. unabridged ed. (NGF Info Pacs Ser.). (Illus.). 134p. (Orig.). 1995. pap. 45.00 (*0-9638647-7-7*) Natl Golf.

***Tournaments of Value: Sociability & Hierarchy in a Yemeni Town.** Anne Meneley. (Anthropological Horizons Ser.). (Illus.). 248p. 1996. 45.00 (*0-8020-0883-6*); pap. 18.95 (*0-8020-7868-0*) U of Toronto Pr.

Tournants: Conversation en Culture. Deborah H. Morsink. LC 92-24486. 1992. pap. text ed. 34.60 (*0-13-927682-3*) P-H.

Tournesol. Therese De Saint Phalle. (FRE.). 1973. pap. 10.95 (*0-7859-4001-4*) Fr & Eur.

Tourney Fever. Kirk Marshall. (Hoops Ser.: No. 5). 144p. (J). 1989. mass mkt. 3.95 (*0-345-35912-7*) Ballantine.

Tournier Elementaire. Jonathan F. Krell. LC 94-11288. (Purdue Studies in Romance Literatures: Vol. 6). 240p. (FRE.). 1994. 34.95 (*1-55753-056-4*) Purdue U Pr.

Tourniquet. Alice Joanou. 1992. mass mkt. 6.95 (*1-56333-060-1*, Rhinoceros) Masquerade.

Tours. Chris Hoosen & Francis Dix. (Travel Agent Training Ser.). (Illus.). (Orig.). 1989. student ed., pap. 20.00 (*0-917063-17-1*) Travel Text.

Tours & Expeditions. 44p. 1971. pap. 6.70 (*0-8395-3734-4*, 33737) BSA.

Tours & Visits Directory: A Behind-the-Scenes Guide to Factories, Mines, Business Firms, Government Agencies, Cultural & Educational Institutions & Other Facilities Which Receive Visitors. 2nd ed. 416p. 1981. 120.00 (*0-8103-0946-7*) Gale.

***Tours City Plan.** (Grafocarte Maps Ser.). 1995. 8.95 (*2-7416-0041-4*, 80041) Michelin.

Tours for All Seasons. Howard Bryan. (Illus.). 128p. (Orig.). 1986. reprint ed. pap. 4.95 (*0-910467-04-8*) Heritage Assocs.

***Tours in Historic Morris County.** Morris County Historical Soc. Staff. (Illus.). 298p. 1977. reprint ed. pap. 5.00 (*0-614-29778-8*) M C H S.

***Tours of Duty: Carroll County & the Vietnam War.** Gary Jestes & Jay A. Graybeal. LC 97-72059. (Illus.). 200p. 1997. pap. 18.00 (*1-886742-26-X*) Hist Soc Carroll.

Tours of the Black Clock. Steve Erickson. 320p. 1990. pap. 10.00 (*0-380-70944-9*) Avon.

Tours Symposium on Nuclear Physics. M. Ohta & B. Remand. 364p. 1992. text ed. 102.00 (*981-02-0892-8*) World Scientific Pub.

Tours Symposium on Nuclear Physics II: Tours, France, August 30-September 2, 1994. H. Utsunomiya. LC 95-17278. 450p. 1995. text ed. 112.00 (*981-02-2156-8*) World Scientific Pub.

Tourtellotte & Hummel of Idaho: The Standard Practice of Architecture. Patricia Wright & Lisa B. Reitzes. LC 86-32540. (Western Experience Ser.). (Illus.). 119p. reprint ed. pap. 34.00 (*0-7837-7070-7*, 2046882) Bks Demand.

Tous Ceux Qui Tombent. Samuel Beckett. 80p. (FRE.). 1957. pap. 10.95 (*0-7859-0611-8*, F86000) Fr & Eur.

Tous Feux Eteints: Carnets 1965, 1966, 1697, Carnets sans Dates et Carnets 1972. Henry De Montherlant. 192p. (FRE.). 1975. pap. 19.95 (*0-7859-1343-2*, 2070293025) Fr & Eur.

Tous les Animaux - All the Animals. (Gallimard - Encyclopedie Vis. Bilingue Ser.). 63p. (ENG & FRE.). (J). 1991. 19.95 (*2-07-057512-8*) Schoenhof.

Tous les Chats ne Sont pas en Peluche. Remo Forlani. 348p. (FRE.). 1990. pap. 11.95 (*0-7859-2589-9*, 2070382486) Fr & Eur.

Tous les Hommes Sont Mortels. Simone De Beauvoir. 544p. (FRE.). 1974. pap. 15.95 (*0-8288-3656-6*, F85820) Fr & Eur.

Tous les Hommes Sont Mortels. Simone De Beauvoir. (Folio Ser.: No. 533). 544p. (FRE.). (J). 1974. pap. 12.50 (*2-07-036533-6*) Schoenhof.

Tous les Poemes. 3rd ed. Ed. by Andre O. Hurtgen. 256p. 1992. 22.61 (*0-8013-0854-2*, 78942) Longman.

Tous N'Etaient Pas des Anges. Joseph Kessel. (FRE.). 1988. pap. 16.95 (*0-7859-3200-3*, 2264011483) Fr & Eur.

Toussaint l'Ouverture. Intro. by G. R. Simpson. 1990. 25.00 (*0-87498-031-3*) Assoc Pubs DC.

Toussaint L'Ouverture: A Biography & Autobiography. Toussaint L'Ouverture. LC 77-152924. (Black Heritage Library Collection). 1977. 32.95 (*0-8369-8768-3*) Ayer.

Toussaint L'Ouverture: The Fight for Haiti's Freedom. Walter D. Myers. LC 95-30046. (Illus.). (J). (gr. 3-7). 1996. 16.00 (*0-689-80126-2*, S&S Bks Young Read) S&S Childrens.

Toussaint l'Ouverture, Lover of Liberty. Laurence Santrey. LC 93-18971. (Illus.). 48p. (J). (gr. 4-6). 1993. pap. 3.95 (*0-8167-2824-0*); lib. bdg. 12.95 (*0-8167-2823-2*) Troll Communs.

Tout a Fait Francais. Ed. by Veronique Morrison et al. (Illus.). (C). 1979. pap. text ed. 17.95 (*0-393-09005-1*) Norton.

Tout Compte Fait. Simone De Beauvoir. (FRE.). 1978. pap. 16.95 (*0-8288-3657-4*) Fr & Eur.

T

Tout Compte Fait. Simone De Beauvoir. (Folio Ser.: No. 1022). 633p. (FRE.). 1978. pap. 13.95 (*2-07-037022-4*) Schoenhof.

Tout Connaitre en S'Amusant: Bateaux. Charles M. Schulz. (Peanuts Ser.). 34p. (FRE.). 1982. 10.95 (*0-8288-4577-8*) Fr & Eur.

Tout Connaitre en S'Amusant: Camions. Charles M. Schulz. (Peanuts Ser.). 32p. (FRE.). (J). 1983. 10.95 (*0-8288-4578-6*) Fr & Eur.

Tout Connaitre en S'Amusant: La Ferme. Charles M. Schulz. (Peanuts Ser.). 34p. (FRE.). (J). 1982. 10.95 (*0-8288-4573-5*) Fr & Eur.

Tout Connaitre en S'Amusant: La Nature. Charles M. Schulz. (Peanuts Ser.). 34p. (FRE.). (J). 1983. 10.95 (*0-8288-4574-3*) Fr & Eur.

Tout Connaitre en S'Amusant: La Plage. Charles M. Schulz. (Peanuts Ser.). 34p. (FRE.). (J). 1982. 10.95 (*0-8288-4575-1*) Fr & Eur.

Tout Connaitre en S'Amusant: Les Avions. Charles M. Schulz. (Peanuts Ser.). 34p. (FRE.). (J). 1982. 10.95 (*0-8288-4576-X*) Fr & Eur.

Tout Connaitre en S'Amusant: Maisons. Charles M. Schulz. (Peanuts Ser.). 32p. (FRE.). (J). 1983. 10.95 (*0-8288-4579-4*) Fr & Eur.

Tout Connaitre en S'Amusant: Saisons. Charles M. Schulz. (Peanuts Ser.). 32p. (FRE.). (J). 1983. 10.95 (*0-8288-4580-8*) Fr & Eur.

Tout de Suite: A la Microwave, 2 vols. Jean K. Durkee. Incl. Vol. I. French, Acadian & Creole Recipes, Delicious, Nutrious & Colorful. (Illus.). 224p. 1977. (*0-318-56953-1*); Vol. II. Mexican, Italian & French Recipes Tested & Tasted by the Author. (Illus.). 236p. 1980. (*0-318-56954-X*); (Illus.). 224p. 1977. write for info. (*0-318-56952-3*) Tout De Suite.

Tout Ensemble. Raymond F. Comeau & Normand J. Lamoureux. LC 95-38460. (ENG & FRE.). (C). 1996. pap. text ed. 45.00 (*0-03-009598-0*) HR&W Schl Div.

Tout Ensemble. Raymond F. Comeau. (ENG & FRE.). (C). 1996. lab manual ed., pap. text ed. 27.75 (*0-03-009599-9*) HB Coll Pubs.

Tout l'Amour Du Monde. Michel Deon. (FRE.). 1978. pap. 11.95 (*0-7859-2215-6*, 207037016X) Fr & Eur.

Tout l'Humour du Monde. Pierre Daninos. 224p. (FRE.). 1967. pap. 24.95 (*0-7859-5491-0*) Fr & Eur.

Tout Pour Plaire. Chester Himes. 245p. (FRE.). 1987. pap. 10.95 (*0-7859-2651-8*, 207037890X) Fr & Eur.

Tout Se Complique. Goscinny Sempe. (FRE.). 1976. pap. 10.95 (*0-8288-3792-9*, F18530) Fr & Eur.

Tout Sonia: Avec Sonia les Autres et Moi, Comment Vivre avec ou sans Sonia. Pierre Daninos. (Illus.). 435p. (FRE.). 1976. 10.95 (*0-8288-9180-X*, F66921) Fr & Eur.

Tout Ubu. Alfred Jarry. 512p. (FRE.). 1962. 13.95 (*0-8288-9834-0*, F106610) Fr & Eur.

Tout Ubu. Alfred Jarry. Incl. Ubu Roi. (*0-318-52307-8*); Ubu Cocu. (*0-318-52308-6*); Ubu Enchaine. (*0-318-52309-4*); Almanachs du Pere Ubu. (*0-318-52310-8*); Ubu sur la Butte. (*0-318-52311-6*); (Coll. Diamant). 16.50 (*0-685-34260-3*) Fr & Eur.

Toutankhamon Dans les Archives Hittites. J. Vergote. vi, 42p. 1961. pap. text ed. 14.00 (*0-614-04005-1*, Pub. by Netherlands Inst NE) Eisenbrauns.

***Toute la Beaute Du Monde.** Jacques Savoie. (Novels in the Roman Jeunesse Ser.). 96p. (FRE.). (J). (gr. 4-7). 1996. pap. 7.95 (*2-89021-243-2*, Pub. by Les Editions CN) Firefly Bks Ltd.

Toute la Verite. Erskine Caldwell. (FRE.). 1984. pap. 11.95 (*0-7859-1997-X*, 2070375714) Fr & Eur.

***Toutes Latitudes.** Ed. by Pierre-Edmond Robert. 159p. (FRE.). 1993. pap. 17.95 (*2-278-04307-2*, Pub. by Edns Didier FR) Hatier Pub.

Toutounier see Duo

Tova & Esty. 1982. pap. 2.95 (*0-87306-247-7*) Feldheim.

Tova & Esty's Purim Surprise. 1982. pap. 2.95 (*0-87306-248-5*) Feldheim.

Tova Lous Yo. Hanna Hutchinson. Tr. by Terry Gadness. (Interlingo Ser.). Orig. Title: Three Bears. (Illus.). 24p. (Orig.). (J). (gr. 1-2). 1995. pap. 2.95 (*0-922852-39-1*) Another Lang Pr.

Tovangar. Anne Galloway. (J). 1978. pap. 3.00 (*0-939046-25-3*) Malki Mus Pr.

Tovar Calendar: An Illustrated Mexican Manuscript ca. 1585, Reproduced with a Commentary & Handlist of Sources on the Mexican 365-Day Year. George Kubler & Charles Gibson. (Connecticut Academy of Arts & Sciences Ser., Trans.: Vol. 11). 1951. pap. 100.00 (*0-685-22860-6*) Elliots Bks.

Tovey - A Free Range Dog. Betty Brooke. (C). 1990. pap. 24.00 (*0-85305-294-8*, Pub. by J Arthur Ltd UK) St Mut.

Tovish. Norman Keyes, Jr. (Illus.). 78p. (Orig.). 1988. pap. 10.00 (*1-879886-26-X*) Addison Gallery.

Tovismadarak. Colleen McCullough. Tr. by Arpad Goncz & Margit Borbas from ENG. 568p. (HUN.). 1984. 20.00 (*0-935484-11-6*) Universe Pub Co.

Toward a Better Understanding: United States-Japan Relations. 1995. lib. bdg. 251.95 (*0-8490-6759-6*) Gordon Pr.

Toward a Better Understanding: United States-Japanese Relations. 1992. lib. bdg. 95.00 (*0-8490-5494-X*) Gordon Pr.

***Toward a Better World: Adventures of a Missionary Engineer.** John Snell. LC 97-60466. 224p. (Orig.). 1997. pap. 13.99 (*1-57921-017-1*) WinePress Pub.

Toward a Biocritical Sociology. John W. Neuhaus. 224p. (C). 1996. pap. text ed. 29.95 (*0-8204-3081-1*) P Lang Pubng.

Toward a Canada-Quebec Union. Philip Resnick. 160p. (Orig.). (C). 1991. pap. text ed. 18.95 (*0-7735-0865-1*, Pub. by McGill CN) U of Toronto Pr.

Toward a Career in Business, 2 Vols. 2nd ed. Kathryn W. Hegar. (C). 1987. pap. 12.76 (*0-395-45293-7*) HM.

Toward a Caring Curriculum: A New Pedagogy for Nursing. Em O. Bevis & Jean Watson. 416p. 1989. 34.95 (*0-88737-440-9*) Natl League Nurse.

Toward a Caring Society. Robert Morris. 1974. 2.50 (*0-686-09284-8*) Univ Bk Serv.

Toward a Caring Society. Samuel P. Oliner. 1994. 22.95 (*0-02-923835-8*) S&S Trade.

Toward a Caring Society: Ideas into Action. Pearl M. Oliner & Samuel P. Oliner. LC 95-3339. 256p. 1995. text ed. 62.95 (*0-275-95198-7*, Praeger Pubs) Greenwood.

Toward a Caring Society: Ideas into Action. Pearl M. Oliver & Samuel P. Oliver. LC 95-3339. 256p. 1995. pap. text ed. 19.95 (*0-275-95453-6*, Praeger Pubs) Greenwood.

Toward a Catholic Constitution. Leonard Swidler. 192p. 1996. pap. text ed. 19.95 (*0-8245-1626-5*) Crossroad NY.

Toward a Chicano Social Science. Irene I. Blea. LC 88-6593. 173p. 1988. text ed. 42.95 (*0-275-92408-4*, C2408, Praeger Pubs); pap. text ed. 18.95 (*0-275-92531-5*, B2531, Praeger Pubs) Greenwood.

Toward a Christian Revolt Against Alien Influences. 1992. lib. bdg. 88.00 (*0-8490-5405-2*) Gordon Pr.

***Toward a Christian Theology of Religious Pluralism.** Jacques Dupuis. LC 97-2515. 700p. 1997. 50.00 (*1-57075-125-0*) Orbis Bks.

Toward a Common Agenda: Linking Gifted Education & School Reform: a Product of the National Training Program for Gifted Education. LC 94-42218. 36p. 1994. pap. text ed. 15.00 (*0-86586-260-5*, P5088) Coun Exc Child.

Toward a Common Destiny: Improving Race & Ethnic Relations in America. Ed. by Willis D. Hawley et al. LC 94-48172. (Education Ser.). 508p. text ed. 45.00 (*0-7879-0097-4*) Jossey-Bass.

Toward a Community Air Transport Policy. Ed. by P. J. Slot & P. D. Dagtoglou. 400p. 1989. 88.00 (*90-6544-407-6*) Kluwer Law Tax Pubs.

Toward a Comparative Structural Theory of the Arts. David Ward-Steinman. (University Research Lectures: No. 3). 212p. 1989. pap. 14.50 (*0-916304-86-8*) SDSU Press.

Toward a Competitive Telecommunications Industry: Selected Papers from the 1994 Telecommunications Policy Research Conference. Ed. by Gerald W. Brock. (Telecommunications Ser.). 400p. 1995. text ed. 79.95 (*0-8058-2030-2*) L Erlbaum Assocs.

Toward a Competitive Telecommunications Industry: Selected Papers from the 1994 Telecommunications Policy Research Conference. Ed. by Gerald W. Brock. (Telecommunications Ser.). 400p. 1995. pap. 39.95 (*0-8058-2031-0*) L Erlbaum Assocs.

Toward a Contemporary Wisdom Christology: A Study of Karl Rahner & Norman Pittenger. Leo D. Lefebure. LC 88-22798. 298p. (Orig.). (C). 1988. pap. text ed. 25.00 (*0-8191-7152-2*); lib. bdg. 45.00 (*0-8191-7151-4*) U Pr of Amer.

Toward a Coordinated Spatial Data Infrastructure for the Nation. National Research Council Staff. 192p. (Orig.). (C). 1993. pap. text ed. 24.00 (*0-309-04899-0*) Natl Acad Pr.

Toward a Critical Politics of Teacher Thinking: Mapping the Postmodern. Joe L. Kincheloe. LC 92-32181. (Critical Studies in Education & Culture). 280p. 1993. text ed. 59.95 (*0-89789-270-4*, H270, Bergin & Garvey); pap. text ed. 17.95 (*0-89789-271-2*, G271, Bergin & Garvey) Greenwood.

Toward a Critique of Production: A Philosophical Inquiry. Pierre Watter. 136p. 1996. pap. 17.00 (*0-8059-3631-9*) Dorrance.

Toward a Cultural Theory of Education & Schooling. Ed. by Frederick Gearing & Lucinda Sangree. (World Anthropology Ser.). xiv, 260p. 1979. text ed. 44.65 (*90-279-7760-7*) Mouton.

Toward a Dangerous World? U. S. National Security Strategy for the Coming Turbulence. Richard L. Kugler. LC 94-36801. 305p. 1995. pap. 20.00 (*0-8330-1592-3*, MR-485-JS) Rand Corp.

Toward a Definition of American Film Noir (1941-1949) A. M. Karimi. Ed. by Garth S. Lowett. LC 75-21431. (Dissertations on Film Ser.). 1976. lib. bdg. 24.95 (*0-405-07534-0*) Ayer.

Toward a Definition of Antisemitism. Gavin I. Langmuir. LC 90-41686. 427p. 1990. 45.00 (*0-520-06144-6*) U CA Pr.

Toward a Definition of Antisemitism. Gavin I. Langmuir. LC 90-41686. 432p. (C). 1996. pap. 17.95 (*0-520-06143-8*) U CA Pr.

Toward a Definition of Clinical Social Work. Ed. by Patricia L. Ewalt. LC 80-81821. 104p. 1980. pap. 11.95 (*0-87101-086-0*) Natl Assn Soc Wkrs.

Toward a Democratic China: The Intellectual Autobiography of Yan Jiaqi. Yan Jiaqi. Tr. by David S. Hong & Denis C. Mair. LC 92-15859. (SHAPS Library of Translations). 272p. 1992. text ed. 36.00 (*0-8248-1484-3*); pap. text ed. 16.95 (*0-8248-1501-7*) UH Pr.

***Toward a Democratic Science: Scientific Narration & Civice Communication.** Richard H. Brown. LC 97-14234. 1998. write for info. (*0-300-06707-0*) Yale U Pr.

Toward a Democratic Work Process. Fred H. Blum. LC 73-11840. 229p. 1974. reprint ed. lib. bdg. 15.00 (*0-8371-7063-X*, BLDW, Greenwood Pr) Greenwood.

Toward a Dependable Peace: A Proposal for an Appropriate Security System. Robert Johansen. 30p. (Orig.). 1978. pap. 15.95 (*0-87855-758-X*) Transaction Pubs.

Toward a Dialogue of Understandings: Loren Eiseley & the Critique of Science. Mary E. Pitts. LC 94-46994. 352p. 1995. 47.50 (*0-934223-37-8*) Lehigh Univ Pr.

Toward a Dimensional Reality. Charles M. Perry. LC 39-11737. 188p. reprint ed. pap. 53.60 (*0-317-09342-8*, 2016249) Bks Demand.

Toward a Drug-Free Generation: A Nation's Responsibilty. 98p. (Orig.). (C). 1995. pap. text ed. 20.00 (*0-7881-1999-0*) DIANE Pub.

Toward a European Nation? Political Trends in Europe - East & West, Center & Periphery. Ed. by Max Haller & Rudolf Richter. LC 93-48346. (Illus.). 320p. (gr. 13). 1995. text ed. 72.95 (*1-56324-384-9*) M E Sharpe.

Toward a Feminist Epistemology. Jane Duran. 256p. (C). 1990. lib. bdg. 58.00 (*0-8476-7635-8*) Rowman.

Toward a Feminist Epistemology. Jane Duran. 288p. 1990. pap. 21.95 (*0-8476-7989-6*) Rowman.

Toward a Feminist Rhetoric: The Writing of Gertrude Buck. Ed. by Joann Campbell. (Series in Composition, Literacy, & Culture). (Illus.). 312p. (C). 1996. 49.95 (*0-8229-3900-2*); pap. 19.95 (*0-8229-5573-3*) U of Pittsburgh Pr.

Toward a Feminist Theory of the State. Catharine A. MacKinnon. LC 89-7540. 304p. 1989. text ed. 27.50 (*0-674-89645-9*) HUP.

Toward a Feminist Theory of the State. Catharine A. MacKinnon. 304p. (C). 1991. pap. text ed. 14.95 (*0-674-89646-7*) HUP.

Toward a Formal Science of Economics. Bernt P. Stigum. 1000p. 1990. 65.00 (*0-262-19284-5*) MIT Pr.

Toward a Fraternal Society: A Study of Gabriel Marcel's Approach to Being, Technology & Intersubjectivity. Donald F. Traub. (American University Studies: Philosophy: Ser. V, Vol. 51). 263p. (C). 1988. text ed. 35.50 (*0-8204-0631-7*) P Lang Pubng.

Toward a Freudian Theory of Literature: With an Analysis of Racine's Phedre. Francesco Orlando. Tr. by Charmaine Lee. LC 78-7577. 224p. reprint ed. pap. 63.90 (*0-8357-6622-5*, 2035267) Bks Demand.

***Toward a Fuel Cell Future: Planning for the Commercialization of Fuel Cells (Sept. 93)** Compiled by Institute of Transportation Studies, Univeristy of CA, Davis Staff & Sacramento Municipal Utility District Staff. (Fuel Cells Information Ser.: Vol. IX). (Illus.). 93p. 1996. lib. bdg. 115.00 (*0-89934-313-9*, B953) Bus Tech Bks.

Toward a Fuller Vision: Orthodoxy & the Anglican Experience. E. C. Miller, Jr. LC 84-61015. 188p. (Orig.). 1984. pap. 8.95 (*0-8192-1351-9*) Morehouse Pub.

Toward a Genealogy of Individualism. Daniel Shanahan. LC 92-10933. (Critical Perspectives on Modern Culture Ser.). 168p. 1992. 25.00 (*0-87023-811-6*) U of Mass Pr.

Toward a General Theory of Action. Ed. by Talcott Parsons & Edward A. Shils. LC 51-14629. 518p. reprint ed. pap. 147.70 (*0-317-09500-5*, 2017682) Bks Demand.

Toward a General Theory of Expertise: Prospects & Limits. Ed. by K. Anders Ericsson & Jacqui Smith. (Illus.). 300p. (C). 1991. text ed. 64.95 (*0-521-40470-3*); pap. text ed. 29.95 (*0-521-40612-9*) Cambridge U Pr.

Toward a General Theory of Systems: One Man's Window on our Universe. Win Wenger. (Library of the Republic of the Sciences). 35p. (Orig.). 1987. 12.95 (*0-931865-10-7*) Psychegenics.

Toward a General Theory of the Paranormal. 3rd ed. Lawrence LeShan. LC 73-80027. (Parapsychological Monographs: No. 9). 1969. pap. 7.00 (*0-912328-13-4*) Parapsych Foun.

Toward a Genetics of Language. Ed. by Mabel L. Rice. 432p. 1996. text ed. 89.95 (*0-8058-1677-1*) L Erlbaum Assocs.

Toward a Genetics of Language. Ed. by Mabel L. Rice. 432p. 1996. pap. 39.95 (*0-8058-1678-X*) L Erlbaum Assocs.

Toward a Global Civil Society. Ed. by Michael Walzer. LC 94-33656. (Friedrich Ebert Stiftung Series on International Political Currents). 344p. 1995. text ed. 39.95 (*1-57181-054-4*) Berghahn Bks.

***Toward a Global Community of Scholars: The Special Partnership Between the Carnegie Foundation for the Advancement of Teaching & China's National Center for Education Development Research, 1988-1997.** Hsi-Kheng Ch'i et al. LC 96-36012. (Illus.). 80p. (Orig.). 1997. pap. 15.00 (*0-931050-61-8*) Carnegie Fnd Advan Teach.

Toward a Glorious Indonesia: Reminiscences & Observations of Dr. Soetomo. Raden Soetomo. Ed. & Tr. by Paul W. Van Der Veur. Tr. by Suharni Soemarmo. LC 86-33257. (Monographs in International Studies, Southeast Asia Ser.: No. 81). 376p. reprint ed. pap. 107.20 (*0-7837-6480-4*, 2046485) Bks Demand.

Toward a Grammar of Abstraction: Modernity, Wittgenstein, & the Paintings of Jackson Pollack. Robert Steiner. (Literature & Philosophy Ser.). 96p. 1992. 16.50 (*0-271-00866-0*) Pa St U Pr.

Toward a Grammar of Passages. Richard M. Coe. LC 87-9894. (Studies in Writing & Rhetoric). 142p. (Orig.). 1987. pap. text ed. 12.95 (*0-8093-1420-7*) S Ill U Pr.

Toward a Green Central America: Integrating Conservation & Development. Ed. by Valerie Barzetti & Yanina Rovinski. LC 92-9644. (Library of Management for Development). (Illus.). xvi, 110p. (Orig.). 1992. pap. 14.95 (*1-56549-006-1*) Kumarian Pr.

Toward a Growing Marriage: Building the Love Relationship of Your Dreams. Gary Chapman. LC 79-21376. (C). 1996. pap. 11.99 (*0-8024-8787-4*) Moody.

Toward a Harmony of Faith & Learning: Essays on Bible College Curriculum. Ed. by Kenneth O. Gangel. 247p. 1983. pap. 13.95 (*0-912407-00-X*, BV4022T68) William Tyndale Col Pr.

***Toward a Healthier Sexuality: A Book of Readings.** Joseph Darden. 144p. (C). 1996. per., pap. text ed. 28.68 (*0-7872-3236-X*) Kendall-Hunt.

Toward a High-Wage, High-Productivity Service Sector. Lester C. Thurow & Louise Waldstein. LC 89-83993. (Illus.). 58p. 1989. 12.00 (*0-944826-06-7*) Economic Policy Inst.

***Toward a History of Epistemic Things: Synthesizing Proteins in the Test Tube.** LC 96-47145. (Writing Science Ser.). 1997. write for info. (*0-8047-2785-6*); pap. write for info. (*0-8047-2786-4*) Stanford U Pr.

Toward a History of Game Theory. Ed. by E. Roy Weintraub. 312p. 1992. text ed. 40.00 (*0-8223-1253-0*) Duke.

Toward a History of the New Left: Essays from Within the Movement. Intro. by R. David Myers. LC 89-25472. 210p. 1989. 50.00 (*0-926019-23-6*) Carlson Pub.

Toward a History of Ukrainian Literature. George G. Grabowicz. (Harvard Ukrainian Studies). 112p. (C). 1981. 5.00 (*0-674-89676-9*) HUP.

Toward a Homeodynamic Society. Robert J. Blakely. 1965. 2.50 (*0-8156-7028-1*, NES 49) Syracuse U Cont Ed.

Toward a Human Curriculum. Denenberg. 1990. pap. 9.99 (*0-89824-612-1*) Trillium Pr.

Toward a Humanist Political Economy. Harold Chorney & Phillip Hansen. 200p. 1992. 38.95 (*1-895431-23-9*, Pub. by Black Rose Bks CN); pap. text ed. 19.95 (*1-895431-22-0*, Pub. by Black Rose Bks CN) Consort Bk Sales.

Toward a Humanitarian Diplomacy: A Primer for Policy. Tom J. Farer. LC 79-3514. (C). 1980. text ed. 36.00 (*0-8147-2565-1*) NYU Pr.

Toward a Jewish America. Eugene Kaellis. Ed. by Rhoda Kaellis. LC 87-12354. (Symposium Ser.: Vol. 20). 216p. 1987. lib. bdg. 89.95 (*0-88946-712-9*) E Mellen.

Toward a Jewish Theology: Methods, Problems, & Possibilities. Byron L. Sherwin. LC 91-38221. 204p. 1992. lib. bdg. 89.95 (*0-7734-9635-1*) E Mellen.

Toward a Just Correctional System. Joseph E. Hickey & Peter L. Scharf. LC 79-88112. (Jossey-Bass Social & Behavioral Science Ser.). 224p. reprint ed. pap. 63.90 (*0-8357-4700-X*, 2052355) Bks Demand.

Toward a Just Social Order. Derek L. Phillips. LC 85-43303. 450p. 1986. pap. text ed. 19.95 (*0-691-02834-6*) Princeton U Pr.

***Toward a Just Social Order.** Derek L. Phillips. LC 85-43303. reprint ed. pap. 134.30 (*0-608-04648-5*, 2065334) Bks Demand.

Toward a Just World. Rajni Kothari. 42p. 1980. pap. 12.95 (*0-911646-18-3*) Transaction Pubs.

Toward a Kinder & Gentler America: Ending Poverty & Homelessness & Fulfilling the American Dream. Richard H. Ropers. (Distinguished Faculty Lecture Ser.). 29p. pap. text ed. write for info. (*0-935615-08-3*) S Utah U Pr.

Toward a Language Policy for Puerto Ricans in the U. S. An Agenda for a Community in Movement. National P. R. Task Force on Educational Policy Staff. 21p. 1982. pap. 3.00 (*1-878483-16-1*) Hunter Coll CEP.

Toward a Larger Theatre: Seven Plays by Mordecai Gorelik. Mordecai Gorelik. LC 87-35224. 384p. (Orig.). (C). 1988. pap. text ed. 28.00 (*0-8191-6846-7*); lib. bdg. 56.50 (*0-8191-6845-9*) U Pr of Amer.

Toward a Liberalism. Richard E. Flathman. LC 88-47922. 248p. 1989. pap. 14.95 (*0-8014-9536-9*) Cornell U Pr.

Toward a Liberation Spirituality. Nestor Jaen. Ed. by Erin Milnes. Tr. by Phillip Berryman from SPA. LC 91-3213. 128p. 1991. pap. 2.00 (*0-8294-0698-0*) Loyola Pr.

Toward a Livable World: Leo Szilard & the Crusade for Nuclear Arms Control. Leo Szilard. Ed. by Hele S. Hawkins et al. 484p. 1987. 50.00 (*0-262-19260-8*) MIT Pr.

Toward a Logic of Meanings. Ed. by Jean Piaget & Rolando Garcia. Tr. by Jack Easley & Phil Davidson. 200p. 1991. text ed. 39.95 (*0-8058-0301-7*) L Erlbaum Assocs.

Toward a Male Spirituality. John T. Carmody. LC 89-50905. x, 128p. 1989. pap. 7.95 (*0-89622-410-4*) Twenty-Third.

Toward a Market-Oriented Housing Sector in Eastern Europe: Developments in Bulgaria, Czechoslovakia, Hungary, Poland, Romania & Yugoslavia, U. I. Reports 90-10. Jeffrey P. Telgarsky & Raymond J. Struyk. LC 90-49256. (Reports: No. 90-10). (Illus.). 258p. (Orig.). (C). 1990. pap. text ed. 18.50 (*0-87766-496-X*); lib. bdg. 46.50 (*0-87766-495-1*) Urban Inst.

Toward a Marxist Anthropology: Problems & Perspectives. Ed. by Stanley Diamond. (World Anthropology Ser.). 492p. 1979. text ed. 69.25 (*90-279-7780-1*) Mouton.

Toward a Marxist Theory of Nationalism. Horace B. Davis. LC 77-91740. 294p. 1980. 17.50 (*0-85345-441-8*); pap. 10.00 (*0-85345-516-3*) Monthly Rev.

Toward a Mature Faith. Erwin R. Goodenough. (Brown Classics in Judaica Ser.). 200p. (C). 1988. reprint ed. pap. text ed. 20.00 (*0-8191-6791-6*) U Pr of Amer.

Toward a Mature Faith: Does Biblical Inerrancy Make Sense? Clayton Sullivan. 135p. (Orig.). 1990. pap. 5.00 (*0-9627617-0-2*) Bapt Today.

Toward a Meaningful Life: The Wisdom of the Rebbe. Simon Jacobson. 293p. 1995. 20.00 (*0-688-14196-X*) Morrow.

Toward a Meaningful Life: The Wisdom of the Rebbe. large type ed. Menachem M. Schneerson. 481p. 1996. 23.95 (*0-7838-1593-X*, GK Hall) Thorndike Pr.

Toward a Medieval Poetics. Paul Zumthor. Tr. by Philip Bennett from FRE. 496p. (C). 1991. text ed. 59.95 (*0-8166-1845-3*) U of Minn Pr.

Toward A Molecular Basis of Alcohol Use & Abuse. Ed. by B. Jansson. LC 94-10167. (EXS Ser.: Vol. 7). 1994. 118.00 (*3-7643-2940-8*) Birkhauser.

Toward A Molecular Basis of Alcohol Use & Abuse. Ed. by B. Jansson. LC 94-10167. (EXS Ser.: Vol. 7). 1994. 103.00 (*0-8176-2940-8*) Birkhauser.

T

An Asterisk (*) at the beginning of an entry indicates that the title is appearing in BIP for the first time.

Toward a More Exact Ecology. Ed. by Peter J. Grubb & John B. Whittaker. (Illus.). 464p. (C). 1989. pap. text ed. 54.95 (*0-632-02685-5*) Blackwell Sci.
Toward a More Inclusive Curriculum: The Integration of Gender, Race, & Class Ephemera, Vol. I, No. 1. Ed. by Colette Hall. 96p. (Orig.). (C). 1989. pap. 16.95 (*0-685-26834-9*) Blls Lettres.
Toward a More Natural Science: Biology & Human Affairs. Leon R. Kass. 370p. 1988. pap. 14.95 (*0-02-917071-0*, Free Press) Free Pr.
Toward a More Perfect Union: Six Essays on the Constitution. Ed. by Neil L. York. LC 88-14507. 188p. 1988. pap. text ed. 18.95 (*0-88706-926-6*) State U NY Pr.
Toward a More Perfect Union: Six Essays on the Constitution. Ed. by Neil L. York. LC 88-14507. 188p. 1989. text ed. 57.50 (*0-88706-925-8*) State U NY Pr.
Toward a More Perfect Union: Virtue & the Formation of American Republics. Ann F. Withington. (Illus.). 336p. 1991. 49.95 (*0-19-506835-1*) OUP.
Toward a More Perfect Union: Virtue & the Formation of American Republics. Ann F. Withington. (Illus.). 304p. (C). 1996. pap. 16.95 (*0-19-510130-8*) OUP.
Toward a More Perfect Union: Writings of Herbert J. Storing. Herbert J. Storing. LC 94-22771. 479p. 1995. pap. text ed. 14.95 (*0-8447-3840-9*) Am Enterprise.
Toward a More Perfect Union: Writings of Herbert J. Storing. Herbert J. Storing. Ed. by Joseph Bessette. LC 94-22771. 479p. 1995. 39.95 (*0-8447-3841-7*) Am Enterprise.
Toward a More Sustainable Agriculture. Raymond P. Poincelot. (Illus.). (C). 1986. text ed. 43.95 (*0-87055-518-9*) AVI.
Toward a National Center for Higher Continuing Education. Robert B. Hudson. 1968. 2.50 (*0-87060-014-1*, OCP 17) Syracuse U Cont Ed.
Toward a National Health Care Survey: A Data System for the 21st Century. National Research Council Staff. Ed. by Gooloo S. Wonderlich. 204p. (C). 1992. pap. text ed. 27.00 (*0-309-04692-0*) Natl Acad Pr.
Toward a National Policy on Drug & AIDS Testing. Ed. by Mathea Falco & Warren I. Cikins. (Dialogues on Public Policy Ser.). 80p. 1989. pap. 10.95 (*0-8157-2733-X*) Brookings.
Toward a National Policy on Energy Resources & Mineral Plant Foods. Ed. by S. P. Ellison, Jr. (Illus.). 128p. 1973. pap. 3.00 (*0-317-05182-2*, SP0004) Bur Econ Geology.
Toward a National Power Policy: The New Deal & the Electric Utility Industry, 1933-1941. Philip J. Funigiello. LC 72-92695. 314p. reprint ed. pap. 89.50 (*0-317-28770-2*, 2020622) Bks Demand.
Toward a National Security Strategy for the 1990s: Assuring 21st Century Competitiveness. Richard M. Cohen & Peter A. Wilson. 300p. 1990. 62.00 (*0-8448-1624-8*, Crane Russak); pap. 34.00 (*0-8448-1625-6*, Crane Russak) Taylor & Francis.
Toward a National Semiconductor Strategy, Vol. 1. (Illus.). 54p. (Orig.). (C). 1993. pap. text ed. 25.00 (*1-56806-889-1*) DIANE Pub.
Toward a National Semiconductor Strategy, Vol. 2. 24p. (Orig.). (C). 1993. pap. text ed. 25.00 (*1-56806-890-5*) DIANE Pub.
Toward a New Africa Policy. Jane W. Jacqz. 71p. 1977. pap. text ed. 15.95 (*0-87855-754-7*) Transaction Pubs.
Toward a New Age in Christian Theology. Richard H. Drummond. LC 85-5155. (American Society of Missiology Ser.: No. 8). 272p. 1985. reprint ed. pap. 77.60 (*0-7837-9829-6*, 2060558) Bks Demand.
Toward a New Arts Order: Process, Power, Change. Nello McDaniel & George Thorn. Ed. by Sharon Block. 88p. (Orig.). (C). 1993. pap. text ed. 10.00 (*1-884345-00-X*) ARTS Action.
Toward a New Beginning in Cooperative Cataloging: The History, Progress, & Future of the Cooperative Cataloging Council. Compiled by David W. Reser. LC 94-42740. 1994. write for info. (*0-8444-0867-0*) Lib Congress.
***Toward a New Behaviorism: The Case Against Perceptual Reductionism.** William R. Uttal. LC 97-19624. 1997. write for info. (*0-8058-2738-2*) L Erlbaum Assocs.
Toward a New Brain: Evolution & the Human Mind. Stuart Litvak & A. Wayne Senzee. 250p. 1985. 17.95 (*0-13-926056-0*) P-H.
Toward a New Central Europe: A Symposium. Francis Wagner. (Illus.). 394p. 1970. 8.50 (*0-87934-002-9*) Danubian.
Toward a New Common Sense: Law, Science & Politics in the Paradigmatic Transition. Boaventura De Sousa Santos. (After the Law Ser.). 500p. (C). 1995. pap. 29.95 (*0-415-90439-0*, A5764) Routledge.
Toward a New Common Sense: Law, Science & Politics in the Paradigmatic Transition. Boaventura De Sousa Santos. (After the Law Ser.). 500p. (C). 1995. text ed. 79.95 (*0-415-90438-2*, A5760) Routledge.
Toward a New Council of Florence: On the Peace of Faith & Other Works by Nicolaus of Cusa. William F. Wertz. LC 92-85238. (Illus.). 500p. (C). 1993. pap. 15.00 (*0-9621095-8-4*) Schiller Inst.
***Toward a New Cuba? Legacies of a Revolution.** Ed. by Miguel A. Centeno & Mauricio Font. LC 96-32581. 250p. 1996. lib. bdg. 45.00 (*1-55587-632-3*, 876323) Lynne Rienner.
Toward a New Deal in Baltimore: People & Government in the Great Depression. Jo Ann E. Argersinger. LC 87-21767. (Illus.). xix, 284p. (C). 1988. 39.95 (*0-8078-1769-4*) U of NC Pr.
***Toward a New Durable & Environmentally Compliant Adhesive Bonding Process for Aluminum Alloys.** Richard Oosting. (Illus.). 273p. (Orig.). 1995. pap. 62.50 (*90-407-1170-4*, Pub. by Delft U Pr NE) Coronet Bks.
Toward a New Earth: Apocalypse in the American Novel. John R. May. LC 72-3510. 264p. 1972. reprint ed. pap. 75.30 (*0-608-00891-5*, 2061685) Bks Demand.
Toward a New Economics: Critical Essays on Ecology, Distribution & Other Themes. Kenneth Boulding. (Economists of the Twentieth Century Ser.). 368p. 1992. text ed. 85.00 (*1-85278-568-3*) E Elgar.
Toward a New Economics: Essays in Post-Keynesian & Institutionalist Theory. Alfred S. Eichner. LC 84-27724. 256p. (gr. 13). 1985. text ed. 62.95 (*0-87332-326-2*); pap. text ed. 26.95 (*0-87332-327-0*) M E Sharpe.
Toward a New Electromagnetics, Pt. III. 38p. 1988. 9.00 (*0-914119-22-2*) Tesla Bk Co.
Toward a New Electromagnetics, Pt. IV. 64p. 1988. 10.25 (*0-914119-23-0*) Tesla Bk Co.
Toward a New Electromagnetics: Vectors & Mechanisms Clarified, 2 vols., Set. (Nikola Tesla Ser.). 1991. lib. bdg. 150.95 (*0-8490-4323-9*) Gordon Pr.
Toward a New Enlightenment: The Philosophy of Paul Kurtz. Paul Kurtz. Ed. by Timothy J. Madigan. LC 93-17058. 376p. (C). 1993. text ed. 39.95 (*1-56000-118-6*) Transaction Pubs.
Toward a New Era in Arts Education: The Interlochen Symposium. Ed. by John McLaughlin. LC 88-16649. 138p. (Orig.). 1988. pap. 12.95 (*0-915400-69-3*, ACA Bks) Am Council Arts.
Toward a New Era in United States Manufacturing: The Need for a National Vision. National Research Council, Manufacturing Studies Board Staff. LC 86-50832. (Illus.). 190p. reprint ed. pap. 54.20 (*0-8357-4222-9*, 2037007) Bks Demand.
Toward a New Foundation for Physics. Joseph H. Spigelman. LC 87-82142. 144p. 1987. 15.00 (*0-9619183-0-6*) Kips Bay Pr.
Toward a New Historicism. Wesley Morris. LC 77-166384. 277p. 1972. reprint ed. pap. 79.00 (*0-7837-9394-4*, 2060139) Bks Demand.
Toward a New Integration of Language & Culture. Ed. by Alan J. Singerman. (Reports of the Northeast Conference on the Teaching of Foreign Languages). 164p. 1988. pap. 10.95 (*0-915432-88-9*) NE Conf Teach Foreign.
Toward a New International Economic System: A Joint Japanese-American View. Committee for Economic Development. LC 74-79477. 64p. 1974. pap. 2.00 (*0-87186-054-6*) Comm Econ Dev.
Toward a New International Marine Order. Finn Laursen. 1982. lib. bdg. 102.00 (*90-247-2597-6*) Kluwer Ac.
Toward a New Interpretation of Plato. Giovanni Reale. Tr. by John R. Catan & Richard Davies. LC 95-34533. 459p. 1997. 44.95 (*0-8132-0847-5*); pap. 29.95 (*0-8132-0854-8*) Cath U Pr.
Toward a New Iron Age? Quantitative Modeling of Resource Exhaustion. Robert B. Gordon et al. (Illus.). 200p. 1987. 33.95 (*0-674-89818-4*) HUP.
***Toward a New Modernism.** Kenneth Cauthen. 184p. 1996. pap. text ed. 24.50 (*0-7618-0521-4*) U Pr of Amer.
***Toward a New Modernism.** Kenneth Cauthen. 184p. 1997. lib. bdg. 44.00 (*0-7618-0520-6*) U Pr of Amer.
Toward a New Music: Music & Electricity. Carlos Chavez. Tr. by Herbert Weinstock from SPA. LC 74-28308. (Music Reprint Ser.). (Illus.). 180p. 1975. reprint ed. lib. bdg. 29.50 (*0-306-70719-5*) Da Capo.
Toward a New Order of Sea Power. Harold H. Sprout. (History - United States Ser.). 336p. 1993. reprint ed. lib. bdg. 89.00 (*0-7812-4859-0*) Rprt Serv.
Toward a New Pentecost, for a New Evangelization: Malines Document I. 2nd ed. Ed. by Kilian McDonnell. LC 92-46910. 80p. 1993. pap. text ed. 5.95 (*0-8146-5846-6*, M Glazier) Liturgical Pr.
Toward a New Personology: An Evolutionary Model. Theodore Millon. (Series on Personality Processes). 200p. 1990. text ed. 39.95 (*0-471-51573-6*) Wiley.
Toward a New Philosophical Basis for Parapsychological Phenomena. Hornell Hart. LC 65-15951. (Parapsychological Monographs: No. 6). 1965. pap. 5.00 (*0-912328-09-6*) Parapsych Foun.
Toward a New Philosophy of Biology: Observations of an Evolutionist. Ernst W. Mayr. (Illus.). 640p. 1989. pap. text ed. 16.95 (*0-674-89666-1*) HUP.
Toward A New Poetics: Contemporary Writing in France. Serge Gavronsky. LC 94-2946. 1994. 55.00 (*0-520-08071-8*); pap. 18.00 (*0-520-08793-3*) U CA Pr.
Toward a New Politics in the South. Jasper B. Shannon. LC 50-6094. 110p. reprint ed. pap. 31.40 (*0-317-29910-7*, 2021782) Bks Demand.
Toward a New Psychology of Gender. Ed. by Gergen. 512p. (C). 1997. text ed. 74.95 (*0-415-91307-1*, Routledge NY) Routledge.
Toward a New Psychology of Gender. Ed. by Mary Gergen. 512p. (C). 1996. pap. 27.95 (*0-415-91308-X*, Routledge NY) Routledge.
Toward a New Psychology of Men: Psychoanalytic & Social Perspectives. Ed. by Robert M. Friedman & Leila Lerner. (Psychoanalytic Review Ser.: Vol. 73, No. 4). 240p. 1987. lib. bdg. 30.00 (*0-89862-581-5*) Guilford Pr.
Toward a New Psychology of Women. 2nd ed. Jean B. Miller. LC 86-47553. 192p. 1997. reprint ed. pap. 12.50 (*0-8070-2909-2*) Beacon Pr.
Toward a New Science of Educational Testing & Assessment. Harold Berlak et al. LC 90-28708. (SUNY Series, Teacher Preparation & Development). (Illus.). 235p. (C). 1992. text ed. 59.50 (*0-7914-0877-9*); pap. text ed. 19.95 (*0-7914-0878-7*) State U NY Pr.
Toward a New Science of Instruction. 1994. lib. bdg. 250.00 (*0-8490-5727-2*) Gordon Pr.
Toward a New Science of Instruction. Kate Maloy. 73p. (Orig.). (C). 1994. pap. text ed. 25.00 (*0-7881-0595-7*) DIANE Pub.
***Toward a New Science of Instruction: Learning Processes in Mathematics, Science, Social Science & the Comprehension of Texts.** 1997. lib. bdg. 251.95 (*0-8490-8114-9*) Gordon Pr.
Toward a New Sensibility: Essays of O. K. Bouwsma. O. K. Bouwsma. Ed. by J. L. Craft & Ronald E. Hustwit. LC 81-16117. 299p. reprint ed. pap. 85.30 (*0-7837-4664-4*, 2044391) Bks Demand.
Toward a New Social Contract: Employment Security for Managers & Professionals. Jerome M. Rosow & Robert Zager. Ed. by Jill Casner-Lotto. (New Roles for Managers Ser.: Pt. IV). 75p. 1991. pap. 95.00 (*0-89361-043-7*) Work in Amer.
Toward a New South? Studies in Post-Civil War Southern Communities. Ed. by Orville V. Burton & Robert C. McMath, Jr. LC 81-1666. (Contributions in American History Ser.: No. 97). (Illus.). xx, 319p. 1982. text ed. 59.95 (*0-313-22996-1*, BNC/) Greenwood.
Toward a New Spring of Humankind. Francis A. Cegielka. LC 84-72170. 1987. 8.95 (*0-8158-0427-X*) Chris Mass.
Toward a New Synthesis: John Fowles, John Gardner, Norman Mailer. Robert J. Begiebing. LC 88-34076. 162p. 1991. 39.00 (*0-8357-1947-2*) Univ Rochester Pr.
***Toward a New Synthesis: John Fowles, John Gardner, Norman Mailer.** Robert J. Begiebing. LC 88-34076. 162p. 1989. reprint ed. pap. 46.20 (*0-608-02655-7*, AU00479) Bks Demand.
Toward a New Taxonomic Framework for Central California Archaeology: Essays. James A. Bennyhoff & David A. Fredrickson. Ed. by Richard E. Hughes. (Contributions of the University of California Archaeologial Research Facility Ser.: No. 52). 128p. 1994. pap. 14.00 (*1-882744-02-0*) U CA Arch Res Fac.
Toward a New Theatre. Edward G. Craig. LC 68-56531. (Illus.). 106p. 1972. 38.95 (*0-405-08399-8*, Pub. by Blom Pubns UK) Ayer.
Toward a New Understanding of Literacy. Ed. by Merald E. Wrolstad & Dennis Fisher. LC 83-24615. 350p. 1985. text ed. 59.95 (*0-275-92072-0*, 2072, Praeger Pubs) Greenwood.
Toward a New World Vol. 1: Powerful Proof of the Existence of God: Non-Denominational - Non-Sectarian. abr. rev. ed. Ernst F. Baumann & Norman Bloom. (Illus.). 300p. 1995. text ed. 20.00 (*0-9648440-2-8*) Coll Of The Canons.
Toward a New World Order: Adjusting India-U. S. Relations. Ed. by Leo E. Rose & Eric Gonsalves. LC 92-70529. (Research Papers & Policy Studies: No. 38). 1992. pap. 15.00 (*1-55729-032-6*) IEAS.
Toward a New World Order: The Countdown to Armageddon. Donald S. McAlvany. 250p. (Orig.). (C). 1990. pap. 8.95 (*0-9624517-9-7*) Hearthstone OK.
Toward a New World Outlook: A Documentary History of Education in the People's Republic of China, 1949-1976. Ed. by Shi Ming Hu & Eli Seifman. LC 76-23977. (Asian Studies: No. 2). 1976. 42.50 (*0-404-15401-8*); pap. 11.95 (*0-404-15404-2*) AMS Pr.
Toward a Nuclear Peace: The Future of Nuclear Weapons. Ed. by Michael J. Mazarr & Alexander T. Lennon. LC 93-28019. 227p. 1994. text ed. 45.00 (*0-312-10404-9*) St Martin.
Toward a Peace Ticket in 1968. Gus Hall. 1967. pap. 0.25 (*0-87898-016-4*) New Outlook.
Toward a Perfected State. Paul Weiss. LC 85-26220. (SUNY Series in Systematic Philosophy). 459p. (Orig.). (C). 1986. text ed. 64.50 (*0-88706-253-9*); pap. text ed. 21.95 (*0-88706-254-7*) State U NY Pr.
Toward a Phenomenology of the Etheric World: Investigations into the Life of Nature & Man. Jochen Bockemuhl et al. Ed. by Malcolm Gardner et al. Tr. by John Meeks from GER. (Illus.). 200p. (Orig.). 1985. pap. 16.95 (*0-88010-115-6*) Anthroposophic.
Toward a Phenomenology of Written Art. Gerald Burns. LC 79-15699. 64p. 1979. 12.50 (*0-914232-36-3*); pap. 4.95 (*0-914232-35-5*) McPherson & Co.
Toward a Philosophy of the Act. M. M. Bakhtin. Ed. by Vadim Liapunov & Michael Holquist. LC 93-7557. (Slavic Ser.: No. 10). 128p. (C). 1993. pap. 10.95 (*0-292-70805-X*); text ed. 25.00 (*0-292-76534-7*) U of Tex Pr.
Toward a Philosophy of the Science of Chiropractic. Joseph C. Keating. (Illus.). 451p. 1993. text ed. 59.95 (*0-9614296-9-0*) Wrld-Wide Bks.
Toward a Philosophy of the Seas. Horace M. Kallen. LC 72-97788. 56p. reprint ed. pap. 25.00 (*0-317-28831-8*, 2017817) Bks Demand.
Toward a Planned Society: From Franklin D. Roosevelt to Richard Nixon. Otis L. Graham, Jr. 376p. 1976. 25.00 (*0-19-501985-7*) OUP.
Toward a Political Economy of Development: A Rational Choice Perspective. Ed. by Robert H. Bates. (California Series on Social Choice & Political Economy: Vol. 14). 1988. pap. 18.00 (*0-520-06052-0*) U CA Pr.
Toward a Political Economy of Development: A Rational Choice Perspective. Ed. by Robert H. Bates. LC 87-10870. (California Series on Social Choice & Political Economy: No. 14). 403p. reprint ed. pap. 114.90 (*0-7837-4763-2*, 2044510) Bks Demand.
Toward a Post-Industrial Psychology: Emerging Perspectives on Technology, Work, Education, & Leisure. Donald A. Mankin. LC 78-5302. 227p. reprint ed. pap. 64.70 (*0-317-28058-9*, 2055773) Bks Demand.
Toward a Postpositivist World: Hermeneutics for Understanding International Relations, Environment, & Other Important Issues of the Twenty-First Century. Katrina Rogers. LC 94-10288. (San Francisco State University Series in Philosophy: Vol. 3). 216p. (C). 1996. text ed. 47.95 (*0-8204-2486-2*) P Lang Pubng.
Toward a Practice of Autonomous Systems: Proceedings of the First European Conference on Artificial Life, Dec. 11-13, 1991, Paris, France. Ed. by Francisco J. Varela & Paul Bourgine. (Illus.). 550p. 1992. pap. 57.50 (*0-262-72019-1*) MIT Pr.
Toward a Process Pneumatology. Blair Reynolds. LC 88-43326. 216p. 1990. 34.50 (*0-941664-97-X*) Susquehanna U Pr.
Toward a Programme of Imperial Life: The British Empire at the Turn of the Century. Ed. by H. John Field. LC 81-2115. (Contributions in Comparative Colonial Studies: No. 9). xiv, 256p. 1982. text ed. 55.00 (*0-313-22917-1*, FIL/, Greenwood Pr) Greenwood.
Toward a Psychology of Art: Collected Essays. Rudolf Arnheim. LC 66-10692. 1966. pap. 14.95 (*0-520-02161-4*) U CA Pr.
Toward a Psychology of Being. 2nd ed. Abraham H. Maslow. 1968. pap. 36.95 (*0-442-03805-4*) Van Nos Reinhold.
Toward a Psychology of Deafness: Theoretical & Empirical Perspectives. Peter V. Paul & Dorothy W. Jackson. LC 92-31126. 334p. 1992. text ed. 66.00 (*0-205-14112-9*, H41122) Allyn.
***Toward a Psychology of Persons.** Ed. by William E. Smythe. 400p. 1998. write for info. (*0-8058-2718-8*) L Erlbaum Assocs.
Toward a Psychology of Situations: An Interactional Perspective. Ed. by David Magnusson. 480p. 1981. text ed. 69.95 (*0-89859-061-2*) L Erlbaum Assocs.
Toward a Public Policy on Mental Health Care of the Elderly. Group for the Advancement of Psychiatry Staff. LC 62-2872. (Group for the Advancement of Psychiatry, Symposium Ser.: Vol. 7, No. 79). 56p. reprint ed. pap. 25.00 (*0-7837-2115-3*, 2042394) Bks Demand.
Toward a Quantitative Methodology for Stylistic Analyses. Agnes M. Bruno. LC 73-80835. (University of California Publications in Social Welfare: Vol. 109). 90p. reprint ed. pap. 25.70 (*0-317-29556-X*, 2021259) Bks Demand.
Toward a Rational Society: Student Protest, Science, & Politics. Jurgen Habermas. Tr. by Jeremy J. Shapiro from GER. LC 73-121827. 132p. 1970. pap. 14.00 (*0-8070-4177-7*) Beacon Pr.
Toward a Rationality of Emotions: An Essay in the Philosophy of Mind. W. George Turski. LC 93-42936. (Series in Continental Thought: Vol. 21). 208p. (C). 1994. text ed. 39.95 (*0-8214-1075-X*) Ohio U Pr.
Toward a Realistic Military Assistance Program. Robert J. Pranger et al. LC 74-29150. (Foreign Affairs Study Ser.: No. 15). 56p. reprint ed. pap. 25.00 (*0-317-08189-6*, 2017151) Bks Demand.
Toward a Reassessment of the Shepherd of Hermas: Its Date & Its Pneumatology. J. Christian Wilson. LC 93-29331. (Biblical Press Ser.: Vol. 18). 192p. 1993. text ed. 79.95 (*0-7734-2382-6*, Mellen Biblical Pr) E Mellen.
Toward a Rebirth of Common Sense in Education. Thomas J. Brown. LC 95-83913. 128p. (Orig.). 1996. pap. 11.95 (*1-56167-246-7*) Am Literary Pr.
Toward a Recovery of Christian Belief. Carl F. Henry. LC 90-80629. 128p. (Orig.). 1990. pap. 9.99 (*0-89107-588-7*) Crossway Bks.
Toward a Reference Grammar of Tok Pisin: An Experiment in Corpus Linguistics. John W. Verhaar. LC 95-7328. (Oceanic Linguistics Special Publication: No. 26). 512p. (C). 1995. pap. text ed. 38.00 (*0-8248-1672-2*) UH Pr.
Toward a Renaissance of Puerto Rico. Anthony M. Stevens-Arroyo & San. 1987. text ed. 46.00 (*0-88033-956-X*, SC53) Col U Pr.
Toward a Renewable Energy Future: The Urban Potential, Austin, Texas. Contrib. by Marlan Blissett. LC 81-82253. (Policy Research Project Reports: No. 44). 139p. 1982. pap. 7.00 (*0-89940-646-7*) LBJ Sch Pub Aff.
Toward a Renewed Catholic Charities Movement: A Partial Reprint. 54p. 1992. 10.00 (*0-318-15959-7*) Catholic Charities.
Toward a Renewed Catholic Charities Movement: A Study of the National Conference of Catholic Charities. 54p. 1972. reprint ed. 15.00 (*0-318-15960-0*) Catholic Charities.
Toward a Renewed Mind. Richard F. Gottier. (Illus.). 276p. 1990. 19.95 (*0-9625671-0-8*) R F Gottier.
Toward a Response to the American Crisis. rev. ed. Glenn N. Schram. 267p. 1993. pap. 12.95 (*0-931888-53-0*) Christendom Pr.
Toward a Restraint-Free Environment: Reducing the Use of Physical & Chemical Restraints in Long-Term & Acute Care Settings. Ed. by Judith V. Braun & Steven Lipson. LC 92-48379. 320p. 1993. pap. 29.95 (*1-878812-12-2*) Hlth Prof Pr.
Toward a Right to Peace: Selected Papers of John H. E. Fried. John H. Fried. LC 93-43733. 1994. lib. bdg. 25.00 (*1-880831-10-4*) Aletheia Pr.
Toward a Safe & Sane Halloween: And Other Tales of Suburbia. William E. Geist. LC 84-40421. 288p. 1985. 16.95 (*0-8129-1150-4*, Times Bks) Random.
Toward a Safer Future-Excellence in Aviation: Proceedings of the 5th Annual European Corporate & Regional Aircraft Operators Seminar, March 2-4, 1993, Amsterdam, Netherlands. Flight Safety Foundation Staff. LC 91-657078. (Flight Safety Digest Ser. Special Supplement: Vol. 12, No. 8, August 1993). (Illus.). 167p. reprint ed. pap. 47.60 (*0-7837-7030-8*, 2046845) Bks Demand.
***Toward a Safer Workplace: Reform & Deregulation of Workers' Compensation.** James R. Chelius & Edward Muscovitch. Ed. by Kathryn Ciffoiluo. LC 96-34775. (Pioneer Paper Ser.: No. 11). 220p. (Orig.). 1996. pap. 15.00 (*0-929930-16-9*) Pioneer Inst.
Toward a Science of Accounting. Robert R. Sterling. LC 80-14502. 247p. (C). 1980. text ed. 20.00 (*0-914348-31-0*) Scholars Bk.

Toward a Science of Consciousness: The First Tucson Discussions & Debates. Ed. by Stuart R. Hameroff et al. (Complex Adaptive Systems Ser.). (Illus.). 832p. 1996. 65.00 (*0-262-08249-7*, Bradford Bks) MIT Pr.

Toward a Science of Family Nursing. Catherine L. Gillis et al. Ed. by Debra Hunter. 501p. (C). 1989. text ed. 50.50 (*0-201-14238-4*) Addison-Wesley.

Toward a Science of Human Nature: Aspirations of Nineteenth Century Psychology. Daniel N. Robinson. LC 81-38458. 256p. 1982. text ed. 52.50 (*0-231-05174-3*) Col U Pr.

Toward a Science of Human Nature: Aspirations of Nineteenth Century Psychology. Daniel N. Robinson. LC 81-38458. 256p. 1982. pap. text ed. 22.00 (*0-231-05175-1*) Col U Pr.

Toward a Science of Man: Essays in the History of Anthropology. Ed. by Timothy H. Thoresen. (World Anthropology Ser.). xiv, 232p. 1975. 43.10 (*90-279-7609-0*) Mouton.

Toward a Science of Vocabulary Development. Joseph P. O'Rourke. LC 73-87530. (Janua Linguarum, Ser.: No. 183). (Illus.). 1974. pap. text ed. 44.65 (*90-279-2663-8*) Mouton.

Toward a Scientific Practice of Science Education. Ed. by Marjorie Gardner et al. 368p. 1990. 99.95 (*0-8058-0345-9*) L Erlbaum Assocs.

Toward a Seamless System for Youth Development: A New Strategy for Integrating Resources, Programs & Institutions. David A. Gruber. 76p. 1994. pap. 10.00 (*1-887410-64-3*) Jobs for Future.

Toward a Semantic Specification of Deep Case. Don L. Nilsen. (Janua Linguarum, Ser. Minor: No. 152). 52p. (Orig.). 1972. text ed. 34.65 (*90-279-2318-3*) Mouton.

Toward a Semiotic Theory of Visual Communication in the Cinema. Gorham A. Kindem. Ed. by Garth S. Jowett. LC 79-6678. (Dissertations on Film, 1980 Ser.). 1980. lib. bdg. 20.95 (*0-405-12912-2*) Ayer.

Toward a Simpler Way of Life: The Arts & Crafts Architects of California. Ed. by Robert Winter. LC 94-43749. 1995. write for info. (*0-89133-243-X*) Natl Trust Hist Pres.

***Toward a Simpler Way of Life: The Arts & Crafts Architects of California.** Ed. by Robert Winter. LC 96-45103. (Illus.). 1997. 45.00 (*0-520-20916-8*) U CA Pr.

Toward a Social Architecture. Andrew Saint. LC 86-28179. 272p. 1987. text ed. 50.00 (*0-300-03830-5*) Yale U Pr.

Toward a Social History of American English. J. L. Dillard. (Contributions to the Sociology of Language Ser.: No. 39). xii, 301p. 1985. 98.50 (*3-11-010584-5*) Mouton.

Toward a Social History of Archaeology in the United States. Thomas C. Patterson. Ed. by Jeffrey Quilter. (Case Studies in Archaeology). 231p. (C). 1994. pap. text ed. write for info. (*0-15-500824-2*) HB Coll Pubs.

Toward a Social History of the American Civil War: Exploratory Essays. Ed. by Maris Vinovskis. (Illus.). 192p. (C). 1990. text ed. 54.95 (*0-521-39523-2*); pap. text ed. 15.95 (*0-521-39559-3*) Cambridge U Pr.

***Toward a Social Technology of Peace: A Sociology of Conflict Resolution. Reginald D. Olson. 340p. (Orig.). 1996. pap. text ed. 35.95 (*0-9653403-0-9*) R Olson.**

This book is based on three premises. First, there are many different ways to wage struggles & attain peace. (A "tool-box" of options is available.) Second, there is a cultural lag between these material & social techniques. (This is revealed in the "old" & "new" scenarios of conflict resolution). Third, the resolution of struggles at the interpersonal level has its parallels at the inter-organizational & international levels (with corresponding choices to be made regarding the importance of both integrative & instrumental activities). Chapters include: SOCIOLOGY OF CONFLICT -- Cultural Lag in Conflict Resolution; Nature of Conflict; Power -- Means & Ends; Functions of Social Conflict; Causes of Violence; VIOLENCE & SOCIETY -- Arms Race; Militarism; Pacifism; Just War & the Crusade; INTERPERSONAL CONFLICT RESOLUTION -- Personal Styles; Negotiation; Mediation; Arbitration & Adjudication; TRADITIONAL METHODS OF RESOLVING INTERNATIONAL CONFLICTS -- Warfare; United Nations; Normative & Functional Integration; Disarmament; NON VIOLENCE, A CREATIVE RESOLUTION TO CONFLICT -- its Proponents; Tactics; & Strategy; Poland - a Case Study; Civilian Nonviolent National Defense; TRENDS TOWARD A WORLD OF PEACE -- United States Institute of Peace; Convergence of Conflict Resolution Techniques; & Careers in Conflict Resolution. Interdisciplinary, seven appendices (including Nobel Peace Prize recipients), 12 figures, 6 tables, 600 reference entries, questions for discussion & investigation for each chapter. To order contact: REGINALD OLSON, Publisher, 6172 Vereker Drive, Oxford OH 45056. 513-523-1304. *Publisher Provided Annotation.*

Toward a Sociology of Education. Ed. by John Beck et al. LC 77-80869. Orig. Title: World's Apart: Readings for a Sociology of Education. 570p. 1978. reprint ed. pap. text ed. 24.95 (*0-87855-643-5*) Transaction Pubs.

Toward a Sociology of the Novel. Lucien Goldmann. (Social Science Paperbacks Ser.). 196p. 1986. pap. 9.95 (*0-422-76350-0*, NO. 1066, Tavistock) Routledge Chapman & Hall.

Toward a Solar Civilization. Omraam M. Aivanhov. (Izvor Collection: Vol. 201). (Illus.). 148p. 1982. pap. 6.95 (*0-911857-00-1*) Prosveta USA.

Toward a Solution. Israel Goldstein. LC 79-128248. (Essay Index Reprint Ser.). 1977. 23.95 (*0-8369-1877-0*) Ayer.

Toward a Sound Philosophy of Nursing. Ed. by June F. Kikuchi & Helen Simmons. LC 93-34604. (C). 1993. text ed. 42.00 (*0-8039-5422-0*) Sage.

***Toward a Sound Philosophy of Nursing.** Ed. by June F. Kikuchi & Helen Simmons. LC 93-34604. (C). 1993. pap. text ed. 18.50 (*0-8039-5423-9*) Sage.

Toward a Sound World Order: A Multidimensional, Hierarchical Ethical Theory. Donald C. Lee. LC 91-40942. (Contributions in Philosophy Ser.: No. 49). 240p. 1992. text ed. 45.00 (*0-313-27903-9*, LTA, Greenwood Pr) Greenwood.

Toward a Speech Act Theory of Literary Discourse. Mary L. Pratt. LC 76-26424. 255p. reprint ed. pap. 72.70 (*0-685-44461-9*, 2056732) Bks Demand.

Toward a State of Esteem: The Final Report of the California Task Force to Promote Self-Esteem & Personal & Social Responsibility. (Illus.). 160p. (Orig.). (C). 1996. pap. 30.00 (*0-7881-2720-9*) DIANE Pub.

Toward a State of Esteem: The Final Report of the California Task Force to Promote Self-Esteem & Personal & Social Responsibility. Andrew M. Mecca et al. (Illus.). 160p. 1990. pap. 8.00 (*0-8011-0846-2*) Calif Education.

Toward a Strategy for the Management of Peace: U. S. Foreign Policy in the 1980's. Harlan Cleveland. 1983. 1.00 (*1-55614-011-8*) U of SD Gov Res Bur.

Toward a Strategy for Urban Integration: Lessons in School & Housing Policy from Twelve Cities: A Report to the Ford Foundation. Ford Foundation Staff & Gary Orfield. LC 81-19447. 87p. (Orig.). 1982. pap. text ed. write for info. (*0-916584-19-4*) Ford Found.

Toward a Structural Psychology of Cinema. John M. Carroll. (Approaches to Semiotics Ser.: No. 55). 224p. 1980. 43.10 (*90-279-3447-9*) Mouton.

Toward a Structural Theory of Action: Network Models of Social Structure, Perception & Action. Ronald S. Burt. (Quantitative Studies in Social Relations). 1982. text ed. 66.00 (*0-12-147150-0*) Acad Pr.

Toward a Superconsciousness: Meditational Theory & Practice. Hiroshi Motoyama. Tr. by Shigenori Nagatomo & Clifford R. Ames. LC 89-81298. (Illus.). 164p. (Orig.). 1990. reprint ed. pap. 46.80 (*0-608-01784-1*, 2062442) Bks Demand.

Toward a Sustainable Maine: The Politics, Economics, & Ethics of Sustainability. Ed. by Richard Barringer. (Orig.). 1993. pap. 10.00 (*0-939561-18-2*) Univ South ME.

Toward a Sustainable Society: An Economic, Social, & Environmental Agenda for Our Children's Future. James Garbarino. LC 91-51218. 260p. 1992. 19.95 (*1-879360-15-2*) Noble Pr.

Toward a System of "Fair & Effective Representation" 129p. 1977. 1.00 (*0-914389-14-9*) Common Cause.

Toward a Systems Theory of Organization. Jamshid Gharajedaghi. (Systems Inquiry Ser.). 116p. 1985. pap. text ed. 13.95 (*0-914105-35-3*) Intersystems Pubns.

Toward a Tenderer Humanity & a Nobler Womanhood: African American Women's Clubs in Turn-of-the-Century Chicago. Anne M. Knupfer. (Illus.). 230p. (C). 1997. 50.00 (*0-8147-4671-3*); pap. 18.95 (*0-8147-4691-8*) NYU Pr.

Toward a Theater of the Oppressed: The Dramaturgy of John Arden. Javed Malick. LC 95-17397. (Theater: Theory - Text - Performance Ser.). 1995. text ed. 39.50 (*0-472-10587-6*) U of Mich Pr.

Toward a Theological Encounter: Jewish Understandings of Christianity. Ed. by Leon Klenicki. LC 91-3305. (Stimulus Bks.). 176p. 1991. pap. 8.95 (*0-8091-3256-7*) Paulist Pr.

Toward a Theology of Beauty. John Navone & Robert Stefanotti. 96p. (Orig.). 1996. pap. 14.95 (*0-8146-2272-0*, Liturg Pr Bks) Liturgical Pr.

Toward a Theology of Inculturation. Aylward Shorter. LC 88-17030. 256p. (Orig.). 1989. pap. 20.00 (*0-88344-536-0*, 536-0) Orbis Bks.

Toward a Theology of Nature: Essays on Science & Faith. Wolfhart Pannenberg. Ed. by Ted Peters. LC 93-19480. 208p. (Orig.). 1993. pap. 20.00 (*0-664-25384-9*) Westminster John Knox.

Toward a Theology of Radical Involvement: The Theological Legacy of Martin Luther King, Jr. Luther D. Ivory. 256p. (Orig.). 1997. pap. 16.95 (*0-687-01453-0*) Abingdon.

Toward a Theology of Struggle. Eleazar S. Fernandez. LC 94-10605. 194p. (Orig.). 1994. pap. 19.50 (*0-88344-982-X*) Orbis Bks.

***Toward a Theology of the Body.** Mary T. Prokes. 196p. 1996. pap. 23.95 (*0-567-08531-7*, Pub. by T & T Clark UK) Bks Intl VA.

***Toward a Theology of the Body.** Mary T. Prokes. 208p. 1997. pap. text ed. 21.00 (*0-8028-4339-5*) Eerdmans.

Toward a Theology of the Corporation. rev. ed. Michael Novak. 66p. (C). 1991. pap. text ed. 7.25 (*0-8447-3744-5*) Am Enterprise.

Toward a Theory of Cognitive Poetics. Reuven Tsur. LC 92-30150. (North-Holland Linguistic Ser.: Vol. 55). 574p. 1992. 186.50 (*0-444-88996-5*, North Holland) Elsevier.

Toward a Theory of Context in Linguistics & Literature: Proceedings of a Conference of the Kelemen Mikes Hungarian Cultural Society, Maastricht, September 21-25, 1971. Ed. by Adam Makkai. (De Proprietatibus Litterarum, Ser. Minor: No. 18). pap. 40.00 (*90-279-3273-5*) Mouton.

Toward a Theory of Cultural Linguistics. Gary B. Palmer. (Illus.). 368p. (Orig.). (C). 1996. pap. 21.95 (*0-292-76569-X*); text ed. 45.00 (*0-292-76568-1*) U of Tex Pr.

Toward a Theory of Eurocommunism: The Relationship of Eurocommunism to Eurosocialism. Armen Antonian. LC 86-19395. (Contributions in Political Science Ser.: No. 166). 199p. 1987. text ed. 49.95 (*0-313-25295-5*, ATT/, Greenwood Pr) Greenwood.

Toward a Theory of Historical Narrative: A Case Study in Perso-Islamicate Historiography. Marilyn R. Waldman. LC 79-886. (Illus.). 228p. 1980. 42.50 (*0-8142-0297-7*) Ohio St U Pr.

Toward a Theory of Instruction. Jerome S. Bruner. LC 66-13179. (Illus.). 186p. 1974. pap. 11.60 (*0-674-89701-3*) Belknap Pr.

Toward a Theory of Programmed Learning Foreign Language. K. Bung. (Janua Linguarum, Series Didactica: No. 1). 1973. text ed. 55.40 (*90-279-2383-3*) Mouton.

Toward a Theory of Psychosomatic Disorders: Proceedings of the European Conference on Psychosomatic Research, 11th, Heidelberg, September 14-17, 1976. European Conference on Psychosomatic Research Staff. Ed. by Walter Brautigam & Michael Von Rad. (Journal: Psychotherapy & Psychosomatics: Vol. 28, Nos. 1-4). 1977. 78.50 (*3-8055-2747-0*) S Karger.

Toward a Theory of Radical Origin: Essays on Modern German Thought. John Pizer. LC 94-45932. (Modern German Culture & Literature Ser.). xi, 215p. 1995. text ed. 40.00 (*0-8032-3711-1*) U of Nebr Pr.

Toward a Theory of Trade Union Internationalism. John Logue. LC 80-153679. (University of Gothenberg (Sweden), Research Section Post-War History Publications Ser.: No. 7). 66p. (Orig.). 1980. pap. 2.95 (*0-933522-02-9*) Kent Popular.

Toward a Theory on Biological-Physical Interactions in the World Ocean. Ed. by Bruce J. Rothschild. (C). 1988. lib. bdg. 265.50 (*90-277-2765-1*) Kluwer Ac.

Toward a Third Century of Excellence: An Informal History of the J. B. Lippincott Company on the Occasion of Its Two-Hundredth Anniversary. J. Stuart Freeman, Jr. LC 92-10615. 1992. 25.00 (*0-397-51298-8*) Lppncott-Raven.

Toward a Thomist Theology. Joyce A. Little. LC 87-34963. (Toronto Studies in Theology: Vol. 34). 576p. 1988. lib. bdg. 119.95 (*0-88946-779-X*) E Mellen.

Toward a Transpersonal Ecology: Developing New Foundations for Environmentalism. Warwick Fox. LC 95-10627. 380p. 1995. pap. 16.95 (*0-7914-2776-5*); text ed. 49.50 (*0-7914-2775-7*) State U NY Pr.

***Toward a True Alliance: Restructuring U. S. - Japan Security Relations.** Mike Mochizuki. LC 97-21062. 1997. write for info. (*0-8157-5800-6*); pap. write for info. (*0-8157-5801-4*) Brookings.

Toward a Truer Life. Jonathan D. Spence. 96p. 1991. pap. 19.95 (*0-89381-477-6*) Frnds Photography.

Toward a Typology of European Languages. Ed. by Bechert et al. (Empirical Approaches to Language Typology Ser.: No. 8). x, 388p. (C). 1990. lib. bdg. 121.55 (*3-11-012108-5*) Mouton.

Toward a Typology of Juvenile Offenders: Implications for Therapy & Prevention. Sheldon Glueck & Eleanor Glueck. LC 71-115014. 200p. 1970. text ed. 56.00 (*0-8089-0648-8*, 791600, Grune) Saunders.

Toward a Typology of Opiate Users. William Bates & Betty Crowther. 160p. 1974. pap. text ed. 13.95 (*0-87073-960-3*) Schenkman Bks Inc.

Toward a U. S. Grand Strategy. Ed. by Gregory D. Foster. 400p. 1987. pap. write for info. (*0-312-00832-5*) St Martin.

Toward a Unified Ecology. Timothy F. Allen & Thomas W. Hoekstra. 400p. 1991. text ed. 63.00 (*0-231-06918-9*) Col U Pr.

Toward a Unified Ecology. Timothy F. Allen & Thomas W. Hoekstra. Ed. by T. F. Allen & David W. Roberts. (Complexity in Ecological Systems Ser.). 384p. 1993. pap. 29.50 (*0-231-06919-7*) Col U Pr.

Toward a Unified Theory of Consciousness from an Information Science Viewpoint, Artemis Smith: Artemis Smith: the Collected C. U. N. Y. Lectures, 1965-1974 Presented in the Midst of a Religious-Political Controversy. Artemis Smith, pseud. (Unification of Science Ser.). (Illus.). 200p. (Orig.). (C). 1997. reprint ed. pap. 25.00 (*1-878998-24-2*) Savant Garde.

Toward a Unified Theory of Problem Solving: Views from the Content Domains. Ed. by Mike U. Smith. 176p. (C). 1990. pap. 24.50 (*0-8058-0511-7*); text ed. 45.00 (*0-8058-0510-9*) L Erlbaum Assocs.

Toward a United States of Russia: Plans & Projects of Federal Reconstruction of Russia in the Nineteenth Century. Dimitri Von Mohrenschildt. LC 79-56853. (Illus.). 312p. 1981. 39.50 (*0-8386-3013-8*) Fairleigh Dickinson.

Toward a Unity of Knowledge. Ed. by Marjorie Grene. LC 69-17280. (Psychological Issues Monograph: No. 22, Vol. 6, No. 2). 302p. 1969. 42.50 (*0-8236-6610-7*) Intl Univs Pr.

Toward a Usable Past: Liberty under State Constitutions. Ed. by Paul Finkelman & Stephen E. Gottlieb. LC 90-49667. 400p. 1991. 45.00 (*0-8203-1305-X*) U of Ga Pr.

Toward a Viable Lebanon. Intro. by Halim Barakat. 395p. 1988. 27.95 (*0-614-02965-1*); pap. text ed. 17.95 (*0-932568-13-0*) GU Ctr CAS.

Toward a Visible Constituency for Health: A Guide to Citizen Action on Health Legislation. United Hospital Fund Staff. 64p. 1980. 5.00 (*0-934459-28-2*) United Hosp Fund.

Toward a Warless World: The Travail of the American Peace Movement, 1887-1914. David S. Patterson. LC 75-28916. 350p. reprint ed. pap. 99.80 (*0-317-27843-6*, 2056050) Bks Demand.

Toward a Well-Fed World. Don Paarlberg. LC 87-36152. (Henry A. Wallace Series on Agricultural History & Rural Studies). 288p. 1988. reprint ed. pap. 82.10 (*0-608-00113-9*, 2060878) Bks Demand.

Toward a Working-Class Canon: Literary Criticism in British Working-Class Periodicals 1816-1858. Paul T. Murphy. (Studies in Victorian Life & Literature). 213p. 1995. text ed. 39.50 (*0-8142-0654-9*) Ohio St U Pr.

Toward a Working Philosophy of Adult Education. Jerold W. Apps. LC 73-7425. (Occasional Papers). 65p. 1973. pap. 5.00 (*0-87060-059-1*, OCP 36) Syracuse U Cont Ed.

Toward a World of Economic Stability: Optimal Monetary Framework & Policy. Ed. by Yoshio Suzuki & Mitsuaki Okabe. 350p. 1988. 49.50 (*0-86008-422-1*, Pub. by U of Tokyo JA) Col U Pr.

Toward Academic Competence: Theory & Classroom Practice Preparing ESL Students for Content Courses. H. Douglas Adamson. 208p. (C). 1993. pap. text ed. 32.50 (*0-8013-0602-7*) Longman.

Toward Achieving Equity for Women in Social Work Education: A Conceptual Frame of Reference & Guidelines for Organizing Equity Efforts. 1981. 6.60 (*0-318-35378-4*) Coun Soc Wk Ed.

Toward Active Living: Proceedings of the International Conference on Physical Activity, Fitness & Health. Ed. by H. Arthur Quinney et al. LC 93-29972. (Illus.). 312p. 1994. pap. text ed. 39.00 (*0-87322-523-6*, BQUI0523) Human Kinetics.

Toward Adolescence: The Middle School Years: 79th Yearbook, Pt. 1. Ed. by Mauritz Johnson. LC 79-91183. (National Society for the Study of Education Publication Ser.). xviii, 356p. 1985. pap. text ed. 10.00 (*0-226-60089-0*) U Ch Pr.

Toward Affirmative Action & Racial-Ethnic Pluralism: How to Train in Organizations. John W. Work. LC 88-63890. 141p. (Orig.). 1989. pap. text ed. 24.95 (*0-911057-01-3*) Belvedere Pr.

Toward Amnesia. Sarah Van Arsdale. 192p. 1996. 21.95 (*1-57322-017-5*, Riverhead Books) Putnam Pub Group.

***Toward Amnesia.** Sarah Van Arsdale. 192p. 1997. reprint ed. pap. 11.00 (*1-57322-577-0*, Riverhd Trade) Berkley Pub.

Toward an Adult Faith: Talking about the Big Questions. Eugene A. Walsh. (Illus.). 208p. (Orig.). 1994. pap. 12.95 (*0-915531-23-2*) OR Catholic.

Toward an Aesthetic Criticism of Technology. Wolhee Choe. (Worcester Polytechnic Institute Studies in Science, Technology, & Culture: Vol. 2). 218p. (C). 1989. text ed. 39.95 (*0-8204-0654-6*) P Lang Pubng.

Toward an Aesthetics of the Puppet: Puppetry As a Theatrical Art. Steve Tillis. LC 91-43366. (Contributions in Drama & Theatre Studies: No. 47). 200p. 1992. text ed. 49.95 (*0-313-28359-1*, TTA/, Greenwood Pr) Greenwood.

Toward an African Christian Theology of the Kingdom of God: The Kingship of Onyame. Emmanuel Asante. LC 94-11493. 212p. 1995. text ed. 89.95 (*0-7734-2291-9*, Mellen Univ Pr) E Mellen.

Toward an African Christianity: Inculturation Applied. Eugene Hillman. LC 92-39526. 112p. 1993. pap. 6.95 (*0-8091-3381-4*) Paulist Pr.

Toward an Alternative Security System. Robert Johansen. 57p. 1983. pap. text ed. 12.95 (*0-685-54934-8*) Transaction Pubs.

***Toward an American Identity: Selections from the Wichita Art Museum Collection of American Art.** Novelene Ross. Ed. by David Cateforis. (Illus.). 288p. (Orig.). 1997. pap. 40.00 (*0-939324-51-2*) Wichita Art Mus.

Toward an American Revolution: Exposing the Constitution & Other Illusions. Jerry Fresia. LC 08-14784. 250p. 1988. 35.00 (*0-89608-298-9*); pap. 12.00 (*0-89608-297-0*) South End Pr.

Toward an American Sociology: Questioning the European Construct. Gordon D. Morgan. LC 96-20692. 216p. 1997. text ed. 57.95 (*0-275-94999-0*, Praeger Pubs) Greenwood.

Toward an American Theology. Herbert W. Richardson. 182p. 1967. lib. bdg. 79.95 (*0-88946-026-0*) E Mellen.

Toward an Authentic Church: Orthodox Christians Discuss Their Conversion. Ed. & Intro. by Thomas Doulis. 116p. (Orig.). 1996. pap. 14.95 (*1-880971-10-0*) Light&Life Pub Co MN.

Toward an Authentic Interpretation of the Organ Works of Cesar Franck. Rollin Smith. LC 83-8273. (Juilliard Performance Guides Ser.: No. 1). (Illus.). 191p. 1983. lib. bdg. 54.00 (*0-918728-25-8*) Pendragon NY.

Toward an Ecological Assessment of Reading Progress. Ed. by Mary Jett-Simpson. 114p. 1990. pap. text ed. 6.00 (*1-888714-02-6*) Wiscon St Rdng.

Toward an Ecological Society. Murray Bookchin. 315p. 1980. 37.95 (*0-919618-99-5*, Pub. by Black Rose Bks CN); pap. 18.95 (*0-919618-98-7*, Pub. by Black Rose Bks CN) Consort Bk Sales.

Toward an Ecology of the Brain. R. Walsh. (Illus.). 285p. 1981. text ed. 29.95 (*0-88331-208-5*) Luce.

Toward an Ecumenical Fundamental Theology. Randy L. Maddox. LC 84-13838. (American Academy of Religion, Studies in Religion). 178p. 1984. 20.95 (*0-89130-771-0*, 01 01 47) Scholars Pr GA.

T

Toward an Educational Model of Nursing Effectiveness. Joanne C. McCloskey. LC 83-9288. (Studies in Nursing Management: No. 11). 187p. reprint ed. pap. 53.30 (0-685-20811-7, 2070025) Bks Demand.

Toward an Electronic Patient Record '95: Eleventh International Symposium on the Creation of Electronic Health Records & Global Conference on Patient Cards, 2 Vols., Set. Ed. by C. Peter Waegemann. (Illus.). 1040p. (Orig.). 1995. pap. 89.95 (0-9640667-5-0) Medical Recs.

Toward an Electronic Patient Record '96: International Symposium on the Creation of Electronic Health Records & Global Conference on Patient Cards. Ed. by C. Peter Waegemann. (Illus.). (Orig.). 1996. pap. text ed. write for info. (0-9640667-7-7) Medical Recs.

Toward an Entangling Alliance: American Isolationism & Europe, 1901-1950. Ronald E. Powaski. LC 90-45604. (Contributions to the Study of World History Ser.: No. 22). 312p. 1991. text ed. 59.95 (0-313-27274-3, PEH, Greenwood Pr) Greenwood.

Toward an Environmental Strategy for Asia. Carter Brandon & Ramesh Ramankutty. LC 93-44599. (Discussion Paper Ser.: No. 224). 223p. 1994. 11.95 (0-8213-2735-6, 12735) World Bank.

Toward an Environmental Strategy for Asia: A Summary of a World Bank Discussion Paper No. 224. Carter Brandon & Ramesh Ramankutty. 40p. 1993. 6.95 (0-8213-2737-2, 12737) World Bank.

Toward an Ethic & Etiquette for Electronic Mail. Shapiro & Anderson. 122p. 1995. pap. 14.95 (1-57555-033-4); audio compact disk 5.95 (1-57555-034-2) Cedar Bay Pr.

Toward an Ethic of Higher Education. Mortimer R. Kadish. LC 90-27058. 224p. 1991. 35.00 (0-8047-1883-0) Stanford U Pr.

Toward an Exegetical Theology: Biblical Exegesis for Preaching & Teaching. Walter C. Kaiser, Jr. LC 80-68986. 224p. (C). 1981. 19.99 (0-8010-5425-7) Baker Bks.

Toward an Explanation of National Price Levels. Irving B. Kravis & Robert E. Lipsey. LC 83-18546. (Studies in International Finance: No. 52). 36p. 1983. pap. text ed. 11.00 (0-88165-224-5) Princeton U Int Finance Econ.

Toward an Improved Fips Cost-Benefit Methodology: Descriptive Models, Data Processing, Software Development & Maintenance, 2 Vols. 1986. lib. bdg. 400.00 (0-8490-3744-1) Gordon Pr.

***Toward an Information Bill of Rights & Responsibility.** Ed. by Charles M. Firestone & Jorge R. Schement. (Communications & Society Program Book Ser.). 143p. 1996. pap. 10.00 (0-89843-172-7) Aspen Inst Human.

Toward an Integrated Medicine: Classics from Psychosomatic Medicine 1959 - 1979. American Psychosomatic Society Staff. 358p. 1995. text ed. 38.50 (0-88048-727-5, 8727) Am Psychiatric.

***Toward an Integrative Explanation of Corporate Financial Performance.** Noel Capon. LC 96-46306. 424p. (C). 1996. lib. bdg. 125.00 (0-7923-9831-9) Kluwer Ac.

***Toward an Intellectual History of Women: Essays by Linda K. Kerber.** Linda K. Kerber. LC 96-45138. (Illus.). 400p. (C). 1997. 49.95 (0-8078-2348-1); pap. 18.95 (0-8078-4654-6) U of NC Pr.

Toward an Islamic Reformation: Civil Liberties, Human Rights & International Law. Abdullahi Ahmed-An-Na'im. LC 89-21828. (Contemporary Issues in the Middle East Ser.). 240p. (C). 1990. text ed. 34.95 (0-8156-2484-0) Syracuse U Pr.

Toward an Islamic Reformation: Civil Liberties, Human Rights, & International Law. Abdullahi Ahmed An-Na'im. (Contemporary Issues in the Middle East Ser.). 270p. (Orig.). (C). 1996. pap. 16.95 (0-8156-2706-8, ANTIP) Syracuse U Pr.

Toward an Old Testament Theology. Walter C. Kaiser, Jr. (Old Testament Studies). 315p. 1991. pap. 24.99 (0-310-37101-5) Zondervan.

Toward an Ontology of Number Mind & Sign. Charles B. Daniels et al. (Scots Philosophical Monographs: No. 10). 176p. 1986. pap. 15.00 (0-685-17182-5, Pub. by Aberdeen U Pr); text ed. 31.95 (0-08-032462-2, R132, K150, Pub. by Aberdeen U Pr) Macmillan.

***Toward an Operational Risk Assessment in Flood Alleviation: Theory, Operationalization & Application.** Hao-Ming Zhou. xiii, 215p. (Orig.). 1995. pap. 62.50 (90-407-1146-1, Pub. by Delft U Pr NE) Coronet Bks.

Toward an Optimal Health Program. 1994. lib. bdg. 250.95 (0-8490-5670-5) Gordon Pr.

Toward an Understanding of Language: Charles Carpenter Fries in Perspective. Ed. by Peter H. Fries. LC 85-9168. (Current Issues in Linguistic Theory Ser.: No. 40). xvi, 384p. 1985. 78.00 (90-272-3534-1) Benjamins North Am.

Toward an Understanding of the A. M. E. Zion Church, Vol. 1: A Manual for Lay Persons, Students, & Others Who Are Interested in Learning about Zion. Robert L. Clayton. 60p. 1988. student ed. 11.50 (0-910363-04-8) EBONICS.

Toward an Understanding of the International Nonprofit Sector. Lester M. Salamon & Helmut K. Anheier. (Working Papers of the Johns Hopkins Comparative Nonprofit Sector Project: No. 1). (Illus.). 24p. 1992. pap. text ed. 6.00 (1-886333-02-5) JH Univ Inst Pol Studies.

Toward an Understanding of the Metropolis, Pts. 1 & 2. Robert M. Haig. LC 75-38130. (Demography Ser.). 1976. reprint ed. 17.95 (0-405-07984-2) Ayer.

Toward an Urban Ohio. John Wunder. (Illus.). 44p. 1977. pap. 2.00 (0-318-00840-8) Ohio Hist Soc.

Toward an Urban View: The Nineteenth-Century American City in Prints. Sally L. Gross. LC 89-50442. (Illus.). 48p. (Orig.). 1989. pap. 5.00 (0-89467-050-6) Yale Art Gallery.

Toward an Urban Vision: Ideas & Institutions in Nineteenth-Century America. Thomas Bender. LC 82-47980. 296p. (Orig.). (C). 1982. pap. text ed. 14.95 (0-8018-2925-9) Johns Hopkins.

***Toward Anti-Adhesion Therapy for Microbial Diseases: Proceedings of the Bat-Sheva Seminar Held in Zichron Yaakov, Israel, February 25-March 1, 1996.** Ed. by Itzhak Kahane & Itzhak Ofek. LC 96-31493. (Advances in Experimental Medicine & Biology Ser.: Vol. 408). 288p. 1996. 89.50 (0-306-45397-5, Plenum Pr) Plenum.

Toward Appomattox. Virginia Scott. 80p. (Orig.). (C). 1993. pap. text ed. 6.95 (0-934238-08-1) Motheroot.

Toward Arab-Israeli Peace: Guidelines for American Policy. Report of a Study Group Staff. LC 88-70490. 49p. 1988. pap. 6.95 (0-8157-7291-2) Brookings.

Toward Awakening an Approach. Jean Vaysse. 1987. pap. 9.95 (0-7100-0715-9, RKP) Routledge.

Toward Balance: Psycho-Physical Integration & Vibrational Therapy. Rita McNamara. LC 88-33816. (Illus.). 196p. 1989. pap. 8.95 (0-87728-693-0) Weiser.

Toward Belief: Essays in the Human Sciences, Social Ethics, & Philosophical Theology. W. Widick Schroeder. LC 95-83405. xiii, 541p. 1996. 34.95 (0-913552-59-3) Exploration Pr.

Toward Benevolent Neutrality: Church, State, & the Supreme Court. 5th ed. Ed. by Robert T. Miller & Ronald B. Flowers. LC 96-18086. 885p. 1996. 75.00 (0-918954-63-0) Baylor Univ Pr.

Toward Better Blood Pressure. Linda Pietz et al. 48p. 1992. student ed. write for info. (1-884153-06-2) Prk Nicollet.

Toward Better Human Relations. Ed. by Lloyd A. Cook. LC 70-90626. (Essay Index Reprint Ser.). 1977. 19.95 (0-8369-1284-5) Ayer.

Toward Better Problems: New Perspectives on Abortion, Animal Rights, the Environment & Justice. Anthony Weston. (Ethics & Action Ser.). 240p. (C). 1992. 54.95 (0-87722-947-3); pap. 17.95 (0-87722-948-1) Temple U Pr.

Toward Black Undergraduate Student Equality in American Higher Education. Ed. by Michael T. Nettles. LC 87-24956. (Contributions to the Study of Education Ser.: No. 25). 240p. 1988. text ed. 55.00 (0-313-25616-0, NBK/, Greenwood Pr) Greenwood.

Toward Chronopharmacology: Proceedings of Satellite Symposium to the 8th International Congress of Pharmacology, Nagasaki, Japan, 27-28 July, 1981. International Congress of Pharmacology Staff. Ed. by R. Takahashi & Franz Halberg. (Illus.). 456p. 1982. 81.00 (0-08-027977-5, Pergamon Pr) Elsevier.

Toward Civil Society in the Middle East? A Primer. Ed. by Jillian Schwedler. 124p. 1995. lib. bdg. 8.95 (1-55587-588-2) Lynne Rienner.

Toward Civilization: A Report on Arts Education. 182p. (Orig.). 1988. pap. 12.95 (0-317-04287-4, 7600) Natl Endow Arts.

Toward Civilization: A Report on Arts Education by the National Endowment for the Arts. Intro. by Frank Hodsoll. (Illus.). 182p. (Orig.). 1988. pap. text ed. 12.00 (0-685-45136-4) Natl Endow Arts.

Toward Civilization: A Report on Arts Education: Writing, Painting, Sculpture, Photography, Video, Crafts, Architecture, Dance, Music, Opera, Theater, Musical Theater, Film, Radio, Television, Music & Graphic Design. 1991. lib. bdg. 75.00 (0-87700-923-6) Revisionist Pr.

Toward Clean & Fuel Efficient Automobiles. OECD Staff. 620p. (Orig.). 1993. pap. 64.00 (92-64-03869-8) OECD.

***Toward Clean & Fuel Efficient Automobiles.** OECD Staff. 620p. (Orig.). 1993. pap. 64.00 (92-64-03868-X) OECD.

Toward Coexistence: An Analysis of the Resolutions of the Palestine National Council. Muhammad Y. Muslih. LC 90-81685. (IPS Papers). 56p. (Orig.). (C). 1990. pap. text ed. 3.95 (0-88728-210-5) Inst Palestine.

Toward Common Sense: Understanding & Including Science Policy in the Environmental Risk Management Debate. Regulatory Impact Analysis Project, Inc. Staff. 300p. (Orig.). 1994. pap. write for info. (0-9643747-0-6) Regulatory Impact.

Toward Comparative Social Welfare. Ed. by Brij Mohan. (Illus.). 192p. (Orig.). (C). 1986. 18.95 (0-87047-025-6); pap. 14.95 (0-87047-026-4) Schenkman Bks Inc.

Toward Competition in Cable Television. Leland L. Johnson. (AEI Studies in Telecommunications Deregulation). (Illus.). 170p. 1994. 27.50 (0-262-10054-1) MIT Pr.

Toward Competition in Local Telephony. William J. Baumol & J. Gregory Sidak. LC 93-28956. (AEI Studies in Telecommunications Deregulation). (Illus.). 175p. 1993. 27.50 (0-262-02369-5) MIT Pr.

***Toward Comprehensive Peace in Southeast Europe: Preventing Conflict in the South Balkans: Report of the South Balkans Working Group.** Center for Preventive Action Staff & Barnett R. Rubin. LC 96-27647. 1996. write for info. (0-87078-402-1) TCFP-PPP.

***Toward Computer Composition.** Dornsife. (C). 1998. pap. text ed. 14.75 (0-15-505395-7) HB Coll Pubs.

Toward Conceptual Codification: In Race & Ethnic Relations. Jonathan Udell. LC 79-84196. 1980. 12.95 (0-87212-119-4) Libra.

Toward Consensus in Foreign & Defense Policy. Ed. by Harold Brown. 78p. (Orig.). (C). 1989. pap. text ed. 12.50 (0-941700-50-X) JH FPI SAIS.

Toward Constitutional Competence: A Casebook for Public Administrators. David H. Rosenbloom & James D. Carroll. 176p. (C). 1989. pap. text ed. 26.20 (0-13-926122-2) P-H.

Toward Continuous Learning. rev. ed. Jerome M. Rosow et al. Ed. by Jill Casner-Lotto. (Training for New Technology Ser.: Part II). 87p. 1991. pap. 95.00 (0-89361-057-7) Work in Amer.

Toward Continuous Misson: Strategizing for the Evangelization of Bolivia. W. Douglas Smith. LC 77-21490. 1978. pap. 5.95 (0-87808-321-9) William Carey Lib.

Toward Curriculum for Being: Voices of Educators. Louise M. Berman et al. LC 90-40121. (SUNY Series in Curriculum Issues & Inquiries). 205p. (C). 1991. text ed. 65.50 (0-7914-0630-X); pap. text ed. 21.95 (0-7914-0631-8) State U NY Pr.

Toward Defensive Restructuring in the Middle East. Carl Conetta et al. (PDA Monograph: No. 1). 39p. 1991. reprint ed. pap. 7.50 (1-881677-02-8) Commonwlth Inst.

Toward Defining Literacy. Ed. by Richard L. Venezky et al. LC 89-37002. 88p. 1990. reprint ed. pap. 25.10 (0-608-00500-2, 2061320) Bks Demand.

Toward Defining the African Aesthetic. Bernadette Cailler et al. Ed. by Lemuel Johnson et al. LC 82-40408. (Annual Selected Papers of the African Literature Association). 140p. 1983. 22.00 (0-89410-356-3); pap. 14.00 (0-89410-357-1) Cornell AS&RC.

***Toward Democracy: A Journey: Reflections, 1940-1997.** Robert A. Dahl. LC 97-12132. 1997. write for info. (0-87772-372-9) UCB IGS.

***Toward Desire.** Linda L. Harper. LC 95-62219. 1996. pap. 10.00 (0-915380-33-1) Word Works.

Toward Development Work: The Workplace As a Learning Environment. Ed. by Michael R. Walton. 115p. (C). 1991. 48.00 (0-7300-1354-5, Pub. by Deakin Univ AT) St Mut.

Toward Economic Liberation: Southern Africa. Ed. by Amon J. Nsekela. (Illus.). 294p. 1981. text ed. 48.00 (0-8476-4741-2) Rowman.

Toward Education with a Global Perspective. 15p. (Orig.). 1980. pap. text ed. 3.00 (0-911696-10-5) Assn Am Coll.

Toward Education with a Global Perspective: A Report. National Assembly on Foreign Language & International Studies Staff. 19p. 1980. reprint ed. pap. 25.00 (0-608-01794-9, 2062447) Bks Demand.

Toward Educational Engineering. John Durnin. LC 81-40101. (Illus.). 134p. (Orig.). (C). 1982. pap. text ed. 17.00 (0-8191-2436-2) U Pr of Amer.

Toward Effective Public School Programs for Deaf Students: Context, Process, & Outcomes. Ed. by Thomas N. Kluwin et al. (Special Education Ser.). 272p. (C). 1992. text ed. 46.00 (0-8077-3160-9); pap. text ed. 22.95 (0-8077-3159-5) Tchrs Coll.

Toward Effective Schooling: The IGE Experience. Thomas A. Romberg. LC 85-3156. (Illus.). 246p. (Orig.). 1985. pap. text ed. 22.50 (0-8191-4581-5); lib. bdg. 48.00 (0-8191-4580-7) U Pr of Amer.

Toward Effective Social Work Practice. Ed. by Morley D. Glicken. LC 74-6248. 300p. (C). 1974. text ed. 39.50 (0-8422-5171-5) Irvington.

Toward Ending Poverty among the Elderly & Disabled Through SSI Reform: Policy & Financing Options. Sheila R. Zedlewski & Jack A. Meyer. LC 88-27840. (Urban Institute Report: No. 89-1). (Illus.). 150p. (Orig.). 1989. pap. text ed. 16.50 (0-87766-450-1); lib. bdg. 46.00 (0-87766-467-6) Urban Inst.

Toward Environmental Strategies for Cities: Policy Considerations for Urban Environmental Management in Developing Countries. Carl Bartone et al. LC 94-13583. (Urban Management Programme Ser.: No. 18). 128p. 1994. 8.95 (0-8213-2827-1, 12827) World Bank.

***Toward Environmentally Sustainable Development in Sub-Saharan Africa: A World Bank Agenda.** 160p. 1996. 20.00 (0-8213-3599-5, 13599) World Bank.

Toward Equal Educational Opportunity: The Report of the Select Committee on Equal Educational Opportunity, U. S. Senate. Intro. by U. S. Congress, Senate Select Committee on Equal Opportunity. LC 74-8765. (AMS Studies in Education: No. 2). 37.50 (0-404-11622-1) AMS Pr.

Toward Equality of Well-Being: Strategies for Improving Minority Health. 1994. lib. bdg. 250.00 (0-8490-8527-6) Gordon Pr.

Toward Equality of Well Being: Strategies for Improving Minority Health: Strategic Planning & Coordination Process. 1995. lib. bdg. 250.00 (0-8490-6551-8) Gordon Pr.

***Toward Equality of Well-Being: Strategies for Improving Minority Health, Strategy Planning & Coordination Process.** 1997. lib. bdg. 251.95 (0-8490-6089-3) Gordon Pr.

Toward Ethnic Diversification in Psychology Education & Training. Ed. by George Stricker et al. 251p. 1990. pap. 29.95 (1-55798-088-8) Am Psychol.

Toward Evening & the Day Far Spent. Stephen J. Frech. LC 96-11210. (Wick Poetry Chapbook Ser.: No. 11). 23p. (Orig.). 1996. pap. 4.75 (0-87338-556-X) Kent St U Pr.

Toward Excellence in Secondary Vocational Education: Developing Pretechnical Curricula. M. Harry Daniels et al. 48p. 1985. 5.50 (0-318-22216-7, IN295) Ctr Educ Trng Employ.

Toward Excellence in Secondary Vocational Education: Elements of Program Quality. Paul B. Campbell & Phyllis Panzano. 35p. 1985. 4.75 (0-318-22217-5, IN291) Ctr Educ Trng Employ.

Toward Excellence in Secondary Vocational Education: Implementing Standards. Tim L. Wentling. 29p. 1985. 4.25 (0-318-22218-3, IN292) Ctr Educ Trng Employ.

Toward Excellence in Secondary Vocational Education: Improving Teaching. Gwen C. Cooke. 43p. 1985. 4.75 (0-318-22219-1, IN293) Ctr Educ Trng Employ.

Toward Excellence in Secondary Vocational Education: Providing Job Training. David W. Stevens. 40p. 1985. 4.75 (0-318-22220-5, IN296) Ctr Educ Trng Employ.

Toward Excellence in Secondary Vocational Education: Using Cognitive Psychology in Curriculum Planning. Janet F. Laster. 65p. 1985. 7.25 (0-318-22221-3, IN297) Ctr Educ Trng Employ.

Toward Excellence in Secondary Vocational Education: Using Evaluation Results. Donald R. Brannon. 38p. 1985. 4.75 (0-318-22222-1, IN294) Ctr Educ Trng Employ.

Toward Explaining Human Culture: A Critical Review of the Findings of Worldwide Cross-Cultural Research. David Levinson & Martin J. Malone. LC 80-83324. (Comparative Studies). 412p. 1980. 25.00 (0-87536-339-3) HRAFP.

Toward Fair Employment. Paul H. Norgren & Samuel E. Hill. LC 64-17756. 296p. 1964. text ed. 59.50 (0-231-02716-8) Col U Pr.

***Toward Finance with Meaning: The Methodology of Finance, What It Is & What It Can Be.** George M. Frankfurter & Elton G. McGoun. LC 96-40849. (Contemporary Studies in Economic & Financial Analysis). 1996. write for info. (0-7623-0163-5) Jai Pr.

Toward Fitness: Guided Exercise for Those with Health Problems. Robert Cantu. LC 79-27686. 258p. 1980. 32.95 (0-87705-496-7) Human Sci Pr.

Toward Foundations of Information Science. Ed. by Laurence W. Heilprin. 232p. 1985. text ed. 55.00 (0-313-25780-9, HTF/, Greenwood Pr); lib. bdg. 34.95 (0-685-30881-2, Greenwood Pr) Greenwood.

Toward Freedom & Dignity: The Humanities & the Idea of Humanity. O. B. Haradison. LC 72-4010. 189p. reprint ed. pap. 53.90 (0-317-30464-X, 2024832) Bks Demand.

Toward Full Communion & Concordat of Agreement. Ed. by William A. Norgren & William G. Rusch. (Lutheran-Episcopal Dialogue Ser.: No. III). 120p. (Orig.). 1991. pap. 4.95 (0-88028-119-7, 1119) Forward Movement.

Toward Full Communion & Concordat of Agreement: Lutheran-Episcopal Dialogue III. William A. Norgren & William G. Rusch. LC 91-12472. 120p. (Orig.). 1992. pap. 4.99 (0-8066-2578-3, 9-2578, Augsburg) Augsburg Fortress.

Toward Full Employment in Our Free Enterprise Economy. Morris A. Copeland. LC 66-16972. (Moorhouse I.X. Millar Lecture Ser.: No. 7). 96p. reprint ed. pap. 27.40 (0-7837-0441-0, 2040764) Bks Demand.

Toward Gender Equality: The Role of Public Policy. LC 95-631. 88p. 1995. 6.95 (0-8213-3337-2, 13337) World Bank.

Toward Gender Equity in the Classroom: Everyday Teachers' Beliefs & Practices. Janice Streitmatter. LC 93-20334. (SUNY Series, Teacher Preparation & Development). 207p. (C). 1994. text ed. 59.50 (0-7914-1803-0); pap. text ed. 19.95 (0-7914-1804-9) State U NY Pr.

Toward Global Equilibrium: Collected Papers. Ed. by Dennis L. Meadows & Donella H. Meadows. LC 72-81804. (Illus.). 358p. 1973. text ed. 45.00 (0-262-13143-9) Prod Press.

Toward Global Planning of Sustainable Use of the Earth: Development of Global Eco-Engineering: A Collection of Contributions Based on Lectures Presented at the 8th Toyota Conference, Mikkabi, Shizuoka, Japan, November 8 to 11, 1994. Ed. by Shunji Murai. LC 95-18909. 484p. 1995. 210.50 (0-444-81904-5) Elsevier.

Toward God: The Ancient Wisdom of Western Prayer. Michael Casey. LC 95-46093. 192p. (Orig.). 1996. pap. 12.95 (0-89243-890-8, Triumph Books) Liguori Pubns.

Toward Gog & Magog Or? A Critical Review of the Literature of Adult Group Discussion. Ed. by F. W. Osinski et al. LC 72-6475. (Occasional Papers: No. 30). 80p. (Orig.). 1972. pap. 2.00 (0-87060-053-2, OCP 30) Syracuse U Cont Ed.

Toward Greater Understanding: Essays in Honor of John Cardinal O'Connor. Ed. by Anthony J. Cernera. x, 149p. 1995. 14.95 (1-888112-00-X) Sacred Hrt Univ.

Toward Growth: A Blueprint for Economic Rebirth in Israel. Ed. by Alvin Rabushka & Steve H. Hanke. 110p. 1988. pap. 19.00 (0-923791-00-0) IASPS.

Toward Healthy Aging. 4th ed. Ebersole. 800p. (C). (gr. 13). 1993. text ed. 56.00 (0-8016-6816-6) Mosby Yr Bk.

***Toward Healthy Aging.** 5th ed. Ebersole. (Illus.). 950p. (C). (gr. 13). 1997. text ed. 56.00 (0-8151-2879-7, 31040) Mosby Yr Bk.

Toward High Precision Machine Translation: Based on Contrastive Textology. John Laffling. LC 91-33903. (Distributed Language Translation Ser.: No. 7). xiv, 178p. (C). 1991. lib. bdg. 75.40 (3-11-013388-1) Mouton.

Toward Holy Ground: Spiritual Directions for the Second Half of Life. Margaret Guenther. 160p. 1995. pap. 10.95 (1-56101-114-2) Cowley Pubns.

Toward Imagination. Rudolf Steiner. Tr. by Sabine H. Seiler from GER. 192p. (Orig.). 1990. 24.95 (0-88010-284-5); pap. 12.95 (0-88010-285-3) Anthroposophic.

Toward Improved Accounting for the Environment. Ed. by Ernst Lutz. LC 93-13831. 334p. 1993. 40.00 (0-8213-2436-5, 12436) World Bank.

***Toward Improved Multilevel Planning for Agricultural & Rural Development in Asia & the Pacific.** 119p. 1985. 14.00 (92-5-102221-6, F1250, Pub. by FAO IT) Bernan Associates.

Toward Inclusive Classrooms. LC 94-5521. (Teacher to Teacher Ser.). 1994. pap. 12.95 (0-8106-2903-8) NEA.

Toward Increased Judicial Activism: The Political Role of the Supreme Court. Arthur S. Miller. LC 81-20201. (Contributions in American Studies: No. 59). xii, 355p. 1982. text ed. 39.95 (0-313-23305-5, MIO/, Greenwood Pr) Greenwood.

Toward Independence: The Use of Instructional Objectives in Teaching Daily Living Skills to the Blind. Anne Yeadon. 122p. 1974. pap. 24.95 (0-89128-064-2) Am Foun Blind.

T

Toward Industrial Democracy: Management & the Workers in Modern Japan. Kunio Odaka. LC 74-82575. (East Asian Monographs: No. 80). 272p. 1975. 18.50 (*0-674-89816-8*) HUP.

Toward Infrastructure Improvement: An Agenda for Research. National Research Council Staff. Ed. by James P. Gould & Andrew C. Lemer. (Studies in Infrastructure Technology & Policy). 144p. (Orig.). (C). 1994. pap. text ed. 30.00 (*0-309-05144-4*) Natl Acad Pr.

Toward Integrated Adult Learning Systems: The Status of State Literacy Efforts. Robert A. Silvanik. Ed. by Gerry Feinstein & Karen Glass. 53p. (Orig.). 1991. pap. text ed. 15.00 (*1-55877-087-9*) Natl Governor.

Toward Interactive & Intelligent Decision Support Systems. Ed. by Y. Sawargi et al. (Lecture Notes in Economics & Mathematical Systems Ser.: Vol. 285). xii, 445p. 1987. 59.95 (*0-387-17718-3*) Spr-Verlag.

Toward Interactive & Intelligent Decision Support Systems. Ed. by Y. Sawargi et al. (Lecture Notes in Economics & Mathematical Systems Ser.: Vol. 286). xii, 450p. 1987. 59.95 (*0-387-17719-1*) Spr-Verlag.

Toward International Descriptive Standards for Archives: Papers Presented at the ICA Invitational Meeting of Experts on Descriptive Standards. National Archives of Canada, Ottawa 4-7, October 1988. (Archivum: 37). 177p. 1993. pap. 50.00 (*3-598-11163-0*) K G Saur.

Toward Internationalism: New Deal Foreign Economic Policy, 1933-39. Ed. by Daniel B. Smith. LC 90-2987. (Foreign Economic Policy of the United States Ser.). 398p. 1990. reprint ed. text ed. 30.00 (*0-8240-7465-3*) Garland.

Toward Internationalism: Readings in Cross-Cultural Communication. 2nd ed. Ed. by Louise F. Luce & Elise F. Smith. 293p. 1986. pap. 27.95 (*0-8384-2689-1*, Newbury) Heinle & Heinle.

Toward Islamic Anthropology. Akbar S. Ahmed. (Islamization of Knowledge Ser.: No. 2). 80p. (C). 1986. pap. text ed. 5.00 (*0-912463-05-8*) IIIT VA.

Toward Islamic English. 3rd ed. Isma'il Raji al Faruqi. LC 88-9287. (Islamization of Knowledge Ser.: No. 3). 64p. (C). 1986. pap. text ed. 5.00 (*0-912463-07-4*) IIIT VA.

Toward Jazz. Andre Hodeir. LC 76-7568. (Roots of Jazz Ser.). 1976. reprint ed. lib. bdg. 25.00 (*0-306-70810-8*) Da Capo.

T

Toward Jerusalem. Amy Carmichael. 1989. pap. 4.95 (*0-87508-080-4*) Chr Lit.

Toward Jewish-Arab Rapprochement: A History of Ihud. Ed. by Bezalel Chaim. 1979. lib. bdg. 44.95 (*0-686-24785-X*) M Buber Pr.

Toward Lawfulness in Schooling: Components in Program Development. Delores Silva. 148p. (Orig.). (C). 1994. pap. text ed. 22.50 (*0-8191-9355-0*); lib. bdg. 46.50 (*0-8191-9354-2*) U Pr of Amer.

Toward Learning Organizations: Integrating Total Quality Control & Systems Thinking. rev. ed. Daniel H. Kim. (Illus.). 17p. (Orig.). 1992. pap. text ed. 10.00 (*1-883823-01-3*) Pegasus Comm.

Toward Learning Robots. Ed. by Walter Van de Velde. (Illus.). 162p. 1993. pap. 23.95 (*0-262-72017-5*) MIT Pr.

Toward Lexington: The Role of the British Army in the Coming of the American Revolution. John W. Shy. LC 65-17160. (Illus.). 473p. reprint ed. pap. 134.90 (*0-317-09999-X*, 2014026) Bks Demand.

Toward Literacy: Theory & Applications for Teaching Writing in the Content Areas. Jean E. Brown et al. 436p. (C). 1993. pap. 31.95 (*0-534-17658-5*) Wadsworth Pub.

Toward Logical Form: An Exploration of the Role of Syntax in Semantics. Lisa A. Reed. Ed. by Laurence Horn. LC 96-34690. (Outstanding Dissertations in Linguistics Ser.). 344p. 1996. text ed. 68.00 (*0-8153-2555-X*) Garland.

Toward Managed Peace: The National Security Interests of the United States, 1759 to the Present. Eugene V. Rostow. LC 92-24550. 352p. (C). 1993. text ed. 40.00 (*0-300-05700-8*) Yale U Pr.

Toward Managed Peace: The National Security Interests of the United States, 1759 to the Present. Eugene V. Rostow. 1995. pap. text ed. 19.00 (*0-300-06316-4*) Yale U Pr.

Toward Maturity. Jaber F. Gubrium & David R. Buckholdt. LC 76-57306. (Jossey-Bass Behavioral Science Ser.). 240p. reprint ed. pap. 68.40 (*0-317-41970-6*, 2025674) Bks Demand.

Toward Modernity: The European Jewish Model. Ed. by Jacob Katz. 246p. (Orig.). 1986. 39.95 (*0-88738-092-1*) Transaction Pubs.

***Toward More Economical Gear Inspection.** F. Bohle. (Technical Papers). 1957. pap. text ed. 30.00 (*1-55589-302-3*) AGMA.

Toward More Glorious Praise: Power Principles for Faith-Filled People. Ed. by Jack W. Hayford. 1994. pap. 6.99 (*0-8407-8518-6*) Nelson.

***Toward More Glorious Praise/Hacia una Slabonza Ma's Gloriosa.** Jack Hayford. 1996. pap. 5.99 (*0-89922-520-9*) Edit Betania.

Toward More Productive Naval Shipbuilding. National Research Council (U. S.), Marine Board Staff. 214p. reprint ed. pap. 61.00 (*0-8357-7704-9*, 2036058) Bks Demand.

Toward Morning-Swimmers. Elaine Terranova. (Hollow Spring Poetry Ser.). 44p. (Orig.). 1980. pap. text ed. 4.00 (*0-685-02323-0*) Hollow Spring Pr.

Toward Multiculturalism: Readings in Multicultural Education. Ed. by Jaime S. Wurzel. LC 88-81392. 240p. 1988. pap. text ed. 24.95 (*0-933662-72-6*) Intercult Pr.

Toward My Father's House: Hope Filled Meditations for the Terminally Ill. Mary J. Mason. LC 92-75942. 54p. (Orig.). 1993. pap. text ed. 3.95 (*0-89243-518-6*) Liguori Pubns.

Toward New Human Rights: The Social Policies of the Kennedy & Johnson Administrations. Ed. by David C. Warner. (Symposia Ser.). 472p. 1977. pap. 5.00 (*0-89940-406-5*) LBJ Sch Pub Aff.

Toward New Towns for America. Clarence S. Stein. (Illus.). 1966. pap. 14.95 (*0-262-69009-8*) MIT Pr.

Toward Nineteen Eighty-Four: The Future of Appalachia? Southern Appalachian Regional Conference Staff. LC 75-521. 1975. pap. 2.95 (*0-686-27853-4*) Appalach Consortium.

Toward Non-Essentialist Sociolinguistics. Karol Janicki. (Contributions to the Sociology of Language Ser.: No. 56). xi, 136p. (C). 1990. lib. bdg. 67.70 (*3-11-012157-3*) Mouton.

Toward Objective Mobility Evaluation: Some Thoughts on a Theory. Leslie Kay. LC 80-489842. 57p. reprint ed. pap. 25.00 (*0-685-16098-X*, 2027353) Bks Demand.

Toward Octavio Paz: A Reading of His Major Poems, 1957-1976. John M. Fein. LC 85-29417. 199p. 1986. reprint ed. pap. 56.80 (*0-7837-9583-1*, 2060332) Bks Demand.

Toward Old Testament Ethics. Walter C. Kaiser, Jr. (Ethics - Old Testament Studies). 357p. 1991. pap. 19.99 (*0-310-37111-2*) Zondervan.

Toward Our Common American Destiny. John M. Cabot. LC 72-90621. (Essay Index Reprint Ser.). 1977. 23.95 (*0-8369-1553-4*) Ayer.

Toward Pacifism. Gunnar Sundberg. (C). 1950. pap. 3.00 (*0-87574-056-1*) Pendle Hill.

Toward Participatory Research. Deepa Narayan. LC 95-45755. (Technical Paper Ser.: No. 307). 276p. 1996. 16.95 (*0-8213-3473-5*) World Bank.

Toward Peace: Prayers for the Widowed. Beverly S. Gordon. 36p. 1990. pap. text ed. 2.95 (*0-86716-129-9*) St Anthony Mess Pr.

Toward Peace & Security in Southern Africa. Ed. by H. Glickman. xvi, 260p. 1990. pap. text ed. 28.00 (*2-88124-381-9*) Gordon & Breach.

Toward Peace, Freedom & Socialism: Main Political Resolution, 21st National Convention, Communist Party U. S. A. 1976. pap. 1.00 (*0-87898-120-9*) New Outlook.

Toward Peace in the Middle East: Perspectives, Principles, & Hope. National Conference of Catholic Bishops Staff. 52p. (Orig.). 1989. pap. 2.95 (*1-55586-325-6*) US Catholic.

Toward Peacemaking: Presbyterians in the South & National Security, 1945-1983. Rick L. Nutt. LC 94-4828. 192p. 1994. pap. text ed. 19.95 (*0-8173-0759-1*) U of Ala Pr.

Toward Pearl Harbor: The Diplomatic Interchange Between Japan & the United States, 1899-1941. Intro. by Ralph E. Schaffer. LC 91-32081. 224p. (C). 1991. pap. text ed. 14.95 (*1-55876-045-8*) Wiener Pubs Inc.

Toward Pearl Harbor: The Diplomatic Interchange Between Japan & the United States, 1899-1941. Intro. by Ralph E. Schaffer. LC 91-32081. 224p. (C). 1991. text ed. 39.95 (*1-55876-046-6*) Wiener Pubs Inc.

Toward Polaris. 2nd rev. ed. Max M. Fain. 171p. (YA). 1990. 8.95 (*0-9618960-4-3*) M M Fain.

Toward Polaris. 3rd ed. Max Fain. 1992. 8.00 (*0-9618960-8-6*) M M Fain.

Toward Political Responsibility. Cecil E. Hinshaw. (C). 1954. pap. 3.00 (*0-87574-080-4*) Pendle Hill.

Toward Proto-Nostratic: A New Approach to the Comparison of Proto-Indo-European & Proto-Afroasiatic. Alan R. Bomhard. (Current Issues in Linguistic Theory Ser.: Vol. 27). xi, 356p. 1984. 71.00 (*90-272-3519-8*) Benjamins North Am.

Toward Psychological Deafness. Paul. 1993. student ed., pap. text ed. 26.00 (*0-205-14609-0*) Allyn.

Toward Quality in Education, the Leader's Odyssey. 1994. lib. bdg. 300.00 (*0-8490-8589-6*) Gordon Pr.

Toward Realistic Reform: A Commentary on Proposals for Change in New York City's Criminal Justice System. Diana R. Gordon. 1981. 3.00 (*0-318-02048-3*) Natl Coun Crime.

Toward Reform of Program Evaluation. Lee J. Cronbach et al. LC 80-8013. (Joint Publication in the Jossey-Bass Series in Social & Behavioral Science & in Higher Education). 462p. reprint ed. pap. 131.70 (*0-8357-4876-6*, 2037808) Bks Demand.

Toward Renewed Economic Growth in Latin America. Bela A. Balassa et al. LC 86-15253. 207p. (Orig.). reprint ed. pap. 59.00 (*0-7837-4216-9*, 2043905) Bks Demand.

Toward Research & Theory Building in the Study of Nonviolent Action. Ronald M. McCarthy & Christopher Kruegler. (Monograph Ser.). 35p. (Orig.). 1993. pap. 3.00 (*1-880813-08-4*) A Einstein Inst.

Toward Resolution? The Falklands-Malvinas Dispute. Ed. by Wayne S. Smith. LC 91-13435. 161p. 1991. lib. bdg. 26.50 (*1-55587-265-4*) Lynne Rienner.

Toward Restoration: The Growth of Political Consciousness in Tokugawa Japan. H. D. Harootunian. 435p. 1991. pap. 16.95 (*0-520-07403-3*) U CA Pr.

Toward Reunion in Philosophy. Gabriel M. White. LC 82-1026. xv, 308p. 1982. reprint ed. text ed. 65.00 (*0-313-23478-7*, WHTR, Greenwood Pr) Greenwood.

Toward Robert Frost: The Reader & the Poet. Judith Oster. LC 90-11277. 352p. 1993. pap. 19.95 (*0-8203-1621-0*) U of Ga Pr.

Toward Samson Agonistes: The Growth of Milton's Mind. Mary A. Radzinowicz. LC 77-85559. (Illus.). 461p. 1978. reprint ed. pap. 131.40 (*0-7837-8180-6*, 2047885) Bks Demand.

Toward Schooling for the Twenty-First Century. Per Dalin & Val D. Rust. (School Development Ser.). (Illus.). 256p. 1996. 90.00 (*0-304-33447-2*); pap. 21.00 (*0-304-33448-0*) Cassell.

Toward Scientifically Based Prevention. 416p. 1990. 40.00 (*92-9078-015-0*) UN.

Toward Second Language Acquisition: A Study of Null-Prep. Elaine C. Klein. LC 93-28052. (Studies in Theoretical Psycholinguistics: Vol. 17). 304p. (C). 1993. lib. bdg. 141.00 (*0-7923-2463-3*) Kluwer Ac.

Toward Self & Sanity: On the Genetic Origins of the Human Character. A. M. Benis. LC 84-26313. 528p. 1985. 39.95 (*0-88437-074-7*) Psych Dimensions.

Toward Shining Castle: A Devotional Allegory. Robert E. Tourville. LC 88-81371. (Illus.). 160p. 1988. pap. 5.95 (*0-912981-20-2*) Hse BonGiovanni.

Toward Social Economy. Howard R. Bowen. LC 76-43973. (Political & Social Economy Ser.). 367p. 1977. reprint ed. 24.95 (*0-8093-0813-4*) S Ill U Pr.

Toward Social Welfare. Clair Wilcox & Onnolee Vodges. (C). 1969. 29.25 (*0-256-00589-3*) Irwin.

Toward Socio-Criticism: Selected Proceedings of the Conference "Luso Brazilian Literatures: a Socio-Critical Approach" Intro. by Roberto Reis. LC 91-563. 325p. (Orig.). 1991. pap. text ed. 25.00 (*0-87918-074-9*) ASU Lat Am St.

Toward Spirituality: The Inner Journey. Jerry Dollard. 17p. 1983. pap. 1.75 (*0-89486-193-X*, 1421B) Hazelden.

Toward Standards. Norman Foerster. LC 66-13476. 1928. 30.00 (*0-8196-0166-7*) Biblo.

Toward Stendhal. H. Levin. LC 75-22213. (Studies in French Literature: No. 45). 1975. lib. bdg. 75.00 (*0-8383-2083-X*) M S G Haskell Hse.

Toward Strategies for Public Administration Development in Latin America. John C. Honey. LC 68-14963. 191p. reprint ed. pap. 54.50 (*0-317-28335-9*, 2022106) Bks Demand.

Toward Student-Centered Foreign-Language Programs. Ed. by Warren C. Born. (Reports of the Northeast Conference on the Teaching of Foreign Languages). 180p. 1974. pap. 10.95 (*0-87352-122-6*) NE Conf Teach Foreign.

Toward Sustainability: A Plan for Collaborative Research on Agriculture & Natural Resource Management. Ed. by Board on Agriculture Staff, National Research Council. 164p. 1991. pap. text ed. 19.00 (*0-309-04540-1*) Natl Acad Pr.

Toward Sustainability: Soil & Water Research Priorities for Developing Countries. National Research Council Staff. 76p. 1991. pap. text ed. 9.95 (*0-309-04641-6*) Natl Acad Pr.

***Toward Sustainable Communities: Resources for Citizens & Their Governments.** Mark Roseland. 1997. 59.00 (*0-86571-373-1*); pap. text ed. 19.95 (*0-86571-374-X*) New Soc Pubs.

Toward Sustainable Development: Concepts, Methods, & Policy. Ed. by Jeroen C. Van Den Bergh & Jan Van Der Straaten. LC 94-36174. 288p. (C). 1994. pap. text ed. 30.00 (*1-55963-349-2*) Island Pr.

Toward Sustainable Development? Struggling over India's Narmada River. Ed. by William F. Fisher. LC 94-27016. (Columbia University Seminars Ser.). 500p. (C). 1995. pap. text ed. 27.95 (*1-56324-525-6*) M E Sharpe.

Toward Sustainable Development? Struggling over India's Narmada River. Ed. by William F. Fisher. LC 94-27016. (Columbia University Seminars Ser.). 500p. (C). (gr. 13). 1995. text ed. 76.95 (*1-56324-341-5*) M E Sharpe.

Toward Sustainable Management of Water Resources. Ismail Serageldin. (Directions in Development Ser.). 40p. 1995. 6.95 (*0-8213-3413-1*, 13413) World Bank.

Toward Telecommunications Strategies in Academic & Research Libraries. T. Kinney. pap. 25.00 (*0-918006-58-9*, OP#14) ARL.

Toward Teraflop Computing & New Grand Challenge Applications. Ed. by R. K. Kalia & P. Vashishta. 383p. (C). 1995. lib. bdg. 98.00 (*1-56072-247-9*) Nova Sci Pubs.

Toward the African Revolution. Frantz Fanon. Tr. by Haakon Chevalier from FRE. LC 87-37247. 108p. 1988. pap. 12.00 (*0-8021-3090-9*, Grove) Grove-Atltic.

Toward the Automatic Factory: A Case Study of Men & Machines. Charles R. Walker. LC 76-45083. (Illus.). 252p. 1977. reprint ed. text ed. 35.00 (*0-8371-9301-X*, WATA, Greenwood Pr) Greenwood.

Toward the Beloved Community: Martin Luther King, Jr. & South Africa. Lewis V. Baldwin. LC 95-18073. (Illus.). 280p. 1995. 24.95 (*0-8298-1102-8*); pap. 18.95 (*0-8298-1108-7*) Pilgrim OH.

Toward the Blue Peninsula. James Williams. 32p. (Orig.). 1995. pap. 3.50 (*0-935331-17-4*) Ampersand RI.

Toward the Brink. Claude Manceron. (French Revolution Ser.: Vol. 4). (Illus.). 1983. 22.95 (*0-394-51533-1*) Knopf.

Toward the Century of Words: Johann Cotta & the Politics of the Public Realm in Germany, 1795-1832. Daniel Moran. 312p. 1990. 47.50 (*0-520-06640-5*) U CA Pr.

Toward the Conquest of Beriberi. Robert R. Williams. LC 61-7397. (Illus.). 360p. 1961. 34.50 (*0-674-89790-0*) HUP.

Toward the Conquest of the Inner Cosmos. Edmond B. Szekely. (Illus.). 64p. 1969. pap. 6.80 (*0-89564-053-8*) IBS Intl.

Toward the Death of Man. William Kluback. LC 90-49502. (American University Studies: Philosophy: Ser. V, Vol. 116). 230p. (C). 1990. text ed. 39.95 (*0-8204-1470-0*) P Lang Pubng.

Toward the Decolonization of African Literature, Vol. I. Chinweizu et al. LC 82-23357. 320p. 1982. pap. 12.95 (*0-88258-123-6*) Howard U Pr.

Toward the Educative Society. Alexander N. Charters. LC 74-149023. (Notes & Essays Ser.: No. 67). 1971. pap. 2.50 (*0-87060-039-7*, NES 67) Syracuse U Cont Ed.

Toward the End: Closure & Structure in the American Short Story. John Gerlach. 208p. 1985. pap. text ed. 16.50 (*0-8173-0234-4*) U of Ala Pr.

Toward the End of the Century: Essays into Poetry. Wayne Dodd. LC 92-15642. 154p. 1992. pap. 13.95 (*0-87745-256-3*); text ed. 24.95 (*0-87745-378-0*) U of Iowa Pr.

***Toward the End of Time.** John Updike. LC 97-5167. 1997. 25.00 (*0-375-40006-0*) Knopf.

Toward the Establishment of Liberal Catholicism in America. Joseph A. Varacalli. LC 82-23811. 326p. (Orig.). 1983. lib. bdg. 56.50 (*0-8191-2974-7*) U Pr of Amer.

***Toward the Final Solution: A History of European Racism.** George L. Mosse. LC 77-24356. (Illus.). 1978. 40.00 (*0-86527-194-1*) Fertig.

***Toward the Final Solution: A History of European Racism.** George L. Mosse. (Illus.). 288p. 1997. reprint ed. pap. 14.95 (*0-614-26153-8*) Fertig.

Toward the Final Solution: A History of European Racism. George L. Mosse. (Illus.). xvi, 277p. 1997. reprint ed. pap. 14.95 (*0-86527-428-2*) Fertig.

Toward the Final Solution: A History of European Racism. George L. Mosse. LC 84-40501. (Illus.). 324p. 1985. reprint ed. pap. text ed. 16.95 (*0-299-10184-3*) U of Wis Pr.

Toward the Flame. Ray Dean. LC 92-75781. 304p. 1993. 22.95 (*1-878398-22-9*) Blue Note Pubns.

Toward the French Revolution: Europe & America in the Eighteenth-Century World. Louis Gottschalk & Donald F. Lach. LC 72-1905. (Illus.). 1973. 39.50 (*0-684-13170-6*) Irvington.

Toward the Fullness of Life: The Fullness of Love. Arnaud Desjardins. Tr. by Kathleen Kennedy from FRE. LC 89-29545. 182p. (C). 1990. pap. 12.95 (*0-934252-55-6*) Hohm Pr.

Toward the Future. Pierre Teilhard De Chardin. Tr. by Rene Hague from FRE. LC 74-23802. 224p. 1975. reprint ed. pap. 4.95 (*0-15-690780-1*, HB310, Harvest Bks) HarBrace.

Toward the Future: Catholic Social Thought & the U. S. Economy, a Lay Letter. Lay Commission on Catholic Social Teaching & the U. S. Economy. 120p. 1985. reprint ed. pap. text ed. 15.00 (*0-8191-4860-1*) U Pr of Amer.

Toward the Goal Supreme. Swami Virajananda. LC 73-87782. 155p. 1973. reprint ed. pap. 4.95 (*0-87481-029-9*) Vedanta Pr.

Toward the Habit of Truth: A Life in Science. Mahlon B. Hoagland. 1994. pap. 12.95 (*0-393-31147-3*) Norton.

***Toward the Inquisition: Essays on Jewish & Converso History in Late Medieval Spain.** B. Netanyahu. 272p. 1997. 32.50 (*0-8014-3410-6*) Cornell U Pr.

Toward the Integration of Psychotherapy. John M. Reisman. LC 77-147236. (Wiley Series on Psychological Disorders). 169p. reprint ed. pap. 48.20 (*0-317-08444-5*, 2011884) Bks Demand.

Toward the Light. Linda Ashear. 52p. (Orig.). 1989. pap. 8.95 (*0-317-93457-0*) Croton Review.

Toward the Making of Thoreau's Modern Reputation: Selected Correspondence of S. A. Jones, A. W. Hosmer, H. S. Salt, H. G. O. Blake & D. Ricketson. Ed. by Fritz Oehlschlaeger & George Hendrick. LC 79-12831. (Illus.). 433p. 1980. text ed. 39.95 (*0-252-00725-5*) U of Ill Pr.

***Toward the Millennium: The Election of 1996.** Larry J. Sabato. 336p. 1997. pap. 17.95 (*0-205-19907-0*) Allyn.

Toward the Multicultural University. Gale A. Young. Ed. by Benjamin P. Bowser et al. LC 94-25046. 224p. 1995. text ed. 49.95 (*0-275-94767-X*, Praeger Pubs) Greenwood.

***Toward the New Degeneracy: An Essay.** Bruce Benderson. LC 96-61925. (Illus.). 64p. 1997. pap. 10.00 (*0-9646466-3-3*) Edgewise Pr.

Toward the New Jerusalem. Alma P. Burton. 160p. 1994. pap. 9.95 (*1-55517-156-7*) CFI Dist.

Toward the New Spain: The Spanish Revolution of 1868 & the First Republic. Joseph A. Brandt. LC 76-54695. (Perspectives in European History Ser.: No. 3). (Illus.). xiii, 435p. 1976. reprint ed. lib. bdg. 49.50 (*0-87991-607-9*) Porcupine Pr.

***Toward the Origins of Christmas.** Susan K. Roll. (Liturgia Condenda Ser.: Vol. 5). 296p. 1995. pap. 35.75 (*90-390-0531-1*, Pub. by KOK Pharos NE) Eisenbrauns.

Toward the Poems of Mallarme. Robert G. Cohn. 1965. pap. 12.00 (*0-520-03846-0*) U CA Pr.

Toward the Poetics of Surrealism. J. H. Matthews. 244p. 1976. 39.95 (*0-8156-0120-4*) Syracuse U Pr.

Toward the Postmodern. Jean-Francois Lyotard. Ed. by Robert Harvey & Mark S. Roberts. LC 92-719. (Philosophy & Literary Theory Ser.). 280p. (C). 1995. pap. 17.50 (*0-391-03890-7*) Humanities.

Toward the Practice of Theory-Based Instruction: Current Cognitive Theories & Their Educational Promise. Ed. by Anne McKeough & Lupart. 208p. (C). 1991. text ed. 32.50 (*0-8058-0773-X*) L Erlbaum Assocs.

Toward the Prevention of Alcohol Problems: Government, Business, & Community Action. National Research Council (U. S.), Panel on Alternative Policies Affecting the Prevention of Alcohol Abuse & Alcoholism Staff. Ed. by Dean R. Gerstein. LC 84-16543. 188p. reprint ed. pap. 53.60 (*0-8357-6816-3*, 2035499) Bks Demand.

***Toward the Primeval Lightning Field.** Will Alexander. 120p. 1997. 10.50 (*1-882022-30-0*) O Bks.

Toward the Principles of Mathematics 1900-1902. Bertrand Russell. Ed. by Gregory H. Moore. LC 93-3505. (Collected Papers of Bertrand Russell: Vol. 3). 960p. (C). 1994. text ed. 180.00 (*0-415-09405-4*, A9411) Routledge.

Toward the Promised Land: From Uncle Tom's Cabin to the Onset of the Civil War (1851-1861) Ed. by Darlene C. Hine et al. (Milestones in Black American History Ser.). (Illus.). 144p. (YA). (gr. 5 up). 1995. pap. 8.95 (*0-7910-2691-4*) Chelsea Hse.

An Asterisk (*) at the beginning of an entry indicates that the title is appearing in BIP for the first time.

Toward the Radical Center: A Karel Capek Reader. Karel Capek. Ed. by Peter Kussi. LC 89-39708. (Garrigue Bks.). 416p. (Orig.). 1990. 23.95 (*0-945774-06-0*, PG5038.C3A25); pap. 12.95 (*0-945774-07-9*, PG5038. C3A2S) Catbird Pr.

***Toward the Resolution of Poverty in America.** Craig White. 358p. (C). 1997. 52.65 (*0-7872-3438-9*) Kendall-Hunt.

Toward the "Rule of Law" in Russia? Political & Legal Reform in the Transition Period. Ed. by Donald D. Barry. LC 92-9677. 430p. (gr. 13). 1992. text ed. 118.00 (*1-56324-065-3*) M E Sharpe.

Toward the Sea. Stanley Middleton. 217p. 1995. 26.00 (*0-09-179158-8*, Pub. by Hutchnson UK) Trafalgar.

***Toward the Sea.** large type ed. Stanley Middleton. LC 97-13096. 1997. write for info. (*0-7862-1128-8*) Thorndike Pr.

Toward the Second Decade: The Impact of the Women's Movement on American Institutions. Ed. by Betty Justice & Renate Pore. LC 80-24764. (Contributions in Women's Studies: No. 25). (Illus.). 272p. 1981. text ed. 59.95 (*0-313-22110-3*, JSD/) Greenwood.

Toward the Setting Sun: A Journey into the American Past. Douglass W. Ward. LC 86-80598. 1986. 10.00 (*0-9609380-0-1*) Sundowner Serv.

Toward the Splendid City. Marjorie Agosin. Tr. by Richard Schaaf. LC 94-6216. 1994. pap. 15.00 (*0-927534-46-0*) Biling Rev-Pr.

Toward the Sunrising. Lynn Morris & Gilbert Morris. LC 95-43937. (Cheney Duval, M. D. Ser.: Vol. 4). 368p. (Orig.). 1996. pap. 9.99 (*1-55661-425-X*) Bethany Hse.

Toward the Thinking Curriculum: Current Cognitive Research. Ed. by Laura Resnick & Leopold Klopfer. (Yearbook, 1989 Ser.). (Illus.). 221p. (Orig.). 1989. pap. 18.95 (*0-87120-156-9*, 610-89012) Assn Supervision.

Toward the Transformation of Art. Justin Schorr. LC 73-8298. 118p. 1974. 15.00 (*0-8386-1382-9*) Fairleigh Dickinson.

Toward the Twenty-First Century: A Reader in World Politics. Ed. by Glenn P. Hastedt & Kay Kinckrehm. LC 93-23913. 438p. (C). 1993. pap. text ed. 36.60 (*0-13-953050-9*) P-H.

Toward the Twenty-First Century: The Challenges for Small Business. Ed. by Martyn Robertson et al. (U. K. Enterprise Management & Research Association Ser.). 295p. 1992. 88.00 (*0-9519230-0-5*, Pub. by P Chapman UK) Taylor & Francis.

Toward the Twenty-First Century: The Future of Speech Communication. Ed. by Julia T. Wood & Richard B. Gregg. LC 95-31231. 208p. (C). 1995. text ed. 49.50 (*1-57273-006-4*) Hampton Pr NJ.

Toward the Twenty-First Century: The Future of Speech Communication. Ed. by Julia T. Wood & Richard B. Gregg. 208p. (C). 1995. pap. text ed. 19.95 (*1-57273-007-2*) Hampton Pr NJ.

Toward the Twenty-First Century: The University Addresses of Daisaku Ikeda. Daisaku Ikeda. 224p. 1995. 29.95 (*0-8348-0334-8*) Weatherhill.

***Toward the Unknown: Martial Artist, What Shall You Become?** Dang. (Bruce Lee Library). 1997. pap. text ed. 12.95 (*0-8048-2099-6*) C E Tuttle.

Toward the Validation of Dynamic Psychotherapy: A Replication. D. H. Malan. LC 76-10182. 308p. 1976. 59.50 (*0-306-30896-7*, Plenum Pr) Plenum.

Toward the World & Wisdom of Wittgenstein's "Tractatus" John Moran. 1973. pap. text ed. 49.25 (*90-279-2394-9*) Mouton.

***Toward the Year 2000: Work in Progress.** Daniel Bell & Stephen R. Graubard. LC 97-14090. (Illus.). 412p. 1997. pap. 17.50 (*0-262-52237-3*) MIT Pr.

***Toward the 21st Century.** Ed. by Leslie H. Tepper. (Mercury Ser.: No. 5). 192p. 1989. pap. 19.95 (*0-660-50292-5*, Pub. by Can Mus Civil CN) U of Wash Pr.

***Toward the 21st Century: Incorporating Genetics into Primary Health Care.** Nancy Touchette. LC 97-19247. 1997. write for info. (*0-87969-499-8*) Cold Spring Harbor.

Toward the 21st Century: New Directions. 176p. Date not set. 15.00 (*0-614-11326-1*) Bagehot Council.

Toward the 21st Century: New Directions. CNL Staff & Justin Winsor. (CNL/World Reports: Vol. VII). (Illus.). 176p. 1994. pap. 18.00 (*0-918680-48-4*) Bagehot Council.

Toward Tomorrow: New Visions for General Music. Ed. by Sandra Stauffer. (Illus.). 144p. (Orig.). (C). 1995. pap. 21.00 (*1-56545-080-9*, 1042) Music Ed Natl.

Toward Transfigured Life. S. Harakas. 1983. pap. 15.95 (*0-937032-28-X*) Light&Life Pub Co MN.

Toward Transformation in Social Knowledge. 2nd ed. Kenneth J. Gergen. 288p. (C). 1994. text ed. 59.95 (*0-8039-8971-7*); pap. text ed. 22.95 (*0-8039-8972-5*) Sage.

Toward Two Societies: The Changing Distributions of Income & Wealth in the U. S. since 1960. Andrew J. Winnick. LC 88-35980. 282p. 1989. text ed. 59.95 (*0-275-92899-3*, C2899, Praeger Pubs) Greenwood.

***Toward 2015: A Church Odyssey.** Richard Kew & Roger J. White. LC 96-38715. 1997. write for info. (*1-56101-137-1*); pap. 12.95 (*1-56101-136-3*) Cowley Pubns.

Toward Understanding Islam: Contemporary Apologetic of Islam & Missionary Policy. Harry G. Dorman. LC 79-176727. (Columbia University. Teachers College. Contributions to Education Ser.: No. 940). reprint ed. 37.50 (*0-404-55940-9*) AMS Pr.

Toward Understanding the Social Impact of Computers. Roy C. Amara. 136p. 1974. 10.50 (*0-318-14427-1*, R29) Inst Future.

Toward Undiscovered Ends. Anna Brinton. (C). 1951. pap. 7.00 (*0-87574-062-6*) Pendle Hill.

Toward Unification in Psychology: The Banff Conference on Theoretical Psychology, 1st, 1965. Banff Conference on Theoretical Psychology Staff. Ed. by Joseph R. Royce. LC 72-505050. 314p. reprint ed. pap. 89.50 (*0-317-08093-8*, 2014393) Bks Demand.

Toward Unity Against World Imperialism. Gus Hall. 1969. pap. 0.35 (*0-87898-040-7*) New Outlook.

Toward Unity among Environmentalists. Bryan G. Norton. (Illus.). 304p. 1994. reprint ed. pap. 18.95 (*0-19-509397-6*) OUP.

Toward Universal Religion: Voices of American & Indian Spirituality. Daniel R. Chandler. LC 95-33968. (Contributions to the Study of Religion Ser.). 272p. 1996. text ed. 65.00 (*0-313-29484-4*, Greenwood Pr) Greenwood.

Toward Useful Performance Measurement: Lessons Learned from Initial Pilot Plans Prepared under the GPRA. unabridged ed. 26p. 1994. pap. 12.00 (*1-57744-003-X*) Nat Acad Public Admin.

Toward Wholeness: Rudolf Steiner Education in America. Mary C. Richards. LC 80-14905. 222p. 1980. pap. 14.95 (*0-8195-6062-6*, Wesleyan Univ Pr) U Pr of New Eng.

Toward Wholeness in Paule Marshall's Fiction. Joyce Pettis. LC 94-48916. 192p. (C). 1995. text ed. 29.50 (*0-8139-1614-3*) U Pr of Va.

Toward Wider Acceptance of U N Treaties. Oscar Schachter et al. LC 79-140127. (UNITAR Studies). 1977. 42.95 (*0-405-02236-0*) Ayer.

Toward Wisdom: Finding Our Way to Inner Peace, Love, & Happiness. Copthorne Macdonald. 208p. (Orig.). 1996. pap. 11.95 (*1-57174-044-9*) Hampton Roads Pub Co.

Toward Women: A Study of the Origins of Western Attitudes Through Greco-Roman Philosophy. Joseph P. Ghougassian. LC 77-92325. 1977. pap. 3.95 (*0-930994-01-9*) Lukas & Sons.

Toward Women in Love: The Emergence of a Lawrentian Aesthetic. Stephen J. Miko. LC 73-151583. (Yale Studies in English: No. 177). 309p. reprint ed. pap. 88. 10 (*0-8357-8354-5*, 2033827) Bks Demand.

Toward World Peace. Henry A. Wallace. 1948. 20.00 (*0-686-17404-6*) R S Barnes.

Toward World Peace. Henry A. Wallace. LC 74-100247. 121p. 1970. reprint ed. text ed. 35.00 (*0-8371-3434-X*, WAWP, Greenwood Pr) Greenwood.

Towards a Better Life: Being a Series of Epistles, or Declamations. Kenneth Burke. 1966. pap. 12.95 (*0-520-04638-2*) U CA Pr.

Towards a Better Understanding of History. Bernard Norling. LC 60-15676. 157p. 1960. pap. 9.50 (*0-268-00284-3*) U of Notre Dame Pr.

***Towards a Calculus of Meaning: Studies in Markedness, Distinctive Features & Deixis.** Ed. by Edna Andrews & Yishai Tobin. LC 96-37217. (Studies in Functional & Structural Linguistics: Vol. 43). xxviii, 432p. 1997. lib. bdg. 99.00 (*1-55619-268-1*) Benjamins North Am.

***Towards a Christian Philosophy.** Joseph Owens. (Studies in Philosophy & the History of Philosophy). 332p. 1990. 44.95 (*0-8132-0708-8*) Cath U Pr.

Towards a Christian Poetics. Michael Edwards. LC 83-20629. 254p. reprint ed. pap. 72.40 (*0-685-23455-X*, 2032725) Bks Demand.

Towards a Citizens Militia: Anarchist Alternatives to NATO & the Warsaw Pact. Ed. by First of May Group. 1984. lib. bdg. 79.95 (*0-87700-631-8*) Revisionist Pr.

Towards a Civil Architecture in America Modulus 23. University of Virginia Staff. (Illus.). 160p. 1995. pap. 24. 95 (*1-56898-037-X*) Princeton Arch.

Towards a Civilisation of Love: Being Church in Today's World. Basil Hume. 177p. Date not set. reprint ed. pap. write for info. (*0-932506-91-7*) St Bedes Pubns.

***Towards a Classless Society?** Helen Jones. LC 97-9747. (State of Welfare Ser.). 240p. (C). 1997. pap. write for info. (*0-415-15331-X*); text ed. write for info. (*0-415-15330-1*) Routledge.

Towards a Comparative Analysis of Peace Movements. Ed. by Katsuya Kodama & Unto Vesa. (Illus.). 296p. 1990. text ed. 52.95 (*1-85521-110-6*, Pub. by Dartmth Pub UK) Ashgate Pub Co.

Towards a Competence Theory of the Firm. Ed. by Nicolai J. Foss & Christian Knudsen. (Studies in Business Organization & Networks Ser.: Vol. 2). 216p. (C). 1996. text ed. 74.95 (*0-415-14472-8*) Routledge.

Towards a Competent Workforce. Bob Mansfield & Lindsay Mitchell. 175p. 1996. text ed. 72.95 (*0-566-07699-3*, Pub. by Gower UK) Ashgate Pub Co.

Towards a Comprehensive Model for Schizophrenic Disorders. Ed. by David B. Feinsilver. (Psychoanalytic Inquiry Bk.: Vol. 5). 416p. (C). 1986. text ed. 49.95 (*0-88163-029-2*) Analytic Pr.

***Towards a Comprehensive Therapy of Schizophrenia.** rev. ed. Ed. by H. D. Brenner et al. (Illus.). 300p. 1997. text ed. 49.00 (*0-88937-175-X*) Hogrefe & Huber Pubs.

Towards a Constitutional Charter for Canada. Albert S. Abel. LC 81-116198. 111p. reprint ed. pap. 31.70 (*0-8357-4133-8*, 2036905) Bks Demand.

Towards a Contextual Grammar of English. Eugene Winter. 224p. 1983. pap. text ed. 11.95 (*0-04-425028-2*) Routledge Chapman & Hall.

Towards a Cosmic Music. Karlteinz Stockhausen. 1993. pap. 15.95 (*1-85230-084-1*) Element MA.

Towards a Critical Sociolinguistics. Ed. by Rajendra Singh. LC 96-3823. (Current Issues in Linguistic Theory Ser.: No. 125). 250p. 1996. lib. bdg. 70.00 (*1-55619-579-6*) Benjamins North Am.

Towards a Critical Sociology of Reading Pedagogy: Papers of the XII World Congress on Reading. Ed. by Carolyn D. Baker & Allan Luke. LC 91-7316. (Pragmatics & Beyond Ser.: No. 19). xxi, 287p. 1991. 71.00 (*1-55619-285-1*); pap. 27.95 (*1-55619-286-X*) Benjamins North Am.

Towards a Critique of Foucault. Ed. by Mike Gane. 1987. pap. text ed. 15.95 (*0-7102-0764-6*, RKP) Routledge.

Towards a CSCW Framework for Scientific Cooperation in Europe. Hannes P. Lubich. LC 94-46548. (Lecture Notes in Computer Science Ser.: Vol. 889). 1995. 45.00 (*3-540-58844-2*) Spr-Verlag.

Towards a Developmental Theory of Andragogy. Nottingham Andragogy Group Staff. (C). 1986. 35.00 (*0-685-67269-7*, Pub. by Univ Nottingham UK) St Mut.

Towards a Developmental Theory of Andragogy. Nottingham Andragogy Group Staff. (C). 1988. text ed. 40.00 (*0-685-22137-7*, Pub. by Univ Nottingham UK) St Mut.

Towards a Developmental Theory of Andragogy. Ed. by Nottingham Andragogy Group Staff. (C). 1986. reprint ed. 25.00 (*0-685-50345-3*, Pub. by Univ Nottingham UK) St Mut.

Towards a Discipline of Nursing. Ed. by Genevieve Gray & Rosalie Pratt. (Illus.). 400p. (Orig.). 1992. pap. text ed. 48.00 (*0-443-04438-4*) Churchill.

Towards A Dynamic African Economy: Selected Speeches & Lectures, 1975-1986. Adebayo Adedeji. Ed. by Jeggan C. Senghor. (Illus.). 729p. (C). 1989. text ed. 55.00 (*0-7146-3349-6*, Pub. by F Cass Pubs UK); pap. text ed. 37.50 (*0-7146-4062-X*, Pub. by F Cass Pubs UK) Intl Spec Bk.

Towards a Dynamic Economics: Some Recent Developments of Economic Theory & Their Application to Policy. Roy F. Harrod. LC 79-20398. 168p. 1980. reprint ed. text ed. 38.50 (*0-313-22089-1*, HATD, Greenwood Pr) Greenwood.

Towards a European Civil Code. Ed. by A. S. Hartkamp et al. LC 93-41423. 474p. (C). 1994. lib. bdg. 176.00 (*0-7923-2625-3*) Kluwer Ac.

Towards a European Foreign Policy: Legal, Economic, & Political Dimensions. Johan K. De Vree et al. LC 87-5612. 1987. lib. bdg. 148.00 (*90-247-3506-8*) Kluwer Ac.

Towards a Feminist Christology: Jesus of Nazareth, European Women, & the Christological Crisis. Julie M. Hopkins. 1995. pap. 15.00 (*0-8028-4074-4*) Eerdmans.

Towards a Feminist Critical Reading of the Gospel According to Matthew. Elaine M. Wainwright. (Beihefte zur Zeitschrift fuer die Neuetestamentliche Wissenschaft Ser.: Vol. 60). xxiii, 410p. (C). 1991. lib. bdg. 127.70 (*3-11-012860-8*) De Gruyter.

***Towards a Feminist Ethics.** Ina Praetorius. 200p. 1997. pap. 32.50 (*90-390-0422-6*, Pub. by KOK Pharos NE) Eisenbrauns.

Towards a Formal Description of Ada. Ed. by B. Bjorner & O. N. Oest. (Lecture Notes in Computer Science Ser.: Vol. 98). 630p. 1980. 39.00 (*0-387-10283-3*) Spr-Verlag.

Towards a Free Society: An Introduction to Markets & the Political System. 2nd ed. Charles W. Wolfram. 1993. pap. text ed. write for info. (*0-07-071523-8*) McGraw.

Towards a Future European Peace Order? Ed. by Karl E. Birnbaum et al. 240p. (C). 1993. text ed. 69.95 (*0-333-54624-5*) St Martin.

Towards a General Comparative Linguistics. Jeffrey Ellis. (Janua Linguarum, Ser. Minor: No. 52). (Orig.). 1966. pap. text ed. 47.70 (*90-279-0584-3*) Mouton.

Towards a Global Village: International Community Development Initiatives. Michael Shuman. LC 94-1728. (C). 66.50 (*0-7453-0861-9*, Pub. by Pluto Pr UK); pap. 17.95 (*0-7453-0862-7*, Pub. by Pluto Pr UK) LPC InBook.

Towards a Good Beginning. G. Burton. 1985. text ed. 22.95 (*0-201-20086-4*) Addison-Wesley.

Towards a Good Beginning: Teaching Early Childhood Mathematics. G. M. Burton et al. 257p. 1984. write for info. (*0-318-61051-5*) Addison-Wesley.

Towards a Healthy Baby: Congenital Disorders & the New Genetics in Primary Health Care. Bernadette Modell & Michael Modell. (Illus.). 430p. 1992. 95.00 (*0-19-262234-X*); pap. 49.95 (*0-19-261486-X*) OUP.

Towards a Healthy District: Organizing & Managing District Health Systems Based on Primary Health Care. E. Tarimo. v, 105p. (CHI, ENG, FRE & SPA.). 1990. pap. text ed. 19.00 (*92-4-154412-0*, 1150353) World Health.

Towards a History of Adult Education in America: The Search for a Unifying Principle. Harold W. Stubblefield. 208p. (C). 1988. text ed. 37.50 (*0-415-00563-9*) Routledge.

***Towards a History of Irish Spirituality.** Peter O'Dwyer. 288p. (Orig.). 1995. pap. 17.95 (*1-85607-124-3*, Pub. by Columba Pr IE) Twenty-Third.

Towards a History of Literary Composition in Medieval Spain. Colbert I. Nepaulsingh. (Romance Ser.). 302p. 1986. text ed. 45.00 (*0-8020-2570-6*) U of Toronto Pr.

Towards a History of the Basque Language. Ed. by Jose I. Hualde et al. LC 95-50363. (Current Issues in Linguistic Theory Ser.: No. 131). 365p. 1996. lib. bdg. 90.00 (*1-55619-585-0*) Benjamins North Am.

***Towards a History of the Spanish Villancico.** Paul R. Laird. LC 97-2393. (Detroit Monographs in Musicology). 1997. write for info. (*0-89990-075-5*) Info Coord.

Towards a Jurisprudence of Injury: A Summary of the Report of the A.B.A.'s Special Committee on the Tort Liability System. Marshall S. Shapo. 19p. 1986. pap. 10.00 (*0-933067-09-7*) Roscoe Pound Found.

Towards a Jurisprudence of Injury: The Continuing Creation of a System of Substantive Justice in American Tort Law: Report to the American Bar Association. American Bar Association, Special Committee on Dispute Resolution & Marshall S. Shapo. LC 85-112535. 996p. 1984. 55.00 (*0-685-10475-3*, 486-0001) Amer Bar Assn.

Towards a Just Immigration Policy. Ed. by Ann Dummett. (C). 1988. 21.00 (*0-900137-26-6*, Pub. by NCCL UK) St Mut.

***Towards a Just Monetary System.** M. Umer Chapra. 292p. 1996. pap. 13.95 (*0-614-21531-5*, 1243) Kazi Pubns.

Towards a Liberating Peace. Rajni Kothari et al. 220p. (Orig.). 1989. pap. 14.50 (*0-945257-00-7*) Apex Pr.

Towards a Literature of Knowledge. Jerome J. McGann. 152p. 1989. 29.95 (*0-226-55839-8*) U Ch Pr.

Towards a Market Economy in Central & Eastern Europe. Ed. by Herbert Giersch. (Illus.). 169p. 1991. 62.10 (*0-387-53922-0*) Spr-Verlag.

Towards a Methodology of Military Force Comparison. Dieter S. Lutz. 255p. 1986. pap. 45.00 (*3-7890-0915-6*, Pub. by Nomos Verlags GW) Intl Bk Import.

Towards a Model of Biochemical Processes. Ed. by Geoffrey T. Evans & Michael J. R. Fasham. LC 93-23008. (NATO ASI Series I: Global Environmental Change: Vol. 10). 1993. 157.00 (*0-387-54583-2*) Spr-Verlag.

Towards a Model of Ocean Biogeochemical Processes. Ed. by Geoffrey T. Evans & Michael J. Fasham. (NATO ASI Series I: Global Environmental Change: Vol. 10). (Illus.). 370p. 1993. write for info. (*3-540-54583-2*) Spr-Verlag.

Towards a Modern Art World. Ed. by Brian Allen. LC 94-61989. (Studies in British Art: No. 1). (Illus.). 240p. 1995. 40.00 (*0-300-06380-6*) Yale U Pr.

Towards a Modern Iran: Studies in Thought, Politics & Society. Ed. by Elie Kedourie & Sylvia G. Haim. 262p. 1980. 37.50 (*0-7146-3145-0*, Pub. by F Cass Pubs UK) Intl Spec Bk.

Towards a More General Theory of Value. Edward H. Chamberlin. LC 82-6259. xii, 318p. 1982. reprint ed. text ed. 65.00 (*0-313-23590-2*, CHTO, Greenwood Pr) Greenwood.

Towards a Mythology: Studies in the Poetry of W. B. Yeats. Peter Ure. LC 85-24696. 125p. 1986. reprint ed. text ed. 49.75 (*0-313-25055-3*, URTM, Greenwood Pr) Greenwood.

Towards a National Nutrition Policy: Guidelines for Countries of the Eastern Mediterranean Region. Ed. by K. Bagchi. 65p. 1990. pap. text ed. 2.00 (*92-9021-118-0*, 1450017) World Health.

Towards a National Spirit. Whitfield J. Bell, Jr. 1979. pap. 3.00 (*0-89073-057-1*) Boston Public Lib.

Towards a "Natural" Narratology. Monika Fludernik. 472p. (C). 1996. text ed. 99.95 (*0-415-12482-4*) Routledge.

T

Towards a New Alchemy Vol. 1: The Millennium Science. Nick Begich. Ed. by Thomas Begich. (Illus.). 208p. (Orig.). 1996. pap. 14.95 (*0-9648812-2-5*) Earthpulse Pr.

Towards a New Architecture. Le Corbusier. (Illus.). 312p. 1970. pap. 36.95 (*0-7506-0627-4*) Buttrwrth-Heinemann.

Towards a New Architecture. Le Corbusier. 320p. 1986. reprint ed. pap. 8.95 (*0-486-25023-7*) Dover.

Towards a New Balance of Power in Asia. Paul Dibb. (Illus.). 96p. 1995. pap. text ed. 23.00 (*0-19-828069-6*) OUP.

Towards a New Bretton Woods: Alternatives for the Global Economy. Stuart Holland. 274p. (Orig.). 1994. pap. 42. 50 (*0-85124-556-0*, Pub. by Spokesman Bks UK) Coronet Bks.

Towards a New Consciousness. R. P. Kaushik. LC 78-59118. 1979. pap. 8.95 (*0-918038-09-X*) Journey Pubns.

Towards a New Development Strategy for Latin America: Pathways from Hirschman's Thought. Intro. by Simon Teitel. 380p. (Orig.). (C). 1992. pap. text ed. 24.00 (*0-940602-44-X*) IADB.

Towards a New Economic Order: Postfordism, Ecology & Democracy. Alain Lipietz. LC 92-11305. (Europe & the International Order Ser.). 196p. (C). 1992. text ed. 45.00 (*0-19-520961-3*); pap. text ed. 17.95 (*0-19-520962-1*) OUP.

Towards a New Educational System: The Victory of the New Right. Clyde Chitty. 225p. 1989. 55.00 (*1-85000-448-X*, Falmer Pr); pap. 33.00 (*1-85000-449-8*, Falmer Pr) Taylor & Francis.

Towards a New Europe: Stops & Starts in Regional Integration. Ed. by Gerald Schneider et al. LC 95-7553. 240p. 1995. text ed. 57.95 (*0-275-94865-X*, Praeger Pubs) Greenwood.

Towards a New Europe: Structural Change in the European Economy. Ed. by Ash Amin & Michael Dietrich. (European Association for Evolutionary Political Economy Ser.). 256p. 1991. text ed. 85.00 (*1-85278-415-6*) E Elgar.

Towards a New Europe: The Restructuring of the European Space Economy. Yehunda Hayuth & Gunnar Tornqvist. 1996. text ed. 90.00 (*0-471-96118-3*) Wiley.

Towards a New Formation: South Indian Society under Vijayanagar Rule. Noboru Karashima. (Illus.). 300p. 1993. 21.00 (*0-19-562861-6*) OUP.

Towards a New Frontier: History of the Bank of Baroda, 1908-1983. Dwijendra Tripathi. (C). 1985. 16.00 (*0-8364-2882-X*, Pub. by Manohar II) S Asia.

***Towards a New Global Framework for High-Technology Competition.** Ed. by Horst Siebert. (C). 1997. 79.50 (*3-16-146711-6*) U of Mich Pr.

Towards a New International Economic Order. Mohammed Bedjaoui. LC 79-22943. Orig. Title: Pour un Nouvel Ordre Economique International. 287p. 1979. pap. 29.95 (*0-8419-0588-6*) Holmes & Meier.

Towards a New Israel: The Jewish State & the Arab Question. Mordechai Nisan. LC 91-11936. (Studies in Modern Society: No. 24). 1992. 42.50 (*0-404-61631-3*) AMS Pr.

***Towards a New Kind of Living: The Werkbund Housing Estate Breslau, 1929.** Andreas Denk. (Illus.). 96p. 1996. pap. 29.95 (*3-7643-5420-8*) Birkhauser.

Towards a New Liberal Internationalism: The International Theory of J. A. Hobson. David Long. (London School of Economics Monographs in International Studies). 276p. (C). 1996. text ed. 54.95 (*0-521-45497-2*) Cambridge U Pr.

Towards a New Map of Automobile Manufacturing in Europe? New Production Concepts & Spatial Restructuring. Ed. by R. Hudson & E. Schamp. (Illus.). 269p. 1996. 135.00 (*3-540-58812-4*) Spr-Verlag.

Towards a New Marxism: Proceedings of the International Telos Conference, 1st, Waterloo, Ont., Oct. 8-11, 1970. International Telos Conference Staff. Ed. by Paul Piccone & Bart Grahl. LC 73-87129. 240p. (C). 1973. 24.00 (*0-914386-03-4*) Telos Pr.

***Towards a New Model of Creole Genesis.** John McWhorter. (Studies in Ethnolinguistics: Vol. 3). 216p. (C). 1997. text ed. 44.95 (*0-8204-3312-8*) P Lang Pubng.

Towards a New Multilateralism: Funding Global Priorities: New & Innovative Financing Mechanisms for Internationally Agreed Programmes. Hans D'Orville & Dragoljub Najman. 60p. 1995. 15.00 (*1-885060-04-1*) H dOrville.

***Towards a New Museum.** Victoria Newhouse. 1997. pap. 29.95 (*1-885254-60-1*) Monacelli Pr.

Towards a New Pharmacotherapy of Pain. Ed. by A. I. Basbaum & Jean-Marie Besson. LC 90-42921. (Dahlem Workshop Reports - Life Sciences). 457p. 1991. text ed. 285.00 (*0-471-92854-2*) Wiley.

Towards a New Poetry. Diane Wakoski. (Poets on Poetry Ser.). 1979. pap. 13.95 (*0-472-06307-3*) U of Mich Pr.

Towards a New Price Revolution. B. Csikos-Nagy. 190p. (C). 1979. 50.00 (*963-05-1851-1*, Pub. by Akad Kiado HU) St Mut.

Towards a New Science of Health. Ed. by Robert Lafaille & Stephen Fulder. LC 93-3282. 208p. (C). 1993. text ed. 74.95 (*0-415-08171-8*) Routledge.

***Towards a New Social Order in Russia: Transforming Structures & Everyday Life.** Timo Piirainen. LC 96-32176. (Illus.). 272p. 1997. text ed. 63.95 (*1-85521-690-6*, Pub. by Dartmth Pub UK) Ashgate Pub Co.

Towards a New Socialism. W. Paul Cockshott & Allin Cottrell. 234p. 1993. 72.50 (*0-85124-544-7*, Pub. by Spokesman Bks UK); pap. 37.50 (*0-85124-545-5*, Pub. by Spokesman Bks UK) Coronet Bks.

Towards a New Theatre: The Lectures of Robert Edmond Jones. Robert E. Jones. Ed. by Delbert Unruh. LC 91-37925. 112p. (Orig.). 1992. pap. 8.95 (*0-87910-152-0*) Limelight Edns.

***Towards a New Theory of Distributive Justice.** Norman E. Bowie. LC 72-150315. 160p. 1971. reprint ed. pap. 45.60 (*0-608-04439-3*, 2064971) Bks Demand.

Towards a New World. Sarvepalli Radhakrishnan. 149p. 1983. 9.00 (*0-86578-202-4*); pap. 4.25 (*0-86578-138-9*) Ind-US Inc.

***Towards a New World View Vol. I: Conversation at the Leading Edge.** unabridged ed. Russell E. DiCarlo. 377p. (Orig.). 1996. pap. text ed. 16.95 (*1-886718-00-8*) Epic Publ.

Towards a Newer World. B. R. Sen. 342p. 1982. 35.00 (*0-907567-26-6*, Tycooly Pub); pap. 10.00 (*0-907567-27-4*, Tycooly Pub) Weidner & Sons.

Towards a Non-Static Theory of Profit Maximization. A. Mukherjee. 1990. 34.00 (*81-7017-274-8*, Pub. by Abhinav II) S Asia.

***Towards a Nuclear Weapon-Free World: Proceedings of the 45th Pugwash Conference, Hiroshima, Japan, 23-29 July 1995.** Ed. by J. Rotblat & M. Konuma. 830p. 1997. 118.00 (*981-02-3179-2*) World Scientific Pub.

Towards a Nuclear-Weapons-Free Zone in Middle East. 57p. 1991. 12.95 (*92-1-142176-4*, 91.IX.3) UN.

Towards a Payments System Law for Developing & Transition Economies. Raj Bhala. LC 95-37718. (Discussion Papers: Vol. 299). 42p. 1995. 7.95 (*0-8213-3438-7*, 13438) Wrld Bank.

Towards a Peace Economy in the United States: Essays on Military Industry, Disarmament & Economic Conversion. Ed. by Gregory A. Bischak. LC 90-32034. 230p. 1991. text ed. 45.00 (*0-312-04731-2*) St Martin.

Towards a People's Liturgy. Mark Elvins. 1994. pap. 12.95 (*0-85244-257-2*, Pub. by Gracewing UK) Morehouse Pub.

Towards a Phenomenological Ethics: Ethos & the Life-World. Werner Marx. LC 90-36907. (SUNY Series in Contemporary Continental Philosophy). 153p. (C). 1992. text ed. 59.50 (*0-7914-0574-5*); pap. text ed. 19.95 (*0-7914-0575-3*) State U NY Pr.

Towards a Philosophy of Critical Mathematics Education. Ole Skovsmose. LC 94-21077. (Mathematics Education Library: No. 15). 256p. 1994. lib. bdg. 106.00 (*0-7923-2932-5*, Pub. by Klwr Acad Pubs NE) Kluwer Ac.

Towards a Philosophy of Social Work in India. Sugata Dasgupta. 272p. 1967. 59.50 (*0-614-01823-4*) Elliots Bks.

Towards a Poetics of Criticism. Ed. by Mark Wallace et al. 230p. (Orig.). (C). 1993. pap. 12.95 (*0-922668-11-6*) SUNYB Poetry Rare Bks.

Towards a Poetics of Fiction: Essays from Novel, a Forum on Fiction, 1967-1976. Mark Spilka. LC 76-48550. 383p. reprint ed. pap. 109.20 (*0-685-16300-8*, 2056242) Bks Demand.

***Towards a Policy for Water Resources Development & Management in the Asian & Pacific Region, Vol. 1.** 1997. pap. 15.00 (*971-561-092-7*, Pub. by Asian Devel Bank PH) Paul & Co Pubs.

***Towards a Policy for Water Resources Development & Management in the Asian & Pacific Region, Vol. 2.** 1997. pap. 15.00 (*971-561-093-5*, Pub. by Asian Devel Bank PH) Paul & Co Pubs.

***Towards a Policy for Water Resources Development & Management in the Asian & Pacific Region, Vol. 3.** 1997. pap. 15.00 (*971-561-094-3*, Pub. by Asian Devel Bank PH) Paul & Co Pubs.

Towards a Political Economy for Africa: The Dialectics of Independence. Timothy M. Shaw. LC 84-8218. 150p. 1985. text ed. 29.95 (*0-312-81043-1*) St Martin.

Towards a Political Economy of Nigeria: Petroleum & Politics at the Semi-Periphery. Julius O. Ihonvbere & Tim Shaw. 224p. 1988. text ed. 54.95 (*0-566-05422-1*, Pub. by Dartmth Pub UK) Ashgate Pub Co.

Towards a Poor Theatre. Jerzy Grotowski. 218p. (C). 1991. reprint ed. pap. 25.95 (*0-413-34910-1*, A0566, Pub. by Methuen UK) Heinemann.

Towards a Post-Apartheid Future: Political & Economic Relations in Southern Africa. Ed. by Gavin Maasdorp & Alan Whiteside. LC 91-30440. 240p. 1992. text ed. 55.00 (*0-312-07496-4*) St Martin.

Towards a Post-Fordist Welfare State? Ed. by Roger Burrows & Brian D. Loader. LC 93-42527. (State of Welfare Ser.). 240p. (C). 1994. pap. 18.95 (*0-415-09967-6*, B4432, Routledge NY) Routledge.

Towards a Post-Fordist Welfare State? Ed. by Roger Burrows & Brian D. Loader. LC 93-42527. (State of Welfare Ser.). 288p. (C). (gr. 13). 1994. text ed. 62.95 (*0-415-09968-4*, B4427, Routledge NY) Routledge.

***Towards a Postmodern Theory of Narrative.** Andrew Gibson. (Postmodern Theory Ser.). 1997. pap. text ed. 28.00 (*0-7486-0841-9*) Col U Pr.

Towards a Practice Led Curriculum. David T. Sawdon et al. (C). 1988. 42.00 (*0-685-28593-6*, Pub. by Natl Inst Soc Work); 45.00 (*0-685-40350-5*, Pub. by Natl Inst Soc Work); 65.00 (*0-7855-0080-4*, Pub. by Natl Inst Soc Work); pap. 21.00 (*0-902789-52-X*, Pub. by Natl Inst Soc Work) St Mut.

Towards a Reading-Writing Classroom. Andrea Butler & Jan Turbill. LC 87-29663. (Illus.). 90p. (Orig.). 1987. reprint ed. pap. 16.00 (*0-435-08461-5*, 08461) Heinemann.

Towards a Reconstructed Past: Historical Texts from Busoga, Uganda. David W. Cohen. (Fontes Historiae Africanae, Series Varia: Vol. III). 250p. 1986. 19.98 (*0-19-726039-X*) David Brown.

Towards a Renewed Priesthood. Arthur Middleton. 140p. (Orig.). 1995. pap. 12.95 (*0-85244-273-4*, Pub. by Gracewing UK) Morehouse Pub.

Towards a Revaluation of Avellaneda's False Quixote. E. T. Aylward. Ed. by Thomas Lathrop et al. (Documentacion Cervantina Ser.: No. 9). 92p. pap. 8.50 (*0-936388-43-9*) Juan de la Cuesta.

Towards a Romantic Conception of Nature: Coleridge's Poetry up to 1803. H. R. Rookmaaker, Jr. LC 84-24633. (Utrecht Publications in Literature: 20). ix, 214p. 1984. 71.00 (*90-272-2205-3*); pap. 37.00 (*90-272-2215-0*) Benjamins North Am.

Towards a Science of Healing, Vol. II: Advanced Human Ecology & Energy Balancing Sciences. deluxe ed. Steven Rochlitz. (Illus.). 100p. (C). 1991. spiral bd. 59.95 (*0-945262-40-X*) HEBS Inc.

Towards a Science of Peace. Theodore F. Lentz. 1955. 4.00 (*0-318-03980-X*) Lentz Peace Res.

Towards a Science of Science Teaching: Cognitive Development & Curriculum Demand. Michael Shayer & Philip Adey. 159p. (Orig.). (C). 1995. pap. text ed. 23.00 (*0-435-57825-1*, 57825) Heinemann.

Towards a Science of Translating. Eugene A. Nida. (Illus.). 1964. 68.00 (*90-04-02605-3*) Adlers Foreign Bks.

Towards a Second Green Revolution: From Chemical to New Biological Tehcnologies in Agriculture in the Tropics. Ed. by G. B. Marini-Bettolo. (Developments in Agricultural & Managed-Forest Ecology Ser.: Vol. 19). 530p. 1988. 282.25 (*0-444-98927-7*) Elsevier.

Towards a Semiotics of Ideology. Carlos A. Reis. LC 92-21173. (Approaches to Semiotics Ser.: No. 109). vii, 163p. (C). 1993. lib. bdg. 90.80 (*3-11-011829-7*) Mouton.

***Towards a Semiotics of the Modern Quebec Novel: Agaguk, by Yves Theriault.** Paul J. Perron. (Toronto Studies in Semiotics). 192p. 1996. 40.00 (*0-8020-0926-3*) U of Toronto Pr.

Towards a Single European Infrastructure: Final Report of the Rare Task Force on the Establishment of the Operational Unit for the Supply of Network & Information Services to the R&D Community. (Illus.). 62p. (Orig.). (C). 1993. pap. text ed. 30.00 (*1-56806-320-2*) DIANE Pub.

Towards a Social Ecology: Contextual Appreciation of the Future in the Present. F. E. Emery & E. L. Trist. LC 74-26842. 256p. 1975. 39.50 (*0-306-30563-1*, Plenum Pr); pap. 19.95 (*0-306-20015-5*, Plenum Pr) Plenum.

Towards a Social Grammar of Language. M. Grayshon. 1977. 31.15 (*90-279-7633-3*) Mouton.

***Towards a Social Science of Language Vol. 2: Social Interaction & Discourse Structures.** Ed. by Gregory Guy et al. LC 97-1998. (Current Issues in Linguistic Theory Ser.: Vol. 128). xv, 295p. 1997. lib. bdg. 75.00 (*0-614-26628-9*) Benjamins North Am.

Towards a Social Science of Language - Papers in Honor of William Labov Vol. 1: Variation & Change in Language & Society. Ed. by Gregory R. Guy et al. LC 95-46466. (Current Issues in Linguistic Theory Ser.: Vol. 127). 420p. 1996. lib. bdg. 89.00 (*1-55619-581-8*) Benjamins North Am.

Towards a Socially Critical Drama Education. Edward Errington. 1992. pap. 32.00 (*0-7300-1476-2*, ECT465, Pub. by Deakin Univ AT) St Mut.

Towards a Society That Serves Its People: The Intellectual Contribution of El Salvador's Murdered Jesuits. Ignacio Ellacuria et al. Ed. by John Hassett & Hugh Lacey. Tr. by James Brockman et al. from SPA. LC 91-37465. (Illus.). 424p. (Orig.). (C). 1991. pap. 25.00 (*0-87840-523-2*) Georgetown U Pr.

Towards a Sociology of Mass Communications. Denis McQuail. 1969. pap. text ed. write for info. (*0-686-66487-6*, 97480) Macmillan.

Towards a Sociology of Schizophrenia: Humanistic Reflections. Keith Doubt. 144p. 1996. 30.00 (*0-8020-0845-3*); pap. 13.95 (*0-8020-7830-3*) U of Toronto Pr.

Towards a Software Factory. Michiel Van Genuchten. LC 92-12505. (DIVS-Diverse Ser.). 192p. (C). 1992. lib. bdg. 102.00 (*0-7923-1751-3*) Kluwer Ac.

Towards a Soviet-American Crisis Prevention Regime: History & Prospects. Alexander L. George. (CISA Working Papers: No. 28). 27p. (Orig.). 1980. pap. 15.00 (*0-86682-027-2*) Ctr Intl Relations.

Towards a Standard English, 1600-1800. Ed. by Dieter Stein & Ingrid T. Van Ostade. LC 93-36930. (Topics in English Linguistics Ser.: No. 11). vi, 325p. (C). 1993. 136.95 (*3-11-013697-X*) Mouton.

Towards a Strategic Management & Decision Technology. John W. Sutherland. (C). 1989. lib. bdg. 132.00 (*0-7923-0245-1*) Kluwer Ac.

Towards a Strategy for Conservation in a World of Technological Change. Colin A. Gannon. (Discussion Paper Ser.: No. 24). 1968. pap. 10.00 (*1-55869-124-3*) Regional Sci Res Inst.

Towards a Structure of Indifference: The Social Origins of Maternal Custody. Debra Friedman. (Sociology & Economics Ser.). 168p. 1995. pap. text ed. 20.95 (*0-202-30496-5*); lib. bdg. 43.95 (*0-202-30495-7*) Aldine de Gruyter.

Towards a Sustainable Economy: The Need for Fundamental Change. Ted Trainer. Date not set. pap. 15.95 (*1-897766-14-9*, Pub. by Jon Pubng UK) LPC InBook.

Towards a Sustainable Urban Environment: The Rio de Janeiro Study. Ed. by Mohan Munasinghe et al. LC 93-6969. (Discussion Paper Ser.: No. 195). 185p. 1993. 10.95 (*0-8213-2388-1*, 12388) World Bank.

Towards a Tantrik Goal. B. Bhattacharya. 224p. 1989. text ed. 30.00 (*81-207-0957-8*, Pub. by Sterling Pubs II) Apt Bks.

Towards a Technology of Peace. Theodore F. Lentz. 1972. pap. 3.00 (*0-933061-11-0*) Lentz Peace Res.

Towards a Theology for Inter-Faith Dialogue. Interfaith Consultative Group, Board for Mission & Unity, Church of England. (Lambeth Study Bks.). 64p. 1986. pap. 2.25 (*0-88028-058-1*, 862) Forward Movement.

Towards a Theology of Religions. Glyn Richards. 208p. 1989. 55.00 (*0-415-02450-1*) Routledge.

Towards a Theology of Story. John Navone. (C). 1988. 39.00 (*0-85439-136-3*, Pub. by St Paul Pubns UK) St Mut.

Towards a Theory & Practice of Cultural Politics: Continuing the Postmodern Debate. Barry Kanpol. Ed. by William T. Pink & George W. Noblit. (Interpretive Perspectives on Education & Policy Ser.). 176p. (C). 1992. pap. 39.50 (*0-89391-910-1*); text ed. 73.25 (*0-89391-822-9*) Ablex Pub.

Towards a Theory of Relativity of Truth in Morality & Religion. Charles Goossens. LC 90-26814. (Problems in Contemporary Philosophy Ser.: Vol. 30). 152p. 1991. lib. bdg. 69.95 (*0-7734-9760-9*) E Mellen.

Towards a Theory of Schooling. Ed. by David Hamilton. (Deakin Studies in Education Ser.). 190p. 1989. 70.00 (*1-85000-480-3*, Falmer Pr); pap. 33.00 (*1-85000-481-1*, Falmer Pr) Taylor & Francis.

Towards a Theory of Text for Contrastive Rhetoric: An Introduction to Issues of Text for Students & Practitioners of Contrastive Rhetoric. James E. Martin. LC 91-40824. (American University Studies: Linguistics: Ser. XIII, Vol. 19). 221p. (C). 1992. text ed. 38.95 (*0-8204-1855-2*) P Lang Pubng.

Towards a Theory of United Nations Peacekeeping. A. B. Fetherston. LC 94-19512. 1994. text ed. 65.00 (*0-312-12275-6*) St Martin.

Towards a Thinking Curriculum. Louis Fillinger. LC 90-63770. 140p. 1991. student ed., spiral bd. 10.95 (*0-88247-854-0*) R & E Pubs.

Towards a Third Theatre. Ian Watson. (Illus.). 216p. 1995. pap. 17.95 (*0-415-12269-4*, C0220) Routledge.

Towards a Third Theatre. Ian Watson. 216p. (C). 1995. pap. 18.95 (*0-415-12764-5*, Routledge NY) Routledge.

Towards a Transatlantic Environmental Policy: Conclusions from an International Round Table Seminar Conducted by The European Institute, Washington D. C., January, 1992. LC 92-71104. 193p. (Orig.). 1992. pap. 15.00 (*0-9628287-2-6*) European Inst.

Towards a Transformative Political Economy of Adult Education: Theoretical & Practical Challenges. Ed. by Paul Wangoola & Frank Youngman. 350p. 1996. text ed. 19.95 (*1-879528-15-0*) LEPS Pr.

Towards a Transnational Perspective on Migration: Race, Class, Ethnicity, & Nationalism Reconsidered. Ed. by Nina G. Schiller et al. LC 92-10551. (Annals Ser.: Vol. 645). 1992. write for info. (*0-89766-703-4*); pap. write for info. (*0-89766-704-2*) NY Acad Sci.

***Towards a Trinitarian Theology of Religions: A Study of Paul Tillich's Thought.** Pan-Chiu Lai. (Studies in Philosophical Theology: Vol. 8). 181p. 1994. pap. 40.50 (*90-390-0025-5*, Pub. by KOK Pharos NE) Eisenbrauns.

Towards a Truer Life: Photographs of China, 1980-1990. Reagan Louie. (Illus.). 96p. 1991. 35.00 (*0-89381-465-2*) Aperture.

Towards a Truly Public Education. John F. Gardner. 29p. 1977. pap. 1.50 (*0-913098-03-5*) Myrin Institute.

Towards a Unified Picture of Nuclear Dynamics. Ed. by Y. Abe et al. (Conference Proceeding Ser.: No. 250). 584p. 1992. 110.00 (*0-88318-930-5*) Am Inst Physics.

Towards a Uniform Civil Code. Vasudha Dhagamwar. (C). 1990. 50.00 (*0-89771-246-3*) St Mut.

Towards a United States of Europe. Ronald W. Mackay. LC 75-31435. 160p. 1976. reprint ed. text ed. 59.75 (*0-8371-8509-2*, MATU, Greenwood Pr) Greenwood.

Towards a Visual Culture: Educating Through Television. Caleb Gattegno. LC 76-91461. 192p. 1969. 10.95 (*0-87825-251-7*) Ed Solutions.

***Towards a War-Free World: Annals of Pugwash, 1994.** Joseph Rotblat. 1995. 36.00 (*981-02-2492-3*) World Scientific Pub.

Towards a World Theology: Faith & the Comparative History of Religion. Wilfred C. Smith. LC 90-212511. 212p. 1989. reprint ed. pap. 60.50 (*0-7837-9841-5*, 2060570) Bks Demand.

Towards Aboriginal Self-Government: Relations Between Status Indian Peoples & the Government of Canada. Anne-Marie Mawhiney. LC 93-18018. 160p. 1993. text ed. 28.00 (*0-8153-0823-X*, 93-18018) Garland.

Towards Acceptance - Some Thoughts: Aging, Pain, Suffering, Death & Immortality. Henry G. Fairbanks. LC 85-72440. 1988. pap. 8.95 (*0-8158-0433-4*) Chris Mass.

Towards Ada 9X. Ed. by Alan Burns. LC 91-59041. (Studies in Computer & Communications Systems: Vol. 2). 201p. (gr. 12). 1992. 70.00 (*90-5199-075-8*, Pub. by IOS Pr NE) IOS Press.

Towards Adminstrative Justice. Henry W. Rawson-Wade. LC 63-9896. (Michigan Legal Publications). vii, 138p. 1985. reprint ed. lib. bdg. 34.00 (*0-89941-390-0*, 303600) W S Hein.

***Towards Advanced Nursing Practice.** write for info. (*0-340-59358-X*, Pub. by E Arnold UK) Routledge Chapman & Hall.

Towards Advanced Practice: Key Concepts for Care. Jane E. Schober & Susan M. Hinchliff. 320p. 1995. pap. 45.00 (*1-56593-592-6*, 1230) Singular Publishing.

Towards African Literary Independence: A Dialogue with Contemporary African Writers. Phanuel A. Egejuru. LC 79-6188. (Contributions in Afro-American & African Studies: No. 53). vii, 173p. 1980. text ed. 52.95 (*0-313-22310-6*, EAL/, Greenwood Pr) Greenwood.

Towards an Aesthetic of Reception. Hans R. Jauss. Tr. by Timothy Bahti from GER. LC 81-16260. (Theory & History of Literature Ser.: Vol. 2). 243p. (C). 1982. pap. text ed. 15.95 (*0-8166-1037-1*) U of Minn Pr.

***Towards an African Narrative Theology.** Joseph G. Healey & Donald Sybertz. LC 96-37715. (Faith & Cultures Ser.). 300p. (Orig.). 1997. pap. 25.00 (*1-57075-121-8*) Orbis Bks.

Towards an Alternative for Central America & the Caribbean. Ed. by George Irvin & Xabier Gorostiaga. (C). 1985. pap. text ed. 14.95 (*0-04-320173-3*) Routledge Chapman & Hall.

Towards an Appreciation of Literature. Frank O'Connor. LC 74-6482. (Studies in Comparative Literature: No. 35). 1974. lib. bdg. 75.00 (*0-8383-1907-6*) M S G Haskell Hse.

Towards an Appreciation of the Theatre. Lennox Robinson. LC 74-6447. (Studies in Drama: No. 39). (C). 1974. lib. bdg. 49.95 (*0-8383-1915-7*) M S G Haskell Hse.

Towards an East European Marxism. Marc Rakovski. LC 77-18171. 1978. text ed. 24.95 (*0-312-81048-2*) St Martin.

Towards An Ecologically Sustainable Growth Society: Physical Foundations, Economic Transitions, & Political Constraints. Bruno Fritsch et al. LC 94-5542. 1994. 79.00 (*0-387-57598-7*) Spr-Verlag.

Towards an Effective Use of Relational Database Management Systems. R. Buitendijk. (Tinbergen Institute Research Ser.). 213p. 1992. pap. 25.00 (*90-5170-084-9*, Pub. by Thesis Pubs NE) IBD Ltd.

Towards an Environmentally Sound & Sustainable Development of Water Resources in Asia & the Pacific. (Water Resources Ser.: No. 71). 231p. 1993. 25.00 (*92-1-119605-1*) UN.

***Towards an Equity-Oriented Policy of Decentralization in Health Systems under Conditions of Turbulence No. 6: The Case of Zambia Forum on Health Sector Refor, Discussion Paper.** 47p. 1997. pap. 10.80 (*0-615-11027-4*, 1936076) World Health.

Towards an Ergonomic Theory of Text Design & Composition. Mats Myrberg. (Upsala Studies in Education: No. 5). 175p. (Orig.). 1978. pap. 29.50 (*91-554-0762-5*) Coronet Bks.

Towards an Explanation of Economic Growth. Ed. by Herbert Giersch. 481p. 1981. lib. bdg. 97.50 (*3-16-343961-6*, Pub. by J C B Mohr GW) Coronet Bks.

Towards an Igbo Literary Standard. P. Akujuobi Nwachukwu. 200p. 1983. pap. 19.50 (*0-7103-0045-X*) Routledge Chapman & Hall.

***Towards an Inclusive Democracy: The Crisis of the Growth Economy & the Need for a New Liberatory Project.** Takis Fotopoulos. LC 96-35201. (Global Issues Ser.). 352p. 1997. 75.00 (*0-304-33627-0*); pap. 19.95 (*0-304-33628-9*) Cassell.

Towards an Indefinite Shore: The Final Months of the Civil War, December 1864-May 1865, Vol. IV. Don Lowry. LC 95-23240. 882p. 1995. 35.00 (*0-7818-0422-1*) Hippocrene Bks.

Towards an Integrated Europe. Richard E. Baldwin. 234p. (C). 1994. pap. 19.95 (*1-898128-13-8*) Brookings.

Towards an Integrated Humanity: Thomas Merton's Journey. Ed. by M. Basil Penington. 1988. pap. 17.95 (*0-87907-603-8*) Cistercian Pubns.

An Asterisk (*) at the beginning of an entry indicates that the title is appearing in BIP for the first time.

Towards an Integrated Impact Assessment of Climate Change: The Mink Study. Ed. by Norman J. Rosenberg. LC 93-26849. 172p. (C). 1993. lib. bdg. 88.50 (0-7923-2448-X) Kluwer Ac.

***Towards an Integrated Management of Tropical Coastal Resources.** Ed. by L. M. Chou et al. (ICLARM Conference Proceedings Ser.: No. 22). 455p. 1991. write for info. (971-10-2268-0, Pub. by ICLARM PH) Intl Spec Bk.

Towards an Integrated Society. Tarlok Singh. LC 76-95507. 554p. 1970. text ed. 55.00 (0-8371-2338-0, SIT/, Greenwood Pr) Greenwood.

***Towards an Intellectual History of Ukraine: An Anthology of Ukrainian Thought from 1710 to 1993.** Ed. by Ralph Lindheim & George S. Luckyj. 480p. 1996. 65.00 (0-8020-0871-2); pap. 24.95 (0-8020-7855-9) U of Toronto Pr.

***Towards an Interest-Free Islamic Economic System.** Waqar M. Khan. 126p. 1996. pap. 8.95 (0-614-21532-3, 1244) Kazi Pubns.

Towards an Islamic Theory of International Relations. A. A. Sulayman. pap. 16.50 (1-56744-106-8) Kazi Pubns.

Towards an Islamic Theory of International Relations: New Directions for Methodology & Thought. 2nd rev. ed. AbdulHamid A. AbuSulayman. (Islamization of Knowledge Ser.: No. 1). 240p. 1993. pap. 12.75 (0-912463-71-6); text ed. 22.75 (0-685-39266-X) IIIT VA.

Towards an Older Australia: Readings in Social Gerontology. rev. ed. Ed. by Anna L. Howe. (Illus.). 356p. (C). 1988. pap. text ed. 19.95 (0-7022-1535-X, Pub. by Univ Queensland Pr AT) Intl Spec Bk.

Towards an Open World Economy. Ed. by Frank McFadzean. LC 72-91277. 264p. 1973. text ed. 29.95 (0-312-81060-1) St Martin.

Towards an Optimum Urban Development. Mariano Ospina. (Illus.). (Orig.). 1995. pap. 17.95 (0-533-11662-7) Vantage.

Towards an Understanding of Juvenile Delinquency. Bernard Lander. LC 72-120208. (Columbia University. Studies in the Social Sciences: No. 578). reprint ed. 20.00 (0-404-51578-9) AMS Pr.

Towards an Understanding of the African Experience from Historical & Contemporary Perspectives. Festus U. Ohaegbulam. 298p. (Orig.). (C). 1990. lib. bdg. 47.00 (0-8191-7940-X) U Pr of Amer.

Towards Ballet: Dance Training for the Very Young. Beryl Manthorp. LC 87-62262. (Illus.). 88p. 1987. 10.95 (0-916622-60-6, Dance Horizons) Princeton Bk Co.

Towards Black Community Development: Moving Beyond the Limitations of the Lecture Model. Manu Ampim. (Critical Issues in the Current Africentric Movement Ser.: Vol. II). (Illus.). 228p. (Orig.). 1993. pap. 11.95 (0-9636447-0-X) Advan The Res.

Towards Capitalist Restoration? Chinese Socialism after Mao. Michel Chossudovsky. LC 86-6684. 272p. 1986. text ed. 45.00 (0-312-81134-9); text ed. 18.95 (0-312-81135-7) St Martin.

Towards Christian Reunion: Vatican I: Obstacles & Opportunities. Luis M. Bermejo. 320p. 1987. reprint ed. pap. text ed. 27.00 (0-8191-6474-7) U Pr of Amer.

***Towards Clean Transport: Fuel Efficient & Clean Motor Vehicles.** 600p. 1996. 94.00 (92-64-14820-5, Pub. by Org for Econ FR) OECD.

Towards Community Education: An Evaluation of Community Schools. John Nisbet et al. 144p. 1980. 20.00 (0-08-025735-6, Pergamon Pr) Elsevier.

Towards Consensus? The 1993 Election & Referendum in New Zealand & the Transition to Proportional Representation. Jack Vowles et al. 280p. 1995. pap. 29.95 (1-86940-123-9, Pub. by Auckland Univ NZ) Paul & Co Pubs.

Towards Coordination of Cancer Research in Europe: Results of the 4th EC Biomedical & Health Research Program. A. J. Vermorken. LC 94-75421. (Biomedical & Health Research Ser.: Vol. 5). 200p. (gr. 12). 1994. 93.00 (90-5199-157-6) IOS Press.

Towards Deeper Space Penetration: Proceedings of the American Astronautical Society Symposium, Montreal, 1964. American Astronautical Society Staff. Ed. by Edward R. Van Driest. (Science & Technology Ser.: Vol. 2). 1964. 20.00 (0-87703-030-8) Univelt Inc.

Towards Democracy & Citizenship-Social Studies Education. Ed. by Rod Charles. (C). 1988. 45.00 (0-7300-0561-5, Pub. by Deakin Univ AT) St Mut.

Towards Democratic Politics: Essays on Chinese Politics by Yan Jiaqi. Ed. by Yan Jiaqi. 364p. (Orig.). (CHI.). 1990. pap. text ed. 14.00 (0-9625118-0-3) Global Pub NJ.

Towards Democratic Schooling: European Experiences. Ed. by Knud Jensen & Stephen Walker. (Innovations in Education Ser.). 224p. 1989. 85.00 (0-335-09568-2, Open Univ Pr); pap. 32.00 (0-335-09567-4, Open Univ Pr) Taylor & Francis.

***Towards Drama As a Method in the Foreign Language Classroom.** Ed. by Manfred Schewe et al. (Bayreuth Contributions to Glottodidactics Ser.: Vol. 3). (Illus.). 356p. 1993. 55.80 (3-631-46066-X) P Lang Pubng.

Towards Dynamic Randomized Algorithms in Computational Geometry. Monique Teillaud. LC 93-23628. 1993. 34.95 (0-387-57503-0) Spr-Verlag.

Towards Earlier Diagnosis: A Guide to Primary Care. 5th ed. Keith Hodgkin. LC 84-7103. (Illus.). 784p. 1985. pap. text ed. 54.00 (0-443-03131-2) Churchill.

Towards Economic Recovery in Sub-Saharan Africa. Ed. by James Pickett & Hans W. Singer. 288p. (C). (gr. 13). 1990. text ed. 99.95 (0-415-05409-5, A4706) Routledge.

Towards Efficiency in Reading: Ten Passages for Practice in Faster & More Efficient Reading for Students & Adults. Gordon R. Wainwright. reprint ed. pap. 26.80 (0-317-07743-0, 2016181) Bks Demand.

Towards Employment Guarantee in India: Indian & International Experiences in Rural Public Works Programmes. Indira Hirway & Piet Terhal. LC 94-21923. (Indo-Dutch Studies on Development Alternatives: Vol. 14). 284p. 1994. 37.50 (0-8039-9192-4) Sage.

Towards Eradication of Child Labour. Ed. by Indira Hirway et al. (C). 1991. text ed. 27.00 (81-204-0594-3, Pub. by Oxford IBH II) S Asia.

Towards European Management. K. Thurley & H. Wirdenius. 192p. (Orig.). 1989. pap. 24.00 (0-273-03125-2, Pub. by Pitman Pub Ltd UK) Trans-Atl Phila.

***Towards Evening: Reflections on Aging, Illness & the Soul's Union with God.** Mary Hope. Ed. by LaVonne Neff. LC 97-628. 220p. (Orig.). 1997. pap. 10.95 (1-55725-183-5) Paraclete MA.

Towards Evolvable Hardware: The Evolutionary Engineering Approach. Ed. by Eduardo Sanchez & Marco Tomassini. LC 96-14199. (Lecture Notes in Computer Science Ser.: Vol. 1062). 249p. 1996. pap. 49.00 (3-540-61093-6) Spr-Verlag.

Towards Excellence: Case Studies of Good School Libraries. Ed. by Margaret M. McDonald. LC 85-44387. (Illus.). 104p. reprint ed. pap. 29.70 (0-7837-5328-4, 2045068) Bks Demand.

Towards Fairer Selection: A Code for Non-Discrimination. IPM Joint Standing Committees on Discrimination Staff. (C). 1978. 51.00 (0-85292-239-6, Pub. by IPM Hse UK) St Mut.

Towards Free Trade in Agriculture. Kirit S. Parikh. (C). 1988. lib. bdg. 116.50 (90-247-3632-3) Kluwer Ac.

***Towards Freedom: A Journey of Discovery Through Rudolf Steiner's Philosophy of Spiritual Activity.** Evelyn F. Capel. 128p. 1993. pap. write for info. (0-904693-53-8, Pub. by Temple Ldge Pub UK) Anthroposophic.

***Towards Freedom: Documents on the Movements for Independence in India 1943-1944.** Ed. by Partha S. Gupta. (Illus.). 3650p. 1998. 210.00 (0-19-563868-9) OUP.

Towards Full Employment: A Policy Appraisal. Ciaran Driver. (Illus.). 252p. 1988. lib. bdg. 49.00 (0-7102-0918-5, RKP) Routledge.

Towards Gender Equity in Mathematics Education: An ICMI Study. Ed. by Gila Hanna. (ICMI Study Ser.). 312p. (C). 1996. pap. text ed. 65.00 (0-7923-3922-3); lib. bdg. 133.00 (0-7923-3921-5) Kluwer Ac.

Towards Gettysburg: A Biography of General John F. Reynolds. Edward J. Nichols. 276p. 1988. reprint ed. 30.00 (0-942211-64-2) Olde Soldier Bks.

Towards Global Localization: The Computing & Communication Industries in Britain & France. Philip Cooke et al. 240p. 1992. 55.00 (1-85728-000-8, Pub. by UCL Pr UK) Taylor & Francis.

Towards Global Localization: The Computing & Communication Industries in Britain & France. Philip Cooke et al. 240p. 1994. pap. 27.50 (1-85728-261-2, Pub. by UCL Pr UK) Taylor & Francis.

Towards Global Multilingualism: European Models & Asian Realities. Ed. by Rosemary Khoo et al. LC 94-3398. 136p. 1994. 29.95 (1-85359-244-7, Pub. by Multilingual Matters UK) Taylor & Francis.

Towards Greater Europe? A Continent Without an Iron Curtain. Ed. by Colin Crouch & David Marquand. 180p. 1993. pap. 20.95 (0-631-18551-8) Blackwell Pubs.

Towards Greater Freedom & Happiness. 1985. pap. 9.95 (0-9601926-0-3) Self-Prog Control.

Towards Greater Freedom & Happiness. 3rd ed. Alfred A. Barrios. LC 78-63152. 1985. 15.95 (0-9601926-1-1) Self-Prog Control.

Towards Herodiade: A Literary Genealogy. Alan R. Chisholm. LC 77-10255. reprint ed. 41.50 (0-404-16310-6) AMS Pr.

Towards Holistic Agriculture: A Scientific Approach. R. W. Widdowson. (Illus.). 194p. 1987. text ed. 39.50 (0-08-034211-6, Pergamon Pr) Elsevier.

Towards Human Unity. Anthony Brooke. 133p. 1976. pap. 7.50 (0-7051-0234-3) Attic Pr.

Towards Human Work: Solutions to Problems in Occupational Health & Safety. Ed. by M. Kumashiro & E. D. Megaw. 438p. 1991. 99.00 (0-7484-0039-7, Pub. by Tay Francis Ltd UK) Taylor & Francis.

Towards Illiberal Democracy in Pacific Asia. Daniel Bell et al. LC 95-4169. 1995. text ed. 59.95 (0-312-12686-7) St Martin.

Towards Inclusive Schools? Ed. by Catherine Clark et al. LC 95-5706. (Special Education Ser.: Vol. 16). 280p. (C). 1995. pap. text ed. 22.95 (0-8077-3461-6) Tchrs Coll.

***Towards Independence.** Paul Scott. 1991. 18.00 (0-7486-6104-2, Pub. by Polygon UK) Subterranean Co.

Towards India's Freedom & Partition. S. R. Mehrotra. 322p. 1979. 24.95 (0-7069-0712-4) Asia Bk Corp.

Towards Interest Free Banking. S. Mahmud Ahmad. 22.00 (0-933511-78-7) Kazi Pubns.

Towards International Guarantees for Religious Liberty. Isaac Lewin. LC 81-52086. 128p. 12.00 (0-88400-078-8) Shengold.

Towards Islamic Anthropology. Akbar S. Ahmad. 80p. (Orig.). 1986. pap. 7.50 (0-317-52455-0) New Era Publns MI.

Towards Islamic Arabic. I. R. Al Farugi. 64p. (Orig.). 1986. pap. 5.00 (0-317-52453-4) New Era Publns MI.

Towards Islamization of Disciplines: Proceedings of the Third International Conference of Islamic Thought. Intro. by IIIT. LC 88-8269. (Islamization of Knowledge Ser.: No. 4). 760p. 1989. text ed. 24.50 (0-912463-21-X); pap. text ed. 12.50 (0-912463-12-0) IIIT VA.

Towards Jeruslem. large type ed. Denise A. Robertson. (Magna Large Print Ser.). 1994. 25.99 (0-7505-0617-2, Pub. by Magna Print Bks UK) Ulverscroft.

Towards Joy Profound. Ruhama Morahg & Mordecai Morahg. Ed. by Larry Freifield. 282p. (Orig.). 1990. pap. 12.95 (0-9625998-0-8) M & R Project.

Towards Justice? Crime & State Control in South Africa. Ed. by Desiree Hansson & Dirk Van Zyl Smit. (Contemporary South African Debates Ser.). (Illus.). 288p. 1990. pap. 24.00 (0-19-570579-3) OUP.

Towards Justice & Virtue: A Constructive Account of Practical Reasoning. Onora O'Neill. 240p. (C). 1996. text ed. 54.95 (0-521-48095-7) Cambridge U Pr.

Towards Justice & Virtue: A Constructive Account of Practical Reasoning. Onora O'Neill. 240p. (C). 1996. pap. text ed. 18.95 (0-521-48559-2) Cambridge U Pr.

Towards Knowledge in Writing: Illustrations from Revision Studies. Jerry Fitzgerald. (Illus.). xvii, 150p. 1991. 87.95 (0-387-97623-X) Spr-Verlag.

Towards Laughter: Paintings by Maggi Hambling. George Melly. (Illus.). 64p. (C). 1993. pap. 27.50 (0-85331-647-3, Pub. by Lund Humphries UK) Antique Collect.

Towards Measures of Spatial Opportunity see Progress in Planning

Towards Measuring the Technological Impact of Multinational Corporations in the Less Developed Countries. Oswald A. Mascarenhas. Ed. by Stuart Bruchey. LC 80-583. (Multinational Corporations Ser.). 1980. lib. bdg. 44.95 (0-405-13375-8) Ayer.

***Towards Migraine 2000.** F. Clifford Rose. LC 96-38504. (Developments in Neurology Ser.). 328p. 1996. 234.75 (0-444-82494-4) Elsevier.

Towards Minimally Invasive Neurosurgery. Ed. by P. K. Pillay et al. (Journal Ser.: Vol. 64, No. 2, 1995). (Illus.). 44p. 1995. pap. 21.75 (3-8055-6269-1) S Karger.

Towards Modern Art: Or, King Solomon's Picture Book. Ludwig Goldscheider. LC 52-9478. 1952. reprint ed. 39.00 (0-403-08924-7) Somerset Pub.

***Towards Molecular Biophysics of Ion Channels.** M. Sokabe et al. LC 97-3992. (Progress in Cell Research Ser.). 324p. 1997. 250.00 (0-444-82554-1) Elsevier.

Towards Moral Perfectionism. Bill Puka. (Harvard Dissertations in Philosophy Ser.). 488p. 1990. reprint ed. text ed. 30.00 (0-8240-3208-X) Garland.

***Towards More Effective Monetary Policy.** Iwao Kuroda. LC 96-34663. 1997. text ed. 79.95 (0-312-16526-9) St Martin.

Towards More Effective Supervision by International Organizations: Essays in Honour of Henry G. Schermers, Vol. I. Niels Blokker. 372p. (C). 1994. lib. bdg. 169.50 (0-7923-3159-1, Pub. by M Nijhoff NE) Kluwer Ac.

Towards Multilateral Investment Rules. 165p. 1996. pap. 31.00 (92-64-14784-5) OECD.

Towards Multiple Perspectives on Literacy: Proceedings from the 61st Claremont Reading Conference Held March 17-18, 1995. 58th ed. Ed. & Intro. by Philip H. Dreyer. 216p. 1995. pap. 20.00 (0-941742-15-6) Claremont Grad.

Towards Myself. Mikhael Armalinsky. 110p. 1981. pap. 7.00 (0-935090-05-3) Almanac Pr.

Towards Nationhood in West Africa. J. William Johnson. 158p. 1971. reprint ed. 37.50 (0-7146-1752-0, Pub. by F Cass Pubs UK) Intl Spec Bk.

Towards Network Globalization. Ed. by Gee S. Poo. 500p. (C). 1991. text ed. 118.00 (981-02-0796-4) World Scientific Pub.

Towards New Forms of Economic Co-operation Between Latin America & Japan: Cuadernos de la Cepal No. 51. 245p. 1988. pap. 6.00 (92-1-121133-6, E.86.II.G.4) UN.

Towards New Worlds in Tunnelling - Hacia Nuevos Mundos en Tuneles: Proceedings of the International Congress, Acapulco, 16-20 May 1992, Memorias del Congreso Internacional, Acapulco, 16-20 Mayo 1992, 3 vols. Ed. by Luis Vieitez-Utesa & Luis E. Montanez-Cartaxo. (Illus.). 1300p. (C). Date not set. Set. text ed. 195.00 (90-5410-050-8, Pub. by A A Balkema NE) Ashgate Pub Co.

Towards Operational Disequilibrium Macro Economics. Jan C. Siebrand. 1979. pap. text ed. 88.00 (90-247-2153-9) Kluwer Ac.

Towards Paradise on Earth: Modern Space Conception in Architecture--A Creation of Renaissance Humanism. Lise Bek. (Analecta Romana Ser.: Suppl. IX). (Illus.). 274p. (Orig.). 1980. pap. 49.50 (87-7492-310-2, Pub. by Odense Universitets Forlag DK) Coronet Bks.

Towards Peace, & Other Essays, Critical or Constructive. Basil De Selincourt. LC 67-30205. (Essay Index Reprint Ser.). 1977. 17.95 (0-8369-0370-6) Ayer.

Towards Perpetual Peace. Nikunja V. Banerjee. 1988. 21.00 (81-208-0536-4, Pub. by Motilal Banarsidass II) S Asia.

Towards Planning for Sustainable Development: A Guide for the Ultimate Environmental Threshold (UET) Method. Ed. by J. Kozlowski & G. Hill. 383p. 1993. 69.95 (1-85628-467-0, Pub. by Avebury Pub UK) Ashgate Pub Co.

***Towards Priorities of Biodiversity Research in Support of Policy & Management of Tropical Rain Forests: A Contribution to the Conservation & Wise Use of Tropical Rain Forests.** E. M. Lammerts Van Bueren & J. F. Duivenvoorden. (Tropenbos Technical Ser.). (Illus.). 32p. 1996. 25.00 (90-5113-029-5, Pub. by Backhuys Pubs NE) Balogh.

Towards Rational Use of High Salinity Tolerant Plants: Agriculture & Forestry under Marginal Soil Water Conditions. Ed. by Helmut Lieth & Ahmed A. Massoum. LC 92-22601. (Tasks for Vegetation Science Ser.: No. 28). 1993. lib. bdg. 277.50 (0-7923-1866-8) Kluwer Ac.

Towards Rational Use of High Salinity Tolerant Plants Vol. 1: Deliberations about High Salinity Tolerant Plants & Ecosystems. Ed. by Helmut Lieth & Ahmed A. Massoum. 1992. lib. bdg. 334.00 (0-7923-1865-X) Kluwer Ac.

Towards Reading: Literacy Development in the Pre-School Years. Linda Miller. LC 95-14679. (Re-Thinking Reading Ser.). 1995. text ed. write for info. (0-335-19216-5, Open Univ Pr); pap. text ed. write for info. (0-335-19215-7, Open Univ Pr) Taylor & Francis.

Towards Reading Freud: Self-Creation in Milton, Wordsworth, Emerson, & Sigmund Freud. Mark Edmundson. 179p. (C). 1990. text ed. 29.95 (0-691-06868-2) Princeton U Pr.

Towards Resident-Oriented Environments. Ed. by Stella Dixon. (C). 1989. 60.00 (0-86242-098-9, Pub. by Age Concern Eng UK) St Mut.

***Towards Security in Medical Telematics: Legal & Technical Aspects.** Ed. by B. Barber et al. (Studies in Health Technology & Informatics: Vol. 27). 262p. (YA). (gr. 12 up). 1996. 98.00 (90-5199-246-7, 246-7) IOS Press.

Towards Self-Managing Schools. Vivian Williams. (Education Management Ser.). (Illus.). 128p. 1995. 60.00 (0-304-32982-7); pap. 20.00 (0-304-32984-3) Cassell.

Towards Self-Reliance: A Programme of Action for Refugees in Eastern & Central Sudan. xx, 571p. (Orig.). 1984. pap. 40.50 (92-2-103750-9) Intl Labour Office.

Towards Social Adjustment: Labour Market Issues in Structural Adjustment. Ed. by Guy Standing & Victor Tokman. vi, 348p. (Orig.). 1991. pap. 27.00 (92-2-107745-4) Intl Labour Office.

Towards Socialism in Tanzania. Ed. by Cranford Pratt & Bismarck U. Mwansasu. LC 78-10350. 1979. pap. 11.95 (0-8020-6433-7) U of Toronto Pr.

Towards Socialism in Tanzania. Ed. by Bismarck U. Mwansasu & Cranford Pratt. LC 78-10350. (Illus.). 253p. reprint ed. pap. 72.20 (0-8357-3662-8, 2036389) Bks Demand.

Towards Solving the Puzzle of Agency Values. Academy of Producer Insurance Studies, Inc. Staff. 100p. (Orig.). 1993. pap. text ed. 10.00 (1-878204-50-5) APIS Inc.

Towards Spiritual Maturity. W. Still. 5.99 (1-85792-015-5, Pub. by Christian Focus UK) Spring Arbor Dist.

Towards SQL Database Language Extensions for Geographic Information Systems. Ed. by Vincent B. Robinson & Henry Tom. LC 94-24762. 1994. write for info. (0-929306-19-8) Silicon Pr.

Towards Still Greater Professionalism. K. Bartlett. (Tolley Medal Ser.). 1971. 1.50 (0-686-52206-0, WPT 4) Syracuse U Cont Ed.

Towards Strategic Information Systems. E. K. Somogyi & R. D. Galliers. (Abacus Bks.). (Illus.). 252, xiip. 1987. text ed. 101.00 (0-85626-460-1) Gordon & Breach.

Towards Strategic Language Learning: Current Research in the Netherlands. Gert Rijlaarsdam & Ron Oostdam. (Orig.). (C). 1995. pap. 24.95 (90-5356-156-0, Pub. by Amsterdam U Pr NE) U of Mich Pr.

Towards Successful Schooling. Hugh Lauder & Wylie. 1990. 75.00 (1-85000-722-5, Falmer Pr); pap. 35.00 (1-85000-723-3, Falmer Pr) Taylor & Francis.

Towards Summer Fair. large type ed. Paula Grayson. (Linford Romance Library). 240p. 1992. pap. 15.99 (0-7089-7204-7, Traitree Bookshop) Ulverscroft.

Towards Sustainable Agricultural Development. Ed. by Michael D. Young. 400p. 1992. text ed. 78.95 (1-85293-137-X, Pub. by Pinter Pubs Ltd UK) CRC Pr.

Towards Sustainable Agriculture Development. Ed. by M. D. Young. 346p. 1994. text ed. 95.00 (0-471-94797-0) Wiley.

Towards Sustainable Development of the Coastal Resources of Lingayen Gulf, Philippines. G. T. Silvestre. 1989. pap. 15.00 (971-10-2245-1, Pub. by ICLARM PH) Intl Spec Bk.

Towards Sustainable Growth: Essays in Fiscal & Financial Sector Reforms in India. Raja J. Chelliah. 236p. 1996. 24.00 (0-19-563946-4) OUP.

***Towards Sustainable Project Development.** Ed. by Frank A. Wilson. LC 96-52675. 1997. 80.00 (1-85898-430-0) E Elgar.

***Towards Sustainable Transport Planning: A Comparison Between Britain & the Netherlands.** Gary Haq. 272p. 1997. text ed. 63.95 (1-85972-382-9, Pub. by Avebury Pub UK) Ashgate Pub Co.

Towards Synergism: The Cosmic Significance of the Human Civilizational Project. Anthony E. Mansueto, Jr. 552p. (Orig.). (C). Date not set. lib. bdg. 67.50 (0-7618-0083-2) U Pr of Amer.

Towards Synergism: The Cosmic Significance of the Human Civilizational Project. Anthony E. Mansueto, Jr. 552p. (Orig.). (C). 1995. pap. text ed. 39.50 (0-7618-0084-0) U Pr of Amer.

Towards the Abolition of Whiteness: Essays on Race, Politics, & Working Class History. David R. Roediger. LC 93-49387. (Haymarket Ser.). 200p. (C). 1994. pap. text ed. 18.00 (0-86091-658-8, Pub. by Vrso UK) Norton.

Towards the Abolition of Whiteness: Essays on Race, Politics, & Working Class History. David R. Roediger. LC 93-49387. (Haymarket Ser.). 200p. (C). (gr. 13). 1994. text ed. 60.00 (0-86091-438-0, Pub. by Vrso UK) Norton.

Towards the Biochip. C. Nicolini. 240p. (C). 1990. text ed. 92.00 (9971-5-0958-X) World Scientific Pub.

Towards the Borderless Mainport Rotterdam. Arjen Van Klink. 153p. 1995. pap. 25.00 (90-5170-367-8, Pub. by Thesis Pubs NE) IBD Ltd.

Towards the Center. Joyce B. Balokovic. 1956. 3.95 (0-910664-23-4) Gotham.

T

***Towards the Close of the Century of Counterrevolutions.** unabridged ed. Shalt M. Main. 160p. 1997. pap. 12.95 (*0-9658580-0-6*) Engger.

Towards the Discovery of Clare of Assisi: Clare Discovers the Love of God in the Church, Vol. II. Regis J. Armstrong & Pacelli Millane. (Clare Centenary Ser.). 188p. 1992. pap. 10.00 (*1-57659-076-3*) Franciscan Inst.

Towards the Discovery of Clare of Assisi: Clare Formed by Francis. Regis J. Armstrong & Pacelli Milland. (Clare Centenary Ser.). 172p. 1992. pap. 8.00 (*1-57659-077-1*) Franciscan Inst.

Towards the Discovery of Clare of Assisi: Clare's Form of Gospel Life, Vol. III. Regis J. Armstrong & Pacelli Millane. (Clare Centenary Ser.). 188p. 1992. pap. 9.00 (*1-57659-075-5*) Franciscan Inst.

Towards the Discovery of Clare of Assisi: Fraternal Life, Vol. IV. Regis J. Armstrong & Pacelli Milland. (Clare Centenary Ser.). 364p. 1992. pap. 10.00 (*1-57659-074-7*) Franciscan Inst.

Towards the Edge of the Universe: A Review of Modern Cosmology. Stuart G. Clark. LC 95-48036. (Astronomy & Astrophysics Ser.). 1996. text ed. 64.95 (*0-471-96248-1*); pap. text ed. 39.95 (*0-471-96249-X*) Wiley.

Towards the End. Joseph Mills. 1992. pap. 13.95 (*0-7486-6031-3*, Pub. by Edinburgh U Pr UK) Col U Pr.

***Towards the End of the Century.** E. A. Markham. 108p. 1989. pap. 14.93 (*0-85646-223-3*, Pub. by Anvil Press UK) Dufour.

Towards the Factory of the Future: Emergence of the Computerized Factory & Its Impact on Society: Presented at the Winter Annual Meeting of the ASME, Chicago, Illinois, November 16-21, 1980. American Society of Mechanical Engineers Staff. Ed. by L. Kops. LC 80-69197. (PED Ser.: Vol. 1). 120p. pap. 34.20 (*0-317-58243-7*, 2056389) Bks Demand.

Towards the Goal Supreme. Virajananda. pap. 2.95 (*0-87481-106-6*, Pub. by Advaita Ashrama II) Vedanta Pr.

Towards the Gulf: A Romance of Louisiana. LC 72-3107. (Black Heritage Library Collection). 1977. reprint ed. 20.95 (*0-8369-9084-6*) Ayer.

Towards the Harnessing of Chaos: Collections of Contributions Based on Lectures Presented at the Seventh Toyota Conference, Mikkabi, Shizuoka, Japan, October 31 to November 3, 1993. Ed. by Masaya Yamaguti. LC 94-26259. 454p. 1994. 191.50 (*0-444-81934-7*) Elsevier.

Towards the Healing of Schism: The Sees of Rome & Constantinople (Ecumenical Documents III) Ed. & Tr. by E. J. Stormon. 576p. 1987. pap. 12.95 (*0-8091-2910-8*) Paulist Pr.

Towards the Holocaust: The Social & Economic Collapse of the Weimar Republic. Ed. by Michael N. Dobkowski & Isidor Wallimann. LC 82-18388. (Illus.). 440p. 1983. text ed. 37.50 (*0-313-22795-0*, DHO/, Greenwood Pr) Greenwood.

Towards the Homeland. Talar Keoseyan. 20p. (Orig.). 1995. pap. write for info. (*1-885206-14-3*, Iliad Pr) Cader Pubng.

Towards the Human. Ed. by Iain C. Smith. (C). 1995. pap. 50.00 (*0-86334-059-8*, Pub. by Saltire Soc) St Mut.

Towards the Learning Company: Concepts & Practices. Ed. by Mike Pedler et al. LC 94-103167. 1994. write for info. (*0-07-707802-0*) McGraw.

Towards the Learning Society. Stewart Ranson. (Education Ser.). 224p. 1994. 70.00 (*0-304-32770-0*); pap. 24.95 (*0-304-32769-7*) Cassell.

Towards the Long-Promised Peace: A History of the Israeli-Palestinian Conflict. Omar Massalha. 330p. 1994. 50.00 (*0-86356-057-1*, Pub. by Saqi Bks UK); pap. 17.95 (*0-86356-065-2*, Pub. by Saqi Bks UK) Interlink Pub.

Towards the Love Divine. rev. ed. Swami P. Saraswati. (Illus.). 132p. 1974. reprint ed. pap. 10.00 (*1-881921-03-4*) Intl Soc Divine Love.

Towards the Managed Economy: Keynes, the Treasury & the Fiscal Policy Debate of the 1930's. Roger Middleton. 288p. 1985. 70.00 (*0-416-35830-6*, 9523) Routledge Chapman & Hall.

Towards the Most Great Justice. 212p. 1995. pap. 16.95 (*1-870989-62-7*) Bahai.

Towards the Museum of the Future: New European Perspectives. Roger Miles & Lauro Zavala. LC 93-12788. 204p. (C). (gr. 13). 1994. 39.95 (*0-415-09498-4*) Routledge.

***Towards the Neurobiology of Chronic Pain.** G. Carli & M. Zimmermann. LC 96-40280. (Progress in Brain Research Ser.). 290p. 1996. 218.75 (*0-444-82149-X*) Elsevier.

Towards the Personal Communications Environment: Green Paper on a Common Approach in the Field of Mobile & Personal Communications in the European Union. (Illus.). 228p. (Orig.). (C). 1994. pap. text ed. 65.00 (*0-7881-1399-2*) DIANE Pub.

Towards the Radio Amateurs Examination. J. Bowyer. (C). 1985. 53.00 (*0-85973-036-0*, Pub. by S Thornes Pubs UK) St Mut.

Towards the Renaissance of Puerto Rican Studies: Ethnic & Area Studies in University Education. Antonio M. Stevens. No. 53. write for info. (*0-318-61103-1*) Brooklyn Coll Pr.

Towards the Self-Regulating Municipality: Free Communes & Administrative Modernization in Scandinavia. Ed. by Harald Baldersheim & Krister Stahlberg. 242p. 1994. 59.95 (*1-85521-553-5*, Pub. by Dartmth Pub UK) Ashgate Pub Co.

Towards the Seventies. Dick Higgins. LC 79-129807. 1969. pap. 0.75 (*0-911856-00-5*) Abyss.

***Towards the Seventies: Art in Italy in the 1970s.** Luciano Caramel. 1997. pap. 35.00 (*88-8158-101-9*, Pub. by Charta IT) Dist Art Pubs.

Towards the Spiritual Convergence of America & Russia: American Mind & Russian Soul, American Individuality & Russian Community, & the Potent Alchemy of National Characteristics. Stephen L. Lapeyrouse. LC 90-92072. 168p. (Orig.). 1991. pap. 12.95 (*0-9628048-0-0*) S Lapeyrouse.

Towards the Spiritualization of Kwanzaa. L. Doyle Colimon. (Illus.). 25p. (Orig.). 1996. pap. write for info. (*0-9651363-2-9*) L D Colimon.

Towards the Sun. Margaret Chatterjee. (Writers Workshop Redbird Ser.). 1975. 8.00 (*0-88253-664-8*); pap. text ed. 3.00 (*0-88253-663-X*) Ind-US Inc.

Towards the Sun: A Poetic Journey. Bryan Arnold. (Illus.). 121p. (Orig.). 1989. 20.00 (*0-9622511-0-0*); pap. 15.00 (*0-9622511-1-9*) Asgard Pub.

Towards the Theoretical Understanding of High Temperature Superconductors: ICTP, Trieste, Italy, June 20-July 29, 1988. Ed. by S. O. Lundqvist et al. (Progress in High Temperature Superconductivity: Vol. XIV). 808p. 1988. pap. 53.00 (*9971-5-0640-8*); text ed. 138.00 (*9971-5-0639-4*) World Scientific Pub.

Towards the Twentieth Century. Harold V. Routh. LC 69-17587. (Essay Index Reprint Ser.). 1977. 21.95 (*0-8369-0091-X*) Ayer.

Towards the Twenty-First Century: Judaism & the Jewish People in Israel & America, Essays in Honor of Rabbi Leon Kronish on the Occasion of His Seventieth Birthday. Ed. by Ronald Kronish. 1988. 25.00 (*0-88125-306-5*) Ktav.

Towards the Use of Noradrenergic Agonists for the Treatment of Pain: Proceedings of the International Symposium on Towards the Use of Noradrenergic Agonists for the Treatment of Pain, Held in Versailles, France, 20-21 March 1992. Ed. by Jean-Marie Besson & Gisele Guilbaud. LC 92-49725. (International Congress Ser.: Vol. 1006). 1992. 138.25 (*0-444-89582-5*, Excerpta Medica) Elsevier.

***Towards the Virtual Organization.** Richard Hale & Peter Whitlam. LC 97-17259. 1997. pap. write for info. (*0-07-709293-7*) McGraw.

***Towards the 21st Century - Books & Media for the Millennium: Selected Papers from the 21st Annual Conference of the International Association of School Librarianship, the Queen's University of Belfast, Belfast, Northern Ireland, U. K., July 20-24, 1992.** 108p. 25.00 (*1-890861-14-6*) IASL.

Towards the 21st Century in Christian Mission. Ed. by James M. Phillips & Robert T. Coote. viii, 376p. (Orig.). 1993. pap. 25.00 (*0-8028-0638-4*) Eerdmans.

Towards Theory of Alternative Society. Narendra K. Singh. 1986. 26.00 (*81-7033-021-1*, Pub. by Rawat II) S Asia.

Towards Theory of Positive Secularism. S. L. Verma. 167p. 1986. 27.00 (*81-7033-018-1*, Pub. by Rawat II) S Asia.

Towards Third Generation Robotics. Ed. by Bernard Espiau. (Illus.). 650p. 1988. 158.95 (*0-387-18404-X*) Spr-Verlag.

Towards Togetherness: The Cooperative Games, Songs, & Activities Handbook. Richard Burrill. (Illus.). 112p. (Orig.). (J). (gr. 3-12). 1994. pap. 10.95 (*1-878464-12-4*) Anthro Co.

Towards Tomorrow: The Story of the African Teachers Association of South Africa. R. L. Peteni. Ed. by Cole Kitchen. LC 78-59714. 1979. pap. 7.95 (*0-917256-08-5*) Ref Pubns.

Towards Total Revolution: Writings of Jayaprakash Narayan, 4 vols., Set. J. P. Narayan. (C). 1978. 34.00 (*0-8364-2547-2*, Pub. by Popular Prakashan II) S Asia.

Towards 2000: The Future of Childhood, Literacy, & Schooling. Ed. by Ed Marum. LC 95-7254. 1995. write for info. (*0-7507-0420-9*, Falmer Pr); pap. write for info. (*0-7507-0421-7*, Falmer Pr) Taylor & Francis.

Towards Understanding Galaxies at Large Redshift. Ed. by Richard G. Kron & Alvio Renzini. (C). 1988. lib. bdg. 157.50 (*90-277-2681-7*) Kluwer Ac.

***Towards Understanding Hindu Myths.** Sadashiv A. Dange. lxiv, 497p. (C). 1996. 60.00 (*81-7305-080-5*, Pub. by Aryan Bks Intl II) Nataraj Bks.

Towards Understanding Islam. A. A. Maududi. pap. 7.50 (*0-933511-79-5*) Kazi Pubns.

Towards Understanding Islam. Abul A. Maududi. Tr. by Khurshid Ahmad from URD. 116p. pap. 5.95 (*0-86037-053-4*, Pub. by Islamic Fnd UK) New Era Publns MI.

Towards Understanding Islam. Sayyid A. Maudidi. Tr. by Khurshid Ahmad from URD. 126p. 1977. pap. 4.00 (*0-89259-151-X*) Am Trust Pubns.

Towards Understanding Islam. Sayyid A. Maududi. Tr. by Khurshid Ahmad from URD. 179p. (Orig.). 1980. pap. 5.95 (*0-939830-22-1*, Pub. by IIFSO KW) New Era Publns MI.

Towards Understanding Islam. Abul A. Al-Maudoodi. Tr. & Intro. by Khurshid Ahmad. 116p. (YA). 1985. reprint ed. pap. write for info. (*1-882837-25-8*) W A M Y Intl.

Towards Understanding Relationships. Robert A. Hinde. LC 79-40921. (European Monographs in Social Psychology: No. 18). 1980. text ed. 60.00 (*0-12-349250-5*) Acad Pr.

Towards Understanding the Basics of Islam: Texts from Qur'an & Hadith. 2nd ed. Kaukab Siddique. 52p. 1986. reprint ed. pap. 2.50 (*0-942978-09-9*) Am Soc Ed & Rel.

Towards Understanding the Bible. Perry B. Yoder & Elizabeth Yoder. LC 78-53649. 1978. pap. 5.95 (*0-87303-006-0*) Faith & Life.

Towards Understanding the Intrinsic in Body Movement. Martha Davis. LC 74-7857. (Body Movement Perspectives in Research Ser.). (Illus.). 192p. 1980. 34.95 (*0-405-06200-1*) Ayer.

***Towards Understanding the Quran, Vols. I-IV.** S. Abul Mawdudi. Tr. by Zafar I. Ansari. 380p. 1996. pap. 16.50 (*0-614-21074-7*, 1248) Kazi Pubns.

Towards Universal Justice: International Penal Court. International Commission of Jurists. 91p. reprint ed. pap. 26.00 (*0-7837-6979-2*, 2046791) Bks Demand.

Towards Verified Systems. Ed. by Jonathan Bowen. LC 94-30630. (Real-Time Safety Critical Systems Ser.: Vol. 2). 322p. 1994. 168.75 (*0-444-89901-4*) Elsevier.

Towards Very Large Knowledge Bases. Mars. LC 95-75768. (gr. 12). 1995. 99.00 (*90-5199-217-3*) IOS Press.

Towards Visitor Impact Management. John Glasson. 208p. 1995. 59.95 (*1-85972-054-4*, Pub. by Avebury Pub UK) Ashgate Pub Co.

Towards Welfare Pluralism: Public Services in a Time of Change. Nirmala Rao. (Illus.). 224p. 1996. 66.95 (*1-85521-727-9*, Pub. by Dartmth Pub UK); pap. 24.95 (*1-85521-732-5*, Pub. by Dartmth Pub UK) Ashgate Pub Co.

Towards World Class Manufacturing 1993: Proceedings of the IFIP TC5 - WG5.3 Conference on Towards World Class Manufacturing 1993, Litchfield Park, Arizona, USA. Ed. by Michael J. Wozny & Gustav Olling. LC 94-10007. 468p. 1994. pap. 155.75 (*0-444-81850-2*, North Holland) Elsevier.

Towards World Peace Through Legal Controls in the Air & Outer Space: A Bibliographic Survey of Japanese Studies & Practices in the Aviation Industry & Space Exploration, with Special Reference to Legal, Political, & Economic Aspects. Young H. Yoo. LC 79-116630. 1973. Provisional edition. 10.00 (*0-912580-02-X*) Far Eastern Res.

Towards Zero. Agatha Christie & Gerald Verner. 1957. pap. 5.25 (*0-8222-1162-9*) Dramatists Play.

Towards 1995: The Prospects for Ending the Proliferation of Nuclear Weapons. David Fischer. (UNIDIR Ser.). 304p. 1993. 59.95 (*1-85521-322-2*, Pub. by Dartmth Pub UK) Ashgate Pub Co.

***Towards 2000: Public Policy in Nevada Pak.** Dennis Soden & Eric Herzik. (C). Date not set. write for info. (*0-7872-3379-X*) Kendall-Hunt.

Towboat on the Ohio. James E. Casto. (Illus.). 208p. 1995. 22.95 (*0-8131-1916-2*) U Pr of Ky.

Towboatman's Guide to Federal Regulations. John R. Sutton. Ed. by Richard A. Block. 195p. (Orig.). 1995. pap. text ed. 30.00 (*1-879778-40-8*, BK-0507) Marine Educ.

Tower. Arlette Lavie. LC 90-1372. (J). (ps-3). 1990. 11.99 (*0-85953-392-1*); pap. 5.99 (*0-85953-393-X*) Childs Play.

Tower. Matthew Maguire. (American Theater in Literature Ser.). 88p. (Orig.). 1991. pap. 8.95 (*1-55713-133-3*) Sun & Moon CA.

Tower. Lene Mayer-Skumanz. (J). (gr. 2-5). 1993. 12.95 (*965-465-000-2*) Pitspopany.

Tower. Peeters & Peeters Schuiten. Tr. by Jean-Marc Lofficier & R. Lofficier from FRE. (Stories of the Fantastic Ser.). 112p. 1993. pap. 14.95 (*1-56163-070-5*) NBM.

Tower Abbey. Isabelle Holland. 1979. pap. 1.95 (*0-449-24044-4*, Crest) Fawcett.

Tower & Dungeon: A Study of Place & Power in American Society. Gloria L. House. (Illus.). 154p. (Orig.). (C). 1991. pap. text ed. write for info. (*0-9615977-5-5*) Casa Unidad.

Tower & the Abyss: An Inquiry into the Transformation of the Individual. Erich Kahler. 401p. 1989. pap. 24.95 (*0-88738-788-8*) Transaction Pubs.

Tower & the Bridge: The New Art of Structural Engineering. David P. Billington. LC 85-42667. (Illus.). 328p. 1985. pap. text ed. 19.95 (*0-691-02393-X*) Princeton U Pr.

Tower & the Well: A Psychological Interpretation of the Fairy Tales of Madame D'Aulnoy. Amy DeGraff. LC 83-50517. 136p. (ENG & FRE.). 1984. pap. 12.00 (*0-917786-03-3*) Summa Pubns.

Tower & Tray Design see **Technical Engineering Training Series**

Tower at the Edge of the World. William Heinesen. Tr. by Anne Born. 183p. 1982. 7.95 (*0-906191-64-5*, Pub. by Penumbra Pr CN) U of Toronto Pr.

Tower Block: Modern Public Housing in England, Scotland, Wales, & Northern Ireland. Stefan Muthesius & Miles Glendinning. (Illus.). 288p. 70.00 (*0-300-05444-0*) Yale U Pr.

Tower by the Sea. Meindert Dejong. (Illus.). 1990. 17.00 (*0-8446-6246-1*) Peter Smith.

Tower Clock & How to Make It. E. Ferson. (Illus.). 57p. 1989. pap. 6.00 (*0-930163-30-3*) Arlington Bk.

Tower Genealogy: An Account of the Descendants of John Tower of Hingham, Massachusetts. C. Tower. 701p. 1989. reprint ed. pap. 99.00 (*0-8328-1173-4*); reprint ed. lib. bdg. 107.00 (*0-8328-1172-6*) Higginson Bk Co.

Tower Hill Gifted Research Program. Hughes. 1991. pap. 15.00 (*0-89824-537-0*) Trillium Pr.

Tower of Babel. (Illus.). 144p. 1979. pap. 4.00 (*0-943810-32-9*) Inst Southern Studies.

***Tower of Babel.** Gloria Clanin & Lloyd R. Hight. 32p. 1996. 6.95 (*0-89051-214-0*, TOWBAB) Master Bks.

Tower of Babel. Martha Jander. (Arch Bks.). (Illus.). 24p. (Orig.). (J). (gr. k-4). 1991. pap. 1.99 (*0-570-09026-1*, 59-1449) Concordia.

Tower of Babel. Jack Spicer. LC 93-51062. vi, 170p. (Orig.). 1994. pap. 12.95 (*1-883689-04-X*); lib. bdg. 33.95 (*1-883689-05-8*) Talisman Hse.

Tower of Babel. John Steele. 1995. pap. 5.99 (*1-56504-853-9*, 04853/11008) White Wolf.

Tower of Babel. large type ed. Morris West. 512p. 1986. 27.99 (*0-7089-8311-1*, Charnwood) Ulverscroft.

Tower of Beowol. Parke Godwin. 1996. pap. 5.99 (*0-614-98031-3*, AvoNova) Avon.

Tower of Beowulf. Parke Godwin. 352p. 1996. mass mkt. 5.99 (*0-380-72165-1*, AvoNova) Avon.

Tower of Cirith Ungol & Shelob's Lair. Carl Willner. (Illus.). 32p. (YA). (gr. 10-12). 1984. pap. 7.00 (*0-915795-21-3*, 8030) Iron Crown Ent Inc.

Tower of Doom. Mark Anthony. 1994. pap. 4.95 (*0-7869-0062-8*) TSR Inc.

Tower of Dreams. Kathryn K. Abdoul-Baki. 208p. 1995. 20.00 (*0-89410-816-6*, Three Contnts); pap. 10.00 (*0-89410-817-4*, Three Contnts) Lynne Rienner.

Tower of Evil. Martin James. 368p. (Orig.). 1994. mass mkt., pap. text ed. 4.50 (*0-8439-3608-8*) Dorchester Pub Co.

Tower of Evil. Mary Main. (YA). 1996. pap. 2.95 (*0-8167-3533-6*) Troll Communs.

Tower of Faith in the Heart of the City, 1888-1988: Centennial History of the First Congregational Church of Long Beach, California. Ed. by Faith A. Sand. (Illus.). 128p. 1989. text ed. 25.00 (*0-932727-22-0*) Hope Pub Hse.

Tower of Fear. Glen Cook. 1991. mass mkt. 4.99 (*0-8125-1933-7*) Tor Bks.

Tower of Geburah. John White. LC 78-2078. (Archives of Anthropos Ser.: Vol. 3). (Illus.). 404p. (J). (gr. 4 up). 1978. pap. 11.99 (*0-87784-560-3*, 560) InterVarsity.

Tower of Geburah - Chinese Edition. John White. Tr. by Ruth Chen. 302p. (CHI.). 1984. pap. 7.50 (*1-56582-079-7*) Christ Renew Min.

Tower of Glass. Ivan Angelo. Tr. by Ellen Watson. 1986. mass mkt. 3.95 (*0-380-89607-9*, Bard) Avon.

Tower of London. Leonard E. Fisher. LC 87-1629. (Illus.). 32p. (J). (gr. 1-5). 1987. lib. bdg. 15.95 (*0-02-735370-2*, Mac Bks Young Read) S&S Childrens.

Tower of London. William Heslep. LC 95-1822. 23p. (J). 1995. pap. 6.00 (*0-88734-418-6*) Players Pr.

***Tower of London.** Soseki Natsume. Tr. by Peter Milward & Kii Nakano. LC 93-109654. (Illus.). 80p. 1997. pap. 9.95 (*1-873047-90-8*, Pub. by In Print Pub UK) Weatherhill.

Tower of Myriad Mirrors: A Supplement to Journey to the West. Yueh Tung. Tr. by Shuen-Fu Lin & Larry J. Schulz from CHI. LC 88-70535. 206p. 1978. reprint ed. suppl. ed., pap. 58.80 (*0-608-01779-5*, 2062437) Bks Demand.

Tower of Secrets: A Real Life Spy Thriller. Victor Sheymov. 560p. 1994. mass mkt. 5.99 (*0-06-100832-X*) HarpC.

Tower of Secrets: A Real Life Spy Thriller. Victor Sheymov. LC 93-11386. 420p. 1993. 26.95 (*1-55750-764-3*) Naval Inst Pr.

Tower of Shadows. large type ed. Sara Craven. (Harlequin Ser.). 1994. lib. bdg. 18.95 (*0-263-13648-5*) Thorndike Pr.

Tower of Shadows: (Postcards from Europe) Sara Craven. (Presents Ser.). 1994. mass mkt. 2.99 (*0-373-11708-6*, 1-11708-4) Harlequin Bks.

Tower Room. Geras. 1997. pap. write for info. (*0-15-201518-3*) HarBrace.

Tower Slo-Cook Book. Annette Yates. 120p. 1995. 14.95 (*0-572-01477-5*, Pub. by Foulsham UK) Assoc Pubs Grp.

Tower That Fell. Rosemary L. Haughton. 64p. (Orig.). 1997. pap. 5.95 (*0-8091-3686-4*) Paulist Pr.

Tower, This Is Andy & Other Flying Stories from Northeast Nebraska. Robert L. Carlisle. LC 91-18416. (Illus.). 178p. (Orig.). (YA). 1991. pap. 8.95 (*0-934988-24-2*, CIP) Foun Bks.

Tower to the Sun. Colin Thompson. 1997. lib. bdg. 18.99 (*0-679-98334-1*) Knopf.

Tower to the Sun. Colin Thompson. (J). 1997. 17.00 (*0-679-88334-7*, Bullseye Bks) Random Bks Yng Read.

Tower Treasure. Franklin W. Dixon. LC 91-46833. (Hardy Boys Ser.: No. 1). 214p. (J). 1991. 12.95 (*1-55709-144-7*) Applewood.

Tower Treasure. Franklin W. Dixon. (Hardy Boys Ser.: Vol. 1). 180p. (J). (gr. 5-9). 1927. 5.95 (*0-448-08901-7*, G&D) Putnam Pub Group.

Tower Trick. H. William Stine. (Brains & Parker McGoohan Ser.). 77p. (J). (gr. 4-6). 1993. pap. 3.95 (*1-56801-066-4*) Sundance Pub.

Tower Typing: Using Sears, Roebuck & Co. Business Forms. Theodore W. Ivarie. 1978. text ed. 17.50 (*0-07-032066-7*) McGraw.

Towering Jehovah. Morrow. Date not set. pap. 5.99 (*0-09-926301-7*) Random.

Towerman. Jack Rudman. (Career Examination Ser.: C-811). 1994. pap. 23.95 (*0-8373-0811-9*) Nat Learn.

Towers. 1982. text ed. 33.88 (*0-395-31940-4*) HM.

Towers. Robert Andrews. 1996. pap. 6.50 (*0-671-86652-4*, PB Trade Paper) PB.

Towers: A Historical Survey. Erwin Heinle & Fritz Leonhardt. (Illus.). 343p. 1996. 79.95 (*0-408-04306-7*, Butterwrth Archit) Buttrwrth-Heinemann.

Towers & Domes in Architecture. F. Escrig Pallares. 200p. 1996. 91.00 (*1-85312-437-0*, 4370) Computational Mech MA.

***Towers & Tunnels.** Etta Kaner. (Illus.). 48p. (J). (gr. 3-7). 1995. pap. 9.95 (*1-55074-218-3*, Pub. by Kids Can Pr CN) Genl Dist Srvs.

***Towers at the Edge of a World.** Virgil Burnett. 216p. 1983. pap. 9.95 (*0-88984-082-2*, Pub. by Porcupines Quill CN) Genl Dist Srvs.

Towers, Crosses. E. C. Curtsinger. 1988. pap. 15.00 (*0-941179-07-9*) Latitudes Pr.

Towers in the Light. James Flurer. 1994. pap. 8.95 (*1-55673-931-1*) CSS OH.

Towers in the Midst. Elizabeth Goudge. 386p. 1979. reprint ed. lib. bdg. 16.95 (*0-89966-109-2*) Buccaneer Bks.

Towers in the Mist. Elizabeth Goudge. 1976. 17.95 (*0-8488-1346-4*) Amereon Ltd.

Towers in Time: T in T Amazon Box 12 Decks. Mike Sager. 83.40 (*1-887032-11-8*) Thund Castle.

Towers in Time: T in T Amazon Box 60 Packs. Mike Sager. 87.00 (*1-887032-12-6*) Thund Castle.

An Asterisk (*) at the beginning of an entry indicates that the title is appearing in BIP for the first time.

Towers in Time: T in T Amazon 54 Card Deck. Mike Sager. 6.95 (1-887032-09-6) Thund Castle.

Towers in Time: T in T Amazon 8 Card Pack. Mike Sager. 1.45 (1-887032-10-X) Thund Castle.

Towers in Time: T in T Greek Edition Box of 12 Decks. Mike Sager. 83.40 (1-887032-07-X) Thund Castle.

Towers in Time: T in T Greek Edition Box of 60 Packs. Mike Sager. 87.00 (1-887032-08-8) Thund Castle.

Towers in Time: T in T Greek Edition 54 Card Deck. Mike Sager. 6.95 (1-887032-05-3) Thund Castle.

Towers in Time: T in T Greek Edition 8 Card Pack. Mike Sager. 1.45 (1-887032-06-1) Thund Castle.

Towers in Time: T in T Norse Box of 12 Decks. Mike Sager. 83.40 (1-887032-19-3) Thund Castle.

Towers in Time: T in T Norse Box 60 Packs. Mike Sager. 87.00 (1-887032-20-7) Thund Castle.

Towers in Time: T in T Norse 54 Card Deck. Mike Sager. 6.95 (1-887032-17-7) Thund Castle.

Towers in Time: T in T Norse 8 Card Pack. Mike Sager. 1.45 (1-887032-18-5) Thund Castle.

Towers in Time: T in T Original Edition Box of 12 Decks. Mike Sager. 83.40 (1-887032-03-7) Thund Castle.

Towers in Time: T in T Original Edition Box of 60 Packs. Mike Sager. 87.00 (1-887032-04-5) Thund Castle.

Towers in Time: T in T Original Edition Promo Deck. Mike Sager. (1001 Ser.). 9.95 (1-887032-00-2) Thund Castle.

Towers in Time: T in T Original Edition 54 Card Deck. Mike Sager. 6.95 (1-887032-01-0) Thund Castle.

Towers in Time: T in T Original Edition 8 Card Pack. Mike Sager. 1.45 (1-887032-02-9) Thund Castle.

Towers in Time: T in T Players Guide. Mike Sager. 9.95 (1-887032-21-5) Thund Castle.

Towers in Time: T in T Zodiac Box of 12 Decks. Mike Sager. 83.40 (1-887032-15-0) Thund Castle.

Towers in Time: T in T Zodiac Box 60 Packs. Mike Sager. 87.00 (1-887032-16-9) Thund Castle.

Towers in Time: T in T Zodiac 54 Card Deck. Mike Sager. 6.95 (1-887032-13-4) Thund Castle.

Towers in Time: T in T Zodiac 8 Card Pack. Mike Sager. 1.45 (1-887032-14-2) Thund Castle.

Towers' International MOS Power & Other FET Selector. Ed. by Foulsham, W., & Company Staff. (Orig.). 1994. pap. 57.50 (0-572-01931-9, Pub. by W Foulsham UK) Trans-Atl Phila.

Towers of Debt: The Rise & Fall of the Reichmanns. Peter Foster. 1993. 26.95 (1-55013-445-0) U of Toronto Pr.

Towers of Hovenweep. Ian Thompson. LC 92-83789. 64p. (Orig.). pap. 6.95 (0-937062-19-7) Mesa Verde Museum.

Towers of Silence. Paul Scott. (Raj Quartet Ser.: Vol. III). 400p. 1979. mass mkt. 4.95 (0-380-44198-5) Avon.

Towers of Silence. Paul Scott. (Raj Quartet Ser.). 400p. 1992. pap. 11.00 (0-380-71810-3) Avon.

Towers of Sunset. Lee E. Modesitt, Jr. 576p. 1993. mass mkt. 5.99 (0-8125-1967-1) Tor Bks.

Towers of the Brazos. Orlin Corey. 80p. (Orig.). 1987. pap. text ed. 5.00 (0-685-28900-1) Rivendell Hse Ltd.

Towers of the Sunset. Lee E. Modesitt, Jr. 368p. 1992. 21.95 (0-312-85297-5) Tor Bks.

Towers of Trebizond. Rose Macaulay. 1995. pap. 12.95 (0-7867-0266-4) Carroll & Graf.

Towers Reach High. LC 96-22109. (Building Block Bks.). 1996. write for info. (1-57505-036-6, Carolrhoda) Lerner Group.

Towery Report on Bergen County, New Jersey. Robert J. Masiello & Glen Weisman. (Towery Report on New American Communities Ser.). (Illus.). 144p. 1995. pap. 9.50 (1-881096-20-3) Towery Pub.

Towery Report on DuPage County, Illinois. Jack McGuinn & Tom McNamee. (Towery Report on New American Communities Ser.). (Illus.). 128p. 1995. pap. 9.50 (1-881096-19-X) Towery Pub.

Towery Report on Fairfield County, CT. Kathy Failla & Donna Callighan. (Towery Report on New American Communities Ser.). (Illus.). 272p. (Orig.). 1995. pap. 9.50 (1-881096-24-6) Towery Pub.

Towery Report on Lake County, IL. Tom McNamee & Rich Cahan. (Towery Report on New American Communities Ser.). (Illus.). 192p. (Orig.). 1994. pap. 9.50 (1-881096-12-2) Towery Pub.

Towery Report on Mesa, Arizona. Art Gissendaner & Don B. Stevenson. (The Towery Report on New American Communities Ser.). (Illus.). 96p. (Orig.). 1995. pap. 9.50 (1-881096-17-3) Towery Pub.

***Towery Report on Northern Kentucky.** Jack Hicks & Mary Friedberg. (Towery Report on New American Communities Ser.). 128p. 1996. pap. 9.50 (1-881096-25-4) Towery Pub.

Towing, Vol. 4. Michael Hancox. (Oilfield Seamanship Ser.). (Illus.). 500p. 1994. pap. 185.00 (1-870945-63-8, Pub. by Oilfld Pubns Ltd UK) Am Educ Systs.

***Towing Aloft: Learning to Surface-Tow & Aerotow Hang Gliders, Paragliders & Ultralight Sailplanes.** Dennis Pagen. (Illus.). 320p. (Orig.). 1997. pap. 29.95 (0-936310-13-8) Black Mntn.

Towing Jehovah. James Morrow. LC 93-35022. 1995. pap. 12.00 (0-15-600210-8) HarBrace.

Town. William Faulkner. 1957. 13.95 (0-394-42452-2) Random.

Town. William Faulkner. 384p. 1961. pap. 9.00 (0-394-70184-4, V184, Vin) Random.

Town. Conrad Richter. 1981. lib. bdg. 17.95 (0-89967-048-2) Harmony Raine.

Town. Conrad Richter. LC 90-20736. 297p. 1991. reprint ed. pap. 14.95 (0-8214-0980-8) Ohio U Pr.

Town: Preliminary Materials, Vol. 1. Ed. by Michael Millgate. (William Faulkner Manuscripts). 348p. 1986. text ed. 60.00 (0-8240-6831-9) Garland.

Town: Typescript, Vol. 2. Ed. by Michael Millgate. (William Faulkner Manuscripts). 536p. 1986. text ed. 90.00 (0-8240-6830-0) Garland.

Town Abandoned: Flint, Michigan, Confronts Deindustrialization. Steven P. Dandaneau. (SUNY Series in Popular Culture & Political Change). 259p. 1996. text ed. 59.50 (0-7914-2877-X); pap. text ed. 19.95 (0-7914-2878-8) State U NY Pr.

Town & City Gardener. Ed. by Linda Yang. (Plants & Gardens Ser.). (Illus.). 96p. 1992. per., pap. 7.95 (0-945352-74-3) Bklyn Botanic.

Town & City of Waterbury, Connecticut, from the Aboujinal Period to the Year 1895, 3 vols. Ed. by Joseph Anderson. (Illus.). 1380p. 1994. reprint ed. lib. bdg. 140.00 (0-8328-3903-5) Higginson Bk Co.

***Town & City of Waterbury, from the Aboriginal Period to the Year 1895.** Ed. by Joseph Anderson. (Illus.). 2264p. 1997. reprint ed. lib. bdg. 232.50 (0-8328-5692-4) Higginson Bk Co.

Town & Country. Mark Girouard. (Illus.). 288p. (C). 1992. 50.00 (0-300-05185-9) Yale U Pr.

Town & Country. Alice Provensen & Martin Provensen. LC 93-44749. (Illus.). 32p. (J). (ps-3). 1994. 17.00 (0-15-200182-4, Browndeer Pr) HarBrace.

Town & Country: Essays on the Structure of Local Government in the American Colonies. Ed. by Bruce C. Daniels. LC 77-14834. 293p. 1978. text ed. 35.00 (0-8195-5020-5, Wesleyan Univ Pr) U Pr of New Eng.

Town & Country: Race Relations in an Urban-Rural Context, Arkansas, 1865-1905. John W. Graves. 348p. 1990. 32.00 (1-55728-137-8) U of Ark Pr.

Town & Country Casuals: An Accounting Clerk Practice Set. A. C. Peele. 1985. 11.55 (0-07-049197-6) McGraw.

Town & Country Cookbook, Vol. 1. James Villas. 1988. 10.98 (0-316-90301-9) Little.

Town & Country Creative Breads: A Healthy Tradition for Todays Family. Ferne C. Chapman. Ed. by Karl Schlosser. (Illus.). 160p. 1993. spiral bd. 12.95 (0-9637312-9-7) Jac-Lynn Ent.

Town & Country in Central & Eastern Africa: Studies Presented & Discussed at the International African Seminar, 12th, Lusaka, September 1972. International African Seminar Staff. Ed. by David Parkin. LC 76-363783. 368p. reprint ed. pap. 104.90 (0-8357-3025-5, 2057112) Bks Demand.

Town & Country in Locorotondo. George D. Spindler. LC 92-3298. (Spindler Ser.). (Illus.). 132p. (C). 1992. pap. text ed. 13.50 (0-03-073327-8) HB Coll Pubs.

Town & Country in Pre-Industrial Spain: Cuenca, 1540-1870. David S. Reher. (Cambridge Studies in Population, Economy & Society in Past Time: No. 12). (Illus.). 345p. (C). 1990. text ed. 69.95 (0-521-35292-4) Cambridge U Pr.

Town & Country in Southeastern Anatolia, Vol. 1: Settlement & Land Use at Kurban Hoyuk & Other Sites in the Lower Karababa Basin. T. J. Wilkinson. LC 90-61729. (Oriental Institute Publications: No. 109). (Illus.). 334p. 1990. 66.00 (0-918986-64-8) Orient Inst.

Town & Country in Southeastern Anatolia, Vol. 2: The Stratigraphic Sequence at Kurban Hoyuk, 2 vols., Set. G. Algaze et al. LC 90-61729. (Oriental Institute Publications: No. 110). (Illus.). 647p. 1990. 132.00 (0-918986-65-6) Orient Inst.

Town & Country Planning in Britain. 11th ed. J. B. Collingworth & Vincent Nadin. LC 93-35545. 368p. (C). 1994. pap. text ed. 35.00 (0-415-10708-3, Routledge NY) Routledge.

***Town & Country Planning in Britain.** 12th ed. J. B. Cullingworth & Vincent Nadin. LC 96-52768. 416p. (C). 1997. pap. write for info. (0-415-13913-9); text ed. write for info. (0-415-13912-0) Routledge.

Town & Country under Fascism: The Transformation of Brescia 1915-1926. Alice A. Kelikian. (Illus.). 300p. 1986. text ed. 59.00 (0-19-821970-9) OUP.

Town & Countryside: The English Landowner in the National Economy, 1660-1860. Ed. by C. W. Chalklin & J. R. Wordie. 220p. 1989. 55.00 (0-04-445353-1) Routledge Chapman & Hall.

Town & Countryside in the English Revolution. Ed. by R. C. Richardson. LC 93-76. 288p. (C). 1993. text ed. 59.95 (0-7190-3462-0, Pub. by Manchester Univ Pr UK) St Martin.

Town & Environs: Recreation in Town Planning. Imre Perenyi. 152p. (C). 1978. 85.00 (963-05-1493-1, Pub. by Akad Kiado HU) St Mut.

Town & Gown. Lynn Montross & Lois S. Montross. LC 70-132122. (Short Story Index Reprint Ser.). 1977. 19.95 (0-8369-3679-5) Ayer.

Town & the City. Jack Kerouac. 1976. 21.95 (0-8488-1068-6) Amereon Ltd.

Town & the City. Jack Kerouac. LC 83-8466. 501p. 1970. reprint ed. pap. 16.00 (0-15-690790-9, Harvest Bks) HarBrace.

Town & the River. Robert Collen. (Illus.). 8p. (Orig.). 1993. pap. 1.50 (0-9626308-4-5) Haleys.

Town & the River. rev. ed. Robert Collen. LC 93-79010. (Illus.). 8p. (Orig.). 1994. pap. 1.50 (1-884540-03-1) Haleys.

Town & Village in the Nineteenth Century. J. F. Phillips. (C). 1983. text ed. 45.00 (0-685-22169-5, Pub. by Univ Nottingham UK) St Mut.

***Town Belles.** Pamela Evans. LC 97-12434. 1997. write for info. (0-7862-1115-6) Thorndike Pr.

***Town Belles.** Pamela Evans. 474p. 1997. pap. 11.95 (0-7472-5166-5, Pub. by Headline UK) Trafalgar.

Town Beyond the Wall. Elie Wiesel. LC 81-16546. 179p. (C). reprint ed. pap. 13.00 (0-8052-0697-3) Schocken.

Town Beyond the Wall: A Novel. Elie Wiesel. 192p. 1995. pap. 13.00 (0-8052-1045-8) Schocken.

Town-By-Town Restaurant Survey: Fairfield & Westchester Counties, 1992 Edition. 3rd ed. Ed. by A. G. Ungerland & Roger E. Clark. (Illus.). 145p. 1991. pap. 8.85 (0-9626988-1-4) Town-By-Town.

Town Called Longnose & Other Writings. Eugenia T. Avant. LC 90-84670. (Illus.). 56p. 1990. 15.00 (0-914570-09-9) LAvant Studios.

Town Called Shaoyang: Introducing Industry Appropriate to China. Joseph E. Stepanek. (Illus.). 273p. 1992. pap. 16.50 (1-881031-01-2) Gold Hill CO.

Town Clerk. Jack Rudman. (Career Examination Ser.: C-1854). 1994. pap. 27.95 (0-8373-1854-8) Nat Learn.

Town Clock Burning. 2nd ed. Charles Fort. (Classic Contemporaries Ser.). (Orig.). 1991. reprint ed. pap. 12.95 (0-88748-123-X) Carnegie-Mellon.

Town Creek: A Legacy from the Past. Joffre L. Coe. LC 94-17931. (Illus.). 1995. pap. 18.95 (0-8078-4490-X); text ed. 45.00 (0-8078-2176-4) U of NC Pr.

Town Engineer. Jack Rudman. (Career Examination Ser.: C-2001). 1994. pap. 34.95 (0-8373-2001-1) Nat Learn.

Town Finances of Elizabethan Ipswich: Select Treasurers' & Chamberlains' Accounts. Ed. by John Webb. (Suffolk Records Society Ser.: Vol. 38). (Illus.). 198p. 1996. 35.00 (0-85115-643-6) Boydell & Brewer.

Town Follies. Margaret Westhaven. (Regency Romance Ser.). 224p. (Orig.). 1992. pap. 3.99 (0-451-17302-3, Sig) NAL-Dutton.

***Town Government in Rhode Island.** W. E. Foster. 36p. 1997. reprint ed. pap. 7.50 (0-8328-6473-0) Higginson Bk Co.

Town Hall, Saynatsalo: Saynatsalo, Finland 1951 Alvar Aalto. Richard Weston. (Architecture in Detail Ser.). (Illus.). 60p. (C). 1993. pap. 29.95 (0-7148-2775-4, Pub. by Phaidon Press UK) Chronicle Bks.

Town History of Weare, NH from 1888. Helen E. Dearborn. (Illus.). 305p. 1993. reprint ed. lib. bdg. 35.00 (0-8328-3185-9) Higginson Bk Co.

Town House. Moss. 1996. 39.95 (0-8050-1398-9) H Holt & Co.

Town House. Gwenda Smith. 172p. 1993. pap. 15.00 (0-9634233-0-4) Strafford Hist Soc.

Town House. Norah Lofts. reprint ed. lib. bdg. 27.95 (0-89190-230-9, Rivercity Pr) Amereon Ltd.

Town House, Country House: Recollections of a Quebec Childhood. Hazel Boswell. (Illus.). 152p. (C). 1990. 29.95 (0-7735-0721-3, Pub. by McGill CN) U of Toronto Pr.

Town House in Jerusalem. Arieh Larkey. 376p. 1996. 19.95 (965-229-153-6) Gefen Bks.

Town in Medieval Hungary. Lajos Gerevich. 1991. text ed. 44.00 (0-88033-194-1) Col U Pr.

Town in the Ruhr: A Social History of Bochum, 1860-1914. David F. Crew. LC 78-31526. 289p. 1979. text ed. 49.50 (0-231-04300-7) Col U Pr.

Town in the Ruhr: A Social History of Bochum, 1860-1914. David F. Crew. LC 78-31526. 289p. 1986. pap. text ed. 18.00 (0-231-04301-5) Col U Pr.

Town in Tragedy, Vol. Two: The Boyertown Opera House Fire. Mary J. Schneider. (Illus.). 248p. (Orig.). 1992. pap. write for info. (0-9629218-1-5) MJS Pubns.

Town in Transition: 1914-1977 see History of Hudson, New Hampshire: 1673-1913

Town into City: Springfield, Massachusetts & the Meaning of Community, 1840-1880. Michael H. Frisch. LC 72-178075. (Studies in Urban History). (Illus.). 317p. 1980. pap. 13.95 (0-674-89826-5) HUP.

Town Investigator. Jack Rudman. (Career Examination Ser.: C-3067). 1994. pap. 29.95 (0-8373-3067-X) Nat Learn.

Town Is Aaron. Yereth K. Knowles. LC 88-51226. 279p. (Orig.). 1989. pap. 10.00 (0-916383-79-2) Aegina Pr.

Town Law, New York State. annuals New York State Legislature Staff. 350p. 1997. Updated annually. ring bd. 15.95 (0-930137-41-8) Looseleaf Law.

***Town Leaders - Littleton, North Carolina, 1790-1920.** Rebecca L. Dozier. LC 96-43882. 1996. write for info. (0-87152-505-4) Reprint.

Town Library of Ipswich Provided for the Use of the Town Preachers in 1599: A History & Catalogue. John Blatchly. (Illus.). 214p. 1989. 70.00 (0-85115-517-0) Boydell & Brewer.

Town Life in the Fifteenth Century, 2 vols. Alice S. Green. LC 70-171443. 930p. 1972. reprint ed. Set. 44.95 (0-405-08575-3, Pub. by Blom Pubns UK) Ayer.

Town Life in the Fifteenth Century, 2 vols., 1. Alice S. Green. LC 70-171443. 920p. 1972. reprint ed. 23.95 (0-405-08576-1, Pub. by Blom Pubns UK) Ayer.

Town Life in the Fifteenth Century, 2 vols., 2. Alice S. Green. LC 70-171443. 920p. 1972. reprint ed. 23.95 (0-405-08577-X, Pub. by Blom Pubns UK) Ayer.

Town Like Alice. Nevil Shute. 23.95 (0-8488-0848-7) Amereon Ltd.

Town Like Alice. Nevil Shute. 288p. 1987. mass mkt. 5.99 (0-345-35374-9) Ballantine.

Town Maintenance Supervisor. Jack Rudman. (Career Examination Ser.: C-2764). 1994. pap. 29.95 (0-8373-2764-4) Nat Learn.

Town Meeting Time: A Handbook of Parliamentary Law. 2nd ed. Massachusetts Moderators Association Staff. LC 84-4354. 202p. 1984. lib. bdg. 23.50 (0-89874-754-6) Krieger.

Town Minutes: Town of Carmel, Putnam County, New York, 1795-1839. Marilyn C. Greene. 183p. 1990. lib. bdg. 26.90 (1-56012-106-8, 99) Kinship Rhinebeck.

Town Mouse & Country Mouse. (Read Along With Me Ser.). (Illus.). 24p. (J). (ps-3). 1989. write for info. (1-56288-161-2) Checkerboard.

Town Mouse & the Country Mouse. Aesop. LC 78-18062. (Illus.). 32p. (J). (gr. k-3). 1979. lib. bdg. 11.89 (0-89375-131-6) Troll Communs.

Town Mouse & the Country Mouse. Aesop. LC 78-18062. (Illus.). 32p. (J). (gr. k-3). 1997. pap. 3.95 (0-89375-109-X) Troll Communs.

Town Mouse & the Country Mouse. Illus. & Retold by Helen Craig. LC 91-58761. 32p. (J). (ps up). 1992. 13.95 (1-56402-102-5) Candlewick Pr.

Town Mouse & the Country Mouse. Helen Craig. LC 91-58761. (J). (ps-3). 1995. pap. 5.99 (1-56402-467-9) Candlewick Pr.

Town Mouse & the Country Mouse. Illus. by Holly Hannon. LC 94-9789. (Bank Street Ready-to-Read Ser.). (J). 1995. pap. 3.99 (0-553-37572-5) Bantam.

Town Mouse & the Country Mouse. Illus. by Holly Hannon. LC 96-10175. (Bank Street Ready-to-Read Ser.). (J). 1996. lib. bdg. 17.27 (0-8368-1622-6) Gareth Stevens Inc.

Town Mouse, & the Country Mouse. Vicky Ireland. 38p. (Orig.). (J). (gr. k-3). 1987. pap. 5.00 (0-87602-266-2) Anchorage.

Town Mouse & the Country Mouse. Illus. & Adapted by Janet Stevens. LC 86-14276. 32p. (J). (ps-3). 1989. pap. 5.95 (0-8234-0733-0) Holiday.

Town Mouse & the Country Mouse; The Boy Who Cried Wolf, 2 bks. in 1. (Aesop's Fables - Two in One Tales Ser.). (Illus.). 24p. (Orig.). (J). (gr. 1-4). 1993. pap. 2.50 (1-56144-303-4, Honey Bear Bks) Modern Pub NYC.

Town Mouse, Country Mouse. Jan Brett. LC 93-41227. (Illus.). 32p. (J). (ps-3). 1994. lib. bdg. 15.95 (0-399-22622-2, Putnam) Putnam Pub Group.

Town Mouse, Country Mouse. Carol Jones. LC 94-14411. (Illus.). 32p. (J). (gr. k-3). 1995. 14.95 (0-395-71129-0) HM.

Town of Ballymuck. Victor Power. LC 84-52121. (Illus.). 176p. (Orig.). 1984. pap. 9.50 (0-930501-00-4) Swallows Tale Pr.

Town of Ballymuck. Victor Power. LC 84-52121. (Illus.). 162p. (Orig.). 1985. lib. bdg. 15.95 (0-930501-04-7) Swallows Tale Pr.

Town of Hercules: A Buried Treasure Trove. expanded rev. ed. Joseph J. Deiss. LC 94-41648. (Illus.). 192p. (YA). 1995. 24.95 (0-89236-222-7, J P Getty Museum) J P Getty Trust.

Town of Islip: A History of Its Communities & Schools. Patrick J. Curran. (Orig.). pap. text ed. write for info. (0-9615532-0-0) Town Islip.

***Town of Milan.** J. A. Ryan. (Illus.). 96p. 1997. reprint ed. pap. 17.50 (0-8328-6347-5) Higginson Bk Co.

Town of Moravia, New York. James A. Wright. 289p. 1993. reprint ed. lib. bdg. 35.00 (0-8328-2841-6) Higginson Bk Co.

Town of No & My Brother Running: Dual Volume. Wesley McNair. LC 95-35338. 1997. pap. 15.95 (1-56792-056-X) Godine.

Town of Roxbury. Francis S. Drake. (Notable American Authors Ser.). 1992. reprint ed. lib. bdg. 75.00 (0-7812-2690-2) Rprt Serv.

Town of Roxbury, MA: Its Memorable Persons & Places, Its History & Antiquities, with Numerous Illustrations of Its Old Landmarks & Noted Personages. Francis S. Drake. (Illus.). 493p. (Orig.). 1995. pap. text ed. 32.00 (0-7884-0148-3) Heritage Bk.

Town of San Felipe & Colonial Cacao Economics. Eugenio Pinero. LC 94-71251. (Transactions Ser.: Vol. 84, Pt. 3). (Illus.). 190p. (C). 1994. pap. 20.00 (0-87169-843-9, T843-pie) Am Philos.

Town of Spafford, Onondaga County, New York. George K. Collins. 280p. 1993. reprint ed. lib. bdg. 33.00 (0-8328-2968-4) Higginson Bk Co.

Town of St. Johnsbury, VT, a Review of One Hundred Twenty-Five Years. Edward T. Fairbanks. (Illus.). 592p. 1992. reprint ed. lib. bdg. 55.00 (0-8328-2259-0) Higginson Bk Co.

Town of Tombarel. William J. Locke. LC 71-150548. (Short Story Index Reprint Ser.). 1977. reprint ed. 20.95 (0-8369-3845-3) Ayer.

Town of Weston, Massachusetts: Births, Deaths & Marriages, 1707-1850. Ed. by Mary F. Pierce. 649p. 1993. reprint ed. lib. bdg. 66.00 (0-8328-3145-X) Higginson Bk Co.

Town of Yarmouth, Massachusetts: A History, 1639-1989. Marion Vuilleumier. (Illus.). 320p. 1989. 35.00 (0-9625068-0-X) Hist Soc Yarmouth.

Town of York, Eighteen Fifteen to Eighteen Thirty-Four: A Further Collection of Documents of Early Toronto. Ed. by Edith G. Firth. (Champlain Society, Toronto, Publications, Ontario Ser.: No. 8). 479p. reprint ed. pap. 136.60 (0-685-10713-2, 2023615) Bks Demand.

Town of York, Seventeen Ninety-Three to Eighteen Fifteen: A Collection of Documents of Early Toronto. Ed. by Edith G. Firth. LC 62-4422. (Champlain Society, Toronto, Publications, Ontario Ser.: No. 5). 462p. reprint ed. pap. 131.70 (0-317-26912-7, 2023614) Bks Demand.

Town on Sandy Bay: A History of Rockport Massachusetts. Marshall W. Swan. LC 80-15578. (Illus.). 456p. 1980. 15.00 (0-914016-72-5) Phoenix Pub.

Town on the Grow, the History of Blanchard, Louisiana. 1997. 6.00 (0-910653-24-0, 8332Q, Red River Pr) Archival Servs.

***Town on the Hassayampa: A History of Wickenburg, Arizona.** Mark E. Pry. (Illus.). x, 157p. 1997. pap. 12.95 (0-9657377-0-5) Desert Cab.

***Town Origins & Development in Early England: C. 400-950 A. D.** Daniel G. Russo. LC 96-35354. (Contributions to the Study of World History Ser.: Vol. 58). 1997. text ed. write for info. (0-313-30079-8, Greenwood Pr) Greenwood.

Town Park & Other Stories. Hermann Grab. Tr. by Quintin Hoare. 256p. 1988. 18.95 (0-86091-189-6, Pub. by Verso UK) Routledge Chapman & Hall.

Town Parrot. Penelope Bennett. LC 94-6409. (Read & Wonder Bks.). (Illus.). (J). (gr. k-3). 1995. 14.95 (1-56402-484-9) Candlewick Pr.

***Town Planning & British Colonialism.** Robert Home. (Illus.). 240p. 1996. 65.00 (*0-419-20230-7*, E & FN Spon) Routledge Chapman & Hall.

Town Planning Appeals: A Citizen's Guide. P. D. Day & S. E. Nall. 84p. (C). 1990. pap. 30.00 (*0-86439-075-0*, Pub. by Boolarong Pubns AT) St Mut.

Town Planning Education. Agustin Rodrigues-Bachiller. 240p. 1988. text ed. 68.95 (*0-566-05500-7*, Pub. by Avebury Pub UK) Ashgate Pub Co.

Town Planning Education in the 1970s. A. H. Thomas & W. K. Thomas. (C). 1981. 35.00 (*0-685-30289-X*, Pub. by Oxford Polytechnic UK) St Mut.

Town Planning Glossary: English, French, German, Italian, Spanish. Marco Venturi. 277p. (ENG, FRE, GER, ITA & SPA.). 1990. 150.00 (*0-7859-9957-4*) Fr & Eur.

Town Planning Glossary - Stadtplanungsglossar - Glossaire d'Urbanisme - Glosario de UrbanAsmo - Glossario du Urbanistica: Ten Thousand Multilingual Terms in One Alphabet for European Town Planners. Marco Venturi. 277p. (ENG, FRE, GER, ITA & SPA.). 1990. lib. bdg. 70.00 (*3-598-10903-2*) K G Saur.

Town Planning in Ancient Dekkan. C. P. Ayyar. (C). 1994. text ed. 17.50 (*81-206-0972-7*, Pub. by Asian Educ Servs II) S Asia.

Town Planning in Britain since 1900: The Rise & Fall of the Planning Ideal. Gordon E. Cherry. LC 96-8104. (Making Contemporary Britain Ser.). 224p. 1996. 59.95 (*0-631-19993-4*); pap. 21.95 (*0-631-19994-2*) Blackwell Pubs.

Town Planning in Early South India. C. P. Ayyar. 197p. 1987. 17.50 (*0-8364-2083-7*, Pub. by Mittal II) S Asia.

Town Planning in Frontier America. John W. Reps. LC 68-20877. 336p. 1981. reprint ed. pap. 16.95 (*0-8262-0316-7*) U of Mo Pr.

Town Planning in London: The Eighteenth & Nineteenth Centuries. Donald J. Olsen. LC 82-50440. (Illus.). 246p. 1982. pap. 22.00 (*0-300-02915-2*, Y-443) Yale U Pr.

Town Planning in Practice. 2nd ed. Raymond Unwin. LC 68-56507. (Illus.). 1972. reprint ed. 36.95 (*0-405-09036-6*) Ayer.

Town Planning in Practice: An Introduction to the Art of Designing Cities & Suburbs. Raymond Unwin. LC 94-5726. (Illus.). 456p. 1994. reprint ed. 75.00 (*1-56898-004-3*) Princeton Arch.

***Town Planning in the 21st Century.** Ed. by Andy Blowers & Bob Evans. 256p. (C). 1997. pap. 22.95 (*0-415-10526-9*); text ed. 69.95 (*0-415-10525-0*) Routledge.

Town Planning Responses to City Change. Vincent Nadin & Joe Doak. 252p. 1991. text ed. 63.95 (*1-85628-161-2*, Pub. by Avebury Pub UK) Ashgate Pub Co.

Town Planning under Military Occupation: An Explanation of the Law & Practice of Town Planning. Anthony Coon. 180p. 1992. 59.95 (*1-85521-287-0*, Pub. by Dartmth Pub UK) Ashgate Pub Co.

Town Proprietors in Vermont. Florence M. Woodard. LC 68-58646. (Columbia University. Studies in the Social Sciences: No. 418). reprint ed. 21.50 (*0-404-51418-9*) AMS Pr.

Town Proprietors of the New England Colonies. R. H. Akagi. 1963. 14.50 (*0-8446-1012-7*) Peter Smith.

***Town Records of Derby, 1655-1710.** Compiled by Nancy O. Phillips. 496p. 1997. reprint ed. lib. bdg. 52.50 (*0-8328-5635-5*) Higginson Bk Co.

***Town Records of Roxbury, Massachusetts, 1647 to 1730: Being Volume One of the Original.** Robert J. Dunkle & Ann S. Lainhart. LC 97-12907. 1997. write for info. (*0-88082-065-9*) New Eng Hist.

***Town Register of Ashland, Plymouth, Sandwich, Campton, Holderness, Center Harbor, Moultonboro, 1908. (Town Histories & Cencuses)** 266p. 1997. reprint ed. lib. bdg. 35.00 (*0-8328-5973-7*) Higginson Bk Co.

***Town Register of Canterbury, Northwood, Epsom, Loudon, Chichester & Deerfield, 1909 (Town Histories & Censuses)** 239p. 1997. reprint ed. lib. bdg. 29.00 (*0-8328-5981-8*) Higginson Bk Co.

***Town Register of Henniker, Bradford, Warner & Hopkinton, 1908 (Town Histories & Censuses)** 212p. 1997. reprint ed. lib. bdg. 27.00 (*0-8328-5994-X*) Higginson Bk Co.

***Town Register of Marlboro, Troy, Jaffrey & Swanzey, 1908 (Town Histories & Censuses)** 216p. 1997. reprint ed. lib. bdg. 27.50 (*0-8328-6011-5*) Higginson Bk Co.

***Town Register of Meredith, Tilton, Gilmanton, Gilford, Belmont, New Hampton, 1908.** (Illus.). 252p. 1997. reprint ed. lib. bdg. 32.00 (*0-8328-6012-3*) Higginson Bk Co.

***Town Register of Poland, Raymond & Casco, 1906 (Town Histories & Directories)** Compiled by Mitchell & Davis. (Illus.). 141p. 1997. reprint ed. pap. 19.00 (*0-8328-5897-8*) Higginson Bk Co.

***Town Register of Wolfboro, Ossipee, Effingham, Tuftonboro, Tamworth, Freedom, 1908 (Town Histories & Censuses)** 256p. 1997. reprint ed. lib. bdg. 32.00 (*0-8328-6030-1*) Higginson Bk Co.

Town Smokes. Pinckney Benedict. LC 87-5684. 168p. (Orig.). 1987. pap. 9.95 (*0-86538-058-9*) Ontario Rev NJ.

***Town Social.** Trana M. Simmons. 1996. mass mkt. 5.99 (*0-515-11971-7*) Jove Pubns.

Town Tamer. large type ed. Frank Gruber. (Linford Western Library). 368p. 1992. pap. 15.99 (*0-7089-7179-2*, Trailtree Bookshop) Ulverscroft.

Town Team: The Folklore of Town Team Baseball. Harry G. Santos. (Illus.). 120p. (Orig.). (J). 1988. pap. 12.95 (*0-940151-09-X*) Statesman-Exam.

Town That Country Built: Welcome to Branson, Missouri. Bruce Cook. 280p. (Orig.). 1993. mass mkt. 4.99 (*0-380-77095-4*) Avon.

Town That Didn't Exist. Pierre Christin. Ed. by Bernd Metz. Tr. by Tom Leighton from FRE. 56p. (Orig.). 1988. pap. 11.95 (*0-87416-051-0*) Catalan Communs.

Town That Got Out of Town. Robert Priest. LC 88-46108. (Illus.). 32p. (J). 1989. 14.95 (*0-87923-786-4*) Godine.

Town That Started the Civil War. Nathan H. Brandt, Jr. (Illus.). 352p. 1990. 34.50 (*0-8156-0243-X*) Syracuse U Pr.

Town That Wouldn't Die. Robert E. Haltiner. (Illus.). 144p. 1986. 16.95 (*0-9617779-0-7*) J Besser Mus.

Town They Called the World Charters Towers. L. Lawson & H. Hardy. Ed. by Don Roderick. 64p. (C). 1990. 69.00 (*0-908175-94-9*, Pub. by Boolarong Pubns AT) St Mut.

Town Traveller. George Gissing. LC 68-54268. reprint ed. 18.00 (*0-404-02813-6*) AMS Pr.

Town Within a City: A History of Five Points South Neighborhood. Ann M. Burkhardt. Ed. by Alice M. Bowsher. (Illus.). 92p. 1982. pap. 10.00 (*0-943994-13-6*) Birmingham Hist Soc.

***Town without a Zip.** McGrady. 1997. mass mkt. 5.99 (*0-671-86942-6*) S&S Trade.

Towne: Letters & Diary of Laura M. Towne, Written from the Sea Islands of So. Carolina, 1862-1884. Ed. by Rupert S. Holland. (Illus.). 310p. 1995. reprint ed. pap. 29.00 (*0-8328-4853-0*); reprint ed. lib. bdg. 39.00 (*0-8328-4852-2*) Higginson Bk Co.

Towne Family in Early Massachusetts Vital Records from Printed Sources. Evelyn C. Lane. 103p. 1991. pap. 15.00 (*0-9626201-1-4*) E C Lane.

Towneley Cycle. A. C. Cawley & Martin Stevens. LC 75-42854. 332p. 1976. pap. 11.97 (*0-87328-113-6*) Huntington Lib.

Towneley Plays. Ed. by George England. 418p. 1966. text ed. 25.00 (*0-910278-87-3*) Boulevard.

Townhouses & Condominiums: Residents' Likes & Dislikes; A Special Report. Carl Norcross. LC 73-82886. (Illus.). 111p. reprint ed. pap. 31.70 (*0-8357-3192-8*, 2039464) Bks Demand.

Townlife in Fourteenth Century Scotland. Elizabeth Ewan. 1991. text ed. 50.00 (*0-7486-0128-7*, Pub. by Edinburgh U Pr UK) Col U Pr.

Townlife in Fourteenth Century Scotland. Elizabeth Ewan. (Illus.). 208p. 1992. pap. 16.50 (*0-7486-0151-1*, Pub. by Edinburgh U Pr UK) Col U Pr.

Townline Road: Lines from the Beginning - the Place - the Time. Esther E. Buskohl. (Illus.). 1996. pap. write for info. (*0-9614991-2-5*) EEBART.

***Towns along the Towpath.** Kate Mulligan. (Illus.). 128p. (Orig.). 1997. pap. 14.00 (*0-9655552-0-8*) Wakefield Pr.

Towns & Buildings. Steen E. Rasmussen. 1969. pap. 18.00 (*0-262-68011-4*) MIT Pr.

Towns & Cities. Rodney Aldis. LC 91-35801. (Ecology Watch Ser.). (Illus.). 48p. (J). (gr. 5 up). 1992. lib. bdg. 13.95 (*0-87518-496-0*, Dillon Silver Burdett) Silver Burdett Pr.

***Towns & Cities.** Patience Coster. LC 97-16182. (Step-by-Step Geography Ser.). (Illus.). (J). 1998. write for info. (*0-516-20355-X*) Childrens.

***Towns & Cities.** Claire Llewellyn. LC 96-52728. (Illus.). (J). 1997. lib. bdg. write for info. (*1-57572-197-X*) Rigby Interact Libr.

Towns & Cities. Emrys Jones. LC 80-24687. (Illus.). viii, 152p. 1981. reprint ed. text ed. 49.75 (*0-313-22724-1*, JOTC, Greenwood Pr) Greenwood.

Towns & Cities: Close-Up on Urban Wildlife. Christine Hatt. (Alpha Bks.). (Illus.). 45p. (J). (gr. 5-8). 1996. 19.95 (*0-237-51460-5*, Pub. by Evans Bros Ltd UK) Trafalgar.

Towns & Temples along the Mississippi. Ed. by David H. Dye & Cheryl A. Cox. LC 89-32994. (Illus.). 312p. 1990. pap. text ed. 29.95 (*0-8173-0455-X*) U of Ala Pr.

Towns & Townspeople in the Fifteenth Century. Ed. by J. A. Thomson. (Illus.). 208p. 1988. 35.00 (*0-86299-469-1*, Pub. by Sutton Pubng UK) Bks Intl VA.

Towns & Urban Society in Early Nineteenth-Century Hungary. V. Bacskai. 151p. (C). 1989. pap. 60.00 (*963-05-5259-0*, Pub. by Akad Kiado HU) St Mut.

***Towns & Villages of the Lower Ohio.** Darrel E. Bigham. (Ohio River Valley Ser.). (Illus.). 400p. (C). 1998. text ed. 39.95 (*0-8131-2042-X*) U Pr of Ky.

Towns Down Underground see Books for Young Explorers

Towns Facing Railroads. Jo McDougall. 64p. 1991. pap. 10.00 (*1-55728-199-8*) U of Ark Pr.

Towns for People: Transforming Urban Life. Ken Worpole. 112p. 1992. 80.00 (*0-335-09965-3*, Open Univ Pr); pap. 27.00 (*0-335-09964-5*, Open Univ Pr) Taylor & Francis.

***Towns in Late Antiquity: Iol Caesarea & Its Context.** Timothy W. Potter. (Ian Sanders Memorial Fund, Occasional Publications: No. 2). (Illus.). 122p. 1995. pap. 22.00 (*0-9521073-1-7*, Pub. by Oxbow Bks UK) David Brown.

Towns in Medieval Hungary. Laszlo Gerevich. 151p. 1990. 90.00 (*963-05-5519-0*, Pub. by Akad Kiado HU) St Mut.

Towns in the Viking Age. Helen Clarke & Bjorn Ambrosiani. LC 90-63782. (Illus.). 219p. 1991. text ed. 45.00 (*0-312-06086-6*) St Martin.

Towns in the Viking Age. Helen Clarke & Bjorn Ambrosiani. 210p. 1994. pap. 21.00 (*0-7185-1792-X*) St Martin.

Towns in Transition: Urban Evolution in Late Antiquity & the Early Middle Ages. Ed. by Neil Christie & S. T. Loseby. (Illus.). 325p. 1996. text ed. 76.95 (*1-85928-107-9*, Pub. by Scolar Pr UK) Ashgate Pub Co.

Towns in Tudor & Stuart Britain. Sybil M. Jack. LC 96-6360. (Social History in Perspective Ser.). 1997. text ed. 49.95 (*0-312-16210-3*) St Martin.

Towns of Ancient Rus. M. Tikhomirov. 503p. (C). 1997. reprint ed. text ed. 50.00 (*0-89241-536-3*) Caratzas.

Towns of Destiny. Hilaire Belloc. LC 72-101273. (BCL Ser. I). (Illus.). reprint ed. 44.50 (*0-404-00745-7*) AMS Pr.

***Towns of Roman Britain.** John Wacher. 480p. (C). 1997. pap. 49.95 (*0-415-17041-9*, Routledge NY) Routledge.

Towns of the Monadnock Region, NH. R. Stephenson. (Images of America Ser.). 1994. pap. 14.99 (*0-7524-0073-8*, Arcdia) Chalford.

Towns of the Renaissance: Travellers in Northern Italy. David D. Hume. LC 95-6847. (Illus.). 240p. 1995. 25.00 (*1-880158-07-8*) J N Townsend.

Towns on Teacher Training, 2 vols. Elmer L. Towns. Ed. by Sharon L. Anthony. 166p. 1989. ring bd. 199.95 incl. vhs (*0-941005-24-0*) Chrch Grwth VA.

***Towns, Plans & Society in Modern Britain.** Helen Meller. (New Studies in Economic & Social History: Vol. 31). 148p. (C). 1997. text ed. 44.95 (*0-521-57227-4*) Cambridge U Pr.

***Towns, Plans & Society in Modern Britain.** Helen Meller. (New Studies in Economic & Social History: Vol. 31). 148p. (C). 1997. pap. text ed. 12.95 (*0-521-57644-X*) Cambridge U Pr.

Towns' Sunday School Encyclopedia: A Practical Guide for Sunday School Workers. Elmer L. Towns. LC 92-28605. 639p. 1993. pap. 14.99 (*0-8423-7303-9*) Tyndale.

Towns, Villages, & Countryside of Celtic Europe. Francoise Audouze & Olivier Buchsenschutz. Tr. by Henry Cleere. LC 91-37593. (Illus.). 258p. 1992. text ed. 49.95 (*0-253-31082-2*) Ind U Pr.

Townsend: A Memorial of John, Henry & Richard Townsend & Their Descendants with 1969 Index. rev. ed. W. A. Townsend. 296p. 1991. reprint ed. pap. 47.00 (*0-8328-1788-0*); reprint ed. lib. bdg. 57.00 (*0-8328-1787-2*) Higginson Bk Co.

Townsend - Townshend, 1066-1909: The History, Genealogy & Alliances of the English & American House of Townsend. rev. ed. Margaret Townsend. (Illus.). 125p. 1992. reprint ed. pap. 19.50 (*0-8328-2743-6*); reprint ed. lib. bdg. 29.50 (*0-8328-2742-8*) Higginson Bk Co.

Townsend Harris: First American Envoy in Japan. William E. Griffis. LC 74-175698. (Select Bibliographies Reprint Ser.). 1977. reprint ed. 23.95 (*0-8369-6613-9*) Ayer.

Townsend Harris: First American Envoy to Japan. William E. Griffis. (Notable American Authors Ser.). 1992. reprint ed. lib. bdg. 75.00 (*0-7812-2963-4*) Rprt Serv.

Townsend Thematic Reader. Christopher G. Hayes & Patricia J. McAlexander. 256p. 1995. pap. text ed. 12.00 (*0-944210-69-4*) Townsend NJ.

Townshend Duties Crisis: The Second Phase of the American Revolution 1767-1773. Peter D. Thomas. 290p. 1987. 75.00 (*0-19-822967-4*) OUP.

Townshends & Their World: Gentry, Law, & the Land in Norfolk C. 1450-1551. C. E. Moreton. (Oxford Historical Monographs). (Illus.). 320p. 1992. 79.00 (*0-19-820299-7*) OUP.

Township Laws of Ohio 1995. 602p. 1995. pap. 40.00 (*1-884669-08-5*) Conway Greene.

Township Politics: Civic Struggles for a New South Africa. Mzwanele Mayekiso. (Illus.). 288p. (Orig.). (C). 1995. pap. text ed. 18.00 (*0-85345-966-5*) Monthly Rev.

Township Politics: Civic Struggles for a New South Africa. Mzwanele Mayekiso. (Illus.). 288p. (Orig.). (C). 1995. text ed. 15.00 (*0-85345-965-7*) Monthly Rev.

Township Thirty-Four, 7 vols., Set. Harold K. Hochschild. (Illus.). 1962. pap. 44.95 (*0-8156-8026-0*, Adirondack Mus) Syracuse U Pr.

Township Thirty-Four Series, 7 vols. rev. ed. Harold K. Hochschild. (Illus.). 1952. Set. boxed 44.95 (*0-910020-13-2*) Adirondack Mus.

Townships. Ed. by Michael Martone. LC 91-25925. (Bur Oak Original Ser.). (Illus.). 243p. 1992. 32.95 (*0-87745-354-3*); pap. 14.95 (*0-87745-355-1*) U of Iowa Pr.

***Townsite Settlement & Dispossession in the Cherokee Nation, 1866-1907.** Brad A. Bays. LC 97-17753. (Native Americans Ser.). 1997. write for info. (*0-8153-2912-1*) Garland.

Towpath. Arch Merrill. (Arch Merrill's New York Ser.: Vol. 4). (Illus.). 208p. 1989. reprint ed. pap. 12.95 (*1-55787-001-2*, 76038, Empire State Bks) Hrt of the Lakes.

Towpath Guide to the Chesapeake & Ohio Canal. Thomas F. Hahn. (Illus.). 226p. 1996. pap. 15.00 (*0-933788-66-5*) Am Canal & Transport.

Towpath to Freedom. Georgia A. Johnson. 144p. (Orig.). (YA). (gr. 9-12). 1988. pap. 7.95 (*0-9626450-0-1*) G A Johnson Pub.

Towpath Topsy: The Story of the Ohio Canal at Dresden. Leland Beers. Ed. & Intro. by Proctor Jones. LC 94-78060. 260p. (Orig.). (YA). 1994. pap. 9.95 (*1-885446-00-4*) Proctor Jones.

Towpaths to Tugboats, 1992: A History of American Canal Engineering. William H. Shank et al. 1995. 8.00 (*0-933788-40-1*) Am Canal & Transport.

Toxemia Explained. rev. ed. J. H. Tilden. 187p. 1960. reprint ed. spiral bd. 12.50 (*0-7873-1111-1*) Hlth Research.

Toxemia Explained: The True Interpretation of the Cause of Disease (1926) J. H. Tilden. 137p. 1996. pap. 16.95 (*1-56459-869-1*) Kessinger Pub.

Toxic. Robert W. Witt. LC 94-90553. 152p. (Orig.). (YA). 1995. pap. 10.00 (*1-56002-515-8*, Univ Edtns) Aegina Pr.

Toxic Action of Marine & Terrestrial Alkaloids. Ed. by Murray S. Blum. (Illus.). 328p. (C). 1995. text ed. 89.95 (*1-880293-04-8*) Alaken.

Toxic Air Emissions from Wastewater Treatment Facilities. Water Environment Federation Staff & American Society of Civil Engineers Staff. 220p. 1995. pap. 68.00 (*0-7844-0064-4*) Am Soc Civil Eng.

Toxic Air Emissions from Wastewater Treatment Facilities: A Special Publication. Ed. by Task Force on Air Toxics Staff. LC 93-50199. 1994. 45.00 (*1-881369-37-4*) Water Environ.

Toxic Air Pollution Handbook. Ed. by David R. Patrick. LC 93-21545. (Environmental Engineering Ser.). 1994. text ed. 114.95 (*0-442-00903-8*) Van Nos Reinhold.

Toxic & Carcinogenic Effects of Solid Particles in the Respiratory Tract. Ed. by Ulrich Mohr et al. LC 94-75676. (Illus.). 652p. 1994. 95.00 (*0-944398-14-6*) ILSI.

Toxic & Hazardous Industrial Chemicals Safety Manual. International Technical Information Institute Staff. 450p. 1995. pap. 119.00 (*0-318-04390-4*) Media Intl Promo.

Toxic & Hazardous Materials: A Sourcebook & Guide to Information Sources. Ed. by James K. Webster. LC 86-25710. 444p. 1987. text ed. 79.50 (*0-313-24575-4*, WTH/, Greenwood Pr) Greenwood.

***Toxic Anger.** Doyle W. Gentry. Date not set. write for info. (*0-688-15500-6*) Morrow.

Toxic Carpet, No. III. Glenn Beebe. 368p. 1991. pap. 12.95 (*0-9637095-0-X*) AOPR.

Toxic Chemical & Explosives Facilities: Safety & Engineering Design. LC 79-9760. (Symposium Ser.: No. 96). 1979. 43.95 (*0-8412-0481-0*) Am Chemical.

***Toxic Chemical & Explosives Facilities: Safety & Engineering Design.** Ed. by Ralph A. Scott, Jr. LC 79-9760. (ACS Symposium Ser.: Vol. 96). 361p. 1979. reprint ed. pap. 102.90 (*0-608-03092-9*, 2063544) Bks Demand.

Toxic Chemical Emissions: A Compliance Guide for the Community Right-to-Know Act. W. Randy Kubetin. 1988. 60.00 (*0-87179-995-2*) BNA Plus.

Toxic Chemical Release Inventory: Directory of Public Libraries. 162p. (Orig.). (C). 1993. pap. text ed. 30.00 (*1-56806-528-0*) DIANE Pub.

Toxic Chemicals, Health & the Environment. Ed. by Lester B. Lave & Arthur C. Upton. LC 86-46276. (Johns Hopkins Series in Environmental Toxicology). 336p. 1987. pap. text ed. 18.95 (*0-8018-3474-0*) Johns Hopkins.

Toxic Chemicals in the Workplace: A Manager's Guide to: Recognition - Evaluation - Control. T. M. Fraser. 192p. 1996. pap. 18.95 (*0-88415-871-3*, 5871) Gulf Pub.

Toxic Circles: Environmental Hazards from the Workplace into the Community. Ed. by Helen E. Sheehan & Richard P. Wedeen. LC 92-48258. (Illus.). 290p. (C). 1993. text ed. 45.00 (*0-8135-1990-X*) Rutgers U Pr.

Toxic Cities: And the Fight to Save the Kurnell Peninsula. Gary J. Smith. 165p. 1990. pap. 22.95 (*0-86840-204-4*, Pub. by New South Wales Univ Pr AT) Intl Spec Bk.

Toxic Compounds of Foods. Pavidek. 280p. 1995. 184.00 (*0-8493-4623-1*) CRC Pr.

Toxic Contaminants & Ecosystem Health: A Great Lakes Focus. Ed. by Marlene S. Evans. LC 87-22996. (Advances in Environmental Science & Technology Ser.). 602p. 1988. text ed. 199.00 (*0-471-85556-1*) Wiley.

Toxic Contamination in Large Lakes, Vol. I. Norbert W. Schmidtke. 1988. 84.00 (*0-87371-089-4*, L089) Lewis Pubs.

Toxic Contamination in Large Lakes, Vol. II. Norbert W. Schmidtke. 1988. 84.00 (*0-87371-090-8*, L090) Lewis Pubs.

Toxic Contamination in Large Lakes, Vol. III. Norbert W. Schmidtke. 1988. 84.00 (*0-87371-091-6*, L091) Lewis Pubs.

Toxic Contamination in Large Lakes, Vol. IV. Norbert W. Schmidtke. 1988. 84.00 (*0-87371-092-4*, L092) Lewis Pubs.

Toxic Cops. D. J. Arneson. LC 90-13102. (Venture Bks.). (Illus.). 112p. (YA). (gr. 7-12). 1991. lib. bdg. 22.00 (*0-531-12525-4*) Watts.

Toxic Debts & the Superfund Dilemma. Harold C. Barnett. LC 93-32059. xviii, 334p. (C). 1994. text ed. 49.95 (*0-8078-2124-1*); pap. text ed. 19.95 (*0-8078-4435-7*) U of NC Pr.

***Toxic Deception: How the Chemical Industry Manipulates Science, Subverts the Law & Threatens Your Health.** Marianne Lavelle & Dan Fagin. LC 96-41045. (Illus.). 336p. 1996. 24.95 (*1-55972-385-8*, Birch Ln Pr) Carol Pub Group.

Toxic Emergencies. Ed. by William Hanson, Jr. LC 84-7615. (Clinics in Emergency Medicine Ser.: No. 5). 331p. reprint ed. pap. 94.40 (*0-7837-6261-5*, 2045973) Bks Demand.

***Toxic Faith: Understanding the Fine Line Between Healthy Faith & Spiritual Abuse.** Stephen Arterburn & Jack Felton. LC 97-21648. 320p. 1997. pap. 12.99 (*0-7852-7221-6*) Nelson.

Toxic Fame: Celebrities Speak on Stardom. Joey Berlin & Furtaw. LC 96-2885. (Illus.). 450p. 1996. 19.95 (*0-7876-0874-2*) Visible Ink Pr.

Toxic Food: What You Need to Know to Feed Your Family Safely. Carl Lowe & Philip Lief Group Inc. Staff. 128p. 1990. mass mkt. 3.95 (*0-380-76001-0*) Avon.

***Toxic Friends.** Florence Isaacs. Date not set. write for info. (*0-688-15442-5*) Morrow.

***Toxic Gas Monitors.** Richard K. Miller et al. (Market Research Survey Ser.: No. 255). 50p. 1996. 200.00 (*1-55865-273-6*) Future Tech Surveys.

Toxic Gas Releases in Earthquakes: Existing Programs, Sources, & Mitigation Strategies. 374p. 1991. ring bd. 20.00 (*0-317-05679-4*, P91002EQK) Assn Bay Area.

Toxic, Hazardous, & Title 3 Air Pollutants. Gerald A. Rich. 320p. 1995. 29.95 (*0-934165-56-4*, 6556X) Gulf Pub.

Toxic Immune Syndrome Cookbook: Yeast-Free Hypoallergenic Recipes to Support Your Immune System. rev. ed. William R. Kellas. (Illus.). 192p. 1995. pap. 16.95 (*0-9636491-0-8*) Comprehen Hlth.

Toxic Injury of the Liver, 2 pts., Pt. A. Ed. by Emmanuel Farber & Murray M. Fisher. LC 79-17469. (Liver, Normal Function & Disease Ser.: No. 2). (Illus.). 496p. reprint ed. pap. 134.00 (*0-7837-0627-8*, 2040971) Bks Demand.

An Asterisk (*) at the beginning of an entry indicates that the title is appearing in BIP for the first time.

Toxic Injury of the Liver, 2 pts., Pt. B. Ed. by Emmanuel Farber & Murray M. Fisher. LC 79-17469. (Liver, Normal Function & Disease Ser.: No. 2). (Illus.). 410p. reprint ed. pap. 116.90 (*0-7837-0628-6*) Bks Demand.

Toxic Leaders: When Organizations Go Bad. Marcia L. Whicker. LC 95-44311. 200p. 1996. text ed. 55.00 (*0-89930-998-4*, Quorum Bks) Greenwood.

Toxic Leak! Russell Wright. (Event-Based Science Ser.: 570H50). (Illus.). (Orig.). 1996. teacher ed., text ed. 19. 95 incl. vhs (*0-201-49436-1*) Addison-Wesley.

Toxic Leak! Russell Wright. Ed. by Katarina Stenstedt. (Event-Based Science Ser.). (Illus.). (Orig.). (YA). (gr. 6-9). 1996. wbk. ed., pap. text ed. 7.95 (*0-201-49433-7*) Addison-Wesley.

Toxic Leak!, Class Set. Russell Wright. (Event-Based Science Ser.). (Illus.). (Orig.). (J). (gr. 6-9). 1995. teacher ed., wbk. ed., pap. text ed. 115.00 (*0-201-49437-X*) Addison-Wesley.

Toxic Literacies: Controlling the Minds & Imagination of the American People. Denny Taylor. LC 96-21843. 1996. 24.95 (*0-435-08137-3*) Heinemann.

Toxic Love: A Chilling True Story of Twisted Passion & Death. Tomas Guillen. 368p. 1995. mass mkt. 5.99 (*0-440-21793-8*) Dell.

***Toxic Love: The Illusion of Self-Worth.** Malcolm Smith. Date not set. mass mkt. 3.99 (*1-880089-12-2*) Albury Pub.

Toxic Materials. Richard Amdur. (Earth at Risk Ser.). (Illus.). 112p. (J). (gr. 5 up). 1993. lib. bdg. 19.95 (*0-7910-1574-2*) Chelsea Hse.

Toxic Materials in the Atmosphere, Sampling & Analysis, Vol. STP 786. Ed. by B. Himmelsbach. 174p. 1982. 26. 00 (*0-8031-0603-3*, 04-786000-17) ASTM.

Toxic Metal Chemistry in Marine Environments. Ed. by Sadiq. (Environmental Science & Pollution Ser.: Vol. 1). 400p. 1992. 155.00 (*0-8247-8647-5*) Dekker.

Toxic Metal Syndrome: How Metal Poisonings Can Affect Your Brain. H. Richard Casdorph & Morton Walker. LC 94-28053. 430p. pap. 14.95 (*0-89529-649-7*) Avery Pub.

Toxic Metals & Their Analysis. Eleanor Berman. LC 79-41781. (Heyden International Topics in Science Ser.). (Illus.). 303p. reprint ed. pap. 86.40 (*0-317-58705-6*, 2029641) Bks Demand.

Toxic Metals in Soil-Plant Systems. Ed. by S. M. Ross. 400p. 1994. text ed. 165.00 (*0-471-94279-0*) Wiley.

Toxic Microcystis. Ed. by M. F. Watanabe et al. LC 95-15052. 304p. 1995. 209.95 (*0-8493-7693-9*, 7693) CRC Pr.

Toxic Nation: That Fight to Save Our Communities from Chemical Contamination. Fred Setterberg & Lonny Shavelson. 320p. 1993. text ed. 22.95 (*0-471-57545-3*) Wiley.

Toxic Nephropathies: Proceedings. Congress on Toxic Nephropathies, 6th, Parma, June 1977. Ed. by G. M. Berlyne et al. (Contributions to Nephrology Ser.: Vol. 10). (Illus.). 1978. 39.25 (*3-8055-2832-9*) S Karger.

Toxic Nightmare: Ecocide in the U. S. S. R. & Eastern Europe. Gary E. McCuen. Ed. by Ronald P. Swanson. (Ideas in Conflict Ser.). (Illus.). 134p. 1993. lib. bdg. 12. 95 (*0-86596-090-9*) G E M.

Toxic Oil Syndrome: Current Knowledge & Future Perspectives. (WHO Regional Publications, European Ser.: No. 42). xvii, 163p. (ENG & SPA.). 1992. pap. text ed. 31.00 (*92-890-1305-2*, 1310042) World Health.

***Toxic Oil Syndrome Mass Food Poisoning in Spain.** 1984. pap. text ed. 12.00 (*92-890-1021-5*) World Health.

Toxic Organic Chemicals in Porous Media. Ed. by Z. Gerstl et al. (Ecological Studies: Vol. 73). (Illus.). 250p. 1989. 119.00 (*0-387-50799-X*) Spr-Verlag.

Toxic Organic Vapors in the Workplace: Collection & Analysis. Frank E. Jones. 224p. 1993. 66.95 (*0-87371-900-X*, L900) Lewis Pubs.

Toxic Parents: Overcoming Their Hurtful Legacy & Reclaiming Your Life. Susan Foward & Craig Buck. 336p. 1990. mass mkt. 6.99 (*0-553-28434-7*) Bantam.

***Toxic People.** Glass. LC 96-48919. 1997. pap. 14.95 (*0-312-15232-9*) St Martin.

Toxic People: 10 Ways Dealing with People Who Make Your Life Miserable. Glass. 1995. 22.00 (*0-671-89028-X*) S&S Trade.

Toxic People: 10 Ways of Dealing with People Who Make Your Life Miserable. Lillian Glass. LC 95-1431. 1995. 22.00 (*0-684-80315-1*) S&S Trade.

Toxic Phytoplankton Blooms in the Sea: Proceedings of the Fifth International Conference on Toxic Marine Phytoplankton, Newport, Rhode Island, United States, 28 October-1 November 1991. Ed. by Theodore J. Smayda & Yuzuru Shimizu. LC 93-18985. (Developments in Marine Biology Ser.: Vol. 3). 976p. 1993. 255.75 (*0-444-89719-4*) Elsevier.

Toxic Plants. Ed. by A. Douglas Kinghorn. LC 79-16180. 1979. text ed. 48.50 (*0-231-04686-3*) Col U Pr.

Toxic Politics: Responding to Chemical Disasters. Michael R. Reich. LC 91-55054. 392p. 1991. 47.50 (*0-8014-2434-8*); pap. 18.95 (*0-8014-9986-0*) Cornell U Pr.

Toxic Properties Handbook of Monomers & Additives. Victor O. Sheftel. 384p. 1995. 85.00 (*1-56670-075-2*, L1075) Lewis Pubs.

Toxic Properties of Pesticides. Ed. by Nicholas P. Cheremisinoff & King. (Environmental Science & Pollution Ser.: Vol. 12). 344p. 1994. 135.00 (*0-8247-9253-X*) Dekker.

Toxic Psychiatry: Why Therapy, Empathy & Love Must Replace the Drugs, Electroshock Therapy & Biochemical Theories of the "New Psychiatry" Peter R. Breggin. 480p. 1994. pap. 15.95 (*0-312-11366-8*) St Martin.

Toxic Psychiatry Vol. 1: Psychiatry's Assault on the Brain with Drugs & Electroshock. Peter R. Breggin. LC 91-113. 1991. 24.95 (*0-312-05975-2*) St Martin.

Toxic Revenge. Franklin W. Dixon. (Hardy Boys Ser.: No. 83). (YA). (gr. 6 up). 1994. mass mkt. 3.99 (*0-671-79467-1*, Archway) PB.

Toxic Risks: Science, Regulation, & Perception. Ronald E. Gots. 288p. 1992. 59.95 (*0-87371-510-1*, L510) Lewis Pubs.

Toxic Shock Syndrome. Merlin S. Bergdoll & P. Joan Chesney. (Illus.). 240p. 1990. 129.00 (*0-8493-6671-2*, R) CRC Pr.

Toxic Shock Syndrome: Assessment of Current Information & Future Research Needs: Report of a Study. Institute of Medicine (U. S.), Division of Health Sciences Policy Staff. LC 82-60420. (Publication IOM Ser.: No. 82-02). 126p. reprint ed. pap. 36.00 (*0-8357-6820-1*, 2035502) Bks Demand.

Toxic Sludge Is Good for You! Lies, Damn Lies & the Public Relations Industry. John Stauber & Sheldon Rampton. (Illus.). 240p. (C). 1995. 29.95 (*1-56751-061-2*); pap. text ed. 16.95 (*1-56751-060-4*) Common Courage.

Toxic Struggles: The Theory & Practice of Environmental Justice. Ed. by Richard Hofrichter. 272p. 1993. pap. 16. 95 (*0-86571-270-0*); lib. bdg. 39.95 (*0-86571-269-7*) New Soc Pubs.

Toxic Substance Storage Tank Containment. Ecology & Environment, Inc. Staff. LC 84-22697. (Pollution Technology Review Ser.: No. 116). (Illus.). 274p. 1985. 36.00 (*0-8155-1018-7*) Noyes.

Toxic Substances: Crop Plants. D'Mello. 1991. 160.00 (*0-85186-863-0*) CRC Pr.

Toxic Substances & Human Risk: Principles of Data Interpretation. Ed. by Robert G. Tardiff & Joseph V. Rodricks. LC 87-18660. (Life Science Monographs). (Illus.). 460p. 1987. 105.00 (*0-306-42529-7*, Plenum Pr) Plenum.

Toxic Substances & Mental Retardation: Neurobehavioral Toxicology & Teratology. Ed. by S. Schroeder. LC 87-1776. (Monographs of the American Association on Mental Retardation: No. 8). 188p. (C). 1987. pap. 8.00 (*0-940898-15-2*) Am Assn Mental.

Toxic Substances Control Act: Legislative Changes Could Make the Act More Effective. (Illus.). 68p. (Orig.). (C). 1994. pap. text ed. 25.00 (*0-7881-1514-6*) DIANE Pub.

Toxic Substances Control Act Compliance Guide & Service, 3 vols. John R. Wheeler. LC 88-80678. 1200p. 1997. 495.00 (*0-945940-88-2*) Environment Bks.

Toxic Substances Controls Guide. 2nd ed. Mary D. Worobec & Cheryl Hogue. LC 92-17102. 273p. 1992. pap. 45.00 (*0-87179-752-6*, 0752) BNA Books.

Toxic Substances in Agricultural Water Supply & Drainage, 3 vols. 1989. Set. 90.00 (*0-685-56567-X*) US Comm Irrigation.

Toxic Substances in Agricultural Water Supply & Drainage: Defining the Problems, Proceedings of the USCID Regional Meetings, 1986. 372p. 1986. 40.00 (*0-9618257-0-7*) US Comm Irrigation.

Toxic Substances in Agricultural Water Supply & Drainage - An International Environmental Perspective: Proceedings of the Second Pan-American Regional Conference on Irrigation & Drainage. 1989. 40.00 (*0-9618257-4-X*) US Comm Irrigation.

Toxic Substances in Agricultural Water Supply & Drainage - Searching for Solutions: Proceedings of the USCID 1987 National Meeting. Ed. by Susan S. Anderson & Joseph B. Summers. 176p. (Orig.). 1988. pap. 36.00 (*0-9618257-2-3*) US Comm Irrigation.

Toxic Substances in Municipal Wastewaters. Ruffier. 240p. 1991. 66.95 (*0-87371-533-0*, L533) Lewis Pubs.

Toxic Substances in the Environment. Bettina M. Francis. LC 92-26896. (Environmental Science & Technology Ser.). 360p. 1994. text ed. 52.95 (*0-471-50781-4*) Wiley.

Toxic Terror: The Truth Behind the Cancer Scares. Elizabeth M. Whelan. (Consumer Health Ser.). 476p. (C). 1993. 27.95 (*0-87975-788-4*) Prometheus Bks.

Toxic Threat: How Hazardous Substances Poison Our Lives. rev. ed. Stephen J. Zipko. Ed. by Jane Steltenpohl. (Illus.). 208p. (YA). (gr. 7 up). 1990. pap. 5.95 (*0-671-69331-X*, Julian Messner) Silver Burdett Pr.

***Toxic Tort & Hazardous Substance Litigation.** L. Neal Ellis, Jr. & Charles D. Case. 702p. 1995. 105.00 (*1-55834-257-5*, 61676) MICHIE.

***Toxic Tort Annual: 1996.** (Annual Ser.). 500p. 1996. 95.00 (*0-9636246-1-X*) Andrews Pubns.

Toxic Tort Case Essentials: Strategies, Experts, Motions, & ADR. (Litigation & Administrative Practice Course Handbook, 1983-84 Ser.: Vol. 446). 600p. 1992. 70.00 (*0-685-65524-5*, H4-5144) PLI.

Toxic Tort Litigation Manual. Michael Dore. 1988. pap. 125.00 (*0-87632-623-8*) Clark Boardman Callaghan.

Toxic Torts. Charles Pugh & Martyn Day. (Environmental Law Ser.). 220p. 1992. pap. 80.00 (*1-874698-00-7*, Pub. by Cameron May UK) Gaunt.

Toxic Torts: A Complete Personal Injury Guide, 2 vols. Larry Cetrulo. 1993. ring bd. 240.00 (*0-685-68855-0*) Clark Boardman Callaghan.

Toxic Torts: Litigation of Hazardous Substance Cases. Gary Z. Nothstein. LC 83-27128. (Trial Practice Ser.). 776p. 1984. text ed. 95.00 (*0-07-047454-0*) Shepards.

Toxic Torts & Product Liability: Changing Tactics for Changing Times. Ed. by Michael A. Brown. LC 89-7365. 1989. 95.00 (*1-55871-117-1*, BSP 102) BNA Plus.

Toxic Torts by Government. Bruce L. Benson. (Independent Policy Reports). 52p. (Orig.). 1996. pap. 6.95 (*0-945999-53-4*) Independent Inst.

Toxic Torts Deskbook. Madden. 240p. 1992. 84.95 (*0-87371-508-X*, L508) Lewis Pubs.

Toxic Torts in a Nutshell. Jean M. Eggen. LC 95-36804. (Nutshell Ser.). 361p. 1995. pap. 17.50 (*0-314-06542-3*) West Pub.

Toxic Trends: Are These Subtle Delusions Controlling Your Life? Madlyn L. Hamblin & Cari Haus. LC 96-13494. 1996. pap. 4.99 (*0-8163-1336-9*) Pacific Pr Pub Assn.

Toxic Waste. Jenkins. (Troubled Society Ser.: Set II). (YA). 1991. 12.95 (*0-86593-111-9*) Rourke Corp.

Toxic Waste: A Bibliography. Ed. by Joan Nordquist. (Contemporary Social Issues: A Bibliographic Ser.: No. 11). 60p. (Orig.). 1988. pap. 15.00 (*0-937855-21-9*) Ref Rsch Serv.

Toxic Waste: New Strategies for Controlling Toxic Contamination. Ed. by Bruce W. Piasecki. LC 83-24510. (Quorum Ser.). (Illus.). xix, 239p. 1984. text ed. 59.95 (*0-89930-056-1*, PIT/, Quorum Bks) Greenwood.

Toxic Waste Management. Englande & Eckenfelder. (Water Science & Technology Ser.). 298p. 1992. pap. 126.00 (*0-08-042046-X*, Pergamon Pr) Elsevier.

Toxic Waste Minimization in the Printed Circuit Board Industry. T. J. Nunno et al. LC 88-22630. (Pollution Technology Review Ser.: No. 162). (Illus.). 162p. 1989. 39.00 (*0-8155-1183-3*) Noyes.

Toxic Waste Time Bomb. LC 91-50342. (Environment Alert! Ser.). (Illus.). 32p. (J). (gr. 3-8). 1993. lib. bdg. 18. 60 (*0-8368-0699-9*) Gareth Stevens Inc.

Toxic Wastes. J. M. Patten. (Eye On the Environment Ser.). (J). (gr. 2-6). 1995. write for info. (*1-55916-100-0*) Rourke Bk Co.

Toxic Wastes: The Fouling of America. Knowledge Unlimited Staff. (Illus.). 24p. (J). (gr. 4-12). 1984. teacher ed. 27.00 incl. audio, flmstrp (*0-915291-31-2*) Know Unltd.

***Toxic Work.** Barbara B. Reinhold. 1997. pap. 12.95 (*0-452-27275-0*, Plume) NAL-Dutton.

Toxic Work: Overcoming Stress, Overload, & Burnout & Revitalizing Your Career. Ed. by Barbara B. Reinhold. LC 95-26490. 288p. 1996. pap. 23.95 (*0-525-93875-3*, Dutton) NAL-Dutton.

Toxic Work: Women Workers at GTE Lenkurt. Steve Fox. (Labor & Social Change Ser.). (C). 1991. 39.95 (*0-87722-816-7*) Temple U Pr.

Toxic Work: Women Workers at GTE Lenkurt. Steve Fox. (Labor & Social Change Ser.). (C). 1992. pap. 16.95 (*0-87722-895-7*) Temple U Pr.

***Toxicants in the Aqueous Ecosystem.** T. R. Crompton. LC 96-37346. 1997. write for info. (*0-471-97272-X*) Wiley.

Toxicants of Plant Origin, 4 Vols. Peter R. Cheeke. 288p. 1989. Vol. II, 304p. 228.95 (*0-8493-6991-6*, SF757) CRC Pr.

Toxicants of Plant Origin, 4 Vols., Vol. I. Peter R. Cheeke. 336p. 1989. 242.00 (*0-8493-6990-8*, SF757) CRC Pr.

Toxicants of Plant Origin, 4 Vols., Vol. III. Peter R. Cheeke. 288p. 1989. 216.95 (*0-8493-6992-4*) CRC Pr.

Toxicants of Plant Origin, 4 Vols., Vol. IV. Peter R. Cheeke. 240p. 1989. 207.00 (*0-8493-6993-2*, SF757) CRC Pr.

Toxicity & Metabolism of Explosives. Jehuda Yinon. 192p. 1990. 121.95 (*0-8493-5128-6*, RA1270) CRC Pr.

Toxicity of Anticancer Drugs: A Study in Human Toxicity. Ed. by Garth Powis & M. Hackar. 256p. 1991. text ed. 55.00 (*0-07-105305-0*, Pub. by PPI UK) McGraw.

Toxicity of Heavy Metals, Pt. 1. Oehme. (Hazardous & Toxic Substances Ser.: Vol. 2). 528p. 1978. 190.00 (*0-8247-6718-7*) Dekker.

Toxicity of Heavy Metals in the Environment, Pt. 2. Oehme. (Hazardous & Toxic Substances Ser.: Vol. 2). 472p. 1979. 190.00 (*0-8247-6719-5*) Dekker.

Toxicity of Hormones in Perinatal Life. Ed. by Takao Mori & Hiroshi Nagasawa. 208p. 1988. 114.00 (*0-8493-6862-6*, RG627, CRC Reprint) Franklin.

Toxicity of Houseplants. Ed. by David G. Spoerke & Susan C. Smolinske. 635p. 1990. 205.95 (*0-8493-6655-0*, RA1250) CRC Pr.

Toxicity of Methyl Mercury. Ed. by Christine U. Eccles & Zoltan Annau. LC 86-46278. (Johns Hopkins Series in Environmental Toxicology). 256p. 1987. text ed. 70.00 (*0-8018-3449-X*) Johns Hopkins.

Toxicity of Nitroaromatic Compounds. Ed. by Douglas E. Rickert. LC 84-8937. (Chemical Industry Institute of Toxicology Ser.). (Illus.). 295p. 1985. 104.00 (*0-89116-304-2*) Hemisp Pub.

Toxicity of Pesticides to Fish, Vol. I. Ed. by A. S. Murty. 192p. 1986. 111.00 (*0-8493-6058-7*, SH174) CRC Pr.

Toxicity of Pesticides to Fish, Vol. II. Ed. by A. S. Murty. 192p. 1986. 92.00 (*0-8493-6059-5*, SH174) CRC Pr.

Toxicity of Plutonium, Americium & Curium. J. C. Nenot & J. W. Stather. (Commission of the European Communities Ser.: EUR 6157). (Illus.). 1979. pap. 103. 00 (*0-08-023440-2*, Pub. by Pergamon Repr UK) Franklin.

Toxicity Reduction, Vol. 3: Evaluation & Control. Ed. by Davis L. Ford. LC 92-53519. (Water Quality Management Library). 350p. 1992. text ed. 89.95 (*0-87762-905-6*) Technomic.

Toxicity Screening Procedures Using Bacterial Systems. Liu & Dutka. (Drug & Chemical Toxicology Ser.: Vol. 1). 496p. 1984. 185.00 (*0-8247-7171-0*) Dekker.

Toxicity Testing: New Approaches & Applications in Human Risk Assessment. fac. ed. Ed. by Albert P. Li et al. LC 84-27634. 300p. pap. 85.50 (*0-7837-7281-5*, 2047025) Bks Demand.

Toxicity Testing: Strategies to Determine Needs & Priorities. National Research Council Staff. 382p. 1984. pap. text ed. 34.95 (*0-309-03433-7*) Natl Acad Pr.

Toxicity Testing Digest. 150p. 1992. pap. 55.00 (*1-881369-17-X*) Water Environ.

Toxicity Testing of Dental Materials. Ed. by Harold R. Stanley. 176p. 1985. 104.00 (*0-8493-5916-3*, RA1270, CRC Reprint) Franklin.

Toxicity Testing Using Microorganisms, Vol. I. Bernard J. Dutka & Gabriel Bitton. 168p. 1986. 103.00 (*0-8493-5256-8*, RA1199, CRC Reprint) Franklin.

Toxicity Testing Using Microorganisms, Vol. II. Bernard J. Dutka & Gabriel Bitton. 240p. 1986. 123.00 (*0-8493-5257-6*, RA1199, CRC Reprint) Franklin.

Toxicokinetics & New Drug Development. Avraham Yacobi. 1989. text ed. 50.00 (*0-07-105333-6*) McGraw.

Toxicologic & Pharmacologic Principles in Pediatrics. Sam Kacew & Simon Lock. 310p. 1988. 94.95 (*0-89116-631-9*) Hemisp Pub.

***Toxicologic Assessment of the Army's Zinc Cadmium Sulfide Dispersion Tests.** 350p. 1997. pap. 49.00 (*0-309-05783-3*) Natl Acad Pr.

Toxicological Analysis. 2nd ed. Muller. LC 70-31715. Date not set. write for info. (*0-471-91846-6*) Wiley.

***Toxicological & Performance Aspects of Oxygenated Motor Vehicle Fuels.** National Research Council Staff. 176p. (Orig.). 1996. pap. text ed. 35.00 (*0-309-05545-8*) Natl Acad Pr.

***Toxicological Appraisal of Halogenated Aromatic Compounds Following Groundwater Pollution: Report on a WHO Working Group.** (EURO Nonserial Publication Ser.). 58p. 1980. 8.00 (*92-9020-196-7*, 1340001) World Health.

Toxicological Aspects of Energy Production. Charles L. Sanders. 256p. (C). 1985. 38.95 (*0-02-948960-1*, Free Press) Free Pr.

Toxicological Chemistry: A Guide to Toxic Substances in Chemistry. Stanley E. Manahan. (Illus.). 310p. 1988. 76.00 (*0-87371-149-1*, RA1219) Lewis Pubs.

Toxicological Chemistry: A Guide to Toxic Substances in Chemistry. 2nd ed. Stanley E. Manahan. (Illus.). 464p. 1992. 74.95 (*0-87371-621-3*, L621) Lewis Pubs.

***Toxicological Evaluation of Certain Food Additives: Fourty-Sixth Meeting of the Joint FAO/WHO Expert Committee on Food Additives (JECFA)** WHO Staff. (WHO Food Additives Ser.: No. 37). 106p. 1996. 45.00 (*92-4-166037-6*) World Health.

Toxicological Evaluation of Certain Food Additives & Contaminants. Contrib. by FAO-WHO Expert Committie on Food Additives (JECFA) Staff. (WHO Food Additives Ser.: No. 32). vii, 301p. 1993. pap. text ed. 45.00 (*92-4-166032-5*, 1270032) World Health.

Toxicological Evaluation of Certain Food Additives & Contaminants, 22. FAO-WHO Expert Committee on Food Additives. (Illus.). 298p. 1988. pap. text ed. 44.95 (*0-521-36928-2*) Cambridge U Pr.

Toxicological Evaluation of Certain Food Additives & Contaminants, Vol. 21. Joint FAO-WHO Expert Committee on Food Additives Staff. 282p. 1987. pap. 42.95 (*0-521-35985-6*) Cambridge U Pr.

Toxicological Evaluation of Certain Food Additives & Contaminants: Prepared by the 33rd Meeting of the Joint FAO-WHO Expert Committee on Food Additives. Joint FAO-WHO Expert Committee on Food Additives Staff. (WHO Food Additives Ser.: No. 24). 362p. (C). 1989. pap. 37.95 (*0-521-38894-5*) Cambridge U Pr.

***Toxicological Evaluation of Certain Food Additives & Contaminants: 35th Meeting of the Joint FAO/WHO Expert Committee on Food Additives.** WHO Staff. (WHO Food Additives Ser.: No. 26). 198p. 1990. 22.00 (*92-4-166026-0*) World Health.

***Toxicological Evaluation of Certain Food Additives & Contaminants: 44th Meeting of the Joint FAO-WHO Expert Committee on Food Additives (JECFA)** (Food Additives Ser.: Vol. 35). 465p. 1996. pap. 80.00 (*92-4-166035-X*, 1270035) World Health.

Toxicological Evaluation of Certain Food Additives & Naturally Occurring Toxicants. Contrib. by FAO-WHO Expert Committee on Food Additives. (WHO Food Additives Ser.: No. 30). vii, 399p. 1993. pap. text ed. 45. 00 (*92-4-166030-9*, 1270030) World Health.

Toxicological Evaluation of Certain Veterinary Drug Residues in Food. Contrib. by FAO-WHO Expert Committee on Food Additives. (WHO Food Additives Ser.: No. 27). vii, 227p. 1991. pap. text ed. 25.00 (*92-4-166027-9*, 1270027) World Health.

Toxicological Evaluation of Certain Veterinary Drug Residues in Food. Contrib. by FAO-WHO Expert Committee on Food Additives. (WHO Food Additives Ser.: No. 29). vii, 237p. 1992. pap. text ed. 40.00 (*92-4-166029-5*, 1270029) World Health.

Toxicological Evaluation of Certain Veterinary Drug Residues in Food. Contrib. by FAO-WHO Expert Committee on Food Additives. (WHO Food Additives Ser.: No. 31). vii, 216p. 1993. pap. text ed. 40.00 (*92-4-166031-7*, 1270031) World Health.

Toxicological Evaluation of Certain Veterinary Drug Residues in Food. Contrib. by FAO-WHO Expert Committee on Food Additives. (WHO Food Additives Ser.: No. 33). vi, 152p. 1994. pap. text ed. 40.00 (*92-4-166033-3*, 1270033) World Health.

Toxicological Evaluation of Certain Veterinary Drug Residues in Food. Contrib. by Forty-Third Meeting of Joint FAO-WHO Expert Committee of Food Additives (JECFA) Staff. (WHO Food Additives Ser.: No. 34). vi, 173p. 1995. pap. text ed. 45.00 (*92-4-166034-1*, 1270034) World Health.

***Toxicological Evaluation of Certain Veterinary Drug Residues in Food: Meeting of the Joint FAO/WHO Expert Committee on Food Additives (JECFA)** WHO Staff. (WHO Food Additives Ser.: No. 39). 1997. 45.00 (*92-4-166039-2*) World Health.

***Toxicological Evaluation of Certain Veterinary Drug Residues in Food: 34th Meeting of the Joint FAO/WHO Expert Committee on Food Additives.** WHO Staff. (WHO Food Additives Ser.: No. 25). 175p. 1990. 22.00 (*92-4-166025-2*) World Health.

T

An Asterisk (*) at the beginning of an entry indicates that the title is appearing in BIP for the first time.

***Toxicological Evaluation of Certain Veterinary Drug Residues in Food: 45th Meeting of the Joint FAO-WHO Expert Committee on Food Additives (JECFA)** (Food Additives Ser.: Vol. 36). 157p. 1996. pap. 45.00 (*92-4-166036-8*, 1270036) World Health.

Toxicological Evaluation of Some Enzymes, Modified Starches & Certain Other Substances. FAO-WHO Expert Committee on Food Additives. (WHO Food Additives Ser.: Vol. 1). 109p. 1972. pap. text ed. 5.40 (*92-4-166001-5*, 1270001) World Health.

Toxicological Evaluation of Some Food Colours, Enzymes, Flavour Enhancers, Thickening Agents & Certain Other Food Additives. (Food Additive Ser.: No. 6). 1975. pap. text ed. 13.00 (*92-4-166006-6*, 1270006) World Health.

Toxicological Evaluation of Some Food Colours, Thickening Agents & Certain Other Substances. (Food Additive Ser.: No. 8). 1975. pap. text ed. 12.00 (*92-4-166008-2*, 1270008) World Health.

Toxicological Evaluations Vol. 2: Potential Health Hazards of Existing Chemicals. Ed. by B. G. Chemie. (Illus.). 224p. 1991. 64.95 (*0-387-53435-0*) Spr-Verlag.

***Toxicological Evaluations Vol. 11: Potential Health Hazards of Existing Chemicals.** Ed. by Berufsgenossenschaft der Chemischen Industrie Staff. (Illus.). vi, 180p. 1997. 52.00 (*3-540-61391-9*) Spr-Verlag.

Toxicological Evaluations Four: Potential Health Hazards of Existing Chemicals. BG Chemie Staff. (Illus.). 336p. 1992. 62.95 (*0-387-54984-6*) Spr-Verlag.

Toxicological Evaluations Three: Potential Health Hazards of Existing Chemicals. Ed. by B. G. Chemie. (Illus.). 192p. 1991. 54.95 (*0-387-54331-7*) Spr-Verlag.

Toxicological Evaluations VII: Potential Health Hazards of Existing Chemicals. Ed. by BG Chemie Staff. 205p. 1994. 62.95 (*0-387-57300-3*) Spr-Verlag.

***Toxicological Evaluations 10.** 268p. 1996. 59.95 (*3-540-60683-1*) Spr-Verlag.

Toxicological Evaluations 5: Potential Health Hazards of Existing Chemicals. Ed. by B. G. Chemie. vii, 193p. 1993. 62.95 (*0-387-56138-2*) Spr-Verlag.

Toxicological Evaluations 6: Potential Health Hazards of Existing Chemicals. 244p. 1993. 62.95 (*0-387-56980-4*) Spr-Verlag.

Toxicological Evaluations 8: Potential Health Hazards of Existing Chemicals. Ed. by B. G. Chemie & Heidelberg. 300p. 1994. 62.95 (*0-387-58287-8*) Spr-Verlag.

Toxicological Evaluations 9: Potential Health Hazards of Existing Chemicals. Ed. by B. G. Chemie. (Illus.). 171p. 1995. 53.95 (*3-540-59148-6*) Spr-Verlag.

Toxicological Problems see Pharmacology & the Future of Man: Proceedings of the International Congress on Pharmacology, 5th, San Francisco, 1972

Toxicological Profile for Mercury. 1995. lib. bdg. 299.75 (*0-8490-8378-8*) Gordon Pr.

Toxicological Risk Assessment: Biological & Statistical Criteria, 2 vols., Vol. I. D. Krewski & D. B. Clayson. Ed. by I. C. Munro et al. 244p. 1985. 138.00 (*0-8493-5976-7*, RA1199, CRC Reprint) Franklin.

Toxicological Risk Assessment: Biological & Statistical Criteria, 2 vols., Vol. II. Ed. by I. C. Munro et al. LC 84-12679. 276p. 1985. 156.00 (*0-8493-5977-5*, RA1199, CRC Reprint) Franklin.

Toxicologist As Expert Witness: A Hint Book For Courtroom Procedure. Arthur Furst. LC 96-21820. 150p. 1996. 59.95 (*1-56032-531-3*) Taylor & Francis.

Toxicologist As Expert Witness: A Hint Book for Courtroom Procedure. Arthur Furst. 150p. 1996. pap. 24.95 (*1-56032-590-9*) Hemisp Pub.

***Toxicology.** 1994. 160.00 (*1-56238-204-7*, SC13-L) Natl Comm Clin Lab Stds.

Toxicology. Ford. 1998. text ed. write for info. (*0-7216-5485-1*) Saunders.

Toxicology. Ed. by Thomas J. Haley & William O. Berndt. 697p. 1988. pap. 74.95 (*0-89116-810-9*) Hemisp Pub.

Toxicology. Gary D. Osweiler. LC 94-49123. (National Veterinary Medical Series for Independent Study). 1995. 24.50 (*0-683-06664-1*) Williams & Wilkins.

Toxicology: A Primer on Toxicology Principles & Applications. Michael A. Kamrin. (Illus.). 160p. 1988. 59.95 (*0-87371-133-5*, L133) Lewis Pubs.

Toxicology - from Cells to Man: Proceedings of the 1995 EUROTOX Congress Meeting Held in Prague, Czech Republic, August 27-30, 1995. Ed. by J. P. Seiler et al. LC 95-47133. (Archives of Toxicology Ser.: Supplement No. 18). 1996. write for info. (*0-387-60673-4*); 157.00 (*3-540-60673-4*) Spr-Verlag.

Toxicology & Biological Monitoring of Metals in Humans--Including Feasability & Need. B. L. Carson et al. (Illus.). 360p. 1986. 190.00 (*0-87371-072-X*, RA1231, CRC Reprint) Franklin.

***Toxicology & Environmental Health Information Resources: The Role of the National Library of Medicine.** Ed. by Catharyn T. Liverman et al. 176p. (Orig.). 1997. pap. 32.00 (*0-309-05686-1*, Joseph Henry Pr) Natl Acad Pr.

Toxicology & Metabolism of Hydrazine. Timbrell. 1995. write for info. (*0-8493-6946-0*) CRC Pr.

Toxicology Annual, 2 vols., Vol. 2. Ed. by Charles L. Winek et al. LC 76-641009. (Illus.). 288p. 1977. reprint ed. pap. 77.80 (*0-7837-0675-8*, 2041010) Bks Demand.

Toxicology Annual, 2 vols., Vol. 3. Ed. by Charles L. Winek et al. LC 76-641009. (Illus.). 356p. 1979. reprint ed. pap. 101.50 (*0-7837-0676-6*) Bks Demand.

Toxicology Annual, 1974. Ed. by Charles L. Winek et al. LC 75-6778. (Illus.). 341p. reprint ed. pap. 97.20 (*0-7837-0706-1*, 2041038) Bks Demand.

***Toxicology, Biochemistry & Molecular Biology of Herbicide.** Ed. by R. M. Roe et al. LC 96-79142. 350p. (YA). (gr. 12 up). Date not set. 82.00 (*90-5199-311-0*, 311-0) IOS Press.

Toxicology Desk Reference: The Toxic Exposure & Medical Monitoring Index. Robert P. Ryan & Claude E. Terry. 1996. cd-rom 425.00 (*1-56032-588-7*) Taylor & Francis.

Toxicology Desk Reference: The Toxic Exposure & Medical Monitoring Index, 3 vols., Set. Robert P. Ryan & Claude E. Terry. 2226p. 1996. pap. text ed. 425.00 (*1-56032-579-8*); pap. text ed. 510.00 incl. cd-rom (*1-56032-605-0*) Taylor & Francis.

Toxicology in the Tropics. Ed. by R. L. Smith & E. A. Babaunumi. 280p. 1980. 68.00 (*0-85066-194-3*) Taylor & Francis.

Toxicology in the Use, Misuse, & Abuse of Food, Drugs & Chemicals. Ed. by P. L. Chambers et al. (Archives of Toxicology Ser.: Suppl. 6). (Illus.). 380p. 1983. pap. 85.00 (*0-387-12392-X*) Spr-Verlag.

Toxicology in Transition: Proceedings of the 1994 EUROTOX Congress Meeting Held in Basel, Switzerland, August 21-24, 1994. Ed. by G. H. Degen et al. LC 94-43580. (Archives of Toxicology Ser.: Vol. 17). 1995. 136.00 (*3-540-58781-0*) Spr-Verlag.

Toxicology Laboratory Design & Management for the 80's & Beyond. Ed. by A. S. Tegeris. (Concepts in Toxicology Ser.: Vol. 1). (Illus.). xii, 320p. 1984. 119.25 (*3-8055-3797-2*) S Karger.

Toxicology of Aflatoxins: Human Health, Veterinary & Agricultural Significance. Ed. by David L. Eaton & John D. Groopman. (Illus.). 544p. 1993. text ed. 69.00 (*0-12-228255-8*) Acad Pr.

Toxicology of Aquatic Pollution: Physiological, Molecular & Cellular Approaches. Ed. by E. W. Taylor. (Society for Experimental Biology Seminar Ser.: No. 57). (Illus.). 220p. (C). 1996. text ed. 85.00 (*0-521-45524-3*) Cambridge U Pr.

Toxicology of Chemical Mixtures: Case Studies, Mechanisms & Novel Approaches. Ed. by Raymond S. Yang. (Illus.). 720p. 1994. text ed. 179.00 (*0-12-768350-X*) Acad Pr.

Toxicology of CNS Depressants. Ho. 280p. 1987. 157.00 (*0-8493-6477-9*) CRC Pr.

Toxicology of Contact Hypersensitivity. Ed. by Ian Kimber & Thomas Maurer. 130p. 1996. 79.95 (*0-7484-0349-3*) Taylor & Francis.

Toxicology of Industrial Compounds. Ed. by Helmut Thomas et al. 448p. 1995. 99.00 (*0-7484-0239-X*, Pub. by Taylor Francis Ltd UK) Taylor & Francis.

Toxicology of Insecticides. 2nd ed. Fumio Matusmura. LC 85-12371. 618p. 1985. 75.00 (*0-306-41979-3*, Plenum Pr) Plenum.

Toxicology of Metals, Vol. 1. Ed. by Louis W. Chang et al. LC 95-42586. 1232p. 1996. 125.00 (*0-87371-803-8*, L803) Lewis Pubs.

Toxicology of Metals: Biochemical Aspects. N. Ballatori. Ed. by Robert Goyer & George M. Cherian. LC 94-26484. 1995. 393.95 (*0-387-58281-9*) Spr-Verlag.

Toxicology of Molluscicides. Ed. by G. Webbe. (International Encyclopedia of Pharmacology & Therapeutics Ser.: No. 125). (Illus.). 174p. 1987. 158.25 (*0-08-034209-4*, Pergamon Pr) Elsevier.

Toxicology of Pesticides: Experimental, Clinical & Regulatory Perspectives. Ed. by L. G. Costa et al. (NATO ASI Series H: Vol. 13). 335p. 1987. 121.00 (*0-387-16093-0*) Spr-Verlag.

Toxicology of Pesticides in Animals. Dilshith. 264p. 1990. 206.00 (*0-8493-6907-X*, RA1270) CRC Pr.

Toxicology of Radioactive Substances, 2 vols. Ed. by A. A. Letavet & E. B. Kurlyandskaya. Incl. Vol. 4. Thorium-232 & Uranium-238. 1970. 73.00 (*0-08-013413-0*); Vol. 5. Zinc-65. 1970. 84.00 (*0-08-013414-9*); write for info. (*0-318-55235-3*, Pub. by Pergamon Repr UK) Franklin.

Toxicology of the Blood & Bone Marrow. Ed. by Richard D. Irons. LC 85-1919. (Target Organ Toxicology Ser.). (Illus.). 192p. reprint ed. pap. 54.80 (*0-7837-7123-1*, 2046952) Bks Demand.

Toxicology of the Eye: Effects on the Eyes & Visual System from Chemicals, Drugs, Metals & Minerals, Plants, Toxins & Venoms; Also, Systemic Side Effects from Eye Medications. 4th ed. W. Morton Grant & Joel S. Schuman. LC 93-12521. 1620p. (C). 1993. 252.95 (*0-398-05860-1*) C C Thomas.

Toxicology of the Immune System. Robert Burrell. 1992. text ed. 83.95 (*0-442-00836-8*) Van Nos Reinhold.

Toxicology of the Liver. 2nd ed. Gabriel L. Plaa & William R. Hewitt. (Target Organ Toxicology Ser.). 500p. 1993. text ed. 121.00 (*0-88167-886-4*) Lppncott-Raven.

Toxicology of the Lung. Ed. by Donald E. Gardner et al. LC 88-11639. (Target Organ Toxicology Ser.). (Illus.). 539p. reprint ed. pap. 153.70 (*0-7837-7091-X*, 2046916) Bks Demand.

Toxicology of the Male & Female Reproductive System. Ed. by Peter K. Working. (Chemical Industry Institute of Toxicology Ser.). 384p. 1989. 109.00 (*0-89116-583-5*) Hemisp Pub.

Toxicology of the Nasal Passage. Ed. by Craig S. Barrow. (CIIT Toxicology Ser.). 1986. 115.00 (*0-89116-397-2*) Hemisp Pub.

Toxicology Risk Assessment. Fan. Ed. by Chang. 888p. 1995. 195.00 (*0-8247-9490-7*) Dekker.

Toxics: A Case Study, 1979. 1979. 3.25 (*0-943136-19-9*) Ctr Analysis Public Issues.

Toxics: Taking Charge. Leslie Comnes & Carolie Sly. Ed. by John E. Bateson. LC 89-37364. (Illus.). 64p. (Orig.). 1989. write for info. (*0-88067-001-0*) Alameda Cnty Supr Schls.

Toxics A to Z: A Guide to Everyday Pollution Hazards. John Harte et al. LC 90-25860. (Illus.). 576p. 1991. 75.00 (*0-520-07223-5*); pap. 22.50 (*0-520-07224-3*) U CA Pr.

Toxics & Health: The Potential Long-Term Effects of Industrial Activity. Cheryl S. Silver & Dale S. Rothman. 75p. (Orig.). 1995. pap. 14.95 (*1-56973-027-X*) World Resources Inst.

Toxics Away! The Alameda County Pilot Collection Program for Small Quantity Generators of Hazardous Wastes. 190p. 1988. 20.00 (*0-317-05689-1*, P88001WAT) Assn Bay Area.

Toxics Crisis: What the States Should Do. Jeffrey Tryens. 100p. 1983. 8.95 (*0-89788-072-2*) CPA Washington.

Toxics in the Community, 2 vols., Set. 1995. lib. bdg. 601.99 (*0-8490-7543-2*) Gordon Pr.

Toxics in the Community: National & Local Perspectives. (Illus.). 500p. (Orig.). (C). 1995. pap. text ed. 50.00 (*0-7881-2513-3*) DIANE Pub.

Toxics, Management & Reduction: Building Sustainable Communities, an Environmental Guide for Local Government. Center for the Study of Law & Politics Staff. 182p. 1991. 40.00 (*1-880386-03-8*) Ctr Study Law.

***Toxics Release Inventory (1992) Public Data Release.** (Illus.). 500p. 1996. reprint ed. pap. 50.00 (*0-7881-3177-X*) DIANE Pub.

Toxics Watch 1995. Inform, Inc. Staff. 816p. (Orig.). 1995. pap. 125.00 (*0-918780-64-0*) INFORM NY.

Toxigenic Fusarium Species: Identity & Mycotoxicology. W. F. Marasas et al. LC 82-42779. 350p. 1984. 45.00 (*0-271-00348-0*) Pa St U Pr.

Toxikologische, Endokrinologische und Klinische Aspekte bei der Pruefung eines neuen Neuroleptikums. Ein wissenschaftliches Gespraech. Ed. by Cilag-Chemie. (International Pharmacopsychiatry Ser.: Vol. 13, Suppl. 1). (Illus.). 1978. pap. 23.25 (*3-8055-2931-7*) S Karger.

***Toxin.** Robin Cook. 384p. 1998. 24.95 (*0-399-14316-5*) Putnam Pub Group.

Toxin-Induced Models of Neurological Disorders. M. L. Woodruff & A. J. Nonneman. (Illus.). 290p. 1994. 75.00 (*0-306-44614-6*, Plenum Pr) Plenum.

Toxins & Enzymes: Microbial Composition: Amino Acids, Proteins & Nucleic Acids, Vol. 8. 2nd ed. Allen I. Laskin & Hubert A. Lechevalier. LC 77-12460. (Handbook of Microbiology Ser.). 1000p. 1987. 242.00 (*0-8493-7208-9*, QR6) Franklin.

Toxins & Exocytosis. Ed. by Dusan Suput & Robert Zorec. LC 93-46350. (Annals Ser.: Vol. 710). 1994. write for info. (*0-89766-851-0*); pap. 100.00 (*0-89766-852-9*) NY Acad Sci.

***Toxins & Signal Transduction, Vol. 1.** Ed. by Yehuda Gutman & Philip Lazarovici. (Cellular & Molecular Mechanisms of Toxin Action Ser.). 520p. 1997. 150.00 (*90-5702-078-5*, Harwood Acad Pubs) Gordon & Breach.

Toxins & Targets: Effects of Natural & Synthetic Poisons on Living Cells & Fragile Ecosystems. Ed. by Dianne Watters. 199p. 1992. text ed. 79.00 (*3-7186-5194-7*, Harwood Acad Pubs) Gordon & Breach.

Toxins as Tools in Neurochemistry. Ed. by F. Hucho & Y. A. Ovchinnikov. xiv, 368p. 1983. 138.50 (*3-11-009593-9*) De Gruyter.

***Toxins in Plant Disease Development & Evolving Biotechnology.** Ed. by R. K. Upadhyay & K. G. Mukerji. (Illus.). 260p. (C). 1997. 79.00 (*1-886106-75-4*) Science Pubs.

Toxins of Animal & Plant Origin, 3 vols., Vol. 3. Ed. by A. DeVries & E. Kochva. LC 71-130967. (Illus.). 1088p. 1973. Set. text ed. 701.00 (*0-677-14710-4*) Gordon & Breach.

Toxizitat von Zink, Schwefel und Stickstoffverbindungen auf Flechten-Symbionten. J. T. Marti. (Bibliotheca Lichenologica Ser.: No. 21). (Illus.). 130p. 1985. pap. text ed. 30.00 (*3-7682-1426-5*) Lubrecht & Cramer.

Toxological Evaluation of Certain Food Additives & Contaminants, Thirty-Seventh Meeting. (WHO Food Additives Ser.: No. 28). vii, 437p. (C). 1991. pap. text ed. 35.00 (*92-4-166028-7*, 1270028) World Health.

Toxophilus: Archery - Theory & Practice, 2 vols. in 1. Roger Asham & Horace Ford. Ed. by Dean V. Manley. (Legends of the Longbow Ser.: Vol. 6). (Illus.). (YA). (gr. 10 up). 1992. reprint ed. 39.95 (*1-56416-092-0*) Derrydale Pr.

Toxophilus, Fifteen Forty-Five. Roger Ascham. 1988. reprint ed. lib. bdg. 49.00 (*0-7812-0203-5*) Rprt Serv.

Toxophilus, 1545. Roger Ascham. Ed. by Edward Arber. LC 73-131612. 1971. reprint ed. 29.00 (*0-403-00499-3*) Scholarly.

Toxoplasmosis. Ed. by Judith E. Smith. LC 93-35674. (NATO ASI Series H: Cell Biology: Vol. 78). 1994. 158.95 (*0-387-57305-4*) Spr-Verlag.

Toxoplasmosis: Proceedings of the WHO Expert Committee of Investigators, Geneva, 1968. WHO Staff. (Technical Report Ser.: No. 431). 1969. pap. text ed. 5.00 (*92-4-120431-1*, 1100431) World Health.

Toxoplasmosis of Animals & Man. J. P. Dubey & C. P. Beattie. 288p. 1988. 214.95 (*0-8493-4618-5*, SF809) CRC Pr.

Toy & Game Inventor's Guide. 2nd ed. Gregory J. Battersby & Charles W. Grimes. 240p. 1996. pap. 15.95 (*1-888206-01-2*) Kent Communs.

***Toy & Miniature Sewing Machines Bk. II: Identification & Value Guide, Vol. 2.** Glenda Thomas. (Illus.). 304p. (Orig.). 1997. pap. 24.95 (*0-89145-788-7*, 4876) Collector Bks.

Toy Autos: 1890-1939. Peter Ottenheimer. Ed. by Allen Levy. (Illus.). 168p. pap. 25.00 (*1-872727-61-1*, Pub. by New Cavendish UK) Pincushion Pr.

Toy Bear. Ron Reese. Ed. by Alton Jordan. (I Can Eat an Elephant Ser.). (Illus.). (J). (gr. k-3). 1984. 7.95 (*0-89868-016-6*, Read Res); pap. 3.95 (*0-89868-049-2*, Read Res) ARO Pub.

Toy Boats. Basil Harley. 1989. pap. 35.00 (*0-85263-851-5*, Pub. by Shire UK) St Mut.

Toy Bop: Kid Classics of the 50's & 60's. Tom Frey. (Illus.). 180p. 1994. pap. 29.95 (*0-9639700-1-1*); text ed. 39.95 (*0-9639700-0-3*) Fuzzy Dice.

Toy Box Science, 4 vols., Set. Chris Ollerenshaw & Pat Triggs. (Illus.). (J). (gr. 3 up). 1994. lib. bdg. 74.40 (*0-8368-1118-6*) Gareth Stevens Inc.

Toy Brother. William Steig. LC 95-69464. (Michael di Capua Bks.). (Illus.). 32p. (J). (ps-1). 1996. 14.95 (*0-06-205078-8*) HarpC Child Bks.

Toy Brother. William Steig. LC 95-69464. (Michael di Capua Bks.). (Illus.). 32p. (J). (ps up). 1996. lib. bdg. 14.89 (*0-06-205079-6*) HarpC Child Bks.

Toy Campaign. John Bibee. LC 87-3261. (Spirit Flyer Ser.: Vol. 2). (Illus.). 225p. (Orig.). (J). (gr. 4-8). 1987. pap. 6.99 (*0-8308-1201-6*, 1201) InterVarsity.

Toy Car Stickers. Lisa A. Greene. (Illus.). (J). (gr. k-3). 1993. pap. 1.00 (*0-486-27692-9*) Dover.

Toy Cars & Trucks. Richard O'Brien. 448p. 1994. pap. 22.95 (*0-89689-103-8*) Bks Americana.

Toy Cart. Sudraka. (Writers Workshop Bluebird Ser.). 80p. 1979. 14.00 (*0-86578-053-6*); 8.00 (*0-86578-052-8*) Ind-US Inc.

Toy Cemetery. William W. Johnstone. 432p. 1987. mass mkt. 3.95 (*0-8217-2228-X*, Zebra Kensgtn) Kensgtn Pub Corp.

***Toy Chest.** (Fisher-Price Paint with Water Ser.). (Illus.). 32p. (J). (gr. k-2). 1997. pap. write for info. (*1-56144-943-1*, Honey Bear Bks) Modern Pub NYC.

Toy Chest. Stevanne Auerbach. (Illus.). 256p. 1986. pap. 9.95 (*0-8184-0405-1*) Carol Pub Group.

Toy Circus. Jan Wahl. LC 85-30186. (Illus.). 32p. (J). (ps-3). 1986. 14.00 (*0-15-200609-5*, Gulliver Bks) HarBrace.

Toy Cupboard. Lee Jordan. 192p. 1990. 17.95 (*0-8027-5775-8*) Walker & Co.

Toy Cupboard. large type ed. Lee Jordan. 1991. 25.99 (*0-7089-2520-0*) Ulverscroft.

Toy Dogs: Their Points in Health & Disease: The Italian Greyhound, Toy Bull Dog, Schipperke, Chow, Maltese, Yorkie, Spaniel, Toy Poodle, Clydesdale Terrier. Frank T. Barton. 1992. lib. bdg. 79.95 (*0-8490-5217-3*) Gordon Pr.

Toy Fox Terrier. Sherry Baker-Kreuger. 1994. 9.95 (*0-86622-868-3*, KW-222) TFH Pubns.

Toy Fox Terrier. Eliza L. Hopkins & Cathy J. Flamholtz. (Illus.). 124p. (Orig.). 1988. pap. 9.95 (*0-940269-01-5*) OTR Pubns.

***Toy Guns: Involvement in Crime & Encounters with the Police.** David L. Carter et al. LC 90-61772. (Illus.). 50p. (Orig.). 1990. pap. 5.50 (*1-878734-21-0*) Police Exec Res.

***Toy Guns: Involvement in Crime & Encounters with the Police.** David L. Carter et al. (Illus.). 47p. (Orig.). 1996. reprint ed. pap. text ed. 25.00 (*0-7881-3671-2*) DIANE Pub.

Toy Knits: More Than 30 Irresistible & Easy-to-Knit Patterns. Debbie Bliss. LC 95-1007. 1995. pap. 18.95 (*0-312-11901-1*) St Martin.

Toy Making on a Budget. Nancy E. Carlberg. 40p. 1993. pap. 5.00 (*0-944878-28-8*) Carlberg Pr.

Toy Palace: A Libretto for Animals, People & Machines. Charles Doria. 32p. (Orig.). 1991. pap. 9.00 (*1-880516-02-0*) Left Hand Bks.

Toy Price Guide: Post World War II. Harry L. Rinker. (Illus.). 320p. (Orig.). 1997. pap. 17.95 (*0-930625-30-7*, Antque Trdr Bks) Antique Trader Bks.

Toy Price Guide: Toys of the Pre-World War II Era. Harry L. Rinker. (Illus.). 320p. (Orig.). 1997. pap. 17.95 (*0-930625-31-5*, Antque Trdr Bks) Antique Trader Bks.

Toy Sewing Machines. Glenda Thomas. 1995. pap. 18.95 (*0-89145-622-8*) Collector Bks.

Toy-Shop, a Dramatick Satire: And the King & the Miller of Mansfield, a Dramatick Tale. Robert Dodsley. LC 92-23038. (Augustan Reprints Ser.: Nos. 218-219). 1983. reprint ed. 21.50 (*0-404-70218-X*) AMS Pr.

Toy Shop Mystery. Flora G. Jacobs. (Illus.). 96p. (J). 1960. 5.95 (*0-686-31595-2*) Wash Dolls Hse.

***Toy Shop of Terror.** Laban C. Hill. (Choose Your Own Nightmare Ser.: No. 18). 96p. (Orig.). (J). (gr. 3-7). 1997. pap. 3.50 (*0-553-48458-3*) BDD Bks Young Read.

Toy-Shop Surprise. Suzy McPartland. (Pee Wee Pops Ser.). (Illus.). 12p. (J). (ps). 1994. bds. 4.95 (*0-689-71749-0*, Aladdin Paperbacks) S&S Childrens.

Toy Shop Tales. Veda Linforth. (J). 1993. 7.95 (*0-533-10266-9*) Vantage.

Toy Shop 1997 Annual. Toy Shop Staff. 1996. pap. text ed. 9.95 (*0-87341-472-1*) Krause Pubns.

***Toy Soldier.** Random House Value Publishing Staff. 1997. 14.99 (*0-517-18774-4*) Random Hse Value.

Toy Soldiers. Bernard Goldstein & Estelle T. Goldstein. (Illus.). 48p. 1982. 24.00 (*0-88014-047-X*) Mosaic Pr OH.

Toy Soldiers. Paul Lenardo. (Dr. Who New Adventures Ser.). 1995. mass mkt. 5.95 (*0-426-20452-2*, Pub. by Virgin Pub UK) London Brdge.

Toy Soldiers. James Opie. 1989. pap. 25.00 (*0-85263-632-6*, Pub. by Shire UK) St Mut.

***Toy Soldiers.** Random House Value Publishing Staff. Date not set. 14.99 (*0-517-18472-9*) Random Hse Value.

***Toy Soldiers.** M. Wesley Swearinger. Date not set. write for info. (*0-688-03656-2*) Morrow.

Toy Soldiers: Identification & Price Guide. Bertel Bruun. (Illus.). 304p. (Orig.). 1994. pap. 12.50 (*0-380-77128-4*, Confident Collect) Avon.

***Toy Steam Accessories.** Marcus Rooks. 1996. pap. 25.00 (*0-7478-0313-7*, Pub. by Shire UK) St Mut.

Toy Steam Engines. Bob Gordon. 1989. pap. 25.00 (*0-85263-775-6*, Pub. by Shire UK) St Mut.

Toy Story. 96p. (J). 1996. 7.98 (*1-57082-460-6*) Mouse Works.

Toy Story. (J). 1996. 7.98 (*1-57082-343-X*) Mouse Works.

Toy Story. Mouse Works Staff. 24p. (J). 1996. 6.98 (*1-57082-278-6*) Mouse Works.

An Asterisk (*) at the beginning of an entry indicates that the title is appearing in BIP for the first time.

Toy Story. Walt Disney Staff. 32p. (J). 1996. pap. text ed. 4.95 (0-7868-4122-2) Hyprn Child.

Toy Story: A Pop-up Book. Illus. by Brown, Wells, & Jacobs Staff. LC 95-74735. 10p. (J). 1995. 13.95 (0-7868-3084-0) Disney Pr.

Toy Story: A Postcard Book. (Illus.). 64p. 1995. pap. 8.95 (0-7868-8138-0) Hyperion.

Toy Story: An Animated Flip Book. (Illus.). 96p. 1995. pap. 3.95 (0-7868-8139-9) Hyperion.

Toy Story: I Come in Peace. Jan Carr. 64p. (J). (gr. 2-5). 1996. pap. text ed. 3.50 (0-7868-4108-7) Disney Pr.

Toy Story: The Art & Making of the Animated Film. John Lasseter & Steve Daly. (Illus.). 136p. 1995. 39.95 (0-7868-6180-0) Hyperion.

Toy Story: The Art & Making of the Animated Film. John Lasseter. (Disney Miniatures Ser.). (Illus.). 192p. 1996. 10.95 (0-7868-6254-8) Hyperion.

Toy Story: The Secret Life of Toys. Ali Hokin. LC 95-61486. (Illus.). 128p. (J). 1995. pap. 5.95 (0-7868-4057-9) Disney Pr.

Toy Story - Disney's. Retold by Betty Birney. (Look-Look Bks.). (Illus.). 24p. (J). (ps-3). 1995. pap. 2.25 (0-307-12908-X, Golden Books) Western Pub.

Toy Story Flip Book. 1996. 2.98 (1-57082-412-6) Mouse Works.

Toy Story Joke Book. Barbara Bazaldua. (J). 1996. pap. text ed. 2.95 (0-307-12943-8, Golden Books) Western Pub.

Toy Story Junior: Junior Novelization. Cathy E. Dubowski. LC 95-69981. (Illus.). 96p. (J). (gr. 2-7). 1995. 4.95 (0-7868-4056-0) Disney Pr.

Toy Story Official Game Book. Rhonda Von & BradyGAMES Staff. (Illus.). 112p. (Orig.). 1995. 9.99 (1-56686-447-X) Brady Pub.

Toy Story Word Books. Mouse Works Staff. (J). 1995. 6.98 (1-57082-291-3) Mouse Works.

Toy Sword. large type ed. Elizabeth Cadell. LC 94-22015. 1995. pap. 19.95 (0-7862-0291-2) Thorndike Pr.

*Toy Terror: Batteries Included. R. L. Stine. (Goosebumps Ser.: No. 20). (J). 1997. pap. text ed. 3.99 (0-590-93492-9, Apple Paperbacks) Scholastic Inc.

Toy Theaters. deluxe ed. Valentine J. Poska. (Illus.). 48p. 1994. 45.00 (0-88014-057-7) Mosaic Pr OH.

Toy Theatres of the World. Peter Baldwin. (Illus.). 176p. 1993. 39.95 (0-302-00614-1, Pub. by Zwemmer Bks UK) Sothebys Pubns.

Toy Tractors. Vincent Manocchi & Rob L. Wagner. (Enthusiast Color Ser.). (Illus.). 96p. 1996. pap. 12.95 (0-7603-0167-0) Motorbooks Intl.

Toy Train Department: Electric Train Catalog Pages from the Legendary Sears Christmas Wishbooks of the 1950s & 1960s. Ed. by Thomas W. Holland. LC 95-78549. (Illus.). 160p. 1995. pap. 19.95 (1-887790-00-4) Windmill Press.

Toy Trains. David Salisbury. 1989. pap. 25.00 (0-7478-0087-1, Pub. by Shire UK) St Mut.

Toy Trains of Yesteryear. Case Kowal. LC 73-188178. (Hobby Bks.: No. C-67). (Illus.). 52p. 1990. pap. 5.00 (0-911868-67-4, C67) Carstens Pubns.

Toy Trouble. Marty Engle & Barnes. (Strange Matter Ser.: No. 13). 140p. (J). (gr. 4 up). 1996. pap. 3.50 (1-56714-052-1) Montage Bks.

*Toy Truck Collectors Official Price Guide. 7th rev. ed. Michael V. Harwood. Orig. Title: Toy Truck Collectors Official Price Guide. (Illus.). 60p. (Orig.). 1997. pap. 14.95 (0-9630345-3-7) F S B O.

Toy Truck Collectors Official Price Guide see Toy Truck Collectors Official Price Guide

Toy Trumpet. 2nd ed. Illus. by Ann Grifalconi. LC 94-34503. (J). (ps-3). 1995. 15.95 (0-316-32858-8) Little.

Toybox. White Wolf Staff & Jackie Cassada. (Immortal Eyes Ser.: Bk. 1). 1995. pap. 5.99 (1-56504-860-1, 11401) White Wolf.

Toying Around with Science: The Physics Behind Toys & Gags. Bob Friedhoffer. (Illus.). 96p. (J). (gr. 7-9). 1995. pap. 8.00 (0-531-15743-1) Watts.

Toying Around with Science: The Physics Behind Toys & Gags. Robert Friedhoffer. (Illus.). 128p. (J). (gr. 7-9). 1995. lib. bdg. 20.00 (0-531-11215-2) Watts.

*Toyko: The Shogun's City at the 21st Century. 2nd ed. Roman Cybriwsky. pap. text ed. 35.00 (0-471-97187-1) Wiley.

Toyko Museum Guide: Comp Gde. Tom Flannigan & Ellen Flannigan. 208p. 1993. pap. 14.95 (0-8048-1892-4) C E Tuttle.

Toyland. Kirk Henneberry. LC 93-61286. 61p. (Orig.). 1993. pap. 10.00 (1-882825-19-5) Hse of Prayer.

Toymaker. Jones. 5.00 (0-686-00485-X); pap. 2.00 (0-686-00486-8) Fantasy Pub Co.

Toymaker. Martin Waddell. LC 91-58762. (Illus.). 32p. (J). (ps up). 1992. 13.95 (1-56402-103-3) Candlewick Pr.

Toymaking & Children's Furniture Simplified. rev. ed. Donald R. Brann. LC 77-89943. 1982. pap. 9.95 (0-87733-771-3) Easi-Bild.

Toymaking with Children. Freya Jaffke. (J). 1988. pap. 10.95 (0-86315-069-1, 20244, Pub. by Floris Bks UK) Gryphon Hse.

Toynbee: A Reappraisal. Ed. by C. T. McIntire & Marvin Perry. 40.00 (0-8020-5785-3) U of Toronto Pr.

Toynbee & History: Critical Essays & Reviews. Ed. by Ashley Montagu. (Extending Horizons Ser.). 385p. (C). 1956. 7.00 (0-87558-026-2) Porter Sargent.

Toynbee at Home. John W. Smurr. LC 88-71449. 1990. 39.95 (0-8158-0451-2) Chris Mass.

Toynbee Convector. Ray Bradbury. LC 87-46189. 1988. 17.95 (0-394-54703-9) Knopf.

Toynbee Convector. Ray Bradbury. 1988. 17.95 (0-318-32850-X) NAL-Dutton.

Toynbee Hall & Social Reform, 1880-1914: The Search for Community. Standish Meacham. LC 86-28269. (Illus.). 233p. reprint ed. pap. 66.50 (0-7837-4536-2, 2080263) Bks Demand.

Toynbee's Approach to World Politics, Vol. 5. H. L. Mason. LC 60-202. 1958. 11.00 (0-930598-04-0) Tulane Stud Pol.

Toynbee's Study of History. Francis Neilson. 1979. lib. bdg. 250.00 (0-685-96644-5) Revisionist Pr.

Toyo Ito. Charles Jencks. (Architectural Monographs: No. 36). (Illus.). 144p. 1995. pap. 38.00 (1-85490-270-9) Academy Ed UK.

Toyohiko Kagawa: An Apostle of Love & Social Justice. Robert D. Schildgen. LC 88-20316. (Illus.). 341p. 1988. 18.95 (0-9620537-0-8); pap. 12.95 (0-9620537-1-6) Centenary Bks.

Toyota Camry, 1983-92. 784p. 1992. pap. 21.95 (0-8019-8265-0) Chilton.

Toyota Camry, 1983-92. rev. ed. Chilton Automotives Editorial Staff. 496p. 1992. pap. 16.95 (0-8019-8311-8) Chilton.

*Toyota Celica-Supra (RWD), 1971-1987. Chilton Publishing Staff. (Total Car Care Ser.). 1997. pap. text ed. 28.95 (0-8019-8980-9) Chilton.

*Toyota Celica 1971-85. (Automobile Repair Manuals Ser.). (Illus.). pap. 16.95 (1-56392-045-X, MBI 111212AM) Haynes Pubns.

Toyota Celica, 1986-93. Chilton Automotives Editorial Staff. 832p. 1993. pap. 21.95 (0-8019-8413-0) Chilton.

*Toyota Corolla FWD 1984-92. (Automobile Repair Manuals Ser.). (Illus.). pap. 16.95 (1-56392-064-6, MBI 109194AM) Haynes Pubns.

Toyota Corolla Service Manual 1.8 Models: 1980-1983. Bentley, Robert, Inc. Staff. LC 83-62734. (Illus.). 640p. (Orig.). 1984. pap. 29.95 (0-8376-0246-7) Bentley.

Toyota Corolla 1600 Service Manual, 1973-1979. Bentley, Robert, Inc. Staff. LC 79-53189. (Illus.). (Orig.). 1979. pap. 29.95 (0-8376-0242-4) Bentley.

Toyota Corolla 1.8 Service Manual, 1980 & 1981. Robert Bentley. 1981. 1.95 (0-8376-0245-9) Bentley.

Toyota Corolla 1970-87. Chilton Automotives Editorial Staff. 600p. 1995. pap. 21.95 (0-8019-8586-2) Chilton.

*Toyota Corolla, 1988-1997. Chilton Book Co. Staff. (New Total Car Care Ser.). 1997. pap. text ed. write for info. (0-8019-8827-6) Chilton.

Toyota Corolla, 1990-93. Chilton Automotives Editorial Staff. 592p. 1993. pap. 21.95 (0-8019-8414-9) Chilton.

Toyota Corolla, 1990-93. Chilton Automotives Editorial Staff. 304p. 1994. pap. 16.95 (0-8019-8434-3) Chilton.

*Toyota Management System: Linking the Seven Key Functional Areas. Yasuhiro Monden. LC 92-27133. 245p. 1996. pap. 30.00 (1-56327-139-7) Prod Press.

Toyota Pick-Ups-Land Cruiser-4Runner 1989-95. Chilton Automotives Editorial Staff. 800p. 0196. pap. 22.95 (0-8019-8682-6) Chilton.

Toyota Pickup, 4Runner Service Manual: 1978-1988 Including Gasoline, Diesel, & Turbo Diesel, 4-cylinder & 6-cylinder Engines. Robert Bentley, Inc. Staff. (Orig.). 39.95 (0-8376-0258-0) Bentley.

*Toyota Pickups 1979-95. (Automobile Repair Manuals Ser.). (Illus.). pap. 16.95 (1-56392-151-0, MBI 105009AM) Haynes Pubns.

Toyota Production System: An Integrated Approach to Just-in-Time. 2nd ed. Yasuhiro Monden. LC 92-27711. 425p. 1993. 53.95 (0-89806-129-6) Eng Mgmt Pr.

Toyota Production System: Beyond Large-Scale Production. Taiichi Ohno. LC 87-43172. (Illus.). 162p. 1988. 45.00 (0-915299-14-3) Prod Press.

Toyota Standard Four Speed Transmission Explained. Manny Kaneblei. LC 85-701502. (Orig.). 1985. student ed. 8.00 (0-8064-0187-7, 469); audio, vhs 269.00 (0-8064-0188-5) Bergwall.

Toyota Tercel 1984-94. Chilton Automotives Editorial Staff. (Total Car Care Ser.). 536p. 1995. pap. 21.95 (0-8019-8595-1) Chilton.

Toyota Tercel 1984-94. Chilton Automotives Editorial Staff. 450p. 1995. pap. 16.95 (0-8019-8599-4) Chilton.

Toyota Truck & Land Cruiser Owner's Bible: A Hands-on Guide to Getting the Most from Your Toyota. Moses Ludel. LC 95-51695. 1995. pap. text ed. 29.95 (0-8376-0159-2) Bentley.

Toyota Trucks 1970-88. (Total Car Care Ser.). 624p. 1994. pap. 21.95 (0-8019-8578-1) Chilton.

Toyota Trucks, 1989-1991. (Total Car Care Ser.). 896p. 1991. pap. 21.95 (0-8019-8163-8) Chilton.

Toyota Trucks, 1989-1991. 408p. 1991. pap. 16.95 (0-8019-8164-6) Chilton.

*Toyota, 1970-1982: Cressida, Corona, Crown & MKII. Chilton Book Co. Staff. (New Total Car Care Ser.). 1997. pap. text ed. write for info. (0-8019-9081-5) Chilton.

*Toyota, 1983-1990: Cressida-Van. Chilton Book Co. Staff. (New Total Car Care Ser.). 1997. pap. text ed. write for info. (0-8019-9066-1) Chilton.

*Toyotomi Blades: A Ken Tanaka Mystery. Dale Furutani. LC 97-20033. 1997. write for info. (0-312-17050-5) St Martin.

Toys. (Americana Bks.). (Illus.). 1975. 3.00 (0-911410-40-6) Applied Arts.

Toys. LC 91-60534. (What's Inside? Ser.). (Illus.). 24p. (J). (ps-3). 1991. 8.95 (1-879431-08-4) DK Pub Inc.

Toys. (Things to Learn Board Book Ser.). 10p. (J). (ps-3). Date not set. bds. 2.95 (1-56987-275-9) Landoll.

*Toys. (Fit-A-Shape Ser.). (J). (ps-k). 1997. 5.95 (0-614-29008-2) Running Pr.

Toys. Pamela C. Beall & Susan H. Nipp. (Wee Sing Sounds & Songs Board Book & Cassette Ser.). (Illus.). 10p. (J). (ps). 1996. bds. 8.95 incl. audio (0-8431-3984-6, Wee Sing) Price Stern Sloan.

Toys. Roma Bishop. (Nursery Board Mini Pop Bks.). (Illus.). 14p. (J). (ps). 1991. pap. 2.95 (0-671-74831-9, Litl Simon S&S) S&S Childrens.

*Toys. Karen Bryant-Mole. LC 96-37243. (Picture This! Ser.). (J). 1997. lib. bdg. write for info. (1-57572-057-4) Rigby Interact Libr.

Toys. Meryl Doney. LC 95-10735. (World Crafts Ser.). (Illus.). 32p. (J). (gr. 4-7). 1996. lib. bdg. 18.00 (0-531-14400-3) Watts.

*Toys. Meryl Doney. (World Crafts Ser.). 1997. pap. text ed. 5.95 (0-531-15873-X) Watts.

Toys. Lorenz Books Staff. 24p. (J). 1996. 3.95 (1-85967-129-2, Lorenz Bks) Anness Pub.

Toys. Chris Oxlade. LC 95-23173. (Through Time Ser.). (J). 1996. lib. bdg. 24.26 (0-8172-4139-6) Raintree Steck-V.

Toys, 10 vols., Set. (Smithsonian Coloring Bks.). (Illus.). 32p. (J). (ps-8). pap. 29.50 (0-87474-615-9) Smithsonian.

Toys: An Integrated Unit. Kathy Rogers. (Primary Thematic Units Ser.). (Illus.). 96p. (Orig.). 1993. pap. 12.95 (0-944459-86-2) ECS Lrn Systs.

Toys: Antique to Modern. David Longest. (Illus.). 240p. 1994. 24.95 (0-89145-596-5) Collector Bks.

*Toys & Designs Book. (Beatrix Potter Collection). (Illus.). 128p. 12.98 (0-7651-0114-9) Smithmark.

*Toys & Games. 1997. 12.00 (0-679-88423-8) Knopf.

Toys & Games. (Ladybird Stories Ser.). (Illus.). (ARA.). (J). (gr. 4-6). 1987. 4.50 (0-86685-241-7) Intl Bk Ctr.

*Toys & Games. LC 96-48747. (Design & Create Ser.). (J). 1997. lib. bdg. write for info. (0-8172-4885-4) Raintree Steck-V.

Toys & Games for Children to Make. Gerri Jenny & Sherrie Gould. (Projects for Parents Ser.). (Illus.). 128p. (Orig.). 1990. pap. 10.95 (1-878767-81-X) Murdoch Bks.

Toys & Games into the Nineteen Nineties: The Complete Toys & Games Report. Euromonitor Staff. (C). 1990. 4,790.00 (0-685-37363-0, Pub. by Euromonitor Pubns UK) Gale.

*Toys & Games of Early America: A How-To Book. Charles W. Overstreet. Ed. by Denise Knight. (Illus.). 220p. (Orig.). 1997. pap. 15.95 (0-943604-54-0, BOO/31) Eagles View.

*Toys & Play: A Guide to Fun & Development for Children with Impaired Vision. Mary A. Lang et al. (Illus.). 56p. 1995. 9.95 (0-9603444-6-2, P580) Lighthouse NYC.

Toys & Play for the Handicapped Child. Barbara Riddick. (Illus.). 224p. 1982. pap. 27.50 (0-7099-0292-1, Pub. by Croom Helm UK) Routledge Chapman & Hall.

Toys Antique & Collectible. David Longest. 1995. pap. 14.95 (0-89145-402-0) Collector Bks.

Toys As Culture. Brian Sutton-Smith. LC 85-20563. 290p. 1992. pap. 24.95 (0-89876-203-0) Gardner Pr.

Toys Everywhere. Cynthia H. Greising & David Greising. LC 95-16256. (World of Difference Ser.). (Illus.). 32p. (J). (gr. 3-7). 1995. lib. bdg. 19.50 (0-516-08178-0) Childrens.

Toys Everywhere. Cynthia David Greising. (World of Difference Ser.). (Illus.). 32p. (J). (gr. 3-7). 1996. reprint ed. pap. 6.95 (0-516-48178-9) Childrens.

Toys from Occupied Japan. Anthony Marsella. LC 95-69835. (Illus.). 144p. (Orig.). 1995. pap. 29.95 (0-88740-875-3) Schiffer.

Toys Go to War: World War II Military Toys, Games, Puzzles & Books. Jack Matthews. Ed. by Candace A. Chenoweth. LC 94-73995. (Illus.). 272p. (Orig.). (C). 1995. pap. 29.95 (0-929521-95-1) Pictorial Hist.

*Toys in Space: Exploring Science with the Astronauts. Carolyn Sumners. LC 97-12351. (Illus.). 324p. 1997. teacher ed., pap. text ed. 29.95 (0-07-069489-3) McGraw.

Toys in Space: Exploring Science with the Astronauts. Carolyn Sumners. LC 93-21036. pap. 10.95 (0-8306-4534-9) McGraw-Hill Prof.

Toys in Space: Exploring Science with the Astronauts. Carolyn Sumners. LC 93-21036. text ed. 17.95 (0-8306-4533-0) TAB Bks.

Toys in the Attic. Lillian Hellman. 1959. pap. 5.25 (0-8222-1163-7) Dramatists Play.

Toys in the Attic: Acting Edition see Four Contemporary American Plays

Toys in the Haunted Castle. Pat Zawadsky. (Illus.). 36p. 1977. pap. 3.25 (0-88680-192-3); Piano-Vocal Score. pap. 7.50 (0-88680-193-1) I E Clark.

Toys of Other Days. F. Nevill Jackson. LC 68-57989. (Illus.). 1972. reprint ed. 24.95 (0-405-08663-6, Pub. by Blom Pubns UK) Ayer.

Toys of Princes. Ghislain De Diesbach. Tr. & Intro. by Richard Howard. LC 92-81006. 200p. (Orig.). (C). 1992. pap. 12.95 (0-9627987-2-X) Turtle Point Pr.

*Toys of the Sixties: A Pictorial Price Guide. 4th ed. William R. Bruegman, III. Ed. by Joanne M. Bruegman. (Illus.). 209p. 1996. pap. 19.95 (0-9632637-7-3) Toy Scouts.

Toys, Play, & Child Development. Ed. by Jeffrey H. Goldstein. (Illus.). 175p. (C). 1994. text ed. 49.95 (0-521-45062-4); pap. text ed. 14.95 (0-521-45564-2) Cambridge U Pr.

Toys R Us Toy Guide. Sandy Macdonald. 1996. mass mkt. 6.99 (0-671-52598-0) PB.

Toys, Scientific & Musical Instruments: Vehicles of Transportation see Encyclopedie Des Arts Decoratifs et Industriels Modernes

Toys Take over Christmas. Patricia Clapp. 1977. 3.75 (0-87129-545-8, T46) Dramatic Pub.

Toys That Talk: Over Three Hundred Pullstring Dolls & Toys - 1960's to Today. Joe A. Johnson & Dana McGuinn. 209p. 1991. pap. 12.95 (1-880163-00-4) Firefly Pub.

Toys to Go: A Guide to the Use of Realia in Public Libraries. Ed. by Faith H. Hektoen & James R. Rinehart. (Illus.). 25p. reprint ed. pap. 25.00 (0-7837-5952-5, 2045752) Bks Demand.

*Toys to Make. Smithmark Staff. 1996. 9.98 (0-7651-9760-X) Smithmark.

*Toys We Play With. Sally Hewitt & Jane Rowe. LC 96-30861. (Have You Noticed? Ser.). (J). 1997. lib. bdg. write for info. (0-8172-4602-9) Raintree Steck-V.

Toys with Nine Lives: A Social History of American Toys. Andrew McClary. LC 96-21550. (Illus.). 258p. (J). 1997. lib. bdg. 35.00 (0-208-02386-0, Linnet Bks) Shoe String.

Toys Wooden: Beautiful Small Unique Toys, Handcrafted with Simple Tools. J. James Hasenau. LC 84-61368. 1985. pap. 12.95 (0-913042-16-1) Holland Hse Pr.

Toyshop 1996 Annual. 4th ed. Toyshop Magazine Staff. (Illus.). 80p. 1995. pap. text ed. 9.95 (0-87341-409-8, TS96) Krause Pubns.

*Tozer on Entertainment & Worship. Compiled by James L. Snyder. 1997. pap. 8.99 (0-87509-715-4) Chr Pubns.

Tozer Pulpit: Selections from His Pulpit Ministry, 2 vols., Set. 3rd ed. Aiden W. Tozer. 1200p. 1994. 39.99 (0-87509-572-0, 0015720) Chr Pubns.

Tozzer Library. 2nd ed. Library of the Peabody Museum of Archaeology & Ethnology, Harvard University Staff. (Library Reference Ser.). 1988. 7,260.00 (0-8161-1731-4) G K Hall.

Tozzetti. (Phytopathological Classics Ser.). 139p. 1952. 15.00 (0-89054-010-1) Am Phytopathol Soc.

TP Software Development for OpenVMS: ACMS, DECforms, SQL, Rdb & CDD. John M. Willis. LC 93-8679. 384p. (Orig.). 1994. pap. text ed. 35.00 (1-878956-34-5) CBM Bks.

TPM - Total Productive Maintenance: The Western Way. Peter Willmott. LC 94-12560. (Illus.). 296p. 1995. 90.95 (0-7506-1925-2) Buttrwrth-Heinemann.

TPM Case Studies. Nikkan K. Shimbun. LC 94-31518. (Factory Management Notebook Ser.). (Illus.). 195p. (JPN.). 1995. 30.00 (1-56327-066-8) Prod Press.

TPM for America: What It Is & Why You Need It. Herbert R. Steinbacher & Norma L. Steinbacher. LC 92-31388. (Illus.). 169p. 1993. 25.00 (1-56327-044-7) Prod Press.

TPM for Every Operator. Japan Institute of Plant Maintenance Staff. (Shopfloor Ser.). (Illus.). 137p. 1996. reprint ed. pap. 25.00 (1-56327-080-3) Prod Press.

*TPM for Every Operator Learning Package. (Illus.). 1997. ring bd. 295.00 (1-56327-164-8) Prod Press.

TPM for Supervisors. Kunio Shirose. 1996. pap. text ed. 25.00 (1-56327-161-3) Prod Press.

TPM for Workshop Leaders. Kunio Shirose. Tr. by Bruce Talbot from JPN. LC 91-26611. 164p. 1992. 40.00 (0-915299-92-5) Prod Press.

TPM Implementation: A Japanese Approach. Masaji Tajiri. 1992. text ed. 49.00 (0-07-062834-3) McGraw.

TPM in Process Industries. Ed. by Tokutaro Suzuki. (Illus.). 392p. 1994. 85.00 (1-56327-036-6, 70366) Prod Press.

TPM Para Mandos Intermedios. Kunio Shirose. 155p. 1992. pap. 40.00 (84-87022-11-1) Prod Press.

TPM Para Operarios. Kunio Shirose. 97p. (Orig.). (SPA.). 1994. pap. 17.00 (84-87022-12-X) Prod Press.

TPM Team Guide - Shopfloor Series. Japan Institute of Plant Maintenance Staff. Ed. by Kunio Shirose. (Illus.). 169p. 1996. pap. 25.00 (1-56327-079-X) Prod Press.

TPM That Works: The Theory & Design of Total Productive Maintenance. Bill N. Maggard. LC 92-41792. (Illus.). 202p. (C). 1992. text ed. 39.95 (1-882258-01-0, TPMTW) TPM Pr.

*Tponohp Bephoctu. Georgi P. Vins. 315p. 1997. write for info. (0-9648588-1-9) Russian Gospel.

TPR Is More Than Commands - At All Levels. Contee Seely & Elizabeth Romijn. 184p. 1995. pap. text ed. 14.95 (0-929724-14-3) Command Performance.

TPR Student Kit Stories. Joan M. Rosen. (Illus.). 80p. 1994. pap. 10.95 (1-56018-420-5) Sky Oaks Prodns.

TQ Twenty: Twenty Years of Triquarterly. Ed. by Reginald Gibbons. LC 85-60910. (Illus.). 1983. 28.00 (0-916366-31-6) Pushcart Pr.

TQC Solutions: The Fourteen-Step Process, 2 vols. Ed. by JUSE Problem Solving Research Group Staff. (Illus.). 430p. 1991. Set. 50.00 (0-915299-79-8) Prod Press.

TQE Principal: A Transformed Leader. Richard Sagor & Bruce G. Barnett. LC 93-40956. (Total Quality Education for the World's Best Schools Ser.: Vol. 4). 168p. 1994. pap. 18.95 (0-8039-6123-5) Corwin Pr.

*TQM: A Basic Text. Larry McCloskey & Dennis Collett. 150p. 1993. pap. write for info. (1-879364-35-2) GOAL-QPC.

*TQM: A Pictorial Guide for Managers. John Oakland & Peter Morris. 90p. 1997. pap. 19.95 (0-7506-2324-1) Buttrwrth-Heinemann.

TQM: A Primer for Implementation. Lesley Muno-Faure & Malcolm Muno-Faure. 300p. 1994. text ed. 30.00 (0-7863-0138-4) Irwin Prof Pubng.

TQM: A Step-by-Step Guide to Implementation. Charles N. Weaver. 235p. 1991. 39.00 (0-87389-116-3, H0644) ASQC Qual Pr.

*T.Q.M: An Integrated Approach. Samuel Ho. (Quality Management Ser.). 1995. 55.00 (0-7494-1561-4) Kogan Page Ltd.

TQM: Does It Always Work? John MacDonald. 1994. 150.00 (0-946655-77-4, Pub. by Stanley Thornes UK) Trans-Atl Phila.

TQM: Leadership for the Quality Transformation. Richard S. Johnson. LC 92-18532. (Johnson TQM Ser.: Vol. 1). 342p. 1993. 45.00 (0-87389-186-4, H0731) ASQC Qual Pr.

TQM: Management Processes for Quality Operations. Richard S. Johnson. LC 92-34009. (ASQC Total Quality Management Ser.: Vol. 2). 336p. 1993. 45.00 (0-87389-226-7, H0732) ASQC Qual Pr.

TQM: Mechanics of Quality Processes. Richard S. Johnson & Lawrence E. Kazense. LC 92-25408. (Johnson TQM Ser.: Vol. 3). 268p. 1993. 45.00 (0-87389-225-9, H0733) ASQC Qual Pr.

TQM: Quality Training Practices. Richard S. Johnson. LC 92-42759. (Johnson TQM Ser.: Vol. 4). 265p. 1993. 45.00 (0-87389-234-8, H0734) ASQC Qual Pr.

TQM - 50 Ways to Make It Work for You. JoAnn Haberer & MaryLou Webb. Ed. by Sara Schneider. LC 93-73149. (Fifty-Minute Ser.). (Illus.). 97p. (Orig.). 1994. pap. 10.95 (1-56052-256-9) Crisp Pubns.

TQM Almanac. Timeplace Inc. Staff. 768p. 1994. text ed. 75.00 (0-7863-0242-9) Irwin Prof Pubng.

TQM America: How America's Most Successful Companies Profit from Total Quality Management. Eric E. Anschutz. LC 95-4163. 232p. (Orig.). 1995. pap. 19.95 (1-881117-13-8) McGuinn & McGuire.

TQM & ISO 9000 for Architects & Designers. C. Nelson. LC 95-45348. (Illus.). 1995. text ed. 45.00 (0-07-046277-1) McGraw.

***TQM & Partnering.** 1996. pap. 15.00 (1-879304-51-1, J389) AIA DC.

TQM Approach to Achieving Manufacturing Excellence. A. Richard Shores. (Illus.). 318p. 1990. text ed. 34.95 (0-527-91632-3, 916323) Qual Resc.

TQM Basics. Lowell J. Arthur. (C). 1997. pap. text ed. write for info. (0-201-63487-2) Addison-Wesley.

***TQM Engineering Handbook.** Stamatis. LC 97-13117. (Quality & Reliability Ser.: Vol. 52). 608p. 1997. 135.00 (0-8247-0083-X) Dekker.

***TQM Facilitator's Guide.** Jerome S. Arcaro. (Illus.). 200p. (Orig.). 1997. pap. 29.95 (1-57444-089-6) St Lucie Pr.

TQM Field Manual. James H. Saylor. 288p. 1991. 34.95 (0-8306-2409-0) McGraw-Hill Prof.

TQM for Engineering: Applying Quality Principles to Product Design & Development. Ed. by Patrick J. Sweeney. LC 93-9945. 159p. 1993. 29.95 (0-527-91718-4) Qual Resc.

TQM for Purchasing Management. James F. Cali. 1992. text ed. 29.95 (0-07-009623-6) McGraw.

TQM for Sales & Marketing Management. James W. Cortada. LC 93-37. 240p. 1993. text ed. 24.95 (0-07-023752-2) McGraw.

TQM for Technical Groups: Total Quality Principles for Product Development. Kiyoshi Uchimaru et al. Ed. by Diane Asay. Tr. by Scott Decker from JPN. (Illus.). 256p. 1993. 40.00 (1-56327-005-6) Prod Press.

TQM for Training. Elaine Biech. 1994. text ed. 29.95 (0-07-005210-7) McGraw.

TQM in Action: A Practical Approach to Continuous Performance Improvement. John Pike & Richard Barnes. LC 93-34332. 1993. write for info. (0-412-48790-X) Chapman & Hall.

TQM in Service Industries: A Practitioner's Manual. Ian Graham. (C). 1994. 150.00 (0-946655-65-0, Pub. by Stanley Thornes UK) Trans-Atl Phila.

TQM Simplified. 2nd ed. J. H. Saylor. (Illus.). 320p. 1996. text ed. 44.00 (0-07-057678-5) McGraw.

TQM Transformation: A Model for Organizational Change. Ed. by John Persico, Jr. 224p. 1992. text ed. 24.95 (0-527-91654-4, 916544) Qual Resc.

TQM Trilogy: Using ISO 9000, the Deming Prize, & the Baldrige Award to Establish a System for Total Quality Management. Francis X. Mahoney & Carl G. Thor. 224p. 1994. 29.95 (0-8144-5105-5) AMACOM.

TQManager: A Practical Guide for Managing in a Total Quality Organization. Warren H. Schmidt & Jerome P. Finnigan. LC 93-4588. (Management Ser.). 192p. 27.00 (1-55542-559-3) Jossey-Bass.

TQS: Total Quality Sales. Jack Bernstein. 224p. (Orig.). 1997. pap. 19.95 (0-9616226-7-9) JB & Me.

TQS Factor & You: Learn to Lead Yourself, Manage Your Boss, Delight Your Customer. G. Ronald Gilbert. 260p. 1992. pap. 14.95 (0-9630251-0-4) Busn Perf.

TR for Triumph. Chris Harvey. (Illus.). 229p. 31.95 (0-902280-94-5, P094, Pub. by Oxford Ill Pr) Haynes Pubns.

Tra Due Secoli: Il Tardo Ottocento e il Primo Novecento Nella Critica Italiana Dell'Ultimo Ventennio. Ed. by Leonard G. Sbrocchi & Francesco Loriggio. (Biblioteca di Quaderni d'Italianistica Ser.). 184p. (Orig.). (C). 1988. pap. 15.00 (0-9691979-4-2, Pub. by Can Soc Ital Stu CN) Speedimpex.

TRAA: Therapeutic Recreation Activity Assessment. M. A. Hoss. Ed. by Joan Burlingame. 27p. (Orig.). 1993. ring bd. 240.00 incl. vhs (1-882883-15-2) Idyll Arbor.

Trabajador Cubano En El Estado De Obreros y Campesinos. Efren Cordova. LC 89-81223. (Coleccion Cuba y Sus Jueces). 219p. (Orig.). (SPA.). 1990. pap. 16.00 (0-89729-553-6) Ediciones.

Trabajadores Frente a la Crisis. Emilio Maspero. (Coleccion CLAT Ser.). 124p. (Orig.). (SPA.). 1986. pap. 6.00 (0-917049-04-7) Saeta.

Trabajadores Puertorriquenos y el Partido Socialista, 1932 a 1940. Blanca Silvestrini De Pacheco. Orig. Title: Puerto Rican Workers & the Socialist Party, 1932-1940. (Illus.). (SPA.). 1979. pap. 6.00 (0-8477-0858-6) U of PR Pr.

***Trabajando Tu Llamado a las Naciones - Working Your Callway to the Nations.** Lewis. 205p. (SPA.). 1995. write for info. (1-56063-975-X) Editorial Unilit.

Trabajo del Pastor Evangelico. Seth Mswell & Donald Crider. Tr. & Adapted by David Tinoco. (SPA.). 1982. 9.25 (1-55955-106-2) CRC Wrld Lit.

Trabajo Social Se Manifiesta. 60p. 1992. 14.95 (0-87101-222-7) Natl Assn Soc Wkrs.

Trabajos Arqueologicos en el Centro de la Ciudad de Mexico. 2nd ed. Ed. by Eduardo Matos. 584p. 1990. pap. 14.00 (968-6487-42-5, IN021) UPLAAP.

***Trabajos Desconocidos y Olvidados de Jose Maria Heredia.** Angel A. Laurencio. (SPA.). pap. 9.00 (0-89729-140-9) Ediciones.

***Trabajos Manuales de los Tiempos Biblicos.** Hickerson. (SPA.). (J). 1995. write for info. (0-614-27146-0) Editorial Unilit.

***Trabajos Manuales de los Tiempos Biblicos - Bible Times: Crafts for Kids.** Hickerson. (SPA.). 1995. write for info. (0-614-24404-8) Editorial Unilit.

Trabantenstadt. Rene De Goscinny & M. Uderzo. (Illus.). (GER.). (J). 19.95 (0-8288-4910-2) Fr & Eur.

Trabelin' On: The Slave Journey to an Afro-Baptist Faith. Mechal Sobel. LC 77-84775. (Contributions in Afro-American & African Studies: No. 36). 454p. 1979. text ed. 79.50 (0-8371-9887-9, STO/, Greenwood Pr) Greenwood.

TrAC - Trends in Analytical Chemistry. (TrAC Compendium Ser.: Vol. 14). 540p. 1995. 581.50 (0-444-82388-3) Elsevier.

TrAC - Trends in Analytical Chemistry: Reference Edition. (TrAC Compendium Ser.: Vol. 12). 510p. 1994. 442.00 (0-444-81805-7) Elsevier.

TrAC - Trends in Analytical Chemistry: Reference Edition. (TrAC Compendium Ser.: Vol. 13). 664p. 1995. 458.25 (0-444-82110-4) Elsevier.

TrAC Directory of Hypenated Techniques: Supplement No. 2. Z. Deyl. 178p. 1994. pap. 86.50 (0-444-82126-0) Elsevier.

***TRAC 94: Theoretical Roman Archaeology.** Ed. by Sally Cottam et al. 150p. 1995. pap. 18.00 (0-946897-86-7, Pub. by Oxbow Bks UK) David Brown.

***TRAC-Trends in Analytical Chemistry: Reference Edition.** (TRAC Compendium Ser.: Vol. 15). 878p. 1997. 623.75 (0-444-82662-9) Elsevier.

Trace. Albert Lorenz. LC 92-46409. (Illus.). 304p. 1993. pap. 35.00 (0-8230-0172-5, Whitney Lib) Watsn-Guptill.

***Trace a Moment's Closure for Clues.** Steve Carll. 40p. (Orig.). 1996. pap. write for info. (0-9651401-1-3) Logodaedalus.

Trace Amines: Comparative & Clinical Neurobiology. Ed. by Alan A. Boulton et al. LC 88-6847. (Experimental & Clinical Neuroscience Ser.). (Illus.). 496p. 1988. 99.50 (0-89603-144-6) Humana.

Trace Amines & the Brain: Proceedings of a Study Group Held at the Fourteenth Annual Meeting of the American College of Neuropsychopharmacology, San Juan, Puerto Rico. Ed. by Earl Usdin & Merton Sandler. LC 76-12282. (Psychopharmacology Ser.: No. 1). (Illus.). 319p. reprint ed. pap. 91.00 (0-7837-0671-5, 2041006) Bks Demand.

Trace Analysis with Microcolumn Liquid Chromatography. Ed. by Krejci. (Chromatographic Science Ser.: Vol. 59). 224p. 1992. 140.00 (0-8247-8641-6) Dekker.

Trace & Forty-Seven Miles of Rope. Warren Murphy. (Trace Ser.: No. 2). 1984. pap. 2.95 (0-317-00847-1, Sig) NAL-Dutton.

Trace & Reactive Metals - Processing & Technology: Proceedings of the International Symposium on Extraction & Processing of Trace & Reactive Metals, Sponsored by the Extraction & Processing Et Al. Ed. by R. G. Reddy & B. Mishra. LC 94-73543. 291p. 1995. 74.00 (0-87339-280-9, 2809) Minerals Metals.

Trace & Transformation: American Criticism of Photography in the Modernist Period. Joel Eisinger. LC 94-18753. 320p. 1995. 45.00 (0-8263-1623-9) U of NM Pr.

Trace & Ultratrace Analysis by HPLC. Satinder Ahuja. LC 91-7276. (Chemical Analysis: A Series of Monographs on Analytical Chemistry & Its Applications). 432p. 1991. text ed. 99.95 (0-471-51419-5) Wiley.

***Trace & Write (Language)** Jo E. Moore. (Reading & Writing Ser.). (Illus.). 32p. (J). (ps-k). 1996. teacher ed., pap. 2.95 (1-55799-400-5, 4002) Evan-Moor Corp.

Trace Atmospheric Constituents: Properties, Transformations & Fates. Stephen E. Schwartz. LC 82-16095. (Advances in Environmental Science & Technology Ser.). 564p. 1983. 85.00 (0-471-87640-2) Krieger.

Trace Contaminants from Coal. Ed. by S. Torrey. LC 78-61890. (Pollution Technology Review Ser.: No. 50). 249p. 1979. 39.00 (0-8155-0724-0) Noyes.

Trace Determination of Pesticides & Their Degradation in Water. D. Barcelo & M.-C. Hennion. 1996. write for info. (0-614-17889-4) Elsevier.

Trace Element Analysis in Biological Specimens. Ed. by R. F. Herber & M. Stoeppler. LC 94-11681. (Techniques & Instrumentation in Analytical Chemistry Ser.: Vol. 15). 590p. 1994. 311.25 (0-444-89867-0) Elsevier.

Trace Element Analytical Chemistry in Medicine & Biology, Vol. 1. Ed. by Peter Schramel. 1000p. 1980. 161.55 (3-11-008357-4) De Gruyter.

Trace Element Analytical Chemistry in Medicine & Biology, Vol. 2. Ed. by Peter Braetter & Peter Schramel. 1189p. 1983. 253.85 (3-11-008681-6) De Gruyter.

Trace Element Analytical Chemistry in Medicine & Biology Vol. 4: Proceedings of the 4th International Workshop, Neuherberg, Federal Republic of Germany, 1986. Ed. by P. Baretter & Peter Schramel. xiii, 630p. 1987. lib. bdg. 240.00 (3-11-010905-0) De Gruyter.

Trace Element Analytical Chemistry in Medicine & Biology Vol. 5: Proceedings of the Fifth International Workshop, Neuherberg, Federal Republic of Germany, April 1988. Ed. by Peter Bratter & Peter Schramel. xx, 666p. (C). 1990. lib. bdg. 235.00 (3-11-011340-6) De Gruyter.

Trace Element Analytical Chemistry in Medicine & Biology, Vol. 3: Proceedings of the 3rd International Workshop. Ed. by P. Braetter & Peter Schramel. LC 80-26803. (Illus.). xvi, 763p. 1984. 219.25 (3-11-009821-0) De Gruyter.

Trace-Element Contamination of the Environment: Fundamental Aspects of Pollution Control & Environmental Science, 7. rev. ed. D. Purves. 244p. 1985. 133.25 (0-444-42503-9) Elsevier.

Trace Element Geochemistry in Health & Disease. Ed. by Jacob Freedman. LC 75-3801. (Geological Society of America, Special Paper Ser.: No. 155). 126p. reprint ed. pap. 36.00 (0-685-16455-1, 2027368) Bks Demand.

Trace Element Medicine & Chelation Therapy. David M. Taylor & David R. Williams. (Royal Society of Chemistry Paperbacks Ser.). 124p. 1995. pap. 29.95 (0-85404-503-1) CRC Pr.

Trace Element Metabolism in Animals--2: Proceedings of the International Symposium, 2nd, University of Wisconsin, Madison, 1973. International Symposium on Trace Element Metabolism in Animals Staff. Ed. by W. G. Hoekstra & J. W. Suttie. LC 74-11167. 801p. reprint ed. pap. 180.00 (0-317-41887-4, 2025746) Bks Demand.

Trace Element Speciation: Analytical Methods & Problems. Batley. 360p. 1989. 241.95 (0-8493-4712-2) CRC Pr.

Trace Elements & Iron in Human Metabolism. Ananda S. Prasad. LC 78-13446. (Topics in Hematology Ser.). 408p. reprint ed. pap. 116.30 (0-317-26186-X, 2052077) Bks Demand.

Trace Elements & Man. Henry A. Schroeder. LC 72-85731. (Illus.). 192p. 1973. pap. 7.95 (0-8159-6907-4) Devin.

Trace Elements from a Recurring Kingdom. William P. Root. LC 94-71360. 1994. 25.00 (1-881090-12-4); pap. 15.00 (1-881090-11-6) Confluence Pr.

Trace Elements, Hair Analysis & Nutrition: Fact & Myth. Richard A. Passwater & Elmer M. Cranton. LC 81-83892. 1983. 18.95 (0-87983-348-3); pap. 14.95 (0-87983-265-7) Keats.

Trace Elements in Clinical Medicine: Proceedings of the Second Meeting of the International Society for Trace Element Research in Humans (ISTERH), August 28-September 1, 1989, Tokyo. Ed. by H. Tomita. (Illus.). 522p. 1990. 96.00 (0-387-70060-9) Spr-Verlag.

Trace Elements in Coal, Vol. 2. V. Valkovic. LC 82-4386. 1983. 165.00 (0-8493-5492-7, CRC Reprint) Franklin.

Trace Elements in Coal & Coal Combustion Residues. Ed. by Robert F. Keefer & Kenneth S. Sajwan. LC 93-17908. (Advances in Trace Substances Research Ser.). 336p. 1993. 97.95 (0-87371-890-9, L890) Lewis Pubs.

Trace Elements in Crop Production. P. C. Srivastava & U. C. Gupta. (Illus.). 300p. 1996. lib. bdg. 82.00 (1-886106-62-2) Science Pubs.

Trace Elements in Health & Disease. Aito & J. Jarvisalo. 1991. 132.00 (0-85186-976-9) CRC Pr.

Trace Elements in Health & Disease. Ed. by H. Bostrom & N. Ljungstedt. (Illus.). 285p. 1985. text ed. 78.00 (91-22-00733-4) Coronet Bks.

Trace Elements in Health Biology: Index of Modern Information. Nevil Y. Farrugia. LC 88-47954. 150p. 1988. 44.50 (0-88164-994-5); pap. 39.50 (0-88164-995-3) ABBE Pubs Assn.

Trace Elements in Human & Animal Nutrition, Vol. 1. 5th ed. Walter Mertz. 480p. 1987. text ed. 99.00 (0-12-491251-6) Acad Pr.

Trace Elements in Human & Animal Nutrition, Vol. 2. 5th ed. Walter Mertz. 1986. text ed. 99.00 (0-12-491252-4) Acad Pr.

Trace Elements in Human Nutrition: Proceedings of the WHO Expert Committee, Geneva, 1973. WHO Staff. (Technical Report Ser.: No. 532). 1973. pap. text ed. 7.00 (92-4-120532-6, 1100532) World Health.

Trace Elements in Human Plasma or Serum. Ed. by Jacques Versieck. 224p. 1988. 135.00 (0-8493-6810-3, QP99, CRC Reprint) Franklin.

Trace Elements in Laboratory Rodents. Ed. by Ronald R. Watson. LC 96-15926. (Methods in Nutrition Research Ser.). 416p. 1996. 69.95 (0-8493-9611-5) CRC Pr.

Trace Elements in Man & Animals 6. 6th ed. Ed. by Lucille S. Hurley et al. (Illus.). 676p. 1988. 135.00 (0-306-43004-5, Plenum Pr) Plenum.

Trace Elements in Natural Waters. Salbu. 314p. 1994. 89.95 (0-8493-6304-7) CRC Pr.

Trace Elements in Nutrition of Children. Ed. by Ranjit K. Chandra. LC 85-10649. (Nestle Nutrition Workshop Ser.: Vol. 8). 320p. 1985. reprint ed. pap. 91.20 (0-608-00441-3, 2061156) Bks Demand.

Trace Elements in Nutrition of Children Two. Ranjit K. Chandra. (Nestle Nutrition Workshop Ser.: Vol. 23). 248p. 1991. text ed. 61.00 (0-88167-741-8, 2209) Lppncott-Raven.

Trace Elements in Relation to Cardiovascular Diseases: Status of the Joint WHO-IAEA Research Programme. Ed. by R. Masironi. (Offset Publication Ser.: No. 5). 1974. pap. text ed. 7.00 (92-4-170005-X, 1120005) World Health.

Trace Elements in Renal Insufficiency. Ed. by E. Quellhorst et al. (Contributions to Nephrology Ser.: Vol. 38). (Illus.). x, 206p. 1984. 91.25 (3-8055-3676-3) S Karger.

Trace Elements in Soils & Plants. Ed. by Alina K. Pendias & Henryk K. Pendias. 336p. 1984. 176.00 (0-8493-6639-9, S592) CRC Pr.

Trace Elements in Soils & Plants. 2nd ed. Ed. by Alina Kabata-Pendias & Henryk Pendias. 384p. 1991. 219.95 (0-8493-6643-7, S592) CRC Pr.

Trace Elements in Soils of the South Texas Uranium District: Concentrations, Origin, & Environmental Significance. C. D. Henry & R. R. Kapadia. (Report of Investigations Ser.: RI 101). (Illus.). 52p. 1980. pap. 2.00 (0-318-03243-0) Bur Econ Geology.

***Trace Elements in the Environment.** Ed. by Evaldo L. Kothny. LC 73-87347. (Advances in Chemistry Ser.: Vol. 123). 159p. 1973. reprint ed. pap. 45.40 (0-608-03900-4, 2064347) Bks Demand.

Trace Elements in the Terrestrial Environment. D. C. Adriano. (Illus.). xix, 533p. 1985. 178.95 (0-387-96158-5) Spr-Verlag.

Trace Elements, Micronutrients & Free Radicals. Ed. by Ivor E. Dreosti. LC 91-13721. (Contemporary Issues in Biomedicine, Ethics & Society Ser.). (Illus.). 239p. 1991. 79.50 (0-89603-188-8) Humana.

Trace Fossil Concepts. Ed. by Paul B. Basan. (Society of Economic Paleontologists & Mineralogists, Special Publication Ser.: No. 5). (Illus.). 185p. reprint ed. pap. 52.80 (0-317-58122-8, 2029675) Bks Demand.

Trace Fossils: Biology & Taphonomy. Richard Bromley. (Special Topics in Palaeontology Ser.). (Illus.). 310p. (C). 1990. text ed. 65.00 (0-04-445303-5); pap. text ed. 29.95 (0-04-445686-7) Routledge Chapman & Hall.

***Trace Fossils: Biology, Taphonomy & Applications.** 2nd ed. Bromley. (Illus.). 384p. (Orig.). 1996. pap. text ed. 43.00 (0-412-61480-4, Chap & Hall NY) Chapman & Hall.

Trace Gas Emissions by Plants. Ed. by Thomas D. Sharkey et al. (Physiological Ecology Ser.). (Illus.). 365p. 1991. text ed. 109.00 (0-12-639010-X) Acad Pr.

Trace Metal Analysis & Speciation Journal of Chromatography Library, Vol. 47. I. S. Krull. 302p. 1991. 185.25 (0-444-88209-X) Elsevier.

Trace Metal Removal from Aqueous Solution, No. 61. Thompson. 1987. 105.00 (0-85186-646-8) CRC Pr.

Trace Metals & Fluoride in Bones & Teeth. Priest & Vyver. 400p. 1990. 254.00 (0-8493-6190-7, QP88) CRC Pr.

Trace Metals in Combustion Systems. David A. Tillman. (Illus.). 276p. 1994. text ed. 79.00 (0-12-691265-3) Acad Pr.

Trace Minerals in Foods. Smith. (Food Science & Technology Ser.: Vol. 28). 488p. 1988. 210.00 (0-8247-7835-9) Dekker.

Trace of Desert Waters. Samuel G. Houghton. (Illus.). 296p. 1994. pap. 14.95 (0-87417-234-9) U of Nev Pr.

Trace of Political Representation. Brian Seitz. LC 94-10611. (SUNY Series in Radical, Social & Political Theory). 232p. 1995. text ed. 57.50 (0-7914-2365-4); pap. text ed. 18.95 (0-7914-2366-2) State U NY Pr.

Trace Residue Analysis: Chemometric Estimations of Sampling, Amount, & Error. Ed. by Davie A. Kurtz. (ACS Symposium Ser.: No. 284). 284p. 1985. lib. bdg. 65.95 (0-8412-0925-1) Am Chemical.

***Trace Residue Analysis: Chemometric Estimations of Sampling, Amount, & Error.** Ed. by David A. Kurtz. LC 85-11226. (ACS Symposium Ser.: Vol. 284). 1985. reprint ed. pap. 84.40 (0-608-03913-6, 2064360) Bks Demand.

Trace Resource Book: 1991-92 Edition: Assistive Technologies for Communication, Control & Computer Access. Ed. by Jane R. Berliss et al. (Illus.). 900p. 1991. pap. 50.00 (0-945459-02-5) Trace Res & Dev.

Trace Resource Book: 1996-97 Edition: Assistive Technologies for Communication, Control & Computer Access. Ed. by Peter A. Borden. (Illus.). 950p. (Orig.). 1995. pap. 50.00 (0-945459-04-1) Trace Res & Dev.

Trace Resource Book, 1993-94: Assistive Technologies for Communication, Control & Computer Access. Ed. by Peter A. Borden et al. (Illus.). 950p. (Orig.). 1992. pap. 50.00 (0-945459-03-3) Trace Res & Dev.

Trace Rings of Generic Two by Two Matrices. Lieven LeBruyn. LC 87-1810. (Memoirs of the American Mathematical Society Ser.: Vol. 363). 100p. 1987. pap. 18.00 (0-8218-2425-2, MEMO/66/363C) Am Math.

Trace Su Camino Al Exito. Glenn Bland. 99p. (SPA.). 1990. pap. 2.49 (1-56063-025-6, 498057) Editorial Unilit.

Trace Substances & Health, Pt. 1, 1976: A Handbook. Ed. by Paul M. Newberne. LC 75-25167. (Illus.). 412p. reprint ed. pap. 117.50 (0-7837-0705-3, 2041037) Bks Demand.

Trace System: How to Get Organized, How to Stay Organized. James P. King. 1986. pap. 9.95 (0-936895-01-2) Brown House.

Trace Theory & VLSI Design. Jan L. Van de Snepscheut. (Lecture Notes in Computer Science Ser.: Vol. 200). vi, 140p. 1985. 25.00 (0-387-15988-6) Spr-Verlag.

Trace Theory for Automatic Hierarchical Verification of Speed Independent Circuits. David L. Dill. 200p. 1989. 32.50 (0-262-04101-4) MIT Pr.

Traceability & Quality Control in the Measurement of Environmental Radioactivity: Seminar Sponsored by the International Committee for Radionuclide Metrology in Braunschweig, June 18-19, 1979. 80p. 1980. pap. 18.25 (0-08-026253-8, Pergamon Pr) Elsevier.

***Traceable Calibration of Master Gears at PTB.** Wolfgang Beyer. (1996 Fall Technical Meeting Ser.: Vol. 4). 6p. 1996. pap. text ed. 30.00 (1-55589-671-5) AGMA.

Traceable Faces for Cloth Dolls. Barb Spencer. Ed. by Kim Shields. (Illus.). 64p. (Orig.). 1995. pap. 9.95 (1-879825-16-3) Jones Publish.

Traceable Temperatures: An Introduction of Temperatures, Measurement & Calibration. J. V. Nicholas. 358p. 1994. text ed. 115.00 (0-471-93803-3) Wiley.

Tracer Hydrology: Proceedings of the Sixth International Symposium on Water Tracing Karlsruhe - Germany 21-26 September 1992. Ed. by H. Hotzel & A. Werner. (Illus.). 477p. (C). 1992. text ed. 110.00 (90-5410-084-2, Pub. by A A Balkema NE) Ashgate Pub Co.

Tracer, Inc. Jeff Andrus. 1994. text ed. 20.00 (0-684-19705-7) S&S Trade.

Tracer Manual on Crops & Soils. (Technical Reports: No. 171). (Illus.). 227p. 1976. pap. 60.00 (92-0-115076-8, IDC171, Pub. by IAEA AU) Bernan Associates.

Tracer Techniques in Sediment Transport. (Technical Reports: No. 145). (Illus.). 234p. (Orig.). 1973. pap. 35.00 (92-0-145073-7, IDC145, Pub. by IAEA AU) Bernan Associates.

An Asterisk (*) at the beginning of an entry indicates that the title is appearing in BIP for the first time.

Traceries. Gertrude Johnson. Ed. by Janet Leih. 96p. (Orig.). 1993. pap. 9.00 (*1-877649-20-1*) Tesseract SD.

Tracers. Vincent Caristi et al. 71p. 1987. pap. 5.25 (*0-8222-1164-5*) Dramatists Play.

Tracers in the Ocean. Ed. by H. Charnock et al. 552p. 1990. pap. text ed. 29.95 (*0-691-02443-X*) Princeton U Pr.

Tracers in the Oil Field. B. Zemel. 514p. 1994. 231.50 (*0-444-88968-X*) Elsevier.

Traces. Aaron Rosen. LC 91-13792. 77p. 1991. pap. 10.95 (*1-878818-10-4*) Sheep Meadow.

Traces. Mary S. Tyler. (Illus.). 46p. 1994. 35.00 (*1-880515-51-2*) Schl Mus Fine.

***Traces: Journey to Lost Frontiers.** Mitchell. 1996. 22.95 (*0-8050-1981-2*) H Holt & Co.

Traces: The Story of Lexington's Past. Dag Ryen. (Illus.). 177p. (J). (gr. 4 up). 1987. text ed. 13.95 (*0-912839-08-2*) Lexington-Fayette.

Traces & Their Antecedents. Samuel D. Epstein. (Illus.). 216p. 1991. 45.00 (*0-19-506485-2*) OUP.

Traces Behind the Esmeraldas Shore: Prehistory of the Santiago-Cayapas Region, Ecuador. Warren R. DeBoer. LC 95-8371. (Illus.). 240p. (Orig.). (SPA.). (C). 1996. pap. text ed. 29.95 (*0-8173-0792-3*) U of Ala Pr.

Traces-Fire. Winslow Durgin. 4.00 (*0-686-15294-8*) Great Raven Pr.

Traces of an Omnivore. Paul Shepard. 307p. 1996. 24.95 (*1-55963-431-6*) Island Pr.

Traces of Another Time: History & Politics in Postwar British Fiction. Margaret Scanlan. 215p. 1990. text ed. 35.00 (*0-691-06824-0*) Princeton U Pr.

Traces of Bygone Biospheres. Andrey Lapo. (Illus.). 356p. 1988. pap. 8.95 (*0-907791-06-9*) Synerg AZ.

Traces of Dance: Choreographers' Drawings & Notations. Paul Virilio. 1994. pap. text ed. 39.95 (*2-906571-28-8*, Pub. by Editions Dis Voir FR) Dist Art Pubs.

Traces of Differential Forms & Hochschild-Homology. R. Hubl. (Lecture Notes in Mathematics Ser.: Vol. 1368). iii, 111p. 1989. 39.95 (*0-387-50985-2*) Spr-Verlag.

Traces of God: Understanding God's Presence in the World Today. Peter Malone. 64p. (Orig.). 1991. pap. 6.95 (*0-8146-2074-4*) Liturgical Pr.

Traces of God in a Frequently Hostile World. Diogenes Allen. LC 80-51570. 108p. (Orig.). 1981. pap. 8.95 (*0-936384-03-4*) Cowley Pubns.

Traces of Guilt: Crime Science & the Fight for Justice. Hugh Miller. 200p. 1996. 20.00 (*1-57500-006-7*, Viewer Bks) TV Bks.

***Traces of Light: Sermons & Bible Studies.** Gerd Theissen. 240p. (Orig.). (C). 1996. pap. 24.00 (*0-334-02629-6*, SCM Pr) TPI PA.

Traces of Prehistory: Papers in Honor of William G. Haag. Ed. by Frederick H. West & Robert W. Neuman. LC 81-81201. (Geoscience & Man Ser.: Vol. 22). (Illus.). 134p. 1981. pap. 14.00 (*0-938909-30-4*) Geosci Pubns LSU.

Traces of the Brush: Studies in Chinese Calligraphy. Shen Fu. LC 76-49688. (Illus.). 328p. reprint ed. pap. 93.50 (*0-8357-6407-9*, 2035768) Bks Demand.

Traces of the Light. Charlie Camp. (Illus.). 344p. (Orig.). 1996. pap. 14.95 (*0-89896-154-8*) Larksdale.

Traces of the Oregon Trail. Robert Priest. (Northwest Mythic Landscape Ser.). (Illus.). 28p. 1993. 5.95 (*0-912365-80-3*) Sasquatch Bks.

Traces of the Past. Lambert. LC 97-11454. (C). 1997. write for info. (*0-201-40928-3*) Addison-Wesley.

Traces of the Past. Alan T. Synenki. 56p. 1994. pap. 4.95 (*0-915992-61-2*) Eastern Acorn.

Traces of Treasure: Quest for God in the Commonplace. Joanne Lehman. LC 93-36493. 160p. (Orig.). 1994. pap. 7.99 (*0-8361-3655-1*) Herald Pr.

Traces of War: Poetry, Photography & the Crisis of the Union. Timothy Sweet. LC 89-38436. (Parallax: Re-Visions of Culture & Society Ser.). (Illus.). 272p. 1990. text ed. 39.95 (*0-8018-3959-9*) Johns Hopkins.

Traces on the Appalachians: A Natural History of Serpentine in Eastern North America. Kevin T. Dann. (Illus.). 150p. (Orig.). (C). 1988. pap. 13.95 (*0-8135-1324-3*) Rutgers U Pr.

Traces on the Rhodian Shore: Nature & Culture in Western Thought from Ancient Times to the End of the Eighteenth Century. 5th ed. Clarence J. Glacken. LC 72-95298. 800p. 1967. reprint ed. 65.00 (*0-520-02367-6*) U CA Pr.

Traces on the Rhodian Shore: Nature & Culture in Western Thought from Ancient Times to the End of the Eighteenth Century. Clarence J. Glacken. LC 67-10970. 1967. reprint ed. pap. 32.50 (*0-520-03216-0*) U CA Pr.

Tracey: A Mother's Journal of Teenage Addiction. M. A. Anderson. 115p. 1988. 15.95 (*0-930773-07-1*); pap. 7.95 (*0-930773-08-X*) Black Heron Pr.

Tracey's Mess. Elise Peterson. (Illus.). 32p. (J). (ps-2). 1996. pap. 14.95 (*1-879085-94-1*) Whsprng Coyote Pr.

Tracey's Tough Choice. Suzanne Weyn. LC 93-25185. (Cover Kids Ser.). (Illus.). 128p. (J). (gr. 4-8). 1993. pap. 3.95 (*0-8167-3238-8*) Troll Communs.

Tracheal Intubation. Cros. 1992. 70.00 (*0-683-08584-0*) Williams & Wilkins.

Tracheal Reconstruction in Infancy. Thom E. Lobe. 1991. text ed. 110.00 (*0-7216-5779-6*) Saunders.

Tracheotomy. Ed. by Eugene N. Myers et al. (Illus.). 318p. 1985. text ed. 49.95 (*0-443-08381-9*) Churchill.

***Tracheotomy.** 3rd rev. ed. Johannes J. Fagan et al. LC 96-52775. (SIPac - Self-Instructional Package Ser.). (Illus.). 60p. 1997. pap. text ed. 25.00 (*1-56772-053-6*) AAO-HNS.

Trachiniae. Sophocles. Ed. by P. E. Easterling. LC 81-21680. (Cambridge Greek & Latin Classics Ser.). 256p. 1982. text ed. 65.00 (*0-521-20087-3*); pap. text ed. 22.95 (*0-521-28776-6*) Cambridge U Pr.

Trachtenberg Speed System of Basic Mathematics. Tr. by Ann Cutler & Rudolph McShane. LC 81-13439. 270p. 1982. reprint ed. text ed. 49.75 (*0-313-23200-8*, CUTS, Greenwood Pr) Greenwood.

***Traci on the Spot.** Marie Ferrarella. (Yours Truly Ser.). 1997. mass mkt. 3.50 (*0-373-52039-5*, 1-520394) Silhouette.

Tracie: From Here to Heaven. Harold Sofie & John Morgan. 160p. 1989. pap. 5.95 (*0-88144-147-3*) Christian Pub.

Tracing a River's Toxic Pollution: A Case Study of the Hudson, 2 vols., Vol. 1. Steven O. Rohmann & Nancy Lilienthal. LC 85-60234. 218p. 1985. Phase I, 1985, 162p. write for info. (*0-918780-30-6*) INFORM NY.

Tracing a River's Toxic Pollution: A Case Study of the Hudson, 2 vols., Vol. 2. Steven O. Rohmann & Nancy Lilienthal. LC 85-60234. 162p. 1987. Set. pap. 20.00 (*0-918780-40-3*) INFORM NY.

Tracing Archaeology's Past: The Historiography of Archaeology. Ed. by Andrew L. Christenson. LC 88-27278. (Publications in Archaeology). (Illus.). 288p. (C). 1989. 34.95 (*0-8093-1523-8*) S Ill U Pr.

Tracing Back the Radiance: Chinul's Korean Way of Zen. abr. ed. Robert E. Buswell, Jr. LC 91-28980. (Classics in East Asian Buddhism Ser.). (C). 1991. pap. text ed. 18.00 (*0-8248-1427-4*) UH Pr.

Tracing Biological Evolution in Protein & Gene Structures: Proceedings of the 20th Taniguchi International Symposium, Division of Biophysics, Held in Nagoya, Japan, 31 October-4 November 1994. Paul Schimmel. 322p. 1995. 184.75 (*0-444-82187-2*) Elsevier.

Tracing Chains-of-Thought: Fuzzy Methods in Cognitive Diagnosis, Vol. 7. Ed. by J. Kacprzyk. XVIII, 230p. 1996. 95.00 (*3-7908-0922-5*) Spr-Verlag.

Tracing, Charting & Writing Your Family History. rev. ed. Lois M. Skalka. LC 75-15954. 48p. 1994. pap. 5.95 (*0-87576-186-0*) Pilot Bks.

Tracing Common Themes: Comparative Courses in the Study of Religion. John B. Carman & Steven P. Hopkins. 318p. 1991. 44.95 (*1-55540-563-0*, 00 01 16); pap. 34.95 (*1-55540-564-9*, 00 01 16) Scholars Pr GA.

Tracing Cultures. Rebecca Solnit et al. Ed. by Michael Read & Steven Jenkins. (Points of Entry Ser.). (Illus.). 96p. (Orig.). (C). 1995. pap. 18.95 (*0-933286-69-4*) Frnds Photography.

Tracing Cultures: Art History, Criticism, Critical Fiction. Alexander Alberro et al. 176p. 1995. pap. 17.95 (*0-87427-092-8*) Dist Art Pubs.

Tracing Cultures: Art History Criticism Critical Fiction. Alexander Alberro et al. (Illus.). 176p. 1994. pap. 15.95 (*0-614-14990-8*) Whitney Mus.

Tracing EMFs in Building Wiring & Grounding. Karl Riley. (Illus.). 126p. (Orig.). 1995. pap. 27.50 (*0-9646790-0-0*) Magnetic Sci.

Tracing File for Interior & Architectural Rendering. Richard M. McGarry. (Illus.). 280p. 1988. pap. 42.95 (*0-442-20530-9*) Van Nos Reinhold.

Tracing It Home: A Chinese Journey. Lynn Pan. Ed. by Paul De Angelis. LC 93-20563. 240p. 1993. 22.00 (*1-56836-009-6*) Kodansha.

Tracing It Home: A Chinese Journey. Lynn Pan. 240p. 1995. reprint ed. pap. 14.00 (*1-56836-043-6*) Kodansha.

Tracing Life's Footprints. Jerry D. Lehman. LC 88-91214. 1989. 10.00 (*0-87212-218-2*) Libra.

Tracing Literary Theory. Ed. by Joseph Natoli. LC 86-24982. 400p. 1987. pap. 14.95 (*0-252-01384-0*) U of Ill Pr.

***Tracing Memory: Glossary of Graphic Signs & Symbols in African Art & Culture.** Clementine M. Faik-Nzuji. (Mercury Ser.). (Illus.). 216p. 1997. pap. 24.95 (*0-660-15965-1*, Pub. by Can Mus Civil CN) U of Wash Pr.

Tracing Minnesota's Old Government Roads. Grover Singley. LC 74-4149. (Minnesota Historic Sites Pamphlet Ser.: No. 10). 60p. reprint ed. pap. 25.00 (*0-8357-3318-1*, 2039542) Bks Demand.

Tracing Missing Heirs. Ralph D. Thomas. (Private Investigation Ser.). 90p. 1996. pap. text ed. 35.00 (*0-918487-91-9*) Thomas Pubns TX.

Tracing Missing Persons: An Introduction to Agencies & Methods in England & Wales. Colin D. Rogers. 208p. 1988. text ed. 24.95 (*0-7190-1901-X*, Pub. by Manchester Univ Pr UK) St Martin.

Tracing Neural Connections with Horseradish Peroxidase. M-Marsel Mesulam. (IBRO Handbook Ser.: Methods in the Neurosciences). 251p. 1982. pap. text ed. 140.00 (*0-471-10029-3*, Wiley-Interscience) Wiley.

Tracing New Orbits: Competition & Cooperation in Satellite Development. Donna A. Demac. LC 86-9593. (Columbia Studies in Business, Government & Society). 320p. 1986. text ed. 56.00 (*0-231-06344-X*) Col U Pr.

Tracing of Angels. large type ed. Minton. 1995. 25.99 (*0-7505-0806-X*, Pub. by Magna Print Bks UK) Ulverscroft.

Tracing Our English Roots. Sharon Moscinski. LC 94-26925. (American Origins Ser.). (Illus.). (J). 1995. 12.95 (*1-56261-188-7*) John Muir.

Tracing Our German Roots. Leda Silver. (American Origins Ser.). (Illus.). 48p. (J). (gr. 3-7). 1993. text ed. 12.95 (*1-56261-150-X*) John Muir.

Tracing Our Irish Roots. Sharon Moscinski. LC 93-2070. (American Origins Ser.). (Illus.). 48p. (J). 1993. text ed. 12.95 (*1-56261-148-8*) John Muir.

Tracing Our Italian Roots. Kathleen Lee. (American Origins Ser.). (Illus.). 48p. (J). (gr. 3-7). 1993. text ed. 12.95 (*1-56261-149-6*) John Muir.

Tracing Our Japanese Roots. Gary Kawaguchi. (American Origins Ser.). (Illus.). 48p. (J). (gr. 3-7). 1994. 12.95 (*1-56261-160-7*) John Muir.

Tracing Our Jewish Roots. Miriam Sagan. (American Origins Ser.). (Illus.). 48p. (J). (gr. 3-7). 1993. text ed. 12.95 (*1-56261-151-8*) John Muir.

Tracing Our Polish Roots. Sharon Moscinski. (American Origins Ser.). (Illus.). 48p. (J). (gr. 3-7). 1994. 12.95 (*1-56261-161-5*) John Muir.

Tracing Romania's Heterogeneous German Minority from Its Origins to the Diaspora. Jacob Steigerwald. LC 85-231201. (Illus.). 61p. 1985. pap. 4.95 (*0-9615505-1-1*) Trans Inter Serv.

***Tracing Shadows.** Rick Schaub. 1997. 69.95 (*1-57553-354-5*) Nat Lib Poetry.

***Tracing Subversive Currents in Goethe's Wilhelm Meister's Apprenticeship.** John Blair. LC 96-46641. (GERM Ser.). x, 200p. 1997. 54.95 (*1-57113-092-6*) Camden Hse.

Tracing T. S. Eliot's Spirit: Essays on His Poetry & Thought. A. David Moody. LC 95-47586. 172p. (C). 1996. text ed. 49.95 (*0-521-48060-4*) Cambridge U Pr.

Tracing the History of Eukaryotic Cells: The Enigmatic Smile. Betsey D. Dyer & Robert A. Obar. LC 93-26798. (Critical Moments in Paleobiology & Earth History Ser.). 335p. 1984. 61.00 (*0-231-07592-8*) Col U Pr.

Tracing the History of Eukaryotic Cells: The Enigmatic Smile. Betsey D. Dyer & Robert A. Obar. LC 93-26798. (Critical Moments in Paleobiology & Earth History Ser.). 335p. 1994. pap. 26.00 (*0-231-07593-6*) Col U Pr.

Tracing the Immigrant Ancestor. Arlene H. Eakle. 73p. 1973. pap. 18.00 (*0-940764-11-3*) Genealog Inst.

Tracing the Past at Honaunau. Dorothy B. Barrere. (Illus.). 28p. (Orig.). 1994. pap. text ed. 4.75 (*0-940295-15-6*) HI Natural Hist.

***Tracing the Past in Lexington, Massachusetts.** Edwin B. Worthen. LC 96-90883. 1997. 18.95 (*0-533-12208-2*) Vantage.

Tracing the Paths: Reading Isn't Equal Writing the Martyrology. Ed. by Roy Miki. (NFS Canada Ser.). 344p. 1993. pap. 16.95 (*0-88922-256-8*) Genl Dist Srvs.

Tracing the Rainbow. Mary H. Jones. LC 95-80719. 80p. 1996. 13.95 (*0-8233-0505-8*) Golden Quill.

Tracing the Semiotic Boundaries of Politics. Ed. by Pertti Ahonen. LC 93-25329. (Approaches to Semiotics Ser.: No. 111). (Illus.). ix, 399p. (C). 1993. lib. bdg. 160.00 (*3-11-013533-7*) Mouton.

Tracing the Spirit: Ethnographic Essays on Haitian Art. Karen M. Brown. LC 95-74922. (Illus.). 112p. 1996. pap. 29.95 (*0-295-97504-0*) U of Wash Pr.

Tracing the Threads: Studies in the Vitality of Jewish Pseudepigrapha. John C. Reeves. LC 94-25032. (SBL Early Judaism & Its Literature Ser.). 310p. 1994. pap. 19.95 (*1-55540-995-4*) Scholars Pr GA.

Tracing the Threads: Studies in the Vitality of Jewish Pseudepigrapha. Ed. by John C. Reeves. LC 94-25032. (SBL Early Judaism & Its Literature Ser.). 310p. 1994. 29.95 (*1-55540-994-6*, 063506) Scholars Pr GA.

Tracing the Universe, Finding Myself: A Journal & Writing Quest. B. Nina Holzer. LC 93-32585. 1994. pap. 11.00 (*0-517-88096-2*, Bell Tower) Crown Pub Group.

***Tracing Your Ancestors in Northern Ireland.** Ian Maxwell. (Illus.). 160p. 1997. pap. 14.95 (*0-11-495823-8*, Pub. by Statnry Ofc UK) Seven Hills Bk.

Tracing Your Ancestry: Step-by-Step Guide to Researching Your Family History. F. Wilbur Helmbold. LC 76-14109. (Illus.). 1978. pap. 9.95 (*0-8487-0486-X*) Oxmoor Hse.

Tracing Your Ancestry Logbook. F. Wilbur Helmbold. LC 76-14113. (Illus.). 256p. 1978. pap. 9.95 (*0-8487-0414-2*) Oxmoor Hse.

Tracing Your British Ancestors. Colin R. Chapman. 108p. 1996. reprint ed. pap. 15.00 (*0-8063-1503-2*) Genealog Pub.

Tracing Your Civil War Ancestor. Bertram H. Groene. 1989. pap. 10.00 (*0-345-36192-X*, Ballantine Trade) Ballantine.

Tracing Your Civil War Ancestor. 2nd rev. ed. Bertram H. Groene. LC 94-47605. (Illus.). 1996. 14.95 (*0-89587-123-8*) Blair.

Tracing Your Czech & Slovak Roots. Maralyn A. Wellauer. 77p. 1980. pap. 10.00 (*0-932019-04-8*) Roots Intl.

Tracing Your English Ancestors: A Manual for Analysing & Solving Genealogical Problems in England & Wales, 1538 to the Present Day. Colin D. Rogers. 196p. 1989. text ed. 35.00 (*0-7190-3172-9*, Pub. by Manchester Univ Pr UK) St Martin.

Tracing Your Family History. (C). 1987. 30.00 (*0-317-89896-5*, Pub. by Birmingham Midland Soc UK) St Mut.

Tracing Your Family Roots: The Ancestor Hunt. Frances D. Robotti. write for info. (*0-935497-03-X*) Fountainhead.

Tracing Your Greek Ancestry - Reference to Cyprus, Vol. 1. Antonia S. Mattheou. (Illus.). 54p. (Orig.). 1992. pap. 12.00 (*0-9635648-0-3*) A S Mattheou.

Tracing Your Irish Ancestors. John Grenham. (Illus.). 320p. (Orig.). 1993. pap. 19.95 (*0-8063-1369-2*, 2385) Genealog Pub.

Tracing Your Irish Roots. Christine Kinealy. (Pocket Guide Ser.). 72p. (Orig.). 1991. pap. 7.95 (*0-86281-278-X*, Pub. by Appletree Pr IE) Irish Bks Media.

Tracing Your Mississippi Ancestors. Anne S. Lipscomb & Kathleen Hutchison. (Illus.). 160p. 1994. 32.50 (*0-87805-697-1*); pap. 14.95 (*0-87805-698-X*) U Pr of Miss.

Tracing Your Roots. Ed. by O. J. Fargo. (History of Iowa Ser.). (Illus.). 51p. (Orig.). (J). (gr. 4-9). 1988. pap. text ed. 1.50 (*0-924702-08-7*) Grn Valley Area.

***Tracing Your Roots: Locating Your Ancestors through Landscape & History.** Meg Wheeler. 1996. 15.98 (*0-7651-9774-X*) Smithmark.

***Tracing Your Scottish Ancestry.** 2nd ed. Kathleen B. Cory. 1996. pap. 16.00 (*0-7486-6215-4*, Pub. by Polygon UK) Subterranean Co.

***Tracing Your Scottish Ancestry.** 2nd ed. Kathleen B. Cory. 195p. 1997. pap. 16.95 (*0-8063-1534-2*) Genealog Pub.

Tracing Your Scottish Ancestry. Kathleen B. Cory. 195p. 1993. reprint ed. 16.95 (*0-8063-6054-2*) Genealog Pub.

Tracings: A Book of Partial Portraits. Paul Horgan. LC 93-12381. 1993. 22.00 (*0-374-27859-8*) FS&G.

Tracings of Light: Sir John Herschel & the Camera Lucida. Larry J. Schaaf. LC 89-85802. (Illus.). 120p. 1989. 45.00 (*0-933286-55-4*) Frnds Photography.

Track. Tony Ward. LC 95-39278. (Olympic Library). (J). 1996. lib. bdg. write for info. (*1-57572-037-X*) Rigby Interact Libr.

***Track & Field.** (Composite Guide to...Ser.). (Illus.). 64p. (YA). (gr. 3 up). 1998. lib. bdg. 15.95 (*0-7910-4720-2*) Chelsea Hse.

Track & Field. Donna Bailey. LC 90-23053. (Sports World Ser.). (Illus.). 32p. (J). (gr. 1-4). 1991. pap. 3.95 (*0-8114-4747-2*); lib. bdg. 21.40 (*0-8114-2901-6*) Raintree Steck-V.

Track & Field. Dewayne J. Johnson & Joey Haines. (Illus.). 78p. (Orig.). (C). 1982. pap. text ed. 8.95 (*0-89641-093-5*) American Pr.

Track & Field. Mark Littleton. (Sports Heroes Ser.). 112p. 1995. pap. 5.99 (*0-310-49581-4*) Zondervan.

Track & Field. Doug Marx. LC 93-27154. (J). 1993. write for info. (*0-86593-345-6*) Rourke Corp.

Track & Field. Burt Rosenthal. LC 93-23281. (How to Play the All-Star Way Ser.). (J). 1993. lib. bdg. 24.26 (*0-8114-5778-8*) Raintree Steck-V.

Track & Field. David Smale. (The Summer Olympics Ser.). 32p. (J). (gr. 4-8). 1995. 14.79 (*1-887068-01-5*) Smart Apple.

Track & Field. Tony Ward. (Successful Sports Ser.). (J). 1996. lib. bdg. write for info. (*1-57572-072-8*) Rigby Interact Libr.

***Track & Field.** Tony Ward. (Successful Sports Ser.). (J). 1997. lib. bdg. write for info. (*1-57572-201-1*) Rigby Interact Libr.

Track & Field: A Step-By-Step Guide. Gary Wright. LC 89-27344. (Be the Best! Ser.). (Illus.). 64p. (J). (gr. 4-8). 1990. lib. bdg. 11.89 (*0-8167-1947-0*) Troll Communs.

Track & Field: A Step-By-Step Guide. Gary Wright. LC 89-27344. (Be the Best! Ser.). (Illus.). 64p. (J). (gr. 4-8). 1997. pap. 3.95 (*0-8167-1948-9*) Troll Communs.

Track & Field see Sport Signs

Track & Field Championship. Steve Potts. (Great Moments in Sports Ser.). (J). (gr. 5 up). 1992. lib. bdg. 14.95 (*0-88682-533-4*) Creative Ed.

Track & Field Drills for Women, 3 bks. Sherry Calvert et al. 66p. (Orig.). 1983. pap. 19.95 (*0-932741-94-0*) Championship Bks & Vid Prodns.

Track & Field Fundamentals for Teacher & Coach. 4th ed. John T. Powell. (Illus.). 1987. spiral bd. 19.80 (*0-87563-294-7*) Stipes.

Track & Field Masters Ranking Book 1981: Men & Women Ages 30-89; U. S. A., Canada & Mexico. Haig E. Bohigian. 96p. (Orig.). 1982. pap. 15.00 (*0-933390-06-8*) Valian Assocs.

Track & Field Masters Ranking Book 1982: Men & Women Ages 30-89, U. S. A., Canada & Mexico. Haig E. Bohigian. 96p. (Orig.). 1981. pap. 10.00 (*0-686-91816-9*) Valian Assocs.

Track & Field Masters Ranking Book 1982: Men & Women Ages 30-89, U. S. A., Canada & Mexico. Haig E. Bohigian. 96p. (Orig.). 1983. pap. 19.95 (*0-933390-05-X*) Valian Assocs.

***Track & Field News' Big Red Book: Metric Coversion Tables & Other Essential Data for the Track Fan, Coach & Official.** Track & Field News Staff. 133p. (Orig.). 1995. spiral bd., pap. 15.00 (*0-911521-40-2*) Tafnews.

Track & Field Record Holders: Profiles of the Men & Women Who Set World, Olympic & American Marks, 1946 Through 1995. David Baldwin. LC 96-3026. 344p. 1996. lib. bdg. 48.50 (*0-7864-0249-0*) McFarland & Co.

Track & Field Training Diary: Your Personal Workout Record. Jerry W. Stanley. (YA). (gr. 7-12). 1988. spiral bd. 7.95 (*0-685-44186-5*) Sports Diary Pub.

Track & Trailcraft. E. Jaeger. 1985. 12.95 (*0-02-558830-3*) Macmillan.

Track Athletics. Robert Sandelson. LC 90-27449. (Olympic Sports Ser.). (Illus.). 48p. (J). (gr. 6). 1991. lib. bdg. 13.95 (*0-89686-671-8*, Crstwood Hse) Silver Burdett Pr.

Track Athletics. Nick Whitehead. (EP Sports Ser.). (Illus.). 1976. 7.95 (*0-7158-0586-X*) Charles River Bks.

***Track Conditions: A Memoir.** Michael Klein. LC 96-37647. 192p. 1997. 22.00 (*0-89255-225-5*) Persea Bks.

Track Cyclopedia 1985. 10th ed. Ed. by H. C. Archdeacon & Ken Ellsworth. (Illus.). 1985. 60.00 (*0-911382-02-X*) Simmons Boardman.

Track Design. Ed. by Harold Carstens. (Hobby Bks.: No. C88). (Illus.). 72p. 1996. pap. 11.95 (*0-911868-88-7*, C88) Carstens Pubns.

Track Down Your Ancestors. large type ed. Estell Catlett. 192p. 1990. 19.95 (*1-85089-380-2*, Pub. by ISIS UK) Transaction Pubs.

Track Equipment Maintainer. Jack Rudman. (Career Examination Ser.: C-3307). 1994. pap. 23.95 (*0-8373-3307-5*) Nat Learn.

Track Finder: A Guide to Mammal Tracks of Eastern North America. Dorcas S. Miller. (Illus.). 62p. 1981. pap. 3.00 (*0-912550-12-0*) Nature Study.

Track Layout & Accessory Manual for Lionel Trains. Albert C. Ruocchio & Maury D. Klein. (Illus.). 1979. pap. 3.00 (*0-934580-08-1*, K-4) MDK Inc.

T

Track o' the Bear. James L. Berkman. (Patriot Ser.: Vol. 6, No. 3). (Illus.). (Orig.). 1989. pap. 10.00 (*0-943662-12-5*, 2-766-522) Runaway Pubns.

Track of a Killer. large type ed. Stephen Overholser. (Sagebrush Large Print Westerns Ser.). 168p. 1996. lib. bdg. 17.95 (*1-57490-016-1*) T T Beeler.

Track of Man, Adventures of an Anthropologist: Volume 2: The White House Years, 1941-1945. Henry Field. 134p. 10.95 (*0-916224-83-X*) Banyan Bks.

Track of Real Desire. Beverly Lowry. LC 93-34755. 1994. 21.00 (*0-679-42939-5*) Knopf.

Track of the Albatross. Rudolph Mellard. (Illus.). 1974. 15.00 (*0-685-50194-9*) A Jones.

Track of the Assassin. Paul R. Rothweiler. 352p. 1987. mass mkt. 3.95 (*0-380-89898-5*) Avon.

Track of the Bear. Don Coldsmith. 240p. 1995. pap. 4.99 (*0-553-56362-9*) Bantam.

Track of the Cat. Nevada Barr. (Anna Pigeon Ser.: No. 1). 320p. 1994. reprint ed. mass mkt. 6.50 (*0-380-72164-3*) Avon.

Track of the Cat. Walter Van Tilburg Clark. LC 93-17052. (Western Literature Ser.). 424p. 1993. reprint ed. pap. 14.95 (*0-87417-230-6*) U of Nev Pr.

Track of the Coyote. Todd Wilkinson. LC 95-15125. (Illus.). 144p. 1995. pap. 14.95 (*1-55971-471-9*) NorthWord.

Track of the Golden Bear: The California Maritime Academy Schoolships. Walter W. Jaffee. LC 96-77093. (Illus.). 224p. 1996. 40.00 (*0-9637586-8-3*) Glencannon Pr.

Track of the Gray Wolf: U-Boat Warfare on the U. S. Eastern Seaboard, 1942-1945. Gary Gentile. (Illus.). 312p. (Orig.). 1989. mass mkt. 4.50 (*0-380-75685-4*) Avon.

Track of the Grizzly. Frank C. Craighead, Jr. LC 78-8563. (Paperback Library). (Illus.). 272p. 1982. reprint ed. pap. 16.00 (*0-87156-322-3*) Sierra.

Track of the Kodiak. Marvin H. Clark, Jr. (Illus.). 224p. 1984. 39.95 (*0-937708-01-1*) Great Northwest.

***Track of the Lion.** Capstick. Date not set. write for info. (*0-312-18198-1*) St Martin.

Track of the Mystic: The Spirituality of Jessica Powers. Marcianne Kappes. LC 93-46599. 192p. (Orig.). 1994. pap. 12.95 (*1-55612-659-X*) Sheed & Ward MO.

Track of the Repetend: Syntactic & Lexical Repetition in Modern Poetry. Laury Magnus. LC 86-47850. (Ars Poetica Ser.: No. 4). 1989. 37.50 (*0-404-62504-5*) AMS Pr.

Track of the Scorpion. Val Davis. 320p. 1996. 22.95 (*0-312-14437-7*) St Martin.

***Track of the Tiger.** Maurice Hornocker. LC 97-19069. 1997. 30.00 (*0-87156-973-6*) Sierra.

Track of the White Wolf. Jennifer Roberson. (Chronicles of the Cheysuli Ser.: Bk. 4). 1987. mass mkt. 5.99 (*0-88677-193-5*) DAW Bks.

Track of the Zombie. Franklin W. Dixon. (Hardy Boys Casefiles Ser.: No. 71). (J). (gr. 3-6). 1986. pap. 3.50 (*0-671-62623-X*) PB.

Track Planning Ideas from Model Railroader. Ed. by Bob Hayden. LC 80-84022. (Illus.). 96p. (Orig.). 1981. per. 12.95 (*0-89024-555-X*, 12050) Kalmbach.

Track Record: The Story of the Caterpillar Occupation. Charles Woolfson & John Foster. 304p. 1989. 45.00 (*0-86091-236-1*, Pub. by Verso UK); pap. 16.95 (*0-685-24723-6*, Pub. by Verso UK) Routledge Chapman & Hall.

Track Starters Guide. 1990. 8.00 (*0-88314-432-8*) AAHPERD.

Track Talk. rev. ed. Mabel Butker & Burton Butker. Ed. by Christy Duquette-May. (Illus.). 64p. 1987. reprint ed. pap. 4.95 (*0-944012-02-7*) D M Communications.

Track Technique. Ed. by Track & Field News Staff. 10.00 (*0-317-65150-1*) Athletics Cong.

Track Technology: Proceedings of a Conference Organized by the Institution of Civil Engineers. 280p. 1985. 52.00 (*0-7277-0228-9*, Pub. by T Telford UK) Am Soc Civil Eng.

Track the Men Down. Lee Martin. 1993. 17.95 (*0-8034-9029-1*) Bouregy.

Track to Bralgu. B. Wongar. 120p. (Orig.). 1993. pap. 10.00 (*0-207-17148-3*, Pub. by Angus & Robertson AT) HarpC.

Track to Unknown Water: Proceedings of the Second Pacific Rim Conference on Children's Literature. Ed. by Stella Lees. LC 87-12852. (Illus.). 420p. 1987. reprint ed. 37.50 (*0-8108-2006-4*) Scarecrow.

Track Worker. Hy Hammer. 1987. 10.00 (*0-13-915331-4*, Arco) Macmillan Gen Ref.

Trackdown at Immigrant Lake. R. C. House. Ed. by Doug Gran. 224p. (Orig.). 1993. pap. 3.50 (*0-671-76042-4*) PB.

***Tracked by the Wolf Pack.** Lee Roddy. LC 97-10869. (Ladd Family Adventure Ser.: Bk. 15). (YA). 1997. pap. 5.99 (*1-56179-548-8*) Focus Family.

***Tracked in the Whites.** Tom Eslick. 272p. 1997. 21.95 (*1-885173-32-6*) Write Way.

Tracked Vehicles. John Nicholaus. (Army Library). (Illus.). 48p. (J). (gr. 3-8). 1989. lib. bdg. 18.60 (*0-86592-422-8*); lib. bdg. 13.95 (*0-685-58579-4*) Rourke Corp.

Tracker. Gary Paulsen. LC 83-22447. 96p. (J). (gr. 6-8). 1984. lib. bdg. 15.00 (*0-02-770220-0*, Bradbury S&S) S&S Childrens.

Tracker. Gary Paulsen. (J). (gr. 5-9). reprint ed. pap. 3.95 (*0-317-62280-3*, Puffin) Puffin Bks.

Tracker: Sentries. Gary Paulsen. 90p. (J). 1995. 3.95 (*0-689-80412-1*) S&S Childrens.

Tracker Tom see Take Along Stories

Trackers. Jake McMasters. (White Apache Ser.: Vol. 8). 176p. (Orig.). 1995. mass mkt., pap. text ed. 3.99 (*0-8439-3830-7*) Dorchester Pub Co.

***Trackfacts: Examination of Data Bases.** Daniel Dipleco. (Illus.). 178p. (Orig.). 1997. pap. write for info. (*1-57502-392-X*, PO1288) Morris Pubng.

Tracking: A Blueprint for Learning How. Jack Kearney. LC 77-18472. 1977. 12.95 (*0-317-04619-5*) Pathways Pr.

***Tracking: A Blueprint for Learning How.** 6th ed. Photos by Mackintosh Studios Staff et al. LC 77-18472. (Illus.). 148p. 1978. reprint ed. pap. 12.95 (*0-9658881-1-8*) Pathways Pr.

Tracking: Conflicts & Resolutions. Ann T. Lockwood. LC 96-28060. (CIE Ser.). 80p. 1996. 28.95 (*0-8039-6480-3*); pap. 12.95 (*0-8039-6268-1*) Corwin Pr.

Tracking: Poems. Virginia R. Terris. LC 76-13194. 84p. 1976. 9.95 (*0-252-00603-8*) U of Ill Pr.

Tracking America's Economy. 2nd ed. Norman Frumkin. LC 91-38370. 368p. (gr. 13). 1992. text ed. 56.95 (*1-56324-002-5*); pap. text ed. 25.95 (*1-56324-003-3*) M E Sharpe.

***Tracking America's Economy.** 3rd abr. ed. Norman Frumkin. 368p. (C). (gr. 13). 1997. text ed. 71.95 (*0-7656-0001-3*) M E Sharpe.

***Tracking America's Economy.** 3rd ed. Norman Frumkin. 368p. (C). (gr. 13). 1997. pap. text ed. 28.95 (*0-7656-0002-1*) M E Sharpe.

Tracking & Data Association. Yaakov Bar-Shalom & Thomas E. Fortmann. (Mathematics in Science & Engineering Ser.: Vol. 179). 353p. 1987. text ed. 81.00 (*0-12-079760-7*) Acad Pr.

Tracking & Locating Systems. Ray Lavas. Ed. by Bob Berkel. (CCS SecuritySource Library: Vol. X). (Illus.). 720p. 1995. 300.00 (*1-884674-10-0*) CCS Security.

Tracking & the Art of Seeing: How to Read Animal Tracks & Signs. Paul Rezendes. LC 92-10734. (Illus.). 320p. 1992. 29.95 (*0-944475-33-7*, Pub. by Camden Hse CN); pap. 19.95 (*0-944475-29-9*, Pub. by Camden Hse CN) Firefly Bks Ltd.

Tracking Dinosaurs: A New Look at an Ancient World. Martin Lockley. (Illus.). 249p. (C). 1991. pap. text ed. 18.95 (*0-521-42598-0*) Cambridge U Pr.

Tracking Dinosaurs: A New Look at an Ancient World. Martin Lockley. (Illus.). 249p. (C). 1991. text ed. 59.95 (*0-521-39463-5*) Cambridge U Pr.

Tracking Dog: Theory & Methods. Glen R. Johnson. LC 75-14693. (Illus.). 240p. 1975. 19.95 (*0-914124-04-8*) Arner Pubns.

Tracking down Coyote. Mike Helm. (Illus.). 202p. 1990. pap. 14.95 (*0-931742-16-1*) Rainy Day Oreg.

Tracking Down Hidden Food Allergy. 2nd ed. William G. Crook. (Illus.). 104p. (Orig.). 1980. pap. 6.95 (*0-933478-05-4*) Prof Bks Future Health.

Tracking Down Oregon. Ralph Friedman. LC 76-6647. (Illus.). 1978. pap. 9.95 (*0-87004-257-2*) Caxton.

Tracking down the Killer. Gyeorgos C. Hatonn. 236p. (Orig.). 1995. pap. 6.00 (*1-56935-083-3*) Phoenix Source.

Tracking down the Savior. Brian R. Keller. 32p. (Orig.). (J). (gr. 4-9). 1991. pap. 2.99 (*0-8100-0380-5*, 06N0684) Northwest Pub.

Tracking Down Trivia. Barbara Slater & Ron Slater. 48p. (J). (gr. 5-12). 1982. 7.99 (*0-86653-078-9*, GA 423) Good Apple.

Tracking Familiar Animals. John Ferrand, Jr. LC 92-13445. (Audubon Society Pocket Guides Ser.). 1993. pap. 9.00 (*0-679-74148-8*) Knopf.

***Tracking Foodborne Pathogens from Farm to Table: Data Needs to Evaluate Control Options.** (Illus.). 188p. (C). 1997. reprint ed. pap. 40.00 (*0-7881-3700-X*) DIANE Pub.

Tracking God in Italy. Louise Kennelly. 40p. 1995. pap. 6.00 (*1-880286-21-1*) Singular Speech Pr.

Tracking K-12 Education Spending in California: Who, Where, & How Much? Cathy S. Krop et al. LC 94-46755. 122p. 1995. pap. text ed. 13.00 (*0-8330-1624-5*, MR-548-SFR) Rand Corp.

Tracking Mackenzie to the Sea: Coast to Coast in Eighteen Splashdowns. Robert J. Hing. LC 91-77487. (Illus.). 234p. (Orig.). 1992. pap. 19.95 (*0-9631460-0-9*) Anchor Watch.

Tracking Mode. John B. Springs, III. 192p. (Orig.). 1992. mass mkt. 3.95 (*0-87067-388-2*) Holloway.

Tracking Nuclear Proliferation: A Guide in Maps & Charts, 1995. Leonard S. Spector et al. LC 95-13251. (Illus.). 194p. (C). 1995. pap. 12.95 (*0-87003-061-2*) Carnegie Endow.

***Tracking Nuclear Proliferation, 1996: A Guide in Maps & Charts.** Leonard S. Spector & Gregory P. Webb. (Illus.). 208p. 1996. pap. 14.95 (*0-87003-113-9*) Carnegie Endow.

Tracking Technologies for Radioactive Waste Shipments. (State Legislative Reports: Vol. 15, No. 4). 8p. 1990. 5.00 (*1-55516-260-6*, 7302-1504) Natl Conf State Legis.

Tracking the American Dream: Fifty Years of Housing History, 1940 to 1990. 1996. lib. bdg. 253.99 (*0-8490-5996-8*) Gordon Pr.

Tracking the "Bear" The Wooden Ship Manned by Iron Men. Kathy Hunter. (Illus.). 36p. (Orig.). 1986. pap. 4.95 (*0-9619906-0-0*) Lazy Mountn Pr.

Tracking the Elusive Human, Vol. I: A Practical Guide to C. G. Jung's Psychological Types, W. H. Sheldon's Body & Temperament Types, & Their Integration. Tyra Arraj & James Arraj. LC 87-30213. (Illus.). 184p. (Orig.). 1988. pap. 12.00 (*0-914073-16-8*) Inner Growth Bks.

Tracking the Elusive Human, Vol. 2: An Advanced Guide to the Typological Worlds of C. G. Jung, W. H. Sheldon, Their Integration & the Biochemical Typology of the Future. James Arraj. LC 87-30213. (Illus.). 336p. (Orig.). 1990. pap. 14.00 (*0-914073-36-2*) Inner Growth Bks.

Tracking the Facts: How to Develop Research Skills. Claire McInerney. (Study Skills Ser.). (Illus.). 64p. (J). (gr. 4 up). 1990. lib. bdg. 14.95 (*0-8225-2426-0*, Lerner Publctns) Lerner Group.

Tracking the Flood Survivors. Jean Hunt. (Illus.). 290p. (Orig.). 1991. pap. 25.00 (*0-9626812-0-2*) Hunt Asso LA.

Tracking the Glorious Lord: Vital Scientific Proofs of the Existence of God. Vinson Brown. LC 87-1689. (Paperback Ser.). (Illus.). 128p. (Orig.). 1987. pap. 6.95 (*0-8022-2519-5*) Naturegraph.

Tracking the Gods: The Place of Myth in Modern Life. James Hollis. (Illus.). 160p. 1995. pap. 16.00 (*0-919123-69-4*, Pub. by Inner City CN) BookWorld Dist.

Tracking the Group Sales Trail for Profit. Howard J. Hinton. Ed. by Joe Plachno. LC 94-45419. 64p. 1995. pap. 13.00 (*0-933449-25-9*) Transport Trails.

Tracking the Holocaust. Gerda Haas. LC 94-46003. (Illus.). 176p. (YA). (gr. 6 up). 1995. lib. bdg. 22.95 (*0-8225-3157-7*, Runestone Pr) Lerner Group.

Tracking the Sasquatch: How to Track the Elusive Pacific Northwest Hominoid, by a Professional Tracker. Barbara Wasson, pseud. 23p. (Orig.). 1994. pap. 6.00 (*0-9614105-2-3*) B Butler.

***Tracking the Serpent: Journeys to Four Continents.** Janine P. Vega. LC 97-4109. 256p. (Orig.). 1997. per. 12.95 (*0-87286-327-1*) City Lights.

Tracking the Snow-Shoe Itinerant. Kent Gunnufson. Ed. by John Dyer. LC 80-54041. (Illus.). 128p. 1981. text ed. 18.95 (*0-9605366-0-4*); pap. text ed. 11.95 (*0-9605366-1-2*) Snowstorm.

Tracking the Vanishing Frogs: An Ecological Mystery. Kathryn Phillips. (Illus.). 256p. 1994. 22.95 (*0-312-10973-3*, Thomas Dunne Bks) St Martin.

Tracking the Vanishing Frogs: An Ecological Mystery. Kathryn Phillips. (Illus.). 256p. 1995. pap. 11.95 (*0-14-024646-0*, Penguin Bks) Viking Penguin.

Tracking the Vital Signs of Materials Management: 1988 Annual Conference Proceedings. 99p. 1988. 40.00 (*0-318-41016-8*, 142816) ASHMM.

Tracking Thomas the Tank Engine & His Friends: A Book with Finger Tabs. W. Awdry. LC 91-67876. (Illus.). 16p. (J). (ps-1). 1992. 8.99 (*0-679-83458-3*) Random Bks Yng Read.

Tracking Toxic Substances at Industrial Facilities: Engineering Mass Balance vs. Materials Accounting. Committee to Evaluate Mass Balance Information for Facilities Handling Toxic Substances, National Research Council Staff. 198p. 1990. pap. text ed. 21.00 (*0-309-04086-8*) Natl Acad Pr.

Tracking, Tracing, Marking, Pacing: (Movement Drawings) Ellen Schwartz et al. (Illus.). 64p. 1982. 10.00 (*0-685-70723-7*) Gal Assn NY.

Tracking Wounded Deer: How to Find & Tag Deer Shot with Bow or Gun. Richard P. Smith. LC 88-9700. 168p. (Orig.). 1988. pap. 47.90 (*0-608-00479-0*, 2061298) Bks Demand.

Tracking Your Life & Times Vol. 1: A New Concept for Writing Your Life Story with Historical Sketches for Each Year of the Twentieth Century. Rex D. Bordugh. Ed. by Kathleen Herbison. LC 95-77805. (Illus.). 220p. 1995. ring bd. 23.95 (*1-880988-03-8*) Amer W Bks.

Tracking Your School's Success: A Guide to Sensible Evaluation. Joan L. Herman & Lynn Winters. 168p. 1992. student ed., pap. text ed. 24.95 (*0-8039-6024-7*, D1478) Corwin Pr.

Tracking Your Walk: The Young Person's Prayer Diary. 230p. 1994. pap. 12.99 (*0-927545-70-5*) YWAM Pub.

Trackings: Composers Speak with Richard Dufallo. Richard Dufallo. (Illus.). 432p. 1989. 40.00 (*0-19-505816-X*) OUP.

***Trackings: The Body's Memory, the Heart's Fiction.** Bill Morgan. 48p. (Orig.). 1998. pap. 5.00 (*1-880743-08-6*) Dead Metaphor.

Trackless Trolleys of Rhode Island. Richard L. Wonson. (Bulletin Ser.: No. 18). (Illus.). 96p. (Orig.). 1983. pap. 9.95 (*0-938315-01-3*) Boston St Rwy.

Trackless Wastes & Stars to Steer By: Christian Identity in a Homeless Age. Michael A. King. LC 89-26865. 192p. (Orig.). 1990. pap. 14.99 (*0-8361-3513-X*) Herald Pr.

Trackman. Jack Rudman. (Career Examination Ser.: C-1066). 1994. pap. 23.95 (*0-8373-1066-0*) Nat Learn.

***Tracks.** Aharon Appelfeld. 1998. write for info. (*0-8052-4158-2*) Schocken.

Tracks. Gary Crew. LC 96-24263. (Illus.). 32p. (J). (ps up). 1996. lib. bdg. 18.60 (*0-8368-1665-X*) Gareth Stevens Inc.

Tracks. Robyn Davidson. 1995. pap. 12.00 (*0-679-76287-6*) Random.

Tracks. David Galef. LC 95-13264. (Illus.). 32p. (J). 1996. 16.00 (*0-688-13343-6*, Morrow Junior) Morrow.

Tracks. David Galef. LC 95-13264. (Illus.). 1996. lib. bdg. 15.93 (*0-688-13344-4*, Morrow Junior) Morrow.

Tracks. Robert Locke. (J). (gr. 5 up). 1986. 14.95 (*0-395-40571-8*) HM.

Tracks. J. D. Whitney. 1969. 4.00 (*0-685-01016-3*) Elizabeth Pr.

Tracks. Louise Erdrich. LC 89-45123. 240p. 1989. reprint ed. pap. 12.50 (*0-06-097245-9*, PL 7245, PL) HarpC.

Tracks: Poems about People. Ruth Richardson. LC 88-72339. (Illus.). 93p. (Orig.). 1989. pap. 7.00 (*0-916383-73-3*) Aegina Pr.

Tracks Across Alaska: A Dog Sled Journey. Alastair Scott. LC 90-1022. 247p. 1991. pap. 10.95 (*0-87113-470-5*, Atlntc Mnthly) Grove-Atltic.

Tracks & Landfalls of Bering & Chirikof on the Northwest Coast of America. George Davidson. 44p. 1994. 11.95 (*0-87770-112-1*) Ye Galleon.

***Tracks & Sidetracks of Families.** 2nd ed. Mila Goldner et al. 120p. 1996. pap. write for info. (*0-9657106-7-X*) Zona Incerta.

***Tracks & Trails: An Insider's Guide to the Best Cross-Country Skiing in the Northeast.** Leggett & Teachout. Ed. by Pamela Gerloff. (Illus.). 275p. 1995. pap. 14.95 (*0-933603-41-X*) Dawbert Pr.

Tracks from the Junction: Historical Anecdotes of San Anselmo. Larine A. Brown. 208p. 1992. pap. 18.95 (*0-9632390-0-7*) Marin Light.

Track's Greatest Champions. Cordner Nelson. (Illus.). 385p. (Orig.). 1986. pap. 12.00 (*0-911521-19-4*) Tafnews.

***Track's Greatest Women.** Jon Hendershott. (Illus.). 243p. (Orig.). 1987. pap. 12.00 (*0-911521-22-4*) Tafnews.

Tracks in Oregon. Robert A. Davies. pap. 10.00 (*0-9622738-3-X*) Mr Cogito Pr.

Tracks in the Dust. Stanley W. Hoffman. (Orig.). 1996. pap. 12.95 (*0-533-11674-0*) Vantage.

Tracks in the Sand. Loreen Leedy. LC 92-3405. 32p. (J). (ps-3). 1993. 15.95 (*0-385-30658-X*) Doubleday.

Tracks in the Sky: Wildlife & Wetlands of the Pacific Flyway. Photos by Tupper A. Blake. (Illus.). 166p. 1991. 17.99 (*0-517-05552-X*) Random Hse Value.

***Tracks in the Snow.** Lucy Bledsoe. LC 96-52915. 96p. 1997. pap. 14.95 (*0-8234-1309-8*) Holiday.

Tracks in the Snow. Donna E. Chotvacs. (J). (gr. 4-7). 1996. pap. text ed. 4.95 (*0-9644076-1-2*) Calliope Pub.

Tracks in the Snow. Heribert Horneck. Ed. by Richard G. Young. LC 89-11890. (Illus.). 24p. (J). (gr. 1-3). 1989. lib. bdg. 14.60 (*0-944483-53-4*) Garrett Ed Corp.

Tracks in the Snow. Ruthven Todd. LC 76-51349. (English Literature Ser.: No. 33). 1977. lib. bdg. 42.95 (*0-8383-2159-3*) M S G Haskell Hse.

Tracks in the Snowy Forests. 3rd ed. Po Chu. Tr. by Sidney Shapiro et al. from CHI. (Illus.). 559p. (C). 1978. pap. 7.95 (*0-917056-72-8*, Pub. by Foreign Lang Pr CH) Cheng & Tsui.

***Tracks in the Straw: Tales Spun from the Manger.** 2nd rev. ed. Ted Loder. 176p. (Orig.). 1997. pap. 12.95 (*1-880913-29-1*) Innisfree Pr.

Tracks in the Wilderness of Dreaming: Exploring Interior Landscape Through Practical Dreamwork. Robert Bosnak. 208p. 1996. 21.95 (*0-385-31526-0*) Delacorte.

***Tracks in the Wilderness of Dreaming: Exploring Interior Landscape Through Practical Dreamwork.** Robert Bosnak. 256p. 1997. pap. 11.95 (*0-385-31529-5*, Delta) Dell.

***Tracks North: The Railroad Bracero Program of World War II.** Barbara A. Driscoll. (CMAS Border & Migration Studies Ser.). 224p. 1997. pap. 14.95 (*0-292-71592-7*) U of Tex Pr.

***Tracks North: The Railroad Bracero Program of World War II.** Barbara A. Driscoll. (CMAS Border & Migration Studies Ser.). 224p. 1997. 30.00 (*0-292-71593-5*) U of Tex Pr.

Tracks of a Fellow Struggler: How to Handle Grief. rev. ed. John Claypool. LC 95-6933. 1995. pap. 10.00 (*0-914520-35-0*) Insight Pr.

Tracks of Angels. Kelly Dwyer. 272p. 1995. pap. 11.99 (*0-446-67052-9*) Warner Bks.

Tracks of Angels. large type ed. Kelly Dwyer. LC 94-921. 1994. lib. bdg. 23.95 (*0-7862-0193-2*) Thorndike Pr.

Tracks of Dancing Light: A Native American Approach to Understanding Your Name. Joseph E. Rael & Lindsay Sutton. LC 93-41375. (Earth Quest Ser.). 1994. pap. 12.95 (*1-85230-434-0*) Element MA.

Tracks of Deceit. Alan Morris & Gilbert Morris. LC 95-46656. (Katy Steele Adventures Ser.: No. 1). 256p. 1996. pap. 10.99 (*0-8423-2039-3*) Tyndale.

Tracks of Eternity: Birthday Date Book. Carolyn J. Palmer. 192p. 1994. 12.95 (*0-9643952-0-7*) Eternity MI.

Tracks of Gypsy Angels. L. Bradley Law. LC 86-70545. 50p. (Orig.). 1986. pap. 6.95 (*0-933865-03-1*) Doris Pubns.

Tracks on My Heart. Dorothy M. Edwards. 160p. 1993. pap. 9.95 (*0-9634916-0-1*) D M Edwards.

Tracks, Scats, & Other Traces: A Field Guide to Australian Mammals. 2nd ed. Barbara Triggs. (Illus.). 304p. (C). 1996. pap. text ed. 34.95 (*0-19-553643-6*) OUP.

Tracks, Scats, & Signs. Leslie A. Dendy. LC 95-6207. (Take-Along Guide Ser.). (Illus.). 48p. (J). (gr. 1-3). 1995. 9.95 (*1-55971-481-6*) NorthWord.

Tracks, Trails & Tales in Clallam County State of Washington. Harriet U. Fish. (Illus.). 214p. (Orig.). 1985. reprint ed. 9.57 (*0-9612344-0-7*) H U Fish.

Tracks We Leave: Poems on Endangered Wildlife of North America. Barbara Helfgott-Hyett. (Illus.). 120p. 1996. 13.95 (*0-252-06575-1*) U of Ill Pr.

Tracks We Leave: Poems on Endangered Wildlife of North America. Barbara H. Hyett. LC 95-41830. (Illus.). 120p. 1996. text ed. 24.95 (*0-252-02235-1*) U of Ill Pr.

Trackside: Preserving Railroad Station Warehouse Districts: A Comparative Study of Seven Cities. Don C. Miles et al. Ed. by Lawrence Kreisman. (Illus.). 140p. (Orig.). 1988. pap. write for info. (*0-9621572-0-1*) City Tacoma Hist Preserv.

Trackside Maryland from Railyard to Main Line. Jacques Kelly & James P. Gallagher. (Illus.). 224p. 1992. text ed. 49.95 (*0-89778-290-9*, 10-7810, Greenberg Books) Kalmbach.

***Trackwork for Model Railroaders.** Paul Mallery. (Hobby Bks.: No. C86). (Illus.). 116p. 1997. 13.95 (*0-911868-90-9*, C86) Carstens Pubns.

Trackwork for Model Railroaders. 3rd ed. Paul Mallery. (Hobby Bks.: No. C86). (Illus.). 116p. 1994. 13.95 (*0-911868-86-0*, C86) Carstens Pubns.

Tract: Questions on Divorce & Remarriage. Thomas B. Warren. 1984. pap. 0.60 (*0-934916-04-7*); pap. 6.00 (*0-685-07105-7*); pap. 40.00 (*0-934716-04-8*) Natl Christian Pr.

An Asterisk (*) at the beginning of an entry indicates that the title is appearing in BIP for the first time.

Tract Against Usurie. Thomas Culpeper. LC 74-80170. (English Experience Ser.: No. 649). 22p. 1974. reprint ed. 15.00 (*90-221-0649-7*) Walter J Johnson.

Tract on Monetary Reform see Collected Writings

Tract on Panot. George J. Skapski. 1995. 24.95 (*0-533-11259-1*) Vantage.

Tract on Prayer. Shalom Dov Ber Schneersohn. Tr. by Lazer Danzinger. LC 92-19383. 1992. 11.90 (*0-8266-0436-6*) Kehot Pubn Soc.

Tractable Reasoning in Artificial Intelligence. Marco Cadoli. LC 95-23193. (Lecture Notes in Computer Science Ser.: Vol. 941). 1995. 49.00 (*3-540-60058-2*) Spr-Verlag.

Tractado de Vicios e Virtudes: An Edition with Introduction & Glossary. Cleveland Johnson. 220p. 49.00 (*0-916379-50-7*) Scripta.

Tractate Avodah Zarah, Horayoth, Eduyoth, & Avoth: Hebrew Text, English Translation. Tr. by I. Epstein. 1988. 27.50 (*0-900689-89-7*) Soncino Pr.

Tractate Baba Bathra: Hebrew Text, English Translation. Tr. by I. Epstein. 1989. 35.00 (*0-900689-64-1*) Soncino Pr.

Tractate Baba Kamma. I. Epstein. 1990. 27.50 (*1-871055-35-0*) Soncino Pr.

Tractate Bekoroth-Arakin: Hebrew Text, English Translation. Tr. by I. Epstein. 1989. 27.50 (*0-900689-99-4*) Soncino Pr.

Tractate Berakhos: Commentary & Study Guide. Nachman Cohen. 600p. (C). 1989. write for info. (*1-877650-00-5*) Torah Lishmah.

Tractate Berakoth: Hebrew Text, English Translation. Tr. by I. Epstein. 1990. 27.50 (*0-900689-56-0*) Soncino Pr.

Tractate Erubin: Hebrew Text, English Translation. Tr. by I. Epstein. 1983. 27.50 (*0-900689-41-2*) Soncino Pr.

Tractate Gittin: Hebrew Text, English Translation. Tr. by I. Epstein. 1977. 27.50 (*1-871055-30-X*) Soncino Pr.

Tractate Hullin: Hebrew Text, English Translation. Tr. by I. Epstein. 1989. 27.50 (*0-900689-17-X*) Soncino Pr.

Tractate Kethuboth: Hebrew Text, English Translation. Tr. by I. Epstein. 1989. 27.50 (*1-871055-10-5*) Soncino Pr.

Tractate Kiddushin: Hebrew Text, English Translation. Tr. by I. Epstein. 1990. 27.50 (*1-871055-40-7*) Soncino Pr.

Tractate Kiddushin According to Meiri: Translation of Classic Commentary to Tractate Kiddushin. O. Fogel. 1989. 22.95 (*0-87306-522-0*) Feldheim.

Tractate Menahoth: Hebrew Text, English Translation. Tr. by I. Epstein. 1989. 27.50 (*0-900689-98-6*) Soncino Pr.

Tractate Mourning: Regulations Relating to Death, Burial, & Mourning. Tr. by Dov Zlotnick & Eduard Y. Kutscher. (Judaica Ser.: No. 17). 1966. 42.50 (*0-300-01069-9*) Yale U Pr.

Tractate Nazir-Sotah: Hebrew Text, English Translation. Tr. by I. Epstein. 1985. 27.50 (*0-900689-95-1*) Soncino Pr.

Tractate Nedarim. I. Epstein. 1985. 27.50 (*0-900689-90-0*) Soncino Pr.

Tractate Niddah. Ed. by I. Epstein. 1989. 27.50 (*0-900689-94-3*) Soncino Pr.

Tractate Pesachim: Hebrew Text, English Translation. Tr. by I. Epstein. 1983. 27.50 (*0-900689-81-1*) Soncino Pr.

Tractate Rosh Hashana, Bezah, Shekalim: Hebrew Text, English Translation. Tr. by I. Epstein. 1983. 27.50 (*0-900689-82-X*) Soncino Pr.

Tractate Sanhedrin: Hebrew Text, English Translation. Tr. by I. Epstein. 1994. 27.50 (*0-900689-88-9*) Soncino Pr.

Tractate Shevouth-Makkoth: Hebrew Text, English Translation. Tr. by I. Epstein. 1987. 27.50 (*0-900689-96-X*) Soncino Pr.

Tractate Sukkah-Moed-Katan: Hebrew Text, English Translation. Tr. by I. Epstein. 1990. 27.50 (*0-900689-83-8*) Soncino Pr.

Tractate Taanit, Megillah, Chagiga: Hebrew Text, English Translation. Tr. by I. Epstein. 1984. 27.50 (*0-900689-84-6*) Soncino Pr.

Tractate Temurah - Kerithoth-Meilah-Kinnim-Tamid-Middoth: Hebrew Text, English Translation. Tr. by I. Epstein. 1989. 27.50 (*0-900689-61-7*) Soncino Pr.

Tractate Yebamoth: Hebrew Text, English Translation. Tr. by I. Epstein. 86p. 1994. 27.50 (*0-900689-97-8*) Soncino Pr.

Tractate Yoma: Hebrew Text, English Translation. Ed. & Tr. by I. Epstein. 1989. 27.50 (*1-871055-25-3*) Soncino Pr.

Tractate Zebahim: Hebrew Text, English Translation. Tr. by I. Epstein. 1988. 27.50 (*0-900689-93-5*) Soncino Pr.

Tractates & Sermons. Richard Hooker. Ed. by W. Speed Hill. (Folger Library Edition of the Works of Richard Hooker: Vol. 5). (Illus.). 976p. 1990. text ed. 122.00 (*0-674-63217-6*) Belknap Pr.

Tractates on the Gospel of John, 1-10. Augustine, Saint. Tr. by John W. Rettig. LC 87-18387. (Fathers of the Church Ser.: Vol. 78). 236p. 1988. 31.95 (*0-8132-0078-4*) Cath U Pr.

Tractates on the Gospel of John, 11-27. Augustine, Saint. Tr. by John W. Rettig. LC 87-18387. (Fathers of the Church Ser.: Vol. 79). 306p. 1988. 31.95 (*0-8132-0079-2*) Cath U Pr.

Tractates on the Gospel of John, 112-124. St. Augustine. Tr. by John W. Rettig. LC 87-18387. (Fathers of the Church Ser.). 301p. 1995. 36.95 (*0-8132-0092-X*) Cath U Pr.

Tractates on the Gospel of John, 28-54. St. Augustine. Tr. by John W. Rettig from LAT. LC 87-18387. (Fathers of the Church Ser.: Vol. 88). 326p. 1993. 36.95 (*0-8132-0088-1*) Cath U Pr.

Tractates on the Gospel of John, 55-111. St. Augustine. Tr. by John W. Rettig from LAT. LC 87-18387. (Fathers of the Church Ser.: Vol. 90). 328p. 1994. 36.95 (*0-8132-0090-3*) Cath U Pr.

Tractato di Musica. fac. ed. Giovanni Spataro. (Monuments of Music & Music Literature in Facsimile, II Ser.: No. 88). (Illus.). 1979. lib. bdg. 40.00 (*0-8450-2288-1*) Broude.

Tractatus Brevior see Walter Burleigh De Puritate Artis Logicae Tractus Langios

Tractatus De Intellectus Emendatione. Benedict De Spinoza. LC 78-94284. (Select Bibliographies Reprint Ser.). 1977. 19.95 (*0-8369-5057-7*) Ayer.

Tractatus Figurarum: Subtilitas in the Notation of the Late Fourteenth Century. Philip Schreur. LC 89-22569. (Greek & Latin Music Theory Ser.). (Illus.). xii, 122p. 1989. text ed. 30.00 (*0-8032-4203-4*) U of Nebr Pr.

Tractatus Logico Philosophicus. Ludwig Wittgenstein. 261p. 1981. pap. 15.95 (*0-415-05186-X*) Routledge Chapman & Hall.

Tractatus Logico-Philosophicus: English Translation. Ludwig Wittgenstein. Ed. by D. F. Pears & B. F. McGuinness. LC 95-4149. 188p. (gr. 13). 1994. pap. 15.95 (*0-415-02825-6*, C0592) Routledge.

Tractatus Logico-Philosophicus: German Text with English Translation. Ludwig Wittgenstein. Tr. by C. K. Ogden. 208p. 1981. pap. 12.95 (*0-685-04401-7*, RKP) Routledge.

***Tractatus Methodo-Logicus.** Matthias Luserke. (Philosophische Texte und Studien: Vol. 19). x, 74p. (GER.). 1988. write for info. (*3-487-09135-6*) G Olms Pubs.

Tractatus Super Psalmum Vicesimum of Richard Rolle of Hampole. James C. Dolan. LC 91-23525. (Texts & Studies in Religion: Vol. 57). 124p. 1991. lib. bdg. 59.95 (*0-7734-9666-1*) E Mellen.

Tractatus Theologico-Politicus. 2nd ed. Baruch Spinoza. Tr. by Samuel Shirley from LAT. LC 89-17307. vi, 316p. 1989. 117.75 (*90-04-09099-1*) E J Brill.

Tractatus Theologico-Politicus. 2nd ed. Baruch Spinoza. Tr. by Samuel Shirley from LAT. LC 89-17307. vi, 316p. 1991. pap. 50.50 (*90-04-09550-0*) E J Brill.

Tracting Made Easy. C. M. Melonakos. 48p. 1987. pap. 3.95 (*0-9616024-1-4*) Paramount Bks.

Traction Classics: The High Speed & Deluxe Interurban Cars, Vol. 2. William D. Middleton. LC 83-18482. (Illus.). 230p. 1985. 38.95 (*0-87095-089-4*) Gldn West Bks.

Traction Drives: Selection & Application. Heilich & Shube. (Mechanical Engineering Ser.: Vol. 24). 360p. 1983. 125.00 (*0-8247-7018-8*) Dekker.

Traction Extra, No. 1. 1985. 27.95 (*0-9610414-3-9*) Traction Yrbk.

Traction Extra, No. 2. 1986. 59.95 (*0-9610414-5-5*) Traction Yrbk.

Traction in Franklin County Vermont - St. Albans Street Railway St. Albans & Swanton Traction Company: St. Albans Street Railway, St. Albans & Swanton Traction Company. James R. McFarlane. Ed. by Marion Harris. LC 94-14087. (Illus.). 48p. 1994. pap. 16.50 (*0-933449-21-6*) Transport Trails.

Traction on the Grand. John Mills. (Illus.). 96p. 10.00 (*0-919130-27-5*, Pub. by Boston Mills Pr CN) Genl Dist Srvs.

Traction Planbook. 2nd ed. Harold H. Carstens. (Hobby Bks.: No. C-16). (Illus.). 100p. 1968. pap. 9.95 (*0-911868-16-X*, C16) Carstens Pubns.

Traction Yearbook, 1983. Joseph P. Saitta. (Illus.). 128p. 1983. pap. 18.95 (*0-9610414-1-2*) Traction Yrbk.

Traction Yearbook, 1984. 1985. 27.95 (*0-685-35123-8*) Traction Yrbk.

Traction Yearbook, 1985. 1986. 39.95 (*0-9610414-4-7*) Traction Yrbk.

Traction Yearbook, 1986. 1988. 39.95 (*0-9610414-6-3*) Traction Yrbk.

Traction Yearbook, 1987. 1991. 39.95 (*0-9610414-7-1*) Traction Yrbk.

Traction Yearbook, 1988. 1990. write for info. (*0-318-67007-0*) Traction Yrbk.

Traction Yearbook, 1989. 1990. write for info. (*0-318-67008-9*) Traction Yrbk.

Traction Yearbook, 1990, Vol. 1. 1991. write for info. (*0-9610414-8-X*) Traction Yrbk.

Tractor. (Things That Go Shaped Board Bks.). (Illus.). 10p. (J). 1996. 3.95 (*0-7894-1137-7*) DK Pub Inc.

Tractor. Craig Brown. LC 94-19367. (Illus.). 24p. (J). (ps up). 1995. 16.00 (*0-688-10499-1*); lib. bdg. 15.93 (*0-688-10500-9*) Greenwillow.

Tractor. Claire Llewellyn. LC 94-24403. (Mighty Machines Ser.). (Illus.). 24p. (J). (ps-3). 1995. 9.95 (*1-56458-515-8*) DK Pub Inc.

Tractor & Farm Implement & Lubrication Guide, 1986. (Illus.). 192p. student ed. 39.40 (*0-88098-082-6*, H M Gousha) P-H Gen Ref & Trav.

Tractor & Self Propelled Farm Implement Guide, 1987. rev. ed. Ed. by Daniel Doornbos. (Illus.). 192p. 1986. student ed. 41.35 (*0-88098-092-3*, H M Gousha) P-H Gen Ref & Trav.

Tractor & Small Engine Maintenance. 5th ed. Arlen D. Brown & R. Mack Strickland. 383p. 1983. 26.60 (*0-8134-2258-2*); teacher ed. 4.95 (*0-8134-2335-X*) Interstate.

Tractor del Granjero. Wendy Kanno. Tr. by Gloria Schaffer-Melendez. (Libro de Viente Palabras Ser.). (Illus.). (SPA.). (J). (gr. k-3). 1994. pap. 3.95 (*0-89868-270-3*, Read Res); lib. bdg. 9.95 (*0-89868-269-X*, Read Res) ARO Pub.

Tractor Factory: A Pop-up Book. Elinor Bagenal. (Illus.). 10p. (J). 1994. 14.95 (*0-307-17640-1*) Western Pub.

Tractor Goes Farming. Roy Harrington. LC 95-77925. (Illus.). 32p. (Orig.). (J). (gr. k-3). 1995. 6.95 (*0-614-10660-5*, H1095) Am Soc Ag Eng.

Tractor Heritage. Duncan Wherrett & Trevor Innes. (Color Library). (Illus.). 128p. 1994. pap. 15.95 (*1-85532-411-3*, Pub. by Osprey Pubng Ltd UK) Motorbooks Intl.

Tractor-Implement Systems. Ralph Alcock. (Illus.). 1986. text ed. 43.95 (*0-87055-522-7*) AVI.

Tractor in Trouble. Heather Amery. (Farmyard Tales Ser.). (Illus.). 16p. (J). (ps-3). 1992. pap. 3.95 (*0-7460-0588-1*) EDC.

Tractor in Trouble Sticker Book. Judy Tatchell. (Farmyard Tales Sticker Storybook Ser.). (Illus.). 16p. (J). (ps up). 1996. pap. 5.95 (*0-7460-2432-0*, Usborne) EDC.

Tractor Operator. Jack Rudman. (Career Examination Ser.: C-827). 1994. pap. 23.95 (*0-8373-0827-5*) Nat Learn.

Tractor Trailer. Joanne Barkan. (Truckin' Board Bks.). (J). 1996. bds. 4.99 (*0-689-81148-9*) S&S Childrens.

Tractor-Trailer Operator. Jack Rudman. (Career Examination Ser.: C-1519). 1994. pap. 23.95 (*0-8373-1519-0*) Nat Learn.

***Tractor Trouble.** Steve Augarde. LC 96-52154. (J). 1997. pap. 14.99 (*0-525-67561-2*) NAL-Dutton.

***Tractors.** Date not set. 30.00 (*0-8464-4427-5*) Beekman Pubs.

Tractors. Peter Brady. (Beginning Reader Science Bks.). 24p. (J). (ps-4). 1996. lib. bdg. 17.80 (*1-56065-348-5*) Capstone Pr.

***Tractors.** Peter Brady. (Early Reader Science Bks.). (Illus.). 24p. (J). (gr. k-3). 1996. 13.25 (*0-516-20119-0*) Childrens.

Tractors. Gil Chandler. LC 95-7121. (Cruisin' Ser.). 48p. (J). (gr. 3-9). 1995. lib. bdg. 17.80 (*1-56065-254-3*) Capstone Pr.

***Tractors.** Gil Chandler. (Cruisin' Ser.). (Illus.). 48p. (J). (gr. 3-6). 1995. 18.40 (*0-516-35254-7*) Childrens.

***Tractors.** Ed. by Carol Cuellar. 44p. (Orig.). (C). 1995. pap. text ed. 14.95 (*0-89724-571-7*, VF2176) Warner Brothers.

Tractors. C. Young. (Young Machines Ser.). (Illus.). 32p. (J). (ps-2). 1992. lib. bdg. 14.95 (*0-88110-553-8*, Usborne) EDC.

Tractors. C. Young. (Machines Board Bks.). (Illus.). 12p. (J). (ps). 1993. bds. 4.95 (*0-7460-1097-4*) EDC.

Tractors. Caroline Young. (Young Machines Ser.). (Illus.). 32p. (J). (ps-2). 1992. pap. 6.95 (*0-7460-0671-3*, Usborne) EDC.

Tractors. 3rd rev. ed. Ed. by Deere & Company Staff. (Fundamentals of Machine Operation Ser.). (Illus.). 119p. 1994. Instr.'s guide incl. transparency masters. teacher ed., pap. text ed. 33.20 incl. trans. (*0-86691-160-X*, FMO10503T); Student guide. student ed., pap. text ed. 13.25 (*0-86691-159-6*, FMO10603W); pap. text ed. 34.95 (*0-86691-212-6*, FMO10103BX) Deere & Co.

***Tractors.** 3rd rev. ed. Ed. by Deere & Company Staff. (Fundamentals of Machine Operation Ser.). 92p. 1994. 92.95 incl. sl. (*0-614-24209-6*, FMO10203S) Deere & Co.

Tractors: How They Work & What They Do. Michael Williams. (Illus.). 96p. 1992. text ed. 19.95 (*0-85236-239-0*, Pub. by Farming Pr UK) Diamond Farm Bk.

Tractors & Trucks. Robert Crowther. LC 95-71701. (Illus.). 12p. (J). (ps-2). 1996. 7.99 (*0-7636-0009-1*) Candlewick Pr.

***Tractors at Work.** Stuart Gibbard. (Illus.). 156p. 1995. 29.95 (*0-85236-316-8*, Vol. 2, Pub. by Farming Pr UK) Diamond Farm Bk.

Tractors at Work: A Pictorial Review 1904-94. Stuart Gibbard. (Illus.). 128p. 1994. text ed. 29.95 (*0-85236-284-6*, Pub. by Farming Pr UK) Diamond Farm Bk.

Tractors Since Eighteen Eighty-Nine. Michael Williams. (Illus.). 136p. 1991. 29.95 (*0-85236-223-4*, Pub. by Farming Pr UK) Diamond Farm Bk.

Tracts. David Ferguson. Ed. by David Laing. LC 70-168016. (Bannatyne Club, Edinburgh. Publications: No. 110). reprint ed. 32.50 (*0-404-52864-3*) AMS Pr.

Tracts. Gilbert Skeyne. (Bannatyne Club, Edinburgh. Publications: No. 108). reprint ed. 31.50 (*0-404-52862-7*) AMS Pr.

Tracts Against New England see Library of American Puritan Writings. The Seventeenth Century: The Seventeenth Century

Tracts & Other Papers. Peter Force. (Notable American Authors Ser.). 1992. reprint ed. lib. bdg. 75.00 (*0-7812-2867-0*) Rprt Serv.

Tracts & Other Papers Relating Principally to the Origin, Settlement & Progress of the Colonies in North America, Vol. 1, 2, 3. Ed. by Peter Force. 1990. 15.50 (*0-8446-1188-3*) Peter Smith.

Tracts & Other Publications on Metallic & Paper Currency: With Further Reflections on the State of the Currency (1837), 2 vols. in 1. Samuel J. Overstone. LC 67-20089. (Library of Money & Banking History). viii, 649p. 1972. reprint ed. 57.50 (*0-678-00902-3*) Kelley.

Tracts for the New Times: No. 1 Letter to a Swedenborgian. Henry James, Sr. LC 72-916. (Selected Works of Henry James, Sr.: Vol. 9). 1983. reprint ed. 35.00 (*0-404-10089-9*) AMS Pr.

Tracts for the Times, 6 Vols, Set. Ed. by John H. Newman et al. 1841. lib. bdg. 450.00 (*0-404-04710-6*) AMS Pr.

Tracts for Today. Moncure D. Conway. (Works of Moncure Daniel Conway Ser.). 1990. reprint ed. lib. bdg. 79.00 (*0-7812-2327-X*) Rprt Serv.

Tracts of the American Revolution, 1763-1776. Ed. by Merrill Jensen. LC 66-26805. (Orig.). 1967. pap. 11.95 (*0-672-60046-3*, AHS35, Bobbs) Macmillan.

Tracts on Our Present Money System & National Bankruptcy: Comprising Strictures on the Price & Trade of Corn. Peter R. Hoare. LC 67-27467. (Reprints of Economic Classics Ser.). 331p. 1969. reprint ed. 49.50 (*0-678-00574-5*) Kelley.

Tracts on Sundry Topics of Political Economy. Oliver Putnam. LC 68-56567. (Reprints of Economic Classics Ser.). viii, 156p. 1970. reprint ed. 35.00 (*0-678-00600-8*) Kelley.

Tractus Simplex de Cortice Peruuiano. Saul Jarcho. (Illus.). 140p. 1992. 19.95 (*0-614-03128-1*) F A Countway.

Tracy. Mark Dunster. (Rin Ser.: Pt. 54). (Orig.). 1981. pap. 4.00 (*0-89642-079-5*) Linden Pubs.

Tracy Chapman. 76p. 1988. per. 14.95 (*0-7935-0264-0*, 00356378) H Leonard.

Tracy Chapman: Crossroads. 80p. 1990. per. 14.95 (*0-7935-0290-X*, 00490245) H Leonard.

Tracy Diamonds. Mary J. Holmes. (Notable American Authors Ser.). 1992. reprint ed. lib. bdg. 75.00 (*0-7812-3151-5*) Rprt Serv.

Tracy Genealogy: Being Some Descendants of Stephen Tracy of Plymouth Colony, 1623; Also Ancestral Sketches & Chart. Sherman W. Tracy. (Illus.). 242p. 1995. reprint ed. pap. 37.00 (*0-8328-4946-4*); reprint ed. lib. bdg. 47.00 (*0-8328-4945-6*) Higginson Bk Co.

Tracy Knows Picasso: Children's Art History Read-Along Book. Carmen Vila. (Illus.). (J). (gr. 1-6). write for info. incl. audio (*0-9635047-0-3*) VILA Grp.

Tracy Lawrence Greatest Hits. 14.95 (*0-7935-5272-9*, 00306051) H Leonard.

***Tracy Log Book: A Month in Summer.** Ed. by Anne Mazlish. (Illus.). 1997. 19.95 (*0-934745-22-6*) Acadia Pub Co.

***Tracy Log Book: A Month in Summer.** Ed. by Anne Mazlish. (Illus.). 1997. pap. 14.95 (*0-934745-25-0*) Acadia Pub Co.

Tracy's Mess. Elise Petersen. (J). (ps-2). 1996. 14.95 (*0-614-15585-1*) Whsprng Coyote Pr.

Tradability of Banking Services: Impact & Implications. (Illus.). 195p. (Orig.). (C). 1995. pap. 65.00 (*0-7881-1653-3*) DIANE Pub.

Tradability of Banking Services: Impact & Implications. 195p. 1995. 50.00 (*92-1-104433-2*) ASME Pr.

Trade. Eileen Lucas. LC 95-7292. (Native Latin American Cultures Ser.). (J). (gr. 2-6). 1995. write for info. (*0-86625-555-9*) Rourke Pubns.

Trade. Winthrop. 1999. 1.00 (*0-316-94751-2*) Little.

Trade: Opposing Viewpoints. Ed. by William Dudley. LC 90-24087. (Opposing Viewpoints Ser.). (Illus.). 264p. (YA). (gr. 10 up). 1991. pap. 12.96 (*0-89908-151-7*); lib. bdg. 20.96 (*0-89908-176-2*) Greenhaven.

Trade Vol. 2: 1994 Supplement. Clubb. 1994. 75.00 (*0-316-14770-2*); 75.00 (*0-316-14771-0*) Little.

Trade Agreements Program of the United States: Annual Reports to the President, 4 vols., Set. Ed. by Bernard D. Reams, Jr. LC 89-83415. 3074p. 1989. lib. bdg. 395.00 (*0-89941-711-6*, 306080) W S Hein.

Trade, Aid & Development: Essays in Honor of Hans Linnemann. Jan W. Gunning et al. LC 93-13664. 1994. text ed. 85.00 (*0-312-10186-4*) St Martin.

Trade, Aid & Global Interdependence. George Cho. LC 94-44561. (Introductions to Development Ser.). 176p. (C). 1995. pap. 13.95 (*0-415-09159-4*) Routledge.

Trade among Multinationals: Intra-Industry Trade & National Competitiveness. D. C. MacCharles. 224p. 1987. lib. bdg. 65.00 (*0-7099-4618-X*, Pub. by Croom Helm UK) Routledge Chapman & Hall.

Trade Amongst Growing Economies. Ian Steedman. LC 78-73818. 168p. 1980. text ed. 44.95 (*0-521-22671-6*) Cambridge U Pr.

Trade & Aid: Eisenhower's Foreign Economic Policy, 1953 - 1961. Burton I. Kaufman. LC 81-15594. 325p. 1982. text ed. 43.00 (*0-8018-2623-3*) Johns Hopkins.

Trade & Civilisation in the Indian Ocean: An Economic History from the Rise of Islam to 1750. K. N. Chaudhuri. (Illus.). 256p. 1985. pap. text ed. 25.95 (*0-521-28542-9*) Cambridge U Pr.

Trade & Commercial Activities of Southern India in the Malayo-Indonesian World, Vol. 1: Up to 1511 A. D. Himansu B. Sarkar. 420p. 1986. 32.50 (*0-317-53507-2*, Pub. by Firma KLM II) S Asia.

Trade & Competition Policies: Comparing Objectives & Methods. OECD Staff. 40p. (Orig.). 1994. pap. 7.00 (*92-64-14157-X*) OECD.

Trade & Conquest: Studies on the Rise of British Dominance in India. P. J. Marshall. (Collected Studies: No. CS 409). 320p. 1993. 84.95 (*0-86078-373-1*, Pub. by Variorum UK) Ashgate Pub Co.

Trade & Cooperation in South Asia: A Nepalese Perspective. Y. P. Pant. (C). 1992. 15.95 (*0-7069-5694-X*, Pub. by Vikas II) S Asia.

Trade & Currency in Early Oregon. James H. Gilbert. LC 77-168145. (Columbia University. Studies in the Social Sciences: No. 68). reprint ed. 30.00 (*0-404-51068-X*) AMS Pr.

Trade & Development: Nepal's Experiences. B. Pant. 1994. pap. 60.00 (*0-7855-0488-5*, Pub. by Ratna Pustak Bhandar) St Mut.

Trade & Development in Sub-Saharan Africa. Ed. by J. H. Frimpong-Ansah et al. 272p. 1991. text ed. 59.95 (*0-7190-3478-7*, Pub. by Manchester Univ Pr UK) St Martin.

Trade & Development Report. 209p. 1992. 42.00 (*92-1-112309-7*) UN.

Trade & Development Report & Overview. 173p. 1994. 45.00 (*92-1-112360-7*) UN.

Trade & Development Report, 1988. 292p. 1988. pap. 20.00 (*92-1-112248-1*, 88.II.D.8) UN.

Trade & Development Report, 1989. 40.00 (*92-1-112280-5*, E.89.II.D.14) UN.

Trade & Development Report, 1990. 200p. 1990. 40.00 (*92-1-112291-0*, 90.II.D.6) UN.

***Trade & Development Report, 1996.** United Nations Conference on Trade & Development Staff. 180p. 1996. pap. 48.00 (*92-1-112399-2*, HF91) UN.

Trade & Diplomacy in India-China Relations: A Study of Bengal During the 15th Century. H. P. Ray. 1993. text ed. 25.00 (*81-7027-202-5*, Pub. by Radiant Pubs II) S Asia.

Trade & Diplomacy on the China Coast: The Opening of the Treaty Ports, 1842-1854, 2 vols. in 1. John K. Fairbank. LC 65-100264. (Historical Studies: No. 62-63). 608p. 1953. Set. 22.50 (*0-674-89835-4*) HUP.

Trade & Diplomacy on the China Coast: The Opening of the Treaty Ports, 1842-1854. John K. Fairbank. LC 69-10365. (Illus.). xviii, 583p. 1953. pap. 22.50 (*0-8047-0648-4*) Stanford U Pr.

Trade & Economic Development: India, Pakistan & Bangladesh. Krishnalekha Sood. 288p. (C). 1990. text ed. 25.00 (*0-8039-9618-7*) Sage.

Trade & Economic Development in Small Open Economies: The Case of the Caribbean Countries. Arnold M. McIntyre. LC 94-32931. 200p. 1995. text ed. 57.95 (*0-275-94745-9*, Praeger Pubs) Greenwood.

Trade & Economic Structure: Models & Methods. Richard E. Caves. LC 60-5389. (Economic Studies: No. 115). (Illus.). 325p. 1960. 22.50 (*0-674-89881-8*) HUP.

Trade & Empire: The British Customs Service in Colonial America, 1660-1775. Thomas C. Barrow. LC 67-11666. 348p. 1967. 34.50 (*0-674-89925-3*) HUP.

Trade & Empire in Muscat & Zanzibar: The Roots of British Domination. M. Reda Bhacker. LC 91-47666. (Exeter Series on Arabic & Islamic Studies). 224p. (C). (gr. 13). 1992. text ed. 89.95 (*0-415-07997-7*, A7590) Routledge.

Trade & Employment: A Study of the Effects of Trade Expansion on Employment in Developing & Developed Countries (WEP Study) Harold F. Lydall. x, 140p. 1975. 24.75 (*92-2-101240-9*); pap. 15.75 (*92-2-101239-5*) Intl Labour Office.

Trade & Employment in Asia & the Pacific: Proceedings of the Eighth Pacific Trade & Development Conference, Pattaya, Thailand, July 10-14, 1976. Pacific Trade & Development Conference Staff. Ed. by Narongchai Akrasanee et al. 469p. reprint ed. pap. 133.70 (*0-7837-1304-5*, 2041452) Bks Demand.

Trade & Employment in Developing Countries: Factor Supply & Substitution, Vol. 2. Ed. by Anne O. Krueger. LC 80-15826. (National Bureau of Economic Research Project Report Ser.). 282p. (C). 1982. lib. bdg. 35.00 (*0-226-45493-2*) U Ch Pr.

Trade & Employment in Developing Countries: Synthesis & Conclusions, Vol. 3. Ed. by Anne O. Krueger. (National Bureau of Economic Research Ser.). x, 232p. 1988. pap. text ed. 16.00 (*0-226-45495-9*) U Ch Pr.

Trade & Employment in Developing Countries, Vol. 1: Individual Studies. Anne O. Krueger et al. LC 80-15826. (National Bureau of Economic Research Ser.). (Illus.). 560p. 1980. lib. bdg. 66.00 (*0-226-45492-4*) U Ch Pr.

Trade & Environment: The Regulatory Controversy & a Theoretical & Empirical Assessment of Unilateral Environmental Action. Ed. by K. Steininger. 219p. 1995. 54.00 (*3-7908-0814-8*) Spr-Verlag.

Trade & Environmental Law in the European Community. Andreas R. Ziegler. (Oxford European Community Law Ser.). 344p. 1997. 90.00 (*0-19-826246-9*) OUP.

***Trade & Exchange in Prehistoric Europe.** Christopher Scarre. (Oxbow Monographs in Archaeology: No. 33). (Illus.). 255p. 1993. pap. 60.00 (*0-946897-62-X*, Pub. by Oxbow Bks UK) David Brown.

Trade & Export Finance Handbook. Ed. by First Washington Associates Staff. 1994. ring bd. 300.00 (*1-85564-288-3*, Pub. by Euromoney UK) Am Educ Systs.

Trade & Finance in Colonial India 1750-1860. Ed. by Asiya Siddiqi. (Oxford in India Readings Ser.: Themes in Indian History). 396p. 1995. 35.00 (*0-19-563130-7*) OUP.

Trade & Finance in Portuguese India. Celsa Pinto. (C). 1994. text ed. 40.00 (*81-7022-507-8*, Pub. by Concept II) S Asia.

Trade & Growth: Dilemmas in Trade Policy. Ed. by Manuel R. Agosin & Diana Tussie. LC 93-1303. 1993. text ed. 85.00 (*0-312-09987-8*) St Martin.

Trade & Gunboats: The United States & Brazil in the Age of Empire. Steven C. Topik. LC 96-10467. 1996. write for info. (*0-8047-2602-7*) Stanford U Pr.

Trade & Imperialism in Southern Nigeria, 1881-1929. W. I. Ofonagoro. LC 78-64521. 263p. 1979. text ed. 23.95 (*0-88357-049-1*) NOK Pubs.

Trade & Industrial Resources of the Common Market & EFTA Countries: A Comparative Statistical Analysis. A. E. Walsh & John Paxton. 176p. 1970. text ed. 40.00 (*0-8377-1302-1*) Rothman.

***Trade & Industrialization.** Ed. by Deepak Nayyar. (Oxford in India Readings). 350p. 1997. 24.95 (*0-19-563532-9*) OUP.

***Trade & Innovation: Theory & Evidence.** Katharine Wakelin. LC 97-22603. 1997. write for info. (*1-85898-677-X*) E Elgar.

***Trade & Investment Complementarities in North-East Asia: Proceedings - Papers of the Roundtable on Economic Cooperation of Possibilities.** (Studies in Trade & Investment: No. 18). 248p. Date not set. pap. 30.00 (*92-1-119725-2*, HD9987) UN.

***Trade & Investment in Asia.** Ed. by Edward B. Flowers et al. (Illus.). 236p. (Orig.). 1997. pap. 25.00 (*0-9657171-0-0*) St Johns U Global Educ.

Trade & Investment in the Asia-Pacific Region. Henri C. De Bettignies. LC 95-24872. (Research in the Asian-Pacific Business with the INSEAD Euro-Asia Centre: Vol. 1). 224p. 1996. 63.95 (*0-415-12321-6*, Pub. by Intl Thomson Busn UK) Inter Thomson.

Trade & Investment in the 1990s: Experts Debate Japan-U. S. Issues. Ed. by Myra Aronson. 128p. (C). 1996. 25.00 (*0-8147-0641-X*) NYU Pr.

Trade & Investment Law in Hong Kong. Philip St. J Smart et al. 1993. boxed 150.00 (*0-409-99630-0*, SI) MICHIE.

Trade & Investment Opportunities in China: The Current Commercial & Legal Framework. Danian Zhang et al. LC 91-44992. 280p. 1992. text ed. 55.00 (*0-89930-566-0*, ZLE/, Quorum Bks) Greenwood.

Trade & Investment Policies in the Americas. Conference on Trade Policies in the Americas Staff. Ed. by Stephen E. Guisinger. LC 73-84723. (Jno. E. Owens Memorial Foundation Publication Ser.). 113p. reprint ed. pap. 32.30 (*0-8357-7058-3*, 2033435) Bks Demand.

Trade & Investment Reference Manual. 96p. (Orig.). 1996. per., pap. write for info. (*0-9652718-0-3*) Busn Rndtable.

Trade & Investment Relations among the United States, Canada, & Japan. Ed. by Robert M. Stern. LC 89-31248. (Illus.). 456p. 1989. 66.00 (*0-226-77317-5*) U Ch Pr.

Trade & Labour Standards: A Review of the Issues. 36p. (Orig.). (FRE.). 1995. pap. 14.00 (*92-64-04353-5*, Pub. by Org for Econ FR) OECD.

Trade & Merchandise Marks Act, 1982: With Supplement. 2nd rev. ed. V. D. Kushreshtha. (C). 1990. reprint ed. 140.00 (*0-685-39534-0*) St Mut.

Trade & Migration: NAFTA & Agriculture. Philip L. Martin. LC 93-2922. (Policy Analyses in International Economics Ser.: No. 38). 158p. 1993. pap. 15.00 (*0-88132-201-6*) Inst Intl Eco.

Trade & Navigation of Great Britain Considered. 4th ed. Joshua Gee. LC 71-97977. (Reprints of Economic Classics Ser.). xxxix, 239p. 1969. reprint ed. 39.50 (*0-678-00576-1*) Kelley.

Trade & Navigation of Great Britain Considered: Shewing That Surest Way for a Nation to Increase in Riches, Is to Prevent the Importation of Such Foreign Commodities As May Be Rais'd at Home. Joshua Gee. LC 75-141123. (Research Library of Colonial Americana). 1972. reprint ed. 23.95 (*0-405-03335-4*) Ayer.

Trade & Payments after Soviet Disintegration. John Williamson. LC 92-21821. (Policy Analyses in International Economics Ser.: No. 37). 76p. 1992. pap. 12.00 (*0-88132-173-7*) Inst Intl Eco.

Trade & Payments Arrangements for States of the Former U. S. S. R. Constantine Michalopoulos & David G. Tarr. LC 92-31863. (Studies of Economies in Transformation: No. 2). 53p. 1992. 6.95 (*0-8213-2260-5*, 12260) World Bank.

Trade & Payments Arrangements for States of the Former U. S. S. R. Constantine Michalopoulos & David G. Tarr. (Studies of Economies in Transformation: No. 2R). 49p. (RUS.). 1993. 6.95 (*0-8213-2422-5*, 12422) World Bank.

***Trade & Payments in Central & Eastern Europe's Transforming Economies.** Lucjan T. Orlowski & Dominick Salvatore. LC 96-29276. (Handbook of Comparative Economic Policies Ser.). 416p. 1997. text ed. 115.00 (*0-313-29764-9*, Greenwood Pr) Greenwood.

Trade & Politics in a Shona Kingdom: The Manyika & Their African & Portuguese Neighbors, 1575-1902. H. H. Bhila. (Studies in Zimbabwean History). 307p. reprint ed. pap. 87.50 (*0-317-27757-X*, 2025233) Bks Demand.

Trade & Politics in Ancient Greece. J. Hasbroeck. Tr. by L. M. Fraser et al. xii, 187p. 1978. 20.00 (*0-89005-240-9*) Ares.

Trade & Politics in Ancient Greece. Johannes Hasebroek. LC 65-15245. 1933. pap. 18.00 (*0-8196-0150-0*) Biblo.

Trade & Politics in the Indian Ocean: Historical & Contemporary Perspectives. Ed. by Gorgio Borsa. (C). 1991. 25.00 (*81-85425-11-6*, Pub. by Manohar II) S Asia.

Trade & Politics in the Niger Delta, 1830-1885: An Introduction to the Economic & Political History of Nigeria. Kenneth O. Dike. LC 81-13381. (Oxford Studies in African Affairs). vi, 250p. 1982. reprint ed. text ed. 59.75 (*0-313-23297-0*, DITR) Greenwood.

Trade & Poor Economies. Ed. by Sheila Smith & John Toye. 166p. 1979. 37.50 (*0-7146-3137-X*, Pub. by F Cass Pubs UK) Intl Spec Bk.

Trade & Professional Associations in California: A Directory. 6th ed. LC 95-34816. (California Information Guides Ser.). 1996. pap. 50.00 (*1-880028-05-0*) Cal Inst Public.

Trade & Professional Associations in California: A Directory. 6th ed. Ed. by Jennifer T. Caughman. LC 91-9749. (California Information Guides Ser.). 1996. pap. 50.00 (*0-912102-95-0*) Cal Inst Public.

Trade & Project Finance in Emerging Markets. Michael Rowe. 280p. 1995. 170.00 (*1-85564-387-1*, Pub. by Euromoney UK) Am Educ Systs.

Trade & Protectionism. Ed. by Takatoshi Ito & Anne O. Krueger. LC 92-39852. (National Bureau of Economic Research East Asia Seminar on Economics Ser.: Vol. 2). (Illus.). 460p. (C). 1993. 74.95 (*0-226-38668-6*) U Ch Pr.

Trade & Security: U. S. Policies at Cross-Purposes. Henry R. Nau. 128p. 1995. 29.95 (*0-8447-7056-6*, AEI Pr); pap. 9.95 (*0-8447-7038-8*) Am Enterprise.

Trade & Society: The Amoy Network on the China Coast, 1683-1735. Ng Chin-Keong. 346p. 1984. 49.50 (*9971-69-068-3*, Pub. by Sgapore Univ SI) Coronet Bks.

Trade & Structural Adjustment see Positive Approach to the International Economic Order

Trade & Structural Change. Leslie Stein. LC 83-40181. 192p. 1984. text ed. 29.95 (*0-312-81205-1*) St Martin.

Trade & Structural Change in Pacific Asia. Ed. by Colin I. Bradford, Jr. & William H. Branson. LC 86-19293. (National Bureau of Economic Research Conference Report Ser.). 576p. (C). 1987. lib. bdg. 72.00 (*0-226-07025-5*) U Ch Pr.

Trade & Sustainable Development: A Survey of the Issues & a New Research Agenda. (Illus.). 139p. (Orig.). (C). 1994. pap. text ed. 50.00 (*0-7881-1047-0*) DIANE Pub.

Trade & Technical English. Robert E. Barry. 464p. 1994. pap. text ed. 52.00 (*0-13-606047-1*) P-H.

Trade & Technology in Soviet-Western Relations. Philip Hanson. LC 80-69940. 300p. 1981. text ed. 59.50 (*0-231-05276-6*) Col U Pr.

Trade & the American Dream: A Social History of Postwar Trade Policy. Susan A. Aaronson. (Illus.). 264p. 1996. text ed. 45.00 (*0-8131-1955-3*) U Pr of Ky.

Trade & the American Dream: A Social History of Postwar Trade Policy. Susan A. Aaronson. LC 95-51058. (Illus.). 264p. 1996. pap. 15.95 (*0-8131-0874-8*) U Pr of Ky.

***Trade & the Environment: A Comparative Study of EC & U. S. Law.** Damien Geradin. (Studies in International & Comparative Law). 280p. (C). 1997. text ed. 69.95 (*0-521-59012-4*) Cambridge U Pr.

Trade & the Environment: Law, Economics, & Policy. Ed. by Durwood Zaelke et al. (Illus.). 270p. 1993. pap. 24.95 (*1-55963-268-2*); text ed. 49.95 (*1-55963-267-4*) Island Pr.

Trade & the Environment: The Search for Balance, 2 vols., Vols. 1 & 2. Ed. by James Cameron et al. (Environmental Law Ser.). 1200p. 1994. 275.00 (*1-874698-55-4*, Pub. by Cameron May UK) Gaunt.

Trade & the Industrial Revolution, 1700-1850, Vol. 2. Ed. by Stanley L. Engerman. LC 95-36557. (Growth of the World Economy Ser.). (Illus.). 936p. 1996. 290.00 (*1-85898-007-0*) E Elgar.

Trade & the Poor: The Impact of International Trade on Developing Countries. John Madeley. LC 92-39846. 224p. 1993. text ed. 39.95 (*0-312-09236-9*) St Martin.

Trade & the Poor: The Impact of International Trade on Developing Countries. 2nd ed. John Madely. 230p. (Orig.). 1996. pap. 23.95 (*1-85339-324-X*, Pub. by Intermed Tech UK) Women Ink.

Trade & Trade Barriers in the Pacific. Philip G. Wright. LC 75-30090. (Institute of Pacific Relations Ser.). reprint ed. 43.50 (*0-404-59571-5*) AMS Pr.

Trade & Traders in Muslim Spain: The Commercial Realignment of the Iberian Peninsula, 900-1500. Olivia R. Constable. (Cambridge Studies in Medieval Life & Thought: No. 24). (Illus.). 320p. (C). 1994. text ed. 64.95 (*0-521-43075-5*) Cambridge U Pr.

***Trade & Traders in Muslim Spain: The Commercial Realignment of the Iberian Peninsula, 900-1500.** Olivia R. Constable. (Cambridge Studies in Medieval Life & Thought: No. 24). (Illus.). 348p. 1996. pap. text ed. 22.95 (*0-521-56503-0*) Cambridge U Pr.

Trade & Traders in Western India. V. K. Jain. (C). 1990. 38.00 (*0-685-39094-2*, Pub. by Munshiram Manoharial II) S Asia.

Trade & Transformation in Korea, 1876-1945. Dennis L. McNamara. (Transitions: Asia & Asian America Ser.). 228p. (C). 1996. text ed. 59.00 (*0-8133-8994-1*) Westview.

Trade & Transitions: A Comparative Analysis of Adjustment Policies. Michael J. Trebilcock et al. 240p. (C). 1990. text ed. 74.95 (*0-415-04977-6*, A4663) Routledge.

Trade & Travel in South America. F. Alcock. 1976. lib. bdg. 59.95 (*0-8490-2754-3*) Gordon Pr.

Trade & Urban Development in Poland: An Economic Geography of Cracow, from Its Origins to 1795. F. W. Carter. LC 92-27971. (Cambridge Studies in Historical Geography: No. 20). (Illus.). 432p. (C). 1994. text ed. 85.00 (*0-521-41239-0*) Cambridge U Pr.

Trade & Wages: Leveling Wages Down? Jagdish Bhagwatt & Marvin H. Kosters. LC 94-13297. 150p. 1994. 29.95 (*0-8447-3858-1*, AEI Pr) Am Enterprise.

Trade Aspects of the Internationalization of Mexican Agriculture: Consequences for Mexico's Food Crisis. Steven E. Sanderson. (Monographs: No. 10). 84p. (Orig.). (C). 1983. pap. 7.50 (*0-935391-48-7*, MN-10) UCSD Ctr US-Mex.

Trade Association Activities. Irving S. Paull et al. (Business Enterprises Reprint Ser.). viii, 381p. 1983. reprint ed. lib. bdg. 45.00 (*0-89941-209-2*, 302950) W S Hein.

Trade Associations & Professional. 10th ed. Braun. 1991. 140.00 (*0-8103-8385-3*) Gale.

Trade Associations & Professional Bodies of the United Kingdom. 8th ed. Patricia Millard. 600p. 1987. 78.00 (*0-08-033390-7*, Pergamon Pr) Elsevier.

Trade Associations & Professional Bodies of the United Kingdom. 9th ed. Ed. by Patricia Millard. LC 88-19516. (Trade Association & Professional Bodies Ser.). 530p. 1988. 40.00 (*0-08-034876-9*, Pergamon Pr) Elsevier.

Trade Associations & Professional Bodies of the United Kingdom. 11th ed. Ed. by Patricia Millard. 624p. 1993. 145.00 (*1-873477-55-4*, Gale Res Intl) Gale.

Trade Associations & Professional Bodies of the United Kingdom. 12th ed. Ed. by Millard. 648p. 1994. 150.00 (*1-873477-21-X*, Gale Res Intl) Gale.

Trade Associations & Professional Bodies of the United States. 7th ed. Patricia Millard. 1984. 46.00 (*0-08-023024-5*, Pergamon Pr) Elsevier.

Trade Associations & the Antitrust Laws. Basil J. Mezines. (Corporate Practice Portfolio Ser.: No. 32). 1983. 92.00 (*0-318-33054-7*) BNA Books.

***Trade Associations & the Antitrust Laws.** Basil J. Mezines. (Corporate Practice Ser.: No. 32). 1993. 95.00 (*1-55871-298-4*) BNA.

***Trade Associations & Uniform Costing in the British Printing Industry, 1900-1963.** Ed. by Stephen P. Walker & Falconer Mitchell. LC 97-23319. (New Works in Accounting History). 230p. 1997. 47.00 (*0-8153-3024-3*) Garland.

Trade Associations in Business History. Ed. by Hiroaki Yamazaki & Matao Miyamoto. 326p. 1988. 47.50 (*0-86008-420-5*, Pub. by U of Tokyo JA) Col U Pr.

Trade Associations in Law & Business. Benjamin S. Kirsh & Harold R. Shapiro. (Business Enterprises Reprint Ser.). 399p. 1986. reprint ed. lib. bdg. 47.50 (*0-89941-442-7*, 303810) W S Hein.

Trade Associations, Their Economic Significance & Legal Status: Their Economic Significance & Legal Status. 2nd rev. ed. National Industrial Conference Board, Inc. Staff. LC 25-12032. xiv, 388p. 1982. reprint ed. lib. bdg. 47.50 (*0-89941-164-9*, 302310) W S Hein.

Trade Balances During Business Cycles: U. S. & Britain since 1880. Ilse Mintz. (Occasional Papers: No. 67). 111p. 1959. reprint ed. 28.90 (*0-87014-381-6*); reprint ed. mic. film 20.00 (*0-685-61322-4*) Natl Bur Econ Res.

Trade Barriers: International Trade Documents: Selected Papers, 4 bks. U. S. Tariff Commission. 1980. reprint ed. Set. lib. bdg. 240.00 (*0-89941-144-4*, 201060) W S Hein.

Trade Blocs: The Future of Economic Regionalism. Ed. by Vincent Cable & David Henderson. 208p. (C). 1994. pap. 18.95 (*0-905031-81-4*) Brookings.

Trade Book Marketing. Ed. by Robert A. Carter. 320p. 1983. pap. 24.95 (*0-8352-1693-4*) Bowker.

***Trade Book Publishing, 1996: Analysis by Category.** 3rd ed. Charles Dianis et al. (Illus.). 257p. 1996. 995.00 (*0-88709-131-8*) Simba Info Inc.

Trade Catalogs in the Hagley Museum & Library. Nina D. Walls. (Illus.). 104p. 1987. pap. 7.50 (*0-914650-26-2*) Hagley Museum.

Trade Catalogues at Winterthur: A Guide to Literature of Merchandising, 1750 to 1980. Compiled by E. Richard McKinstry. LC 93-13919. (Winterthur Bk.). 1993. reprint ed. 100.00 (*1-55655-480-X*) U Pubns Amer.

Trade Catalogues 1542 to 1842. Theodore R. Crom. LC 88-93066. (Illus.). xi, 392p. 1989. text ed. 165.00 (*0-9604888-3-9*) T R Crom.

Trade, Commerce...of the Empire see British Empire

***Trade, Commodities & Shipping in the Medieval Mediterranean.** David Jacoby. (Variorum Collected Studies: Vol. 572). 350p. 1997. 98.95 (*0-86078-620-X*, Pub. by Ashgate UK) Ashgate Pub Co.

Trade Conflicts & U. S. - Mexican Relations. John F. Purcell. (Research Reports: No. 38). 49p. (Orig.). (C). 1982. pap. 5.00 (*0-935391-37-1*, RR-38) UCSD Ctr US-Mex.

Trade Contacts in China. Kagan Page. 357p. 1987. 110.00 (*1-85091-340-4*, 073029-M99348) Gale.

Trade Cycle: An Essay. Roy F. Harrod. LC 65-25859. (Reprints of Economic Classics Ser.). xi, 234p. 1965. reprint ed. 35.00 (*0-678-00114-6*) Kelley.

***Trade Data Elements Directory: Trade Facilitation Recommendations, Vol. 3.** Economic Commission for Europe. 333p. pap. 60.00 (*92-1-116650-0*) UN.

Trade Data Elements Directory (UNTDED 1990) 310p. 1990. 95.00 (*92-1-116473-7*, 90.II.E.8) UN.

Trade Data Elements Directory (UNTDED 1993) Trade Facilitation: 1993. 272p. 1994. 95.00 (*92-1-116585-7*, E.94.II.E.4) UN.

Trade, Debt & Growth in Latin America. Ed. by Antonio Jorge et al. 176p. 1984. 74.00 (*0-08-030981-X*, Pergamon Pr) Elsevier.

Trade, Development & Foreign Debt: A History of Theories of Polarisation & Convergence in the International Economy, Vol. 1. Michael Hudson. 306p. (C). 63.00 (*0-7453-0484-2*, Pub. by Pluto Pr UK); pap. 19.95 (*0-7453-0489-3*, Pub. by Pluto Pr UK) LPC InBook.

Trade, Development & Foreign Debt: A History of Theories of Polarisation & Convergence in the International Economy, Vol. 1, Vol. 2. Michael Hudson. 212p. (C). 63.00 (*0-7453-0577-6*, Pub. by Pluto Pr UK); pap. 19.95 (*0-7453-0666-7*, Pub. by Pluto Pr UK) LPC InBook.

Trade, Development, & Political Economy: Selected Essays of Ronald Findlay. Ronald Findlay. (Economists of the Twentieth Century Ser.). 480p. 1993. 85.00 (*1-85278-982-4*) E Elgar.

Trade, Devotion & Governance: Papers in Later Medieval English History. Dorothy Clayton & Peter McNiven. 192p. (C). 1994. text ed. 60.00 (*0-7509-0598-0*, Pub. by Sutton Pubng UK) Bks Intl VA.

Trade, Devotion, & Governance: Papers in Later Medieval History. Ed. by Dorothy J. Clayton et al. LC 94-22173. 1994. 77.00 (*0-7509-0594-8*, Pub. by Sutton Pubng UK) Bks Intl VA.

Trade Directories of the World, 1987. LC 52-6569. 1990. write for info. (*0-87514-003-3*) Croner.

Trade Dress Protection. William E. Levin. LC 96-15608. 1996. ring bd. write for info. (*0-8366-1031-8*) Clark Boardman Callaghan.

Trade Employment & Industrialisation in Singapore. Linda Lim & Pang Eng Fong. (Employment, Adjustment & Industrialisation Ser.: No. 2). vi, 110p. 1986. pap. 22.50 (*92-2-105231-1*) Intl Labour Office.

***Trade, Employment, & Labour Standards: A Study of Core Workers' Rights & International Trade.** OECD Staff. 252p. (Orig.). 1996. pap. 48.00 (*92-64-15270-9*, 22-96-03-1) OECD.

Trade, Employment, & Welfare: A Comparative Study of Trade & Labour Market Policies in Sweden & New Zealand, 1880-1980. Deborah Mabbett. (Illus.). 216p. 1995. 52.00 (*0-19-828379-2*) OUP.

Trade, Environment & Sustainable Development: A South Asian Perspective. Ed. by Grant Hewison & Maree Underhill. LC 96-11318. 208p. 1997. text ed. 69.95 (*0-312-16022-4*) St Martin.

Trade Fair Design. Rotovision S. A. Staff. 1996. pap. text ed. 35.00 (*0-8230-6503-0*) Watsn-Guptill.

Trade Fairs in Japan 1996-97. 292p. 1996. text ed. 41.00 (*4-8224-0739-X*, Pub. by JETRO JA) Taylor & Francis.

Trade, Finance & Developing Countries: Strategies & Constraints in the 1990s. Sheila Page. 426p. (C). 1989. lib. bdg. 76.50 (*0-389-20890-6*, N 8446) B&N Imports.

An Asterisk (*) at the beginning of an entry indicates that the title is appearing in BIP for the first time.

Trade, Finance, & Development in Pakistan. J. Russell Andrus & Azizali F. Mohammed. xii, 289p. 1966. 42.50 (*0-8047-0126-1*) Stanford U Pr.

Trade Financing. Ed. by Euromoney Staff. 1985. 210.00 (*0-686-79057-X*) St Mut.

Trade Flows & Trade Policy after Nineteen Ninety-Two. Ed. by L. Alan Winters. LC 92-27968. (Illus.). 312p. (C). 1993. text ed. 59.95 (*0-521-44020-3*) Cambridge U Pr.

Trade for Freedom. Morris Brafman & David Schimel. LC 75-26371. 96p. 1975. 16.95 (*0-88400-043-5*) Shengold.

Trade Friction & Economic Policy: Problems & Prospects for Japan & the United States. Ed. by Ryuzo Sato & Paul Wachtel. (Illus.). 304p. 1987. text ed. 69.95 (*0-521-34446-8*) Cambridge U Pr.

Trade, Growth, & Development: The Role of Politics & Institutions - Proceedings of the 12th Arne Ryde Symposium, 13-14 June 1991, in Honour of Bo Sodersten. Ed. by Gote Hansson. LC 93-19274. (Illus.). 336p. (C). (gr. 13). 1993. text ed. 74.95 (*0-415-08760-0*, B2396) Routledge.

***Trade, Growth & Technical Change.** Ed. by Daniele Archibugi & Jonathan Michie. 300p. (C). 1997. text ed. 59.95 (*0-521-55393-8*) Cambridge U Pr.

***Trade, Growth & Technical Change.** Ed. by Daniele Archibugi & Jonathan Michie. 300p. (C). 1997. pap. text ed. 19.95 (*0-521-55641-4*) Cambridge U Pr.

***Trade Growth in Transition Economies: Export Impediments for Central & Eastern Europe.** Ed. by Richard N. Cooper & Janos Gacs. 384p. 1997. 85.00 (*1-85898-608-7*) E Elgar.

Trade in Death: An Economics Mystery. Scott Brunger. LC 93-23202. 192p. (Orig.). 1993. pap. 7.95 (*0-377-00265-8*) Friendship Pr.

Trade in Domestic Workers: Causes, Mechanisms & Consequences of International Migration. Ed. by Noaleen Heyzer et al. 240p. (C). 1994. text ed. 59.95 (*1-85649-285-0*, Pub. by Zed Bks Ltd UK) Humanities.

Trade in Domestic Workers: Causes, Mechanisms & Consequences of International Migration. Ed. by Noaleen Heyzer et al. 247p. (C). 1994. pap. 25.00 (*1-85649-286-9*, Pub. by Zed Bks Ltd UK) Humanities.

Trade in Information, Computer & Communication Service. OECD Staff. (Information Computer Communications Policy Ser.: No. 21). 56p. (Orig.). 1990. pap. 13.00 (*92-64-13327-5*) OECD.

Trade in Manufactured Products with Developing Countries: Reinforcing North-South Partnership. Albert Fishlow et al. (Triangle Papers: Vol. 21). 1981. 6.00 (*0-930503-29-5*) Trilateral Comm.

Trade in Manufactures. A. C. Hotson & K. L. Gardiner. (Bank of England. Discussion Papers. Technical Ser.: No. 5). 40p. reprint ed. pap. 25.00 (*0-318-34923-X*, 2031457) Bks Demand.

Trade-in Mother. Marisabina Russo. LC 91-47681. (Illus.). 32p. (J). (ps up). 1993. 14.00 (*0-688-11416-4*); lib. bdg. 13.93 (*0-688-11417-2*) Greenwillow.

Trade in Services: A Theoretical Analysis. James R. Melvin. 195p. 1989. pap. text ed. 29.95 (*0-88645-090-X*, Pub. by Inst Res Pub CN) Ashgate Pub Co.

Trade in Services & Imperfect Competition: Application to International Aviation. Ethan Weisman. (C). 1990. lib. bdg. 94.50 (*0-7923-0900-6*) Kluwer Ac.

***Trade in the Ancient Near East.** Ed. by J. D. Hawkins. (Illus.). 230p. 1977. reprint ed. pap. 32.50 (*0-614-21866-7*, Pub. by Brit Sch Archaeol Iraq UK) David Brown.

Trade in the Asian Pacific Region. Ed. by A. M. Babkina. (Illus.). 237p. (C). 1996. lib. bdg. 59.00 (*1-56072-358-0*) Nova Sci Pubs.

Trade in the Eastern Seas, 1793-1813. C. Northcote Parkinson. (Illus.). 437p. 1966. 35.00 (*0-7146-1348-7*, Pub. by F Cass Pubs UK) Intl Spec Bk.

Trade in the New Independent States. Ed. by Constantine Michalopoulos & David G. Tarr. LC 94-35297. (Studies of Economies in Transformation: No. 15). 274p. 1995. 17.95 (*0-8213-3077-2*, 13077) World Bank.

Trade in the New Independent States. Constantine Michalopoulos & David G. Tarr. (Studies of Economies in Transformation: No. 13). 274p. (RUS.). 1995. 17.95 (*0-8213-3236-8*, 13236) World Bank.

Trade in the Pre-Modern Era, 1400-1700, 2 vols., Set. Ed. by Douglas A. Irwin. LC 95-36559. (Growth of the World Economy Ser.: Vol. 1). (Illus.). 952p. 1996. 290.00 (*1-85278-989-1*) E Elgar.

Trade in Transit. Visser. 1986. lib. bdg. 101.50 (*90-247-3305-7*, Pub. by M Nijhoff NE) Kluwer Ac.

Trade, Industrial, & Professional Periodicals of the United States. Ed. by Kathleen L. Endres. LC 93-11531. (Historical Guides to the World's Periodicals & Newspapers Ser.). 496p. 1994. text ed. 105.00 (*0-313-28042-8*, Greenwood Pr) Greenwood.

***Trade, Industrial, & Technical Careers, 175 titles in 7 vols., Set.** (Education for Success Ser.). 1994. spiral bd. 188.00 (*0-87063-519-0*, TI94) Vocational Biographies.

***Trade, Industrial, & Technical Careers, 175 titles in 7 vols., Set.** (Education for Success Ser.). 1994. 188.00 (*0-87063-527-1*, TI94) Vocational Biographies.

***Trade, Industrial, & Technical Careers, 175 titles in 7 vols., Set.** (Education for Success Ser.). 1995. spiral bd. 188.00 (*0-87063-603-0*, TI95) Vocational Biographies.

***Trade, Industrial, & Technical Careers, 175 titles in 7 vols., Set.** (Education for Success Ser.). 1995. 188.00 (*0-87063-604-9*, TI95) Vocational Biographies.

Trade, Industrial Cooperation & Technology Transfer with the Former Socialist Countries of Eastern Europe: The British Experience. Caroline M. Hay & Malcolm R. Hill. (Illus.). 131p. 1993. 49.95 (*1-85628-502-2*, Pub. by Avebury Pub UK) Ashgate Pub Co.

Trade, Industrial Policy & International Competition, Vol. 13. Richard G. Harris. (Collected Research Studies of the Royal Commission..: No. 13). 192p. 1985. 14.95 (*0-8020-7255-0*) U of Toronto Pr.

Trade, Industrialization & Integration in Twentieth Century Central America. Ed. by Irma T. De Alonso. LC 93-23678. 304p. 1994. text ed. 65.00 (*0-275-94804-8*, Praeger Pubs) Greenwood.

Trade, Inflation & the Dollar. 2nd rev. ed. Thibaut de Saint Phalle. LC 84-6991. 464p. 1984. text ed. 65.00 (*0-275-91144-6*, C1144, Praeger Pubs) Greenwood.

Trade, Innovation, Environment. Ed. by Carlo Carraro. LC 94-3702. (Economics, Energy & Environment Ser.: Vol. 2). 416p. (C). 1994. lib. bdg. 137.50 (*0-7923-3033-1*) Kluwer Ac.

Trade is a Two-Way Street. 99p. 1981. pap. 5.00 (*0-685-07136-7*, 521-0030) Amer Bar Assn.

Trade Is Everybody's Business. Susan A. Arronson. LC 95-42266. 64p. (YA). (gr. 7-12). 1996. pap. 9.95 (*0-932765-72-6*) Close Up Fnd.

Trade Is Everybody's Business. Susan A. Arronson. Ed. by Charles Sass. LC 95-42266. 40p. 1996. teacher ed., pap. 9.95 (*0-614-08835-6*) Close Up Fnd.

Trade Issues in the Caribbean, Vol. 7. Ed. by Irma Tirado de Alonso. LC 92-15396. (Caribbean Studies: Vol. 7). 231, xvp. 1992. text ed. 55.00 (*2-88124-550-1*); pap. text ed. 26.00 (*2-88124-555-2*) Gordon & Breach.

Trade Issues in the New Independent States. Constantine Michalopoulos. LC 93-22695. (Studies of Economics in Transformation Paper: No. 7). 39p. 1993. 6.95 (*0-8213-2483-7*, 12483) World Bank.

***Trade Japan.** Barbara Bader. Date not set. lib. bdg. write for info. (*0-688-05151-0*) Greenwillow.

***Trade Japan.** Barbara Bader. (J). Date not set. write for info. (*0-688-05150-2*) Greenwillow.

Trade, Jobs & Income Distribution. William R. Cline. (Orig.). Date not set. pap. write for info. (*0-88132-216-4*) Inst Intl Eco.

Trade Laws & Institutions: Good Practices & the World Trade Organization. Bernard M. Hoekman. LC 95-7272. (Discussion Papers: Vol. 282). 124p. 1995. 8.95 (*0-8213-3217-1*, 13217) World Bank.

Trade Liberalisation: Global Economic Implications. OECD Staff. 242p. (Orig.). 1993. pap. 43.00 (*92-64-13962-1*) OECD.

***Trade Liberalisation Policies in Mexico.** OECD Staff. 160p. (Orig.). 1996. pap. 24.00 (*92-64-15316-0*, 22-96-05-1) OECD.

Trade Liberalization among Major World Trading Areas. John Whalley. (Illus.). 328p. 1984. 35.00 (*0-262-23120-4*) MIT Pr.

Trade Liberalization & the Canadian Pulp & Paper Industry. William E. Haviland et al. LC 70-351140. (Canada in the Atlantic Economy Ser.: No. 5). 116p. reprint ed. pap. 33.10 (*0-8357-4025-0*, 2036717) Bks Demand.

Trade Liberalization in Chile. 125p. 1991. 125.00 (*92-1-112312-7*, E.91.II.D.18) UN.

***Trade Liberalization in Sri Lanka: Exports, Technology & Industrial Policy.** Ganeshan Wignaraja. LC 97-22914. 1997. write for info. (*0-312-17731-3*) St Martin.

Trade Liberalization in the Western Hemisphere. Ed. by ECLAC Staff & IDB (Inter-American Development Bank) Staff. 502p. (Orig.). (C). 1995. pap. text ed. write for info. (*0-9645938-0-7*) ECLAC.

Trade Liberalization in the 1990's. Neelamber Hatti & Hans Singer. (New World Order Ser.: Vol. 8). 1990. 95.00 (*81-85182-46-9*, Pub. by Indus Pub II) S Asia.

Trade Like Any Other: Female Singers & Dancers in Egypt. Kathy Van Nieuwkerk. LC 94-26452. (Illus.). 240p. 1995. pap. 15.95 (*0-292-78723-5*); text ed. 35.00 (*0-292-78720-0*) U of Tex Pr.

***Trade Mark Laws of the World & Unfair Trade.** B. Singer. LC 97-1958. 685p. 1997. reprint ed. lib. bdg. 115.00 (*0-8377-2661-1*) Rothman.

Trade Marketing Strategies: The Partnership Between Manufacturers, Brands & Retailers. 2nd ed. Geoffrey Randall. (Professional Development Ser.). 250p. 1994. pap. 39.95 (*0-7506-2012-9*) Buttrwrth-Heinemann.

Trade Marketing Strategy. Gary Davies. 1993. 88.00 (*1-85396-213-9*, Pub. by Paul Chapman UK) Taylor & Francis.

Trade, Markets & Welfare. Kelvin J. Lancaster. LC 95-38731. (Illus.). 288p. 1996. 95.00 (*1-85278-975-1*) E Elgar.

Trade Marks Act 1994. David Kitchin & James Mellor. (Current Law Statutes Reprint Ser.). 1994. pap. 40.00 (*0-614-03040-4*, Pub. by Sweet & Maxwll UK); text ed. 40.00 (*0-614-02492-7*) Gaunt.

Trade Marks Acts & Regulations Consolidated, 1994-95 Edition. 1994. pap. 28.00 (*0-433-39156-1*, CN) MICHIE.

Trade Marks & Symbols of the World, Vol. 1: The Alphabet in Design. Yasaburo Kuwayama. (Design Sourcebook Ser.). (Illus.). 192p. 1989. pap. 24.95 (*4-7601-0451-8*, 30132) Rockport Pubs.

Trade, Mercantile Capital & Economic Development. Mihir Rakshit. 1993. pap. 10.00 (*0-86311-368-0*, Pub. by Orient Longman Ltd II) Apt Bks.

***Trade Name Origins.** LC 97-20606. (Artful Wordsmith Ser.). 1997. pap. 12.95 (*0-8442-0904-X*) NTC Pub Grp.

***Trade Names Dictionary.** 3rd ed. 1981. 225.00 (*0-8103-0696-4*, 00000497, Gale Res Intl) Gale.

***Trade Names Dictionary.** 5th ed. 1986. 285.00 (*0-8103-0686-7*, 00006690, Gale Res Intl) Gale.

Trade Names Dictionary, 2 vols. 6th ed. Ed. by Donna Wood. 1600p. 1987. 300.00 (*0-8103-1596-3*) Gale.

Trade Names Dictionary. 7th ed. Ed. by Donna Wood. 1989. 320.00 (*0-8103-2941-7*) Gale.

***Trade Names Dictionary: Company Index.** 5th ed. 1986. 290.00 (*0-8103-0687-5*, 00007139, Gale Res Intl) Gale.

Trade Names Dictionary: Company Index, 2 vols. 6th ed. Ed. by Donna Wood. 1500p. 1987. 310.00 (*0-8103-1598-X*) Gale.

Trade Names Dictionary: Company Index. 7th ed. Ed. by Donna Wood. 1989. 320.00 (*0-8103-2942-5*) Gale.

Trade Negotiations in the OECD: Structures, Institutions & States. David J. Blair. 280p. 1992. 93.50 (*0-7103-0432-3*, A7586) Routledge Chapman & Hall.

Trade Negotiations in the Tokyo Round: A Quantitative Assessment. William R. Cline et al. LC 77-91799. 314p. 1978. 28.95 (*0-8157-1472-6*) Brookings.

***Trade of the Tricks.** William D. Noe. 320p. (Orig.). 1998. mass mkt. 8.99 (*1-889501-86-7*, Stargate Pr) Sovereign.

Trade-Off. Maxine O'Callaghan. (Mystery Ser.). 1996. mass mkt. 4.99 (*0-373-26191-8*, 1-26191-6, Wrldwide Lib) Harlequin Bks.

Trade-Offs: Negotiating the Omnibus Trade & Competitiveness Act. Susan C. Schwab. LC 94-10392. 275p. 1994. 35.00 (*0-87584-510-X*) Harvard Busn.

Trade-Offs: Negotiating the Omnibus Trade & Competitiveness Act. Susan C. Schwab. 1994. text ed. 35.00 (*0-07-103606-7*) McGraw.

Trade-Offs: The Impact of New Trade Rules on Developing Countries. Oxfam Staff. (Books from Community Aid Abroad). (C). 1994. pap. 11.95 (*1-875870-04-0*, Pub. by Oxfam UK) Humanities.

Trade on the Guinea Coast, 1657-1666: The Correspondence of the English East India Company. Ed. by Margaret Makepeace. LC 91-34443. (African Primary Texts Ser.: No. 5). 158p. (Orig.). 1991. pap. 26.00 (*0-942615-11-5*) U Wis African Stud.

Trade, Payments & Adjustments in Central & Eastern Europe. John Flemming. Ed. by E. M. Rollo. 1992. pap. 18.95 (*0-905031-50-4*) Brookings.

Trade Performance & Policy in the New Independent States. Constantine Michalopoulos & David G. Tarr. LC 96-12272. (Directions in Development Ser.). 36p. 1996. 10.95 (*0-8213-3615-0*, 13615) World Bank.

Trade Performance & Policy in the New Independent States: Russian Edition. Constantine Michalopoulos & David G. Tarr. 52p. 1996. pap. 10.95 (*0-8213-3687-8*, 13687) World Bank.

Trade, Planning & Rural Development: Essays in Honour of Nurul Islam. Ed. by Azizur R. Khan & Rehman Sobhan. LC 90-32086. 220p. 1990. text ed. 55.00 (*0-312-04512-3*) St Martin.

Trade, Plunder & Settlement: Maritime Enterprise & the Genesis of the British Empire, 1480-1630. Kenneth R. Andrews. 404p. 1985. pap. text ed. 24.95 (*0-521-27698-5*) Cambridge U Pr.

Trade Policies & Developing Nations. Anne O. Krueger. (Integrating National Economies Ser.). 124p. (C). 1995. 34.95 (*0-8157-5056-0*); pap. 14.95 (*0-8157-5055-2*) Brookings.

Trade Policies & Industrialization in a Small Country: The Case of Israel. Richard W. Pomfret. 220p. 1976. lib. bdg. 53.50 (*3-16-338831-0*, Pub. by J C B Mohr GW) Coronet Bks.

Trade Policies for a Better Future. Gatt. 1987. lib. bdg. 84.00 (*0-89838-925-9*) Kluwer Ac.

Trade Policies for International Competitiveness. Ed. by Robert C. Feenstra. LC 89-33917. (National Bureau of Economic Research Conference Report Ser.). (Illus.). 272p. 1989. lib. bdg. 42.00 (*0-226-23949-7*) U Ch Pr.

***Trade Policies in Latin America & the Caribbean: Priorities, Progress & Prospects.** Sarath Rajapatirana. LC 97-11094. (Illus.). xix, 237p. (Orig.). 1997. pap. 19.95 (*0-9656930-0-7*) Intl Ctr Economic.

Trade Policies Towards Developing Countries. Ed. by Akira Hirata & Ippei Yamazawa. LC 92-18929. 1993. text ed. 75.00 (*0-312-08557-5*) St Martin.

Trade Policy Ahead: Three Tracks & One Question. Ernest H. Preeg. LC 95-15804. (Significant Issues Ser.: vol. 17, no. 2). 85p. (C). 1995. pap. 11.95 (*0-89206-309-2*) CSI Studies.

Trade Policy & Corporate Business Decisions. Ed. by Tamir Agmon & Christine R. Hekman. (Illus.). 256p. 1990. 42.00 (*0-19-505538-1*) OUP.

***Trade Policy & Economic Welfare.** 2nd ed. W. Max Corden. (Illus.). 320p. 1997. pap. 19.95 (*0-19-877534-2*) OUP.

***Trade Policy & Economic Welfare.** 2nd ed. W. Max Corden. (Illus.). 320p. 1997. 85.00 (*0-19-829223-6*) OUP.

Trade Policy & Industrialization in Turbulent Times. Ed. by Gerald K. Helleiner. LC 93-26896. 496p. (C). (gr. 13). 1994. text ed. 110.00 (*0-415-10711-3*, Routledge NY) Routledge.

Trade Policy & Market Structure. Elhanan Helpman & Paul R. Krugman. 224p. 1989. 30.00 (*0-262-08182-2*) MIT Pr.

Trade Policy & Market Structure. Elhanan Helpman & Paul R. Krugman. (Illus.). 208p. 1989. reprint ed. pap. 17.95 (*0-262-58098-5*) MIT Pr.

***Trade Policy & the Transition Process.** OECD Staff. 252p. (Orig.). 1996. pap. 49.00 (*92-64-14866-3*, Pub. by Org for Econ FR) OECD.

Trade Policy Developments in Industrial Countries. L. L. Perez et al. (Occasional Papers: No. 5). 56p. 1981. pap. 5.00 (*1-55775-082-3*) Intl Monetary.

Trade Policy for Free Societies: The Case Against Protectionism. Robert W. McGee. LC 93-42760. 216p. 1994. text ed. 55.00 (*0-89930-898-8*, Quorum Bks) Greenwood.

Trade Policy in a Changing World Economy. Robert E. Baldwin. LC 88-20881. (Illus.). xii, 288p. 1989. 47.95 (*0-226-03611-1*) U Ch Pr.

Trade Policy in the 1980s. Ed. by William R. Cline. LC 83-4310. 812p. 1983. pap. 180.00 (*0-7837-8496-1*, 2049303) Bks Demand.

Trade Policy in the 1980's: An Agenda for Canadian-U.S. Relations. Rodney D. Grey. LC 82-106955. (Policy Commentary Ser.: No. 3). 89p. 1981. reprint ed. pap. 25.40 (*0-608-01365-X*, 2062104) Bks Demand.

Trade Policy, Industrialization, & Development: New Perspectives. Gerald K. Helleiner. (WIDER Studies in Development Economics). (Illus.). 288p. 1991. 85.00 (*0-19-820294-6*) OUP.

Trade Policy Issues & Developments. Shailendra J. Anjaria et al. LC 85-14544. (Occasional Paper Ser.: No. 38). 161p. 1985. pap. 7.50 (*0-939934-46-9*) Intl Monetary.

Trade Policy Issues & Empirical Analysis. Ed. by Robert E. Baldwin. (National Bureau of Economic Research Conference Report Ser.). (Illus.). 392p. 1988. lib. bdg. 55.50 (*0-226-03607-3*) U Ch Pr.

***Trade Policy Issues (Seminar Volume)** LC 97-12466. 1997. write for info. (*1-55775-621-X*) Intl Monetary.

Trade Policy Making in Canada: Are We Doing it Right? W. R. Hines. 111p. 1985. pap. text ed. 10.00 (*0-88645-019-5*, Pub. by Inst Res Pub CN) Ashgate Pub Co.

Trade Policy of the Nineteen Eighties. C. Fred Bergsten & William R. Cline. (Policy Analyses in International Economics Ser.: No. 3). 84p. reprint ed. pap. 25.00 (*0-317-20818-7*, 2024793) Bks Demand.

Trade Policy Reform in Developing Countries Since 1985: A Review of the Evidence. Judith M. Dean et al. (Discussion Papers: No. 267). 114p. 1994. 8.95 (*0-8213-3102-7*, 13102) World Bank.

Trade Policy Reforms under Adjustment Programs. World Bank Staff. LC 92-18830. (Operations Evaluation Study Ser.). 171p. 1992. 10.95 (*0-8213-2157-9*, 12157) World Bank.

***Trade Policy Review (GATT) Czech Republic 1996, 2 vols.** GATT Staff. 1996. pap. 55.00 (*92-870-1157-5*, WTO575, Pub. by Wrld Trade SZ) Bernan Associates.

***Trade Policy Review (GATT) Dominican Republic 1996, 2 vols.** WTO Staff. 1996. pap. 55.00 (*92-870-1158-3*, WTO/1996-900, Pub. by Wrld Trade SZ) Bernan Associates.

***Trade Policy Review (GATT) Mauritius 1995, 2 vols. in 1.** GATT Staff. 1996. pap. 55.00 (*92-870-1152-4*, WTO/1995-15, Pub. by Wrld Trade SZ) Bernan Associates.

***Trade Policy Review (GATT) Slovak Republic 1995, 2 vols.** GATT Staff. 1995. pap. 55.00 (*92-870-1155-9*, WTO/1995-18, Pub. by Wrld Trade SZ) Bernan Associates.

***Trade Policy Review (GATT) Switzerland, 1996, 2 vols.** GATT Staff. 1996. pap. 55.00 (*92-870-1160-5*, WTO/605, Pub. by Wrld Trade SZ) Bernan Associates.

***Trade Policy Review (GATT) Thailand 1995, 2 vols.** GATT Staff. 1995. pap. 55.00 (*92-870-1153-2*, WTO/1995-16, Pub. by Wrld Trade SZ) Bernan Associates.

Trade Practices & Consumer Protection. 3rd ed. G. G. Taperell et al. 1983. 109.00 (*0-409-49111-X*, AT); Australia. pap. 87.00 (*0-409-49121-7*, A.T.) MICHIE.

Trade Practices & Traditions: Origin & Development in India. Vipin K. Garg. 1985. 17.50 (*0-8364-1434-9*, Pub. by Allied II) S Asia.

Trade Problems Between Japan & Western Europe. Masamichi Hanabusa. LC 79-88567. (Illus.). 138p. 1979. text ed. 49.95 (*0-275-90360-5*, C0360, Praeger Pubs) Greenwood.

Trade Protection in the European Community. Ludger Schuknecht. LC 92-442. 228p. 1992. text ed. 53.00 (*3-7186-5287-0*) Gordon & Breach.

Trade Protection in the United States. Charles K. Rowley et al. LC 95-7195. (John Locke Ser.). (Illus.). 368p. 1995. 90.00 (*1-85898-198-0*) E Elgar.

Trade Reform: Lessons from Eight Countries. Geoffrey Shepherd & Carlos G. Langoni. 136p. 1991. pap. 12.95 (*1-55815-086-2*) ICS Pr.

Trade Reform Legislation, 1988: A Legislative History of the Omnibus Trade & Competitiveness Act of 1988, 10 vols. Bernard D. Reams, Jr. & Mary A. Nelson. LC 91-75494. 1991. Set. 985.00 (*0-89941-777-9*, 306760) W S Hein.

Trade Regulation: Cases & Materials on. 3rd ed. Milton Handler et al. (University Casebook Ser.). 1100p. 1990. text ed. 44.50 (*0-88277-795-5*) Foundation Pr.

Trade Regulation: Cases & Materials, 1994 Supplement. 3rd ed. Milton Handler et al. (University Casebook Ser.). 315p. 1994. 11.95 (*1-56662-225-5*) Foundation Pr.

Trade Regulation: Teacher's manual to Accompany. 3rd ed. Milton Handler et al. (University Casebook Ser.). 186p. 1990. pap. text ed. write for info. (*0-88277-856-0*) Foundation Pr.

Trade Regulation, Antitrust & Economics: A Bibliography, 1981-1987, 4 vols., Set. Ed. by Peter D. Ward & Margaret A. Goldblatt. 3400p. 1988. 395.00 (*0-89941-638-1*, 305570) W S Hein.

Trade Regulation by Negotiation: Federal Trade Commission Consent Decrees. Talbot Lindstrom & Kevin P. Tighe. LC 73-93919. 1181p. reprint ed. pap. 180.00 (*0-317-26772-8*, 2024341) Bks Demand.

Trade Regulation, 1995: Supplement to Cases & Materials On. 3rd ed. Milton Handler et al. (University Casebook Ser.). 374p. (C). 1995. pap. text ed. 12.50 (*1-56662-293-X*) Foundation Pr.

Trade Related Aspects of Intellectual Property. Ed. by Lonnie T. Brown & Eric A. Szweda. LC 90-82986. vii, 398p. 1990. lib. bdg. 55.00 (*0-89941-747-7*, 306220) W S Hein.

***Trade Related Investments.** Stewart. 1993. pap. text ed. 77.50 (*90-6544-759-8*) Kluwer Ac.

Trade Restraints & the Competitive Status of the Textile, Apparel, & Nonrubber - Footwear Industries. (Illus.). 78p. (Orig.). (C). 1992. pap. text ed. 65.00 (*1-56806-086-6*) DIANE Pub.

Trade Routes: The Manager's Network of Relationships. Robert E. Kaplan & Mignon S. Mazique. (Technical Reports: No. 122G). 26p. 1983. pap. 10.00 (*0-912879-20-3*) Ctr Creat Leader.

Trade Routes & Commerce of the Roman Empire. M. P. Charlesworth. 320p. 1986. pap. 25.00 (*0-89005-444-4*) Ares.

Trade Routes & Economic Exchange among the Indians of California. fac. ed. James T. Davis. (Reports of the University of California Archaeological Survey: No. 54). (Illus.). 78p. 1961. reprint ed. pap. 7.15 (*1-55567-370-8*) Coyote Press.

Trade Routes to Sustained Economic Growth. Ed. by Amnuay Viravan. LC 87-3494. 178p. 1988. text ed. 49. 95 (*0-312-01263-2*) St Martin.

***Trade Secret Protection & Exploitation.** Alan S. Gutterman & Jerry Cohen. 450p. 1997. 115.00 (*1-57018-057-1*, 1057) BNA Books.

Trade Secret Protection & Litigation: Protecting Confidential Business & Technical Information. (Patents, Copyrights, Trademarks, & Literary Property Ser.). 704p. 1992. pap. 70.00 (*0-685-69507-7*) PLI.

Trade Secrets. Winifred Conkling. 1995. pap. 11.00 (*0-684-81182-0*, Fireside) S&S Trade.

Trade Secrets. Eva Shaw. 1994. pap. 9.95 (*1-56924-895-8*) Marlowe & Co.

Trade Secrets. Maynard F. Thompson. Ed. by Jane Chelius. 256p. (Orig.). 1994. mass mkt. 4.99 (*0-671-86788-1*) PB.

***Trade Secrets.** Maynard F. Thomson. 244p. 3.98 (*0-8317-2322-X*) Smithmark.

Trade Secrets: A Practitioner's Guide. Henry H. Perritt, Jr. 700p. 1994. 125.00 (*0-614-17115-6*, G1-1021) PLI.

***Trade Secrets: A State-by-State Survey.** 1997. 165.00 (*1-57018-084-9*, 1084) BNA Books.

Trade Secrets: Answers to the Most Commonly Asked Exporting Questions. Sarah S. McCue & Julie Clowes. 200p. 1994. pap. 14.95 (*1-886641-00-5*) MI Small Busn.

Trade Secrets: Course Manual. Kenneth B. Weckstein & Brian B. Bannon. 199p. write for info. (*0-318-61825-7*) Fed Pubns Inc.

Trade Secrets: Natural Flower Arranging. Pure Madderlake et al. LC 92-29775. 1994. 40.00 (*0-517-59332-7*, C P Pubs) Crown Pub Group.

Trade Secrets: Protecting Your Business's Confidential Information. Nishan Swais. 144p. (Orig.). 1996. pap. 9.95 (*1-55180-053-5*) Self-Counsel Pr.

Trade Secrets: Protection & Remedies. Roy E. Hofer. (Corporate Practice Ser.: No. 43). 1985. 92.00 (*1-55871-235-6*) BNA.

Trade Secrets: Twenty-Five Proven Success Tools for Working, Dealing & Winning with People. Martha Langdon-Dahm. LC 85-82343. 211p. (Orig.). 1986. pap. 14.95 (*0-936585-00-5*) Learn Deve.

Trade Secrets Bk. 1. 140p. 1995. pap. 19.95 (*0-9644752-0-0*) Stewart MacDonald.

***Trade Secrets for Gorgeous Rooms: A Compendium of Designer Techniques & Stylish Ideas.** Dylan Landis. LC 97-816. 1997. write for info. (*0-440-50774-X*) Dell.

Trade Secrets Handbook: Strategies & Techniques for Safeguarding Corporate Information. Dennis Unkovic. 229p. 1985. 39.95 (*0-13-925926-0*, Busn) P-H.

Trade Secrets Law, 3 vols. Melvin F. Jager. LC 85-16654. (IP Ser.). 1985. Set. ring bd. 425.00 (*0-87632-480-4*) Clark Boardman Callaghan.

Trade Secrets of Retail Stars. Debbie Allen. Ed. by Design & Type Staff. 120p. (Orig.). 1996. pap. 19.95 (*0-9650965-4-8*) Image Dynamics.

Trade Shocks: Consequences & Policy Responses Theory & Evidence from Africa, Asia & Latin America. Paul Collier & Jan W. Gunning. LC 94-15540. (Occasional Papers Ser.: No. 51). 1994. pap. 6.95 (*1-55815-326-8*) ICS Pr.

Trade Shop Assistant. Jack Rudman. (Career Examination Ser.: C-3296). 1994. pap. 27.95 (*0-8373-3296-6*) Nat Learn.

Trade Shop Manager. Jack Rudman. (Career Examination Ser.: C-3043). 1994. pap. 34.95 (*0-8373-3043-2*) Nat Learn.

Trade Show & Exhibition Calendars: A Where to Find or Locate Workbook. rev. ed. 1991. ring bd. 24.95 (*0-911569-65-0*) Prosperity & Profits.

Trade Show Basics. Norman Abelson. 140p. 1987. 22.95 (*0-913247-07-3*); pap. 15.95 (*0-685-18704-7*) Commerce Comns.

Trade Show Exhibiting. Diane K. Weintraub. 1991. 14.95 (*0-8306-3585-8*) McGraw-Hill Prof.

Trade Show Exhibiting: The Insider's Guide for Entrepreneurs. Dian E. Weintraub. 1991. text ed. 14.95 (*0-07-157615-0*) McGraw.

***Trade Show Worldwide.** 12th ed. 1997. 255.00 (*0-7876-1120-4*, 00156255, Gale Res Intl) Gale.

Trade Shows: The Small Business Guide to Successful Exhibiting. Diane K. Weintraub. (Illus.). 220p. 1991. pap. 14.95 (*0-8306-0477-4*, 3585) McGraw-Hill Prof.

Trade Shows & Professional Exhibits Directory. 2nd ed. Ed. by Robert J. Elster. LC 84-6101. 915p. 1986. 150.00 (*0-8103-2113-0*) Gale.

Trade Shows & Professional Exhibits Directory. 3rd ed. Martin Connors & Charity A. Dorgan. 1988. 159.95 (*0-8103-2748-1*) Gale.

Trade Shows & Professional Exhibits Directory: Supplement. 2nd ed. Ed. by Robert J. Elster. 300p. 1987. 80.00 (*0-8103-2124-6*) Gale.

Trade Shows Worldwide. 4th ed. Ed. by Charity A. Dorgan & Martin Conners. 1700p. 1989. 170.00 (*0-8103-4872-1*, Gale Res Intl) Gale.

Trade Shows Worldwide. 5th ed. 1990. 179.00 (*0-8103-4874-8*) Gale.

Trade Shows Worldwide. 6th ed. Webster. 1991. 189.00 (*0-8103-7629-6*) Gale.

Trade Shows Worldwide. 7th ed. Webster. 1992. 2.95 (*0-8103-7630-X*) Gale.

Trade Shows Worldwide. 8th ed. Webster. 1993. 220.00 (*0-8103-8079-X*) Gale.

***Trade Shows Worldwide.** 9th ed. 1994. 225.00 (*0-8103-8840-5*, 00001624, Gale Res Intl) Gale.

***Trade Shows Worldwide.** 13th ed. 1998. 255.00 (*0-7876-1252-9*, 00156429, Gale Res Intl) Gale.

Trade Shows Worldwide: An International Directory of Events, Facilities & Supplies. 10th ed. Annamarie L. Sheldon. 1600p. 1995. 245.00 (*0-8103-5675-9*, 004534) Gale.

***Trade Shows Worldwide 1997: An International Directory of Events, Facilities & Suppliers.** 11th ed. 1743p. 1996. 255.00 (*0-8103-6159-0*, GML00197-004535) Gale.

Trade Tactics. Ed Barr. LC 94-90112. 176p. (Orig.). 1995. pap. 9.85 (*1-56002-441-0*, Univ Edtns) Aegina Pr.

Trade Talks with Mexico: A Time for Realism. Peter Morici. 124p. (Orig.). 1991. pap. text ed. 15.00 (*0-89068-110-4*, CIR 22 (NPA253)) Natl Planning.

Trade, Technology, & International Competitiveness. Irfan Ul Haque et al. LC 95-33307. (EDI Development Studies Ser.). 228p. 1996. 16.95 (*0-8213-3418-2*) World Bank.

Trade, Technology & Soviet-American Relations. Ed. by Bruce Parrott. LC 84-48549. (CSIS Publication Series on the Soviet Union in the 1980's; Midland Bks.). (Illus.). 414p. 1985. 35.00 (*0-253-36025-0*); pap. 18.95 (*0-253-20351-1*, MB 351) Ind U Pr.

Trade, the Engine of Growth in the Pacific Basin. Peter C. Chow & Mitchell H. Kellman. LC 92-27965. 184p. 1993. 42.00 (*0-19-507895-0*) OUP.

Trade the Oex. 3rd ed. Arthur Darack. 247p. 1995. 29.95 (*1-56625-032-3*) Bonus Books.

Trade Theory & Economic Reform: North, South, & East: Essays in Honor of Bela Balassa. Ed. by Jaime De Melo & Andre Sapir. (Illus.). 384p. 1991. 55.95 (*1-55786-256-7*) Blackwell Pubs.

Trade Through the Himalayas. Schuyler Camman. LC 74-90477. 186p. 1970. reprint ed. text ed. 75.00 (*0-8371-3260-6*, CAHI, Greenwood Pr) Greenwood.

Trade Tokens of Illinois. 2nd rev. ed. Ore Vacketta. (Illus.). 576p. 1983. 29.95 (*0-912317-05-1*) World Exo.

Trade, Transfers & Development: Problems & Prospects for the 21st Century. Ed. by S. Mansoob Murshed & Kunibert Raffer. (Illus.). 272p. 1994. 85.00 (*1-85278-796-1*) E Elgar.

Trade, Transport & Society in the Ancient World: A Sourcebook. Fik J. Meijer & Onno Van Nifj. LC 91-46010. 256p. (C). 1992. pap. 17.95 (*0-415-00345-8*, A7617) Routledge.

Trade Trap. Belinda Coote & Caroline LeQuesne. 256p. (C). 1996. pap. 17.50 (*0-85598-351-5*, Pub. by Oxfam UK) Humanities.

Trade, Tribute, & Transportation: The Sixteenth-Century Political Economy of the Valley of Mexico. Ross Hassig. LC 84-25762. 1993. pap. 14.95 (*0-8061-2563-2*) U of Okla Pr.

Trade Union & Social History. H. E. Musson. 224p. 1974. 37.50 (*0-7146-3031-4*, Pub. by F Cass Pubs UK) Intl Spec Bk.

Trade Union Behaviour, Pay Bargaining, & Economic Performance. R. J. Flanagan et al. LC 92-41369. (FIGF Studies in Labor Markets & Economic Policy). (Illus.). 176p. 1993. 45.00 (*0-19-828798-4*) OUP.

Trade Union Democracy & Industrial Relations. Ed. by Roger Blanpain. (Bulletin of Comparative Labour Relations Ser.: Vol. 17). 220p. 1989. pap. 62.00 (*90-6544-394-0*) Kluwer Law Tax Pubs.

Trade Union Democracy in Western Europe. Walter Galenson. LC 75-45493. 96p. 1976. reprint ed. text ed. 38.50 (*0-8371-8752-4*, GATU, Greenwood Pr) Greenwood.

Trade Union Democracy, Members' Rights & the Law. Patrick Elias & K. D. Ewing. Ed. by Bob Hepple & Paul O'Higgins. LC 87-7645. (Studies in Labour & Social Law). 300p. 1987. 110.00 (*0-7201-0729-6*, Mansell Pub); pap. text ed. 50.00 (*0-7201-1871-9*, Mansell Pub) Cassell.

Trade Union Financial Administration. Don H. Taylor. 64p. 1988. pap. 5.40 (*92-2-102711-2*) Intl Labour Office.

Trade Union Gospel: Christianity & Labor in Industrial Philadelphia, 1865-1915. Ken Fones-Wolf. (American Civilization Ser.). 260p. (C). 1990. 34.95 (*0-87722-652-0*) Temple U Pr.

Trade Union Growth & Decline: An International Study. Walter Galenson. LC 93-40199. 176p. 1994. text ed. 52. 95 (*0-275-94325-9*, Praeger Pubs) Greenwood.

Trade Union Growth & Decline in the Netherlands. Annette Van den Berg. 210p. 1995. pap. 25.00 (*90-5170-345-7*, Pub. by Thesis Pubs NE) IBD Ltd.

Trade Union Handbook. 5th ed. Arthur I. Marsh. 400p. 1991. text ed. 99.95 (*0-566-02975-8*, Pub. by Gower UK) Ashgate Pub Co.

Trade Union Law. Bryan Perrins. 1985. 70.00 (*0-406-25830-9*, UK); pap. 48.00 (*0-406-25831-7*, UK) MICHIE.

Trade Union Leadership in India: A Sociological Perspective. Edwin Masihi. 1986. 19.00 (*0-8364-1530-2*, Pub. by Ajanta II) S Asia.

Trade Union-Management Relations in India. T. Tripathi. (C). 1988. 375.00 (*0-685-27895-6*) St Mut.

Trade Union Membership, 1897-1962. Leo Troy. (Occasional Papers: No. 92). 93p. 1965. reprint ed. 24. 20 (*0-87014-406-5*) Natl Bur Econ Res.

Trade Union Mergers & Labor Conglomerates. Gideon Chitayat. LC 79-2966. (Praeger Special Studies). 240p. 1979. text ed. 55.00 (*0-275-90340-0*, C0340, Praeger Pubs) Greenwood.

Trade Union Movement & the National Movement. Kiran Saxena. 1990. 21.00 (*0-317-99588-X*, Pub. by S Asia Pubs II) S Asia.

Trade Union Movement in India: Role of M. N. Roy. Dipti K. Roy. 1990. 17.50 (*81-85195-28-5*, Pub. by Minerva II) S Asia.

Trade Union Officers: A Study of Full-Time Officers, Branch Secretaries & Shop Stewards in British Trade Unions. Hugh A. Clegg et al. LC 61-65475. 281p. 1961. 33.95 (*0-674-89970-9*) HUP.

Trade Union Policies in the Massachusetts Shoe Industry. Thomas L. Norton. LC 78-76630. (Columbia University. Studies in the Social Sciences: No. 372). reprint ed. 27. 50 (*0-404-51372-7*) AMS Pr.

Trade Union Politics: American Unions & Economic Change, 1960s-1990s. Ed. by Glenn Perusek & Kent Worcester. LC 94-37802. 264p. (C). 1995. pap. 17.50 (*0-391-03887-7*) Humanities.

Trade Union Politics: American Unions & Economic Change, 1960s-1990s. Ed. by Glenn Perusek & Kent Worcester. LC 94-37802. 264p. (C). 1995. text ed. 49.95 (*0-391-03886-9*) Humanities.

Trade Union Question in British Politics: Government & Unions since 1945. Robert Taylor. LC 92-39484. (Making Contemporary Britain Ser.). 320p. 1993. 50.95 (*0-631-16626-2*); pap. 23.95 (*0-631-16627-0*) Blackwell Pubs.

Trade Union Security Law. Phillipa Weeks. 288p. 1995. 49. 00 (*1-86287-167-1*, Pub. by Federation Pr AU) Gaunt.

Trade Union Situation & Industrial Relations in Austria: Report of an ILO Mission. xiii, 107p. (Orig.). 1986. pap. 18.00 (*92-2-105659-7*) Intl Labour Office.

Trade Union Situation & Industrial Relations in Spain: Report of an ILO Mission. xiii, 138p. (Orig.). 1985. pap. text ed. 18.00 (*92-2-105202-8*) Intl Labour Office.

Trade Union Situation & Industrial Relations in Yugoslavia: Report of an ILO Mission. xii, 104p. (Orig.). 1985. pap. 18.00 (*92-2-105201-X*) Intl Labour Office.

Trade Union Strategy in the Common Market: The Programme of the Belgian Trade Unions. Ed. by Ken Coates. 149p. 1971. 33.50 (*0-685-71539-6*, Pub. by Spokesman Bks UK) Coronet Bks.

Trade Union View of U. S. Manpower Policy. William W. Winpisinger. LC 80-81536. (British-North American Committee Ser.). 52p. 1980. 3.00 (*0-89068-052-3*) Natl Planning.

Trade Unionism & Industrial Relations in the Commonwealth Caribbean: History, Contemporary Practice & Prospect. Lawrence A. Nurse. LC 91-38212. (Contributions in Legal Studies: No. 40). 168p. 1992. text ed. 45.00 (*0-313-28380-X*, NTU, Greenwood Pr) Greenwood.

Trade Unionism & Labor Problems. Ed. by John R. Commons. LC 66-21664. (Library of American Labor History). xiv, 628p. 1967. reprint ed. 65.00 (*0-678-00221-5*) Kelley.

Trade Unionism & Labor Problems, 2nd Series. Ed. by John R. Commons. LC 66-21665. (Library of American Labor History). xiii, 838p. 1967. reprint ed. 75.00 (*0-678-00287-8*) Kelley.

Trade Unionism in Recession. Ed. by Duncan Gallie et al. (Social Change & Economic Life Initiative Ser.). (Illus.). 384p. 1996. 80.00 (*0-19-827920-5*) OUP.

Trade Unionists: How the Public Order Proposals Affect You. Marie Staunton. 1988. 21.00 (*0-946088-18-7*, Pub. by NCCL UK) St Mut.

Trade Unionists Against Terror: Guatemala City, 1954-1985. Deborah Levenson-Estrada. LC 93-32054. (Illus.). 310p. (C). 1994. text ed. 49.95 (*0-8078-2131-4*); pap. text ed. 17.95 (*0-8078-4440-3*) U of NC Pr.

Trade Unionists & the Law. Jennifer Horne. (C). 1983. pap. 50.00 (*0-7219-0940-X*, Pub. by Scientific UK) St Mut.

***Trade Unions.** Jackson. 1989. pap. text ed. write for info. (*0-582-02040-9*, Pub. by Longman UK) Longman.

Trade Unions Act, 1926. 2nd ed. U. K. Choudhary. (C). 1991. 110.00 (*0-685-39533-2*) St Mut.

***Trade Unions & Child Labour.** Alec Fyfe & Michele Jankanish. 80p. 1996. pap. 18.00 (*92-2-109514-2*) Intl Labour Office.

Trade Unions & Collective Bargaining in the Netherlands. Rob van de Wijngaert. (Tinbergen Institute Research Ser.: No. 78, Series A). 230p. 1994. pap. 25.00 (*90-5170-293-0*, Pub. by Thesis Pubs NE) IBD Ltd.

Trade Unions & Community: The German Working Class in New York City, 1870-1900. Dorothee Schneider. LC 93-24325. (Working Class in American History Ser.). (Illus.). 296p. 1994. text ed. 34.95 (*0-252-02057-X*) U of Ill Pr.

Trade Unions & Democratic Participation in Europe. Ed. by Gerard Kester & Henri Pinaud. 320p. 1996. 68.95 (*1-85972-302-0*, Pub. by Avebury Pub UK) Ashgate Pub Co.

Trade Unions & Migrant Workers: A Workers' Education Guide. Harold Dunning. vi, 40p. (Orig.). 1985. pap. 9.00 (*92-2-105241-9*) Intl Labour Office.

Trade Unions & Politics: A Comparative Introduction. Andrew J. Taylor. LC 89-5930. (Illus.). 240p. 1989. text ed. 45.00 (*0-312-03172-6*) St Martin.

Trade Unions & Politics in Ceylon. Robert N. Kearney. LC 76-115495. 209p. reprint ed. pap. 59.60 (*0-318-34919-1*, 2031439) Bks Demand.

Trade Unions & Politics in Western Europe. Ed. by Jack Hayward. 138p. 1980. 37.50 (*0-7146-3155-8*, Pub. by F Cass Pubs UK) Intl Spec Bk.

Trade Unions & Social Research. Keith Forrester & Colin Thorne. (Avebury Business School Library). 227p. 1993. 59.95 (*1-85628-354-2*, Pub. by Avebury Pub UK) Ashgate Pub Co.

Trade Unions & Socialist Poli. John Kelly. 352p. 1988. text ed. 50.00 (*0-86091-206-X*, Pub. by Verso UK); pap. text ed. 16.95 (*0-86091-924-2*, Pub. by Verso UK) Routledge Chapman & Hall.

Trade Unions & the British Electorate. Paul Webb. 140p. 1992. 58.95 (*1-85521-217-X*, Pub. by Dartmth Pub UK) Ashgate Pub Co.

Trade Unions & the ILO: A Workers' Education Manual. 2nd rev. ed. x, 151p. 1988. pap. 13.50 (*92-2-106321-6*) Intl Labour Office.

Trade Unions & the Labour Party since 1945. Martin Harrison. LC 60-4363. 360p. reprint ed. pap. 102.60 (*0-7837-3624-X*, 2043490) Bks Demand.

Trade Unions & the Law in New York: A Study of Some Legal Phases of Labor Organizations. George G. Groat. LC 68-56659. (Columbia University. Studies in the Social Sciences: No. 51). reprint ed. 30.00 (*0-404-51051-5*) AMS Pr.

Trade Unions & the New Industrialization of the Third World. Ed. by Roger Southall. LC 87-40608. (Social & Labor History Ser.). 392p. (C). 1988. 49.95 (*0-8229-1152-3*) U of Pittsburgh Pr.

Trade Unions & the Professional Engineer. Will Howie. 78p. 1977. 4.75 (*0-7277-0044-8*, Pub. by T Telford UK) Am Soc Civil Eng.

Trade Unions & the State. Walter Johnson. 200p. 1978. 19. 95 (*0-919618-77-4*, Pub. by Black Rose Bks CN); pap. 9.95 (*0-919618-76-6*, Pub. by Black Rose Bks CN) Consort Bk Sales.

Trade Unions & the State in Peninsular Malaysia. Jomo K. Sundaram & Patricia Todd. (South-East Asian Social Science Monographs). 224p. 1995. 42.00 (*967-65-3050-6*) OUP.

Trade Unions & Vocational Training: A Workers' Education Guide. Harold Dunning. ii, 83p. (Orig.). 1984. pap. 9.00 (*92-2-103522-0*) Intl Labour Office.

Trade Unions, Employers & the Law. 2nd ed. Gillian S. Morris & Timothy J. Archer. 1993. boxed 135.00 (*0-406-02448-0*, UK) MICHIE.

Trade Unions in Britain. 2nd ed. Elizabeth Gard. 1989. pap. 8.50 (*0-521-35842-6*) Cambridge U Pr.

Trade Unions in Britain Today. 2nd ed. John McIlroy. (Illus.). 304p. 1995. text ed. 59.95 (*0-7190-3982-7*, Pub. by Manchester Univ Pr UK); text ed. 19.95 (*0-7190-3983-5*, Pub. by Manchester Univ Pr UK) St Martin.

Trade Unions in China: 1949 to the Present. Lee L. To. 218p. (Orig.). 1986. pap. 36.00 (*9971-69-093-4*, Pub. by Sgapore Univ SI) Coronet Bks.

Trade Unions in Communist States. Alex Pravda & Blair A. Ruble. LC 85-30717. 250p. (C). 1986. text ed. 49.95 (*0-04-331108-3*) Routledge Chapman & Hall.

Trade Unions in Construction: Construction Guide. Will Howie. 32p. 1981. 10.00 (*0-7277-0092-8*, Pub. by T Telford UK) Am Soc Civil Eng.

Trade Unions in Russia. Linda J. Cook. LC 97-8847. 120p. (C). 1995. pap. 9.95 (*0-87078-377-7*) TCFP-PPP.

Trade Unions in the Early Eighteen Thirties. LC 72-2549. (British Labour Struggles Before 1850 Ser.). 1974. 20.95 (*0-405-04440-2*) Ayer.

Trade Unions in the Epoch of Imperialist Decay. Leon Trotsky & Karl Marx. Ed. by John Riddell. LC 90-70744. (Illus.). 156p. (Orig.). (C). 1990. pap. 14.95 (*0-87348-583-1*); lib. bdg. 40.00 (*0-87348-584-X*) Pathfinder NY.

Trade Unions in the European Union: A Handbook. Ed. by Wolfgang Lecher. 288p. (C). 1994. pap. 29.95 (*0-85315-766-9*, Pub. by Lawrence & Wishart UK) NYU Pr.

***Trade Unions in Twentieth-Century Britain.** John Lovell. 112p. 1996. pap. 12.50 (*1-85728-250-7*, Pub. by UCL Pr UK) Taylor & Francis.

Trade Unions of the World. Ed. by Alan J. Day & Ciaran O. Maolain. 500p. 1987. 90.00 (*0-8103-2193-9*, Pub. by Longman Grp UK) Gale.

Trade Unions of the World. 2nd ed. 500p. 1989. 85.00 (*1-55862-014-1*) St James Pr.

Trade Unions of the World. 3rd ed. 1992. 130.00 (*0-582-08194-7*, Pub. by Longman Grp UK) Gale.

Trade Unions under the Combination Acts 1799-1823. LC 72-2550. (British Labour Struggles Before 1850 Ser.). 1974. 23.95 (*0-405-04441-0*) Ayer.

Trade, Urbanisation & the Family: Studies in the History of Medieval Flanders. David Nicholas. (Collected Studies: No. CS531). 350p. 1996. 94.95 (*0-86078-585-8*, Pub. by Variorum UK) Ashgate Pub Co.

Trade Warriors: An Inside Look at Trade Activists in Congress-& How to Reach Them. WIRES, Ltd. Staff. Ed. by WIRES Ltd. Editors. (Illus.). 230p. 1986. pap. 19.95 (*0-9616173-0-6*, JK1013.W43) Whalen Co.

Trade Warriors: The Guide to the Politics of Trade & Foreign Investment. Ed. by Richard J. Whalen & R. Christopher Whalen. LC 90-70292. 467p. (Orig.). 1990. pap. 38.50 (*0-9616173-1-4*) Whalen Co.

Trade Warriors: The Guide to the Politics of Trade & Foreign Investment. 2nd ed. Ed. by Richard J. Whalen & R. Christopher Whalen. LC 90-70292. 478p. (Orig.). (C). 1990. pap. text ed. 34.95 (*0-685-37413-0*) Whalen Co.

Trade Wars: The Theory & Practice of International Commercial Rivalry. John A. Conybeare. (Political Economy of International Change Ser.). (Illus.). 352p. 1987. text ed. 49.50 (*0-231-06234-6*) Col U Pr.

Trade Wars Against America: A History of United States Trade & Monetary Policy. William J. Gill. LC 89-29765. 336p. 1990. text ed. 59.95 (*0-275-93316-4*, C3316, Greenwood Pr) Greenwood.

T

An Asterisk (*) at the beginning of an entry indicates that the title is appearing in BIP for the first time.

Trade, Welfare, & Economic Policies: Essays in Honor of Murray C. Kemp. Ed. by Horst Herberg & Ngo Van Long. LC 92-43038. (Studies In International Trade Policy). 350p. (C). 1993. text ed. 75.00 (*0-472-10364-4*) U of Mich Pr.

Trade Winds. Janet Quin-Hamlin. Ed. by Creative Media Applications Staff. 256p. (Orig.). 1993. pap. text ed. write for info. (*1-884066-00-3*) NBC Inc.

Trade Winds: The Lure of the China Trade 16th-19th Centuries. Catherine Coleman Brawer & Geri Wu. (Illus.). 24p. 1985. 6.00 (*0-915171-01-5*) Katonah Gal.

Trade Winds on the Niger: The Saga of the Royal Niger Company 1830-1971. Geoff Baker. 224p. 1997. text ed. 39.50 (*1-86064-014-1*) St Martin.

Trade with Japan: Has the Door Opened Wider? Ed. by Paul R. Krugman. x, 350p. 1995. pap. text ed. 17.95 (*0-226-45459-2*) U Ch Pr.

Trade with Latin America: Opportunities for the States. (State-Federal Issue Brief Ser.: Vol. 3, No. 4). 19p. 1990. 6.50 (*1-55516-886-8*, 8500-0304) Natl Conf State Legis.

***Trade Yearbook 1988, Vol. 42.** (Statistics Ser.: No. 91). 388p. 1990. 45.00 (*92-5-002901-2*, Pub. by FAO IT) Bernan Associates.

***Trade Yearbook 1989, Vol. 43.** (Statistics Ser.: No. 96). 380p. 1990. 45.00 (*92-5-002971-3*, Pub. by FAO IT) Bernan Associates.

***Trade Yearbook 1990, Vol. 44.** (Statistics Ser.: No. 102). 377p. 1991. 50.00 (*92-5-003085-1*, F0851, Pub. by FAO IT) Bernan Associates.

***Trade Yearbook 1992, Vol. 46.** (Statistics Ser.: No. 115). 396p. 1993. 45.00 (*92-5-003365-6*, F33656, Pub. by FAO IT) Bernan Associates.

Tradecraft: A Sourcebook of Competitive Intelligence Tactics. Ed. by D. C. Sawyer. 68p. 1995. pap. write for info. (*0-9645424-0-4*) Info Plus NY.

***Traded Options Simplified.** 4th ed. Brian J. Millard. pap. text ed. 55.00 (*0-471-96658-4*) Wiley.

Traded Secrets. Victoria Presley. 352p. (Orig.). 1996. mass mkt., pap. text ed. 4.99 (*0-505-52092-3*, Love Spell) Dorchester Pub Co.

Trademaker Guide for Entrepreneurs. Robert E. Lee. 200p. 1996. 29.95 (*1-888206-04-7*); pap. text ed. 15.95 (*1-888206-05-5*) Kent Communs.

Trademark: How to Name Your Business & Product. 2nd ed. Stephen Elias & Kate McGrath. Ed. by Ralph Warner. 1996. pap. 29.95 (*0-87337-311-1*) Nolo Pr.

***Trademark: How to Name Your Business & Product.** 3rd ed. Kate McGrath. 1997. pap. text ed. 29.95 (*0-87337-396-0*) Nolo Pr.

***Trademark Administration.** Glenn S. Bacal et al. 334p. 1990. ring bd. 71.95 (*0-939190-04-4*) Intl Trademark.

Trademark & Unfair Competition Law: Cases & Materials. Jane C. Ginsburg et al. 724p. 1991. 46.00 (*0-87473-670-6*) MICHIE.

Trademark Designs of the Twenties. Ed. by Leslie Cabarga & Marcie Cabarga. (Illus.). 112p. (Orig.). pap. 3.50 (*0-486-26804-7*) Dover.

Trademark Designs of the Twenties. Leslie Carbarga. 1991. pap. 6.95 (*0-486-26858-6*) Dover.

Trademark Designs of the World. Yusaku Kamekura. (Illus.). 160p. 1981. reprint ed. pap. 6.95 (*0-486-24191-2*) Dover.

Trademark Dilution. Tony Martino. LC 95-43641. 160p. 1996. text ed. 90.00 (*0-19-826071-7*) OUP.

Trademark for Success - You. Darryl R. Webster. 140p. 1991. 12.00 (*0-9624825-6-0*) Achivmnt USA.

Trademark Guide: A Friendly Handbook for Protecting & Profiting from Trademarks. Lee Wilson. 192p. (Orig.). 1997. pap. 18.95 (*1-880559-59-5*) Allworth Pr.

***Trademark Index of U. S. Patent & Trademark Office Federal Records: 1997 Edition, 2 vols.** Thomson & Thomson Staff. Ed. by Cheryl A. Paul & Andrea L. Francisco. 3800p. 1997. pap. 265.00 (*1-57123-037-8*) Thomson & Thomson.

Trademark Law: A Practitioner's Guide. Siegrun D. Kane. 449p. 1991. text ed. 125.00 (*0-87224-034-7*, G1-1017) PLI.

Trademark Law: A Practitioner's Guide. 2nd ed. Siegrun D. Kane. 449p. 1991. 125.00 (*0-614-17114-8*, G1-1017) PLI.

Trademark Law: A Practitioner's Guide & 1989 Supplement. 428p. 1987. 15.00 (*0-685-70149-2*) PLI.

***Trademark Law in Indochina: Practice & Procedures in Vietnam, Cambodia & Laos.** F. Jeannie Smith. 202p. 1994. pap. 35.00 (*0-939190-10-9*) Intl Trademark.

Trademark Law Practice Forms: Rules, Annotations, Commentary, 3 vols. Barry Kramer & Allen D. Brufsky. LC 85-30913. (IP Ser.). 1986. Set. ring bd. 425.00 (*0-87632-490-1*) Clark Boardman Callaghan.

Trademark Law Practice Forms: Rules, Annotations, Commentary. 2nd ed. Barry Kramer & Allen D. Brufsky. LC 96-21017. 1996. write for info. (*0-8366-1059-8*) Clark Boardman Callaghan.

Trademark Law Practice Forms: Rules, Annotations, Commentary, 3 vols., Set with forms on disk. Barry Kramer & Allen D. Brufsky. (IP Ser.). 1986. 525.00 incl. disk (*0-614-07309-X*) Clark Boardman Callaghan.

Trademark of God. George L. Murphy. LC 86-5402. 138p. (Orig.). 1986. pap. 6.95 (*0-8192-1382-9*) Morehouse Pub.

Trademark Protection & Practice, 7 vols. Jerome Gilson. 1974. Set. Updates available. ring bd. write for info. (*0-8205-1726-7*) Bender.

Trademark Register of the United States. 2200p. (Orig.). (C). 1996. pap. 355.00 (*0-614-14547-3*) Trademark Reg.

Trademark Register of the United States: 1881-1995. rev. ed. Cyril W. Sernak. 1996. pap. 355.00 (*0-911522-60-3*, 0082-5786) Trademark Reg.

Trademark Registration Practice. James E. Hawes. LC 86-29896. (IP Ser.). 1987. ring bd. 145.00 (*0-87632-534-7*) Clark Boardman Callaghan.

***Trademark Registration Practice.** 2nd ed. James E. Hawes. LC 97-25960. (Intellectual Property Library). 1997. write for info. (*0-8366-1141-1*) Clark Boardman Callaghan.

***Trademark Searching: A Practical & Strategic Guide to the Clearance of New Marks in the U. S.** Glenn A. Gundersen. 164p. 1994. 59.95 (*0-939190-08-7*) Intl Trademark.

Trademark Surveys. Phyllis J. Welter. LC 93-21570. (IP Ser.). 1993. ring bd. 135.00 (*0-87632-909-1*) Clark Boardman Callaghan.

Trademark Valuation. Gordon V. Smith. LC 96-21260. (Intellectual Property Library Ser.). 1996. text ed. 75.00 (*0-471-14112-7*) Wiley.

Trademarks. Hillard & Evan G. Pattishall. 1987. write for info. (*0-8205-0501-3*, 725) Bender.

Trademarks. R. Swinehart. (Design & Graphic Design Ser.). 1992. pap. write for info. (*0-442-00793-0*) Van Nos Reinhold.

Trademarks. Roy Ehrhardt. (Illus.). 128p. 1976. reprint ed. spiral bd. 25.00 (*0-913902-06-3*) Heart Am Pr.

***Trademarks, Vol. 1.** Art Direction Staff. 1988. 19.00 (*0-688-08632-2*) Morrow.

***Trademarks, Vol. 2.** Art Direction Staff. 1988. 19.00 (*0-688-08633-0*) Morrow.

***Trademarks, Vol. 3.** Art Direction Staff. 1988. 19.00 (*0-688-08634-9*) Morrow.

***Trademarks, Vol. 4.** Art Direction Staff. 1988. 19.00 (*0-688-08635-7*) Morrow.

***Trademarks, Vol. 5.** Art Direction Staff. 1988. 19.00 (*0-688-08637-3*) Morrow.

***Trademarks, Vol. 6.** Art Direction Staff. 1988. 19.00 (*0-688-08638-1*) Morrow.

***Trademarks, Vol. 7.** Art Direction Staff. 1988. 19.00 (*0-688-08639-X*) Morrow.

***Trademarks, Vol. 8.** Art Direction Staff. 1988. 19.00 (*0-688-08640-3*) Morrow.

***Trademarks, Vol. 9.** Art Direction Staff. 1988. 19.00 (*0-688-08641-1*) Morrow.

***Trademarks, Vol. 10.** Art Direction Staff. 1987. 19.00 (*0-688-07575-4*) Morrow.

***Trademarks, Vol. 11.** 1989. 27.50 (*0-688-09227-6*) Morrow.

Trademarks: Annotations from the ALR System. Ed. by Lawyers Cooperative Publishing Staff. LC 90-63738. (Critical Issues Ser.). 1991. ring bd. 112.50 (*0-317-03033-7*) Lawyers Cooperative.

Trademarks: Legal & Business Aspects. Ed. by Dennis Campbell et al. LC 94-27720. 1994. write for info. (*90-6544-859-4*) Kluwer Law Tax Pubs.

Trademarks & Related Unfair Competition: Selection & Protection. 2nd ed. Francis W. Campbell & Jerry Cohen. (Corporate Practice Ser.: No. 18). 1991. ring bd. 95.00 (*1-55871-106-6*) BNA.

Trademarks & Symbols of the World: European Trademarks, Vol. 4. Yasaburo Kuwayama. (Illus.). 200p. 1992. pap. 24.95 (*1-56496-018-8*, 30435) Rockport Pubs.

Trademarks & Symbols of the World, Vol. 1: The Alphabet in Design. Yasaburo Kuwayama. (Design Sourcebook Ser.). (Illus.). 192p. 1989. pap. 24.99 (*0-935603-96-4*) Rockport Pubs.

Trademarks & Symbols of the World, Vol. 3: Pictogram & Sign Design. (Illus.). 232p. 1989. pap. 24.95 (*0-935603-30-1*, 30172) Rockport Pubs.

Trademarks & Symbols of the World 2. Yasaburo Kuwayama. (Illus.). 459p. 89.95 (*4-7601-0480-1*, 30211) Rockport Pubs.

Trademarks & the Arts. William M. Borchard. 1990. pap. text ed. 12.50 (*0-685-59975-2*) Col U Pr.

Trademarks & the Arts. William M. Borchard. 100p. (C). 1988. pap. text ed. write for info. (*0-318-64034-1*) CUSLCLA.

Trademarks & the Arts. William M. Borchard. 86p. 1989. pap. 12.00 (*0-929912-00-4*, 7780) CUSLCLA.

Trademarks in Developing Countries. Ed. by Surendra J. Patel. 122p. 1979. pap. 29.00 (*0-08-025223-0*, Pergamon Pr) Elsevier.

Trademarks of the Forties & Fifties. Eric Baker et al. LC 88-6142. (Illus.). 144p. 1988. pap. 14.95 (*0-87701-485-X*) Chronicle Bks.

Trademarks of the Jewelery & Kindred Trades. Jewelers' Circular-Keystone Staff. (Illus.). 325p. 1988. pap. 19.95 (*0-930163-09-5*) Arlington Bk.

Trademarks of the Twenties & Thirties. Eric Baker & Tyler Blik. LC 85-11355. (Illus.). 144p. 1985. pap. 14.95 (*0-87701-360-8*) Chronicle Bks.

***Trademarks of the '60s & '70s.** Tyler Blik. LC 97-9340. 1998. pap. write for info. (*0-8118-1698-2*) Chronicle Bks.

Trademarks on Greek Vases. Johnston. 1980. pap. 75.00 (*0-85668-259-4*, Pub. by Aris & Phillips UK) David Brown.

Trademarks Throughout the World. 4th ed. Ed. by Alan Jacobs. LC 79-137. (IP Ser.). 1979. ring bd. 195.00 (*0-87632-126-0*) Clark Boardman Callaghan.

Tradeoff Between Cost & Risk in Hazardous Waste Management. Kenneth S. Sewall. LC 90-47328. (Environment: Problems & Solutions Ser.: Vol. 16). 255p. 1990. text ed. 20.00 (*0-8240-2526-1*) Garland.

Tradeoff Between Number of Children & Child Schooling: Evidence from Cote d'Ivoire & Ghana. Mark Montgomery et al. LC 94-23764. (LSMS Working Paper Ser.: Vol. 112). 108p. 1995. 8.95 (*0-8213-3123-X*, 13123) World Bank.

Tradeoffs: Imperatives of Choice in a High-Tech World. Edward Wenk, Jr. LC 86-45441. 256p. 1989. reprint ed. pap. text ed. 14.95 (*0-8018-3942-4*) Johns Hopkins.

***Tradeoffs in Balancing Multiple Objectives of an Integrated Agricultural Economic & Environmental System.** P. G. Lakshminarayan. LC 96-85287. (Card Monographs: Vol. 96-M8). (Illus.). 142p. (Orig.). 1996. pap. 15.00 (*0-936911-08-5*) Ctr Agri & Rural Dev.

***Trader.** Charles De Lint. LC 96-30646. 352p. 1997. 24.95 (*0-312-85847-7*) Tor Bks.

Trader Clark: Six Decades of Racing Lore. John H. Clark. 336p. 1991. 22.95 (*1-879850-00-1*) Thrghbred Times.

Trader on the American Frontier: Myth's Victim. Howard R. Lamar. LC 76-51650. (Elma Dill Russell Spencer Series in the West & Southwest: No.2). (Illus.). 56p. 1977. 12.95 (*0-89096-033-X*) Tex A&M Univ Pr.

Trader Vic: Methods of a Wall Street Master. Victor Sperandeo. LC 90-25716. 290p. 1991. text ed. 32.50 (*0-471-53576-1*) Wiley.

Trader Vic: Methods of a Wall Street Master. Victor Sperandeo & T. Sullivan Brown. 290p. 1993. pap. text ed. 17.95 (*0-471-30497-2*) Wiley.

Trader Vic II: Principles of Professional Speculation. Victor Sperandeo. 275p. 1994. text ed. 39.95 (*0-471-53577-X*) Wiley.

Trader Wooly & the Ghost in the Colonel's Jeep. Tom Townsend. (Illus.). 110p. (J). (gr. 6-8). 1991. 12.95 (*0-89015-807-X*) Sunbelt Media.

Trader Wooly & the Secret of the Lost Nazi Treasure. Tom Townsend. Ed. by Melissa Roberts. (Illus.). 120p. (J). (gr. 4-7). 1987. 12.95 (*0-89015-602-6*); pap. 5.95 (*0-89015-634-4*) Sunbelt Media.

Trader Wooly & the Terrorist. Townsend. 1988. pap. 7.95 (*0-89015-670-0*) Sunbelt Media.

Traders. William Brashler. 1990. reprint ed. mass mkt. 4.95 (*1-55817-460-5*, Pinncle Kensgtn) Kensgtn Pub Corp.

Traders. Sonny Kleinfield. 214p. 1993. reprint ed. pap. 16.95 (*0-934380-22-8*, 67) Traders Pr.

Traders: The Jobs, the Products, the Markets. David M. Weiss. 1990. pap. 19.95 (*0-13-926320-9*) NY Inst Finance.

Traders & Gentlefolk: The Livingstons of New York, 1675-1790. Cynthia A. Kierner. LC 91-55565. (Illus.). 312p. 1992. 42.50 (*0-8014-2638-3*) Cornell U Pr.

Traders & Merchants: An Introduction to International Commodity Trading. Philippe Chalmin. 310, xiip. (C). 1987. text ed. 109.00 (*3-7186-0435-3*) Gordon & Breach.

Traders & Raiders on China's Northern Frontier. Jenny F. So & Emma C. Bunker. (Illus.). 224p. (C). 1995. pap. 35.00 (*0-295-97473-7*) U of Wash Pr.

Traders & Transports: The Jews of Colonial Maryland. Eric L. Goldstein. 96p. 1993. pap. 7.50 (*1-883312-01-9*) Jew Hist Soc MD.

Traders & Travellers. Claire Craig. LC 95-32624. (Illus.). (J). (gr. 4-7). Date not set. write for info. (*0-8094-9373-X*) Time-Life.

Trader's Edge, Vol. 13. Ed. by Carol Hirsch. 396p. (Orig.). 1996. pap. 64.95 (*1-888349-01-8*) Katydid.

***Trader's Edge, Vol. XIV.** Ed. by Carol Hirsch. 402p. (Orig.). 1997. 64.95 (*1-888349-04-2*) Katydid.

Trader's Edge: Cashing in on the Winning Strategies of Floor Traders, Commercials & Market. Grant Noble. 1994. text ed. 34.95 (*1-55738-599-8*) Irwin Prof Pubng.

Traders Guide to Technical Analysis. C. Colburn Hardy. 208p. 1984. 25.00 (*0-934380-06-6*, 25) Traders Pr.

Traders in a Brave New World: The Uruguay Round & the Future of the International Trading System. Ernest H. Preeg. LC 95-18585. 304p. 1995. 29.95 (*0-226-67959-4*) U Ch Pr.

Traders in Time: A Dream-Quest Adventure. Janie L. Panagopoulos. 200p. (J). (gr. 3-6). 1993. 14.95 (*0-938682-24-5*) River Rd Pubns.

Traders in Time: A Dream-Quest Adventure. Janie L. Panagopoulos. (J). (gr. 3-6). 1994. pap. 7.95 (*0-938682-27-X*) River Rd Pubns.

Traders Instruction Book. Burton H. Pugh. (Illus.). 1980. pap. 25.00 (*0-939093-08-1*) Lambert Gann Pub.

Traders, Planters & Slaves: Market Behavior in Early English America. David W. Galenson. (Illus.). 256p. 1986. text ed. 69.95 (*0-521-30845-3*) Cambridge U Pr.

Trader's Tales: A Chronicle of Wall Street Myths, Legends, & Outright Lies. Ron Insana. LC 96-3501. 208p. 1996. text ed. 24.95 (*0-471-12999-2*) Wiley.

***Traders' Tales: British Traders' Narratives of Cultural Encounters in the Columbia Plateau, 1807-1846.** Elizabeth Vibert. LC 96-42235. 384p. 1997. 29.95 (*0-8061-2932-8*) U of Okla Pr.

Trader's Tax Survival Guide. Ted Tesser. 304p. 1994. text ed. 55.00 (*0-471-08229-5*) Wiley.

***Trader's Tax Survival Guide, Vol. 612.** rev. ed. Ted Tesser. LC 96-53213. 1997. 75.00 (*0-471-17965-5*) Wiley.

Trades & Crafts in Medieval Manuscripts. Patricia Basing. (Illus.). 123p. (C). 1990. 30.00 (*1-56131-002-6*) New Amsterdam Bks.

Trades & Industrial Education. Jack Rudman. (National Teacher Examination Ser.: NT-22). 1994. pap. 23.95 (*0-8373-8432-X*) Nat Learn.

Trades & Occupations: A Pictorial Archive from Early Sources. Carol B. Grafton. 1990. pap. 10.95 (*0-486-26362-2*) Dover.

Trades & Traditions: Of Old China. (Exotic Miniatures Ser.). (Illus.). 100p. 1995. 14.95 (*981-00-4212-4*) Heian Intl.

***Trades (Construction)** LC 97-22130. (Careers in Focus Ser.). 192p. (YA). (gr. 9-12). 1997. write for info. (*0-89434-218-5*) Ferguson.

Trade's Hidden Costs: Worker Rights in a Changing World Economy. John Cavanagh et al. 66p. 1988. pap. 3.95 (*1-880103-00-1*) Intl Labor Rghts.

Trades' Societies & Strikes: Report of the Committee on Trades' Societies Presented at the 4th Annual Meeting, Glasgow, Sept. 1860. National Association for the Promotion of Social Science Trades' Societies Committee. LC 67-20514. (Reprints of Economic Classics Ser.). xxi, 651p. 1968. reprint ed. 65.00 (*0-678-00347-5*) Kelley.

Tradeshow Week Data Book 1997. Ed. by Bowker, R. R., Staff. 1996. pap. 355.00 (*0-8352-3848-2*) Bowker.

***Tradeshow Week Data Book 1998.** Ed. by Bowker, R. R., Staff. 2000p. (Orig.). 1997. pap. 369.00 (*0-8352-3932-2*) Bowker.

***Tradesmen & Traders: The World of the Guilds in Venice & Europe, c. 1250-c. 1650.** Richard MacKenney. LC 89-10963. 1990. write for info. (*0-415-02656-3*) Routledge.

Tradewind Terror, Vol. 1. Paul Leighty. 225p. 1995. 16.95 (*0-9649584-0-6*) Caravan Pr.

Tradewinds. Annee Cartier. 416p. 1995. mass mkt. 4.99 (*0-8217-0099-5*, Zebra Kensgtn) Kensgtn Pub Corp.

***Tradewinds.** large type ed. Annee Cartier. (Black Satin Romance Ser.). 455p. 1996. 25.99 (*1-86110-008-6*) Ulverscroft.

Tradewinds: Poetry in English from Different Cultures. Compiled by R. B. Heath. 192p. 1989. pap. 10.52 (*0-582-02195-2*, 78700) Longman.

Tradewinds & Coconuts. J. Brennan. 320p. 1997. 25.00 (*0-06-016905-2*, HarpT) HarpC.

***Tradicion y Cambio: Lecturas Sobre la Cultura Latinoamericana Contemporanea.** 2nd ed. Denis L. Heyck. 1996. pap. text ed. write for info. (*0-07-028607-8*) McGraw.

Tradicionalismo y Literatura En Valle-Inclan: (1889-1910) Margarita Santos Zas. LC 92-64367. 410p. 1993. pap. 40.00 (*0-89295-068-4*) Society Sp & Sp-Am.

Tradiciones del Pueblo: Traditions of Three Mexican Feast Days in Southwest Detroit. Intro. by Margarita Valdez & Laurie K. Sommers. (Illus.). 80p. 1990. pap. text ed. 10.00 (*0-9615977-3-9*) Casa Unidad.

Tradiciones Orales en la Historiografia de Fines de la Edad Media. Mercedes Vaquero. (Spanish Ser.: No. 55). xii, 146p. (SPA.). 1990. text ed. 15.00 (*0-940639-44-0*) Hispanic Seminary.

Trading. Brian Williams. LC 92-27031. (Ways of Life Ser.). (Illus.). 48p. (J). (gr. 5-8). 1993. lib. bdg. 22.13 (*0-8114-4787-1*) Raintree Steck-V.

Trading Advantage: Specific Techniques for Pinpointing High, Low, & Trend Change Points. Joseph T. Duffy. 1992. pap. 95.00 (*0-930233-51-4*) Windsor.

Trading & Investing in Bond Options: Risk Management, Arbitrage & Value Investing. Anthony M. Wong. LC 90-12216. 262p. 1991. text ed. 55.00 (*0-471-52560-X*) Wiley.

Trading & Securitization of Senior Bank Loans. Ed. by Frank J. Fabozzi & John Carlson. 450p. 1992. text ed. 75.00 (*1-55738-293-X*) Irwin Prof Pubng.

Trading & Valuation Techniques, Set. 263p. 250.00 (*1-871682-97-5*, Pub. by Euromoney UK) Am Educ Systs.

Trading Applications of Japanese Candlestick Charting. Gary S. Wagner & Bradley L. Matheny. (Finance Editions Ser.). 285p. 1993. text ed. 59.50 (*0-471-58728-1*) Wiley.

***Trading Arrangements in the Pacific Rim: ASEAN & APEC, 2 bdrs.** Ed. by Paul Davidson. 1995. ring bd. 375.00 (*0-379-00855-6*) Oceana.

Trading Asia-Pacific Financial Futures Markets. Will Slatyer & Edna Carew. 224p. (Orig.). 1993. pap. text ed. 29.95 (*1-86373-393-0*, Pub. by Allen Unwin AT) Paul & Co Pubs.

Trading Away Jobs: The Effects of the U. S. Merchandise Trade Deficit on Employment. Faye Duchin & Glenn-Marie Lange. (Working Papers: No. 102). 1990. 10.00 (*0-944826-26-1*) Economic Policy Inst.

Trading Away the Future: Child Labor in India's Export Industries. Pharis Harvey & Lauren Riggin. 124p. 1994. pap. 10.00 (*1-880103-04-4*) Intl Labor Rghts.

Trading Away U. S. Food Safety. Public Citizen Environmental Working Group Staff et al. 100p. (C). 1994. pap. text ed. 20.00 (*0-937188-54-9*) Pub Citizen Inc.

***Trading Beyond the Mountains: The British Fur Trade on the Pacific, 1793-1843.** Richard S. Mackie. (Illus.). 368p. 1997. pap. 22.50 (*0-7748-0613-3*, Pub. by U BC Pr) U of Wash Pr.

***Trading Beyond the Mountains: The British Fur Trade on the Pacific, 1793-1843.** Richard S. Mackie. 440p. 1997. 75.00 (*0-7748-0559-5*, Pub. by U BC Pr) U of Wash Pr.

Trading Chaos: Applying Expert Techniques to Maximize Your Profits. Bill Williams. LC 95-2730. (Finance Editions Ser.). 265p. 1995. text ed. 55.00 (*0-471-11929-6*) Wiley.

Trading Cultures in the Classroom: Two American Teachers in China. Lois Muehl & Siegmar Muehl. 288p. (Orig.). 1993. pap. 14.95 (*0-8248-1442-8*, Kolowalu Bk) UH Pr.

Trading Currency Cross Rates. Gary Klopfenstein & Jon Stein. LC 93-20090. (Traders Library). 176p. 1993. text ed. 45.00 (*0-471-56948-8*) Wiley.

Trading Edge: Neural, Genetic & Fuzzy Systems for Chaotic & Financial Markets. Ed. by Guido J. Deboeck. (Finance Editions Ser.). 416p. 1994. text ed. 65.00 (*0-471-31100-6*) Wiley.

***Trading Electricity in the New Era of Deregulation.** Albert Bassano & Ed Leefeldt. (Bloomberg Professional Library). 288p. 1998. 29.95 (*1-57660-013-0*) Bloomberg NJ.

Trading Energy Futures: A Manual for Energy Industry Professionals. Stewart L. Brown & Steven Errera. LC 86-12379. 214p. 1987. text ed. 55.00 (*0-89930-160-6*, BTE, Quorum Bks) Greenwood.

Trading Financial Futures: Markets, Methods, Strategies, & Tactics. John W. Labuszewski & John E. Nyhoff. LC 87-28570. 242p. 1988. text ed. 45.00 (*0-471-60675-8*) Wiley.

***Trading Financial Futures: Markets, Methods, Strategies, & Tactics.** 2nd ed. John W. Labuszewski & John E. Nyhoff. (Wiley Finance Editions Ser.). text ed. 49.95 (*0-471-30394-1*) Wiley.

Trading for a Living: Psychology, Trading Tactics, Money Management. Alexander Elder. LC 92-35165. 304p. 1993. text ed. 55.00 (*0-471-59224-2*); student ed., suppl. ed., pap. text ed. 29.95 (*0-471-59225-0*) Wiley.

Trading for Growth: The Next Round of Trade Negotiations. Gary C. Hufbauer & Jeffrey J. Schott. LC 85-18104. (Policy Analyses in International Economics Ser.: No. 11). 112p. (Orig.). 1985. pap. 32.00 (*0-7837-8495-3*, 2049302) Bks Demand.

Trading for Profit with Precision Timing. Don Vodopich. (C). 1989. 40.00 (*0-317-93645-X*) Precision Timing.

Trading for Profit with Precision Timing. 4th ed. Don Vodopich. (Illus.). 92p. (C). reprint ed. spiral bd. 40.00 (*0-9622544-0-1*) Precision Timing.

Trading Free: The GATT & U. S. Trade Policy. Patrick Low. LC 93-12630. 310p. (C). 1993. pap. 14.95 (*0-87078-351-3*) TCFP-PPP.

Trading Freedom: How Free Trade Affects Our Lives, Work & Environment. Ed. by Cavanagh et al. 140p. 1991. pap. 5.00 (*0-935028-59-5*) Inst Food & Develop.

Trading Freedom: How Free Trade Affects Our Lives, Work & Environment. John Cavanagh et al. 130p. (C). 1992. pap. 10.00 (*0-685-60300-8*) Inst Policy Stud.

Trading Game. Alfred Slote. LC 89-12851. 208p. (J). (gr. 3-7). 1990. lib. bdg. 14.89 (*0-397-32398-0*, Lipp Jr Bks) HarpC Child Bks.

Trading Game. Alfred Slote. LC 89-12851. (Trophy Bk.). 208p. (J). (gr. 3-7). 1992. pap. 4.50 (*0-06-440438-2*, Trophy) HarpC Child Bks.

Trading Game. large type ed. Alfred Slote. 1993. 54.00 (*0-614-09857-2*, L-33674-00) Am Printing Hse.

Trading Game: Inside Lobbying for the North American Free Trade. Center for Public Integrity Staff. 108p. 1995. pap. 10.00 (*1-882583-02-7*) U Pr of Amer.

Trading in Choppy Markets: Breakthrough Techniques for Exploiting Non-Trending Markets. Robert M. Barnes. 528p. 1996. text ed. 50.00 (*0-7863-1007-3*) Irwin Prof Pubng.

Trading in International Bond Futures & Options. Ian Weitzel. 192p. 1997. 169.95 (*1-85573-189-4*, Pub. by Woodhead Pubng UK) Am Educ Systs.

Trading in Metals. 2nd ed. Trevor Tarring & Geoff Pinney. 275p. 1989. text ed. 83.00 (*0-947671-29-3*) Metal Bulletin.

Trading in Metals Futures & Options. Vivian Davies. (Illus.). 192p. 1997. 165.00 (*1-85573-150-9*, Pub. by Woodhead Pubng UK) Am Educ Systs.

Trading in Oil Futures. 2nd ed. Sally Clubley. 144p. 1990. 42.95 (*0-89397-360-2*) Nichols Pub.

Trading in Options on Futures. James T. Colburn. 1990. 34.95 (*0-13-638552-4*) NY Inst Finance.

Trading in Santa Fe: John M. Kingsbury's Correspondence with James Josiah Webb, 1853-1861. Ed. by Jane L. Elder & David J. Weber. LC 95-43120. (DeGolyer Library: Vol. 5). (Illus.). 368p. 1996. 40.00 (*0-87074-389-9*); pap. 19.95 (*0-87074-390-2*) SMU Press.

Trading in Soft Commodity Futures. Bernard C. Savaiko. 116p. 1986. text ed. 68.50 (*0-471-81778-3*) Wiley.

Trading in the European Union: A Guide to Business & Taxation. 2nd ed. John Dixon. 480p. (C). 1996. pap. 195.00 (*0-85459-964-9*, Pub. by Tolley Pubng UK) St Mut.

***Trading Index Options.** James B. Bittman. 1998. 34.95 incl. disk (*0-7863-1230-0*) Irwin.

Trading Industries, Trading Regions. Ed. by Helzi Noponen et al. (Perspectives on Economic Change Ser.). 290p. 1993. pap. text ed. 19.95 (*0-89862-753-2*); lib. bdg. 42.00 (*0-89862-296-4*) Guilford Pr.

Trading Nations: Jews & Venetians in the Early-Modern Eastern Mediterranean. Benjamin Arbel. (Brill's Series in Jewish Studies: Vol. 14). 1995. 81.50 (*90-04-10057-1*) E J Brill.

***Trading Natural Gas: Cash Futures Options & Swaps.** Fletcher J. Sturm. LC 96-51043. 1996. write for info. (*0-87814-709-8*) PennWell Bks.

Trading on the Seattle Mercs: How to Trade Forward Contract Options on the Seattle Mercantile Exchange. David R. Capasso. 206p. 1994. text ed. 59.95 (*0-471-06326-6*) Wiley.

Trading on Tomorrow's Headlines: How to Make Extraordinary Profits by Following the Stock Purchases. Mark W. Arnold & Kevin Preble. (Illus.). 134p. (Orig.). 1994. pap. 39.95 (*0-9650256-0-8*) TTH Inc.

Trading 101: How to Trade Like a Pro. Sunny Harris. LC 96-10258. 224p. 1996. text ed. 29.95 (*0-471-14445-2*) Wiley.

***Trading Options on Futures.** 2nd ed. John W. Labuszewski & John E. Nyhoff. 288p. 1996. 60.00 (*0-471-02509-7*) Wiley.

Trading Options on Futures: Markets, Methods, Strategies, & Tactics. John W. Labuszewski & John E. Nyhoff. LC 87-29656. 264p. 1988. text ed. 39.95 (*0-471-60676-6*) Wiley.

Trading Options on Futures: Markets, Methods, Strategies & Tactics. 2nd ed. John W. Labuszwski. 288p. 1996. text ed. 39.95 (*0-471-30393-3*) Wiley.

Trading Partners: Australia & Asia 1790-1993. Sandra Tweedie. 1995. pap. 34.95 (*0-86840-166-8*, Pub. by New South Wales Univ Pr AT) Intl Spec Bk.

Trading Partners or Trading Blows? Market Access in EC-U. S. Relations. Michael Woolcock. (Chatham House Papers). 144p. 1992. pap. 14.95 (*0-87609-119-2*) Coun Foreign.

Trading Peasants & Urbanization in Eighteenth-Century Russia: The Central Industrial Region. Daniel Morrison. (Modern European History Ser.). 440p. 1987. text ed. 15.00 (*0-8240-8059-9*) Garland.

Trading Performance in Forward Markets: Information versus Normal Backwardation. Gordon M. Phillips & Robert Weiner. (Illus.). 45p. (Orig.). (C). 1993. pap. text ed. 20.00 (*1-56806-913-8*) DIANE Pub.

Trading Places: Caring for Elderly Parents. Henry Holstege. LC 96-12780. (Issues in Christian Living Ser.). 92p. (Orig.). 1996. pap. 7.15 (*1-56212-171-5*) CRC Pubns.

Trading Places: How We Are Giving Our Future to Japan & How to Reclaim It. Clyde V. Prestowitz, Jr. LC 87-47775. 592p. 1993. reprint ed. pap. 18.00 (*0-465-08679-9*) Basic.

Trading Places: The Intersecting Histories of Judaism & Christianity. Bruce Chilton & Jacob Neusner. LC 96-44694. 296p. (Orig.). 1996. pap. 16.95 (*0-8298-1141-9*) Pilgrim OH.

Trading Places Sourcebook: The Intersecting Histories of Judaism & Christianity. Ed. by Bruce Chilton & Jacob Neusner. LC 96-44694. 304p. (Orig.). 1997. pap. 16.95 (*0-8298-1154-0*) Pilgrim OH.

Trading Post. Larry Ketron. 1981. pap. 5.25 (*0-8222-1165-3*) Dramatists Play.

Trading Post Game: Using Base Ten Blocks in the Primary Grades. William L. Swart. 9p. 1991. pap. text ed. 4.00 (*1-883547-03-2*) Tricon Pub.

Trading Post Guidebook: Where to Find the Trading Posts, Galleries, Auctions, Artists, & Museums of the Four Corners Region. Patrick Eddington & Susan Makov. (Illus.). 264p. (Orig.). 1995. pap. 17.95 (*0-87358-612-3*) Northland AZ.

***Trading Post Guidebook: Where to Find the Trading Posts, Galleries, Auctions, Artists & Museums of the Four Corners Region.** 2nd ed. Susan Makov & Patrick Eddington. LC 97-3348. 1997. write for info. (*0-87358-690-5*) Northland AZ.

***Trading Reality: A Novel.** Michael Ridpath. 352p. 1997. 25.00 (*0-06-017629-6*) HarpC.

Trading Room: Louis Sullivan & the Chicago Stock Exchange. 2nd ed. John Vinci. LC 89-17615. (Illus.). 72p. 1989. reprint ed. pap. 9.95 (*0-86559-082-6*) Art Inst Chi.

Trading Rule That Can Make You Rich: Precision Bid Commodity Trading. Edward D. Dobson. LC 79-64620. (Illus.). 1979. 29.95 (*0-934380-03-1*, 5) Traders Pr.

Trading Rules. William F. Eng. 266p. 1989. 29.95 (*0-88462-920-1*, 5608-2501) Dearborn Finan.

Trading Rules Vol. II: More Strategies for Success. William F. Eng. 284p. 1995. 29.95 (*0-7931-1242-7*, 5680-1301) Dearborn Finan.

***Trading S&P Futures & Options: A Survival Manual & Study Guide.** Humphrey E. Lloyd. 136p. 1997. reprint ed. pap. 49.00 (*0-934380-34-1*, 1111) Traders Pr.

Trading Stocks on the Over-the-Counter Market. New York Institute of Finance Staff. 1988. 21.50 (*0-13-926007-2*) NY Inst Finance.

Trading System after the Uruguay Round. John Whalley. 220p. 1996. pap. 25.00 (*0-88132-131-1*) Inst Intl Eco.

***Trading System Analysis.** Robert M. Barnes. LC 96-53447. 192p. 1997. 60.00 (*0-7863-1098-7*) Irwin Prof Pubng.

Trading System Development 101. Joe Krutsinger. 1993. 49.95 (*0-7602-0108-0*) Irwin Prof Pubng.

Trading System Development 102. Joe Krutsinger. 1993. 49.95 (*0-7602-0109-9*) Irwin Prof Pubng.

Trading System Development 103. Joe Krutsinger. 1993. 49.95 (*0-7602-0110-2*) Irwin Prof Pubng.

Trading Systems: Secrets of the Masters. Joe Krutisinger. LC 97-9644. 1996. 50.00 (*1-55738-912-8*) Irwin Prof Pubng.

Trading Systems Tool Kit: How to Build, Test & Apply Money Making Stock & Futures Trading. Joe Krutsinger. 1993. text ed. 55.00 (*1-55738-534-3*) Irwin Prof Pubng.

Trading Technology: Europe & Japan in the Middle East. Thomas L. Ilgen & T. J. Pempel. LC 86-21197. 215p. 1986. text ed. 55.00 (*0-275-92483-1*, C2483, Praeger Pubs) Greenwood.

***Trading the Fundamentals.** Michael P. Niemira. 1997. 40.00 (*0-7863-1100-2*) Irwin Prof Pubng.

Trading the Fundamentals: The Trader's Complete Guide to Interpreting Economic Indicators & Monetary Policy. Michael P. Niemira & Gerald F. Zukowski. 300p. 1993. text ed. 37.50 (*1-55738-450-9*) Irwin Prof Pubng.

Trading the Future: The Concentration of Economic Power in Our Food System. James Wessel & Mort Hantman. (Illus.). 260p. 1983. pap. 8.95 (*0-935028-13-7*) Inst Food & Develop.

***Trading the Plan: Wealth Building, Money Management & Risk Control Strategies.** Robert Deel. LC 97-8981. (Traders Advantage Ser.). 288p. 1997. 49.95 (*0-471-16979-X*) Wiley.

Trading the Regression Channel: Defining & Predicting Stock Price Trends. Gilbert L. Raff. Ed. by Steven B. Achelis & John C. Slauson. (University Ser.). (Illus.). 145p. Date not set. 39.95 (*1-885439-01-6*) Equis International.

Trading the Silver Seed: Local Knowledge & Market Moralities in Aquaculture Development. David J. Lewis et al. (Orig.). 1996. pap. 32.50 (*1-85339-342-8*, Pub. by Intermed Tech UK) Women Ink.

***Trading the Yield Curve: How Changes in the Price of Money Predict Movements in the World's Market.** Martha Eden. 1997. 55.00 (*0-7863-0995-4*) Irwin Prof Pubng.

***Trading Up: Consumer & Enviormental Regulation in a Global Economy.** David Vogel. 1997. pap. text ed. 17.95 (*0-674-90084-7*) HUP.

Trading Up: Consumer & Environmental Regulation in a Global Economy. David Vogel. LC 95-11865. 336p. (C). 1995. text ed. 39.95 (*0-674-90083-9*) HUP.

Trading Up: How Cargill, the World's Largest Grain Company, is Changing Canadian Agriculture. Brewster Kneen. 144p. 1990. pap. 11.95 (*1-55021-060-2*, Pub. by NC Press CN) U of Toronto Pr.

Trading Water: An Economic Framework for Water Marketing. Rodney T. Smith. LC 88-25627. 95p. 1988. 16.95 (*0-934842-54-X*) CSPA.

Trading Western Softwood Lumber: The Basics. Dave Leckey. 192p. (Orig.). 1989. pap. 24.95 (*0-9621022-0-2*) Highland Oregon.

***Trading with America.** David N. Kay & Ernest Kay. 175p. 1997. pap. 29.95 (*0-566-07685-3*, Pub. by Gower UK) Ashgate Pub Co.

Trading with Canada: The Canada-U. S. Free Trade Agreement - A Twentieth Century Fund Paper. Gilbert R. Winham. 81p. 1988. 18.95 (*0-87078-251-7*); pap. 8.95 (*0-87078-250-9*) TCFP-PPP.

Trading with Iran: Post-Revolution Law & Practice. S. H. Amin. 1987. 150.00 (*0-946706-38-7*, Pub. by Royston Ltd) St Mut.

Trading with Mexico: Petrochemicals & Plastics. (U. S.-Mexico Trade Ser.). 138p. 1994. 1,500.00 (*1-56965-209-0*, GB-17-OB) BCC.

Trading with Mexico: Telecommunications-Consumer Electronics. (U. S.-Mexico Trade Ser.). 1994. 1,500.00 (*1-56965-212-0*, GB-170C) BCC.

Trading with Mexico: The Auto Parts Industry. 1994. 1,500.00 (*1-56965-206-6*, GB-170A) BCC.

***Trading with Oscillators: Pinpointing Market Extremes - Theory & Practice.** Mark Etzkorn. LC 97-22410. (Trader's Exhange Ser.). 176p. 1997. pap. 39.95 (*0-471-15538-1*) Wiley.

Trading with Saudi Arabia: A Guide to the Shipping, Trade, Investment & Tax Laws of Saudi Arabia. Leslie A. Glick. LC 79-55002. 620p. 1980. text ed. 87.50 (*0-916672-43-3*) Rowman.

Trading with the Bolsheviks: The Politics of East-West Trade, 1920-1939. Andrew J. Williams. LC 92-29431. 240p. (C). 1992. text ed. 79.95 (*0-7190-3330-6*, Pub. by Manchester Univ Pr UK) St Martin.

Trading with the Elliott Wave Principle: A Practical Guide. David H. Weis. (Illus.). 160p. (Orig.). (C). 1988. pap. 65.00 (*0-9621350-0-3*) Tape Readers Pr.

Trading with the Enemy: A Yankee Travels Through Castro's Cuba. Tom Miller. 352p. 1992. text ed. 24.00 (*0-689-12094-X*, Pub. by Ctrl Bur voor Schimmel NE) Macmillan.

Trading with the Enemy: A Yankee Travels Through Castro's Cuba. Tom Miller. (Illus.). 384p. 1996. pap. 15.00 (*0-465-08678-0*) Basic.

Trading with the Enemy: Britain's Arming of Iraq. John Sweeney. (Illus.). 197p. (Orig.). 1993. pap. 19.95 (*0-330-33128-0*, Pub. by Pan Books UK) Trans-Atl Phila.

Trading with the Future & Futures Trading. Leonardo Auernheimer. Ed. by Steve Pejovich & Henry Dethloff. (Series on Public Issues: No. 14). 23p. 1985. pap. 2.00 (*0-86599-050-6*) PERC.

Trading with the Natives: A Guide to the Small Shops of Albuquerque. Chris S. Barley. Ed. by Elise Mayer. (Illus.). 160p. (Orig.). 1990. pap. 9.95 (*0-9627497-0-2*) Dancing Desert.

Trading with the Odds: Using the Power of Statistics to Profit in the Futures Market. Cynthia Kase. 200p. 1996. per. 45.00 (*1-55738-911-X*) Irwin Prof Pubng.

Trading with Uncertainty: Foreign Investment Trends in the Soviet Union. Ed. by Mark Meredith. 87, viiip. 1991. text ed. 242.00 (*2-88316-007-4*) Gordon & Breach.

Trading Without Fear: Eliminating Emotional Decisions with Arms Trading. Richard Arms. LC 96-10229. 288p. 1996. text ed. 49.95 (*0-471-13748-0*) Wiley.

Trading Words: Poetry, Typography, & Illustrated Books in the Modern Literary Economy. Claire H. Badaracco. LC 94-45323. (Illus.). 232p. 1995. text ed. 35.00 (*0-8018-4859-8*) Johns Hopkins.

Trading Your Worry for Wonder: A Woman's Guide to Overcoming Anxiety. Cheri Fuller. 176p. 1996. pap. 12.99 (*0-8054-6192-2*, 4261-92) Broadman.

Traditio: An Introduction to the Latin Language. 2nd ed. Patricia Johnston. (Illus.). 430p. (C). 1997. pap. text ed. 32.95 (*0-941051-95-1*) Focus Pub-R Pullins.

Traditio: An Introduction to the Latin Language & Its Influence. Patricia A. Johnston. 663p. (C). 1988. text ed. 59.00 (*0-13-088006-X*) P-H.

***Tradition.** Charles W. Chesnutt. (X Press Black Classics Ser.). 231p. 1996. pap. 9.95 (*1-874509-12-3*, Pub. by X Pr UK) LPC InBook.

Tradition. A. F. Moritz. LC 85-43203. (Contemporary Poets Ser.). 128p. 1986. pap. 10.95 (*0-691-01427-2*) Princeton U Pr.

Tradition: Akashic Brotherhood. White Wolf Staff & Emory Barnes. 72p. 1994. per., pap. 10.00 (*1-56504-410-X*, 4057(4410)) White Wolf.

Tradition: Celestial Chorus. Jim Estes & Phil Brucato. (Mage Ser.). (Illus.). 72p. (Orig.). 1996. pap. 10.00 (*1-56504-411-8*, 4008) White Wolf.

Tradition: Convention & Intervention. Ed. by Lucien Steil. (Architectural Design Profiles Ser.). (Illus.). 80p. 1987. pap. 19.95 (*0-312-81229-9*) St Martin.

Tradition: Cult of Ecstasy. Phil Brucato. (Mage Ser.). (Illus.). 72p. (Orig.), (YA). 1996. suppl. ed., pap. 10.00 (*1-56504-412-6*, 4061) White Wolf.

***Tradition: Dreamspeakers.** Phil Brucato et al. (Mage Ser.). (Illus.). 72p. (Orig.). 1997. pap. 10.00 (*1-56504-413-4*, 4062) White Wolf.

***Tradition: Euthanatos.** Phil Brucato et al. (Mage Ser.). (Illus.). 72p. (Orig.). 1997. pap. 10.00 (*1-56504-414-2*, 4063) White Wolf.

Tradition! Jewish Wisdom for Everyday Life. Ed. by Suzanne S. Zenkel. (Gift Editions Ser.). (Illus.). 64p. 1996. 7.99 (*0-88088-862-8*) Peter Pauper.

***Tradition: Order of Hermes.** Beth Fischi. (Mage Ser.). (Illus.). (Orig.). 1997. pap. 10.00 (*1-56504-416-9*, 4064) White Wolf.

Tradition: Sons of Ether. White Wolf Staff & Bill Bridges. 72p. 1994. per., pap. 10.00 (*1-56504-138-0*, 4058) White Wolf.

Tradition: Verbena. Sam Chupp & Nicky Rea. (Mage Ser.). 72p. 1994. per., pap. 10.00 (*1-56504-128-3*, 4059) White Wolf.

Tradition - Transition - New Vision: Exhibition of Phillips Academy Alumni. Chrisopher C. Cook. (Illus.). 88p. (Orig.). 1983. pap. 15.00 (*1-879886-24-3*) Addison Gallery.

Tradition Als Interpretation in der Chronik: Konig Josaphat Als Paradigma Chronisticher Hermeneutik und Theologie. Kim Strubind. (Beihefte zur Zeitschrift fuer die Alttestamentliche Wissenschaft Ser.: Band 201). xiii, 220p. (GER.). (C). 1991. lib. bdg. 75.40 (*3-11-012791-1*) De Gruyter.

Tradition & Adaptation: Life in a Modern Yucatan Maya Village. Irwin Press. LC 75-71. (Illus.). 288p. 1975. text ed. 55.00 (*0-8371-7954-8*, PYM/, Greenwood Pr) Greenwood.

***Tradition & Adaptation: Writing in the Disciplines.** Dean Ward. LC 96-44134. xxv, 548p. 1997. pap. text ed. 27.95 (*1-55934-460-1*, 1460) Mayfield Pub.

Tradition & Argument in Classical Indian Linguistics. Johannes Bronkhorst. 232p. 1985. lib. bdg. 107.50 (*90-277-2040-1*, D Reidel) Kluwer Ac.

Tradition & Authenticity in the Search for Ecumenic Wisdom. Thomas Langan. 256p. (C). 1992. text ed. 34.95 (*0-8262-0800-2*) U of Mo Pr.

Tradition & Authority in the Reformation. Scott H. Hendrix. (Collected Studies: No. CS535). 352p. 1996. 89.95 (*0-86078-590-4*, Pub. by Variorum UK) Ashgate Pub Co.

Tradition & Avant Garde. Jelena Milojkovic-Djuric. 1988. 42.00 (*0-685-42856-7*) East Eur Monographs.

Tradition & Avant Garde: Literature & Arts in Serbian Culture, 1900-1918. Jelena Milojkovic-Djuric. (East European Monographs: No. 234). 224p. 1988. text ed. 55.50 (*0-88033-131-3*) East Eur Monographs.

Tradition & Avante-Garde: The Arts in Serbian Culture Between the Two World Wars. Jelena Milojkovic-Djuric. 175p. 1984. text ed. 48.50 (*0-88033-052-X*) East Eur Monographs.

Tradition & Change. Arthur Waugh. LC 79-93385. (Essay Index Reprint Ser.). 1977. 21.95 (*0-8369-1316-7*) Ayer.

Tradition & Change: Essays in Honour of Marjorie Chibnall. Ed. by Diana Greenway et al. 412p. 1985. 79.95 (*0-521-25793-X*) Cambridge U Pr.

Tradition & Change in a Turkish Town. 2nd ed. Paul J. Magnarella. (Illus.). 210p. 1982. 19.95 (*0-87073-153-X*); pap. 15.95 (*0-87073-152-1*) Schenkman Bks Inc.

Tradition & Change in Australian Law. Patrick Parkinson. 280p. 1995. pap. 39.00 (*0-455-21292-9*, Pub. by Law Bk Co AT) Gaunt.

Tradition & Change in Jewish Experience: B. G. Rudolph Lectures in Judaic Studies. Ed. by A. Leland Jamison. (C). 1978. pap. 9.95 (*0-8156-8097-X*) Syracuse U Pr.

Tradition & Change in Modern Morocco. E. Jefferson Murphy. (Instructional Unit Based on Film Study). 12p. 1974. 2.50 (*0-317-65384-9*) I N Thut World Educ Ctr.

Tradition & Change in Postindustrial Japan: The Roles of the Political Parties. Roger Benjamin & Kan Ori. LC 80-28559. 192p. 1981. text ed. 39.95 (*0-275-90583-7*, C0583, Praeger Pubs) Greenwood.

***Tradition & Change in Psychoanalysis.** Roy Schafer. LC 96-46630. 272p. 1997. 42.50 (*0-8236-6632-8*, BN06632) Intl Univs Pr.

Tradition & Change in the Asian Family. Ed. by Lee-Jay Cho & Moto Yada. 664p. (C). 1994. text ed. 48.00 (*0-86638-161-9*) EW Ctr HI.

Tradition & Change in the Asian Family. Ed. by Lee-Jay Cho & Moto Yada. 664p. (C). 1995. pap. text ed. 34.95 (*0-86638-174-0*) EW Ctr HI.

Tradition & Change in the Northwest Coast: The Makah, Nuu-chah-nulth, Southern Kwakiutl, & Nuxalk. Ruth Kirk. (Illus.). 256p. 1986. pap. 29.95 (*0-295-96628-9*) U of Wash Pr.

Tradition & Christianity: The Colonial Transformation of a Solomon Islands Society. Ben Burt. LC 93-23801. (Studies in Anthropology & History: Vol. 10). 1994. text ed. 58.00 (*3-7186-5449-0*) Gordon & Breach.

Tradition & Composition in the Parables of Enoch. David W. Suter. LC 79-17441. (Society of Biblical Literature. Dissertation Ser.: No. 47). 252p. reprint ed. pap. 71.90 (*0-7837-5462-0*, 2045227) Bks Demand.

Tradition & Contract: The Problem of Order. Elizabeth Colson. LC 74-82603. 152p. (C). 1974. lib. bdg. 23.95 (*0-202-01131-3*) Aldine de Gruyter.

Tradition & Creativity: Contributions to East Asian Civilization. Ed. by Ching-I Tu. 192p. (Orig.). 1988. pap. 24.95 (*0-88738-738-1*) Transaction Pubs.

Tradition & Creativity: The Engelhard of Konrad von Wurzburg - Its Strucutre & its Sources. Peter H. Oettli. (Australian & New Zealand Studies in German Language & Literature: Vol. 14). 194p. 1986. text ed. 20.55 (*0-8204-0302-4*) P Lang Pubng.

Tradition & Crisis: Jewish Society at the End of the Middle Ages. Jacob Katz. Tr. & Afterword by Bernard D. Cooperman. LC 92-11910. 416p. (C). 1993. 45.00 (*0-8147-4637-3*) NYU Pr.

Tradition & Design in the Iliad. Cecil M. Bowra. LC 77-3065. 278p. 1977. reprint ed. text ed. 38.50 (*0-8371-9561-6*, BOTD, Greenwood Pr) Greenwood.

An Asterisk (*) at the beginning of an entry indicates that the title is appearing in BIP for the first time.

Tradition & Development. S. C. Dube. (C). 1995. text ed. 32.00 (*0-7069-8956-2*, Pub. by Vikas II); pap. text ed. 12.00 (*0-7069-8339-4*, Pub. by Vikas II) S Asia.

Tradition & Diversity: Christianity in a World Context to 1500. Ed. by Karen L. Jolly. LC 96-40287. (Sources & Studies in World History Ser.). 512p. (C). (gr. 13). 1997. pap. text ed. 28.95 (*1-56324-468-3*) M E Sharpe.

Tradition & Diversity: Christianity in a World Context to 1500. Ed. by Karen L. Jolly. LC 96-40287. (Sources & Studies in World History Ser.). 512p. (C). (gr. 13-13). 1997. text ed. 64.95 (*1-56324-467-5*) M E Sharpe.

Tradition & Enlightenment in the Tuscan Academies: 1690-1800. Eric W. Cochrane. LC 60-14232. 292p. reprint ed. pap. 83.30 (*0-317-09759-8*, 2020045) Bks Demand.

Tradition and Exegesis in Early Christian Writers. C. P. Bammel. (Collected Studies: Vol. 500). 328p. 1995. 87.50 (*0-86078-494-0*, Pub. by Variorum UK) Ashgate Pub Co.

Tradition & Experiment in Modern Sculpture. Charles Seymour, Jr. LC 70-91378. (Contemporary Art Ser.). 1970. reprint ed. 17.95 (*0-405-00737-X*) Ayer.

Tradition & Experiment in Present Day Literature. T. S. Eliot. 1972. lib. bdg. 250.00 (*0-87968-044-X*) Gordon Pr.

Tradition & Experiment in Present-Day Literature. City Literary Institute of London Staff. LC 68-20290. (Essay Index Reprint Ser.). 1977. reprint ed. 18.95 (*0-8369-0307-2*) Ayer.

Tradition & Experiment in Present-Day Literature. London City Literary Institute Staff. LC 68-761. (Studies in Comparative Literature: No. 35). (C). 1972. reprint ed. lib. bdg. 75.00 (*0-8383-0544-X*) M S G Haskell Hse.

Tradition & Exploration: Collected Papers on Theology & the Church. Henry Chadwick. 1995. 58.00 (*1-85311-082-5*, Pub. by Canterbury Press Norwich UK) Morehouse Pub.

Tradition & History of the Early Churches of Christ in Central Europe. Hans Grimm. pap. 1.00 (*0-88027-095-0*) Firm Foun Pub.

Tradition & Incarnation: Foundations of Christian Theology. William L. Portier. LC 93-42702. 1994. 14.95 (*0-8091-3467-5*) Paulist Pr.

Tradition & Individuality: Essays. J. C. Nyiri. (Synthese Library). 192p. (C). 1992. lib. bdg. 102.00 (*0-7923-1566-9*, Pub. by Klwr Acad Pubs NE) Kluwer Ac.

Tradition & Influence in Anglo-Irish Poetry. Ed. by Terence Brown & Nicholas Grene. LC 88-29243. 224p. (C). 1988. lib. bdg. 46.00 (*0-389-20817-5*, N8375) B&N Imports.

Tradition & Innovation: A Basket History of the Indians of the Yosemite- Mono Lake Area. Craig D. Bates & Martha J. Lee. (Illus.). 225p. (C). 1991. 49.95 (*0-939666-54-5*) Yosemite Assn.

Tradition & Innovation: General Education & the Reintegration of the University, a Columbia Report. Robert L. Belknap & Richard Kuhns. LC 77-3315. 130p. 1977. text ed. 45.00 (*0-231-04322-8*); pap. text ed. 17.00 (*0-231-04323-6*) Col U Pr.

Tradition & Innovation: Newton's Metaphysics of Nature. J. E. McGuire. LC 95-30104. (University of Western Ontario Series in Phylosophy of Science: Vol. 5). 304p. (C). 1995. lib. bdg. 140.00 (*0-7923-3617-8*, Pub. by Klwr Acad Pubs NE) Kluwer Ac.

Tradition & Innovation: Reflections on Latin American Jewish Writing. Ed. by Robert DiAntonio & Nora Glickman. LC 92-25845. (SUNY Series in Modern Jewish Literature & Culture). 225p. 1993. text ed. 64.50 (*0-7914-1509-0*); pap. text ed. 21.95 (*0-7914-1510-4*) State U NY Pr.

Tradition & Innovation: The Pottery of New Mexico's Pueblos. Linda B. Eaton. 34p. 1993. pap. 6.95 (*0-89734-102-3*) Mus Northern Ariz.

Tradition & Innovation in American Free Verse: Whitman to Duncan. E. Bollobas. (Studies in Modern Philology: Vol. 3). 328p. (C). 1986. pap. 48.00 (*963-05-4139-4*, Pub. by Akad Kiado HU) St Mut.

Tradition & Innovation in Contemporary Austria. Ed. by Kurt Steiner et al. LC 82-60869. 222p. 1982. pap. 15.00 (*0-930664-05-1*) SPOSS.

Tradition & Innovation in Haggai & Zechariah 1-8. Janet A. Tollington. (JSOT Supplement Ser.: No. 150). 220p. 1993. 52.50 (*1-85075-384-9*, Pub. by Sheffield Acad UK) CUP Services.

Tradition & Innovation in Late Antiquity. Ed. by F. M. Clover & R. S. Humphreys. LC 88-40427. (Wisconsin Studies in Classics). (Illus.). 366p. reprint ed. pap. 104.40 (*0-7837-6661-0*, 2046273) Bks Demand.

Tradition & Innovation in Modern English Dictionaries. Henri Bejoint. (Studies in Lexicography & Lexicology). 288p. 1994. 55.00 (*0-19-823919-X*) OUP.

Tradition & Innovation in New Deal Art. Belisario R. Contreras. LC 81-65861. (Illus.). 256p. 1984. 45.00 (*0-8387-5032-X*) Bucknell U Pr.

Tradition & Innovation in Psychoanalytic Education: Clark Conference on Psychoanalytic Training for Psychologists. Murray Meisels. 312p. 1989. 59.95 (*0-8058-0386-6*) L Erlbaum Assocs.

Tradition & Innovation: Progressivism in Primary Education since 1945' see Curriculum Change in the Primary School since 1945: Dissemination of the Progressive Ideal

Tradition & Jazz. Fred L. Pattee. LC 68-22937. (Essay Index Reprint Ser.). 1977. reprint ed. 23.95 (*0-8369-0776-0*) Ayer.

Tradition & Modern Japan. Ed. by P. G. O'Neill. 320p. (C). 1981. text ed. 37.00 (*0-904404-36-6*, Pub. by Curzon Press UK) UH Pr.

Tradition & Modern Society: A Symposium at the Royal Academy of Letters, History & Antiquities, Stockholm, 1987. Ed. by Sven Gustavsson. 220p. (Orig.). 1989. pap. 46.50 (*91-7402-202-4*, Pub. by Umea U Bibl SW) Coronet Bks.

***Tradition & Modernity: Philosophical Reflections on the African Experience.** Kwame Gyekye. 368p. 1997. 45.00 (*0-19-511225-3*); pap. 19.95 (*0-19-511226-1*) OUP.

Tradition & Modernity in Arabic Language & Literature. Ed. by J. R. Smart. 384p. 1996. 98.00 (*0-7007-0411-6*, Pub. by Curzon Pr UK) Paul & Co Pubs.

***Tradition & Modernity in Arabic Literature.** Issa J. Boullata et al. LC 97-6667. 1997. write for info. (*1-55728-447-4*) U of Ark Pr.

Tradition & Modernity in the African Short Story: An Introduction to a Literature in Search of Critics. F. Odun Balogun. LC 90-42616. (Contributions in Afro-American & African Studies: No. 141). 208p. 1991. text ed. 49.95 (*0-313-27637-4*, BTM/, Greenwood Pr) Greenwood.

Tradition & Modernity in the Mediterranean: The Wedding As Symbolic Struggle. Vassos Argyrou. (Studies in Social & Cultural Anthropology: Vol. 101). (Illus.). 224p. (C). 1996. text ed. 44.95 (*0-521-56095-0*) Cambridge U Pr.

Tradition & Modernity Reconsidered. Reinhard Bendix. (Reprint Series in Sociology). (C). 1993. reprint ed. pap. text ed. 4.50 (*0-8290-2693-2*, S-665) Irvington.

Tradition & Modernization in China & Japan. Peter R. Moody, Jr. LC 94-16413. 360p. 1995. pap. text ed. write for info. (*0-534-24546-3*) HarBrace.

Tradition & Politics: The Religious Parties of Israel. Gary S. Schiff. LC 77-5723. (Modern Middle East Ser.: No. 9). 562p. reprint ed. pap. 160.20 (*0-7837-3654-1*, 2043525) Bks Demand.

Tradition & Progress. Gilbert Murray. LC 68-20323. (Essay Index Reprint Ser.). 1977. 19.95 (*0-8369-0728-0*) Ayer.

Tradition & Progress. Gilbert Murray. LC 68-20323. (Essay Index Reprint Ser.). 221p. reprint ed. lib. bdg. 16.00 (*0-8290-0490-4*) Irvington.

Tradition & Progress in the African Village: Non-Capitalist Reform of Rural Communities in Mali - The Sociological Problems. Klaus Ernst. LC 74-22292. 350p. 1977. text ed. 39.95 (*0-312-81235-3*) St Martin.

Tradition & Re-Interpretation in Jewish & Early Christian Literature: Essays in Honour of Jurgen C. H. Lebram. J. W. Van Henten et al. (Studia Post-Biblica Ser.: Vol. 36). viii, 313p. 1986. 119.50 (*90-04-07752-9*) E J Brill.

Tradition & Reflection: Explorations in Indian Thought. Wilhelm Halbfass. LC 89-29795. 425p. 1990. pap. text ed. 21.95 (*0-7914-0362-9*) State U NY Pr.

Tradition & Reflection: Explorations in Indian Thought. Wilhelm Halbfass. LC 89-29795. 425p. 1991. text ed. 64.50 (*0-7914-0361-0*) State U NY Pr.

Tradition & Reform: Land Tenure & Rural Development in South-East Asia. Mark Cleary & Peter Eaton. (South-East Asian Social Science Monographs). 160p. (C). 1996. 39.95 (*967-65-3108-1*) OUP.

Tradition & Renewal: Contemporary Art in the German Democratic Republic. David Elliott & Gabrielle Wittrin. 1984. pap. 32.00 (*0-905836-43-X*, Pub. by Museum Modern Art UK) St Mut.

Tradition & Renewal: Essays on Twentieth-Century Latin American Literature & Culture. Ed. by Merlin H. Forster. LC 74-31179. (Office of International Programs & Studies Ser.). 248p. 1975. 24.95 (*0-252-00440-X*) U of Ill Pr.

Tradition & Renewal in "La Gloria de Don Ramiro" Gabriella Ibieta. 27.50 (*0-916379-29-9*) Scripta.

Tradition & Revolution. Jiddu Krishnamurti. 357p. 1972. 12.95 (*0-318-37042-5*) Asia Bk Corp.

Tradition & Technique in 'El Libro del Cavallero Zifar' Roger M. Walker. (Monagrafias A Ser.: No. 36). 252p. (C). 1974. pap. 45.00 (*0-900411-86-4*, Pub. by Tamesis Bks Ltd UK) Boydell & Brewer.

Tradition & the Talents of Women. Ed. by Florence Howe. 400p. 1990. text ed. 44.95 (*0-252-01685-8*); pap. text ed. 17.50 (*0-252-06106-3*) U of Ill Pr.

***Tradition & Theme in the Annals of Tacitus.** Judith Ginsbur. Date not set. write for info. (*0-88143-017-X*) Ayer.

Tradition & Theme in the "Annals" of Tacitus. rev. ed. Judith Ginsberg. Ed. by W. R. Connor. LC 80-2651. (Monographs in Classical Studies). 1981. lib. bdg. 20.00 (*0-405-14038-X*) Ayer.

Tradition & Transformation: Portuguese Feasting in New Bedford. Stephen L. Cabral. LC 88-46205. (Immigrant Communities & Ethnic Minorities in the U. S. & Canada Ser.: No. 47). 1989. 45.00 (*0-404-19457-5*) AMS Pr.

Tradition & Transformation in Catholic Culture: The Priests of Saint Sulpice in the United States from 1791 to the Present. Christopher J. Kauffman. 366p. (C). 1987. 29.95 (*0-02-917211-X*, Free Press) Free Pr.

Tradition & Transformation in Eastern Nigeria: A Sociopolitical History of Owerri & Its Hinterland, 1902-1947. Felix K. Ekechi. LC 88-30111. 268p. 1989. reprint ed. pap. 74.70 (*0-7837-9316-2*, 2060056) Bks Demand.

Tradition & Transformation in Medieval Byzantium. Paul Magdalino. (Collected Studies: No. CS 343). 350p. 1991. text ed. 97.95 (*0-86078-295-6*, Pub. by Variorum UK) Ashgate Pub Co.

Tradition & Transition: Amish Mennonites & Old Order Amish, 1800-1900. 2nd ed. Paton Yoder. LC 90-47207. (Studies in Anabaptist & Mennonite History: Vol. 31). (Illus.). 360p. 1994. pap. 15.99 (*0-8361-3115-0*) Herald Pr.

Tradition & Transition in East Africa: Studies of the Tribal Element in the Modern Era. Ed. by P. H. Gulliver. LC 78-84787. 384p. reprint ed. pap. 109.50 (*0-685-44491-0*, 2031505) Bks Demand.

Tradition & Transition in South Africa. Ed. by Andrew D. Spiegel & Patrick A. McAllister. 288p. (C). 1992. 49.95 (*1-56000-050-3*) Transaction Pubs.

Tradition & Trauma: Studies in the Fiction of S. J. Agnon. Ed. by David Patterson & Glenda Abramson. LC 93-43704. (Modern Hebrew Classics Ser.). 216p. (C). 1994. pap. text ed. 22.00 (*0-8133-2025-9*) Westview.

Tradition as Selectivity: Scripture, Mishnah, Tosefta, & Midrash in the Talmut of Babylonia. Jacob Neusner. 248p. 1990. 59.95 (*1-55540-478-2*, 240009) Scholars Pr GA.

Tradition As Truth & Communication: A Cognitive Description of Traditional Discourse. Pascal Boyer. (Cambridge Studies in Social & Cultural Anthropology: No. 68). 168p. (C). 1990. text ed. 54.95 (*0-521-37417-0*) Cambridge U Pr.

Tradition, Change, & Modernity. S. N. Eisenstadt. LC 83-11273. 382p. (C). 1983. reprint ed. text ed. 44.50 (*0-89874-642-6*) Krieger.

Tradition Chevaleresque des Arabes. Boutros G. Wacyf. LC 79-8374. reprint ed. 41.50 (*0-404-18356-5*) AMS Pr.

Tradition Day by Day. Ed. & Intro. by John E. Rotelle. 430p. 1994. pap. 12.95 (*0-941491-74-9*) Augustinian Pr.

Tradition de l'Ennui Splenetique en France de Christine de Pisan a Baudelaire, Vol. 16. Frantz LeConte. (Reading Plus Ser.). 280p. (FRE.). (C). 1995. text ed. 51.95 (*0-8204-2498-6*) P Lang Pubng.

***Tradition, Dissent & Ideology: Essays in Honour of Romila Thapar.** Ed. by R. Champakalakshmi & S. Gopal. (Illus.). 448p. 1996. 35.00 (*0-19-563867-0*) OUP.

Tradition et Actualite Chez Isidore de Seville. Jaques Fontaine. (Collected Studies: No. CS281). 350p. (FRE.). (C). 1988. reprint ed. lib. bdg. 99.95 (*0-86078-229-8*, Pub. by Variorum UK) Ashgate Pub Co.

Tradition Family Property: Half a Century of Epic Anticommunism. LC 81-50133. (All about the TFP Ser.). (Illus.). 468p. (Orig.). (C). 1981. 16.95 (*1-877905-13-5*); pap. 11.95 (*1-877905-12-7*) Am Soc Defense TFP.

Tradition, Harmony, & Transcendence. George F. McLean. LC 93-4607. (Cultural Heritage & Contemporary Life Series I. Culture & Values: Vol. 4). 1993. 45.00 (*1-56518-030-5*); pap. 17.50 (*1-56518-031-3*) Coun Res Values.

Tradition History & the Psalms of Asaph. Harry P. Nasuti. LC 86-25232. (Society of Biblical Literature Dissertation Ser.). 230p. 1989. pap. 14.95 (*0-89130-971-3*, 06 01 88) Scholars Pr GA.

Tradition im Umbruch: Zur Sophokles-Rezeption im Deutschen Vormarz. Gabriele S. May. (American University Studies: Germanic Languages & Literature: Ser. I, Vol. 76). 163p. (C). 1989. text ed. 32.95 (*0-8204-1007-1*) P Lang Pubng.

Tradition in a Rootless World: Women Turn to Orthodox Judaism. Lynn Davidman. LC 90-25881. 265p. 1991. 30.00 (*0-520-07282-0*) U CA Pr.

Tradition in a Rootless World: Women Turn to Orthodox Judaism. Lynn Davidman. 1993. pap. 14.95 (*0-520-07545-5*) U CA Pr.

Tradition in Greek Religion. Bernard C. Dietrich. xvi, 213p. 1986. 86.15 (*3-11-010695-7*) De Gruyter.

Tradition in Late Antique Sculpture: Conservation, Modernization, Production. Niels Hannestad. (Acta Jutlandica Ser.: No. 69, Pt. 2). (Illus.). 176p. (C). 1994. pap. text ed. 33.00 (*87-7288-442-8*, Pub. by Aarhus Univ Pr DK) David Brown.

Tradition in Modern Times: Graduate Liberal Studies Today. Ed. by Charles B. Hands. LC 88-17232. 158p. (Orig.). (C). 1988. pap. text ed. 17.50 (*0-8191-7070-4*) U Pr of Amer.

Tradition in the Eastern Orthodox Church. pap. 0.50 (*0-89981-104-3*) Eastern Orthodox.

Tradition in the Kitchen Two: The Authentic Guide to Kosher Cooking. North Suburban Bethel Sisterhood Staff. Ed. by Eenie Frost. (Illus.). 328p. 1993. 19.95 (*0-9635594-0-0*) N Suburban BES.

Tradition in the Making of Modern Poetry Vol. 1. Howard Sergeant. 1951. 49.50 (*0-614-01808-0*) Elliots Bks.

Tradition in Transition: Orthodoxy, Halakhah, & the Boundaries of Modern Jewish Identity. David Ellenson. LC 89-32311. (Studies in Judaism). 202p. (C). 1989. lib. bdg. 41.50 (*0-8191-7452-1*, Studies in Judaism) U Pr of Amer.

Tradition in Transition: Women Writers, Marginal Texts, & the Eighteenth-Century Canon. Alvaro Ribeiro & James G. Basker. (Illus.). 370p. 1996. 75.00 (*0-19-818288-0*) OUP.

Tradition, Innovation, & Romantic Images: The Architecture of Historic Knoxville. William R. McNabb. 80p. 1991. 18.95 (*1-880174-00-6*) U TN F H McClung.

Tradition, Innovation, Conflict: Jewishness & Judaism in Contemporary Israel. Ed. by Zvi Sobel & Benjamin Beit-Hallahmi. LC 90-35232. (SUNY Series in Israeli Studies). 324p. (C). 1991. text ed. 64.50 (*0-7914-0554-0*); pap. text ed. 21.95 (*0-7914-0555-9*) State U NY Pr.

Tradition, Innovation, Continuity: Native Art in the Public Eye. Susan W. Fair. LC 92-32191. (Illus.). (Orig.). pap. 24.00 (*0-910615-10-1*) Alaska St Coun.

Tradition, Interpretation, & Science: Political Theory in the American Academy. Ed. by John S. Nelson. LC 86-7098. (SUNY Series in Political Theory: Contemporary Issues). 372p. (C). 1986. text ed. 64.50 (*0-88706-371-3*) State U NY Pr.

Tradition, Interpretation, & Science: Political Theory in the American Academy. Ed. by John S. Nelson. LC 86-7098. (SUNY Series in Political Theory: Contemporary Issues). 372p. (C). 1986. pap. text ed. 21.95 (*0-88706-373-X*) State U NY Pr.

***Tradition Lives: A 75 Year History of the Ellensburg Rodeo.** John Ludtka. (Illus.). 192p. 1997. write for info. (*0-9658735-0-1*) Ellensburg.

***Tradition, Location & Community: Place-Making & Development.** Ed. by Adenrele Awotona & Mecdet Teymur. (Ethnoscapes Ser.). 352p. 1997. 76.95 (*1-85972-320-9*, Pub. by Avebury Pub UK) Ashgate Pub Co.

Tradition Matters: Modern Gaucho Identity in Brazil. Ruben Oliven. Tr. by Carmen C. Tesser. (Illus.). 160p. 1996. pap. 17.50 (*0-231-10425-1*) Col U Pr.

Tradition, Modernity & Religious Authority in the Twentieth Century. Moshe Z. Sokol. LC 96-12065. 1996. pap. write for info. (*1-56821-908-3*) Aronson.

Tradition of Advaita: Essays in Honour of Bhasyabhavajna VR Kalyanasundara Sastri. Balasubramanian. (C). 1994. 28.00 (*81-215-0588-7*, Pub. by Munshiram Manoharial II) S Asia.

Tradition of Australian Cooking. Gollan. (Australian National University Press Ser.). 1983. pap. 18.00 (*0-08-032939-X*, Pergamon Pr) Elsevier.

Tradition of Care. Helen Gregory. 180p. (C). 1990. 90.00 (*0-86439-064-5*, Pub. by Boolarong Pubns AT) St Mut.

Tradition of Choice: Planned Parenthood at 75. Planned Parenthood Federation of America, Inc. Staff. LC 91-75358. (Illus.). 108p. 1991. 19.95 (*0-934586-71-3*) Plan Parent.

Tradition of Constructivism. Stephen Bann. (Quality Paperbacks Ser.). (Illus.). 384p. 1990. reprint ed. pap. 13.95 (*0-306-80396-8*) Da Capo.

Tradition of Craftsmanship in Mexican Homes. Patricia W. O'Gorman. (Illus.). 272p. 1988. 37.50 (*0-8038-0047-9*) Archit CT.

Tradition of Excellence: The Sesquicentennial History of the University at Albany, 1884 to 1994. Kendall A. Birr. LC 94-2894. 1994. write for info. (*0-89865-889-6*) Donning Co.

Tradition of Excellence: Winneconne Community School District, 1848-1996. Ed. by Polly Zimmerman. LC 96-2993. (Illus.). 224p. (Orig.). 1996. pap. 35.00 (*0-938627-32-5*) New Past Pr.

Tradition of Excellence Vol. I: 100 Years of Alma College Football: A Centennial Salute to the Champions. Todd E. Harburn & Charles A. Gray. LC 94-72618. (Illus.). 229p. 1994. spiral bd. 15.00 (*0-614-14181-8*) T & G Harburn.

***Tradition of Female Transvestism in Early Modern Europe.** Rudolf M. Dekker. 1997. text ed. 17.95 (*0-312-17334-2*) St Martin.

Tradition of Fine Bookbinding in the Twentieth Century. Compiled by B. G. Callery & E. A. Mosimann. (Illus.). 120p. 1979. 25.00 (*0-913196-28-2*) Hunt Inst Botanical.

Tradition of Human Rights in China & Vietnam. Nguyen Ngoc Huy & Stephen B. Young. (Lac-Viet Ser.: No. 10). 480p. 1990. pap. 20.00 (*0-685-63100-1*) Yale U SE Asia.

Tradition of Modern Architecture see History of Modern Architecture

Tradition of Natural Law: A Philosopher's Reflections. Yves R. Simon. Ed. by Vukan Kuic. LC 92-5460. xxxii, 194p. 1992. pap. 19.95 (*0-8232-0641-6*) Fordham.

Tradition of Natural Law: A Philosopher's Reflections. Yves R. Simon. Ed. by Vukan Kuic. LC 64-24756. 206p. reprint ed. pap. 58.80 (*0-7837-0473-9*, 2040796) Bks Demand.

Tradition of Political Hedonism: From Hobbes to J. S. Mill. Frederick Vaughan. LC 81-72097. 283p. reprint ed. pap. 80.70 (*0-7837-5621-6*, 2045530) Bks Demand.

Tradition of Pride. Janet Dailey. (Americana Ser.: No. 874). 1992. mass mkt. 3.59 (*0-373-89874-6*) Harlequin Bks.

***Tradition of Return: The Implicit History of Modern Literature.** Jeffrey M. Perl. LC 84-42567. (Illus.). 338p. 1984. reprint ed. pap. 96.40 (*0-608-02548-8*, 2063192) Bks Demand.

Tradition of Science: Landmarks of Western Science in the Collections of the Library of Congress. Leonard C. Bruno. LC 86-600088. 351p. 1987. 30.00 (*0-8444-0528-0*, 030-000-00183-4) Lib Congress.

***Tradition of Scottish Philosophy.** Alexander Broadie. 1990. 20.00 (*0-7486-6029-1*, Pub. by Polygon UK) Subterranean Co.

Tradition of Scottish Philosophy: A New Perspective on the Enlightenment. Alexander Broadie. 192p. (C). 1990. lib. bdg. 53.00 (*0-389-20921-X*) Rowman.

Tradition of Silence in Myth & Legend. A. H. Gebhard-L'Estrange. 1977. lib. bdg. 59.95 (*0-8490-2755-1*) Gordon Pr.

Tradition of Subversion: The Prose Poem in English from Wilde to Ashbery. Margueritte S. Murphy. LC 91-40282. 264p. (C). 1992. lib. bdg. 30.00 (*0-87023-781-0*) U of Mass Pr.

Tradition of Teachers: Sankara & the Jagadgurus Today. (C). 1995. reprint ed. 16.50 (*81-208-0932-7*, Pub. by Motilal Banarsidass II) S Asia.

***Tradition of Technology: Landmarks of Western Technology.** 1997. lib. bdg. 259.99 (*0-8490-6155-5*) Gordon Pr.

Tradition of Technology: Landmarks of Western Technology in the Collections of the Library of Congress. Leonard C. Bruno. LC 93-16406. 1993. write for info. (*0-8444-0781-X*) Lib Congress.

Tradition of the Himalayan Masters. Pandit R. Tigunait. LC 93-11991. (Illus.). 230p. (Orig.). 1993. pap. 14.95 (*0-89389-134-7*) Himalayan Inst.

Tradition of the Law & Law of the Tradition: Law, State & Social Control in China. Xin Ren. LC 96-20676. (Contributions in Criminology & Penology Ser.: No. 50). 192p. 1997. text ed. 59.95 (*0-313-29096-2*, Greenwood Pr) Greenwood.

T

Tradition of the New. Harold Rosenberg. LC 72-134130. (Essay Index Reprint Ser.). 1977. 21.95 (*0-8369-2127-5*) Ayer.

Tradition of the New. Harold Rosenberg. 286p. 1994. reprint ed. pap. 14.95 (*0-306-80596-0*) Da Capo.

Tradition of the Novela in Spain: From Pedro Mexia (1540) to Lope De Vega's Novelas a Marcia Leonarda 1621-24. Yvonne M. Yarbro-Bejarano. LC 91-11531. (Harvard Romance Languages Ser.). 288p. 1991. reprint ed. text ed. 30.00 (*0-8240-0497-3*) Garland.

Tradition of the Thompson River Indians of British Columbia. J. A. Teit. (AFS Memoirs Ser.). 1974. reprint ed. 30.00 (*0-527-01058-8*) Periodicals Srv.

Tradition of the Topics in the Middle Ages. N. J. Green-Pedersen. (Analytica Ser.). 459p. 1985. lib. bdg. 119.00 (*3-88405-046-X*) Philosophia Pr.

Tradition of Three Tropes. Joseph A. Diamond. (Wissenschaftliche Abhandlungen-Musicological Studies: Vol. 54). 127p. (ENG.). 1991. 46.00 (*0-931902-67-3*) Inst Mediaeval Mus.

Tradition of Wood-Carving & Stair-Making. Ed. by G. Lister Sutcliffe. (Modern Carpenter Joiner & Cabinet-Maker Ser.: Vol. 6). (Illus.). 152p. 1990. reprint ed. 19.95 (*0-918678-60-9*) Natl Hist Soc.

Tradition Renewed: The Oxford Movement Conference Papers. Ed. by Geoffrey Rowell. LC 85-32078. (Princeton Theological Monographs: No. 3). (Orig.). 1986. pap. 20.00 (*0-915138-82-4*) Pickwick.

***Tradition That Has No Name: Nurturing the Development of People, Families & Communities.** Mary Field Belenky et al. LC 96-53583. 384p. 1997. 28.00 (*0-465-02605-2*) Basic.

Tradition That You Received from Us: Two Thessalonians in the Pauline Tradition. Glenn S. Holland. 190p. 1987. lib. bdg. 64.00 (*3-16-145203-8*, Pub. by J C B Mohr GW) Coronet Bks.

Tradition Transformed: The Jewish Experience in America. Gerald Sorin. LC 96-28303. (American Moment Ser.). 304p. 1997. text ed. 40.00 (*0-8018-5446-6*); pap. text ed. 14.95 (*0-8018-5447-4*) Johns Hopkins.

Tradition, Transmission, Transformation: Proceedings of Two Conferences on Premodern Science Held at the University of Oklahoma. F. J. Ragep & S. P. Ragep. 1996. 122.50 (*90-04-10119-5*) E J Brill.

Tradition und Translation: Zum Problem der interkulturellen Uebersetzbarkeit Religioeser Phaenomene. Ed. by Christoph Elsas et al. xxxvi, 565p. (GER.). (C). 1994. lib. bdg. 229.25 (*3-11-013930-8*, 126-94) De Gruyter.

Tradition, Values, & Socio-Economic Development. Joseph J. Spengler et al. Ed. by Ralph Braibanti. LC 60-15267. (Duke University, Commonwealth-Studies Center, Publication Ser.: No. 13). 313p. reprint ed. pap. 89.30 (*0-317-20092-5*, 2023372) Bks Demand.

Tradition Versus Democracy in the South Pacific: Fiji, Tonga & Western Samoa. Stephanie Lawson. (Asia-Pacific Studies: No. 2). (Illus.). 240p. (C). 1996. text ed. 59.95 (*0-521-49638-1*) Cambridge U Pr.

Tradition Versus Revolution: Russia & the Balkans in 1917. Robert H. Johnston. (East European Monographs: No. 28). 1977. text ed. 61.00 (*0-914710-21-4*) East Eur Monographs.

Tradition Via Heidegger: An Essay on the Meaning of Being in the Philosophy of Martin Heidegger. J. N. Deely. 222p. 1971. pap. text ed. 59.00 (*90-247-5111-X*, Pub. by M Nijhoff NE) Kluwer Ac.

Tradition with a Twist: Variations on Your Favorite Quilts. Blanche Young & Dalene Y. Stone. Ed. by Joyce Lytle & Barbara K. Kuhn. LC 95-38142. (Illus.). 128p. (Orig.). 1995. pap. 24.95 (*1-57120-002-9*, 10124) C & T Pub.

***Traditional Aboriginal Society: A Reader.** 2nd ed. W. H. Edwards. 320p. 1997. pap. 39.95 (*0-7329-4082-6*, Pub. by Macmill Educ AT) Paul & Co Pubs.

***Traditional Aboriginal Society: A Reader.** 2nd ed. W. H. Edwards. 320p. 1997. 79.95 (*0-7329-4094-X*, Pub. by Macmill Educ AT) Paul & Co Pubs.

Traditional Acupuncture: The Law of Five Elements. 3rd ed. Diane M. Connelly. (Illus.). 157p. pap. 12.00 (*0-912379-01-4*) Ctr Traditional Acupuncture.

Traditional Acupuncture: The Law of the Five Elements. Dianne M. Connelly. 1994. pap. 12.00 (*0-912381-03-5*) Trad Acupuncture.

Traditional Africa. Louis Minks. LC 95-20851. (World History Ser.). (Illus.). 96p. (J). (gr. 6-10). 1996. lib. bdg. 17.96 (*1-56006-239-8*) Lucent Bks.

***Traditional African Designs.** Gregory Mirow. (Illus.). 48p. 1997. pap. 5.95 (*0-486-29622-9*) Dover.

Traditional Aikido, 5 vols. M. Saito. 45.00 (*0-318-56395-9*) Wehman.

Traditional American Folk Songs from the Anne & Frank Warner Collection. Anne Warner. LC 84-95. (Illus.). 526p. 1984. pap. 29.95 (*0-8156-0185-9*) Syracuse U Pr.

Traditional & Analytical Philosophy: Lectures on the Philosophy of Language. Ernst Tugendhat. Tr. by P. A. Gorner from GER. LC 81-15509. 450p. 1982. 84.95 (*0-521-22236-2*) Cambridge U Pr.

***Traditional & Archaeology: Early Maritime Contacts in the Indian Ocean.** Ed. by Himanshu P. Ray & J. F. Salles. (C). 1996. 80.00 (*81-7304-145-8*, Pub. by Manohar II) S Asia.

Traditional & Contemporary Guitar Finger-Picking Styles. Happy Traum. (Illus.). 71p. 1969. pap. 14.95 (*0-8256-0103-7*, OK62091, Oak) Music Sales.

Traditional & Folk Designs. Gill Bridgewater & Allan Bridgewater. (Illus.). 64p. (Orig.). 1990. pap. 9.95 (*0-85532-654-9*, 654-9, Pub. by Search Pr UK) A Schwartz & Co.

Traditional & Modern Medical Systems. Ed. by Ray Elling. (Illus.). 100p. 1981. pap. 18.00 (*0-08-028097-8*, Pergamon Pr) Elsevier.

Traditional & Non-Traditional Robotic Sensors. T. C. Henderson. (NATO ASI Series F: Computer & Systems Science: Vol. 63). viii, 468p. 1990. 107.95 (*0-387-53007-X*) Spr-Verlag.

***Traditional & Popular Wedding Music.** Ed. by Carol Cuellar. (Orig.). (C). 1997. pap. text ed. 16.95 (*1-57623-971-3*, MF9720) Warner Brothers.

Traditional Anglo-American Folk Music: An Annotated Discography of Published Sound Recordings. Norm Cohen. LC 93-26934. (Library of Music Ethnology: Vol. 2). 543p. 1993. text ed. 95.00 (*0-8153-0377-7*, H1469) Garland.

Traditional Animal Designs & Motifs for Artists & Craftspeople. Madeleine Orban-Szontagh. LC 92-43113. (Pictorial Archive Ser.). 1993. pap. write for info. (*0-486-27485-3*) Dover.

***Traditional Arabic Cooking.** Miriam A. Hashimi. 192p. 1996. 35.00 (*0-614-21525-0*, 1249) Kazi Pubns.

Traditional Architecture in the Gilbert Islands: A Cultural Perspective. John Hockings. (Illus.). 250p. (Orig.). 1989. pap. text ed. 32.95 (*0-7022-2179-1*, Pub. by Univ Queensland Pr AT) Intl Spec Bk.

Traditional Architecture of Mexico. Photos by Mariana Yampolsky. LC 93-60430. (Illus.). 208p. 1993. 40.00 (*0-500-34128-1*) Thames Hudson.

Traditional Architecture of the Kathmandu Valley. Wolfgang Korn. 1989. 125.00 (*0-7855-0305-6*, Pub. by Ratna Pustak Bhandar); 125.00 (*0-7855-0323-4*, Pub. by Ratna Pustak Bhandar) St Mut.

Traditional Architecture of the Kathmandu Valley. Wolfgang Korn. 125p. (C). 1989. 250.00 (*0-89771-122-X*, Pub. by Ratna Pustak Bhandar) St Mut.

Traditional Art & Symbolism. Ananda K. Coomaraswamy. Ed. by Roger Lipsey. (Bollingen Ser.: No. 89). (Illus.). 620p. 1977. pap. text ed. 26.95 (*0-691-01869-3*) Princeton U Pr.

Traditional Art of Africa. Thierry Gentis. (Illus.). 12p. (Orig.). 1983. pap. 3.00 (*0-912089-01-6*) Haffenreffer Mus Anthro.

Traditional Art of the Mask: Carving a Transformation Mask. Lelooska. (Illus.). 80p. 1996. 19.95 (*0-7643-0028-8*) Schiffer.

Traditional Art of the Nigerian Peoples: The Ratner Collection. Henry J. Drewal. (Illus.). 1977. 7.00 (*0-686-25965-3*) Mus African Art.

Traditional Artist in African Societies. Ed. by Warren L. D'Azevedo. LC 79-160126. (Illus.). 478p. 1989. pap. 16.95 (*0-253-20518-2*, MB-518) Ind U Pr.

Traditional Arts & Crafts of Japan. Christopher Dresser. LC 93-23730. Orig. Title: Japan: Its Architecture, Art & Art Manufactures. (Illus.). 480p. 1994. reprint ed. pap. 11.95 (*0-486-27992-8*) Dover.

Traditional Arts & Crafts of Nepal. C. L. Gajural & Vaidya. 1994. pap. 60.00 (*0-7855-0487-7*, Pub. by Ratna Pustak Bhandar) St Mut.

Traditional Arts & Crafts of Nepal. C. L. Gajurel & K. K. Vaidka. 1984. text ed. 32.50 (*0-685-14066-0*) Coronet Bks.

Traditional Arts of Spanish New Mexico: The Hispanic Heritage Wing at the Museum of International Folk Art. Robin F. Gavin. (Illus.). 104p. 1994. bds. 19.95 (*0-89013-258-5*) Museum NM Pr.

Traditional Autoharp. Clayton Jones & Barbara Koehler. 1993. 9.95 (*0-87166-276-0*, 93389); audio 10.98 (*0-87166-277-9*, 93389C); audio 19.95 (*0-87166-278-7*, 93389P) Mel Bay.

Traditional Balinese Culture: Essays. Jane Belo. LC 68-54454. 495p. reprint ed. pap. 141.10 (*0-317-08157-8*, 2006119) Bks Demand.

Traditional Ballads of Virginia: Collected Under the Auspices of the Virginia Folk- Lore Society. LC 78-79458. 652p. reprint ed. pap. 180.00 (*0-8357-2569-3*, 2040259) Bks Demand.

Traditional Bargello: Stitches, Techniques, & Dozens of Pattern & Project Ideas. Dorothy Phelan. (Illus.). 96p. (Orig.). 1991. pap. 15.95 (*0-312-06882-4*) St Martin.

Traditional Basque Cooking: History & Preparation. Jose M. Busca Isusi. LC 87-10741. (Basque Ser.). (Illus.). 212p. (C). 1993. pap. 19.95 (*0-87417-202-0*) U of Nev Pr.

Traditional Beancurd Manufacture. Natasha J. Johnson. 38p. (Orig.). 1994. pap. 11.50 (*1-85339-270-7*, Pub. by Intermed Tech UK) Women Ink.

***Traditional Birth Attendant in Seven Countries: The Case Studies in Utilization & Training.** A. Mangay-Maglacas & H. Pizurki. (Public Health Papers: No. 75). 211p. 1981. pap. text ed. 15.00 (*92-4-130075-2*, 1110075) World Health.

Traditional Birth Attendants: A Joint WHO-UNFPA-UNICEF Statement. 18p. (ENG, FRE & SPA.). 1992. pap. text ed. 9.00 (*92-4-156150-5*, 1150388) World Health.

Traditional Black Music, 13 vols., Set. Ed. by Kenneth B. Clark. (Illus.). 80p. (YA). (gr. 5 up). 1993. lib. bdg. 220.35 (*0-7910-1826-1*) Chelsea Hse.

Traditional Blocks Meet Applique: Combine Piecing & Applique to Create Exciting Secondary Quilt Designs! Deborah J. Moffett-Hall. (Illus.). 96p. (Orig.). 1996. pap. 19.95 (*1-56477-123-7*, B240) That Patchwork.

***Traditional Boatbuilding Made Easy: Build a Traditional Skiff for Oar or Sail.** Richard Kolin. (Illus.). 96p. 1996. pap. 19.95 (*0-937822-40-X*) WoodenBoat Pubns.

Traditional Bobbin Lace: Patterns in Torchin, Guipure & Indria. Gertrude Biedermann & Martha Anderson. Ed. by Jules Kliot & Kaethe Kliot. 1975. reprint ed. pap. 21.00 (*0-916896-07-2*) Lacis Pubns.

Traditional Bowyer's Bible, Vol. 1. Jim Hamm. (Illus.). 326p. 1993. 19.95 (*1-55821-206-X*) Lyons & Burford.

Traditional Bowyers of America: The Bowhunting & Bowmaking World of the Nation's Top Crafters of Longbows & Recurves. Dan Bertalan. LC 89-85279. (Illus.). 528p. 1995. 29.95 (*0-9623955-0-1*) Envisage Unlimited.

Traditional British Ballads. Ed. by Bartlett J. Whiting. LC 55-10557. (Crofts Classics Ser.). 160p. (C). 1955. pap. text ed. write for info. (*0-88295-016-9*) Harlan Davidson.

Traditional Buildings of England. Anthony Quiney. LC 89-51819. (Illus.). 224p. 1990. 29.95 (*0-500-34110-9*) Thames Hudson.

Traditional Buildings of England. Anthony Quiney. LC 89-51819. (Illus.). 224p. 1995. per., pap. 18.95 (*0-500-27661-7*) Thames Hudson.

Traditional Catholic Prayers. Charles Dollen. LC 89-62496. 176p. 1990. 13.95 (*0-87973-440-X*, 440) Our Sunday Visitor.

Traditional Catholic Religious Orders: Living in Community. Edward A. Wynne. 224p. 1987. 39.95 (*0-88738-129-4*) Transaction Pubs.

Traditional Cheesemaking: An Introduction. Josef Duback. 112p. (Orig.). 1988. pap. 13.50 (*0-942850-18-1*) Bootstrap Pr.

Traditional Chikankari Embroidery Patterns of India. Pradumna Tana & Rosalba Tana. (International Design Library). 48p. (Orig.). 1988. pap. 5.95 (*0-88045-089-4*) Stemmer Hse.

Traditional China. Islay Doncaster. Ed. by Margaret Killingray & Edmund O'Connor. (World History Program Ser.). (Illus.). (YA). (gr. 6-11). 1980. reprint ed. pap. text ed. 4.72 (*0-89908-007-3*) Greenhaven.

Traditional Chinese Acupuncture, Vol. 1: Meridians & Points. J. R. Worsley. (Illus.). 328p. 1910. pap. 100.00 (*0-906540-03-8*) Element MA.

Traditional Chinese Clan Rules. Hui-Chen Wang Liu. (Illus.). 15.00 (*0-685-71737-2*) J J Augustin.

Traditional Chinese Clan Rules. Hui-Chen Wang Liu. (Illus.). 264p. 1985. pap. 14.00 (*0-89986-375-2*) Oriental Bk Store.

Traditional Chinese Clothing: In Hong Kong & South China, 1840-1980. Valery M. Garrett. (Images of Asia Ser.). (Illus.). 96p. 1988. 17.95 (*0-19-584174-3*) OUP.

Traditional Chinese Cut-Paper Designs. Bernard Melchers. LC 77-88654. (Pictorial Archive Ser.). (Illus.). 1978. reprint ed. pap. 4.95 (*0-486-23581-5*) Dover.

Traditional Chinese Designs. Ed. by Stanley Appelbaum. (Design Library). 48p. (Orig.). 1987. pap. 3.95 (*0-486-25347-3*) Dover.

Traditional Chinese Fiction & Fiction Commentary: Reading & Writing Between the Lines. David L. Rolston. LC 96-12369. 1997. write for info. (*0-8047-2720-1*) Stanford U Pr.

Traditional Chinese Fitness Exercises. China Sports Editorial Board Staff. Ed. by New World Press Staff. (China Spotlight Ser.). (Illus.). 135p. (Orig.). 1984. pap. 4.95 (*0-8351-1407-4*) China Bks.

Traditional Chinese Folktales. Tr. by Yin-lien C. Chin et al. from CHI. LC 88-31129. (Illus.). 192p. (YA). (gr. 8-12). 1989. 37.95 (*0-87332-507-9*) M E Sharpe.

Traditional Chinese Herbal Science: Herbs, Strategies, & Case Studies, 2 vols., Set. 4th ed. Roger W. Wicke. (Illus.). (C). 1994. pap. text ed. 98.00 (*1-885779-02-X*) Rocky Mtn Herbal.

Traditional Chinese Herbal Science Vol. 1: The Language & Patterns of Life. 5th ed. Roger W. Wicke. (Illus.). 282p. (C). 1994. pap. text ed. 60.00 (*1-885779-00-3*) Rocky Mtn Herbal.

Traditional Chinese Herbal Science Vol. 2: Herbs, Strategies, & Case Studies. 4th ed. Roger W. Wicke. (Illus.). 293p. (C). 1994. pap. text ed. 60.00 (*1-885779-01-1*) Rocky Mtn Herbal.

Traditional Chinese Humor: A Study in Art & Literature. Henry W. Wells. LC 78-143248. (Illus.). 260p. reprint ed. pap. 74.10 (*0-317-10154-4*, 2055231) Bks Demand.

Traditional Chinese Lattice Designs. Muncie Hendler. LC 95-7441. (Design Library). 1995. pap. write for info. (*0-486-28699-1*) Dover.

Traditional Chinese Legal Thought: The Pre-Ch'in Period. Joseph D. Lowe. LC 84-80994. (Illus.). 101p. 1984. pap. 30.00 (*0-9605506-8-2*) Lowe Pub.

Traditional Chinese Medicine. Sheila McNamara. LC 95-45945. 320p. 1996. pap. 14.00 (*0-465-00629-9*) Basic.

***Traditional Chinese Medicine: The A-Z Guide to Natural Healing from the Orient.** Carol Hart & Magnolia Goh. Date not set. write for info. (*0-440-22436-5*) Dell.

Traditional Chinese Penal Law. Geoffrey MacCormack. 1991. text ed. 69.00 (*0-7486-0211-9*, Pub. by Edinburgh U Pr UK) Col U Pr.

Traditional Chinese Plays, Vol. 1: Ssfu Lang Visits His Mother (Ssu Lang T'an Mu), The Butterfly Dream (Hu Tieh Meng) Adolphe C. Scott. LC 66-22854. (Illus.). 187p. reprint ed. pap. 53.30 (*0-8357-3571-0*, 2034278) Bks Demand.

Traditional Chinese Plays, Vol. 3: Picking up the Jade Bracelet, Shih Yu-cho; a Girl Setting out for Trial, Nu Ch'i-chieh. Adolphe C. Scott. LC 66-22854. (Illus.). 111p. reprint ed. pap. 31.70 (*0-7837-4617-2*, 2044338) Bks Demand.

Traditional Chinese Poetry & Poetics: Omen of the World. Stephen Owen. LC 83-40269. 320p. 1985. text ed. 27.50 (*0-299-09420-0*) U of Wis Pr.

Traditional Chinese State in Ming Times (1368-1644) fac. ed. Charles O. Hucker. LC 61-15391. 91p. 1961. pap. 26.00 (*0-7837-7551-2*, 2047304) Bks Demand.

Traditional Chinese Stories: Themes & Variations. Ed. by Y. W. Ma & Joseph S. Lau. LC 86-71550. (C & T Asian Literature Ser.). 619p. (C). 1991. reprint ed. pap. text ed. 22.95 (*0-88727-071-9*) Cheng & Tsui.

Traditional Chinese Tales. Tr. by Wang Chi-Chen. LC 69-14138. 225p. 1969. reprint ed. text ed. 55.00 (*0-8371-0739-3*, WACT, Greenwood Pr) Greenwood.

***Traditional Chinese Therapeutic Exercises - Standing Pole.** (Illus.). 89p. 1994. pap. 6.95 (*7-119-00696-7*, Pub. by Foreign Lang CH) China Bks.

Traditional Chinese Thought: The Four Schools. Don Y. Lee. (C). 1990. 43.50 (*0-939758-17-2*) Eastern Pr.

***Traditional Christmas Carols: For Piano Solo or Duet.** Carole Flatau. Orig. Title: One or Two for Christmas. 28p. (Orig.). (J). (gr. k-5). 1997. pap. 5.95 (*0-7692-0125-3*, EL9743) Warner Brothers.

Traditional Christmas Cooking, Crafts & Gifts. DeCosse, Cy, Incorporated Staff. LC 93-50059. 320p. 1994. 32.95 (*0-86573-939-0*) Cowles Creative.

***Traditional Christmas Crafts.** Deborah Schneebeli-Morrell. LC 97-17025. 1997. write for info. (*0-8160-3719-1*) Facts on File.

***Traditional Christmas Standards.** 32p. (Orig.). 1993. pap. write for info. (*1-890281-04-2*, X093) J T Pubns.

***Traditional Christmas Two: Cooking, Crafts & Gifts.** Cowles Creative Pub. Staff. LC 97-9479. (Illus.). 320p. 1997. write for info. (*0-86573-899-8*) Cowles Creative.

Traditional Costumes of Morocco. Jean Besancenot. Tr. by Caroline Stone. 206p. 1990. 87.50 (*0-7103-0359-9*, A3922) Routledge Chapman & Hall.

Traditional, Country & Electric Slide Guitar. Arlen Roth. (Illus.). 128p. 1975. pap. 17.95 (*0-8256-0162-2*, OK62836, Oak) Music Sales.

Traditional Country Craftsmen. rev. ed. J. Geraint Jenkins. (Illus.). 1979. reprint ed. pap. 10.95 (*0-7100-0239-4*, RKP) Routledge.

Traditional Country Style. Elizabeth Wilhide. 180p. 1996. pap. 25.00 (*0-7893-0068-0*) St Martin.

Traditional Country Winemaking. Paul Turner. 1996. pap. text ed. 19.95 (*0-572-02180-1*, Pub. by W Foulsham UK) Trans-Atl Phila.

Traditional Crafts from Africa. Florence Temko. LC 95-8109. (Culture Crafts Ser.). (J). 1996. lib. bdg. 21.50 (*0-8225-2936-X*, Lerner Publctns) Lerner Group.

Traditional Crafts from Mexico & Central America. Florence Temko. LC 95-46583. (Culture Crafts Ser.). (Illus.). (J). 1996. 21.50 (*0-8225-2935-1*, Lerner Publctns) Lerner Group.

Traditional Crafts from Native North America. Florence Temko. LC 96-4973. (Culture Crafts Ser.). (Illus.). (J). 1996. 21.50 (*0-8225-2934-3*, Lerner Publctns) Lerner Group.

Traditional Crafts of Saudi Arabia. John Topham. 1983. 55.00 (*0-86685-532-7*) Intl Bk Ctr.

Traditional Crafts of Saudi Arabia. 2nd rev. ed. John Topham. (Illus.). 192p. 1988. boxed 55.00 (*0-905743-30-X*, Pub. by Stacey Intl UK) Intl Bk Ctr.

Traditional Culture & Modern Systems: Administering Primary Education in Bangladesh. Muhammad H. Hossain. LC 94-17645. 238p. 1994. 32.50 (*0-8191-9581-2*) U Pr of Amer.

Traditional Curing & Crop Fertility Rituals Among Otomi Indians of the Sierra de Puebla, Mexico: The Lopez Manuscripts. Alan R. Sandstrom. (Occasional Papers & Monographs: No. 3). (Illus.). vi, 104p. 1981. 4.00 (*0-9605982-0-0*) W H Mathers Mus.

Traditional Dancing in Scotland. T. M. Flett & J. P. Flett. (Illus.). 313p. (C). 1985. pap. text ed. 8.95 (*0-7102-0731-X*, RKP) Routledge.

Traditional Designs from India for Artists & Craftsmen. Pradumna Tana & Rosalba Tana. (Illus.). 112p. pap. 10.95 (*0-486-24129-7*) Dover.

Traditional Designs in Hardanger Embroidery. Ed. by Jules Kliot & Kaethe Kliot. 1992. 12.00 (*0-916896-41-2*) Lacis Pubns.

Traditional Designs of Armenia & the Near East. Ramona Jablonski. LC 79-15212. (International Design Library). (Illus.). 56p. (Orig.). 1979. pap. 5.95 (*0-916144-41-0*) Stemmer Hse.

Traditional Desserts. Anness Publishing Staff. (Creative Cooking Library). 1995. 12.98 (*0-8317-7409-6*) Smithmark.

Traditional Details for Building Restoration, Renovation & Rehabilitation: From the 1932-1951 Editions of Architectural Graphic Standards. Charles G. Ramsey et al. Ed. by John Hoke & Stephen Kliment. 285p. 1991. text ed. 125.00 (*0-471-52956-7*) Wiley.

***Traditional Doorways Stained Glass Pattern Book.** Carolyn Relei. LC 97-5735. 64p. 1997. pap. 6.95 (*0-486-29692-X*) Dover.

Traditional Dress. Adolf Hungrywolf. LC 90-42386. (Illus.). 80p. 1990. pap. 6.95 (*0-913990-72-8*) Book Pub Co.

Traditional Edgings to Crochet. Ed. by Rita Weiss. 48p. 1987. pap. 3.95 (*0-486-25238-8*) Dover.

Traditional Egyptian Christianity: A History of the Coptic Orthodox Church. Theodore H. Partrick. LC 96-84373. 256p. (Orig.). 1996. pap. 14.95 (*0-9652396-0-8*) Fisher Park.

Traditional Embroideries of India. Shailaja D. Naik. (C). 1996. 28.00 (*81-7024-731-4*, Pub. by Ashish II) S Asia.

Traditional English Gardens. Arabella Lennox-Boyd & Clay Perry. (Country Ser.). (Illus.). 160p. 1996. pap. 17.95 (*0-297-79368-3*, Weidenfeld) Trafalgar.

Traditional Entrance Ways. Mike Tecton. C-8. (Illus.). 64p. (Orig.). 1988. pap. write for info. (*0-318-64051-1*) M Tecton Pub.

Traditional Epics: A Literary Companion. Guida M. Jackson. (Illus.). 752p. 1996. pap. 22.50 (*0-19-510276-2*) OUP.

Traditional Ethiopian Church Education. Imbakom A. Kalewold. LC 70-93506. (Columbia University, Center for Education in Asia, Publications). 57p. reprint ed. pap. 25.00 (*0-317-41927-7*, 2026028) Bks Demand.

An Asterisk (*) at the beginning of an entry indicates that the title is appearing in BIP for the first time.

Traditional Festivals in Thailand. Ruth Gerson. (Images of Asia Ser.). (Illus.). 108p. 1996. 24.95 (967-65-3111-1) OUP.

Traditional Floral Charted Designs for Borders & Bands. Elizabeth F. Nyhan. (Needlecraft Ser.). (Illus.). 48p. (Orig.). 1991. pap. 2.95 (0-486-26696-6) Dover.

***Traditional Floral Designs.** Madeleine Orban-Szontagh. (Illus.). pap. 8.95 (0-486-26106-9) Dover.

Traditional Flower Remedies of Edward Bach: A Self Help Guide. Leslie J. Kaslof. (Good Health Guide Ser.). 32p. (Orig.). 1988. pap. 2.95 (0-87983-624-5) Keats.

***Traditional Folk Costumes Paper Dolls.** Kathy Allert. (Illus.). pap. 4.95 (0-486-24571-3) Dover.

Traditional Folksongs - Ballads of Scotland 1. Ed. by John Loesburg. 1994. 7.95 (0-946005-78-8, OS00093) Omnibus NY.

Traditional Folksongs - Ballads of Scotland 2. 1994. 7.95 (0-946005-79-6, OS00094) Omnibus NY.

Traditional Folksongs-Ballads of Scotland, No. 3. 1994. 7.95 (0-946050-80-5, OS00095) Omnibus NY.

Traditional Food East & West of the Pennienes. Ed. by C. Anne Wilson. 220p. 1992. text ed. 27.50 (0-7486-0118-X, Pub. by Edinburgh U Pr UK) Col U Pr.

Traditional Food from Scotland: The Edinburgh Book of Plain Cookery Recipes. 336p. 1996. pap. 11.95 (0-7818-0514-7) Hippocrene Bks.

***Traditional Food from Wales.** rev. ed. Bobby Freeman. LC 97-973. (Original Cookbook Ser.). (Illus.). 332p. 1997. 24.95 (0-7818-0527-9) Hippocrene Bks.

Traditional Food Technologies. Peter Fellows. 288p. (Orig.). 1996. pap. 47.50 (1-85339-228-6, Pub. by Intermed Tech UK) Women Ink.

***Traditional Foods Are Your Best Medicine: Improving Health & Longevity with Native Nutrition.** Ronald F. Schmid. LC 97-1070. 1997. write for info. (0-89281-735-6) Healing Arts.

Traditional Furniture Projects. Percy W. Blandford. 1991. 22.95 (0-8306-2159-8); pap. 12.95 (0-8306-2158-X) McGraw-Hill Prof.

Traditional Garage Plans One to Four Car - Rooms Above - 90 Plans: Collection A4. (Illus.). (Orig.). 1993. pap. 20.00 (0-922070-10-5, COLLECTION A4) M Tecton Pub.

Traditional Garden Woodwork. Peter Holland. (Illus.). 128p. 1996. pap. 16.95 (0-7063-7451-7, Pub. by Ward Lock UK) Sterling.

Traditional Grammar: A Short Summary. rev. ed. Jewell A. Friend. LC 75-30861. 32p. 1976. teacher ed. 6.95 (0-8093-0847-9) S Ill U Pr.

Traditional Hardanger Embroidery. Ed. by Priscilla Publishing Co. Staff. 32p. 1985. reprint ed. pap. 2.95 (0-486-24906-9) Dover.

Traditional Healers & Childhood in Zimbabwe. Pamela Reynolds. LC 94-47391. (Illus.). 320p. (C). 1995. text ed. 39.95 (0-8214-1121-7); pap. text ed. 17.95 (0-8214-1122-5) Ohio U Pr.

***Traditional Healer's Handbook.** Hakim Chishti. 395p. 1996. pap. 16.95 (0-614-21561-7, 1250) Kazi Pubns.

Traditional Healer's Handbook: A Classic Guide to the Medicine of Avicenna. rev. ed. Hakim G. Chishti. (Illus.). 385p. 1991. pap. 19.95 (0-89281-438-1) Inner Tradit.

Traditional History of the Chinese Script: From a Seventeenth Century Jesuit Manuscript. Knud Lundbaek. (Illus.). 64p. (C). 1988. 33.00 (87-7288-179-8, Pub. by Aarhus Univ Pr DK) David Brown.

***Traditional Holiday Ethnic Recipes.** Duane R. Lund. (Illus.). 144p. 1996. pap. write for info. (1-885061-17-X) Adventure Pubns.

Traditional Home Plans. (Design America Ser.). (Illus.). 224p. 1995. pap. 8.95 (0-934039-42-9, DA1003) Natl Plan Serv.

***Traditional Home Plans.** (Illus.). 192p. 1997. reprint ed. pap. 10.00 (0-7881-3956-8) DIANE Pub.

Traditional Home Plans, Vol. III. Jeff Spring. 1986. pap. 4.95 (0-9614407-0-8) Drafting Design.

***Traditional Home Remedies: Time-Tested Methods for Staying Well the Natural Way.** rev. ed. Martha White & Old Farmers' Almanac Editors. LC 96-52374. (Old Farmer's Almanac Home Library). (Illus.). 160p. 1997. write for info. (0-7835-4868-0) Time-Life.

Traditional Home Winemaking. Paul Turner & Ann Turner. (Illus.). 120p. 1990. pap. 14.95 (0-572-01608-5, Pub. by Foulsham UK) Assoc Pubs Grp.

Traditional Houses of Rural Britain. Matthew Rice. (Illus.). 160p. 1992. 29.95 (1-55859-338-1, Cross Riv Pr) Abbeville Pr.

Traditional Houses of Rural France. Bill Laws. (Illus.). 160p. 1991. 27.50 (1-55859-222-9) Abbeville Pr.

Traditional Houses of Rural Italy. Paul Duncan. (Illus.). 160p. 1993. 27.50 (1-55859-637-2) Abbeville Pr.

Traditional Houses of Rural Spain. Bill Laws. (Illus.). 160p. 1995. 27.50 (0-7892-0057-0) Abbeville Pr.

Traditional Hungarian Songs. limited ed. Tr. by W. D. Snodgrass from HUN. (Poetry Ser.). (Illus.). 1978. 125.00 (0-931356-01-6) Seluzicki Fine Bks.

Traditional Hyms: Illustrated Selections. Ebury Press Staff. (Illus.). 256p. 1996. 27.95 (0-8050-4843-X) H Holt & Co.

Traditional Indian Agriculture: An Annotated Bibliography. K. Vijayalakshmi. (C). 1993. 14.00 (81-224-0584-3) S Asia.

Traditional Indian Bead & Leather Crafts. Monte Smith & Michele Van Sickle. (Traditional Indian Crafts Ser.). (Illus.). 100p. (Orig.). 1987. per. 9.95 (0-943604-14-1, BOO/11) Eagles View.

Traditional Indian Crafts. Monte Smith. (Illus.). 96p. (Orig.). 1987. per. 9.95 (0-943604-13-3, BOO/10) Eagles View.

Traditional Indian Melodies for the Sitar. Harold Schram. 1969. pap. 5.00 (0-686-09077-2, 61478-930) Peer-Southrn.

Traditional Indian Textiles. John Gillow & Nicholas Barnard. LC 90-70203. (Illus.). 160p. 1993. pap. 22.50 (0-500-27709-5) Thames Hudson.

Traditional Indonesian Textiles. John Gillow. LC 92-70863. (Illus.). 160p. 1995. pap. 22.50 (0-500-27820-2) Thames Hudson.

Traditional Interpretation of the Apocalypse of St. John in the Ethiopian Orthodox Church. Roger Cowley. LC 80-19834. (University of Cambridge Oriental Publications: No. 33). 480p. 1983. 89.95 (0-521-24561-3) Cambridge U Pr.

Traditional Irish Fairy Tales. unabridged ed. James Stephens. (Illus.). 256p. 1996. reprint ed. pap. text ed. 9.95 (0-486-29166-9) Dover.

***Traditional Irish Laws.** Mary D. Daley. 1998. 10.95 (0-8118-1995-7) Chronicle Bks.

Traditional Irish Literature & Its Backgrounds: A Brief Introduction. rev. ed. George B. Saul. LC 71-120997. 115p. 1975. 23.50 (0-8387-7686-8) Bucknell U Pr.

***Traditional Islam in the Modern World.** Seyyed H. Nasr. 335p. 1996. pap. 29.00 (0-614-21451-3, 1251) Kazi Pubns.

Traditional Islam in the Modern World. Seyyed H. Nasr. 320p. 1987. text ed. 49.50 (0-7103-0177-4) Routledge Chapman & Hall.

Traditional Islam in the Modern World. Seyyed H. Nasr. 335p. 1989. pap. 29.00 (0-7103-0332-7) Routledge Chapman & Hall.

Traditional Island Knitting. Pam Dawson. Ed. by Rosalind Dace. (Illus.). 144p. 1989. pap. 19.95 (0-85532-657-3, Pub. by Search Pr UK) A Schwartz & Co.

Traditional Japan. Don Nardo. LC 94-8376. (World History Ser.). (Illus.). 128p. (J). (gr. 6-9). 1995. lib. bdg. 17.96 (1-56006-244-4) Lucent Bks.

Traditional Japanese Annual Brothel Festival. Jitsupenshva. (Asian Folklore & Social Life Monographs: No. 99). (JPN.). 1977. 14.00 (0-89986-329-9) Oriental Bk Store.

***Traditional Japanese Crest Designs.** Hornung. (Illus.). pap. 4.95 (0-486-25243-4) Dover.

Traditional Japanese Design Motifs. Illus. by Joseph D'Addetta. (Pictorial Archive Ser.). 96p. pap. 5.95 (0-486-24629-9) Dover.

Traditional Japanese Furniture. Kazuko Koizumi. Tr. by Alfred Birnbaum from JPN. LC 85-40067. (Illus.). 224p. 1986. 85.00 (0-87011-722-X) Kodansha.

Traditional Japanese Poetry: An Anthology. Tr. & Intro. by Steven D. Carter. (Illus.). 534p. 1991. 65.00 (0-8047-1562-9) Stanford U Pr.

Traditional Japanese Poetry: An Anthology. Ed. & Tr. by Steven D. Carter from JPN. (Illus.). 534p. (C). 1993. pap. 22.50 (0-8047-2212-9) Stanford U Pr.

Traditional Japanese Stencil Designs. Ed. by Clarence P. Hornung. (Pictorial Archive Ser.). 128p. 1985. pap. 6.95 (0-486-24791-0) Dover.

***Traditional Japanese Theater: An Anthology of Plays.** Karen Brazell. 1998. 49.50 (0-231-10872-9) Col U Pr.

Traditional Jewellery & Ornament of the Sudan. Clara Semple. (Illus.). 400p. 1993. 69.95 (0-7103-0242-8, A0254) Routledge Chapman & Hall.

***Traditional Jewelry of India.** Oppi Untracht. LC 96-28472. (Illus.). 432p. 1997. 85.00 (0-8109-3886-3) Abrams.

Traditional Jewish Cooking. Betty S. Goldberg. LC 93-44920. 420p. 1994. 26.95 (0-8246-0365-6) Jonathan David.

***Traditional Jewish Cooking.** Betty S. Goldberg. 1997. pap. text ed. 22.00 (0-8246-0405-9) Jonathan David.

Traditional Jewish Family in Historical Perspective. Jacob Katz. 1983. pap. 1.00 (0-87495-048-1) Am Jewish Comm.

Traditional Jewish Law of Sale: Shulhan Arukh, Hoshen Misshpat, Chapters 189-240. Joseph E. Karo. Tr. & Anno. by Stephen M. Passamaneck. LC 83-4287. (Monographs of the Hebrew Union College: No. 9). 344p. 1983. reprint ed. pap. 98.10 (0-608-02088-5, 2062741) Bks Demand.

Traditional Karate-do, Vol. 4. Morihiro Higaonna. 1990. pap. 28.00 (0-87040-848-8) Japan Pubns USA.

Traditional Karate-Do-Okinawa Goju Ryu: Performances of the Kata, Vol. 2. Morio Higaonna. (Illus.). 200p. (Orig.). 1987. pap. 28.00 (0-87040-596-9) Japan Pubns USA.

Traditional Karate-Do, Vol. 3: Applications of the Kata. Morio Higaonna. 160p. 1990. pap. 28.00 (0-87040-597-7) Japan Pubns USA.

Traditional Karatedo: Okinawa Goju-Ryu, Vol. 1. Morio Higaonna. (Fundamental Techniques Ser.). (Illus.). 200p. (Orig.). 1985. pap. 28.00 (0-87040-595-0) Japan Pubns USA.

Traditional Knitting Patterns from Scandinavia, the British Isles, France, Italy & Other European Countries. James Norbury. LC 73-79490. (Illus.). 240p. 1973. reprint ed. pap. 7.95 (0-486-21013-8) Dover.

Traditional Knowledge & Sustainable Development: Proceedings of the 1993 United Nations International Year of the World's Indigenous Peoples' Conference Held at the World Bank, Washington, D. C., September 27-28, 1993. United Nations International Year of the World's Indigenous Peoples' Conference Staff. Ed. by Shelton H. Davis et al. LC 94-48104. (Environmentally Sustainable Development Occasional Papers: No. 4). 68p. 1995. 7.95 (0-8213-3188-4, 13188) World Bank.

Traditional Korean Art. Kim Won-yong et al. Ed. by Korean National Commission for UNESCO. (Korean Art, Folklore, Language, & Thought Ser.: No. 1). (Illus.). viii, 153p. 1983. 20.00 (0-89209-014-6) Pace Intl Res.

Traditional Korean Cooking: Snacks & Basic Side Dishes, 3 vols., Vol. 3. Chin-hwa Noh. (Illus.). 64p. 1985. 16.95 (0-930878-48-5) Hollym Intl.

Traditional Korean Designs. Madeleine Orban-Szontagh. 1991. pap. 3.95 (0-486-26646-X) Dover.

Traditional Korean Music. Yi Hye-gu et al. Ed. by Korean National Commission for UNESCO. (Korean Art, Folklore, Language, & Thought Ser.: No. 3). (Illus.). viii, 228p. 1983. 20.00 (0-89209-016-2) Pace Intl Res.

Traditional Korean Painting. Ch'oe Sun-u et al. Ed. by Korean National Commission for UNESCO. (Korean Art, Folklore, Language, & Thought Ser.: No. 2). (Illus.). viii, 177p. 1983. 20.00 (0-89209-015-4) Pace Intl Res.

Traditional Korean Painting: A Lost Art Rediscovered. Zo Za-Zong & U. Fan Lee. Ed. by Suzuki & Barry. (Illus.). 176p. 1990. 65.00 (0-87011-997-4) Kodansha.

Traditional Korean Theatre. Oh-Kon Cho. LC 87-71272. (Studies in Korean Religions & Culture: Vol. 2). (Illus.). 364p. 1988. reprint ed. pap. 103.80 (0-608-01783-3, 2062441) Bks Demand.

Traditional Latin Roman Catholic Mass. Pope Pius V. Tr. by Gommar A. De Pauw from LAT. (Illus.). 98p. (Orig.). 1989. ring bd. 10.00 (0-685-25984-6) CTM Pubns.

Traditional Latin Roman Catholic Mass for the Faithful Departed. Pope Pius V. Tr. & Illus. by Gommar A. De Pauw. 78p. 1989. ring bd. 20.00 (0-685-25985-4) CTM Pubns.

Traditional Lifeways to the Southern Maori. James H. Beattie. 640p. 1994. pap. 59.95 (0-908569-79-3, Pub. by U Otago Pr NZ) Intl Spec Bk.

Traditional Literature of Cambodia: A Prelimanary Guide. Judith M. Jacob. (London Oriental Ser.; School of Oriental & African Studies Ser.: Vol. 40). 296p. (C). 1996. 52.00 (0-19-713612-5) OUP.

Traditional Literatures of the American Indian: Texts & Interpretations. Ed. by Karl Kroeber. LC 80-18338. x, 162p. 1981. pap. text ed. 10.00 (0-8032-7753-9, Bison Books) U of Nebr Pr.

Traditional Literatures of the American Indian: Texts & Interpretations. 2nd ed. Ed. by Karl Kroeber. LC 96-23682. ix, 161p. 1997. pap. 12.00 (0-8032-7782-2, Bison Books); text ed. 35.00 (0-8032-2733-7) U of Nebr Pr.

***Traditional Media for Gender Communication.** Pamela Brooke. (Illus.). 78p. (Orig.). 1996. pap. 15.00 (1-888753-06-4) PACT Pubns.

Traditional Medical Systems in East Asia. Seung-Pyo Hong. (Bibliographies in Technology & Social Change Ser.: No. 3). 44p. (Orig.). (C). 1988. pap. 6.00 (0-945271-06-9) ISU-CIKARD.

Traditional Medicine in Contemporary China. Nathan Sivin. (Science, Medicine, & Technology in East Asia Ser.: No. 2). 549p. 1987. text ed. 60.00 (0-89264-073-1) Ctr Chinese Studies.

***Traditional Metalworking in Kenya.** Jean Brown. (Oxbow Monographs in Archaeology; Cambridge Monographs in African Archaeology: Nos. 44 & 38). (Illus.). 192p. 1995. pap. 45.00 (0-946897-99-9, Pub. by Oxbow Bks UK) David Brown.

Traditional Moral Values in the Age of Technology. Hans Mark et al. (Andrew R. Cecil Lectures on Moral Values in a Free Society: Vol. VIII). 210p. 1987. text ed. 16.50 (0-292-78098-2) U of Tex Pr.

Traditional Moroccan Cooking Recipes. Z. Guinaudeau. 1996. 13.95 (1-897959-13-3, Pub. by Serif UK) LPC InBook.

Traditional Music in Ireland. Tomas Cainainn. 1994. 14.95 (0-946005-73-7, OS00048) Omnibus NY.

Traditional Music in Ireland. Tomas O'Canainn. (Illus.). 1978. pap. 13.95 (0-7100-0021-9, RKP) Routledge.

Traditional Music in Modern Java: Gamelan in Changing Society. Judith O. Becker. LC 80-19180. (Illus.). 271p. reprint ed. pap. 77.30 (0-685-23809-1, 2032916) Bks Demand.

Traditional Music of America. Ira W. Ford. LC 78-2026. (Music Reprint Ser.: 1978). 1978. reprint ed. lib. bdg. 49.50 (0-306-77588-3) Da Capo.

Traditional Music of the Lao: Kaen Playing & Mawlum Singing in Northeast Thailand. Terry E. Miller. LC 84-22538. (Contributions in Intercultural & Comparative Studies: No. 13). xv, 333p. 1985. text ed. 69.50 (0-313-24765-X, MKP/, Greenwood Pr) Greenwood.

Traditional Narratives of the Arikara Indians, 2 vols. Douglas R. Parks. LC 90-12889. (Studies in the Anthropology of North American Indians). 1991. audio 20.00 (0-8032-3697-2) U of Nebr Pr.

Traditional Narratives of the Arikara Indians, 2 vols., Set. Douglas R. Parks. LC 90-12889. (Studies in the Anthropology of North American Indians). (Illus.). 1991. text ed. 125.00 (0-8032-3698-0) U of Nebr Pr.

Traditional Narratives of the Arikara Indians, 2 vols., Vol. 2: Stories of Other Narrators. Douglas R. Parks. LC 90-12889. (Studies in the Anthropology of North American Indians). xiv, 659p. 1991. text ed. 70.00 (0-8032-3692-1) U of Nebr Pr.

Traditional Narratives of the Arikara Indians, 2 vols., Vol. 3: Stories of Alfred Morsette. Douglas R. Parks. LC 90-12889. (Studies in the Anthropology of North American Indians). (Illus.). xxvi, 468p. 1991. text ed. 40.00 (0-8032-3694-8) U of Nebr Pr.

Traditional Narratives of the Arikara Indians, 2 vols., Vol. 4: Stories of Other Narrators. Douglas R. Parks. LC 90-12889. (Studies in the Anthropology of North American Indians). (Illus.). xvii, 431p. 1991. text ed. 40.00 (0-8032-3695-6) U of Nebr Pr.

Traditional Narratives of the Arikara Indians: English Translations, 2 vols., Set. Douglas R. Parks. LC 90-12889. (Studies in the Anthropology of North American Indians). 1992. text ed. 75.00 (0-8032-3696-4) U of Nebr Pr.

Traditional Narratives of the Arikara Indians: English Translations, 2 vols., Vol. 1: Stories of Alfred Morsette. Douglas R. Parks. LC 90-12889. (Studies in the Anthropology of North American Indians). xxiv, 684p. 1991. text ed. 70.00 (0-8032-3691-3) U of Nebr Pr.

Traditional Native American Healing & Child Sexual Abuse. Ed. by David W. Lloyd. 62p. (Orig.). (C). 1994. pap. text ed. 30.00 (0-7881-1306-2) DIANE Pub.

Traditional Ninja Weapons & Ninjutsu Techniques. Charles Daniel. LC 85-52270. 147p. (Orig.). 1986. pap. 7.95 (0-86568-075-2, 108) Unique Pubns.

Traditional Ninjutsu. Bo F. Munthe. pap. 18.95 (0-901764-95-7, 93225) Talman.

Traditional Ojibwa Religion & Its Historical Changes. Christopher Vecsey. LC 83-72209. (American Philosophical Society, Memoirs Ser.: No. 152). (Illus.). 244p. reprint ed. pap. 69.60 (0-7837-4332-7, 2044043) Bks Demand.

Traditional Oral Epic: "Beowulf", the "Odyssey" & the Serbo-Croatian Return Song. John M. Foley. LC 88-29596. 680p. 1990. 65.00 (0-520-06409-7); pap. 17.00 (0-520-08436-5) U CA Pr.

Traditional Papermaking & Paper Cult Figures of Mexico. Alan R. Sandstrom & Pamela E. Sandstrom. LC 85-40947. (Illus.). 336p. 1986. 29.95 (0-8061-1972-1) U of Okla Pr.

Traditional Patchwork Patterns: Full-Size Cut-Outs & Instructions for 12 Quilts. Carol B. Grafton. (Illus.). 64p. (Orig.). 1974. pap. 4.95 (0-486-23015-5) Dover.

***Traditional Peoples & Biodiversity: Conservation in Large Tropical Landscapes.** Ed. by Kent H. Redford & Jane A. Mansour. (Illus.). 267p. (Orig.). (C). 1996. pap. text ed. 19.95 (1-886765-02-2, America Verde) Nature VA.

Traditional Performance of South Kamrup. Dhaneswar Kalita. (C). 1991. 14.00 (81-212-0335-X, Pub. by Gian Publng Hse II) S Asia.

Traditional Performing Arts. Varsha Das. (C). 1992. 15.00 (81-224-0407-3) S Asia.

Traditional Plant Foods of Canadian Indigenous Peoples: Nutrition, Botany & Use, Vol. 8. Harriet V. Kuhnlein. (Food & Nutrition in History & Anthro Ser.). 633p. 1991. text ed. 118.00 (2-88124-465-3) Gordon & Breach.

Traditional Politics & Regime Change in Brazil. Frances Hagopian. (Studies in Comparative Politics). (Illus.). 384p. (C). 1996. text ed. 64.95 (0-521-41429-6) Cambridge U Pr.

***Traditional Portuguese Recipes from Provincetown.** 2nd rev. ed. Mary A. Cook. Ed. by Gillian Drake. LC 97-40526. (Illus.). 96p. 1997. 9.50 (0-9609814-3-8) Shank Painter Pub.

Traditional Potter in Nineteenth-Century Illinois: Archaeological Investigations at Two Kiln Sites in Upper Alton. John A. Walthall et al. (Reports of Investigations Ser.: No. 46). 68p. 1991. pap. 8.00 (0-89792-131-3) Ill St Museum.

Traditional Potters of Seagrove, North Carolina: And Surrounding Areas from the 1800s to the Present. Robert C. Lock. (Illus.). 224p. 1994. 34.95 (0-9641247-0-X) Antiques & Collect.

Traditional Pottery of Alabama. E. Henry Willett & Joey Brackner. Ed. by Margaret L. Ausfeld. LC 83-11409. (Illus.). 70p. (ps-12). 1983. pap. 10.00 (0-89280-020-8) Montgomery Mus.

Traditional Pottery Techniques of Pakistan: Field & Laboratory Studies. Owen S. Rye & Clifford Evans. LC 75-619168. (Smithsonian Contributions to Anthropology Ser.: no. 21). 301p. reprint ed. pap. 85.80 (0-317-28428-2, 2020314) Bks Demand.

Traditional Prayer in the Psalms - & Literarische Studien zur Josephsgeschichte. Aejmelaeus & Schmidt. (Beiheft zur Zeitschrift fuer die Alttestamentliche Wissenschaft Ser.: Vol. 167). vi, 310p. (C). 1986. lib. bdg. 126.95 (3-11-010480-6) De Gruyter.

Traditional Prayerbook for Shabbath & Festivals. rev. ed. Ed. by Rabbinical Council of America. Tr. by David De Sola Poole. 879p. 1960. 15.00 (0-87441-118-1) Behrman.

***Traditional Psychoethics & Personality Paradigm, God's Will Be Done, Vol. I.** Laleh Bakhtiar. 174p. 1996. pap. 19.95 (0-614-21562-5, 348) Kazi Pubns.

Traditional Quest. D. Cohn-Sherbok. 60.00 (1-85075-279-6, Pub. by Sheffield Acad UK) CUP Services.

***Traditional Quilts: A Book of Postcards.** Ed. by Sally Schneider. (Illus.). 64p. (Orig.). 1997. pap. 9.95 (1-56477-199-7, PC100) That Patchwork.

***Traditional Quilts: Today's Techniques.** Debra Wagner. LC 96-29945. 1997. write for info. (0-8019-8660-5) Chilton.

Traditional Quilts II. Sharon Hultgren. 64p. 14.95 (1-881588-25-4) EZ Quilting.

***Traditional Quilts with Painless Borders.** Sally Schneider & Barbara Eikmeier. Ed. by Janet White. (Illus.). 72p. (Orig.). 1997. pap. 17.95 (1-56477-203-9, B315) That Patchwork.

***Traditional Recipes of Laos.** 2nd ed. Phia Sing. Ed. by Alan Davison. Tr. by Phouangphet Vannithone & Boon S. Klausner. (Illus.). 192p. 1995. pap. 18.50 (0-907325-60-2, Pub. by Prospect UK) Food Words.

Traditional Recipes of Old England. 128p. 1996. pap. 9.95 (0-7818-0489-2) Hippocrene Bks.

Traditional Religion & Guerrilla Warfare in Modern Africa. Stephen L. Weigert. 1996. text ed. 49.95 (0-312-12715-4) St Martin.

Traditional Samoan Music. Richard Moyle. (Illus.). 288p. 1989. 65.00 (1-86940-027-5) OUP.

Traditional Santa Carving with Tom Wolfe. Tom Wolfe & Douglas Congdon-Martin. LC 91-61156. (Illus.). 64p. (Orig.). 1991. pap. 12.95 (0-88740-366-2) Schiffer.

Traditional Sculpture from Upper Volta. (Illus.). (Orig.). 1979. 3.00 (0-686-27122-X) Mus African Art.

Traditional Silk & Metal Thread Techniques on Canvas. Jane D. Zimmerman. 206p. 1995. pap. text ed. 37.95 (*0-9646219-0-8*) J D Zimmerman.

***Traditional Songs from Latin America.** Ed. by Debbie Cavalier. 28p. (Orig.). 1995. pap. text ed. 5.95 (*0-89724-671-3*, AF9526) Warner Brothers.

***Traditional Songs of Singing Cultures.** Warner Brothers Staff. 1997. pap. text ed. 19.95 (*1-57623-859-8*, BMR051523CD) Warner Brothers.

Traditional Songs of the Maori. Mervyn McLean & Margaret Orbell. 324p. 1990. 27.95 (*1-86940-048-8*, Pub. by Auckland Univ NZ) Paul & Co Pubs.

Traditional South African Cookery. Hildegonda Duckitt. 184p. 1996. pap. 10.95 (*0-7818-0490-6*) Hippocrene Bks.

Traditional Stables & Barns: Collection A100. (Illus.). (Orig.). 1994. pap. 25.00 (*0-922070-06-7*, COLLECTION A100) M Tecton Pub.

Traditional Stained Glass Patterns. Ed Sibbett, Jr. 1988. pap. 4.95 (*0-486-25794-0*) Dover.

Traditional Stories & Foods: An American Indian Remembers. Joan L. Woodruff. Ed. by Yoly Zentella. (Illus.). 60p. (Orig.). 1991. pap. 10.95 (*0-943557-02-X*) Esoterica Pr.

Traditional Tatting Patterns. Rita Weiss. 48p. (Orig.). 1986. pap. 2.95 (*0-486-25066-0*) Dover.

Traditional Technological Structures & Cultures of the Pacific 5 Papers: From the Symposium Technology & Cultural Change in the Pacific, XVII Pacific Science Congress Honolulu, Hawaii, May 27-June 2, 1991. Ed. by Rebecca A. Stephenson et al. (Educational Ser.: No. 18). 87p. 1994. pap. 10.00 (*1-878453-19-X*) Univ Guam MAR Ctr.

Traditional Textiles of Central Asia. Janet Harvey. LC 95-60479. (Illus.). 160p. 1996. 40.00 (*0-500-01670-4*) Thames Hudson.

Traditional Textiles of Central Asia. Janet Harvey. LC 95-60479. (Illus.). 160p. 1997. reprint ed. pap. 24.95 (*0-500-27875-X*) Thames Hudson.

***Traditional Textiles of the Andes: Life & Cloth in the Highlands.** Ed. by Lynn A. Meisch. LC 97-60320. 144p. (Orig.). 1997. pap. 24.95 (*0-500-27985-3*) Thames Hudson.

Traditional Textiles of Tunisia & Related North African Weaving. Irmtraud Reswick. (Illus.). 272p. 1985. pap. 24.95 (*0-295-96281-X*) U of Wash Pr.

Traditional Textiles of West Timor: Regional Variations in Historical Perspective. Mark I. Jacobson & Ruth M. Yeager. 178p. 1995. pap. text ed. 20.00 (*0-9635296-0-9*) Batuan Biru Prods.

Traditional Textiles of West Timor: Regional Variations in Historical Perspective. 2nd rev. ed. Ruth M. Yeager & Mark I. Jacobson. 200p. 1996. pap. text ed. 20.00 (*0-9635296-1-7*) Batuan Biru Prods.

Traditional Theism & Its Modern Alternatives. Ed. by Svend Andersen. (Acta Jutlandica Ser.: Vol. 70:1). 240p. (Orig.). (C). 1994. pap. 27.00 (*87-7288-482-7*, Pub. by Aarhus Univ Pr DK) David Brown.

Traditional Theory of Literature. Ray F. Livingston. LC 62-10830. 198p. reprint ed. pap. 56.50 (*0-317-41714-2*, 2055889) Bks Demand.

***Traditional Thoughts & Practices in Korea.** Ed. by Eui-Young Yu & Earl H. Phillips. 183p. 1983. pap. 15.00 (*0-8420-2224-4*) Scholarly Res Inc.

Traditional Ties: Cultural Awareness & Listening Skills. S. Begin et al. 112p. 1992. pap. text ed. 13.50 (*0-8013-0816-X*, 78878); audio 37.95 (*0-8013-0922-0*, 78884); audio 46.50 (*0-8013-0817-8*, 79184) Longman.

Traditional Tole Painting: With Authentic Antique Designs & Working Diagrams for Stenciling & Brush-Stroke Painting. Roberta R. Blanchard. LC 77-78208. (Illus.). 1977. reprint ed. pap. 5.95 (*0-486-23531-9*) Dover.

Traditional Tole Painting, with Authentic Antique Designs & Working Diagrams for Stenciling & Brush-Stroke Painting. Roberta R. Blanchard. 1990. 20.25 (*0-8446-5559-7*) Peter Smith.

Traditional Tunes of the Child Ballads: With Their Texts According to the Extant Records of Great Britain & America, Vol. 1. Bertrand H. Bronson. LC 57-5468. 503p. 1959. reprint ed. pap. 143.40 (*0-608-02231-4*, 2011482) Bks Demand.

Traditional Tunes of the Child Ballads: With Their Texts According to the Extant Records of Great Britain & America, Vol. 2. Bertrand H. Bronson. LC 57-5468. 585p. 1959. reprint ed. pap. 165.80 (*0-608-02232-2*, 2011482) Bks Demand.

***Traditional Values in Action Resource Directory, 1997-1998.** 2nd rev. ed. Ed. by Robert W. Klous. 1044p. 1996. 49.95 (*0-9647443-1-7*) Chrst Values.

Traditional Vegetarian Cooking: Recipes from Europe's Famous Cranks Restaurants. David Canter et al. (Illus.). 192p. 1991. reprint ed. pap. 14.95 (*0-89281-425-X*, Heal Arts VT) Inner Tradit.

Traditional Victorian White Work to Knit & Crochet for the Home. Shelagh Hollingsworth. (Illus.). 128p. 1988. pap. 12.95 (*0-312-01253-5*) St Martin.

***Traditional Welsh Cookery.** Geoffrey O. Taylor. 1997. pap. text ed. 1.95 (*0-7090-5968-X*, Hale-Parkwest) Parkwest Pubns.

Traditional Wicca. Keith Morgan. (Orig.). 1994. pap. 7.95 (*1-872189-25-3*, Pub. by Mandrake Pr UK) Holmes Pub.

Traditional Windsor Chair Making with Jim Rendi. Douglas Congdon-Martin. LC 93-83051. (Illus.). 128p. (Orig.). 1993. pap. 19.95 (*0-88740-503-7*) Schiffer.

***Traditional Wisdom for Heart Care.** H. S. Wasir. (C). 1995. 7.00 (*0-7069-9739-5*, Pub. by Vikas II) S Asia.

Traditional Woodland Crafts. Raymond Tabor. (Illus.). 160p. 1994. pap. 34.95 (*0-7134-7500-5*, Pub. by Batsford UK) Trafalgar.

***Traditional Woodwork.** Mario Rodriguez. (Illus.). 192p. 1998. 28.95 (*1-56158-176-3*, 070303) Taunton.

***Traditional World Music Influences in Contemporary Solo Piano Literature: A Selected Bibliographic Survey & Review.** Elizabeth C. Axford. LC 97-19901. 1997. write for info. (*0-8108-3380-8*) Scarecrow.

Traditionalism, Nationalism, & Feminism: Women Writers of Quebec. Ed. by Paula G. Lewis. LC 84-10854. (Contributions in Women's Studies: No. 53). (Illus.). xli, 280p. 1985. text ed. 59.95 (*0-313-24510-X*, LTF/, Greenwood Pr) Greenwood.

Traditionalism vs Modernism at Death: Allegorical Tales of Africa. John E. Njoku. LC 88-14075. (African Studies: Vol. 11). 150p. 1989. lib. bdg. 69.95 (*0-88946-188-0*) E Mellen.

Traditionalists & Revivalists in Jazz. Chip Deffaa. LC 93-1875. (Studies in Jazz: No. 16). (Illus.). 401p. 1993. Acid-free paper. 42.50 (*0-8108-2704-2*) Scarecrow.

Traditionality & Genre in Middle English Romance. Carol Fewster. 176p. 1987. 70.00 (*0-85991-229-9*) Boydell & Brewer.

Traditionally Yours. Gail Kelley. LC 86-43230. 184p. 1987. pap. text ed. 8.95 (*0-89390-103-2*) Resource Pubns.

Traditionary Anecdotes of Shakespeare. John Dowdall. Ed. by J. Payne Collier. LC 70-164782. reprint ed. 37.50 (*0-404-02165-4*) AMS Pr.

***Traditionellen Gesange Des Israelitischen Gottesdienstes In Deutschland.** Jakob Schonberg. xi, 94p. (GER.). 1971. reprint ed. write for info. (*3-487-04065-4*) G Olms Pubs.

Traditioneller Stoff und Individuelle Gestaltung, Untersuchungen Zu Alkaios und Sappho. Dirk Meyerhoff. (Beitrage Zur Altertumswissenschaft Ser.: Band 3). viii, 264p. (GER.). 1984. write for info. (*3-487-07463-X*) G Olms Pubs.

Traditions. Asante. 1997. 40.00 (*0-02-503511-8*, Free Press) Free Pr.

Traditions. Shirley Greenslade. 50p. 1997. pap. write for info. (*1-886799-06-7*) Agape Word.

Traditions. Tina Salser. 230p. 1992. 13.95 (*0-929271-01-7*) D Gibson.

Traditions: A Tribute to Wedding Cake Decorating. Raymond Lippert & Richard A. Segal, Jr. (Orig.). 1990. write for info. (*0-9627704-0-X*) Bakery Crafts.

Traditions: Beadwork of the Native American. Lynn Harrison. 20p. 1990. pap. 9.95 (*0-910524-17-3*) Eastern Wash.

Traditions: Healthy Home Cooking. Barbara J. Kobsar. LC 90-91871. (Illus.). 175p. (Orig.). 1990. pap. 14.95 (*0-9619459-1-5*) Cottage Kitchen.

***Tradition(s) Refiguring Community & Virtue in Classical German Thought.** Stephen H. Watson. LC 97-1225. (Studies in Continental Thought). 1997. write for info. (*0-253-33328-8*); pap. write for info. (*0-253-21152-2*) Ind U Pr.

Traditions & Innovations. 1990. 42.50 (*0-87413-355-6*) U Delaware Pr.

Traditions & Innovations: Essays on British Literature of the Middle Ages & the Renaissance. Ed. by David G. Allen & Robert A. White. LC 88-40599. (Illus.). 272p. 1990. 39.50 (*0-685-32622-5*) Bucknell U Pr.

Traditions & Innovations: Essays on British Literature of the Middle Ages & the Renaissance. Ed. by David G. Allen & Robert A. White. LC 88-40599. (Illus.). 272p. 1990. 39.50 (*0-685-31211-9*) Susquehanna U Pr.

Traditions & Innovations: Essays on British Literature of the Middle Ages & the Renaissance. Ed. by David G. Allen & Robert A. White. LC 88-40599. (Illus.). 272p. 1990. 39.50 (*0-685-31249-6*) U Delaware Pr.

Traditions & Memories of American Yachting: The Fiftieth Anniversary Edition. William P. Stephens. (Illus.). 456p. 1989. 49.95 (*0-937822-20-5*) McGraw-Hill Prof.

Traditions & Present Problems of Czech Political Culture: Czech Philosophical Studies, I. Ed. by Michael Vejrazka & Milosav Bednar. LC 93-11930. (Cultural Heritage & Contemporary Change Series VI: Foundations of Moral Education.: Vol. IVA,3). 250p. (Orig.). 1994. 45.00 (*1-56518-056-9*); pap. 17.50 (*1-56518-057-7*) Coun Res Values.

Traditions & Records of Southwest Harbor & Somesville, Mt. Desert Island, Maine. Seth S. Thornton. (Illus.). 346p. 1994. reprint ed. lib. bdg. 39.00 (*0-8328-4359-8*) Higginson Bk Co.

Traditions & Reminiscences of Concord, Massachusetts, 1779-1878. Edward Jarvis. Ed. by Sarah Chapin. LC 93-20179. (Illus.). 304p. (C). 1993. Alk. paper. lib. bdg. 35.00 (*0-87023-849-3*) U of Mass Pr.

Traditions & Superstitions of the New Zealanders. 2nd ed. Edward Shortland. LC 75-35270. reprint ed. 55.00 (*0-404-14439-X*) AMS Pr.

Traditions & Trends in Indian Music. V. Agarwal. 82p. 1975. 7.95 (*0-318-36333-X*) Asia Bk Corp.

Traditions & Values: American Diplomacy, 1790-1865. Ed. by Norman A. Graebner & Kenneth W. Thompson. LC 85-7334. (American Values Projected Abroad Ser.: Vol. VII). 192p. (Orig.). 1985. pap. text ed. 19.50 (*0-8191-4389-8*) U Pr of Amer.

Traditions & Values: American Diplomacy, 1945 to the Present. Kenneth W. Thompson. LC 84-13146. (American Values Projected Abroad Ser.: Vol. 9). 1984. pap. 24.00 (*0-8191-4154-2*) U Pr of Amer.

Traditions & Values in Politics & Diplomacy: Theory & Practice. Kenneth W. Thompson. LC 91-39876. (Political Traditions in Foreign Policy Ser.). 456p. (C). 1992. text ed. 55.00 (*0-8071-1742-0*); pap. text ed. 18.95 (*0-8071-1746-3*) La State U Pr.

Traditions in American Basketry. Barbara Beckos. (Illus.). 11p. 1977. 10.00 (*0-685-70735-0*) Gal Assn NY.

Traditions in American Literature. Joseph E. Mersand. (BCL1-PS American Literature Ser.). 247p. 1993. reprint ed. lib. bdg. 79.00 (*0-7812-6566-5*) Rprt Serv.

Traditions in Mysticism. M. P. Pandit. 1987. text ed. 45.00 (*81-207-0669-2*, Pub. by Sterling Pubs II) Apt Bks.

Traditions in New Freedom: Studying Religion in Russian & Ukrainian Higher Education Today. Jonathan Sutton. 1996. 24.95 (*0-9517853-7-0*, Pub. by Drake Intl Serv UK) Intl Spec Bk.

Traditions in Occultism. N. P. Pandit. 108p. 1987. text ed. 15.95 (*81-207-0660-9*, Pub. by Sterling Pubs II) Apt Bks.

Traditions in Transformation: Turning Points in Biblical Faith. Ed. by Baruch Halpern & Jon D. Levenson. LC 80-29112. xiv, 446p. 1981. 39.50 (*0-931464-06-4*) Eisenbrauns.

Traditions in Transition: Jewish Culture in Philadelphia, 1840-1940. (Illus.). 16.00 (*0-614-14843-X*) Balch Inst Ethnic Studies.

Traditions in Transition: Jewish Culture in Philadelphia 1840-1940. Intro. by Gail F. Stern. LC 89-60258. (Illus.). 134p. (Orig.). (C). 1989. pap. text ed. 20.00 (*0-937437-06-9*) Balch IES Pr.

Traditions, Myths & Memories, 1693-1993: Celebrating the Tercentenary of the College of William & Mary in Virginia. W. Wilford Kale. Ed. by S. Dean Olson et al. (Illus.). 84p. 1992. 35.00 (*0-9615670-2-3*, King & Queen Pr) Soc Alu Wm.

Traditions of African Education. Intro. & Notes by David G. Scanlon. LC 64-12575. (Classics in Education Ser.: No. 16). 195p. (Orig.). reprint ed. pap. 55.60 (*0-8357-3035-2*, 2039282) Bks Demand.

Traditions of Asian Art. Michael Brand. LC 95-61181. (Illus.). 96p. (Orig.). 1996. pap. 19.95 (*0-500-97432-2*) Thames Hudson.

Traditions of Belief in Late Byzantine Demonology. Richard P. Greenfield. lxxxvi, 369p. 1988. pap. 98.00 (*90-256-0962-7*, Pub. by A M Hakkert NE) Benjamins North Am.

Traditions of Bread & Violence. Catherine Sasanov. LC 95-61373. (Stahlecker Ser.). 64p. 1996. pap. 12.95 (*1-884800-09-2*) Four Way Bks.

Traditions of Eleazar Ben Azariah. Tzvee Zahavy. LC 76-46373. (Brown Judaic Studies: No. 2). 381p. reprint ed. pap. 108.60 (*0-7837-5435-3*, 2045200) Bks Demand.

***Traditions of Essay, Vol. 1.** Atwan Mcquade. Date not set. pap. text ed. write for info. (*0-312-02016-3*) St Martin.

Traditions of Experiment from the Enlightenment to the Present: Essays in Honor of Peter Demetz. Ed. by Nancy Kaiser & David E. Wellbery. LC 92-27453. 350p. (C). 1992. text ed. 57.50 (*0-472-10309-1*) U of Mich Pr.

Traditions of Freemasonry & Its Coincidences with the Ancient Mysteries. A. T. Pierson. 384p. 1996. reprint ed. pap. 27.00 (*1-56459-534-X*) Kessinger Pub.

Traditions of Glastonbury. E. Raymond Capt. LC 82-72525. (Illus.). 128p. (Orig.). 1983. pap. 6.00 (*0-934666-10-5*) Artisan Sales.

Traditions of Honor. Dave Hollis & Dotty Hollis. Ed. by Mary S. Woodburn. 297p. (Orig.). (YA). (gr. 8-12). 1994. pap. 12.95 (*0-9640894-1-6*) BPCOA.

Traditions of Igbo Origin: A Study of Pre-Colonial Population Movements in Africa. rev. ed. John N. Oriji. LC 93-43268. (Am. Univ. Studies, XI: Vol. 48). 234p. (C). 1994. pap. text ed. 24.95 (*0-8204-2481-1*) P Lang Pubng.

Traditions of International Ethics. Ed. by Terry Nardin & David R. Mapel. (Studies in International Relations: No. 17). 342p. (C). 1993. pap. text ed. 19.95 (*0-521-45757-2*) Cambridge U Pr.

Traditions of Islam. Alfred Guillaume. LC 79-52552. (Islam Ser.). 1980. reprint ed. lib. bdg. 22.95 (*0-8369-9260-1*) Ayer.

Traditions of Meditation in Chinese Buddhism. Ed. by Peter N. Gregory. LC 86-19243. (Studies in East Asian Buddhism: No. 4). 272p. 1986. pap. text ed. 18.00 (*0-8248-1088-0*) UH Pr.

***Traditions of Men Versus the Word of God.** Alvin Jennings. (Orig.). 1979. pap. 4.95 (*0-933672-37-3*, C-1049) Star Bible.

***Traditions of Origin & Their Interpretation: The Mijikenda of Kenya.** Thomas T. Spear. LC 81-22325. (Papers in International Studies: No. 42). 176p. reprint ed. pap. 50.20 (*0-608-04104-1*, 2064836) Bks Demand.

Traditions of Spiritual Guidance: Spiritual Direction in the Tradition Collected from "The Way" Lavinia Byrne. 213p. (Orig.). 1991. pap. 11.95 (*0-8146-2005-1*) Liturgical Pr.

Traditions of the Arapaho. G. A. Dorsey & A. L. Kroeber. (Chicago Field Museum of Natural History Fieldiana Anthropology Ser.: Vol. 5). 1903. 55.00 (*0-527-01865-1*) Periodicals Srv.

***Traditions of the Arapaho.** George A. Dorsey & Alfred L. Kroeber. (Sources of American Indian Oral Literature Ser.). 496p. 1997. pap. text ed. 19.95 (*0-8032-6608-1*) U of Nebr Pr.

Traditions of the Arapaho: Collected under the Auspices of the Field Columbian Museum & of the American Museum of Natural History. George A. Dorsey & Alfred L. Kroeber. LC 04-12211. (Field Columbian Museum, Publication 81, Anthropological Ser.: Vol. 5). 485p. 1903. reprint ed. pap. 138.30 (*0-608-02120-2*, 2062769) Bks Demand.

***Traditions of the Caddo.** George A. Dorsey. (Sources of American Indian Oral Literature Ser.). 152p. 1997. pap. text ed. 8.95 (*0-8032-6602-2*) U of Nebr Pr.

Traditions of the Caddo. George A. Dorsey. LC 74-7956. reprint ed. 29.50 (*0-404-11845-3*) AMS Pr.

Traditions of the Chilcotin Indians. Livingston Farrand. LC 73-3516. (Jesup North Pacific Expedition. Publications: Vol. 2, Pt. 1). reprint ed. 32.50 (*0-404-58102-1*) AMS Pr.

Traditions of the Earliest Visits of Foreigners to North America. Reuben T. Durrett. (Notable American Authors Ser.). 1992. reprint ed. lib. bdg. 75.00 (*0-7812-2726-7*) Rprt Serv.

Traditions of the Hopi: The Stanley McCormic Hopi Expedition. Tr. by Henry R. Voth. LC 74-9014. reprint ed. 39.00 (*0-404-11911-5*) AMS Pr.

Traditions of the Land: The History of Gregg County, Texas. Eugene W. McWhorter. LC 89-80785. (Illus.). 128p. (C). 1989. 29.95 (*0-9623844-0-2*) Gregg Cty Hist Found.

***Traditions of the Magi: Zoroastrianism in Greek & Latin Literature.** Albert D. Jong. LC 97-14806. (Religions in the Greco-Roman World Ser.). 1997. write for info. (*90-04-10844-0*) E J Brill.

Traditions of the North American Indians, 3 vols. J. A. Jones. 1972. 300.00 (*0-8490-1224-4*) Gordon Pr.

Traditions of the Osage. George A. Dorsey. LC 74-7957. reprint ed. 29.50 (*0-404-11846-1*) AMS Pr.

***Traditions of the Osage.** George A. Dorsey. LC 04-12210. (Field Columbian Museum Anthropological Ser.: Vol. 7, No. 1). 60p. 1904. reprint ed. pap. 25.00 (*0-608-02696-4*, 2063349) Bks Demand.

Traditions of the Prophet, Vol. 1. Javad Nurbakhsh & Leonard Lewisehn. Ed. by Jeffrey Rothschild et al. Tr. by Ali-Reza Nurbakhsh. 101p. (ARA, ENG & PER.). 1981. reprint ed. pap. 0.95 (*0-933546-06-8*) KNP.

Traditions of the Prophet, Vol. 2. Javad Nurbakhsh. Tr. by Leonard Lewisohn & Terry Graham. 96p. (ARA, ENG & PER.). 1983. pap. 0.95 (*0-933546-10-6*) KNP.

Traditions of the Quinault Indians. Livingston Farrand & W. S. Kahnweiler. LC 73-3518. (Jesup North Pacific Expedition. Publications: Vol. 2, Pt. 3). reprint ed. 37.50 (*0-404-58119-6*) AMS Pr.

Traditions of the Tinguian. Fay C. Cole. LC 78-67698. (Folktale Ser.). reprint ed. 22.50 (*0-404-16069-7*) AMS Pr.

***Traditions of the Tinguian: A Study in Philippine Folklore. The R. F. Cummings Philippine Expedition.** Fay-Cooper Cole. LC 15-8602. (Field Museum of Natural History Anthropological Ser.: Vol. 14, No. 1). 226p. 1915. reprint ed. pap. 64.50 (*0-608-02707-3*, 2063372) Bks Demand.

Traditions of the Tinguian, a Study in Philippine Folk-Lore: The Tinguian Social Religious & Economic Life of a Philippine Tribe. F. C. Cole. (Chicago Field Museum of Natural History Fieldiana Anthropology Ser.: Vol. 14). 1974. reprint ed. 60.00 (*0-527-01874-0*) Periodicals Srv.

Traditions, Superstitions, & Folk-Lore: Chiefly Lancashire & the North of England: Their Affinity to Others in Widely-Distributed Localities: Their Eastern Origin & Mythical Significance. Charles Hardwick. Ed. by Richard M. Dorson. LC 80-794. (Folklore of the World Ser.). 1981. reprint ed. lib. bdg. 31.95 (*0-405-13333-2*) Ayer.

Traditions, Voices, & Dreams: The American Novel since the 1960s. Ed. by Melvin J. Friedman & Ben Siegel. LC 94-44373. 336p. 1995. 47.50 (*0-87413-556-7*) U Delaware Pr.

Traduccion e Interpretacion: Cuaderno de Ejercicios. Mary F. Ayala. 98p. (C). 1994. 20.00 (*1-881604-14-4*) Scopcraeft.

Traduccion, Escritura y Violencia Colonizadora: Un Estudio de la Obra del Inca Garcilaso. Susana Jafalvi-Leiva. (Foreign & Comparative Studies Program, Latin American Ser.: No. 7). (Orig.). (SPA.). (C). 1984. pap. text ed. 6.00 (*0-915984-98-9*) Syracuse U Foreign Comp.

Traducciones de Shakespeare en Espana: El Ejemplo de Othello. Esther V. Ros. (Coleccion Interdisciplinar: No. 2). (Illus.). 302p. (SPA.). (C). 1988. lib. bdg. 25.00 (*0-937509-03-5*) Edit Arcos.

Traducteur Huguenot: Peirre Coste. Margaret E. Rumbold. LC 90-34363. (American University Studies: Romance Languages & Literature: Ser. II, Vol. 140). 190p. (C). 1990. text ed. 36.95 (*0-8204-1270-8*) P Lang Pubng.

Traduction: Theorie et Methode. Charles R. Taber & Eugene A. Nida. 1971. pap. 10.00 (*0-8267-0022-5*, 103907, Pub. by United Bible GW) Am Bible.

Traduction Scientifique et Technique. 2nd ed. J. Maillot. 280p. (FRE.). 1981. 49.95 (*0-8288-2105-4*, M14402) Fr & Eur.

Traductions de Jacob Bohme, 4 vols., Set. Louis-Claude De Saint-Martin. Ed. by Robert Amadou. reprint ed. write for info. (*0-318-71412-4*) G Olms Pubs.

Traductions de Jacob Bohme, 4 vols., Vol. V. Louis-Claude De Saint-Martin. Ed. by Robert Amadou. reprint ed. Vol. 1: Quarante Questions, 1807, viii, 486p. write for info. (*0-318-71413-2*); reprint ed. Vol. 2: De la Triple Vie, 1809, viii, 552p. write for info. (*0-318-71414-0*); reprint ed. Vol. 3: L'Aurore Naissante, 1800, 608p. write for info. (*0-318-71415-9*); reprint ed. Vol. 4: Des Trois Principes, 1802, xxii, 758p. write for info. (*0-318-71416-7*) G Olms Pubs.

Traduire l'Anglais. Henri Van Hoof. 216p. (ENG & FRE.). 1989. lib. bdg. 45.00 (*0-8288-3358-3*) Fr & Eur.

Tradution. unabridged ed. Ann Erickson. (Modern Poetry in English Ser.: No. 45). (Illus.). 36p. (Orig.). 1995. pap. 5.00 (*1-879457-48-2*) Norton Coker Pr.

***Trae Tus Panes y Peces al Senor.** Judith K. Kristy & Modesto Espinoza. 60p. (SPA.). pap. 7.95 (*0-88177-189-9*, DR189) Discipleship Res.

Trafalgar. Richard Balkwill. LC 93-2650. (Great Battles & Sieges Ser.). (Illus.). 32p. (YA). (gr. 6 up). 1993. lib. bdg. 13.95 (*0-02-726326-6*, New Dscvry Bks) Silver Burdett Pr.

Trafalgar: Countdown to Battle. Alan Schom. 448p. 1992. 15.95 (*0-19-507518-8*) OUP.

***Trafalgar: The Nelson Touch.** David Howarth. (Great Battles Ser.). 1997. pap. 21.95 (*1-900624-03-6*, Pub. by Windrush Pr UK) Interlink Pub.

Trafalgar & the Spanish Navy. John D. Harbron. LC 88-61414. (Illus.). 208p. 1988. 37.95 (*0-87021-695-3*) Naval Inst Pr.

Trafalgar Roll. Robert H. Mackenzie. 354p. 1989. 27.95 (*0-87021-990-1*) Naval Inst Pr.

An Asterisk (*) at the beginning of an entry indicates that the title is appearing in BIP for the first time.

Trafalgar Rose. large type ed. Clare F. Holmes. (Linford Romance Library). 320p. 1996. pap. 15.99 (*0-7089-7842-8*, Linford) Ulverscroft.

Trafalgar Square: Emblem of Empire. Mace. (C). 1976. pap. 22.50 (*0-85315-367-1*, Pub. by Lawrence & Wishart UK) NYU Pr.

Trafalgar 1805. David F. Marley. 1995. pap. 14.95 (*1-85532-479-2*, Pub. by Osprey UK) Stackpole.

Traffic. Mark Foreman. (Illus.). 32p. (J). (ps-k). 1995. 16.95 (*1-85793-206-4*, Pub. by Pavilion UK) Trafalgar.

Traffic. Nancy Loewen. LC 95-25897. (Safety Sense Ser.). (Illus.). 24p. (J). (gr. k-3). 1996. lib. bdg. 18.50 (*1-56766-254-4*) Childs World.

Traffic. Gil Ott. 24p. (Orig.). 1985. pap. 2.50 (*0-935162-06-2*) Singing Horse.

Traffic. Tom Smith. LC 83-51446. (Illus.). 92p. 1983. pap. 6.00 (*0-912292-74-1*) Smith.

Traffic: A Book of Opposites. Betsy Maestro & Giulio Maestro. LC 80-29641. (Illus.). 32p. (J). (ps-1). 1991. 16.00 (*0-517-54427-X*) Crown Bks Yng Read.

Traffic Accident Analysis & Roadway Visibility. (Research Record Ser.: No. 1172). 97p. 1988. 13.00 (*0-309-04709-9*) Transport Res Bd.

Traffic Accident Analysis, Visibility Factors, & Motorist Information Needs. (Research Record Ser.: No. 1111). 149p. 1987. 20.00 (*0-309-04463-4*) Transport Res Bd.

Traffic Accident Fatalities City of St. Louis, MO 1935-1945. Irene Terhoff. 108p. 1993. 13.95 (*0-9629830-1-2*, 93105) Inkwell MO.

Traffic Accident Field Measurements & Scale Diagrams Manual. R. W. Rivers. (Illus.). 154p. 1983. spiral bd., pap. 31.95 (*0-398-04845-2*) C C Thomas.

Traffic Accident Investigation & Physical Evidence. D. R. McGrew. (Illus.). 132p. 1975. spiral bd., pap. 27.95 (*0-398-03503-2*) C C Thomas.

Traffic Accident Investigation Manual. 9th ed. J. Stannard Baker & Lynn B. Fricke. 420p. 1986. 55.00 (*0-912642-06-8*) Traffic Inst.

Traffic Accident Investigators' Book of Formulae & Tables. R. W. Rivers. (Illus.). 160p. 1981. spiral bd., pap. 38.95 (*0-398-04537-2*) C C Thomas.

Traffic Accident Investigator's Manual: A Levels 1 & 2 Reference, Training & Investigation Manual. 2nd ed. R. W. Rivers. LC 94-40334. Orig. Title: On-Scene Traffic Accident Investigator's Manual. (Illus.). 238p. (C). 1995. text ed. 59.95 (*0-398-05967-5*); pap. text ed. 39.95 (*0-398-05968-3*) C C Thomas.

Traffic Accident Reconstruction: Legal Issues in the 1990's. Carol H. Garcia & Craig J. Trocino. 80p. (C). 1991. pap. text ed. 14.95 (*1-884566-10-3*) Inst Police Tech.

Traffic Accident Reconstruction: Volume 2 of the Traffic Accident Investigation Manual. Lynn B. Fricke. LC 90-60196. 453p. (C). 1990. text ed. 75.00 (*0-912642-07-6*) Traffic Inst.

Traffic Analysis & the Zendian Problem. Lambros D. Callimahos. 261p. (Orig.). (C). 1989. pap. 32.80 (*0-89412-161-8*) Aegean Park Pr.

Traffic & Grade Crossing Control Devices. (Transportation Research Record Ser.: No. 1244). 72p. 1989. 12.00 (*0-309-04970-9*) Transport Res Bd.

Traffic & Highway Engineering. Garber. (West - Engineering Ser.). 1996. text ed. 59.00 (*0-534-93823-X*) PWS Pubs.

Traffic & Laughter. Ted Mooney. 1992. pap. 12.00 (*0-679-73884-3*, Vin) Random.

Traffic & Park Officer. Jack Rudman. (Career Examination Ser.: C-1689). 1994. pap. 23.95 (*0-8373-1689-8*) Nat Learn.

Traffic & Politics: The Construction & Management of Rochester Bridge, AD 43-1993. Ed. by Nigel Yates & James M. Gibson. LC 93-50852. (Kent History Project Ser.: Vol. 1). (Illus.). 432p. (C). 1994. 45.00 (*0-85115-356-9*, Boydell Pr) Boydell & Brewer.

Traffic & the Police: Variations in Law-Enforcement Policy. John A. Gardiner. LC 69-18030. (Joint Center for Urban Studies). 184p. 1969. 25.00 (*0-674-90140-1*) HUP.

***Traffic & Transport Psychology - Theory & Application: Proceedings of the 1996 International Conference on Traffic & Transport Psychology.** Ed. by Talib Rothengatter & Enrique J. Carbonell Vaya. 350p. Date not set. text ed. write for info. (*0-08-042786-3*, Pergamon Pr) Elsevier.

***Traffic & Transport Systems: English-German, German-English.** William Leutzbach. 143p. (ENG & GER.). 1991. 125.00 (*0-7859-9999-X*) Fr & Eur.

Traffic Assignment Techniques. Roy Thomas. 396p. 1991. text ed. 104.95 (*1-85628-166-3*, Pub. by Avebury Technical UK) Ashgate Pub Co.

Traffic Congestion: Activities to Reduce Travel Demand & Air Pollution Are Not Widely Implemented. (Illus.). 88p. (Orig.). (C). 1993. pap. text ed. 20.00 (*1-56806-617-1*) DIANE Pub.

Traffic Congestion & Suburban Activity Centers. (Transportation Research Circular Ser.: No. 359). 110p. 1990. 14.00 (*0-685-38590-6*) Transport Res Bd.

***Traffic Congestion & Traffic Safety in the 21st Century: Proceedings of the Conference, Chicago, Illinois, June 8-11, 1997.** R. F. Benekohal & American Society of Civil Engineers Staff. 1997. write for info. (*0-7844-0243-4*) Am Soc Civil Eng.

Traffic Control Agent. Jack Rudman. (Career Examination Ser.: C-1750). 1994. reprint ed. pap. 23.95 (*0-8373-1750-9*) Nat Learn.

Traffic Control Devices & Highway Visibility. LC 92-40450. 1992. 20.00 (*0-309-05409-5*, R1368) Transport Res Bd.

Traffic Control Devices & Rail-Highway Grade Crossings. (Research Record Ser.: No. 1114). 155p. 1987. 21.50 (*0-309-04466-9*) Transport Res Bd.

Traffic Control Devices for Highways, Work Zones, & Railroad Grade Crossings. (Transportation Research Record Ser.: No. 1254). 90p. 1990. 16.00 (*0-309-05006-5*) Transport Res Bd.

Traffic Control Devices, Visibility, & Traffic Signal Systems (TRR 1421) Ed. by Naomi Kassabian. (Transportation Research Record Ser.). (Illus.). 120p. 1994. pap. text ed. 26.00 (*0-309-05574-1*) Natl Res Coun.

Traffic Control in Oversaturated Street Networks. (National Cooperative Highway Research Program Report Ser.: No. 194). 152p. 1978. 9.60 (*0-309-02854-X*) Transport Res Bd.

Traffic Control Inspector. Jack Rudman. (Career Examination Ser.: C-812). 1994. pap. 27.95 (*0-8373-0812-7*) Nat Learn.

Traffic Control Methods. Sam Yagar & Edwin Rowe. 424p. pap. text ed. 50.00 (*0-939204-41-X*) Eng Found.

Traffic Control Systems. 1983. 50.00 (*0-318-18032-4*, TS 1-1983) Natl Elec Mfrs.

Traffic Court: How To Win. James Glass. (Illus.). 208p. 1988. 12.95 (*0-9615419-4-6*) Allenby Pr.

Traffic Court Kit. 40p. (Orig.). 1995. pap. 19.95 (*1-56382-110-9*) E-Z Legal.

Traffic Court Procedure & Administration. 2nd ed. LC 82-73591. 249p. 1982. 20.00 (*0-89707-053-4*, 523-0012) Amer Bar Assn.

Traffic Data Collection: Conference Proceedings. 178p. 1978. 40.00 (*0-7277-0061-8*, Pub. by T Telford UK) Am Soc Civil Eng.

Traffic Data Collection & Analysis: Methods & Procedures. (National Cooperative Highway Research Program Report Ser.: No. 130). 58p. 1986. 8.40 (*0-309-04406-5*) Transport Res Bd.

Traffic Device Maintainer. Jack Rudman. (Career Examination Ser.: C-813). 1994. pap. 23.95 (*0-8373-0813-5*) Nat Learn.

Traffic Device Maintainer Trainee. Jack Rudman. (Career Examination Ser.: C-814). 1994. pap. 23.95 (*0-8373-0814-3*) Nat Learn.

Traffic Education for Young Pedestrians: A Selection of Papers Adapted from the Proceedings of the 1978 OECD Workshop on Training Objectives for Child Pedestrians. John A. Michon. (Accident Analysis & Prevention Ser.: No. 13). 138p. 1983. pap. 31.00 (*0-08-030224-6*, Pergamon Pr) Elsevier.

Traffic Enforcement Agent. Hy Hammer. LC 83-15697. 208p. (Orig.). 1984. pap. 9.95 (*0-668-05771-8*, 5771, Arco) Macmillan Gen Ref.

Traffic Enforcement Agent. Jack Rudman. (Career Examination Ser.: C-2407). 1994. pap. 23.95 (*0-8373-2407-6*) Nat Learn.

Traffic Engineer. Jack Rudman. (Career Examination Ser.: C-1520). 1994. pap. 29.95 (*0-8373-1520-4*) Nat Learn.

Traffic Engineer I. Jack Rudman. (Career Examination Ser.: C-1886). 1994. pap. 29.95 (*0-8373-1886-6*) Nat Learn.

Traffic Engineering. William R. McShane & Roger P. Roess. 704p. 1990. text ed. 95.00 (*0-13-926148-6*) P-H.

Traffic Escapes: Westchester, Fairfield, NYC. Michael J. Kelly. (Illus.). 49p. (Orig.). 1991. pap. 8.95 (*0-9629965-0-5*) M J Kelly.

Traffic Flow & Highway Capacity. Ed. by Susan Brown. LC 93-35536. (Transportation Research Record Ser.: No. 1398). (Illus.). 144p. 1993. pap. text ed. 28.00 (*0-309-05467-2*) Transport Res Bd.

Traffic Flow Fundamentals. Adolf D. May. 726p. 1989. text ed. 89.00 (*0-13-926072-2*) P-H.

Traffic Flow in Switching Systems. Gerard Hebuterne. LC 87-71224. (Artech House Telecommunications Library). (Illus.). 272p. reprint ed. pap. 77.60 (*0-7837-1801-2*, 2042002) Bks Demand.

Traffic Flow Theory. (Special Reports: No. 165). 240p. 1976. 20.00 (*0-309-02459-5*) Transport Res Bd.

Traffic in Culture: Refiguring Anthropology & Art. Ed. by George E. Marcus & Fred R. Myers. LC 94-39487. 1995. 48.00 (*0-520-08846-8*); pap. 17.95 (*0-520-08847-6*) U CA Pr.

Traffic in Narcotics. H. J. Anslinger & William F. Tompkins. Ed. by Gerald N. Grob. LC 80-1211. (Addiction in America Ser.). 1981. reprint ed. lib. bdg. 33.95 (*0-405-13567-X*) Ayer.

Traffic in Narcotics & Drug Addiction. S. K. Ghosh. (C). 1987. 25.00 (*81-7024-157-X*, Pub. by Ashish II) S Asia.

Traffic in Praise: Pindar & the Poetics of Social Economy. Leslie Kurke. LC 90-55722. (Myth & Poetics Ser.). 320p. 1991. 47.50 (*0-8014-2350-3*) Cornell U Pr.

Traffic in Women & Other Essays on Feminism. Emma Goldman. Ed. by Alix K. Shulman. LC 90-19844. (Illus.). 63p. (Orig.). (C). 1971. pap. 4.25 (*0-87810-001-6*) Times Change.

Traffic Incident. Roger Rittner. (Read-along Radio Dramas Ser.). (YA). (gr. 6-11). 1982. 35.00 (*1-878298-10-0*) Balance Pub.

Traffic Investigation & Enforcement. 3rd rev. ed. Donald O. Schultz & Derald D. Hunt. LC 94-69410. (Illus.). 293p. (C). 1995. pap. 27.95 (*0-942728-65-3*) Copperhouse.

Traffic Jam. Bronwen Scarffe. LC 92-31956. (Voyages Ser.). (Illus.). (J). 1993. 3.75 (*0-383-03599-6*) SRA McGraw.

Traffic Jam see Set 7

Traffic Law. Malcolm M. Britts. vii, 397p. 1990. pap. 28.00 (*0-455-20988-X*, Pub. by Law Bk Co AT) Gaunt.

Traffic Law: NSW. 3rd ed. Malcolm M. Britts. 445p. 1992. pap. 41.00 (*0-455-21166-3*, Pub. by Law Bk Co AT) Gaunt.

Traffic Law & Practice in Wisconsin, 2 vols. 2nd rev. ed. Barry S. Cohen et al. LC 94-24027. 1050p. 1995. ring bd. 149.00 (*0-945574-65-7*) State Bar WI CLE Bk Div.

***Traffic Law for Illinois Police.** Albert M. Johnston, Jr. 444p. 1996. pap. text ed. 29.00 (*0-87563-641-1*) Stipes.

Traffic Law NSW. 4th ed. Malcolm M. Britts. 1994. pap. 35.00 (*0-455-21259-7*, Pub. by Law Bk Co AT) Gaunt.

Traffic Laws, Traffic Courts, Your Rights: A Revolution with Pen & Paper. Gary L. Hicks. (Road Warrior Militia Ser.). 118p. 1995. pap. 18.95 (*0-9649613-0-X*) Star Chamber.

Traffic Management: Issues & Techniques. Ed. by Sam Yagar et al. 350p. 1992. pap. 50.00 (*0-939204-48-7*) Eng Found.

Traffic Management: Planning, Operations, & Control. C. John Langley, Jr. et al. (Illus.). 515p. (C). 1991. reprint ed. text ed. 45.95 (*0-88133-617-3*) Waveland Pr.

Traffic Management & Collision Investigation. Warren E. Clark. (Illus.). 320p. (C). 1981. text ed. 58.51 (*0-13-926162-1*) P-H.

Traffic Management for Freeway Emergencies & Special Events. (Transportation Research Circular Ser.: No. 344). 51p. 1989. 6.00 (*0-685-38591-4*) Transport Res Bd.

Traffic Monitoring & Control Systems. Ed. by Sam Yagar. LC 85-70350. 214p. 1985. pap. 50.00 (*0-939204-24-X*, 83-11) Eng Found.

Traffic Noise Regulation: A Comparative Study of the American & German Experience. Stephen G. Wood. LC 81-84065. x, 372p. 1982. lib. bdg. 43.50 (*0-89941-108-8*, 302470) W S Hein.

Traffic of Ideas Between India & America. Ed. by Robert Crunden. 1985. 37.50 (*0-8364-1317-2*, Pub. by Chanakya II) S Asia.

Traffic Offences: An Examination of the Principles of Law Governing Offences Committed by Motorists on the Roads of Australia. 2nd ed. Douglas Brown. 302p. 1988. 75.00 (*0-409-49517-4*, AT) MICHIE.

Traffic Operations. LC 92-32759. 157p. 1992. 28.00 (*0-309-05223-8*, R1360) Transport Res Bd.

Traffic Processes in Queueing Networks: A Markov Renewal Approach. Ralph L. Disney & Peter C. Kiessler. LC 86-46275. (Johns Hopkins Series in the Mathematical Sciences: No. 4). 272p. 1987. text ed. 49.50 (*0-8018-3454-6*) Johns Hopkins.

Traffic Radar Handbook. Donald S. Sawicki. Ed. by Bob Grove. (Illus.). 100p. (C). 1993. 14.95 (*0-944543-08-1*, BOK75) Grove Enterp.

Traffic Recorder. Jack Rudman. (Career Examination Ser.: C-1521). 1994. pap. 27.95 (*0-8373-1521-2*) Nat Learn.

Traffic Restraints in Residential Areas, Vol. II. George G. Wynne. (Learning from Abroad Ser.). 40p. (C). 1980. pap. 19.95 (*0-685-06643-6*) Transaction Pubs.

Traffic Rules of N.Y.C. 65p. 1997. ring bd. 6.95 (*0-930137-48-5*) Looseleaf Law.

Traffic Safety. (Illus.). 64p. (J). (gr. 6-12). 1975. pap. 2.40 (*0-8395-3391-8*, 33391) BSA.

Traffic Safety & the Driver. Leonard Evans. 424p. 1991. text ed. 67.95 (*0-442-00163-0*) Van Nos Reinhold.

Traffic Safety Reform in the United States & Great Britain. Jerome S. Legge, Jr. LC 90-49091. (Policy & Institutional Studies). 198p. (C). 1991. 49.95 (*0-8229-3662-3*) U of Pittsburgh Pr.

Traffic Signal Maintenance Supervisor. (Career Examination Ser.: C-3757). pap. 29.95 (*0-8373-3757-7*) Nat Learn.

***Traffic Smart.** Patricia Ruben. (J). Date not set. write for info. (*0-688-01614-6*); write for info. (*0-688-05261-4*); lib. bdg. write for info. (*0-688-01615-4*); lib. bdg. write for info. (*0-688-05262-2*) Lothrop.

Traffic Supervisor. Jack Rudman. (Career Examination Ser.: C-2627). 1994. pap. 29.95 (*0-8373-2627-3*) Nat Learn.

Traffic System Design Handbook: Timesaving Telecommunication Traffic Tables & Programs. James R. Boucher. LC 92-30770. (Illus.). 200p. (C). 1993. pap. 49.95 (*0-7803-0428-4*, PP0325-1) Inst Electrical.

Traffic Technician. Jack Rudman. (Career Examination Ser.: C-1522). 1994. pap. 27.95 (*0-8373-1522-0*) Nat Learn.

Traffic Technician I. Jack Rudman. (Career Examination Ser.: C-2335). 1994. pap. 27.95 (*0-8373-2335-5*) Nat Learn.

Traffic Technician II. Jack Rudman. (Career Examination Ser.: C-2336). 1994. pap. 29.95 (*0-8373-2336-3*) Nat Learn.

Traffic Technician III. Jack Rudman. (Career Examination Ser.: C-1887). 1994. pap. 29.95 (*0-8373-1887-4*) Nat Learn.

Traffic Technician Trainee. Jack Rudman. (Career Examination Ser.: C-3269). 1994. pap. 23.95 (*0-8373-3269-9*) Nat Learn.

Traffic, the Best of Smiling Phases. 136p. 1993. otabind 19.95 (*0-7935-1660-9*, 00673227) H Leonard.

Traffic Theories for New Telecommunications Services: Proceedings of the ITC Specialists Seminar, Adelaide, Australia, 25-29 Sept., 1989. Ed. by N. M. Van Dijk et al. 468p. 1991. 184.50 (*0-444-88988-4*, North Holland) Elsevier.

Traffic Ticket Defense. Chris Sutherland & Mark D. Sutherland. 184p. 1993. pap. 14.95 (*1-56625-025-0*) Bonus Books.

Traffic Ticket Defense for the Trucker. Mark D. Sutherland & Florine Sutherland. LC 95-15004. (Illus.). 161p. 1995. pap. 14.95 (*1-56625-048-X*) Bonus Books.

Traffic Tickets, Fines & Other Annoying Things. Tim Matheson. 72p. 1984. pap. 4.95 (*0-8065-0883-3*, Citadel Pr) Carol Pub Group.

Traffic World's Questions & Answers, Vol. 28. Traffic World Editors. 576p. 1982. text ed. 24.50 (*0-87408-024-X*) Intl Thom Trans Pr.

Traffic World's Questions & Answers, Vol. 29. Colin Barrett. 1985. 35.00 (*0-87408-035-5*) Intl Thom Trans Pr.

Traffickers: Drug Markets & Law Enforcement. Nicholas Dorn et al. 224p. (C). 1991. pap. text ed. 19.95 (*0-415-03537-6*, A5965) Routledge.

Trafficking. Berkeley Rice. 1991. mass mkt. 5.95 (*0-312-92523-9*) St Martin.

Trafficking in Burmese Women & Girls in Thailand. Ed. by Human Rights Watch Staff. 160p. (Orig.). 1993. pap. 15.00 (*1-56432-107-X*) Hum Rts Watch.

Trafficking in Drug Users: Professional Exchange Networks in the Control of Deviance. James R. Beniger. LC 83-5251. (American Sociological Assn. Rose Monograph Ser.). 224p. 1984. text ed. 54.95 (*0-521-25753-0*); pap. text ed. 18.95 (*0-521-27680-2*) Cambridge U Pr.

Trafficking in Women & Children in India: Sexual Exploitation & Sale. M. Rita Rozario. 1988. 22.00 (*0-317-90858-8*, Pub. by Uppal Pub Hse II) S Asia.

Trafficking of Bacterial Toxins. Ed. by Catharine Saelinger. 184p. 1989. 153.00 (*0-8493-4787-4*, QP632) CRC Pr.

Trafficking of Intercellular Membranes: From Molecular Sorting to Membrane Fusion. Ed. by Maria C. Pedroso de Lima et al. LC 94-49441. (NATO ASI Series: Subseries H: Cell Biology: Vol. 91). 1995. 188.95 (*3-540-58915-5*) Spr-Verlag.

Traffics & Discoveries. Rudyard Kipling. Ed. & Intro. by Hermione Lee. 1,352p. 1991. pap. 9.95 (*0-14-018375-2*, Penguin Classics) Viking Penguin.

***Traficante.** J. Kregel. (SPA.). 1.50 (*0-8297-0306-3*) Life Pubs Intl.

Trafiquants Italiens Dans L'orient Hellenique. Jean Hatzfeld. LC 75-7322. (Roman History Ser.). (FRE.). 1975. reprint ed. 34.95 (*0-405-07086-1*) Ayer.

Tragedi vom Grossen Abentmal see Saemtliche Schriften

Tragedia Josephina. M. De Carvajal. Ed. by S. E. Gillet. (Elliott Monographs: Vol. 28). 1974. reprint ed. 35.00 (*0-527-02631-X*) Periodicals Srv.

Tragedian: An Essay on the Histrionic Genius of Junius Brutus Booth. Thomas R. Gould. LC 70-87122. 190p. 1972. 18.95 (*0-405-08567-2*, Pub. by Blom Pubns UK) Ayer.

Tragedian in Spite of Himself see Seagull

Tragedias. Esquilo. pap. 1.95 (*0-685-11603-4*) Fr & Eur.

Tragedie Completes Tome I. Euripides. 701p. (FRE.). 1989. pap. 16.95 (*0-7859-2578-3*, 2070381919) Fr & Eur.

Tragedie Completes Tome II. Euripides. 715p. (FRE.). 1989. pap. 16.95 (*0-7859-2579-1*, 2070381927) Fr & Eur.

Tragedie du Roi Christophe. Aime Cesaire. 160p. (FRE.). 1970. pap. 12.95 (*0-7859-3452-9*) Fr & Eur.

Tragedie of Anthonie, & Cleopatra. M.H. Publications Staff. 300p. 1990. 175.00 (*1-872680-06-2*, Pub. by M H Pubns UK) St Mut.

Tragedie of Anthonie & Cleopatra. William Shakespeare. Ed. & Intro. by John Turner. LC 95-3141. (Shakespearean Originals--First Editions Ser.). 1995. pap. 12.95 (*0-13-355595-X*) P-H.

Tragedie of Cymbeline: Reprint from 1st Folio, 1623, with Collations of the 2nd, 3rd, & 4th Folios. William Shakespeare. Ed. by W. J. Craig. (New Shakespeare Society, London, Ser. 2: No. 11). 1974. reprint ed. pap. 35.00 (*0-8115-0236-8*) Periodicals Srv.

Tragedie of Darius. William Alexander. LC 72-6936. (English Experience Ser.: No. 293). 80p. 1971. reprint ed. 25.00 (*90-221-0293-9*) Walter J Johnson.

Tragedie of Hamlet. George MacDonald. (George MacDonald Original Works: Series VI). 1995. reprint ed. 18.00 (*1-881084-38-8*) Johannesen.

Tragedie of Hamlet, Prince of Denmarke. M.H. Publications Staff. 272p. 1990. 175.00 (*1-872680-01-1*, Pub. by M H Pubns UK) St Mut.

Tragedie of Julius Caesar. M.H. Publications Staff. 280p. 1990. 175.00 (*1-872680-09-7*, Pub. by M H Pubns UK) St Mut.

***Tragedie of Julius Caesar.** William Shakespeare & Neil Freeman. LC 97-9577. (Applause Shakespeare Library). 1997. pap. write for info. (*1-55783-289-7*) Applause Theatre Bk Pubs.

Tragedie of King Lear. M.H. Publications Staff. 225p. 1990. 175.00 (*1-872680-10-0*, Pub. by M H Pubns UK) St Mut.

Tragedie of Macbeth. M.H. Publications Staff. 207p. 1990. 125.00 (*1-872680-12-7*, Pub. by M H Pubns UK) St Mut.

Tragedie of Macbeth. William William. Ed. by James Rigney. LC 96-2694. (Shakespearean Originals--First Editions Ser.). 1996. pap. 12.95 (*0-13-355439-2*) P-H.

Tragedie of Romeo & Juliet. M.H. Publications Staff. 238p. 1990. 125.00 (*1-872680-05-4*, Pub. by M H Pubns UK) St Mut.

Tragedie of Troylus & Cressida. M.H. Publications Staff. 1990. 95.00 (*1-872680-17-8*, Pub. by M H Pubns UK) St Mut.

Tragedie Sans Masque: Notes de Theatre. Henry De Montherlant. 16.50 (*0-685-36990-0*) Fr & Eur.

Tragedies, 2 vols. Aeschylus. Incl. Vol. 1. Suppliant Maidens, Persians, Prometheus, Seven Against Thebes. 464p. 1922. 18.95 (*0-674-99160-5*); Vol. 2. Agamemnon, Libation Bearers, Eumenides' Fragments. 618p. 1922. 18.95 (*0-674-99161-3*); (Loeb Classical Library: Nos. 145-146). 18.95 (*0-318-53197-6*) HUP.

Tragedies. Eschyle. (FRE.). 1982. pap. 11.95 (*0-7859-2457-4*, 2070373649) Fr & Eur.

Tragedies. Lucius A. Seneca. (Classical Texts Ser.). 448p. 1986. 35.00 (*0-19-814657-4*) OUP.

Tragedies. William Shakespeare. Ed. by Stanley Wells et al. (Oxford Shakespeare Ser.). 416p. 1994. pap. 13.95 (*0-19-818274-0*) OUP.

Tragedies, 2 vols. Sophocles. (Loeb Classical Library: No. 20-21). text ed. write for info. (*0-318-53199-2*) HUP.

Tragedies, 2 vols., 1. Lucius A. Seneca. (Loeb Classical Library: No. 62, 78). 586p. 1917. text ed. 18.95 (*0-674-99069-2*) HUP.

Tragedies, 2 vols., 2. Lucius A. Seneca. (Loeb Classical Library: No. 62, 78). 548p. 1917. text ed. 18.95 (*0-674-99070-6*) HUP.

Tragedies, Vol. I. William Shakespeare. LC 92-52907. 608p. 1992. 20.00 (*0-679-41742-7*, Everymans Lib) Knopf.

Tragedies, Vol. 2. William Shakespeare. 1993. 20.00 (0-679-42306-0, Everymans Lib) Knopf.

Tragedies, 2 vols., Vols. VIII-IX. Lucius A. Seneca. (Loeb Classical Library: No. 62, 78). text ed. write for info. (0-318-53198-4) HUP.

Tragedies de la Foi. Romain Rolland. 296p. (FRE.). 1970. pap. 11.95 (0-7859-5467-8) Fr & Eur.

Tragedies of Ennius: The Fragments. Quintus Ennius. Ed. by H. D. Jocelyn. LC 67-11525. (Cambridge Classical Texts & Commentaries Ser.: No. 10). 481p. reprint ed. pap. 137.10 (0-317-29380-X, 2024481) Bks Demand.

Tragedies of Euripides in English Verse, 3 Vols. Euripides. Ed. by Arthur S. Way. 1977. 59.95 (0-8369-6973-1, 7854) Ayer.

***Tragedies of G. B. Giraldi Cinthio: The Transformation of Narrative Source into Stage Play.** Mary G. Morrison. LC 97-10516. (Studies in Italian Literature: No. 4). (Illus.). 412p. 1997. text ed. 109.95 (0-7734-8636-4) E Mellen.

Tragedies of Herod & Mariamne. Maurice J. Valency. LC 70-8450. reprint ed. 27.50 (0-404-06750-6) AMS Pr.

Tragedies of L. Annaeus Seneca, the Philospher. Lucius A. Seneca. LC 70-158326. (Augustan Translators Ser.). 1976. reprint ed. 67.50 (0-404-54136-4) AMS Pr.

Tragedies of Our Own Making: How Private Choices Have Created Public Bankruptcy. Richard Neely. 184p. 1994. 19.95 (0-252-02038-3) U of Ill Pr.

Tragedies of Sophocles. Sophocles. Tr. by Richard C. Jebb. LC 71-39209. (Select Bibliographies Reprint Ser.). 1977. reprint ed. 35.95 (0-8369-6811-5) Ayer.

Tragedies of Tyrants: Political Thought & Theater in the English Renaissance. Rebecca W. Bushnell. LC 89-77175. 216p. 1990. 35.00 (0-8014-2271-X) Cornell U Pr.

Tragedies of William Shakespeare. William Shakespeare. 1280p. 1994. 22.00 (0-679-60129-5, Modern Lib) Random.

***Tragedy.** John Drakakis. LC 97-10456. (Longman Critical Readers Ser.). 1998. write for info. (0-582-20997-8); pap. write for info. (0-582-20998-6) Longman.

Tragedy. Clifford Leech. (Critical Idiom Ser.: Vol. 1). (C). 1969. pap. 8.50 (0-416-15720-3, NO. 2291) Routledge Chapman & Hall.

Tragedy. Maurice Valency. 128p. (C). 1990. 17.95 (1-56131-009-3) New Amsterdam Bks.

Tragedy. Ashley H. Thorndike. (BCL1-PR English Literature Ser.). 390p. 1992. reprint ed. lib. bdg. 89.00 (0-7812-7098-7) Rprt Serv.

Tragedy: Finding a Hidden Meaning: How to Transform the Tragedies in Your Life into Personal Growth. Trudy Carlson. LC 95-94111. 144p. (Orig.). 1997. pap. 14.95 (0-9642443-3-0) Benline Pr.

Tragedy: Modern Essays in Criticism. Ed. by Laurence A. Michel & Richard B. Sewall. LC 77-13779. 340p. 1978. reprint ed. text ed. 55.00 (0-8371-9876-3, MITR, Greenwood Pr) Greenwood.

Tragedy: Plays, Theory & Criticism. Ed. by Richard Levin & David Levin. (Harbrace Sourcebooks Ser.). 217p. (Orig.). (C). 1960. pap. text ed. 17.50 (0-15-592346-3) HB Coll Pubs.

Tragedy Against Psychology. Ed. by Brynmill Pr. Ltd. Staff. (C). 1989. 60.00 (0-907839-11-8, Pub. by Brynmill Pr Ltd UK) St Mut.

Tragedy & After: Euripides, Shakespeare, Goethe. Ekbert Faas. 1986. pap. 24.95 (0-7735-0605-5, Pub. by McGill CN) U of Toronto Pr.

Tragedy & After: Euripides, Shakespeare, Goethe. Ekbert Faas. LC 84-673369. 233p. reprint ed. pap. 66.50 (0-7837-6909-1, 2046739) Bks Demand.

Tragedy & Biblical Narrative: Arrows of the Almighty. J. Cheryl Exum. 224p. (C). 1992. text ed. 54.95 (0-521-41073-8) Cambridge U Pr.

Tragedy & Biblical Narrative: Arrows of the Almighty. J. Cheryl Exum. 220p. 1996. pap. text ed. 17.95 (0-521-56506-5) Cambridge U Pr.

Tragedy & Civilization: An Interpretation of Sophocles. Charles Segal. LC 80-19765. (Modern Classical Lectures: No. 26). 519p. 1981. 34.95 (0-674-90206-8) HUP.

Tragedy & Comedy. Walter Kerr. (Quality Paperbacks Ser.). 350p. 1985. reprint ed. pap. 9.95 (0-306-80249-X) Da Capo.

***Tragedy & Comedy: A Systematic Study & a Critique of Hegel.** Mark W. Roche. LC 97-986. (Hegelian Studies). 320p. (C). 1997. pap. text ed. 21.95 (0-7914-3546-6) State U NY Pr.

***Tragedy & Comedy: A Systematic Study & a Critique of Hegel.** Mark W. Roche. LC 97-986. (SUNY Series in Hegelian Studies). 320p. (C). 1997. text ed. 65.50 (0-7914-3545-8) State U NY Pr.

Tragedy & Comedy from Dante to Pseudo-Dante. fac. ed. Henry A. Kelly. LC 88-21089. (University of California Publications in Entomology: No. 121). 144p. 1989. reprint ed. pap. 41.10 (0-7837-8131-8, 2047938) Bks Demand.

Tragedy & Comedy of Life: Plato's Philebus. Plato. Tr. by Seth Benardete. LC 92-44620. (Illus.). 264p. (C). 1993. 37.50 (0-226-04239-1) U Ch Pr.

Tragedy & Enlightenment: Athenian Political Thought & the Dilemmas of Modernity. Christopher Rocco. LC 96-11600. (Classics & Contemporary Thought Ser.: 4). 240p. (C). 1997. 40.00 (0-520-20494-8) U CA Pr.

Tragedy & Hope: A History of the World in Our Time. Carroll Quigley. 1348p. 1966. text ed. 39.95 (0-945001-10-X) GSG & Assocs.

Tragedy & Metatheater. Lionel Abel. 200p. 1997. 24.00 (0-8419-1352-8) Holmes & Meier.

Tragedy & Philosophy. Ed. by N. Georgopoulos. LC 92-37143. 288p. 1993. text ed. 35.00 (0-312-08938-4) St Martin.

Tragedy & Philosophy. Walter Kaufmann. LC 78-73428. 406p. 1968. pap. text ed. 17.95 (0-691-02005-1) Princeton U Pr.

Tragedy & Social Evolution. Eva Figes. 170p. 1990. pap. 12.95 (0-89255-148-8) Persea Bks.

Tragedy & Social Evolution. Eva Figes. 1976. pap. 10.95 (0-7145-3639-3) Riverrun NY.

Tragedy & the Tragic: Greek Theatre & Beyond. Ed. by M. S. Silk. LC 95-25867. 576p. (C). 1996. 90.00 (0-19-814951-4, Clarendon Pr) OUP.

Tragedy & Theory: The Problem of Conflict since Aristotle. Michelle Gellrich. LC 87-25868. 311p. reprint ed. pap. 88.70 (0-7837-6764-1, 2046594) Bks Demand.

Tragedy & Tragic Theory: An Analytical Guide. Richard H. Palmer. LC 91-46861. 252p. 1992. text ed. 59.95 (0-313-28203-X, PTT, Greenwood Pr) Greenwood.

Tragedy & Treason. Janice S. Hofmann. LC 95-94659. (Illus.). 64p. (YA). (gr. 5-12). 1995. 12.95 (0-9647764-0-5) J S Hofmann.

Tragedy & Triumph, 3 vols., Set. Susan White-Bowden. (Illus.). pap. write for info. (0-9633762-3-3) White-Bowden Assocs.

***Tragedy & Triumph: Poetry & Essays of the Affected.** Ed. by Nubia Levon. Date not set. 24.99 (1-890254-27-4) Innov Pub Concepts.

Tragedy & Truth: Studies in the Development of a Renaissance & Neoclassical Discourse. Timothy J. Reiss. LC 80-10413. 344p. reprint ed. pap. 98.10 (0-7837-4549-4, 2080338) Bks Demand.

Tragedy as a Critique of Virtue: The Novel & Ethical Reflection. John D. Barbour. LC 83-20028. (Studies in Humanities). 214p. (C). 1984. pap. text ed. 16.95 (0-89130-662-5, 00 01 02) Scholars Pr GA.

Tragedy at Taos: The Revolt of 1847. James A. Crutchfield. LC 94-49513. 208p. 1995. pap. 12.95 (1-55622-385-4, Rep of TX Pr) Wordware Pub.

Tragedy-Contradiction & Repression. Richard Kuhns. LC 90-20279. 190p. 1991. 31.95 (0-226-45826-1) U Ch Pr.

***Tragedy in Athens: Performance Space & Theatrical Meaning.** David Wiles. (Illus.). 256p. (C). 1997. text ed. 59.95 (0-521-46268-1) Cambridge U Pr.

Tragedy in East Timor: Report on the Trials in Dili & Jakarta. International Commission of Jurists. (Illus.). 75p. 1992. reprint ed. pap. 25.00 (0-7837-6981-4, 2046793) Bks Demand.

Tragedy in Paradise: Family & Gender Politics in German Bourgeois Tragedy 1750-1850. Gail K. Hart. (GERM Ser.). xiv, 1536p. (C). 1996. 52.95 (1-57113-037-3) Camden Hse.

Tragedy in the Church: The Missing Gifts. rev. ed. Aiden W. Tozer. 150p. (C). 1990. pap. 8.99 (0-87509-424-4) Chr Pubns.

Tragedy in the House of Brodeln: Fantasy Game Adventure. Brian Jelko. 56p. 1995. pap. 9.95 (1-889182-01-X) Kenzer & Co.

Tragedy of Abundance: Myth Restoration in American Culture. Jerome Steffen. 1993. 19.95 (0-87081-272-6) Univ Pr Colo.

Tragedy of Afghanistan: A First-Hand Account. Raja Anwar. Tr. by Khalid Hasan. 384p. 1989. 35.00 (0-86091-208-6, A2665, Pub. by Verso UK); pap. text ed. 17.95 (0-86091-979-X, A3738, Pub. by Verso UK) Routledge Chapman & Hall.

Tragedy of American Compassion. Marvin N. Olasky. 299p. 1995. pap. 14.95 (0-89526-725-X) Regnery Pub.

Tragedy of American Diplomacy. William A. Williams. 1988. pap. 11.95 (0-393-30493-0) Norton.

Tragedy of Belief: Division, Politics, & Religion in Ireland. John Fulton. (Illus.). 272p. 1991. 75.00 (0-19-827316-9) OUP.

Tragedy of Black Lung: Federal Compensation for Occupational Disease. Peter S. Barth. LC 87-8332. 292p. 1987. 24.00 (0-88099-045-7); pap. 14.00 (0-88099-044-9) W E Upjohn.

Tragedy of Bolivia: A People Crucified. Gutierrez A. Ostria. Tr. from by Eithne Golden from SPA. LC 81-2424. Orig. Title: Un Pueblo en la Cruz. 224p. 1981. reprint ed. text ed. 35.00 (0-313-22935-X, GUTB, Greenwood Pr) Greenwood.

Tragedy of Bukharin. Donny Gluckstein. LC 93-34928. pap. 18.95 (0-7453-0773-6, Pub. by Pluto Pr UK) LPC InBook.

Tragedy of Bukharin. Donny Gluckstein. LC 93-34928. (C). 60.00 (0-7453-0772-8, Pub. by Pluto Pr UK) LPC InBook.

Tragedy of Cambodian History: Politics, War, & Revolution Since 1945. David P. Chandler. (Illus.). 416p. 1993. pap. 19.00 (0-300-05752-0) Yale U Pr.

Tragedy of Central Europe. rev. ed. Stephen Borsody. LC 80-51032. (Yale Russian & East European Publications: No. 2). (Illus.). xviii, 274p. 1980. 18.50 (0-936586-01-X) Slavica.

Tragedy of Central Europe: Nazi & Soviet Conquest & Aftermath. Stephen Borsody. LC 80-51032. (Russian & East European Publications: No. 2). 274p. 1980. 18.50 (0-685-09610-6) Yale Russian.

Tragedy of Childhood. Alberto Savinio. Tr. by John Shepley from ITA. LC 91-61536. 131p. 1991. 25.95 (0-910395-73-X) Marlboro Pr.

Tragedy of Childhood. Alberto Savinio. Tr. by John Shepley from ITA. LC 91-61536. 131p. 1993. pap. 10.95 (0-910395-74-8) Marlboro Pr.

Tragedy of Chile. Robert J. Alexander. LC 77-91101. (Contributions in Political Science Ser.: No. 8). 509p. 1978. text ed. 75.00 (0-313-20034-3, ATC/, Greenwood Pr) Greenwood.

Tragedy of Compromise. Fred Moritz. Ed. by Mark Sidwell. (Orig.). 1994. pap. 11.95 (0-89084-757-6, 079053) Bob Jones Univ Pr.

Tragedy of Dido, Queen of Carthage see Life of Marlowe

Tragedy of Errors. Queen. Date not set. 15.95 (0-312-00060-X) St Martin.

Tragedy of Europe. Francis Neilson. 1971. 300.00 (0-87700-003-4) Revisionist Pr.

Tragedy of Evolution: Our Biological Heritage & Irony of Western Civilization. Michio Kitahara. LC 91-10180. 208p. 1991. text ed. 49.95 (0-275-94041-1, C4041, Praeger Pubs) Greenwood.

Tragedy of German-America. John A. Hawgood. 1940. 20.00 (0-686-17392-9) R S Barnes.

Tragedy of German-America: The Germans in the United States of America During the Nineteenth Century & after. John A. Hawgood. LC 71-129401. (American Immigration Collection. Series 2). 1976. reprint ed. 21.95 (0-405-00554-7) Ayer.

Tragedy of Hamlet: A Critical Edition of the Second Quarto. Ed. by Thomas M. Parrott & Hardin Craig. LC 75-42328. 256p. 1976. reprint ed. 50.00 (0-87752-172-7) Gordian.

Tragedy of HMS Dasher. John Steele. 192p. 1995. 65.00 (1-874640-41-6, Pub. by Argyll Pubng UK) St Mut.

Tragedy of Human Effort. C. H. Douglas. 1991. lib. bdg. 75.00 (0-8490-4401-4) Gordon Pr.

Tragedy of Ignoring the Creator: And Other Essays on Christian Life & Ministry. Maurice R. Irvin. 126p. (Orig.). 1995. pap. 6.99 (0-87509-619-0, 0016190) Chr Pubns.

Tragedy of Jane Shore. Nicholas Rowe. Ed. & Intro. by William-Alan Landes. LC 95-25451. 1995. pap. 7.00 (0-88734-295-7) Players Pr.

Tragedy of Jane Shore. Nicholas Rowe. Ed. by Harry W. Pedicord. LC 73-85439. (Regents Restoration Drama Ser.). xxviii, 97p. 1974. pap. text ed. 8.95 (0-8032-5381-8, Bison Books) U of Nebr Pr.

***Tragedy of Julius Caesar.** 97th ed. William Shakespeare. 1997. pap. text ed. 7.75 (0-03-052229-3) HR&W Schl Div.

Tragedy of Julius Caesar see Bibliographies to Supplement the New Variorum Editions of Shakespeare

Tragedy of King Lear. William Shakespeare. Ed. by Jay L. Halio. (New Cambridge Shakespeare Ser.). (Illus.). 300p. (C). 1992. text ed. 39.95 (0-521-33111-0); pap. text ed. 10.95 (0-521-33729-1) Cambridge U Pr.

Tragedy of King Richard the Third. Ed. & Illus. by J. Drakakis. LC 96-6896. (Shakespearean Originals Ser.). 1996. 12.95 (0-13-441023-8) P-H.

Tragedy of Leschi. Ezra Meeker. 1991. pap. 10.95 (0-685-49164-1) Hist Soc Seattle.

Tragedy of Libby & Andersonville Prison Camps. 5th ed. Daniel P. Brown. LC 79-54263. (U. S. History Civil War Ser.: No. II1102). (Illus.). 1991. reprint ed. pap. 3.95 (0-930860-01-2) Golden West Hist.

***Tragedy of Lin Biao.** Frederick C. Tiewes & Warren Sun. 248p. 1996. pap. write for info. (962-209-416-3, Pub. by Hong Kong Univ Pr HK) Coronet Bks.

Tragedy of Lin Biao: Riding the Tiger During the Cultural Revolution, 1966-1971. Frederick C. Teiwes & Warren Sun. 1996. text ed. 30.00 (0-8248-1811-3) UH Pr.

Tragedy of Lynching. Arthur F. Raper. LC 72-90191. (Mass Violence in America Ser.). 1969. reprint ed. 19.95 (0-405-01334-5) Ayer.

Tragedy of Lynching. Arthur F. Raper. LC 69-14943. (Criminology, Law Enforcement, & Social Problems Ser.: No. 25). 1969. reprint ed. 16.00 (0-87585-025-1) Patterson Smith.

Tragedy of Lynching. Arthur F. Raper. LC 69-16568. (Illus.). 499p. 1969. reprint ed. text ed. 35.00 (0-8371-1145-5, RAL&, Greenwood Pr) Greenwood.

***Tragedy of Macbeth.** William Shakespeare & Neil Freeman. LC 97-9576. (Applause Shakespeare Library). 1997. pap. write for info. (1-55783-290-0) Applause Theatre Bk Pubs.

***Tragedy of MacBeth.** 97th ed. William Shakespeare. 1997. pap. text ed. 7.75 (0-03-052233-1) HR&W Schl Div.

Tragedy of Man. Imre Madach. 148p. 1989. text ed. 29.50 (0-88033-169-0) East Eur Monographs.

Tragedy of Man. Imre Madach. 1973. 300.00 (0-8490-1225-2) Gordon Pr.

***Tragedy of Man.** Imre Madach. (Illus.). 272p. 1989. reprint ed. pap. 54.00 (963-13-3994-7, Pub. by Corvina Bks HU) St Mut.

Tragedy of Mariam, the Fair Queen of Jewry: Elizabeth Cary, Lady Falkland, with "The Lady Falkland: Her Life", by One of Her Daughters. Elizabeth Cary. Ed. by Barry Weller & Margaret W. Ferguson. LC 92-36294. 1993. 45.00 (0-520-07967-1); pap. 16.00 (0-520-07969-8) U CA Pr.

Tragedy of Mesopotamia. George Buchanan. LC 71-180324. (Mid-East Studies). reprint ed. 39.50 (0-404-56218-3) AMS Pr.

Tragedy of Morant Bay: A Narrative of the Disturbances in the Island of Jamaica in 1865. Edward B. Underhill. LC 73-157378. (Black Heritage Library Collection). 1977. 20.95 (0-8369-8816-7) Ayer.

Tragedy of Nijinsky. Anatole Bourman. LC 70-98822. 291p. 1970. reprint ed. text ed. 35.00 (0-8371-2965-6, BOTN, Greenwood Pr) Greenwood.

Tragedy of Origins: Pierre Corneille & Historical Perspective. John D. Lyons. LC 95-33608. 1996. 37.50 (0-8047-2616-7) Stanford U Pr.

Tragedy of Othello, the Moore of Venice. Ed. & Intro. by Andrew Murphy. LC 94-42994. (Shakespearean Originals--First Edition Ser.). 144p. 1996. pap. 12.95 (0-13-355488-0) P-H.

Tragedy of Pelee: A Narrative of Personal Experience & Observation in Martinique. George F. Kennan. LC 69-18984. (Illus.). 257p. 1970. reprint ed. text ed. 45.00 (0-8371-0932-9, KEP&, Greenwood Pr) Greenwood.

Tragedy of Philotas by Samuel Daniel. Lawrence A. Michel. (Yale Studies in English: No. 110). xiv, 185p. (C). 1970. reprint ed. lib. bdg. 31.00 (0-208-00923-X, Archon Bks) Shoe String.

Tragedy of Platitudinous Piety. Bill Best. (Illus.). 14p. (Orig.). 1982. pap. 2.50 (0-685-24883-6) Kentucke Imprints.

Tragedy of Political Science. David Ricci. LC 84-3510. 352p. 1987. pap. 17.00 (0-300-03760-0, Y-631) Yale U Pr.

Tragedy of Political Science: Politics, Scholarship, & Democracy. David M. Ricci. LC 84-3510. 352p. 1984. 45.00 (0-300-03088-6) Yale U Pr.

Tragedy of Political Theory: The Road Not Taken. J. Peter Euben. 325p. (Orig.). 1990. pap. text ed. 17.95 (0-691-02314-X) Princeton U Pr.

***Tragedy of Pudd'nhead Wilson & the Comedy Those Extraordinary Twins (1894)** Ed. by Shelley F. Fishkin. (Oxford Mark Twain). 512p. 1997. lib. bdg. 22.00 (0-19-511415-9) OUP.

Tragedy of Quebec. Robert Sellar. LC 72-1429. (Select Bibliographies Reprint Ser.). 1977. reprint ed. 19.95 (0-8369-6836-0) Ayer.

Tragedy of Quebec: The Expulsion of its Protestant Farmers. Robert Sellar. LC 73-90925. (Social History of Canada Ser.: No. 17). 419p. reprint ed. pap. 119.50 (0-685-15910-8, 2026388) Bks Demand.

Tragedy of Richard the Third. M.H. Publications Staff. 277p. 1990. 125.00 (1-872680-03-8, Pub. by M H Pubns UK) St Mut.

***Tragedy of Romeo & Juliet.** William Shakespeare & Neil Freeman. LC 97-10058. (Applause Shakespeare Library). 1997. pap. write for info. (1-55783-294-3) Applause Theatre Bk Pubs.

Tragedy of Sir Francis Bacon. Harold Bayley. LC 70-133281. (English Biography Ser.: No. 31). 1970. reprint ed. lib. bdg. 59.95 (0-8383-1180-6) M S G Haskell Hse.

Tragedy of Sir John French. George H. Cassar. LC 82-49302. (Illus.). 320p. 1985. 42.50 (0-87413-241-X) U Delaware Pr.

Tragedy of Sohrab & Rostam: From the Persian National Epic, the Shahname of Abdol-Qasem Ferdowsi. rev. ed. Abol-Qasem Ferdowski. Tr. by Jerome W. Clinton from PER. LC 96-19208. (Publications on the Near East: Vol. 3). 224p. 1996. pap. text ed. 14.95 (0-295-97567-9) U of Wash Pr.

Tragedy of Statesmanship: Bethmann Hollweg As War Chancellor (1914-1917) see Sword & the Scepter: The Problem of Militarism in Germany

Tragedy of Technology. Stephen Hill. 294p. (C). pap. 19.95 (1-85305-069-5, Pub. by Pluto Pr UK) LPC InBook.

Tragedy of Tenaya. Allan Shields. (Indian Culture Ser.). (J). (gr. 6). 1974. pap. 5.95 (0-89992-043-8) Coun India Ed.

Tragedy of Tenaya: A Yosemite Indian Story. Allan Shields. LC 92-97499. (Illus.). 95p. (Orig.). 1992. pap. 5.95 (1-882803-01-9) Jerseydale Ranch.

Tragedy of the Blackfoot. Walter McClintock. (Illus.). 53p. 1970. reprint ed. pap. 5.00 (0-916561-63-1) Southwest Mus.

Tragedy of the Chinese Revolution. 3rd rev. ed. Harold R. Isaacs. LC 61-11101. xxii, 394p. 1961. 52.50 (0-8047-0415-5); pap. 17.95 (0-8047-0416-3) Stanford U Pr.

Tragedy of the Jews in Hungary: Essays & Documents. Ed. by Randolph L. Braham. (East European Monographs: No. 208). 328p. 1987. text ed. 52.50 (0-88033-105-4) East Eur Monographs.

Tragedy of the Moisty Morning. Jessica A. Salmonson. (Illus.). 1978. 2.95 (0-914580-10-8) Angst World.

Tragedy of the Negro in America. 2nd ed. P. Thomas Stanford. LC 75-178483. (Black Heritage Library Collection). 1977. reprint ed. 28.95 (0-8369-8932-5) Ayer.

Tragedy of the Reformation: Being the Authentic Narrative of the History & Burning of the "Christianismi Restitutio", 1553, with a Succinct Account of the Theological Controversy Between Michael Servetus, Its Author, & the Reformer, John Calvin. David Cuthbertson. LC 83-45608. reprint ed. 37.50 (0-404-19826-0) AMS Pr.

Tragedy of the Soviet Germans. John Philipps. LC 83-61289. (Illus.). 190p. (Orig.). 1983. pap. 6.50 (0-9611412-0-4) John Philipps.

Tragedy of the Tragedies for the Life & Death of Tom Thumb the Great with the Annotations of H. Scribblerus Secundus. Henry Fielding. Ed. by James T. Hillhouse. LC 71-131704. 1971. reprint ed. 59.00 (0-403-00591-4) Scholarly.

Tragedy of the Victorian Novel. Jeanette M. King. LC 77-77762. 182p. 1980. pap. text ed. 24.95 (0-521-29744-3) Cambridge U Pr.

Tragedy of the Wahk-Shum: The Death of Andrew J. Bolon, Yakima Indian Agent As Told by Sue-el-lil, Eyewitness; Also, The Suicide of Gen. Geo. A. Custer As Told by Owl Child, Eyewitness. Lucullus V. McWhorter. Ed. by Donald M. Hines. LC 94-79277. (Illus.). 105p. 1995. pap. text ed. 10.95 (0-9629539-4-6) Great Eagle Pub.

Tragedy of Tragedies. Henry Fielding. 1988. reprint ed. lib. bdg. 75.00 (0-7812-0462-3) Rprt Serv.

Tragedy of Vietnam. Patrick J. Hearden. (C). 1991. text ed. 24.50 (0-673-52126-5) Addson-Wesley Educ.

Tragedy of Vietnam. Patrick J. Hearden. 192p. reprint ed. pap. 22.95 (1-886746-45-1, 93493) Talman.

Tragedy of Vinnytsia: Materials on Stalin's Policy of Extermination in Ukraine (1936-1938) Ed. by Ihor Kamenetsky. LC 89-868535. (Illus.). 286p. 1990. text ed. 35.00 (1-879070-08-1) Ukrainian Hist.

Tragedy of White Injustice. Marcus Garvey. 24p. 1978. reprint ed. pap. 2.00 (0-933121-08-3) Black Classic.

An Asterisk (*) at the beginning of an entry indicates that the title is appearing in BIP for the first time.

Tragedy of White Injustice. Marcus Garvey. LC 75-122992. 22p. (C). 1927. reprint ed. text ed. 75.00 (*0-8383-1125-3*) M S G Haskell Hse.

Tragedy of X. Ellery Queen. 256p. 1986. pap. 5.95 (*0-930330-43-9*) Intl Polygonics.

Tragedy of Yugoslavia: The Failure of Democratic Transformation. Ed. by James H. Seroka & Vukasin Pavlovic. LC 92-23052. 256p. (gr. 13). 1992. text ed. 59.95 (*1-56324-035-1*); pap. text ed. 25.95 (*1-56324-392-X*) M E Sharpe.

Tragedy of Z. Ellery Queen. (Library of Crime Classics). 192p. 1987. pap. 4.95 (*0-930330-58-7*) Intl Polygonics.

Tragedy Queens of the Georgian Era. John Fyvie. LC 78-91503. 326p. 1972. 23.95 (*0-405-08544-3*) Ayer.

Tragedy, Tradition, Transformism: The Ethics of Paul Ramsey. D. Stephen Long. LC 93-29459. 221p. (C). 1993. text ed. 63.00 (*0-8133-8747-7*) Westview.

Tragedye of Solyman & Perseda. John J. Murray. LC 91-1465. (Renaissance Imagination Ser.). 168p. 1991. text ed. 20.00 (*0-8153-0457-9*) Garland.

Tragedy's Child. Lavada Zeek. Tr. by Bill Harris. (Orig.). 1984. pap. 4.00 (*0-9611220-2-1*) Crnrstn Cmns.

Tragedy's End: Closure & Innovation in Euripidean Drama. Francis M. Dunn. 264p. (C). 1996. 45.00 (*0-19-508344-X*) OUP.

Trager Mentastics: Movement As a Way to Agelessness. 2nd ed. Milton Trager & Cathy Guadagno. Ed. by George Quasha. LC 87-23454. (Illus.). 120p. (C). 1989. reprint ed. text ed. 19.95 (*0-318-41713-8*); reprint ed. pap. text ed. 14.95 (*0-88268-067-6*) Station Hill Pr.

Tragi-Comic Professional: Basic Considerations for Ethical Reflective-Generative Practice. Paul R. Dokecki. LC 96-9981. 180p. (C). 1996. text ed. 29.95 (*0-8207-0269-2*); pap. text ed. 16.95 (*0-8207-0270-6*) Duquesne.

Tragic Alphabet: Shakespeare's Drama of Language. Lawrence Danson. LC 74-79902. 212p. reprint ed. pap. 60.50 (*0-8357-8768-0*, 2033702) Bks Demand.

Tragic Ambiguity: Anthropology, Philosophy & Sophocles' Antigone. T. C. Oudemans & A. P. Lardinois. (Brill's Studies in Intellectual History: Vol. 4). 280p. 1987. 89.00 (*90-04-08417-7*) E J Brill.

Tragic & the Sublime in Medieval Literature. Piero Boitani. 352p. (C). 1989. text ed. 75.00 (*0-521-35476-5*) Cambridge U Pr.

Tragic Beginning: The Taiwan Uprising of February 28, 1947. Lai Tse-Han et al. LC 90-39218. (Illus.). 288p. 1991. 39.50 (*0-8047-1829-6*) Stanford U Pr.

Tragic Cavalier: Governor Manuel Salcedo of Texas, 1808-1813. Felix D. Almaraz, Jr. LC 91-22811. (Illus.). 224p. 1992. pap. 15.95 (*0-89096-503-X*) Tex A&M Univ Pr.

***Tragic Charge of the Light Horse at Gallipoli.** Paul Burness. 1996. pap. text ed. 16.95 (*0-86417-782-8*, Pub. by Kangaroo Pr AT) Seven Hills Bk.

Tragic Choices. Guido Calabresi & Philip Bobbitt. (C). 1978. pap. text ed. 8.95 (*0-393-09085-X*) Norton.

Tragic Comedians: A Study in a Well-Known Story. (Revised Edition) George Meredith. LC 74-29508. (Modern Jewish Experience Ser.). 1975. reprint ed. 17.95 (*0-405-06735-6*) Ayer.

Tragic Deception: FDR & America's Involvement in World War II. Hamilton Fish. 1983. 14.95 (*0-8159-6917-1*) Devin.

Tragic Demise of a Faithful Court Official. Fritz Herzmanovsky-Orlando. Tr. by David A. Veeder. LC 96-28006. (Studies in Austrian Literature, Culture, & Thought). 1997. pap. 14.50 (*1-57241-035-3*) Ariadne CA.

Tragic Descent: America in 2020. Hamilton H. Howze. 88p. 1993. 15.95 (*1-56530-019-X*) Summit TX.

Tragic Drama & the Family: Psychoanalytic Studies from Aeschylus to Becheld. Bennett Simon. LC 88-3200. (C). 1988. 32.50 (*0-300-04132-2*) Yale U Pr.

Tragic Drama & the Family: Psychoanalytic Studies from Aeschylus to Beckett. Bennett Simon. 287p. (C). 1993. pap. 17.00 (*0-300-05805-5*) Yale U Pr.

Tragic Drama of William Butler Yeats: Figures in a Dance. Leonard E. Nathan. LC 65-16513. 319p. reprint ed. pap. 91.00 (*0-8357-4570-8*, 2037480) Bks Demand.

***Tragic Dynasty: A History of the Romanovs.** John Bergamini. (Illus.). 544p. 1997. reprint ed. write for info. (*1-56852-160-X*, Konecky & Konecky) W S Konecky Assocs.

Tragic Era: The Revolution after Lincoln. Claude G. Bowers. (History - United States Ser.). 567p. 1992. reprint ed. lib. bdg. 99.00 (*0-7812-6201-1*) Rprt Serv.

***Tragic Failure.** Tom Wicker. 1997. pap. write for info. (*0-688-15560-X*, Quill) Morrow.

Tragic Failure: Racial Integration in America. Tom Wicker. LC 95-43162. 208p. 1996. 25.00 (*0-688-10629-3*) Morrow.

Tragic Fate of Hungary: A Country Carved up Alive at Trianon. Ives De Daruvar. (Illus.). boxed 10.00 (*0-912404-03-5*) Alpha Pubns.

Tragic Grace: The Catholic Church & Child Sexual Abuse. Stephen J. Rossetti. LC 96-22804. 136p. (Orig.). 1996. pap. text ed. 10.95 (*0-8146-2434-0*, Liturg Pr Bks) Liturgical Pr.

Tragic Illusion: Educational Testing. Raven. 1991. pap. 10.00 (*0-89824-523-0*) Trillium Pr.

Tragic Kingdom: Inside Disney: An Expose. 288p. Date not set. pap. 22.95 (*0-7871-1103-1*, Dove Bks) Dove Audio.

***Tragic Kingdom: Inside Michael Eisner's Disney.** Kathleen Harkey-Smith. 1997. 22.95 (*1-55972-444-7*, Birch Ln Pr) Carol Pub Group.

Tragic Knowledge: Yeat's Autobiography & Hermeneutics. Daniel T. O'Hara. LC 80-26825. 224p. 1981. text ed. 49.50 (*0-231-05204-9*) Col U Pr.

Tragic Life: Bessie Head & Literature in Southern Africa. Ed. by Cecil Abrahams. LC 90-81309. (C). 1990. 29.95 (*0-86543-176-0*); pap. 9.95 (*0-86543-177-9*) Africa World.

Tragic Lucidity: Discourse of Recuperation in Unamuno & Camus. Keith W. Hansen. LC 92-46265. (Currents in Comparative Romance Languages & Literatures Ser.: Vol. 2). 187p. (C). 1993. text ed. 44.95 (*0-8204-1909-5*) P Lang Pubng.

Tragic Magic: A Novel. Wesley Brown. LC 94-32220. 1994. pap. 14.00 (*0-88001-401-6*) Ecco Pr.

Tragic Magic: The Life & Crimes of a Heroin Addict. Stuart L. Hills & Ron Santiago. 200p. 1992. text ed. 28.95 (*0-8304-1354-5*); pap. text ed. 19.95 (*0-8304-1317-0*) Nelson-Hall.

Tragic Mask: A Study of Faulkner's Heroes. John L. Longley. LC 63-22806. 254p. reprint ed. pap. 72.40 (*0-8357-4414-0*, 2037234) Bks Demand.

Tragic Method & Tragic Theology: Evil in Contemporary Drama & Religious Thought. Larry D. Bouchard. LC 88-21827. 240p. 1989. lib. bdg. 32.50 (*0-271-00655-2*) Pa St U Pr.

Tragic Middle: Racine, Aristotle, Euripides. Richard E. Goodkin. LC 91-3595. 222p. (C). 1991. 37.00 (*0-299-13080-0*) U of Wis Pr.

Tragic Mountains: The Hmong, the Americans, & the Secret Wars for Laos, 1942-1992. Jane Hamilton-Merritt. LC 92-28970. 612p. 1993. 29.95 (*0-253-32731-8*) Ind U Pr.

Tragic Muse. Henry James. Ed. & Intro. by Philip Horne. 576p. 1995. pap. 12.95 (*0-14-043389-9*, Penguin Classics) Viking Penguin.

Tragic Muse, Vol. 1. Henry James. LC 77-158786. (Novels & Tales of Henry James Ser.: Vol. 7). 440p. 1977. reprint ed. lib. bdg. 37.50 (*0-678-02807-9*) Kelley.

Tragic Muse, Vol. 2. Henry James. LC 77-158786. (Novels & Tales of Henry James Ser.: Vol. 8). xxi, 373p. 1977. reprint ed. lib. bdg. 37.50 (*0-678-02808-7*) Kelley.

Tragic Muse: Rachel of the Comedie-Francaise. Rachel M. Brownstein. LC 94-30101. (Illus.). 344p. 1995. pap. text ed. 16.95 (*0-8223-1571-8*) Duke.

Tragic Muse of John Ford. George F. Sensabaugh. LC 64-14714. 1972. reprint ed. 22.95 (*0-405-08949-X*, Pub. by Blom Pubns UK) Ayer.

Tragic Myth: Lorca & Cante Jondo. Edward F. Stanton. LC 77-84067. (Studies in Romance Languages: No. 20). 152p. 1979. 16.00 (*0-8131-1378-4*) U Pr of Ky.

Tragic Paradox: Myth & Ritual in Greek Tragedy. J. P. Guepin. 397p. 1968. lib. bdg. 87.50 (*0-685-13797-X*, Pub. by AM Hakkert NE) Coronet Bks.

Tragic Philosopher: Friedrich Nietzsche. F. A. Lea. LC 93-9875. 354p. (C). 1993. reprint ed. pap. 29.95 (*0-485-12095-X*, Pub. by Athlone Pr UK) Humanities.

Tragic Plane. H. A. Mason. 200p. 1985. 55.00 (*0-19-812843-6*) OUP.

Tragic Pleasures: Aristotle on Plot & Emotion. Elizabeth Belfiore. 408p. 1992. text ed. 57.50 (*0-691-06899-2*) Princeton U Pr.

Tragic Posture & Tragic Vision: Against the Modern Failure of Nerve. Louis A. Ruprecht, Jr. 288p. (C). 1994. 29.95 (*0-8264-0686-6*) Continuum.

Tragic Psalms. Francis Sullivan. 1987. pap. 7.95 (*0-912405-35-X*) Pastoral Pr.

Tragic Realism in English Literature, 1720-1820. Gerald M. Garmon. (American University Studies: English Language & Literature: Ser. 4, Vol. 72). 235p. 1988. 33.50 (*0-8204-0640-6*) P Lang Pubng.

Tragic Rhetoric: An Interpretation of Sophocles' Trachiniae. Bruce Heiden. (Hermeneutic Commentaries Ser.: Vol. 1). 216p. (C). 1989. text ed. 39.95 (*0-8204-0951-0*) P Lang Pubng.

Tragic School Bus. Tom B. Stone. (Graveyard School Ser.: No. 14). 128p. (J). (gr. 3-7). 1996. pap. 3.99 (*0-553-48490-7*, Skylark BDD) BDD Bks Young Read.

Tragic Sense of Life. Miguel De Unamuno. Tr. by J. Crawford Flitch. 1921. pap. 6.95 (*0-486-20257-7*) Dover.

Tragic Tale of French Citizenship Policy. Bruce H. Smith. 70p. 1991. pap. 34.95 (*0-9627882-3-6*) Bradley Mann.

Tragic Themes in Western Literature: Seven Essays by Bernard Knox & Others. Ed. by Cleanth Brooks. LC 55-5516. 184p. reprint ed. pap. 52.50 (*0-8357-8769-9*, 2033682) Bks Demand.

Tragic Theory in the Critical Works of Thomas Rymer, John Dennis, & John Dryden. Joan C. Grace. LC 73-2892. 143p. 1975. 26.50 (*0-8386-1312-8*) Fairleigh Dickinson.

Tragic Victory: The Doctrine of Subjective Salvation in the Poetry of W. B. Yeats. Larry Brunner. LC 86-50163. 181p. 1986. 18.50 (*0-87875-315-X*) Whitston Pub.

Tragic Vision Vol. 1: The Confrontation of Extremity. Murray Krieger. 295p. 1973. pap. 14.95 (*0-8018-1550-9*) Johns Hopkins.

Tragic Vision & Divine Compassion: A Contemporary Theodicy. Wendy Farley. 252p. (Orig.). 1990. pap. 20.00 (*0-664-25096-3*) Westminster John Knox.

***Tragic Vision in Romeo & Juliet.** James Seward. Date not set. write for info. (*0-8434-0470-1*, Pub. by McGrath NH) Ayer.

Tragic Ways of Killing a Woman. Nicole Loraux. Tr. by Anthony Forster. LC 87-390. 112p. 1987. 23.00 (*0-674-90225-4*) HUP.

Tragic Ways of Killing a Woman. Nicole Loraux. 112p. (C). 1991. pap. 12.50 (*0-674-90226-2*) HUP.

Tragic Week: A Study of Anti-Clericalism in Spain. Joan C. Ullman. LC 67-27082. 453p. 1968. reprint ed. pap. 129.20 (*0-7837-4194-4*, 2059044) Bks Demand.

Tragic Wisdom & Beyond. Gabriel Marcel. Tr. by Stephen Jolin & Peter McCormick from FRE. LC 72-96700. (Studies in Phenomenology & Existential Philosophy). 256p. (C). 1973. pap. 24.95 (*0-8101-0614-0*) Northwestern U Pr.

Tragic Years, 1860-1865: A Documentary History of the American Civil War. Paul M. Angle & Earl S. Miers. 1108p. 1992. 23.95 (*0-306-80462-X*) Da Capo.

Tragicae Dictionis Index, Spectans ad Tragicorum Graecorum Fragmenta. August Nauck. xxxii, 738p. 1962. reprint ed. write for info. (*0-318-70981-3*); reprint ed. write for info. (*0-318-72057-4*) G Olms Pubs.

Tragical Comedy or Comical Tragedy of Punch & Judy. Ed. by Karl Leabo. LC 83-70096. (Illus.). 1983. pap. 2.50 (*0-87830-582-3*, Thtre Arts Bks) Routledge.

Tragical History of Doctor Faustus. Christopher Marlowe. Ed. by Paul H. Kocher. (Crofts Classics Ser.). 96p. 1950. pap. text ed. write for info. (*0-88295-054-1*) Harlan Davidson.

Tragical History of Doctor Faustus. Christopher Marlowe. Ed. by Frederick S. Boas. (Works & Life of Christopher Marlowe Ser.: Vol. 5). 221p. 1966. reprint ed. 50.00 (*0-87752-190-5*); reprint ed. pap. 12.50 (*0-685-01942-X*) Gordian.

Tragical History of Dr. Faustus. Christopher Marlowe. Ed. by Hope. (Australian National University Press Ser.). 1982. text ed. 35.00 (*0-08-032953-5*, Pergamon Pr) Elsevier.

***Tragical History of the Life & Death of Doctor Faustus.** Christopher Marlowe. Ed. by William-Alan Landes. LC 97-1018. 55p. (Orig.). 1997. pap. 7.00 (*0-88734-721-5*) Players Pr.

Tragicall Historie of Hamlet Prince of Denmarke. Ed. by Graham Holderness & Bryan Loughrey. 300p. (C). 1992. text ed. 62.50 (*0-389-20999-6*) B&N Imports.

Tragicall Historye of Romeus & Juliet. Arthur Broke. LC 78-26035. (English Experience Ser.: No. 134). 168p. 1969. reprint ed. 21.00 (*90-221-0134-7*) Walter J Johnson.

***Tragically Hip - Day for Night.** The Tragically Hip Staff. 128p. (Orig.). 1997. pap. 19.95 (*0-7692-0257-8*, CCC125) Warner Brothers.

***Tragically Hip - Trouble at the Henhouse.** Ed. by Michael Lefferts. 116p. (Orig.). (C). 1996. pap. text ed. 19.95 (*0-7692-0826-6*, CCC118) Warner Brothers.

Tragicomedy & Novelistic Discourse in Celestina. Dorothy S. Severin. (Cambridge Iberian & Latin American Studies). (Illus.). 160p. (C). 1989. text ed. 59.95 (*0-521-35085-9*) Cambridge U Pr.

Tragicomedy in the Courts. Ralph Slovenko. 1974. pap. 5.95 (*0-87511-112-2*) Claitors.

Tragicomedy of Classical Thermodynamics: Proceedings of CISM, Department of Solids, 1971. CISM (International Center for Mechanical Sciences), Department of Mechanics of Solids Staff. Ed. by Clifford A. Truesdell. (CISM Publications: No. 70). (Illus.). 41p. 1973. 15.95 (*0-387-81114-1*) Spr-Verlag.

Tragicomic Novel: Studies in a Fictional Mode from Meredith to Joyce. Randall Craig. LC 87-40544. 192p. 1989. 32.50 (*0-87413-339-4*) U Delaware Pr.

Tragicomic Passion: Clowns, Fools & Madmen in Drama, Film & Literature. Faye Ran-Moseley. LC 92-27556. (American University Studies: Comparative Literature: Ser. III, Vol. 40). 208p. (C). 1993. text ed. 43.95 (*0-8204-1551-0*) P Lang Pubng.

Tragicomical History of Thermodynamics, Eighteen Twenty-Two to Eighteen Fifty-Four. Clifford A. Truesdell. LC 79-11925. (Studies in the History of Mathematics & Physical Sciences: Vol. 4). 1980. 130.95 (*0-387-90403-4*) Spr-Verlag.

Tragicorum Graecorum Fragmenta. August Nauck. xxvi, 1048p. 1983. reprint ed. write for info. (*3-487-00622-7*); reprint ed. Supplement, 44p. suppl. ed. write for info. (*0-318-70982-1*) G Olms Pubs.

Tragiques, 4 tomes. Agrippa D'Aubigne. Ed. by M. Garnier & Jean Plattard. (Soc. des Textes Francais Modernes Ser.). Set. 84.50 (*0-685-34180-1*) Fr & Eur.

Tragiques Grecs: Eschyle - Sophocle. deluxe ed. Ed. by Raphael Dreyfus. 1552p. (FRE.). 1967. 125.00 (*0-7859-3801-X*, 2070105679) Fr & Eur.

Tragiques Grecs: Eschyle-Sophocle. 1544p. 41.50 (*0-686-56590-8*) Fr & Eur.

Tragiques Grecs: Euripide-Theatre Complet. 1502p. 45.00 (*0-686-56589-4*) Fr & Eur.

Tragoediae. Aeschylus. Ed. by Ulrich Von Wilamowitz-Moellendorff. xxxv, 382p. (GER.). 1958. 120.00 (*3-296-10300-7*) G Olms Pubs.

Tragoediae, Vol. I: Observationes Criticas Continens. Lucius A. Seneca. viii, 232p. 1963. write for info. (*3-296-15501-5*) G Olms Pubs.

Tragoediae, Vol. II: Tragoedias Et Octaviam Continens. Lucius A. Seneca. xxx, 406p. 1963. write for info. (*3-296-15502-3*) G Olms Pubs.

Traherne in Dialogue: Heidegger, Lacan, & Derrida. A. Leigh DeNeef. LC 87-31952. ix, 312p. (C). 1988. text ed. 49.95 (*0-8223-0832-0*) Duke.

***Trahison Du Vampire.** Denis Cote. (Novels in the Roman Jeunesse Ser.). 96p. (FRE.). (J). (gr. 4-7). 1996. pap. 7.95 (*2-89021-238-6*, Pub. by Les Editions CN) Firefly Bks Ltd.

Traicion A la Sangre. Raul T. Estrella. LC 89-80763. (Coleccion Caniqui). 81p. (Orig.). (SPA.). 1991. pap. 9.95 (*0-89729-543-9*) Ediciones.

***Traicion Inocente - Wild Innocence.** Ann Major. (Deseo Ser.). 1997. mass mkt. 3.50 (*0-373-35171-2*, 1-351717) Harlequin Bks.

Traiciones-Haven's Call. Robin Elliot. 1996. mass mkt. 3.50 (*0-373-35135-6*) Harlequin Bks.

Traidor, Inconfeso y Martir. Jose Zorrilla. Ed. by Roberto Calvo Sanz. (Nueva Austral Ser.: No. 160). (SPA.). 1991. pap. text ed. 24.95 (*84-239-1960-9*) Elliots Bks.

Trail & Camp Fire: A Book of the Boone & Crockett Club. Ed. by George B. Grinnell & Theodore Roosevelt. (Illus.). 354p. reprint ed. pap. 19.95 (*0-940864-14-2*) Boone & Crockett.

***Trail Atlas of Michigan: Nature, Mountain Biking, Hiking, Cross Country Skiing.** 2nd ed. Dennis R. Hansen. (Illus.). 650p. 1997. pap. 29.95 (*0-930098-06-4*) Hansen Pub MI.

Trail Blazer: History of S.E. Idaho, Daughters of Pioneers. rev. ed. Ed. by Newell Hart. 1976. 11.00 (*0-941462-02-1*) Cache Valley.

Trail Blazers. Date not set. pap. 2.50 (*0-590-03307-7*) Scholastic Inc.

Trail Blazers of Advertising: Stories of the Romance & Adventure of the Old-Time Advertising Game. Chalmers L. Pancoast. LC 75-39264. (Getting & Spending: The Consumer's Dilemma Ser.). (Illus.). 1976. reprint ed. 26.95 (*0-405-08037-9*) Ayer.

Trail-Blazers of Science: Life Stories of Some Half-Forgotten Pioneers of Modern Research. Martin Gumpert. Tr. by Edwin L. Shuman. LC 68-29212. (Essay Index Reprint Ser.). 1977. reprint ed. 20.95 (*0-8369-0501-6*) Ayer.

***Trail Book: For Boise & the Surrounding Area.** Peak Media, Inc. Staff. 210p. 1995. ring bd. 24.95 (*0-9639134-5-X*) Peak Media.

***Trail Book: For Lake Tahoe & the Surrounding Area.** Peak Media, Inc. Staff. 210p. 1997. ring bd. 24.95 (*1-889364-00-2*) Peak Media.

***Trail Book: For Monterey & the Surrounding Area.** Peak Media, Inc. Staff. 210p. 1996. ring bd. 24.95 (*0-9639134-8-4*) Peak Media.

***Trail Book: For Portland & the Surrounding Area.** Peak Media, Inc. Staff. 210p. 1996. ring bd. 24.95 (*0-9639134-6-8*) Peak Media.

***Trail Book: For San Francisco & the Surrounding Area.** Peak Media, Inc. Staff. 210p. 1996. ring bd. 24.95 (*0-9639134-9-2*) Peak Media.

***Trail Book: For Seattle & the Surrounding Area.** Peak Media, Inc. Staff. 210p. 1996. ring bd. 24.95 (*0-9639134-7-6*) Peak Media.

***Trail Book: For Sun Valley & the Surrounding Area.** Peak Media, Inc. Staff. 210p. 1995. ring bd. 24.95 (*0-9639134-4-1*) Peak Media.

Trail Boss from Texas. large type ed. Barry Cord. (Linford Western Library). 288p. 1989. pap. 15.99 (*0-7089-6708-6*, Linford) Ulverscroft.

Trail Boss's Cowboy Cookbook. LC 88-60338. 336p. 1985. reprint ed. spiral bd., pap. 14.95 (*0-9603692-6-0*) Falcon Pr MT.

Trail Building & Maintenance. 2nd ed. Robert D. Proudman & Reuben Rajala. LC 82-121206. (Illus.). 304p. 1981. pap. 12.95 (*0-910146-30-6*) AMC Books.

Trail Creek County, Missouri. Mina Hickman & Sherry Lovell. (Illus.). 178p. 1993. 35.00 (*0-88107-233-8*) Curtis Media.

Trail Design, Construction & Maintenance. Robert D. Proudman & William Birchard, Jr. (Illus.). 176p. 1996. reprint ed. pap. 8.95 (*0-917953-07-X*) Appalachian Trail.

Trail Drive. James Rice. LC 96-23057. (Illus.). 32p. (J). (gr. k-5). 1996. 14.95 (*1-56554-163-4*) Pelican.

Trail Driver. Zane Grey. 304p. 1991. mass mkt. 3.99 (*0-06-100154-6*, Harp PBks) HarpC.

Trail Drivers of Texas. Ed. by J. Marvin Hunter. (Illus.). 1117p. 1985. reprint ed. 40.00 (*0-292-78076-1*) U of Tex Pr.

Trail Drivers of Texas. Compiled by J. Marvin Hunter. (Illus.). 1117p. (C). 1993. reprint ed. pap. 24.95 (*0-292-73076-4*) U of Tex Pr.

Trail Drivers of Texas, 2 vols. J. Marvin Hunter. 1993. reprint ed. Set. lib. bdg. 150.00 (*0-7812-5938-X*) Rprt Serv.

***Trail Dust.** Don Kennington & Phil Kennington. (Illus.). xii, 121p. 1992. pap. 10.00 (*1-890672-02-5*) Phil Don.

***Trail Dust.** Don Kennington & Phil Kennington. (Illus.). xv, 179p. 1995. pap. 10.00 (*1-890672-03-3*) Phil Don.

***Trail Dust.** Don Kennington & Phil Kennington. (Illus.). 1998. pap. 10.00 (*1-890672-04-1*) Phil Don.

Trail Dust. Gene Martin. 1988. pap. 3.75 (*0-9606648-0-7*) Martin Assocs.

Trail Dust. large type ed. Clarence E. Mulford. Date not set. lib. bdg. 24.95 (*0-88411-240-3*, Aeonian Pr) Amereon Ltd.

***Trail Dust, Vol I.** Don Kennington & Phil Kennington. (Illus.). xv, 153p. 1988. pap. 10.00 (*1-890672-00-9*) Phil Don.

***Trail Dust, Vol. II.** Don Kennington & Phil Kennington. (Illus.). xvii, 161p. 1990. pap. 10.00 (*1-890672-01-7*) Phil Don.

Trail Dust see Hopalong Cassidy Series

Trail Dust & Saddle Leather. Jo Mora. LC 86-19303. (Illus.). x, 246p. 1987. pap. 10.95 (*0-8032-8145-5*, Bison Books) U of Nebr Pr.

Trail Ends at Hell. large type ed. John Benteen. 1991. pap. 15.99 (*0-7089-6957-7*) Ulverscroft.

***Trail Fever: Spin Doctors, Rented Strangers, Thumb Wrestlers, Toe Suckers, Grizzly Bears, & Other Creatures on the Road to the White House.** Michael Lewis. 299p. 1997. 25.00 (*0-679-44660-5*) Knopf.

Trail Fever: The Life of a Texas Cowboy. D. J. Lightfoot. LC 92-5458. (Illus.). (YA). 1992. 11.00 (*0-688-11537-3*) Lothrop.

Trail from St. Augustine. Lee Gramling. LC 93-5214. 264p. 1993. 14.95 (*1-56164-047-6*); pap. 8.95 (*1-56164-042-5*) Pineapple Pr.

Trail Guide: The Locator. 2nd ed. Cheryl Erlenback. 64p. Date not set. pap. 2.95 (*0-614-10204-9*) Trail Guide.

***Trail Guide Handbook: Cuyahoga Valley National Recreation Area.** 2nd rev. ed. Peg Bobel. Ed. & Illus. by Rob Bobel. LC 92-114089. 190p. 1997. pap. 14.95 (*0-9630416-1-4*) Cuyahoga Valley.

Trail Guide to Bob Marshall Country. Eric K. Molvar. (Falcon Guides Ser.). (Illus.). 294p. (Orig.). 1994. pap. 19.95 (*1-56044-254-9*) Falcon Pr MT.

T

Trail Guide to Los Padres National Forest. (Illus.). 132p. (YA). (gr. 8 up). pap. 14.95 (0-9650652-0-0) Sierra Club Ventana.

Trail Guide to Microsoft Network: A Rapid-Reading Reference to Using & Cruising the Microsoft Network Online Service. Melody Newrock. 1996. pap. 12.95 (0-201-48943-0) Addison-Wesley.

Trail Guide to Pecos Wilderness: Santa Fe National Forest. Ed. by Stephen G. Maurer. (National Forest Visitors Guide Ser.). (Illus.). 192p. 1991. pap. 9.95 (1-879343-01-0) SW NCH Assn.

Trail Guide to Prodigy: A Rapid-Reading Reference to Using & Cruising the Prodigy Online. Caroline M. Halliday. 1995. pap. 12.95 (0-201-40972-0) Addison-Wesley.

Trail Home: Essays. John Daniel. 272p. 1994. pap. 13.00 (0-679-75438-5) Pantheon.

***Trail Is Never Cold: Life & Times of Sheriff Jess Sweeten.** 284p. (Orig.). 1997. pap. 14.95 (0-9648819-1-8, 500) Ballycastle.

Trail Makers of the Middle Border. Hamlin Garland. (Collected Works of Hamlin Garland). 1988. reprint ed. lib. bdg. 59.00 (0-7812-1249-9) Rprt Serv.

Trail Markers of the Middle Border see Collected Works of Hamlin Garland

Trail North. Hawk Greenway. LC 81-2954. (Illus.). 191p. (Orig.). 1981. pap. 9.95 (0-933280-04-1) Island Pr.

***Trail North: Stories of Texas' Yesterdays.** 2nd ed. Charlotte Baker. (J). (gr. 4-7). 1997. pap. 8.95 (1-57168-066-7) Sunbelt Media.

Trail of an Artist-Naturalist: Autobiography of Ernest Thompson Seton. Ernest T. Seton. Ed. by Keir B. Sterling. LC 77-81134. (Biologists & Their World Ser.). (Illus.). 1978. reprint ed. lib. bdg. 40.95 (0-405-10734-X) Ayer.

Trail of an Artist-Naturalist: The Autobiography of Ernest Thompson Seton. Ernest T. Seton. (American Biography Ser.). 412p. 1991. reprint ed. lib. bdg. 89.00 (0-7812-8349-3) Rprt Serv.

Trail of Apple Blossoms. Irene Hunt. LC 92-46739. (Illus.). 64p. (J). (gr. 4-6). 1993. pap. 6.95 (0-8136-7220-1) Silver Burdett Pr.

Trail of Commerce & Conquest: A Brief History of the Road to Santa Fe. Jack D. Rittenhouse. (Illus.). 30p. (Orig.). 1987. pap. 1.95 (0-938463-03-9) Western Bks.

Trail of Corn: A True Mystery. Keith Walker. (Illus.). 770p. 1995. 24.95 (1-885793-00-6) Gldn Door Pr.

Trail of Cthulhu. August Derleth. 256p. 1996. mass mkt. 4.95 (0-7867-0341-5) Carroll & Graf.

Trail of Darkness. Darlene D. Bolesny. 1996. pap. 5.99 (0-7869-0517-4) TSR Inc.

***Trail of Darkness.** Carn Jensen. 270p. (Orig.). 1997. pap. 12.95 (1-881542-35-1) Book World Inc.

Trail of Education in Two Cities Omaha & Manila. Natividad T. Nacianceno & Floyd T. Waterman. 100p. (Orig.). 1985. pap. 6.00 (1-55719-057-7) U NE CPAR.

Trail of Flame. Jennifer T. Thompson. 192p. 1995. pap. 11.95 (0-89815-750-1) Ten Speed Pr.

Trail of Fu Manchu. Sax Rohmer. 25.95 (0-8488-0317-5) Amereon Ltd.

Trail of Fu Manchu. Sax Rohmer. 1985. pap. 3.50 (0-8217-1619-0) Kensgtn Pub Corp.

Trail of Heart's Blood Wherever We Go. Robert Olmstead. 1990. 19.95 (0-394-57539-3) Random.

Trail of Heart's Blood Wherever We Go. Robert Olmstead. 416p. 1992. reprint ed. pap. 11.00 (0-380-71548-1) Avon.

***Trail of Hope: The Story of the Mormon Trail.** William W. Slaughter & Michael Landon. LC 97-12727. 1997. write for info. (1-57345-251-3) Deseret Bk.

Trail of Lewis & Clark: 1804-1904, 2 vols. Olin D. Wheeler. LC 75-177829. reprint ed. Set. 125.00 (0-404-06926-6) AMS Pr.

Trail of Lies. Carolyn Keene. Ed. by Ann Greenberg. (Nancy Drew Files Ser.: No. 53). 160p. (Orig.). (YA). (gr. 6 up). 1990. pap. 3.75 (0-671-70030-8, Archway) PB.

Trail of Lonesome Pine. John Fox. 1976. 26.95 (0-8488-1328-6) Amereon Ltd.

Trail of Love. Amanda Browning. (Presents Ser.). 1995. pap. 3.25 (0-373-11742-6, 1-11742-3) Harlequin Bks.

Trail of Memories: The Quotations of Louis L'Amour. Compiled by Angelique L'Amour. LC 88-965. 224p. 1988. 12.95 (0-553-05271-3) Bantam.

Trail of Memories: The Quotations of Louis L'Amour. large type ed. Compiled by Angelique L'Amour. (General Ser.). 216p. 1989. lib. bdg. 21.95 (0-8161-4728-0, GK Hall) Thorndike Pr.

Trail of Murder. Christine Andreae. (Mystery Ser.). 1995. mass mkt. 3.99 (0-373-26183-7, 1-26183-3, Wrldwide Lib) Harlequin Bks.

Trail of Mythmaker. Tracy Dunham. LC 95-94893. 192p. 1995. 17.95 (0-8034-9151-4) Bouregy.

***Trail of Rogues.** large type ed. Fred Grove. LC 96-36486. 322p. 1997. 18.95 (0-7862-0900-3, Thorndike Lrg Prnt) Thorndike Pr.

Trail of Secrets. Eileen Goudge. 1997. mass mkt. 6.99 (0-451-18774-1, Sig) NAL-Dutton.

Trail of Secrets. Eileen Goudge. LC 95-39411. 464p. 1996. pap. 23.95 (0-670-86191-X, Viking) Viking Penguin.

Trail of Secrets. large type ed. Eileen Goudge. LC 96-16743. 1996. 26.95 (1-56895-325-9) Wheeler Pub.

Trail of Tears. David Fremon. (American Events Ser.). (Illus.). 96p. (YA). (gr. 6 up). 1994. lib. bdg. 14.95 (0-02-735745-7, New Dscvry Bks) Silver Burdett Pr.

Trail of Tears. Gloria Jahoda. LC 95-10144. 1995. 9.99 (0-517-14677-0) Random.

***Trail of Tears.** Tony Johnston. LC 96-6597. (Illus.). (J). 1998. write for info. (0-590-48519-9, Blue Sky Press) Scholastic Inc.

Trail of Tears. R. Conrad Stein. LC 92-33422. (Cornerstones of Freedom Ser.). (Illus.). 32p. (J). (gr. 3-6). 1993. pap. 4.95 (0-516-46666-6); lib. bdg. 18.00 (0-516-06666-8) Childrens.

Trail of Tears: The Cherokee Journey from Home. Marlene T. Brill. LC 94-16988. (Spotlight on American History Ser.). (Illus.). 64p. (J). (gr. 4-6). 1995. lib. bdg. 16.40 (1-56294-486-X) Millbrook Pr.

Trail of Tears: The Rise & Fall of the Cherokee Nation. John Ehle. 432p. 1989. pap. 12.95 (0-385-23954-8, Anchor NY) Doubleday.

Trail of Tears Across Missouri. Joan Gilbert. (Missouri Heritage Readers Ser.). (Illus.). 136p. (C). 1995. pap. 8.95 (0-8262-1063-5) U of Mo Pr.

Trail of the Dangerous Gun. Lee Martin. 1995. 17.95 (0-8034-9099-2, 094641) Bouregy.

Trail of the Dove. Dorothy Friedman. 150p. (Orig.). 1995. pap. 10.95 (0-943873-39-8) Elder Bks.

Trail of the Dragon. Susan Kelly. 282p. 1988. 17.95 (0-8027-5696-4) Walker & Co.

Trail of the Eagle: Hunting Alaska with Master Guide Bud Conkle. Bud Conkle & Jim Rearden. (Illus.). 252p. 1990. 29.50 (0-937708-24-0) Great Northwest.

Trail of the First Wagons over the Sierra Nevada. 3rd ed. Charles K. Graydon. LC 88-5924. (Illus.). 80p. 1994. pap. 16.95 (1-880397-07-2) Patrice Pr.

Trail of the Fox. David Irving. (YA). (gr. 7 up). 1978. mass mkt. 5.95 (0-380-40022-7) Avon.

Trail of the Fox. David Irving. 624p. 1990. pap. 12.95 (0-380-70940-6) Avon.

Trail of the Goldseekers. Hamlin Garland. (Collected Works of Hamlin Garland). 1988. reprint ed. lib. bdg. 59.00 (0-7812-1227-8) Rprt Serv.

Trail of the Goldseekers see Collected Works of Hamlin Garland

Trail of the Hare: Environment & Stress in a Sub-Arctic Community. 2nd ed. Joel S. Savishinsky. LC 93-38945. (Library of Anthropology). 272p. 1994. text ed. 50.00 (2-88124-647-8); pap. text ed. 22.00 (2-88124-618-4) Gordon & Breach.

Trail of the Huguenots: In Europe, the United States, South Africa, & Canada. G. Elmore Reaman. (Illus.). 318p. 1993. reprint ed. 25.00 (0-8063-0290-9, 4810) Genealog Pub.

Trail of the Hunter's Horn. 2nd ed. Billy C. Clark. Ed. by James M. Gifford & Patricia A. Hall. LC 95-7143. (Illus.). 80p. (J). (gr. 4 up). 1995. pap. 6.00 (0-945084-48-X) J Stuart Found.

Trail of the Lonesome Pine. John Fox. 1976. lib. bdg. 27.95 (0-89968-040-2, Lghtyr Pr) Buccaneer Bks.

Trail of the Lonesome Pine. John Fox, Jr. LC 84-2234. 440p. 1984. reprint ed. 30.00 (0-8131-1508-6); reprint ed. pap. 16.00 (0-8131-0156-5) U Pr of Ky.

Trail of the Moon: South African Poems. John Brander. (Illus.). 105p. (Orig.). 1992. pap. write for info. (0-9624205-3-0) Inevitable Pr.

Trail of the Mountain Man. 1991. mass mkt. 3.50 (0-8217-3676-0, Zebra Kensgtn) Kensgtn Pub Corp.

Trail of the Mountain Man. William W. Johnstone. 1995. mass mkt. 4.50 (0-8217-5151-4, Zebra Kensgtn) Kensgtn Pub Corp.

***Trail of the Mountain Man.** William W. Johnstone. 272p. 1996. mass mkt. 4.99 (0-8217-5609-5, Zebra Kensgtn) Kensgtn Pub Corp.

Trail of The Octopus: The DEA-CIA Cover-up at Lockerbie. Donald Goddard & Lester Coleman. (Illus.). 288p. 1995. 22.95 (1-882206-11-8); pap. 13.95 (1-882206-10-X) Argonaut Pr.

Trail of the Pack Peddler. Sam Mims. 40p. pap. 2.50 (0-911116-45-1) Pelican.

Trail of the Sandhill Stag. Ernest T. Seton. (Illus.). 93p. (YA). 1994. pap. 11.95 (1-885529-03-1) Stevens Pub.

Trail of the Screaming Teenager. Patricia R. Giff & Blanche Sims. (Polka Dot Ser.: No. 7). 80p. (Orig.). (J). 1990. pap. 3.99 (0-440-40312-X) Dell.

Trail of the Snake from Big Bend to Baja. Michael A. Williamson. LC 85-26138. (Illus.). 128p. (Orig.). 1986. pap. 10.95 (0-86534-077-3) Sunstone Pr.

Trail of the Spanish Bit. Don Coldsmith. 192p. 1987. mass mkt. 4.99 (0-553-26397-8) Bantam.

***Trail of the Wild West.** Ed. by National Geographic Society Staff. 1997. 30.00 (0-7922-7021-5) Natl Geog.

***Trail of the Wild West.** Paul R. Walker. LC 97-14043. 1997. write for info. (0-7922-7019-3) Natl Geog.

***Trail of the Wolf.** R. D. Lawrence. 1997. pap. text ed. 19.95 (1-55209-186-4) Firefly Bks Ltd.

Trail of Thread: A Woman's Westward Journey. Linda K. Hubalek. LC 95-78434. (Trail of Thread Ser.: Bk. 1). (Illus.). 124p. (Orig.). 1995. pap. 9.95 (1-886652-06-6) Butterfld Bks.

Trail of Time: Time Measurement with Incense Clocks in East Asia. Silvio A. Bedini. (Needham Research Institute Studies). (Illus.). 300p. (C). 1994. text ed. 130.00 (0-521-37482-0) Cambridge U Pr.

Trail of '42: A Pictorial History of the Alaska Highway. rev. ed. Stan B. Cohen. (Illus.). 1988. pap. 7.95 (0-933126-06-9) Pictorial Hist.

Trail on Which They Wept: The Story of a Cherokee Girl. (Her Story Ser.). 64p. (J). (gr. 4-6). 1992. pap. 3.95 (0-382-24353-6); lib. bdg. 9.95 (0-382-24331-5) Silver Burdett Pr.

***Trail Rider.** Jill Stover. Date not set. write for info. (0-688-13899-3); lib. bdg. write for info. (0-688-13900-0) Lothrop.

***Trail Riding & Pack Trips in Washington.** Dick Woodfin & LaDonna Woodfin. (Illus.). 256p. 1997. pap. write for info. (0-939116-44-8) Frontier OR.

Trail Riding Book. 90p. 3.95 (0-318-14509-X) Intl Arabian.

***Trail Riding Western Montana.** Carellen Barnett. LC 96-49969. (Illus.). 160p. 1997. pap. 14.95 (1-56044-336-7) Falcon Pr MT.

***Trail-Side Vol. 1: Florida.** Joan L. Scalpon. (Illus.). 64p. 1997. pap. 8.95 (0-929198-16-6) Mini DayTrip Bks.

Trail Smoke. Ernest Haycox. 1989. mass mkt. 2.95 (1-55817-161-4, Pinncle Kensgtn) Kensgtn Pub Corp.

Trail Talk. Bobby J. Copeland. LC 96-84162. (Illus.). 168p. 1996. pap. 12.50 (0-944019-20-X) Empire NC.

***Trail Through Leaves: The Journal As a Path to Place.** Hannah Hinchman. 1997. 24.95 (0-393-04101-8) Norton.

***Trail to Buddha's Mirror.** Don Winslow. 1997. mass mkt. 5.99 (0-614-27787-6) St Martin.

***Trail to Buddha's Mirror, Vol. 1.** Winslow. 1997. mass mkt. 5.99 (0-312-96309-2) St Martin.

Trail to Crazy Man. Louis L'Amour. 368p. 1986. pap. 4.50 (0-553-28035-X) Bantam.

Trail to Disaster. Patricia J. Richmond. 1992. pap. 11.95 (0-87081-275-0) Univ Pr Colo.

Trail to El Paso. Lloyd E. Miller, Jr. (Western Classic Premier Bks.). 225p. (Orig.). 1995. pap. 4.95 (0-9639322-3-3) Literary Prods.

Trail to Forever. Elizabeth Gregg. 1997. pap. 5.99 (0-451-40637-0, Onyx) NAL-Dutton.

Trail to Heaven: Knowledge & Narrative in a Northern Native Community. Robin Ridington. LC 88-17098. (Illus.). 317p. 1988. text ed. 33.95 (0-87745-212-1) U of Iowa Pr.

Trail to Heaven: Knowledge & Narrative in a Northern Native Community. Robin Ridington. LC 88-17098. (Illus.). 317p. 1992. reprint ed. pap. 11.95 (0-87745-391-8) U of Iowa Pr.

Trail to Honk Ballard's Bones. Sam Brown. 192p. 1990. 17.95 (0-8027-4101-0) Walker & Co.

Trail to Honk Ballard's Bones. large type ed. Sam Brown. LC 90-41904. 349p. 1990. reprint ed. lib. bdg. 15.95 (1-56054-043-5) Thorndike Pr.

Trail to Medicine Lodge. Tracy Dunham. 192p. 1994. 17.95 (0-8034-9069-0) Bouregy.

Trail to Nemesis. large type ed. Elliot Long. (Linford Western Large Print Ser.). 1994. pap. 15.99 (0-7089-7642-5) Ulverscroft.

Trail to North Star Gold: True Story of the Alaska-Klondike Gold Rush. 2nd ed. Ella L. Martinsen. LC 70-98194. (Illus.). 378p. 1991. reprint ed. pap. 14.95 (0-8323-0242-2) Binford Mort.

Trail to Ogallala. Benjamin Capps. LC 85-4721. (Texas Tradition Ser.: No. 3). 286p. 1985. reprint ed. 16.95 (0-87565-012-0); reprint ed. pap. 9.95 (0-87565-013-9) Tex Christian.

Trail to Riches. E. Paul Braxton. 240p. 1995. pap. 9.95 (0-939017-02-4) Hermit Pr FL.

Trail to San Jacinto. Archie P. McDonald. (Texas History Ser.). (Illus.). 45p. 1982. pap. text ed. 8.95 (0-89641-074-9) American Pr.

Trail to Seven Pines. Louis L'Amour. 1993. pap. 4.99 (0-553-56178-2) Bantam.

Trail to Seven Pines. large type ed. Louis L'Amour. LC 93-45637. 1994. pap. 19.95 (0-8161-5799-5, GK Hall) Thorndike Pr.

Trail to Temptation. Rae Muir. 1996. pap. 4.99 (0-373-28945-6, 1-28945-3) Harlequin Bks.

***Trail to the Klondike.** Don McCune. LC 97-735. (Illus.). 144p. (Orig.). 1997. 35.00 (0-87422-143-9); pap. 19.95 (0-87422-144-7) Wash St U Pr.

Trail to Timberline. large type ed. Stephen Calder. (Bonanza Ser.: Vol. 6). 340p. 1996. 19.95 (0-7838-1828-9, GK Hall) Thorndike Pr.

Trail to Tomorrow. Anita Niles-Beattie. LC 92-91104. (Illus.). 72p. 1993. pap. 9.00 (1-56002-278-7, Univ Edtns) Aegina Pr.

***Trail to Trouble.** large type ed. Lauran Paine. (Linford Western Library). 272p. 1996. pap. 15.99 (0-7089-7950-5, Linford) Ulverscroft.

Trail to Vicksburg: A Western Duo. large type ed. Lewis B. Patten. LC 96-53881. 238p. Date not set. 17.95 (0-7862-0741-8, Thorndike Lrg Prnt); 20.00 (0-7862-0764-7, Thorndike Lrg Prnt) Thorndike Pr.

Trail to Wrangell: The Adventures of Dusty Sourdough, Vol. 2. Glen Guy. (Illus.). 105p. (Orig.). 1995. pap. 7.95 (0-9644491-3-7) Old Alaska.

Trail Tools - Desolation Wilderness: Trail Maps, Trail Profits, Mileage Charts, & Destination Charts for Hikers & Backpackers. Dennis V. O'Neill. LC 95-92647. (Illus.). 180p. (Orig.). 1996. per., pap. 16.95 (0-931285-04-6) ONeill Soft.

Trail Tools: Yosemite Valley: Trail Maps, Trail Profiles, Mileage Charts, & Destination Charts for Hikers & Backpackers. Dennis V. O'Neil. (Illus.). 112p. (Orig.). 1996. pap. 12.95 (0-931285-05-4) ONeill Soft.

Trail Town. Ernest Haycox. 1989. mass mkt. 2.95 (1-55817-293-9, Pinncle Kensgtn) Kensgtn Pub Corp.

Trail West. David Thompson. (Wilderness Giant Edition Ser.). 368p. (Orig.). 1996. mass mkt. 5.99 (0-8439-3938-9) Dorchester Pub Co.

Trail West. large type ed. Cy James. (Linford Western Library). 336p. 1986. pap. 15.99 (0-7089-6207-6, Linford) Ulverscroft.

Trail West: A Bibliography-Index to Western American Trails, 1841-1869. John M. Townley. (Illus.). 350p. (C). 1988. 29.95 (0-913381-05-5) Great Basin Studies Ctr.

Trailblazer Fun Honors I: Birds, Buttons, Computers, Dress, Kites & Stamps. L. S. Gattis, III. (Illus.). 20p. (Orig.). (J). (ps-5). 1986. teacher ed., pap. 5.00 (0-936241-08-X) Cheetah Pub.

Trailblazer Fun Honors II: Cooking, Dogs, Flowers, Hiking, Seeds & Trees. L. S. Gattis, III. (Illus.). 20p. (Orig.). (J). (ps-5). 1987. teacher ed., pap. 5.00 (0-936241-43-8) Cheetah Pub.

Trailblazer (Urban Cowboys) Vicki L. Thompson. 1995. mass mkt. 3.25 (0-373-25655-8) Harlequin Bks.

***Trailblazers, 10 bks.** (American Women of Achievement Ser.). (YA). (gr. 5 up). 199.50 (0-7910-3503-4) Chelsea Hse.

Trailblazers. H. Upton. (Wild West in American History Ser.). (Illus.). 32p. (J). (gr. 3-8). 1990. lib. bdg. 18.00 (0-86625-369-6); lib. bdg. 13.50 (0-685-58653-7) Rourke Corp.

Trailblazers: The Men & Women Who Forged the West. Constance Jones. 144p. 1995. 16.98 (1-56799-179-3, MetroBooks) M Friedman Pub Grp Inc.

Trailblazers for Translators: The Influence of the "Chichicastenago Twelve" Anna M. Dahlquist. LC 91-65732. 1995. pap. 10.95 (0-87808-205-0) William Carey Lib.

***Trailblazers of the Wild West Series, 6 vols.** (Illus.). (J). (gr. 4-10). 1995. lib. bdg. 89.70 (0-89490-563-5) Enslow Pubs.

***Traildust: Cowboys, Cattle & Country, the Art of James Reynolds.** Donald Hedgpeth & James Reynolds. LC 97-15123. 1997. write for info. (0-86713-038-5) Greenwich Wrkshop.

***Traildust: Cowboys, Cattle & Country: The Art of James Reynolds.** Don Hedgpeth. (Illus.). 156p. 1997. 39.95 (0-86713-035-0) Greenwich Wrkshop.

Trailer Boater's Basic Handbook. William S. Carpenter et al. LC 93-91422. 150p. 1993. pap. 19.95 (1-883818-02-8) Gemini Marine.

***Trailer Life Campground-RV Park & Services Directory.** Trailer Life Editors. 1996. pap. text ed. 14.95 (0-934798-42-7) TL Enterprises.

Trailer Life's RV Repair & Maintenance Manual. 2nd ed. Bob Livingston. LC 89-4637. 1989. pap. 29.95 (0-934798-12-5) TL Enterprises.

***Trailer Life's 1996 Towing Guide.** Trailer Life Editors. 64p. (Orig.). 1996. pap. 7.95 (0-934798-41-9) TL Enterprises.

***Trailer Lifes 1997 Towing Guide.** Trailer Life Magazine Staff. 1997. pap. 7.95 (0-934798-47-8) TL Enterprises.

Trailer-Loading Success: A Step-by-Step Guide for Training Horses to Load. Diane Longanecker. LC 92-91182. (Illus.). 103p. (Orig.). 1993. spiral bd. 28.50 (0-9635320-0-6) Roustabout Pr.

Trailer Trash from Tennessee. David Hunter. 224p. 1995. pap. 9.95 (1-55853-346-X) Rutledge Hill Pr.

Trailer Underride: Conspicuity, Human Factors, & Rear Bumpers. Joseph E. Badger. (Illus.). 22p. (C). 1993. pap. text ed. 12.95 (1-884566-14-6) Inst Police Tech.

Trailerboat Guide. Joe A. Skorupa. LC 93-958. 1993. pap. 15.00 (0-688-12338-4) Hearst Marine Bks.

Trailerboats-West. (Illus.). 7.95 (0-393-60021-1) Norton.

***Trailerpark.** Russell Banks. 240p. 1996. 33.00 (0-8095-9197-9) Borgo Pr.

Trailerpark. Russell Banks. LC 95-53310. 1996. write for info. (0-614-95862-8, PL) HarpC.

Trailerpark. Russell Banks. LC 95-53310. 240p. 1996. pap. 12.00 (0-06-097706-X) HarpC.

Trailers. Carol Burch-Brown & David Rigsbee. LC 96-6014. (Illus.). 112p. (Orig.). 1996. pap. 16.95 (0-8139-1680-1) U Pr of Va.

Trailers: How to Buy & Evaluate. 2nd ed. M. M. Smith. (Illus.). 182p. (Orig.). 1988. pap. text ed. 12.95 (0-914483-07-2) Techni-Visions.

Trailers: How to Design & Build, Vol. 1: Basics. M. M. Smith. (Illus.). 1995. spiral bd. 24.95 (0-914483-31-5) Techni-Visions.

Trailers: How to Design & Build, Vol. 2: Structures. M. M. Smith. (Illus.). 1996. spiral bd. 29.95 (0-914483-32-3) Techni-Visions.

Trailers: How to Design & Build, Vol. 3: Performance. M. M. Smith. (Illus.). 1999. spiral bd. 31.95 (0-914483-33-1) Techni-Visions.

Trailers: How to Tow & Maintain. M. M. Smith. (Illus.). (Orig.). 1982. pap. text ed. 9.95 (0-914483-15-3) Techni-Visions.

Trailin' Max Brand. LC 94-13998. xv, 375p. 1994. text ed. 25.00 (0-8032-1247-X) U of Nebr Pr.

Trailing a Bear: Adventures of Fred Bear & Bob Munger. Robert S. Munger. (Illus.). 353p. (Orig.). 1995. lib. bdg. 19.95 (0-9645143-0-3) Munger Pub.

Trailing Back. Charles A. Seltzer. 320p. 1975. reprint ed. lib. bdg. 24.95 (0-88411-107-5) Amereon Ltd.

Trailing Billy the Kid. Philip J. Rasch. Ed. by Robert K. DeArment. LC 95-12960. (Outlaw-Lawman Research Studies: Vol. 1). 232p. 1995. 29.95 (0-935269-19-3) Western Pubns.

Trailing Clouds of Glory. William Wordsworth. (Poetry Ser.). (Illus.). 96p. 1996. 19.95 (1-85793-649-3, Pub. by Pavilion UK) Trafalgar.

Trailing Louis L'Amour in New Mexico. Bert Murphy. Ed. by Appleyard Communications Staff. (Trailing Louis L'Amour Ser.: Vol. 1). (Illus.). 200p. (Orig.). 1996. 19.95 (0-9650298-0-8) MBAR Pubng.

Trailing the Cowboy: His Life & Lore As Told by Frontier Journalists. Ed. by Clifford P. Westermeier. LC 77-13831. (Illus.). 414p. 1978. reprint ed. text ed. 38.50 (0-8371-9866-6, WETC, Greenwood Pr) Greenwood.

Trailing the Pioneers: A Guide to Utah's Emigrant Trails, 1829-1869. Ed. by Peter H. DeLafosse. LC 94-825. (Illus.). 112p. 1994. pap. 10.95 (0-87421-172-7) Utah St U Pr.

Trailing the Pioneers: A Guide to Utah's Emigrant Trails, 1829-1869. limited ed. Ed. by Peter H. DeLafosse. LC 94-825. (Illus.). 112p. 1994. boxed 50.00 (0-87421-175-1) Utah St U Pr.

Trailing Whitetails. John Trout, Jr. LC 87-22137. (Illus.). 207p. (Orig.). 1987. pap. 8.95 (0-945980-14-0) Nrth Country Pr.

Trailing You. Kimberly Blaeser. 1994. pap. 9.95 (0-912678-88-7) Greenfld Rev Lit.

An Asterisk (*) at the beginning of an entry indicates that the title is appearing in BIP for the first time.

***Trailmen's Truce.** large type ed. John Roberts. (Dales Large Print Ser.). 203p. 1997. pap. 18.99 (*1-85389-734-5*, Dales) Ulverscroft.

Trailrider's Guide to Texas. Mary E. Goldman. (Illus.). 280p. (Orig.). 1992. pap. 14.95 (*1-55622-317-X*, Rep of TX Pr) Wordware Pub.

Trails. Mark Dunster. 32p. (Orig.). 1991. pap. 5.00 (*0-89642-191-0*) Linden Pubs.

Trails: Reflections of a Pilgrimage. Donald C. Jackson. (Illus.). 180p. 1984. 14.95 (*0-87397-261-9*, Strode Pubs) Circle Bk Service.

Trails: Toward a New Western History. Ed. by Patricia N. Limerick et al. LC 91-25640. (Illus.). 250p. 1991. pap. 12.95 (*0-7006-0501-0*) U Pr of KS.

Trails: Toward a New Western History. Ed. by Patricia N. Limerick et al. LC 91-25640. (Illus.). 250p. 1991. 29.95 (*0-7006-0500-2*) U Pr of KS.

Trails Across America: Traveler's Guide to Our National Scenic & Historic Trails. Aurthur P. Miller & Marjorie L. Miller. (Illus.). 336p. (Orig.). 1996. pap. 19.95 (*1-55591-235-4*) Fulcrum Pub.

Trails among the Columbine: 1989. Sundance Staff. Ed. by Russ Collman. (Illus.). 192p. 1989. reprint ed. 37.00 (*0-913582-11-5*, 0215) Sundance.

Trails among the Columbine: 91/92. Ed. by Russ Collman. (Illus.). 320p. 1992. 37.00 (*0-913582-54-9*, 0247) Sundance.

Trails among the Columbine: 93/94. Ed. by Russ Collman. (Illus.). 192p. 1994. 37.00 (*0-913582-59-X*, 0251) Sundance.

Trails among the Columbine Nineteen Eighty-Eight Creede, Lake City. Sundance Publications, Ltd. Staff. (Illus.). 192p. 1988. 37.00 (*0-913582-44-1*) Sundance.

Trails among the Columbine, 1987: A Colorado High Country Anthology. Sundance Publications Ltd. Staff. (Alamosa-Durango Ser.). (Illus.). 160p. 1987. 37.00 (*0-913582-08-5*) Sundance.

Trails Among the Columbine 1990. Sundance Staff. (Illus.). 192p. 1990. 37.00 (*0-913582-51-4*) Sundance.

Trails among the Columbine 95/96: The Calumet Branch & the Turret Mining Area. Dick Dixon. Ed. by Russ Collman. (Illus.). 320p. 1996. 37.00 (*0-913582-62-X*, 0255) Sundance.

Trails & Trails of the Berrys. Ione B. Jones. 32p. 1985. 5.95 (*0-943480-62-0*) Friis-Pioneer Pr.

Trails & Trials of a Texas Ranger. William W. Sterling. (Illus.). 1979. pap. 26.95 (*0-8061-1574-2*) U of Okla Pr.

Trail's End. David Thompson. (Wilderness Ser.: No. 22). 176p. (Orig.). 1995. mass mkt., pap. 3.99 (*0-8439-3849-8*) Dorchester Pub Co.

Trails Filled with Lighted Notions. William Harrold. 64p. 1988. pap. 5.95 (*0-932616-22-4*) Brick Hse Bks.

Trails for the Twenty-First Century: Planning, Design, & Management Manual for Multi-Use Trails. Ed. by Karen-Lee Ryan. LC 93-8433. (Rails-to-Trails Conservancy Ser.). (Illus.). 290p. 1993. pap. 24.95 (*1-55963-238-0*); text ed. 49.95 (*1-55963-237-2*) Island Pr.

Trails from Steppingstones to Kerbstones. Russell A. Apole. LC 66-4453. (Bernice P. Bishop Museum Special Publications: No. 53). (Illus.). 85p. reprint ed. pap. 25.00 (*0-685-20289-5*, 2030322) Bks Demand.

Trails Guide to Pikes Peak County. 5th ed. Zoltan Malocsay & Topo Maps U. S. Staff. (Illus.). 1991. pap. write for info. (*0-9629250-3-9*) Squeezy Pr.

Trails I Rode. Con Price. (American Autobiography Ser.). 262p. 1995. reprint ed. lib. bdg. 79.00 (*0-7812-8621-2*) Rprt Serv.

Trails in Darkness No. 6. Robert E. Howard. (Reh Library: Vol. VI). 240p. 1996. mass mkt. 5.99 (*0-671-87726-7*, Baen Books) Baen Bks.

Trails in No-Man's Land: Essays in Cultural & Literary History. Karl S. Guthke. LC 93-26248. (GERM Ser.). 258p. 1993. 55.00 (*1-879751-54-2*) Camden Hse.

Trails of a Wanderer: The Keith W. Avery Story. Rhonda S. Stearns. LC 95-76609. (Illus.). 168p. 1995. pap. 29.95 (*0-9624489-7-4*) G Logsdon Bks.

Trails of a Wanderer: The Keith W. Avery Story. limited ed. Rhonda S. Stearns. LC 95-76609. (Illus.). 168p. 1995. 250.00 (*0-9624489-8-2*) G Logsdon Bks.

Trails of an Arkie Cowboy. (Illus.). 94p. (Orig.). 1996. pap. 19.95 (*0-938041-72-X*) Arc Pr AR.

Trails of Destiny. Neil Duke. LC 91-65536. 362p. 1992. pap. 10.95 (*1-55523-440-2*) Winston-Derek.

Trails of History: The Story of Mount Desert Island's Paths from Norumbega to Acadia. Tom St. Germain. (Illus.). 192p. (Orig.). 1993. per. 14.95 (*0-9629997-3-3*) Parkman Pubns.

***Trails of Laughter/Trails of Tears: A Spiritual Journey into the American Wilderness.** Lorin D. Swinehart. (Orig.). 1996. pap. 11.95 (*0-9654511-0-0*) L D Swinehart.

Trails of Tears: American Indians Driven from Their Lands. rev. ed. Jeanne Williams. LC 91-28849. (Illus.). 192p. (YA). (gr. 7 up). 1992. reprint ed. 16.95 (*0-937460-76-1*) Hendrick-Long.

Trails of the Angeles. 6th ed. John W. Robinson. LC 83-51479. (Illus.). 248p. (Orig.). 1990. pap. 12.95 (*0-89997-110-5*) Wilderness Pr.

Trails of the Big South Fork National River & Recreation Area: A Guide for Hikers, Bikers, & Horse Riders. 3rd ed. Russ Manning & Sondra Jamieson. (Tag-Along Bks.). (Illus.). 256p. 1995. pap. 12.95 (*0-9625122-5-7*) Mtn Laurel Pl.

Trails of the Frank Church - River of No Return Wilderness. Margaret C. Fuller. (Illus.). 348p. 1987. pap. 14.95 (*0-913140-45-7*) Signpost Bk Pub.

Trails of the Sawtooth & White Cloud Mountains. rev. ed. Margaret C. Fuller. LC 88-31851. (Illus.). (Orig.). 1988. pap. 12.95 (*0-913140-47-3*) Signpost Bk Pub.

Trails of the Smoky Hill. Wayne C. Lee. LC 79-67199. (Illus.). 235p. (Orig.). 1980. pap. 12.95 (*0-87004-276-9*) Caxton.

***Trails of the Triad: 100 Hikes in the Winston-Salem/Greensboro/High Point Area.** Allen De Hart. LC 96-53451. (Illus.). (Orig.). 1997. pap. 11.95 (*0-89587-161-0*) Blair.

***Trails of the Triangle: 170 Hikes in the Raleigh/Durham/Chapel Hill Area.** Allen De Hart. LC 96-39789. (Illus.). (Orig.). 1997. pap. 11.95 (*0-89587-160-2*) Blair.

Trails of Two Cities: A Walker's Guide to Yokohama, Kamakura & Vicinity. John Carroll. Ed. by Hilary Sagar. (Illus.). 320p. 1994. pap. 20.00 (*4-7700-1837-1*) Kodansha.

Trails of Virginia: Hiking the Old Dominion. rev. ed. Allen DeHart. LC 94-33818. (Illus.). 430p. (C). 1995. pap. 18.50 (*0-8078-4508-6*) U of NC Pr.

Trails of Western Idaho. rev. ed. Margaret C. Fuller. LC 82-5621. (Illus.). 280p. 1992. reprint ed. pap. 14.95 (*0-913140-48-1*) Signpost Bk Pub.

Trails of Yesterday. John Bratt. LC 79-26411. (Illus.). xx, 320p. 1996. pap. 12.00 (*0-8032-6055-5*, Bison Books) U of Nebr Pr.

***Trails of '98.** Pierre Berton. (Great Klondike Gold Rush Ser.). 88p. (J). (gr. 6-9). pap. 4.99 (*0-7710-1444-9*) McCland & Stewart.

Trails Plowed Under: Stories of the Old West. Charles M. Russell. LC 96-8324. xxxiv, 221p. 1996. pap. 12.00 (*0-8032-8961-8*, Bison Books) U of Nebr Pr.

Trails, Rails, & War: The Life of General G. M. Dodge. J. R. Perkins. Ed. by Stuart Bruchey. LC 80-1338. (Railroads Ser.). (Illus.). 1981. reprint ed. lib. bdg. 38.95 (*0-405-13810-5*) Ayer.

Trails South: The Wagon-Road Economy in the Dodge City-Panhandle Region. C. Robert Haywood. LC 85-40946. (Illus.). 336p. 1986. 24.95 (*0-8061-1987-X*) U of Okla Pr.

***Trails, Tails & Tide Pools in Pails (&) Nature Songs for Walk Alongs.** 3rd ed. Docents of Nursery Nature Walks Staff. (Illus.). 112p. (J). Date not set. 15.95 incl. audio (*0-9632753-5-6*) Nursery Nature.

Trails, Tails & Tidepools in Pails: Over 100 Fun & Easy Nature Activities for Families & Teachers to Share with Babies & Young Children. 3rd ed. Docents of Nursery Nature Staff. (Illus.). 112p. (Orig.). 1995. reprint ed. pap. 10.95 (*0-9632753-2-1*) Nursery Nature.

Trails, Tails & Tidepools in Pails: Over 100 Nature Activities for Families with Babies & Young Children. Docents of Nursery Nature Walks Staff. (Illus.). 112p. (Orig.). 1992. pap. 9.95 (*0-9632753-0-5*) Nursery Nature.

Trails That Daddy Walked Vol. 2: The Journey. Mildred C. Gandy & Ina C. Brantley. (Illus.). 179p. (Orig.). (J). 1995. pap. 10.00 (*0-9642549-1-3*, 7566-2) Childbrant.

Trails to Explore in Great Basin National Park. Rose Houk. (Illus.). 45p. 1989. pap. 7.95 (*0-614-06142-3*) Falcon Pr MT.

Trails to Marcy. A. S. Hopkins. 21p. 1993. reprint ed. lib. bdg. 69.00 (*0-7812-5256-3*) Rprt Serv.

Trails to Poosey. Olive R. Cook. LC 86-8602. (Illus.). 200p. (Orig.). (J). (gr. 3-6). 1986. pap. 5.95 (*0-930079-01-9*) Misty Hill Pr.

Trails to Successful Trapping. V. E. Lynch. 170p. 1935. pap. 4.00 (*0-936622-23-7*) A R Harding Pub.

Trails to Texas: Southern Roots of Western Cattle Ranching. Terry G. Jordan. LC 80-14169. (Illus.). 238p. reprint ed. pap. 67.90 (*0-7837-4642-3*, 2044366) Bks Demand.

***Trails to the Far West: Beyond the Mississippi.** LC 96-39483. (American Trails Ser.). (J). 1997. lib. bdg. 27.11 (*0-8172-4072-1*) Raintree Steck-V.

Trails to Timberline: In West Central British Columbia. rev. ed. Einar Bliz. (Illus.). 201p. (Orig.). 1989. pap. 17.50 (*0-88925-969-0*) Gordon Soules Bk.

Trails to Tropical Treasures: A Tour of Asean's Cultural Heritage. Ed. by David Sassoon. (Illus.). 64p. (Orig.). 1992. pap. 20.00 (*0-9627931-1-6*) World Monuments.

Trails, Trails & Tidepools in Pails: Over One Hundred Fun & Easy Nature Activities for Families & Teachers to Share with Babies & Young Children. 2nd ed. Illus. by Marlena Day. 112p. 1994. reprint ed. pap. text ed. 9.95 (*0-9632753-1-3*) Nursery Nature.

Trailside Botany: 101 Favorite Trees, Ferns, & Wildflowers of the Upper Midwest. John Bates. LC 95-14380. (Illus.). 240p. (Orig.). 1995. pap. 12.95 (*1-57025-070-7*) Pfeifer-Hamilton.

Trailside Notes: A Naturalist's Companion to Adirondack Plants. Ruth Schottman. LC 96-3458. (Illus.). 128p. 1997. pap. 12.95 (*0-935272-81-X*) ADK Mtn Club.
TRAILSIDE NOTES brings together over thirty essays on Adirondack plants written by educator & naturalist Ruth Schottman. Born of a passionate interest in wildflowers & other plants, these essays combine scientific detail with careful field observation, research, anecdotal information, & folklore. Each essay is accompanied by a detailed line illustration. The collection includes field tips & selected references. Order from Adirondack Mountain Club, 814 Goggins Rd., Lake George, NY 12845-4117; 518-668-4447; FAX: 518-668-3746; 800-395-8080; E-mail: pubs@adk.org ***Publisher Provided Annotation.***

Trailside Plants of Hawaii's National Parks. rev. ed. Charles H. Lamoureux. (Illus.). 80p. 1996. reprint ed. pap. 12.95 (*0-940295-09-1*) HI Natural Hist.

Trailside Sales Marketing Kit. Date not set. pap. write for info. (*0-393-99159-8*) Norton.

Trailside's Hints & Tips for Outdoor Living. Backpacker Magazine Editors. (Illus.). 128p. (Orig.). 1993. pap. 9.95 (*0-87596-170-3*) Rodale Pr Inc.

Trailside's Trail Food. Backpacker Magazine Editors. (Illus.). 128p. (Orig.). 1993. pap. 9.95 (*0-87596-169-X*) Rodale Pr Inc.

Trailsman: Number 171. Jon Sharpe. 1996. pap. 4.99 (*0-451-18539-0*, Sig) NAL-Dutton.

Trailsman: Number 173. Jon Sharpe. 1996. pap. 4.99 (*0-451-18541-2*, Sig) NAL-Dutton.

Trailsman: Number 174. Jon Sharpe. 1996. pap. 4.99 (*0-451-18542-0*, Sig) NAL-Dutton.

Trailsman: Tomahawk Justice, No. 141. Jon Sharpe. 176p. 1993. pap. 3.50 (*0-451-17752-5*, Sig) NAL-Dutton.

Trailsman No. 158: Texas Terror. Jon Sharpe. 176p. (Orig.). 1995. pap. 3.99 (*0-451-18215-4*, Sig) NAL-Dutton.

Trailsman No. 159: North Country Guns. Jon Sharpe. 176p. (Orig.). 1995. pap. 3.99 (*0-451-18216-2*, Sig) NAL-Dutton.

Trailsman No. 160: The Tornado Trail. Jon Sharpe. 176p. (Orig.). 1995. mass mkt., pap. 3.99 (*0-451-18271-5*) NAL-Dutton.

Trailsman 182. Jon Messmann. 1997. pap. 4.99 (*0-451-18740-7*, Sig) NAL-Dutton.

Trailsman 183. Jon Sharpe. 1997. pap. 4.99 (*0-451-18762-8*, Sig) NAL-Dutton.

***Trailsman 180.** (Trailsman Ser.: No. 180). 1996. mass mkt. 4.99 (*0-451-18760-1*, Sig) NAL-Dutton.

***Trailsman 181.** Jon Sharpe. (Trailsman Ser.: No. 181). 1997. mass mkt. 4.99 (*0-451-18669-9*, Sig) NAL-Dutton.

Trailsman 184. Jon Sharpe. 1997. pap. 4.99 (*0-451-19160-9*, Sig) NAL-Dutton.

***Trailsman 185.** Jon Sharpe. (Trailsman Ser.: No. 185). 1997. mass mkt. 4.99 (*0-451-19137-4*, Sig) NAL-Dutton.

***Trailsman 186.** Jon Sharpe. (Trailsman Ser.: No. 186). 1997. mass mkt. 4.99 (*0-451-18763-6*, Sig) NAL-Dutton.

***Trailsman 187.** Jon Sharpe. (Trailsman Ser.). 1997. mass mkt. 4.99 (*0-451-19161-7*, Sig) NAL-Dutton.

***Trailsman 190.** Jon Sharpe. 1997. mass mkt. 4.99 (*0-451-19163-3*, Sig) NAL-Dutton.

***Trailsman 191.** Jon Sharpe. 1997. mass mkt. 4.99 (*0-451-19146-3*, Sig) NAL-Dutton.

***Trailsman 192.** Jon Sharpe. 1997. mass mkt. 4.99 (*0-451-19235-4*, Sig) NAL-Dutton.

Train. Charlotte B. Blizard. 1995. 8.95 (*0-533-11383-0*) Vantage.

Train. John Coiley. LC 92-4711. (Eyewitness Bks.). (Illus.). 64p. (J). (gr. 5 up). 1992. 19.00 (*0-679-81684-4*); lib. bdg. 20.99 (*0-679-91684-9*) Knopf Bks Yng Read.

***Train.** Patricia T. Cousin et al. (Visions: African-American Experiences: No. 30). (Illus.). 8p. (Orig.). (J). (gr. k-1). 1996. pap. text ed. 3.00 (*1-57518-029-4*) Arborlake.

Train. Chris L. Demarest. LC 95-6637. (Illus.). 16p. (J). (ps). 1996. pap. 4.95 (*0-15-200809-8*, Red Wagon Bks) HarBrace.

Train. Diane Hoh. 192p. (J). (gr. 7-9). 1992. 3.99 (*0-590-45640-7*, 068, Point) Scholastic Inc.

Train. David McPhail. (J). (gr. 3-6). 1977. lib. bdg. 15.95 (*0-316-56316-1*, Joy St Bks) Little.

Train. David McPhail. (J). (ps-3). 1990. write for info. (*0-318-66965-X*, Joy St Bks); mass mkt. 5.95 (*0-316-56331-5*, Joy St Bks) Little.

Train. David McPhail. 1990. 4.95 (*0-316-88847-8*) Little.

Train. Georges Simenon. (FRE.). 1991. pap. 11.95 (*0-7859-3248-8*, 2266045849) Fr & Eur.

Train. Charles Temple. LC 94-28256. (Illus.). 32p. (J). (ps-3). 1996. 14.95 (*0-395-69826-X*) HM.

Train Accident Reconstruction & FELA & Railroad Litigation. 2nd ed. James R. Loumiet & William G. Jungbauer. (Illus.). 760p. 1995. text ed. 115.00 (*0-913875-18-X*, 0969) Lawyers & Judges.

Train Boy. Horatio Alger, Jr. (Works of Horatio Alger Jr.). 1989. reprint ed. lib. bdg. 79.00 (*0-685-27541-8*) Rprt Serv.

Train Country. Donald Mackay & Lorne Perry. (Illus.). 192p. 1995. pap. 24.95 (*0-911581-37-5*) Heimburger Hse Pub.

Train de 8h 47. Georges Courteline. 256p. 1959. 14.95 (*0-7859-0695-9*, F97630) Fr & Eur.

Train Dispatcher. Jack Rudman. (Career Examination Ser.: C-815). 1994. pap. 23.95 (*0-8373-0815-1*) Nat Learn.

Train Doesn't Stop in Wagner, Montana Anymore & Neither Do I: Travels in America. Joseph G. Kelly. LC 94-39152. 240p. 1994. pap. 12.95 (*0-9639290-1-1*) Good Times.

Train Etait a l'Heure Suivi De Quatorze Nouvelles. Heinrich Boll. (FRE.). 1983. pap. 11.95 (*0-7859-1971-6*, 2070374599) Fr & Eur.

Train Go Sorry: Inside a Deaf World. Leah H. Cohen. 1995. pap. 14.00 (*0-679-76165-9*, Vin) Random.

***Train Hard, Win Easy: The Kenyan Way.** Toby Tanser. (Illus.). 196p. 1997. pap. 20.00 (*0-911521-50-X*) Tafnews.

Train Home. large type ed. Susan R. Shreve. 304p. 1994. lib. bdg. 20.95 (*0-7862-0090-1*) Thorndike Pr.

Train Leaves the Station. Eve Merriam. (Illus.). (J). (PS-3). 1994. pap. 5.95 (*0-8050-3547-8*) H Holt & Co.

Train No. 8. Julian McCaull. LC 87-30756. 1989. 22.95 (*0-87949-279-1*) Ashley Bks.

Train Operator. Jack Rudman. (Career Examination Ser.: C-1068). 1994. pap. 23.95 (*0-8373-1068-7*) Nat Learn.

Train Ride. Ted Berrigan. 48p. (Orig.). 1978. pap. 6.00 (*0-931428-21-1*) Vehicle Edns.

Train Ride. June Crebbin. LC 94-15156. (Illus.). (J). (ps up). 1995. 14.95 (*1-56402-546-2*) Candlewick Pr.

Train Ride. J. David Loeb. (Illus.). 24p. (Orig.). (J). (ps-3). 1994. pap. 3.95 (*1-885744-02-1*) Otter Creek.

Train Ride. June Crebbin. LC 94-15156. (Illus.). 32p. (J). 1996. reprint ed. pap. 5.99 (*1-56402-842-9*) Candlewick Pr.

Train Ride see Phonics Is My Way Series

Train Robberies, Train Robbers, & the Holdup Men. William A. Pinkerton. LC 74-15748. (Popular Culture in America Ser.). (Illus.). 88p. 1980. reprint ed. 15.95 (*0-405-06383-0*) Ayer.

Train Robbers. large type ed. John Dyson. (Dales Large Print Ser.). 229p. 1995. pap. 17.99 (*1-85389-522-9*, Dales) Ulverscroft.

***Train Robbery & Other Stories.** Allen. 1993. pap. text ed. write for info. (*0-17-556007-2*) Addison-Wesley.

Train Robbing Bunch. Rick Miller. LC 82-22204. (Early West Ser.). (Illus.). 175p. 1983. 18.95 (*0-932702-25-2*); pap. 8.50 (*0-932702-27-9*) Creative Texas.

Train Robbing Bunch. deluxe ed. Rick Miller. LC 82-22204. (Early West Ser.). (Illus.). 175p. 1983. ring bd. 75.00 (*0-932702-26-0*) Creative Texas.

Train Running for the Confederacy: An Eyewitness Memoir, 1861-1865. Ed. by Walbrook D. Swank. LC 90-90102. (Illus.). 74p. (C). 1992. pap. 9.95 (*0-942597-42-7*, Burd St Pr) White Mane Pub.

Train Service Supervisor. (Career Examination Ser.: C-3758). pap. 27.95 (*0-8373-3758-5*) Nat Learn.

Train Song. Diane Siebert. LC 88-389. (Illus.). 32p. (J). (ps-3). 1990. lib. bdg. 14.89 (*0-690-04728-2*, Crowell Jr Bks) HarpC Child Bks.

Train Song. Diane Siebert. LC 88-389. (Trophy Picture Bk.). (Illus.). 32p. (J). (gr. k-3). 1993. pap. 5.95 (*0-06-443340-4*, Trophy) HarpC Child Bks.

Train Songs. Jerry Silverman. 15.00 (*1-56222-235-X*, 94556) Mel Bay.

Train Stopped at Domodossola. Jack Royce & John D. Mitchell. LC 94-70382. (Orig.). 1993. pap. text ed. 6.95 (*1-884953-00-X*) Eaton St Pr.

***Train Stops Here.** Don Trosper. (History of Tumwater: Vol. 4). (Illus.). 90p. (Orig.). 1995. pap. 7.00 (*1-890717-03-7*) Tumwater Hist.

Train That Never Ran. George K. Bowers. LC 91-65707. 276p. 1991. 10.95 (*1-55523-439-9*) Winston-Derek.

Train the Trainer. Penny L. Ittner & Alex F. Douds. (Orig.). 1988. Set. pap. 139.95 (*0-685-20034-5*); teacher ed., ring bd. 139.95 (*0-87425-088-9*); student ed., ring bd. write for info. (*0-87425-089-7*) HRD Press.

Train the Trainer Conference. BSA Staff. (Illus.). 164p. 1993. pap. 10.00 (*0-8395-4168-6*, 34168) BSA.

Train to Estelline. Jane R. Wood. 240p. 1987. 19.95 (*0-936650-05-2*) E C Temple.

Train to Estelline. Jane R. Wood. 240p. 1988. pap. 11.95 (*0-385-31289-X*, Delta) Dell.

Train to Estelline. large type ed. Jane R. Wood. LC 94-5386. (Americana Ser.). 1995. 21.95 (*0-7862-0321-8*) Thorndike Pr.

Train to Kiu (El Cero Transparente) Alfonso Vallejo. Tr. by H. Rick Hite. LC 95-61854. (Contemporary Spanish Plays Ser.: Vol. 9). 1996. pap. write for info. (*0-9631212-8-6*) Estreno.

Train to Lulu's. Elizabeth F. Howard. LC 93-25565. (Illus.). 32p. (J). (gr. k-2). 1994. reprint ed. pap. 4.95 (*0-689-71797-0*, Mac Bks Young Read) S&S Childrens.

Train to Pakistan. Khushwant Singh. Orig. Title: Mano Majra. 181p. 1990. 9.95 (*0-318-36927-3*) Asia Bk Corp.

Train to Pakistan. Khushwant Singh. LC 80-8920. Orig. Title: Mano Majra. 192p. 1990. pap. 8.95 (*0-8021-3221-9*, Grove) Grove-Atltic.

Train to Pakistan. Khushwant Singh. Orig. Title: Mano Majra. (C). 1988. 8.50 (*0-86131-985-0*) S Asia.

Train to Pakistan. Khushwant Singh. LC 75-15688. Orig. Title: Mano Majra. 181p. 1975. reprint ed. text ed. 38.50 (*0-8371-8226-3*, SIMM, Greenwood Pr) Greenwood.

Train to Somewhere. Eve Bunting. LC 95-6787. (Illus.). 32p. (J). (gr. k-3). 1996. 15.00 (*0-395-71325-0*, Clarion Bks) HM.

Train to the City. 1993. pap. 4.95 (*1-55037-283-1*, Pub. by Annick CN); lib. bdg. 14.95 (*1-55037-282-3*, Pub. by Annick CN) Firefly Bks Ltd.

Train up a Child. Kathleen Demaray. (Illus.). 24p. 1974. spiral bd. 6.95 (*0-89367-059-6*) Light & Life Comm.

Train up a Child. Clifton M. Kelly & Sherman P. Wantz. LC 82-84318. 110p. (Orig.). 1983. pap. 4.95 (*0-685-06652-5*) Highlands Pub.

Train up a Child. Jean Lubin. 1994. pap. 14.99 (*1-56507-217-0*) Harvest Hse.

Train up a Child. Chuck Sturgeon. 32p. (Orig.). 1979. pap. 4.99 (*0-89274-120-1*) Harrison Hse.

Train up a Child. Rolf Zettersten. 180p. 1994. mass mkt. 5.99 (*0-8423-7313-6*) Tyndale.

Train up a Child see Instruye al Nino

Train Was on Time. Heinrich Boll. Tr. by Leila Vennewitz from GER. (European Classics Ser.). 120p. (C). 1994. 29.95 (*0-8101-1156-X*); pap. 9.95 (*0-8101-1123-3*) Northwestern U Pr.

Train Whistle Guitar. Albert Murray. (Northeastern Library of Black Literature). 183p. 1989. reprint ed. pap. text ed. 12.95 (*1-55553-051-6*) NE U Pr.

Train Whistles. Sarah A. Fifield. LC 81-51156. (Collaboration of Southwest Writers & Artists Ser.). (Illus.). 53p. 1981. pap. 10.00 (*0-686-96957-X*) SarSan Pub.

Train Wrecks. R. C. Reed. 1988. 10.99 (*0-517-32897-6*) Random Hse Value.

***Train Wrecks: A Pictorial History of Accidents on the Main Line.** Robert C. Reed. LC 96-9539. 184p. (gr. 10). 1997. pap. 19.95 (*0-7643-0136-5*) Schiffer.

***Train Your Brain for a Track Career.** Jacqueline Renaud. 1997. pap. text ed. 14.95 (*0-572-02290-5*, Pub. by W Foulsham UK) Trans-Atl Phila.

Train Your Cat. Terry Jester. 128p. (Orig.). 1992. mass mkt. 4.50 (*0-380-76485-7*) Avon.

T

Train Your Dog. Don Harper. 1991. 12.98 (*1-55521-715-X*) Bk Sales Inc.

Train Your Dog the Easy Way. Danny Wilson & Sylvia Wilson. LC 96-25425. (Illus.). 108p. 1996. pap. 10.95 (*0-8069-9499-1*) Sterling.

***Train Your Own Mini.** Cynthia Tunstall. Ed. by Toni M. Leland. LC 95-74741. (Illus.). 88p. (Orig.). 1997. pap. 17.95 (*1-887932-01-1*, TRN, Small Horse Pr) Equine Graph Pubng.

Trained Eye: An Introduction to Astronomical Observing. Leon Palmer. (Illus.). 274p. (C). 1991. pap. text ed. 9.50 (*0-03-047363-2*) SCP.

Trained Eye: Introduction to Astronomy. 2nd ed. Palmer. 2000. pap. text ed. write for info. (*0-03-001367-4*) HB Coll Pubs.

***Trained Manpower for Agricultural & Rural Development.** 132p. 1980. 17.00 (*92-5-100861-2*, Pub. by FAO IT) Bernan Associates.

Trained Mind. (Fitness, Health & Nutrition Ser.). (Illus.). 144p. 1988. 17.27 (*0-8094-6118-8*); lib. bdg. 23.27 (*0-8094-6119-6*) Time-Life.

Trainee. Jack Rudman. (Career Examination Ser.: C-816). 1994. pap. 23.95 (*0-8373-0816-X*) Nat Learn.

Trainee's Companion to General Practice. Ed. by Joe Rosenthal et al. LC 93-3406. 320p. 1993. text ed. 44.95 (*0-443-04703-0*) Churchill.

Trainer. Sara Adamson. (Marketplace Ser.). (Orig.). 1995. mass mkt. 6.95 (*1-56333-249-3*, Rhinoceros) Masquerade.

Trainer. Marcia Hunter. 72p. 1995. per., pap. text ed. 13.95 (*0-7872-0439-0*) Kendall-Hunt.

Trainer's Companion to Advanced Automotive Emissions Systems. Andrew Douglas. (IT-Automotive Technology Ser.). 689p. 1996. teacher ed. 395.00 incl. vhs (*0-8273-7876-9*) Delmar.

Trainer's Complete Guide to Management & Supervisory Development. Carolyn Nilson. LC 92-15854. 1992. write for info. (*0-13-410663-6*) P-H.

Trainer's Dictionary: HRD Terms, Abbreviations, & Acronyms. Angus Reynolds. 350p. 1993. pap. 19.95 (*0-87425-219-9*) HRD Press.

Trainer's Guide: A Practical Manual for the Design, Delivery, & Evaluation of Training. Sullivan et al. 224p. 1990. 127.00 (*0-8342-0116-X*, 20116) Aspen Pub.

***Trainers' Guide: Concepts, Principles & Methods of Training, with Special Reference to Agricultural Development, Vol. 1.** 427p. 1993. 60.00 (*92-5-103348-X*, Pub. by FAO IT) Bernan Associates.

Trainer's Guide: For Enhancing the Lives of Adults with Disabilities. 2nd rev. ed. Dale DiLeo. LC 93-61404. 112p. 1993. pap. 20.00 (*1-883302-04-8*) Trning Res.

Trainer's Guide to Caring for Children in Family Child Care. Diane T. Dodge et al. 240p. (C). 1994. spiral bd. 23.95 (*1-879537-11-7*) Tchng Strtgs.

Trainer's Guide to Caring for Children in School-Age Programs. Derry G. Koralek & Debra D. Foulks. (Illus.). 272p. (Orig.). (C). 1995. pap. text ed. 23.95 (*1-879537-16-8*) Tchng Strtgs.

Trainer's Guide to Caring for Infants & Toddlers. Diane T. Dodge & Derry G. Koralek. 190p. (Orig.). (C). 1991. pap. text ed. 23.95 (*1-879537-03-6*) Tchng Strtgs.

Trainer's Guide to Caring for Preschool Children. 2nd rev. ed. Derry G. Koralek et al. LC 96-61877. (C). 1997. otabind 23.95 (*1-879537-28-1*) Tchng Strtgs.

***Trainer's Guide to Running Effective Team Meetings.** Ave S. Butler. 1996. text ed. 69.95 (*0-07-913129-8*) McGraw.

Trainer's Guide to the Creative Curriculum for Family Child Care. Diane T. Dodge & Laura J. Colker. (Illus.). 128p. (Orig.). (C). 1991. spiral bd. 22.95 (*0-9602892-8-3*) Tchng Strtgs.

Trainer's Guide to Title XX Planning: Bd. with, Take a Giant Step Backward, a Needs Assessment Methodology, 2 vols, 1. Ed. by Susan Herzog. 1977. pap. text ed. 10.00 (*0-686-22965-7*) Univ Bk Serv.

Trainer's Guide to Title XX Planning: Bd. with, Take a Giant Step Backward, a Needs Assessment Methodology, 2 vols, 2. Ed. by Susan Herzog. 1977. pap. text ed. 5.00 (*0-686-22966-5*) Univ Bk Serv.

Trainer's Handbook: The AMA Guide to Effective Training. 2nd ed. Garry Mitchell. LC 92-27379. 432p. 1992. 75.00 (*0-8144-5062-8*) AMACOM.

***Trainer's Handbook: The Ama Guide to Effective Training.** 3rd rev. ed. Gary Mitchell. 428p. 1997. 75.00 (*0-8144-0341-7*) AMACOM.

Trainer's Handbook: The AMA Guide to Effective Training. Garry Mitchell. LC 86-47819. 361p. reprint ed. pap. 102.90 (*0-7837-4238-X*, 2043927) Bks Demand.

Trainer's Handbook: What Infant-Family Specialists Need to Know & How to Teach It. Ed. by Nancy Rushmer & Valerie Schuyler. (Early Intervention Ser.). 90p. (C). 1993. 45.00 (*1-883204-00-3*) Infant Hearing Resc.

Trainer's Manual: Project S.I.T.E.: Training Skills Handbook. rev. ed. Barbara Berman & Fredda J. Friederwitzer. 126p. (C). 1991. pap. text ed. 25.00 (*0-685-51624-5*) Educ Support.

Trainer's Manual: Tools for Missionaries. Grant Von Harrison & Conrad Gottfredson. (Missionary Success Ser.). 77p. (Orig.). 1991. pap. write for info. (*0-910558-02-7*) Ensign Pub.

Trainer's Manual for One Day Workshop & Experimental Lab. Ed. by Margot Fritz. 1980. 7.50 (*0-686-31461-1*) Parents Anon.

Trainer's Manual for Training the Staff in Esteem-Building Development. Michele Borba. 408p. 1994. ring bd. 129.95 (*1-880396-03-3*, JP9078-8) Jalmar Pr.

Trainer's Professional Development Handbook. Ray Bard et al. LC 87-45507. (Management Ser.). 346p. text ed. 42.95 (*1-55542-067-2*) Jossey-Bass.

Trainer's Questionnaire Kit: 21 Simple Feedback Questionnaires to Inspire Learning. Peter Honey. 320p. 1996. ring bd. 99.95 (*0-07-913067-4*) McGraw.

Trainer's Stat Pak (Kit) rev. ed. Edward E. Hubbard. 50p. 1992. pap. 99.95 (*1-883733-04-9*) Global Insghts.

***Trainers Tool Kit.** Cy Charney & Kathy Conway. LC 97-23134. 208p. 1997. pap. 18.95 (*0-8144-7944-8*) AMACOM.

Trainer's Toolkit More Needs Assessment Instruments. Ed. & Intro. by John Wilcox. LC 94-70188. (ASTD Trainer's Toolkits Ser.). 200p. 1994. pap. 59.00 (*1-56286-003-8*) Am Soc Train & Devel.

Trainiacs! Eric Weiner. (Cliffhangers Ser.: No. 6). 128p. (Orig.). (YA). 1996. mass mkt. 3.99 (*0-425-15639-7*) Berkley Pub.

***Training.** 1984. 33.95 (*0-387-13406-9*) Spr-Verlag.

***Training: A Do-It-Yourself Guide for Managers.** Alan George. LC 97-11021. 1997. write for info. (*0-566-07840-6*, Pub. by Gower UK) Ashgate Pub Co.

Training: Issues & Answers for the Eighties. Michael Marquardt & Robert W. Stump. 1982. pap. 6.00 (*0-87771-030-9*) Grad School.

Training--The Competitive Edge: Introducing New Technology into the Workplace. Jerome M. Rosow et al. LC 88-42797. (Management Ser.). 269p. 33.95 (*1-55542-109-1*) Work in Amer.

Training a Dog to Live in Your Home: Combined Edition. John D. Weiss. LC 80-67749. (Illus.). 112p. (Orig.). 1991. pap. 9.95 (*0-9604576-2-3*) Animal Owners.

Training a Dog to Live in Your Home: Insight Behavior Modification, Bk. Two. John Weiss. LC 80-67749. (Illus.). 84p. (Orig.). 1983. pap. 6.95 (*0-9604576-1-5*) Animal Owners.

***Training a Tiger: A Father's Account of How to Raise a Winner in Both Golf & Life.** Earl Woods & Pete McDaniel. LC 96-39797. 1997. 18.00 (*0-06-270178-9*) HarpC.

Training Adults: Life Long Learning. Robert E. Ripley & Marie J. Ripley. (Illus.). 180p. 1993. pap. 19.95 (*0-9621133-7-9*, WB011) Carefree Pr.

Training Adults for Youth Ministry. Robert J. McCarty & Lynn Tooma. Ed. by Robert P. Stamschror. 131p. (Orig.). 1990. Training manual. spiral bd. 14.95 (*0-88489-238-7*) St Marys.

Training Advisor. Ed. by Andrew T. Shields & Health for Life Staff. 302p. 1989. pap. 29.95 (*0-944831-22-2*) Health Life.

Training Aids. Elwyn H. Edwards. 100p. (C). 1990. 28.00 (*0-85131-528-3*, Pub. by J A Allen & Co UK) St Mut.

Training & Careers for the Professional Musician. Gerald McDonald. 112p. 1979. 35.00 (*0-905418-03-4*, Pub. by Gresham Bks UK) St Mut.

Training & Conditioning of Athletes. 2nd ed. Max M. Novich & Buddy Taylor. LC 82-17988. (Illus.). 335p. reprint ed. pap. 95.50 (*0-8357-7651-4*, 2056977) Bks Demand.

Training & Continuing Education: A Handbook for Health Care Institutions. 261p. 1970. 17.50 (*0-87914-006-2*) Hosp Res & Educ.

Training & Continuing Education in Early Intervention. Ed. by James A. Blackman. LC 94-24185. (Infants & Young Children Ser.). 240p. 1995. pap. 30.00 (*0-8342-0650-1*) Aspen Pub.

Training & Development. Ed. by Peter Cappelli. LC 93-37289. (International Library of Management). 512p. 1994. 149.95 (*1-85521-353-2*, Pub. by Dartmth Pub UK) Ashgate Pub Co.

Training & Development. Rosemary Harrison. 392p. (C). 1988. 95.00 (*0-85292-392-9*, Pub. by IPM Hse UK) St Mut.

Training & Development. Ed. by IPM Personnel Management Services Ltd. Staff. 150p. (C). 1992. pap. text ed. 110.00 (*0-85292-455-0*, Pub. by IPM Hse UK) St Mut.

Training & Development: A Guide for Professionals. Rummler & George S. Odiorne. 472p. 1988. 55.00 (*0-685-67146-1*, 5287) Commerce.

Training & Development for Women. Beryl Morris. 64p. 1993. pap. 35.00 (*1-85604-080-1*, LAP0801, Pub. by Library Association UK) Bernan Associates.

Training & Development Handbook. 4th ed. Robert L. Craig. 900p. 1996. text ed. 89.50 (*0-07-013359-X*) McGraw.

Training & Development in Australia. A. Smith. 300p. 1992. pap. 52.00 (*0-409-30354-2*, Austral) MICHIE.

Training & Development in Organizations. Goldstein, Irwin L., & Associates. LC 89-45587. (Management-Industrial-Organizational Psychology Ser.). 555p. text ed. 39.95 (*1-55542-186-5*) Jossey-Bass.

Training & Development of School Principals: A Handbook. Ward Sybouts & Frederick C. Wendel. LC 94-11222. (Educators' Reference Collection). 384p. 1994. text ed. 79.50 (*0-313-28556-X*, Greenwood Pr) Greenwood.

***Training & Development Organization Directory.** 6th ed. 1994. 375.00 (*0-8103-8827-8*, 00001225, Gale Res Intl) Gale.

Training & Development Organizations Directory. 3rd ed. Ed. by Paul Wasserman. 1214p. 1983. 270.00 (*0-8103-0432-5*) Gale.

Training & Development Organizations Directory. 4th ed. Ed. by Janice McLean. 684p. 1988. 295.00 (*0-8103-4348-7*) Gale.

Training & Development Organizations Directory. 5th ed. 1991. 310.00 (*0-8103-4349-5*) Gale.

Training & Development Programs. (Personnel Policies Forum Surveys Ser.: No 140). 61p. 1985. 30.00 (*0-87179-980-4*) BNA.

Training & Development Sourcebook. 2nd ed. Craig E. Schneier et al. 500p. 1994. pap. 44.95 (*0-87425-247-4*) HRD Press.

Training & Development Strategic Plan Workbook. Ray Svenson. 1992. 59.95 (*0-13-853862-X*, Busn) P-H.

***Training & Development Yearbook.** Carolyn Nilson. 1997. 79.95 (*0-13-494899-8*) P-H.

Training & Development Yearbook - 1991. Richard B. Frantzreb. 603p. 1991. 79.95 (*0-13-928011-1*, 140704) P-H.

Training & Development Yearbook, 1990. Richard B. Frantzreb. 608p. 1990. 79.95 (*0-13-927500-2*) P-H.

Training & Development Yearbook, 1992-1993. Richard B. Frantzreb. 1992. 79.95 (*0-13-921891-2*) P-H.

Training & Development Yearbook 1995-1996. Richard B. Frantzreb. 1995. text ed. 79.95 (*0-13-206038-8*) P-H.

Training & Development Yearbook, 1996-1997. Carolyn Nilson. 550p. 1996. 79.95 (*0-13-461831-9*) P-H.

Training & Educating the Work Force in the Nineties: The Rationale for Public-Private Collaboration. Thomas J. Smith & Carolyn Trist. (Information Ser.: No. 331). 56p. 1988. 6.00 (*0-318-42048-1*) Ctr Educ Trng Employ.

***Training & Education in Occupational Health: Report of a WHO Study Group.** WHO Staff. (Technical Report Ser.: No. 762). 0047p. 1988. 6.00 (*92-4-120762-0*) World Health.

Training & Explaining: How to Be the Dog Trainer You Want to Be. Job Michael Evans. (Illus.). 240p. 1994. pap. 25.00 (*0-87605-781-4*) Howell Bk.

Training & Fighting Skills. Benny Urquidez. Ed. by Stuart Sobel & Emil Farkas. LC 80-54831. (Illus.). 200p. (Orig.). 1981. pap. 14.95 (*0-86568-015-9*, 402) Unique Pubns.

Training & Habilitating Developmentally Disabled People: An Introduction. Richard M. Wielkieqicz & Christiane R. Calvert. LC 89-10125. 211p. reprint ed. pap. 60.20 (*0-7837-6724-2*, 2046351) Bks Demand.

Training & Hiring of Journalists. Lee B. Becker et al. Ed. by Melvin J. Voigt. LC 86-17419. (Communication & Information Science Ser.). 192p. 1987. text ed. 73.25 (*0-89391-337-5*) Ablex Pub.

Training & Its Alternatives. Ed. by Dennis Gleeson. 224p. 1990. 90.00 (*0-335-09332-9*); pap. 32.00 (*0-335-09331-0*) Taylor & Francis.

Training & Jobs for the Urban Poor. Committee for Economic Development. LC 78-130757. 78p. 1970. pap. 1.50 (*0-87186-037-6*) Comm Econ Dev.

Training & Legal Issues: The Law & How It Relates to Training. Patricia S. Eyers & William M. Moreland. 100p. 1994. pap. 14.95 (*0-87425-996-7*) HRD Press.

Training & Orienting Employees Leader's Guide. Cuna & Ewing. (Merit Ser.). 166p. 1992. pap. 25.00 (*0-8403-7838-6*) Kendall-Hunt.

***Training & Preparation of Teachers for Medical Schools with Special Regard to the Needs of Developing Countries.** (Technical Report Ser.: No. 337). 26p. 1966. pap. text ed. 3.00 (*92-4-120337-4*) World Health.

Training & Preparation of Teachers for Schools of Medicine & of Allied Health Sciences: Proceedings of the WHO Scientific Group, Geneva, 1972. WHO Staff. (Technical Report Ser.: No. 521). 1973. pap. text ed. 4.00 (*92-4-120521-0*, 1100521) World Health.

Training & Productivity in Eastern Africa. T. L. Maliyamkono et al. (Eastern African Universities Research Project Ser.). 400p. (C). 1982. text ed. 60.00 (*0-435-89582-6*, 89582) Heinemann.

Training & Pruning Apple & Pear Trees. C. G. Forshey et al. (Illus.). 176p. (Orig.). 1992. pap. text ed. 30.00 (*0-9615027-1-1*) Am Soc Horticult.

Training & Recordkeeping: OSHA/EPA/DOT Cross-Reference Manual, 48M. rev. ed. E. Mary Schreiber & Keller, J. J., & Associates, Inc. Staff. LC 92-72359. 460p. 1996. ring bd. 139.00 (*1-877798-11-8*, 48M) J J Keller.

Training & Reference Manual for Traffic Accident Investigation. 2nd rev. ed. R. W. Rivers. (Illus.). 558p. (C). 1995. pap. text ed. 45.00 (*1-884566-18-9*) Inst Police Tech.

Training & Safety Officer. Jack Rudman. (Career Examination Ser.: C-3491). 1994. pap. 34.95 (*0-8373-3491-8*) Nat Learn.

Training & Supervision for Counselling in Action. Ed. by Windy Dryden & Brian Thorne. (Counselling in Action Ser.: Vol. 14). 192p. (C). 1991. 49.95 (*0-8039-8335-2*); pap. 21.50 (*0-8039-8336-0*) Sage.

Training & Teaching the Mental Health Professional: An In-Depth Approach. Jed A. Yalof. LC 95-21425. 320p. 1996. pap. 40.00 (*1-56821-710-2*) Aronson.

Training & Technology for Safety at Sea: Summary Proceedings. Pref. by Jerry Dzugan. (Alaska Sea Grant Report: No. 92-01). 60p. (Orig.). 1992. pap. 7.00 (*1-56612-011-X*) AK Sea Grant CP.

Training & the Private Sector: International Comparisons. Ed. by Lisa M. Lynch. LC 93-46425. (National Bureau of Economic Research Comparative Labor Markets Ser.). 336p. (C). 1994. 47.00 (*0-226-49810-7*) U Ch Pr.

***Training & Use of Dental Auxiliary Personnel.** H. Alfred. (Public Health in Europe Ser.: No. 7). 70p. 1977. 9.00 (*92-9020-126-6*, 1320007) World Health.

***Training & Utilization of Auxiliary Personnel for Rural Health Teams in Developing Countries: Report of a WHO Expert Committee.** (Technical Report Ser.: No. 633). 35p. 1979. pap. text ed. 5.00 (*92-4-120633-0*, 1100633) World Health.

Training & Utilization of Feldshers in the U. S. S. R. (Public Health Papers: No. 56). 1974. pap. text ed. 5.00 (*92-4-130056-6*, 1110056) World Health.

Training & Work of An Initiate. Dion Fortune. 125p. 1995. pap. 14.95 (*1-56459-475-0*) Kessinger Pub.

Training & Working Dogs: For Quiet Confident Control of Stock. 2nd ed. Scott Lithgow. (Orig.). 1991. pap. 18.95 (*0-7022-2394-8*, Pub. by Univ Queensland Pr AT) Intl Spec Bk.

***Training Annual, 1.** Pfeiffer Staff. 1997. 89.95 (*0-7879-1103-8*, Pfffr & Co); pap. 39.95 (*0-7879-1104-6*, Pfffr & Co) Jossey-Bass.

Training at Home to be a Locksmith. James Magorian. LC 80-68264. 112p. 1981. pap. 6.00 (*0-930674-05-7*) Black Oak.

***Training Behavioral Healthcare Professionals: Higher Learning in an Era of Managed Care.** James M. Schuster et al. LC 96-41553. (Managed Behavioral Healthcare Library). 180p. 1997. 32.95 (*0-7879-0795-2*) Jossey-Bass.

Training Behaviour Therapists: Methods, Evaluation & Implementation with Parents, Nurses & Teachers. Derek Milne. 324p. 1986. text ed. 15.00 (*0-914797-22-0*) Brookline Bks.

Training Best Practices. Dennis J. Kravetz. 270p. 1997. 495.00 (*0-927764-01-6*) Kravetz & Assocs.

Training Busy Staff to Succeed with Volunteers: The 55 Minute In-Service Training Series. Betty Stallings. 350p. (Orig.). 1996. pap. 125.00 (*0-9634560-1-6*) Blding Better Skills.

Training by Design Basic Package. (Training by Design Ser.). 1994. 175.00 (*1-56420-040-X*, 2040-X) New Readers.

Training by Design Complete Package. (Training by Design Ser.). 1994. 750.00 (*1-56420-050-7*, 2050-7) New Readers.

Training by Design Videotape Library. (Training by Design Ser.). 1994. 575.00 (*1-56420-049-3*, 2049-3) New Readers.

Training Camp for the Army of God. Norvel Hayes. 32p. (Orig.). 1995. mass mkt. 4.99 (*0-89274-842-7*, HH-842) Harrison Hse.

Training Christians to Counsel. H. Norman Wright. 236p. 1983. reprint ed. student ed., pap. 16.99 (*0-89081-422-8*) Harvest Hse.

***Training Complex Cognitive Skills: A Four-Component Instructional Design Model for Technical Training.** Jeroen J. Van Merrienboer. LC 97-4229. (Illus.). 350p. 1997. 59.95 (*0-87778-298-9*) Educ Tech Pubns.

Training, Conditioning, & the Care of Injuries. Knute K. Rockne & Ernest Meanwell. (Illus.). 200p. write for info. (*0-930405-68-4*) Norman SF.

Training Coordinator. Jack Rudman. (Career Examination Ser.: C-3257). 1994. pap. 39.95 (*0-8373-3257-5*) Nat Learn.

Training Cost Analysis: A How-to Guide for Trainers & Managers. rev. ed. Glenn E. Head. LC 93-74581. (Illus.). 145p. 1993. reprint ed. pap. 30.00 (*1-56286-000-3*) Am Soc Train & Devel.

Training Cost Analysis: A Practical Guide. Glenn E. Head. (Illus.). 144p. (Orig.). 1985. 19.95 (*0-932949-33-9*) ICOM Boulder.

***Training Counselors: The Assessment of Competence.** Sue Wheeler. (Counselor Trainer & Supervisor Ser.). (Illus.). 1996. pap. 21.95 (*0-304-33349-2*); text ed. 75.00 (*0-304-33348-4*) Cassell.

Training Course for TEFL. Peter Hubbard et al. (Illus.). 1983. pap. 14.50 (*0-19-432710-8*) OUP.

***Training Course for the Extension Seminary.** William H. Smallman. 75p. (SPA.). 1975. 4.95 (*1-879892-24-3*) Editorial Bautista.

Training Delivery Series, 7 bks., Set. IPM Staff. (C). 1994. student ed. 640.26 incl. audio (*0-08-042173-3*, Pub. by IPM Hse UK) St Mut.

Training Design & Management Series, 6 bks., Set. IPM Staff. (C). 1994. student ed. 559.50 incl. audio (*0-614-03375-6*, Pub. by IPM Hse UK) St Mut.

Training Development Specialist. Jack Rudman. (Career Examination Ser.: C-3495). 1994. pap. 34.95 (*0-8373-3495-0*) Nat Learn.

Training Diary. Runner's World Editors. (Runner's World Ser.). 1978. pap. 6.95 (*0-02-499620-3*, Macmillan Coll) P-H.

Training Directory for Business & Industry. Connors. 1988. 62.00 (*0-8103-2232-3*) Gale.

Training Economics: The Science of Cost, Benefits. 3rd ed. Clark. (HB - Economics Ser.). 1993. 332.95 (*0-538-61761-6*) S-W Pub.

Training Educators of Adults: The Theory & Practice of Graduate Adult Education. Ed. by Stephen D. Brookfield. 256p. (C). 1988. lib. bdg. 37.50 (*0-415-00564-7*) Routledge.

Training Effectiveness Handbook: A High-Results System for Design, Delivery, & Evaluation. Lester T. Shapiro. LC 94-42613. 1995. text ed. 69.95 (*0-07-057109-0*) McGraw.

Training Employees with Disabilities: Strategies to Enhance Learning & Development for an Expanding Part of Your Workforce. William R. Tracey. LC 94-26610. 368p. 1994. 59.95 (*0-8144-0220-8*) AMACOM.

Training Enhancement in Government Organizations. Ronald R. Sims. LC 92-37465. 256p. 1993. text ed. 59.95 (*0-89930-757-4*, SQU/, Quorum Bks) Greenwood.

Training Entrepreneurs for Small Business Creation: Lessons from Experience. Kenneth Loucks. (Management Development Ser.: No. 26). xi, 137p. (Orig.). 1990. pap. 20.25 (*92-2-106343-7*) Intl Labour Office.

Training Evaluation Process: A Practical Approach to Evaluating Corporate Training Programs. David J. Basarab, Sr. & Darrell K. Root. LC 92-25675. (Evaluation in Education & Human Services Ser.). 288p. (C). 1992. lib. bdg. 90.00 (*0-7923-9266-3*) Kluwer Ac.

Training Families to Do an Intervention: A Professional's Guide. Ed. by Alexandra Robbin et al. 152p. (Orig.). 1996. pap. 15.95 (*1-56246-116-8*, P552) Johnsn Inst.

Training Fire Department Personnel to Make Dwelling Fire Safety Surveys. 19p. 1993. 16.75 (*0-685-64957-1*, 1452-93) Natl Fire Prot.

***Training for a Rapidly Changing Workplace: Applications of Psychological Research.** Miguel A. Quinones & Addie Ehrenstein. LC 96-29550. 1996. 19.95 (*1-55798-386-0*) Am Psychol.

An Asterisk (*) at the beginning of an entry indicates that the title is appearing in BIP for the first time.

Training for Adult Education. K. T. Elsdon. 202p. (C). 1975. text ed. 45.00 (*0-685-22166-0*, Pub. by Univ Nottingham UK) St Mut.

***Training for Agriculture & Rural Development.** (Economic & Social Development Papers: Vol. 54). 163p. 1996. pap. 25.00 (*92-5-103726-4*, F37264, Pub. by FAO IT) Bernan Associates.

***Training for Agriculture & Rural Development, 1989-90: FAO/Unesco/ILO.** (Economic & Social Development Papers: No. 48). 148p. 1990. 25.00 (*92-5-002988-8*, F9888, Pub. by FAO IT) Bernan Associates.

Training for an Effective Life. Charles W. Eliot. LC 70-105009. (Essay Index Reprint Ser.). 1977. 16.95 (*0-8369-1461-9*) Ayer.

Training for Appraisal & Professional Development. Jeff Jones & John Mathias. (Cassell Practical Handbooks Ser.). (Illus.). 160p. 1995. pap. 32.00 (*0-304-32969-X*) Cassell.

Training for Assertiveness. Seifert. 380p. 1995. ring bd. 169.95 (*0-566-07516-4*, Pub. by Gower UK) Ashgate Pub Co.

Training for Change Agents: A Guide to the Design of Training Programs in Education & Other Fields. Ronald G. Havelock. LC 72-86637. (Illus.). 263p. reprint ed. pap. 75.00 (*0-7837-5687-9*, 2044987) Bks Demand.

Training for Change Agents: A Guide to Training Programs in Education & Other Fields. Ronald G. Havelock & Mary C. Havelock. LC 72-86337. 262p. 1973. 18.00 (*0-87944-126-7*) Inst Soc Res.

Training for Communication: A Trainer's Manual. John Adair & David Despres. 89p. (C). 1985. ring bd. 225.00 (*0-85171-082-4*, Pub. by IPM Hse UK) St Mut.

Training for Cycling: The Ultimate Guide to Improved Performance. Davis Phinney & Connie Carpenter. (Illus.). 256p. (Orig.). 1992. pap. 13.95 (*0-399-51731-6*, Perigee Bks) Berkley Pub.

***Training for Decentralized Planning: Lessons from Experience, Vol. 1.** 64p. 1993. 10.00 (*92-5-103420-6*, F34206, Pub. by FAO IT) Bernan Associates.

Training for Development. 2nd fac. ed. Rolf P. Lynton & Udai Pareek. LC 89-7989. (Kumarian Press Library of Management for Development). (Illus.). 364p. 1990. pap. 103.80 (*0-7837-7584-9*, 2047337) Bks Demand.

Training for Diversity of Ministry. Patrick Vaughan. 106p. (C). 1983. text ed. 40.00 (*0-685-22148-2*, Pub. by Univ Nottingham UK) St Mut.

Training for Employment in Western Europe & the United States. Linda Clarke et al. LC 94-34106. 288p. 1995. 80.00 (*1-85278-863-1*) E Elgar.

Training for Empowerment. Sarah Cook. 484p. 1994. 238.95 (*0-566-07514-8*, Pub. by Gower UK) Ashgate Pub Co.

Training for Endurance. Philip B. Maffetone. Ed. by Matthew Fitzgerald. LC 96-83504. 160p. (Orig.). 1996. pap. 12.95 (*0-9642062-1-8*) D Barmore Prods.

Training for Environmental & Safety Compliance. Jim Newton. 300p. 1995. ring bd. 60.00 (*1-888555-06-8*) MGR Pr.

Training for Impact: How to Link Training to Business Needs & Measure the Results. Dana G. Robinson & James C. Robinson. LC 88-46088. (Management Ser.). 336p. text ed. 32.95 (*1-55542-153-9*) Jossey-Bass.

***Training for It Library Training Guide.** Richard Briscombe. 71p. 1997. pap. 40.00 (*1-85604-186-7*, LAP1867, Pub. by Library Association UK) Bernan Associates.

Training for Job Developers: A Job Developer's Guide. Denise Bissonnette-Lamendella & Richard Pimentel. 104p. (C). 1987. student ed. 19.95 (*0-942071-09-3*) M Wright & Assocs.

Training for Job Developers: A Supervisor's Guide. Denise Bissonnette-Lamendella & Richard Pimentel. 129p. (C). 1987. reprint ed. teacher ed. 94.50 (*0-942071-03-4*) M Wright & Assocs.

Training for Life. 5th ed. Fred J. Hecklinger. 304p. 1995. per., pap. 25.14 (*0-8403-8663-X*) Kendall-Hunt.

***Training for Life: A Practical Guide to Career & Life Planning.** Fred J. Hecklinger & Bernadette Black. 350p. 1996. per., pap. text ed. 24.95 (*0-7872-2801-X*) Kendall-Hunt.

Training for Non-Trainers: A Do-It-Yourself Guide for Managers. Carolyn Nilson. 240p. 1991. pap. 16.95 (*0-8144-7775-5*) AMACOM.

Training for Non-Trainers: A Practical Guide. J. Delgado Figueroa. LC 94-32317. 101p. 1996. pap. 14.95 (*0-87425-981-9*) HRD Press.

Training for Older People: A Handbook. P. Plett et al. v, 217p. (Orig.). 1991. pap. 22.50 (*92-2-107294-0*) Intl Labour Office.

Training for Organizations. Bridget O'Connor et al. (KU - Office Procedures Ser.). 358p. 1995. pap. 42.95 (*0-538-71122-1*) S-W Pub.

Training for Performance: Principles of Applied Human Learning. Ed. by John E. Morrison. LC 90-22211. (Series on Studies in Human Performance & Cognition: No. 1507). 311p. 1991. text ed. 140.00 (*0-471-92248-X*) Wiley.

Training for Professional Child Care. Beverly Gulley et al. LC 86-26151. (Illus.). 222p. 1987. text ed. 24.95 (*0-8093-1331-6*) S Ill U Pr.

***Training for Professionals Who Work with Gay & Lesbians in Educational & Workplace Settings.** Hilda F. Besner & Charlotte I. Spungin. LC 97-20520. 1997. pap. write for info. (*1-56032-566-6*) Hemisp Pub.

Training for Profit: A Guide to the Integration of Training in an Organization's Success. 2nd ed. Philip Darling. LC 93-2921. (McGraw-Hill Training Ser.). 1993. pap. text ed. 24.95 (*0-07-707786-5*) McGraw.

***Training for Project Management: A Collection of Ready to Use Activities & Exercises, Vol. 1.** Ian Stokes. 200p. 1997. ring bd. 199.95 (*0-566-07778-7*, Pub. by Gower UK) Ashgate Pub Co.

***Training for Project Management: A Collection of Ready to Use Activities & Exercises, Vol. 2.** Ian Stokes. 200p. 1997. ring bd. 239.95 (*0-566-07780-9*, Pub. by Gower UK) Ashgate Pub Co.

Training for Quality: Improving Early Childhood Programs Through Systematic Inservice Training. Ann S. Epstein. LC 93-8514. (Monographs of the High/Scope Educational Research Foundation: Vol. 9). 160p. 1993. 19.95 (*0-929816-56-0*) High-Scope.

Training for Results: Teaching Adults to Be Independant, Assertive Learners. 2nd rev. ed. Bob Mosher et al. (Illus.). vii, 138p. (Orig.). 1996. pap. 19.95 (*1-889176-00-1*) Logical Opers.

Training for Retail Sales & Profit. Judith J. Howe. LC 81-66236. 253p. reprint ed. pap. 72.20 (*0-317-39666-8*, 2023558) Bks Demand.

Training for School Improvement: Understanding Context & Change. H. Dickson Corbett & Joseph J. D'Amico. 205p. 1985. pap. 24.95 (*1-56602-010-7*) Research Better.

Training for Service Delivery to Minority Clients. Ed. by Emelicia Mizio & Anita J. Delaney. LC 80-23468. 208p. reprint ed. pap. 59.30 (*0-8357-8513-0*, 2034810) Bks Demand.

***Training for Speed & Endurance.** Peter Reaburn & David Jenkins. (Illus.). 192p. (Orig.). 1997. pap. 13.95 (*1-86448-120-X*, Pub. by Allen & Unwin Aust Pty AT) IPG Chicago.

Training for Sport & Activity: The Physiological Basis of the Condition Process. 3rd ed. Jack H. Wilmore & David L. Costill. LC 93-2145. 436p. 1993. text ed. 30.00 (*0-87322-557-0*, BWIL0557) Human Kinetics.

Training for Student Leaders. Joseph Murray. 384p. (C). 1996. per. 29.34 (*0-8403-9436-5*) Kendall-Hunt.

Training for the Alter Experience. Mark Schaufler. 22p. 1994. teacher ed. 5.00 (*1-886904-14-6*); student ed. 2.00 (*1-886904-13-8*) MST Minist.

Training for the Future: The Rise & Fall of the Manpower Services Commission. Pat Ainley & Mark Corney. 160p. 1990. pap. text ed. 24.95 (*0-304-31861-2*) Cassell.

Training for the Future, 1990: A Seminar for Training Professionals: Westin Peachtree Plaza, Atlanta, GA, April 26-27. Technical Association of the Pulp & Paper Industry Staff. (TAPPI Notes Ser.). (Illus.). 39p. reprint ed. pap. 25.00 (*0-8357-4216-4*, 2036998) Bks Demand.

Training for the Healthcare Manufacturing Industries: Tools & Techniques to Improve Performance. James L. Vesper. (Illus.). 413p. 1993. 98.75 (*0-935184-43-0*) Interpharm.

***Training for the Hospitality Industry.** 2nd ed. Lewis C. Forrest, Jr. LC 89-23747. (Illus.). 414p. 1996. pap. write for info. (*0-86612-105-6*) Educ Inst Am Hotel.

Training for the Public Profession of the Law. Alfred Z. Reed. LC 75-22837. (America in Two Centuries Ser.). 1976. reprint ed. 42.95 (*0-405-07708-4*) Ayer.

Training for the Public Profession of the Law. Alfred Z. Reed. Ed. by R. H. Helmholz & Bernard D. Reams, Jr. LC 86-62932. (Historical Writings in Law & Jurisprudence Ser.: No. 2). xviii, 498p. 1986. reprint ed. lib. bdg. 45.00 (*0-89941-516-4*, 304520) W S Hein.

Training for the Theatre. Michel Saint-Denis. Ed. by Suria Saint-Denis. (Illus.). 1982. pap. 12.95 (*0-87830-576-9*, Thtre Arts Bks) Routledge.

Training for Total Quality Management. Caryl Burton & Anton Franckeiss. 1994. ring bd. 212.95 (*0-566-07311-0*, Pub. by Gower UK) Ashgate Pub Co.

Training for TPM: A Manufacturing Success Story. Ed. by Nachi-Fujikoshi. LC 90-40276. (Illus.). 274p. 1990. 50.00 (*0-915299-34-8*) Prod Press.

Training for Tracklayers: A Manual for Everyone Who Works with Tracking Dogs. Joyce D. Geier. 120p. 1991. pap. 8.95 (*0-9631118-0-9*) J D Geier.

Training for Trade: Community College Programs to Promote Export. Ed. by Mary L. Fifield & Lourdene Huhra. 200p. (C). 1991. pap. text ed. 22.50 (*0-87117-222-4*, 1318) Am Assn Comm Coll.

Training for Transformation. Anne Hope & Sally Timmel. 514p. (Orig.). 1996. pap. 37.95 (*1-85339-353-3*, Pub. by Intermed Tech UK) Women Ink.

Training for Work in the Informal Sector. Ed. by Fred Fluitman. xii, 224p. (Orig.). 1989. pap. 27.00 (*92-2-106506-5*) Intl Labour Office.

Training for Young Distance Runners. Laurence S. Greene & Russell R. Pate. LC 96-26110. (Illus.). 208p. (Orig.). 1996. pap. 18.95 (*0-87322-406-X*, PGRE0406) Human Kinetics.

Training for Your Next Career. K. Korving. (C). 1989. text ed. 29.95 (*0-948032-29-4*, Pub. by Rosters Ltd) St Mut.

Training Foreign Language Teachers: A Reflective Approach. Michael J. Wallace. (Teacher Training & Development Ser.). 176p. (C). 1991. text ed. 47.95 (*0-521-35636-9*); pap. text ed. 18.95 (*0-521-35654-7*) Cambridge U Pr.

***Training Games: Coaching Runners Creatively.** 2nd ed. Eric Anderson. (Illus.). 160p. (Orig.). 1996. pap. 15.00 (*0-911521-47-X*) Tafnews.

Training Games for Assertiveness & Conflict Resolution: 50 Ready to Use Activities. Sue Bishop. 250p. 1996. ring bd. 99.95 (*0-07-913052-6*) McGraw.

Training Games for Career Development. James J. Kirk & Lynne D. Kirk. LC 95-3943. (Illus.). 1995. pap. text ed. 24.95 (*0-07-034790-5*) McGraw.

Training Games for Interpersonal Skills: 107 Experiential Learning Activities for Trainers. Philip Burnard. 250p. 1996. ring bd. 99.95 (*0-07-009186-2*) McGraw.

Training Games for the Learning Organization: 50 Experiential Learning Activities. Lynne Kirk & James Kirk. (Illus.). 270p. 1996. pap. text ed. 34.95 (*0-07-034924-X*) McGraw.

Training Games for the Learning Organization: 50 Experiential Learning Activities. Lynne Kirk & James Kirk. (Illus.). 270p. 1997. text ed. 89.95 (*0-07-034923-1*) McGraw.

Training God's Army: The American Bible School, 1880-1940. Virginia L. Brereton. LC 89-46007. 214p. 1990. 29.95 (*0-253-31266-3*) Ind U Pr.

Training Grouse & Woodcock Dogs. Logan J. Bennett. (Illus.). 146p. 1989. reprint ed. 24.95 (*0-936075-17-1*) Gunnerman Pr.

Training Guarantee Register. Kimberley C. Smith. (C). 1989. 170.00 (*1-875114-13-0*, Pub. by Blackstone Pr UK) Gaunt.

Training Guarantee Register. 2nd ed. Kimberley C. Smith. 150p. 1991. ring bd. 135.00 (*1-875114-23-8*, Blckstone AT) Gaunt.

Training Guide for Foodservice Personnel in Programs for Young Children. 200p. 1987. write for info. (*1-55672-028-9*) US HHS.

Training Guide for Islamic Workers. 3rd ed. Hisham Altalib. LC 91-12896. (Human Development Ser.: No. 1). (Illus.). 397p. 1993. pap. 25.00 (*1-56564-120-5*) IIIT VA.

***Training Guide for the Head Start Learning Community, 9 vols.** 1997. lib. bdg. 2,729.99 (*0-8490-8235-8*) Gordon Pr.

Training Guide to Cerebral Palsy Sports. 3rd ed. Ed. by Jeffery A. Jones. LC 87-3081. (Illus.). 256p. 1988. pap. text ed. 25.00 (*0-87322-125-7*, BJON0125) Human Kinetics.

Training Health Workers to Recognize, Treat, Refer & Educate. Paul Courtright & Susan Lewallen. 60p. 1993. pap. text ed. 23.00 (*981-02-1329-8*) World Scientific Pub.

Training, Human Decision Making & Control. Ed. by J. Patrick & K. D. Duncan. 408p. 1988. 183.75 (*0-444-70381-0*, North Holland) Elsevier.

Training Human Intelligence: Developing Exploratory & Aesthetic Skills. Robert M. Travers. LC 83-82786. (Illus.). (C). 1985. pap. 19.95 (*0-918452-51-1*, 511) Learning Pubns.

Training in America: The Organization & Strategic Role of Training. Anthony Carnevale et al. LC 89-28662. (Management Ser.). 450p. text ed. 32.95 (*1-55542-203-9*) Jossey-Bass.

Training in Anti-Lock Brake Systems. Scharff. (Automotive Technology Ser.). 1992. pap. 32.09 (*0-8273-5599-8*) Delmar.

Training in Christianity & the Edifying Discourse Which Accompanied It. Soren Kierkegaard. Tr. & Intro. by Walter Lowrie. 303p. reprint ed. pap. 86.40 (*0-8357-4650-X*, 2037581) Bks Demand.

Training in Community Living Model: A Decade of Experience. Ed. by Leonard I. Stein & Mary A. Test. LC 84-82375. (New Directions for Mental Health Services Ser.: No. MHS 26). (Orig.). 1985. pap. 19.00 (*0-87589-760-6*) Jossey-Bass.

Training in Conservation: A Symposium on the Occasion of the Dedication of the Stephen Chan House. Intro. by Norbert S. Baer. (Illus.). iv, 92p. (Orig.). (C). 1989. pap. text ed. write for info. (*0-9623175-0-0*) NYU Inst Fine.

***Training in Environmental Management - Industry & Sustainability/Corporate, Pt. 1.** 260p. 1996. pap. 40.00 (*92-827-6927-5*, SY95-96-253-ENC, Pub. by Europ Com UK) Bernan Associates.

Training in European Enterprises. Frederic Meyers. (Monograph & Research Ser.: No. 14). 173p. 1969. 5.00 (*0-89215-015-7*) U Cal LA Indus Rel.

Training in Family Planning for Health Personnel. (Public Health in Europe Ser.: No. 20). 105p. 1985. pap. text ed. 10.00 (*92-890-1156-4*, 1320020) World Health.

Training in Family Support: Towards a Conceptual Framework. Christine Vogel. 40p. 1993. pap. 10.00 (*1-885429-05-3*) Family Resource.

Training in Human Services, Vol. I. Ed. by Thomas D. Morton & Ronald K. Green. 223p. (Orig.). 1978. pap. text ed. 5.00 (*0-89695-002-6*) U Tenn CSW.

Training in Industry & Commerce. Edwin J. Singer. 160p. (C). 1988. 50.00 (*0-85292-156-X*, Pub. by IPM Hse UK) St Mut.

Training in Injection Molding. Walter Michaeli et al. Tr. by Kurt Alex from GER. LC 95-11657. 172p. (C). 1995. pap. text ed. 29.95 (*1-56990-135-X*) Hanser-Gardner.

Training in Interpersonal Skills: TIPS for Managing People at Work. 2nd ed. Stephen P. Robbins & Phillip L. Hunsaker. 1995. pap. text ed. 37.20 (*0-13-435827-9*) P-H.

Training in Legal Ethics, Pt. C. 1986. Part C. pap. 7.50 (*0-317-03745-5*, 42,725C) NCLS Inc.

Training in Legal Ethics, Pt. A. 1986. Part A. pap. 3.50 (*0-317-03743-9*, 42,725A) NCLS Inc.

Training in Legal Ethics, Pt. B. 1986. Part B. pap. 5.50 (*0-317-03744-7*, 42,725B) NCLS Inc.

Training in Marriage Environment Handbook. Dinkmeye. 1987. 14.95 (*0-913476-64-1*, 6002) Am Guidance.

Training in Medical Psychotherapy: Cross-Cultural Diversity. Ed. by H. Costa & P. Herrmann. (Psychotherapy & Psychosomatics Journal: Vol. 53, No. 1-4, 1990). (Illus.). 208p. 1990. pap. 150.50 (*3-8055-5321-8*) S Karger.

Training in No Time: Controlling Behavior Through Daily Interactions. Amy Ammen. (Illus.). 1995. pap. 14.95 (*0-87605-778-4*) Howell Bk.

Training in Objective Educational Measurements for Elementary School Teachers. Maxwell G. Park. LC 70-177143. (Columbia University. Teachers College. Contributions to Education Ser.: No. 520). (C). reprint ed. 37.50 (*0-404-55520-9*) AMS Pr.

Training in Organizations. 3rd ed. Irwin L. Goldstein. LC 92-3484. 320p. (C). 1993. pap. 33.95 (*0-534-16452-8*) Brooks-Cole.

Training in Organizations. 4th ed. Goldstein. (Miscellaneous/Catalogs Ser.). Date not set. pap. 22.00 (*0-534-34554-9*) Course Tech.

Training in Plastics Technology: A Text & Workbook. Walter Michaeli et al. LC 95-11658. 192p. (C). 1995. pap. text ed. 29.95 (*1-56990-134-1*) Hanser-Gardner.

Training in Population: The United Nations Fellowship Programme 1953-1983. 95p. 10.00 (*92-1-123112-4*, E.89.II.H.3) UN.

***Training in Practice.** Steve Truelove. LC 96-40884. (Illus.). 220p. (Orig.). 1997. pap. text ed. 32.95 (*0-631-20251-X*) Blackwell Pubs.

Training in Radiological Protection for Nuclear Programs. (Technical Reports: No. 166). 116p. 1975. pap. 25.00 (*92-0-125075-4*, IDC166, Pub. by IAEA AU) Bernan Associates.

Training in the Automated Office: A Decision-Maker's Guide to Systems Planning & Implementation. Randy J. Goldfield. LC 86-30605. 256p. 1987. text ed. 59.95 (*0-89930-112-6*, EOF/, Quorum Bks) Greenwood.

Training in the Community for People with Disabilities. G. Nelson et al. (Illus.). 684p. (ARA, CHI, ENG, FRE & SPA.). 1989. pap. text ed. 72.00 (*92-4-154401-5*, 1150330) World Health.

Training in the Furniture Industry. Timothy J. Lauber. LC 95-42465. 144p. (Orig.). 1996. pap. text ed. 280.00 (*0-921577-57-5*) AKTRIN.

***Training Information Directory.** annuals 10.00 (*0-614-18723-0*) Natl Conf Stds Labs.

Training Intervention for Control of SBA Loan Defaults. J. Dennis Coates. LC 92-33006. (Studies in Entrepreneurship). 136p. 1992. text ed. 44.00 (*0-8153-0992-9*) Garland.

Training Interventions. John Kenney & Margaret Reid. 384p. (C). 1988. 84.00 (*0-85292-409-7*, Pub. by IPM Hse UK) St Mut.

Training Interventions. 3rd ed. Margaret Reid et al. 456p. (C). 1992. pap. text ed. 95.00 (*0-85292-480-1*, Pub. by IPM Hse UK) St Mut.

Training Interventions: Managing Employee Development. Margaret A. Reid & Harry Barrington. 456p. (C). 1994. pap. 45.00 (*0-85292-566-2*, Pub. by IPM Hse UK) St Mut.

Training Interventions in Job Skill Development. James E. Gardner. LC 80-23810. (Illus.). 224p. 1981. 15.16 (*0-201-03097-7*) Addison-Wesley.

Training Investment: Banking on People for Superior Results. Margaret R. Keene. 250p. 1990. 55.00 (*1-55623-318-3*) Irwin Prof Pubng.

Training Issues & Strategies in Libraries. Ed. by Paul M. Gherman & Francis O. Painter. LC 90-4221. (Journal of Library Administration: Vol. 12, No. 2). 95p. 1990. text ed. 24.95 (*0-86656-937-5*) Haworth Pr.

Training Issues in Incremental Learning: Papers from the 1993 Spring Symposium. Ed. by Antoine Cornuejols. (Technical Reports). (Illus.). 157p. 1993. spiral bd. 25.00 (*0-929280-44-X*) AAAI Pr.

Training Know-How for Cross-Cultural & Diversity Trainers. Ed. by L. Robert Kohls & Herbert L. Brussow. 1995. write for info. (*1-887493-04-2*) Adult Lrng Systs.

Training Leaders for Family Life Education. Beth C. Fallon. LC 82-10200. (Workshop Models for Family Life Education Ser.). 124p. 1982. spiral bd. 17.95 (*0-87304-188-7*) Families Intl.

Training Life: Living & Learning in the Substance Abuse Field. William L. White et al. Ed. by Randall Webber. 214p. (C). 1994. pap. 16.00 (*0-938475-04-5*) Lighthouse Inst.

Training Made Easy. Carolyn Torma. LC 94-79509. (Illus.). 80p. (Orig.). 1994. pap. text ed. 8.00 (*1-884829-08-2*) Planners Pr.

Training Manager Competencies: The Standards. Shirley Miller et al. 128p. 1989. ring bd. 125.00 (*1-881326-05-5*) IBSTPI.

Training Manager Competencies: The Standards. 2nd ed. Judith A. Hale. Ed. by Craig A. Polak. 125.00 (*1-881326-10-1*) IBSTPI.

Training Managers So They Can Really Manage: Confessions of a Frustrated Trainer. Thomas L. Quick. LC 90-28765. (Management Ser.). 214p. text ed. 28.95 (*1-55542-341-8*) Jossey-Bass.

***Training Managers to Train: A Practical Guide to Improve Employee Performance.** (Staff Training & Development Ser.). 88p. 1993. 18.00 (*0-614-23464-6*, 2473) Am Assn Coll Registrars.

Training Managers to Train: A Practical Guide to Improving Employee Performance. rev. ed. Herman Zaccarelli & David K. Hayes. LC 96-85348. (Fifty-Minute Ser.). (Illus.). 100p. 1996. pap. 10.95 (*1-56052-411-1*) Crisp Pubns.

***Training Manual.** Project Success Enrichment Staff. 116p. 1996. pap. text ed., spiral bd. 45.00 (*0-7872-2641-6*) Kendall-Hunt.

Training Manual & Video for Dementia Care Specialists. Jean M. Stehman et al. LC 95-44411. (Illus.). 232p. (C). 1996. text ed. 95.00 (*0-8018-5268-4*) Johns Hopkins.

Training Manual for Americans with Disabilities Act Compliance in Parks & Recreation Settings. Carol Stensrud. LC 93-61009. (Illus.). 176p. 1993. pap. text ed. 24.95 (*0-910251-63-0*) Venture Pub PA.

Training Manual for Central Service Technicians. American Society for Healthcare Central Service Personnel Staff. LC 86-3332. (Illus.). 278p. 1986. pap. text ed. 70.00 (*0-87258-442-9*, 031802) Am Hospital.

Training Manual for Central Service Technicians: Instructor's Manual. American Society for Healthcare Central Service Personnel Staff. (Illus.). 94p. (Orig.). 1991. pap. text ed. 35.00 (*0-87258-615-4*, 031084) Am Hospital.

Training Manual for Central Service Technicians: Workbook. American Society for Healthcare Central Service Personnel Staff. (Illus.). 173p. (C). 1994. 35.00 (*0-87258-678-2*, 031803) Am Hospital.

Training Manual for Enteral Feeding. Richard E. Dean. LC 90-62727. 96p. 1990. pap. 22.95 (*0-944496-17-2*) Precept Pr.

Training Manual for Law Enforcement Officers. Russell L. Bintliff. 330p. 1990. text ed. 49.95 (*0-13-926890-1*) P-H.

Training Manual for SENG Guided Discussion Groups. James T. Webb & Arlene R. Devries. 85p. 1994. pap. 22.00 (*0-910707-22-7*) Gifted Psych Pr.

Training Manual for Small Group Leaders. Julie A. Gorman. (Groupbuilders Series for Adults). 127p. 1991. pap. 8.99 (*0-89693-266-4*, 6-1266) SP Pubns.

Training Manual for the Gentle Art of Verbal Self-Defense, Pt. 1. 1993. 15.00 (*1-878709-02-X*) Ozark Ctr Lang Studies Pr.

Training Manual for the Gentle Art of Verbal Self-Defense, Pt. 2. 1993. 15.00 (*1-878709-03-8*) Ozark Ctr Lang Studies Pr.

Training Manual for Total Parenteral Nutrition. Richard E. Dean. LC 90-62754. 140p. 1990. pap. 22.95 (*0-944496-18-0*) Precept Pr.

Training Manual in Applied Medical Anthropology. Ed. by Carole E. Hill. 1991. pap. 20.00 (*0-913167-46-0*) Am Anthro Assn.

Training Materials for Animal Facility Personnel: Bibliography, January 1990-January 1995. Michael D. Kreger. 33p. (Orig.). (C). 1995. pap. text ed. 25.00 (*0-7881-1982-6*) DIANE Pub.

Training Methods for Management & Development. R. K. Samanta. 138p. (C). 1993. 45.00 (*81-85880-10-7*, Pub. by Print Hse II) St Mut.

Training Methods That Work: A Handbook for Trainers. Lois B. Hart. Ed. by Michael G. Crisp. LC 90-84925. (Fifty-Minute Ser.). (Illus.). 96p. (Orig.). 1991. pap. 10.95 (*1-56052-082-5*) Crisp Pubns.

Training Mules & Donkeys: A Logical Approach to Longears. Meredith S. Hodges. LC 92-9170. 222p. 1993. 34.95 (*0-931866-58-8*) Alpine Pubns.

Training Needs: Assessment & Monitoring. L. Richter. viii, 83p. (Orig.). 1990. pap. 15.75 (*92-2-105458-6*) Intl Labour Office.

Training Needs Analysis: A Resource for Identifying Training Needs, Selecting Training Strategies & Developing Training Plans. Sharon Bartram & Brenda Gibson. LC 94-9877. 176p. 1994. 66.95 (*0-566-07561-X*, Pub. by Gower UK); ring bd. 83.95 (*0-566-07437-0*, Pub. by Gower UK) Ashgate Pub Co.

***Training Needs Analysis: A Resource for Identifying Training Needs, Selecting Training Strategies, & Developing Training Plans.** 2nd ed. Sharon Bartram & Brenda Gibson. LC 96-40148. 244p. 1997. text ed. 88.95 (*0-566-07916-X*, Pub. by Gower UK) Ashgate Pub Co.

***Training Needs Analysis: A Resource for Identifying Training Needs, Selecting Training Strategies, & Developing Training Plans.** 2nd ed. Sharon Bartram & Brenda Gibson. LC 96-40148. 244p. 1997. ring bd. 136.95 (*0-566-07917-8*, Pub. by Gower UK) Ashgate Pub Co.

Training Needs Analysis: Library Training Guide. Michael Williamson. 64p. 1993. pap. 35.00 (*1-85604-077-1*, LAP0771, Pub. by Library Association UK) Bernan Associates.

Training Needs Analysis & Evaluation. Frances Bee & Roland Bee. 200p. 1993. pap. 125.00 (*0-85292-547-6*, Pub. by IPM Hse UK) St Mut.

Training Needs Assessment. Allison Rossett. LC 87-9070. (Illus.). 281p. 1987. 42.95 (*0-87778-195-8*) Educ Tech Pubns.

Training New Admissions Recruiters: A Guide for Survival & Success. Christine Wilkinson & Roger Swanson. 88p. 1993. pap. 25.00 (*0-89964-299-3*, 29202) Coun Adv & Supp Ed.

Training New York. 58p. 1988. pap. 9.00 (*0-685-54048-0*, 43,705) NCLS Inc.

Training Notes for Brokers: Introduction to Marine Insurance. Robert H. Brown. (C). 1987. 80.00 (*0-948691-26-3*, Pub. by Witherby & Co UK) St Mut.

Training Nutrition: The Diet & Nutrition Guide for Peak Performance. Ed Burke et al. LC 92-53280. (Illus.). 180p. (Orig.). (C). 1996. pap. text ed. 20.00 (*1-884125-22-0*) Cooper Pubng.

Training of an American: The Earlier Life & Letters of Walter H. Page. LC 90-45587. (Illus.). 464p. 1990. reprint ed. 34.95 (*0-87797-187-0*) Cherokee.

Training of an Army: Camp Curtin & the North's Civil War. William J. Miller. LC 90-31770. (Illus.). 350p. (C). 1990. 27.95 (*0-942597-15-X*) White Mane Pub.

Training of an Orator, 4 vols. Quintilian. No. 124-127. write for info. (*0-318-53200-X*) HUP.

Training of an Orator, 4 vols., 1. Quintilian. (Loeb Classical Library: No. 124-127). 568p. 1920. 18.95 (*0-674-99138-9*) HUP.

Training of an Orator, 4 vols., 2. Quintilian. (Loeb Classical Library: No. 124-127). 538p. 1921. 18.95 (*0-674-99139-7*) HUP.

Training of an Orator, 4 vols., 3. Quintilian. (Loeb Classical Library: No. 124-127). 504p. 1921. 18.95 (*0-674-99140-0*) HUP.

Training of an Orator, 4 vols., 4. Quintilian. (Loeb Classical Library: No. 124-127). 556p. 1922. 18.95 (*0-674-99141-9*) HUP.

Training of Children. 2nd ed. William Booth. 260p. 1997. reprint ed. pap. 8.99 (*0-88019-154-6*) Schmul Pub Co.

Training of Children. Helen H. Jackson. (Notable American Authors Ser.). 1992. reprint ed. lib. bdg. 75.00 (*0-7812-3355-0*) Rprt Serv.

Training of Children in the New Thought. Francis Partlow. 88p. 1997. pap. 7.00 (*0-89540-273-4*, SB-273) Sun Pub.

Training of Communist Cadres in Laos: The Notes of Do Xuan Tao, Vietnamese Economics Specialist Assigned to the Pathet Lao in Xieng Khouang, Laos, 1968. Ed. by Joel M. Halpern & William S. Turley. 103p. 1990. reprint ed. pap. 12.50 (*0-923135-15-4*) Dalley Bk Service.

Training of Elementary & Secondary Teachers in Sweden. Axel G. Peterson. LC 70-177151. (Columbia University. Teachers College. Contributions to Education Ser.: No. 575). (C). reprint ed. 37.50 (*0-404-55575-6*) AMS Pr.

Training of Good Physicians: Critical Factors in Career Choices. Fremont J. Lyden et al. LC 68-21977. (Commonwealth Fund Publications). 262p. 1968. 32.00 (*0-674-90285-8*) HUP.

Training of Government Accountants & Auditors. 59p. 1989. 10.00 (*92-1-123111-6*) UN.

***Training of Health Laboratory Personnel (Technical Staff) Fourth Report of the WHO Expert Committee on Health Laboratory Services, 1966.** (Technical Report Ser.). 0031p. 1966. pap. text ed. 3.00 (*92-4-120345-5*, 1100345) World Health.

Training of High School Teachers in Louisiana. James M. Smith. LC 74-177771. (Columbia University. Teachers College. Contributions to Education Ser.: No. 247). reprint ed. 37.50 (*0-404-55247-1*) AMS Pr.

***Training of Medical Assistants & Similar Personnel: Seventeenth Report of the WHO Expert Committee on Professional & Technical Education of Medical & Auxiliary Personnel.** (Technical Report Ser.: No. 385). 0026p. 1968. pap. text ed. 3.00 (*92-4-120385-4*, 1100385) World Health.

Training of Modern Foreign Language Teachers for the Secondary Schools in the United States. Hugh Stuart. LC 70-177738. (Columbia University. Teachers College. Contributions to Education Ser.: No. 256). reprint ed. 37.50 (*0-404-55256-0*) AMS Pr.

***Training of NOH Actors & the Dove.** David Griffiths. (Mask Ser.). 1997. pap. text ed. 21.00 (*3-7186-5716-3*, Harwood Acad Pubs) Gordon & Breach.

***Training of Noh Actors & the Dove.** David Griffiths. (Mask Ser.). 1997. text ed. 64.00 (*3-7186-5715-5*, Harwood Acad Pubs) Gordon & Breach.

***Training of Occupational Health Personnel: Report on a Consultation.** (Euro Reports & Studies Ser.: No. 58). 22p. 1982. pap. text ed. 4.00 (*92-890-1224-2*) World Health.

Training of Part-Time Teachers of Adults. B. Daines Graham, Jr. (C). 1982. 45.00 (*0-902031-79-1*, Pub. by Univ Nottingham UK) St Mut.

Training of Part-Time Teachers of Adults. T. J. Graham et al. 228p. (C). 1982. text ed. 60.00 (*0-685-22159-8*, Pub. by Univ Nottingham UK) St Mut.

Training of Primary Physicians. Ed. by Stephen J. Kunitz et al. LC 85-22745. (Illus.). 428p. (Orig.). 1986. pap. text ed. 34.00 (*0-8191-5031-2*); lib. bdg. 64.50 (*0-8191-5030-4*) U Pr of Amer.

***Training of Psychiatrists.** (Technical Report Ser.: No. 252). 39p. 1963. pap. text ed. 3.00 (*92-4-120252-1*) World Health.

Training of Research Workers in the Medical Sciences: Proceedings of the CIOMS Round Table conference, Geneva, 1970. CIOMS Round Table Conference Staff. 186p. 1972. pap. text ed. 24.00 (*92-4-156040-1*, 1830005) World Health.

Training of Sanitary Engineers in Europe. Ed. by Robert B. Dean. 198p. 1985. pap. text ed. 16.00 (*92-890-1022-3*, 1340025) World Health.

Training of Sci-Tech Librarians & Library Users. Ed. by Ellis Mount. LC 81-6975. (Science & Technology Libraries: Vol. 1, No. 3). 72p. 1981. pap. text ed. 22.95 (*0-917724-75-5*) Haworth Pr.

Training of Secondary School Heads in Europe. Buckley. (C). 1985. pap. text ed. 20.00 (*0-7005-0691-8*) Routledge.

Training of Teachers in England & Wales. Peter Sandiford. LC 71-177225. (Columbia University. Teachers College. Contributions to Education Ser.: No. 32). reprint ed. 37.50 (*0-404-55032-0*) AMS Pr.

Training of Teachers in the United States of America. Amy Bramwell. 1976. lib. bdg. 59.95 (*0-8490-2756-X*) Gordon Pr.

Training of Teachers, 1849-1947: A History of the Church Colleges in Cheltenham. Charles More. 232p. 1992. 45.00 (*1-85285-077-9*) Hambledon Press.

***Training of Terminal Staff Involved in Loading & Discharging Gas Carriers.** SIGTTO Staff. 1996. pap. 270.00 (*1-85609-092-2*, Pub. by Witherby & Co UK) St Mut.

Training of the Left Hand Opus 89: 49 Exercises 25 Piano Studies. H. Berens. 32p. 1986. pap. 7.95 (*0-7935-5224-9*) H Leonard.

***Training of the Physician for Family Practice.** (Technical Report Ser.: No. 257). 39p. 1963. pap. text ed. 3.00 (*92-4-120257-2*) World Health.

Training of the Twelve. Alexander B. Bruce. LC 73-129738. 566p. 1979. pap. 15.99 (*0-8254-2236-1*, Kregel Class) Kregel.

Training of the Will. Johann Lindworsky. Tr. by A. Steiner & E. A. Fitzpatrick. 192p. 1995. reprint ed. text ed. 19.95 (*0-912141-31-X*) Roman Cath Bks.

Training of the Zen Buddhist Monk. Daisetz T. Suzuki. (Illus.). 160p. 1994. reprint ed. pap. 12.95 (*0-8048-3042-8*) C E Tuttle.

Training of Trainers. K. T. Elsdon. 140p. (C). 1984. text ed. 65.00 (*0-685-22132-6*, Pub. by Univ Nottingham UK) St Mut.

Training of Trainers. Konrad Elsdon. (C). 1984. 39.00 (*0-906389-08-9*, Pub. by Univ Nottingham UK) St Mut.

Training Officer. Jack Rudman. (Career Examination Ser.: C-1523). 1994. pap. 34.95 (*0-8373-1523-9*) Nat Learn.

Training Officer's Guide to Discussion. Ian Debenham. (C). 1969. pap. 30.00 (*0-85171-009-3*, Pub. by IPM Hse UK) St Mut.

***Training Older Dogs.** Contrib. by Herbert Axelrod. (Cats & Dogs). (Illus.). (YA). (gr. 3 up). 1998. lib. bdg. 19.95 (*0-7910-4817-9*) Chelsea Hse.

Training on AIDS for Personnel in Drug Treatment Centres. v, 27p. (ENG & GER.). 1988. pap. text ed. 8.00 (*92-890-1056-8*, 1340039) World Health.

Training Onboard. L. A. Holder. 75p. 1991. 160.00 (*1-85609-028-0*, Pub. by Witherby & Co UK) St Mut.

***Training Operations Reengineering Survey (TORS)** Donald Shandler. pap. 6.95 (*1-56052-416-2*) Crisp Pubns.

Training Others: Learning on-the-Job. Donald F. Barkman. 65p. 1992. 19.95 (*1-883655-03-X*) Busn Ctr.

Training Our Five Spiritual Senses: To Develop Discernment. Marilyn J. Wright. 50p. 1994. pap. 4.50 (*0-9632748-6-4*) Majesty Pubns.

Training Paraprofessionals for Reference Service: A How-to-Do-It Manual for Librarians. Judith K. Ohles & Julie A. McDaniel. (How-to-Do-It Ser.). 184p. 1993. pap. 42.50 (*1-55570-084-5*) Neal-Schuman.

Training Physicians: The Case of Internal Medicine. Claire H. Kohrman et al. (Health Ser.). 504p. text ed. 49.95 (*0-7879-0038-9*) Jossey-Bass.

Training Plans. (Open Learning for Supervisory Management). 1986. pap. text ed. 19.50 (*0-08-070100-0*, Pergamon Pr) Elsevier.

Training Plans. Nebsm Staff. (Open Learning for Supervisory Management Ser.). 1985. pap. text ed. 19.50 (*0-08-033392-3*, Pergamon Pr) Elsevier.

Training Pointing Dogs. Paul Long. (Illus.). 128p. 1985. pap. 12.95 (*0-941130-08-8*) Lyons & Burford.

***Training Problem Dogs.** Louis Vine. (Illus.). 256p. 1997. pap. 16.95 (*0-7938-0474-4*, TS-283) TFH Pubns.

Training Problems in the Far East see Second Session of the Permanent Migration Committee

Training Professionals for Rural Mental Health. Ed. by H. A. Dengerink & H. J. Cross. LC 81-16288. 143p. reprint ed. pap. 40.80 (*0-8357-3797-7*, 2036524) Bks Demand.

***Training Program for Individuals Working with Older American Indians Who Are Blind & Visually Impaired.** K. White et al. 64p. 1991. pap. text ed. write for info. (*1-888557-52-4*) No Ariz Univ.

Training Program for Operation of Emergency Vehicles, 3 vols. in 1. 1992. lib. bdg. 375.00 (*0-8490-8864-X*) Gordon Pr.

Training Program for Teams at Work. Suzanne W. Zoglio. LC 93-94078. (Illus.). 144p. 1993. teacher ed., ring bd. 179.95 (*0-941668-05-3*) Tower Hill Pr.

Training Program Workbook & Kit. Carolyn Nilson. 384p. 1989. text ed. 69.95 (*0-13-926247-4*) P-H.

Training Programs & Tuition Aid Plans. (Personnel Policies Forum Surveys Ser.: No. 123). 1978. 30.00 (*0-686-88635-6*) BNA.

Training Programs for Health Care Workers: Food Service Workers. Incl. Being a Food Service Worker. 276p. 1967. student ed. 13.95 (*0-685-02354-0*, 546002); Training the Food Service Worker. 155p. 1967. teacher ed. 9.95 (*0-685-02355-9*, 546003); 1967. write for info. (*0-318-53453-3*) Hosp Res & Educ.

Training Programs for Health Care Workers: Housekeeping Aides. Incl. Being a Housekeeping Aide. 320p. 1967. student ed. 11.95 (*0-685-02356-7*, 585785); Training the Housekeeping Aide. 271p. 1967. teacher ed. 9.95 (*0-685-02357-5*, 585786); 1967. write for info. (*0-318-53454-1*) Hosp Res & Educ.

Training Programs for Health Care Workers: Pediatric Nursing Aides - Caring for Children in the Hospital. 1973. student ed. 6.95 (*0-685-02358-3*, 654772) Hosp Res & Educ.

Training Programs in Assistive Technology: 1992 Guide. Lynn R. Bryant. 87p. 1992. pap. 15.00 (*0-9635859-1-6*) RehabTech.

Training Psychiatrists for the '90s: Issues & Recommendations. Ed. by Carol C. Nadelson & Carolyn B. Robinowitz. (Issues in Psychiatry Ser.). 219p. 1987. pap. text ed. 21.00 (*0-88048-142-0*, 8142) Am Psychiatric.

Training Readiness in the Army Reserve Components. J. Michael Polich et al. LC 94-32569. 1994. pap. 15.00 (*0-8330-1586-9*, MR-474-A) Rand Corp.

Training Record. 40p. 1976. 7.00 (*0-7277-0076-6*, Pub. by T Telford UK) Am Soc Civil Eng.

Training Reference for Oil Spill Response. 1996. lib. bdg. 251.95 (*0-8490-6890-8*) Gordon Pr.

Training Reports & Records: 1989. 1989. 20.25 (*0-317-07397-4*, 1401-89) Natl Fire Prot.

Training Research & Practice. Ed. by John Patrick. (Illus.). 585p. 1992. text ed. 78.00 (*0-12-546660-9*) Acad Pr.

***Training Resource Book for Agro-Ecosystems Mapping.** Compiled by C. Lightfoot et al. 55p. 1989. write for info. (*0-614-23053-5*, Pub. by ICLARM PH) Intl Spec Bk.

***Training Resource Book for Farming Systems Diagnosis.** Compiled by C. Lightfoot et al. 62p. 1990. per. write for info. (*971-10-4222-3*, Pub. by ICLARM PH) Intl Spec Bk.

***Training Resource Book for Participatory Experimental Design.** Compiled by C. Lightfoot et al. 73p. 1991. per. write for info. (*0-614-23054-3*, Pub. by ICLARM PH) Intl Spec Bk.

Training Resource Directory, 1989: A Guide to Training Programs for the Communications Industries. Ed. by Dana Eggert. (Illus.). 700p. 1989. pap. 56.00 (*0-9621723-0-8*) Perf Plus.

Training Resources for the Produce Industry. Anne L. Day & Carolyn Myles. 92p. 1992. ring bd. write for info. (*0-9632546-0-X*) U Fresh Fruit & Veg.

Training Retrievers: Methods & Concepts of 20 Top Professionals. Bill Hillmann. LC 79-63126. 19.50 (*0-686-24829-5*) Seattle Pub Co.

Training Russian Mediators: Advent of a New Era? Ira B. Lobel & Louis J. Manchise. (Current Issues Ser.: No. 19). 1993. 5.00 (*0-89215-182-X*) U Cal LA Indus Rel.

Training Sales Associates for Success. Michael Jewell. Ed. by Christopher Bettin. 150p. (Orig.). (C). 1991. pap. text ed. 22.00 (*0-913652-76-8*) Realtors Natl.

Training School Age Child Care Teachers. Betsy Arns. 284p. 1991. 135.00 (*0-9622108-1-1*) Schl-Age Wkshops Pr.

Training Schools for Delinquent Girls. Margaret Reeves. 1992. lib. bdg. 79.95 (*0-8490-5298-X*) Gordon Pr.

Training Seminar - Offset Printing: Instructor's Manual. Illus. by George Farnsworth. 56p. (C). 1993. text ed. 47.50 (*0-9637163-0-1*) ATI Grap Arts.

Training Seminar - Offset Printing: Student Handbook. (Illus.). 38p. (C). 22.50 (*0-9637163-1-X*) ATI Grap Arts.

Training Sessions. (Open Learning for Supervisory Management Ser.). 1986. pap. text ed. 19.50 (*0-08-070103-5*, Pergamon Pr) Elsevier.

Training Sessions. Nebsm Staff. (Open Learning for Supervisory Management Ser.). 1985. pap. text ed. 19.50 (*0-08-033393-1*, Pergamon Pr) Elsevier.

Training Showjumpers. Anthony Paalman. 352p. 1990. 62.00 (*0-85131-260-8*, Pub. by J A Allen & Co UK) St Mut.

Training Skills for Supervisors. Robert W. Lucas. LC 94-4999. (Business Skills Express Ser.). 112p. 1994. text ed. 10.00 (*0-7863-0313-1*) Irwin Prof Pubng.

Training Soccer Champions. Anson Dorrance. Ed. by Tim Nash. (Illus.). 160p. 1996. 33.00 (*1-887791-01-9*) JTC Sports.

Training Social Workers for Groupwork. Allan Brown et al. (C). 1987. text ed. 35.00 (*0-902789-50-3*, Pub. by Natl Inst Soc Work) St Mut.

Training Spaniels. Joe Irving. (Illus.). 176p. 1993. 29.95 (*1-85310-419-1*, Pub. by Swan Hill UK) Voyageur Pr.

Training Specialist. Jack Rudman. (Career Examination Ser.: C-2337). 1994. pap. 34.95 (*0-8373-2337-1*) Nat Learn.

Training Specialist I. Jack Rudman. (Career Examination Ser.: C-2338). 1994. pap. 34.95 (*0-8373-2338-X*) Nat Learn.

Training Specialist II. Jack Rudman. (Career Examination Ser.: C-1768). 1994. reprint ed. pap. 39.95 (*0-8373-1768-1*) Nat Learn.

Training Standard on Initial Fire Attack. National Fire Protection Association Staff. 1988. 16.75 (*0-317-63547-6*, 1410-88) Natl Fire Prot.

Training Strategies for Dressage Riders. Charles De Kunffy. (Illus.). 240p. 1994. pap. 30.00 (*0-87605-972-8*) Howell Bk.

Training Student Library Assistants. Morell D. Boone et al. LC 90-27837. 140p. (C). 1991. pap. text ed. 25.00 (*0-8389-0561-7*, 0561-7) ALA.

Training Student Library Staff. Lesley S. Farmer. LC 96-51148. (Professional Growth Ser.). 192p. 1997. pap. 29.95 (*0-938865-56-0*) Linworth Pub.

Training Teachers: A Harvest of Theory & Practice. Margie Carter & Deb Curtis. LC 94-38144. (Illus.). 288p. (Orig.). 1995. pap. 32.95 (*0-934140-82-0*, 1311) Redleaf Pr.

Training Teachers of Adults: Models & Innovative Programs. Stanley M. Grabowski. LC 76-23432. (Occasional Papers: No. 46). 75p. 1976. pap. text ed. 3.50 (*0-87060-071-0*, OCP 46) Syracuse U Cont Ed.

Training Teachers of the Gifted & Talented. Margaret Lindsey. Ed. by Abraham J. Tannenbaum. LC 80-11867. (Perspectives on Gifted & Talented Education Ser.). 60p. (Orig.). 1980. pap. text ed. 8.95 (*0-8077-2590-0*) Tchrs Coll.

Training Teachers of the Gifted & Talented. Margaret Lindsey. LC 80-11867. (Perspectives on Gifted & Talented Education Ser.). 72p. (Orig.). 1980. reprint ed. pap. 25.00 (*0-608-00540-1*, 2061419) Bks Demand.

Training Technician. Jack Rudman. (Career Examination Ser.: C-1524). 1994. pap. 34.95 (*0-8373-1524-7*) Nat Learn.

Training Technician (Police) Jack Rudman. (Career Examination Ser.: C-417). 1994. pap. 39.95 (*0-8373-0417-2*) Nat Learn.

Training Techniques in Brief: A Guide to Teaching Methods for the Non-Professional. Stan Smith. 1988. 13.70 (*0-945795-03-3*) MBA Pub.

***Training Techniques in Cardiac Rehabilitation.** Paul Fardy. LC 97-16033. (Illus.). 152p. (Orig.). 1997. pap. text ed. write for info. (*0-87322-536-8*) Human Kinetics.

Training Technology System. abr. ed. Richard A. Swanson & Gary R. Sisson. 61p. 1985. pap. text ed. 4.95 (*0-318-19529-1*) Paradigm Corp.

Training Tenor Voices. Richard Miller. 173p. 1993. 38.00 (*0-02-871397-4*) Schirmer Bks.

Training That Makes a Difference: Teachers, Educators, Administrators, Pastors. Anne Gilbert. 91p. 1991. pap. 12.95 (*1-877871-16-8*, 4110) Ed Ministries.

Training That Works! Charles Cadwell. Ed. by Bonnie Sanford. LC 95-75606. (AMI How-to Ser.). 101p. 1995. per. 12.95 (*1-884926-36-3*) Amer Media.

An Asterisk (*) at the beginning of an entry indicates that the title is appearing in BIP for the first time.

Training the American Workforce: The Mark of Excellence Conference Proceedings, November 14-16, 1990, San Francisco, California. Ed. by Karen Glass. 200p. (Orig.). 1990. pap. text ed. 15.00 (*1-55877-078-X*) Natl Governor.

Training the Body for China: Sports in the Moral Order of the People's Republic. Susan Brownell. LC 94-49561. 406p. 1995. pap. text ed. 18.95 (*0-226-07647-4*) U Ch Pr.

Training the Body for China: Sports in the Moral Order of the People's Republic. Susan Brownell. LC 94-49561. 360p. 1995. lib. bdg. 49.95 (*0-226-07646-6*) U Ch Pr.

Training the Bourgeoisie: The University of Toulouse in the Nineteenth Century-Faculties & Students in Provincial France. John M. Burney. (Modern European History Ser.). 392p. 1987. text ed. 15.00 (*0-8240-8033-5*) Garland.

Training the Counsellor: An Integrative Model. Mary Connor. LC 94-16169. 240p. (C). 1994. pap. 18.95 (*0-415-10219-7*, B4079) Routledge.

Training the Counsellor: An Integrative Model. Mary Connor. LC 94-16169. 240p. (C). (gr. 13). 1994. text ed. 62.95 (*0-415-10218-9*, B4075) Routledge.

***Training the Dressage Horse: Novice to Medium Level.** Tricia Gardiner. 1997. pap. text ed. 19.95 (*0-7063-7644-7*, Pub. by Ward Lock UK) Sterling.

Training the Event Horse. Virginia Leng. (Illus.). 224p. 1991. 24.95 (*0-943955-38-6*, Trafalgar Sq Pub) Trafalgar.

Training the Food Service Worker. Hospital Research & Educational Trust of the AHA Staff. (Illus.). 1967. pap. 9.95 (*0-87618-047-0*) P-H.

Training the Food Service Worker: Instructor's Guide. 155p. 1967. write for info. (*0-318-59928-7*, 9776) Hosp Res & Educ.

Training the Food Service Worker see Training Programs for Health Care Workers: Food Service Workers

***Training the German Shepherd Dog.** John Cree. (Illus.). 192p. 1997. 39.95 (*1-85223-955-7*, Pub. by Crowood Pr UK) Trafalgar.

Training the Housekeeping Aide: Instructor's Guide. 271p. 1967. 9.95 (*0-685-43355-2*) Hosp Res & Educ.

Training the Housekeeping Aide see Training Programs for Health Care Workers: Housekeeping Aides

Training the Hunting Retriever. Jerome B. Robinson. 232p. 1993. 22.95 (*1-55821-263-9*) Lyons & Burford.

Training the Hunting Retriever. Bill Tarrant. (Illus.). 256p. 1991. pap. 25.95 (*0-87605-575-7*) Howell Bk.

Training the Mind: And Cultivating Loving-Kindness. Chogyam Trungpa. LC 93-520. 168p. (Orig.). 1993. pap. 9.00 (*0-87773-954-4*) Shambhala Pubns.

***Training the Mind & Hand to Draw: The Wholebrain, Self-Teaching ArtBerst Method of Building Artistic Ability & Increasing Intelligence.** 1997. spiral bd. 14.00 (*0-9614126-7-4*) Natl Lilac Pub.

Training the Mind in the Great Way. Glenn H. Mullin. 96p. 1993. pap. 12.95 (*0-937938-96-3*) Snow Lion Pubns.

Training the Mind of Your Gun Dog. J. A. Kersley & F. Haworth. (Illus.). 1977. 18.00 (*0-7207-0948-2*) Transatl Arts.

Training the Pointer-Retriever Gundog. Michael Brander. (Illus.). 176p. 1992. 27.95 (*1-85310-238-5*, Pub. by Swan Hill UK) Voyageur Pr.

Training the Roman Cavalry. Ann Hyland. (Illus.). 224p. 1993. text ed. 52.00 (*0-86299-984-7*, Pub. by Sutton Pubng UK) Bks Intl VA.

Training the Roughshooter's Dog. P. R. Moxon. (Illus.). 176p. 1994. 26.95 (*1-85310-501-5*, Pub. by Swan Hill UK) Voyageur Pr.

Training the Sales Team. David Hillier. 165p. 1994. 63.95 (*0-566-07495-8*, Pub. by Gower UK) Ashgate Pub Co.

***Training the Sheep Dog.** Thomas Longton & Barbara Sykes. (Illus.). 160p. 1997. 35.00 (*1-86126-031-8*, Pub. by Crowood Pr UK) Trafalgar.

***Training the Speaking Voice.** H. D. Flowers. 140p. 1996. pap. text ed. 22.95 (*1-56226-300-5*) CT Pub.

Training the Speaking Voice. 3rd ed. Virgil A. Anderson. (Illus.). 494p. (C). 1977. text ed. 41.95 (*0-19-502150-9*) OUP.

Training the Teacher as a Champion. Joseph K. Hasenstab & Connie C. Wilson. 184p. (Orig.). (C). 1989. pap. 15.95 (*0-9621766-0-5*) Perf Lrn Systs.

Training the Technical Work Force. Anthony P. Carnevale et al. LC 89-48806. (Management Ser.). 220p. text ed. 32.95 (*1-55542-201-2*) Jossey-Bass.

Training the Three-Day-Event Horse & Rider. James C. Wofford. LC 94-32577. 272p. 1995. 27.95 (*0-385-42520-1*) Doubleday.

Training the Time Sense: Hypnotic & Conditioning Approaches. Philip G. Zimbardo et al. 219p. (C). 1994. pap. text ed. 65.00 (*1-885679-06-8*) Morgan Fnd Pubs.

Training the Translator. Paul Kussmaul. (Translation Library: No. 10). x, 178p. 1995. 43.00 (*1-55619-690-3*) Benjamins North Am.

***Training the Translator.** Paul Kussmaul. x, 178p. pap. 29.95 (*1-55619-704-7*) Benjamins North Am.

Training the Versatile Retriever to Hunt Upland Birds. Bill Tarrant. LC 96-60858. (Illus.). 268p. 1996. 29.95 (*1-885106-28-9*) Wild Adven Pr.

Training the Young Horse: The First Two Years. Anthony Crossley. (Illus.). 191p. 1994. pap. 14.95 (*0-09-178224-4*, Pub. by S Paul UK) Trafalgar.

Training Theory & Practice. Ed. by W. Brendan Reddy & Clenard C. Henderson, Jr. LC 87-62132. 300p. (Orig.). 1987. pap. text ed. 19.00 (*0-9610392-4-8*) NTL Inst.

Training Theory for Martial Arts. Tony Gummerson. pap. 19.95 (*0-7136-3400-6*, 92771, Pub. by A&C Black UK) Talman.

Training Therapy: Prophylaxis & Rehabilitation. 2nd rev. ed. Gustavsen Rolf & Renate Streeck. Tr. & Adapted by Wolfgang G. Gilliar. LC 92-48359. (Flexibook Ser.). (Illus.). 240p. 1993. pap. text ed. 27.00 (*0-86577-483-8*) Thieme Med Pubs.

Training Thoroughbred Horses. Preston M. Burch & Alex Bower. LC 92-25146. 1992. 19.95 (*0-929346-19-X*) R Meerdink Co Ltd.

Training Through Dialogue: Promoting Effective Learning & Change with Adults. Jane K. Vella. (Higher & Adult Education Ser.). 224p. text ed. 27.95 (*0-7879-0135-0*) Jossey-Bass.

Training Tips: Materials for Training Early Intervention Special Education Personnel. Infant Hearing Resource Staff. (Early Intervention Series II). 30p. (Orig.). (C). 1994. pap. text ed. 20.00 (*1-883204-06-2*) Infant Hearing Resc.

Training to Be Like Bruce Lee. Jesse R. Glover. 200p. 1990. pap. 25.00 (*0-9602328-5-0*) Glover Pubns.

Training to Proficiency. (Instrument Pilots Library: Vol. VI). Date not set. 23.95 (*1-879620-27-8*) Belvoir Pubns.

Training Today: Careers Tomorrow. Ed. by Paul Downes. 1994. 122.95 (*1-55631-020-X*) Chron Guide.

Training Too Much? A Sceptical Look at the Economics of Skill Provision in the U. K. J. R. Shackleton. 86p. (C). 1992. text ed. 59.95 (*0-255-36307-9*, Pub. by Inst Economic Affairs UK) St Mut.

Training Trances: Multi-Level Communication in Therapy & Training. John Overdurf & Julie Silverthorn. 260p. (Orig.). 1996. pap. 19.95 (*1-55552-069-3*) Metamorphous Pr.

Training Translators & Conference Interpreters. Wilhelm K. Weber. (Language in Education Ser.: No. 58). 70p. 1986. pap. text ed. write for info. (*0-13-926924-X*) P-H.

Training Trilogy: Assessing Needs. Dick Leatherman. 72p. 1990. 10.00 (*0-87425-141-9*) HRD Press.

Training Trilogy: Designing Programs. Dick Leatherman. 136p. 1990. 15.00 (*0-87425-142-7*) HRD Press.

Training Trilogy: Facilitation Skills. Dick Leatherman. 96p. 1990. 10.00 (*0-87425-143-5*) HRD Press.

***Training Truck Drivers.** OECD Staff. (Road Transport Research Ser.). 98p. (Orig.). 1996. pap. 28.00 (*92-64-15275-X*, 77-96-02-1) OECD.

Training Users & Producers in Compiling Statistics & Indicators on Women in Development. (Studies in Methods, Series F: No. F45). 141p. 1987. 17.00 (*92-1-161284-5*, E.87.XVII.6) UN.

***Training Verification for Laboratory Personnel: Approved Guideline (1995)** Contrib. by David E. Nevalainen. 1995. 85.00 (*1-56238-286-1*, GP21-A) Natl Comm Clin Lab Stds.

***Training Wheels.** 2nd rev. ed. Donna R. Fisher. (Illus.). 349p. 1996. teacher ed., pap. 49.95 (*0-913717-00-2*, 1278) Hewitt Res Fnd.

Training Wheels & Here I Grow Songbook. Donna R. Fisher. 16p. (J). (gr. k-1). 1995. pap. 5.95 incl. audio (*0-913717-60-6*, 1990) Hewitt Res Fnd.

Training Wheels Coloring Book. Ed. by Donna R. Fisher. 84p. (J). 1991. pap. 5.95 (*0-913717-26-6*, 1277) Hewitt Res Fnd.

Training with Bits: Bitting Techniques to Make Training Understandable for the Horse. William G. Langdon, Jr. LC 93-199250. (Illus.). 100p. (Orig.). 1992. spiral bd. 29.95 (*1-883714-05-2*) Langdon Ent.

Training with NLP: Neuro-linguistic Programming. Joseph O'Connor & John Seymour. (Illus.). 224p. 1994. pap. 16.00 (*0-7225-2853-1*) Thorsons SF.

Training with Outdoor Activities. Carmine M. Consalvo. 344p. 1993. ring bd. 125.95 (*1-85904-041-1*, Pub. by Gower UK) Ashgate Pub Co.

Training with the Champions: Body Building Principle, Weekly Training Formats & Routines. Paul Ward. (Illus.). 350p. pap. 39.95 (*0-614-04687-4*) QPT Pubns.

Training with Video. Steve R. Cartwright. LC 86-2902. (Illus.). 168p. 1986. 42.95 (*0-86729-132-X*, Focal) Buttrwrth-Heinemann.

Training Workhorses: Training Teamsters. L. R. Miller. (Illus.). 352p. (Orig.). 1994. pap. 24.95 (*1-885210-00-0*) Small Farmers.

Training Workhorses: Training Teamsters. L. R. Miller. (Illus.). 352p. (Orig.). 1994. 43.95 (*1-885210-01-9*) Small Farmers.

Training Workshop for Supervisors: Building the Essential Skills. Frank Atkinson. LC 94-22347. 1995. 59.95 (*0-566-07610-1*, Pub. by Gower UK) Ashgate Pub Co.

Training Young Horses. Pony Club Training Committee. (Illus.). 112p. 1990. 18.95 (*0-900226-37-4*, Pub. by Brit Horse Soc & Pony Club UK) Half Halt Pr.

Training Your Colt to Ride & Drive: A Complete Guide for Pleasure or Show. rev. ed. Marilyn C. Childs & Rick M. Wallen. LC 93-28286. 1993. 19.95 (*0-943955-83-1*, Trafalgar Sq Pub) Trafalgar.

Training Your Creative Mind. Arthur B. VanGundy. 206p. 1991. pap. 14.95 (*0-943456-36-3*) Bearly Ltd.

Training Your Dog. Diane Ashton. (Illus.). 160p. 1994. pap. 22.95 (*1-85223-833-X*, Pub. by Crowood Pr UK) Trafalgar.

***Training Your Dog.** Dk Publishing, Inc. Staff. LC 96-6586. (101 Essential Tips Ser.: Vol. 26). 72p. 1997. pap. 6.95 (*0-7894-1460-0*) DK Pub Inc.

Training Your Dog. Barbara Woodhouse. (Barbara Woodhouse on...Ser.). (Illus.). 64p. 1994. 7.95 (*0-948955-57-0*) Seven Hills Bk.

Training Your Dog: A Day-by-Day Program. Kathleen Berman & Bill Landesman. LC 93-44536. (Illus.). 160p. 1994. pap. 14.95 (*0-8069-0576-X*) Sterling.

Training Your Dog: A Guide to a More Compatible Relationship. Elizabeth Ballinger. 120p. 1983. pap. write for info. (*0-318-57590-6*) Old Farm Ken.

Training Your Dog: The Step-by-Step Manual. Joachim J. Volhard & Gail T. Fisher. LC 82-21327. (Illus.). 240p. 1983. pap. 18.95 (*0-87605-775-X*) Howell Bk.

Training Your Dog for Sports & Other Activities. Charlotte Schwartz. (Illus.). 160p. 1996. 19.95 (*0-7938-2079-0*, TS258) TFH Pubns.

Training Your Hand Fed Parrot. Delia Berlin. (Illus.). 128p. 1996. 23.95 (*0-7938-2184-3*, TS242) TFH Pubns.

Training Your Horse with Lunge & Long Reins. Christopher Coldrey & Victoria Coldrey. (Illus.). 160p. 1996. 24.95 (*1-85223-944-1*, Pub. by Crowood Pr UK) Trafalgar.

Training Your Parrot. Kevin Murphy. (Illus.). 192p. 1983. 23.95 (*0-87666-872-4*, H-1056) TFH Pubns.

Training Your Retriever. rev. ed. James L. Free. (Illus.). 368p. 1991. 18.95 (*0-399-13620-7*, Putnam) Putnam Pub Group.

***Training, 1997 Annual, Vol. 1.** Pfeiffer & Company Staff. 1997. pap. text ed. 39.95 (*0-88390-491-8*, Pfffr & Co) Jossey-Bass.

Trainmaster. Jack Rudman. (Career Examination Ser.: C-817). 1994. pap. 23.95 (*0-8373-0817-8*) Nat Learn.

Trains. LC 95-15135. (Look Inside Cross-Sections Ser.). (Illus.). 32p. (YA). (gr. 5 up). 1995. pap. 5.95 (*0-7894-0319-6*, 5-70669) DK Pub Inc.

Trains. LC 92-12351. (Eye Openers Ser.). (Illus.). 24p. (J). (ps-k). 1992. pap. 8.99 (*0-689-71647-8*, Litl Simon S&S) S&S Childrens.

***Trains.** Ariel Books Staff. 1996. 3.95 (*0-8362-0995-8*, Arie Bks) Andrews & McMeel.

***Trains.** Wendy Barish & Gallimard Jeunesse. LC 97-15428. (First Discovery Bks.). (Illus.). 1998. write for info. (*0-590-38156-3*) Scholastic Inc.

Trains. Byron Barton. LC 85-47898. (Illus.). 32p. (J). (ps). 1986. 6.95 (*0-694-00061-2*, Crowell Jr Bks); lib. bdg. 13.89 (*0-690-04534-4*, Crowell Jr Bks) HarpC Child Bks.

Trains. Byron Barton. (Illus.). 28p. (J). (ps). 1994. 2.95 (*0-694-00601-7*, Festival) HarpC Child Bks.

***Trains.** Amanda Bennett. (Unit Study Adventures Ser.). 104p. Date not set. pap. 13.99 (*1-888306-11-4*, Home School Pr) GCB.

Trains. Mike Bowler. LC 94-9029. (Pointers Ser.). (Illus.). (J). 1994. lib. bdg. 22.83 (*0-8114-6192-0*) Raintree Steck-V.

Trains. Mike Bowler. (J). 1996. pap. text ed. 4.95 (*0-8114-9365-2*) Raintree Steck-V.

Trains. Ray Broekel. (New True Bks.). (Illus.). 48p. (J). (gr. k-4). 1981. pap. 5.50 (*0-516-41652-9*) Childrens.

Trains. J. Cooper. (Traveling Machines Ser.). (J). 1991. 8.95 (*0-86592-490-2*) Rourke Enter.

Trains. Gabriele. (J). 1986. pap. 1.95 (*0-911211-63-2*) Penny Lane Pubns.

Trains. Gail Gibbons. LC 86-19595. (Illus.). 32p. (J). (ps-3). 1987. lib. bdg. 15.95 (*0-8234-0640-7*) Holiday.

Trains. Gail Gibbons. LC 86-19595. (Illus.). 32p. (J). (ps-3). 1988. pap. 6.95 (*0-8234-0699-7*) Holiday.

***Trains.** Michael Johnstone et al. (Illus.). (J). pap. 8.99 (*0-590-24654-2*) Scholastic Inc.

Trains. Seymour V. Reit. (J). (ps-3). 1990. write for info. (*0-307-17869-2*) Western Pub.

Trains. Joy Richardson. LC 93-49731. (Picture Science Ser.). (Illus.). 32p. (J). 1994. lib. bdg. 20.00 (*0-531-14327-9*) Watts.

Trains. Anne Rockwell. (J). 1993. pap. 4.99 (*0-14-054979-X*, Puff Unicorn) Puffin Bks.

***Trains.** Snapshot Staff. (Shape Board Books Ser.). 1997. 3.95 (*0-7894-2211-5*) DK Pub Inc.

Trains. Philip Steele. LC 90-41179. (Pocket Facts Ser.). (Illus.). 32p. (J). (gr. 5-6). 1991. lib. bdg. 11.95 (*0-89686-523-1*, Crstwood Hse) Silver Burdett Pr.

Trains. Darlene R. Stille. LC 96-25728. (True Bk.). (J). 1997. lib. bdg. 19.00 (*0-516-20342-8*) Childrens.

Trains. limited ed. William Heyen. (Metacom Limited Edition Ser.: No. 2). 24p. 1981. 25.00 (*0-911381-01-5*) Metacom Pr.

Trains: Richard Scarry. Richard Scarry. (Golden Little Look-Look Bks.). (Illus.). 24p. (J). (ps). 1992. pap. 1.49 (*0-307-11536-4*, 11536, Golden Pr) Western Pub.

Trains & Railroads. Sydney Wood. LC 91-58201. (See & Explore Library). (Illus.). 64p. (J). (gr. 3 up). 1992. 12.95 (*1-56458-001-6*); 12.99 (*1-56458-002-4*) DK Pub Inc.

Trains & Railroads. rev. ed. Howard W. Kanetzke. LC 87-20813. (Read about Science Ser.). (Illus.). 48p. (J). (gr. 2-6). 1987. pap. 4.95 (*0-8114-8222-7*) Raintree Steck-V.

Train's Done Been & Gone: An Annapolis Portrait 1859-1910. rev. ed. Marion E. Warren & Mame Warren. LC 81-50974. (Illus.). 1981. reprint ed. 19.95 (*0-9606060-0-9*) M E Warren.

Trains Etroitement Surveilles. Bohumil Hrabal. (FRE.). 1984. pap. 10.95 (*0-7859-2485-X*, 2070375293) Fr & Eur.

Trains from Grandfather's Attic. Peter H. Riddle. (Illus.). 144p. 1991. pap. text ed. 22.95 (*0-89778-215-1*, 10-7585, Greenberg Books) Kalmbach.

Trains of America. 2nd rev. ed. Donald J. Heimburger. LC 89-84380. (Illus.). 204p. 1992. 44.95 (*0-911581-13-8*) Heimburger Hse Pub.

Trains of Discovery: Western Railroads & the National Parks. limited rev. ed. Alfred E. Runte. 96p. 1993. 65.00 (*1-879373-74-2*) R Rinehart.

Trains of Discovery: Western Railroads & the National Parks. rev. ed. Alfred E. Runte. 96p. 1993. pap. 19.95 (*1-879373-68-8*) R Rinehart.

Trains of Discovery: Western Railroads & the National Parks. 3rd rev. ed. Alfred E. Runte. 96p. 1993. 35.00 (*1-879373-69-6*) R Rinehart.

Trains of Northern New England. John Krause & Fred Bailey. 1977. pap. 8.95 (*0-915276-17-8*) Quadrant Pr.

***Trains of the Old West.** Brian Solomon. LC 97-13126. 1997. write for info. (*1-56799-478-4*, MetroBooks) M Friedman Pub Grp Inc.

Trains of Wisconsin. Malcolm Rosholt. 176p. 1992. text ed. 29.95 (*0-9635065-0-1*) Nat Railrd Mus.

Trains of Wisconsin. Malcolm Rosholt. LC 85-90436. (Illus.). 176p. 1985. 29.95 (*0-910417-06-7*) Rosholt Hse.

Trains, Planes, & Automobiles: Full-Size Designs, Ready to Cut. John A. Nelson. (Scroll Saw Pattern Bks.). (Illus.). 96p. 1995. pap. 14.95 (*0-8117-3072-7*) Stackpole.

Trains Sl-ay Huns. Crag Hill. (Chapbook Ser.). 17p. 1990. pap. 5.00 (*0-945112-10-6*) Generator Pr.

***Trains, Tracks & Tall Timber: The History, Making & Modeling of Lumber & Paper.** Matt Coleman. (Illus.). 144p. 1997. text ed. 49.98 (*0-941952-49-5*) W K Walthers.

Trains, Trails & Tin Lizzies: Glacier National Park, 1932-1934. George A. Grant. LC 87-7433. (Illus.). 72p. 1987. 32.50 (*0-916792-05-6*) Glacier Nat Hist Assn.

***Trains Traveling Through Time.** Neil Morris. LC 96-51499. (J). 1997. pap. write for info. (*0-382-39794-0*); lib. bdg. write for info. (*0-382-39793-2*) Silver Burdett Pr.

Trains Trestles & Tunnels: Railroads of the Southern Appalachians. 3rd ed. Lou Harshaw. LC 77-77409. (Illus.). 93p. 1989. reprint ed. pap. write for info. (*0-9623532-0-5*) NRHS Asheville Chapter.

***Trains West: Stories of Children Who Rode the Orphan Trains West from New York City 1854-1929.** Carole Johnston. (Illus.). 170p. 1997. pap. 9.95 (*1-57166-073-9*) Quixote Pr IA.

Trainspotting. John Hodge. LC 97-11201. (Illus.). 128p. 1996. 9.95 (*0-7868-8221-2*) Hyperion.

Trainspotting. Irvine Welsh. Date not set. pap. 5.99 (*0-7493-2173-3*) Heinemann.

Trainspotting. Irvine Welsh. 340p. 1996. pap. 13.00 (*0-393-31480-4*, Norton Paperbks) Norton.

***Trainspotting & Headstate.** Irvine Welsh. 1997. pap. 13.95 (*0-7493-9573-7*) Heinemann.

Trainspotting & Shallow Grave. John Hodge. 1996. pap. text ed. 13.95 (*0-571-17968-1*) Faber & Faber.

Trainwail Loneliness. David A. Wilson. (Illus.). 48p. (Orig.). 1991. pap. 5.00 (*0-934852-35-9*) Lorien Hse.

Traipsin Woman. Jeannette B. Thomas. (American Biography Ser.). 277p. 1991. reprint ed. lib. bdg. 69.00 (*0-7812-8382-5*) Rprt Serv.

Trait-Names: Psycho-Lexical Study. Gordon W. Allport. Bd. with Psychological Studies of Heiman Variability. (Psychological Monographs General & Applied: Vol. 97). 1974. reprint ed. Set pap. 8.00 (*0-8115-1446-3*) Periodicals Srv.

***Traite de Catastrophe.** P. Huguenard. 1000p. pap. 199.00 (*2-906077-89-5*) Elsevier.

Traite de Civisme. Boris Vian. (FRE.). 1987. pap. 18.95 (*0-7859-3198-8*, 2264010762) Fr & Eur.

Traite De Fauconnerie: Treatise of Falconry. H. Schlegel & A. H. Wulverhorst. Tr. by Thomas Hanlon. (Illus.). 1973. 32.50 (*0-913930-01-6*) Chasse Pubns.

Traite de Gastro-Enterologie, 2 vols. J. J. Bernier et al. (Illus.). 1600p. (FRE.). 1984. Set. 295.00 (*2-257-10431-5*) S M P F Inc.

Traite de la Relieure des Livres. Jean-Vincent C. De Gauffecourt. 134p. 1987. 60.00 (*0-614-16152-5*) Oak Knoll.

Traite de la Relieure des Livres. Jean-Vincent C. De Gauffecourt. Tr. by Claude Benaiteau. 140p. (ENG & FRE.). 1987. reprint ed. 100.00 (*0-935072-13-6*) W T Taylor.

Traite de L'Accord de L'Espinette. 2nd ed. Jean Denis. LC 68-16229. (Music Ser.). 1969. reprint ed. 21.50 (*0-306-70950-3*) Da Capo.

Traite de l'Esprit de l'Homme et de Ses Facultes ou Fonctions et de Son Union avec le Corps. Louis De La Forge. (Historia Philosophiae Ser.). xliv, 455p. 1984. reprint ed. write for info. (*3-487-07476-1*) G Olms Pubs.

Traite de l'Harmonie Reduite a Ses Principes Naturels see Monuments of Music & Music Literature in Facsimile

Traite de Pierre d'Ailly sur la Consolation de Boece, Qu 1. Marguerite Chappuis. LC 92-37652. (Bochumer Studien zur Philosophie Ser.: Band 20). xli, 236p. (FRE.). 1993. 83.00 (*90-6032-338-6*, Pub. by B R Gruener NE) Benjamins North Am.

Traite de Pisicultur see Textbook of Fish Culture: Breeding & Cultivation of Fish

Traite de Prononciation Francaise. Pierre Fouche. 528p. 1959. 14.95 (*0-8288-7475-1*) Fr & Eur.

Traite de Reciprocite, 1854: Textes. Pierre Trudel & Claude Belanger. LC 73-348505. (Cahiers d'Histoire - Historical Studies: Vol. 1). 134p. (FRE.). 1968. reprint ed. pap. 38.20 (*0-608-02194-6*, 2062864) Bks Demand.

Traite De Saisons. Hector Bianciotti. 256p. (FRE.). 1984. pap. 11.95 (*0-7859-1998-8*, 2070375730) Fr & Eur.

Traite de Savior-Vivre a l'usage des Jeunes Generationse see Revolution of Everyday Life

Traite de Style. Louis Aragon. (FRE.). 1980. pap. 16.95 (*0-7859-3377-8*, 207020989X) Fr & Eur.

Traite d'Epigraphie Grecque. Salomon Reinbach. xliv, 560p. reprint ed. write for info. (*0-318-71401-9*); reprint ed. write for info. (*0-318-72106-6*) G Olms Pubs.

Traite des Couleurs pour la Peinture en Email et Sur la Porcelaine. Didier D. Arclais De Montamy. iii, 287p. 1981. reprint ed. 71.00 (*3-487-07062-6*) G Olms Pubs.

Traite Des Degenerescences Physiques, Intellectuelles et Morales De L'espece Humaine, 2 Vols. Benedict A. Morel. LC 75-16721. (Classics in Psychiatry Ser.). (Illus.). (FRE.). 1976. reprint ed. 62.95 (*0-405-07446-8*) Ayer.

Traite des Maladies Du Cerveau et De Ses Membranes: Maladies Mentales. Antoine L. Bayle. LC 75-16682. (Classics in Psychiatry Ser.). (FRE.). 1976. reprint ed. 51.95 (*0-405-07414-X*) Ayer.

T

Traite des tournois, joustes, carrousels et autres spectacles publics. Claude-Francois Menestrier. LC 76-43926. (Music & Theatre in France in the 17th & 18th Centuries Ser.). reprint ed. 84.50 (*0-404-60174-X*) AMS Pr.

Traite d'orchestration d'Hector Berlioz. Richard Strauss. Tr. by Ernest Closson. LC 74-24236. reprint ed. 34.50 (*0-404-13104-2*) AMS Pr.

Traite D'organogenie Comparee de la Fleur. I. B. Payer. 1966. reprint ed. 132.00 (*3-7682-0346-8*) Lubrecht & Cramer.

Traite du Poeme Epique, 2 vols. Rene Le Bossu. 646p. reprint ed. write for info. (*0-318-71365-9*) G Olms Pubs.

Traite du Poeme Epique, pour l'Intelligence de l'Eneide de Virgile. Michel De Marolles. x, 123p. 1974. reprint ed. write for info. (*3-487-05265-2*) G Olms Pubs.

Traite du recitatif dans la lecture, dans l'action publique, dans la declamation, et dans le chant. Jean L. Grimarest. LC 76-43921. (Music & Theatre in France in the 17th & 18th Centuries Ser.). 1977. reprint ed. 37.50 (*0-404-60164-2*) AMS Pr.

Traite Elementaire de Comptabilite: Elementary Treatise on Accounting. J. G. Courcelle-Seneuil. Ed. by Richard P. Brief. (Dimensions of Accounting Theory & Practice Ser.). (FRE.). 1980. reprint ed. lib. bdg. 24.95 (*0-405-13513-0*) Ayer.

Traite Elementaire De Paleontologie Histoire Naturelle Des Animaux Fossiles Consideres Ans Leur S Rapports Zoologiques et Geologiques, 4 Vols. Francois J. Pictet. Ed. by Stephen J. Gould. LC 79-8344. (History of Paleontology Ser.). (Illus.). (FRE.). 1980. reprint ed. Set. lib. bdg. 191.95 (*0-405-12734-0*) Ayer.

Traite Elementaire De Paleontologie Histoire Naturelle Des Animaux Fossiles Consideres Ans Leur S Rapports Zoologiques et Geologiques, 4 Vols., Vol. 1. Francois J. Pictet. Ed. by Stephen J. Gould. LC 79-8344. (History of Paleontology Ser.). (Illus.). (FRE.). 1980. reprint ed. lib. bdg. 47.95 (*0-405-12735-9*) Ayer.

Traite Elementaire De Paleontologie Histoire Naturelle Des Animaux Fossiles Consideres Ans Leur S Rapports Zoologiques et Geologiques, 4 Vols., Vol. 2. Francois J. Pictet. Ed. by Stephen J. Gould. LC 79-8344. (History of Paleontology Ser.). (Illus.). (FRE.). 1980. reprint ed. lib. bdg. 47.95 (*0-405-12736-7*) Ayer.

Traite Elementaire De Paleontologie Histoire Naturelle Des Animaux Fossiles Consideres Ans Leur S Rapports Zoologiques et Geologiques, 4 Vols., Vol. 3. Francois J. Pictet. Ed. by Stephen J. Gould. LC 79-8344. (History of Paleontology Ser.). (Illus.). (FRE.). 1980. reprint ed. lib. bdg. 47.95 (*0-405-12737-5*) Ayer.

Traite Elementaire De Paleontologie Histoire Naturelle Des Animaux Fossiles Consideres Ans Leur S Rapports Zoologiques et Geologiques, 4 Vols., Vol. 4. Francois J. Pictet. Ed. by Stephen J. Gould. LC 79-8344. (History of Paleontology Ser.). (Illus.). (FRE.). 1980. reprint ed. lib. bdg. 47.95 (*0-405-12738-3*) Ayer.

Traite Elementaire Theorique et Pretique De l'Art De La Danse see Elementary Treatise upon the Theory & Practice of the Art of Dancing

Traite General des Elemens du Chant see Monuments of Music & Music Literature in Facsimile

Traite Historique et Pratique de la Gravure en Bois, 2 vols. J. B. Papillon. 1125p. 1985. pap. text ed. 325.00 (*2-903928-30-4*) Gordon & Breach.

Traite Maladies des Os et des Articulations Mise a Jour 1985. S. De Seze & A. Ryckewaert. (Collection Medico-Chirurgicale). (Illus.). 168p. (FRE.). 1985. 36.00 (*0-318-04694-6*) S M P F Inc.

Traite Medico-Philosophique Sur L'alienation Mentale. 2nd ed. Philippe Pinel. LC 75-16727. (Classics in Psychiatry Ser.). (FRE.). 1976. reprint ed. 46.95 (*0-405-07450-6*) Ayer.

Traite Neo-Manicheen du XIIIe siecle. Liber de Duobus Principiis Staff. LC 78-63185. (Heresies of the Early Christian & Medieval Era Ser.: Second Ser.). 1979. reprint ed. 49.50 (*0-404-16224-X*) AMS Pr.

Traite Philosophique de la Foiblesse de l'Esprit Humain. Pierre D. Huet. xl, 296p. 1974. reprint ed. write for info. (*3-487-04889-2*) G Olms Pubs.

Traite sur la Tolerance. Francois-Marie De Voltaire. (FRE.). 1998. pap. 10.95 (*0-7859-2998-3*) Fr & Eur.

Traite sur l'Art de la Guerre. B. Stuart. (International Archives of the History of Ideas Ser.: No. 85). 1977. pap. text ed. 82.50 (*90-247-1871-6*) Kluwer Ac.

Traite Touchant...L'Escrite Francoise. Meigret. Ed. by Cameron. (Exeter French Texts Ser.: Vol. 33). 121p. (FRE.). Date not set. pap. text ed. 19.95 (*0-85989-039-2*, Pub. by Univ Exeter Pr UK) Northwestern U Pr.

Traite...Du Rire. De Sivry. Ed. by Brooks. (Exeter French Texts Ser.: Vol. 61). 92p. (FRE.). Date not set. pap. text ed. 19.95 (*0-85989-222-0*, Pub. by Univ Exeter Pr UK) Northwestern U Pr.

Traitement De la Criminalite Au Canada. Alice Parizeau & Denis Szabo. LC 77-479632. 436p. (FRE.). reprint ed. pap. 124.00 (*0-7837-6948-2*, 2046777) Bks Demand.

Traites des Pierres Precieuses et de la Maniere de le Employer en Parure see Five Hundred Fifty Authentic Rococo Designs & Motifs for Artists & Craftspeople

Traitmatch. Whiting. pap. 9.95 (*0-937480-02-9*) Newcastle Pub.

Traitor. Andre Gorz. Tr. by Richard Howard. 320p. 1988. text ed. 42.50 (*0-86091-228-0*, Pub. by Verso UK) Routledge Chapman & Hall.

Traitor. Andre Gorz. Tr. by Richard Howard. 320p. 1988. pap. 20.00 (*0-86091-941-2*, Pub. by Vrso UK) Norton.

Traitor. James Shirley. Ed. by John S. Carter. LC 65-11520. (Regents Renaissance Drama Ser.). 129p. 1965. reprint ed. pap. 36.80 (*0-608-02144-X*, 2062813) Bks Demand.

Traitor, Bk. 2. Joe B. Johnson. Ed. by Sarah Norris. 325p. 14.95 (*0-9622969-1-0*) JBJ True Pr.

Traitor: The Case of Benedict Arnold. Jean Fritz. (Illus.). (Orig.). (J). (gr. 3-7). 1981. 16.95 (*0-399-20834-8*, Putnam) Putnam Pub Group.

***Traitor: The Case of Benedict Arnold.** Jean Fritz. 192p. (Orig.). (YA). (gr. 5 up). 1997. pap. 5.95 (*0-698-11553-8*, Paperstar) Putnam Pub Group.

***Traitor among Us.** Elizabeth Van Steenwyk. 1997. pap. write for info. (*0-8028-5157-6*) Eerdmans.

***Traitor among Us.** Elizabeth VanSteenwyk. (J). 1997. write for info. (*0-8028-5150-9*) Eerdmans.

Traitor & the Spy: Benedict Arnold & John Andre. James T. Flexner. (New York Classics Ser.). (Illus.). 480p. (Orig.). 1991. reprint ed. pap. 15.95 (*0-8156-0263-4*) Syracuse U Pr.

Traitor Heart. large type ed. Nara Lake. 352p. 1995. 25.99 (*0-7089-3334-3*) Ulverscroft.

***Traitor in the Tower: John Bunyan.** Dave Jackson & Neta Jackson. LC 96-45854. (Trailblazer Bks.). (Illus.). (J). (gr. 3-8). 1997. pap. 5.99 (*1-55661-741-0*) Bethany Hse.

Traitor to the Living. Philip Jose Farmer. 288p. 1993. mass mkt. 4.99 (*0-8125-2397-0*) Tor Bks.

Traitor to the Race. Scott Darieck. 1996. pap. 10.95 (*0-452-27335-8*, Plume) NAL-Dutton.

Traitor to the Race. Darieck Scott. 1995. write for info. (*0-615-00242-0*, Dutton) NAL-Dutton.

Traitor to the Race. Darieck Scott. 1995. 20.00 (*0-525-93912-1*) Facts on File.

Traitor Trade. J. Bernard Hutton. (Illus.). 1963. 12.95 (*0-8392-1120-1*) Astor-Honor.

Traitor Trilogy, Vol. 1. Joe B. Johnson. Ed. by S. Morewitz. 205p. 1989. 14.95 (*0-9622969-0-2*) JBJ True Pr.

Traitor Tyrant Assassin. Mark Shane. 218p. 1993. 29.95 (*0-9640805-0-8*) Union Rebel.

Traitor Winds. L. A. Glaf. Ed. by Kevin Ryan. (Star Trek Ser.: No. 70). 288p. (Orig.). 1994. mass mkt. 5.50 (*0-671-86913-2*) PB.

Traitorous Hearts. Susan K. Law. 416p. 1994. mass mkt. 4.50 (*0-06-108183-3*, Harp PBks) HarpC.

Traitorous Hero: The Life & Fortunes of Benedict Arnold. Willard M. Wallace. LC 74-117896. (Select Bibliographies Reprint Ser.). 1980. 31.95 (*0-8369-5349-5*) Ayer.

Traitors. Kristine K. Rusch. 288p. (Orig.). 1994. pap. 4.99 (*0-451-45415-4*, ROC) NAL-Dutton.

Traitors. Stephen Sewell. 104p. (C). 1995. pap. 16.50 (*0-86819-413-1*) Aubrey Bks.

Traitors. large type ed. Peter Chester. (Linford Mystery Library). 288p. 1989. pap. 15.99 (*0-7089-6737-X*, Linford) Ulverscroft.

Traitors. large type ed. Vivian Stuart. 784p. 1983. 27.99 (*0-7089-8137-2*) Ulverscroft.

Traitors Crime. large type ed. Roderic Jeffries. 324p. 1995. pap. 17.99 (*1-85389-501-6*, Dales) Ulverscroft.

Traitor's Daughter. Anna Lorme. Tr. by Robert Bononno from FRE. LC 91-39756. (French Expressions Ser.). 208p. 1993. 18.95 (*0-8419-1294-7*) Holmes & Meier.

Traitor's Gate. Anne Perry. 1996. mass mkt. 6.99 (*0-449-22439-2*) Fawcett.

Traitor's Kiss. Joy Tucker. 384p. (Orig.). 1993. mass mkt. 4.50 (*0-380-76446-6*) Avon.

Traitors of the Crown. Joel H. Sherman. Date not set. pap. write for info. (*0-345-40388-6*) Ballantine.

***Traitor's Purse.** Margery Allingham. 224p. 1997. mass mkt. 4.95 (*0-7867-0447-0*) Carroll & Graf.

Traitor's Purse. Margery Allingham. 176p. 1993. 17.95 (*1-56723-019-9*) Yestermorrow.

Traitor's Purse. large type ed. Margery Allingham. LC 91-41613. 333p. 1992. reprint ed. lib. bdg. 20.95 (*1-56054-324-8*) Thorndike Pr.

Traitor's Purse. Margery Allingham. 176p. reprint ed. lib. bdg. 16.95 (*0-89190-199-X*, Rivercity Pr) Amereon Ltd.

Traitor's Purse. Margery Allingham. 1994. reprint ed. lib. bdg. 24.95 (*1-56849-251-0*) Buccaneer Bks.

Traitors to the Masculine Cause: The Men's Campaigns for Women's Rights. Sylvia Strauss. LC 81-20299. (Contributions in Women's Studies: No. 35). (Illus.). xix, 290p. 1982. text ed. 55.00 (*0-313-22238-X*, STM/, Greenwood Pr) Greenwood.

Traits & Stories of the Irish Peasantry, I. William Carleton. (Illus.). (C). 1990. text ed. 72.00 (*0-389-20908-2*) B&N Imports.

Traits & Stories of the Irish Peasantry, II. William Carleton. (Illus.). (C). 1990. text ed. 72.00 (*0-389-20909-0*); pap. text ed. 22.00 (*0-389-20942-2*) B&N Imports.

Traits & Stories of the Irish Peasantry: With Illustrations by Phiz, Wrightson Lee & Others, 4 Vols. William Carleton. LC 79-163022. (Short Story Index Reprint Ser.). (Illus.). 1977. reprint ed. Set. 88.95 (*0-8369-3936-0*) Ayer.

Traits d'Union. Ralph Hester et al. 512p. (C). 1988. audio 18.36 (*0-318-32630-2*) HM.

Traits et Portraits. Natalie C. Barney. LC 75-12303. (Homosexuality: Lesbians & Gay Men in Society, History & Literature Ser.). (FRE.). 1975. reprint ed. 16.95 (*0-405-07395-X*) Ayer.

Traits of a Healthy Family. Dolores Curran. 336p. 1984. mass mkt. 5.99 (*0-345-31750-5*) Ballantine.

***Traits of a Healthy Spirituality.** Melannie Svoboda. LC 96-60346. 144p. (Orig.). 1997. pap. 9.95 (*0-89622-698-0*) Twenty-Third.

Traits of a Lasting Marriage. Jim Conway & Sally Conway. LC 91-21244. 200p. (Orig.). 1991. pap. 10.99 (*0-8308-1293-8*, 1293, Saltshaker Bk) InterVarsity.

Traits of a Winner: The Formula for Developing Thoroughbred Racehorses. Carl Nefzger. (Illus.). 320p. 1994. 30.00 (*0-929346-33-5*) R Meerdink Co Ltd.

Traits of American Indian Life. Peter S. Ogden. 1987. 19.95 (*0-87770-389-2*) Ye Galleon.

Traits of American Indian Life & Character. Peter S. Ogden. (Illus.). 128p. 1995. pap. text ed. 6.95 (*0-486-28436-0*) Dover.

Traits of American Indian Life & Character. 2nd ed. Peter S. Ogden. reprint ed. 34.50 (*0-404-07149-X*) AMS Pr.

Traits of an Intercessor. Mildred C. Harris. 40p. (Orig.). 1991. 4.00 (*0-9631183-0-7*) God First.

Traitte de la Nature et de la Grace. Pierre Jurieu. 419p. 1973. reprint ed. write for info. (*3-487-05105-2*) G Olms Pubs.

***Trajan: Optimus Princeps: A Life & Times.** Bennett. LC 96-40044. (Roman Imperial Biographies Ser.). 1997. write for info. (*0-415-16524-5*) Routledge.

***Trajan, Optimus Princeps: A Life & Times.** Julian Bennett. 1996. 35.00 (*0-253-33216-8*) Ind U Pr.

***Trajan's Army on Trajan's Column.** Ian Richmond. (Illus.). 56p. 1982. pap. 9.00 (*0-904152-05-7*, Pub. by British Schl Rome UK) David Brown.

Trajan's Column. S. S. Ferre & F. A. Lepper. (Illus.). 384p. 1988. 45.00 (*0-86299-467-5*, Pub. by Sutton Pubng UK) Bks Intl VA.

Trajan's Parthian War. rev. ed. F. A. Lepper. xv, 262p. (ENG & GRE.). (C). 1994. text ed. 30.00 (*0-89005-530-0*) Ares.

Trajectories. Ricoeur. 1996. 39.95 (*0-226-71337-7*) U Ch Pr.

Trajectories & Rays: The Path - Summation in Quantum Mechanics & Optics. A. Ranfagni. Ed. by D. Mugnai et al. 240p. (C). 1990. text ed. 70.00 (*9971-5-0781-1*) World Scientific Pub.

Trajectories in the Study of Religion: Addresses at the Seventy-Fifth Anniversary of the American Academy of Religion. Ed. by Ray L. Hart. LC 86-20272. (Studies in Religious & Theological Scholarship). 317p. 1987. 30.95 (*1-55540-064-7*, 01 99 99) Scholars Pr GA.

Trajectories of the Fantastic: Selected Essays from the Fourteenth International Conference on the Fantastic in the Arts. Ed. by Michael A. Morrison. LC 96-8428. (Contributions to the Study of Science Fiction & Fantasy: Vol. 70). 240p. 1997. text ed. 59.95 (*0-313-29646-4*, Greenwood Pr) Greenwood.

Trajectories Through Knowledge Space: A Dynamic Framework for Machine Comprehension. Lawrence A. Bookman. (Kluwer International Series in Engineering & Computer Science). 296p. (C). 1994. lib. bdg. 105.00 (*0-7923-9487-9*) Kluwer Ac.

Trajectory: Fueling the Future & Preserving the Black Literary Past-Essays in Criticism (1962-1986) Ruthe T. Sheffrey. (Illus.). 160p. 1986. 20.00 (*0-9610324-6-4*) Morgan State.

Trajectory Spaces, Generalized Functions & Unbounded Operators. S. J. Van Eijndhoven & J. De Graaf. (Lecture Notes in Mathematics Ser.: Vol. 1162). iv, 272p. 1985. 42.95 (*0-387-16065-5*) Spr-Verlag.

Trakehnen Horses. Herbert Rudofsky. (Breed Ser.). 1977. pap. 4.95 (*0-88376-011-8*) Dreenan Pr.

Trakehner. Eberhard Von Velsen & Erhard Schulte. 140p. 1990. 44.00 (*0-85131-479-1*, Pub. by J A Allen & Co UK) St Mut.

Tram: The Frank Trumbauer Story. Philip R. Evans & Larry F. Kiner. LC 94-706. (Studies in Jazz: No. 18). 1994. 79.50 (*0-8108-2851-0*) Scarecrow.

Tram to Bondi Beach. Elizabeth Hathorn. (Illus.). 32p. (J). (gr. 4-8). 1989. 12.95 (*0-916291-20-0*) Kane-Miller Bk.

***Tramaine Hawkins: Songbook.** 84p. 1997. pap. 14.95 (*0-8256-1485-6*, AM 931227) Music Sales.

Trammeled. Bart Quinet. 20p. 1992. pap. 5.00 (*1-885710-07-0*) Geekspeak Unique.

Trammels of Tradition: Social Democracy in Britain, France, & Germany. Carl C. Hodge. LC 93-31626. (Contributions in Political Science Ser.: No. 342). 200p. 1994. text ed. 59.95 (*0-313-28783-X*, Greenwood Pr) Greenwood.

***Tramp.** Larry E. Denson. 1996. write for info. (*0-9654617-0-X*) MPA Pub.

***Tramp.** Marine D. Kellog. LC 96-29719. 256p. 1997. 21.95 (*0-385-48859-9*) Doubleday.

Tramp. Jack London. (Illus.). 51p. 1984. pap. 1.95 (*0-932458-24-6*) Star Rover.

Tramp: The Life of Charlie Chaplin. Joyce Milton. LC 95-48438. (Illus.). 578p. 1996. 32.00 (*0-06-017052-2*) HarpC.

Tramp Abroad. Mark Twain & H. Hill. LC 97-13725. 1997. pap. 14.95 (*0-14-043608-1*) Viking Penguin.

Tramp Abroad. Mark Twain, pseud. (Works of Mark Twain). 1988. reprint ed. lib. bdg. 59.00 (*0-317-90249-0*) Rprt Serv.

Tramp Abroad, 1. Mark Twain, pseud. (Works of Mark Twain). 1988. reprint ed. write for info. (*0-7812-1108-5*) Rprt Serv.

Tramp Abroad, 2. Mark Twain, pseud. (Works of Mark Twain). 1988. reprint ed. write for info. (*0-7812-1109-3*) Rprt Serv.

***Tramp Abroad (1880)** Ed. by Shelley F. Fishkin. (Oxford Mark Twain). 720p. 1997. lib. bdg. 30.00 (*0-19-511408-6*) OUP.

Tramp Across the Continent. Charles F. Lummis. LC 81-16194. xxvi, 270p. 1982. reprint ed. pap. 8.95 (*0-8032-7908-6*, Bison Books) U of Nebr Pr.

Tramp for the Lord. Corrie Ten Boom. 1986. mass mkt. 5.50 (*0-515-08993-1*) Jove Pubns.

Tramp for the Lord. Corrie Ten Boom. 1974. pap. 6.95 (*0-87508-028-6*) Chr Lit.

Tramp for the Lord. Corrie Ten Boom & Jamie Buckingham. (Illus.). 200p. 1984. pap. 8.99 (*0-8007-0769-9*) Revell.

***Tramp Freighters.** (Star Wars Galaxy Guides Ser.: No. 6). 15.00 (*0-87431-212-4*, 40095) West End Games.

Tramp in Armour. Colin Forbes. 286p. (Orig.). 1971. pap. 14.95 (*0-330-02686-0*, Pub. by Pan Books UK) Trans-Atl Phila.

Tramp Printers. John M. Howells & Marion Dearman. 260p. 1996. pap. 18.95 (*0-9650979-0-0*) Discov Pr CA.

Tramp Royal: The True Story of Trader Horn. Tim Couzens. (Illus.). 624p. (C). 1993. pap. text ed. 19.95 (*0-86975-416-5*, Pub. by Ravan Pr ZA) Ohio U Pr.

***Tramp Royale.** Robert A. Heinlein. 384p. 1996. pap. 15.00 (*0-441-00409-1*) Ace Bks.

***Tramp Shipping Dynasty - Burrell & Son of Glasgow, 1850-1939: A History of Ownership, Finance & Profit.** R. A. Cage. LC 96-43408. (Contributions in Economics & Economic History Ser.: Vol. 184). 275p. 1997. text ed. 69.50 (*0-313-30346-0*, Greenwood Pr) Greenwood.

Tramp, Tramp, Tramp, the Girls Are Marching: A Self-Styled Report on the Women's Liberation Movement. Bernard M. Bane. 80p. 1982. pap. 5.00 (*0-930924-15-0*) BMB Pub Co.

Trampa. Myrna Casas. Bd. with Impromptu De San Juan. (UPREX, Teatro y Cine Ser.: No. 36). 179p. (C). 1975. Set pap. 1.50 (*0-8477-0036-4*) U of PR Pr.

***Trampa.** Lois Mowday. Date not set. write for info. (*0-614-26584-3*) Editorial Unilit.

***Trampa.** Rabey. 276p. (SPA.). pap. write for info. (*1-56063-554-1*) Editorial Unilit.

Trampa del Amor. Catherine Spencer. (Harlequin Bianca Ser.: No. 368). 1996. mass mkt. 3.50 (*0-373-33368-4*, 1-33368-1) Harlequin Bks.

Tramping in Europe. (One-of-a-Kind Travel Guides Ser.). 7.95 (*0-317-52027-X*) P-H.

Tramping in New Zealand: A Walking Guide. 3rd ed. Jim DuFresne & Jeff Williams. (Illus.). 320p. 1995. pap. 13.95 (*0-86442-253-9*) Lonely Planet.

Tramping on Life: An Autobiographical Narrative. Harry Kemp. 1993. reprint ed. lib. bdg. 89.00 (*0-7812-5383-7*) Rprt Serv.

Tramping out the Vintage. Frank Bardacke. Date not set. pap. write for info. (*0-8050-4444-2*) H Holt & Co.

Tramping out the Vintage. Frank Bardacke. 1997. write for info. (*0-8050-4443-4*) H Holt & Co.

Tramping Out the Vintage: The Civil War Diaries & Letters of Eugene Kingman. Eugene C. Kingman. Ed. by Helene C. Phelan. (Illus.). 388p. 1983. pap. 9.95 (*0-9605836-4-5*) Phelan.

Tramping to Success: Story of the Great Eastern Shipping Company Limited. S. N. Sanklecha. (C). 1994. 32.00 (*81-7154-784-2*, Pub. by Popular Prakashan II) S Asia.

Tramping with Tramps: Studies & Sketches of Vagabond Life. Josiah F. Willard. LC 72-129317. (Criminology, Law Enforcement, & Social Problems Ser.: No. 140). (Illus.). 414p. 1972. reprint ed. lib. bdg. 18.00 (*0-87585-140-1*) Patterson Smith.

Trampled Grass: Tributary States & Self-reliance in the Indian Ocean Zone of Peace. George W. Shepherd, Jr. LC 86-17116. 187p. 1987. pap. text ed. 14.95 (*0-275-92608-7*, B2608, Praeger Pubs) Greenwood.

Trampled Grass: Tributary States & Self-reliance in the Indian Ocean Zone of Peace. George W. Shepherd, Jr. LC 86-27116. (Contributions in Political Science Ser.: No. 169). 191p. 1987. text ed. 55.00 (*0-313-25772-8*, SFQ, Greenwood Pr) Greenwood.

Trampling Herd: The Story of the Cattle Range in America. Paul I. Wellman. LC 88-5946. (Illus.). 433p. 1988. reprint ed. pap. 10.95 (*0-8032-9723-8*, Bison Books) U of Nebr Pr.

Trampolining. Jeff T. Hennessy. (Physical Education Activities Ser.). 70p. (C). 1968. per. write for info. (*0-697-07034-4*) Wm C Brown Pubs.

Trampolining. Erika Phelps & Brian Phelps. (Skills of the Game Ser.). (Illus.). 112p. 1991. pap. 19.95 (*1-85223-363-X*, Pub. by Crowood Pr UK) Trafalgar.

Tramps & Ladies. James Bisset & P. R. Stephensen. LC 59-12193. (Illus.). 1959. 42.95 (*0-87599-014-2*) S G Phillips.

Tramps & Reformers, 1873-1916: The Discovery of Unemployment in New York. Paul T. Ringenbach. LC 77-175610. (Contributions in American History Ser.: No. 27). (Illus.). 224p. 1973. text ed. 59.95 (*0-8371-6266-1*, RAT/, Greenwood Pr) Greenwood.

Tramps, Workmates, & Revolutionaries: Working-Class Stories of the 1920s. Ed. by Gustav Klaus. (C). 1993. text ed. 44.00 (*0-85172-030-7*); pap. text ed. 16.95 (*0-85172-031-5*) Westview.

Tramps, Workmates & Revolutionaries: Working Class Stories of the 1920's. Ed. by Gustav Klaus. (C). 49.00 (*1-85172-030-8*, Pub. by Pluto Pr UK) LPC InBook.

Tramps, Workmates & Revolutionaries: Working Class Stories of the 1920's. Ed. by Gustav Klaus. (C). pap. 17.50 (*1-85172-031-6*, Pub. by Pluto Pr UK) LPC InBook.

Trams on the Road. David Gladwin. (Illus.). 128p. 1991. pap. 34.95 (*0-7134-6125-X*, Pub. by Batsford UK) Trafalgar.

Tramways & Trolleys: The Rise of Urban Mass Transport in Europe. John P. McKay. LC 76-3746. reprint ed. pap. 80.70 (*0-608-02229-2*, 2060132) Bks Demand.

Tramways of Chile, 1858-1978. Allen Morrison. LC 92-73238. (Illus.). 144p. (Orig.). 1992. pap. 20.00 (*0-9622348-2-6*) Bonde Pr.

Tran. Jerry Pournelle & Roland Green. 688p. 1996. mass mkt. 6.99 (*0-671-87741-0*) Baen Bks.

Trance. Richard Kessler. 1993. 22.00 (*0-7278-4426-1*) Severn Hse.

Trance: From Magic to Technology. Dennis R. Wier. LC 95-62295. (Illus.). 184p. (Orig.). (C). 1996. 30.00 (*1-888428-37-6*); pap. 20.00 (*1-888428-38-4*) Trans Media MI.

Trance & Recalcitrance: The Private Voice in the Public Realm. Frances Butler et al. (Illus.). 48p. (Orig.). 1995. pap. 15.00 (*0-918395-16-X*) Poltroon Pr.

Trance & Treatment: Clinical Uses of Hypnosis. Herbert Spiegel & David Spiegel. LC 86-20627. (Illus.). 382p. 1987. pap. 24.00 (*0-88048-264-8*, 8264) Am Psychiatric.

T

An Asterisk (*) at the beginning of an entry indicates that the title is appearing in BIP for the first time.

Trance Dance: The Dance of Life. Frank Natale. LC 95-12177. 1995. pap. 22.95 incl. audio compact disk (*1-85230-702-1*) Element MA.

Trance-Formations: Neuro-Linguistic Programming & the Structure of Hypnosis. John Grinder & Richard Bandler. Ed. by Connirae Andreas. 252p. (Orig.). 1981. 14.00 (*0-911226-22-2*); pap. 10.50 (*0-911226-23-0*) Real People.

Trance, Healing, & Hallucination: Three Field Studies in Religious Experience. F. D. Goodman et al. LC 80-20043. 414p. 1982. reprint ed. text ed. 42.00 (*0-89874-246-3*) Krieger.

***Trance Mission.** (FunFax Horror Ser.). (Illus.). 144p. (J). (gr. 3-9). 1996. pap. 2.95 (*0-7894-1155-5*) DK Pub Inc.

Trance on Trial. Alan W. Scheflin & Jerrold L. Shapiro. LC 88-1674. (Guilford Clinical & Experimental Hypnosis Ser.). 338p. 1989. pap. text ed. 21.95 (*0-89862-340-5*); lib. bdg. 47.50 (*0-89862-749-4*) Guilford Pr.

Trance State: How People Change. Steven Goldsmith. 140p. 1986. text ed. 16.95 (*0-8290-1465-9*) Irvington.

Trancers: The Adventures of Jack Deth. S. A. Bennett. (Illus.). 50p. 1991. pap. 4.95 (*1-56398-018-5*) Malibu Comics Ent.

Trances People Live: Healing Approaches in Quantum Psychology. Stephen Wolinsky & Margart O. Ryan. LC 91-72049. 272p. 1991. 24.95 (*0-9626184-1-1*, Bramble Bks); pap. 14.95 (*0-9626184-2-X*, Bramble Bks) Bramble Co.

Trancework: An Introduction to the Practice of Clinical Hypnosis. 2nd enl. rev. ed. Michael D. Yapko. LC 89-22173. 464p. 1990. text ed. 44.95 (*0-87630-568-0*) Brunner-Mazel.

Tranches de Vie: Authentic Readings for Basic Skill Development. Brown & Young. 1987. pap. 37.95 (*0-8384-1517-2*) Heinle & Heinle.

***Trancing the Witch's Wheel: A Guide to Magical Meditation.** Yasmine Galenorn. LC 97-19479. (Illus.). 240p. (Orig.). 1997. pap. 12.95 (*1-56718-303-4*) Llewellyn Pubns.

Tranction Collector's Library. (Illus.). pap. 12.00 (*0-00-000108-2*, Pub. by Boston Mills Pr CN) Genl Dist Srvs.

Tranformation of Contemporary Conservatism. Ed. by Brian Girvin. (Modern Politics Ser.: Vol. 22). 256p. (C). 1988. text ed. 47.50 (*0-8039-8145-7*); pap. text ed. 18.95 (*0-8039-8146-5*) Sage.

Trang Mat. Nghieu Minh. 140p. 1992. 15.00 (*0-9635574-2-4*) Alpha Bks VA.

Tranquebar: A Guide to the Coins of Danish India Circa 1620 to 1845. John C. Gray. LC 74-84564. (Illus.). 96p. 1975. 10.00 (*0-88000-054-6*) Quarterman.

Tranquebar: A Season in South India. Georgina Harding. 205p. 1994. 34.95 (*0-340-54904-1*, Pub. by H & S UK) Trafalgar.

Tranquil Ecstasy: Mark Twain's Pastorale Neigung und Ihre Literarische Gestaltung. Karl-Otto Strohmidel. (Bochumer Anglistische Studien: No. 20). 302p. 1986. pap. 41.00 (*90-6032-293-2*, Pub. by B R Gruener NE) Benjamins North Am.

Tranquil Lake of Love: Love Letters. Carl Cook. LC 92-85179. 80p. (Orig.). 1993. pap. 8.00 (*1-880729-04-0*) Vega Pr.

Tranquil Moments. (Words of Comfort Ser.). (Illus.). 64p. 1993. 6.95 (*0-7117-0346-9*, Pub. by Jarrold Pub UK) Seven Hills Bk.

Tranquil Sitting: A Taoist Journal on the Theory, Practice, & Benefits of Meditation, by Yin Shih Tzu. Shu Fu Hwang & Cheny Crow. (Illus.). 162p. (Orig.). 1995. pap. 9.50 (*0-938045-12-1*) Dragon Door.

Tranquility: Pathways to Inner Peace. LC 93-18822. 256p. 1993. pap. 9.95 (*0-553-37035-9*) Bantam.

Tranquility: The Piano Solos of Phil Coulter. (Illus.). 64p. 1986. pap. 15.95 (*0-7119-0944-X*, AM63280) Music Sales.

***Tranquility Alternative.** Allen Steele. 320p. 1997. mass mkt. 5.99 (*0-441-00433-4*) Ace Bks.

Tranquility Alternative. Allen M. Steele. LC 95-21056. 320p. (Orig.). 1996. 21.95 (*0-441-00299-4*) Ace Bks.

Tranquilizer Use & Well-Being: A Longitudinal Study of Social & Psychological Effects. Robert D. Caplan et al. (ISR Research Report Ser.). 442p. (Orig.). 1984. pap. text ed. 25.00 (*0-87944-296-4*) Inst Soc Res.

Tranquilizer Use & Well-Being: A Longitudinal Study of Social & Psychological Effects. Robert D. Caplan et al. LC 84-9116. (Institute for Social Research, Research Report Ser.). 440p. (Orig.). reprint ed. pap. 125.40 (*0-7837-5250-4*, 2044986) Bks Demand.

Tranquilizers. Lawrence Clayton. LC 96-26949. (Drug Library). 104p. (YA). (gr. 6 up). 1997. lib. bdg. 18.95 (*0-89490-849-9*) Enslow Pubs.

Tranquillisation. James G. Speight. 111p. 1990. pap. 7.95 (*0-85207-228-7*, Pub. by C W Daniel UK) Natl Bk Netwk.

Tranquillisation: The Non-Addictive Way. Phyllis Speight. 100p. (Orig.). pap. 11.95 (*0-8464-4302-3*) Beekman Pubs.

Tranquillisers: Social, Psychological & Clinical Perspectives. Jonathan Gabe & Paul Williams. 350p. 1986. 57.50 (*0-422-79930-0*, 1025, Pub. by Tavistock UK) Routledge Chapman & Hall.

Tranquillity Base & Other Stories. Asa Baber. LC 79-89138. 141p. 1979. pap. 6.00 (*0-931362-01-6*) Fiction Intl.

***Trans, No. 2.** 168p. 1996. pap. 15.00 (*1-888209-01-1*, 620541) PASSIM.

***Trans, No. 3.** 168p. 1996. pap. 15.00 (*1-888209-02-X*, 620544) PASSIM.

Trans-Alaska Pipeline: Actions to Improve Safety Are under Way. (Illus.). 59p. (Orig.). (C). 1996. pap. 20.00 (*0-7881-2940-6*) DIANE Pub.

Trans-Alaska Pipeline Controversy: Technology, Conservation, & the Frontier. Peter A. Coates. LC 89-45420. (Illus.). 448p. 1991. 57.50 (*0-934223-10-6*) Lehigh Univ Pr.

Trans-Alaska Pipeline Controversy: Technology, Conservation, & the Frontier. Peter A. Coates. LC 93-32931. (Illus.). vii, 447p. 1993. pap. 25.00 (*0-912006-67-6*) U of Alaska Pr.

Trans-Allegheny Pioneers: Historical Sketches of the First White Settlements West of the Alleghenies 1748 & After. John P. Hale. (Illus.). 339p. 1988. reprint ed. pap. 20.00 (*1-55613-128-3*) Heritage Bk.

Trans-Allegheny Pioneers: Historical Sketches of the First White Settlements West of the Alleghenies. 3rd ed. John P. Hale. LC 89-92007. (Illus.). 528p. 1989. reprint ed. 20.00 (*0-9617146-1-1*); reprint ed. pap. 12.00 (*0-9617146-2-X*) R I Steele.

Trans-Appalachian Frontier: People, Societies, & Institutions, 1775-1850. Malcolm J. Rohrbough. 403p. (C). 1990. pap. 28.95 (*0-534-12336-8*) Wadsworth Pub.

Trans-Atlantic Conservative Protestantism in the Evangelical Free & Mission Covenant Traditions. Frederick Hale. Ed. by Franklyn D. Scott. LC 78-15183. (Scandinavians in America Ser.). 1979. lib. bdg. 33.95 (*0-405-11638-1*) Ayer.

Trans-Atlantic Historical Solidarity. Charles F. Adams, Jr. (Works of Charles Francis Adams Jr. (1835-1915)). 1989. reprint ed. lib. bdg. 79.00 (*0-7812-1418-1*) Rprt Serv.

Trans-Atlantica: Essays on Scandinavians Migration & Culture. Ed. by Franklyn D. Scott. LC 78-15849. (Scandinavians in America Ser.). (Illus.). 1979. lib. bdg. 31.95 (*0-405-11659-4*) Ayer.

Trans-Atlantique. Witold Gombrowicz. (FRE.). 1990. pap. 11.95 (*0-7859-2598-8*, 2070382974) Fr & Eur.

Trans-Atlantyk. Witold Gombrowicz. Tr. by Nina Karsov & Frances Carroll. LC 93-11880. 152p. (C). 1994. 23.00 (*0-300-05384-3*) Yale U Pr.

Trans-Atlantyk. Witold Gombrowicz. 1995. pap. 10.00 (*0-300-06503-5*) Yale U Pr.

***Trans-Border Terrorism: Internationalisation of the Kashmir Tangle.** B. P. Saha. 1996. 36.00 (*81-241-0377-1*, Pub. by Har-Anand Pubns II) S Asia.

Trans-Canada Rail Guide. Melissa Graham. 1996. pap. text ed. 14.95 (*1-873756-05-4*, Pub. by Trlblazer Pubn UK) Seven Hills Bk.

Trans-Career Investigations. Hendrix. (Education Ser.). 1990. 74.95 (*0-8273-3969-0*) Delmar.

Trans-Continental Railroad. Marilyn Miller. LC 85-40167. (Turning Points in American History Ser.). (Illus.). 64p. (YA). (gr. 5 up). 1985. pap. 7.95 (*0-382-09912-5*) Silver Burdett Pr.

***Trans-European Telecommunication Networks: The Challenges for Industrial Policy.** Colin Turner. LC 97-3705. 216p. (C). 1997. text ed. write for info. (*0-415-16186-X*) Routledge.

***Trans Fatty Acids & Coronary Heart Disease Risk.** R. J. Nicolosi & Penny M. Kris-Etherton. 24p. 1995. pap. 12. 50 (*0-944398-67-7*, 398677) ILSI.

Trans-Formation in Everyday Life: A Short Cut to Relaxation & Problem Solving. Kate Cohen-Posey. LC 94-78440. 102p. (Orig.). 1994. pap. 9.95 (*1-885961-00-6*) Leightons Sales.

***Trans-Futilism: The Philosophy of Living In-Between.** (Illus.). 40p. (Orig.). 1996. pap. write for info. (*0-9658270-0-3*) Trans-Futilism.

Trans-Himalaya: Discoveries & Adventures in Tibet, 3 vols. Sven A. Hedin. (C). 1990. reprint ed. Set. 120.00 (*81-212-0340-6*, Pub. by Gian Publng Hse II) S Asia.

Trans-Himalaya, Discoveries & Adventures in Tibet, 2 vols. Sven A. Hedin. LC 68-55194. 1970. reprint ed. Set. text ed. 135.00 (*0-8371-3895-7*, HETH) Greenwood.

Trans-Himalaya, Discoveries & Adventures in Tibet, 2 vols., 1. Sven A. Hedin. LC 68-55194. 1970. reprint ed. text ed. 75.00 (*0-8371-0470-X*, HETA) Greenwood.

Trans-Himalaya, Discoveries & Adventures in Tibet, 2 vols., Vol. 2. Sven A. Hedin. LC 68-55194. 1970. reprint ed. text ed. 75.00 (*0-8371-0815-2*, HETA) Greenwood.

Trans-Himalayan Trade - A Retrospect (1774-1914) In Quest of Tibet's Identity. Phanindra N. Chakravarti. (C). 1990. 20.00 (*81-85132-10-0*, Pub. by Classics India Pubns II) S Asia.

***Trans-Making Connections 1996, No. 1.** McCloskey. (Global ESL/ELT Ser.). 1996. text ed. 104.95 (*0-8384-7002-5*) Heinle & Heinle.

***Trans-Making Connections 1996, No. 2.** McCloskey. (Adult ESL Ser.). 1996. text ed. 104.95 (*0-8384-7014-9*) Heinle & Heinle.

***Trans Method of Circuit Analysis.** Harrison. (C). 1990. pap. write for info. (*0-15-504282-3*) HB Coll Pubs.

Trans-Mississippi Mails after the Fall of Vicksburg. Richard Krieger. Ed. by John F. Dunn. (Philatelic Foundation Monographs: No. 1). (Illus.). 76p. (Orig.). 1984. pap. 7.00 (*0-911989-13-7*) Philatelic Found.

Trans-Mississippi West, 1804-1912 Pt. I: A Guide to Records of the Department of State for the Territorial Period. Compiled by Robert M. Kvasnicka. 140p. 1992. pap. text ed. 12.00 (*1-880875-00-4*, 200018) National Archives & Recs.

Trans-Mississippi West, 1804-1912 Pt. II: A Guide to Records of the Department of Justice for the Territorial Period. 140p. 1994. pap. text ed. 12.00 (*1-880875-02-0*) National Archives & Recs.

***Trans-Oceanic Marketing Channel: A New Tool for Understanding Tropical Africa's Export Agriculture.** H. Laurens Van der Laan. LC 97-1160. (Illus.). 272p. 1997. lib. bdg. 49.95 (*0-7890-0116-0*, Intl Busn Pr) Haworth Pr.

Trans. of Ike Garuda, No. 1. Elaine Lee & James Sherman. 48p. 1991. 3.95 (*0-87135-775-5*) Marvel Entmnt.

Trans. of Ike Garuda, No. 2. Elaine Lee & James Sherman. 48p. 1992. 3.95 (*0-87135-776-3*) Marvel Entmnt.

Trans-Pacific Echoes & Resonance; Listening Once Again. J. Needham. 132p. 1991. pap. text ed. 7.00 (*0-9625118-8-9*) World Scientific Pub.

Trans-Pacific Echoes & Resonances: Listening Once Again. Joseph Needham & Gwei-Djen. 106p. 1985. text ed. 30. 00 (*9971-950-86-3*) World Scientific Pub.

Trans-parent: Sexual Politics in the Language of Emerson. Eric Cheyfitz. LC 80-25750. 206p. reprint ed. pap. 58.80 (*0-8357-6606-3*, 2035251) Bks Demand.

Trans Parent Thread: Asian Philosophy in Recent American Art. Gail Gelburd & Geri De Paoli. LC 90-84218. (Illus.). 124p. (C). 1990. pap. 28.95 (*0-8122-1376-9*, Hofstra U Hofstra Mus); lib. bdg. 42.95 (*0-8122-3094-9*, Hofstra U Hofstra Mus) U of Pa Pr.

***Trans-Scriptions.** (Illus.). 126p. (Orig.). 1996. pap. 9.95 (*1-57502-375-X*, P01197) Morris Pubng.

Trans-Siberian Express. Ed. by Victor Kuranov. LC 79-3106. (Illus.). 376p. 1980. 29.95 (*0-943071-10-0*) Sphinx Pr.

***Trans-Siberian Handbook.** 4th ed. Bryn Thomas. (World Rail Guides Ser.). (Illus.). 416p. 1997. pap. 17.95 (*1-873756-16-X*, Pub. by Trlblazer Pubn UK) Seven Hills Bk.

Trans-Siberian Rail Guide. 4th ed. Robert Strauss. (Illus.). 256p. (Orig.). 1995. pap. 17.95 (*0-9520900-1-5*) Hunter NJ.

Trans-Siberian Railway. Cornelia Veenendaal. LC 73-86246. (Illus.). 64p. 1973. pap. 3.95 (*0-914086-01-4*) Alicejamesbooks.

***Trans-Social Problems.** 8th ed. Kornblum. 1995. pap. 79. 00 (*0-13-121757-7*) P-H.

Transacciones Financieras Internationales: Aspectos Seleccionados. Ed. by Emilio J. Cardenas et al. 292p. 1984. write for info. (*0-940602-22-9*) IADB.

***Transact SQL.** William C. Amo. 1997. pap. 39.99 (*0-7645-8048-5*) IDG Bks.

Transaction Cost Economics, 2 vols. Ed. by Oliver E. Williamson & Scott E. Masten. (International Library of Critical Writings in Economics Ser.: Vol. 54). 1392p. 1995. 420.00 (*1-85278-952-2*) E Elgar.

Transaction Cost Economics: Recent Developments. Ed. by Claude Menard. LC 96-26476. 192p. 1997. 65.00 (*1-85898-483-1*) E Elgar.

Transaction Cost Economics & Beyond. Ed. by John Groenewegen. LC 95-24150. (Recent Economic Thought Ser.). 400p. (C). 1996. lib. bdg. 99.95 (*0-7923-9611-1*) Kluwer Ac.

Transaction Cost Economics & Beyond: Towards a New Economics of the Firm. Michael Dietrich. LC 93-24592. 208p. (C). 1994. pap. 18.95 (*0-415-07156-9*) Routledge.

Transaction in Hearts. Edgar E. Saltus. LC 68-54294. reprint ed. 37.50 (*0-404-05515-X*) AMS Pr.

***Transaction Management.** Chorofas. Date not set. text ed. write for info. (*0-312-21018-3*) St Martin.

Transaction of Free Men: The Birth & Course of the Declaration of Independence. Intro. by David F. Hawke. (Quality Paperbacks Ser.). (Illus.). 296p. 1989. pap. 12.95 (*0-306-80352-6*) Da Capo.

Transaction of the American Society of Civil Engineers, Vol. 151. 474p. 1987. 65.00 (*0-87262-581-8*) Am Soc Civil Eng.

Transaction Processing: Concepts & Techniques. Jim Gray & Andreas Reuter. LC 92-25954. (Morgan Kaufmann Series in Data Management Systems). 1992. 84.95 (*1-55860-190-2*) Morgan Kaufmann.

Transaction Processing Systems. E. V. Krishnamurthy & V. K. Murthy. 176p. 1991. pap. text ed. 34.95 (*0-13-928128-2*) P-H.

Transactional Analysis: A Handbook for Trainers. Julie Hay. 208p. (C). 1991. pap. 69.00 (*0-07-707470-X*, Pub. by IPM Hse UK) St Mut.

Transactional Analysis at Work. Keith Carby & Manab Thakur. 98p. (C). 1976. 60.00 (*0-85292-133-0*) St Mut.

Transactional Analysis Counselling in Action. Ian Stewart. (Counselling in Action Ser.). 160p. (C). 1989. text ed. 49.95 (*0-8039-8190-2*); pap. text ed. 21.50 (*0-8039-8191-0*) Sage.

Transactional Analysis in Health Care. Jean Elder. LC 78-57376. 1978. pap. text ed. write for info. (*0-201-01512-9*, Health Sci) Addison-Wesley.

Transactional Analysis on the Job & Communicating with Subordinates. rev. ed. Charles Albano. Ed. by Thomasine Rendero. LC 75-20236. 183p. reprint ed. pap. 52.20 (*0-317-27194-6*, 2023928) Bks Demand.

Transactional Analysis Psychotherapy: An Integrated Approach. Petremeuska Clarkson. 368p. (C). 1993. pap. 24.95 (*0-415-08699-X*, B2554) Routledge.

Transactional Filing: A Timesaving, Record Keeping System for Computerized Agencies. Academy of Producer Insurance Studies, Inc. Staff & R. David Tebben. 24p. (Orig.). 1989. pap. text ed. 10.00 (*1-878204-14-9*) APIS Inc.

Transactional Guide to the Uniform Commercial Code, 2 vols. 2nd ed. Richard Alderman & Richard F. Dole. 1349p. 1983. 217.00 (*0-8318-0400-9*, B400/B581) Am Law Inst.

Transactional Guide to the Uniform Commercial Code: 1987 Supplement, 2 vols. 2nd ed. Richard Alderman & Richard F. Dole. 1349p. 1987. Supplement 1987. suppl. ed., pap. 28.00 (*0-8318-0581-1*, B581) Am Law Inst.

Transactional Manager: How to Solve People Problems with Transactional Analysis. Abe Wagner. 208p. 1992. pap. 11.95 (*0-926632-07-8*) A Wagner & Assocs.

Transactioneer with Some of His Philosophical Fancies: In Two Dialogues. William King. LC 92-23640. (Augustan Reprints Ser.: Nos. 251-252). 1988. reprint ed. 21.50 (*0-404-70251-1*, PR3539) AMS Pr.

Transactions, 6 Vols. Ossianic Society of Dublin Staff. LC 78-144462. reprint ed. Set. 72.50 (*0-404-09070-2*) AMS Pr.

Transactions: International Vacuum Congress, 3rd, Stuttgart, 1965, Vol. 1-2, Pts. 1-2. Ed. by H. Adam. 1967. 108.00 (*0-08-012127-6*, Pub. by Pergamon Repr UK) Franklin.

Transactions: Proceedings of the American Association for the Study & Prevention of Infant Mortality Meeting, 1st, New Haven, 1909. American Association for the Study & Prevention of Infant Mortality Meeting Staff. LC 74-1663. (Children & Youth Ser.). 356p. 1974. reprint ed. 29.95 (*0-405-05944-2*) Ayer.

Transactions: The Interplay Between Individual, Family, & Society. John Spiegel. LC 84-45129. 480p. 1983. 50.00 (*0-87668-699-4*) Aronson.

Transactions: Twelfth Congress on Irrigation & Drainage, Fort Collins, Colorado, 1984, 2 vols. 1984. 300.00 (*0-685-14748-7*) US Comm Irrigation.

Transactions: 1984 Reports of Mortality, Morbidity & Other Experience. 1988. text ed. 50.00 (*0-938959-11-5*) Soc Actuaries.

Transactions: 1985-1986-1987 Reports of Mortality, Morbidity & Other Experience. text ed. 50.00 (*0-938959-16-6*) Soc Actuaries.

Transactions: 1988-1989-1990 Reports of Mortality, Morbidity & Other Experience. text ed. 50.00 (*0-938959-21-2*) Soc Actuaries.

Transactions: 1991-1992 Reports of Mortality, Morbidity & Other Experience. text ed. 50.00 (*0-938959-29-8*) Soc Actuaries.

Transactions - Fifteenth Congress on Irrigation & Drainage, The Hague, 1993: "Water Management in the Next Century", Vol. 1A-1J. 395.00 (*81-85068-34-8*) US Comm Irrigation.

Transactions - Fourteenth Congress on Irrigation & Drainage, Rio de Janeiro, 1990, Set. 1990. 338.00 (*81-85068-27-5*) US Comm Irrigation.

Transactions - Thirteenth Congress on Irrigation & Drainage, Casablanca, 1987, Set, Vols. IA, IB, IC, ID & II. 1987. Set. 270.00 (*0-685-56568-8*) US Comm Irrigation.

***Transactions from 'A Symposium on Quality Function Deployment'** (Illus.). 449p. (Orig.). 1989. reprint ed. pap. 75.00 (*1-889477-01-X*, 1QFDS) QFD Inst.

***Transactions from the Eighth Symposium on Quality Function Deployment: Concurrent with International Symposium on QFD '96.** (Illus.). 599p. (Orig.). 1996. pap. 75.00 (*1-889477-08-7*, 8QFDS) QFD Inst.

***Transactions from the Fifth Symposium on Quality Function Deployment.** (Illus.). 549p. (Orig.). 1993. pap. 75.00 (*1-889477-05-2*, 5QFDS) QFD Inst.

***Transactions from the Fourth Symposium on Quality Function Deployment.** (Illus.). 604p. (Orig.). 1992. pap. 75.00 (*1-889477-04-4*, 4QFDS) QFD Inst.

***Transactions from the Second Symposium on Quality Function Deployment.** (Illus.). 459p. (Orig.). 1990. pap. 75.00 (*1-889477-02-8*, 2QFDS) QFD Inst.

***Transactions from the Seventh Symposium on Quality Deployment.** (Illus.). 645p. (Orig.). 1995. pap. 75.00 (*1-889477-07-9*, 7QFDS) QFD Inst.

***Transactions from the Sixth Symposium on Quality Function Deployment.** (Illus.). 615p. (Orig.). 1994. pap. 75.00 (*1-889477-06-0*, 6QFDS) QFD Inst.

***Transactions from the Third Symposium on Quality Function Demployment.** (Illus.). 521p. (Orig.). 1991. pap. 75.00 (*1-889477-03-6*, 3QFDS) QFD Inst.

Transactions in a Foreign Currency. Deborah Eisenberg. LC 85-45591. 212p. 1986. 15.95 (*0-394-54598-2*) Knopf.

Transactions in Families. John Papajohn & John Spiegel. LC 74-6740. (Jossey-Bass Behavioral Science Ser.). 335p. reprint ed. pap. 95.50 (*0-685-16151-X*, 2027764) Bks Demand.

Transactions in Families: Resolving Cultural & Generational Conflicts. John Papajohn & John Spiegel. LC 95-4759. (Master Works). 336p. 1995. reprint ed. pap. 30.00 (*1-56821-575-4*) Aronson.

Transactions in Kinship: Adoption & Fosterage in Oceania. Ed. by Ivan Brady. LC 76-10342. (ASAO Monographs: No. 4). 322p. reprint ed. pap. 91.80 (*0-7837-1305-3*, 2041453) Bks Demand.

***Transactions in Real Property in Germany.** 400p. 1994. pap. 135.00 (*0-614-26860-5*) Commerce.

Transactions of AACE International, 1993. Ed. by Brian J. Walker. 1993. 59.95 (*0-930284-54-2*) AACE Intl.

Transactions of AACE International, 1994. Ed. by Brian J. Walker. (Illus.). 472p. (Orig.). 1994. pap. 79.95 (*1-885517-00-9*) AACE Intl.

Transactions of Technical Conference on Metric Mechanical Fasteners. 122p. 1975. pap. text ed. 12.00 (*0-685-62576-1*, E00092) ASME.

Transactions of the American Association of Cost Engineers, 1979. Kenneth K. Humphreys. Ed. by Curtis M. Sides. (Illus.). 1979. 40.00 (*0-930284-04-6*); pap. text ed. 30.00 (*0-930284-03-8*) Morgantown Print & Bind.

Transactions of the American Association of Cost Engineers, 1990. Ed. by B. Humphreys. (Illus.). 459p. 1990. pap. 34.95 (*0-930284-43-7*) AACE Intl.

Transactions of the American Association of Cost Engineers, 1991. Ed. by B. Humphreys. (Illus.). 507p. 1991. pap. 34.95 (*0-930284-47-X*) AACE Intl.

Transactions of the American Association of Cost Engineers, 1992, 2 vols., Set. Ed. by B. Humphreys. (Illus.). 1992. 34.95 (*0-930284-49-6*) AACE Intl.

Transactions of the American Society of Civil Engineers, Vol. 141. 795p. 1977. 60.00 (*0-87262-341-6*) Am Soc Civil Eng.

Transactions of the American Society of Civil Engineers, Vol. 144. Compiled by American Society of Civil Engineers Staff. 791p. 1980. 60.00 (*0-87262-236-3*) Am Soc Civil Eng.

Transactions of the American Society of Civil Engineers, Vol. 145. 1068p. 1981. 60.00 (0-87262-340-8) Am Soc Civil Eng.

Transactions of the American Society of Civil Engineers, Vol. 146. Compiled by American Society of Civil Engineers Staff. 1056p. 1982. 60.00 (0-87262-309-2) Am Soc Civil Eng.

Transactions of the American Society of Civil Engineers, Vol. 147. 492p. 1983. 60.00 (0-87262-355-6) Am Soc Civil Eng.

Transactions of the American Society of Civil Engineers, Vol. 148. 480p. 1984. 60.00 (0-87262-394-7) Am Soc Civil Eng.

Transactions of the American Society of Civil Engineers, Vol. 149. 490p. 1985. 65.00 (0-87262-440-4) Am Soc Civil Eng.

Transactions of the American Society of Civil Engineers, Vol. 150. 484p. 1986. 65.00 (0-87262-514-1) Am Soc Civil Eng.

Transactions of the American Society of Civil Engineers, Vol. 152. 537p. 1988. 65.00 (0-87262-636-9) Am Soc Civil Eng.

Transactions of the American Society of Civil Engineers, Vol. 153. 574p. 1989. text ed. 75.00 (0-87262-692-X) Am Soc Civil Eng.

Transactions of the American Society of Civil Engineers, Vol. 154. 693p. 1990. text ed. 100.00 (0-87262-745-4) Am Soc Civil Eng.

Transactions of the American Society of Civil Engineers, Vol. 155. 729p. 1991. text ed. 108.00 (0-87262-823-X) Am Soc Civil Eng.

Transactions of the American Society of Civil Engineers, Vol. 156. 690p. 1992. text ed. 120.00 (0-87262-883-3) Am Soc Civil Eng.

Transactions of the American Society of Civil Engineers Vol. 159: January-December, 1994. 758p. 1995. 150.00 (0-7844-0069-5) Am Soc Civil Eng.

Transactions of the American Society of Civil Engineers Vol. 160: January-December, 1995. 747p. 1996. 160.00 (0-7844-0149-7) Am Soc Civil Eng.

Transactions of the American Society of Civil Engineers, Vol. 142, 1978. 808p. text ed. 60.00 (0-87262-234-7) Am Soc Civil Eng.

Transactions of the American Society of Civil Engineers, Vol. 143. 805p. 1979. text ed. 60.00 (0-87262-235-5) Am Soc Civil Eng.

Transactions of the Blavatsky Lodge of the T.S. Reprinted Verbatum from the Original Edition. Helena P. Blavatsky. xxiv, 149p. 1923. 5.00 (0-938998-05-6) Theosophy.

Transactions of the Eighth National Vacuum Symposium of the American Vacuum Society: Second International Congress of Vacuum Science & Technology, Washington, D. C. October, 1961. International Organization of Vacuum Sicence & Technology Staff & L. Preuss. LC 59-1422. (American Vacuum Society Ser.: Vol. 2). 1962. 306.00 (0-08-009121-0, Pub. by Pergamon Repr UK) Franklin.

Transactions of the Historical Society of Berks County, Vol. 2. Historical Society of Berks County, PA, Staff. (Illus.). 470p. 1995. reprint ed. pap. 29.00 (0-7884-0276-5) Heritage Bk.

Transactions of the Illinois State Historical Society: Selected Papers from the Fifth & Sixth Illinois History Symposium of the Illinois State Historical Society. Ed. by Mary E. McElligott & Patrick H. O'Neal. LC 89-28563. 132p. (Orig.). 1988. pap. text ed. 12.50 (0-912226-21-8) Ill St Hist Soc.

Transactions of the Illinois State Historical Society: Selected Papers from the Seventh Annual History Symposium & the Eighth Annual History Symposium. Ed. by Mary E. McElligott. LC 89-28563. 90p. 1989. pap. 12.50 (0-912226-25-0) Ill St Hist Soc.

Transactions of the International Astronomical Union. Ed. by Jean-Pierre Swings. 1986. lib. bdg. 225.50 (90-277-2321-4) Kluwer Ac.

Transactions of the International Astronomical Union, Vol. 17b. Ed. by Patrick A. Wayman. 536p. 1980. lib. bdg. 171.00 (90-277-1159-3) Kluwer Ac.

Transactions of the International Astronomical Union, Vol. 18b. Ed. by Richard M. West. 1983. lib. bdg. 187.00 (90-277-1563-7) Kluwer Ac.

Transactions of the International Astronomical Union: Proceedings of the General Assembly of I.A.U., 13th, Prague, 1967, Vol. 14b. International Astronomical Union Staff. Ed. by C. De Jager & A. Jappels. LC 30-10103. 378p. 1971. lib. bdg. 112.00 (90-277-0190-3) Kluwer Ac.

Transactions of the International Astronomical Union: Proceedings of the General Assembly of I.A.U., 13th, Prague, 1967, Vol. 15b. International Astronomical Union Staff & Extraordinary General Assembly, Poland, 1973. Ed. by G. Contopoulos & Arnost Jappel. LC 73-81827. 334p. 1974. lib. bdg. 165.00 (90-277-0451-1) Kluwer Ac.

Transactions of the International Astronomical Union: Proceedings of the 21st General Assembly, Buenos Aires, 1991, Vol. XXI B. Ed. by Jacqueline Bergeron. LC 92-25559. 952p. 1992. lib. bdg. 306.00 (0-7923-1914-1) Kluwer Ac.

Transactions of the International Astronomical Union: Reports on Astronomy, Vol. 13a. International Astronomical Union Staff. Ed. by L. Perek. 1047p. 1968. lib. bdg. 171.00 (90-277-0138-5) Kluwer Ac.

Transactions of the International Astronomical Union: Reports on Astronomy, Vol. 14a. Ed. by C. De Jager. LC 30-10103. 566p. 1970. lib. bdg. 129.50 (90-277-0154-7) Kluwer Ac.

Transactions of the International Astronomical Union: Reports on Astronomy, Vol. 15a. Ed. by C. De Jager. LC 73-81827. 762p. 1973. lib. bdg. 269.50 (90-277-0340-X) Kluwer Ac.

Transactions of the International Astronomical Union Vol. XXIIB: Proceedings of the Twenty-Second General Assembly The Hague '1994. Ed. by Immo Appenzeller. (International Astronomical Union Transactions Ser.: Vol. 22b). 944p. (C). 1996. lib. bdg. 287.00 (0-7923-3842-1) Kluwer Ac.

Transactions of the International Astronomical Union, Vol. XXB: Proceedings of the Twentieth General Assembly, Baltimore, 1988. Ed. by Derek McNally. (C). 1990. lib. bdg. 317.00 (0-7923-0550-7) Kluwer Ac.

Transactions of the International Vacuum Congress, 3rd, Stuttgart, June 1965, Vol. 2: Sessions 1-4. H. Adam. LC 59-6851. 1967. 368.00 (0-08-011763-5, Pub. by Pergamon Repr UK) Franklin.

Transactions of the International Vacuum Congress, 3rd, 1965, Vol. 2: Sessions 5-8. H. Adam. 129.00 (0-08-012126-8, Pub. by Pergamon Repr UK) Franklin.

***Transactions of the Iron & Steel Society.** Iron & Steel Society of AIME Staff. LC 83-122618. (Illus.). 109p. pap. 31.10 (0-608-04801-1, 2033007) Bks Demand.

Transactions of the Iron & Steel Society of AIME, Vol. 5. AIME, Iron & Steel Society Staff. LC 83-643272. (Illus.). 116p. reprint ed. pap. 33.10 (0-8357-8393-6, 2033007) Bks Demand.

Transactions of the Iron & Steel Society of AIME, Vol. 10. Iron & Steel Society of AIME Staff. LC 83-122618. (Illus.). 138p. reprint ed. pap. 39.40 (0-8357-6300-5, 2033007) Bks Demand.

Transactions of the Iron & Steel Society of AIME Vol. 12. fac. ed. Iron & Steel Society of AIME Staff. LC 83-122618. (Illus.). 240p. 1991. pap. 68.40 (0-7837-7304-8, 2033007) Bks Demand.

Transactions of the Iron & Steel Society of AIME Vol. 14. fac. ed. Iron & Steel Society of AIME Staff. LC 83-122618. (Illus.). 124p. 1993. pap. 35.40 (0-7837-7305-6, 2033007) Bks Demand.

Transactions of the Iron & Steel Society of AIME, 1987, Vol. 8. Iron & Steel Society of AIME Staff. LC 83-643272. (Illus.). 68p. reprint ed. pap. 25.00 (0-685-44475-9, 2033007) Bks Demand.

Transactions of the Iron & Steel Society, 1985, Vol. 6. 84p. 1985. 52.00 (0-911277-05-6) ISS Found.

Transactions of the Iron & Steel Society, 1986, Vol 7. 54p. 1986. 52.00 (0-911277-06-4) ISS Found.

Transactions of the Japanese Society for Non-Destructive Inspection, Vol. 4. LC 90-13821. 81p. 1992. text ed. 97.00 (2-88124-852-7) Gordon & Breach.

Transactions of the JSNDI, Vol. 2. H. Kato. 133p. 1991. text ed. 171.00 (2-88124-755-5) Gordon & Breach.

Transactions of the JSNDI, Vol. 3. H. Kato. 128p. 1991. text ed. 169.00 (2-88124-793-8) Gordon & Breach.

Transactions of the JSNDI Five, Vol. 5. Ed. by Ichirou Yamaguchi. 88p. 1993. text ed. 107.00 (2-88124-929-9) Gordon & Breach.

Transactions of the Moscow Mathematical Society. American Mathematical Society Staff. LC 65-4713. 390p. reprint ed. pap. 111.20 (0-7837-1793-8, 2041994) Bks Demand.

***Transactions of the Moscow Mathematical Society, Vol. 12.** LC 65-7413. 524p. 1965. 78.00 (0-8218-1612-8, MOSCOW/12) Am Math.

***Transactions of the Moscow Mathematical Society, Vol. 13.** LC 65-7413. 384p. 1967. 66.00 (0-8218-1613-6, MOSCOW/13) Am Math.

***Transactions of the Moscow Mathematical Society, Vol. 14.** LC 65-7413. 368p. 1967. 66.00 (0-8218-1614-4, MOSCOW/14) Am Math.

Transactions of the Moscow Mathematical Society, Vol. 15. LC 65-7413. 508p. 1968. 78.00 (0-8218-1615-2, MOSCOW/15) Am Math.

***Transactions of the Moscow Mathematical Society, Vol. 16.** LC 65-7413. 373p. 1969. 67.00 (0-8218-1616-0, MOSCOW/16) Am Math.

***Transactions of the Moscow Mathematical Society, Vol. 17.** LC 65-7413. 386p. 1969. write for info. (0-8218-1617-9, MOSCOW/17) Am Math.

***Transactions of the Moscow Mathematical Society, Vol. 18.** LC 65-7413. 392p. 1969. 62.00 (0-8218-1618-7, MOSCOW/18) Am Math.

***Transactions of the Moscow Mathematical Society, Vol. 19.** LC 65-7413. 331p. 1969. 57.00 (0-8218-1619-5, MOSCOW/19) Am Math.

***Transactions of the Moscow Mathematical Society, Vol. 20.** LC 65-7413. 283p. 1971. 82.00 (0-8218-1620-9, MOSCOW/20) Am Math.

***Transactions of the Moscow Mathematical Society, Vol. 21.** LC 65-7413. 316p. 1971. 70.00 (0-8218-1621-7, MOSCOW/21) Am Math.

***Transactions of the Moscow Mathematical Society, Vol. 22.** LC 65-7413. 280p. 1972. 66.00 (0-8218-1622-5, MOSCOW/22) Am Math.

Transactions of the North American Manufacturing Research Institute of SME 1995. LC 89-656337. 362p. 1995. 45.00 (0-87263-460-4) SME.

Transactions of the North American Manufacturing Research Institution of SME 1989: Papers Presented at NAMRC XVII, May 24-26, 1989, Ohio State University, Columbus, OH. North American Manufacturing Research Conference (14th: 1986: University of Minnesota, Minneapolis) Staff. LC 89-60331. (Illus.). 396p. 1989. reprint ed. pap. 112.90 (0-7837-9726-5, 2060457) Bks Demand.

Transactions of the North American Manufacturing Research Institution of SME 1991 (NAMRC) Intro. by Richard E. DeVor. (Illus.). 372p. 1991. 80.00 (0-87263-404-3) SME.

Transactions of the Royal Historical Society. (RHS Transactions Sixth Ser.: Vol. 2). 256p. (C). 27.00 (0-86193-131-9) David Brown.

Transactions of the Royal Historical Society. (Transactions Fifth Ser.: Vol. 40). 256p. 27.00 (0-86193-124-6) David Brown.

Transactions of the Royal Historical Society. (Transactions Fifth Ser.: Vol. I). 272p. 27.00 (0-86193-134-3) David Brown.

Transactions of the Royal Historical Society, Vol. 34. (Transactions Fifth Ser.: Vol. 34). 27.00 (0-86193-104-1) David Brown.

Transactions of the Royal Historical Society, Vol. 37. (Transactions Fifth Ser.: Vol. 37). 200p. 27.00 (0-86193-115-7) David Brown.

Transactions of the Royal Historical Society, Vol. 39. (Transactions Fifth Ser.: Vol. 39). 81p. 27.00 (0-86193-121-1) David Brown.

Transactions of the Society of Actuaries, Pts. I & II, Vol. XL. (Illus.). 1988. text ed. 55.00 (0-938959-09-3) Soc Actuaries.

Transactions of the Society of Actuaries, Vol. XXXIII. 1981. 55.00 (0-938959-06-9) Soc Actuaries.

Transactions of the Society of Actuaries, Vol. XXXV. Incl. Vol. XXXVI. . 1984. (0-318-60287-3); 1983. 55.00 (0-938959-01-8) Soc Actuaries.

Transactions of the Society of Actuaries, Vol. XXXVI. 632p. 1984. text ed. 55.00 (0-938959-02-6) Soc Actuaries.

Transactions of the Society of Actuaries, Vol. XXXVII. 1985. 55.00 (0-938959-03-4) Soc Actuaries.

Transactions of the Society of Actuaries, Vol. XXXVIII. 1986. 55.00 (0-938959-04-2) Soc Actuaries.

Transactions of the Society of Actuaries, Vol. XXXIX. 1987. 55.00 (0-938959-05-0) Soc Actuaries.

Transactions of the Society of Actuaries, Vol. XLI. 1989. text ed. 55.00 (0-938959-15-8) Soc Actuaries.

Transactions of the Society of Actuaries, Vol. XLII. 1990. text ed. 55.00 (0-938959-19-0) Soc Actuaries.

Transactions of the Society of Actuaries, Vol. XLIII. (Illus.). 1991. text ed. 55.00 (0-938959-22-0) Soc Actuaries.

Transactions of the Society of Actuaries, Vol. XLIV. 1992. text ed. 55.00 (0-938959-31-X) Soc Actuaries.

Transactions of the Society of Actuaries, Vol. XLV. 1993. 55.00 (0-938959-33-6) Soc Actuaries.

Transactions of the Society of Actuaries, Vol. XLVI. 1995. 55.00 (0-938959-37-9) Soc Actuaries.

***Transactions of the Society of Actuaries, Vol. XLVII.** 1997. 55.00 (0-938959-41-7) Soc Actuaries.

Transactions of the Society of Actuaries, XXXIV. Society Of Actuaries Staff. 1982. 55.00 (0-938959-07-7) Soc Actuaries.

Transactions of the 52nd North American Wildlife & Natural Resources Conference. 780p. 1987. 25.00 (0-318-23696-6) Wildlife Mgmt.

***Transactions RHS 5, Vol. 20.** (Transactions Fifth Ser.). 27.00 (0-901050-65-2) David Brown.

***Transactions RHS 5, Vol. 21.** (Transactions Fifth Ser.). 27.00 (0-901050-05-9) David Brown.

***Transactions RHS 5, Vol. 22.** (Transactions Fifth Ser.). 27.00 (0-901050-07-5) David Brown.

***Transactions RHS 5, Vol. 23.** (Transactions Fifth Ser.). 27.00 (0-901050-19-9) David Brown.

***Transactions RHS 5, Vol. 24.** (Transactions Fifth Ser.). 27.00 (0-901050-22-9) David Brown.

***Transactions RHS 5, Vol. 25.** (Transactions Fifth Ser.). 27.00 (0-901050-26-1) David Brown.

***Transactions RHS 5, Vol. 27.** (Transactions Fifth Ser.). 27.00 (0-901050-38-5) David Brown.

***Transactions RHS 5, Vol. 28.** (Transactions Fifth Ser.). 27.00 (0-901050-42-3) David Brown.

***Transactions RHS 5, Vol. 29.** (Transactions Fifth Ser.). 27.00 (0-901050-54-7) David Brown.

***Transactions RHS 5, Vol. 30.** (Transactions Fifth Ser.). 27.00 (0-901050-68-7) David Brown.

***Transactions RHS 5, Vol. 32.** (Transactions Fifth Ser.). 27.00 (0-86193-096-7) David Brown.

***Transactions RHS 5, Vol. 33.** (Transactions Fifth Ser.). 27.00 (0-86193-099-1) David Brown.

***Transactions RHS 5, Vol. 35.** (Transactions Fifth Ser.). 27.00 (0-86193-107-6) David Brown.

***Transactions RHS 5, Vol. 36.** (Transactions Fifth Ser.). 27.00 (0-86193-109-2) David Brown.

***Transactions RHS 5, Vol. 38.** (Transactions Fifth Ser.). 27.00 (0-86193-118-1) David Brown.

***Transactions RHS 6, Vol. 3.** (Transactions Fifth Ser.). 27.00 (0-86193-136-X) David Brown.

Transactions, Society of Actuaries, Index to Vol. XXXVI-XL, Inclusive. 1990. text ed. 9.00 (0-938959-17-4) Soc Actuaries.

Transactions, 1991. (Transactions Ser.: Vol. 15). 499p. 1991. 50.00 (0-934412-69-3) Geothermal.

Transactions, 1992. (Transactions Ser.: Vol. 16). 668p. 1992. 50.00 (0-934412-70-7) Geothermal.

Transactions, 1992: Robotics Research. Bartholomew O. Nnaji. 476p. 1992. pap. text ed. 88.00 (0-87263-429-9) SME.

Transactions, 1993. (Transactions Ser: Vol. 17). 552p. 1993. write for info. (0-934412-71-5) Geothermal.

Transactions, 1993-94 Reports of Mortality, Morbidity & Other Experience. 1996. 50.00 (0-938959-38-7) Soc Actuaries.

Transactions, 1994. (Transactions Ser.: Vol. 18). 644p. 1994. write for info. (0-934412-72-3) Geothermal.

Transatlantic Alliance on the Eve of the New Millennium. Snezana Trifunovska. LC 96-18258. 1996. 195.00 (90-411-0243-4) Kluwer Law Tax Pubs.

***Transatlantic Armament Cooperation: Into the 21st Century.** Ed. by Robert P. Grant. (Conference Report Ser.). 62p. (Orig.). 1996. pap. 15.95 (0-9629930-6-9) US Crest.

Transatlantic Brethren: Rev. Samuel Jones (1735-1814) & His Friends: Baptists in Wales, Pennsylvania & Beyond. Hywel M. Davies. LC 94-30666. 368p. 1995. 49.50 (0-934223-32-7) Lehigh Univ Pr.

Transatlantic Connections: Nordic Migrations to the New World after 1800. Hans Norman & Harald Runblom. (Norwegian University Press Publication). (Illus.). 335p. 1988. 49.50 (82-00-06988-5) Scandnvan Univ Pr.

Transatlantic Dialogue: Selected American Correspondence of Edmund Gosse. Edmund Gosse. Ed. by Michael Millgate. LC 65-16471. 359p. reprint ed. pap. 102.40 (0-318-34939-6, 2030733) Bks Demand.

Transatlantic Encounters: Europeans & Andeans in the Sixteenth Century. Ed. by Kenneth J. Andrien & Rolena Adorno. (Illus.). 353p. 1991. 50.00 (0-520-07228-6) U CA Pr.

Transatlantic Foreign Investment: Evolving International Rules & Trends in Domestic Regulations: Conclusions from an International Round Table Seminar. Intro. by Jacqueline Grapin. LC 93-72139. 52p. (Orig.). 1992. pap. 7.00 (0-9628287-3-4) European Inst.

***Transatlantic Images & Perceptions: Germany & America since 1776.** Ed. by David E. Barclay & Elisabeth Glaser-Schmidt. (Publications of the German Historical Institute, Washington, D. C.). (Illus.). 400p. (C). 1997. text ed. 64.95 (0-521-58091-9) Cambridge U Pr.

Transatlantic Manners: Social Patterns in Nineteenth-Century Anglo-American Travel Literature. Christopher Mulvey. (Illus.). 260p. (C). 1990. text ed. 64.95 (0-521-30366-4) Cambridge U Pr.

Transatlantic Paddle Steamers. H. Phillip Spratt. (C). 1987. 48.00 (0-85174-158-4, Pub. by Brwn Son Ferg) St Mut.

Transatlantic Persuasion: The Liberal-Democratic Mind in the Age of Gladstone. Robert Kelley. 456p. 1989. pap. 29.95 (0-88738-635-0) Transaction Pubs.

***Transatlantic Radicals & the Early American Republic.** Michael Durey. LC 96-49216. 540p. 1997. 45.00 (0-7006-0823-0) U Pr of KS.

Transatlantic Relationship. Wiener. 1997. text ed. 59.95 (0-312-16203-0) St Martin.

Transatlantic Revivalism: Popular Evangelicalism in Britain & America, 1790-1865. Richard Carwardine. LC 77-94740. (Contributions in American History Ser.: No. 75). 249p. 1978. text ed. 49.95 (0-313-20308-3, CTR/, Greenwood Pr) Greenwood.

Transatlantic Sketches. Henry James. LC 72-310. (Essay Index Reprint Ser.). 1977. reprint ed. 23.95 (0-8369-2797-4) Ayer.

Transatlantic Technology Agenda: New Policy Dimensions: Report of the European Institute Project on Transatlantic Technology Cooperation (PROTEC) Seminar. Ed. by Shaazka M. Beyerle. 46p. (Orig.). 1995. pap. 15.00 (0-9628287-9-3) European Inst.

Transatlantic Trends in Retailing: Takeovers & Flow of Know-How. Madhav B. Kacker. LC 84-15928. xv, 165p. 1985. text ed. 55.00 (0-89930-036-7, KEI/, Quorum Bks) Greenwood.

Transatlantic with Street: A Two-Hour Video Film. Gavin Shore. (C). 1989. 224.00 (0-685-40369-6, Pub. by Imray Laurie Norie & Wilson UK) St Mut.

TRANSAX Ninety-Two: Practicing for Disaster. Alex White-Tail Feather. (State Legislative Reports: Vol. 18, No. 13). 4p. 1993. 5.00 (1-55516-338-6, 7302-1813) Natl Conf State Legis.

Transax-93: A Waste Isolation Pilot Plant Transportation Emergency Exercise Program: Summary Report. 53p. (Orig.). (C). 1994. pap. text ed. 25.00 (0-7881-1502-2) DIANE Pub.

Transbluesency: The Selected Poems of Amiri Baraka/Leroi Jones. Amiri Baraka, pseud. Ed. by Paul Vangelisti. 171p. 1995. 32.95 (1-56886-013-7); pap. 17.95 (1-56886-014-5) Marsilio Pubs.

Transborder Data Flows & Mexico. 150p. 1991. 27.50 (92-1-104347-6, 90.II.A.17) UN.

Transborder Flow of Personal Data Within the EC. A. C. Nugter. (Computer - Law Ser.: Vol. 6). 456p. 1990. pap. 94.00 (90-6544-513-7) Kluwer Law Tax Pubs.

Transboundary Air Pollution: International Legal Aspects of the Co-Operation of States. Ed. by K. Flinterman et al. 1986. lib. bdg. 159.00 (90-247-3285-9) Kluwer Ac.

Transboundary Air Polution Effects & Control. (Air Pollution Studies: No. 3). 35p. 1987. pap. 11.00 (92-1-116374-9, E.86.II.E.23) UN.

Transboundary Environmental Interference & the Origin of State Liability. Rene Lefeber. LC 96-20679. (Developments in International Law Ser.). 365p. 1996. 195.00 (90-411-0275-2) Kluwer Law Tax Pubs.

Transboundary Income & Expenditure Flows in Regional Input-output Models. Adam Z. Rose & Benjamin H. Stevens. (Discussion Paper Ser.: No. 133). 32p. (C). 1989. pap. 10.00 (1-55869-138-3) Regional Sci Res Inst.

Transboundary Movements & Disposal of Hazardous Wastes in International Law: Basic Documents. Ed. by Barbara Kwiatkowska. (International Environmental Law & Policy Ser.). 1488p. (C). 1993. lib. bdg. 445.00 (0-7923-1667-3, Pub. by Graham & Trotman UK) Kluwer Ac.

Transboundary Movements of Hazardous Wastes at the Interface of Environment & Trade. (Environment & Trade Ser.: No. 7). 96p. 1995. 10.00 (92-1-127011-1) UN.

Transboundary Regulation of Hazardous Waste Management along the U. S.-Mexico Border. Lizbeth G. Ellis. 29p. (Orig.). (C). 1993. pap. text ed. 12.50 (0-937795-14-3) Border Res Inst.

An Asterisk (*) at the beginning of an entry indicates that the title is appearing in BIP for the first time.

Transboundary Water Resources Management: Institutional & Engineering Approaches. Ed. by Jacques Ganoulis et al. LC 95-52380. (NATO ASI Series 2: Vol. 7). 470p. 1996. 220.00 (*3-540-60714-5*) Spr-Verlag.

***Transbrasil: An Airline & Its Aircraft.** R. E. Davies. (Great Airlines of the World Ser.). (Illus.). 64p. 1997. 30.00 (*1-888962-01-1*) Paladwr Pr.

Transcatheter Therapy in Pediatric Cardiology. Ed. by P. Syamasundar Rao. 528p. 1993. text ed. 159.95 (*0-471-58827-X*) Wiley.

***Transcations RHS 5, Vol. 26.** (Transactions Fifth Ser.). 27.00 (*0-901050-28-8*) David Brown.

Transcaucasia & Ararat Being Notes of a Vacation Tour in the Autumn of 1876. James B. Bryce. LC 73-115509. (Russia Observed, Series I). 1970. reprint ed. 29.95 (*0-405-03007-X*) Ayer.

Transcaucasia, Nationalism & Social Change: Essays in the History of Armenia, Azerbaijan, & Georgia. rev. ed. Ronald G. Suny. LC 96-4588. (Illus.). 70.00 (*0-472-09617-6*); pap. 27.95 (*0-472-06617-X*) U of Mich Pr.

Transcaucasian Boundaries. Ed. by John F. Wright et al. 256p. 1996. text ed. 39.95 (*0-312-12912-2*) St Martin.

Transcaucasus in Transition: Nation-Building & Conflict. Shireen T. Hunter. (CSIS Significant Issues Ser.). 240p. (C). 1994. pap. text ed. 19.95 (*0-89206-247-9*) CSI Studies.

Transceiver System Design for Digital Communications. Scott R. Bullock. Ed. by Gary A. Breed & Crawford Hammond. (Illus.). 432p. 1995. 54.00 (*1-884932-46-0*) Noble Pubng.

Transcendance de l'Ego: Esquisse d'une Description Phenomenoligique. 3rd ed. Jean-Paul Sartre. Ed. by S. Le Bon. (Illus.). 136p. (FRE.). 1988. pap. 16.95 (*0-7859-1538-9*, 2711606767) Fr & Eur.

Transcendance de L'ego: Esquisse d'une Description Phenomenologique. Jean-Paul Sartre. pap. 5.50 (*0-685-36566-2*) Fr & Eur.

Transcendence. Art Becker. 16p. 1995. pap. 7.95 (*0-9646065-0-X*) A Becker Photo.

Transcendence: The Birth of Homo Novus. M. F. Taylor. LC 91-76848. 128p. (Orig.). 1991. pap. 9.95 (*0-9631530-0-5*) Eclipse Pr.

Transcendence & Divine Passion: The Queen Mother of the West in Medieval China. Suzanne E. Cahill. LC 92-26835. (Illus.). 326p. 1995. 45.00 (*0-8047-2112-2*); pap. 16.95 (*0-8047-2584-5*) Stanford U Pr.

Transcendence & Immanence in the Philosophy of Michael Polanyi & Christian Theism. R. T. Allen. LC 92-30298. (Rutherford Studies in Contemporary Theology: Vol. 5). 204p. 1992. text ed. 89.95 (*0-7734-1635-8*) E Mellen.

Transcendence & Mature Thought in Adulthood: The Further Reaches of Adult Development. Ed. by Melvin E. Miller & Susanne Cook-Greuter. 300p. (C). 1994. pap. text ed. 24.95 (*0-8476-7919-5*); lib. bdg. 62.50 (*0-8476-7918-7*) Rowman.

Transcendence & the Sacred, Vol. 2. Ed. by Alan M. Olson & Leroy S. Rouner. LC 81-50456. (Boston University Studies in Philosophy & Religion: Vol. 2). 256p. (C). 1981. text ed. 34.50 (*0-268-01841-3*) U of Notre Dame Pr.

Transcendence & the Sacred, Vol. 2. Ed. by Alan M. Olson & Leroy S. Rouner. LC 81-50456. (Boston University Studies in Philosophy & Religion: Vol. 2). (C). 1994. reprint ed. pap. text ed. 13.00 (*0-268-01888-X*) U of Notre Dame Pr.

Transcendence & Wittgenstein's Tractatus. Michael P. Hodges. 172p. 1990. 39.95 (*0-87722-692-X*) Temple U Pr.

Transcendence in Relationships: Existentialism & Psychotherapy. Robert Willis. (Frontiers in Psychotherapy Ser.). 240p. 1994. pap. 39.50 (*1-56750-074-9*); text ed. 73.25 (*1-56750-073-0*) Ablex Pub.

Transcendence in Society Suppl. 1: Case Studies. Ed. by Craig Calhoun. (Comparative Social Research Ser.). 252p. 1990. 73.25 (*1-55938-070-5*) Jai Pr.

Transcendence of Loss over the Life-Span. Patricia Weenolsen. LC 66-56391. (Death Education, Aging & Health Care Ser.). 500p. 1988. 109.00 (*0-89116-736-6*); pap. text ed. 49.95 (*0-89116-582-7*) Hemisp Pub.

Transcendence of the Ego. Jean-Paul Sartre. 119p. (Orig.). 1991. pap. text ed. 7.95 (*0-8090-1545-5*) Hill & Wang.

Transcendence of the World: Phenomenological Studies. Richard Holmes. 120p. (C). 1995. text ed. 29.95 (*0-88920-241-9*) Wilfrid Laurier.

Transcendence Therapy. Adrian Van Kaam. (Formative Spirituality Ser.: Vol. 7). 336p. 1995. 35.00 (*0-8245-1512-9*) Crossroad NY.

Transcendence with the Human Body in Art: George Segal, Stephen De Staebler, Jasper Johns, & Christo. Doug Adams. (Illus.). 159p. 1995. reprint ed. 18.95 (*0-8245-1104-2*) Sharing Co.

Transcendency. Gerald Stutsman. LC 81-69736. 96p. 1982. pap. 4.75 (*0-87516-466-8*) DeVorss.

Transcendent Adventure: Studies of Religion in Science Fiction-Fantasy. Ed. by Robert Reilly. LC 84-542. (Contributions to the Study of Science Fiction & Fantasy Ser.: No. 12). x, 266p. 1985. text ed. 59.95 (*0-313-23062-5*, RET/, Greenwood Pr) Greenwood.

Transcendent Child: Tales of Triumph over the Past. Lillian B. Rubin. LC 95-24895. 240p. 1996. 22.00 (*0-465-08669-1*) HarpC.

Transcendent Child: Tales of Triumph over the Past. Lillian B. Rubin. 1996. write for info. (*0-614-97003-2*) Basic.

***Transcendent Child: Tales of Triumph Over the Past.** Lillian B. Rubin. 240p. 1997. pap. 12.50 (*0-06-097720-5*, PL) HarpC.

Transcendent Collector. Donald S. Vogel. Ed. by Peggy Goad. (Adventure with Joe & Heather Ser.: No. 3). (Illus.). 240p. 1992. 20.00 (*1-879154-09-9*) Vlly Hse Gllry.

Transcendent Daughters in Jewett's Country of the Pointed Firs. Joseph Church. LC 94-214. 1995. 34.50 (*0-8386-3560-1*) Fairleigh Dickinson.

Transcendent Experience in Sports. Michael Murphy & Rhea A. White. LC 94-44134. 288p. 1995. pap. 11.95 (*0-14-019492-4*, Arkana) Viking Penguin.

Transcendent Formation. Adrian Van Kaam. (Formative Spirituality Ser.: Vol. 6). 360p. 1995. 35.00 (*0-8245-1511-0*) Crossroad NY.

Transcendent God of Eugnostos: An Exegetical Contribution to the Study of the Knostic Texts of Nag Hammadi with a Retroversion of the Lost Original Greek Text of Eugnostos the Blessed. Demetrios Trakatellis. Tr. by Charles Sarelis from GRE. 229p. (C). 1991. 19.95 (*0-917651-87-1*); pap. 14.95 (*0-917651-89-8*) Holy Cross Orthodox.

***Transcendent Individual: Essays Toward a Literary & Liberal Anthropology.** Nigel Rapport. LC 97-7414. 248p. (C). 1997. pap. write for info. (*0-415-16967-4*); text ed. write for info. (*0-415-16966-6*) Routledge.

Transcendent Love: The Fifth Passage of Marriage - Beyond the Thirty-Fifth Anniversary, the Growth Stage That Can Glorify Your Union. Brian Newman et al. LC 92-33182. 1993. 9.99 (*0-8407-4553-2*) Nelson.

Transcendent Nation. Chris Foster. 31p. (Orig.). 1987. pap. 4.50 (*0-9690341-1-3*, B12) Foundation Hse.

Transcendent Reason: James Marsh & the Forms of Romantic Thought. Peter C. Carafiol. LC 82-13617. xviii, 222p. 1982. 49.95 (*0-8130-0732-1*) U Press Fla.

Transcendent Science: Kant's Conception of Biological Methodology. Clark Zumbach. 178p. 1984. lib. bdg. 89.00 (*90-247-2904-1*, Pub. by M Nijhoff NE) Kluwer Ac.

***Transcendent Unity of Religions.** Frithjof Schuon. 174p. 1996. pap. 12.00 (*0-614-21687-7*, 1252) Kazi Pubns.

Transcendent Unity of Religions. rev. ed. Frithjof Schuon. LC 84-239. 165p. (C). 1984. reprint ed. pap. 10.00 (*0-8356-0587-6*, Quest) Theos Pub Hse.

Transcendent Wisdom. Tenzin Gyatso. Tr. & Anno. by B. Alan Wallace. LC 94-7562. 96p. 1994. pap. 12.95 (*1-55939-030-1*) Snow Lion Pubns.

Transcendental Anarchy Confessions of a Metaphysical Tourist. Choyce. 1994. per. 11.95 (*1-55082-073-7*, Pub. by Quarry Pr CN) LPC InBook.

Transcendental Arguments & Science: Essays in Epistemology. Ed. by Rolf-Peter Horstmann et al. (Synthese Library: No. 133). 322p. 1979. lib. bdg. 88.00 (*90-277-0963-7*, D Reidel) Kluwer Ac.

Transcendental Art of Emil Bisttram. Walt Wiggins. (Illus.). 96p. 1988. 50.00 (*0-934116-08-3*); pap. 30.00 (*0-685-24105-X*) Pintores Pr.

Transcendental Dancing. Margaret J. Phillippou. 1982. pap. 3.00 (*0-941500-29-2*) Sharing Co.

Transcendental Diary, Vol. 1: Travels with His Divine Grace A. C. Bhaktivedanta Swami Prabhupada, November 1975-April 1976. Hari S. Dasa. 660p. (Orig.). 1992. 25.00 (*0-9633355-0-2*); pap. 15.00 (*0-9633355-1-0*) Lotus Imprints.

Transcendental Diary, Vol. 2: Travels with His Divine Grace A. C. Bhaktivedanta Swami Prabhupada, April 1976-June 1976. Hari S. Dasa. Ed. by Suzzanne Gilbakian. 600p. (Orig.). 1993. 30.00 (*0-9633355-3-7*); pap. 20.00 (*0-9633355-4-5*) Lotus Imprints.

Transcendental Diary, Vol. 3: Travels with His Divine Grave A. C. Bhaktivedanta Swami Praghupada. Hari S. Dasa. Ed. by Suzzanne Gilbakian. (Illus.). 540p. (Orig.). (C). 1994. text ed. 30.00 (*0-9633355-5-3*); pap. text ed. 20.00 (*0-9633355-6-1*) Lotus Imprints.

Transcendental Imagination: An Essay in Philosophical Theology. Charles E. Winquist. 96p. 1972. pap. text ed. 47.00 (*90-247-1330-7*, Pub. by M Nijhoff NE) Kluwer Ac.

Transcendental Magic. Eliphas Levi. Tr. by A. E. Waite from FRE. LC 72-16629. (Illus.). 438p. 1968. pap. 17.50 (*0-87728-079-7*) Weiser.

Transcendental Magic, Its Doctrine & Ritual. Eliphas Levi. 420p. 1976. reprint ed. spiral bd. 24.50 (*0-7873-0556-1*) Hlth Research.

Transcendental Meditation. Marharishi Mahesh Yogi. 320p. 1973. pap. 4.95 (*0-451-14081-8*, Sig) NAL-Dutton.

Transcendental Meditation. Robert Roth. 1988. pap. 5.95 (*1-55611-085-5*, Primus Lib Contemp) D I Fine.

Transcendental Meditation. rev. ed. Robert Roth. LC 94-71116. 160p. 1994. pap. 10.95 (*1-55611-403-6*, Primus) D I Fine.

Transcendental Meditation: Science of Being & Art of Living. Maharishi Mahesh Yogi. (New Age Ser.). 320p. 1988. pap. 4.95 (*0-317-67301-7*, Sig) NAL-Dutton.

Transcendental Meditation Program for Business People. Robert B. Kory. LC 76-3696. (AMA Management Briefing Ser.). 91p. reprint ed. pap. 26.00 (*0-317-27195-4*, 2023929) Bks Demand.

***Transcendental Metaphysics.** Richard Sylvan. 500p. 1997. 85.00 (*1-874267-32-4*, Pub. by White Horse Pr UK) Paul & Co Pubs.

***Transcendental Methods in Algebraic Geometry: Lectures Given at the 3rd Session of the Centro Internazionale Matematico Estivo (C. I. M. E.) Held in Cetraro, Italy, July 4-12, 1994, Vol. 164.** Jean-Pierre Demailly et al. LC 96-49601. (Lecture Notes in Mathematics Ser.). 1996. pap. 52.00 (*3-540-62038-9*) Spr-Verlag.

Transcendental Murder. Jane Langton. 256p. 1990. pap. 6.95 (*0-14-014852-3*, Penguin Bks) Viking Penguin.

Transcendental Murder. Jane Langton. 256p. 1990. pap. 3.95 (*0-14-011384-3*, Penguin Bks) Viking Penguin.

Transcendental Number Theory. Alan Baker. 164p. (C). 1990. pap. text ed. 20.95 (*0-521-39791-X*) Cambridge U Pr.

Transcendental Numbers. Andrei B. Shidlovskii. (Studies in Mathematics: Vol. 12). xx, 466p. (C). 1989. lib. bdg. 103.95 (*3-11-011568-9*) De Gruyter.

Transcendental Philosophy & Everyday Experience. Ed. by Tom Rockmore & Vladimir Zeman. LC 96-37869. 224p. (C). 1997. text ed. 55.00 (*0-391-04024-3*) Humanities.

Transcendental Physics: An Account of Experimental Investigations. Johann C. Zollner. Tr. by Charles C. Massey. LC 75-36924. (Occult Ser.). 1976. reprint ed. 19.95 (*0-405-07978-8*) Ayer.

Transcendental Physics (1881) Johann C. Zollner. 220p. 1996. pap. 18.95 (*1-56459-866-7*) Kessinger Pub.

Transcendental Psychosis: The Lyrics of Transmigration. Blacky Hix. 40p. 1994. pap. 8.00 (*1-885466-00-5*) Smoke The Soul.

Transcendental Saunterer: Thoreau & the Search for Self. David C. Smith. LC 91-14635. (Illus.). 320p. 1996. 24.95 (*0-913720-74-7*) Beil.

Transcendental Style in Film: Ozu, Bresson & Dreyer. Paul Schrader. (Quality Paperbacks Ser.). (Illus.). 200p. 1988. reprint ed. pap. 13.95 (*0-306-80335-6*) Da Capo.

Transcendental Temptation: A Critique of Religion & the Paranormal. 2nd ed. Paul Kurtz. 500p. (C). 1991. reprint ed. pap. 21.95 (*0-87975-645-4*) Prometheus Bks.

Transcendental Turn: The Foundation of Kant's Idealism. Moltke S. Gram. LC 84-22047. xii, 260p. 1985. 38.95 (*0-8130-0787-9*) U Press Fla.

Transcendental Typology. Dirk Goertz. (Illus.). 252p. (Orig.). 1990. pap. 12.99 (*1-56043-011-7*) Destiny Image.

***Transcendental Universe: Six Lectures on Occult Science, Theosophy, & the Catholic Faith.** C. G. Harrison. Ed. & Intro. by Christopher Bamford. 224p. 1993. pap. write for info. (*0-904693-44-9*, Pub. by Temple Ldge Pub UK) Anthroposophic.

Transcendental Universe: Six Lectures on Occult Science, Theosophy, & the Catholic Faith: Delivered Before the Berean Society. C. G. Harrison. Ed. & Intro. by Christopher Bamford. LC 93-348. (Esoteric Society Ser.). 1993. pap. 18.95 (*0-940262-58-4*) Lindisfarne Bks.

***Transcendental Utopias: Individual & Community at Brook Farm, Fruitlands, & Walden.** Richard Francis. LC 96-46314. (Illus.). 264p. 1996. 32.50 (*0-8014-3093-3*) Cornell U Pr.

Transcendental Wife: The Life of Abigail May Alcott. Cynthia H. Barton. LC 96-16217. 196p. 1996. pap. text ed. 29.50 (*0-7618-0387-4*); lib. bdg. 52.50 (*0-7618-0386-6*) U Pr of Amer.

Transcendental Wild Oats. Louisa May Alcott. LC 76-355426. (Illus.). 92p. 1981. 6.95 (*0-916782-21-2*) Harvard Common Pr.

Transcendental Wild Oats: And Excerpts from the Fruitlands Diary. Louisa May Alcott. LC 76-355426. 1995. pap. text ed. 6.95 (*1-55832-039-3*) Harvard Common Pr.

Transcendentalism & Equality. William B. Greene. LC 81-8972. 1981. 50.00 (*0-8201-1366-2*) Schol Facsimiles.

Transcendentalism & the Western Messenger: A History of the Magazine & Its Contributors, 1835-1841. Robert D. Habich. LC 83-49358. (Illus.). 208p. 1985. 32.50 (*0-8386-3204-1*) Fairleigh Dickinson.

Transcendentalism in New England: A History. Octavius B. Frothingham. (Notable American Authors Ser.). 1992. reprint ed. lib. bdg. 75.00 (*0-7812-2906-5*) Rprt Serv.

Transcendentalist Constant in American Literature. Roger Asselineau. (Gotham Library). (C). 1981. text ed. 40.00 (*0-8147-0572-3*); pap. text ed. 12.00 (*0-8147-0573-1*) NYU Pr.

Transcendentalist Hermeneutics: Institutional Authority & the Higher Criticism of the Bible. Richard A. Grusin. LC 90-35091. 216p. (C). 1990. text ed. 37.95 (*0-8223-1059-7*) Duke.

***Transcendentalists.** Thomas S. Kuhn. (Illus.). 1997. 9.98 (*1-56731-215-2*, MJF Bks) Fine Comms.

Transcendentalists: A Review of Research & Criticism. Ed. by Joel Myerson. LC 83-19442. (Reviews of Research Ser.: No. 7). xix, 534p. 1984. pap. 25.00 (*0-87352-261-3*, Z540P) Modern Lang.

Transcendentalists: An Anthology. Ed. by Perry G. Miller. LC 50-7360. 521p. 1950. pap. 18.50 (*0-674-90333-1*) HUP.

Transcending Addiction & Other Afflictions: Lifehealing. Angela Browne-Miller. LC 93-2901. (Frontiers in Psychotherapy Ser.). 1993. pap. 39.50 (*0-89391-903-9*); text ed. 73.25 (*0-89391-900-4*) Ablex Pub.

Transcending AIDS: Nurses & HIV Patients in New York City. Peggy McGarrahan. LC 93-26279. (Studies in Health, Illness, & Caregiving). 200p. (Orig.). (C). 1994. text ed. 32.95 (*0-8122-3203-8*); pap. text ed. 14.95 (*0-8122-1418-8*) U of Pa Pr.

Transcending All Understanding: The Meaning of Christian Faith Today. Walter Kasper. Tr. by Boniface Ramsey from GER. LC 89-83497. 124p. (Orig.). 1989. pap. text ed. 9.95 (*0-89870-256-9*) Ignatius Pr.

Transcending Angels: Rainer Maria Rilke's Duino Elegies. Kathleen L. Komar. LC 86-30863. 300p. 1987. reprint ed. pap. 85.50 (*0-608-02052-4*, 2062705) Bks Demand.

Transcending Boundaries: Multi-Disciplinary Approaches to the Study of Gender. Ed. by Pamela R. Frese & John M. Coggeshall. LC 90-39154. 224p. 1990. text ed. 49.95 (*0-89789-230-5*, H230, Bergin & Garvey); pap. text ed. 17.95 (*0-89789-231-3*, G231, Bergin & Garvey) Greenwood.

***Transcending Boundaries: Selected Poems by S. Grey Brewer.** S. Grey Brewer. 24p. (Orig.). 1996. pap. 7.00 (*1-879025-09-4*) Christopher-Burghardt.

Transcending Exile: Conrad, Nabokov, I. B. Singer. Asher Z. Milbauer. LC 84-22104. 155p. 1985. 34.95 (*0-8130-0815-8*) U Press Fla.

Transcending Gender: The Male/Female Double in Women's Fiction. Joanne Blum. LC 88-15592. 102p. 1991. 39.00 (*0-8357-1886-7*) Univ Rochester Pr.

***Transcending Loss: Understanding the Lifelong Impact of Grief & How to Make It Meaningful.** Ashley Prend. 304p. 1997. pap. 12.00 (*0-425-15775-X*, Berkley Trade) Berkley Pub.

Transcending Madness: The Experience of the Six Bardos. Chogyam Trungpa. LC 91-50879. (Dharma Ocean Ser.). 288p. (Orig.). 1992. pap. 20.00 (*0-87773-637-5*) Shambhala Pubns.

Transcending Stereotypes: Discovering Japanese Culture & Education. Ed. by Barbara Finkelstein et al. LC 90-24661. 224p. (Orig.). (C). 1991. pap. text ed. 29.95 (*0-933662-93-9*) Intercult Pr.

Transcending the Psychoneurotic Disturbances: New Approaches in Psychospirituality & Personality Development. Edward B. Bynum. LC 92-1578. 1993. pap. 19.95 (*1-56023-028-2*) Harrington Pk.

Transcending the Psychoneurotic Disturbances: New Approaches in Psychospirituality & Personality Development. Edward B. Bynum. LC 92-1577. (Illus.). 414p. 1994. lib. bdg. 49.95 (*1-56024-338-4*) Haworth Pr.

Transcending the State-Global Divide: A Neostructuralist Agenda in International Relations. Ed. by Ronen P. Palan & Barry Gills. LC 93-8935. (Critical Perspectives on World Politics Ser.). 286p. 1994. lib. bdg. 48.00 (*1-55587-395-2*) Lynne Rienner.

Transcending the Talented Tenth: Race Leaders & American Intellectualism. Joy James. LC 96-21488. 256p. 1996. pap. 16.95 (*0-415-91763-8*) Routledge.

Transcending the Talented Tenth: Race Leaders & American Intellectualism. Joy James. LC 96-21488. 196p. (C). 1996. text ed. 65.00 (*0-415-91762-X*) Routledge.

Transcending the West: Mao's Vision of Socialism & the Legitimization of Teng Hsiao-Ping's Modernization Program. Thomas A. Metzger. LC 96-7880. (Hoover Essays Ser.: No. 15). 1996. pap. 5.00 (*0-8179-3782-X*) Hoover Inst Pr.

***Transcending Traditions.** Dan Hardin. 160p. (Orig.). 1996. pap. 8.95 (*1-56794-100-1*, C-2398) Star Bible.

Transcending Turmoil: Painting at the Close of China's Empire, 1796-1911. Claudia Brown & Ju-Hsi Chou. LC 92-50375. (Illus.). 368p. 1992. pap. 49.95 (*0-910407-26-6*) Phoenix Art.

Transcending Turmoil: Survivors of Dysfunctional Families. Donna F. Lamar. (Illus.). 320p. 1992. 27.95 (*0-306-44127-6*, Plenum Insight) Plenum.

Transcending Turmoil: Survivors of Dysfunctional Families. Donna F. LaMar. Ed. by Bonnie Tilson. 328p. (Orig.). Date not set. pap. 13.95 (*1-884570-39-9*) Research Triangle.

Transcending unto Heaven. August K. Anderson. (Illus.). 200p. (Orig.). 1994. pap. 9.95 (*0-9640610-4-X*) Cheval Intl.

Transcontinental: An Investigation of Reality. Guy Brett. (Illus.). 112p. (gr. 13). 1990. pap. 23.00 (*0-86091-511-5*, A4983, Pub. by Vrso UK) Norton.

Transcontinental Railroad. Peter Anderson. LC 95-33593. (Cornerstones of Freedom Ser.). (Illus.). 32p. (J). (gr. 3-6). 1996. lib. bdg. 18.00 (*0-516-06635-8*) Childrens.

Transcontinental Railroad. Peter Anderson. LC 95-33593. (Cornerstones of Freedom Ser.). (Illus.). 32p. (J). (gr. 3-6). 1996. pap. 4.95 (*0-516-26035-9*) Childrens.

Transcontinental Railroad: A Thematic Unit. Mary E. Sterling. (Thematic Units Ser.). (Illus.). 80p. 1993. student ed. 9.95 (*1-55734-295-4*) Tchr Create Mat.

Transcontinental Railroad: America at Its Best? Robert Young. (J). 1996. pap. 5.95 (*0-382-39172-1*) Silver Burdett Pr.

Transcontinental Railroad: America at Its Best? Robert Young. (Both Sides Ser.). (J). 1996. lib. bdg. 13.95 (*0-87518-611-4*, Dillon Silver Burdett) Silver Burdett Pr.

Transcontinental Railroad: Triumph of a Dream. Dan Elish. LC 92-39995. (Spotlight on American History Ser.). (Illus.). 64p. (J). (gr. 4-6). pap. 5.95 (*1-56294-746-X*) Millbrook Pr.

Transcontinental Railroad: Triumph of a Dream. Dan Elish. LC 92-39995. (Spotlight on American History Ser.). (Illus.). 64p. (J). (gr. 4-6). 1993. lib. bdg. 16.40 (*1-56294-337-5*) Millbrook Pr.

***Transcontinental Railroad in American History.** LC 96-45525. (In American History Ser.). (J). 1997. lib. bdg. 18.95 (*0-89490-882-0*) Enslow Pubs.

Transcontinental Railroad Legislation, 1835-1862. Thamar E. Dufwa. Ed. by Stuart Bruchey. LC 80-1279. (Railroads Ser.). 1981. lib. bdg. 20.95 (*0-405-13754-0*) Ayer.

Transcontinental Rails. Thomas K. Hinckley. LC 71-43562. (Wild & Woolly West Ser., No. 12). (Illus.). (Orig.). 1969. pap. 4.00 (*0-910584-13-3*) Filter.

Transcranial Doppler. David W. Newell & Rune Aaslid. 288p. 1991. text ed. 173.50 (*0-88167-836-8*) Lppncott-Raven.

Transcranial Doppler Imaging: Techniques & Interpretation. Ed. by Mira L. Katz & Anthony J. Comerota. (Illus.). 250p. 1996. 69.00 (*1-56757-062-3*) Appleton Comms.

Transcranial Doppler Sonography. Ed. by R. Aaslid. (Illus.). 190p. 1992. 55.92 (*0-387-81935-5*) Spr-Verlag.

Transcranial Doppler Ultrasonography. Wechsler & Babikian. 323p. (gr. 13). 1992. text ed. 95.00 (*1-55664-394-2*) Mosby Yr Bk.

Transcreation: Two Essays. P. Lal. 29p. 1973. 8.00 (*0-88253-269-3*) Ind-US Inc.

T

Transcribing & Editing Oral History. Willa K. Baum. LC 77-3340. (American Association for State & Local History Book Ser.). (Illus.). 128p. 1991. reprint ed. pap. 14.95 (*0-910050-26-0*) AltaMira Pr.

Transcribing Machine Operator. Jack Rudman. (Career Examination Ser.: C-1067). 1994. pap. 23.95 (*0-8373-1067-9*) Nat Learn.

Transcribing Typist. Jack Rudman. (Career Examination Ser.: C-818). 1994. pap. 23.95 (*0-8373-0818-6*) Nat Learn.

Transcript. Judith Doyle. 12p. (Orig.). 1981. pap. 3.00 (*0-917061-08-X*) Top Stories.

Transcript: Testimony of Dr. Robert Buckhout in the Case of State of Michigan V. Hall & McGill. R. Buckhout. (Monographs: No. CR-24). 1978. 10.00 (*1-55524-025-9*) Ctr Respon Psych.

Transcript & Simulation Materials: To Accompany Tape II: Mediation, the Red Devil Dog Lease, Instructor's Manual with A. Leonard L. Riskin. (Dispute Resolution & Lawyers Videotape Ser.). 68p. (C). 1992. pap. text ed. write for info. (*0-314-01009-2*) West Pub.

Transcript & Simulation Materials, Tape II: Transaction Negotiation the Carton Contract, Instructor's Manual with A. Leonard L. Riskin. (Dispute Resolution & Lawyers Videotape Ser.). 47p. (C). 1992. pap. text ed. write for info. (*0-314-01008-4*) West Pub.

Transcript & Simulation Materials to Accompany Tape I: Dispute Negotiation Thompson vs. Decker, a Medical Malpractice Claim, Instructor's Manual with A. Leonard L. Riskin. (Dispute Resolution & Lawyers Videotape Ser.). 78p. (C). 1992. pap. text ed. write for info. (*0-314-01007-6*) West Pub.

Transcript & Simulation Materials to Accompany Tape IV: Overview of ADR: The Roark vs. Daily Bugle Libel Claim, Instructor's Manual with A. Leonard L. Riskin. (Dispute Resolution & Lawyers Videotape Ser.). 74p. (C). 1992. pap. text ed. write for info. (*0-314-01010-6*) West Pub.

Transcript Exercises for Learning Evidence. Paul Bruce Bergman. 274p. (C). 1992. pap. 17.50 (*0-314-01143-9*) West Pub.

Transcript Exercises for Learning Evidence, Teacher's Manual to Accompany. Paul B. Bergman. 20p. (C). 1992. pap. text ed. write for info. (*0-314-01307-5*) West Pub.

Transcript of the Anglo-Norman Passages in Liber Albus, Glossaries, Appendices, & Index see Munimenta Gildhallae Londoniensis: Liber Albus, Liber Custumarum, et Liber Horn

Transcript of the First Volume, 1538-1636, of the Parish Register of Chesham, in the County of Buckingham. J. W. Garrett-Pegge. 438p. 1993. reprint ed. pap. text ed. 28.00 (*1-55613-863-6*) Heritage Bk.

Transcript of the 1800, 1810 & 1820 Federal Census of Schoharie County, New York. Virginia P. Partridge & Susan F. Watkins. 251p. 1992. lib. bdg. 49.95 (*1-56012-112-2*, 114) Kinship Rhinebeck.

Transcript of the 1830 & 1840 Federal Census of Schoharie County, New York. Virginia P. Partridge & Susan F. Watkins. 350p. 1991. lib. bdg. 69.95 (*1-56012-113-0*, 106) Kinship Rhinebeck.

Transcript of Three Registers of Passengers from Great Yarmouth to Holland & New England, 1637-1639. Charles B. Jewson. 98p. 1990. reprint ed. 12.00 (*0-685-60502-7*, 3000) Clearfield Co.

***Transcript of Workshop on Flow Standards April 7, 1995 University of California, Davis.** (Illus.). 84p. 1997. pap. text ed. write for info. (*1-887192-05-0*) U Cal CWWR.

Transcription: Mechanisms & Regulation. Ed. by Ronald C. Conaway & Joan W. Conaway. LC 93-29738. (Series on Molecular & Cellular Biology: Vol. 3). 592p. 1994. text ed. 129.00 (*0-7817-0126-0*) Lppncott-Raven.

Transcription & Analysis of Jane Austen's Last Work, Sanditon. Teran L. Sacco. LC 94-46935. 200p. 1995. text ed. 79.95 (*0-7734-8995-9*) E Mellen.

Transcription & Splicing: Frontiers of Molecular Biology. Ed. by B. David Hames & David M. Glover. (Frontiers in Molecular Biology Ser.). (Illus.). 224p. (C). 1988. text ed. 46.00 (*1-85221-080-X*, IRL Pr); pap. text ed. 32.00 (*1-85221-076-1*, IRL Pr) OUP.

Transcription & Translation: A Practical Approach. Ed. by B. David Hames & S. J. Higgins. (Practical Approach Ser.). 348p. 1984. pap. 45.00 (*0-904147-52-5*, IRL Pr) OUP.

Transcription & Transliteration: An Annotated Bibliography on Conversion of Scripts. Hans Wellisch. LC 74-77274. 133p. 1994. pap. 11.95 (*0-8325-9294-3*, Natl Textbk) NTC Pub Grp.

Transcription & Visual Poetics in the Early Italian Lyric. H. Wayne Storey. LC 93-19648. (Studies in Medieval Literature: Vol. 7). 504p. 1993. text ed. 15.00 (*0-8153-1245-8*) Garland.

Transcription Dictation. Louis A. Leslie & Charles E. Zoubek. 1956. text ed. 32.75 (*0-07-037276-4*) McGraw.

Transcription English for the Spanish Speaking Student. Sarah P. Gonzalez. 135p. (SPA.). 1984. 6.00 (*0-8477-2608-8*) U of PR Pr.

Transcription Factors: A Practical Approach. Ed. by David S. Latchman. LC 92-48702. (Practical Approach Ser.). 224p. (C). 1993. 90.00 (*0-19-963342-8*, IRL Pr); pap. 50.00 (*0-19-963341-X*, IRL Pr) OUP.

Transcription Factors: Essential Data. Ed. by J. Locker. (Essential Data Ser.). 128p. 1996. pap. text ed. 19.95 (*0-471-95339-3*) Wiley.

***Transcription Factors & Cell Aging.** Ed. by A. Y. Liu et al. (Journal: Biological Signals: Vol. 5, No. 3, 1996). (Illus.). 70p. 1996. pap. 28.00 (*3-8055-6366-3*) S Karger.

Transcription Factors & the Control of DNA Replication. David S. Pederson & Nicholas H. Heintz. (Molecular Biology Intelligence Unit Ser.). 125p. 1994. 89.95 (*1-57059-069-9*, LN9069) R G Landes.

***Transcription Factors in Eukaryotes.** Athanasios Papavassiliou. 200p. 1997. 89.95 (*0-412-12501-3*) R G Landes.

Transcription Factors in Immunology. Ed. by H. W. Ziegler-Heitbrock. (Immunobiology Ser.: Vol. 193, Nos. 2-4). (Illus.). 250p. 1995. pap. 85.00 (*3-437-30813-0*, Pub. by G Fischer Verlag GW) Lubrecht & Cramer.

Transcription for Medical Office Assistant. Baker. 1998. 99.95 (*0-8273-7907-2*) Delmar.

Transcription for Medical Office Assistant. Baker. (C). 1998. teacher ed. 16.00 (*0-8273-7906-4*) Delmar.

Transcription for Medical Office Assistants. Baker. (C). 1998. 35.95 (*0-8273-7905-6*) Delmar.

***Transcription of Genetic Material.** Cold Spring Harbor Symposia on Quantitative Biology Staff. LC 34-8174. (Cold Spring Harbor Symposia on Quantitative Biology Ser.). (Illus.). 910p. 1971. reprint ed. pap. 180.00 (*0-608-04165-3*, 2064898) Bks Demand.

Transcription of Wunders Cemetery, Chicago, Illinois. Ed. by Gail Santroch. 106p. 1985. pap. 7.50 (*1-881125-10-6*) Chi Geneal Soc.

Transcription Skills for Business. 3rd ed. Louis Meyer & Ruth C. Moyer. 1988. pap. text ed. 23.95 (*0-471-85452-2*) P-H.

Transcription Skills for Business. 4th ed. Linda Mallinson et al. LC 92-16455. 161p. 1993. pap. text ed. 34.80 (*0-13-928029-4*) P-H.

***Transcription Skills for Business.** 5th ed. Lois Meyer et al. LC 97-18746. 1998. 29.33 (*0-13-639550-3*) P-H.

Transcription Skills for Information Processing, Module 4. Anne E. Schatz & Beverley M. Funk. 1981. wbk. ed., text ed. 7.36 (*0-07-055203-7*) McGraw.

Transcription Skills for Information Processing, Module 5. Anne E. Schatz & Beverley M. Funk. 1982. wbk. ed., text ed. 7.36 (*0-07-055204-5*) McGraw.

Transcription Skills for Information Processing, Module 6. Anne E. Schatz & Beverley M. Funk. 1982. student ed., text ed. 7.36 (*0-07-055205-3*) McGraw.

Transcription Skills for Information Processing, Module 7. Anne E. Schatz & Beverley M. Funk. 1982. student ed., text ed. 7.36 (*0-07-055206-1*) McGraw.

Transcription Skills for Information Processing, Module 8. Anne E. Schatz & Beverley M. Funk. 1982. student ed., text ed. 7.36 (*0-07-055207-X*) McGraw.

Transcription Skills for Information Processing, Unit 1. Anne E. Schatz & Beverley M. Funk. 96p. (C). 1981. text ed. 7.36 (*0-07-055200-2*) McGraw.

Transcription Skills for Information Processing, Unit 2. Anne E. Schatz & Beverley M. Funk. 112p. (C). 1981. text ed. 7.36 (*0-07-055201-0*) McGraw.

Transcription Skills for Information Processing Unit 3: Incorporating a Sequence Language Arts Program. Anne E. Schatz & Beverley M. Funk. (Illus.). 112p. 1981. text ed. 7.36 (*0-07-055202-9*) McGraw.

Transcriptional Regulation. Ed. by Steven L. McKnight & Keith R. Yamamoto. LC 92-31461. (Monographs: Vol. 22). 1335p. 1993. 160.00 (*0-87969-410-6*); pap. 95.00 (*0-87969-425-4*) Cold Spring Harbor.

Transcripts from Study Abroad Programs: A Workbook. Ed. by Eleanor Kramutschke & Thomas Roberts. 59p. 1986. student ed. 12.00 (*0-912207-20-5*) NAFSA Washington.

Transcripts of the Registers of the Worshipful Company of Stationers, London: 1554-1640 & 1640-1708, 4 vols. Edward Arber. 1967. write for info. (*0-8446-1449-1*) Peter Smith.

Transcripts of Will Book I: Mobile County Alabama, 1813-1837. Clinton P. King & Meriem A. Barlow. LC 87-81858. 200p. 1988. 20.00 (*0-943609-01-1*) AL Ancestors.

Transcripts of Will Book II: Mobile County Alabama, 1837-1857. Clinton P. King & Meriem A. Barlow. LC 87-81858. 305p. 1989. 30.00 (*0-943609-03-8*) AL Ancestors.

Transcualisticas: Bilingual Edition. Ernest M. Robson. Tr. by Lucy Lopez De Thorgood. LC 78-65323. (Illus.). (ENG & SPA.). 1978. pap. 8.95 (*0-934982-04-X*) Primary Pr.

Transcualisticas: Bilingual Edition. deluxe ed. Ernest M. Robson. Tr. by Lucy Lopez De Thorgood. LC 78-65323. (Illus.). (ENG & SPA.). 1978. 25.00 (*0-934982-03-1*) Primary Pr.

Transcultural Aspects of Psychiatric Art: Proceedings of the International Congress of Psychopathology of Expression, 7th, Boston, Mass., Oct., 1973. International Congress of Psychopathology of Expression Staff. Ed. by Irene Jakab. (Journal: Psychiatry & Art: Vol. 4). 1975. 102.50 (*3-8055-2138-3*) S Karger.

***Transcultural Child Development: A Context for Psychological Assessment & Treatment.** Ed. by Gloria Johnson-Powell et al. LC 97-8358. 320p. 1997. 59.95 (*0-471-17479-3*) Wiley.

Transcultural Concepts in Nursing Care. 2nd ed. Margaret M. Andrews & Joyceen S. Boyle. LC 94-27740. 496p. 1994. pap. text ed. 28.95 (*0-397-55115-0*) Lppncott-Raven.

Transcultural Counseling: Bilateral & International Perspectives. Ed. by John McFadden. LC 93-7970. 347p. 1993. pap. text ed. 35.95 (*1-55620-121-4*, 72540) Am Coun Assn.

Transcultural Counseling: Needs, Programs, & Techniques. Garry R. Walz & Libby Benjamin. LC 77-26253. (New Vistas in Counseling Ser.: Vol. VII). 243p. 1978. 42.95 (*0-87705-320-0*) Human Sci Pr.

Transcultural Counselling in Action. Patricia D'Ardennes & Aruna Mahtani. (Counselling in Action Ser.: Vol. 6). 144p. (C). 1989. text ed. 49.95 (*0-8039-8110-4*); pap. text ed. 21.50 (*0-8039-8111-2*) Sage.

Transcultural Dimensions in Medical Ethics. Ed. by Edmund D. Pellegrino et al. 225p. 1992. 35.00 (*1-55572-015-3*) Univ Pub Group.

Transcultural Education Model: A Guide for Developing ESL Bilingual & LEP Programs for K-12 & Adult Populations. Judy P. Donaldson. LC 84-80658. 176p. (Orig.). 1988. pap. text ed. 19.95 (*0-918452-60-0*, 600) Learning Pubns.

Transcultural Health Care. George Henderson & Martha Primeaux. 1981. 24.50 (*0-201-03237-6*, Health Sci); pap. write for info. (*0-201-03452-2*, Health Sci) Addison-Wesley.

Transcultural Health Care: A Culturally Competent Approach. Ed. by Larry D. Purnell & Betty J. Paulanka. LC 97-5282. (Illus.). 525p. (C). 1997. pap. text ed. 29.95 (*0-8036-0208-1*) Davis Co.

Transcultural Leadership: Empowering the Diverse Workforce. George F. Simons et al. LC 92-21508. (Managing Cultural Differences Ser.). 384p. 1993. 28.95 (*0-87201-299-9*) Gulf Pub.

***Transcultural Management: A New Approach for Global Organizations.** Atusushi Funakawa. 1997. 26.95 (*0-7879-0323-X*) Jossey-Bass.

Transcultural Management: How to Unlock Global Resources. Albert Koopman. (Developmental Management Ser.). 250p. 1991. 41.95 (*0-631-17804-X*) Blackwell Pubs.

Transcultural Management: How to Unlock Global Resources. Albert Koopman & Ronnie Lessem. (Developmental Management Ser.). 250p. 1994. pap. 26.95 (*0-631-19314-6*) Blackwell Pubs.

Transcultural Mosaic: Folk Art from the Collection of Mingei International Museum. Ed. by Martha W. Longenecker. (Illus.). 168p. 1993. 45.00 (*0-914155-03-2*) Mingei Intl Mus.

Transcultural Nursing: A Book of Readings. Ed. by Pamela J. Brink. 289p. (C). 1990. reprint ed. pap. text ed. 12.95 (*0-88133-486-3*) Waveland Pr.

Transcultural Nursing: Assessment & Intervention. 2nd ed. Joyce N. Giger. 568p. (C). (gr. 13). 1995. pap. text ed. 36.00 (*0-8016-7411-5*) Mosby Yr Bk.

Transcultural Nursing: Concepts, Theories, & Practices. Madeleine Leininger. 532p. 1994. pap. text ed. 25.95 (*1-57074-121-2*) Greyden Pr.

***Transcultural Odysseys: The Evolving Global Consciousness.** Germaine Shames. 1997. mass mkt. 18.95 (*0-614-26003-5*) Intercult Pr.

Transcultural Picture Word List: For Teaching English to Children from any of Twelve Language Backgrounds, Vol. II. Judy P. Donaldson. LC 78-58532. 204p. (Orig.). 1983. pap. text ed. 21.95 (*0-918452-38-4*, 384) Learning Pubns.

Transcultural Picture Word List: For Teaching English to Children from Any of Twenty One Language Backgrounds, Vol. I. Judy P. Donaldson. LC 78-58532. 1980. pap. text ed. 24.95 (*0-918452-10-4*, 104) Learning Pubns.

Transcultural Poetics: Corporative Studies of the Cantos by Ezra Pound & Bachittra Natak. Gurbachan Singh. 200p. (C). 1987. 25.00 (*81-202-0178-7*, Pub. by Ajanta II) S Asia.

Transcultural Space & Transcultural Beings. David Tomas. LC 96-10224. (Institutional Structures of Feeling Ser.). 1996. text ed. 55.00 (*0-8133-1974-9*) Westview.

Transcultural Study Guide. 5th ed. Volunteers in Asia Staff. Ed. by Bradley Palmquist & Kenneth Darrow. 1997. pap. 7.95 (*0-917704-01-0*) Volunteers Asia Pr.

Transculturation: The Cultural Factor in Translation & Other Communication Tasks. R. Daniel Shaw. LC 88-71335. (Illus.). 312p. (Orig.). 1988. pap. text ed. 10.95 (*0-87808-216-6*) William Carey Lib.

Transculturation & Resistance in Lusophone African Narrative. Phyllis Peres. LC 96-20868. 1997. 49.95 (*0-8130-1492-1*) U Press Fla.

Transcutaneous Electrical Nerve Stimulators. 10p. 1986. pap. 70.00 (*0-910275-60-2*, NS4-209) Assn Adv Med Instrn.

Transcutaneous Monitoring of Oxygen. (Illus.). 1978. pap. 26.50 (*3-8055-2883-3*) S Karger.

***Transdermal & Topical Drug Delivery Systems.** Ed. by Tapash K. Ghosh et al. LC 97-3050. (Illus.). 420p. 1997. 219.00 (*1-57491-041-8*) Interpharm.

Transdermal Controlled Systemic Medications. Chien. (Drugs & the Pharmaceutical Sciences Ser.: Vol. 31). 464p. 1987. 175.00 (*0-8247-7760-3*) Dekker.

Transdermal Delivery of Drugs, 3 vols. Agis F. Kydonieus. Ed. by Bret Berner. 300p. 1987. Set. 499.85 (*0-8493-6483-3*, RS201) CRC Pr.

Transdermal Delivery of Drugs. Agis F. Kydonieus & B. Berner. LC 86-2585. 216p. 1986. 125.00 (*0-8493-6484-1*, CRC Reprint) Franklin.

Transdermal Delivery of Drugs, Vol. II. Agis F. Kydonieus. 168p. 1987. 191.00 (*0-8493-6485-X*) CRC Pr.

Transdermal Delivery of Drugs, Vol. 3. Agis F. Kydonieus & B. Berner. LC 86-2585. 1987. 101.00 (*0-8493-6486-8*, CRC Reprint) Franklin.

Transdermal Drug Delivery: Developmental Issues & Research Initiatives. Hadgraft & Guy. (Drugs & the Pharmaceutical Sciences Ser.: Vol. 35). 340p. 1988. 155.00 (*0-8247-7991-6*) Dekker.

Transdermal Drug Delivery: Seminar Notes - October 1994. 1994. 154.95 (*1-56676-237-5*) Technomic.

Transdermal Fentanyl. Ed. by K. A. Lehmann & D. Zech. (Illus.). 192p. 1991. 69.95 (*0-387-54440-2*) Spr-Verlag.

Transdermal Hormone Replacement. Ed. by M. I. Whitehead & L. Schenkel. (Illus.). 94p. 1990. pap. 32.00 (*1-85070-847-9*) Prthnon Pub.

Transdifferentiation: Flexibility in Cell Differentiation. T. S. Okada. (Illus.). 248p. 1991. 105.00 (*0-19-854281-X*) OUP.

Transdimensional Teenage Mutant Ninja Turtles. Erick Wujcik. Ed. by Alex Marciniszyn. (Teenage Mutant Ninja Turtles RPG Adventures Ser.). (Illus.). 112p. (Orig.). (YA). (gr. 8 up). 1989. pap. 11.95 (*0-916211-35-5*, 508) Palladium Bks.

Transdisciplinary Play-Based Assessment: A Functional Approach to Working with Young Children. rev. ed. Lovett. LC 89-70795. 224p. (Orig.). 1993. spiral bd. 39.00 (*1-55766-162-6*, 1626) P H Brookes.

Transdisciplinary Play-Based Assessment & Intervention: Child & Program Summary Forms. Linder. 58p. 1993. 27.00 (*1-55766-163-4*) P H Brookes.

Transdisciplinary Play-Based Intervention: Guidelines for Developing a Meaningful Curriculum for Young Children. Toni W. Linder. LC 93-426. 1993. 49.00 (*1-55766-130-8*) P H Brookes.

Transdisciplinary Vocational Assessment: Issues in School-based Programs. Edward M. Levinson. LC 92-53226. 1993. pap. 42.50 (*0-88422-118-0*) Clinical Psych.

Transducer & Transmitter Installation for Nuclear Safety Applications: 1994. Date not set. 40.00 (*1-55617-542-6*) ISA.

Transducer Design Handbook: Applications & Theory. Alexander D. Khazan. LC 93-22873. 572p. (C). 1993. text ed. 86.00 (*0-13-929480-5*) P-H.

Transducer Fundamentals, Vol. 19. Lab-Volt Systems, Inc. Staff. (F.A.C.E.T. Ser.). (Illus.). 146p. (Orig.). (C). 1995. teacher ed., pap. text ed. write for info. (*0-86657-091-8*, TM90878-10); student ed., pap. text ed. write for info. (*0-86657-081-0*, TM90878-00) Lab-Volt.

Transducer Handbook: User's Directory of Electrical Transducers. H. B. Boyle. (Illus.). 240p. 1993. 57.95 (*0-7506-1194-4*) Buttrwrth-Heinemann.

Transducer Interfacing Handbook: A Guide to Analog Signal Conditioning. Ed. by Daniel H. Sheingold. LC 80-65520. (Illus.). 260p. 1980. 14.50 (*0-916550-05-2*) Analog Devices.

Transducers & Sensors: Self Study Course Package. John Webster. (Illus.). 1989. 199.00 (*0-87942-461-3*, HL4119) Inst Electrical.

Transducers in Measurement & Control. 3rd ed. P. H. Sydenham. (Illus.). 124p. 1984. pap. 50.00 (*0-85274-777-2*) IOP Pub.

Transducers in Mechanical & Electronic Design. Trietley. (Mechanical Engineering Ser.: Vol. 51). 392p. 1986. 145.00 (*0-8247-7598-8*) Dekker.

Transducing. George-Therese Dickenson. LC 85-62145. (Segue Bks.). 150p. (Orig.). 1985. pap. text ed. 7.50 (*0-937804-17-7*) Segue NYC.

Transduction in Biological Systems. C. Hidalgo et al. LC 90-35639. (Centro de Estudios Cientificos de Santiago Ser.). (Illus.). 530p. 1990. 125.00 (*0-306-43439-3*, Plenum Pr) Plenum.

Transect Through the New England Appalachians. Ed. by Lyons. (IGC Field Trip Guidebooks Ser.). 72p. 1989. 21.00 (*0-87590-607-9*, T162) Am Geophysical.

***Transect Through Time: The Archaeological Landscape of the Shell North Western Ethylene Pipeline.** Ed. by Janet Lambert et al. (Lancaster Imprint Ser.: No. 1). (Illus.). 1995. pap. 36.00 (*0-901800-74-0*, Pub. by Lancaster U Archaeol UK) David Brown.

Transentence. Damian Lopes. 28p. (Orig.). 1994. pap. 3.00 (*1-57141-005-8*) Runaway Spoon.

Transescence- The Child in the Middle see New Child in the Middle

Transesophageal Echocardiography. De Bruijn. 1991. 133.00 (*0-316-17816-0*) Little.

Transesophageal Echocardiography. Ed. by R. Erbel et al. (Illus.). 385p. 1991. 211.00 (*0-387-50507-5*) Spr-Verlag.

Transesophageal Echocardiography. Ed. by William K. Freeman et al. LC 93-5357. 624p. 1994. text ed. 195.00 (*0-316-29293-1*) Lppncott-Raven.

Transesophageal Echocardiography. C. Carl Jaffe & Patrick J. Lynch. (C). 1992. 500.00 incl. disk (*1-56815-014-8*) Mosby Yr Bk.

Transesophageal Echocardiography. Ed. by Gerald Maurer. (Illus.). 304p. 1993. text ed. 149.00 (*0-07-040988-9*) McGraw-Hill HPD.

Transesophageal Echocardiography. Jonathan F. Plehn. LC 95-37081. 608p. (gr. 13). 1997. text ed. 195.00 (*0-412-04451-X*) Chapman & Hall.

Transesophageal Echocardiography: A New Monitoring Technique. N. Kolev et al. LC 94-42060. 1996. 85.00 (*3-211-82650-5*) Spr-Verlag.

Transesophageal Echocardiography: Basic Principles & Clinical Applications. Arthur J. Labovitz & Anthony Pearson. (Illus.). 135p. 1992. pap. text ed. 45.00 (*0-8121-1578-3*) Williams & Wilkins.

Transesophageal Echocardiography: Clinical & Intraoperative Applications. Ed. by Jose C. Missri. LC 92-23799. (Illus.). 248p. 1993. text ed. 124.95 (*0-443-08852-7*) Churchill.

Transesophageal Echocardiography in Congenital Heart Disease. Ed. by Oliver Stumper & George R. Sutherland. (Illus.). 296p. 1994. 165.00 (*0-340-55653-6*, Pub. by Ed Arnold UK) OUP.

Transfer Across the Primate & Non Primate Placenta. Ed. by M. Young & H. Wallenburg. 264p. 1981. text ed. 89.50 (*0-275-91354-6*, C1354, Praeger Pubs) Greenwood.

Transfer Activities: Thinking Skill Vocabulary Development. Patty Mayo & Nancy Gajewski. (Illus.). 202p. (YA). (gr. 5-12). 1987. pap. text ed. 33.00 (*0-930599-13-6*) Thinking Pubns.

Transfer & Development of Technology in Developing Countries: A Compendium of Policy Issues. 64p. 1989. 19.00 (*92-1-112284-8*, 89.II.D.17) UN.

Transfer & Interference in Language: A Selected Bibliography. Hans W. Dechert et al. LC 84-16830. (Library & Information Sources in Linguistics: 14). xiv, 488p. 1984. 91.00 (*90-272-3735-2*) Benjamins North Am.

An Asterisk (*) at the beginning of an entry indicates that the title is appearing in BIP for the first time.

Transfer & Measurement of Chemicals. James N. Spencer. (Modular Laboratory Program in Chemistry Ser.). 12p. (C). 1990. pap. text ed. 1.35 (*0-87540-382-4*, TECH 382-4) Chem Educ Res.

*__Transfer & Mortage Recording Taxes in New York Title Closings, 1996.__ annuals David M. Goldberg. 383p. 1996. pap. 100.00 (*1-55834-290-7*, 62550-12) MICHIE.

Transfer & Mortgage Recording Taxes in New York Title Closings, 1995 Edition. David M. Goldberg. 383p. 1994. pap. 95.00 (*1-55834-123-4*) MICHIE.

Transfer, Articulation & Collaboration: Twenty-Five Years Later. Dorothy Knoell. 1990. pap. 18.50 (*0-87117-211-9*, 1131) Am Assn Comm Coll.

Transfer Challenge: Overcoming Barriers, Maintaining Commitment. Harold Wechsler. v, 74p. 1990. pap. text ed. 12.00 (*0-911696-46-6*) Assn Am Coll.

*__Transfer Credit Practices of Designated Educational Institutions (1994-96)__ Ed. by James Christensen. 176p. 1994. 20.00 (*0-614-23455-7*, 3008) Am Assn Coll Registrars.

Transfer Energy of Semi-Transparent Solids. G. N. Marchenko & A. A. Petrov. 1990. 75.00 (*0-89116-753-6*) CRC Pr.

Transfer Function Techniques for Control Engineers. D. R. Towill. LC 74-21807. (Illus.). 521p. reprint ed. pap. 148.50 (*0-317-41718-5*, 2025727) Bks Demand.

Transfer Functions & Solute Movement Through Soil Theory & Applications. W. A. Jury & K. Roth. 232p. 1990. 61.00 (*0-8176-2509-7*) Birkhauser.

Transfer in Language Production. Ed. by Hans W. Dechert & Manfred Raupach. LC 88-33377. 296p. (C). 1989. text ed. 73.25 (*0-89391-399-5*) Ablex Pub.

Transfer in Power of Africa: Decolonization 1940-1960. Prosser Gifford & William R. Louis. 989p. (C). 1988. reprint ed. 24.00 (*0-300-04348-1*) Yale U Pr.

Transfer, Making It Work: A Community College Report. Ed. by Richard A. Donovan et al. 80p. reprint ed. pap. 25.00 (*0-7837-2487-X*, 2042649) Bks Demand.

Transfer Matrix Method. Alexander Tesar & Ludovit Fillo. (C). 1988. lib. bdg. 143.50 (*90-277-2590-X*) Kluwer Ac.

Transfer, Memory & Creativity: After-Learning As Perceptual Process. George M. Haslerud. LC 72-79096. 191p. reprint ed. pap. 54.50 (*0-317-41715-0*, 2055873) Bks Demand.

Transfer of Arms, Leverage, & Peace in the Middle East. Nitza Nachmias. LC 88-17777. (Contributions in Military Studies: No. 83). 208p. 1988. text ed. 49.95 (*0-313-26300-0*, NAT/, Greenwood Pr) Greenwood.

Transfer of Assets into & Out of a Taxing Jurisdiction. (Cahiers de Droit Fiscal International Ser.: Vol. LXXIa). 550p. 1986. pap. 100.00 (*90-6544-258-8*) Kluwer Law Tax Pubs.

Transfer of Care: Psychiatric Deinstitutionalization & Its Aftermath. Phil Brown. 292p. (C). 1988. pap. text ed. 13.95 (*0-415-00188-9*) Routledge.

Transfer of Chattels in Private International Law: A Comparative Study. G. A. Zaphiriou. (University of London Legal Ser.: No. IV). xix, 227p. 1981. reprint ed. lib. bdg. 26.00 (*0-8377-1325-0*) Rothman.

Transfer of Cognitive Skill. Mark K. Singley & John R. Anderson. LC 88-28404. (Cognitive Science Ser.: No. 9). (Illus.). 320p. 1989. 37.00 (*0-674-90340-4*) HUP.

Transfer of Development Rights: A New Technique of Land Use Regulation. Ed. by Jerome G. Rose. 356p. 1975. boxed 29.95 (*0-87855-119-0*) Transaction Pubs.

Transfer of Development Rights: Buckingham Township (Bucks County, PA) & Other Experiences. Robert E. Coughlin. Ed. by Benjamin H. Stevens. (Discussion Paper Ser.: No. 126). 61p. (Orig.). 1981. pap. 10.00 (*1-55869-003-4*) Regional Sci Res Inst.

Transfer of Ideas: Historical Essays. Ed. by Craufurd C. Goodwin & I. B. Holley, Jr. LC 68-26691. 191p. reprint ed. pap. 54.50 (*0-317-26757-4*, 2023390) Bks Demand.

Transfer of Industrial Technologies to Early America. Darwin H. Stapleton. LC 86-72882. (Memoirs Ser.: Vol. 177). (Illus.). (C). 1987. 18.00 (*0-87169-177-9*, M177-STD) Am Philos.

Transfer of Industrial Technology to the Manufacturing Sector: The Case of Malaysia. Maisom Bt Abdullah. (Studies in Technology & Social Change: No. 1). 86p. (Orig.). (C). 1988. pap. 8.00 (*0-945271-01-8*) ISU-CIKARD.

Transfer of International Technology: Europe, Japan & the U. S. A. in the Twentieth Century. David J. Jeremy. 240p. 1992. text ed. 85.00 (*1-85278-453-9*) E Elgar.

Transfer of Japanese Technology & Management to the ASEAN Countries. Ed. by Shoichi Yamashita & Nobuo Kawabe. 312p. 1991. text ed. 57.50 (*0-86008-463-9*) Col U Pr.

Transfer of Land in Victoria. S. Robinson. lxv, 517p. 1979. 123.00 (*0-455-19746-6*, Pub. by Law Bk Co AT) Gaunt.

Transfer of Learning: Contemporary Research & Applications. Ed. by Stephen M. Cormier & Joseph D. Hagman. (Educational Technology Ser.). 281p. 1987. text ed. 71.00 (*0-12-188950-5*) Acad Pr.

Transfer of Management Technology to Developing Nations: The Role of Multinational Oil Firms in Saudi Arabia. Ibrahim A. Al-Moneef. Ed. by Stuart Brouchey. LC 80-564. (Multinational Corporations Ser.). 1981. lib. bdg. 56.95 (*0-405-13361-8*) Ayer.

Transfer of Marine Technology to Developing Nations in International Law: Occasional Paper No. 32. Ed. by B. Boczek. 79p. 1982. 3.75 (*0-911189-04-1*) Law Sea Inst.

Transfer of Nuclear Technology. P. J. Howe. 1977. pap. 43.00 (*0-08-022132-7*, Pergamon Pr) Elsevier.

Transfer of Power. Ilija Poplasen. (Illus.). 401p. 1984. 20.00 (*0-935352-15-5*) MIR PA.

Transfer of Property. Vepa P. Sarathi. (C). 1990. 65.00 (*0-685-37469-6*) St Mut.

Transfer of Scholarly Scientific & Technical Information Between North & South America: Proceedings of a Conference. Ed. by Victor Rosenberg & Gretchen Whitney. LC 86-15625. (Illus.). 739p. 1986. 59.50 (*0-8108-1935-X*) Scarecrow.

Transfer of Spectral Line Radiation. C. J. Cannon. (Illus.). 650p. 1985. text ed. 130.00 (*0-521-25995-9*) Cambridge U Pr.

*__Transfer of Technology.__ Istvan Gazda. 168p. 1996. pap. 70.00 (*90-411-0044-X*) Kluwer Law Tax Pubs.

Transfer of Technology for Deep Sea-Bed Mining: The 1982 Law of the Sea Convention & Beyond. Yuwen Li Dordrecht. (Publications on Ocean Development: Vol. 25). 1994. lib. bdg. 132.00 (*0-7923-3212-1*) Kluwer Ac.

Transfer of Technology in Indian Agriculture: Experience of Agricultural Universities. Ed. by N. C. Nath. (C). 1992. 18.00 (*81-85182-70-1*, Pub. by Indus Pub II) S Asia.

Transfer of Technology within Multinational Corporations: An Exploratory Analysis. Jean-Pierre Jeannet. Ed. by Stuart Bruchey. LC 80-577. (Multinational Corporations Ser.). 1981. lib. bdg. 25.95 (*0-405-13370-7*) Ayer.

Transfer of Training & Retroaction see Two Studies in Mental Tests

Transfer of Water Resources Knowledge: Proceedings of the International Conference, 1st, Colorado State University, Sept. 14-16, 1972. International Conference on Transfer of Water Resources Knowledge Staff. Ed. by Evan Vlachos. LC 73-80678. 1973. 25.00 (*0-918334-05-5*) WRP.

*__Transfer of Wealth.__ Ed. by Raymond W. Merritt & Clifford R. Ennico. 165p. 1993. pap. 32.00 (*0-614-26658-0*, 4230) NYS Bar.

Transfer on Trial: Intelligence, Cognition, & Construction. Douglas K. Detterman & Robert J. Sternberg. 304p. (C). 1993. pap. 39.50 (*0-89391-826-1*) Ablex Pub.

Transfer on Trial: Intelligence, Cognition, & Construction. Ed. by Douglas K. Detterman & Robert J. Sternberg. 304p. (C). 1993. text ed. 78.50 (*0-89391-825-3*) Ablex Pub.

*__Transfer Please: Memories of Riding the Streetcar.__ James W. Garvey. (Illus.). (Orig.). 1996. pap. 4.95 (*0-939332-24-8*) J Pohl Assocs.

Transfer Pricing. Clive R. Emmanuel & Messaoud Mehafdi. (Advanced Management Accounting & Finance Ser.). (Illus.). 192p. 1994. pap. text ed. 16.00 (*0-12-238330-3*) Acad Pr.

Transfer Pricing. Colin Masters & Alan Stroud. 151p. 1991. boxed 170.00 (*0-406-00112-X*, U.K.) MICHIE.

Transfer Pricing & Multi-National Enterprises. 1979. 15.00 (*92-64-11947-7*) OECD.

Transfer Pricing & Multinational Enterprises: Three Taxation Issues. OECD Staff. 92p. (Orig.). 1984. pap. 20.00 (*92-64-12626-0*) OECD.

Transfer Pricing & Valuation in Corporate Taxation: Federal Legislation vs. Administrative Practice. Elizabeth King. LC 93-28693. 304p. (C). 1993. lib. bdg. 111.00 (*0-7923-9392-9*) Kluwer Ac.

Transfer Pricing for Intangibles. Comment by Fred C. De Hosson. 92p. 1990. pap. 35.00 (*90-6544-425-4*) Kluwer Law Tax Pubs.

Transfer Pricing Guidelines for Multinational Enterprises & Tax Administrations. OECD Staff. 150p. (Orig.). 1995. pap. 63.00 (*92-64-14533-8*, Pub. by Org for Econ FR) OECD.

Transfer Pricing Handbook. Robert Feinschreiber. 648p. 1993. text ed. 150.00 (*0-471-59597-7*) Wiley.

Transfer Pricing Handbook. Robert Feinschreiber. 127p. 1994. suppl. ed., pap. text ed. 50.00 (*0-471-01227-0*) Wiley.

*__Transfer Pricing Handbook, 2 vols.__ 2nd ed. Ed. by Robert Feinschreiber. LC 97-9319. 992p. 1998. 250.00 (*0-471-17599-4*) Wiley.

*__Transfer Pricing Handbook, Vol. 1.__ 2nd ed. Ed. by Robert Feinschreiber. LC 97-9319. 1998. write for info. (*0-471-17600-1*) Wiley.

*__Transfer Pricing Handbook, Vol. 2.__ 2nd ed. Ed. by Robert Feinschreiber. LC 97-9319. 1998. write for info. (*0-471-17601-X*) Wiley.

*__Transfer Pricing Handbook: 1996 Cumulative Supplement, Vol. 2.__ Ed. by Robert Feinschreiber. LC 96-24720. 1996. pap. text ed. 70.00 (*0-471-16618-9*) Wiley.

Transfer Pricing in the Absence of Comparable Market Prices, Vol. LXXVIIa. International Fiscal Association Staff. 680p. 1992. pap. 84.00 (*90-6544-618-4*) Kluwer Law Tax Pubs.

Transfer Pricing in the Nineteen Nineties: Tax Management Perspectives. Roger Y. Tang. LC 92-31713. 168p. 1993. text ed. 47.95 (*0-89930-776-0*, TTG, Quorum Bks) Greenwood.

Transfer Pricing Practices in the United States & Japan. Roger Y. Tang. LC 78-19780. (Praeger Special Studies). 144p. 1979. text ed. 55.00 (*0-275-90429-6*, C0429, Praeger Pubs) Greenwood.

Transfer Pricing under U. S. Law. 195.00 (*1-85271-274-0*, Pub. by IBC Finan Pubng UK) IBC Pubns.

Transfer RNA: Biological Aspects. Ed. by Dieter Soll et al. LC 79-17578. (Cold Spring Harbor Monograph Ser.: No. 9B). 590p. reprint ed. pap. 168.20 (*0-7837-6440-5*, 2046440) Bks Demand.

Transfer RNA in Protein Synthesis. 448p. 1992. 210.00 (*0-8493-5698-9*, QP263) CRC Pr.

Transfer RNAs & Other Soluble RNAs. Cherayil. 184p. 1990. 153.00 (*0-8493-5744-6*, QP623) CRC Pr.

*__Transfer School Curriculum, Vol. 1.__ Hollins. Date not set. pap. text ed. write for info. (*0-312-11939-9*) St Martin.

Transfer Spending, Taxes, & the American Welfare State. Wallace C. Peterson. (C). 1990. lib. bdg. 75.00 (*0-7923-9077-6*) Kluwer Ac.

Transfer Student's Guide to Changing Colleges. Sidonia Dalby & Sally Rubenstone. LC 92-35581. 1993. pap. 12.00 (*0-671-84851-8*, Arco) Macmillan Gen Ref.

Transferability of Social Technology: Explorations in the Knowledge Structures of the Helping Professions & Their Transfer. Pranab Chatterjee. LC 89-12648. (Studies in Health & Human Services: Vol. 16). 244p. 1990. lib. bdg. 89.95 (*0-88946-141-4*) E Mellen.

*__Transferbeziehungen Zwischen den Generationen: Unter Besonderer Berucksichtigung der Intragenerationalen Verteilungswirkungen.__ Alexander Becker. (Illus.). 353p. (GER.). 1996. 61.95 (*3-631-30151-0*) P Lang Pubng.

Transference: Its Structure & Function in Psychoanalytic Therapy. Benjamin Wolstein. LC 95-16993. 292p. 1995. pap. 30.00 (*1-56821-626-2*) Aronson.

Transference & Countertransference. Heinrich Racker. 216p. 1968. 33.00 (*0-8236-6640-9*) Intl Univs Pr.

Transference & Empathy in Asian American Psychotherapy: Cultural Values & Treatment Needs. Jean L. Chin et al. LC 92-48757. 168p. 1993. text ed. 49.95 (*0-275-94493-X*, C4493, Praeger Pubs) Greenwood.

Transference & Its Context: Selected Papers on Psychoanalysis. Leo Stone. LC 83-25807. 470p. 1984. 50.00 (*0-87668-655-2*) Aronson.

Transference & Transcendence: Ernest Becker's Contribution to Psychotherapy. Daniel Liechty. LC 94-39365. 224p. 1995. 35.00 (*1-56821-434-0*) Aronson.

Transference/ Countertransference. Ed. by Nathan Schwartz-Salant & Murray Stein. LC 91-40546. (Chiron Clinical Ser.: Vol. 1984). (Illus.). 200p. (Orig.). 1992. pap. 24.95 (*0-933029-63-2*) Chiron Pubns.

Transference in Brief Psychotherapy: An Approach to the Study of Psychoanalytic Process. Stanley Grand et al. LC 84-24422. 154p. reprint ed. pap. 43.90 (*0-8357-2738-6*, 2039847) Bks Demand.

Transference in Psychotherapy: Clinical Management. Ed. by Evelyne A. Schwaber. LC 84-12958. 181p. (C). 1986. 30.00 (*0-8236-6625-5*, 06625) Intl Univs Pr.

Transference Methods in Analysis. Ronald Coifman & Guido Weiss. LC 77-24098. (CBMS Regional Conference Series in Mathematics: No. 31). 59p. 1977. pap. 21.00 (*0-8218-1681-0*, CBMS/31) Am Math.

Transference Neurosis & Psychoanalytic Experience: Perspectives on Contemporary Clinical Practice. Gail S. Reed. LC 94-1406. 240p. 1994. 32.50 (*0-300-05957-4*) Yale U Pr.

Transference Neurosis & Transference Psychosis. Margaret I. Little. LC 80-66925. 352p. 1993. pap. 30.00 (*1-56821-074-4*) Aronson.

*__Transfering Wealth & Management.__ Fowler. Date not set. pap. text ed. 49.00 (*0-15-601985-X*) Profess Pubns.

Transferrin: The Iron Carrier. Alan J. Welch. 304p. 1992. 166.00 (*0-8493-6793-X*, QP552) CRC Pr.

Transferring a Tradition: C Abd Al Ra'uf Al-Singkili's Rendering into Malay of the Jalalayn. unabridged ed. Peter Riddell. (Monographs: Vol. 31). 320p. (Orig.). 1990. pap. text ed. 25.00 (*0-944613-10-1*) UC Berkeley Ctrs SE Asia.

Transferring Data to & from Windows. Richard P. Braden. LC 94-17675. (Hands-on Windows Programming Ser.: Bk. 4). 160p. (Orig.). 1994. pap. 15.95 (*1-55622-435-4*) Wordware Pub.

Transferring Hazardous Technologies & Substances: The International Legal Challenge. Ed. by Gunther Handl & Robert E. Lutz. (C). 1990. lib. bdg. 122.50 (*0-86010-704-3*) Kluwer Ac.

Transferring Juveniles to Criminal Courts: Trends & Implications for Criminal Justice. Dean J. Champion & G. Larry Mays. LC 90-40798. 208p. 1991. text ed. 49.95 (*0-275-93534-5*, C3534, Praeger Pubs) Greenwood.

Transferring Models to Users. Ed. by Eric B. Janes & William R. Hotchkiss. LC 90-84161. (Technical Publications: No. 90-3). (Illus.). 404p. (Orig.). 1991. pap. 55.00 (*1-882132-12-2*) Am Water Resources.

Transferring Models to Users: Proceedings of the Symposium Held November 4-8, 1990, at the Hyatt Regency Denver, Denver, Colorado. American Water Resources Association Staff. Ed. by Eric B. Janes & William R. Hotchkiss. LC 90-84161. (American Water Resources Association Technical Publication Ser.: Vol. TPS-90-3). (Illus.). 416p. 1990. reprint ed. pap. 118.60 (*0-7837-9219-0*, 2049970) Bks Demand.

Transferring Responsibility: The Dangers of Transition: Report of the Miller Center Commission on Presidential Transitions & Foreign Policy. Miller Center Commission. LC 86-5536. 9.00 (*0-8191-5344-3*) U Pr of Amer.

Transferring Technologies for the Hardwood Industry: Wetwood Detection, Biocides, Cutting Optimization & Value-Added Wood Products. Christopher W. Murdoch et al. (Illus.). 70p. (Orig.). (C). 1994. pap. text ed. 50.00 (*0-7881-0547-7*) DIANE Pub.

Transferring Technology for Small Scale Farming. Ed. by N. R. Usherwood. (Illus.). 1981. pap. 5.50 (*0-89118-066-4*) Am Soc Agron.

Transferring Technology in the Personal Social Services. Emilia E. Martinez-Brawley & Sybil M. Delevan. LC 93-16123. 210p. (C). 1993. 24.95 (*0-87101-226-X*) Natl Assn Soc Wkrs.

Transferring Technology to China: Prosper Giquel & the Self-Strengthening Movement. Steven A. Leibo. LC 85-60380. (China Research Monographs: No. 28). 175p. 1985. pap. 7.50 (*0-912966-76-9*) IEAS.

Transferring the Privately-Held Business: Creating a Succession Plan to Meet Your Changing Tax, Estate & Business Needs. Irving L. Blackman. 400p. 1993. text ed. 75.00 (*1-55738-433-9*) Irwin Prof Pubng.

*__Transferring to a United States Medical School.__ 2nd rev. ed. Stanley Zaslau. 125p. (C). 1996. pap. text ed. 25.00 (*1-886468-11-7*) FMSG.

Transferring to America: Jewish Interpretations of American Dreams. Rael Meyerowitz. LC 94-43358. (SUNY Series in Psychoanalysis & Culture). 302p. (C). 1995. text ed. 59.50 (*0-7914-2607-6*); pap. text ed. 19.95 (*0-7914-2608-4*) State U NY Pr.

Transferring Your Business When You Have Two or More Children. Irving L. Blackman & Brian T. Whitlock. (Special Report Ser.: No. 12). 57p. 1991. pap. 25.00 (*0-916181-26-X*) Blackman Kallick Bartelstein.

Transfers: Three Plays. Conrad Bromberg. 1970. pap. 5.25 (*0-8222-1166-1*) Dramatists Play.

Transfers of Property in Eleventh-Century Norman Law. Emily Z. Tabuteau. LC 87-21736. (Studies in Legal History). x, 445p. (C). 1988. text ed. 70.00 (*0-8078-1774-0*) U of NC Pr.

Transfiguracion. Catharose De Petri. (SPA.). 1987. pap. 7.00 (*90-70196-84-0*) Rosycross Pr.

Transfiguration. Frank Celis. LC 90-72003. 145p. (Orig.). 1992. pap. 8.00 (*1-56002-084-9*, Univ Edtns) Aegina Pr.

Transfiguration. Catharose De Petri. (Rose Ser.: No. 1). 1986. pap. 6.00 (*90-70196-40-9*) Rosycross Pr.

Transfiguration. Ed. by Wolfgang Hageney. (Illus.). 112p. (ENG, FRE, GER, ITA & SPA.). 1983. pap. 21.95 (*88-7070-036-4*) Belvedere USA.

Transfiguration: Elements of Science & Christian Faith. Ed. by Marianne Postiglione. (Illus.). iii, 294p. (Orig.). 1993. pap. 15.95 (*0-9625431-7-9*) ITEST Faith.

Transfiguration: Introduction to the Contemplation of Icons. Maria G. Muzj. Tr. by Kenneth D. Whitehead. LC 91-2341. (Illus.). 179p. 1991. 19.95 (*0-8198-7350-0*) Pauline Bks.

Transfiguration: Poetic Metaphor & the Languages of Religious Belief. Frank B. Brown. LC 82-24714. (Studies in Religion). x, 230p. 1983. 34.95 (*0-8078-1560-8*) U of NC Pr.

Transfiguration by Cyrnai. Carolyn Fok. (Illus.). 72p. 1996. write for info. incl. cd-rom (*0-9651307-0-3*, T-01) Titanium CA.

Transfiguration Catechesis: A New Vision Based on the Liturgy & the "Catechism of the Catholic Church" Dominic F. Ashkar. LC 95-50111. 216p. 1996. pap. 19.95 (*0-89390-342-6*) Resource Pubns.

Transfiguration Diet. Littlegreen, Inc. Think Tank Staff. LC 85-91090. (Illus.). 176p. (Orig.). 1986. pap. 7.95 (*0-936863-04-8*, Littlegreen) Chris Pub UT.

Transfiguration of Benno Blimpie. Albert Innaurato. 1977. pap. 3.25 (*0-8222-1167-X*) Dramatists Play.

Transfiguration of Christ. Monks of New Skete Staff. Tr. by Laurence Mancuso. (Liturgical Music Series I: Great Feasts: Vol. 1). 40p. 1986. pap. text ed. 12.00 (*0-935129-02-2*) Monks of New Skete.

Transfiguration of Christ in Scripture & Tradition. John A. McGuckin. LC 86-23892. (Studies in Bible & Early Christianity: Vol. 9). 352p. 1986. lib. bdg. 99.95 (*0-88946-609-2*) E Mellen.

Transfiguration of History at the Center of Dante's Paradise. Jeffrey T. Schnapp. LC 85-43309. 264p. 1986. text ed. 45.00 (*0-691-06679-5*) Princeton U Pr.

Transfiguration of Man. Frithjof Schuon. LC 95-10140. (Library of Traditional Wisdom). 110p. (Orig.). 1995. pap. 12.00 (*0-941532-19-4*) Wrld Wisdom Bks.

Transfiguration of Mission: Biblical, Theological, & Historical Foundations. Ed. by Wilbert R. Shenk. LC 92-37009. 256p. (Orig.). 1993. pap. 16.99 (*0-8361-3610-1*) Herald Pr.

Transfiguration of the Commonplace: A Philosophy of Art. Arthur C. Danto. 222p. 1983. pap. 12.95 (*0-674-90346-3*) HUP.

Transfigurations: Studies in the Dynamics of Byzantine Iconography. Anthony Cutler. LC 75-1482. (Illus.). 226p. 1976. 35.00 (*0-271-01194-7*) Pa St U Pr.

Transfigurations, Art Critical Essays, on the Modern Period. Nicolas Calas. LC 85-16353. (Contemporary American Art Critics Ser.: No. 7). 291p. reprint ed. pap. 83.00 (*0-8357-1690-2*, 2070535) Bks Demand.

Transfigurations of the Maghreb: Feminism, Decolonization, & Literatures. Winifred Woodhull. LC 92-46725. 260p. 1993. text ed. 44.95 (*0-8166-2054-7*); pap. text ed. 17.95 (*0-8166-2055-5*) U of Minn Pr.

Transfigure System. Health for Life Staff. (Illus.). 127p. 1989. pap. 19.95 (*0-944831-21-4*) Health Life.

Transfigure System Two. Jerry Robinson & Robert Miller. (Illus.). 132p. (Orig.). 1990. pap. 19.95 (*0-944831-24-9*) Health Life.

Transfigured Hart. Jane Yolen. LC 97-5765. 1997. pap. write for info. (*0-15-201195-1*) HarBrace.

Transfigured Rites in Seventeenth-Century English Poetry. A. B. Chambers. 296p. (C). 1992. text ed. 39.95 (*0-8262-0808-8*) U of Mo Pr.

Transfigured World: Walter Pater's Aesthetic Historicism. Carolyn Williams. LC 89-42883. 312p. 1990. 42.50 (*0-8014-2151-9*) Cornell U Pr.

*__Transfiguring Sword: The Just War of the Women's Social & Political Union.__ Cheryl R. Jorgensen-Earp. LC 96-34736. (Studies in Rhetoric & Communication). 208p. 29.95 (*0-8173-0870-9*) U of Ala Pr.

Transfiniteness for Graphs, Networks, & Walks. Armen H. Zemanian. LC 95-24601. 264p. 1995. 79.50 (*0-8176-3818-0*); text ed. write for info. (*3-7643-3818-0*) Birkhauser.

Transfixed by Light. Kathryn Davidson & Elizabeth Glassman. Ed. & Selected by Beaumont Newhall. LC 81-80810. 46p. (C). 1981. pap. 7.50 (*0-939594-00-5*) Menil Collect.

Transfixion. W. Sabrina. 16p. (Orig.). 1993. pap. 2.00 (*1-884047-54-8*) Mass Extinct.

*__Transform! The Final Fitness Solution.__ Phil Kaplan. Orig. Title: Mind-Muscle: Fitness for All of You. (Illus.). 365p. (Orig.). 1997. pap. 39.95 (*1-887463-14-3*) Grt Atltc.

Transform Analysis. Markowitz. (Electronics Technology Ser.). 1998. teacher ed. 12.00 (*0-8273-6948-4*); text ed. 68.95 (*0-8273-6947-6*) Delmar.

Transform Analysis of Generalized Functions. O. P. Misra & J. L. Lavoine. (Mathematical Studies: Vol. 119). 332p. 1986. pap. 117.50 (*0-444-87885-8*, North Holland) Elsevier.

Transform Circuit Analysis for Engineering & Technology. 3rd ed. William D. Stanley. LC 96-18725. 464p. (C). 1996. 87.00 (*0-13-492430-4*) P-H.

Transform Methods for Solving Partial Differential Equations. Dean G. Duffy. LC 93-40215. 512p. 1994. 71.95 (*0-8493-7374-3*) CRC Pr.

Transform Methods in Applied Mathematics: An Introduction. Peter Lancaster & Kestutis Salkauskas. LC 95-48302. (Canadian Mathematical Society Ser. & Advanced Texts). 1996. text ed. 59.95 (*0-471-00810-9*) Wiley.

Transform Methods in Circuit Analysis. Cecil A. Harrison. 800p. (C). 1990. text ed. 51.00 (*0-03-020724-X*) SCP.

Transform My Spirit: Prayers by Baha'u'llah. Baha'u'llah. 73p. 1992. pap. 3.50 (*0-87743-238-4*) Bahai.

Transform Techniques in Chemistry. Ed. by Peter R. Griffiths. LC 77-29271. (Modern Analytical Chemistry Ser.). (Illus.). 403p. reprint ed. pap. 114.90 (*0-317-09433-5*, 2019649) Bks Demand.

Transform Your Emotional DNA: Understanding the Blueprint of Your Life. Theresa Dale. (Illus.). iv, 140p. (Orig.). 1996. 19.95 (*0-9652947-6-5*, 001) Wellness Ctr.

Transform Your Life. Barbara King. LC 94-42495. 208p. (Orig.). 1995. pap. 12.00 (*0-399-51932-7*, Perigee Bks) Berkley Pub.

Transform Your Life: A Step-by-Step Programme for Change. Diana Cooper. 176p. (Orig.). 1995. pap. 14.95 (*0-7499-1310-X*, Pub. by Piatkus Bks UK) London Brdge.

Transformados en Su Semejanza. T. S. Nee. Orig. Title: Transformed into His Image. 144p. (SPA.). 1992. mass mkt. 4.99 (*0-8254-1506-3*, Edit Portavoz) Kregel.

Transformal Organization: A Business Paradigm for the 1990s. Louis DeThomasis et al. (Illus.). vii, 171p. (Orig.). 1991. pap. 11.95 (*0-9631835-0-8*) Metanoia Grp.

Transformation. John G. Bennett. LC 78-60760. 6.95 (*0-900306-07-6*) Claymont Comm.

T

Transformation. Marc Berrenson. 352p. 1993. mass mkt. 4.50 (*0-8217-4294-9*, Zebra Kensgtn) Kensgtn Pub Corp.

Transformation. W. Blaser. Orig. Title: Livio Vacchini. 168p. 1994. 89.50 (*0-8176-2987-4*) Spr-Verlag.

Transformation: ("Metamorphosis") & Others Stories. Franz Kafka. Ed. & Tr. by Malcolm Pasley. 256p. 1995. pap. 10.95 (*0-14-018478-3*, Penguin Classics) Viking Penguin.

Transformation: A Rites of Passage Manual for African American Girls. 2nd ed. Maxori Moore et al. (Illus.). 83p. 1987. reprint ed. pap. 15.00 (*0-9621527-0-6*) Stars Pr.

Transformation: Poems January to March 1981. John Logan. 22p. (Orig.). 1983. pap. 6.95 (*0-942908-06-6*) Pancake Pr.

Transformation: The Breakthrough. Whitley Strieber. 288p. 1989. mass mkt. 6.99 (*0-380-70535-4*) Avon.

Transformation: The Poetry of Spiritual Consciousness. Illus. by Bill Arkle. 180p. (C). 1988. pap. 40.00 (*0-947612-28-9*, Pub. by Rivelin Grapheme Pr) St Mut.

Transformation: Understanding the Three Levels of Masculine Consciousness. Robert A. Johnson. LC 89-45560. 128p. 1993. reprint ed. pap. 11.00 (*0-06-250543-2*) Harper SF.

Transformation & Continuity in Revolutionary Ethiopia. Christopher Clapham. (African Studies: No. 61). (Illus.). 304p. 1988. text ed. 75.00 (*0-521-33441-1*) Cambridge U Pr.

Transformation & Continuity in Revolutionary Ethiopia. Christopher Clapham. (African Studies: No. 61). (Illus.). 304p. (C). 1990. pap. 22.95 (*0-521-39650-6*) Cambridge U Pr.

Transformation & Convergence in the Frame of Knowledge: Exploration in the Interrelations of Scientific & Theological Enterprise. Thomas F. Torrance. LC 83-16463. 367p. reprint ed. pap. 104.60 (*0-685-15968-X*, 2027552) Bks Demand.

Transformation & Emerging Markets. George Macesich. LC 96-16273. 144p. 1996. text ed. 52.95 (*0-275-95518-4*, Praeger Pubs) Greenwood.

Transformation & Healing: Sutra on the Four Establishments of Mindfulness. Thich Nhat Hanh. Tr. by Annabel Laity. LC 90-49512. 179p. 1990. per. 10.00 (*0-938077-34-1*) Parallax Pr.

Transformation & Reaction: America, 1921-1945. Glen Jeansonne. LC 93-25508. (C). 1994. text ed. 37.50 (*0-06-500142-7*) Addson-Wesley Educ.

Transformation & Reaction: America 1921-1945. Glen Jeansonne. 204p. reprint ed. pap. 35.00 (*1-886746-44-3*, 93492) Talman.

Transformation & Recovery: A Guide for the Design & Development of Acupuncture-Based Chemical Dependency Treatment Programs. Alex Brumbaugh. 650p. 1994. pap. 39.00 (*0-9639791-0-8*) Stillpoint Pr.

Transformation & Resiliency in Africa. Ed. by Pearl T. Robinson & Elliott P. Skinner. LC 82-23211. 336p. 1982. 21.95 (*0-88258-054-X*) Howard U Pr.

Transformation & Struggle: Cuba Faces the 1990s. Ed. by Sandor Halebsky & John M. Kirk. LC 89-39648. 324p. 1990. text ed. 59.95 (*0-275-93227-3*, C3227, Praeger Pubs); pap. text ed. 21.95 (*0-275-93228-1*, Praeger Pubs) Greenwood.

Transformation & Survival: In Search of Humane World Order. Rajni Kothari. 234p. 1989. 27.50 (*0-945257-17-1*) Apex Pr.

***Transformation & Tradition in the Sciences: Essays in Honor of I. Bernard Cohen.** 592p. 1985. text ed. 85.00 (*0-521-26724-2*) Cambridge U Pr.

Transformation & Trend of Buddhism in the 20th Century. Satchidananda Dhar. 189p. 22.00 (*0-8364-1951-0*, KL Mukhopadhyay) S Asia.

Transformation & Weighting in Regression. R. J. Carroll & D. Ruppert. (Monographs in Statistics & Applied Probability). 300p. (gr. 13). 1988. text ed. 51.95 (*0-412-01421-1*, 9962, Chap & Hall NY) Chapman & Hall.

Transformation Assay of Established Cell Lines: Mechanisms & Application. Ed. by T. Kakunaga & H. Yamasaki. (IARC Scientific Publications: No. 67). (Illus.). 230p. 1986. 40.00 (*0-19-723067-9*) OUP.

Transformation-Associated Cellular p53 Protein. Ed. by George Klein. LC 82-11209. (Advances in Viral Oncology Ser.: No. 2). (Illus.). 152p. 1982. reprint ed. pap. 43.40 (*0-608-00660-2*, 2061248) Bks Demand.

***Transformation-Based Reactive Systems Development: 4th International Amast Workshop on Real-Time Systems & Concurrent & Distributed Software, Arts'97, Palma, Mallorca, Spain, May 21-23, 1997, Proceedings, Vol. 123.** Miquel Bertran & Theodor Rus. LC 97-20858. (Lecture Notes in Computer Science). 1997. pap. write for info. (*3-540-63010-4*) Spr-Verlag.

***Transformation, Cooperation, & Conversion: Proceedings of the NATO Advanced Research Workshop on Scientific & Technical Cooperation of the Baltic States in the New Europe & the Conversion of Their Industry, Vilnius, Lithuania, June 5-8, 1995.** Elmar Altvater & Lithuanian European Institute Staff. Ed. by Kazimiera Prunskiene. LC 96-30326. (NATO ASI Series, Partnership SubSeries 4: Science & Technology Policy). 168p. (C). 1996. lib. bdg. 99.00 (*0-7923-4178-3*) Kluwer Ac.

Transformation des klassischen Seinsverstandnisses: Studien zur Vorgeschichte des Neuzeitlichen Seinsbegriffs im Mittelalter. Rolf Schonberger. (Quellen und Studien zur Philosophie Ser.: Band 21). xii, 423p. 1985. 173.10 (*3-11-010296-X*) De Gruyter.

Transformation Factor. Allerd Stikker. (Chrysalis Bks.). 176p. 1988. pap. 9.95 (*0-916349-56-X*) Amity Hse Inc.

Transformation Factor: Towards an Ecological Consciousness. Allerd Stikker. 176p. 1993. pap. 13.95 (*1-85230-271-2*) Element MA.

Transformation-Fr Landscape. write for info. (*0-8387-5202-0*) Bucknell U Pr.

Transformation from Below: Local Power & the Political Economy of Post-Communist Transitions. Ed. by John Gibson & Philip Hanson. LC 95-42287. (Studies of Communism in Transition). (Illus.). 344p. 1996. 80.00 (*1-85898-122-0*) E Elgar.

Transformation Geometry: An Introduction to Symmetry. G. E. Martin. (Undergraduate Texts in Mathematics Ser.). (Illus.). 240p. 1996. 39.95 (*0-387-90636-3*) Spr-Verlag.

Transformation Groups. Ed. by Katsuo Kawakubo. (Lecture Notes in Mathematics Ser.: Vol. 1375). vii, 394p. 1989. 50.95 (*0-387-51218-7*) Spr-Verlag.

Transformation Groups: De Gruyter Studies in Mathematics, Vol. 8. Tammo D. Tom. x, 312p. 1987. text ed. 82.95 (*3-11-009745-1*) De Gruyter.

Transformation Groups & Algebraic K-Theory. W. A. Luck. (Lecture Notes in Mathematics Ser.: Vol. 1408). xii, 443p. 1989. 73.95 (*0-387-51846-0*) Spr-Verlag.

Transformation Groups in Differential Geometry. S. Kobayashi. LC 94-41257. (Classics in Mathematics Ser.). 1995. 35.00 (*3-540-58659-8*) Spr-Verlag.

Transformation Groups on Manifolds. Ted Petrie & John D. Randall. LC 84-5855. (Monographs & Textbooks in Pure & Applied Mathematics: No. 82). 280p. reprint ed. pap. 79.80 (*0-7837-3384-4*, 2043342) Bks Demand.

Transformation Groups Poznan 1985. Ed. by S. Jackowski & K. Pawalowski. (Lecture Notes in Mathematics Ser.: Vol. 1217). xiv, 396p. 1986. pap. 43.40 (*0-387-16824-9*) Spr-Verlag.

Transformation Imperative: Achieving Market Dominance Through Radical Change. Thomas E. Vollmann. 1996. text ed. 27.95 (*0-07-103675-X*) McGraw.

Transformation in Clinical & Developmental Psychology. Ed. by D. A. Kramer & M. J. Bopp. (Illus.). 270p. 1989. 106.95 (*0-387-96901-2*) Spr-Verlag.

Transformation in Late Eighteenth Century Art. R. Rosenblum. 344p. 1967. text ed. 65.00 (*0-691-03846-5*); pap. text ed. 21.95 (*0-691-00302-5*) Princeton U Pr.

Transformation in Metals. Paul G. Shewmon. 394p. 39.95 (*0-930745-11-6*) Williams Bk Co.

Transformation in Modern Europe. Donaldson. (Australian National University Press Ser.). 1996. pap. text ed. write for info. (*0-08-032843-1*, Pergamon Pr) Elsevier.

Transformation in the Writing: A Case of Surrender-&-Catch. Kurt H. Wolff. LC 94-35596. (Boston Studies in the Philosophy of Science: Vol. 166). 236p. 1995. lib. bdg. 99.00 (*0-7923-3178-8*, Pub. by Klwr Acad Pubs NE) Kluwer Ac.

***Transformation, Livio Vacchini.** Werner Blaser. 168p. 1996. 98.00 (*3-7643-2987-4*) Birkhauser.

Transformation Management in Postcommunist Countries: Organizational Requirements for a Market Economy. Ed. by Refik Nino Culpan & Brij Kumar. LC 94-31461. 272p. 1995. text ed. 65.00 (*0-89930-840-6*, Quorum Bks) Greenwood.

Transformation Methods for Partial Differential Equations. Dominic G. Edelen & Jian-hua Wang. LC 92-9941. 400p. 1992. text ed. 74.00 (*981-02-0933-9*) World Scientific Pub.

Transformation, Miracles, & Mischief: The Mountain Priest Plays of Kyogen. Carolyn A. Morley. (Cornell East Asia Ser.: No. 62). (Illus.). 248p. (Orig.). (C). 1993. pap. 12.00 (*0-939657-62-7*) Cornell East Asia Pgm.

Transformation of a Peasant Economy: Townspeople & Villagers in the Lutterworth Area, 1500-1700. John Goodacre. (Communities, Contexts & Cultures, Leicester Studies in English Local History). (Illus.). 345p. 1994. 84.95 (*1-85928-073-0*, Pub. by Scolar Pr UK) Ashgate Pub Co.

Transformation of Agriculture in the West. David Grigg. (New Perspectives on the Past Ser.). 176p. (C). 1992. pap. text ed. 23.95 (*0-631-17094-4*) Blackwell Pubs.

Transformation of American Capitalism: From Competitive Market Structures to Centralized Private Sector Planning. John R. Munkirs. LC 83-27093. 246p. (gr. 13). 1985. text ed. 42.50 (*0-87332-247-9*); pap. text ed. 29.95 (*0-87332-270-3*) M E Sharpe.

Transformation of American Catholic Sisters. Lora A. Quinonez & Mary D. Turner. (Women in the Political Economy Ser.). (C). 1991. 44.95 (*0-87722-865-5*) Temple U Pr.

Transformation of American Catholic Sisters. Lora A. Quinonez & Mary D. Turner. 224p. 1993. pap. 16.95 (*1-56639-074-5*) Temple U Pr.

Transformation of American Industrial Relations. 2nd ed. Thomas A. Kochan et al. LC 94-34375. 320p. 1994. pap. 19.95 (*0-87546-320-7*, ILR Press) Cornell U Pr.

Transformation of American Law: 1780-1860. Morton J. Horwitz. 384p. 1992. 35.00 (*0-19-507829-2*) OUP.

Transformation of American Law, Seventeen Eighty to Eighteen Sixty. Morton J. Horwitz. LC 76-26500. 384p. 1979. pap. 17.95 (*0-674-90371-4*) HUP.

Transformation of American Law, 1870-1960: The Crisis of Legal Orthodoxy. Morton J. Horwitz. 384p. 1994. reprint ed. pap. 14.95 (*0-19-509259-7*) OUP.

Transformation of American Politics: The New Washington & the Rise of Think Tanks. David M. Ricci. 320p. 1994. pap. 17.00 (*0-300-06123-4*) Yale U Pr.

Transformation of American Politics: The New Washington & the Rise of Washington Think Tanks. David M. Ricci. LC 92-36419. 280p. (C). 1993. text ed. 35.00 (*0-300-05340-1*) Yale U Pr.

Transformation of American Quakerism: Orthodox Friends, 1800-1907. Thomas D. Hamm. LC 86-46236. (Religion in North America Ser.). (Illus.). 288p. 1988. text ed. 31.50 (*0-253-36004-8*) Ind U Pr.

Transformation of American Quakerism: Orthodox Friends, 1800-1907. Thomas D. Hamm. LC 86-46236. (Religion in North America Ser.). (Illus.). 288p. 1992. reprint ed. pap. text ed. 13.95 (*0-253-20718-5*, MB-718) Ind U Pr.

Transformation of an Indian Labor Market: The Case of Pune. Richard D. Lambert et al. LC 86-26900. (University of Pennsylvania Studies on South Asia: No. 3). x, 249p. 1986. 65.00 (*0-915027-63-1*) Benjamins North Am.

Transformation of Anglicanism: From State Church to Global Communion. William L. Sachs. LC 92-11486. 320p. (C). 1993. text ed. 64.95 (*0-521-39143-1*) Cambridge U Pr.

***Transformation of Authorship in America.** Grantland S. Rice. LC 96-43890. 1996. pap. text ed. 17.95 (*0-226-71124-2*) U Ch Pr.

***Transformation of Authorship in America.** Grantland S. Rice. LC 96-43890. 1997. lib. bdg. 42.00 (*0-226-71123-4*) U Ch Pr.

Transformation of Britain 1830-1939. G. E. Mingay. (Making of Britain Ser.). (Illus.). 233p. (C). 1986. 49.95 (*0-7100-9762-X*, RKP) Routledge.

Transformation of British Politics 1860-1995. Brian Harrison. (Illus.). 632p. (C). 1996. pap. 19.95 (*0-19-873121-3*) OUP.

Transformation of British Politics 1860-1995. Brian Harrison. (Illus.). 632p. (C). 1996. 90.00 (*0-19-873122-1*) OUP.

Transformation of Buildings & the City Renaissance 1300-1550: A Graphic Introduction. Howard Saalman. LC 96-86043. (Illus.). xix, 155p. (Orig.). 1996. pap. 24.95 (*1-884470-01-7*) Astrion Pubng.

***Transformation of Capitalist Society.** Zellig S. Harris. LC 96-44876. 256p. 1997. 62.50 (*0-8476-8411-3*); pap. 23.95 (*0-8476-8412-1*) Rowman.

Transformation of Charity in Postrevolutionary New England. Conrad E. Wright. (New England Studies). 384p. 1992. text ed. 50.00 (*1-55553-123-7*) NE U Pr.

Transformation of Cinema, 1907-1915. Eileen Bowser. LC 93-41317. 1994. 17.00 (*0-520-08534-5*) U CA Pr.

Transformation of Consciousness in Myth: Integrating the Thought of Jung & Campbell. John W. Tigue. LC 93-12339. (Reshaping of Psychoanalysis Ser.: Vol. 4). 168p. (C). 1994. text ed. 39.95 (*0-8204-2130-8*) P Lang Pubng.

Transformation of Corporate Control. Neil Fligstein. Date not set. pap. 21.00 (*0-674-90359-5*) HUP.

Transformation of Corporate Control. Neil Fligstein. (Illus.). 391p. 1990. 42.50 (*0-674-90358-7*) HUP.

Transformation of Criminal Justice: Philadelphia, 1800-1880. Allen Steinberg. LC 89-5485. (Studies in Legal History). x, 326p. (C). 1989. text ed. 17.95 (*0-8078-1844-5*) U of NC Pr.

Transformation of Culture: Christian Social Ethics after H. Richard Niebuhr. Charles Scriven. LC 87-33935. 224p. (Orig.). 1988. pap. 10.99 (*0-8361-3101-0*) Andrews Univ Pr.

Transformation of Culture: Christian Social Ethics after H. Richard Niebuhr. Charles Scriven. LC 87-33935. 224p. (Orig.). reprint ed. pap. 63.90 (*0-7837-5109-5*, 2044808) Bks Demand.

Transformation of Democracy. Vilfredo Pareto. Ed. by Charles Powers. Tr. by Renata Girola from ITA. 128p. (Orig.). 1984. pap. 18.95 (*0-87855-949-3*) Transaction Pubs.

Transformation of Dogma: An Introduction to Kark Rahner on Doctrine. Mary E. Hines. 1989. pap. 7.95 (*0-8091-3072-6*) Paulist Pr.

Transformation of Eastern Europe: Joining the European Integration Movement. Jozef M. Van Brabant, pseud. (Illus.). 677p. (C). 1994. lib. bdg. 79.00 (*1-56072-206-1*) Nova Sci Pubs.

***Transformation of Economic Systems in Central Europe.** Herman W. Hoen. 256p. 1998. 70.00 (*1-85898-271-5*) E Elgar.

***Transformation of Egypt.** Mark N. Cooper. LC 82-15317. 282p. 1982. reprint ed. pap. 80.40 (*0-608-03648-X*, 2064474) Bks Demand.

***Transformation of Emily.** Nigel McParr. (Orig.). 1997. mass mkt. 6.50 (*1-56333-519-0*) Masquerade.

Transformation of England: Essays in the Economic & Social History of England in the Eighteenth Century. Peter Mathias. LC 80-10813. 302p. 1980. text ed. 49.50 (*0-231-05046-1*) Col U Pr.

Transformation of European Agriculture in the 19th Century: The Case of the Netherlands. Jan L. Van Zanden. 500p. 1993. pap. text ed. 49.50 (*90-5383-186-X*, Pub. by VU Univ Pr NE) Paul & Co Pubs.

Transformation of European Politics 1763-1848. Paul W. Schroeder. (History of Modern Europe Ser.). 980p. 1994. 59.00 (*0-19-822119-3*) OUP.

***Transformation of European Politics 1763-1848.** Paul W. Schroeder. (Oxford History of Modern Europe Ser.). (Illus.). 916p. 1996. pap. 24.95 (*0-19-820654-2*) OUP.

Transformation of European Social Democracy. Herbert Kitschelt. (Studies in Comparative Politics). (Illus.). 368p. (C). 1994. text ed. 59.95 (*0-521-45106-X*); pap. text ed. 18.95 (*0-521-45715-7*) Cambridge U Pr.

Transformation of Failure: A Critical Analysis of Character Presentation in the Novels of Wolfgang Koeppen. Carole Hanbidge. LC 83-48752. (American University Studies: Germanic Languages & Literature: Ser. I, Vol. 25). 283p. (Orig.). (C). 1983. pap. text ed. 25.80 (*0-8204-0047-5*) P Lang Pubng.

Transformation of Family Law: State, Law, & Family in the United States & Western Europe. Mary A. Glendon. LC 88-31842. (Illus.). 336p. 1989. 34.95 (*0-226-29969-4*) U Ch Pr.

Transformation of Family Law: State, Law, & Family in the United States & Western Europe. Mary A. Glendon. xvi, 320p. 1996. pap. text ed. 16.95 (*0-226-29970-8*) U Ch Pr.

Transformation of Firms & Markets: A Network Approach to Economic Transformation Processes in East Germany. Horst Albach. (Studia Oeconomiae Negotiorum: No. 34). (Illus.). 114p. (Orig.). 1994. pap. 36.50 (*91-554-3236-0*) Coronet Bks.

Transformation of German Academic Medicine, 1750-1820. Thomas H. Broman. (Cambridge History of Medicine Ser.). 256p. (C). 1996. text ed. 54.95 (*0-521-55231-1*) Cambridge U Pr.

Transformation of Hera: A Study of Ritual, Hero, & the Goddess in the Iliad. Joan V. O'Brien. LC 92-37157. (Greek Studies: Interdisciplinary Approaches). 240p. (Orig.). (C). 1993. pap. text ed. 23.95 (*0-8476-7808-3*) Rowman.

Transformation of Hera: A Study of Ritual, Hero, & the Goddess in the Iliad. Joan V. O'Brien. LC 92-37157. (Greek Studies: Interdisciplinary Approaches). 240p. (Orig.). (C). 1993. lib. bdg. 58.00 (*0-8476-7807-5*) Rowman.

Transformation of Higher Learning, 1860-1930: Expansion, Diversification, Social Opening & Professionalization in England, Germany, Russia & the United States. Ed. by Konrad H. Jarausch. LC 82-17629. 376p. (C). 1983. 36.00 (*0-226-39367-4*) U Ch Pr.

Transformation of Human Diploid Fibroblasts. Ed. by Milo. 304p. 1990. 202.00 (*0-8493-4956-7*, RC268) CRC Pr.

Transformation of Human Epithelial Cells. Milo. 336p. 1992. 206.00 (*0-8493-6382-9*, RC280) CRC Pr.

Transformation of Intellectual Life in Victorian England. T. W. Heyck. LC 89-123150. 262p. (C). 1989. reprint ed. pap. text ed. 23.95 (*0-925065-22-6*) Lyceum IL.

Transformation of Intimacy: Sexuality, Love, & Eroticism in Modern Societies. Anthony Giddens. LC 92-80406. 212p. (C). 1992. 35.00 (*0-8047-2090-8*) Stanford U Pr.

Transformation of Intimacy: Sexuality, Love, & Eroticism in Modern Societies. Anthony Giddens. 212p. (C). 1993. pap. 12.95 (*0-8047-2214-5*) Stanford U Pr.

Transformation of Italian Communism. Leonard Weinberg. LC 94-8721. 170p. (C). 1994. 34.95 (*1-56000-180-1*) Transaction Pubs.

Transformation of Job: A Tale of the High Sierras. Frederick V. Fisher. LC 70-137729. (American Fiction Reprint Ser.). 1977. 17.95 (*0-8369-7028-4*) Ayer.

Transformation of John Foster Dulles: From Prophet of Realism to Priest of Nationalism. Mark G. Toulouse. LC 85-10467. (Illus.). xii, 278p. 1985. 29.95 (*0-86554-160-4*, MUP-H150) Mercer Univ Pr.

Transformation of Judaism from Philosophy to Religion. Jacob Neusner. 368p. 1992. text ed. 34.95 (*0-252-01805-2*) U of Ill Pr.

Transformation of Liberalism in Late Nineteenth-Century Mexico. Charles A. Hale. (American History, Literature & Religion Ser.). 296p. (C). 1990. text ed. 47.50 (*0-691-07814-9*) Princeton U Pr.

Transformation of Libido: A Seminar on Jung's Symbols of Transformation. Edward F. Edinger. 80p. 1994. pap. 12.00 (*0-9642221-0-8*) C G Jung Bkstore.

Transformation of Man. rev. ed. Rosemary Haughton. 288p. 1980. pap. 14.95 (*0-87243-102-9*) Templegate.

Transformation of Man: A Blueprint for Creative Living. George A. Jones. vii, 65p. (Orig.). 1975. 5.00 (*0-89142-015-0*); pap. 2.00 (*0-89142-016-9*) Sant Bani Ash.

Transformation of Management. Mike Davidson. LC 95-25906. 256p. 1996. 28.95 (*0-7506-9774-1*) Buttrwrth-Heinemann.

An Asterisk (*) at the beginning of an entry indicates that the title is appearing in BIP for the first time.

Transformation of Management. Mike Davidson. 256p. 1996. pap. 17.95 (*0-7506-9814-4*) Buttrwrth-Heinemann.

*****Transformation of Meaning in Psychological Therapies: Integrating Theory & Practice.** Michael J. Power & Chris Brewin. LC 96-48034. 1997. pap. write for info. (*0-471-97005-0*) Wiley.

*****Transformation of Meaning in the Psychological Therapies: Reconciling Theory & Practice.** Mick Power & Chris Brewin. LC 96-48034. (Clinical Psychology Ser.). 1997. text ed. 65.00 (*0-471-95826-3*) Wiley.

Transformation of Mexican Agriculture: International Structure & the Politics of Rural Change. Steven E. Sanderson. LC 85-42701. 304p. 1986. pap. text ed. 17.95 (*0-691-02239-9*) Princeton U Pr.

*****Transformation of Modern France.** William B. Cohen. 256p. (C). 1996. pap. text ed. 24.36 (*0-669-41678-9*) HM College Div.

Transformation of Moravian Bethlehem: From Communal Mission to Family Economy. Beverly P. Smaby. LC 88-26128. (Illus.). 290p. (C). 1988. text ed. 41.95 (*0-8122-8130-6*) U of Pa Pr.

Transformation of Myth Through Time. Joseph Campbell. 263p. 1991. reprint ed. lib. bdg. 47.00 (*0-8095-9133-2*) Borgo Pr.

Transformation of Natural Philosophy: The Case of Philip Melanchthon. Sachiko Kusukawa. (Ideas in Context Ser.: No. 34). (Illus.). 272p. (C). 1995. text ed. 59.95 (*0-521-47347-0*) Cambridge U Pr.

Transformation of Nature in Art. Ananda K. Coomaraswamy. 1937. pap. 6.95 (*0-486-20368-9*) Dover.

Transformation of Nature in Art. Ananda K. Coomaraswamy. (C). 1994. text ed. 16.00 (*81-215-0325-6*, Pub. by Munshiram Manoharial II) S Asia.

Transformation of Nature in Art. Ed. by Kapila Vatsyayan. (C). 1995. 30.00 (*81-207-1643-4*, Pub. by Sterling Plns Pvt II) S Asia.

Transformation of New Deal Liberalism. Alan Brinkley. LC 94-21478. 1995. 27.50 (*0-394-53573-1*) Knopf.

Transformation of Nicaragua, 1519-1548. Dan Stanislawski. LC 82-49326. (University of California Publications: No. 54). 170p. 1983. pap. 48.50 (*0-7837-8430-9*, 2049232) Bks Demand.

Transformation of Old Age Security: Class & Politics in the American Welfare State. Jill S. Quadagno. (Illus.). 270p. 1988. 35.95 (*0-226-69923-4*) U Ch Pr.

Transformation of Organometallics into Common & Exotic Materials: Design & Activation. Ed. by Richard M. Laine. (C). 1988. lib. bdg. 157.50 (*90-247-3661-7*) Kluwer Ac.

Transformation of Plants & Soil Microorganisms. Ed. by Kan Wang et al. (Plant & Microbial Biotechnology Research Ser.: No. 3). (Illus.). 230p. (C). 1995. text ed. 90.00 (*0-521-45089-6*) Cambridge U Pr.

Transformation of Political Culture: Massachusetts Parties, 1790s-1840s. Ronald P. Formisano. (Illus.). 510p. 1984. pap. 18.95 (*0-19-503509-7*) OUP.

Transformation of Political Culture in Cuba. Richard R. Fagen. LC 77-83117. (Illus.). xii, 270p. 1969. reprint ed. 39.50 (*0-8047-0702-2*); reprint ed. pap. 12.95 (*0-8047-0814-2*) Stanford U Pr.

Transformation of Property Rights in the Gold Coast: An Empirical Analysis Applying Rational Choice Theory. Kathryn Firmin-Sellers. (Political Economy of Institutions & Decisions Ser.). (Illus.). 150p. (C). 1996. text ed. 54.95 (*0-521-55503-5*) Cambridge U Pr.

Transformation of Rage: Mourning & Creativity in George Eliot's Fiction. Peggy F. Johnstone. (Literature & Psychoanalysis Ser.). 224p. (C). 1994. 45.00 (*0-8147-4194-0*) NYU Pr.

*****Transformation of Rage: Mourning & Creativity in George Eliot's Fiction.** Peggy F. Johnstone. (Literature & Psychoanalysis Ser.). 1997. pap. text ed. 20.00 (*0-8147-4235-1*) NYU Pr.

Transformation of Railroad Stations. Louis K. Loewenstein. (Railway History Monograph). (Illus.). 20p. 1992. pap. 9.00 (*0-916170-43-8*) J-B Pub.

Transformation of Rhode Island, 1790-1860. Peter J. Coleman. LC 84-27932. xiv, 314p. 1985. reprint ed. text ed. 69.50 (*0-313-24796-X*, COTR, Greenwood Pr) Greenwood.

Transformation of Rural Life: Southern Illinois, 1890-1990. Jane Adams. LC 94-4176. (Studies in Rural Culture). (Illus.). 352p. 1994. pap. text ed. 19.95 (*0-8078-4479-9*); lib. bdg. 49.95 (*0-8078-2168-3*) U of NC Pr.

*****Transformation of Rural Mexico: Reforming the Ejido Sector.** Ed. by Wayne A. Cornelius & David Myhre. 1997. pap. write for info. (*1-878367-31-5*) UCSD Ctr US-Mex.

Transformation of Rural Scotland: Social Change & the Agrarian Economy, 1660-1815. T. M. Devine. LC 94-184650. 275p. 1994. 65.00 (*0-7486-0452-9*, Pub. by Edinburgh U Pr UK) Col U Pr.

Transformation of Science & Technology into Productive Power, 2 vols., Set. Ed. by Li Ming. 2119p. 1991. 620.00 (*0-7484-0004-4*, Pub. by Tay Francis Ltd UK) Taylor & Francis.

Transformation of Security of the Asia-Pacific Region. Ed. by Desmond Ball. LC 95-20638. (Illus.). 220p. (C). 1996. 39.50 (*0-7146-4661-X*, Pub. by F Cass Pubs UK); pap. 19.50 (*0-7146-4190-1*, Pub. by F Cass Pubs UK) Intl Spec Bk.

Transformation of Sikh Society. Ethne K. Marenco. 342p. 1976. 24.95 (*0-318-36785-8*) Asia Bk Corp.

Transformation of Sikh Society. Ethne K. Marenco. (Illus.). 342p. 1972. pap. 16.95 (*0-913244-08-2*) Hapi Pr.

Transformation of Sin: Studies in Donne, Herbert, Vaughan & Traherne. Patrick Grant. LC 73-93174. 254p. reprint ed. pap. 72.40 (*0-317-26444-3*, 2023850) Bks Demand.

Transformation of South Korea: Reform & Reconstitution in the Sixth Republic under Roe Tae Woo, 1987-1992. Robert E. Bedeski. LC 93-30537. 208p. (C). 1994. pap. 16.95 (*0-415-10604-4*, Routledge NY) Routledge.

Transformation of South Korea: Reform & Reconstitution in the Sixth Republic under Roe Tae Woo, 1987-1992. Robert E. Bedeski. LC 93-30537. 208p. (C). (gr. 13). 1994. text ed. 79.95 (*0-415-05750-7*, Routledge NY) Routledge.

Transformation of Southern Politics: Social Change & Political Consequence since 1945. Jack Bass & Walter DeVries. LC 95-2855. 544p. 1995. pap. 25.00 (*0-8203-1728-4*) U of Ga Pr.

*****Transformation of the Agri-Food System in Central & Eastern Europe & the New Independent States.** J. E. Hobbs et al. 384p. 1997. 100.00 (*0-85199-176-9*, Pub. by CAB Intntl UK) OUP.

Transformation of the American Economy, 1865-1914: An Essay in Interpretation. Robert Higgs. LC 74-165949. (Wiley Series in American Economic History). (Illus.). 158p. reprint ed. pap. 45.10 (*0-7837-3493-X*, 2057826) Bks Demand.

Transformation of the American Manufacturing Paradigm. P. Timothy Bushnell. LC 94-487. (Studies on Industrial Productivity). 296p. 1994. text ed. 49.00 (*0-8153-1530-9*) Garland.

Transformation of the Avant-Garde: The New York Art World, 1940-1985. Diana Crane. LC 87-5013. (Illus.). x, 204p. (C). 1989. pap. text ed. 13.95 (*0-226-11790-1*) U Ch Pr.

Transformation of the Banking Industry. Business Communications Co., Inc. Staff. 214p. 1990. 2,450.00 (*0-89336-661-7*, G-113B) BCC.

Transformation of the Christian Right. Matthew C. Moen. LC 91-31447. 224p. 1992. text ed. 26.95 (*0-8173-0574-2*) U of Ala Pr.

Transformation of the Communist Economies: Against the Mainstream. Ed. by Chang Ha-Joon & Peter Nolan. LC 94-30590. 1995. text ed. 75.00 (*0-312-12323-X*) St Martin.

Transformation of the Decline & Fall of the Roman Empire. David Womersley. (Cambridge Studies in Eighteenth Century English Literature & Thought: No. 1). 320p. 1988. text ed. 69.95 (*0-521-35036-0*) Cambridge U Pr.

Transformation of the English Cultural Ethos in Colonial America: Maryland 1634-1720. Michal J. Rozbicki. LC 88-14399. 232p. (C). 1988. lib. bdg. 41.50 (*0-8191-7048-8*) U Pr of Amer.

Transformation of the English Novel, 1890-1930. Daniel R. Schwarz. 224p. 1989. text ed. 39.95 (*0-312-02371-5*) St Martin.

Transformation of the English Novel, 1890-1930 Vol. 1. Daniel R. Schwarz. 1995. text ed. 18.95 (*0-312-12283-7*) St Martin.

*****Transformation of the French Demographic Landscape, 1806-1906.** Noel Bonneuil. 232p. 1997. 55.00 (*0-19-823340-X*) OUP.

Transformation of the God Image. Edward Edinger. pap. 16.00 (*0-919123-55-4*, Pub. by Inner City CN) BookWorld Dist.

Transformation of the Heart: Stories By Devotees of Sathya Sai Baba. Compiled by Judy Warner. LC 89-77667. 200p. (Orig.). 1990. pap. 9.95 (*0-87728-716-3*) Weiser.

Transformation of the Hummingbird: Cultural Roots of a Zinacantecan Mythical Poem. Eva Hunt. LC 76-12909. (Symbol, Myth & Ritual Ser.). (Illus.). 417p. 1977. 45.00 (*0-8014-1022-3*) Cornell U Pr.

Transformation of the Inner Man. John Sandford & Paula Sandford. LC 82-72007. 432p. 1982. reprint ed. pap. 10.95 (*0-932081-13-4*) Victory Hse.

Transformation of the Japanese Economy. Ed. by Kazuo Sato. 352p. (gr. 13). 1998. text ed. 64.95 (*1-56324-775-5*, East Gate Bk) M E Sharpe.

Transformation of the Japanese Economy. Ed. by Kazuo Sato. 352p. (gr. 13). 1998. pap. text ed. 24.95 (*1-56324-776-3*, East Gate Bk) M E Sharpe.

Transformation of the Jews. Calvin Goldscheider & Alan S. Zuckerman. LC 84-198. (Chicago Studies in the History of Judaism). xii, 292p. (C). 1986. pap. text ed. 13.95 (*0-226-30148-6*) U Ch Pr.

*****Transformation of the Roman World: AD 400-900.** Ed. by Leslie Webster & Michelle Brown. LC 96-50246. (Illus.). 1997. pap. 25.00 (*0-520-21060-3*) U CA Pr.

Transformation of the School: Progressivism in American Education, 1876-1957. Lawrence A. Cremin. 1964. pap. text ed. 5.95 (*0-07-553704-4*) McGraw.

Transformation of the School: Progressivism in American Education 1876-1957. Lawrence A. Cremin. 1964. pap. 9.56 (*0-394-70519-X*) Random.

Transformation of the U. S. Senate. Barbara Sinclair. LC 88-46070. 240p. 1989. text ed. 45.00 (*0-8018-3766-9*) Johns Hopkins.

Transformation of the U. S. Senate. Barbara Sinclair. LC 88-46070. 248p. 1990. reprint ed. pap. text ed. 14.95 (*0-8018-4110-0*) Johns Hopkins.

Transformation of the Woman Suffrage Movement: The Case of Illinois, 1850-1920. Steven M. Buechler. (Douglass Series on Women's Lives & the Meaning of Gender). 280p. (C). 1986. text ed. 35.00 (*0-8135-1131-3*) Rutgers U Pr.

Transformation of the World Economy: New Directions & New Interests. Tamas Szentes. LC 88-31887. 144p. (C). 1988. pap. 15.00 (*0-86232-727-X*, Pub. by Zed Bks Ltd UK); text ed. 49.95 (*0-86232-726-1*, Pub. by Zed Bks Ltd UK) Humanities.

Transformation of the Year One Thousand: The Village of Lournand from Antiquity to Feudalism. Guy Bois. Tr. by Jean Birrell. LC 92-1488. 1992. text ed. 79.95 (*0-7190-3565-1*, Pub. by Manchester Univ Pr UK); text ed. 24.95 (*0-7190-3566-X*, Pub. by Manchester Univ Pr UK) St Martin.

*****Transformation of Theology, 1830-1890: Positivism & Protestant Thought in Britain & America.** Charles D. Cashdollar. LC 88-25442. 501p. 1989. reprint ed. pap. 142.80 (*0-608-03305-7*, 2064017) Bks Demand.

Transformation of Threadneedle Street: The Deregulation & Reregulation of Britain's Financial Services. James J. Fishman. LC 92-73987. 316p. 1993. 45.00 (*0-89089-517-1*) Carolina Acad Pr.

Transformation of Urban Housing: The Experience of Upgrading in Cartagena. Wolfgang P. Strassmann. LC 81-48176. 239p. reprint ed. pap. 68.20 (*0-7837-4268-1*, 2043960) Bks Demand.

Transformation of Virginia, 1740-1790. Rhys Isaac. LC 81-10393. (Institute of Early American History & Culture Ser.). xxxii, 451p. 1982. 45.50 (*0-8078-1489-X*) U of NC Pr.

Transformation of Virginia, 1740-1790. Rhys Isaac. (C). 1988. pap. text ed. 12.95 (*0-393-95693-8*) Norton.

Transformation of Wall Street: A History of the Securities & Exchange Commission & Modern Corporate Finance. rev. ed. Joel Seligman. LC 95-13762. 1995. text ed. 75.00 (*1-55553-231-4*) NE U Pr.

Transformation of War. Martin L. Van Creveld. 256p. 1991. 29.95 (*0-02-933155-2*, Free Press) Free Pr.

Transformation of Western Europe. William Wallace. LC 90-34196. (Chatham House Papers). 148p. 1990. pap. 14.95 (*0-87609-084-6*) Coun Foreign.

Transformation of Western Pennsylvania, 1770-1800. Robert E. Harper. LC 90-28574. (Social & Labor History Ser.). 288p. 1991. 49.95 (*0-8229-3678-X*) U of Pittsburgh Pr.

Transformation of Work? Ed. by Stephen Wood. 384p. 1989. 55.00 (*0-04-445356-6*); pap. 22.95 (*0-04-445357-4*) Routledge Chapman & Hall.

Transformation of Work. Ed. by Stephen Wood. 384p. (C). 1989. pap. 22.95 (*0-415-07869-5*, Routledge NY) Routledge.

Transformation of Your Life in Twenty-Four Hours. Brown Landone. 16p. 1976. reprint ed. spiral bd. 4.50 (*0-7873-0531-6*) Hlth Research.

Transformation Process in Joyce's Ulysses. Elliott B. Gose. LC 80-506247. 248p. reprint ed. pap. 70.70 (*0-8357-8355-3*, 2034031) Bks Demand.

Transformation Thinking. Joyce Wycoff. Ed. by Tim Richardson. 304p. (Orig.). 1995. pap. 12.00 (*0-425-14374-0*, Berkley Trade) Berkley Pub.

Transformation Through Birth: A Woman's Guide. Claudia Panuthos. LC 83-15559. (Illus.). 208p. 1984. pap. text ed. 14.95 (*0-89789-038-8*, Bergin & Garvey) Greenwood.

Transformation Through Bodywork: Using Touch Therapy to Find Inner Peace. Dan Menkin. (Illus.). 252p. (Orig.). 1996. pap. 16.00 (*1-879181-34-7*) Bear & Co.

Transformation Through Flowers: Spiritual & Physical Healing. Kathleen Lemler. (Illus.). 128p. (Orig.). 1993. pap. 5.95 (*0-9635987-0-8*) Express of Nature.

*****Transformation Through Insight: Enneatypes in Clinical Practice.** Claudio Naranjo. LC 97-1010. 450p. (Orig.). 1997. pap. 24.95 (*0-934252-73-4*) Hohm Pr.

Transformation Through Menopause. Marian Van Eyck McCain. LC 91-12685. 200p. 1991. text ed. 49.95 (*0-89789-268-2*, H268, Bergin & Garvey) Greenwood.

Transformation Through Menopause. Marian Van Eyck McCain. 200p. 1991. pap. text ed. 12.95 (*0-89789-269-0*, Bergin & Garvey) Greenwood.

Transformation Toughening of Ceramics. David J. Green et al. LC 88-25805. 256p. 1989. 139.00 (*0-8493-6594-5*, TA455, CRC Reprint) Franklin.

Transformation with Industrialization in Peninsular Malaysia. Ed. by Harold Brookfield. (South-East Asian Social Science Monographs). (Illus.). 320p. (C). 1994. 60.00 (*967-65-3030-1*, 8940) OUP.

Transformation Workbook: Colour Healing & Yoga. Pauline Wills & Theodore Gimbel. (Illus.). 224p. (Orig.). 1992. pap. 27.50 (*0-572-01599-2*, Pub. by W Foulsham UK) Trans-Atl Phila.

Transformational Analysis of the Syntax of Aelfric's "Lives of the Saints" J. A. Johnson. (Janua Linguarum, Series Practica: No. 212). 1975. pap. text ed. 32.35 (*90-279-3084-8*) Mouton.

Transformational & Structural Morphology: In Defense of Structuralism. Alphonse Juilland. (Stanford French & Italian Studies: No. 5). vi, 78p. 1978. pap. 46.50 (*0-915838-33-8*) Anma Libri.

Transformational Breathwork: The Basics of Renewal & Rebirth. Patricia Price. 100p. (Orig.). 1989. pap. text ed. 6.50 (*0-926625-88-8*) Trilogy Pubns.

Transformational Dreaming. Jill Morris. 1996. mass mkt. 5.99 (*0-449-22362-0*) Fawcett.

Transformational Grammar: A First Course. Andrew Radford. (Cambridge Textbooks in Linguistics Ser.). 600p. 1988. pap. text ed. 29.95 (*0-521-34750-5*) Cambridge U Pr.

Transformational Grammar: Essays for the Left Hand. James W. Ney. (Edward Sapir Monograph Ser. in Language, Culture & Cognition: No. 16). vi, 169p. (Orig.). 1988. pap. 24.00 (*0-933104-26-X*) Jupiter Pr.

Transformational Grammar & the Rumanian Language. Ed. by S. Alexandrescu. 97p. (Orig.). 1977. pap. 12.00 (*90-316-0144-6*) Benjamins North Am.

Transformational Grammar & Written Sentences. Marianna W. Davis. (Janua Linguarum, Series Didactica: No. 2). 1973. pap. text ed. 33.85 (*90-279-2384-1*) Mouton.

Transformational Grammar of Russian Adjectives. Leonard H. Babby. LC 73-83929. (Janua Linguarum, Ser. Practica: No. 235). 242p. (C). 1975. pap. text ed. 75.40 (*90-279-3022-8*) Mouton.

Transformational Growth & Effective Demand: Economics after the Capital Critique. Edward J. Nell. 675p. (C). 1991. 100.00 (*0-8147-5769-3*) NYU Pr.

*****Transformational Growth & the Business Cycle.** Edward J. Nell. LC 96-50075. 272p. (C). 1997. text ed. write for info. (*0-415-14855-3*) Routledge.

Transformational Leader. Noel M. Tichy & Mary A. Devanna. 306p. 1990. pap. text ed. 19.95 (*0-471-62334-2*) Wiley.

Transformational Leadership. Phillip V. Lewis. 256p. (Orig.). 1996. pap. 19.99 (*0-8054-1239-5*, 4212-39) Broadman.

Transformational Leadership: Renewing Fundamental Values & Achieving New Relationships in Health Care. Ed. by Eric B. Linne et al. LC 95-35494. 303p. 1995. pap. 40.00 (*1-55648-144-6*, 001116) AHPI.

Transformational Leadership in Government. Jerry W. Koehler & Joseph M. Pankowski. (Illus.). 175p. 1996. 39.95 (*1-57444-030-6*) St Lucie Pr.

Transformational Leadership in Nursing. Ed. by Ann Marriner-Tomey. LC 92-15283. 197p. (C). (gr. 13). 1992. pap. text ed. 36.00 (*0-8016-6875-1*) Mosby Yr Bk.

Transformational Learning: Renewing Your Company Through Knowledge & Skills. Daniel R. Tobin. LC 95-39107. 304p. 1996. text ed. 29.95 (*0-471-13289-6*) Wiley.

Transformational Learning: Renewing Your Company Through People & Knowledge. Daniel R. Tobin. 300p. 1995. 30.00 (*0-939246-81-3*) Wiley.

Transformational Mentoring. Julie Hay. LC 95-22721. 1995. write for info. (*0-07-707627-3*) McGraw.

Transformational Nursing Leadership: A Vision for the Future. Anne M. Barker. 288p. (C). 1992. reprint ed. pap. text ed. 26.95 (*0-88737-551-0*, 15-2473) Natl League Nurse.

*****Transformational Reiki: Trans-Reiki.** Karyn Mitchell. 250p. (Orig.). 1997. pap. 19.96 (*0-9640822-6-8*) Mind Rivers.

Transformational Syntax: The Grammar of Modern American English. Baxter Hathaway. LC 67-11889. 327p. reprint ed. pap. 93.20 (*0-317-09517-X*, 2012465) Bks Demand.

Transformational Syntax & Model Theoretic Semantics. James McCloskey. (Synthese Language Library: No. 9). 1979. pap. text ed. 44.00 (*90-277-1026-0*); lib. bdg. 100.50 (*90-277-1025-2*) Kluwer Ac.

Transformational Tarot. Arnell Ando. 96p. 1995. pap. 24.95 (*0-9649386-3-4*) Ink Well.

Transformational Tarot. Shirley Gotthold. (Illus.). 1995. boxed 49.95 (*0-9644672-0-8*) Foolscap Pr.

Transformational Tarot: An Appropriate Tool for a Time of Transition. Shirley Gotthold. (Illus.). 180p. 1995. pap. 22.95 (*0-9644672-1-6*) Foolscap Pr.

Transformational Tarot: The 100-Card Deck. Illus. by Peggy Gotthold. 1995. boxed 29.95 (*0-9644672-2-4*) Foolscap Pr.

*****Transformations.** W. R. Bion. Date not set. pap. 30.00 (*1-56821-864-8*) Aronson.

Transformations. Wilfred R. Bion. LC 84-45130. 192p. 1983. 25.00 (*0-87668-723-0*) Aronson.

*****Transformations.** T. Cochran & J. Zaleski. Date not set. 3.99 (*0-517-17626-2*) Random Hse Value.

*****Transformations.** John Nelson. 304p. 1997. pap. 12.95 (*1-57174-077-5*) Hampton Roads Pub Co.

Transformations. Anne Sexton. 1972. pap. 11.95 (*0-395-12722-X*) HM.

Transformations. Time-Life Books Editors. Ed. by Jim Hicks. (Mysteries of the Unknown Ser.). (Illus.). 144p. 1989. 14.95 (*0-8094-6364-4*); lib. bdg. write for info. (*0-8094-6365-2*) Time-Life.

Transformations: Art & Society in the Modern Era. Lou A. Culley. 256p. (C). 1992. per., pap. text ed. 35.64 (*0-8403-8367-3*) Kendall-Hunt.

Transformations: Awakening to the Sacred in Ourselves. Tracy Cochran & Jeff Zaleski. 208p. 1995. 21.00 (*0-517-70150-2*) Random Hse Value.

Transformations: Countertransference During the Psychoanalytic Treatment of Incest, Real & Imagined. Elaine V. Siegel. 216p. 1996. 32.50 (*0-88163-117-5*) Analytic Pr.

Transformations: Critical & Speculative Essays on Art. Roger E. Fry. LC 68-14904. (Essay Index Reprint Ser.). 1977. 35.95 (*0-8369-0464-8*) Ayer.

Transformations: Migration, Family Life, & Achievement Motivation among Latino Adolescents. Carola Suarez-Orozco & Marcelo Suarez-Orozco. 334p. 45.00 (*0-8047-2550-0*); pap. 16.95 (*0-8047-2551-9*) Stanford U Pr.

Transformations: Recollective Imagination & Sexual Difference. Drucilla Cornell. 264p. (C). 1993. pap. 16.95 (*0-415-90747-0*, B0259, Routledge NY) Routledge.

Transformations: The Next Step. John Nelson. 280p. 1988. pap. 8.95 (*0-89865-549-8*) Hampton Roads Pub Co.

Transformations Administration Guide. Center for Occupational Research & Development Staff. 275p. 1992. pap. text ed. 49.50 (*1-55502-466-1*) CORD Commns.

Transformations & Texts: G. B. Shaw's "Buoyant Billions" Steven Joyce. (ENGL Ser.: Vol. 8). (Illus.). xiv, 136p. 1991. 55.00 (*0-938100-94-7*) Camden Hse.

Transformations & Their Use in the Resolution of Syntactic Homomorphy, Prepositional of Constructions in Contemporary Standard Russian. D. Barton Johnson. (Janua Linguarum, Ser. Practica: No. 95). (Orig.). 1970. pap. text ed. 59.25 (*90-279-1525-3*) Mouton.

Transformations East & West: The New Industrial Structures. Ed. by Michael A. Gurdon & Ronald Savitt. 65p. (Orig.). (C). 1993. pap. text ed. write for info. (0-944799-02-7) U VT Schl Busn Admin.

Transformations I: 1973-74. Ellen Lanyon. 1977. pap. 12.50 (0-89439-005-8) Printed Matter.

Transformations in American Medicine: From Benjamin Rush to William Osler. Lester S. King. LC 90-4662. 256p. 1990. text ed. 44.00 (0-8018-4057-0) Johns Hopkins.

Transformations in Cleveland Art, 1796-1946: Community & Diversity in Early Modern America. William Robinson & David Steinberg. LC 96-11969. (Illus.). 304p. 1996. pap. 29.95 (0-940717-33-6); text ed. 50.00 (0-940717-34-4) Cleveland Mus Art.

Transformations in Consciousness: The Metaphysics & Epistemology. Franklin Merrell-Wolff. LC 95-13896. 326p. (C). 1995. pap. 19.95 (0-7914-2676-9); text ed. 59.50 (0-7914-2675-0) State U NY Pr.

Transformations in Design: A Formal Approach to Stylistic Change & Innovation in the Visual Arts. Terry W. Knight. LC 92-23445. (Illus.). 288p. (C). 1994. text ed. 95.00 (0-521-38460-5) Cambridge U Pr.

Transformations in French Business: Political, Economic, & Cultural Changes from 1981-1987. Ed. by Judith G. Frommer & Janice McCormick. LC 88-18506. 207p. 1989. text ed. 65.00 (0-89930-387-0, FND/, Quorum Bks) Greenwood.

*Transformations in Global & Organizational Systems: Changing Boundaries in the 90s (Proceedings of the 10th Scientific Meeting of the A. K. Rice Institute) Ed. by Solomon Cytrynbaum & Susan A. Lee. LC 93-84339. 170p. 1993. 28.00 (0-614-19469-5) Rice Inst.

Transformations in Irish Culture. Luke Gibbons. LC 96-11708. (Critical Conditions Ser.). (C). 1996. pap. text ed. 20.00 (0-268-01893-6) U of Notre Dame Pr.

Transformations in Literature & Film: Selected Papers from the Sixth Annual Florida State University Conference on Literature & Film. Ed. by Leon Golden. LC 82-20195. 114p. 1982. pap. 14.95 (0-8130-0744-5) U Press Fla.

Transformations in Personhood & Culture: The Languages of History, Aesthetics, & Ethics. Ed. by Christie McDonald & Gary Wihl. LC 93-23859. (Literature & Philosophy Ser.). (Illus.). 224p. (C). 1994. 35.00 (0-271-01010-X); pap. 16.95 (0-271-01011-8) Pa St U Pr.

Transformations in Slavery: A History of Slavery in Africa. Paul E. Lovejoy. LC 82-1284. (African Studies: No. 36). (Illus.). 336p. 1983. pap. text ed. 24.95 (0-521-28646-8) Cambridge U Pr.

*Transformations in Social Security Systems. (International Institute of Administrative Sciences Monographs: No. 3). 140p. Date not set. pap. 50.00 (90-5199-338-2) IOS Press.

Transformations in the Global Political Economy. Ed. by Dennis C. Pirages & Christine Sylvester. LC 89-28541. (International Political Economy Ser.). 236p. 1990. text ed. 49.95 (0-312-04075-X) St Martin.

Transformations into Color: The Art of Stan Brodsky. Judy K. Collischan Van Wagner. LC 90-85139. (Illus.). 32p. (Orig.). 1991. pap. text ed. 8.00 (1-879195-06-2) Heckscher Mus.

Transformations of Circe: The History of an Enchantress. Judith Yarnall. LC 93-14024. (Illus.). 224p. 1994. text ed. 39.95 (0-252-02063-4); pap. text ed. 14.95 (0-252-06356-2) U of Ill Pr.

Transformations of Consciousness: Conventional & Contemplative Perspectives on Development. Ken Wilber et al. LC 85-2486. 325p. (Orig.). 1986. pap. 30.00 (0-394-74202-8) Shambhala Pubns.

Transformations of Godot. Frederick Busi. LC 79-4002. 160p. 1980. 17.00 (0-8131-1392-X) U Pr of Ky.

*Transformations of Language in Modern Dystopias. David W. Sisk. LC 97-9378. (Contributions to the Study of Science Fiction & Fantasy: Vol. 75). 1997. text ed. write for info. (0-313-30411-4, Greenwood Pr) Greenwood.

Transformations of Man. Lewis Mumford. 1990. 22.00 (0-8446-4590-7) Peter Smith.

Transformations of Myth Through Time. PBS Adult Learning Service Staff. (Illus.). 496p. (C). 1989. teacher ed. write for info. (0-15-592337-4); pap. text ed. 20.00 (0-15-592335-8); Study guide, 183 pgs. student ed., pap. text ed. 18.00 (0-15-592336-6) HB Coll Pubs.

Transformations of Myths Through Time. Joseph Campbell. LC 89-45788. 270p. (Orig.). 1990. pap. 19.00 (0-06-096463-4, PL) HarpC.

Transformations of the American Party System: Political Coalitions from the New Deal to the 1970's. Everett C. Ladd, Jr. & Charles D. Hadley. (Illus.). 371p. (C). 1975. pap. text ed. 6.95 (0-393-09203-8) Norton.

Transformations of the Animal World: Being the Authorized Translation of "Les Transformations Du Monde Animal. Charles Deperet. Ed. by Stephen J. Gould. LC 79-8330. (History of Paleontology Ser.). 1980. reprint ed. lib. bdg. 35.95 (0-405-12711-1) Ayer.

Transformations of the Court Style: Gothic Art in Europe 1270-1330. Brown University, Department of Art Staff. LC 77-70260. (Illus.). 163p. (Orig.). 1977. pap. text ed. 20.00 (0-933519-08-7) D W Bell Gallery.

Transformations of the War Oracle in Old Testament Prophecy see Prophecy & War in Ancient Israel: Studies in the Oracles Against the Nations

Transformations of the Word: Spenser, Herbert, Vaughan. John W. Wall, Jr. LC 86-24969. 440p. 1988. 50.00 (0-8203-0930-3) U of Ga Pr.

*Transformations of Utopia: Changing Views of the Perfect Society. George E. Slusser et al. LC 96-53072. (AMS Studies in Cultural History). 1997. write for info. (0-404-64255-1) AMS Pr.

Transformations Through Drama: A Teacher's Guide to Educational Drama, Grads K-8. Jerneral W. Cranston. 335p. (C). 1995. pap. text ed. 18.00 (0-9648006-0-8) Jenfred Pr.

Transformations Through Space & Time. Ed. by Daniel A. Griffith & Robert P. Haining. 1986. lib. bdg. 188.00 (90-247-3362-6) Kluwer Ac.

Transformationsgruppen, 3 Vols. 2nd ed. Sophus Lie. LC 76-113135. 1970. Set. 125.00 (0-8284-0232-9) Chelsea Pub.

Transformative Curriculum Leadership. James G. Henderson & Richard D. Hawthorne. LC 94-31454. 1995. pap. text ed. 30.00 (0-02-353514-8, Macmillan Coll) P-H.

Transformative Dimensions of Adult Learning. Jack Mezirow. LC 90-24155. (Higher & Adult Education Ser.). 269p. text ed. 30.95 (1-55542-339-6) Jossey-Bass.

Transformative Getaways: Spiritual Growth, Self Discovery, & Holistic Healing. rev. ed. John Benson. (Illus.). 288p. 1996. pap. 15.00 (0-8050-4479-5, Owl) H Holt & Co.

Transformative Politics: The Future of Socialism in Western Europe. Anthony Butler. LC 95-4166. 1995. text ed. 65.00 (0-312-12673-5) St Martin.

Transformative Rituals: Celebrations for Personal Growth. David Williamson & Gay L. Williamson. 180p. (Orig.). 1994. pap. 10.00 (1-55874-293-X, 293X) Health Comm.

Transformative Vision: Reflections on the Nature & History of Human Expression. Jose Arguelles. (Illus.). 364p. (C). 1992. reprint ed. pap. 14.95 (0-9631750-0-9) Muse Pubns.

Transformed. Talibah F. Modupe. Ed. by T. Munirah Harris. (Illus.). 123p. (Orig.). 1995. pap. 13.95 (1-887442-04-9) Modupe Pr.

Transformed by Love: The Way of Mary Magdalen. Margaret Magdelen. LC 90-61562. 96p. (Orig.). 1990. pap. 5.95 (0-9623410-5-3) Resurrection.

*Transformed by the Divine Power. S. A. Freeman. 84p. (Orig.). 1994. pap. 2.95 (1-56794-079-X, C-2374) Star Bible.

Transformed by the Light: The Powerful Effect of Near-Death Experiences on People's Lives. Melvin Morse & Paul Perry. 1994. reprint ed. mass mkt. 5.99 (0-8041-1183-9) Ivy Books.

*Transformed by Truth. Joseph Tkach. LC 97-17764. 220p. 1997. 19.99 (1-57673-181-2, Multnomah Bks) Multnomah Pubs.

Transformed Cell: Unlocking the Mysteries of Cancer. Steven Rosenberg & John M. Barry. viii, 376p. 1993. reprint ed. pap. 12.50 (0-380-72115-5) Avon.

Transformed Cladistics, Taxonomy & Evolution. N. R. Scott-Ram. 250p. (C). 1990. text ed. 59.95 (0-521-34086-1) Cambridge U Pr.

Transformed into His Image see Transformados en Su Semejanza

Transformed Judgment: Toward a Trinitarian Account of the Moral Life. L. Gregory Jones. LC 89-40755. 208p. (C). 1990. text ed. 26.50 (0-268-01872-3) U of Notre Dame Pr.

Transformed Living. Eric Geiger. LC 90-93078. 60p. (Orig.). 1990. pap. 5.95 (0-9623784-0-2) E L Geiger.

Transformed Mind: Transformed Life. Larry R. Helms. 124p. (Orig.). 1995. pap. write for info. (1-885591-56-X) Morris Pubng.

Transformed Phenotype. Ed. by Arnold J. Levine et al. LC 83-26318. (Cancer Cells Ser.: No. 1). 320p. reprint ed. pap. 91.20 (0-7837-2003-3, 2042277) Bks Demand.

Transformed Self: The Psychology of Religious Conversion. Christian Ullman. (Emotions, Personality, & Psychotherapy Ser.). (Illus.). 298p. 1989. 42.50 (0-306-43134-3, Plenum Pr) Plenum.

Transformed Temperaments. Tim LaHaye. 293p. 1993. mass mkt. 5.99 (0-8423-7304-7) Tyndale.

Transformer: The Lou Reed Story. Victor Bockris. 400p. 1995. 25.00 (0-684-80366-6) S&S Trade.

*Transformer: The Lou Reed Story. Victor Bockris. LC 96-43856. (Illus.). 464p. 1997. reprint ed. pap. 15.95 (0-306-80752-1) Da Capo.

Transformer & Inductor Design Handbook. 2nd ed. C. McLyman. (Electrical Engineering & Electronics Ser.: Vol. 49). 432p. 1988. 75.00 (0-8247-7828-6) Dekker.

Transformer Exam Calculations. rev. ed. Tom Henry. (Illus.). 117p. (Orig.). (C). 1989. reprint ed. pap. text ed. 18.00 (0-945495-14-5) T Henrys CECB.

Transformers. 275p. 1995. 1,995.00 (0-614-06126-1, LE609) Lead Edge Reports.

Transformers. Center for Occupational Research & Development Staff. (EUTEC Power Plant Operator Curriculum Ser.). (Illus.). 40p. (C). 1986. pap. text ed. write for info. (1-55502-243-X) CORD Commns.

*Transformers. K. R. Edwards. LC 96-42900. (Illus.). 316p. 1996. pap. 29.96 (0-8269-1603-1) Am Technical.

Transformers. Herman. (Electrical Trades Ser.). 1997. teacher ed. 12.00 (0-8273-7210-8) Delmar.

Transformers: The Artists of Self-Creation. Jacquelyn Small. LC 91-10347. 304p. 1994. reprint ed. pap. 15.95 (0-87516-673-3) DeVorss.

Transformers & Motors. George P. Shultz. 320p. 1991. 29.95 (0-672-30131-8) Buttrwrth-Heinemann.

Transformers GRT Car Rally. (J). 1984. pap. 1.50 (0-87135-015-7) Marvel Entmnt.

Transformers Universe. 128p. 1987. pap. 5.95 (0-87135-296-6) Marvel Entmnt.

Transforming a Bureaucracy: The Experience of the Philippine National Irrigation Administration. Ed. by Frances F. Korten & Robert Y. Siy, Jr. LC 88-13221. (Library of Management for Development, Case Study Ser.). (Illus.). xv, 175p. (C). 1988. lib. bdg. 26.50 (0-931816-73-4) Kumarian Pr.

Transforming a People of God. Denham Grierson. 1991. pap. 9.50 (0-85819-464-3, Pub. by JBCE AT) Morehouse Pub.

Transforming a Rape Culture. Ed. by Emilie Buchwald et al. LC 93-5693. 484p. 1993. 23.95 (0-915943-06-9) Milkweed Ed.

Transforming a Rape Culture. Ed. by Emilie Buchwald et al. 484p. 1995. pap. 18.95 (1-57131-204-8) Milkweed Ed.

Transforming Abuse: Nonviolent Resistance & Recovery. K. Louise Schmidt. 192p. 1995. pap. 14.95 (0-86571-314-6) New Soc Pubs.

Transforming Abuse: Nonviolent Resistance & Recovery. K. Louise Schmidt. 192p. 1995. lib. bdg. 39.95 (0-86571-313-8) New Soc Pubs.

Transforming Agrarian Economies: Opportunities Seized, Opportunities Missed. Thomas P. Tomich et al. 496p. 1995. pap. 25.00 (0-8014-8245-3) Cornell U Pr.

Transforming Agriculture in Taiwan: The Experience of the Joint Commission on Rural Reconstruction. Joseph A. Yager. LC 88-47769. (Food Systems & Agrarian Change Ser.). 320p. 1988. 45.00 (0-8014-2112-8) Cornell U Pr.

Transforming America from the Inside Out. Kay C. James & David Kou. 192p. 1995. pap. 16.99 (0-310-48440-5) Zondervan.

Transforming America's Schools: An Administrators' Call to Action. John Murphy & Jeffry Schiller. LC 92-21020. 319p. 1992. 32.95 (0-8126-9203-9) Open Court.

Transforming America's Schools: An Administrators' Call to Action. John Murphy & Jeffry Schiller. LC 92-21020. 319p. 1995. pap. 18.95 (0-8126-9255-1) Open Court.

Transforming America's Schools: An Rx for Getting Past Blame. Gerald Bracey. 127p. 1994. pap. 17.95 (0-87652-211-8, 21-00470) Am Assn Sch Admin.

Transforming Auto Assembly: Experience in Automation & Work Organization. Koichi S. Shimokawa. LC 96-29828. (Illus.). 400p. 1997. 79.95 (3-540-60506-1) Spr-Verlag.

Transforming Bible Study: A Leader's Guide. enl. rev. ed. Walter Wink. LC 89-29889. 192p. 1990. pap. 13.95 (0-687-42498-4) Abingdon.

Transforming Bible Study with Children: A Guide for Learning Together. Patricia Van Ness. 128p. 1991. pap. 11.95 (0-687-42502-6) Abingdon.

Transforming Body Image: Learning to Love the Body You Have. Marcia G. Hutchinson. LC 85-17524. 170p. (Orig.). 1985. pap. 10.95 (0-89594-172-4) Crossing Pr.

*Transforming Business Families. 4th ed. Gerald Le Van. Ed. by Margaret Marchuk. LC 96-95206. Orig. Title: Getting to Win - Win in Family Business. 320p. 1996. reprint ed. pap. 17.95 (0-9655448-0-X) Le Van Co.

Transforming Capitalism & Patriarchy: Gender & Development in Africa. April A. Gordon. LC 95-41235. (Women & Change in the Developing World Ser.). 219p. 1995. pap. text ed. 19.95 (1-55587-629-3) Lynne Rienner.

Transforming Capitalism & Patriarchy: Gender & Development in Africa. April A. Gordon. LC 95-41235. (Women & Change in the Developing World Ser.). 219p. 1996. lib. bdg. 45.00 (1-55587-402-9) Lynne Rienner.

Transforming Central Government: The Next Steps Initiative. Patricia Greer. LC 93-38386. 160p. (C). 1994. 79.00 (0-335-19115-0, Open Univ Pr); pap. 27.50 (0-335-19114-2, Open Univ Pr) Taylor & Francis.

Transforming Childhood: A Handbook for Personal Growth. Strephon Kaplan-Williams. (Illus.). 256p. 1990. pap. 15.95 (1-85230-152-X) Element MA.

Transforming Children's Mathematics Education: International Perspective. Ed. by T. Wood & Leslie P. Steffe. 512p. (C). 1990. pap. 39.95 (0-8058-0605-9); text ed. 99.95 (0-8058-0604-0) L Erlbaum Assocs.

Transforming Christianity: Ten Pathways to a New Reformation. Stephen Glauz-Todrank. LC 95-4698. 132p. 1995. 15.95 (0-8245-1525-0) Crossroad NY.

Transforming Church Boards into Communities of Spiritual Leaders. Charles M. Olsen. 1995. pap. 15.25 (1-56699-148-X, AL158) Alban Inst.

Transforming Church Boards into Communities of Spiritual Leaders. Charles M. Olson. pap. 15.25 (1-56991-48X-8) Alban Inst.

*Transforming Cities: Contested Governance & New Spatial Divisions. Nick Jewson & Susanne Macgregor. LC 96-2937. 248p. (C). 1997. pap. write for info. (0-415-14604-6); text ed. write for info. (0-415-14603-8) Routledge.

Transforming Communication, Transforming Business: Building Responsive & Responsible Workplaces. Stanley A. Deetz. LC 94-44000. (Communication Series). 1995. text ed. 45.00 (1-57273-036-6); pap. text ed. 20.95 (1-57273-037-4) Hampton Pr NJ.

Transforming Company Culture. David Drennan. 1992. text ed. 32.95 (0-07-707660-5) McGraw.

Transforming Computer Technology: Information Processing for the Pentagon, 1962-1986. Arthur L. Norberg & Judy E. O'Neill. LC 95-23820. (Studies in the History of Technology). 384p. (C). 1996. text ed. 49.95 (0-8018-5152-1) Johns Hopkins.

Transforming Congregations for the Future. Loren B. Mead. (Once & Future Church Ser.: Vol. 3). 11.95 (1-56699-126-9, AL152) Alban Inst.

Transforming Corporate Leadership. Patrick Mileham & Keith Spacie. (Illus.). 225p. 1996. 25.00 (0-273-61457-6) Pitman Publng.

Transforming Curriculum for a Culturally Diverse Society. Ed. by Etta R. Hollins. 304p. 1996. pap. 24.95 (0-8058-8033-X) L Erlbaum Assocs.

Transforming Democracy: Legislative Campaign Committees & Political Parties. Daniel M. Shea. LC 94-32958. 238p. (C). 1995. text ed. 49.50 (0-7914-2551-7); pap. text ed. 16.95 (0-7914-2552-5) State U NY Pr.

Transforming Depression: Healing the Soul Through Creativity. David H. Rosen. 304p. 1996. pap. 14.95 (0-14-019537-8, Penguin Bks) Viking Penguin.

Transforming Desire: Erotic Knowledge in Books III & IV of the Faerie Queene. Lauren Silberman. LC 94-13630. 1995. 42.00 (0-520-08486-1) U CA Pr.

Transforming Development: Women, Poverty & Politics. Margaret Snyder. 313p. (Orig.). 1995. pap. 32.50 (1-85339-302-9, Pub. by Intermed Tech UK) Women Ink.

*Transforming Earth - Transforming Self. Carlo Pietzner. LC 96-30202. 224p. (Orig.). 1997. pap. 16.95 (0-88010-428-7) Anthroposophic.

Transforming Economic Systems. 1996. 58.00 (0-387-00585-4) Spr-Verlag.

Transforming Economic Systems: The Case of Poland. Ed. by M. Kremer & M. Weber. (Contributions to Economics Ser.). (Illus.). xviii, 179p. 1992. pap. 42.00 (0-387-91415-3) Spr-Verlag.

Transforming Economies & European Integration. Ed. by Rumen Dobrinsky et al. LC 95-6825. 352p. 1995. 95.00 (1-85898-204-9) E Elgar.

Transforming Education: Overcoming Barriers. Jane L. David & Paul D. Goren. Ed. by Gerry Feinstein. 48p. (Orig.). 1993. pap. text ed. 15.00 (1-55877-216-2) Natl Governor.

Transforming Education: The New Three R's. Andy LePage. LC 87-18534. 218p. (Orig.). 1987. pap. 14.95 (0-941079-03-1) Oakmore Hse.

Transforming Education Through the Arts. Laura L. Loyacono. 38p. 1995. 15.00 (1-55516-221-5, 2111) Natl Conf State Legis.

Transforming Education Through Total Quality Management: A Practitioners Guide. Franklin P. Schargel. LC 93-46527. (Illus.). 210p. 1994. 35.95 (1-883001-07-2) Eye On Educ.

Transforming Educational Administration: Meaning, Community & Excellence. Robert J. Starratt. LC 95-34015. 1996. pap. text ed. write for info. (0-07-061239-0) McGraw.

*Transforming Fabrics. Carolyn Dahl. (Illus.). 192p. 1997. 192.00 (1-57432-700-3, 4919, Am Quilters Soc) Collector Bks.

Transforming Faith. T. David Sustar. 1992. pap. 6.99 (0-87148-860-4) Pathway Pr.

Transforming Faith: Explorations of Twentieth-Century American Evangelism. David H. Watt. LC 90-29098. 200p. (C). 1991. text ed. 40.00 (0-8135-1716-8); pap. text ed. 15.00 (0-8135-1717-6) Rutgers U Pr.

Transforming Faith: The Sacred & Secular in Modern American History. Ed. by M. L. Bradbury & James B. Gilbert. LC 89-7478. (Contributions to the Study of Religion Ser.: No. 23). 205p. 1989. text ed. 49.95 (0-313-25707-8, BYG, Greenwood Pr) Greenwood.

Transforming Families & Communities: Christian Hope in a World of Change. Alan Nicholas et al. 86p. 1987. pap. 5.00 (0-88028-072-7, 922) Forward Movement.

Transforming Free Speech: The Ambiguous Legacy of Civil Libertarianism. Mark A. Graber. LC 90-11066. 349p. 1991. 48.00 (0-520-06919-6) U CA Pr.

Transforming Free Speech: The Ambiguous Legacy of Civil Libertarianism. Mark A. Graber. (C). 1991. pap. 15.95 (0-520-08033-5) U CA Pr.

Transforming Friendship. Leslie D. Weatherhead. (Classic Ser.). 1990. reprint ed. pap. 4.95 (0-687-42511-5) Abingdon.

Transforming Genres: New Approaches to British Fiction of the 1890s. Ed. by Nikki L. Manos & Meri-Jane Rochelson. LC 94-9855. 1994. text ed. 45.00 (0-312-12154-7) St Martin.

*Transforming God: An Interpretation of Suffering & Evil. Tyron L. Inbody. LC 96-37844. 256p. (Orig.). 1997. pap. 23.00 (0-664-25711-9) Westminster John Knox.

*Transforming Government: Lessons from the Reinventing Laboratories. Patricia Ingraham. 1997. 29.95 (0-7879-0931-9) Jossey-Bass.

Transforming Grace: Christian Tradition & Women's Experience. Anne E. Carr. 288p. 1996. pap. text ed. 19.95 (0-8264-0873-7) Continuum.

Transforming Grace: Living Confidently in God's Unfailing Love. Jerry Bridges. LC 91-61390. 224p. 1993. pap. 12.00 (0-89109-656-6) NavPress.

Transforming Grace Discussion Guide: Living Confidently in God's Unfailing Love. Jerry Bridges. 224p. 1993. pap. 7.00 (0-89109-644-2) NavPress.

Transforming Hand of Revolution: Reconsidering the American Revolution As a Social Movement. Ed. by Ronald Hoffman & Peter J. Albert. 576p. 1995. text ed. 47.50 (0-8139-1561-9) U Pr of Va.

Transforming Hard-Talk into Heart-Speak: An Interactive Conflict Resolution Manual & Ecumenical Workbook for Interreligious Encounter & Dialogue. Anastasios Zavales. 106p. (Orig.). (C). 1994. pap. 34.95 (1-884090-01-X) Ecumenics Intl.

*Transforming Hate to Love: An Outcome Study of the Peper Harow Adolescent Treatment Process. Melvyn Rose. LC 96-46581. 192p. (C). 1997. pap. write for info. (0-415-13832-9); text ed. write for info. (0-415-13831-0) Routledge.

Transforming Health: Christian Approaches to Healing & Wholeness. Ed. by Eric Ram. 3505p. 1995. 21.95 (0-912552-89-1) MARC.

Transforming Health Care Through Information: Case Studies. Ed. by Nancy M. Lorenzi et al. LC 95-17731. (Computers in Health Care Ser.). (Illus.). 504p. 1995. 54.00 (0-387-94455-9) Spr-Verlag.

Transforming Healthcare Organizations: How to Achieve & Sustain Organizational Excellence. Ellen Marszalek-Gaucher & Richard J. Coffey. LC 90-4777. (Health-Management Ser.). 308p. text ed. 36.95 (1-55542-250-0) Jossey-Bass.

Transforming High Schools: A Constructivist Agenda. John M. Jenkins. 179p. 1996. pap. 39.95 (1-56676-378-9, 763789) Technomic.

T

An Asterisk (*) at the beginning of an entry indicates that the title is appearing in BIP for the first time.

Transforming Higher Education. Lee Harvey & Peter T. Knight. LC 96-8124. 192p. 1996. 95.00 (*0-335-19590-3*, Open Univ Pr); pap. 34.00 (*0-335-19589-X*, Open Univ Pr) Taylor & Francis.

Transforming Higher Education: A Vision for Learning in the 21st Century. unabridged ed. Michael G. Dolence & Donald M. Norris. (Illus.). 100p. (Orig.). 1995. pap. 40.00 (*0-9601608-0-9*) Soc Coll & Univ Planning.

Transforming Higher Education: Views from Leaders Around the World. Fred M. Hayward. Ed. by Madeleine F. Green. LC 96-51510. 328p. 1997. boxed 39.95 (*0-89774-891-3*) Oryx Pr.

***Transforming Human Culture: Social Evolution & the Planetary Crisis.** Jay Earley. LC 97-2331. (SUNY Series in Constructive Postmodern Thought). 256p. (C). 1997. text ed. 59.50 (*0-7914-3373-0*); pap. text ed. 19.95 (*0-7914-3374-9*) State U NY Pr.

Transforming Humanity: The Visionary Writings of Soedjatmoko. Ed. by Kathleen Newland & Kamala C. Soedjatmoko. LC 93-5181. (Library of Management for Development). 224p. 1994. 42.00 (*1-56549-025-8*); pap. 18.95 (*1-56549-026-6*) Kumarian Pr.

Transforming Identities: Context, Power & Ideology in a Therapeutic Community. Barbara Frankel. (American University Studies Anthropology & Sociology: Ser. XI, Vol. 14). 319p. (C). 1989. text ed. 47.50 (*0-8204-0536-1*) P Lang Pubng.

Transforming Image: A Study of Shelley's Major Poetry. Jean Hall. LC 80-12748. 180p. 1980. text ed. 21.95 (*0-252-00766-2*) U of Ill Pr.

Transforming Knowledge. Elizabeth K. Minnich. 240p. 1990. 44.95 (*0-87722-695-4*) Temple U Pr.

Transforming Knowledge. Elizabeth K. Minnich. 240p. 1991. pap. 19.95 (*0-87722-880-9*) Temple U Pr.

Transforming Labor: Labour Tradition & the Labor Decade in Australia. Peter Beilharz. LC 93-37970. 244p. (C). 1993. pap. write for info. (*0-521-43821-7*) Cambridge U Pr.

Transforming Labor: Labour Tradition & the Labor Decade in Australia. Peter Beilharz. LC 93-37970. 244p. (C). 1994. text ed. 64.95 (*0-521-43237-5*) Cambridge U Pr.

***Transforming Leadership: Equipping Yourself & Others to Build the Leadership Organization.** Terry Anderson. (Illus.). 250p. 1997. 39.95 (*1-57444-109-4*) St Lucie Pr.

***Transforming Leadership: From Vision to Results.** 2nd ed. John Adams. 300p. 1997. pap. text ed. 26.95 (*0-917917-11-1*) Miles River.

Transforming Leadership: Jesus' Way of Creating Vision, Shaping Values & Empowering Change. Leighton Ford. LC 91-34428. 320p. 1993. pap. 12.99 (*0-8308-1652-6*, 1652) InterVarsity.

Transforming Leadership: New Skills for an Extraordinary Future. Terry D. Anderson. 300p. 1992. pap. 19.95 (*0-87425-181-8*) HRD Press.

Transforming Light: Intellectual Conversion in the Early Lonergan. Richard M. Liddy. 248p. (Orig.). 1993. pap. text ed. 14.95 (*0-8146-5839-3*, M Glazier) Liturgical Pr.

***Transforming Madness.** Jay Neugeboren. Date not set. write for info. (*0-688-15655-X*) Morrow.

***Transforming Medicaid.** League of Women Voters Education Fund Staff. 19p. 1996. 3.99 (*0-89959-399-2*, 1047) LWVUS.

Transforming Men: Changing Patterns of Dependency & Dominance in Gender Relations. Geoff Dench. 275p. (C). 1996. text ed. 34.95 (*1-56000-232-8*) Transaction Pubs.

Transforming Middle Level Education: Perspectives & Possibilities. Judith L. Irvin. 352p. (C). 1991. text ed. 55.95 (*0-205-13472-6*, Longwood Div) Allyn.

Transforming Middle Schools: A Guide to Whole-School Change. Barry Raebeck. LC 92-64255. 180p. 1992. pap. text ed. 39.95 (*0-87762-958-7*) Technomic.

Transforming Mind. 2nd ed. Laurence Bendit & Phoebe Bendit. LC 74-103415. 161p. 1983. reprint ed. pap. 5.75 (*0-8356-0012-2*, Quest) Theos Pub Hse.

Transforming Mind: A Critical Cognitive Activity. Gloria Gannaway. LC 93-11854. (Language & Ideology Ser.). 200p. 1994. text ed. 55.00 (*0-89789-279-8*, Bergin & Garvey); pap. text ed. 14.95 (*0-89789-280-1*, Bergin & Garvey) Greenwood.

Transforming Mission: Paradigm Shifts in Theology of Mission. David J. Bosch. LC 90-21619. (American Society of Missiology Ser.). 1991. pap. 25.00 (*0-88344-719-3*) Orbis Bks.

Transforming Modernity: Popular Culture in Mexico. Nestor Garcia Canclini. Tr. by Lidia Lozano from SPA. LC 92-47426. (Translations from Latin America Ser.). 144p. (C). 1993. pap. 11.95 (*0-292-72759-3*); text ed. 27.50 (*0-292-72758-5*) U of Tex Pr.

Transforming Moment. 2nd ed. James E. Loder. 256p. 1989. reprint ed. pap. text ed. 18.95 (*0-939443-17-1*) Helmers Howard Pub.

Transforming Nat Res for Human Development. 87p. 1985. 15.00 (*92-808-0469-3*, E 85.III.A.1) UN.

Transforming Number One. 4th ed. Ron Smothermon. LC 81-14356. 200p. (Orig.). 1982. pap. 15.00 (*0-932654-04-5*) Context Pubns.

Transforming Nursery Education. Peter Moss & Helen Penn. 192p. 1996. pap. 24.95 (*1-85396-308-9*, Pub. by Paul Chapman UK) Taylor & Francis.

Transforming of the Kirk: Victorian Scotland's Religious Revolution. A. C. Cheyne. 244p. (C). 1988. pap. text ed. 30.00 (*0-7152-0545-5*) St Mut.

Transforming Organizations. Ed. by Thomas A. Kochan & Michael Useem. (Illus.). 480p. 1992. 38.00 (*0-19-506504-2*) OUP.

Transforming Organizations Through Groupware, Lotus Notes in Action: Lotus Notes in Action. Ed. by P. Lloyd & R. Whitehead. 197p. 1996. pap. text ed. 39.95 (*3-540-19961-6*) Spr-Verlag.

Transforming Organizations with Information Technology: Proceedings of the IFIP WG8.2 Working Conference on Information Technology & New Emergent Forms of Organization, Ann Arbor, Michigan, U. S. A., 11-13 August, 1994, A-49. IFIP WG8.2 Working Conference on Information Technology & New Emergent Forms of Organization Staff. Ed. by Richard Baskerville et al. LC 94-21612. (IFIP Transactions, Computer Science & Technology Ser.). 484p. 1994. pap. 162.50 (*0-444-81945-2*) Elsevier.

***Transforming Pain into Power: Making the Most of Your Emotions.** Doris I. Helge. LC 96-69333. (Illus.). 384p. (Orig.). 1997. 21.95 (*1-885598-87-4*); pap. 16.95 (*1-885598-88-2*) Shimoda Pub.

Transforming Paris: The Life & Labors of Baron Haussmann. David P. Jordan. 1995. 28.00 (*0-02-916531-8*, Free Press) Free Pr.

Transforming Paris: The Life & Labours of Baron Haussmann. David P. Jordan. (Illus.). 504p. 1996. pap. 17.95 (*0-226-41038-2*) U Ch Pr.

***Transforming Parish Life: A Spirituality of Parish Leadership for the Twenty-First Century.** Center for Learning Network Staff. 99p. 1996. teacher ed., spiral bd. 15.95 (*1-56077-373-1*) Ctr Learning.

Transforming Payment Systems: Meeting the Needs of Emerging Market Economies. Setsuya Sato & David B. Humphrey. LC 95-23991. (Discussion Papers: Vol. 291). 52p. 1995. 6.95 (*0-8213-3355-0*, 13355) World Bank.

Transforming Power: Domination, Empowerment, & Education. Seth Kreisberg. LC 90-38497. (SUNY Series, Teacher Empowerment & School Reform). 264p. (C). 1991. pap. text ed. 21.95 (*0-7914-0664-4*) State U NY Pr.

Transforming Power: Domination, Empowerment, & Education. Seth Kreisberg. LC 90-38497. (SUNY Series, Teacher Empowerment & School Reform). 264p. (C). 1992. text ed. 64.50 (*0-7914-0663-6*) State U NY Pr.

Transforming Power: The Politics of Electricity Planning. Aynsley Kellow. (Illus.). 320p. (C). 1995. text ed. 59.95 (*0-521-47122-2*) Cambridge U Pr.

***Transforming Power of Fasting & Prayer: Personal Accounts of Spiritual Renewal.** Bill Bright. LC 97-16983. 1997. write for info. (*1-56399-090-3*) NewLife Pubns.

Transforming Power of Grace. Thomas C. Oden. 0879p. (Orig.). 1993. pap. 16.95 (*0-687-42260-4*) Abingdon.

Transforming Power of Prayer: Deepening Your Friendship with God. James Houston. 1996. pap. 13.00 (*0-89109-937-9*) NavPress.

***Transforming Power of the Nuns: Women, Religion, & Cultural Change in Ireland, 1750-1900.** Mary P. Magray. (Illus.). 224p. 1997. 39.95 (*0-19-511299-7*) OUP.

Transforming Principle: Discovering That Genes Are Made of DNA. Maclyn McCarty. LC 84-20544. (Illus.). 288p. 1986. pap. 9.95 (*0-393-30450-7*) Norton.

***Transforming Privacy: A Transpersonal Philosophy of Rights.** Stefano Scoglio. LC 97-9180. (Praeger Series in Transformational Politics & Political Science). 1997. text ed. write for info. (*0-275-95607-5*, Praeger Pubs) Greenwood.

Transforming Problems into Happiness. Lama Zopa. Ed. by Ailsa Cameron & Robina Courtin. LC 92-1423. 104p. 1994. pap. 10.00 (*0-86171-038-X*) Wisdom MA.

Transforming Proteins of DNA Tumor Viruses. Ed. by R. Knippers & A. J. Levine. (Current Topics in Microbiology & Immunology Ser.: Vol. 144). (Illus.). 290p. 1989. 135.00 (*0-387-50909-7*) Spr-Verlag.

***Transforming Public Education: A New Course for America's Future.** Evans Clincy. LC 96-3467. 224p. (C). 1996. text ed. 43.00 (*0-8077-3569-8*); pap. text ed. 18.95 (*0-8077-3568-X*) Tchrs Coll.

Transforming Public Policy: Dynamics of Policy Entrepreneurship & Innovation. Nancy C. Roberts & Paula J. King. (Public Administration Ser.). 302p. 1996. 28.95 (*0-7879-0202-0*) Jossey-Bass.

Transforming Qualitative Data: Description, Analysis, & Interpretation. Harry F. Wolcott. 380p. (C). 1994. text ed. 62.00 (*0-8039-5280-5*); pap. text ed. 27.50 (*0-8039-5281-3*) Sage.

Transforming RN Education: Dialogue & Debate. Ed. by Nancy L. Dickelmann & Marsha L. Rather. (Illus.). 416p. (C). 1993. pap. text ed. 39.95 (*0-88737-573-1*, 14-2511) Natl League Nurse.

Transforming Rural Life: Dairying Families & Agricultural Change, 1820-1885. Sally A. McMurry. (Revisiting Rural America Ser.). 296p. 1995. text ed. 39.95 (*0-8018-4889-X*) Johns Hopkins.

Transforming Russia & China: Revolutionary Struggle in the Twentieth Century. William G. Rosenberg & Marilyn B. Young. 416p. 1982. pap. text ed. 19.95 (*0-19-502966-6*) OUP.

Transforming Russian Enterprises: From State Control to Employee Ownership. Ed. by John Logue et al. LC 95-6666. (Contributions in Economics & Economic History Ser.: No. 168). 312p. 1995. text ed. 65.00 (*0-313-28748-1*, Greenwood Pr) Greenwood.

Transforming School Culture: Stories, Symbols, Values & the Leader's Role. Stephen Stolp & Stuart C. Smith. 1995. pap. 12.50 (*0-86552-132-8*) U of Oreg ERIC.

Transforming School Cultures. Martin L. Maehr & Carol Midgley. (Lives in Context Ser.). (C). 1996. text ed. 60.00 (*0-8133-2743-1*) Westview.

Transforming School Cultures. Martin L. Maehr & Carol Midgley. (Lives in Context Ser.). (C). 1996. pap. text ed. 19.95 (*0-8133-2744-X*) Westview.

Transforming Schools. Ed. by Peter W. Cookson, Jr. & Barbara Schneider. LC 94-36371. (Reference Library of Social Science: Vol. 888). 632p. 1995. text ed. 99.00 (*0-8153-1257-1*, SS888) Garland.

Transforming Schools. Ed. by Peter W. Cookson, Jr. & Barbara Schneider. LC 94-36371. (Reference Library of Social Science: Vol. 888). 632p. 1995. pap. text ed. 21.95 (*0-8153-1533-3*, SS888) Garland.

Transforming Schools Through Collaborative Leadership. Helen Telford. 256p. 1996. 69.95 (*0-7507-0566-3*, Falmer Pr); pap. 24.95 (*0-7507-0567-1*, Falmer Pr) Taylor & Francis.

Transforming Scrooge: Dickens' Blueprint for a Spiritual Awakening. Joseph D. Cusumano. LC 96-22000. (Illus.). 312p. (Orig.). 1996. pap. 17.95 (*1-56718-198-8*) Llewellyn Pubns.

Transforming Self & World: Themes from the Sutra of Golden Light. Sangharakshita. 240p. (Orig.). 1996. pap. 21.95 (*0-904766-73-X*) Windhorse Pubns.

Transforming Settler States: Communal Conflict & Internal Security in Northern Ireland & Zimbabwe. Ronald Weitzler. LC 89-20692. 265p. 1990. 37.50 (*0-520-06490-9*) U CA Pr.

Transforming Sexuality: The Archetypal World of Anima & Animus. Barry Ulanov & Ann B. Ulanov. LC 94-11013. 1994. pap. 19.00 (*0-87773-986-2*) Shambhala Pubns.

Transforming Social Representations: A Social Psychology of Common Sense & Science. S. Caroline Purkhardt. LC 92-47076. 224p. (C). (gr. 13). 1993. text ed. 69.95 (*0-415-07960-8*, B0863, Routledge NY) Routledge.

Transforming Socialist Economies: The Case of Poland & Czechoslovakia. Martin R. Myant. LC 93-2692. (Studies of Communism in Transition). 320p. 1993. 80.00 (*1-85278-786-4*) E Elgar.

Transforming Societies, Transforming Anthropology. Ed. by Emilio F. Moran. 1996. 49.50 (*0-472-10574-4*) U of Mich Pr.

Transforming Southern African Agriculture. Ed. by Ann Seidman et al. LC 90-83793. 275p. 1992. 45.95 (*0-86543-131-0*); pap. 16.95 (*0-86543-132-9*) Africa World.

Transforming State Education Agencies to Support Education Reform. Jane L. Davie. 56p. (Orig.). 1994. pap. text ed. 15.00 (*1-55877-198-0*) Natl Governor.

Transforming State-Society Relations in Mexico: The National Solidarity Strategy. Ed. by Wayne Cornelius et al. (Contemporary Perspectives Ser.: No. 6). 364p. (C). 1994. pap. 21.95 (*1-878367-14-5*) UCSD Ctr US-Mex.

Transforming Stress into Power. Tager & Willard. (gr. 13). 1988. 12.95 (*0-8151-9590-7*) Mosby Yr Bk.

Transforming Stress into Power: The Energy Director System. Mark J. Tager & Stephen Willard. (Illus.). 155p. (Orig.). 1988. pap. 12.95 (*1-56066-002-3*) Great Performance.

Transforming Stress Training Manual. Tager & Willard. 1988. text ed. 195.00 (*1-56066-131-3*) Great Performance.

Transforming Teaching with Technology. Kamala Anandam. (Educom Strategies Ser.). (Illus.). (C). 1991. text ed. 43.25 (*0-201-50641-6*) Addison-Wesley.

Transforming Technology: An Agenda for Environmentally Sustainable Growth in the Twenty-First Century. George R. Heaton et al. 40p. 1991. Large format. pap. 14.95 (*0-915825-68-6*, HETTP) World Resources Inst.

Transforming Texts: Classical Images in New Contexts. Ed. by Robert P. Metzger. LC 91-58592. 1993. 24.50 (*0-8387-5216-0*) Bucknell U Pr.

Transforming the Bottom Line: Managing Performance with the Real Numbers. Tony Hope & Jeremy Hope. 256p. 1996. 27.50 (*0-87584-746-3*) Harvard Busn.

***Transforming the Bottom Line: Managing Performance with the Real Numbers.** Tony Hope & Jeremy Hope. 1996. text ed. 27.50 (*0-07-103847-7*) McGraw.

***Transforming the Business: The IT Contribution.** Robert Moreton & Myrvin Chester. LC 96-27235. (Information Systems Ser.). 1996. pap. write for info. (*0-07-709243-0*) McGraw.

***Transforming the Character of Public Organizations: Techniques for Change Agents.** A. Carol Rusaw. LC 97-20730. 1998. text ed. write for info. (*1-56720-103-2*, Quorum Bks) Greenwood.

***Transforming the Cinderella Dream: From Frances Burney to Charlotte Bronte.** Huang Mei. 200p. 35.00 (*0-8135-1522-X*) Rutgers U Pr.

***Transforming the Civil Service: Building the Workforce of the Future.** 36p. (Orig.). (C). 1996. pap. 20.00 (*0-7881-3113-3*) DIANE Pub.

Transforming the Common-Place: Selections from Laurie Olin's Sketchbooks. Laurie Olin. (Illus.). 72p. (Orig.). 1997. 24.95 (*1-878271-88-1*) Princeton Arch.

***Transforming the Company.** Colin Coulson-Thomas. (Business & Management Ser.). 1992. pap. 24.95 (*0-7494-0671-2*) Kogan Page Ltd.

Transforming the Core: State Industrial Enterprises in Russia, Central Europe & China. Maurice Ernst et al. 288p. (C). 1995. pap. text ed. 24.00 (*0-8133-2705-9*) Westview.

***Transforming the Cotton Frontier: Madison County, Alabama, 1800-1840.** Daniel S. Dupre. LC 97-16094. (Illus.). 344p. 1997. text ed. 40.00 (*0-8071-2193-2*) La State U Pr.

Transforming the Crisis-Prone Organization: Preventing Individual, Organizational, & Environmental Tragedies. Thierry C. Pauchant & Ian I. Mitroff. LC 91-37910. (Management Ser.). 275p. 32.95 (*1-55542-407-4*) Jossey-Bass.

***Transforming the Crown: African, Asian & Caribbean Artists in Britain, 1966-1996.** Mora Beauchamp-Byrd. Ed. by M. Franklin Sirmans. (Illus.). 180p. pap. 39.95 (*0-9654082-0-5*) U Ch Pr.

Transforming the Curriculum: Ethnic Studies & Women's Studies. Ed. by Johnnella E. Butler & John C. Walter. LC 90-37670. 416p. (C). 1991. pap. text ed. 21.95 (*0-7914-0587-7*) State U NY Pr.

Transforming the Curriculum: Ethnic Studies & Women's Studies. Ed. by Johnnella E. Butler & John C. Walter. LC 90-37670. 416p. (C). 1991. text ed. 64.50 (*0-7914-0586-9*) State U NY Pr.

***Transforming the Curriculum for Multicultural Understandings: A Practitioner's Handbook.** James B. Boyer & H. Prentice Baptiste. LC 96-30455. 1996. 19.95 (*1-880192-19-5*) Caddo Gap Pr.

Transforming the Daily Grind: Life with God Is an Adventure. Stuart Briscoe. 144p. 1995. pap. 8.99 (*0-87788-504-4*) Shaw Pubs.

***Transforming the Delivery of Health Care.** Timothy Carse & Jeffrey Slater. 1995. text ed. 95.00 (*0-07-413100-1*) Irwin.

***Transforming the Delivery of Health Care: The Integration Process.** 2nd ed. Keith M. Korenchuk. 436p. 1994. 55.00 (*1-56829-040-3*, 4607) Med Group Mgmt.

Transforming the Enterprise Through COOPERATION: An Object Oriented Solution. NCR Corporation Staff et al. 160p. 1992. pap. text ed. 21.40 (*0-13-088451-0*) P-H.

Transforming the Global Corporation: How the World's Leading Companies Create & Manage Continuous Change. 1994. 295.00 (*0-85058-834-0*) Economist Intell.

Transforming the Hermeneutic Context: From Nietzsche to Nancy. Ed. by Gayle L. Ormiston & Alan D. Schrift. LC 89-4172. (SUNY Series, Intersections: Philosophy & Critical Theory). 306p. 1989. text ed. 59.50 (*0-7914-0134-0*); pap. text ed. 19.95 (*0-7914-0135-9*) State U NY Pr.

Transforming the Images: Ergativity & Transitivity in Inuktitut (Eskimo) Elke Nowak. LC 96-15691. (Empirical Approaches to Language Typology Ser.: Vol. 15). xii, 312p. (C). 1996. lib. bdg. 168.90 (*3-11-014980-X*) Mouton.

Transforming the Inner & Outer Family: Humanistic & Spiritual Approaches to Mind-Body Systems Therapy. Sheldon Z. Kramer. LC 94-47538. (Illus.). 212p. 1995. lib. bdg. 34.95 (*1-56024-947-1*) Haworth Pr.

Transforming the Inner & Outer Family: Humanistic & Spiritual Approaches to Mind-Body Systems Therapy. Sheldon Z. Kramer. LC 94-47538. 1995. pap. 14.95 (*1-56024-968-4*) Haworth Pr.

***Transforming the Latin American Automobile Industry: Union, Workers, & the Politics of Restructuring.** Ed. by John P. Tuman & John T. Morris. 250p. 1997. text ed. 64.95 (*0-7656-0199-0*) M E Sharpe.

***Transforming the Local Exchange Network: Analyses & Forecasts of Technology Change: 1997 Edition.** Lawrence K. Vanston & Ray L. Hodges. 150p. 1996. pap. 1,495.00 (*1-884154-08-5*) Tech Futures.

***Transforming the Local Telephone Network: Analyses & Forecasts of Technology Change: 1994 Edition.** Lawrence K. Vanston. 200p. 1994. pap. 995.00 (*0-614-18101-1*) Tech Futures.

Transforming the Mature Information Technology Organization: Reenergizing & Motivating People. Robert A. Zawacki et al. 208p. (C). 1995. pap. 38.95 (*0-9646910-0-0*) EagleStar.

Transforming the Mind, Healing the World: (Wit Lecture) Joseph Goldstein. LC 94-15319. 64p. 1994. pap. 3.95 (*0-8091-3484-5*) Paulist Pr.

Transforming the Organization. Francis J. Gouillart & James N. Kelly. LC 95-5486. (Illus.). 336p. 1995. text ed. 24.95 (*0-07-034067-6*) McGraw.

Transforming the Organization. Francis J. Gouillart & James N. Kelly. (Illus.). 336p. 1996. pap. text ed. 14.95 (*0-07-024492-8*) McGraw.

Transforming the Pain: A Workbook on Vicarious Traumatization. Karen W. Saakvitne et al. 159p. 1996. pap. 17.00 (*0-393-70233-2*) Norton.

Transforming the Parish: Models for the Future. Thomas P. Sweetser & Patricia M. Forster. 256p. (Orig.). 1993. pap. 18.95 (*1-55612-654-9*) Sheed & Ward MO.

Transforming the Past: Tradition & Kinship among Japanese Americans. Sylvia J. Yanagisako. LC 83-42541. 304p. 1985. 47.50 (*0-8047-1199-2*); pap. 14.95 (*0-8047-2017-7*) Stanford U Pr.

Transforming the State Role in Undergraduate Education: Time for a Different View. 26p. 1986. 12.50 (*0-318-22555-7*, PS-86-3) Ed Comm States.

Transforming the Structure of the Freight Transport Sector. OECD Staff. (EMCT Round Table Ser.: No. 99). 172p. (Orig.). 1995. pap. 45.00 (*92-821-1206-3*, Pub. by Org for Econ FR) OECD.

Transforming the U. S. Financial System: Equity & Efficiency for the 21st Century. Ed. by Gary A. Dymski et al. LC 93-23796. (Economic Policy Institute Ser.). 384p. (C). (gr. 13). 1993. text ed. 74.95 (*1-56324-268-0*); pap. text ed. 30.95 (*1-56324-269-9*) M E Sharpe.

Transforming the Warfare State: Global Militarism & Economic Conversion. Ed. by Gary E. McCuen. (Ideas in Conflict Ser.). (Illus.). 155p. 1992. lib. bdg. 12.95 (*0-86596-083-6*) G E M.

Transforming the Way We Work: The Power of the Collaborative Workplace. Edward M. Marshall. 224p. 1995. 22.95 (*0-8144-0255-0*) AMACOM.

Transforming the Western Image in Twentieth Century American Art. Ed. by Katherine P. Hough & Michael Zakian. LC 91-38799. (Illus.). 112p. 1992. pap. 29.95 (*0-295-97194-0*) U of Wash Pr.

Transforming the World Economy. (United Nations University (UNU) Publications). 300p. 1989. 20.00 (*92-808-0496-0*, E.88.III.A.10) UN.

Transforming Therapy: A New Approach to Hypnotherapy. 2nd ed. Gil Boyne. 400p. 1989. 37.50 (*0-930298-13-6*) Westwood Pub Co.

T

An Asterisk (*) at the beginning of an entry indicates that the title is appearing in BIP for the first time.

Transforming Tradition: Folk Music Revivals Examined. Ed. by Neil V. Rosenberg. LC 92-26727. (Music in American Life, Folklore & Society Ser.). 336p. (C). 1993. text ed. 29.95 (*0-252-01982-2*) U of Ill Pr.

Transforming Traditional Agriculture. Theodore W. Schultz. LC 75-26314. (World Food Supply Ser.). (Illus.). 1980. reprint ed. 23.95 (*0-405-07792-0*) Ayer.

Transforming Traditional Unit Teaching. William J. Stewart. 87p. 1982. pap. text ed. 8.95 (*0-89641-107-9*) American Pr.

Transforming Traditions in American Biology, 1880-1915. Jane Maienschein. LC 90-15623. (Illus.). 288p. 1991. text ed. 48.00 (*0-8018-4126-7*) Johns Hopkins.

Transforming Trauma: A Guide to Understanding & Treating Adult Survivors of Child Sexual Abuse. Anna C. Salter. LC 95-7710. (Illus.). 353p. 1995. 49.95 (*0-8039-5508-1*); pap. 22.95 (*0-8039-5509-X*) Sage.

***Transforming Trauma - EDMR: The Revolutionary New Therapy for Freeing the Mind, Clearing the Body, & Opening the Mind.** Laurel Parnell. 208p. (C). 1997. 21.00 (*0-393-04053-4*) Norton.

Transforming Trouble. M. Duckworth. (Tapestry Collection). 96p. 1996. pap. 6.50 (*1-56476-416-8*, 6-3416, Victor Bks) Chariot Victor.

Transforming Urban Education. Joseph Kretovics & Edward Nussel. LC 93-16023. 420p. 1993. pap. text ed. 54.00 (*0-205-14568-X*) Allyn.

Transforming Vision: Imagination & Will in Kierkegaardian Faith. M. Jamie Ferreira. 176p. 1991. 49.95 (*0-19-826331-7*) OUP.

Transforming Vision: Shaping a Christian World View. Brian J. Walsh & J. Richard Middleton. LC 84-15646. 214p. (Orig.). 1984. pap. 12.99 (*0-87784-973-0*, 973) InterVarsity.

Transforming Vision: Writers on Art. Intro. by Edward Hirsch. LC 94-17323. (Illus.). 144p. 1994. 27.95 (*0-8212-2126-4*) Art Inst Chi.

***Transforming Vision: Writers on Art.** Intro. by Edward Hirsch. (Illus.). 144p. 12.98 (*0-8317-6654-9*) Smithmark.

Transforming Visions: Feminist Critiques in Communication Studies. Sheryl P. Bowen & Nancy Wyatt. Ed. by Lana Rakow. LC 92-38173. (Communication Series: Feminist Perspectives). 288p. (C). 1993. text ed. 59.50 (*1-881303-06-3*); pap. text ed. 26.50 (*1-881303-07-1*) Hampton Pr NJ.

T

Transforming Women's Work: New England Lives in the Industrial Revolution. Thomas Dublin. LC 93-40054. (Illus.). 344p. 1994. 42.50 (*0-8014-2844-0*) Cornell U Pr.

Transforming Women's Work: New England Lives in the Industrial Revolution. Thomas Dublin. (Illus.). 344p. 1995. pap. 15.95 (*0-8014-8090-6*) Cornell U Pr.

Transforming Words: Six Essays on Preaching. Ed. by William F. Schulz. 136p. (Orig.). 1996. pap. 14.00 (*1-55896-272-7*, 5324, Skinner Hse Bks) Unitarian Univ.

***Transforming Work.** 2nd ed. John Adams. 300p. 1997. pap. text ed. 24.95 (*0-917917-12-X*) Miles River.

Transforming Your Business with Lotus. David Marshak. 1996. 29.95 (*0-13-472671-5*) P-H.

***Transforming Your Chronic Pain.** Jeff Kane. 1992. 11.95 incl. audio compact disk (*1-879237-29-6*) New Harbinger.

Transforming Your Community: Empowering for Change. Allen B. Moore & Rusty Brooks. LC 96-14555. (Professional Practices in Adult Education & Human Resource Development Ser.). (Illus.). 202p. (C). 1996. 26.50 (*0-89464-899-3*) Krieger.

***Transforming Your Dragons.** Sonia Cafe. (Illus.). (Orig.). 1998. pap. write for info. (*1-57863-012-6*) Weiser.

Transforming Your Dragons: How to Turn Fear Patterns into Personal Power. Jose Stevens. Ed. by Gail Vivino. LC 94-16002. (Illus.). 416p. (Orig.). 1994. pap. 14.95 (*1-879181-17-7*) Bear & Co.

Transforming Your Healthstyle: A Primer. Elaine L. Willis. 49p. (Orig.). 1989. pap. 5.00 (*0-926454-04-8*) Found Wellness.

Transforming Your Life with Astrology. Tiffany Holmes. LC 85-73305. 192p. 1986. 18.95 (*0-86690-307-0*, H2350-014) Am Fed Astrologers.

Transforming Your Marriage: A Guide to the Process of Opening the Doors in Your Relationship. Judy Schwab & Walter Schwab. 136p. 1996. 16.00 (*0-8059-3877-X*) Dorrance.

Transforming Your Temperament. Tim LaHaye. 1991. 9.98 (*0-88486-040-X*, Inspirational Pr) Arrowood Pr.

***Transforming Your Workplace for Christ.** William H. Nix. LC 96-51759. 224p. (Orig.). 1997. pap. 12.99 (*0-8054-6290-2*) Broadman.

***Transforming Your WWW Server with SGML.** Text Science Inc. Staff. 1997. pap. 49.95 (*0-13-616822-1*) P-H.

***Transformist Illusion.** D. Dewar. 1996. pap. 25.95 (*0-614-21246-4*, 1253) Kazi Pubns.

Transformist Illusion. 2nd ed. James R. Wetmore. (Illus.). 306p. 1995. reprint ed. pap. text ed. 22.95 (*0-900588-18-7*) S Perennis.

Transforms. Illus. by Bill Colrus. 6p. (Orig.). (J). (gr. k-3). 1996. mass mkt. 2.99 (*1-56293-839-8*) McClanahan Bk.

Transforms & Applications Handbook. Ed. by Alexander D. Poularikas. LC 95-2513. (Electrical Engineering Handbook Ser.). 1,288p. 1995. 99.95 (*0-8493-8342-0*, 8342) CRC Pr.

Transforms II. Illus. by Bill Colrus. 6p. (Orig.). (J). (gr. k-3). 1996. mass mkt. 2.99 (*1-56293-840-1*) McClanahan Bk.

Transforms in Signals & Systems. Peter Kraniauskas. (C). 1992. text ed. 54.95 (*0-201-19694-8*) Addison-Wesley.

Transfrontier Mobility of Law. Ed. by A. J. De Roo et al. LC 95-46976. 120p. 1996. pap. 42.00 (*90-411-0170-5*) Kluwer Law Tax Pubs.

Transfrontier Movements of Hazardous Wastes: 1991 Statistics. OECD Staff. 20p. (Orig.). 1994. pap. 9.00 (*92-64-14191-X*) OECD.

***Transfrontier Movements of Hazardous Wastes: 1992-1993 Statistics.** OECD Staff. 24p. (Orig.). 1997. pap. 8.00 (*92-64-15470-1*, 97-97-05-1, Pub. by Org for Econ FR) OECD.

Transfrontier Pollution & International Law. Ed. by Centre d'Etude et de Recherche de Droit International et Relations Internationales Staff. 1986. pap. text ed. 35.00 (*90-247-3394-4*) Kluwer Ac.

Transfrontier Reserves for Peace & Nature: A Contribution to Human Security. 128p. 1995. 25.00 (*92-807-1409-0*) UN.

Transfusion: Or the Orphans of Unwalden. W. M. Godwin. 252p. 1987. text ed. 35.00 (*0-87556-695-2*) Saifer.

Transfusion & Hemaopoietic Stem Cells: Proceedings of the 6th Hokkaido Symposium on Transfusional Medicine, July 22-23, Sapporo, Japan, 1994. Sadayoski Sekiguchi. (Illus.). 256p. 1996. 99.95 (*0-86542-911-1*) Blackwell Sci.

Transfusion-Associated AIDS Litigation. Robert K. Jenner. 364p. 1995. text ed. 65.00 (*0-913875-14-7*, 1078) Lawyers & Judges.

Transfusion Immunology & Medicine: Proceedings of the Twelfth International Convocation on Immunology. Ed. by Carel J. Van Oss. LC 94-23955. 480p. 1995. 185.00 (*0-8247-9640-3*) Dekker.

Transfusion Management of Some Common Heritable Blood Disorders. Ed. by Emanuel Hackel et al. LC 92-49941. 99p. 1992. 9.00 (*1-56395-010-3*) Am Assn Blood.

Transfusion Medicine - Fact & Fiction: Proceedings of the 16th Annual Symposium on Blood Transfusion, Groningen, 1991, Organized by the Red Cross Blood Bank Groningen-Drenthe. Ed. by C. T. Sibinga et al. LC 92-12547. (Developments in Hematology & Immunology Ser.: Vol. 27). 240p. (C). 1992. lib. bdg. 77.50 (*0-7923-1732-7*) Kluwer Ac.

Transfusion Practice in Cardiac Surgery. Michael L. Baldwin & Sanford R. Kurtz. LC 91-4865. (Illus.). 58p. (C). 1991. text ed. 9.00 (*1-56395-005-7*) Am Assn Blood.

***Transfusion Reactions.** Ed. by Mark A. Popovsky. (Illus.). 404p. 1996. 99.00 (*1-56395-055-3*, PC97-PR9602) Am Assn Blood.

***Transfusion Service Manual of SOPs, Training Guides, & Competence Assessment Tools.** (Orig.). 1996. pap. text ed. 50.00 (*1-56395-070-7*, PC97-OP9602) Am Assn Blood.

Transfusion Therapy: From Donor to Patient. Ed. by Christina A. Kasprisin & Linda A. Chambers. LC 92-49978. 67p. 1992. 9.00 (*1-56395-014-6*) Am Assn Blood.

Transfusion Therapy: Guidelines for Practice. Ed. by Stephanie H. Summers. LC 90-955. 180p. (C). 1990. text ed. 9.00 (*0-915355-85-X*) Am Assn Blood.

Transfusion Therapy in Infants & Children. Ed. by Naomi L. Luban. LC 90-4280. (Series in Contemporary Medicine & Public Health). (Illus.). 288p. 1990. text ed. 65.00 (*0-8018-4028-7*) Johns Hopkins.

Transfusion Transmitted Infections. Dennis M. Smith et al. LC 91-4561. 330p. 1991. 65.00 (*0-89189-289-3*) Am Soc Clinical.

Transfusionsmedizin Aktuell: Infektionen, Thrombozyten, Granulozyten. Ed. by V. Kretschmer & W. Stangel. (Beitraege zur Infusionstherapie und Klinische Ernaehrung Ser.: Vol. 15). (Illus.). viii, 294p. 1986. 53.75 (*3-8055-4340-9*) S Karger.

Transfusionsmedizin und Schock. H. Reissigl & D. Schoenitzer. (Handbuch der Infusionstherapie und Klinischen Ernaehrung Ser.: Band 3). xii, 256p. 1986. 100.00 (*3-8055-3744-1*) S Karger.

Transfusionsmedizin 1986 - Infektionen, Autotransfusion, Lymphokine. Ed. by V. Kretschmer & W. Stangel. (Beitraege zur Infusionstherapie und Klinische Ernaehrung Ser.: Vol. 18). (Illus.). xii, 412p. 1987. 80.00 (*3-8055-4696-3*) S Karger.

Transfusionsmedizin 1987 - Notfall - und Massivtransfusion, Autoimmunhaemolysen, Infektionen, Stammzelluebertragung. Ed. by V. Kretschmer et al. (Contributions to Infusion Therapy Ser.: Vol. 21). (Illus.). xiv, 360p. 1988. 67.25 (*3-8055-4840-0*) S Karger.

Transfusionsmedizin 1988: Infektionen, Plasmaprodukte, Transplantationen, Antikoerper. Ed. by V. Kretschmer et al. (Beitraege zur Infusionstherapie Ser.: Vol. 24). (Illus.). viii, 242p. 1989. 63.25 (*3-8055-5055-3*) S Karger.

Transfusionsmedizin, 1989-1990. Ed. by V. Kretschmer et al. (Beitraege zur Infusionstherapie, Contributions to Infusion Therapy Ser.: Vol. 26). (Illus.). viii, 454p. 1990. 105.25 (*3-8055-5251-3*) S Karger.

Transfusionsmedizin, 1990-91. Ed. by V. Kretschmer et al. (Beitraege zur Infusionstherapie, Contributions to Infusion Therapy Ser.: Vol. 28). (Illus.). xii, 378p. 1991. 105.25 (*3-8055-5478-8*) S Karger.

Transfusionsmedizin, 1991-92. Ed. by V. Kretschmer et al. (Beitraege zur Infusionstherapie, Contributions to Infusion Therapy Ser.: Vol. 30). (Illus.). xiv, 482p. 1993. 105.25 (*3-8055-5687-X*) S Karger.

Transfusionsmedizin, 1992-93. Ed. by V. Kretschmer et al. (Beitraege zur Infusionstherapie, Contributions to Infusion Therapy Ser.: Vol. 31). (Illus.). x, 230p. 1993. 81.75 (*3-8055-5841-4*) S Karger.

Transfusionsmedizin 1993-1994. Ed. by W. Sibrowski et al. (Beitraege Zur Infusinstherapie und Transfusionsmedizin. Band 32 Contributions to Infusion Therapy & Transfusion Medicine Ser.). (Illus.). xii, 536p. 1994. 132.00 (*3-8055-6025-7*) S Karger.

Transfusionsmedizin 1995/96: 28. Kongress der Deutschen Gesellschaft fur Transfusionmedizin und Immunhaematologie, Wien, 1995. Ed. by W. Sibrowski et al. (Beitraege zur Infusionsmedizin und Transfusionsmedizin (Contributions to Infusion Therapy & Transfusion Medicine) Ser.: Vol. 33). (Illus.). x, 268p. 1996. 156.50 (*3-8055-6345-0*) S Karger.

***Transgender Care: Recommended Guidelines, Practical Information & Personal Accounts.** Gianna E. Israel & Donald E. Tarver. LC 97-17280. 1997. write for info. (*1-56639-571-2*) Temple U Pr.

Transgender Liberation: A Movement Whose Time Has Come. Leslie Feinberg. 1992. pap. 2.50 (*0-89567-105-0*) World View Forum.

Transgender Nation. Gordene O. MacKenzie. LC 94-71363. (Illus.). 182p. (C). 1994. 41.95 (*0-87972-596-6*); pap. 14.95 (*0-87972-597-4*) Bowling Green Univ Popular Press.

***Transgender Warriors: Making History from Joan of Arc to Dennis Rodman.** Leslie Feinberg. LC 96-37682. 1997. pap. 16.00 (*0-8070-7941-3*) Beacon Pr.

Transgender Warriors: Making History from Joan of Arc to RuPaul. Leslie Feinberg. LC 95-33421. (Illus.). 224p. 1996. 27.50 (*0-8070-7940-5*) Beacon Pr.

Transgenerational Design: Products for an Aging Population. James J. Pirkl. LC 93-9870. 260p. 1994. text ed. 54.95 (*0-442-01065-6*) Van Nos Reinhold.

Transgenerational Family Therapies. Laura G. Roberto. LC 92-1530. (Guilford Family Therapy Ser.). 219p. 1992. lib. bdg. 27.95 (*0-89862-107-0*) Guilford Pr.

Transgenesis: Applications of Gene Transfer. Ed. by J. Murray. LC 91-48077. 331p. 1992. text ed. 120.00 (*0-471-93294-9*, Wiley-L) Wiley.

Transgenesis & Targeted Mutagenesis in Immunology. Ed. by Horst Bleuthmann & Pamela Ohashi. LC 93-43197. (Illus.). 316p. 1994. text ed. 65.00 (*0-12-105760-7*) Acad Pr.

Transgenesis Techniques: Principles & Protocols. Ed. by David Murphy & David A. Carter. LC 93-6775. (Methods in Molecular Biology Ser.: Vol. 18). (Illus.). 480p. 1993. spiral bd. 69.50 (*0-89603-245-0*) Humana.

Transgenic Animal Technology: A Laboratory Handbook. Ed. by Carl A. Pinkert. (Illus.). 364p. 1994. pap. 42.00 (*0-12-557165-8*) Acad Pr.

Transgenic Animals. Ed. by F. Grosveld & George V. Kollias. (Illus.). 277p. 1992. text ed. 59.95 (*0-12-304530-4*) Acad Pr.

***Transgenic Animals: Bibliography January 1991-February 1994.** Raymond Dobert. 56p. (Orig.). (C). 1996. pap. text ed. 30.00 (*0-7881-2804-3*) DIANE Pub.

***Transgenic Animals: Generation & Use.** Ed. by Louis M. Houdebine. 592p. 1997. text ed. 280.00 (*90-5702-068-8*, Harwood Acad Pubs) Gordon & Breach.

***Transgenic Animals: Generation & Use.** Ed. by Louis M. Houdebine. 592p. 1997. pap. text ed. 90.00 (*90-5702-069-6*, Harwood Acad Pubs) Gordon & Breach.

Transgenic Animals: Proceedings of the Symposium on Transgenic Technology in Medicine & Agriculture. Neal L. First & Florence P. Haseltine. (Biotechnology Ser.). (Illus.). 416p. 1990. 59.95 (*0-409-90189-X*) Buttrwrth-Heinemann.

Transgenic Animals As Model Systems for Human Diseases. Ed. by Erwin Wagner & Franz Theuring. LC 93-18847. (Schering Foundation Workshop Ser.: Vol. 6). 1995. 82.95 (*0-387-56281-8*) Spr-Verlag.

Transgenic Fish. Ed. by C. L. Hew & G. L. Fletcher. 280p. 1992. text ed. 81.00 (*981-02-0997-5*) World Scientific Pub.

Transgenic Fish Research: A Bibliography. 52p. (Orig.). (C). 1994. pap. text ed. 20.00 (*0-7881-0607-4*) DIANE Pub.

Transgenic Mice & Mutants in MHC Research. Ed. by I. K. Egorov & C. David. (Illus.). 310p. 1990. 88.00 (*0-387-52201-8*) Spr-Verlag.

Transgenic Mice As in Vivo Model for Self-Reactivity. D. Ferrick. (Medical Intelligence Unit Ser.). 100p. 1993. 89.95 (*1-879702-46-0*) R G Landes.

Transgenic Modification of Germline & Somatic Cells. Ed. by R. B. Flavell & R. B. Heap. LC 93-33047. 119p. (gr. 13). 1994. text ed. 71.95 (*0-412-55510-7*, Chap & Hall NY) Chapman & Hall.

***Transgenic Mouse Model for Alzheimer's Disease.** Dieder Moechars. (Acta Biomedica Lovaniensia Ser.: No. 122). (Illus.). 113p. (Orig.). 1996. pap. 43.50 (*90-6186-727-4*, Pub. by Leuven Univ BE) Coronet Bks.

Transgenic Organisms: Biological & Social Implications. Ed. by J. Tomiuk et al. LC 96-6480. (Advances in Life Sciences Ser.). 1996. 83.95 (*0-8176-5262-0*); 83.95 (*3-7643-5262-0*) Birkhauser.

Transgenic Organisms: Risk Assessment of Deliberate Release. Ed. by J. Tomiuk & K. W. Wohrmann. LC 93-19390. vii, 271p. 1993. 59.00 (*0-8176-2834-7*) Birkhauser.

Transgenic Organisms & Biosafety: Horizontal Gene Transfer, Stability of DNA, & Expression of Transgenes. Ed. by E. R. Schmidt & T. Hankeln. LC 96-14200. (Illus.). 344p. 1996. pap. 119.00 (*3-540-61077-4*) Spr-Verlag.

Transgenic Plants: A Production System for Industrial & Pharmaceutical Proteins. Meran R. Owen & J. Pen. LC 96-21457. 1996. text ed. 125.00 (*0-471-96443-3*); pap. text ed. 52.95 (*0-471-96444-1*) Wiley.

Transgenic Plants: Fundamentals & Applications. Ed. by Andrew Hiatt. LC 92-26046. (Books in Soils, Plants & the Environment: Vol. 24). 360p. 1992. 170.00 (*0-8247-8766-8*) Dekker.

***Transgenic Plants: Intellectual Properties & Commercialisation of Transgenic Plants.** 300p. Date not set. text ed. 33.00 (*1-86094-062-5*) World Scientific Pub.

Transgenic Plants: Present Status & Social & Economic Impacts, Vol. 2. Ed. by Shain-dow Kung & Ray Wu. (Illus.). 265p. 1992. text ed. 89.00 (*0-12-428782-4*) Acad Pr.

Transgenic Plants, Vol. 1: Engineering & Utilization. Ed. by Shain-dow Kung & Ray Wu. (Illus.). 383p. 1992. text ed. 89.00 (*0-12-428781-6*) Acad Pr.

Transgenic Xenopus: Microinjection Methods & Developmental Neurobiology. Hermona Soreq & Shlomo Seidman. (Neuromethods Ser.: No. 28). (Illus.). 216p. 1996. 79.50 (*0-89603-457-7*) Humana.

Transglutaminase. Ed. by Victor A. Najjar & Laszlo Lorand. (Developments in Molecular & Cellular Bio-Chemistry Ser.). 1984. lib. bdg. 116.50 (*0-89838-593-8*) Kluwer Ac.

***Transgressing Boundaries: New Directions in the Study of Culture in Africa.** Ed. by Brenda Cooper & Andrew Steyn. 240p. 1997. pap. text ed. 27.95 (*0-8214-1183-7*) Ohio U Pr.

***Transgressing Discourses: Communication & the Voice of Other.** Ed. by Michael Huspek & Gary P. Radford. LC 97-2267. (SUNY Series, Human Communication Processes). 320p. (C). 1997. text ed. 62.50 (*0-7914-3353-6*); pap. text ed. 20.95 (*0-7914-3354-4*) State U NY Pr.

Transgression & Self-Punishment in Isaac Bashevis Singer's Searches. Frances V. Gibbons. LC 93-50937. (Twentieth-Century American Jewish Writers Ser.: Vol. 6). 168p. (C). 1995. text ed. 41.95 (*0-8204-2489-7*) P Lang Pubng.

Transgressions: The Iowa Anthology of Innovative Fiction. Ed. by Lee Montgomery et al. LC 94-60574. 274p. (Orig.). 1994. pap. 19.95 (*0-87745-474-4*) U of Iowa Pr.

Transgressions of Reading: Narrative Engagement As Exile & Return. Robert D. Newman. LC 92-13546. (Post-Contemporary Interventions Ser.). (Illus.). 192p. 1992. text ed. 43.95 (*0-8223-1280-8*); pap. text ed. 16.95 (*0-8223-1296-4*) Duke.

Transgressive Corporeality: The Body, Poststructuralism & the Theological Imagination. Diane L. MacDonald. LC 94-24727. 170p. 1995. text ed. 57.50 (*0-7914-2487-1*); pap. text ed. 18.95 (*0-7914-2488-X*) State U NY Pr.

Transgressive Readings: The Texts of Franz Kafka & Max Planck. Valerie D. Greenberg. 180p. 1990. text ed. 34.50 (*0-472-10158-7*) U of Mich Pr.

Transgressors. Jim Thompson. 1994. pap. 9.00 (*0-679-74016-3*) Random.

Transhuman Condition: A Report on Machines, Technics & Evolution. Keith Ansell-Pearson. LC 96-20530. 224p. (C). 1997. pap. write for info. (*0-415-15435-9*); text ed. write for info. (*0-415-15434-0*) Routledge.

***Transicion y Transaccion: La Revista Cubana Casa de las Americas (1960-1976)** Nadia Lie. 318p. (Orig.). (SPA.). (C). 1996. pap. 30.00 (*0-935318-23-2*) Edins Hispamerica.

Transiciones, Migraciones. Julio Matas. LC 93-72085. (Coleccion Caniqui). 149p. (Orig.). (SPA.). 1993. pap. 16.00 (*0-89729-693-1*) Ediciones.

***Transient Amnesia: Clinical & Neuropsychological Aspects.** John R. Hodges. (Major Problems in Neurology Ser.: Vol. 24). (Illus.). 171p. 1991. write for info. (*0-7020-1553-9*, Pub. by W B Saunders UK) Saunders.

Transient & Permanent in Liberal Religion: Collected Papers of the 1995 Convocation. Ed. by Dan O'Neal et al. 1995. pap. 16.00 (*1-55896-330-8*, Skinner Hse Bks) Unitarian Univ.

Transient Criminality: A Model of Stress-Induced Crime. Anthony R. Mawson. LC 87-11741. 352p. 1987. text ed. 65.00 (*0-275-92552-8*, C2552, Praeger Pubs) Greenwood.

***Transient Enzyme Kinetics.** Bagshaw. (Illus.). 200p. (Orig.). 1997. pap. text ed. write for info. (*0-412-60310-1*, Chap & Hall NY) Chapman & Hall.

Transient Flow in Natural Gas Transmission Systems. American Gas Association, Transient Flow Committee et al. 273p. 1964. 5.00 (*0-318-12725-3*, L20030) Am Gas Assn.

Transient Global Amnesia & Related Disorders. Ed. by Hans J. Markowitsch. LC 90-4811. (Illus.). 260p. 1990. text ed. 58.00 (*0-920887-70-8*) Hogrefe & Huber Pubs.

Transient Ground Water Hydraulics. Robert E. Glover. 1978. pap. 35.00 (*0-918334-24-1*) WRP.

Transient Guest & Other Episodes. Edgar E. Saltus. LC 76-116007. reprint ed. 37.50 (*0-404-05509-5*) AMS Pr.

***Transient Ischaemic Attacks of the Brain & Eye.** Graeme J. Hankey & Charles P. Warlow. (Major Problems in Neurology Ser.: Vol. 27). (Illus.). 422p. 1994. write for info. (*0-7020-1590-3*, Pub. by W B Saunders UK) Saunders.

Transient Ischemic Attacks. Ed. by Peter J. Morris & Charles P. Warlow. LC 82-9668. (Science & Practice of Surgery Ser.: No. 3). (Illus.). 430p. reprint ed. pap. 122.60 (*0-7837-0923-4*, 2041228) Bks Demand.

Transient Lens Synthesis. Baum & Stone. 1990. 68.95 (*0-89116-986-5*) Hemisp Pub.

Transient Nativity: A Christmas Story. Frederick A. Raborg, Jr. (Amelia Chapbooks Ser.). 8p. 1987. pap. 4.00 (*0-936545-07-0*) Amelia.

Transient Phenomena in Multiphase Flow: Proceedings of the International Centre for Heat & Mass Transfer. Ed. by Naim H. Afgan. 400p. 1988. 302.00 (*0-89116-682-3*) Hemisp Pub.

Transient Phenomena in Nuclear Reactor Systems. Ed. by P. F. Peterson & J. H. Kim. (HTD Series, Vol. 245: NE: Vol. 11). 148p. 1993. 40.00 (*0-7918-1158-1*, G00802) ASME.

Transient Poet: William Allan Retrospective. William Allan et al. 1993. write for info. (*0-318-72127-9*) Crocker Art Mus.

Transient Protection, Grounding, & Shielding of Electronic Traffic Control Equipment. (National Cooperative Highway Research Program Report Ser.: No. 317). 84p. 1989. 11.00 (*0-309-04614-9*) Transport Res Bd.

Transient Sex. Brent Reiten. 60p. (Orig.). 1989. pap. 8.00 (*0-317-94038-4*) Scalding Pr.

Transient Simulation Methods for Gas Networks. Andrzej J. Osiadacz. 300p. 1993. text ed. write for info. (*0-13-927963-6*) P-H.

Transient Stability Analysis of Synchronous Motors. J. Cemus & V. Hamata. (Studies in Electrical & Electronic Engineering: No. 36). 266p. 1991. 163.25 (*0-444-98866-1*) Elsevier.

Transient Stability of Power Systems: Theory & Practice. M. Pavella & P. G. Murthy. LC 93-32934. 403p. 1994. text ed. 110.00 (*0-471-94213-8*) Wiley.

Transient Techniques in Electrochemistry. Ed. by Digby D. Macdonald. LC 77-24603. 330p. 1977. 75.00 (*0-306-31010-4*, Plenum Pr) Plenum.

Transient Techniques in NMR of Solids: An Introduction to Theory & Practice. B. C. Gerstein & C. R. Dybowski. 1985. text ed. 121.00 (*0-12-281180-1*) Acad Pr.

Transient Temperatures in Engineering & Science. G. Klingenberg & B. Lawton. LC 96-96. (Illus.). 600p. (C). 1996. 150.00 (*0-19-856260-8*) OUP.

Transient Thermal Hydraulics, Heat Transfer, & Coupled Vessel & Piping Responses. Ed. by Y. S. Shin et al. LC 94-71577. (Proceedings of the 1995 ASME/JSME Pressure Vessels & Piping Conference Ser.: Vol. 311). 120p. 1995. 80.00 (*0-7918-1342-8*, H00974) ASME.

Transient Thermal Hydraulics, Heat Transfer, Fluid-Structure Interaction & Structural Dynamics: Proceedings of the Pressure Vessels & Piping Conference, Minneapolis, MN, 1994. Y. W. Shin. LC 94-71577. (PVP Ser.: Vol. 270). 159p. 1994. pap. 50.00 (*0-7918-1193-X*) ASME.

***Transient Thermal Processing Techniques in Electronic Materials.** Ed. by N. M. Ravindra & R. K. Singh. (Illus.). 179p. 1996. 48.00 (*0-87339-331-7*) Minerals Metals.

***Transient Tunnel Effect & Sommerfeld Problem: Waves in Semi-Infinite Structures.** F. Ali Mehmeti. (Mathematical Research Ser.: Vol. 91). 200p. 1996. pap. 59.95 (*3-05-501707-2*, Pub. by Akademie Verlag GW) Wiley.

Transient Unemployed. John N. Webb. LC 71-166337. (FDR & the Era of the New Deal Ser.). 1971. reprint ed. lib. bdg. 20.00 (*0-306-70335-1*) Da Capo.

Transient Waves in Layered Media. M. Tygel & P. Hubral. (Methods in Geochemistry & Geophysics Ser.: No. 26). 342p. 1987. 144.50 (*0-444-42808-9*) Elsevier.

***Transient Ways.** Jessica E. Hahn. (Illus.). 96p. (Orig.). 1996. pap. 5.99 (*1-890054-03-8*) Passing Through.

Transients: Paintings by Thomas S. Buechner. Intro. by Kenneth H. Lindquist. (Orig.). 1985. pap. 14.95 (*1-877885-04-5*) Arnot Art.

Transients & Other Disqueting Stories. Darrell Schweitzer. LC 91-75681. (Illus.). 191p. 1993. 26.50 (*0-932445-56-X*); pap. 8.95 (*0-932445-55-1*) Ganley Pub.

Transients & Other Disqueting Stories. limited ed. Darrell Schweitzer. LC 91-75681. (Illus.). 191p. 1993. boxed 42.50 (*0-932445-57-8*) Ganley Pub.

Transients, Settlers, & Refugees. Vaughan Robinson. (Illus.). 264p. 1986. 55.00 (*0-19-878009-5*) OUP.

Transistion from School to Work in Europe. Ed. by Peter Grootings & Michael Stefanov. 256p. (C). 1988. lib. bdg. 49.95 (*0-415-00576-0*) Routledge.

Transistor Amplifier Circuits. Buck Engineering Staff. Ed. by Buck Engineering Tech. Writers. (F. A. C. E. T. Ser.: Vol. 6). (Illus.). 108p. 1989. teacher ed., pap. text ed. 11.00 (*0-86657-019-5*); ring bd. 13.00 (*0-86657-018-7*) Lab-Volt.

Transistor Circuit Action. 2nd ed. H. C. Veatch. (Illus.). (C). 1976. text ed. 39.95 (*0-07-067383-7*) McGraw.

Transistor Circuit Approximations. 3rd ed. Albert P. Malvino. LC 79-18580. (Illus.). 1980. text ed. 42.95 (*0-07-039878-X*) McGraw.

Transistor Circuit Design. Vincent F. Leonard, Jr. (Engineering Design Ser.). (Illus.). 583p. (C). 1983. teacher ed. 9.95 (*0-87119-018-4*); student ed. 10.95 (*0-87119-017-6*); pap. text ed. 19.95 (*0-87119-016-8*); ring bd. 59.95 (*0-87119-015-X*, EE-1002) Heathkit-Zenith Ed.

Transistor Circuit Techniques. 2nd ed. Gordon J. Ritchie. 1987. pap. 34.95 (*0-278-00034-7*) Chapman & Hall.

Transistor Circuit Techniques: Discrete & Integrated. 3rd ed. Gordon J. Ritchie. LC 92-44028. (Tutorial Guides in Electronic Engineering Ser.: Vol. 1). 240p. (gr. 13). 1993. pap. text ed. 30.95 (*0-412-46470-5*) Chapman & Hall.

Transistor Feedback Circuits. Buck Engineering Staff. Ed. by Buck Engineering Tech. Writers. (F. A. C. E. T. Ser.: Vol. 8). (Illus.). 88p. 1989. teacher ed., pap. text ed. 11.00 (*0-86657-023-3*); ring bd. 13.00 (*0-86657-022-5*) Lab-Volt.

Transistor Fundamentals. Training & Retraining Inc. Staff. LC 68-21313. 1968. 10.35 (*0-672-20744-3*, Bobbs); teacher ed. 5.00 (*0-672-20647-1*, Bobbs) Macmillan.

Transistor Fundamentals, Bk. 2. Training & Retraining Inc. Staff. LC 68-21313. 1968. Bk 2. 10.35 (*0-672-20745-1*, Bobbs) Macmillan.

Transistor Power Amplifiers. Buck Engineering Staff. Ed. by Buck Engineering Tech. Writers. (F. A. C. E. T. Ser.: Vol. 7). (Illus.). 152p. 1989. ring bd. 12.00 (*0-86657-020-9*) Lab-Volt.

Transistor Power Amplifiers. Buck Engineering Staff. Ed. by Buck Engineering Tech. Writers. (F. A. C. E. T. Ser.: Vol. 7). (Illus.). 76p. 1990. teacher ed., pap. text ed. 11.00 (*0-86657-021-7*) Lab-Volt.

Transistor Radios: A Wallace-Homestead Price Guide. David Lane. 176p. 1994. pap. 19.95 (*0-87069-712-9*) Chilton.

Transistors. Richard Hunter. LC 84-730278. (Orig.). 1984. student ed. 7.00 (*0-8064-0313-6*, 807); audio, vhs 329.00 (*0-8064-0314-4*) Bergwall.

***Transistors: From Crystal to IC's.** 250p. 1998. lib. bdg. 34.00 (*981-02-2743-4*) World Scientific Pub.

Transistors: Fundamentals for the Integrated-Circuit Engineer. R. M. Warner, Jr. & B. L. Grung. LC 88-17417. 896p. 1990. reprint ed. lib. bdg. 76.50 (*0-89464-323-1*) Krieger.

***Transit.** Jean-Francois Lyotard. 1997. 35.00 (*3-89322-894-2*, Pub. by Edition Cantz GW) Dist Art Pubs.

TransiT: A Novel. Rosaire Appel. 133p. 1993. 18.95 (*0-932511-70-8*); pap. 8.95 (*0-932511-71-6*) Fiction Coll.

Transit & Transportation: Study of Port & Industrial Areas, Vol. 6. (Metropolitan America Ser.). 230p. 1974. 29.95 (*0-405-05419-X*) Ayer.

Transit Bus Energy Efficiency & Productivity - Bus Equipment Selection Handbook. (National Cooperative Transit Research Program Synthesis Ser.: No. 1). 55p. 1982. 7.20 (*0-309-03417-5*) Transport Res Bd.

Transit Bus Maintenance. (Research Record Ser.: No. 1140). 51p. 1987. 7.50 (*0-309-04651-3*) Transport Res Bd.

Transit Capital Investment to Reduce Operating Deficits-Alternative Bus Replacement Strategies. (National Cooperative Transit Research Program Synthesis Ser.: No. 15). 69p. 1988. 10.40 (*0-309-04571-1*) Transport Res Bd.

Transit Captain. Jack Rudman. (Career Examination Ser.: C-819). 1994. pap. 39.95 (*0-8373-0819-4*) Nat Learn.

Transit Circle: Biography of William Simms, 1793-1860. Eleanor Mennim. (C). 1989. pap. 35.00 (*1-85072-101-7*, Pub. by W Sessions UK) St Mut.

Transit Electrical Helper Series. Jack Rudman. (Career Examination Ser.: C-1963). 1994. pap. 23.95 (*0-8373-1963-3*) Nat Learn.

Transit, Land Use & Urban Form. Wayne O. Attoe. (Illus.). 200p. 1988. text ed. 20.00 (*0-934951-01-2*) Ctr Study of Amer Archit.

Transit Lieutenant. Jack Rudman. (Career Examination Ser.: C-820). 1994. pap. 34.95 (*0-8373-0820-8*) Nat Learn.

***Transit Lounge: Wake-Up Calls & Travelers' Tales from the Future.** Ed. by Ashley Crawford & Ray Edgar. 192p. (Orig.). 1997. pap. 28.00 (*90-5704-111-1*, Pub. by Craftsman Hse VB) IPG Chicago.

Transit Management Analyst. Jack Rudman. (Career Examination Ser.: C-2028). 1994. pap. 34.95 (*0-8373-2028-3*) Nat Learn.

Transit Management Analyst Trainee. Jack Rudman. (Career Examination Ser.: C-3228). 1994. reprint ed. pap. 29.95 (*0-8373-3228-1*) Nat Learn.

Transit Management & Replacement Capital Planning. (Research Record Ser.: No. 1165). 121p. 1988. 18.50 (*0-309-04706-4*) Transport Res Bd.

Transit Management in the Northwest Passage: Problems & Prospects. Ed. by C. Lamson & D. Vanderzwaag. (Studies in Polar Research). (Illus.). 200p. 1988. 99.95 (*0-521-32065-8*) Cambridge U Pr.

Transit Management, Marketing, & Performance. (Research Record Ser.: No. 1144). 97p. 1987. 13.00 (*0-309-04521-5*) Transport Res Bd.

Transit Manager's Guide to Portable Fire Extinguishers for Transit Vehicles. Erskine S. Walther. 22p. 1995. spiral bd. 20.00 (*1-885327-08-0*) Walther Cnslt.

Transit of Civilization from England to America in the Seventeenth Century. Edward Eggleston. (BCL1 - U. S. History Ser.). 344p. 1991. reprint ed. lib. bdg. 89.00 (*0-7812-6008-6*) Rprt Serv.

Transit of Saturn. Marc Robertson. 74p. 1976. 10.50 (*0-86690-149-3*, R1406-014) Am Fed Astrologers.

Transit of "Small, Merry" Anglo-American Culture: Sir John BarleyCorne & Sir Richard Rum (& Captain Whiskey) Joel Bernard. 57p. 1990. pap. 8.00 (*0-944026-24-9*) Am Antiquarian.

Transit of Venus. Shirley Hazzard. 352p. 1990. pap. 11.95 (*0-14-010747-9*, Penguin Bks) Viking Penguin.

Transit Patrolman. Jack Rudman. (Career Examination Ser.: C-821). 1994. pap. 23.95 (*0-8373-0821-6*) Nat Learn.

Transit Politics in South Asia. Roop S. Baraith. 1989. 36.00 (*0-8364-2539-1*, Commonwealth) S Asia.

Transit Postmark Collector Bound, Vol. 8. 33.00 (*0-318-18051-0*) Mobile PO.

Transit Problems of Three Asian Land-Locked Countries: Afghanistan, Nepal & Laos. Martin I. Glassner. (Occasional Papers-Reprints Series in Contemporary Asian Studies: No. 4-1983 (57)). 55p. (Orig.). 1983. pap. text ed. 3.00 (*0-942182-56-1*) U MD Law.

Transit Property Protection Agent. Jack Rudman. (Career Examination Ser.: C-2397). 1994. pap. 23.95 (*0-8373-2397-5*) Nat Learn.

Transit Property Protection Supervisor. (Career Examination Ser.: C-3593). 1994. pap. 27.95 (*0-8373-3593-0*) Nat Learn.

Transit Security Procedures Guide. lib. bdg. 267.00 (*0-8490-8357-5*) Gordon Pr.

Transit Sergeant. Jack Rudman. (Career Examination Ser.: C-822). 1994. pap. 34.95 (*0-8373-0822-4*) Nat Learn.

Transit System Manager. Jack Rudman. (Career Examination Ser.: C-539). 1994. pap. 39.95 (*0-8373-0539-X*) Nat Learn.

Transit System Security Program Planning Guide. 1995. lib. bdg. 252.95 (*0-8490-8358-3*) Gordon Pr.

Transit Time Effects in Unipolar Solid-State Devices. D. Dascalu. (Abacus Bks.). 396p. 1974. text ed. 92.00 (*0-85626-007-X*) Gordon & Breach.

Transit to Narcissus: A Facsimile of the Original Typescript. Norman Mailer. LC 77-24755. xiv, 848p. 1978. lib. bdg. 49.50 (*0-86527-315-4*) Fertig.

Transit Villages in the 21st Century. Michael S. Bernick & Robert B. Cervero. LC 96-34617. (Illus.). 254p. 1996. text ed. 42.95 (*0-07-005475-4*) McGraw.

Transition: An Author Index. Charles L. Silet. LC 79-67477. 186p. 1979. 15.00 (*0-87875-168-8*) Whitston Pub.

Transition: An Introduction to Urban College Student Life. Ed. by Robert DeLucia. 1992. 30.00 (*0-536-58155-X*) Ginn Pr.

Transition: Decouverte du Texte Litteraire. 2nd ed. Hage et al. (Illus.). 176p. (FRE.). (C). 1994. pap. text ed. 36.20 (*0-13-157348-9*) P-H.

***Transition: Essays on Contemporary Literature.** Edwin Muir. 218p. Date not set. 20.95 (*0-8369-2666-8*) Ayer.

Transition: Essays on Contemporary Literature. Edwin Muir. (BCL1-PR English Literature Ser.). 218p. 1992. reprint ed. lib. bdg. 79.00 (*0-7812-7061-8*) Rprt Serv.

***Transition: Issue 69.** Ed. by K. Anthony Appiah et al. 245p. 1996. pap. 10.00 (*0-8223-6439-5*) Duke.

***Transition: Planning for the Post-School Adjustment of Individuals with Disabilities.** Edward Levinson. 1997. 60.00 (*0-8133-2515-3*) Westview.

Transition: Questions & Answers. 48p. 1986. pap. 25.00 (*0-86688-110-7*) Joint Comm Hlthcare.

Transition - School to Work: Models for Effective Transition Planning. Fred J. Krieg. 167p. 1995. pap. text ed. 24.95 (*0-932955-97-5*) Natl Assn Schl Psych.

Transition - Taking over a Management Account. 54p. 1992. pap. 24.95 (*0-685-71662-7*, 79701); pap. 34.95 incl. 5.25 hd (*0-685-71663-5*, 797) Inst Real Estate.

Transition & Instability in Central Asia: The Fergana Valley. Yuriy G. Kulchik. 60p. 1996. pap. text ed. 12.95 (*1-899658-16-5*, Pub. by Royal Inst Intl Affairs UK) Brookings.

***Transition & Price Stabilization Policies in East European Agriculture.** 63p. 1994. 9.00 (*92-5-103488-5*, F34885, Pub. by FAO IT) Bernan Associates.

Transition & Students with Learning Disabilities: Facilitating the Movement from School to Adult Life. Ed. by James R. Patton & Ginger Blalock. LC 95-52856. 309p. 1996. pap. 32.00 (*0-89079-696-3*) PRO-ED.

***Transition & Sustainability: Actors & Interests in Eastern European Environmental Policies.** Bernd Baumgartl. LC 97-10312. (International Environmental Law & Policy Ser.). 1997. write for info. (*90-411-0681-2*) Kluwer Law Tax Pubs.

Transition & Tradition in Moral Theology. Charles E. Curran. LC 78-20877. 272p. 1979. text ed. 15.00 (*0-268-01837-5*) U of Notre Dame Pr.

Transition & Turmoil in the Atlantic Alliance. Ed. by Robert A. Levine. 250p. 1991. 47.00 (*0-8448-1701-5*, Crane Russak); pap. 29.00 (*0-8448-1702-3*, Crane Russak) Taylor & Francis.

***Transition at the Local Level: The Czech Republic, Hungary, Poland, & the Slovak Republic.** 176p. (Orig.). 1996. pap. 29.00 (*92-64-15363-2*, 14-96-20-1, Pub. by Org for Econ FR) OECD.

Transition Behavior Scale IEP & Intervention Manual. Stephen B. McCarney. 230p. (Orig.). 1989. pap. 20.00 (*1-878372-14-9*) Hawthorne Educ Servs.

***Transition Demo in Paraguay.** Lambert. LC 97-9651. 1997. text ed. 69.95 (*0-312-17523-X*) St Martin.

Transition Equation: A Proven Strategy for Organizational Change. J. Allan McCarthy. 217p. 23.00 (*0-02-920485-2*, Lexington) Jossey-Bass.

Transition, Explained: Earth Questions - Spirit Answers As Presented by the Spirit World through the Automatic Writings of Frances Bird. Frances Bird. LC 87-22788. 172p. (Orig.). 1990. pap. 16.95 (*1-55768-700-5*) LC Pub.

Transition form School to Work: States Are Developing New Strategies to Prepare Students for Jobs. 56p. (Orig.). (C). 1994. pap. text ed. 20.00 (*0-7881-0732-1*) DIANE Pub.

Transition from Capitalism to Feudalism. Rodney H. Hilton et al. 175p. (C). 1984. pap. text ed. 18.00 (*0-86091-701-0*, Pub. by Vrso UK) Norton.

Transition from Capitalism to Socialism. John D. Stephens. LC 86-1329. 248p. 1986. pap. text ed. 11.95 (*0-252-01323-9*) U of Ill Pr.

Transition from Developer Control. rev. ed. Amanda G. Hyatt. (GAP Report Ser.: Vol. 3). (C). 1996. pap. 17.50 (*0-944715-20-6*) CAI.

Transition from Infancy to Language: Acquiring the Power of Expression. Lois Bloom. LC 92-47407. (Illus.). 384p. (C). 1993. text ed. 54.95 (*0-521-44031-9*) Cambridge U Pr.

Transition from Infancy to Language: Acquiring the Power of Expression. Lois Bloom. (Illus.). 363p. (C). 1995. pap. text ed. 17.95 (*0-521-48379-4*) Cambridge U Pr.

Transition from Military to Civilian Life: How to Plan a Bright Future Now for You & Your Family. Merle Dethlefsen & James D. Canfield. LC 84-10536. (Illus.). 256p. (Orig.). 1984. reprint ed. pap. 73.00 (*0-608-00472-3*, 2061291) Bks Demand.

Transition from Prelinguistic to Linguistic Communication. Ed. by Roberta M. Golinkoff. 344p. (C). 1983. text ed. 69.95 (*0-89859-257-7*) L Erlbaum Assocs.

Transition from School to Adult Life. Ed. by Frank R. Rusch et al. 400p. (C). 1991. text ed. 49.95 (*0-9625233-4-8*) Sycamore Pub.

Transition from School to Adult Life. 2nd ed. Frank R. Rusch & Janis C. Rusch. (Special Education Ser.). (C). 1997. pap. text ed. 49.95 (*0-534-34432-1*) Wadsworth Pub.

Transition from Shamanism to Russian Orthodoxy in Alaska. S. A. Mousalimas. LC 94-36777. 272p. (C). 1995. 49.95 (*1-57181-006-4*) Berghahn Bks.

Transition from Socialism in Eastern Europe: Domestic Restructuring & Foreign Trade. Ed. by Arye L. Hillman & Branko Milanovic. LC 92-1684. (Regional & Sectoral Studies). 352p. 1992. 20.95 (*0-8213-2148-X*, 12148) World Bank.

Transition from State Socialism in Eastern Europe Vol. 14: The Case of Hungary. Ed. by Craig Calhoun. (Comparative Social Research Ser.). 232p. 1994. 73.25 (*1-55938-527-8*) Jai Pr.

Transition from War to Peace in Sub-Saharan Africa. Nat J. Colletta et al. LC 96-10245. (Directions in Development Ser.). 96p. 1996. 10.95 (*0-8213-3581-2*, 13581) World Bank.

Transition from Work to Retirement. OECD Staff. (Social Policy Studies: No. 16). 178p. (Orig.). 1995. pap. 43.00 (*92-64-14555-9*, Pub. by Org for Econ FR) OECD.

Transition Game: An Inside Look at Life with the Chicago Bulls. Melissa Isaacson. LC 94-68642. (Illus.). 250p. 1994. 19.95 (*1-57167-005-X*) Sagamore Pub.

Transition Guide for College Juniors & Seniors: How to Prepare for the Future. Carol Weinberg. (Illus.). 320p. (C). 1996. 45.00 (*0-8147-9285-5*) NYU Pr.

Transition Guide for College Juniors & Seniors: How to Prepare for the Future. Carol Weinberg. (Illus.). 320p. (C). 1996. pap. 14.95 (*0-8147-9306-1*) NYU Pr.

Transition, How to Become a Salon Professional. Louise Cotter & Frances L. DuBose. (Cosmetology Ser.). 352p. 1996. 24.95 (*1-56253-263-4*) Milady Pub.

Transition in African Beliefs: Traditional Religion & Christian Change: A Study in Sukumaland, Tanzania, East Africa. Ralph E. Tanner. LC 67-21411. 270p. reprint ed. pap. 77.00 (*0-317-26638-1*, 2025117) Bks Demand.

***Transition in Burundi: The Context for a Homecoming.** (Issue Papers). 1993. pap. 4.00 (*0-614-25346-2*) US Comm Refugees.

Transition in Central & Eastern Europe - Implications for EU-LDC Relations: Implilcations for EU-LDC Relations. Ed. by Arie Kuyvenhoven et al. LC 95-49482. (Diverse Ser.). 352p. (C). 1996. lib. bdg. 130.00 (*0-7923-3875-8*) Kluwer Ac.

Transition in Cuba: New Challenges for U. S. Policy. Cuban Research Institute Staff & Florida International University Staff. 674p. 1993. pap. 35.00 (*1-879862-05-0*) FL Intl U Latin.

T

Transition in Eastern Europe, 2 vols., Set. Ed. by Olivier J. Blanchard et al. LC 93-36585. (National Bureau of Economic Research Project Report Ser.). 384p. 1994. 39.95 (*0-226-05660-0*) U Ch Pr.

Transition in Eastern Europe: Restructuring, Vol. 2. Ed. by Jean O. Blanchard et al. 384p. (C). 1994. 48.00 (*0-226-05662-7*) U Ch Pr.

Transition in Illinois from British to American Government. Robert L. Schuyler. reprint ed. 24.50 (*0-404-05627-X*) AMS Pr.

Transition in Open Dualistic Economies: Theory & Southeast Asian Experience. Douglas S. Paauw & John C. Fei. LC 73-77163. (Illus.). 312p. 1973. 47.00 (*0-300-01641-7*) Yale U Pr.

Transition in Spain: From Franco to Democracy. Victor Alba. Tr. by Barbara Lotito. LC 77-28117. 334p. 1978. 44.95 (*0-87855-225-1*) Transaction Pubs.

***Transition in the Baltic States: Microlevel Studies.** Neil Hood et al. LC 96-38948. 1997. text ed. 55.00 (*0-312-17235-4*) St Martin.

Transition in the Nuclear Industry: Proceedings of a Symposium Sponsored by the Construction & Energy Division. Ed. by James H. Olyniec. 237p. 1985. 26.00 (*0-87262-443-9*) Am Soc Civil Eng.

Transition in Virginia from Colony to Commonwealth. Charles R. Lingley. LC 10-14656. (Columbia University. Studies in the Social Sciences: No. 96). reprint ed. 37.50 (*0-404-51096-5*) AMS Pr.

Transition Ion Electron Paramagnetic Resonance. J. R. Pilbrow. (Illus.). 738p. 1991. 210.00 (*0-19-855214-9*) OUP.

Transition Magician: Strategies for Guiding Your Children in Early Childhood Programs. Nola Larson et al. (Illus.). 136p. (Orig.). 1994. pap. 18.95 (*0-934140-81-2*, 3029) Redleaf Pr.

Transition Math. Martha Palmer. Ed. by Joan Hoffman. (I Know It! Bks.). (Illus.). 32p. (J). (gr. k-1). 1979. student ed. 1.99 (*0-938256-27-0*) Sch Zone Pub Co.

Transition Mathematics. 2nd ed. University of Chicago School Mathematic Project Staff. 1995. text ed. 37.27 (*0-673-45745-1*) Addson-Wesley Educ.

Transition Mathematics. 2nd ed. University of Chicago School Mathematic Project Staff. 1995. teacher ed., text ed. 50.32 (*0-673-45748-6*) Addson-Wesley Educ.

Transition Mechanisms in Child Development: The Longitudinal Perspective. Ed. by Anik De Ribaupierre. (Illus.). 300p. (C). 1989. text ed. 74.95 (*0-521-37138-4*) Cambridge U Pr.

Transition Metal Carbene Complexes: Dedicated to Professor E. O. Fischer. D. Seyferth et al. 265p. 1983. 105.00 (*0-89573-073-1*, VCH) Wiley.

Transition Metal Carbyne Complexes: Proceedings of the NATO Advanced Research Workshop, Wildbad Kreuth, Germany, September 17-October 2, 1992. Ed. by F. R. Kreibl. (NATO Advanced Study Institutes Ser.). 292p. (C). 1993. lib. bdg. 137.00 (*0-7923-2212-6*) Kluwer Ac.

Transition Metal Catalyzed Polymerizations: Ziegler-Natta & Metathesis Polymerizations. Ed. by Roderic P. Quirk. (Illus.). 880p. (C). 1989. text ed. 105.00 (*0-521-33289-3*) Cambridge U Pr.

Transition Metal Catalyzed Polymerizations-Alkenes & Dienes: Papers Presented at Eleventh Midland Macromolecular Meeting, Midland, Michigan, August 1981, Vol. 4. Ed. by R. P. Quirk. (MMI Press Symposium Ser.). 1349p. 1983. text ed. 494.00 (3-7186-0143-5, Harwood Acad Pubs) Gordon & Breach.

Transition Metal Chemistry. A. Mueller & E. Diemann. (Illus.). 338p. 1981. pap. 90.00 (0-89573-039-1, VCH) Wiley.

Transition Metal Chemistry, 1. Ed. by Richard L. Carlin. LC 65-27431. 319p. 1965. pap. 91.00 (0-8357-8000-7, 2027127) Bks Demand.

Transition Metal Chemistry, 2. Ed. by Richard L. Carlin. LC 65-27431. 360p. 1966. pap. 102.60 (0-8357-8001-5, 2027127) Bks Demand.

Transition Metal Chemistry, 3. Ed. by Richard L. Carlin. LC 65-27431. 371p. 1967. pap. 105.80 (0-8357-8002-3, 2017696) Bks Demand.

Transition Metal Chemistry, 4. Ed. by Richard L. Carlin. LC 65-27431. 365p. 1968. pap. 104.10 (0-8357-8003-1, 2027127) Bks Demand.

Transition Metal Chemistry, 5. Ed. by Richard L. Carlin. LC 65-27431. 317p. 1969. pap. 90.40 (0-8357-8004-X, 2027127) Bks Demand.

Transition Metal Chemistry, 7. Ed. by Richard L. Carlin. LC 65-27431. 378p. 1972. pap. 107.80 (0-8357-8005-8, 2027127) Bks Demand.

Transition Metal Chemistry, Vol. 6. Ed. by Richard L. Carlin. LC 65-27431. 340p. 1970. reprint ed. pap. 96.90 (0-7837-0018-0, 2027127) Bks Demand.

Transition Metal Chemistry, Vols. 1-2. Ed. by Fred Basolo et al. LC 72-95642. (ACS Reprint Collection). reprint ed. pap. 12.95 (0-8412-0356-3) Am Chemical.

***Transition Metal Chemistry: The Valence Shell in d-Block Chemistry.** M. Gerloch & E. C. Constable. (Illus.). xi, 211p. 1994. 75.00 (3-527-29218-7, VCH) Wiley.

Transition Metal Chemistry: The Valence Shell in d-Block Chemistry. M. Gerloch & E. C. Constable. (Illus.). xi, 211p. 1994. pap. 35.00 (3-527-29219-5, VCH) Wiley.

Transition Metal Chemistry Vol. 9 - 1985. fac. ed. Ed. by Gordon A. Melson & Brian N. Figgis. LC 65-27431. 320p. 1985. pap. 91.20 (0-7837-8638-7, 2027127) Bks Demand.

Transition Metal Chemistry, Vol. 8: 1982. Ed. by Gordon A. Melson & Brian N. Figgis. LC 65-27431. (Illus.). 478p. 1982. reprint ed. pap. 136.30 (0-7837-0915-3, 2041220) Bks Demand.

Transition Metal Cluster Carbonyls. Raithby. 200p. 1993. 55.00 (0-13-927989-X) P-H.

Transition Metal Clusters. fac. ed. Ed. by Brian F. Johnson. LC 80-40496. (Illus.). 693p. 1980. pap. 180.00 (0-7837-7651-9, 2047404) Bks Demand.

Transition Metal Complexes: Structure & Spectra. M. H. Gubelman et al. (Structure & Bonding Ser.: Vol. 55). (Illus.). 210p. 1983. 79.95 (0-387-12833-6) Spr-Verlag.

Transition Metal Complexes As Drugs & Chemotherapeutic Agents. Nicholas Farrell. (C). 1989. lib. bdg. 158.50 (90-277-2828-3) Kluwer Ac.

Transition Metal Hydrides. Ed. by Alain Dedieu. (Illus.). x, 400p. 1991. 95.00 (0-89573-781-7, VCH) Wiley.

Transition Metal Impurities in Semiconductors. V. N. Fleurov & K. A. Kikoin. 360p. 1994. text ed. 71.00 (981-02-1883-4) World Scientific Pub.

Transition Metal Mediated Organic Syntheses. Ed. by D. W. Slocum & O. R. Hughes. LC 79-24735. (Annals Ser.: Vol. 333). 301p. 1980. 57.00 (0-89766-039-0); pap. write for info. (0-89766-038-2) NY Acad Sci.

Transition Metal Nuclear Magnetic Resonance. P. S. Pregosin. (Studies in Inorganic Chemistry: Vol. 13). 352p. 1991. 255.00 (0-444-88176-X, SIC 13) Elsevier.

Transition Metal Organometallics for Organic Synthesis. F. J. McQuillin et al. (Illus.). 672p. (C). 1992. text ed. 215.00 (0-521-33353-9) Cambridge U Pr.

Transition Metal Oxides. C. N. Rao & Bernard Raveau. LC 95-10717. (Illus.). xii, 340p. 1995. 120.00 (1-56081-647-3, VCH) Wiley.

Transition Metal Oxides: An Introduction to Their Electronic Structure & Properties. P. A. Cox. (International Series of Monographs on Chemistry: Vol. 27). 296p. 1995. pap. 45.00 (0-19-855925-9) OUP.

***Transition Metal Sulfur Chemistry: Biological & Industrial Significance.** Ed. by Edward I. Stiefel & Kazuko Matsumoto. LC 96-45738. (Symposium Ser.: No. 653). (Illus.). 336p. 1996. 109.95 (0-8412-3476-0) Am Chemical.

Transition Metals & Organometallics as Catalysts for Olefin Polymerization. Ed. by W. Kaminsky & Hans-Werner Sinn. (Illus.). 450p. 1988. 118.95 (0-387-18548-8) Spr-Verlag.

Transition Metals in Homogeneous Catalysis. Ed. by G. N. Schrauzer. LC 74-162281. (Illus.). 429p. reprint ed. pap. 122.30 (0-7837-0916-1, 2041221) Bks Demand.

***Transition Metals in Organic Synthesis: A Practical Approach.** Ed. by Susan Gibson. (The Practical Approach in Chemistry Ser.). (Illus.). 208p. 1997. pap. 55.00 (0-19-855845-7) OUP.

***Transition Metals in Organic Synthesis: A Practical Approach.** Ed. by Susan Gibson. (The Practical Approach in Chemistry Ser.). (Illus.). 208p. 1997. 110.00 (0-19-855846-5) OUP.

Transition Metals in the Synthesis of Complex Organic Molecules. Louis S. Hegedus. LC 93-85291. (Illus.). 340p. (C). 1994. pap. text ed. 44.00 (0-935702-28-8) Univ Sci Bks.

Transition Metals in Total Synthesis. Peter J. Harrington. LC 89-38139. 484p. 1990. text ed. 110.00 (0-471-61300-2) Wiley.

Transition of Finance in Japan & the United States: A Comparative Perspective. Thomas F. Cargill & Shoichi Royama. (Publication Ser.: No. 372). 242p. (C). 1988. text ed. 25.95 (0-8179-8721-5); pap. text ed. 18.95 (0-8179-8722-3) Hoover Inst Pr.

Transition of Legacy Systems to a Distributed Architecture. Narsim Ganti & William Brayman. LC 94-23583. 336p. 1995. text ed. 36.95 (0-471-06080-1) Wiley.

Transition of Socialist Economies: Lessons from Asia & Europe. (CSIS Report Ser.). 34p. (Orig.). (C). 1994. pap. 10.95 (0-89206-270-3) CSI Studies.

Transition of the Human Dentition. Ed. by Frans P. Linden. (Craniofacial Growth Monograph Ser.: Vol. 13). (Illus.). 150p. reprint ed. pap. 42.80 (0-685-24149-1, 2033022) Bks Demand.

Transition of Titus Crow. rev. ed. Brian Lumley. LC 88-81855. 192p. 1992. reprint ed. 25.00 (0-932445-45-4); reprint ed. 40.00 (0-932445-46-2) Ganley Pub.

Transition or Translation? Friend Stuart. 28p. 1982. pap. 4.95 (0-912132-14-0) Dominion Pr.

Transition Planning in the Schools: Using the Enderle-Severson Transition Rating Scale. rev. ed. Susan J. Severson et al. (Illus.). 64p. (Orig.). 1997. pap. text ed. 11.95 (1-886979-10-3) Practicl Pr.

Transition Planning Portfolio. 95th ed. Fowler. 1995. pap. 312.00 (0-15-601897-7) HB Legal.

Transition Preserving Functions & Infinite Automata see Introduction to the Theory of AUTOMATA

Transition Programs for Students with Moderate - Severe Disabilities. John McDonnell et al. 448p. 1996. text ed. 59.95 (0-534-34080-6) Brooks-Cole.

Transition Radiation & Transition Scattering. V. L. Ginzburg & V. N. Tsytovich. (Plasma Physics Ser.). (Illus.). 448p. 1990. 192.00 (0-85274-003-4) IOP Pub.

***Transition Report: 1997 Update.** EBRD Staff. 232p. 1997. pap. 35.00 (1-898802-06-8, HM02068, Pub. by Stationery Ofc UK) Bernan Associates.

Transition Report 1995: Investment & Enterprise Development. European Bank. 232p. 1995. pap. 49.00 (1-898802-02-5, HM02025, Pub. by Stationery Ofc UK) Bernan Associates.

***Transition Report, 1996: Infrastructure & Savings.** EBRD Staff. 210p. 1996. pap. 50.00 (1-898802-04-1, HM802041, Pub. by Stationery Ofc UK) Bernan Associates.

Transition, Special Needs & Vocational Education. Patricia L. Sitlington. (Eric Information Analysis Ser.). 37p. 1986. 5.25 (0-318-22355-4, IN 309) Ctr Educ Trng Employ.

Transition Stories: Twenty-Three Stories from 'Transition' Ed. by Eugene Jolas & Robert Sage. LC 78-37569. (Short Story Index Reprint Ser.). 1977. reprint ed. 23.95 (0-8369-4128-4) Ayer.

Transition Strategies for Persons with Learning Disabilities. Ed. by Craig A. Michaels. LC 94-2164. (Illus.). 284p. (Orig.). (C). 1994. pap. text ed. 32.50 (1-56593-165-3, 0476) Singular Publishing.

Transition Survival Training: Information Technology in the '90s: Proceedings. (Illus.). 165p. (Orig.). (C). 1994. pap. text ed. 60.00 (0-7881-1406-9) DIANE Pub.

Transition Time. Ilija Poplasen. (Illus.). 392p. 1984. 20.00 (0-935352-14-7) MIR PA.

Transition Time: Let's Do Something Different. Jean Feldman. LC 95-17456. (Illus.). (Orig.). 1995. pap. 19.95 (0-87659-173-X) Gryphon Hse.

Transition to a Free Market: Deregulation of the Air Cargo Industry. Andrew S. Carron. LC 81-10244. (Studies in the Regulation of Economic Activity). 45p. 1981. pap. 8.95 (0-8157-1297-9) Brookings.

Transition to a Global Society. Ed. by Iraj Ayman. 176p. 1994. pap. 12.95 (1-85168-039-X) Onewrld Pubns.

Transition to a Market Economy, 2 vols. OECD Staff. 700p. (Orig.). (ENG & FRE.). 1992. pap. 72.00 (92-64-03520-6) OECD.

Transition to a Market Economy: Transformation & Reform in the Baltic States. Ed. by Tarmo Haavisto. LC 96-23174. 288p. 1997. 80.00 (1-85898-393-2) E Elgar.

Transition to Adulthood During Military Service: The Israeli Case. Amia Lieblich. LC 89-30041. (SUNY Series in Israeli Studies). 221p. 1989. text ed. 64.50 (0-7914-0146-4); pap. text ed. 21.95 (0-7914-0147-2) State U NY Pr.

Transition to Advanced Mathematics. 3rd ed. St. Andre et al. LC 89-9989. 300p. (C). 1990. text ed. 60.95 (0-534-12234-5) Brooks-Cole.

Transition to Advanced Mathematics. 4th ed. Standre & Smith. (Mathematics Ser.). 1997. text ed. 60.95 (0-534-34028-8) Brooks-Cole.

Transition to Agile Manufacturing: Staying Flexible for Competitive Advantage. Marilyn R. Block. Ed. by Joseph C. Montgomery & Lawrence O. Levine. 306p. 1996. 37.00 (0-87389-347-6, H0898) ASQC Qual Pr.

Transition to Capitalism? The Communist Legacy in Eastern Europe. Ed. by Janos M. Kovacs. 276p. (C). 1994. 39.95 (1-56000-167-4) Transaction Pubs.

Transition to Chaos: In Conservative Classical Systems: Quantum Manifestations. L. E. Reichl. (Institute for Nonlinear Science Ser.). (Illus.). xv, 551p. 1994. 49.95 (0-387-97753-8) Spr-Verlag.

Transition to Chaos in Classical & Quantum Mechanics: Lectures Given at the 3rd Session of the Centro Internazionale Matematico Estivo (C.I.M.E.) Held in Montecatini, Italy, July 6-13, 1991. Ed. by S. Graffi. (Lecture Notes in Mathematics Ser.: Vol. 1589). 192p. 1994. 35.95 (3-540-58416-1) Spr-Verlag.

Transition to College Mathematics. Franklin D. Demana et al. (Illus.). 592p. 1984. write for info. (0-201-11153-5); teacher ed. write for info. (0-201-11154-3) Addison-Wesley.

Transition to College Mathematics. 2nd ed. Franklin Demana. (C). 1990. text ed. 68.95 (0-201-51523-7) Addison-Wesley.

Transition to Democracy: Political Change in the Soviet Union, 1987-1991. Giulietto Chiesa & Douglas T. Northrop. LC 92-56901. (Nelson A. Rockefeller Series in Social Science & Public Policy). (Illus.). 322p. (C). 1993. pap. 19.95 (0-87451-615-3); text ed. 50.00 (0-87451-614-5) U Pr of New Eng.

Transition to Democracy: Proceedings of a Workshop. National Research Council, Commission of Behavioral & Social Sciences & Education Staff. 104p. 1991. pap. text ed. 19.00 (0-309-04441-3) Natl Acad Pr.

Transition to Democracy in Eastern Europe. Klaus Von Beyme. 1997. text ed. 59.95 (0-312-15884-X) St Martin.

Transition To Democracy in Latin America: The Role of the Military. Bruce W. Farcau. LC 96-5538. 200p. 1996. text ed. 55.00 (0-275-95636-9, Praeger Pubs) Greenwood.

Transition to Democracy in Nepal. Louise Brown. (Politics in Asia Ser.). 232p. (C). 1995. text ed. 74.95 (0-415-08576-4, Routledge NY) Routledge.

Transition to Democracy in Poland. Ed. by Richard F. Staar. LC 93-26014. 1993. text ed. 45.00 (0-312-10000-0) St Martin.

Transition to Deregulation: Developing Economic Standards for Public Policies. William B. Tye. LC 90-48950. 576p. 1991. text ed. 75.00 (0-89930-582-2, TRR/, Quorum Bks) Greenwood.

Transition to Egalitarian Development. Keith Griffin & Jeffrey James. 1981. text ed. 29.95 (0-312-81465-8) St Martin.

Transition to EMU in the Maastricht Treaty. Lorenzo Bini-Smaghi et al. LC 94-23847. (Essays in International Finance Ser.: No. 194). 74p. 1994. pap. 8.00 (0-88165-101-X) Princeton U Int Finan Econ.

Transition to European Monetary Union. Alberto Giovannini. Ed. by Margaret B. Riccardi. LC 90-23597. (Essays in International Finance Ser.: No. 178). 28p. 1990. pap. text ed. 8.00 (0-88165-085-4) Princeton U Int Finan Econ.

Transition to Flexibility. Ed. by Daniel C. Knudsen. LC 96-9476. 200p. (C). 1996. lib. bdg. 105.00 (0-7923-9760-6) Kluwer Ac.

Transition to Global Rivalry: Alliance Diplomacy & the Quadruple Entente, 1895-1907. John A. White. (Illus.). 384p. (C). 1995. text ed. 59.95 (0-521-47445-0) Cambridge U Pr.

Transition to Independence in Namibia. Lionel Cliffe et al. LC 93-33326. 290p. 1994. lib. bdg. 49.95 (1-55587-420-7) Lynne Rienner.

Transition to Manhood: Through Rites of Passage. W. C. Myles. Tr. by Edward Cook. (Illus.). 165p. (C). 1993. pap. write for info. (0-9638582-0-3) Stud Ninety.

Transition to Market: Studies in Fiscal Reform. Ed. by Vito Tanzi. LC 93-19120. 387p. 1993. pap. 30.00 (1-55775-275-3) Intl Monetary.

Transition to Modernity: Essays on Power, Wealth & Belief. Ed. by John A. Hall & I. C. Jarvie. (Illus.). 360p. (C). 1992. text ed. 80.00 (0-521-38202-5) Cambridge U Pr.

Transition to Neo-Confucianism: Shao Yung on Knowledge & Symbols of Reality. Anne D. Birdwhistell. 336p. 1989. 42.50 (0-8047-1550-5) Stanford U Pr.

Transition to Palestinian Self-Government: Practical Steps Toward Israeli-Palestinian Peace. Ann M. Lesch. (Illus.). 160p. (C). 1992. 29.95 (0-253-33326-1, MB-794); pap. 11.95 (0-253-20794-0) Ind U Pr.

Transition to Parenthood: Current Theory & Research. Ed. by Gerald Y. Michaels & Wendy A. Goldberg. (Cambridge Studies in Social & Emotional Development). (Illus.). 350p. 1993. 54.95 (0-521-35418-8) Cambridge U Pr.

Transition to Parenthood: How a First Child Changes a Marriage - Why Some Couples Grow Closer. Jay Belsky. 304p. 1995. pap. 12.95 (0-440-50698-0) Dell.

***Transition to Parenthood: How Infants Change Families.** Ralph LaRossa & Maureen M. LaRossa. LC 80-26766. (Sage Library of Social Research: Vol. 119). 262p. 1981. reprint ed. pap. 74.70 (0-608-03381-2, 2059645) Bks Demand.

***Transition to Parenthood: Understanding & Adjusting to the Changes Couples Face.** Kristine C. Palmer. (Illus.). 150p. (Orig.). 1996. pap. 12.95 (0-9654639-0-7) Bright Fame.

***Transition to Preschool.** E. Romer. 78p. 1995. pap. text ed. write for info. (1-888557-32-X, 100002) No Ariz Univ.

Transition to Responsible Government: British Policy in British North America 1815-1850. Phillip A. Buckner. LC 84-12811. (Contributions in Comparative Colonial Studies: No. 17). xi, 358p. 1985. text ed. 59.95 (0-313-24630-0, BTV/) Greenwood.

***Transition to Single Seat Gliders Made Easy.** 2nd unabridged ed. Robert Wander. (Gliding Made Easy! Ser.: Vol. 6). 52p. (Orig.). 1996. mass mkt. 8.95 (0-614-29370-7) Soaring Bks.

Transition to Socialism in China. Ed. by Mark Selden & Victor D. Lippit. LC 82-5503. (Illus.). 336p. 1982. reprint ed. pap. 95.80 (0-7837-9973-X, 2060700) Bks Demand.

Transition to Stable Employment: The Experiences of U. S. Youth in Their Early Labor Market Career. Jacob J. Klerman & Lynn A. Karoly. LC 95-17301. 152p. 1995. pap. text ed. 13.00 (0-8330-1644-X, MR-564-NCRVEUCB) Rand Corp.

Transition to Sustainable Waste Management: A Simulation Gaming Approach. Robert J. Lempert & William L. Schwabe. LC 93-14765. 1993. pap. 13.00 (0-8330-1339-4, MR-183-EAC) Rand Corp.

Transition to Teaching: A Guide for the Beginning Teacher. 66p. 1983. 5.00 (0-88314-247-3) AAHPERD.

Transition to Technocracy: The Structural Origins of the Soviet Administrative State. Don K. Rowney. LC 88-47925. (Cornell Studies in Soviet History & Science). 264p. 1989. 39.95 (0-8014-2183-7) Cornell U Pr.

Transition to the Market Economy: Critical Perspectives on the World Economy, 4 vols., Set. Ed. by Paul Hare & Junior Davis. LC 96-2569. 1400p. (C). 1997. boxed, text ed. 620.00 (0-415-12434-4) Routledge.

Transition to the 21st Century Vol. 2: Prospects & Policies for Economic & Urban-Regional Transformation. Ed. by Donald A. Hicks & Norman J. Glickman. LC 82-81209. (Contemporary Studies in Sociology). 384p. 1983. 73.25 (0-89232-321-3) Jai Pr.

Transition to Vegetarianism: An Evolutionary Step. Rudolph Ballentine. LC 87-23618. 309p. 1987. pap. 15.95 (0-89389-104-5) Himalayan Inst.

Transition to Windows 95 for Windows 3.X Users. Shelley O'Hara. 1995. pap. text ed. 27.99 (1-57576-251-X) Que Educ & Trng.

Transition to Windows 95 for 3.X Users, IM. Sue Plumley. 1996. teacher ed., ring bd. 49.99 (1-57576-252-8) Que Educ & Trng.

***Transition Towards Democracy in Post-1990 Zaire: Contradictions & Dilemma.** Mondonga M. Mokoli. LC 96-53469. 284p. 1997. 69.95 (1-57309-144-8); pap. 49.95 (1-57309-143-X) Intl Scholars.

Transition, Turbulence & Combustion, 2. Ed. by T. B. Gatski et al. LC 94-32719. (ICASE-LaRC Interdisciplinary Series in Science & Engineering: 2). 1994. write for info. (0-7923-3086-2) Kluwer Ac.

Transition, Turbulence & Combustion, 2 vols., Vol. 2. Ed. by T. B. Gatski et al. LC 94-32719. (CASE-LaRC Interdisciplinary Science & Engineering Ser.). 1994. lib. bdg. 204.50 (0-7923-3084-6) Kluwer Ac.

Transition, Turbulence & Noise, 287. Reda R. Mankbadi. LC 94-21221. (International Engineering & Computer Science, VLSI, Computer Architecture, & Digital Screen Processing Ser.). 400p. (C). 1994. lib. bdg. 146.00 (0-7923-9481-X) Kluwer Ac.

Transition Without End: Nigerian Politics & Civil Society under Babangida. Ed. by Larry Diamond et al. 500p. 1997. 55.00 (1-55587-591-2) Lynne Rienner.

Transition Zoning. Arthur C. Comey. LC 73-2903. (Metropolitan America Ser.). (Illus.). 184p. 1974. reprint ed. 12.95 (0-405-05392-4) Ayer.

Transition 2 - Terminating a Management Account. 50p. 1993. pap. 24.95 (0-685-71660-0, 71401); pap. 34.95 incl. 5.25 hd (0-685-71661-9, 714) Inst Real Estate.

Transitional & Turbulent Compressible Flows - 1995. Ed. by L. D. Kral et al. LC 95-71638. (1995 ASME/JSME Fluids Engineering Conference Ser.: FED-Vol. 224). 224p. 1995. 112.00 (0-7918-1479-3, G00974) ASME.

Transitional & Turbulent Compressible Flows 1993. Ed. by L. D. Kral & T. A. Zang. LC 93-71638. (FED Ser.: Vol. 151). 263p. 1993. pap. 45.00 (0-7918-0959-5, H00791) ASME.

***Transitional Boundary Layers in Aeronautics.** R. A. Henkes & J. L. Van Ingen. (Verhandelingen der Koninklijke Nederlandse Akademie van Wetenschappen, Afd. Letterkunde, Nieuwe Reeks Ser.: Vol. 46). 484p. pap. 59.50 (0-444-85812-1) Elsevier.

Transitional Care: The Problem of Alternate Level of Care in New York City. Dana G. Safran & Elizabeth A. Eastwood. (Papers: No. 13). 48p. 1989. 5.00 (0-934459-60-6) United Hosp Fund.

Transitional Chemistry. McMurry. 1995. 130.00 (0-13-350505-7) P-H.

***Transitional Chinese Cinemas: Identity, Nationhood, Gender.** Hsiao-Peng L. Sheldon. (Illus.). 432p. 1997. pap. text ed. 28.00 (0-8248-1845-8) UH Pr.

Transitional Economic Systems: The Polish-Czech Example. Dorothy W. Douglas. LC 73-178717. 407p. reprint ed. pap. 116.00 (0-318-34964-7, 2030761) Bks Demand.

Transitional Home Designs, No. A104. Ed. by National Plan Service Staff. (Illus.). 32p. reprint ed. 4.95 (0-934039-35-6) Natl Plan Serv.

***Transitional Justice & the Rule of Law in New Democracies.** A. James McAdams. LC 97-5313. (Title from the Helen Kellogg Institute for International Studies). 1997. write for info. (0-268-04202-0); pap. write for info. (0-268-04203-9) U of Notre Dame Pr.

***Transitional Justice & the Rule of Law in New Democracies.** Ed. by A. James McAdams. (Orig.). 1997. pap. 18.00 (0-614-27589-X) U of Notre Dame Pr.

Transitional Justice: How Emerging Democracies Reckon with Former Regimes Vol. I: General Considerations. Ed. by Neil J. Kritz. LC 95-24363. 1995. 70.00 (1-878379-47-X); pap. text ed. 40.00 (1-878379-43-7) US Inst Peace.

Transitional Justice: How Emerging Democracies Reckon with Former Regimes Vol. II: Country Studies. Ed. by Neil J. Kritz. LC 95-24363. 1995. 80.00 (1-878379-48-8); pap. text ed. 47.50 (1-878379-44-5) US Inst Peace.

Transitional Justice: How Emerging Democracies Reckon with Former Regimes Vol. III: Laws, Rulings, & Reports. Ed. by Neil J. Kritz. LC 95-24363. 1995. 80.00 (1-878379-49-6); pap. text ed. 47.50 (1-878379-45-3) US Inst Peace.

Transitional Light: Facing Death with Dignity. Leslie Brown & Alan Brown. LC 83-61016. (Illus.). 60p. 1983. pap. 7.95 (0-934306-04-4) Springfield.

Transitional Man: The Anatomy of a Miracle. Franklin Earnest, III. LC 81-68047. 76p. 1981. pap. 7.00 (0-914480-06-5) Far West Edns.

Transitional Mathematics. Sam Thompson et al. 435p. (C). 1990. text ed. 34.75 (0-15-592345-5) HB Coll Pubs.

Transitional Metal Oxides: Surface Chemistry & Catalysis. H. H. Kung. (Studies in Surface Science & Catalysis: No. 45). 286p. 1989. 183.50 (*0-444-87394-5*) Elsevier.

Transitional Objects & Potential Spaces: Literary Uses of D. W. Winnicott. Ed. by Peter L. Rudnytsky et al. LC 92-43907. (Psychoanalysis & Culture Ser.). 315p. (C). 1993. text ed. 49.50 (*0-231-07572-3*) Col U Pr.

Transitional Program for Socialist Revolution. 3rd ed. Leon Trotsky. LC 77-78023. 269p. 1977. pap. 20.95 (*0-87348-524-6*) Pathfinder NY.

***Transitional Regional Overview.** 1997. write for info. (*0-614-25461-2*) Econ Intel.

Transitional Space in Mental Breakdown & Creative Integration. Peter L. Giovacchini. (Master Works). 1996. 40.00 (*1-56821-776-5*) Aronson.

Transitional Storm, Vol. 1. 78p. 1977. 2.50 (*0-317-34112-X*, 01766500) Edison Electric.

Transitioning Exceptional Child & Youth into the Community: Research & Practice. Ed. by Ennio Cipani. LC 88-852. (Child & Youth Services Ser.: Vol. 10, No. 2). (Illus.). 202p. 1989. text ed. 39.95 (*0-86656-733-X*) Haworth Pr.

Transitioning from Individual to Family Counseling. Ed. by Charles H. Huber. LC 93-37731. (Family Ser.: No. 2). 143p. 1994. pap. text ed. 17.95 (*1-55620-132-X*, 72563) Am Coun Assn.

Transitioning "Special" Children into Elementary School. Jayne D. Weber. 56p. (Orig.). 1994. pap. 8.50 (*1-883862-04-3*) Bks Beyond Brdrs.

***Transitioning to Object Technology: A 12 Step Approach.** Carl Argila. (C). 1997. text ed. 27.00 (*0-13-491945-9*) P-H.

Transitioning to Open Systems: Concepts, Methods, & Architecture. Steven L. Shaffer. 245p. 1996. pap. 34.95 (*1-55860-313-1*) Morgan Kaufmann.

Transitions. Bates. 1993. teacher ed., pap. text ed. 0.54 (*0-312-04116-0*) St Martin.

Transitions. Bates. 1996. pap. text ed. 15.00 (*0-312-13373-1*) St Martin.

Transitions. Dave Gannaway. LC 95-68720. 148p. (Orig.). 1995. pap. 10.95 (*0-87516-680-6*) DeVorss.

***Transitions.** Richard Isralowitz & Jonathan Friedlander. LC 97-14065. 1997. write for info. (*965-229-164-1*) Gefen Bks.

Transitions. Harriet E. McDuffie. 432p. 1996. per. 39.84 (*0-8403-9019-X*) Kendall-Hunt.

Transitions. Sylvia Reichman. Ed. by David Stewart & Lee Stewart. LC 87-63157. 160p. (Orig.). 1987. pap. 9.95 (*0-934426-15-5*) NAPSAC Reprods.

***Transitions, Vol. 1.** 2nd ed. Bates. Date not set. pap. text ed. write for info. (*0-312-13375-8*) St Martin.

***Transitions: Easy Ways to Adapt to Changes in Your Day.** Jeri A. Carroll. Ed. by Judy Mitchell. (Illus.). 144p. (Orig.). 1997. teacher ed., pap. 13.95 (*1-57310-070-6*) Teachng & Lrning Co.

***Transitions: Education & Employment.** Joseph Rotter & Walter Bailey. 204p. (C). 1996. per., pap. text ed. 37.74 (*0-7872-2711-0*) Kendall-Hunt.

Transitions: Exeter Remembered. Ed. by Christine Robinson et al. 195p. 1990. 15.95 (*0-939618-06-0*); pap. 9.95 (*0-939618-07-9*) Phillips Exeter.

Transitions: From Literature to Literacy. Regie Routman. LC 88-4379. 352p. (Orig.). (C). 1988. pap. 20.00 (*0-435-08467-4*, 08467) Heinemann.

Transitions: From Reading to Writing. Barbara F. Clouse. LC 93-28684. 1993. pap. text ed. write for info. (*0-07-011427-7*) McGraw.

***Transitions: From Reading to Writing.** 2nd ed. Barbara F. Clouse. LC 97-5812. 1997. pap. text ed. write for info. (*0-07-011876-0*) McGraw.

Transitions: Handbook of Managed Care for Inpatient to Outpatient Treatment. Ed. by Douglas H. Ruben & Chris E. Stout. LC 92-45144. 184p. 1993. text ed. 59.95 (*0-275-94064-0*, C4064, Praeger Pubs) Greenwood.

***Transitions: Lives in America.** Irina Raicu & Greg Grewell. LC 97-12825. 1997. write for info. (*1-55934-958-1*) Mayfield Pub.

Transitions: Making Sense of Life's Changes. William Bridges. 160p. 1980. pap. 13.00 (*0-201-00082-2*) Addison-Wesley.

Transitions: Military Pathways to Civilian Careers. Robert Macdonald. Ed. by Roger Rosen. (Military Opportunities Ser.). (YA). (gr. 7-12). 1988. lib. bdg. 15.95 (*0-8239-0777-5*) Rosen Group.

Transitions: Narratives in Modern Irish Culture. Richard Kearney. LC 87-31878. 318p. 1988. text ed. 59.95 (*0-7190-1926-5*, Pub. by Manchester Univ Pr UK) St Martin.

Transitions: New Australian Feminism. Ed. by Barbara Caine & Rosemary Pringle. LC 94-47582. 1995. text ed. 49.95 (*0-312-12547-X*) St Martin.

Transitions: New Australian Feminism. Ed. by Barbara Caine & Rosemary Pringle. LC 94-47582. 1995. pap. write for info. (*0-312-12548-8*) St Martin.

Transitions: Successfully Managing Changes in Your Career. Stephen Strasser & John Sena. 272p. 1988. pap. 17.50 (*0-13-929266-7*, Busn) P-H.

***Transitions: Teaching Writing in Computer-Supported & Traditional Classrooms.** LC 97-23867. 1998. text ed. 73.25 (*1-56750-352-7*) Ablex Pub.

***Transitions: Teaching Writing in Computer-Supported & Traditional Classrooms.** LC 97-23867. 1998. pap. 39.50 (*1-56750-353-5*) Ablex Pub.

***Transitions: The Challenge of Change.** Barrie Hopson. 1993. pap. text ed. 7.95 (*0-13-603010-6*) P-H.

Transitions: The Emergence, Growth & Development of the School of Social Welfare. Shirley Patterson & Ben Zimmerman. (Illus.). xii, 192p. (Orig.). 1987. pap. 12.95 (*0-9619225-0-8*) U KS Schl Soc Welfare.

Transitions: Unlocking the Creative Quilter Within. Andrea Balosky. Ed. by Laura M. Reinstatler. LC 96-26498. (Illus.). 80p. (Orig.). 1996. pap. 19.95 (*1-56477-170-9*, B284) That Patchwork.

Transitions & Relaxations to Zwitterionic Polymerization see Encyclopedia of Polymer Science & Engineering

***Transitions Environments Translations: International Feminisms in Contemporary Politics.** Ed. by Cora Kaplan & Joan W. Scott. 556p. 1997. pap. 18.95 (*0-415-91541-4*, Routledge NY) Routledge.

***Transitions Environments Translations: International Feminisms in Contemporary Politics.** Ed. by Joan W. Scott & Cora Kaplan. 556p. (C). 1997. text ed. 65.00 (*0-415-91540-6*, Routledge NY) Routledge.

Transitions for Persons with Deaf-Blindness & Other Profound Handicaps: State of the Art. Ed. by Angela Covert & H. D. Fredericks. 180p. (Orig.). 1987. 10.00 (*0-944232-00-0*) Teaching Res.

Transitions from Authoritarian Rule: Comparative Perspectives. Ed. by Guillermo O'Donnell et al. LC 86-2710. 240p. 1986. pap. text ed. 13.50 (*0-8018-3192-X*) Johns Hopkins.

Transitions from Authoritarian Rule: Latin America. Ed. by Guillermo O'Donnell et al. LC 86-2711. 272p. 1986. pap. text ed. 13.50 (*0-8018-3188-1*) Johns Hopkins.

Transitions from Authoritarian Rule: Southern Europe. Ed. by Guillermo O'Donnell et al. LC 86-2713. 232p. 1986. pap. text ed. 14.50 (*0-8018-3190-3*) Johns Hopkins.

Transitions from Authoritarian Rule: Tentative Conclusions about Uncertain Democracies. Ed. by Guillermo O'Donnell & Philippe C. Schmitter. LC 86-2714. 96p. 1986. pap. text ed. 9.95 (*0-8018-2682-9*) Johns Hopkins.

Transitions from Communism in Russia & Eastern Europe: Analysis & Perspectives. Ed. by Constantine C. Menges. LC 93-6192. 320p. 1993. 62.50 (*0-8191-9296-1*); pap. 28.50 (*0-8191-9297-X*) U Pr of Amer.

Transitions from Dictatorship to Democracy: Comparative Studies of Spain, Portugal, & Greece. Ronald H. Chilcote et al. (Illus.). 270p. (C). 1990. text ed. 52.00 (*0-8448-1675-2*, Crane Russak); pap. text ed. 36.00 (*0-8448-1676-0*, Crane Russak) Taylor & Francis.

***Transitions from State Socialism: Economic & Political Change in China & Hungary.** Yanqi Tong. LC 97-25283. 280p. 1997. 59.95 (*0-8476-8434-2*); pap. 22.95 (*0-8476-8435-0*) Rowman.

Transitions in a Woman's Life: Major Life Events in Developmental Context. Ramona T. Mercer et al. (Focus on Women Ser.). 224p. 1989. 27.95 (*0-8261-6560-5*) Springer Pub.

Transitions in Continental Philosophy. Ed. by Arleen B. Dallery et al. LC 93-1254. (Selected Studies in Phenomenology & Existential Philosophy). 353p. 1994. text ed. 59.50 (*0-7914-1849-9*); pap. text ed. 19.95 (*0-7914-1850-2*) State U NY Pr.

Transitions in Critical Phenomena. Domb. 1983. text ed. 185.00 (*0-12-220308-9*) Acad Pr.

Transitions in Development: The Role of Aid & Commercial Flows. Ed. by Uma Lele & Ijaz Nabi. LC 89-26922. 535p. 1990. 34.95 (*1-55815-078-1*); pap. 14.95 (*1-55815-093-5*) ICS Pr.

Transitions in Engineering: Guillaume Henri Dufour & the Early 19th Century Cable Suspension Bridges. Tom F. Peters. 252p. 1987. 122.00 (*0-8176-1929-1*) Birkhauser.

***Transitions in Engineering: Guillaume Herni Dufour & the Early 19th Century Cable Suspension B.** Tom F. Peters. 1996. 122.00 (*3-7643-1929-1*) Birkhauser.

Transitions in Land & Housing: Bulgaria, the Czech Republic, & Poland. Ann L. Strong et al. LC 96-17339. 298p. 1996. text ed. 49.95 (*0-312-15906-4*) St Martin.

Transitions in Mental Retardation Vol. 1: Advocacy, Technology, & Science. James Mulick & Bruce L. Mallory. 320p. 1985. text ed. 78.50 (*0-89391-236-0*) Ablex Pub.

Transitions in Mental Retardation Vol. 2: Issues in Therapeutic Intervention. Ed. by Richard Antonak & James Mulick. 288p. 1987. text ed. 78.50 (*0-89391-327-8*) Ablex Pub.

Transitions in Mental Retardation Vol. 3: The Community Imperative Revisited. Ed. by James Mulick & Richard Antonak. 272p. 1987. text ed. 78.50 (*0-89391-408-8*) Ablex Pub.

Transitions in Mental Retardation Vol. 4: Applications & Implications of Technology. Ed. by Richard Antonak & James Mulick. 288p. (C). 1989. text ed. 78.50 (*0-89391-458-4*) Ablex Pub.

Transitions in Oligomer & Polymer Systems. Ed. by H. G. Kilian & M. Pietralla. (Progress in Colloid & Polymer Science Ser.: Vol. 96). 72p. 1994. 62.95 (*0-387-91485-4*) Spr-Verlag.

***Transitions in Work & Learning: Implications for Assessment.** Ed. by Alan Lesgold et al. 400p. 1997. pap. 48.00 (*0-309-06365-5*) Natl Acad Pr.

Transitions of Aging. Ed. by Nancy Datan. LC 80-528. 1980. text ed. 57.00 (*0-12-203580-1*) Acad Pr.

Transitions Through Adolescence: Interpersonal Domains & Context. Ed. by Julia A. Graber et al. 408p. 1996. text ed. 79.95 (*0-8058-1594-5*) L Erlbaum Assocs.

Transitions Through Adult Life. Charles M. Sell. 240p. 1991. pap. 16.99 (*0-310-53661-8*) Zondervan.

***Transitions to a Heart-Centered World: Through the Kundaline Yoga & Meditations of Yogi Bhajan.** Rattana, pseud. & Ann M. Maxwell. (Illus.). 200p. 1995. spiral bd. 25.00 (*1-888029-02-1*, Yoga Tech Pr) Heart Quest.

***Transitions to Capitalism in Early Modern Europe.** Robert S. DuPlessis. (New Approaches to European History Ser.: Vol. 10). (Illus.). 356p. (C). 1997. text ed. 59.95 (*0-521-39465-1*) Cambridge U Pr.

***Transitions to Capitalism in Early Modern Europe.** Robert S. DuPlessis. (New Approaches to European History Ser.: Vol. 10). (Illus.). 356p. (C). 1997. pap. text ed. 18.95 (*0-521-39773-1*) Cambridge U Pr.

Transitions to Democracy: Comparative Perspectives from Southern Europe, Latin America & Eastern Europe. Ed. by Geoffrey Pridham. LC 94-47359. (International Library of Politics & Comparative Government). 1995. 149.95 (*1-85521-424-5*, Pub. by Dartmth Pub UK) Ashgate Pub Co.

Transitions to Empire: Essays in Greco-Roman History, 360-146 B. C., in Honor of E. Badian. E. Badian et al. Ed. by Robert W. Wallace & Edward M. Harris. LC 96-18192. (Oklahoma Series in Classical Culture: Vol. 21). 512p. 1996. text ed. 49.95 (*0-8061-2863-1*) U of Okla Pr.

Transitions to Leisure: Conceptual & Human Issues. Ed. by B. G. Gunter et al. 334p. (Orig.). 1985. pap. text ed. 25.50 (*0-8191-4770-2*); lib. bdg. 55.50 (*0-8191-4769-9*) U Pr of Amer.

Transitions to Parenthood. Ed. by Robin J. Palkovitz & Marvin B. Sussman. LC 88-853. (Marriage & Family Review Ser.: Vol. 12, Nos. 3-4). (Illus.). 396p. 1988. text ed. 49.95 (*0-86656-787-9*) Haworth Pr.

Transitions to School. Elizabeth Stief. 40p. (Orig.). 1994. pap. text ed. 15.00 (*1-55877-197-2*) Natl Governor.

Transitive Vampire: A Handbook of Grammar for the Innocent, the Eager & the Doomed. Karen E. Gordon. LC 83-40086. (Illus.). 144p. 1984. 13.00 (*0-8129-1101-6*, Times Bks) Random.

Transitivity: Grammatical Relations in Government-Binding Theory. 2nd ed. T. Hoekstra. (Linguistic Models Ser.). xii, 311p. 1987. reprint ed. pap. 69.25 (*90-6765-013-7*) Mouton.

Transitivity & Discourse Continuity in Chamorro Narratives. Ann M. Cooreman. (Empirical Approaches to Language Typology Ser.: No. 4). 246p. 1987. lib. bdg. 81.50 (*3-11-011307-4*) Mouton.

Transito De la Mirada. Carlos M. Luis. (Illus.). 266p. (Orig.). 1991. pap. 12.00 (*0-917049-56-X*) Saeta.

Transitory Gardens. Diana Balmori & Margaret Morton. (Illus.). 160p. 1993. 30.00 (*0-300-05772-5*) Yale U Pr.

Transitory Gardens, Uprooted Lives. Diana Balmori. 1995. pap. text ed. 16.00 (*0-300-06301-6*) Yale U Pr.

Transits. Reinhold Ebertin. 136p. 1971. 11.00 (*0-86690-094-2*, E1101-014) Am Fed Astrologers.

Transits. Jean H. Meeus. 1990. pap. 14.95 (*0-943396-26-3*) Willmann-Bell.

Transits: The Time of Your Life. Betty Lundsted. LC 83-159289. 188p. 1980. pap. 8.95 (*0-87728-503-9*) Weiser.

***Transits from Beginning to End.** 2nd rev. ed. Sophia Mason. (Illus.). 72p. 1996. spiral bd. 16.00 (*1-889805-02-5*) A-C Tapes.

Transits of the West - Dasas of the East see How to Predict Your Future: Secrets of Eastern & Western Astrology

Transits of Venus. Harry Wool. Ed. by I. Bernard Cohen. LC 80-2150. (Development of Science Ser.). (Illus.). 1981. lib. bdg. 27.95 (*0-405-13959-4*) Ayer.

Transjugular Intrahepatic Portal-Systemic Shunts: (TIPS) Ed. by Harold O. Conn et al. LC 95-48166. (Illus.). 400p. 1996. 108.00 (*0-89640-300-9*) Igaku-Shoin.

***Translabyrinthine Acoustic Neurinoma Surgery: A Surgical Manual.** Mirko Tos & J. Thomsen. (Illus.). 79p. 1991. 39.00 (*0-86577-397-1*) Thieme Med Pubs.

Translatability of Cultures: Figurations of the Space Between. Ed. by Sanford Budick & Wolfgang Iser. (Irvine Studies in the Humanities). (Illus.). 362p. pap. 17.95 (*0-8047-2561-6*) Stanford U Pr.

Translatability of Cultures: Figurations of the Space Between. Ed. by Sanford Budick & Wolfgang Iser. (Irvine Studies in the Humanities). (Illus.). 362p. (C). 45.00 (*0-8047-2484-9*) Stanford U Pr.

***Translate or Communicate: English As a Foreign Language in Japanese Schools.** George Moore & Judith Lamie. 198p. (C). 1997. lib. bdg. 59.00 (*1-56072-418-8*) Nova Sci Pubs.

***Translate This Darkness: The Life of Chritiana Morgan, the Veiled Woman in Jung's Circle.** Claire Douglas. 1997. pap. text ed. 16.95 (*0-691-01735-2*) Princeton U Pr.

Translated Woman: Crossing the Border with Esperanza's Story. Ruth Behar. LC 92-5588. 400p. 1994. pap. 15.00 (*0-8070-7053-X*) Beacon Pr.

Translated World: A Postmodern Tour of Libraries in Literature. Debra A. Castillo. LC 84-17200. x, 358p. 1985. pap. 29.95 (*0-8130-0792-5*) U Press Fla.

Translating an International Education to a National Environment: Papers Presented at the International Doctoral Student Conference Sponsored by the Doctoral Guild at the University of Pittsburgh School of Library & Information Science, September, 13-25, 1988. Julie I. Tallman. Ed. by Joseph B. Ojiambo. LC 89-49418. 259p. 1990. 29.50 (*0-8108-2072-2*) Scarecrow.

Translating Buddhism from Tibetan: An Introduction to the Tibetan Literary Language & the Translation of Buddhist Texts from Tibetan. Joe Wilson, Jr. 96p. 1992. 50.00 (*0-937938-34-3*) Snow Lion Pubns.

Translating by Factors. Christoph Gutknecht & Lutz J. Rolle. LC 95-32086. (SUNY Series in Linguistics). 346p. 1996. text ed. 62.50 (*0-7914-2957-1*); pap. text ed. 23.95 (*0-7914-2958-X*) State U NY Pr.

Translating Chinese. Wayne Schlepp. (Language & Literature Ser.: Vol. 1). 1964. pap. 3.50 (*0-900891-00-9*) Oleander Pr.

Translating Chinese Literature. Ed. by Eugene Eoyang & Lin Yao-fu. LC 94-18309. 352p. 1995. text ed. 29.95 (*0-253-31958-7*) Ind U Pr.

Translating for King James: Notes Made by a Translator of King James's Bible. Ward S. Allen. LC 69-17535. 164p. 1993. reprint ed. pap. 19.95 (*0-8265-1246-1*) Vanderbilt U Pr.

Translating Freud. Ed. by Darius G. Ornston, Jr. LC 92-9151. 272p. (C). 1993. 35.00 (*0-300-05454-8*) Yale U Pr.

Translating Genesis. Deborah Godin. 82p. 1986. 7.95 (*0-920806-43-0*, Pub. by Penumbra Pr CN) U of Toronto Pr.

***Translating History: The Top Russian Interpreter's Twenty-Five Years on the Front Line of Diplomacy.** Igor Korchilov. LC 96-51575. 1997. write for info. (*0-684-81418-8*) Scribner Intl.

***Translating Ireland: Translation, Languages, Culture.** Michael Cronin. 1996. 46.95 (*1-85918-018-3*, Pub. by Cork Univ IE); pap. 27.95 (*1-85918-019-1*, Pub. by Cork Univ IE) Intl Spec Bk.

Translating L.A. A Tour of the Rainbow City. Peter Theroux. 272p. 1995. pap. 12.00 (*0-393-31394-8*, Norton Paperbks) Norton.

***Translating Literature.** Susan Bassnett. (English Association Ser.). 160p. 1997. 49.50 (*0-85991-522-0*, DS Brewer) Boydell & Brewer.

Translating Literature: Translational Practice, Literary Theory, Comparative Literature. Andre Lefevere. LC 92-20469. vii, 165p. (C). 1992. pap. 15.50 (*0-87352-394-6*, S760P); lib. bdg. 37.50 (*0-87352-393-8*, S760C) Modern Lang.

Translating Neruda: The Way to Macchu Picchu. John Felstiner. LC 79-67773. (Illus.). xii, 284p. 1980. 42.50 (*0-8047-1079-1*); pap. 14.95 (*0-8047-1327-8*) Stanford U Pr.

Translating Organizational Change. Ed. by Barbara Czarniawska & Guje Sevon. (De Gruyter Studies in Organization: No. 56). xii, 284p. (C). 1996. pap. text ed. 29.95 (*3-11-014868-4*) De Gruyter.

Translating Organizational Change. Ed. by Barbara Czarniawska & Guje Sevon. (Studies in Organization: Vol. 56). xii, 284p. 1996. text ed. 79.95 (*3-11-014869-2*) De Gruyter.

Translating Poetic Discourse: Questions of Feminist Strategies in Adrienne Rich. Myriam Diaz-Diocaretz. LC 84-28245. (Critical Theory Ser.: No. 2). vii, 167p. 1985. 55.00 (*0-915027-52-6*); pap. 29.00 (*0-915027-53-4*) Benjamins North Am.

Translating Poetry: The Double Labyrinth. Ed. by Daniel Weissbort. LC 88-50870. 262p. 1989. text ed. 32.95 (*0-87745-225-3*) U of Iowa Pr.

Translating Relational Queries into Iterative Programs. J. C. Freytag. (Lecture Notes in Computer Science Ser.: Vol. 261). xi, 131p. 1987. 26.00 (*0-387-18000-1*) Spr-Verlag.

Translating Religious Texts: Translation, Transgression & Interpretation. Ed. by David Jasper. (Studies in Literature & Religion). 192p. (C). 1993. text ed. 49.95 (*0-312-08668-7*) St Martin.

Translating Research into Practice (TRIP) Classwide Peer Tutoring. Tom Lovitt et al. 44p. (Orig.). 1996. ring bd. 39.50 incl. vhs (*1-57035-086-8*, 38CLAS) Sopris.

Translating Research into Practice (TRIP) Cooperative Learning. Tom Lovitt et al. 60p. (Orig.). 1996. ring bd. 39.50 incl. vhs (*1-57035-081-7*, 38COOP) Sopris.

Translating Research into Practice (TRIP) Graphic Organizers. Tom Lovitt et al. 62p. (Orig.). 1996. ring bd. 39.50 incl. vhs (*1-57035-083-3*, 38GRAP) Sopris.

Translating Research into Practice (TRIP) Learning Strategies. Tom Lovitt et al. (Illus.). 190p. 1992. teacher ed., ring bd. 129.00 incl. vhs (*0-944584-63-2*, 38LS) Sopris.

Translating Research into Practice (TRIP) Reading Strategies. Tom Lovitt et al. 52p. (Orig.). 1996. ring bd. 39.50 incl. vhs (*1-57035-082-5*, 38RS) Sopris.

Translating Research into Practice (TRIP) Self-Management. Tom Lovitt et al. 54p. (Orig.). 1996. ring bd. 39.50 incl. vhs (*1-57035-079-5*, 38MGT) Sopris.

Translating Research into Practice (TRIP) Social Skills. Tom Lovitt et al. 68p. (Orig.). 1996. ring bd. 39.50 incl. vhs (*1-275-080-9*, 38SKILL) Sopris.

Translating Research into Practice (TRIP) Study Guides. Tom Lovitt et al. 40p. (Orig.). 1996. ring bd. 39.50 incl. vhs (*1-57035-084-1*, 38STUD) Sopris.

Translating Research into Practice (TRIP) Teaching Strategies. Tom Lovitt et al. (Illus.). 160p. 1992. teacher ed., ring bd. 129.00 incl. vhs (*0-944584-59-4*, 38TS) Sopris.

Translating Research into Practice (TRIP) Vocabulary Practice Sheets. Tom Lovitt et al. 64p. (Orig.). 1996. ring bd. 39.50 incl. vhs (*1-57035-085-X*, 38VOC) Sopris.

Translating Slavery: Gender & Race in French Women's Writing, 1783-1823. Ed. by Doris Y. Kadish & Francoise Massardier-Kenney. LC 93-34207. (Translation Studies Ser.: No. 2). 368p. (FRE.). 1994. 32.00 (*0-87338-498-9*) Kent St U Pr.

***Translating Style: The English Modernists & Their Italian Translations.** Tim Parks. LC 97-3591. 256p. 1997. 40.00 (*0-304-70098-3*) Cassell.

Translating the Classics of Judaism: In Theory & in Practice. Jacob Neusner. LC 89-6281. (Brown Judaic Studies). 158p. 1989. 46.95 (*1-55540-353-0*, 14 01 76) Scholars Pr GA.

Translating the Curriculum. Edgerton. 224p. (C). 1996. text ed. 59.95 (*0-415-91400-0*, Routledge NY) Routledge.

Translating the Curriculum. Susan H. Edgerton. 224p. (C). 1996. pap. 17.95 (*0-415-91401-9*, Routledge NY) Routledge.

Translating the Enlightenment: Scottish Civic Discourse in Eighteenth-Century Germany. Fania Oz-Salzberger. (Oxford Historical Monographs). 360p. 1995. 59.00 (*0-19-820519-8*) OUP.

Translating the Message: The Missionary Impact on Culture. Lamin Sanneh. LC 88-36508. (American Society of Missiology Ser.). (Illus.). 310p. 1989. pap. 20.00 (*0-88344-361-9*) Orbis Bks.

An Asterisk (*) at the beginning of an entry indicates that the title is appearing in BIP for the first time.

Translating the Orient: The Reception of Sakuntala in Nineteenth-Century Europe. Dorothy M. Figueira. LC 89-39698. (SUNY Series in Hindu Studies). 260p. 1991. text ed. 59.50 (*0-7914-0327-0*); pap. text ed. 19.95 (*0-7914-0328-9*) State U NY Pr.

Translating the Scriptures into Modern Greek. 2nd rev. ed. Nomikos M. Vaporis. 1994. pap. 17.95 (*1-885652-00-3*) Holy Cross Orthodox.

Translating the Sugilanon: Re-framing the Sign. Corazon D. Villareal. 408p. (Orig.). 1995. pap. text ed. 20.00 (*971-542-037-0*, Pub. by U of Philippines Pr PH) UH Pr.

Translatio Studii: Manuscript & Library Studies Honoring Oliver L. Kapsner, OSB. Ed. by Julian G. Plante. LC 73-76553. xii, 288p. (GER & SPA.). 1972. 20.00 (*0-940250-75-6*) Hill Monastic.

Translation. 1989. 12.95 (*0-19-437104-2*) OUP.

Translation: A Means to an End. Ed. by Shirley Larsen. (Dolphin Ser.: No. 18). (Illus.). 128p. (C). 1990. pap. 19.95 (*0-614-11377-6*, Pub. by Aarhus Univ Pr DK) David Brown.

Translation: Literary, Linguistic & Philosophical Approaches. Ed. by William Frawley. LC 82-40479. (Illus.). 224p. 1984. 36.50 (*0-87413-226-6*) U Delaware Pr.

Translation: Theory & Practice, Tension & Interdependence. Ed. by Mildred L. Larson. (American Translators Association Scholarly Monograph Ser.: Vol. V). viii, 270p. 1991. lib. bdg. 45.00 (*0-614-16446-X*) Benjamins North Am.

Translation - History - Culture: A Sourcebook. Ed. by Andre Lefevre. LC 92-6010. (Translation Studies). 256p. (C). 1992. pap. text ed. 15.95 (*0-415-07698-6*, A9621) Routledge.

Translation - History - Culture: A Sourcebook. Ed. by Andre Lefevre. LC 92-6010. (Translation Studies). 256p. (C). (gr. 13). 1992. text ed. 85.00 (*0-415-07697-8*, A9617) Routledge.

Translation, an Elizabethan Art. Francis O. Matthiessen. (BCL1-PR English Literature Ser.). 232p. 1992. reprint ed. lib. bdg. 79.00 (*0-7812-7034-0*) Rprt Serv.

Translation & Critical Study of Ten Pre-Islamic Odes: Traces in the Sand. Christopher Nouryeh. LC 93-26256. 264p. 1993. text ed. 89.95 (*0-7734-9319-0*) E Mellen.

Translation & Interpretation in Principle & Practice: From English into Chinese & from Chinese into English. Joseph D. Lowe. LC 88-90988. (Illus.). xviii, 475p. 1994. 90.00 (*0-930325-00-1*) Lowe Pub.

Translation & Interpreting: Bridging East & West. Ed. by Richard K. Seymour & C. C. Liu. (Literary Studies: East & West: Vol. 8). 176p. 1994. pap. text ed. 16.00 (*0-8248-1603-X*) Coll Lang Ling & Lit.

Translation & Literature, Vol. 1. Ed. by Robert Cummings & Stuart Gillespie. 224p. 1993. pap. 29.95 (*0-7486-0310-7*, Pub. by Edinburgh U Pr UK) Col U Pr.

Translation & Literature, Vol. 2. Ed. by Robert Cummings & Stuart Gillespie. 224p. 1994. pap. 40.00 (*0-7486-0366-2*, Pub. by Edinburgh U Pr UK) Col U Pr.

Translation & Literature, Vol. 3. Ed. by Stuart Gillespie. 240p. 1994. pap. 35.00 (*0-7486-0426-X*, Pub. by Edinburgh U Pr UK) Col U Pr.

Translation & Poetization in the Quaderna via. Study & Edition of the Libro de Miseria d'omme. Jane Ellen Connolly. (Spanish Ser.: No. 33). 260p. 1987. 20.00 (*0-942260-81-3*) Hispanic Seminary.

***Translation & Subjectivity: On Japan & Cultural Nationalism.** Naoki Sakai. LC 97-11443. (Public Worlds Ser.). 1997. write for info. (*0-8166-2862-9*); pap. write for info. (*0-8166-2863-7*) U of Minn Pr.

Translation & Taboo. Douglas Robinson. LC 95-39478. 250p. 1996. pap. 18.50 (*0-87580-571-X*); lib. bdg. 35.00 (*0-87580-209-5*) N Ill U Pr.

Translation & Text Transfer: An Essay on the Principles of Intercultural Communication. Anthony Pym. LC 92-15375. 1992. write for info. (*3-631-44995-X*) P Lang Pubng.

Translation & the Law. Ed. by Marshall Morris. (American Translators Association Scholarly Monograph Ser.: Vol. 8). viii, 334p. 1995. lib. bdg. 75.00 (*1-55619-627-X*) Benjamins North Am.

Translation & the Nature of Philosophy: A New Theory of Words. Andrew Benjamin. 224p. 1989. 49.95 (*0-415-01059-4*, A3531); pap. 14.95 (*0-415-04485-5*, A3535) Routledge.

Translation & the Transmission of the Culture 1300-1600. Ed. by Jeanette M. Beer & Kenneth Lloyd-Jones. LC 95-30225. (Studies in Medieval Culture: Vol. 35). 1995. pap. 18.00 (*1-879288-56-7*); boxed 38.00 (*1-879288-55-9*) Medieval Inst.

Translation & Translating. Roger Bell. (Applied Linguistics & Language Ser.). 416p. (C). 1991. pap. text ed. 29.55 (*0-582-01648-7*) Longman.

***Translation As Intercultural Communication: Selected Papers from the EST Congress - Prague 1995.** Ed. by Mary Snell-Hornby et al. LC 97-21369. (Benjamins Translation Library: Vol. 20). 354p. 1997. lib. bdg. 79.00 (*1-55619-702-0*) Benjamins North Am.

Translation As Social Action: Russian & Bulgarian Perspectives. Ed. by Palma Zlateva. LC 92-28387. (Translation Studies). 144p. (C). 1993. pap. text ed. 24.95 (*0-415-07696-X*, B0615, Routledge NY) Routledge.

Translation As Social Action: Russian & Bulgarian Perspectives. Ed. by Palma Zlateva. LC 92-28387. (Translation Studies). 144p. (C). (gr. 13). 1993. text ed. 74.95 (*0-415-07695-1*, B0611, Routledge NY) Routledge.

Translation As Text. Gregory M. Shreve. LC 92-7731. (Translation Studies Ser.: No. 1). 184p. (C). 1992. 27.00 (*0-87338-469-5*) Kent St U Pr.

Translation Begins. Jacqueline Risset. Tr. by Jennifer Moxley from FRE. (Serie d'Ecriture Ser.: Vol. 10). 96p. (Orig.). 1996. pap. 10.00 (*1-886224-09-9*) Burning Deck.

Translation Determined. Robert Kirk. 236p. 1986. 65.00 (*0-19-824921-7*) OUP.

Translation Group & Particle Representations in Quantum Field Theory. Hans-Jurgen Borchers. LC 96-16949. (Lecture Notes in Physics Ser.: Vol. 40). 131p. 1996. 43.00 (*3-540-61140-1*) Spr-Verlag.

Translation Guide to Nineteenth Century Polish-Language Civil-Registration Documents (Birth, Marriage & Death Records) 2nd ed. Judith R. Frazin. (Illus.). 160p. 1988. pap. 25.00 (*0-9613512-1-7*) Jewish Genealogical.

Translation, History & Culture. Ed. by Susan Bassnett & Andre Lefevre. 224p. 1995. pap. 21.95 (*0-304-33622-X*) Cassell.

Translation, History & Culture. Ed. by Susan Bassnett & Andre Lefevre. 256p. 1990. text ed. 49.00 (*0-86187-100-6*) St Martin.

Translation in Eukaryotes. Hans Trachsel. 432p. 1991. 197.00 (*0-8493-8816-3*, QP) CRC Pr.

Translation Lattices. Richard S. Pierce. (Memoirs Ser.: No. 1/32). 66p. 1983. reprint ed. pap. 22.00 (*0-8218-1232-7*, MEMO 1/32) Am Math.

***Translation Manual for "a New English Translation of the Septuagint" (NETS)** Albert Pietersma. 60p. 1996. ring bd. 15.00 (*0-9653269-0-X*) Uncial Bks.

Translation of All the Greek, Latin, Italian, & French Quotations: Which Occur in Blackstone's Commentaries on the Laws of England; & Also in the Notes of the Editions by Christian, Archbold, & Williams. J. W. Jones. iv, 250p. 1993. reprint ed. 65.00 (*0-8377-2308-6*) Rothman.

Translation of Babel. Scott Cairns. LC 89-37663. (Contemporary Poetry Ser.). 80p. 1990. pap. 14.95 (*0-8203-1200-2*) U of Ga Pr.

Translation of Computer Languages. Frederick W. Weingarten. LC 72-83240. 330p. (C). 1973. text ed. 24.95 (*0-8162-9423-2*) Holden-Day.

Translation of Euripides' "Hecuba" Euripides. Tr. by Kiki Gounaridou & Joel Tansey from GRE. LC 95-3012. 84p. 1995. text ed. 49.95 (*0-7734-8974-6*) E Mellen.

Translation of Film/Video Terms into French. Verne Carlson. LC 84-203565. (Video Terms into Ser.: Vol. 1). 180p. (Orig.). (ENG & FRE.). 1984. pap. 17.95 (*0-943288-00-2*, Double C Pub) Caverne Pub.

Translation of Film/Video Terms into German. Verne Carlson. LC 84-203565. (Video Terms into Ser.: Vol. 2). 180p. (Orig.). (ENG & GER.). 1984. pap. 17.95 (*0-943288-01-0*, Double C Pub) Caverne Pub.

Translation of Film/Video Terms into Italian. Verne Carlson. LC 84-203565. (Video Terms into Ser.: Vol. 3). 180p. (Orig.). (ENG & ITA.). 1984. pap. 17.95 (*0-943288-02-9*, Double C Pub) Caverne Pub.

Translation of Film/Video Terms into Japanese. Verne Carlson. LC 84-203565. (Video Terms into Ser.: Vol. 5). 180p. (Orig.). (ENG & JPN.). 1984. pap. 17.95 (*0-943288-04-5*, Double C Pub) Caverne Pub.

Translation of Film/Video Terms into Series (French, German, Italian, Spanish, Japanese), 5 vols. Verne Carlson. LC 84-203565. (Translation of Film/Video Terms into Ser.). (ENG, FRE, GER, ITA, JPN & SPA.). 1984. pap. 89.75 (*0-943288-05-3*, Double C Pub) Caverne Pub.

Translation of Film/Video Terms into Spanish. Verne Carlson. LC 84-203565. (Video Terms into Ser.: Vol. 4). 180p. (Orig.). (ENG & SPA.). 1984. pap. 17.95 (*0-943288-03-7*, Double C Pub) Caverne Pub.

Translation of Glanville: (A Treatise on the Laws & Customs of the Kingdom of England) Ranulph De Glanville. Tr. by John Beames from LAT. xl, 362p. 1980. reprint ed. lib. bdg. 30.00 (*0-8377-0313-1*) Rothman.

***Translation of Guy Vaes' October Long Sunday.** Guy Vaes. Tr. by Philip Mosley from FRE. (Belgian Francophone Library: Vol. 7). 288p. (C). 1996. text ed. 51.95 (*0-8204-3140-0*) P Lang Pubng.

Translation of Jerome's Chronicon with Historical Commentary. Malcolm D. Donalson. LC 95-35398. 184p. (C). 1996. 79.95 (*0-7734-2258-7*, Mellen Univ Pr) E Mellen.

Translation of Lao Tzu's "Tao Te Ching" & Wang Pi's "Commentary." Paul J. Lin. (Michigan Monographs in Chinese Studies: No. 30). 232p. (Orig.). 1997. pap. text ed. 15.00 (*0-89264-030-8*) Ctr Chinese Studies.

***Translation of Manuel Scorza's The Sleepless Rider.** Manuel Scorza. Tr. by Anna-Marie Aldaz from SPA. (Wor(l)ds of Change Ser.: Vol. 31). 192p. (C). 1996. text ed. 42.95 (*0-8204-3375-6*) P Lang Pubng.

Translation of Scripture: Proceedings of a Conference at the Annenberg Research Institute, May 15-17, 1989. David M. Goldenberg et al. (JQR Supplement Ser.). vi, 285p. 1990. pap. text ed. 22.50 (*0-685-57084-3*, Ctr Judaic Studies) Eisenbrauns.

Translation of the Meanings of Hadith from Muslim & Bukhari (Lu'Lu wa Maarjan), Vols. I & II. Maulana Qadri. 562p. 1985. 69.00 (*1-56744-405-9*) Kazi Pubns.

Translation of the Orpheus of Angelo Politian & the Aminta of Torquato Tasso. Angelo A. Poliziano. LC 86-3172. 198p. 1986. reprint ed. text ed. 49.75 (*0-313-25211-4*, LOTR, Greenwood Pr) Greenwood.

Translation of the Precious Relics of Our Father among the Saints Nicholas, Archbishop of Myra in Lycia from Myra, to Bari in Italy: Account of the Translation, & the Liturgical Service for Its Commemoration. Tr. by Isaac E. Lambertsen from RUS. (Illus.). 32p. (Orig.). 1987. pap. 2.50 (*0-912927-26-7*, X026) St John Kronstadt.

Translation Planes. Ed. by H. Lueneburg. 256p. 1980. 92.95 (*0-387-09614-0*) Spr-Verlag.

Translation Planes: Foundations & Construction Principles, Vol. VI. Norbert Knarr. Ed. by A. Dold & F. Takens. LC 95-35774. (Lecture Notes in Mathematics Ser.: Vol. 1611). 112p. 1995. 29.95 (*3-540-60208-9*) Spr-Verlag.

Translation, Poetics, & the Stage: Six French Hamlets. Romy Heylen. LC 92-11713. 240p. (C). (gr. 13). 1993. text ed. 59.95 (*0-415-07689-7*, A9648, Routledge NY) Routledge.

Translation, Power, Subversion. Ed. by Roman Alvarez & M. Carmen Vidal. LC 95-50708. (Topics in Translation Ser.: Vol. 8). 160p. 1996. 69.00 (*1-85359-351-6*, Pub. by Multilingual Matters UK); pap. 24.95 (*1-85359-350-8*, Pub. by Multilingual Matters UK) Taylor & Francis.

Translation, Rewriting & the Manipulation of Literary Fame. Andre Lefevre. LC 92-7608. 208p. (C). 1992. pap. 16.95 (*0-415-07700-1*, A9570) Routledge.

Translation, Rewriting & the Manipulation of Literary Fame. Andre Lefevre. LC 92-7608. (Translation Studies). 208p. (C). (gr. 13). 1992. text ed. 69.95 (*0-415-07699-4*, A9566) Routledge.

Translation Series, 4 vols., Set. Viking Society for Northern Research Staff. reprint ed. 174.00 (*0-404-60010-7*) AMS Pr.

Translation Spectrum: Essays in Theory & Practice. Ed. by Marilyn G. Rose. LC 80-20302. 172p. 1980. pap. text ed. 14.95 (*0-87395-437-8*) State U NY Pr.

Translation Studies. rev. ed. Susan Bassnett. (New Accents Ser.). 192p. (C). 1991. pap. 16.95 (*0-415-06528-3*, A6321) Routledge.

Translation Studies: An Integrated Approach. Mary Snell-Hornby. LC 88-7606. x, 163p. (C). 1988. 56.00 (*1-55619-051-4*) Benjamins North Am.

Translation Studies: An Integrated Approach. 2nd rev. ed. Mary Snell-Hornby. LC 88-7606. x, 170p. (C). 1995. pap. 17.95 (*1-55619-052-2*) Benjamins North Am.

Translation Studies: An Interdiscipline: Selected Papers from the Translation Studies Congress, Vienna, 9-12 September 1992. Ed. by Mary Snell-Hornby et al. LC 93-42309. (Translation Library: No. 2). viii, 440p. 1994. lib. bdg. 95.00 (*1-55619-478-1*) Benjamins North Am.

Translation Technique in the Peshitta to Job: A Model for Evaluating a Text with Documentation from the Peshitta to Job. Heidi M. Szpek. LC 92-34963. (Dissertation Ser.: No. 137). 329p. 1992. 29.95 (*1-55540-761-7*, 06 21 37); pap. 19.95 (*1-55540-762-5*) Scholars Pr GA.

Translation Textbook. Madeleine Sergent & Kay Wilkins. LC 85-17989. 140p. 1986. pap. text ed. 15.00 (*0-8191-4960-8*) U Pr of Amer.

Translation Theory & Practice: Reassembling the Tower. Frederic Will. LC 92-41890. 216p. 1993. text ed. 89.95 (*0-7734-9234-8*) E Mellen.

***Translation Theory & Practice in the Middle Ages.** Janet Beer. LC 97-12898. (Studies in Medieval Culture). 1997. write for info. (*1-879288-81-8*); pap. write for info. (*1-879288-82-6*) Medieval Inst.

Translational Apparatus: Structure, Function, Regulation, Evolution. Ed. by K. H. Nierhaus et al. 1994. 165.00 (*0-306-44538-7*, Plenum Pr) Plenum.

Translational Apparatus of Photosynthetic Organelles. Ed. by R. Mache et al. (NATO ASI Series H: Cell Biology: Vol. 55). (Illus.). 241p. 1991. 119.95 (*0-387-51779-0*) Spr-Verlag.

Translational Control. Ed. by John W. Hershey et al. (Monographs: Vol. 30). (Illus.). 650p. (Orig.). (C). 1995. text ed. 115.00 (*0-87969-458-0*) Cold Spring Harbor.

Translational Control. Ed. by Michael B. Mathews. (Current Communications in Molecular Biology Ser.). 192p. (Orig.). 1986. pap. text ed. 27.00 (*0-87969-191-3*) Cold Spring Harbor.

Translational Regulation of Gene Expression 1. Ed. by J. Ilan. LC 87-15322. (Illus.). 510p. 1987. 105.00 (*0-306-42640-4*, Plenum Pr) Plenum.

Translational Regulation of Gene Expression 2. Ed. by J. Ilan. (Illus.). 490p. (C). 1993. 105.00 (*0-306-44374-0*, Plenum Pr) Plenum.

Translational Technique of the Greek Septuagint for the Hebrew Verbs & Participles in Psalms 3-41. John H. Sailhamer. (Studies in Biblical Greek: Vol. 2). 230p. (C). 1989. text ed. 43.95 (*0-8204-1030-6*) P Lang Pubng.

Translationes Operum Sinensium des Gesneriaceis--I. L. E. Skog & H. M. Wetzel. LC 86-16368. (Contributions from the New York Botanical Garden Ser.: Vol. 16). (Illus.). 140p. 1986. pap. text ed. 10.20 (*0-89327-305-8*) NY Botanical.

Translations. Paul Auster. 350p. 1996. 28.00 (*1-56886-032-3*) Marsilio Pubs.

Translations. Paul Auster. 350p. 1996. pap. 14.95 (*1-56886-033-1*) Marsilio Pubs.

Translations. Brian Friel. 72p. (Orig.). 1995. pap. 10.95 (*0-571-11742-2*) Faber & Faber.

Translations. Henry David Thoreau. Ed. by Elizabeth Witherell. LC 83-42589. (Writings of Henry D. Thoreau). (Illus.). 300p. 1986. text ed. 45.00 (*0-691-06531-4*) Princeton U Pr.

Translations. rev. ed. Ezra Pound. LC 53-11965. 1953. pap. 12.95 (*0-8112-0164-3*, NDP145) New Directions.

Translations: Experiments in Reading. Henri Michaux et al. Ed. by Don Wellman et al. Tr. by Charles Simic et al. from CHI. (Illus.). 272p. (Orig.). 1983. pap. 12.00 (*0-942030-03-6*) O ARS.

Translations: Series 2, Vol. 6. American Mathematical Society Staff. 487p. pap. 138.80 (*0-317-58776-5*, 2029659) Bks Demand.

Translations: Turner & Printmaking. Eric M. Lee. LC 93-60992. (Illus.). 48p. (Orig.). 1993. pap. 8.95 (*0-930606-71-X*) Yale Ctr Brit Art.

Translations, "A" Saul Yurkievich et al. Ed. by Don Wellman. Tr. by Cola Franzen. (Translations: Experiments in Reading Ser.). (Illus.). 72p. (Orig.). 1983. pap. 4.50 (*0-942030-04-4*) O ARS.

Translations & Annotations of Choval Repertoire: Sacred Latin Texts, Vol. I. Compiled by Ron Jeffers. 279p. (C). 1988. text ed. 38.95 (*0-9621532-0-6*); pap. text ed. 29.50 (*0-9621532-1-4*) Earthsongs.

Translations & Other Rhymes. Henry C. Lea. 1973. 59.95 (*0-8490-1226-0*) Gordon Pr.

Translations & Reprints from the Original Sources of European History, 6 Vols. rev. ed. Pennsylvania University - Department of History Staff. LC 75-143179. reprint ed. Set. lib. bdg. 207.00 (*0-404-08970-4*) AMS Pr.

Translations, "B" Joseph Guglielmi. Ed. by Don Wellman. Tr. by Christopher Duncan. (Translations: Experiments in Writing Ser.). (Illus.). 96p. (Orig.). 1983. pap. 4.50 (*0-942030-05-2*) O ARS.

***Translations by Baba.** H. Youngs. Date not set. pap. 4.40 (*0-614-19094-0*, BW-205) Sathya Sai Bk Ctr.

Translations, "C" Bruce Andrews et al. Ed. by Don Wellman et al. Tr. by Jerome Rothenberg et al. (Translations: Experiments in Reading Ser.). (Illus.). 104p. (Orig.). 1983. pap. 4.50 (*0-942030-06-0*) O ARS.

Translations from C. Baudelaire. Richard H. Shepherd. LC 77-11485. reprint ed. 34.50 (*0-404-16345-9*) AMS Pr.

***Translations from Drawing to Building & Other Essays.** Robin Evans. LC 96-47544. (Illus.). 296p. 1997. pap. 25.00 (*0-262-55027-X*) MIT Pr.

Translations from Hispanic Poets. 1938. 10.00 (*0-87535-045-3*) Hispanic Soc.

Translations from the Dark. Michele A. Belluomini. LC 93-71697. 58p. (Orig.). 1993. pap. 8.95 (*0-9636617-3-6*) Blue Deer.

Translations from the Finnish: First FATA Annual. Ed. by Steve Stone. (FATA Translation Annuals Ser.). 34p. 1990. pap. 5.00 (*1-880474-01-8*) FATA.

Translations from the Finnish: Second FATA Annual. Ed. by Steve Stone. (FATA Translation Annuals Ser.). 59p. 1991. pap. 7.00 (*1-880474-02-6*) FATA.

Translations from the Icelandic. Ed. & Tr. by W. C. Green. 1976. lib. bdg. 59.95 (*0-8490-2757-8*) Gordon Pr.

Translations from the Natural World: Poems. Les Murray. LC 93-11183. 1994. 21.00 (*0-374-27870-9*) FS&G.

Translations from the Poetry. Rainer M. Rilke. Tr. by M. D. Norton. 256p. 1993. pap. 9.95 (*0-393-31038-8*) Norton.

Translations from the Unconscious. Clyde F. Smith. 32p. 1986. pap. 5.00 (*0-929170-10-5*) Paper Plant.

***Translations into English.** Denis Devlin & Roger Little. 354p. 9200. pap. 19.95 (*1-873790-18-X*) Dufour.

Translations of Beowulf: A Critical Biography. Chauncey B. Tinker. LC 67-21717. 148p. 1967. reprint ed. 40.00 (*0-87752-114-X*) Gordian.

Translations of German Poetry in American Magazines. E. Z. Davis. 1973. 59.95 (*0-8490-1227-9*) Gordon Pr.

Translations of Hindi Works into English: A Bibliography. Dipali Ghosh. 176p. (C). 1995. 28.00 (*81-215-0695-6*, Pub. by Munshiram Manoharial II) S Asia.

Translations of Power: Narcissism & the Unconscious in Epic History. Elizabeth J. Bellamy. LC 91-55549. 290p. 1992. pap. 16.95 (*0-8014-9990-9*) Cornell U Pr.

Translations of the Carnival Comedies of Hans Sachs, 1494-1576. Ed. by Robert Alyett. LC 94-17946. (Studies in German Language & Literature: Vol. 16). (Illus.). 217p. 1995. text ed. 89.95 (*0-7734-1342-1*) E Mellen.

Translations of the Gospel Back into Tongues. C. D. Wright. LC 82-17047. 84p. 1983. text ed. 44.50 (*0-87395-652-4*); pap. text ed. 14.95 (*0-87395-685-0*) State U NY Pr.

Translations Without Originals. Julio Marzan. 50p. 1986. pap. 3.95 (*0-918408-23-7*) Reed & Cannon.

Translations/Transformations - Gender & Culture in Film & Literature East & West: Selected Conference Papers. Ed. by Valerie Wayne & Cornelia N. Moore. LC 93-12952. (Literary Studies: East & West: Vol. 7). 1993. pap. text ed. 15.00 (*0-8248-1565-3*) UH Pr.

Translator. Pat Goodheart. 160p. 1983. reprint ed. pap. 10.00 (*0-941324-07-9*) Van Vactor & Goodheart.

Translator As Communicator. Basil Hatim & Ian Mason. LC 96-15699. 256p. (C). 1997. pap. write for info. (*0-415-11737-2*); text ed. write for info. (*0-415-11736-4*) Routledge.

Translator Big Book: Licensee Manual & Site Book, 2. Jim McDonald et al. Incl. Translator Big Book No. 2: Licensee Manual, TV & FM Translators. (Illus.). 100p. student ed. 99.00 (*0-614-04925-3*); (*0-938023-18-7*) Wind River Inst Pr.

Translator Big Book, No. 2, Licensee Manual, TV & FM Translators see Translator Big Book: Licensee Manual & Site Book

Translator in the Text: On Reading Russian Literature in English. Rachel May. LC 94-22792. (Studies in Russian Literature & Theory). 209p. 1994. pap. text ed. 15.95 (*0-8101-1158-6*) Northwestern U Pr.

Translator in the Text: On Reading Russian Literature in English. Rachel May. LC 94-22792. (Studies in Russian Literature & Theory). 220p. (C). 1994. text ed. 49.95 (*0-8101-1157-8*) Northwestern U Pr.

Translator-Warrior Speaks: A Personal History of the American Translators Association, 1959-1970. Bernard Bierman. Ed. by Evelyn Rothstein. (Illus.). 220p. (Orig.). 1987. pap. text ed. 19.95 (*0-913935-43-3*) ERA-CCR.

Translator's Freedom. C. A. Hargreaves. pap. 18.50 (*1-85075-400-4*, Pub. by Sheffield Acad UK) CUP Services.

Translator's Handbook: With Special Reference to Conference Translation from French & Spanish. Frederick Fuller. LC 83-22107. 160p. 1984. 25.00 (*0-271-00368-5*) Pa St U Pr.

Translator's Handbook on Leviticus see Handbook on Leviticus

An Asterisk (*) at the beginning of an entry indicates that the title is appearing in BIP for the first time.

Translators Handbook on Paul's First Letter to the Corinthians see Handbook on Paul's First Letter to the Corinthians
Translator's Handbook on Paul's Letter to the Ephesians see Handbook on Paul's Letter to the Ephesians
Translator's Handbook on Paul's Letter to the Galatians see Handbook on Paul's Letter to the Galatians
Translator's Handbook on Paul's Letter to the Philippians see Handbook on Paul's Letters to the Philippians
Translators Handbook on Paul's Letter to the Romans see Handbook on Paul's Letter to the Romans
Translators Handbook on Paul's Letter to the Thessalonians see Handbook on Paul's Letters to the Thessalonians
Translator's Handbook on Paul's Letters to the Colossians & to Philemon see Handbook on Paul's Letters to the Colossians & to Philemon
Translator's Handbook on Psalms see Handbook on Psalms
Translator's Handbook on the Acts of the Apostles see Handbook on the Acts of the Apostles
Translator's Handbook on the Book of Amos see Handbook on the Book of Amos
Translator's Handbook on the Book of Joshua see Handbook on the Book of Joshua
Translator's Handbook on the Book of Ruth see Handbook on the Book of Ruth
Translators Handbook on the Books of Nahum, Habakkuk & Zephaniah see Handbook on the Books of Nahum, Habakkuk, & Zephaniah
Translators Handbook on the First Letter from Peter see Handbook on the First Letter from Peter
Translator's Handbook on the Gospel of John see Handbook on the Gospel of John
Translator's Handbook on the Gospel of Mark see Handbook on the Gospel of Mark
Translator's Handbook on the Gospel of Mark see Handbook on the Gospel of Luke
Translator's Handbook on the Gospel of Matthew see Handbook on the Gospel of Matthew
Translator's Handbook on the Letter to the Hebrews see Handbook on the Letter to the Hebrews
Translators Handbook on the Letters of John see Handbook on the Letters of John
Translator's Handbook 1997. Morry Sofer. 450p. (Orig.). 1996. pap. 24.95 (*1-887563-02-4*) Schreiber Pub.
Translator's Handbook 1997. Morry Sofer. 450p. 1996. pap. 24.95 (*1-887563-22-9*) Schreiber Pub.
Translator's Invisibility. Lawrence Venuti. LC 94-6477. (Translation Studies). 336p. (C). 1994. pap. 18.95 (*0-415-11538-8*, B4758) Routledge.
Translator's Invisibility. Lawrence Venuti. LC 94-6477. (Translation Studies). 336p. (C). (gr. 13). 1994. text ed. 69.95 (*0-415-11537-X*, B4754) Routledge.
Translator's Son. Joseph Bruchac. Ed. by Stanley H. Barkan. (Cross-Cultural Review Chapbook Ser.: No. 10: Native American Abenaki Poetry 1). (Illus.). 40p. 1980. 15.00 (*0-89304-833-X*, CCC135); pap. 5.00 (*0-89304-809-7*); audio 10.00 (*0-685-01277-8*) Cross-Cultrl NY.
Translators Through History. Ed. by Jean Delisle & Judith Woodsworth. LC 95-49054. (Translation Library: Vol. 13). xvi, 346p. 1996. pap. 31.95 (*1-55619-697-0*); lib. bdg. 85.00 (*1-55619-694-6*) Benjamins North Am.
Translator's Turn. Douglas Robinson. LC 90-4629. (Parallax: Re-Visions of Culture & Society Ser.). 368p. 1991. text ed. 52.00 (*0-8018-4046-5*); pap. text ed. 16.95 (*0-8018-4047-3*) Johns Hopkins.
Translator's Workbench: Tools & Terminology for Translation & Text Preprocessing in Europe. Ed. by K. Ahmad et al. (Research Reports ESPRIT: Vol. 1). 185p. 1996. pap. 39.00 (*0-387-57645-2*) Spr-Verlag.
Translingual Practice: Literature, National Culture, & Modernity - China, 1900-1937. Lydia H. Liu. LC 94-45961. (Illus.). 368p. 1995. 60.00 (*0-8047-2534-9*); pap. 19.95 (*0-8047-2535-7*) Stanford U Pr.
Transliterated Haggadah: Passover Haggadah. deluxe ed. Ed. by Gabriel Pollak. 18.50 (*0-87559-082-9*) Shalom.
Translucent Blues: A Collection of Short Stories. Thom Hunter. LC 81-78304. 1992. pap. 9.95 (*1-879603-15-2*) Los Hombres.
Translucent Gears. Richard Silberg. 64p. 1982. pap. 4.95 (*0-938190-06-7*) North Atlantic.
Transmemberment of Song: Hart Crane's Anatomies of Rhetoric & Desire. Lee Edelman. LC 87-16187. 312p. 1987. 39.50 (*0-8047-1413-4*) Stanford U Pr.
Transmembrane Potentials & Characteristics of Immune & Tumor Cells. Ed. by Richard C. Niemtzow. 176p. 1985. 101.00 (*0-8493-5688-1*, RC267, CRC Reprint) Franklin.
Transmembrane Signaling & Sensation. Ed. by Fumio Oosawa et al. (Taniguchi Symposia on Brain Sciences Ser.: No. 7). 278p. 1984. lib. bdg. 112.00 (*90-6764-041-7*, Pub. by VSP NE) Coronet Bks.
***Transmembrane Signaling Protocols.** Ed. by Dafna Bar-Sagi. (Methods in Molecular Biology Ser.: Vol. 84). (Illus.). 320p. 1997. 99.50 (*0-89603-488-7*); spiral bd. 59.50 (*0-89603-432-1*) Humana.
Transmembrane Signalling, Intracellular Messengers & Implications for Drug Development. Ed. by S. R. Nahorski. LC 89-24919. 248p. 1990. text ed. 159.00 (*0-471-92432-6*) Wiley.
Transmigrasi - Indonesian Resettlement Policy, 1965-1985: Myths & Realities. Mariel Otten. (IWGIA Document Ser.: No. 57). (Illus.). 254p. (Orig.). 1986. pap. text ed. 49.00 (*0-317-65617-1*) Coronet Bks.
Transmigration in Indonesia. Dietrich Kebschull. 162p. 1986. pap. text ed. 24.95 (*3-87895-314-3*) Transaction Pubs.
Transmigration of Souls. William Barton. 352p. (Orig.). 1996. mass mkt. 5.99 (*0-446-60167-5*, Aspect) Warner Bks.
Transmigration of the Seven Brahmans. Henry David Thoreau. LC 72-3516. (American Literature Ser.: No. 49). Orig. Title: Harivansa. (C). 1972. reprint ed. lib. bdg. 29.95 (*0-8383-1563-1*) M S G Haskell Hse.
Transmigration of Timothy Archer. Philip K. Dick. LC 90-55675. 256p. 1991. pap. 12.00 (*0-679-73444-9*, Publishers Media) Random.
Transmigration Solo. Joseph Ceravolo. LC 79-1068. 45p. (Orig.). 1979. pap. 4.00 (*0-915124-21-1*, Toothpaste) Coffee Hse.
Transmissible Spongiform Enecephalopathies: Impact on Animal & Human Health. Ed. by F. Brown. (Developments in Biological Standardization Ser.: Vol. 80). (Illus.). x, 234p. 1993. pap. 191.50 (*3-8055-5831-7*) S Karger.
***Transmissible Subacute Spongiform Encephalopathies: Prion Diseases.** Ed. by L. Court & B. Bodet. 508p. 1996. pap. 139.00 (*2-906077-91-7*) Elsevier.
Transmission. Atima Srivastava. (Orig.). 1993. pap. 11.99 (*1-85242-228-9*) Serpents Tail.
Transmission. 2nd ed. Stewart O'Nan. LC 87-30635. (Illus.). 26p. 1987. pap. text ed. 2.00 (*0-943123-04-6*) Arjuna Lib Pr.
Transmission: A Meditation for the New Age. 3rd rev. ed. Benjamin Creme. 145p. 1988. pap. 6.00 (*0-936604-09-3*) Tara Ctr.
Transmission: Communication Skills for Technicians. Long. (Illus.). 1980. teacher ed. write for info. (*0-8359-7818-4*, Reston) P-H.
Transmission: Toward a Post-Television Culture. 2nd ed. Ed. by Peter D'Agostino & David Tafler. (Communication & Human Values Ser.: Vol. 16). 258p. 1994. 52.00 (*0-8039-4268-0*); pap. 24.95 (*0-8039-4269-9*) Sage.
***Transmission & Controls Problems.** 1996. 55.00 (*1-56091-843-8*, SP-1191) Soc Auto Engineers.
Transmission & Distribution Electrical Engineer. Colin Bayliss. (Illus.). 672p. 1996. 150.00 (*0-7506-2287-3*) Buttrwrth-Heinemann.
Transmission & Driveline Advancements. (SAE Worldwide Passenger Car Conference & Exposition, 1993 Ser.). 1993. pap. 19.00 (*1-56091-437-8*, SP-998) Soc Auto Engineers.
Transmission & Driveline Design. 92p. 1991. pap. 19.00 (*1-56091-171-9*, SP-879) Soc Auto Engineers.
Transmission & Driveline Developments: SAE International Congress & Exposition 1994, 19 papers. (Special Publications). 187p. 1994. pap. 56.00 (*1-56091-484-X*, SP-1032) Soc Auto Engineers.
Transmission & Driveline Developments for Trucks. 80p. 1991. pap. 19.00 (*1-56091-196-4*, SP-893) Soc Auto Engineers.
Transmission & Driveline Systems Symposium: Efficiency, Components, & Materials-1996 International Congress & Exposition. (Special Publications). 34p. 1996. pap. 99.00 (*1-56091-784-9*, SP-1154) Soc Auto Engineers.
***Transmission & Signaling Basics.** Jack Dempsey. 135p. (Orig.). 1997. pap. 29.95 (*0-87288-649-2*) Intertec IL.
Transmission Basics. Jack L. Dempsey. LC 89-45512. (Illus.). 83p. 1989. 29.95 (*0-917845-09-9*) Intertec IL.
Transmission de Savoir en Islam (VIIe-XVIIIe Siecles) Georges Vajda. Ed. by Nicole Cottart. (Collected Studies: No. CS181). 330p. (FRE.). (C). 1983. reprint ed. lib. bdg. 105.00 (*0-86078-129-1*, Pub. by Variorum UK) Ashgate Pub Co.
Transmission des Textes Philosophiques et Ecientifiques au Moyen Age. Marie-Therese D'Alverny. Ed. by Charles Burnett. (Collected Studies: CS 463). 368p. 1994. 103.95 (*0-86078-448-7*, Pub. by Variorum UK) Ashgate Pub Co.
Transmission Development of TEXTRON Lycoming's Geared Fan Engines. A. G. Meyer. (Fall Technical Meeting Papers 88FTM14). (Illus.). 1988. pap. text ed. 30.00 (*1-55589-519-0*) AGMA.
Transmission Diagnostic Manual, 1988-93. Chilton Automotives Editorial Staff. 1368p. 1993. text ed. 97.00 (*0-8019-8473-4*) Chilton.
Transmission Electron Energy Loss Spectrometry in Materials Science. Ed. by C. Ahn et al. (Illus.). 352p. 1992. 30.00 (*0-87339-180-2*, 1802) Minerals Metals.
Transmission Electron Microscopy: A Textbook for Materials Science. David B. Williams & C. Barry Carter. (Illus.). 710p. (C). 1996. 95.00 (*0-306-45247-2*, Plenum Pr) Plenum.
Transmission Electron Microscopy: A Textbook for Materials Science. David B. Williams & C. Barry Carter. (Illus.). 710p. (C). 1996. pap. 66.00 (*0-306-45324-X*, Plenum Pr) Plenum.
Transmission Electron Microscopy: Physics of Image Formation & Microanalysis. 3rd ed. Ludwig Reimer. LC 93-27996. (Optical Sciences Ser.: Vol. 36). 1993. 69.00 (*0-387-56849-2*) Spr-Verlag.
***Transmission Electron Microscopy: Physics of Image Formation & Microanalysis.** 4th ed. Ludwig Reimer. LC 97-6983. (Series in Optical Sciences). 1997. write for info. (*3-540-62568-2*) Spr-Verlag.
Transmission Electron Microscopy of Materials. Gareth Thomas & Michael J. Goringe. (Illus.). 404p. (C). 1990. reprint ed. text ed. 65.00 (*1-878907-15-8*) TechBooks.
Transmission Electron Microscopy of Minerals & Rocks. Alex C. McLaren. (Topics in Mineral Physics & Chemistry Ser.: No. 2). (Illus.). 350p. (C). 1991. text ed. 89.95 (*0-521-35098-0*) Cambridge U Pr.
Transmission Equipment. (Principles of Steam Generation Ser.: Module 18). (Illus.). 60p. 1982. spiral bd. 22.50 (*0-87683-268-0*) GP Courseware.
***Transmission Line Construction: 1994 Edition.** 107.00 (*1-55937-439-X*, SH17483) IEEE Standards.
Transmission Line Design Handbook. Brian C. Wadell. (Microwave Library). 512p. 1991. text ed. 77.00 (*0-89006-436-9*) Artech Hse.
Transmission-Line Modeling Method: TLM. Christos Christopoulos. LC 94-45582. (IEEE-OUP Series on Electromagnetic Waves Theory). 232p. 1995. 69.95 (*0-7803-1017-9*, PC3665) Inst Electrical.
Transmission-Line Modeling Method: TLM. Christos. (IEEE/OUP Series on Electromagnetic Wave Theory). (Illus.). 232p. (C). 1995. 65.00 (*0-19-856533-X*) OUP.
Transmission Line Transformers. Jerry Sevick. (Illus.). 250p. 1996. 34.00 (*1-884932-66-5*) Noble Pubng.
Transmission Lines & Wave Propagation. 3rd ed. Magnusson & Alexa. 250p. 1991. 64.95 (*0-8493-4279-1*, TK3221) CRC Pr.
Transmission Lines for Communications. 2nd ed. C. W. Davidson. 244p. 1989. pap. text ed. 79.95 (*0-470-21337-X*) Halsted Pr.
Transmission Lines for Digital & Communication Networks: An Introduction to Transmission Lines, High-Frequency, & High-Speed Pulse Characteristics & Applications. Richard E. Matick. LC 94-32639. 392p. 1995. 69.95 (*0-7803-1121-3*, PC4853) Inst Electrical.
Transmission Lines for Digital & Communications Networks: An Introduction to Transmission Lines, High-Frequency & High-Speed Pulse Characteristics & Applications. Richard E. Matick. LC 68-30561. 382p. reprint ed. pap. 108.90 (*0-317-09847-0*, 2052038) Bks Demand.
***Transmission Network Protection.** Paithanakar. (Power Engineering Ser.). 400p. 1997. write for info. (*0-8247-9911-9*) Dekker.
Transmission Networking: SONET & the Synchronous Digital Hierarchy. Michael J. Sexton & Andrew B. Reid. (Telecommunications Library). 340p. 1992. text ed. 75.00 (*0-89006-551-9*) Artech Hse.
Transmission of Culture in Early Modern Europe. Ed. by Anthony Grafton & Ann Blair. LC 89-70750. (Shelby Cullom Davis Center Ser.). (Illus.). 336p. (C). 1990. text ed. 39.95 (*0-8122-8191-8*) U of Pa Pr.
Transmission of Depression in Families & Children: Assessment & Intervention. Ed. by Pirooz G. Sholevar. LC 93-24688. 368p. 1994. 40.00 (*1-56821-088-4*) Aronson.
Transmission of Doubt: Talks & Essays on the Transcendence of Scientific Materialism Through Radical Understanding. Da Free John. 484p. (Orig.). 1984. pap. 10.95 (*0-913922-77-3*) Dawn Horse Pr.
Transmission of Epidemic Influenza. R. E. Hope-Simpson. (Illus.). 230p. 1991. 49.50 (*0-306-44073-3*, Plenum Pr) Plenum.
Transmission of Ideas in the Lutheran Reformation. Ed. by Helga Robinson-Hammerstein. 240p. 1988. 39.50 (*0-7165-2376-0*, Pub. by Irish Acad Pr IE) Intl Spec Bk.
Transmission of Knowledge in Medieval Cairo: A Social History of Islamic Education. Jonathan Berkey. (Near East Studies). 244p. 1992. text ed. 45.00 (*0-691-03191-6*) Princeton U Pr.
Transmission of Knowledge in South Asia: Essays on Education, Religion, History, & Politics. Nigel Crook. (Studies on South Asia). (Illus.). 348p. (C). 1996. 29.95 (*0-19-563644-9*) OUP.
***Transmission of Light.** Keizan. 1996. pap. 20.95 (*0-8348-0262-7*) Weatherhill.
Transmission of Light (Denkoroku) Zen in the Art of Enlightenment. Keizan. Tr. & Intro. by Thomas Cleary. LC 89-28491. 234p. 1990. pap. 14.95 (*0-86547-433-8*, North Pt Pr) FS&G.
Transmission of Money. David Hillier. 97p. 1990. pap. 125.00 (*0-85297-363-2*, Pub. by Inst Bankers UK) St Mut.
***Transmission of Sikh Heritage in the Diaspora.** Ed. by P. Singh & N. G. Barrier. (C). 1996. 34.00 (*81-7304-155-5*, Pub. by Manohar II) S Asia.
Transmission of the Flame: A Collection of Talks with Jean Klein on Non-Duality. Jean Klein. LC 90-83516. 298p. (Orig.). 1990. 14.95 (*1-877769-22-3*) Third Millennium.
Transmission of the Lamp. Rajneesh Osho Staff. Ed. by Deva Ashik. (Talks in Uruguay Ser.). 464p. 1989. 24.95 (*3-89338-049-3*, Pub. by Rebel Hse GW) Osho America.
Transmission of the Lamp: Early Masters. rev. ed. Tr. by Sohaku Ogata. LC 89-8125. 475p. 1990. pap. 19.95 (*0-89341-565-0*, Longwood Academic) Hollowbrook.
Transmission of the Punica of Silius Italicus. Patrick McGushin. iv, 165p. 1985. 27.00 (*90-256-0895-7*, Pub. by A M Hakkert NE) Benjamins North Am.
Transmission of the Text of Lucan in the Ninth Century. Harold C. Gotoff. LC 72-133212. (Loeb Classical Monographs). 223p. 1971. 23.95 (*0-674-90466-4*) HUP.
Transmission Planning, Siting & Certification in the 1990s: Problems, Prospects & Policies. 300p. 1990. 130.00 (*0-317-03100-7*) Consumer Energy Coun.
Transmission Pricing & Stranded Costs in the Electric Power Industry. William J. Baumol & J. Gregory Sidak. LC 95-14087. 200p. 1995. 49.95 (*0-8447-3922-7*) Am Enterprise.
Transmission Principles for Technicians. 2nd ed. D. C. Green. (Illus.). 224p. 1995. pap. 39.50 (*0-582-24515-X*, Pub. by Longman Group UK) Trans-Atl Phila.
Transmission System Interface. Center for Occupational Research & Development Staff. (EUTEC Power Plant Operator Curriculum Ser.). (Illus.). 42p. (C). 1987. pap. text ed. write for info. (*1-55502-246-4*) CORD Commns.
Transmission Systems. Ed. by J. E. Flood & P. Cochrane. (I. E. E. Telecommunications Ser.: No. 27). 524p. (Orig.). 1995. pap. 45.00 (*0-86341-310-2*, TE027Z) Inst Elect Eng.
Transmission Systems, No. 27. Ed. by J. E. Flood & P. Cochrane. (Telecommunications Ser.). (Orig.). 1991. text ed. 109.00 (*0-86341-148-7*, TE027) Inst Elect Eng.
Transmission Systems: Engineering Seminar II. 2nd ed. Eugene W. Riley & Victor E. Acuna. LC 76-15104. (ABC of the Telephone Ser.: Vol. 8). (Illus.). 68p. (C). 1984. pap. text ed. 13.95 (*1-56016-007-1*) ABC TeleTraining.
Transmissions, Steering & Brakes see Truck Guide
Transmit 95: Visual Telephone Directory. Carolyn P. Speranza. 1995. pap. 35.00 (*1-885522-00-2*) Telecommunity Pr.
Transmitelo. (SPA.). 1993. write for info. (*0-916856-63-1*) AAWS.
Transmitted-Picture Assessment. John Allnatt. LC 82-21895. (Illus.). 319p. reprint ed. pap. 91.00 (*0-8357-3572-9*, 2034210) Bks Demand.
Transmitter Hunting: Radio Direction Finding Simplified. Thomas N. Curlee & Joseph D. Moell. 1987. pap. text ed. 19.95 (*0-07-156006-8*) McGraw.
Transmitter Hunting: Radio Direction Finding Simplified. Joseph D. Modell et al. (Illus.). 336p. (Orig.). 1987. pap. 19.95 (*0-8306-2701-4*) McGraw-Hill Prof.
Transmitting Loop Antenna Computer Aided Design Software. Ted Hart. 1989. 17.75 incl. disk (*0-685-28860-9*) Franklin-Belle.
Transmitting World News: A Study of Telecommunications & the Press. Francis Williams. LC 72-4686. (International Propaganda & Communications Ser.). (Illus.). 95p. 1972. reprint ed. 15.95 (*0-405-04770-3*) Ayer.
Transmural Plasma Flow in Atherogenesis. H. Jellinek et al. 190p. (C). 1983. 75.00 (*963-05-3205-0*, Pub. by Akad Kiado HU) St Mut.
Transmutation. Robert G. Chaney. (Adventures in Esoteric Learning Ser.). 56p. 1969. pap. 4.95 (*0-918936-17-9*) Astara.
Transmutation, Natural & Artificial. Thaddeus J. Trenn. LC 82-106284. (Nobel Prize Topics in Chemistry Ser.). (Illus.). 144p. reprint ed. pap. 41.10 (*0-8357-7059-1*, 2033357) Bks Demand.
Transmutation Notebooks: Poems in the Voices of Charles & Emma Darwin. Anne Becker. Ed. by Grace Cavalieri & Cindy Comitz. 120p. (Orig.). 1995. pap. 10.00 (*0-938572-12-1*) Bunny Crocodile.
Transmutation of Attitudes. Deborah Morea. 1979. pap. 6.50 (*0-9603022-1-2*) Davida Pubns.
Transmutation Operators & Mean Periodic Functions Associated ITH Differential Operators, Vol. 4. Khalife Trimeche. (Mathematical Reports: Vol. 4, No. 1). xviii, 282p. 1988. pap. text ed. 62.00 (*3-7186-4822-9*) Gordon & Breach.
***Transmutation Theory.** Sitnik. 1996. write for info. (*0-582-10294-4*, Pub. by Longman UK) Longman.
Transmutations: Understanding Literary & Pictorial Caricature. Kenneth T. Rivers. 330p. (Orig.). (C). 1991. pap. text ed. 28.00 (*0-8191-8329-6*); lib. bdg. 49.00 (*0-8191-8328-8*) U Pr of Amer.
Transnational Accounting, 2 Vols. Kpmg Peat Marwick Staff. 3225p. 1995. 490.00 (*1-56159-168-8*, Stockton Pr) Groves Dictionaries.
Transnational Bank Behaviour & the International Debt Crisis (Est. e Inf. 76) 208p. 6.00 (*92-1-121150-6*, E.89.II.G.12) UN.
Transnational Banks, & the Dynamics of Peruvian Foreign Debt & Inflation. J. Manuel Uriarte. LC 84-26307. 208p. 1985. text ed. 55.00 (*0-275-90104-1*, C0104, Praeger Pubs) Greenwood.
Transnational Banks & the External Indebtedness of Developing Countries: Impact of Regulatory Changes. 48p. Date not set. 12.50 (*92-1-104388-3*) UN.
Transnational Banks & the International Debt Crisis. 157p. 1990. 22.50 (*92-1-104349-2*) UN.
Transnational Business Information - A Manual of Needs & Sources. 228p. 1991. 45.00 (*92-1-104371-9*, 91.II.A.13) UN.
Transnational Business Problems. Detlev F. Vagts. (University Casebook Ser.). 529p. 1991. reprint ed. text ed. 30.50 (*0-88277-323-2*) Foundation Pr.
Transnational Capitalism & Hydropolitics in Argentina: The Yacyreta High Dam. Gustavo L. Ribeiro. LC 93-33426. (Center for Latin American Studies, University of Florida). (Illus.). 216p. (C). 1994. bds. 39.95 (*0-8130-1280-5*) U Press Fla.
Transnational Citizenship: Membership & Rights in International Migration. Rainer Baubock. 360p. 1994. 70.00 (*1-85278-942-5*) E Elgar.
Transnational Communications: Wiring the Third World. Gerald Sussman & John A. Lent. (Communication & Human Values Ser.: Vol. 7). (Illus.). 338p. (C). 1991. text ed. 52.00 (*0-8039-3765-2*); pap. text ed. 24.95 (*0-8039-3766-0*) Sage.
Transnational Communications: Wiring the Third World. Ed. by Gerald Sussman & John A. Lent. LC 90-25943. (Communication & Human Values Ser.). (Illus.). 343p. 1991. pap. 97.80 (*0-7837-8969-6*, 2049750) Bks Demand.
Transnational Conglomerates & the Economics of Dependent Development: A Case Study of the International Electrical Oligopoly & Brazils Electrical Industry. Ingo I. Walter. LC 78-13842. (Contemporary Studies in Economic & Financial Analysis: Vol. 23). 420p. 1980. 73.25 (*0-89232-110-5*) Jai Pr.
Transnational Connections: Culture, People, Places. Ulf Hannerz. LC 95-46217. 216p. (C). 1996. pap. 17.95 (*0-415-14309-8*); text ed. 65.00 (*0-415-14308-X*) Routledge.
Transnational Contracts; Applicable Law & Settlement of Disputes: A Study in Conflict Avoidance, Law & Practice, 6 vols. Georges R. Delaume. 1983. Set. ring bd. 945.00 (*0-379-10200-5*) Oceana.
Transnational Corporations: A Selective Bibliography, Vol. 2. 617p. 1991. 75.00 (*92-1-004032-5*) UN.
Transnational Corporations: A Selective Bibliography, Vol. III. 727p. 1992. 75.00 (*92-1-004033-3*, B.93.II.A.16) UN.
Transnational Corporations: A Selective Bibliography, 1983-1987, Vol. II. 462p. (ENG & FRE.). 1988. 49.00 (*92-1-004031-7*, EF.88.II.A.10) UN.

Transnational Corporations: Technology Transfer. Ed. by John Cantwell. LC 93-15973. (United Nations Library on Transnational Corporations: Vol. 18). 1994. write for info. (0-415-08545-4) Routledge.

Transnational Corporations - A Selective Bibliography, 1983-1987. 442p. 1988. 45.00 (92-1-004030-9, EF.88.II.A.9) UN.

*__Transnational Corporations & Business Strategy.__ Ed. by Donald J. Lecraw & Allen J. Morrison. (Readings in Transnational Corporations Ser.). 402p. 1996. pap. 29.95 (0-415-14109-5) Routledge.

*__Transnational Corporations & Economic Development.__ Ed. by Sanjaya Lall. (Readings in Transnational Corporations Ser.). 428p. 1996. pap. 29.95 (0-415-14110-9) Routledge.

Transnational Corporations & Human Resources. Ed. by Peter Enderwick. LC 93-19489. (United Nations Library on Transnational Corporations). 1993. write for info. (0-415-08552-7) Routledge.

Transnational Corporations & Industrial Hazards Disclosure. 102p. 1991. 17.50 (92-1-104375-1, E.9.II.A.18) UN.

Transnational Corporations & Industrialization. Ed. by Daniel Chudnovsky. LC 93-18761. (United Nations Library on Transnational Corporations: Vol. 11). 1993. write for info. (0-415-08544-6) Routledge.

Transnational Corporations & Innovatory Activities. Ed. by Seymour J. Rubin & Don Wallace, Jr. LC 93-15972. (United Nations Library on Transnational Corporations: Vol. 17). 1994. write for info. (0-415-08550-0) Routledge.

Transnational Corporations & International Economic Relations: Recent Developments & Selected Issues. 150p. 7.50 (92-1-104322-0, E.89.II.A.15) UN.

Transnational Corporations & Legal Issues. Edward K. Chen. LC 93-15974. (United Nations Library on Transnational Corporations: Vol. 19). 1994. write for info. (0-415-08549-7) Routledge.

Transnational Corporations & Manufacturing Exports from Developed Countries. 419p. 1995. 35.00 (92-1-127048-0, E.95.II.F.84) UN.

Transnational Corporations & Manufacturing Exports from Developing Countries. 130p. 1990. 25.00 (92-1-104351-4, 90.II.A.21) UN.

Transnational Corporations & Non-Fuel Primary Commodities in Developing Countries. 89p. 1987. 10.00 (92-1-104211-9, E.87.II.A.17) UN.

Transnational Corporations & Regional Economic Integration. Ed. by Peter Robson. LC 93-18758. (United Nations Library on Transnational Corporations: Vol. 9). 1993. write for info. (0-415-08542-X, Routledge NY) Routledge.

Transnational Corporations & Technology Transfer. 156p. 1995. 20.00 (92-1-127031-6) UN.

Transnational Corporations & Technology Transfer: Effects & Policy Issues. 77p. 1987. 11.00 (92-1-104199-6, E.87.II.A.4) UN.

Transnational Corporations & the Electronics Industries of ASEAN Economies. (UNCTC Current Studies A: No. 5). 55p. 1987. 10.00 (92-1-104207-0, E.87.II.A.13) UN.

Transnational Corporations & the Exploitation of Natural Resources. Ed. by Bruce McKern. LC 93-18760. (United Nations Library on Transnational Corporations: Vol. 10). 1993. write for info. (0-415-08543-8) Routledge.

*__Transnational Corporations & the Global Economy.__ Richard Kozul-Wright & Bob Rowthorn. LC 97-22917. 1997. write for info. (0-312-17724-0) St Martin.

Transnational Corporations & the Growth of Services: Some Conceptual & Theoretical Issues. 80p. 1989. 12.00 (92-1-104311-5, 89.II.A.5) UN.

Transnational Corporations & the Latin American Automobile Industry. Rhys Jenkins. LC 86-1500. (Latin American Ser.). (Illus.). 288p. 1986. 49.95 (0-8229-1145-0) U of Pittsburgh Pr.

Transnational Corporations & the Transfer of New & Emerging Technologies to Developing Countries. 150p. 1990. 27.50 (92-1-104350-6, 90.II.A.20) UN.

Transnational Corporations & Uneven Development. Rhys Jenkins. LC 87-12351. 250p. 1988. pap. 15.95 (0-416-73350-6); text ed. 75.00 (0-416-73340-9) Routledge Chapman & Hall.

Transnational Corporations, Armaments & Developments. Helena Tuomi & Raimo Vayrynen. LC 81-18444. 1982. text ed. 35.00 (0-312-81473-9) St Martin.

Transnational Corporations from Developing Countries: Impact on Their Home Countries. 102p. 1993. 15.00 (92-1-104410-3, E.93.II.A.8) UN.

Transnational Corporations in a Developing Country: The Indian Experience. John Martinussen. 228p. (C). 1988. text ed. 24.00 (0-8039-9584-9) Sage.

Transnational Corporations in Biotechnology. 136p. 1988. 17.00 (92-1-104222-4, E.88.II.A.4) UN.

Transnational Corporations In Services. Ed. by Karl P. Sauvant & Padma Mallampally. LC 93-18759. (United Nations Library on Transnational Corporations: Vol. 12). 1993. write for info. (0-415-08548-9) Routledge.

Transnational Corporations in South Africa. 286p. 1991. 22.00 (0-685-41905-3, 91.II.A.9) UN.

Transnational Corporations in South Africa: List of Companies with Investments & Disinvestments. 286p. 1990. 22.00 (0-685-50216-3) UN.

Transnational Corporations in South Africa & Namibia: A Selective Bibliography. 98p. 1989. 12.00 (92-1-104320-4, 89.II.A.13) UN.

Transnational Corporations in South Africa & Namibia: United Nations Public Hearings, 4 vols. 1671p. Set. 200.00 (0-685-50217-1) UN.

Transnational Corporations in South Africa & Namibia: United Nations Public Hearings, 4 vols., Vol. I. 427p. 65.00 (92-1-104179-1) UN.

Transnational Corporations in South Africa & Namibia: United Nations Public Hearings, 4 vols., Vol. II. 282p. write for info. (92-1-104180-5) UN.

Transnational Corporations in South Africa & Namibia: United Nations Public Hearings, 4 vols., Vol. III. 518p. write for info. (92-1-104181-3) UN.

Transnational Corporations in South Africa & Namibia: United Nations Public Hearings, 4 vols., Vol. IV. 444p. 65.00 (92-1-104182-1) UN.

Transnational Corporations in South Africa & Namibia - Second United Nations Public Hearings, Vol. One: Report of the Panel of Eminent Persons, Background Documentation. 174p. 1989. 19.00 (92-1-104335-2, 90.II.A.6) UN.

Transnational Corporations in South Africa & Namibia - Second United Nations Public Hearings, Vol. Two: Statements & Submissions. 201p. 1989. 21.00 (92-1-104341-7, 90.II.A.12) UN.

Transnational Corporations in Southeast Asia: An Institutional Approach to Industrial Organization. Hans Jansson. (New Horizons in International Business Ser.). 208p. 1994. 75.00 (1-85278-983-2) E Elgar.

Transnational Corporations in the Construction & Design Engineering Industry: Engineering Industry. 69p. 9.00 (92-1-104312-3, E.89.II.A.6) UN.

Transnational Corporations in the International Semiconductor Industry, No. 16. 471p. 41.00 (92-1-104174-0, E.86.II.A.1) UN.

Transnational Corporations in the Man-Made Fibre, Textile & Clothing Industries. 154p. 1987. 19.00 (92-1-104205-4, E.87.II.A.11) UN.

Transnational Corporations in the Plastics Industry. 167p. 1990. 20.00 (92-1-104327-1, 90.II.A.1) UN.

Transnational Corporations, Services & the Uruguay Round. 266p. 1990. 28.50 (92-1-104340-9, 90.II.A.11) UN.

Transnational Corporations vs. the State: The Political Economy of the Mexican Auto Industry. Douglas C. Bennett & Kenneth E. Sharpe. LC 85-42674. 392p. 1985. pap. text ed. 17.95 (0-691-02237-2) Princeton U Pr.

Transnational Crime: Investigative Responses. Ed. by Harold E. Smith. (Studies in Terrorism). 1989. pap. text ed. 7.50 (0-942511-22-0) OICJ.

Transnational Crime & Criminal Law. Andre Bossard. 100p. pap. 7.00 (0-942511-33-6) OICJ.

Transnational Dispute Resolution, 1984. Ed. by Gregory P. Crinion. (Wisconsin International Law Journal, 1982 Ser.). 300p. (Orig.). 1985. pap. text ed. 8.00 (0-933431-02-3) U Wisc Law Madison.

Transnational Drug Problem: The Final Report of the CSIS Transnational Drug Challenge. Stephen Flynn & Gregory M. Grant. 60p. (Orig.). 1993. pap. 8.95 (0-89206-212-6) CSI Studies.

Transnational Enterprises in a New International System. Klaus W. Grewlich. 240p. 1981. lib. bdg. 87.00 (90-286-0650-5) Kluwer Ac.

Transnational Environmental Law & Its Impact on Corporate Behavior. Ed. by Eric J. Urbani et al. LC 93-50724. (Illus.). 366p. 1994. text ed. 75.00 (1-56425-031-8) Juris Pubng.

Transnational Environmental Liability & Insurance. Ed. by Ralph P. Kroner. LC 92-32774. (International Bar Association Ser.). 1993. lib. bdg. 176.00 (1-85333-778-1, Pub. by Graham & Trotman UK) Kluwer Ac.

Transnational Industrial Relations. Hans Gunter. 1972. text ed. 39.95 (0-312-81480-1) St Martin.

Transnational Investments in Mobile Telephone Systems: Toward Global Telephone Companies?, Vol. P-94-7. unabridged ed. Christopher W. Mines. (Illus.). 53p. (Orig.). 1994. pap. text ed. write for info. (1-879716-17-8) Ctr Info Policy.

Transnational Joint Ventures, 2 vols., No. 66. Ed. by Peter B. Fitzpatrick. 1000p. 1989. Set. ring bd. 215.00 (0-929576-45-4) Busn Laws Inc.

Transnational Legal Practice: A Guide to Selected Countries, 2 vols. Ed. by D. Campbell. 410p. 122.50 (90-6544-028-3) Kluwer Ac.

Transnational Legal Practice in the EEC & the United States. Linda S. Spedding. 386p. 1987. lib. bdg. 55.00 (0-941320-36-7) Transnatl Pubs.

Transnational Legal Problems: Materials & Text. 4th ed. Detlev F. Vagts et al. (University Casebook Ser.). 1179p. 1994. text ed. 46.00 (1-56662-159-3) Foundation Pr.

Transnational Legal Problems: Materials & Text, Documentary Supplement. 4th ed. Henry J. Steiner et al. 154p. 1994. pap. text ed. 10.95 (1-56662-163-1) Foundation Pr.

*__Transnational Litigation.__ Louise E. Teitz. 550p. 1996. 105.00 (1-55834-345-8, 67485) MICHIE.

*__Transnational Litigation: A Practitioner's Guide.__ Richard H. Kreindler. LC 97-9283. 1997. write for info. (0-379-21365-6) Oceana.

Transnational Litigation & Commercial Arbitration under American, European & International Law. Joseph M. Lookofsky. 800p. 1991. 65.00 (0-929179-66-8) Juris Pubng.

Transnational Management: Text, Cases, & Readings in Cross Border Management. Christopher A. Bartlett & Sumantra Ghoshal. 928p. (C). 1991. text ed. 72.25 (0-256-08485-8) Irwin.

Transnational Management: Text Cases & Readings in Cross Border Management. 2nd ed. Christopher A. Barlett & Sumantra Ghoshal. 200p. (C). 1995. ring bd. 72.25 (0-256-14138-X) Irwin.

Transnational Management: Text Cases & Readings in Cross Border Management. 2nd ed. Christopher A. Bartlett & Sumantra Ghoshal. 1995. write for info. (0-256-16553-X) Irwin Prof Pubng.

Transnational Management, International: Text Cases & Readings in Cross Border Management. Christopher A. Bartlett & Sumantra Ghoshal. (C). 1991. student ed., text ed. 31.50 (0-256-11746-2) Irwin.

Transnational Marriages in the Steel Industry: Experience & Lessons for Global Business. Garth L. Mangum et al. LC 95-45964. 216p. 1996. text ed. 59.95 (1-56720-040-0, Quorum Bks) Greenwood.

Transnational Media & Third World Development: The Structure & Impact of Imperialism. William H. Meyer. LC 88-10239. (Contributions to the Study of Mass Media & Communications Ser.: No. 11). 146p. 1988. text ed. 55.00 (0-313-26264-0, MYN/, Greenwood Pr) Greenwood.

Transnational Media Corporation: Global Messages & Free Market Competition. Richard A. Gershon. LC 96-20813. (Communication Ser.). 264p. (C). 1996. 49.95 (0-8058-1255-5) L Erlbaum Assocs.

*__Transnational Media Corporation: Global Messages & Free Market Competition.__ Richard A. Gershon. 1996. pap. 22.50 (0-8058-2425-1) L Erlbaum Assocs.

Transnational Monopoly Capitalism. Keith Cowling & Roger Sugden. LC 87-4965. 265p. 1987. text ed. 45.00 (0-312-00954-2) St Martin.

Transnational Oil: Issues, Policies & Perspectives. Zuhayr Mikdashi. LC 85-30364. 280p. 1986. text ed. 39.95 (0-312-81482-8) St Martin.

Transnational Parties: Organizing the World's Precincts. Ed. by Ralph M. Goldman. LC 83-12369. (Illus.). 374p. (C). 1983. pap. text ed. 28.00 (0-8191-3401-5) U Pr of Amer.

*__Transnational Person.__ Campbell. 1992. pap. text ed. 96.50 (90-6544-604-4) Kluwer Ac.

Transnational Relations & World Politics. Ed. by Robert O. Keohane & Joseph S. Nye, Jr. LC 76-178076. (Center for International Affairs Ser.). (Illus.). 460p. 1972. pap. 17.95 (0-674-90482-6) HUP.

*__Transnational Religion, the State, & Global Civil Society.__ James P. Piscatori. Ed. by Susanne H. Rudolph. (C). 1996. text ed. 67.50 (0-8133-2767-9); pap. text ed. 21.00 (0-8133-2768-7) Westview.

Transnational Retailing. Ed. by Erdener Kaynak. 374p. (C). 1988. lib. bdg. 125.00 (3-11-010801-1) De Gruyter.

Transnational Service Corporations & Developing Countries: Impact & Policy Issues. 55p. 1989. 7.50 (92-1-104321-2, 89.II.A.14) UN.

Transnational Terrorism: A Chronology of Events, 1968-1979. Edward F. Mickolus. LC 79-6829. xxxviii, 967p. 1980. text ed. 135.00 (0-313-22206-1, MTT/, Greenwood Pr) Greenwood.

Transnational Tort Litigation: Jurisdictional Principles. Ed. by Campbell McLachlan & Peter Nygh. 300p. 1996. 90.00 (0-19-825919-0) OUP.

Transnationals. Profulla Roychoudhury. 1983. 12.50 (0-8364-0949-3, Pub. by Mukhopadhyaya II) S Asia.

Transnationals & Governments: Recent Policies in Japan, France, Germany, the United States & Britain. David Bailey et al. LC 93-38032. 256p. (C). (gr. 13). 1994. text ed. 74.95 (0-415-09825-4, B3710) Routledge.

Transnationals & the Third World: The Struggle for Culture. Armand Mattelart. (Illus.). 192p. 1985. text ed. 34.95 (0-89789-030-2, Bergin & Garvey); pap. text ed. 14.95 (0-89789-100-7, Bergin & Garvey) Greenwood.

Transonic Aerodynamics. J. D. Cole & L. P. Cook. (Applied Mathematics & Mechanics Ser.: Vol. 30). 474p. 1986. 145.25 (0-444-87958-7, North Holland) Elsevier.

Transonic Aerodynamics: Problems in Asymptotic Theory. L. P. Cook. LC 93-3092. (Frontiers in Applied Mathematics Ser.: No. 12). x, 90p. 1993. pap. 28.50 (0-89871-310-2) Soc Indus-Appl Math.

Transonic Vortical Gas Flows. O. M. Belotserkovskii & E. G. Shifrin. 392p. 1994. text ed. 165.00 (0-471-95066-1) Wiley.

Transosseous Osteosynthesis: Theoretical & Clinical Aspects of the Regeneration & Growth of Tissue. G. A. Ilizarov. (Illus.). 816p. 1991. 298.00 (0-387-53534-9) Spr-Verlag.

Transpacific Steam: The Story of Steam Navigation from the Pacific Coast of North America to the Far East & the Antipodes, 1867-1941. E. Mowbray Tate. LC 84-45642. (Illus.). 272p. 1986. 39.95 (0-8453-4792-6, Cornwall Bks) Assoc Univ Prs.

*__Transparence of November Snow.__ Roo Borson & Kim Maltman. 68p. 1985. pap. 12.95 (0-919627-30-7, Pub. by Quarry Pr CN) LPC InBook.

Transparencies. Vesle Fenstermaker. 48p. (Orig.). 1985. pap. 5.95 (0-935306-36-6) Barnwood Pr.

Transparencies. S. Fox. 1978. pap. 2.95 (0-942396-23-5) Blackberry ME.

Transparencies: Remembrances of My Father. Jesse Stuart & Jane Stuart. 1985. pap. 9.95 (0-89097-026-2) Downtown Bks.

*__Transparencies, Love Poems for the New Age.__ Karla Andersdatter. 118p. 1978. per., pap. write for info. (0-935430-05-9) In Between.

Transparencies to Accompany Sorensen & Luckmann's Basic Nursing: A Psychophysiologic Approach. 3rd ed. Verolyn B. Bolander. 160p. 1994. write for info. incl. trans. (0-7216-4745-6) Saunders.

*__Transparency.__ Colin Rowe et al. LC 97-4294. 1997. write for info. (0-8176-5615-4); pap. 24.95 (3-7643-5615-4) Birkhauser.

*__Transparency.__ Colin Rowe et al. (Illus.). 132p. (GER.). 1997. pap. 24.95 (3-7643-5614-6) Birkhauser.

Transparency. Edward Stever. 28p. 1990. pap. 5.00 (0-925062-02-2) Writers Ink Pr.

Transparency. Edward Stever. 28p. 1990. 10.00 (0-925062-03-0) Writers Ink Pr.

*__Transparency & Refraction of the Cornea.__ Janos Feher. (Pathophysiology of the Eye Ser.: Vol. 3). 230p. 1996. pap. 38.00 (963-05-6996-5, Pub. by A K HU) Intl Spec Bk.

Transparency in Armaments: Regional Dialogue & Disarmament. (Disarmament Topical Papers: No. 20). 224p. Date not set. pap. 13.50 (92-1-142212-4, E.94.IX.12) UN.

Transparency in Armaments: The Mediterranean Region. (Disarmament Topical Papers: No. 15). 118p. Date not set. pap. 13.50 (92-1-142198-5, E.93.IX.13) UN.

Transparency in International Arms Transfer. (Disarmament Topical Papers: No. 3). 193p. 1990. 13.50 (92-1-142160-8, 90.IX.9) UN.

Transparency Making Made Easy: A Programmed Primer. (Illus.). 1977. 3.75 (0-9601006-2-8) G T Yeamans.

*__Transparency Masters SPC Essentials & Productivity Improvement: A Manufacturing Approach.__ Frank Tumbelty. 407p. (Orig.). 1996. pap. 28.00 incl. trans. (0-87389-373-5, H0938) ASQC Qual Pr.

Transparency Masters to Accompany Fundamentals of Quality Auditing. B. Scott Parsowith. 197p. 1995. pap. 18.00 (0-87389-342-5, H0794A) ASQC Qual Pr.

Transparency of Evil: Essays on Extreme Phenomena. Jean Baudrillard. Tr. by J. St. John Baddeley. 200p. (C). (gr. 13). 1993. text ed. 60.00 (0-86091-387-2, A9737, Pub. by Vrso UK); pap. text ed. 19.00 (0-86091-588-3, A9741, Pub. by Vrso UK) Norton.

*__Transparency of Spectacle: Meditations on the Moving Image.__ Wheeler W. Dixon. (SUNY Series in Postmodern Culture). 224p. (C). 1998. text ed. 59.50 (0-7914-3781-7) State U NY Pr.

*__Transparency of Spectacle: Meditations on the Moving Image.__ Wheeler W. Dixon. (SUNY Series in Postmodern Culture). 224p. (C). 1998. pap. text ed. 19.95 (0-7914-3782-5) State U NY Pr.

Transparent Body. Lisa Bernstein. LC 88-10656. (Wesleyan New Poets Ser.). 64p. 1989. pap. 11.95 (0-8195-1163-3, Wesleyan Univ Pr) U Pr of New Eng.

Transparent Eye: Reflections on Translation, Chinese Literature, & Comparative Poetics. Eugene C. Eoyang. LC 92-33366. (SHAPS Library of Translations). 352p. 1993. text ed. 39.00 (0-8248-1429-0) UH Pr.

Transparent Gestures. Rodney Jones. 68p. 1989. pap. 9.95 (0-395-51063-5) HM.

Transparent God. Claude Esteban. Tr. by David Cloutier from FRE. LC 80-84603. (Modern Poets in Translation Ser.: Vol. II). ix, 107p. (Orig.). (C). 1983. 17.00 (0-916426-07-6); pap. 7.95 (0-916426-08-4) KOSMOS.

*__Transparent Hero.__ James Forte. 26p. (Orig.). 1995. pap. 12.95 (1-889560-08-1) Wildflower Pub.

Transparent I Vol. 2: Self-Subject in European Cinema. Stephen R. Snyder. LC 93-51022. (Comparative Literary & Film Studies: Vol. 2). 202p. (C). 1994. text ed. 47.95 (0-8204-2282-7) P Lang Pubng.

Transparent Illusion: Image & Ideology in French Text & Film. Rebecca M. Pauly. LC 92-16539. (Art of Interpretation Ser.: Vol. 3). 495p. (Orig.). (FRE.). (C). 1993. pap. text ed. 41.95 (0-8204-1930-3) P Lang Pubng.

Transparent Jewel. Mabel Collins. 142p. 1913. reprint ed. spiral bd. 8.50 (0-7873-1231-2) Hlth Research.

Transparent Jewel (1913) Mabel Collins. 142p. 1996. pap. 17.95 (1-56459-914-0) Kessinger Pub.

Transparent Jungle. George Snelling. 100p. (Orig.). 1986. pap. text ed. 4.95 (0-935805-00-1) Innerlogic Cir.

*__Transparent Lyric: Reading & Meaning in the Poetry of Stevens & Williams.__ David Walker. LC 84-1986. 224p. 1984. reprint ed. pap. 63.90 (0-608-03343-X, 2064055) Bks Demand.

Transparent Man. Anthony Hecht. 1992. pap. 16.00 (0-679-73358-2) Knopf.

Transparent Minds: Narrative Modes for Presenting Consciousness in Fiction. Dorritt Cohn. LC 78-51161. 344p. 1984. pap. text ed. 18.95 (0-691-10156-6) Princeton U Pr.

Transparent Plastics: Broadening the Base of Materials & Applications. M. Schlecter. 204p. 1994. 2,650.00 (0-89336-706-0, P-053N) BCC.

Transparent Prolog Machine: Visualizing Logic Programs. Marc Eisenstadt et al. 200p. 1991. lib. bdg. 88.50 (0-7923-1447-6) Kluwer Ac.

*__Transparent Realities: The Anthroposophical Impulse in the Environmental Movement & the 33-Year Rhythm in the History of the Anthroposophical Society.__ Hans P. Van Manen. Tr. by Ursula Gleed et al. 64p. 1994. pap. write for info. (0-904693-62-7, Pub. by Temple Ldge Pub UK) Anthroposophic.

Transparent Self: Self-Disclosure & Well-Being. 2nd ed. Sidney M. Jourard. 1971. pap. 36.95 (0-442-24192-5) Van Nos Reinhold.

Transparent Simulacra: Spanish Fiction, 1902-1926. Robert C. Spires. LC 88-4882. 192p. 1989. text ed. 27.50 (0-8262-0695-6) U of Mo Pr.

*__Transparent Soapmaking: A Complete Guide to Making Natural See-Through Soap.__ Catherine Failor. LC 96-93093. (Illus.). 154p. (Orig.). 1997. pap. 14.95 (0-9656390-0-2) Rose City Pr.

*__Transparent Society.__ David Brin. 1998. write for info. (0-201-32802-X) Addison-Wesley.

Transparent Society. Gianni Vattimo. Tr. by David Webb. LC 92-10839. (Parallax: Re-Visions of Culture & Society Ser.). 144p. 1992. text ed. 32.50 (0-8018-4527-0); pap. text ed. 12.95 (0-8018-4528-9) Johns Hopkins.

Transparent Tape: Over 350 Super, Simple & Surprising Uses You've Probably Never Thought Of. Vicki Lansky. (Illus.). 108p. 1995. pap. 6.95 (0-916773-44-2) Book Peddlers.

Transparent Things. Vladimir Nabokov. (Vintage International Ser.). 1989. pap. 11.00 (0-679-72541-5, Vin) Random.

Transparent Tree: Fictions. Robert Kelly. LC 85-2951. 200p. 1985. 20.00 (*0-914232-68-1*); pap. 10.00 (*0-914232-70-3*) McPherson & Co.

Transparent Tree: Fictions. deluxe ed. Robert Kelly. LC 85-2951. 200p. 1985. 50.00 (*0-914232-69-X*) McPherson & Co.

Transparent Watercolor: My Second Career. William H. Condit. (Illus.). 128p. 1990. text ed. 29.95 (*0-9624318-0-X*) Sand Dllr CO.

Transparent Watercolor: Painting Methods & Materials. Inessa Derkatsch. (Illus.). 1980. text ed. 25.95 (*0-13-930321-9*, Spectrum IN) Macmillan Gen Ref.

Transparent Watercolor Wheel. James Kosvanec. (Illus.). 144p. 1994. 29.95 (*0-8230-5436-5*, Watsn-Guptill) Watsn-Guptill.

Transparenz der Wirklichkeit: Edzard Schaper und die innere Spannung in der christlichen Literatur des zwanzigstes Jahrhunderts. Irene Sonderegger-Kummer. (Quellen und Forschungen zur Sprach und Kulturgeschichte der Germanischen Voelker Ser.: No. 37). (C). 1971. 123.10 (*3-11-001845-4*) De Gruyter.

Transpersonal: Psychotherapy & Counselling. John Rowan. LC 92-15268. (Illus.). 304p. (C). (gr. 13). 1993. pap. 16.95 (*0-415-05362-5*, A7787, Routledge NY); text ed. 69.95 (*0-415-05361-7*, A7783, Routledge NY) Routledge.

Transpersonal Actor: Reinterpreting Stanislavski. rev. ed. Ned Manderino. 240p. (Orig.). 1989. pap. 14.95 (*0-9601194-5-0*) Manderino Bks.

Transpersonal Psychology for Daily Life. Paul Philips. LC 80-66662. (Illus.). 98p. (Orig.). 1984. pap. 8.95 (*0-930149-01-7*) AAP Calif.

Transpersonal Psychology in Psychoanalytic Perspective. Michael Washburn. LC 93-38025. 367p. (C). 1994. text ed. 59.50 (*0-7914-1953-3*); pap. text ed. 19.95 (*0-7914-1954-1*) State U NY Pr.

Transpersonal Psychotherapy. 2nd ed. Ed. by Seymour Boorstein. LC 95-44527. (SUNY Series in the Philosophy of Psychology). 587p. 1996. text ed. 59.50 (*0-7914-2835-4*); pap. text ed. 19.95 (*0-7914-2836-2*) State U NY Pr.

Transplacental Carcinogenesis: Proceedings of a Meeting Held at the Medizinische Hochschule, Hannover, Federal Republic of Germany, 6-7 October 1971. International Agency for Research on Cancer Staff. Ed. by L. Tomatis & Ulrich Mohr. LC 73-173464. (IARC Scientific Publications: No. 4). 192p. reprint ed. pap. 54.80 (*0-7837-3991-5*, 2043822) Bks Demand.

***Transplant Infections.** Bowden & Raleigh. 1998. text ed. write for info. (*0-397-58776-7*) Lppncott-Raven.

Transplant International: Proceedings of the Fifth Congress of the European Society for Organ Transplantation Maastricht, October 7-10, 1991. John Wallwork. (Official Journal of the European Society for Organ Transplantation: Vol. 5, Suppl. 1, 1992). xx, 729p. 1992. 176.00 (*0-387-55342-8*) Spr-Verlag.

Transplant International: Proceedings of the 6th ESOT Congress, Rodos, October 25-28, 1993. Ed. by C. Hammer Munich et al. (Official Journal of the European Society for Organ Transplantation). 705p. 1994. 168.00 (*0-387-57835-8*) Spr-Verlag.

***Transplant International - Official Journal of the European Society for Organ Transplantation: Proceedings of the 7th ESOT Congress, Vienna, October 3-7, 1995.** Ed. by F. Muhlbacher et al. (Illus.). 530p. 1996. suppl. ed., pap. 157.00 (*3-540-61024-3*) Spr-Verlag.

Transplant Pathology: Clinical & Anatomic Principles. Ed. by Peter C. Kolbeck et al. LC 93-1867. 327p. 1994. 125.00 (*0-89189-364-4*) Am Soc Clinical.

Transplant Production Systems: Proceedings of the International Symposium on Transplant Production Systems, Yokohama, Japan, 21-26 July 1992. Toyoki Kozai. LC 92-15554. 344p. (C). 1992. lib. bdg. 153.00 (*0-7923-1797-1*) Kluwer Ac.

Transplant Protocols. Ed. by Alexander M. Walker. LC 90-3166. 328p. (Orig.). 1990. 45.00 (*0-917227-05-0*) Epidemiology.

Transplant Success Stories 1993. Paul I. Terasaki. 1993. 5.00 (*1-880318-00-8*) UCLA Tissue.

***Transplant Surgery.** Ed. by John Forsythe. (Companion Guide to Specialist Surgical Practice Ser.: Vol. 7). (Illus.). 280p. 1997. write for info. (*0-7020-2146-6*, Pub. by W B Saunders UK) Saunders.

Transplant Vascular Sclerosis. Charles Orosz. (Medicine Ser.). 251p. 1996. text ed. 89.95 (*0-412-10121-1*) Chapman & Hall.

Transplant Vascular Sclerosis. Charles Orosz. LC 95-31248. (Medical Intelligence Unit Ser.). 222p. 1996. 89.95 (*1-57059-287-X*) R G Landes.

Transplantation. 1995. 45.95 (*3-211-82648-3*) Spr-Verlag.

Transplantation. Ed. by Graeme R. Catto. (New Clinical Applications Nephrology Ser.). (C). 1989. lib. bdg. 100.50 (*0-7462-0116-8*) Kluwer Ac.

Transplantation. Ed. by M. Gumpel. (Journal: Developmental Neuroscience: Vol. 14, No. 2, 1992). (Illus.). 112p. 1992. pap. 41.75 (*3-8055-5658-6*) S Karger.

Transplantation. John S. Najarian & Richard L. Simmons. LC 73-135689. (Illus.). 811p. reprint ed. 180.00 (*0-8357-9424-5*, 2014566) Bks Demand.

Transplantation: Anaesthesia & Critical Care Procedures at the University of Pittsburgh. Leonard Firestone. 656p. 1997. 45.00 (*0-7506-9565-X*) Buttrwrth-Heinemann.

Transplantation: In Focus. J. Fabre. (In Focus Ser.). (Illus.). 85p. (C). Date not set. pap. text ed. 13.95 (*0-19-963193-X*, IRL Pr) OUP.

Transplantation & Developmental Biology of the Liver. Ed. by H. S. Rosenberg. (Perspectives in Pediatric Pathology Ser.: Vol. 14). xii, 220p. 1991. 240.00 (*3-8055-5156-8*) S Karger.

***Transplantation & Replacement of Thoracic Organs: The Present Status of Biological & Mechanical Replacement of the Heart & Lungs.** Ed. by D. K. Cooper et al. 830p. 1997. lib. bdg. 350.00 (*0-7923-8898-4*) Kluwer Ac.

Transplantation Antigens: A Study in Serological Data Analysis. Neville Selwood & Alan Hedges. LC 78-5708. 153p. reprint ed. 43.70 (*0-8357-9995-6*, 2016180) Bks Demand.

Transplantation Biology: Cellular & Molecular Aspects. Nicholas Tilney. 778p. 1996. text ed. 159.00 (*0-397-51683-5*) Lppncott-Raven.

Transplantation Biology: Cellular & Molecular Aspects. Ed. by Nicholas L. Tilney et al. 1996. write for info. (*0-516-83503-3*) Lppncott-Raven.

Transplantation Drug Reference Guide. Ed. by Hans Sollinger. LC 94-7784. 1994. write for info. (*1-57059-162-8*) R G Landes.

Transplantation Immunology. Ed. by Fritz H. Bach & Hugh Auchincloss. LC 94-49601. 409p. 1995. text ed. 84.95 (*0-471-30448-4*) Wiley.

Transplantation in Primates. Ed. by G. P. Murphy. (Primates in Medicine Ser.: Vol. 7). 1972. 47.25 (*3-8055-1408-5*) S Karger.

Transplantation in the Nineteen Eighties: Recent Advances. Ed. by Rex Jamison. LC 84-6783. 128p. 1984. text ed. 45.00 (*0-275-91436-4*, C1436, Praeger Pubs) Greenwood.

Transplantation into the Mammalaian CNS. Ed. by Don M. Gash & John R. Sladek, Jr. (Progress in Brain Research Ser.: No. 78). 664p. 1989. 361.25 (*0-444-81012-9*) Elsevier.

Transplantation Nursing. Ed. by Marie T. Nolan & Sharon M. Agustine. LC 94-31323. 1994. text ed. 54.95 (*0-8385-8989-8*, A8989-4) Appleton & Lange.

Transplantation of Muscles in Animals. A. N. Studitsky. (C). 1988. 18.50 (*81-7087-023-2*, Pub. by Oxford IBH II) S Asia.

Transplantation of Neural Tissue into Spinal Cord. Gerta Vrbova. 1994. 89.95 (*1-57059-037-0*) R G Landes.

Transplantation of Neural Tissue into the Spinal Cord. Gerta Vrbova et al. (Neuroscience Intelligence Unit Ser.). 128p. 1994. 89.95 (*1-57059-169-5*, LN9037) R G Landes.

Transplantation of Ovarian & Testicular Tissues. Robert G. Gosden. (Medical Intelligence Unit Ser.). 158p. 1996. 89.95 (*1-57059-336-1*) R G Landes.

Transplantation of the Liver. Ronald W. Busutil & Goran B. Klintmalm. Ed. by Lisette Bralow. (Illus.). 784p. 1996. text ed. 260.00 (*0-7216-4942-4*) Saunders.

Transplantation of the Liver. 2nd ed. Willis C. Maddrey & Michael F. Sorrell. LC 94-25108. (Illus.). 640p. (C). 1994. text ed. 150.00 (*0-8385-8990-1*, A8990-2) Appleton & Lange.

Transplantation Reviews. 2nd ed. Morris & Tilney. 240p. 1988. text ed. 79.00 (*0-7216-2869-9*) Saunders.

Transplantation Reviews, Vol. 3. Morris & Tilney. (Illus.). 240p. 1989. text ed. 86.00 (*0-7216-3288-2*) Saunders.

Transplantation Techniques & Use of Cryopreserved Allograft Cardiac Valves & Vascular Tissue. Ed. by David R. Clarke. (Illus.). 237p. (C). 1989. pap. 345.00 (*0-944903-03-7*) Adams Pub Group.

Transplantation Theorems & Multiplier Theorems for Jacobi Series. Benjamin Muckenhoupt. LC 86-22270. (Memoirs of the American Mathematical Society Ser.: No. 64/356). 86p. 1986. pap. text ed. 18.00 (*0-8218-2418-X*, MEMO/64/356) Am Math.

Transplantation Therapeutics. Ed. by A. P. Monacco. (Journal: Nephron: Vol. 46, Suppl. 1, 1987). (Illus.). iv, 60p. 1987. pap. 18.50 (*3-8055-4642-4*) S Karger.

Transplantation Tolerance Induction. J. Wesley Alexander. (Medical Intelligence Unit Ser.). 275p. 1996. 89.95 (*1-57059-282-9*) R G Landes.

Transplantation Tolerance Induction. J. Wexley Alexander & Robert A. Good. (Medical Intelligence Unit Ser.). 280p. 1996. text ed. 79.95 (*0-412-10161-0*) Van Nos Reinhold.

Transplanted: A History of Immigrants in Urban America. John E. Bodnar. LC 84-48041. (Interdisciplinary Studies in History). (Illus.). 320p. 1985. pap. 12.95 (*0-253-20416-X*) Ind U Pr.

Transplanted: A History of Immigrants in Urban America. John E. Bodnar. LC 84-48041. (Interdisciplinary Studies in History). (Illus.). 320p. 1985. 35.00 (*0-253-31347-3*) Ind U Pr.

Transplanted & Artificial Body Organs. Arnold Madison. LC 81-3805. (Illus.). 128p. (YA). (gr. 7 up). 1981. 10.95 (*0-8253-0050-9*) Beaufort Bks NY.

***Transplanted Executive: Why You Need to Understand How Workers in Other Countries See the World Differently.** P. Christopher Earley & Miriam Erez. (Illus.). 208p. 1997. 25.00 (*0-19-508795-X*) OUP.

Transplanted Family: A Study of Social Adjustment of the Polish Immigrant Family to the United States after the Second World War. Danuta Mostwin. Ed. by Francesco Cordasco. LC 80-881. (American Ethnic Groups Ser.). 1981. lib. bdg. 42.95 (*0-405-13442-8*) Ayer.

Transplanted Gardener. Charles Elliott. 224p. 1995. 22.95 (*1-55821-417-8*) Lyons & Burford.

***Transplanted Gardener.** Charles Elliott. 224p. 1997. pap. 14.95 (*1-55821-556-5*) Lyons & Burford.

Transplanted Kids. Sharon Miller. pap. 6.95 (*0-87377-010-2*) GAM Pubns.

Transplanted Woman: A Study of French-American Marriages in France. Gabrielle Varro. LC 87-29093. 272p. 1988. text ed. 49.95 (*0-275-92856-X*, C2856, Praeger Pubs) Greenwood.

Transplanting Religious Traditions: Asian Indians in America. John Y. Fenton. LC 88-15561. (Illus.). 283p. 1988. text ed. 55.00 (*0-275-92676-1*, C2676, Praeger Pubs) Greenwood.

Transplants: Dutch Tulips & Oriental Poppies. Amy J. VanOoyen. (Woodpecker Ser.: Vol. 4). (Illus.). 200p. (Orig.). 1997. pap. 14.95 (*1-889363-03-0*) Woodpecker Bks.

Transplants: Unwrapping the Second Gift of Life - The Inside Story of Organ Transplants As Told by Recipients & Their Families, Donor Families, & Health Professionals. Pat S. Helmberger. 208p. 1992. pap. 10.95 (*1-56561-004-0*) Chronimed.

Transplants & Implants in Otology. Ed. by G. Babighian et al. LC 88-12784. (Illus.). 402p. 1988. text ed. 156.50 (*90-6299-047-9*, Pub. by Kugler NE) Kugler Pubns.

Transplants & Implants in Otology: Proceedings of the Third International Symposium on Transplants & Implants in Otology, Bordeaux, France, June 10-14, 1995. Ed. by M. Portmann et al. LC 96-4640. 1996. 159.00 (*90-6299-142-4*) Kugler Pubns.

Transplants & Implants in Otology II. Ed. by N. Yanagihara et al. LC 92-10385. (Illus.). 413p. 1992. lib. bdg. 141.00 (*90-6299-084-3*, Pub. by Kugler NE) Kugler Pubns.

***Transpluto.** David Dukelow. 31p. 1996. pap. 4.95 (*0-935127-26-7*) ACS Pubns.

***Transpluto or Shall We Call Him Bacchus?** John Hawkins. 1996. 14.95 (*0-86690-386-0*, H1182-014) Am Fed Astrologers.

***Transplutonium Elements: Production & Recovery.** Ed. by James D. Navratil & Wallace W. Schulz. LC 81-7999. (ACS Symposium Ser.: Vol. 161). 314p. 1981. reprint ed. pap. 89.50 (*0-608-03049-X*, 2063502) Bks Demand.

Transplutonium Elements--Production & Recovery. Ed. by Wallace W. Schultz & James D. Navratil. LC 81-7999. (ACS Symposium Ser.: No. 161). 1981. 43.95 (*0-8412-0638-4*) Am Chemical.

***Transporation: Blimps.** Childrens Press Staff. (New True Books Ser.). 1997. pap. 6.95 (*0-516-26163-0*) Childrens.

***Transporation: From Cars to Planes.** Gare Thompson. (You Are There Ser.). 1997. pap. 6.95 (*0-516-26055-3*) Childrens.

***Transporation: Helicopters.** Childrens Press Staff. (New True Books Ser.). 1997. pap. 6.95 (*0-516-26171-1*) Childrens.

***Transporation: Trains.** Childrens Press Staff. (New True Books Ser.). 1997. pap. 6.95 (*0-516-26178-9*) Childrens.

***Transporation: Trucks.** Childrens Press Staff. (True Books Ser.). 1997. pap. 6.95 (*0-516-26179-7*) Childrens.

Transport. H. Hayes. (Down to Earth Ser.). (C). 1983. 45.00 (*0-09-149151-7*, Pub. by S Thornes Pubs UK) St Mut.

Transport: Creative Image Bank. 96p. 1992. pap. 19.95 (*88-7070-157-3*) Belvedere USA.

Transport: How It Works. Ian Graham. (Illus.). 48p. (J). 1995. 14.95 (*0-8069-0956-0*) Sterling.

***Transport - New Problems, New Solutions: 13th International Symposium on Theory & Practice in Transport Economics.** OECD ECMT Staff. 720p. (Orig.). 1996. pap. 112.00 (*92-821-1212-8*, Pub. by Org for Econ FR) OECD.

Transport Acts 1981 & 1982: Penalty Points-Drink & Driving-Fixed Penalties. Peter S. Wallis. 115p. 1985. 90.00 (*0-906840-92-9*, Pub. by Fourmat Pub UK) St Mut.

Transport Analysis Using Boundary Elements. P. W. Partridge. 1993. student ed., ring bd. 506.00 incl. disk (*1-56252-122-5*, 1940) Computational Mech MA.

Transport & Bioenergetics In Biomembranes. Ed. by Ryo Sato & Yasuo Kagawa. 262p. 1982. 65.00 (*0-306-41282-9*, Plenum Pr) Plenum.

Transport & Chemical Rate Phenomena. Nickolas J. Themelis. 256p. 1995. text ed. 82.00 (*2-88449-127-9*) Gordon & Breach.

Transport & Communication in India Prior to Steam Locomotion Vol. 2: Water Transport. Jen Deloche. Tr. by James Walker from FRE. (French Studies on South Asian Culture & Society; Oxford India Paperbacks: Vol. VIII). 302p. 1995. 32.00 (*0-19-563243-5*) OUP.

Transport & Communication Innovation in Europe. G. A. Giannopolous et al. LC 93-10001. 369p. 1993. text ed. 59.95 (*0-470-22000-7*, Belhaven) Halsted Pr.

Transport & Communications: Aspects of Britain. Central Office of Info. (Aspects of Britain Ser.). (Illus.). 88p. 1997. pap. 9.95 (*0-11-701698-5*, HM16985, Pub. by Statnry Ofc UK) Seven Hills Bk.

***Transport & Communications Bulletin for Asia & the Pacific.** 37p. 1996. pap. text ed. 15.00 (*92-1-119723-6*, HF5718) UN.

Transport & Communications Bulletin for Asia & the Pacific, No. 60. 34p. 1989. 6.00 (*92-1-119543-8*, 89.II.F.8) UN.

Transport & Communications Bulletin for Asia & the Pacific, No. 61. 66p. 1991. 9.00 (*92-1-119567-5*) UN.

Transport & Communications Bulletin for Asia & the Pacific, No. 63. annuals 27p. 1993. 9.00 (*92-1-119619-1*) UN.

Transport & Communications Bulletin for Asia & the Pacific, No. 64. annuals 34p. 1994. 15.00 (*92-1-119644-2*) UN.

Transport & Communications in India Prior to Steam Locomotion, Vol. I: Land Transport. Jean Deloche. (French Studies on South Asian Culture & Society: Vol. VIII). 352p. 1994. Vol. I Land Transport. 35.00 (*0-19-563141-2*) OUP.

Transport & Communications Innovation in Europe. Ed. by G. Giannopoulos & A. Gillespie. LC 93-10001. 369p. 1993. text ed. 85.00 (*0-471-94814-4*) Wiley.

Transport & Confinement in Toroidal Devices: Second Workshop on Magnetic Confinement Fusion. Ed. by C. Alejaldre & B. A. Carreras. (Illus.). 176p. 1992. pap. 84.00 (*0-7503-0184-8*) IOP Pub.

Transport & Developing Countries. David Hilling. LC 95-47892. 368p. (C). 1996. pap. 22.95 (*0-415-13655-5*); text ed. 69.95 (*0-415-13654-7*) Routledge.

Transport & Development in the Third World. David Simon. LC 95-40958. (Introductions to Development Ser.). 208p. (C). 1996. pap. 14.95 (*0-415-11905-7*) Routledge.

Transport & Diffusion Across Cell Membranes. Wilfred D. Stein. 1986. text ed. 149.00 (*0-12-664660-0*) Acad Pr.

Transport & Distribution. Don Benson & Geoffrey Whitehead. 345p. (C). 1989. 100.00 (*0-685-46420-2*, Pub. by Inst Pur & Supply UK) St Mut.

Transport & Distribution. G. J. Murphy. 200p. 1972. 32.00 (*0-8464-1437-6*) Beekman Pubs.

Transport & Distribution Manager's Guide to 1992. D. Lowe. 206p. (C). 1989. 180.00 (*0-685-39893-5*, Pub. by Inst Pur & Supply UK) St Mut.

Transport & Economic Development in the New Central & Eastern Europe. Ed. by Derek Hall. 253p. 1993. text ed. 54.95 (*0-470-22003-1*) Halsted Pr.

Transport & Economic Development in the New Central & Eastern Europe. Derek R. Hall. 253p. 1993. text ed. 80.00 (*0-471-94629-X*) Wiley.

Transport & Energy: Conference Proceedings. 132p. 1981. 46.00 (*0-7277-0125-8*, Pub. by T Telford UK) Am Soc Civil Eng.

Transport & Inherited Disease. Ed. by N. R. Belton & C. Toothill. 1982. lib. bdg. 151.50 (*0-85200-391-9*) Kluwer Ac.

Transport & Land Use. Ed. by Joseph Berechman et al. LC 96-32420. (Modern Classics in Regional Science Ser.: No. 2). 736p. 1996. 230.00 (*1-85898-109-3*) E Elgar.

Transport & Optical Properties of Nonideal Plasma. M. M. Popovich & I. T. Iakubov. 325p. 1995. 79.50 (*0-306-44938-2*) Plenum.

Transport & Public Policy Planning. Ed. by D. Banister & P. Hall. 484p. 1981. text ed. 100.00 (*0-7201-1580-9*, Mansell Pub) Cassell.

Transport & Reactive Processes in Aquifers: Proceedings of the International Symposium, Zurich, April 1994. T. Dracos. (Illus.). 500p. (C). 1994. text ed. 115.00 (*90-5410-368-X*, Pub. by A A Balkema NE) Ashgate Pub Co.

Transport & Receptor Proteins of Plant Membranes: Molecular Structure & Function. Ed. by D. T. Cooke & D. T. Clarkson. (Illus.). 207p. (C). 1992. 75.00 (*0-306-44221-3*, Plenum Pr) Plenum.

Transport & Relaxation in Random Materials: Proceedings of the Third NBS Conference on Transport & Relaxation in Random Materials, October 15-17, 1985, Maryland. Michael F. Shlesinger. 425p. 1986. pap. 45.00 (*9971-5-0134-1*); text ed. 110.00 (*9971-5-0133-3*) World Scientific Pub.

Transport & Remediation of Subsurface Contaminants: Colloidal, Interfacial, & Surfactant Phenomena. Ed. by David A. Sabatini & Robert C. Knox. LC 92-11468. (Symposium Ser.: Vol. 491). (Illus.). 252p. 1992. 69.95 (*0-8412-2223-1*) Am Chemical.

***Transport & Storage of Radioactive Materials.** Ed. by R. W. Carlson. 83p. 1996. pap. text ed. 70.00 (*0-7918-1781-4*, TS283) ASME Pr.

Transport & Storage of Radioactive Materials: Proceedings of the Pressure Vessel & Piping Conference, Minneapolis, MN, 1994. Ed. by R. W. Carlson. LC 94-71747. (PVP Ser.: Vol. 284). 53p. 1994. pap. 25.00 (*0-7918-1357-6*) ASME.

Transport & Storage of Radioactive Materials - 1995. Ed. by R. W. Carlson et al. LC 94-71747. (Proceedings of the 1995 ASME/JSME Pressure Vessels & Piping Conference Ser.: PVP-Vol. 307). 192p. 1995. 100.00 (*0-7918-1338-X*, H00970) ASME.

Transport & the Environment: The Linacre Lectures 1994-1995. Ed. by Bryan Cartledge. (Illus.). 168p. 1996. 50.00 (*0-19-854934-2*) OUP.

Transport & the Environment: The Royal Commission on Environmental Pollution Report. Royal Commission on Environmental Pollution. (Illus.). 344p. 1996. pap. 12.95 (*0-19-826065-2*) OUP.

Transport & the Farmer. Shaw & Sons Ltd. Staff. 1988. 100.00 (*0-7219-1150-1*, Pub. by Scientific UK); pap. 50.00 (*0-317-92362-5*, Pub. by Scientific UK) St Mut.

Transport & the State of Trade in Britain. Thor Hultgren & William I. Greenwald. (Occasional Papers: No. 40). 127p. 1953. reprint ed. 33.10 (*0-87014-442-1*); reprint ed. mic. film 20.00 (*0-685-61291-0*) Natl Bur Econ Res.

Transport & Thermal Properties of f-Electron Systems. Ed. by G. Oomi et al. 1993. 89.50 (*0-306-44531-X*, Plenum Pr) Plenum.

Transport & Transformation of Contaminants Near the Sediment-Water Interface. Joseph V. DePinto. 368p. 1993. 77.95 (*0-87371-887-9*, L887) Lewis Pubs.

***Transport & Urban Development.** D. Banister. (Illus.). 304p. 1995. text ed. 77.50 (*0-419-20390-7*, E & FN Spon) Routledge Chapman & Hall.

Transport ATPases, Vol. 402. 120.00 (*0-89766-196-6*) NY Acad Sci.

Transport Border Guide: U. S. - Canadian Compliance Manual, 43M. rev. ed. Keller, J. J. & Assocs., Inc. Staff. LC 91-61951. 280p. 1992. ring bd. 99.00 (*0-934674-98-1*, 43M) J J Keller.

Transport Carrier Costing, Vol. 9. Wayne K. Talley. (Transportation Studies: Vol. 9). 390p. 1988. text ed. 105.00 (*2-88124-650-8*) Gordon & Breach.

Transport Category Aircraft Systems. Tom Wild. LC 91-144966. (Illus.). 336p. 1990. pap. text ed. 22.95 (*0-89100-363-0*, EA-363) IAP.

Transport, Chaos & Plasma Physics. S. Benkadda et al. 420p. 1994. text ed. 109.00 (*981-02-1619-X*) World Scientific Pub.

***Transport, Chaos & Plasma Physics II.** 460p. 1996. lib. bdg. 69.00 (*981-02-2696-9*) World Scientific Pub.

Transport Concepts in European Cities. Dieter Apel & Timothy M. Pharoah. (Avebury Studies in Green Research). 320p. 1996. 72.95 (*1-85972-094-3*, Pub. by Avebury Pub UK) Ashgate Pub Co.

Transport Coordination & Social Policy. John Sutton. 231p. 1988. text ed. 68.95 (*0-566-05596-1*, Pub. by Avebury Pub UK) Ashgate Pub Co.

Transport, Correlation & Structural Defects: Advances in Disordered Semiconductors, Vol. 3. H. Fritzsche. 316p. 1990. pap. 37.00 (*9971-5-0974-1*); text ed. 101.00 (*9971-5-0973-3*) World Scientific Pub.

Transport Decisions in an Age of Uncertainty. Ed. by Evert J. Visser. 1978. lib. bdg. 194.00 (*90-247-2061-3*) Kluwer Ac.

Transport Economics. P. C. Stubbs et al. (Studies in Economics). (Illus.). 1980. pap. text ed. 16.95 (*0-04-338089-1*) Routledge Chapman & Hall.

Transport Economics. 2nd ed. Kenneth Button. (Illus.). 288p. (Orig.). 1993. 85.00 (*1-85278-521-7*); pap. text ed. 25.00 (*1-85278-523-3*) E Elgar.

Transport Economics: Past Trends & Future Prospects. OECD Staff. (ECMT Round Table Ser.: No. 100). 266p. (ENG & FRE.). 1996. pap. 58.00 (*92-821-1208-X*, Pub. by Org for Econ FR) OECD.

***Transport Economics: Selected Readings.** Ed. by Tae H. Oum et al. 1997. pap. text ed. 40.00 (*90-5702-186-2*, Harwood Acad Pubs) Gordon & Breach.

Transport Energy in Africa. J. Baguant & M. Teferra. Ed. by M. R. Bhagavan. (African Energy Policy Research Network Ser.). (Illus.). 144p. (C). 1996. 55.00 (*1-85649-461-6*, Pub. by Zed Bks Ltd UK) Humanities.

Transport Energy in Africa: ; J. Baguant & M. Teferra. Ed. by M. R. Bhagavan. LC 96-23126. (African Energy Policy Research Network Ser.). (Illus.). 144p. (C). 1996. pap. 17.50 (*1-85649-462-4*, Pub. by Zed Bks Ltd UK) Humanities.

Transport Finance Directory, 1996. 1996. 70.00 (*0-614-17083-4*, Pub. by IFR Pub UK) Am Educ Systs.

Transport for a Sustainable Future: The Case for Europe. John Whitelegg & Helmut Holzafel. 202p. 1993. pap. text ed. 39.95 (*0-470-22018-X*) Halsted Pr.

Transport for a Sustainable Future: The Case for Europe. John Whitelegg. LC 93-14989. 202p. 1993. pap. text ed. 52.95 (*0-471-94791-1*) Wiley.

Transport for Society: Conference Proceedings. 181p. 1976. 55.00 (*0-7277-0015-4*, Pub. by T Telford UK) Am Soc Civil Eng.

Transport Growth in Question. OECD Staff. 653p. (Orig.). 1993. pap. 80.00 (*92-821-1180-6*) OECD.

Transport History, Vol. 2, Nos. 1-3. Ed. by Baron F. Duckham & J. R. Hume. LC 69-10856. (Illus.). 1970. 24.95 (*0-678-05668-4*) Kelley.

Transport in a Unified Europe: Policies & Challenges. Ed. by David Banister & Joseph Berechman. LC 93-36449. (Studies in Regional Science & Urban Economics: Vol. 24). 446p. 1993. 129.75 (*0-444-81702-6*, North Holland) Elsevier.

***Transport in Ancient Egypt.** Robert B. Partridge. (Illus.). 160p. 1996. 34.95 (*0-948695-42-0*, Pub. by Rubicon Pr UK); pap. 25.95 (*0-948695-43-9*, Pub. by Rubicon Pr UK) David Brown.

Transport in Biomembranes: Model Systems & Reconstitution. Ed. by Renzo Antolini et al. LC 82-12364. (Illus.). 288p. 1982. reprint ed. pap. 82.10 (*0-608-00648-3*, 2061236) Bks Demand.

***Transport in Europe.** Christian Gerondeau. LC 97-9806. (Wireless - Transportation Technology Ser.). 496p. 1997. 69.00 (*0-89006-931-X*) Artech Hse.

Transport in Fluidized Particle Systems. Ed. by L. K. Doraiswamy & Arun S. Mujumdar. (Transport Processes in Engineering Ser.: No. 1). 546p. 1989. 214.50 (*0-444-87138-1*) Elsevier.

***Transport in Nanostructures.** David K. Ferry & Stephen M. Goodnick. (Studies in Semiconductor Physics & Microelectronic Engineering: Vol. 6). (Illus.). 560p. (C). 1997. text ed. 100.00 (*0-521-46141-3*) Cambridge U Pr.

Transport in Nonstoichiometric Compounds. Ed. by George Simkovich & Vladimir S. Stubican. (NATO ASI Series B: Physics: Vol. 129). 574p. 1985. 115.00 (*0-306-42086-4*, Plenum Pr) Plenum.

Transport in Plants. U. Luettge & N. Higinbotham. (Illus.). 1979. 107.95 (*0-387-90383-6*) Spr-Verlag.

Transport in Plants: Intracellular Transport & Exchange Mechanisms, No. 3. Ed. by C. Ralph Stocking & V. Heber. (Encyclopedia of Plant Physiology Ser.). 1977. 133.00 (*0-387-07818-5*) Spr-Verlag.

Transport in Plants: Pholoem Transport. Ed. by M. H. Zimmermann & J. A. Milburn. LC 75-20178. (Encyclopedia of Plant Physiology Ser.: Vol. 1). (Illus.). 550p. 1976. 171.95 (*0-387-07314-0*) Spr-Verlag.

Transport in Plants Two, Pts. A & B. Incl. Pt. A. Cells. Frwd. by R. A. Robertson. (Illus.). 440p. 1976. 141.95 (*0-387-07452-X*); Pt. B. Tissues & Plants. Ed. by U. Luettge & M. G. Pitman. (Illus.). 480p. 1976. 153.95 (*0-387-07453-8*); (Encyclopedia of Plant Physiology Ser.: Vol. 2). 1976. write for info. (*0-318-55830-0*) Spr-Verlag.

Transport in the Industrial Revolution. Ed. by Derek H. Aldcroft & Michael J. Freeman. LC 82-62266. 228p. 1988. text ed. 29.95 (*0-7190-0979-0*, Pub. by Manchester Univ Pr UK) St Martin.

Transport in the Information Age: Wheels & Wires. Ed. by Mark E. Hepworth & Ken Ducatel. (Illus.). 224p. 1992. text ed. 59.00 (*1-85293-220-1*) St Martin.

Transport in the Liver: Proceedings of the 74th Falk Symposium Held in Heidelberg, Germany, January 27-18, 1994. Ed. by D. Keppler & K. Jungermann. LC 94-17600. 1994. lib. bdg. 95.00 (*0-7923-8858-5*) Kluwer Ac.

Transport in the Nineties - The Shaping of Europe. Terence Bendixson. 64p. (C). 1989. text ed. 130.00 (*0-85406-430-3*, Pub. by Surveyors Pubns) St Mut.

Transport in Transition: Aspects of British & European Experience. Ed. by James McConville & John Sheldracke. 211p. (C). 1995. text ed. 59.95 (*1-85628-664-9*, Pub. by Avebury Pub UK) Ashgate Pub Co.

Transport in Transition: Lessons from the History of Energy Policy. Stephen Peake. 144p. (C). 1994. pap. 19.95 (*1-85383-209-X*) Brookings.

Transport in Transition: The Evolution of Traditional Shipping in China. Tr. by Andrew Watson from JPN. (Michigan Abstracts of Chinese & Japanese Works on Chinese History: No. 3). 96p. 1972. pap. text ed. 15.00 (*0-89264-903-8*) Ctr Chinese Studies.

Transport in Transition: The Reorganization of the Federal Transport Portfolio. John W. Langford. LC 76-381003. (Canadian Public Administration Ser.). 283p. reprint ed. pap. 80.70 (*0-7837-1165-4*, 2041694) Bks Demand.

Transport in Victorian Britain. Ed. by Michael J. Freeman & Derek H. Aldcroft. LC 88-6844. 388p. 1991. reprint ed. text ed. 24.95 (*0-7190-2333-5*, Pub. by Manchester Univ Pr UK) St Martin.

Transport Information: 1993. 117p. 1993. 35.00 (*92-1-116580-6*) UN.

Transport Information Nineteen Ninety. 1990. 23.00 (*92-1-116487-7*, E 90.II.E.30) UN.

Transport Infrastructure in Central & Eastern European Countries: Selection Criteria & Funding. 140p. (Orig.). 1995. pap. 40.00 (*92-821-1203-9*, Pub. by Org for Econ FR) OECD.

Transport, Land-Use & the Environment. Ed. by Yoshitsugu Hayashi & John R. Roy. LC 96-16238. (Transportation, Research, Economics & Policy Ser.: Vol. 4). 448p. (C). 1996. lib. bdg. 110.00 (*0-7923-3728-X*) Kluwer Ac.

Transport Law. Ed. by Marc A. Huybrechts. 1991. ring bd. write for info. (*0-318-68490-X*) Kluwer Law Tax Pubs.

Transport Law of the European Community. Rosa Greaves. LC 90-25268. (European Community Law Ser.). 240p. (C). 1991. text ed. 85.00 (*0-485-70006-9*, Pub. by Athlone Pr UK) Humanities.

Transport Machines. Norman Barrett. LC 93-33235. (Visual Guides Ser.). (Illus.). 48p. (J). (gr. 5-7). 1994. lib. bdg. 22.00 (*0-531-14298-1*) Watts.

***Transport Manager's & Operator's Handbook 97.** 27th ed. David Lowe. (Transport & Logistics Ser.). 1996. pap. 50.00 (*0-7494-2136-3*) Kogan Page Ltd.

Transport Mechanisms in Membrane Separation Processes. J. G. Bitter. (Chemical Engineering Ser.). (Illus.). 190p. 1991. 75.00 (*0-306-43849-6*, Plenum Pr) Plenum.

Transport Medal Roll. Roberts Staff. (C). 1989. 95.00 (*1-873058-15-2*, Pub. by Roberts UK) St Mut.

Transport Modeling for Environmental Engineers & Scientists. Mark Clark. LC 96-4814. (Environmental Science & Technology Ser.). 1996. text ed. 69.95 (*0-471-12348-X*) Wiley.

Transport Modelling: Sensitivity Analysis & Policy Testing **see Progress in Planning**

Transport Models for Inland & Coastal Waters: Proceedings of a Symposium on Predictive Ability. Ed. by Hugo B. Fischer. LC 81-10990. 1981. text ed. 118.00 (*0-12-258152-0*) Acad Pr.

Transport of Animals Intended for Breeding, Production & Slaughter. Ed. by R. Moss. 1982. lib. bdg. 100.50 (*90-247-2679-4*) Kluwer Ac.

Transport of Hazardous Materials: Proceedings of a Symposium Sponsored by the Council of Engineering Institutions & the Council for Science & Technology Institutes. 160p. 1978. 25.00 (*0-7277-0058-8*, Pub. by T Telford UK) Am Soc Civil Eng.

Transport of Neurotransmitters. Ed. by D. M. Paton. (Journal: Pharmacology: Vol. 21, No. 2). (Illus.). 74p. 1980. pap. 19.25 (*3-8055-1316-X*) S Karger.

***Transport of Photoassimilates.** Baker. (C). 1996. text ed. 169.95 (*0-582-46234-7*, Pub. by Longman UK) Longman.

Transport of Suspended Solids in Open Channels: Proceedings of Euromech 192, Munich - Neubibiberg, 11-15 June 1985. Ed. by W. Bechteler. 278p. (C). 1986. text ed. 105.00 (*90-6191-644-5*, Pub. by A A Balkema NE) Ashgate Pub Co.

Transport of Vegetables in Papua New Guinea. K. J. Scott & G. Atkinson. (C). 1989. text ed. 78.00 (*0-949511-96-X*, Pub. by ACIAR) St Mut.

Transport Organisation in a Great City: The Case of London. Michael F. Collins & Timothy M. Pharoah. LC 74-77339. 660p. reprint ed. pap. 180.00 (*0-317-29604-3*, 2021877) Bks Demand.

Transport Packaging for Radioactive Materials: Proceedings of the International Atomic Energy Agency Seminar, Vienna, Austria. International Atomic Energy Agency Staff. (Proceedings Ser.). (Illus.). 546p. 1977. pap. 120.00 (*92-0-020576-3*, ISP437, Pub. by IAEA AU) Bernan Associates.

Transport Phenomena. R. Byron Bird et al. 808p. 1960. text ed. 57.50 (*0-471-07392-X*) Wiley.

Transport Phenomena: A Unified Approach. R. S. Brodkey & H. C. Hershey. (Chemical Engineering Ser.). 864p. (C). 1988. text ed. write for info. (*0-07-007963-3*) McGraw.

Transport Phenomena - Special Topics. Ed. by R. J. Gordon. LC 80-25573. (AIChEMI Modular Instruction C Series: Vol. 6). 54p. 1987. pap. 44.00 (*0-8169-0397-2*, J-31) Am Inst Chem Eng.

Transport Phenomena Dynamic Design, 2 vols. Kim & Yang. 1989. 396.00 (*1-56032-057-5*) Hemisp Pub.

Transport Phenomena in Combustion: Proceedings of the Eighth International Symposium on Transport Phenomena in Combustion (ISTP-VIII) Held in San Francisco, California, July 16-20, 1995, 2 vols., Set. Ed. by S. H. Chan. LC 96-14300. 1700p. 1996. text ed. 299.00 (*1-56032-456-2*, Pub. by Tay Francis Ltd UK) Taylor & Francis.

Transport Phenomena in Fluids. Ed. by Howard J. M. Hanley. LC 70-78831. 521p. reprint ed. pap. 148.50 (*0-317-08382-1*, 2055041) Bks Demand.

Transport Phenomena in Heat & Mass Transfer: Proceedings of the Fourth International Symposium on Transport Phenomena in Heat & Mass Transfer (ISTP-IV), Sydney, Australia, 14-19 July, 1991, Organized under the Auspices of the Pacific Center of Thermal-Fluid Engineering. Ed. by J. A. Reizes. LC 92-36403. 1992. 499.50 (*0-444-89851-4*) Elsevier.

Transport Phenomena in Manufacturing & Materials Processing. Wen-Jei Yang et al. LC 94-3120. (Transport Processes in Engineering Ser.: Vol. 6). 192p. 1994. 184.75 (*0-444-89358-X*) Elsevier.

Transport Phenomena in Materials Processing. Sindo Kou. LC 95-49988. 664p. 1996. text ed. 79.95 (*0-471-07667-8*) Wiley.

Transport Phenomena in Materials Processing. D. R. Poirier & G. H. Geiger. LC 94-76335. (Illus.). 645p. 1994. text ed. 72.00 (*0-87339-272-8*, 2728) Minerals Metals.

Transport Phenomena in Materials Processing. Ed. by C. L. Tucker et al. (HTD Ser.: Vol. 10). 124p. 1983. pap. text ed. 9.00 (*0-317-02657-7*, H00283) ASME.

Transport Phenomena in Materials Processing - Solutions Manual. D. R. Poirier & G. H. Geiger. 25.00 (*0-87339-275-2*, 2752) Minerals Metals.

***Transport Phenomena in Materials Processing & Manufacturing: Proceedings, International Mechanical Engineering Congress & Exposition, Atlanta, GA, 1996.** Ed. by A. S. Lavine et al. LC 96-78667. 331p. 1996. pap. 96.00 (*0-7918-1524-2*, TS183) ASME.

Transport Phenomena in Materials Processing & Manufacturing - 1994. (HTD Ser.: Vol. 280). 148p. 1994. 40.00 (*0-7918-1279-0*, H00911) ASME.

Transport Phenomena in Mesoscopic Systems: Proceedings of the 14th Taniguchi Symposium, Shima, Japan, November 10-14, 1991. H. Fukuyama & T. Ando. LC 92-28119. (Solid-State Sciences Ser.: Vol. 109). xi, 283p. 1992. 97.95 (*0-387-55794-6*) Spr-Verlag.

Transport Phenomena in Metallurgy. G. H. Geiger & D. R. Poirier. LC 75-164648. (C). 1973. text ed. 63.50 (*0-201-02352-0*) Addison-Wesley.

Transport Phenomena in Nonconventional Manufacturing & Materials Processing. Ed. by C. L. Chan et al. LC 93-73717. 149p. 1993. pap. 47.50 (*0-7918-1004-6*) ASME.

Transport Phenomena in Polymeric Systems, No. 1. R. A. Mashelkar et al. (C). 1988. 52.50 (*0-85226-542-5*) S Asia.

Transport Phenomena in Polymeric Systems, No. 2. Ed. by M. R. Kamal. (Advances in Transport Processes Ser.: Vol. 6). 1989. 52.50 (*81-224-0185-6*) S Asia.

Transport Phenomena in Rotating Machinery: Proceedings of 2nd International Symposia on Transport Phenomena, Thermodynamics & Design of Rotating Machinery, Pt. 1 of 2 part set. Ed. by Jong H. Kim & Wen-Jei Yang. (Illus.). 1989. 198.00 (*1-56032-013-3*) Hemisp Pub.

Transport Phenomena in Solidification: Proceedings: International Mechanical Engineering Congress & Exposition (1994: Chicago, IL) Ed. by C. Beckermann et al. LC 94-78966. (HTD - AMD Ser.: Vol. 284, Vol. 182). 279p. 1995. pap. 90.00 (*0-7918-1392-4*, G00887) ASME Pr.

Transport Phenomena in Thermal Control: Cooling Technologies for Electronic Equipment & Rotating Machinery. Ed. by Guang-Jyh Hwang. (Illus.). 900p. 1989. 198.00 (*0-89116-888-5*) Hemisp Pub.

Transport Phenomena in Thermal Engineering, 2 vols., Set. Joon S. Lee et al. LC 93-39130. 1544p. 1995. 225.00 (*1-56700-015-0*) Begell Hse.

Transport Phenomena in Thermal-Fluids Engineering, 2 vols., Set. Ed. by S. H. Winoto et al. (Illus.). 1600p. 1996. write for info. (*0-9652469-0-6*) Pac Ctr Thermal.

Transport Phenomena in Turbulent Flows: Proceedings of International Symposia on Transport Phenomena. Ed. by Masaru Hirata. 500p. 1988. 236.00 (*0-89116-742-0*) Hemisp Pub.

Transport Phenomena of Foods & Biologic Materials. Gekas. 256p. 1992. 121.95 (*0-8493-7901-6*) CRC Pr.

Transport Phenomena Problem Solver. rev. ed. Research & Education Association Staff. LC 84-61816. (Illus.). 864p. 1994. pap. text ed. 29.95 (*0-87891-562-1*) Res & Educ.

Transport Phenomena with Drops & Bubbles. S. S. Sadhal et al. LC 96-18415. (Mechanical Engineering Ser.). 512p. 1996. 79.00 (*0-387-94678-0*) Spr-Verlag.

Transport Phenomena-1973: AIP Conference Proceedings, No. 11. AIP Conference. Ed. by J. Kestin. LC 73-80682. 346p. 1973. 14.00 (*0-88318-110-X*) Am Inst Physics.

Transport Planning: An International Appraisal. David Banister. LC 93-33231. 1993. write for info. (*0-419-18930-0*, E & FN Spon) Routledge Chapman & Hall.

***Transport Planning & Traffic Engineering.** write for info. (*0-340-66279-4*, Pub. by E Arnold UK) Routledge Chapman & Hall.

***Transport Planning & Traffic Engineering.** 2nd ed. Ed. by Colm A. O'Flaherty. pap. text ed. 69.95 (*0-470-23619-1*) Wiley.

Transport Policies & Practices in Britain's Conurbations (1967-1986) M. Jones. (C). 1986. 29.00 (*0-685-30254-7*, Pub. by Oxford Polytechnic UK) St Mut.

Transport Policy. Kerry Hamilton. (Spicers European Policy Reports). 160p. (C). 1990. pap. text ed. 150.00 (*0-415-03831-6*, A4378) Routledge.

Transport Policy & Environment. Jean-Philippe Barde & Kenneth Button. 1989. 22.00 (*1-85383-075-5*, Pub. by Erthscan Pubns UK) Island Pr.

Transport Policy & Planning: An Integrated Analytical Approach. Brian T. Bayliss. (EDI Technical Materials Ser.). 80p. 1992. pap. 6.95 (*0-8213-1944-2*, 11944) World Bank.

Transport Policy in the EEC. John Whitelegg. (Routledge EEC Ser.). (Illus.). 208p. 1989. 49.95 (*0-415-01258-9*) Routledge.

Transport Processes & Unit Operations. 3rd ed. Christie J. Geankoplis. 928p. 1993. text ed. 83.00 (*0-13-930439-8*) P-H.

Transport Processes in Boiling & Two-Phase Systems Including Near-Critical Fluids. Yih-Yun Hsu & Robert W. Graham. LC 75-38662. (McGraw-Hill - Hemisphere Series in Thermal & Fluids Engineering). (Illus.). 1976. text ed. 43.00 (*0-07-030637-0*) McGraw.

Transport Processes in Boiling & Two-Phase Systems, Including Near-Critical Fluids. Yih-Yun Hsu & Robert W. Graham. LC 75-38662. (Series in Thermal & Fluids Engineering). 558p. reprint ed. pap. 159.10 (*0-317-08866-1*, 2055327) Bks Demand.

Transport Processes in Boiling & 2-Phase Systems. Yih-Yun Hsu & Robert W. Graham. 606p. 1986. 48.00 (*0-89448-030-8*, 300021) Am Nuclear Soc.

Transport Processes in Bubbles, Drops, & Particles. D. De Kee & R. P. Chhabra. 275p. 1991. 84.95 (*0-89116-999-7*) Hemisp Pub.

***Transport Processes in Eukaryotic & Prokaryotic Organisms.** Wilhelmus N. Konings et al. LC 96-27380. (Handbook of Biological Physics Ser.: Vol. 2). 956p. 1996. 299.50 (*0-444-82442-1*) Elsevier.

Transport Processes in Porous Media. Ed. by Jacob Bear & M. Yavuz Corapcioglu. 840p. (C). 1991. lib. bdg. 306.50 (*0-7923-1363-1*) Kluwer Ac.

Transport Processes in the Middle Atmosphere. Ed. by Guido Visconti & Rolando V. Garcia. (C). 1987. lib. bdg. 206.00 (*90-277-2587-X*) Kluwer Ac.

Transport Processes in Wood. J. F. Siau. LC 83-10457. (Wood Science Ser.). (Illus.). 245p. 1983. 129.95 (*0-387-12574-4*) Spr-Verlag.

Transport Properties & Related Thermodynamic Data of Binary Mixtures, Vol. 1. Bruce E. Gammon et al. LC 93-33434. 994p. 1993. 300.00 (*0-8169-0580-0*, X-125) Am Inst Chem Eng.

Transport Properties & Related Thermodynamic Data of Binary Mixtures, Vol. 2. Bruce E. Gammon et al. LC 93-33434. 584p. 1994. 275.00 (*0-8169-0622-X*, X-126) Am Inst Chem Eng.

***Transport Properties & Related Thermodynamic Data of Binary Mixtures, Vol. 3.** 1996. 325.00 (*0-8169-0699-8*, X-127) Am Inst Chem Eng.

***Transport Properties & Related Thermodynamic Data of Binary Mixtures, Vol. 4.** 1997. write for info. (*0-8169-0725-0*, X-128) Am Inst Chem Eng.

***Transport Properties & Related Thermodynamic Data of Binary Mixtures, Vol. 5.** 1997. write for info. (*0-8169-0735-8*, X-129) Am Inst Chem Eng.

Transport Properties in Polymers. J. Stastna & D. De Kee. LC 94-62157. 311p. 1995. text ed. 89.95 (*1-56676-282-0*) Technomic.

Transport Properties of Dense Plasmas, Vol. 47. Ed. by W. Ebeling et al. (Experientia Supplementa Ser.). 184p. 1984. 45.95 (*3-7643-1554-7*) Birkhauser.

Transport Properties of Density. 1984. 65.00 (*0-8176-1554-7*) Birkhauser.

Transport Properties of Fluids: Their Correlation, Prediction & Estimation. Ed. by Jurgen Millat et al. (Illus.). 456p. (C). 1996. text ed. 90.00 (*0-521-46178-2*) Cambridge U Pr.

Transport Properties of Fluids: Thermal Conductivity, Viscosity & Diffusion Coefficient. Ed. by Joseph Kestin & W. A. Wakeham. (CINDAS Data Series on Material Properties: Vol. I-1). 350p. 1988. 159.00 (*0-89116-833-8*) Hemisp Pub.

Transport Properties of Ions in Gases. Edward A. Mason & Earl W. McDaniel. 560p. 1988. text ed. 149.00 (*0-471-88385-9*) Wiley.

Transport Properties of Superconductors: Prog in Hts, Vol. 25. R. Nicolsky. 808p. 1990. text ed. 151.00 (*981-02-0211-3*) World Scientific Pub.

***Transport, Regulation & Control.** 86p. 1995. pap. text ed. 18.95 (*0-521-42202-7*) Cambridge U Pr.

***Transport Regulation Matters.** James McConville. LC 96-44707. 192p. 1997. 90.00 (*1-85567-386-X*, Pub. by Pntr Pubs UK) Bks Intl VA.

Transport, Relaxation, & Kinetic Processes in Electrolyte Solutions. P. Turq et al. (Lecture Notes in Chemistry Ser.: Vol. 57). (Illus.). 206p. 1992. 49.95 (*0-387-55002-X*) Spr-Verlag.

Transport Scheduling & Routing: An Introduction to Quantitative Methods. H. I. Stern. 1981. write for info. (*0-07-061196-3*) McGraw.

Transport Simulation in Microelectronics. Alfred Kersch & William J. Morokoff. LC 94-47303. (Progress in Numerical Simulation for Microelectronics Ser.: Vol. 3). 1995. write for info. (*3-7643-5168-3*, Pub. by Birkhauser Vlg SZ) Birkhauser.

Transport Simulation in Microelectronics. Alfred Kersch & William J. Morokoff. LC 94-47303. (Progress in Numerical Simulation for Microelectronics Ser.: Vol. 3). 1995. 89.00 (*0-8176-5168-3*, Pub. by Birkhauser Vlg SZ) Birkhauser.

Transport Statistics of Great Britain 1995. H. M. S. O. Staff. 248p. 1995. 60.00 (*0-11-551716-2*, HM17162, Pub. by Stationery Ofc UK) Bernan Associates.

An Asterisk (*) at the beginning of an entry indicates that the title is appearing in BIP for the first time.

***Transport Statistics of Great Britain, 1996.** HMSO Staff. 248p. 1996. pap. 70.00 (0-11-551823-1, HM18231, Pub. by Stationery Ofc UK) Bernan Associates.

Transport Strategies for the Russian Federation. Jane Holt. LC 93-32003. (Studies of Economics in Transformation Paper: No. 9). 272p. 1993. 14.95 (0-8213-2625-2, 126252) World Bank.

Transport Supply Analysis. (Transportation Research Record Ser.: No. 1251). 73p. 1989. 12.00 (0-309-05002-2) Transport Res Bd.

Transport Systems in Plants. Jeffrey Moorby. LC 80-41374. (Integrated Themes in Biology Ser.). (Illus.). 175p. reprint ed. pap. 49.90 (0-8357-3573-7, 2034503) Bks Demand.

***Transport Systems, Policy & Planning: A Geographical Approach.** R. S. Tolley. 1995. pap. 32.95 (0-582-00562-0, Pub. by Longman UK) Longman.

Transport, the Environment & Economic Policy. Kenneth Button. 184p. 1993. 75.00 (1-85278-443-1) E Elgar.

Transport, the Environment & Sustainable Development. Ed. by Kenneth J. Button & David Banister. LC 92-39738. 1992. write for info. (0-419-17870-8, E & FN Spon) Routledge Chapman & Hall.

Transport Theory. James J. Duderstadt & William R. Martin. LC 78-13672. (Wiley-Interscience Publications). 623p. reprint ed. pap. 177.60 (0-317-39631-5, 2025186) Bks Demand.

Transport Theory: Proceedings of the SIAM-AMS Symposia, New York, April, 1967. Society for Industrial & Applied Mathematics Staff et al. Ed. by I. K. Abu-Shumays et al. LC 68-23112. (SIAM-AMS Proceedings Ser.: Vol. 1). 327p. 1969. 42.00 (0-8218-1320-X, SIAMS/1) Am Math.

Transport Theory, Invariant Imbedding, & Integral Equations: Proceedings in Honor of G. M. Wing's 65th Birthday. Nelson et al. (Lecture Notes in Pure & Applied Mathematics Ser.: Vol. 115). 480p. 1989. 175.00 (0-8247-8158-9) Dekker.

Transport Through Membranes: Carriers, Channels & Pumps. Ed. by Alberte Pullman et al. (C). 1988. lib. bdg. 252.00 (90-277-2831-3) Kluwer Ac.

***Transport Toys.** Random House Value Publishing Staff. 1997. 14.99 (0-517-18471-0) Random Hse Value.

Transport Tycoon Strategies & Secrets. Lee Buchanan. LC 95-68656. 186p. 1995. 14.99 (0-7821-1752-X, Strategies & Secrets) Sybex.

Transport 7-41-R. T. Degens. 176p. (YA). (gr. 7 up). 1991. pap. 3.95 (0-14-034789-5, Puffin) Puffin Bks.

Transportation. (Ultimate Sticker Bks.). (Illus.). 20p. (J). 1994. pap. 6.95 (1-56458-479-8) DK Pub Inc.

Transportation. (Encyclopaedia Britannica Fascinating Facts Ser.). (Illus.). 32p. (J). 1993. 8.98 (1-56173-314-8) Pubns Intl Ltd.

Transportation. LC 92-24929. (Understanding Science & Nature Ser.). 176p. (J). 1993. 17.95 (0-8094-9700-X); lib. bdg. 24.60 (0-8094-9701-8) Time-Life.

Transportation. (Butterfly Bks.). (Illus.). (ARA.). 12.95 (0-614-09290-6, LDL6161, Pub. by Librairie du Liban FR) Intl Bk Ctr.

***Transportation.** LC 97-10078. (Then & Now Ser.). (Illus.). 32p. (YA). (gr. 4 up). 1997. lib. bdg. 16.40 (0-7613-0604-8, Copper Beech Bks) Millbrook Pr.

Transportation. Robert Gardner. (Yesterday's Science, Today's Technology Ser.). (Illus.). 96p. (J). (gr. 5-8). 1994. lib. bdg. 16.98 (0-8050-2853-6) TFC Bks NY.

***Transportation.** Ed. by Eleanor C. Goldstein. (Social Issues Resources Ser.: Vol. 5). 1996. 38.00 (0-89777-196-6) Sirs Inc.

Transportation. Ian Graham. LC 92-20740. (Facing the Future Ser.). 48p. (J). (gr. 5 up). 1992. lib. bdg. 22.80 (0-8114-2807-9) Raintree Steck-V.

Transportation. Illus. by Robert R. Ingpen. LC 94-36365. (Ideas That Changed the World). 96p. (YA). (gr. 5 up). 1995. lib. bdg. 19.95 (0-7910-2768-6) Chelsea Hse.

***Transportation.** Robin Kerrod. (Let's Investigate Science Ser.). (Illus.). 64p. (YA). (gr. 5 up). 1996. lib. bdg. 17.95 (1-85435-629-1) Marshall Cavendish.

Transportation. Linda Leuzzi. LC 94-17183. (Life in America 100 Years Ago Ser.). (Illus.). (YA). (gr. 5 up). 1995. lib. bdg. 19.95 (0-7910-2840-2) Chelsea Hse.

***Transportation.** Julian Rowe. LC 96-27560. (Science Encounters Ser.). (J). 1997. write for info. (1-57572-087-6) Rigby Interact Libr.

***Transportation.** Gare Thompson. (You Are There Ser.). (Illus.). (J). 1997. lib. bdg. 17.30 (0-516-20705-9) Childrens.

Transportation. Kim M. Thompson & Karen M. Hilderbrand. (Early Childhood Ser.). (Illus.). 24p. (J). (ps-2). 1995. pap. 9.98 incl. audio (1-882331-84-2, Twin416) Twin Sisters.

Transportation. rev. ed. (Understanding Computers Ser.). (Illus.). 128p. 1991. 19.93 (0-8094-7606-1); lib. bdg. 25.93 (0-8094-7607-X) Time-Life.

Transportation. 3rd ed. Robert C. Lieb. (C). 1985. teacher ed. write for info. (0-8359-7824-9, Reston); text ed. write for info. (0-8359-7823-0, Reston) P-H.

Transportation. 4th ed. John J. Coyle et al. Ed. by Fenton. LC 93-23611. 550p. (C). 1993. text ed. 62.50 (0-314-02853-6) West Pub.

***Transportation.** 5th ed. Coyle & Bardi. (C). Date not set. text ed. 59.95 (0-538-88180-1) S-W Pub.

Transportation, Vol. 3. Ed. by Eleanor C. Goldstein. (Social Issues Resources Ser.). 1990. Incl. 1985-1989 Supplements. suppl. ed. 95.00 (0-89777-082-X) Sirs Inc.

Transportation: A Pictorial Archive From 19th Century Sources with 400 Copyright-Free Illustrations for Artists & Designs. Ed. by Jim Harter. (Illus.). 160p. (Orig.). 1983. pap. 7.95 (0-486-24499-7) Dover.

Transportation: A Resource Guide to Who's Doing What in California. Ed. by Ilze M. Gotelli. LC 89-39399. (California Information Guides Ser.). 48p. (Orig.). 1990. pap. 20.00 (0-912102-89-6) Cal Inst Public.

Transportation: A Salute to Black Inventors. rev. ed. Ann C. Howell. Ed. by Evelyn L. Ivery. (Black Inventors Activity Bks.). (Illus.). 24p. (J). (gr. 3-7). 1992. reprint ed. pap. text ed. 1.50 (1-877804-00-2) Chandler White.

Transportation: America's Lifeline. Ed. by Cornelia Cessna. (Information Plus Ser.). 140p. 1995. pap. text ed. 22.95 (1-57302-006-0) Info Plus TX.

Transportation: Basic Terms. Douglas Moore & Harris Winitz. (All about Language Ser.). (Illus.). 35p. (Orig.). 1987. pap. text ed. 22.00 incl. audio (0-939990-51-2) Intl Linguistics.

Transportation: Educational Coloring Book. Spizzirri Publishing Co. Staff. Ed. by Linda Spizzirri. (Illus.). 32p. (J). (gr. 1-8). 1981. pap. 1.99 (0-86545-038-2) Spizzirri.

Transportation: Getting from One Place to Another. 2nd rev. ed. Ed. by Margaret Mitchell et al. (Compact Reference Ser.). (Illus.). 60p. 1996. pap. text ed. 12.95 (1-57302-023-0) Info Plus TX.

Transportation: Management, Economics, Policy. John L. Hazard. LC 77-22414. (Illus.). 607p. 1977. text ed. 18.00 (0-87033-229-5) Cornell Maritime.

Transportation: Steam Trains to Space Planes. June English. LC 94-29245. (Kid's Encyclopedia Ser.). (J). (gr. 1-8). 1994. pap. write for info. (0-590-27553-4) Scholastic Inc.

Transportation Vol. 4: Incl. 1990-1994 Supplements. Ed. by Eleanor C. Goldstein. (Social Issues Resources Ser.). 1995. 95.00 (0-89777-160-5) Sirs Inc.

Transportation - Food - Safety - Old West - Working Easier - Communication - Black Women: A Salute to Black Inventors. rev. ed. Ann C. Howell. Ed. by Evelyn L. Ivery. (Black Inventors Activity Bks.). (Illus.). 24p. (J). (gr. 3-7). 1992. reprint ed. pap. text ed. 10.50 (1-877804-10-X) Chandler White.

Transportation - Nautical Education for Offshore Extractive Industries. 2nd ed. G. H. Hoffmann et al. (Nautical Education for Offshore Extractive Industries Ser.). (Illus.). 206p. 1985. reprint ed. pap. 16.00 (0-934114-71-4, BK-113) Marine Educ.

***Transportation - Sky & Earth.** (Bip Quiz Ser.). (J). 1997. pap. 10.95 (0-8069-8140-7) Sterling.

Transportation Accounting & Control: Guidelines for Distribution & Financial Management. Ernst & Young Staff & Cleveland Consulting Association. 232p. pap. 40.00 (0-86641-092-9, 83143) Inst Mgmt Account.

Transportation Act 1920. Rogers Macveagh. Ed. by Stuart Bruchey. LC 80-1330. (Railroads Ser.). 1981. reprint ed. lib. bdg. 93.95 (0-405-13804-0) Ayer.

***Transportation Action: A Local Input Model to Engage Community Transportation Planning.** Timothy O. Borich & Janet Ayres. Ed. by Julie Stewart. 148p. 1996. pap. text ed. 15.00 (0-936913-11-8, RRD 174) NCRCRD.

Transportation Analyst. Jack Rudman. (Career Examination Ser.: C-3380). 1994. pap. 29.95 (0-8373-3380-6) Nat Learn.

Transportation & Behavior. Ed. by Irwin Altman et al. LC 76-382942. (Human Behavior & Environment Ser.: Vol. 5). 304p. (C). 1982. 65.00 (0-306-40773-6, Plenum Pr) Plenum.

***Transportation & Communication.** Patience Coster. LC 97-1979. (Step-by-Step Geography Ser.). (Illus.). (J). 1997. write for info. (0-516-20352-5) Childrens.

Transportation & Communication. Ed. & Intro. by Neil L. Shumsky. LC 95-36145. (American Cities Ser.: Vol. 6). (Illus.). 424p. 1995. reprint ed. text ed. 95.00 (0-8153-2191-0) Garland.

Transportation & Communication Policy. Ed. by Alan Altshuler. (C). 1977. pap. 15.00 (0-918592-22-4) Pol Studies.

Transportation & Economic Development 1990: Proceedings of a Conference. (Transportation Research Record Ser.: No. 1274). 290p. 1990. 40.00 (0-309-05024-3) Transport Res Bd.

Transportation & Economic Opportunity. (Illus.). 96p. 1974. 10.00 (0-318-16388-8, 119) Regional Plan Assn.

Transportation & Economic Stagnation in Spain, 1750-1850. David R. Ringrose. LC 78-101131. 213p. reprint ed. pap. 60.80 (0-317-20423-8, 2023441) Bks Demand.

Transportation & Energy. (Research Record Ser.: No. 1155). 68p. 1987. 10.50 (0-309-04662-9) Transport Res Bd.

Transportation & Energy. Compiled by American Society of Civil Engineers Staff. 456p. 1978. pap. 17.00 (0-87262-135-9) Am Soc Civil Eng.

Transportation & Energy: Strategies for a Sustainable Transportation System. Ed. by Daniel Sperling & Susan Shaheen. 400p. (Orig.). (C). 1995. pap. 31.00 (0-918249-20-1) Am Coun Energy.

Transportation & Global Climate Change. Ed. by David L. Greene & Danilo J. Santini. LC 93-15469. (Illus.). 357p. (Orig.). (C). 1993. pap. 31.00 (0-918249-17-1) Am Coun Energy.

***Transportation & Growth: Myth & Fact.** Robert T. Dunphy et al. 16p. 1996. pap. text ed. 12.95 (0-87420-788-6, T15) Urban Land.

Transportation & Handling of Meat & Meat Products. ICHCA Staff. (C). 1976. 310.00 (0-685-37345-2, Pub. by ICHCA UK) St Mut.

Transportation & Land Development. (Special Reports: No. 183). 49p. 1978. 3.60 (0-309-02803-5) Transport Res Bd.

***Transportation & Land Use Innovations: When You Can't Build Your Way Out of Congestion.** rev. ed. Reid Ewing. LC 97-71137. (Illus.). 112p. 1997. pap. write for info. (1-884829-12-0) Planners Pr.

***Transportation & Land Use Innovations: When You Can't Build Your Way Out of Congestion.** rev. ed. Reid Ewing. LC 97-71137. (Illus.). 112p. 1997. lib. bdg. write for info. (1-884829-13-9) Planners Pr.

***Transportation & Logistics Basics.** R. Neil Southern. (Illus.). ix, 400p. 1996. 39.95 (0-9655014-0-X) Continental Traffic.

Transportation & Logistics in the Army. 1996. lib. bdg. 250.95 (0-8490-6896-7) Gordon Pr.

***Transportation & Service Policy: Introduction to Planning & Design Projects.** J. Schoon. (Illus.). 160p. (C). (gr. 13 up). 1996. text ed. 36.95 (0-412-07481-8) Chapman & Hall.

Transportation & the 1977 Clean Air Act Amendments. LC 80-66291. 440p. 1980. pap. 37.00 (0-87262-242-8) Am Soc Civil Eng.

Transportation & Traffic Management, 4 vols. 16th ed. E. Albert Ovens. Ed. by Robert M. Butler et al. LC 74-19874. (Illus.). 1191p. 1981. Set. pap. text ed. 85.00 (0-87408-012-6) Intl Thom Trans Pr.

Transportation & Traffic Management, 4 vols., Vol. I. 16th ed. E. Albert Ovens. Ed. by Robert M. Butler et al. LC 74-19874. (Illus.). 273p. 1981. pap. text ed. 23.00 (0-87408-029-0) Intl Thom Trans Pr.

Transportation & Traffic Management, 4 vols., Vol. II. 16th ed. E. Albert Ovens. Ed. by Robert M. Butler et al. LC 74-19874. (Illus.). 262p. 1981. pap. text ed. 23.00 (0-87408-030-4) Intl Thom Trans Pr.

Transportation & Traffic Management, 4 vols., Vol. III. 16th ed. E. Albert Ovens. Ed. by Robert M. Butler et al. LC 74-19874. (Illus.). 310p. 1981. pap. text ed. 23.00 (0-87408-031-2) Intl Thom Trans Pr.

Transportation & Traffic Management, 4 vols., Vol. IV. 16th ed. E. Albert Ovens. Ed. by Robert M. Butler et al. LC 74-19874. (Illus.). 346p. 1981. pap. text ed. 23.00 (0-87408-032-0) Intl Thom Trans Pr.

Transportation & Traffic Theory: Proceedings of the 12th International Symposium on the Theory of Traffic Flow & Transportation, Berkeley, CA, U. S. A., 21-23 July--A Symposium in Honor of Gordon F. Newell. Ed. by Carlos F. Daganzo. LC 93-1826. 614p. 1993. Alk. paper. 286.00 (0-444-89439-X) Elsevier.

Transportation & Traffic Theory: Proceedings of the 13th International Symposium on Transportation & Traffic Theory, Lyon, France, 24-26 July 1996. Ed. by Jean-Baptiste Lesort. 772p. 1996. text ed. 173.00 (0-08-042586-0, Pergamon Pr) Elsevier.

Transportation & Traffic Theory: Proceedings of the 9th International Symposium, Delft, 1984. Ed. by J. Volmuller & R. Hamerslag. 608p. 1984. lib. bdg. 135.00 (90-6764-008-5, Pub. by VSP NE) Coronet Bks.

Transportation & Urban Land. Lowdon Wingo, Jr. LC 77-86416. (Resources for the Future Ser.). 144p. reprint ed. 47.50 (0-404-60346-7) AMS Pr.

Transportation & Urban Land. Lowdon Wingo. LC 61-13662. 142p. reprint ed. pap. 40.50 (0-7837-3040-3, 2042886) Bks Demand.

***Transportation & Village: Find African Travel.** pap. 7.95 (0-8213-3747-5, 13747) World Bank.

Transportation & World Development. Wilfred Owen. LC 87-4154. 176p. 1987. text ed. 28.50 (0-8018-3495-3) Johns Hopkins.

Transportation Assistant. Jack Rudman. (Career Examination Ser.: C-2358). 1994. pap. 27.95 (0-8373-2358-4) Nat Learn.

Transportation Buttons, Vol. I: Railroads. Donald P. Van Court. LC 87-90092. (Transportation Uniform Buttons Ser.). (Illus.). 280p. 1987. 34.50 (0-9618301-0-7) D P Van Court.

Transportation, Clear Air, & Energy Efficiency: A Look at Overlapping Federal Legislation. Jackie Cummins & Eric Skiiema. (State Legislative Reports: Vol. 18, No. 11). 3p. 1993. 5.00 (1-55516-337-8, 7302-1811) Natl Conf State Legis.

Transportation Company Insolvencies. (Commercial Law & Practice Ser.). 414p. 1992. pap. text ed. 70.00 (0-685-56871-7, A4-4371) PLI.

Transportation Conformity. Sean Cavanagh. 5p. 1995. 5.00 (0-614-10576-5, 7302-2005) Natl Conf State Legis.

Transportation Congress: Civil Engineers - Key to the World Infrastructure: Proceedings of the 1995 Conference, San Diego, California, October 22-26, 1995, 2 Vols. Ed. by B. Kent Lall & Daniel L. Jones, Jr. 2229p. 1995. 209.00 (0-7844-0129-2) Am Soc Civil Eng.

Transportation Construction, Nineteen Ninety. (Transportation Research Record Ser.: No. 1282). 144p. 1990. 23.00 (0-309-05059-6) Transport Res Bd.

Transportation Construction, Nineteen Ninety. (Transportation Research Record Ser.: No. 1285). 117p. 1990. 18.00 (0-309-05054-5) Transport Res Bd.

Transportation Data. (Research Record Ser.: No. 1134). 64p. 1987. 10.50 (0-309-04518-5) Transport Res Bd.

Transportation Data & Information Systems. (Transportation Research Record Ser.: No. 1271). 88p. 1990. 16.00 (0-309-05053-7) Transport Res Bd.

Transportation Data 1989. (Transportation Research Record Ser.: No. 1236). 66p. 1989. 12.00 (0-309-04958-X) Transport Res Bd.

Transportation Demand Management: A Cautious Look. Jeffrey M. Zupan. LC 92-24160. (Transportation Research Record Ser.: No. 1346). 73p. 1992. 20.00 (0-309-05209-2) Transport Res Bd.

Transportation Deregulation: What's Deregulated & What Isn't. Daniel Sweeney et al. LC 86-60020. 309p. 1986. 50.00 (0-9616271-0-7) NASSTRAC.

Transportation Economics. National Bureau of Economic Research Staff. (Universities-National Bureau Conference Ser.: No. 17). 482p. 1965. 124.80 (0-87014-308-5) Natl Bur Econ Res.

Transportation Economics: A Conference of the Universities-National Bureau Committee for Economic Research. National Bureau of Economic Research Staff. LC 65-11221. (National Bureau of Economic Research. Special Conference Ser.: No. 17). (Illus.). 480p. reprint ed. pap. 136.80 (0-8357-7584-4, 2056905) Bks Demand.

Transportation Economics: A Guide to Information Sources. Ed. by James P. Rakowski. LC 73-17584. (Economics Information Guide Ser.: Vol. 5). 232p. 1976. 68.00 (0-8103-1307-3) Gale.

Transportation Economics: Issues & Impacts. (Research Record Ser.: No. 1116). 90p. 1987. 13.00 (0-309-04467-7) Transport Res Bd.

Transportation Education & Training: Meeting the Challenge. (Special Reports: No. 210). 205p. 1985. 16.00 (0-309-03914-2) Transport Res Bd.

Transportation, Efficiency & Alternatives: Building Sustainable Communities, an Environmental Guide for Local Government. Center for the Study of Law & Politics Staff. 92p. 1991. 40.00 (1-880386-04-6) Ctr Study Law.

Transportation, Energy & Environment: Balancing Goals & Identifying Policies. 215p. 1995. 195.00 (0-614-06983-1) Consumer Energy Coun.

***Transportation, Energy, & Environment: How Far Will Technology Take Us?** Ed. by John DeCicco & Mark Delucchi. 300p. (C). 1997. per., pap. 33.00 (0-918249-28-7) Am Coun Energy.

Transportation, Energy & Environment Annotated Bibliography. 120p. 1995. write for info. (0-614-06984-X) Consumer Energy Coun.

Transportation, Energy & Power. 2nd ed. Anthony E. Schwaller. (Tech & Industrial Education Ser.). 1998. teacher ed. 15.95 (0-8273-6910-7); text ed. 38.00 (0-8273-6909-3) Delmar.

***Transportation, Energy, & Power.** 2nd ed. Anthony E. Schwaller. (TP - Technology Education Ser.). Date not set. text ed. 42.95 (0-538-67615-9) S-W Pub.

***Transportation, Energy, & Power: Instructor's Guide.** 2nd ed. Anthony E. Schwaller. (TP - Technology Education Ser.). Date not set. pap. 33.95 (0-538-67617-5) S-W Pub.

***Transportation, Energy, & Power Workbook.** 2nd ed. Anthony E. Schwaller. (TP - Technology Education Ser.). Date not set. wbk. ed., pap. 17.95 (0-538-67616-7) S-W Pub.

Transportation Energy & the Future. Lloyd J. Money. (Illus.). 144p. (C). 1984. text ed. 38.00 (0-13-930230-1) P-H.

***Transportation Engineering.** Bartholomew. (C). 1998. text ed. write for info. (0-321-01060-4) Addson-Wesley Educ.

Transportation Engineering: An Introduction. C. Jotin Khisty. 768p. 1990. text ed. 95.00 (0-13-929274-8) P-H.

***Transportation Engineering: An Introduction.** 2nd ed. C. Jotin Khisty & B. Kent Lall. (Illus.). 752p. (C). 1997. text ed. 90.00 (0-13-157355-1) P-H.

***Transportation Engineering: Planning & Design.** 4th ed. Paul H. Wright & Norman J. Ashford. LC 97-15256. 640p. 1997. text ed. write for info. (0-471-17396-7) Wiley.

Transportation Engineering & Planning. 2nd ed. C. S. Papacostas & P. D. Prevedouros. 656p. 1992. text ed. 95.00 (0-13-958075-1) P-H.

Transportation Engineering Basics. A. S. Murthy & R. Henry Mohle. LC 93-15229. 52p. 1993. 16.00 (0-87262-881-7) Am Soc Civil Eng.

Transportation Engineering, Planning & Design. 3rd ed. Paul H. Wright & Norman J. Ashford. LC 88-26090. 776p. 1989. Net. text ed. 54.50 (0-471-83874-8) Wiley.

***Transportation Enhancements: Status of the $2.4 Billion Authorized for Nonmotorized Transportation.** (Illus.). 56p. (Orig.). (C). 1996. pap. 25.00 (0-7881-3670-4) DIANE Pub.

Transportation Equipment Lighting. 100p. 1990. 1,600.00 (0-945235-29-1) Lead Edge Reports.

***Transportation Facilities.** Meisei Co., Ltd. Editors. (Illus.). 224p. 1997. 85.00 (4-938812-26-6, Pub. by Meisei Co Ltd JA) Bks Nippan.

Transportation Facilities Through Difficult Terrain. Ed. by Jonathan T. Wu & Robert K. Barrett. 611p. 1993. 125.00 (90-5410-343-4, Pub. by A A Balkema NE) Ashgate Pub Co.

Transportation Finance & Economic Analysis Issues. (Research Record Ser.: No. 1197). 76p. 1988. 12.00 (0-309-04766-8) Transport Res Bd.

***Transportation for a Sustainable Environment, Vol. 251.** National Research Council (U. S.) Staff. LC 97-19443. (Special Report Ser.). 1997. write for info. (0-309-05969-0) Natl Acad Pr.

Transportation for Cities: The Role of Federal Policy. Wilfred Owen. LC 75-44508. 70p. 1976. pap. 8.95 (0-8157-6773-0) Brookings.

Transportation for Marketing & Business Students. Paul T. McElhiney. (Quality Paperback Ser.: No. 290). 232p. (Orig.). 1975. pap. 9.95 (0-8226-0290-3) Littlefield.

Transportation for the Next Century. William B. Johnston. 19p. (Orig.). 1990. pap. text ed. 2.95 (1-55813-033-0) Hudson Instit IN.

Transportation for the Nuclear Industry. Ed. by D. G. Walton & S. M. Blackburn. LC 89-39478. (Illus.). 425p. 1989. 120.00 (0-306-43379-6, Plenum Pr) Plenum.

Transportation from Bicycle to Spacecraft see Macmillan Encyclopedia of Science

Transportation Futures: An Option for Tomorrow? 146p. 1988. 25.00 (0-934292-07-8) Natl Waterways.

Transportation Geography: A Bibliography. 3rd ed. William R. Siddall. 1972. reprint ed. 2.50 (0-318-22154-3) KSU.

Transportation Geography: A Bibliography. 3rd ed. William R. Siddall. LC 73-633686. (Libraries Bibliography: No. 1). 1972. reprint ed. 2.50 (0-686-20817-X) KSU.

Transportation Health & Safety Representative. Jack Rudman. (Career Examination Ser.: C-3379). 1994. pap. 29.95 (*0-8373-3379-2*) Nat Learn.

Transportation in America. William L. Richter. LC 95-13170. (ABC-CLIO Companions Ser.). (Illus.). 653p. (YA). (gr. 8 up). 1995. lib. bdg. 57.00 (*0-87436-789-1*) ABC-CLIO.

Transportation in America: Users, Carriers, Government. 2nd ed. Donald V. Harper. (Illus.). 624p. (C). 1982. text ed. write for info. (*0-13-930297-2*) P-H.

Transportation in an Aging Society: Improving Mobility & Safety for Older People, Vols. 1 & 2, Vol. 2. (Special Reports: No. 218). 528p. 1988. 39.00 (*0-309-04754-4*) Transport Res Bd.

Transportation in Eastern Europe. Bogdan Mieczkowski. (East European Monographs: No. 38). 221p. 1978. text ed. 60.00 (*0-914710-31-1*) East Eur Monographs.

Transportation in Iowa: A Historical Summary. William H. Thompson. (Illus.). 315p. 1989. 25.00 (*0-9623167-0-9*) IA Dept Transportation.

Transportation in Pencil. Gene Franks. (How to Draw & Paint Ser.). (Illus.). 32p. (Orig.). 1990. pap. 6.95 (*1-56010-067-2*, HT-230) W Foster Pub.

Transportation Industries, 1889-1946: A Study of Output, Employment & Productivity. Harold Barger. LC 75-19692. (National Bureau of Economic Research Ser.). (Illus.). 1975. reprint ed. 23.95 (*0-405-07573-1*) Ayer.

Transportation Industries, 1889-1946: A Study of Output, Employment, & Productivity. Harold Barger. (General Ser.: No. 51). 304p. 1951. reprint ed. 79.10 (*0-87014-050-7*) Natl Bur Econ Res.

Transportation Information Sources. Ed. by Kenneth N. Metcalf. LC 65-24657. (Management Information Guide Ser.: No. 8). 308p. 1965. 68.00 (*0-8103-0808-8*) Gale.

Transportation Infostructures: The Development of Intelligent Transportation Systems. John Diebold. LC 95-2213. 224p. 1995. text ed. 59.95 (*0-275-95155-3*, Praeger Pubs); pap. text ed. 17.95 (*0-275-95156-1*, Praeger Pubs) Greenwood.

Transportation Infrastructure: Environmental Challenges in Poland & Neighboring Countries. Ed. by Richard M. Gutkowski & Jan Kmita. LC 95-39338. (NATO ASI Series, Patnership 2: Vol. 5). 472p. 1996. 236.00 (*3-540-60601-7*) Spr-Verlag.

Transportation Infrastructure: The Nation's Highway Bridges Remain at Risk from Earthquakes. (Illus.). 40p. (Orig.). (C). 1993. pap. text ed. 25.00 (*1-56806-980-4*) DIANE Pub.

Transportation Landscape & Environmental Design. rev. ed. AASHTO Staff. (Planning & Environment Ser.). (Illus.). 184p. (C). 1991. pap. text ed. 48.50 (*1-56051-009-9*, HLED-2) AASHTO.

Transportation Logistics. (Research Record Ser.: No. 1120). 67p. 1987. 10.50 (*0-309-04473-1*) Transport Res Bd.

Transportation-Logistics Dictionary. 2nd ed. Ed. by Joseph L. Cavinato. 323p. 1982. 14.00 (*0-87408-022-3*) Intl Thom Trans Pr.

***Transportation Logistics Dictionary.** 3rd ed. Ed. by J. Cavinato. (Illus.). 311p. (C). 1989. pap. text ed. 47.95 (*0-87408-050-9*) Intl Thom Trans Pr.

Transportation Management for Major Highway Reconstruction. (Special Reports: No. 212). 128p. 1987. 16.00 (*0-309-04452-9*) Transport Res Bd.

Transportation Management, HOV Systems, & Geometric Design & Effects, 1990. (Transportation Research Record Ser.: No. 1280). 236p. 1990. 34.00 (*0-309-05058-8*) Transport Res Bd.

Transportation Management Through Partnerships. Robert T. Dunphy & Ben C. Lin. LC 89-52210. 224p. 1991. 45.95 (*0-87420-698-7*, T10) Urban Land.

Transportation-Markings: A Study in Communication Monograph Series, 9 bks. Incl. First Studies in Transportation-Markings Vol. I, Pt. A: Foundations. 2nd enl. rev. ed. Brian Clearman. LC 91-46071. (Illus.). 167p. 1991. pap. 15.95 (*0-918941-02-4*); First Studies in Transportation-Markings Vol. I, Pt. B: The U. S. 2nd enl. rev. ed. Brian Clearman. LC 91-46071. (Illus.). 207p. 1992. pap. 17.95 (*0-918941-05-9*); First Studies in Transportation-Markings Vol. 1, Pts. C & D: International Marine Aids to Navigation. 2nd rev. ed. Brian Clearman. LC 88-8960. (Illus.). 240p. 1988. pap. 14.95 (*0-918941-01-6*); Further Studies in Transportation-Markings Vol. II, Pt. E: International Traffic Control Devices. Brian Clearman. LC 80-6184. (Illus.). 269p. (Orig.). 1984. pap. 9.95 (*0-918941-00-8*); Further Studies in Transportation-Markings Vol. II, Pt. F: International Railway Signals. Brian Clearman. LC 91-67255. (Illus.). 291p. (Orig.). 1991. pap. 18.95 (*0-918941-03-2*); Further Studies in Transportation-Markings Vol. II, Pt. G: International Aeronautical Navigation Aids. Brian Clearman. LC 94-76173. (Illus.). 214p. (Orig.). 1994. pap. 18.95 (*0-918941-08-3*); Further Studies in Transportation-Markings Vol. II, Pt. H: A General Classification of International Transportation-Markings. Brian Clearman. LC 94-41752. (Orig.). 1994. pap. text ed. 9.95 (*0-918941-09-1*); Additional Studies in Transportation-Markings Vol. III, Pt. I: Database of Transportation Markings Phenomena: Marine. LC 97-25496. 1997. pap. (*0-918941-10-5*); Final Studies in Transportation-Markings Vol. IV, Pt. J: Transportation Markings: Messages, Meanings, Generating Agents & their Developments, 1750-2000. Date not set. pap. (*0-918941-12-1*); write for info. (*0-918941-11-3*) Mt Angel Abbey.

Transportation Milestones & Breakthroughs. Richard Steins. (Twenty Events Ser.). (Illus.). 48p. (J). (gr. 4-8). 1994. lib. bdg. 24.26 (*0-8114-4935-1*) Raintree Steck-V.

***Transportation Modelling for Tomorrow: Rudi-Mental Contributions.** Ed. by Piet H. Bovy. xviii, 284p. (Orig.). 1996. pap. 67.50 (*90-407-1317-0*, Pub. by Delft U Pr NE) Coronet Bks.

Transportation Needs, Priorities, & Financing. (Research Record Ser.: No. 1124). 80p. 1987. 12.00 (*0-309-04504-5*) Transport Res Bd.

Transportation Needs Study & Financial Constraints. (National Cooperative Highway Research Program Report Ser.: No. 72). 54p. 1980. 6.40 (*0-309-03152-4*) Transport Res Bd.

***Transportation Network Analysis.** M. Bell & Y. Lida. text ed. 90.00 (*0-471-96493-X*) Wiley.

Transportation Networks: A Quantitative Treatment. Dusan Teodorovic. (Transportation Studies: Vol. 6). 220p. 1986. text ed. 178.00 (*0-677-21380-8*) Gordon & Breach.

***Transportation Networks, Recent Methodological Advances: Selected Proceedings of the 4th Euro Transportation Meeting.** Ed. by Michael G. H. Bell. 300p. Date not set. text ed. write for info. (*0-08-043052-X*, Pergamon Pr) Elsevier.

***Transportation Noise Control: NOISE-CON 77.** Ed. by George C. Maling, Jr. (Noise-Con Ser.). ix, 502p. pap. 35.00 (*0-614-25015-3*) Noise Control.

Transportation of Dangerous Goods in Canada: A Practical Guide to the Law. Douma. 144p. 1990. pap. 46.00 (*0-409-89390-0*) MICHIE.

Transportation of Hazardous Materials: A Compliance & Practice Guide for Safe Transportation of Hazardous Materials. 2nd ed. Rea, Cross & Auchincloss Staff. 300p. 1992. pap. text ed. 79.00 (*0-86587-286-4*) Gov Insts.

Transportation of Hazardous Materials: A Guide to Compliance. Nicholas P. Cheremisinoff. LC 94-3866. (Illus.). 262p. 1994. 54.00 (*0-8155-1350-X*) Noyes.

Transportation of Hazardous Materials: Issues in Law, Social Science, & Engineering Ser. Ed. by Leon N. Moses & Dan Lindstrom. LC 93-20447. 368p. (C). 1993. lib. bdg. 111.00 (*0-7923-9340-6*) Kluwer Ac.

Transportation of Hazardous Materials 1989. (Transportation Research Record Ser.: No. 1245). 64p. 1989. 12.00 (*0-309-04967-9*) Transport Res Bd.

Transportation of Hazardous Materials, 1990. (Transportation Research Record Ser.: No. 1264). 85p. 1990. 16.00 (*0-309-05021-9*) Transport Res Bd.

Transportation of Soviet Energy Resources. Matthew J. Sagers & Milford B. Green. LC 86-15508. 200p. 1986. 56.00 (*0-8476-7504-1*, R7504) Rowman.

Transportation Office Assistant. (Career Examination Ser.: C-3674). pap. 23.95 (*0-8373-3674-0*) Nat Learn.

Transportation on Land & Sea. Nigel Hawkes. (New Technology Ser.). (Illus.). 32p. (J). (gr. 5-8). 1994. lib. bdg. 13.98 (*0-8050-3415-3*) TFC Bks NY.

Transportation on the Western Front. A. M. Henniker. (Great War Ser.: No. 22). (Illus.). 592p. reprint ed. 49.95 (*0-89839-179-2*) Battery Pr.

Transportation Physical Exam & Health Assessment. 2nd ed. Jarvis. 1996. 150.00 (*0-7216-6539-X*) Saunders.

Transportation Planning Aide. Jack Rudman. (Career Examination Ser.: C-2846). 1994. pap. 27.95 (*0-8373-2846-2*) Nat Learn.

Transportation Planning & Air Quality: Proceedings of the National Conference. Ed. by Roger L. Wayson. LC 92-11204. 360p. 1992. pap. text ed. 34.00 (*0-87262-815-9*) Am Soc Civil Eng.

Transportation Planning & Air Quality II: Proceedings of the National Conference, Sheraton Tara Hotel & Resort, Denver, Massachusets, May 24-26, 1993. American Society of Civil Engineers, Urban Transportation Division Staff. Ed. by Thomas F. Wholley. LC 94-5431. 1994. write for info. (*0-87262-914-7*) Am Soc Civil Eng.

Transportation Planning & Automated Guideways. (Research Record Ser.: No. 1167). 58p. 1988. 9.00 (*0-309-04708-0*) Transport Res Bd.

Transportation Planning & Policy: The Role of Analytical Methods in Government. D. N. Starkie. 154p. 1976. pap. 31.00 (*0-08-020908-4*, Pergamon Pr) Elsevier.

Transportation Planning & Policy Decision Making: Behavioral Science Contributions. Richard M. Michaels. LC 79-24820. 264p. 1980. text ed. 59.95 (*0-275-90524-1*, C0524, Praeger Pubs) Greenwood.

Transportation Planning & Public Policy see Progress in Planning

Transportation Planning for Small Urban Areas. (National Cooperative Highway Research Program Report Ser.: No. 167). 71p. 1976. 4.80 (*0-309-02506-0*) Transport Res Bd.

Transportation Planning Handbook. Institute of Transportation Engineers Staff. 704p. 1992. text ed. 91.00 (*0-13-928052-9*) P-H.

Transportation Planning in the Boston Metropolitan Area: A Selected Bibliography, 1930-1982. Toby Pearlstein. LC 83-20954. (CPL Bibliographies Ser.: No. 128). 1983. 10.00 (*0-317-00897-8*, Sage Prdcls Pr) Sage.

Transportation Planning in the Boston Metropolitan Area: A Selected Bibliography, 1930-1982. Toby Pearlstein. (CPL Bibliographies Ser.: No. 128). 53p. 1983. 10.00 (*0-86602-128-0*, Sage Prdcls Pr) Sage.

Transportation Planning on Trial: The Clean Air Act & Travel Forecasting. Mark Garrett & Martin Wachs. LC 95-50228. (Metropolis & Region Ser.: Vol. T). 312p. (C). 1996. 42.00 (*0-8039-7352-7*); pap. 19.95 (*0-8039-7353-5*) Sage.

Transportation Policy. Ed. by Margk Maggio & T. H. Maze. (Orig.). 1993. pap. 15.00 (*0-944285-33-3*) Pol Studies.

Transportation Policy Issues for the 1980's. Gayton E. Germane. (Illus.). 512p. (C). 1983. teacher ed. write for info. (*0-318-57292-3*) Addison-Wesley.

Transportation Professionals: Future Needs & Opportunities. (Special Reports: No. 207). 299p. 1985. 18.00 (*0-309-03813-8*) Transport Res Bd.

Transportation Program Aide. (Career Examination Ser.: C-3774). pap. 27.95 (*0-8373-3774-7*) Nat Learn.

Transportation Questions & Answers, Vol. 30. Colin Barrett. 400p. 1991. 59.95 (*0-9630797-0-0*) Loft Pr.

Transportation Rates & Economic Development in Northern Ontario. N. C. Bonsor. LC 77-369766. (Ontario Economic Council Research Studies: No. 7). (Illus.). 99p. reprint ed. pap. 28.30 (*0-8357-4016-1*, 2036706) Bks Demand.

Transportation Regulatory Policy, 1994-1995. 200p. 1995. 35.00 (*0-317-05198-9*) NARUC.

***Transportation-Related Air Quality & Energy.** Transportation Research Board Staff. (Transportation Research Record, No. 1520 Ser.). 172p. 1996. pap. 37.00 (*0-309-06215-2*, HE336) Natl Acad Pr.

Transportation Restructuring: The Legal Challenges. 247p. 1995. 65.00 (*1-56986-263-X*, TRA-95-247) Federal Bar.

Transportation Revolution: 1815-1860. George R. Taylor. LC 89-10686. (Economic History of the United States Ser.). 454p. (gr. 13). 1977. pap. text ed. 25.95 (*0-87332-101-4*) M E Sharpe.

Transportation Safety in an Age of Deregulation. Ed. by Leon N. Moses & Ian Savage. (Illus.). 368p. 1989. 59.00 (*0-19-505797-X*) OUP.

Transportation Safety Law Practice Manual, 2 vols. William E. Kenworthy. 800p. 1989. ring bd. 175.00 (*0-88063-286-0*, 82467) MICHIE.

Transportation Service to Small Rural Communities: Effects of Deregulation. John F. Due et al. LC 89-11151. (Illus.). 231p. 1990. reprint ed. pap. 65.90 (*0-608-00094-9*, 2060859) Bks Demand.

Transportation Signal & Control Equipment 1991-1996 Analysis: Traffic Signals, Railroad Grade Crossing Signals, Lighted Buoys & Maritime Beacons & Airport Lighting Equipment. Dennis M. Zogbi. (Illus.). 220p. (Orig.). 1991. pap. 1,800.00 (*1-878218-15-8*) World Info Tech.

Transportation Specialist. Jack Rudman. (Career Examination Ser.: C-2479). 1994. pap. 29.95 (*0-8373-2479-3*) Nat Learn.

***Transportation Statistics.** 1997. lib. bdg. 250.95 (*0-8490-7686-2*) Gordon Pr.

Transportation Supervisor. Jack Rudman. (Career Examination Ser.: C-2738). 1994. pap. 29.95 (*0-8373-2738-5*) Nat Learn.

Transportation Supply Models. Ed. by Michael Florian & Marc Gaudry. 225p. 1981. pap. 34.00 (*0-08-026075-6*, Pergamon Pr) Elsevier.

Transportation System Management, Parking & Travel Demand Management (TRR 1404) Ed. by Luanne Crayton. (Transportation Research Record Ser.). (Illus.). 1100p. 1993. pap. text ed. 25.00 (*0-309-05550-4*) Transport Res Bd.

Transportation Systems: Theory & Application of Advanced Technology: Proceedings, 2 vols. IFAC Symposium on Transportation Systems (1994: Tianjin, PRC) Staff. Ed. by B. Liu & J. M. Blosseville. LC 95-19831. (IPPV Ser.). 1068p. 1995. pap. 186.50 (*0-08-042226-8*, Pergamon Pr) Elsevier.

Transportation Systems: 1994 International Mechanical Engineering Congress & Exposition, Chicago, Illinois - November 6-11, 1994. (DSC - Design Engineering Ser.: Vol. 54, Vol. 76). 400p. 1994. 104.00 (*0-7918-1403-3*, G00898) ASME.

Transportation Systems - 1992. Ed. by G. Rizzoni et al. (DSC Ser.: Vol. 44). 464p. 1992. 72.50 (*0-7918-1119-0*, G00763) ASME.

Transportation Systems & Service Policy: Introduction to Planning & Design Policy. John D. Schoon. 1996. pap. write for info. (*0-04-120741-6*) Routledge Chapman & Hall.

***Transportation Systems Explained.** Donald J. Jambro. Ed. by Lynn Rice. (Illus.). 42p. (YA). (gr. 10 up). 1988. wbk. ed., pap. 7.00 (*0-8064-1250-X*, T10) Bergwall.

Transportation Systems Explained. Donald J. Jambro. (Technology Education Ser.). 42p. (YA). (gr. 10 up). 1988. student ed. write for info. (*0-8064-0392-6*, T10) Bergwall.

Transportation, Techknowledge Reference Series. Anthony E. Schwaller. (TP - Technology Education Ser.). 176p. (J). (gr. k-12). 1996. pap. 21.95 (*0-538-64478-8*) S-W Pub.

Transportation, Technology, & Society: Future Options. Ed. by Gerald J. Karaska & Judith B. Gertler. 10.00 (*0-914206-16-8*) Clark U Pr.

Transportation Telecommunications. (National Cooperative Highway Research Program Report Ser.: No. 165). 92p. 1990. 10.00 (*0-309-04913-X*) Transport Res Bd.

Transportation Theme Set, 4 bks. (Beginners Ser.). 1991. Land Transport. pap. 10.52 (*0-8123-6954-8*); Sea Transport. pap. 10.52 (*0-8123-6956-4*); Trains. pap. 10.52 (*0-8123-6998-X*); Bicycles. pap. 10.52 (*0-8123-6985-8*) McDougal-Littell.

Transportation to the Seaboard: The Communication Revolution & American Foreign Policy, 1860-1900. Howard B. Schonberger. LC 75-105979. (Contributions in American History Ser.: No. 8). 265p. 1971. text ed. 39.95 (*0-8371-3306-8*, SCT/, Greenwood Pr) Greenwood.

Transportation to Work, 1990. Pennsylvania State Data Center Staff. 193p. 1993. pap. text ed. 25.00 (*0-939667-20-7*) Penn State Data Ctr.

***Transportation Tunnels.** S. Ponnuswamy & D. Johnson Victor. (Illus.). 182p. (C). 1996. text ed. 70.00 (*90-5410-296-9*, Pub. by A A Balkema NE) Ashgate Pub Co.

Transportation U. S. A. Frederick J. Stephenson, Jr. LC 84-24403. (Illus.). 672p. (C). 1987. text ed. 39.96 (*0-201-07800-7*) Addison-Wesley.

Transportation Uniform Buttons - Transit. Donald P. Van Court. LC 87-9092. (Transportation Uniform Buttons Ser.: Vol. II). (Illus.). 306p. 1991. 39.50 (*0-9618301-1-5*) D P Van Court.

***Transporte y la Navegacion - Transportation.** (Enciclopedia Ilustrada de Ciencia y Naturaleza - Understanding Science & Nature Ser.). (Illus.). 152p. (SPA.). (YA). (gr. 6 up). 17.95 (*0-7835-3379-9*) Time-Life.

Transported Life: Memories of Kindertransport: The Oral History of Thea Eden. Ed. by Irene Reti & Valerie J. Chase. (Illus.). 96p. (Orig.). 1995. pap. text ed. 9.00 (*0-939821-07-9*) HerBooks.

Transported of Kwardebele: A South African Odyssey. David Goldblatt. (Illus.). 84p. 1989. pap. 14.95 (*0-89381-385-0*) Aperture.

Transported Styles in Shakespeare & Milton. Harold Toliver. LC 88-12614. 283p. 1989. lib. bdg. 35.00 (*0-271-00646-3*) Pa St U Pr.

Transported to Van Diemen's Land. Judith O'Neill. (Cambridge Introduction to World History Topic Bks.). (Illus.). 48p. (YA). (gr. 7 up). 1977. pap. 7.95 (*0-521-21231-6*) Cambridge U Pr.

***Transporting Hazardous Materials: Law & Compliance, Vol. 1.** Albert V. Hartl. 1992. text ed. 120.00 (*0-471-59115-7*) Wiley.

Transporting Hazardous Materials: Law & Compliance, 2 vols., Vol. 2. Albert V. Hartl. (Environmental Law Library). 1040p. 1992. Set. text ed. 240.00 (*0-471-57413-9*) Wiley.

***Transporting Hazardous Materials: Law & Compliance, Vol. 2.** Albert V. Hartl. 1992. text ed. 120.00 (*0-471-59116-5*) Wiley.

Transporting Hazardous Materials: Law & Compliance, 2 vols., Vol. 2. Albert V. Hartl et al. 152p. 1994. suppl. ed., pap. text ed. 65.00 (*0-471-07652-X*) Wiley.

Transporting Hazardous Wastes & Other Hazardous Materials: A Guide to DOT Regulations. 424p. 1996. 75.00 (*0-614-17890-8*) Elsevier.

***Transporting Radioactive Spent Fuel.** League of Women Voters Education Fund Staff. 1996. 5.95 (*0-89959-394-1*, 1052) LWVUS.

***Transports: Travel, Pleasure & Imaginative Geography, 1600-1830.** Ed. by Chloe Chard & Helen Langdon. LC 96-28226. (Studies in British Art). (Illus.). 296p. 1996. 50.00 (*0-300-06382-2*) Yale U Pr.

Transports Maritimes: Termes Techniques, Juridiques & Commerciaux-Lexique Anglais-Francais. 658p. 1992. 55.00 (*92-1-000044-7*, B.GV.92.0.19) UN.

Transposable Elements & Evolution. Ed. by John F. McDonald. LC 93-17743. (Contemporary Issues in Genetics & Evolution Ser.: Vol. 1). 350p. (C). 1993. lib. bdg. 207.00 (*0-7923-2338-6*) Kluwer Ac.

Transposable Elements in Plants: Sponsored CRIS/ICAR Projects & Bibliography. Andrew Kalinski. 175p. (Orig.). (C). 1995. pap. text ed. 35.00 (*0-7881-1989-3*) DIANE Pub.

Transposed Heads. Thomas Mann. 1959. pap. 9.00 (*0-394-70086-4*, Vin) Random.

Transposing Drama: Studies in Representation. Egil Tornqvist. LC 90-8761. (New Directions in Theatre Ser.). 200p. 1991. text ed. 39.95 (*0-312-04728-2*) St Martin.

Transposition. Ed. by A. J. Kingsman et al. (Society for General Microbiology Symposium Ser.: No. 43). 384p. 1988. text ed. 100.00 (*0-521-35464-1*) Cambridge U Pr.

Transposition of the Great Arteries: Twenty-Five Years after Rashkind Balloon Septostomy. Ed. by M. L. Vogel & K. Buhlmeyer. 160p. 1992. 45.00 (*0-387-91420-X*) Spr-Verlag.

Transputer - Occam Japan Five: Proceedings of the 5th Transputer - Occam International Conference 10-11 June 1993, Osaka, Japan. Ed. by S. Noguchi & M. Yamamoto. LC 92-63412. (Transputer & Occam Engineering Ser.: Vol. 35). 266p. (gr. 12). 1993. pap. 105.00 (*90-5199-125-8*, Pub. by IOS Pr NE) IOS Press.

Transputer - Occam Japan Four: Proceedings of the Fourth T-O International Conference, June 4-5, 1992, Tokyo, Japan. Ed. by S. Noguchi & H. Umeo. LC 92-53262. (Transputer & Occam Engineering Ser.: Vol. 27). 278p. (gr. 12). 1992. pap. 105.00 (*90-5199-093-6*) IOS Press.

Transputer - Occam Japan Three: Proceedings of the Third Transputer-Occam International Conference, Tokyo, Japan, May 17-18, 1990. Ed. by Toshiyasu L. Kunii & D. May. (Transputer & Occam Engineering Ser.). x, 308p. (YA). (gr. 12). 1990. pap. 89.00 (*90-5199-032-4*, Pub. by IOS Pr NE) IOS Press.

Transputer - Occam Japan 6: Proceedings of the 6th International Conference Jun 14-17, 1993, Tokyo, Japan. S. Noguchi et al. LC 94-77314. (Transputer & Occam Engineering Ser.: Vol. 39). 330p. (gr. 12). 1994. pap. 99.00 (*90-5199-174-6*) IOS Press.

Transputer & Occam Developments. Nixon. LC 95-75772. (Transputer & Occam Engineering Ser.). 69.50 (*90-5199-222-X*) IOS Press.

Transputer & Occam Research: New Directions. Ed. by Jon Kerridge. LC 92-56598. (Transputer & Occam Engineering Ser.: Vol. 33). 262p. (gr. 12). 1993. pap. 83.00 (*90-5199-121-5*, Pub. by IOS Pr NE) IOS Press.

Transputer Applications. Gordon Harp. 272p. (C). 1989. text ed. 260.00 (*0-273-02852-9*, Pub. by Pitman Pubng UK) St Mut.

An Asterisk (*) at the beginning of an entry indicates that the title is appearing in BIP for the first time.

Transputer Applications - Progress & Prospects: Proceedings of the Closing Symposium of the SERC-DTI Initiative in the Engineering Applications of Transputers, 30-31 March 1992, Reading, UK. Ed. by M. R. Jane et al. LC 91-59037. (Transputer & Occam Engineering Ser.: Vol. 23). 234p. (gr. 12). 1992. 79.00 (*90-5199-079-0*, Pub. by IOS Pr NE) IOS Press.

Transputer Applications & Systems '93: Proceedings of the World Transputer Congress '93 - Transputer Anwender Treffen Conference 1993, Aachen, Germany, September 20-22, 1993. R. Grebe et al. LC 93-79653. (Transputer & Occam Engineering Ser.: Vol. 36). 1317p. (gr. 12). 1993. 185.00 (*90-5199-140-1*, Pub. by IOS Pr NE) IOS Press.

Transputer Applications & Systems '94: Proceedings of the 1994 World Transputer Congress, Cernobbio, Italy, Sept. 5-7, 1994. M. R. Jane et al. LC 94-77525. (Transputer & Occam Engineering Ser.: Vol. 41). 1009p. (gr. 12). 1994. 130.00 (*90-5199-177-0*) IOS Press.

***Transputer Applications & Systems '95.** Ed. by B. M. Cook et al. LC 95-7902. 614p. (YA). (gr. 12 up). 1995. 127.00 (*90-5199-235-1*, 235-1) IOS Press.

Transputer in Australasia: Proceedings of the Third Australian Transputer & Occam User Group Conference, Sydney, Australia, June 28-29, 1990. Ed. by T. Bossomaier et al. (Transputer & Occam Engineering Ser.). 170p. (YA). (gr. 12). 1990. pap. 60.00 (*90-5199-034-0*, Pub. by IOS Pr NE) IOS Press.

Transputer in Australasia Two: ATOUG-4. Ed. by John Hulskamp et al. LC 91-77700. (Transputer & Occam Engineering Ser.). 208p. (YA). (gr. 12). 1991. pap. 65.00 (*90-5199-068-5*, AT006-4, Pub. by IOS Pr NE) IOS Press.

Transputer Research & Applications 1: Proceedings of the 1st North American Transputers Users Group Meeting, Salt Lake City, Utah, April 15-16, 1989. Ed. by G. S. Stiles. (Transputer & Occam Engineering Ser.). 166p. 1990. 60.00 (*90-5199-026-X*, Pub. by IOS Pr NE) IOS Press.

Transputer Research & Applications 2: Proceedings of the Second North American Transputer Users Group Meeting, Durham, NC, October 18-19, 1989. Ed. by J. A. Board, Jr. (Transputer & Occam Engineering Ser.). 462p. (gr. 12). 1990. pap. 115.00 (*90-5199-027-8*, Pub. by IOS Pr NE) IOS Press.

Transputer Research & Applications 3: Proceedings of the Third Conference of the North American Transputer Users Group, April 26-27, 1990. Ed. by A. S. Wagner. (Transputer & Occam Engineering Ser.). 342p. (gr. 12). 1990. pap. 95.00 (*90-5199-030-8*, Pub. by IOS Pr NE) IOS Press.

Transputer Research & Applications 4: Proceedings of the Fourth North American Transputer Users Group Meeting, Ithaca, NY, October 11-12, 1990. Ed. by D. L. Fielding. (Transputer & Occam Engineering Ser.). 250p. (gr. 12). 1990. pap. 69.00 (*90-5199-040-5*, Pub. by IOS Pr NE) IOS Press.

Transputer Research & Applications 5: Proceedings of the Fifth Conference of the North American Transputer Users Group, April 5-7, 1992, Baltimore, MD. E. Shore. LC 91-59034. (Transputer & Occam Engineering Ser.: Vol. 24). 345p. (YA). (gr. 12). 1992. 98.00 (*90-5199-078-2*, Pub. by IOS Pr NE) IOS Press.

Transputer Research & Applications 6: Proceedings of the Sixth North American Transputer Users Group (NATUG-6) Ed. by S. Atkins & A. S. Wagner. (Transputer & Ocean Engineering Ser.: Vol. 34). 363p. (gr. 12). 1993. pap. 117.00 (*90-5199-120-7*, Pub. by IOS Pr NE) IOS Press.

Transputer Research & Applications 7: Proceedings of the 7th Conference of the North American Transputer Users Group, Oct 23-25, 1994, Athens, GA. H. R. Arabnia. LC 94-78470. (Transputer & Occam Engineering Ser.: Vol. 42). 349p. (gr. 12). 1994. pap. 99.00 (*90-5199-187-8*) IOS Press.

Transputer Systems - Ongoing Research. Ed. by Alastair Allen. LC 92-52507. (Transputer & Occam Engineering Ser.: Vol. 25). 274p. (gr. 12). 1992. 90.00 (*90-5199-085-5*, Pub. by IOS Pr NE) IOS Press.

Transputer Technical Notes. Inmos Limited Staff. 300p. 1989. pap. text ed. 28.80 (*0-13-929126-1*) P-H.

Transputers & Parallel Applications. Ed. by John Hulskamp & David Jones. (Transputer & Occam Engineering Ser.: Vol. 31). 227p. (gr. 12). 1992. pap. 80.00 (*90-5199-115-0*, Pub. by IOS Pr NE) IOS Press.

Transputers, 1992: Advanced Research & Industrial Applications, Proceedings of the International Conference, 20-22 May 1992, Bensancon, France. Ed. by Monique Becker et al. LC 91-59039. (Transputer & Occam Engineering Ser.: Vol. 26). 381p. (YA). (gr. 12). 1992. 105.00 (*90-5199-081-2*, Pub. by IOS Pr NE) IOS Press.

Transputers '94: Advanced Research & Industrial Applications: Proceedings of the International Conference Actes de la Conference International, Seriens, France, Sept. 21-23, 1994. M. Becker et al. LC 94-77519. (Transputer & Occam Engineering Ser.: Vol. 40). 316p. (YA). (gr. 12). 1994. 99.00 (*90-5199-179-7*) IOS Press.

Transputing for Numerical & Neural Network Applications. Ed. by G. L. Reijns & J. Luo. LC 92-73167. (Transputer & Occam Engineering Ser.: Vol. 30). 264p. (gr. 12). 1992. pap. 79.00 (*90-5199-100-2*) IOS Press.

Transputing Ninety-One: Proceedings of the First World Conference, Sunnyvale, CA, April 22-26, 1991. Ed. by P. Welch et al. (Transputer & Occam Engineering Ser.). 908p. (YA). (gr. 12). 1991. 150.00 (*90-5199-045-6*, Pub. by IOS Pr NE) IOS Press.

Transracial Adoptees & Their Families: A Study of Identity & Commitment. Rita J. Simon & Howard Altstein. LC 86-30332. 163p. 1987. text ed. 45.00 (*0-275-92398-3*, C2398, Praeger Pubs) Greenwood.

Transracial Adoption: A Bibliography. Kathleen K. Harris. (C). 1989. 50.00 (*0-903534-59-2*, Pub. by Brit Ag for Adopt & Fost UK) St Mut.

Transracial Adoption: Children & Parents Speak. Constance Pohl & Kathleen K. Harris. LC 92-10991. (Changing Family Ser.). (Illus.). 128p. (YA). (gr. 9-12). 1992. lib. bdg. 22.70 (*0-531-11134-2*) Watts.

Transracial & Inracial Adoptees: The Adolescent Years. Ruth G. McRoy & Louis A. Zurcher, Jr. 168p. 1983. pap. 19.95 (*0-398-06282-X*); text ed. 31.95 (*0-398-04840-1*) C C Thomas.

Transsexual Empire: The Making of the She-Male. Janice G. Raymond. LC 93-46771. (Athene Ser.: No. 39). 256p. (C). 1994. pap. text ed. 17.95 (*0-8077-6272-5*) Tchrs Coll.

Transsexualism & Sex Reassignment. Ed. by Richard Green et al. LC 69-15761. (Illus.). 536p. reprint ed. pap. 152.80 (*0-317-07865-8*, 2013133) Bks Demand.

Transsexualism in Society: A Sociology of Male-to-Female Transsexuals. Frank Lewins. 184p. 1995. 49.95 (*0-7329-3043-X*); pap. 24.95 (*0-7329-3044-8*) Paul & Co Pubs.

Transsexuality in the Male: The Spectrum of Gender Dysphoria. Erwin K. Koranyi. (Illus.). 192p. 1979. 36.95 (*0-398-03924-0*) C C Thomas.

Transsexuals: Candid Answers to Private Questions. Gerald Ramsey. 192p. (Orig.). 1996. pap. 24.95 (*0-89594-790-0*) Crossing Pr.

Transsexual's Survival Guide II. Joann A. Stringer. 60p. 1992. pap. 10.00 (*1-880715-09-0*) Creat Des Srvs.

Transsexual's Survival Guide, Vol. 1: Transition & Beyond. JoAnn A. Stringer. 68p. 1990. pap. 15.00 (*1-880715-04-X*) Creat Des Srvs.

Transtemporal Surgery of the Internal Auditory Canal: Proceedings. International Otoneurological Symposium Staff. Ed. by C. R. Pfaltz & Ugo Fisch. (Advances in Oto-Rhino-Laryngology Ser.: Vol. 17). 1970. 66.50 (*3-8055-0237-0*) S Karger.

Transtextualities: Of Cycles & Cyclicity in Medieval French Literature. Ed. by Sara Sturm-Maddox & Donald Maddox. (Medieval & Renaissance Texts & Studies). 210p. 1996. 24.00 (*0-86698-189-6*, MR149) MRTS.

Transtheoretical Approach: Crossing Traditional Boundaries of Therapy. James O. Prochaska & Carlo C. DiClemente. 204p. (C). 1994. reprint ed. lib. bdg. 25.00 (*0-89464-848-9*) Krieger.

Transthoracic Echocardiography. C. Carl Jaffe & Patrick J. Lynch. (C). 1992. 500.00 incl. disk (*1-56815-015-6*) Mosby Yr Bk.

Transuming Passion: Ganymede & the Erotics of Humanism. Leonard Barkan. LC 90-37800. (Illus.). 168p. 1991. 27.50 (*0-8047-1851-2*) Stanford U Pr.

Transurane-Transuranium Elements. Planck, Max, Society for the Advancement of Science, Gmelin Institute for Inorganic Chemistry Staff. (Gmelin Handbuch der Anorganischen Chemie Ser.: Vol. 20d, Pt. 2). (Illus.). 278p. 1975. 425.00 (*0-387-93288-7*) Spr-Verlag.

Transuranic Elements in the Environment: A Summary of Environmental Research on Transuranium Radionuclides Funded by the U. S. Department of Energy Through Calendar Year 1979. DOE Technical Information Center. Ed. by Wayne C. Hanson. LC 80-607069. 744p. 1980. 26.75 (*0-87079-119-2*, DOE/TIC-22800); fiche 9.00 (*0-87079-331-4*, DOE/TIC-22800) DOE.

Transuranium Elements: A Half Century. Ed. by Lester R. Morss & Jean Fuger. LC 92-7475. (Illus.). 590p. 1992. 99.95 (*0-8412-2219-3*) Am Chemical.

Transuranium Elements: Index. 1979. 360.00 (*0-387-93389-1*) Spr-Verlag.

Transurethral Resection. 3rd ed. J. P. Blandy & Richard G. Notley. (Illus.). 176p. 1993. 110.00 (*0-7506-1327-0*) Buttrwrth-Heinemann.

Transurethral Surgery. W. Mauermayer. (Illus.). 477p. 1982. 535.00 (*0-387-11869-1*) Spr-Verlag.

Transvaal Episode. Harry Bloom. 24.95 (*0-8488-0918-1*) Amereon Ltd.

Transvaal Episode. Harry Bloom. LC 81-51098. 363p. 1981. reprint ed. 22.00 (*0-933256-24-8*); reprint ed. pap. 16.00 (*0-933256-25-6*) Second Chance.

Transvaginal Colour Doppler: The Scientific Basis & Practical Application of Colour Doppler in Gynaecology. Ed. by Tom H. Bourne et al. LC 95-2189. (Illus.). 208p. 1995. 140.00 (*3-540-58432-3*) Spr-Verlag.

Transvaginal Sono. Sautter. 248p. (gr. 13). 1991. 74.00 (*1-55664-360-8*) Mosby Yr Bk.

***Transvaginal Sonography.** 2nd ed. I. E. Timor-Trishsch & Rottem. (Illus.). 521p. (C). (gr. 13 up). 1991. text ed. 83.95 (*0-412-04651-2*) Chapman & Hall.

Transvaginal Sonography: A Clinical Atlas. 2nd ed. Arthur C. Fleischer & Donna M. Kepple. LC 95-7919. 448p. 1995. text ed. 99.00 (*0-397-51513-8*) Lppncott-Raven.

Transvaginal Sonography in Infertility. Bill Yee. LC 95-17693. (Illus.). 224p. 1995. text ed. 89.00 (*0-7817-0305-0*) Lppncott-Raven.

Transvaginal Ultrasound. Melvin G. Dodson. (Illus.). 284p. 1991. text ed. 76.00 (*0-443-08761-X*) Churchill.

Transvaginal Ultrasound. David A. Nyberg et al. LC 92-8483. 368p. (C). (gr. 13). 1992. text ed. 150.00 (*0-8016-3709-0*) Mosby Yr Bk.

Transvaginal Ultrasound. 2nd ed. Melvin G. Dodson. (Illus.). 352p. 1994. 89.95 (*0-443-08953-1*) Churchill.

***Transvaluations: Nietzsche in France 1872-1972.** Douglas Smith. (Oxford Modern Languages & Literature Monographs). 260p. 1996. 67.00 (*0-19-815919-6*) OUP.

Transverse Paraphysics: The New Science of Space, Time & Gravity Control. J. G. Gallimore. LC 82-50823. (Illus.). 359p. (Orig.). 1982. pap. text ed. 35.00 (*0-9603536-4-X*) Tesla Bk Co.

Transvestism: A Handbook for Psychologists, Psychiatrists & Counsellors. Harry Brierley. (Illus.). 160p. 1979. 126.00 (*0-08-022268-4*, Pub. by Pergamon Repr UK) Franklin.

Transvestite & the Transexual: A Case Study of Public Categories & Private Indentities. Dave King. 229p. 1993. text ed. 59.95 (*1-85628-134-5*, Pub. by Avebury Pub UK) Ashgate Pub Co.

Transvestite Memoirs: And the Story of the Marquise-Marquis de Banneville. Abbe De Choisy. Tr. & Intro. by R. H. Scott. (Illus.). 142p. 9400. pap. 18.95 (*0-7206-0915-1*, Pub. by P Owen Ltd UK) Dufour.

Transvestites: The Erotic Drive to Cross Dress. Magnus Hirschfeid. Tr. by Michael A. Lombardi-Nash. 424p. (C). 1991. 43.95 (*0-87975-665-9*) Prometheus Bks.

Transvestites & Transsexuals: Toward a Theory of Cross-Gender Behavior. R. F. Docter. LC 88-19586. (Perspectives in Sexuality Ser.). (Illus.). 266p. 1988. 39.50 (*0-306-42878-4*, Plenum Pr) Plenum.

Transwhichics. Ernest M. Robson. LC 74-121306. 1970. 17.00 (*0-8023-1249-7*); pap. 8.95 (*0-8023-1250-0*) Primary Pr.

Transylvania: History & Reality. Milton G. Lehrer. Ed. & Frwd. by David Martin. LC 86-25861. 320p. 1987. 18.95 (*0-910155-04-6*) Bartleby Pr.

Transylvania: The Hungarian Minority in Romania. Julia Nanay. LC 76-19730. (Behind the Iron Curtain Ser.: No. 11). 1976. pap. 5.00 (*0-87934-014-2*) Danubian.

Transylvania & Beyond. Dervla Murphy. 256p. 1993. 21.95 (*0-87951-472-8*) Overlook Pr.

Transylvania & Beyond. Dervla Murphy. 256p. 1995. pap. 13.95 (*0-87951-603-8*) Overlook Pr.

Transylvania & Beyond. large type ed. Dervla Murphy. (Charnwood Library). 400p. 1993. 27.99 (*0-7089-8730-3*, Trail West Pubs) Ulverscroft.

Transylvania & Hungarian Revisionism: (A Discussion of Present-Day Developments) Traian Golea. 200p. 1988. write for info. (*0-937019-08-9*); pap. 18.00 (*0-937019-09-7*) Romanian Hist.

***Transylvania by Night.** Nicky Rea et al. (Vampire). (Illus.). (Orig.). 1997. pap. 18.00 (*1-56504-287-5*, 2808) White Wolf.

Transylvania Station. Donald E. Westlake & Abby Westlake. (Orig.). 1987. pap. 6.95 (*0-89366-273-9*) Ultramarine Pub.

Transylvania, the Hungarian-Rumanian Conflict: A Symposium. A. Haraszti et al. Ed. by A. Wass De Czege. 1979. 18.00 (*0-87934-021-5*) Danubian.

Transylvania, Tutor to the West. 2nd rev. ed. John D. Wright. LC 79-57567. (Illus.). 463p. 1980. reprint ed. pap. 132.00 (*0-7837-9588-2*, 2060337) Bks Demand.

Transylvanian Hungarian Folk Art. A. Wass De Czege et al. (Illus.). 80p. 1983. 16.00 (*0-87934-029-0*) Danubian.

Transylvanian Library: A Consumer's Guide to Vampire Fiction. Greg Cox. Ed. by Daryl F. Mallett. LC 88-36553. (Borgo Literary Guides Ser.: No. 8). 264p. (C). 1993. pap. 23.00 (*0-89370-435-0*); lib. bdg. 33.00 (*0-89370-335-4*) Borgo Pr.

***Transylvanian Roots: The True Life Adventure of a Hungarian-American.** Michael Kosztarab. (Illus.). (Orig.). 1997. pap. 18.95 (*0-936015-72-1*) Pocahontas Pr.

Transylvanian Villagers: Three Centuries of Political, Economic & Ethnic Change. Katherine Verdery. LC 82-17411. (Illus.). 400p. (C). 1983. 48.00 (*0-520-04879-2*) U CA Pr.

Transzendentale Dialektik: Ein Kommentar zu Kants Kritik der reinen Vernunft, 4 pts. Heinz Heimsoeth. Incl. Pt. 1. Ideenlehre und Paralogismen. xii, 198p. 1966. pap. 28.00 (*3-11-005164-8*); Pt. 2. Vierfache Vernunftantinomie: Natur und Freiheit; intelligibler und empirischer Charakter. iv, 209p. 1967. pap. 28.00 (*3-11-005165-6*); Pt. 3. Ideal der reinen Vernunft: Die spekulativen Beweisarten vom Dasein Gottes; Dialektischer Schein und Leitideen der Forschung. vi, 235p. 1969. pap. 28.00 (*3-11-005166-4*); Pt. 4. Methodenlehre. 1971. pap. 28.00 (*3-11-003362-3*); (GER.). (C). Set pap. write for info. (*0-318-51650-0*) De Gruyter.

Transzendentale Prinzip der Urteilskraft: Eine Unterschung Zur Funktion und Struktur der Reflektierenden Urteilskraft Bei Kant. Peter Joachim. (Kantstudien Ergaenzungsheft Ser.: No. 126). xiii, 277p. (GER.). (C). 1992. lib. bdg. 90.80 (*3-11-013375-X*) De Gruyter.

Transzendentalienlehre der alten Ontologie, Pt. 1: Transzendentalienlehre im Corpus Aristotelicum. Karl Baerthlein. 415p. (C). 1972. 108.50 (*3-11-004021-2*) De Gruyter.

Tranvia a la Malvarrosa. Manuel Vicent. (FRE.). 1995. pap. 14.95 (*0-679-76523-9*) Random.

Tranx: Minor Tranquilizers, Major Problems. rev. ed. Jim Parker. (Illus.). 1991. pap. 2.00 (*0-89230-180-5*) Do It Now.

***Tranzit: A Bridge in Advance Russian Language Studies.** Daphne West & Michael Ransome. 1996. pap. 19.95 (*1-900405-00-8*, Pub. by Drake Intl Serv UK) Intl Spec Bk.

Trap. James Goldsmith. 1995. pap. text ed. 11.95 (*0-7867-0263-X*) Carroll & Graf.

Trap. Tabitha King. 352p. 1986. pap. 5.99 (*0-451-16030-4*, Sig) NAL-Dutton.

Trap. Ana M. Matute. Tr. by Maria Jose De La Camara & Robert Nugent from SPA. LC 96-17096. (Discoveries Ser.). 160p. (Orig.). (C). 1996. pap. 15.95 (*0-935480-81-1*) Lat Am Lit Rev Pr.

Trap. John E. Treherne. 176p. 1986. 14.95 (*0-8253-0390-7*) Beaufort Bks NY.

Trap. Rink Van Der Velde. Tr. by Henry J. Baron from FRI. 144p. 1995. pap. 8.95 (*0-9645502-0-2*) Redux Pubns.

***Trap.** Rink Van der Velde. LC 96-27256. 1997. write for info. (*1-877946-80-X*) Permanent Pr.

Trap: The Case Against Free Trade. James Goldsmith. LC 94-37295. 200p. 1994. 20.00 (*0-7867-0185-4*) Carroll & Graf.

Trap at Comanche Bend. large type ed. Max Brand. LC 93-7031. 335p. 1993. Alk. paper. lib. bdg. 19.95 (*1-56054-700-6*) Thorndike Pr.

Trap at Comanche Bend. Max Brand. 256p. 1994. reprint ed. mass mkt., pap. text ed. 3.99 (*0-8439-3622-3*) Dorchester Pub Co.

Trap Door & Other Stories to Twist Your Mind. Don Wulffson. (Screamers Ser.: No. 1). (J). (gr. 3-7). 1995. pap. 3.50 (*0-8167-3721-5*) Troll Communs.

Trap Doors & Trojan Horses. Lawrence M. Smith & Iris W. Collett. LC 89-81733. 1991. pap. text ed. 9.95 (*0-913878-45-6*) T Horton & Dghts.

Trap for Buchanan. large type ed. Jonas Ward. (Linford Western Library). 256p. 1989. pap. 15.99 (*0-7089-6715-9*, Linford) Ulverscroft.

***Trap for Cinderella.** Sebastien Japisot. Tr. by Helen Weaver. LC 97-15740. 1997. pap. 10.95 (*0-452-27779-5*, Plume) NAL-Dutton.

Trap for Fools. Amanda Cross. 224p. 1990. mass mkt. 5.95 (*0-345-35947-X*) Ballantine.

Trap for Sam Dodge. large type ed. Harry Whittington. (Linford Western Library). 1991. pap. 15.99 (*0-7089-6964-X*) Ulverscroft.

***Trap Live.** Carl Hiaasen. 1998. pap. write for info. (*0-375-70069-2*, Vin) Random.

Trap Responses of Flying Insects: The Influence of Trap Design on Capture Efficiency. Ed. by R. C. Muirhead-Thomson. (Illus.). 287p. 1991. text ed. 79.00 (*0-12-509755-7*) Acad Pr.

Trap with a Green Fence: Survival in Treblinka. Richard Glazar. Tr. by Roslyn Theobald. (Jewish Lives Ser.). 250p. 1995. 49.95 (*0-8101-1184-5*); pap. 16.95 (*0-8101-1169-1*) Northwestern U Pr.

Trapdoor Spiders. James E. Gerholdt. LC 95-14021. (Spiders Ser.). (J). (gr. k-3). 1995. lib. bdg. 13.99 (*1-56239-509-2*) Abdo & Dghtrs.

Trapdoor Spiders. L. Martin. (Spider Discovery Library). (Illus.). 24p. (J). (gr. k-5). 1988. lib. bdg. 11.94 (*0-86592-963-7*); lib. bdg. 8.95 (*0-685-58303-1*) Rourke Corp.

Trapdoor Springfield. Malden D. Waite & Bernard Ernst. 1985. 39.95 (*0-917714-20-2*) Gun Room.

***Trapdoor to Heaven.** Lesley Choyce. 1997. pap. 12.95 (*1-55082-157-1*, Pub. by Quarry Pr CN) LPC InBook.

Trapline Twins. Miki Collins & Julie Collins. LC 88-34231. (Illus.). 224p. (Orig.). (YA). (gr. 7). 1989. pap. 12.95 (*0-88240-332-X*) Alaska Northwest.

Traplines: Stories. Eden Robinson. 224p. 1996. 23.00 (*0-8050-4446-9*) H Holt & Co.

Trapnall Legacy. Jan Calloway. LC 81-67266. (Illus.). 112p. (Orig.). 1981. 9.95 (*0-9606278-0-4*); pap. 5.95 (*0-9606278-1-2*) AR Commemorative.

Trapped. Sandra L. Elkington. LC 96-84278. 224p. (Orig.). 1996. pap. 15.95 (*1-56167-306-4*) Am Literary Pr.

Trapped. rev. ed. Eunice Boeve. (Orig.). (YA). (gr. 6-9). 1996. reprint ed. pap. 5.00 (*0-88092-160-9*) Royal Fireworks.

Trapped! The Story of Floyd Collins. Robert K. Murray & Roger W. Brucker. LC 82-40177. (Illus.). 344p. 1982. reprint ed. pap. 19.95 (*0-8131-0153-0*) U Pr of Ky.

Trapped at the Bottom of the Sea. Frank E. Peretti. (Cooper Kids Adventure Ser.: No. 4). (J). (gr. 4-7). 1990. pap. 5.99 (*0-89107-594-1*) Crossway Bks.

Trapped Between Floors. Dick Squires. LC 89-92193. (Family Edition Ser.). (Illus.). 216p. (Orig.). 1989. per. 6.00 (*0-9624138-0-1*) D Squires.

***Trapped Beyond the Magic Attic.** Sheri C. Sinykin. Ed. by Judit Bodnar. (Magic Attic Club Ser.). (Illus.). 72p. (J). (gr. 2 up). 1997. 12.95 (*1-57513-102-1*) Magic Attic.

Trapped Beyond the Magic Attic see Magic Attic Club Series

Trapped by a Treacherous Twin. Charles H. Randall & Joan L. Bushnell. 1982. 5.00 (*0-87129-498-2*, T56) Dramatic Pub.

***Trapped by an Earthquake.** Kathryn Dahlstrom. (Good News Club Ser.). Date not set. pap. 4.99 (*1-55976-827-4*) CEF Press.

Trapped by Coal. Constance Horne. (Illus.). 144p. (Orig.). (YA). (gr. 8-12). 1994. pap. 6.95 (*0-88865-091-4*, Pub. by Pacific Educ Pr CN) Orca Bk Pubs.

***Trapped by Love: When Your Partner Has a Drinking Problem.** Sara M. & Johnson Institute (Minneapolis, Minn.) Staff. LC 97-7459. 1997. write for info. (*1-56246-141-9*, Johnson Inst) GWC Inc.

Trapped by Memory. Edith Bajema. (Open Door Bks.). (Illus.). 68p. (Orig.). 1992. pap. text ed. 3.95 (*1-56212-013-1*, 1740-2120) CRC Pubns.

Trapped by Success: The Eisenhower Administration & Vietnam. David L. Anderson. Ed. by William E. Leuchtenburg. (Contemporary American History Ser.). 296p. (C). 1991. text ed. 49.50 (*0-231-07374-7*) Col U Pr.

Trapped by Success: The Eisenhower Administration & Vietnam. David L. Anderson. Ed. by William E. Leuchtenburg. (Contemporary American History Ser.). 296p. (C). 1993. pap. 17.00 (*0-231-07375-5*) Col U Pr.

***Trapped by the Ice! Shackleton's Amazing Antarctic Adventure.** Michael McCurdy. LC 97-6976. (Illus.). 40p. (J). (gr. 1-5). 1997. 16.95 (*0-8027-8438-0*); lib. bdg. 17.85 (*0-8027-8439-9*) Walker & Co.

Trapped by the Mountain Storm. Aileen Fisher. 134p. 1992. 6.00 (*0-317-05258-6*) Rod & Staff.

Trapped Charges. Ed. by F. Kieffer. 236p. 1976. pap. 42.00 (0-08-019961-5, Pergamon Pr) Elsevier.

Trapped In A Cave! A True Story. Deborah Morris. LC 92-40731. (J). 1993. 7.99 (0-8054-4003-8, 4240-03) Broadman.

***Trapped in a Tiny Town.** A. G. Cascone. 1997. pap. 3.50 (0-8167-4395-9) Troll Communs.

Trapped in Apartheid: A Socio-Theological History of the English-Speaking Churches in South Africa. Charles Villa-Vicencio. LC 88-5348. 264p. reprint ed. pap. 75.30 (0-7837-5508-2, 2045278) Bks Demand.

Trapped in Bat Wing Hall. R. L. Stine. (Give Yourself Goosebumps Ser.: No. 3). (J). 1995. pap. 3.99 (0-590-56646-6) Scholastic Inc.

Trapped in Death Cave. Bill Wallace. LC 83-48962. 176p. (J). (gr. 4-7). 1984. 15.95 (0-8234-0516-8) Holiday.

Trapped in Death Cave. Bill Wallace. (J). (gr. 3-6). Date not set. pap. 3.50 (0-671-69014-0, PB Trade Paper) PB.

Trapped in Hill House. David LaRochelle. (Mad Mysteries Ser.). (J). (gr. 2 up). 1996. pap. 2.95 (0-8431-3945-5) Price Stern Sloan.

Trapped in Pharaoh's Tomb. Peter R. Doyle. (Daring Adventure Ser.: Vol. 2). 1993. pap. 5.99 (1-56179-143-1) Focus Family.

Trapped in Poverty: Labour-Market Decisions in Low-Income Households. Bill Jordan et al. 256p. (C). (gr. 13). 1991. text ed. 74.95 (0-415-06867-3, A6458) Routledge.

Trapped in Slickrock Canyon. Gloria Skurzynski. LC 83-14988. (Mountain West Adventure Ser.). (Illus.). 128p. (J). (gr. 4-6). 1984. 16.00 (0-688-02688-5) Lothrop.

Trapped in Tar: Fossils from the Ice Age. Caroline Arnold. LC 86-17614. (Illus.). 64p. (J). (gr. 3-6). 1900. pap. 6.95 (0-395-54783-0, Clarion Bks) HM.

***Trapped in the Arctic.** Pierre Berton. (Exploring the Frozen North Ser.). 88p. (J). (gr. 6-9). pap. 4.99 (0-7710-1447-3) McCland & Stewart.

Trapped in the Ashes. William W. Johnstone. 1989. mass mkt. 3.95 (0-8217-2626-9, Zebra Kensgtn) Kensgtn Pub Corp.

Trapped in the Lawyers' Den with Bloodsuckers. Thelma N. McKoy. 230p. 1988. pap. 12.00 (0-9649430-0-X) T N McKoy.

Trapped in the Mirror: Adult Children of Narcissistic Parents in Their Struggle for Self. Elan Golomb. 272p. 1995. pap. 10.00 (0-688-14071-8, Quill) Morrow.

***Trapped in the Net: The Unintended Consequences of Computerization.** Gene I. Rochlin. LC 96-41003. 310p. 1997. text ed. 29.95 (0-691-01080-3) Princeton U Pr.

Trapped in the Slickrock Canyon. Gloria Skurzynski. Ed. by Amy Cohn. LC 83-14988. (Illus.). 128p. (J). (gr. 7 up). 1994. reprint ed. pap. 4.95 (0-688-13621-4) Morrow.

Trapped in Toyland. Francine Pascal. (Sweet Valley Kids Super Ser.: No. 8). 96p. (J). (ps-3). 1994. pap. 3.99 (0-553-48251-3) Bantam.

Trapped Strawberry: Poems. Petru Cardu. Tr. by B. Walker & D. Marinkov from CRO. 96p. (Orig.). 9000. pap. 16.95 (0-948259-83-3, Pub. by Forest Bks UK) Dufour.

Trapped under Ice: Death Row Anthology. U. S. Prisoners Staff. Ed. by Julie Zimmerman. LC 95-79754. (Illus.). 80p. (Orig.). 1995. pap. 8.00 (1-879418-19-3) Biddle Pub.

Trapped Woman: Catch-22 in Deviance & Control. Ed. by Josefina Figuira-McDonough & Rosemary Sarri. LC 86-27967. (Sage Sourcebooks for the Human Services Ser.: No. 4). 459p. 1987. reprint ed. pap. 130.90 (0-608-01508-3, 2059552) Bks Demand.

Trapper. Stephen Cosgrove. (Serendipity Bks.). (Illus.). 32p. (Orig.). (J). (gr. 1-4). 1981. pap. 3.95 (0-8431-0587-9) Price Stern Sloan.

Trappers & Traders. Gail Stewart. (Wild West in American History Ser.). (Illus.). 32p. (J). (gr. 3-8). 1990. lib. bdg. 18.00 (0-86625-401-3); lib. bdg. 13.50 (0-685-58655-3) Rourke Corp.

Trappers & Traders. Jane V. Barker. Ed. by Sybil Downing. (Colorado Heritage Ser.). (Illus.). 36p. (J). (gr. k-6). reprint ed. pap. 3.95 (1-878611-03-8) Silver Rim Pr.

Trapper's Bible: Traps, Snares, & Pathguards. Dale Martin. (Illus.). 72p. 1987. pap. 8.00 (0-87364-406-9) Paladin Pr.

Trapper's Blood. David Thompson. (Wilderness Ser.: No. 17). 176p. (Orig.). 1994. mass mkt., pap. text ed. 3.50 (0-8439-3566-9) Dorchester Pub Co.

Trapper's Companion. (Illus.). 155p. pap. 4.00 (0-936622-24-5) A R Harding Pub.

Trappers Handbook. A. R. Harding. 64p. 1951. pap. 3.00 (0-936622-25-3) A R Harding Pub.

Trapper's Moon. Jory Sherman. 1995. 4.99 (0-8125-8877-0) Forge NYC.

Trappers of New York. Jeptha R. Simms. 287p. 1993. reprint ed. lib. bdg. 79.00 (0-7812-5198-2) Rprt Serv.

Trappers of New York: A Biography of Nicholas Stoner & Nathaniel Foster. Jeptha R. Simms. LC 79-25915. (Illus.). 308p. 1987. reprint ed. 24.00 (0-916346-38-2) Purple Mnt Pr.

Trappers of the Far West: Sixteen Biographical Sketches. Ed. by Leroy R. Hafen. LC 83-5824. (Illus.). xviii, 334p. 1983. reprint ed. pap. 10.95 (0-8032-7218-9, Bison Books) U of Nebr Pr.

Trapping As a Profession. A. R. Harding. 95p. 1975. pap. 3.00 (0-936622-26-1) A R Harding Pub.

Trappings of Experience. James D. Quinn. LC 94-90893. 120p. (Orig.). 1996. pap. 9.00 (1-56002-553-0, Univ Edtns) Aegina Pr.

Trappings of Gold. Manoje Basu. Tr. by S. L. Ghosh. 176p. 1969. pap. 2.00 (0-88253-013-5) Ind-US Inc.

Trappings of Power: Ballistic Missiles in the Third World. Janne E. Nolan. 209p. 1991. 32.95 (0-8157-6096-5); pap. 12.95 (0-8157-6095-7) Brookings.

Trappings of the Great Basin Buckaroo. Caroline J. Hadley. LC 93-22217. (Illus.). 216p. (C). 1993. 44.95 (0-87417-223-3) U of Nev Pr.

***Trappist: Living in the Land of Desire.** Michael Downey. LC 97-19977. (Illus.). 128p. 1998. 29.95 (0-8091-0491-1) Paulist Pr.

Traprock: Connecticut Rock Climbs. Ken Nichols. LC 81-71989. (Illus.). 479p. 1990. 20.00 (0-930410-14-9) Amer Alpine Club.

Traps. Caryl Churchill. 67p. 1989. pap. 11.95 (1-85459-095-2, Pub. by N Hern Bks UK) Theatre Comm.

Traps. Sondra S. Olsen. LC 91-19062. (Iowa Short Fiction Award Ser.). 159p. 1991. 22.95 (0-87745-346-2) U of Iowa Pr.

Traps & Seals: Stratigraphy-Capillary Traps, Vol. 2. Ed. by Norman H. Foster & Edward A. Beaumont. (Treatise of Petroleum Geology Ser.: No. 7). (Illus.). 410p. 1988. 15.00 (0-89181-406-X, 730) AAPG.

Traps & Seals: Structural-Fault-Seal & Hydrodynamic Traps, Vol. 1. Ed. by Norman H. Foster & Edward A. Beaumont. (Treatise of Petroleum Geology Reprint Ser.: No. 6). (Illus.). 554p. 1988. pap. 10.00 (0-89181-405-1, 727) AAPG.

Traps for the Young. Anthony Comstock. Ed. by Robert H. Bremner. LC 67-17306. (John Harvard Library). (Illus.). 293p. 1967. 29.95 (0-674-90555-5) HUP.

***Trapshooter's Bible - Precision Shooting.** James Russell. (Illus.). 120p. (Orig.). 1998. pap. write for info. (0-916367-10-X) J R Pub.

***Trapshooting Is a Game of Opposites.** Dick Bennett. (Illus.). 132p. (Orig.). 1996. pap. 19.95 (0-925012-05-X) Shotgun Sports.

Trapshooting Secrets. James Russell. (Illus.). 154p. (Orig.). 1997. pap. 34.95 (0-916367-09-6) J R Pub.

Trapunto & Stippling. John F. Flynn. 1994. 15.95 (0-614-04276-3) Flynn Quilt Frame.

Trapunto by Machine. Hari Walner. Ed. by Elizabeth Aneloski & Diana Roberts. (Illus.). 96p. (Orig.). 1996. pap. 21.95 (1-57120-006-1, 10130) C & T Pub.

***Traquenard.** large type ed. Jean Larteguy. 256p. 1996. pap. 25.99 (2-258-00152-8) Ulverscroft.

Tras el Alma de America Latina - Searching for the Soul of Latin America. Arnoldo Canclini. 192p. (Orig.). (SPA.). 1992. pap. 7.50 (0-311-09139-3) Casa Bautista.

Trasfondo Constitucional De Puerto Rico: Primera Parte, 1887-1914. 3rd ed. Reece B. Bothwell. 65p. (C). 1971. pap. 2.00 (0-8477-0821-7) U of PR Pr.

Trash. Dorothy Allison. LC 88-30175. 176p. (Orig.). 1988. pap. 10.95 (0-932379-51-6); lib. bdg. 22.95 (0-932379-52-4) Firebrand Bks.

***Trash.** Cherie Bennett & Jeff Gottesfeld. (Trash Ser.: No. 1). 224p. (YA). 1997. mass mkt. 3.99 (0-425-15851-9) Berkley Pub.

Trash. Ed. by John W. Dagion. (True Revelations & Strange Happenings Ser.: Vol. 1). (Illus.). 192p. (Orig.). 1985. pap. 10.95 (0-917342-07-0) Leyland Pubns.

Trash. J. M. Patten. LC 94-42670. (Eye on the Environment Ser.). (J). (gr. 2-6). 1995. write for info. (1-55916-101-9) Rourke Bk Co.

Trash! Charlotte Wilcox. (Carolrhoda Photo Bks.). (Illus.). 40p. (J). (ps-5). 1988. lib. bdg. 14.96 (0-87614-311-7, Carolrhoda) Lerner Group.

Trash. Amy Yamada. 384p. 1996. pap. 11.95 (0-14-025418-8, Penguin Bks) Viking Penguin.

Trash! Charlotte Wilcox. (Photo Bks.). (Illus.). 40p. (J). (ps-5). 1989. reprint ed. pap. 5.95 (0-87614-511-X, Lerner Publctns) Lerner Group.

Trash: A Novel. Amy Yamada. Ed. by Chikako Noma & Susan Bell. Tr. by Sonya L. Johnson. 384p. 1995. 18.00 (1-56836-018-5) Kodansha.

***Trash: Dirty Big Secrets.** Cherie Bennett & Jeff Gottesfeld. (Trash Ser.: No. 4). 176p. 1997. mass mkt. 3.99 (0-425-16044-0) Berkley Pub.

***Trash: Good Girls, Bad Boys.** Cherie Bennett & Jeff Gottesfeld. (Trash Ser.: No. 3). 176p. 1997. mass mkt. 3.99 (0-425-15937-X) Berkley Pub.

***Trash: Love, Lies, & Video.** Cherie Bennett & Jeff Gottesfeld. (Trash Ser.: No. 2). 224p. 1997. mass mkt. 3.99 (0-425-15907-8) Berkley Pub.

***Trash No. 5.** Cherie Bennett & Jeff Gottesfeld. 176p. 1997. mass mkt. 3.99 (0-425-16087-4) Berkley Pub.

***Trash No. 6.** Cherie Bennett & Jeff Gottesfeld. 1998. mass mkt. write for info. (0-425-16188-9) Berkley Pub.

***Trash Aesthetics.** Deborah Cartmell. 1997. pap. text ed. 15.95 (0-7453-1202-0, Pub. by Pluto Pr UK) LPC InBook.

***Trash Aesthetics: Popular Culture & Its Audience.** LC 96-45671. (Film/Fiction Ser.). 1997. write for info. (0-7453-1203-9, Pub. by Pluto Pr UK) LPC InBook.

Trash & Treasure. Patricia Lakin. LC 93-49844. (My School Ser.). (Illus.). (J). 1994. lib. bdg. 21.40 (0-8114-3865-1) Raintree Steck-V.

Trash & Treasure: The Complete Book about Garage Sales. Jack Wilkie & Chris Wilkie. LC 87-73354. (Illus.). 96p. (Orig.). 1988. pap. 7.95 (0-945221-00-2) Bent Twig.

Trash Artists Workshop. Linda Allison. LC 80-84184. (Crafts Workshop Ser.). (J). (gr. 3-8). 1981. pap. 9.99 (0-8224-9780-8) Fearon Teach Aids.

Trash Bash. Judy Delton. (Pee Wee Scouts Ser.: No. 16). 96p. (J). (ps-3). 1992. mass mkt. 3.99 (0-440-40592-0, YB BDD) BDD Bks Young Read.

Trash Busters Series, 6 vols., Set. Jamie Daniel & Veronica Bonar. (Illus.). (J). (gr. 2 up). 1994. lib. bdg. 111.60 (0-8368-1055-4) Gareth Stevens Inc.

***Trash Conflicts: A Science & Social Studies Curriculum on the Ethics of Disposal.** Amy Ballin et al. (Illus.). 220p. (Orig.). 1993. pap. 25.00 (0-942349-06-7) Eductrs Soc Respons.

Trash into Treasure: Recycling Ideas for Library-Media Centers Containing 100 Easy-to-Do Ideas. Eleanor Silverman. LC 87-36449. (Illus.). 176p. 1988. 24.00 (0-8108-2101-X) Scarecrow.

Trash Marks the Spot. Richard Jarboe. LC 88-72336. 51p. (Orig.). 1989. pap. 7.00 (0-916383-76-8) Aegina Pr.

Trash or Treasure: How to Fine the Best Buyers of Antiques, Collectibles & Other Undiscovered Treasures. Tony Hyman. (Where to Sell Ser.). 560p. (Orig.). 1994. pap. 29.95 (0-937111-03-1) Treasure Hunt Pubns.

Trash or Treasure II: How to Find the Best Buyers of Antiques, Collectibles, & Other Undiscovered Treasures. Tony Hyman. 640p. (Orig.). 1997. pap. 29.95 (0-937111-06-6) Treasure Hunt Pubns.

Trash Talk. Hank Herman. (Super Hoops Ser.: No. 3). 96p. (J). 1996. mass mkt. 3.50 (0-553-48275-0, Skylark BDD) BDD Bks Young Read.

Trash to Cash: How Businesses Can Save Money & Increase Profits. Fran Berman. 260p. 1996. pap. 29.95 (1-884015-96-4) St Lucie Pr.

Trash to Cash: New Business Opportunities in the Post-Consumer Waste Stream. Susan Williams. 150p. (Orig.). 1991. pap. 20.00 (0-931035-84-8) IRRC Inc DC.

Trash to Treasure. (Americana Bks.). (Illus.). 1979. 3.00 (0-911410-48-1) Applied Arts.

***Trash to Treasure.** Leisure Arts Staff. 1997. 19.95 (1-57486-048-8) Leisure AR.

***Trash-Trash: Love, Lies & Video, Sunset Forever.** Cherie Bennett. 1997. mass mkt. 71.82 (0-425-16014-9) Berkley Pub.

Trash! Trash! Trash! Shelly Nielsen. Ed. by Julie Berg. LC 93-18952. (Target Earth Ser.). (J). 1993. pap. 7.49 (1-56239-408-8); lib. bdg. 15.98 (1-56239-192-5) Abdo & Dghtrs.

Trash Trio: Three Screenplays. 2nd ed. John Waters. 1996. pap. 12.95 (1-56025-127-1) Thunders Mouth.

Trash Trucks. Daniel Kirk. LC 95-47881. (Illus.). 32p. (J). (ps-3). 1997. 15.95 (0-399-22927-2, Putnam) Putnam Pub Group.

Trash Unlimited: Linking Environmental Studies with Everyday Life. Bev McKay. (Illus.). 64p. (Orig.). 1993. teacher ed. 8.95 (0-86530-276-6) Incentive Pubns.

Trashcan Kids. Richard Benedict. LC 92-19499. 53p. (Orig.). 1992. pap. 11.95 (0-87120-194-1, 611-92132) Assn Supervision.

Trashing of America. Caras. 1992. write for info. (0-201-52367-1) Addison-Wesley.

Trashing of America. Charles Pirmell. 1975. 7.00 (0-686-11117-6); pap. 3.50 (0-686-11118-4) Kulchur Foun.

Trashing the Economy: How Runaway Environmentalism Is Wrecking America. Ron Arnold & Alan Gottlieb. 672p. (Orig.). 1993. pap. 19.95 (0-939571-13-7) Free Enter Pr.

Trashing the Economy: How Runaway Environmentalism Is Wrecking America. 2nd ed. Ron Arnold & Alan Gottlieb. 670p. (Orig.). 1994. pap. 19.95 (0-939571-17-X) Free Enter Pr.

Trashing the Planet: How Science Can Help Us Deal with Acid Rain, Depletion of the Ozone, & Nuclear Waste (Among Other Things) Dixy L. Ray & Louis R. Guzzo. LC 90-8344. 210p. 1990. 19.95 (0-89526-544-3) Regnery Pub.

Trashman Lives! Spain. Ed. by Robert Fiore. (Illus.). 144p. (Orig.). 1989. pap. 12.95 (0-930193-74-1) Fantagraph Bks.

Trashproof Resumes: Your Guide to Cracking the Job Market. Timothy Haft. (Princeton Review Ser.). 1995. pap. 12.00 (0-679-75911-5) Random.

Trask. Don Berry. LC 60-5835. 376p. 1976. reprint ed. pap. 3.95 (0-89174-001-5) Comstock Edns.

Trastamaras de Castilla y Aragon en el Siglo XV. Ramon Menendez Pidal. Ed. by L. S. Fernandez et al. (Historia de Espana Ser.: Vol. 17). 1026p. (SPA.). 1992. 195.00 (0-7859-0558-8, 842394817X) Fr & Eur.

***Tratado: Le Gustaria Conocer a Dios...?** Bright. 16p. (SPA.). pap. write for info. (1-56063-923-7) Editorial Unilit.

***Tratado - Tract: Cuatro Leyes Espirituales - Four Spiritual Laws.** Bill Bright. 65p. (SPA.). write for info. (1-56063-928-8) Editorial Unilit.

Tratado de Cooperacion Amazonica Primer Encuentro Internacional de Organismos de Desarrollo de la Region Amazonica. 7.00 (0-8270-2292-1) OAS.

Tratado de Cooperacion Amazonica Primer Seminario Internacional de Hidrologia y Climatologia de la Amazonia. 7.00 (0-8270-2133-X) OAS.

Tratado de Cooperacion Amazonica Seminario sobre Transporte Fluvial. 7.00 (0-8270-2473-8) OAS.

Tratado de Cooperacion Amazonica Seminario sobre Transporte por Carreteras en la Amazonia. 7.00 (0-8270-2304-9) OAS.

Tratado de Enfermeria Medico Quirurgica. 6th ed. Lillian S. Brunner. 1989. text ed. 79.95 (0-07-104007-2) McGraw.

Tratado de Enfermeria Practica. 4th ed. Beverly W. Dugas. 1986. pap. text ed. 39.95 (0-07-104008-0) McGraw.

Tratado De Instrumentos Negociables. 2nd enl. rev. ed. Basilio Santiago Romero. LC 79-22321. (Illus.). 1043p. 1981. 35.00 (0-8477-2636-3) U of PR Pr.

Tratado de la Epidemia e de la Pestilenc: Biblioteca Nacional de Madrid, I-51. Vasco De Taranto. Ed. by Maria Purificacion Zabia. (Medieval Spanish Medical Texts Ser.: No. 16). 6p. (SPA.). 1987. 10.00 incl. fiche (0-940639-12-2) Hispanic Seminary.

Tratado de la Phisonomia: Biblioteca Nacional, Madrid, I-51. Vernon Hicks. Ed. by Maria Nieves-Sanchez & Tim Dennison. (Medieval Spanish Medical Texts Ser.: No. 14). 8p. (SPA.). 1987. 10.00 incl. fiche (0-940639-10-6) Hispanic Seminary.

Tratado de Paleografia Espanola, 3 vols., 1-Texto. 3rd ed. Agustin Millares Carlos. 1176p. 1989. write for info. (0-318-65348-6) Elliots Bks.

Tratado de Paleografia Espanola, 3 vols., 2-Laminas. 3rd ed. Carlos A. Millares. 1176p. 1989. write for info. (0-318-65349-4) Elliots Bks.

Tratado de Paleografia Espanola, 3 vols., 3-Laminas. 3rd ed. Carlos A. Millares. 1176p. 1989. write for info. (0-318-65350-8) Elliots Bks.

Tratado de Paleografia Espanola, 3 vols., Set. 3rd ed. Carlos A. Millares. 1176p. 1989. 975.00 (84-239-4986-9) Elliots Bks.

Tratado de Sociologia. Eugenio Maria De Hostos. LC 87-25566. 358p. 1989. 12.95 (0-8477-3606-7); pap. 7.50 (0-8477-3605-9) U of PR Pr.

Tratado Del Esphera y Del Arte Del Marear. Francisco Faleiro. 55.00 (0-8201-1480-4) Schol Facsimiles.

Tratado Interamericano De Asistencia Reciproca. Incl. Vol. 1. Aplicaciones, 1948-1959. 5.00 (0-8270-0670-5); Vol. 2. Aplicaciones, 1960-1972. 5.00 (0-8270-0675-6); Vol. 3. Aplicaciones, 1973-1976. (ENG & SPA.). 2.00 (0-685-03625-1); (Serie de Tratados Multilaterales, Convenciones y Acuerdos). (SPA.). write for info. (0-318-54749-X) OAS.

Tratado Nuevo: Alvarez Chanca, Biblioteca Nacional, Madrid, I-51. Ed. by Maria Purificacion Zabia. (Medieval Spanish Medical Texts Ser.: No. 19). 6p. (SPA.). 1987. 10.00 incl. fiche (0-940639-15-7) Hispanic Seminary.

Tratado Sobre el Titulo de Duque. Juan De Mena. Ed. by Louise V. Fainberg. (Textos B Ser.: No. 16). 134p. (SPA.). (C). 1976. 35.00 (0-7293-0009-9, Pub. by Tamesis Bks Ltd UK) Boydell & Brewer.

Tratado Sobre la Predicacion. J. A. Broadus. Tr. by Ernesto Barocio. Orig. Title: On the Preparation & Delivery of Sermons. 336p. 1985. reprint ed. pap. 10.99 (0-311-42034-6) Casa Bautista.

Tratado TeUrico, Practico y Critico De Derecho Privado De PuertoriqueOo. Eduardo V. Bote. 1992. 800.00 (0-614-05985-2) MICHIE.

Tratado Util. Licenciado Fores: Biblioteca Nacional de Madrid, I-51. Ed. by Maria Purificacion Zabia. (Medieval Spanish Medical Texts Ser.: No. 17). 6p. (SPA.). 1987. 10.00 incl. fiche (0-940639-13-0) Hispanic Seminary.

Tratados E Convencoes Firmados Na Sexta Conferencia Internacional Americana. (Treaty Ser.: No. 35). (POR.). 1928. pap. 1.00 (0-8270-0450-8) OAS.

Tratados Sobre el Canal de Panama Suscritos Entre la Republica de Panama y los Estados Unidos de America. OAS, General Secretariat, Bureau of Legal Affairs Staff. (Serie Sobre Tratados: No. 57 & 57a). 157p. (C). 1979. text ed. 9.00 (0-685-03626-X) OAS.

Tratados y Convenciones Interamerianos. Oas General Secretariat Staff. (Serie Sobre Tratados: No. 9). 303p. (C). 1980. 15.00 (0-685-03627-8) OAS.

Tratameinto Medico Emerg Adultos. Vogel & David H. Manhoff. 1991. pap. 7.95 (0-916363-09-0) EMT Inc.

Tratamiento de las Fracturas de la Mandibula los Maxilares el Cigoma. Antonio Reyes-Guerra. LC 77-551324. 193p. (SPA.). 1969. 25.00 (0-317-04088-X); pap. 20.00 (0-317-04089-8) Am Soc Ad Anesthesia Dentistry.

Tratamiento Medico de Emergencia para Infantes. Stephen Vogel & David H. Manhoff. 1990. pap. 7.95 (0-916363-03-1) EMT Inc.

Tratamiento Medico de Emergencia para Ninos. Stephen Vogel & David H. Manhoff. 1990. pap. 7.95 (0-916363-02-3) EMT Inc.

***Tratando Con Deseo Incontrolado.** M. McMinn. 225p. (SPA.). 1995. pap. write for info. (0-614-27147-9) Editorial Unilit.

***Tratando con Deseo Incontrolado - Dealing with Desires You Cannot Control.** M. McMinn. 225p. (SPA.). 1995. write for info. (0-614-24405-6) Editorial Unilit.

***Tratando Con Los Deseos Que Usted No Puede Controlar.** McMinn. (Serie Realidades - Realities Ser.). 28p. (SPA.). pap. write for info. (1-56063-999-7) Editorial Unilit.

Trate Bien a Su Bebe Brochure. (SPA.). 1994. 0.50 (0-8151-3867-9) Mosby Yr Bk.

***Tratelo Con Oracion.** C. Stanley. (SPA.). 6.95 (0-8297-1906-7) Life Pubs Intl.

Trato Hecho!, Vol. 1. John McMinn. 1995. lab manual ed., wbk. ed., pap. text ed. 14.80 (0-13-459140-2) P-H.

Trato Hecho, Vol. 2. McMinn. 256p. (C). 1995. pap. text ed. 32.80 (0-13-459116-X) P-H.

Trato Hecho!, Vol. 2. John McMinn. 1995. lab manual ed., wbk. ed., pap. text ed. 14.80 (0-13-459173-9) P-H.

Trato Hecho! Spanish for Real Life. John McMinn et al. 1995. teacher ed. write for info. (0-13-446949-6) P-H.

Trato Hecho! Spanish for Real Life. John McMinn et al. 1995. text ed. 56.00 (0-13-327974-X) P-H.

Trato Hecho! Spanish for Real Life, Pt. 2. abr. ed. John McMinn et al. 1995. pap. text ed. 28.00 (0-13-447012-5) P-H.

Trato Hecho! Spanish for Real Life, Vol. 1. abr. ed. John McMinn et al. 256p. (C). 1995. pap. text ed. 32.80 (0-13-459108-9) P-H.

Trattato di Musica see Monuments of Music & Music Literature in Facsimile

Trattato...di Canto Figurato. fac. ed. Pietro Aaron. (Monuments of Music & Music Literature in Facsimile Ser., Series II: Vol. 129). 1979. lib. bdg. 40.00 (0-8450-2329-2) Broude.

Trattoria. Patricia Wells. LC 93-16679. 1993. 25.00 (0-688-10532-7) Morrow.

Trattoria Cooking. Biba Caggiano. 352p. 1992. 25.00 (0-02-520252-9) Macmillan.

Trattoria Pasta. Loukie Werle. LC 95-9540. 96p. 1996. 12.95 (0-8120-9534-0) Barron.

An Asterisk (*) at the beginning of an entry indicates that the title is appearing in BIP for the first time.

Trauma. M. Houts. 1959. write for info. (*0-8205-1740-2*) Bender.

Trauma. Jakobiec. 1995. 39.00 (*0-316-06076-3*) Little.

***Trauma.** Skinner. (Companion Series to Bailey & Love's Short Practice of Surgery). (Illus.). 512p. (C). 1997. text ed. 110.00 (*0-412-61940-7*, Chap & Hall NY); text ed. write for info. (*0-412-61950-4*, Chap & Hall NY) Chapman & Hall.

Trauma. 3rd ed. Moore et al. (Illus.). (C). 1995. text ed. 165.00 (*0-8385-9010-1*, A9010-8) Appleton & Lange.

Trauma: Emergency Surgery & Critical Care, 2 vols. Ed. by John H. Siegel. (Illus.). 1206p. 1987. text ed. 169.00 (*0-443-08330-4*) Churchill.

Trauma: Explorations in Memory. Cathy Caruth. 328p. 1995. text ed. 48.50 (*0-8018-5009-6*); pap. text ed. 15.95 (*0-8018-5007-X*) Johns Hopkins.

Trauma: Pathogenesis & Treatment. Westaby. (Illus.). 400p. 1989. 165.00 (*0-433-35502-6*) Buttrwrth-Heinemann.

Trauma: The Pain That Stays. Robert M. Hicks. 256p. (gr. 10). 1996. pap. 10.99 (*0-8007-5596-0*) Revell.

***Trauma Vol. 8: Perspectives on Theory, Research, & Intervention.** Ed. by Dante Cicchetti & Sheree L. Toth. (Rochester Symposium on Developmental Psychopathology Ser.: Vol. 1056-6511). 576p. 1997. 99. 50 (*1-878822-97-7*) Univ Rochester Pr.

Trauma, Amnesia & the Denial of Abuse. R. Falconer et al. 1995. 24.95 (*0-614-04198-8*) Family Violence.

Trauma & Dreams. Ed. by Deirdre Barrett. LC 96-13023. 288p. 1996. 35.00 (*0-674-90552-0*) HUP.

Trauma & Healing under State Terrorism. Inger Agger & Soren B. Jensen. LC 95-42699. 240p. (C). 1996. pap. 25. 00 (*1-85649-384-9*, Pub. by Zed Bks Ltd UK); text ed. 59.95 (*1-85649-383-0*, Pub. by Zed Bks Ltd UK) Humanities.

Trauma & Its Metabolic Problems. Ed. by R. N. Barton. (British Medical Bulletin Ser.: Vol. 41, No. 3). (Illus.). 104p. 1985. 56.00 (*0-443-03250-5*) Churchill.

Trauma & Its Wake, Vol. 1: The Study & Treatment of Post-Traumatic Stress Disorder. Ed. by Charles R. Figley. LC 84-29344. (Psychosocial Stress Ser.: No. 4). 484p. 1985. text ed. 50.95 (*0-87630-385-8*) Brunner-Mazel.

Trauma & Its Wake, Vol. 2: Traumatic Stress Theory, Research, & Intervention. Ed. by Charles R. Figley. LC 84-29344. (Psychosocial Stress Ser.: No. 8). 368p. 1986. text ed. 49.95 (*0-87630-431-5*) Brunner-Mazel.

Trauma & Mastery in Life & Art: With an Original New Docudrama. Gilbert J. Rose. LC 96-23726. 1996. pap. 24.95 (*0-8236-8319-2*) Intl Univs Pr.

***Trauma & Memory: Clinical & Legal Controversies.** Ed. by Paul S. Applebaum et al. (Illus.). 512p. 1997. 55.00 (*0-19-510065-4*) OUP.

Trauma & Mobile Radiography. Michael W. Drafke. LC 89-17230. (Illus.). 347p. 1990. spiral bd., pap. 23.95 (*0-8036-2805-6*) Davis Co.

Trauma & Rebirth: Intergenerational Effects of the Holocaust. John J. Sigal & Morton Weinfeld. LC 88-34027. 221p. 1989. text ed. 55.00 (*0-275-92906-X*, C2906, Praeger Pubs) Greenwood.

***Trauma & Recovery: The Aftermath of Violence, from Domestic Abuse to Political Terror.** Judith Herman. 288p. 1997. pap. 14.00 (*0-465-08730-2*) Basic.

Trauma & Self. Charles B. Strozier & Michael Flynn. LC 96-1354. 280p. 1996. 58.50 (*0-8476-8228-5*); pap. 22.95 (*0-8476-8229-3*) Rowman.

Trauma & Survival: Post-Traumatic & Dissociative Disorders in Women. Elizabeth A. Waites. 280p. (C). 1993. 32.95 (*0-393-70150-6*) Norton.

Trauma & Symbolism. Bernard D. Fine & Herbert F. Waldhorn. LC 73-6942. (Kris Study Group Monograph: No. 5). 1973. 25.00 (*0-8236-6643-3*) Intl Univs Pr.

Trauma & the Therapist: Countertransference & Vicarious Traumatization in Psychotherapy with Incest Survivors. Laurie A. Pearlman & Karen W. Saakvitne. 320p. 1995. 40.00 (*0-393-70183-2*) Norton.

Trauma & the Vietnam War Generation: Report of Findings from the National Vietnam Veterans Readjustment Study. Intro. by Richard A. Kulka et al. LC 89-71185. (Brunner-Mazel Psychosocial Stress Ser.: No. 18). (Illus.). 352p. 1990. text ed. 34.95 (*0-87630-573-7*) Brunner-Mazel.

***Trauma & Transformation: A Traumatic Incident Reduction Manual.** Gerald D. French & Frank A. Gerbode. 208p. 1998. text ed. 39.95 (*1-57224-078-4*) New Harbinger.

Trauma & Transformation: Growing in the Aftermath of Suffering. Richard G. Tedeschi. LC 95-11803. 163p. (C). 1995. 39.95 (*0-8039-5256-2*) Sage.

Trauma & Transformation: Growing in the Aftermath of Suffering. Richard G. Tedeschi. LC 95-11803. 144p. (C). 1995. pap. 18.50 (*0-8039-5257-0*) Sage.

***Trauma Anesthesia & Critical Care of Neurological Injury.** Ed. by Kenneth J. Abrams & Christopher M. Grande. LC 97-14865. (TraumaCare Ser.). (Illus.). 576p. 1997. 98.00 (*0-87993-625-8*) Futura Pub.

Trauma Care Systems: Clinical, Financial, & Political Considerations. Ed. by John G. West et al. LC 83-11223. 208p. 1983. text ed. 59.95 (*0-275-91418-6*, C1418, Praeger Pubs) Greenwood.

***Trauma Center.** J. Lloyd & E. Herman. 1997. mass mkt. 5.99 (*0-8041-1546-X*) Ivy Books.

***Trauma Code: On the Scene with Fire & Rescue.** Sonny Shepherd. (Illus.). 130p. (Orig.). 1996. pap. 24.95 (*0-9655450-6-7*) Raven Ent.

***Trauma, Dissociation, & Impulse Dyscontrol in Eating Disorders.** Johan Vanderlinden & Walter Vandereycken. 256p. 1997. write for info. (*0-87630-843-4*) Brunner-Mazel.

Trauma, Growth, & Personality. Phyllis Greenacre. LC 71-75188. 1969. reprint ed. 50.00 (*0-8236-6645-X*) Intl Univs Pr.

Trauma Handbook. David V. Feliciano. 1997. pap. text ed. 30.00 (*0-8385-9011-X*) P-H.

Trauma in the Lives of Children: Crisis & Stress Management Techniques for Counselors & Other Professionals. Kendall Johnson. LC 88-32037. 256p. 1989. pap. 15.95 (*0-89793-056-8*) Hunter Hse.

Trauma in the Lives of Children: Crisis & Stress Management Techniques for Teachers, Counselors & Student Service Professionals. Kendall Johnson. 256p. (C). 1990. reprint ed. lib. bdg. 41.00 (*0-8095-6318-5*) Borgo Pr.

***Trauma in the Workplace: The Book about Chronic Work Trauma.** Linda Stennett-Brewer. 255p. (Orig.). 1997. pap. 21.95 (*0-9658056-0-3*) Nepenthe Pubns.

***Trauma Informatics.** Kimball I. Maull & Jeffrey S. Augenstein. LC 97-8491. (Computers in Health Care Ser.). 312p. 1996. 59.00 (*0-387-94359-5*) Spr-Verlag.

Trauma Management. David J. Kreis & Geraldo Gomez. 600p. 1989. 120.00 (*0-316-50371-1*) Little.

***Trauma Manual.** Andrew Peitzman et al. (Illus.). 250p. 1997. spiral bd. 32.95 (*0-316-69834-2*) Lppncott-Raven.

***Trauma, Memory, & Dissociation.** Ed. by J. Douglas Bremner & Charles R. Marmar. LC 97-3211. (Progress in Psychiatry Ser.). 439p. 1997. text ed. 54.00 (*0-88048-753-4*, 8753) Am Psychiatric.

Trauma Novel: Contemporary Symbolic Depictions of Collective Disaster. Ronald Granofsky. (American University Studies: Ser. III, Vol. 55). 216p. (C). 1995. text ed. 40.95 (*0-8204-2736-5*) P Lang Pubng.

Trauma Nursing: Comprehensive Curriculum. Bayley. (Nursing-Health Science Ser.). 1992. pap. text ed. 45.00 (*0-86720-331-5*) Jones & Bartlett.

Trauma Nursing: Comprehensive Curriculum. Bayley. 1992. 52.50 (*0-86720-628-4*) Jones & Bartlett.

Trauma Nursing: From Resuscitation Through Rehabilitation. 2nd ed. Virginia D. Cardona et al. LC 92-49094. (Illus.). 1104p. 1993. text ed. 99.00 (*0-7216-4333-7*) Saunders.

Trauma Nursing: Principles & Practice. Barbara A. Knezevich. (Illus.). 640p. 1986. text ed. 54.95 (*0-8385-9006-3*, A9006-6) Appleton & Lange.

Trauma Nursing: The Art & Science. Janet A. Neff. LC 92-16291. 808p. (C). (gr. 13). 1992. text ed. 57.95 (*0-8016-6655-4*) Mosby Yr Bk.

Trauma of Birth. Otto Rank. LC 93-21385. (Illus.). 256p. reprint ed. pap. 7.95 (*0-486-27974-X*) Dover.

Trauma of Decolonization: The Dutch & West New Guinea. Arend Lijphart. LC 66-12506. (Yale Studies in Political Science). 316p. reprint ed. pap. 90.10 (*0-317-11338-0*, 2022014) Bks Demand.

Trauma of Moving: Psychological Issues for Women. Audrey T. McCollum. (Library of Social Research: Vol. 182). 312p. (C). 1990. text ed. 54.00 (*0-8039-3699-0*); pap. text ed. 24.95 (*0-8039-3700-8*) Sage.

Trauma of the Foot & Ankle. Bruce Sangeorzan. 400p. 1996. text ed. write for info. (*0-7817-0300-X*) Lppncott-Raven.

Trauma of the Middle Ear. Michael Strohm. (Advances in Oto-Rhino-Laryngology Ser.: Vol. 35). (Illus.). x, 254p. 1986. 139.25 (*3-8055-4087-6*) S Karger.

Trauma of the Nose & Paranasal Sinuses. Robert H. Mathog et al. Ed. by Howard Levine. LC 94-26571. (Rhinology & Sinusology Ser.). (Illus.). 184p. 1994. 69. 00 (*0-86577-526-5*) Thieme Med Pubs.

Trauma of the Spine. B. Wimmer et al. (Radiology of the Spine Ser.). (Illus.). 120p. 1990. 118.00 (*0-387-50977-1*) Spr-Verlag.

Trauma of Time: A Psychoanalytic Investigation. Irvine Schiffer. LC 77-92182. 279p. 1978. 40.00 (*0-8236-6646-8*) Intl Univs Pr.

Trauma of Transgression: Psychotherapy of Incest Victims. Ed. by Selma Kramer & Salman Akhtar. LC 91-4565. 200p. 1991. 27.50 (*0-87668-554-8*) Aronson.

***Trauma of Transition: The Psycho-Social Cost of Ethiopian Immigration to Israel.** Ruben Schindler & David Ribner. 128p. 1997. text ed. 55.95 (*1-85972-453-1*, Pub. by Avebury Pub UK) Ashgate Pub Co.

Trauma of Transparency - Chinese Edition. Grant Howard. Tr. by Daniel Chen. 232p. (CHI.). 1988. pap. 5.50 (*1-56582-091-6*) Christ Renew Min.

Trauma of War: Stress & Recovery in Vietnam Veterans. Ed. by Stephen M. Sonnenberg et al. LC 85-6094. 454p. 1985. text ed. 48.00 (*0-88048-048-3*, 8048) Am Psychiatric.

Trauma Organised Systems: Physical & Sexual Abuse in Families. Arnon Bentovim. 144p. 1992. pap. text ed. 25.95 (*1-85575-012-0*, Pub. by Karnac Bks UK) Brunner-Mazel.

Trauma Radiology. Ed. by James J. McCort. (Illus.). 483p. 1990. text ed. 135.00 (*0-443-08645-1*) Churchill.

***Trauma Radiology Companion: Methods, Guidelines & Imaging Fundamentals.** Eric J. Stern. LC 97-4092. (Illus.). 400p. 1997. pap. text ed. 65.00 (*0-397-51733-5*) Lppncott-Raven.

Trauma Ready Reference. Susan B. Sheehy. 44p. (C). (gr. 13). 1994. spiral bd. 15.00 (*0-8151-7823-9*) Mosby Yr Bk.

Trauma Research Methodology. Ed. by Eve B. Carlson. LC 95-26829. viii, 291p. (Orig.). 1996. pap. text ed. 18.95 (*0-9629164-8-X*, CATR) Sidran Pr.

Trauma Response: Treatment for Emotional Injury. Diane S. Everstine & Louis Everstine. 240p. (C). 1993. 27.95 (*0-393-70123-9*) Norton.

Trauma, Sepsis, & Shock: The Physiological Basis of Therapy. Clowes. (Science & Practice of Surgery Ser.: Vol. 15). 608p. 1988. 175.00 (*0-8247-7502-3*) Dekker.

Trauma Surgery. Donovan. 350p. (C). (gr. 13). 1994. text ed. 99.00 (*0-8016-6677-5*) Mosby Yr Bk.

***Trauma Surgery.** 4th ed. Donald D. Trunkey et al. (Rob & Smith's Operative Surgery Ser.). (Illus.). 482p. (C). 1993. text ed. write for info. (*0-407-00677-X*, Chap & Hall NY) Chapman & Hall.

***Trauma Surgery & Surgical Critical Care: The Requisitese.** Hiatt et al. (Illus.). 544p. (C). (gr. 13 up). 1998. text ed. 65.00 (*0-8151-2624-7*, 31643) Mosby Yr Bk.

Trauma to the Genito-Urinary Tract: A Practical Guide to Management. Nicholas Cetti & Roger S. Kirby. LC 96-39334. 208p. 1996. 50.00 (*0-7506-1587-7*) Buttrwrth-Heinemann.

***Trauma to the Middle & Inner Ear.** Michael D. Dilea et al. LC 96-50974. (Self-Instructional Package Ser.). (Illus.). 60p. (Orig.). 1997. pap. text ed. 25.00 (*1-56772-054-4*, 5506300) AAO-HNS.

Trauma, Transformation, & Healing: An Integrative Approach to Theory, Research, & Post-Traumatic Therapy. John P. Wilson. LC 89-639. (Psychosocial Stress Ser.: No. 14). 368p. 1989. text ed. 47.95 (*0-87630-540-0*) Brunner-Mazel.

Trauma Update for the EMT. Kimball I. Maull et al. 272p. 1992. pap. 24.00 (*0-89303-889-X*, 740503) P-H.

Trauma Victim: Practical Suggestions. Hyer, Lee, & Associates Staff. 768p. (C). 1994. 45.95 (*1-55959-047-5*) Accel Devel.

Traumatic Abuse & Neglect of Children. Gertrude Williams & John Money. LC 79-3684. 1980. pap. 19.95 (*0-8018-2926-7*) Johns Hopkins.

Traumatic & Reconstructive Urology. Jack W. McAninch. Ed. by Richard Zorab. LC 95-10055. 640p. 1996. text ed. 155.00 (*0-7216-3886-4*) Saunders.

Traumatic Aphasia: Its Syndromes, Psychology & Treatment. A. R. Luria. Tr. by Douglas Bowden. LC 68-17903. (Janua Linguarum, Ser. Major: No. 5). 1970. text ed. 101.55 (*90-279-0717-X*) Mouton.

Traumatic Brain Edema. Ed. by F. Cohadon et al. (FIDIA Research Ser.). 195p. 1987. 82.00 (*0-387-96507-6*) Spr-Verlag.

Traumatic Brain Injury. Paul Bach-y-Rita. LC 88-71751. (Illus.). 331p. 1989. 74.95 (*0-939957-18-3*) Demos Vermande.

Traumatic Brain Injury: Evaluation & Litigation. Richard W. Petrocelli et al. 643p. 1994. 95.00 (*1-55834-172-2*) MICHIE.

Traumatic Brain Injury: Mechanisms of Damage, Assessment, Intervention, & Outcome. Ed. by Erin D. Bigler. LC 90-3855. 458p. 1990. text ed. 41.00 (*0-89079-201-1*, 1484) PRO-ED.

Traumatic Brain Injury: Pathophysiology & Neuropsychological Evaluation, Vol. 1. Ralph M. Reitan & Deborah Wolfson. LC 86-60951. (Illus.). 425p. 1986. text ed. 59.95 (*0-934515-06-9*) Neuropsych Pr.

Traumatic Brain Injury: Recovery & Rehabilitation, Vol. 2. Ralph M. Reitan & Deborah Wolfson. LC 86-60952. (Illus.). 400p. 1987. text ed. 59.95 (*0-934515-07-7*) Neuropsych Pr.

Traumatic Brain Injury Activities: Back into Life. Andrew K. Gruen & Lynn S. Gruen. LC 93-46707. 1994. pap. 39.00 (*0-930599-95-0*) Thinking Pubns.

Traumatic Brain Injury & Neuropsychological Impairment. R. S. Parker. xii, 452p. 1990. 95.95 (*0-387-97239-0*) Spr-Verlag.

Traumatic Brain Injury in Children & Adolescents: A Sourcebook for Teachers & Other School Personnel. Mary P. Mira et al. LC 92-3454. 152p. (Orig.). 1992. pap. text ed. 21.00 (*0-89079-531-2*, 4037) PRO-ED.

Traumatic Brain Injury Rehabilitation. Ed. by Mark J. Ashley & David K. Krych. LC 95-7284. 480p. 1995. 95. 00 (*0-8493-9463-5*, 9463) CRC Pr.

Traumatic Brain Injury Rehabilitation: A Guide for Speech-Language Pathologists. Gillis. 320p. 1996. 40.00 (*0-7506-9650-8*) Buttrwrth-Heinemann.

***Traumatic Brain Injury Rehabilitation: Children & Adolescents.** 2nd ed. Mark Ylvisaker. LC 97-26005. 1997. write for info. (*0-7506-9972-8*) Buttrwrth-Heinemann.

Traumatic Brain Injury Rehabilitation: Services, Treatments & Outcomes. Ed. by M. Anne Chamberlain et al. 312p. 1995. pap. 60.50 (*1-56593-307-9*, 0631) Singular Publishing.

Traumatic Brain Injury Vocational Rehabilitation: Job Placement Models. Paul Wehman et al. Ed. by Robert Fraser & David Clemmons. LC 91-75927. (Traumatic Brain Injury Rehabilitation Training Ser.). 74p. (Orig.). 1991. spiral bd. 22.95 (*1-878205-22-6*) GR Press.

***Traumatic Disability Syndromes.** Laurence Miller. Date not set. 32.00 (*0-393-70256-1*) Norton.

Traumatic Disorders of the Ankle. Ed. by W. C. Hamilton. (Illus.). 300p. 1984. 196.00 (*0-387-90831-5*) Spr-Verlag.

Traumatic Disorders of the Knee. Ed. by John M. Siliski. LC 93-46007. (Illus.). 456p. 1994. 160.00 (*0-387-94171-1*) Spr-Verlag.

Traumatic Experiences of Nurses: When Your Profession Becomes a Nightmare. Huub Buyssen. 112p. 1996. pap. 16.95 (*1-85302-377-9*, Pub. by J Kingsley Pubs UK) Taylor & Francis.

Traumatic Head Injury in Children. Ed. by Sarah H. Broman & Mary E. Michel. (Illus.). 256p. 1995. 47.50 (*0-19-509428-X*) OUP.

Traumatic Hip Dislocation in Childhood. A. Barquet. (Illus.). 160p. 1987. 93.95 (*0-387-17009-X*) Spr-Verlag.

Traumatic Stress. George Tribune. Ed. by Joyce Carbone. (Illus.). 52p. (Orig.). 1995. pap. 4.95 (*1-878116-48-7*) JVC Bks.

Traumatic Stress: From Theory to Practice. Ed. by John R. Freedy & Stevan E. Hobfoll. (Series on Stress & Coping). 402p. (C). 1995. 59.50 (*0-306-45020-8*, Plenum Pr) Plenum.

Traumatic Stress: The Effects of Overwhelming Experience on Mind, Body, & Society. Ed. by Bessel A. Van der Kolk et al. LC 96-10818. 1996. lib. bdg. 55.00 (*1-57230-088-4*) Guilford Pr.

Traumatic Stress in Critical Occupations: Recognition, Consequences, & Treatment. Douglas Paton & John M. Violanti. LC 95-47069. (Illus.). 260p. 1996. 59.95 (*0-398-06577-2*); pap. 39.95 (*0-398-06578-0*) C C Thomas.

Traumatic Subarachnoid Haemorrhage. A. Kakarieka. LC 96-3359. 128p. 1996. pap. 29.95 (*3-540-60771-4*) Spr-Verlag.

Traumatized Hand & Wrist: Radiographic & Anatomic Correlation. Gelula. (Illus.). 288p. 1991. text ed. 87.00 (*0-7216-1217-2*) Saunders.

Traumatologie und Rehabilitation, No. 2: Organverletzungen. Ed. by U. Laffer et al. (Basler Beitraege zur Chirurgie Ser.: Vol. 4). (Illus.). vi, 118p. 1992. 77.50 (*3-8055-5459-1*) S Karger.

Traumatology As Treated by Traditional Chinese Medicine: A Comprehensive Text. Lee Lo. 80p. (Orig.). (C). 1989. pap. text ed. 24.95 (*0-685-29019-0*) Zee Lo.

Traumatology of the Skull Base: Anatomy, Clinical & Radiological Diagnosis, Operative Treatment. Ed. by Madjid Samii & J. Brihaye. (Illus.). 260p. 1983. 79.95 (*0-387-12528-0*) Spr-Verlag.

Travail see Quatre Evangiles

Travail & Triumph. Michael Phillips & Judith Pella. (Russians Ser.: Vol. 3). 400p. (Orig.). 1992. pap. 10.99 (*1-55661-174-9*) Bethany Hse.

Travail & Triumph: Black Life & Culture in the South Since the Civil War. Arnold H. Taylor. LC 76-5264. (Contributions in Afro-American & African Studies: No. 26). 326p. (Orig.). 1977. text ed. 55.00 (*0-8371-8912-8*, TTT/, Greenwood Pr) Greenwood.

Travail de la Femme dans la Grece Ancienne. Pieter Herfst. Ed. by Moses Finley. LC 79-4982. (Ancient Economic History Ser.). (FRE.). 1979. reprint ed. lib. bdg. 23.95 (*0-405-12368-X*) Ayer.

Travail et Ses Representations. Ed. by M Cartier. 313p. 1984. pap. write for info. (*0-318-65450-4*) Gordon & Breach.

Travail in an Arab Land. Samuel A. Romanelli. LC 88-3931. (Judaic Studies Ser.). (Illus.). 238p. 1989. reprint ed. pap. 67.90 (*0-608-01679-9*, 2062335) Bks Demand.

Travail of Nature: The Ambiguous Ecological Promise of Christian Theology. H. Paul Santmire. LC 84-47934. 288p. (Orig.). 1991. pap. 20.00 (*0-8006-1806-8*, 1-1806, Fortress Pr) Augsburg Fortress.

Travail of the Flag. Shelli J. Baker. LC 89-63069. (Illus.). 96p. 1989. pap. 5.95 (*0-89221-176-8*) New Leaf.

Travailleurs de la Mer. Victor Hugo. (Illus.). 60p. (FRE.). 1966. 15.95 (*0-7859-0057-8*, M11199) Fr & Eur.

Travailleurs de la Mer. Victor Hugo. (Folio Ser.: No. 1197). (FRE.). pap. 12.95 (*2-07-037197-2*) Schoenhof.

Travaux. Georges Navel. (FRE.). 1979. pap. 10.95 (*0-7859-4127-4*) Fr & Eur.

Travaux d'Approche. Michel Butor. 1972. pap. 10.95 (*0-7859-2771-9*, F90050) Fr & Eur.

Travaux Pra. Hoffmann. 1973. pap. 11.95 (*0-684-13577-9*) S&S Trade.

Travaux Publics des Etats-Unis Amerique en 1870 Souvenirs d'Une Mission. J. Malezieux & E. Malezieux. (Industrial Antiquities Ser.). (Illus.). 256p. (FRE.). (C). 1989. reprint ed. 150.00 (*1-85297-014-6*, Pub. by Archival Facs UK) St Mut.

Travel. Blythe Camenson. LC 94-43362. (VGM Career Portraits Ser.). 96p. 1995. 13.95 (*0-8442-4365-5*) NTC Pub Grp.

***Travel.** Bobbie Kalman. (Historical Etchings Gallery Ser.). (Illus.). 32p. (J). 1997. pap. 7.95 (*0-86505-916-0*) Crabtree Pub Co.

Travel? Hanif Kureishi. 1999. pap. 18.95 (*0-670-82322-8*) Viking Penguin.

Travel. Sue Sheldon. (Illus.). 160p. 1991. 40.00 (*0-86299-903-0*, Pub. by Sutton Pubng UK) Bks Intl VA.

Travel: Anything Book. 1993. 7.99 (*0-517-10007-X*) Random Hse Value.

Travel: Careers in Travel. Deborah Crisfield. LC 93-15211. (Now Hiring Ser.). (Illus.). 48p. (J). (gr. 5-6). 1994. lib. bdg. 14.95 (*0-89686-790-0*, Crstwood Hse) Silver Burdett Pr.

Travel Accounts of Indiana, 1679-1961. Shirley S. McCord. 331p. 1970. 13.50 (*1-885323-24-7*) IN Hist Bureau.

Travel Adventures & Trivia Map: California. Steve Rice. 1986. 2.95 (*0-912831-04-9*) Map Ink.

Travel Adventures on the Company's Nickel: Fun on Business Trips. Frank Perkins. LC 95-92462. (Illus.). 1996. pap. 14.95 (*0-9648512-0-2*) Oak Pubng.

Travel Agency Accounting Procedures. James M. Poynter. 320p. 1991. text ed. 34.50 (*0-8273-3389-7*) Delmar.

Travel Agency Accounting Procedures. James M. Poynter. 320p. 1991. teacher ed. 11.95 (*0-8273-3390-0*) Delmar.

Travel Agency Bookkeeping Made Simple. 2nd ed. Douglas Thompson & Mary Miller-Marshall. 200p. 1991. ring bd. 45.00 (*0-936831-04-9*) Dendrobium Bks.

Travel Agency Management. George C. Brownell. LC 75-15476. 1975. pap. 12.50 (*0-87651-206-6*) Southern U Pr.

Travel Agency Management. Fuller. (Hospitality, Travel & Tourism Ser.). 1994. pap. 25.25 (*0-538-70693-7*) S-W Pub.

Travel Agent. Wilma Boyd. (Illus.). 256p. 1989. pap. 15.95 (*0-13-930058-9*) P-H.

Travel Agent: Dealer in Dreams. 2nd ed. Aryear Gregory. (Illus.). 270p. 1985. pap. 19.95 (*0-8403-3539-3*, Ntl Pubs Blck) P-H.

Travel Agent: Dealer in Dreams. 4th ed. Aryear Gregory. 375p. 1992. pap. text ed. 55.00 (*0-13-948340-3*) P-H.

***Travel Agent in Cyber School: The Internet & the Library Media Program.** John F. LeBaron et al. LC 96-31826. 200p. 1996. pap. text ed. 25.00 (*1-56308-333-7*) Libs Unl.

Travel Agent Official Travel Industry Directory. Ed. by Eric Friedheim. 320p. 1994. spiral bd. 19.95 (*1-56333-995-1*) Masquerade.

Travel Agents: From Caravans & Clippers to the Concorde. Eric Friedheim. (Illus.). 288p. 1992. 23.00 (*0-9632300-0-X*) E Friedheim.

Travel Air: Wings Over the Prairie. Ed. by Edward H. Phillips. LC 82-82791. (Illus.). 128p. 1992. 21.95 (*0-911139-00-1*) Flying Bks.

Travel Air: Wings over the Prairie. Edward H. Philips. (Illus.). 128p. reprint ed. pap. 21.95 (*0-911139-17-6*) Flying Bks.

Travel Alarm. limited ed. Naomi Shihab-Nye. (New Texas Poetry Sampler Ser.). 32p. 1992. 10.00 (*0-930324-27-7*) Wings Pr.

Travel Alone & Love It: A Flight Attendant's Guide to Solo Travel. Sharon Wingler. (Illus.). 160p. (Orig.). 1996. pap. 14.95 (*1-886094-35-7*) Chicago Spectrum.

Travel America: California. Photos by Christian Heeb. (Illus.). 96p. 1995. 27.95 (*1-55868-297-X*) Gr Arts Ctr Pub.

Travel Analysis Methods for the 1980s. (Special Reports: No. 201). 202p. 1983. 24.80 (*0-309-03609-7*) Transport Res Bd.

Travel & Adventure in South-East Africa: Being the Narrative of the Last Eleven Years Spent by This Author on the Zambesi & Its Tributaries. Frederick C. Selous. LC 72-5527. (Black Heritage Library Collection). 1977. reprint ed. 54.95 (*0-8369-9148-6*) Ayer.

Travel & Drama in Shakespeare's Time. Michele M. Willems. 278p. (C). 1996. text ed. 54.95 (*0-521-47500-7*) Cambridge U Pr.

Travel & Entertainment: Business or Pleasure? 64p. 1995. pap. 6.50 (*0-318-33158-6*, 5435) Commerce.

Travel & Entertainment Deduction Guide: With Answers to Vital Questions on How to Nail Down Big Cash Savings under the All-New T&E Setup. Executive Reports Corporation Editorial Staff. LC 85-1619. 1985. 35.00 (*0-13-930090-2*) Exec Reports.

Travel & Hospitality Career Directory. 2nd ed. R. Fry. 1992. 17.95 (*0-8103-9427-8*) Visible Ink Pr.

Travel & Hospitality Career Directory. 2nd ed. Ed. by Bradley J. Morgan. (Career Advisor Ser.). 300p. 1992. 39.00 (*0-8103-5605-8*, 101577) Visible Ink Pr.

Travel & Hospitality Online: A Guide to Online Services. Gary Holleman. LC 95-40400. (Hospitality, Travel & Tourism Ser.). 288p. 1996. pap. 29.95 (*0-442-02187-9*) Van Nos Reinhold.

Travel & Learn: The New Guide to Educational Travel. 2nd enl. rev. ed. Evelyn Kaye. LC 91-76693. (Illus.). 350p. (Orig.). 1992. pap. 12.95 (*0-9626231-2-1*) Blue Panda.

Travel & Learn: Where to Go for Everything You'd Love to Know. 3rd rev. ed. Evelyn Kaye. LC 94-70200. (Travel Resource Guides Ser.). (Illus.). 250p. (Orig.). Date not set. 19.95 (*0-9626231-5-6*) Blue Panda.

***Travel & Leisure.** MacMillan. 1997. pap. text ed. 334.80 (*0-02-862094-1*) Macmillan.

Travel & Leisure Graphics: A Pamphlet Collection Featuring Hotels, Package Tours &... P.I.E. Books Editorial Staff. (Illus.). 224p. 1996. 85.00 (*4-938586-87-8*, Pub. by PIE Bks JA) Bks Nippan.

Travel & Leisure Guide: London. 1996. 13.95 (*0-614-12825-0*) Macmillan.

Travel & Leisure Guide: New York. 1996. 13.95 (*0-614-12826-9*) Macmillan.

Travel & Leusire Guide: Washington, D. C. 1996. 13.95 (*0-614-12824-2*) Macmillan.

Travel & Older Adults. Allison St. Claire. LC 90-24411. (Choices & Challenges: An Older Adult Reference Ser.). 300p. 1991. lib. bdg. 45.00 (*0-87436-573-2*) ABC-CLIO.

Travel & Roads in England. Virginia A. LaMar. LC 61-1916. (Folger Guides to the Age of Shakespeare Ser.). 1961. 4.95 (*0-918016-23-1*) Folger Bks.

***Travel & Site Guide to Birds of Costa Rica with Side Trips to Panama.** Aaron D. Sckerak. (Illus.). 256p. (Orig.). 1996. pap. 16.95 (*1-55105-084-6*) Lone Pine.

Travel & Sports. 4th ed. John C. Dean. 300p. 1990. pap. 2.95 (*0-942427-05-X*) Travel & Sports SF.

Travel & Sports Guide. John C. Dean. (Illus.). 336p. (Orig.). 1988. pap. 9.95 (*0-942427-02-5*) Travel & Sports SF.

Travel & Sports Guide. 3rd ed. John Dean et al. Ed. by Karla Jacobs & Dorthy Huysman. 256p. (Orig.). 1989. pap. 2.95 (*0-942427-04-1*) Travel & Sports SF.

Travel & the Sense of Wonder. John M. Brinnin. LC 92-2906. 3.95 (*0-8444-0743-7*) Lib Congress.

Travel & the Single Male: The World's Best Destinations for the Single Male. Bruce Cassirer. 256p. 1992. pap. 14.95 (*0-9634234-0-1*) TSM Pub.

Travel & Tourism: A Legislators' Guide. 116p. 1991. 20.00 (*1-55516-219-3*, 2109) Natl Conf State Legis.

Travel & Tourism: An Introduction to Travel Agency Operations. Armin D. Lehmann. LC 77-12589. 1978. pap. write for info. (*0-672-97090-2*) Macmillan.

Travel & Tourism- - Resorts-Air-Cruise-Hotels-Casinos. 4th rev. ed. Richard M. Zink. (Illus.). 64p. (YA). (gr. 9 up). 1994. pap. 14.95 (*0-939469-42-1*) Zinks Career Guide.

Travel & Tourism Careers Guide Book. Lulu Lizon. Ed. by Janet Parkerson. (Illus.). 133p. (Orig.). (C). 1987. pap. 19.95 (*0-935423-05-2*) Educ Pubns.

Travel & Tourism Data. Euromonitor Staff. 320p. 1988. 160.00 (*0-86338-131-6*, Pub. by Euromonitor Pubns UK) Gale.

Travel & Tourism in Michigan: A Statistical Profile. 2nd ed. Ed. & Intro. by Daniel M. Spotts. (Illus.). 570p. (C). 1991. pap. 40.00 (*0-9645518-0-2*) MSU Trvl Tourism.

Travel & Tourism Industry: Strategies for the Future. Ed. by A. Hodgson. LC 86-25296. (Illus.). 168p. 1987. pap. text ed. 32.95 (*0-08-033893-3*, Prgamon Press) Buttrwrth-Heinemann.

Travel & Tourism Laws in Australia & New Zealand. Gary N. Heilbronn. 500p. 1991. 133.00 (*1-86287-039-X*, Pub. by Federation Pr AU) Gaunt.

Travel & Tourism Marketing Techniques. 2nd ed. 280p. 1988. text ed. 33.95 (*0-8273-3300-5*) Delmar.

Travel & Tourism Marketing Techniques. 2nd ed. Reilly. (Hospitality, Travel & Tourism Ser.). 1988. teacher ed., pap. 11.50 (*0-8273-3301-3*) Delmar.

Travel & Transport. H. Edom. (Explainers Ser.). (Illus.). 24p. (J). (gr. 2-4). 1990. pap. 4.50 (*0-7460-0446-X*); lib. bdg. 12.95 (*0-88110-401-9*) EDC.

Travel & Transportation. Sharon Smith. (Social Studies Ser.). 24p. (gr. 5-9). 1976. student ed. 5.00 (*0-8209-0247-0*, SS-14) ESP.

Travel & Travellers of the Middle Ages. Ed. by Arthur P. Newton. LC 67-23252. (History of Civilization Ser.). 1977. 17.95 (*0-8369-0743-4*) Ayer.

Travel & Travellers of the Middle Ages. Arthur P. Newton. 1972. 59.95 (*0-8490-1228-7*) Gordon Pr.

Travel & Tropical Medicine Manual. 2nd ed. Elaine C. Jong & Russell McMullen. (Illus.). 448p. 1995. pap. text ed. 49.50 (*0-7216-4214-4*) Saunders.

Travel & Vacation Advertising Cuts from the Twenties & Thirties. Ed. by Trina Robbins & Casey Robbins. LC 94-13334. (Pictorial Archive Ser.). 1994. pap. write for info. (*0-486-28199-X*) Dover.

Travel & Vacation Discount Guide. Paige Palmer. LC 86-30514. 64p. 1994. pap. 5.95 (*0-87576-189-5*) Pilot Bks.

***Travel & Vacation Phone Book U. S. A. 1997: A Pocket Guide to 100 Major Travel Destinations in the United States.** 1997. pap. 50.00 (*0-7808-0295-0*) Omnigraphics Inc.

Travel Arizona. rev. ed. Joseph Stocker. 128p. 1984. pap. 10.95 (*0-916179-03-6*) Ariz Hwy.

Travel Arizona: The Back Roads. James E. Cook et al. Ed. by Dean Smith & Wesley Holden. (Illus.). 136p. (Orig.). 1989. pap. 10.95 (*0-916179-19-2*) Ariz Hwy.

***Travel Arizona: The Scenic Byways.** Paula Searcy. 1997. pap. text ed. 14.95 (*0-916179-62-1*) Ariz Hwy.

Travel As Metaphor: From Montaigne to Rousseau. Georges Van Den Abbeele. 224p. (C). 1991. pap. text ed. 15.95 (*0-8166-1934-4*) U of Minn Pr.

***Travel Atlas of South Africa.** Globetrotter Staff. 1997. pap. text ed. 12.95 (*1-85368-847-9*) Globe Pequot.

***Travel Bargains: How to Pay Less & Travel More.** Art Evans. LC 96-70724. (Illus.). 216p. (Orig.). 1997. pap. 9.95 (*0-9626508-9-7*) Photo Data Res.

Travel Basics. Catherine Watson. (Illus.). 130p. (Orig.). 1984. pap. 5.95 (*0-932272-09-6*) Minneapolis Tribune.

Travel Behaviour Research: Fifth International Conference on Travel Behaviour. International Association for Travel Behaviour Staff. (Illus.). 296p. 1990. text ed. 78.95 (*0-566-07062-6*, Pub. by Avebury Pub UK) Ashgate Pub Co.

Travel Blurt! The Webster's Game of Word Racing! Tim Walsh. Date not set. write for info. (*0-9646973-1-9*) Keys Pub.

Travel Book: A Vacation Journal. Carol Inouye. (Illus.). 160p. 1985. 16.95 (*0-8109-1683-5*) Abrams.

Travel Book: Guide to the Travel Guides. 2nd ed. Jon O. Heise & Julia R. Rinehart. LC 93-15822. 404p. 1993. 42.50 (*0-8108-2697-6*) Scarecrow.

Travel Book of Johann Rauh: From Lochau, Bavaria to Hagerstown, Indiana 1840-1860. Charles Teetor. (Illus.). 128p. 1991. pap. 6.00 (*0-9628651-1-7*) Teetor Twn Pr.

Travel Bug. L. Schwartz. LC 92-74104. (Educational Travel Ser.). 120p. (J). (gr. 2-9). 1993. 9.95 (*0-88160-256-6*, LW203) Learning Wks.

Travel Bugs: Arizona. Sun Tree Publishing Staff. 1995. pap. 18.00 (*0-671-50349-9*) S&S Trade.

Travel Bugs: Bahamas. Sun Tree Publishing Staff. 1995. pap. 18.00 (*0-671-50345-6*) S&S Trade.

Travel Bugs: Bermuda. Sun Tree Publishing Staff. 1995. pap. 18.00 (*0-671-50343-X*) S&S Trade.

Travel Bugs: Caribbean. 1994. pap. 18.00 (*0-671-88281-3*, P-H Travel) P-H Gen Ref & Trav.

Travel Bugs: Colorado. Sun Tree Publishing Staff. 1995. pap. 18.00 (*0-671-50315-4*) S&S Trade.

Travel Bugs: Costa Rica. Sun Tree Publishing Staff. 1995. pap. 18.00 (*0-671-50304-9*) S&S Trade.

Travel Bugs: Czech Republic & Slovenia. Sun Tree Publishing Staff. 1995. pap. 18.00 (*0-671-50325-1*) S&S Trade.

Travel Bugs: Egypt. Sun Tree Publishing Staff. 1995. pap. 18.00 (*0-671-50314-6*) S&S Trade.

Travel Bugs: Guatemala & Belize. Sun Tree Publishing Staff. 1995. pap. 18.00 (*0-671-50332-4*) S&S Trade.

Travel Bugs: Israel. Sun Tree Publishing Staff. 1995. pap. 18.00 (*0-671-50322-7*) S&S Trade.

Travel Bugs: Netherlands. Sun Tree Publishing Staff. 1995. pap. 18.00 (*0-671-50316-2*) S&S Trade.

Travel Bugs: Switzerland. Sun Tree Publishing Staff. 1995. pap. 18.00 (*0-671-50311-1*) S&S Trade.

Travel Bugs: Virgin Islands. Sun Tree Publishing Staff. 1995. pap. 18.00 (*0-671-50331-6*) S&S Trade.

Travel by Cargo Ship. Hugo Verlomme. (Cadogan Guides Ser.). (Illus.). 336p. (Orig.). 1995. pap. 14.95 (*1-86011-035-5*, Pub. by Cadogan Bks UK) Globe Pequot.

Travel by Charter. J. James Hasenau. LC 74-27858. 100p. (Orig.). 1975. pap. 9.55 (*0-913042-04-8*) Holland Hse Pr.

Travel by Road Through the Ages. R. J. Unstead. (Junior Reference Ser.). (Illus.). (J). (gr. 7-10). 1983. 14.95 (*0-7136-1812-4*) Dufour.

Travel by Sea. Robert Hoare. Ed. by R. J. Unstead. (Junior Reference Ser.). (J). (gr. 7 up). 1975. 14.95 (*0-7136-0119-1*) Dufour.

Travel Career Development. 5th ed. Patricia Gagnan & Karen Silva. LC 92-10507. Orig. Title: Travel Career Development. 325p. (C). 1992. text ed. 45.95 (*0-256-11977-5*) Irwin.

***Travel Career Development.** 6th rev. ed. Patricia J. Gagnon & Bruno Ociepka. (Illus.). 300p. (C). 1997. lthr. 46.95 (*0-931202-21-3*) Inst Cert Trav Agts.

***Travel Career Development.** 6th rev. ed. Patricia J. Gagnon & Bruno Ociepka. (Illus.). (C). 1997. teacher ed. write for info. (*0-931202-22-1*) Inst Cert Trav Agts.

***Travel Career Development.** 6th rev. ed. Patricia J. Gagnon & Bruno Ociepka. (Illus.). (C). 1997. student ed., wbk. ed. 19.95 (*0-931202-23-X*) Inst Cert Trav Agts.

Travel Career Development see Travel Career Development

Travel Careers & How to Get Started. Dorian Robb, pseud. 74p. (Orig.). (C). 1989. pap. 9.95 (*0-9622910-0-5*) Gar Pub Co.

Travel Characteristics at Large-Scale Suburban Activity Centers. (National Cooperative Highway Research Program Report: No. 323). 106p. 1989. 11.00 (*0-309-04620-3*) Transport Res Bd.

Travel-Concerning Health Benefits & Dangers, Risks, Warnings & Strategies for Survival & Enjoyment: Index of New Information. Wendy J. Pepper. (Illus.). 150p. 1994. 44.50 (*0-7883-0016-4*); pap. 39.50 (*0-7883-0017-2*) ABBE Pubs Assn.

Travel Consultant's On-Site Inspection Journal. rev. ed. Gerald E. Mitchell. (Illus.). 192p. 1990. reprint ed. student ed. 30.00 (*0-945439-00-8*) G E Mitchell & Assocs.

Travel Crosswords for Kids. Ed. by Keesing U. K. Ltd. Staff. 96p. (Orig.). (J). 1993. pap. 9.95 (*0-572-01786-3*, Pub. by W Foulsham UK) Trans-Atl Phila.

Travel Demand Forecasting, Travel Behavior, & Telecommunications. LC 92-30914. 100p. 1992. 21.00 (*0-309-05221-1*, R1357) Transport Res Bd.

Travel Diaries of Peter Pears, 1936-1978. Peter Pears. Ed. by Philip Reed. (Aldeburgh Studies in Music: No. 2). (Illus.). 272p. (C). 1995. 45.00 (*0-85115-364-X*) Boydell & Brewer.

Travel-Diaries of William Beckford of Fonthill, 2 vols. William Beckford. (BCL1-PR English Literature Ser.). 1992. reprint ed. Set. lib. bdg. 150.00 (*0-7812-7435-4*) Rprt Serv.

Travel Diary of Peter Tolstoi: A Muscovite in Modern Europe. Peter Tolstoi. Tr. & Intro. by Max J. Okenfuss. LC 87-17616. 1988. text ed. 35.00 (*0-87580-130-7*) N Ill U Pr.

Travel Dice. Thomas W. Shapcott. LC 86-30755. (Poetry Ser.). 84p. (Orig.). 1987. pap. text ed. 14.95 (*0-7022-2077-9*, Pub. by Univ Queensland Pr AT) Intl Spec Bk.

***Travel Dictionary.** Claudine Dervaes. 336p. 1996. pap. 15.95 (*0-933143-53-2*) Solitaire Pub.

***Travel, Entertainment, & Gifts.** 3rd ed. Richard W. Maches. 181p. (C). 1996. pap. text ed. 69.95 (*1-878025-98-8*) Western Schls.

Travel Fact & Travel Fiction: Studies on Fiction, Literary Tradition, Scholarly Discovery, & Observation in Travel Writing. Ed. by Zweder R. Von Martels. LC 94-27051. (Studies in Intellectual History: 55). 1994. 90.00 (*90-04-10112-8*) E J Brill.

Travel Far, Pay No Fare. Anne M. Lindbergh. LC 91-35886. 192p. (J). (gr. 5-8). 1992. lib. bdg. 14.89 (*0-06-021776-6*) HarpC Child Bks.

Travel Fitness. Rebecca M. Johnson & William C. Tulin. LC 95-1294. (Illus.). 216p. (Orig.). 1995. pap. 14.95 (*0-87322-655-0*, PJOH0655) Human Kinetics.

Travel for Free. 1991. 12.95 (*0-685-50664-9*) Agora Inc MD.

Travel for Free: How to Accumulate Frequent Flyer Miles for Your Vacation. Eric Gelb. (Illus.). 32p. (Orig.). 1997. pap. 7.95 (*0-9631289-9-X*) Career Advan.

***Travel for Fun & Profit.** (Illus.). 350p. 1997. pap. 24.95 (*1-56559-909-8*) HGI Mrktng.

Travel for the Disabled: A Handbook of Travel Resources & 500 Worldwide Access Guides. large type ed. Helen Hecker. LC 85-16471. (Illus.). 192p. (Orig.). 1985. pap. 19.95 (*0-933261-00-4*) Twin Peaks Pr.

Travel for Two: The Art of Compromise. Margot S. Biestman. (Illus.). 192p. (Orig.). 1986. pap. 10.95 (*0-936865-07-5*) Pergot Pr.

Travel Fun, 6 Vols. (J). 1996. pap. 15.95 (*0-7894-0571-7*) DK Pub Inc.

***Travel Fun.** DK Publishing, Inc. Staff. (Sticker Bks.). 1997. pap. text ed. 6.95 (*0-7894-1525-9*) DK Pub Inc.

Travel Games. Amoco Pathfinder Staff. 1992. pap. 2.25 (*0-671-84035-5*) Mac Pub USA.

Travel Games. Edmund Beaver. (J). (gr. 4 up). 1974. pap. 1.00 (*0-910208-01-8*) Beavers.

Travel Games. T. Potter & M. Butterfield. (Illus.). 64p. (J). (gr. 2 up). 1986. pap. 8.95 (*0-86020-999-7*, Usborne) EDC.

Travel Games: Vol. 1, Family. Judith E. Donaldson & George H. Brown. (Illus.). 36p. (Orig.). reprint ed. pap. text ed. 1.50 (*0-939942-05-4*) Larkspur.

Travel Games: Vol. 2, Five to Ten Years. Judith E. Donaldson. Ed. by George H. Brown. (Illus.). 36p. (J). (gr. k-5). reprint ed. pap. text ed. 1.50 (*0-939942-06-2*) Larkspur.

Travel Games: Vol. 3, Sports. George H. Brown. Ed. by Judith E. Donaldson. (Illus.). 36p. reprint ed. pap. text ed. 1.50 (*0-939942-07-0*) Larkspur.

Travel Games for the Family. Marie E. Boatness. Ed. by Mary Westheimer. LC 93-90005. (Illus.). 144p. (Orig.). (J). (gr. 1-8). 1993. pap. 6.95 (*0-9635619-0-1*) Canyon Creek.

Travel Gems. Charles R. Hayes. 86p. (Orig.). 1982. pap. text ed. write for info. (*0-9621710-1-8*) C R Hayes.

Travel, Gender & Imperialism: Mary Kingsley & West Africa. Alison Blunt. LC 94-2306. (Mappings: Society - Theory - Space Ser.). 190p. 1994. pap. text ed. 18.95 (*0-89862-546-7*); lib. bdg. 42.00 (*0-89862-347-2*) Guilford Pr.

Travel Geography. 2nd ed. Rosemary Burton. 512p. (Orig.). 1994. pap. 52.50 (*0-273-60203-9*, Pub. by Pitman Pub Ltd UK) Trans-Atl Phila.

Travel Geography for Tourism Bk. 1: United Kingdom. Pauline Horner. 128p. 1993. pap. 39.00 (*0-7487-1557-6*, Pub. by Stanley Thornes UK) Trans-Atl Phila.

Travel Geography for Tourism Pt. 1: United Kingdom. Pauline Horner. 128p. (C). 1993. pap. 49.00 (*0-7478-1557-7*, Pub. by S Thornes Pubs UK) St Mut.

Travel Geography for Tourism Pt. 2: Worldwide. Pauline Horner. 128p. (C). 1993. pap. 59.00 (*0-7478-1558-5*, Pub. by S Thornes Pubs UK) St Mut.

Travel Geography for Tourism Pt. 2: Worldwide. Pauline Horner. 128p. 1993. 39.00 (*0-7487-1558-4*, Pub. by Stanley Thornes UK) Trans-Atl Phila.

Travel Guide Indonesia. Richard I. Mann. (Holiday Sports of Tomorrow Ser.). (Illus.). 200p. 1991. pap. 14.95 (*981-00-2393-6*) Intl Spec Bk.

Travel Guide Thailand. (Holiday Spots of Tomorrow Ser.). (Illus.). 200p. 1991. pap. 14.95 (*981-00-2390-1*) Intl Spec Bk.

Travel Guide to Black Historical Sites & Landmarks in North Carolina. Lenwood G. Davis. LC 91-70215. (Illus.). 240p. (Orig.). 1991. pap. 9.95 (*1-878177-02-8*) Bandit Bks.

***Travel Guide to Botswana.** Globetrotter Staff. 1997. pap. text ed. 10.95 (*1-85368-567-4*) Globe Pequot.

Travel Guide to British/American English. Norman Moss. 172p. 1994. pap. 4.95 (*0-8442-9512-4*, Passport Bks) NTC Pub Grp.

***Travel Guide to Florida.** Globetrotter Staff. 1997. pap. text ed. 10.95 (*1-85368-432-5*) Globe Pequot.

Travel Guide to Israel. Rob Lindsted. (Illus.). 126p. (Orig.). (C). 1990. pap. 5.95 (*0-9624517-5-4*) Hearthstone OK.

Travel Guide to Jewish Europe. 2nd ed. Ben G. Frank. LC 94-34689. (Illus.). 600p. (Orig.). 1996. pap. 18.95 (*1-56554-037-9*) Pelican.

***Travel Guide to Madagascar.** Globetrotter Staff. 1997. pap. text ed. 10.95 (*1-85368-551-8*) Globe Pequot.

***Travel Guide to Mozambique.** Globetrotter Staff. 1997. pap. text ed. 10.95 (*1-85368-425-2*) Globe Pequot.

Travel Guide to South Africa. Les De Villiers et al. (Illus.). 256p. (Orig.). 1992. pap. 13.50 (*0-916673-07-3*) Business Bks CT.

Travel Guide to the Natchez Trace Parkway Between Natchez, MS, & Nashville, TN. Ilene J. Cornwell. LC 83-51206. (Illus.). 104p. (Orig.). 1984. pap. 7.95 (*0-915575-00-0*) Southern Resources.

Travel Guide to the Scientific Sited of the British Isles: A Guide to the People, Places & Landmarks of Science. Charles Tanford & Jacqueline Reynolds. LC 94-42176. 344p. 1995. pap. text ed. 16.95 (*0-471-95270-2*) Wiley.

***Travel Guide to Tribal Casinos in the Pacific Northwest.** Jim Roll. 1996. pap. 12.95 (*0-89716-624-8*) P B Pubng.

Travel Health Clinic Pocket Guide to Healthy Travel. Lawrence Bryson. 222p. (Orig.). 1994. pap. 13.95 (*0-9624945-4-2*) Silvercat Pubns.

***Travel Here & There.** Anita Zelman. LC 97-8429. (Illus.). 160p. (Orig.). 1998. pap. 12.95 (*1-56474-231-8*) Fithian Pr.

***Travel Impressions: The Discovery of Golden Civilizations.** Lucina B. Moxley. LC 96-78246. 75p. (Orig.). 1996. pap. 8.95 (*1-878208-93-4*) Guild Pr IN.

Travel in Aquatint & Lithography, 1770-1860: A Bibliographical Catalogue, 2 vols. J. R. Abbey. (Illus.). 1991. reprint ed. Set Vol. 1 352p., Vol. 2 1464p. 325.00 (*1-55660-133-6*) A Wofsy Fine Arts.

Travel in Aquatint & Lithography, 1770-1860 Vol. II: Asia, Oceania, Antarctica, America: A Bibliographical Catalogue. J. R. Abbey. (Illus.). 464p. 1991. reprint ed. 175.00 (*1-55660-132-8*) A Wofsy Fine Arts.

Travel in Aquatint & Lithography, 1770-1860, Vol. 1: World, Europe, Africa, Vol. 1. J. R. Abbey. (Abbey Collection of Colour-Plate Books in Aquatint & Lithography, 1770-1860). (Illus.). 352p. 1991. reprint ed. 175.00 (*1-55660-131-X*) A Wofsy Fine Arts.

Travel in Asia: A Guide to Information Sources. Ed. by Neal L. Edgar & Wendy Y. Ma. (Geography & Travel Information Guide Ser.: Vol. 6). 432p. 1983. 68.00 (*0-8103-1470-3*) Gale.

Travel in Canada: A Guide to Information Sources. Ed. by Nora T. Corley. (Geography & Travel Information Guide Ser.: Vol. 4). 320p. 1983. 68.00 (*0-8103-1493-2*) Gale.

Travel in Early Modern Europe. Antoni Maczak. Tr. by Ursula Phillips from POL. 368p. 1995. 66.95 (*0-7456-0840-X*) Blackwell Pubs.

Travel in England in the Seventeenth Century. Joan Parkes. LC 70-109817. 354p. 1970. reprint ed. text ed. 59.75 (*0-8371-4308-X*, PATE, Greenwood Pr) Greenwood.

Travel in Europe, 1804-1805, 3 vols. in 1. Washington Irving. reprint ed. lib. bdg. 99.00 (*0-7812-0320-1*) Rprt Serv.

Travel in Oceania, Australia & New Zealand: A Guide to Information Sources. Ed. by Robert E. Burton. LC 80-15333. (Geography & Travel Information Guide Ser.: Vol. 2). 148p. 1980. 68.00 (*0-8103-1421-5*) Gale.

Travel in the Ancient World. Lionel Casson. LC 93-30502. 400p. 1994. pap. 15.95 (*0-8018-4808-3*) Johns Hopkins.

***Travel in the Digital Age.** Linsey McNeil. (Work in the Digital Age Ser.). 1997. pap. text ed. 19.95 (*0-906097-64-9*, Pub. by Bowerdean Pubng UK) LPC InBook.

An Asterisk (*) at the beginning of an entry indicates that the title is appearing in BIP for the first time.

Travel in the First Century after Christ. C. A. Skeel. 1977. lib. bdg. 59.95 (*0-8490-2758-6*) Gordon Pr.

Travel in the United States: A Guide to Information Sources. Ed. by Joyce A. Post & Jeremiah Post. (Geography & Travel Information Guide Ser.: Vol. 3). 608p. 1981. 68.00 (*0-8103-1423-1*) Gale.

Travel in Time: Unitarian Universalism for Grades 5 & 6. Lois E. Ecklund. Ed. by Elizabeth Anastos & Mary J. Curry. 128p. (Orig.). 1991. teacher ed., pap. 20.00 (*1-55896-082-1*) Unitarian Univ.

Travel in Vogue. LC 82-25610. (Quality Paperbacks Ser.). (Illus.). 255p. 1983. reprint ed. pap. 12.95 (*0-306-80185-X*) Da Capo.

Travel Industry. 2nd ed. Chuck Y. Gee et al. (Illus.). 352p. (C). 1989. text ed. 46.95 (*0-442-22825-2*); Tchr's. manual. teacher ed. 21.95 (*0-442-31904-5*) Van Nos Reinhold.

Travel Industry, vol. 3. 3rd ed. Chuck Y. Gee et al. 448p. (C). 1997. text ed. 49.95 (*0-442-02297-2*) Van Nos Reinhold.

Travel Industry Business Management. Ed. by Nona S. Starr. 1985. pap. text ed. 35.00 (*0-931202-10-8*) Inst Cert Trav Agts.

Travel Industry Business Management. rev. ed. Ed. by John P. Butters & Roberta A. Lew. (Illus.). 414p. (Orig.). 1992. pap. 25.00 (*0-931202-20-5*) Inst Cert Trav Agts.

Travel Industry Guidelines for Employment. Chris Hoosen & Francis Dix. (Travel Agent Training Ser.). (Illus.). (Orig.). 1990. student ed., pap. 20.00 (*0-917063-24-4*) Travel Text.

Travel Industry in Britain. Pauline Horner. 192p. (Orig.). 1991. pap. 39.00 (*0-7487-0599-6*, Pub. by Stanley Thornes UK) Trans-Atl Phila.

Travel Industry Marketing. Ed. by John P. Butters & Roberta A. Lew. (Illus.). 405p. (Orig.). (C). 1990. pap. 35.00 (*0-931202-19-1*) Inst Cert Trav Agts.

Travel Industry World Yearbook: The Big Picture. Thomas Bridges et al. (Illus.). 180p. (Orig.). 1996. pap. write for info. (*0-614-12929-X*) Child & Waters Inc.

Travel Industry World Yearbook: The Big Picture, Vol. 29. Somerset R. Waters. 136p. (Orig.). (C). 1985. pap. 49.00 (*0-9611200-2-9*) Child & Waters Inc.

Travel Industry World Yearbook: The Big Picture, Vol. 30. Somerset R. Waters. 140p. (Orig.). 1986. pap. 56.00 (*0-9611200-3-7*) Child & Waters Inc.

Travel Industry World Yearbook: The Big Picture, Vol. 31. Somerset R. Waters. (Orig.). 1987. pap. 66.00 (*0-9611200-4-5*) Child & Waters Inc.

Travel Industry World Yearbook: The Big Picture, Vol. 32. Somerset R. Waters. (Orig.). 1988. pap. 69.00 (*0-9611200-5-3*) Child & Waters Inc.

***Travel Industry World Yearbook: The Big Picture, Vol. 39.** Somerset R. Waters. Ed. by Thomas Bridges. (Illus.). (Orig.). pap. text ed. 89.00 (*1-883933-02-1*) Child & Waters Inc.

***Travel Industry World Yearbook: The Big Picture, Vol. 40.** Somerset R. Waters. Ed. by Thomas Bridges. (Illus.). 164p. (Orig.). 1997. pap. text ed. 89.00 (*1-883933-03-X*) Child & Waters Inc.

Travel Industry World Yearbook: The Big Picture, Vol.33. Somerset R. Waters. (Orig.). 1989. pap. 75.00 (*0-9611200-6-1*) Child & Waters Inc.

Travel Industry World Yearbook, Vol. 37, 1993: The Big Picture. Somerset R. Waters. Ed. by Thomas Bridges. (Illus.). 158p. 1993. pap. 79.00 (*1-883933-00-5*) Child & Waters Inc.

Travel Industry World Yearbook, 1994-95 Vol. 38: The Big Picture. Somerset R. Waters. Ed. by Thomas Bridges. (Illus.). 173p. 1995. pap. 79.00 (*1-883933-01-3*) Child & Waters Inc.

Travel Information Aide. Jack Rudman. (Career Examination Ser.: C-3486). 1994. pap. 27.95 (*0-8373-3486-1*) Nat Learn.

Travel Is Not Just for Sightseeing: Insightseeing. Patsy S. Saiki. (Illus.). 1993. pap. 10.00 (*0-614-04515-0*) Kisaku.

Travel Journal. 160p. 1994. pap. 8.95 (*0-89815-647-5*) Ten Speed Pr.

Travel Journal. Melanie M. Tallon. (Illus.). 112p. (Orig.). 1995. ring bd. 16.50 (*0-9646869-0-2*) Global Expressions.

Travel Journal: Africa. Mark W. Nolting. (Illus.). 160p. (Orig.). 1988. pap. 12.95 (*0-939895-01-3*) Global Travel Pubs.

Travel Journal Africa. 3rd ed. Mark W. Nolting. 1994. pap. 12.95 (*0-939895-06-4*) Global Travel Pubs.

Travel Journal-Europe & North Africa. R. Bruce Allison. 1979. pap. 5.95 (*0-913370-03-7*, Sol Press) Wisconsin Bks.

Travel Journals: Carnets de Voyage. Pierre Dessureault. 95p. 1995. 32.95 (*0-88884-569-3*) U Ch Pr.

***Travel Jumble: Puzzles on the Move.** (Illus.). 192p. (Orig.). 1997. pap. 9.95 (*1-57243-198-9*) Triumph Bks.

Travel Korea Your Way. Richard Saccone. LC 94-75557. (Illus.). 128p. 1994. pap. text ed. 29.95 incl. audio (*1-56591-037-0*) Hollym Intl.

Travel Korea Your Way: Sixty Must-See Places in Korea. Richard Saccone. LC 94-77533. (Illus.). 213p. (Orig.). 1994. 22.95 (*1-56591-012-5*) Hollym Intl.

Travel Law. Thomas A. Dickerson. 700p. 1986. reprint ed. ring bd. 98.00 (*0-318-21442-3*, 00565) NY Law Pub.

***Travel Law: Cases & Materials.** Robert M. Jarvis et al. (Illus.). (C). 1997. text ed. write for info. (*0-89089-802-2*) Carolina Acad Pr.

Travel Letter, 1871. Michael Reese, II. 1988. write for info. (*0-318-65536-5*) Cloister Pr.

Travel Letters. Sangharakshita. 224p. (Orig.). 1985. pap. 9.95 (*0-904766-17-9*, Pub. by Windhorse UK) Windhorse Pubns.

Travel Letters from New Zealand, Australia, & Africa. E. W. Howe. (Collected Works of E. W. Howe). 1988. reprint ed. lib. bdg. 59.00 (*0-7812-1294-4*) Rprt Serv.

Travel Letters from New Zealand, Australia & Africa see Collected Works of E. W. Howe

Travel Light: How to Go Anywhere in the World with Only One Suitcase. Joy Nyquist. 300p. 1996. 15.95 (*1-879899-02-7*) Newjoy Pr.

Travel Literature & the Evolution of the Novel. Percy G. Adams. LC 83-19683. 380p. reprint ed. pap. 108.30 (*0-8357-4290-3*, 2037089) Bks Demand.

Travel Managers Personnel Manual. 2nd ed. Stevens. (Hospitality, Travel & Tourism Ser.). 1989. 33.00 (*0-8273-4036-2*) Delmar.

Travel Medicine. Ed. by R. H. Behrens & K. P. McAdam. (British Medical Bulletin Ser.: Vol. 49, 2). (Illus.). 320p. 1993. text ed. 120.00 (*0-443-04925-4*) Churchill.

Travel Medicine. Ed. by R. Steffen et al. (Illus.). 350p. 1989. 127.00 (*0-387-19356-1*) Spr-Verlag.

Travel Money. E. Elkington. (C). 1989. text ed. 50.00 (*0-948032-72-3*, Pub. by Rosters Ltd) St Mut.

Travel Notes. Gomer Press Staff. 64p. 1992. pap. 20.00 (*0-86383-734-4*, Pub. by Gomer Pr UK) St Mut.

***Travel Odyssey: The Academy Pacific Story.** William A. Schoneberger. LC 97-3366. 1997. write for info. (*0-89865-989-2*) Donning Co.

Travel-Ogs: The Do-It-Yourself Survival Kit for Traveling with Parents, Siblings, & Dirty Socks. Ann Brown & Mary Bold. (Children's Resources Ser.). 80p. (Orig.). (J). (gr. 1-6). 1988. student ed. 6.95 (*0-938267-06-X*) Bold Prodns.

Travel on Your Own: Go Now, Here's How; An Adventure in Discovery, Solo Travel Can Be Fun. Marilyn N. Clark. 224p. 1994. pap. 12.95 (*1-884617-24-7*) Primrose.

Travel Perspectives: A Guide to Becoming a Travel Agent. Susan Rice & Ginger Todd. 300p. 1991. pap. 47.95 (*0-8273-4570-4*) Delmar.

Travel Perspectives: A Guide to Becoming a Travel Agent. Susan Rice & Ginger Todd. 300p. 1992. teacher ed., pap. 12.95 (*0-8273-4571-2*) Delmar.

Travel Perspectives: A Guide to Becoming a Travel Agent. 2nd ed. Rice. (Hospitality, Travel & Tourism Ser.). 64p. 1996. teacher ed. 19.00 (*0-8273-6534-9*) Delmar.

Travel Perspectives: A Guide to Becoming a Travel Agent. 2nd ed. Ginger Todd & Susan Rice. LC 94-45008. 1996. pap. 43.95 (*0-8273-6533-0*) Delmar.

Travel Perspectives: A Guide to Becoming a Travel Agent Update Two. Ginger Todd & Susan Rice. 1992. 8.50 (*0-8273-5775-3*) Delmar.

Travel Perspectives PCDI Edition. Rice & Todd. (Hospitality, Travel & Tourism Ser.). 1991. pap. 17.00 (*0-8273-4884-3*) Delmar.

Travel Perspectives Update One. Susan Rice & Ginger Todd. 1992. pap. 8.00 (*0-8273-4569-0*) Delmar.

Travel Photographer's Handbook: Professional Techniques - The National Geographic Way. Albert Moldvay & Erika Fabian. (Illus.). 104p. (Orig.). 1995. spiral bd., pap. 14.95 (*0-9638417-2-6*) Eriako Assocs.

Travel Photography: A Complete Guide to How to Shoot & Sell. Susan McCartney. LC 91-77926. (Illus.). 384p. 1992. pap. 22.95 (*1-880559-00-5*) Allworth Pr.

Travel Photography Using Existing Light. Ed. by Chester C. Carr. LC 88-92326. (Orig.). 1989. pap. 12.95 (*0-922958-04-1*) H W Parker.

Travel Reservations. Murdock Travel Systems Staff. 309p. (C). 1992. pap. text ed. 35.00 (*1-879982-11-0*) Educ Systs.

***Travel Rights.** 2nd ed. Charles Leocha. 192p. 1997. pap. 9.95 (*0-915009-57-9*) World Leis Corp.

Travel Safely at Home & Abroad: Don't Be a Target! 3rd rev. ed. Raymond W. Worring et al. Ed. by Marita Martiniak. LC 95-62066. (Illus.). 136p. 1996. pap. 12.95 (*0-940659-10-7*) Uniquest Pubns.

Travel Safety: Don't Be a Target! Whitney Hibbard et al. (Orig.). 1987. pap. 6.95 (*0-940659-05-0*) Uniquest Pubns.

Travel Safety: How to Travel Safely at Home & Abroad. rev. ed. Hibbard Whitney et al. LC 87-81342. 84p. 1991. pap. 7.95 (*0-685-41346-2*) Uniquest Pubns.

Travel Safety: How to Travel Safely at Home & Abroad. 2nd ed. Whitney Hibbard et al. LC 87-81342. Orig. Title: Travel Safety: Don't Be a Target!. 84p. 1987. pap. 6.95 (*0-940659-06-9*) Uniquest Pubns.

Travel Safety: Don't Be a Target! see Travel Safety: How to Travel Safely at Home & Abroad

Travel Scams & Cons: Getting There a Lot Cheaper Than You're Supposed To. Henry L. Eisenson. (Illus.). 160p. (Orig.). 1995. pap. 12.95 (*1-56866-093-6*) Index Pub Grp.

Travel Secrets: A Guide for Practical Travelers. Todd Hewett. 210p. (Orig.). 1995. pap. 14.95 (*0-9646624-0-X*) New Generation Pub.

Travel Selling Skills. Carl L. Bryant et al. 112p. 1992. pap. 22.95 (*0-538-70553-1*) S-W Pub.

Travel Selling Skills. Chris Hoosen & Francis Dix. (Travel Agent Training Ser.). (Illus.). (Orig.). 1989. student ed., pap. 20.00 (*0-917063-21-X*) Travel Text.

Travel Smarts: Getting the Most for Your Travel Dollar. Herbert Teison & Nancy Dunnan. LC 94-40246. (Illus.). 368p. (Orig.). 1995. pap. 12.95 (*1-56440-370-X*) Globe Pequot.

***Travel Smarts: Getting the Most for Your Travel Dollar.** 2nd rev. ed. Nancy Dunnan & Herbert Teison. (Illus.). 144p. (Orig.). 1997. pap. 14.95 (*0-7627-0141-2*) Globe Pequot.

Travel Tales: A Mobility Storybook. Julia Halpern-Gold et al. LC 88-62588. (Illus.). 107p. (Orig.). (J). (ps-3). 1988. pap. text ed. 20.00 (*0-922637-00-8*) Most Mobil.

Travel the Winds: A Beginning Mystery, Vol. 1. Ti Mar. Ed. by Mary L. Green. (Illus.). 186p. 1996. pap. 19.95 (*0-9651538-0-0*) Trvl the Winds. There is a need for humans to increase their conscious awareness, gain control over telepathic communications, change energy to stop unwanted encounters & recognize all contacts. With this control will come a knowledge of all life forms. The importance of Light Being communication is understood through energy, earth & human changes. TRAVEL THE WINDS has seventeen portraits of light beings, nine maps of ancient lands & illustrations of a dome, double carrier & outer shell of a UFO. Today Ti Mar is an author, lecturer, artist & remembers many encounters. Ti Mar's work includes intuitive insights into contacts & memory counseling to help people remember encounters. She does psychic readings. Ti Mar is also available for workshops & seminars on UFOs & can be contacted through Travel the Winds Publishing, P.O. Box 781628, Wichita, KS 67278-1628. The topics of gods & life in Space has received so much of man's attention, speculation & conversation that this trend of thought can be traced from the earliest limit of earth time into the present. Even with the imposed limit, all people should know of the presence & location of all other life forms. $19.95 (plus $4.00 shipping & handling), KS residents add $1.18 tax, Visa, MasterCard & American Express orders please FAX your order: 1-316-683-6021. Please include Card Number, Expiration Date, & the Name on the Card. ***Publisher Provided Annotation.***

Travel-the-World Cookbook: For Kids of All Ages. Pamela Marx. (Illus.). (J). (gr. 3-6). 1996. pap. 12.95 (*0-673-36254-X*, GoodYrBooks) Addson-Wesley Educ.

Travel the World Free as an International Tour Director: How to Be an International Tour Director, 5, 1. Gerald E. Mitchell. 300p. 1995. 59.95 (*0-945439-13-X*) G E Mitchell & Assocs.

***Travel Through Time.** Dorling Kindersley Staff. (Funfax Eyewitness Library). (J). 1997. pap. 1.95 (*0-7894-1838-X*) DK Pub Inc.

***Travel Time.** (My First Backseat Bks.). (Illus.). (J). (ps-2). 1997. pap. 3.95 (*0-614-28917-3*) Rand McNally.

Travel Tips: Travel Made Fun & Easy for Business & Pleasure. Global Inc. Staff & James D. Durdy. (Illus.). 80p. (Orig.). 1995. pap. 4.95 (*1-887430-14-8*) Global Inc.

Travel Tips for Older Americans. 1990. lib. bdg. 74.00 (*0-8490-4028-0*) Gordon Pr.

Travel Tips for Older Americans. 1994. lib. bdg. 250.00 (*0-8490-6485-6*) Gordon Pr.

Travel Tips for Teachers. Sunni Bloyd. 132p. (Orig.). 1991. pap. 8.95 (*0-929923-43-X*) Lowell Hse.

Travel Tips for the Nineties. Don Weiss & Phyliss W. Weiss. LC 89-26988. (Illus.). 160p. (Orig.). 1990. pap. 11.99 (*0-934802-58-0*) ICS Bks.

Travel to Cusco, Peru. James Tiskell. 1992. 24.95 (*1-85043-172-8*, Pub. by I B Tauris UK) St Martin.

Travel to Prague. Christine Adams. 1992. 24.95 (*1-85043-312-7*, Pub. by I B Tauris UK) St Martin.

***Travel to Success, Success System, Pt. 1.** (Illus.). 250p. (Orig.). 1995. mass mkt. write for info. (*0-9658371-0-6*) M Goloversic.

***Travel to the Stars.** limited ed. Akbar F. Brinsmade. (Illus.). 169p. 1996. 30.00 (*1-889930-15-6*) J M Phillips Pub.

Travel, Tourism, & Hospitality Law. Alexander Anolik. (Illus.). 100p. (Orig.). 1988. pap. 12.00 (*0-935920-60-9*, Ntl Pubs Blck) P-H.

Travel, Tourism, & Hospitality Research: A Handbook for Managers & Researchers. 2nd ed. J. R. Ritchie & Charles R. Goeldner. 614p. 1994. text ed. 59.95 (*0-471-58248-4*) Wiley.

Travel, Trade, & Temptation: The Dutch Italianate Harbor Scene, 1640-1680. Christine S. Schloss. LC 82-1864. (Studies in Baroque Art History: No. 3). (Illus.). 213p. reprint ed. pap. 60.80 (*0-8357-1309-1*, 2070249) Bks Demand.

Travel-Trailer Homesteading under $5,000. Brian D. Kelling. 1995. pap. text ed. 8.00 (*1-55950-132-4*) Loompanics.

Travel Training Workbook, Section One: Introduction to Travel & Geography. Claudine Dervaes. (Illus.). 320p. 1995. pap. 19.95 (*0-933143-44-3*) Solitaire Pub.

***Travel Training Workbook Set, Set.** Claudine Dervaes. (Illus.). 1300p. (C). 1996. pap. 129.95 (*0-933143-50-8*) Solitaire Pub.

***Travel Training Workbook, 1996 Section 1: Introduction to Travel & Geography.** 320p. 1996. pap. 19.95 (*0-933143-52-4*) Solitaire Pub.

***Travel Training Workbook, 1996 Section 6: Review, Sales Techniques & Business Communications.** Claudine Dervaes. 200p. 1996. pap. 24.95 (*0-933143-22-2*) Solitaire Pub.

Travel Training Workbook, 1996, Section 3: Hotels, Car Rentals, Packages, Tours & Motorcoach & Rail (Supplemental Sales) Claudine Dervaes. (Illus.). 176p. 1995. 18.95 (*0-933143-36-2*) Solitaire Pub.

Travel Training Workbook, 1996, Section 4, International Travel. Claudine Dervaes. (Illus.). 256p. 1996. 24.95 (*0-933143-24-9*) Solitaire Pub.

Travel Training Workbook, 1996, Section 5: Cruises. Claudine Dervaes. (Illus.). 144p. 1996. 15.95 (*0-933143-23-0*) Solitaire Pub.

***Travel Training Workbook, 1997-1999 Section 2: Domestic Travel & Ticketing.** 260p. 1996. pap. 29.95 (*0-933143-51-6*) Solitaire Pub.

Travel Treats: Fun for Kids on the Move, 3 bks., Set. Barbara Helwig & Susan Stewart. (Little Books for Kids). (Illus.). 90p. (J). (gr. 2-6). 1993. spiral bd. 19.95 (*1-881285-07-3*) Arbus Pub.

Travel Trivia Handbook of Oddball European Sights. Nino Lo Bello. (Illus.). 224p. 1992. pap. 12.95 (*0-8065-1333-0*, Citadel Pr) Carol Pub Group.

Travel U. S. A. Magazine: A Document Pro. 8th ed. Gorman & Mass. (TA - Typing/Keyboarding Ser.). 1993. 21.95 (*0-538-61136-7*) S-W Pub.

Travel Vermont: The Best of the Green Mountain State. 2nd rev. ed. Andrew L. Nemethy. 1992. pap. 16.95 (*0-936896-19-1*) VT Life Mag.

Travel Vermont: The Best of the Green Mountain State. 3rd ed. Andrew L. Nemethy. LC 95-38316. (Illus.). 1995. pap. text ed. 19.95 (*0-936896-39-6*) VT Life Mag.

Travel Well. Audrey Kaplan & Norman Kaplan. 1988. pap. 5.95 (*0-929240-06-5*) EMIS.

***Travel Westward 1853: The Journal of R. M. Hawley.** R. M. Hawley. Ed. by Jim Gentry. (Illus.). 100p. (Orig.). 1997. pap. 5.95 (*0-9657023-0-8*) Full Court.

***Travel While You Work.** Kay Peterson & Joe Peterson. 160p. 1996. 10.95 (*0-614-30366-4*) RoVers Pubns.

Travel with Children. 3rd ed. Maureen Wheeler. (Illus.). 160p. (Orig.). 1995. pap. 11.95 (*0-86442-299-7*) Lonely Planet.

Travel with Inner Perceptiveness. Flower A. Newhouse. (Illus.). 112p. (Orig.). 1979. pap. text ed. 9.00 (*0-910378-16-9*) Christward.

***Travel with or Without Pets: 25,000 Pets-R-Permitted Accomodations, Petsitters, Kennels & More!** 6th ed. ACI Staff. Ed. by M. E. Nelson. (Illus.). 512p. 1997. pap. 13.95 (*1-56471-797-6*) Annenberg.

Travel Wonderful Wyoming with Jesse Jackalope. Karey H. Stebner. 28p. (J). (ps-4). 1992. pap. 3.00 (*0-9632746-3-5*) Karey Kreations.

Travel Writer's Guide: How to Earn at Least Twice What You Spend on Travel by Writing Newspaper & Magazine Articles. Gordon Burgett. (Illus.). 304p. (Orig.). 1991. pap. 14.95 (*1-55958-115-8*) Prima Pub.

Travel Writer's Guide: How to Earn at Least Twice What You Spend on Travel by Writing Newspaper & Magazine Articles. 2nd rev. ed. Gordon Burgett. LC 94-20626. (Orig.). 1994. pap. 14.95 (*1-55958-561-7*) Prima Pub.

Travel Writer's Handbook: How to Write & Sell Your Own Travel Experiences. 4th ed. Louise P. Zobel. LC 96-54866. 1997. pap. 15.95 (*1-57284-005-6*) Surrey Bks.

Travel Writing. Blanton. LC 97-18791. 1996. 23.95 (*0-8057-0967-3*, Twayne) Scribnrs Ref.

Travel Writing: A Guide to Research, Writing & Selling. L. Peat O'Neil. LC 95-34121. 256p. 1996. 18.99 (*0-89879-671-7*, Wrtrs Digest Bks) F & W Pubns Inc.

Travel Writing for Profit & Pleasure. Perry Garfinkel. 1989. pap. 8.95 (*0-452-26159-7*, Plume) NAL-Dutton.

Travel 1001 Jobs: Travel 1001 Jobs in a Glamour Industry. James Flanagan. (Illus.). 128p. 1991. pap. 19.95 (*0-9630950-0-5*) Jimdandee.

Traveler. Don Coldsmith. (Spanish Bit Saga Ser.: No. 2). 352p. 1991. 5.50 (*0-553-28868-7*) Bantam.

Traveler. Elaine Fox. 368p. (Orig.). 1996. mass mkt., pap. text ed. 4.99 (*0-505-52074-5*) Dorchester Pub Co.

Traveler. John Katzenbach. 432p. 1988. mass mkt. 6.99 (*0-345-34709-9*) Ballantine.

Traveler. Antal Szerb. Tr. by Peter Hargitai from HUN. LC 93-84996. 279p. (Orig.). 1994. pap. 15.00 (*0-915951-21-5*) Puski-Corvin.

Traveler: A Voyager's Notebook. Illus. by Helen Buttfield. 160p. 1996. spiral bd. 17.95 (*1-55670-475-5*) Stewart Tabori & Chang.

Traveler: An American Odyssey in the Himalayas. Eric Hansen. LC 93-18400. (Illus.). 160p. 1993. 25.00 (*0-87156-521-8*) Sierra.

Traveler: An American Odyssey in the Himalayas. Eric Hansen. LC 93-18400. 1995. pap. 18.00 (*0-87156-350-9*) Sierra.

Traveler: Manuscript Edition. Marc Connelly. 1939. pap. 13.00 (*0-8222-1418-0*) Dramatists Play.

Traveler: River of Love. Sue Dean. (Illus.). 96p. (Orig.). 1995. pap. 10.95 (*1-884385-17-6*) Painted Wheel.

Traveler: Shining Wealth. Sue Dean. (Illus.). 96p. (Orig.). 1996. pap. 10.95 (*1-884385-18-4*) Painted Wheel.

Traveler - Glowing Power. Sue Dean. (Illus.). 96p. (Orig.). 1993. pap. 10.95 (*1-884385-15-X*) Painted Wheel.

Traveler - Spirit of Play. Sue Dean. (Illus.). 96p. (Orig.). 1994. pap. 10.95 (*1-884385-16-8*) Painted Wheel.

***Traveler: A Magical Journey.** James Keller. LC 97-17590. 1997. 15.95 (*0-86713-042-3*) Greenwich Wrkshop.

Traveler & the End of Time: The Secret Life of Ken Page. Ken Page & Simon P. Hemingway. Ed. by Mary D. Page. (The Traveler Ser.). 195p. (Orig.). 1996. pap. text ed. 11.95 (*0-9649703-1-7*) Clr Light Arts.

Traveler Disguised: The Rise of Modern Yiddish Fiction in the Nineteenth Century. Dan Miron. 373p. 1995. pap. 16.95 (*0-8156-0330-4*) Syracuse U Pr.

Traveler From Altruria. Levy. 1996. pap. text ed. 7.50 (*0-312-11799-X*) St Martin.

Traveler from Altruria. William Dean Howells. (Notable American Authors Ser.). 1992. reprint ed. lib. bdg. 75.00 (*0-7812-3249-X*) Rprt Serv.

Traveler in Indian Territory: The Journal of Ethan Allan Hitchcock, Late Major-General in the U. S. Army. Ethan A. Hitchcock. Ed. by Grant Foreman. LC 30-31133. 270p. reprint ed. pap. 77.00 (*0-317-29297-8*, 2055513) Bks Demand.

Traveler in Indian Territory: The Journal of Ethan Allen Hitchcock. Ethan A. Hitchcock. Ed. by Grant Foreman. LC 95-46136. (American Exploration & Travel Ser.: Vol. 75). (Illus.). 288p. 1996. pap. 17.95 (*0-8061-2840-2*) U of Okla Pr.

Traveler in the Dark. Marsha Norman. 1988. pap. 5.25 (*0-8222-1168-8*) Dramatists Play.

Traveler in the Life & Works of George Sand. Ed. by Tamara Alvarez-Detrell & Michael G. Paulson. LC 93-60502. 174p. 1994. 25.00 (*0-87875-441-5*) Whitston Pub.

Traveler Ken Page & the Fallen Angel: An Adventure Story. Daniel L. Rogers & Mary D. Page. (Traveler Ser.). 196p. (Orig.). 1995. pap. text ed. 11.95 (*0-9649703-0-9*) Clr Light Arts.

Traveler of the Crossroads: The Life of Adventurer Nicol Smith. Sharon Karr. LC 94-77271. (Illus.). 367p. (Orig.). 1995. pap. 19.95 (*0-9639864-1-4*) Log Cabin Manuscripts.

Traveler Toward the Dawn: The Spiritual Journal of John Eagan, S.J. John Eagan. 200p. (Orig.). 1990. pap. 2.50 (*0-8294-0647-6*) Loyola Pr.

Travelers. Stephen Kear. Ed. by Judy Hilvosky. LC 89-287. 1989. 13.95 (*0-87949-288-0*) Ashley Bks.

Traveler's Advisory. Donald L. Berry. LC 90-6095. (Poetry Ser.: Vol. 9). 68p. 1990. lib. bdg. 24.95 (*0-88946-879-6*) E Mellen.

Traveler's Advisory. Steven Sher. 56p. (Orig.). 1994. pap. 8.95 (*0-916155-24-2*) Trout Creek.

Travelers Affordable Accommodations: Washington State. Elaine C. Ingle. LC 95-70498. 348p. 1995. pap. 12.95 (*0-9639064-1-0*) Cottage Computer.

Traveler's Alaska. Altus L. Simpson. Ed. by Wordsmith. (Illus.). 162p. (Orig.). 1988. pap. 9.95 (*0-9621293-0-5*) Travelers WA.

Traveler's Almanac: Planning Your Vacation Around the Weather. Harold W. Bernard, Jr. LC 86-70329. (Illus.). 216p. 1987. 14.95 (*0-913215-18-X*) Riverdale Co.

Traveler's Almanac - Europe: Iceland to Israel . . . Planning Your Vacation Around the Weather. Harold W. Bernard, Jr. 177p. 1991. 14.95 (*0-913215-49-X*) Riverdale Co.

Travelers Among the Cucapa. Anita Alvarez De Williams. (Baja California Travels Ser.: No. 34). 1975. 30.00 (*0-87093-234-9*) Dawsons.

Travelers & Outlaws see Black Rebellion

Traveler's Atlas. Vivian Lewis. (Illus.). 230p. (Orig.). (C). 1988. pap. 9.95 (*0-945332-13-0*) Agora Inc MD.

Traveler's Book of Verse. Ed. by Frederick E. Emmons & T. W. Huntington, Jr. LC 77-108582. (Granger Index Reprint Ser.). 1977. 25.95 (*0-8369-6110-2*) Ayer.

Traveler's Companion to Montana History. Carroll Van West. LC 85-31072. (Illus.). 256p. 1986. pap. 10.95 (*0-917298-12-8*) MT Hist Soc.

Traveler's Diarrhea: Recent Advances. Ed. by C. Scarpignato & P. Rampal. (Journal Ser.: Vol. 41, Suppl. 1, 1995). (Illus.). iv, 82p. 1995. pap. 24.50 (*3-8055-6125-3*) S Karger.

Traveler's Diary. Jill B. Firestone. 1988. 5.99 (*0-517-65574-8*) Random Hse Value.

Traveler's Diary. Ed. by Running Press Staff. (Portable Diary Ser.). (Illus.). 144p. 1989. 11.95 (*0-89471-783-9*) Running Pr.

Traveler's Dictionary. Constantine et al. 1985. pap. 7.95 (*0-8120-3557-7*) Barron.

***Traveler's Eye.** Lisl Dennis. Date not set. 9.99 (*0-517-19246-2*) Random Hse Value.

Traveler's Eye: A Guide to Still & Video Travel Photography. Dennis List. 192p. 1996. 40.00 (*0-517-70573-7*, C P Pubs) Crown Pub Group.

Traveler's French Dictionary. Cortina. 1993. pap. 6.95 (*0-8050-2909-5*) H Holt & Co.

Travelers from an Antique Land. R. Martin Helick. (Series of 15 Paperbound Chapbooks: Bk. 1). 24p. (GAE.). 1988. pap. 2.00 (*0-912710-12-8*) Regent Graphic Serv.

Travelers from Olympus. Nellie McCaslin. 55p. (Orig.). 1996. pap. 5.00 (*0-88734-475-5*) Players Pr.

Traveler's German Dictionary. Cortina. 1993. pap. 5.95 (*0-8050-2910-9*) H Holt & Co.

Traveler's Guide to American Gardens. rev. ed. Ed. by Mary H. Ray & Robert P. Nicholls. (Illus.). xv, 375p. 1988. 12.95 (*0-8078-1787-2*) U of NC Pr.

***Traveler's Guide to Caribbean History.** Don Dachner. (Illus.). 350p. (Orig.). 1997. per. 17.95 (*0-9657780-0-2*) Travelers Pr.

Traveler's Guide to Chinese History. Madge Huntington. LC 86-4767. (Illus.). 240p. 1987. pap. 12.95 (*0-8050-0097-6*, Owl) H Holt & Co.

Travelers' Guide to Christian Radio Broadcasts. Charles E. Hugenberger. 28p. 1994. pap. 3.95 (*1-885057-05-9*) C E Hugenberger.

***Traveler's Guide to Death Valley National Park.** Cliff Lawson. (Illus.). 40p. (Orig.). 1996. pap. 7.95 (*1-878900-30-7*) DVNH Assn.

Traveler's Guide to European Camping: Explore Europe Economically at Your Own Pace Using RV or Tent. Mike W. Church & Terri L. Church. (Illus.). 416p. (Orig.). 1996. pap. 19.95 (*0-9652968-0-6*) Rolling Homes.

Traveler's Guide to Japanese Pilgrimages. Ed Readicker-Henderson. (Illus.). 240p. (Orig.). 1994. pap. 14.95 (*0-8348-0291-0*) Weatherhill.

***Traveler's Guide to Jewish Germany.** Peter Hirsch & Billie A. Lopez. (Illus.). 272p. 1997. pap. 22.50 (*1-56554-254-1*) Pelican.

Travelers' Guide to Latin American Customs & Manners. Nancy L. Braganti & Elizabeth Devine. (Illus.). 240p. 1989. pap. 13.95 (*0-312-02303-0*) St Martin.

***Traveler's Guide to Mexican Camping: Explore Mexico with Your RV or Tent.** Mike Church. 1997. pap. text ed. 19.95 (*0-9652968-1-4*) Rolling Homes.

Traveler's Guide to Middle Eastern & North African Customs & Manners. Elizabeth Devine. 1991. pap. 13.95 (*0-312-05523-4*) St Martin.

Traveler's Guide to Monument Valley. Stewart Aitchison. LC 93-15911. (Illus.). 64p. (Orig.). 1993. pap. 3.95 (*0-89658-225-6*) Voyageur Pr.

Traveler's Guide to Museum Exhibitions, 1996: U. S. Edition. Ed. by Susan S. Rappaport. (Illus.). 160p. (Orig.). 1995. pap. 12.95 (*0-923041-00-1*) Mus Guide Pubns Inc.

Traveler's Guide to Native America: The Great Lakes States. Hayward Allen & Pemina Yellow Bird. 192p. 1992. pap. 16.95 (*1-55971-139-6*) NorthWord.

Traveler's Guide to Native America: The Southwest Region. Hayward Allen. Ed. by Greg Linder. (Origins Ser.). (Illus.). (Orig.). 1993. pap. 16.95 (*1-55971-158-2*) NorthWord.

Traveler's Guide to Pioneer Jewish Cemeteries of the California Gold Rush. Susan Morris. LC 95-80185. (Illus.). 107p. (Orig.). 1996. pap. 12.95 (*0-943376-63-7*) Magnes Mus.

Traveler's Guide to Places We've All Been Before. S. Bortone. 149p. 1991. pap. text ed. write for info. (*0-318-68834-4*) KME Seabks.

Traveler's Guide to Spacetime: An Introduction to the Special Theory of Relativity. Thomas A. Moore. LC 94-39850. 1995. pap. text ed. write for info. (*0-07-043027-6*) McGraw.

Travelers' Guide to Sports Halls of Fame. Gerald Snyder & Thomas Blanchfield. (Illus.). 137p. (Orig.). 1994. pap. 13.95 (*0-9639696-0-9*) Cherry Val Pub.

Traveler's Guide to the Galapagos Islands. 2nd ed. Barry Boyce. LC 93-79633. (Illus.). 256p. (Orig.). 1994. pap. 15.95 (*0-9626142-1-1*) Galapagos Travel.

Traveler's Guide to the Great Art Treasures of Europe. Davis L. Morton. 575p. 1987. 50.00 (*0-8161-8733-9*, Hall Reference) Macmillan.

Traveler's Guide to the Great Sioux War: The Battlefields, Forts & Related Sites of America's Greatest Indian War. Paul L. Hedren. (Illus.). 128p. (Orig.). 1996. pap. 10.95 (*0-917298-38-1*) MT Hist Soc.

Traveler's Guide to the Great Sioux War: The Battlefields, Forts & Related Sites of America's Greatest Indian War. limited ed. Paul L. Hedren. (Illus.). 128p. (Orig.). 1996. 70.00 (*0-917298-39-X*) MT Hist Soc.

Travelers Guide to the Historic Columbia River Highway. Ken Monske & Diana Moore. (Illus.). 52p. pap. 2.95 (*1-883606-26-8*) Intl Lov Touch.

Traveler's Guide to the History of Biology & Medicine. Eric T. Pengelley & Daphne Pengelley. 238p. 1986. pap. text ed. 12.50 (*0-9616695-0-0*) Trevor Hill Pr.

Traveler's Guide to the Hudson River Valley. 3rd ed. Tim Mulligan. 1995. pap. 14.00 (*0-679-76175-6*) Random.

Traveler's Guide to the Lewis & Clark Trail. Julie Fanselow. LC 94-4106. (Falcon Guides Ser.). 266p. (Orig.). 1994. pap. 12.95 (*1-56044-224-7*) Falcon Pr MT.

***Traveler's Guide to the Lewis & Clark Trail.** Barbara Fifer & Vicky Soderberg. (Illus.). 272p. (Orig.). 1997. pap. 16.95 (*1-56037-117-X*) Am Wrld Geog.

Traveler's Guide to the Pony Express Trail. Joe Benson. LC 95-8232. 140p. 1995. pap. 12.95 (*1-56044-233-6*) Falcon Pr MT.

Traveler's Guide to the Solar System. Patricia Barnes-Svarney. LC 93-17313. 80p. (J). 1994. pap. 9.95 (*0-8069-8675-1*) Sterling.

Travelers' Guide to U. S. Certified Doctors Abroad. LC 76-10128. 1976. 9.95 (*0-672-50833-8*, Bobbs) Macmillan.

Traveler's Guide to World Radio 1996. Ed. by Andrew G. Sennitt. 200p. 1995. pap. 9.95 (*0-8230-5962-6*, RAC Bks) Watsn-Guptill.

Traveler's Guide to 100 Eastern Great Lakes Lighthouses: American & Canadian Lighthouses of the Eastern Great Lakes. Penrose Family Staff. (Illus.). 136p. (Orig.). 1994. pap. 14.95 (*0-923756-09-4*) Friede Pubns.

Traveler's Guide to 1116 Michigan Lighthouses. Laurie Penrose. (Illus.). 136p. 1992. pap. 14.95 (*0-923756-03-5*) Friede Pubns.

Travelers Guide to 116 Western Great Lakes Lighthouses. Penrose Family Staff. (Illus.). 176p. (Orig.). 1995. pap. 14.95 (*0-923756-12-4*) Friede Pubns.

Traveler's Handbook: The Essential Guide for Every Traveler. LC 94-34543. (Illus.). 900p. 1994. pap. 19.95 (*1-56440-482-X*) Globe Pequot.

***Traveler's Handbook: The Essential Guide for International Travelers.** 7th rev. ed. Wexas, Ltd. Staff. 900p. 1997. 19.95 (*0-7627-0145-5*) Globe Pequot.

Travelers' Health: How to Stay Healthy All over the World. Ed. by Richard Dawood. LC 92-37815. 512p. 1993. pap. 18.00 (*0-679-74608-0*) Random.

Traveler's Health Companion. John J. Connolly. 158p. (Orig.). 1995. pap. 8.95 (*1-883769-75-2*) Castle Connolly Med.

Traveler's Health Guide: Practical Advice for a Safe Trip. 2nd ed. Erwin J. Haas. Ed. by Lawrence E. Pawl. LC 90-90096. (Illus.). 176p. 1990. pap. 7.95 (*0-9625931-6-8*) Travelers Hlth Pubns.

Travelers Health Handbook: How to Prepare for Carefree Travel. Joy Nyquist. 80p. 1992. per. 7.95 (*1-879899-01-9*) Newjoy Pr.

Travelers' Highway Safety Book. Charles E. Hugenberger. LC 93-91616. 104p. 1993. pap. 12.95 (*1-885057-03-2*) C E Hugenberger.

Traveler's History of Washington. Bill Gulick. LC 96-3586. (Illus.). 550p. (Orig.). 1996. pap. 19.95 (*0-87004-371-4*, 037140) Caxton.

Travelers Hotline Directory. Dorothy DuBois. 288p. (Orig.). 1991. pap. 15.95 (*1-880581-88-4*) Visions Res.

Travelers, Immigrants, Inmates. Frances Bartkowski. LC 94-32674. 1995. text ed. 44.95 (*0-8166-2361-9*); pap. text ed. 17.95 (*0-8166-2362-7*) U of Minn Pr.

***Travelers in an Antique Land.** William Studebaker & Russell Hepworth. LC 96-38996. 1997. 49.95 (*0-89301-203-3*) U of Idaho Pr.

Travelers in Disguise: Narratives of Eastern Travel. rev. ed. Lincoln D. Hammond & Ludovico De Varthema. Ed. by Poggio Bracciolini. Tr. by John W. Jones. LC 63-2569. (Texts from the Romance Languages Ser.: Vol. 1). 271p. 1990. pap. 3.25 (*0-674-90645-4*) HUP.

Traveler's I.Q. Test: Rate Your Globetrotting Knowledge. George Blagowidow. 194p. 1987. pap. 6.95 (*0-87052-307-4*) Hippocrene Bks.

Traveler's Italian Dictionary. Cortina. 1993. pap. 5.95 (*0-8050-2911-7*) H Holt & Co.

Traveler's Italian Dictionary: English-Italian, Italian-English. rev. ed. Dilaver Berberi. LC 93-19015. 1993. pap. 6.95 (*0-8327-0724-4*) Cortina.

Traveler's Journal. 96p. 1996. pap. 5.95 (*1-56138-697-9*) Running Pr.

Traveler's Journal: Los Angeles. (Illus.). 101p. (Orig.). 1994. pap. 12.00 (*0-9631662-1-2*) Travelers Jrnl.

Traveler's Journey Through Time & Space. Julia A. Pogue & Eileen M. Jones. 130p. (Orig.). 1989. pap. write for info. (*0-9622814-1-7*) Anonymous & Assocs.

Traveler's Joy. Juliette De Bairacli-Levy. LC 78-61327. 1979. 11.95 (*0-87983-182-0*) Keats.

Traveler's Joy. Juliette De Bairacli Levy. LC 94-25343. (Illus.). 224p. 1994. pap. 11.95 (*0-87983-651-2*) Keats.

Traveler's Key to Ancient Egypt: A Guide to the Sacred Places of Ancient Egypt. John A. West. (Illus.). 480p. (Orig.). 1996. pap. 18.00 (*0-8356-0724-0*) Theos Pub Hse.

Traveler's Key to Ancient Greece: A Guide to the Sacred Places of Ancient Greece. Richard G. Geldard. LC 88-45268. (Illus.). 416p. 1989. 18.95 (*0-394-55631-3*) Knopf.

Traveler's Legend & Lore. Ronald Fritze. 1996. lib. bdg. 50.00 (*0-87436-759-X*) ABC-CLIO.

Traveler's Little Book of Wisdom. David Scott & William W. Forgey. (Little Book of Wisdom Ser.). 160p. (Orig.). 1996. pap. 5.95 (*1-57034-036-6*) ICS Bks.

***Traveler's Narrative: Written to Illustrate the Episode of the Bab.** rev. ed. Abdu'l-Baha. Tr. by Edward G. Browne from PER. LC 79-19025. 110p. 1980. 11.00 (*0-87743-143-4*, 106-027) Bahai.

Travelers of a Hundred Ages: The Japanese As Revealed Through 1,000 Years of Diaries. Donald Keene. 480p. 1989. 34.50 (*0-8050-0751-2*) H Holt & Co.

Travelers of a Hundred Ages: The Japanese As Revealed Through 1,000 Years of Diaries. Donald Keene. 480p. 1992. pap. 24.95 (*0-8050-1655-4*, Owl) H Holt & Co.

Travelers on the Western Frontier. Ed. by John F. McDermott. LC 77-100375. (Illus.). 363p. reprint ed. 103.50 (*0-8357-9700-7*, 2014920) Bks Demand.

Traveler's Phrasebook. Constantine et al. 1985. pap. 8.95 (*0-8120-3558-5*) Barron.

***Traveler's Pictorial Communication Guide.** Marty Katz. (Illus.). 72p. 1994. pap. 6.95 (*0-8059-3511-8*) Dorrance.

Traveler's Psalm: A 40-Day Spiritual Journey. Louise Chapman et al. 96p. 1993. pap. 6.99 (*0-8341-1513-1*) Beacon Hill.

Traveler's Radio Guide: Arizona, Utah, Colorado & New Mexico. Peter Crowell & Patricia Crowell. (Orig.). 1993. pap. text ed. 2.95 (*1-880962-03-9*) TRG Pubns.

Traveler's Radio Guide: California & Nevada. Peter Crowell & Patricia Crowell. 32p. (Orig.). 1992. pap. text ed. 2.95 (*1-880962-00-4*) TRG Pubns.

Traveler's Radio Guide: Idaho - Montana - Wyoming. Peter Crowell & Patricia Crowell. (Orig.). 1993. pap. 2.95 (*1-880962-02-0*) TRG Pubns.

Traveler's Radio Guide: Washington & Oregon. Peter Crowell & Patricia Crowell. 30p. (Orig.). 1992. pap. 2.95 (*1-880962-01-2*) TRG Pubns.

Traveler's Reading Guide: Ready-Made Reading Lists for the Armchair Traveler. rev. ed. Ed. by Maggy Simony. 528p. 1992. lib. bdg. 50.00 (*0-8160-2648-3*) Facts on File.

Traveler's Reading Guide: Ready-Made Reading Lists for the Armchair Traveler. rev. ed. Ed. by Maggy Simony. 528p. 1994. reprint ed. pap. 19.95 (*0-8160-2657-2*) Facts on File.

***Travelers Rose.** Jane Yolen. (J). Date not set. 14.95 (*0-399-21985-4*) Putnam Pub Group.

Travelers' Self Care Manual. William W. Forgey. LC 90-4970. (Illus.). 128p. (Orig.). 1990. pap. 6.95 (*0-934802-63-7*) ICS Bks.

Traveler's Shirt Pocket Handbook of Spanish Grammar. Charles E. Hugenberger. 56p. (ENG & SPA.). 1992. pap. 3.95 (*1-885057-01-6*) C E Hugenberger.

Traveler's Sourcebook: A Practical Guide to Information on Recreational & Business Travel in the United States. Ed. by Darren L. Smith. LC 96-9740. 350p. 1996. lib. bdg. 48.00 (*0-7808-0174-1*) Omnigraphics Inc.

Traveler's Spanish Dictionary. Cortina. 1993. pap. 5.95 (*0-8050-2908-7*) H Holt & Co.

***Traveler's Tales: Finding the World's Best Bird Shooting, with Some Fly-Fishing on the Side.** Michael McIntosh. LC 97-24322. (Illus.). 288p. 1997. 22.95 (*0-89272-420-X*, Silver Quill Pr) Down East.

Travelers' Tales Guides: A Woman's World. Ed. by Marybeth Bond. (Illus.). 417p. (Orig.). 1995. pap. 17.95 (*1-885211-06-6*) Trvlers Tale.

Travelers' Tales Guides Brazil. Ed. by Scott Doggett & Annette Haddad. (Travelers' Tales Guides Ser.). (Illus.). 400p. (Orig.). 1997. pap. 17.95 (*1-885211-11-2*) Trvlers Tale.

Travelers' Tales Guides Food. Ed. by Richard Sterling. (Travelers' Tales Guides Ser.). 1996. pap. 17.95 (*1-885211-09-0*) Trvlers Tale.

Travelers' Tales Guides France. Ed. by James O'Reilly et al. (Travelers' Tales Guides Ser.). (Illus.). 432p. (Orig.). 1995. pap. 17.95 (*1-885211-02-3*) Trvlers Tale.

Travelers' Tales Guides Greece. Ed. by Brian Alexander. (Travelers' Tales Guides Ser.). (Illus.). 400p. (Orig.). Date not set. pap. 17.95 (*1-885211-12-0*) Trvlers Tale.

Travelers' Tales Guides Hong Kong. Ed. by James O'Reilly et al. (Travelers' Tales Guides Ser.). 400p. 1997. pap. 17.95 (*1-885211-03-1*) Trvlers Tale.

Travelers' Tales Guides India. Ed. by James O'Reilly & Larry Habegger. (Travelers' Tales Guides Ser.). 477p. 1995. pap. 17.95 (*1-885211-01-5*) Trvlers Tale.

***Travelers' Tales Guides Italy: True Stories of Life on the Road.** Ed. by Anne Calcagno. (Travelers' Tales Guides Ser.). (Illus.). 350p. (Orig.). 1997. pap. 17.95 (*1-885211-16-3*, 16-3) Trvlers Tale.

***Travelers' Tales Guides Love & Romance: True Stories of Life on the Road.** Ed. by Judy Wylie. (Travelers' Tales Guides Ser.). (Illus.). 350p. (Orig.). 1997. pap. 17.95 (*1-885211-18-X*, 18-X) Trvlers Tale.

Travelers' Tales Guides Mexico. Ed. by James O'Reilly & Larry Habegger. (Travelers' Tales Guides Ser.). 426p. 1994. pap. 17.95 (*1-885211-00-7*) Trvlers Tale.

***Travelers' Tales Guides Nepal: True Stories of Life on the Road.** Ed. by Raj B. Khadka. (Travelers' Tales Guides Ser.). (Illus.). 300p. (Orig.). 1997. pap. 17.95 (*1-885211-14-7*) Trvlers Tale.

Travelers' Tales Guides Paris. Ed. by James O'Reilly et al. (Travelers' Tales Guides Ser.). (Illus.). 400p. (Orig.). 1997. pap. 17.95 (*1-885211-10-4*) Trvlers Tale.

Travelers' Tales Guides San Francisco. Ed. by James O'Reilly et al. (Travelers' Tales Guides Ser.). 420p. 1996. pap. 17.95 (*1-885211-08-2*) Trvlers Tale.

Travelers' Tales Guides Spain. Ed. by Lucy McCauley. (Travelers' Tales Guides Ser.). 440p. 1995. pap. 17.95 (*1-885211-07-4*) Trvlers Tale.

Travelers' Tales Guides Thailand. rev. ed. Ed. by James O'Reilly & Larry Habegger. (Travelers' Tales Guides Ser.). (Illus.). 405p. 1993. pap. 17.95 (*1-885211-05-8*) Trvlers Tale.

***Travelers' Tales Guides, The Road Within: True Stories of Transformation Around the World.** (Travelers' Tales Guides Ser.). (Illus.). 350p. (Orig.). 1997. pap. 17.95 (*1-885211-19-8*, 19-8) Trvlers Tale.

Travelers Through Time: Back to the Titanic. Beatrice Gormley. 144p. (J). (gr. 4-7). 1994. pap. 3.99 (*0-590-46226-1*) Scholastic Inc.

Travelers to an Antique Land: The History & Literature of Travel to Greece. Robert Eisner. (Illus.). 336p. 1993. pap. 17.95 (*0-472-08220-5*) U of Mich Pr.

Traveler's Tool Kit: How to Travel Absolutely Anywhere. Rob Sangster. (Illus.). 340p. (Orig.). 1996. pap. 15.95 (*0-89732-201-0*) Menasha Ridge.

Traveler's Tree. Bruno Bontempelli. Tr. by Linda Coverdale. 256p. 1994. 20.00 (*1-56584-150-6*) New Press NY.

Traveler's Trivia Test: 1101 Questions & Answers for the Sophisticated Globetrotter. rev. ed. George Blagowidow. 224p. 1991. pap. text ed. 6.95 (*0-87052-915-3*) Hippocrene Bks.

Traveler's Weather Guide. Tom Loffman. LC 90-70281. 96p. (Orig.). 1996. pap. 8.95 (*0-89815-831-1*) Ten Speed Pr.

Traveler's Workbook: Based on the People's Travel Book Index. Frieda Carrol. 50p. (C). 1983. ring bd. 25.95 (*0-939476-52-5*, Biblio Pr) Prosperity & Profits.

Traveler's World. Sebo. (C). 1991. pap. 35.95 (*0-538-70087-4*, JC45AB/) S-W Pub.

Traveler's World: A Dictionary of Industry & Destination Literacy. Illus. & Des. by Sybil Norwood. LC 95-16338. (C). 1995. pap. text ed. 22.20 (*0-13-228651-3*) P-H.

Traveler's World: Destination Geography. Sebo. (Hospitality, Travel & Tourism Ser.). 1991. teacher ed. 54.95 (*0-538-70088-2*) S-W Pub.

Traveler's World Atlas & Guide. 1995. pap. text ed. 9.95 (*0-528-83781-8*) Rand McNally.

Traveler's World Atlas & Guide. Rand McNally Staff. LC 93-11580. 1993. 14.95 (*0-528-83626-9*); pap. 9.95 (*0-528-83625-0*) Rand McNally.

***Traveler's World Atlas & Guide.** Rand McNally Staff. 1996. 14.95 (*0-528-83719-2*) Rand McNally.

Travelin' Light. Mike Allen. LC 95-94875. (Orig.). pap. 10.00 (*0-9648689-0-3*) Lght Lines Pr.

Travelin' On: The Slave Journey to an Afro-Baptist Faith. Mechal Sobel. (Andrew E. Murray, Journal of American History). (Illus.). 344p. 1988. reprint ed. pap. text ed. 17.95 (*0-691-00603-2*) Princeton U Pr.

***Travelin' Sam: America's Sports Ambassador.** Bill Heller. 158p. 1995. 19.95 (*0-931541-57-3*) Mancorp Pub.

Travelin' Talk Directory. Rick Crowder. (Illus.). 530p. (Orig.). 1993. pap. text ed. 35.00 (*0-9635818-4-8*) Travelin Talk.

Traveling. Nancy King. (Orig.). 1982. pap. 2.00 (*0-936563-01-X*) Signpost.

Traveling Again, Dad? Michael K. Lorelli. Ed. by Dylan Struzan. LC 95-60604. (Illus.). 32p. (J). (ps-7). 1995. 17.95 (*0-9646302-0-6*) Awesome Bks.

Traveling Alone. 1989. 9.95 (*0-930399-16-1*) BackPax Int.

Traveling America: An Activity Book for the Whole Family. Michael E. Redman et al. 56p. (Orig.). 1993. pap. write for info. (*0-9637442-0-8*) Mstr Designs.

Traveling Around Aquidneck Island 1890-1930: How We Got Around. James E. Garman. (Illus.). 152p. (Orig.). 1995. pap. text ed. write for info. (*0-9631722-6-3*) Hamilton Print.

Traveling Around Mt. St. Helens. Dan Youra & Pat Thompson. (Illus.). 64p. (Orig.). 1981. pap. 2.50 (*0-940828-01-4*) D Youra Studios.

Traveling Around Mt. St. Helens. 3rd ed. Dan Youra & Pat Thompson. (Illus.). 64p. (Orig.). 1981. pap. 3.50 (*0-940828-03-0*) D Youra Studios.

Traveling Around Mt. St. Helens: 400 Mile Scenic Loop. 2nd ed. Dan Youra & Pat Thompson. (Illus.). 64p. 1981. pap. 3.50 (*0-940828-02-2*) D Youra Studios.

Traveling Around the Human Genome: An In Situ Investigation. Bertrand Jordan. 188p. 1993. pap. 50.00 (*2-7420-0030-5*) IBD Ltd.

Traveling at High Speeds. John Rybicki. (New Issues Press Poetry Ser.). 64p. (Orig.). 1996. 22.00 (*0-932826-44-X*); pap. 12.00 (*0-932826-45-8*) New Issues MI.

Traveling at Home. Wendell Berry. LC 89-32376. (Press of Appletree - Alley Edition Ser.). (Illus.). 64p. 1989. reprint ed. 13.95 (*0-86547-417-6*, North Pt Pr) FS&G.

***Traveling at Warp 7: A Search for Star Trek.** Jim Duriga. 110p. (Orig.). 1997. pap. text ed. 7.95 (*1-889991-02-3*) Seneca-Secor.

Traveling Backward. Toby Forward. LC 93-32514. (Illus.). (J). 1994. 15.00 (*0-688-13076-3*, Tambourine Bks) Morrow.

Traveling Backward. Toby Forward. (Illus.). 160p. (J). (gr. 3-7). 1996. pap. 3.99 (*0-14-037875-8*, Puffin) Puffin Bks.

Traveling Backward. Toby Forward. (Illus.). (J). (gr. 3-7). reprint ed. pap. 3.99 (*0-614-15702-1*) Puffin Bks.

Traveling Basket Vol. II: And the Missing Hour. S. J. Wiseman & Kelly B. Sagert. LC 96-72330. (Illus.). 160p. Date not set. 21.95 (*0-9646803-7-8*) Plant Speak Prods.

Traveling Basket: or Mrs. Carey's Christmas Call. Kathi Belford. LC 95-68984. (Illus.). 1995. 19.95 (*0-9646803-6-X*) Plant Speak Prods.

Traveling Bird. Robert Burch. (J). (gr. 1-4). 1959. 9.95 (*0-8392-3038-9*) Astor-Honor.

Traveling Black Holes. Slightly Off Center Writers Group Staff. (Orig.). 1995. pap. 8.95 (*1-56721-110-0*) Twenty-Fifth Cent Pr.

Traveling by Bike. Ed. by Bike World Staff. 1982. pap. 3.95 (*0-02-499830-3*, Macmillan Coll) P-H.

***Traveling California's Gold Rush Country.** Leslie A. Kelly. LC 97-15108. 160p. (Orig.). 1997. pap. 14.95 (*1-56044-484-3*) Falcon Pr MT.

Traveling Chef: Low Fat Recipes You Can Make Anywhere. Constance L. Gallo. 120p. (Orig.). 1996. pap. 9.95 (*0-9652522-0-5*) Gallos Galley.

Traveling Companions. Friedrich Gorenstein. 1991. 21.95 (*0-15-191074-X*) HarBrace.

***Traveling Europe's Trains.** 4th ed. Jay Brunhouse. LC 96-45611. 1997. pap. 14.95 (*1-56554-261-4*) Pelican.

Traveling Gourmet Visits Turtle Back Farm Inn. Susan Fletcher. (Illus.). 128p. (Orig.). 1990. pap. 9.95 (*0-942133-60-9*) Sweet Forever Pub.

Traveling Gourmets Visit the Carter House. Mark Carter & D. K. Shumway. (Traveling Gourmets Ser.). (Illus.). 128p. (Orig.). 1991. pap. 10.95 (*0-942133-63-3*) Sweet Forever Pub.

Traveling Hints & Tips. Pamela C. Grossman. 62p. (Orig.). Date not set. pap. 5.95 (*0-9649022-0-6*) P C Grossman.

Traveling I-80 with Otto: Travel Guide. 3rd ed. Clark K. Parks. 384p. 1993. pap. text ed. 12.95 (*1-878959-01-8*) Trav Guide Pubns.

Traveling In. Douglas V. Steere. Ed. by E. Glenn Hinson. 1995. pap. 3.00 (*0-87574-324-2*) Pendle Hill.

Traveling in Africa. Gwen Cottman. 36p. 1982. pap. 3.50 (*0-912444-24-X*) DARE Bks.

Traveling in Mark Twain. Richard Bridgman. (Quantum Bks.: No. 30). (Illus.). 176p. 1987. 35.00 (*0-520-05952-2*) U CA Pr.

***Traveling in Notions: The Stories of Gordon Penn.** Michael J. Rosen. 1996. 15.95 (*1-57003-156-8*) U of SC Pr.

***Traveling in Notions: The Story of Gordon Penn.** Michael J. Rosen. LC 96-35684. 1996. pap. text ed. 9.95 (*1-57003-157-6*) U of SC Pr.

Traveling in South Carolina: A Selective Guide to Where to Go, What to See, What to Do. Sara Pitzer. LC 93-6535. (Illus.). 165p. (Orig.). 1993. 10.95 (*0-87249-868-9*) U of SC Pr.

Traveling in Space. Sue Becklake. LC 90-11017. (Exploring the Universe Ser.). (Illus.). 32p. (J). (gr. 4-6). 1991. lib. bdg. 13.95 (*0-8167-2136-X*) Troll Communs.

Traveling in Space. Sue Becklake. LC 90-11017. (Exploring the Universe Ser.). (Illus.). 32p. (J). (gr. 4-6). 1996. pap. 4.95 (*0-8167-2137-8*) Troll Communs.

***Traveling in the Gait of a Fox.** Dacia Maraini. Tr. by Genni Gunn. 96p. 1993. pap. 12.95 (*1-55082-055-9*, Pub. by Quarry Pr CN) LPC InBook.

***Traveling Inland.** Flora Foss. LC 94-68735. (Illus.). 92p. (Orig.). 1994. pap. 8.95 (*0-9627031-7-6*) Stone & Scott Pubs.

Traveling Jamaica with Knife, Fork & Spoon: A Rightous Guide to Jamaican Cooking. Robb Walsh & Jay McCarthy. LC 94-2445. 232p. 1995. pap. 16.95 (*0-89594-698-X*) Crossing Pr.

Traveling Jewish in America: For Business & Pleasure. rev. ed. Brynna C. Bloomfield et al. 472p. 1987. pap. 9.95 (*0-9617104-1-1*) Wandering You Pr.

Traveling Jewish in America: The Complete Guide for Business & Pleasure. 3rd ed. Ellen Chernofsky. 1991. pap. 11.95 (*0-9617104-2-X*) Wandering You Pr.

Traveling Jewish in America: The Complete Guide for 1986 for Business & Pleasure. Brynna C. Bloomfield & Jane M. Moskowitz. 407p. (Orig.). 1986. pap. 9.95 (*0-9617104-0-3*) Wandering You Pr.

Traveling Kentucky Back Roads: Old-History & Tall Tales. Sharon H. Fowler. Ed. by Gooch-on Fowler. (Illus.). 54p. 1995. 12.95 (*0-9651588-0-2*) Fowler & Gooch.

Traveling Lady. Horton Foote. 1955. pap. 5.25 (*0-8222-1169-6*) Dramatists Play.

Traveling Light. Lawrence G. Enscoe. 1992. 9.99 (*0-685-68687-6*, MP-670); cd-rom 29.99 (*0-685-68688-4*, MU-9144T) Lillenas.

Traveling Light. Steve Toth. 1977. pap. 4.95 (*0-912652-04-7*) Blue Wind.

Traveling Light. Steve Toth. LC 76-29720. (Illus.). 1977. pap. 9.95 (*0-912652-19-5*) Blue Wind.

Traveling Light: An Introduction to Philosophy. Jorn K. Bramann. LC 91-62676. (Illus.). 170p. (Orig.). (C). 1992. pap. text ed. 15.00 (*0-945073-13-5*) Nightsun MD.

Traveling Light: Contentment Amid the Burden of Life's Expectations. Kurt D. Bruner. 153p. (Orig.). Date not set. pap. 10.99 (*0-8024-8539-1*) Moody.

***Traveling Light: Mark's Complete Gospel Told in 70 Scenes & Monologues.** 91p. 1992. 9.99 (*0-8341-9596-8*) Lillenas.

Traveling Light: Modern Meditations on St. Paul's Letter of Freedom. Eugene H. Peterson. LC 88-11258. 204p. 1988. reprint ed. pap. 15.95 (*0-939443-08-2*) Helmers Howard Pub.

Traveling Light: Monologues. Jim Stowell. LC 88-42976. 126p. (Orig.). 1988. pap. 8.95 (*0-915943-31-X*) Milkweed Ed.

Traveling Light: Poems. Norma Almquist. 64p. (Orig.). 1997. pap. 9.00 (*1-56474-192-3*) Fithian Pr.

Traveling ...Like Everybody Else: A Practical Guide for Disabled Travelers. Jacqueline Freedman & Susan Gersten. 224p. 1987. pap. 11.95 (*0-915361-77-9*) Hemed Bks.

Traveling Like Everybody Else: A Practical Guide for Disabled Travelers. Jacqueline Freedman & Susan Gersten. 224p. (gr. 12 up). 1987. reprint ed. pap. 11.95 (*0-318-32656-6*, Watts) Hemed Bks.

Traveling Machines Series, 6 bks. J. Cooper. (J). 1991. Set. 53.70 (*0-86592-489-9*) Rourke Enter.

Traveling Man. Leigh Michaels. 1994. 2.99 (*0-373-03311-7*) Harlequin Bks.

Traveling Man: The Life Story of Henry Watkins Allen. Vincent Cassidy & Amos Simpson. (J). 1967. 6.50 (*0-87511-017-7*) Claitors.

Traveling Mercies. David Williams. LC 92-38738. 80p. (Orig.). 1993. pap. 9.95 (*0-914086-98-7*) Alicejamesbooks.

Traveling on into the Light. Martha Brooks. 160p. (YA). (gr. 7 up). 1996. pap. 3.99 (*0-14-037867-7*, Puffin) Puffin Bks.

Traveling on into the Light: And Other Stories. Martha Brooks. LC 94-9136. 144p. (YA). (gr. 7 up). 1994. 15.95 (*0-531-06863-3*); lib. bdg. 16.99 (*0-531-08713-1*) Orchard Bks Watts.

Traveling on Your Own. Eleanor Berman. 1990. 12.95 (*0-517-57454-3*, C P Pubs) Crown Pub Group.

Traveling Photographer's Guide to San Francisco: How to Find & Photograph the Classic San Francisco Scenes. Mary A. Schatz. LC 85-52229. (Illus.). 34p. (Orig.). 1986. pap. 4.95 (*0-9616197-0-8*) Travel Photo.

Traveling Pillow. Beverly Brown. LC 94-75990. (Illus.). 32p. (J). (ps-2). 1994. 12.95 (*1-880851-12-1*) Greene Bark Pr.

Traveling Salesman, Vol. 840. Gerhard Reinelt. LC 94-31562. (Lecture Notes in Computer Science). 1994. 39.95 (*0-387-58334-3*) Spr-Verlag.

Traveling Salesman Problem. E. L. Lawler et al. LC 85-3158. (Discrete Mathematics Ser.). 465p. 1985. text ed. 179.00 (*0-471-90413-9*) Wiley.

***Traveling Solo: Advice & Ideas for More Than 250 Great Vacations.** Eleanor Berman. LC 97-1531. (Illus.). 320p. 1997. pap. 16.95 (*0-7627-0044-0*) Globe Pequot.

***Traveling the - New, Historic Route 66 of Illinois.** John Weiss. Ed. & Photos by Lenore Weiss. (Illus.). 100p. (Orig.). 1997. pap. 12.95 (*0-9604576-3-1*) Animal Owners.

Traveling the High Way Home: Ralph Stanley & the World of Traditional Bluegrass Music. John Wright. (Music in American Life Ser.). (Illus.). 292p. 1993. 27.50 (*0-252-02024-3*) U of Ill Pr.

Traveling the High Way Home: Ralph Stanley & the World of Traditional Bluegrass Music. John Wright. 304p. 1995. 15.95 (*0-252-06478-X*) U of Ill Pr.

Traveling the Information FREEway: A Primer on Using Local Computer Bulletin Boards to Communicate Around the World. LC 94-90373. (Illus.). 64p. (Orig.). 1994. pap. 8.95 (*0-9642807-0-1*) Wolff Pubns.

Traveling the Microsoft Network: Things to Do, Places to Go, People to Meet on the MSN. Stephen W. Sagman. (Independent Ser.). 352p. 1995. 19.95 (*1-55615-817-3*) Microsoft.

Traveling the Natchez Trace. Lori Finley. LC 95-6023. (Illus.). 233p. (Orig.). 1995. pap. 12.95 (*0-89587-130-0*) Blair.

Traveling the National Road: Across the Centuries on America's First Highway. Intro. by Merritt Ierley. (Illus.). 270p. 1993. pap. 14.95 (*0-87951-495-7*) Overlook Pr.

Traveling the National Road: Two Centuries on America's First Highway. Merritt Ierley. (Illus.). 288p. 1990. 21.95 (*0-87951-394-2*) Overlook Pr.

Traveling the Oregon Trail. Julie Fanselow. (Falcon Guides Ser.). 1996. pap. 12.95 (*1-56044-391-X*) Falcon Pr MT.

Traveling the Path of Love: Sayings of Sufi Masters. Ed. by Llewellyn Vaughan-Lee. LC 94-78690. 245p. (Orig.). 1995. pap. 12.95 (*0-9634574-2-X*) Golden Sufi Ctr.

***Traveling the Southern Highlands: A Complete Vacation Guide to the Mountains of N.E. Georgia, East Tennessee, Western North Carolina, & Southwestern Virginia.** Cathy Summerlin & Vernon Summerlin. LC 97-9487. (Illus.). 320p. 1997. pap. 14.95 (*1-55853-484-9*) Rutledge Hill Pr.

Traveling the Trace. Cathy Summerlin. LC 95-3793. 315p. 1995. pap. 14.95 (*1-55853-340-0*) Rutledge Hill Pr.

Traveling the Trans-Canada: From Newfoundland to British Columbia. William L. Howarth. Ed. by Donald J. Crump. (Special Publications Series 22: No. 3). (Illus.). 200p. 1987. lib. bdg. 12.95 (*0-87044-631-2*) Natl Geog.

Traveling the Trans-Canada: From Newfoundland to British Columbia. William L. Howarth. Ed. by Donald J. Crump. LC 87-28145. (Special Publications Series 22: No. 3). (Illus.). 200p. 1995. 16.00 (*0-87044-626-6*) Natl Geog.

Traveling the Way. Drusilla McGowen. 1977. 6.55 (*0-686-20047-0*) Rod & Staff.

Traveling Through Idioms: An Exercise Guidebook to the World of American Idioms. Judi Kadden. (Orig.). 1995. pap. text ed. 17.95 (*0-472-08354-6*) U of Mich Pr.

Traveling Through Time: A Guide to Michigan's Historical Markers. Ed. by Laura R. Ashlee. (Illus.). 336p. (Orig.). 1992. pap. text ed. 14.95 (*0-935719-18-0*) MI Hist Mag.

Traveling Through Time & Space: A Study Guide. Michael Golden. (Thematic Units Ser.). (J). (gr. 5-8). 1991. pap. text ed. 20.95 (*0-88122-563-0*) Lrn Links.

Traveling Through Tippecanoe: A Pictorial History. Paula Woods & Fern Martin. (Indiana Pictorial History Ser.). (Illus.). 1992. write for info. (*0-943963-25-7*) G Bradley.

***Traveling to Europe Like a Pro.** Analu. 528p. (Orig.). 1997. pap. text ed. 18.95 (*1-879899-06-X*) Newjoy Pr.

Traveling to Tondo: A Tale of the Nkundo of Zaire. Illus. by Will Hillenbrand. LC 90-39419. 40p. (J). (gr. k-4). 1991. lib. bdg. 14.99 (*0-679-90081-0*) Knopf Bks Yng Read.

Traveling to Tondo: A Tale of the Nkundo of Zaire. Illus. by Will Hillenbrand. LC 90-39419. (Dragonfly Bks.). 40p. (J). (ps-3). 1994. pap. 5.99 (*0-679-85309-X*) Knopf Bks Yng Read.

Traveling Toward the Heart. Judith Goren. 64p. (Orig.). 1994. pap. 10.00 (*1-56439-036-5*) Ridgeway.

Traveling Wave Antennas. Carleton H. Walter. LC 89-64104. 448p. 1990. reprint ed. 29.95 (*0-932146-51-1*) Peninsula CA.

Traveling Wave Solutions of Parabolic Systems. A. I. Volpert et al. (Translations of Mathematical Monographs: Vol. 140). 448p. 1994. 142.00 (*0-8218-4609-4*, MMONO/140) Am Math.

***Traveling with Angels.** Linda Harrell. 112p. (Orig.). 1997. pap. 7.99 (*1-884369-49-9*, EBED Pubns) McDougal Pubng.

Traveling with Children in the U. S. A. A Guide to Pleasure, Adventure, Discovery. Leila Hadley. LC 77-79233. (Americans-Discover-America Ser.). 1977. pap. 4.95 (*0-688-03132-3*, Quill) Morrow.

Traveling with Heart: A Handbook for the Socially Conscious Tourist. Lisa French. 240p. 1995. 20.00 (*1-885420-24-2*) Peradam Pr.

Traveling with Hermes: Hermeneutics & Rhetoric. Bruce Krajewski. LC 92-5080. 176p. (C). 1993. 22.50 (*0-87023-815-9*) U of Mass Pr.

Traveling with Impunity: Journey of the Heart. Rani Ziegler. 264p. (Orig.). 1989. pap. 9.95 (*0-9622035-1-3*) Universal Oregon.

Traveling with Kids - One Hundred One Tips for a Great Trip. Jay A. Parry. (Illus.). 193p. (Orig.). 1989. pap. text ed. 7.95 (*0-944803-69-5*) Brite Music.

Traveling with Power: The Exploration & Development of Perception. Ken Eagle Feather. 248p. 1992. pap. 12.95 (*1-878901-28-1*) Hampton Roads Pub Co.

Traveling with Tangerines: Refreshing Biblical Truth for Women Journeying Through Family Life. Barbara Crider. Ed. by Susan Hansen. 64p. (Orig.). 1996. pap. 5.95 (*1-56309-166-6*) Womans Mission Union.

Traveling with the Dead. Barbara Hambly. 352p. 1995. 22.00 (*0-345-38102-5*, Del Rey) Ballantine.

***Traveling with the Dead.** Barbara Hambly. 1996. mass mkt. 5.99 (*0-345-40740-7*, Del Rey) Ballantine.

Traveling with the Family. 1989. 9.95 (*0-930399-15-3*) BackPax Int.

Traveling with the Nicelies. Sandra J. Ross. LC 94-94426. (Nicelies Ser.). (Illus.). 64p. (J). (ps-2). 1994. pap. 5.95 (*1-881235-03-3*) Creat Opport.

Traveling with Your Sketchbook: A Step-by-Step Guide to Travel Sketching with Emphasis on Pen-&-Ink. Joyce Ryan. LC 90-83216. (Illus.). 200p. (Orig.). 1990. pap. 19.95 (*0-939077-02-7*) Butterfly Bks.

Traveling Women. Opal P. Adisa & Devorah Major. LC 89-83489. (Illus.). 103p. (Orig.). 1989. pap. 6.95 (*0-932693-01-6*) Jukebox Press.

Travelingue. Marcel Ayme. 288p. (FRE.). 1973. pap. 12.95 (*0-7859-3565-7*, F84350) Fr & Eur.

Traveller: Stories of Two Continents. Victor Kelleher. 218p. 1988. pap. 14.95 (*0-7022-2103-1*, Pub. by Univ Queensland Pr AT) Intl Spec Bk.

Traveller in China. Christina Dodwell. (Illus.). 160p. 1986. 15.95 (*0-8253-0371-0*) Beaufort Bks NY.

Traveller in Little Things. William H. Hudson. reprint ed. 64.50 (*0-404-03412-8*) AMS Pr.

Traveller in Space: In Search of Female Identity in Tibetan Buddhism. June Campbell. LC 95-50614. 240p. 1996. 27.50 (*0-8076-1406-8*) Braziller.

Traveller on Horseback. large type ed. Christina Dodwell. 1989. 25.99 (*0-7089-2102-7*) Ulverscroft.

Traveller on Horseback: In Eastern Turkey & Iran. Christina Dodwell. (Illus.). 192p. 1989. 18.95 (*0-8027-1078-6*) Walker & Co.

Traveller Tales of the Pan-American Countries. Hezekiah Butterworth. LC 71-130986. (Illus.). reprint ed. 37.50 (*0-404-01255-8*) AMS Pr.

Traveller Without a Map. Chien Hsiao. Tr. by Jeffrey C. Kinkley from CHI. LC 93-28197. (Illus.). 302p. (C). 1993. 45.00 (*0-8047-2237-4*); pap. 14.95 (*0-8047-2238-2*) Stanford U Pr.

Travellers. (Junior African Writers Ser.). (Illus.). 128p. (J). (gr. 7-8). 1995. pap. 4.99 (*0-7910-3165-9*) Chelsea Hse.

Traveller's Alphabet. Marty Cohen. Ed. by Vi Gale. LC 79-84509. (First Bk.). (Illus.). 1979. pap. 5.00 (*0-915986-16-7*) Prescott St Pr.

Traveller's Alphabet. limited ed. Marty Cohen. Ed. by Vi Gale. LC 79-84509. (First Bk.). (Illus.). 1979. 20.00 (*0-915986-15-9*) Prescott St Pr.

***Travellers & Ireland: Whose Country, Whose History?** Jim Maclaughlin. (Undercurrents Ser.). 90p. 1995. pap. text ed. 7.50 (*1-85918-094-9*, Pub. by Cork Univ IE) Intl Spec Bk.

Travellers & Ireland: Whose History, Whose Country? Jim M. Laughlin. 80p. 1995. pap. 7.50 (*1-85918-090-6*, Pub. by Cork Univ IE) Intl Spec Bk.

Traveller's Bed & Breakfast. rev. ed. Jean Knight. 80p. 1985. 4.95 (*0-9613481-0-0*) Travellers Bed.

Traveller's Breviant, or an Historical Description of the Most Famous Kingdomes. Giovanni Botero. LC 72-175. (English Experience Ser.: No. 143). 180p. 1969. reprint ed. 35.00 (*90-221-0143-6*) Walter J Johnson.

Travellers Dictionary of Quotations. Peter Yapp. 1986. pap. 19.95 (*0-7102-0672-0*, RKP) Routledge.

Traveller's Dictionary of Quotations: Who Said What, about Where. Ed. by Peter Yapp. 1022p. 1985. pap. 25.00 (*0-415-02760-8*) Routledge.

Traveller's Guide. 1990. reprint ed. pap. 9.99 (*0-88019-273-9*) Schmul Pub Co.

***Traveller's Guide: An English Coursebook Phrasebook for Speakers of English as a Second Language Who Are Travelling or Plan to Travel to the U. S. A.** Stephen J. Sinsley. LC 91-10769. 1991. 8.95 (*0-02-411035-3*) Macmillan.

Traveller's Guide to Aboriginal B. C. Cheryl Coull. 1996. pap. text ed. 14.95 (*1-55110-402-4*, Pub. by Whitecap Bks CN) Gr Arts Ctr Pub.

Travellers' Guide to Asian Customs & Manners. Elizabeth Devine & Nancy L. Braganti. (Illus.). 352p. 1986. pap. 13.95 (*0-312-81610-3*) St Martin.

Traveller's Guide to Celtic Britain. Anne Ross & Michael Cyprien. (Traveller's Guide Ser.). (Illus.). 128p. 1985. 14.95 (*0-918678-06-4*) Natl Hist Soc.

Traveller's Guide to Early Medieval Britain. Anthony Goodman. Ed. by Michael Cyprien. (Traveller's Guide Ser.). 1986. 14.95 (*0-918678-16-1*) Natl Hist Soc.

Traveller's Guide to Historic British Columbia. Rosemary Neering. 1994. pap. text ed. 14.95 (*1-55110-095-9*, Pub. by Whitecap Bks CN) Gr Arts Ctr Pub.

Traveller's Guide to Homoeopathy. Phyllis Speight. 64p. (Orig.). 1990. pap. 12.95 (*0-8464-1337-X*) Beekman Pubs.

Travellers Guide to Homoeopathy. Phyllis Speight. 111p. 1989. pap. 5.95 (*0-85207-212-0*, Pub. by C W Daniel UK) Natl Bk Netwk.

Traveller's Guide to Places of Worship. Charles Kightly. 1986. 14.95 (*0-918678-18-8*) Natl Hist Soc.

Traveller's Guide to Roman Britain. Patrick Ottaway. 1986. 14.95 (*0-918678-19-6*) Natl Hist Soc.

Traveller's Guide to Royal Roads. Charles Kightly. (Illus.). 128p. 1985. 14.95 (*0-918678-09-9*) Natl Hist Soc.

Traveller's Guide to South Africa. Peter Joyce. (Illus.). 376p. 1992. pap. 10.95 (*1-56757-016-X*) Appleton Comms.

Traveller's Guide to Spurgeon Country. Eric W. Hayden. 1974. pap. 3.00 (*1-56186-415-3*) Pilgrim Pubns.

Traveller's Guide to the Best Cathouses in Nevada. rev. ed. Jerry R. Schwartz. (Illus.). 192p. 1995. pap. 14.95 (*0-9613653-0-7*) Straight Pubs.

Traveller's Guide to the Food of France. Glynn Christian. LC 86-80099. (Illus.). 192p. 1986. pap. 9.95 (*0-03-008529-2*, Owl) H Holt & Co.

Traveller's Guide to the Scotland of Robert the Bruce. Nigel Tranter. LC 85-21914. (Illus.). 127p. 1985. 14.95 (*0-918678-10-2*) Natl Hist Soc.

Travellers' Health: How to Stay Healthy Abroad. 3rd ed. Ed. by Richard Dawood. LC 92-9169. (C). 1992. write for info. (*0-19-262247-1*) OUP.

Traveller's History of China. Stephen G. Haw. LC 95-6927. (Traveller's History Ser.). 320p. 1995. pap. 14.95 (*1-56656-180-9*) Interlink Pub.

***Traveller's History of China.** 2nd ed. Stephen G. Haw. (Traveller's History Ser.). (Illus.). 320p. 1997. pap. 14.95 (*1-56656-257-0*) Interlink Pub.

Traveller's History of Egypt. Michael Hagg. (Traveller's History Ser.). (Illus.). 320p. Date not set. pap. 14.95 (*0-940793-72-5*) Interlink Pub.

Traveller's History of France. 3rd ed. Robert Cole. LC 89-15346. (Traveller's History Ser.). (Illus.). 240p. 1995. pap. 12.95 (*1-56656-177-9*) Interlink Pub.

***Traveller's History of France.** 4th ed. Robert Cole. (Traveller's History Ser.). (Illus.). 240p. 1997. pap. 12.95 (*1-56656-222-8*) Interlink Pub.

Traveller's History of Greece. 2nd ed. Timothy Boatswain & Colin Nicolson. LC 89-15341. (Traveller's History Ser.). (Illus.). 320p. 1995. pap. 14.95 (*1-56656-178-7*) Interlink Pub.

Traveller's History of Greece see Pelican History of Greece

Traveller's History of India. Sinharaja Tammita-Delgoda. LC 94-36800. (Traveller's History Ser.). 288p. 1994. pap. 14.95 (*1-56656-161-2*) Interlink Pub.

Traveller's History of Ireland. 2nd ed. Peter Neville. LC 92-5756. (Traveller's History Ser.). (Illus.). 288p. (Orig.). 1995. pap. 14.95 (*1-56656-181-7*) Interlink Pub.

***Traveller's History of Ireland.** 3rd ed. Peter Neville. (Traveller's History Ser.). (Illus.). 288p. 1997. pap. 14.95 (*1-56656-259-7*) Interlink Pub.

Traveller's History of Italy. 3rd ed. Valerio Lintner. LC 89-15345. (Traveller's History Ser.). (Illus.). 288p. 1995. pap. 14.95 (*1-56656-182-5*) Interlink Pub.

***Traveller's History of Italy.** 4th ed. Valerio Lintner. (Traveller's History Ser.). (Illus.). 288p. 1997. pap. 14.95 (*1-56656-258-9*) Interlink Pub.

Traveller's History of Japan. Richard Tames. LC 93-8074. (Traveller's History Ser.). (Illus.). 288p. (Orig.). 1994. pap. 13.95 (*1-56656-138-8*) Interlink Pub.

*Travellers History of Japan. 2nd ed. Peter Neville. 1997. pap. text ed. 13.95 (1-56656-260-0) Interlink Pub.

Traveller's History of London. Richard Tames. LC 92-5755. (Traveller's History Ser.). (Illus.). 320p. (Orig.). 1992. pap. 13.95 (1-56656-109-4) Interlink Pub.

***Traveller's History of North Africa.** Barnaby Rogerson. (Traveller's History Ser.). 1997. pap. text ed. 14.95 (1-56656-252-X) Interlink Pub.

Traveller's History of Paris. Robert Cole. LC 94-7120. (Traveller's History Ser.). 320p. 1994. pap. 13.95 (1-56656-150-7) Interlink Pub.

***Travellers History of Russia.** 3rd ed. Peter Neville. 1997. pap. 13.95 (1-56656-273-2) Interlink Pub.

Traveller's History of Russia & the U. S. S. R. 2nd rev. ed. Peter Neville. LC 90-34708. (Traveller's History Ser.). (Illus.). 336p. (Orig.). 1994. pap. 13.95 (1-56656-143-4) Interlink Pub.

Traveller's History of Scotland. 2nd rev. ed. Andrew Fisher. LC 90-34709. (Traveller's History Ser.). (Illus.). 306p. 1994. pap. 13.95 (1-56656-149-3) Interlink Pub.

***Traveller's History of Scotland.** 3rd ed. Andrew Fisher. (Traveller's History Ser.). (Illus.). 256p. 1997. pap. 13.95 (1-56656-211-2) Interlink Pub.

Traveller's History of Spain. 2nd rev. ed. Juan Lalaguna. LC 89-15344. (Traveller's History Ser.). (Illus.). 304p. 1994. pap. 13.95 (1-56656-148-5) Interlink Pub.

Traveller's History of Spain. 3rd ed. Juan Lalaguna. LC 91-7597. (Traveller's History Ser.). (Illus.). 304p. 1997. pap. 14.95 (1-56656-203-1) Interlink Pub.

Traveller's History of Turkey. 2nd ed. Richard Stoneman. LC 92-42424. (Traveller's History Ser.). (Illus.). 256p. 1996. pap. 13.95 (1-56656-209-0) Interlink Pub.

***Travellers in a Landscape: Visitors' Impressions of the Darling Downs 1827-1954.** Maurice French. (Illus.). 314p. 1994. pap. 44.95 (0-949414-53-0, Pub. by U Sthrn Queenslnd AT) Aubrey Bks.

Travellers in Eighteenth-Century England. Rosamond Bayne-Powell. LC 74-174875. (Illus.). 241p. 1972. reprint ed. 23.95 (0-405-08245-2, Pub. by Blom Pubns UK) Ayer.

***Travellers in Magic.** Goldstein. 1997. pap. 15.95 (0-312-86301-2) St Martin.

Travellers in Magic. Lisa Goldstein. 288p. 1994. 21.95 (0-312-85790-X) Tor Bks.

***Traveller's India: An Anthology.** Ed. by H. K. Kaul. 1997. pap. 15.95 (0-19-563926-X) OUP.

Travellers, Journeys, Tourists. Ed. by David Walker & Julia Horne. 148p. 1994. 39.95 (0-7855-0335-8, Pub. by Deakin Univ AT) St Mut.

Travellers Laffbook: 50 Reasons to Stay Home, Starting with Alabama. Michelle Beaudry. (Illus.). 128p. 1995. pap. 9.95 (0-9644347-0-9) Laffbooks.

Traveller's Literary Companion: Caribbean. Ed. by James Ferguson. 350p. 1997. pap. 22.95 (0-8442-8964-7, Passport Bks) NTC Pub Grp.

Traveller's Literary Companion: France. Ed. by John Edmondson. 350p. 1997. pap. 17.95 (0-8442-8965-5, Passport Bks) NTC Pub Grp.

Travellers Medical Services Directory: 1993 Edition. Ed. by Milan Korcok. 144p. 1992. pap. 7.95 (0-9635675-0-0) Intl Med Srvs.

Travellers' Money. John Booker. (Illus.). 160p. 1994. text ed. 30.00 (0-7509-0597-2, Pub. by Sutton Pubng UK) Bks Intl VA.

Traveller's Notebook. Leslie Forbes. 1992. 16.00 (0-517-58905-2, Ebury Pr Stationery) Crown Pub Group.

Traveller's Quest: Original Contributions Towards a Philosophy of Travel. Maurice A. Michael. LC 72-5673. (Essay Index Reprint Ser.). 1977. reprint ed. 24.95 (0-8369-7297-X) Ayer.

Traveller's Rest. Philip Gosse. LC 70-84308. (Essay Index Reprint Ser.). 1977. 20.95 (0-8369-1132-6) Ayer.

Traveller's Road. Margaret P. Kowarick. 135p. (Orig.). 1994. pap. write for info. (0-9642230-0-7) J Maciel.

Traveller's Scotland: A Practical Guide. Katie Wood. 336p. 1994. pap. 14.95 (1-85158-519-2, Pub. by Mnstream UK) Trafalgar.

Travellers' Songs: From England & Scotland. Ed. by Ewan MacColl & Peggy Seeger. LC 76-2854. 399p. 1977. reprint ed. pap. 113.80 (0-608-01433-8, 2062195) Bks Demand.

Traveller's Tales. Enid M. Dinnis. LC 72-5908. (Short Story Index Reprint Ser.). 1977. reprint ed. 16.95 (0-8369-4211-6) Ayer.

Travellers' Tales: Narratives of Home & Displacement. George Robertson et al. LC 93-23698. (Futures, New Perspectives for Cultural Analysis Ser.). 272p. (C). 1994. pap. 16.95 (0-415-07016-3, B3899) Routledge.

Travellers' Tales: Narratives of Home & Displacement. George Robertson et al. LC 93-23698. (Futures, New Perspectives for Cultural Analysis Ser.). 272p. (C). (gr. 13). 1994. text ed. 62.95 (0-415-07015-5, B3895) Routledge.

***Traveller's Wine Guide to France.** Christopher Fielden. LC 96-45974. (Traveller's Wine Guides). 1997. pap. 17.95 (1-56656-250-3) Interlink Pub.

***Traveller's Wine Guide to Germany.** Hans Ambrosi & Kerry B. Stewart. LC 96-45977. (Traveller's Wine Guides). 1997. pap. 17.95 (1-56656-223-6) Interlink Pub.

***Traveller's Wine Guide to Italy.** Stephen Hobley. LC 96-45975. (Traveller's Wine Guides). 1997. pap. 17.95 (1-56656-251-1) Interlink Pub.

***Traveller's Wine Guide to Spain.** Desmond Begg. LC 96-45976. (Traveller's Wine Guides). 1997. pap. write for info. (1-56656-224-4) Interlink Pub.

Traveller's Yellow Pages. Seth Godin. 278p. 1996. pap. 9.95 (0-395-79285-1) HM.

Traveller's Yellow Pages: Moscow Map 1995. InFoservices International Staff. 1995. 4.95 (1-881832-04-X) InfoSrvs Int.

Traveller's Yellow Pages & Handbook for Moscow 1997-98. Ed. by Michael R. Dohan. (Traveller's Yellow Pages Ser.). 640p. 1997. pap. 12.95 (1-881832-08-2) InfoSrvs Int.

Traveller's Yellow Pages & Handbook for Northwest Russia, 1997-1998. Ed. by Michael R. Dohan. (Traveller's Yellow Pages Ser.). 384p. 1997. pap. 9.95 (1-881832-09-0) InfoSrvs Int.

Traveller's Yellow Pages & Handbook for St. Petersburg 1997-98. Ed. by Michael R. Dohan. (Traveller's Yellow Pages Ser.). 456p. 1997. pap. 9.95 (1-881832-07-4) InfoSrvs Int.

Travellers's Guide to Norman Britain. Trevor Rowley. (Traveller's Guide Ser.). (Illus.). 128p. 1986. 14.95 (0-918678-11-0) Natl Hist Soc.

Travelling: Three Months on the NBA Road. John E. Nordahl. (Illus.). 304p. 1995. 14.95 (0-02-860438-5) Macmillan.

Travelling along with Methodism: A Personal Retrospect. Frank Garforth. 207p. (C). 1990. pap. 50.00 (0-948340-01-0, Pub. by Christygate Pr UK) St Mut.

***Travelling Bear.** Marilyn Woody. (Illus.). 16p. (J). (ps-1). 1998. bds. 14.99 (1-57673-153-7, Gold & Honey) Multnomah Pubs.

Travelling Companions. Henry James. LC 75-37552. (Short Story Index Reprint Ser.). 1977. reprint ed. 19.95 (0-8369-4111-X) Ayer.

Travelling Free: How to Recover from the Past by Changing Your Beliefs. Mandy Evans. LC 90-91423. 128p. (Orig.). 1990. pap. 9.95 (1-878639-04-8) Yes You Can Pr.

Travelling in Family: Selected Poems. Carlos D. De Andrade. 1995. pap. 13.00 (0-88001-434-2) Ecco Pr.

Travelling in the Family. Carlos Drummond. Ed. by Thomas Colchie. Tr. by Elizabeth Bishop et al. pap. 19.95 (0-394-52478-0) Random.

Travelling Kind. Janet Dailey. (Americana Ser.: No. 862). 1991. mass mkt. 3.50 (0-373-89862-2) Harlequin Bks.

Travelling Light. Bill Barich. (Nonfiction Ser.). 1985. pap. 11.00 (0-14-007418-X, Penguin Bks) Viking Penguin.

Travelling Light. Sandra Field. (Presents Ser.). 1994. mass mkt. 2.99 (0-373-11646-2, 1-11646-6) Harlequin Bks.

Travelling Light. large type ed. Sandra Field. (Harlequin Ser.). 1994. lib. bdg. 19.95 (0-263-13656-6) Thorndike Pr.

***Travelling Musicians.** unabridged ed. P. K. Page. (Illus.). 32p. (J). (gr. k-2). 1991. 12.95 (1-55074-039-3, Pub. by Kids Can Pr CN) Genl Dist Srvs.

Travelling My Shadow. Sue B. Walker. LC 82-80016. (Illus.). 60p. 1982. pap. text ed. 5.00 (0-942544-02-1) Negative Capability Pr.

Travelling Painter: A Companion, Tutor & Guide. Paul Millichip. (Illus.). 224p. 1991. 34.95 (0-7134-6451-8, Pub. by Batsford UK) Trafalgar.

Travelling Sketches. Anthony Trollope. Ed. by N. John Hall. LC 80-1884. (Selected Works of Anthony Trollope). 1981. reprint ed. lib. bdg. 18.95 (0-405-14147-5) Ayer.

Travelling the Miracle Road. Betty Palmer. LC 88-90635. (Orig.). 1988. pap. 5.95 (0-910487-16-2) Royalty Pub.

Travelling the Miracle Road. Betty Palmer. Ed. by Nita Scoggan. LC 88-90635. (Illus.). 224p. (Orig.). 1988. 10.00 (0-910487-17-0) Royalty Pub.

***Travelling the Oregon Trail.** Julie Fanselow. LC 97-284. 1996. pap. text ed. 12.95 (1-56044-477-0) Falcon Pr MT.

Travelling to England to Find Your Roots (Cheap) Nancy E. Carlberg. 200p. (Orig.). 1989. pap. 15.00 (0-944878-06-7) Carlberg Pr.

***Travelling with Cats.** Contrib. by Herbert Axelrod. (Cats & Dogs). (Illus.). (YA). (gr. 3 up). 1998. lib. bdg. 19.95 (0-7910-4805-5) Chelsea Hse.

***Travelling with Dogs.** Contrib. by Herbert Axelrod. (Cats & Dogs). (Illus.). (YA). (gr. 3 up). 1998. lib. bdg. 19.95 (0-7910-4816-0) Chelsea Hse.

Travelling with Women. Harry Polkinhorn. 56p. 1983. pap. 5.00 (0-317-63763-0) Atticus Pr.

Travelling Without a Valid Ticket. Howard Sergeant. (C). 1988. 25.00 (0-904524-39-6, Pub. by Rivelin Grapheme Pr) St Mut.

Travelmates: 105 Fun Games Kids Can Play in the Car or on the Go. Story Evans & Lise O'Haire. 96p. 1997. pap. 8.00 (0-517-88760-6) Random Hse Value.

Travelog. Charles Harbutt. 1974. pap. 10.95 (0-262-58026-8) MIT Pr.

Travelogues. Peter Frank. LC 82-80710. (Contemporary Literature Ser.: No. 12). 48p. (Orig.). 1982. pap. 4.00 (0-940650-15-0) Sun & Moon CA.

Travels. William Bartram. 1928. pap. 7.95 (0-486-20013-2) Dover.

Travels. William Bartram. (Illus.). 432p. 1988. pap. 13.95 (0-14-025300-9, Penguin Bks) Viking Penguin.

Travels. Michael Crichton. LC 87-46040. 1988. 25.50 (0-394-56236-4) Knopf.

Travels. Michael Crichton. 1989. mass mkt. 6.99 (0-345-35932-1) Ballantine.

Travels. Michael Crichton. 400p. 1993. pap. 10.00 (0-345-37966-7, Ballantine Trade) Ballantine.

Travels. W. S. Merwin. 1994. pap. 14.00 (0-679-75277-3) Random.

Travels. Marco Polo. 26.95 (0-8488-0187-3) Amereon Ltd.

Travels. Marco Polo. Tr. & Intro. by Ronald Latham. (Classics Ser.). 384p. 1958. pap. 11.95 (0-14-044057-7, Penguin Classics) Viking Penguin.

Travels. Marco Polo. Ed. by T. Wright. Tr. by Marsden. LC 68-57871. (Bohn's Antiquarian Library). reprint ed. 57.00 (0-404-50023-4) AMS Pr.

Travels: Bilingual Edition. Yehuda Amichai. Tr. by Ruth Nevo from HEB. LC 85-27814. 137p. (Orig.). (ENG & HEB.). 1986. 13.95 (0-935296-62-X); pap. 11.95 (0-935296-63-8) Sheep Meadow.

***Travels: Poems by Joanna Biggar.** Joanna Biggar. Ed. by R. D. Baker. (Poetry Chapbook Ser.). (Illus.). 28p. (Orig.). 1996. pap. 4.00 (1-887641-12-2) Argonne Hotel Pr.

Travels Along the Edge. Noland. LC 97-11594. 1997. pap. 14.00 (0-679-76344-9) Random.

Travels & Adventures: In Canada & the Indian Territories: Between the Years 1760 & 1776. Alexander Henry. Ed. & Illus. by James Bain. LC 72-108491. 375p. 1972. reprint ed. 79.00 (0-403-00393-8) Scholarly.

Travels & Adventures of Celebrated Travelers. Henry Howe. (Notable American Authors Ser.). 1992. reprint ed. lib. bdg. 75.00 (0-7812-3204-X) Rprt Serv.

Travels & Adventures of Pero Tafur (1435-149) Ed. & Tr. by Malcolm Letts from SPA. (Curzon Travellers Ser.). (C). 1996. text ed. 65.00 (0-7007-0348-9, Pub. by Curzon Pr UK) Paul & Co Pubs.

Travels & Archaeology in South Chile. Junius B. Bird. LC 87-30245. (Illus.). 278p. 1988. text ed. 32.95 (0-87745-202-4) U of Iowa Pr.

Travels & Discoveries in the Levant, 2 vols. in 1. Charly T. Newton. (Illus.). xxvi, 635p. 1990. reprint ed. 102.70 (3-487-09149-6) G Olms Pubs.

Travels & Life in Ashanti & Jaman. Richard A. Freedman. 559p. 1967. reprint ed. 59.50 (0-7146-1808-X, BHA-01808, Pub. by F Cass Pubs UK) Intl Spec Bk.

Travels & Other Writings. William Bartram. Ed. by Thomas P. Slaughter. LC 95-49282. (Illus.). 700p. 1996. 37.50 (1-883011-11-6) Library of America.

Travels & Politics in the Near East. William Miller. LC 70-135822. (Eastern Europe Collection). 1971. reprint ed. 33.95 (0-405-02764-8) Ayer.

Travels & Researches among the Lakes & Mountains of Eastern & Central Africa. J. F. Elton. Ed. by H. B. Cotterill. (Illus.). 417p. 1968. 55.00 (0-7146-1806-3, Pub. by F Cass Pubs UK) Intl Spec Bk.

Travels & Researches in Asia Minor, More Particularly in the Province of Lycia. Charles Fellows. (Illus.). xvi, 510p. 1975. reprint ed. lib. bdg. 57.20 (3-487-05488-4) G Olms Pubs.

Travels & Researches in Caffraria. Stephan Kay. 1834. 49.00 (0-403-00374-1) Scholarly.

Travels & Researches in Crete, 2 vols. in 1. T. A. Spratt. (Illus.). 848p. 1984. reprint ed. lib. bdg. 137.50 (90-256-0893-0, Pub. by AM Hakkert NE) Coronet Bks.

Travels Back in Time. Vezic Melegari. 1997. 2.99 (0-517-18454-0) Random Hse Value.

Travels During the Years 1787, 1788 & 1789, 2 Vols, Set. 2nd ed. Arthur Young. LC 79-115008. reprint ed. 265.00 (0-404-07068-X) AMS Pr.

Travels for a Donkey. Elisabeth D. Svendson. (Illus.). 80p. text ed. 15.95 (0-905483-78-2, Pub. by Whittet Bks UK) Diamond Farm Bk.

Travels for Two: Stories & Lies from My Childhood. Stephane Poulin. (Illus.). 32p. (J). (ps-2). 1991. pap. 5.95 (1-55037-204-1, Pub. by Annick CN); lib. bdg. 15.95 (1-55037-205-X, Pub. by Annick CN) Firefly Bks Ltd.

Travels in a Stone Canoe. H. Arden. 22.00 (0-06-016965-6, HarpT) HarpC.

Travels in a Strange State: Cycling Across the U. S. A. Joise Dew. 1996. pap. text ed. 7.95 (0-316-18222-2) Little.

Travels in a Thin Country. large type ed. Sara Wheeler. 576p. 1995. 25.99 (0-7089-3422-6) Ulverscroft.

Travels in Alaska. Katherine McNamara. Date not set. pap. 18.00 (0-670-82920-X) Viking Penguin.

***Travels in Alaska.** John Muir. 1997. pap. 11.95 (0-14-026832-4) Viking Penguin.

Travels in Alaska. Intro. by Richard Nelson. (Illus.). 336p. 1993. pap. 12.00 (0-14-017021-9, Penguin Bks) Viking Penguin.

Travels in Alaska. John Muir. LC 77-19358. (Illus.). reprint ed. 32.50 (0-404-16075-1) AMS Pr.

Travels in Alaska. John Muir. LC 77-19358. 1979. reprint ed. pap. 11.95 (0-395-28522-4) HM.

Travels in Alaska. John Muir. 1988. reprint ed. lib. bdg. 49.00 (0-7812-0154-3) Rprt Serv.

Travels in Alaska. John Muir. (BCL1 - United States Local History Ser.). 326p. 1991. reprint ed. lib. bdg. 89.00 (0-7812-6345-X) Rprt Serv.

Travels in Alaska. John Muir. LC 70-145196. 1915. reprint ed. 59.00 (0-403-01120-5) Scholarly.

Travels in Alaska. John Muir. LC 87-26311. (John Muir Library). 352p. 1988. reprint ed. pap. 10.00 (0-87156-783-0) Sierra.

Travels in America: From the Voyages of Discovery to the Present: An Annotated Bibliography of Travel Articles in Periodicals, 1955-1980. Garold L. Cole. LC 84-40273. 344p. 1985. 65.00 (0-8061-1791-5) U of Okla Pr.

Travels in America, 1851-1855. Rosalie Roos. Ed. by Carl L. Anderson. LC 81-187. 170p. 1982. 19.95 (0-8093-1018-X) S Ill U Pr.

Travels in Arabia. Burckhardt J. Lewis. 478p. (C). 1992. 125.00 (0-685-67239-5, Pub. by Darf Pubs Ltd UK) St Mut.

Travels in Arabia. B. Taylor. 336p. 1986. 200.00 (1-85077-084-0, Pub. by Darf Pubs Ltd UK) St Mut.

Travels in Arabia Deserta, 2 vols. Charles M. Doughty. xxxiv, 1345p. reprint ed. write for info. (0-318-71502-3) G Olms Pubs.

Travels in Arabia Deserts, 2 vols., 1. Charles M. Doughty. (Illus.). 1980. reprint ed. pap. 15.95 (0-486-23825-3) Dover.

Travels in Arabia Deserts, 2 vols., 2. Charles M. Doughty. (Illus.). 1980. reprint ed. pap. 15.95 (0-486-23826-1) Dover.

Travels in Arabia, 1845-1848. Georg A. Wallin. (Arabia Past & Present Ser.: Vol. 8). (Illus.). 1979. 26.95 (0-900891-53-X) Oleander Pr.

Travels in Britain, 1794-1795: The Diary of John Aspinwall, Great-Grandfather of Franklin Delano Roosevelt, with a Brief History of His Aspinwall Forebears. John Aspinwall. Ed. by Aileen S. Collins. LC 94-23232. 1994. 23.95 (0-9638487-6-3) Parsons Pr VA.

Travels in Canoe Country. Photos by Gerald Brimacombe. (Illus.). 144p. 1992. 35.00 (0-8212-1893-X) Bulfinch Pr.

Travels in Central Asia. Arminius Vambery. LC 73-115592. (Russia Observed, Series I). 1970. reprint ed. 37.95 (0-405-03073-8) Ayer.

Travels in Chili & La Plata, 2 Vols, Set. John Miers. LC 76-128416. reprint ed. 115.00 (0-404-04317-8) AMS Pr.

***Travels in Dreams: An Autobiography.** Bill Mollison. (Illus.). 863p. 1996. pap. text ed. 49.95 (0-908228-11-2, Pub. by Tagari Pubns AT) Permaculture.

Travels in Eastern Africa, 2 vols. Lyons McLeod. 1971. reprint ed. Set. 115.00 (0-7146-1832-2, Pub. by F Cass Pubs UK) Intl Spec Bk.

Travels in Egypt, Vol. 1. V. Denon. 346p. 1986. 180.00 (1-85077-098-0, Pub. by Darf Pubs Ltd UK) St Mut.

Travels in Egypt, Vol. 2. V. Denon. 332p. 1986. 180.00 (1-85077-099-9, Pub. by Darf Pubs Ltd UK) St Mut.

Travels in Egypt, Vols. 1 & 2. V. Denon. 1986. write for info. (0-318-62292-0, Pub. by Darf Pubs Ltd UK) St Mut.

Travels in Egypt & Nubia, Syria & Asia Minor. C. Irby & J. Mangles. 614p. 1985. 350.00 (1-85077-082-4, Pub. by Darf Pubs Ltd UK) St Mut.

Travels in Egypt, Arabia Petraea &the Holy Land, 2 Vols. Stephen Olin. Ed. by Moshe Davis. LC 77-70727. (America & the Holy Land Ser.). 1977. lib. bdg. 81.95 (0-405-10273-9) Ayer.

Travels in Hyperreality: Essays. Umberto Eco. Tr. by William Weaver. 1990. pap. 11.00 (0-15-691321-6) HarBrace.

Travels in Imperial China: The Intrepid Explorations & Discoveries of Pere Armand David. George Bishop. (Illus.). 192p. 1996. pap. 17.95 (0-304-34802-3, Pub. by Cassell UK) Sterling.

***Travels in India: Jean-Baptiste Tavernier, 2 vols., Set.** V. Ball. Ed. by William Crooke. (C). 1995. 58.00 (81-215-0682-4, Pub. by Munshiram Manoharial II) S Asia.

Travels in India, Ceylon & Borneo. Basil Hall. Ed. by Hugh G. Rawlinson. LC 76-174846. 274p. 1972. reprint ed. 24.95 (0-405-08593-1, Pub. by Blom Pubns UK) Ayer.

Travels in India Ceylon & Borneo. Basil Hall. Ed. by H. G. Rawlinson. (C). 1995. reprint ed. 42.00 (81-206-1022-9, Pub. by Asian Educ Servs II) S Asia.

Travels in India Including Sinde & the Punjab, 2 vols. Leopold Von Orlinch. 315p. 67.50 (0-8364-1630-9, Pub. by Usha II) S Asia.

Travels in Kamtchatka & Siberia: With a Narrative of a Residence in China. Peter Dobell. LC 78-115529. (Russia Observed Ser., No. 1). 1970. reprint ed. 36.95 (0-405-03021-5) Ayer.

Travels in Kamtschatka, During the Years 1787 & 1788. Jean De Lesseps. LC 72-115557. (Russia Observed, Series I). 1970. reprint ed. 35.95 (0-405-03043-6) Ayer.

Travels in Kashmir & the Panjab. Charles Hugel. Tr. by T. B. Jervis. (C). 1995. reprint ed. 44.00 (81-206-1047-4, Pub. by Asian Educ Servs II) S Asia.

Travels in Madeira, Sierra Leone, Teneriffe, St. Jago, Cape Coast, Fernando Po, Princes Island, Ect. Etc. 2nd ed. James Holman. LC 72-5529. (Black Heritage Library Collection). 1977. reprint ed. 39.95 (0-8369-9142-7) Ayer.

Travels in Mexico & California. A. B. Clarke. Ed. by Anne M. Perry. LC 88-1490. (Elma Dill Russell Spencer Series in the West & Southwest: No. 10). (Illus.). 176p. 1988. 19.95 (0-89096-354-1) Tex A&M Univ Pr.

Travels in Mexico, South America, 2 vols. Godfrey T. Vigne. LC 70-177865. (Illus.). reprint ed. 115.00 (0-404-06766-2) AMS Pr.

Travels in My Homeland: A Portuguese Classic. Almeida Garrett. Tr. & Intro. by John M. Parker. LC 87-61378. (Unesco Collection of Representative Works, Series of Translations from the Literature of the Union of Soviet Socialist Republics). 256p. 8700. 30.00 (0-7206-0663-2, Pub. by P Owen Ltd UK) Dufour.

Travels in Nepal & Sikkim, 1875-76. Richard Temple. 148p. (C). 1977. 62.50 (0-89771-103-3, Pub. by Ratna Pustak Bhandar) St Mut.

Travels in New England. Thea Wheelwright. 1989. 9.99 (0-517-69046-2) Random Hse Value.

Travels in New England & New York. Timothy Dwight. (Notable American Authors Ser.). 1992. reprint ed. lib. bdg. 75.00 (0-7812-2744-5) Rprt Serv.

Travels in North Africa. Darf Publishers Ltd. Staff. (C). 1988. 135.00 (1-85077-200-2, Pub. by Darf Pubs Ltd UK) St Mut.

Travels in North America, 3 vols., Set. Peter Kalm. 1993. reprint ed. lib. bdg. 225.00 (0-7812-5130-3) Rprt Serv.

Travels in North America, During the Years 1834-36, Including a Summer with the Pawnees. 2nd ed. Charles A. Murray. LC 68-54845. (American Scene Ser.). 878p. 1974. reprint ed. lib. bdg. 85.00 (0-306-71021-8) Da Capo.

Travels in North-America, in the Years 1780-1782, 2 Vols, 1. Francois J. De Chastellux. LC 67-29046. (Eyewitness Accounts of the American Revolution Ser., No. 1). 1968. reprint ed. 39.95 (0-405-01135-0) Ayer.

Travels in North-America, in the Years 1780-1782, 2 Vols, Set. Francois J. De Chastellux. LC 67-29046. (Eyewitness Accounts of the American Revolution Ser., No. 1). 1968. reprint ed. 20.95 (0-405-01109-1) Ayer.

Travels in North-America, in the Years 1780-1782, 2 Vols, Vol. 2. Francois J. De Chastellux. LC 67-29046. (Eyewitness Accounts of the American Revolution Ser., No. 1). 1968. reprint ed. 20.95 (0-405-01127-X) Ayer.

An Asterisk (*) at the beginning of an entry indicates that the title is appearing in BIP for the first time.

Travels in North America in the Years 1827-1828, 3 vols., Set. Basil Hall. 1993. reprint ed. lib. bdg. 225.00 (*0-7812-5123-0*) Rprt Serv.

Travels in North America, the Years, 1841-2: Geological Observations on the United States, Canada & Nova Scotia, 2 Vols. Charles Lyell. Ed. by Claude C. Albritton, Jr. LC 77-6525. (History of Geology Ser.). (Illus.). 1978. reprint ed. lib. bdg. 44.95 (*0-405-10447-2*) Ayer.

Travels in North America, 1827-1828, 3 Vols. Basil Hall. LC 73-13135. (Foreign Travelers in America, 1810-1935 Ser.). (Illus.). 1318p. 1974. reprint ed. 95.95 (*0-405-05457-2*) Ayer.

Travels in Nubia. J. L. Burchardt. 656p. 1990. 140.00 (*1-85077-172-3*, Pub. by Darf Pubs Ltd UK) St Mut.

Travels in Nubia. John L. Buckhardt. 498p. reprint ed. lib. bdg. 79.00 (*0-7812-0234-5*) Rprt Serv.

Travels in Nubia. John L. Burckhardt. LC 74-15014. reprint ed. 71.50 (*0-404-12009-1*) AMS Pr.

Travels in Oceania: Memoirs of a Whaling Ship's Doctor. Louis Thiercelin. Tr. by Christiane Mortelier. 350p. 1996. pap. 34.95 (*0-908569-71-8*, Pub. by U Otago Pr NZ) Intl Spec Bk.

Travels in Oman. Philip Ward. (Arabia Past & Present Ser.: Vol. 21). (Illus.). 584p. 1986. 55.00 (*0-906672-51-1*) Oleander Pr.

Travels in Persia, Sixteen Seventy-Three - Sixteen Seventy-Seven. John Chardin. (Illus.). 336p. 1988. reprint ed. pap. 7.95 (*0-486-25636-7*) Dover.

Travels in Persia, 1627-1629. Thomas Herbert. Ed. by William Foster. LC 78-39468. (Select Bibliographies Reprint Ser.). 1977. reprint ed. 23.95 (*0-8369-9912-6*) Ayer.

Travels in Philadelphia. Christopher Morley. 1993. reprint ed. lib. bdg. 89.00 (*0-7812-5492-2*) Rprt Serv.

Travels in Poland & Russia. William Coxe. LC 73-115524. (Russia Observed Ser.). 1970. reprint ed. 58.95 (*0-405-03017-7*) Ayer.

Travels in Russia. William R. Wilson. LC 75-115598. (Russia Observed, Series I). 1970. reprint ed. 41.95 (*0-405-03071-1*) Ayer.

Travels in Russia, the Krimea, the Caucasus & Georgia. Robert Lyall. LC 74-115560. (Russia Observed Ser., No. 1). 1970. reprint ed. 52.95 (*0-405-03046-0*) Ayer.

Travels in Siam, Cambodia & Laos 1858-1860, 2 vols. Henri Mouhot. (Oxford in Asia Hardback Reprints Ser.). (Illus.). 632p. 1991. Set. 69.00 (*0-19-588951-7*) OUP.

Travels in Siberia. S. S. Hill. LC 71-115546. (Russia Observed, Series I). 1970. reprint ed. 46.95 (*0-405-03034-7*) Ayer.

Travels in Siberia: Including Excursions Northwards, Down the Obi, to the Polar Circle, & Southwards, to the Chinese Frontier. Adolph Erman. LC 70-115535. (Russia Observed Ser., No. 1). 1970. reprint ed. 56.95 (*0-405-03025-8*) Ayer.

Travels in South America, 2 vols. rev. ed. Paul Marcoy. Incl. Vol. 2. Travels in South America. rev. ed. (Illus.). 504p. 1996. reprint ed. (*1-887954-13-9*); Vol. 1. Travels in South America. rev. ed. (Illus.). 536p. 1996. reprint ed. (*1-887954-12-0*); reprint ed. 24.95 (*1-887954-11-2*) Athena FL.

Travels in South America, 2 vols, Set. Francois R. De Pons. LC 71-128420. reprint ed. 145.00 (*0-404-02115-8*) AMS Pr.

Travels in South America see Travels in South America

***Travels in Southern Abyssinia.** Charles Johnston. Date not set. write for info. (*0-405-30028-X*); write for info. (*0-405-30112-X*) Ayer.

Travels in Southern Abyssinia: Through the Country of Adal to the Kingdom of Shoa, 2 Vols., Set. Charles Johnston. LC 72-3885. (Black Heritage Library Collection). 1977. reprint ed. 75.95 (*0-8369-9099-4*) Ayer.

Travels in Syria & Holy Land. J. L. Burckhardt. 668p. (C). 1992. 140.00 (*1-85077-189-8*, Pub. by Darf Pubs Ltd UK) St Mut.

Travels in Syria & the Holy Land. John L. Burckhardt. LC 77-87614. (Illus.). 720p. 1983. reprint ed. 76.50 (*0-404-16437-4*) AMS Pr.

Travels in Tartary Thibet & China, 1844-1846, 2 vols. Huc & Gabet. Ed. by Paul Pelliot. Tr. by William C. Hazlitt. (C). 1988. reprint ed. Set. 50.00 (*81-206-0396-6*, Pub. by Asian Educ Servs II) S Asia.

Travels in Tartary, Thibet & China, 1844-1846. Evariste-Regis Huc & Joseph Gabet. 864p. 1987. reprint ed. pap. 16.95 (*0-486-25438-0*) Dover.

Travels in the American West: Photographs by Len Jenshel. Ed. by Constance Sullivan. (Photographers at Work Ser.). (Illus.). 60p. (Orig.). 1992. pap. 15.95 (*1-56098-148-2*) Smithsonian.

Travels in the Colonies in 1773-1775 Described in the Letters of William Mylne. Ed. by Ted Ruddock. LC 91-37478. (Illus.). 168p. 1993. 30.00 (*0-8203-1426-9*) U of Ga Pr.

Travels in the Confederate States: A Bibliography. E. Merton Coulter. LC 94-17847. 304p. 1994. pap. 14.95 (*0-8071-1952-0*) La State U Pr.

Travels in the Confederate States: A Bibliography. E. Merton Coulter. xiv, 289p. 1981. reprint ed. 30.00 (*0-916107-02-7*) Broadfoot.

Travels in the Congo. Andre Gide. 305p. 1997. pap. 25.00 (*0-87556-024-5*) Saifer.

Travels in the Congo. Andre Gide. 1994. pap. 13.00 (*0-88001-365-6*) Ecco Pr.

Travels in the Drifting Dawn. Kenneth White. 160p. 1992. 29.95 (*1-85158-240-1*, Pub. by Mnstream UK) Trafalgar.

Travels in the Free States of Central America, 2 Vols, Set. Karl Scherzer. LC 79-128430. 1970. reprint ed. 87.50 (*0-404-05600-8*) AMS Pr.

Travels in the Great Desert of Sahara, 1845-1846, 2 vols. James Richardson. (Illus.). 1970. reprint ed. Set. 125.00 (*0-7146-1850-0*, BHA-01850, Pub. by F Cass Pubs UK) Intl Spec Bk.

Travels in the Great Sahara, Vol. 1. James Richardson. (C). 1988. 135.00 (*1-85077-192-8*, Pub. by Darf Pubs Ltd UK) St Mut.

Travels in the Great Sahara, Vol. 2. James Richardson. (C). 1988. 135.00 (*1-85077-193-6*, Pub. by Darf Pubs Ltd UK) St Mut.

Travels in the Great Western Prairies, 2 vols. in 1. Thomas J. Farnham. LC 68-16231. (American Scene Ser.). 612p. 1973. reprint ed. lib. bdg. 75.00 (*0-306-71012-9*) Da Capo.

Travels in the Great Western Prairies, the Anahuac & Rocky Mountains, & in the Oregon Territory: An 1839 Wagon Train Journal. Thomas J. Farnham. (American Biography Ser.). 108p. 1991. reprint ed. lib. bdg. 59.00 (*0-7812-8127-X*) Rprt Serv.

***Travels in the Interior Districts of Africa.** (Illus.). 372p. Date not set. 45.95 (*0-405-01718-9*) Arno Press.

Travels in the Interior Districts of Africa. Mungo Park & James Rennell. 1977. 18.95 (*0-405-18974-5*, 16889) Ayer.

Travels in the Interior Inhabited Parts of North America in the Years 1791 & 1792, Vol. 23. Patrick Campbell. Ed. by H. H. Langton. LC 68-28611. 326p. 1968. reprint ed. text ed. 75.00 (*0-8371-5061-2*, CATI, Greenwood Pr) Greenwood.

Travels in the Interior of Africa. G. Mollien. Ed. by T. E. Bowdich. (Illus.). 408p. 1967. 60.00 (*0-7146-1077-1*, Pub. by F Cass Pubs UK) Intl Spec Bk.

***Travels in the Interior of Africa 1849-1863, 2 vols.** James Chapman. Ed. by E. C. Tabler. (South African Biographical & Historical Studies: No. 10). 540p. 1971. 115.00 (*0-86961-003-1*, Pub. by A A Balkema NE) Ashgate Pub Co.

Travels in the Interior of Brazil. George Gardner. LC 75-128421. reprint ed. 62.50 (*0-404-02678-8*) AMS Pr.

Travels in the Interior of Mexico in 1825, 1826, 1827 & 1828: In Baja California & Around the Sea of Cortes. R. W. Hardy. (Beautiful Rio Grande Classics Ser.). 606p. 1977. reprint ed. 30.00 (*0-87380-146-6*) Rio Grande.

Travels in the Interiors of America in the Years 1809, 1810, & 1811. John Bradbury. LC 85-24615. 320p. reprint ed. pap. 91.20 (*0-7837-4650-4*, 2044374) Bks Demand.

Travels in the Ionian Isles, Albania, Thessaly, Macedonia, etc. Henry Holland. 1971. 18.95 (*0-405-18970-2*, 16885) Ayer.

***Travels in the Ionian Isles, Albania, Thessaly, Macedonia, Etc.** Henry Holland. (Illus.). 551p. Date not set. 55.95 (*0-405-01714-6*) Arno Press.

Travels in the Land of the Gods: The Japan Diaries of Richard Gordon Smith. Richard G. Smith. Ed. by Victoria Manthorpe. (Illus.). 224p. 1986. 25.00 (*0-685-16943-X*) P-H.

Travels in the Mogul Empire AD 1656-1668. Francois Bernier. 1989. reprint ed. 18.00 (*81-85395-12-8*, Pub. by Low Price II) S Asia.

***Travels in the Mogul Empire 1656-1668.** Francois Bernier. 1996. 44.00 (*81-206-1169-1*, Pub. by Asian Educ Servs II) S Asia.

Travels in the Mughal Empire AD 1656-1668. 2nd ed. Francois Bernier. Tr. by Archibald Constable. (Illus.). 500p. reprint ed. text ed. 47.50 (*0-685-13398-2*) Coronet Bks.

Travels in the New South: A Bibliography, 2 vols. Thomas D. Clark. LC 62-10772. (American Exploration & Travel Ser.: No. 36). (Illus.). 284p. reprint ed. Vol. 1, The Postwar South, 1865-1900: An Era of Reconstruction & Readjustment. pap. 81.00 (*0-685-20364-6*, 2029819); reprint ed. Vol. 2, The Twentieth-Century South, 1900-1955: An Era of Change, Depression & Emergence. pap. 90.10 (*0-685-20365-4*, 2029819) Bks Demand.

Travels in the North of Germany, 2 vols., Set. Thomas Hodgskin. LC 68-55735. (Reprints of Economic Classics Ser.). 1969. reprint ed. 95.00 (*0-678-00587-7*) Kelley.

Travels in the Old South: A Bibliography, 1. Ed. by Thomas D. Clark. LC 56-8016. (American Exploration & Travel Ser.: No. 19). reprint ed. pap. 85.80 (*0-317-10655-4*, 2016201) Bks Demand.

Travels in the Old South: A Bibliography, 2. Ed. by Thomas D. Clark. LC 56-8016. (American Exploration & Travel Ser.: No. 19). reprint ed. pap. 75.50 (*0-317-10656-2*) Bks Demand.

Travels in the Old South: A Bibliography, 3. Ed. by Thomas D. Clark. LC 56-8016. (American Exploration & Travel Ser.: No. 19). reprint ed. pap. 104.30 (*0-317-10657-0*) Bks Demand.

***Travels in the Skin Trade: Tourism & the Sex Industry.** Jeremy Seabrook. LC 96-34398. 1997. 37.50 (*0-7453-1115-6*); pap. 14.95 (*0-7453-1116-4*) LPC InBook.

Travels in the Slavonic Provinces of Turkey-In-Europe. Georgena M. Mackenzie & A. P. Irby. LC 78-135816. (Eastern Europe Collection). 1971. reprint ed. 44.95 (*0-405-02758-3*) Ayer.

Travels in the Trench Between Child Welfare Theory & Practice: A Case Study of Failed Promises & Prospects for Renewal. Ed. by George Thomas. LC 94-15563. (Child & Youth Services Ser.). (Illus.). 220p. 1994. lib. bdg. 39.95 (*1-56024-691-X*) Haworth Pr.

Travels in the Unknown East. John Grant. 1992. 27.00 (*0-86304-071-3*, Pub. by Octagon Pr UK) ISHK.

Travels in the West: Cuba with Notices of Porto Rico & the Slave Trade. David Turnbull. LC 76-177576. reprint ed. 46.50 (*0-404-06528-7*) AMS Pr.

Travels in Three Continents, Europe, Africa, Asia. James M. Buckley. LC 72-5586. (Black Heritage Library Collection). 1977. reprint ed. 60.95 (*0-8369-9136-2*) Ayer.

Travels in to Bokhara Being the Account of a Journey from India to Cabool, Tartary & Persia: Also, Narrative of a Voyage on the Indus from the Sea to Lahore, 3 vols., Set. Alexander Burnes. (C). 1992. reprint ed. 72.50 (*81-206-0792-9*, Pub. by Asian Educ Servs II) S Asia.

***Travels in Turkey, Asia Minor, Syria & Egypt.** William Whittman. (Illus.). 595p. Date not set. 38.95 (*0-405-01733-2*) Arno Press.

Travels in Upper & Lower Egypt, 3 Vols. Vivant Denon. LC 73-6275. (Middle East Ser.). 1973. reprint ed. 94.95 (*0-405-05331-2*) Ayer.

Travels in Various Parts of Peru, 2 Vols, Set. Edmond Temple. LC 76-12824. reprint ed. 52.00 (*0-404-06359-4*) AMS Pr.

Travels in West Africa. Mary Kingsley. Ed. by Elspeth Huxley. 310p. 1993. pap. 6.95 (*0-460-87394-6*, Everyman's Classic Lib) C E Tuttle.

Travels in Western Africa in 1845 & 1846, 2 vols. John Duncan. 1968. reprint ed. Set. 95.00 (*0-7146-1804-7*, Pub. by F Cass Pubs UK) Intl Spec Bk.

***Travels in Western India.** James Tod. 1996. 52.50 (*81-215-0767-7*, Pub. by M Manoharial II) Coronet Bks.

Travels into Dalmatia. Alberto Fortis. LC 70-135806. (Eastern Europe Collection). 1971. reprint ed. 41.95 (*0-405-02748-6*) Ayer.

Travels into Poland. William Coxe. LC 76-135802. (Eastern Europe Collection). (Illus.). 226p. 1971. reprint ed. 18.95 (*0-405-02744-3*) Ayer.

Travels of a Genre: The Modern Novel & Ideology. Mary N. Layoun. 318p. 1990. text ed. 42.50 (*0-691-06834-8*) Princeton U Pr.

Travels of a Photographer in China, 1933-1946. Hedda Morrison. (Illus.). 276p. 1987. 29.95 (*0-19-584098-4*) OUP.

***Travels of a Poet.** Anne P. Boucher. (Orig.). 1996. pap. write for info. (*1-57553-437-1*) Watermrk Pr.

Travels of Alexine. Penelope Gladstone. (Illus.). 1971. 18.00 (*0-7195-2044-4*) Transatl Arts.

Travels of an Alchemist. Li Chih-Ch'ang. LC 75-36233. reprint ed. 24.50 (*0-404-14481-0*) AMS Pr.

Travels of an Alechemist, the Journey of the Taoist Ch'ang-ch'un from China to the Hindukush at the Summons of Chingiz Khan. Arthur Waley. (Illus.). 166p. reprint ed. 17.00 (*957-638-064-2*, HSE014, Pub. by SMC Pub CC) Oriental Bk Store.

Travels of an Olive Eater from Pit to Pit Plus How to Cure an Olive. Virginia P. Ryder. (Illus.). 57p. (Orig.). 1991. pap. 15.95 (*0-935098-03-8*) Amigo Pr.

Travels of Babar. Jean De Brunhoff. (Illus.). (J). (ps). 1966. 14.00 (*0-394-80576-3*) Random Bks Yng Read.

Travels of Babar. Jean De Brunhoff. (Illus.). (J). (ps). 1967. lib. bdg. 11.99 (*0-394-90576-8*) Random Bks Yng Read.

Travels of Ben Sira. Stanley Nelson. LC 77-82687. 70p. (Orig.). 1978. pap. 6.00 (*0-912292-44-X*) Smith.

Travels of Certaine Englishmen into Africa, Asia & to the Blacke Sea, Finished 1608. William Biddulph & Peter Biddulph. LC 72-6344. (English Experience Ser.: No. 22). 144p. 1968. reprint ed. 25.00 (*90-221-0022-7*) Walter J Johnson.

Travels of Dean Mahomet: An Eighteenth-Century Journey Through India. Dean Mahomet. Ed. by Michael H. Fisher. LC 96-19700. (Illus.). 1997. 45.00 (*0-520-20716-5*); pap. 16.95 (*0-520-20717-3*) U CA Pr.

Travels of Fah-Hian & Sung Yun: Buddhist Pilgrims, from China to India, 400 A. D. & 518 A. D. Tr. by Samuel Beal. (C). 1993. reprint ed. 17.50 (*81-206-0824-0*, Pub. by Asian Educ Servs II) S Asia.

Travels of Faith. Faith A. Sand. LC 85-17751. (Illus.). 128p. (Orig.). 1986. pap. 10.95 (*0-932727-03-4*); lib. bdg. 15.95 (*0-932727-46-8*) Hope Pub Hse.

Travels of Frank Forrester. Carl C. Osgood. (Illus.). 198p. (Orig.). 1993. pap. 15.00 (*0-9638587-0-X*) Vista Hse.

Travels of Horatio. Foreman. 1970. pap. 3.95 (*0-394-80448-1*) Pantheon.

Travels of Ibn Battuta, 1325-1354 AD, 3 vols., Set. Ed. by Hamilton A. Gibb. (C). 1993. 78.50 (*81-215-0614-X*, Pub. by Munshiram Manoharial II) S Asia.

Travels of Ibn Batuta. S. Lee. 264p. 1985. 210.00 (*1-85077-035-2*, Pub. by Darf Pubs Ltd UK) St Mut.

Travels of Ibn Jubayr. 2nd ed. Muhammad Ibn Ahmad. Ed. by William Wright. LC 77-173005. reprint ed. 46.50 (*0-404-03480-2*) AMS Pr.

Travels of Jaimie McPheeters. Robert L. Taylor. 37.95 (*0-8488-1483-5*) Amereon Ltd.

Travels of Jaimie McPheeters. Robert L. Taylor. 550p. 1991. reprint ed. lib. bdg. 36.95 (*0-89966-835-6*) Buccaneer Bks.

Travels of Jamie McPheeters. Robert L. Taylor. 1993. 100.95 (*1-56054-867-3*) Thorndike Pr.

Travels of Jedediah Smith. Maurice S. Sullivan. LC 91-46728. (Illus.). xvi, 229p. 1992. reprint ed. pap. 9.95 (*0-8032-9206-6*, Bison Books) U of Nebr Pr.

Travels of Lao Can. E. Liu. 180p. 1995. lib. bdg. 29.00 (*0-8095-4520-9*) Borgo Pr.

Travels of Lao Ts'an. Liu T'ieh-yun. Tr. by Harold Shadick from CHI. (Modern Asian Literature Ser.). 304p. 1990. pap. text ed. 15.50 (*0-231-07255-4*) Col U Pr.

Travels of Lao Ts'an. E. Liu. Tr. & Intro. by Harold Shadick. LC 86-1867. 301p. 1986. reprint ed. text ed. 59.75 (*0-313-25164-9*, LITR, Greenwood Pr) Greenwood.

Travels of Macarius: Extracts from the Diary of the Travels of Macarius, Patriarch of Antioch. Ed. by Laura Ridding. LC 77-115577. (Russia Observed Ser.). 1971. reprint ed. 15.95 (*0-405-03089-4*) Ayer.

Travels of Marco Polo. Mary Hull. LC 94-2924. (World History Ser.). (Illus.). 112p. (J). (gr. 6-9). 1995. lib. bdg. 17.96 (*1-56006-238-X*) Lucent Bks.

Travels of Marco Polo. Marco Polo. (Airmont Classics Ser.). (YA). (gr. 9 up). 1968. mass mkt. 1.50 (*0-8049-0186-4*, CL-186) Airmont.

Travels of Marco Polo. Marco Polo. Tr. by Ronald Latham from FRE. 318p. 1982. 35.00 (*0-89835-058-1*) Abaris Bks.

Travels of Marco Polo. Marco Polo. 1982. reprint ed. lib. bdg. 18.95 (*0-89967-045-8*) Harmony Raine.

Travels of Marco Polo: The Complete Yule-Cordier Edition, 2 vols., 1. 3rd rev. ed. Marco Polo et al. (Illus.). 1680p. 1993. reprint ed. pap. 17.95 (*0-486-27586-8*) Dover.

Travels of Marco Polo: The Complete Yule-Cordier Edition, 2 vols., 2. rev. ed. Marco Polo et al. (Illus.). 1680p. 1993. reprint ed. pap. 17.95 (*0-486-27587-6*) Dover.

Travels of Mendes Pinto. Fernao M. Pinto. Ed. & Tr. by Rebecca D. Catz. LC 88-39778. (Illus.). 752p. 1989. 60.00 (*0-226-66951-3*) U Ch Pr.

Travels of Olearius in Seventeenth-Century Russia. Adam Olearius. Ed. & Tr. by Samuel H. Baron. (Illus.). xvi, 352p. 1967. 49.50 (*0-8047-0219-5*) Stanford U Pr.

Travels of Pedro Teixeira with His "Kings of Harmuz" & Extracts from His "Kings of Persia" Ed. by William F. Sinclair & Donald Ferguson. (Hakluyt Society Second Ser.: Vol. 9). 400p. 1996. 63.00 (*0-85115-957-5*, Pub. by Hakluyt Soc UK) Boydell & Brewer.

Travels of Peter Mundy. John Keast. (C). 1989. 40.00 (*0-907566-75-8*, Pub. by Dyllansow Truran UK) St Mut.

Travels of Peter Mundy 1608-1667 No. II: Travels in Asia, 1628-1634. (Hakluyt Society Second Ser.: Vol. 35). (Illus.). 516p. 1996. 63.00 (*0-85115-972-9*, Pub. by Hakluyt Soc UK) Boydell & Brewer.

Travels of Peter Mundy 1608-1667 No. III: Travels in England, India, China, etc. 1634-1638. Peter Mundy. Ed. by Richard C. Temple. (Hakluyt Society Second Ser.: Vol. 45). (Illus.). 622p. 1996. 81.00 (*0-85115-979-6*, Pub. by Hakluyt Soc UK) Boydell & Brewer.

Travels of Pietro Dellavalle in India. Edward Grey. (C). 1991. reprint ed. Set. text ed. 45.00 (*81-206-0676-0*, Pub. by Asian Educ Servs II) S Asia.

Travels of Sir Johb Mandeville. John Mandeville. Tr. & Intro. by Charles Moseley. (Classics Ser.). 208p. 1984. pap. 11.95 (*0-14-044435-1*, Penguin Classics) Viking Penguin.

Travels of Sir John Mandeville. Josef Krasa. Tr. by Peter Kussi from CZE. LC 83-12283. (Illus.). 112p. 1983. boxed 65.00 (*0-8076-1054-2*) Braziller.

Travels of Sir John Mandeville. deluxe ed. Josef Krasa. Tr. by Peter Kussi from CZE. (Illus.). 112p. 1995. 35.00 (*0-8076-1388-6*) Braziller.

Travels of the Abbe Carre in India & the Near East, 1672 to 1674, 3 vols., Set. Abbe Carre. 1990. reprint ed. 120.00 (*81-206-0596-9*, Pub. by Asian Educ Servs II) S Asia.

Travels of the Itinerant Freda Aharon. Myra Sklarew. (Orig.). 1985. pap. 10.00 (*0-931956-22-6*) Water Mark.

Travels of the Jesuits, 2 vols., Set. J. Lockman. (C). 1995. reprint ed. 72.00 (*81-206-1060-1*, Pub. by Asian Educ Servs II) S Asia.

Travels of the Mind. Renato Silva de Mendonca e Vasconcelos. LC 96-11073. 220p. 1996. 18.95 (*0-944957-85-4*) Rivercross Pub.

Travels of the Naturalist Charles A. Lesueur in North America, 1815-1837. Ernest T. Hamy. Ed. by H. F. Raup. LC 67-65271. 118p. reprint ed. pap. 33.70 (*0-685-43701-9*, 2027305) Bks Demand.

Travels of W. W. Brown: Narratives of William Wells Brown, the American Fugitive in Europe, Sketches of Places & People Abroad. William W. Brown. Ed. by Paul Jefferson. LC 91-8667. (Illus.). 320p. (C). 1991. pap. text ed. 14.95 (*1-55876-043-1*) Wiener Pubs Inc.

Travels of William Bartram. William Bartram. (American Biography Ser.). 414p. 1991. reprint ed. lib. bdg. 89.00 (*0-7812-8013-3*) Rprt Serv.

Travels on My Elephant. Mark Shand. (Illus.). 200p. 1992. 22.95 (*0-87951-454-X*) Overlook Pr.

Travels on the Lower Mississippi, 1879-1880: A Memoir by Ernst von Hess-Wartegg. Ed. & Tr. by Frederic Trautmann. LC 89-4847. (Illus.). 280p. 1990. 32.50 (*0-8262-0709-X*) U of Mo Pr.

Travels, Researches, & Missionary Labours During an Eighteen Years' Residence in Eastern Africa. 2nd rev. ed. J. Ludwig Krapf. (Illus.). 566p. 1968. reprint ed. 59.50 (*0-7146-1872-1*, Pub. by F Cass Pubs UK) Intl Spec Bk.

Travels Through Central Africa to Timbuctoo, 1. Rene Caillie. 483p. (C). 1992. 125.00 (*1-85077-196-0*, Pub. by Darf Pubs Ltd UK) St Mut.

Travels Through Central Africa to Timbuctoo, 2. Rene Caillie. 515p. (C). 1992. 125.00 (*1-85077-199-5*, Pub. by Darf Pubs Ltd UK) St Mut.

Travels Through Germany, Russia & Poland in the Years 1769 & 1770. Joseph Marshall. LC 77-135821. (Eastern Europe Collection). 1971. reprint ed. 19.95 (*0-405-02763-X*) Ayer.

Travels Through North & South Carolina. William Bartram. 1972. 250.00 (*0-8490-1229-5*) Gordon Pr.

Travels Through Part of the Russian Empire & the Country of Poland: Along the Southern Shores of the Baltic. Robert M. Johnston. LC 72-115549. (Russia Observed, Series I). 1970. reprint ed. 23.95 (*0-405-03036-3*) Ayer.

Travels Through Sacred India. Roger Housden. 304p. 1996. pap. 16.00 (*1-85538-497-3*) Harper SF.

Travels Through Sacred India. Roger House. 304p. 1996. pap. 16.00 (*1-85538-494-9*) Harper SF.

Travels Through Syria & Egypt, Vol. 1. C. F. Volney. 420p. reprint ed. 45.00 (*0-933121-67-9*) Black Classic.

Travels Through Syria & Egypt, Vol. 2. C. F. Volney. 516p. reprint ed. 45.00 (*0-933121-68-7*) Black Classic.

Travels Through the English Sentence: Study & Practice in English Syntax. Chenliang Sheng & Eugene Hammond. LC 95-38085. 250p. (Orig.). (C). 1995. pap. text ed. 26.50 (*0-7618-0118-9*) U Pr of Amer.

Travels Through the Interior Parts of America in a Series of Letters by an Officer, 2 Vols., Set. Thomas Anbury. LC 75-76553. (Eyewitness Accounts of the American Revolution Ser., No. 1). (Illus.). 1969. reprint ed. 45.95 (*0-405-01140-7*) Ayer.

Travels Through the Interior Parts of America in a Series of Letters by an Officer, 2 Vols., Vol. 1. Thomas Anbury. LC 75-76553. (Eyewitness Accounts of the American Revolution Ser., No. 1). (Illus.). 1969. reprint ed. 22.95 (*0-405-01141-5*) Ayer.

Travels Through the Interior Parts of America in a Series of Letters by an Officer, 2 Vols., Vol. 2. Thomas Anbury. LC 75-76553. (Eyewitness Accounts of the American Revolution Ser., No. 1). (Illus.). 1969. reprint ed. 22.95 (*0-405-01142-3*) Ayer.

Travels Through the Middle Settlements of North America in the Years 1759 & 1760: With Observations upon the State of the Colonies. 3rd ed. Andrew Burnaby. LC 68-55496. 265p. 1970. reprint ed. 39.50 (*0-678-00682-2*) Kelley.

Travels Through the Southern Provinces of the Russian Empire Performed in the Years 1793 & 1794, 2 Vols, 1. P. S. Pallas. LC 72-115573. (Russia Observed, Series I). 1970. reprint ed. 35.95 (*0-405-03238-2*) Ayer.

Travels Through the Southern Provinces of the Russian Empire Performed in the Years 1793 & 1794, 2 Vols, Set. P. S. Pallas. LC 72-115573. (Russia Observed, Series I). 1971. reprint ed. 66.95 (*0-405-03055-X*) Ayer.

Travels Through the Southern Provinces of the Russian Empire Performed in the Years 1793 & 1794, 2 Vols, Vol. 2. P. S. Pallas. LC 72-115573. (Russia Observed, Series I). 1970. reprint ed. 35.95 (*0-405-03239-0*) Ayer.

Travels Through the States of North America: And the Provinces of Upper & Lower Canada During the Years 1795, 1796 & 1797, 2 vols. 4th ed. Issac Weld. LC 68-58663. 1970. reprint ed. Set. 95.00 (*0-678-00535-4*) Kelley.

Travels to Russia, Tartary & Turkey. Edward D. Clarke. LC 75-115520. (Russia Observed, Series I). 1970. reprint ed. 35.95 (*0-405-03015-0*) Ayer.

Travels to the Islands of the Pacific Ocean. J. A. Moerenhout. Tr. by Arthur R. Borden, Jr. LC 92-26842. 564p. (Orig.). (C). lib. bdg. 68.00 (*0-8191-8898-0*) U Pr of Amer.

Travels to the Islands of the Pacific Ocean. J. A. Moerenhout. Tr. by Arthur R. Borden, Jr. LC 92-26842. 564p. (Orig.). (C). 1993. pap. text ed. 39.50 (*0-8191-8899-9*) U Pr of Amer.

Travels to the West of the Allegheny Mountains in the States of Ohio, Kentucky & Tennessee. Francois A. Michaux. 1993. reprint ed. lib. bdg. 89.00 (*0-7812-5390-X*) Rprt Serv.

Travels with a Donkey, an Inland Voyage, the Silverado Squatters. Robert Louis Stevenson. Ed. by Trevor Royle. 299p. 1993. pap. 6.95 (*0-460-87278-8*, Everyman's Classic Lib) C E Tuttle.

Travels with a Donkey, & an Inland Voyage. Robert Louis Stevenson. (BCL1-PR English Literature Ser.). 297p. 1992. reprint ed. lib. bdg. 79.00 (*0-7812-7667-5*) Rprt Serv.

Travels with a Donkey in the Cevennes. Robert Louis Stevenson. 1996. write for info. (*0-8101-6005-6*); pap. 12.95 (*0-8101-6006-4*) Northwestern U Pr.

Travels with a Donkey in the Cevennes & Selected Travel Writings. Ed. by Emma Letley. (World's Classics Ser.). 304p. 1993. pap. 9.95 (*0-19-282629-8*) OUP.

Travels with a Hungry Bear: A Journey to the Russian Heartland. Mark Kramer. 352p. 1996. 24.95 (*0-395-42670-7*) HM.

Travels with a Laptop. Michael Hewitt. (Illus.). 192p. 1996. pap. 16.95 (*1-85032-164-7*) ITCP.

Travels with a Pram & Hot Flush & the Toy Boy. Sara Yeomans. pap. 11.95 (*0-7043-4338-X*, Pub. by Womens Press UK) Trafalgar.

Travels with a Stethoscope: A Physician Looks at the 20th Century. Ronald Girdwood. 250p. (C). 1989. text ed. 45.00 (*0-85976-334-X*, Pub. by J Donald UK) St Mut.

Travels with a Troubadour: A Journey Through the Middle Ages. Debra Shepherd-Wundrow. (Past Ports Ser.). 300p. (J). (gr. 4-8). 1996. ring bd. 79.95 (*1-885360-12-6*, Past Ports) Demco WI.

Travels with Alice. Calvin Trillin. 1990. pap. 9.00 (*0-380-71209-1*) Avon.

Travels with Charley. John Steinbeck. 1997. pap. 10.95 (*0-14-018741-3*) Viking Penguin.

Travels with Charley in Search of America. John Steinbeck. 288p. 1980. pap. 6.95 (*0-14-005320-4*, Penguin Bks) Viking Penguin.

Travels with Diana Hunter. Regine Sands. 173p. (Orig.). 1991. reprint ed. pap. 7.95 (*1-55583-304-7*) Alyson Pubns.

Travels with Dinosaurs. Vezic Melegari. 1997. 2.99 (*0-517-18453-2*) Random Hse Value.

Travels with Dr. Pepper. Pepper Worthington. (Illus.). 211p. (Orig.). 1990. pap. text ed. 14.95 (*0-9627087-1-2*) Mt Olive Coll Pr.

Travels with Dubinsky & Clive. David Gurewich. 262p. 16.95 (*0-317-64614-1*) Viking Penguin.

Travels with Lizbeth. Lars Eighner. 288p. 1993. 19.95 (*0-312-09926-6*) St Martin.

Travels with Lizbeth: Three Years on the Road & on the Streets. Lars Eighner. 288p. 1994. reprint ed. pap. 11.00 (*0-449-90943-3*) Fawcett.

Travels with My Aunt. Graham Greene. 1977. mass mkt. 5.95 (*0-14-003221-5*, Penguin Bks) Viking Penguin.

Travels with My Aunt. Graham Greene. (Twentieth-Century Classics Ser.). 272p. 1991. pap. 11.95 (*0-14-018501-1*, Penguin Classics) Viking Penguin.

Travels with My Aunt. Giles Havergal. 1994. pap. 5.95 (*0-87129-137-1*, T89) Dramatic Pub.

Travels with My Aunt. Graham Greene. 275p. 1992. reprint ed. lib. bdg. 19.95 (*0-89966-924-7*) Buccaneer Bks.

Travels with My Briefcase Vol. 1: Around the World-On Expenses. Peter Biddlecombe. 1996. pap. 12.95 (*0-316-07664-3*) Little.

Travels with Pegasus: A Microlight Journey Across West Africa. Christina Dodwell. 208p. 1990. 19.95 (*0-8027-1125-1*) Walker & Co.

Travels with Peppy: A Motorcycle Adventure Across the Country. Dean S. Lawrence. LC 94-90172. 250p. 1994. pap. 12.95 (*0-9641348-0-2*) Triad Pubng.

Travels with Rainie Marie. Patricia M. Martin. LC 96-20005. 192p. (J). (gr. 4-8). 1997. 15.95 (*0-7868-0257-X*); lib. bdg. 15.89 (*0-7868-2212-0*) Hyprn Child.

Travels with Tess & Tim. Marc Gave. LC 89-16401. (Illus.). 48p. (J). (ps-3). 1990. 5.95 (*0-8193-1192-8*) Parents.

Travels with Tiny Teddy: Cape Cod: The Great Escape. Thomas Truelson. (Illus.). 40p. (Orig.). (J). (gr. 1-3). 1988. pap. 3.95 (*0-945692-00-5*) Lighthse Bks MA.

Travelscan: Good Frequencies Across America, & Beyond! Henry L. Eisenson. LC 95-81310. (Illus.). 150p. (Orig.). 1997. pap. 9.95 (*1-56866-084-7*) Index Pub Grp.

Traveltalk Phrase Book: French. 1989. 15.00 incl. audio (*0-517-56995-7*, Living Language); pap. 7.00 (*0-517-56993-0*, Living Language) Crown Pub Group.

Traveltalk Phrasebook: Japanese Dictionary. Terry Kawashima. (ENG & JPN.). 1993. pap. 7.00 (*0-517-58733-5*, Living Language) Crown Pub Group.

Travelwise: Tips for International Travel: Being Secure in Your Travels. Scottie Giebink, pseud. (Illus.). 50p. (Orig.). 1996. pap. write for info. (*0-9652830-0-3*) Focus Internatl.

***Travers Corners.** Scott Waldie. LC 96-34406. 192p. 1997. 25.00 (*1-55821-533-6*) Lyons & Burford.

***Traverse City: And the Beautiful Surrounding Area.** Rebecca Austin & Jennifer Nelson. (Illus.). ix, 80p. (Orig.). 1997. pap. 16.95 (*0-9657153-0-2*) Austin & Nelson.

Traverse City Postcard History. Lawrence M. Wakefield. 1992. pap. 12.00 (*0-9618903-3-9*) L M Wakefield.

Traverse of the Gods. large type ed. Bob Langley. 464p. 1982. 25.99 (*0-7089-0879-9*) Ulverscroft.

Traverse Region Book. John S. Penrod. 1992. pap. 5.00 (*0-942618-37-8*) Penrod-Hiawatha.

***Traversee des Ideologies et Exploration des Identites dans les Ecritures de Femmes au Quebec (1970-1980)** Benedicte N. Mauguiere. (Francophone Cultures & Literatures Ser.: Vol. 17). 400p. (FRE.). (C). 1997. text ed. 59.95 (*0-8204-3021-8*) P Lang Pubng.

***Traversing Philosophical Boundaries.** Max Hallman. LC 97-16312. (Philosophy Ser.). 725p. (C). 1997. pap. text ed. 36.95 (*0-534-26706-8*) Wadsworth Pub.

***Traves de la Semana con Gato y Perro.** Rozanne L. Williams. Ed. by Christine Hood. Tr. by Rancho Park Publishing Staff. (Fun & Fantasy Spanish Learn to Read Ser.). (Illus.). 16p. (Orig.). (SPA.). (J). (ps-2). 1996. pap. 2.49 (*1-57471-152-0*, 4070) Creat Teach Pr.

Traves de una Rendija. Luis A. Aguilar. Ed. by SLUSA, Inc. Staff. 80p. (Orig.). (SPA.). 1986. 6.00 (*0-917129-04-0*) SLUSA.

Travesia Secreta. Carlos Victoria. LC 94-70351. (Coleccion Caniqui). 477p. (Orig.). (SPA.). 1994. pap. 22.95 (*0-89729-729-6*) Ediciones.

Travessia: A Portuguese Language Textbook, Vol. 1. Jon M. Tolman et al. (Illus.). 300p. (Orig.). (C). 1988. student ed., pap. 10.95 (*0-87840-229-2*); pap. text ed. 18.95 (*0-87840-227-6*) Georgetown U Pr.

Travessia: A Portuguese Language Textbook, Vol. 2. Jon M. Tolman et al. (Illus.). 300p. (Orig.). (C). 1989. student ed., pap. 10.95 (*0-87840-230-6*); pap. text ed. 18.95 (*0-87840-228-4*) Georgetown U Pr.

Travessia: A Portuguese Language Textbook, Vols. 1 & 2. Jon M. Tolman et al. (Illus.). 300p. (Orig.). (C). 1988. vhs 350.00 (*0-87840-238-1*) Georgetown U Pr.

Travessia Manual de Laboratorio. Ricardo M. Paiva & Jon M. Tolman. (Travessia, Portuguese Language Textbook Program Ser.). 248p. (Orig.). (C). 1991. student ed., pap. 13.00 (*0-87840-235-7*) Georgetown U Pr.

Travessia Manual de Laboratorio. Jon M. Tolman. (Travessia Portuguese Language Textbook Program Ser.). (Orig.). (C). 1989. 215.00 incl. audio (*0-87840-236-5*) Georgetown U Pr.

Travesties. Tom Stoppard. LC 75-13552. 100p. 1989. pap. 10.00 (*0-8021-5089-6*, Grove) Grove-Atltic.

Travesty. John Hawkes. LC 75-26764. 128p. 1976. pap. 9.95 (*0-8112-0640-8*, NDP430) New Directions.

Travesty: A True Crime Story. Executive Intelligence Review Editors. (Illus.). 300p. (Orig.). 1993. pap. 10.00 (*0-943235-09-X*) Exec Intel Review.

Travesuras De Snoopy. Charles M. Schulz. 64p. 1971. 4.95 (*0-686-56192-9*) Fr & Eur.

Traviata. Giuseppe Verdi. Ed. by Nicholas John. Tr. by Edmund Tracey from ITA. (English National Opera Guide Series: Bilingual Libretto, Articles: No. 5). (Illus.). 1981. pap. 9.95 (*0-7145-3848-5*) Riverrun NY.

Traviata: Libretto. Giuseppe Verdi. 56p. 1986. pap. 4.95 (*0-7935-2618-3*, 50340110) H Leonard.

Traviata: Melodramma in Three Acts by Francesco Maria Piave, 2 vols., Set. Giuseppe Verdi. Ed. by Fabrizio Della Seta. 608p. 1994. lib. bdg. 300.00 (*0-226-85316-0*) U Ch Pr.

Traviata in Full Score. Giuseppe Verdi. 1990. pap. 15.95 (*0-486-26321-5*) Dover.

Travis & the Better Mousetrap. Deborah Dennard. LC 94-16642. (Illus.). 32p. (J). (gr. k-4). 1996. pap. 14.99 (*0-525-65178-0*, Cobblehill Bks) Dutton Child Bks.

Travis & Trish Bk. 2: A Beyond the Call Novel. Richard C. Nelson. LC 94-90483. (Illus.). 192p. (Orig.). 1995. pap. 10.00 (*1-56002-495-X*) Aegina Pr.

***Travis B. Stevenson.** Ray B. Dickey. 227p. (Orig.). 1997. mass mkt. 4.99 (*1-55197-995-0*, Pub. by Comnwlth Pub CN) Partners Pubs Grp.

Travis County, Texas Census, 1890 Pt. I: Uniquely Reconstructed & Annotated. Compiled by Mary C. Moody. LC 91-76865. 418p. (Orig.). 1991. Part I. pap. 57.95 (*0-9615836-6-5*) Blackstone Pub.

Travis County, Texas Census, 1890 Pt. II: Uniquely Reconstructed & Annotated. Compiled by Mary C. Moody. LC 91-76865. 418p. (Orig.). 1991. Part II. pap. write for info. (*0-9615836-7-3*) Blackstone Pub.

Travis: I Got Lots of Neat Stuff: Children Living with Muscular Dystrophy. Kathy L. Gordon. (Illus.). 24p. (Orig.). (J). 1995. pap. write for info. (*1-56167-226-2*) Am Literary Pr.

Travis Tritt: Country Club. 136p. 1992. per. 17.95 (*0-7935-1022-8*, 00308113) H Leonard.

Travis Tritt: Ten Feet Tall & Bullet Proof. 64p. 1994. otabind 14.95 (*0-7935-3679-0*, 00308253) H Leonard.

Travis Tritt: Trouble. 64p. 1993. otabind 14.95 (*0-7935-1943-8*, 00308166) H Leonard.

Travis Tritt Songbook, No. 290. 80p. 1992. pap. 7.95 (*0-7935-1342-1*, 00243089) H Leonard.

Travis Tritt Songbook, No. 302. 80p. 1992. pap. 8.95 (*0-7935-1340-5*, 00102222) H Leonard.

Travolta. Dave Thompson. (Illus.). 256p. (Orig.). 1996. pap. 12.95 (*0-87833-949-3*) Taylor Pub.

***Trawl Fisheries in the Gulf of Thailand.** M. Boonyubol & S. Pramokchutima. Tr. by T. Bhukaswan. (ICLARM Translations Ser.: No. 4). 12p. 1984. write for info. (*971-10-2213-3*, Pub. by ICLARM PH) Intl Spec Bk.

***Trawling: The Rise & Fall of British Trawl Fishery.** Robb Robinson. (Illus.). 272p. 1996. 59.95 (*0-85989-480-0*, Pub. by Univ Exeter Pr UK) Northwestern U Pr.

TraX: Simulation & Analysis of Dynamical Systems. Victor Levitin. Ed. by Jeffrey A. Millstein. 73p. 1990. 345.00 (*1-884977-10-3*); teacher ed. 695.00 (*1-884977-11-1*) Applied Biomath.

Tray Distillation Columns. Equipment Testing Procedures Committee Staff. 26p. 1987. pap. 60.00 (*0-8169-0404-9*, E-24) Am Inst Chem Eng.

Tray Gourmet: Be Your Own Chef in the College Cafeteria. Larry Berger & Lynn Harris. LC 91-75630. (Illus.). 192p. 1992. 10.95 (*0-9627403-2-2*) Lake Isle Pr.

Trayecto: The Trek. Ann Jonas. Tr. by Teresa Mlawer from ENG. (Illus.). 32p. (J). (gr. 5-7). 1991. lib. bdg. 13.95 (*0-9625162-3-6*) Lectorum Pubns.

Trayectoria de la Novela Hispanoamericana Actual (del "Realismo Magico" a los Anos Ochenta) Dario Y. Villanueva. (Nueva Austral Ser.: No. 222). (SPA.). 1991. pap. text ed. 34.95 (*84-239-7222-4*) Elliots Bks.

Trayne: John Trayne & Some of His Descendants. S. T. Hand. (Illus.). 198p. 1991. reprint ed. pap. 29.50 (*0-8328-2188-8*); reprint ed. lib. bdg. 39.50 (*0-8328-2187-X*) Higginson Bk Co.

Traza Bien la Palabra de Verdad. C. I. Scofield. Orig. Title: Rightly Dividing the Word of Truth. 96p. (SPA.). 1971. mass mkt. 3.99 (*0-8254-1660-4*, Edit Portavoz) Kregel.

Trazodone, New Avenues in Psycho-Pharmaco-Therapy: Proceedings of the International Symposium, Montreal, October, 1973. Ed. by T. Ban & B. Silvestrini. (Modern Problems of Pharmacopsychiatry Ser.: Vol. 9). 250p. 1974. 60.00 (*3-8055-1718-1*) S Karger.

TRB Culture: The First Farmers of the North European Plain. Magdelina Midgeley. (Illus.). 424p. 1993. 95.00 (*0-7486-0348-4*, Pub. by Edinburgh U Pr UK) Col U Pr.

TRB Distinguished Lecture, 1992. Carl L. Monismith. LC 92-29494. 100p. 1992. 21.00 (*0-309-05218-1*, R1354) Transport Res Bd.

Tre Arianne di Claudio Monteverdi. Nella Anfuso & Annibale Gianuario. LC 77-452198. (Nuova Metodologia, Studi Musicologici: No. 5). (Illus.). 37p. (Orig.). (ITA.). 1975. pap. 8.00 (*0-934082-14-6*, Pub. by SP Quaranta Quattro IT) Theodore Front.

Tre Orsi: The Three Bears. Hanna Hutchinson. Tr. by Victoria Amico from ENG. (Interlingo Ser.). (Illus.). 22p. (Orig.). (ITA.). (J). (gr. k-12). 1990. pap. 2.95 (*0-922852-09-X*) Another Lang Pr.

***Treacherous Attempts.** Giese. Date not set. text ed. write for info. (*0-312-16604-4*) St Martin.

Treacherous Beauties. Cheryl Emerson. (Silhouette Promo Ser.). 1994. mass mkt. 3.99 (*0-373-48288-4*, 1-48288-4) Harlequin Bks.

Treacherous Beauties. Cheryl Emerson. (Shadows Ser.). 1993. mass mkt. 3.50 (*0-373-27019-4*, 5-27019-4) Silhouette.

Treacherous Longings. Anne Mather. (Presents Ser.). 1995. mass mkt. 3.25 (*0-373-11759-0*, 1-11759-7) Harlequin Bks.

Treacherous Longings. large type ed. Anne Mather. (Harlequin Romance Ser.). 1995. 19.95 (*0-263-14321-X*, Pub. by Mills & Boon UK) Thorndike Pr.

Treacherous Road see Walker Mysteries

***Treacherous Season.** large type ed. Irene Northan. (Large Print Ser.). 288p. 1996. 25.99 (*0-7089-3558-3*) Ulverscroft.

Treacherous Trail. large type ed. M. Duggan. (Linford Western Library). 288p. 1992. pap. 15.99 (*0-7089-7251-9*, Trailtree Bookshop) Ulverscroft.

Treacherous Traitors. Nathan Aaseng. LC 96-29861. (Profiles Ser.). (Illus.). 160p. (YA). (gr. 5-12). 1997. lib. bdg. 16.95 (*1-881508-38-2*) Oliver Pr MN.

Treachery. Johnny Quarles. (Orig.). 1996. mass mkt. 5.99 (*0-380-78325-8*) Avon.

Treachery & Innocence: Psychology & Racial Difference in South Africa. N. Chabani Manganyi. 164p. 1992. 50.00 (*1-873836-05-8*, Pub. by H Zell Pubs UK) Bowker-Saur.

***Treachery at the River Canyon.** Stephen A. Bly. LC 96-40088. (Lewis & Clark Squad Adventure Ser.: 3). 160p. (Orig.). (J). (gr. 4-9). 1997. pap. 4.99 (*0-89107-941-6*) Crossway Bks.

Treachery in D. C. Dick Beyer. LC 95-60256. 330p. 1995. pap. 3.95 (*0-9635404-2-4*) TwoForYou Bks.

Treachery in Dallas. Walt Brown. 448p. 26.95 (*0-7867-0238-9*) Carroll & Graf.

Treachery of Time. Anna Gilbert. 432p. 1996. 24.95 (*0-312-14055-X*) St Martin.

Treachery of Time. large type ed. Anna Gilbert. 1996. pap. 20.95 (*0-7838-1663-4*, GK Hall) Thorndike Pr.

Treacle on the Tongue. Ruth M. Parks. Ed. by Roger E. Egan, Sr. (Illus.). 80p. (Orig.). 1994. pap. 12.00 (*0-9632687-3-2*) PenRose Pub.

Treacle Story Series, Vol. One (1-4) Tom Ahern et al. LC 76-43558. (Illus.). 172p. 1976. 10.00 (*0-914232-14-2*) McPherson & Co.

Treacle Story Series, Vol. Two (5-10) Jaimy Gordon et al. LC 76-43558. (Illus.). 304p. 1980. 15.00 (*0-914232-34-7*) McPherson & Co.

Tread Lightly My Dear. Eric Bercovici. 1990. 17.95 (*1-55972-027-1*, Birch Ln Pr) Carol Pub Group.

Tread Softly, Nurse. large type ed. Lynne A. Collins. (Linford Romance Library). 304p. 1992. pap. 15.99 (*0-7089-7273-X*, Linford) Ulverscroft.

Tread upon the Lion. Gilbert Morris. (Liberty Bell Ser.: No. 3). 304p. 1996. pap. 9.99 (*1-55661-567-1*) Bethany Hse.

Tread Warily at Midnight. large type ed. Margaret A. Carr. (Linford Mystery Library). 1988. pap. 15.99 (*0-7089-6508-3*) Ulverscroft.

Treading Different Paths: Informatization in Asian Nations. Ed. by Georgette Wang. LC 94-10147. 288p. 1994. pap. 39.50 (*1-56750-048-X*) Ablex Pub.

Treading Different Paths: Informatization in Asian Nations. Ed. by Georgette Wang. LC 94-10147. 288p. 1994. text ed. 73.25 (*1-56750-047-1*) Ablex Pub.

Treading in the Past: Sandal of the Anaszi. Ed. by Kathy Kankainen. LC 94-25169. (Illus.). 216p. 1995. 50.00 (*0-87480-470-1*); pap. 29.95 (*0-87480-471-X*) U of Utah Pr.

Treading Lightly with Pack Animals: A Guide to Low-Impact Travel in the Backcountry. Dan Aadland. Ed. by Daniel Greer. (Illus.). 152p. (Orig.). 1993. pap. 15.00 (*0-87842-297-8*) Mountain Pr.

Treading the Ebony Path: Ideology & Violence in Contemporary Afro-Colombian Prose Fiction. Marvin A. Lewis. LC 86-30901. 152p. 1988. text ed. 24.95 (*0-8262-0638-7*) U of Mo Pr.

Treading the Maze: An Artist's Journey Through Breast Cancer. Susan E. King. LC 96-26778. 1997. 17.95 (*0-8118-1605-2*) Chronicle Bks.

Treadmill to Oblivion. (Money Reform Ser.). 1994. lib. bdg. 250.95 (*0-8490-5652-7*) Gordon Pr.

Treadmill Walking: A Motivational Resource for Treadmill Training. R. Sweetgall & Robert Neeves. 96p. 1989. pap. 9.95 (*0-939041-08-1*) Creative Walking.

Treads & Threads. Janet Cassagio. 128p. (C). 1989. per. 16.95 (*0-256-07654-5*, 46-2786-01) Irwin.

Treadwell: Photographs. Andrea Modica. 88p. 1996. 40.00 (*0-8118-1118-2*) Chronicle Bks.

Trease & Evans Pharmacognosy. 14th ed. Evans. 1996. text ed. 75.00 (*0-7020-1899-6*) Saunders.

Treason. Orson Scott Card. 1990. mass mkt. 5.99 (*0-312-92109-8*) St Martin.

Treason: Famous English Treason Trials. Alan Wharam. (Illus.). 192p. 1996. 33.95 (*0-7509-0991-9*, Pub. by Sutton Pubng UK) Bks Intl VA.

Treason: The New World Order. Gurudas. (Illus.). 300p. (Orig.). 1996. pap. 14.95 (*0-945946-14-7*) Cassandra Pr.

Treason at Michilimackinac. Ed. by David Armour. LC 67-81179. (Illus.). 103p. 1967. pap. 6.00 (*0-911872-32-9*) Mackinac St Hist Pks.

Treason in the Blood: H. St. John Riley, Kim Philby & the Spy Case of the Century. Anthony C. Brown. 1994. 29.95 (*0-395-63119-X*) HM.

Treason in Tudor England: Politics & Paranoia. Lacey B. Smith. LC 85-43200. 352p. 1986. 49.50 (*0-691-05463-0*) Princeton U Pr.

Treason of Isengard: History of the Lord of the Rings, Pt. 2. J. R. R. Tolkien & Christopher Tolkien. (Illus.). 544p. 1989. 29.95 (*0-395-51562-9*) HM.

Treason of the Bar. Warren Hinckle. (Argonaut Ser.: No. 5). 1995. pap. text ed. 11.95 (*1-882206-09-6*) Argonaut Pr.

Treason of the People. Ferdinand Lundberg. LC 73-19114. 370p. 1974. reprint ed. text ed. 69.50 (*0-8371-7307-8*, LUTP, Greenwood Pr) Greenwood.

Treason, Tradition & the Intellectual: Julien Benda & Political Discourse. Ray Nichols. LC 78-7785. x, 270p. 1979. 29.95 (*0-7006-0175-9*) U Pr of KS.

Treason Trials, Seventeen Ninety-Four. Alan Wharam. LC 92-15182. 1992. 79.00 (*0-7185-1445-9*) St Martin.

Treason's Harbour. Patrick O'Brian. 1992. pap. 12.95 (*0-393-30863-4*) Norton.

Treason's Harbour. Patrick O'Brian. 1994. 22.50 (*0-393-03709-6*) Norton.

Treasure. Lisa F. Bergren. 273p. (Orig.). 1994. pap. 8.99 (*0-88070-725-9*, Palisades OR) Multnomah Pubs.

***Treasure.** Lisa T. Bergren. LC 96-51930. 1997. 22.95 (*0-7838-8066-9*) G K Hall.

***Treasure.** Lisa T. Bergren. 273p. (Orig.). 1994. pap. 8.99 (*0-614-31005-9*, Palisades OR) Multnomah Pubs.

Treasure. Clive Cussler. Ed. by Paul McCarthy. 560p. 1989. pap. 7.99 (*0-671-70465-6*) PB.

Treasure. Uri Shulevitz. LC 78-12952. (Illus.). 32p. (J). (ps-3). 1979. 16.00 (*0-374-37740-5*) FS&G.

Treasure. Uri Shulevitz. (Sunburst Ser.). (Illus.). 32p. (J). (gr. k-3). 1986. pap. 5.95 (*0-374-47955-0*, Sunburst Bks) FS&G.

***Treasure! Bonanzas Worth a Billion Bucks.** Carson. 182p. 1996. pap. 10.00 (*0-918080-37-1*) Treas Chest Bks.

Treasure: The Trials of a Teenage Terror & Her Mom. Gina Davidson. LC 94-67617. 218p. (Orig.). 1994. pap. 12.95 (*1-57143-023-7*, Zenobia Pr) RDR Bks.

An Asterisk (*) at the beginning of an entry indicates that the title is appearing in BIP for the first time.

***Treasure & Other Poems.** RoseMarie A. Reyes. (Illus.). 28p. (Orig.). 1996. pap. 6.95 (0-9654775-0-9) R M A R Publns.

Treasure & Scavenger Hunts: How to Plan, Create, & Give Them. Gordon Burgett. (Illus.). 128p. 1994. pap. 9.95 (0-910167-25-7) Comm Unltd CA.

Treasure at Dolphin Bay. Franklin W. Dixon. Ed. by Ruth Ashby. (HB Ser.: No. 129). 160p. (Orig.). (J). (gr. 3-6). 1994. pap. 3.99 (0-671-87213-3, Minstrel Bks) PB.

Treasure at Morning Gulch. Joan R. Biggar. (Adventure Quest Ser.). (Illus.). 152p. (Orig.). (J). (gr. 5-8). 1991. pap. 4.99 (0-570-04193-7, 56-1652) Concordia.

Treasure Beyond the Ranges: Violetta Books First Annual Poetry Anthology. Ed. by Kathleen Gilbert. (Illus.). 31p. (Orig.). 1985. pap. 4.00 (0-915913-05-4) Violetta Bks.

Treasure Bird. Peni R. Griffin. 144p. (J). (gr. 3-7). 1994. pap. 3.99 (0-14-036653-9) Puffin Bks.

Treasure Bird. Peni R. Griffin. LC 91-42773. 144p. (J). (gr. 4-7). 1992. lib. bdg. 14.00 (0-689-50554-X, McElderry) S&S Childrens.

Treasure! Bonanzas Worth a Billion Bucks. Xanthus Carson. 182p. 1974. reprint ed. pap. 15.95 (0-941620-66-2) Carson Ent.

Treasure Box. Orson Scott Card. LC 96-16248. 320p. 1996. 24.00 (0-06-017654-7) HarpC.

***Treasure Box.** Orson Scott Card. 1997. mass mkt. write for info. (0-06-109398-X, Harp PBks) HarpC.

***Treasure Box: A Novel.** large type ed. Orson Scott Card. LC 96-34828. (Cloak & Dagger Ser.). 485p. 1996. 23.95 (0-7862-0887-2, Thorndike Lrg Prnt) Thorndike Pr.

***Treasure by Post.** David Williams. 1992. pap. 4.99 (0-00-647253-2, Pub. by HarpC UK) HarpC.

Treasure by the Bay: The Historic Architecture of Sandusky, Ohio. Ellie Damm. LC 87-47807. (Illus.). 192p. 1989. 45.00 (0-8387-5133-4) Bucknell U Pr.

Treasure Chest. Johann P. Hebel. (Illus.). 204p. 1994. 39.95 (1-870352-43-2, Pub. by Libris UK) Paul & Co Pubs.

Treasure Chest. Johann P. Hebel. Tr. & Intro. by John Hibberd. (Classics Ser.). 208p. 1995. pap. 10.95 (0-14-044639-7, Penguin Classics) Viking Penguin.

Treasure Chest: A Chinese Tale. Retold by Rosalind C. Wang. LC 93-20744. (Illus.). 32p. (J). (ps-3). 1995. lib. bdg. 15.95 (0-8234-1114-1) Holiday.

Treasure Chest: A Teacher Advisory Source Book. Cheryl Hoversten et al. (Illus.). 268p. 1991. ring bd. 28.00 (1-56090-056-3) Natl Middle Schl.

***Treasure Chest: An Anthology of Contemplative Prose.** James D. Adams. 402p. Date not set. 23.95 (0-8369-2883-0) Ayer.

Treasure Chest: Practice Exercises for "Wee Folks Readers" Charlotte M. Hill & Fred Hill. Ed. by Elaine A. Young. LC 93-71070. (Illus.). 90p. (Orig.). (J). (gr. 1-3). 1993. student ed. 6.95 (0-9620182-8-7) Charill Pubs.

Treasure Chest of Tales. Paul Stroyer. (Illus.). (J). (gr. 3 up). 1959. 12.95 (0-8392-3039-7) Astor-Honor.

Treasure Chest of Wisdom, Jewels of Thought. Henry Wagner. 1967. 7.50 (0-911584-02-1) Green Dolphin.

***Treasure Coast Black Heritage: A Pictorial History.** Audria V. Moore et al. LC 96-40908. 1996. write for info. (0-89865-983-3) Donning Co.

Treasure Coast Magazine, 1994: The Best of South Florida from North Palm Beach to Vero Beach. (Illus.). 112p. 1994. 5.95 (1-883117-04-6) Mohr Graphics.

Treasure Coast Magazine, 1995: The Best of South Florida from North Palm Beach to Vero Beach. (Illus.). 112p. 1995. 5.95 (1-883117-05-4) Mohr Graphics.

Treasure Dive. Desjarlais. (New Readers Ser.). 1993. pap. text ed. write for info. (0-15-599353-4) HB Schl Dept.

Treasure Diver's Guide. John S. Potter. (Illus.). 590p. 1988. pap. 19.95 (0-912451-22-X) Florida Classics.

Treasure Express: The Epic Days of Wells Fargo. Neill C. Wilson. (Illus.). 352p. 1987. reprint ed. pap. 12.00 (0-87380-157-1) Rio Grande.

Treasure for Life. large type ed. Anne Weale. 304p. 1986. 25.99 (0-7089-1478-0) Ulverscroft.

***Treasure for Our Sand Castle.** Chuck Robinson & Debbie Robinson. LC 96-72259. (Illus.). 24p. (J). (gr. k-3). 1997. 16.95 (0-9647267-7-7) Old Squan Vill Pub.

Treasure from British Waters. John Howland. LC 90-61318. (Illus.). 160p. 1991. pap. 7.95 (0-915920-72-7) Ram Pub.

Treasure Galleons. (Illus.). 259p. 1990. pap. 15.95 (0-912451-17-3) Florida Classics.

***Treasure Guide to Idaho.** H. Glenn Carson. 127p. 1996. pap. 11.95 (0-941620-64-6) Carson Ent.

Treasure Guide to Nebraska, Kansas, North & South Dakota. Thomas Penfield. (Treasure Guide Ser.). 87p. 1971. pap. 7.95 (0-941620-18-2) Carson Ent.

Treasure Guide to Nevada. Thomas Penfield. (Treasure Guide Ser.). 74p. 1974. pap. 8.95 (0-941620-15-8) Carson Ent.

Treasure Guide to New Mexico. Thomas Penfield. (Treasure Guide Ser.). 104p. 1974. pap. 8.95 (0-941620-24-7) Carson Ent.

***Treasure Guide to Texas.** Thomas Peufield. 141p. 1988. pap. 9.95 (0-614-24177-4) Carson Ent.

Treasure Hard to Attain: Images of Archaeology in Popular Film with a Filmogoraphy. David H. Day. 176p. 1997. 42.50 (0-8108-3171-6) Scarecrow.

Treasure Hidden. Thomas Trueblood. LC 85-10954. 1985. 7.50 (0-89536-777-2, 5880) CSS OH.

Treasure House of Early American Rooms. John A. Sweeney & Henry F. Du Pont. (Illus.). 1983. pap. 9.95 (0-393-30039-0) Norton.

Treasure House of Good Books. James A. Stewart. pap. 1.50 (1-56632-064-X) Revival Lit.

Treasure House of Martin Hews. E. Phillips Oppenheim. reprint ed. lib. bdg. 26.95 (0-89190-415-8, Rivercity Pr) Amereon Ltd.

Treasure Hunt. Roger Barr. 1992. pap. 11.95 (0-9634408-0-2) Medallion MN.

***Treasure Hunt.** Roger Befelar. (Great Adventures Ser.). (Illus.). 24p. (Orig.). (J). (ps up). 1997. pap. 2.99 (0-88743-460-6, 06790) Sch Zone Pub Co.

***Treasure Hunt.** Bill Cosby. LC 96-52072. (Little Bill Bk.). (Illus.). (J). 1997. 3.99 (0-590-95618-3) Scholastic Inc.

***Treasure Hunt.** Bill Cosby. LC 96-52072. (Little Bill Book Ser.). (Illus.). (J). 1997. 13.95 (0-590-16399-X) Scholastic Inc.

Treasure Hunt. Disney Studios Staff. (Mickey Mouse Ser.). (Illus.). 10p. (J). (ps-3). 1994. 6.98 (1-57082-094-5) Mouse Works.

Treasure Hunt. Richard Scarry. (J). 1995. pap. 2.95 (0-689-80367-2) S&S Childrens.

Treasure Hunt. Richard Scarry. (J). 1995. 2.95 (0-689-80747-3) S&S Childrens.

Treasure Hunt. Sullivan. (Illus.). 160p. 1993. pap. 9.95 (0-912451-30-0) Florida Classics.

Treasure Hunt. large type ed. Molly Keane. 272p. 1992. 24.95 (1-85089-554-6, Pub. by ISIS UK) Transaction Pubs.

***Treasure Hunt: A New York Times Reporter Tracks the Quedlinburg Hoard.** William H. Honan. LC 96-39303. 1997. write for info. (0-88064-174-6) Fromm Intl Pub.

***Treasure Hunt: A "New York Times" Reporter Tracks the Quedlinburg Hoard.** William H. Honan. (Illus.). 256p. 1996. 24.95 (0-614-24433-1) Fromm Intl Pub.

***Treasure Hunt: Fifty Games for Beginning Readers & Busy Parents.** Steve Cohen. (Learn-to-Read Ser.). 1997. pap. text ed. 71.60 (0-7611-0857-2) Workman Pub.

Treasure Hunt: The Sixteen-Year Search for the Lost Treasure Ship Atocha. George Sullivan. LC 87-8791. (Illus.). 128p. (J). (gr. 4-6). 1987. 13.95 (0-8050-0569-2, Bks Young Read) H Holt & Co.

Treasure Hunt: 10 Stepping Stones to a New & More Confident You! Pam Grout. Ed. by Kelly Scanlon & Jane D. Guthrie. (Illus.). 58p. 1995. pap. 10.95 (1-878542-97-4, 12-0021) SkillPath Pubns.

Treasure Hunt Activity Book. Jeffrey Hunt. (Orig.). (J). 1994. pap. 2.99 (0-8125-9440-1) Tor Bks.

Treasure Hunt in the Creepy Mansion: A Puzzle & Role-Playing Adventure. Dan Abnett. (J). 1995. 5.99 (0-517-14026-8) Random Hse Value.

Treasure Hunt in the Lost City: A Puzzle & Role-Playing Adventure. Dan Abnett. (J). 1996. 5.99 (0-517-14188-4) Random Hse Value.

Treasure Hunter: Undiscovered Treasures of the Southeast. Jerry Williams. LC 92-3510. 1992. 18.95 (0-87844-112-3); pap. 9.95 (0-87844-113-1) Sandlapper Pub Co.

Treasure Hunter's Guide to Historic Middle Tennessee & South Central Kentucky Antiques, Flea Markets & Junk Stores: Also Old Diners, Bed & Breakfast Inns & Much More. Maude G. Kiser. 288p. (Orig.). 1994. pap. 10.95 (0-9635078-1-8) Gold-Kiser.

Treasure Hunter's Guide to Historic Middle Tennessee & South Central Kentucky Antiques, Flea Markets, Junk Stores & More. rev. ed. Maude G. Kiser. 288p. (Orig.). 1995. pap. 11.95 (0-9635078-2-6) Gold-Kiser.

Treasure Hunter's Guide to Morocco: A Common Sense Approach to Sightseeing, Shopping & Etiquette in the Land Known As Maghreb-al-Aqsa: Islam's Far West. Alf Taylor & Ruth Rotert. Tr. by Rohn Eloul & Isabelle Houthakker. (Illus.). 192p. (Orig.). (ENG & FRE.). 1991. pap. text ed. write for info. (0-9628915-0-9) Scenic Pubns.

Treasure Hunter's Information Source Guide. Barry W. Wainwright. 96p. 1995. pap. 12.95 (0-9647768-0-4) Dynamic Fortune Bks.

Treasure Hunting: A Modern Search for Adventure. H. Glenn Carson. (Illus.). 82p. 1981. reprint ed. pap. 7.95 (0-941620-05-0) Carson Ent.

Treasure Hunting: The Treasure Hunter's Own Book of Land Caches & Bullion Wrecks. Harold T. Wilkins. (Illus.). 402p. 1989. reprint ed. pap. 15.00 (0-87380-169-5) Rio Grande.

Treasure Hunting Annual, Vol. 1. Compiled by H. Glenn Carson. (Illus.). 160p. 1979. pap. 7.95 (0-941620-11-5) Carson Ent.

Treasure Hunting Annual, Vol. 2. Compiled by H. Glenn Carson. (Illus.). 164p. 1980. pap. 7.95 (0-941620-22-0) Carson Ent.

Treasure Hunting Bibliography & Index to Periodical Articles. John H. Reed. 425p. (Orig.). 1989. pap. 15.95 (0-940519-04-6) Res Discover Pubns.

***Treasure Hunting for Fun & Profit.** Charles Garrett. 1997. pap. text ed. 10.95 (0-915920-90-5) Ram Pub.

Treasure Hunting for Fun & Profit: A Hobby That Can Pay for Itself. Charles Garrett. Ed. by Hal Dawson. (Illus.). 150p. 1997. pap. 9.95 (0-915920-87-5) Ram Pub.

Treasure in Clay. Fulton J. Sheen. LC 92-75068. (Illus.). 362p. 1993. reprint ed. pap. 14.95 (0-89870-420-0) Ignatius Pr.

Treasure in Heaven Katharine Drexel. Felicity O'Brien. 120p. (C). 1990. 45.00 (0-85439-323-4, Pub. by St Paul Pubns UK) St Mut.

Treasure in Louisiana: Treasure Hunters Guide to the Bayou State. John Miller. 290p. (Orig.). 1996. pap. 18.95 (1-57502-237-0, P0911) Morris Pubng.

Treasure in Roubles. David Williams. 224p. 1988. pap. 2.95 (0-380-70546-X) Avon.

Treasure in the Attic. Christina Chapman. LC 92-35814. (Publish-a-Book Contest Ser.). (Illus.). 32p. (J). (gr. 4-6). 1992. lib. bdg. 22.83 (0-8114-3582-2) Raintree Steck-V.

Treasure in the Attic. Christina Chapman. (Publish-a-Book Ser.). (J). (ps-3). 1994. pap. 4.95 (0-8114-7777-0) Raintree Steck-V.

Treasure in the Jungle Mist. Bill J. Harrison. (Illus.). 270p. 1994. reprint ed. pap. 4.95 (0-9640938-0-4) S by S Develop.

Treasure in the Little Trunk. Helen F. Orton. (Illus.). 208p. (J). (gr. 4). 1989. reprint ed. text ed. 5.95 (1-878233-00-9) Niagara Cnty Hist Soc.

Treasure in the Okinagan, Vol. 1. Sandra Hilderbrand. (Illus.). 592p. (Orig.). 1991. pap. 29.95 (0-940151-11-1) Statesman-Exam.

Treasure in the Royal Tower. Carolyn Keene. (Nancy Drew Ser.: No. 128). (J). (gr. 3-6). 1995. pap. 3.99 (0-671-50502-5) PB.

Treasure in the Sand: How & Where to Find Hundreds of Gold & Silver Rings, Hundreds of Silver Coins & Hundreds of Dollars. Preston Parris. LC 89-80193. 225p. 1992. pap. 19.95 (0-9631917-0-5) THR Hunter Pub.

Treasure in the Stream: The Story of a Gold Rush Girl. Dorothy Hoobler & Thomas Hoobler. (Her Story Ser.). (Illus.). 64p. (J). (gr. 4-6). 1991. pap. 3.95 (0-382-24346-3); lib. bdg. 9.95 (0-382-24144-4) Silver Burdett Pr.

***Treasure in the Tiny Blue Tin.** Dede F. Ducharme. LC 97-15419. (J). 1997. pap. write for info. (0-87565-180-1) Tex Christian.

Treasure in the Yukon. Jeri Massi. Ed. by Carla Vogt. (Light Line Ser.). (Illus.). 128p. (Orig.). (J). (gr. 4-6). 1986. pap. 6.49 (0-89084-365-1, 031070) Bob Jones Univ Pr.

***Treasure Island.** (Nelson Readers Ser.). (J). Date not set. pap. text ed. write for info. (0-17-556699-2) Addison-Wesley.

Treasure Island. (Illus.). 24p. (J). (gr. k up). 1993. pap. 2.50 (1-56144-103-1, Honey Bear Bks) Modern Pub NYC.

Treasure Island. write for info. (0-318-54498-9) NAL-Dutton.

Treasure Island. 1993. pap. 5.25 (0-19-585273-7) OUP.

Treasure Island. 1994. pap. 19.95 (0-7871-0133-8, Dove Bks) Dove Audio.

***Treasure Island.** (Classics Illustrated Study Guides Ser.). (Illus.). (Orig.). 1997. mass mkt. write for info. (1-57840-031-7) Acclaim Bks.

Treasure Island. Raymond Alwin-Hill. LC 91-52607. (Orig.). (YA). 1991. pap. 6.00 (0-88734-412-7) Players Pr.

***Treasure Island.** Casey Brady. (Baywatch Junior Lifeguard Bks.). 1997. pap. 3.99 (0-679-88417-3, Bullseye Bks) Random Bks Yng Read.

Treasure Island. Enchanted Tales Staff. 96p. 1996. mass mkt. 3.50 (0-06-106435-1, Harp PBks) HarpC.

Treasure Island. Created by Harcourt Brace Staff. 1990. student ed., teacher ed., pap. 22.75 (0-15-348527-2) HR&W Schl Div.

Treasure Island. Created by Harcourt Brace Staff. 1990. student ed., pap. 10.00 (0-15-348521-3) HR&W Schl Div.

Treasure Island. Aurand Harris. (J). (gr. 4 up). 1983. pap. 5.00 (0-87602-253-0) Anchorage.

Treasure Island. Holt. 1989. student ed., pap. 10.00 (0-03-023437-9) HR&W Schl Div.

Treasure Island. Ed. by William A. Kottmeyer. 1972. text ed. 7.96 (0-07-034020-X) McGraw.

Treasure Island. Meinkoff. 1995. 24.95 (0-8057-8804-2, Twayne) Scribnrs Ref.

Treasure Island. Illus. by Neil Reed. 96p. (J). (gr. 2-6). 1996. 9.98 (1-85854-190-5) Brimax Bks.

Treasure Island. Justin Scott. 240p. 1994. 19.95 (0-312-11368-4) St Martin.

Treasure Island. Marcia Sohl & Gerald Dackerman. (Now Age Illustrated Ser.). 16p. (J). (gr. 4-10). 1976. pap. 2.95 (0-88301-106-9); student ed., pap. 1.25 (0-88301-185-9) Pendulum Pr.

***Treasure Island.** Stevenson. 1997. pap. text ed. 7.75 (0-03-051503-3) HR&W Schl Div.

Treasure Island. Robert Louis Stevenson. LC 92-53174. (Illus.). 240p. (J). 1992. 12.95 (0-679-41800-8, Evrymans Lib Childs) Knopf.

Treasure Island. Robert Louis Stevenson. (Illus.). 208p. (YA). (gr. 7-12). 1982. mass mkt. 3.95 (0-553-21249-4, Bantam Classics) Bantam.

Treasure Island. Robert Louis Stevenson. 1996. pap. 19.95 (0-7871-0016-1, Dove Bks) Dove Audio.

Treasure Island. Robert Louis Stevenson. (Illus.). (J). 1992. write for info. (0-89434-128-6) Ferguson.

Treasure Island. Robert Louis Stevenson. (Classics Illustrated Ser.). (Illus.). 52p. (J). (gr. 4-7). 1991. pap. 4.95 (1-57209-015-4) First Classics.

Treasure Island. Robert Louis Stevenson. Ed. by Mapes Monde Editore Staff. (Illus.). 190p. 1989. pap. write for info. (0-926330-01-2) Mapes Monde.

Treasure Island. Robert Louis Stevenson. (YA). (gr. 7 up). 1965. pap. 1.75 (0-451-51917-5, Sig Classics) NAL-Dutton.

Treasure Island. Robert Louis Stevenson. (J). (gr. 6). 1965. pap. 3.95 (0-451-52189-7, Sig Classics) NAL-Dutton.

Treasure Island. Robert Louis Stevenson. Ed. by Emma Letley. (WC-P Ser.). 250p. (YA). (gr. 7-12). 1985. pap. 5.95 (0-19-281681-0) OUP.

Treasure Island. Robert Louis Stevenson. (Classics Ser.). (Illus.). 52p. (J). 1994. 3.50 (0-7214-1658-6, Ladybrd) Penguin.

Treasure Island. Robert Louis Stevenson. (Shipwreck Edition Ser.: Vol. 1). (Illus.). 208p. 19.95 (1-883684-07-2) Peninsula MA.

Treasure Island. Robert Louis Stevenson. (Regents Illustrated Classics Ser.). (YA). (gr. 7-12). 1987. pap. text ed. 3.75 (0-13-930629-3, 20521) Prentice ESL.

Treasure Island. Robert Louis Stevenson. (Storybooks Ser.). 224p. (J). (gr. 2-5). 1984. pap. 2.95 (0-14-035016-0, Puffin) Puffin Bks.

Treasure Island. Robert Louis Stevenson. 224p. (YA). (gr. 5 up). 1994. pap. 3.99 (0-14-036672-5) Puffin Bks.

Treasure Island. Robert Louis Stevenson. LC 93-50905. (Illustrated Junior Library). (J). 1994. 15.95 (0-448-40562-8, G&D) Putnam Pub Group.

Treasure Island. Robert Louis Stevenson. LC 79-24100. (Short Classics Ser.). (Illus.). (J). (gr. 4-12). 1983. lib. bdg. 22.80 (0-8172-1655-3) Raintree Steck-V.

Treasure Island. Robert Louis Stevenson. (J). (gr. 4-7). 1993. pap. 4.95 (0-8114-6844-5) Raintree Steck-V.

Treasure Island. Robert Louis Stevenson. LC 89-70039. (Bullseye Step into Classics Ser.). (Illus.). 96p. (J). (gr. 2-6). 1990. pap. 3.99 (0-679-80402-1, Bullseye Bks); lib. bdg. 5.99 (0-679-90402-6) Random Bks Yng Read.

Treasure Island. Robert Louis Stevenson. (Children's Classics Ser.). 1989. 12.99 (0-517-61816-8) Random Hse Value.

Treasure Island. Robert Louis Stevenson. 224p. (J). (gr. 7-9). 1988. pap. 2.95 (0-590-44501-4) Scholastic Inc.

Treasure Island. Robert Louis Stevenson. LC 81-8788. (Scribner's Illustrated Classics Ser.). (Illus.). 296p. (J). (gr. 3 up). 1981. lib. bdg. 26.00 (0-684-17160-0, C Scribner Sons Young) S&S Childrens.

Treasure Island. Robert Louis Stevenson. (J). 1985. 15.45 (0-671-52760-6) S&S Trade.

Treasure Island. Robert Louis Stevenson. (Classic Story Bks.). (J). (gr. 4 up). 1994. 4.98 (0-8317-1649-5) Smithmark.

Treasure Island. Robert Louis Stevenson. 272p. (YA). 1990. pap. 2.99 (0-8125-0508-5) Tor Bks.

Treasure Island. Robert Louis Stevenson. (Illus.). 192p. (J). (gr. 4 up). 1994. 24.95 (1-85145-962-6, Pub. by Pavilion UK) Trafalgar.

Treasure Island. Robert Louis Stevenson. (Illus.). 192p. (YA). (gr. 5 up). 1995. pap. 19.95 (1-85793-488-1, Pub. by Pavilion UK) Trafalgar.

Treasure Island. Robert Louis Stevenson. pap. 2.95 (0-89375-353-X) Troll Communs.

Treasure Island. Robert Louis Stevenson. Ed. by Earle Hitchner. LC 89-20561. (Illustrated Classics Ser.). (Illus.). 48p. (J). (gr. 3-6). 1990. lib. bdg. 12.89 (0-8167-1877-6) Troll Communs.

Treasure Island. Robert Louis Stevenson. (Deluxe Watermill Classic Ser.). 304p. (YA). 1992. 9.49 (0-8167-2560-8); pap. 2.95 (0-8167-2561-6) Troll Communs.

Treasure Island. Robert Louis Stevenson. Ed. by Earle Hitchner. LC 89-20561. (Illustrated Classics Ser.). (Illus.). 48p. (J). (gr. 3-6). 1996. pap. 4.95 (0-8167-1878-4) Troll Communs.

Treasure Island. Robert Louis Stevenson. (Airmont Classics Ser.). (YA). (gr. 7 up). 1962. mass mkt. 3.50 (0-8049-0002-7, CL-2) Airmont.

Treasure Island. Robert Louis Stevenson. Ed. by Nicholas McGuinn. (Literature Ser.). (Illus.). 224p. (C). 1995. pap. text ed. 7.95 (0-521-48568-1) Cambridge U Pr.

Treasure Island. Robert Louis Stevenson. (Literary Classics Ser.). 208p. 1995. 5.98 (1-56138-510-7) Courage Bks.

***Treasure Island.** Robert Louis Stevenson. 304p. (YA). (gr. 10 up). 1996. pap. 14.95 (0-9652952-3-0) Doyle Studio.

Treasure Island. Robert Louis Stevenson. (First Illustrated Classics Ser.). (Illus.). 240p. (J). (ps-6). Date not set. pap. text ed. 2.95 (1-56987-405-0) Landoll.

Treasure Island. Robert Louis Stevenson. (Illus.). 56p. (J). (gr. 2-4). 1996. pap. 2.99 (0-7214-5609-X, Ladybrd) Penguin.

Treasure Island. Robert Louis Stevenson. LC 95-71030. (Shipwreck Edition Ser.: Vol. I). (Illus.). 240p. 1995. 14.95 (1-883684-05-6) Peninsula MA.

Treasure Island. Robert Louis Stevenson. 1996. pap. 6.95 (0-7871-1071-X) Viking Penguin.

Treasure Island. Robert Louis Stevenson. (The Whole Story Ser.). (Illus.). 304p. (YA). (gr. 7 up). 1996. pap. 23.99 (0-670-86920-1) Viking Child Bks.

Treasure Island. Robert Louis Stevenson. (Classics Ser.). (Illus.). 224p. (J). (ps-6). Date not set. pap. text ed. 3.95 (1-56987-414-X) Landoll.

Treasure Island. Robert Louis Stevenson. (Illustrated Classics Ser.). (Illus.). 240p. (J). (ps-6). Date not set. text ed. 9.95 (1-56987-393-3) Landoll.

***Treasure Island.** Robert Louis Stevenson. (Young Collector's Illustrated Classics Ser.). (Illus.). 192p. (J). (gr. 3-7). write for info. (1-56156-456-7) Kidsbks.

***Treasure Island.** Robert Louis Stevenson. LC 95-77836. (Classroom Reading Plays Ser.). 32p. (YA). (gr. 6-12). 1995. pap. 3.95 (0-7854-1120-8, 40208) Am Guidance.

***Treasure Island.** Robert Louis Stevenson. Ed. by Malvina Vogel. (Great Illustrated Classics Ser.: Vol. 7). (Illus.). 240p. (J). (gr. 3-6). 1989. 9.95 (0-86611-958-2) Playmore Inc.

***Treasure Island.** abr. ed. Robert Louis Stevenson. Ed. by Michael J. Marshall. (Core Classics Ser.). (Illus.). 160p. (J). (gr. 4-6). 1997. lib. bdg. write for info. (1-890517-05-4) Core Knowledge.

***Treasure Island.** abr. ed. Robert Louis Stevenson. Ed. by Michael J. Marshall. (Core Classics Ser.: Vol. 3). (Illus.). 160p. (J). (gr. 4-6). 1997. pap. 5.95 (1-890517-04-6) Core Knowledge.

Treasure Island. adapted ed. Robert Louis Stevenson. 1991. pap. 5.25 (0-8222-1170-X) Dramatists Play.

Treasure Island. deluxe ed. Robert Louis Stevenson. (Whole Story Ser.). (Illus.). 304p. (YA). (gr. 7 up). 1996. pap. 15.99 (0-670-86795-0) Viking Child Bks.

Treasure Island. large type ed. Robert Louis Stevenson. 304p. 1983. 27.99 (0-7089-8147-X) Ulverscroft.

***Treasure Island.** large type ed. Robert Louis Stevenson. 349p. 1993. lib. bdg. 24.00 (0-939495-84-8) North Bks.

Treasure Island. Robert Louis Stevenson. (J). (gr. 5-6). Date not set. reprint ed. lib. bdg. 22.95 (0-89190-236-8, Am Repr) Amereon Ltd.

Treasure Island. Robert Louis Stevenson. LC 92-29791. (Thrift Editions Ser.). 160p. (J). 1993. reprint ed. pap. 1.00 (0-486-27559-0) Dover.

Treasure Island, 2 cassettes, Set. (Read-Along Ser.). (YA). 1994. student ed., pap. 34.95 incl. audio (*0-88432-972-0*, S23919) Audio-Forum.

Treasure Island: A Study Guide. James H. Macon. (Novel-Ties Ser.). 1989. student ed., teacher ed., pap. text ed. 15.95 (*0-88122-060-4*) Lrn Links.

***Treasure Island: Treasure Island.** 2nd rev. ed. Robert Louis Stevenson. (Longman Fiction Ser.). 1996. pap. text ed. 7.49 (*0-582-27529-6*, Pub. by Longman UK) Longman.

Treasure Island, Adapted for the Stage. Robert Louis Stevenson. (Illus.). 36p. (Orig.). 1995. pap. 4.00 (*0-88680-413-2*, 413-2) I E Clark.

Treasure Island & Kidnapped Notes. O. L. Mishk. 73p. (Orig.). (C). 1974. pap. text ed. 3.95 (*0-8220-1306-1*) Cliffs.

***Treasure Island Readalong.** Robert Louis Stevenson. (Illustrated Classics Collection 1). 64p. 1994. pap. 14.95 incl. audio (*0-7854-0713-8*, 40363) Am Guidance.

***Treasure Island/Kidnapped.** Robert Lewis Stevenson. (Classic Library Collection). 1996. 12.98 (*0-7651-9985-8*) Smithmark.

Treasure Islands: A Robert Louis Stevenson Centenary Anthology. Ed. by Jenni Calder. (Illus.). 88p. 1995. pap. 14.95 (*0-948636-59-9*, 6599, Woodstocker Bks); audio 8.95 (*0-614-06902-5*, 599C, Woodstocker Bks) A Schwartz & Co.

Treasure Islands: The Fascinating World of Pirates, Buried Treasure, & Fortune Hunters. Cameron Platt & John Wright. LC 94-34454. 1995. pap. 15.95 (*1-55591-190-0*) Fulcrum Pub.

Treasure Keeper. Anita Williams. Ed. by Debbie Parker. LC 95-32151. (Pennant Ser.). (Illus.). 89p. (Orig.). (J). (gr. 2-3). 1995. pap. 7.95 (*0-89084-835-1*, 091710) Bob Jones Univ Pr.

Treasure Laws of the United States. Roger W. Grim. 208p. pap. text ed. 16.95 (*0-9636458-0-3*) R W Grim.

Treasure Map. Houghton Mifflin Company Staff. (Mathematics Big Book Ser.). (J). 1994. pap. 41.04 (*0-395-70372-7*) HM.

Treasure Maps & Charts in the Library of Congress: A Descriptive List by a Reference Librarian. Ed. by Richard S. Ladd. LC 64-60033. 1988. pap. 5.00 (*0-87380-161-X*) Rio Grande.

Treasure Mountain. Louis L'Amour. 208p. (Orig.). 1984. 3.99 (*0-553-27689-1*) Bantam.

Treasure Mountain. Evelyn S. Lampman. (Eager Beaver Bks.). (Illus.). 207p. (J). (gr. 4). 1990. reprint ed. pap. 5.95 (*0-87595-231-3*) Oregon Hist.

Treasure Mountain Home Park City Revisited. rev. ed. George Thompson & Fraser Buck. (Illus.). 141p. 1993. reprint ed. pap. 16.95 (*0-942688-89-9*) Dream Garden.

Treasure Nap. Juanita Havill. (Illus.). 32p. (J). (gr. k-3). 1992. 15.00 (*0-395-57817-5*) HM.

***Treasure of Alpheus Winterborn.** John Bellairs. LC 96-40082. (Illus.). (J). 1997. pap. 3.99 (*0-14-038009-4*) Puffin Bks.

***Treasure of Bessledorf Hill.** Phyllis R. Naylor. LC 96-30514. (J). 1998. 15.00 (*0-689-81337-6*, Atheneum Bks Young) S&S Childrens.

***Treasure of Bessledorf Hill.** Roberts. (J). Date not set. mass mkt. 4.50 (*0-689-81856-4*) S&S Childrens.

Treasure of Bridge Tips: Four Hundred Fifty Tips to Improve Your Partner's Game. Edwin B. Kantar. (Kantar on Bridge Ser.). 172p. 1991. pap. 10.95 (*0-9630970-0-8*) E Kantar.

Treasure of Camuy's Cave. Victor M. Misla. (Illus.). 30p. (Orig.). (YA). (gr. 6-7). 1987. pap. 5.00 (*0-9626870-1-4*) NW Monarch Pr.

Treasure of Charter Oak: Growing up in the Masonic Home for Children, 1928-1938. Ivan G. Reynolds & Helen Reynolds. LC 89-34633. (Illus.). 80p. (Orig.). 1989. pap. 7.95 (*0-931832-34-9*) Fithian Pr.

Treasure of Cozy Cove. Tony Ross. (J). (ps-3). 1990. 14.00 (*0-374-37744-8*) FS&G.

***Treasure of Darkness.** Sylvia Pearce. 178p. (Orig.). 1997. pap. 6.00 (*1-57502-395-4*, P01232) Morris Pubng.

Treasure of Death Valley. Francine Pascal. (Sweet Valley High Ser.: No. 115). 208p. (YA). (gr. 7-12). 1995. mass mkt. 3.99 (*0-553-56633-4*) Bantam.

Treasure of Earthen Vessels: Explorations in Theological Anthropology. Ed. by Brian H. Childs & David W. Waanders. LC 94-524. 256p. (Orig.). 1994. pap. 20.00 (*0-664-25493-4*) Westminster John Knox.

Treasure of El Dorado. 4th rev. ed. Joseph Whitfield. LC 86-50360. (Illus.). 216p. 1977. reprint ed. 15.95 (*0-912119-02-0*) Treasure Publications.

Treasure of El Lahun: Metropolitan Museum of Art (Department of Egyptian Art Publications, Vol. 4) Herbert E. Winlock. LC 73-168416. (Metropolitan Museum of Art Publications in Reprint). (Illus.). 130p. 1973. reprint ed. 24.95 (*0-405-02254-9*) Ayer.

Treasure of El Patron. Gary Paulsen. (Adventure Ser.: 10). 96p. (J). 1996. pap. 3.99 (*0-440-41048-7*) Dell.

Treasure of Euonymus: Conteyninge the Hid Secretes of Nature. Conrad Gesner. Tr. by P. Morwyng. LC 63-6477. (English Experience Ser.: No. 97). 408p. 1969. reprint ed. 45.00 (*90-221-0097-9*) Walter J Johnson.

Treasure of Hymns. Amos R. Wells. LC 70-128330. (Essay Index Reprint Ser.). 1977. 22.95 (*0-8369-2096-1*) Ayer.

Treasure of Jericho Mountain. large type ed. Cameron Judd. LC 90-40663. 239p. 1990. reprint ed. lib. bdg. 16.95 (*1-56054-042-7*) Thorndike Pr.

Treasure of Love. large type ed. Delia Foster. (Linford Romance Library). 264p. 1984. pap. 15.99 (*0-7089-6033-2*) Ulverscroft.

Treasure of Pawley's Island. Celia C. Halford. LC 86-25997. (Illus.). 190p. (Orig.). 1987. pap. 7.95 (*0-87844-068-2*) Sandlapper Pub Co.

Treasure of Pelican Cove. Milly Howard. Ed. by Laurie Garner. (Light Line Ser.). (Illus.). 104p. (Orig.). (J). 1988. pap. 6.49 (*0-89084-464-X*, 043182) Bob Jones Univ Pr.

Treasure of Plunderell Manor. Bruce Clements. 192p. (YA). (gr. 7 up). 1991. pap. 3.95 (*0-374-47962-3*) FS&G.

Treasure of Sierra Madre. Ed. by James Naremore. LC 78-53298. (Screenplay Ser.). (Illus.). 206p. 1979. 11.95 (*0-299-07680-6*); pap. 6.95 (*0-299-07684-9*) U of Wis Pr.

***Treasure of Skeleton Reef.** Brad Strickland & Tom Fuller. (Wishbone Mysteries Ser.). (Illus.). 128p. (Orig.). (J). (gr. 3-6). 1997. mass mkt. 3.99 (*1-57064-279-6*, Big Red) Lyrick Pub.

Treasure of Stonewycke. Michael Phillips & Judith Pella. (Stonewycke Legacy Ser.). 400p. (Orig.). 1988. pap. 9.99 (*0-87123-902-7*) Bethany Hse.

Treasure of Stonewycke. Michael Phillips & Judith Pella. (Stonewycke Legacy Ser.: Bk. 3). 462p. (Orig.). 1995. mass mkt. 6.99 (*1-55661-634-1*) Bethany Hse.

Treasure of Taos: Tales of Northern New Mexico. Reed Stevens. (Illus.). 128p. (Orig.). 1992. pap. 9.95 (*0-933553-08-0*) Mariposa Print Pub.

***Treasure of the Atocha.** 2nd ed. R. Duncan Mathewson, III. (Orig.). 1998. pap. 18.95 (*0-88415-875-6*, 5875) Gulf Pub.

Treasure of the Atocha: A Sixteen Year Undersea Adventure. P. Matthewson. LC 85-30978. (Illus.). 192p. 1987. 19.95 (*0-525-24497-2*, 9EP1, Pisces Bks) Gulf Pub.

Treasure of the Brasada. large type ed. Les Savage, Jr. LC 93-7034. 1993. Alk. paper. pap. 15.95 (*1-56054-697-2*) Thorndike Pr.

Treasure of the City of the Ladies: Or the Book of Three Virtues. Christine De Pisan. Tr. & Intro. by Sarah Lawson. (Classics Ser.). 192p. 1985. pap. 9.95 (*0-14-044453-X*, Penguin Classics) Viking Penguin.

Treasure of the Concepcion. William M. Mathers. (Illus.). 164p. (C). 1994. 24.50 (*0-931234-56-5*, D666) Best Pub Co.

***Treasure of the Hidden Tomb.** 216p. (J). 1997. write for info. (*0-7814-3003-8*, Chariot Bks) Chariot Victor.

Treasure of the Humble. Maurice Maeterlinck. Tr. by Alfred Sutro. LC 77-10276. reprint ed. 27.50 (*0-404-16328-9*) AMS Pr.

Treasure of the Land of Darkness: The Fur Trade & Its Significance for Medieval Russia. Janet L. Martin. (Illus.). 296p. 1987. text ed. 69.95 (*0-521-32019-4*) Cambridge U Pr.

***Treasure of the Long Sault.** Monica Hughes. 1996. pap. 4.95 (*0-7736-7277-X*) Putnam Pub Group.

Treasure of the Lost Lagoon. Geoffrey Hayes. LC 90-40118. (Step into Reading Bks.). (Illus.). 48p. (Orig.). (J). (gr. 2-3). 1991. pap. 3.99 (*0-679-81484-1*); lib. bdg. 9.99 (*0-679-91484-6*) Random Bks Yng Read.

Treasure of the Magi: A Story of Modern Zoroastrianism. James H. Moulton. LC 73-173004. reprint ed. 41.50 (*0-404-04508-1*) AMS Pr.

Treasure of the Magi: A Study of Modern Zoroastrianism. James H. Moulton. 1973. lib. bdg. 59.95 (*0-8490-2759-4*) Gordon Pr.

Treasure of the Magi: A Study of Modern Zoroastrianism. James H. Moulton. 280p. 1996. reprint ed. pap. 24.95 (*1-56459-612-5*) Kessinger Pub.

Treasure of the Mayans. William Hezlep. LC 94-27107. 28p. (Orig.). (J). (gr. 3-8). 1995. pap. 5.00 (*0-88734-405-4*) Players Pr.

Treasure of the Merrilee. Charles Mills. LC 93-6803. 1993. pap. 5.99 (*0-8280-7117-9*) Review & Herald.

Treasure of the Sangre De Cristos: Tales & Traditions of the Spanish Southwest. Arthur L. Campa. LC 94-8093. (Illus.). 223p. 1994. pap. 12.95 (*0-8061-1176-3*) U of Okla Pr.

Treasure of the Sierra Madre. B. Traven. (American Century Ser.). 308p. 1984. pap. 10.95 (*0-374-52149-2*, Noonday) FS&G.

Treasure of the Sierra Madre. large type ed. B. Traven. LC 93-40835. 1994. lib. bdg. 22.95 (*0-7862-0100-2*) Thorndike Pr.

Treasure of the Sierra Madre. B. Traven. LC 79-10456. 1980. reprint ed. lib. bdg. 20.00 (*0-8376-0436-2*) Bentley.

Treasure of the Tear. Karl Pilzer. (Illus.). 40p. (J). pap. write for info. (*0-936015-51-9*) Pocahontas Pr.

Treasure of the Vanquished: A Novel of Visigothic Spain. Bernard Reilly. 256p. 1993. 19.95 (*0-938289-27-6*, 7332) Combined Pub.

***Treasure of Timbuktu.** Catherine Palmer. LC 96-32139. (HeartQuest Ser.: No. 1). 1997. pap. 10.99 (*0-8423-5775-0*) Tyndale.

Treasure of Trash: A Recycling Story. Linda Mandel & Hedi M. Mandel. LC 92-41222. (Illus.). 48p. (J). (gr. 4 up). 12.95 (*0-89529-575-X*) Avery Pub.

Treasure of Venice. 1996. pap. 49.99 (*88-86502-20-6*, Pub. by Canal & Stamperia UK) Antique Collect.

Treasure of Victoria Peak. Phil A. Koury. LC 85-52375. 200p. 1986. pap. 9.95 (*0-88740-060-4*) Schiffer.

***Treasure of Zanzibar.** Palmer. LC 96-37222. (Heartquest Ser.: No. 2). 1997. pap. 10.99 (*0-8423-5776-9*) Tyndale.

Treasure on Earth: A Country House Christmas. Phyllis E. Sandeman. (Illus.). 114p. 1996. pap. 8.95 (*0-7078-0175-3*, Pub. by Natl Trust UK) Trafalgar.

Treasure Quest PLAE Score: A Thematic Play & Learning Program for Children of All Abilities. Susan M. Goltsman et al. LC 94-32791. (Illus.). 1994. pap. 14.95 (*0-944661-06-8*) MIG Comns.

Treasure Recovery from Sand & Sea. rev. ed. Charles Garrett. Ed. by Hal Dawson. LC 89-63316. (Illus.). 466p. 1990. pap. 14.95 (*0-915920-70-0*) Ram Pub.

Treasure Search for Godly Wisdom. Dorothy Hellstern. 160p. 1995. pap. text ed. 9.99 (*1-56322-044-X*); teacher ed., ring bd. 19.99 (*1-56322-045-8*) V Hensley.

***Treasure Secrets of the Lost Dutchman.** Charles A. Kenworthy. (Illus.). 96p. (Orig.). 1997. pap. 14.95 (*0-9632156-3-9*) Quest Pubns.

Treasure Ship. E. J. Hall. 64p. 1984. text ed. 2.99 (*0-07-025751-5*) McGraw.

Treasure Ship, Rory Aforesaid, The Happy War: Three Plays. John Brandane. LC 79-50019. (One-Act Plays in Reprint Ser.). 1980. reprint ed. 25.00 (*0-8486-2043-7*) Roth Pub Inc.

Treasure Signs, Symbols, Shadow & Sun Signs. Charles A. Kenworthy. (Illus.). 64p. 1991. pap. 10.95 (*0-9632156-0-4*) Quest Pubns.

Treasure State Treasury: Banks, Bankers & Banking in Montana, 1863-1984. William C. Skidmore. (Illus.). 200p. 1985. 29.95 (*0-9612006-0-X*) Montana Bankers.

Treasure Store. Ed. by Robert Backhouse. 272p. 1996. pap. 13.99 (*0-551-02992-7*) Zondervan.

Treasure Tales: Shipwrecks & Salvage. Thomas H. Sebring. (Illus.). 150p. 1986. lib. bdg. 24.95 (*0-9617735-0-2*) T H Sebring.

Treasure Tales of the Rockies. 4th rev. ed. Perry Eberhart. LC 89-22037. (Illus.). 315p. 1990. pap. 17.95 (*0-8040-0935-X*) Swallow.

Treasure, the Business & Technology. Phillip S. Olin. (Illus.). 188p. (Orig.). 1991. pap. 19.95 (*1-880502-00-3*) Omicron Grp.

Treasure the Moment. Ed. by Shirley J. Mikkelson. (Orig.). 1996. pap. 24.95 (*0-943536-84-7*) Quill Bks.

Treasure Trails. J. Tykr. (J). (ps-3). 1993. pap. 4.50 (*0-7460-1321-3*, Usborne) EDC.

Treasure Trails of the Southwest. Marc Simmons. LC 93-42191. (Illus.). 177p. (C). 1994. pap. 8.95 (*0-8263-1509-7*) U of NM Pr.

Treasure Tree. John Trent et al. 128p. (J). (gr. k-3). 1992. 15.99 (*0-8499-0936-8*) Word Pub.

***Treasure Tree Collection from World Book, 22 vols.** 704p. (J). (ps-3). 1996. 160.00 (*0-614-23190-6*, 6163) World Bk.

***Treasure Trove.** Christopher Patterson. 1997. mass mkt. 4.99 (*1-55197-285-9*, Pub. by Comnwlth Pub CN) Partners Pubs Grp.

***Treasure Trove of Fitly Words.** Kathleen McCarroll. 70p. 1996. pap. write for info. (*1-57502-262-1*, P0945) Morris Pubng.

Treasure-Trove of Protection & Blessings: The Seven Chapter Prayer of Orgyen Rinpoche. Tr. by Mike Dickman. 288p. (Orig.). 1997. pap. 12.95 (*1-887276-05-X*, Coolgrve Pr) Cool Grove Pub.

Treasure Vault. Steven D. Howard. (Illus.). 1984. 6.95 (*0-940244-81-0*) Flying Buffalo.

Treasure Vault of Atlantis. Olof W. Anderson. Ed. by R. Reginald & Douglas Melville. LC 77-84194. (Lost Race & Adult Fantasy Ser.). 1978. reprint ed. lib. bdg. 29.95 (*0-405-10952-0*) Ayer.

Treasure Worth Seeking. Sandra Brown. 288p. 1992. mass mkt. 5.99 (*0-446-36073-2*) Warner Bks.

***Treasure Worth Seeking.** Sandra Brown. 1997. mass mkt. 3.99 (*0-446-60567-0*) Warner Bks.

Treasure Worth Seeking. large type ed. Sandra Brown. LC 93-20592. 1994. pap. 18.95 (*1-56054-787-1*) Thorndike Pr.

Treasure Worth the Effort: Navigating the Pathway Toward Wholeness. Dudley Hall. (Christian Maturity Ser.). 108p. 1996. pap. 7.00 (*1-888946-02-4*) Succssfl Liv Chrstian.

Treasured Age: Spirituality for Seniors. James F. Finley. LC 88-36695. 120p. (Orig.). 1989. pap. 5.95 (*0-8189-0554-9*) Alba.

***Treasured Christmas Memories.** Emilie Barnes. (Illus.). 48p. 1996. 19.99 (*1-56507-519-6*) Harvest Hse.

Treasured Earth: Hattie Cosgrove's Mimbres Archaeology in the American Southwest. Carolyn O. Davis. (Illus.). 216p. (Orig.). 1995. pap. 24.95 (*0-9635092-1-7*) Sanpete Pubns.

Treasured Friends: Celebrating the Joys of Friendship. Illus. by Sandra Kuck. 32p. 1996. 12.99 (*1-56507-445-9*) Harvest Hse.

Treasured Friendship. Carrie Bender. LC 95-47390. (Miriam's Journal Ser.: No. 4). 160p. (Orig.). 1996. pap. 7.99 (*0-8361-9033-5*) Herald Pr.

Treasured Heritage. Jean F. Carlo & Rose A. Fosdick. Ed. by Terry P. Dickey & Andrea P. Krumhardt. (Illus.). 61p. (Orig.). 1988. pap. 12.50 (*0-931163-04-8*) U Alaska Museum.

***Treasured Italian Recipes, Bk. II.** Ed. by Miele C. Battaglini. (Illus.). 146p. (Orig.). 1996. pap. 11.95 (*0-9627620-1-6*) ERRC.

Treasured Italian Recipes: A Collection of Three Hundred Never Before Published Recipes. East Rochester Rotary Club Staff. Ed. by Miele C. Battaglini. (Illus.). 223p. (Orig.). 1989. pap. 11.95 (*0-9627620-0-8*) ERRC.

Treasured Landmarks of Indian Hill. Virginia S. White. 113p. 1993. 25.00 (*0-9644666-0-0*) Indian Hill Hist Soc.

Treasured Mailbox. Caroline Linse. LC 97-600. 1997. teacher ed., pap. 13.95 (*0-435-08139-X*) Heinemann.

Treasured Memories. Anita M. Hicks. 36p. spiral bd., pap. 7.00 (*0-9648955-0-1*) View Two Concepts.

Treasured Memories: A Book to Recover the Memories of a Loved One Lost. Warren Wiard. 105p. (Orig.). 1995. wbk. ed., spiral bd., pap. 15.95 (*1-885473-08-7*) Wood NBarnes.

Treasured Memories of My Grandma. Bernice Kepple. (Illus.). 112p. 1995. 12.95 (*0-929915-14-3*) Headline Bks.

***Treasured Memory Journal & Scrapbook.** 60p. 1997. spiral bd. 36.95 (*0-9658998-1-0*) Treas Memory.

Treasured Mennonite Recipes, Favorite Recipes from Mennonite Relief Sale Volunteers. 224p. 1993. pap. 11.95 (*1-56523-025-6*) Fox Chapel Pub.

Treasured Poems of America, Fall 1990. Ed. by William H. Trent. LC 90-60054. (Illus.). 400p. 1990. lib. bdg. 59.95 (*0-923242-07-4*) Sparrowgrass Poetry.

Treasured Poems of America, Fall 1991. Ed. by William H. Trent. LC 91-60034. (Illus.). 340p. 1991. lib. bdg. 59.95 (*0-923242-13-9*) Sparrowgrass Poetry.

Treasured Poems of America, Fall 1992. Ed. by Patricia Hamilton. LC 90-640795. (Illus.). 194p. 1992. lib. bdg. 59.95 (*0-923242-19-8*) Sparrowgrass Poetry.

Treasured Poems of America, Fall 1993. Ed. by Patricia Hamilton. LC 90-640795. (Illus.). 400p. 1993. lib. bdg. 39.95 (*0-923242-27-9*) Sparrowgrass Poetry.

Treasured Poems of America, Fall 1994. Ed. by Patricia Hamilton. LC 90-640795. (Illus.). 324p. 1994. lib. bdg. 39.95 (*0-923242-33-3*) Sparrowgrass Poetry.

Treasured Poems of America, Fall 1995. Ed. by Patricia Hamilton. LC 90-640795. (Illus.). 452p. 1995. lib. bdg. 39.95 (*0-923242-41-4*) Sparrowgrass Poetry.

Treasured Poems of America, Fall 1996. Ed. by Patricia Hamilton. LC 91-60034. (Illus.). 352p. 1996. lib. bdg. 39.95 (*0-923242-48-1*) Sparrowgrass Poetry.

Treasured Poems of America, Summer 1990. Ed. by William H. Trent. LC 89-63046. (Illus.). 330p. 1990. lib. bdg. 59.95 (*0-923242-05-8*) Sparrowgrass Poetry.

Treasured Poems of America, Summer 1991. Ed. by William H. Trent. LC 90-63197. (Illus.). 340p. 1991. lib. bdg. 59.95 (*0-923242-11-2*) Sparrowgrass Poetry.

Treasured Poems of America, Summer, 1992. Ed. by Patricia Hamilton. LC 90-640795. (Illus.). 340p. 1992. lib. bdg. 49.00 (*0-923242-17-1*) Sparrowgrass Poetry.

Treasured Poems of America, Summer 1994. Ed. by Patricia Hamilton. LC 90-640795. (Illus.). 348p. 1994. lib. bdg. 39.95 (*0-923242-31-7*) Sparrowgrass Poetry.

Treasured Poems of America, Summer 1995. Ed. by Patricia Hamilton. LC 90-640795. (Illus.). 534p. 1995. lib. bdg. 39.95 (*0-923242-37-6*) Sparrowgrass Poetry.

Treasured Poems of America, Summer 1996. Ed. by Patricia Hamilton. LC 90-640795. (Illus.). 598p. 1996. 39.95 (*0-923242-46-5*) Sparrowgrass Poetry.

Treasured Poems of America, Winter 1990. Ed. by William H. Trent. LC 89-61322. (Illus.). 224p. 1989. lib. bdg. 59.95 (*0-923242-03-1*) Sparrowgrass Poetry.

Treasured Poems of America, Winter 1991. Ed. by William H. Trent. LC 90-61947. (Illus.). 336p. 1990. lib. bdg. 59.95 (*0-923242-09-0*) Sparrowgrass Poetry.

Treasured Poems of America, Winter 1992. Ed. by Patricia Hamilton. LC 91-61546. (Illus.). 344p. 1991. lib. bdg. 49.00 (*0-923242-15-5*) Sparrowgrass Poetry.

Treasured Poems of America, Winter 1993. Ed. by Patricia Hamilton. LC 90-640795. (Illus.). 332p. 1992. lib. bdg. 59.95 (*0-923242-21-X*) Sparrowgrass Poetry.

Treasured Poems of America, Winter 1994. Ed. by Patricia Hamilton. LC 90-640795. (Illus.). 384p. 1993. lib. bdg. 59.95 (*0-923242-29-5*) Sparrowgrass Poetry.

Treasured Poems of America, Winter 1995. Ed. by Patricia Hamilton. LC 90-640795. (Illus.). 374p. 1994. lib. bdg. 39.95 (*0-923242-35-X*) Sparrowgrass Poetry.

Treasured Poems of America, Winter 1996. Patricia Hamilton. LC 90-640795. (Illus.). 392p. 1995. lib. bdg. 39.95 (*0-923242-44-9*) Sparrowgrass Poetry.

Treasured Poems of America, Winter 1997. Ed. by Patricia Hamilton. LC 90-640795. (Illus.). 448p. 1996. lib. bdg. 39.95 (*0-923242-50-3*) Sparrowgrass Poetry.

Treasured Poems That Touch the Heart. Mary Sanford Laurence. 256p. 1995. 12.00 (*0-88486-116-3*, Bristol Park Bks) Arrowood Pr.

Treasured Polish Christmas Customs & Traditions. 1972. 16.95 (*0-685-37594-3*) Polanie.

Treasured Polish Folk Rhyhms, Songs & Games. 1976. 7.95 (*0-685-84287-8*) Polanie.

Treasured Polish Recipes for Americans. 1948. 7.95 (*0-685-22650-6*) Polanie.

Treasured Polish Songs for Americans. (ENG & POL.). 1953. reprint ed. 21.95 (*0-685-22652-2*) Polanie.

Treasured Recipes: An Organizer of Edible Nostalgia. Carriage House Staff. 1993. 19.95 (*0-89786-148-5*) CHP Ltd Redding.

Treasured Recipes & Cooking Secrets of the Bayou see Bayou la Batre Treasured Seafood Recipes

Treasured Recipes from the Charleston Cake Lady: Fast, Fabulous, Easy-to-Make Cakes for Every Occasion. Teresa Pregnall. LC 95-47441. 1996. 17.00 (*0-688-13931-0*) Hearst Bks.

Treasured Recipes from the Shipwreck Coast. Jan M. Holt. 150p. 1996. pap. 14.95 (*0-9651844-0-4*) Grt Lks Shipwreck.

Treasured Romance Vol. 1: On Wings of Love; Love's Late Spring; Fountain of Love. Velma S. Daniels et al. 450p. 1996. 19.99 (*0-310-20952-8*) Zondervan.

***Treasured Stories of Christmas.** Guidepost Editors. 1997. 9.99 (*0-88486-180-5*, Inspirational Pr) Arrowood Pr.

Treasured Time with Your Toddler: A Monthly Guide to Activities. Jan Brennan. (Illus.). 208p. 1991. pap. 14.95 (*0-87483-127-X*) August Hse.

***Treasured Token.** Ed. by Deborah LaBoo. 1997. 69.95 (*1-57553-421-5*) Nat Lib Poetry.

Treasured Vows. Cathy Maxwell. 352p. 1996. mass mkt. 4.99 (*0-06-108415-8*) HarpC.

Treasurer's & Controller's Desk Book. Daniel L. Gotthilf. 512p. 1977. text ed. 59.95 (*0-13-930727-3*) P-H.

***Treasurer's & Controller's Desk Book.** 2nd ed. Daniel L. Gotthilf. LC 96-51049. 640p. 1997. 75.00 (*0-8144-0340-9*) AMACOM.

Treasurer's & Controller's New Equipment Leasing Guide. Albert R. McMeen, III. LC 84-6994. 251p. 1984. 59.95 (*0-13-930876-8*, Busn) P-H.

Treasurer's Guide. E R C Editorial Staff. 1976. 131.50 (*0-13-930503-3*) P-H.

Treasurer's Guide. Executive Reports Corporation Editorial Staff. 1976. 97.50 (*0-685-01590-4*) Exec Reports.

An Asterisk (*) at the beginning of an entry indicates that the title is appearing in BIP for the first time.

***Treasurer's Handbook of Financial Management.** Ed. by Basil B. Mavrovitis. Date not set. write for info. (*0-614-30098-3*) Treasry Mgmt.

Treasurer's Handbook of Financial Management: Applying the Theories, Concepts & Quantitative Methods of Corporate Finance. Dubos J. Masson. Ed. by John G. Oros et al. (Illus.). 447p. 1995. 69.95 (*1-55738-884-9*) Treasry Mgmt.

Treasurer's Office Inventory. enl. rev. ed. Rev. by John S. Salmon. xx, 55p. 1981. pap. 7.95 (*0-88490-103-3*) Library of VA.

Treasures. Darwin Gross. LC 88-90607. 150p. (Orig.). 1988. pap. 6.95 (*0-931689-11-2*) D Gross.

Treasures. Johanna Kingsley. 1991. mass mkt. 5.99 (*0-446-36123-2*) Warner Bks.

***Treasures.** Northland Publishing Staff. 1997. pap. text ed. 12.95 (*0-87358-702-2*) Northland AZ.

Treasures. Belva Plain. 432p. 1992. 21.00 (*0-385-29927-3*) Delacorte.

Treasures. Belva Plain. 528p. 1993. mass mkt. 6.99 (*0-440-21400-9*) Dell.

Treasures. Jo-Ann Power. 324p. 1996. mass mkt. 5.99 (*0-671-52995-1*, PB Trade Paper) PB.

Treasures. large type ed. Belva Plain. LC 93-1991. 1993. pap. 19.95 (*0-8161-5803-7*, GK Hall) Thorndike Pr.

Treasures: Historic Architecture of Greater Orlando. Illus. by Pamela Harris. 95p. (Orig.). 1993. pap. 19.95 (*0-9652696-0-4*) Orlando Lndmrks.

Treasures: Stories & Art by Students in Oregon. Ed. by Chris Weber. (Illus.). 256p. (Orig.). 1985. pap. 10.95 (*0-9616058-0-4*) OR Students Writing.

Treasures: 300 Best Excavated Antiques from China. Ed. by Cultural Relics Exchange Center of the PRC Staff. (Illus.). 331p. 1992. 90.00 (*0-934643-01-6*) Cypress Co.

Treasures & Pleasures of Australia: Best of the Best. Ronald L. Krannich & Caryl R. Krannich. 250p. (Orig.). 1997. pap. 15.95 (*1-57023-060-9*) Impact VA.

***Treasures & Pleasures of China.** Ronald L. Krannich. (Impact Guides Ser.). 1997. pap. text ed. 14.95 (*1-57023-077-3*) Impact VA.

***Treasures & Pleasures of Hong Kong: Best of the Best.** 4th ed. Ronald L. Krannich. LC 97-3718. (Impact Guides Ser.). 1997. pap. text ed. 14.95 (*1-57023-075-7*) Impact VA.

Treasures & Pleasures of India: Best of the Best. Ronald L. Krannich & Caryl R. Krannich. 150p. (Orig.). Date not set. pap. 14.95 (*1-57023-056-0*) Impact VA.

Treasures & Pleasures of Indonesia: Best of the Best. 2nd ed. Ronald L. Krannich & Caryl R. Krannich. 50p. 1995. pap. 14.95 (*1-57023-045-5*) Impact VA.

Treasures & Pleasures of Italy: Best of the Best. Ronald L. Krannich & Caryl R. Krannich. LC 96-44838. 150p. (Orig.). 1996. pap. 14.95 (*1-57023-058-7*) Impact VA.

Treasures & Pleasures of Paris & the French Riviera: Best of the Best. Ronald L. Krannich & Caryl R. Krannich. 150p. (Orig.). 1996. pap. 14.95 (*1-57023-057-9*) Impact VA.

***Treasures & Pleasures of Singapore: Best of the Best.** Ron Krannich. (Impact Guides Ser.). 1997. pap. text ed. 14.95 (*1-57023-083-8*) Impact VA.

Treasures & Pleasures of Singapore & Malaysia: Best of the Best. 2nd ed. Ronald L. Krannich & Caryl R. Krannich. 150p. 1995. pap. 14.95 (*1-57023-044-7*) Impact VA.

***Treasures & Pleasures of Thailand.** Ronald L. Krannich. (Impact Guides Ser.). 1997. pap. text ed. 14.95 (*1-57023-076-5*) Impact VA.

Treasures & Pleasures of Thailand: Best of the Best. Ronald L. Krannich & Caryl R. Krannich. 260p. (Orig.). 1995. pap. 14.95 (*1-57023-043-9*) Impact VA.

Treasures & Pleasures of the Caribbean: Best of the Best. 2nd ed. John W. Edmiston & Nancy B. Edmiston. 230p. 1995. pap. 16.95 (*1-57023-046-3*) Impact VA.

Treasures & Rarities - Renaissance, Mannerist & Baroque: A Picture Book. LC 72-198355. (Illus.). 39p. 1971. pap. 1.50 (*0-911886-21-4*) Walters Art.

Treasures Beyond the Snows. Marie A. Gouffe. LC 77-95392. Orig. Title: Jigme. (Illus.). (J). (gr. 3-9). 1970. 3.75 (*0-8356-0026-2*, Quest) Theos Pub Hse.

Treasure's Disguise. Edlena Washington. 24p. 1996. pap. 8.00 (*0-8059-3844-3*) Dorrance.

Treasures for Teachers. Victoria Estrem. (Small Wonders Ser.). 120p. 1996. spiral bd. write for info. (*1-879127-70-9*) Lighten Up Enter.

Treasures for Teachers. Janet C. Teitsort. LC 94-16001. 144p. (gr. 10). 1994. 9.99 (*0-8010-8917-4*) Baker Bks.

Treasures for the Christmas Tree: 101 Festive Ornaments to Make & Enjoy. Carol Taylor. LC 94-13705. (Illus.). 128p. 1994. 27.95 (*0-8069-0806-8*) Sterling.

Treasures for the Christmas Tree: 101 Festive Ornaments to Make & Enjoy. Carol Taylor. (Illus.). 128p. (Orig.). 1995. pap. 14.95 (*0-8069-0807-6*) Lark Books.

Treasures for the Heart. Lex W. Adams. 100p. (Orig.). 1994. pap. write for info. (*0-9643206-0-6*) Spirit of Truth.

Treasures from an Ancient Land: The Art of Jordan. Ed. by Piotr Bienkowski. (Illus.). 192p. 1996. pap. 22.95 (*0-7509-1238-3*, Pub. by Sutton Pubng UK) Bks Intl VA.

Treasures from Grandma. Arleta Richardson. LC 84-12736. (Grandma's Attic Ser.). 128p. (J). (gr. 3-7). 1994. pap. 4.99 (*0-7814-0088-0*, 59345, Chariot Bks) Chariot Victor.

***Treasures from Heaven.** Nawracas. 1997. pap. 14.95 (*0-670-87289-X*) Viking Penguin.

Treasures from India: The Clive Collection at Powis Castle. Mildred Archer et al. LC 87-12234. (Illus.). 144p. 1987. 25.00 (*0-941533-01-8*) New Amsterdam Bks.

***Treasures from Italy's Great Libraries.** Lorenzo Crinelli. (Illus.). 288p. 1997. 65.00 (*0-86565-986-9*) Vendome.

***Treasures from My Utmost for His Highest.** Oswald Chambers. 128p. 1997. lthr. 7.97 (*1-57748-078-3*) Barbour & Co.

Treasures from Near Eastern Looms. Ernest H. Roberts. LC 81-68474. (Illus.). 1981. pap. 10.00 (*0-916606-02-3*) Bowdoin Coll.

Treasures from Our West. Buffalo Bill Historical Center Staff. (Illus.). 60p. (C). 1995. pap. 15.00 (*0-295-97488-5*) U of Wash Pr.

Treasures from Paul's Letters, Vol. I. Anthony M. Coniaris. 1978. pap. 15.95 (*0-937032-05-0*) Light&Life Pub Co MN.

Treasures from Paul's Letters, Vol. II. Anthony M. Coniaris. 1979. pap. 15.95 (*0-937032-06-9*) Light&Life Pub Co MN.

Treasures from the Baptist Heritage: The Library of Baptist Classics. Ed. by Timothy George & Denise George. 288p. 1997. 24.99 (*0-8054-1252-2*, 4212-52) Broadman.

Treasures from the Beginning of the World. Jeff Lewis. (Illus.). 140p. (Orig.). 1994. pap. 10.95 (*1-886028-13-3*) Savage Pr.

Treasures from the Buffalo Bill Museum. Buffalo Bill Historical Center Staff. (Illus.). 64p. (C). 1995. pap. 20.00 (*0-295-97489-3*) U of Wash Pr.

Treasures from the Chrysler Museum at Norfolk & Walter P. Chrysler, Jr. Mario Amaya. LC 77-81411. (Illus.). 124p. 1977. pap. 8.50 (*0-940744-14-7*) Chrysler Museum.

Treasures from the Embroiderers' Guild Collection. (Illus.). 192p. 1995. pap. 19.95 (*0-7153-0372-4*, Pub. by D & C Pub UK) Sterling.

Treasures from the Film Archives: A Catalog of Short Silent Fiction Films Held by FIAF Archives. Ronald S. Magliozzi. LC 88-13500. 856p. 1988. 62.50 (*0-8108-2180-X*) Scarecrow.

Treasures from the Fitzwilliam Museum: The Increase of Learning & Other Great Objects. Ed. by R. A. Crighton. (Fitzwilliam Museum Publications). (Illus.). 208p. (C). 1989. text ed. 80.00 (*0-521-37130-9*) Cambridge U Pr.

Treasures from the Garden. Pat Andreatta. 34p. 1990. student ed. 14.95 (*0-9616848-4-4*) Heirloom Stitches.

***Treasures from the Heart.** Gladys C. Mopales. 11p. 1996. wbk. ed. 5.00 (*0-9649937-1-6*) P M Pubng.

***Treasures from the Hymnal.** Gail Smith. 1993. pap. 17.95 incl. audio (*0-7866-1093-X*, 94691P) Mel Bay.

Treasures from the Language of Jesus. Rocco A. Errico. LC 87-70912. 131p. 1987. pap. 10.95 (*0-87516-594-X*) DeVorss.

Treasures from the Master's Heart. Greg Reid. 107p. (Orig.). 1991. pap. 10.00 (*1-877858-39-0*, TFTMH) Amer Focus Pub.

Treasures from the Meher Baba Journals. Meher Baba et al. Ed. by Jane B. Haynes. LC 79-92169. (Illus.). 246p. 1980. pap. 8.95 (*0-913078-37-9*) Sheriar Pr.

Treasures from the National Library of Ireland. Ed. by Noel Kissane. (Illus.). 254p. 1995. pap. 24.95 (*0-9517823-4-7*, Pub. by Natl Lib Ireland IE) Syracuse U Pr.

Treasures from the National Library of Ireland. Ed. by Noel Kissane. (Illus.). 254p. 1995. text ed. 65.00 (*0-9517823-5-5*, Pub. by Natl Lib Ireland IE) Syracuse U Pr.

Treasures from the National Museum of American Art. William Kloss. LC 85-61846. (Illus.). 256p. 1986. 42.00 (*0-87474-594-2*, KLTN) Smithsonian.

Treasures from The New York Public Library. Ed. by Richard Newman. (Illus.). 134p. (Orig.). 1985. pap. 19.95 (*0-87104-286-X*) NY Pub Lib.

Treasures from the Rietberg Museum. Helmut Brinker & Eberhard Fischer. LC 80-12528. (Illus.). 176p. 1980. 19.95 (*0-87848-055-2*) Asia Soc.

Treasures from the Sea. Susan Alcon. 24p. 1995. pap. text ed. 5.95 (*0-87487-743-1*) Summy-Birchard.

Treasures in Cross-Stitch: 50 Projects Inspired by Antique Needlework. Jane Greenoff. LC 95-52797. (Illus.). 160p. 1996. 24.95 (*0-8442-2606-8*) Quilt Digest Pr.

Treasures in Earthen Vessels: The Vows. Joyce Ridick. (C). 1988. 39.00 (*0-685-22287-X*, Pub. by St Paul Pubns UK) St Mut.

Treasures in Heaven. Huldah Buntain. 240p. (Orig.). 1989. mass mkt. 3.99 (*0-88368-217-6*) Whitaker Hse.

***Treasures in Heaven: Armenian Illuminated Manuscripts.** Ed. by T. F. Mathews & R. S. Wieck. 296p. 1994. text ed. 75.00 (*0-691-03752-3*) Princeton U Pr.

Treasures in Heaven: Armenian Illuminated Manuscripts. Ed. by Thomas F. Mathews & Roger S. Wieck. LC 93-40269. 1994. write for info. (*0-87598-100-3*) Pierpont Morgan.

Treasures in Heaven: Armenian Illuminated Manuscripts. Thomas F. Mathews. 296p. 1994. pap. text ed. 39.50 (*0-691-03751-5*) Princeton U Pr.

Treasures in Heaven: Inspiration to You. Dewilda M. Williams. LC 95-68158. 188p. (Orig.). pap. 7.00 (*1-886493-00-6*) NBC Study Pub.

Treasures in Miniature. Sybil Harp. Ed. by Terry Spohn. LC 92-43720. (Illus.). 104p. (Orig.). 1993. per. 16.95 (*0-89024-144-9*, 12113) Kalmbach.

***Treasures in the Darkness: Stories from Behind Broken Walls.** 86p. 1995. 6.25 (*0-8341-1556-5*) Nazarene.

***Treasures in the Dust.** Tracey Porter. LC 96-54860. (Joanna Cotler Bks.). (Illus.). 128p. (J). (gr. 3-5). 1997. 14.95 (*0-06-027563-4*); lib. bdg. 14.89 (*0-06-027564-2*) HarpC Child Bks.

Treasures in the Sand: What Archaeology Tells Us about the Bible. Orley Berg. LC 92-14845. 1993. pap. 3.97 (*0-8163-1110-2*) Pacific Pr Pub Assn.

Treasures in the Sea see Books for Young Explorers

Treasures in the Trunk: Quilts of the Oregon Trail. Mary B. Cross. LC 92-45831. (Illus.). 192p. 1993. pap. 19.95 (*1-55853-237-4*) Rutledge Hill Pr.

Treasures in the Wind. Bill Panko & Margaret Panko. 200p. (Orig.). Date not set. pap. 14.95 (*1-885342-14-4*) Creative Ways.

Treasures Lost, Treasures Found. Nora Roberts. (NR Flowers Ser.: No. 40). 1994. mass mkt. 3.59 (*0-373-51040-3*, 1-51040-3) Silhouette.

***Treasures Middle Earth.** 1994. 20.00 (*1-55806-211-4*) Iron Crown Ent Inc.

Treasures New & Old: Recent Contributions to Matthean Studies. Ed. by David R. Bauer & Mark A. Powell. LC 95-51504. (Society of Biblical Literature Symposium Ser.: No. 1). 440p. (C). 1996. 49.95 (*0-7885-0220-4*, 06 07 01); pap. 34.95 (*0-7885-0221-2*, 06 07 01) Scholars Pr GA.

Treasures of American Architecture in Geneva, New York. H. Edmund Wirtz. LC 87-80227. (Illus.). (Orig.). 1986. pap. 5.00 (*0-9613821-2-0*) Geneva Hist Soc Mus.

Treasures of American West: Selections from the Collection of Harrison Eiteljorg. Harrison Eiteljorg. (Illus.). 176p. 1982. 45.00 (*0-9607596-0-3*) Eiteljorg Pubns.

***Treasures of Ancient Coinage: From the Private Collections of American Numismatic Society Members.** Catharine C. Lorber. (Illus.). 128p. (Orig.). 1996. pap. 19.95 (*0-9636738-3-1*) Classical Numismatic Grp.

Treasures of Ancient Indian Astronomy. Ed. by K. D. Abhyankar. (C). 1993. 17.00 (*81-202-0354-2*, Pub. by Ajanta II) S Asia.

Treasures of Animal Illustrations. Carol B. Grafton. 1988. pap. 6.95 (*0-486-25805-X*) Dover.

Treasures of Asian Art: The Asia Society's Mr. & Mrs. John D Rockefeller 3rd Collection. Denise P. Leidy. LC 94-9437. (Illus.). 320p. 1994. 65.00 (*1-55859-863-4*) Abbeville Pr.

Treasures of Asian Art from the Idemitsu Collection. Amy R. Newland et al. LC 81-52557. (Illus.). 204p. 1981. pap. 13.95 (*0-932216-06-4*) Seattle Art.

Treasures of Beloit College: 100 Works from the Logan Museum of Anthropology & the Wright Museum of Art. Intro. by Henry Moy. (Illus.). 100p. (Orig.). 1995. pap. 12.95 (*1-884941-03-6*) Beloit Coll.

Treasures of Britain. Reader's Digest Editors. (Illus.). 680p. 1991. 45.00 (*0-276-42022-5*, Random) RD Assn.

Treasures of British Art: Tate Gallery. Robert Upstone. (Tiny Folios Ser.). (Illus.). 320p. 1996. pap. 11.95 (*1-55859-772-7*) Abbeville Pr.

Treasures of Buddhism. Frithjof Schuon. LC 92-43915. (Library of Traditional Wisdom). 90p. (Orig.). 1993. pap. 12.00 (*0-941532-15-1*) Wrld Wisdom Bks.

Treasures of Canada. Alan E. Samuel et al. 1993. write for info. (*0-88866-640-3*) Edgar Kent.

Treasures of Childhood: Books, Toys & Games from the Opie Collection. Iona A. Opie et al. (Illus.). 192p. 1995. pap. 29.95 (*1-85793-624-8*, Pub. by Pavilion UK) Trafalgar.

Treasures of Childhood: The Hattie Collection, 4 vols., with Charm Necklace. Marie Frost. (J). 1994. pap. 19.99 (*1-56179-269-1*) Focus Family.

Treasures of China: An Armchair Journey to 352 Legendary Landmarks. Reader's Digest Editors. (Illus.). 336p. 1989. 29.95 (*0-89577-325-2*, Random) RD Assn.

Treasures of Darkness. Paul W. Carlin, Sr. (Illus.). 158p. (Orig.). 1989. pap. text ed. 7.95 (*0-317-93532-1*) Kerusso Co.

Treasures of Darkness: A History of Mesopotamian Religion. Thorkild Jacobsen. LC 75-27576. (Illus.). 1978. pap. 17.00 (*0-300-02291-3*) Yale U Pr.

Treasures of Disney Animation Art. Selected by Robert E. Abrams. (Tiny Folios Ser.). (Illus.). 256p. 1992. pap. 11.95 (*1-55859-335-7*) Abbeville Pr.

Treasures of Disney Animation Art. Selected by Robert E. Abrams. (Illus.). 320p. 1992. 49.98 (*0-89660-031-9*, Artabras) Abbeville Pr.

Treasures of East Toledo: A History of the Schools, Churches, Houses, & Other Landmarks of the East Side. Larry R. Michaels. (Illus.). 164p. 1997. 15.00 (*1-883829-15-1*); pap. 10.00 (*1-883829-17-8*) Bihl Hse Pub.

Treasures of Encouragement: Women Helping Women in the Church. Sharon W. Betters. 208p. (Orig.). 1996. pap. 9.99 (*0-87552-097-9*, Pub. by Evangelical Pr) Presby & Reformed.

Treasures of Eton College Library. Paul Quarrie. (Illus.). 122p. 1990. 24.95 (*0-87598-089-9*) Pierpont Morgan.

***Treasures of Existence.** Margaret James. (Magna Large Print Ser.). 532p. 1997. 27.50 (*0-7505-1033-1*) Ulverscroft.

***Treasures of Fantasy.** Ed. by Margaret Weis & Tracy Hickman. (Orig.). 1997. pap. 14.00 (*0-614-27312-9*, HarperPrism) HarpC.

Treasures of Folk Art: The Museum of American Folk Art. Lee Kogan & Barbara Cate. LC 94-12272. (Tiny Folios Ser.). (Illus.). 360p. 1996. pap. 11.95 (*1-55859-560-0*) Abbeville Pr.

Treasures of Galveston Bay. Carroll Lewis. (Illus.). 1966. 13.95 (*0-87244-052-4*) Texian.

Treasures of Georgie. Georgie A. Sadler. 92p. pap. write for info. (*0-9648518-0-6*) G A Sadler.

Treasures of Gold Reading Program. Doris Hoyt & Scarlet Malecha. (Illus.). (Orig.). 1987. pap. text ed. 75.00 (*0-9622364-0-3*) Adona Pub.

Treasures of Gold Reading Program, Vol. 1. Doris Hoyt & Scarlet Malecha. (Illus.). 174p. (Orig.). 1987. teacher ed. write for info. (*0-9622364-1-1*) Adona Pub.

Treasures of Gold Reading Program, Vol. 2: Read a Song. Doris Hoyt & Scarlet Malecha. (Illus.). 166p. (Orig.). 1987. Vol. 2 Read a Song, 166p. student ed. write for info. (*0-9622364-2-X*) Adona Pub.

Treasures of Gold Reading Program, Vol. 3: Little Book Library. Doris Hoyt & Scarlet Malecha. (Illus.). 290p. (Orig.). 1987. Vol. 3 Little Book Library, 290p. write for info. (*0-9622364-3-8*) Adona Pub.

Treasures of Hawaiian History: From the Collection of the Hawaiian Historical Society. David W. Forbes. (Illus.). 126p. (Orig.). (C). 1993. pap. text ed. 25.00 (*0-945048-03-3*) HI Hist Soc.

Treasures of History: Historic Buildings in Chaves County 1870-1935. Ed. by William E. Gibbs et al. LC 85-72824. (Illus.). 144p. (Orig.). 1986. pap. 6.95 (*0-9615310-2-9*) Hist Soc SE NM.

Treasures of History Three: Southeast New Mexico People, Places, & Events. Ernestine C. Williams. (Illus.). viii, 248p. 1995. 25.00 (*0-9615310-5-3*); pap. 15.00 (*0-9615310-6-1*) Hist Soc SE NM.

Treasures of History Two: Chaves County Vignettes. Elvis E. Fleming & Ernestine C. Williams. (Illus.). viii, 205p. 1991. 13.95 (*0-9615310-3-7*); pap. 9.95 (*0-9615310-4-5*) Hist Soc SE NM.

Treasures of Impressionism & Post-Impressionism from the National Gallery of Art. Florence Coman. LC 93-10768. (Tiny Folios Ser.). (Illus.). 320p. 1996. pap. 11.95 (*1-55859-561-9*) Abbeville Pr.

Treasures of Indian Textiles. Calico Museum, Ahmedabad Staff. (Illus.). 148p. 1980. 49.95 (*0-940500-44-2*) Asia Bk Corp.

Treasures of Inspiration. Vivian Carrington. 70p. (Orig.). 1992. pap. 5.00 (*0-9628859-0-8*) V Carrington.

Treasures of Inspiration: A Woman's Guide to Daily Living. Ed. by Paul C. Brownlow. 7.99 (*1-877719-39-0*) Brownlow Pub Co.

Treasures of Iowa. Ed. by Charles W. Roberts & Mary Hirsch. (Illus.). 76p. (Orig.). 1987. pap. 4.95 (*0-317-61645-5*) Mid Am Pub.

Treasures of Jesus: A Meditation on the Sermon on the Mount. Alan Robinson. 144p. 1994. pap. 13.95 (*0-85439-466-4*, Pub. by St Paul Pubns UK) St Mut.

***Treasures of Jewish Traditional Art.** Furman & Grossman. 1997. 100.00 (*0-88363-047-8*) H L Levin.

Treasures of Love & Inspiration. Marjorie Barrows. LC 85-70378. 1993. 8.98 (*0-88365-698-1*) Galahad Bks.

Treasures of Middle Earth. Jessica M. Ney. (Middle Earth Ser.). (Illus.). 144p. (Orig.). (C). 1989. pap. 15.00 (*1-55806-048-0*, 8006) Iron Crown Ent Inc.

Treasures of Simple Living: A Family's Search for a Simpler & More Meaningful Life in the Middle of a Forest. Tyra Arraj & James Arraj. LC 87-5990. (Illus.). 216p. (Orig.). 1987. pap. 8.00 (*0-914073-04-4*) Inner Growth Bks.

Treasures of St. Paul: Selected Themes from Paul's Theology & Ethics. Alan Robinson. 224p. 1994. pap. 19.95 (*0-85439-500-8*, Pub. by St Paul Pubns UK) St Mut.

Treasures of State: Fine & Decorative Arts in Diplomatic Reception Rooms. Clement E. Conger. 1991. 95.00 (*0-8109-3911-8*) Abrams.

Treasures of the American West. 1989. 27.50 (*0-517-69517-0*) Random Hse Value.

Treasures of the Ashmolean. Christopher White & S. David Piper. (Illus.). 120p. 1995. pap. 17.95 (*1-85444-059-4*, TREA, Pub. by Ashmolean Mus UK) A Schwartz & Co.

Treasures of the Bloodstock Breeder's Review. Ed. by Miles Napier. 700p. 1990. 100.00 (*0-85131-502-X*, Pub. by J A Allen & Co UK) St Mut.

***Treasures of the Chinese Scholar: Form, Function, & Symbolism.** Jing P. Fang & J. May Barrett. LC 97-19300. 1997. pap. write for info. (*0-8348-0399-2*) Weatherhill.

Treasures of the Confederate Coast: The "Real Rhett Butler" & Other Revelations. Edward L. Spence. (Illus.). 528p. 1995. 29.95 (*1-886391-00-9*); pap. 19.95 (*1-886391-01-7*) Narwhal Pr.

Treasures of the Fitzwilliam Museum. Pevensey Pr. Staff. (C). 1987. text ed. 60.00 (*0-907115-19-5*, Pub. by Pevensey UK); pap. text ed. 40.00 (*0-907115-16-0*, Pub. by Pevensey UK) St Mut.

Treasures of the Great Temple. Eduardo M. Moctezuma. (Illus.). 180p. 1990. 39.95 (*0-9625399-6-1*) ALTI Pub.

Treasures of the Heart. Donna F. Crow. LC 94-16564. (Cambridge Chronicles Ser.: Bk. 2). 224p. 1994. pap. 9.99 (*0-89107-807-X*) Crossway Bks.

Treasures of the Heart. Velma A. Hamilton. 1995. pap. 10.95 (*0-533-11485-3*) Vantage.

Treasures of the Heart. Connie Mason. 448p. (Orig.). 1993. mass mkt., pap. text ed. 5.99 (*0-8439-3539-1*, Leisure Bks) Dorchester Pub Co.

***Treasures of the Heart.** large type ed. Donna F. Crow. LC 97-7223. (Candlelights Ser.). 319p. 1997. 19.95 (*0-7862-1094-X*, Thorndike Lrg Prnt) Thorndike Pr.

Treasures of the Heart: Sufi Stories for Young Children. M. R. Muhaiyaddeen. Ed. by Christine Steele. Tr. by Usha Balamore. (Illus.). 110p. (J). (ps). 1993. 15.00 (*0-914390-33-3*) Fellowship Pr PA.

***Treasures of the Heart: Sufi Stories for Young Children.** M. R. Muhaiyaddeen. (Illus.). 97p. (J). 1996. 15.00 (*0-614-21043-7*, 1257) Kazi Pubns.

Treasures of the Hermitage. Boris Piotrouski. 1990. 39.99 (*0-517-02725-9*) Random Hse Value.

Treasures of the Hermitage. Mikhail B. Piotrovsky. LC 96-13374. (Tiny Folio Ser.). (Illus.). 288p. 1996. pap. 11.95 (*0-7892-0104-6*) Abbeville Pr.

***Treasures of the Hermitage.** Intro. by Vitaly A. Suslov. (Illus.). 288p. (SPA.). 1996. pap. 11.95 (*84-376-1421-X*) Abbeville Pr.

Treasures of the Holy Land: A Visit to the Places of Christian Origins. Veselin Kesich & Lydia W. Kesich. LC 85-18403. (Illus.). (Orig.). 1985. pap. 8.95 (*0-88141-045-4*) St Vladimirs.

***Treasures of the Hopi.** Theda Bassman. LC 96-53291. (Illus.). 112p. 1997. pap. 12.95 (*0-87358-672-7*) Northland AZ.

Treasures of the Israel Museum, Jerusalem. Israel Museum Staff. (Illus.). 120p. 1985. 35.00 (*0-295-96444-8*) U of Wash Pr.

An Asterisk (*) at the beginning of an entry indicates that the title is appearing in BIP for the first time.

T

Treasures of the Italian Table. Burton Anderson. LC 93-14272. 1994. 20.00 (*0-688-11557-8*) Morrow.

Treasures of the Jewish Museum. Vivian B. Mann & Norman L. Kleeblatt. LC 85-28913. (Illus.). 216p. 1986. pap. 19.95 (*0-87663-890-6*); text ed. 35.00 (*0-87663-493-5*) Universe.

Treasures of the Library: Trinity College Dublin. Ed. by Peter Fox. (Illus.). 258p. 1986. pap. 24.95 (*0-901714-46-1*, 4661, Woodstocker Bks) A Schwartz & Co.

Treasures of the Lost Races. Rene Noorbergen. LC 82-4209. 1982. 13.95 (*0-672-52696-4*, Bobbs) Macmillan.

Treasures of the Louvre. (Illus.). 30p. 1995. pap. 7.95 (*1-55859-909-6*) Abbeville Pr.

Treasures of the Louvre. Michel Laclotte. LC 92-38308. (Tiny Folios Ser.). (Illus.). 424p. 1996. pap. 11.95 (*1-55859-477-9*) Abbeville Pr.

***Treasures of the Louvre.** Michel Laclotte. (Tiny Folios Ser.). 1997. 11.95 (*0-7892-0406-1*) Abbeville Pr.

***Treasures of the Louvre.** Michel Laclotte. (Illus.). 424p. (JPN.). 1996. pap. 11.95 (*1-55859-779-4*) Abbeville Pr.

Treasures of the Medici. Anna M. Massinelli & Filippo Tuena. LC 92-12965. 240p. 1992. 45.00 (*0-86565-135-3*) Vendome.

Treasures of the Mound Builders. Lar Hothem. (Illus.). 146p. 1989. pap. text ed. 11.95 (*0-9617041-1-X*) Hothem Hse.

Treasures of the Musee D'Orsay. (Illus.). 30p. 1995. pap. 7.95 (*1-55859-984-3*) Abbeville Pr.

Treasures of the Musee d'Orsay. Intro. by Francoise Cachin. LC 94-11326. (Tiny Folios Ser.). (Illus.). 368p. 1996. pap. 11.95 (*1-55859-783-2*) Abbeville Pr.

Treasures of the Musee d'Orsay. rev. ed. Intro. by Francoise Cachin. LC 94-39367. (Illus.). 204p. 1995. 24.98 (*0-89660-054-8*, Artabras) Abbeville Pr.

***Treasures of the Musee D'Orsay: Mini Edition.** Mussee D'Orsay. (Tiny Folios Ser.). 1997. 11.95 (*0-7892-0408-8*) Abbeville Pr.

Treasures of the Musee Picasso. Gerard Regnier. (Tiny Folios Ser.). (Illus.). 320p. 1996. pap. 11.95 (*1-55859-836-7*) Abbeville Pr.

Treasures of the Museum of Fine Arts, Boston. Malcolm Rogers & Gilian Wohlauer. LC 96-13377. (Tiny Folio Ser.). (Illus.). 320p. 1996. pap. 11.95 (*0-7892-0146-1*) Abbeville Pr.

Treasures of the National Air & Space Museum. National Air & Space Museum Staff & Martin O. Harwit. LC 94-41496. (Tiny Folios Ser.). (Illus.). 320p. 1996. pap. 11.95 (*1-55859-822-7*) Abbeville Pr.

Treasures of the National Archives. National Archives of Canada Staff. (Illus.). 368p. 1992. 50.00 (*0-8020-5022-0*) U of Toronto Pr.

Treasures of the National Gallery, London. Erika Langmuir. LC 96-3919. (Tiny Folio Ser.). (Illus.). 288p. 1996. pap. 11.95 (*0-7892-0148-8*) Abbeville Pr.

***Treasures of the National Gallery, London.** Frwd. by Neil MacGregor. (Illus.). 288p. (SPA.). 1996. pap. 11.95 (*84-376-1419-8*) Abbeville Pr.

Treasures of the National Library of Scotland - Perpetual Diary. HMSO Staff. 128p. 1993. 19.95 (*0-11-494236-6*, HM42366, Pub. by Stationery Ofc UK) Bernan Associates.

Treasures of the National Museum of the American Indian. W. Richard West, Jr. et al. LC 95-38529. (Tiny Folios Ser.). (Illus.). 320p. 1996. pap. 11.95 (*0-7892-0105-4*) Abbeville Pr.

***Treasures of the Navajo.** Theda Bassman. LC 96-53299. (Illus.). 112p. 1997. pap. 12.95 (*0-87358-673-5*) Northland AZ.

Treasures of the Night: Collected Poems of Jean Genet. Jean Genet. Tr. by Steven Finch from FRE. (Illus.). 120p. (Orig.). 1981. 25.00 (*0-917342-75-5*); pap. 6.95 (*0-917342-76-3*) Gay Sunshine.

Treasures of the Old West: Paintings & Sculpture from the Thomas Gilrease Institute of American History & Art. Peter H. Hassrick. LC 93-20836. (Illus.). 128p. 1994. pap. 17.98 (*0-8109-8133-5*, Abradale Pr) Abrams.

Treasures of the Oregon Country: No. IV. Maynard C. Drawson. (Illus.). 1977. pap. 9.95 (*0-934476-03-9*) Dee Pub Co.

Treasures of the Parthenon & Erechtheion. Diane Harris. (Oxford Monographs on Classical Archaeology). (Illus.). 328p. 1996. text ed. 100.00 (*0-19-814940-9*) OUP.

Treasures of the Prado. Felipe V. Llombart. (Tiny Folios Ser.). (Illus.). 312p. 1996. pap. 11.95 (*1-55859-558-9*) Abbeville Pr.

Treasures of the Psychic Realm. Jack J. Studer. (Illus.). 1976. pap. 3.95 (*0-87516-226-6*) DeVorss.

Treasures of the Royal Horticultural Society. Brent Elliott. (Illus.). 160p. 1994. 39.95 (*0-88192-297-8*) Timber.

Treasures of the Smithsonian. Edwards Park. LC 83-40203. (Illus.). 496p. 1983. 42.96 (*0-89599-012-1*) Smithsonian Bks.

Treasures of the Smithsonian. Edwards Park. LC 94-19263. (Illus.). 1994. reprint ed. 39.99 (*0-517-11955-2*) Random Hse Value.

Treasures of the Smokies: Tempting Recipes from East Tennessee. rev. ed. 328p. 1986. 18.95 (*0-9642075-0-8*) Jr Leag Johnson Cty.

Treasures of the Snow. Patricia M. St. John. (Patricia St. John Bks.). (J). (gr. 5-8). 1950. mass mkt. 5.99 (*0-8024-0008-6*) Moody.

***Treasures of the Throne.** Tyrone Lawrence. (Illus.). 70p. 1997. pap. 9.95 (*0-9658676-0-9*) Dataway Inc.

Treasures of the Tsar: Court Culture of Peter the Great from the Kremlin. P. De Buck. (Illus.). 296p. 1996. 40.00 (*90-6918-161-4*, Pub. by Mus Boymans-van Beuningen NE) U of Wash Pr.

Treasures of the Uffizi. (Illus.). 144p. 1996. 35.00 (*0-7892-0234-4*) Abbeville Pr.

Treasures of the Uffizi: Florence. Caterina Caneva. LC 93-36611. (Tiny Folios Ser.). (Illus.). 320p. 1994. pap. 11.95 (*1-55859-559-7*) Abbeville Pr.

Treasures of the Unicorn: The Return to the Sacred Quest. Ted Andrews. Ed. by Pagan Alexander. (Illus.). 250p. 1996. 19.95 (*1-888767-26-X*); pap. 12.95 (*1-888767-25-1*) Life Magic.

Treasures of the Vatican. M. Calvesi. 39.95 (*0-517-62643-8*) Random Hse Value.

***Treasures of the Zuni.** Theda Bassman. LC 96-36125. (Illus.). 116p. 1997. pap. 12.95 (*0-87358-674-3*) Northland AZ.

Treasures of Tibetan Art: The Collections of the Jacques Marchais Museum of Tibetan Art. Barbara Lipton & Nima D. Ragnubs. (Illus.). 320p. 1996. pap. 29.95 (*0-19-509714-9*) OUP.

***Treasures of Time.** Naomi Davis. (Orig.). 1997. mass mkt. 5.99 (*1-55237-105-0*, Pub. by Comnwlth Pub CN) Partners Pubs Grp.

Treasures of Time: A Fully Illustrated Guide to Prehistoric Ceramics of the Southwest. James R. Cunkle. LC 94-16275. 1994. pap. 14.95 (*0-914846-92-2*) Golden West Pub.

Treasures of Trinkamalee. Tim Leslie-Spinks. (J). (gr. 4-7). 1993. lib. bdg. 15.95 (*1-55037-320-X*, Pub. by Annick CN) Firefly Bks Ltd.

Treasures of Trinkamalee. Tim Leslie-Spinks. (J). (gr. 4-7). 1993. pap. 5.95 (*1-55037-323-4*, Pub. by Annick CN) Firefly Bks Ltd.

Treasures of Tutankhamen. Illus. by Tony Smith. (Butterfly Bks.). 48p. (J). (gr. 3-5). 1987. 8.95 (*0-86685-453-3*) Intl Bk Ctr.

Treasures of Venice: Paintings from the Museum of Fine Arts, Budapest. Ed. by George S. Keyes et al. (Illus.). 232p. 1995. 49.50 (*0-8109-3880-4*) Abrams.

Treasures of Wisdom: Studies in Colossians & Philemon. Homer A. Kent, Jr. pap. 8.99 (*0-88469-062-8*) BMH Bks.

Treasures of Witch Hat Mountain. Lou Kassem. 112p. (Orig.). (J). 1992. pap. 2.99 (*0-380-76519-5*, Camelot) Avon.

Treasures of 19th- & 20th-Century Painting: The Art Institute of Chicago. Intro. by James N. Wood. LC 93-22630. (Tiny Folios Ser.). (Illus.). 336p. (Orig.). 1996. pap. 11.95 (*1-55859-603-8*) Abbeville Pr.

***Treasures of 19th & 20th Century Painting.** James Wood. (Tiny Folios Ser.). 1997. 11.95 (*0-7892-0402-9*) Abbeville Pr.

Treasures on Earth. James L. Brown. 1979. pap. 7.80 (*0-685-00099-0*) Academy Santa Clara.

Treasures on Earth. James L. Brown. LC 79-54075. 282p. 1979. pap. 7.50 (*0-317-00106-X*) J L Brown.

Treasures on Earth. William Walden. 1965. pap. 5.25 (*0-8222-1171-8*) Dramatists Play.

Treasures on New Mexico Trails: Discover New Deal Art & Architecture. Ed. & Compiled by Kathryn A. Flynn. LC 94-36562. (Illus.). 320p. (Orig.). 1994. pap. 18.95 (*0-86534-236-9*) Sunstone Pr.

Treasures on Tampa Bay: Tampa, Saint Petersburg, Clearwater. Steve Otto & Greater Tampa Chamber of Commerce Staff. LC 96-277. (Urban Tapestry Ser.). 224p. 1996. 39.50 (*1-881096-31-9*) Towery Pub.

Treasures on the Shore. Raizy Kessler. 126p. 9.95 (*1-56062-233-4*); pap. 7.95 (*1-56062-234-2*) CIS Comm.

Treasures 2: Stories & Art by Students in Oregon. Ed. by Chris Weber. 256p. (Orig.). (J). (gr. k-12). 1988. pap. 11.95 (*0-9616058-1-2*) OR Students Writing.

Treasures 3: Stories & Art by Students in Japan & Oregon. Tr. by Wayne Lammers & Clinton D. Morrison. (Illus.). 258p. (Orig.). (J). (gr. k-12). 1994. pap. 13.95 (*0-9616058-6-3*) OR Students Writing.

Treasurie or Store-House of Similies. Robert Cawdrey. LC 75-171738. (English Experience Ser.: No. 365). 880p. 1971. reprint ed. 150.00 (*90-221-0365-X*) Walter J Johnson.

Treasuries Made Easy: How to Loan Money to Uncle Sam Just Like the Fat Cats. R. David Dornbusch. LC 95-92721. (Illus.). 120p. (Orig.). pap. 24.95 (*0-930627-14-8*) Paradigm Comm.

Treasuring the Chesapeake: A Partnership Between Business, Government, & the People. Bruce Galloway. (Illus.). 128p. 1995. 34.95 (*1-882933-06-0*) Cherbo Pub Grp.

***Treasury.** Ronald Dahl. 1997. pap. 35.00 (*0-670-87769-7*) Viking Penguin.

Treasury. William Shakespeare. Ed. by Levi Fox. (Shakespeare Collection). 160p. 1993. 4.95 (*0-85306-946-8*, Pub. by Jarrold Pub UK); 5.95 (*0-85306-947-6*, Pub. by Jarrold Pub UK) Seven Hills Bk.

***Treasury & Public Policy Making.** Richard A. Chapman. LC 97-7500. 240p. (C). 1998. text ed. write for info. (*0-415-09639-1*) Routledge.

Treasury & Whitehall: The Planning & Control of Public Expenditure, 1976-1993. Colin Thain & Maurice Wright. (Illus.). 590p. 1995. 98.00 (*0-19-827784-9*) OUP.

Treasury Auction Results As Interest Rate Predictors. rev. ed. James A. Larson. LC 93-41567. (Financial Sector of the American Economy Ser.). 152p. 1994. text ed. 47.00 (*0-8153-1682-8*) Garland.

Treasury Bond Basis: An In-Depth Analysis for Hedgers, Speculators & Arbitrageurs. rev. ed. Galen D. Burghardt & Terrence M. Belton. 225p. 1993. text ed. 65.00 (*1-55738-479-7*) Irwin Prof Pubng.

Treasury Division Three of the Organization Executive Course see Organization Executive Course

Treasury Enforcement Agent. Jack Rudman. (Career Examination Ser.: C-823). 1994. pap. 27.95 (*0-8373-0823-2*) Nat Learn.

Treasury for the Free World. Ed. by Ben Raeburn. LC 72-5771. (Essay Index Reprint Ser.). 1977. reprint ed. 27.95 (*0-8369-7293-7*) Ayer.

Treasury Management: International Banking Operations. Alasdair Watson & Ron Altringham. 1985. 145.00 (*0-85297-142-7*, Pub. by Inst Bankers UK) St Mut.

Treasury Management Handbook for Small Cities & Other Governmental Units. Municipal Finance Officers Association Staff. LC 78-71725. (Illus.). 93p. 1978. 15.00 (*0-686-84374-6*) Municipal.

***Treasury of African-American Christmas Stories.** Bettye Collier-Thomas. LC 97-5459. 1997. write for info. (*0-8050-5122-8*) TFC Bks NY.

Treasury of African-American Folklore: The Oral Literature, Traditions, Recollections. Harold Courlander. (Illus.). 618p. (Orig.). 1995. pap. 14.95 (*1-56924-811-7*) Marlowe & Co.

Treasury of African Art from the Harrison Eiteljorg Collection. Theodore Celenko. LC 82-47954. (Illus.). 240p. 1984. 57.50 (*0-253-11057-2*) Ind U Pr.

Treasury of African Folklore: The Oral Literature, Traditions, Myths, Legends, Epics, Tales, Recollections, Wisdom, Sayings, & Humor of Africa. Harold Courlander. (Illus.). 617p. 1995. pap. 14.95 (*1-56924-816-8*) Marlowe & Co.

Treasury of African Love Poems, Quotations, & Proverbs. Ed. by Nicholas Awde. LC 97-19296. 128p. 1997. 11.95 (*0-7818-0483-3*) Hippocrene Bks.

***Treasury of Afro-American Folklore.** Harold Courlander. 1996. 10.98 (*0-7651-9733-2*) Smithmark.

Treasury of Albert Schweitzer. Albert Schweitzer. Ed. by Thomas Kiernan. LC 73-136651. (Biography Index Reprint Ser.). 1977. 23.95 (*0-8369-8046-8*) Ayer.

Treasury of Alphabets & Lettering. Jan Tschichold. 240p. 1992. pap. 29.95 (*0-8306-3486-X*, 0734) McGraw-Hill Prof.

***Treasury of Alphabets & Lettering: A Handbook of Type & Lettering.** Jan Tschichold. 240p. Date not set. write for info. (*0-85331-620-1*, Pub. by Lund Humphries UK) Antique Collect.

Treasury of Alphabets & Lettering: A Source Book of the Best Letter Forms of Past & Present for Sign Painters, Graphic Artists, Commercial Artists, Typographers, Printers, Sculptors, Architects, & Schools of Art & Design. Jan Tschichold. LC 94-35996. (Illus.). 236p. 1995. pap. 35.00 (*0-393-70197-2*, Norton Paperbks) Norton.

Treasury of American Anecdotes. B. A. Botkin. 1989. 7.98 (*0-88365-616-7*) Galahad Bks.

Treasury of American Design & Antiques. Clarence P. Hornung. (Illus.). 888p. 1989. 39.99 (*0-517-16908-8*) Random Hse Value.

***Treasury of American Design & Antiques: A Pictorial Survey of Popular Folk Arts Based upon Watercolor Renderings in the Index of American Design at the National Gallery of Art.** Clarence P. Hornung. (Illus.). 846p. 1997. pap. 34.98 (*0-8109-8183-1*, Abradale Pr) Abrams.

Treasury of American Folklore. Benjamin A. Botkin. 1989. 14.99 (*0-517-67978-7*) Random Hse Value.

Treasury of American Horror Stories. Charles G. Waugh. 1988. 9.99 (*0-517-48075-1*) Random Hse Value.

Treasury of American-Jewish Folklore. Steve Koppman & Lionel Koppman. LC 96-941. 414p. 1997. 40.00 (*1-56821-620-3*) Aronson.

Treasury of American Pen & Ink Illustration: 222 Drawings by 99 Artists, 1890-1930. Ed. by Fridolf Johnson. (Illus.). 176p. (C). 1982. pap. 7.95 (*0-486-24280-3*) Dover.

Treasury of American Sacred Song. W. G. Horder. LC 74-76944. (Granger Index Reprint Ser.). 1977. 20.95 (*0-8369-6019-X*) Ayer.

Treasury of American Scrimshaw. Michael McManus. 1997. pap. 34.95 (*0-670-86234-7*) Viking Penguin.

***Treasury of American Superstition.** Claudia Delys. 1997. 9.99 (*0-517-18130-4*) Random Hse Value.

Treasury of American Verse. Walter Learned. LC 74-86799. (Granger Index Reprint Ser.). 1977. 29.95 (*0-8369-6081-5*) Ayer.

Treasury of American Writers from Harpers Magazine. 1985. 7.98 (*0-517-48074-3*) Random Hse Value.

Treasury of Amish Quilts. deluxe ed. Kenneth Pellman & Rachel T. Pellman. LC 90-82488. (Illus.). 128p. 1990. pap. 19.95 (*1-56148-000-2*) Good Bks PA.

Treasury of Animal Stories. E. Louise Malley. 1994. 10.98 (*0-7858-0213-4*) Bk Sales Inc.

Treasury of Animal Stories. E. Louise Mally. 1976. 25.95 (*0-8488-0764-2*) Amereon Ltd.

Treasury of Animal Stories. Ed. by John C. Miles. LC 90-11158. (Illus.). 96p. (J). (gr. 2-5). 1991. lib. bdg. 15.50 (*0-8167-2240-4*) Troll Communs.

Treasury of Animal Stories. Ed. by John C. Miles. LC 90-11158. (Illus.). 96p. (J). (gr. 2-5). 1997. pap. 6.95 (*0-8167-2241-2*) Troll Communs.

Treasury of Animal Stories. Ed. by Jane Olliver. LC 92-53110. (Treasury of Stories Ser.). (Illus.). 160p. (Orig.). (J). (gr. k-5). 1992. pap. 6.95 (*1-85697-831-1*, Kingfisher LKC) LKC.

Treasury of Aphoristic Jewels: The Subhasitaratnanidhi of Sa Skya Pandita in Tibetan & Mongolian. James E. Bosson. (Uralic & Altaic Ser.: Vol. 92). 1969. pap. text ed. 19.00 (*0-87750-080-0*) Res Inst Inner Asian Studies.

Treasury of Applique Quilt Patterns. Maggie Malone. LC 95-40526. (Illus.). 144p. 1996. 24.95 (*0-8069-0746-0*) Sterling.

Treasury of Arab Names, 4 vols., Set. Sultan Qaboos University Staff. 2631p. (ARA.). 120.00 (*0-86685-559-9*, LDL5599, Pub. by Librairie du Liban FR) Intl Bk Ctr.

Treasury of Arabic Love Poems Quotations & Proverbs. Ed. by Farid Bitar. (Hippocrene Treasury of Love Ser.). 128p. 1995. 11.95 (*0-7818-0395-0*) Hippocrene Bks.

Treasury of Art Nouveau Design & Ornament. Carol B. Grafton. (Pictorial Archive Ser.). (Illus.). 144p. (Orig.). 1980. pap. 8.95 (*0-486-24001-0*) Dover.

Treasury of Asian Literature. John D. Yohannan. 1995. pap. 10.95 (*0-452-01148-5*, Mer) NAL-Dutton.

Treasury of Audubon Birds in Full Color: Two Hundred Twenty-Four Plates from The Birds of America. John J. Audubon. LC 93-9698. Orig. Title: Birds of America - Selections. (Illus.). 16p. 1993. reprint ed. pap. 15.95 (*0-486-27604-X*) Dover.

Treasury of Australian Verse. rev. ed. Ed. by Beatrice Davis. (Illus.). 336p. 1996. 75.00 (*0-7305-8905-6*, Pub. by Drake Intl Serv UK); pap. 55.00 (*0-7305-8906-4*, Pub. by Drake Intl Serv UK) Intl Spec Bk.

Treasury of Authentic Art Nouveau: Alphabets, Decorative Initials, Monograms, Frames & Ornaments. Ed. by L. Petzendorfer. (Lettering, Calligraphy, Typography Ser.). 160p. 1984. reprint ed. pap. 9.95 (*0-486-24653-1*) Dover.

Treasury of Ba-Suto Lore, 2 vols. in 1. E. Jacottet. LC 78-67723. (Folktale Ser.). reprint ed. 45.00 (*0-404-16098-0*) AMS Pr.

Treasury of Baby Names. Alan Benjamin. 1991. pap. 3.95 (*0-451-16561-6*, Sig) NAL-Dutton.

Treasury of Baby Names. enl. ed. Ed. by Alan Benjamin. 1983. pap. 4.99 (*0-451-16944-1*, Sig) NAL-Dutton.

Treasury of Barbecue Recipes, 3 bks. in 1. (Illus.). 288p. 1993. spiral bd. 19.98 (*1-56173-599-X*, 2018000) Pubns Intl Ltd.

Treasury of Bed & Breakfast. 2nd ed. American Bed & Breakfast Association Staff. Ed. by Sarah W. Sonke. (Illus.). 201p. 1986. pap. 14.95 (*0-934473-01-3*) Am Bed & Breakfast.

Treasury of Bed & Breakfast. 2nd rev. ed. American Bed & Breakfast Association Staff. 201p. 1986. pap. 14.95 (*0-915765-23-3*) Am Bed & Breakfast.

Treasury of Bed & Breakfast. 3rd rev. ed. American Bed & Breakfast Association Staff. 189p. 1987. pap. 14.95 (*0-317-91103-1*) Am Bed & Breakfast.

Treasury of Bedtime Stories. Illus. by Hilda Offen. 160p. (J). (ps-3). 1981. pap. 14.00 (*0-671-44463-8*, S&S Bks Young Read) S&S Childrens.

Treasury of Bedtime Stories. Illus. by Annabel Spenceley. LC 92-43152. (Treasury of Stories Ser.). 160p. (J). (gr. k-4). 1993. pap. 6.95 (*1-85697-931-8*, Kingfisher LKC) LKC.

Treasury of Best Loved Songs: 114 All-Time Family Favorites. Reader's Digest Editors. LC 71-183858. (Illus.). 288p. 1981. spiral bd. 29.95 (*0-89577-007-5*, Random) RD Assn.

Treasury of Bible Illustrations. Ed. by Zodhiates & Peters. (Bible Illustrations Ser.: Vol. 443). (Illus.). (Orig.). 1995. 19.99 (*0-89957-227-8*) AMG Pubs.

Treasury of Bible Subjects. Weaver. 1986. 6.95 (*0-317-01453-6*) Rod & Staff.

Treasury of Book Ornament & Decoration. Carol B. Grafton. 1986. pap. 6.95 (*0-486-25167-5*) Dover.

Treasury of Bookplates from the Renaissance to the Present. Fridolf Johnson. (Illus.). 1978. pap. 6.95 (*0-486-23485-1*) Dover.

Treasury of Bridge Playing Tips: Five Hundred Forty Bidding Tips to Improve Your Partner's Game. Edwin B. Kantar. 1993. pap. 10.95 (*1-882180-06-2*) Griffin CA.

Treasury of British Humor. Ed. by Morris Bishop. (Granger Index Reprint Ser.). 1977. 38.95 (*0-8369-6194-3*) Ayer.

***Treasury of Business Humor.** Ed. by James E. Myers. (Orig.). Date not set. pap. 12.95 (*0-942936-28-0*) Lincoln-Herndon Pr.

***Treasury of Business Quotation.** Michael C. Thornsett. 1997. pap. 12.00 (*0-345-41941-3*) Ballantine.

Treasury of Business Quotations. Michael C. Thomsett. LC 89-27903. 228p. 1990. lib. bdg. 32.50 (*0-89950-469-8*) McFarland & Co.

Treasury of Business Quotations. Michael C. Thomsett. 1991. mass mkt. 5.99 (*0-345-37399-5*) Ballantine.

Treasury of Calligraphy: Two Hundred Nineteen Great Examples, 1522-1840. Jan Tschichold. 244p. 1984. pap. 11.95 (*0-486-24700-7*) Dover.

Treasury of Campbell's Recipes, 3 bks. in 1. (Illus.). 288p. 1993. spiral bd. 19.98 (*0-7853-0082-1*, 2000900) Pubns Intl Ltd.

Treasury of Canadian Verse. Theodore H. Rand. LC 76-75717. (Granger Index Reprint Ser.). 1977. 23.95 (*0-8369-6039-4*) Ayer.

Treasury of Carolina Tales. Webb Garrison. LC 88-3188. 1996. pap. text ed. 8.95 (*1-55853-449-0*) Rutledge Hill Pr.

Treasury of Cartoon Classics: Walt Disney's Silly Symphonies. Ed. by Darlene Geis. LC 95-12134. Orig. Title: Walt Disney's Treasury of Silly Symphonies. (Illus.). 256p. (J). 1995. 29.95 (*0-7868-3085-9*) Disney Pr.

Treasury of Catholic Prayer. National Conference of Catholic Bishops & United States Catholic Conference Administrative Board Staff. 80p. (Orig.). 1989. pap. 3.95 (*1-55586-296-9*) US Catholic.

Treasury of Catholic Wisdom. Ed. by John A. Hardon. 737p. (Orig.). pap. 24.95 (*0-89870-539-8*) Ignatius Pr.

Treasury of Charted Designs for Needleworkers. Georgia Gorham & Jeanne M. Warth. (Illus.). 1978. pap. 2.50 (*0-486-23558-0*) Dover.

***Treasury of Chassidic Tales, 2 vols., Set.** S. Y. Zevin. Tr. by Uri Kaploun. boxed 52.99 (*0-89906-904-5*) Mesorah Pubns.

Treasury of Chassidic Tales on the Torah. Shlomo Y. Zevin. Tr. by Uri Kaploun. (ArtScroll Judaica Classics Ser.). 352p. 24.99 (*0-89906-900-2*, TREH) Mesorah Pubns.

Treasury of Children's Classics in Spanish & English. (Illus.). 176p. (J). (gr. 4 up). 1995. pap. 7.95 (*0-8442-7145-4*, Natl Textbk) NTC Pub Grp.

An Asterisk (*) at the beginning of an entry indicates that the title is appearing in BIP for the first time.

Treasury of Children's Literature. Armand Eisen. LC 92-2847. (Illus.). 304p. (J). (gr. 3-7). 1992. 24.95 (0-395-53349-X) HM.

Treasury of Children's Poetry. LC 93-85533. (Miniature Editions Ser.). (Illus.). 136p. (J). 1994. 4.95 (1-56138-362-7) Running Pr.

Treasury of Chinese Cooking. 14.98 (0-7853-0798-2) Pubns Intl Ltd.

Treasury of Chinese Design Motifs. Joseph D'Addetta. (Illus.). 108p. pap. 6.95 (0-486-24167-X) Dover.

Treasury of Chocolate Recipes, 3 bks. in 1. (Illus.). 288p. 1993. spiral bd. 19.98 (1-56173-659-7, 2019500) Pubns Intl Ltd.

Treasury of Christian Spiritual Classics: Complete & Unabridged with Contemporary Introductions. Timothy Weber. LC 94-33206. 1994. 24.99 (0-7852-8084-7) Nelson.

Treasury of Christmas. 1994. 14.98 (0-7853-0792-3) Pubns Intl Ltd.

Treasury of Christmas. Ed. by John C. Miles. LC 90-39372. (Illus.). 96p. (J). (gr. 2-5). 1991. pap. 6.95 (0-8167-2237-4); lib. bdg. 15.50 (0-8167-2236-6) Troll Communs.

Treasury of Christmas: Stories for Families. 64p. 1994. 4.50 (0-687-07821-0) Dimen for Liv.

Treasury of Christmas Classics. Charles Dickens et al. 176p. 1994. 14.99 (0-87788-819-1) Shaw Pubs.

*Treasury of Christmas Classics. Honor Books Staff. 1997. 14.99 (1-56292-360-9) Honor Bks OK.

Treasury of Christmas Classics. large type ed. 1995. pap. 12.95 (0-8027-2691-7) Walker & Co.

Treasury of Christmas Cookies, 3 bks. in 1. (Illus.). 288p. 1993. spiral bd. 19.98 (0-7853-0309-X, 2023200) Pubns Intl Ltd.

Treasury of Christmas Crafts. (Illus.). 192p. 1993. spiral bd. 19.95 (0-7853-0286-7, 9027500) Pubns Intl Ltd.

Treasury of Christmas Ornaments by the Editors of Crafts Magazine. Ed. by Judith Brossart. (Illus.). 96p. 1991. text ed. write for info. (0-9621148-4-7); pap. text ed. write for info. (0-9621148-5-5) PJS Pubns.

Treasury of Christmas Recipe Collection, 3 bks. in 1. (Illus.). 288p. 1993. spiral bd. 19.98 (1-56173-235-4, 2008601) Pubns Intl Ltd.

Treasury of Christmas Recipes. (Favorite All Time Recipes Ser.). (Illus.). 96p. 1993. 7.98 (0-7853-0313-8, 2019102) Pubns Intl Ltd.

Treasury of Christmas Recipes. Publications International Staff. 1989. 5.99 (0-517-69242-2) Random Hse Value.

Treasury of Christmas Stories. Webb Garrison. 1994. 9.98 (0-88365-869-0) Galahad Bks.

Treasury of Christmas Stories. Beverley Mathias. LC 93-50708. (Illus.). 160p. (J). (ps-3). 1994. pap. 6.95 (1-85697-985-7, Kingfisher LKC) LKC.

Treasury of Christmas Stories. Henry Van Dyke. Ed. by James S. Bell, Jr. LC 92-46869. 168p. 1993. 14.99 (0-87788-817-5) Shaw Pubs.

Treasury of Christmas Tales: The Christmas Mouse; Christmas Carols; Jingle Bells; The Magic Toy Shop; Frosty's Snowy Day; Santa Claus Is Coming to Town, 6 bks., Set. (Illus.). 24p. (J). 1993. boxed 9.98 (0-7853-0277-8) Pubns Intl Ltd.

Treasury of Civil War Stories. Ed. by Martin H. Greenburg & Bill Pronzini. 1991. 9.99 (0-517-06013-2) Random Hse Value.

Treasury of Civil War Tales. Webb Garrison. 320p. 1990. mass mkt. 5.99 (0-345-36262-4) Ballantine.

Treasury of Civil War Tales. Webb Garrison. LC 88-23826. (Illus.). 1988. 14.95 (0-934395-95-0) Rutledge Hill Pr.

Treasury of Classic French Love Short Stories. LC 97-8212. (Hippocrene Bilingual Love Short Stories Ser.). 128p. (ENG & FRE.). 1997. 11.95 (0-7818-0511-2) Hippocrene Bks.

Treasury of Classic Polish Love Short Stories: Short Stories in Polish & English. LC 97-15376. 128p. (ENG & POL.). 1997. 11.95 (0-7818-0513-9) Hippocrene Bks.

*Treasury of Classic Russian Love Short Stories. Auton Chekhov. Date not set. 11.95 (0-7818-0601-1) Hippocrene Bks.

*Treasury of Clean Children's Jokes. 2nd rev. ed. Tad D. Bonham. LC 96-53374. 144p. (J). 1997. pap. 5.99 (0-8054-6364-X) Broadman.

Treasury of Clean Church Jokes. Tal D. Bonham. LC 85-26837. 128p. 1986. pap. 4.99 (0-8054-5719-4, 4257-19) Broadman.

*Treasury of Clean Church Jokes. 2nd rev. ed. Tad D. Bonham. LC 96-29826. 144p. 1997. pap. 5.99 (0-8054-6363-1) Broadman.

Treasury of Clean Country Jokes. Tal D. Bonham. LC 85-28045. 128p. 1986. pap. 4.99 (0-8054-5717-8, 4257-17) Broadman.

*Treasury of Clean Country Jokes. 2nd rev. ed. Tad D. Bonham. LC 96-53377. 144p. 1997. pap. 5.99 (0-8054-6362-3) Broadman.

Treasury of Clean Jokes. Tal D. Bonham. LC 80-67639. 160p. (Orig.). 1981. pap. 4.99 (0-8054-5703-8, 4257-03) Broadman.

*Treasury of Clean Jokes. 2nd rev. ed. Tad D. Bonham. LC 96-53378. 144p. 1997. pap. 5.99 (0-8054-6360-7) Broadman.

Treasury of Clean Jokes for Children. Tal D. Bonham. (Orig.). (J). (gr. 1-6). 1987. pap. 4.99 (0-8054-5721-6, 4257-21) Broadman.

Treasury of Clean Senior Adult Jokes. Tal D. Bonham & Jack Gulledge. (Orig.). 1989. pap. 4.99 (0-8054-5736-4, 4257-36) Broadman.

*Treasury of Clean Seniors' Jokes. 2nd rev. ed. Tad D. Bonham & Jack Gulledge. LC 96-53375. 144p. (Orig.). 1997. pap. 5.99 (0-8054-6365-8) Broadman.

*Treasury of Clean Teenagers' Jokes. 2nd rev. ed. Tad D. Bonham. LC 96-53376. 144p. 1997. pap. 5.99 (0-8054-6361-5) Broadman.

Treasury of Cocktail Humor. Ed. by James E. Myers, Sr. 300p. 1995. pap. 10.95 (0-942936-27-2) Lincoln-Herndon Pr.

Treasury of Comfort. Ed. by Sidney Greenberg. 1967. 12.50 (0-87677-022-7) Hartmore.

Treasury of Comfort. Ed. by Sidney S. Greenberg. 1972. pap. 10.00 (0-87980-167-0) Wilshire.

Treasury of Country Heritage. Decosse. (SPA.). 1995. 24.95 (2-89429-591-X) Cowles Creative.

*Treasury of Country Recipes. Land O Lakes Staff. 1994. 24.95 (2-89429-058-6, Pub. by Tormont Pubns CN) Cowles Creative.

Treasury of Critical & Creative Thinking Activities. Ed. by Janet Reed & Linette Ellis. (Macmillan Instant Activities Program Ser.). (Illus.). 408p. 1993. ring bd. 29.95 (1-56784-701-3) Newbridge Comms.

*Treasury of Czech Love Poems, Quotations, & Proverbs. Ed. by Marcela Rydloua-Erlich. 128p. 1997. 11.95 (0-7818-0571-6) Hippocrene Bks.

*Treasury of David. C. H. Spurgeon & Roy H. Clarke. LC 97-14594. 1997. write for info. (0-7852-1158-6) Nelson.

Treasury of David. Charles H. Spurgeon. LC 76-12085. 704p. 1977. pap. 19.99 (0-8254-3684-2) Kregel.

Treasury of David, 7 vols., Set. C. H. Spurgen. 1983. 90.00 (1-56186-118-9) Pilgrim Pubns.

Treasury of David - A Commentary on the Psalms, 3 vols. Charles H. Spurgeon. 2912p. 1988. 59.95 (0-917006-25-9) Hendrickson MA.

Treasury of Design for Artists & Craftsmen. Gregory Mirow. LC 69-18877. (Pictorial Archive Ser.). 1969. reprint ed. pap. 5.95 (0-486-22002-8) Dover.

Treasury of Designs for Lace Net Embroidery. Ed. by Rita Weiss. (Embroidery, Needlepoint, Charted Designs Ser.). 48p. 1985. pap. 2.95 (0-486-24840-2) Dover.

Treasury of Desserts. (Illus.). 384p. 1993. 39.95 (0-7853-0198-4, 2022800) Pubns Intl Ltd.

Treasury of Devotion. deluxe ed. (C). 1990. ring bd. 50.00 (0-85305-247-6, Pub. by J Arthur Ltd UK) St Mut.

Treasury of Disney Little Golden Books. (Deluxe Golden Bks.). (J). (ps-2). 1972. write for info. (0-307-17865-X) Western Pub.

Treasury of Disney Little Golden Books: 22 Best-Loved Disney Stories. (Illus.). 96p. (J). (ps-1). 1991. 10.95 (0-307-15509-9, Golden Pr) Western Pub.

*Treasury of Dragon Stories. Illus. by Mark Robertson. (Treasury of Stories Ser.). 160p. (J). (gr. k-4). 1997. pap. 6.95 (0-7534-5114-X) LKC.

Treasury of Early Christianity. Ed. & Intro. by Anne Fremantle. xiv, 625p. 1995. reprint ed. text ed. 29.95 (0-912141-22-0) Roman Cath Bks.

Treasury of Encyclopedia Britannica. 1990. 27.50 (0-07-019421-1) McGraw.

Treasury of English Verse: New & Old. Ed. by A. S. Collins. LC 79-168778. (Granger Index Reprint Ser.). 1977. reprint ed. 24.95 (0-8369-6298-2) Ayer.

Treasury of Evangelical Writings: Valiant for the Truth. Ed. by David O. Fuller. Orig. Title: Valiant for the Truth. 460p. (Orig.). 1996. reprint ed. pap. 18.95 (0-944355-27-7) IBTS.

Treasury of Fairy Tales. Annie-Claude Martin. 400p. 1994. 14.98 (0-8317-3398-5) Smithmark.

*Treasury of Fairy Tales: Classic Bedtime Stories. Annie-Claude Martin. 1996. 14.98 (0-7651-9659-X) Smithmark.

Treasury of Fantastic & Mythological Creatures: 1,087 Renderings from Historic Sources. Richard Huber. (Illus.). 160p. (Orig.). 1981. pap. 7.95 (0-486-24174-2) Dover.

*Treasury of Fantasy. Margaret Weis & Martin Greenberg. Date not set. mass mkt. write for info. (0-06-105240-X, HarperPrism) HarpC.

*Treasury of Fantasy. Margaret Weis. Ed. by Martin H. Greenberg. mass mkt. write for info. (0-06-105630-8, HarperPrism) HarpC.

*Treasury of Fantasy. Margaret Weis. Ed. by Martin H. Greenberg. 1997. pap. write for info. (0-06-105327-9, HarperPrism) HarpC.

Treasury of Fantasy. Williams. 1995. 11.99 (0-517-14649-5) Random Hse Value.

Treasury of Farm & Ranch Humor. James E. Myers. (Illus.). 325p. 1989. pap. 10.95 (0-942936-15-9) Lincoln-Herndon Pr.

Treasury of Farm Women's Humor. Ed. by Eileen Mears. 300p. 1994. pap. 12.95 (0-942936-25-6) Lincoln-Herndon Pr.

Treasury of Fine Construction Design: 104 Detailed Plates of Early Twentieth Century Interior & Exterior Elements. Philip G. Knobloch. (Illus.). 128p. 1995. pap. 19.95 (1-879335-64-6) Astragal Pr.

Treasury of Finnish Love Poems Quotations & Proverbs. Ed. by Borje Vahamaki. (Hippocrene Treasury of Love Ser.). 128p. 1995. 11.95 (0-7818-0397-7) Hippocrene Bks.

Treasury of Flannelboard Stories. Jeanette G. Bay. (Illus.). 200p. (J). (ps-3). 1995. student ed. 15.95 (0-917846-51-6, 34021, Alleyside) Highsmith Pr.

Treasury of Floral Designs & Initials for Artists & Craftspeople. Ed. by Mary C. Waldrep. (Pictorial Archive Ser.). 1995. pap. write for info. (0-486-28808-0) Dover.

Treasury of Florida Tales. Webb Garrison. LC 89-10610. (Illus.). 176p. 1989. 10.95 (1-55853-038-X) Rutledge Hill Pr.

Treasury of Flower Designs for Artists, Embroiderers & Craftsmen: 100 Garden Favorites. Susan Gaber. (Illus.). 80p. (Orig.). 1981. pap. 4.95 (0-486-24096-7) Dover.

Treasury of Flower Fairies. deluxe ed. Cicely M. Barker. (Illus.). 128p. (J). 1992. pap. 19.95 (0-7232-3796-4, Warne) Viking Child Bks.

Treasury of Flute Music: In Progressive Order for Beginning Flutists. 48p. 1986. pap. 10.95 (0-7935-5418-7, 50333630) H Leonard.

Treasury of French Love Poems Quotations & Proverbs. Ed. by Richard Branyon. 128p. 1994. 11.95 (0-7818-0307-1) Hippocrene Bks.

Treasury of Funny Stories. Illus. by Frank James. LC 94-30242. (J). (gr. k-5). 1995. pap. 6.95 (1-85697-544-4, Kingfisher LKC) LKC.

Treasury of Georgia Tales. Webb Garrison. LC 87-23255. (Illus.). 160p. 1987. 9.95 (0-934395-66-7) Rutledge Hill Pr.

Treasury of German Love Poems Quotations & Proverbs. Ed. by Marlen Wolfram. 128p. 1994. 11.95 (0-7818-0296-2) Hippocrene Bks.

Treasury of German Trademarks: 1850-1925, Vol. 1. 2nd ed. Leslie Cabarga. (Illus.). 160p. 1990. 24.75 (0-910158-89-4) Art Dir.

Treasury of German Trademarks: 1925-1950, Vol. 2. Leslie Cabarga. LC 81-71799. 156p. 1985. 24.75 (0-88108-007-1) Art Dir.

Treasury of Ghost Stories. Illus. by Tomy Morris. LC 96-1907. 160p. (J). (gr. k-4). 1996. 5.95 (0-7534-5027-5, Kingfisher LKC) LKC.

Treasury of Giant & Monster Stories. Ed. by Jane Olliver. LC 92-53112. (Treasury of Stories Ser.). (Illus.). 160p. (Orig.). (J). (gr. k-5). 1992. pap. 5.95 (1-85697-832-X, Kingfisher LKC) LKC.

Treasury of Great Adirondack Stories. John Vinton. LC 91-29637. (Illus.). 155p. 1991. 35.00 (0-932052-34-7); pap. 19.95 (0-932052-35-5) North Country.

Treasury of Great Humor. Al Sarrantonio. 1996. 8.99 (0-517-18150-9) Random Hse Value.

Treasury of Great Hymns: And Their Stories. Guye Johnson. 382p. (Orig.). 1985. pap. 14.95 (0-89084-249-3, 030478) Bob Jones Univ Pr.

Treasury of Great Poems. Louis Untermeyer. 1992. 14.98 (0-88365-796-1) Galahad Bks.

Treasury of Great Preaching, 13 vols. Ed. by Clyde E. Fant, Jr. & William M. Pinson, Jr. LC 95-16191. Orig. Title: 20 Centuries of Great Preaching. 1995. 299.99 (0-8499-5121-6) Word Pub.

Treasury of Great Recipes. Vincent Price & Mary Price. (Illus.). 1995. reprint ed. lib. bdg. 75.00 (1-56849-540-4) Buccaneer Bks.

Treasury of Hawaiian Words in One Hundred & One Categories. Harold W. Kent. LC 86-788. 504p. (C). 1993. pap. text ed. 25.00 (0-8248-1604-8) UH Pr.

Treasury of Helpful Verse. Ed. by John W. Chadwick & Annie H. Chadwick. LC 73-76933. (Granger Index Reprint Ser.). 1977. 19.95 (0-8369-6007-6) Ayer.

Treasury of His Promises. Graham Miller. 386p. (Orig.). 1986. pap. 18.99 (0-85151-472-3) Banner of Truth.

Treasury of Historic Folk Ornament in Full Color. Ed. by Helmuth Bossert. LC 96-4257. (Illus.). 1996. pap. 16.95 (0-486-29094-8) Dover.

Treasury of Historic Pattern & Design. J. Engelhorn. 1990. pap. 9.95 (0-486-26274-X) Dover.

Treasury of Home Business Opportunities. 1987. lib. bdg. 79.00 (0-8490-3882-0) Gordon Pr.

Treasury of Humor. Eric Johnson. 286p. 1990. mass mkt. 4.99 (0-8041-0587-1) Ivy Books.

Treasury of Humor: An Indexed Collection of Anecdotes. Eric W. Johnson. (Illus.). 269p. 1989. 29.95 (0-87975-515-6) Prometheus Bks.

Treasury of Humor II. Eric Johnson. (Orig.). 1994. mass mkt. 4.50 (0-8041-1186-3) Ivy Books.

Treasury of Humorous Poetry. Ed. by Frederic L. Knowles. LC 71-75713. (Granger Index Reprint Ser.). 1977. 24.95 (0-8369-6023-8) Ayer.

Treasury of Hungarian Love Poems, Quotations & Proverbs. Ed. & Tr. by Katherine G. Gatto from HUN. LC 96-15658. 128p. (HUN.). 1996. 11.95 (0-7818-0477-9) Hippocrene Bks.

Treasury of Hunting & Fishing Humor. Ed. by James E. Myers. (Illus.). 320p. 1990. pap. 10.95 (0-942936-19-1) Lincoln-Herndon Pr.

Treasury of Husband & Wife Humor. Ed. by James E. Myers. 350p. (Orig.). 1993. pap. 10.95 (0-942936-22-1) Lincoln-Herndon Pr.

Treasury of Hymn Stories. Wilbur Konekl. 1990. pap. 7.99 (0-88019-254-2) Schmul Pub Co.

Treasury of Hymn Stories: Brief Biographies of 120 Hymnwriters with Their Best Hymns. Amos R. Wells. 392p. (gr. 10). 1992. reprint ed. pap. 14.99 (0-8010-9718-5) Baker Bks.

Treasury of Illuminated Borders in Full Color. Ed. by Carol B. Grafton. (Pictorial Archive Ser.). (Illus.). 48p. (Orig.). 1988. pap. 6.95 (0-486-25699-5) Dover.

Treasury of Indian Coins. Ed. by Martha L. Carter. (C). 1994. 78.00 (81-85026-25-4, Pub. by Marg) S Asia.

Treasury of Indian Tales: Book I. Alaka Shankar. (Illus.). (YA). (gr. 8-12). 1979. 4.95 (0-89744-170-2) Auromere.

Treasury of Indian Tales: Book II. Alaka Shankar. (Illus.). (YA). (gr. 8-12). 1979. 4.95 (0-89744-171-0) Auromere.

Treasury of Inspiration: Illustrations, Quotations, Poems & Selections. Herbert V. Prochnow. LC 58-12417. (Speakers & Toastmasters Library). (Illus.). 120p. 1991. reprint ed. pap. 7.99 (0-8010-6868-1) Baker Bks.

Treasury of Inspirational Anecdotes, Quotations, & Illustrations: 1875 Illustrations on Nearly 250 Topics. Ed. by E. Paul Hovey. LC 59-8725. 320p. (C). (gr. 13). 1994. reprint ed. pap. 11.99 (0-8007-5539-1) Revell.

Treasury of Irish Folklore. Padraic Colum. 640p. 1985. reprint ed. 12.99 (0-517-42046-5) Random Hse Value.

Treasury of Irish Folklore Deluxe Edition. Padraic Column. 1988. 12.99 (0-517-67612-5) Random Hse Value.

Treasury of Irish Myth, Legend, & Folklore. William Butler Yeats. 1988. 11.99 (0-517-48904-X) Random Hse Value.

Treasury of Irish Stories. Illus. by Ian Newsham. LC 95-3009. (J). (gr. k-5). 1995. pap. 5.95 (1-85697-595-9, Kingfisher LKC) LKC.

*Treasury of Irish Verse. BHB International Staff. 1997. 12.95 (1-85833-702-X) BHB Intl.

Treasury of Irish Verse. David Gibbon. 1993. 10.98 (1-55521-888-1) Bk Sales Inc.

Treasury of Ironwork Designs: Four Hundred Sixty-Nine Examples from Historical Sources. Compiled by Carol B. Grafton. LC 92-10134. (Pictorial Archive Ser.). 1992. pap. write for info. (0-486-27126-9) Dover.

Treasury of Italian Love Poems Quotations & Proverbs. (Hippocrene Treasury of Love Poems Ser.). 128p. (ITA.). 1995. 11.95 (0-7818-0352-7) Hippocrene Bks.

Treasury of Jamaican Poetry. Ed. by John E. McFarlane. 1977. lib. bdg. 59.95 (0-8490-2760-8) Gordon Pr.

Treasury of Japanese Designs & Motifs for Artists & Craftsmen. Ed. by Carol B. Grafton. (Illus.). 96p. (Orig.). 1982. pap. 5.95 (0-486-24435-0) Dover.

Treasury of Jazz. Ed. by Eddie Condon & Richard Gehman. LC 75-2693. 488p. 1975. reprint ed. text ed. 75.00 (0-8371-8032-5, COTJ, Greenwood Pr) Greenwood.

Treasury of Jewels & Gems. M. Curran. 1960. 14.95 (0-87523-139-X) Emerson.

Treasury of Jewish Anecdotes. Lawrence J. Epstein. LC 89-393. 308p. 1995. pap. 24.95 (1-56821-513-4) Aronson.

Treasury of Jewish Folklore. Ed. by Nathan Ausubel. 768p. 1989. 22.00 (0-517-50293-3, Crown) Crown Pub Group.

*Treasury of Jewish Holidays: History, Legends, Traditions. Hyman E. Goldin. LC 97-5270. (Illus.). 308p. 1997. reprint ed. lib. bdg. 40.00 (0-7808-0266-7) Omnigraphics Inc.

Treasury of Jewish Humor. Nathan Ausubel. 1993. 12.98 (0-88365-842-9) Galahad Bks.

Treasury of Jewish Inspirational Stories. Lawrence J. Epstein. LC 92-23252. 296p. 1993. 30.00 (0-87668-596-3) Aronson.

Treasury of Jewish Love Poems Quotations & Proverbs. Ed. by David Gross. 128p. 1995. 11.95 (0-7818-0308-X) Hippocrene Bks.

*Treasury of Jewish Poetry. Nathen Ausubel. 471p. Date not set. 30.95 (0-8369-6178-1) Ayer.

Treasury of Jewish Quotations. Ed. by Joseph L. Baron. LC 85-3857. 648p. 1991. 40.00 (0-87668-894-6) Aronson.

Treasury of Jewish Quotations. Ed. by Joseph L. Baron. LC 85-3857. 648p. 1996. pap. 40.00 (1-56821-948-2) Aronson.

Treasury of Jewish Stories. Illus. by Jane Cope. LC 96-363. 160p. (J). (gr. k-4). 1996. pap. 5.95 (0-7534-5028-3, Kingfisher LKC) LKC.

Treasury of Joy & Enthusiasm. Norman Vincent Peale. 1987. mass mkt. 5.99 (0-449-21483-4) Fawcett.

*Treasury of Joy & Enthusiasm. Norman Vincent Peale. 1996. pap. 10.00 (0-449-91208-6) Fawcett.

Treasury of Kahlil Gibran. Kahlil Gibran. Ed. by Martin L. Wolf. Tr. by Anthony R. Ferris from ARA. 448p. 1974. pap. 12.95 (0-8065-0410-2, Citadel Pr) Carol Pub Group.

Treasury of Literature: Anthologies, 6 vols., Set. 93th ed. (J). (gr. 1). 1993. pap. 155.75 (0-15-304239-7) HarBrace.

Treasury of Literature for Children. 1988. 8.98 (0-671-07049-5) S&S Trade.

Treasury of Little Golden Books. Ed. by Ellen L. Buell. (Deluxe Golden Bks.). 120p. (J). (ps-2). 1989. write for info. (0-307-86540-1) Western Pub.

Treasury of Living Faith: Catholic Devotions for Every Day of the Year. Ed. by James E. Adams. (Illus.). 384p. 1991. 12.95 (0-9629585-1-4) Crtve Commns MO.

*Treasury of Love Proverbs from Many Lands. Ed. by Hippocrene Editorial Staff. Date not set. 17.50 (0-7818-0563-5) Hippocrene Bks.

*Treasury of Love Quotations from Many Lands. Ed. by Hippocrene Editorial Staff. (Illus.). 120p. 1997. 17.50 (0-7818-0574-0) Hippocrene Bks.

Treasury of Mahayana Sutras: Selections from the Maharatnakuta Sutra. Ed. by Garma C. C. Chang. Tr. by Buddhist Association of the United States from CHI. LC 82-42776. (Institute for Advanced Study of World Religions Ser.). 512p. (C). 1983. 45.00 (0-271-00341-3) Pa St U Pr.

Treasury of Medical Humor. Ed. by James E. Myers. 350p. (Orig.). 1992. pap. 10.95 (0-942936-21-3) Lincoln-Herndon Pr.

Treasury of Mennonite Quilts. deluxe ed. Kenneth Pellman & Rachael T. Pellman. LC 92-26505. (Illus.). 128p. 1992. pap. 19.95 (1-56148-059-2) Good Bks PA.

Treasury of Mexican Cuisine. Delores Rojas. 1994. 9.98 (0-8317-5167-3) Smithmark.

Treasury of Military Humor. Ed. by James E. Myers et al. (Illus.). 350p. (Orig.). 1989. pap. 10.95 (0-942936-16-7) Lincoln-Herndon Pr.

*Treasury of Mom, Pop & Kids' Humor. Ed. by James E. Myers. (Illus.). 225p. (Orig.). 1997. pap. 10.95 (0-942936-29-9) Lincoln-Herndon Pr.

Treasury of Mother Goose. Illus. by Hilda Offen. (J). (gr. 1 up). 1984. pap. 14.00 (0-671-50118-6, S&S Bks Young Read) S&S Childrens.

Treasury of Mother Goose: A Pop-up Book. Elizabeth Falconer. (Illus.). 18p. (J). (ps-1). 1992. pap. 11.95 (0-689-71505-6, Aladdin Paperbacks) S&S Childrens.

*Treasury of Mother's Prayers. Helen Allingham. 96p. Date not set. 10.99 (1-56292-268-8) Honor Bks OK.

Treasury of Natural First Aid Remedies from A-Z. James Kusick. 1994. pap. text ed. 11.95 (0-13-063181-7) P-H.

Treasury of Nebraska Pioneer Folklore. Illus. by Jack Brodie. LC 66-10876. xviii, 391p. 1966. reprint ed. pap. 16.95 (0-8032-9707-6, Bison Books) U of Nebr Pr.

Treasury of New England Folklore. Benjamin A. Botkin. 1989. 12.99 (0-517-67977-9) Random Hse Value.

Treasury of New Testament Synonyms. Stewart Custer. 161p. 1975. pap. 11.95 (*0-89084-025-3*, 002345) Bob Jones Univ Pr.

Treasury of North American Birdlore. Ed. by Paul S. Eriksson & Alan Pistorius. LC 87-27287. 400p. 1994. reprint ed. pap. 14.95 (*0-8397-8373-6*) Eriksson.

Treasury of Novenas. Lawrence G. Lovasik. 352p. 1986. vinyl bd. 7.75 (*0-89942-345-0*, 345/22) Catholic Bk Pub.

Treasury of Office Humor. Ed. by Mary E. Hirsch. 300p. 1994. pap. 10.95 (*0-942936-26-4*) Lincoln-Herndon Pr.

Treasury of Ohio Tales. Webb Garrison. LC 93-29073. 1996. pap. text ed. 8.95 (*1-55853-450-4*) Rutledge Hill Pr.

Treasury of Old Testament Stories. Ed. by Maggie Pearson & Kate Aldous. LC 95-1351. 1995. pap. 5.95 (*1-85697-594-0*, Kingfisher LKC) LKC.

Treasury of Orthodox Hymnology: The Triodion. Savas J. Savas. 1983. pap. 7.95 (*0-937032-32-8*) Light&Life Pub Co MN.

Treasury of Our Western Heritage: The Favell Museum of Western Art & Indian Artifacts. (Illus.). 1986. 19.75 (*0-317-57138-9*) Favell Mus.

Treasury of Patchwork Borders: 92 Foolproof Tricks. Elizabeth F. Nyhan. 1990. pap. 3.95 (*0-486-26183-2*) Dover.

Treasury of Patchwork Quilt Sets. Elizabeth F. Nyhan. LC 94-17258. 1994. write for info. (*0-486-28148-5*) Dover.

Treasury of Pennsylvania Tales. Webb Garrison. LC 95-50653. 224p. 1996. pap. text ed. 8.95 (*1-55853-388-5*) Rutledge Hill Pr.

***Treasury of Pet Stories.** Suzanne Carnell. LC 96-34092. (Illus.). (J). 1997. 6.95 (*0-7534-5074-7*, Kingfisher LKC) LKC.

Treasury of Peter Rabbit & Other Stories. Beatrix Potter. LC 94-35477. (Illus.). (J). (gr. k up). 1984. 7.99 (*0-517-23948-5*) Random Hse Value.

Treasury of Pineapple Designs for Crocheting. Ed. by Linda Macho. (Illus.). 48p. (Orig.). 1983. pap. 2.95 (*0-486-24494-6*) Dover.

***Treasury of Polish Aphorisms: A Bilingual Edition.** Tr. by Jacek Galazka & Helen S. Zand. (Illus.). 140p. (ENG & POL.). 1997. 12.95 (*0-7818-0549-X*, 647) Hippocrene Bks.

Treasury of Polish Love Poems, Quotations & Proverbs. Ed. by Miroslaw Lipinski. 128p. 1995. 11.95 (*0-7818-0297-0*) Hippocrene Bks.

Treasury of Pony Stories. Illus. by Anthony Lewis. LC 96-1906. (J). (gr. k-4). 1996. 6.95 (*0-7534-5029-1*, Kingfisher LKC) LKC.

Treasury of Popular Classics. Ed. by Denes Agay. (Illus.). 112p. 1987. pap. 11.95 (*0-8256-2096-1*, AM40361) Music Sales.

Treasury of Positive Answers. Vernon Howard. 1977. pap. 7.00 (*0-911203-25-7*) New Life.

Treasury of Prayer. E. M. Bounds. LC 53-9865. 192p. 1961. pap. 8.99 (*0-87123-543-9*) Bethany Hse.

Treasury of Prayers. 32p. 1973. pap. 0.50 (*0-8146-0807-8*) Liturgical Pr.

***Treasury of Presidential Quotations.** William J. Federer. (Illus.). 192p. (Orig.). 1996. pap. 9.95 (*0-9653557-0-5*) AmeriSearch.

Treasury of Princesses: Princess Tales from Around the World. Shirley Climo. LC 95-31062. (Illus.). 80p. (J). (ps up). 1996. 16.95 (*0-06-024532-8*) HarpC Child Bks.

Treasury of Princesses: Princess Tales from Around the World. Shirley Climo. LC 95-31062. (Illus.). 80p. (J). (ps up). 1996. lib. bdg. 16.89 (*0-06-024533-6*) HarpC Child Bks.

Treasury of Quilt Designs. Linda G. Emery. 1990. pap. 14.95 (*0-89145-948-0*) Collector Bks.

Treasury of Quilt Labels. Susan McKelvey. Ed. by Louise O. Townsend. LC 92-46212. (Illus.). 80p. (Orig.). 1995. pap. 17.95 (*0-914881-60-4*, 10080) C & T Pub.

Treasury of Quilting Patterns. Cheryl Fall. LC 94-30299. (Illus.). 144p. (Orig.). 1995. 19.95 (*0-8069-1272-3*) Sterling.

Treasury of Quilting Patterns. Cheryl Fall. (Illus.). 144p. (Orig.). 1996. pap. 12.95 (*0-8069-1273-1*) Sterling.

Treasury of Quotes. Jim Rohn. 120p. 1996. 20.00 (*1-55874-394-4*) Health Comm.

Treasury of Railroad Folklore. Benjamin A. Botkin. 1989. 10.99 (*0-517-16868-5*) Random Hse Value.

Treasury of Raw Foods. Edmond B. Szekely. (Illus.). 48p. 1981. pap. 3.50 (*0-89564-042-2*) IBS Intl.

Treasury of Reels. Jim Brown. (From the Collections of the American Museum of Fly Fishing). (Illus.). 1990. 50.00 (*0-685-30055-2*) Amer Mus Fly Fishing.

Treasury of Religious Humor. Ed. by James E. Myers, Sr. (Illus.). 300p. 1994. pap. 10.95 (*0-942936-24-8*) Lincoln-Herndon Pr.

Treasury of Religious Quotations. Gerald Tomlinson. 1991. pap. 14.95 (*0-13-276411-3*) P-H.

Treasury of Roman Love Poems Quotations & Proverbs. Ed. by Richard Branyon. 128p. 1994. 11.95 (*0-7818-0309-8*) Hippocrene Bks.

Treasury of Russian Love Poems, Quotations & Proverbs. (Treasury of Love Poems Ser.). 1996. audio 12.95 (*0-7818-0364-0*) Hippocrene Bks.

Treasury of Russian Love Poems, Quotations, & Proverbs. Victoria Andreyeva. 128p. 1995. 11.95 (*0-7818-0298-9*) Hippocrene Bks.

Treasury of Russian Verse. Ed. by Avrahm Yarmolinsky. LC 79-80370. (Granger Index Reprint Ser.). 1977. 23.95 (*0-8369-6093-9*) Ayer.

***Treasury of School "Daze" Humor.** Paul A. McClure. 200p. (Orig.). 1997. pap. 10.95 (*0-942936-30-2*) Lincoln-Herndon Pr.

Treasury of Science Jokes. Morris Goran. (Illus.). 136p. (Orig.). 1987. pap. 9.95 (*0-942936-09-4*) Lincoln-Herndon Pr.

Treasury of Scripture Knowledge. R. A. Torrey. 784p. 1993. 22.99 (*0-8007-0324-3*) Revell.

Treasury of Scripture Knowledge. R. A. Torrey. 784p. 1988. 19.95 (*0-917006-22-4*) Hendrickson MA.

Treasury of Scripture Knowledge. Intro. by R. A. Torrey. 778p. 1993. 15.99 (*0-529-07667-5*, TSK1) World Publng.

Treasury of Senior Humor. Ed. by James E. Myers. 350p. (Orig.). 1992. pap. 10.95 (*0-942936-20-5*) Lincoln-Herndon Pr.

Treasury of Sephardic Laws & Customs. Herbert C. Dobrinsky. 1986. 29.50 (*0-88125-031-7*) Ktav.

Treasury of Sholom Aleichem Children's Stories. Aliza Shevrin. LC 96-14590. (Illus.). 368p. (J). 1996. 30.00 (*1-56821-926-1*) Aronson.

***Treasury of Sholom Aleichem Children's Stories.** Aliza Shevrin. LC 96-14590. (Illus.). 368p. 1997. pap. 25.00 (*0-7657-9965-0*) Aronson.

Treasury of Short Magical Stories. Bill Hodges. Ed. by Dahk Knox. (Illus.). 6p. (Orig.). 1997. 10.95 (*1-881116-86-7*) Black Forest Pr. TREASURY OF SHORT MAGICAL STORIES by Bill Hodges is filled with a collection of interesting magical tales. The author takes the reader into a world of unexpected happenings & events. The twists in the stories make them truly unique & different. When the reader sits down to relish the magical stories, he or she is surprised by what actually happens & who is involved, leaving the reader wanting more. Although the reader can never really be sure what will occur next, they can only make an educated guess. The characters are one of a kind.. .they jump out at the reader & present a challenge of whether what he or she is reading can actually exist. These stories are reminiscent of the Twilight Zone. The TREASURY OF SHORT MAGICAL STORIES ISBN: 1-881116-86-7 can be directly purchased for $10.95 plus shipping & handling from Black Forest Book Promotions, Deborah Johnson, National Marketing Director, 539 Telegraph Canyon Road #521, Chula Vista, CA 91910. Phone 619-426-1862, FAX 619-426-1795, E-mail BFP@Flash.net or www.Flash.net/~dbk.** ***Publisher Provided Annotation.

Treasury of Smocking Designs. Allyne S. Holland. 48p. (Orig.). 1985. pap. 3.50 (*0-486-24991-3*) Dover.

Treasury of Snake Lore: From the Garden of Eden to Snakes of Today in Mythology, Fable, Stories, Essays, Poetry, Drama, Religion, & Personal Adventures. Ed. by Brandt Aymar. LC 89-63102. 448p. 1998. reprint ed. lib. bdg. 48.00 (*1-55888-853-5*) Omnigraphics Inc.

Treasury of Southern Baking: Luscious Cakes, Cobblers, Pies, Custards, Muffins, Biscuits, & Breads in the Tradition of the American South. Prudence Hilburn. LC 92-53401. 304p. 1993. pap. 15.00 (*0-06-096597-5*, PL) HarpC.

Treasury of Southern Folklore. B. A. Botkin. 1988. 12.99 (*0-517-64136-4*) Random Hse Value.

Treasury of Spanish Love Poems, Quotations, & Proverbs. (Hippocrene Treasury of Love Poems Ser.). 128p. (SPA.). 1995. pap. 11.95 (*0-7818-0358-6*) Hippocrene Bks.

Treasury of Spanish Love Stories. LC 97-15375. 128p. (ENG & SPA.). 1997. 11.95 (*0-7818-0512-0*) Hippocrene Bks.

Treasury of Spiritual Wisdom: A Collection of 10,000 Powerful Quotations for Transforming Your Life. 2nd ed. Andy Zubko. LC 95-33635. 506p. (Orig.). 1996. pap. 19.95 (*1-884997-10-4*) Blue Dove Pr.

Treasury of Spooky Stories. Ed. by Jane Olliver. LC 92-53111. (Treasury of Stories Ser.). (Illus.). 160p. (Orig.). (J). (gr. k-5). 1992. pap. 5.95 (*1-85697-830-3*, Kingfisher LKC) LKC.

Treasury of Sports Humor. (J). pap. 1.75 (*0-590-05007-9*) Scholastic Inc.

Treasury of Standards, Vol. 1. (Ultimate Ser.). 287p. 1986. pap. 17.95 (*0-88188-527-4*, 00361431) H Leonard.

Treasury of Standards, Vol. 2. 287p. 1986. pap. 17.95 (*0-88188-529-0*, 00361433) H Leonard.

Treasury of Standards, Vol. 3. 287p. 1986. pap. 17.95 (*0-88188-531-2*, 00361435) H Leonard.

Treasury of Stencil Designs for Artists & Craftsmen. Ed. by Martin J. Isaacson & Dorothy A. Rennie. LC 75-46105. (Pictorial Archive Ser.). (Illus.). 64p. (Orig.). 1976. pap. 5.95 (*0-486-23307-3*) Dover.

Treasury of Stencil Designs for Artists & Craftsmen. Martin J. Isaacson & Dorothy A. Rennie. 1990. 13.00 (*0-8446-5469-8*) Peter Smith.

Treasury of Stories for Eight Year Olds. Illus. by Mick Reid. LC 94-30241. (J). 1995. pap. 6.95 (*1-85697-545-2*, Kingfisher LKC) LKC.

Treasury of Stories for Five Year Olds. Ed. by Edward Blishen & Nancy Blishen. LC 92-53107. (Treasury of Stories Ser.). (Illus.). 160p. (Orig.). (J). (gr. k-5). 1992. pap. 6.95 (*1-85697-827-3*, Kingfisher LKC) LKC.

Treasury of Stories for Four Year Olds. Nancy Blishen & Edward Blishen. LC 94-2337. (Illus.). (J). 1994. pap. 6.95 (*1-85697-984-9*, Kingfisher LKC) LKC.

Treasury of Stories for Seven Year Olds. Ed. by Edward Blishen & Nancy Blishen. LC 92-53109. (Treasury of Stories Ser.). (Illus.). 160p. (Orig.). (J). (gr. k-5). 1992. pap. 5.95 (*1-85697-829-X*, Kingfisher LKC) LKC.

Treasury of Stories for Six Year Olds. Ed. by Edward Blishen & Nancy Blishen. LC 92-53108. (Treasury of Stories Ser.). (Illus.). 160p. (Orig.). (J). (gr. k-5). 1992. pap. 6.95 (*1-85697-828-1*, Kingfisher LKC) LKC.

Treasury of Stories from Around the World. Illus. by Victor Ambrus. LC 92-43153. (Treasury of Stories Ser.). 160p. (J). (gr. k-4). 1993. pap. 6.95 (*1-85697-932-6*, Kingfisher LKC) LKC.

Treasury of Stories from Hans Christian Andersen. Hans Christian Andersen. LC 95-36161. (Treasury of Stories Ser.). (Illus.). 160p. (J). (gr. k-4). 1996. pap. 5.95 (*1-85697-676-9*, Kingfisher LKC) LKC.

Treasury of Stories from the Brothers Grimm. Jenny Koralek. (Treasury of Stories Ser.). (Illus.). 160p. (J). (gr. k-4). 1996. pap. 5.95 (*1-85697-677-7*, Kingfisher LKC) LKC.

Treasury of Successful Appeal Letters. Ed. by Joseph Dermer. 176p. 1985. pap. 49.50 (*0-914977-07-5*, 600028) Fund Raising.

***Treasury of Tales.** Smithmark Staff. 1996. 14.98 (*0-7651-9779-0*) Smithmark.

Treasury of Tantric Ideas: A Study of the Samrajyalaksmipithika. Artatrana Sarangi. (C). 1993. 44.00 (*81-85094-65-9*, Pub. by Punthi Pus II) S Asia.

***Treasury of Tatting Patterns, 3 vols., Set.** Orr et al. (Illus.). pap. 9.95 (*0-486-25426-7*) Dover.

Treasury of Tennessee Tales. James Ewing. LC 96-29912. 192p. 1997. pap. 8.95 (*1-55853-451-2*) Rutledge Hill Pr.

***Treasury of Tested Collections.** 1996. pap. text ed. 24.95 (*0-15-606574-6*) Profess Pubns.

***Treasury of Texas Tales.** Webb Garrison. (Illus.). 192p. (Orig.). 1997. pap. 8.95 (*1-55853-537-3*) Rutledge Hill Pr.

Treasury of Texas Trivia. Bill Cannon. LC 96-40199. 224p. (Orig.). 1997. pap. 12.95 (*1-55622-526-1*, Rep of TX Pr) Wordware Pub.

Treasury of the Art of Living. Ed. by Sidney Greenberg. 1964. 12.50 (*0-87677-019-7*) Hartmore.

Treasury of the Art of Living. Sidney Greenberg. 1972. pap. 10.00 (*0-87980-168-9*) Wilshire.

Treasury of the Familiar. Ralph L. Woods. 762p. 1991. reprint ed. lib. bdg. 48.95 (*0-89966-824-0*) Buccaneer Bks.

***Treasury of the Great Children's Book Illustrators.** Susan E. Meyer. (Illus.). 272p. 1997. pap. 24.95 (*0-8109-2694-6*) Abrams.

Treasury of the Sierra Nevada. Robert Reid. LC 82-62811. (Illus.). 256p. (Orig.). 1983. 19.95 (*0-89997-032-X*); pap. 15.95 (*0-89997-023-0*) Wilderness Pr.

Treasury of the World's Best Loved Poems. 1988. 4.99 (*0-517-63753-7*) Random Hse Value.

Treasury of the World's Great Sermons. Compiled by Warren W. Wiersbe. LC 77-72366. 662p. 1977. pap. 22.99 (*0-8254-4002-5*) Kregel.

Treasury of Thoughts on Jewish Prayer. Ed. by Sidney Greenberg. LC 89-31455. 256p. 1990. 30.00 (*0-87668-865-2*) Aronson.

Treasury of Thoughts on Jewish Prayer. Sidney Greenberg. LC 89-31455. (Illus.). 256p. 1996. pap. 25.00 (*1-56821-937-7*) Aronson.

Treasury of Tips for the Antiquarian Bookseller. Hoffman Research Services Staff. 24p. (Orig.). 1983. pap. 9.95 (*0-910203-00-8*) Hoffman Res.

Treasury of Traditional Stained Glass Designs. Ann V. Winterbotham. (Illus.). 80p. (Orig.). 1981. pap. 4.95 (*0-486-24084-3*) Dover.

Treasury of Traditional Wisdom, Vol. 1. Whitall N. Perry. 111p. 1991. pap. 18.95 (*1-870196-08-2*, Pub. by Islamic Texts UK) Intl Spec Bk.

Treasury of Trellaye. Brian Wyant & Eric Wyant. (Illus.). 96p. 1997. pap. 9.95 (*1-883788-20-X*) Event Horzn.

***Treasury of Trickster Tales.** Valerie Marsh. LC 97-5208. 1997. pap. write for info. (*0-917846-91-5*) Highsmith Pr.

Treasury of Trueness: Gems of Wisdom. Vernon Howard. 257p. 1995. pap. 11.95 (*0-911203-33-8*) New Life.

Treasury of Turkish Designs: Six Hundred Seventy Motifs from Iznik Pottery. Azade Akar. (Pictorial Archive Ser.). (Illus.). 128p. 1987. pap. 7.95 (*0-486-25594-8*) Dover.

Treasury of Turkish Folktales for Children. Barbara K. Walker. LC 88-6859. xii, 155p. (J). (gr. 3 up). 1988. lib. bdg. 22.50 (*0-208-02206-6*, Linnet Bks) Shoe String.

***Treasury of 20th Century Child.** Ed. by Simon Boughton. (J). 1998. write for info. (*0-679-88647-8*) Knopf Bks Yng Read.

***Treasury of Ukrainian Love Poems, Quotations & Proverbs.** Ed. by Helene Turkewicz-Sanko. LC 97-4349. (Treasury of Love Ser.). 128p. 1997. 11.95 (*0-7818-0517-1*, 650) Hippocrene Bks.

***Treasury of Unearned Gifts: Rebbe Nachman's Path to Happiness & Contentment in Life.** Chaim Kramer. Ed. by Ozer Bergman. 98p. 1996. pap. 10.00 (*0-930213-56-4*) Breslov Res Inst.

Treasury of Urdu Rubaiyat. K. C. Kanda. 1993. 30.00 (*81-207-1502-0*, Pub. by Sterling Pubs II) Apt Bks.

Treasury of Victorian Murder. Rick Geary. 64p. (Orig.). 1987. pap. 6.95 (*0-918348-41-2*, Comics Lit) NBM.

***Treasury of Victorian Murder: The Borden Tragedy.** Rick Geary. (Illus.). 64p. 1997. pap. 9.95 (*1-56163-189-2*, Comics Lit) NBM.

Treasury of Victorian Murder Vol. 2: Jack the Ripper. Rick Geary. 64p. (J). 1995. 14.95 (*1-56163-124-8*, Comics Lit) NBM.

Treasury of Victorian Printers' Frames, Ornaments, & Initials. Carol B. Grafton. 128p. 1984. pap. 6.95 (*0-486-24703-1*) Dover.

Treasury of Virginia Tales. Webb Garrison. LC 90-24434. 1996. pap. text ed. 8.95 (*1-55853-452-0*) Rutledge Hill Pr.

Treasury of White House Tales. rev. ed. Webb Garrison. LC 89-6252. 248p. 1996. pap. text ed. 9.95 (*1-55853-382-6*) Rutledge Hill Pr.

Treasury of Winnie-the-Pooh, 4 bks., Set. Incl. Winnie-the-Pooh. A. A. Milne. 1987. pap. (*0-318-51662-4*); House at Pooh Corner. A. A. Milne. 1987. pap. (*0-318-51663-2*); Now We Are Six. (*0-318-51664-0*); When We Were Very Young. (*0-318-51665-9*); (Illus.). (J). 1987. Boxed set. boxed 13.00 (*0-440-49580-6*) Dell.

Treasury of Wisdom: A Daily Devotional Journal. deluxe ed. Ken Abraham et al. 384p. 1996. bond lthr. 19.97 (*1-55748-906-8*) Barbour & Co.

Treasury of Wise Action: Jataka Tales for Young Readers. LC 93-883. (Traditional Tales - Adaptations Ser.). (Illus.). 157p. (Orig.). (J). (gr. 4-7). 1993. pap. 10.95 (*0-89800-224-9*) Dharma Pub.

Treasury of Wit & Wisdom. Ed. by F. Seymour Smith. 80p. 6600. 4.95 (*0-212-35832-4*) Dufour.

Treasury of Witchcraft: A Source Book of Magic Arts. Harry E. Wedeck. (Illus.). 288p. 1992. pap. 10.95 (*0-8065-1384-5*, Citadel Pr) Carol Pub Group.

Treasury of Witches & Wizards. David Bennett. LC 95-36026. (Treasury of Stories Ser.). (Illus.). 160p. (J). (gr. k-4). 1996. pap. 5.95 (*1-85697-678-5*, Kingfisher LKC) LKC.

Treasury of Women Saints. Rhonda D. Chervin. 400p. (Orig.). 1991. pap. 12.99 (*0-89283-707-1*, Charis) Servant.

Treasury of Worship. Helena Dickinson. 1972. 59.95 (*0-8490-1230-9*) Gordon Pr.

Treasury of Writings of Kahlil Gibran. Kahlil Gibran. 1989. 12.98 (*0-89009-389-X*) Bk Sales Inc.

Treasury of Yiddish Stories. rev. ed. Ed. by Irving Howe & Eliezer Greenberg. 640p. 1990. reprint ed. pap. 19.95 (*0-14-014419-6*, Penguin Bks) Viking Penguin.

***Treasury of 20th Century Child.** Dimon Boughton. 1998. lib. bdg. write for info. (*0-679-98647-2*) Knopf Bks Yng Read.

Treasury Operations & Foreign Exchange Challenge: A Guide to Risk Management Strategies for the New World Markets. Dimitris N. Chorafas. LC 91-35940. (Finance Editions Ser.). 304p. 1992. text ed. 49.95 (*0-471-54393-4*) Wiley.

Treasury Risk Management - Training Manual, Set. 200p. 1991. 250.00 (*1-871682-55-X*, Pub. by Euromoney UK) Am Educ Systs.

Treasury Rules: Recurrent Themes in British Economic Policy. Adrian Ham. 15.95 (*0-7043-2267-6*, Pub. by Quartet UK) Charles River Bks.

***Treasury Securities & Derivatives.** Frank J. Fabozzi. (Illus.). 1997. 53.00 (*1-883249-23-6*) F J Fabozzi.

TREAT: A New & Efficient Match Algorithm for AI Production Systems. Daniel Miranker. (Research Notes in Artificial Intelligence Ser.). 140p. 1989. 29.95 (*0-934613-71-0*) Morgan Kaufmann.

Treat: A New & Efficient Match Algorithm for AI Production Systems. Daniel Miranker. 144p. (C). 1989. pap. text ed. 200.00 (*0-273-08793-2*, Pub. by Pitman Pubng UK) St Mut.

Treat Family: A Genealogy of Trott, Tratt, & Treat for Fifteen Generations & Four Hundred Fifty Years in England & America. J. H. Treat. (Illus.). 649p. 1989. reprint ed. pap. 97.00 (*0-8328-1179-3*); reprint ed. lib. bdg. 105.00 (*0-8328-1178-5*) Higginson Bk Co.

Treat Family in America, 1622-1922: Line of Benjamin Franklin Treat. Bob Treat. (Illus.). 70p. 1994. reprint ed. pap. 14.00 (*0-8328-4161-7*) Higginson Bk Co.

Treat It Gentle: An Autobiography. Sidney Bechet. LC 74-23412. (Roots of Jazz Ser.). (Illus.). vi, 245p. 1978. reprint ed. pap. 12.95 (*0-306-80086-1*) Da Capo.

Treat It Right: A Local Official's Guide to Small Town Wastewater Treatment. National Association of Towns & Townships Staff. (Illus.). 64p. (Orig.). 1989. pap. 8.00 (*0-925532-02-9*) Natl Assn Town & Twps.

Treat Me Right: Essays in Medical Law & Ethics. Ian Kennedy. (Illus.). 448p. 1991. reprint ed. pap. 29.95 (*0-19-825558-6*) OUP.

***Treat Shop.** Ed. by Eleanor Johnson & Leland Jacobs. 10.00 (*0-614-30544-6*) NAVH.

Treat, the Cavalry Saber: Treat & Joseph Brown Civil War History & Legacy. Bob Treat. (Illus.). 62p. 1994. reprint ed. pap. 12.50 (*0-8328-4160-9*) Higginson Bk Co.

Treat Them Like Animals. Rae S. Stewart. 1992. mass mkt. 3.50 (*0-87067-372-6*, BH372-6) Holloway.

Treat Your Face Like a Salad! Skin Care Naturally, Blemish & Wrinkle-Free, Recipes & Gourmet Hints for a Fabu-lishous Face. Julia M. Busch. LC 93-90245. (Illus.). 256p. (Orig.). 1993. per. 14.95 (*0-9632907-8-9*) Anti Aging Pr.

Treat Your Own Back. 6th ed. Robin A. McKenzie. (Illus.). 73p. (SPA.). 1989. reprint ed. Spanish ed. pap. text ed. 10.00 (*0-473-00065-2*, Pub. by Spinal Pubns Ltd NZ) Orthopedic Phys.

Treat Your Own Back. 7th ed. Robin A. McKenzie. (Illus.). 73p. 1989. reprint ed. pap. text ed. 10.00 (*0-9597746-6-1*, Pub. by Spinal Pubns Ltd NZ) Orthopedic Phys.

Treat Your Own Neck. 3rd ed. Robin A. McKenzie. (Illus.). 61p. 1989. reprint ed. pap. text ed. 10.00 (*0-473-00209-4*, Pub. by Spinal Pubns Ltd NZ) Orthopedic Phys.

Treat Yourself Gift Pack. Date not set. spiral bd. write for info. (*1-879127-37-7*) Lighten Up Enter.

Treat Yourself Shopping List. 75p. 1992. write for info. (*1-879127-20-2*) Lighten Up Enter.

***Treat Yourself to Life.** Raymond C. Barker. LC 87-30216. 120p. 1996. reprint ed. pap 9.95 (*0-87516-700-4*) DeVorss.

Treat Yourself to the Best Cookbook. 1994. pap. 14.95 (*0-9613428-0-3*) Jr Leag Wheeling.

An Asterisk (*) at the beginning of an entry indicates that the title is appearing in BIP for the first time.

Treaties & Agreements & the Proceedings of the Treaties & Agreements of the Tribes & Bands of the Sioux Nation. (American Indian Treaty Ser.: No. 1). 20.00 (*0-944253-17-2*) Inst Dev Indian Law.

Treaties & Agreements of the Chippewa Indians. (American Indian Treaty Ser.: No. 7). 15.00 (*0-317-57356-X*) Inst Dev Indian Law.

Treaties & Agreements of the Eastern Oklahoma Indians. (American Indian Treaty Ser.: No. 4). 12.00 (*0-944253-14-8*) Inst Dev Indian Law.

Treaties & Agreements of the Five Civilized Tribes. (American Indian Treaty Ser.: No. 6). 20.00 (*0-944253-16-4*) Inst Dev Indian Law.

Treaties & Agreements of the Indian Tribes of the Great Lakes Region. (American Indian Treaty Ser.: No. 8). 10.00 (*0-944253-18-0*) Inst Dev Indian Law.

Treaties & Agreements of the Indian Tribes of the Northern Plains. (American Indian Treaty Ser.: No. 3). 15.00 (*0-944253-13-X*) Inst Dev Indian Law.

Treaties & Agreements of the Indian Tribes of the Pacific Northwest. (American Indian Treaty Ser.: No. 2). 12.00 (*0-944253-12-1*) Inst Dev Indian Law.

Treaties & Agreements of the Indian Tribes of the Southwest. (American Indian Treaty Ser.: No. 5). 15.00 (*0-944253-15-6*) Inst Dev Indian Law.

Treaties & Alliances of the World. Ed. by Nicholas Rengger. 580p. 1995. 195.00 (*0-614-14334-9*, Stockton Pr) Groves Dictionaries.

Treaties & Alliances of the World. 5th ed. 495p. 1990. text ed. 120.00 (*0-685-47377-5*, Pub. by Longman Grp UK) Gale.

Treaties & Alliances of the World. 5th ed. Nicholas Rengger. 1991. 120.00 (*0-582-05733-7*) Longman.

Treaties & Alliances of the World, 8 Vols., Vol. 1. 94th ed. Henry W. Degenhardt. 1995. 3,200.00 (*0-8103-9915-6*, 076413, Pub. by Longman Grp UK) Gale.

Treaties & Conventions Signed at the Second International Conference on American States. (Treaty Ser.). 82p. 1902. 1.00 (*0-8270-0430-3*) OAS.

Treaties & Engagements Relating to Arabia & the Persian Gulf. Ed. by C. U. Aitchison. 350p. (C). 1987. reprint ed. lib. bdg. 95.00 (*1-85207-076-5*, Pub. by Archive Editions UK) N Ross.

Treaties & Federal Constitutions. James M. Hendry. LC 75-1361. 186p. 1975. reprint ed. text ed. 49.75 (*0-8371-8010-4*, HETF, Greenwood Pr) Greenwood.

Treaties & Indigenous Peoples. Ian Brownlie. Ed. by F. M. Brookfield. 160p. 1992. 49.95 (*0-19-825716-3*) OUP.

Treaties & Other International Agreements: The Role of the U. S. Senate. 1994. lib. bdg. 275.75 (*0-8490-5810-4*) Gordon Pr.

Treaties Between the Empire of China & Foreign Powers. Ed. by William F. Mayers. 1976. lib. bdg. 59.95 (*0-8490-2761-6*) Gordon Pr.

Treaties Concerning the Non-Navigational Uses of International Watercourses: Europe. (Legislative Studies: No. 50). 523p. 1993. pap. 55.00 (*92-5-003010-X*, F3010X, Pub. by FAO IT) Bernan Associates.

Treaties, Conventions, International Acts, Protocols, Agreements Between the U. S. & Other Powers, 1910-1938, 4 vols. U. S. Treaties Staff. LC 10-35763. 1968. reprint ed. Set. 395.00 (*0-685-38432-2*) Scholarly.

Treaties, Conventions, International Acts, Protocols & Agreements Between the United States of America & Other Powers, 4 vols. LC 68-55144. 1970. reprint ed. Set. text ed. 395.00 (*0-8371-2514-6*, TRCI) Greenwood.

Treaties, Conventions, International Acts, Protocols & Agreements Between the United States of America & Other Powers, 4 vols., 1. LC 68-55144. 1970. reprint ed. text ed. 125.00 (*0-8371-0724-5*, TRCA) Greenwood.

Treaties, Conventions, International Acts, Protocols & Agreements Between the United States of America & Other Powers, 4 vols., Vol. 2. LC 68-55144. 1970. reprint ed. text ed. 125.00 (*0-8371-0855-1*, TRCB) Greenwood.

Treaties, Conventions, International Acts, Protocols & Agreements Between the United States of America & Other Powers, 4 vols., Vol. 3. LC 68-55144. 1970. reprint ed. text ed. 125.00 (*0-8371-0856-X*, TRCC) Greenwood.

Treaties, Conventions, International Acts, Protocols & Agreements Between the United States of America & Other Powers, 4 vols., Vol. 4. LC 68-55144. 1970. reprint ed. text ed. 125.00 (*0-8371-0857-8*, TRCD) Greenwood.

Treaties for the Eighteen Sixties with the Southern Cheyenne & Arapaho. Raymond J. DeMaille. 15.00 (*0-944253-58-X*) Inst Dev Indian Law.

Treaties in Force: A List of Treaties & Other International Agreements of the U. S. in Force on January 1, 1994. Department of State Office of Legal Affairs Staff. 460p. 1994. pap. 28.00 (*0-89059-025-7*) Bernan Pr.

Treaties in Force: A List of Treaties & Other International Agreements of the U. S. in Force on January 1, 1995. 468p. (Orig.). (C). 1995. pap. text ed. 50.00 (*0-7881-2426-9*) DIANE Pub.

Treaties in Force: A List of Treaties & Other International Agreements of the United States Currently in Force, 2 vols., Set. 1995. lib. bdg. 602.99 (*0-8490-6709-X*) Gordon Pr.

***Treaties in Force U. S. '96.** U. S. Government Staff. 1994. pap. 32.00 (*0-614-30820-8*) Claitors.

Treaties of Puget Sound, 1854-1855. Robert B. Lane & Barbara Lane. (Treaty Manuscripts Ser.: No. 6). 60p. 12.50 (*0-944253-28-8*) Inst Dev Indian Law.

Treaties of Seventeen Seventy-Eight: Proceedings of French Treaties, 1774-1792 (Louis XVI) & United States Treaties, Feb. 7, 1778. Gilbert Chinard. 1979. 15.95 (*0-405-10595-9*) Ayer.

Treaties of Seventeen Seventy-Eight, & Allied Documents. (BCL1 - U. S. History Ser.). 70p. 1991. reprint ed. lib. bdg. 59.00 (*0-7812-6117-1*) Rprt Serv.

Treaties of Seventeen Seventy-Eight & Allied Documents. Ed. by Gilbert Chinard. LC 73-181911. (BCL Ser.: No. I). reprint ed. 24.50 (*0-404-52421-4*) AMS Pr.

Treaties of the War of the Spanish Succession: An Historical & Critical Dictionary. Ed. by Linda Frey & Marsha Frey. LC 95-3804. 608p. 1995. text ed. 125.00 (*0-313-27884-9*, Greenwood Pr) Greenwood.

Treaties on Analytical Chemistry: Theory & Practice, Pt. 1, Vol. 7. Ed. by Izaak M. Kolthoff & Philip J. Elving. LC 78-1707. reprint ed. pap. 160.00 (*0-318-34743-1*, 2032002) Bks Demand.

Treaties on the Panama Canal Signed Between the United States of American & the Republic of Panama. (Treaty Ser.). 254p. 1979. 9.00 (*0-685-18416-1*) OAS.

Treaties on Utilization of International Water Courses for Other Purposes Than Navigation: Africa. 130p. 1984. 13.50 (*92-1-104225-9*) UN.

Treaties, Their Making & Enforcement. Samuel B. Crandall. LC 74-76672. (Columbia University. Studies in the Social Sciences: No. 54). reprint ed. 42.50 (*0-404-51054-X*) AMS Pr.

Treating Abuse in Families: A Feminist & Community Approach. Elaine Leeder. LC 94-15849. 232p. 1994. 41.95 (*0-8261-8530-4*) Springer Pub.

Treating Abused Adolescents. Eliana Gil. LC 96-12550. 228p. 1996. lib. bdg. 42.00 (*1-57230-114-7*) Guilford Pr.

Treating Abused Adolescents. Eliana Gil. LC 96-12550. 228p. 1996. pap. text ed. 18.95 (*1-57230-115-5*) Guilford Pr.

Treating Abused Adolescents: A Program for Providing Individual & Group Therapy. Darlene A. Merchant. 1990. pap. text ed. 14.95 (*1-55691-017-7*, 177) Learning Pubns.

Treating Acromegaly: 100 Years On. Ed. by J. A. Wass. 221p. 1994. pap. 29.95 (*1-898099-05-7*) Blackwell Sci.

Treating Addicted Survivors of Trauma. Katie Evans & J. Michael Sullivan. 282p. 1994. pap. text ed. 19.95 (*0-89862-324-3*, 2324); lib. bdg. 40.00 (*0-89862-306-5*, 2306) Guilford Pr.

Treating Addictive Behaviors: Processes of Change. Ed. by William R. Miller & Nick H. Heather. (Applied Clinical Psychology Ser.). 450p. 1986. 65.00 (*0-306-42248-4*, Plenum Pr) Plenum.

Treating Adolescent Sex Offenders in the Community. Charlene Steen & Barbara Monnette. (Illus.). 212p. 1989. pap. 33.95 (*0-398-06441-5*) C C Thomas.

Treating Adolescent Sex Offenders in the Community. Charlene Steen & Barbara Monnette. (Illus.). 212p. (C). 1989. text ed. 49.95 (*0-398-05521-1*) C C Thomas.

Treating Adolescent Substance Abuse: Understanding the Fundamental Elements. George R. Ross. LC 93-11215. 238p. 1993. text ed. 47.95 (*0-205-15255-4*, Longwood Div) Allyn.

Treating Adolescents. Ed. by Nans Steiner. (Library of Current Clinical Technique). 432p. (Orig.). 1996. pap. 27.95 (*0-7879-0206-3*) Jossey-Bass.

Treating Adult Children of Alcholics: A Developmental Perspective. Stephanie Brown. (Personality Processes Ser.). 333p. 1988. text ed. 65.00 (*0-471-85300-3*) Wiley.

***Treating Adult Children of Alcoholics: A Developmental Perspective.** Stephanie Brown. 1996. pap. text ed. 29.95 (*0-471-15559-4*) Wiley.

Treating Adult Survivors of Childhood Sexual Abuse. William C. Nichols. LC 91-50913. (Practitioner's Resource Ser.). 80p. 1992. pap. 15.20 (*0-943158-68-0*, TASBP, Prof Resc Pr) Pro Resource.

Treating AIDS with Chinese Medicine. Mary K. Ryan & Arthur Shattuck. LC 93-85212. 384p. 1993. pap. 29.95 (*1-881896-07-2*) Pacific View Pr.

Treating Alcohol & Drug Users in the Community. 2nd ed. T. A. Waller. 288p. 1997. pap. 34.95 (*0-632-03575-7*) Blackwell Sci.

Treating Alcohol Dependence: A Coping Skills Training Guide. Peter M. Monti et al. LC 88-36838. (Treatment Manuals for Practitioners Ser.). 240p. 1989. pap. text ed. 20.95 (*0-89862-215-8*); lib. bdg. 45.00 (*0-89862-204-2*) Guilford Pr.

Treating Alcohol Problems: Marital & Family Interventions. Ed. by Timothy J. O'Farrell. LC 93-3061. (Substance Abuse Ser.). 446p. 1993. lib. bdg. 41.95 (*0-89862-195-X*) Guilford Pr.

Treating Alcoholism. Ed. by Stephanie Brown. LC 94-39887. (Social & Behavioral Sciences-Health Ser.). 440p. 34.95 (*0-7879-0068-0*) Jossey-Bass.

***Treating Alcoholism: An Alcoholics Anonymous Approach.** Norman K. Denzin. LC 87-4846. (Sage Human Services Guides Ser.: No. 46). 149p. 1987. reprint ed. pap. 42.50 (*0-608-04307-9*, 2065086) Bks Demand.

Treating Alcoholism & Drug Abuse among Homeless Men & Women: Nine Community Demonstration Grants. Milton Argerion & Dennis McCarty. LC 90-4301. (Alcoholism Treatment Quarterly Ser.: Vol. 7, No. 1). (Illus.). 164p. 1990. text ed. 29.95 (*0-86656-992-8*) Haworth Pr.

Treating Alzheimer's & Other Dementias: Recent Research Advances. Ed. by Manfred Bergener & Sanford I. Finkel. LC 94-45399. 1995. 61.95 (*0-8261-8930-X*) Springer Pub.

Treating & Drying Trees on the Stump. P. S. Zakharov. LC 61-9225. (Illus.). 35p. reprint ed. pap. 25.00 (*0-317-08275-2*, 2020664) Bks Demand.

Treating & Overcoming Anorexia Nervosa. Steven Levenkron. 240p. 1988. mass mkt. 5.99 (*0-446-34416-8*) Warner Bks.

Treating & Preventing Obesity. William G. Johnson. (Advances in Eating Disorders Ser.: Vol. 1). 1987. 73.25 (*0-89232-814-2*) Jai Pr.

Treating Anger, Anxiety, & Depression in Children & Adolescents: A Cognitive-Behavioral Perspective. Jerry Wilde. LC 95-36561. 187p. 1995. 39.95 (*1-56032-481-3*); pap. 19.95 (*1-56032-482-1*) Accel Devel.

***Treating Anxiety Disorders.** Walton T. Roth & Irvin D. Yalom. LC 96-28708. (Library of Current Clinical Technique). 1996. write for info. (*0-7879-0316-7*) Jossey-Bass.

***Treating Anxiety Disorders Across Cultures.** Steven Friedman. LC 97-13509. 1997. write for info. (*1-57230-237-2*) Guilford Pr.

***Treating Anxiety Disorders with a Cognitive-Behavioral Approach & the Eye-Movement Technique: A Viewer's Guide.** unabridged ed. Larry D. Smyth. 51p. (Orig.). 1996. pap. 6.00 (*1-889287-01-6*) RTR Publng.

Treating Arthritis: Medicine, Myth, & Magic. Felix Fernandez-Madrid. LC 89-9140. (Illus.). 312p. 1989. 22.95 (*0-306-43185-8*, Plenum Insight) Plenum.

Treating Attachment Abuse: A Compassionate Approach. Steven Stosny. LC 95-7295. (Illus.). 304p. 1995. 44.95 (*0-8261-8960-1*) Springer Pub.

Treating Auditory Processing Difficulties in Children. Christine Sloan. (Illus.). 229p. (Orig.). (C). 1991. reprint ed. pap. text ed. 34.95 (*1-879105-15-2*, A068) Singular Publishing.

Treating Bites & Stings. Jennifer Holvoet et al. (Taking Care of Simple Injuries Ser.). (Illus.). 80p. (Orig.). 1979. Set. pap. 149.00 (*0-685-05761-5*) PRO-ED.

Treating Borderline Patients: The Major Clinical Explorers. Ed. by Joseph LeBoit & Attilio Capponi. LC 95-4050. 538p. 1995. pap. 45.00 (*1-56821-525-8*) Aronson.

Treating Bruises & Nosebleeds. Jennifer Holvoet et al. (Taking Care of Simple Injuries Ser.). (Illus.). 64p. (Orig.). 1979. Set. pap. text ed. 149.00 (*0-685-05762-3*) PRO-ED.

Treating Burns. Jennifer Holvoet et al. (Taking Care of Simple Injuries Ser.). (Illus.). 64p. (Orig.). 1979. Set. pap. text ed. 149.00 (*0-685-05763-1*) PRO-ED.

Treating Cancer with Chinese Herbs. Hong-yen Hsu. 346p. 1993. pap. 12.95 (*0-941942-04-X*) Orient Heal Arts.

Treating Cerebral Palsy: For Clinicians by Clinicians. Ed. by Eugene T. McDonald. LC 86-22568. (For Clinicians by Clinicians Ser.). (Illus.). 312p. 1987. pap. text ed. 31.00 (*0-89079-141-4*, 1412) PRO-ED.

Treating Character Disorders. Peter L. Giovacchini. LC 93-37631. 552p. 1994. pap. 45.00 (*1-56821-158-9*) Aronson.

Treating Child Abuse & Family Violence in Hospitals: A Program for Training & Services. Kathleen M. White et al. 186p. 35.00 (*0-669-20822-1*, Lexington) Jossey-Bass.

Treating Child-Abusive Families: Intervention Based on Skills Training Principles. Jeffrey A. Kelly. (Applied Clinical Psychology Ser.). 234p. 1983. 42.50 (*0-306-41417-1*, Plenum Pr) Plenum.

Treating Child Sex Offenders & Their Victims: A Practical Guide. Anna C. Salter. 320p. (C). 1988. text ed. 52.00 (*0-8039-3181-6*); pap. text ed. 24.00 (*0-8039-3182-4*) Sage.

Treating Children in Groups: A Behavioral Approach. Sheldon D. Rose. LC 78-189609. (Jossey-Bass Behavioral Science Ser.). 239p. reprint ed. pap. 68.20 (*0-8357-6890-2*, 2037942) Bks Demand.

Treating Chronic Pain: The Healing Partnership. A. M. Friedman. (Illus.). 335p. 1992. 27.50 (*0-306-44121-7*, Plenum Insight) Plenum.

Treating Chronically Mentally Ill Women. Leona L. Bachrach & Carol C. Nadelson. LC 87-31830. (Clinical Practice Ser.: No. 1). 184p. 1988. text ed. 25.00 (*0-88048-144-7*, 8144) Am Psychiatric.

Treating Coexisting Psychiatric & Addictive Disorders: A Practical Guide. Ed. by Norman S. Miller. LC 94-4696. 1994. 24.95 (*0-89486-972-8*, 1499) Hazelden.

Treating Conduct & Oppositional. Horne. (Practitioner Guidebook Ser.). (C). 1992. pap. text ed. 31.50 (*0-205-14371-7*, H4371, Longwood Div) Allyn.

Treating Couples. Ed. by Hilda Kessler. (Library of Current Clinical Technique). 304p. (Orig.). 1996. pap. 26.95 (*0-7879-0205-5*) Jossey-Bass.

Treating Couples: The Intersystem Model of the Marriage Council of Philadelphia. Ed. by Gerald R. Weeks. LC 88-24231. 368p. 1989. text ed. 42.95 (*0-87630-534-6*) Brunner-Mazel.

***Treating Depressed Children: A Therapeutic Manual of Cognitive Behavioral Interventions.** Charma D. Dudley. 160p. 1996. text ed. 39.95 (*1-57224-061-X*) New Harbinger.

Treating Depression. Ed. by Ira D. Glick. LC 95-16853. (Library of Current Clinical Technique). 244p. 32.95 (*0-7879-0144-X*) Jossey-Bass.

Treating Depression in Children. Johnny L. Matson. (Practitioner Guidebook Ser.). (C). 1992. text ed. 46.50 (*0-205-14415-2*, H4415, Longwood Div); pap. text ed. 31.50 (*0-205-14414-4*, H4414, Longwood Div) Allyn.

Treating Difficult Personality Disorders. Michael Rosenbluth & Irvin D. Yalom. LC 96-8761. (Jossey-Bass Library of Current Clinical Technique). 219p. 1996. pap. 24.95 (*0-7879-0315-9*) Jossey-Bass.

Treating Disordered Speech Motor Control: For Clinicians by Clinicians. Ed. by Deanie Vogel & Michael Cannito. LC 90-9167. (For Clinicians by Clinicians Ser.). 410p. 1991. pap. text ed. 36.00 (*0-89079-299-2*, 1943) PRO-ED.

Treating Dissociative Identity Disorder. Ed. by James L. Spira. (Psychology Ser.). 416p. 34.95 (*0-7879-0157-1*) Jossey-Bass.

Treating Dissociative Identity Disorder. James L. Spira. (Jossey-Bass Library of Current Clinical Technique). 1995. write for info. (*0-614-08075-4*) Jossey-Bass.

***Treating Dissociative Identity Disorder.** James L. Spira. (Jossey Bass Library Of Current Clinical). 1996. pap. text ed. 27.95 (*0-7879-0329-9*) Jossey-Bass.

Treating Drug Abusers: New Directions. Gerald A. Bennett. 200p. 1989. 49.50 (*0-415-02039-5*, A3461); pap. 15.95 (*0-415-05837-6*, A5206) Routledge.

***Treating Drug Abusers Effectively.** Ed. by Daniel M. Fox et al. (Illus.). 448p. (C). 1996. text ed. 59.95 (*1-57718-041-0*) Blackwell Pubs.

Treating Drug Abusers Effectively: Researchers Talk with Policy Makers. Harry Nelson. (Illus.). 18p. (Orig.). 1996. pap. write for info. (*1-887748-01-6*) Milbank Memorial.

Treating Drug Problems, Vol. 1. Institute of Medicine Staff. Ed. by Dean R. Gerstein & Henrick J. Harwood. 356p. 1990. text ed. 29.95 (*0-309-04285-2*) Natl Acad Pr.

Treating Drug Problems, Vol. 2. Ed. by Dean R. Gerstein & Henrick J. Harwood. LC 90-6633. 328p. 1992. reprint ed. pap. 93.50 (*0-608-02331-0*, 2062972) Bks Demand.

Treating Eating Disorders. Ed. by Joellen Werne. (Psychology Ser.). 416p. 34.95 (*0-7879-0159-8*) Jossey-Bass.

***Treating Eating Disorders.** Joellen Werne. 1996. pap. text ed. 27.95 (*0-7879-0330-2*) Jossey-Bass.

Treating Families of Brain Injury Survivors. Paul R. Sachs. LC 91-4612. (Series on Rehabilitation: Vol. 9). 232p. 1991. 33.95 (*0-8261-6920-1*) Springer Pub.

Treating Family of Origin Problems: A Cognitive Approach. Richard C. Bedrosian & George D. Bozicas. LC 93-33386. 384p. 1994. lib. bdg. 38.95 (*0-89862-178-X*) Guilford Pr.

Treating Fearful Dental Patients: A Patient Management Handbook. 2nd ed. Philip Weinstein et al. (Illus.). 359p. (C). 1995. pap. write for info. (*1-880291-01-0*) Cont Dental Educ.

Treating Food Allergy, My Way! see Food Allergy Book: The Foods That Cause You Pain & Discomfort & How to Eliminate Them from Your Diet

Treating IBD: A Patient's Guide to the Medical & Surgical Management of Inflammatory Bowel Disease. Ed. by Lawrence J. Brandt & Penny Steiner-Grossman. (Illus.). 219p. 1989. pap. text ed. 19.00 (*0-88167-532-6*, 1996) Lppncott-Raven.

Treating Incest: A Multiple System Perspective. Terry S. Trepper. LC 87-33344. 1987. pap. 10.95 (*0-86656-739-9*) Haworth Pr.

Treating Incest: A Multiple Systems Perspective. Ed. by Terry S. Trepper & Mary Jo Barrett. LC 86-4719. (Journal of Psychotherapy & the Family: Vol. 2, No. 2). 126p. 1986. text ed. 34.95 (*0-86656-512-4*) Haworth Pr.

Treating Industrial Waste Interferences at Publicly-Owned Treatment Works. Edward D. Wetzel & Scott B. Murphy. LC 90-24376. (Pollution Technology Review Ser.: No. 203). (Illus.). 381p. 1991. 54.00 (*0-8155-1282-1*) Noyes.

***Treating Intellectually Disabled Sex Offenders: A Model Residential Program.** J. Haaven et al. Ed. by Evan Bear. 152p. (Orig.). 1990. pap. 24.00 (*1-884444-30-X*) Safer Soc.

Treating Male Infertility: New Possibilities. Ed. by G. M. Colpi & M. Balerna. (Progress in Reproductive Biology & Medicine Ser.: Vol. 16). (Illus.). xx, 314p. 1994. 259.25 (*3-8055-5892-9*) S Karger.

Treating Malpractice: Report of the Twentieth Century Fund Task Force on Medical Malpractice Insurance. 70p. (Orig.). (C). 1986. pap. text ed. 7.50 (*0-87078-173-1*) TCFP-PPP.

Treating Memory Impairments: A Memory Book & Other Strategies. Vicki S. Dohrman. 210p. 1994. pap. text ed. 45.00 (*0-88450-178-7*, 3041) Commun Skill.

Treating Men Who Batter: Theory, Practice, & Programs. Ed. by P. Lynn Caesar & L. Kevin Hamberger. (Focus on Men Ser.: Vol. 5). 288p. 1989. 35.95 (*0-8261-6340-8*) Springer Pub.

Treating Menstrual Cramps Naturally. Susan M. Lark. Ed. by Phyllis Herman. (Women's Ser.). 48p. 1996. 3.95 (*0-87983-712-8*) Keats.

Treating Mentally Ill Substance Abusers. Rosenberg. Date not set. write for info. (*1-56372-039-6*) Buttrwrth-Heinemann.

***Treating Mind & Body: Essays in the History of Science, Professions, & Society under Extreme Conditions.** Geoffrey Cocks. LC 97-20184. 1997. write for info. (*1-56000-310-3*) Transaction Pubs.

Treating Nicotine Addiction: A Challenge for the Recovery Professional. Vincent C. Pletcher et al. 60p. (Orig.). 1990. pap. 7.95 (*0-89486-715-6*, 5531B) Hazelden.

Treating Obsessive-Compulsive. Samuel M. Turner. (Practitioner Guidebook Ser.). (C). 1988. text ed. 46.50 (*0-205-14489-6*, H4489, Longwood Div) Allyn.

Treating Oilfield Emulsions. 4th ed. Ron Baker. Ed. by Kathy Bork. (Illus.). 115p. 1990. pap. text ed. 25.00 (*0-88698-137-9*, 3.50040) PETEX.

***Treating Panic Disorder & Agoraphobia: A Step-by-Step Clinical Guide.** Elke Zuercher-White. 208p. 1997. text ed. 44.95 (*1-57224-084-9*) New Harbinger.

***Treating Patients with Memories of Abuse: Legal Risk Management.** Samuel Knapp & Leon Vandecreek. LC 97-15987. 1997. write for info. (*1-55798-441-7*) Am Psychol.

Treating People in Families. William C. Nichols. (Family Therapy Ser.). (Illus.). 1995. lib. bdg. 35.00 (*1-57230-036-1*, 0036) Guilford Pr.

***Treating People with Chronic Disease: A Psychological Guide.** Carol D. Goodheart & Martha H. Lansing. (Psychologists in Independent Practice Book Ser.). 229p. (Orig.). 1996. pap. text ed. 24.95 (*1-55798-387-9*, 431-7750) Am Psychol.

Treating Personality Disorders. Ed. by David A. Adler. LC 87-646993. (New Directions for Mental Health Services Ser.: No. 47). 1990. 19.00 (*1-55542-811-8*) Jossey-Bass.

Treating Phonological Disorders in Children: Metaphon - Theory to Practice. 2nd ed. Janet Howell & Elizabeth Dean. 222p. (Orig.). 1994. pap. text ed. 52.50 (*1-56593-386-9*, 0815) Singular Publishing.

Treating PTSD: Cognitive-Behavioral Strategies. Ed. by David W. Foy. LC 92-1463. (Treatment Manuals for Practitioners Ser.). 172p. 1992. pap. text ed. 19.95 (*0-89862-220-4*); lib. bdg. 45.00 (*0-89862-209-3*) Guilford Pr.

Treating Resistant Depression. Ed. by Joseph Zohar & R. H. Belmaker. LC 85-14424. 496p. 1987. text ed. 50.00 (*0-89335-225-X*) PMA Pub Corp.

Treating Schizophrenia. Werner M. Mendel. LC 88-46080. (Social & Behavioral Sciences Ser.). 264p. 34.95 (*1-55542-151-2*) Jossey-Bass.

Treating Schizophrenia. Ed. by Sophia Vinogradov. LC 94-44052. (Social & Behavioral Sciences-Health Ser.). 392p. 29.95 (*0-7879-0079-6*) Jossey-Bass.

***Treating School-Age Children.** Hans Steiner & Irvin D. Yalom. LC 97-20811. (Volume in the Jossey-Bass Library of Current Clinical Technique). 1997. pap. write for info. (*0-7879-0877-0*); pap. write for info. (*0-7879-0878-9*) Jossey-Bass.

***Treating Sex Offenders in Correctional Institutions & Outpatient Clinics: A Guide to Clinical Practice.** William E. Prendergast. 220p. 1991. pap. 19.95 (*1-56024-207-8*) Haworth Pr.

Treating Sex Offenders in Correctional Institutions & Outpatient Clinics: A Guide to Clinical Practice. William E. Prendergast. 220p. 1991. 49.95 (*1-56024-206-X*) Haworth Pr.

Treating Sexual Disorders. Randolph S. Charlton. LC 96-8762. (Jossey-Bass Library of Current Clinical Technique). 1996. write for info. (*0-7879-0311-6*) Jossey-Bass.

Treating Sexual Distress: Integrative Systems Therapy. Jane D. Woody. 272p. (C). 1992. text ed. 48.00 (*0-8039-4199-4*); pap. text ed. 22.95 (*0-8039-4200-1*) Sage.

Treating Sexual Problems in Medical Practice. David K. Kentsmith & Merrill T. Eaton. LC 78-16836. (Illus.). 1979. pap. text ed. 15.95 (*0-668-04050-5*, Arco) Macmillan Gen Ref.

Treating Sexually Abused Children & Their Families. Beverly James & Maria Nasjleti. 168p. 1983. pap. 19.95 (*0-89106-023-5*, 7310) Davies-Black.

Treating Sinus, Migraine, & Cluster Headaches, My Way! Vol. II: An Allergist's Approach to Headache Treatment. William E. Walsh. LC 93-90632. (The Food Allergy Book Ser.). 269p. (Orig.). 1993. pap. 12.95 (*0-9631544-5-1*) ACA Pubns.

Treating Stress in Families. Ed. by Charles R. Figley. LC 88-8554. (Psychosocial Stress Ser.: No. 13). 300p. 1989. text ed. 45.95 (*0-87630-530-3*) Brunner-Mazel.

Treating Substance Abuse: Theory & Technique. Ed. by Frederick Rotgers et al. (Guilford Substance Abuse Ser.). 328p. 1995. lib. bdg. 35.00 (*1-57230-025-6*, 0025) Guilford Pr.

Treating Suicidelike Behavior in a Preschooler. Paul V. Trad. LC 89-36105. 490p. 1990. 60.00 (*0-8236-6649-2*, BN 06649) Intl Univs Pr.

Treating Survivors of Satanist Abuse. Ed. by Valerie Sinason. LC 93-41461. 332p. (C). 1994. pap. 19.95 (*0-415-10543-9*); text ed. 62.95 (*0-415-10542-0*) Routledge.

Treating Survivors of Satanist Abuse: An Invisible Trauma. Valerie Sinason. 320p. (C). 1994. pap. text ed. 18.95 (*0-415-10608-7*) Routledge.

Treating Survivors of Satanist Abuse: Invisible Trauma. Ed. by Valerie Sinason. 320p. (C). 1994. pap. 18.95 (*0-415-10607-9*, Routledge NY) Routledge.

Treating Teenage Drug Abuse in a Day Care Setting. William Feigelman. LC 89-26538. 160p. 1990. text ed. 49.95 (*0-275-93379-2*, C3379, Greenwood Pr) Greenwood.

Treating the Adult Survivor of Childhood Sexual Abuse: A Psychoanalytic Perspective. Jody M. Davies & Mary G. Frawley. LC 93-34377. 304p. 1994. 37.00 (*0-465-06633-X*) Basic.

***Treating the African American Male Substance Abuser.** Mark Sanders. 104p. 1996. pap. 9.95 (*0-614-21700-8*, 1259) Kazi Pubns.

Treating the African American Male Substance Abuser. Mark Sanders. 100p. 1993. pap. text ed. 10.00 (*0-9637910-0-1*) Wnds of Change.

Treating the Alcoholic: A Developmental Model of Recovery. Stephanie Brown. LC 85-3172. (Personality Processes Ser.). 348p. 1985. text ed. 62.50 (*0-471-81736-8*) Wiley.

***Treating the Alcoholic: A Developmental Model of Recovery.** Stephanie Brown. 1996. pap. text ed. 29.95 (*0-471-16163-2*) Wiley.

Treating the Alcoholic: A Social Work Challange: A Special Issue of Social Casework. 72p. 1989. pap. 8.00 (*0-87304-234-4*) Families Intl.

Treating the Changing Family: Handling Normative & Unusual Events. Michele Harway. LC 95-11794. (Couples & Family Dynamics & Treatment Ser.). 384p. 1995. text ed. 47.50 (*0-471-07905-7*) Wiley.

Treating the Chemically Dependent & Their Families. Ed. by Dennis C. Daley & Miriam S. Raskin. (Sourcebooks for the Human Services Ser.: Vol. 16). (Illus.). 244p. (C). 1990. text ed. 52.00 (*0-8039-3297-9*); pap. text ed. 24.95 (*0-8039-3298-7*) Sage.

Treating the Criminal Offender. 3rd ed. A. B. Smith & Louis Berlin. LC 88-16877. (Criminal Justice & Public Safety Ser.). (Illus.). 444p. 1988. 55.00 (*0-306-42885-7*, Plenum Pr) Plenum.

***Treating the Disorder, Treating the Family.** Ed. by Jim Orford. LC 87-3159. 310p. 1987. reprint ed. pap. 88.40 (*0-608-03672-2*, 2064498) Bks Demand.

Treating the Earth as If We Plan to Stay: A Resource Guide to Individual Action. Anita Bash et al. (Illus.). 28p. (Orig.). 1990. pap. 3.00 (*0-9626493-0-9*) Beyond War Fndtn.

Treating the Elderly. Ed. by Javaid I. Sheikh & Irvin D. Yalom. (Jossey-Bass Library of Current Clinical Technique Ser.). 264p. (Orig.). 1996. pap. 24.95 (*0-7879-0219-5*) Jossey-Bass.

Treating the Elderly with Psychotherapy. Molyn Leszcz. Ed. by Joel Sadavoy. LC 86-10487. 390p. 1987. 57.50 (*0-8236-6647-6*, BN-06647) Intl Univs Pr.

Treating the Headache Patient. Ed. by Roger K. Cady & Anthony W. Fox. LC 94-25658. 384p. 1994. 135.00 (*0-8247-9109-6*) Dekker.

Treating the Homeless: Urban Psychiatry's Challenge. Ed. by Billy E. Jones. LC 85-30626. (Clinical Insights Ser.). 126p. reprint ed. pap. 36.00 (*0-8357-7833-9*, 2036207) Bks Demand.

Treating the Homeless Mentally Ill: A Task Force Report of the American Psychiatric Association. Ed. by H. Richard Lamb et al. LC 92-10470. 315p. 1992. text ed. 35.00 (*0-89042-236-2*, 2236) Am Psychiatric.

Treating the Long-Term Mentally Ill. H. Richard Lamb. LC 82-48391. (Social & Behavioral Science Ser.). 270p. 1982. 36.95 (*0-87589-553-0*) Jossey-Bass.

Treating the Long-Term Mentally Ill. H. Richard Lamb. LC 82-48391. (Jossey-Bass Social & Behavioral Science Ser.). 270p. reprint ed. pap. 77.00 (*0-7837-6514-2*, 2045626) Bks Demand.

Treating the Mentally Disabled. Ed. by Gary E. McCuen. (Ideas in Conflict Ser.). (Illus.). 140p. 1988. lib. bdg. 12.95 (*0-86596-066-6*) G E M.

Treating the Neurotic Patient in Brief Psychotherapy. Ed. by Althea J. Horner. LC 93-74779. 256p. 1994. pap. 25.00 (*1-56821-212-7*) Aronson.

Treating the Poor: A Personal Sojourn Through the Rise & Fall of Community Mental Health. 2nd ed. Matthew P. Dumont. Ed. by Judy Kaplan. LC 92-97289. 149p. (Orig.). 1994. 26.95 (*0-9634975-1-0*) Dymphna Pr.

Treating the Poor: A Personal Sojourn Through the Rise & Fall of Community Mental Health. 2nd ed. Matthew P. Dumont. Ed. by Judy Kaplan. LC 92-97289. 149p. (Orig.). 1994. pap. 15.95 (*0-9634975-0-2*) Dymphna Pr.

The author, a well known activist, writer & psychiatrist, played a significant role in the community mental health movement of the 60s & 70s. The book describes its antecedents & subsequent destruction against the social, economic & political events of recent American history. As a practitioner of 16 years in a low-income, immigrant community, he tells vivid stories which demonstrate how poverty drives people crazy & how the prevention & control of mental illness requires community organization, pollution control, jobs & housing as much as case finding & treatment. Documented with research & personal experience, the book is also a critique of biological psychiatry with its emphasis on genetic etiologies & reliance on drugs. It warns against privatization, managed care, & the continued medical hegemony of mental health as part of current models of health care "reform." Call or write for information to order: Dymphna Press, Box 44, Belmont, MA 02178. 617-489-2126. ***Publisher Provided Annotation.***

***Treating the Psychological Consequences of HIV.** Michael F. O'Connor & Irvin D. Yalom. LC 96-31519. (Library of Current Clinical Technique). 1996. write for info. (*0-7879-0314-0*) Jossey-Bass.

Treating the Remarried Family. Clifford J. Sager et al. LC 82-17811. 406p. 1986. text ed. 47.95 (*0-87630-323-8*) Brunner-Mazel.

Treating the School Age Stutterer: A Guide for Clinicians, No. 14. Carl W. Dell, Jr. LC 79-67284. 110p. (Orig.). pap. 2.00 (*0-933388-11-X*) Stuttering Fnd Am.

Treating the Self: Elements of Clinical Self-Psychology. Ernest S. Wolf. LC 88-4860. 194p. 1988. lib. bdg. 27.50 (*0-89862-717-6*) Guilford Pr.

Treating the Sexual Offender. Barry M. Maletzky. 320p. (C). 1990. text ed. 49.95 (*0-8039-3662-1*); pap. text ed. 23.50 (*0-8039-3663-X*) Sage.

Treating the Troubled Family. Nathan W. Ackerman. LC 94-71150. 320p. 1994. pap. 35.00 (*1-56821-268-2*) Aronson.

Treating the Unmanageable Adolescent: A Guide to Oppositional Defiant & Conduct Disorders. Neil I. Bernstein. LC 96-15620. 368p. 1997. 40.00 (*1-56821-630-0*) Aronson.

Treating the Whole Patient: BPH & Beyond. Ed. by J. E. Altwein & R. S. Kirby. (Journal Ser.: Vol. 29, Suppl. 1, 1996). (Illus.). iv, 52p. 1996. pap. 21.75 (*3-8055-6295-0*) S Karger.

Treating the Young Male Victim of Sexual Assault: Issues & Intervention Strategies. Eugene Porter. LC 86-60720. (Illus.). 86p. 1994. reprint ed. pap. 12.50 (*1-884444-08-3*) Safer Soc.

Treating Traumatized Children: New Insights & Creative Interventions. Beverly James. 320p. 1989. 36.95 (*0-669-20994-5*) Free Pr.

Treating Troubled Adolescents: A Family Therapy Approach. H. Charles Fishman. LC 87-47838. 336p. 1988. 39.00 (*0-465-08742-6*) Basic.

Treating Troubled Children & Their Families. Ellen F. Wachtel. LC 94-8553. 320p. 1994. lib. bdg. 32.50 (*0-89862-007-4*, C2007) Guilford Pr.

Treating Type A Behavior - & Your Heart. Meyer Friedman & Diane Ulmer. (Heart Care Titles Ser.). 1985. mass mkt. 5.95 (*0-449-20826-5*, Crest) Fawcett.

Treating Victims of Child Sexual Abuse: Implications for Clinical Practice. Ed. by John Briere. LC 87-646993. (New Directions for Mental Health Services Ser.: No. 51). 1991. 19.00 (*1-55542-775-8*) Jossey-Bass.

***Treating Victims of Torture: Theoretical, Cross-Cultural, & Clinical Implications.** Elsass. LC 97-21088. 1997. 40.00 (*0-8147-2201-6*) NYU Pr.

Treating Vision Problems in the Older Adult. Melore. 192p. (gr. 13). 1996. pap. text ed. 36.95 (*0-8151-5700-2*) Mosby Yr Bk.

Treating Women Molested in Childhood. Catherine Classen. LC 94-39886. (Social & Behavioral Sciences-Health Ser.). 276p. 29.95 (*0-7879-0078-8*) Jossey-Bass.

Treating Women's Fear of Failure. Ed. by Esther D. Rothblum & Ellen Cole. LC 87-25134. (Women & Therapy Ser.: Vol. 6, No. 3). 105p. 1988. text ed. 29.95 (*0-86656-676-7*) Haworth Pr.

Treating Women's Fear of Failure: From Worry to Enlightenment. Ed. by Esther D. Rothblum & Ellen Cole. LC 87-25132. (Women & Therapy Ser.: Vol. 6, No. 3). 105p. 1988. pap. text ed. 9.95 (*0-918393-41-8*) Harrington Pk.

Treatise: Arms Race. Spencer Walaitis. Ed. by David Wilde. (Sun Also Sets Ser.). (Illus.). 235p. (Orig.). 1993. pap. text ed. write for info. (*1-882204-04-2*) Wilde Pub.

Treatise see Technique of Etching

Treatise Against Dicing, Dancing, Plays & Interludes. John Northbrooke. LC 77-149667. reprint ed. 29.50 (*0-404-04793-9*) AMS Pr.

Treatise Against Judicial Astrology, 2 pts. John Chamber. LC 77-6872. (English Experience Ser.: No. 860). 1977. reprint ed. lib. bdg. 20.00 (*90-221-0860-0*) Walter J Johnson.

Treatise Concerning Enthusiasme. Meric Casaubon. LC 77-119864. 1970. reprint ed. 50.00 (*0-8201-1077-9*) Schol Facsimiles.

Treatise Concerning Eternal & Immutable Morality & a Treatise of Freewill. Ralph Cudworth. (Collected Works: Vol. II). viii, 95p. 1979. reprint ed. 110.00 (*3-487-06010-8*) G Olms Pubs.

Treatise Concerning Political Enquiry & the Liberty of the Press. Tunis Wortman. LC 78-122162. (Civil Liberties in American History Ser.). 1970. reprint ed. lib. bdg. 39.50 (*0-306-71967-3*) Da Capo.

Treatise Concerning Religious Affections. Jonathan Edwards. (Notable American Authors Ser.). 1992. reprint ed. lib. bdg. 75.00 (*0-7812-2768-2*) Rprt Serv.

Treatise, Concerning the Causes of the Magnificence & Greatness of Cities. Giovanni Botero. LC 79-84090. (English Experience Ser.: No. 910). 128p. 1979. reprint ed. lib. bdg. 25.00 (*90-221-0910-0*) Walter J Johnson.

Treatise Concerning the Division Between the Spirituality & Temporality. German C. Saint. LC 72-6027. (English Experience Ser.: No. 453). 94p. 1972. reprint ed. 20.00 (*90-221-0453-2*) Walter J Johnson.

Treatise Concerning the Medicinal Philosophic Stone. Paracelsus. 1989. pap. 3.95 (*1-55818-161-X*) Holmes Pub.

Treatise Concerning the Motion of the Sea & Winds: Together with, De Motu Marium et Ventorum. Issak Vossius. LC 93-29679. 1993. 75.00 (*0-8201-1486-3*) Schol Facsimiles.

Treatise Concerning the Principles of Human Knowledge. George Berkeley. Ed. & Intro. by Kenneth Winkler. LC 82-2876. (HPC Classics Ser.). 156p. (C). 1982. pap. text ed. 5.95 (*0-915145-39-1*); lib. bdg. 21.95 (*0-915145-40-5*) Hackett Pub.

Treatise Concerning the Principles of Human Knowledge: Three Dialogues Between Hylas & Philonous. George Berkeley. 288p. (C). 1985. pap. 8.00 (*0-87548-446-8*) Open Court.

Treatise How by the Worde of God, Christian Mens Almose Ought to Be Distributed. Martin Bucer. LC 76-57360. (English Experience Ser.). 1977. reprint ed. lib. bdg. 10.00 (*90-221-0779-5*) Walter J Johnson.

Treatise in Thirty Verses on Mere-Consciousness. Swati Ganguly. (C). 1992. 22.00 (*81-208-0924-6*, Pub. by Motilal Banarsidass II) S Asia.

Treatise in 30 Verses on Mere Consciousness - A Critical English Translation of Vijnaptimatratatrimsika. Swati Ganguly. (C). 1992. 16.00 (*0-8364-2801-3*, Pub. by Motilal Banarsidass II) S Asia.

Treatise of Civil Government & a Letter Concerning Toleration. John Locke. Ed. by Charles L. Sherman. 1965. pap. text ed. 10.95 (*0-89197-519-5*) Irvington.

Treatise of Commerce. Wheeler John. Ed. by Mira Wilkins. LC 76-29979. (European Business Ser.). 1977. reprint ed. lib. bdg. 41.95 (*0-405-09745-X*) Ayer.

Treatise of Earthly-Mindedness. Jeremiah Burroughs. Ed. by Don Kistler. 219p. 1991. reprint ed. 18.95 (*1-877611-38-7*) Soli Deo Gloria.

Treatise of Ecclesiastical Discipline. Matthew Sutcliffe. LC 73-7082. (English Experience Ser.: No. 626). 1973. reprint ed. 21.00 (*90-221-0626-8*) Walter J Johnson.

Treatise of Femme Coverts: Or, the Lady's Law. Intro. by Lance E. Dickson. viii, 280p. 1974. reprint ed. text ed. 22.50 (*0-8377-2129-6*) Rothman.

***Treatise of Freewill: An Introduction to Cudworth's Treatise Concerning Eternal & Immutable Morality 1838/1891 Editions.** W. R. Scott. 182p. 1996. reprint ed. write for info. (*1-85506-125-2*) Bks Intl VA.

Treatise of Health & Long Life with the Future Means of Attaining It. Leonard Lessius & Luigi Cornaro. Ed. by Robert J. Kastenbaum. Tr. by Timothy Smith. LC 78-22206. (Aging & Old Age Ser.). 1979. reprint ed. lib. bdg. 17.95 (*0-405-11821-X*) Ayer.

Treatise of Human Nature. David Hume. Ed. by L. A. Selby-Bigge & Peter H. Nidditch. 764p. 1978. pap. text ed. 17.95 (*0-19-824588-2*) OUP.

Treatise of Human Nature. David Hume. Ed. & Intro. by Ernest C. Mossner. (Classics Ser.). 688p. 1986. pap. 9.95 (*0-14-043244-2*, Penguin Classics) Viking Penguin.

Treatise of Human Nature. David Hume. 1990. reprint ed. lib. bdg. 25.95 (*0-89966-655-8*) Buccaneer Bks.

Treatise of Lorenzo Valla on the Donation of Constantine: Text & Translation into English. Christopher B. Coleman. (Renaissance Society of America Reprint Text Ser.). 188p. 1993. pap. 16.95 (*0-8020-7734-X*) U of Toronto Pr.

Treatise of Morall Philosophie. rev. ed. William Baldwin. LC 67-10126. 1967. reprint ed. 50.00 (*0-8201-1003-5*) Schol Facsimiles.

Treatise of Musick, Speculative, Practical & Historical. Alexander Malcolm. LC 69-16676. (Music Ser.). 1970. reprint ed. lib. bdg. 75.00 (*0-306-71099-4*) Da Capo.

Treatise of One Hundred & Thirteen Diseases of the Eyes. Richard Banister. LC 79-37135. (English Experience Ser.: No. 297). 480p. 1971. reprint ed. 35.00 (*90-221-0297-1*) Walter J Johnson.

Treatise of Orders & Plain Dignities. Charles Loyseau. Ed. by Howell A. Lloyd. (Cambridge Texts in the History of Political Thought Ser.). 288p. (C). 1994. text ed. 65.00 (*0-521-40519-X*) Cambridge U Pr.

Treatise of Orders & Plain Dignities. Charles Loyseau. Ed. by Howell A. Lloyd. (Cambridge Texts in the History of Political Thought Ser.). 288p. (C). 1994. pap. text ed. 22.95 (*0-521-45624-X*) Cambridge U Pr.

Treatise of Schemes & Tropes. Richard Sherry. LC 61-5030. 1977. reprint ed. 50.00 (*0-8201-1258-5*) Schol Facsimiles.

Treatise of the Canker of Englands Common Wealth. Gerard Malynes. LC 77-7412. (English Experience Ser.: No. 880). 1977. reprint ed. lib. bdg. 15.00 (*90-221-0880-5*) Walter J Johnson.

Treatise of the Contract of Partnership by Pothier. Owen D. Tudor. LC 94-77469. xii, 116p. 1994. reprint ed. 35.00 (*0-89941-897-X*, 308390) W S Hein.

Treatise of the Donation of Gyfts & Endowment of Possessyons Gyven & Graunted Unto Sylvester Pope of Rome by Constantyne Emperour of Rome. Constantine I. Tr. by William Marshall. LC 79-84096. (English Experience Ser.: No. 916). 152p. 1979. reprint ed. lib. bdg. 35.00 (*90-221-0916-X*) Walter J Johnson.

Treatise of the First Part of Chirurgerie. Alexander Read. LC 76-57411. (English Experience Ser.: No. 826). 1977. reprint ed. lib. bdg. 24.00 (*90-221-0826-0*) Walter J Johnson.

Treatise of the Hypochondriack & Hysterick Diseases. Bernard Mandeville. LC 76-45623. 1976. reprint ed. 60.00 (*0-8201-1277-1*) Schol Facsimiles.

Treatise of the Hypochondriack & Hysterick Passions. Bernard De Mandeville. LC 75-16717. (Classics in Psychiatry Ser.). 1976. reprint ed. 25.95 (*0-405-07445-X*) Ayer.

Treatise of the Law of Judgments, 3 vols., Set. 5th ed. A. C. Freeman. Ed. by Edward W. Tuttle. 3760p. 1993. reprint ed. 295.00 (*0-9630106-6-2*) Lawbk Exchange.

Treatise of the Law Relative to Merchant Ships & Seamen. 14th ed. Charles Abbott et al. cii, 1356p. 1993. reprint ed. 150.00 (*0-8377-1908-9*) Rothman.

Treatise of the Lawes of the Forest. John Manwood. LC 76-57398. (English Experience Ser.: No. 814). 1977. reprint ed. lib. bdg. 60.00 (*90-221-0814-7*) Walter J Johnson.

Treatise of the Natural Grounds & Principles of Harmony see Monuments of Music & Music Literature in Facsimile

Treatise of the Organ of Hearing. Guichard J. Duverney. LC 77-147969. reprint ed. 41.50 (*0-404-08221-1*) AMS Pr.

Treatise of the Passions & Faculties of the Soule of Man. Edward Reynolds. LC 79-161935. (History of Psychology Ser.). 1971. 75.00 (*0-8201-1095-7*) Schol Facsimiles.

Treatise of the Plague: Containing the Nature, Signes & Accidents of the Same. Thomas Lodge. LC 79-84119. (English Experience Ser.: No. 938). 92p. 1979. reprint ed. lib. bdg. 20.00 (*90-221-0938-0*) Walter J Johnson.

Treatise of the Pleas of the Crown: Or, a System of the Principal... William G. Hawkins. LC 70-37977. (American Law Series: The Formative Law). 876p. 1972. reprint ed. 64.95 (*0-405-04020-2*) Ayer.

Treatise of the Pool: Al-Mawala al Hawdiyya. Obadyah Maimonides. Tr. by Paul Fenton. 1981. 23.00 (*0-900860-87-1*, Pub. by Octagon Pr UK) ISHK.

Treatise of the Relative Rights & Duties of Belligerent & Neutral Powers in Maritime Affairs: In Which the Principles of Armed Neutralities & the Opinions of Hubner & Schlegel Are Fully Discussed. Robert Ward. viii, 180p. 1988. reprint ed. lib. bdg. 27.50 (*0-8377-1347-1*) Rothman.

Treatise of the Structure & Preservation of the Violin. Jacob A. Otto. 1976. lib. bdg. 45.00 (*0-403-03760-3*) Scholarly.

Treatise of the Structure & Preservation of the Violin. Jacob A. Otto. 1988. reprint ed. lib. bdg. 59.00 (*0-7812-0345-7*) Rprt Serv.

***Treatise of the Three Impostors & the Problem of Enlightenment.** Abraham Anderson. LC 97-7424. 192p. 1997. 52.50 (*0-8476-8430-X*); pap. 21.95 (*0-8476-8431-8*) Rowman.

Treatise of Usurie. Roger Fenton. LC 74-28855. (English Experience Ser.: No. 736). 1975. reprint ed. 20.00 (90-221-0736-1) Walter J Johnson.

Treatise of Weights, Mets & Measures of Scotland. Alexander Huntar. LC 74-80191. (English Experience Ser.: No. 671). 58p. 1974. reprint ed. 15.00 (90-221-0671-3) Walter J Johnson.

Treatise on Adhesion & Adhesives, Vol. 3. Robert L. Patrick. LC 66-11285. 271p. reprint ed. pap. 77.30 (0-8357-3575-3, 2026808) Bks Demand.

Treatise on Adhesion & Adhesives, Vol. 5. Patrick. 416p. 1981. 195.00 (0-8247-1399-0) Dekker.

Treatise on Adhesion & Adhesives, Vol. 6. Patrick. 296p. 1988. 150.00 (0-8247-7587-2) Dekker.

Treatise on Adhesion & Adhesives, Vol. 7. Ed. by J. Dean Minford. 528p. 1991. 225.00 (0-8247-8112-0) Dekker.

Treatise on Adhesion & Adhesives, Vol. 2: Materials. Ed. by Robert L. Patrick. LC 66-11285. (Illus.). 568p. reprint ed. pap. 161.90 (0-8357-3574-5, 2026808) Bks Demand.

Treatise on American Citizenship. John S. Wise. (Studies in Constitutional Law). viii, 340p. 1981. reprint ed. lib. bdg. 30.00 (0-8377-1306-4) Rothman.

Treatise on Analysis, Vol. 1. Jean A. Dieudonne. (Pure & Applied Mathematics Ser.). 1960. text ed. 118.00 (0-12-215550-5) Acad Pr.

Treatise on Analytical Chemistry: Theory & Practice, Thermal Methods, Vol. 13. 2nd ed. Ed. by James D. Winefordner et al. LC 78-1707. 432p. 1993. text ed. 140.00 (0-471-80647-1) Wiley.

Treatise on Analytical Chemistry Vol. 2: Theory & Practice - Part One, Vol. 11. 2nd ed. Ed. by James D. Winefordner & Maurice M. Bursey. LC 78-1707. 311p. 1989. text ed. 150.00 (0-471-50938-8) Wiley.

Treatise on Analytical Chemistry, Pt. 1, Vol. 2: Theory & Practice. 2nd ed. Ed. by Izaak M. Kolthoff & Philip J. Elving. LC 78-1707. (Illus.). 815p. reprint ed. pap. 180.00 (0-685-20440-5, 2056452) Bks Demand.

Treatise on Analytical Chemistry, Pt. 2, Vol. 15: Analytical Chemistry of Inorganic & Organic Compounds. Izaak M. Kolthoff & Philip J. Elving. LC 78-1707. (Illus.). 509p. reprint ed. pap. 152.00 (0-685-20441-3, 2056453) Bks Demand.

Treatise on Analytical Chemistry, Vol. 7, Pt. 1: Theory & Practice. Ed. by Izaak M. Kolthoff & Philip J. Elving. LC 78-1707. (Illus.). 846p. reprint ed. pap. 180.00 (0-685-23668-4, 2032002) Bks Demand.

Treatise on Analytical Dynamics. L. A. Pars. LC 79-87498. 1979. reprint ed. 95.00 (0-918024-07-2) Ox Bow.

Treatise on Ancient Hindu Music. A. Bhattacharya. 176p. 1978. 12.95 (0-318-36325-9) Asia Bk Corp.

Treatise on Ancient Indian Music. Arun Bhattacharya. 1978. 12.00 (0-8364-0051-8) S Asia.

Treatise on Aphasia & Other Speech Defects. Henry C. Bastian. LC 78-72786. (Brainedness, Handedness, & Mental Abilities Ser.). reprint ed. 49.50 (0-404-60851-5) AMS Pr.

Treatise on Architecture: Being the Treatise by Antonio di Piero Averlino, Known As Filarete, Vol. 1: Translation. Antonio A. Filarete. Tr. by John R. Spencer. LC 65-12547. (Yale Publications in the History of Art: No. 16). reprint ed. Vol. 1 (Translation). pap. 112.50 (0-317-10501-9, 2013374) Bks Demand.

Treatise on Architecture: Being the Treatise by Antonio di Piero Averlino, Known As Filarete, Vol. 2: Facsimile. Antonio A. Filarete. Tr. by John R. Spencer. LC 65-12547. (Yale Publications in the History of Art: No. 16). reprint ed. Vol. 2 (Facsimile). pap. 52.50 (0-317-10502-7) Bks Demand.

Treatise on Atonement. Hosea Ballou. Ed. by Ernest Cassara. 1986. pap. 8.00 (0-933840-26-8, 6062, Skinner Hse Bks) Unitarian Univ.

***Treatise on Attorneys & Counsellors at Law: Comprising the Rules & Legal Principles Applicable to the Vocation of the Lawyer, & Those Governing...** Edward P. Weeks. LC 97-1956. xvi, 698p. 1997. reprint ed. lib. bdg. 75.00 (0-8377-2786-3) Rothman.

Treatise on Basic Philosophy, 8 vols. Mario Bunge. 1900. Set. pap. text ed. 295.00 (0-7923-0552-3, D Reidel); Set. lib. bdg. 595.00 (0-7923-0551-5, D Reidel) Kluwer Ac.

Treatise on Basic Philosophy: Epistemology & Methodology I. Mario Bunge. 424p. 1983. lib. bdg. 187.00 (90-277-1511-4, D Reidel) Kluwer Ac.

Treatise on Basic Philosophy: Epistemology & Methodology II, Vol. 6. Mario Bunge. 308p. 1983. pap. text ed. 78.50 (90-277-1635-8, D Reidel); lib. bdg. 146.00 (90-277-1634-X, D Reidel) Kluwer Ac.

Treatise on Basic Philosophy Vol. 8: Ethics: The Good & the Right. Mario Bunge. 448p. (C). 1989. lib. bdg. 198.00 (90-277-2839-9, D Reidel) Kluwer Ac.

Treatise on Basic Philosophy, Vol. 3: Ontology I--the Furniture of the World. Mario Bunge. 364p. 1977. lib. bdg. 141.50 (90-277-0780-4, D Reidel) Kluwer Ac.

Treatise on Basic Philosophy, Vol. 7: Epistemology & Methodology III: Philosophy of Science & Technology Pt I: Formal & Physical Sciences. Mario Bunge. 272p. 1985. pap. text ed. 57.50 (90-277-1904-7, D Reidel); lib. bdg. 112.00 (90-277-1903-9, D Reidel) Kluwer Ac.

Treatise on Basic Philosophy, Vol. 7: Epistemology & Methodology III: Philosophy of Science & Technology Pt. II: Life Science, Social Science & Technology. Mario Bunge. 352p. 1985. lib. bdg. 138.00 (90-277-1913-6, D Reidel) Kluwer Ac.

Treatise on Basic Philosophy, Vol. 7: Epistemology & Methodology III: Philosophy of Science & Technology Pt. II: Life Science, Social Science & Technology. Mario Bunge. 353p. 1985. pap. text ed. 67.50 (90-277-1914-4, D Reidel) Kluwer Ac.

Treatise on Byzantine Music. S. G. Hatherly. 162p. 1991. reprint ed. text ed. 89.00 (0-7812-9323-5) Rprt Serv.

Treatise on Carriages. unabridged ed. William Felton. (Illus.). 720p. 1996. reprint ed. 65.00 (1-879335-70-0) Astragal Pr.

Treatise on Chemistry. John W. Draper. (Notable American Authors Ser.). 1992. reprint ed. lib. bdg. 75.00 (0-7812-2697-X) Rprt Serv.

Treatise on Children's Disease. T. Datta. (C). 1984. 40.00 (0-685-36185-3, Pub. by Current Dist II) St Mut.

Treatise on Children's Diseases. Tirthankar Datta. 1984. 75.00 (0-317-38808-8, Pub. by Current Dist II) St Mut.

Treatise on Christian Perfection. Richard Treffry. 1992. reprint ed. pap. 9.99 (0-88019-286-0) Schmul Pub Co.

***Treatise on Citizenship by Birth & by Naturalization: With Reference to the Law of Nations...** Alexander P. Morse. LC 97-1953. xxviii, 385p. 1997. reprint ed. lib. bdg. 55.00 (0-8377-2483-X) Rothman.

Treatise on Civil Architecture. 3rd ed. William Chambers. LC 68-17154. (Illus.). 1972. reprint ed. 42.95 (0-405-08349-1, Pub. by Blom Pubns UK) Ayer.

Treatise on Civil Government, 3 pts. in 1, Set. Josiah Tucker. LC 65-26384. v, 428p. 1967. reprint ed. 49.50 (0-678-00217-7) Kelley.

Treatise on Clean Surface Technology, Vol. 1. Ed. by K. L. Mittal. 326p. 1987. 95.00 (0-306-42420-7, Plenum Pr) Plenum.

Treatise on Coatings, Vol. 2, Part 1. Ed. by Raymond R. Myers & J. S. Long. LC 67-21701. reprint ed. pap. 160.00 (0-685-16095-5, 2026411) Bks Demand.

Treatise on Communication by Telegraph. Morris Gray. LC 12-14201. 1988. reprint ed. 18.45 (0-685-17219-8) Little.

Treatise on Constitutional Conventions Their History, Powers & Modes of Proceeding. John A. Jameson. LC 73-166332. (American Constitutional & Legal History Ser.). 1972. reprint ed. lib. bdg. 75.00 (0-306-70243-6) Da Capo.

Treatise on Constitutional Law: Substance & Procedure, 1. 2nd ed. John E. Nowak & Ronald D. Rotunda. (Practice Ser.: Vols. 1-3). 1992. text ed. write for info. (0-314-00803-9) West Pub.

Treatise on Constitutional Law: Substance & Procedure, 2. 2nd ed. John E. Nowak & Ronald D. Rotunda. (Practice Ser.: Vols. 1-3). 1992. text ed. write for info. (0-314-00804-7) West Pub.

Treatise on Constitutional Law: Substance & Procedure, 3. 2nd ed. John E. Nowak & Ronald D. Rotunda. (Practice Ser.: Vols. 1-3). 1992. text ed. write for info. (0-314-00805-5) West Pub.

Treatise on Contempt Including Civil & Criminal Contempts of Judicial Tribunals, Justices of the Peace, Legislative Bodies, Municipal Boards, Committees, Notaries, Commissioners, Referees & Other Officers Exercising Judicial & Quasi-judicial Functions: With Practice & Forms. Stewart Rapalje. xliv, 273p. 1981. reprint ed. lib. bdg. 32.50 (0-8377-1030-8) Rothman.

Treatise on Controlled Drug Delivery: Fundamentals - Optimization - Applications. Ed. by Agis F. Kydonieus. 568p. 1991. 195.00 (0-8247-8519-3) Dekker.

Treatise on Cosmic Fire. Alice A. Bailey. LC 51-6116. 1925. 60.00 (0-85330-017-8) Lucis.

Treatise on Cosmic Fire. Alice A. Bailey. LC 51-6116. 1973. pap. 36.00 (0-85330-117-4) Lucis.

Treatise on Court Marshall. J. Payne Adye. 284p. reprint ed. 44.00 (0-932051-70-7) Rprt Serv.

Treatise on Criminal Law. K. K. Dutta. 625p. (C). 1984. 240.00 (0-317-54744-5) St Mut.

Treatise on Criminal Law & Criminal Procedure. Charles E. Chadman. LC 77-156008. (Foundations of Criminal Justice Ser.). reprint ed. 72.50 (0-404-09108-3) AMS Pr.

Treatise on Cryptography: With Problems in French. Andre Lange & E. A. Soudart. 181p. 1981. pap. 26.80 (0-89412-055-7) Aegean Park Pr.

Treatise on Currency & Banking. 2nd ed. Condy Raguet. LC 65-26375. (Library of Money & Banking History). xiv, 323p. 1967. reprint ed. 45.00 (0-678-00215-0) Kelley.

Treatise on Daguerreotype, Pts. 1-4. Levi L. Hill & W. McCartey, Jr. LC 72-9210. (Literature of Photography Ser.). 1973. reprint ed. 18.95 (0-405-04918-8) Ayer.

Treatise on Deeds. Robert F. Norton et al. LC 81-83533. 854p. 1981. reprint ed. 99.00 (0-912004-17-7) Gaunt.

Treatise on Differential Equations. 6th unabridged ed. Andrew R. Forsyth. LC 96-22069. 602p. reprint ed. pap. text ed. 14.95 (0-486-69314-7) Dover.

Treatise on Disputed Handwriting & the Determination of Genuine from Forged Signatures. W. E. Hagan. LC 76-38666. reprint ed. 42.50 (0-404-09175-X) AMS Pr.

Treatise on Domestic Education. Daniel A. Payne. LC 75-157373. (Black Heritage Library Collection). 1977. 21.95 (0-8369-8811-6) Ayer.

***Treatise on Education: 1790 Edition.** George Chapman. (Classics in Education Ser.). 298p. 1996. reprint ed. write for info. (1-85506-275-5) Bks Intl VA.

Treatise on Elders. J. M. Baker. 24p. 1992. pap. 0.95 (1-56794-011-0, D2275) Star Bible.

Treatise on Environmental Law, 5 vols. Frank P. Grad. 1973. Updates. ring bd. write for info. (0-8205-1323-7) Bender.

Treatise on Equity Jurisprudence: As Administered in the United States of America. Adapted for All the States, 5 vols., Set. 5th ed. John N. Pomeroy. Ed. by Spencer W. Symons. 4756p. 1994. reprint ed. 450.00 (1-886363-05-6) Lawbk Exchange.

Treatise on Ethics (1684) Nicolas Malebranche. Tr. & Intro. by Craig Walton. LC 92-13823. (International Archives of the History of Ideas Ser.: Vol. 133). 240p. 1992. lib. bdg. 129.50 (0-7923-1763-7, Pub. by Klwr Acad Pubs NE) Kluwer Ac.

***Treatise on Extradition & Interstate Rendition: With Appendices Containing the Treaties & Statutes..., 2 vols., Set.** John B. Moore. LC 96-42915. 1624p. 1996. reprint ed. lib. bdg. 165.00 (0-8377-2482-1) Rothman.

Treatise on Facts As Subjects of Inquiry by a Jury. 3rd ed. James Ram & John N. Townshend. 486p. 1982. reprint ed. lib. bdg. 35.00 (0-8377-1033-2) Rothman.

Treatise on Fugue. Andre Gedalge. Tr. by A. Levin. 1964. 35.00 (0-910648-02-6) Gamut Music.

Treatise on Glaucoma. 2nd ed. Robert H. Elliot. LC 78-20807. (Classics in Ophthalmology Ser.). (Illus.). 680p. 1979. reprint ed. lib. bdg. 54.00 (0-88275-842-X) Krieger.

Treatise on God As First Principle. rev. ed. John D. Scotus & Allan Wolter. LC 65-28880. 373p. 1983. pap. 15.00 (0-8199-0860-6, Frncscn Herld) Franciscan Pr.

Treatise on Groups of Elements: Abhidharma-Dhatukaya Pada-Sastra: With Chinese Text, English Translation & Notes, Based on Sanskrit & Pali Sources on Buddhism. Swati Guguly. x, 144p. 1994. 16.00 (81-86339-06-X, Pub. by Estrn Bk Linkers II) Nataraj Bks.

Treatise on Happiness. St. Thomas Aquinas. Tr. by John A. Oesterle. LC 83-17091. 224p. (C). 1983. pap. text ed. 11.50 (0-268-01849-9, 85-18490) U of Notre Dame Pr.

Treatise on Harmony. Jean-Philippe Rameau. Tr. by Philip Gossett. 11.95 (0-486-22461-9) Dover.

Treatise on Harmony: Containing the Chief Rules for Composing in Two, Three & Four Parts. 2nd ed. John C. Pepusch. 227p. 1976. reprint ed. 50.70 (3-487-05930-4) G Olms Pubs.

Treatise on Harmony see Monuments of Music & Music Literature in Facsimile

Treatise on Harpsichord Tuning by Jean Denis. Ed. & Tr. by Vincent J. Panetta. (Cambridge Musical Texts & Monographs). 120p. 1987. pap. text ed. 20.95 (0-521-31402-X) Cambridge U Pr.

Treatise on Heavy-Ion Science, Vol. 1: Elastic & Quasi-Elastic Phenomena. Ed. by D. Allan Bromley. LC 84-8384. 750p. 1984. 145.00 (0-306-41571-2, Plenum Pr) Plenum.

Treatise on Heavy-Ion Science, Vol. 2: Fusion & Quasi-Fusion Phenomena. Ed. by D. Allan Bromley. 752p. 1985. 145.00 (0-306-41572-0, Plenum Pr) Plenum.

Treatise on Heavy-Ion Science, Vol. 3: Compound Systems Phenomena. Ed. by D. Allan Bromley. 610p. 1985. 135.00 (0-306-41573-9, Plenum Pr) Plenum.

Treatise on Heavy-Ion Science, Vol. 4: Extreme Nuclear States. D. Allan Bromley. 722p. 1985. 135.00 (0-306-41574-7, Plenum Pr) Plenum.

Treatise on Heavy-Ion Science, Vol. 5: High-Energy Atomic Physics. Ed. by D. Allan Bromley. 518p. 1985. 125.00 (0-306-41575-5, Plenum Pr) Plenum.

Treatise on Heavy-Ion Science, Vol. 6: Astrophysics, Chemistry, & Condensed Matter. Ed. by D. Allan Bromley. 452p. 1985. 115.00 (0-306-41786-3, Plenum Pr) Plenum.

Treatise on Heavy Ion Science, Vol. 7: Instrumentation & Techniques. Ed. by D. Allan Bromley. 494p. 1985. 120.00 (0-306-41787-1, Plenum Pr) Plenum.

Treatise on Heavy Ion Science, Vol. 8: Nuclei Far from Stability. Ed. by D. Allan Bromley. (Illus.). 752p. 1989. 145.00 (0-306-42949-7, Plenum Pr) Plenum.

Treatise on Heliochromy. Levi Hill. LC 71-173025. 175p. 1972. reprint ed. text ed. 15.00 (0-87601-005-2) Carnation.

Treatise on Hindu Law. S. Venkataraman. (Orient Longman Law Library). 550p. 1980. pap. text ed. 18.95 (0-86131-211-2, Pub. by Orient Longman Ltd II) Apt Bks.

Treatise on Human Nature. David Hume. (Great Books in Philosophy). 639p. (C). 1991. pap. 9.95 (0-87975-743-4) Prometheus Bks.

Treatise on Human Nature, 3 vols., Set. David Hume. LC 78-67528. (Scottish Enlightenment Ser.). reprint ed. 97.50 (0-404-17653-4) AMS Pr.

Treatise on Hygiene. William Hammond. (American Civil War Medical Ser.: No. 5). (Illus.). 604p. 1991. reprint ed. 60.00 (0-930405-38-2) Norman SF.

Treatise on Hygiene & Public Health, 2 Vols. Albert H. Buck. Ed. by Barbara G. Rosenkrantz. LC 76-25654. (Public Health in America Ser.). 1977. reprint ed. Set. lib. bdg. 116.95 (0-405-09810-3) Ayer.

Treatise on Hygiene & Public Health, 2 Vols., Vol. 1. Albert H. Buck. Ed. by Barbara G. Rosenkrantz. LC 76-25654. (Public Health in America Ser.). 1977. reprint ed. lib. bdg. 58.95 (0-405-09811-1); reprint ed. lib. bdg. 58.95 (0-405-09812-X) Ayer.

Treatise on Insanity see Responsibility in Mental Disease

Treatise on Insanity & Other Disorders Affecting the Mind. James C. Prichard. LC 73-2412. (Mental Illness & Social Policy; the American Experience Ser.). 1973. reprint ed. 26.95 (0-405-05222-7) Ayer.

Treatise on Insanity in Its Medical Relations. William A. Hammond. LC 73-2402. (Mental Illness & Social Policy; the American Experience Ser.). 1973. reprint ed. 50.95 (0-405-05208-1) Ayer.

Treatise on Instrumentation. Hector Berlioz & Richard Strauss. (Illus.). 432p. reprint ed. pap. 18.95 (0-486-26903-5) Dover.

Treatise on Interior Peace. Ambroise De Lombez. Tr. by Elizabeth A. Seton from FRE. LC 95-45564. 200p. (Orig.). 1996. pap. 10.95 (0-8189-0715-0) Alba.

Treatise on International Law Including American Diplomacy. Cushman K. Davis. xiii, 368p. 1982. reprint ed. lib. bdg. 30.00 (0-8377-0441-3) Rothman.

Treatise on Invertebrate Paleontology. Ed. by Raymond C. Moore. LC 53-12913. 267p. reprint ed. pap. 76.10 (0-7837-1257-X, 2041394) Bks Demand.

Treatise on Invertebrate Paleontology Pt. L: Mollusca 4 Ammonoidea. (Illus.). 393p. 1996. 75.00 (0-8137-3112-7) Geol Soc.

Treatise on Invertebrate Paleontology, Part E: Archaeocyatha. enl. rev. ed. Dorothy Hill. Ed. by Curt Teichert. LC 53-12913. (Illus.). 188p. 1972. 31.25 (0-8137-3105-4) Geol Soc.

Treatise on Invertebrate Paleontology, Part G: Bryoza, Vol. 1. rev. ed. Ed. by Richard A. Robinson. 641p. 1983. 52.00 (0-8137-3107-0) Geol Soc.

Treatise on Invertebrate Paleontology, Pt. A: Introduction: Fossilization (Taphonomy), Biogeography, & Biostratigraphy. Ed. by Richard A. Robison & Curt Tiechert. LC 53-12913. 1979. 47.50 (0-8137-3001-5) Geol Soc.

Treatise on Invertebrate Paleontology, Pt. C: Protista 2: Sarcodina, Chiefly "Thecamoebians" & Foraminiferida, 2 vols. Alfred R. Loeblich, Jr. & Helen Tappan. Ed. by Raymond C. Moore. LC 53-12913. 936p. 1964. 43.00 (0-8137-3003-1) Geol Soc.

Treatise on Invertebrate Paleontology, Pt. D: Protista 3 (Chiefly Radiolaria, Tintinnina) Ed. by Raymond C. Moore. LC 53-12913. (Illus.). 207p. 1954. reprint ed. 25.00 (0-8137-3004-X) Geol Soc.

Treatise on Invertebrate Paleontology, Pt. F: Coelenterata. Ed. by Raymond C. Moore. LC 53-12913. (Illus.). 508p. 1956. 27.50 (0-8137-3006-6) Geol Soc.

Treatise on Invertebrate Paleontology, Pt. F, Suppl. 1: Coelenterata (Rugosa & Tabulata), 2 vols. Dorothy Hill. LC 53-12913. (Illus.). 762p. 1981. 44.00 (0-8137-3029-5) Geol Soc.

Treatise on Invertebrate Paleontology, Pt. H: Brachiopoda, 2 vols. Ed. by Raymond C. Moore. LC 53-12913. (Illus.). 959p. 1965. reprint ed. 65.00 (0-8137-3008-2) Geol Soc.

Treatise on Invertebrate Paleontology, Pt. I: Mollusca 1. Ed. by Raymond C. Moore. LC 53-12913. (Illus.). 374p. 1960. 43.75 (0-8137-3009-0) Geol Soc.

Treatise on Invertebrate Paleontology, Pt. K: Mollusca 3. Ed. by Raymond C. Moore. LC 53-12913. (Illus.). 547p. 1964. 44.00 (0-8137-3011-2) Geol Soc.

Treatise on Invertebrate Paleontology, Pt. L: Mollusca 4. Ed. by Raymond C. Moore. (Illus.). 511p. 1957. 55.00 (0-8137-3012-0) Geol Soc.

Treatise on Invertebrate Paleontology, Pt. N: Mollusca 6, Bivalvia, Vol. 3 (Oysters) Henryk B. Stenzel. Ed. by Raymond C. Moore. LC 53-12913. (Illus.). 275p. 1971. 23.50 (0-8137-3026-0) Geol Soc.

Treatise on Invertebrate Paleontology, Pt. N: Mollusca 6, Bivalvia, Vols. 1-2. Ed. by Raymond C. Moore. LC 53-12913. (Illus.). 989p. 1969. 44.25 (0-8137-3014-7) Geol Soc.

Treatise on Invertebrate Paleontology, Pt. O: Arthropoda 1. Ed. by Raymond C. Moore. LC 53-12913. (Illus.). 579p. 1959. 27.50 (0-8137-3015-5) Geol Soc.

Treatise on Invertebrate Paleontology, Pt. P: Arthropoda 2. Ed. by Raymond C. Moore. LC 53-12913. (Illus.). 198p. 1955. 24.50 (0-8137-3016-3) Geol Soc.

Treatise on Invertebrate Paleontology, Pt. Q: Arthropoda 3: Crustacea: Ostracoda. Ed. by Raymond C. Moore. LC 53-12913. (Illus.). 465p. 1961. 26.75 (0-8137-3017-1) Geol Soc.

Treatise on Invertebrate Paleontology, Pt. R: Arthropoda 4: Crustacea (Except Ostracoda): Myriapoda, Vols. 1-2. Ed. by Raymond C. Moore & Curt Teichert. LC 53-12913. (Illus.). 687p. 1969. 32.00 (0-8137-3018-X) Geol Soc.

Treatise on Invertebrate Paleontology, Pt. R: Hexapoda 1, 2 vols. Ed. by R. L. Kaesler. (Illus.). 677p. 1992. Set. 87.50 (0-8137-3019-8) Geol Soc.

Treatise on Invertebrate Paleontology, Pt. S: Echinodermata 1: General Characters Homalozoa-Crinozoa (Except Crinoidea), 2 vols. Ed. by Raymond C. Moore. LC 53-12913. (Illus.). 679p. 1967. 32.00 (0-8137-3020-1) Geol Soc.

Treatise on Invertebrate Paleontology, Pt. T: Echinodermata 2: Crinoidea, 3 vols. Ed. by Raymond C. Moore & Curt Teichert. LC 53-12913. (Illus.). 1978. Set. 61.00 (0-8137-3021-X) Geol Soc.

Treatise on Invertebrate Paleontology, Pt. U: Echinodermata 3: Asterozoa-Echinozoa, 2 vols. Raymond C. Moore. LC 53-12913. (Illus.). 725p. 1966. reprint ed. 62.00 (0-8137-3022-8) Geol Soc.

Treatise on Invertebrate Paleontology, Pt. V: Graptolithina. rev. ed. O. M. Bulman. Ed. by Raymond C. Moore. LC 53-12913. (Illus.). 195p. 1970. 16.75 (0-8137-3123-2) Geol Soc.

Treatise on Invertebrate Paleontology, Pt. W: Miscellanea. Ed. by Raymond C. Moore. LC 53-12913. (Illus.). 284p. 1962. 18.00 (0-8137-3024-4) Geol Soc.

Treatise on Invertebrate Paleontology, Pt. W, Suppl. 2: Conodonta. Ed. by Richard A. Robinson. LC 53-12913. (Illus.). 230p. 1982. 22.00 (0-8137-3028-7) Geol Soc.

Treatise on Invertebrate Paleontology, Pt. W., Suppl. 1: Miscellanea: Trace Fossils & Problematica. 2nd enl. rev. ed. Walter Hartzschel. LC 53-12913. (Illus.). 290p. 1975. 30.00 (0-8137-3027-9) Geol Soc.

Treatise on Judicial Evidence, Extracted from the Manuscripts of Jeremy Bentham. M. Dumont. xvi, 366p. 1981. reprint ed. lib. bdg. 35.00 (0-8377-0318-2) Rothman.

Treatise on Lathes & Turning. W. Henry Northcott. LC 87-3618. (Illus.). 298p. 1988. reprint ed. pap. 14.95 (0-941936-10-4) Linden Pub Fresno.

Treatise on Laughter. Laurent Joubert. Tr. & Anno. by Gregory D. De Rocher. LC 79-16796. 172p. 1980. pap. 49.10 (0-7837-8199-7, 2059197) Bks Demand.

Treatise on Law. St. Thomas Aquinas. 116p. (Orig.). 1996. pap. 9.95 (0-89526-705-5, Gateway Editions) Regnery Pub.

Treatise on Law: Summa Theologiae, I-II; 88-90-97. St. Thomas Aquinas. Tr. by R. J. Henle from LAT. LC 92-56861. (Notre Dame Studies in Law & Contemporary Issues: Vol. 4). (C). 1993. text ed. 40.50 (0-268-01880-4); pap. text ed. 23.00 (0-268-01881-2) U of Notre Dame Pr.

T

Treatise on Laws. Gratian. Tr. by James Gordley & Augustine Thompson from LAT. LC 93-19237. (Studies in Medieval & Early Modern Canon Law: Vol. 2). 131p. (Orig.). (C). 1993. pap. 14.95 (*0-8132-0786-X*) Cath U Pr.

Treatise on Life Insurance Accounts: Forming Pt. II on "Life Insurance in 1872", 2 Vols. Thomas B. Sprague. Ed. by Richard P. Brief. LC 80-1526. (Dimensions of Accounting Theory & Practice Ser.). 1980. reprint ed. lib. bdg. 30.95 (*0-405-13547-5*) Ayer.

Treatise on Limnology: The Zoobenthos, Vol. 4. G. Evelyn Hutchinson & Yvette H. Edmonson. 968p. 1993. text ed. 165.00 (*0-471-54294-6*) Wiley.

Treatise on Lovesickness. Jacques Ferrand. Ed. by Donald A. Beecher & Massimo Ciavolella. 742p. 1989. text ed. 55.00 (*0-8156-2467-0*) Syracuse U Pr.

Treatise on Man. St. Thomas Aquinas & James F. Anderson. LC 81-6631. 178p. 1981. text ed. 38.50 (*0-313-22186-3*, TATM, Greenwood Pr) Greenwood.

Treatise on Man & the Development of His Faculties, 1842. Lambert A. Quetelet. LC 77-81364. (History of Psychology Ser.). (Illus.). 1969. 50.00 (*0-8201-1061-2*) Schol Facsimiles.

Treatise on Marine Ecology & Paleoecology. National Research Council, Committee on Vision Staff. Ed. by Joel W. Hedgpeth. LC 57-4669. (Geological Society of America, Memoir Ser.: No. 67, Vol. 1). 1352p. pap. 180.00 (*0-318-34695-8*, 2031784) Bks Demand.

Treatise on Materials Science & Technology, Vol. 31: Aluminum Alloys: Contemporary Research & Applications. Ed. by Herbert Herman et al. 702p. 1989. text ed. 223.00 (*0-12-341831-3*) Acad Pr.

Treatise on Mechanics: 1989. Henry Kater & D. Lardner. 290p. 1990. reprint ed. pap. 25.00 (*0-87556-761-4*) Saifer.

Treatise on Media & Methods Used in Bacteriological Techniques. 2nd ed. V. Iswaran. 189p. 1980. 12.00 (*0-88065-132-6*, Messers Today & Tomorrow) Scholarly Pubns.

Treatise on Meekness & Quietness of Spirit. Henry Matthew. 144p. 20.95 (*1-57358-022-8*) Soli Deo Gloria.

Treatise on Mental Diseases. Henry J. Berkley. Ed. by Gerald N. Grob. LC 78-22549. (Historical Issues in Mental Health Ser.). (Illus.). 1980. reprint ed. lib. bdg. 50.95 (*0-405-11903-8*) Ayer.

Treatise on Military Matters & Warfare, Vol. 2. Pierino Belli. LC 95-77297. (Classics in International Law Reprint Ser.: No. 18). 1995. reprint ed. 115.00 (*1-57588-262-0*, 310360) W S Hein.

Treatise on Modern Instrumentation & Orchestration. Hector Berlioz. 1976. 69.00 (*0-403-06679-4*, Regency) Scholarly.

Treatise on Modern Instrumentation & Orchestration. Hector Berlioz. 1988. reprint ed. lib. bdg. 79.00 (*0-7812-0266-3*) Rprt Serv.

Treatise on Money, 2 vols., Set. John Maynard Keynes. LC 75-41162. reprint ed. write for info. (*0-404-15000-4*) AMS Pr.

Treatise on Money Reform. (Money Reform Ser.). 1994. lib. bdg. 250.00 (*0-8490-5655-1*) Gordon Pr.

Treatise on Money, the Applied Theory of Money see Collected Writings

Treatise on Money, the Pure Theory of Money see Collected Writings

Treatise on Natural History. John W. Draper. (Notable American Authors Ser.). 1992. reprint ed. lib. bdg. 75.00 (*0-7812-2698-8*) Rprt Serv.

Treatise on Nature & Grace. Nicolas Malebranche. Tr. & Intro. by Patrick Riley. 224p. 1992. 65.00 (*0-19-824832-6*) OUP.

Treatise on New York Environmental Law. New York State Bar Association Staff. Ed. by Nicholas A. Robinson & James D. Hopkins. LC 92-53528. 1000p. 1992. 95.00 (*0-685-56517-3*) NYS Bar.

Treatise on Partisan Warfare. Johann Ewald. LC 91-21190. (Contributions in Military Studies: No. 116). 192p. 1991. text ed. 55.00 (*0-313-27350-2*, EEP, Greenwood Pr) Greenwood.

Treatise on Photography. N. P. Lerebours. LC 72-9215. (Literature of Photography Ser.). 1973. reprint ed. 19.95 (*0-405-04923-4*) Ayer.

Treatise on Photogravure. Herbert Denison. Ed. by Nathan Lyons. (Reprint & Research Ser.). (Illus.). 142p. 1974. reprint ed. 11.95 (*0-87992-004-1*); reprint ed. pap. 6.50 (*0-685-05260-5*) Visual Studies.

Treatise on Poisons in Relation to Medical Jurisprudence, Physiology & the Practice of Physic. Robert Christison. LC 79-156011. reprint ed. 67.50 (*0-404-09111-3*) AMS Pr.

Treatise on Political Economy. George Opdyke. LC 68-56559. (Reprints of Economic Classics Ser.). xxxiv, 339p. 1973. reprint ed. 49.50 (*0-678-00802-7*) Kelley.

Treatise on Political Economy: Or the Production, Distribution & Consumption of Wealth. Jean-Baptiste Say. LC 63-23524. (Reprints of Economic Classics Ser.). lx, 488p. 1971. reprint ed. 49.50 (*0-678-00028-X*) Kelley.

Treatise on Practical Seamanship. William Hutchinson. 1979. reprint ed. 60.00 (*0-85967-566-1*, Pub. by Scolar Pr UK) Ashgate Pub Co.

Treatise on Prayer: An Explanation of the Services of the Orthodox Church. Symeon of Thessalonike. Tr. by H. L. Simmons from GRE. (Archbishop Iakovos Library of Ecclesiastical & Historical Sources: No. 9). Orig. Title: Peri Theias Kai Hieras Proseuches. (Orig.). 1984. pap. text ed. 4.00 (*0-917653-06-8*) Hellenic Coll Pr.

Treatise on Private International Law, or the Conflict of Laws with Principal Reference to Its Practice in the English & Other Cognate Systems of Jurisprudence, & Numerous References to American Authorities. John Westlake. 251p. 1986. reprint ed. lib. bdg. 32.50 (*0-8377-2732-4*) Rothman.

Treatise on Probability. John Maynard Keynes. LC 75-41163. reprint ed. write for info. (*0-404-14563-9*) AMS Pr.

Treatise on Probability see Collected Writings

Treatise on Purgatory see Fire of Love!: Understanding Purgatory

Treatise on Rhetoric. Aristotle. Tr. by Theodore Buckley from GRE. LC 95-11390. (Great Books in Philosophy). 275p. 1995. pap. 7.95 (*0-87975-976-3*) Prometheus Bks.

Treatise on Sanctification. James Fraser. 925p. 1992. reprint ed. 29.95 (*0-9632557-1-1*) Old Paths Pubns.

Treatise on Social Justice Vol. 1: Theories of Justice 1989. Brian Barry. (California Series on Social Choice & Political Economy: Vol. 16). 1989. 55.00 (*0-520-03866-5*) U CA Pr.

Treatise on Social Justice Vol. 1: Theories of Justice 1989. Brian Barry. (California Series on Social Choice & Political Economy: Vol. 16). 443p. 1989. reprint ed. pap. 16.00 (*0-520-07649-4*) U CA Pr.

Treatise on Social Security & Labour Law. S. C. Srivastava. 1985. 180.00 (*0-317-57707-7*) St Mut.

***Treatise on Social Theory.** W. G. Runciman. 400p. (C). Date not set. pap. write for info. (*0-521-59459-6*) Cambridge U Pr.

***Treatise on Social Theory Vol. 3: Applied Social Theory.** W. G. Runciman. 400p. (C). 1997. write for info. (*0-521-24960-0*) Cambridge U Pr.

***Treatise on Social Theory Vol. 3: Applied Social Theory.** W. G. Runciman. 400p. (C). 1997. pap. write for info. (*0-521-58801-4*) Cambridge U Pr.

Treatise on Solar Energy: Fundamentals of Solar Energy, Vol. 1. H. P. Garg. LC 81-21951. 607p. reprint ed. pap. 173.00 (*0-685-23359-6*, 2032291) Bks Demand.

Treatise on Stair Building & Hand Railing. William Mowat & Alexander Mowat. LC 85-6916. 390p. 1985. reprint ed. pap. 24.95 (*0-941936-02-3*) Linden Pub Fresno.

Treatise on State & Federal Control of Persons & Property in the United States, 2 vols., Set. 2nd ed. Christopher G. Tiedeman. LC 72-38673. reprint ed. 115.00 (*0-404-09185-7*) AMS Pr.

Treatise on Style (Traite du Style) Louis Aragon. Tr. by Alyson Waters from FRE. LC 90-12894. (French Modernist Library). xx, 119p. 1991. text ed. 25.00 (*0-8032-1024-8*) U of Nebr Pr.

Treatise on Sunday Laws: The Sabbath-the Lord's Day, Its History & Observance, Civil & Criminal. George E. Harris. xxiii, 338p. 1980. reprint ed. lib. bdg. 32.50 (*0-8377-2232-2*) Rothman.

Treatise on the Admissibility of Parol Evidence in Respect to Written Instruments. Irving Browne. xlviii, 510p. 1982. reprint ed. lib. bdg. 38.50 (*0-8377-0325-5*) Rothman.

Treatise on the American Law of Landlord & Tenant. John N. Taylor. Ed. by R. H. Helmholz & Bernard D. Reams, Jr. LC 80-84857. (Historical Writings in Law & Jurisprudence Ser.: No. 14, Bk. 17). xxv, 477p. 1981. reprint ed. lib. bdg. 52.00 (*0-89941-069-3*, 302420) W S Hein.

Treatise on the American Law Relating to Mines & Mineral Lands Within the Public Land States & Territories & Governing the Acquisition & Enjoyment of Mining Rights in Lands of the Public Domain, 2 vols. 2nd ed. Curtis H. Lindley. LC 72-2853. (Use & Abuse of America's Natural Resources Ser.). 1972. reprint ed. 145.95 (*0-405-04517-4*) Ayer.

Treatise on the American Law Relating to Mines & Mineral Lands Within the Public Land States & Territories & Governing the Acquisition & Enjoyment of Mining Rights in Lands of the Public Domain, 3 vols. 3rd ed. Curtis H. Lindley. cclii, 2810p. 1988. reprint ed. Set, Vol. 1, ccIii, 730p., Vol.2, 954p., Vol.3, 1126p. lib. bdg. 195.00 (*0-8377-2411-2*) Rothman.

Treatise on the American Law Relating to Mines & Mineral Lands Within the Public Land States & Territories & Governing the Acquisition & Enjoyment of Mining Rights in Lands of the Public Domain, 2 vols, 1. 2nd ed. Curtis H. Lindley. LC 72-2853. (Use & Abuse of America's Natural Resources Ser.). 1972. reprint ed. 72.95 (*0-405-04546-8*) Ayer.

Treatise on the American Law Relating to Mines & Mineral Lands Within the Public Land States & Territories & Governing the Acquisition & Enjoyment of Mining Rights in Lands of the Public Domain, 2 vols, Vol. 2. 2nd ed. Curtis H. Lindley. LC 72-2853. (Use & Abuse of America's Natural Resources Ser.). 1972. reprint ed. 72.95 (*0-405-04547-6*) Ayer.

Treatise on the Analytical Dynamics of Particles & Rigid Bodies. Edmund T. Whittaker. (Cambridge Mathematical Library). 456p. 1989. pap. text ed. 34.95 (*0-521-35883-3*) Cambridge U Pr.

Treatise on the Analytical Dynamics of Particles & Rigid Bodies: With an Introduction to the Problem of Three Bodies. 4th ed. Edmund T. Whittaker. LC 83-45485. 1937. 78.50 (*0-404-20288-8*) AMS Pr.

Treatise on the Art of Dancing see Monuments of Music & Music Literature in Facsimile

Treatise on the Blessed Body see Treatise on the Passion: Complete Works of St. Thomas More

Treatise on the Canon of Medicine of Avicenna. Avicenna. LC 73-12409. reprint ed. 145.00 (*0-404-11231-5*) AMS Pr.

Treatise on the Chemical Constitution of the Brain. J. L. Thudichum. xxiii, 262p. (C). 1962. reprint ed. 36.00 (*0-208-00575-7*, Archon Bks) Shoe String.

Treatise on the Circle & the Sphere. Julian L. Coolidge. LC 78-128872. 1971. text ed. 45.00 (*0-8284-0236-1*) Chelsea Pub.

Treatise on the Circumstances Which Determine the Rate of Wages & the Conditions of the Labouring Classes. John R. McCulloch. LC 64-56231. (Reprints of Economic Classics Ser.). x, 114p. 1967. reprint ed. 29.50 (*0-678-00005-0*) Kelley.

Treatise on the Coins of the Realm: In a Letter to the King. Charles J. Liverpool. LC 67-29513. (Reprints of Economic Classics Ser.). xii, 295p. 1968. reprint ed. 45.00 (*0-678-00412-9*) Kelley.

Treatise on the Commerce & Police of the River Thames. Patrick Colquhoun. LC 69-14917. (Criminology, Law Enforcement, & Social Problems Ser.: No. 41). 1969. reprint ed. 35.00 (*0-87585-041-3*) Patterson Smith.

Treatise on the Conflict of Laws, or Private International Law: Including a Comparative View of Anglo-American, Roman, German, & French Jurisprudence. Francis Wharton. xxxii, 758p. 1991. reprint ed. lib. bdg. 75.00 (*0-8377-2749-9*) Rothman.

Treatise on the Construction of the Statutes, 13 Eliz. C.5. & 27 Eliz. C.4. Relating to Voluntary & Fraudulent Conveyances, & on the Nature & Force of Different Considerations to Support Deeds & Other Legal Instruments, in the Courts of Law & Equity. 2nd ed. William Roberts. xv, 667p. 1979. reprint ed. lib. bdg. 35.00 (*0-8377-1028-6*) Rothman.

Treatise on the Construction, Preservation, Repair, & Improvement of the Violin: Supplement by J. F. Hanks. Jacob A. Otto & J. F. Hanks. (Illus.). 48p. 1995. reprint ed. pap. 8.95 (*0-931877-26-1*) Captain Fiddle Pubns.

Treatise on the Criminal Law As Now Administered in the United States, 2 vols., Set. Incl. Vol. 1. Criminal Law - United States. Emlin McClain. LC 74-156026. (*0-404-09166-0*); Vol. 2. Criminal Procedure. LC 74-156026. (*0-404-09167-9*); LC 74-156026. reprint ed. 125.00 (*0-404-09127-X*) AMS Pr.

Treatise on the Criminal Law of the United States: Comprising a Digest of the Penal Statutes of the General Government, & of Massachusetts, New York... Francis Wharton. viii, 688p. 1996. reprint ed. lib. bdg. 87.50 (*0-8377-2784-7*) Rothman.

Treatise on the Doctrine of Ultra Vires: Being an Investigation of the Principles Which Limit the Powers & Liabilities of Corporations, Quasi-Corporate Bodies & Non-Sovereign Legislatures. Howard A. Street. LC 81-83532. 679p. 1981. reprint ed. 94.00 (*0-912004-18-5*) Gaunt.

Treatise on the Family. enl. ed. Gary S. Becker. LC 90-4975. (Illus.). 424p. 1994. 55.50 (*0-674-90698-5*, BECTRR) HUP.

Treatise on the Family. enl. ed. Gary S. Becker. 424p. 1993. pap. 21.00 (*0-674-90699-3*) HUP.

Treatise on the Forces Which Produce the Organization of Plants. John W. Draper. (Notable American Authors Ser.). 1992. reprint ed. lib. bdg. 75.00 (*0-7812-2696-1*) Rprt Serv.

Treatise on the Fugue. Andre Gedalge. Tr. by Ferdinand Davis. LC 65-11241. 442p. reprint ed. 126.00 (*0-8357-9744-9*, 2016219) Bks Demand.

Treatise on the Fundamental Principles of Violin Playing. 2nd ed. Leopold Mozart. Tr. by Editha Knocker. (Early Music Ser.). (Illus.). 272p. (C). 1985. pap. 45.00 (*0-19-318513-X*) OUP.

***Treatise on the Gods.** 2nd ed. H. L. Mencken. LC 96-51594. (Maryland Paperback Bookshelf Ser.). 375p. 1997. reprint ed. pap. 15.95 (*0-8018-5654-X*) Johns Hopkins.

Treatise on the Heathen Superstitions that Today Live among the Indians Native to this Day in New Spain, 1629. Hernando Ruiz de Alarcon. Ed. by J. Richard Andrews & Ross Hassig. LC 83-47842. (Civilization of the American Indian Ser.: Vol. 164). (Illus.). 540p. 1987. pap. 24.95 (*0-8061-2031-2*) U of Okla Pr.

Treatise on the Law & Practice of Injunctions. 6th ed. William W. Kerr & John M. Paterson. LC 81-1500. lxiv, 743p. 1981. reprint ed. 105.00 (*0-912004-16-9*, Pub. by Sweet & Maxwll UK) Gaunt.

Treatise on the Law & Practice of Receivers (Clark on Receivers) 3rd ed. Ralph E. Clark. 2372p. 1992. reprint ed. 350.00 (*0-89941-811-2*, 307670) W S Hein.

Treatise on the Law of Arson. Arthur F. Curtis. lxviii, 689p. 1936. 52.00 (*0-89941-371-4*, 500290) W S Hein.

Treatise on the Law of Carriers of Goods & Passengers, by Land & by Water. Joseph K. Angell. LC 72-37694. (American Law: The Formative Years). 796p. 1972. reprint ed. 50.95 (*0-405-03991-3*) Ayer.

Treatise on the Law of Citizenship in the United States. Prentiss Webster. xxiii, 338p. 1980. reprint ed. lib. bdg. 30.00 (*0-8377-1307-2*) Rothman.

Treatise on the Law of Contracts Not Under Seal. William W. Story. LC 71-37988. (American Law: The Formative Years). 522p. 1972. reprint ed. 33.95 (*0-405-04033-4*) Ayer.

***Treatise on the Law of Crimes.** William L. Clark et al. xxxiv, 906p. 1996. reprint ed. lib. bdg. 87.50 (*0-8377-2059-1*) Rothman.

Treatise on the Law of Descents, in the Several United States of America. Tapping Reeve. Ed. by R. H. Helmholz & Bernard D. Reams, Jr. LC 80-84864. (Historical Writings in Law & Jurisprudence Ser.: No. 12, Bk. 15). iv, 515p. 1981. reprint ed. lib. bdg. 52.00 (*0-89941-067-7*, 301330) W S Hein.

Treatise on the Law of Estoppel & Its Application in Practice. Melville M. Bigelow. lxiv, 656p. 1991. reprint ed. lib. bdg. 67.50 (*0-8377-1923-2*) Rothman.

Treatise on the Law of Evidence, 3 Vols. Simon Greenleaf. LC 73-37975. (American Law: The Formative Years). 2070p. 1972. reprint ed. Set. 132.95 (*0-405-04015-6*) Ayer.

Treatise on the Law of Evidence, 3 Vols., Vol. 1. Simon Greenleaf. LC 73-37975. (American Law: The Formative Years). 2070p. 1972. reprint ed. 44.95 (*0-405-04016-4*) Ayer.

Treatise on the Law of Evidence, 3 Vols., Vol. 2. Simon Greenleaf. LC 73-37975. (American Law: The Formative Years). 2070p. 1972. reprint ed. 44.95 (*0-405-04017-2*) Ayer.

Treatise on the Law of Evidence, 3 Vols., Vol. 3. Simon Greenleaf. LC 73-37975. (American Law: The Formative Years). 2070p. 1972. reprint ed. 44.95 (*0-405-04018-0*) Ayer.

Treatise on the Law of Fire & Life Insurance. Joseph K. Angell. LC 76-37965. (American Law: The Formative Years). 600p. 1972. reprint ed. 39.95 (*0-405-03992-1*) Ayer.

Treatise on the Law of Highways. 3rd ed. George F. Choate. Ed. by R. H. Helmholz & Bernard D. Reams, Jr. LC 86-62941. (Historical Writings in Law & Jurisprudence Ser.: No. 9). xl, 625p. 1986. reprint ed. lib. bdg. 52.50 (*0-89941-524-5*, 304600) W S Hein.

Treatise on the Law of Indirect & Collateral Evidence. John H. Gillett. xlvi, 407p. 1994. reprint ed. lib. bdg. 47.50 (*0-8377-2214-4*) Rothman.

Treatise on the Law of Libel & the Liberty of the Press, Showing the Origin, Use & Abuse of the Law of Libel. Thomas Cooper. LC 78-125688. (American Journalists Ser.). 1977. reprint ed. 23.95 (*0-405-01665-4*) Ayer.

Treatise on the Law of Master & Servant. Horace G. Wood. Ed. by R. H. Helmholz & Bernard D. Reams, Jr. LC 80-84866. (Historical Writings in Law & Jurisprudence Ser.: No. 15, Bk. 18). xxxiv, 956p. 1981. reprint ed. lib. bdg. 55.00 (*0-89941-070-7*, 302460) W S Hein.

Treatise on the Law of Principal & Agent: And of Sales by Auction, 2 vols. Samuel Livermore & Bernard D. Reams, Jr. Ed. by R. H. Helmholz. LC 86-62943. (Historical Writings in Law & Jurisprudence Ser.: No. 11). 1986. reprint ed. Set. lib. bdg. 95.00 (*0-89941-526-1*, 304620) W S Hein.

Treatise on the Law of Principal & Agent, Chiefly with Reference to Mercantile Transactions. 2nd ed. William Paley. xvi, 202p. 1982. reprint ed. lib. bdg. 25.00 (*0-8377-1010-3*) Rothman.

Treatise on the Law of Private Corporations, 2 vols. Henry O. Taylor. 1976. Set. lib. bdg. 200.00 (*0-8490-2762-4*) Gordon Pr.

Treatise on the Law of Private Corporations, Aggregate. Joseph K. Angell & Samuel Ames. LC 70-37966. (American Law: The Formative Years). 600p. 1972. reprint ed. 39.95 (*0-405-03993-X*) Ayer.

Treatise on the Law of Property in Intellectual Productions in Great Britain & the United States. Eaton S. Drone. liv, 774p. 1972. reprint ed. lib. bdg. 45.00 (*0-8377-2027-3*) Rothman.

Treatise on the Law of Securities Regulation, Vol. 1. 3rd ed. Thomas L. Hazen. (Practitioner Treatise Ser.). 644p. (C). 1995. text ed. write for info. (*0-314-06192-4*) West Pub.

Treatise on the Law of Securities Regulation, Vol. 2. 3rd ed. Thomas L. Hazen. (Practitioner Treatise Ser.). 981p. (C). 1995. text ed. write for info. (*0-314-06193-2*) West Pub.

Treatise on the Law of Securities Regulation, Vol. 3. 3rd ed. Thomas L. Hazen. (Practitioner Treatise Ser.). 500p. (C). 1995. text ed. write for info. (*0-614-07013-9*) West Pub.

Treatise on the Law of Torts or the Wrongs Which Arise Independent of Contract. Thomas M. Cooley. ci, 755p. 1993. reprint ed. lib. bdg. 85.00 (*0-8377-2049-4*) Rothman.

Treatise on the Law of Warranties in the Sale of Chattels. Arthur Biddle. xx, 308p. 1981. reprint ed. lib. bdg. 30.00 (*0-8377-0316-6*) Rothman.

Treatise on the Law Relative to Sales of Personal Property. George Long. xvi, 288p. 1982. reprint ed. lib. bdg. 30.00 (*0-8377-2403-1*) Rothman.

***Treatise on the Legal Remedies of Mandamus & Prohibition, Habeas Corpus, Certiorari, & Quo Warranto.** 3rd enl. rev. ed. Horace G. Wood. LC 97-4206. xlvii, 276p. 1997. reprint ed. lib. bdg. 42.50 (*0-8377-2787-1*) Rothman.

Treatise on the Liability of Stockholders in Corporations. Seymour D. Thompson. xxxix, 528p. 1983. reprint ed. lib. bdg. 42.50 (*0-8377-1130-4*) Rothman.

Treatise on the Limitations of Police Power in the United States. C. G. Tiedeman. LC 73-150421. (American Constitutional & Legal History Ser). 1971. reprint ed. lib. bdg. 75.00 (*0-306-70104-9*) Da Capo.

Treatise on the Line Complex. Charles H. Jessop. LC 68-55945. 1969. reprint ed. 24.95 (*0-8284-0223-X*) Chelsea Pub.

Treatise on the Management of Pregnant & Lying-In Women. Charles White. LC 86-6600. 1988. 15.00 (*0-88135-081-8*) Watson Pub Intl.

Treatise on the Mathematical Theory of Elasticity. 4th ed. Augustus E. Love. (Illus.). 1927. pap. text ed. 14.95 (*0-486-60174-9*) Dover.

Treatise on the Measure of Damages, or an Inquiry into the Principles Which Govern the Amount of Compensation Recovered in Suits at Law. Theodore Sedgwick. LC 77-37984. (American Law: The Formative Years). 648p. 1972. reprint ed. 41.95 (*0-405-04027-X*) Ayer.

Treatise on the Medical Jurisprudence of Insanity. 5th ed. Isaac Ray. LC 75-16732. (Classics in Psychiatry Ser.). 1977. reprint ed. 54.95 (*0-405-07453-0*) Ayer.

Treatise on the Medical Jurisprudence of Insanity. Isaac Ray. (Historical Foundations of Forensic Psychiatry & Psychology Ser.). xvi, 480p. 1983. reprint ed. lib. bdg. 45.00 (*0-306-76181-5*) Da Capo.

An Asterisk (*) at the beginning of an entry indicates that the title is appearing in BIP for the first time.

Treatise on the Method of Government Surveying. Shobal V. Clevenger. 1978. reprint ed. pap. 12.00 (*0-686-25541-0*) CARBEN Survey.

Treatise on the Methods of Observation & Reasoning in Politics, 2 Vols. George C. Lewis. LC 73-14166. (Perspectives in Social Inquiry Ser.). 984p. 1974. reprint ed. 59.95 (*0-405-05511-0*) Ayer.

Treatise on the Military Band. H. E. Adkins. 1977. lib. bdg. 59.95 (*0-8490-2763-2*) Gordon Pr.

Treatise on the Millennium. Samuel Hopkins. LC 70-38450. (Religion in America, Ser. 2). 162p. 1972. reprint ed. 17.95 (*0-405-04070-9*) Ayer.

Treatise on the Nature, Symptoms, Causes & Treatment of Insanity. William C. Ellis. LC 75-16700. (Classics in Psychiatry Ser.). 1976. reprint ed. 30.95 (*0-405-07427-1*) Ayer.

Treatise on the Novel. Robert Liddell. LC 83-45913. reprint ed. 21.00 (*0-404-20160-1*) AMS Pr.

Treatise on the Operation & Construction of Retroactive Laws, As Affected by Constitutional Limitations & Judicial Interpretations. William P. Wade. xlviii, 391p. 1982. reprint ed. lib. bdg. 35.00 (*0-8377-1319-6*) Rothman.

Treatise on the Organization, Jurisdiction & Practice of the Courts of the United States. Alfred Conkling. LC 85-80031. 538p. 1985. reprint ed. 99.00 (*0-912004-27-4*) Gaunt.

Treatise on the Organization, Jurisdiction & Practice of the Courts of the United States: With an Appendix of Practical Forms. 4th rev. ed. Alfred Conkling. LC 86-83210. xii, 882p. 1987. reprint ed. 105.00 (*0-912004-61-4*) Gaunt.

Treatise on the Passion: Complete Works of St. Thomas More, Vol. 13. Thomas More. Ed. by Garry E. Haupt. Incl. Treatise on the Passion. LC 63-7949. 1976. (*0-318-56514-5*); Treatise on the Blessed Body. LC 63-7949. 1976. (*0-318-56515-3*); Instructions & Prayers. LC 63-7949. 1976. (*0-318-56516-1*); LC 63-7949. 1976. text ed. 80.00 (*0-300-01794-4*) Yale U Pr.

Treatise on the Passion see Treatise on the Passion: Complete Works of St. Thomas More

Treatise on the Passions, So Far As They Regard the Stage. Samuel Foote. LC 72-144608. reprint ed. 27.50 (*0-404-02448-3*) AMS Pr.

Treatise on the Patriarchal, or Co-Operative System of Society. 2nd ed. Zaphaniah Kingsley. LC 78-126240. (Select Bibliographies Reprint Ser.). reprint ed. 10.00 (*0-8369-5467-X*) Ayer.

Treatise on the Police & Crimes of the Metropolis. John Wade & J. J. Tobia. LC 71-129306. (Criminology, Law Enforcement, & Social Problems Ser.: No. 128). 410p. 1972. reprint ed. 24.00 (*0-87585-128-2*) Patterson Smith.

Treatise on the Police of the Metropolis. 7th ed. Patrick Colquhoun. LC 69-14918. (Criminology, Law Enforcement, & Social Problems Ser.: No. 42). 1969. reprint ed. 35.00 (*0-87585-042-1*) Patterson Smith.

Treatise on the Practice of the Supreme Court of Judicature of the State of New York in Civil Actions. William Wyche. LC 70-37993. (American Law: The Formative Years). 374p. 1972. reprint ed. 26.95 (*0-405-04040-7*) Ayer.

Treatise on the Principles & Practical Influence of Taxation & the Funding System. 2nd ed. John R. McCulloch. LC 67-28411. (Reprints of Economic Classics Ser.). xvi, 552p. 1968. reprint ed. 57.50 (*0-678-00331-9*) Kelley.

***Treatise on the Principles & Practice of the Action of Ejectment, & the Resulting Action for Mesne Profits.** John Adams. LC 97-25982. lxxi, 620p. 1997. reprint ed. lib. bdg. 127.50 (*0-8377-1913-5*) Rothman.

Treatise on the Principles of American Constitutional Law & Legislation: The Constitutional Convention; Its History, Powers & Modes of Proceeding. 2nd ed. John A. Jameson. xix, 561p. 1981. reprint ed. lib. bdg. 42.50 (*0-8377-0734-X*) Rothman.

Treatise on the Principles of Pleading, in Civil Actions. James Gould. LC 70-37974. (American Law: The Formative Years). 540p. 1972. reprint ed. 34.95 (*0-405-04014-8*) Ayer.

Treatise on the Provincial Dialect of Scotland by Sylvester Douglas (Lord Glenberrie) Ed. by Charles Jones. 220p. 1991. text ed. 59.00 (*0-7486-0300-X*, Pub. by Edinburgh U Pr UK) Col U Pr.

Treatise on the Right of Property in Tide Waters & in the Soil & Shores Thereof. Joseph K. Angell. 435p. 1983. reprint ed. lib. bdg. 37.50 (*0-8377-0214-3*) Rothman.

***Treatise on the Rule of Saint Augustine.** Ange Le Proust. Ed. by John E. Rotelle. 290p. (Orig.). 1996. pap. write for info. (*0-941491-99-4*) Augustinian Pr.

Treatise on the Rules Which Govern the Interpretation & Construction of Statutory & Constitutional Law. 2nd ed. Theodore Sedgwick. Ed. by John N. Pomeroy. xlviii, 692p. 1981. reprint ed. lib. bdg. 49.50 (*0-8377-1115-0*) Rothman.

Treatise on the Seven Rays, 5 vols. Alice A. Bailey. Incl. Esoteric Psychology I. LC 53-19914. 1979. 27.00 (*0-85330-018-6*); Esoteric Psychology I. LC 53-19914. 1971. pap. 14.00 (*0-85330-118-2*); Esoteric Psychology II. LC 53-19914. 1981. 35.00 (*0-85330-019-4*); Esoteric Psychology II. LC 53-19914. 1981. pap. 22.00 (*0-85330-119-0*); Vol. III. Esoteric Astrology. LC 53-19914. 1975. 33.00 (*0-85330-020-8*); Vol. III. Esoteric Astrology. LC 53-19914. 1975. pap. 20.00 (*0-85330-120-4*); Vol. IV. Esoteric Healing. LC 53-19914. 1978. 33.00 (*0-85330-021-6*); Vol. IV. Esoteric Healing. LC 53-19914. 1971. pap. 20.00 (*0-85330-121-2*); Vol. V. Rays & the Initiations. LC 53-19914. 1981. 35.00 (*0-85330-022-4*); Vol. V. Rays & the Initiations. LC 53-19914. 1972. pap. 22.00 (*0-85330-122-0*); LC 53-19914. Set pap. write for info. (*0-318-54146-7*) Lucis.

Treatise on the Shift Operator. N. K. Nikol'skii. Tr. by J. Peetre from RUS. LC 84-26869. (Grundlehren der Mathematischen Wissenschaften Ser.: Vol. 273). (Illus.). 504p. 1986. 182.95 (*0-387-15021-8*) Spr-Verlag.

***Treatise on the Soul.** 2nd ed. Edward Reynolds. (Works of Edward Reynolds: Vol. 6). 380p. 1996. reprint ed. 29.95 (*1-57358-048-1*) Soli Deo Gloria.

Treatise on the Specific Performance of Contracts. 3rd ed. John N. Pomeroy & John C. Mann. Ed. by R. H. Hemholz & Bernard D. Reams, Jr. LC 86-62940. (Historical Writings in Law & Jurisprudence Ser.: No. 8). xl, 1045p. 1986. reprint ed. lib. bdg. 65.00 (*0-89941-523-7*, 304590) W S Hein.

Treatise on the Spleen & Stomach: A Translation of the Pi Wei Lun. Li Dong-Yuan. Ed. by Bob Flaws. Tr. by Yang Shou-Zhong & Li Jian-Yong from CHI. LC 92-75135. 275p. 1993. pap. 22.95 (*0-936185-41-4*) Blue Poppy Pr.

Treatise on the Study & Practice of the Law: With Directions for a Course of Law Studies. John Williams. iv, 208p. 1996. reprint ed. lib. bdg. 35.00 (*0-8377-2782-0*) Rothman.

Treatise on the Teeth. John A. Skinner. (Illus.). 1967. reprint ed. 15.00 (*0-87266-027-3*) Argosy.

Treatise on the Theory & Practice of Landscape Gardening Adapted to North America. Andrew J. Downing. (Illus.). 1976. reprint ed. 20.00 (*0-913728-23-3*) Theophrastus.

Treatise on the Theory & Practice of Landscape Gardening, Adapted to North America. Andrew J. Downing. LC 91-4356. (Dumbarton Oaks Reprints & Facsimiles in Landscape Architecture Ser.: No. 2). (Illus.). 576p. 1991. reprint ed. 60.00 (*0-88402-192-0*, DOTR) Dumbarton Oaks.

Treatise on the Theory & Practice of Landscape Gardening Adapted to North America. Andrew J. Downing. 576p. 1993. reprint ed. lib. bdg. 99.00 (*0-685-61624-X*) Rprt Serv.

Treatise on the Theory of Bessel Functions. 2nd ed. G. N. Watson. (Cambridge Mathematical Library). (Illus.). 804p. (C). 1995. pap. text ed. 33.95 (*0-521-48391-3*) Cambridge U Pr.

Treatise on the Theory of the First Amendment. Nimmer. 1984. Student Edition. student ed. write for info. (*0-8205-0286-3*, 516) Bender.

***Treatise on the True Art of Making Musical Instruments: A Practical Introduction to the Forgotten Craft of Enhancing Sound.** Keith R. Hill. (Illus.). xvi, 540p. 1997. 125.00 (*0-9657240-0-X*) Dioptra Pr.

Treatise on the Unconstitutionality of American Slavery: Together with the Powers & Duties of the Federal Government, in Relation to That Subject. Joel Tiffany. LC 78-83905. (Black Heritage Library Collection). 1977. 12.95 (*0-8369-8666-0*) Ayer.

Treatise on the Use of the Tenses in Hebrew & Some Other Syntactical Questions. 4th ed. S. R. Driver. 361p. 1997. pap. 30.00 (*0-8028-4160-0*) Eerdmans.

Treatise on the Virtues. St. Thomas Aquinas. Tr. by John A. Oesterle. LC 84-10691. 171p. (C). 1984. pap. text ed. 11.50 (*0-268-01855-3*) U of Notre Dame Pr.

Treatise on Theatres. George Saunders. Incl. . LC 68-21227. 1968. (*0-318-50910-5*); LC 68-21227. (Illus.). 1972. 31.95 (*0-405-08917-1*) Ayer.

***Treatise on Thermodynamics.** Max Planck. pap. 9.95 (*0-486-66371-X*) Dover.

Treatise on Thoroughbred Selection. Donald Lesh. 80p. 1990. pap. 21.00 (*0-85131-296-9*, Pub. by J A Allen & Co UK) St Mut.

Treatise on Toleration & Other Essays. Voltaire. (Great Minds Ser.). 128p. (C). 1994. pap. 8.95 (*0-87975-881-3*) Prometheus Bks.

Treatise on Trial by Jury: Including Questions of Law & Fact. With an Introductory Chapter on the Origin & History of Jury Trial. John Proffatt. viii, 608p. 1986. reprint ed. lib. bdg. 47.50 (*0-8377-2506-2*) Rothman.

Treatise on Trigonometric Series, Vol. 1. N. Bary & M. Mullins. LC 63-12682. 1964. 246.00 (*0-08-010002-3*, Pub. by Pergamon Repr UK) Franklin.

Treatise on Trigonometric Series, Vol. 2. N. Bary & M. Mullins. LC 63-12682. 1964. 246.00 (*0-08-011307-9*, Pub. by Pergamon Repr UK) Franklin.

Treatise on White Magic. Alice A. Bailey. LC 34-4815. 1934. 33.00 (*0-85330-023-2*) Lucis.

Treatise on White Magic. Alice A. Bailey. LC 34-4815. 1970. pap. 20.00 (*0-85330-123-9*) Lucis.

Treatise Touching the Inconveniences, That the Importation of Tobacco Out of Spaine, Hath Brought into This Land. Edward Bennett. LC 77-6856. (English Experience Ser.: No. 846). 1977. reprint ed. lib. bdg. 15.00 (*90-221-0846-5*) Walter J Johnson.

Treatise Upon Cable or Rope Traction As Applied to the Working of Street & Other Railways. J. Bucknall Smith & George W. Hilton. LC 76-53131. (Illus.). 1978. reprint ed. 14.50 (*0-913896-08-X*) Owlswick Pr.

Treatise Upon the Law of Eminent Domain. Henery E. Mills. lxvii, 404p. 1982. reprint ed. lib. bdg. 35.00 (*0-8377-0841-9*) Rothman.

Treatise Wherein Is Declared the Sufficiencie of English Medicines, for Cure of All Diseases, Cured with Medicine. Timothy Bright. LC 77-6860. (English Experience Ser.: No. 854). 1977. reprint ed. lib. bdg. 15.00 (*90-221-0854-6*) Walter J Johnson.

Treatises. St. Cyprian. Tr. by Roy J. Deferrari et al. LC 77-81349. (Fathers of the Church Ser.: Vol. 36). 372p. 1958. 21.95 (*0-8132-0036-9*) Cath U Pr.

Treatises & Essays on Subjects Connected with Economical Policy: With Biographical Sketches of Quesnay, Adam Smith & Ricardo. John R. McCulloch. LC 67-20088. (Reprints of Economic Classics Ser.). vii, 487p. 1967. reprint ed. 57.50 (*0-678-00255-X*) Kelley.

Treatises & the Pastoral Prayer. Aelred of Rievaulx. pap. 5.00 (*0-87907-902-9*) Cistercian Pubns.

Treatises I: Apologia, Precept & Dispensation. Bernard of Clairvaux. (Cistercian Fathers Ser.: No. 1). 190p. 7.95 (*0-87907-101-X*) Cistercian Pubns.

Treatises of Benvenuto Cellini on Goldsmithing & Sculpture. Benvenuto Cellini. Tr. by C. R. Ashbee. (Illus.). 1966. pap. 6.95 (*0-486-21568-7*) Dover.

Treatises of Later Han: Their Author, Sources, Contents & Place in Chinese Historiography. B. J. Mansvelt-Beck. LC 90-2156. (Sinica Leidensia Ser.: Vol. 21). xii, 296p. 1990. pap. 75.50 (*90-04-08895-4*) E J Brill.

Treatises on Various Subjects. Augustine, Saint. Tr. by Mary S. Muldowney et al. LC 65-18319. (Fathers of the Church Ser.: Vol. 16). 479p. 1952. 26.95 (*0-8132-0016-4*) Cath U Pr.

Treatment. Martin Crimp. 96p. 1993. pap. 12.95 (*1-85459-240-8*, Pub. by N Hern Bks UK) Theatre Comm.

Treatment Algorithms. Ed. by A. J. Rush. LC 97-21357. (Modern Problems of Pharmacopsychiatry Ser.: Vol. 25, 1996). (Illus.). x, 190p. 1996. 191.50 (*3-8055-6223-3*) S Karger.

Treatment Alternatives to Street Crime: TASC Programs. 2nd ed. (Illus.). 64p. (Orig.). (C). 1995. pap. text ed. 25.00 (*0-7881-2098-0*) DIANE Pub.

Treatment Alternatives to Street Crime, TASC: History, Experiences, & Issues. James A. Inciardi & Duane C. McBride. 65p. (Orig.). (C). 1994. pap. text ed. 30.00 (*0-7881-0451-9*) DIANE Pub.

Treatment & Care in Old Age Psychiatry. Ed. by Raymond Levy et al. LC 93-3405. 256p. 1993. pap. 85.00 (*1-871816-17-3*, Pub. by Wrightson Biomed UK) Taylor & Francis.

Treatment & Choices for Alcoholism & Substance Abuse. Ed. by Harvey B. Milkman & Lloyd I. Sederer. 395p. 45.90 (*0-669-20019-0*, Lexington) Jossey-Bass.

Treatment & Disposal Methods for Waste Chemicals. (IRPTC Data Profile Ser.: No. 5). 303p. 1986. 50.00 (*92-807-1106-7*, E.85.III.D.2) UN.

Treatment & Disposal of Clinical Waste: Handbook, No. 3. Laura DeChaine et al. Ed. by Brian P. Favno. 120p. 1994. pap. 125.00 (*0-948237-18-X*, Pub. by H&H Sci Cnslts UK) St Mut.

***Treatment & Disposal of Pesticide Wastes.** Ed. by Raymond F. Krueger & James N. Seiber. LC 84-12327. (ACS Symposium Ser.: No. 259). (Illus.). 376p. 1984. reprint ed. pap. 107.20 (*0-608-03136-4*, 2063589) Bks Demand.

Treatment & Disposal of Radioactive Wastes. C. Amphlett & J. Dunworth. Vol. 2. 1961. write for info. (*0-318-69653-3*, Pub. by Pergamon Repr UK) Franklin.

***Treatment & Disposal of Wastes: Report of a WHO Scientific Group, 1967.** (Technical Report Ser.: No. 367). 0030p. 1967. pap. text ed. 3.00 (*92-4-120367-6*, 1100367) World Health.

Treatment & Handling of Wastes. A. D. Bradshaw et al. (Technology in the Third Millennium Ser.). (Illus.). 320p. (gr. 13). 1991. text ed. 80.95 (*0-412-39390-5*) Chapman & Hall.

Treatment & Minimization of Heavy Metal-Containing Wastes, 1995: Proceedings: International Symposium Sponsored by the Extraction & Processing Division of TMS (1995: Las Vegas, Nevada) Proceedings. Ed. by John P. Hager et al. LC 94-74342. 263p. 1995. 86.00 (*0-87339-287-6*, 2876) Minerals Metals.

Treatment & Prevention of Alcohol Problems. W. Miles Cox. (Personality, Psychopathology & Psychotherapy Ser.). 1986. text ed. 49.95 (*0-12-194470-0*) Acad Pr.

Treatment & Prevention of Childhood Sexual Abuse. Ed. by Sandra A. Burkhardt & Anthony F. Rotatori. 220p. 1995. 29.50 (*1-56032-320-5*) Taylor & Francis.

Treatment & Prognosis: OB Gyn. Grudzinskas. 257p. 1988. pap. 70.00 (*0-433-12645-0*) Buttrwrth-Heinemann.

Treatment & Prognosis: Surgery. Hawkins. 277p. 1986. 70.00 (*0-433-13394-5*) Buttrwrth-Heinemann.

Treatment & Rehabilitation of the Chronic Alcoholic see Biology of Alcoholism

Treatment & Security Needs of Special Hospital Patients. Tony Maden et al. 150p. 1995. pap. text ed. 150.00 (*1-56593-501-2*, 1160) Singular Publishing.

Treatment Approaches for Alcohol & Drug Dependence: An Introductory Guide. Tracey J. Jarvis et al. LC 94-35185. 176p. 1995. pap. text ed. 45.00 (*0-471-95373-3*) Wiley.

Treatment Approaches with Suicidal Adolescents. Ed. by James K. Zimmerman & Gregory M. Asnis. LC 94-30990. (Publication Series of the Department of Psychiatry Albert Einstein College of Medicine of Yeshiva University: Vol. 11). 288p. 1995. text ed. 50.00 (*0-471-10236-9*) Wiley.

Treatment Aspects of Drug Dependence. Arnold J. Schecter. (Uniscience Ser.). 1978. 148.00 (*0-8493-5476-5*, RC566, CRC Reprint) Franklin.

Treatment by Manipulation. H. Jackson Burrows & W. D. Coltart. 36p. 1970. reprint ed. spiral bd. 8.00 (*0-7873-0135-3*) Hlth Research.

Treatment by Neuropathy & the Encyclopedia of Physical & Manipulative Therapeutics. Thomas T. Lake. 684p. 1972. reprint ed. spiral bd. 38.50 (*0-7873-0519-7*) Hlth Research.

***Treatment Compliance & the Therapeutic Alliance.** Ed. by Barry Blackwell. (Chronic Mental Illness Ser.: Vol. 5). 368p. 1997. text ed. 58.00 (*90-5699-525-1*, Harwood Acad Pubs) Gordon & Breach.

***Treatment Compliance & the Therapeutic Alliance.** Ed. by Barry Blackwell. (Chronic Mental Illness Ser.). 1997. text ed. 60.00 (*90-5702-546-9*, Harwood Acad Pubs) Gordon & Breach.

Treatment Costs for Very Low Birthweight Infants: The California Medicaid Experience. Jeannette A. Rogowski. 66p. (Orig.). Date not set. pap. text ed. 13.00 (*0-8330-2345-4*) Rand Corp.

Treatment Dentures for Edentulous Prosthodontic Patients. Toshihiro Hirai et al. LC 95-77085. (Dental Technique Ser.: Vol. 6). (Illus.). 43p. (Orig.). 1995. pap. 30.00 (*1-56386-033-3*) Ishiyaku Euro.

Treatment, Disposal & Management of Human Wastes: Proceedings of an IAWPRC Conference Held in Tokyo, Japan, 30 September-4 October 1985. Ed. by J. Matusmoto & T. Matusuo. LC 82-645900. (Water Science & Technology Ser.: No. 18). (Illus.). 444p. 1987. pap. 105.00 (*0-08-035192-1*, Pergamon Pr) Elsevier.

Treatment Disposal Re-Use of Building Demolition & Site Cleaning Wastes from Nuclear. H. Wingender et al. 210p. 1994. pap. 30.00 (*92-826-8134-3*, CD-NA-15188-ENC, Pub. by Europ Com UK) Bernan Associates.

Treatment Effectiveness Handbook: A Reference Guide to the Key Research Reviews in Mental Health & Substance Abuse. Howard B. Pikoff. LC 96-84425. 192p. 1996. 65.00 (*0-9640981-0-5*) Data for Decisions.

Treatment for Abused & Neglected Children: Infancy to Age 18. Anthony J. Urquiza. 120p. (Orig.). (C). 1995. pap. text ed. 25.00 (*0-7881-1661-4*) DIANE Pub.

Treatment for Adolescent Substance Abusers. 1991. lib. bdg. 250.00 (*0-8490-5046-4*) Gordon Pr.

Treatment for Adolescent Substance Abusers. 1992. lib. bdg. 250.00 (*0-8490-5495-8*) Gordon Pr.

Treatment in Crisis Situations. Naomi Golan. LC 77-85350. (Treatment Approaches in the Human Services Ser.). 1978. 35.00 (*0-02-912060-8*, Free Press) Free Pr.

Treatment in Dermatology. Ed. by Julian L. Verbov. (New Clinical Applications Dermatology Ser.). 1987. lib. bdg. 82.00 (*0-85200-955-0*) Kluwer Ac.

Treatment in Dermatology. rev. ed. Barbara Leppard & Richard Ashton. Ed. by Joshua Wieder & Nicholas J. Lowe. LC 94-40427. 1995. 39.95 (*1-85775-135-3*, Radcliffe Med Pr); text ed. 115.00 (*1-85775-130-2*, Radcliffe Med Pr) Scovill Paterson.

Treatment in Dermatology. 2nd ed. Barbara Leppard & Richard Ashton. 1995. pap. 39.95 (*1-870905-52-0*, Radcliffe Med Pr) Scovill Paterson.

Treatment Interventions In Human Sexuality. Ed. by Carol C. Nadelson & David B. Marcotte. LC 83-4078. (Critical Issues in Psychiatry Ser.). 502p. 1983. 89.50 (*0-306-41082-6*, Plenum Pr) Plenum.

Treatment Issues & Innovations in Mental Retardation. Ed. by Johnny L. Matson & Frank Andrasik. (Applied Clinical Psychology Ser.). 666p. 1983. 95.00 (*0-306-40935-6*, Plenum Pr) Plenum.

Treatment Modalities in Lung Cancer. Ed. by R. Arriagada & T. Le Chevalier. (Antibiotics & Chemotherapy Ser.: Vol. 41). (Illus.). xii, 248p. 1988. 158.50 (*3-8055-4775-7*) S Karger.

Treatment of Adult Survivors of Childhood Abuse. Eliana Gil. LC 88-80275. 250p. (Orig.). (C). 1988. pap. 18.95 (*0-9613205-6-7*, 0007) Launch Pr.

Treatment of Adult Survivors of Incest. Ed. by Patricia L. Paddison. LC 92-17653. (Clinical Practice Ser.: No. 27). 148p. 1993. text ed. 27.50 (*0-88048-469-1*, 8469) Am Psychiatric.

Treatment of Affective Disorders in the Elderly. Ed. by Charles A. Shamoian. LC 85-6103. (Progress in Psychiatry Ser.: No. 3). 84p. 1985. text ed. 22.00 (*0-88048-086-6*, 8086) Am Psychiatric.

Treatment of Age-Related Cognitive Dysfunction: Pharmacological & Clinical Evaluation. Ed. by Giorgio Racagni et al. (International Academy for Biomedical & Drug Research Ser.: Vol. 2). (Illus.). vi, 154p. 1992. 121.00 (*3-8055-5551-2*) S Karger.

Treatment of Airborne Radioactive Wastes. (Proceedings Ser.). (Illus.). 818p. 1968. pap. 85.00 (*92-0-020068-0*, ISP195, Pub. by IAEA AU) Bernan Associates.

Treatment of Alcoholism & Other Addictions: A Self-Psychology Approach. Jerome D. Levin. LC 87-19563. 448p. 1994. pap. 35.00 (*0-87668-521-1*) Aronson.

Treatment of Anxiety. Ed. by R. Noyes, Jr. et al. (Handbook of Anxiety Ser.: Vol. 4). 558p. 1990. 300.00 (*0-444-81261-X*) Elsevier.

Treatment of Anxiety Disorders: Clinician's Guide & Treatment Manuals. Gavin Andrews et al. (Illus.). 400p. (C). 1995. text ed. 85.00 (*0-521-46521-4*); pap. text ed. 39.95 (*0-521-46927-9*) Cambridge U Pr.

Treatment of Anxiety Disorders: Patient Manuals. Gavin Andrews et al. 250p. (C). 1995. pap. text ed. 22.61 (*0-521-46958-9*) Cambridge U Pr.

Treatment of Aphasia: From Theory to Practice. Ed. by Chris Code & Dave J. Muller. 250p. (Orig.). (C). 1995. pap. text ed. 45.00 (*1-56593-255-2*, 0430) Singular Publishing.

***Treatment of Behaviour Problems in Dogs & Cats: A Guide for the Small Animal Veterinarian.** Henry R. Askew. (Illus.). 448p. (C). 1996. text ed. 49.95 (*0-632-04108-0*) Iowa St U Pr.

Treatment of Black Alcoholics. Ed. by Frances L. Brisbane & Maxine Womble. LC 85-13975. (Alcoholism Treatment Quarterly Ser.: Vol. 2, No. 3-4). 270p. 1985. text ed. 49.95 (*0-86656-403-9*) Haworth Pr.

Treatment of Bleeding Disorders with Blood Components. Ed. by Eberhard F. Mammen et al. (Reviews of Hematology: Vol. I). 1980. 49.95 (*0-915340-01-1*) PJD Pubns.

Treatment of Burns: Principles & Practice. William W. Monafo & Carlos Pappalardo. LC 71-138827. (Illus.). 286p. 1971. 19.10 (*0-87527-055-7*) Green.

Treatment of Cancer. 2nd ed. Ed. by Karol Sikora & K. Halnan. (Illus.). 936p. 1989. 251.95 (*0-412-29400-1*) Chapman & Hall.

Treatment of Cancer. 3rd ed. P. Price. 1160p. (gr. 13). 1995. text ed. 230.00 (*0-412-56010-0*) Chapman & Hall.

An Asterisk (*) at the beginning of an entry indicates that the title is appearing in BIP for the first time.

Treatment of Cats by Homoeopathy. K. Sheppard. 1979. pap. 3.95 (*0-85032-120-4*) Formur Intl.

Treatment of Cattle by Homeopathy. Macleod. 129p. 1981. pap. 17.95 (*0-85207-247-3*, Pub. by C W Daniel UK) Natl Bk Netwk.

***Treatment of Cattle by Homoeopathy.** MacLeod. Date not set. pap. 26.95 (*0-8464-1210-1*) Beekman Pubs.

Treatment of Cattle by Homoeopathy. George MacLeod. 160p. (Orig.). pap. 26.95 (*0-8464-4303-1*) Beekman Pubs.

Treatment of Cerebral Infarction. J. Suzuki. (Illus.). 400p. 1987. 120.00 (*0-387-81933-9*) Spr-Verlag.

Treatment of Cerebral Palsy in Motor Delay. 3rd ed. Sophie Levitt. (Illus.). 312p. 1995. pap. 36.95 (*0-632-03873-X*, Pub. by Blckwell Sci Pubns UK) Blackwell Sci.

Treatment of Chemical Agent Casualties & Conventional Military Chemical Injuries. 1991. lib. bdg. 79.95 (*0-8490-4087-6*) Gordon Pr.

Treatment of Chemical Agent Casualties & Conventional Military Chemical Injuries. 1995. lib. bdg. 261.75 (*0-8490-6590-9*) Gordon Pr.

Treatment of Chemical Agent Casualties & Conventional Military Chemical Injuries. 1995. lib. bdg. 255.75 (*0-8490-6628-X*) Gordon Pr.

Treatment of Child & Adult Survivors see Child Abuse: A Multidisciplinary Survey

Treatment of Childhood Disorders. Ed. by Eric J. Mash & Russell A. Barkley. LC 88-24464. 568p. 1989. lib. bdg. 55.00 (*0-89862-743-5*) Guilford Pr.

Treatment of Children & Adolescents in Residential & Inpatient Settings. Robert D. Lyman & Nancy R. Campbell. LC 96-10054. (Developmental Clinical Psychology & Psychiatry Ser.: Vol. 36). 144p. 1996. 39.95 (*0-8039-7046-3*); pap. 17.95 (*0-8039-7047-1*) Sage.

Treatment of Children Through Social Group Work: A Developmental Approach. James A. Garland & Ralph L. Kolodny. 1980. text ed. 20.00 (*0-89182-016-7*); pap. text ed. 10.00 (*0-89182-017-5*) Charles River Bks.

Treatment of Chronic Pain. Ed. by Mark Mumenthaler. 337p. 1990. text ed. 120.00 (*3-7186-5026-6*, Harwood Acad Pubs); pap. text ed. 77.00 (*3-7186-5027-4*, Harwood Acad Pubs) Gordon & Breach.

Treatment of Cocaine Abuse: An Annotated Bibliography. John J. Miletich. LC 91-35403. (Bibliographies & Indexes in Medical Studies: No. 9). 256p. 1992. text ed. 55.00 (*0-313-27839-3*, MTQ/, Greenwood Pr) Greenwood.

Treatment of Collective Co-ordinates in Many-Body Systems. Ed. by D. R. Bes & J. Kurchan. (Lecture Notes in Physics Ser.: Vol. 34). 128p. (C). 1990. text ed. 36.00 (*981-02-0306-3*); pap. text ed. 21.00 (*981-02-0307-1*) World Scientific Pub.

Treatment of Communication Disorders in Culturally & Linguistically Diverse Populations. Orlando Taylor. LC 82-22431. 209p. (Orig.). (C). 1986. 32.50 (*0-89079-365-4*, 1558) Buttrwrth-Heinemann.

Treatment of Complicated Epilepsies in Adults. Ed. by P. Berner & L. W. Diehl. (Bibliotheca Psychiatrica Ser.: No. 158). (Illus.). 1978. 46.50 (*3-8055-2814-0*) S Karger.

Treatment of Complicated Mourning. Therese A. Rando. LC 90-64044. 768p. (Orig.). (C). 1992. text ed. 39.95 (*0-87822-329-0*, 4428) Res Press.

Treatment of Convulsive Status Epilepticus. Working Group on Status Epilepticus Staff. 32p. (Orig.). 1995. pap. write for info. (*0-916570-21-5*) Epilepsy Foundation of America.

Treatment of Dementias: A New Generation of Progress. Ed. by E. M. Meyer et al. (Advances in Behavioral Biology Ser.: Vol. 40). (Illus.). 528p. (C). 1992. 120.00 (*0-306-44228-0*, Plenum Pr) Plenum.

***Treatment of Depression: A Holistic Approach.** David McMillin. LC 97-8533. (Edgar Cayce Health Ser.). 352p. (Orig.). 1997. pap. 16.95 (*0-87604-386-4*, 498) ARE Pr.

***Treatment of Depression: Old Controversies & New Approaches.** Ed. by Paula J. Clayton & James E. Barrett. LC 81-40379. (American Psychopathological Association Ser.). reprint ed. pap. 100.40 (*0-608-04739-2*, 2065460) Bks Demand.

Treatment of Depression & Related Moods: A Manual for Psychotherapists. Daniel W. Badal. LC 87-33665. 451p. 1988. 50.00 (*0-87668-981-0*) Aronson.

Treatment of Depression & Related Moods: A Manual for Psychotherapists. Daniel W. Badal. 1995. pap. text ed. 40.00 (*1-56821-716-1*) Aronson.

Treatment of Depression in Managed Care. Mark Mays & James W. Croake. Ed. by S. Richard Sauber. LC 96-36748. (Mental Health Practice under Managed Health Care Ser.: Vol. 7). 256p. 1997. 27.95 (*0-87630-829-9*) Brunner-Mazel.

Treatment of Diabetic Neuropathy. David F. Horrobin. 139p. 1992. text ed. 65.00 (*0-443-04774-X*) Churchill.

Treatment of Disease in TCM Vol. 1: Diseases of the Head & Face Including Mental/Emotional Disorders. Philippe Sionneau & Lu Gang. Ed. by Bob Flaws. LC 95-83249. 260p. 1996. pap. text ed. 21.95 (*0-936185-69-4*) Blue Poppy Pr.

Treatment of Disease in TCM Vol. II: Diseases of the Eyes, Ears, Nose, & Throat. Philippe Sionneau & Lu Gang. Ed. by Bob Flaws. LC 95-83249. 290p. (Orig.). 1996. per., pap. text ed. 21.95 (*0-936185-73-2*) Blue Poppy Pr.

***Treatment of Disease in TCM Vol. III: Disease of the Mouth, Lips, Tongue, Teeth & Gums.** Philippe Sionneau & Lii Gang. Ed. by Bob Flaws. LC 95-83249. 256p. (Orig.). 1997. pap. 21.95 (*0-936185-79-1*) Blue Poppy Pr.

Treatment of Disease with Acupuncture: Complete Course in Acupuncture, Vol. II. James Tin Yao So. Ed. by Richard Feit. 379p. (C). 1987. text ed. 35.00 (*0-912111-08-9*) Paradigm Publns.

Treatment of Dogs by Homoeopathy. K. Sheppard. 1981. pap. 3.95 (*0-85032-079-8*) Formur Intl.

***Treatment of Drinking Problems: A Guide for the Helping Professions.** Griffith Edwards et al. (Illus.). 350p. (C). 1997. text ed. 80.00 (*0-521-49696-9*) Cambridge U Pr.

***Treatment of Drinking Problems: A Guide for the Helping Professions.** Griffith Edwards et al. (Illus.). 350p. (C). 1997. pap. text ed. 32.95 (*0-521-49793-0*) Cambridge U Pr.

Treatment of DSM-IV Psychiatric Disorders. 3rd rev. ed. William H. Reid et al. LC 96-7478. 750p. 1997. write for info. (*0-87630-765-9*) Brunner-Mazel.

Treatment of Early Breast Cancer: A Systematic Overview of All Available Randomized Trials of Adjuvant Endocrine & Cytotoxic Therapy, Vol. 1: Worldwide Evidence, 1985-1990. Early Breast Cancer Trialists' Collaborative Group Staff. (Illus.). 224p. 1990. 58.00 (*0-19-262015-0*); pap. 17.95 (*0-19-262014-2*) OUP.

Treatment of Early Stage Breast Cancer. 1994. lib. bdg. 250.00 (*0-8490-8523-3*) Gordon Pr.

Treatment of Emotional Disorders. Seymour L. Halleck. LC 77-18374. 544p. 1978. 45.00 (*0-87668-263-8*) Aronson.

Treatment of End-Stage Coronary Artery Disease. P. J. Walter. (Advances in Cardiology Ser.: Vol. 36). (Illus.). x, 306p. 1988. 151.25 (*3-8055-4717-X*) S Karger.

Treatment of Endometriosis & Other Disorders & Infections, Vol. 4. Ed. by Y. Boutaleb & A. Gzouli. (Recent Developments in Fertility & Sterility Ser.). (Illus.). 250p. (C). 1991. 85.00 (*1-85070-287-X*) Prthnon Pub.

Treatment of Epilepsy. Ed. by Simon D. Shorvon et al. LC 95-36763. (Illus.). 900p. 1996. 195.00 (*0-632-03782-2*) Blackwell Sci.

Treatment of Epilepsy: Principles & Practice. Elaine Wyllie. LC 92-49990. (Illus.). 1100p. 1992. text ed. 105.00 (*0-8121-1504-X*) Williams & Wilkins.

***Treatment of Epilepsy: Principles & Practice.** 2nd ed. Ed. by Elaine Wyllie. 1188p. 1996. 139.00 (*0-683-09285-5*) Williams & Wilkins.

Treatment of Equine Fractures. H. R. Denny. 168p. 1991. 44.95 (*0-7236-0943-8*) Blackwell Sci.

***Treatment of External Diseases with Acupuncture Moxibustion.** Yan Cui-Lan. Ed. by Bob Flaws. Tr. by Yang Shou-Zhong from CHI. LC 96-80188. 250p. (Orig.). 1997. pap. 29.95 (*0-936185-80-5*) Blue Poppy Pr.

Treatment of External Hazards in Probabilistic Safety Assessment for Nuclear Power. IAEA Staff. (Safety Ser.: No. 50-P-7). 58p. 1995. pap. 30.00 (*92-0-104794-0*, STI/PUB/968, Pub. by IAEA AU) Bernan Associates.

Treatment of Facial Cleft Deformities: An Illustrated Guide. Kurt W. Butow. LC 94-72969. (Illus.). 146p. 1995. pap. 30.00 (*1-56386-032-5*) Ishiyaku Euro.

Treatment of Families in Conflict: The Clinical Study of Family Process. Group for the Advancement of Psychiatry Staff. LC 84-45131. 352p. 1983. 30.00 (*0-87668-724-9*) Aronson.

Treatment of Family Violence: Sourcebook. Robert T. Ammerman. LC 89-39492. (Personality Processes Ser.). 461p. 1990. text ed. 92.50 (*0-471-61023-2*) Wiley.

Treatment of Final Vowels in Early Neo-Babylonian. James P. Hyatt. LC 78-63567. (Yale Oriental Series: Researches: No. 23). reprint ed. 20.00 (*0-404-60323-8*) AMS Pr.

Treatment of Fractures in Children & Adolescents. Ed. by B. G. Weber. LC 79-16985. (Illus.). 1979. 271.00 (*0-387-09313-3*) Spr-Verlag.

***Treatment of Fractures in the Elderly.** Ed. by Kenneth J. Koval et al. (Illus.). 350p. 1997. text ed. 125.00 (*0-397-51825-0*) Lppncott-Raven.

Treatment of Functional Somatic Symptoms. Ed. by Richard Mayou et al. (Illus.). 472p. (C). 1995. text ed. 89.50 (*0-19-262499-7*) OUP.

Treatment of Gaseous Effluents at Nuclear Facilities, Vol. 2. Ed. by W. R. A. Goossens et al. (Radioactive Waste Management Ser.). 537p. 1991. text ed. 176.00 (*3-7186-0525-2*) Gordon & Breach.

Treatment of Genetic Diseases. Ed. by Robert J. Desnick. (Illus.). 350p. 1991. text ed. 79.00 (*0-443-08773-3*) Churchill.

Treatment of Haemoglobinopathies & Allied Disorders: Proceedings of the WHO Scientific Group, Geneva, 1971. WHO Staff. (Technical Report Ser.: No. 509). 1972. pap. text ed. 5.00 (*92-4-120509-1*, 1100509) World Health.

Treatment of Hand Injuries: Preservation & Restoration of Function. Elden C. Weckesser. LC 72-86353. 284p. reprint ed. pap. 81.00 (*0-317-58154-6*, 2029741) Bks Demand.

Treatment of Hazardous Petrochemical & Petroleum Wastes: Current, New & Emerging Technologies. Dudley J. Burton & K. Ravishankar. LC 89-39093. (Illus.). 268p. 1990. 56.00 (*0-8155-1215-5*) Noyes.

Treatment of Hazardous Waste Leachate: Unit Operations & Costs. J. L. McArdle et al. LC 87-34715. (Pollution Technology Review Ser.: No. 151). (Illus.). 111p. 1988. 36.00 (*0-8155-1160-4*) Noyes.

Treatment of Heart Disease in the Adult. 2nd ed. Ira L. Rubin et al. LC 79-175466. 522p. reprint ed. pap. 148.80 (*0-317-26706-X*, 2056008) Bks Demand.

Treatment of Homosexuals with Mental Health Disorders. Ed. by Michael Ross & John P. DeCecco. LC 87-30826. (Journal of Homosexuality Ser.: No. 15, No. 1-2). (Illus.). 222p. 1988. pap. 17.95 (*0-918393-47-7*) Harrington Pk.

Treatment of Horses by Acupuncture. 2nd ed. Erwin Westermayer. (Illus.). 40p. 1985. 37.95 (*0-8464-4304-X*) Beekman Pubs.

Treatment of Horses by Homeopathy. George Macleod. 130p. 1977. pap. 17.95 (*0-85207-249-X*, Pub. by C W Daniel UK) Natl Bk Netwk.

Treatment of Horses by Homeopathy. rev. ed. G. MacLeod. 182p. 1993. pap. 26.95 (*0-8464-1284-5*) Beekman Pubs.

***Treatment of Hospitalized Cystic Fibrosis Patient.** Ed. by Orentsein & Stern. (Lung Biology in Health & Disease Ser.). 448p. 1997. write for info. (*0-8247-9500-8*) Dekker.

Treatment of Hyperlipoproteinemia. Ed. by Lars A. Carlson & Anders G. Olsson. LC 83-42855. 304p. 1984. reprint ed. pap. 86.70 (*0-608-00360-3*, 2061077) Bks Demand.

Treatment of Imprecise Goals: The Case of the Regional Science. Horst Zimmerman. (Discussion Paper Ser.: No. 9). 1966. pap. 10.00 (*1-55869-125-1*) Regional Sci Res Inst.

Treatment of Indians by the Criminal Justice System. 51p. (Orig.). (C). 1993. pap. text ed. 25.00 (*1-56806-856-5*) DIANE Pub.

Treatment of Infantile Hydrocephalus, 2 vols. Concezio Di Rocco. LC 86-24451. 1987. Set. 205.00 (*0-8493-5720-9*, RJ469, CRC Reprint) Franklin.

Treatment of Infantile Hydrocephalus, Vol. 1. C. Di Rocco. LC 86-24451. 1987. 96.00 (*0-8493-5721-7*, RJ496, CRC Reprint) Franklin.

Treatment of Infantile Hydrocephalus, 2 vols., Vol. I. Concezio Di Rocco. 160p. 1987. write for info. (*0-318-62350-1*) CRC Pr.

Treatment of Infantile Hydrocephalus, 2 vols., Vol. II. Concezio Di Rocco. 160p. 1987. write for info. (*0-318-62351-X*) CRC Pr.

Treatment of Infantile Hydrocephalus, Vol. 2. Concezio Di Rocco. LC 86-24451. 184p. 1987. reprint ed. 109.00 (*0-8493-5722-5*, CRC Reprint) Franklin.

Treatment of Infants, Child & Adolescents. Burg. 432p. 1990. pap. text ed. 35.00 (*0-7216-2139-2*) Saunders.

Treatment of Infertility, Vol. 1. Ed. by Y. Boutaleb & A. Gzouli. (Recent Developments in Fertility & Sterility Ser.). (Illus.). 250p. (C). 1991. 85.00 (*1-85070-284-5*) Prthnon Pub.

Treatment of Insanity. John M. Galt. LC 73-2397. (Mental Illness & Social Policy; the American Experience Ser.). 1973. reprint ed. 35.95 (*0-405-05205-7*) Ayer.

Treatment of Intangibles: A Banker's View. T. H. Donaldson. LC 92-5286. 164p. 1993. text ed. 69.95 (*0-312-07981-8*) St Martin.

Treatment of Integral Equations by Numerical Methods. Christopher T. Baker & Geoffrey F. Miller. 1983. text ed. 117.00 (*0-12-074120-2*) Acad Pr.

Treatment of Liquid Aluminum-Silicon Alloys. 272p. boxed 75.00 (*0-87433-121-8*, NF9001) Am Foundrymen.

Treatment of Low Carbon Steel. 1996. lib. bdg. 249.75 (*0-8490-8346-X*) Gordon Pr.

Treatment of Mandibular Fractures. 2nd ed. Jonas T. Johnson et al. LC 95-8250. (Self-Instructional Package Ser.). (Illus.). 112p. (Orig.). (C). 1995. pap. text ed. 25.00 (*1-56772-018-8*) AAO-HNS.

Treatment of Market Power: Antitrust Regulation & Public Enterprise. William G. Shepherd. LC 75-19459. 326p. 1975. text ed. 49.00 (*0-231-03773-2*) Col U Pr.

Treatment of Mental Disorders. Ed. by John H. Greist et al. 584p. (C). 1982. pap. text ed. 32.50 (*0-19-503107-5*) OUP.

Treatment of Mental Disorders: A Review of Effectiveness. Ed. by Norman Sartorius et al. LC 93-2989. 7p. 1993. text ed. 69.95 (*0-88048-975-8*, 8975) Am Psychiatric.

Treatment of Metal Wastestreams. 2nd ed. Kenneth D. Kerri. (Illus.). 130p. (C). 1993. pap. text ed. 10.00 (*1-884701-07-8*) CA St U Ofc Water.

Treatment of Metastasis: Problems & Prospects. K. Hellman & S. A. Eccles. 430p. 1985. 110.00 (*0-85066-294-X*) Taylor & Francis.

Treatment of Microbial Contaminants in Potable Water Supplies: Technologies & Costs. Jerrold J. Troyan & Sigurd P. Hansen. LC 89-16034. (Pollution Technology Review Ser.: No. 171). (Illus.). 335p. 1990. 45.00 (*0-8155-1214-7*) Noyes.

Treatment of Migraine: Pharmacological & Biofeedback Considerations. Ed. by Roy J. Mathew. (Illus.). 170p. 1981. text ed. 27.50 (*0-88331-209-3*) Luce.

Treatment of Movement Disorders. Ed. by Roger Kurlan. (Illus.). 500p. 1994. text ed. 79.50 (*0-397-51326-7*) Lppncott-Raven.

Treatment of Multiple Personality Disorder. Ed. by Bennett G. Braun. LC 86-10903. 258p. 1985. pap. text ed. 22.50 (*0-88048-096-3*, 8096) Am Psychiatric.

Treatment of Multiple Sclerosis: Trial Design, Results & Future Perspectives. Ed. by R. A. Rudick et al. (Clinical Medicine & the Nervous System Ser.). (Illus.). xviii, 313p. 1992. 150.00 (*0-387-19683-8*) Spr-Verlag.

***Treatment of Multiple Sclerosis: Trial Design, Results, & Future Perspectives.** Richard A. Rudick & Donald E. Goodkin. (Clinical Medicine & the Nervous System Ser.). 290p. 1991. 145.00 (*3-540-19683-8*) Spr-Verlag.

Treatment of Nature in English Poetry Between Pope & Wordsworth. Myra Reynolds. LC 66-29468. 388p. 1966. reprint ed. 50.00 (*0-87752-091-7*) Gordian.

Treatment of Nature in German Literature from Guenther to Goethe's Werner. Max Batt. 1976. lib. bdg. 59.95 (*0-8490-2764-0*) Gordon Pr.

Treatment of Neuromuscular Diseases. Ed. by Robert C. Griggs & Richard T. Moxley. LC 75-43197. (Advances in Neurology Ser.: No. 17). (Illus.). 384p. reprint ed. pap. 109.50 (*0-7837-7110-X*, 2046939) Bks Demand.

Treatment of Neurosis in the Young: A Psychoanalytic Perspective. Ed. by M. Hossein Etezady. LC 93-231. 320p. 1993. 50.00 (*0-87668-500-9*) Aronson.

Treatment of Obsessive & Compulsive Behaviors. Leon Salzman. LC 94-38376. 274p. 1995. reprint ed. pap. text ed. 40.00 (*1-56821-422-7*) Aronson.

Treatment of Obsessive Compulsive Disorder. Gail S. Steketee. LC 93-15832. (Treatment Manuals for Practitioners Ser.). 224p. 1993. lib. bdg. 39.95 (*0-89862-184-4*) Guilford Pr.

Treatment of Obsessive Compulsive Disorder. Gail S. Steketee. LC 93-15832. (Treatment Manuals for Practitioners Ser.). 1996. pap. text ed. 19.95 (*0-89862-911-X*, 2911) Guilford Pr.

Treatment of Offenders & Families see Child Abuse: A Multidisciplinary Survey

Treatment of Oil-Containing Wastewater. V. V. Pushkarev et al. LC 83-70667. viii, 214p. 1983. 42.50 (*0-89864-004-0*) Allerton Pr.

Treatment of Opiate Addiction Using Methadone: A Counselor's Manual. Michael J. McCann et al. 335p. (Orig.). (C). 1995. pap. text ed. 50.00 (*0-7881-2534-6*) DIANE Pub.

Treatment of Panic Disorder: A Consensus Development Conference. Ed. by Barry E. Wolfe & Jack D. Maser. LC 93-17653. 377p. 1994. Alk. paper. text ed. 45.00 (*0-88048-685-6*, 8685) Am Psychiatric.

Treatment of Parkinson's Disease. Ed. by N. Yanagisawa. (Journal: European Neurology Ser.: Vol. 36, Suppl. 1, 1996). (Illus.). iv, 62p. 1996. pap. 27.00 (*3-8055-6327-2*) S Karger.

Treatment of Patients in the Borderline Spectrum. William W. Meissner. LC 88-10526. 648p. 1995. pap. 50.00 (*1-56821-495-2*) Aronson.

Treatment of Precancerous Lesions & Early Breast Cancer: Diagnosis & Management. Irving M. Ariel & Anthony C. Cahan. 416p. 1993. 89.00 (*0-683-00255-4*) Williams & Wilkins.

***Treatment of Pressure Ulcers: Clinical Prctice Guideline.** Nancy Bergstrom. (Illus.). 154p. (C). 1997. reprint ed. pap. text ed. 40.00 (*0-7881-2418-8*) DIANE Pub.

***Treatment of Primary Glomerulonephritis.** Claudion Ponticelli & Richard J. Glassock. (Oxford Clinical Nephrology Ser.). (Illus.). 272p. 1997. text ed. 110.00 (*0-19-262666-3*) OUP.

Treatment of Primitive Mental States. Peter Giovacchini. 536p. 1996. pap. 50.00 (*1-56821-808-7*) Aronson.

Treatment of Problem Foundations for Highway Embankments. (National Cooperative Highway Research Program Report Ser.: No. 147). 72p. 1989. 9.00 (*0-309-04557-6*) Transport Res Bd.

Treatment of Psychiatric Disorders: Revised for the DSM-III-R. enl. rev. ed. William H. Reid. LC 88-19468. 438p. 1989. text ed. 43.95 (*0-87630-536-2*) Brunner-Mazel.

Treatment of Radiation Injuries. Ed. by D. Browne et al. LC 90-14216. (Illus.). 260p. 1990. 79.50 (*0-306-43729-5*, Plenum Pr) Plenum.

Treatment of Rape Victims. Lawrence G. Calhoun. (Practitioner Guidebook Ser.). (C). 1992. pap. text ed. 31.50 (*0-205-14296-6*, H4296, Longwood Div) Allyn.

Treatment of Renal Anemia: Mini-Symposium on Recombinant Human Erythropoietin - Journal: Blood Purification, Vol. 8, No. 5, 1990. Ed. by B. Canaud & K. M. Koch. (Illus.). 76p. 1991. pap. 40.00 (*3-8055-5344-7*) S Karger.

Treatment of Renal Anemia with Recombinant Human Erythropoietin. Ed. by K. M. Koch. (Contributions to Nephrology Ser.: Vol. 66). (Illus.). viii, 212p. 1988. 126.50 (*3-8055-4764-1*) S Karger.

Treatment of Schizophrenia. Leland E. Hinsie. Ed. by Gerald N. Grob. LC 78-22565. (Historical Issues in Mental Health Ser.). 1980. reprint ed. lib. bdg. 18.95 (*0-405-11919-4*) Ayer.

***Treatment of Schizophrenia: A Holistic Approach Based on the Readings of Edgar Cayce.** David McMillin. LC 97-8463. (Edgar Cayce Health Ser.). 521p. (Orig.). 1997. pap. 16.95 (*0-87604-384-8*, 493) ARE Pr.

Treatment of Serious Infections in the 1990s. Ed. by Merle A. Sande & Richard K. Root. (Contemporary Issues in Infectious Diseases Ser.: Vol. 9). (Illus.). 243p. 1992. text ed. 69.00 (*0-443-08799-7*) Churchill.

Treatment of Severe Dyslipoproteinemia in the Prevention of Coronary Heart Disease. Ed. by A. M. Gotto, Jr. et al. (Illus.). x, 366p. 1992. 105.25 (*3-8055-5539-3*) S Karger.

Treatment of Severe Dyslipoproteinemia in the Prevention of Coronary Heart Disease: Fourth International Symposium, Munich, October 1992. Ed. by A. M. Gotto, Jr. et al. (Illus.). x, 242p. 1993. 216.75 (*3-8055-5843-0*) S Karger.

Treatment of Severe Hypercholesterolemia in the Prevention of Coronary Heart Disease. Ed. by A. M. Grotto et al. (Contributions to Infusion Therapy Ser.: Vol. 23). (Illus.). viii, 198p. 1988. 50.50 (*3-8055-4905-9*) S Karger.

Treatment of Severe Hypercholesterolemia in the Prevention of Coronary Heart Disease - 2. M. Mancini et al. Ed. by A. M. Gotto, Jr. et al. viii, 274p. 1990. 68.75 (*3-8055-5085-5*) S Karger.

Treatment of Sex Offenders in Social Work & Mental Health Settings. Ed. by Daniel L. Whitaker. LC 88-16422. (Journal of Social Work & Human Sexuality: Vol. 7, No. 2). (Illus.). 161p. 1989. text ed. 39.95 (*0-86656-791-7*) Haworth Pr.

Treatment of Sexual Dysfunction: A Basic Approach. William E. Hartman & Marilyn A. Fithian. LC 84-45132. 306p. 1994. pap. text ed. 32.00 (*1-56821-368-9*) Aronson.

Treatment of Sexual Dysfunction: A Bio-Psycho Social Approach. William E. Hartman & Marilyn A. Fithian. LC 72-93106. (Illus.). 282p. 1972. 14.95 (*0-9600626-1-0*) Ctr Marital Sexual.

An Asterisk (*) at the beginning of an entry indicates that the title is appearing in BIP for the first time.

Treatment of Sexual Problems in Individual & Couples Therapy. R. A. Brown & J. R. Field. LC 88-319. 460p. 1988. 47.50 (*0-89335-301-9*) PMA Pub Corp.

Treatment of Shakespeare's Text by His Earlier Editors, 1709-1768. Ronald B. McKerrow. LC 79-109656. (Select Bibliographies Reprint Ser.). 1977. 15.95 (*0-8369-5265-0*) Ayer.

Treatment of Shame & Guilt in Alcoholism Counseling. Ed. by Patricia S. Potter-Efron. LC 87-29724. (Alcoholism Treatment Quarterly Ser.: Vol. 4, No. 2). (Illus.). 218p. 1989. pap. 14.95 (*0-86656-941-3*); text ed. 39.95 (*0-86656-718-6*) Haworth Pr.

Treatment of Shock: Principles & Practice. 2nd ed. John Barrett & Lloyd M. Nyhus. LC 85-18170. 254p. reprint ed. pap. 72.40 (*0-7837-2690-2*, 2043068) Bks Demand.

Treatment of Skin Diseases: A Manual. Charles Sheard. LC 78-53581. (Illus.). 414p. reprint ed. pap. 118.00 (*0-8357-6758-2*, 2035419) Bks Demand.

Treatment of Small Bowel Diseases: Proceedings of the Hepato-Gastroenterology Symposium, University Hospital Center of Nice, 1st, August 1972. Hepato-Gastroenterology Symposium Staff. Ed. by J. Delmont. (Illus.). 200p. 1973. 35.25 (*3-8055-1490-5*) S Karger.

Treatment of Soft Tissue Sarcomas. Ed. by Herbert M. Pinedo & Jaap Verweij. (Cancer Treatment & Research Ser.). (C). 1988. lib. bdg. 94.00 (*0-89838-391-9*) Kluwer Ac.

***Treatment of Spent Chemical Oxygen Demand Solutions for Safe Disposal.** Thomas R. Holm. (Illus.). 28p. (Orig.). (C). 1996. pap. 20.00 (*0-7881-3690-9*) DIANE Pub.

Treatment of Substance Abuse: Psychosocial Occupational Therapy Approaches. Ed. by Diane Gibson. LC 88-21309. (Occupational Therapy in Mental Health Ser.: Vol. 8, No. 2). (Illus.). 80p. 1989. text ed. 19.95 (*0-86656-838-7*) Haworth Pr.

Treatment of Suicidal People. Ed. by Robert A. Neimeyer et al. 240p. 1994. 54.95 (*1-56032-287-X*) Hemisp Pub.

Treatment of the Addictions: Applications of Outcome Research for Clinical Management. Ed. & Intro. by Norman S. Miller. LC 94-22157. (Alcoholism Treatment Quarterly Ser.: Vol. 12, No. 2). (Illus.). 135p. 1994. lib. bdg. 39.95 (*1-56024-686-3*) Haworth Pr.

Treatment of the Addictions: Applications of Outcome Research for Clinical Management. Intro. by Norman S. Miller. LC 94-22157. (Alcoholism Treatment Quarterly Ser.: Vol. 12, No. 2). (Illus.). 135p. 1994. pap. 12.95 (*1-56023-064-9*) Haworth Pr.

Treatment of the Alcohol-Abusing Offender. Robert R. Ross & Lynn O. Lightfoot. 164p. 1985. pap. 18.95 (*0-398-06410-5*) C C Thomas.

Treatment of the Alcohol-Abusing Offender. Robert R. Ross & Lynn O. Lightfoot. 164p. (C). 1985. 31.95 (*0-398-05090-2*) C C Thomas.

Treatment of the Borderline Adolescent: A Developmental Approach. James F. Masterson. LC 85-4236. 305p. 1985. reprint ed. text ed. 38.95 (*0-87630-394-7*) Brunner-Mazel.

Treatment of the Borderline Patient: Applying Fairbairn's Object Relations Theory in the Clinical Setting. David P. Celani. LC 92-1699. 200p. 1993. 30.00 (*0-8236-6644-1*) Intl Univs Pr.

Treatment of the Borderline Personality. Patricia M. Chatham. LC 84-20425. 585p. 1985. 55.00 (*0-87668-754-0*) Aronson.

Treatment of the Capital Sins. R. J. Ianucci. LC 70-140024. (Catholic University Studies in German: No. 17). reprint ed. 37.50 (*0-404-50237-7*) AMS Pr.

Treatment of the Chemically Dependent Homeless: Fourteen American Projects. Ed. by Kendon J. Conrad et al. LC 95-4175. 1995. 19.95 (*1-56023-066-5*) Harrington Pk.

Treatment of the Chemically Dependent Homeless: Theory & Implementation in Fourteen American Projects. Ed. by Cheryl I. Hultmand & John S. Lyons. LC 93-29552. (Alcoholism Treatment Quarterly Ser.: Vol. 10, Nos. 3 & 4). (Illus.). 261p. 1993. lib. bdg. 49.95 (*1-56024-476-3*) Haworth Pr.

Treatment of the Chronic Schizophrenic Patient. Ed. by Diane Gibson. LC 86-18451. (Occupational Therapy in Mental Health Ser.: Vol. 6, No. 2). 87p. 1986. text ed. 32.95 (*0-86656-578-7*) Haworth Pr.

Treatment of the Edentulous Patient. Victor O. Lucia. LC 85-30060. (Illus.). 248p. 1986. text ed. 148.00 (*0-86715-122-6*, 1226) Quint Pub Co.

Treatment of the Holocaust in Textbooks: The Federal Republic of Germany, Israel, the United States. Walter Renn et al. (Holocaust Studies). 333p. 1987. text ed. 55.50 (*0-88033-955-1*) East Eur Monographs.

Treatment of the Insane Without Mechanical Restraints. John Conolly. LC 73-2392. (Mental Illness & Social Policy; the American Experience Ser.). 1973. reprint ed. 28.95 (*0-405-05200-6*) Ayer.

Treatment of the Jews in the Christian Writers of the First Three Centuries, Vol. 81. Robert Wilde. (Patristic Studies). 255p. 1983. reprint ed. 38.00 (*0-939738-28-7*) Zubal Inc.

Treatment of the Juvenile Sex Offender Substitute: Neurological & Psychiatric Impairments. Matthew L. Ferrara & Sherry McDonald. LC 95-14354. 1995. pap. 45.00 (*1-56821-566-5*) Aronson.

Treatment of the Masochistic Personality: An Interactional-Object Relations Approach to Psychotherapy. Cheryl G. Hughes & Marolyn Wells. LC 94-34953. 288p. 1995. text ed. 40.00 (*1-56821-384-0*) Aronson.

Treatment of the Narcissistic Neuroses. Hyman Spotnitz & Phyllis W. Meadow. LC 94-36858. 304p. 1995. pap. text ed. 35.00 (*1-56821-416-2*) Aronson.

Treatment of the Obsessive Personality. Leon Salzman. LC 84-46127. 544p. 1992. reprint ed. 45.00 (*0-87668-881-4*) Aronson.

Treatment of the Obsessive Personality, Vol. 1. Leon Salzman. 1983. pap. text ed. 36.00 (*0-87668-392-8*) Aronson.

Treatment of the Postmenopausal Woman: Basic & Clinical Aspects. Ed. by Rogerio A. Lobo. 464p. 1993. text ed. 145.00 (*0-7817-0113-9*) Lppncott-Raven.

Treatment of the Pregnant Addict. Janice Pringle et al. 135p. 1994. pap. 49.50 (*1-884937-16-0*) Manisses Communs.

Treatment of the Rheumatic Diseases: Companion to the Textbook of Rheumatology. Ed. by Michael H. Weisman & Michael E. Weinblatt. LC 94-28994. Orig. Title: Drug Therapy of the Rheumatic Diseases. (Illus.). 384p. 1994. text ed. 55.00 (*0-7216-5382-0*) Saunders.

Treatment of the Seriously Ill Psychiatric Patient. Ed. by Alexander Gralnick. 133p. (C). 1984. text ed. 28.00 (*0-8147-2998-3*) NYU Pr.

Treatment of the Seriously Obese Patient. Ed. by Thomas A. Wadden & Theodore B. VanItallie. LC 92-1459. 524p. 1992. lib. bdg. 55.00 (*0-89862-879-2*) Guilford Pr.

Treatment of the Severely Disturbed Adolescent. Donald B. Rinsley. LC 80-66922. 364p. 1994. pap. 35.00 (*1-56821-222-4*) Aronson.

Treatment of Tinnitus. Vernon. LC 97-19661. 1997. pap. 26.95 (*0-205-18269-0*) P-H.

Treatment of Traumatized Incisor in the Child Patient. Ronald Johnson. Ed. by D. Walter Cohen. (Continuing Dental Education Ser.). (Illus.). 116p. 1981. pap. text ed. 22.00 (*0-931386-29-2*) Quint Pub Co.

Treatment of Tuberculosis: Guidelines for National Programmes. vii, 43p. (ENG, FRE & SPA.). 1993. pap. text ed. 9.00 (*92-4-154451-1*, 1150397) World Health.

Treatment of Water by Granular Activated Carbon. Ed. by Michael J. McGuire & Irwin H. Suffet. LC 82-22662. (Advances in Chemistry Ser.: No. 202). 600p. 1983. lib. bdg. 68.95 (*0-8412-0665-1*) Am Chemical.

***Treatment of Water by Granular Activated Carbon.** Irwin H. Suffet. LC 82-22662. (Advances in Chemistry Ser.: Vol. 202). 616p. 1983. reprint ed. pap. 175.60 (*0-608-03506-8*, 2064225) Bks Demand.

Treatment of Water, Electrolyte, & Acid-Base Disorders in the Surgical Patient. L. Beaty Pemberton & Deloras Pemberton. 432p. 1993. pap. text ed. 32.00 (*0-07-049363-4*) McGraw-Hill HPD.

Treatment Options in Addiction: Medical Management of Alcohol & Opiate Abuse. Ed. by Colin Brewer. LC 94-137578. 120p. 1993. reprint ed. pap. 34.20 (*0-608-01826-0*, 2062475) Bks Demand.

Treatment Options in Early Intervention. Ed. by James A. Blackman. LC 94-38449. (Infants & Young Children Ser.). 240p. 1995. 31.00 (*0-8342-0645-5*) Aspen Pub.

Treatment Outcomes in Psychotherapy & Psychiatric Interventions. Len Sperry et al. (Mental Health Practice under Managed Care Ser.: Vol. 6). 256p. 1996. pap. 27.95 (*0-87630-826-4*) Brunner-Mazel.

Treatment Perspectives in Urologic Oncology. Richard D. Williams & Peter Carroll. 1990. text ed. 52.50 (*0-07-105330-1*) McGraw.

Treatment Perspectives in Urologic Oncology. Richard D. Williams. Ed. by Peter R. Carroll. (Illus.). 256p. 1990. 52.50 (*0-08-040298-4*, Pub. by PPI UK) McGraw.

Treatment Planning & Dose Calculation & Treatment Planning in Radiation Oncology. Gunilla C. Bentel et al. (Illus.). 265p. 1982. text ed. 54.00 (*0-08-027176-6*, H230, Pergamon Pr); pap. text ed. 24.00 (*0-08-027175-8*, Pergamon Pr) Elsevier.

Treatment Planning & Dose Calculation in Radiation Oncology. 4th ed. Gunilla C. Bentel et al. 352p. 1989. pap. text ed. 42.00 (*0-07-105246-1*) McGraw-Hill HPD.

Treatment Planning for Pedodontic Patients. A. Blinkhorn. (Illus.). 152p. 1992. text ed. 62.00 (*1-85097-014-9*) Quint Pub Co.

Treatment Planning for Psychotherapists. Richard B. Makover. 256p. 1996. text ed. 35.00 (*0-88048-743-7*, 8743) Am Psychiatric.

Treatment Planning in Psychiatry. Ed. by Jerry M. Lewis & Gene Usdin. LC 82-3985. 453p. reprint ed. pap. 129.20 (*0-8357-7792-8*, 2036153) Bks Demand.

***Treatment Planning in Radiation Oncology.** Faiz M. Khan & Roger A. Potish. LC 97-6377. 1997. write for info. (*0-683-04607-1*) Williams & Wilkins.

Treatment Planning in the Radiation Therapy of Cancer. Ed. by J. M. Vaeth & J. Meyer. (Frontiers of Radiation Therapy & Oncology Ser.: Vol. 21). (Illus.). x, 342p. 1987. 260.00 (*3-8055-4377-8*) S Karger.

Treatment Plant Hydraulics for Environmental Engineers. Larry D. Benefield et al. (Illus.). 240p. (C). 1984. text ed. 76.00 (*0-13-930248-4*) P-H.

Treatment Practices of New England Surface Water Supplies. New England Water Works Association Staff. 80p. 1994. 22.50 (*1-881198-01-4*) New Eng Water Wks.

Treatment Procedures in Communicative Disorders. 2nd ed. M. N. Hegde. LC 92-3401. (Illus.). 336p. (C). 1993. text ed. 36.00 (*0-89079-563-0*, 6529) PRO-ED.

Treatment Process Digest. 335p. 1993. pap. 70.00 (*1-881369-28-5*) Water Environ.

Treatment Resistance: A Guide for Practitioners. Salvatore Cullari. 1996. text ed. 43.50 (*0-205-15572-3*) Allyn.

***Treatment Resource Manual for Speech-Language Pathologists.** Froma P. Roth & Colleen K. Worthington. LC 96-26450. 326p. 1996. 45.00 (*1-56593-636-1*, 1318) Singular Publishing.

Treatment Services for Adolescent Substance Abusers. 1986. lib. bdg. 79.95 (*0-8490-3496-5*) Gordon Pr.

***Treatment Strategies for Abused Adolescents: From Victim to Survivor.** Cheryl L. Karp et al. LC 97-21010. (Interpersonal Violence Ser.). 1997. write for info. (*0-7619-0950-8*) Sage.

Treatment Strategies for Abused Children: From Victim to Survivor. Cheryl L. Karp & Traci L. Butler. (Interpersonal Violence: the Practice Ser.: Vol. 13). 288p. (C). 1996. 52.00 (*0-8039-7217-2*); pap. 24.95 (*0-8039-7218-0*) Sage.

Treatment Strategies for Chronic Renal Failure: Limitations of Resources & Priorities, the Dilemma of the Nineties. Ed. by C. Zoccali. (Contributions to Nephrology Ser.: Vol. 109). (Illus.). x, 120p. 1994. 107.00 (*3-8055-5868-6*) S Karger.

***Treatment Strategies for Patients with Psychiatric Comorbidity.** Ed. by Scott Wetzler & William C. Sanderson. LC 96-34774. (Publication Series of the Department of Psychiatry Albert Einstein College of Medicine of Yeshiva University). 350p. 1997. text ed. 47.50 (*0-471-11773-0*) Wiley.

Treatment Strategies for Refractory Depression. Ed. by Steven P. Roose & Alexander H. Glassman. LC 90-10. (Progress in Psychiatry Ser.: No. 25). 226p. 1990. text ed. 33.00 (*0-88048-184-6*, 8184) Am Psychiatric.

Treatment Strategies in Child & Adolescent Psychiatry. Ed. by J. G. Simeon & H. B. Ferguson. LC 90-7429. (Illus.). 250p. 1990. 42.50 (*0-306-43466-0*, Plenum Pr) Plenum.

Treatment Team Foster Care. 4th ed. Braley & Thompson, Inc. Staff. (Illus.). 100p. pap. 6.00 (*1-883239-00-1*) Braley & Thompson.

Treatment Team Foster Care. 5th ed. Braley & Thompson, Inc. Staff. (Illus.). 100p. pap. 6.00 (*1-883239-01-X*) Braley & Thompson.

Treatment Techniques for Common Mental Disorders. Joan Atwood & Robert Chester. LC 87-17471. 352p. 1993. pap. 40.00 (*1-56821-136-8*) Aronson.

Treatment Techniques of Harry Stack Sullivan. A. H. Chapman. LC 95-36655. 256p. 1995. 35.00 (*1-56821-673-4*) Aronson.

Treatment Technologies. 2nd ed. EPA Staff. 230p. 1991. pap. text ed. 79.00 (*0-86587-263-5*) Gov Insts.

Treatment Technologies for Solvent Containing Wastes. M. Breton et al. LC 87-34853. (Pollution Technology Review Ser.: No. 149). (Illus.). 753p. 1988. 64.00 (*0-8155-1158-2*) Noyes.

Treatment Unit Clerk. Jack Rudman. (Career Examination Ser.: C-319). 1994. pap. 23.95 (*0-8373-0319-2*) Nat Learn.

Treatment Wetlands: Theory & Implementation. Robert H. Kadlec & Robert L. Knight. 928p. 1995. 79.95 (*0-87371-930-1*, L930) Lewis Pubs.

Treatment with GnRH Analogs: Controversies & Perspectives - Proceedings of a Symposium Held in Bologna, Italy, 15-16 September 1995. Ed. by Marco Filicori & Carlo Flamigni. LC 96-33672. (Illus.). 260p. 1996. text ed. 68.00 (*1-85070-690-5*) Prthnon Pub.

Treatment Without Consent: Law, Psychiatry & the Treatment of Mentally Disordered People since 1845. Phil Fennell. LC 95-21254. (Social Ethics & Policy Ser.). 288p. (C). 1995. text ed. 74.95 (*0-415-07787-7*) Routledge.

Treatments for the Alzheimer Patient: The Long Haul. Ed. by Lissy F. Jarvik & Carol H. Winograd. 288p. 1988. 33.95 (*0-8261-6000-X*) Springer Pub.

Treatments of Psychiatric Disorders, 2 vols., Set. 2nd ed. Ed. by Glen O. Gabbard. 2800p. 1995. boxed 250.00 (*0-88048-700-3*, 8700) Am Psychiatric.

Treatments of Psychiatric Disorders: A Task Force Report of the American Psychiatric Association, Index. LC 89-248. 297p. 1989. reprint ed. pap. 84.70 (*0-608-02034-6*, 2062687) Bks Demand.

Treatments of Psychiatric Disorders: A Task Force Report of the American Psychiatric Association, Vol. 1. LC 89-248. 840p. 1989. reprint ed. pap. 180.00 (*0-608-02031-1*, 2062687) Bks Demand.

Treatments of Psychiatric Disorders Vol. 2: A Task Force Report of the American Psychiatric Association, Vol. 2. LC 89-248. 969p. 1989. reprint ed. pap. 180.00 (*0-608-02032-X*, 2062687) Bks Demand.

Treatments of Psychiatric Disorders Vol. 3: A Task Force Report of the American Psychiatric Association, Vol. 3. LC 89-248. 1134p. 1989. reprint ed. pap. 180.00 (*0-608-02033-8*, 2062687) Bks Demand.

***Treatments That Work: A Review of the Outcome Studies on Psychotherapies & Drugs.** Peter E. Nathan & Jack M. Gorman. (Illus.). 688p. 1997. 75.00 (*0-19-510227-4*) OUP.

Treats for My Sweets. Gail C. Jaye. (Illus.). 128p. 1981. pap. 6.50 (*0-686-31566-9*) G C Jaye.

Treats Nutritional Treats: A Dynamite Cookbook for Nutritional Sweet Treats, Drinks, Breads & Muffins. Wendy Morrison. 72p. 1980. spiral bd. 7.95 (*0-920490-05-0*, Pub. by Detselig CN) Temeron Bks.

Treats of Quotas in International Trade: Their Effect on the Exporting Country. Gerard L. Stockhausen. LC 87-23682. (Contributions in Economics & Economic History Ser.: No. 78). (Illus.). 170p. 1988. text ed. 45.00 (*0-313-25785-X*, SQT/, Greenwood Pr) Greenwood.

Treaty at Doona. Anne McCaffrey. Ed. by Jody L. Nye. 352p. (Orig.). 1994. mass mkt. 5.99 (*0-441-00089-4*) Ace Bks.

Treaty at Fort Laramie. John Legg. (Forts of Freedom Ser.). 304p. 1994. mass mkt. 4.99 (*0-312-95128-0*) St Martin.

Treaty Conflict & Political Consideration: The Dialectic of Duplicity. Guyora Binder. LC 88-11756. 234p. 1988. text ed. 55.00 (*0-275-93046-7*, C3046, Praeger Pubs) Greenwood.

Treaty-Making & Australia: Globalisation Versus Sovereignty? Ed. by Philip Alston & Madelaine Chiam. 309p. 1995. pap. 29.95 (*1-86287-195-7*, Pub. by Federation Pr AU) Gaunt.

Treaty of Bayonne with Preliminary Treaties of Trancoso. Ed. by Palmer & Powell. (Exeter Hispanic Text Ser.: No. 47). 92p. Date not set. pap. text ed. 18.95 (*0-85989-316-2*, Pub. by Univ Exeter Pr UK) Northwestern U Pr.

Treaty of Brest-Litovsk. Mary E. Fischer. (Pew Case Studies in International Affairs). 50p. (C). 1995. pap. text ed. 3.50 (*1-56927-466-5*, GU Schl Foreign) Geo U Inst Dplmcy.

Treaty of Eighteen Forty-Two Between the United States & the Chippewa Indians of the Mississippi & Lake Superior. Robert Keller. (Treaty Manuscripts Ser.: No. 32). 58p. 12.50 (*0-944253-54-7*) Inst Dev Indian Law.

Treaty of Eighteen Thirty-Six Between the Ottawa & Chippewa Nations of Indians & the U. S. Government. Robert Keller. (Treaty Manuscripts Ser.: No. 31). 55p. 12.50 (*0-317-57475-2*) Inst Dev Indian Law.

Treaty of Guadalupe Hidalgo: A Legacy of Conflict. Richard Griswold del Castillo. LC 89-38642. (Illus.). 268p. 1992. pap. 14.95 (*0-8061-2478-4*) U of Okla Pr.

***Treaty of Maastricht.** 1994. 136.00 (*0-582-20906-4*, 00109047, Pub. by Longman Grp UK) Gale.

Treaty of Medicine Lodge: A Programmed Text. Lynn Kickingbird & Curtis Berkey. (Treaty Manuscripts Ser.: No. 20). 22p. 7.50 (*0-944253-42-3*) Inst Dev Indian Law.

Treaty of Medicine Lodge, 1867, Between the United States & the Kiowa, Comanche & Apache Indians. R. J. DeMallie & Lynn Kickingbird. (Treaty Manuscripts Ser.: No. 26). 65p. 15.00 (*0-944253-48-2*) Inst Dev Indian Law.

Treaty of Nineteen Eleven & the Immigration & Alien Land Law Issue Between the U. S. & Japan, 1911-1913. Teruko O. Kachi. Ed. by Roger Daniels. LC 78-54821. (Asian Experience in North America Ser.). 1979. lib. bdg. 25.95 (*0-405-11277-7*) Ayer.

Treaty of Trianon & European Peace: Four Lectures Delivered in London in November 1933. Stephen Bethlen. LC 73-135795. (Eastern Europe Collection). 1971. reprint ed. 16.95 (*0-405-02737-0*) Ayer.

Treaty of Union of Scotland & England. Ed. by George S. Pryde. LC 78-24202. 120p. 1979. reprint ed. text ed. 45.00 (*0-313-20829-8*, SCTR, Greenwood Pr) Greenwood.

Treaty of Versailles & After, Annotations of the Text & Treaty. U. S. Department of State Staff. 1968. reprint ed. 49.00 (*0-403-00054-8*) Scholarly.

Treaty of Waitangi. T. Lindsay Buick. LC 72-1294. (Select Bibliographies Reprint Ser.). 1977. reprint ed. 31.95 (*0-8369-6822-0*) Ayer.

Treaty of Washington: Its Negotiation, Execution & the Discussions Relating Thereto. Caleb Cushing. LC 72-114872. (Select Bibliographies Reprint Ser.). 1977. 21.95 (*0-8369-5277-4*) Ayer.

Treaty on the Little Arkansas River, 1865. R. J. DeMallie & Lynn Kickingbird. (Treaty Manuscripts Ser.: No. 25). 55p. 12.50 (*0-944253-47-4*) Inst Dev Indian Law.

Treaty Ports in China: A Study in Diplomacy. En-Sai Tai. LC 75-32311. (Studies in Chinese History & Civilization). 202p. 1976. text ed. 55.00 (*0-313-26975-0*, U6975, Greenwood Pr) Greenwood.

Treaty Power under the Constitution of the United States: Commentaries on the Treaty Clauses of the Constitution; Construction of Treaties... Robert T. Devlin. lxx, 864p. 1996. reprint ed. lib. bdg. 125.00 (*0-8377-2041-9*) Rothman.

Treaty Shopping. Deloitte et al. 350p. 1988. pap. 67.00 (*90-6544-335-5*) Kluwer Law Tax Pubs.

***Treaty Talks in British Columbia: Negotiating a Mutually Beneficial Future.** Christopher McKee. 144p. 1996. 65.00 (*0-7748-0586-2*, Pub. by U BC Pr) U of Wash Pr.

***Treaty Talks in British Columbia: Negotiating a Mutually Beneficial Future.** Christopher McKee. 144p. 1997. pap. 19.95 (*0-7748-0587-0*, Pub. by U BC Pr) U of Wash Pr.

Treaty Veto of the American Senate. Denna F. Fleming. LC 76-168039. reprint ed. 45.00 (*0-404-02409-2*) AMS Pr.

Treaty with the Makah. Kenneth C. Hansen. (Treaty Manuscripts Ser.: No. 8). 30p. 10.00 (*0-944253-30-X*) Inst Dev Indian Law.

Treaty with the Quinaielt & Quileute Indian. Lynn Kickingbird & Curtis Berkey. (Treaty Manuscripts Ser.: No. 7). 21p. 7.50 (*0-944253-29-6*) Inst Dev Indian Law.

***Treaty's Law.** Rusch. (Star Trek the Original Ser.). 1997. mass mkt. 5.99 (*0-671-00424-7*, Star Trek) PB.

Treatyse of Fysshinge with an Angle. Thomas Satchell. (English Dialect Society Publications: No. 41a). 1974. reprint ed. pap. 25.00 (*0-8115-0467-0*) Periodicals Srv.

Treble Chance Murder. large type ed. Victor Gunn. 1977. 25.99 (*0-7089-0008-9*) Ulverscroft.

Treble Clef & Notes. Mary L. Walker. (Music Ser.). 24p. (gr. 1 up). 1980. student ed. 5.00 (*0-8209-0274-8*, MU-3) ESP.

Treblinka. Jean-Francois Steiner. LC 93-38845. 1994. pap. 13.95 (*0-452-01124-8*, Mer) NAL-Dutton.

Treblinka. Jean-Francois Steiner. 415p. reprint ed. pap. 13.95 (*0-686-95096-8*) ADL.

Treblinka. Jean-Francois Steiner. Tr. by Helen Weaver. LC 96-76465. (Library of the Holocaust). 416p. 1996. reprint ed. 8.98 (*1-56731-142-3*, MJF Bks) Fine Comms.

Treblinka Virus. Robert B. Litman. LC 90-82034. 289p. 1991. pap. 8.95 (*0-918921-02-3*) Ivy League Pr.

Trece Cuentos Nerviosos: Narraciones Burlescas y Diabolicas. Luis A. Casas. LC 89-80763. (Coleccion Caniqui). 143p. (Orig.). (SPA.). 1990. pap. 12.00 (*0-89729-501-3*) Ediciones.

Trece Lecciones de Doctrina Biblica. Denver Sizemore. Tr. by Raul Martinez from ENG. 124p. (SPA.). 1984. pap. 4.99 (*0-89900-300-1*) College Pr Pub.

Trechos de "Meu Caminho Para Rotary" Paul Harris. 58p. (POR.). 1984. 3.00 (*0-915062-20-8*) Rotary Intl.

T

Tredway: History of the Tredway Family. W. T. Tredway. (Illus.). xiv, 418p. 1993. reprint ed. pap. 65.00 (0-8328-3753-9); reprint ed. lib. bdg. 75.00 (0-8328-3752-0) Higginson Bk Co.

Tree. David Burnie. LC 88-1572. (Eyewitness Bks.). (Illus.). 64p. (J). (gr. 5 up). 1988. 19.00 (0-394-89617-3) Knopf Bks Yng Read.

Tree. David Burnie. LC 88-1572. (Eyewitness Bks.). (Illus.). 64p. (J). (gr. 5 up). 1988. lib. bdg. 20.99 (0-394-99617-8) Knopf Bks Yng Read.

Tree. Pascale De Bourgoing. (First Discovery Bks.). (Illus.). 24p. (J). 1992. 11.95 (0-590-45265-7, Cartwheel) Scholastic Inc.

Tree. Stephen Dolinar. LC 92-85413. 231p. 1993. 10.95 (1-55523-555-7) Winston-Derek.

Tree. Jane B. Montero. (Illus.). 16p. (Orig.). (J). (ps-6). 1995. pap. 5.00 (0-9650829-0-3) J B Montero.

Tree. Tim Vyner. LC 94-30417. (J). 1995. 12.95 (0-8120-6492-5); pap. 5.95 (0-8120-9170-1) Barron.

Tree. John Fowles. 125p. 1983. reprint ed. 13.50 (0-88001-033-9) Ecco Pr.

***Tree: Essays & Pieces.** Deena Metzger. LC 96-50153. (Orig.). 1997. pap. 15.95 (1-55643-245-3) North Atlantic.

Tree: Five, the Snake, the Apple. Ed. by David Meltzer. (Illus.). 200p. (Orig.). 1975. pap. 15.00 (0-686-10822-1) Tree Bks.

Tree: Four, Raa. Ed. by David Meltzer. (Illus.). (Orig.). 1974. pap. 15.00 (0-686-17262-0) Tree Bks.

Tree: Six, Messiah. Ed. by David Meltzer. (Illus.). (Orig.). 1978. pap. 10.00 (0-686-31720-3) Tree Bks.

Tree: Spirit Deer. Jim Meirose. Ed. & Illus. by Artemis Smith. (On-Demand Collectors' Editions Ser.). 900p. 1998. per. 100.00 (1-878998-26-9) Savant Garde.

Tree: The Complete Book of Saxon Witchcraft. Raymond Buckland. LC 74-79397. (Illus.). 168p. 1974. pap. 8.95 (0-87728-258-7) Weiser.

Tree: Three, Shekinah. Ed. by David Meltzer. (Illus.). (Orig.). 1973. pap. 15.00 (0-686-27969-7) Tree Bks.

Tree: Two, Yetzirah. Ed. by David Meltzer. (Illus.). (Orig.). 1972. pap. 15.00 (0-686-27968-9) Tree Bks.

Tree, a Rock, a Cloud. Carson McCullers. (Creative Short Stories Ser.). (YA). (gr. 4-12). 1989. 13.95 (0-88682-349-8, 97225-098) Creative Ed.

Tree Adventures at Tahoe. Rod Haulenbeek. (Illus.). 224p. (Orig.). 1996. pap. 9.95 (1-885155-03-4) Wide-Eyed.

Tree Adventures in Yosemite Valley. Rod Haulenbeek. LC 94-90129. (Illus.). 160p. (Orig.). 1994. pap. 7.95 (1-885155-02-6) Wide-Eyed.

Tree Almanac: A Year-Round Activity Guide. Monica Russo. LC 92-41347. (Illus.). (J). (gr. 3 up). 1993. 16.95 (0-8069-1252-9) Sterling.

Tree Almanac: A Year-Round Activity Guide. Monica Russo. (Illus.). 136p. 1994. pap. 9.95 (0-8069-1253-7) Sterling.

Tree Anatomy. Alex L. Shigo. (Dr. Shigo's Tree Ser.). (Illus.). 104p. (C). 1994. 79.00 (0-943563-14-3) Shigo & Trees Assocs.

Tree & Baby. Illus. by Vicki Wehrman. 1989. boxed 12.95 (0-943114-25-X, BA105) Childbirth Graphics.

***Tree & Graph Processing in SQL.** David Rozenshtein et al. Ed. by Tom Bondur. Date not set. mass mkt. 24.95 (0-9649812-3-8) SQL Forum.

Tree & Its Forest: The Weave of the Woods, from Chloroplast to Biome. Jon R. Luoma. 1997. 25.00 (0-8050-1491-8) H Holt & Co.

Tree & Serpent Worship. J. W. Lake. 1994. reprint ed. pap. 7.95 (1-55818-274-8, Sure Fire) Holmes Pub.

Tree & Shrub Expert. D. G. Hessayon. (Expert Ser.). (Illus.). 128p. (Orig.). 1990. pap. 12.95 (0-903505-17-7, Pub. by Expert Bks UK) Sterling.

Tree & the Canoe: History & Ethnogeography of Tanna. Joel Bonnemaison. Tr. by Josee Penot-Demetry from FRE. LC 94-14319. (Illus.). 392p. (C). 1994. reprint ed. text ed. 36.00 (0-8248-1525-4) UH Pr.

Tree & the Environment: An Indian Scenario. A. B. Chaudhuri. (Illus.). xvii, 602p. 1993. 59.00 (81-7024-562-1, Pub. by Ashish Pub Hse II) Nataraj Bks.

Tree & the Vine. Dola De Jong. Tr. by Ilona Kinzer from DUT. 150p. 1996. reprint ed. pap. 9.95 (1-55861-141-X); reprint ed. lib. bdg. 27.50 (1-55861-140-1) Feminist Pr.

Tree Automata. F. Gecseg & M. Steinby. 234p. (C). 1984. 78.00 (963-05-3170-4, Pub. by Akad Kiado HU) St Mut.

Tree Automata & Languages. Ed. by Maurice Nivat & Andreas Podelski. LC 92-17937. (Studies in Computer Sicence & Artificial Intelligence: Vol. 10). 486p. 1992. 165.50 (0-444-89026-2, North Holland) Elsevier.

Tree Basics: What Every Person Needs to Know about Trees. Alex L. Shigo. (Dr. Shigo's Tree Ser.). (Illus.). 40p. (Orig.). 1996. pap. text ed. 7.00 (0-943563-16-X) Shigo & Trees Assocs.

Tree-Bird. Lalitha Venkateswaran. 8.00 (0-89253-749-3); text ed. 4.80 (0-89253-750-7) Ind-US Inc.

Tree Book: Teaching Responsible Enviromental Education, Vol. 1. Toni Christenson et al. (Illus.). 78p. (Orig.). 1981. teacher ed. 6.95 (0-686-36286-1) Creative Curriculum.

Tree Book: The Indispensable Guide to Tree Facts, Crafts & Lore. J. Edward Milner. (Illus.). 192p. 1994. 39.95 (1-85585-132-6) Trafalgar.

Tree Breeding: Principles & Strategies. G. Namkoong et al. (Monographs on Theoretical & Applied Genetics: Vol. 11). (Illus.). 190p. 1988. 128.95 (0-387-96747-8) Spr-Verlag.

Tree by a Stream. E. Smith. 10.99 (1-85792-124-0, Pub. by Christian Focus UK) Spring Arbor Dist.

Tree by Leaf. Cynthia Voigt. 176p. 1989. mass mkt. 4.50 (0-449-70334-7, Juniper) Fawcett.

Tree by Leaf. Cynthia Voigt. LC 87-17512. 208p. (J). (gr. 4-8). 1988. lib. bdg. 15.95 (0-689-31403-5, Atheneum Bks Young) S&S Childrens.

Tree Care. rev. ed. John M. Haller. LC 76-50995. (Illus.). 1986. pap. 18.00 (0-02-062870-6) Macmillan.

Tree Celebrations! Tree Planting Ceremonies, Songs, Poems, Stories, & Activities. 2nd ed. Scott H. Alyn. LC 93-74729. (Illus.). 80p. 1993. pap. 14.95 (1-884607-77-2) Blooming Pr.

Tree Climber: A Play in Two Acts. 2nd ed. Tawfiq Al-Hakim. Tr. by Denys Johnson-Davis from ARA. LC 82-74256. (Illus.). 87p. 1994. 18.00 (0-89410-204-4, Three Contnts); pap. 10.00 (0-89410-205-2, Three Contnts) Lynne Rienner.

Tree Climber's Guide. Sharon Lilly. (Illus.). (C). 1994. pap. 40.00 (1-881956-08-3) Int Soc Arboricult.

Tree Climbing. Susan Mernit. 60p. (Orig.). 1981. pap. 3.00 (0-87924-036-9) Membrane Pr.

Tree-Crop Interactions: A Physiological Approach. Ed. by Chin K. Ong & P. A. Huxley. 408p. 1996. pap. 45.00 (0-85198-987-X, Pub. by CAB Intntl UK) OUP.

Tree Crop Physiology. Ed. by M. R. Sethuraj & A. S. Raghavendra. (Developments in Agricultural & Managed-Forest Ecology Ser.: No. 18). 362p. 1987. 167.50 (0-444-42841-0) Elsevier.

Tree Crops: A Permanent Agriculture. rev. ed. J. Russell Smith. (Illus.). 408p. 1987. reprint ed. pap. 24.95 (0-8159-6908-2) Devin.

Tree Crops: A Permanent Agriculture. J. Russell Smith & Wendell Berry. LC 87-82037. (Conservation Classics Ser.). (Illus.). 408p. (C). 1987. reprint ed. pap. 19.95 (0-933280-44-0) Island Pr.

Tree Detailing. Michael Littlewood. (Illus.). 193p. 1988. 47.95 (0-408-50002-6) Buttrwrth-Heinemann.

Tree Disease Concepts. 2nd rev. ed. Paul D. Manion. 1990. text ed. 67.51 (0-13-929423-6, 510101) P-H.

Tree Diseases & Disorders: Causes, Biology, & Control in Forest & Amenity Trees. Heinz Butin. Ed. by D. Lonsdale. Tr. by R. G. Strouts. (Illus.). 248p. 1995. 75.00 (0-19-854932-6) OUP.

Tree Diseases of Eastern Canada. Canadian Forestry Service Staff. 172p. (Orig.). 1994. pap. 51.95 (0-317-06257-3, Pub. by Canada Commun Grp CN) Accents Pubns.

Tree Ecology & Preservation. A. Bernatzky. (Developments in Agricultural & Managed-Forest Ecology Ser.: Vol. 2). 358p. 1978. 163.25 (0-444-41606-4) Elsevier.

Tree Elf & Other Folktales: Illustrated Tales for Children. Ed. by Lissa Gars. (Illus.). 60p. (J). (gr. 2-6). 1993. pap. 9.95 (1-882427-01-7) Aspasia Inc.

Tree Farm: Replanting a Life. Robert Treuer. (Illus.). 249p. 1996. reprint ed. pap. 14.00 (1-886913-06-4) Hungry Mind.

***Tree Fever.** Karen Hood-Caddy. 275p. (Orig.). 1997. pap. 14.95 (0-929141-53-9, Pub. by Napoleon Pubng CN) ACCESS Pubs Network.

Tree Finder: A Manual for Identifying Trees by Their Leaves East of Rockies. May T. Watts. (Illus.). 62p. 1991. pap. 3.00 (0-912550-01-5) Nature Study.

Tree for Me. Norma LeValley. LC 87-70974. (Illus.). 50p. (J). (ps-2). 1987. pap. 5.95 (0-9618740-0-7) Caring Tree.

Tree! For Me! Frankie Maynard. (Illus.). 60p. 1986. 15.00 (0-912783-02-8) Upton & Sons.

Tree! for Me! Frankie Maynard. LC 86-51132. (Illus.). 68p. 1986. 15.00 (0-912783-07-9) Upton & Sons.

Tree for Poverty. Margaret Laurence. 160p. (C). 1993. pap. 16.00 (1-55022-177-9, Pub. by ECW Press CN) Genl Dist Srvs.

Tree Form, Size & Colour. Bodfan Gruffydd. 243p. 1994. reprint ed. pap. 26.00 (0-419-19610-2, E & FN Spon) Routledge Chapman & Hall.

Tree Fort Wars. Mark Littleton. LC 56-94101. 208p. (J). (gr. 4 up). 1993. pap. 5.99 (1-55513-764-4, Chariot Bks) Chariot Victor.

Tree Frogs. Sylvia A. Johnson. LC 86-2721. (Lerner Natural Science Bks.). (Illus.). 48p. (J). (gr. 4 up). 1986. lib. bdg. 21.50 (0-8225-1467-2, Lerner Publctns) Lerner Group.

Tree from Me: Gentle Reflections for a Friend. Burkhard Herbote. (Illus.). 32p. 1994. 16.95 (0-85572-233-9, Pub. by Hill Content Pubng AT) Seven Hills Bk.

Tree Fruit Irrigation: A Comprehensive Manual of Deciduous Tree Fruit Irrigation Needs. Ed. by Kathleen M. Williams & Thomas W. Ley. LC 94-36397. (Illus.). 240p. (Orig.). 1994. pap. 17.00 (0-9630659-5-5) Good Fruit Grow.

Tree Fruit Nutrition. Ed. by Allen B. Peterson. LC 93-45012. (Illus.). 224p. (Orig.). 1994. pap. 15.00 (0-9630659-4-7) Good Fruit Grow.

***Tree Fruit Physiology: Growth & Development: A Comprehensive Manual for Deciduous Tree Fruit Growth & Development Needs.** Ed. by Karen M. Maib et al. LC 96-46960. 216p. (Orig.). 1996. pap. 17.00 (0-9630659-6-3) Good Fruit Grow.

Tree Full of Mitzvos. Dina H. Rosenfeld. (Illus.). 48p. (J). 1985. reprint ed. 10.00 (0-8266-0363-7, Merkos LInyonei Chinuch) Kehot Pubn Soc.

Tree Giants. Bill Schnieder. LC 88-80225. (Interpreting the Great Outdoors Ser.). (Illus.). 32p. (J). 1988. pap. 5.95 (0-937959-40-5) Falcon Pr MT.

Tree Grows in Brooklyn. Betty Smith. 432p. 1993. pap. 7.00 (0-06-080126-3, P126, PL) HarpC.

Tree Grows in Brooklyn. large type ed. Betty Smith. LC 93-13153. 1993. lib. bdg. 21.95 (0-8161-5813-4, GK Hall) Thorndike Pr.

Tree Grows in Brooklyn. Betty Smith. 321p. 1981. reprint ed. lib. bdg. 27.95 (0-89966-303-6) Buccaneer Bks.

Tree Growth. Theodore T. Kozlowski. LC 69-9752. (Illus.). 452p. 1962. reprint ed. pap. 128.90 (0-7837-3453-0, 2057779) Bks Demand.

Tree Growth & Environmental Stress. Theodore T. Kozlowski. LC 78-10815. (George S. Long Publications). (Illus.). 184p. 1979. 20.00 (0-295-95636-4) U of Wash Pr.

Tree Habit in Land Plants: A Functional Comparison of Trunk Construction with a Brief Introduction into the Biomechanics of Trees. A. Adolf Seilacher. (Lecture Notes in Earth Sciences Ser.: Vol. 28). v, 161p. 1990. 32.95 (0-387-52374-X) Spr-Verlag.

Tree Homes. Jean C. Echols. Ed. by Lincoln Bergman & Carl Babcock. (Great Explorations in Math & Science (GEMS) Ser.). (Illus.). 88p. (Orig.). (J). (ps-1). 1993. teacher ed., pap. 13.50 (0-912511-87-7) Lawrence Science.

Tree House Book. David Stiles. 80p. 1992. pap. 7.50 (0-380-76900-X) Avon.

Tree House Detective Club. Elizabeth Bolton. LC 84-8762. (Illus.). 48p. (J). (gr. 2-4). 1985. pap. 3.50 (0-8167-0405-8); lib. bdg. 11.50 (0-8167-0404-X) Troll Communs.

Tree House Fun. Rose Greydanus. (Illus.). 32p. (J). (gr. k-2). 1996. pap. 2.50 (0-89375-291-6) Troll Communs.

Tree House Kids Journal. Carol Gorman. (Tree House Kids Ser.). (Illus.). 96p. (Orig.). (J). (gr. 2-5). 1994. pap. 3.99 (0-570-04763-3, 56-1782) Concordia.

Tree House Mystery. Paul Hutchens. (Sugar Creek Gang Ser.: Vol. 22). (J). (gr. 2-7). 1972. mass mkt., pap. 3.99 (0-8024-4835-6) Moody.

Tree House Mystery. Gertrude C. Warner. LC 77-91744. (Boxcar Children Mysteries Ser.: No. 14). (Illus.). 128p. (J). (gr. 2-7). 1969. pap. 3.50 (0-8075-8087-2); lib. bdg. 13.95 (0-8075-8086-4) A Whitman.

Tree House Mystery. Bob Wright. Tr. by Phyllis Bourne & Eugenia Tusquets. (Tom & Ricky Spanish-English Readers Ser.). (Illus.). 96p. (ENG & SPA.). (J). (gr. 1-5). 1988. pap. 4.95 (0-87879-665-7) High Noon Bks.

***Tree Huggers: Victory, Defeat, & Renewal in the Northwest Ancient Forest Campaign.** Kathie Durbin. (Illus.). 304p. 1996. 24.95 (0-89886-488-7) Mountaineers.

Tree I. D. Kit. 3rd ed. Ed. by Robert F. Wilson. (Illus.). 42p. 1997. pap. 24.95 (0-9635744-0-X) Lawrence Co.

Tree Identification Book. George W. Symonds. LC 58-5359. 272p. 1973. pap. 17.95 (0-688-05039-5, Quill) Morrow.

***Tree in a Forest.** Jan Thornhill. (Illus.). 32p. (YA). (gr. 3 up). 1996. 14.95 (0-920775-64-0, Pub. by Greey dePencier CN); pap. 5.95 (1-895688-18-3, Pub. by Greey dePencier CN) Firefly Bks Ltd.

Tree in a Forest. Jan Thornhill. LC 91-25857. (Illus.). 40p. (J). (ps-3). 1992. pap. 15.00 (0-671-75901-9, S&S Bks Young Read) S&S Childrens.

Tree in Art. Ed. by Stephen Longstreet. (Master Draughtsman Ser.). (Illus.). (Orig.). 1966. 10.95 (0-87505-047-6); pap. 4.95 (0-87505-200-2) Borden.

Tree in Sprocket's Pocket: Stories about God's Green Earth. Paulette Nehemias. LC 92-26033. (God's Green Earth Ser.). (Illus.). 128p. (Orig.). (J). (gr. 3-5). 1993. pap. 4.99 (0-570-04730-7, 56-1696) Concordia.

Tree in the Ancient Forest. Carol Reed-Jones. (Illus.). 32p. (J). (ps-5). 1995. 16.95 (1-883220-32-7); pap. 7.95 (1-883220-31-9) Dawn CA.

***Tree in the Forest.** Jan Thornhill. 40p. (J). 1996. pap. 5.95 (0-382-24374-9) Silver Burdett Pr.

Tree in the Moon & Other Legends of Plants & Trees. Rosalind Kerven. (Illus.). 32p. (J). 1989. text ed. 17.95 (0-521-34269-4) Cambridge U Pr.

Tree in the Trail. Holling C. Holling. (Illus.). (J). (gr. 4-6). 17.95 (0-395-18228-X) HM.

Tree in the Trail. Holling C. Holling. (Illus.). 64p. (J). (gr. 4-6). 1990. pap. 8.95 (0-395-54534-X) HM.

Tree in the Wind. large type ed. Mary Muller. 394p. 1981. 25.99 (0-7089-0606-0) Ulverscroft.

Tree in the Wood: An Old Nursery Song. Illus. & Adapted by Christopher Manson. LC 92-23524. 32p. (J). (gr. k-3). Date not set. 14.95 (1-55858-192-8); lib. bdg. 14.88 (1-55858-193-6) North-South Bks NYC.

Tree Is a Tree. King Vidor. LC 89-84948. (Illus.). 316p. 1989. pap. 13.95 (0-573-60602-1) S French Trade.

Tree Is Growing. Arthur Dorros. LC 96-10844. (Illus.). (J). 1997. 15.95 (0-590-45300-9) Scholastic Inc.

Tree Is Known by Its Fruit. Aurelia R. Downey. 200p. (YA). (gr. 9-12). 1996. pap. write for info. (0-9641602-2-6) A R Downey.

Tree Is Lighted. Ellen Davies-Rogers. LC 84-90673. (Illus.). 1984. 5.00 (0-317-19588-3) Plantation.

Tree Is Nice. Janice M. Udry. LC 56-5153. (Illus.). 32p. (J). (ps-1). 1956. 14.95 (0-06-026155-2) HarpC Child Bks.

Tree Is Nice. Janice M. Udry. LC 56-5153. (Illus.). 32p. (J). (ps-1). 1957. lib. bdg. 14.89 (0-06-026156-0) HarpC Child Bks.

Tree Is Nice. Janice M. Udry. LC 56-5153. (Trophy Picture Bk.). (Illus.). 32p. (J). (ps-3). 1987. pap. 4.95 (0-06-443147-9, Trophy) HarpC Child Bks.

Tree Is Older Than You Are: A Bilingual Gathering of Poems & Stories from Mexico with Paintings by Mexican Artists. Naomi Shihab-Nye. LC 95-1565. (J). (gr. 3 up). 1995. 19.95 (0-689-80297-8, S&S Bks Young Read) S&S Childrens.

Tree Is Special. Catherine G. Campbell. 1992. pap. 2.95 (0-87813-537-5) Christian Light.

Tree Life. Theresa Greenaway. LC 92-52824. (Look Closer Ser.). (Illus.). 32p. (J). (gr. 1-4). 1992. 9.95 (1-56458-132-2) DK Pub Inc.

Tree Life of Argyll. Picton Publishing Staff. 1987. 25.00 (0-317-90397-7, Pub. by Picton UK) St Mut.

Tree Maintenance. 6th ed. Pascal P. Pirone et al. (Illus.). 528p. 1988. 49.95 (0-19-504370-7) OUP.

Tree Management in Farmer Strategies: Responses to Agricultural Intensification. Ed. by J. E. Arnold & Peter A. Dewees. (Illus.). 282p. 1995. 115.00 (0-19-858414-8) OUP.

Tree Mazes: An Educational-Activity Coloring Book. Spizzirri Publishing Co. Staff. (Illus.). 32p. (J). (gr. 1-8). 1989. pap. 1.25 (0-86545-143-5) Spizzirri.

Tree Medicine, Tree Magic. Ellen E. Hopman. (Illus.). 176p. 1992. pap. 12.95 (0-919345-55-7) Phoenix WA.

Tree Models of Similarity & Association. James E. Corter. LC 95-50165. (Quantitative Applications in the Social Science Ser.: Vol. 112). 96p. (C). 1996. pap. 9.95 (0-8039-5707-6) Sage.

Tree of Appomattox. Joseph A. Altsheler. 1993. reprint ed. lib. bdg. 21.95 (0-89968-568-4) Buccaneer Bks.

Tree of Appomattox: A Story of the Civil War's Close. Joseph A. Altsheler. (Joseph A. Altsheler Civil War Ser.). 1985. 23.95 (0-8488-0073-7, American Hse) Amereon Ltd.

Tree of Birds. Susan Meddaugh. (Illus.). 32p. (J). (gr. k-3). 1990. 13.95 (0-395-53147-0) HM.

Tree of Birds. Susan Meddaugh. (J). (ps-3). 1994. pap. 4.95 (0-395-68978-3) HM.

Tree of Cranes. Allen Say. (Illus.). 32p. (J). (gr. k-3). 1991. 17.95 (0-395-52024-X, Sandpiper) HM.

***Tree of Crows.** Lewis Davies. 102p. 1996. pap. 9.95 (0-9521558-3-4) Dufour.

Tree of Death. Marcia Muller. 208p. 1996. mass mkt. 5.99 (0-446-40420-9, Mysterious Paperbk) Warner Bks.

Tree of Dreams: Ten Tales from the Garden of Night. Laurence Yep. LC 94-11250. (Illus.). 96p. (YA). (gr. 8-12). 1996. pap. 5.95 (0-8167-3499-2) BrdgeWater.

Tree of Dreams: Ten Tales from the Garden of Night. Laurence Yep. LC 94-11250. (Illus.). 96p. (J). 1997. pap. 13.95 (0-8167-3498-4) BrdgeWater.

***Tree of Gnosis.** Askari. pap. 20.00 (0-06-060246-5) HarpC.

Tree of Hands. Ruth Rendell. LC 85-8148. 320p. 1986. mass mkt. 5.99 (0-345-31200-7) Ballantine.

Tree of Heaven. James McKean. LC 94-49018. (Iowa Poetry Prize Ser.). 84p. (Orig.). 1995. pap. 10.95 (0-87745-505-8) U of Iowa Pr.

Tree of Heaven: A Novel. R. C. Binstock. LC 94-41552. 220p. 1996. pap. 12.00 (1-56947-069-3) Soho Press.

Tree of Hope. Jessica Goronwy. 1985. 20.00 (0-7223-1827-8, Pub. by A H S Ltd UK) St Mut.

Tree of Knowledge. Louis A. Gottschalk. LC 85-71701. (Illus.). 236p. (J). (gr. 8 up). 1985. text ed. 12.50 (0-939373-01-7) Art Reprod.

Tree of Knowledge & Other Essays. George H. Von Wright. LC 92-42036. (Philosophy of History & Culture Ser.: No. 11). 254p. 1993. 93.00 (90-04-09764-3) E J Brill.

Tree of Knowledge of Good & Evil. 3rd ed. Omraam M. Aivanhov. (Izvor Collection: Vol. 210). (Illus.). 160p. (Orig.). 1988. pap. 6.95 (2-85566-283-4, Pub. by Prosveta FR) Prosveta USA.

Tree of Liberty. Elizabeth Page. 1000p. 1990. reprint ed. lib. bdg. 57.95 (0-89966-658-2) Buccaneer Bks.

Tree of Liberty: A Documentary History of Rebellion & Political Crime in America. Ed. by Nicholas N. Kittrie & Eldon D. Wedlock, Jr. LC 85-24068. 768p. reprint ed. pap. 180.00 (0-7837-4401-3, 2044141) Bks Demand.

Tree of Liberty: Radicalism, Catholicism, & the Construction of Irish Identity, 1760-1830. Kevin Whelan. LC 96-11876. (Critical Conditions Ser.). (C). 1996. pap. text ed. 20.00 (0-268-01894-4) U of Notre Dame Pr.

Tree of Lies: Become Who You Are. Christopher S. Hyatt. LC 91-60058. 224p. (Orig.). 1992. pap. 12.95 (1-56184-008-4) New Falcon Pubns.

Tree of Life. (Illus.). 280p. (Orig.). 1996. pap. 46.00 (0-9652863-0-4) Am Visionary.

Tree Of Life. Witness Lee. 156p. per. 6.00 (0-87083-300-6, 07018001) Living Stream Ministry.

Tree of Life. Mosie Lister. 1985. 4.99 (0-685-68635-3, ME-38) Lillenas.

Tree of Life. George W. Carey. 60p. 1985. reprint ed. spiral bd. 12.50 (0-7873-1225-8) Hlth Research.

Tree of Life. Isaac Jennings. 279p. 1993. reprint ed. spiral bd. 25.00 (0-7873-0472-7) Hlth Research.

Tree of Life: A Novel. M. David Detweiler. LC 95-8864. (Fiction Bk.). 540p. 1995. 24.95 (0-8117-1600-7) Stackpole.

***Tree of Life: An Exploration of Biblical Wisdom Literature.** 2nd ed. Roland E. Murphy. LC 96-28479. 248p. 1996. pap. 22.00 (0-8028-4192-9) Eerdmans.

Tree of Life: Image for the Cosmos. Roger Cook. LC 88-50248. (Art & Imagination Ser.). (Illus.). 128p. (Orig.). 1988. pap. 15.95 (0-500-81007-9) Thames Hudson.

Tree of Life: Paths in Jungian Individuation. J. Marvin Spiegelman. LC 74-81034. 368p. (Orig.). 1993. pap. 14.95 (1-56184-062-9) New Falcon Pubns.

***Tree of Life: Spiritual Duet.** Rochelle L. Holt & Marie Asner. (Duets Ser.). (Illus.). 64p. (Orig.). 1997. pap. 13.00 (0-934536-61-9) Rose Shell Pr.

***Tree of Life: Stories of Civil War.** Mario Bencastro. LC 96-49351. 1997. pap. 11.95 (1-55885-186-0) Arte Publico.

Tree of Life: The Wonders of Evolution. Ellen Jackson. (Young Readers Ser.). (Illus.). 40p. (J). (gr. k-3). 1993. 14.95 (0-87975-819-8) Prometheus Bks.

Tree of Life: The World of the African Baobab. Barbara Bash. (Illus.). 32p. (J). (gr. 1-5). 1994. 5.95 (0-316-08322-4) Little.

Tree of Life, a Study in Magic. Israel Regardie. LC 70-16403. 284p. 1972. reprint ed. pap. 14.95 (0-87728-149-1) Weiser.

***Tree of Life & the Holy Grail.** Sylvia Francke & Thomas Cawthorne. (Illus.). 288p. 1996. pap. write for info. (0-904693-79-1, Pub. by Temple Ldge Pub UK) Anthroposophic.

An Asterisk (*) at the beginning of an entry indicates that the title is appearing in BIP for the first time.

Tree of Life, or, Human Degeneracy, Its Nature & Remedy as Based on the Elevating Principle of Orthopathy. Isaac Jennings. 1991. lib. bdg. 88.95 (*0-8490-5038-3*) Gordon Pr.

Tree of Love: Ramon Llull's "Tree of the Philosophy of Love" Ramon Llull. (Historical & Scholarly Resources Ser.). 100p. 1997. pap. 19.95 (*1-883938-11-2*) Dry Bones Pr.

Tree of Mythology, Its Growth & Fruitage. Charles Mills. 1976. lib. bdg. 59.95 (*0-8490-2765-9*) Gordon Pr.

Tree of Northern Bengal. A. M. Cowan. 178p. 1979. 125.00 (*0-685-54031-6*, Pub. by Intl Bk Distr II) St Mut.

***Tree of Red Stars.** Tessa Bridal. LC 96-40156. 250p. 1997. 21.95 (*1-57131-013-4*) Milkweed Ed.

Tree of Rights: Patient's Rights on a Broken Limb. Sandra K. Wagner. 1995. 10.95 (*0-533-11512-4*) Vantage.

Tree of Shelter. 1979. pap. 5.95 (*0-685-05241-9*) Vedanta Ctr.

Tree of Song. 2nd rev. ed. Federico Garcia Lorca. Tr. by Alan Brilliant from SPA. LC 70-134743. (Keepsake Ser.: Vol. 3). (Illus.). 36p. (ENG & SPA.). 1973. 17.50 (*0-87775-046-7*); pap. 7.50 (*0-87775-047-5*) Unicorn Pr.

Tree of the Christian Faith. Jacob Boehme. 1993. reprint ed. pap. 8.95 (*1-55818-190-3*, Sure Fire) Holmes Pub.

***Tree of the Seventh Heaven.** Milton Hatoum. 210p. 3.98 (*0-8317-5853-8*) Smithmark.

Tree of Time: A Story of a Special Sequoia. Kathy Baron. (Illus.). 40p. (J). (gr. 4-7). 1994. pap. 7.95 (*0-939666-73-1*) Yosemite Assn.

Tree of Yoga. B. K. Iyengar. LC 88-18587. 206p. (Orig.). 1989. pap. 12.00 (*0-87773-464-X*) Shambhala Pubns.

***Tree, One Life That Made a Difference.** Norman Kjono. (Illus.). 328p. 1997. 11.95 (*1-57532-078-9*) Press-Tige Pub.

***Tree or Three? An Elementary Pronunciation Course.** 128p. 1982. pap. text ed. 12.95 (*0-521-28293-4*) Cambridge U Pr.

Tree People. Naomi M. Stokes. 384p. 1996. mass mkt. write for info. (*0-614-05516-4*) Forge NYC.

Tree People. Naomi M. Stokes. 544p. 1996. mass mkt. 6.99 (*0-8125-3510-3*) Tor Bks.

Tree Place: And Other Poems. Constance Levy. LC 93-20586. (Illus.). 48p. (J). (gr. k-5). 1994. lib. bdg. 14.00 (*0-689-50599-X*, McElderry) S&S Childrens.

Tree Plantation & Environment Awareness. Lalit M. Mathur. (Illus.). xvi, 443p. 1993. 59.00 (*81-7024-489-7*, Pub. by Ashish Pub Hse II) Nataraj Bks.

Tree Planting on Mined Lands in the Midwest: A Handbook. W. Clark Ashby & Willis G. Vogel. (Illus.). 115p. 1994. lib. bdg. write for info. (*1-885189-01-X*) Coal Res Ctr.

Tree Planting Practices for Arid Zones. F. A. O. Staff. 226p. (C). 1989. text ed. 225.00 (*0-89771-617-5*, Pub. by Intl Bk Distr II) St Mut.

Tree Planting Practices in Temperate Asia: Burma India Pakistan. F. A. O. Staff. 150p. 1989. 88.00 (*81-7089-106-X*, Pub. by Intl Bk Distr II) St Mut.

Tree Poachers. Pierre Coran. (Child's World Library). (Illus.). 32p. (J). (gr. k-5). 1991. lib. bdg. 18.50 (*0-89565-746-5*) Childs World.

Tree Protection. V. K. Gupta & N. K. Sharma. (C). 1988. 62.00 (*0-8364-2436-0*, Pub. by Oxford IBH II) S Asia.

Tree Pruner Supervisor. Jack Rudman. (Career Examination Ser.: C-3049). 1994. pap. 29.95 (*0-8373-3049-1*) Nat Learn.

Tree Pruning: A Worldwide Photo Guide. Alex L. Shigo. (Dr. Shigo's Tree Ser.). (Illus.). 192p. 1989. text ed. 39.00 (*0-943563-08-9*) Shigo & Trees Assocs.

Tree-Pruning Guidelines. John Britton & Richard Harris. (Illus.). 20p. (Orig.). 1994. pap. 5.00 (*1-881956-07-5*) Int Soc Arboricult.

Tree Resources & Environmental Policy: A Stakeholder Approach. R. J. Grimble et al. 1994. pap. 25.00 (*0-85954-380-3*, Pub. by Nat Res Inst UK) St Mut.

Tree Rings. Fritz H. Schweingruber. (C). 1988. lib. bdg. 265.50 (*90-277-2445-8*) Kluwer Ac.

Tree Rings & Telescopes: The Scientific Career of A. E. Douglass. George E. Webb. LC 83-1152. 242p. 1983. 33.50 (*0-8165-0798-8*) U of Ariz Pr.

Tree Rings As Indicators of Ecosystem Health. Timothy E. Lewis. 224p. 1994. 104.95 (*0-8493-7651-3*, 7651) CRC Pr.

Tree Rings, Environment & Humanity: Proceedings of the International Conference, Tucson, Arizona, 17-21 May 1994. Ed. by Jeffrey S. Dean et al. LC 96-25331. (Illus.). 889p. (Orig.). 1996. pap. text ed. 65.00 (*0-9638314-2-9*) Radiocarbon.

***Tree Roots & Buildings.** Cutler. 1989. pap. text ed. write for info. (*0-582-03410-8*, Pub. by Longman UK) Longman.

***Tree Seed Problems, with Special Reference to Africa: Proceedings of the IUFRO Symposium, Ouagadougou, Burkina Faso, 23-28 November 1993.** L. M. Some & M. D. De Kam. (Illus.). 478p. 1993. 130.00 (*90-73348-26-9*, Pub. by Backhuys Pubs NE) Balogh.

Tree Spree. Barbara Helwig & Susan Stewart. (Little Books for Kids). (Illus.). 56p. (J). (gr. 2-5). 1991. spiral bd. 4.95 (*1-881285-01-4*) Arbus Pub.

Tree Spree. rev. ed. Barbara Helwig & Susan Stewart. (Little Books for Kids). (Illus.). 90p. (J). (gr. 2-6). 1992. spiral bd. 4.95 (*1-881285-05-7*) Arbus Pub.

Tree Still Stands. Mae Briskin. 256p. 1992. pap. 8.95 (*0-393-30876-6*) Norton.

Tree Stump. 2nd ed. Chris Forbes. (Let Me Read Ser.). (Illus.). 8p. (J). (ps). 1994. text ed. 2.95 (*0-673-36191-8*, GoodYrBooks) Addson-Wesley Educ.

Tree Surgeon's Gift. Edward C. Lynskey. 1990. 22.50 (*0-916379-75-2*) Scripta.

Tree-Talk. Marie-France Boyer. LC 96-60251. (Illus.). 112p. 1996. 19.95 (*0-500-01729-8*) Thames Hudson.

Tree Talk: The People & Politics of Timber. Ray Raphael. LC 81-2835. (Illus.). 287p. (Orig.). 1981. pap. 14.95 (*0-933280-10-6*) Island Pr.

***Tree That Came to Stay.** Anna Quindlen. LC 97-12239. (Illus.). (J). 1997. pap. 14.99 (*0-670-87704-2*) Viking Penguin.

Tree That Owns Itself: And Other Adventure Tales from Out of the Past. Loretta C. Hammer & Gail Karwoski. (Illus.). 128p. (Orig.). (J). (gr. 3-7). 1996. pap. 8.95 (*1-56145-120-7*) Peachtree Pubs.

Tree That Rains: The Flood Myth of the Huichol Indians of Mexico. Illus. by Durga Bernhard. LC 93-8294. 32p. (J). (ps-3). 1994. lib. bdg. 15.95 (*0-8234-1108-7*) Holiday.

Tree That Survived the Winter. Mary Fahy. (Illus.). 288p. (YA). (gr. 8-12). 1989. 8.95 (*0-8091-0432-6*) Paulist Pr.

Tree That Would Not Die. Ellen Levine. LC 94-8394. (Illus.). 32p. (J). (gr. 2-4). 1995. 14.95 (*0-590-43724-0*, Scholastic Hardcover) Scholastic Inc.

Tree Trimmer. Jack Rudman. (Career Examination Ser.: C-1526). 1994. pap. 23.95 (*0-8373-1526-3*) Nat Learn.

Tree Trimmer: A Search Tool for Multiple Tree Explosions in Medical Subject Headings, 1987. Ed. by William A. Clintworth. 359p. (Orig.). 1986. pap. 35.00 (*0-945293-00-3*) Clintworth Pubns.

Tree Trimmer: A Search Tool for Multiple Tree Explosions in Medical Subject Headings, 1987. 2nd ed. Ed. by William A. Clintworth. 370p. (Orig.). 1987. pap. 35.00 (*0-945293-01-1*) Clintworth Pubns.

Tree Trimmer: A Search Tool for Multiple Tree Explosions in Medical Subject Headings, 1987. 3rd ed. Ed. by William A. Clintworth. 388p. (Orig.). 1988. pap. 35.00 (*0-945293-02-X*) Clintworth Pubns.

Tree Trimmer: A Search Tool for Multiple Tree Explosions in Medical Subject Headings, 1987. 4th ed. Ed. by William A. Clintworth. 422p. (Orig.). 1989. pap. 35.00 (*0-945293-03-8*) Clintworth Pubns.

Tree Trimmer: A Search Tool for Multiple Tree Explosions in Medical Subject Headings, 1987. 5th ed. Ed. by William A. Clintworth. 468p. (Orig.). 1990. pap. 42.00 (*0-945293-04-6*) Clintworth Pubns.

Tree Trimmer Foreman. Jack Rudman. (Career Examination Ser.: C-2574). 1994. pap. 27.95 (*0-8373-2574-9*) Nat Learn.

Tree Trunk Traffic. Bianca Lavies. (Illus.). 32p. (J). (ps-2). 1993. pap. 4.99 (*0-14-054837-8*) Puffin Bks.

Tree, Turf & Ornamental Pesticide Guide. rev. ed. W. T. Thomson. 160p. 1994. pap. text ed. 18.50 (*0-913702-46-3*) Thomson Pubns.

Tree Vipers. Sherie Bargar & Johnson. (Snake Discovery Library: Set II). (Illus.). 24p. (J). (gr. 1-4). 1987. lib. bdg. 11.94 (*0-86592-245-4*) Rourke Corp.

Tree Vipers. Sherie Bargar & Johnson. (Snake Discovery Library: Set. II). (Illus.). 24p. (J). (gr. 1-4). 1987. lib. bdg. 8.95 (*0-685-67604-8*) Rourke Corp.

Tree Vipers. Sherie Bargar & L. Johnson. (J). 1997. pap. 2.50 (*0-8167-1451-7*) Troll Communs.

Tree Where Man Was Born. Peter Matthiessen. 1996. 22.25 (*0-8446-6892-3*) Peter Smith.

Tree Where Man Was Born. Peter Matthiessen. (Nature Classics Ser.). 448p. 1995. pap. 12.95 (*0-14-023934-0*, Penguin Bks) Viking Penguin.

Tree Where Man Was Born. Peter Matthiessen. 353p. 1983. reprint ed. pap. 8.95 (*0-525-48032-3*, Obelisk) NAL-Dutton.

Tree Where Man Was Born. Peter Matthiessen. (Illus.). 248p. 1996. reprint ed. 19.98 (*1-56731-102-4*, MJF Bks) Fine Comms.

Tree Witch: A Poem & Play (First of All a Poem) Peter R. Viereck. LC 70-178794. 126p. 1973. reprint ed. text ed. 35.00 (*0-8371-6282-3*, VTWI, Greenwood Pr) Greenwood.

Tree with Arms. James Saba. (Orig.). (J). (gr. 1-7). 1997. pap. 5.00 (*0-87602-342-1*) Anchorage.

Tree Within: Bilingual Edition. Octavio Paz. Tr. by Eliot Weinberger. LC 88-19666. 176p. 1988. pap. 9.95 (*0-8112-1071-5*, NDP661) New Directions.

Tree Worship in Ancient India. B. C. Sinha. xv, 103p. 1979. 15.00 (*1-55528-057-9*, Pub. by Today & Tomorrows P & P II) Scholarly Pubns.

Treefrogs. James E. Gerholdt. LC 94-18099. (Amazing Amphibians Ser.). (J). 1994. lib. bdg. 14.98 (*1-56239-311-1*) Abdo & Dghtrs.

Treeful of Pigs. Arnold Lobel. LC 78-1810. (Illus.). 32p. (J). (gr. k-3). 1979. lib. bdg. 15.93 (*0-688-84177-5*) Greenwillow.

Treeful of Pigs. Lober. 1988. pap. (*0-590-48979-8*) Scholastic Inc.

Treehouse: New & Selected Poems. William Kloefkorn. 240p. (Orig.). 1996. pap. 15.00 (*1-877727-65-2*) White Pine.

Treehouse Kids. Tamar Kamins. (B. Y. Times Kid Sisters Ser.: No. 2). (J). (gr. 4-7). Date not set. pap. 7.95 (*0-944070-92-2*) Targum Pr.

Treehouse Tales. Anne Isaacs. (J). 1997. pap. 14.99 (*0-525-45611-2*) NAL-Dutton.

Treehouses. Peter Nelson. LC 93-32568. 1994. pap. 19.95 (*0-395-62949-7*) HM.

Treeless Plains. Glen Rounds. (Illus.). (J). 1994. pap. 6.95 (*0-8234-1085-4*) Holiday.

Treeless Plains. Glen Rounds. (Illus.). 96p. (J). (gr. 5 up). 1994. reprint ed. 15.95 (*0-8234-1084-6*) Holiday.

Treelike: The Poetry of Kinoshita Yuji. Ed. by Thomas Fitzsimmons. Tr. by Robert Epp from JPN. LC 82-81181. (Asian Poetry in Translation: Japan Ser.: No. 4). (Illus.). 294p. (Orig.). (ENG & JPN.). 1989. pap. 20.00 (*0-942668-04-9*) Katydid Bks.

Treeman. Carmen A. Deedy. LC 93-1667. (Illus.). (J). 1993. 16.95 (*1-56145-077-4*) Peachtree Pubs.

Treemonisha. Angela S. Medearis. (Illus.). 40p. (J). (gr. k-4). 1995. 15.95 (*0-8050-1748-8*) H Holt & Co.

Treemonisha: Vocal Selections. (Illus.). 072p. 1981. pap. 9.95 (*0-88188-118-X*, 00312440) H Leonard.

Trees. (Flora - In Focus Ser.). 1996. 12.98 (*0-8317-6124-5*) Smithmark.

Trees. Ivan M. Anatta. LC 92-32286. (Nature Bks.). 32p. (J). (gr. 2-6). 1993. lib. bdg. 22.79 (*1-56766-002-9*) Childs World.

Trees. Ed. by Y. S. Bajaj. LC 85-17309. (Biotechnology in Agriculture & Forestry Ser.: Vol. 1). (Illus.). 550p. 1985. 344.95 (*0-387-15581-3*) Spr-Verlag.

Trees. Harry Behn. LC 91-25179. (Illus.). 32p. (J). (ps-2). 1992. 14.95 (*0-8050-1926-X*, B Martin BYR) H Holt & Co.

Trees. Harry Behn. (Illus.). (J). (PS-3). 1994. pap. 5.95 (*0-8050-3550-8*, Bks Young Read) H Holt & Co.

Trees. Karen Bryant-Mole. (See for Yourself Ser.). (J). 1996. lib. bdg. 19.97 (*0-8172-4212-0*) Raintree Steck-V.

Trees. Andrew Charman. (Fact Finders Ser.). (Illus.). 48p. (Orig.). (J). (gr. 2 up). 1992. pap. 6.95 (*0-563-35017-2*, BBC-Parkwest) Parkwest Pubns.

Trees. Allen J. Coombes. LC 92-52782. (Eyewitness Handbks.). (Illus.). 320p. 1992. 29.95 (*1-56458-075-X*); pap. 17.95 (*1-56458-072-5*) DK Pub Inc.

Trees. J. Cooper. (Earth's Garden Ser.). (J). 1991. 8.95 (*0-86592-621-2*) Rourke Enter.

***Trees.** Jason Cooper. LC 97-16927. (Guide to State Symbols Ser.). 1997. write for info. (*1-57103-195-2*) Rourke Pr.

***Trees.** Dorling Kindersley Staff. (Eyewitness Explorers Ser.). (Illus.). 64p. (J). 1997. pap. 5.95 (*0-7894-1679-4*) DK Pub Inc.

***Trees.** John Feltwell. (Eyewitness Explorers Ser.). (Illus.). (J). (gr. 1 up). 1997. pap. 5.95 (*0-614-28712-X*) DK Pub Inc.

Trees. Linda Gamlin. LC 92-54310. (Eyewitness Explorers Ser.). (Illus.). 64p. (J). (gr. 3 up). 1993. 9.95 (*1-56458-230-2*) DK Pub Inc.

Trees. Frederick J. Garner. (How to Draw & Paint Ser.). (Illus.). 32p. (Orig.). 1989. pap. 6.95 (*0-929261-24-0*, HT3) W Foster Pub.

Trees. Galen Gates et al. (American Garden Guides Ser.). 224p. 1996. pap. 25.00 (*0-679-75862-3*) Pantheon.

Trees. Peggy Gavan. LC 95-4868. (First-Start Science Ser.). (Illus.). 32p. (J). (gr. k-2). 1995. lib. bdg. 9.79 (*0-8167-3856-4*) Troll Communs.

Trees. Peggy Gavan. LC 95-4868. (First-Start Science Ser.). (Illus.). 32p. (J). (gr. k-2). 1996. pap. 2.95 (*0-8167-3857-2*) Troll Communs.

Trees. Sharon Gordon. LC 82-20291. (Now I Know Ser.). (Illus.). 32p. (J). (gr. k-2). 1996. pap. 3.50 (*0-8167-0879-7*) Troll Communs.

Trees. Theresa Greenaway. LC 94-32038. (DK Pockets Ser.). (Illus.). 160p. (YA). (gr. 7 up). 1995. pap. 5.95 (*1-56458-884-X*) DK Pub Inc.

Trees. Ed. by Kristin Joyce. LC 95-11940. (Cultivated Gardner Ser.). (Illus.). 96p. 1997. 18.95 (*0-00-225040-3*) Collins SF.

***Trees.** Chris Oxlade. (Learn about Ser.). (Illus.). 64p. (J). (gr. 3-7). 1997. 7.95 (*1-85967-313-9*, Lorenz Bks) Anness Pub.

Trees. Jonathan Pine. LC 93-3136. (Nature Studies). (Illus.). 48p. (J). (gr. 2-5). 1995. lib. bdg. 14.89 (*0-06-021469-4*) HarpC Child Bks.

Trees. Henry Pluckrose. LC 93-44699. (Walkabout Ser.). (J). 1994. lib. bdg. 17.60 (*0-516-08121-7*) Childrens.

Trees. Henry Pluckrose. (Walkabout Ser.). (J). (ps-2). 1994. pap. 4.95 (*0-516-40121-1*) Childrens.

Trees. Conrad Richter. 1940. 18.95 (*0-394-44951-7*) Knopf.

Trees. Ed. by Angela Royston. LC 93-46145. (Science Nature Guides Ser.). (Illus.). 81p. (J). (gr. 3-6). 1994. 12.95 (*1-85028-265-X*) Thunder Bay CA.

Trees. Andres L. Ruiz. LC 96-25740. (Cycles of Life Ser.). (Illus.). 32p. (J). 1996. 12.95 (*0-8069-9327-8*) Sterling.

Trees. Jean-Pierre Serre. 140p. 1980. 39.00 (*0-387-10103-9*) Spr-Verlag.

Trees. Thompson. (First Nature Bks.). (J). (gr. 2-5). 1980. pap. 3.95 (*0-86020-473-1*, Usborne); lib. bdg. 11.95 (*0-88110-071-4*, Usborne) EDC.

Trees. Herbert S. Zim & Alexander C. Martin. (Golden Guide Ser.). (Illus.). 160p. (YA). (gr. 6 up). 1952. pap. 5.50 (*0-307-24056-8*, Golden Pr) Western Pub.

Trees. 3rd ed. Howard Miller. (Pictured Key Nature Ser.). 276p. (C). 1978. spiral bd. write for info. (*0-697-04896-9*) Wm C Brown Pubs.

Trees. Charles Fenyvesi. 192p. 1993. reprint ed. pap. 8.00 (*0-380-72020-5*) Avon.

Trees. Conrad Richter. LC 90-19936. 167p. 1991. reprint ed. pap. 12.95 (*0-8214-0978-6*) Ohio U Pr.

Trees, No. III. Ed. by Y. P. Bajaj. (Biotechnology in Agriculture & Forestry Ser.). (Illus.). 512p. 1991. 405.95 (*0-387-52576-9*) Spr-Verlag.

Trees: A Celebration in Photography. Photos by Graeme Matthews & David Bellamy. LC 94-4807. 1994. 60.00 (*0-517-59963-5*, C P Pubs) Crown Pub Group.

Trees: A Gardener's Guide. Judith D. Zuk. (Illus.). 96p. 1992. per., pap. 7.95 (*0-945352-75-1*) Bklyn Botanic.

***Trees: Flashguides.** George A. Petrides. 1996. pap. 7.95 (*0-395-82998-4*) HM.

Trees: The Green Testament. Ya'akov Kirschen. 192p. (YA). 1993. pap. text ed. 14.95 (*0-9641252-1-8*) Vital Media.

Trees: The Mechanical Design. G. Claus Mattheck. (Illus.). 125p. 1996. 39.00 (*0-387-54276-0*) Spr-Verlag.

***Trees: Workshop in Versailles, June 14-16, 1995.** Brigitte Chauvin et al. LC 96-39024. (Progress in Probability Ser.). 1996. write for info. (*0-8176-5453-4*) Birkhauser.

***Trees: Workshop in Versailles, June 14-16, 1995.** Brigitte Chauvin et al. LC 96-39024. (Progress in Probability Ser.). 168p. 1996. 78.00 (*3-7643-5453-4*) Birkhauser.

Trees - It's Our Planet Activity Book. Kathy B. Smith. (Illus.). 32p. (Orig.). (J). (gr. k-6). 1992. pap. 2.95 (*1-879424-38-X*) Nickel Pr.

Trees & Deer. Richard Prior. (Illus.). 216p. 1994. 40.00 (*1-85310-432-9*, Pub. by Swan Hill UK) Voyageur Pr.

Trees & Flowers. (Ultimate Sticker Bks.). (Illus.). 20p. (J). (ps-3). 1995. pap. 6.95 (*0-7894-0009-X*) DK Pub Inc.

Trees & Forests: From Algae to Sequoias: the History, Life, & Richness of Forests. Scholastic Staff. (Voyages of Discovery Ser.: No. 5). 48p. (J). (gr. 4-6). 1995. bds., spiral bd. 19.95 (*0-590-47639-4*, Blue Sky Press) Scholastic Inc.

Trees & Forests of the World, 2 vols. Ed. by Bayard Hora. LC 90-36009. (Illus.). 290p. (J). 1990. lib. bdg. 79.95 (*1-85435-330-6*) Marshall Cavendish.

Trees & Hierarchical Structures: Proceedings of a Conference Held at Bielefeld, FRG, Fall 1987. Ed. by A. Dress et al. (Lecture Notes in Biomathematics Ser.: Vol. 84). vi, 137p. 1990. 34.95 (*0-387-52453-3*) Spr-Verlag.

Trees & Leader: Two Short Plays. Israel Horovitz. 1970. pap. 3.25 (*0-8222-0647-1*) Dramatists Play.

Trees & Leaves. Althea. LC 89-20308. (Nature Club Ser.). (Illus.). 32p. (J). (gr. 3-6). 1990. pap. 4.95 (*0-8167-1968-3*) Troll Communs.

Trees & Other Poems. Joyce Kilmer. LC 82-14061. 1982. pap. write for info. (*0-89783-024-5*) Larlin Corp.

Trees & Other Poems: Candles That Burn, 2 bks. in 1. Joyce Kilmer & Aline M. Kilmer. 128p. 1994. reprint ed. pap. 13.95 (*0-87797-267-2*) Cherokee.

Trees & Other Woody Plants of Maine. Fay Hyland & Ferdinand H. Steinmetz. LC 78-18706. 72p. 1978. reprint ed. pap. 8.95 (*0-89621-018-9*) U Maine Pr.

Trees & Proximity Representations. Jean-Pierre Barthelemy & Alain Guenoche. LC 91-13808. (Interscience Series in Discrete Mathematics). 238p. 1991. text ed. 129.00 (*0-471-92263-3*) Wiley.

***Trees & Shrubs.** Cathy Haas. Ed. by Nancy Arbuckle. (Easy-Step Ser.). (Illus.). 64p. (Orig.). 1997. pap. 6.95 (*0-89721-328-9*, 05452) Ortho Info.

***Trees & Shrubs for Landscaping.** T. La Dell. (Illus.). 400p. 1997. text ed. write for info. (*0-419-20800-3*, E & FN Spon) Routledge Chapman & Hall.

Trees & Shrubs for Pacific Northwest Gardens. 2nd ed. John Grant & Carol Grant. Ed. by Brian O. Mulligan et al. LC 89-31343. (Illus.). 456p. 1990. 29.95 (*0-88192-145-9*) Timber.

Trees & Shrubs for Pacific Northwest Gardens. 2nd ed. John A. Grant & Carol L. Grant. (Illus.). 456p. 1994. pap. 19.95 (*0-88192-303-6*) Timber.

Trees & Shrubs for Temperate Climates. 3rd ed. Gordon Courtright. LC 87-36433. (Illus.). 250p. 1988. 49.95 (*0-88192-097-5*) Timber.

Trees & Shrubs for the Northern Plains. Donald G. Hoag. LC 65-65406. (Illus.). 376p. 1965. pap. 12.50 (*0-911042-10-5*) NDSU Inst Reg.

***Trees & Shrubs of Alberta.** Kathleen Wilkinson. 1995. pap. 15.95 (*0-919433-39-1*) Lone Pine.

Trees & Shrubs of British Columbia. T. Christopher Brayshaw. (Royal British Columbia Museum Handbook Ser.). (Illus.). 400p. 1996. pap. 24.95 (*0-7748-0564-1*, Pub. by U BC Pr) U of Wash Pr.

Trees & Shrubs of Colorado: From Plains to Tundra. Jack L. Carter. (Illus.). 165p. (Orig.). 1988. pap. 13.95 (*0-9619945-0-9*) Mimbres.

Trees & Shrubs of Europe. S. Priszter. 300p. (ENG, FRE, GER, HUN, ITA, RUS & SPA.). 1983. 95.00 (*0-8288-0070-7*, M15341) Fr & Eur.

Trees & Shrubs of Kentucky. 2nd ed. Mary E. Wharton. (Illus.). 592p. 1994. 29.95 (*0-8131-1294-X*) U Pr of Ky.

Trees & Shrubs of Mexico, 5 vols. Paul C. Standley. 1976. Set. lib. bdg. 1,250.00 (*0-8490-2766-7*) Gordon Pr.

Trees & Shrubs of Mexico. Paul C. Standley. (Contributions to U. S. National Herb Ser.: No. 23, 1-5). 1722p. 1982. reprint ed. lib. bdg. 175.00 (*3-7682-1288-2*) Lubrecht & Cramer.

***Trees & Shrubs of New Mexico.** Jack L. Carter. (Illus.). vi, 520p. (Orig.). 1997. pap. 29.95 (*0-9658404-0-9*) Mimbres.

Trees & Shrubs of New Zealand. rev. ed. A. L. Poole & N. M. Adams. 1990. 29.95 (*0-477-02603-6*, Pub. by Manaaki Whenua NZ) Balogh.

Trees & Shrubs of the Adirondacks. Alan Bessette & Bill Chapman. 150p. 1990. pap. 13.95 (*0-932052-75-4*) North Country.

Trees & Shrubs of the Natal Drakensberg. 2nd ed. Olive M. Hilliard. (Ukhahlamba Ser.: No. 1). (Illus.). 48p. 1992. pap. 10.25 (*0-86980-882-6*, Pub. by Univ Natal Pr SA); pap. 11.95 (*0-86980-470-7*, Pub. by Univ Natal Pr SA) Intl Spec Bk.

***Trees & Shrubs of the Sahel: Their Characteristics & Uses.** H. J. Von Maydell. (Illus.). 525p. 1990. 61.00 (*3-8236-1198-4*, Pub. by Backhuys Pubs NE) Balogh.

***Trees & Shrubs of the Trans-Pecos & Adjacent Areas.** 2nd rev. ed. A. Michael Powell. LC 97-13155. (Illus.). 464p. 1998. 75.00 (*0-292-76579-7*) U of Tex Pr.

Trees & Shrubs of the Trans-Pecos & Adjacent Areas. 2nd rev. ed. A. Michael Powell et al. LC 97-13155. (Illus.). 464p. 1998. pap. 34.95 (*0-292-76573-8*) U of Tex Pr.

Trees & Shrubs of the Upper Midwest. Carl O. Rosendahl. LC 55-8489. (Illus.). 419p. reprint ed. pap. 119.50 (*0-318-39693-9*, 2033288) Bks Demand.

Trees & Shrubs of Virginia. Oscar W. Gupton & Fred C. Swope. LC 80-21585. (Illus.). 205p. 1981. 14.95 (*0-8139-0886-8*) U Pr of Va.

***Trees & Shrubs of Washington.** C. P. Lyons. (Illus.). 176p. (Orig.). 1997. pap. write for info. (*1-55105-094-3*) Lone Pine.

Trees & Tenure: An Annotated Bibliography for Agroforesters & Others. Louise Fortmann & James Riddell. (Illus.). xvii, 135p. (Orig.). 1985. 8.00 (*0-934519-00-5*) U of Wis Land.

Trees & Wood in Dendrochronology: Morphological, Anatomical, & Tree-ring Analytical Characteristics of Trees Frequently Used in Dendrochronology. Fritz H. Schweingruber. Tr. by Susan Johnson. LC 92-46678. (Wood Science Ser.). (ENG & GER.). 1993. 256.95 (*0-387-54915-3*) Spr-Verlag.

Trees Are Lonely Company. Howard O'Hagan. 1994. pap. 16.95 (*0-88922-327-0*) Genl Dist Srvs.

Trees Are Terrific. National Wildlife Federation Staff. (J). (gr. k-8). 1991. pap. 7.95 (*0-945051-43-3*, 75021) Natl Wildlife.

Trees Became Torches: Selected Poems. Edwin Rolfe. Ed. by Cary Nelson & Jefferson Hendricks. LC 94-6722. (American Poetry Recovery Ser.). write for info. (*0-252-02131-2*) U of Ill Pr.

Trees Became Torches: Selected Poems. Edwin Rolfe. Ed. by Cary Nelson & Jefferson Hendricks. LC 94-6722. (American Poetry Recovery Ser.). 168p. 1995. 13.95 (*0-252-06417-8*) U of Ill Pr.

Trees Call for What They Need. Melissa Kwasny. LC 93-26213. 256p. (Orig.). 1993. 21.95 (*0-933216-97-1*); pap. 10.95 (*0-933216-96-3*) Spinsters Ink.

Trees, Coffee, & the Eyes of Deer: New & Selected Poems. 2nd rev. ed. Jack Grapes. 160p. 1993. reprint ed. pap. 12.50 (*0-941017-20-6*) Bombshelter Pr.

Trees Collection. Jerrold Ziff. (Illus.). 56p. 1993. pap. write for info. (*1-883015-02-2*) Krannert Art.

Trees' Ears: A Counselor's Story. Bruce B. Fisher. 256p. (YA). (gr. 10-12). 1997. pap. 17.00 (*0-8059-3317-4*) Dorrance.

Trees Every Boy & Girl Should Know. American Forestry Association Staff. (J). (gr. 1-6). 4.50 (*0-686-26729-X*, 31) Am Forests.

Trees for... An Illustrated Guide to Pruning. Gilman. LC 96-27725. (Illus.). (C). 1997. pap. text ed. 25.95 (*0-8273-8040-2*) Delmar.

Trees for American Gardens. 3rd ed. Donald Wyman. 576p. 1990. 50.00 (*0-02-632201-3*) Macmillan.

Trees for Architecture & Landscape. 2nd ed. R. Zion. 1994. text ed. 64.95 (*0-442-01314-0*) Van Nos Reinhold.

Trees for Fuelwood: A Step Toward Energy Diversity. Ed. by James R. Fazio. 80p. 1992. 9.95 (*0-9634657-0-8*) Natl Arbor Day.

Trees for Healing: Harmonizing with Nature for Personal Growth & Planetary Balance. Pamela L. Chase & Jonathan Pawlik. 256p. (Orig.). 1991. pap. 12.95 (*0-87877-157-3*) Newcastle Pub.

Trees for Pathfinders: A Basic Youth Enrichment Skill Honor Packet. L. S. Gattis, III. (Illus.). 20p. (Orig.). (J). (gr. 5 up). 1988. teacher ed., pap. 5.00 (*0-936241-36-5*) Cheetah Pub.

Trees for the Rocky Mountain & Plains States. Gayle Weinstein. (Illus.). 300p. 1996. pap. text ed. 30.00 (*0-9629743-2-3*) Shereth Grp.

Trees for Urban & Suburban Landscapes. Edward E. Gilman. LC 96-17000. (Agriculture Ser.). 672p. 1997. 49.95 (*0-8273-7053-9*) Delmar.

Trees for Your Garden. Roy Lancaster. (Illus.). 1993. 35.00 (*0-85628-232-4*, Pub. by Aidan Ellis Pub UK) Antique Collect.

Trees, Gardener's Collection. Better Homes & Gardens Editors. (Better Homes & Gardens Ser.). (Illus.). 64p. 1995. pap. 4.95 (*0-696-02586-8*) Meredith Bks.

Trees II. Ed. by Y. P. Bajaj. (Biotechnology in Agriculture & Forestry Ser.: Vol. 5). (Illus.). 640p. 1989. 328.95 (*0-387-19158-5*) Spr-Verlag.

Trees in Algebra & Programming - CAAP '96: 21st International Colloquium, Linkoping, Sweden, April 22-24, 1996, Proceedings. Ed. by Helene Kirchner. LC 96-17669. (Lecture Notes in Computer Science Ser.: Vol. 1059). 331p. 1996. pap. 56.00 (*3-540-61064-2*) Spr-Verlag.

Trees in Algebra & Programming, CAAP '94: Nineteenth International Coloquium, Edinburgh, U.K., April 1994. Ed. by Sophie Tison. LC 94-8473. (Lecture Notes in Computer Science Ser.: Vol. 787). 1994. 55.95 (*0-387-57879-X*) Spr-Verlag.

Trees in Britain, Europe & North America. Roger Phillips & Sheila Grant. Ed. by Tom Wellsted. (Illus.). 224p. (Orig.). 1978. pap. 52.50 (*0-330-25480-4*, Pub. by Pan Books UK) Trans-Atl Phila.

Trees in Hong Kong: Species for Landscape Planting. C. Y. Jim. 442p. (C). 1990. pap. text ed. 90.00 (*962-209-264-0*, Pub. by Hong Kong U Pr HK) St Mut.

***Trees in Idaho.** Sherman Brough & Darrell Weber. (Illus.). 315p. 1997. pap. 19.00 (*0-9635617-1-5*) Brstlecone Pr.

***Trees in My Forest.** Bernd Heinrich. LC 97-16885. 288p. 1997. 23.00 (*0-06-017446-3*) HarpC.

***Trees in Oil.** Parramon's Editorial Team Staff. LC 97-9416. (Easy Painting & Drawing Ser.). 1997. pap. text ed. 13.95 (*0-7641-0106-4*) Barron.

Trees in Society in Rural Karnataka, India. C. Bostock-Wood. (Illus.). 223p. 1993. pap. 60.00 (*0-902500-47-3*, Pub. by Nat Res Inst UK) St Mut.

***Trees in the Landscape.** 2nd rev. ed. Graham S. Thomas. LC 97-7951. (Illus.). 216p. 1997. 35.00 (*0-89831-035-0*) Sagapr.

***Trees in the Urban Landscape: Principles & Practice.** Bradshaw et al. (Illus.). 288p. 1995. text ed. 59.95 (*0-419-20100-9*, E & FN Spon) Routledge Chapman & Hall.

Trees in Urban Design. 2nd ed. Henry Arnold. LC 92-11127. 1993. text ed. 44.95 (*0-442-00889-9*) Van Nos Reinhold.

***Trees IV, Vol. 35.** Ed. by Y. P. Bajaj. 432p. 1996. 298.50 (*3-540-60547-9*) Spr-Verlag.

Trees Kneel at Christmas. Maud H. Lovelace. LC 94-10512. (J). 1994. lib. bdg. 16.98 (*1-56239-999-3*) Abdo & Dghtrs.

Trees, Land, & Labor. Peter A. Dewees. LC 93-43865. (Environment Paper Ser.: No. 4). 62p. 1994. 6.95 (*0-8213-2733-X*, 12733) World Bank.

Trees, Leaves, & Bark. Diane L. Burns. LC 95-6695. (Take-Along Guide Ser.). (Illus.). 48p. (J). (gr. 1-3). 1995. 9.95 (*1-55971-477-8*) NorthWord.

Trees of Arizona: Arizona Trees. (Illus.). 32p. 1994. pap. 1.25 (*0-935810-18-8*) Primer Pubs.

Trees of Bombay. R. R. Fernandez. 1987. 450.00 (*0-685-21761-2*, Pub. by Intl Bk Distr II) St Mut.

Trees of Calcutta & Its Neighbourhood. A. P. Benthall. 515p. (C). 1988. 90.00 (*0-685-22292-6*, Pub. by Scientific UK) St Mut.

Trees of California. Willis L. Jepson. 1992. reprint ed. lib. bdg. 75.00 (*0-7812-5057-9*) Rprt Serv.

Trees of Central Texas. Robert A. Vines. (Illus.). 423p. 1984. pap. 14.95 (*0-292-78058-3*) U of Tex Pr.

Trees of East Texas. Robert A. Vines. (Illus.). 556p. 1977. pap. 16.95 (*0-292-78017-6*) U of Tex Pr.

Trees of Everglades National Park & the Florida Keys. rev. ed. George B. Stevenson. (Illus.). 32p. 1992. pap. 2.95 (*0-945142-04-8*) FL Natl Parks.

Trees of Florida. Gil Nelson. LC 93-41607. (Illus.). 352p. 1994. 29.95 (*1-56164-053-0*); pap. 19.95 (*1-56164-055-7*) Pineapple Pr.

Trees of Georgia & Adjacent States. Claud L. Brown & L. Katherine Kirkman. (Illus.). 372p. 1990. 39.95 (*0-88192-148-3*) Timber.

Trees of Greater Portland. Phyllis C. Reynolds & Elizabeth F. Dimon. LC 92-19585. (Illus.). 216p. 1993. pap. 19.95 (*0-88192-263-3*) Timber.

Trees of Hawai'i. Angela K. Kepler. LC 90-39868. (Illus.). 96p. (Orig.). 1990. pap. 12.95 (*0-8248-1329-4*, Kolowalu Bk) UH Pr.

Trees of Heaven. Jesse Stuart. LC 80-51020. 344p. 1980. reprint ed. pap. 14.95 (*0-8131-0150-6*) U Pr of Ky.

Trees of India, a Popular Handbook. C. McCann. (C). 1988. text ed. 85.00 (*0-685-44243-8*, Pub. by Scientific UK) St Mut.

Trees of Ireland. Charles Nelson. (Illus.). 240p. 1993. 75.00 (*1-874675-24-4*, Pub. by Lilliput Pr Ltd IE); pap. 36.95 (*1-874675-25-2*, Pub. by Lilliput Pr Ltd IE) Irish Bks Media.

Trees of Life: Essays in Philosophy of Biology. Ed. by Paul Griffiths. (Australasian Studies in History & Philosophy of Science). 288p. (C). 1992. lib. bdg. 129.50 (*0-7923-1709-2*, Pub. by Klwr Acad Pubs NE) Kluwer Ac.

Trees of Life: Saving Tropical Forests & Their Biological Wealth. World Resources Institute Staff et al. LC 90-21623. (Illus.). 218p. 1991. pap. 12.00 (*0-8070-8505-7*) Beacon Pr.

Trees of Michigan & the Upper Great Lakes. rev. ed. Norman F. Smith. (Illus.). 178p. 1995. pap. 21.95 (*1-882376-08-0*) Thunder Bay Pr.

***Trees of Mississippi - & Other Woody Plants.** George H. Dukes, Jr. LC 96-92727. (Illus.). 276p. 1996. 19.95 (*0-9655380-0-1*) Poplar Petal.

Trees of New Mexico: New Mexico Trees. (Illus.). 32p. 1985. reprint ed. pap. 1.25 (*0-935810-23-4*) Primer Pubs.

Trees of Newport: On the Estates of the Preservation Society of Newport County. Richard L. Champlin. (Illus.). 94p. 1976. pap. 4.00 (*0-917012-24-0*) Preserv Soc Newport.

Trees of North America. C. Frank Brockman. Ed. by Herbert S. Zim & George S. Fichter. (Golden Field Guide Ser.). (Illus.). (YA). (gr. 9 up). 1968. pap. 11.95 (*0-307-13658-2*) Western Pub.

Trees of North America. Alan Mitchell. (Illus.). 208p. 1987. 35.00 (*0-8160-1806-5*) Facts on File.

***Trees of North America.** Alan Mitchell. (Spotter's Guides Ser.). (Illus.). 64p. 1993. pap. 4.95 (*0-7460-1627-1*, Usborne) EDC.

Trees of North America & Europe. Roger Phillips. 1978. pap. 27.50 (*0-394-73541-2*) Random.

Trees of North Texas. Robert A. Vines. (Elma Dill Russell Spencer Foundation Ser.: No. 14). (Illus.). 486p. 1982. 24.95 (*0-292-78018-4*); pap. 14.95 (*0-292-78019-2*) U of Tex Pr.

Trees of Northern Bengal. A. M. Cowan. 178p. (C). 1979. text ed. 125.00 (*0-89771-589-6*, Pub. by Intl Bk Distr II) St Mut.

Trees of Northern Bengal. A. M. Cowan. 178p. 1993. 88.00 (*81-7089-188-4*, Pub. by Intl Bk Distr II) St Mut.

Trees of Northern Florida. Herman Kurz & Robert K. Godfrey. LC 62-17479. (Illus.). xxxiv, 311p. 1962. pap. 24.95 (*0-8130-0666-X*) U Press Fla.

Trees of Nova Scotia: A Guide to the Native & Exotic Species. Gary L. Saunders. (Illus.). 112p. (Orig.). 1996. pap. 9.95 (*1-55109-123-2*) Chelsea Green Pub.

Trees of San Marino. Wendy M. Stubley. (Illus.). 120p. 1989. pap. 8.95 (*0-87328-129-2*) Huntington Lib.

Trees of Santa Barbara. Katherine K. Muller et al. (Illus.). 1974. 10.00 (*0-916436-00-4*) Santa Barb Botanic.

Trees of Seattle: The Complete Tree-Finder's Guide to 740 Varieties. Arthur L. Jacobson. LC 89-91264. (Illus.). 464p. 1990. pap. 16.95 (*0-912365-34-X*) Sasquatch Bks.

Trees of Somalia: Oxfam Research Discussion Papers. Des Mahoney. (Oxfam Research Papers). 196p. (C). 1990. 15.95 (*0-85598-109-1*, Pub. by Oxfam UK) Humanities.

***Trees of Southern Africa, 3 vols.** Eve Palmer & Norah Pitman. 2302p. 1972. 535.00 (*0-86961-033-3*, Pub. by A A Balkema NE) Ashgate Pub Co.

***Trees of the Balikpapan-Samarinda Area, East Kalimantan, Indonesia: A Manual to 280 Selected Species.** P. J. Kessler & K. Sidiyasa. (Tropenbos Technical Ser.: No. 7). (Illus.). 448p. 1994. pap. 78.00 (*90-5113-019-8*, Pub. by Backhuys Pubs NE) Balogh.

***Trees of the California Sierra Nevada: A New & Simple Way to Identify & Enjoy Some of the World's Most Beautiful & Impressive Forest Trees in a Mountain Setting of Incomparable Majesty.** George A. Petrides. LC 95-60999. (Backpacker Field Guide Ser.). (Illus.). 80p. (Orig.). 1996. pap. 9.95 (*0-9646674-0-1*) Explr Pr MI.

***Trees of the Central Hardwood Forests of North America: An Identification & Cultivation Guide.** Donald J. Leopold et al. LC 97-6200. 1998. write for info. (*0-88192-406-7*) Timber.

Trees of the Dancing Goats. Patricia Polacco. (J). 1996. 16.00 (*0-689-80862-3*) S&S Childrens.

***Trees of the Dancing Goats.** Patricia Polacco. (J). 1997. pap. 22.00 incl. audio compact disk (*0-689-81193-4*) S&S Childrens.

Trees of the Eastern & Central United States & Canada. William M. Harlow. (Illus.). 1942. pap. 4.50 (*0-486-20395-6*) Dover.

***Trees of the Field.** 1983. pap. 1.20 (*0-8341-9109-1*) Lillenas.

Trees of the Great Basin: A Natural History. Ronald M. Lanner. LC 83-21714. (Max C. Fleischmann Series in Great Basin Natural History). 273p. 1984. reprint ed. pap. 77.90 (*0-608-01262-9*, 2062011) Bks Demand.

Trees of the Northern United States & Canada. John L. Farrar. 512p. 1995. 39.95 (*0-8138-2740-X*, Pub. by Fitzhenry & Whiteside CN) Iowa St U Pr.

***Trees of the Oregon Campus.** Knapp. pap. 12.95 (*0-88246-161-3*) Oreg St U Bkstrs.

***Trees of the Pacific Northwest.** Martha Pedersen. (Illus.). 72p. (Orig.). 1996. pap. write for info. (*0-9639462-1-8*) Portland Garden.

***Trees of the Pacific Northwest: Including Oregon, Washington, Idaho, NW. Montana, British Columbia, Yukon, & Alaska.** George A. Petrides. LC 96-61922. (Backpacker Field Guide Ser.). (Illus.). 100p. (Orig.). Date not set. pap. 10.95 (*0-9646674-1-X*) Explr Pr MI.

Trees of the San Jacinto Mountains. Illus. by Ernest Maxwell. 32p. 1976. pap. 1.75 (*0-913612-02-2*) Strawberry Valley.

Trees of the Smokies. Steve Kemp. Ed. by Ed Clebsch & Don DeFoe. LC 93-91420. (Illus.). 128p. (Orig.). 1993. pap. 8.95 (*0-937207-09-8*) GSMNH.

Trees of the Southeastern United States. Wilbur H. Duncan & Marion B. Duncan. LC 87-5837. (Illus.). 336p. 1992. pap. 19.95 (*0-8203-1469-2*) U of Ga Pr.

Trees of the Tropics. Jennifer Cochrane. LC 90-10023. (Green World Ser.). (Illus.). 48p. (J). (gr. 5-9). 1990. lib. bdg. 24.26 (*0-8114-2731-5*) Raintree Steck-V.

Trees of the West. Mabel Crittenden. 220p. 1992. pap. 14.95 (*0-88839-269-9*) Hancock House.

***Trees of Time.** Edna A. Zeavin. 156p. 1996. pap. 8.95 (*0-9654277-0-6*) Casa Publishing.

Trees of Utah. Darrell J. Weber & Sherman Brough. (Illus.). 148p. (Orig.). 1993. pap. 10.00 (*0-9635617-0-7*) Brstlecone Pr.

Trees of Vancouver: A Guide to the Common & Unusual Trees of the City. Gerald Straley. (Illus.). 288p. 1992. pap. 19.95 (*0-7748-0406-8*, Pub. by U BC Pr) U of Wash Pr.

Trees on Marginal Land. S. S. Sagwai. 1993. pap. 200.00 (*81-7233-070-7*, Pub. by Scientific Pubs II) St Mut.

Trees, People & Power: Social Dimensions of Deforestation & Forest Protecction in Central America. E. S. Utting. 256p. (Orig.). 1992. 24.95 (*1-85383-162-X*, Pub. by Erthscan Pubns UK) Island Pr.

Trees Planting Practices for Arid Zones. FAO Staff. 226p. 1989. 188.00 (*81-7089-105-1*, Pub. by Intl Bk Distr II) St Mut.

Trees, Shrubs, & Cacti of South Texas. James H. Everitt. 1993. pap. 18.95 (*0-89672-253-8*) Tex Tech Univ Pr.

Trees Shrubs & Economic Herbs of the Southern Circle Central Province. S. S. Haines. 384p. 1984. 125.00 (*81-7089-019-5*, Pub. by Intl Bk Distr II) St Mut.

***Trees Shrubs & Flowers To Know in British Columbia & Washington.** C. P. Lyons. 1997. pap. 15.95 (*1-55105-044-7*) Lone Pine.

Trees, Shrubs & Flowers to Know in Washington & British Columbia, Vol. 1. rev. ed. William J. Merilees. (Illus.). 376p. (Orig.). 1995. pap. 15.95 (*1-55105-062-5*, 1-55105) Lone Pine.

Trees, Shrubs, & Plants of Virgil. John Sargeaunt. LC 79-99669. (Select Bibliographies Reprint Ser.). 1977. 21.95 (*0-8369-5098-4*) Ayer.

Trees, Shrubs, & Vines. Bonnie L. Appleton & Alfred F. Scheider. (Rodale's Successful Organic Gardening Ser.). (Illus.). 1993. 24.95 (*0-87596-561-X*); pap. 14.95 (*0-87596-562-8*) Rodale Pr Inc.

Trees, Shrubs, & Vines: A Pictorial Guide to the Ornamental Woody Plants of the Northern United States, Exclusive of Conifers. Arthur T. Viertel. (Illus.). (C). 1970. pap. 18.95 (*0-8156-0068-2*) Syracuse U Pr.

Trees, Shrubs & Vines of Arkansas. Carl G. Hunter. LC 89-62892. (Illus.). 207p. 1995. 29.50 (*0-912456-16-7*); pap. 22.50 (*0-912456-17-5*) Ozark Soc Bks.

Trees, Shrubs, & Vines on the University of Notre Dame Campus. Barbara J. Hellenthal et al. LC 93-24764. (Sesquicentennial Bk.). (Orig.). (C). 1993. pap. text ed. 23.00 (*0-268-01878-2*) U of Notre Dame Pr.

Trees, Shrubs, & Woody Vines in Kansas. Homer A. Stephens. LC 69-10357. (Illus.). vi, 250p. 1969. pap. 14.95 (*0-7006-0057-4*) U Pr of KS.

Trees, Shrubs, & Woody Vines of Great Smoky Mountains National Park. Arthur Stupka. LC 64-25370. (Illus.). 196p. 1964. 21.00 (*0-87049-478-3*); pap. 12.95 (*0-87049-053-2*) U of Tenn Pr.

Trees, Shrubs, & Woody Vines of Northern Florida & Adjacent Georgia & Alabama. Robert K. Godfrey. LC 87-35840. 728p. 1988. 65.00 (*0-8203-1035-2*) U of Ga Pr.

Trees, Shrubs, & Woody Vines of the Southwest. Robert A. Vines. (Illus.). 1116p. 1960. 75.00 (*0-292-73414-X*) U of Tex Pr.

Trees Stand Shining: Poetry of the North American Indians. Hettie Jones. LC 79-142452. (Illus.). 32p. (J). (gr. k up). 1993. pap. 13.99 (*0-8037-9083-X*) Dial Bks Young.

Tree's Tale. Lark Carrier. LC 95-10855. (Illus.). 32p. (J). (ps-3). 1996. pap. 14.99 (*0-8037-1202-2*); pap. 14.89 (*0-8037-1203-0*) Dial Bks Young.

Trees Through the Road. Dan Raphael. (Illus.). 36p. (Orig.). 1997. pap. 6.00 (*1-878888-23-4*) Nine Muses.

Trees, Why Do You Wait? America's Changing Rural Culture. Richard Critchfield. LC 90-20898. 265p. (Orig.). 1991. 29.95 (*1-55963-029-9*); pap. 15.95 (*1-55963-028-0*) Island Pr.

***Treestand Strategies.** Gene Wensel & Barry Wensel. Ed. by Craig Boddington. (Whitetail Secrets Ser.: No. 2). (Illus.). 186p. (YA). (gr. 10 up). 1994. 17.95 (*1-56416-152-8*) Derrydale Pr.

Treestone: Piano Vocal Reduction. S. Albert. 136p. 1993. per. 50.00 (*0-7935-2916-6*) H Leonard.

Treewidth: Computations & Approximations. Ton Kloks. LC 94-31558. (Lecture Notes in Computer Science Ser.: 842). 1994. 37.00 (*0-387-58356-4*) Spr-Verlag.

Treffende Ausdruck. 2nd ed. Bridgette M. Turneaure. (C). Date not set. pap. text ed. 28.95 (*0-393-96823-5*, Norton Paperbks); pap. text ed. write for info. (*0-393-96830-8*) Norton.

Treffende Fremdwort: Woerterbuch Deutsch-Fremd. Reinhard Von Normann. 378p. (GER.). 1991. 45.00 (*0-7859-8506-9*, 3821812621) Fr & Eur.

Treffende Reim. 7th ed. Karl Peltzer. 148p. (GER.). 1993. 39.95 (*0-7859-8690-1*, 372256123x) Fr & Eur.

Treffende Wort. 23th ed. Karl Peltzer. 792696p. (GER.). 1993. 75.00 (*0-8288-1980-7*, M15518) Fr & Eur.

Treffpunkt Deutsch: Grundstufe. 2nd ed. E. Rosemarie Widmaier & Fritz T. Widmaier. LC 94-24506. 1994. text ed. 61.33 (*0-13-106691-9*) P-H.

Trefoil 'Round the World. rev. ed. World Association of Girl Guides & Girl Scouts Staff. (Illus.). 304p. (YA). (gr. 4-12). 1992. 9.25 (*0-900827-50-5*, 23-967) Girl Scouts USA.

Tregantle & Scraesdon: Their Forts & Railway. Philip Payton. (C). 1989. 35.00 (*1-85022-038-7*, Pub. by Dyllansow Truran UK) St Mut.

Tregaran. large type ed. Mary Lide. (General Ser.). 300p. 1990. lib. bdg. 18.95 (*0-8161-4980-1*, GK Hall) Thorndike Pr.

Tregarn Autumn. Dee Wyatt. (Rainbow Romances Ser.). 160p. 1995. 14.95 (*0-7090-5519-6*, 930, Hale-Parkwest) Parkwest Pubns.

Tregua. Mario Benedetti. 1995. pap. 12.50 (*0-679-76095-4*) Random.

Tregurran Man. large type ed. Marjorie Warby. 400p. 1987. 25.99 (*0-7089-1648-1*) Ulverscroft.

***Trei Assar/The Twelve Prophets: Hoshea, Yoel, Amos, Ovadiah.** Matis Roberts. 22.99 (*0-89906-017-X*, TW1H); pap. 18.99 (*0-89906-018-8*, TW1P) Mesorah Pubns.

Treinta Poemas de Amor Para Maria. Oscar R. Benitez. 60p. 1992. pap. 4.95 (*1-881619-03-6*) Edit Encuentro.

***Treinta Poemas de Amor para Maria.** 3rd ed. Oscar R. Benitez. (Illus.). 62p. (SPA.). 1997. pap. 5.99 (*1-890701-03-3*) La Mancha.

Treize Enigmes, la Folle d'Itteville, les Treize Mysteres. Georges Simenon. 1047p. (FRE.). 1992. 49.95 (*0-7859-0487-5*, 2258032733) Fr & Eur.

Treize Histoires. William Faulkner. (FRE.). 1991. pap. 14.95 (*0-7859-2619-4*, 2070384144) Fr & Eur.

Treize Lecons En Doctrine Chretienne (Thirteen Lessons in Christian Doctrine) Denver Sizemore. 138p. (FRE.). 1991. pap. 4.99 (*0-89900-396-6*) College Pr Pub.

Treizieme Cesar. Henry De Montherlant. 13.95 (*0-685-36991-9*) Fr & Eur.

Treizieme Cesar. Henry De Montherlant. 200p. (FRE.). 1970. pap. 14.95 (*0-7859-1335-1*, 2070272222) Fr & Eur.

Trek. Ann Jonas. LC 84-25962. (Illus.). 32p. (J). (gr. k-3). 1985. 16.00 (*0-688-04799-8*); lib. bdg. 15.93 (*0-688-04800-5*) Greenwillow.

Trek. Ann Jonas. LC 84-25962. (Illus.). 32p. (J). (ps up). 1989. pap. 3.95 (*0-688-08742-6*, Mulberry) Morrow.

Trek! Man Alone in the Arizona Wild. Geoffrey Platts. Ed. by Jack Grenard. (Illus.). 208p. (Orig.). 1991. pap. 10.50 (*0-9631487-0-2*) Carefree Comm.

Trek Classic: Twenty-Five Years Later. Edward Gross. (History of Trek Ser.: Vol. 1). (Illus.). 128p. (Orig.). 1991. pap. 12.95 (*0-9627508-9-1*) Image NY.

Trek for Trinie. Wiesje De Lange. 116p. 1995. pap. text ed. 9.95 (*965-229-124-2*, Pub. by Gefen Pub Hse IS) Gefen Bks.

Trek for Trivia. Loretta B. Minn. (Illus.). 48p. (J). (gr. 3-8). 1985. student ed. 7.99 (*0-86653-291-9*, GA 646) Good Apple.

***Trek Navigator: The Ultimate Guide to the Entire Trek Saga.** Mark A. Altman. 1997. pap. text ed. 13.95 (*0-316-03812-1*) Little.

Trek of James MacDonald New Concord, Ohio to California 1850. Edgar W. Stanton, III. (Illus.). 148p. (Orig.). 1989. pap. text ed. write for info. (*0-9621919-0-6*) E W Stanton.

Trek of the Grey Eagle. Darrell M. Galloway. 368p. 1995. mass mkt. 5.99 (*1-896329-49-7*, Pub. by Comnwlth Pub CN) Partners Pubs Grp.

Trek to Equality. Barnett J. Grier, Sr. LC 95-73038. (Illus.). 247p. 1996. pap. 18.95 (*0-935661-23-9*) Riverside Mus Pr.

Trek to Kraagen-Cor. Dennis L. McKiernan. (Silver Call Duology Ser.: No. 1). 1987. pap. 2.95 (*0-451-14787-1*, Sig) NAL-Dutton.

An Asterisk (*) at the beginning of an entry indicates that the title is appearing in BIP for the first time.

Trek to Kraagen-Cor. Dennis L. McKiernan. (Silver Call Duology Ser.: No. 1). (YA). (gr. 9-12). 1989. pap. 3.95 (*0-451-15563-7*, Sig) NAL-Dutton.

Trek to Kraagen-Cor. Dennis L. McKiernan. (Silver Call Duology Ser.: No. 1). 256p. 1987. pap. 4.99 (*0-451-45165-1*, ROC) NAL-Dutton.

Trek to Mustang. S. Armington. (C). 1992. 21.00 (*0-7855-0217-3*, Pub. by Ratna Pustak Bhandar) St Mut.

Trek West: My Pioneer Sticker Book. Richard N. Holzapfel. 1996. pap. 8.95 (*1-57008-260-X*) Bookcraft Inc.

Trekka Round the World: Seabook, No. 10. John Guzzwell. (Illus.). 1979. pap. 6.95 (*0-679-51380-9*) McKay.

Trekker's Guide to Collectibles. Jeffrey B. Snyder. LC 95-25792. (Illus.). 160p. 1996. pap. 29.95 (*0-88740-965-2*) Schiffer.

***Trekker's Guide to Deep Space Nine.** Hal J. Schuster. 1997. pap. 16.00 (*0-7615-0574-1*) Prima Pub.

***Trekker's Guide to the Next Generation - Complete, Unauthorized & Uncensored.** Hal J. Schuster. LC 96-41950. 288p. 1996. pap. 14.99 (*0-7615-0573-3*) Prima Pub.

Trekker's Guide to Voyager: Complete, Unauthorized, & Uncensored. Hal J. Schuster. LC 96-8195. 208p. 1996. per. 14.99 (*0-7615-0572-5*) Prima Pub.

Trekking: Searching for Love & Self-Esteem. Glenn Wilkerson. 144p. (Orig.). 1991. pap. 10.99 (*0-8272-3628-X*) Chalice Pr.

Trekking & Climbing in the Himalaya. Jonathan Chester. (Illus.). 224p. (Orig.). 1989. pap. 24.95 (*0-938567-17-9*) Cloudcap.

***Trekking in Bolivia: A Traveler's Guide.** Yossi Brain. LC 97-2348. (Trekking in...Ser.). (Illus.). 208p. (Orig.). 1997. pap. 16.95 (*0-89886-501-8*) Mountaineers.

Trekking in East Africa: A Walking Guide. David Else. (Illus.). 296p. (Orig.). 1993. pap. 13.95 (*0-86442-186-9*) Lonely Planet.

***Trekking in East Africa: Walking Guide.** 2nd ed. David Else. (Illus.). 304p. 1998. pap. 17.95 (*0-86442-541-4*) Lonely Planet.

Trekking in Greece: A Walking Guide. Marc Dubin & Michael Cullen. (Illus.). 360p. (Orig.). 1993. pap. 15.95 (*0-86442-159-1*) Lonely Planet.

Trekking in Nepal. rev. ed. Toru Nakano. Tr. by Diane T. Ooka from JPN. (Illus.). 232p. 1990. pap. 29.95 (*0-89346-251-9*) Heian Intl.

***Trekking in Nepal: A Traveler's Guide.** 7th ed. Stephen Bezruchka. 1997. pap. text ed. 18.95 (*0-89886-535-2*) Mountaineers.

Trekking in Russia & Central Asia, a Traveler's Guide: Urals, Pamirs, Caucasus, Siberia, Lake Baikal, Crimean Peninsula, Kamchatka Peninsula. Frith Maier. (Illus.). 320p. 1994. pap. 16.95 (*0-89886-355-4*) Mountaineers.

Trekking in Spain: A Walking Guide. Marc Dubin. (Illus.). 208p. (Orig.). 1990. pap. 11.95 (*0-86442-088-9*) Lonely Planet.

Trekking in the Annapurna Region. 2nd ed. Bryn Thomas. (Orig.). 1996. pap. text ed. 14.95 (*1-873756-07-0*, Pub. by Trlblazer Pubn UK) Seven Hills Bk.

Trekking in the Everest Region. 2nd ed. Jamie McGuinness. (Orig.). 1996. pap. text ed. 14.95 (*1-873756-08-9*, Pub. by Trlblazer Pubn UK) Seven Hills Bk.

***Trekking in the Indian Himalaya: Walking Guide.** 3rd ed. Garry Weare. (Illus.). 272p. 1997. pap. 17.95 (*0-86442-357-8*) Lonely Planet.

Trekking in the Karakoram & Hindukush. John Mock & Kimberly O'Neil. (Illus.). 304p. 1996. pap. 16.95 (*0-86442-360-8*) Lonely Planet.

Trekking in the Nepal Himalaya: A Walking Guide. 6th ed. Stan Armington. (Illus.). 392p. 1994. pap. 14.95 (*0-86442-231-8*) Lonely Planet.

***Trekking in the Nepal Himalaya: Walking Guide.** 7th ed. Stan Armington. (Illus.). 400p. 1997. pap. 17.95 (*0-86442-511-2*) Lonely Planet.

***Trekking in the Patagonian Andes: Walking Guide.** 2nd ed. Clem Lindenmayer. (Illus.). 224p. 1998. pap. 15.95 (*0-86442-477-9*) Lonely Planet.

Trekking in Tibet: A Traveler's Guide. Gary McCue. LC 91-24874. (Illus.). 240p. 1991. pap. 16.95 (*0-89886-239-6*) Mountaineers.

Trekking Mount Everest. R. Uchida. (C). 1991. 137.00 (*0-7855-0218-1*, Pub. by Ratna Pustak Bhandar) St Mut.

Trekking Peaks of Nepal. Bill O'Connor. (Illus.). 224p. 1989. pap. 24.95 (*0-938567-28-4*) Cloudcap.

Treks into the Past. Dee Smith. 142p. 1990. 10.00 (*0-8187-0122-6*) Harlo Press.

Treks into the Past: Historical Sketches of the Thumb. Dee Smith. (Illus.). 140p. 1989. text ed. 10.00 (*0-9616538-6-8*); pap. text ed. 7.50 (*0-9616538-5-X*) Heritage Val Pub.

Treks Not Taken. Steven R. Boyett. 170p. (Orig.). 1996. pap. 12.95 (*1-882813-05-7*) Sneaker Pr.

Treks to the Top of the World. Andy Clausen. 1995. pap. write for info. (*0-929730-57-7*) Zeitgeist Pr.

Trektoons. Mark Lister et al. (Illus.). 100p. (Orig.). 1991. pap. 7.95 (*0-9629570-0-3*) Starland.

Trekways of the Wind. Nils-Aslak Valkeapaa. Tr. by Ralph Salisbury et al. (Illus.). 320p. 1994. 20.00 (*82-90625-21-9*) U of Ariz Pr.

Trelawny of the "Wells" & Other Plays. Arthur W. Pinero. Ed. & Intro. by Jacky Bratton. (World's Classics Ser.). 352p. 1995. 59.00 (*0-19-812148-2*); pap. 11.95 (*0-19-282568-2*) OUP.

***Trellis Coding.** Christian Schlegel. LC 96-43184. 304p. 1997. 79.95 (*0-7803-1052-7*, PC4069) Inst Electrical.

Trellis Cookbook. Marcel Desaulniers. 368p. 1992. pap. 15.00 (*0-671-74842-4*, Fireside) S&S Trade.

***Trellis Decoding of Block Codes: A Practical Approach.** Bahram Honary & Garik Markarian. LC 96-40193. (International Series in Engineering & Computer Science, Natural Language Processing & Machine Translation). 288p. (C). 1997. lib. bdg. 88.50 (*0-7923-9860-2*) Kluwer Ac.

Trellisane Confrontation. David Dvorkin. (Star Trek Ser.: No. 14). (Orig.). 1989. mass mkt. 4.50 (*0-671-70095-2*) PB.

Trellising: How to Grow Climbing Vegetables, Fruits, Flowers, Vines & Trees. Rhonda M. Hart. Ed. by Connie Oxley. LC 91-50606. (Illus.). 160p. 1992. pap. 10.95 (*0-88266-765-3*) Storey Comm Inc.

Treloar Genealogy: Tree of Treloar. Orson L. Treloar. (Illus.). 309p. 1995. reprint ed. pap. 47.50 (*0-8328-4894-8*); reprint ed. lib. bdg. 57.50 (*0-8328-4893-X*) Higginson Bk Co.

Tremaine: Or, the Man of Refinement, 3 vols. in 2. Robert P. Ward. LC 79-8212. reprint ed. Set. 84.50 (*0-404-62155-4*) AMS Pr.

Tremaine Collection: Twentieth Century Masters - The Spirit of Modernism. LC 83-51420. (Illus.). 188p. 1984. 14.95 (*0-317-13593-7*); pap. 9.95 (*0-317-13594-5*) Wadsworth Atheneum.

Tremaine Site Complex: Oneota Occupation In the La Crosse Locality, Wisconsin. Jodie O'Gorman. LC 93-38782. 1993. write for info. (*0-87020-273-1*) State Hist Soc Wis.

Trematodes, Their Life Cycles, Biology & Evolution. T. A. Ginetinskaya. (C). 1989. 52.50 (*81-205-0075-X*, Pub. by Oxford IBH II) S Asia.

***Tremble.** C. D. Wright. 1997. pap. 12.00 (*0-88001-512-8*) Ecco Pr.

Tremble: Poems. C. D. Wright. LC 95-44779. 72p. 1996. 20.00 (*0-88001-458-X*) Ecco Pr.

Tremble from the Wind. Jason S. Cherry. LC 89-50188. (Illus.). 43p. (Orig.). (gr. 7-12). 1990. pap. 5.95 (*0-916383-87-3*) Aegina Pr.

Tremble Purple: Seven Poems. Alurista. (Illus.). 29p. (Orig.). (C). 1986. pap. 3.00 (*0-945308-00-0*) Getting Together Pubns.

Tremblin' Earth. W. Horace Carter. LC 94-93941. 260p. (Orig.). 1994. pap. 13.95 (*0-937866-47-4*) Atlantic Pub Co.

Trembling Beauty. Jennifer Dunning. 480p. (YA). 1996. 30.00 (*0-201-62607-1*) Addison-Wesley.

Trembling Hearts in the Bodies of Dogs: New & Selected Poems. Selima Hill et al. 144p. 9500. pap. 18.95 (*1-85224-288-4*) Dufour.

Trembling Hills. Norman A. Fox. 176p. 1987. pap. 2.75 (*0-380-70299-1*) Avon.

***Trembling Ladders, No. 1.** Ed. by Tania Elizov. 1993. pap. 5.00 (*1-880855-02-X*) Fifth Planet.

***Trembling Ladders, Nos. 2 & 3.** Ed. by Tania Elizov. 1996. pap. 8.00 (*1-880855-04-6*) Fifth Planet.

Trembling of a Leaf. W. Somerset Maugham. 302p. 1985. reprint ed. mass mkt. 4.95 (*0-935180-21-4*) Mutual Pub HI.

Trembling with Wonder. Phyllis J. Sloan et al. (J). (gr. 4 up). 1990. 3.00 (*0-940248-80-8*) Guild Pr.

Tremco Health, Safety & Environment Audit Working Copy. Date not set. spiral bd. write for info. (*0-88061-187-1*) Intl Loss Cntrl.

Tremco Health, Safety & Environmental Audit Field Verification. Date not set. spiral bd. write for info. (*0-88061-188-X*) Intl Loss Cntrl.

Tremco Health, Safety & Environmental Audit Reference Manual. Date not set. ring bd. write for info. (*0-88061-186-3*) Intl Loss Cntrl.

Tremellales. Bernard Lowy. LC 79-26289. (Flora Neotropica Monographs: No. 6S). 18p. (Orig.). 1980. suppl. ed., pap. 4.50 (*0-89327-220-5*) NY Botanical.

Tremellales. Bernard Lowy. LC 76-130518. (Flora Neotropica Monographs: No. 6). (Illus.). 153p. (Orig.). 1971. reprint ed. pap. text ed. 9.75 (*0-89327-321-X*) NY Botanical.

***Tremendous Number 10: Amazing Facts about the Number Ten.** Kitty Higgins. (Birthday Book Ser.). 1998. 6.95 (*0-8362-3221-6*) Andrews & McMeel.

Tremendous Tree Book. Barbara Brenner & May Garelick. LC 91-73753. (Illus.). 40p. (J). (ps-3). 1992. 15.95 (*1-878093-56-8*) Boyds Mills Pr.

Tremendous Tree Book. Garelick. 1979. 10.95 (*0-590-07590-X*) Scholastic Inc.

Tremendous Trifles. Lewis B. Sage. LC 78-69886. 108p. 1978. pap. 10.00 (*0-912760-82-6*) Valkyrie Pub Hse.

Tremendum: A Theological Interpretation of the Holocaust. Arthur A. Cohen. 120p. 1993. reprint ed. pap. text ed. 12.95 (*0-8264-0634-3*) Continuum.

Trementina Revisited. Beryl C. Roper. 82p. 1994. 24.95 (*1-885812-00-0*) Aquamarine.

Tremolo of Light. Nancy Pulley. (Indiana Poetry Chapbook Contest Ser.: No. 2). 40p. 1992. pap. 3.95 (*1-880649-28-4*) Writ Ctr Pr.

Tremor. Rodger J. Elble & William C. Koller. (Series in Contemporary Medicine & Public Health). 232p. 1990. text ed. 65.00 (*0-8018-4024-4*) Johns Hopkins.

Tremor. Winston Graham. 256p. 1996. 22.95 (*0-312-14056-8*) St Martin.

Tremor. large type ed. Winston Graham. 1997. pap. 21.95 (*0-7862-0827-9*, Thorndike Lrg Prnt) Thorndike Pr.

Tremor in the Morning - Alex Katz - Vincent Katz. limited ed. Vincent Katz. Ed. by Mario Diacono. (Illus.). 26p. 1987. 400.00 (*0-935875-06-9*) P Blum Edit.

Tremor of Bliss. Elie. 1995. pap. write for info. (*0-15-600230-2*) HarBrace.

Tremor of Bliss: Contemporary Writers on the Saints. Paul Elie. LC 94-22332. 1994. 22.00 (*0-15-100101-4*) HarBrace.

Tremor of Bliss: Contemporary Writers on the Saints. Ed. by Paul Elie. LC 94-22332. 352p. 1995. pap. 12.00 (*1-57322-513-4*, Riverhd Trade) Berkley Pub.

Tremor of Forgery. Patricia Highsmith. LC 88-28478. 264p. 1988. reprint ed. pap. 12.00 (*0-87113-258-3*, Atlntc Mnthly) Grove-Atltic.

Tremor of Racehorses: Selected Poems. Sylva Fischerova. Tr. by Jarmila Milner & Ian Milner. LC 90-80813. 80p. 9000. pap. 14.95 (*1-85224-106-3*, Pub. by Bloodaxe Bks UK) Dufour.

Tremors & Faultlines: Photopoems of San Francisco. 72p. (Orig.). 1995. pap. 4.95 (*1-888451-02-5*) Akashic Bks.

Tremors from the Fault Line. Tamarra Kaida. LC 88-51232. (Illus.). 60p. 1989. pap. 15.00 (*0-89822-056-4*) Visual Studies.

Tremors from the Fault Line. Tamarra Kaida. LC 88-51232. (Illus.). 60p. 1989. pap. write for info. (*0-89822-053-X*) Visual Studies.

***Tremors of the Jungle.** B. M. Kayira. (Three Continents Ser.). 146p. 1997. pap. 10.95 (*0-89410-856-5*) Lynne Rienner.

***Tremors Vibrations Enough to Change the World.** Contrib. by Marcella Taylor et al. (Illus.). 158p. 1995. per. 14.95 (*1-882699-04-1*) Heywood Pr.

Tremulous Hand of Worcester: A Study of Old English in the Thirteenth Century. Christine Franzen. (Oxford English Monographs). (Illus.). 264p. 1991. 90.00 (*0-19-811742-6*) OUP.

Tremulous Private Body: Essays on Subjection. Francis Barker. (Body in Theory: Histories of Cultural Materialism Ser.). 124p. (C). 1995. text ed. 37.50 (*0-472-09552-8*); pap. text ed. 14.95 (*0-472-06552-1*) U of Mich Pr.

Trench Excavation & Support. J. K. Budleigh. 80p. 1989. pap. text ed. 22.00 (*0-7277-1347-7*, Pub. by T Telford UK) Am Soc Civil Eng.

***Trench-Fever: Poems.** John Latham. LC 92-21182. 72p. 1996. pap. 12.95 (*0-7734-2675-2*, Mellen Poetry Pr) E Mellen.

Trench Town Rock. Kamau Brathwaite. (Lost Roads Ser.: No. 40). 88p. (Orig.). 1994. pap. 10.95 (*0-918786-45-2*) Lost Roads.

***Trenchless Pipeline Projects: Proceedings of the Conference, Boston, Massachusetts, June 8-11, 1997.** Lynn E. Osborn & American Society of Civil Engineers Staff. LC 97-16274. 1997. write for info. (*0-7844-0244-2*) Am Soc Civil Eng.

***Trenchless Technology.** Richard K. Miller & Christy H. Gunter. (Market Research Survey Ser.: No. 316). 50p. 1996. 200.00 (*1-55865-339-2*) Future Tech Surveys.

Trend in On-Line Computer Control Systems: 21-24 April, 1975. Conference on Trend in On-Line Computer Control Systems, 2nd., University of Sheffield, 1975. LC 76-355944. (Institution of Electrical Engineers Conference Report Ser.: 127). (Illus.). 290p. reprint ed. pap. 82.70 (*0-317-10838-7*, 2012129) Bks Demand.

***Trend in Women Studies.** Raj Pruthi & Bela R. Sharma. (C). 1995. 29.00 (*81-7488-082-8*, Pub. by Anmol II) S Asia.

Trend of Economic Thinking: Essays on Political Economists & Economic History. Friedrich A. Hayek. (Collected Works of F. A. Hayek). xii, 398p. 1991. 46.00 (*0-226-32067-7*) U Ch Pr.

Trend of Government Activity in the United States since 1900. Solomon Fabricant & Robert E. Lipsey. (General Ser.: No. 56). 288p. 1952. reprint ed. 74.90 (*0-87014-055-8*) Natl Bur Econ Res.

Trend of the Races. George E. Haynes. LC 73-89408. (Black Heritage Library Collection). 1977. 17.95 (*0-8369-8592-3*) Ayer.

Trend Report see Social Science Research on Higher Education & Universities

Trend Setters: Purpose for Living, 3 pts. Sara L. Ensor. Ed. by Vera Frampton. (World That Works & Reaching Out Ser.). (Illus.). 176p. (Orig.). 1989. pap. text ed. 11.00 (*1-85239-506-0*) Grosvenor USA.

Trends & Changes in Drug Research & Development. Ed. by S. R. Walker & B. C. Walker. 120p. (C). 1989. lib. bdg. 92.00 (*0-85200-839-2*) Kluwer Ac.

Trends & Cycles in Capital Formation by United States Railroads, 1870-1950. Melville J. Ulmer. (Occasional Papers: No. 43). 80p. 1954. reprint ed. 20.80 (*0-87014-357-3*); reprint ed. mic. film 20.00 (*0-685-61294-5*) Natl Bur Econ Res.

Trends & Cycles in Corporate Bond Financing. W. Braddock Hickman. (Occasional Papers: No. 37). 49p. 1952. reprint ed. 20.00 (*0-87014-352-2*) Natl Bur Econ Res.

Trends & Cycles in the Commercial Paper Market. Richard T. Selden. (Occasional Papers: No. 85). 133p. 1963. reprint ed. 34.60 (*0-87014-399-9*) Natl Bur Econ Res.

Trends & Development in the Eighties: Proceedings of the International Workshop on Bielefeld Encounters in Physics & Mathematics IV. Ed. by Sergio A. Albeverio. 436p. 1985. 70.00 (*9971-966-77-8*) World Scientific Pub.

Trends & Developments in Business Administration Programs. Donald L. Joyal. LC 81-15339. 188p. 1982. text ed. 35.00 (*0-275-90828-3*, C0828, Praeger Pubs) Greenwood.

Trends & Developments in Ordinary Differential Equations. P. F. Hsieh & Y. Alavi. 420p. 1994. text ed. 109.00 (*981-02-1530-4*) World Scientific Pub.

Trends & Directions in Hydrology. Stephens J. Burges. (Special Publications). 192p. 13.50 (*0-317-66489-1*) Am Geophysical.

Trends & Future Perspectives in Peptide & Protein Drug Delivery. Ed. by V. Lee. (Drug Targeting & Delivery Ser.). 340p. 1995. text ed. 120.00 (*3-7186-5641-8*, Harwood Acad Pubs) Gordon & Breach.

***Trends & Innovations in Master-Planned Communities.** Urban Land Institute Staff. 150p. (Orig.). 1997. pap. 58.95 (*0-87420-800-9*, T02) Urban Land.

Trends & Issues: Criminal & Juvenile Justice in Illinois. Illinois Criminal Justice Information Authority Staff. (Illus.). 123p. (Orig.). 1987. pap. text ed. write for info. (*0-942715-00-4*) IL Criminal Just.

Trends & Issues Eighty-Nine: Criminal & Juvenile Justice in Illinois. Focus on Drugs, AIDS, DUI. Illinois Criminal Justice Information Authority Staff. (Illus.). 230p. (Orig.). 1987. pap. text ed. write for info. (*0-942715-01-2*) IL Criminal Just.

Trends & Issues in Adult Education, 1988. Susan Imel. (Information Ser.: No. 330). 28p. 1988. 4.75 (*0-318-42047-3*) Ctr Educ Trng Employ.

Trends & Issues in Career Education 1988. Ida Halasz. (Information Ser.: No. 332). 29p. 1988. 4.75 (*0-318-42049-X*) Ctr Educ Trng Employ.

Trends & Issues in Contemporary Arab Thought. Issa J. Boullata. LC 89-31277. (SUNY Series in Middle Eastern Studies). 219p. (C). 1990. pap. text ed. 24.95 (*0-7914-0195-2*) State U NY Pr.

Trends & Issues in Contemporary Arab Thought. Issa J. Boullata. LC 89-31277. (SUNY Series in Middle Eastern Studies). 219p. (C). 1990. text ed. 69.50 (*0-7914-0194-4*) State U NY Pr.

Trends & Issues in Nursing. Marilyn H. Oermann. 1993. write for info. (*0-397-54919-9*) Lppncott-Raven.

Trends & Issues in Professional Nursing. Lois J. Rew. (Nursing Education Ser.). (C). 1998. 31.95 (*0-8273-7879-3*) Delmar.

Trends & Issues in Theoretical Psychology. Ed. by Ian Lubek et al. 412p. 1995. pap. 69.95 (*0-8261-8810-9*) Springer Pub.

Trends & Issues in Vocational Education, 1988. Wesley E. Budke. (Information Ser.: No. 334). 32p. 1988. 4.75 (*0-318-42051-1*) Ctr Educ Trng Employ.

Trends & Issues Ninety - Criminal & Juvenile Justice in Illinois: Focus on Criminal Justice Financing. Pref. by James Thompson & J. David Coldren. (Illus.). 289p. (Orig.). pap. text ed. write for info. (*0-942715-02-0*) IL Criminal Just.

Trends & Issues Ninety-One: Education & Criminal Justice in Illinois. Illinois Criminal Justice Information Authority Staff. (Illus.). 203p. (Orig.). 1991. pap. text ed. write for info. (*0-942715-03-9*) IL Criminal Just.

***Trends & Patterns.** Local Examinations Syndicate Staff. (Modular Sciences Ser.). 80p. 1997. pap. text ed. 13.95 (*0-521-42206-X*) Cambridge U Pr.

Trends & Patterns of Poverty along the U. S.-Mexico Border. Ellwyn R. Stoddard & John Hedderson. 63p. (Orig.). (C). 1986. pap. text ed. 10.00 (*0-937795-08-9*) Border Res Inst.

Trends & Perspectives in Applied Mathematics. Ed. by Lawrence Sirovich. LC 93-46063. (Applied Mathematical Sciences Ser.: Vol. 100). (Illus.). 376p. 1994. 59.95 (*0-387-94201-7*) Spr-Verlag.

Trends & Perspectives in Empirical Social Research. Ed. by Ingwer Borg & Peter Mohler. LC 94-26590. 375p. 1994. lib. bdg. 114.95 (*3-11-014311-9*) De Gruyter.

Trends & Perspectives in Empirical Social Research. Ed. by Ingwer Borg & Peter Mohler. LC 94-26590. 375p. (C). 1994. pap. text ed. 53.95 (*3-11-014312-7*) De Gruyter.

Trends & Perspectives in Parasitology, Vol. 2. Ed. by D. W. Crompton & B. A. Newton. LC 81-642963. 101p. reprint ed. pap. 28.80 (*0-685-16293-1*, 2027281) Bks Demand.

Trends & Practices. Ed. by Ron J. McBeath et al. (Instructional Media & Technology Ser.: Vol. 1). 210p. (Orig.). (C). 1983. pap. text ed. 11.50 (*0-89503-041-1*) Baywood Pub.

Trends & Progress in System Identification. Ed. by P. Eykhoff. LC 80-41994. (IFAC Series for Graduate, Research Workers & Practicing Engineers: Vol. 1). (Illus.). 410p. 1981. 186.00 (*0-08-025683-X*, Pub. by Pergamon Repr UK) Franklin.

Trends & Regional Variations in Amphetamine-Related Emergency Admissions Vol. 1: California, 1984-1993. James K. Cunningham & Margaret A. Thielemeir. (Illus.). 98p. (Orig.). 1995. reprint ed. pap. 16.00 (*0-9651259-3-9*) Public Statistics.

Trends & the Future of University Education in Kenya. Ed. by Paul P. Achola et al. 134p. 1990. pap. text ed. 10.95 (*9966-835-84-9*) Prof World Peace.

Trends & Traditions in Japanese Art. (Illus.). 36p. 1984. 3.00 (*0-912303-34-4*) Michigan Mus.

Trends & Variations in Fertility in the United States. Clyde V. Kiser et al. LC 68-25613. (Vital & Health Statistics Monographs, American Public Health Association). (Illus.). 368p. 1968. 32.00 (*0-674-90780-9*) HUP.

Trends in Advanced Avionics. Jim Curran. LC 92-5963. (Illus.). 200p. 1992. text ed. 35.95 (*0-8138-0749-2*) Iowa St U Pr.

Trends in African Contemporary Art. Kojo Fosu. LC 79-51527. (Illus.). 1980. 45.00 (*0-933184-02-6*); pap. 35.00 (*0-933184-03-4*) Flame Intl.

Trends in Agency Compensation: 1994. Bill Weilbacher. (Illus.). 1995. pap. 37.50 (*1-56318-019-7*) Assn Natl Advertisers.

Trends in American Economic Growth, 1929-1982. Edward F. Denison. LC 85-17413. 141p. 1985. pap. 16.95 (*0-8157-1809-8*) Brookings.

Trends in American Higher Education. Joseph Ben-David. LC 78-177370. (Midway Reprint Ser.). xii, 150p. 1981. pap. text ed. 11.00 (*0-226-04225-1*) U Ch Pr.

Trends in Animal Cell Culture Technology: Proceedings of Annual Meeting of the Japanese Association for Animal Cell Technology, 2nd, Tsukuba, Ibaraki, Japan, Nov. 20-22, 1989. Ed. by Hiroki Murakami. 342p. 1990. 95.00 (*3-527-28199-1*, VCH) Wiley.

Trends in Applications of Mathematics to Mechanics. Ed. by J. F. Biesseling & Wiktor Eckhaus. (Illus.). ix, 361p. 1988. 71.95 (*0-387-50075-8*) Spr-Verlag.

***Trends in Applications of Mathematics to Mechanics.** Manual D. Marques. 1995. 91.87 (*0-582-24874-4*, Pub. by Longman UK) Longman.

Trends in Applications of Pure Mathematics to Mechanics. Ed. by E. Kroner & K. Kirchgassner. (Lecture Notes in Physics Ser.: Vol. 249). viii, 523p. 1986. 64.95 (*0-387-16467-7*) Spr-Verlag.

Trends in Applied Theoretical Chemistry. Luis A. Montero & Yves G. Smeyers. LC 92-12289. (Topics in Molecular Organization & Engineering Ser.: Vol. 9). 224p. (C). 1992. lib. bdg. 137.50 (*0-7923-1745-9*) Kluwer Ac.

Trends in Art Education from Diverse Cultures. Ed. by Heta Kauppinen & Read Diket. 213p. (Orig.). 1995. pap. text ed. 27.00 (*0-937652-79-2*, 230) Natl Art Ed.

Trends in Artificial Intelligence: 2nd Congress of the Italian Association for Artificial Intelligence, AI-IA Palermo, Italy, October 29-31, 1991 Proceedings. Ed. by E. Ardizzone et al. (Lecture Notes in Artificial Intelligence: Vol. 549). xiv, 479p. 1991. 47.95 (*0-387-54712-6*) Spr-Verlag.

Trends in Artist Occupations, 1970-1990. Ed. by Diane C. Ellis & John C. Beresford. 1994. write for info. (*0-615-00261-7*) Natl Endow Arts.

Trends in Astroparticle Physics. Ed. by M. Laraneta & Roberto D. Peccei. 600p. (C). 1991. text ed. 130.00 (*981-02-0825-1*) World Scientific Pub.

Trends in Auto Injury Claims Pt. 1: Analysis of Claim Frequency. 2nd ed. Insurance Research Council Staff. 32p. 1995. pap. text ed. 10.00 (*1-56594-003-2*) Ins Res Coun.

Trends in Auto Injury Claims Pt. 2: Analysis of Claim Costs. 2nd ed. Insurance Research Council, Inc. Staff. 32p. 1995. pap. text ed. 10.00 (*1-56594-005-9*) Ins Res Coun.

Trends in Automatic Pharmacology, Vol. 3. Ed. by Stanley Kalsner. 366p. 1985. 120.00 (*0-85066-327-X*) Taylor & Francis.

Trends in Baha'i Education: Proceedings of the 2nd Symposium on Baha'i Education 1989. Hooshang Nikjoo. 238p. 1990. pap. 5.50 (*1-870987-11-X*) Bahai.

Trends in Bile Acid Research. Ed. by G. Paumgartner et al. (Falk Symposium Ser.). (C). 1989. lib. bdg. 173.00 (*0-7462-0112-5*) Kluwer Ac.

Trends in Bioenergetics & Biotechnological Processes: Proceedings of the Workshop on Recent Advances. G. S. Singhal & T. Ramasarma. (Illus.). 270p. 1992. 59.00 (*1-55528-253-9*, Pub. by Today & Tomorrows P & P II) Scholarly Pubns.

Trends in British Public Policy. Brian W. Hogwood. 224p. 1992. 80.00 (*0-335-15630-4*, Open Univ Pr); pap. 27.00 (*0-335-15629-0*, Open Univ Pr) Taylor & Francis.

Trends in Business Ethics: Implications for Decision Making. Cees Van Dam & Luud M. Stallaert. (Nijenrode Studies in Business: Vol. 3). 190p. 1978. lib. bdg. 65.00 (*90-207-0691-8*, Pub. by M Nijhoff NE) Kluwer Ac.

***Trends in Business Organization: Do Participation & Cooperation Increase Competitiveness? An International Workshop.** Ed. by Horst Siebert. (Kiel Institute of World Economics Ser.). 292p. 1995. 87.50 (*3-16-146391-9*, Pub. by J C B Mohr GW) Coronet Bks.

Trends in Cancer Incidence & Mortality. Ed. by R. Doll et al. (Cancer Surveys Ser.: Vol. 19/20). (Illus.). 583p. (C). 1994. 144.00 (*0-87969-391-6*) Cold Spring Harbor.

Trends in Cancer Incidences: Causes & Practical Implications. Knut Magnus. 1982. text ed. 79.50 (*0-07-039501-2*) McGraw.

Trends in Cancer Research. 84p. (ENG, FRE & RUS.). 1966. pap. text ed. 5.40 (*92-4-156000-2*, 1150151) World Health.

Trends in Chemical Consulting. Ed. by Charles S. Sodano & David M. Sturmer. LC 91-20718. (Illus.). 165p. 1991. pap. 29.95 (*0-8412-2106-5*) Am Chemical.

Trends in Chromosome Research. Ed. by T. Sharma. (Illus.). 400p. 1990. 158.95 (*0-387-51903-3*) Spr-Verlag.

Trends in Chronobiology: Proceedings of the 18th Conference of the International Society for Chronobiology, Held in Conjunction with the Third Annual Meeting of the European Society for Chronobiology, Leiden, The Netherlands, 12-17 July 1987. Ed. by W. Hekkens et al. (Advances in the Biosciences Ser.). (Illus.). 393p. 1988. 140.00 (*0-08-036865-4*, Pergamon Pr) Elsevier.

Trends in Civil Jury Verdicts since 1985. Erik Moller. LC 96-19851. xxi, 84p. (Orig.). 1996. pap. 15.00 (*0-8330-2360-8*, MR-694-ICJ) Rand Corp.

Trends in Cognitive & Behavioural Therapies. Paul M. Salkovskis. LC 95-31227. 162p. 1996. text ed. 55.00 (*0-471-96172-8*) Wiley.

***Trends in Collider Spin Physics.** 450p. 1997. lib. bdg. 68.00 (*981-02-2868-6*) World Scientific Pub.

***Trends in Colloid & Interface Science, No. X.** Ed. by C. Solans et al. (Progress in Colloid & Polymer Science Ser.: Vol. 100). 372p. 1996. 159.50 (*3-7985-1056-3*) Spr-Verlag.

Trends in Colloid & Interface Science II. Ed. by V. Degiorgio. (Progress in Colloid & Polymer Science Ser.: Vol. 76). 320p. 1988. 129.00 (*0-387-91335-1*) Spr-Verlag.

Trends in Colloid & Interface Science III. Ed. by J. Bothorel & J. Dufoure. (Progress in Colloid & Polymer Science Ser.: Vol. 79). 356p. 1989. 158.00 (*0-387-91364-5*) Spr-Verlag.

Trends in Colloid & Interface Science IV. Ed. by M. Zulauf et al. (Progress in Colloid & Polymer Science Ser.: Vol. 81). 260p. 1990. 115.00 (*0-387-91368-8*) Spr-Verlag.

Trends in Colloid & Interface Science IX. G. Porte & G. Lagaly. (Progress in Colloid & Polymer Science Ser.: Vol. 98). 311p. 1995. 155.95 (*3-7985-1031-8*) Spr-Verlag.

Trends in Colloid & Interface Science V. Ed. by M. Corti & F. Mallamace. (Progress in Colloid & Polymer Science Ser.: Vol. 84). 250p. 1991. 169.00 (*0-387-91399-8*) Spr-Verlag.

Trends in Colloid & Interface Science VI. Ed. by C. Helm et al. (Progress in Colloid & Polymer Science Ser.: Vol. 89). 372p. 1992. 153.00 (*0-387-91410-2*) Spr-Verlag.

Trends in Colloid & Interface Science VII. Ed. by P. Laggner & O. Glatter. (Progress in Colloid & Polymer Science Ser.: Vol. 93). 412p. 1994. 159.95 (*0-387-91454-4*) Spr-Verlag.

Trends in Colloid & Interface Science VIII. Ed. by Ronald H. Ottewill & A. R. Rennie. (Progress in Colloid & Polymer Science Ser.: Vol. 97). 340p. 1994. 152.95 (*3-7985-0984-0*) Spr-Verlag.

Trends in Computer Algebra. R. Janssen. (Lecture Notes in Computer Science Ser.: Vol. 296). v, 197p. 1988. pap. 33.00 (*0-387-18928-9*) Spr-Verlag.

Trends in Computerized Structural Analysis & Synthesis, Vol. 10, No. 1-2. A. K. Noor & H. G. McComb, Jr. 1978. 83.00 (*0-08-023261-2*, Ed Skills Dallas) Elsevier.

Trends in Computerized Structural Analysis & Synthesis, Vol. 10, No. 1-2. A. K. Noor & H. G. McComb, Jr. 1981. pap. 91.00 (*0-08-028707-7*, Pergamon Pr) Elsevier.

Trends in Construction Equipment Markets. 175p. 1991. 1,950.00 (*0-945235-54-2*) Lead Edge Reports.

Trends in Consumer Behavior Research. Robert A. Peterson. LC 76-45657. (American Marketing Association Monograph Ser.: No. 6). 46p. reprint ed. pap. 25.00 (*0-317-28135-6*, 2022481) Bks Demand.

***Trends in Contemporary Trust Law.** Ed. by A. J. Oakley. 388p. 1997. 85.00 (*0-19-826286-8*) OUP.

Trends in Control: A European Perspective. Alberto Isidori. (Illus.). 432p. 1995. 97.95 (*3-540-19967-5*) Spr-Verlag.

***Trends in Control & Measurement Education.** Derek A. Linkens & D. P. Atherton. (IFAC Symposia Ser.: Vol. 8905). 258p. 1989. 127.25 (*0-08-035736-9*, Pergamon Pr) Elsevier.

Trends in Coronary Heart Disease Mortality: The Influence of Medical Care. Ed. by Millicent W. Higgins & Russell V. Luepker. (Illus.). 320p. 1988. 45.00 (*0-19-505297-8*) OUP.

Trends in Corporate Advertising Practices, 1994. 1994. pap. 27.50 (*1-56318-013-8*) Assn Natl Advertisers.

Trends in Corporate Bond Quality. Thomas R. Atkinson & Elizabeth T. Simpson. (Financial Research Program V: Studies in Corporate Bond Financing: No. 4). 122p. 1967. reprint ed. 31.80 (*0-87014-148-1*) Natl Bur Econ Res.

Trends in Crime & Criminal Justice, in the Context of Socio-Economic Change: 1970-1985 Edition. 108p. 1992. 20.00 (*92-1-130150-5*) UN.

Trends in Database Design & Customer Services. Ed. by Wendy Schipper & Betty Unruh. (Report Series, 1990: No. 3). 80p. 1990. pap. text ed. 30.00 (*0-942308-27-1*) NFAIS.

***Trends in der Linguistischen Datenverarbeitung.** Contrib. by Peter Hellwig & Hubert Lehmann. (Sprache und Computer Ser.: Bd. 1). viii, 188p. (GER.). 1986. write for info. (*3-487-07679-9*) G Olms Pubs.

Trends in Dermatoglyphic Research. Ed. by Norris M. Durham & Chris C. Plato. (Studies in Human Biology). 328p. 1990. lib. bdg. 112.00 (*0-7923-0963-4*) Kluwer Ac.

Trends in Developing Economies Vol. 1: Extracts: Eastern Europe & Central Asia. 1995. 12.95 (*0-8213-3282-1*, 13282) World Bank.

Trends in Developing Economies Vol. 2: Extracts: Emerging Capital Markets. 1995. 12.95 (*0-8213-3283-X*, 13283) World Bank.

***Trends in Developing Economies 1996: Profiles Recent Economic Trends in the World Bank's 117 Borrowing Members.** 590p. 1996. 50.00 (*0-8213-3572-3*, 13572) World Bank.

Trends in Development Bank Lending 1995: A Professional Reference Guide, Including Projected Lending Figures to FY 1998. Nicholas H. Ludlow & Benjamin C. Pappas. LC 94-71589. (Illus.). 358p. 1995. pap. 303.00 (*0-943781-08-6*) Develop Bank.

Trends in Discrete Mathematics. Ed. by W. Deuber et al. LC 95-8188. (Topics in Discrete Mathematics Ser.: Vol. 9). 398p. 1995. 210.50 (*0-444-82192-9*) Elsevier.

***Trends in Distributed Systems: Corba & Beyond - International Workshop Treds '96, Aachen, Germany, October 1-2, 1996 : Proceedings.** Claudia Linnhoff-Popien & Bernd E. Meyer. LC 96-41958. (Lecture Notes in Computer Science Ser.: Vol. 1161). 289p. 1996. text ed. 49.00 (*3-540-61842-2*) Spr-Verlag.

Trends in Drug Research: Proceedings of the Seventh Noordwikerhout-Camerino Symposium Noordwijkerhout, The Netherlands, 5-8 Sept., 1989. Ed. by V. Claassen. (Pharmacochemistry Library: No. 13). 430p. 1990. 202.50 (*0-444-88614-1*) Elsevier.

Trends in Dyeing & Finishing: A Global View. (Symposium Papers). 67p. 1986. 15.00 (*0-318-12154-9*) AATCC.

Trends in Ecological Physical Chemistry: Proceedings of the Second International Workshop on Ecological Physical Chemistry, Milan, Italy, 25-29 May 1992. Ed. by L. Bonati et al. LC 92-39682. 366p. 1993. 238.50 (*0-444-89646-5*) Elsevier.

Trends in Economic Development Organizations: A Survey of Selected Metropolitan Areas. Kenneth Poole. Ed. by Jenny Murphy. 580p. (Orig.). 1991. pap. 225.00 (*0-317-04832-5*) Natl Coun Econ Dev.

***Trends in Education Access & Financing During the Transition in Central & Eastern Europe.** Bruno Laporte & Dena Ringold. (Technical Papers: No. 361). 56p. 1997. 20.00 (*0-8213-3912-5*, 13912) World Bank.

Trends in Educational Occupations. Marjorie Rankin. LC 74-177179. (Columbia University. Teachers College. Contributions to Education Ser.: No. 412). reprint ed. 37.50 (*0-404-55412-1*) AMS Pr.

***Trends in Educational Technology 1995.** Donald P. Ely. 79p. (Orig.). 1996. pap. 10.00 (*0-937597-40-6*) ERIC Clear.

***Trends in Eicosanoid Biology.** Ed. by Bengt Samuelsson et al. (Advances in Prostaglandin, Thromboxane, & Leukotriene Research Ser.: Vol. 20). reprint ed. pap. 78.70 (*0-608-04668-X*, 2065389) Bks Demand.

Trends in Electric Utility Research: Proceedings of the Electric Utility Research Conference, Chicago, April 1984. Ed. by C. Bullard & P. Wameldorff. 500p. 1984. pap. 170.00 (*0-08-030982-8*) Elsevier.

Trends in Electrochemical Biosensors: Proceedings of the Conference. G. Costa. 216p. 1993. text ed. 95.00 (*981-02-1247-X*) World Scientific Pub.

Trends in Employee Counseling Programs. Brenda McGowan. (Studies in Productivity: Highlights of the Literature Ser.: No. 37). 55p. 1984. pap. 55.00 (*0-08-032361-8*, PS37) Work in Amer.

Trends in Employment & Earnings for Nineteen Graduating Classes of a Teachers College: As Shown by the Record of the 1927-1936 Classes of the New Jersey State Teachers College at Newark, New Jersey. John S. French. LC 79-176786. (Columbia University. Teachers College. Contributions to Education Ser.: No. 911). reprint ed. 37.50 (*0-404-55911-5*) AMS Pr.

Trends in Employment in the Service Industries. George J. Stigler. (General Ser.: No. 59). 187p. 1956. reprint ed. 48.70 (*0-87014-058-2*) Natl Bur Econ Res.

Trends in Energy Use in Industrial Societies: An Overview. Joy Dunkerley. LC 80-8022. (Resources for the Future Ser.: No. R-19). 167p. reprint ed. pap. 47.60 (*0-685-23698-6*, 2032150) Bks Demand.

***Trends in English & American Studies: Literature & the Imagination.** Ed. by Sabine Coelsch-Foisner et al. LC 96-44223. 468p. 1996. text ed. 109.95 (*0-7734-8747-6*) E Mellen.

***Trends in English & American Studies: Literature & the Imagination.** Sabine Foisner et al. LC 96-44223. (ENG & GER.). 1996. pap. write for info. (*0-7734-8751-4*) E Mellen.

Trends in Enzyme Histochemistry & Cytochemistry. CIBA Foundation Staff. LC 80-11757. (CIBA Foundation Symposium: New Ser.: No. 73). 322p. reprint ed. pap. 91.80 (*0-317-29754-6*, 2022192) Bks Demand.

Trends in Enzymology: Proceedings, 2 vols. Ed. by L. J. Vitale & V. Simeon. Incl. Industrial & Clinical Enzymology. 1980. 60.00 (*0-08-024418-1*); (FEBS Ser.: Vols. 60 & 61). (Illus.). 730p. 1980. write for info. (*0-318-55236-1*, Pub. by Pergamon Repr UK) Franklin.

Trends in Europe & North America Statistical Yearbook of the ECE No. 1: 1995. 148p. 1995. 35.00 (*92-1-116626-8*) UN.

Trends in European Social Policy: Essays in Memory of Malcolm Mead. Ed. by Jeff Kenner. 320p. 1995. text ed. 63.95 (*1-85521-704-X*, Pub. by Dartmth Pub UK) Ashgate Pub Co.

Trends in Family Welfare Planning. M. Z. Khan. (C). 1992. 20.00 (*81-210-0287-7*, Pub. by Inter-India Pubns) S Asia.

Trends in Female & Male Age at Marriage & Celibacy in Asia. Peter Xenos & Socorro A. Gultiano. LC 92-27059. (Papers of the Program on Population: No. 120). vi, 46p. (Orig.). 1992. pap. 3.00 (*0-86638-153-8*) EW Ctr HI.

Trends in Financial Decision Making: Planning & Capital Investment Decisions. Cees Van Dam. (Nijenrode Studies in Business: Vol. 2). 1978. lib. bdg. 64.00 (*90-207-0692-6*) Kluwer Ac.

Trends in Financing European Local Governments. Ed. by John Gibson & Richard Batley. LC 92-40702. 1993. 37.50 (*0-7146-4513-3*, Pub. by F Cass Pubs UK) Intl Spec Bk.

Trends in Flavour Research: Proceedings of the 7th Weurman Flavour Research Symposium, Noordwijkerhout, The Netherlands, 15-18 June, 1993. Ed. by H. Maarse & D. G. Van der Heij. LC 93-50139. (Developments in Food Science Ser.: No. 35). 528p. 1994. 204.50 (*0-444-81587-2*) Elsevier.

Trends in Foreign Language Requirements & Placement **see Foreign Languages: Reading, Literature, Requirements**

Trends in Government Financing. Morris A. Copeland. LC 75-19710. (National Bureau of Economic Research Ser.). (Illus.). 1975. reprint ed. 20.95 (*0-405-07590-1*) Ayer.

Trends in Government Financing. Morris A. Copeland. (Studies in Capital Formation & Financing: No. 7). 236p. 1961. reprint ed. 61.40 (*0-87014-105-8*); reprint ed. mic. film 30.70 (*0-685-61327-5*) Natl Bur Econ Res.

Trends in Haemostasis 1995. Hajna Losonczy & Marianna David. 204p. 1995. pap. 30.00 (*963-05-6844-6*, Pub. by A K HU) Intl Spec Bk.

Trends in Health Benefits. 1994. lib. bdg. 300.00 (*0-8490-9049-0*) Gordon Pr.

Trends in Health Care Provider Liability II: An Analysis of Jury Verdicts. Brian Shenker. LC 92-36273. 1992. 49.50 (*0-934753-81-4*) LRP Pubns.

Trends in Health Spending: An Update. (Illus.). 80p. (Orig.). (C). 1993. pap. text ed. 40.00 (*1-56806-549-3*) DIANE Pub.

Trends in Health Spending: An Update. (Orig.). 1994. lib. bdg. 250.00 (*0-8490-5745-0*) Gordon Pr.

***Trends in Health Status, Services, & Finance: The Transition in Central & Eastern Europe.** Ellen Goldstein et al. (Technical Paper Ser.: No. 341). 56p. 1996. pap. 7.95 (*0-8213-3751-3*, 13751) World Bank.

***Trends in Health Status, Services, & Finance: The Transition in Central & Eastern Europe, Statistical Annex, Vol. II.** Gnanaraj Chellaraj et al. (Technical Paper Ser.: No. 348). 152p. 1997. pap. 9.95 (*0-8213-3828-5*, 13828) World Bank.

Trends in Hospital Procedures Performed on Black Patients & White Patients. 1995. lib. bdg. 250.95 (*0-8490-6842-8*) Gordon Pr.

Trends in Hospital Utilization: United States, 1988-92. Brenda Gillum et al. LC 96-8988. 1996. write for info. (*0-8406-0516-1*) Natl Ctr Health Stats.

Trends in Income: An Analysis of Income Tax Returns for San Francisco Bay Area Counties, 1978-1990. 68p. 1993. 35.00 (*0-317-05666-2*, P93001PRO) Assn Bay Area.

Trends in Indian Economy, 6 vols. Ed. by Devandra Thakur. (C). 1993. Set. 225.00 (*81-7100-453-9*, Pub. by Deep II) S Asia.

Trends in Industrial Location & Their Impact on Regional Economic Development. Benjamin H. Stevens et al. (Discussion Paper Ser.: No. 31). 1969. pap. 10.00 (*1-55869-126-X*) Regional Sci Res Inst.

Trends in Infant Mortality by Cause of Death & Other Characteristics, 1960-88. (Illus.). 53p. (Orig.). (C). 1994. pap. text ed. 25.00 (*0-7881-1009-8*) DIANE Pub.

Trends in Infant Mortality by Causes of Death & Other Characteristics 1960-88. 1994. lib. bdg. 250.00 (*0-8490-5744-2*) Gordon Pr.

Trends in Inflammation Research Two. R. Hirschelmann. Ed. by H. Bekemeier. (Agents & Actions Supplements Ser.: Vol. 10). 315p. 1982. 79.50 (*0-8176-1344-7*) Birkhauser.

Trends in Inflammatory Bowel Disease Therapy. Ed. by C. N. Williams. (Falk Symposium Ser.). 480p. 1991. lib. bdg. 190.50 (*0-7923-8952-2*) Kluwer Ac.

Trends in Inflammatory Bowel Disease Therapy, 1992. Ed. by C. N. Williams. (Falk Symposium Ser.). 384p. (C). 1993. lib. bdg. 144.00 (*0-7923-8827-5*) Kluwer Ac.

***Trends in Inflammatory Bowel Disease Therapy 1996.** Ed. by R. S. McLeod et al. 320p. 1997. lib. bdg. 135.00 (*0-7923-8718-X*) Kluwer Ac.

Trends in Information Systems: TC 8 Anthology. Ed. by B. Langefors et al. 450p. 1986. 113.75 (*0-444-87949-8*, North Holland) Elsevier.

Trends in Information Technology: A Handbook for Senior Management Who Must Understand Information Technology in a Competitive Context. Andersen, Arthur, & Co. Staff. 128p. (Orig.). (JPN.). (C). 1988. pap. text ed. write for info. (*0-942319-02-8*) A Andersen.

Trends in Information Technology: A Handbook for Senior Management Who Must Understand Information Technology in a Competitive Context. 3rd ed. Andersen, Arthur & Co. (Illus.). 88p. (Orig.). (C). 1987. pap. 9.95 (*0-942319-00-1*) A Andersen.

Trends in Information Transfer. Ed. by Philip J. Hills. LC 82-3021. vii, 191p. 1982. text ed. 49.95 (*0-313-23600-3*, HIT/, Greenwood Pr) Greenwood.

Trends in Interfacial Electrochemistry. Ed. by A. Fernando Silva. 1986. lib. bdg. 212.50 (*90-277-2271-4*) Kluwer Ac.

Trends in International Distribution of Gross World Product National Accounts Statistics: Special Issue. 336p. 1992. 50.00 (*92-1-161346-9*, E.92.XVII.7) UN.

Trends in International Migration - Annual Report 1994. 244p. (Orig.). 1995. pap. 60.00 (*92-64-14463-3*, Pub. by Org for Econ FR) OECD.

Trends in Israeli Democracy: The Public's View. Yochanan Peres & Ephraim Yuchtman-Yaar. LC 91-43887. (Israel Democracy Institute Policy Studies). 62p. 1992. pap. text ed. 9.95 (*1-55587-308-1*) Lynne Rienner.

Trends in Khmer Art. Jean Boisselier. Ed. by Natasha Eilenberg. Tr. by Melvin Elliott from FRE. (Studies on Southeast Asia: No. 6). (Illus.). 124p. 1989. pap. text ed. 15.00 (*0-87727-705-2*) Cornell SE Asia.

Trends in Law Library Management & Technology: 1987-1992. 75.00 (*0-8377-9248-7*) Rothman.

Trends in Lower Power Electronics. B. Razavi. (Current Topics in Electronics & System). 200p. 1994. text ed. 48.00 (*981-02-1863-X*) World Scientific Pub.

Trends in Managerial & Financial Accounting: Income Determining & Financial Reporting. Cees Van Dam. (Nijenrode Studies in Business: Vol. 1). 1978. lib. bdg. 64.00 (*90-207-0693-4*) Kluwer Ac.

Trends in Manpower & Educational Development: A British Perspective. Keith Hampson. 18p. 1985. 2.75 (*0-318-22225-6*, OC104) Ctr Educ Trng Employ.

Trends in Mathematical Optimization. K. H. Hoffmann et al. (International Series of Numerical Mathematics: No. 84). 390p. 1988. 106.50 (*0-8176-1919-4*) Birkhauser.

Trends in Medicinal Chemistry. Sarel. 1992. 132.00 (*0-632-03364-9*) CRC Pr.

Trends in Memory Development Research. Ed. by M. T. Chi. (Contributions to Human Development Ser.: Vol. 9). (Illus.). xii, 128p. 1983. pap. 39.25 (*3-8055-3661-5*) S Karger.

Trends in Mission: Toward the Third Millennium. Ed. by William Jenkinson & Helene O'Sullivan. LC 91-18469. 450p. 1991. pap. 27.50 (*0-88344-766-5*) Orbis Bks.

Trends in Modern American Society. Intro. by Clarence R. Morris. LC 86-22762. (Benjamin Franklin Lectures of the University of Pennsylvania, 7th Series). 191p. 1986. reprint ed. text ed. 49.75 (*0-313-22106-5*, MOTM, Greenwood Pr) Greenwood.

Trends in Modern Indian Art. S. K. Bhattacharya. 84p. (C). 1994. 90.00 (*81-85880-21-2*, Pub. by Print Hse II) St Mut.

An Asterisk (*) at the beginning of an entry indicates that the title is appearing in BIP for the first time.

Trends in Natural Language Generation: An Artificial Intelligence Perspective: Fourth European Workshop, EWNLG '93, Pisa, Italy, April 1993: Selected Papers. Ed. by Giovanni Adorni & Michael Zock. (Lecture Notes in Computer Science Ser.: Vol. 1036). 390p. 1996. pap. text ed. 60.00 (*3-540-60800-1*) Spr-Verlag.

Trends in Natural Resource Commodities: Statistics of Prices, Output, Consumption, Foreign Trade, & Employment in the United States, 1870-1957. Neal Potter & Francis T. Christy. Ed. by Pauline Manning. LC 62-11711. 580p. reprint ed. pap. 165.30 (*0-317-26474-5*, 2023809) Bks Demand.

***Trends in NDE Science & Technology: Proceedings of the 14th World Conference on Non-Destructive Testing, New Delhi, 8-13 December 1996.** Ed. by C. G. Krishnadas Nair et al. (Illus.). 2800p. (C). 1997. text ed. 195.00 (*90-5410-740-5*, Pub. by A A Balkema NE) Ashgate Pub Co.

Trends in Neuroimmunology. Ed. by M. G. Marrosu et al. LC 90-6764. (Illus.). 178p. 1990. 55.00 (*0-306-43510-1*, Plenum Pr) Plenum.

Trends in Non-Crystalline Solids: Proceedings of the 3rd International Workshop on Non-Crystalline Solids. A. Conde et al. 450p. 1992. text ed. 124.00 (*981-02-1035-3*) World Scientific Pub.

***Trends in Nuclear Research Institutes.** OECD NEA Staff. 200p. (Orig.). 1996. pap. 68.00 (*92-64-14781-0*, Pub. by Org for Econ FR) OECD.

Trends in Optical Fibre Metrology & Standards: Proceedings of the NATO Advanced Study Institute, Viana do Castelo, Portugal, June 27 - July 8, 1994. Oliverio D. Soares. LC 95-5544. (NATO ASI, Series E, Applied Sciences: Vol. 285). 844p. (C). 1995. lib. bdg. 317.00 (*0-7923-3402-7*) Kluwer Ac.

Trends in Optics: Research, Developments & Applications. Ed. by Anna Corsortini. (Lasers & Optical Engineering Ser.). (Illus.). 608p. 1996. boxed 89.95 (*0-12-186030-2*) Acad Pr.

Trends in Oral Contraception. Ed. by R. F. Harrison et al. 70p. 1983. lib. bdg. 49.00 (*0-85200-771-X*) Kluwer Ac.

Trends in Organ Transplantation. Barbara A. Williams. LC 95-24993. (Illus.). 272p. 1996. 49.95 (*0-8261-9150-9*) Springer Pub.

Trends in Organizational Behavior, Vol. 1. Ed. by Cary L. Cooper & Denise M. Rousseau. 141p. 1994. pap. text ed. 39.95 (*0-471-94344-4*) Wiley.

Trends in Organizational Behavior, Vol. 2. Ed. by Cary L. Cooper & Denise M. Rousseau. (Trends in Organizational Behavior Ser.). 1996. pap. text ed. 34.95 (*0-471-95692-9*) Wiley.

Trends in Organizational Behavior, Vol. 3. Ed. by Cary L. Cooper & Denise M. Rousseau. (Trends in Organizational Behavior Ser.). Date not set. pap. text ed. 39.95 (*0-471-16527-1*); pap. text ed. 39.95 (*0-471-96585-5*) Wiley.

Trends in Output & Employment. George J. Stigler. (Twenty-Fifth Anniversary Ser.: No. 4). 77p. 1947. reprint ed. 20.10 (*0-87014-116-3*); reprint ed. mic. film 20.00 (*0-685-61267-8*) Natl Bur Econ Res.

Trends in Pensions. 1991. lib. bdg. 79.95 (*0-8490-4359-X*) Gordon Pr.

Trends in Pensions, 2 vols., Set. 1996. lib. bdg. 750.95 (*0-8490-6029-X*) Gordon Pr.

Trends in Pensions: A Reference Guide on Federal Government Statistics on Pension Plans. 1990. lib. bdg. 75.00 (*0-8490-4009-4*) Gordon Pr.

Trends in Philanthropy: A Study in a Typical American City. Willford I. King & Kate E. Huntley. (General Ser.: No. 12). 76p. 1928. reprint ed. 20.00 (*0-87014-011-6*); reprint ed. mic. film 20.00 (*0-685-61142-6*) Natl Bur Econ Res.

Trends in Population Policy. 387p. 1992. 44.00 (*92-1-151187-9*) UN.

***Trends in Private Investment in Developing Countries: Statistics for 1970-94.** Frederick Z. Jaspersen et al. (IFC Discussion Paper Ser.: No. 28). 58p. 1996. 7.95 (*0-8213-3557-X*, 13557) World Bank.

***Trends in Private Investment in Developing Countries: Statistics for 1970-95.** Lawrence Bouton & Mariusz Sumlinski. (IFC Discussion Papers: No. 31). 52p. 1997. 7.95 (*0-8213-3874-9*, 13874) World Bank.

Trends in Private Investment in Developing Countries 1995: Statistics for 1980-93. Jack D. Glen & Mariusz A. Sumlinski. (IFC Discussion Paper Ser.: No. 25). 46p. 1995. 6.95 (*0-8213-3183-3*, 13183) World Bank.

Trends in Productivity Quality & Worker Attitude. Gary Blau. (Studies in Productivity: Highlights of the Literature Ser.: Vol. 3). 36p. 1978. pap. 55.00 (*0-318-41889-4*) Work in Amer.

Trends in Protestant Social Idealism. Neal Hughley. LC 74-167359. (Essay Index Reprint Ser.). 1977. reprint ed. 20.95 (*0-8369-2771-0*) Ayer.

Trends in Public Opinion: A Compendium of Survey Data. Richard G. Niemi et al. LC 89-2213. (Documentary Reference Collections). 344p. 1989. text ed. 79.50 (*0-313-25426-5*, NTP/, Greenwood Pr) Greenwood.

Trends in Public Sector Pay: A Study of Nine OECD Countries 1985-1990. OECD Staff. 130p. (Orig.). 1994. pap. 18.00 (*92-64-14143-X*) OECD.

Trends in Public Sector Pay in OECD Countries. 165p. (Orig.). 1995. pap. 40.00 (*92-64-14643-1*, Pub. by Org for Econ FR) OECD.

Trends in Radiation Dosimetry. Ed. by W. L. McLaughlin. (Illus.). 320p. 1983. pap. 28.00 (*0-08-029143-0*, Pergamon Pr) Elsevier.

Trends in Radiation Processing: Transactions of the Third International Meeting on Radiation Processing, Held in Tokyo, Japan, October 1980, 3 vols. Ed. by J. Silverman. 1350p. 1982. pap. 155.00 (*0-08-026512-X*, C145, E110, Pergamon Pr) Elsevier.

Trends in Radio Station Sales 1991-1993. National Association of Broadcasters Staff. 160p. (Orig.). 1993. pap. 225.00 (*0-89324-201-2*) Natl Assn Broadcasters.

***Trends in Receptor Research.** P. Angeli et al. (Pharmacochemistry Library: Vol. 18). x, 434p. 1992. 272.50 (*0-444-88931-0*) Elsevier.

Trends in Receptor Research: Proceedings of the Ninth Noordwijkerhout-Camerino Symposium, Noordwijkerhout, The Netherlands, 23-27 May 1993. Ed. by V. Claassen. LC 93-40990. (Pharmacochemistry Library: Vol. 20). 334p. 1993. 307.00 (*0-444-89664-3*) Elsevier.

Trends in Research & Treatment of Joint Diseases. Ed. by Kazushi Hirohata et al. (Illus.). 192p. 1992. 123.00 (*0-387-70095-1*) Spr-Verlag.

Trends in Research on Human Settlements in ECE Countries. 45p. 1990. 10.00 (*92-1-116474-5*, 90.II.E.9) UN.

Trends in Romance Linguistics & Philology, Vol. 2. Ed. by Rebecca Posner & John Green. (Synchronic Romance Linguistics Ser.). 422p. 1981. 123.10 (*90-279-7896-4*) Mouton.

Trends in Romance Linguistics & Philology: Romance Comparative & Historical Linguistics. John N. Green. Ed. by Rebecca Posner. (Trends in Linguistics, Studies & Monographs: No. 12). 386p. 1980. 113.85 (*90-279-7886-7*) Mouton.

Trends in Romance Linguistics & Philology, Vol. 5: Bilingualism & Linguistic Conflict in Romance. Ed. by Rebecca Posner & John Green. (Trends in Linguistics, Studies & Monographs: No. 71). x, 630p. (C). 1993. lib. bdg. 221.55 (*3-11-011724-X*) Mouton.

Trends in Schenkerian Research. Ed. by Allen Cadwallader. 168p. 1990. text ed. 45.00 (*0-02-870551-3*) Schirmer Bks.

Trends in Social Work, Eighteen Seventy-Four to Nineteen Fifty-Six: A History Based on the Proceedings of the National Conference of Social Work. 2nd ed. Frank J. Bruno. LC 80-19210. xviii, 462p. 1980. reprint ed. text ed. 79.50 (*0-313-22665-2*, BRTI) Greenwood.

Trends in Software Process. Alfonso Fuggetta & A. Wolfe. 200p. 1996. pap. text ed. 50.00 (*0-471-95854-9*) Wiley.

Trends in Solid Mechanics. Ed. by J. F. Besseling & A. M. Van Der Heijden. 256p. 1980. lib. bdg. 115.50 (*90-286-0699-8*) Kluwer Ac.

Trends in Soviet Theoretical Linguistics. Ed. by Ferenc Kiefer. LC 72-95890. (Foundations of Language Supplementary Ser.: No. 18). 1973. lib. bdg. 165.00 (*90-277-0274-8*) Kluwer Ac.

Trends in Specialization: Tomorrow's Medicine. Ed. by Donald G. Langsley & James H. Darragh. LC 85-73107. (Illus.). 128p. 1985. lib. bdg. 29.95 (*0-934277-06-0*) Am Bd Med Spec.

***Trends in State Coordination & Governance: Historical & Current Perspectives.** Rhonda M. Epper & Alene B. Russell. 50p. 1996. pap. 15.00 (*0-614-23674-6*) SHEEO.

***Trends in Structural Mechanics: Theory, Practice & Education.** J. Roorda & N. K. Srivastava. LC 97-20237. (Solid Mechanics & Its Applications Ser.). 1997. text ed. write for info. (*0-7923-4603-3*) Kluwer Ac.

Trends in Student Personnel Work As Represented in the Positions of Dean of Women & Dean of Girls in Colleges & Universities, Normal Schools, Teachers Colleges, & High Schools. Ruth Strang et al. LC 79-177732. (Columbia University. Teachers College. Contributions to Education Ser.: No. 787). reprint ed. 37.50 (*0-404-55787-2*) AMS Pr.

Trends in Supercomputing. Ed. by Y. Kanada & C. K. Yuen. 216p. (C). 1988. text ed. 89.00 (*9971-5-0831-1*) World Scientific Pub.

Trends in Synthetic Carbohydrate Chemistry. Ed. by Derek Horton et al. LC 88-39237. (ACS Symposium Ser.: No. 386). (Illus.). xi, 345p. 1989. 69.95 (*0-8412-1563-4*) Am Chemical.

***Trends in Synthetic Carbohydrate Chemistry.** Ed. by Derek Horton et al. LC 88-39237. (ACS Symposium Ser.: No. 386). (Illus.). 359p. 1989. reprint ed. pap. 102.40 (*0-608-03141-0*, 2063594) Bks Demand.

Trends in Teaching Genetics. Ed. by Daniel Bergsma. (Alan R. Liss Ser.: Vol. 13, No. 6). 1977. 23.00 (*0-686-23125-2*) March of Dimes.

Trends in Testing & Instrumentation: 1996 International Congress & Exposition. (Special Publications). 109p. 1996. pap. 38.00 (*1-56091-760-1*, SP-1130) Soc Auto Engineers.

Trends in the American Economy in the Nineteenth Century. (Studies in Income & Wealth: No. 24). 791p. 1960. reprint ed. 160.00 (*0-87014-180-5*) Natl Bur Econ Res.

Trends in the American Economy in the Nineteenth Century. Conference on Research in Income & Wealth. LC 75-19709. (National Bureau of Economic Research Ser.). (Illus.). 1975. reprint ed. 64.95 (*0-405-07588-X*) Ayer.

Trends in the Criminal Enforcement of Environmental Laws. Thomas J. Kelly, Jr. & Valerie K. Mann. (Environmental Management Guides Ser.). 18p. 1994. pap. text ed. 17.50 (*0-86587-440-9*) Gov Insts.

Trends in the Enforcement of Non-Money Judgments & Orders. Ed. by U. Jacobsson & J. Jacob. 304p. 1988. pap. 68.00 (*90-6544-336-3*) Kluwer Law Tax Pubs.

Trends in the Global Balance of Airpower. Christopher J. Bowie et al. LC 94-42440. xxv, 111p. 1995. pap. 15.00 (*0-8330-1601-6*, MR-478-1-AF) Rand Corp.

Trends in the Global Balance of Airpower: Supporting Data. Christopher J. Bowie et al. LC 94-42441. v, 115p. 1995. pap. text ed. 13.00 (*0-8330-1602-4*, MR-478/2-AF) Rand Corp.

***Trends in the Golf Industry 1986-1995.** 3rd rev. ed. 50p. 1996. pap. 200.00 (*1-57701-056-6*) Natl Golf.

Trends in the Health of Older Americans: U. S., 1994. R. A. Cohen & J. F. Van Nostrand. (Illus.). 326p. (Orig.). 1996. pap. text ed. 45.00 (*0-7881-2796-9*) DIANE Pub.

Trends in the Health of Older Americans: United States, 1994. Ed. by R. A. Cohen et al. LC 94-44483. (Vital & Health Statistics, Series 3, Analytical & Epidemiological Studies: No. 30). 328p. 1995. 21.00 (*0-8406-0504-8*) Natl Ctr Health Stats.

Trends in the Historiography of Science. Ed. by Kostas Gavroglu. LC 93-7415. (Boston Studies in the Philosophy of Science: Vol. 151). 452p. (C). 1994. lib. bdg. 172.50 (*0-7923-2255-X*, Pub. by Klwr Acad Pubs NE) Kluwer Ac.

Trends in the Management of Systemic Fungal Infections. Ed. by D. W. Denning. (Journal: Chemotherapy: Vol. 38, Suppl. 1, 1992). (Illus.). iv, 96p. 1992. pap. 30.50 (*3-8055-5627-6*) S Karger.

Trends in the Relocation of U. S. Manufacturing. Christina M. Kelton. LC 83-9117. (Research in Business Economics & Public Policy Ser.: No. 6). 194p. reprint ed. pap. 55.30 (*0-8357-1445-4*, 2070398) Bks Demand.

Trends in the Soviet Oil & Gas Industry. Robert W. Campbell. LC 76-15940. (Resources for the Future Ser.). (Illus.). 144p. 1977. 12.00 (*0-8018-1870-2*) Johns Hopkins.

Trends in the Soviet Oil & Gas Industry. Robert W. Campbell. LC 76-15940. 141p. reprint ed. pap. 40.20 (*0-685-20399-9*, 2030193) Bks Demand.

Trends in the Study of Morbidity & Mortality. D. Curiel et al. (Public Health Papers: No. 27). 196p. (ENG, FRE, RUS & SPA.). 1965. pap. text ed. 8.00 (*92-4-130027-2*, 1110027) World Health.

***Trends in the Transport Sector, 1970-1995.** ECMT Staff. 60p. (Orig.). 1997. pap. 9.00 (*92-821-1220-9*, 75-97-01-1, Pub. by Org for Econ FR) OECD.

***Trends in the Well-Being of America's Children & Youth.** 1997. lib. bdg. 251.95 (*0-8490-8244-7*) Gordon Pr.

Trends in the World Aluminum Industry. Sterling Brubaker. LC 67-16035. 274p. reprint ed. pap. 78.10 (*0-317-26024-3*, 2023790) Bks Demand.

Trends in Theoretical Physics, Vol. 1. Ed. by Paul J. Ellis & Y. C. Tang. 432p. (C). 1990. 54.95 (*0-201-50393-X*, Adv Bk Prog) Addison-Wesley.

Trends in Theoretical Physics, Vol. 2. Paul J. Ellis & Y. C. Tang. 352p. (C). 1991. 49.95 (*0-201-52251-9*, Adv Bk Prog) Addison-Wesley.

Trends in Theory & Practice of Nonlinear Differential Equations. V. Lakshmikantham. (Lecture Notes in Pure & Applied Mathematics Ser.: Vol. 90). 592p. 1984. 155.00 (*0-8247-7130-3*) Dekker.

Trends in U. S.-Caribbean Relations. Ed. by Anthony P. Maingot. LC 93-85876. (Annals of the American Academy of Political & Social Science Ser.: Vol. 533). 1994. 28.00 (*0-8039-5588-X*); pap. 18.00 (*0-8039-5589-8*) Am Acad Pol Soc Sci.

***Trends in U. S. Health Care.** 4th ed. American Medical Association Staff. 100p. pap. 34.95 (*0-614-19685-X*, OP190295WE) AMA.

Trends in Urban Library Management: Proceedings of the Urban Library Management Institute Held in October, 1988 at the University of Wisconsin-Milwaukee. Ed. by Mohammed M. Aman et al. LC 89-10285. 180p. 1989. 26.00 (*0-8108-2245-8*) Scarecrow.

Trends in Urbanisation in India. Raj Bala. 1986. 49.50 (*81-7033-012-2*, Pub. by Rawat II) S Asia.

Trends in Vertebrate Morphology: Proceedings of the Second International Symposium on Vertebrate Morphology Vienna, August 25-29, 1986. Ed. by Heinz Splechtna & Helga Hilgers. LC 89-11933. (Progress in Zoology/Fortschritte der Zoologie Ser.: Vol. 35). 647p. 1989. 160.00 (*0-89574-288-8*) G F Verlag.

Trends in Welding Research: Proceedings of the 4th International Conference. 950p. 1995. 136.00 (*0-87170-567-2*, 6448) ASM.

Trends in White Attitudes Toward Negroes. Mildred Schwartz. (Report Ser.: No. 119). 1967. 3.00 (*0-932132-11-1*) Natl Opinion Res.

Trends in World Natural Gas Trade: Papers Presented at a Conference Organised by the Energy Economics Group on 25 October 1989, Including a Paper Presented to the Society of Petroleum Engineers on the Topic of Some Aspects of a Major Hydrocarbon Development. Institute of Petroleum, London Staff. Ed. by T. S. Radford. LC 91-17903. (Illus.). 141p. reprint ed. pap. 40.20 (*0-7837-6848-6*, 2046677) Bks Demand.

Trends in World Social Development: The Social Progress of Nations, 1980-1986. Richard J. Estes. LC 87-36132. 238p. 1988. text ed. 55.00 (*0-275-92613-3*, C2613, Praeger Pubs) Greenwood.

Trends Influence Curriculum. 2nd ed. Ed. by Lutian R. Wootton & John C. Reynolds. 1974. 29.50 (*0-8422-5177-4*) Irvington.

Trends of History in Quran: Sunnat Hai Tarikh Dar Quran. rev. ed. Ayatullah M. Sadr. Tr. by Islamic Seminary Staff from ARA. 224p. (C). reprint ed. pap. 8.00 (*0-941724-56-5*) Islamic Seminary.

Trends of Mental Disease. American Psychopathological Association Staff. Ed. by Gerald N. Grob. LC 78-22547. (Historical Issues in Mental Health Ser.). (Illus.). 1980. reprint ed. lib. bdg. 17.95 (*0-405-11901-1*) Ayer.

Trends of Occupational Mobility among Migrants. Sunanda Pande. 232p. (C). 1986. 31.00 (*81-7033-023-8*, Pub. by Rawat II) S Asia.

Trends of Professional Opportunities in the Liberal Arts College. Merle S. Kuder. LC 74-176940. (Columbia University. Teachers College. Contributions to Education Ser.: No. 717). reprint ed. 37.50 (*0-404-55717-1*) AMS Pr.

Trends of Urbanization in Taiwan, 2 vols. in one. Lung Kwan-Hai. (Asian Folklore & Social Life Monographs: Nos. 39-40). (CHI.). 1972. 17.00 (*0-89986-039-7*) Oriental Bk Store.

***Trends, Risks, & Interventions in Lethal Violence: Proceedings of the Third Annual Spring Symposium of the Homicide Research Working Group.** Ed. by Carolyn Block & Richard Block. (Illus.). 370p. (C). 1997. reprint ed. pap. text ed. 50.00 (*0-7881-3494-9*) DIANE Pub.

Trends Selected & Annotated Bibliographies Analyses, 3 vols., Set. J. Durand-Drouhin & Lili-Marie Szwengrub. LC 80-41523. (Rural Community Studies in Europe). reprint ed. 372.00 (*0-08-032651-X*, Pub. by Pergamon Repr UK) Franklin.

Trends, Techniques & Problems in Theoretical Computer Science. Ed. by A. Kelemenova & J. Kelemen. (Lecture Notes in Computer Science Ser.: Vol. 281). vi, 213p. 1987. 33.00 (*0-387-18535-6*) Spr-Verlag.

Trends Toward the Year 2000 see Recreation Markets: Trends Toward the Year 2000

Trends Transforming South Africa: Insights, Information & Ideas. Ed. by Tony Manning. 188p. (C). 1991. pap. text ed. 26.00 (*0-7021-2682-9*, Pub. by Juta & Co SA) Intl Spec Bk.

Trend's Who's Who in Recycling Worldwide (WIW) Vol. 1: Plastics & Others. rev. ed. Jessica Bonzon. xxxvii, 400p. (C). 1996. 99.00 (*1-889370-00-2*) Trend Assocs.

Trend's Who's Who in Recycling Worldwide (WIW) Vol. 2: Textiles & Others. 5th rev. ed. Jessica Bonzon. xxxvii, 400p. (C). 1996. 99.00 (*1-889370-01-0*) Trend Assocs.

Trend's Who's Who in Recycling Worldwide (WIW) Vol. 3: Glass & Others. rev. ed. Jessica Bonzon. xxxvii, 400p. (C). 1996. 99.00 (*1-889370-02-9*) Trend Assocs.

Trend's Who's Who in Recycling Worldwide (WIW) Vol. 4: Paper & Others. rev. ed. Jessica Bonzon. xxxvii, 400p. (C). 1996. write for info. (*1-889370-03-7*) Trend Assocs.

Trend's Who's Who in Recycling Worldwide (WIW) Vol. 5: Metals & Others. rev. ed. Jessica Bonzon. xxxvii, 400p. (C). 1996. 99.00 (*1-889370-04-5*) Trend Assocs.

Trends 2000: How to Prepare for & Profit from the Changes of the 21st Century. Gerald Celente. LC 96-20082. 352p. 1997. 24.00 (*0-446-51901-4*) Warner Bks.

***Trends 2000: How to Prepare for & Profit from the Changes of the 21st Century.** Gerald Celente. 352p. 1998. pap. 14.99 (*0-446-67331-5*) Warner Bks.

Trendy Traveler. Ann R. Cooper. (Illus.). 140p. (Orig.). 1989. pap. text ed. write for info. (*0-910463-10-7*) Edit Heliodor.

***Trene, King & Autocrat.** A. Gabriella Kolias. 188p. (Orig.). 1997. pap. write for info. (*0-9658524-0-7*) G K K.

Trenes (Trains) J. Cooper. (Spanish Language Books, Set 5: Maquinas de Viaje (Traveling Machines)). (J). 1991. 8.95 (*0-86592-515-1*) Rourke Enter.

Trenfell Castle. large type ed. Helga Moray. 416p. 1989. 25.99 (*0-7089-2016-0*) Ulverscroft.

Trenhaile: Genealogy & History of the Descendants & Ancestors of George Trenhaile (1812-78) & Mary Stephens (Stevens) (1814-78) of England, Who Emigrated to America, 1874, & Settled in Iowa Co., Wis. Fred E. Sawyer. (Illus.). 65p. 1995. reprint ed. pap. 13.00 (*0-8328-4855-7*); reprint ed. lib. bdg. 23.00 (*0-8328-4854-9*) Higginson Bk Co.

Trenhawk. large type ed. Mary Williams. 558p. 1994. 25.99 (*0-7505-0528-1*, Pub. by Magna Print Bks UK) Ulverscroft.

Trent. Mark Dunster. 33p. (Orig.). 1982. pap. 4.00 (*0-89642-091-4*) Linden Pubs.

Trent Affair: A Diplomatic Crisis. Norman B. Ferris. LC 76-28304. 293p. reprint ed. pap. 83.60 (*0-8357-7060-5*, 2033365) Bks Demand.

***Trent Dimas.** Valerie Menard. LC 97-21984. (Real Life Reader Biographies Ser.). (Illus.). 32p. (J). (gr. k-4). 1997. lib. bdg. 15.95 (*1-883845-50-5*) M Lane Pubs.

Trent Frayne's All Stars. Trent Frayne. 288p. 1996. 27.95 (*0-385-25540-3*) Doubleday.

Trent, Museo Provinciale d'arte, Biblioteca Musicale L. Feininger N.S. Ed. by Alexander Silbiger. (Seventeenth-Century Keyboard Music Ser.: Vol. 16). 225p. 1988. text ed. 30.00 (*0-8240-8015-7*) Garland.

Trent-Severn Guide. Larry Wright. 1995. 15.00 (*1-55046-132-X*, Pub. by Boston Mills Pr CN) Genl Dist Srvs.

Trent 1475: Stories of a Ritual Murder Trail. R. Po-Chia Hsia. 1996. pap. 13.00 (*0-300-06872-7*) Yale U Pr.

Trent 1475: Stories of a Ritual Murder Trial. R. Po-Chia Hsia. 192p. (C). 1992. text ed. 30.00 (*0-300-05106-9*) Yale U Pr.

Trente-Sept Sous de Monsieur Montaudouin. Eugene Labiche. 9.95 (*0-686-54256-8*) Fr & Eur.

Trente-Sixieme Dessous. Pierre Daninos. (FRE.). 1990. pap. 10.95 (*0-7859-5492-9*) Fr & Eur.

***Trentepohliales: Cephaleuros, Phycopeltis, & Stomatochroon: Morphology, Taxonomy, & Ecology.** R. H. Thompson & D. E. Wujek. (Illus.). 160p. (C). 1997. 93.00 (*1-886106-83-5*) Science Pubs.

Trenton: Poems. Grace Cavalieri. Ed. by Herman M. Ward. 66p. (Orig.). 1990. pap. 10.00 (*0-9610346-0-2*) Belle Mead Pr.

Trent's Last Case. E. C. Bentley. 1976. lib. bdg. 18.95 (*0-89968-165-4*, Lghtyr Pr) Buccaneer Bks.

***Trent's Last Case.** E. C. Bentley. 4.95 (*0-7867-0770-4*) Carroll & Graf.

Trent's Last Case. E. C. Bentley. 256p. 1991. pap. 4.95 (*0-88184-770-4*) Carroll & Graf.

Trent's Last Case. E. C. Bentley. Ed. by Chris Baldick & David Trotter. (Oxford Popular Fiction Ser.). 288p. 1995. pap. 7.95 (*0-19-282422-8*) OUP.

***Trent's Last Case.** E. C. Bentley. LC 96-53232. (Mystery Classics Ser.). 192p. 1997. reprint ed. pap. text ed. 2.00 (*0-486-29687-3*) Dover.

Trent's Own Case. E. C. Bentley & H. Warner Allen. 324p. 1988. reprint ed. pap. 3.95 (*0-88184-349-0*) Carroll & Graf.

Treponema Pallidum: A Bibliographical Review of the Morphology, Culture & Survival of T. Pallidum & Associated Organisms. (WHO Bulletin Supplement Ser.: Vol. 35). 1966. pap. text ed. 12.00 (*92-4-068351-8*, 1033501) World Health.

***Treponemal Infections.** (Technical Report Ser.: No. 674). 75p. 1982. pap. text ed. 6.00 (*92-4-120674-8*) World Health.

Treponematoses Research: Proceedings of the WHO Scientific Group, Geneva, 1969. WHO Staff. (Technical Report Ser.: No. 455). 91p. 1970. pap. text ed. 7.00 (*92-4-120455-9*, 1100455) World Health.

Trepostomatus Ectoprocta (Bryozoa) from the Lower Chickamauga Group, Wills Valey, Alabama, No. 267 see Bulletins of American Paleontology: Vol. 60

Treppen und Rampen - Staircases see Glossarium Artis, a Specialized & Systematic Dictionary

***Tres Amigos.** Park W. Kerr. 1997. write for info. (*0-688-15553-7*) Morrow.

Tres Bandidos - The Three Robbers. Tomi Ungerer. Tr. by Miguel Azaola. (Illus.). 36p. (SPA.). (J). (gr. 2-4). 1990. pap. write for info. (*84-204-5084-7*) Santillana.

Tres Caras Del Amor. Josh McDowell & Paul Lewis. 96p. 1983. 3.50 (*0-88113-289-6*) Edit Betania.

Tres Cerditos. (Spanish Well Loved Tales Ser.: No. 700-2). (SPA.). (J). (gr. 1). 1990. boxed 3.50 (*0-7214-1408-7*, Ladybrd) Penguin.

Tres Cerditos - Little Book. Addison-Wesley Staff. (Spanish Elementary Ser.). (Illus.). 16p. (SPA.). (J). (gr. k-3). 1989. pap. text ed. 4.50 (*0-201-19710-3*) Addison-Wesley.

Tres Cerditos Big Book. Addison-Wesley Staff. (Spanish Elementary Ser.). (Illus.). 16p. (SPA.). (J). (gr. k-3). 1989. pap. text ed. 31.75 (*0-201-19938-6*) Addison-Wesley.

Tres Chivitos. Patricia McKissack & Fredrick McKissack. LC 86-33450. (Start-off Stories - Spanish Ser.). (Illus.). 32p. (SPA.). (J). (ps-2). 1988. lib. bdg. 14.70 (*0-516-32366-0*) Childrens.

Tres Chivos Testarudos. First Fairy Tales Staff. 1995. pap. text ed. 8.50 (*1-56014-457-2*) Santillana.

Tres Cochinitos. 24p. (SPA.). (J). (ps-3). 1993. pap. 1.95 (*0-307-70099-2*, Golden Pr); pap. 4.50 (*0-307-91598-0*, Golden Pr) Western Pub.

Tres Comedias: Edicion Facsimil (Valencia, 1559) Juan de Timoneda. 172p. (SPA.). 1968. pap. 79.50 (*0-614-00130-7*) Elliots Bks.

Tres Cuentos. 2nd ed. Carlos Garcia-Prada & William E. Wilson. LC 59-4973. (SPA.). (C). 1959. pap. 28.36 (*0-395-04482-0*) HM.

Tres Dramas Romanticos. Jose M. Zorilla et al. LC 73-111116. (Play Anthology Reprint Ser.). 1977. 22.95 (*0-8369-8209-6*) Ayer.

Tres en Busca de Aventuras. Patricia M. St. John. Orig. Title: Three Go Searching. 128p. (SPA.). 1990. mass mkt. 3.99 (*0-8254-1683-3*, Edit Portavoz) Kregel.

Tres en un Arbol - Three up a Tree. James Marshall. Tr. by Ana B. Baro. (Illus.). 48p. (SPA.). (J). (gr. 2-4). 1990. pap. write for info. (*84-204-4637-8*) Santillana.

Tres Farsas Contemporaneas y un Secuestro. Antonio M. Ballesteros. Ed. by Angel R. Maroto & Charles E. Whitehead. (Orig.). (YA). (gr. 10-12). 1980. pap. text ed. 5.95 (*0-88334-125-5*) Longman.

Tres Goldaras En la Poesia Del Siglo XX. Jose L. Goldaras et al. LC 80-7043. (Coleccion Espejo de Paciencia). (Illus.). 143p. (Orig.). (SPA.). 1981. pap. 7.95 (*0-89729-280-4*) Ediciones.

Tres-haut. Maurice Blanchot. (Imaginaire Ser.). (FRE.). pap. 13.95 (*2-07-071447-0*) Schoenhof.

Tres Lent Hommage a Messiaen: For Cello & Piano. J. Tower. 8p. 1995. pap. 7.50 (*0-7935-3856-4*, 50482270) H Leonard.

Tres Llaves del Exito. Betty W. Pena. Tr. by Ana M. Montoya. (Illus.). 64p. 1992. pap. text ed. 6.75 (*1-882462-00-9*) Surpass Your Limit.

***Tres Meses en la Escuela de Juan.** Justo L. Goonzalez. (SPA.). 1997. pap. 5.95 (*0-687-02208-8*) Abingdon.

***Tres Meses en la Escuela de la Prision.** Justo L. Gonzalez. (SPA.). 1997. pap. 5.95 (*0-687-02718-7*) Abingdon.

***Tres Meses en la Escuela de Mateo.** Justo L. Gonzalez. 176p. (SPA.). 1996. pap. 5.95 (*0-687-02176-6*) Abingdon.

***Tres Meses en la Escuela de Patmos.** Justo L. Gonzalez. (SPA.). 1997. pap. 5.95 (*0-687-03328-4*) Abingdon.

***Tres Meses en la Escuela del Espiritu.** Justo L. Gonzalez. 176p. (SPA.). 1997. pap. 5.95 (*0-687-02568-0*) Abingdon.

Tres Novelas Ejemplares. Manuel Vazquez Montalban. (Nueva Austral Ser.: No. 48). (SPA.). 1991. pap. text ed. 24.95 (*84-239-1848-3*) Elliots Bks.

Tres Novelas Ejemplares y Prologo. Unamuno. 141p. (SPA.). 1972. 13.95 (*0-8288-7015-2*) Fr & Eur.

Tres Novelas Ejemplares y un Prologo. Miguel De Unamuno. Ed. by Ciriaco Moron Arroyo. (Nueva Austral Ser.: Vol. 141). (SPA.). 1991. pap. text ed. 9.95 (*84-239-1941-2*) Elliots Bks.

Tres Novelas Ejemplares y un Prologo. Miguel De Unamuno. (SPA.). 9.95 (*0-8288-2580-7*) Fr & Eur.

Tres Novelas Ejemplares y un Prologo. 18th ed. Miguel De Unamuno. 176p. (SPA.). 1990. pap. 8.95 (*0-7859-5005-2*) Fr & Eur.

Tres Osos. 24p. (SPA.). (J). (ps-3). 1993. pap. 1.95 (*0-307-70050-X*, Golden Pr) Western Pub.

Tres Osos. 2nd ed. Hanna Hutchinson. (Interlingo Ser.). Orig. Title: Three Bears. (Illus.). 24p. (Orig.). (SPA.). (J). (gr. 1-2). 1995. reprint ed. pap. 2.95 (*0-922852-06-5*) Another Lang Pr.

Tres Osos, Tres Tamanos, Vol. 4: Pasitos Spanish Language Development Books. Darlyne F. Schott. (Pasitos Hacia la Lectura Ser.). 25p. (J). (gr. k-1). 1990. pap. text ed. 11.00 (*1-56537-053-8*) D F Schott Educ.

Tres Pasos Adelante, Dos Para Atras. Charles R. Swindoll. 176p. 1983. 4.95 (*0-88113-363-9*) Edit Betania.

Tres Pequenos Jabalies - The Three Little Javelinas. Susan Lowell. (Illus.). 32p. (ENG & SPA.). (J). (ps up). 1996. lib. bdg. 14.95 (*0-87358-661-1*) Northland AZ.

Tres Perritos: Big Book. Angela F. Aymerich. (Que Maravilla! Ser.). (Illus.). 16p. (Orig.). (SPA.). (J). (gr. 1-3). 1991. pap. text ed. 29.95 (*1-56334-021-6*) Hampton-Brown.

Tres Perritos: Small Book. Angela F. Aymerich. (Que Maravilla! Ser.). (Illus.). 16p. (Orig.). (SPA.). (J). (gr. 1-3). 1991. pap. text ed. 6.00 (*1-56334-035-6*) Hampton-Brown.

Tres Riches Heures: The Medieval Seasons. Millard Meiss & Longnon. 1995. 10.95 (*0-8076-1399-1*) Braziller.

Tres Riches Heures of Jean, Duke of Berry. Millard Meiss. LC 73-90120. (Illus.). 290p. 1969. boxed 100.00 (*0-8076-0512-3*) Braziller.

Tres Riches Heures of Jean, Duke of Berry. Millard Meiss. LC 73-90120. (Illus.). 290p. 1989. pap. 24.95 (*0-8076-1220-0*) Braziller.

Tres Semillas Para una Mejor Alimentacion: Un Manual De Agricultura Familiar. Mary A. Wooliever. (Illus.). 171p. (SPA.). 1990. spiral bd. 25.00 (*0-932857-12-4*) Ag Access.

Tres Sombreros de Copa. Miguel Mihura. Ed. by Antonio Tordera. (Nueva Austral Ser.: Vol. 63). (SPA.). 1991. pap. text ed. 11.95 (*84-239-1863-7*) Elliots Bks.

Tres Sombreros de Copa. 15th ed. Miguel Mihura. 136p. (SPA.). 1991. pap. 11.95 (*0-7859-5135-0*) Fr & Eur.

Tres Sombreros de Copa - Maribel y la Extrana Familia. 11th ed. Miguel Mihura. 206p. (SPA.). 1988. pap. 10.95 (*0-7859-5137-7*) Fr & Eur.

Tres Ursi. Hanna Hutchinson. Tr. by LeaAnn A. Osburn. (Interlingo Ser.). Orig. Title: Three Bears. (Illus.). 24p. (Orig.). (LAT.). (J). (gr. 1-2). 1995. pap. 2.95 (*0-922852-38-3*) Another Lang Pr.

***Tres Vidas Paralelas: Biografias de Francisco Arango y Parreno, Felix Varela y Jose Antonio Saco.** Nicasio S. Sainz. (SPA.). pap. 13.00 (*0-89729-049-6*) Ediciones.

Tres Visiones Del Amor en la Obra de Jose Marti. Louis Pujol. LC 88-83427. (Coleccion Polymita). 87p. (SPA.). 1989. pap. 9.95 (*0-89729-517-X*) Ediciones.

Trescientos Millones y Tu, Tomo 1. 7th ed. Antonio Garcia del Toro. 244p. (SPA.). (C). 1992. reprint ed. pap. text ed. 11.95 (*1-56328-024-8*) Edit Plaza Mayor.

Trescientos Millones y Tu, Vol. 2: Manual para el Estudio del Espanol como Lengua Vernacula. 6th ed. Antonio Garcia del Toro et al. 244p. (SPA.). (C). 1991. reprint ed. pap. text ed. 11.95 (*1-56328-019-1*) Edit Plaza Mayor.

Tresor d'Arlatan. Anatole France. 160p. (FRE.). 1987. 11.95 (*0-7859-1207-X*, 203870242X) Fr & Eur.

Tresor de Felibridge: Dictionnaire Provencal-Francais, 2 vols. Frederic Mistral. 2375p. (FRE.). Set. 250.00 (*0-686-56736-6*, M-6414) Fr & Eur.

Tresor de la Francaise: Dictionnaire du XIXe et du XXe Siecles (1789-1960), 4 vols. Centre de Recherche Pour un Tresor de la Langue Francaise Staff. Set. 175.00 (*0-685-36650-2*) Fr & Eur.

***Tresor de Livres Rares et Precieux: Ou Nouveau Dictionnaire Bibliographique, 4 vols.** Johann G. Graesse. Incl. Vol. 4. Tresor de Livres Rares et Precieux. (FRE.). 500p. 1995. reprint ed. Not sold separately (*1-888262-99-0*); Vol. 3. Tresor de Livres Rares et Precieux. (FRE.). 543p. 1995. reprint ed. Not sold separately (*1-888262-98-2*); Vol. 2. Tresor de Livres Rares et Precieux. (FRE.). 704p. 1995. reprint ed. Not sold separately (*0-614-21979-5*); Vol. 1. Tresor de Livres Rares et Precieux. (FRE.). 648p. 1995. reprint ed. Not sold separately (*1-888262-96-6*); 350.00 (*0-614-22198-6*) Martino Pubng.

Tresor de Livres Rares et Precieux see Tresor de Livres Rares et Precieux: Ou Nouveau Dictionnaire Bibliographique

***Tresor de Mon Pere.** Marie-Danielle Croteau. (Novels in the Premier Roman Ser.). 64p. (FRE.). (J). (gr. 2-5). 1996. pap. 7.95 (*2-89021-246-7*, Pub. by Les Editions CN) Firefly Bks Ltd.

Tresor De Rackham le Rouge. Herge. (Illus.). 62p. (FRE.). (J). (gr. 7-9). 19.95 (*0-8288-5003-8*) Fr & Eur.

Tresor des Humbles. Maurice Maeterlinck. 180p. (FRE.). 1986. pap. 13.95 (*0-7859-4662-4*) Fr & Eur.

Tresor des Livres Rares et Precieux ou Nouveau Dictionnaire Bibliographique, 8 vols. fac. ed. Jean-Georges Graesse. (FRE.). 1993. 1,495.00 (*0-7859-7714-7*, 2051013004) Fr & Eur.

Tresor des pianistes, 23 vols. Ed. by Aristide Farrenc & Louise Farrenc. LC 77-8873. (Music Reprint Ser.). (Illus.). 1978. reprint ed. Set. lib. bdg. 950.00 (*0-306-77380-5*) Da Capo.

Tresor d'Orphee. Antoine Francisque. 1967. reprint ed. pap. 15.00 (*0-8450-0104-3*) Broude.

Tresors a Prendre. Violette Leduc. (FRE.). 1978. pap. 10.95 (*0-7859-4101-0*) Fr & Eur.

Tresors de la Mer Rouge. Romain Gary. pap. 9.50 (*0-685-34128-3*) Fr & Eur.

Tresors de la Renaissance, la Sculpture en Italie et en France. Francois Gebelin. (Merveille de L'Art Collection). (Illus.). 186p. (FRE.). 1950. lib. bdg. 12.95 (*0-8288-3949-2*) Fr & Eur.

Tresors de l'Espagne. Alexandre Cirici-Pellicer. (Tresors du Monde Ser.). (Illus.). 242p. (FRE.). 1965. lib. bdg. 95.00 (*0-8288-3995-6*) Fr & Eur.

Tresors de Turque. Akurgal, Mango & Ettinghausen Staff. 252p. (FRE.). 1966. 95.00 (*0-8288-4002-4*) Fr & Eur.

Tresors des Musees de Province, 5 tomes. Set. 209.95 (*0-685-35924-7*) Fr & Eur.

Trespass - Summary Procedure for Possession of Land. Peter Birts & Alan Willis. 155p. 1987. pap. 50.00 (*0-406-10481-6*, U.K.) MICHIE.

Trespass of the Sign: Deconstruction, Theology & Philosophy. Kevin Hart. 304p. (C). 1991. pap. 19.95 (*0-521-42382-1*) Cambridge U Pr.

Trespass to Try Title. Harold F. Thurow. 210p. 1994. ring bd. 115.00 (*0-614-05986-0*) MICHIE.

Trespass to Try Title, 1988-1990. Harold F. Thurow. 230p. 1990. ring bd. 115.00 (*0-409-25336-7*) MICHIE.

Trespass to Try Title, 1988-1990. Harold F. Thurow. 1994. suppl. ed., ring bd. 55.00 (*0-685-70862-4*) MICHIE.

Trespasser. D. H. Lawrence. Ed. by Elizabeth Mansfield. LC 80-41663. (Cambridge Edition of the Works of D. H. Lawrence). 350p. 1982. pap. text ed. 29.95 (*0-521-29424-X*) Cambridge U Pr.

Trespasser. D. H. Lawrence. (Classics Ser.). 224p. 1990. mass mkt. 6.95 (*0-14-018210-1*, Penguin Classics) Viking Penguin.

Trespasser. D. H. Lawrence. Ed. by Elizabeth Mansfield. 288p. 1995. pap. 9.95 (*0-14-018800-2*, Penguin Classics) Viking Penguin.

Trespasser. Gilbert Parker. 1976. lib. bdg. 13.85 (*0-89968-083-6*, Lghtyr Pr) Buccaneer Bks.

Trespasser. R. T. Smith. LC 96-24788. 72p. (C). 1996. text ed. 16.95 (*0-8071-2052-9*) La State U Pr.

Trespasser. R. T. Smith. LC 95-24788. (C). 1996. pap. 9.95 (*0-8071-2053-7*) La State U Pr.

Trespasser. D. H. Lawrence. 350p. 1989. reprint ed. lib. bdg. 29.95 (*0-89966-645-0*) Buccaneer Bks.

Trespasser. D. H. Lawrence. 1988. reprint ed. lib. bdg. 49.00 (*0-7812-0179-9*) Rprt Serv.

Trespasser. D. H. Lawrence. 1971. reprint ed. 49.00 (*0-403-01067-5*) Scholarly.

Trespassers. Zilpha K. Snyder. LC 93-31168. 208p. (J). 1995. 15.95 (*0-385-31055-2*) Delacorte.

Trespassers. Zilpha K. Snyder. 208p. (J). 1996. pap. 3.99 (*0-440-41277-3*) Dell.

***Trespassers.** Meredith S. Willis. (Illus.). 320p. (Orig.). 1997. reprint ed. pap. 10.00 (*0-9654043-2-3*, 500-1000) Hamilton Stone.

Trespassers on the Roof of the World: The Secret Exploration of Tibet. Peter Hopkirk. 288p. 1995. reprint ed. pap. 14.00 (*1-56836-050-9*) Kodansha.

Trespasses. Caroline Bridgwood. 1989. 18.95 (*0-517-57468-3*, Crown) Crown Pub Group.

Trespasses. Howard Swindle. 1997. pap. 12.95 (*0-14-024971-0*) Viking Penguin.

Trespasses. Martin Turner. 96p. (Orig.). 1992. pap. 10.95 (*0-571-16723-3*) Faber & Faber.

Trespasses: Portrait of a Serial Rapist. Howard Swindle. LC 95-21276. 320p. 1996. pap. 22.95 (*0-670-85879-X*, Viking) Viking Penguin.

***Trespassing.** John H. Mitchell. 1998. write for info. (*0-201-44214-0*) Addison-Wesley.

***Trespassing.** Sam Pickering. 14.95 (*1-875560-30-0*, Pub. by Univ of West Aust Pr AT) Intl Spec Bk.

Trespassing. Samuel F. Pickering, Jr. LC 93-38325. 260p. (C). 1994. 24.00 (*0-87451-640-4*) U Pr of New Eng.

***Trespassing: My Sojourn in the Halls of Privilege.** Gwendolyn M. Parker. LC 97-19951. 1997. 23.00 (*0-395-82297-1*) HM.

Trespassing in Eden. Walter D. Wagoner. 122p. (Orig.). 1995. pap. 11.75 (*1-881907-24-4*) Two Bytes Pub.

Trespassing Innocence. Virginia Cerenio. 72p. 1989. 8.95 (*0-9609630-5-7*) Kearny St Wkshop.

Trespassing Stoplights & Attitudes. Mary McGrath. (Illus.). 44p. (Orig.). 1980. pap. 5.00 (*0-930012-43-7*) J Mudfoot.

Tress, Arthur: Talisman. Marco Livingstone. (Illus.). 156p. (C). 1986. pap. 48.00 (*0-905836-55-3*, Pub. by Museum Modern Art UK) St Mut.

Trestoulas. Henri Bosco. 320p. (FRE.). 1979. pap. 11.95 (*0-7859-1903-1*, 2070371468) Fr & Eur.

Tretii Rim. Georgii Ivanov. Ed. by Vadim Kreid. LC 87-4114. 380p. (RUS.). 1987. pap. 14.00 (*0-938920-77-4*) Hermitage.

Tretinoin - Actions, Harmful Reactions, & Variations in Therapy: Index of New Information with Authors, Subjects, & References. rev. ed. American Health Research Institute Staff. LC 96-3122. 151p. 1996. 47.50 (*0-7883-1046-1*); pap. 44.50 (*0-7883-1047-X*) ABBE Pubs Assn.

Tretise of Miraclis Pleyinge. Ed. by Clifford Davidson. (Early Drama, Art & Music Monograph: Vol. 19). 1993. pap. 15.00 (*1-879288-32-X*); boxed 36.00 (*1-879288-31-1*) Medieval Inst.

Tretyakov Art Gallery Guide. V. Volodarsky. 184p. (C). 1988. 50.00 (*0-569-12579-0*, Pub. by Collets) St Mut.

Tretyakov Gallery, Moscow: A Panorama of Russian & Soviet Art, Painting, Graphic Art, Sculpture. Natalia L. Adaskina. (Illus.). 376p. 1983. 308.00 (*0-317-57473-6*) St Mut.

Tretyse of Loue. Ed. by J. H. Fisher. (EETS Original Ser.: No. 223). 1970. reprint ed. 30.00 (*0-19-722223-4*, Pub. by EETS UK) Boydell & Brewer.

Treuhandanstalt: The Impossible Challenge. Ed. by Wolfram Fischer et al. LC 94-39186. 1997. write for info. (*3-05-002746-0*, VCH) Wiley.

***Treupflichten bei der Stimmrechtsausubung & Eigenhaftung des Stimmrechtsvertreters.** Tom Beckerhoff. 240p. (GER.). 1996. 44.95 (*3-631-30915-5*) P Lang Pubng.

Trevallion. Gloria Cook. 512p. 1995. pap. 10.95 (*0-7472-4708-0*, Pub. by Headline UK) Trafalgar.

Trevarton Inheritance. Malcolm Macdonald. LC 96-20035. 400p. 1996. 24.95 (*0-312-14748-1*) St Martin.

Trevayne. Robert Ludlum. 480p. 1992. mass mkt. 7.50 (*0-553-28179-8*) Bantam.

Treve. Albert P. Terhune. (J). 1992. reprint ed. lib. bdg. 24.95 (*0-89966-996-4*) Buccaneer Bks.

Trever Gallery: A Public Hanging. John Trever. 192p. 1992. 19.95 (*0-9635314-0-9*); pap. 12.95 (*0-9635314-1-7*) Jrnl Pub NM.

Treves: A Mystery Unravelled. Stephen Trombley. 224p. 1989. 47.50 (*0-415-03423-X*) Routledge.

Trevethick's Occupational Health Hazards: A Practical Industrial Guide. 2nd ed. Peter B. Cook. 181p. 1995. pap. 65.00 (*0-7506-1794-2*) Buttrwrth-Heinemann.

Trevi Fountain. John A. Pinto. LC 85-2480. 376p. 1986. 45.00 (*0-300-03335-4*) Yale U Pr.

Trevithick. large type ed. Pamela Hill. (Linford Romance Library). 320p. 1992. pap. 15.99 (*0-7089-7275-6*, Linford) Ulverscroft.

Trevor: The Saga of the Red Boots. McClellan Falk. Ed. by Margaret Tropp. (Illus.). 64p. (Orig.). 1994. pap. 8.99 (*0-9641531-0-6*) M Falk.

Trevor & Tiffany, the Tyrannosaurus Twins, Learn to Stop Bullying: A Group Activities Manual to Teach K-6 Children How to Replace Aggressive Behavior with Assertive Behavior, 6 vols., Set. Teresa M. Schmidt. LC 96-1684. (Building Trust, Making Friends Ser.: Vol. 6). (Illus.). 235p. (Orig.). 1996. teacher ed. 59.95 (*1-56246-117-6*, P559) Johnsn Inst.

Trevor Griffiths Plays 1: Occupations; The Party Comedians; & Real Dreams. Trevor Griffiths. 256p. (Orig.). 1996. pap. text ed. 13.95 (*0-571-17742-5*) Faber & Faber.

Trevor Howard. Michael Munn. LC 90-41123. (Illus.). 196p. 1990. 19.95 (*0-8128-4006-2*, Scrbrough Hse) Madison Bks UPA.

Trevor Howard: A Gentleman & a Player. Vivienne Knight. (Illus.). 288p. 1987. 17.95 (*0-8253-0430-X*) Beaufort Bks NY.

***Trevor Southey: Reconciliation.** Trevor Southey. LC 97-16889. 1997. write for info. (*1-56085-091-4*) Signature Bks.

Trevor, the Traveling Tree. large type ed. Gail E. Lucas. LC 96-2053. (Illus.). 32p. (J). (ps-3). 1997. 15.95 (*1-887813-24-1*) Cucumber Island.

Trevor's Red Spots: Chicken Pox Time. Tedi T. Wixom. (Illus.). 32p. (Orig.). (J). (ps-8). 1996. pap. 5.95 (*1-885227-46-9*) TNT Bks.

***Trevor's Story: Growing up Biracial.** Bethany Kandel. LC 96-44523. (Illus.). (J). 1997. write for info. (*0-8225-2583-6*) Lerner Group.

Trevose Head to Bull Point. Wilson Ltd. Staff & Imray L. Norie. (C). 1986. 60.00 (*0-685-40433-1*, Pub. by Imray Laurie Norie & Wilson UK) St Mut.

Trewe Mirrour of Glase Wherin We Maye Beholde the Wofull State of Thys Our Realme of Englande. Laurence Saunders. LC 74-28884. (English Experience Ser.: No. 761). 1975. reprint ed. 15.00 (*90-221-0761-2*) Walter J Johnson.

Trex. Mark Dunster. 24p. (Orig.). 1994. pap. 5.00 (*0-89642-235-6*) Linden Pubs.

Trey-Beaux. Lanier DeVours. Ed. by Linda Cowan. 215p. (Orig.). 1990. pap. 4.95 (*0-9624545-0-8*) Lanier-DeVours.

***Tri-Allate Health & Safety Guide.** (Health & Safety Guides Ser.: No. 89). 20p. 1994. pap. text ed. 5.00 (*92-4-151089-7*, 1860089) World Health.

Tri & Tetra-hydric Alcohols, Their Oxidation Products & Derivatives see Rodd's Chemistry of Carbon Compounds

Tri-Ang Railways, 1950-1965. Pat Hammond. (Illus.). 432p. 1993. 75.00 (*0-904568-57-1*) Pincushion Pr.

Tri Bros. Sadie T. Pitts. (J). 1994. 7.95 (*0-533-10929-9*) Vantage.

Tri-Chevy Red Book. Peter C. Sessler. (Red Book). (Illus.). 96p. 1992. pap. 10.95 (*0-87938-625-8*) Motorbooks Intl.

Tri-Cities. San Antonio Cartographers Staff. 1996. 2.95 (*0-671-56295-9*) Macmillan.

Tri-Color Diet: A Miracle Breakthrough in Diet & Nutrition for a Longer, Healthier Life. Martin Katahn. 240p. 1996. 23.00 (*0-393-03920-X*) Norton.

Tri-Hamlets-Port Crescent, Gettysburg & Joyce see Fish Tales of Port Angeles

Tri-Jets. Robbie Shaw. (Illus.). 128p. 1996. pap. 18.95 (*1-85532-592-6*, Pub. by Osprey Pubng Ltd UK) Motorbooks Intl.

Tri-Linear Edition of Lazarillo de Tormes of 1554, Burgos, Alcala de Henares, Amberes. Ed. by J. V. Ricapito. xviii, 82p. 1987. 12.50 (*0-942260-91-0*) Hispanic Seminary.

Tri Log: Diary & Guide for the Triathlete & Duathlete. Tim Houts & Jan Bass. (SportsLog Ser.). (Illus.). 176p. 1995. reprint ed. ring bd. 12.95 (*1-57028-054-1*) Masters Pr IN.

Tri-n-butyl Phosphate. (Environmental Health Criteria Ser.: No. 112). 80p. (ENG, FRE & SPA.). 1990. pap. text ed. 19.00 (*92-4-157112-8*, 1160112) World Health.

Tri-Nim: The Game for Compleat Strategists. Bruce Hicks & Hervey Hicks. 1969. 10.00 (*0-911624-35-X*) Wffn Proof.

Tri Star Tyrants: America's Crooked Sheriffs. Martin D. Yant. 300p. (Orig.). 1995. pap. write for info. (*0-9642780-1-4*) Public Eye Pubns.

Tri-State Tornado: The Story of America's Greatest Tornado Disaster. Peter S. Felknor. LC 91-45860. (Illus.). 150p. 1992. pap. 17.95 (*0-8138-0623-2*) Iowa St U Pr.

***Tri Timeshare Vacation Ownership Resort Directory: 1997-1998 Edition.** 100p. (Orig.). 1997. pap. 12.95 (*1-888176-11-3*) TRI Pubng.

TRI Timeshare Vacation Ownership Resort Directory 1995-1996 Edition. Mario A. Collura & Viccie Mac. 81p. (Orig.). 1995. pap. 12.95 (*1-888176-10-5*) TRI Pubng.

An Asterisk (*) at the beginning of an entry indicates that the title is appearing in BIP for the first time.

Tri Ursoj. Hanna Hutchinson. Tr. by David Crowell. (Interlingo Ser.). Orig. Title: The Three Bears. (Illus.). 24p. (Orig.). (ESP.). (J). (gr. 1-2). 1995. pap. 2.95 (*0-922852-40-5*) Another Lang Pr.

Tri-Via Sermons: For Lenten Reflection & Renewal. Robert R. Gillogly. 130p. (Orig.). 1993. pap. 5.00 (*0-9634870-2-7*) Asterisk Pubns.

Tri-X Chronicles. Bil Paul. LC 73-86842. (Illus.). 1972. pap. 3.45 (*0-9600650-0-8*) Alchemist-Light.

Triad. Derek Lambert. 207p. 1991. 18.95 (*0-8027-1176-6*) Walker & Co.

Triad: The Evolution of Treatment for Chemical Dependency. Cynthia Downing. 1989. pap. 6.50 (*0-8309-0543-X*) Herald Hse.

Triad Cards: Navigational Tools for the Dimension of Meaning. Stephen I. McIntosh. (Illus.). 130p. 1996. pap. 29.95 (*0-9647645-8-X*) Now & Zen.

Triad Guide: A Guide to Touring & Dining in the Triad. Blair Gaines et al. 160p. (Orig.). 1992. pap. 9.95 (*0-9633889-0-8*) Radio Sta WGLD.

Triad Hauntings: Ghost Stories from Winston-Salem, Greensboro, High Point, & Surrounding Areas. Burt Calloway & Jennifer FitzSimons. LC 90-83941. (Illus.). 96p. (Orig.). 1990. pap. 5.95 (*1-878177-00-1*) Bandit Bks.

***Triad Interlock: Strata Art Quilt.** Marilyn Doheny. Ed. & Illus. by Chuck Eng. 12p. (Orig.). 1991. pap. 10.95 (*0-945169-08-6*) Doheny Pubns.

Triad of Evil: Politics, Plagues, Murder. Bill Uselton. 100p. (Orig.). 1991. pap. 5.95 (*1-879366-16-9*) Hearthstone OK.

Triad of Knives. Tom Cooper. 384p. 1986. mass mkt. 3.50 (*0-373-97020-X*) Harlequin Bks.

Triad Optical Illusions & How to Design Them. Harry Turner. LC 77-81212. (Illus.). 1977. pap. 3.95 (*0-486-23549-1*) Dover.

Triad Power: The Coming Shape of Global Competition. Kenichi Ohmae. LC 84-26068. 192p. (C). 1985. 35.00 (*0-02-923470-0*, Free Press) Free Pr.

Triad Reader. Ed. by Joseph S. Renzulli & Sally M. Reis. 218p. 1986. pap. 22.95 (*0-936386-35-5*) Creative Learning.

Triad System. Walter G. Allan. Ed. by Silent Partners, Inc. Staff. (Illus.). 21p. (Orig.). 1987. 139.95 incl. disk (*0-9619483-0-2*) W G Allan.

Triad Worlds. F. M. Busby. 384p. (Orig.). 1996. mass mkt. 5.99 (*0-380-78468-8*, AvoNova) Avon.

Triadic Archetype in Keats' Poetry. Pepper Worthington. (Illus.). 232p. (Orig.). 1992. pap. 14.95 (*1-880994-01-1*) Mt Olive Coll Pr.

Triadic Avenues of India's Cultural Prospects: Philosophy, Physics & Politics. Anil K. Sarkar. (C). 1995. 30.00 (*81-7003-177-X*, Pub. by S Asia Pubns II) S Asia.

Triadic Avenues of India's Cultural Prospects: Philosophy, Physics, & Politics. Anil K. Sarkar. 324p. 1995. reprint ed. pap. 92.40 (*0-608-01606-3*, AU00478) Bks Demand.

Triadic Heart of Siva: Kaula Tantricism of Abhinavagupta in the Non-Dual Shaivism of Kashmir. Paul E. Muller-Ortega. LC 87-30953. (SUNY Series in the Shaiva Traditions of Kashmir). 330p. 1988. pap. text ed. 17.95 (*0-88706-787-5*) State U NY Pr.

Triadic Heart of Siva: Kaula Tantricism of Abhinavagupta in the Non-Dual Shaivism of Kashmir. Paul E. Muller-Ortega. LC 87-30953. (SUNY Series in the Shaiva Traditions of Kashmir). 330p. 1988. text ed. 51.50 (*0-88706-786-7*) State U NY Pr.

Triadic Mysticism. Paul E. Murphy. 1986. 23.00 (*0-685-17541-3*, Pub. by Motilal Banarsidass II) S Asia.

Triads: The Wisdom of the Welsh Witches. Rhuddlwm Gawr. LC 85-73755. (Illus.). 140p. (Orig.). (J). 1989. reprint ed. 14.95 (*0-931760-45-3*, CP 10123); reprint ed. pap. 10.95 (*0-931760-23-2*) Camelot GA.

Triads & Trinity. J. Gwyn Griffiths. 376p. 1996. 85.00 (*0-7083-1281-0*, Pub. by Univ Wales Pr UK) Paul & Co Pubs.

***Triads in the Veda.** J. Gonda. (Verhandelingen der Koninklijke Nederlandse Akademie van Wetenschappen, Afd. Letterkunde, Nieuwe Reeks Ser.: No. 91). 246p. 1976. pap. text ed. 50.00 (*0-7204-8310-7*) Elsevier.

Triads of Ireland. Ed. by Kuno Meyer. LC 78-72688. (Royal Irish Academy. Todd Lecture Ser.: Vol. 13). reprint ed. 27.50 (*0-404-60573-7*) AMS Pr.

Triage: Meeting the Challenge. 2nd rev. ed. (Orig.). 1997. 43.00 (*0-935890-13-0*) Emerg Nurses IL. This manual provides a comprehensive review of the important aspects of triage including types of systems, personnel requirements, the triage process, implementation, evaluation, legal considerations, environment & space planning, & detailed appendices including sample policy & procedures, triage nurses' job descriptions, sample documentation records, triage orientation plan, & ENA position statements on Staffing & Productivity in the Emergency Care Setting, Telephone Advice, Violence in the Emergency Care Setting & Access to Health Care. The manual provides the information needed to implement a triage problem in the emergency department based on the needs of the individual institution & its resources. For complete order information, contact: Emergency Nurses Association, 216 Higgins Road, Park Ridge, IL 60068, 800-243-8362. Price: $43.** ***Publisher Provided Annotation.

***Triage for Failing States.** 44p. 1994. pap. text ed. 30.00 (*1-57979-166-2*) BPI Info Servs.

Triage for Failing States. Edward Marks & William Lewis. 52p. (Orig.). (C). 1994. pap. text ed. 30.00 (*0-7881-1192-2*) DIANE Pub.

Triage in Emergency Practice. Gail Handysides. 400p. (C). (gr. 13). 1995. pap. text ed. 34.95 (*0-8016-7892-7*) Mosby Yr Bk.

Triage Spanish: Basic Conversation for Health Professionals. Irwin Stern. LC 93-86874. x, 149p. (SPA.). 1994. pap. text ed. 19.95 incl. audio (*0-9638926-0-6*) Span-Text Bks.

Trial. Parnell Hall. 320p. 1996. 21.95 (*0-89296-570-3*) Mysterious Pr.

Trial. Parnell Hall. 288p. 1997. mass mkt. 5.99 (*0-446-40396-2*, Mysterious Paperbk) Warner Bks.

Trial. Charles E. Harman. (Illus.). 721p. (Orig.). 1995. pap. 29.50 (*0-9649391-0-X*) Old Ct Pr.

Trial. Clifford Irving. 384p. 1991. mass mkt. 5.99 (*0-440-21017-8*) Dell.

Trial. Franz Kafka. 1992. 17.00 (*0-679-40994-7*, Everymans Lib) Knopf.

***Trial.** Franz Kafka. Date not set. lib. bdg. 24.95 (*0-8488-1392-8*) Amereon Ltd.

Trial. Franz Kafka. 288p. 1995. pap. 11.00 (*0-8052-1040-7*) Schocken.

***Trial.** Franz Kafka. 1997. pap. write for info. (*0-8052-0999-9*) Schocken.

Trial. Judy McGorray. 67p. 1995. pap. text ed. write for info. (*1-888200-02-2*) JayMac Commun.

Trial. Charlotte M. Yonge. (Pocket Classics Ser.). 384p. 1996. pap. 12.95 (*0-7509-1117-4*, Pub. by Sutton Pubng UK) Bks Intl VA.

Trial. rev. ed. Franz Kafka. 1937. 16.95 (*0-394-44955-X*) Knopf.

Trial. Lindsay P. Dew. LC 84-12711. 237p. 1994. reprint ed. pap. 9.95 (*0-87579-157-3*) Deseret Bk.

Trial. Franz Kafka. 179p. 1983. reprint ed. lib. bdg. 23.95 (*0-89966-453-9*) Buccaneer Bks.

Trial: A Procedural Description & Case Study. Howard Myers & Jan Pudlow. Ed. by Hannan. 234p. (C). 1991. pap. text ed. 30.00 (*0-314-82441-3*) West Pub.

Trial: Ordeal of the U. S. S. Enterprise, 14 January 1969. Michael J. Carlin. (Illus.). 256p. Date not set. 29.95 (*0-9647533-0-8*) Tuscarora Pr.

***Trial: Strategy & Psychology.** John N. Iannuzzi. 400p. 59.95 (*0-13-953670-1*) P-H.

Trial: Theories, Tactics, Techniques. John O. Sonsteng. (American Casebook Ser.). 711p. 1991. reprint ed. pap. text ed. 30.50 (*0-314-71601-7*) West Pub.

Trial Advocacy. Marilyn J. Berger. 1989. 48.00 (*0-316-09165-0*) Little.

Trial Advocacy. 2nd ed. James W. Jeans. 587p. 1993. pap. 30.00 (*0-314-01904-9*) West Pub.

Trial Advocacy: A Systematic Approach. Leonard Packel & Delores B. Spina. LC 84-70166. 207p. 1995. reprint ed. pap. text ed. 35.00 (*0-8318-0453-X*, B548) Am Law Inst.

Trial Advocacy: Inferences, Arguments & Techniques, Teacher's Manual to Accompany. Albert J. Moore et al. 318p. 1995. teacher ed. write for info. (*0-314-07879-7*) West Pub.

Trial Advocacy: Inferences, Arguments & Trial Techniques. Albert J. Moore et al. LC 95-37257. (American Casebook Ser.). 330p. 1995. pap. text ed. 24.50 (*0-314-06530-X*) West Pub.

Trial Advocacy in a Nutshell. 2nd ed. Paul Bergman. (Nutshell Ser.). 354p. 1991. reprint ed. pap. text ed. 16.00 (*0-314-66493-9*) West Pub.

Trial Advocate Quarterly: 1981-1996, 15 vols. Bound Set. 600.00 (*0-8377-9164-2*) Rothman.

Trial after Triumph: East Asia after the Cold War. W. E. Odom. 151p. (Orig.) (C). 1992. pap. text ed. 12.95 (*1-55813-042-X*) Hudson Instit IN.

Trial & Death of Jesus. Haim Cohn. 1977. 19.95 (*0-87068-443-4*); 19.95 (*0-87068-432-9*) Ktav.

***Trial & Death of Socrates.** 213p. 1972. 17.95 (*0-8369-6891-3*) Ayer.

Trial & Death of Socrates. Plato. Tr. by G. M. Grube from GRE. LC 75-33058. (HPC Classics Ser.). 64p. (Orig.). (C). 1980. pap. 3.95 (*0-915144-15-8*) Hackett Pub.

Trial & Death of Socrates: Four Dialogues. Plato. (Thrift Editions Ser.). 128p. 1992. reprint ed. pap. 1.00 (*0-486-27066-1*) Dover.

Trial & Error. Don Lane. 325p. (C). 1990. 90.00 (*0-86439-154-4*, Pub. by Boolarong Pubns AT) St Mut.

Trial & Error. Jess E. Stewart. LC 80-54882. 1981. reprint ed. pap. 10.95 (*0-9601574-2-5*) Woodford Mem.

***Trial & Error: An Oxford Anthology of Legal Stories.** Ed. by Fred R. Shapiro & Jane Garry. 496p. 1997. 30.00 (*0-19-509547-2*) OUP.

***Trial & Error: Israel's Route from War to De-Escalation.** Yagil Levy. LC 96-42064. (Israeli Studies). 282p. (C). 1997. pap. text ed. 18.95 (*0-7914-3430-3*) State U NY Pr.

***Trial & Error: Israel's Route from War to De-Escalation.** Yagil Levy. LC 96-42064. (SUNY Series in Israeli Studies). 282p. (C). 1997. text ed. 57.50 (*0-7914-3429-X*) State U NY Pr.

Trial & Error: The Autobiography of Chaim Weizmann. Chaim Weizmann. LC 70-156215. 498p. 1972. reprint ed. text ed. 35.00 (*0-8371-6166-5*, WETE, Greenwood Pr) Greenwood.

Trial & Imprisonment of Jonathan Walker at Pensacola, Florida, for Aiding Slaves to Escape from Bondage, with an Appendix Containing a Sketch of His Life. Jonathan Walker. LC 74-19173. (Floridiana Facsimile & Reprint Ser.). 1974. reprint ed. 17.95 (*0-8130-0371-7*) U Press Fla.

Trial & Practice Skills in a Nutshell. 2nd ed. Kenney F. Hegland. LC 94-5048. (Nutshell Ser.). 347p. 1994. pap. 16.00 (*0-314-03642-3*) West Pub.

***Trial & Tribulations.** Diane Carey. (Star Trek Ser.). 1996. mass mkt. 3.99 (*0-671-00902-8*) PB.

Trial & Triumph Vol. 1: The Saga of the Presidential Second Terms. Alfred J. Zacher. LC 95-73089. (Illus.). 348p. 1996. 24.95 (*0-9651087-0-8*) Presidential Pr.

***Trial at Grand Marais.** Gene Andereck. LC 97-68211. 304p. 1997. 15.00 (*1-890826-01-4*) Rock Creek Pr.

Trial Attorney's Evidence Code Notebook: March 1992 Update. 3rd annot. ed. Ed. by John K. Chapin. LC 82-73213. 252p. 1992. Annotated. ring bd. 45.00 (*0-88124-481-3*, CP-30298) Cont Ed Bar-CA.

Trial Attorney's Evidence Code Notebook: March 1993 Update. 3rd annot. ed. Ed. by John K. Chapin. LC 82-73213. 275p. 1993. ring bd. 46.00 (*0-88124-602-6*, CP-30299) Cont Ed Bar-CA.

Trial Attorney's Evidence Code Notebook: March 1994 Update. 3rd annot. ed. Ed. by John K. Chapin. LC 82-73213. 314p. 1994. 48.00 (*0-88124-721-9*, CP-30291) Cont Ed Bar-CA.

Trial Attorney's Evidence Code Notebook Annotated. 3rd ed. California Continuing Education of the Bar Staff. LC 82-73213. 483p. 1982. 60.00 (*0-88124-107-5*, CP-30290) Cont Ed Bar-CA.

Trial Attorney's Evidence Code Notebook, Annotated: April 1991 Update. 3rd ed. Ed. by John K. Chapin. LC 82-73213. 250p. 1991. ring bd. 45.00 (*0-88124-384-1*, CP-30297) Cont Ed Bar-CA.

Trial Attorney's Guide to Insurance Coverage & Bad Faith. Paul J. Skok. 477p. 1994. text ed. 135.00 (*0-471-59220-X*) Wiley.

***Trial Attorney's Guide to Insurance Coverage & Bad Faith - 1997 Cumulative Supplement.** Paul J. Skok. pap. text ed. write for info. (*0-471-17474-2*) Wiley.

Trial Balance: The Collected Short Stories of William March. William March. LC 87-5900. (Library of Alabama Classics). 536p. 1987. reprint ed. pap. 16.95 (*0-8173-0372-3*) U of Ala Pr.

Trial Begins. Abram Tertz & Andre Sinyavsky. Tr. by Max Hayward & George Denis. 220p. 1982. pap. 12.95 (*0-520-04677-3*) U CA Pr.

Trial Book, Childhood Sexual Abuse, Repressed Memory. William B. Craig. 275p. 1994. student ed. 125.00 (*1-885689-03-9*) Spread the Wrd.

***Trial by Error.** Garland. (Star Trek Deep Space Nine Ser.: No. 20). 1997. mass mkt. 5.99 (*0-671-00251-1*) PB.

***Trial by Error: Drama in Dust Valley.** 1997. 8.99 (*0-8341-9598-4*) Lillenas.

Trial by Fire. Harold Coyle. 21.50 (*0-671-95493-8*) S&S Trade.

Trial by Fire. Faye Morgan, pseud. 192p. 1994. mass mkt., pap. text ed. 3.99 (*0-8439-3717-3*) Dorchester Pub Co.

Trial by Fire. Nancy Taylor Rosenberg. LC 95-34478. 352p. 1996. pap. 22.95 (*0-525-93767-6*) NAL-Dutton.

Trial by Fire. Nancy Taylor Rosenberg. 1996. pap. 6.99 (*0-451-18005-4*, Sig) NAL-Dutton.

Trial by Fire. Anne S. White. 108p. (Orig.). 1975. pap. 3.95 (*0-89228-045-X*) Impact Christian.

Trial by Fire. Anne S. White. LC 75-625. 108p. (Orig.). 1975. pap. 3.50 (*0-9605178-1-2*) Victorious Ministry.

Trial by Fire. large type ed. Nancy Taylor Rosenberg. LC 96-2290. (Large Print Bks.). 1996. 26.95 (*1-56895-305-4*) Wheeler Pub.

Trial by Fire. large type ed. David Whitehead. (Linford Western Library). 288p. 1995. pap. 15.99 (*0-7089-7707-3*, Linford) Ulverscroft.

Trial by Fire. Harold Coyle. Ed. by Paul McCarthy. 544p. 1993. reprint ed. pap. 6.50 (*0-671-79658-5*) PB.

Trial By Fire: Nineteen Seventy-Two Easter Offensive... Dale Andrade. (Illus.). 600p. 1994. 24.95 (*0-7818-0286-5*) Hippocrene Bks.

Trial by Fire: The True Story of a Woman's Ordeal at the Hands of the Law. Gerry L. Spence. 1996. pap. 14.00 (*0-688-14838-7*, Quill) Morrow.

Trial by Friendship: Anglo-American Relations, 1917-1918. David R. Woodward. LC 92-36875. (Illus.). 288p. (C). 1993. text ed. 34.00 (*0-8131-1833-6*) U Pr of Ky.

Trial by Fury. J. A. Jance. (J. P. Beaumont Ser.). 224p. 1986. mass mkt. 6.50 (*0-380-75138-0*) Avon.

Trial by Fury. Craig Rice. LC 91-70598. 255p. 1991. pap. 5.95 (*1-55882-091-4*, Lib Crime Classics) Intl Polygonics.

Trial by Fury. large type ed. Elizabeth X. Ferrars. 1991. 25.99 (*0-7089-2348-8*) Ulverscroft.

Trial by Jury. (Vocal Score Ser.). 096p. 1986. pap. 13.95 (*0-88188-728-5*, 50337590) H Leonard.

Trial by Jury. Arthur Sullivan & William S. Gilbert. Ed. by Steven Ledbetter. (The Savoy Operas. A Critical Edition Ser.: No. 1). (Illus.). 1994. lib. bdg. 200.00 (*0-8450-3001-9*) Broude.

Trial by Jury. Robert Von Moschzisker. LC 95-76901. x, 452p. 1995. reprint ed. 78.00 (*0-89941-971-2*, 308750) W S Hein.

Trial by Love. large type ed. Susanne McCarthy. 231p. 1995. 25.99 (*0-7505-0830-2*, Pub. by Magna Print Bks UK) Ulverscroft.

Trial by Marriage. Lindsay Armstrong. 1996. 3.50 (*0-373-11798-1*, 1-11798-5) Harlequin Bks.

Trial by Marriage. large type ed. Lindsay Armstrong. (Harlequin Romance Ser.). 1995. 20.95 (*0-263-14149-7*, Pub. by Mills & Boon UK) Thorndike Pr.

Trial by Poison. Dave Jackson & Neta Jackson. (Trailblazer Bks.: Vol. 12). (J). (gr. 4-7). 1994. pap. 5.99 (*1-55661-274-5*) Bethany Hse.

Trial by Prejudice. Arthur G. Hays. LC 79-109550. (Civil Liberties in American History Ser.). 1970. reprint ed. lib. bdg. 45.00 (*0-306-71904-5*) Da Capo.

Trial by Television & Other Encounters see In Great Decades

Trial by Trail: Backpacking in the Smoky Mountains. Johnny Molloy. LC 95-4393. (Illus.). 192p. 1996. pap. 14.95 (*0-87049-913-0*) U of Tenn Pr.

Trial by Wilderness. Houghton Mifflin Company Staff. (Literature Experience 1993 Ser.). (J). (gr. 7). 1992. pap. 9.84 (*0-395-61840-1*) HM.

Trial Communication Skills. 2nd ed. Roberto Aron et al. LC 96-6406. (Trial Practice Ser.). (Illus.). 1996. ring bd. write for info. (*0-07-172600-4*) Clark Boardman Callaghan.

Trial Court Budgeting. Robert W. Tobin. (Court Management Library: Vol. 1). (Illus.). 114p. (Orig.). 1996. pap. 18.00 (*0-89656-164-X*) Natl Ctr St Courts.

Trial Ethics. Richard H. Underwood & William H. Fortune. 800p. 1988. 145.00 (*0-316-88810-9*) Little.

Trial Evidence: Making & Meeting Objections. 2nd ed. Anthony J. Bocchino et al. 190p. 1990. pap. 21.95 (*1-55681-233-7*); teacher ed., pap. 8.95 (*1-55681-235-3*) Natl Inst Trial Ad.

Trial Evidence Foundations. John A. Tarantino. LC 86-216436. 1986. 89.98 (*0-938065-15-7*) James Pub Santa Ana.

Trial for Love. large type ed. Doris Howe. 1990. 25.99 (*0-7089-2221-X*) Ulverscroft.

Trial-Forewards to My "Parallel-Text Edition of Chaucer's Minor Poems" for the Chaucer Society. Frederick J. Furnivall. (BCL1-PR English Literature Ser.). 148p. 1992. reprint ed. lib. bdg. 69.00 (*0-7812-7175-4*) Rprt Serv.

Trial Guide to America Online. Jonathan Price. LC 94-13867. (C). 1995. pap. text ed. 12.95 (*0-201-40833-3*) Addison-Wesley.

Trial Guide to CompuServe. Ed Tittel & Robert Wiggins. LC 94-12112. 1995. pap. 12.95 (*0-201-40834-1*) Addison-Wesley.

Trial Handbook. 2nd ed. Kent Sinclair. 650p. 1990. ring bd. 135.00 (*0-614-17123-7*, H6-1540) PLI.

Trial Handbook for Alabama Lawyers. LC 82-81573. 110.00 (*0-318-11925-0*) Lawyers Cooperative.

Trial Handbook for Alabama Lawyers. 1993. suppl. ed. 62.50 (*0-317-03264-X*) Lawyers Cooperative.

Trial Handbook for Arkansas Lawyers. John W. Hall, Jr. LC 93-77178. 1986. 125.00 (*0-318-19875-4*) Lawyers Cooperative.

Trial Handbook for Connecticut Lawyers. John T. Asselin. LC 86-83060. 1987. 115.00 (*0-317-01510-9*) Lawyers Cooperative.

Trial Handbook for Connecticut Lawyers. John T. Asselin. LC 86-83060. 1993. Suppl. 1993. suppl. ed. 55.00 (*0-317-03312-3*) Lawyers Cooperative.

Trial Handbook for Florida Lawyers. 2nd ed. William M. Hicks. LC 74-121653. 479p. 105.00 (*0-317-00562-6*) Lawyers Cooperative.

Trial Handbook for Florida Lawyers. 2nd ed. William M. Hicks. LC 74-121653. 479p. 1993. Suppl. 1993. suppl. ed. 57.50 (*0-317-04333-1*) Lawyers Cooperative.

***Trial Handbook for Florida Lawyers.** 3rd ed. William M. Hicks. Ed. by Carol Campaigne. LC 95-81521. 700p. 1995. text ed. write for info. (*0-7620-0022-8*) Lawyers Cooperative.

Trial Handbook for Georgia Lawyers. Jack Kleiner. LC 73-92581. 433p. 1993. Suppl. 1993. suppl. ed. 50.00 (*0-317-04331-5*) Lawyers Cooperative.

Trial Handbook for Georgia Lawyers. 2nd ed. Jack Kleiner. LC 93-86160. 433p. 110.00 (*0-317-03198-8*) Lawyers Cooperative.

Trial Handbook for Illinois Lawyers, 2 vols. 6th ed. Robert S. Hunter. (Illinois Practice Library). 1993. suppl. ed. 60.00 (*0-317-03778-1*) Lawyers Cooperative.

Trial Handbook for Illinois Lawyers, 2 vols., Set. 6th ed. Robert S. Hunter. LC 89-85753. (Illinois Practice Library). 1989. 180.00 (*0-318-50064-7*) Lawyers Cooperative.

Trial Handbook for Indiana Lawyers. 2nd ed. LC 93-78231. 110.00 (*0-318-11933-1*) Lawyers Cooperative.

Trial Handbook for Kentucky Lawyers. 2nd ed. Thomas L. Osborne. LC 92-73548. 1992. 125.00 (*0-317-05373-6*) Lawyers Cooperative.

Trial Handbook for Louisiana Lawyers. 2nd ed. Eldon Fallon. LC 92-81228. 1992. 110.00 (*0-317-05360-4*) Lawyers Cooperative.

Trial Handbook for Louisiana Lawyers. 2nd ed. Eldon Fallon. 1993. Suppl. 1993. suppl. ed. 35.00 (*0-317-05708-1*) Lawyers Cooperative.

Trial Handbook for Maryland Lawyers. 2nd ed. Jacob A. Stein. LC 85-82441. (Maryland Practice Library). 1991. Suppl. 1991. suppl. ed. 55.00 (*0-317-03294-1*) Lawyers Cooperative.

Trial Handbook for Maryland Lawyers. 3rd ed. Jacob A. Stein. LC 85-82441. (Maryland Practice Library). 1986. 115.00 (*0-317-01286-X*) Lawyers Cooperative.

Trial Handbook for Massachusetts Lawyers. 2nd ed. Edward M. Swartz. LC 90-60500. 416p. 1990. 115.00 (*0-317-00466-2*) Lawyers Cooperative.

Trial Handbook for Massachusetts Lawyers. 2nd ed. Edward M. Swartz. LC 90-60500. 416p. 1993. Suppl. 1993. suppl. ed. 45.00 (*0-317-03179-1*) Lawyers Cooperative.

Trial Handbook for Michigan Lawyers. 2nd ed. Harry M. Philo. LC 87-82165. 369p. 1993. Suppl. 1993. suppl. ed. 55.00 (*0-317-03182-1*) Lawyers Cooperative.

Trial Handbook for Michigan Lawyers. 3rd ed. Harry M. Philo. LC 95-80184. 1270p. 1995. text ed. 125.00 (*0-7620-0006-6*) Lawyers Cooperative.

Trial Handbook for Mississippi Lawyers. Stanford Young. LC 86-80878. 1993. Suppl. 1993. suppl. ed. 52.50 (*0-317-03304-2*) Lawyers Cooperative.

Trial Handbook for Missouri Lawyers. J. William Turley. LC 84-82477. 1985. 110.00 (*0-318-04387-4*) Lawyers Cooperative.

Trial Handbook for Missouri Lawyers. J. William Turley. LC 84-82477. 1993. Suppl. 1993. suppl. ed. 50.00 (*0-317-04340-4*) Lawyers Cooperative.

T

Trial Handbook for New Jersey Lawyers. 2nd ed. William S. Greenberg. LC 89-63222. 1991. Suppl. 1991. suppl. ed. 55.00 (*0-317-03779-X*) Lawyers Cooperative.

Trial Handbook for New Jersey Lawyers. 3rd ed. William S. Greenberg. LC 93-80362. 115.00 (*0-318-50066-3*) Lawyers Cooperative.

Trial Handbook for New Mexico Lawyers. J. Duke Thornton. LC 92-71853. 1992. 110.00 (*0-317-05370-1*) Lawyers Cooperative.

Trial Handbook for New York Lawyers. 2nd ed. Aaron J. Broder. LC 85-82119. 1986. 115.00 (*0-318-19876-2*) Lawyers Cooperative.

Trial Handbook for New York Lawyers. 2nd ed. Aaron J. Broder. LC 85-82119. 1991. Suppl. 1991. suppl. ed. 40.00 (*0-317-03286-0*) Lawyers Cooperative.

***Trial Handbook for New York Lawyers.** 3rd ed. Aaron J. Broder. LC 96-75045. (New York Practice Library). 980p. 1996. text ed. write for info. (*0-7620-0040-6*) Lawyers Cooperative.

Trial Handbook for Ohio Lawyers. 3rd ed. Richard M. Markus & George H. Palmer. LC 90-64031. 354p. 125.00 (*0-317-00553-7*) Lawyers Cooperative.

Trial Handbook for Ohio Lawyers. 3rd ed. Richard M. Markus & George H. Palmer. LC 72-97628. 354p. 1993. Suppl. 1993. suppl. ed. 52.50 (*0-317-05566-6*) Lawyers Cooperative.

Trial Handbook for Pennsylvania Lawyers. 2nd ed. Emil L. Iannelli & Lynne P. Iannelli. LC 90-61768. 1990. 115.00 (*0-317-00585-5*) Lawyers Cooperative.

Trial Handbook for Pennsylvania Lawyers. 2nd ed. Emil L. Iannelli & Lynne P. Iannelli. LC 90-61768. 1993. Suppl. 1993. suppl. ed. 55.00 (*0-317-04334-X*) Lawyers Cooperative.

Trial Handbook for Tennessee Lawyers. Robert E. Burch. LC 79-83775. 450p. 1993. Suppl. 1993. suppl. ed. 52.50 (*0-317-03164-3*) Lawyers Cooperative.

Trial Handbook for Tennessee Lawyers. 2nd ed. Robert E. Burch. LC 95-76595. 450p. 125.00 (*0-317-00394-1*) Lawyers Cooperative.

Trial Handbook for Virginia Lawyers. Craig D. Johnston. LC 85-82118. 1993. Suppl. 1993. suppl. ed. 52.50 (*0-317-04344-7*) Lawyers Cooperative.

Trial Handbook for Virginia Lawyers. 2nd ed. Craig D. Johnston. LC 95-80284. 800p. 1995. text ed. 120.00 (*0-7620-0007-4*) Lawyers Cooperative.

Trial Handbook for Wisconsin Lawyers. Ted M. Warshafsky. LC 81-82645. 125.00 (*0-317-00426-3*) Lawyers Cooperative.

Trial Handbook for Wisconsin Lawyers. Ted M. Warshafsky. LC 81-82645. 1991. Suppl. 1991. suppl. ed. 50.00 (*0-317-03170-8*) Lawyers Cooperative.

***Trial Handbook for Wisconsin Lawyers.** Ted M. Warshafsky. LC 96-77169. (Wisconsin Practice Systems Library). 950p. 1996. text ed. write for info. (*0-7620-0083-X*) Lawyers Cooperative.

***Trial in Serra.** W. E. Dunkle. 451p. (Orig.). 1997. mass mkt. 5.99 (*1-55197-553-X*, Pub. by Comnwlth Pub CN) Partners Pubs Grp.

Trial in the Sun. large type ed. Kay Thorpe. 288p. 1995. 21.50 (*0-263-14156-X*, Pub. by M & B UK) Ulverscroft.

Trial Judge: The Candid, Behind the Bench Story of Justice Bernard Botein. Bernard Botein. (American Constitutional & Legal History Ser). 337p. 1974. reprint ed. lib. bdg. 39.50 (*0-306-70630-X*) Da Capo.

Trial Judges Manual of Charges. 3rd expanded ed. Roland Ford & Andrew V. Clements. vii, 204p. 1959. 30.00 (*0-89941-600-4*, 500350) W S Hein.

Trial Language: Differential Discourse Processing & Discursive Formation. Gail Stygall. LC 94-31090. (Pragmatics & Beyond New Ser.: No. 26). xii, 226p. 1994. lib. bdg. 59.00 (*1-55619-294-0*) Benjamins North Am.

Trial Lawyer. Stanley M. Rosenblatt. LC 84-73. 416p. 1984. 19.95 (*0-8184-0360-8*); pap. 9.95 (*0-8184-0361-6*) Carol Pub Group.

Trial Lawyers: The Nation's Top Litigators Tell How They Win. Emily Couric. 384p. 1990. pap. 14.95 (*0-312-05172-7*) St Martin.

Trial Lawyer's Book: Preparing & Winning Cases. Jonathan M. Purver et al. LC 90-60301. 1990. 100.00 (*0-317-02942-8*) Lawyers Cooperative.

Trial Lawyer's Book: Preparing & Winning Cases. Jonathan M. Purver et al. 1993. Suppl. 1993. suppl. ed. 32.50 (*0-317-04629-2*) Lawyers Cooperative.

Trial Lawyer's Guide, 33 vols. Ed. by John J. Kennelly. 1, 100.00 (*0-685-14564-6*); 118.00 (*0-685-14565-4*) Clark Boardman Callaghan.

Trial Manual Five for the Defense of Criminal Cases: Proceedings Between Arraignment & Trial, Vol. II. 5th ed. Anthony G. Amsterdam. 343p. 1989. text ed. 94.00 (*0-8318-0613-3*, B613) Am Law Inst.

Trial Manual Five for the Defense of Criminal Cases: Trial & Posttrial Proceedings, Vol. III. 5th ed. Anthony G. Amsterdam. LC 88-71176. 356p. 1989. text ed. 94.00 (*0-8318-0614-1*, B614) Am Law Inst.

Trial Manual Five for the Defense of Criminal Cases Vol. I: Proceedings Through Arraignment. 5th ed. Anthony G. Amsterdam. 403p. 1988. text ed. 94.00 (*0-8318-0582-X*, B582) Am Law Inst.

Trial Manual for Defense Attorneys in Juvenile Court, 2 vols. Randy Hertz et al. LC 90-85891. 1199p. 1991. ring bd. 250.00 (*0-8318-0537-4*, B537) Am Law Inst.

Trial Manual for Proving Hedonic Damages. Laurence Bodine. LC 92-74523. 325p. 1993. 85.00 (*0-915544-23-7*) Lawpress CA.

Trial Manual Four for the Defense of Criminal Cases, 2 vols. 4th ed. Anthony G. Amsterdam. LC 84-70792. 950p. 1984. ring bd. 87.00 (*0-8318-0440-8*, B440) Am Law Inst.

Trial Notebook. Thomas A. Mauet. 1994. lib. bdg. 80.00 (*0-316-55109-0*) Little.

Trial Notes. Herberth Czermak. (Orig.). 1976. pap. text ed. 4.50 (*0-8220-1304-5*) Cliffs.

***Trial of a Drug Case.** 206p. 1994. 30.00 (*0-614-26665-3*, 1032) NYS Bar.

***Trial of a Drug Case.** 206p. 1994. 92.00 incl. audio (*0-614-26666-1*, 20321) NYS Bar.

***Trial of a Felony Case.** 295p. 1993. 30.00 (*0-614-26669-6*, 19347) NYS Bar.

***Trial of a Felony Case.** 295p. 1993. 92.00 incl. audio (*0-614-26670-X*, 29347) NYS Bar.

***Trial of a Felony Case.** 295p. 1993. 175.00 incl. vhs (*0-614-26671-8*, 39347) NYS Bar.

***Trial of A. J. Monson.** Ed. by John W. More. (Notable British Trials Ser.). vii, 472p. 1995. reprint ed. 145.00 (*1-56169-152-6*) Gaunt.

Trial of Abigail Goodman. large type ed. Howard Fast. LC 93-35742. 1994. lib. bdg. 22.95 (*0-8161-5904-1*, GK Hall) Thorndike Pr.

***Trial of Abraham Thornton.** Ed. by John Hall. (Notable British Trials Ser.). x, 183p. 1995. reprint ed. 58.00 (*1-56169-129-1*) Gaunt.

***Trial of Adelaide Bartlett.** Ed. by John Hall. (Notable British Trials Ser.). 402p. 1995. reprint ed. 124.00 (*1-56169-147-X*) Gaunt.

Trial of Adolf Eichmann: Record of the Proceedings, 9 vols. (C). 1995. Set. 445.00 (*0-317-05840-1*, Pub. by Israel State Archives IS) Gefen Bks.

***Trial of Alex Kelly.** Samuel Schreiner. 1998. pap. 23.95 (*1-55611-527-X*) D I Fine.

***Trial of Alfred Arthur Rouse.** Ed. by Helena Normanton. (Notable British Trials Ser.). xlviii, 316p. 1995. reprint ed. 110.00 (*1-56169-177-1*) Gaunt.

***Trial of Alma Victoria Rattenbury & George P. Roy Stoner.** Ed. by F. Tennyson Jesse. (Notable British Trials Ser.). 298p. 1995. reprint ed. 94.00 (*1-56169-180-1*) Gaunt.

Trial of an Action. John Sopinka. 280p. 1982. 76.00 (*0-409-86854-X*) MICHIE.

Trial of an Administration Case. William J. Kolasky. 112p. write for info. (*0-318-60937-1*) HarBrace.

Trial of Andrew Johnson on Impeachment, 3 vols. 1970. reprint ed. lib. bdg. 120.00 (*0-89941-606-3*, 500560) W S Hein.

***Trial of Anna Cotman.** Vivien Alcock. LC 96-31658. (J). 1997. pap. 6.95 (*0-395-81649-1*) HM.

***Trial of August Sangret.** Ed. by Macdonald Critchley. (Notable British Trials Ser.). xxiv, 233p. 1995. reprint ed. 78.00 (*1-56169-194-1*) Gaunt.

Trial of Bat Shea. Jack Casey. (Illus.). 372p. 19.95 (*0-9639886-0-3*) Diamond Rock.

Trial of Bat Shea. limited ed. Jack Casey. (Illus.). 372p. 29.95 (*0-9639886-1-1*) Diamond Rock.

***Trial of Benjamin Knowles.** Albert Lieck. (Notable British Trials Ser.). 215p. 1995. reprint ed. 69.00 (*1-56169-175-5*) Gaunt.

Trial of Beyers Naude: Christian Witness & the Rule of Law. Ed. by International Commission of Jurists. 195p. 1994. pap. 20.00 (*0-85532-355-8*, Pub. by Srch Pr UK) St Mut.

***Trial of Billy Byrne of Ballymanus.** Ed. by Jim Rees. 80p. (Orig.). 1996. pap. 11.95 (*0-9519239-4-3*, Pub. by Dee-Jay IE) Irish Bks Media.

Trial of Billy the Kid. Bobby E. Hefner. (Illus.). 95p. (YA). write for info. (*1-886709-08-4*) Outlaw Publ.

Trial of Bruno Richard Hauptmann. (Criminology Ser.). 1992. lib. bdg. 300.00 (*0-8490-5302-1*) Gordon Pr.

***Trial of Buck Ruxton.** 2nd ed. Ed. by R. H. Blundell & G. Haswell Wilson. (Notable British Trials Ser.). lxxxvii, 457p. 1995. reprint ed. 165.00 (*1-56169-181-X*) Gaunt.

Trial of C. B. Reynolds. Robert G. Ingersoll. 44p. 1986. 4.00 (*0-910309-25-6*, 5532) Am Atheist.

***Trial of Captain Kidd.** Ed. by Graham Brooks. (Notable British Trials Ser.). x, 223p. 1995. reprint ed. 70.00 (*1-56169-116-X*) Gaunt.

***Trial of Captain Porteous.** Ed. by William Roughead. (Notable British Trials Ser.). 366p. 1995. reprint ed. 114.00 (*1-56169-118-6*) Gaunt.

Trial of Chaka Dlamini: An Economic Scenario for the New South Africa. Stephen Meintjes & Michael Jacques. 120p. 1990. pap. 14.00 (*0-9583105-1-3*) Schalkenbach.

Trial of Charles I. large type ed. C. V. Wedgwood. (Shadows of the Crown Ser.). 1974. 25.99 (*0-85456-616-3*) Ulverscroft.

Trial of Charles I: A Documentary History. Ed. by David Lagomarsino & Charles T. Wood. LC 89-40356. (Illus.). 167p. 1989. pap. 15.95 (*0-87451-499-1*) U Pr of New Eng.

Trial of Chivalry. LC 77-133748. (Tudor Facsimile Texts. Old English Plays Ser.: No. 104). reprint ed. 49.50 (*0-404-53404-X*) AMS Pr.

***Trial of Christopher Craig & Derek William Bentley.** Ed. by H. Montgomery Hyde. (Notable British Trials Ser.). xi, 264p. 1995. reprint ed. 83.00 (*1-56169-193-3*) Gaunt.

Trial of Christopher Okigbo. Ali A. Mazrui. (African Writers Ser.). 145p. (C). 1971. pap. 8.95 (*0-435-90097-8*, 90097) Heinemann.

Trial of Cristobal Colon: An Historical Play. Crystal D. Morrison. LC 93-84327. 160p. (Orig.). 1996. pap. 15.98 (*1-879289-04-0*) Native Sun Pubs.

Trial of Cristopher Okigbo. Ali A. Mazrui. LC 78-180662. 160p. 1972. 15.95 (*0-89388-024-8*) Okpaku Communications.

Trial of Curiosity: Henry James, William James, & the Challenge of Modernity. Ross Posnock. 382p. 1991. 65.00 (*0-19-506606-5*); pap. 29.95 (*0-19-507124-7*) OUP.

Trial of D. M. Bennett: Upon the Charge of Depositing Prohibited Matter in the Mail. Bennett M. De Robigne. LC 72-8110. (Civil Liberties in American History Ser.). 202p. 1973. reprint ed. lib. bdg. 27.50 (*0-306-70525-7*) Da Capo.

***Trial of Deacon Brodie.** 2nd ed. William Roughead. (Notable British Trials Ser.). 283p. 1995. reprint ed. 87.00 (*1-56169-127-5*) Gaunt.

Trial of Dedan Kimathi. Ngugi Wa Thiong'o et al. (African Writers Ser.). 85p. (C). 1977. pap. 9.95 (*0-435-90191-5*, 90191) Heinemann.

Trial of Democracy: Black Suffrage & Northern Republicans, 1860-1910. Xi Wang. LC 95-46628. (Studies in the Legal History of the South). (C). 1997. 58.00 (*0-8203-1837-X*) U of Ga Pr.

Trial of Dr. Jekyll: An Adaptation of Robert Louis Stevenson's "The Strange Case of Dr. Jekyll & Mr. Hyde", a Play in two Acts. William L. Slout. LC 93-10112. (Clipper Studies in the Theatre: No. 7). x, 75p. 1993. pap. 15.00 (*0-8095-6253-7*, Emeritus Ent); lib. bdg. 25.00 (*0-8095-6252-9*, Emeritus Ent) Borgo Pr.

***Trial of Dr. Pritchard.** Ed. by William Roughead. (Notable British Trials Ser.). 343p. 1995. reprint ed. 107.00 (*1-56169-139-9*) Gaunt.

***Trial of Dr. Smethurst.** Ed. by Leonard A. Barry. (Notable British Trials Ser.). xiii, 259p. 1995. reprint ed. 82.00 (*1-56169-136-4*) Gaunt.

Trial of Duncan Terig. Duncan Terig. LC 79-176140. (Bannatyne Club, Edinburgh. Publications: No. 40). reprint ed. 32.50 (*0-404-52746-9*) AMS Pr.

Trial of Elizabeth Cree: A Novel of the Limehouse Murders. Peter Ackroyd. 272p. 1995. 22.00 (*0-385-47707-4*, N A Talese) Doubleday.

***Trial of Eugene Marie Chantrelle.** 2nd ed. Ed. by A. Duncan Smith. (Notable British Trials Ser.). 243p. 1995. reprint ed. 76.00 (*1-56169-142-9*) Gaunt.

Trial of Faith: Discussions Concerning Mormonism & Neo-Mormonism. William Call. 215p. (Orig.). pap. write for info. (*0-916095-11-8*) Pubs Pr UT.

***Trial of Faith: Discussions Concerning Mormonism & Neo-Mormonism.** William Call. LC 86-62317. 208p. (Orig.). 1986. pap. text ed. 10.95 (*0-9634732-7-1*) Freethinker.

Trial of Faith: Religion & Politics in Tocqueville's. Doris S. Goldstein. LC 75-4753. 156p. reprint ed. pap. 44.50 (*0-685-15413-0*, 2026263) Bks Demand.

***Trial of Faith of St. Therese of Lisieux.** Frederick L. Miller. LC 97-23190. 200p. (Orig.). 1997. pap. 12.95 (*0-8189-0799-1*) Alba.

Trial of Father Dillingham. John Broderick. 224p. 1981. 14.95 (*0-7145-2747-5*) M Boyars Pubs.

***Trial of Field & Gray.** Ed. by Winifred Duke. (Notable British Trials Ser.). vi, 302p. 1995. reprint ed. 93.00 (*1-56169-168-2*) Gaunt.

***Trial of Franz Muller.** Ed. by H. B. Irving. (Notable British Trials Ser.). xlviii, 194p. 1995. reprint ed. 73.00 (*1-56169-138-0*) Gaunt.

***Trial of Frederick Bywaters & Edith Thompson.** Ed. by Filson Young. (Notable British Trials Ser.). xxxii, 261p. 1995. reprint ed. 89.00 (*1-56169-169-0*) Gaunt.

***Trial of Frederick Guy Browne & William Henry Kennedy.** Ed. by W. Teignmouth Shore. (Notable British Trials Ser.). x, 218p. 1995. reprint ed. 69.00 (*1-56169-174-7*) Gaunt.

***Trial of George Chapman.** Hargrave L. Adam. (Notable British Trials Ser.). x, 223p. 1995. reprint ed. 71.00 (*1-56169-155-0*) Gaunt.

***Trial of George Henry Lamson.** Ed. by Hargrave L. Adam. (Notable British Trials Ser.). 192p. 1995. reprint ed. 62.00 (*1-56169-146-1*) Gaunt.

***Trial of George Joseph Smith.** Ed. by Eric R. Watson. (Notable British Trials Ser.). x, 329p. 1995. reprint ed. 103.00 (*1-56169-165-8*) Gaunt.

Trial of Gilles De Rais. Georges Bataille. Tr. by Richard Robinson from FRE. 285p. (Orig.). (C). 1991. pap. 12.95 (*1-878923-02-1*) Amok Bks.

Trial of God: A Play. Elie Wiesel. LC 95-20799. 192p. 1995. reprint ed. pap. 12.00 (*0-8052-1053-9*) Schocken.

Trial of Goldilocks - Musical. Joseph Robinett & Robert Chauls. 40p. 1991. pap. 5.00 (*0-87129-030-8*, T08) Dramatic Pub.

Trial of Goldilocks - Straight. Joseph Robinette. 34p. 1990. pap. 5.00 (*0-87129-003-0*, T81) Dramatic Pub.

***Trial of Gustav Rau, Otto Monsson & Willem Smith: The "Veronica" Trial.** Ed. by G. W. Keeton & John Cameron. (Notable British Trials Ser.). 248p. 1995. reprint ed. 78.00 (*1-56169-157-7*) Gaunt.

***Trial of Guy Fawkes & Others: (The Gunpowder Plot)** Ed. by Donald Carswell. (Notable British Trials Ser.). vi, 191p. 1995. reprint ed. 70.00 (*1-56169-113-5*) Gaunt.

***Trial of Harold Greenwood.** Ed. by Winifred Duke. (Notable British Trials Ser.). xi, 347p. 1995. reprint ed. 145.00 (*1-56169-167-4*) Gaunt.

***Trial of Hawley Harvey Crippen.** 2nd ed. Ed. by Filson Young. (Notable British Trials Ser.). xxxv, 211p. 1995. reprint ed. 74.00 (*1-56169-161-5*) Gaunt.

***Trial of Henry Fauntleroy.** Ed. by Horace Bleackley. (Notable British Trials Ser.). 269p. 1995. reprint ed. 84.00 (*1-56169-130-5*) Gaunt.

***Trial of Herbert Rowse Armstrong.** Ed. by Filson Young. (Notable British Trials Ser.). x, 396p. 1995. reprint ed. 123.00 (*1-56169-171-2*) Gaunt.

***Trial of J. A. Dickman.** Ed. by S. O. Rowan-Hamilton. (Notable British Trials Ser.). vii, 208p. 1995. reprint ed. 66.00 (*1-56169-162-3*) Gaunt.

Trial of J. S. Mack Sullivan. 1989. write for info. (*0-318-65388-5*) Pr MacDonald & Reinecke.

***Trial of Jack Sheppard.** Horace Bleackley. (Notable British Trials Ser.). vi, 260p. 1995. reprint ed. 81.00 (*1-56169-117-8*) Gaunt.

***Trial of James Blomfield Rush.** Ed. by W. Teignmouth Shore. (Notable British Trials Ser.). 272p. 1995. reprint ed. 85.00 (*1-56169-133-X*) Gaunt.

***Trial of James Camb: (The Port-Hole Murder)** Geoffrey Clark. (Notable British Trials Ser.). 255p. 1995. reprint ed. 80.00 (*1-56169-188-7*) Gaunt.

***Trial of James Stewart: (The Appin Murder)** Ed. by David N. Mackay. (Notable British Trials Ser.). xxiv, 390p. 1995. reprint ed. 124.00 (*1-56169-122-4*) Gaunt.

***Trial of Jean Pierre Vaquier.** Ed. by R. H. Blundell & R. E. Seaton. (Notable British Trials Ser.). xxiv, 208p. 1995. reprint ed. 70.00 (*1-56169-172-0*) Gaunt.

***Trial of Jeannie Donald.** (Notable British Trials Ser.). 305p. 1995. reprint ed. 91.00 (*1-56169-179-8*) Gaunt.

Trial of Jessica Wakefield. Francine Pascal. (Sweet Valley University Ser.: 26). 240p. (YA). 1996. mass mkt. 3.99 (*0-553-57007-2*) Bantam.

***Trial of Jesus.** Simon Legasse. 208p. (Orig.). 1997. pap. 27.00 (*0-334-02679-2*, SCM Pr) TPI PA.

Trial of Jesus. Giovanni Rosadi. 1977. lib. bdg. 59.95 (*0-8490-2767-5*) Gordon Pr.

Trial of Jesus. Alan Watson. LC 94-39088. 176p. 1995. 24.95 (*0-8203-1717-9*) U of Ga Pr.

Trial of Jesus Christ. Aristarchus Vassilakos. Ed. by Orthodox Christian Educational Society Staff. 64p. (Orig.). 1950. pap. 3.95 (*0-938366-47-5*) Orthodox Chr.

***Trial of Jesus Continues.** Rudolf Pesch. Tr. by Doris G. Wagner from GER. LC 96-47382. (Princeton Theological Monographs: Vol. 43). 106p. 1996. pap. 12.00 (*1-55635-033-3*) Pickwick.

Trial of Jesus from a Lawyer's Standpoint, 2 vols., Set. Walter M. Chandler. LC 83-82312. 1983. reprint ed. 160.00 (*0-89941-294-7*, 302980) W S Hein.

***Trial of Joan of Arc.** Don Nardo. LC 97-9871. (Famous Trials Ser.). (J). 1997. lib. bdg. 17.96 (*1-56006-466-8*) Lucent Bks.

***Trial of Joan of Arc.** Marina Warner. Ed. by Monica Furlong. (Visionary Women Ser.). 175p. (Orig.). pap. 11.95 (*0-85305-354-5*, Pub. by James Arthur UK) Morehouse Pub.

***Trial of John Donald Merrett.** Ed. by William Roughead. (Notable British Trials Ser.). x, 326p. 1995. reprint ed. 102.00 (*1-56169-173-9*) Gaunt.

***Trial of John George Haigh: (The Acid Bath Murder)** Ed. by Lord Dunboyne. (Notable British Trials Ser.). 271p. 1995. reprint ed. 81.00 (*1-56169-190-9*) Gaunt.

***Trial of John Thomas Straffen.** Ed. by Letitia Fairfield & Eric P. Fullbrook. (Notable British Trials Ser.). xiii, 298p. 1995. reprint ed. 94.00 (*1-56169-191-7*) Gaunt.

Trial of John W. Hinckley, Jr. A Case Study in the Insanity Defense. Peter W. Low et al. (University Casebook Ser.). 137p. 1986. pap. text ed. 10.50 (*0-88277-333-X*) Foundation Pr.

***Trial of John Watson Laurie: (The Arran Murder)** Ed. by William Roughead. (Notable British Trials Ser.). x, 284p. 1995. reprint ed. 89.00 (*1-56169-149-6*) Gaunt.

Trial of Jorge de Almeida by the Inquisition in Mexico. Cyrus Adler. (Studies in Judaica & the Holocaust). 80p. pap. write for info. (*0-89370-241-2*); lib. bdg. write for info. (*0-89370-141-6*) Borgo Pr.

Trial of Judaism in Contemporary Jewish Writing. Josephine Z. Knopp. LC 74-18319. (Illus.). 174p. reprint ed. pap. 49.60 (*0-8357-3576-1*, 2034447) Bks Demand.

***Trial of Kate Webster.** Ed. by Elliot O'Donnell. (Notable British Trials Ser.). x, 213p. 1995. reprint ed. 68.00 (*1-56169-143-7*) Gaunt.

***Trial of Katharine Nairn.** Ed. by William Roughead. (Notable British Trials Ser.). xiii, 257p. 1995. reprint ed. 82.00 (*1-56169-124-0*) Gaunt.

***Trial of King Charles the First.** Ed. by J. G. Muddiman. (Notable British Trials Ser.). xvii, 282p. 1995. reprint ed. 90.00 (*1-56169-114-3*) Gaunt.

Trial of Levi Weeks. Estelle F. Kleiger. (Illus.). 244p. 1989. 20.00 (*0-89733-297-0*) Academy Chi Pubs.

Trial of Love, Custom Pub. Kumar. 1994. pap. text ed. write for info. (*0-07-051505-0*) McGraw.

Trial of Macias in Equatorial Guinea: The Story of a Dictatorship. Alejandro Artucio. 70p. reprint ed. pap. 25.00 (*0-685-23721-4*, 2032709) Bks Demand.

Trial of Madam Caillaux. Edward Berenson. LC 91-2689. (Illus.). 296p. 1992. 29.95 (*0-520-07347-9*); pap. 13.95 (*0-520-08428-4*) U CA Pr.

***Trial of Madeleine Smith.** Ed. by A. Duncan Smith. (Notable British Trials Ser.). xi, 371p. 1995. reprint ed. 115.00 (*1-56169-135-6*) Gaunt.

Trial of Magic. Tom McGowen. (Age of Magic Trilogy Ser.: Bk. 2). 144p. (J). (gr. 5-9). 1992. pap. 15.00 (*0-525-67376-8*, Lodestar Bks) Dutton Child Bks.

***Trial of Mary Blandy.** Ed. by William Roughead. (Notable British Trials Ser.). 210p. 1995. 67.00 (*1-56169-121-6*) Gaunt.

Trial of Mary Lou. Ron Carter. (Settlement Trilogy Ser.: Vol. 1). 98p. 1996. 12.95 (*0-9643672-5-4*) Mountain Pr.

***Trial of Mary Queen of Scots.** Lewis. Date not set. pap. text ed. write for info. (*0-312-15439-9*) St Martin.

***Trial of Mary Queen of Scots.** Ed. by A. Francis Steuart. (Notable British Trials Ser.). xvi, 184p. 1995. reprint ed. 60.00 (*1-56169-112-7*) Gaunt.

***Trial of Mrs. Maybrick.** 2nd ed. Ed. by H. B. Irving. (Notable British Trials Ser.). 354p. 1995. reprint ed. 110.00 (*1-56169-148-8*) Gaunt.

***Trial of Mrs. M'Lachlan.** Ed. by William Roughead. (Notable British Trials Ser.). 338p. 1995. reprint ed. 132.00 (*1-56169-137-2*) Gaunt.

Trial of Ned Kelly. J. H. Phillips. xiii, 135p. 1987. 19.50 (*0-455-20759-3*, Pub. by Law Bk Co AT) Gaunt.

***Trial of Neville George Clevely Heath.** Ed. by Macdonald Critchley. (Notable British Trials Ser.). 239p. 1995. reprint ed. 75.00 (*1-56169-186-0*) Gaunt.

***Trial of Oscar Slater.** Ed. by William Roughead. (Notable British Trials Ser.). lxxx, 320p. 1995. reprint ed. 121.00 (*1-56169-160-7*) Gaunt.

Trial of Patrick Sellar. Ian Grimble. (C). 1995. pap. 39.95 (*0-85411-053-4*, Pub. by Saltire Soc) St Mut.

An Asterisk (*) at the beginning of an entry indicates that the title is appearing in BIP for the first time.

***Trial of Peter Barnes & Others: (The I. R. A. Coventry Explosion of 1939)** Ed. by Letitia Fairfield. (Notable British Trials Ser.). xiii, 284p. 1995. reprint ed. 66.00 (*1-56169-184-4*) Gaunt.

***Trial of Peter Griffiths: (The Blackburn Baby Murder)** Ed. by George Goodwin. (Notable British Trials Ser.). 219p. 1995. reprint ed. 66.00 (*1-56169-189-5*) Gaunt.

Trial of Peter Zenger. Ed. by Vincent Buranelli. LC 75-31814. (Illus.). 152p. 1975. reprint ed. text ed. 35.00 (*0-8371-8444-4*, ZEPZ, Greenwood Pr) Greenwood.

***Trial of Pythagoras & Other Poems.** William Davey. 101p. (Orig.). 1996. pap. 14.95 (*1-897722-44-3*, Pub. by Alyscamps Pr FR) Gotham.

Trial of Richard M. Nixon. Richard Doyle. 288p. Date not set. 24.95 (*0-89526-446-3*, Gateway Editions) Regnery Pub.

Trial of Richard the Third. Richard Drewett & Mark Redhead. (Illus.). 170p. 1989. pap. 14.00 (*0-86299-198-6*, Pub. by Sutton Pubng UK) Bks Intl VA.

***Trial of Rizal.** Ed. by Horacio De la Costa. 202p. 1997. pap. text ed. 15.00 (*971-550-208-3*, Pub. by Ateneo de Manila Univ Pr PH) UH Pr.

***Trial of Robert Wood: (The Camden Town Case)** Ed. by Basil Hogarth. (Notable British Trials Ser.). vi, 268p. 1995. reprint ed. 84.00 (*1-56169-159-3*) Gaunt.

***Trial of Ronald True.** Ed. by Donald Carswell. (Notable British Trials Ser.). x, 295p. 1995. reprint ed. 93.00 (*1-56169-170-4*) Gaunt.

Trial of Samuel Chase, an Associate Justice of the Supreme Court Impeached by the House of Representatives, 2 vols. Samuel Chase. LC 69-11324. (Law, Politics & History Ser.). 1970. reprint ed. Set. lib. bdg. 79.50 (*0-306-71181-8*) Da Capo.

***Trial of Samuel Herbert Dougal.** Ed. by F. Tennyson Jesse. (Notable British Trials Ser.). xii, 236p. 1995. reprint ed. 72.00 (*1-56169-156-9*) Gaunt.

Trial of Scott Nearing & the American Socialist Society. LC 76-122159. (Civil Liberties in American History Ser.). 1970. reprint ed. lib. bdg. 29.50 (*0-306-71966-5*) Da Capo.

Trial of Sergeant Cimo. large type ed. T. M. Dolan. 150p. 1996. pap. 17.99 (*1-85389-597-0*, Dales) Ulverscroft.

***Trial of Sidney Harry Fox.** Ed. by F. Tennyson Jesse. (Notable British Trials Ser.). xii, 299p. 1995. reprint ed. 93.00 (*1-56169-176-3*) Gaunt.

***Trial of Simon, Lord Lovat of the '45.** Ed. by David N. Mackay. (Notable British Trials Ser.). lv, 314p. 1995. reprint ed. 112.00 (*1-56169-120-8*) Gaunt.

***Trial of Sir Roger Casement.** Ed. by H. Montgomery Hyde. (Notable British Trials Ser.). clix, 323p. 1995. reprint ed. 146.00 (*1-56169-166-6*) Gaunt.

Trial of Socrates. Don Nardo. LC 96-20407. (Famous Trials Ser.). (Illus.). (YA). 1996. lib. bdg. 17.96 (*1-56006-267-3*) Lucent Bks.

Trial of Socrates. I. F. Stone. 296p. 1989. pap. 12.95 (*0-385-26032-6*, Anchor NY) Doubleday.

Trial of Soren Qvist. Janet Lewis. LC 72-94405. 256p. 1959. pap. 12.95 (*0-8040-0297-5*) Swallow.

Trial of St. Paul: A Judicial Exegesis of the Second Half of the Acts of the Apostles. H. W. Tajra. (WissUNT Neuen Testament Ser.: No. 35). 230p. 1989. lib. bdg. 57.50 (*3-16-145443-X*, Pub. by J C B Mohr GW) Coronet Bks.

***Trial of Steinie Morrison.** Ed. by H. Fletcher Moulton. (Notable British Trials Ser.). xxxi, 282p. 1995. reprint ed. 95.00 (*1-56169-163-1*) Gaunt.

Trial of Stephen: The First Christian Martyr. Alan Watson. LC 96-1955. 1996. 24.95 (*0-8203-1855-8*) U of Ga Pr.

Trial of Strength: Wilhelm Furtwangler in the Third Reich. Fred K. Prieberg. Tr. by Christopher Dolan. 394p. 1994. text ed. 35.00 (*1-55553-196-2*) NE U Pr.

Trial of the Assassin Guiteau: Psychiatry & the Law in the Gilded Age. Charles E. Rosenberg. LC 68-16713. 1976. pap. 14.95 (*0-226-72717-3*, P682) U Ch Pr.

Trial of the British Soldiers. LC 75-79023. (Black Heritage Library Collection). 1977. 21.95 (*0-8369-8670-9*) Ayer.

Trial of the Century: Obstruction of Justice - Viewpoint of a Trial Watcher. Loretta Justice. Ed. by Adolfo Caso. LC 96-20135. (Illus.). 450p. (Orig.). 1997. pap. 17.95 (*0-8283-2015-2*) Branden Pub Co.

Trial of the Century: People of the State of California vs. Orenthal James Simpson. Frank M. Schmalleger. (Illus.). 432p. 1996. pap. 19.95 (*0-13-651829-X*) P-H.

Trial of the Century: The People of the State of California vs. Orenthal James Simpson. Frank M. Schmalleger. LC 95-52152. 432p. (C). 1996. pap. text ed. 32.00 (*0-13-235953-7*) P-H.

Trial of the Christmas Bells. Nancy Forquer. 1984. pap. 4.95 (*0-912963-05-0*) Eldridge Pub.

***Trial of the City of Glascow Bank Directors.** Ed. by William Wallace. (Notable British Trials Ser.). vii, 472p. 1995. reprint ed. 145.00 (*1-56169-144-5*) Gaunt.

Trial of the Constitution. Sidney G. Fisher. LC 69-18977. 391p. 1969. reprint ed. text ed. 45.00 (*0-8371-0896-9*, FIC&, Greenwood Pr) Greenwood.

Trial of the Dainty Maids. Julie A. Waterman. 12p. (Orig.). 1982. The Trial of the Dainty Maids. pap. 1.25 (*0-943334-05-5*) Carmonelle Pubns.

***Trial of the Duchess of Kingston.** Ed. by Lewis Melville. (Notable British Trials Ser.). x, 328p. 1995. reprint ed. 102.00 (*1-56169-126-7*) Gaunt.

***Trial of the Generals: Selected Journalism 1980-1990.** Colm Toibin. 198p. 9000. pap. 12.95 (*1-85186-081-9*) Dufour.

***Trial of the Germans: An Account of the Twenty-Two Defendants before the International Military Tribunal at Nuremberg.** Eugene Davidson. LC 97-21795. 1997. pap. write for info. (*0-8262-1139-9*) U of Mo Pr.

Trial of the Innocents. Sara Mitchell. LC 95-468. (Shadowcatchers Ser.). 336p. 1995. pap. 9.99 (*1-55661-497-7*) Bethany Hse.

Trial of the IRA Five: Documentary. Ed. by Thomas J. Cox. (Illus.). 363p. (Orig.). (C). 1992. vinyl bd. 27.50 (*1-879710-05-6*) Riverside FL.

Trial of the Major War Criminals Before the International Military Tribunal, 44 vols. Nuremberg War Trials Staff. LC 70-145536. reprint ed. Set. write for info. (*0-404-53650-6*) AMS Pr.

Trial of the Major War Criminals Before the International Military Tribunal: Nuremberg 14 November 1945-1 October 1946, 42 vols., Set. 1995. reprint ed. 2,750.00 (*1-57588-003-2*, 309090) W S Hein.

Trial of the Man Who Said He Was God. D. E. Harding. 384p. 1993. pap. 12.00 (*0-685-66268-3*, Arkana) Viking Penguin.

***Trial of the Seddons.** Ed. by Gilson Young. (Notable British Trials Ser.). x, 420p. 1995. reprint ed. 130.00 (*1-56169-164-X*) Gaunt.

Trial of the Seventh Carrier. Peter Albano. 1990. mass mkt. 3.95 (*0-8217-3213-7*, Zebra Kensgtn) Kensgtn Pub Corp.

***Trial of the Stauntons.** Ed. by J. B. Atlay. (Notable British Trials Ser.). 332p. 1995. reprint ed. 103.00 (*1-56169-141-0*) Gaunt.

Trial of the Templars. Malcolm C. Barber. (Canto Book Ser.). 320p. (C). 1993. pap. text ed. 11.95 (*0-521-45727-0*) Cambridge U Pr.

Trial of the Templars. Edward J. Martin. LC 76-29845. reprint ed. 29.50 (*0-404-15424-7*) AMS Pr.

***Trial of the Wainwrights.** Ed. by H. B. Irving. (Notable British Trials Ser.). xliv, 235p. 1995. reprint ed. 84.00 (*1-56169-140-2*) Gaunt.

Trial of Theodore Parker: For the Misdemeanor of a Speech in Fanenil Hall Against Kidnapping. Theodore Parker. LC 70-154087. (Black Heritage Library Collection). 1977. 28.95 (*0-8369-8798-5*) Ayer.

Trial of Theodore Parker, with the Defence by Theodore Parker. Theodore Parker. (American Biography Ser.). 221p. 1991. reprint ed. lib. bdg. 69.00 (*0-7812-8306-X*) Rprt Serv.

***Trial of Thomas John Ley & Lawrence John Smith: (The Chalk Pit Murder)** Ed. by F. Tennyson Jesse. (Notable British Trials Ser.). li, 313p. 1995. reprint ed. 110.00 (*1-56169-187-9*) Gaunt.

***Trial of Thomas Neill Cream.** Ed. by W. Teignmouth Shore. (Notable British Trials Ser.). x, 207p. 1995. reprint ed. 66.00 (*1-56169-151-8*) Gaunt.

***Trial of Thurtell & Hunt.** Ed. by Eric R. Watson. (Notable British Trials Ser.). x, 217p. 1995. reprint ed. 69.00 (*1-56169-131-3*) Gaunt.

Trial of Tom Sawyer. Virginia G. Koste. (J). (gr. 4 up). 1978. 5.00 (*0-87602-213-1*) Anchorage.

Trial of Treasure. LC 70-133749. (Tudor Facsimile Texts. Old English Plays Ser.: No. 38). reprint ed. 49.50 (*0-404-53338-8*) AMS Pr.

Trial of U. S. Grant: The Pacific Coast Years, 1852-1854. Charles G. Ellington. LC 86-50835. (Frontier Military Ser.: XIV). (Illus.). 248p. 1987. 27.50 (*0-87062-169-6*) A H Clark.

Trial of Walter Graham Rowland see Henry Cecil Reprint Series

Trial of William Drennan. Ed. by John Larkin. 144p. 1991. 14.95 (*0-7165-2457-0*, Pub. by Irish Acad Pr IE) Intl Spec Bk.

***Trial of William Gardiner: (The Peasenhall Case)** Ed. by William Henderson. (Notable British Trials Ser.). 332p. 1995. reprint ed. 121.00 (*1-56169-154-2*) Gaunt.

***Trial of William Joyce.** Ed. by J. W. Hall. (Notable British Trials Ser.). xii, 312p. 1995. reprint ed. 97.00 (*1-56169-185-2*) Gaunt.

***Trial of William Palmer.** Ed. by George H. Knott. (Notable British Trials Ser.). x, 320p. 1995. reprint ed. 98.00 (*1-56169-134-8*) Gaunt.

***Trial of Witches: A Seventeenth Century Witchcraft Prosecution.** Gilbert Geis & Ivan Bunn. LC 97-8354. 1997. write for info. (*0-415-17108-3*); pap. write for info. (*0-415-17109-1*) Routledge.

Trial of Woman. Diana Basham. (Women's Classics Ser.). (Illus.). 246p. (C). 1992. 40.00 (*0-8147-1174-X*) NYU Pr.

Trial on Trial. Lawrence Dennis & Maximillian St. George. 502p. 1984. pap. 9.98 (*0-939484-20-X*) Legion Survival.

Trial on Trial. Lawrence Dennis. 1978. lib. bdg. 75.00 (*0-87700-292-4*) Revisionist Pr.

***Trial Practice.** Lawrence A. Dubin & Thomas F. Guernsey. LC 92-167121. 200p. 1991. pap. text ed. 25.00 (*0-87084-248-X*) Anderson Pub Co.

Trial Practice. 3rd ed. Blanchard. Date not set. teacher ed., pap. text ed. write for info. (*0-314-68774-2*) West Pub.

Trial Practice: Problems & Case Files. Edward Stein & Lawrence Dubin. LC 89-48318. 288p. 1989. teacher ed., pap. text ed. 39.95 (*0-87084-224-2*) Anderson Pub Co.

Trial Practice: Problems & Case Files with Video Presentation. Edward R. Stein & Lawrence A. Dubin. 288p. 1989. pap. 645.00 incl. bmax (*0-87084-221-8*) Anderson Pub Co.

Trial Practice & Procedure in Alabama. 2nd ed. Grover S. McLeod. 786p. 1991. text ed. 79.00 (*1-884150-20-9*) Manchester AL.

Trial Practice Cases & Materials. Joseph R. Nolan. LC 80-29182. (American Casebook Ser.). 518p. 1981. text ed. 41.50 (*0-8299-2129-X*) West Pub.

Trial Practice Checklists. Douglas Danner & John W. Toothman. LC 89-85093. 1990. 95.00 (*0-317-01808-6*) Lawyers Cooperative.

Trial Practice Checklists. Douglas Danner & John W. Toothman. LC 89-85093. 1993. Suppl. 1993. suppl. ed. 45.00 (*0-317-01809-4*) Lawyers Cooperative.

Trial Practices & Procedures. Pamela E. Hill. 400p. (C). 1993. pap. text ed. 40.00 (*1-884028-04-7*) SL Pubs.

Trial Preparation for Prosecutors. M. D. Marcus. 199p. 1994. suppl. ed., pap. 70.00 (*0-471-03340-5*) Wiley.

Trial Preparation for Prosecutors. Michael D. Marcus. (Trial Practice Library). 467p. 1989. text ed. 130.00 (*0-471-84895-6*) Wiley.

Trial Process. Ed. by Bruce D. Sales. LC 80-20487. (Perspectives in Law & Psychology Ser.: Vol. 2). 522p. 1981. 75.00 (*0-306-40491-5*, Plenum Pr) Plenum.

Trial Process: Law, Tactics, & Ethics. J. Alexander Tanford. (Contemporary Legal Education Ser.). (Illus.). 570p. 1983. 32.00 (*0-87215-668-0*) MICHIE.

Trial Psychology: Communication & Persuasion in the Courtroom. Margaret C. Roberts. 490p. 1987. boxed 95.00 (*0-409-25105-4*) MICHIE.

Trial Run. Dick Francis. 1987. mass mkt. 5.95 (*0-449-21273-4*) Fawcett.

Trial Tactics. Mark A. Dombroff. 1983. 25.00 (*1-55917-750-0*, 999); audio 125.00 (*1-55917-748-9*); vhs 395.00 (*1-55917-749-7*) Natl Prac Inst.

Trial Tactics. Irving Younger. write for info. (*0-316-97720-9*) Little.

Trial Tactics & Methods. 2nd ed. Robert E. Keeton. 480p. 1973. 42.00 (*0-316-48572-1*) Little.

Trial Tech. 4th ed. Thomas A. Mauet. 1996. 32.95 (*0-316-55061-2*) Little.

***Trial Technique & Evidence.** Michael R. Fontham. 810p. 1995. 95.00 (*1-55834-258-3*, 61963) MICHIE.

Trial Techniques. Irving Younger. Ed. by Robert Oliphant. LC 78-71017. 98p. 1978. 15.00 (*0-686-31598-7*); audio 125.00 (*1-55917-751-9*); vhs 450.00 (*1-55917-752-7*) Natl Prac Inst.

Trial Techniques: A Compendium of Course Materials. 7th ed. 1990. 25.00 (*0-317-03018-3*) Natl Coll DA.

Trial Techniques: Opening Statements & Closing Arguments. Ed. by Grace W. Holmes & Mary I. Hiniker. LC 87-82961. 454p. 1987. pap. 65.00 (*0-685-22724-3*, 87-027) U MI Law CLE.

Trial, Tribulation & Triumph: Before, During, & after Antichrist. Desmond A. Birch. LC 96-68461. 635p. (Orig.). 1996. pap. text ed. 19.50 (*1-882972-73-2*) Queenship Pub.

Trial Within a Reasonable Time: Working Paper Prepared for the Law Reform Commission of Canada. Law Reform Commission of Canada Staff. 122p. (Orig.). 1994. pap. 38.95 (*0-660-59103-0*, Pub. by Canada Commun Grp CN) Accents Pubns.

Trialbook: A Total System For Preparation & Presentation of a Case. John O. Sonsteng et al. LC 84-15292. (Hornbook Series, Student Edition). 404p. (C). 1984. reprint ed. pap. 28.00 (*0-314-85865-2*) West Pub.

Trialbook: Forms. West Publishing Company Editorial Staff. 99p. 1985. pap. text ed. write for info. (*0-314-95553-4*) West Pub.

Trialogue of Abrahamic Faiths. I. R. Al Farugi. 88p. (Orig.). 1986. pap. 7.50 (*0-317-52454-2*) New Era Publns MI.

Trialogue of Abrahamic Faiths. 3rd ed. Frwd. by Isma'il Raji al Faruqi. LC 91-2836. (Issues of Islamic Thought Ser.: No. 1). 96p. (C). 1986. pap. text ed. 5.00 (*0-912463-06-6*) IIIT VA.

Trialogue of the Abrahamic Faiths: Papers Presented to the Islamic Studies Group of American Academy of Religion. 4th ed. Ed. by Ismail R. Al-Faruqi. LC 95-5120. (Issues of Islamic Thought Ser.: No. 1). 1995. 7.50 (*0-915957-25-6*) amana pubns.

Trialogues at the Edge of the West: Chaos, Creativity, & the Resacralization of the World. Ralph Abraham et al. (Illus.). 208p. (Orig.). 1992. pap. 14.95 (*0-939680-97-1*) Bear & Co.

Trials. Kristine Albert & Nancy Polette. (Illus.). 48p. (Orig.). 1991. pap. 5.95 (*0-913839-99-X*) Pieces of Lrning.

Trials. Anne T. Wallach. LC 96-22023. 384p. 1996. pap. 24.95 (*0-525-94091-X*) NAL-Dutton.

Trials - Don't Resent Them As Intruders. Juanita Purcell. (Women's Ser.). 96p. (Orig.). 1991. pap. text ed. 5.95 (*0-87227-161-7*, RBP5184) Reg Baptist.

Trials & Court Procedures Worldwide. Ed. by Charles Platto. (International Bar Association Ser.). 480p. (C). 1991. lib. bdg. 202.00 (*1-85333-608-4*, Pub. by Graham & Trotman UK) Kluwer Ac.

Trials & Other Tribulations. Damon Runyon. 23.95 (*0-8488-1619-6*) Amereon Ltd.

Trials & Punishments. R. A. Duff. LC 85-15128. (Cambridge Studies in Philosophy). 220p. 1986. 59.95 (*0-521-30818-6*) Cambridge U Pr.

Trials & Punishments. R. A. Duff. (Cambridge Studies in Philosophy). 336p. (C). 1991. pap. text ed. 20.95 (*0-521-40761-3*) Cambridge U Pr.

Trials & the Sacrifice. Vicente Segrelles. (Mercenary Ser.). 96p. 1988. pap. 14.95 (*0-918348-49-8*) NBM.

Trials & Tribulations: Appealing Legal Humor. Intro. by Daniel R. White. LC 89-15865. (Illus.). 320p. 1989. 19.95 (*0-945774-05-2*, PN6231.L4T75) Catbird Pr.

Trials & Tribulations: Looking for a Miracle. Telester F. Kelly-Powell. 66p. 1991. pap. text ed. 10.95 (*0-9614788-2-9*, 333A) Tivoli Pub.

Trials & Tribulations of a Rancher's Son of the Great Southwest. Perry E. Herron. 50p. 1992. pap. 5.95 (*0-9634601-0-2*) Herron Ent.

Trials & Tribulations of Little Red Riding Hood: Versions of the Tale in Sociocultural Context. 2nd ed. Jack D. Zipes. LC 93-19319. (Illus.). 400p. (gr. 13). 1993. reprint ed. pap. 18.95 (*0-415-90835-3*, B2306, Routledge NY) Routledge.

Trials & Tribulations of Little Red Riding Hood: Versions of the Tale in Sociocultural Context. 2nd ed. Jack D. Zipes. LC 93-19319. (Illus.). 400p. (C). (gr. 13). 1993. reprint ed. text ed. 59.95 (*0-415-90834-5*, B2302, Routledge NY) Routledge.

Trials & Tribulations of Staggerlee Booker T. Brown: A Play in Two Acts. Don Evans. 1985. pap. 5.25 (*0-8222-1172-6*) Dramatists Play.

Trials & Triumphs: A Colorado Portrait of the Great Depression, with FSA Photographs. Stephen J. Leonard. (Illus.). 272p. 1993. 35.00 (*0-87081-311-0*) Univ Pr Colo.

Trials & Triumphs: George Washington's Foreign Policy. Frank T. Reuter. LC 83-675. (A.M. Pate, Jr., Series on the American Presidency: No. 2). 250p. (C). 1983. 19.50 (*0-912646-70-5*) Tex Christian.

Trials & Triumphs: George Washington's Foreign Policy. Frank T. Reuter. LC 83-675. (A.M. Pate, Jr., Series on the American Presidency: No. 2). 250p. (C). 1988. pap. 8.95 (*0-87565-038-4*) Tex Christian.

Trials & Triumphs: Women of the American Civil War. Marilyn M. Culpepper. 1994. pap. 18.95 (*0-87013-368-3*) Mich St U Pr.

Trials & Triumphs of Eva Grant. Effie M. Williams. 94p. pap. 1.00 (*0-686-29173-5*) Faith Pub Hse.

Trials & Triumphs of Mrs. Jessie Penn-Lewis: Jessie Penn-Lewis & Friends. Brynmor P. Jones. (Orig.). 1997. pap. 9.95 (*0-88270-727-2*, Logos NJ) Bridge-Logos.

Trials for Acute Stroke Therapy. Ed. by J. Bogousslavsky et al. (Journal Ser.: Vol. 5, Suppl. 1, 1995). (Illus.). iv, 34p. 1995. pap. 15.75 (*3-8055-6228-4*) S Karger.

Trials for Love. large type ed. Margaret Fenton. 1990. pap. 15.99 (*0-7089-6877-5*, Trailtree Bookshop) Ulverscroft.

***Trials from Classical Athens.** Christopher Carey. LC 96-47561. 288p. (C). 1997. pap. write for info. (*0-415-10761-X*); text ed. write for info. (*0-415-10760-1*) Routledge.

Trials in Burma. Maurice Collis. LC 74-179181. reprint ed. 32.50 (*0-404-54812-1*) AMS Pr.

Trials in Power: Cain, Kirner & Victoria 1982-1992. Ed. by Mark Considine & Brian Costar. 292p. 1992. pap. 19.95 (*0-522-84537-1*, Pub. by Melbourne Univ Pr AT) Paul & Co Pubs.

Trials in the Late Roman Republic, 149 B. C. to 50 B. C. Michael C. Alexander. (Phoenix Supplementary Volumes Ser.). 224p. 1990. 47.50 (*0-8020-5787-X*) U of Toronto Pr.

Trials in Vascular Surgery. Greenhalgh. 1996. text ed. 115.00 (*0-7020-2090-7*) HarBrace.

Trials of Ada Adams. Philippa Ruth. write for info. (*0-318-58991-5*) World Pr Ltd.

Trials of American History. Arbetman. Date not set. teacher ed., pap. text ed. 15.95 (*0-314-90077-2*) West Pub.

Trials of an Ordinary Doctor: Joannes Groenevelt in Seventeenth-Century London. Harold J. Cook. LC 93-39733. (Illus.). 301p. 1994. 45.00 (*0-8018-4778-8*) Johns Hopkins.

Trials of Authorship: Anterior Forms & Poetic Reconstruction from Wyatt to Shakespeare. Jonathan Crewe. 1990. 38.00 (*0-520-06693-6*) U CA Pr.

Trials of Brother Jero & The Strong Breed. Wole Soyinka. 1969. pap. 5.25 (*0-8222-1090-8*) Dramatists Play.

Trials of Character: The Eloquence of Ciceronian Ethos. James M. May. LC 87-13884. viii, 216p. (C). 1988. 37.50 (*0-8078-1759-7*) U of NC Pr.

***Trials of Charles Frederick Peace.** Ed. by W. Teignmouth Shore. (Notable British Trials Ser.). xi, 197p. 1995. reprint ed. 64.00 (*1-56169-145-3*) Gaunt.

Trials of Desire: Renaissance Defenses of Poetry. Margaret W. Ferguson. LC 82-8525. (Illus.). 280p. 1983. text ed. 40.00 (*0-300-02787-7*) Yale U Pr.

Trials of Discipleship: The Story of William Clayton, a Mormon. James B. Allen. LC 86-11328. (Illus.). 402p. 1987. text ed. 29.95 (*0-252-01369-7*) U of Ill Pr.

***Trials of Discipleship: The Story of William Clayton, a Mormon Pioneer.** James B. Allen. LC 97-13360. (BYU Studies). 1997. write for info. (*0-8425-2346-4*) Brig Yng Univ.

Trials of Ezra Pound. Timothy Findley. Date not set. 15.95 (*0-921368-50-X*, Pub. by Blizzard Pub CN) Genl Dist Srvs.

Trials of FAT. Grover S. McLeod. 260p. 1989. 19.95 (*0-87651-949-4*) Southern U Pr.

Trials of FAT: An Illustrious Member of the Criminal Bar. Grover S. McLeod. 251p. 1989. 19.95 (*1-884150-07-1*) Manchester AL.

Trials of Frances Howard: Fact & Fiction in the Court of King James. David Lindley. LC 93-654. 224p. (C). (gr. 13). 1993. 45.00 (*0-415-05206-8*, B2563) Routledge.

Trials of Frances Howard: Fact & Fiction in the Court of St. James. David Lindley. 256p. (C). 1996. pap. 17.95 (*0-415-14424-8*) Routledge.

***Trials of Frederick Nodder: The Mona Tinsley Case.** Ed. by Winifred Duke. (Notable British Trials Ser.). xiii, 242p. 1995. reprint ed. 77.00 (*1-56169-182-8*) Gaunt.

***Trials of Friendship.** Hucker. LC 97-25071. 1997. 21.95 (*0-312-17051-3*) St Martin.

Trials of Great Bible Characters. Clarence E. Macartney. 160p. 1996. pap. 9.99 (*0-8254-3285-5*) Kregel.

Trials of Israel Lipski: A True Story of a Victorian Murder in the East End of London. Martin L. Friedland. (Illus.). 224p. 1985. 14.95 (*0-8253-0278-1*) Beaufort Bks NY.

Trials of J. J. Rawlings: Echoes of the 31st December Revolution. Kojo Yankah. 110p. (Orig.). 1992. pap. 8.95 (*1-56411-039-7*) Untd Bros & Sis.

Trials of Labour: The Re-Emergence of Midwifery. Brian Burtch. LC 93-49582. (Critical Perspectives on Public Affairs Ser.). 288p. 1994. 49.95 (*0-7735-1141-5*, Pub. by McGill CN); pap. 19.95 (*0-7735-1143-1*, Pub. by McGill CN) U of Toronto Pr.

Trials of Maria Barbella: The True Story of a 19th Century Crime of Passion. Idanna Pucci. Tr. by Stefania Fumo from ITA. (Illus.). 344p. 1996. 22.00 (*1-56858-061-4*) Random.

T

Trials of Maria Barbella: The True Story of a 19th Century Crime of Passion. Idanna Pucci. Tr. by Stefania Fumo. 1997. pap. 13.00 (0-679-77604-4) Random.

***Trials of Masculinity: Policing Sexual Boundaries, 1870-1930.** Angus McLaren. LC 96-29523. (Chicago Series on Sexuality, History, & Society). 288p. 1997. 24.95 (0-226-50067-5) U Ch Pr.

Trials of Molly Sheldon. Julian F. Thompson. LC 95-2815. 176p. (YA). (gr. 7 up). 1995. 16.95 (0-8050-3382-3) H Holt & Co.

Trials of Molly Sheldon. Julian F. Thompson. 1997. pap. 4.99 (0-14-038425-1) Viking Penguin.

Trials of Mrs. Lincoln. Samuel A. Schreiner, Jr. LC 86-82181. (Illus.). 336p. 1987. pap. 18.95 (1-55611-009-X) D I Fine.

Trials of Oscar Wilde. H. Montgomery Hyde. (Illus.). 327p. 1973. reprint ed. pap. 7.95 (0-486-20216-X) Dover.

***Trials of Oscar Wilde: Deviance, Morality & Late-Victorian Society.** Michael S. Foldy. LC 97-24369. 1997. 30.00 (0-300-07112-4) Yale U Pr.

***Trials of Oscar Wilde: Regina (Wilde) vs. Queensberry - Regina vs. Wilde & Taylor.** Ed. by H. Montgomery Hyde. (Notable British Trials Ser.). 384p. 1995. reprint ed. 120.00 (1-56169-153-4) Gaunt.

***Trials of Patrick Carraher.** Ed. by George Blake. (Notable British Trials Ser.). xii, 278p. 1995. reprint ed. 88.00 (1-56169-183-6) Gaunt.

Trials of Persiles & Sigismunda: A Northern Story. Miguel de Cervantes Saavedra. Tr. by Celia R. Weller & Clark A. Colahan from SPA. 450p. (C). 1989. 45.00 (0-520-06315-5) U CA Pr.

Trials of Prophylactic Agents for the Control of Communicable Diseases: A Guide to Their Organization & Evaluation. T. M. Pollock. (Monograph Ser.: No. 52). 92p. (ENG, FRE, RUS & SPA.). 1966. pap. text ed. 7.00 (92-4-140052-8, 1140052) World Health.

Trial(s) of Psychoanalysis. Francoise Meltzer. 296p. 1988. pap. text ed. 17.00 (0-226-51970-8) U Ch Pr.

Trial(s) of Psychoanalysis. Francoise Meltzer. 306p. 1988. lib. bdg. 34.00 (0-226-51969-4) U Ch Pr.

Trials of Rumpole. John Mortimer. 206p. 1981. mass mkt. 6.00 (0-14-005162-7, Penguin Bks) Viking Penguin.

***Trials of Rumpole.** John Mortimer. 1981. pap. 9.95 (0-14-024697-5, Penguin Bks) Viking Penguin.

Trials of the Earth: The Autobiography of Mary Hamilton. Mary Hamilton. Ed. by Helen D. Davis. LC 92-17772. (Illus.). 224p. 1992. 25.00 (0-87805-579-7) U Pr of Miss.

Trials of the Earth: The Autobiography of Mary Hamilton. Mary Hamilton. Ed. by Helen D. Davis. 286p. reprint ed. text ed. 13.95 (0-87805-671-8) U Pr of Miss.

Trials of the Human Heart, 4 vols. in 2, Set. Susanna Rowson. LC 78-64091. reprint ed. 75.00 (0-404-17360-8) AMS Pr.

Trials of the Self: Heroic Ordeals in the Epic Tradition. George D. Lord. LC 83-11727. x, 249p. (C). 1983. lib. bdg. 35.00 (0-208-02013-6, Archon Bks) Shoe String.

Trials of Thinking, Feeling & Willing. Carl Unger. 1980. pap. 2.50 (0-916786-47-1, Saint George Pubns) R Steiner Col Pubns.

***Trials of Timothy John Evans & John Reginald Halliday Christie.** Ed. by F. Tennyson Jesse. (Notable British Trials Ser.). 379p. 1995. reprint ed. 145.00 (1-56169-192-5) Gaunt.

Trials on Trial: The Pure Theory of Legal Procedure. Gordon Tullock. LC 80-13113. 264p. 1980. text ed. 49.50 (0-231-04952-8) Col U Pr.

Trials, Tribulation, & Celebrations: African-American Perspectives on Health, Illness, Aging, & Loss. Ed. by Marian G. Secundy. LC 91-37596. 352p. 1991. pap. 19.95 (1-877864-00-5) Intercult Pr.

Trials, Tribulations & Tributes: Story Poems - The Great Alaska Highway Fiftieth Anniversary Edition. Raynold I. Savela. 56p. 1991. pap. 8.00 (0-9631523-0-0) R I Savela.

Triangle. Sondra Marshak. (Star Trek Ser.: No. 9). (Orig.). 1991. mass mkt. 5.50 (0-671-74351-1) PB.

Triangle. Sondra Marshak. 1986. mass mkt. 3.50 (0-671-62748-1) PB.

***Triangle.** Irene Pence. 320p. 1998. mass mkt. 5.99 (0-7860-0473-8, Pinncle Kensgtn) Kensgtn Pub Corp.

Triangle. Jon Ripslinger. 224p. (YA). (gr. 7 up). 1994. 11.00 (0-15-200048-8); pap. 4.00 (0-15-200049-6) HarBrace.

Triangle: Busy Railroading in Southern Illinois. Stanley A. Changnon. 104p. 1992. 25.00 (0-9631811-0-6) S A Changnon.

Triangle Broadcasting Company: A Word Information Processing Simulation. Betty S. Johnson & Gayle A. Nagai. 192p. (Orig.). (C). 1985. teacher ed. write for info. (0-672-98565-9); student ed. write for info. (0-672-98563-2); pap. text ed. write for info. (0-672-98562-4); audio write for info. (0-672-98564-0) Macmillan.

Triangle Factory Fire. Victoria Sherrow. LC 95-14523. (Spotlight on American History Ser.). (Illus.). 64p. (J). (gr. 4-6). 1995. lib. bdg. 16.40 (1-56294-572-6) Millbrook Pr.

Triangle Fire. Leon Stein. 224p. 1985. pap. 7.95 (0-88184-126-9) Carroll & Graf.

Triangle Fire. limited ed. Mary Fell. (U. S. A. Poetry Chapbook Ser.: No. 2). 12p. (Orig.). 1983. pap. 2.50 (0-937724-02-5); pap. 5.00 (0-685-06689-4) Shadow Pr.

Triangle Game: Breaking Communication Triangles in Recovery. rev. ed. Sandra Inskeep-Fox. 1996. pap. 0.50 (0-89230-211-9) Do It Now.

Triangle Murder. large type ed. Lauran Paine. 202p. 1996. pap. 20.95 (0-7838-1898-X, GK Hall) Thorndike Pr.

Triangle News Special. Troll Associates Staff. 1996. pap. 188.50 (0-8167-4230-8) Troll Communs.

Triangle Noir: Laclos, Goysa, Saint-Just. Andre Malraux. 13.15 (0-685-34272-7) Fr & Eur.

***Triangle of Death.** Levine Michael. 1997. mass mkt. 6.99 (0-440-22111-0) Dell.

Triangle of Death: Deep Cover II. Michael Levine & Laura Kavanau. LC 95-50361. 336p. 1996. 23.95 (0-385-31475-2) Delacorte.

Triangle Power: A Source of Staying Power in Marriage. E. Scott Mabry. LC 94-65479. 210p. (Orig.). 1994. pap. 11.95 (0-9639732-0-7) St Croix Pubns.

Triangle Shirtwaist. Barbara D. Goldin. Date not set. pap. 10.95 (0-670-83753-9) Viking Penguin.

Triangle Shirtwaist. Barbara D. Goldin. 1997. pap. 3.99 (0-14-034685-6, Viking) Viking Penguin.

Triangle Shirtwaist Fire: Mini-Play. (Women's Studies). (J). (gr. 5 up). 1975. 6.50 (0-89550-369-7) Stevens & Shea.

Triangle Short Cut Layout. 4th ed. Joseph J. Kaberlein. 1986. pap. 27.32 (0-02-819430-6) Macmillan.

Triangle, Square, Circle. large type ed. William Wegman. LC 94-69096. (Illus.). 16p. (J). 1995. 6.95 (0-7868-0104-2) Hyprn Child.

***Triangle/Raleigh/Durham Dine-a-Mate Book.** 280p. 1996. pap. text ed. 30.00 (1-57393-059-8) Dine-A-Mate.

Triangles. Mary C. Penders. LC 91-35690. (Quilts from Simple Shapes Ser.). (Illus.). 32p. 1992. pap. 9.95 (0-8442-2634-3) Quilt Digest Pr.

***Triangles.** Garry Puffer. (J). 1985. write for info. (0-688-02004-6) Lothrop.

***Triangles.** Gary Puffer. (J). Date not set. lib. bdg. write for info. (0-688-02009-7) Lothrop.

Triangles. Sandy Riggs. LC 96-3173. (Discovering Shapes Ser.). (Illus.). (J). (gr. 3 up). 1996. lib. bdg. 14.95 (0-7614-0459-7, Benchmark NY) Marshall Cavendish.

Triangles. Marion Smoothey. LC 92-12156. (Let's Investigate Ser.). (Illus.). (J). (gr. 4-8). 1992. 17.95 (1-85435-461-2) Marshall Cavendish.

***Triangles.** unabridged ed. Catherine S. Ross. (Shapes in Math, Science & Nature Ser.). (Illus.). 64p. (J). (gr. 4-9). 1994. pap. 9.95 (1-55074-194-2, Pub. by Kids Can Pr CN) Genl Dist Srvs.

***Triangles: What You Need to Know about Affairs.** Lana Staheli. 272p. 1997. 23.00 (0-06-018758-1) HarpC.

Triangles of Fire. 2nd ed. Torkom Saraydarian. LC 77-82155. 1989. pap. 12.00 (0-911794-35-2) Aqua Educ.

Triangles, Parallel Lines, Similar Polygons see Key to Geometry Series

Triangular Algebras & Ideals of Nest Algebras. John L. Orr. (Memoirs of the American Mathematical Society Ser.: No. 562). 1995. 28.00 (0-8218-0405-7, MEMO/117/562) Am Math.

Triangular & Jordan Representations of Linear Operators. M. S. Brodskii. LC 74-162998. (Translations of Mathematical Monographs: Vol. 32). 246p. 1971. 47.00 (0-8218-1582-2, MMONO/32) Am Math.

Triangular Arbitrage in the Foreign Exchange Market: Inefficiencies, Technology, & Investment Opportunities. Marios Mavrides. LC 91-47075. 200p. 1992. text ed. 55.00 (0-89930-718-3, Quorum Bks) Greenwood.

Triangular Clause Relationship in Aelfric's Lives of Saints & in Other Works. Ed. by Ruth Waterhouse. LC 83-5399. (American University Studies: English Language & Literature: Ser. IV, Vol. 1). 119p. (Orig.). (C). 1983. pap. text ed. 12.10 (0-8204-0007-6) P Lang Pubng.

Triangular Norm-Based Measures & Games with Fuzzy Coalitions. Dan Butnariu & Erich P. Klement. LC 93-24820. (Theory & Decision Library, Series C, Game Theory, Mathematical Programming, & Operations Research: Vol. 10). 212p. (C). 1993. lib. bdg. 133.00 (0-7923-2369-6) Kluwer Ac.

Triangular Products of Group Representations & Their Applications. Samuel M. Vovsi. (Progress in Mathematics Ser.: No. 17). 150p. (C). 1981. 40.50 (0-8176-3062-7) Birkhauser.

Triangular Trade & the Atlantic Economy of the Eighteenth Century: A Simple General-Equilibrium Model. Ronald Findlay. LC 90-4037. (Essays in International Finance Ser.: No. 177). 36p. 1990. pap. text ed. 8.00 (0-88165-084-6) Princeton U Int Finan Econ.

Triangulated Categories in the Representation Theory of Finite-Dimensional Algebras. D. Happel. (London Mathematical Society Lecture Note Ser.: Series 119). 200p. 1988. pap. text ed. 39.95 (0-521-33922-7) Cambridge U Pr.

***Triangulating Positions: Poststructuralism, Feminism, & Religion.** Carol W. White. (Society/Religion - Religion/Society Ser.). 152p. 1997. 45.00 (0-391-04069-3) Humanities.

***Triangulating Positions: Poststructuralism, Feminism, & Religion.** Carol W. White. (Society/Religion - Religion/Society Ser.). 152p. 1997. pap. 15.00 (0-391-04070-7) Humanities.

Triangulation from a Known Point. Ruth Danon. (Orig.). 1990. 16.95 (0-929654-97-8, North Star Line); pap. 8.95 (0-929654-93-5, North Star Line) Blue Moon Bks.

Triangulations & Simplicial Methods. C. Dang & W. Trockel. Ed. by G. Fandel. (Lecture Notes in Economics & Mathematical Systems Ser.: Vol. 421). (Illus.). X, 196p. 1995. 59.00 (3-540-58838-8) Spr-Verlag.

Triangulo: Aplicaciones Practicas de la Lengua Espanola. rev. ed. Barbara Gatski & John McMullan. (Illus.). 194p. (SPA.). (YA). (gr. 11-12). 1995. student ed., pap. text ed. 17.27 (1-877653-34-9, 25A) Wayside Pub.

Triangulo: Aplicaciones Practicas de la Lengua Espanola. 2nd rev. ed. Barbara Gatski & John McMullan. (SPA.). (YA). (gr. 11-12). 1995. teacher ed., pap. 9.33 (1-877653-28-4, 26) Wayside Pub.

Trianon & East Central Europe: Antecedents & Repercussions. Ed. by Bela K. Kiraly & Laszlo Veszpremy. (Atlantic Studies on Society in Change). 321p. 1995. 45.00 (0-88033-315-4) East Eur Monographs.

Trianon & the Protection of Minorities. Jozsef Galantai. (Atlantic Studies on Society & Change: No. 70). 260p. (C). 1993. text ed. 38.50 (0-88033-249-2, 352) Col U Pr.

Triarthrus Eatoni (Trilobita), Vol. 53, Anatomy of Its Exoskeletal, Skeletomuscular, & Digestive Systems see Palaeontographica Americana: Vol. 9

Triassic Dinosaur Coelophysis. Edwin H. Colbert. (Bulletin Ser.). 174p. 1989. pap. 14.95 (0-89734-097-3, BS-57) Mus Northern Ariz.

Triassic Floras of Eurasia. I. A. Dobruskina. (Schriftenreihe der Erdwissenschaftlichen Kommissionen Ser.: Bd. 10). 425p. 1997. pap. 96.00 (0-387-86557-8) Spr-Verlag.

Triassic-Jurassic Rifting: Continental Breakup & the Origin of the Atlantic Passive Margins, 2 vols. Ed. by W. Manspeizer. (Developments in Geotectonics Ser.: No. 22). 998p. 1989. 519.75 (0-444-42903-4) Elsevier.

***Triassische Megalodontaceae.** E. Vegh-Neubrandt. 1983. pap. 180.00 (963-05-2659-X, Pub. by Akad Kiado HU) St Mut.

Triathalon Training. Almekinders et al. 281p. 1991. pap. 19.95 (0-88725-161-7) Hunter Textbks.

Triathlon. Ed. by Carla J. Crane. (Next Level Preteen Electives Ser.). (Illus.). 128p. 1996. teacher ed. 14.99 (0-7847-0502-X, 42102) Standard Pub.

Triathlon. Bill Lund. LC 96-9295. (Extreme Sports Ser.). 1996. write for info. (1-56065-430-9) Capstone Pr.

***Triathlon.** Bill Lund. (Extreme Sports Ser.). (Illus.). 48p. (J). (gr. 3-7). 1996. 18.40 (0-516-20257-X) Childrens.

Triathlon: Achieving Your Personal Best. Rod Cedaro. LC 93-4007. 300p. 19.95 (0-8160-2948-2) Facts on File.

Triathloning for Ordinary Mortals. Steven Jonas. (Illus.). 1986. pap. 12.95 (0-393-30279-2) Norton.

Triathlons for Fun. Sally Edwards. (Illus.). 125p. (Orig.). 1992. pap. 6.95 (1-880682-02-8) Winning Intl.

Triathlons for Kids. Sally Edwards. (Illus.). 128p. (Orig.). 1992. pap. 6.95 (1-880682-01-X) Winning Intl.

Triathlons for Women. Sally Edwards. (Illus.). 152p. (Orig.). 1992. pap. 6.95 (1-880682-00-1) Winning Intl.

Triax & the NGR. Kevin Siembieda & Kevin Long. Ed. by Alex Marciniszyn et al. (Rifts World Bks.: No. 5). (Illus.). 224p. (Orig.). (YA). (gr. 8 up). 1994. pap. 20.95 (0-916211-60-6, 810) Palladium Bks.

Triazenes: Chemical, Biological, & Clinical Aspects. Ed. by T. Giraldi et al. LC 90-14271. (Illus.). 220p. 1990. 79.50 (0-306-43667-1, Plenum Pr) Plenum.

Tribal & Chiefly Warfare in South America. Elsa M. Redmond. Ed. by Joyce Marcus. LC 94-18061. (Memoirs Series, Prehistory & Human Ecology of the Valley of Oaxaca: No. 28, Vol. 5). 1994. 25.00 (0-915703-35-1) U Mich Mus Anthro.

Tribal & Peasant Life in Nineteenth Century India. V. Ball. 1986. reprint ed. 60.00 (0-8364-1583-3, Pub. by Usha II) S Asia.

Tribal Art & Craft. A. K. Das. (C). 1993. 44.00 (0-8364-2877-3, Pub. by Agam II) S Asia.

Tribal Arts & Crafts of Madhya Pradesh. Manohar Ashi. (Illus.). 160p. Date not set. 39.50 (0-944142-71-0, Pub. by Mapin Pubng II) Antique Collect.

Tribal Colleges: Shaping the Future of Native America. Frwd. by Ernest L. Boyer. LC 89-27994. 103p. 1989. pap. text ed. 8.00 (0-931050-36-7) Carnegie Fnd Advan Teach.

***Tribal Colleges Revisited: A New Era in Indian Higher Education.** Corporate Publication Staff. LC 97-13002. 100p. (Orig.). 1997. pap. 15.00 (0-931050-63-4) Carnegie Fnd Advan Teach.

Tribal Cooperative System: A Study of North-East India. S. Mahalingam. (C). 1992. text ed. 21.00 (81-7033-169-2, Pub. by Rawat II) S Asia.

Tribal Crafts of Uganda, by M. T. & K. P. Wachsmann. Margaret Trowell. LC 74-15098. (Illus.). reprint ed. 57.50 (0-404-12147-0) AMS Pr.

Tribal Culture: Economy & Health. Shashi Bairathi. (C). 1991. 18.00 (0-8364-2803-X, Pub. by Rawat II) S Asia.

Tribal Culture & History of Arunachal Pradesh. J. N. Chowdbury. (C). 1990. 26.00 (81-7035-095-6, Pub. by Daya Pub Hse II) S Asia.

Tribal Cultures & Change. Rs. K. Mann. (C). 1989. 42.00 (0-685-32674-8, Pub. by Mittal II) S Asia.

Tribal Custom in Anglo-Saxon Law Being an Essay Supplemental to 'The English Village Community' & 'The Tribal System in Wales' Frederic Seebohm. xvi, 538p. 1972. reprint ed. lib. bdg. 25.00 (0-8377-2605-0) Rothman.

Tribal Customary Laws of North East India. Shibani Roy & S. H. Rizvi. (C). 1990. text ed. 27.00 (81-7018-586-6, Pub. by BR Pub II) S Asia.

Tribal Demography in India. Lalitendu Jagatleg. (C). 1991. 29.00 (81-7024-445-5, Pub. by Ashish II) S Asia.

Tribal Demography of Gonds. B. G. Banerjee & Kiran Bhatia. (C). 1988. 21.50 (81-212-0237-X, Pub. by Gian Publng Hse II) S Asia.

Tribal Design. Deborah Christine & Stevie Mack. (Programs Ser.). 50p. (J). (gr. 4-12). 1988. pap. 249.00 (0-945666-09-8) Crizmac.

Tribal Development & Administration, 1986. S. S. Negi. 167p. (C). 1986. 125.00 (81-7089-038-1, Pub. by Intl Bk Distr II) St Mut.

Tribal Development in India. Ed. by B. Jena & Rabindra N. Pati. (C). 1989. 34.00 (81-7024-228-2, Pub. by Ashish II) S Asia.

Tribal Development in India: A Trend Report. M. Satyananarayana. 1990. 23.50 (81-210-0243-5, Pub. by Inter-India Pubns) S Asia.

Tribal Development in India: Myth & Reality. L. K. Mahapatra. (C). 1994. 15.00 (0-7069-7351-8, Pub. by Vikas II) S Asia.

Tribal Development in India, No. Two: Problems & Prospects. rev. ed. Ed. by Buddhadeb Chaudhuri. (C). 1990. 74.00 (81-210-0254-0, Pub. by Inter-India Pubns) S Asia.

Tribal Development Without Tears. M. L. Patel. (C). 1994. 38.00 (81-210-0320-2, Pub. by Inter-India Pubns) S Asia.

Tribal Dispossession & the Ottawa Indian University Fraud. William E. Unrau & H. Craig Miner. LC 84-19534. (Illus.). 224p. 1985. 32.95 (0-8061-1896-2) U of Okla Pr.

Tribal Distribution in Oregon. J. V. Berreman. LC 37-20181. (American Anthropological Association Memoirs Ser.). 1974. reprint ed. pap. 25.00 (0-527-00546-0) Periodicals Srv.

Tribal Economy: Problems & Prospects. V. S. Ramamani. 1988. 34.00 (0-317-90510-4, Pub. by Chugh Pubns II) S Asia.

Tribal Economy & Society. M. S. Jairth. (C). 1991. 13.50 (81-7099-299-0, Pub. by Mittal II) S Asia.

Tribal Ecosystem & Malnutrition in India. Ed. by P. D. Tiwari & A. N. Sharma. 1989. 38.00 (81-85119-74-0, Pub. by Northern Bk Ctr II) S Asia.

Tribal Education in India: A Case Study of Orrissa. Satyavrata R. Patel. (C). 1991. 14.00 (81-7099-292-3, Pub. by Mittal II) S Asia.

Tribal Elites & Social Transformation. K. K. Misra. (C). 1994. 18.00 (81-210-0319-9, Pub. by Inter-India Pubns) S Asia.

Tribal Encounter with Industry. A. R. Srivastava. (Sociological Publications in Honour of Dr. K. Ishwaran: No. 5). 1990. text ed. 25.00 (81-85047-56-1, Pub. by Reliance Pub Hse II) Apt Bks.

Tribal Ethnicity, Class & Integration. S. L. Doshi. 1990. 29.00 (81-7033-093-9, Pub. by Rawat II) S Asia.

Tribal Ethnography Customary Law & Change. Ed. by K. S. Singh. (C). 1993. 52.00 (81-7022-471-3, Pub. by Concept II) S Asia.

Tribal Eye: Antique Kilims of Anatolia. Peter Davies. LC 92-43327. (Illus.). 144p. 1993. pap. 29.95 (0-8478-1705-9) Rizzoli Intl.

Tribal Food Habits. P. V. Rajyalakshmi. (C). 1991. 18.50 (81-212-0337-6, Pub. by Gian Publng Hse II) S Asia.

Tribal Government of the Oglala Sioux of Pine Ridge, South Dakota. Ira H. Grinnell. 1967. 5.00 (1-55614-012-6) U of SD Gov Res Bur.

Tribal History: (A New Interpretation) Hira L. Shukra. (C). 1988. 29.00 (81-7018-471-1) S Asia.

Tribal Identities: Historical Perspectives on Nationalism, Europe, & Sport. Ed. by James A. Mangan. (International Journal of the History of Sport Ser.). 260p. (C). 1996. 35.00 (0-7146-4666-0, Pub. by F Cass Pubs UK); pap. 19.50 (0-7146-4201-0, Pub. by F Cass Pubs UK) Intl Spec Bk.

Tribal Identity: A Language & Communication Perspective. Lachman M. Khubchandani. (C). 1992. 16.00 (81-85182-77-9, Pub. by Manohar II) S Asia.

Tribal Identity & the Modern World. Suresh Sharma. LC 93-50134. 216p. 1994. 26.95 (0-8039-9155-X) AltaMira Pr.

Tribal India. K. S. Padhy & P. C. Satapathy. (C). 1988. 18.00 (81-7024-225-8, Pub. by Ashish II) S Asia.

Tribal India: Problem Development Prospect, 2 vols. Ed. by Manis K. Raha & P. C. Commar. 400p. 1989. Set. write for info. (81-212-0273-6, Pub. by Gian Publng Hse II) S Asia.

Tribal Innovators: Tswana Chiefs & Social Change, 1795-1940. Isaac Schapera. (London School of Economics Monographs on Social Anthropology: No. 43). 280p. (C). 1970. text ed. 46.50 (0-485-19543-7, Pub. by Athlone Pr UK) Humanities.

Tribal Issues: A Non-Conventional Approach. Neeti Mahanti. (C). 1994. 14.00 (81-210-0332-6, Pub. by Inter-India Pubns) S Asia.

Tribal Languages of Himachal Pradesh, 2 pts., 2. D. D. Sharma. (Studies in Tibeto-Himalayan Languages). (C). 1992. text ed. 70.00 (81-7099-102-1, Pub. by Mittal II) S Asia.

Tribal Languages of Himachal Pradesh, 2 pts., Set. D. D. Sharma. (Studies in Tibeto-Himalayan Languages). (C). 1992. text ed. write for info. (81-7099-048-3, Pub. by Mittal II) S Asia.

Tribal Law. Scott Prentzas. LC 94-5531. (Native American Culture Ser.). (J). 1994. write for info. (0-86625-536-2) Rourke Corp.

Tribal Law. Terri Willis. LC 95-870. (Native Central & South American Cultures Ser.). (J). (gr. 2-6). 1995. write for info. (0-86625-554-0) Rourke Pubns.

Tribal Life & Forests No. 1: Tribal Life in India. Ed. by Devendra Thakur & D. N. Thakur. (C). 1995. 34.00 (81-7100-625-6) S Asia.

Tribal Living Book: 150 Things to Do & Make from Traditional Cultures. rev. ed. David Levinson & David Sherwood. LC 93-10533. (Illus.). 240p. 1993. pap. 16.95 (1-55566-104-1) Johnson Bks.

Tribal Migration in Himalayan Frontiers. R. P. Khatana. (C). 1992. 30.00 (81-85326-46-0, Pub. by Vintage II) S Asia.

Tribal Movements in India, Vol. 1. Ed. by K. S. Singh. 1982. 25.00 (0-8364-0901-9, Pub. by Manohar II) S Asia.

Tribal Movements in India, Vol. 2. K. S. Singh. 1983. 27.00 (0-8364-1027-0, Pub. by Manohar II) S Asia.

Tribal Myths of Orissa. Verrier Elwin. Ed. by Richard M. Dorson. LC 80-746. (Folklore of the World Ser.). 1981. reprint ed. lib. bdg. 81.95 (0-405-13312-X) Ayer.

Tribal Paintings & Sculptures. Umesh C. Misra. (C). 1989. 25.00 (81-7018-543-2, Pub. by BR Pub II) S Asia.

Tribal Peoples & Development Issues: A Global Overview. John H. Bodley. LC 87-12508. 420p. (C). 1988. pap. text ed. 34.95 (0-87484-786-9, 786) Mayfield Pub.

Tribal Peoples & Economic Development: Human Ecologic Considerations. Robert Goodland. 118p. 1982. 7.95 (0-8213-0010-5, 10010) World Bank.

An Asterisk (*) at the beginning of an entry indicates that the title is appearing in BIP for the first time.

Tribal Politics & State Systems in Pre-Colonial & Eastern & Northeastern India. Surajit Sinha. 366p. (C). 1987. 22.50 (*81-7074-014-2*, Pub. by KP Bagchi IA) S Asia.

Tribal Research in India: Approach, Constraints, Structure & Techniques. M. L. Patel. (C). 1994. text ed. 34.00 (*81-210-0318-0*, Pub. by Inter-India Pubns) S Asia.

Tribal Revolt of Chotanagpur, Nineteen Thirty-One to Nineteen Thirty-Two. Jagdish C. Jha. 356p. 1987. 14.00 (*0-8364-2045-4*, Pub. by Usha II) S Asia.

Tribal Rhythms - Creating the Village: A Curriculum Guide for Building Community with Children. Susan E. Porter et al. 98p. 1995. teacher ed., pap. 18.95 (*0-9649688-0-0*) Cprtive Artists.

***Tribal Rugs.** Jenny Housego. LC 90-34710. (Illus.). 180p. 1996. pap. text ed. 19.95 (*1-56656-218-X*) Interlink Pub.

***Tribal Rugs.** James Opie. 1997. 95.00 (*1-85669-025-3*, Pub. by L King Publing UK) Bks Nippan.

Tribal Rugs: A Buyer's Guide. Lee Allane. LC 96-60258. (Illus.). 144p. (Orig.). 1996. pap. 17.95 (*0-500-27897-0*) Thames Hudson.

Tribal Rugs: Nomadic & Village Weavers from the Near East & Central Asia. James Opie. Ed. by Spencer Gill & Sophie Collins. LC 92-72906. (Illus.). 328p. 1992. 95.00 (*0-9633689-0-7*) Tolstoy Pr.

Tribal Rugs of Southern Persia. James Opie. LC 81-90582. 223p. 1981. text ed. 110.00 (*0-9611144-0-1*) J Opie Oriental.

Tribal Scars & Other Stories. Sembene Ousmane. Tr. by Len Ortzen. LC 87-25035. (African Writers Ser.). 117p. (C). 1987. pap. 8.95 (*0-435-90142-7*, 90142) Heinemann.

Tribal Sculpture from the Barbier Mueller Collection. Douglas Newton. LC 95-12486. (Illus.). 348p. 1995. 80.00 (*0-86565-962-1*) Vendome.

Tribal Secrets: Recovering American Indian Intellectual Traditions. Robert A. Warrior. LC 94-26219. 1994. pap. text ed. 16.95 (*0-8166-2379-1*) U of Minn Pr.

Tribal Situation & Development in Central India. S. K. Tiwan. 149p. 1995. pap. 100.00 (*81-85880-60-3*, Pub. by Print Hse II) St Mut.

Tribal Situation in Forest Villages: Changing Subsistence Strategies & Adaptation. R. R. Prasad. (C). 1993. 27.50 (*81-7141-234-3*, Pub. by Discovery Pub Hse II) S Asia.

Tribal Situation in India. Ed. by K. Suresh Singh. 1986. reprint ed. 47.50 (*0-685-17543-X*, Pub. by Motilal Banarsidass II) S Asia.

Tribal Situation in West Bengal. Manis K. Raha. (C). 1990. 47.50 (*0-8364-2648-7*, Pub. by Firma KLM II) S Asia.

Tribal Society in India. K. S. Singh. 1986. 32.00 (*0-8364-1541-8*, Pub. by Manohar II) S Asia.

Tribal Songs of Northeast India Choudhury, Amalendu B Kar. 1985. 10.00 (*0-8364-1259-1*, Pub. by Mukhopadhyaya II) S Asia.

Tribal Studies in Northern Nigeria, 2 vols. Charles K. Meek. LC 74-15066. reprint ed. Set. 155.00 (*0-404-12107-1*) AMS Pr.

Tribal Style: Selections from the African Collection at the Peabody Museum of Salem. John R. Grimes. (Illus.). 1984. pap. 15.00 (*0-87577-150-5*, Peabody Museum) Peabody Essex Mus.

Tribal Thought & Culture. Ed. by Baidyanath Saraswati. 1991. text ed. 26.00 (*81-7022-340-7*, Pub. by Concept II) S Asia.

Tribal Traditions of Kenya: Kenyan Arts from the Collection of Irene Sedgwick Briedis. Esther Bockhoff & Nancy I. Fleming. Ed. by Lucy Ireland & Carolyn Platt. (Illus.). 40p. (Orig.). 1986. pap. 7.50 (*1-878600-04-4*) Cleve Mus Nat Hist.

Tribal Transformation in India, Vol. I: Economy & Agrarian Issues. Ed. by Duddhadeb Chaudhuri. (C). 1992. 58.00 (*81-210-0272-9*, Pub. by Inter-India Pubns) S Asia.

Tribal Transformation in India, Vol. II: Socio-Economic & Ecological Development. Ed. by Duddhadeb Chaudhuri. (C). 1992. 40.00 (*0-8364-2822-6*, Pub. by Inter-India Pubns) S Asia.

Tribal Transformation in India, Vol. III: Ethnopolitics & Identity Crisis. Ed. by Duddhadeb Chaudhuri. (C). 1992. 60.00 (*0-8364-2823-4*, Pub. by Inter-India Pubns) S Asia.

Tribal Transformation in India, Vol. IV: Education & Literacy Programmes. Ed. by Duddhadeb Chaudhuri. (C). 1992. 34.00 (*81-210-0275-3*, Pub. by Inter-India Pubns) S Asia.

Tribal Warfare in Organizations. Peg C. Neuhauser. 240p. 1990. pap. 17.50 (*0-88730-444-3*) Harper Busn.

Tribal Wars of the Southern Plains. Stan Hoig. LC 92-54154. 272p. 1993. 27.95 (*0-8061-2463-6*) U of Okla Pr.

Tribal Water Management Handbook. American Indian Resources Institute Staff. (Illus.). 208p. (Orig.). (C). 1988. pap. text ed. 24.00 (*0-939890-08-9*) Am Indian LTP.

Tribal Welfare Development & Administration. S. S. Negi. 167p. (C). 1986. text ed. 125.00 (*0-685-52015-3*, Pub. by Intl Bk Distr II) St Mut.

Tribal Wisdom: Lardil, Keepers of the Dreamtime; Maasai, People of Cattle; Yanomami, Masters of the Spirit World, 3 vols., Set. David McKnight et al. (Little Wisdom Library). (Illus.). 192p. 1995. boxed 29.95 (*0-8118-0843-2*) Chronicle Bks.

Tribal Woman Labourers: Aspects of Economic & Physical Exploitation. Sushama S. Prasad. 1988. 36.00 (*81-212-0193-4*, Pub. by Gian Publng Hse II) S Asia.

***Tribal Women: On the Threshold of Twenty First Century.** Kamlesh Mann. 174p. 1995. pap. 150.00 (*81-85880-88-3*, Pub. by Print Hse II) St Mut.

Tribal Women & Development. Ed. by J. P. Singh et al. (C). 1988. 34.00 (*81-7033-048-3*, Pub. by Rawat II) S Asia.

Tribal Women in Changing Society. K. Mann. 178p. 1987. 21.00 (*0-8364-2034-9*, Pub. by Mittal II) S Asia.

Tribal Women of India. S. S. Shashi. 163p. 1978. 16.95 (*0-318-37314-9*) Asia Bk Corp.

***Tribal Writes: The Correspondence Guide for Native Americans.** 2nd ed. Linda J. Rasmussen. LC 95-68649. VII, 196p. (Orig.). 1995. reprint ed. pap. 22.95 (*0-9657905-0-9*) Native Amer Path.

Tribaliks: Contemporary Congolese Stories. Henri Lopes. Tr. by Andrea Leskes from FRE. (African Writers Ser.). Orig. Title: Tribaliques. 112p. (Orig.). (C). 1987. pap. 8.95 (*0-435-90762-X*, 90762) Heinemann.

Tribaliques see Tribaliks: Contemporary Congolese Stories

Tribalism & Society in Islamic Iran 1500-1629. Ed. by James J. Reid. (Studies in Near Eastern Culture & Society Ser.: Vol. 4). 215p. 1983. pap. 23.00 (*0-89003-124-X*) Undena Pubns.

Tribalism in India. Kamaladevi Chattopadhyaya. 302p. 1978. 19.95 (*0-318-36985-0*) Asia Bk Corp.

Tribally Controlled Colleges: Making Good Medicine. Wayne J. Stein. LC 92-7326. (American Indian Studies: Vol. 3). (Illus.). 180p. (C). 1993. text ed. 35.95 (*0-8204-1772-6*) P Lang Pubng.

Tribally Controlled Indian College. Norman T. Oppelt. 1990. pap. 20.00 (*0-912586-67-2*) Navajo Coll Pr.

Tribals & Christian Missionaries. Shyam Lal. (C). 1994. text ed. 22.00 (*81-85445-58-3*, Pub. by Manas Pubns II) S Asia.

Tribals & Their Culture in Arunachal Pradesh & Tripura, Vol. 2. G. K. Ghosh. 154p. 1992. 12.50 (*81-7024-427-7*, Pub. by Ashish Pub Hse II) Nataraj Bks.

Tribals & Their Culture in Assam, Meghalaya & Mizoram, Vol. 1. G. K. Ghosh. 143p. 1992. 12.50 (*81-7024-397-1*, Pub. by Ashish Pub Hse II) Nataraj Bks.

Tribals & Their Culture in Manipur & Nagaland, Vol. 3. G. K. Ghosh. 223p. 1992. 17.00 (*81-7024-455-2*, Pub. by Ashish Pub Hse II) Nataraj Bks.

Tribals from Tradition to Transition: A Study of Yanadi Tribe to Andhra Pradesh. G. Stanley Jaya Kumar. 126p. 1995. pap. 100.00 (*81-85880-81-6*, Pub. by Print Hse II) St Mut.

Tribals in India. Ed. by Amar Kumar Singh. (C). 1995. 36.00 (*81-241-0330-5*, Pub. by Har-Anand Pubns II) S Asia.

Tribals of Andaman & Nicobar Islands. Hari H. Das & Rabindranath Rath. (C). 1991. text ed. 22.50 (*81-7024-367-X*, Pub. by Ashish II) S Asia.

Tribals of India. Sunil Janah. (Illus.). 144p. (C). 1994. 45.00 (*0-19-562862-4*, 3583) OUP.

Tribals of Orissa: The Changing Socio-Economic Profile. Ed. by B. C. Ray. 170p. 1989. 16.00 (*81-212-0270-1*, Pub. by Gian Publng Hse II) S Asia.

Tribals, Rehabilitation, & Development. K. C. Alexander et al. (C). 1991. text ed. 20.00 (*0-685-53666-1*, Pub. by Rawat II) S Asia.

Tribe. R. D. Zimmerman. 288p. 1996. mass mkt. 5.50 (*0-440-21870-5*) Dell.

***Tribe: A Todd Mills Mystery.** R. D. Zimmerman. (Todd Mills Mystery Ser.). 288p. 1997. pap. 10.95 (*0-385-32002-7*) Doubleday.

Tribe Alasmidontini: Unionidae Anodontinae. Arthur Clarke. LC 80-23747. (Smithsonian Contributions to Zoology Ser.: No. 326). 79p. reprint ed. pap. 25.00 (*0-317-26683-7*, 2025112) Bks Demand.

Tribe & Class in Monrovia. Merran Fraenkel. LC 64-6843. 266p. reprint ed. pap. 75.90 (*0-8357-6955-0*, 2039014) Bks Demand.

Tribe & Polity in Late Prehistoric Europe: Demography, Production, & Exchange in the Evolution of Complex Social Systems. Ed. by D. B. Gibson & M. N. Geselowitz. LC 88-9940. (Illus.). 248p. 1988. 59.50 (*0-306-42913-6*, Plenum Pr) Plenum.

***Tribe Apart: An Uncommon Journey Inside American Adolescence.** Patricia Hersch. 1998. write for info. (*0-449-90767-8*) Fawcett.

Tribe of Dina: A Jewish Women's Anthology. rev. ed. Ed. by Melanie K. Kantrowitz & Irena Klepfisz. LC 88-43319. (Illus.). 360p. 1989. reprint ed. pap. 17.00 (*0-8070-3605-6*) Beacon Pr.

Tribe of John: Ashbery & Contemporary Poetry. Ed. by Susan M. Schultz. LC 94-28820. (Illus.). 288p. (Orig.). 1995. pap. text ed. 28.95 (*0-8173-0767-2*) U of Ala Pr.

Tribe of Tiger. large type ed. Elizabeth M. Thomas. 1995. 22.95 (*0-7838-1169-1*, GK Hall) Thorndike Pr.

Tribe of Tiger: Cats and Their Culture. Elizabeth M. Thomas. 240p. 1994. 20.00 (*0-671-79965-7*) S&S Trade.

Tribe of Tiger: Cats & Their Culture. Elizabeth M. Thomas. 1995. pap. 12.00 (*0-684-80454-9*, Touchstone Bks) S&S Trade.

Tribe of Warrior Women: Breast Cancer Survivors. Melissa Springer. LC 96-7083. (Illus.). 72p. 1996. 39.95 (*1-57587-049-5*) Crane Hill AL.

Tribe Returned. Janet Cunningham. Ed. by Winafred B. Lucas. (Illus.). 200p. 1994. 18.85 (*1-882530-09-8*) Deep Forest Pr.

Tribe That Hides from Man. Adrian Cowell. (Illus.). 265p. 1996. pap. 16.95 (*0-7126-5959-5*, Pub. by Pimlico) Trafalgar.

***TriBeCa Cookbook.** Mary Cleaver et al. 1997. pap. 16.95 (*0-89815-912-1*) Ten Speed Pr.

Tribes. Art Wolf. LC 96-50275. 1997. 45.00 (*0-517-70368-8*) Random Hse Value.

Tribes: A New Way of Learning & Being Together. 3rd rev. ed. Jeanne Gibbs. (Illus.). 432p. 1995. pap. 31.95 (*0-932762-09-3*, 100) CtrSource Systs. TRIBES, A NEW WAY OF LEARNING & BEING TOGETHER, details an inspiring process transforming educational systems. Educators & parents who are concerned with preparing students to do well in today's world of rapid change, information & complex issues will appreciate the integrated approach to learning critical thinking & collaborative social skills. The focus of TRIBES is nothing less than the development of each & every child within the school community. The approach transforms traditional "teacher-talk" classrooms into student centered classrooms using cooperative learning methods, ways to reach students of multiple learning styles & the supportive learning environment, called TRIBES. The book details how to build the caring environment by facilitating a three-stage group development process: inclusion (everyone belongs), influence (everyone contributes) & community (learning together). Students enjoy on-going membership in a tribe of peers throughout the year & become accountable to each other for accomplishing learning tasks. TRIBES is used by thousands of educational systems with multicultural preschool through adult populations. Over time the process lessens behavior problems, increases academic achievement, & improves staff morale & intergroup relations. The book contains 432 pages, 168 activities/curricula structures, delightful graphics & photos, & a resource section. Volume discounts available from publisher: CenterSource Systems, 305 Tesconi Circle, Santa Rosa, CA 95401; 707-577-8233.

Publisher Provided Annotation.

Tribes: How Race, Religion, & Family Determine Success in the New Global Economy. Joel Kotkin. LC 92-53638. 1992. 24.00 (*0-679-41282-4*) Random.

Tribes: How Race, Religion & Identity Determine Success in the New Global. Joel Kotkin. 1994. pap. 13.00 (*0-679-75299-4*) Random.

Tribes & Castes of Bombay Presidency, 3 vols., Set. R. E. Enthoeven. (C). 1990. 140.00 (*81-206-0630-2*, Pub. by Asian Educ Servs II) S Asia.

Tribes & Castes of Manipur: Description & Select Biography. Sipra Sen. (C). 1992. 40.00 (*81-7099-310-5*, Pub. by Mittal II) S Asia.

Tribes & Customs of Hy Many Commonly Called O'Kellys Country. deluxe ed. John O'Donovan. (Old Ireland Ser.). (Illus.). vi, 221p. 1992. reprint ed. lib. bdg. 100.00 (*0-940134-39-X*) Irish Genealog.

***Tribes & State Formation in the Middle East.** Ed. by Philip S. Khoury. 350p. 1996. pap. 15.50 (*0-614-21171-9*, 1261) Kazi Pubns.

Tribes & State Formation in the Middle East. Ed. by Philip S. Khoury & Joseph Kostiner. LC 90-35640. 400p. 1991. 50.00 (*0-520-07079-8*); pap. 16.00 (*0-520-07080-1*) U CA Pr.

Tribes & Trailblazers see Story of Colorado

Tribes & Tribulations: Misconceptions about American Indians & Their Histories. Laurence M. Hauptman. LC 94-40042. 184p. 1995. 37.50 (*0-8263-1581-X*); pap. 15.95 (*0-8263-1582-8*) U of NM Pr.

Tribes at Risk: The Wisconsin Tribes Comparative Risk Project. (Illus.). 133p. (Orig.). (C). 1994. pap. text ed. 30.00 (*0-7881-1522-7*) DIANE Pub.

Tribes Castes & Harijans. Ed. by Bam D. Sharda. (C). 1991. 28.00 (*81-202-0351-8*, Pub. by Ajanta II) S Asia.

Tribes, Clans & Castles of Nepal. V. Vansittari. (C). 1991. text ed. 39.00 (*0-7855-0164-9*, Pub. by Ratna Pustak Bhandar) St Mut.

Tribes, Government, & History in Yemen. Paul Dresch. (Illus.). 472p. 1994. pap. 26.00 (*0-19-827790-3*) OUP.

Tribe's Home Plates. Cleveland Indians Wives' Association Staff. LC 92-23879. 1992. write for info. (*0-87197-343-X*) Favorite Recipes.

Tribes in Oman. John Carter. 176p. (C). 1995. 96.00 (*0-907151-02-7*, Pub. by IMMEL Pubng UK) St Mut.

Tribes of California. Stephen Powers. LC 74-7994. reprint ed. 67.50 (*0-404-11881-X*) AMS Pr.

Tribes of California. Stephen Powers. LC 75-13150. 1977. reprint ed. pap. 15.95 (*0-520-03172-5*) U CA Pr.

Tribes of India: The Struggle for Survival. Christoph Von Furer-Haimendorf. LC 80-28647. (Illus.). 360p. 1982. 50.00 (*0-520-04315-4*) U CA Pr.

Tribes of India, Nepal, Tibet Borderland: A Study of Cultural Transformation. B. S. Bisht. (C). 1994. 24.00 (*81-212-0454-2*, Pub. by Gian Publng Hse II) S Asia.

Tribes of India Nepal Tibet Borderland: A Study of Cultural Transformation. R. S. Bisht. 1994. pap. 72.00 (*0-7855-0489-3*, Pub. by Ratna Pustak Bhandar) St Mut.

Tribes of Indo-Burma Border. S. N. Barua. (C). 1991. 36.00 (*81-7099-308-3*, Pub. by Mittal II) S Asia.

Tribes of Nagaland. Sipra Sen. 1987. 44.00 (*0-8364-2220-1*, Pub. by Mittal II) S Asia.

Tribes of North East India. Sudhangshu B. Saha. (C). 1987. 27.50 (*0-8364-2127-2*, KL Mukhopadhyay) S Asia.

Tribes of North-East India. Sarthak Sengupta. (C). 1994. 22.50 (*81-212-0463-1*, Pub. by Gian Publng Hse II) S Asia.

Tribes of Northeast India. Ed. by Sebastian Karotemprel. 1984. 32.50 (*0-8364-1135-8*, Pub. by Mukhopadhyaya II) S Asia.

Tribes of Northern & Central Kordofan. H. A. Macmichael. 260p. 1967. reprint ed. 57.50 (*0-7146-1113-1*, Pub. by F Cass Pubs UK) Intl Spec Bk.

***Tribes of Palos Verdes.** Nicholson. LC 97-12429. 1997. 19.95 (*0-312-15677-4*) St Martin.

Tribes of the Buffalo: A Swiss Artist on the American Frontier. Ed. by Megan Harding. (Illus.). 64p. (Orig.). 1994. pap. text ed. 15.00 (*1-878600-07-9*) Cleve Mus Nat Hist.

Tribes of the Extreme Northwest, Alaska, the Aleutians & Adjacent Territories. George Gibbs et al. (Illus.). 156p. reprint ed. pap. 9.95 (*0-8466-4018-X*, I18) Shorey.

***Tribes of the Heartless Wastes.** TSR Inc. Staff. 1997. 20.00 (*0-7869-0773-8*) TSR Inc.

Tribes of the Liberian Hinterland. George Schwab. Ed. by G. W. Harley. (HU PMP Ser.). (Illus.). 1947. 100.00 (*0-527-01278-5*) Periodicals Srv.

Tribes of the Niger Delta: Their Religion & Customs. Margery F. Perham. 1976. lib. bdg. 59.95 (*0-8490-2768-3*) Gordon Pr.

Tribes of the Niger Delta: Their Religions & Customs. Percy A. Talbot. (Illus.). 350p. 1967. reprint ed. 57.50 (*0-7146-1013-5*, Pub. by F Cass Pubs UK) Intl Spec Bk.

Tribes of the Sahara. Lloyd C. Briggs. LC 60-7988. 328p. reprint ed. pap. 93.50 (*0-317-10935-9*, 2006009) Bks Demand.

Tribes of the Southern Plains, Vol. 19. Time-Life Books Editors. Ed. by Henry Woodhead. LC 95-8790. (American Indians Ser.). (Illus.). 184p. 1995. 19.95 (*0-8094-9595-3*) Time-Life.

Tribes of the Southern Woodlands. Time-Life Books Editors. LC 93-40640. (American Indians Ser.). 176p. 1994. 19.95 (*0-8094-9550-3*); lib. bdg. write for info. (*0-8094-9551-1*) Time-Life.

Tribes of Tripura: Description, Ethnology, & Bibliography. Sipra Sen. (C). 1993. 34.00 (*81-212-0448-8*, Pub. by Gian Publng Hse II) S Asia.

Tribes of Yahweh: A Sociology of the Religion of Liberated Israel, 1250-1050 B.C. Norman K. Gottwald. LC 78-24333. 944p. (Orig.). 1979. pap. 50.00 (*0-88344-499-2*) Orbis Bks.

Tribes on the Hill: The United States Congress - Rituals & Realities. rev. ed. Jack M. Weatherford. LC 85-3864. 320p. 1985. text ed. 55.00 (*0-89789-071-X*, Bergin & Garvey); pap. text ed. 24.95 (*0-89789-072-8*, Bergin & Garvey) Greenwood.

Tribes That Slumber: Indians of the Tennessee Region. Thomas M. Lewis & Madeline Kneberg. LC 58-12085. (Illus.). 208p. 1958. pap. 16.95 (*0-87049-021-4*) U of Tenn Pr.

Tribes with Flags: A Dangerous Passage Through the Chaos of the Middle East. Charles Glass. LC 89-157. 1991. pap. 12.95 (*0-87113-457-8*, Atlntc Mnthly) Grove-Atltic.

Tribhuvan University Charter: An Act Promulgated for the Establishment & Organization of a Teaching & Affiliating University. 39p. 1959. 7.50 (*0-318-23190-5*) Am-Nepal Ed.

Tribiological Design of Machine Elements: Proceedings of the 15th Leeds-Lyon Symposium on Tribilogy, Leeds, UK, 6-9 Sept., 1988. Ed. by Duncan Dowson et al. (Tribology Ser.: No. 14). 522p. 1989. 257.00 (*0-444-87435-6*) Elsevier.

Tribiology in Machine Design. T. A. Stolarski. (Illus.). 312p. 1990. 70.00 (*0-8311-1102-X*) Indus Pr.

Tribiology of Miniature Systems. Z. Rymuza. (Tribology Ser.: No. 13). 565p. 1989. 232.00 (*0-444-87401-1*) Elsevier.

Tribo Babo: Chan Sanba. Jean A. Duge. Ed. by Emmanuel W. Vedrine et al. (Illus.). 71p. 1995. pap. write for info. (*1-885566-05-0*) Oresjozef.

Tribological Insights & Performance Characteristics of Modern Engine Lubricants. (International Fuels & Lubricants Meeting & Exposition, 1993 Ser.). 334p. 1993. pap. 85.00 (*1-56091-435-1*, SP-996) Soc Auto Engineers.

Tribological Materials & NDE. Ed. by Robert L. Fusaro et al. LC 92-52644. (Flight-Vehicle Materials, Structures, & Dynamics Ser.: Vol. 4). 426p. 1992. 100.00 (*0-7918-0662-6*, 100325) ASME.

Tribological Mechanisms & Wear Problems in Materials: Proceedings of a Conference Held in Conjunction with Materials Week '87, Cincinnati, OH, 10-15 October 1987. Ed. by Prasad S. Godavarti et al. LC 87-73381. (Illus.). 187p. reprint ed. pap. 53.30 (*0-8357-4094-3*, 2036860) Bks Demand.

Tribological Modeling for Mechanical Designers. Ed. by Kenneth C. Ludema & Raymond G. Bayer. LC 91-8238. (Special Technical Publication Ser.: No. STP 1105). (Illus.). 195p. 1991. text ed. 76.00 (*0-8031-1412-5*, 04-011050-27) ASTM.

Tribological Processes in Contact Areas of Lubricated Solid Bodies see Eurotrib, '81: Proceedings of the Third International Tribology Congress, Warsaw

Tribological Processes in Solid Body Contact Areas see Eurotrib, '81: Proceedings of the Third International Tribology Congress, Warsaw

***Tribology.** write for info. (*0-340-58719-9*, Pub. by E Arnold UK) Routledge Chapman & Hall.

Tribology: A Source Guide. 1991. lib. bdg. 79.75 (*0-8490-4906-7*) Gordon Pr.

Tribology: Friction & Wear of Engineering Materials. I. M. Hutchings. 1992. 58.00 (*0-8493-7764-1*, TJ1075) CRC Pr.

Tribology: Wear Test Selection for Design & Application. Ed. by A. W. Ruff & Raymond G. Bayer. LC 93-37460. (Special Technical Publication: Vol. 1199). (Illus.). 185p. 1993. text ed. 46.00 (*0-8031-1856-2*, 04-011990-27) ASTM.

Tribology & Mechanics of Magnetic Storage Devices. Bharat Bhushan. (Illus.). xviii, 1019p. 1989. 169.00 (*0-387-96926-8*) Spr-Verlag.

***Tribology & Mechanics of Magnetic Storage Devices.** 2nd ed. Bharat Bhushan. 1152p. 1996. 149.95 (*0-7803-3406-X*, PC5676) Inst Electrical.

Tribology & Mechanics of Magnetic Storage Devices. 2nd ed. Bharat Bhushan. (Illus.). 1144p. 1996. 149.00 (*0-387-94627-6*) Spr-Verlag.

Tribology & Mechanics of Magnetic Storage Systems, 25 papers. 191p. 1984. 80.00 (*0-318-17681-5*, SP-16) Soc Tribologists.

T

Tribology & the Liquid-Crystalline State. Ed. by Girma Biresaw. LC 90-14427. (ACS Symposium Ser.: No. 441). (Illus.). 144p. 1990. 39.95 (0-8412-1874-9) Am Chemical.

Tribology Handbook. 2nd ed. Ed. by Michael J. Neal. 640p. 1996. pap. 145.00 (0-7506-1198-7) Buttrwrth-Heinemann.

Tribology in Machine Design. T. A. Stolarski. Date not set. pap. write for info. (0-7506-1968-6) Buttrwrth-Heinemann.

Tribology in Manufacturing Processes. 209p. 1994. pap. 84.00 (0-7918-1211-1) ASME.

Tribology in Manufacturing Processes: 1994 International Mechanical Engineering Congress & Exposition, Chicago, Illinois - November 6-11, 1994. (CRTD - TRIB Ser.: Vol. 30, Vol. 5, Vol. 69). 216p. 1994. 84.00 (0-614-05619-5, I00374) ASME.

*Tribology in Metalworking: Friction, Lubrication & Wear. John A. Schey. LC 82-73612. (Illus.). 752p. 1983. reprint ed. pap. 180.00 (0-608-02619-0, 2063277) Bks Demand.

Tribology in Particulate Technology. Ed. by B. J. Briscoe & M. J. Adams. (Illus.). 496p. 1987. 204.00 (0-85274-425-0) IOP Pub.

Tribology in the U. S. A. & the Former Soviet Union: Studies & Applications. Ed. by V. A. Belyi et al. LC 93-49725. 1994. 95.00 (0-89864-065-2) Allerton Pr.

*Tribology of Composite Materials: Proceedings of a Conference Held May 1-3, 1990, in Oak Ridge, TN. ASM International Staff. Ed. by P. K. Rohatgi et al. LC 90-83193. (Illus.). 376p. 1990. reprint ed. pap. 107.20 (0-608-02630-1, 2063288) Bks Demand.

*Tribology of Contact-Near Contact Recording for Ultra High Density Magnetic Storage: Proceedings. Ed. by C. S. Bhatia & Aric K. Menon. (TRIB Ser.: Vol. 6). 65p. pap. 60.00 (0-7918-1515-3) ASME.

Tribology of Engines & Engine Oils: Eighteen Papers. 1993. 29.00 (1-56091-344-4, SP-959) Soc Auto Engineers.

*Tribology of Hydraulic Pump Testing, STP 1310, Vol. 131. 2nd ed. Ed. by George E. Totten et al. LC 96-40253. 380p. 1997. text ed. 57.00 (0-8031-2422-8, 04-013100-12) ASTM.

Tribology of Plastic Materials: Their Characteristics & Applications to Sliding Components. Y. Yamaguchi. (Tribology Ser.: No. 16). 362p. 1990. 189.50 (0-444-87445-3) Elsevier.

Tribology Symposium, 1994, Vol. 61. Ed. by H. Masudi. LC 93-74682. 140p. 1994. pap. 37.50 (0-7918-1189-1) ASME.

Tribology Symposium, 1995: Proceedings: The Energy & Environmental EXPO '95 - the Energy-Sources Technology Conference & Exhibition (1995: Houston, TX) Ed. by H. Masudi. LC 93-74682. (PD Ser.: Vol. 72). 177p. 1995. pap. 86.00 (0-7918-1297-9, H00929) ASME.

Tribond. Tim Walsh et al. (Orig.). (C). 1989. pap. 29.97 (0-9628275-1-7) Big Fun A Go Go.

*Tribophyceae (Xanthophyceae) Tyge Christensen. (Seaweeds of the British Isles Ser.: Vol. 4). (Illus.). 38p. 1997. pap. 12.95 (0-11-310004-3, Pub. by Statnry Ofc UK) Seven Hills Bk.

Tribu de Wagap (Nouvelle-Caledonie) A. Colomb. LC 75-32812. reprint ed. 44.50 (0-404-14116-1) AMS Pr.

Tribu des Immotels: Petit Dictionnaire de l'Acadamie Francais, Voyage a l'Interieur de l'Academie Francaise. Nicolas Silatsa. 96p. (FRE.). 1989. 59.95 (0-7859-8234-5, 2905291109) Fr & Eur.

Tribuhaven University & Its educational Activities. Madan R. Poudel. 210p. 1989. pap. 18.00 (0-317-04776-0) Am-Nepal Ed.

*Tribul. Frederick Tristan. Date not set. write for info. (0-688-05760-8) Morrow.

*Tribulacion. Thomas Ice. (Profecia Ser.). (SPA.). 1997. pap. 2.99 (0-8254-1342-7, Edit Portavoz) Kregel.

Tribulat Bonhomet. Auguste de Villiers De L'Isle-Adam. 192p. 19.95 (0-686-55725-5) Fr & Eur.

Tribulation & the Church. Chuck Smith. 64p. (Orig.). 1980. pap. 1.50 (0-936728-01-9) Word for Today.

*Tribulation Force. Tim LaHaye & Jerry B. Jenkins. 450p. 1996. 19.99 (0-8423-2913-7); audio 14.99 (0-8423-1787-2) Tyndale.

*Tribulation Force. Tim LaHaye & Jerry B. Jenkins. 1996. pap. 12.99 (0-8423-2921-8) Tyndale.

Tribulation Period Will Last Longer Than 7 Years. Walter E. Adams. (Orig.). 1988. pap. 3.95 (0-937408-99-9) GMI Pubns Inc.

Tribulation Temple. Gordon Lindsay. (Revelation Ser.: Vol. 5). 1962. 1.95 (0-89985-038-3) Christ for the Nations.

Tribulation 99: Alien Anomalies under America. Craig Baldwin. 72p. 1992. pap. 9.99 (0-9642284-1-6) Ediciones La Calavera.

Tribulations d'un Chinois en Chine. Jules Verne. (Illus.). 8.95 (0-686-55957-6) Fr & Eur.

Tribulations d'un Chinois en Chine. 4th ed. Jules Verne. 192p. 1976. 10.95 (0-686-55956-8) Fr & Eur.

*Tribulations of a Chinese Gentleman. Jules Verne. lib. bdg. 22.95 (0-8488-2058-4) Amereon Ltd.

Tribulations of Veneguay. Jim Stickter. LC 78-53364. (Illus.). (Orig.). 1978. pap. 7.50 (0-930770-08-0) Hemisphere Hse.

Tribunal de Cristo. Rick C. Howard. Tr. by Percy Quanrud & Alexandro Sarmiento from ENG. 124p. (SPA.). pap. 4.00 (0-9628091-2-8) Naioth Sound & Pub.

Tribunal of the Heart. Hope B. Mirilyubov. LC 95-91042. 1996. 19.95 (0-533-11829-8) Vantage.

Tribunaux Civils de Paris Pendant la Revolution: 1791-1800, 2 vols., Set. Aristide Douarche. LC 71-164777. (Collection de Documents Relatifs a l'Histoire de Paris Pendant la Revolution Francaise). reprint ed. 270.00 (0-404-52553-9) AMS Pr.

Tribune Almanac & Political Register for 1876. Ed. by David M. White. LC 74-15751. (Popular Culture in America Ser.). 112p. 1975. reprint ed. 16.95 (0-405-06385-7) Ayer.

Tribune Essays. Charles T. Congdon. LC 79-154147. (Select Bibliographies Reprint Ser.). 1977. reprint ed. 38.95 (0-8369-5763-6) Ayer.

Tribune Primer. Eugene Field. (Classics of Modern American Humor Ser.). (Illus.). reprint ed. 27.50 (0-404-19930-5) AMS Pr.

Tribune Sesquicentenial. Chicago Tribune Staff. LC 96-51735. 1996. write for info. (0-8092-3155-7) Contemp Bks.

Tribune Story. Etienne Dupuch. (Illus.). 1968. 12.00 (0-685-20643-2) Transatl Arts.

Triburst: (The Arms Trilogy) (Executioner Ser.). 1995. mass mkt. 3.50 (0-373-61196-X, 1-61196-1) Harlequin Bks.

Tributaries: An Anthology: Writer to Writer. Ed. by Barry Dempster. 112p. 1995. lib. bdg. 27.00 (0-8095-4590-X) Borgo Pr.

Tributaries - An Anthology: Writer to Writer. Barry Dempster. 112p. pap. 8.95 (0-88962-089-X) Mosaic.

*Tributary. Cid Corman. Ed. by Philippe Briet. (Illus.). 64p. (Orig.). (C). Date not set. pap. text ed. 10.00 (0-9646466-2-5) Edgewise Pr.

*Tribute: Poems by Bess Kingsbury. Bess Kingsbury. Ed. by Vicki K. Flanagan. (Illus.). 96p. (Orig.). 1996. pap. write for info. (0-940169-24-X) Liturgical Pubns.

Tribute: Selected Stories of Katharine Susannah Prichard. Katharine S. Prichard. Ed. by Ric Throssell. (Orig.). 1989. pap. 16.95 (0-7022-2166-X, Pub. by Univ Queensland Pr AT) Intl Spec Bk.

Tribute for the Negro. Wilson S. Armistead. (Black Heritage Library Collection). 1977. 43.95 (0-8369-8503-6) Ayer.

Tribute for Violin & Piano. S. Albert. 16p. 1995. pap. 20.00 (0-7935-4383-5, 50482201) H Leonard.

Tribute of His Peers: Elegies for Robinson Jeffers. William P. Root et al. 85p. (Orig.). 1989. pap. write for info. (0-9622774-0-1) Tor Hse Pr.

Tribute of Massachusetts Being the Addresses Delivered at Boston & Cambridge, February 4, 1901 in Commemoration of the One Hundredth Anniversary of His Elevation to the Bench as Chief Justice of the Supreme Court of the United States. Ed. by Marquis F. Dickinson & John Marshall. xvii, 120p. 1988. reprint ed. lib. bdg. 27.50 (0-8377-2305-1) Rothman.

Tribute to a Champion: A Fight for Life. Joseph J. Portera. LC 81-84291. (Illus.). 145p. (Orig.). 1981. 10.95 (0-941602-00-1); pap. 8.95 (0-941602-01-X) Iapetus Pr.

Tribute to A. Edward Newton. A. Edward Newton. 1972. 59.95 (0-8490-1231-7) Gordon Pr.

Tribute to Africa: The Photography & Collection of Eliot Elisofon. Eliot Elisofon & Warren M. Robbins. (Illus.). 1974. 9.00 (0-686-25967-X) Mus African Art.

*Tribute to an Antiquary: Essays Presented to Marc Fitch. Ed. by F. Emmison & Roy Stephens. (Illus.). 332p. 1976. 28.00 (0-904920-00-3, Pub. by Leopards Head Pr UK) David Brown.

Tribute to Beauty. Herta Wittgenstein. (Illus.). 1977. pap. 1.50 (0-916388-14-X) Nautilus NJ.

Tribute to Benjamin Britten on His Fiftieth Birthday. Anthony Gishford. 195p. 1990. reprint ed. lib. bdg. 59.00 (0-7812-9210-7) Rprt Serv.

Tribute to Charlotte Forten 1837-1914. Roberta H. Wright. 1993. write for info. (0-9629468-2-6) Charro Bk.

*Tribute to Dad. Ed. by Elizabeth Belew. 128p. 1997. pap. 5.95 (1-889116-13-0) Penbrooke Pub.

Tribute to Emil Grosswald: Number Theory & Related Analysis. Ed. by Marvin Knopp & Mark Sheingorn. LC 92-39436. (Contemporary Mathematics Ser.: Vol. 143). 612p. 1993. pap. 79.00 (0-8218-5155-1, CONM/143) Am Math.

Tribute to Freud: Writing on the Wall. 2nd ed. Hilda Doolittle. LC 84-3317. 208p. 1984. reprint ed. pap. 9.95 (0-8112-0897-4, NDP572) New Directions.

Tribute to Friendship: We All Have One of Many. (Illus.). 132p. (Orig.). 1996. pap. write for info. (0-9651201-0-4) One of Many.

Tribute to Golf: A Celebration in Art, Literature & Photography. Tom Stewart. (Illus.). 240p. 1990. 59.95 (0-9625276-0-2) T P Stewart Pub.

Tribute to Grandma Moses. (Illus.). 1955. pap. 5.00 (0-910810-15-X) Johannes.

Tribute to Hermann Weigand. Ed. by A. Leslie et al. 144p. 1982. pap. 9.95 (0-911173-00-5) Dimension Pr.

Tribute to Ilya Bakelman. Ed. by I. R. Bakelman et al. (Discourses in Mathematics & Its Applications Ser.). vi, 138p. (Orig.). (C). 1994. pap. 12.00 (0-9630728-2-X) TX A&M Dept Math.

Tribute to John G. Jackson. John G. Jackson et al. 22p. (Orig.). 1991. pap. 2.95 (1-56411-006-0) Untd Bros & Sis.

*Tribute to Mom. Ed. by Elizabeth Belew. 128p. 1997. pap. 5.95 (1-889116-12-2) Penbrooke Pub.

*Tribute to Moms. Ruth Senter et al. LC 96-6712. 192p. 1997. pap. 10.99 (1-57673-133-2, Multnomah Bks) Multnomah Pubs.

*Tribute to Mothers: Reflections on Motherhood. Ariel Books Staff. 128p. 1997. 5.95 (0-8362-2951-7, Arie Bks) Andrews & McMeel.

Tribute to Papa & Other Poems. Mamta Kalia. 8.00 (0-89253-691-8); text ed. 4.80 (0-89253-692-6) Ind-US Inc.

Tribute to Paul Erdos. Ed. by A. Baker et al. (Illus.). 400p. (C). 1991. text ed. 100.00 (0-521-38101-0) Cambridge U Pr.

Tribute to Robert A. Koch: Studies in the Northern Renaissance. Gregory Clark et al. LC 94-22519. (Illus.). 193p. 1995. 42.50 (0-691-04340-X) Princeton A & A.

Tribute to Roman Jakobson 1896-1982. LC 83-23844. 96p. 1983. pap. 36.55 (3-11-009796-6) Mouton.

Tribute to Sandra A. Wadsworth, A. I. A. Ed. by Bernard H. Pucker & Ilaria L. St. Florian. (Illus.). (Orig.). 1995. pap. write for info. (0-9635318-1-6) Pucker Art Pubn.

Tribute to Teddy Bear Artists. 2nd ed. Linda Mallins. (Illus.). 192p. 1996. 29.95 (0-87588-427-X) Hobby Hse.

Tribute to the Book: Works by Contemporary Colombian Artists. Carmen M. Jaramillo. Tr. by Ana Neri & Christian H. Faune. (Illus.). 30p. (Orig.). 1996. pap. write for info. (1-883592-10-0) Perm Mission.

Tribute to the Gods: Treasures of the Museo del Oro. Ed. by Armand J. Labbe. Tr. by Maria Inga & Hanka De Rhodes from SPA. (Illus.). 92p. 1992. pap. 25.00 (0-9633959-1-2) Bowers Mus.

Tribute to the Group Settlers. Philip E. Blond. (Staples South West Region Publication Ser.). pap. 9.95 (0-85564-279-3, Pub. by Staples AT) Intl Spec Bk.

Tribute to the Hound. Laura Qa. LC 95-92588. 64p. (Orig.). 1995. pap. 11.95 (0-9637704-2-X) Red Dragon VA.

Tribute to the Past-Legacy for the Future. Donna Scott et al. (Illus.). 321p. 1990. 25.00 (0-9626510-0-1) D Scott.

Tribute to the Women of Santa Fe. William Constandse. 149p. (Orig.). 1983. pap. 6.95 (0-911527-01-X) Utama Pubns Inc.

Tribute to Toshiro Mifune. David Owens. (Illus.). 32p. 1984. pap. 3.50 (0-317-65759-3) Japan Soc.

Tribute to Trucking (SE) Southeast Region, Vol. 2. Jack Thiessen. 184p. 1989. 34.95 (0-89781-333-2) Am Historical Pr.

Tribute to Woody Guthrie & Leadbelly. Will Schmid. 48p. (Orig.). (J). (gr. 4-12). 1991. student ed., pap. 8.50 (0-940796-84-8, 3064) Music Ed Natl.

Tribute to Woody Guthrie & Leadbelly: Teacher's Guide. Will Schmind. (Illus.). 64p. (Orig.). (C). 1990. pap. 16.00 (0-940796-85-6, 3065) Music Ed Natl.

*Tributes. Martine Bellen. (Conjunctions Ser.: Vol. 29). 1997. pap. text ed. 12.00 (0-941964-45-0) Conjunctions.

*Tributes: Interpreters of Our Cultural Tradition. E. H. Gombrich. (Illus.). 272p. Date not set. 29.95 (0-7148-2338-4, Pub. by Phaidon Press UK) Chronicle Bks.

Tributes: Interpreters of Our Cultural Tradition. Ernest H. Gombrich. LC 83-43149. (Illus.). 272p. 1984. 49.95 (0-8014-1703-1) Cornell U Pr.

Tributes from the Press: Editorial Comments on the Life & Work of Mary Baker Eddy. 199p. 1993. 12.95 (0-87510-233-6) Christian Sci.

*Tributes to Iowa Teachers. Ed. by William Sherman. (Illus.). 208p. (Orig.). 1996. pap. text ed. 19.95 (0-8138-0908-8) Iowa St U Pr.

Tributors, Supporters & Merchant Capital: Mining & Underdevelopment in Sierra Leone. Alfred Zack-Williams. (Making of Modern Africa Ser.). 202p. 1994. 68.95 (1-85628-466-2, Pub. by Avebury Pub UK) Ashgate Pub Co.

Tributyltin: Case Study of an Environmental Contaminant. Stephen J. De Mora. (Cambridge Environmental Chemistry Ser.: No. 8). (Illus.). 272p. (C). 1996. text ed. 79.95 (0-521-47046-3) Cambridge U Pr.

Tributyltin Compounds. (Environmental Health Criteria Ser.: No. 116). 273p. (ENG, FRE & SPA.). 1990. pap. text ed. 46.00 (92-4-157116-0, 1160116) World Health.

Tricentennial Celebration: Norfolk, 1682-1982. LC 81-71829. (Illus.). 208p. 1982. pap. 15.00 (0-940744-36-8) Chrysler Museum.

Tricentennial People: Human Applications of the New Genetics. Ed. by Marguerite Neumann. LC 78-8420. 114p. 1978. reprint ed. pap. 32.50 (0-608-00108-2, 2060873) Bks Demand.

*Triceratops. (Microfaxc Ser.). (J). 1997. pap. text ed. 0.99 (0-7894-2118-6) DK Pub Inc.

Triceratops. Stuart A. Kallen. LC 94-7796. (If the Dinosaurs Could Talk Ser.). (J). (gr. 2 up). 1994. 14.98 (1-56239-288-3) Abdo & Dghtrs.

Triceratops. William Lindsay. LC 92-54308. (American Museum of Natural History Ser.). (Illus.). 32p. (J). (gr. 3 up). 1993. 12.95 (1-56458-226-4) DK Pub Inc.

Triceratops. Janet Riehecky. LC 88-508. (Dinosaur Bks.). (Illus.). 32p. (J). (gr. k-4). 1988. lib. bdg. 21.36 (0-89565-422-9); lib. bdg. 21.36 (1-56766-122-X) Childs World.

Triceratops. Sheehan. (Dinosaur Library: Set I). (Illus.). 24p. (J). 1981. lib. bdg. 14.00 (0-86592-113-X) Rourke Enter.

*Triceratops: The Horned Dinosaur. Janet Riehecky. LC 96-49421. (Dinosaur Days Ser.: Group 1). (Illus.). (J). (ps up). 1997. lib. bdg. 14.95 (0-7614-0602-6, Benchmark NY) Marshall Cavendish.

Triceratops: The Last Dinosaur. Elizabeth Sandell. Ed. by Marjorie Oelerich & Howard Schroeder. LC 88-952. (Dinosaur Discovery Era Ser.). (Illus.). 32p. (J). (gr. k-5). 1988. pap. 5.95 (0-944280-07-2); lib. bdg. 12.95 (0-944280-01-3) Bancroft-Sage.

Triceratops & Other Cretaceous Plant-Eaters. Daniel Cohen. (Dinosaurs of North America Ser.). (Illus.). 48p. (J). (gr. 3-9). 1996. 17.80 (1-56065-289-6) Capstone Pr.

Triceratops & Other Cretaceous Plant Eaters. Daniel Cohen. (Illus.). 48p. (J). (gr. 3-7). 1995. 13.35 (0-516-35289-X) Childrens.

Tricheuse. Guy Des Cars. 320p. (FRE.). 1989. pap. 10.95 (0-7859-4800-7) Fr & Eur.

Trichinella & Trichinosis. Ed. by William C. Campbell. LC 82-2390. 606p. 1983. 125.00 (0-306-41140-7, Plenum Pr) Plenum.

Trichlorfon. (Environmental Health Criteria Ser.: No. 132). 162p. (ENG, FRE & SPA.). 1992. pap. text ed. 36.00 (92-4-157132-2, 1160132) World Health.

*Trichlorfon Health & Safety Guide. (Health & Safety Guides Ser.: No. 66). 14p. 1991. pap. text ed. 5.00 (92-4-151066-8, 1860066) World Health.

Trichloroethylene. (Environmental Health Criteria Ser.: No. 50). 133p. 1985. pap. text ed. 21.00 (92-4-154190-3, 1160050) World Health.

Trichlorogermane - a New Superacid in Organic Chemistry: Reaction with Aromatic Compounds, Vol. 12. S. P. Kolesnikov & O. M. Nefedov. (SSR Chemistry Reviews Ser.: Vol. 12, Pt. 2). 62p. 1988. pap. text ed. 47.00 (3-7186-4851-2) Gordon & Breach.

Trichomoniasis. Ed. by H. Ruettgers. (Journal: Gynaekologische Rundschau: Vol. 22, Suppl. 2). (Illus.). viii, 92p. 1983. pap. 22.50 (3-8055-3646-1) S Karger.

Trichomoniasis. Ed. by H. Ruettgers. (Journal: Gynaekologische Rundschau: Vol. 23, Suppl. 2, 1983). (Illus.). iv, 92p. 1983. pap. 22.50 (3-8055-3751-4) S Karger.

Trichomycetes. R. W. Lichtwardt. (Illus.). 410p. 1986. 129.00 (0-387-96237-9) Spr-Verlag.

Trichoptera, Fourth International Symposium: Proceedings: Clemson, South Carolina, 11-16 July 1983. Ed. by John C. Morse. (Entomologica Ser.: No. 30). 512p. 1984. lib. bdg. 212.50 (90-6193-003-0) Kluwer Ac.

Trichothecene Mycotoxicosis: Pathophysiologic Effects, 2 Vols. Ed. by Val R. Beasley. 1989. 123.95 (0-685-67694-3, RA1242) CRC Pr.

Trichothecene Mycotoxicosis: Pathophysiologic Effects, 2 Vols., Vol. I. Ed. by Val R. Beasley. 208p. 1989. 109.00 (0-8493-5088-3, RA1242, CRC Reprint) Franklin.

Trichothecene Mycotoxicosis: Pathophysiologic Effects, 2 Vols., Vol. II. Ed. by Val R. Beasley. 224p. 1989. 121.00 (0-8493-5089-1, RA1242, CRC Reprint) Franklin.

Trichothecenes & Other Mycotoxins: Proceedings of the International Mycotoxin Symposium, Sydney, Australia, August 1984, Vol. 198. Ed. by John Lacey. LC 85-16907. (Progress in Mycotoxins Research Ser.). 598p. 1986. text ed. 429.00 (0-471-90751-0) Wiley.

*Trichotillomania: A Guide. Jeffrey L. Anders & James W. Jefferson. vii, 45p. 1994. pap. 4.50 (1-890802-10-7) Dean Fnd for HRE.

Tricia & the Money Mystery. Elaine L. Schulte. (Twelve Candles Club Ser.: Vol. 9). 128p. (Orig.). (J). (gr. 3-8). 1996. pap. 5.99 (1-55661-537-X, Hampshire MN) Bethany Hse.

Tricia Guild in Town: Contemporary Design for Urban Living. Elspeth Thompson & Tricia Guild. LC 96-68509. (Illus.). 192p. 1996. 40.00 (0-8478-1977-9) Rizzoli Intl.

Tricia Guild's Country Color. Des. by Tricia Guild. LC 94-8259. 160p. 1994. 45.00 (0-8478-1833-0) Rizzoli Intl.

Tricia's Got Trouble. Elaine L. Schulte. (Twelve Candles Club Ser.: Vol. 4). 128p. (J). (gr. 3-8). 1993. pap. 5.99 (1-55661-253-2) Bethany Hse.

Trick. Tri-City Elementary School, Miss Lox's 1994-95 Third-Grade Class Staff. (Wee Write Bks.: No. 22). (Illus.). 35p. (J). (ps-3). 1995. pap. 8.95 (1-884987-76-1) WeWrite.

Trick: New Stories. Fielding Dawson. LC 90-23890. (Illus.). 160p. (Orig.). 1991. 25.00 (0-87685-819-1); pap. 12.50 (0-87685-818-3) Black Sparrow.

Trick: New Stories, signed ed. deluxe ed. Fielding Dawson. LC 90-23890. (Illus.). 160p. (Orig.). 1991. 35.00 (0-87685-820-5) Black Sparrow.

Trick & Fancy Riding. Frank E. Dean. LC 76-354166. 269p. reprint ed. pap. 76.70 (0-317-55780-7, 2029303) Bks Demand.

Trick Baby. Iceberg Slim & Robert Beck. 320p. 1996. reprint ed. mass mkt. 6.99 (0-87067-977-5, BH977-5) Holloway.

Trick Cinematography: The Oscar Special-Effects Movies. R. M. Hayes. LC 84-43219. (Illus.). 380p. 1986. lib. bdg. 49.95 (0-89950-157-5) McFarland & Co.

Trick for Magic Bunny. Rocco Rotunno & Betsy Rotunno. (Stamptime Stories Ser.). (Illus.). 12p. (J). (gr. 2-6). 1992. Mixed Media Pkg. incls. stamp pad, stamps & box of 4 crayons. 7.00 (1-881980-02-2) Noteworthy.

*Trick is in the Training. Cheryl Smith. Date not set. write for info. (0-8069-9718-4) Sterling.

Trick Is to Keep Breathing. Janice Galloway. LC 93-21201. 236p. 1994. 19.95 (1-56478-046-5) Dalkey Arch.

Trick Is to Keep Breathing. Janice Galloway. LC 93-21201. 236p. 1995. pap. 11.95 (1-56478-081-3) Dalkey Arch.

Trick Is to Stay on the Inside. Julie Herrod. 1980. 2.00 (0-936814-00-4) New Collage.

Trick 'n' Trouble. Janet H. McHenry. Ed. by Sue Reck. LC 94-6635. (Golden Rule Duo Ser.). 48p. (J). (gr. 2-4). 1994. pap. 3.99 (0-7814-0171-2, Chariot Bks) Chariot Victor.

Trick of Singularity: "Twelfth Night" & the Performance Editions. Laurie E. Osborne. LC 95-49374. (Studies in Theatre History & Culture). (Illus.). 226p. 1996. text ed. 32.95 (0-87745-544-9) U of Iowa Pr.

Trick of the Eye. Jane S. Hitchcock. 384p. 1993. pap. 5.50 (0-451-17673-1, Sig) NAL-Dutton.

Trick of the Eye. Jane S. Hitchcock. 1993. pap. write for info. (0-451-17480-1, Sig) NAL-Dutton.

Trick of the Light. Kent R. Brown. 37p. 1996. pap. 3.00 (0-87129-662-4, TA3) Dramatic Pub.

*Trick of the Light. Patricia Robinson. 214p. 3.98 (0-8317-5136-3) Smithmark.

Trick of the Light. Stephen Smoke. 171p. 1989. pap. 9.95 (0-941831-34-5) Beyond Words Pub.

*Trick of the Trade. Ralph W. Cotton. 1997. pap. 5.99 (0-671-57034-X) PB.

Trick or Eeek! And Other Ha Ha Halloween Riddles. Katy Hall & Lisa Eisenberg. (Lift-the-Flap Riddle Bk.). (Illus.). 16p. (J). (gr. k-3). 1996. 5.95 (0-694-00693-9, Festival) HarpC Child Bks.

Trick or Treason: The October Surprise Mystery. Robert Parry. 380p. 1993. 24.95 (*1-879823-08-X*) Sheridan Sq Pr.

Trick or Treat. (J). 1993. pap. 137.50 (*0-590-66826-9*) Scholastic Inc.

Trick or Treat. Ellen Appleby. (Yummy Board Bks.). (Illus.). 5p. (J). 1993. bds. 3.98 (*0-8317-9657-X*) Smithmark.

Trick or Treat. Richie T. Cusick. 224p. (YA). (gr. 7-9). 1989. pap. 3.50 (*0-590-44235-X*) Scholastic Inc.

Trick or Treat. Lesley Glaister. 192p. 1992. text ed. 19.00 (*0-689-12140-7*, Pub. by Ctrl Bur voor Schimmel NE) Macmillan.

***Trick or Treat.** Stobie Piel et al. 400p. (Orig.). 1997. mass mkt. 5.99 (*0-505-52220-9*, Love Spell) Dorchester Pub Co.

Trick or Treat: The History of Halloween. Bill Uselton. 22p. (Orig.). 1994. pap. 2.50 (*1-879366-89-4*) Hearthstone OK.

Trick or Treat, Great Pumpkin. Charles M. Schulz. (Illus.). 24p. (J). (ps-3). 1996. 16.95 (*0-694-00898-2*, Festival) HarpC Child Bks.

Trick or Treat Halloween. Sharon Peters. (Illus.). 32p. (J). (gr. k-2). 1980. lib. bdg. 9.79 (*0-89375-392-0*) Troll Communs.

Trick or Treat Halloween. Sharon Peters. (Illus.). 32p. (J). (gr. k-2). 1997. pap. 2.50 (*0-89375-292-4*) Troll Communs.

Trick or Treat, Little Critter. Gina Mayer. (Illus.). 24p. (J). (ps-3). 1993. pap. 2.25 (*0-307-12791-5*, Golden Books) Western Pub.

***Trick or Treat Murder.** Leslie Meier. 256p. 1997. mass mkt. 5.99 (*1-57566-219-1*, Knsington) Kensgtn Pub Corp.

***Trick Or Treat, Smell My Feet.** Diane Degroat. (J). Date not set. write for info. (*0-688-15766-1*, Morrow Junior); lib. bdg. write for info. (*0-688-15767-X*, Morrow Junior) Morrow.

Trick or Treat Surprise. (J). 1996. 7.98 (*1-57082-455-X*) Mouse Works.

Trick or Treat Taffy. Jamie L. Foehl. LC 89-92436. (Illus.). 40p. (Orig.). (J). (ps-6). 1989. write for info. (*0-9625337-0-X*) B Bk Pub Co.

Trick or Trouble. Ilene Cooper. 128p. (J). (gr. 3-7). 1994. pap. 13.99 (*0-670-85057-8*) Viking Child Bks.

Trick or Trouble. Ilene Cooper. (J). (gr. 4 up). 1994. write for info. (*0-318-72462-6*) Viking Penguin.

Trick or Trouble? Ilene Cooper. (Holiday 5 Ser.: Bk. 1). 160p. (J). (gr. 3-7). 1995. pap. 3.99 (*0-14-036517-6*) Puffin Bks.

Trick Origami. Yoshihide Momotani. (Illus.). 69p. 1994. pap. 15.00 (*0-87040-929-8*) Japan Pubns USA.

Trick Paper Tears with Gospel Truth, No. 10. Arnold C. Westphal. 1977. per. 4.95 (*0-915398-10-9*) Visual Evangels.

Trick Photography. Herb Taylor et al. LC 81-71309. (Modern Photo Guides Ser.). (Illus.). 120p. (Orig.). 1982. pap. 7.95 (*0-385-18154-X*) Avalon Comm.

Trick Question. Tony Dunbar. LC 96-19038. 256p. 1997. 22.95 (*0-399-14184-7*, Putnam) Putnam Pub Group.

***Trick Question.** Tony Dunbar. (Cloak & Dagger Ser.). 332p. 1997. 23.95 (*0-7862-1086-9*) Thorndike Pr.

***Trick Questions.** Tony Dunbar. 1997. mass mkt. write for info. (*0-425-16092-0*, Prime Crime) Berkley Pub.

Trick Ridin' Rowdy. Gloria Roesch. (Wee Write Bks.: No. 25). (Illus.). 30p. (J). (gr. 1-4). 1995. pap. 8.95 (*1-884987-85-0*) WeWrite.

Trick Roping. Chester Byers. (Buckaroos Ser.). 32p. (J). 1996. pap. 1.50 (*1-55709-368-7*) Applewood.

Trick Shooter. Kit Dalton. (Buckskin Ser.: No. 34). 176p. (Orig.). 1992. mass mkt., pap. text ed. 3.50 (*0-8439-3360-7*) Dorchester Pub Co.

Trick Shot. Jack Cummings. LC 95-46723. 180p. 1996. 19.95 (*0-8027-4153-3*) Walker & Co.

***Trick Shot.** large type ed. Jack Cummings. LC 96-36487. 284p. 1997. 18.95 (*0-7862-0907-0*, Thorndike Lrg Prnt) Thorndike Pr.

Trick to Money Is Having Some! Stuart Wilde. LC 89-36920. (Illus.). 220p. (Orig.). 1989. pap. 10.95 (*0-930603-48-6*) White Dove NM.

Trick to Money Is Having Some. Stuart Wilde. 215p. 1995. pap. 10.95 (*1-56170-168-8*, 192) Hay House.

Trick Train Ride. Brown. (Kate & Tracy Ser.). (J). (gr. 4-8). 1989. pap. 1.95 (*0-87386-065-9*); lib. bdg. 8.49 (*0-685-70384-3*) Jan Prods.

Trickeries of Scapin. Moliere. Tr. by Tunc Yalman. 1989. pap. 5.25 (*0-8222-1173-4*) Dramatists Play.

Trickiest Thing in Feathers. Corey Ford. Ed. by Laurie Morrow. LC 96-60843. (Illus.). 192p. 1996. 29.95 (*1-885106-21-1*) Wild Adven Pr.

Trickiest Thing in Feathers. limited ed. Corey Ford. Ed. by Laurie Morrow. (Illus.). 208p. 1996. lthr. 95.00 (*1-885106-42-4*) Wild Adven Pr.

***Trickle Irrigation for Crop Production.** F. S. Nakayama & D. A. Bucks. (Developments in Agricultural Engineering Ser.: Vol. 9). 383p. 1986. 153.25 (*0-444-42615-9*) Elsevier.

Trickle Treat: Diaperless Infant Toilet Training. Laurie Boucke. Ed. by Colin White. LC RJ476.E6B68 1991. (Illus.). 85p. (Orig.). 1991. pap. 7.50 (*0-9625006-2-3*) White-Boucke.

***Tricknology of the Enemy.** Elijah Muhammad. Ed. by Nasie Hakim. 24p. (Orig.). 1997. pap. 3.95 (*1-884855-21-0*) Secretarius.

Tricks. Ed McBain. 256p. 1989. reprint ed. mass mkt. 5.99 (*0-380-70383-1*) Avon.

***Tricks: More Than 125 Ways to Make Good Sex Better.** Jay Wiseman. 128p. (Orig.). 1996. pap. 11.95 (*0-9639763-2-X*) Greenery Pr.

Tricks: Twenty-Five Encounters. Albert Camus. (High Risk Ser.). 1996. pap. 13.99 (*1-85242-414-1*, High Risk Bks) Serpents Tail.

***Tricks Vol. 2: Another 125 Ways to Make Good Sex Better.** Jay Wiseman. (Tricks Ser.). 128p. (Orig.). 1996. pap. text ed. 11.95 (*0-9639763-3-8*) Greenery Pr.

Tricks & Amusements. Robert M. Abraham. Orig. Title: Diversions & Pastimes with Cards, Strings, Coins, Paper & Matches. (Illus.). 122p. 1933. pap. 3.95 (*0-486-21127-4*) Dover.

Tricks & Games on the Pool Table. Fred Herrman. Orig. Title: Fun on the Pool Table, Illustrated. 95p. pap. 2.95 (*0-486-21814-7*) Dover.

Tricks & Games with Paper. Paul Jackson. (J). (gr. 4-7). 1992. mass mkt. 3.95 (*0-207-17721-X*, Pub. by Angus & Robertson AT) HarpC.

Tricks Animals Play see Books for Young Explorers

Tricks for the Wild Fiddler, Bk. I. Yoon-Il Auh. (Auh School of Violin Ser.). 35p. (J). (gr. 1-12). 1985. student ed. 10.00 (*1-882858-28-X*) Yoon-il Auh.

Tricks for the Wild Fiddler, Bk. II. Yoon-Il Auh. (Auh School of Violin Ser.). 35p. (J). (gr. 1-12). 1985. student ed. 10.00 (*1-882858-29-8*) Yoon-il Auh.

Tricks for VICs. Sam D. Roberts. 1984. 9.95 (*3-88963-176-2*) Blue Cat.

Tricks, Games & Puzzles with Matches. Maxey Brooke. (Illus.). 64p. 1973. pap. 2.95 (*0-486-20178-3*) Dover.

Tricks of the Burglar Alarm Trade. Mike Kessler. (Illus.). 96p. 1990. pap. 15.00 (*0-87364-550-2*) Paladin Pr.

Tricks of the Floor Trader: Insider Trading Techniques for the Off-the-Floor Trader. Neal Weintraub. 160p. 1995. text ed. 40.00 (*1-55738-913-6*) Irwin Prof Pubng.

Tricks of the Game Programming Gurus. Ken Allen et al. (Illus.). 1200p. (Orig.). 1994. Incl. CD-ROM. 45.00 (*0-672-30507-0*) Sams.

Tricks of the Game Programming Gurus. 2nd ed. Sams Development Group Staff & Andre Lamothe. (Illus.). 900p. Date not set. 45.00 (*0-672-30846-0*) Sams.

Tricks of the Image Processing Gurus. 1998. 49.99 (*0-672-30753-7*) Sams.

Tricks of the Imagination. Robert E. Neale. (Illus.). 215p. 1991. 30.00 (*0-945296-04-5*) Hermetic Pr.

Tricks of the Java Programming Gurus. Glenn Vanderburg. 880p. 1996. pap. text ed. 39.99 incl. cd-rom (*1-57521-102-5*, SamsNet Bks) Sams.

Tricks of the Mac Game Programming Gurus. Bill Dugan et al. (Illus.). 900p. (Orig.). 1995. 50.00 (*1-56830-183-9*, Alpha Ref) Macmillan Gen Ref.

***Tricks of the Trade.** Becker. LC 97-19618. 1997. 32.00 (*0-226-04123-9*); pap. 12.95 (*0-226-04124-7*) U Ch Pr.

***Tricks of the Trade.** Cheryln Biggs. (Loveswept Ser.: No. 834). 240p. 1997. mass mkt. 3.50 (*0-553-44590-1*, Loveswept) Bantam.

***Tricks of the Trade.** Mark Dempsey. 1997. pap. 14.95 (*1-57112-084-X*, Park Avenue) JIST Works.

Tricks of the Trade. Franklin W. Dixon. Ed. by Ann Greenberg. (Hardy Boys Mystery Stories Ser.: No. 104). 160p. (Orig.). (J). (gr. 3-6). pap. 3.99 (*0-671-69273-9*, Minstrel Bks) PB.

***Tricks of the Trade.** Gayle Graham. 116p. (J). 1995. pap. 12.00 (*1-880892-24-3*) Com Sense FL.

Tricks of the Trade. Dean Lundell. 26p. 1995. text ed. write for info. (*0-9649955-2-2*) Osiris Trading.

Tricks of the Trade. Dean Lundell. 26p. 1995. pap. text ed. write for info. (*0-9649955-3-0*) Osiris Trading.

***Tricks of the Trade.** William J. Mann. LC 97-3955. 1997. pap. 22.95 (*0-525-94335-8*) NAL-Dutton.

***Tricks of the Trade: How to Get in & Stay in Managed Care Networks.** Helen K. Davis. Ed. by Donald P. Wilcox et al. 60p. (Orig.). 1996. pap. 29.00 (*0-9640262-5-2*) TX Med Assn.

Tricks of the Trade! Practical Problem Solving Techniques & Shortcuts Used in Accounting. John M. Karnatz. (Illus.). 104p. (Orig.). 1994. pap. 14.95 (*0-9638990-0-7*) Prospect Pub.

Tricks of the Trade: 101 Psychological Techniques to Help Children Grow & Change. Lawrence E. Shapiro. (Illus.). 180p. (Orig.). (C). 1995. pap. text ed. 24.95 (*1-882732-20-0*) Ctr Applied Psy.

Tricks of the Trade for Divers. John M. Malatich & Wayne C. Tucker. LC 85-47839. (Illus.). (Orig.). 1986. reprint ed. pap. 72.70 (*0-7837-9072-4*, 2049821) Bks Demand.

Tricks of the Trade for Kids: 48 Experts Reveal the Secrets Behind What They Do Best. Jerry Dunn. (Illus.). 150p. (J). 1994. pap. 8.95 (*0-395-65027-5*) HM.

Tricks of the Trade with Cards. Charles Lund. Ed. by Mary Laycock. (Illus.). 64p. (J). (gr. 2-9). 1978. pap. text ed. 8.50 (*0-918932-57-2*, AE-1398) Activity Resources.

Tricks of the Trades: Building Methods & Materials. Fine Homebuilding Magazine Editors. (Illus.). 224p. 1994. pap. 10.95 (*1-56158-077-5*) Taunton.

Tricks of the Trades: Jigs, Tools, & Other Labor-Saving Devices. LC 93-48878. (Illus.). 224p. 1994. pap. 10.95 (*1-56158-076-7*) Taunton.

***Tricks of the Trail: A Guide to Modern Backpacking.** 2nd ed. Roy Santoro. LC 96-39514. (Illus.). 192p. (Orig.). 1996. pap. 9.95 (*0-87961-243-6*) Naturegraph.

Tricks of the Visual Basic 4 Gurus. James Bettone. 744p. 1996. pap. text ed. 49.99 incl. cd-rom (*0-672-30929-7*) Sams.

Tricks of Vision. James Taylor. LC 85-80049. (Illus.). 60p. (Orig.). 1985. pap. 5.95 (*0-933837-50-X*) Seventh Son Pr.

Tricks, Stunts, & Good Clean Fun. Bob Phillips. 144p. (Orig.). (YA). 1996. pap. 6.99 (*1-56507-490-4*) Harvest Hse.

***Tricks That Stick.** Ronnie Moore. (Illus.). 124p. (Orig.). 1996. pap. 15.95 (*0-9649694-0-8*) MC Pubng.

Tricks We Played in Iowa. Judy Combs. (Illus.). 186p. (Orig.). 1990. pap. 9.95 (*1-878488-56-2*) Quixote Pr IA.

Tricks with Chintz: Using Large Prints to Add New Magic to Traditional Quilt Blocks. Nancy Breland. LC 93-47384. 1994. 14.95 (*0-89145-834-4*) Collector Bks.

Tricks Your Cat Can Do. Gilbert W. Langley. (Orig.). 1991. 4.98 (*1-55521-755-9*) Bk Sales Inc.

Trickshot. Randolph Harris. 256p. (Orig.). 1991. mass mkt. 2.95 (*0-87067-724-1*, BH724) Holloway.

Trickster. Muriel Gray. LC 94-43306. 464p. 1995. 23.50 (*0-385-47786-4*) Doubleday.

***Trickster.** Muriel Gray. 1997. mass mkt. write for info. (*0-614-20524-7*, St Martins Paperbacks) St Martin.

***Trickster.** Muriel Gray. 1997. mass mkt. 6.99 (*0-312-96100-6*) St Martin.

Trickster: A Study in American Indian Mythology. Paul A. Radin. LC 74-88986. 212p. 1987. pap. 13.00 (*0-8052-0351-6*) Schocken.

Trickster: A Study in American Indian Mythology. Paul A. Radin. LC 74-88986. 211p. 1969. reprint ed. text ed. 38.50 (*0-8371-2112-4*, RATT, Greenwood Pr) Greenwood.

Trickster: A Transformation Archetype. Suzanne Lundquist. LC 90-29311. 128p. 1991. lib. bdg. 59.95 (*0-7734-9958-X*) E Mellen.

***Trickster & the Fainting Birds.** Howard A. Norman. LC 97-9457. (Illus.). (J). 1998. write for info. (*0-15-200888-8*) HarBrace.

***Trickster & the Troll.** Virginia D. Sneve. LC 96-36879. (Illus.). 104p. (J). 1997. 22.00 (*0-8032-4261-1*) U of Nebr Pr.

Trickster Gods. Will Brame. Date not set. pap. write for info. (*0-345-39146-2*) Ballantine.

Trickster in Land of Dreams. Zeese Papanikolas. LC 94-36924. x, 186p. (C). 1995. 22.50 (*0-8032-3703-0*) U of Nebr Pr.

Trickster in West Africa: A Study of Mythic Irony & Sacred Delight. Robert D. Pelton. LC 77-75396. (Hermeneutics: Studies in the History of Religions: No. 8). 1980. pap. 13.00 (*0-520-06791-6*) U CA Pr.

Trickster, Magician & Grieving Man: Reconnecting Men with Earth. Glen Mazis. 328p. (Orig.). 1994. pap. 12.95 (*1-879181-11-8*) Bear & Co.

***Trickster Makes This World: Mischief, Myth & Art.** Lewis Hyde. 1998. 26.00 (*0-374-27928-4*) FS&G.

Trickster of Liberty: Tribal Heirs to a Wild Baronage. Gerald Vizenor. LC 87-22167. (Emergent Literatures Ser.). xviii, 158p. (Orig.). 1988. pap. 11.95 (*0-8166-1630-2*) U of Minn Pr.

Trickster of Seville & the Stone Guest. De Molina. Ed. by Edwards. (Hispanic Classics Ser.). 1986. 49.95 (*0-85668-300-0*, Pub. by Aris & Phillips UK); pap. 22.00 (*0-85668-301-9*, Pub. by Aris & Phillips UK) David Brown.

Trickster Tales. Jonathan Greene. (Morning Coffee Chapbook Ser.). (Illus.). 11p. (Orig.). 1985. pap. 7.50 (*0-915124-80-7*) Coffee Hse.

Trickster Tales: Forty Tales from Around the World. Retold by Josepha Sherman. LC 95-51702. 1996. 28.95 (*0-87483-449-X*) August Hse.

Trickster Tales: Forty Tales from Around the World. Retold by Josepha Sherman. LC 95-51702. 1996. pap. 18.95 (*0-87483-450-3*) August Hse.

Tricksterism in Turn-of-the-Century American Literature: A Multicultural Perspective. Ed. by Elizabeth Ammons & Annette White-Parks. LC 94-20520. 217p. 1994. 35.00 (*0-87451-680-3*) U Pr of New Eng.

***Tricksters & Estates: On the Ideology of Restoration Comedy.** J. Douglas Canfield. LC 96-48626. 1997. 44.95 (*0-8131-2012-8*) U Pr of Ky.

Tricky Alex. Morgan Matthews. LC 85-14018. (Illus.). 48p. (Orig.). (J). (gr. 1-3). 1986. pap. 3.50 (*0-8167-0599-2*) Troll Communs.

Tricky Brain Ticklers & Mazes. (Trailblazer's Ser.). (Illus.). 24p. (J). (gr. 4-7). 1994. pap. 3.95 (*1-56144-387-5*, Honey Bear Bks) Modern Pub NYC.

Tricky Business. Franklin W. Dixon. Ed. by Ann Greenberg. (Hardy Boys Mystery Stories Ser.: No. 88). 160p. (J). (gr. 3-6). pap. 3.99 (*0-671-64973-6*, Minstrel Bks) PB.

Tricky Business Letters: Persuasive Tactics on Paper. Gordon Wainwright. (Institute of Management Ser.). 192p. (Orig.). 1993. pap. 42.50 (*0-273-60162-8*, Pub. by Pitman Pub Ltd UK) Trans-Atl Phila.

***Tricky Dick & the Pink Lady: Richard Nixon vs. Helen Gahagan Douglas - Sexual Polotics & the Red Scare, 1950.** Greg Mitchell. LC 96-43670. 1997. 25.00 (*0-679-41621-8*) Random.

Tricky Ground. Indira Parthasarathy. (Indian Novels Ser.). 191p. 1975. pap. 4.95 (*0-86578-110-9*) Ind-US Inc.

Tricky Logic Puzzles. Norman D. Willis. LC 95-36264. (Illus.). 96p. 1995. pap. 5.95 (*0-8069-3805-6*) Sterling.

Tricky Puppies: Math. McClanahan Book Co., Inc. Staff. (Flap Bks.). (J). (ps-3). 1994. 4.95 (*1-56293-435-X*) McClanahan Bk.

***Tricky, Sneaky Puzzle Pictures.** Doug Anderson. (Illus.). 128p. 1997. pap. 5.95 (*0-8069-9608-0*) Sterling.

***Tricky Tribal Discourse: The Poetry, Short Stories, & Fus Fixico Letters of Creek Writer Alex Posey.** Alexia M. Kosmider. LC 97-2337. 1998. text ed. write for info. (*0-89301-201-7*) U of Idaho Pr.

Tricky Tricks. Stuart A. Kallen. LC 92-14775. (J). 1992. lib. bdg. 13.98 (*1-56239-127-5*) Abdo & Dghtrs.

***Tricky Troll.** Bartel. 1997. pap. write for info. (*0-395-88079-3*) HM.

***Tricky Twisters.** World Book, Inc. Staff. LC 97-6018. (Mind Benders Ser.). (J). 1997. pap. write for info. (*0-7166-4109-7*) World Bk.

Tricolor over the Taurus: The Franco-Turkish War for Cilicia, Crucible of the National Liberation Movement. Robert F. Zeidner. LC 93-38309. (American University Studies: Vol. 149). 1994. write for info. (*0-8204-2316-5*) P Lang Pubng.

Tricolore, Level 1. Honnor et al. 1993. pap. 23.95 (*0-17-439336-9*) Heinle & Heinle.

Tricolore, Level 2. Honnor et al. Date not set. pap. 23.95 (*0-17-439356-3*) Heinle & Heinle.

Tricolore, Level 3. Honnor et al. Date not set. pap. 23.95 (*0-17-439376-8*) Heinle & Heinle.

Tricolore, Level 4A. Honnor et al. 1995. pap. 20.95 (*0-17-439392-X*) Heinle & Heinle.

Tricolore: Level Four, Bk. 4B. 2nd ed. Honnor. (Secondary French Ser.). 1993. student ed., pap. 18.95 (*0-17-439675-9*) Heinle & Heinle.

Tricolore: Level 4a. 2nd ed. Honnor. (Secondary French Ser.). 1993. student ed., pap. 18.95 (*0-17-439674-0*) Heinle & Heinle.

Tricon Navigation: Geometry, Problem Solving & a Bit of Geography. William L. Swart. 52p. 1988. pap. text ed. 16.75 (*1-883547-00-8*) Tricon Pub.

Tricon Navigation: Geometry, Problem Solving & a Bit of Geography. William L. Swart. 70p. 1992. pap. text ed. 12.75 (*1-883547-04-0*) Tricon Pub.

Tricontinental: The Rise & Fall of a Merchant Bank. Hugo Armstrong & Dick Gross. 384p. 1995. 39.95 (*0-522-84658-0*, Pub. by Melbourne Univ Pr AT) Paul & Co Pubs.

Tricontinental Symposium on Autoimmune Skin Diseases, Proceedings, Kyodai Kaikan, Kyoto - Japan, November 1, 1993. Ed. by T. Nishikawa et al. (Journal: Dermatology Ser.: Vol. 189, Suppl. 1, 1994). (Illus.). xii, 138p. 1994. pap. 62.75 (*3-8055-5993-3*) S Karger.

***Tricot, Piano et Jeu Video.** Sonia Sarafati. (Novels in the Premier Roman Ser.). 64p. (FRE.). (J). (gr. 2-5). 1996. pap. 7.95 (*2-89021-181-9*, Pub. by Les Editions CN) Firefly Bks Ltd.

Tricresyl Phosphate. (Environmental Health Criteria Ser.: No. 110). 122p. (ENG, FRE & SPA.). 1990. pap. text ed. 24.00 (*92-4-157110-1*, 1160110) World Health.

Tridemensional Optical Spectroscopic Methods in Astrophysics. Ed. by G. Comte & M. Marcelin. (ASP Conference Series Proceedings: Vol. 71). 398p. 1995. 28.00 (*0-937707-90-2*) Astron Soc Pacific.

Trident. D. Douglas Dalgleish et al. LC 83-16777. (Science & International Affairs Ser.). (Illus.). 384p. 1984. 34.95 (*0-8093-1126-7*) S Ill U Pr.

Trident: A Trading Strategy. Charles L. Lindsay. 1991. 50.00 (*0-930233-48-4*) Windsor.

Trident Facilities. Ed. by F. D. Yell. (Site Investigation in Construction Ser.: No. 1). 184p. 1994. 48.00 (*0-7277-1992-0*) Am Soc Civil Eng.

***Trident Guide to British Virgin Islands Trusts.** 1996. reprint ed. 67.00 (*1-899217-00-2*, Pub. by Chancellor Pubns UK) Intl Spec Bk.

Trident of Wisdom: Translation of Paratrisika-vivarana. Abhinavagupta. Tr. by Jaideva Singh. LC 89-4425. (SUNY Series in Tantric Studies). 405p. 1989. text ed. 50.50 (*0-7914-0180-4*) State U NY Pr.

Trident of Wisdom: Translation of Paratrisika-vivarana. Abhinavagupta. Tr. by Jaideva Singh. LC 89-4425. (SUNY Series in Tantric Studies). 405p. 1989. pap. text ed. 16.95 (*0-7914-0181-2*) State U NY Pr.

***Trident Practical Guide to Offshore Trusts.** 2nd ed. Ed. by International Trident Trust Group Staff. 1996. reprint ed. 142.00 (*1-899217-01-0*, Pub. by Chancellor Pubns UK) Intl Spec Bk.

***Tridentine Mass.** 6th ed. Michael Davies. 66p. 1985. reprint ed. pap. 4.25 (*0-935952-03-9*) Angelus Pr.

Triduum Book. Ed. by Modern Liturgy Editors. LC 96-44051. Orig. Title: Holy Week Book. (Illus.). 176p. 1997. pap. 24.95 (*0-89390-394-9*) Resource Pubns.

Triduum Sourcebook, 3 vols., Set. 2nd rev. ed. Ed. by Joan Halmo et al. (Illus.). 500p. 1996. pap. 40.00 (*1-56854-099-X*, TRID/R) Liturgy Tr Pubns.

Tried & Transfigured. Leonard Ravenhill. LC 81-71752. 160p. 1963. pap. 7.99 (*0-87123-544-7*) Bethany Hse.

Tried & True: A Century of Rural Recipes. Mary Barile. (Illus.). 120p. 1987. spiral bd. write for info. (*0-937213-03-9*) Heritage NY.

Tried & True: Eleven Principles of Church Growth from Frazer Memorial United Methodist Church. John E. Mathison. LC 92-71309. 128p. 1992. pap. 8.95 (*0-88177-117-1*, DR117) Discipleship Res.

Tried & True Art: Successful Projects for the Elementary Grades. Kristine Martin. LC 89-82079. (Illus.). 52p. 1990. pap. 7.95 (*0-9624597-8-X*) Aberdeen Pr.

Tried & True: Native American Women Confronting Colonization see Young Oxford History of Women in the United States

Triennial Review of Mineral Development Activities in the ESCAP Region, 1985-1987. 53p. 1987. 9.00 (*92-1-119550-0*, 89.II.F.16) UN.

Trienta Dias a la Pie de la Cruz - Thirty Days at the Foot of the Cross. Ed. by Thomas A. Jones & Sheila P. Jones. 117p. (SPA.). 1994. pap. 5.99 (*1-884553-39-7*) Discipleshp.

***Trieste.** Theodore Meth. 90p. 1997. pap. 12.50 (*1-57502-482-9*, PO1446) Morris Pubng.

Trieste Negotiations. Leonard Unger & Kristina Segulja. (FPI Case Studies: No. 16). (Illus.). 64p. (C). 1990. pap. text ed. 16.25 (*0-941700-58-5*); lib. bdg. 31.50 (*0-941700-57-7*) JH FPI SAIS.

Trieste One Hundred One Designi. Marie Z. Greene-Mercier. (Orig.). (ITA.). 1969. pap. 6.00 (*0-910790-17-5*) Intl Bk Co IL.

Triethyl Phosphate: Phosphoric Acid Triethyl Ester. GDCh-Advisory Committee on Existing Chemicals of Environmental Relevance Staff. Tr. by P. Karbe from GER. LC 93-2638. (BUA Reports: Vol. 37). (ENG & GER.). 1993. write for info. (*1-56081-731-3*, VCH) Wiley.

Trifle, a Coddle, a Fry: An Irish Literary Cookbook. Jane O'Mara & Fionnuala O'Reilly. (Illus.). 192p. 1996. pap. 12.95 (*1-55921-084-2*) Moyer Bell.

T

Trifling Affair. Olivia Sumner. 1992. mass mkt. 3.50 (0-8217-3758-9, Zebra Kensgtn) Kensgtn Pub Corp.

***Trifunto Sabre la Depresion.** Tim La Haye. 1.50 (0-8297-1931-8); pap. 6.95 (0-8297-0515-5) Life Pubs Intl.

Trigeminal Neuralgia. Richard L. Rovit et al. (Illus.). 218p. 1990. 85.00 (0-683-07393-1) Williams & Wilkins.

Trigeminal Neuralgia. Zakrzewska. 1995. text ed. 72.50 (0-7020-1696-9) Saunders.

Trigeminal Neuralgia: Current Concepts Regarding Pathogenesis & Treatment. Gerhard H. Fromm & Barry J. Sessle. (Illus.). 256p. 1990. text ed. 75.00 (0-409-90126-1) Buttrwrth-Heinemann.

***Trigeminal System in Man.** K. G. Usunoff et al. LC 97-11159. (Advances in Anatomy, Embryology & Cell Biology Ser.: Vol. 136). (Illus.). x, 87p. 1997. pap. 65.00 (3-540-62786-3) Spr-Verlag.

Trigg in Tibet. Stuart Allen. 171p. 1993. pap. 6.95 (1-55939-016-6) Snow Lion Pubns.

***Trigger.** Elizabeth A. Krajeck. 48p. (Orig.). 1994. pap. 3.95 (1-880649-32-2) Writ Ctr Pr.

Trigger Dance. Diane Glancy. 250p. 1990. 18.95 (0-932511-35-X); pap. 8.95 (0-932511-36-8) Fiction Coll.

***Trigger Effect.** Dewey Gram. 1996. mass mkt. 5.99 (1-57297-244-0) Blvd Books.

***Trigger Factors in Transfusion Medicine: Proceedings of the Twentieth International Symposium on Blood Transfusion, Groningen 1995, Organized by the Red Cross Blood Bank, Noord-Nederland, Groningen.** Ed. by C. T. Smit. LC 96-29622. (Developments in Hematology & Immunology Ser.). 272p. (C). 1996. lib. bdg. 90.00 (0-7923-4255-0) Kluwer Ac.

Trigger in Europe. large type ed. William Holt. 1971. 25.99 (0-85456-029-7) Ulverscroft.

Trigger-Man. large type ed. Basil Copper. (Linford Mystery Library). 320p. 1994. pap. 15.99 (0-7089-7561-5, Linford) Ulverscroft.

Trigger Points: Understanding Myofascial Pain & Discomfort. Anatomical Chart Company Staff. (Illus.). (Orig.). 1994. pap. 39.95 (0-9603730-6-3) Anatomical Chart.

Trigger Pull. Paul Malone. (Agents Bks.: No. 1). 1991. mass mkt. 3.50 (0-373-63801-9) Harlequin Bks.

Trigger Talk. large type ed. Nelson Nye. LC 92-30141. (Nightingale Ser.). 224p. 1993. lib. bdg. 14.95 (0-8161-5631-X, GK Hall) Thorndike Pr.

Trigger Trail to Boot Hill. large type ed. Ross Harlan. (Linford Western Library). 272p. 1996. pap. 15.99 (0-7089-7825-8, Linford) Ulverscroft.

Triggering of Acute Coronary Syndromes: Implications for Prevention. Ed. by Stefan N. Willich & James E. Muller. LC 95-21135. (Developments in Cardiovascular Medicine Ser.: Vol. 170). 424p. (C). 1995. lib. bdg. 189.00 (0-7923-3605-4) Kluwer Ac.

Triggering of Ovulation in Stimulated Cycles: CG or LH? The Proceedings of an International Symposium Held under the Auspices of the French Endocrinology Society. Ed. by J. C. Emperaire. LC 93-46967. (Studies in Profertility Ser.: Vol. 1). 1994. 65.00 (1-85070-539-9) Prthnon Pub.

Triggering Town: Lectures & Essays on Poetry & Writing. Richard Hugo. 128p. 1992. pap. 9.95 (0-393-30933-9) Norton.

Triggerman: The First Volume of John Ragusa's Mafia Secrets. John Ragusa. 1994. pap. 5.99 (1-56171-335-X) Sure Seller.

Triggerman's Dance. T. Jefferson Parker. 352p. 1996. 21.95 (0-7868-6142-8) Hyperion.

***Triggerman's Dance.** T. Jefferson Parker. 512p. 1998. mass mkt. 6.99 (0-7868-8917-9) Hyperion.

***Triggerman's Dance.** large type ed. T. Jefferson Parker. LC 96-42242. (Cloak & Dagger Ser.). 674p. 1996. 23.95 (0-7862-0897-X, Thorndike Lrg Prnt) Thorndike Pr.

Triggernometry: A Gallery of Gunfighters. Eugene Cunningham. LC 95-38776. (Illus.). 504p. 1996. pap. 18.95 (0-8061-2837-2) U of Okla Pr.

Triggernometry: A Gallery of Gunfighters. Eugene Cunningham. 1993. reprint ed. lib. bdg. 75.00 (0-7812-5923-1) Rprt Serv.

Triggers. Donald Guravich. 32p. 1984. pap. 3.50 (0-939180-25-1) Tombouctou.

Triggers: A New Approach to Self-Motivation. Stanley Mann. 216p. 1986. text ed. 25.95 (0-13-930793-1) P-H.

Triglyceride, High Density Lipoprotein & Coronary Heart Disease. 1994. lib. bdg. 255.75 (0-8490-5630-6) Gordon Pr.

Triglycerides: Their Role in Diabetes & Atherosclerosis. Antonio M. Gotto, Jr. & Rodolfo Paoletti. (Atherosclerosis Reviews Ser.: Vol. 22). 246p. 1991. text ed. 80.50 (0-88167-813-9) Lppncott-Raven.

Trignometry & Its Applications. Larry J. Goldstein. LC 92-39480. 1901. text ed. 44.95 (0-256-10268-6) Irwin.

***Trigonometric Delights.** Eli Maor. LC 97-18001. 1998. write for info. (0-691-05754-0) Princeton U Pr.

Trigonometric Fourier Series & Their Conjugates. Levan V. Zhizhiashvili. LC 96-18939. (Mathematics & Its Applications Ser.). 312p. (C). 1996. lib. bdg. 165.00 (0-7923-4088-4) Kluwer Ac.

Trigonometric Series, Vols. I & II. 2nd ed. A. Zygmund. (Cambridge Mathematical Library). 776p. 1988. pap. text ed. 62.95 (0-521-35885-X) Cambridge U Pr.

Trigonometric Series: A Survey. Ralph L. Jeffery. LC 56-59071. (Canadian Mathematical Congress Lecture Ser.: No. 2). 43p. reprint ed. pap. 25.00 (0-317-08877-7, 2014260) Bks Demand.

Trigonometrie, or the Doctrine of Triangles, 2 pts. Richard Norwood. LC 78-171779. (English Experience Ser.: No. 404). 362p. 1971. reprint ed. 75.00 (90-221-0404-4) Walter J Johnson.

***Trigonometry.** Marivn Bittinger. (C). 1998. text ed. write for info. (0-201-33201-9) Addison-Wesley.

Trigonometry. Marvin L. Bittinger & Judith A. Beecher. (Illus.). (C). 1989. text ed. 33.50 (0-201-09184-4) Addison-Wesley.

***Trigonometry.** Cohen. 1992. student ed. 20.95 (0-314-00348-7) Wadsworth Pub.

Trigonometry. David C. Cohen. Ed. by Marshall. 397p. (C). 1992. text ed. 58.25 (0-314-93166-X) West Pub.

Trigonometry. Coughlin. (C). 1998. text ed. 53.25 (0-03-093715-9) HB Coll Pubs.

Trigonometry. Frank Demana & Bert K. Waits. (Illus.). (C). 1990. teacher ed. 12.95 (0-201-19575-5); text ed. 46.25 (0-201-19572-0); teacher ed. 17.25 (0-201-19574-7); student ed. 12.95 (0-201-19577-1); student ed. 12.95 (0-201-19576-3); 12.95 (0-201-19573-9) Addison-Wesley.

Trigonometry. John R. Durbin. LC 86-28193. 416p. 1987. text ed. 41.00 (0-471-03366-9) Wiley.

Trigonometry. James Gehrmann & Thomas Lester. (College Outline Ser.). 278p. (C). 1984. pap. text ed. 12.25 (0-15-601693-1) HB Coll Pubs.

Trigonometry. Vivian S. Groza & Gene R. Sellers. 300p. (C). 1980. pap. text ed. 41.25 (0-7216-4325-6) SCP.

Trigonometry. Adelbert F. Hackert & Gene R. Sellers. 545p. (C). 1989. pap. text ed. 28.00 (0-15-592358-7) SCP.

Trigonometry. Adelbert F. Hackert & Gene R. Sellers. 545p. (C). 1989. text ed. 43.00 (0-15-592356-0); student ed., pap. text ed. 20.00 (0-15-592357-9) SCP.

Trigonometry. Hayden. 35.97 (0-13-930835-0) P-H.

Trigonometry. Hungerford. (C). 1992. student ed., pap. text ed. 20.75 (0-03-054272-3) HB Coll Pubs.

Trigonometry. Hungerford. (C). 1992. suppl. ed., teacher ed., pap. text ed. 22.75 (0-03-054273-1) HB Coll Pubs.

Trigonometry. Thomas W. Hungerford & Richard Mercer. 560p. (C). 1992. text ed. 47.00 (0-03-054264-2) SCP.

Trigonometry. Stephen B. Jahnke. (Straight Forward Math Ser.). 79p. (YA). (gr. 8-12). 1992. 6.95 (0-931993-45-8, GP-045) Garlic Pr OR.

Trigonometry. Kaufmann. (Mathematics Ser.). 1995. suppl. ed., pap. 16.95 (0-534-93470-6) PWS Pubs.

Trigonometry. Jerome E. Kaufmann. 384p. (C). 1988. text ed. 47.95 (0-534-92106-X) PWS Pubs.

Trigonometry. Jack Rudman. (College Level Examination Ser.: CLEP-28). 1994. pap. 23.95 (0-8373-5328-9) Nat Learn.

Trigonometry. Ralph C. Steinlage. 408p. (C). 1985. text ed. 57.50 (0-314-86662-0) West Pub.

Trigonometry. Ralph C. Steinlage. Date not set. teacher ed., pap. text ed. write for info. (0-314-87263-9); student ed., pap. text ed. 20.50 (0-314-87264-7) West Pub.

Trigonometry. Chris Vancil. (C). Date not set. text ed. 51.25 (0-03-006948-3) HB Coll Pubs.

Trigonometry. Chris Vancil. Date not set. text ed. 56.00 (0-314-61443-5); student ed., pap. text ed. 20.50 (0-314-79012-8); teacher ed., pap. text ed. write for info. (0-314-79013-6) West Pub.

Trigonometry. 2nd ed. John D. Baley & Martin Holstege. 1991. text ed. write for info. (0-07-003567-9) McGraw.

Trigonometry. 2nd ed. John D. Baley & Martin Holstege. 1991. Solutions manual. pap. text ed. write for info. (0-07-003568-7) McGraw.

Trigonometry. 2nd ed. Barklay. (C). 1992. student ed., pap. text ed. 17.50 (0-03-096620-5) HB Coll Pubs.

Trigonometry. 2nd ed. Harley Flanders et al. (C). 1982. text ed. 45.25 (0-03-057802-7) SCP.

Trigonometry. 2nd ed. Marshall D. Hestenes & Richard O. Hill, Jr. (Illus.). 320p. (C). 1986. text ed. write for info. (0-13-930744-3) P-H.

Trigonometry. 2nd ed. Kaufmann. (Mathematics Ser.). 1994. student ed., pap. 20.95 (0-534-92459-X) PWS Pubs.

Trigonometry. 2nd ed. Jerome E. Kaufmann. LC 93-6079. 1994. text ed. 60.95 (0-534-92458-1) PWS Pubs.

Trigonometry. 2nd ed. Roland E. Larson. 400p. (C). 1990. teacher ed. 2.66 (0-669-16267-1); text ed. 61.96 (0-669-16266-3); teacher ed. 21.16 (0-669-16268-X); teacher ed. 21.16 (0-669-19540-5) HM College Div.

Trigonometry. 2nd ed. Charles P. McKeague. 413p. (C). 1988. text ed. 47.00 (0-15-592362-5) SCP.

Trigonometry. 2nd ed. Dennis G. Zill. 464p. (C). 1990. text ed. write for info. (0-07-557099-8); student ed. 19.95 (0-07-557013-0) McGraw.

Trigonometry. 2nd ed. Dennis G. Zill & Jacqueline M. Dewar. 1990. student ed., pap. text ed. write for info. (0-07-557012-2) McGraw.

Trigonometry. 3rd annot. ed. Roland E. Larson & Robert P. Hostetler. 592p. (C). 1993. Instr.'s annotated ed. teacher ed., text ed. 60.36 (0-669-33237-2) HM College Div.

Trigonometry. 3rd ed. Baley & Sarell. 1996. pap. text ed. write for info. (0-07-005188-7) McGraw.

Trigonometry. 3rd ed. Barclay. (C). 1993. student ed., pap. text ed. 21.00 (0-03-096638-8) HB Coll Pubs.

Trigonometry. 3rd ed. Roland E. Larson & Robert P. Hostetler. 592p. (C). 1993. text ed. 61.56 (0-669-28317-7); Instr.'s guide. teacher ed. write for info. (0-669-28318-5); Study & solutions guide. student ed. 21.16 (0-669-28319-3); Test item file/Resource guide. 2.66 (0-669-28321-5); Transparencies. trans. write for info. (0-318-70103-0) HM College Div.

***Trigonometry.** 3rd ed. McKeague. (C). 1994. write for info. (0-03-096562-4) HB Coll Pubs.

Trigonometry. 3rd ed. Charles P. McKeague. (C). 1993. suppl. ed., teacher ed., pap. text ed. 209.50 (0-03-094902-5) HB Coll Pubs.

Trigonometry. 3rd ed. Charles P. McKeague. (C). 1994. teacher ed., pap. text ed. 28.00 (0-03-096680-9) HB Coll Pubs.

Trigonometry. 3rd ed. Charles P. McKeague. (C). 1994. pap. text ed. 33.75 (0-03-096774-0) HB Coll Pubs.

***Trigonometry.** 4th ed. McKeague. (C). 1997. text ed. write for info. (0-03-024783-7) HB Coll Pubs.

***Trigonometry.** 4th ed. McKeague. (C). 1998. teacher ed., pap. text ed. 26.75 (0-03-024969-4); student ed., pap. text ed. write for info. (0-03-024971-6) HB Coll Pubs.

***Trigonometry.** 4th ed. Murphy & Sullivan. 1996. student ed., pap. text ed. 25.00 (0-13-651191-0) P-H.

Trigonometry. 4th ed. Murphy. 1996. student ed., pap. text ed. 25.00 (0-13-456435-9) P-H.

Trigonometry. 4th ed. Sullivan. 1996. text ed. 69.00 (0-13-456419-7) P-H.

Trigonometry. 5th ed. Margaret L. Lial et al. LC 92-13849. (Illus.). (C). 1992. text ed. 40.50 (0-673-46647-7) Addson-Wesley Educ.

Trigonometry. 5th ed. Margaret L. Lial et al. LC 92-22236. (C). 1992. 7.20 (0-673-46753-8) Addson-Wesley Educ.

Trigonometry. 5th ed. Charles D. Miller et al. (C). 1992. student ed. 14.00 (0-673-46815-1) Addson-Wesley Educ.

***Trigonometry.** 6th ed. Ed. by Lial. (C). 1997. text ed. write for info. (0-321-40186-7) Addson-Wesley Educ.

Trigonometry. 6th ed. Margaret L. Lial et al. (C). 1997. text ed. 55.95 (0-673-99553-4) Addson-Wesley Educ.

Trigonometry. Roy Dubisch. LC 55-6084. 410p. reprint ed. pap. 116.90 (0-317-08418-6, 2012451) Bks Demand.

Trigonometry, Testbank. Hungerford. (C). 1991. suppl. ed., teacher ed., pap. text ed. 16.75 (0-03-054257-X) HB Coll Pubs.

Trigonometry: A Functions Approach. Robert J. Mergener. 304p. 1989. per. 37.74 (0-8403-5308-1) Kendall-Hunt.

Trigonometry: A Graphing Approach. Roland E. Larson & Robert P. Hostetler. 500p. (C). 1995. text ed. 61.96 (0-669-28296-0) HM College Div.

Trigonometry: A Modern Approach. 2nd ed. Joseph Elich et al. LC 84-9287. (C). 1985. teacher ed. write for info. (0-201-10524-1); text ed. 51.75 (0-201-10523-3); teacher ed. write for info. (0-201-10526-8) Addison-Wesley.

Trigonometry: A Unitized Approach. Reuben W. Farley et al. (Illus.). (C). 1975. pap. text ed. write for info. (0-13-930909-8) P-H.

Trigonometry: An Analytical Approach. 6th rev. ed. Irving Drooyan & Charles C. Carico. 416p. (C). 1990. text ed. 68.00 (0-02-330621-1, Macmillan Coll) P-H.

***Trigonometry: Solutions Manual.** 6th ed. Lial. (C). 1997. student ed., pap. text ed. 21.50 (0-673-98337-4) Addison-Wesley.

Trigonometry: Student Solutions Manual. 3rd ed. Baley. 1995. pap. text ed. write for info. (0-07-005721-4) McGraw.

Trigonometry: Triangles & Functions. 3rd ed. Mervin L. Keedy & Marvin L. Bittinger. LC 81-14974. 1982. write for info. (0-201-13411-X) Addison-Wesley.

Trigonometry: Triangles & Functions. 4th ed. Mervin L. Keedy & Marvin L. Bittinger. 400p. (C). 1986. teacher ed. write for info. (0-201-13333-4); pap. text ed. 44.25 (0-201-13332-6); teacher ed. write for info. (0-201-13335-0); student ed. write for info. (0-318-59742-X) Addison-Wesley.

Trigonometry & Its Applications. Larry J. Goldstein. 416p. (C). 1993. text ed. write for info. (0-697-21486-9) Wm C Brown Pubs.

Trigonometry & Its Applications. Larry J. Goldstein. 140p. (C). 1993. student ed., per. write for info. (0-697-21487-7) Wm C Brown Pubs.

Trigonometry & Its Applications. C. R. Hirsch & Harold L. Schoen. LC 84-23391. 544p. 1985. text ed. write for info. (0-07-029059-8) McGraw.

Trigonometry Enhanced with Graphing. Michael Sullivan. 1996. pap. text ed. 69.00 (0-13-456401-4) P-H.

Trigonometry Enhanced with Graphs. Murphy & Sullivan. 1996. student ed., pap. text ed. 25.00 (0-13-650953-3) P-H.

Trigonometry Flipper. James H. Gerhold et al. 39p. (YA). (gr. 8 up). 1993. 6.25 (1-878383-20-5) C Lee Pubns.

Trigonometry for College Students. 5th ed. Karl J. Smith. LC 90-43580. 384p. (C). 1990. text ed. 49.95 (0-534-13728-8) Brooks-Cole.

Trigonometry for College Students. 6th ed. Smith. (Mathematics Ser.). 1994. student ed., pap. 22.95 (0-534-16801-9) Brooks-Cole.

Trigonometry for College Students. 6th ed. Karl J. Smith. LC 93-30497. 1994. text ed. 65.95 (0-534-16788-8) Brooks-Cole.

***Trigonometry for College Students.** 7th ed. Smith. (C). 1998. pap. 30.95 (0-534-35299-5) Brooks-Cole.

***Trigonometry for College Students.** 7th ed. Smith. (C). 1998. text ed. 74.95 (0-534-35297-9) Brooks-Cole.

***Trigonometry for College Students.** 7th ed. Smith. (Mathematics Ser.). (C). 1998. text ed. 60.95 (0-534-34807-6) PWS Pubs.

Trigonometry Quick Review. David A. Kay. 1994. Study Guide. student ed., pap. text ed. 7.95 (0-8220-5358-6) Cliffs.

Trigonometry the Easy Way. 2nd ed. Douglas Downing. (Easy Way Ser.). 288p. 1990. pap. text ed. 11.95 (0-8120-4389-8) Barron.

Trigonometry Update. Marvin L. Bittinger. 1993. pap. 4.39 (0-201-60010-2) Addison-Wesley.

Trigonometry Using Calculators. Carlotta J. Elich & Joseph Elich. LC 79-18934. (Illus.). 1980. text ed. write for info. (0-201-03186-8) Addison-Wesley.

***Trigonometry with Additional Topics.** 2nd ed. Ed. by Lial. (C). 1996. text ed. write for info. (0-673-67652-8) Addison-Wesley.

***Trigonometry with Analytic Geometry.** Ed. by Steffensen. (C). 1993. text ed. 33.50 (0-673-99147-4) Addison-Wesley.

Trigonometry with Applications. Dale R. Ewen & Lynn R. Akers. (Illus.). 384p. 1984. write for info. (0-201-11312-0); teacher ed. write for info. (0-201-11314-7) Addison-Wesley.

Trigonometry with Applications. Graham. (C). 1989. teacher ed., pap. 23.00 (0-395-48942-3) HM.

Trigonometry with Applications. Graham. 1986. student ed., text ed. 54.52 (0-395-38539-3) HM.

Trigonometry with Applications. Graham. 1989. student ed., text ed. 54.68 (0-395-46141-3) HM.

Trigonometry with Applications. L. Murphy Johnson & Arnold R. Steffensen. (C). 1987. text ed. 55.50 (0-673-18799-3) Addson-Wesley Educ.

Trigonometry with Applications. 2nd ed. Terry H. Wesner et al. 400p. (C). 1993. text ed. write for info. (0-697-12292-1) Wm C Brown Pubs.

Trigonometry with Applications. 2nd ed. Terry H. Wesner et al. 400p. (C). 1993. spiral bd. write for info. (0-697-16787-9); spiral bd. write for info. (0-697-16788-7) Wm C Brown Pubs.

Trigonometry with Applications. 2nd ed. Terry H. Wesner et al. 400p. (C). 1994. teacher ed., per. write for info. (0-697-16786-0) Wm C Brown Pubs.

***Trigonometry with Technology Updates: A Graphing Approach.** Roland E. Larson et al. 688p. (C). 1997. text ed. 61.56 (0-669-41760-2) HM College Div.

***Trigonometry with Technology Updates: A Graphing Approach: Study & Solutions Guide.** Roland E. Larson et al. (C). 1997. text ed. 15.96 (0-669-28297-9) HM College Div.

Trigonometry 1987. Coxford. 1987. text ed. 54.50 (0-15-359370-9) HR&W Schl Div.

TrigTrainer. Katie De Meulemeester. (Illus.). 1993. pap. text ed. 10.95 (0-914534-10-6) Stokes.

Trihalomethane Reduction in Drinking Water: Technologies, Costs, Effectiveness, Monitoring, Compliance. Ed. by Gordon Culp. LC 84-14906. (Pollution Technology Review Ser.: No. 114). (Illus.). 251p. 1985. 42.00 (0-8155-1002-0) Noyes.

Trikon Deception. Ben Bova & Bill Pogue. 480p. 1993. mass mkt. 5.99 (0-8125-0735-5) Tor Bks.

***Trilateral Commission Report.** Trilateral Commission. (C). 1978. text ed. write for info. (0-8147-8163-2) NYU Pr.

***Trilateral Commission Report.** Trilateral Commission. (C). 1978. pap. text ed. write for info. (0-8147-8164-0) NYU Pr.

***Trilateral Commission Report.** Trilateral Commission. (C). 1981. pap. text ed. write for info. (0-8147-8167-5) NYU Pr.

Trilateral Forum on North Pacific Security. Ed. by Thomas Navratil. LC 95-34882. (CSIS Report Ser.). 27p. (C). 1995. pap. text ed. 10.95 (0-89206-279-7) CSI Studies.

Trilateral Perspectives on International Legal Issues: Relevance of Domestic Law & Policy. Ed. by Michael K. Young & Yuji Iwasawa. 604p. 1996. lib. bdg. 95.00 (1-57105-003-5) Transnatl Pubs.

Trilateralism. 1996. lib. bdg. 255.95 (0-8490-5945-3) Gordon Pr.

***Trilateralism: The Trilateral Commission & Elite Planning for World Management.** Ed. by Holly Sklar. 604p. 48.99 (0-919618-44-8, Pub. by Black Rose Bks CN); pap. 19.99 (0-919618-43-X, Pub. by Black Rose Bks CN) Consort Bk Sales.

Trilateralism: The Trilateral Commission & Elite Planning for World Management. Ed. by Holly Sklar. LC 80-51040. 604p. 1980. 40.00 (0-89608-104-4); pap. 22.00 (0-89608-103-6) South End Pr.

***Trilaterals over America.** Antony C. Sutton. 162p. (Orig.). 1995. pap. 7.00 (0-944379-07-9) CPA Bk Pub.

Trilby. Paul Adshead. (J). 1990. 7.99 (0-85953-513-4) Childs Play.

Trilby. George Du Maurier. 390p. 1994. pap. 7.50 (0-460-87447-0, Everyman's Classic Lib) C E Tuttle.

Trilby. George Du Maurier. Ed. by Elaine Showalter & David Trotter. (Oxford Popular Fiction Ser.). 320p. 1995. pap. 8.95 (0-19-282323-X) OUP.

Trilby. George Du Maurier. Ed. & Intro. by Daniel Pick. (Classics Ser.). 336p. 1995. pap. 7.95 (0-14-043403-8, Penguin Classics) Viking Penguin.

Trilby. George L. Du Maurier. 1976. 26.95 (0-8488-0265-9) Amereon Ltd.

***Trilby.** Diana Palmer. 1996. pap. 2.99 (0-8041-9704-0) Ivy Books.

Trilby. unabridged ed. George Du Maurier. LC 94-29799. (Illus.). 384p. 1995. pap. text ed. 8.95 (0-486-28319-4) Dover.

Trilby. George DuMaurier. 1994. reprint ed. lib. bdg. 32.95 (1-56849-527-7) Buccaneer Bks.

***Trilby & Other Plays.** Ed. & Intro. by George Taylor. (The World's Classics Ser.). 352p. 1996. pap. 13.95 (0-19-282984-X) OUP.

Trilce. Cesar Vallejo. Tr. by Clayton Eshleman from SPA. LC 92-82638. 220p. 1992. 28.00 (0-941419-50-9); pap. 14.00 (0-941419-51-7) Marsilio Pubs.

Trilce. Cesar Vallejo. Tr. by Rebecca Seiferle. LC 92-12484. 171p. (ENG & SPA.). (C). 1992. pap. 12.95 (1-878818-12-0) Sheep Meadow.

Trilce (Selections from the 1922 Edition), Set, No. 38/39 & 40/41. Cesar Vallejo. Tr. by Prospero Saiz from SPA. 48p. (ENG & SPA.). (C). 1990. pap. 11.00 (0-932868-06-1) Abraxas.

Trilce (Selections from the 1922 Edition), Set, No. 40/41 & 38/39. Cesar Vallejo. Tr. & Pref. by Prospero Saiz. 76p. (ENG & SPA.). (C). 1991. pap. 11.00 (0-932868-07-X) Abraxas.

Trilemma of World Oil Politics. Sheikh R. Ali & Jeffrey M. Elliot. LC 84-275. (Great Issues of the Day Ser.: No. 2). 152p. (Orig.). 1991. pap. 19.00 (0-89370-268-4); lib. bdg. 29.00 (0-89370-168-8) Borgo Pr.

Trilingual Agricultral Dictionary: Chinese, English, French. Shenglin Cai. 324p. (CHI, ENG & GER.). 1995. 195.00 (0-7859-9934-5) Fr & Eur.

Trilingual Compendium of the United Nations Terminology, 4 vols., Vol. I. rev. ed. 561p. 1986. 75.00 (92-1-002048-0, E/F/G.86.I.20) UN.

Trilingual Compendium of the United Nations Terminology, Vol. II. rev. ed. 571p. 1987. write for info. (*0-318-62018-9*, E/F/G.86.I.20) UN.
Trilingual Compendium of United Nations Terminology, 4 vols. United Nations Staff. (ENG, FRE & GER.). 1992. 150.00 (*0-8288-7359-3*, 9210020480) Fr & Eur.
Trilingual Cotton Terminologie: Terminologie Cotonniere Trilingue. G. Parry. 87p. (ENG, FRE & SPA.). 1986. pap. 34.95 (*0-8288-0039-1*, M15818) Fr & Eur.
Trilingual Dictionary: Hindi - Bengali - English. Bidhu B. Dasgupta. 1991. 29.95 (*0-8288-8433-1*) Fr & Eur.
Trilingual Dictionary: Hindi - Kashmiri - English, 3 vols. CHD Staff. 1992. reprint ed. Set. 95.00 (*0-8288-8428-5*) Fr & Eur.
Trilingual Dictionary Being a Comprehensive Lexicon in English. Mathura P. Misra. (C). reprint ed. 49.00 (*0-8364-2639-8*, Pub. by Asian Educ Servs II) S Asia.
Trilingual Dictionary of Microbiology: English, French, German. 160p. (ENG, FRE & GER.). 1995. 95.00 (*0-7859-9949-3*) Fr & Eur.
Trilingual Education: Sign Language, Spanish, English. Kathee M. Christensen & C. Ben Christensen. LC 85-70169. (Illus.). (ENG & SPA.). 1985. 16.25 (*0-916304-70-1*) SDSU Press.
Trilingual Legal Dictionary: Drietalige Regswoordeboek. 3rd ed. V. G. Hiemstra & H. L. Gonin. 498p. 1992. text ed. 125.00 (*0-7021-2781-7*, Pub. by Juta SA) Gaunt.
Trilingual Lexicon of Cookie & Pastry Making. M. Dumond. 128p. (ENG, FRE & GER.). 1988. pap. 49.95 (*0-8288-7725-4*) Fr & Eur.
Trilingual Psychological Dictionary: International Union of Psychological Science, Vol. 1. Ed. by H. C. Duijker. 355p. (ENG, FRE & GER.). 1975. 42.00 (*3-456-30558-3*) Hogrefe & Huber Pubs.
Trilingual Psychological Dictionary: International Union of Psychological Science, Vol. 2. Ed. by H. C. Duijker. 341p. (ENG, FRE & GER.). 1975. 42.00 (*3-456-30559-1*) Hogrefe & Huber Pubs.
Trilingual Psychological Dictionary: International Union of Psychological Science, Vol. 3. Ed. by H. C. Duijker. 399p. (ENG, FRE & GER.). 1975. 42.00 (*3-456-30560-5*) Hogrefe & Huber Pubs.
Trilingual Psychological Dictionary, Vol. 3: German-English-French. Francoise Mallet-Joris. 592p. 1978. pap. 55.00 (*0-7859-0061-6*, M12024) Fr & Eur.
***Trilingual Vocabulary of the Environment: English/French/German.** Tahirou Diao. 342p. (ENG, FRE & GER.). 1996. 175.00 (*0-7859-9292-8*) Fr & Eur.
Trillion Dollar Budget: How to Stop the Bankrupting of America. Glenn Pascall. LC 84-40665. (Illus.). 328p. 1985. pap. 14.95 (*0-295-96237-2*) U of Wash Pr.
***Trillion Dollar Enterprise.** Cyrus Friedheim. 1998. write for info. (*0-201-47984-2*) Addison-Wesley.
Trillion Dollar Promise: An Inside Look at Corporate Pension Money & the People Who Manage It. James A. Kujaca. LC 95-25892. 208p. 1996. text ed. 27.50 (*0-7863-0857-5*) Irwin Prof Pubng.
Trillion Year Spree: The History of Science Fiction. Brian W. Aldiss. 528p. 1988. pap. 9.95 (*0-380-70461-7*) Avon.
Trillium: A Guide to the Common Wildflowers of Northeast Wisconsin. Mary B. Good. Ed. by Alan Cook. (Illus.). (Orig.). pap. 9.95 (*0-9627976-0-X*) M B Good.
Trillium Basal Math-Ware: Apple Diskette. Helen Oliver & Bob Oliver. (J). (gr. 1-6). 1985. teacher ed., pap. 29.99 (*0-89824-080-8*) Trillium Pr.
Trillium Trail. Pamela A. Kopen & Dan F. Kopen. LC 93-28228. (Illus.). 32p. (J). (ps-12). 1993. pap. 9.95 (*0-9628914-3-6*) Padakami Pr.
***Trilliums.** Frederick W. Case & Roberta B. Case. LC 96-27583. 220p. 1997. 29.95 (*0-88192-374-5*) Timber.
Trilobites. H. B. Whittington. LC 92-11460. (Fossils Illustrated Ser.: Vol. 2). (Illus.). 280p. (C). 1992. 79.00 (*0-85115-311-9*, Boydell Pr) Boydell & Brewer.
Trilobites. 2nd ed. Riccardo Levi-Setti. LC 92-38716. (Illus.). 352p. (C). 1993. 45.00 (*0-226-47451-8*) U Ch Pr.
Trilobites. 2nd ed. Riccardo Levi-Setti. (Illus.). x, 342p. 1995. pap. 24.95 (*0-226-47452-6*) U Ch Pr.
Trilobites: A Photographic Atlas. Riccardo Levi-Setti. LC 74-7555. (Illus.). 222p. reprint ed. pap. 63.30 (*0-685-23835-0*, 2056616) Bks Demand.
***Trilogy.** Allan Carson. 96p. (Orig.). 1997. pap. 9.95 (*1-882897-06-4*) Lost Coast.
Trilogy. C. Wright. 26.00 (*0-06-055340-5*, HarpT) HarpC.
Trilogy: Armadeus Books 1, 2, & 3. 1988. pap. 40.00 (*0-940539-12-8*) Heridonius.
Trilogy: MARC Retriever Search Report; MEDLARS II Search Report; Guidelines for Research. Ed. by Gloria Vadus. 200p. 1982. 32.95 (*1-877772-07-0*) AHAF.
Trilogy Companion: A Reader's Guide to the Trilogy of Henryk Sienkiewicz. Ed. by Jerzy Krzyzanowski. 80p. (Orig.). 1991. pap. 10.00 (*0-87052-221-3*) Hippocrene Bks.
Trilogy in a Minor Key: Poems on Depression & Manic-Depression. Alex Sawyer et al. (Illus.). 90p. 1991. pap. 8.95 (*0-9632224-0-6*) Trilogy IL.
Trilogy of Deneys Reitz, Commando - Trekking On - No Outspan: A Boer Journal of the Boer War. Deneys Reitz. 971p. 1994. 45.00 (*1-879356-39-2*) Wolfe Pub Co.
***Trilogy of Short Stories.** Edgar Dass. 154p. (Orig.). 1997. mass mkt. 4.99 (*1-55237-150-6*, Pub. by Comnwlth Pub CN) Partners Pubs Grp.
Trilogy of Sonnets. Francis Milton. 64p. (Orig.). 1993. pap. 2.95 (*0-931888-46-8*) Christendom Pr.
Trilogy on Stalinism, 3 Vol. Set. (gr. 13). 1993. text ed. 82.95 (*1-56324-379-2*) M E Sharpe.
***Trilogy, The Walls Do Not Fall, Tribute to the Angels & The Flowering of the Rod.** Hilda Doolittle. LC 73-78848. 172p. 1973. pap. 8.95 (*0-8112-0491-X*, NDP362) New Directions.
Trim a Tree. Barbara Morris. LC 89-81054. (Illus.). 106p. (Orig.). 1989. pap. 9.95 (*0-944419-22-4*) Everett Cos Pub.
Trim & Finish Models. University of Washington, Division of Research, DAE Project Staff. (Instructional Materials for the Dental Health Professions Ser.). (Illus.). 65p. 1982. reprint ed. pap. 25.00 (*0-7837-8946-7*, 2049657) Bks Demand.
Trim & Terrific American Favorites. Holly B. Clegg. 1996. pap. write for info. (*0-517-88739-8*, C P Pubs) Crown Pub Group.
Trim & Terrific American Favorites: Over 250 Easy Everyday Low Fat Recipes. Holly B. Clegg. 224p. 1996. 18.95 (*0-517-70256-8*, C P Pubs) Crown Pub Group.
Trim & Terrific American Favorites: 250 Easy, Everyday Low-Fat Recipes. Holly B. Clegg. 1996. 18.95 (*0-614-95783-4*, Clarkson Potter) Crown Bks Yng Read.
Trim & Terrific Louisiana Kitchen: An Easy & Lighter Approach to Southern Cuisine. Holly B. Clegg. (Illus.). 240p. 1993. 16.95 (*0-9610888-3-4*) H B Clegg.
***Trim & Terrific One Dish Meals.** Holly Clegg. 1997. 18.95 (*0-517-70258-4*, C P Pubs) Crown Pub Group.
Trim & Thin 4-Ingredient Cookbook. Marilyn Miech & Shirley A. McClay. 328p. (Orig.). 1989. pap. 6.95 (*0-89586-724-9*, HP Books) Berkley Pub.
Trim Carpentry Techniques: Installing Doors, Windows, Base & Crown. Craig Savage. 1991. 27.00 (*0-8446-6444-8*) Peter Smith.
Trim Carpentry Techniques: Installing Doors, Windows, Base & Crown. Craig Savage. Ed. by Paul Bertorelli. LC 89-50517. (Illus.). 186p. 1989. pap. 19.95 (*0-942391-08-X*) Taunton.
Trim-Down Version of Miracles in Natoma's Kitchen: Healthier Living with Low-Fat Homestyle Cooking. Natoma Riley. Ed. by Frank Riley. 312p. 1997. pap. 14.95 (*1-886246-07-6*) Alpha LifeSpan.
Trimble (& Palmer) A Genealogical Record of Descendants of William & Ann Trimble of Concord Co., PA & James & Mary Trimble of Chester Co., PA & Others. Lyman L. Palmer. (Illus.). 398p. 1990. reprint ed. pap. 59.50 (*0-8328-1529-2*); reprint ed. lib. bdg. 67.50 (*0-8328-1528-4*) Higginson Bk Co.
Trimbleriff: A Book of Revelation. Laurence Housman. (BCL1-PR English Literature Ser.). 320p. 1992. reprint ed. lib. bdg. 89.00 (*0-7812-7568-7*) Rprt Serv.
Trimblerigg: A Book of Revelation. Laurence Houseman. LC 75-145094. 1971. reprint ed. 29.00 (*0-403-01032-2*) Scholarly.
***Trimellitic Anhydride Health & Safety Guide.** (Health & Safety Guides Ser.: No. 71). 30p. 1992. pap. text ed. 5.00 (*92-4-151071-4*, 1860071) World Health.
Trimetric Secret. Marvin Pietruszka & Paulette Lambert. LC 85-61325. (Illus.). 300p. 1986. 9.95 (*0-934249-01-6*) Quail Valley.
Trimipramin - Schlafentzug - Licht: Neurobiologische & Psychopathologische Verlaufsmessungen bei Depressionstherapie. Edith Holsboer-Trachsler. (Bibliotheca Psychiatrica: No. 166). (Illus.). xii, 138p. 1994. 129.75 (*3-8055-5920-8*) S Karger.
Trimmers, Trucklers & Temporizers: Notes of Murat Halstead from the Political Conventions of 1856. Ed. by William B. Hesseltine & Rex Fisher. LC 61-62506. 114p. 1961. 3.50 (*0-87020-044-5*) State Hist Soc Wis.
Trimming Float to Build Earnings. 104p. 1986. 50.00 (*0-929097-29-7*, 18291) Sav & Comm Bank.
Trimming the Cat's Claws: The Politics of Impunity in Albania. Minnesota Lawyers International Human Rights Committee Staff. (Minnesota International Human Rights Committee Ser.). 44p. (Orig.). 1992. pap. text ed. 8.50 (*0-929293-28-2*) MN Advocates.
Trimountain & Its Copper Mines. (Copper Country Local History Ser.: Vol. 39). (Illus.). 120p. 1991. 3.00 (*0-942363-38-8*) C J Monette.
***Trina Deitas: The Controversy Between Hincmar & Gottschalk.** George H. Tavard. LC 96-35637. 1997. 20.00 (*0-87462-636-6*) Marquette.
***Trina's Special Delivery.** Matt Mitter. (Fisher-Price Sidesqueaker Play Bks.). (Illus.). 16p. (J). (ps). 1998. bds. 3.99 (*1-57584-087-1*) Rdrs Dgst Yng Fam.
Trinet Directory of Leading U. S. Companies. Set. 395.00 (*0-317-57793-X*) Trinet.
Trinet Directory of Leading U. S. Companies, The Second 1500. LC 85-643077. 175.00 (*0-685-73866-3*) Trinet.
Trinet Directory of Leading U. S. Companies, The Top 1500. LC 86-637903. 175.00 (*0-685-73865-5*) Trinet.
Trinet Directory of Leading U. S. Companies, The Tops 1500. LC 85-640131. 175.00 (*0-318-61876-1*) Trinet.
Trinet Directory of Leading U. S. Companies: The Second Fifteen Hundred. LC 82-73381. 1984. 175.00 (*0-86692-001-3*) Trinet.
Trinet Directory of Leading US Companies: The Second 1500. LC 85-643077. 175.00 (*0-317-63821-1*) Trinet.
Trinet Directory of Leading US Companies: The Top 1500. LC 86-647903. 175.00 (*0-317-63826-2*) Trinet.
Trinet Directory of Leading US Companies: The Top 1500 Private. write for info. (*0-318-62390-0*) Trinet.
Trinh Nu: Tho. Pham Van Tien. LC 95-90282. 80p. (VIE.). 1995. pap. 6.50 (*0-9645739-1-1*) Van Pham Found.
Trini. Estela P. Trambley. LC 85-73394. 248p. 1986. pap. text ed. 16.00 (*0-916950-62-X*) Biling Rev-Pr.
Trini. Estela Portillo Trambley. LC 85-73394. 248p. 1986. lib. bdg. 26.00 (*0-916950-61-1*) Biling Rev-Pr.
Trinidad. Donna Bailey. LC 89-28567. (Where We Live Ser.). (Illus.). 32p. (J). (gr. 1-4). 1990. lib. bdg. 21.40 (*0-8114-2550-9*) Raintree Steck-V.
Trinidad & Tobago. Frances Chambers. (World Bibliographical Ser.: No. 74). 213p. 1987. lib. bdg. 55.00 (*1-85109-020-7*) ABC-CLIO.
Trinidad & Tobago. Patricia R. Urosevich. (Let's Visit Places & Peoples of the World Ser.). (Illus.). 88p. (YA). (gr. 5 up). 1988. lib. bdg. 19.95 (*1-55546-778-4*) Chelsea Hse.
***Trinidad & Tobago.** Patricia R. Urosevich. LC 97-22095. (Major World Nations Ser.). 1997. write for info. (*0-7910-4769-5*) Chelsea Hse.
Trinidad & Tobago. Lise Winer. LC 93-6531. (Varieties of English Around the World General Ser.: Vol. T6). xii, 368p. 1993. 79.00 (*1-55619-440-4*); audio 29.00 (*1-55619-441-2*) Benjamins North Am.
Trinidad & Tobago: Democracy & Development in the Caribbean. Scott B. MacDonald. LC 86-539. 240p. 1986. text ed. 55.00 (*0-275-92004-6*, C2004, Praeger Pubs) Greenwood.
Trinidad Awakening: West Indian Literature of the Nineteen-Thirties. Reinhard W. Sander. LC 87-31777. (Contributions in Afro-American & African Studies: No. 114). 180p. 1988. text ed. 45.00 (*0-313-24562-2*, SNT/, Greenwood Pr) Greenwood.
Trinidad Ethnicity. Ed. by Kevin A. Yelvington. LC 92-30207. 292p. (C). 1993. 33.00 (*0-87049-779-0*) U of Tenn Pr.
Trinidad to Carupano. Wilson Ltd. Staff & Imray L. Norie. (C). 1989. 60.00 (*0-685-40377-7*, Pub. by Imray Laurie Norie & Wilson UK) St Mut.
Trinidad Yoruba: From Mother Tongue to Memory. Maureen Warner-Lewis. LC 94-35107. 304p. (CRP, FRE & YOR.). 1996. pap. text ed. 27.95 (*0-8173-0727-3*) U of Ala Pr.
Trinitaria Hermeneutics: The Hermeneutical Significance of Karl Barth's Doctrine of the Trinity. Benjamin C. Leslie. LC 91-17450. (American University Studies: Theology & Religion: Ser. VII, Vol. 66). 286p. (C). 1991. text ed. 47.95 (*0-8204-1461-1*) P Lang Pubng.
Trinitarian & Mystical Theology of St. Symeon the New Theologian. Constantine N. Tsirpanlis. 42p. 1981. pap. 9.00 (*0-686-36331-0*) EO Pr.
Trinitarian Controversy. Ed. & Tr. by William G. Rusch. LC 79-8889. (Sources of Early Christian Thought Ser.). 192p. 1980. pap. 13.00 (*0-8006-1410-0*, 1-1410, Fortress Pr) Augsburg Fortress.
Trinitarian Controversy in the Fourth Century. David K. Bernard. LC 93-16363. 80p. (Orig.). 1993. pap. 5.99 (*1-56722-009-6*) Word Aflame.
Trinitarian Faith: The Evangelical Theology of the Ancient Catholic Church. Thomas F. Torrance. 358p. 1993. pap. text ed. 31.95 (*0-567-29219-3*, Pub. by T & T Clark UK) Bks Intl VA.
Trinitarian Formulae in St. Paul: An Exegetical Investigation into the Meaning & Function of Those Pauline Sayings Which Compositely Make Mention of God, Christ & the Holy Spirit. Joseph Maleparampil. LC 95-39185. 299p. 1995. pap. 57.95 (*0-8204-2943-0*) P Lang Pubng.
Trinitarian Perspectives: Toward Doctrinal Agreement. Thomas F. Torrance. 192p. 1994. text ed. 37.95 (*0-567-09699-8*, Pub. by T & T Clark UK) Bks Intl VA.
Trinitarian Theology East & West: St. Thomas Aquinas - St. Gregory Palamas. Michael J. Fahey & John Meyendorff. LC 77-28080. 43p. 1986. reprint ed. pap. 2.00 (*0-916586-18-9*) Holy Cross Orthodox.
***Trinitarian Theology of Dr. Samuel Clarke (1675-1729) Context, Sources, & Controversy.** Thomas C. Pfizenmaier. LC 96-45397. (Studies in the History of Christian Thought: Vol. 75). 224p. 1997. 83.25 (*90-04-10719-3*) E J Brill.
Trinitarian Theology Today: Essays on Divine Being & Art. Ed. by Christoph Schwobel. 182p. 1996. 35.95 (*0-567-09731-5*, Pub. by T & T Clark UK) Bks Intl VA.
Trinitas: A Theological Encyclopedia of the Holy Trinity. Michael O'Carroll. LC 86-45326. 232p. (Orig.). 1986. 35.00 (*0-8146-5595-5*) Liturgical Pr.
***Trinity.** John Ankerberg & John Weldon. (The Defenders Ser.). 48p. (Orig.). 1997. pap. 2.99 (*1-56507-587-0*) Harvest Hse.
Trinity. Edward H. Bickersteth. LC 59-13770. 182p. 1976. pap. 9.99 (*0-8254-2226-4*, Kregel Class) Kregel.
Trinity. F. Donald Harris & Ronald A. Harris. 32p. 1986. pap. 2.99 (*0-87213-310-9*) Loizeaux.
Trinity. Hilary of Poitiers. Tr. by Stephen McKenna. LC 67-28585. (Fathers of the Church Ser.: Vol. 25). 555p. 1954. 36.95 (*0-8132-0025-3*) Cath U Pr.
Trinity. Susan Ludvigson. LC 96-9573. 376p. 1996. text ed. 16.95 (*0-8071-2115-0*) La State U Pr.
Trinity. Susan Ludvigson. LC 96-9573. 376p. 1996. pap. 9.95 (*0-8071-2116-9*) La State U Pr.
Trinity. Karl Rahner. 140p. 1994. pap. 24.00 (*0-86012-015-5*, Pub. by Srch Pr UK) St Mut.
***Trinity.** Karl Rahner. LC 96-51964. 132p. 1997. pap. 17.95 (*0-8245-1627-3*, Crossrd Herd) Crossroad NY.
Trinity. Leon Uris. 832p. 1983. mass mkt. 7.99 (*0-553-25846-X*) Bantam.
Trinity. 2nd ed. Gordon H. Clark. Ed. & Intro. by John W. Robbins. 157p. 1990. pap. 8.95 (*0-940931-92-3*) Trinity Found.
Trinity. Augustine, Saint. Tr. by Stephen McKenna. LC 63-12482. (Fathers of the Church Ser.: Vol. 45). 557p. 1963. reprint ed. pap. 158.80 (*0-7837-9202-6*, 2049952) Bks Demand.
Trinity: A Church, a Parish, a People. Dena Merriam. LC 96-14804. (Illus.). 152p. 1996. 45.00 (*0-7892-0249-2*, Cross Riv Pr) Abbeville Pr.
Trinity: An Analysis of St. Thomas Aquinas' "Exposito" of the "De Trinitate" of Boethius. Douglas C. Hall. LC 92-10928. (Studien und Texte zur Geistesgeschichte des Mittelalters Ser.: Vol. 33). 131p. 1992. 50.00 (*90-04-09631-0*) E J Brill.
Trinity: Classic & Contemporary Readings. Lewis Ayres. (Blackwell Readings in Modern Theology Ser.). Date not set. 59.95 (*0-631-19954-3*) Blackwell Pubs.
Trinity: Classic & Contemporary Readings. Lewis Ayres. (Blackwell Readings in Modern Theology Ser.). 1997. pap. 22.95 (*0-631-19955-1*) Blackwell Pubs.
Trinity: Evidence & Issues. Robert A. Morey. 580p. 1996. 24.99 (*0-529-10692-2*, TEI) World Publng.
Trinity: Is the Doctrine Biblical - Is It Important? F. Donald Harris & Ronald A. Harris. LC 86-21497. 1986. pap. 14.95 (*0-87213-562-4*) Loizeaux.
Trinity: Saint Augustine, Vol. I/5. 2nd ed. Tr. & Intro. by Edmund Hill. 472p. 1991. 24.95 (*0-911782-89-3*) New City.
Trinity: Saint Augustine, Vol. I/5. 3rd ed. Tr. & Intro. by Edmund Hill. 472p. 1991. pap. 39.00 (*0-911782-96-6*) New City.
Trinity see IVP Booklets
Trinity - Chinese Edition. Robert Crossley. Tr. by John Huang. 52p. (CHI.). 1983. pap. 2.50 (*1-56582-094-0*) Christ Renew Min.
Trinity Alps: A Hiking & Backpacking Guide. 3rd ed. Luther Linkhart. LC 94-27756. 240p. 1994. pap. 15.95 (*0-89997-176-8*) Wilderness Pr.
***Trinity Alps Companion: Hiking, Fishing, & Camping in the Northern California Wilderness.** Wayne F. Moss. (Illus.). 224p. (Orig.). 1997. pap. 14.95 (*0-9639705-3-4*) Ecopress.
Trinity & Culture. Charles S. MacKenzie. (American University Studies: Theology & Religion: Ser. VII, Vol. 34). 150p. (C). 1987. text ed. 25.95 (*0-8204-0492-6*) P Lang Pubng.
Trinity & Eternal Sonship of Christ: A Defense Against "Oneness Pentecostal" Attacks on Historic Christianity. Bob L. Ross. 1993. pap. 12.00 (*1-56186-517-6*) Pilgrim Pubns.
Trinity & Incarnation: The Faith of the Early Church. Basil Studer. 288p. (Orig.). 1994. pap. text ed. 19.95 (*0-8146-5506-8*, M Glazier) Liturgical Pr.
***Trinity & Incarnation in Anglo-Saxon Art & Thought.** Barbara C. Raw. (Studies in Anglo-Saxon England: No. 21). (Illus.). 276p. (C). 1997. text ed. 59.95 (*0-521-55371-7*) Cambridge U Pr.
Trinity & Marriage in Paul: The Establishment of a Communitarian Analogy of the Trinity Grounded in the Theological Shape of Pauline Thought. Earl C. Muller. (American University Studies: Theology & Religion: Ser. VII, Vol. 60). 553p. (C). 1989. text ed. 81.50 (*0-8204-0914-6*) P Lang Pubng.
Trinity & Ministry. Peter Drilling. LC 91-31974. 232p. (Orig.). 1991. pap. 18.00 (*0-8006-2490-4*, 1-2490, Fortress Pr) Augsburg Fortress.
Trinity & Ontology: A Comparative Study of the Theologies of Karl Barth & Wolfhart Pannenberg. Timothy Bradshaw. LC 92-5144. (Rutherford Studies in Contemporary Theology). 472p. 1992. reprint ed. 109.95 (*0-7734-1641-2*) E Mellen.
Trinity & Process: A Critical Examination & Reconstruction of Hartshorne's Di-Polar Theism Towards a Trinitarian Metaphysics. Gregory A. Boyd. LC 91-37789. (American University Studies: Theology & Religion: Ser. VII, Vol. 119). 424p. (C). 1992. text ed. 60.95 (*0-8204-1660-6*) P Lang Pubng.
Trinity & Society. Leonardo Boff. 288p. 1994. pap. 27.00 (*0-86012-161-5*, Pub. by Srch Pr UK) St Mut.
Trinity & Society: Theology & Liberation. Leonardo Boff. Tr. by Paul Burns from POR. LC 88-9884. 236p. (Orig.). 1988. pap. 17.50 (*0-88344-622-7*) Orbis Bks.
Trinity & the Kingdom: The Doctrine of God. Jurgen Moltmann. Tr. by Margaret Kohl from GER. LC 93-29952. (Works of Jurgen Moltmann). 272p. (ENG.). 1993. reprint ed. pap. 18.00 (*0-8006-2825-X*, 1-2825, Fortress Pr) Augsburg Fortress.
***Trinity & the Paschal Mystery: A Development in Recent Catholic Theology.** LC 97-20143. (New Theology Studies). 208p. (Orig.). 1997. pap. 19.95 (*0-8146-5865-2*) Liturgical Pr.
Trinity & the Religious Experience of Man: Icon, Person, Mystery. Raimundo Panikkar. LC 73-77329. 98p. reprint ed. pap. 28.00 (*0-317-26668-3*, 2025122) Bks Demand.
Trinity as History: Saga of the Christian God. Bruno Forte. Tr. by Paul Rotondi. LC 89-32734. 250p. (Orig.). 1989. pap. 14.95 (*0-8189-0552-2*) Alba.
Trinity-by-the-Stove. Ed. by Bee Harper. (Illus.). 320p. 1987. 12.95 (*0-9618615-0-9*) TBTC ECW.
Trinity College Historical Society Historical Papers, Series 1-32. Duke University Staff. LC 74-115989. reprint ed. Set. 900.00 (*0-404-51750-1*) AMS Pr.
Trinity College Historical Society Papers, Series 3: Gov. W. W. Holden & Revolutionary Documents. Duke University Staff. reprint ed. 30.00 (*0-404-51753-6*) AMS Pr.
Trinity College Historical Society Papers, Series 2: Legal & Biographical Studies. Duke University Staff. reprint ed. 30.00 (*0-404-51752-8*) AMS Pr.
Trinity College Historical Society Papers, Series 1: Reconstruction & State Biography. Duke University Staff. reprint ed. 30.00 (*0-404-51751-X*) AMS Pr.
Trinity College Historical Society Papers, Series 4: 1900. Duke University Staff. reprint ed. 30.00 (*0-404-51754-4*) AMS Pr.
Trinity College Historical Society Papers, Series 5: 1905. Duke University Staff. reprint ed. 30.00 (*0-404-51755-2*) AMS Pr.
Trinity College Historical Society Papers, Series 6: 1906. Duke University Staff. reprint ed. 30.00 (*0-404-51756-0*) AMS Pr.
Trinity College Historical Society Papers, Series 7: 1907. Duke University Staff. reprint ed. 30.00 (*0-404-51757-9*) AMS Pr.
Trinity College Historical Society Papers, Series 8: 1908-1909. Duke University Staff. reprint ed. 30.00 (*0-404-51758-7*) AMS Pr.

Trinity College Historical Society Papers, Series 9: 1912. Duke University Staff. reprint ed. 30.00 (*0-404-51759-5*) AMS Pr.

Trinity College Historical Society Papers, Series 10: 1914. Duke University Staff. reprint ed. 30.00 (*0-404-51760-9*) AMS Pr.

Trinity College Historical Society Papers, Series 11: 1915. Duke University Staff. reprint ed. 30.00 (*0-404-51761-7*) AMS Pr.

Trinity College Historical Society Papers, Series 12: 1916. Duke University Staff. reprint ed. 30.00 (*0-404-51762-5*) AMS Pr.

Trinity College Historical Society Papers, Series 13: 1919. Duke University Staff. reprint ed. 30.00 (*0-404-51763-3*) AMS Pr.

Trinity College Historical Society Papers, Series 14: 1922. Duke University Staff. reprint ed. 30.00 (*0-404-51764-1*) AMS Pr.

Trinity College Historical Society Papers, Series 15: 1925. Duke University Staff. reprint ed. 30.00 (*0-404-51765-X*) AMS Pr.

Trinity College Library Dublin: Descriptive Catalogue of the Medieval & Renaissance Latin Manuscripts, 2 vols. Marvin L. Colker. 1646p. 1991. Set. text ed. 390.00 (*0-85967-790-7*, Pub. by Scolar Pr UK) Ashgate Pub Co.

Trinity County Beginnings, Texas. Trinity County Book Committee. (Illus.). 866p. 1986. 65.00 (*0-88107-072-6*) Curtis Media.

Trinity Fields. Bradford Morrow. LC 94-20125. 435p. 1995. pap. 22.95 (*0-670-85728-9*, Viking) Viking Penguin.

Trinity Fields. Bradford Morrow. 448p. 1996. pap. 12.95 (*0-14-024013-6*, Viking) Viking Penguin.

Trinity Foot Beagles. James Knox. 134p. 1990. pap. 40.00 (*0-85131-309-4*, Pub. by J A Allen & Co UK) St Mut.

***Trinity Gene.** Tim Newcomb. 330p. (Orig.). 1995. pap. 12.95 (*1-878117-07-6*) Lagumo Corp.

Trinity Grove. David V. Smith. 288p. 1990. mass mkt. 3.95 (*0-380-75835-0*) Avon.

***Trinity in a Pluralistic Age.** Ed. by Kevin J. Vanhoozer. 160p. 1996. pap. 20.00 (*0-8028-4117-1*) Eerdmans.

Trinity in Asian Perspective. Jung Y. Lee. 1996. pap. 19.95 (*0-687-42637-5*) Abingdon.

Trinity in Process: A Relational Theology of God. Ed. by Joseph A. Bracken & Marjorie Hewitt Suchocki. LC 96-22538. 286p. 1996. 34.95 (*0-8264-0878-8*) Continuum.

Trinity Lutheran Church of Reading, (Baptisms 1751-1790), Pt. 1. Compiled by Schuylkill Roots Staff. 122p. 1990. pap. text ed. 14.00 (*1-55856-054-8*) Closson Pr.

Trinity Lutheran Church of Reading, Berks County, PA, Pt. 4: Burials 1754-1812. Schuylkill Roots Staff. 74p. 1992. pap. text ed. 8.50 (*1-55856-113-7*) Closson Pr.

Trinity Lutheran Church of Reading, Pt. 3: Marriages 1754-1812. Compiled by Schuylkill Roots Staff. 72p. 1990. pap. 8.50 (*1-55856-038-6*) Closson Pr.

Trinity Lutheran Church Records Vol. I: 1730-1767. Debra D. Smith & Frederick S. Weiser. 487p. 1995. reprint ed. text ed. 39.95 (*1-55856-009-2*) Closson Pr.

Trinity Lutheran Church Records Vol. II: 1767-1782. Debra D. Smith & Frederick S. Weiser. (Illus.). 578p. 1995. text ed. 39.95 (*1-55856-214-1*) Closson Pr.

Trinity, or the Tri-Personal Being of God. Joseph A. Synan. 1980. pap. 2.95 (*0-911866-00-0*) LifeSprings Res.

Trinity Psalter: Song Leader's Edition. 1995. spiral bd. 25.00 (*1-884527-11-6*) Crown & Covenant.

Trinity Psalter: Words-Only Psalter. LC 93-74255. 130p. 1994. pap. 5.50 (*1-884527-07-8*) Crown & Covenant.

***Trinity River.** Luther Smith et al. LC 97-318. (Illus.). 110p. 1997. pap. 19.95 (*0-87565-168-2*) Tex Christian.

Trinity Story. Calvin B. Hanson. LC 83-81575. 1983. pap. 6.95 (*7-100-07624-2*) Free Church Pubns.

Trinity Strike. Suzann Ledbetter. 352p. 1996. mass mkt., pap. 5.50 (*0-451-18644-3*, Sig) NAL-Dutton.

Trinity Sunday & Beyond. Ed. by Blair G. Meeks. (Liturgy Ser.). 80p. (Orig.). 1996. pap. 10.95 (*0-918208-72-6*) Liturgical Conf.

Trinity Vector. Steve Perry. 1996. mass mkt. 5.99 (*0-441-00350-8*) Ace Bks.

Trinity's Children: Living along America's Nuclear Highway. Tad Bartimus & Scott McCartney. LC 92-39101. (Illus.). 336p. (C). 1993. pap. 11.95 (*0-8263-1433-3*) U of NM Pr.

Trinker der Lufte. Carl R. Raswan. (Illus.). 154p. 1990. write for info. (*3-487-08140-7*) G Olms Pubs.

Trinkets. Lizbeth Dusseau. (Orig.). 1995. mass mkt. 5.95 (*1-56333-246-9*) Masquerade.

Trinkets & Treasures: A Collection of Favorite Bits of Wisdom. Helen E. Christiansen. 130p. (Orig.). (YA). (gr. 7 up). 1984. reprint ed. pap. 8.50 (*0-9621419-0-9*) H Christiansen.

Trio. Dorothy D. Baker. LC 77-5686. 234p. 1977. text ed. 55.00 (*0-8371-9647-7*, BATR, Greenwood Pr) Greenwood.

Trio. Charles W. Greeley. LC 92-62016. 136p. 1993. pap. 8.00 (*1-56002-228-0*, Univ Edtns) Aegina Pr.

Trio. Osbert Sitwell. LC 78-107738. (Essay Index Reprint Ser.). 1977. 20.95 (*0-8369-1535-6*) Ayer.

Trio, No. 2. 7.95 (*0-7935-4049-6*, 50482307) H Leonard.

Trio: Toni Mirosevich, Charlotte Muse, Edward Smallfield. Toni Mirosevich et al. LC 94-12045. 76p. (Orig.). 1995. pap. 10.00 (*0-9645026-0-7*) Specter Pr.

Trio for Flute, Cello & Piano. B. Martinu. 48p. 1986. pap. 17.95 (*0-7935-5538-8*) H Leonard.

Trio for Viole da Gamba: Op. 3. Peter Ballinger. (Contemporary Consort Ser.: No. 8). i, 22p. 1989. pap. text ed. 10.00 (*1-56571-011-8*) PRB Prods.

Trio Grande: Adios Palomita. Olivier Vatine & Alain Clement. Ed. by Greg S. Baisden. Tr. by Mary Irwin from FRE. (Illus.). 56p. 1995. reprint ed. 14.95 (*1-879450-43-7*) Tundra MA.

Trio in C Minor Opus 66: Violin-Violoncello-Piano. Mandelssohn. 72p. 1986. pap. 16.95 (*0-7935-4990-6*, 50259390) H Leonard.

Trio of Doctors. large type ed. Lindsay Hicks. (Linford Romance Library). 336p. 1992. pap. 15.99 (*0-7089-7241-1*, Trailtree Bookshop) Ulverscroft.

Trio of Treasured Quilts. 2nd rev. ed. Eleanor Burns. (Illus.). 155p. (Orig.). 1989. spiral bd. 12.95 (*0-922705-18-6*) Quilt Day.

Trio of Triceratops. Most. LC 96-23701. 1998. write for info. (*0-15-201448-9*) HarBrace.

Trio Recorder, 2 bks., Bk. 1. Gerald Burakoff & Willy Strickland. 1975. 4.00 (*0-913334-24-3*, CM1028) Consort Music.

Trio Recorder, 2 bks., Bk. 2. Gerald Burakoff & Willy Strickland. 1977. 4.00 (*0-685-74376-4*, CM1042) Consort Music.

Trio Recorder, 2 bks., Bks. 1-2. Gerald Burakoff & Willy Strickland. 1975. 4.00 (*0-685-74375-6*) Consort Music.

Trio Seven Poetry. C. L. Dallat et al. 57p. 9300. pap. 13.95 (*0-85640-486-1*, Pub. by Blackstaff Pr IE) Dufour.

Trio Six. Angela Greene. 72p. 9000. pap. 12.95 (*0-85640-431-4*, Pub. by Blackstaff Pr IE) Dufour.

***Trio Sonata.** Christopher Hogwood. 128p. 1996. 4.95 (*0-563-17095-6*, BB 11135, BBC-Parkwest) Parkwest Pubns.

Trio Sonata: Clarinet Trio. 9.95 (*0-7935-4844-6*, 50482450) H Leonard.

Trio Sonata: Saxophone Trio. 9.95 (*0-7935-4846-2*, 50482452) H Leonard.

Trio Sonata: Violin-Viola-Violincello. 9.95 (*0-7935-4074-7*, 50482374) H Leonard.

Trio Sonata: Woodwind Trio Double Reeds. 9.95 (*0-7935-4845-4*, 50482451) H Leonard.

Trio Waltz. (Ballroom Dance Ser.). 1986. lib. bdg. 79.95 (*0-8490-3417-5*) Gordon Pr.

Trio Waltz. (Ballroom Dance Ser.). 1985. lib. bdg. 250.00 (*0-87700-816-7*) Revisionist Pr.

Trio with Four Players. John Wheatcroft. LC 95-30932. 144p. 1996. 19.95 (*0-8453-4856-6*, Cornwall Bks) Assoc Univ Prs.

Triod' Postnaja see Tserkovno-Pjevcheskiji Sbornik

Triod' Tsvjetnaja see Tserkovno-Pjevcheskiji Sbornik

Triology Plus One. Kendall J. Wentz. 1994. 13.95 (*0-533-11120-X*) Vantage.

Triomphe de la Raison. Romain Rolland. 88p. (FRE.). 1971. pap. 8.95 (*0-7859-5468-6*) Fr & Eur.

Triomphe de la Vie: Supplement aux Vraies Richesses. Jean Giono. (FRE.). 1992. pap. 10.95 (*0-7859-3170-8*, 2253059749) Fr & Eur.

Trionfo di Dori: The 29 Madrigals of the 1592 Collection. Harrison Powley. (Renaissance Voices Ser.). 264p. 1990. pap. 25.00 (*1-888471-05-0*) Gaudia Mus & Arts.

Trios for Trombone: Classica-Ragtime-Jazz. 1990. 6.95 (*0-685-32236-X*, K740) Hansen Ed Mus.

Trip. Ezra Jack Keats. LC 77-24907. (Illus.). 32p. (J). (gr. k-3). 1978. lib. bdg. 15.93 (*0-688-84123-6*) Greenwillow.

Trip. Ezra Jack Keats. LC 77-24907. (J). (ps up). 1987. pap. 4.95 (*0-688-07328-X*, Mulberry) Morrow.

Trip a Go-Go. Harry Barba. (Mini-Book Ser). (Orig.). 1970. pap. 1.50 (*0-911906-03-7*) Harian Creative Bks.

Trip Across the Plains in 1849. Martha M. Morgan. 32p. 1983. pap. 5.95 (*0-87770-295-0*) Ye Galleon.

Trip Around the World. Barbara Schaff & Sue Roth. Ed. by Walter Kelly & Ina M. Levin. (Extended Themes Ser.). (Illus.). 144p. (Orig.). 1993. student ed., pap. 12.95 (*1-55734-600-3*) Tchr Create Mat.

Trip Around the World Quilt. pap. 5.98 (*0-317-03203-8*) Gick.

Trip Around the World Quilt. Eleanor Burns. (Illus.). 55p. (Orig.). 1988. pap. 7.95 (*0-922705-13-5*) Quilt Day.

***Trip Back Home.** Janet S. Wong. LC 97-9692. (Illus.). (J). 1998. write for info. (*0-15-200784-9*) HarBrace.

***Trip Book.** (Illus.). 32p. 1996. pap. 4.95 (*0-913515-03-5*, Elliott Clark) Black Belt Comm.

Trip by Torpedo. Pierre Tamboise. (I Love to Read Collection). (Illus.). 46p. (J). (gr. 2-4). 1992. lib. bdg. 12.79 (*0-89565-894-1*) Childs World.

Trip (China) Reading Level 2. (Fitting In Ser.). 1993. audio 7.00 (*0-88336-772-6*) New Readers.

Trip from the Dalles, Oregon, to Fort Owen, Montana & Overland Diary. Charles A. Frush & William H. Frush. 15p. pap. write for info. (*0-87770-302-7*) Ye Galleon.

Trip on a Jet Plane: Photos & Fun for Boys & Girls. Peggy Space. (Sarah Ser.). (Illus.). 32p. (J). (gr. 3-7). 1981. pap. 2.50 (*0-942772-00-8*) Image Pubns.

Trip Out! 25 Vacations That Will Change Your Life. Karoleigh Krenzel. Ed. by Kay Rickey. (Illus.). 117p. (Orig.). 1996. pap. 15.95 (*1-883962-03-X*) Kristalex Pr.

Trip Through Cambodia. Bridgette Diep. LC 73-159478. (Illus.). 32p. (J). (ps-3). 8.95 (*0-87592-054-3*) Scroll Pr.

Trip Through the New Testament. Elaine Cole & David Cole. 56p. (Orig.). (J). (gr. 1-6). 1994. pap. 15.95 incl. audio (*1-883426-07-3*) Chldrns Outrch.

Trip Through the Old Testament. David Cole & Elaine Cole. 56p. (Orig.). (J). (gr. 1-6). 1994. pap. 15.95 incl. audio (*1-883426-06-5*) Chldrns Outrch.

Trip Through Time & the Santa Cruz Mountains. Billie J. Jensen & Reece C. Jensen. 245p. 1994. pap. text ed. 17.95 (*1-886278-07-5*) Ghastly Gallimaufry.

***Trip Through Tipperary Lakeside: From Nenagh to Ballina-Killaloe & from Nenagh to Portumna by the River Shannon's Lough Derg Scenic Routes.** Nancy Murphy. (Illus.). 96p. (Orig.). 1996. pap. 23.95 (*0-946327-21-1*, Pub. by Relay Pubns IE) Irish Bks Media.

Trip to a Pow Wow. Richard Red Hawk. (Illus.). 45p. (Orig.). (J). (gr. k-3). 1988. pap. 6.95 (*0-940113-14-7*) Sierra Oaks Pub.

Trip to Bethlehem: The Traditional Christmas Story As a Guide to Spiritual Transformation. Hypatia Hasbrouck. Ed. by Carol Lindahl. LC 95-74835. 160p. (Orig.). 1995. pap. 12.95 (*0-89716-604-3*) P B Pubng.

Trip to Bodie Bluff & the Dead Sea of the Westin 1863. J. Ross Browne. (Illus.). 1978. reprint ed. pap. 3.95 (*0-89646-076-2*) Vistabooks.

Trip to Bountiful. Horton Foote. 1954. pap. 5.25 (*0-8222-1174-2*) Dramatists Play.

Trip to Cheyenne: In Search of a City & Self. Rachel Edwards. (Illus.). 125p. 1996. lib. bdg. 22.95 (*1-883033-01-2*) Flats Pub.

***Trip to China: Intermediate Reader of Modern Chinese, 2 vols.** Chih-Ping Chou. 460p. 1996. pap. text ed. 39.50 (*0-691-02883-4*) Princeton U Pr.

***Trip to Chinatown.** Charles H. Hoyt. Ed. & Intro. by Walter J. Meserve. (On Stage, America! Ser.). 33p. 1996. spiral bd. 2.95 (*0-937657-33-6*) Feedbk Theabks & Prospero.

Trip to Cuba. Julia W. Howe. (Notable American Authors Ser.). 1992. reprint ed. lib. bdg. 75.00 (*0-7812-3217-1*) Rprt Serv.

Trip to Italy & France. deluxe ed. Lawrence Ferlinghetti. LC 80-36778. 64p. 1981. 50.00 (*0-8112-0782-X*) New Directions.

Trip to Mars. Fenton Ash. LC 74-15948. (Science Fiction Ser.). (Illus.). 326p. 1975. reprint ed. 26.95 (*0-405-06274-5*) Ayer.

Trip to Mezuza Land. Sara Leiberman. Ed. by Chanah Colish. (Illus.). 48p. (J). 1988. reprint ed. 10.00 (*0-8266-0364-5*, Merkos LInyonei Chinuch) Kehot Pubn Soc.

Trip to Paris. Cedric Vallet. (Illus.). 17p. (J). (gr. k-3). 1992. pap. 15.95 (*1-895583-26-8*) MAYA Pubs.

Trip to Planet Doog. Marcus Porus et al. LC 95-92692. (Gribich & Friends Ser.). (Illus.). 32p. (J). (ps). 1996. 14.95 (*0-9646125-1-8*) Doog Pub Grp.

Trip to the Jungle. Susan Butler. (Illus.). 40p. (Orig.). (J). (ps-2). 1978. pap. 3.95 (*0-931416-00-0*) Open Books.

Trip to the Moon. Richard Scarry. (Busy World of Richard Scarry 8x8s Ser.). (J). (ps-3). 1996. pap. 3.25 (*0-689-80806-2*) S&S Childrens.

Trip to the Prairies & in the Interior of North America 1837-1838 Travel Notes. Francesco Arese. LC 74-12556. (Illus.). 216p. 1974. reprint ed. lib. bdg. 42.00 (*0-8154-0496-4*) Cooper Sq.

Trip to the Rockies. B. R. Corwin. LC 78-39693. (Select Bibliographies Reprint Ser.). 1977. reprint ed. 11.95 (*0-8369-9934-7*) Ayer.

Trip to the West & Texas: Far Western Frontier. Amos A. Parker. LC 72-9463. (Illus.). 1973. reprint ed. 28.95 (*0-405-04991-9*) Ayer.

Trip to the West Indies. E. W. Howe. (Collected Works of E. W. Howe). 1988. reprint ed. lib. bdg. 59.00 (*0-7812-1292-8*) Rprt Serv.

Trip to the West Indies see Collected Works of E. W. Howe

Trip to the Zoo: Feelings Coloring Book. Jim Boulden & Joan Boulden. Ed. by Evelyn M. Ward. (Illus.). 16p. (Orig.). (J). (gr. k-2). 1994. pap. 5.95 (*1-878076-39-6*) Boulden Pub.

Trip to Tulum. Federico Fellini. Ed. by V. Mollica. Tr. by Stefano Gaudiano from ITA. (Illus.). 120p. (Orig.). 1990. pap. 17.95 (*0-87416-123-1*) Catalan Communs.

Trip to Tulum. Milo Manara & Federico Fellini. (Illus.). 120p. (Orig.). 1996. pap. 19.95 (*1-56163-149-3*, Comics Lit) NBM.

Trip to Wonderful Alaska. L. D. MacDowell. 33p. reprint ed. pap. 2.95 (*0-8466-2063-4*, S63) Shorey.

***Trip Tracker.** 1997. pap. 16.95 (*0-528-83843-1*) Rand McNally.

Tripartita: Earth, Dreams, Powers. Maritza Arrastia et al. 120p. (Orig.). 1989. pap. 9.00 (*0-685-26445-9*) Atabex Collection.

Tripartite Life of St. Patrick. pap. text ed. 5.95 (*0-89981-106-X*) Eastern Orthodox.

Tripartite Life of St. Patrick, with Other Documents Related to the Saint with Translation & Indexes, 2 vols. Ed. by Whitley Stokes. (Rolls Ser.: No. 89). 1974. reprint ed. Set. 140.00 (*0-8115-1165-0*) Periodicals Srv.

Tripartite Mimicry in Nature. Stanford Goldman. LC 93-17319. 156p. 1993. text ed. 69.95 (*0-7734-9292-5*) E Mellen.

Tripartite Relationship: Government, Foreign Investors & Local Investors During Egypt's Economic Opening. Kate Gillespie. LC 83-21221. 236p. 1984. text ed. 49.95 (*0-275-91171-3*, C1171, Praeger Pubs) Greenwood.

***TripBuilder: Chicago.** 25p. 1997. pap. 5.95 (*1-56621-209-X*) TripBuilder.

TripBuilder: Holland: Best Museums. TripBuilder, Inc. Staff. 25p. 1993. 5.95 (*1-56621-302-9*) TripBuilder.

TripBuilder: Holland: Charming Villages. TripBuilder, Inc. Staff. 25p. 1993. 5.95 (*1-56621-300-2*) TripBuilder.

TripBuilder: Holland: Easy Day Trips from Amsterdam. TripBuilder, Inc. Staff. 25p. 1993. 5.95 (*1-56621-303-7*) TripBuilder.

TripBuilder: Holland: Flowers & Gardens. TripBuilder, Inc. Staff. 25p. 1993. 5.95 (*1-56621-301-0*) TripBuilder.

TripBuilder: Holland: For History Buffs. TripBuilder, Inc. Staff. 25p. 1993. 5.95 (*1-56621-305-3*) TripBuilder.

TripBuilder: London. Tripbuilder, Inc. Staff. 25p. 1995. 5.95 (*1-56621-025-9*) TripBuilder.

***TripBuilder: New York City.** 25p. 1997. pap. 5.95 (*1-56621-605-9*) TripBuilder.

TripBuilder: New York City: A Child's Guide. TripBuilder, Inc. Staff. 25p. 1994. 4.95 (*1-56621-605-2*) TripBuilder.

TripBuilder: New York City: Best Museums. TripBuilder, Inc. Staff. 25p. 1995. pap. 4.95 (*1-56621-600-1*) TripBuilder.

TripBuilder: New York City: Hidden Treasures. TripBuilder, Inc. Staff. 25p. 1995. pap. 4.95 (*1-56621-603-6*) TripBuilder.

TripBuilder: New York City: New York Landmarks. TripBuilder, Inc. Staff. 25p. 1995. pap. 4.95 (*1-56621-602-8*) TripBuilder.

TripBuilder: New York City: Sports Guide. Tripbuilder, Inc. Staff. 25p. 1994. 4.95 (*1-56621-608-7*) TripBuilder.

TripBuilder: Paris. 25p. 1996. pap. 5.95 (*1-56621-114-X*) TripBuilder.

TripBuilder: Rome. 25p. 1996. pap. 5.95 (*1-56621-800-4*) TripBuilder.

***TripBuilder: San Francisco.** 25p. 1997. pap. 5.95 (*1-56621-513-7*) TripBuilder.

***TripBuilder: Washington, D. C.** 25p. 1997. pap. 5.95 (*1-56621-706-7*) TripBuilder.

TripBuilder: Washington, D. C.: A Child's Guide. TripBuilder, Inc. Staff. 25p. 1994. 4.95 (*1-56621-703-2*) TripBuilder.

TripBuilder: Washington, D. C.: Best Museums. TripBuilder, Inc. Staff. 25p. 1994. 4.95 (*1-56621-700-8*) TripBuilder.

TripBuilder: Washington, D. C.: Hidden Treasures. TripBuilder, Inc. Staff. 25p. 1994. 4.95 (*1-56621-702-4*) TripBuilder.

TripBuilder: Washington, D. C.: Landmarks. TripBuilder, Inc. Staff. 25p. 1994. 4.95 (*1-56621-701-6*) TripBuilder.

TripBuilder - England: Best Museums. TripBuilder, Inc. Staff. 1993. 5.95 (*1-56621-009-7*) TripBuilder.

TripBuilder - England: Cathedrals & Abbeys. TripBuilder, Inc. Staff. 1993. 5.95 (*1-56621-007-0*) TripBuilder.

TripBuilder - England: Charming English Villages. TripBuilder, Inc. Staff. 1993. 5.95 (*1-56621-002-X*) TripBuilder.

TripBuilder - England: Country Gardens. TripBuilder, Inc. Staff. 1993. 5.95 (*1-56621-004-6*) TripBuilder.

TripBuilder - England: Easy Day Trips from London. TripBuilder, Inc. Staff. 1993. 5.95 (*1-56621-008-9*) TripBuilder.

TripBuilder - England: Historic Castles. TripBuilder, Inc. Staff. 1993. 5.95 (*1-56621-003-8*) TripBuilder.

TripBuilder - England: Royalty Watching. TripBuilder, Inc. Staff. 1993. 5.95 (*1-56621-013-5*) TripBuilder.

TripBuilder - England: Stately Homes. TripBuilder, Inc. Staff. 1993. 5.95 (*1-56621-005-4*) TripBuilder.

TripBuilder - France: A Shopper's Guide. TripBuilder, Inc. Staff. 1993. 5.95 (*1-56621-102-6*) TripBuilder.

TripBuilder - France: Best Museums. TripBuilder, Inc. Staff. 1993. 5.95 (*1-56621-105-0*) TripBuilder.

TripBuilder - France: Cathedrals & Abbeys. TripBuilder, Inc. Staff. 1993. 5.95 (*1-56621-107-7*) TripBuilder.

TripBuilder - France: Charming Villages. TripBuilder, Inc. Staff. 1993. 5.95 (*1-56621-100-X*) TripBuilder.

TripBuilder - France: Country Markets. TripBuilder, Inc. Staff. 1993. 5.95 (*1-56621-110-7*) TripBuilder.

TripBuilder - France: Easy Day Trips from Paris. TripBuilder, Inc. Staff. 1993. 5.95 (*1-56621-103-4*) TripBuilder.

TripBuilder - France: Historic Chateaux. TripBuilder, Inc. Staff. 1993. 5.95 (*1-56621-101-8*) TripBuilder.

TripBuilder - France: Wine Routes. TripBuilder, Inc. Staff. 1993. 5.95 (*1-56621-106-9*) TripBuilder.

Tripbuilder Portfolio. Tripbuilder, Inc. Staff. 1994. pap. 6.95 (*1-56621-000-3*) TripBuilder.

Triphenyl Phosphate. (Environmental Health Criteria Ser.: No. 111). 80p. (ENG, FRE & SPA.). 1991. pap. text ed. 19.00 (*92-4-157111-X*, 1160111) World Health.

Triphiodorus - Lexicon in Triphiodorum. Triphiodorus. Ed. by Malcolm Campbell. (Alpha-Omega, Reihe A Ser.: Bd. LXXIII). vi, 216p. (GER.). 1985. write for info. (*3-487-07713-2*) G Olms Pubs.

***Triplanetary: A Tale of Cosmic Adventure.** E. E. Smith. LC 96-32947. (History of Civilization Ser.). 1997. pap. 15.00 (*1-882968-09-3*) Old Earth Bks.

Triple. Ken Follett. 352p. 1980. pap. 4.50 (*0-451-13988-7*, Sig); pap. 5.99 (*0-451-16354-0*) NAL-Dutton.

Triple Bond: Audience, Actors & Renaissance Playwrights. Ed. by Joseph G. Price. LC 74-15140. 256p. 1975. 40.00 (*0-271-01177-7*) Pa St U Pr.

Triple Collision of Modernization. Harlan Cleveland. 17p. 1979. pap. 1.50 (*0-89940-000-0*) LBJ Sch Pub Aff.

Triple-Controlled Timed Writings. 2nd ed. Palmer. (TA - Typing/Keyboarding Ser.). 1983. text ed. 18.95 (*0-538-20050-2*) S-W Pub.

Triple-Controlled Timed Writings. 3rd ed. Agnew. (TA - Typing/Keyboarding Ser.). 1993. text ed. 17.95 (*0-538-61174-X*) S-W Pub.

Triple Coronary Bypass: A Cardiologist Tells about His & How to Prevent Yours. Clifford G. Gaddy. LC 94-17535. 1994. 14.99 (*0-86554-447-6*, MUP-P109) Mercer Univ Pr.

Triple Cross. J. R. Roberts, Jr. (Gunsmith Ser.: No. 176). 192p. 1996. mass mkt. 4.99 (*0-515-11926-1*) Jove Pubns.

Triple Cross. Louis Toscano. 1990. 19.95 (*1-55972-028-X*, Birch Ln Pr) Carol Pub Group.

Triple Cross Fire: J. Edgar Hoover & the Kansas City Union Station Massacre. L. R. Kirchner. LC 95-75439. (Illus.). 220p. (Orig.). 1995. pap. 14.95 (*0-9645134-0-4*) Janlar Bks.

Triple Crown. Jon L. Breen. 192p. 1986. 13.95 (*0-8027-5627-1*) Walker & Co.

Triple Crown. Paul E. Patterson. LC 95-44925. 224p. (Orig.). 1996. pap. 14.95 (*0-86534-240-7*) Sunstone Pr.

Triple Crown: Chicano, Puerto Rican & Cuban American Poetry. Roberto Duran et al. LC 87-70081. 168p. 1987. pap. 14.00 (*0-916950-71-9*) Biling Rev-Pr.

***Triple Date.** Jon Potter. 64p. 1996. pap. 5.00 (*0-87440-024-4*) Bakers Plays.

Triple Demism of Sun Yat-Sen (San Min Chu I) Sun Yat-Sen. LC 78-38069. reprint ed. 92.50 (*0-404-56929-3*) AMS Pr.

Triple Detente. Piers Anthony. 256p. (Orig.). 1988. pap. 3.95 (*0-8125-3129-9*) Tor Bks.

Triple-Entry Bookkeeping & Income Momentum, Vol. 18. Yuji Ijiri. LC 82-71118. (Studies in Accounting Research). 53p. 1982. 12.00 (*0-86539-041-X*) Am Accounting.

Triple Espera: Novelas Cortas de Hispanoamerica. Kadir. Ed. by Alfonso Sastre et al. 235p. (SPA.). (C). 1972. pap. text ed. 13.50 (*0-15-564750-4*) HB Coll Pubs.

Triple Espera: Novelas Cortas de Hispanoamerica. Ed. by Djelal Kadir. 235p. (SPA.). (C). 1976. pap. text ed. 20.00 (*0-15-592353-6*) HB Coll Pubs.

Triple Exposure. Jackie Calhoun. 224p. 1994. pap. 10.95 (*1-56280-067-1*) Naiad Pr.

Triple Exposure. Donna Hilbert et al. Ed. by Kathy Roah. 97p. (Orig.). 1989. pap. 7.95 (*0-9622011-0-3*) Medina CA.

***Triple Feature.** Bagshawe. LC 96-44059. 1997. 23.00 (*0-684-83069-8*) S&S Trade.

Triple Fool: A Critical Evaluation of Constantijn Huygens' Translations of John Donne. Koos Daley. (Bibliotheca Humanistica & Reformatorica Ser.: No. XLVI). 238p. 1990. lib. bdg. 57.50 (*90-6004-405-3*, Pub. by B De Graaf NE) Coronet Bks.

Triple Fugue. Osbert Sitwell. LC 74-134980. (Short Story Index Reprint Ser.). 1977. 20.95 (*0-8369-3710-4*) Ayer.

Triple Fun on the Farm, 3 bks. (Triple Fun Ser.). (Illus.). (J). (ps). 1991. Set. 9.95 (*0-8120-6250-7*) Barron.

Triple Fun on the Train, 3 bks. (Triple Fun Ser.). (Illus.). (J). (ps). 1991. Set. 9.95 (*0-8120-6255-8*) Barron.

Triple Goddess: An Exploration of the Archetypal Feminine. Adam McLean. LC 89-34802. (Hermetic Research Ser.: No. 1). (Illus.). 123p. 1989. pap. 14.95 (*0-933999-78-X*) Phanes Pr.

***Triple-Helical Nucleic Acids.** V. N. Soyfer & V. N. Potaman. (Illus.). 360p. 1995. 79.00 (*3-540-94495-8*) Spr-Verlag.

Triple Helical Nucleic Acids. Valery N. Soyfer & Vladimir N. Potaman. LC 95-12214. (Illus.). 368p. 1995. 86.95 (*0-387-94495-8*) Spr-Verlag.

Triple Hoax. (Nancy Drew Mystery Stories Ser.: No. 57). 192p. (J). 1989. pap. 3.99 (*0-671-69153-8*, Minstrel Bks) PB.

Triple Hoax. Carolyn Keene. (Nancy Drew Boxed Gift Set Ser.: No. 57). (J). (gr. 2-7). 1984. 8.85 (*0-685-09396-4*) S&S Trade.

Triple Jeopardy. large type ed. Richard Speight. 1990. 25.99 (*0-7089-2248-1*) Ulverscroft.

Triple Jeopardy: How Determined Lawyers Fought to Save One Man's Life. Roger Parloff. LC 95-53721. 1996. write for info. (*0-614-95867-9*) Little.

Triple Jeopardy: How Determined Lawyers Fought to Save One Man's Life. Roger Parloff. 464p. 1996. 24.95 (*0-316-69261-1*) Little.

Triple Jump Encyclopedia. Ernie Bullard & Larry Knuth. LC 77-4265. (C). 1977. pap. 9.95 (*0-87095-057-6*, Athletic) Gldn West Bks.

Triple Myth. Stella Alexander. 1987. text ed. 52.50 (*0-88033-122-4*, EE1224) Col U Pr.

Triple Nickles: America's First All-Black Paratroop Unit. Bradley Biggs. LC 85-28732. (Illus.). x, 92p. (C). 1986. pap. 17.50 (*0-208-02402-6*, Archon Bks) Shoe String.

Triple Play. William Maidment. 160p. (Orig.). 1993. pap. 4.95 (*0-9619930-9-X*) Moonfall Pr VA.

***Triple Play: A Jake Hines Mystery.** Elizabeth Gunn. LC 97-8511. 240p. 1997. 20.95 (*0-8027-3307-7*) Walker & Co.

Triple Play Plus! Hebrew. (Living Language Ser.). (HEB.). 1995. 48.00 (*0-517-70350-5*) Crown Pub Group.

Triple Play Plus! Italia. Syracuse Language System Staff. (ITA.). 1996. 48.00 (*0-517-70482-X*) Random.

Triple Play Plus! Japanese. Syracuse Language System Staff. (JPN.). 1996. 48.00 (*0-517-70483-8*) Random.

Triple Play Plus!/2.0: English. 1995. 48.00 (*0-517-70173-1*, Harmony) Crown Pub Group.

Triple Play Plus!/2.0: French. 1995. 48.00 (*0-517-70143-X*, Harmony) Crown Pub Group.

Triple Play Plus!/2.0: German. 1995. 48.00 (*0-517-70144-8*, Harmony) Crown Pub Group.

Triple Play Plus!/2.0: Spanish. 1995. 48.00 (*0-517-70142-1*, Harmony) Crown Pub Group.

Triple Plays. Foster. 1994. pap. text ed. write for info. (*0-07-021666-5*) McGraw.

***Triple Point of Water Cell.** 1992. 10.00 (*0-614-18755-9*, RISP-2) Natl Conf Stds Labs.

***Triple S Murders.** Nelda Worth. LC 96-90424. (Orig.). 1997. pap. 8.95 (*0-533-12041-1*) Vantage.

Triple Snaps: The Latest Word Off the Street on the Hot Game of Snapping...an All-New Book... James Percelay et al. 1996. pap. 9.95 (*0-688-14591-4*, Quill) Morrow.

Triple Soul: Browning's Theory of Knowledge. Norton B. Crowell. 235p. 1963. text ed. 29.50 (*0-8290-0228-6*) Irvington.

Triple Squeezes. Hugh Kelsey. 120p. 1991. 24.95 (*0-575-04718-6*, Pub. by V Gollancz UK) Trafalgar.

Triple State ODMR Spectroscopy: Techniques & Applications to Biophysical Systems. Ed. by Richard H. Clarke. LC 81-10486. (Illus.). 576p. reprint ed. pap. 164.20 (*0-8357-7518-6*, 2036013) Bks Demand.

***Triple Trato.** Barbara Boswell. (SPA.). 1997. mass mkt. 3.50 (*0-373-35187-9*, 1-35187-3) Harlequin Bks.

Triple Treat. Barbara Boswell. (Desire Ser.). 1993. mass mkt. 2.99 (*0-373-05787-3*, 5-05787-2) Silhouette.

Triple Trouble. Michael J. Pellowski. 112p. (Orig.). (J). (gr. 3-5). 1995. pap. 2.99 (*0-87406-724-3*) Willowisp Pr.

Triple Trouble in Hollywood. Michael J. Pellowski. (J). (gr. 3-5). 1996. pap. 3.50 (*0-614-15594-0*) Willowisp Pr.

Triple Way. George T. Peck. LC 77-79824. 321p. (Orig.). 1977. pap. 3.00 (*0-87574-213-0*) Pendle Hill.

***Triple-X International.** Pander Brothers Staff. (Illus.). 134p. 24.95 (*1-56971-218-2*) Dark Horse Pub.

Triple Your Reading Speed: The Acceleread Method. 3rd ed. Wade E. Cutler. 224p. 1993. pap. 12.00 (*0-671-84644-2*, Arco) Macmillan Gen Ref.

Triplecross. Linda Stevens. (Intrigue Ser.). 1993. pap. 2.89 (*0-373-22225-4*, 1-22225-6) Harlequin Bks.

Tripled Sixes - Prop & Guide. Michael Anderson & Melanie Neilson. 32p. 1991. pap. 5.00 (*0-935724-45-1*) Figures.

Tripled Sixes - Prop & Guide. deluxe ed. Michael Anderson & Melanie Neilson. 32p. 1991. pap. 15.00 (*0-935724-76-1*) Figures.

Triplepoint - LSD in Group Therapy: A Life Transformed. Trevor Trueheart. 224p. 1992. pap. 19.95 (*0-9633979-0-7*) Green Fir Pub.

***Triplet Births, Trends & Outcomes, 1971-1994.** Joyce A. Martin et al. LC 96-50049. (Vital & Health Statistics. Series 21, Data on Natality, Marriage, & Divorce). 1997. write for info. (*0-8406-0524-2*) Natl Ctr Health Stats.

Triplet Mania. Susan R. Connolly. LC 95-90369. 86p. (Orig.). 1995. pap. 10.95 (*0-9647132-0-9*) Full Moon Pubng.

Triplet States One. A. Devaquet et al. (Topics in Current Chemistry Ser.: Vol. 54). (Illus.). iv, 164p. 1975. 55.95 (*0-387-07107-5*) Spr-Verlag.

***Triplet Trouble & the Bicycle Race.** Debbie Dadey & Marcia T. Jones. (Triplet Trouble Ser.). (Illus.). (J). (gr. 1-4). 1997. pap. 3.50 (*0-614-29027-9*, Little Apple) Scholastic Inc.

***Triplet Trouble & the Class Trip.** Debbie Dadey. 1997. pap. 3.50 (*0-590-90730-1*) Scholastic Inc.

Triplet Trouble & the Cookie Contest. Debbie Dadey. (J). (gr. 4-7). 1996. pap. text ed. 2.99 (*0-590-90728-X*) Scholastic Inc.

Triplet Trouble & the Field Day Disaster. (Triplet Trouble Ser.). (J). (gr. 1-4). 1996. pap. 2.99 (*0-614-15776-5*, Little Apple) Scholastic Inc.

Triplet Trouble & the Pizza Party. Debbie Dadey & Marcia T. Jones. (J). (gr. 1-3). 1996. pap. 2.99 (*0-590-90729-8*) Scholastic Inc.

Triplet Trouble & the Red Heart Race. Debbie Dadey. (J). 1996. pap. text ed. 2.99 (*0-590-58106-6*) Scholastic Inc.

Triplet Trouble & the Runaway Reindeer. Debbie Dadey. (J). 1995. pap. 2.99 (*0-590-25473-1*) Scholastic Inc.

Triplet Trouble & the Talent Show Mess. Debbie Dadey. 64p. (J). 1995. pap. 3.50 (*0-590-25472-3*) Scholastic Inc.

Tripletrap. William H. Hallahan. 384p. 1990. mass mkt. 4.95 (*0-380-70846-9*) Avon.

Triplets. Felix Pirani. 1999. pap. 3.95 (*0-14-054267-1*) NAL-Dutton.

Triplet's Big Switch. Les Carroll. (Illus.). 154p. 1995. 13.95 (*0-9623065-8-4*) Palmetto Bookworks.

Triplet's Big Switch. Les Carroll. (Illus.). 154p. 1995. pap. 8.95 (*0-9623065-9-2*) Palmetto Bookworks.

Tripll Highlights: A Selection of Presentations, 1991-1993, from the Conference on Teaching Research in Private Law Libraries. Judy Floyd Evans. 89p. 1993. pap. 8.95 (*0-926578-06-5*) LEXIS-NEXIS.

Triploid Oysters: Hatchery Manual for Producing Triploid Oysters. Standish K. Allen, Jr. et al. 32p. 1989. pap. 8.00 (*0-295-77031-7*); vhs 250.00 (*0-295-77034-1*) U of Wash Pr.

Tripmaster Monkey: His Fake Book. Maxine H. Kingston. 1989. 19.95 (*0-394-56831-1*) Knopf.

Tripmaster Monkey: His Fake Book. Maxine H. Kingston. LC 89-40550. (Vintage International Ser.). 352p. 1990. pap. 13.00 (*0-679-72789-2*, Vin) Random.

Tripods Trilogy, Set. 2nd ed. John Christopher. 224p. (YA). (gr. 7 up). 1988. boxed 11.95 (*0-02-042571-6*) Macmillan.

Tripoint. C. J. Cherryh. 384p. (Orig.). 1995. mass mkt. 5.99 (*0-446-60202-7*, Aspect) Warner Bks.

Tripolarism: Regional & Global Economic Cooperation. Tommaso Padoa-Schioppa. (Orig.). 1993. pap. write for info. (*1-56708-089-8*) Grp of Thirty.

Tripoli: A Modern Arab City. John Gulick. LC 67-14340. (Harvard Middle Eastern Studies: No. 12). (Illus.). 272p. reprint ed. pap. 77.60 (*0-7837-4468-4*, 2044176) Bks Demand.

Tripoli: Portrait of a City. Philip Ward. (Libya Past & Present Ser.: Vol. 1). (Illus.). 1965. pap. 12.50 (*0-902675-06-0*) Oleander Pr.

Tripoli Business Issue: (Short TBI), No. 1. Ed. by Jerry Irvine. (Illus.). 32p. (C). 1989. pap. text ed. 15.00 (*0-685-57426-1*) CA Rocketry.

Tripoli Politics Issue: (Short TPI No.1), No. 1. Ed. by Jerry Irvine. (Illus.). 16p. (C). 1990. pap. text ed. 4.95 (*0-685-57425-3*) CA Rocketry.

Tripoli Politics Issue: (Short TPI No.2), No. 2. Ed. by Jerry Irvine. (Illus.). 8p. (C). 1992. pap. text ed. 4.95 (*0-685-57424-5*) CA Rocketry.

Tripoli Politics Issue: (Short TPI No.3), No. 3. Ed. by Jerry Irvine. (Illus.). 16p. (C). 1992. pap. text ed. 4.95 (*0-685-57423-7*) CA Rocketry.

Tripoli the Mysterious. Mabel L. Todd. (C). 1988. 135.00 (*1-85077-202-9*, Pub. by Darf Pubs Ltd UK) St Mut.

Tripolitania. David J. Mattingly. LC 94-46968. (C). 1995. 54.50 (*0-472-10658-9*) U of Mich Pr.

Tripolitania in Transition: Late Roman to Islamic Settlements with a Catalogue of Sites. Isabella Sjostrom. (Worldwide Archaeology Ser.). 350p. 1993. 59.95 (*1-85628-707-6*, Pub. by Avebury Pub UK) Ashgate Pub Co.

Triporteur. Rene Fallet. (FRE.). 1982. pap. 11.95 (*0-7859-2298-9*, 2070362868) Fr & Eur.

Trippensee Transparent Simplified Celestial Globe. T. R. Stoeckley. 17p. 1968. pap. text ed. 6.65 (*0-943956-03-X*) Trippensee Pub.

Tripping Daisy. Ed. by Carol Cuellar. 104p. (Orig.). (YA). 1996. pap. text ed. 22.95 (*1-57623-282-4*, PG9548) Warner Brothers.

Tripping in America. John Bennett. 160p. 1984. pap. 5.95 (*0-912824-33-6*) Vagabond Pr.

Tripping the Clock: A Practical Guide to Anti-Aging & Rejuvenation. Hans J. Kugler. 175p. 1993. write for info. (*1-883201-02-0*) Hlth Quest.

Trippy. Virginia S. Smyth. Ed. by Erika D. Walker. (Illus.). (Orig.). (J). (gr. 1-3). 1989. pap. 5.00 (*0-9624060-0-7*) Mount Falcon.

Trips: How Hallucinogens Work in Your Brain. Cheryl Pellerin. (Illus.). 192p. (Orig.). 1997. pap. 18.95 (*1-888363-34-7*) Seven Stories.

Trips & Tours Manual. Kenneth D. Ostrand. 147p. 29.95 (*0-914951-04-1*) LERN.

Trips & Treats: Kid-Tested Fun in & Near Baltimore. Kathleen M. Shull. LC 92-12631. (Illus.). 216p. 1992. pap. 9.95 (*0-939009-63-3*) EPM Pubns.

Trips & Treks *see* **New Jersey Day Trips: A Guide to Outings in New Jersey, New York, Pennsylvania & Delaware**

Trip's Cinch. Phyllis Nagy. 1995. 3.00 (*0-87129-512-1*, T39) Dramatic Pub.

Trips of the Psyche. Frederic Will. LC 93-7833. 88p. 1993. text ed. 49.95 (*0-7734-3040-7*) E Mellen.

Trips on Twos. Leslie Bergstrom & Kim Bergstrom. (Illus.). 72p. 1987. pap. 4.95 (*0-9612668-2-1*) Talk Town.

Trips on Wheels. Leslie Bergstrom. (Illus.). 128p. 1985. pap. 8.50 (*0-9612668-1-3*) Talk Town.

Triptych. rev. ed. Claude Simon. Tr. by Helen R. Lane from FRE. 180p. 1986. pap. 11.95 (*0-7145-3787-X*) Riverrun NY.

Triptychos by Thrice by Thrice. Roger K. Leonard. 76p. 1993. write for info. (*0-9637851-0-9*) R K Leonard.

Triptychs: Buffalo's Lower West Side Revisited. Photos by Milton Rogovin. 160p. 1994. 40.00 (*0-393-03588-3*) Norton.

Tripura: Historical Documents. Maharaj-Kumar Sahadev Bikram-Kisor & Jagadis Gan-Chaudhuri. (C). 1994. 24.00 (*0-8364-2894-3*, Pub. by Firma KLM II) S Asia.

Tripwire. Jay Brandon. Ed. by Dana Isaacson. 320p. (Orig.). 1992. mass mkt. 4.99 (*0-671-70888-0*) PB.

Tripwire: Korea & U. S. Foreign Policy in a Changed World. Doug Bandow. 260p. 1996. 19.95 (*1-882577-29-9*); pap. text ed. 9.95 (*1-882577-30-2*) Cato Inst.

Trireme Project: Operational Experience 1987-90, Lessons Learnt. Timothy M. Shaw. (Oxbow Monographs in Archaeology: No. 31). (Illus.). 136p. 1993. pap. 35.00 (*0-946897-58-1*, Pub. by Oxbow Bks UK) David Brown.

Trireme Trials 1988. J. F. Coates et al. (Oxbow Monographs in Archaeology: No. 2). (Illus.). 108p. 1990. pap. 22.00 (*0-946897-21-2*, Pub. by Oxbow Bks UK) David Brown.

Tris (2,3-dibromopropyl) Phosphate & Bis (2,3-dibromopropyl) Phosphate. (Environmental Health Criteria Ser.: Vol. 173). 129p. (C). 1995. pap. 28.00 (*92-4-157173-X*, 1160173) World Health.

Trisagion. Hellenic College-Holy Cross Faculty. 16p. 1986. pap. 0.50 (*0-917651-25-1*) Holy Cross Orthodox.

Trisectors. Underwood Dudley. LC 94-75575. 176p. 1994. pap. 18.95 (*0-88385-514-3*, TRI) Math Assn.

Trisha & Stanley, Hsiao-Me Hsiao-De. Stanley Y. Chang. 232p. 1996. 16.00 (*0-8059-3934-2*) Dorrance.

Trishanku. Uma Parameswaran. 1988. 9.50 (*0-920661-04-1*) S Asia.

***Tris's Book.** Tamora Pierce. LC 97-8521. (Circle of Magic Ser.). (J). 1998. write for info. (*0-590-55357-7*) Scholastic Inc.

Trissel's Stability of Compounded Formulations. Lawrence A. Trissel. LC 95-80392. 296p. 1995. 58.50 (*0-917330-74-9*) Am Pharm Assn.

***Trissino's "Sophonisba" & Aretino's "Horatia" Two Italian Renaissance Tragedies.** Giovanni G. Trissino et al. Ed. by Michael Lettieri & Michael Ukas. Tr. by Michael Ukas & Gillian Sharman from ITA. LC 97-5113. 272p. 1997. text ed. 109.95 (*0-7734-8659-3*) E Mellen.

Tristan. Andre Mary. (FRE.). 1973. pap. 11.95 (*0-7859-4014-6*) Fr & Eur.

Tristan. Suzanne Schuurman. 248p. 1987. 19.95 (*0-85398-248-1*); pap. 9.50 (*0-85398-249-X*) G Ronald Pub.

Tristan. Gottfried Von Strassburg. Tr. by A. T. Hatto. (Classics Ser.). 384p. 1960. pap. 11.95 (*0-14-044098-4*, Penguin Classics) Viking Penguin.

Tristan & Iseult. Rosemary Sutcliff. 150p. (J). (gr. 5 up). 1991. pap. 3.95 (*0-374-47982-8*, Sunburst Bks) FS&G.

Tristan & Iseult. Rosemary Sutcliff. (J). 1994. 18.00 (*0-8446-6773-0*) Peter Smith.

Tristan & Iseult, 2 vols., Set. Tr. by Jessie L. Weston from GER. LC 71-141784. reprint ed. 45.00 (*0-404-10038-4*) AMS Pr.

Tristan & Isolde. Gottfried Von Strassburg. Ed. by Francis G. Gentry. (German Library: Vol. 3). 320p. (C). 1988. 29.50 (*0-8264-0314-X*); pap. text ed. 16.95 (*0-8264-0315-8*) Continuum.

Tristan & Isolde. Richard Wagner. Ed. by Nicholas John. Tr. by Andrew Porter from GER. (English National Opera Guide Series: Bilingual Libretto, Articles: No. 6). (Illus.). 1981. pap. 9.95 (*0-7145-3849-3*) Riverrun NY.

Tristan & Isolde: A Casebook. Ed. by Joan T. Grimbert. LC 94-25538. (Arthurian Characters & Themes Ser.: Vol. 2). (Illus.). 638p. 1995. text ed. 70.00 (*0-8153-0654-7*, H1514) Garland.

Tristan & Isolde: Complete Orchestral Score. Richard Wagner. Ed. by Felix Mottl. 672p. 1973. reprint ed. pap. 21.95 (*0-486-22915-7*) Dover.

Tristan & the Round Table: A Translation of La Tabola Ritonda. Tr. by Anne Shaver. LC 82-14140. (Medieval & Renaissance Texts & Studies: Vol. 28). (Illus.). 380p. 1983. 24.00 (*0-86698-053-9*, MR28) MRTS.

Tristan de Luna, Conquistador of the Old South: A Study of Spanish Imperial Strategy. Herbert I. Priestley. LC 80-21168. (Perspectives in American History Ser.: No. 49). (Illus.). 215p. 1980. reprint ed. lib. bdg. 37.50 (*0-87991-375-4*) Porcupine Pr.

Tristan in the Underworld: A Study of Gottfried von Strassburg's Tristan Together with the Tristan of Thomas. Neil Thomas. LC 91-19490. (Studies in Medieval Literature: Vol. 10). 136p. 1991. lib. bdg. 69.95 (*0-7734-9712-9*) E Mellen.

Tristan Legend: A Study in Sources. Sigmund Eisner. LC 69-18373. 207p. reprint ed. 59.00 (*0-8357-9474-1*, 2015293) Bks Demand.

Tristan (Modern French) Tristan et Iseut. Ed. by A. Mary. (Folio Ser.: No. 452). (FRE.). pap. 9.95 (*2-07-036452-6*) Schoenhof.

Tristan Story in German Literature of the Late Middle Ages & Early Renaissance: Tradition & Innovation. William C. McDonald. LC 90-41478. (Studies in German Language & Literature: Vol. 5). 250p. 1990. lib. bdg. 89.95 (*0-88946-075-2*) E Mellen.

Tristan Studies. Renee L. Curtis. (Illus.). 91p. 1985. pap. 19.00 (*0-85991-188-8*) Boydell & Brewer.

Tristan und Isolde: Libretto. Richard Wagner. 64p. (GER.). 1986. pap. 4.95 (*0-7935-1436-3*, 50340430) H Leonard.

Tristan und Isolde in Auswahl. 5th ed. Strassburg Gottfried. Ed. by Friedrich Maurer. (Sammlung Goeschen Ser.: No. 2204). 1977. pap. text ed. 15.25 (*3-11-010853-4*) De Gruyter.

Tristan 1489. fac. ed. Ed. by Cedric E. Pickford. 676p. 1970. Facsimile. 81.00 (*0-85991-157-8*) Boydell & Brewer.

Tristana: Bunuel's Film & Galdos' Novel: A Case Study in the Relation Between Literature & Film. Colin Partridge. LC 94-39161. 244p. 1995. text ed. 89.95 (*0-7734-9089-2*) E Mellen.

Tristania: A Publication of the Tristan-Society Devoted to Tristan-Studies, Vol. 14. Ed. by Albrecht Classen & William C. McDonald. 176p. 1993. text ed. 49.95 (*0-7734-9296-8*) E Mellen.

***Tristania 1996, Vol. XVII.** Ed. by Albrecht Classen & William C. McDonald. 164p. 1996. text ed. 49.95 (*0-7734-8692-5*) E Mellen.

Tristanissimo: The Authorized Biography of Heroic Tenor Lauritz Melchior. Shirlee Emmons. 462p. 1990. text ed. 24.95 (*0-02-873060-7*) Schirmer Bks.

***Tristan's Bedtime Story.** Caroline Formby. LC 96-50251. (J). 1996. pap. 6.99 (*0-85953-946-6*) Childs Play.

Tristan's Temper Tantrum. Caroline Formby. (J). 1996. pap. 6.99 (*0-85953-951-2*) Childs Play.

Tristate Terrors: Famous, Historic, Female Ghosts of Ohio, Indiana & Kentucky. Anne Oscard. Ed. by Raymond Rasmer. (Illus.). 137p. 1996. pap. 9.95 (*0-9645166-1-6*) Hermit Pubns.

Triste Historia De Mi Vida Oscura: A Peticion Popular. Armando Couto. LC 78-70332. 1978. pap. 5.95 (*0-89729-196-4*) Ediciones.

Tristealegria. Francisco Santana. LC 90-22411. 104p. 1991. pap. 10.00 (*0-927534-08-8*) Biling Rev-Pr.

Triste's History. Rial H. Vazquez. Tr. by Jo Labanyi from SPA. (Readers International Ser.). 250p. (Orig.). 1990. 18.95 (*0-930523-71-7*); pap. 10.95 (*0-930523-72-5*) Readers Intl.

Tristes Tropiques. Claude Levi-Strauss. LC 97-11778. 1997. 18.50 (*0-679-60246-1*, Modern Lib) Random.

Tristes Tropiques. Claude Levi-Strauss. (Illus.). 432p. 1992. pap. 16.95 (*0-14-016562-2*, Penguin Bks) Viking Penguin.

Tristes Tropiques. rev. ed. Claude Levi-Strauss. (Illus.). (FRE.). 1984. 17.95 (*2-266-02612-7*) Adlers Foreign Bks.

Tristessa. Jack Kerouac. 96p. 1992. pap. 9.95 (*0-14-016811-7*, Penguin Bks) Viking Penguin.

Tristesse de la Cerf-Volant. Francoise Mallet-Joris. (FRE.). 1989. pap. 12.95 (*0-7859-3279-8*, 2277225967) Fr & Eur.

Tristia. Osip Mandelstam. 1988. pap. 9.95 (*0-88268-069-2*) Station Hill Pr.

Tristia: Poems by Osip Mandelstam. Tr. by Bruce McClelland. LC 86-32305. (Illus.). 120p. 1987. 13.95 (*0-88268-041-2*) Station Hill Pr.

Tristia, & Ex Ponto. Ovid. (Loeb Classical Library: No. 151). 556p. 1931. text ed. 18.95 (*0-674-99167-2*) HUP.

Tristia, Ibis, Ex Ponto, Halieutica, Fragmenta. Ovid. Ed. by S. G. Owen. (Oxford Classical Texts Ser.). 365p. 1922. 27.00 (*0-19-814626-4*) OUP.

Tristia of Ovid. Tr. by David R. Slavitt from LAT. (Illus.). 143p. 1986. 14.95 (*0-934958-04-1*) Bellflower.

Tristram & Coote's Probate Practice. 27th rev. ed. Ed. by R. E. Yeldham et al. 1989. boxed 380.00 (*0-406-40340-6*, U.K.) MICHIE.

Tristram Kennedy & the Revival of Irish Legal Training, 1835-1885. Colum Kenny. 256p. 1996. 45.00 (*0-7165-2591-7*, Pub. by Irish Acad Pr IE) Intl Spec Bk.

Tristram Shandy. Max Byrd. Ed. by Claude Rawson. (Unwin Critical Library). 192p. 1985. text ed. 34.95 (*0-04-800033-7*); pap. text ed. 16.95 (*0-685-09722-6*) Routledge Chapman & Hall.

Tristram Shandy. Ed. by Melvyn New. LC 91-35819. (New Casebooks Ser.). 200p. 1992. text ed. 45.00 (*0-312-07566-9*) St Martin.

Tristram Shandy. Laurence Sterne. (Airmont Classics Ser.). (YA). (gr. 11 up). 1967. mass mkt. 1.95 (*0-8049-0152-X*, CL-152) Airmont.

Tristram Shandy. Laurence Sterne. 752p. 1991. 23.50 (*0-679-40560-7*, Everymans Lib) Knopf.

Tristram Shandy. Laurence Sterne. 512p. 1992. pap. 6.95 (*0-460-87130-7*, Everyman's Classic Lib) C E Tuttle.

Tristram Shandy. Laurence Sterne. 1962. mass mkt. 5.95 (*0-452-00945-6*, Mer) NAL-Dutton.

T

Tristram Shandy. Laurence Sterne. Ed. by Howard Anderson. LC 79-277. (Critical Editions Ser.). (C). 1979. pap. text ed. 17.95 (0-393-95034-4) Norton.

Tristram Shandy. Laurence J. Sterne. 32.95 (0-8488-1469-X) Amereon Ltd.

Tristram Shandy. Ruth Whittaker. 128p. 1989. 75.00 (0-335-15264-3, Open Univ Pr); pap. 22.00 (0-335-15263-5, Open Univ Pr) Taylor & Francis.

Tristram Shandy. Laurence Sterne. (BCL1-PR English Literature Ser.). 591p. 1992. reprint ed. lib. bdg. 99.00 (0-7812-7409-5) Rprt Serv.

Tristram Shandy. Laurence J. Sterne. 540p. 1990. reprint ed. lib. bdg. 31.95 (0-89966-720-1) Buccaneer Bks.

Tristram Shandy: The Games of Pleasure. Richard A. Lanham. LC 70-174461. 184p. reprint ed. pap. 52.50 (0-685-23669-2, 2029048) Bks Demand.

Tristram Shandy, & A Sentimental Journey. Ed. by Laurence J. Sterne. 840p. 1995. 19.50 (0-679-60091-4) Random.

Tristram Shandy Notes. Charles Parish. 1968. pap. 4.50 (0-8220-1311-8) Cliffs.

Triticale. Ed. by R. A. Forsberg. 82p. 1985. 12.00 (0-89118-519-4) Crop Sci Soc Am.

***Triticale: Today & Tomorrow.** Ed. by Henrique Guedes-Pinto. LC 96-27437. (Developments in Plant Breeding Ser.). 912p. (C). 1996. lib. bdg. 371.00 (0-7923-4212-7) Kluwer Ac.

Tritium & Its Compounds. 2nd ed. Eustace A. Evans. LC 75-313264. (Illus.). 838p. reprint ed. pap. 180.00 (0-317-41698-7, 2025716) Bks Demand.

Tritium & Other Radionuclide Labeled Organic Compounds Incorporated in Genetic Material. LC 79-84486. (Report Ser.: No. 63). 147p. 1979. pap. text ed. 35.00 (0-913392-47-2) NCRP Pubns.

Tritium in the Environment. LC 79-63514. (Report Ser.: No. 62). 130p. 1979. pap. text ed. 35.00 (0-913392-46-4) NCRP Pubns.

Tritium Isotope Separation. Vasaru. 320p. 1993. 219.95 (0-8493-4322-4, TK9350) CRC Pr.

Tritium Measurement Techniques. LC 76-16301. (Report Ser.: No. 47). 101p. 1976. pap. text ed. 25.00 (0-913392-29-4) NCRP Pubns.

Triton. Daniel Torres. (Rocco Vargas Adventures Ser.). (Illus.). 50p. (Orig.). 1986. pap. 10.95 (0-87416-025-1) Catalan Communs.

Tritonian Ring. L. Sprague De Camp. LC 76-56969. (Illus.). 1977. reprint ed. 12.50 (0-913896-09-8) Owlswick Pr.

Triton's Price Guide to Comic Cards. Stuart Wells. 152p. 1994. pap. 10.95 (0-87069-727-7) Chilton.

Tritum: Radiation Protection in the Laboratory. P. E. Ballance & A. G. Richards. Ed. by R. N. Thomas. (Handbook Ser.: No. 11). 77p. (C). 1994. pap. 140.00 (0-948237-12-0, Pub. by H&H Sci Cnslts UK) St Mut.

Triumph. Roy Bacon. 1994. 10.98 (0-7858-0005-0) Bk Sales Inc.

Triumph. Ben Bova. 256p. 1994. mass mkt. 4.99 (0-8125-2063-7) Tor Bks.

Triumph. Gene Edwards. LC 94-23227. (The Chronicles of the Door Ser.: No. 4). 208p. 1995. pap. 8.99 (0-8423-6978-3) Tyndale.

Triumph. Arthur Moore. (Orig.). 1979. mass mkt. 2.50 (0-89083-522-5, Zebra Kensgtn) Kensgtn Pub Corp.

Triumph: America Coming Back. Dean Herpick. 200p. 1994. pap. 22.95 (0-9641175-0-9) Herpick.

Triumph: Getting Back to Normal When You Have Cancer. Marion Morra & Eve Potts. 304p. 1990. pap. 9.95 (0-380-75503-3) Avon.

Triumph: Missions Renewal for the Local Church. Howard L. Foltz. 179p. 1994. pap. 8.99 (1-882449-24-X) Messenger Pub.

Triumph: Return of the Legend. David Minton. 1995. 12.98 (0-7858-0309-2) Bk Sales Inc.

Triumph Against Trouble: Finding God's Power in Life's Problems. W. Phillip Keller. LC 95-16952. 144p. 1996. pap. 10.99 (0-8254-2994-3) Kregel.

***Triumph & BSA Triples: The Complete Story of the Trident & Rocket 3.** Mick Duckworth. (Illus.). 192p. 1997. 34.95 (1-86126-018-0, Pub. by Crowood UK) Motorbooks Intl.

Triumph & Catastrophe: The War of 1948, Israeli Independence, & the Refugee Problem. Ed. by Ian S. Lustick. LC 93-50088. (Arab-Israeli Relations Ser.: Vol. 2). (Illus.). 384p. 1994. reprint ed. text ed. 68.00 (0-8153-1582-1) Garland.

Triumph & Erosion in the American Media & Entertainment. Dan Steinbock. LC 94-24600. 352p. 1995. text ed. 75.00 (0-89930-914-3, Quorum Bks) Greenwood.

***Triumph & Glory: Armenian World War II Heroes.** Richard N. Demirjian. Ed. by Satenig Demirjian & Evelyn Garabedian. 480p. 1996. write for info. (0-9622945-1-9) Ararat Heritage.

Triumph & Other Stories. Henry Z. Ucko. LC 93-92736. 93p. (Orig.). 1993. pap. 9.95 (0-9637399-0-5) Sverdlik Pr.

Triumph & Terror: The French Revolution. Steven Otfinoski. LC 92-37131. (World History Library). (Illus.). 128p. (J). (gr. 6-9). 1993. 17.95 (0-8160-2762-5) Facts on File.

Triumph & Tragedy, 6 vols. Winston S. Churchill. 1986. pap. 14.95 (0-395-41060-6) HM.

Triumph & Tragedy see Second World War

Triumph & Tragedy in Formula 1: Story of Professor Sid Watkins. Sid Watkins. (Illus.). 256p. 1996. pap. 24.95 (0-7603-0315-0) Motorbooks Intl.

Triumph at Kitty Hawk: The Wright Brothers & Powered Flight. Thomas C. Parramore. (Illus.). ix, 124p. (Orig.). (YA). (gr. 8-12). 1993. pap. 8.00 (0-86526-259-4) NC Archives.

Triumph at Perth: The America's Cup Story. Bruce Stannard et al. (Illus.). 212p. 1987. 39.95 (0-911378-74-X) Sheridan.

Triumph Bonneville. Richard Bird. (Color Library). (Illus.). 128p. 1994. pap. 15.95 (1-85532-398-2, Pub. by Osprey Pubng Ltd UK) Motorbooks Intl.

Triumph By Name, Triumph By Nature: Triumph by Nature. Bill Piggott. (Illus.). 288p. 1995. 49.95 (1-85443-107-2, Pub. by Autostyle Pubng Ltd UK) Motorbooks Intl.

***Triumph Cars: The Complete Story.** R. Langworth & G. Robson. (Illus.). 352p. 1996. 39.95 (0-947981-28-4, Pub. by Motor Racing UK) Motorbooks Intl.

***Triumph Cars in America.** Mike Cook. (Illus.). 192p. 1997. pap. 24.95 (0-7603-0165-4) Motorbooks Intl.

Triumph GT6 & Vitesse 2 Litre Workshop Manual: 1967-1973. 45.00 (0-8376-0571-7) Bentley.

Triumph GT6 Mk III Driver's Handbook (1973) British Leyland Motors. 66p. (Orig.). 16.00 (0-8376-0536-9) Bentley.

Triumph GT6 Mk III Parts Catalogue: 1971-1973. British Leyland Motors. 140p. (Orig.). 40.00 (0-8376-0523-7) Bentley.

***Triumph Herald & Vitesse: The Complete Story.** Graham Robson. (Illus.). 200p. 1997. 35.95 (1-86126-050-4, Pub. by Crowood UK) Motorbooks Intl.

Triumph in Adversity: Studies in Hungarian Civilization in Honor of Professor Ferenc Somogyi. Ed. by Steven B. Vardy & Agnes H. Vardy. (East European Monographs: No. 253). 616p. 1989. text ed. 91.50 (0-88033-150-X) East Eur Monographs.

Triumph in Death: The Story of the Malagasy Martyrs. F. Graeme Smith. 1987. pap. 6.99 (0-85234-242-X, Pub. by Evangelical Pr) Presby & Reformed.

Triumph in Defeat: Infallibility, Vatican I, & the French Minority Bishops. Margaret O'Gara. LC 87-17889. 296p. 1988. 48.95 (0-8132-0641-3) Cath U Pr.

Triumph in the West. Arthur Bryant. LC 73-22634. (Illus.). 438p. (C). 1974. reprint ed. text ed. 72.50 (0-8371-7344-2, BRTR, Greenwood Pr) Greenwood.

Triumph in the Wilderness. Michael A. Carmody. LC 95-68742. 52p. (Orig.). 1995. pap. 5.00 (0-910487-33-2) Royalty Pub.

Triumph in Tropica. Alex Raymond. Ed. by Dave Schreiner & Peter Poplaski. LC 90-549. (Flash Gordon Ser.: Vol. 6). (Illus.). 96p. 1993. 34.95 (0-87816-198-8); pap. 21.95 (0-87816-199-6) Kitchen Sink.

***Triumph Motorcycles from 1950-1990.** Steve Wilson. (Illus.). 160p. 1997. 27.95 (1-85260-571-5) Haynes Pubns.

Triumph Motorcycles in America. A. Lindsay Brooke & David Gaylin. LC 93-13166. (Illus.). 224p. 1993. pap. 24.95 (0-87938-746-7) Motorbooks Intl.

Triumph of Achilles. Louise Gluck. 64p. 1985. pap. 7.50 (0-88001-082-7) Ecco Pr.

***Triumph of Advertising in American Culture.** James B. Twitchell. 1997. pap. 16.95 (0-231-10325-5) Col U Pr.

Triumph of American Painting: A History of Abstract Expressionism. Irving Sandler. (Icon Editions Ser.). (Illus.). 302p. 1976. pap. text ed. 25.00 (0-06-430075-7, IN-75, Icon Edns) HarpC.

Triumph of Art for the Public, 1785-1848, Vol. I. Elizabeth G. Holt. LC 83-60461. (Illus.). 560p. 1983. pap. text ed. 24.95 (0-691-00349-1) Princeton U Pr.

***Triumph of Augustan Poetics: English Literary Culture from Butler to Johnson.** Blanford Parker. (Studies in Eighteenth-Century English Literature & Thought: Vol. 36). 264p. (C). 1997. text ed. 59.95 (0-521-59088-4) Cambridge U Pr.

Triumph of Ballet in Moliere's Theatre. Robert McBride. LC 92-19477. 380p. 1992. text ed. 99.95 (0-7734-9567-3) E Mellen.

Triumph of Barabbas. Giovanni Giglio. Tr. by E. Mosbacher. LC 74-180401. reprint ed. 42.50 (0-404-56125-X) AMS Pr.

Triumph of Color & Light: Ohio Impressionists & Post-Impressionists. Nannette V. Maciejunes & James M. Keny. Ed. by Norma J. Roberts. (Orig.). 1994. pap. 19.95 (0-918881-32-3) Columbus Mus Art.

Triumph of Conservatism: A Reinterpretation of American History, 1900-1916. Gabriel Kolko. LC 63-16588. 1977. pap. 16.95 (0-02-916650-0, Free Press) Free Pr.

Triumph of Corporate Capitalism in France, 1867-1914. Charles E. Freedeman. (Illus.). 152p. (C). 1993. 59.00 (1-878822-22-5) Boydell & Brewer.

Triumph of Death (1985-1990) (Computer Poetry Ser.). 1,000.00 (0-9604252-3-3) Parpaglion.

Triumph of Democracy in Spain. Paul Preston. 263p. 1986. 35.00 (0-416-36350-4, 9880) Routledge Chapman & Hall.

Triumph of Democracy in Spain. Paul Preston. 288p. 1987. pap. text ed. 14.95 (0-416-90010-0) Routledge Chapman & Hall.

***Triumph of Democracy in Spain.** Paul Preston. 288p. (C). 1987. pap. 17.95 (0-415-04314-X) Routledge.

Triumph of Discovery: Women Scientists Who Won the Nobel Prize. Joan Dash. 160p. (YA). (gr. 9 up). 1990. pap. 8.95 (0-671-69333-6, Julian Messner) Silver Burdett Pr.

Triumph of Elohim: From Yahwisms to Judaisms. Ed. by Diana V. Edelman. LC 95-49398. 262p. 1996. pap. 25.00 (0-8028-4161-9) Eerdmans.

Triumph of Evil. Lawrence Block. 126p. 1994. 3.95 (0-7867-0181-1) Carroll & Graf.

Triumph of Evolution: The Heredity-Environment Controversy, 1900-1941. Hamilton Cravens. LC 88-45394. 376p. 1988. pap. 15.95 (0-8018-3742-1) Johns Hopkins.

Triumph of Faith in a Believer's Life. Charles H. Spurgeon. (Believer's Life Ser.). 156p. (Orig.). 1994. pap. 9.99 (1-883002-08-7) Emerald WA.

Triumph of Form. Wallace C. Brown. LC 73-13452. 212p. 1974. reprint ed. text ed. 35.00 (0-8371-7135-0, BRTF, Greenwood Pr) Greenwood.

Triumph of Freedom, Seventeen Seventy-Five to Seventeen Eighty-Three. John C. Miller. LC 78-23672. (Illus.). 718p. 1979. reprint ed. text ed. 75.00 (0-313-20779-8, MITF, Greenwood Pr) Greenwood.

Triumph of Freedom, 1775-1783. John C. Miller. (History - United States Ser.). 718p. 1993. reprint ed. lib. bdg. 109.00 (0-7812-4833-7) Rprt Serv.

Triumph of God: The Essence of Paul's Thought. J. Christiaan Beker. Tr. by Loren T. Stuckenbruck from GER. LC 90-35463. 144p. 1990. pap. 12.00 (0-8006-2438-6, 1-2438) Augsburg Fortress.

Triumph of His Grace: Preparing Ourselves for the Rapture. Paul M. Sadler. (Illus.). 230p. (C). 1995. text ed. 10.00 (0-9644541-1-4) Berean Bibl Soc.

Triumph of Hope: The 1988 Pro-Life Year in Review & a Look to the Future. Raymond J. Adamek et al. (Pro-Life Year in Review Ser.). 232p. (Orig.). (C). 1989. pap. 4.95 (0-9620037-1-9) NRLC Washington.

***Triumph of Ideals: Love Affair with Every Day.** George Celia. (Illus.). 120p. 1998. 17.00 (0-614-30094-0) G Celia.

Triumph of Individual Style: A Guide to Dressing Your Body, Your Beauty, Your Self. Carla M. Mathis & Helen V. Connor. (Illus.). 192p. (Orig.). 1992. pap. 28.95 (0-9632223-0-9) Timeless Edits.

Triumph of Infidelity. Timothy Dwight. (Notable American Authors Ser.). 1992. reprint ed. lib. bdg. 75.00 (0-7812-2738-0) Rprt Serv.

Triumph of Japan. Edwin P. Hoyt. (War in the Pacific Ser.: No. 1). 1990. mass mkt. 4.50 (0-380-75792-3) Avon.

Triumph of Japanese Style: 16th-Century Art in Japan. Michael R. Cunningham. (Illus.). 168p. 1991. text ed. 50.00 (0-940717-12-3); pap. text ed. 30.00 (0-940717-13-1) Cleveland Mus Art.

***Triumph of Jess Connor.** Bill Turner. 155p. (Orig.). 1997. mass mkt. 4.99 (1-55197-927-6, Pub. by Comnwlth Pub CN) Partners Pubs Grp.

Triumph of Jim Crow: Tennessee Race Relations in the 1880's. Joseph H. Cartwright. LC 76-2009. 300p. reprint ed. pap. 85.50 (0-8357-8602-1, 2034998) Bks Demand.

Triumph of Job. L. Pleming. 1978. 7.95 (0-933062-00-1) R H Sommer.

***Triumph of Justice: Closing the Book on the Simpson Saga.** Daniel Petrocelli. 1998. write for info. (0-609-60170-9) Crown Pub Group.

Triumph of Life. Wilhelm Bolsche. Tr. by May W. Simons from GER. (Science for the Workers Ser.). (Illus.). 157p. 1984. 17.95 (0-88286-085-2) C H Kerr.

Triumph of Literature - The Fate of Literacy: English in the Secondary School Curriculum. John Willinsky. (Language & Literacy Ser.). 240p. (C). 1991. text ed. 48.00 (0-8077-3109-9); pap. text ed. 21.95 (0-8077-3108-0) Tchrs Coll.

***Triumph of Literature/the Fate of Literacy: English in the Secondary School Curriculum.** John Willinsky. LC 91-4072. (Language & Literacy Ser.). 242p. pap. 69.00 (0-608-05101-2, 2065658) Bks Demand.

Triumph of Love. Mariuaux. Tr. by James Magruder from FRE. 1994. pap. 5.25 (0-8222-1415-6) Dramatists Play.

***Triumph of Love & Other Paintings: A Novel.** Michael Westlake. 1997. 22.95 (0-312-15678-2) St Martin.

***Triumph of McLean.** large type ed. George Goodchild. (Ulverscroft Large Print Ser.). 448p. 1997. 27.50 (0-7089-3754-3) Ulverscroft.

***Triumph of Meanness.** Nicolaus Mills. LC 97-3389. 1997. 25.00 (0-395-82296-3) HM.

Triumph of Modernism. Shapiro. 1995. pap. 14.95 (0-8057-9079-9, Twayne) Scribnrs Ref.

Triumph of Modernism. Shapiro. 1996. 24.95 (0-8057-9078-0, Twayne) Scribnrs Ref.

Triumph of Moralism in New England Piety: A Study of Lyman Beecher, Harriet Beecher Stowe & Henry Ward Beecher. John Goodell. 1981. 55.95 (0-405-14113-0) Ayer.

Triumph of Moro Diplomacy: The Maguindanao Sultanate in the 17th Century. Ruurdje Laarhoven. 287p. (Orig.). (C). 1989. pap. 17.50 (971-10-0390-2, Pub. by New Day Pub PH) Cellar.

Triumph of Narrow Gauge. John Kerr. 226p. (C). 1990. 120.00 (0-86439-102-1, Pub. by Boolarong Pubns AT) St Mut.

Triumph of Odysseus: Homer's Odyssey Books 21 & 22. Joint Association of Classical Teachers Staff. (Illus.). 104p. (C). 1996. pap. text ed. 18.95 (0-521-46587-7) Cambridge U Pr.

***Triumph of Our Lady: Preparing for the Third Millennium.** Richard Carroll. 325p. (Orig.). Date not set. pap. text ed. 9.95 (0-9643572-1-6) St Marg Mary Chur.

Triumph of Patience: Medieval & Renaissance Studies. Ed. by Gerald J. Schiffhorst. LC 77-12732. (Illus.). 160p. reprint ed. pap. 45.60 (0-7837-5077-3, 2044775) Bks Demand.

Triumph of Pierrot: The Commedia Dell'Arte & the Modern Imagination. Martin Green & John Swan. LC 92-34785. 344p. (C). 1993. reprint ed. pap. 18.95 (0-271-00928-4) Pa St U Pr.

Triumph of Politics: The Inside Story of the Reagan Revolution. David A. Stockman. (Illus.). 512p. 1987. mass mkt. 4.95 (0-380-70311-4) Avon.

Triumph of Propaganda: Film & National Socialism, 1933-1945. Hilmar Hoffmann. Tr. by Volker R. Berghahn & John Broadwin from GER. LC 95-36005. 256p. 1995. 42.00 (1-57181-066-8) Berghahn Bks.

Triumph of Realism in Elizabethan Drama: 1558-1612. Willard Thorp. LC 70-116556. (Princeton Studies in English: No. 3). 151p. (C). 1970. 45.00 (0-87752-110-7) Gordian.

Triumph of Realism in the Elizabethan Drama: Fifteen Fifty-Eight - Sixteen Twelve. W. Thorp. LC 65-21093. (Studies in Drama: No. 39). 1969. reprint ed. lib. bdg. 75.00 (0-8383-0636-5) M S G Haskell Hse.

Triumph of Resistance. T. H. Keyes. 88p. (Orig.). 1995. pap. 6.00 (1-883821-07-X) Mother Bird.

Triumph of Satan. Harry E. Wedeck. 160p. 1974. reprint ed. pap. 2.95 (0-8065-0422-6, Citadel Pr) Carol Pub Group.

Triumph of Sectionalism: The Transformation of Ohio Politics, 1844-1856. Stephen E. Maizlish. LC 83-11255. 325p. reprint ed. pap. 92.70 (0-7837-1353-3, 2041501) Bks Demand.

Triumph of Subjectivity: An Introduction to Transcendental Phenomenology. 2nd ed. Quentin Lauer. LC 58-12363. xxiv, 182p. 1978. 30.00 (0-8232-0336-0) Fordham.

Triumph of Survival: Story of the Jews 1650-1990. deluxe ed. Berel Wein. 1993. 54.99 (0-89906-498-1) Mesorah Pubns.

Triumph of the American Nation. Todd. 1986. text ed. 63.25 (0-15-375950-X); teacher ed., text ed. 90.25 (0-15-375951-8) HR&W Schl Div.

Triumph of the American Nation 1986. Todd. 1986. wbk. ed., pap. text ed. 13.25 (0-15-375954-2); teacher ed., wbk. ed., pap. text ed. 17.75 (0-15-375955-0) HR&W Schl Div.

Triumph of the American Nation 1986: Readings. Todd. 1986. pap. text ed. 31.75 (0-15-375956-9) HR&W Schl Div.

Triumph of the American Nation 1986: Tests. Todd. 1986. pap. text ed. 10.00 (0-15-375953-4) HR&W Schl Div.

Triumph of the American Spirit: Johnstown, Pennsylvania. Howard Muson. (Johnstown Flood Museum Ser.). 1989. 43.00 (0-8026-0032-8) Univ Pub Assocs.

Triumph of the American Spirit: The Presidential Speeches of Ronald Reagan. Ed. by Emil Arca & Gregory J. Pamel. 362p. 1984. 9.95 (0-685-57961-1) Natl Repro Corp.

Triumph of the Bankers: Money & Banking in the Eighteenth & Nineteenth Centuries. William F. Hixson. LC 93-296. 208p. 1993. text ed. 59.95 (0-275-94607-X, C4607, Praeger Pubs) Greenwood.

Triumph of the Cross: Vocal Score (Lent Cantata) Dale Matthews. 84p. 1986. pap. 9.95 (0-7935-4944-2, 50324260) H Leonard.

Triumph of the Crucified see Triunfo del Crucificado

Triumph of the Darksword. Margaret Weis & Tracy Hickman. (Spectra Ser.). 400p. 1988. mass mkt. 5.99 (0-553-27406-6, Spectra) Bantam.

Triumph of the Dragon. Robin W. Bailey. 320p. (Orig.). 1995. pap. 4.99 (0-451-45437-5, ROC) NAL-Dutton.

Triumph of the Egg. Sherwood Anderson. LC 87-35411. 300p. 1988. reprint ed. pap. 8.95 (0-941423-11-5) FWEW.

Triumph of the Embryo. Lewis Wolpert. (Illus.). 224p. 1991. 25.00 (0-19-854243-7) OUP.

Triumph of the Embryo. Lewis Wolpert. (Illus.). 224p. 1994. reprint ed. pap. 12.95 (0-19-854799-4) OUP.

Triumph of the English Language: A Survey of Opinions Concerning the Vernacular from the Introduction of Printing to the Restoration. Richard F. Jones. xii, 352p. 1953. 47.50 (0-8047-0417-1) Stanford U Pr.

Triumph of the Factory System in England. Hsien-T'Ing Fang. LC 78-15111. (Perspectives in European History Ser.: No. 17). (Illus.). 310p. 1978. reprint ed. lib. bdg. 49.50 (0-87991-624-9) Porcupine Pr.

Triumph of the Goddess: The Canonical Models & Theological Visions of the "Devi-Bhagavata Purana" C. Mackenzie Brown. LC 89-21974. (SUNY Series in Hindu Studies). 327p. 1990. pap. text ed. 21.95 (0-7914-0364-5) State U NY Pr.

Triumph of the Goddess: The Canonical Models & Theological Visions of the "Devi-Bhagavata Purana" C. Mackenzie Brown. LC 89-21974. (SUNY Series in Hindu Studies). 327p. 1990. text ed. 64.50 (0-7914-0363-7) State U NY Pr.

Triumph of the Image: The Media's War in the Persian Gulf, a Global Perspective. Ed. by Hamid Mowlana et al. 269p. (C). 1992. pap. text ed. 22.95 (0-8133-1610-3) Westview.

Triumph of the Intelligent: The Creation of Homo Sapiens Sapiens. Seymour W. Itzkoff. LC 84-19110. (Evolution of Human Intelligence Ser.: Vol. 2). (Illus.). 223p. 1985. 25.00 (0-913993-01-8) Paideia MA.

Triumph of the Intelligent: The Creation of Homo Sapiens Sapiens. Seymour W. Itzkoff. (Evolution of Human Intelligence Ser.: Vol. II). 210p. 1989. 25.00 (0-8204-1305-4) P Lang Pubng.

Triumph of the Irony in the Book of Judges. Lillian R. Klein. (Journal for the Study of the Old Testament Supplement Ser.: Vol. 68). 260p. pap. 14.95 (1-85075-099-8, Pub. by Sheffield Acad UK) CUP Services.

Triumph of the King (Two Samuel) Gordon J. Keddie. 1990. pap. 11.99 (0-85234-272-1, Pub. by Evangelical Pr) Presby & Reformed.

***Triumph of the Lack of Will: International Diplomacy & the Yugoslav War-** James Gow. LC 96-48545. 1997. write for info. (0-231-10916-4) Col U Pr.

Triumph of the Lamb. Ted Grimsrud. LC 87-409. 192p. (Orig.). 1987. pap. 12.99 (0-8361-3438-9) Herald Pr.

Triumph of the Lion. Peter Danielson. (Children of the Lion Ser.: Bk. 19). 304p. 1996. mass mkt. 4.99 (0-553-56148-0, Bantam Domain) Bantam.

Triumph of the Market: Essays on Economics, Politics & the Media. Edward S. Herman. 300p. (Orig.). 1995. pap. 16.00 (0-89608-521-X) South End Pr.

An Asterisk (*) at the beginning of an entry indicates that the title is appearing in BIP for the first time.

Triumph of the Market: Essays on Economics, Politics & the Media. Edward S. Herman. 300p. (Orig.). (C). 1995. text ed. 40.00 (*0-89608-522-8*) South End Pr.

***Triumph of the Market: Essays on Economics, Politics, & the Media.** Edward S. Herman. 286p. 1996. 48.99 (*1-55164-063-5*, Pub. by Black Rose Bks CN); pap. 19.99 (*1-55164-062-7*, Pub. by Black Rose Bks CN) Consort Bk Sales.

Triumph of the Mountain Man. William W. Johnstone. 288p. 1997. mass mkt. 4.99 (*0-8217-5551-X*, Zebra Kensgtn) Kensgtn Pub Corp.

Triumph of the Nomads: A History of Aboriginal Australia. Geoffrey Blainey. LC 75-37122. 304p. 1982. 22.95 (*0-87951-043-9*); pap. 13.95 (*0-87951-084-6*) Overlook Pr.

Triumph of the Scarlet Pimpernel. Emmuska Orczy. 321p. 1983. reprint ed. lib. bdg. 27.95 (*0-89966-460-1*) Buccaneer Bks.

Triumph of the Sparrow: Zen Poems of Shinkichi Takahashi. Shinkichi Takahashi. Tr. by Lucien Stryk & Takashi Ikemoto from JPN. LC 85-2539. 192p. 1986. pap. text ed. 9.95 (*0-252-01229-1*) U of Ill Pr.

Triumph of the Spirit: Ten Stories of Holocaust Survivors. Ed. by Jacob Biber & Mary A. Burgess. LC 93-9208. (Studies in Judaica & the Holocaust: No. 9). 128p. 1994. pap. 17.00 (*0-89370-439-3*); lib. bdg. 27.00 (*0-89370-339-7*) Borgo Pr.

Triumph of the Spirit: Thirteen Stories of Holocaust Survivors. 2nd expanded rev. ed. Ed. by Jacob Biber et al. LC 95-19141. (Studies in Judaica & the Holocaust: No. 9). 1997. 29.00 (*0-8095-0410-3*); pap. 19.00 (*0-8095-1410-9*) Borgo Pr.

Triumph of the Therapeutic: Uses of Faith after Freud. Philip Rieff. xviii, 292p. (C). 1987. reprint ed. pap. text ed. 13.95 (*0-226-71646-5*) U Ch Pr.

***Triumph of the Unicorn.** Scott Sussman. LC 96-92927. (Illus.). 60p. (Orig.). 1997. pap. 9.95 (*1-889691-52-6*) SenSation.

***Triumph of Three Cities: A Comprehensive History of the Church until God Carts Satan into Lake of Fire.** Harold D. Henry. 239p. (Orig.). 1997. pap. text ed. 12.95 (*1-56794-132-X*, C-2468) Star Bible.

Triumph of Time: A Study of the Victorian Concepts of Time, History, Progress, & Decadence. Jerome H. Buckley. LC 66-21333. 198p. reprint ed. pap. 56.50 (*0-7837-4452-8*, 2057982) Bks Demand.

Triumph of Truth: A Life of Martin Luther. (Orig.). 1996. pap. 9.95 (*0-89084-876-9*, 094433) Bob Jones Univ Pr.

Triumph of Wit: Moliere & Restoration Comedy. Harold C. Knutson. (Illus.). 232p. 1988. 42.00 (*0-8142-0438-4*) Ohio St U Pr.

Triumph Out of Tragedy: Turning Obstacles into Opportunities. Ralph E. Woodrow & Arlene Woodrow. (Illus.). 144p. 1996. pap. 7.00 (*0-916938-15-8*) R Woodrow.

Triumph over Darkness: The Life of Louis Braille. large type ed. Lennard Bickel. (Illus.). 324p. 1989. 25.99 (*0-7089-2004-7*) Ulverscroft.

Triumph over Darkness: Understanding & Healing the Trauma of Childhood Sexual Abuse. 2nd ed. Wendy A. Wood. Ed. by Julie Livingston. LC 93-18381. (Illus.). 275p. 1993. reprint ed. pap. 12.95 (*0-941831-86-8*) Beyond Words Pub.

Triumph over Fear: A Book of Help & Hope for People with Anxiety, Panic Attacks, & Phobias. Jerilyn Ross. 320p. 1995. pap. 13.95 (*0-553-37444-3*) Bantam.

***Triumph over Illness: What You Should Know about the Power of Chiropractic Care.** William Gandee. 1997. pap. 12.95 (*0-89529-818-X*) Avery Group Inc.

Triumph over Marcos: A True Story Based on the Lives of Gene Viernes & Silme Domingo, Filipino American Cannery Union Organizers, Their Assassination & the Trial That Followed. Thomas Churchill. LC 94-47968. 1995. write for info. (*0-940880-51-2*) Open Hand.

Triumph over Marcos: A True Story Based on the Lives of Gene Viernes & Silme Domingo, Filipino American Cannery Union Organizers, Their Assassination & the Trial That Followed. Thomas Churchill. LC 94-47968. 1995. pap. 14.95 (*0-940880-52-0*) Open Hand.

Triumph over Silence: Women in Protestant History. Ed. by Richard L. Greaves. LC 85-961. (Contributions to the Study of Religion Ser.: No. 15). xii, 295p. 1985. text ed. 59.95 (*0-313-24799-4*, GTS/, Greenwood Pr) Greenwood.

Triumph Over Suffering. Cleo Pursell. 1982. pap. 1.95 (*0-89265-079-6*) Randall Hse.

Triumph over the Odds: Inspirational Success Stories. Louis Baldwin. LC 94-20162. 1994. 19.95 (*1-55972-238-X*, Birch Ln Pr) Carol Pub Group.

Triumph over Turbulence: Alaska's Luckiest Bush Pilot. Jim Magoffin. (Illus.). 322p. 1993. 29.95 (*0-9637806-0-3*) J Magoffin.

***Triumph over Tyranny, Taxation, & Treason: America's Last Battle of the War Against Totalitarianism.** Jeri Ball. LC 96-96764. ix, 368p. (Orig.). 1996. pap. 14.95 (*0-9653226-0-2*) Am Freedom Pr.

Triumph Racing Motorcycles in America. Lindsay Brooke. (Illus.). 160p. 1996. pap. 24.95 (*0-7603-0174-3*) Motorbooks Intl.

Triumph Speed Tuning. 2nd ed. Stan Shenton. Ed. by Mike Arman. (Illus.). 64p. 1983. reprint ed. pap. 11.00 (*0-933078-09-9*) M Arman.

Triumph Spitfire GT-6. Graham Robson. (Illus.). 128p. 1991. 27.95 (*0-947981-60-8*, Pub. by Motor Racing UK) Motorbooks Intl.

Triumph Spitfire GT6: A Guide to Originality. John Tomason. (Illus.). 128p. 1995. 34.95 (*1-85223-893-3*, Pub. by Crowood UK) Motorbooks Intl.

Triumph Spitfire Guide to Purchase & DIY Restoration. Lindsay Porter. (Illus.). 29.95 (*0-85429-728-6*, F728, Pub. by G T Foulis Ltd) Haynes Pubns.

Triumph Spitfire MK I Driver's Handbook. British Leyland Motors Staff. (Orig.). 16.00 (*0-8376-0560-1*) Bentley.

Triumph Spitfire MK I, MK II , MK III, Herald Vitesse Workshop Manual: 1959-1970. British Leyland Motors Staff. (Orig.). 70.00 (*0-8376-0564-4*) Bentley.

Triumph Spitfire Mk III Driver's Handbook (1964) British Leyland Motors. 80p. (Orig.). 16.00 (*0-8376-0527-X*) Bentley.

Triumph Spitfire Mk IV & 1500 1971-1974 Parts Catalogue. British Leyland Motors. 112p. (Orig.). 40.00 (*0-8376-0515-6*) Bentley.

Triumph Spitfire Restoration. Ed. by Practical CLassics & Car Restorer Editors. (Practical Classics & Car Restorer Ser.). (Illus.). 86p. 1995. pap. 19.95 (*1-873098-33-2*, Pub. by Kelsey Pub Ltd UK) Motorbooks Intl.

Triumph Spitfire 1500, Model Years 1975-1980, the Complete Official: Comprising the Official Driver's Handbook & Workshop Manual. British Leyland Motors Staff. LC 79-53184. (Illus.). 520p. (Orig.). 1980. pap. 55.00 (*0-8376-0122-3*) Bentley.

Triumph Spitfire 1500, 1975-1980. Robert Bentley. 1994. 50.00 (*0-8376-0555-5*) Bentley.

Triumph Sports Cars. Graham Robson. 1989. pap. 25.00 (*0-85263-926-0*, Pub. by Shire UK) St Mut.

Triumph Stag. J. Taylor. (Super Profile CAR Ser.). 11.95 (*0-85429-342-6*, F342, Pub. by G T Foulis Ltd) Haynes Pubns.

Triumph Stag Workshop Manual: 1971-1973. British Leyland Motors. 70.00 (*0-8376-0508-3*) Bentley.

Triumph Through Tears. Mary A. Shepard. Ed. by Kathleen Iddings. LC 88-50916. (Illus.). 72p. (Orig.). 1988. pap. text ed. 10.00 (*0-931721-10-5*) La Jolla Poets.

Triumph TR-6 Restoration. (Illus.). 106p. 1993. pap. 24.95 (*1-873098-27-8*, Pub. by Kelsey Pub Ltd UK) Motorbooks Intl.

Triumph Triples. Andrew Morland. (Osprey Colour Library). (Illus.). 128p. 1995. pap. 15.95 (*1-85532-428-8*) Motorbooks Intl.

***Triumph TRs.** James Taylor. (Illus.). 128p. 1997. pap. 19.95 (*0-7603-0407-6*) Motorbooks Intl.

Triumph TR2 & TR Wor. 1954-61. Robert Bentley. 1994. 45.00 (*0-8376-0594-6*) Bentley.

Triumph TR2 & TR3 Spare Parts Catalogue: 1953-1963. British Leyland Motors. 374p. (Orig.). 55.00 (*0-8376-0533-4*) Bentley.

Triumph TR2-TR8, 1953-81. Walter Zeichner. Tr. by Edward Force from GER. LC 90-60482. (Automotive Ser.). (Illus.). 96p. 1990. 19.95 (*0-88740-250-X*) Schiffer.

Triumph TR2-3-3A. W. G. Piggott. (Super Profile Ser.). (Illus.). 56p. 1987. 11.95 (*0-85429-559-3*, F559, Pub. by G T Foulis Ltd) Haynes Pubns.

Triumph TR250 Driver's Handbook: 1968 Edition. British Leyland Motors. 72p. (Orig.). 16.00 (*0-8376-0559-8*) Bentley.

Triumph TR250 Spare Parts Catalogue: 1968. British Leyland Motors. 259p. (Orig.). 55.00 (*0-8376-0507-5*) Bentley.

Triumph TR4 & TR4A 1961-1968: Official Driver's Handbook, Workshop Manual, Competition Preparation Manual. British Leyland Motors Staff. LC 74-21354. (Illus.). 408p. (Orig.). 1975. pap. 55.00 (*0-8376-0121-5*) Bentley.

Triumph TR4 Driver's Handbook. British Leyland Motors. 68p. 16.00 (*0-8376-0517-2*) Bentley.

Triumph TR4 Spare Parts Catalogue. British Leyland Motors. 319p. (Orig.). 55.00 (*0-8376-0546-6*) Bentley.

***Triumph TR4, 5 & 6 Autofolio.** M. Richards. (Illus.). 72p. Date not set. 19.95 (*0-85429-816-9*, Pub. by G T Foulis Ltd) Haynes Pubns.

Triumph TR4A Driver's Handbook. British Leyland Motors. 64p. (Orig.). 16.00 (*0-8376-0511-3*) Bentley.

Triumph TR4A Spare Parts Catalogue. British Leyland Motors. 336p. (Orig.). 55.00 (*0-8376-0556-3*) Bentley.

Triumph TR6. William Kimberley. 160p. 1995. 41.95 (*1-874105-51-0*, Pub. by Veloce Pub UK) Motorbooks Intl.

Triumph TR6 & TR250, 1967-1976, the Complete Official: Comprising the Official Driver's Handbook & Workshop Manual. British Leyland Motors Staff. LC 77-91592. (Illus.). 608p. (Orig.). 1978. pap. 60.00 (*0-8376-0108-8*) Bentley.

Triumph TR6 Driver's Handbook (U. S. Spec), 1970. British Leyland Motors Staff. 16.00 (*0-8376-0562-8*) Bentley.

Triumph TR6 Driver's Handbook (U. S. Spec), 1973. British Leyland Motors Staff. 16.00 (*0-8376-0558-X*) Bentley.

Triumph TR6 Driver's Handbook (U. S. Spec), 1975. British Leyland Motors. 72p. 16.00 (*0-8376-0550-4*) Bentley.

Triumph TR6 Spare Parts Catalogue: 1969-1973. British Leyland Motors. 264p. 1988. 55.00 (*0-8376-0540-7*) Bentley.

Triumph TR6 Spare Parts Catalogue: 1974-1976. British Leyland Motors. 280p. 55.00 (*0-8376-0553-9*) Bentley.

Triumph TR7 Driver's Handbook, 1976 (U.S. Spec) British Leyland Motors. 16.00 (*0-8376-0514-8*) Bentley.

Triumph TR7 Parts Catalogue: 1975-1978. British Leyland Motors. 288p. 55.00 (*0-8376-0544-X*) Bentley.

Triumph TR7 Spare Parts Catalogue, 1979-1981. British Leyland Motors Staff. 60.00 (*0-8376-0567-9*) Bentley.

Triumph TR7, 1975-1981, the Complete Official: Comprising the Official Driver's Handbook & Repair Operation Manual. British Leyland Motors Staff. LC 78-73515. (Illus.). 544p. (Orig.). 1979. pap. 55.00 (*0-8376-0116-9*) Bentley.

***Triumph Twin Restoration.** Roy Bacon. (Illus.). 240p. 1996. 39.95 (*0-85045-635-5*, Pub. by Osprey Pubng Ltd UK) Motorbooks Intl.

***Triumph Twins & Triples.** Tim Remus. (Enthusiast Color Ser.). (Illus.). 96p. 1997. pap. 12.95 (*0-7603-0312-6*) Motorbooks Intl.

Triumph Without Victory. 1992. write for info. (*0-394-23914-8*, Times Bks) Random.

Triumph Without Victory. U. S. News & World Report Staff. 1993. pap. 14.00 (*0-8129-2145-3*, Times Bks) Random.

Triumph 2000 & 2.5 P. I. The Complete Story. Graham Robson. (Illus.). 192p. 1995. 35.95 (*1-85223-854-2*, Pub. by Crowood UK) Motorbooks Intl.

Triumphal Chariot of Antimony. Basilius Valentinus. 204p. 1992. reprint ed. pap. 17.95 (*1-56459-021-6*) Kessinger Pub.

Triumphal Chariot of Antimony: With the Commentary of Theodore Kerchringius, Doctor of Medicine. Basil Valentine. Ed. by J. D. Holmes. Tr. & Intro. by A. E. Waite. 1991. reprint ed. pap. 14.95 (*1-55818-175-X*) Holmes Pub.

***Triumphal Sun.** Annemarie Schimmel. 240p. 1996. pap. 16.95 (*0-614-21373-8*, 1262) Kazi Pubns.

Triumphal Sun: A Study of the Works of Jalaloddin Rumi. Annemarie Schimmel. LC 93-4382. 513p. (C). 1993. pap. 21.95 (*0-7914-1636-4*); text ed. 64.50 (*0-7914-1635-6*) State U NY Pr.

Triumphant. Created by Keith Laumer. (BOLOS Ser.: Vol. 3). 1995. mass mkt. 5.99 (*0-671-87683-X*) Baen Bks.

Triumphant Capitalism: Henry Clay Frick & the Industrial Transformation of America. Kenneth Warren. LC 95-14572. (Illus.). 448p. 1996. text ed. 35.00 (*0-8229-3889-8*) U of Pittsburgh Pr.

Triumphant Christian Living. Gracia Rinden. 37p. (Orig.). 1991. pap. 3.95 (*0-943167-13-2*) Faith & Fellowship Pr.

Triumphant Church: Dominion over All the Powers of Darkness. Kenneth E. Hagin. 296p. 1993. pap. 6.95 (*0-89276-520-8*) Hagin Ministries.

***Triumphant Hymns for Congregation & Choir.** Date not set. pap. 1.20 (*0-8341-9265-9*) Lillenas.

Triumphant in Suffering. Merle Ruth. 78p. 1991. pap. 3.00 (*0-317-04169-X*) Rod & Staff.

Triumphant Journey: The Saga of Bobby Jones & the Grand Slam of Golf. Richard Miller. LC 93-45456. 272p. 1994. reprint ed. pap. 10.95 (*0-87833-851-9*) Taylor Pub.

Triumphant Living in Turbulent Times. William H. Hinson. LC 92-41894. 144p. (Orig.). 1993. pap. 3.00 (*0-687-42641-3*) Dimen for Liv.

Triumphant Marriage: 100 Extremely Successful Couples Reveal Their Secrets. Neil C. Warren. 1995. audio 15.99 (*1-56179-363-9*) Focus Family.

Triumphant Marriage: 100 Extremely Successful Couples Reveal Their Secrets. Neil C. Warren. LC 95-13726. 1995. 17.99 (*1-56179-362-0*) Focus Family.

Triumphant Return of Christ. Ed. by William T. James. LC 93-87260. (Essays in Apocalypse Ser.: Bk. 2). 400p. (Orig.). 1994. pap. 11.95 (*0-89221-250-0*) New Leaf.

***Triumphant Spirit - Portraits & Stories of Holocaust Survivors...Their Messages of Hope & Compassion.** Nick Del Calzo et al. (Illus.). 172p. 1997. 45.00 (*0-9655260-0-3*); pap. 29.95 (*0-9655260-1-1*) Triump Spirit.

Triumphierende und der Besiegte Tod in der Wort und Bildkunst Des Barock. Friedrich-Wilhelm Wentzlaff-Eggebert. (Illus.). 203p. (GER.). (C). 1975. 176.95 (*3-11-005821-9*) De Gruyter.

Triumphs. Houghton Mifflin Company Staff. (Reading Ser.). (J). 1988. teacher ed., pap. 75.64 (*0-395-43704-0*) HM.

Triumphs. Houghton Mifflin Company Staff. (Reading Ser.). (J). 1988. suppl. ed., teacher ed., pap. 8.00 (*0-395-45596-0*) HM.

Triumphs. Houghton Mifflin Company Staff. (Reading Ser.). (J). 1988. wbk. ed., pap. 15.52 (*0-395-45557-X*) HM.

***Triumphs & Tears: Young People, Markets, & the Transition from School to Work.** Phil Hodkinson et al. (Manchester Metropolitan University Education Ser.). 144p. 1996. pap. 26.95 (*1-85346-442-2*, Pub. by D Fulton UK) Taylor & Francis.

Triumphs & Tragedy: A History of the Mexican People. Ramon E. Ruiz. 512p. 1993. pap. 15.95 (*0-393-31066-3*) Norton.

Triumphs & Trials of an Organ Builder. Jerome Markowitz. (Illus.). 195p. 1989. 20.00 (*0-9624896-0-3*) Vox Humana.

***Triumphs Modern Motorcycles.** John Tipler. (Illus.). 200p. 1997. 35.95 (*1-86126-041-5*, Pub. by Crowood UK) Motorbooks Intl.

Triumphs of Ephraim. James E. McGirt. LC 79-39093. (Black Heritage Library Collection). 1977. reprint ed. 22.95 (*0-8369-9031-5*) Ayer.

***Triumphs of Eugene Valmont.** Robert Barr. (Oxford Popular Fiction Ser.). 256p. 1997. pap. 9.95 (*0-19-283248-4*) OUP.

Triumphs of Eugene Valmont. Robert Barr. 192p. 1985. reprint ed. pap. 5.95 (*0-486-24894-1*) Dover.

Triumphs of God's Revenge Against the Crying & Execrable Sinne of Murther (1639), Bks. I-II, Vol. 1. John Reynolds. Ed. by Joan M. Walmsley. LC 94-38864. 332p. 1995. text ed. 99.95 (*0-7734-8992-4*) E Mellen.

Triumphs of Joseph. Woodson. Orig. Title: The Poverty Pentagon. 1998. 20.00 (*0-684-82742-5*) Free Pr.

Triumphs of Providence: The Assassination Plot, 1696. Jane Garrett. LC 80-49950. 301p. reprint ed. pap. 85.80 (*0-318-34793-8*, 2031656) Bks Demand.

Triumphs of the Spirit in Children's Literature. Ed. by Francelia Butler & Richard W. Rotert. LC 86-20143. xii, 252p. (C). 1986. pap. 27.50 (*0-208-02111-6*, Lib Prof Pubns) Shoe String.

Triumviral Narratives of Appain & Cassius Dio. Alain M. Gowing. (Illus.). 300p. (C). 1992. text ed. 47.50 (*0-472-10294-X*) U of Mich Pr.

Triune Brain in Evolution: Role in Paleocerebral Functions. P. D. MacLean. LC 89-22899. (Illus.). 696p. 1990. 95.00 (*0-306-43168-8*, Plenum Pr) Plenum.

Triune Concept of the Brain & Behavior: Papers Presented at Queen's University, Ontario, 1969. Paul D. McLean. LC 72-90742. 177p. reprint ed. pap. 50.50 (*0-317-27771-5*, 2055959) Bks Demand.

Triune Connection. Thomas D. Cobb. 165p. (Orig.). (C). 1995. pap. 6.95 (*0-9650711-0-3*) Sword & Vine.

Triune God. 90p. 1985. teacher ed., ring bd. 19.95 (*0-910566-24-0*) Evang Trg Assn.

Triune God. rev. ed. Clarence H. Benson. 96p. 1970. pap. text ed. 8.95 (*0-910566-09-7*) Evang Trg Assn.

Triune God: A Biblical, Historical, & Theological Study. Thomas Marsh. LC 94-78128. 208p. (Orig.). 1994. pap. 14.95 (*0-89622-631-X*) Twenty-Third.

Triune God: An Ecumenical Study. Eric L. Mascall. LC 86-30327. (Princeton Theological Monographs: No. 10). 1986. pap. 12.90 (*0-915138-96-4*) Pickwick.

Triune God in Experience. Bill Freeman. LC 92-64296. 390p. (Orig.). 1992. pap. 8.50 (*0-914271-24-5*) Mnstry Wrd.

Triune God To Be Life To The Tripartite Man. Witness Lee. 86p. per. 3.25 (*0-87083-552-1*, 15043001) Living Stream Ministry.

Triune Identity: God According to the Gospel. Robert W. Jenson. LC 81-43091. 207p. reprint ed. pap. 59.00 (*0-317-55553-7*, 2029621) Bks Demand.

Triune Symbol: Persons, Process & Community. Joseph A. Bracken. (Studies in Religion: No. 1). 216p. (Orig.). 1985. lib. bdg. 47.50 (*0-8191-4440-1*) U Pr of Amer.

Triunfo de la Fee en los Reynos del Japon. Lope De Vega. Ed. by J. S. Cummins. (Textos B Ser.: No. 1). (Illus.). 116p. (Orig.). (C). 1965. pap. 36.00 (*0-900411-40-6*, Pub. by Tamesis Bks Ltd UK) Boydell & Brewer.

Triunfo del Crucificado. Erich Sauer. Orig. Title: The Triumph of the Crucified. 288p. (SPA.). 1993. pap. 8.99 (*0-8254-1655-8*, Edit Portavoz) Kregel.

Triunity of the Godhead. Gordon Lindsay. 1986. per. 3.95 (*0-89985-272-6*) Christ for the Nations.

***Triversal Woman.** Lynn H. Fisher. (Illus.). 20p. (Orig.). (C). 1997. pap. 4.95 (*1-880718-18-9*) Genius New.

Triversity Fantasy: Seven Keys to Unlock Prejudice. Stephanie W. Allen. LC 94-73158. 160p. (Orig.). 1995. pap. 14.95 (*0-9644207-0-8*) KiteShade Pubng.

Trivia-Lites. Rosemarie Giroux-Collins. 1986. text ed. 22.80 (*0-201-17617-3*) Addison-Wesley.

Trivia Mania. X. Einstein. 1984. pap. 2.50 (*0-8217-1519-4*) Kensgtn Pub Corp.

Trivia Mania: History & Geography. Xavier Einstein. 1984. mass mkt. 2.50 (*0-317-05598-4*, Zebra Kensgtn) Kensgtn Pub Corp.

Trivia Mania: Literature. X Einstein. 1984. 2.50 (*0-8217-1451-1*) Kensgtn Pub Corp.

Trivia Mania: Literature. Xavier Einstein. 1984. mass mkt. 2.50 (*0-317-05597-6*, Zebra Kensgtn) Kensgtn Pub Corp.

Trivia Mania: Movies. Xavier Einstein. 1984. mass mkt. 2.50 (*0-317-05595-X*, Zebra Kensgtn) Kensgtn Pub Corp.

Trivia Mania: Science & Nature. Xavier Einstein. 1984. mass mkt. 2.50 (*0-317-05599-2*, Zebra Kensgtn) Kensgtn Pub Corp.

Trivia Mania: Sports. Xavier Einstein. 1984. mass mkt. 2.50 (*0-317-05600-X*, Zebra Kensgtn) Kensgtn Pub Corp.

Trivia Mania: Television. Xavier Einstein. 1984. mass mkt. 2.50 (*0-317-05596-8*, Zebra Kensgtn) Kensgtn Pub Corp.

Trivia To Go: The Movies. Becker. 1995. pap. 8.95 (*0-8092-3408-4*) Contemp Bks.

Trivia To Go: TV. Becker. 1995. pap. 8.95 (*0-8092-3409-2*) Contemp Bks.

Trivia Treasury: Trivia & Word Games for Older Adults. Beckie Karras. 64p. (Orig.). 1990. pap. text ed. 9.95 (*1-879633-04-3*) Eldersong.

Trivia You Can Use. David A. Weiss. Ed. by Greenberg Consulting Staff. (Illus.). 185p. (Orig.). 1998. pap. 13.50 (*0-9634299-5-7*) Cumberland Ent.

Trivial Pursuit Encyclopedie Junior: Dictionnaire. Stephane Cremer. 558p. (FRE.). 1989. 75.00 (*0-7859-8135-7*, 2863913247) Fr & Eur.

Trivialization of God: The Dangerous Illusion of a Manageable Deity. Donald W. McCullough. LC 95-14409. 176p. 1995. 16.00 (*0-89109-909-3*) NavPress.

Trivializing America. Norman Corwin. 256p. 1983. 14.95 (*0-8184-0341-1*) Carol Pub Group.

Trivializing America: The Triumph of Mediocrity. Norman Corwin. 1986. pap. 9.95 (*0-8184-0389-6*) Carol Pub Group.

Trix of the Grade. A. Tutor & B. Tutor. 176p. (Orig.). 1996. pap. 15.95 (*0-566-07804-X*, Pub. by Gower UK) Ashgate Pub Co.

Trixie. Rick Brownell. LC 93-169. (J). 1994. write for info. (*0-383-03670-4*) SRA McGraw.

Trixie: The Wonder Dog. Marlene Griffiths. (Orig.). (J). (gr. 3-6). 1996. pap. 6.95 (*0-533-11901-4*) Vantage.

Trixie & Baba. John Antrobus. 93p. 1969. 12.95 (*0-910278-10-5*) Boulevard.

***TRIZ Research Report: An Approach to Systematic Innovation.** 48p. 1996. pap. write for info. (*1-879364-99-9*) GOAL-QPC.

TRM en Industrias de Proceso. Ed. by Tokutaro Suzuki. 385p. (ENG & SPA.). 1995. pap. 85.00 (*84-87022-18-9*) Prod Press.

Troade. Sallebray. Ed. by Phillippo & Supple. (Exeter French Texts Ser.: No. 96). 100p. (FRE.). 1996. pap. text ed. 19.95 (*0-85989-495-9*, Pub. by Univ Exeter Pr UK) Northwestern U Pr.

Trobador Guillem Margret see Trobador Pistoleta

Trobador Pistoleta. Pistoleta. Bd. with Trobador Guillem Margret. LC 80-2184. LC 80-2184. reprint ed. 27.00 (*0-404-19013-8*) AMS Pr.

Trobador Uc Brunec Oder Brunenc in: Abhandlungen Herrn Prof. Adolf Tobler. Carl L. Appel. LC 80-2177. 1981. reprint ed. 17.50 (*0-404-19003-0*) AMS Pr.

Trobrianders of Papua New Guinea. Annette R. Weiner. LC 87-18614. (Case Studies in Cultural Anthropology). 208p. (C). 1988. pap. text ed. 13.50 (*0-03-011919-7*) HB Coll Pubs.

Trocar Study. 2nd ed. George Cristino. Ed. by Donna M. Cristino. (Illus.). 467p. (C). 1995. text ed. 819.00 (*1-886974-12-8*) Inst Knowledge.

***Trocars & Pneumoperitoneum Needles in Minimally Invasive Surgery: Litigation, Legal, Marketing & Design.** George Cristino. Date not set. 465.00 (*1-886974-14-4*) Inst Knowledge.

***Trochemoche.** Luis Rodriguez. 1997. pap. 12.95 (*0-614-29394-4*) Curbstone.

Trock. Mark Dunster. 31p. (Orig.). 1995. pap. 5.00 (*0-89642-269-0*) Linden Pubs.

Troff Typesetting for UNIX Systems. Sandra L. Emerson & Karen Paulsell. (Illus.). 224p. 1987. pap. 32.95 (*0-13-930959-4*) P-H.

Trog Christmas Story. Maureen Fitzgerald. (Illus.). 20p. pap. 1.95 (*0-88962-126-8*) Mosaic.

Trog Family. Maureen Fitzgerald. (Illus.). 21p. pap. 1.95 (*0-88962-116-0*) Mosaic.

Troglobitic Halocyprid Ostracoda of Anchialine Caves in Cuba. Louis S. Kornicker & Jill Yager. LC 95-39169. (Smithsonian Contributions to Zoology Ser.: Vol. 580). 22p. 1996. reprint ed. pap. 25.00 (*0-608-02427-9*, 2063070) Bks Demand.

Trogons of the Arizona Borderlands. rev. ed. Richard C. Taylor. Ed. by Nancie S. Mahan. Orig. Title: The Coppery-Tailed Trogan "Arizona Bird of Paradise". (Illus.). 99p. 1995. pap. 10.95 (*0-918080-78-9*, 20963) Treas Chest Bks.

Troia Bretanica, or Great Britaines Troy. Thomas Heywood. LC 74-80187. (English Experience Ser.: No. 667). 466p. 1974. reprint ed. 75.00 (*90-221-0667-5*) Walter J Johnson.

Troia Britanica: or Great Britain's Troy. Thomas Heywood. (Anglistica & Americana Ser.: No. 83). 466p. 1972. reprint ed. 96.20 (*3-487-04173-1*) G Olms Pubs.

***Troika.** Stepan Chapman. 250p. 1997. pap. 14.99 (*1-890464-02-3*) Ministry of Whimsy.

Troika. Louise Cooper. (Indigo Ser.: No. 5). 1991. mass mkt. 4.50 (*0-8125-0799-1*) Tor Bks.

Troika. Clive Egleton. LC 84-45050. 319p. 1984. 14.95 (*0-689-11479-6*, Atheneum S&S) S&S Trade.

Troika. large type ed. Clive Egleton. 480p. 1985. 27.99 (*0-7089-8301-4*) Ulverscroft.

Troika: A Communicative Approach to Russian Language, Life, & Culture. Marita Nummikoski. LC 95-46413. 608p. 1996. text ed. 42.00 (*0-471-30945-1*) Wiley.

Troika: Introduction to Russian Letters & Sounds. Reason A. Goodwin. LC 80-81788. (Orig.). (gr. 11-12). 1980. text ed. 14.50 (*0-936368-00-4*); pap. text ed. 6.95 (*0-936368-01-2*) Lexik Hse.

Troika Four: Funny How You Remember Things; Pulling up the Dawn; Hidden Seed. Judy Brinkworth et al. 96p. 1992. 5.95 (*0-939395-18-5*) Thorntree Pr.

Troika One. Marilyn Taylor et al. 96p. (Orig.). 1991. pap. 5.95 (*0-939395-13-4*) Thorntree Pr.

Troika Three: Side Effects of Life; The Kitchen of Your Dreams; Color Documentary. Laura Telford et al. 96p. 1992. 5.95 (*0-939395-17-7*) Thorntree Pr.

Troika Two. Carol L. Gloor et al. 96p. (Orig.). 1991. pap. 5.95 (*0-939395-14-2*) Thorntree Pr.

Troiley Lives. Steven Sher. 48p. 1985. 7.95 (*0-931694-28-0*) Wampeter Pr.

Troilus. Mark Dunster. 37p. (Orig.). 1995. pap. 5.00 (*0-89642-291-7*) Linden Pubs.

Troilus & Cressida. William Shakespeare. Ed. by Kenneth Muir. (Oxford English Texts Ser.). (Illus.). 224p. 1984. pap. 6.95 (*0-19-281439-7*) OUP.

Troilus & Cressida. William Shakespeare. (New Penguin Shakespeare Ser.). 240p. 1987. mass mkt. 5.95 (*0-14-070741-7*, Pub. by BBC UK) Parkwest Pubns.

Troilus & Cressida. William Shakespeare. Ed. by Louis B. Wright & Virginia A. La Mar. (Folger Library). 336p. (YA). (gr. 11 up). pap. 3.50 (*0-671-66916-8*, WSP) PB.

Troilus & Cressida. William Shakespeare. Ed. by Kenneth Palmer. LC 83-7987. (Arden Shakespeare Ser.). 300p. 1982. pap. 8.95 (*0-416-17790-5*, NO. 2305) Routledge Chapman & Hall.

Troilus & Cressida. William Shakespeare. Ed. by Kenneth Palmer. LC 83-7987. (Arden Shakespeare Ser.). 300p. 1983. text ed. 45.00 (*0-416-47680-5*, NO. 2298) Routledge Chapman & Hall.

Troilus & Cressida. William Shakespeare. (BBC Television Plays Ser.). 1981. pap. 4.95 (*0-563-20004-9*, Pub. by BBC UK) Parkwest Pubns.

***Troilus & Cressida.** William Shakespeare. (English Text Ser.). 1983. pap. 9.95 (*0-415-02707-1*) Routledge.

***Troilus & Cressida.** William Shakespeare. (English Ser.). (C). Date not set. text ed. 45.00 (*0-17-443570-3*) Wadsworth Pub.

***Troilus & Cressida.** William Shakespeare. (English Ser.). (C). 1983. pap. 9.95 (*0-17-443537-1*) Wadsworth Pub.

Troilus & Cressida. large type ed. William Shakespeare. 1994. pap. 24.95 (*0-7089-4520-1*, Charnwood) Ulverscroft.

Troilus & Cressida. rev. ed. William Shakespeare. Ed. by David Seltzer. 1963. pap. 4.95 (*0-451-52297-4*, Sig Classics) NAL-Dutton.

***Troilus & Cressida: An Annotated Bibliography.** Trevor A. Owen. (Garland Shakespeare Bibliographies Ser.). Date not set. text ed. 120.00 (*0-8240-8514-0*) Garland.

Troilus & Cressida: Modern Text with Introduction. Ed. by A. L. Rowse. LC 86-11032. (Contemporary Shakespeare Ser.). 146p. (Orig.). (C). 1986. pap. text ed. 3.45 (*0-8191-3932-7*) U Pr of Amer.

Troilus & Cressida in Modern English Verse. Geoffrey Chaucer. Tr. by George P. Krapp. 1957. pap. 3.95 (*0-394-70142-9*, Vin) Random.

Troilus & Cressida Notes. James K. Lowers. (Cliffs Notes Ser.). 1982. pap. 4.50 (*0-8220-0091-1*) Cliffs.

Troilus & Criseyde. Geoffrey Chaucer. Ed. by R. A. Shoaf. LC 88-72033. 312p. 1989. 42.00 (*0-937191-10-8*); pap. 16.95 (*0-937191-11-6*) Colleagues Pr Inc.

Troilus & Criseyde. Geoffrey Chaucer. Tr. by Nevill Coghill. (Classics Ser.). 336p. 1971. pap. 9.95 (*0-14-044239-1*, Penguin Classics) Viking Penguin.

***Troilus & Criseyde.** Windeatt. 1990. pap. text ed. write for info. (*0-582-03197-4*) Addison-Wesley.

Troilus-Cressida Story from Chaucer to Shakespeare. Hyder Rollins. LC 76-100782. (English Literature Ser.: No. 33). (C). 1970. reprint ed. lib. bdg. 49.95 (*0-8383-0338-2*) M S G Haskell Hse.

Trois Ages de la Nuit. Francoise Mallet-Joris. (FRE.). 1992. pap. 13.95 (*0-7859-4774-4*) Fr & Eur.

Trois Albums. Victor Hugo. (FRE.). 1963. pap. 38.95 (*0-7859-5341-8*) Fr & Eur.

Trois Cent Dix-Septieme Section. Pierre Schoendoerffer. (FRE.). 1973. pap. 10.95 (*0-7859-4007-3*) Fr & Eur.

Trois Chansonniers Francais Du XV Siecle. Ed. by Eugenie Droz et al. LC 77-26063. (Music Reprint Ser.). 1978. reprint ed. lib. bdg. 35.00 (*0-306-77561-1*) Da Capo.

Trois-Chenes. Maurice Denuziere. 945p. (FRE.). 1989. pap. 13.95 (*0-7859-2126-5*, 2070381846) Fr & Eur.

Trois Contes. Gustave Flaubert. Ed. by Maynial. (Coll. Prestige). 49.95 (*0-685-34905-5*); pap. 29.95 (*0-685-34904-7*) Fr & Eur.

Trois Contes. Gustave Flaubert. (Coll. GF). 192p. (FRE.). 1989. pap. write for info. (*0-7859-4758-2*) Fr & Eur.

Trois Contes. Gustave Flaubert. (Folio Ser.: No. 424). (FRE.). pap. 6.95 (*2-07-036424-0*) Schoenhof.

Trois Contes - la Tentation de St. Antoine. unabridged ed. Gustave Flaubert. (FRE.). pap. 7.95 (*2-87714-219-1*, Pub. by Bookking Intl FR) Distribks Inc.

Trois Contes de Jeunesse. Gustave Flaubert. Ed. by Unwin. (Exeter French Texts Ser.: Vol. 41). 107p. (FRE.). Date not set. pap. text ed. 19.95 (*0-85989-102-X*, Pub. by Univ Exeter Pr UK) Northwestern U Pr.

Trois Crimes de Mes Amis. Georges Simenon. (Folio Ser.: No. 1112). (FRE.). pap. 8.95 (*2-07-037112-3*) Schoenhof.

Trois Crimes De Mes Amis, le Suspect, les Soeurs Lacroix. Georges Simenon. 1021p. (FRE.). 1992. 49.95 (*0-7859-0493-X*, 2258035260) Fr & Eur.

Trois Dialogues de l'Exercise du Saunter of Voltiger en L'Air. Arcangelo Tucarro. (Books of the Monarchs of England). (Illus.). 416p. (FRE.). (C). 1989. reprint ed. 135.00 (*1-85297-009-X*, Pub. by Archival Facs UK) St Mut.

Trois Dumas. Andre Maurois. 25.95 (*0-685-36969-2*) Fr & Eur.

Trois Essais de Montaigne. 4th ed. Michel de Montaigne et al. 150p. 1967. 15.00 (*0-686-54778-0*) Fr & Eur.

Trois Essais sur la Theorie Sexuelle. Sigmund Freud. (FRE.). 1989. pap. 12.95 (*0-7859-2820-0*) Fr & Eur.

Trois Figures Saintes. Paul Claudel. 148p. (FRE.). 1953. 10.95 (*0-7859-1126-X*, 2070215245) Fr & Eur.

Trois Fils De Rois. Ed. by F. J. Furnivall. (EETS, ES Ser.: No. 67). 1974. reprint ed. 40.00 (*0-527-00271-2*) Periodicals Srv.

Trois Maitres. Rene Descartes. (Illus.). 91p. (FRE.). 1991. 34.95 (*0-7859-1203-7*, 2876470195) Fr & Eur.

Trois Mondes. Jacques Attali. 415p. (FRE.). 1983. pap. 17.95 (*0-7859-3116-3*) Fr & Eur.

Trois Mousquetaires. Alexandre Dumas. Ed. by Charles Samaran. (Coll. Prestige). 35.00 (*0-685-34892-X*) Fr & Eur.

Trois Mousquetaires. Alexandre Dumas. (FRE.). 1962. 115.00 (*0-8288-3443-1*, F60650) Fr & Eur.

Trois Mousquetaires, 2 vols. Alexandre Dumas. 1973. pap. 9.95 (*0-318-52312-4*) Fr & Eur.

Trois Mousquetaires. Alexandre Dumas, Sr. Ed. by Charles Samaran. 1961. pap. 9.95 (*0-685-11605-0*) Fr & Eur.

Trois Mousquetaires. unabridged ed. Dumas. (FRE.). pap. 7.95 (*2-87714-198-5*, Pub. by Bookking Intl FR) Distribks Inc.

Trois Mousquetaires, Tome I. Alexandre Dumas. 448p. (FRE.). 1973. pap. 11.95 (*0-7859-1771-3*, 2070365263) Fr & Eur.

Trois Mousquetaires, Tome II. Alexandre Dumas. 448p. (FRE.). 1973. pap. 11.95 (*0-7859-1772-1*, 2070365271) Fr & Eur.

Trois Mousquetaires: Avec Vingt Ans Apres. Alexandre Dumas. 1800p. (FRE.). 1962. 95.00 (*0-7859-1098-0*, 2070101800) Fr & Eur.

Trois Mousquetaires: Vingt ans Apres. deluxe ed. Alexandre Dumas. (Pleiade Ser.). (FRE.). 82.95 (*2-07-010180-0*) Schoenhof.

Trois Mousquetaires & Vingt Ans Apres. Alexandre Dumas. 1800p. 45.00 (*0-686-56508-8*) Fr & Eur.

Trois Nouvelles. Georges Duhamel. (Illus.). 25.00 (*0-686-55198-2*) Fr & Eur.

Trois Ours: The Three Bears. 2nd ed. Emanuel Calamaro. (Interlingo Ser.). (Illus.). 19p. (Orig.). (FRE.). (J). (gr. k-12). 1995. reprint ed. pap. 2.95 (*0-922852-07-3*) Another Lang Pr.

Trois Petits Meurtres...et Puis S'en Va. Pascal Laine. (Folio Ser.: No. 2026). 281p. (FRE.). 1985. pap. 9.95 (*2-07-038114-5*) Schoenhof.

Trois Pieces Medievales: Le Jeu d'Adam, le Miracle de Theophile, la Farce du Cuvier. Ed. by Arthur R. Harden. LC 67-20813. (Medieval French Literature Ser.). (Orig.). (FRE.). 1967. pap. text ed. 9.95 (*0-89197-455-5*) Irvington.

Trois Pieces Surrealistes: Les Maries de la Tour Eiffel; L'Armoire a Glace un Beau Soir; Victor ou les Enfants au Pouvoir. Ed. by Robert G. Marshall & Frederic St Aubyn. LC 75-89864. (Illus.). (FRE.). 1969. pap. text ed. 14.95 (*0-89197-456-3*) Irvington.

Trois Portraits de Femme: La Duchesse de Devonshire, la Comtesse D'Albany, Henriette de France. Andre Maurois. (Coll. Les Soirees du Luxembourg). 21.50 (*0-685-36965-X*) Fr & Eur.

Trois Primitifs. Joris-Karl Huysmans. (Illus.). 188p. (FRE.). 1966. 13.95 (*0-7859-0035-7*, F88140) Fr & Eur.

Trois Recits. Francois Mauriac. 1992. pap. 12.95 (*0-7859-3174-0*, 2253062073) Fr & Eur.

Trois Roses Jaunes. Raymond Carver. 189p. (FRE.). 1990. pap. 10.95 (*0-7859-2135-4*, 2070382257) Fr & Eur.

Troisieme Course de Linguistique Generale (1910-1911) - Saussure's Third Course of Lectures on General Linguistics (1910-1911): Saussure's Third Course of Lectures on General Linguistics (1910-1911) from the Notebooks of Emil Constantin see Saussures 1st, 2nd & 3rd Course of Lectures on General Linguistics

Troisieme Generation. Chester Himes. 473p. (FRE.). 1986. pap. 13.95 (*0-7859-2518-X*, 2070377482) Fr & Eur.

Troisieme livre de chansons see Monuments de la musique francaise au temps de la Renaissance

Troja. Heinrich Schliemann. LC 66-29425. (Illus.). 1972. reprint ed. 40.95 (*0-405-08933-3*, Pub. by Blom Pubns UK) Ayer.

Trojan. James Follett. 1996. mass mkt. 5.99 (*0-7493-2481-3*, Reed Trade) Buttrwrth-Heinemann.

Trojan Generals Talk: Memoirs of the Greek War. Stories. Phillip Parotti. LC 87-34282. (Illinois Short Fiction Ser.). 184p. 1988. 14.95 (*0-252-01510-X*) U of Ill Pr.

Trojan Gold. Elizabeth Peters. 1988. mass mkt. 5.99 (*0-8125-2357-1*) Tor Bks.

Trojan Horse. Illus. & Retold by Warwick Hutton. LC 91-21590. 32p. (J). (gr. 2 up). 1992. lib. bdg. 16.00 (*0-689-50542-6*, McElderry) S&S Childrens.

***Trojan Horse.** Jim Pipe. LC 97-10021. (Mystery History of a--Ser.). (J). 1997. lib. bdg. 17.90 (*0-7613-0614-5*, Copper Beech Bks) Millbrook Pr.

***Trojan Horse.** Robert Sternberg. 1998. write for info. (*0-201-77254-X*) Addison-Wesley.

Trojan Horse. Paul Nizan. 1975. reprint ed. 35.00 (*0-86527-317-0*) Fertig.

Trojan Horse: Alberta & the Future of Canada. Gordon Laxer & Trevor Harrison. LC 95-79349. 335p. 1995. 48.99 (*1-55164-035-X*, Pub. by Black Rose Bks CN); pap. 19.99 (*1-55164-034-1*, Pub. by Black Rose Bks CN) Consort Bk Sales.

Trojan Horse: How the Greeks Won the War. Emily Little. LC 87-43118. (Step into Reading Bks.). (Illus.). 48p. (Orig.). (J). (gr. 2-4). 1988. pap. 3.99 (*0-394-89674-2*) Random Bks Yng Read.

Trojan Horse: How the New Age Movement Infiltrates the Church. Samantha Smith & Brenda Scott. LC 93-77443. 208p. 1993. pap. 10.99 (*1-56384-040-5*) Huntington Hse.

Trojan Horse: Imagery in Psychology, Literature, Art & Politics. Akhter Ahsen. LC 84-72150. 287p. 1984. 35.00 (*0-913412-20-1*) Brandon Hse.

Trojan Horse in America. Martin Dies. Ed. by Gerald Grob. LC 76-46072. (Anti-Movements in America Ser.). 1977. reprint ed. lib. bdg. 31.95 (*0-405-09945-2*) Ayer.

Trojan Horse in the City of God: The Catholic Crisis Explained. Dietrich Von Hildebrand. LC 93-1761. 318p. 1993. 16.95 (*0-918477-18-2*) Sophia Inst Pr.

***Trojan Project.** Edmund Contoski. LC 96-78788. 256p. (Orig.). 1997. pap. 17.95 (*0-9655007-5-6*) Am Liberty Pubs.

Trojan Spaceship. John G. Betancourt. (Star Trek: Deep Space Nine Ser.). 1996. pap. 5.99 (*0-671-00239-2*, Star Trek) PB.

Trojan War. Olivia E. Coolidge. (YA). 1990. pap. 6.95 (*0-395-56151-5*) HM.

Trojan War. Mark Dunster. 20p. (YA). (gr. 9-12). 1996. pap. 5.00 (*0-89642-339-5*) Linden Pubs.

Trojan War. Elizabeth Edmondson. LC 91-31860. (Great Battles & Sieges Ser.). (Illus.). 32p. (YA). (gr. 6 up). 1992. lib. bdg. 13.95 (*0-02-733273-X*, Mac Bks Young Read) S&S Childrens.

Trojan War. Bernard Evslin. 160p. (J). (gr. 7-9). 1988. pap. 2.95 (*0-590-41626-X*) Scholastic Inc.

Trojan War. Houghton Mifflin Company Staff. (Literature Experience 1993 Ser.). (J). (gr. 8). 1992. pap. 9.84 (*0-395-61854-1*) HM.

Trojan War. Houghton Mifflin Company Staff. (Literature Experience 1991 Ser.). (J). (gr. 8). 1990. pap. 9.84 (*0-395-55184-6*) HM.

Trojan War. Ed. by William A. Kottmeyer. 1962. pap. 7.96 (*0-07-033733-0*) McGraw.

Trojan War: Opposing Viewpoints. Gail Stewart. LC 89-11616. (Opposing Viewpoints Ser.). (Illus.). 112p. (YA). (gr. 5-12). 1989. lib. bdg. 17.96 (*0-89908-065-0*) Greenhaven.

Trojan War: The Iliad, Vol. 1. Harry Knill. (J). (gr. 4-9). 1995. pap. 3.95 (*0-88388-179-9*) Bellerophon Bks.

Trojan War: The Iliad, Vol. 2. Harry Knill. (J). (gr. 4-9). 1995. pap. 3.95 (*0-88388-214-0*) Bellerophon Bks.

***Trojan War & the Adventures of Odysseus.** Padria Colum. (Illus.). (J). 1997. write for info. (*0-614-29270-0*) Morrow.

Trojan War in Ancient Art. Susan Woodford. (Illus.). 128p. 1993. 47.50 (*0-8014-2949-8*); pap. 17.95 (*0-8014-8164-3*) Cornell U Pr.

Trojan Women. Euripides. Ed. by Barlow. (Classical Texts Ser.). 1986. 49.95 (*0-85668-228-4*, Pub. by Aris & Phillips UK); pap. 24.95 (*0-85668-229-2*, Pub. by Aris & Phillips UK) David Brown.

Trojan Women. Lucius A. Seneca. LC 86-47636. (Masters of Latin Literature Ser.). 128p. 1986. pap. 8.95 (*0-8014-9431-1*) Cornell U Pr.

Trojan Women see Euripides: Four Tragedies

Trojan Women see Ten Plays of Euripides

Trojdimenzny Clovek. Vladimir Uhri. 92p. (Orig.). (SLO.). 1995. pap. 4.50 (*1-56983-030-4*) New Creat WI.

***Trokeville Way.** Russell Hoban. 1997. pap. 4.99 (*0-679-88560-9*) Knopf Bks Yng Read.

Trokeville Way. Russell Hoban. (J). 1996. 17.00 (*0-679-88148-4*) McKay.

Troll: The Norwegian Troll, Its Terrifying Life & History. Frid Ingulstad. Ed. by Nancy Johnson. Tr. by Joan F. Henriksen from NOR. (Illus.). 96p. 1993. 24.95 (*82-05-21778-5*) Skandisk.

Troll & the Elephant Prince. Max Bush. (J). (gr. 4 up). 1985. pap. 5.00 (*0-87602-254-9*) Anchorage.

Troll Children & the Princess. Eli A. Cantillon. (Illus.). 21p. (J). (ps). 1993. 7.98 (*1-881445-17-8*) Sandvik Pub.

Troll Circle. Sigurd Hoel. Tr. by Sverre Lyngstad from NOR. LC 91-17820. (Modern Scandinavian Literature in Translation Ser.). x, 313p. 1992. text ed. 35.00 (*0-8032-2359-5*) U of Nebr Pr.

Troll Country. Edward Marshall. LC 79-19324. (Easy-to-Read Bks.). (Illus.). 56p. (J). (ps-3). 1980. pap. 4.95 (*0-8037-6210-0*) Dial Bks Young.

Troll Country. James Marshall. Date not set. pap. 11.99 (*0-8037-1669-9*) Dial Bks Young.

Troll Country, Level 3. Edward Marshall. (Easy-to-Read Ser.: Level 3). (Illus.). 56p. (J). (gr. 1-4). 1996. pap. 3.50 (*0-14-038110-4*, Puffin) Puffin Bks.

Troll Family. Gunn A. Frantzen. 1995. 7.95 (*0-533-11256-7*) Vantage.

Troll Games. Mary K. Whittington. LC 90-83. (Illus.). 32p. (J). (gr. k-3). 1991. lib. bdg. 13.95 (*0-689-31630-5*, Atheneum Bks Young) S&S Childrens.

Troll Garden: A Definitive Edition. Willa Cather. Ed. by James L. Woodress. LC 82-20138. xxx, 176p. 1983. text ed. 20.00 (*0-8032-1417-0*) U of Nebr Pr.

Troll in the Hole. Pauline Cartwright. LC 93-9282. (J). 1994. pap. write for info. (*0-383-03722-0*) SRA McGraw.

***Troll King: Glimpses of a Unique Southeast Alaska Lifestyle.** John Sabella. (Illus.). 148p. (Orig.). 1997. pap. 15.95 (*0-925750-19-0*) J Sabella.

Troll of Tree Hill. Judy Large. (Illus.). 72p. 1995. 18.95 (*1-869890-74-4*, Pub. by Hawthorn Press UK) Anthroposophic.

Troll-Quest. Rose Estes. 272p. (Orig.). 1995. pap. text ed. 4.99 (*0-441-00145-9*) Ace Bks.

Troll Student Handbook. Peter Eldin. 1997. pap. 8.95 (*0-8167-2525-X*) Troll Communs.

Troll-Taken. Rose Estes. 272p. (Orig.). 1993. mass mkt. 4.99 (*0-441-82414-5*) Ace Bks.

Troll Tale: Lucky Rainbow. (Magic-Picture Bks.). (Illus.). 24p. (J). 1993. 5.98 (*1-56173-885-9*) Pubns Intl Ltd.

Troll Tale: Magic Hair. (Magic-Picture Bks.). (Illus.). 24p. (J). 1993. 5.98 (*1-56173-884-0*) Pubns Intl Ltd.

Troll Wedding: The Troll Children's Search for the Magic Wedding Flower. Erik Arpi. Tr. by Kari Engen & Kirsten Gracey from SWE. LC 92-60297. (Illus.). 30p. (J). (ps-5). 1992. 12.95 (*1-881278-00-X*) M S Pr.

Troll Young People's Dictionary. David Smith & Derek Newton. LC 89-27331. (Illus.). 128p. (J). (gr. 1-4). 1991. pap. 9.95 (*0-8167-2256-0*); lib. bdg. 15.50 (*0-8167-2255-2*) Troll Communs.

Trolley. (Americana Bks.). (Illus.). 1971. 3.00 (*0-911410-28-7*) Applied Arts.

Trolley Bus, Where It Is & Where It's Going. (Special Reports: No. 200). 64p. 1983. 9.20 (*0-309-03523-6*) Transport Res Bd.

Trolley Talk, Vols. 1-9, Nos. 1-180. Incl. Vol. 7, nos. 121-140, 1977-1980. . 1985. pap. 18.95 (*0-914196-23-5*); Vol. 8, Nos. 141-160. 1980-1983. . 1986. pap. 16.95 (*0-914196-24-3*); Vol. 9, Nos. 161-180. 1984-1987. . 1989. pap. 14.95 (*0-914196-26-X*); Set pap. write for info. (*0-318-55952-8*) JAS Pubng.

Trolley to Yesterday. John Bellairs. 192p. (J). (gr. 4-7). 1990. mass mkt. 4.50 (*0-553-15795-7*) Bantam.

Trolley Trails Through the West Vol. 2: Seattle. (Insight Guides, Windows on the World Ser.). (Illus.). 350p. 1993. pap. 21.95 (*0-395-65989-2*) HM.

Trolley Trips Through the Hudson Valley, 1911. Trolley Press Staff. (Illus.). 24p. 1994. pap. 6.00 (*0-935796-47-9*) Purple Mnt Pr.

Trolley Wars: Streetcar Workers on the Line. Scott Molloy. LC 95-8992. 416p. 1996. text ed. 36.50 (*1-56098-608-5*) Smithsonian.

Trolleycars: Streetcars, Trams & Trolleys of North America. Frank Sullivan & Fred Winkowski. (Illus.). 128p. 1995. pap. 19.95 (*0-87938-972-9*) Motorbooks Intl.

Trolleys & Streetcars on American Picture Postcards. Ed. by Ray D. Applegate. LC 78-64854. (Illus.). 88p. 1979. pap. 8.95 (*0-486-23749-4*) Dover.

Trolleys to Augusta, Maine. O. R. Cummings. (Transportation Bulletin Ser.: No. 76). (Illus.). 1969. 7.50 (*0-910506-03-5*) De Vito.

Trolleys to Beaver Lake: A History of the Chester & Derry Railroad Association, 1891-1928. O. R. Cummings. (Illus.). 34p. (Orig.). 1990. pap. 6.00 (*0-911940-48-0*) Cox.

Trolling Flies for Trout & Salmon. Dick Stewart & Bob Leeman. 128p. 1992. reprint ed. 25.00 (*0-936644-18-4*) Mtn Pond Pub.

Trolling, It's Not Rocket Science. Tim L. Mercer. 48p. 1995. pap. 12.95 (*0-9650937-0-0*) MTM Pubns.

Trollnight. Peter Tremayne. 256p. 1996. 22.00 (*0-7278-4834-8*) Severn Hse.

Trollope: A Biography. N. John Hall. (Illus.). 600p. 1991. 35.00 (*0-19-812627-1*) OUP.

Trollope: A Biography. N. John Hall. LC 92-34889. (Illus.). 624p. (C). 1993. reprint ed. pap. 17.95 (*0-19-283071-6*, 5530) OUP.

Trollope: An Illustrated Biography. C. P. Snow. (Illus.). 232p. 1992. pap. 21.95 (*1-56131-034-4*) New Amsterdam Bks.

An Asterisk (*) at the beginning of an entry indicates that the title is appearing in BIP for the first time.

Trollope: Interviews & Recollections. R. C. Terry. (Illus.). 288p. 1987. text ed. 39.95 (*0-312-00368-4*) St Martin.

Trollope & Comic Pleasure. Christopher Herbert. LC 86-11367. xii, 256p. (C). 1987. 28.95 (*0-226-32741-8*) U Ch Pr.

Trollope & the Law. R. D. McMaster. LC 86-1279. 144p. 1986. text ed. 35.00 (*0-312-81891-2*) St Martin.

Trollope & Vicorian Moral Philosophy. Jane Nardin. LC 95-33251. 181p. 1996. 34.95 (*0-8214-1139-X*) Ohio U Pr.

Trollope & Victorial Moral Philosophy. Jane Nardin. LC 95-33251. 176p. (C). 1996. text ed. 34.95 (*0-8214-1145-4*) Ohio U Pr.

***Trollope & Women.** Margaret Markwick. LC 96-29451. 1997. write for info. (*1-85285-152-X*) Hambledon Press.

Trollope Companion. Richard Mullen. 1997. pap. 19.95 (*0-14-023558-2*) Viking Penguin.

Trollope in the Post Office. Robert H. Super. (C). 1981. text ed. 34.50 (*0-472-10013-0*) U of Mich Pr.

Trollope the Traveller: Selections from Anthony Trollope's Travel Writings. Ed. by Graham Handley. 1993. 19.95 (*1-85196-075-9*, Pub. by Pickering & Chatto UK) Ashgate Pub Co.

Trollope the Traveller: Selections from Anthony Trollope's Travel Writings. Anthony Trollope. LC 94-43052. 284p. 1995. pap. text ed. 14.95 (*1-56663-074-6*, Elephant Paperbacks) I R Dee.

Trollope-to-Reader: A Topical Guide to Digressions in the Novels of Anthony Trollope. Compiled by Mary L. Daniels. LC 83-10873. xxi, 393p. 1983. text ed. 55.00 (*0-313-23877-4*, DTR/, Greenwood Pr) Greenwood.

Trolls. (Look & Find Ser.). (Illus.). 24p. (J). 1993. 7.98 (*1-56173-898-0*) Pubns Intl Ltd.

Trolls. Mark Dunster. 16p. (Orig.). (YA). (gr. 9-12). 1997. pap. 5.00 (*0-89642-342-5*) Linden Pubs.

Trolls & the Shoemaker. Illus. by Emilie Kong. (Sound Story Bks.). 24p. (J). (ps-3). 1992. 20.00 (*0-307-74027-7*, 64027, Golden Books) Western Pub.

Trolls at the Door: A Door County Story. Mark Kopetz. LC 95-10842. (Illus.). 62p. (Orig.). (YA). 1995. pap. 8.95 (*0-940473-29-1*) Wm Caxton.

***Trolls' Cathedral.** Olafur Gunnarsson & David McDuff. 294p. 1996. pap. 14.95 (*1-899197-30-3*) Dufour.

Trolls of Omberg. Paul Karlsson. (Illus.). 40p. 1985. pap. 4.95 (*0-916871-08-8*) Welcome Pr.

Trolls Remembering Norway. Contrib. by Joanne Asala. 167p. 1994. pap. 12.95 (*1-57216-000-4*) Penfield.

Troll's Search for Summer. Nicolas Van Pallandt. (Illus.). 32p. (J). (ps-2). 1994. 15.00 (*0-374-36560-1*) FS&G.

Trombone. Bruce Pearson. (Standard of Excellence Ser.: Bk. 1). 1993. 6.45 (*0-8497-5938-2*, W21TB) Kjos.

Trombone. Bruce Pearson. (Standard of Excellence Ser.: Bk. 2). 1993. 6.45 (*0-8497-5963-3*, W22TB) Kjos.

Trombone. Bruce Pearson. (Standard of Excellence Ser.: Bk. 3). 1996. 6.45 (*0-8497-5987-0*, W23TB) Kjos.

Trombone: Its History & Music, 1697-1811. David M. Guion. (Monographs on Musicology: Vol. 6). 344p. 1988. text ed. 71.00 (*2-88124-211-1*) Gordon & Breach.

Trombone Bk. 1. (Breeze Easy Method Ser.). 2p. 1994. pap. 6.50 (*0-89724-372-2*, BE0012) Warner Brothers.

Trombone Bk. 2. (Breeze Easy Method Ser.). 32p. (Orig.). 1994. pap. 6.50 (*0-89724-373-0*, BE0018) Warner Brothers.

Trombone Chamber Music. 2nd ed. Harry J. Arling. Ed. by Stephen L. Glover. LC 83-19669. (Brass Research Ser.: No. 8). 1983. reprint ed. pap. text ed. 10.00 (*0-914282-29-8*) Brass Pr.

Trombone Pocketbook, Bk. 1. L. Dean Bye. pap. 0.95 (*0-87166-558-1*, 93746) Mel Bay.

Trombone Teaching Techniques. 2nd ed. Donald Knaub. (C). 1977. reprint ed. pap. 12.00 (*0-918194-09-1*) Accura.

Trombone Technique. 2nd ed. Denis Wick. (Illus.). 144p. (C). 1984. pap. 26.95 (*0-19-322378-3*) OUP.

Trombone Technique. 2nd ed. Denis Wick. (Illus.). 144p. 1990. reprint ed. pap. 18.95 (*0-685-46319-2*) OUP.

Trombonisms. Bill Watrous & Alan Raph. (Illus.). 48p. (Orig.). 1983. pap. 11.95 (*0-8258-0342-X*, 05130) Fischer Inc NY.

Trombonist's Handbook: A Complete Guide to Playing & Teaching. Reginald H. Fink. LC 76-55601. (Illus.). 1977. 29.50 (*0-918194-01-6*) Accura.

***Trompe L'Oeil: Murals & Decorative Wall Painting.** Lynette Wrigley. 1997. 35.00 (*0-8478-2045-9*) Rizzoli Intl.

Trompe L'Oeil at Home: Faux Finishes & Fantasy Settings. Karen S. Chambers. LC 91-52799. (Illus.). 224p. 1991. 45.00 (*0-8478-1420-3*) Rizzoli Intl.

Trompeta del Cisne - The Trumpet of the Swan. E. B. White. 1996. pap. text ed. 9.75 (*84-279-3214-6*) Lectorum Pubns.

Trompette dans l'Egypte Ancienne. Hans Hickmann. (Brass Research Ser.: No. 4). (Illus.). 1976. reprint ed. pap. text ed. 10.00 (*0-914282-17-4*) Brass Pr.

Trompeuses Esperances. Michel Deon. (FRE.). 1972. pap. 10.95 (*0-7859-1720-9*, 2070362795) Fr & Eur.

TRON Project Symposium, 11th. LC 10-636749. 192p. 1994. pap. 44.00 (*0-8186-6775-3*) IEEE Comp Soc.

TRON Project Symposium, 12th. LC 10-636749. 160p. 1995. pap. 50.00 (*0-8186-7207-2*, PR07207) IEEE Comp Soc.

Tron Project Symposium, 13th. LC 10-636749. 160p. 1996. pap. 50.00 (*0-8186-7658-2*) IEEE Comp Soc.

TRON Project, 1988. Ed. by K. Sakamura. (Illus.). xi, 384p. 1989. 107.95 (*0-387-70038-2*) Spr-Verlag.

TRON Project 1989: Open-Architecture Computer Systems; Proceedings of the Sixth TRON Project Symposium. Ed. by K. Sakamura. (Illus.). x, 324p. 1990. 93.95 (*0-387-70050-1*) Spr-Verlag.

TRON Project 1990: Open-Architecture Computer Systems. Ed. by K. Sakamura. xi, 436p. 1991. 106.95 (*0-387-70066-8*) Spr-Verlag.

Trono di Legno see Wooden Throne

Troodon. Janet Riehecky. (Dinosaur Bks.). (Illus.). 32p. (J). (gr. k-4). 1990. lib. bdg. 21.36 (*0-89565-636-1*) Childs World.

Troodon, the Smartest Dinosaur. Don Lessem. LC 92-44689. (Illus.). (J). (gr. 2-5). 1995. lib. bdg. 14.96 (*0-87614-798-8*, Carolrhoda) Lerner Group.

Troodonte. Janet Riehecky. (Libros Sobre Dinosaurios! Ser.). (Illus.). 32p. (SPA.). (J). (gr. k-4). 1990. lib. bdg. 21.36 (*1-56766-139-4*) Childs World.

***Troop Committee Guidebook.** Boy Scouts of America Staff. (Illus.). 72p. 1992. pap. 2.35 (*0-8395-4505-3*, 34505) BSA.

Troop Seventeen: The Making of Mounties. James E. McKenzie. (Illus.). 184p. 1992. 49.95 (*1-55059-039-1*) Temeron Bks.

***Trooper.** Leo Handel. Ed. by Willa Gray. 250p. 1997. 21.95 (*1-881636-00-3*) Windsor Hse Pub Grp.

Trooper Down. Marie Bartlett. 288p. 1990. mass mkt. 4.50 (*0-671-67610-5*) PB.

Trooper Down! Life & Death on the Highway Patrol. Marie Bartlett. LC 88-5896. (Illus.). 258p. 1988. 16.95 (*0-912697-81-4*) Algonquin Bks.

Trooper Smith. Richard F. Crockett. 1994. 18.95 (*0-533-11059-9*) Vantage.

Trooper Tales. Will L. Comfort. LC 70-106271. (Short Story Index Reprint Ser.). 1977. 20.95 (*0-8369-3308-7*) Ayer.

Trooper Tales. Will L. Comfort. 1976. reprint ed. lib. bdg. 22.95 (*0-89190-853-6*, Rivercity Pr) Amereon Ltd.

Troopers: Behind the Badge. John Stark. LC 93-85268. (Illus.). 288p. (Orig.). 1993. pap. 15.00 (*0-9637674-0-2*) NJ St Police.

Troopers, Tramps & Other Loose Characters. Damon Runyon. 23.95 (*0-8488-0145-8*) Amereon Ltd.

Troopers with Custer. E. A. Brininstool. (Custer Library). (Illus.). 368p. 1994. 19.95 (*0-8117-1742-9*) Stackpole.

Troopers with Custer: Historic Incidents of the Battle of the Little Big Horn. E. A. Brininstool. LC 88-31143. (Illus.). xii, 343p. 1989. reprint ed. pap. 11.95 (*0-8032-6101-2*, Bison Books) U of Nebr Pr.

Troops in Strikes. Steve Peak. (C). 1988. 59.00 (*0-900137-22-3*, Pub. by NCCL UK) St Mut.

Troparia & Kondakia. Tr. by Laurence Mancuso from GRE. 452p. 1984. 49.50 (*0-9607924-7-3*) Monks of New Skete.

Tropes, Parables, Performatives: Essays on Twentieth-Century Literature. J. Hillis Miller. LC 90-44886. 288p. 1991. text ed. 54.95 (*0-8223-1111-9*) Duke.

Trophees. Jose M. Heredia. LC 75-41134. reprint ed. 41.50 (*0-404-14554-X*) AMS Pr.

Trophic Cascade in Lakes. Ed. by Stephen R. Carpenter & James F. Kitchell. LC 92-36737. (Cambridge Studies in Ecology). (Illus.). 320p. (C). 1993. text ed. 85.00 (*0-521-43145-X*) Cambridge U Pr.

Trophic Cascade in Lakes. Ed. by Stephen R. Carpenter & James F. Kitchell. (Studies in Ecology). (Illus.). 399p. 1996. pap. text ed. 30.95 (*0-521-56684-3*) Cambridge U Pr.

***Trophic Cascades in Nature.** Oksanen. (Population & Community Biology Ser.). (Illus.). 224p. 1997. text ed. 73.95 (*0-412-61290-9*, Chap & Hall NY) Chapman & Hall.

***Trophic Factors & the Nervous System.** Ed. by Lloyd A. Horrocks et al. LC 90-8799. (Fidia Research Foundation Symposium Ser.: Vol. 3). reprint ed. pap. 107.20 (*0-608-04747-3*, 2065568) Bks Demand.

***Trophic Models of Aquatic Ecosystems.** Ed. by Daniel Pauly & V. Christensen. (ICLARM Conference Proceedings Ser.: No. 26). 390p. Date not set. per. write for info. (*971-10-2284-2*, Pub. by ICLARM PH) Intl Spec Bk.

Trophic Relationships in Inland Waters. Ed. by P. Biro & J. F. Talling. (Developments in Hydrobiology Ser.). (C). 1990. lib. bdg. 236.00 (*0-7923-0414-4*) Kluwer Ac.

Trophic Relationships in the Marine Environment: Proceedings of the 24th European Marine Biology Symposium. Margaret Barnes & R. N. Gibson. (Illus.). 700p. 1990. 130.00 (*0-08-037982-6*, Pub. by Aberdeen U Pr) Macmillan.

Trophies. John J. Wooten. 1994. pap. 5.25 (*0-8222-1382-6*) Dramatists Play.

Trophies: Sonnets. Jose-Maria De Heredia. Tr. by Frank Sewall. 1977. lib. bdg. 59.95 (*0-8490-2769-1*) Gordon Pr.

Trophies & Dead Things. Marcia Muller. 272p. 1991. mass mkt. 5.99 (*0-446-40039-4*, Mysterious Paperbk) Warner Bks.

Trophies in the Line of Duty: Essays, Columns & Occasional Letters. Colleen M. Rae. 128p. (Orig.). 1996. pap. 7.95 (*1-880382-02-4*) Haven Hill.

Trophies of Heaven. Ron Knott. Ed. by Mary Wallace. LC 86-26649. 160p. 1986. reprint ed. pap. 6.99 (*0-932581-06-4*) Word Aflame.

Trophies of Time: English Antiquarians of the Seventeenth Century. Graham Parry. (Illus.). 400p. 1996. 85.00 (*0-19-812962-9*) OUP.

Trophoblast Cells: Pathways for Maternal-Embryonic Communication. Ed. by Michael J. Soares et al. LC 93-27722. 1993. 157.00 (*0-387-94070-7*) Spr-Verlag.

Trophoblast Research, Vol. 2: Cellular Biology & Pharmacology of the Placenta, Techniques & Applications. Ed. by Richard K. Miller & Henry A. Thiede. LC 87-6934. 640p. 1987. 130.00 (*0-306-42563-7*, Plenum Med Bk) Plenum.

Trophoblast Research, Vol. 3: Placental Vascularization & Blood Flow: Basic Research & Clinical Applications. Ed. by P. Kaufmann & R. K. Miller. (Illus.). 347p. 1988. 95.00 (*0-306-42910-1*, Plenum Med Bk) Plenum.

Trophoblast Research, Vol. 4: Trophoblast Invasion & Endometerial Receptivity, Novel Aspects of the Cell Biology of Embryo Implantation. Ed. by H. W. Denker & J. D. Aplin. LC 90-7197. (Illus.). 463p. 1990. 135.00 (*0-306-43520-9*, Plenum Pr) Plenum.

Trophy. Dean Hughes. LC 93-42234. 128p. (J). (gr. 3-7). 1994. 13.00 (*0-679-84368-X*) Knopf Bks Yng Read.

Trophy Husband. Lynne Graham. (Presents Ser.). 1996. mass mkt. 3.50 (*0-373-11835-X*, 1-11835-5) Harlequin Bks.

***Trophy Husband.** Lynne Graham. 1996. 20.95 (*0-263-14855-6*, Pub. by Mills & Boon UK) Thorndike Pr.

Trophy Mule Deer: Finding & Evaluating Your Trophy. Lance Stapleton. LC 92-62857. (Illus.). 300p. (Orig.). 1993. pap. 24.95 (*0-9634538-2-3*) Outdoor Exprnces.

Trophy Stripers & Hybrids. Steve Baker & Neil Ward. LC 89-82206. (Illus.). 268p. (Orig.). pap. 14.50 (*0-937866-22-9*) Atlantic Pub Co.

Trophy Wife. Kelly Lange. 1995. 23.00 (*0-684-80191-4*) S&S Trade.

Trophy Wife. Kelly Lange. 1996. pap. 5.99 (*0-451-18812-8*, Sig) NAL-Dutton.

Trophy Wives. Lois Wyse. 384p. 1992. mass mkt. 4.99 (*0-380-71531-7*) Avon.

Tropic Cooking. Joyce L. Young. 288p. 1987. pap. 16.95 (*0-89815-234-8*) Ten Speed Pr.

Tropic Lightning. Henry C. Toll. (Illus.). 136p. 1987. pap. 7.95 (*0-89745-081-7*) Sunflower U Pr.

Tropic of Baseball: Baseball in the Dominican Republic. Rob Ruck. (Illus.). 232p. 1993. pap. 10.95 (*0-88184-876-X*) Carroll & Graf.

Tropic of Baseball: Baseball in the Dominican Republic. Rob Ruck. (Baseball & American Society Ser.). (Illus.). 175p. 1991. lib. bdg. 37.50 (*0-88736-707-0*) Mecklermedia.

Tropic of Cancer. Henry Miller. 288p. (Orig.). 1995. mass mkt. 5.95 (*0-451-52605-8*, Sig) NAL-Dutton.

Tropic of Cancer. Henry Miller. LC 61-15597. 318p. 1987. pap. 11.95 (*0-8021-3178-6*, Grove) Grove-Atltic.

Tropic of Cancer. Henry Miller. LC 82-42868. 1983. 18.00 (*0-394-60435-0*, Modern Lib) Random.

Tropic of Cancer. Henry Miller. 1987. pap. 7.95 (*0-394-62375-4*) Random.

Tropic of Capricorn. Henry Miller. LC 86-33510. 348p. 1987. pap. 11.95 (*0-8021-5182-5*, Grove) Grove-Atltic.

Tropic of Capricorn. Henry Miller. 1987. pap. 7.95 (*0-394-62379-7*) Random.

Tropic of Fear. Carolyn Keene. Ed. by Anne Greenberg. (Nancy Drew & Hardy Boys Supermystery Ser.). 224p. (Orig.). (YA). (gr. 7 up). 1992. mass mkt. 3.99 (*0-671-73126-2*, Archway) PB.

Tropic of Lust. 224p. 1992. pap. 4.50 (*0-88184-830-1*) Carroll & Graf.

***Tropic of Lust.** 4.50 (*0-7867-0830-1*) Carroll & Graf.

***Tropic of Orange.** Karen T. Yamashita. LC 97-15991. 320p. (Orig.). 1997. pap. 14.95 (*1-56689-064-0*) Coffee Hse.

Tropic of Venus. Richard Manton. (Victorian Era Ser.). (Orig.). 1990. mass mkt. 5.95 (*0-929654-69-2*, 86) Blue Moon Bks.

Tropic of Virgo. Tomas W. Gatus. Ed. by Mary E. O'Dell. 62p. (Orig.). 1993. pap. 7.95 (*0-9623666-2-5*) Green Rvr Writers.

Tropic Orchid Nights. Illus. by A. Grimm-Richardson. (Orig.). 1987. pap. 10.00 (*0-937953-06-7*) Tiptoe Lit Serv.

Tropic Regulation of the Basal Ganglia: Focus on Dopamine Neurons. Ed. by K. Fuxe et al. LC 93-34086. (Wenner-Gren International Ser.). 628p. 1994. 196.50 (*0-08-042276-4*, Ed Skills Dallas) Elsevier.

Tropica: Color Cyclopedia of Exotic Plants & Trees. 4th ed. Alfred B. Graf. LC 77-82461. (Illus.). 1154p. (C). 1992. reprint ed. 165.00 (*0-911266-24-0*) Roehrs.

Tropical Acacias in East Asia & the Pacific. Kamis B. Awang & David A. Taylor. (Report on COGREDA Ser.). 106p. (Orig.). 1992. pap. 12.50 (*0-933595-71-9*) Winrock Intl.

Tropical Africa. Tony Binns. LC 93-35489. (Introductions to Development Ser.). (Illus.). 208p. (C). 1993. pap. 14.95 (*0-415-04801-X*, B2449) Routledge.

***Tropical African Development: Geographical Perspectives.** M. B. Gleave. 1992. pap. 38.95 (*0-582-30147-5*, Pub. by Longman UK) Longman.

***Tropical Africa's Emergence As a Banana Supplier in the Inter-War Period.** John Houtkamp. (ASC Research Ser.). 160p. 1996. pap. 38.95 (*1-85972-578-3*, Pub. by Ashgate UK) Ashgate Pub Co.

Tropical Agricultural Hydrology: Watershed Management & Land Use. Ed. by E. W. Russell & Rattan Lal. LC 80-41590. (Wiley-Interscience Publications). 518p. reprint ed. pap. 147.70 (*0-7837-3226-0*, 2043243) Bks Demand.

Tropical Agricultural Hydrology Watershed Management & Land Use. Ed. by Rattan Lal. 482p. 1990. 250.00 (*81-7089-120-5*, Pub. by Intl Bk Distr II) St Mut.

Tropical Alpine Environments: Plant Form & Function. P. W. Rundel et al. (Illus.). 370p. (C). 1994. text ed. 105.00 (*0-521-42089-X*) Cambridge U Pr.

Tropical America. Isaac N. Ford. LC 70-168119. reprint ed. 45.00 (*0-404-02512-9*) AMS Pr.

Tropical & Geographical Medicine. 2nd ed. Ed. by Kenneth S. Warren & Adel A. Mahmoud. (Illus.). 1280p. 1989. text ed. 150.00 (*0-07-068328-X*) McGraw-Hill HPD.

Tropical & Geographical Medicine: Companion Handbook. 2nd ed. Ed. by Adel A. F. Mahmoud. (Companion Handbook Ser.). (Illus.). 464p. 1993. pap. text ed. 29.50 (*0-07-039625-6*) McGraw-Hill HPD.

Tropical & Summer Uniforms of the German Army & Airforce in W. W. II. Jose Figueroa. (Illus.). 128p. (Orig.). 1993. 11.95 (*0-9637201-0-4*) Figueroa Creat.

Tropical Animal Health. 2nd ed. Horst S. Seifert. 548p. (C). 1996. lib. bdg. 180.00 (*0-7923-3821-9*) Kluwer Ac.

Tropical Appetites: Fine Cooking & Dining in Tanzania. Arlin E. Greene & Susan S. Hunter. (Appetites Ser.: Vol. 1). (Illus.). 172p. (Orig.). 1995. pap. 10.00 (*9976-89-084-2*) Gecko Pubng.

Tropical Aquarium Fish: Comprehensive Edition. Chris Andrews & Ulrich Baensch. (Illus.). 280p. 1991. 23.95 (*3-89356-131-5*, 16002) Tetra Pr.

Tropical Archaeobotany: Applications & New Developments. Ed. by Jon G. Hather. LC 93-39367. (One World Archaeology Ser.). (Illus.). 296p. (C). 1994. text ed. 69.95 (*0-415-09784-3*, B4701) Routledge.

Tropical Architecture in the Dry & Humid Zones. 2nd ed. Maxwell E. Fry & Jane B. Drew. LC 80-20394. 264p. 1982. lib. bdg. 30.50 (*0-89874-126-2*) Krieger.

***Tropical Asian Interiors.** Luca I. Tettoni. 1997. 39.95 (*962-593-136-8*) Periplus.

Tropical Atlantic in the Age of Slave Trade. Philip D. Curtin. Ed. by Michael Adas. (Essays on Global & Comparative History Ser.). 60p. 1991. pap. 6.00 (*0-87229-048-4*) Am Hist Assn.

Tropical Belle Epoque: Elite Culture & Society in Turn-of-the-Century Rio de Janeiro. Jeffrey D. Needell. (Cambridge Latin American Studies: No. 62). (Illus.). 300p. 1988. text ed. 80.00 (*0-521-33374-1*) Cambridge U Pr.

Tropical Blossoms of the Caribbean. Dorothy Hargreaves & Bob Hargreaves. LC 60-15513. (Illus.). 1960. pap. 4.95 (*0-910690-03-0*) Ross-Hargreaves.

Tropical Blossoms of the Pacific. Dorothy Hargreaves & Bob Hargreaves. LC 72-113701. (Illus.). 1970. pap. 4.95 (*0-910690-08-1*) Ross-Hargreaves.

Tropical Botanic Gardens: Their Role in Conservation & Development. Ed. by Vernon H. Heywood & P. S. Jackson. (Illus.). 375p. 1991. text ed. 79.00 (*0-12-346850-7*) Acad Pr.

Tropical Botany. Ed. by Kai Larsen & Lauritz B. Holm-Nielson. LC 79-41003. 1980. text ed. 99.00 (*0-12-437350-X*) Acad Pr.

Tropical Casual. (World Textile Collection Ser.: No. 10). (Illus.). 84p. 1993. pap. 39.95 (*4-7636-8104-4*, Pub. by Kyoto Shoin JA) Bks Nippan.

Tropical Chills. Ed. by Timothy R. Sullivan. 1988. mass mkt. 3.95 (*0-380-75500-9*) Avon.

Tropical Circle. Alioum Fantoure. Ed. by A. James Arnold & Kandioura Drame. Tr. by Dorothy S. Blair from FRE. LC 88-26166. (CARAF Bks.). 266p. 1989. text ed. 30.00 (*0-8139-1208-3*); pap. text ed. 15.00 (*0-8139-1209-1*) U Pr of Va.

***Tropical Classical: Essays from Several Directions.** Pico Iyer. LC 96-38578. 1997. 25.00 (*0-679-45432-2*, Vin) Random.

Tropical Climatology: An Introduction to the Climate of the Low Latitudes. 2nd ed. Simon Nieuwolt & Glenn R. Mcgregor. Date not set. text ed. 85.00 (*0-471-96610-X*) Wiley.

Tropical Climatology: An Introduction to the Climate of the Low Latitudes. 2nd ed. Simon Nieuwolt & Glenn R. Mcgregor. Date not set. pap. text ed. 35.00 (*0-471-96611-8*) Wiley.

Tropical Climatology: An Introduction to the Climates of the Low Latitudes. Simon Nieuwolt. LC 76-13454. 217p. reprint ed. pap. 61.90 (*0-318-34859-4*, 2031024) Bks Demand.

Tropical Cocktails. T. Murphy. 233p. 6.95 (*0-507-46051-0*, 214) Am Bartenders.

***Tropical Commodities & Their Markets.** Peter Robbins. 1997. 60.00 (*0-7494-1627-0*) Stylus Pub VA.

Tropical Crops: Monocotyledons. J. W. Purseglove. 618p. 1986. pap. text ed. 76.95 (*0-470-20568-7*) Halsted Pr.

Tropical Cyclones: Their Evolution, Structure & Effects. Richard A. Anthes. (Meteorological Monograph: Vol. 19, No. 41). (Illus.). 208p. 1982. 40.00 (*0-933876-54-8*) Am Meteorological.

Tropical Cyclones of the Pacific. Stephen S. Visher. (BMB Ser.). 1974. reprint ed. 25.00 (*0-527-02123-7*) Periodicals Srv.

Tropical Deco: The Architecture & Design of Old Miami Beach. Laura Cerwinske. LC 80-51596. (Illus.). 96p. (Orig.). 1991. pap. 17.95 (*0-8478-0345-7*) Rizzoli Intl.

Tropical Deforestation. C. J. Jepma. 1995. 28.00 (*1-85383-238-3*, Pub. by Erthscan Pubns UK) Island Pr.

Tropical Deforestation. John Terborgh. Ed. by J. J. Head. (Carolina Biology Readers Ser.). (Illus.). 16p. (Orig.). (YA). (gr. 10 up). 1992. pap. text ed. 2.75 (*0-89278-161-0*, 45-9761) Carolina Biological.

Tropical Deforestation: Small Farmers & Land Clearing in the Ecuadorian Amazon. Thomas K. Rudel & Bruce Horowitz. LC 92-44356. (Cases & Methods in Biological Diversity Ser.). 1993. pap. 25.00 (*0-231-08045-X*) Col U Pr.

Tropical Deforestation: Small Farmers & Land Clearing in the Ecuadorian Amazon. Thomas K. Rudel & Bruce Horowitz. LC 92-44356. (Cases & Methods in Biological Diversity Ser.). 1993. write for info. (*0-231-08044-1*) Col U Pr.

Tropical Deforestation: The Human Dimension. Ed. by Leslie E. Sponsel et al. LC 95-47256. (Methods & Cases in Conservation Science Ser.). 1996. 49.50 (*0-231-10318-2*); pap. 19.50 (*0-231-10319-0*) Col U Pr.

Tropical Deforestation: The Tyranny of Time. Ooi J. Bee. (Orig.). 1993. 55.00 (*9971-69-184-1*, Pub. by Sgapore Univ SI) Coronet Bks.

Tropical Deforestation: The Tyranny of Time. Ooi J. Bee. 190p. (Orig.). 1994. pap. 38.50 (*9971-69-183-3*, Pub. by Sgapore Univ SI) Coronet Bks.

Tropical Deforestation & Species Extinction. T. C. Whitmore. Ed. by Jeffrey A. Sayer. (World Conservation Union (IUCN) Ser.). (Illus.). 208p. (C). (gr. 13). 1992. pap. text ed. 36.95 (*0-412-45520-X*, A7126) Chapman & Hall.

Tropical Dependency: An Outline of the Ancient History of the Western Sudan with an Account of the Modern Settlement of Northern Nigeria. Lady Lugard. 508p. reprint ed. 54.00 (*0-933121-72-5*) Black Classic.

Tropical Depression. Laurence Shames. LC 95-13879. 304p. 1996. 21.95 (*0-7868-6109-6*) Hyperion.

Tropical Depression. Laurence Shames. 368p. 1997. mass mkt. 5.99 (*0-7868-8909-8*) Hyperion.

Tropical Depressions. Elton Glaser. LC 87-30205. (Iowa Poetry Prize Ser.). 98p. 1988. pap. 10.95 (*0-87745-201-6*); text ed. 17.95 (*0-87745-200-8*) U of Iowa Pr.

*__Tropical Desserts.__ Andrew MacLauchlan. LC 97-20911. 1997. 35.00 (*0-02-861300-7*) Macmillan.

Tropical Diaspora: The Jewish Experience in Cuba. Robert M. Levine. LC 93-12542. (Illus.). 400p. (C). 1993. lib. bdg. 39.95 (*0-8130-1218-X*) U Press Fla.

Tropical Disease Research: Progress 1975-94; Highlights 1993-1994. Ed. by R. Walgate. v, 167p. (FRE.). (C). 1995. pap. text ed. 26.00 (*92-4-156179-3*, 1150427) World Health.

Tropical Disease Research: Progress 1991-1992, 11th Report. 140p. (FRE.). (C). 1993. pap. text ed. 26.00 (*92-4-156158-0*, 1150400) World Health.

Tropical Disease Research: Seventh Programme Report, January 1, 1983 - December 31, 1984. 267p. 1985. pap. 45.00 (*92-4-156085-1*, 1150234) World Health.

Tropical Diseases: Responses of Pharmaceutical Companies. Jack N. Behrman. LC 80-20164. (AEI Studies: No. 288). 80p. reprint ed. pap. 25.00 (*0-8357-4537-6*, 2037424) Bks Demand.

Tropical Diseases Research: A Global Partnership Eight Programme Report, the First Ten Years, with Highlights of the 1985-86 Biennium. 202p. 1987. pap. text ed. 45.00 (*92-4-156106-8*, 1150267) World Health.

*__Tropical Ecology.__ Pomeroy & Service. 1987. pap. text ed. write for info. (*0-582-64353-8*, Pub. by Longman UK) Longman.

Tropical Ecology & Physical Edaphology. Rattan Lal. LC 85-16906. 732p. 1987. text ed. 450.00 (*0-471-90815-0*, Wiley-Interscience) Wiley.

Tropical Ecosystems: A Synthesis of Tropical Ecology & Conservation. Ed. by Mundanthra Balakrishnan. (C). 1994. text ed. 58.00 (*81-204-0873-X*, Pub. by Oxford IBH II) S Asia.

*__Tropical Ecosystems: Systems Characteristics, Utilization Patterns & Conservation Issues: Proceedings of the International & Interdisciplinary Symposium, Saarbrucken, Germany, 15-18 June 1989.__ Ed. by W. Erdelen et al. (Illus.). 202p. 1991. pap. 59.00 (*3-8236-1183-6*, Pub. by Backhuys Pubs NE) Balogh.

Tropical Environment. Peter Purari. (Mobi Ser.). 1983. lib. bdg. 345.50 (*90-6193-104-5*) Kluwer Ac.

*__Tropical Environments: The Functioning & Management of Tropical Ecosystems.__ Martin C. Kellman & Rosanne Tackaberry. (Routledge Physical Environment Ser.). 304p. (C). 1997. pap. write for info. (*0-415-11609-0*); text ed. write for info. (*0-415-11608-2*) Routledge.

*__Tropical Estuarine Fish & Fisheries.__ S. J. Blaber. 288p. 1997. text ed. write for info. (*0-412-78500-5*, Chap & Hall NY) Chapman & Hall.

Tropical Exotics. Horace F. Clay & James C. Hubbard. LC 77-7363. (Hawaii Garden Ser.: No. 1). (Illus.). 284p. 1987. reprint ed. pap. 34.95 (*0-8248-1127-5*) UH Pr.

Tropical Field Crops. Ian MacDonald & John Low. (Illus.). 112p. 1991. pap. 13.95 (*0-237-50792-7*, Pub. by Evans Bros Ltd UK) Trafalgar.

Tropical Fish. (Illus.). 80p. 1984. pap. text ed. 6.95 (*0-86622-801-2*, PB-128) TFH Pubns.

Tropical Fish. Herbert R. Axelrod. (Illus.). 1979. 9.95 (*0-87666-510-5*, KW-020) TFH Pubns.

Tropical Fish. Bruce W. Halstead & Bonnie L. Landa. (Golden Guide Ser.). (Illus.). 160p. (YA). (ps-3). 1975. pap. 5.50 (*0-307-24361-3*, Golden Books) Western Pub.

*__Tropical Fish.__ Robert Hirschfeld. LC 97-5948. (Nature's Children Ser.). (J). 1997. write for info. (*0-7172-9077-8*) Grolier Educ.

Tropical Fish. P. Jameson. (Responsible Pet Care Ser.). (Illus.). 32p. (J). (gr. 2-5). 1989. lib. bdg. 15.94 (*0-86625-185-5*); lib. bdg. 11.95 (*0-685-58612-X*) Rourke Corp.

Tropical Fish. Neal Pronek. (Illus.). 64p. 1996. pap. 6.95 (*0-7938-0367-5*, RE618) TFH Pubns.

Tropical Fish: A Complete Introduction. Cliff W. Emmens. 1988. pap. 8.95 (*0-86622-357-6*, CO-029S) TFH Pubns.

Tropical Fish: A Complete Pet Owners Manual. Peter Stadelmann. (Barron's Pet Owner's Manuals Ser.). (Illus.). 64p. 1991. pap. 6.95 (*0-8120-4700-1*) Barron.

Tropical Fish: Color & Story Album. Malcolm Whyte. (Troubador Ser.). (Illus.). 32p. (J). (ps up). 1995. 5.95 (*0-8431-3875-0*, Troubador) Price Stern Sloan.

Tropical Fish: Look & Learn. Mary E. Sweeney. (Illus.). 64p. 1993. 9.95 (*0-7938-0071-4*, KD002) TFH Pubns.

Tropical Fish: The Rising Generation. Wolfgang Sommer. 224p. 1993. 23.95 (*0-86622-579-X*, TT029) TFH Pubns.

*__Tropical Fish: Tropical Fish.__ Illus. by Ruth Heller. (Designs for Coloring Ser.). 64p. (Orig.). (J). 1997. pap. 3.95 (*0-448-41565-8*, G&D) Putnam Pub Group.

Tropical Fish As a Hobby. Mary E. Sweeney. (Illus.). 96p. 1993. 8.95 (*0-86622-520-X*, TT017) TFH Pubns.

Tropical Fish As a New Pet. Herbert R. Axelrod. (Illus.). 64p. 1991. pap. 6.95 (*0-86622-532-3*, TU-020) TFH Pubns.

Tropical Fish Charted Designs. Barbara Christopher. LC 92-24968. (Needlework Ser.). 1992. write for info. (*0-486-27341-5*) Dover.

Tropical Fish-Coloring Book. Stefen Bernath. (J). pap. 2.95 (*0-486-23620-X*) Dover.

Tropical Fish for Those Who Care. Herbert R. Axelrod. (Illus.). 32p. 1994. pap. 4.95 (*0-7938-1379-4*, B102) TFH Pubns.

Tropical Fish Stained Glass Coloring Book. John Green. (Illus.). (J). (gr. k-3). 1991. pap. 1.00 (*0-486-26314-2*) Dover.

Tropical Fish Stickers. Steven J. Petruccio. (Illus.). (J). (gr. k-3). 1994. pap. 1.00 (*0-486-28110-8*) Dover.

Tropical Fishery Products. K. Gopakumar. (Illus.). 250p. 1996. lib. bdg. 70.00 (*1-886106-55-X*) Science Pubs.

Tropical Forages: Their Role in Sustainable Agriculture. L. R. Humphreys. LC 94-25797. 400p. 1995. text ed. 165.00 (*0-470-23433-4*) Wiley.

*__Tropical Forest.__ Renato Massa. LC 96-28547. (Deep Green Planet Ser.). (J). 1997. lib. bdg. 24.26 (*0-8172-4311-9*) Raintree Steck-V.

Tropical Forest & Its Environment. Kenneth A. Longman & I. J. Jenik. LC 73-85681. (Illus.). 160p. (Orig.). 1974. pap. text ed. 11.95 (*0-582-44045-9*) Longman.

*__Tropical Forest & Its Environment.__ 2nd ed. K. A. Longman. (C). 1987. text ed. 79.50 (*0-582-44678-3*, Pub. by Longman UK) Longman.

Tropical Forest Ecosystem Soil Fauna in Sub Tropics. V. K. Bahuguna. (C). 1991. text ed. 175.00 (*0-89771-543-8*, Pub. by Intl Bk Distr II) St Mut.

Tropical Forest Ecosystem Soil Fauna in Sub-Tropics. V. K. Bahuguna. 110p. 1992. 110.00 (*81-7089-138-8*, Pub. by Intl Bk Distr II) St Mut.

Tropical Forest Ecosystems: A State of Knowledge Report. UNESCO UNEP/F.A.O. Staff. 683p. (C). 1990. pap. 750.00 (*81-7089-126-4*, Pub. by Intl Bk Distr II) St Mut.

Tropical Forest Expeditions. Jenny Clive. (C). 1993. 26.00 (*0-907649-63-7*, Pub. by Expedit Advisory Centre UK) St Mut.

Tropical Forest Mammals. Elaine Landau. LC 96-3890. (True Bk.). (Illus.). 48p. (J). 1996. lib. bdg. 19.00 (*0-516-20044-5*) Childrens.

*__Tropical Forest Mammals.__ Elaine Landau. (True Bks.). 48p. (J). 1997. pap. 6.95 (*0-516-26116-9*) Childrens.

Tropical Forest Plant Ecophysiology. Ed. by Stephen S. Mulkey et al. LC 95-6750. 672p. (gr. 13). 1996. text ed. 89.95 (*0-412-03571-5*) Chapman & Hall.

Tropical Forest Produce. D. N. Tewari. 673p. 1994. pap. 375.00 (*81-7089-182-5*, Pub. by Intl Bk Distr II) St Mut.

*__Tropical Forest Remnants: Ecology, Management & Conservation of Fragmented Communities.__ Willaim F. Laurance & Richard O. Bierregaard. LC 96-38038. 1996. lib. bdg. 105.00 (*0-226-46898-4*) U Ch Pr.

*__Tropical Forest Remnants: Ecology, Management & Conservation of Fragmented Communities.__ William F. Laurance & Richard O. Bierregaard. LC 96-38038. 1996. pap. text ed. 38.00 (*0-226-46899-2*) U Ch Pr.

*__Tropical Forest Resources.__ 117p. 1983. 14.00 (*92-5-101187-7*, Pub. by FAO IT) Bernan Associates.

Tropical Forested Watersheds: Hydrologic & Soils Response to Major Uses or Conservations Report. L. S. Hamilton. 168p. 1988. 100.00 (*81-7089-056-X*, Pub. by Intl Bk Distr II) St Mut.

*__Tropical Forestry.__ Redhead. 1993. pap. text ed. write for info. (*0-582-77522-1*, Pub. by Longman UK) Longman.

Tropical Forestry Handbook, 2 vols. Ed. by Laslo Pancel. LC 93-34006. (Illus.). 1900p. 1993. Set. 558.95 (*0-387-56420-9*) Spr-Verlag.

Tropical Forestry in India. D. N. Tewari. 387p. 1992. pap. 425.00 (*81-7089-187-6*, Pub. by Intl Bk Distr II) St Mut.

Tropical Forestry Products of India. D. N. Tewari. 400p. 1992. pap. 425.00 (*0-614-09770-3*, Pub. by Intl Bk Distr II) St Mut.

Tropical Forests. J. Borota. (Developments in Agricultural & Managed Forest Ecology Ser.: Vol. 22). 274p. 1991. 158.25 (*0-444-98768-1*) Elsevier.

Tropical Forests: Botanical Dynamics, Speciation & Diversity. Ed. by Lauritz B. Holm-Nielson et al. 350p. 1989. text ed. 69.00 (*0-12-353550-6*) Acad Pr.

Tropical Forests: Botanical Dynamics, Speciation, & Diversity - Abstracts from the AAU 25th Anniversary Symposium. Ed. by Flemming Skov & Anders Barfod. (AAU Reports: No. 18). 46p. (C). 1988. pap. 12.95 (*87-87600-26-9*, Pub. by Aarhus Univ Pr DK) David Brown.

Tropical Forests: Management & Ecology. Ed. by Ariel E. Lugo & Carol Lowe. LC 94-23823. (Ecological Studies: Vol. 112). 1995. 107.95 (*0-387-94320-X*) Spr-Verlag.

Tropical Forests & Their Crops. Nigel J. Smith et al. LC 92-52772. (Comstock Bk.). (Illus.). 584p. (C). 1992. 75.00 (*0-8014-2771-1*, Comstock Pub); pap. 29.95 (*0-8014-8058-2*, Comstock Pub) Cornell U Pr.

Tropical Forests in Transition: Ecology of Natural & Anthropogenic Disturbance Processes. Ed. by J. G. Goldammer. (Advances in Life Sciences Ser.). 280p. 1992. 99.00 (*0-8176-2601-8*) Spr-Verlag.

Tropical Forests, People & Food: Biocultural Interactions & Applications to Development. Ed. by C. M. Hladik et al. LC 93-28303. (Man & the Biosphere Ser.: Vol. 13). 1993. 105.00 (*92-3-102879-0*, U8728) Bernan Associates.

Tropical Forests, People & Food: Biocultural Interactions & Applications to Development. Ed. by C. M. Hladik et al. (Man & the Biosphere Ser.: Vol. 13). (Illus.). 852p. 1993. 85.00 (*1-85070-380-9*) Prthnon Pub.

Tropical Forrage Lagumes. P. J. Skerman & F.A.O. Staff. 609p. 1987. pap. 325.00 (*81-7089-088-8*, Pub. by Intl Bk Distr II) St Mut.

Tropical Freeze. James W. Hall. 320p. 1991. mass mkt. 6.50 (*0-446-36062-7*) Warner Bks.

Tropical Freshwater Wetlands: A Guide to Current Knowledge & Sustainable Management. Henri Roggeri. (Developments in Hydrobiology Ser.: Vol. 112). 1995. lib. bdg. 134.00 (*0-7923-3785-9*) Kluwer Ac.

Tropical Fruit Cookbook. Charlene K. Smoyer. LC 92-44835. (Illus.). 196p. 1993. 19.95 (*0-8248-1441-X*, Kolowalu Bk) UH Pr.

*__Tropical Fruits.__ 2nd ed. Samson. 1986. pap. text ed. write for info. (*0-582-40409-6*, Pub. by Longman UK) Longman.

Tropical Fruits. 2nd ed. J. A. Samson. (Tropical Agriculture Ser.). 336p. 1986. text ed. 115.00 (*0-470-20679-9*) Halsted Pr.

Tropical Fugue. A. T. Allan. Ed. by Richard S. Danbury, III. 192p. (Orig.). 1995. pap. 8.95 (*0-89754-103-0*) Dan River Pr.

Tropical Gangsters: One Man's Experiences with Development & Decadence in Deepest Africa. Robert Klitgaard. LC 90-80243. 304p. 1991. pap. 16.00 (*0-465-08760-4*) Basic.

Tropical Garden. rev. ed. William Warren. LC 96-60183. (Illus.). 224p. 1997. 55.00 (*0-500-01733-6*) Thames Hudson.

Tropical Gardening. David Bar-Zvi & Kathy Sammis. (American Garden Guides Ser.). 25.00p. 1996. pap. 25.00 (*0-679-75863-1*) Pantheon.

Tropical Gardens. (Flora - In Focus Ser.). 1996. 12.98 (*0-8317-6123-7*) Smithmark.

Tropical Gardens. Leslie Gibbs. 36p. 1993. pap. 13.95 (*0-935133-49-6*) CKE Pubns.

Tropical Geomorphology: A Morphogenetic Study of Rajasthan. H. S. Sharma. 1987. 50.00 (*81-7022-041-6*, Pub. by Concept II) S Asia.

*__Tropical Grasses.__ (Plant Production & Protection Papers: No. 23). 832p. 1990. 150.00 (*92-5-101128-1*, F0281, Pub. by FAO IT) Bernan Associates.

Tropical Grasses. P. J. Skerman & F. Riveros. (C). 1991. 750.00 (*81-7233-033-2*, Pub. by Scientific Pubs II) St Mut.

Tropical Grasses of Southeast Asia: Excluding Bamboos. M. Lazarides. 350p. 1980. lib. bdg. 50.00 (*3-7682-1255-6*) Lubrecht & Cramer.

Tropical Headgear of the German Vol. 2: Wehrmacht in W.W. II. Jose Figueroa. Ed. by Don Kochi. (Illus.). 144p. (Orig.). 1995. 11.95 (*0-9637201-1-2*) Figueroa Creat.

*__Tropical Heat.__ Suzanne Dye. 1997. mass mkt. 1.78 (*0-8217-5772-5*) Kensgtn Pub Corp.

Tropical Heat. John Lutz. 256p. 1987. pap. 3.95 (*0-380-70309-2*) Avon.

*__Tropical Herps.__ John Coborn. (Illus.). 160p. 22.95 (*0-7938-0135-4*, LR-110) TFH Pubns.

Tropical Home Gardens. 255p. 1990. 30.00 (*92-808-0732-3*, E.90.III.A.7) UN.

Tropical Hydrology & Caribbean Water Resources: Proceedings of the International Symposium on Tropical Hydrology & Fourth Caribbean Islands Water Resources Congress. International Symposium on Tropical Hydrology Staff. Ed. by J. Hari Krishna et al. LC 90-81063. (American Water Resources Association Technical Publication Ser.: No. TPS-90-2). (Illus.). 586p. reprint ed. pap. 167.10 (*0-7837-1095-X*, 2041627) Bks Demand.

*__Tropical Lands.__ Senior. Date not set. pap. text ed. write for info. (*0-582-02540-0*, Pub. by Longman UK) Longman.

Tropical Legumes in Animal Nutrition. Ed. by J. P. D'Mello & C. Devendra. 352p. 1995. 105.00 (*0-85198-926-8*) CAB Intl.

Tropical Librarianship. Wilfred J. Plumbe. LC 87-19984. 334p. 1987. 37.50 (*0-8108-2057-9*) Scarecrow.

Tropical Lichens: Their Systematics, Conservation, & Ecology. Ed. by D. J. Galloway. (Systematics Association Special Volume Ser.: Vol. 43). (Illus.). 224p. 1991. 125.00 (*0-19-857720-6*) OUP.

Tropical Mangrove Ecosystems. Ed. by Daniel Alongi & Alistair Robertson. (Coastal & Estuarine Studies: Vol. 41). 1993. 37.00 (*0-87590-255-3*) Am Geophysical.

Tropical Maple Leaf: Indian Perspective in Canadian Literature. Ed. by John L. Hill & Uttam Bhoite. 1989. 20.00 (*0-685-46919-0*, Pub. by Manohar II) S Asia.

Tropical Marine Fish Survival Manual: A Comprehensive Family-by-Family Guide to Keeping Tropical Marine Aquarium Fish. Gordon Kay. LC 95-21172. (Illus.). 160p. 1995. pap. 16.95 (*0-8120-9372-0*) Barron.

Tropical Marine Fishes of Southern Florida & the Bahama Islands. Warren Zeiller. (Illus.). 127p. 1975. 50.00 (*0-8386-7914-5*) Fairleigh Dickinson.

Tropical Marine Life. Dieter Eichler. 224p. (C). 1990. 125.00 (*3-405-14116-8*, Pub. by IMMEL Pubng UK) St Mut.

Tropical Marine Life. Dieter Eichler. 224p. 1995. pap. 48.00 (*1-898162-10-7*, Pub. by IMMEL Pubng UK) St Mut.

Tropical Medicine: A Clinical Text. Kevin M. Cahill & William O'Brien. 272p. 1990. pap. 55.00 (*0-433-00430-4*) Buttrwrth-Heinemann.

Tropical Montane Cloud Forests. Ed. by Lawrence S. Hamilton et al. LC 94-12683. (Ecological Studies). 1994. 107.95 (*0-387-94323-4*) Spr-Verlag.

*__Tropical Multiculturalism: A Comparative History of Race in Brazilian Cinema & Culture.__ Robert Stam. LC 97-20233. 392p. 1997. text ed. 59.95 (*0-8223-2048-7*); pap. text ed. 19.95 (*0-8223-2035-5*) Duke.

Tropical Mycology. Ed. by K. K. Janardhanan et al. 350p. 1996. lib. bdg. 89.00 (*1-886106-63-0*) Science Pubs.

Tropical Nature: Life & Death in the Rain Forests of Central & South America. Adrian Forsyth & Ken Miyata. (Illus.). 248p. 1987. pap. 13.00 (*0-684-18710-8*) S&S Trade.

Tropical Nature, & Other Essays. Alfred R. Wallace. LC 72-1663. reprint ed. 52.50 (*0-404-08187-8*) AMS Pr.

Tropical Nematology. Society of Nematologists Staff. Ed. by Grover C. Smart, Jr. & V. G. Perry. LC 68-28872. (Illus.). 177p. reprint ed. pap. 50.50 (*0-8357-6804-X*, 2035487) Bks Demand.

Tropical Neurology. Shakir. 1995. text ed. 79.00 (*0-7020-1922-4*) Saunders.

Tropical Night Falling. Manuel Puig. Tr. by Suzanne J. Levine. 192p. 1993. pap. 8.95 (*0-393-30908-8*) Norton.

Tropical Pacific Invertebrates: A Field Guide to Marine Invertebrates Occurring on Tropical Pacific Ocean Coral Reefs, Seagrass Beds, & Mangroves. Patrick L. Colin & Charles Arneson. (Illus.). 304p. (Orig.). 1995. pap. text ed. 59.95 (*0-9645625-0-2*) Coral Reef CA.

*__Tropical Pacific Island Environments.__ Chirstopher S. Lobban & Maria Schefter. (Illus.). 450p. (C). 1997. 70.00 (*1-881629-04-X*) Univ Guam Pr.

*__Tropical Pacific Island Environments.__ Chirstopher S. Lobban & Maria Schefter. (Illus.). 450p. (C). 1997. pap. 50.00 (*1-881629-05-8*) Univ Guam Pr.

Tropical Paradise, Gulf Coast Florida. D. C. Kip. (Illus.). 26p. (Orig.). 1985. pap. 5.00 (*0-9614549-1-1*) Maedon.

Tropical Pasture & Fodder Plants: Grasses & Legumes. A. V. Bogden. LC 76-14977. (Tropical Agriculture Ser.). 489p. reprint ed. pap. 139.40 (*0-317-29850-X*, 2019606) Bks Demand.

Tropical Pasture Utilisation. L. R. Humphreys. (Illus.). 227p. (C). 1991. text ed. 90.00 (*0-521-38030-8*) Cambridge U Pr.

Tropical Pathology. 2nd ed. Gerhard Seifert. (Spezielle Pathologische Anatomie Ser.: Vol. 8). (Illus.). 1104p. 1995. 767.00 (*0-387-57673-8*) Spr-Verlag.

Tropical Pathology. 2nd ed. Gerhard Seifert. (Illus.). 1104p. 1996. 698.00 (*3-540-59391-8*) Spr-Verlag.

Tropical Paths: Essays on Modern Brazilian Literature. Ed. by Randal Johnson. LC 91-45265. (Latin American Studies: Vol. 2). 248p. 1992. text ed. 40.00 (*0-8153-0780-2*, H#1555) Garland.

Tropical Pests & Uninvited Guests: Survival Handbook, Vol. I. L. King Tadashi, Jr. 24p. 1994. pap. 6.95 (*0-9639951-0-3*) Trop Pests.

Tropical Plant Biology. Margaret Steenfoft. (C). 1988. pap. 18.50 (*81-224-0066-3*) S Asia.

Tropical Plant Diseases. Ed. by H. David Thurston. 208p. (C). 1989. 135.00 (*81-85046-82-4*, Pub. by Scientific UK) St Mut.

Tropical Plant Diseases. H. David Thurston. LC 84-81534. (Illus.). 208p. 1995. reprint ed. pap. 28.00 (*0-89054-063-2*) Am Phytopathol Soc.

*__Tropical Plant Science.__ Berrie. 1988. pap. text ed. write for info. (*0-582-64705-3*, Pub. by Longman UK) Longman.

Tropical Planting & Gardening. H. S. Barlow. 1994. pap. 125.00 (*81-7233-095-2*, Pub. by Scientific Pubs II) St Mut.

*__Tropical Plants: For Home & Garden.__ William Warren. LC 97-60248. (Illus.). 200p. 1997. 50.00 (*0-500-01795-6*) Thames Hudson.

Tropical Poems from Ghana. Mark D. Hayford. 1983. 20.00 (*0-946270-00-7*, Pub. by Pentland Pr UK) St Mut.

Tropical Polytpores. W. A. Murrill. 1973. reprint ed. 21.00 (*3-7682-0914-8*) Lubrecht & Cramer.

Tropical Products Transport Handbook: The Maintenance of Quality of Fruits, Plants & Flowers During Transportation. 1991. lib. bdg. 79.95 (*0-8490-4395-6*) Gordon Pr.

Tropical Provenance & Progeny Research & International Cooperation. J. Burley & G. Nikles. 1973. 100.00 (*0-85074-022-3*) St Mut.

Tropical Pulses. J. Smartt. LC 76-361820. (Tropical Agriculture Ser.). 358p. reprint ed. pap. 102.10 (*0-317-27857-6*, 2025258) Bks Demand.

*__Tropical Punch: Quilt Designs with a Florida Flavor.__ Marilyn Dorwart. Ed. by Janet White. LC 97-12666. (Illus.). 76p. (Orig.). 1997. pap. 16.95 (*1-56477-133-4*, B250) That Patchwork.

Tropical Rain Forest. M. Jacobs. (Illus.). 300p. 1990. 65.95 (*0-387-17996-8*) Spr-Verlag.

Tropical Rain Forest. Lynn M. Stone. LC 95-46175. (J). 1996. write for info. (*0-86593-424-X*) Rourke Corp.

Tropical Rain Forest: A Study of Irradiation & Ecology at El Verde, Puerto Rico, 3 Vols. AEC Technical Information Center Staff. Ed. by Howard T. Odum & Robert F. Pigeon. LC 70-606844. 1684p. 1970. Set. pap. 49.25 (*0-87079-230-X*, TID-24270); fiche 9.00 (*0-87079-340-3*, TID-24270) DOE.

Tropical Rain Forest: An Ecological Study. 2nd ed. P. W. Richards. LC 93-49019. (Illus.). 600p. (C). 1996. pap. text ed. 49.95 (*0-521-42194-2*) Cambridge U Pr.

Tropical Rain Forest: An Ecological Study. 2nd ed. P. W. Richards. LC 93-49019. (Illus.). 600p. (C). 1996. text ed. 110.00 (*0-521-42054-7*) Cambridge U Pr.

Tropical Rain Forest Ecology. 2nd ed. D. J. Mabberley. (Tertiary Level Biology Ser.). 200p. 1991. 87.50 (*0-412-02881-6*, A6375, Blackie & Son-Chapman NY); pap. 35.00 (*0-412-02891-3*, A6379, Blackie & Son-Chapman NY) Routledge Chapman & Hall.

Tropical Rain Forest Ecosystems: Biogeographical & Ecological Studies. Ed. by Helmut Lieth & Marinus J. Werger. (Ecosystems of the World Ser.: Vol. 14B). 714p. 1989. 405.75 (*0-444-42755-4*) Elsevier.

Tropical Rain Forest Ecosystems, Part A: Structure & Function. Ed. by Frank B. Golley & Marinus J. Werger. (Ecosystems of the World Ser.: Vol. 14A). 382p. 1983. 248.25 (*0-444-41986-1*, I-488-82) Elsevier.

Tropical Rain Forest Engagement Calendar 1989. Peter Carmichael. 1988. 8.95 (*0-318-23875-6*) Basic Found.

Tropical Rain Forest Silviculture: A Research Project Report. T. J. Synnott. 1980. 65.00 (*0-85074-050-9*) St Mut.

Tropical Rain Forests & the World Atmosphere. Ghillean T. Prance. 105p. 1988. pap. 125.00 (*81-7089-057-8*, Pub. by Intl Bk Distr II) St Mut.

Tropical Rain Forests Around the World. Elaine Landau. LC 89-24810. (First Bks.). 64p. (J). (gr. 3-5). 1990. lib. bdg. 21.00 (*0-531-10896-1*) Watts.

Tropical Rain Forests Around the World. Elaine Landau. (First Bks.). (Illus.). 64p. (J). (gr. 5-8). 1991. pap. 6.95 (*0-531-15600-1*) Watts.

***Tropical Rain Forests of Southeast Asia : A Forest Ecologist's View.** Isamu Yamada. LC 97-22345. (Monographs of the Center for Southeast Asia Studies, Kyoto University). 1998. write for info. (*0-8248-1936-5*); pap. write for info. (*0-8248-1937-3*) UH Pr.

Tropical Rain Forests of West Africa: Their Biology, Utilization, Destruction & Conservation. Claude Martin. 235p. 1991. 19.50 (*0-8176-2380-9*) Birkhauser.

Tropical Rain over My Heart. Irene Goh. 1995. 15.95 (*0-533-11374-1*) Vantage.

Tropical Rainfall Measurements: An International Symposium Proceedings. Ed. by John S. Theon & Nobuyoshi Fugono. LC 88-32080. 528p. 1988. 79.00 (*0-937194-14-X*) A Deepak Pub.

Tropical Rainforest. Arnold Newman. (Illus.). 256p. 1990. 45.00 (*0-8160-1944-4*) Facts on File.

Tropical Rainforest. Francesco Petretti. (Illus.). 144p. 1995. 19.98 (*0-8317-8683-3*) Smithmark.

Tropical Rainforest. April P. Sayre. (Exploring Earth's Biomes Ser.). (Illus.). 64p. (J). (gr. 5-8). 1994. lib. bdg. 15.98 (*0-8050-2826-9*) TFC Bks NY.

Tropical Rainforest: Nature of Biodiversity in Borneo at Belalong, Brunei. Earl of Cranbrook & David S. Edwards. (Illus.). 408p. 1995. pap. 27.50 (*981-00-5531-5*) Heian Intl.

Tropical Rainforest Letters. Rick W. Bizzoco. LC 93-74549. 104p. (Orig.). 1994. pap. text ed. 6.95 (*1-884562-00-0*) CA Trader.

Tropical Rainforest Research: Current Issues. Ed. by D. S. Edwards et al. (Monographiae Biologicae: Vol. 74). 1996. lib. bdg. 214.50 (*0-7923-4038-8*) Kluwer Ac.

***Tropical Rainforests.** (Ladybird Explorer Plus Ser.). (J). (gr. 4 up). 1997. 9.99 (*0-614-28834-7*, Ladybrd) Penguin.

Tropical Rainforests. Debbie DePauw. (Illus.). 48p. (J). (gr. 3-6). 1994. pap. text ed. 5.95 (*1-55799-276-2*, EMC 283) Evan-Moor Corp.

Tropical Rainforests. Emilie U. Lepthien. LC 93-3408. (New True Bks.). (Illus.). 48p. (J). (gr. k-4). 1993. pap. 5.50 (*0-516-41198-5*); lib. bdg. 19.00 (*0-516-01198-7*) Childrens.

Tropical Rainforests. Chris C. Park. LC 92-5659. (Illus.). 208p. (C). 1992. pap. 16.95 (*0-415-06239-X*, A7416) Routledge.

Tropical Rainforests. rev. ed. Jean Hamilton. Ed. by Vicki Leon. LC 94-31821. (Close up: A Focus on Nature Ser.). (Illus.). 48p. (YA). (gr. 5 up). 1994. pap. 7.95 (*0-382-24869-4*); lib. bdg. 14.95 (*0-382-24868-6*) Silver Burdett Pr.

Tropical Rainforests: Diversity & Conservation. Ed. by Frank Almeda & Catherine M. Pringle. LC 88-70979. (Memoirs of the California Academy of Sciences Ser.: No. 12). (Illus.). 1988. 30.00 (*0-940228-19-X*) Calif Acad Sci.

Tropical Rainforests: Latin American Nature & Society in Transition. Ed. by Susan E. Place et al. LC 93-4335. (Jaguar Books on Latin America: No. 2). (Illus.). 229p. (C). 1993. text ed. 40.00 (*0-8420-2423-9*) Scholarly Res Inc.

***Tropical Rainforests: The Human Impact.** Grainger. (Illus.). 448p. 1997. text ed. 103.50 (*0-412-61250-X*, Chap & Hall NY); pap. text ed. 51.50 (*0-412-61260-7*, Chap & Hall NY) Chapman & Hall.

***Tropical Reef Fishes.** Tuttle Publishing Staff. (Periplus Nature Ser.). 1997. pap. text ed. 9.95 (*962-593-152-X*, Periplus.

***Tropical Refrigeration & Air Conditioning.** Cottell & Olarewaju. 1984. pap. text ed. write for info. (*0-582-65803-9*, Pub. by Longman UK) Longman.

Tropical Renaissance: North American Artists Exploring Latin America, 1839-1879. Katherine E. Manthorne. (Illus.). 235p. 1989. text ed. 60.00 (*0-87474-714-7*); pap. text ed. 29.95 (*0-87474-715-5*) Smithsonian.

***Tropical Residual Soils.** Ed. by P. G. Fookes. (Geological Society Professional Handbooks Ser.). (Illus.). 184p. 1997. 75.00 (*1-897799-38-1*, Pub. by Geol Soc Pub Hse UK) AAPG.

Tropical Resources: Ecology & Development. Ed. by W. B. Morgan et al. (Resource Management & Optimization Ser.). 306p. 1990. pap. text ed. 44.00 (*3-7186-0514-7*) Gordon & Breach.

***Tropical Root & Tuber Crops: Production, Perspectives & Future Prospects.** 242p. 1994. 30.00 (*92-5-103461-3*, F34613, Pub. by FAO IT) Bernan Associates.

Tropical Savannas. F. Bourliere. (Ecosystems of the World Ser.: Vol. 13). 730p. 1983. 405.75 (*0-444-42035-5*) Elsevier.

Tropical Seasons: A Taste of Life in South Florida. University of Miami, Inc., Beaux Arts of the Lowe Art Museum Staff. Ed. by Linda T. Johnson & Denise F. Fernandez. (Illus.). 1992. spiral bd. write for info. (*0-9607010-4-4*) Beaux Arts.

Tropical Settings. Junior League of Ft. Myers Staff. 1995. 19.95 (*0-9613314-1-0*) Jr Leag Ft Myers.

Tropical Shipwrecks: A Vacationing Divers Guide to the Bahamas & Caribbean. Daniel Berg & Denise Berg. (Illus.). 160p. (Orig.). (YA). 1989. pap. text ed. 12.95 (*0-9616167-2-5*) Aqua Explorers.

Tropical Shorts: Short Stories Set in Brazil. D. B. Finegan et al. 268p. (Orig.). 1995. pap. write for info. (*1-57502-042-4*) Morris Pubng.

Tropical Shrubs. Horace F. Clay & James C. Hubbard. LC 77-7363. (Hawaii Garden Ser.: No. 2). (Illus.). 312p. 1987. reprint ed. pap. 34.95 (*0-8248-1128-3*) UH Pr.

Tropical Silviculture. F. A. O. Staff. (C). 1986. 365.00 (*81-7136-007-6*, Pub. by Periodical Expert II) St Mut.

Tropical Soil Biology & Fertility: A Handbook of Methods. 2nd ed. Ed. by J. M. Anderson & J. S. Ingram. 240p. (Orig.). 1993. pap. 50.00 (*0-85198-821-0*, Pub. by CAB Intntl UK) OUP.

***Tropical Soils & Fertilizer Use.** Ahn. 1992. pap. text ed. write for info. (*0-582-77507-8*, Pub. by Longman UK) Longman.

Tropical Soils of Nigeria in Engineering Practice. S. Ola. 336p. (C). 1983. text ed. 140.00 (*90-6191-264-4*, Pub. by A A Balkema NE) Ashgate Pub Co.

Tropical Soybean Improvement & Production. FAO Staff. (Plant Production & Protection Ser.: 27). 260p. 1994. pap. 65.00 (*92-5-103312-9*, F33129, Pub. by FAO IT) Bernan Associates.

***Tropical Storm.** Linda K. Silva. 1996. pap. text ed. 11.99 (*1-883061-14-8*) Rising NY.

Tropical Style. Jennifer Ash. (Illus.). 180p. 1995. 40.00 (*1-55859-489-2*) Abbeville Pr.

***Tropical Sunset: The World War II Story of a Doctor in the South Pacific.** Dorothy N. Perkins. LC 96-71073. (Illus.). 398p. 1996. 70.00 (*1-890240-00-1*) Neblett Pr.

***Tropical Surgery.** Ed. by Ricardo Cohen et al. LC 96-27741. (Vademecum Series Bks.). (Illus.). xx, 338p. 1997. 98.00 (*3-8055-6497-X*) S Karger.

Tropical Synagogues: Short Stories by Jewish Latin-American Writers. Ed. & Tr. by Ilan Stavans from POR. 252p. 1994. 34.95 (*0-8419-1340-4*) Holmes & Meier.

Tropical Synagogues: Short Stories by Jewish Latin-American Writers. Ilan Stavans. LC 97-733. (Portico Paperback Ser.). 252p. 1997. reprint ed. pap. 17.50 (*0-8419-1341-2*) Holmes & Meier.

Tropical Tastes: And Tantalizing Tales. Carol Garvin. (Illus.). 208p. 1993. 16.95 (*0-9633461-1-3*) Valiant Pr.

Tropical Techniques in Botany. B. K. Prsad. 107p. 1989. pap. 100.00 (*0-614-10280-4*) St Mut.

Tropical Tree Crops. Lawrence K. Opeke. LC 81-11501. 330p. reprint ed. pap. 94.10 (*0-685-23670-6*, 2027895) Bks Demand.

Tropical Trees: Found in the Caribbean, South America, Central America, Mexico. Dorothy Hargreaves & Bob Hargreaves. LC 65-19767. (Illus.). 1965. pap. 4.95 (*0-910690-05-7*) Ross-Hargreaves.

Tropical Trees of Hawaii. Dorothy Hargreaves & Bob Hargreaves. LC 64-23259. (Illus.). 1964. pap. 4.95 (*0-910690-02-2*) Ross-Hargreaves.

Tropical Trees of the Pacific. Dorothy Hargreaves & Bob Hargreaves. LC 72-113702. (Illus.). 1970. pap. 4.95 (*0-910690-09-X*) Ross-Hargreaves.

Tropical Tuber Crops: Problems, Prospects & Future Strategies. Ed. by G. T. Kurup et al. (Illus.). 600p. (C). 1996. lib. bdg. 109.00 (*1-886106-37-1*) Science Pubs.

Tropical Tuber Crops: Yam, Cassava, Sweet Potato, Cocoyams. I. C. Onwueme. LC 77-20932. 248p. reprint ed. 70.70 (*0-8357-9996-4*, 2051823) Bks Demand.

***Tropical Tuna: Surface Fisheries in the Indian Ocean.** 240p. 1989. 30.00 (*92-5-102490-1*, F4901, Pub. by FAO IT) Bernan Associates.

Tropical Vegetable Crops. J. C. Norman. (C). 1992. text ed. 70.00 (*0-7223-2595-9*, Pub. by A H S Ltd UK) St Mut.

***Tropical Vegetables.** Tuttle Publishing Staff. (Periplus Nature Ser.). 1997. pap. text ed. 9.95 (*962-593-149-X*) Periplus.

Tropical Veterinary Medicine: Current Issues & Perspectives. Ed. by Jim C. Williams et al. LC 92-15922. (Annals Ser.: Vol. 653). 1992. write for info. (*0-89766-727-1*); pap. write for info. (*0-89766-728-X*) NY Acad Sci.

Tropical Visions. John Millington. (Illus.). 144p. 1988. text ed. 49.95 (*0-7022-2079-5*, Pub. by Univ Queensland Pr AT) Intl Spec Bk.

Tropical Waters. Leslie Gibbs. 36p. 1994. pap. 13.95 (*0-935133-51-8*) CKE Pubns.

Tropical Zooplankton. H. J. Dumont & J. G. Tundisi. (Developments in Hydrobiology Ser.: No. 23). 344p. 1984. lib. bdg. 224.00 (*90-6193-774-4*) Kluwer Ac.

Tropicalism. Kenward Elmslie. LC 75-26459. 80p. (Orig.). 1976. pap. 5.00 (*0-915990-00-8*) Z Pr.

***Tropicalizations: Transcultural Representations of Latinidad.** Ed. by Francis R. Aparicio & Susana Chavez-Silverman. LC 97-558. (Re-Encounters with Colonialism Ser.). (Illus.). 272p. 1997. pap. 19.95 (*0-87451-817-2*); text ed. 50.00 (*0-87451-816-4*) U Pr of New Eng.

Tropicals. Gordon Courtright. LC 88-23524. (Illus.). 155p. 1988. 39.95 (*0-88192-098-3*) Timber.

Tropicals. Gordon Courtright. (Illus.). 155p. 1995. pap. 24. 95 (*0-88192-332-X*) Timber.

Tropics: Their Resources, People & Future. C. R. Enock. 1976. lib. bdg. 59.95 (*0-8490-2770-5*) Gordon Pr.

Tropics & Economic Development: A Provocative Inquiry into the Poverty of Nations. Andrew M. Kamarck. LC 76-17242. 128p. reprint ed. pap. 36.50 (*0-7837-4274-6*, 2043966) Bks Demand.

Tropics of Discourse: Essays in Cultural Criticism. Hayden White. LC 78-58297. 304p. (C). 1985. reprint ed. pap. 14.95 (*0-8018-2741-8*) Johns Hopkins.

***Tropics of History: Cuba Imagined.** Alan West. LC 96-47628. 232p. 1997. text ed. 55.00 (*0-89789-338-7*, Bergin & Garvey) Greenwood.

Troping the Triad. Wendell Metzger. (Illus.). 60p. (Orig.). 1994. 5.95 (*1-878116-24-X*) JVC Bks.

Tropique du Cancer. Henry Miller. (FRE.). 1972. pap. 13.95 (*0-7859-3997-0*) Fr & Eur.

Tropism. Photos by Ralph Gibson. (Illus.). 160p. 1987. 39. 95 (*0-89381-255-2*) Aperture.

Tropism. Photos by Ralph Gibson. (Illus.). 160p. 1989. pap. 39.95 (*0-89381-274-9*) Aperture.

Tropismes. Nathalie Sarraute. 144p. (FRE.). 1957. pap. 18. 95 (*0-7859-1509-5*, 2707301256) Fr & Eur.

Tropisms. Nathalie Sarraute. Tr. by Maria Jolas. LC 67-18211. 71p. (Orig.). 1967. pap. 5.95 (*0-8076-0412-7*) Braziller.

Tropo, Vol. I. Jon Macy. (Illus.). 132p. (Orig.). 1994. pap. 5.95 (*1-883611-04-0*) Blckbird Comics.

Tropologue. Dawn Kolokithas. 72p. 1986. 30.00 (*0-918395-07-0*); pap. 9.00 (*0-918395-04-6*) Poltroon Pr.

Troposcatter Radio Links. Giovanni Roda. (Telecommunications Engineering Library). 250p. 1988. text ed. 10.00 (*0-89006-293-5*) Artech Hse.

Tropospheric Chemistry of Ozone in the Polar Regions. Ed. by Hiromi Niki & K. H. Becker. LC 93-19454. (NATO ASI Series I: Global Environmental Change: Vol. 7). 1993. 237.95 (*0-387-56683-X*) Spr-Verlag.

Tropospheric Ozone. Ed. by Ivar S. Isaksen. (C). 1988. lib. bdg. 171.00 (*90-277-2676-0*) Kluwer Ac.

Tropospheric Ozone: Human Health & Agricultural Impacts. David J. McKee. 352p. 1993. 84.95 (*0-87371-475-X*, L475) Lewis Pubs.

Tropospheric Radiowave Propagation Beyond the Horizon. F. Ducastel & E. Sofaer. LC 65-16853. (International Series of Monographs in Electromagnective Wave: Vol. 8). 1966. 125.00 (*0-08-010974-8*, Pub. by Pergamon Repr UK) Franklin.

Troppo Man. Gerard Lee. 1990. pap. 14.95 (*0-7022-2299-2*, Pub. by Univ Queensland Pr AT) Intl Spec Bk.

Trorenija Svatago Efrema Sirina, Vol. 1. Saint John Moschus. 475p. reprint ed. 21.00 (*0-317-28899-7*); reprint ed. pap. 16.00 (*0-317-28900-4*) Holy Trinity.

Tros of Samothrace. Talbot Mundy. 1995. reprint ed. lib. bdg. 29.95 (*1-56849-584-6*) Buccaneer Bks.

***Trossachs.** (Illus.). 112p. 1997. pap. 16.95 (*0-11-495166-7*, Pub. by Statnry Ofc UK) Seven Hills Bk.

Trotsky. Dmitri Volkogonov. 1996. 30.00 (*0-02-874119-6*) Free Pr.

Trotsky: A Bibliography. Louis Sinclair. 1372p. 1989. text ed. 209.95 (*0-85967-820-2*, Pub. by Scolar Pr UK) Ashgate Pub Co.

Trotsky: A Biography. Dmitri Volkogonov. 1995. 29.95 (*0-02-933436-5*) S&S Trade.

Trotsky: Memoir & Critique. Albert Glotzer. (Illus.). 343p. 1989. 31.95 (*0-87975-544-X*) Prometheus Bks.

Trotsky: The Eternal Revolutionary. Dmitri Volkogonov. (Illus.). 608p. 1996. 32.50 (*0-684-82293-8*) Free Pr.

Trotsky As an Alternative. Ernest Mandel. 256p. (Orig.). (C). 1995. text ed. 65.00 (*1-85984-995-4*, C0500, Pub. by Vrso UK) Norton.

Trotsky As an Alternative. Ernest Mandel. LC 94-48402. 186p. (Orig.). (C). 1995. pap. text ed. 19.00 (*1-85984-085-X*, C051, Pub. by Vrso UK) Norton.

Trotsky Bibliography. 2nd rev. ed. Ed. by Wolfgang Lubitz. xxxi, 612p. 1988. lib. bdg. 82.00 (*3-598-10754-4*) K G Saur.

Trotsky for Beginners. Ali & Smith. (Documentary Comic Bks.). (Illus.). 1980. 6.95 (*0-906495-28-8*) Writers & Readers.

Trotsky Reappraisal. Ed. by Terry Brotherstone & Paul Dukes. 240p. 1992. 42.50 (*0-7486-0317-4*, Pub. by Edinburgh U Pr UK) Col U Pr.

Trotsky, Trotskyism & the Transition to Socialism. Peter Beilharz. 208p. 1987. 53.00 (*0-389-20698-9*, N 8256) B&N Imports.

***Trotskyism.** Alex Callinicos. Ed. by Frank Parkin. (Concepts in the Social Sciences Ser.). 112p. 1990. 32.50 (*0-335-15624-X*, Open Univ Pr); pap. 9.99 (*0-335-15623-1*, Open Univ Pr) Taylor & Francis.

Trotskyism. Alex Callinicos. (Concepts in Social Thought Ser.). 128p. (C). 1990. pap. text ed. 11.95 (*0-8166-1905-0*) U of Minn Pr.

Trotskyism & Maoism: Theory & Practice in France & the U. S. Belden Fields. (Illus.). 288p. 1984. 26.95 (*0-275-91813-0*, C1813, Praeger Pubs) Greenwood.

Trotskyism & Maoism: Theory & Practice in France & the United States. A. Belden Fields. 363p. Date not set. 12. 00 (*0-936756-29-2*) Autonomedia.

Trotskyism & Maoism: Theory & Practice in France & the United States. Belden Fields. LC 82-23042. 288p. 1989. text ed. 55.00 (*0-275-92035-6*, C2035, Praeger Pubs) Greenwood.

Trotskyism & the Dilemma of Socialism. Christopher Z. Hobson & Ronald D. Tabor. LC 88-3093. (Contributions in Political Science Ser.: No. 215). 568p. 1988. text ed. 85.00 (*0-313-26237-3*, HTY/, Greenwood Pr) Greenwood.

Trotskyism in the United States: Historical Essays & Reconsiderations. George Breitman et al. LC 95-37066. (Revolutionary Studies Ser.). 352p. (C). 1996. text ed. 60.00 (*0-391-03922-9*) Humanities.

Trotskyism vs. Stalinism. David North. 33p. 1987. pap. 1.50 (*0-929087-20-8*) Labor Pubns Inc.

Trotskyist Serials Bibliography: With Locations & Indices. Wolfgang Lubitz & Petra Lubitz. 475p. 1993. 128.00 (*3-598-11157-6*) K G Saur.

Trotsky's Diary in Exile, 1935. Leon Trotsky. 236p. 1976. 29.95 (*0-674-91006-0*) HUP.

Trotsky's Notebooks, 1933-1935: Writings on Lenin, Dialectics, & Evolutionism. Tr. & Anno. by Philip Pomper. LC 85-29955. 160p. 1986. text ed. 42.50 (*0-231-06302-4*) Col U Pr.

Trotsky's Run. Richard Hoyt. 320p. 1988. pap. 3.95 (*0-8125-0485-2*) Tor Bks.

Trotter: The Bounder Goes Abroad. Philip W. Helms & David L. Dettman. (Illus.). 38p. (Orig.). 1995. pap. 5.00 (*1-881799-08-5*) Am Tolkien Soc.

Trotting & Pacing Guide: 1991 Edition. United States Trotting Association Staff. 1991. pap. 12.95 (*0-8065-1243-1*, Citadel Pr) Carol Pub Group.

Trottoirs de Dakar. Bouna M. Seye. (Illus.). 1996. pap. text ed. 16.95 (*2-909571-09-2*, Pub. by Revue Noire FR) Dist Art Pubs.

Trottuar: Tpottyar. A. Lozina-Lozinskij. 65p. (Orig.). 1990. reprint ed. 12.00 (*1-878445-54-5*) Antiquary CT.

***Trotz/Dem Subjekt.** Ugo Perone. (Studies in Philosophical Theology: Vol. 12). 220p. 1997. pap. 34.75 (*90-390-0206-1*, Pub. by KOK Pharos NE) Eisenbrauns.

Trou. Jose Giovanni. 192p. (FRE.). 1973. pap. 11.95 (*0-7859-2632-1*, 207036318X) Fr & Eur.

Trou de l'Enfer. Alexandre Dumas. 364p. (FRE.). 1980. pap. 34.95 (*0-7859-5435-X*) Fr & Eur.

***Troubadour's Song.** Patricia Werner. 320p. 1997. mass mkt. 4.99 (*0-8217-5787-3*, Zebra Kensgtn) Kensgtn Pub Corp.

Troubadour Lyric: A Psychocritical Reading. R. C. Cholakian. 1990. text ed. 59.95 (*0-7190-3215-6*, Pub. by Manchester Univ Pr UK) St Martin.

***Troubadour of Knowledge.** Michel Serres. Tr. by Sheila Glaser & William Paulson. LC 97-8493. (C). 1997. pap. 15.95 (*0-472-06551-3*) U of Mich Pr.

***Troubadour of Knowledge.** Michel Serres. Tr. by Sheila Glaser & William Paulson. LC 97-8493. (C). 1997. text ed. 39.50 (*0-472-09551-X*) U of Mich Pr.

Troubadour of Words. James B. Long. (Orig.). 1996. pap. write for info. (*1-57553-170-4*) Watermrk Pr.

Troubadour Raimon Jordan, Vicomte De Saint-Antonin. Raimon Jordan. LC 80-2189. reprint ed. 25.00 (*0-404-19016-2*) AMS Pr.

Troubadours. Francis Hueffer. LC 74-24121. reprint ed. 45. 00 (*0-404-12979-X*) AMS Pr.

Troubadours: Their Loves & Their Lyrics with Remarks on Their Influence, Social & Literary. John Rutherford. 1977. lib. bdg. 59.95 (*0-8490-2771-3*) Gordon Pr.

Troubadours & Irony. Simon Gaunt. (Cambridge Studies in Medieval Literature: No. 3). 256p. (C). 1989. text ed. 69.95 (*0-521-35439-0*) Cambridge U Pr.

Troubadours at Home: Their Lives, Personalities & Songs, 2 vols. Justin Smith. 1972. Set. lib. bdg. 200.00 (*0-8490-1232-5*) Gordon Pr.

Troubadours, Leur Vies, Leurs Oeuvre, Leur Influence. Joseph Anglade. LC 78-38487. reprint ed. 49.50 (*0-404-08344-7*) AMS Pr.

Troubadour's Quest. Angela E. Hunt. LC 93-40904. (Theyn Chronicles Ser.: Vol. 2). 395p. 1994. pap. 9.99 (*0-8423-1287-0*) Tyndale.

Troubadour's Storybag: Musical Folktales of the World. Ed. & Retold by Norma J. Livo. LC 96-10188. 160p. 1996. 15.95 (*1-55591-953-7*) Fulcrum Pub.

Troubadours, Trumpeters & Troubled Makers: Lyricism, Nationalism & Hybridity in China & Its Others. Gregory Lee. LC 95-5193. (Asia-Pacific Ser.). 296p. 1996. text ed. 45.00 (*0-8223-1659-5*) Duke.

Troubadours, Trumpeters & Troubled Makers: Lyricism, Nationalism & Hybridity in China & Its Others. Gregory B. Lee. LC 95-5193. (Asia-Pacific Ser.). 296p. 1996. pap. text ed. 17.95 (*0-8223-1671-4*) Duke.

Troubairitz. Anne Waldman. (Poetry Ser.). 62p. (Orig.). 1993. pap. 10.00 (*1-880855-01-1*) Fifth Planet.

Trouble. Jane Kurtz. LC 95-39308. (Illus.). (J). 1997. 15.00 (*0-15-200219-7*) HarBrace.

Trouble. Fay Weldon. 224p. 1994. reprint ed. pap. 10.95 (*0-14-015916-9*, Penguin Bks) Viking Penguin.

Trouble - of the Northwest Territory. Katherine Greegor. LC 92-61031. (Illus.). 100p. (Orig.). (J). (gr. 3-8). 1992. pap. 5.95 (*0-9633091-7-X*) Promise Land Pubs.

Trouble & Beauty: Women Encounter Catholic Social Teaching. Maria Riley & Nancy Sylvester. 64p. (Orig.). 1991. pap. text ed. 3.95 (*0-934255-10-5*) Center Concern.

Trouble & Her Friends. Melissa Scott. 384p. 1995. 4.99 (*0-8125-2213-3*) Tor Bks.

Trouble at Bamboo Bay. Ernest Herndon. LC 96-24624. (Eric Sterling, Secret Agent Ser.: Bk. 6). 128p. (YA). (gr. 8-12). 1996. pap. 5.99 (*0-310-20730-4*) Zondervan.

Trouble at Camp Treehouse. Carolyn Keene. (Nancy Drew Ser.). (Illus.). (Orig.). (J). (gr. 2-4). 1995. pap. 3.99 (*0-671-87951-0*, Minstrel Bks) PB.

Trouble at Coyote Canyon. Franklin W. Dixon. Ed. by Ellen Winkler. (Hardy Boys Ser.: No. 119). 160p. (Orig.). (J). (gr. 3-6). 1993. pap. 3.99 (*0-671-79309-8*, Minstrel Bks) PB.

Trouble at Foxhall No. 10. Alison Hart. (Riding Academy Ser.). 132p. (J). 1995. pap. 3.99 (*0-679-87142-X*) Random.

Trouble at Home. Francine Pascal. (Sweet Valley High Ser.: No. 65). 160p. (YA). 1990. pap. 2.99 (*0-553-28518-1*) Bantam.

Trouble at Lone Spur. Roz D. Fox. 1996. mass mkt. 3.99 (*0-373-70716-9*, 1-70716-5) Harlequin Bks.

Trouble at Marsh Harbor. Susan Sharpe. 172p. (J). (gr. 3-7). 1991. pap. 4.99 (*0-14-034788-7*, Puffin) Puffin Bks.

Trouble at Sandhill Ranch, Vol. 5. Hilda Stahl. (Elizabeth Gail Ser.: Vol. 5). 128p. (J). 1989. pap. 5.99 (*0-8423-0814-8*) Tyndale.

Trouble at Star Fort. Idella F. Bodie. (J). (gr. 5-7). 1992. 14.95 (*0-87844-118-2*); pap. 9.95 (*0-87844-119-0*) Sandlapper Pub Co.

Trouble at Tahoe. Carolyn Keene. (Nancy Drew Ser.: No. 118). (YA). (gr. 3-6). 1994. pap. 3.99 (*0-671-79304-7*, Minstrel Bks) PB.

Trouble at Tenkiller. large type ed. Ray Hogan. LC 92-36434. (Western Ser.). 143p. 1993. reprint ed. lib. bdg. 15.95 (*1-56054-575-5*) Thorndike Pr.

Trouble at the Gabourys' Joan L. Oppenheimer. 1987. 16. 95 (*0-8027-0981-8*) Walker & Co.

Trouble at the Glory Barn. Tom C. McKenney. LC 85-51173. (Illus.). 127p. (Orig.). 1985. pap. 6.95 (*0-934527-05-9*) Words Living Minis.

***Trouble at the Haunted House.** Arnold Shapiro. (Diorama Pop-Up Books Ser.). 1997. 5.95 (*0-689-81438-0*) S&S Trade.

Trouble at the Park. Misty Reddington. LC 95-62388. (Illus.). 44p. (J). (gr. k-4). 1996. pap. 6.95 (*1-55523-787-8*) Winston-Derek.

Trouble at the Table: Gathering the Tribes for Worship. Thomas H. Troeger & Carol Doran. 144p. (Orig.). 1992. pap. 11.95 (*0-687-42656-1*) Abingdon.

Trouble at Tie-Down. Lola Guymon. 196p. 1991. pap. 8.95 (*0-9633935-0-2*) Rocket Pr WY.

Trouble at Timpetill. Henry Winterfeld. (Illus.). 192p. (J). (gr. 3-7). 1990. pap. 5.00 (*0-15-290786-6*, Odyssey) HarBrace.

Trouble at Topaz. large type ed. Frank C. Robertson. (Western Ser.). 1975. 25.99 (*0-85456-324-5*) Ulverscroft.

Trouble at Wild River. Lois W. Johnson. (Adventures of the Northwoods Ser.: Bk. 5). 160p. (Orig.). (J). (gr. 3-8). 1991. pap. 5.99 (*1-55661-144-7*) Bethany Hse.

Trouble at Windy Acres. Mary M. Landis. (J). (gr. 5-10). 1976. 7.15 (*0-686-15486-X*) Rod & Staff.

Trouble Begins at Eight: Mark Twain's Lecture Tours. Frederick W. Lorch. LC 68-17493. (Illus.). 391p. reprint ed. pap. 111.50 (*0-685-20389-1*, 2030318) Bks Demand.

Trouble by the Pound. Cathy Stanton. LC 95-78739. 120p. (Orig.). 1995. pap. 7.50 (*1-884540-17-1*) Haleys.

Trouble Dolls. Jimmy Buffett & Savannah J. Buffett. (Illus.). 32p. (J). (gr. 1 up). 1991. 16.00 (*0-15-290790-4*) HarBrace.

Trouble Dolls. Jimmy Buffett. (J). 1997. pap. 6.00 (*0-15-201501-9*) HarBrace.

Trouble Don't Last Always: Soul Prayers. Diana J. Hayes. 80p. (Orig.). 1995. pap. 5.95 (*0-8146-2297-6*, Liturg Pr Bks) Liturgical Pr.

Trouble Double on Yellow Mountain. Mercedes M. Reitz et al. (Yellow Mountain Ser.). (Illus.). 184p. (Orig.). (J). (gr. 3 up). 1990. pap. 9.95 (*0-9625344-1-2*) Creative Multi-Media.

Trouble Down the Creek. Mark R. Littleton. Ed. by LoraBeth Norton. 208p. (J). (gr. 4-6). 1994. pap. 5.99 (*0-7814-0082-1*, Chariot Bks) Chariot Victor.

Trouble Downtown: The Local Context of Twentieth Century America. Henry F. Bedford. (Harbrace History of the United States Ser.). (Illus.). 213p. (C). 1978. pap. text ed. 14.75 (*0-15-592369-2*) HB Coll Pubs.

Trouble Enough: Joseph Smith & the Book of Mormon. Ernest H. Taves. LC 84-42790. (Illus.). 280p. 1984. 32.95 (*0-87975-261-0*) Prometheus Bks.

Trouble for Lucia. E. F. Benson. 1992. reprint ed. lib. bdg. 18.95 (*0-89966-960-3*) Buccaneer Bks.

Trouble for Lucy. Carla Stevens. LC 79-10445. 80p. (J). (gr. 3-6). 1987. pap. 5.95 (*0-89919-523-7*, Clarion Bks) HM.

Trouble for Thomas & Other Stories. W. Awdry. (Thomas the Tank Engine & Friends Book & Cassette Ser.). (Illus.). 32p. (J). (ps-2). 1991. 7.95 incl. audio (*0-679-80106-5*) Random Bks Yng Read.

Trouble for Thomas & Other Stories: Based on the Railway Series. W. Awdry. LC 89-8503. (Thomas the Tank Engine Picturebacks Ser.). (Illus.). 32p. (J). (ps-3). 1989. pap. 3.25 (*0-679-80101-4*) Random Bks Yng Read.

Trouble-Free Menopause: Every Woman's Guide to Living a Fit & Healthy Life. Linda Konner & Judy E. Marshel. 336p. (Orig.). 1995. mass mkt. 5.50 (*0-380-77732-0*) Avon.

Trouble-Free Travel: And What to Do When Things Go Wrong. Stephen Colwell & Ann Shulman. (Illus.). 220p. 1996. pap. text ed. 14.95 (*0-87337-328-6*) Nolo Pr.

Trouble-Free Travel with Children: Helpful Hints for Parents on the Go. 2nd rev. ed. Vicki Lansky. (Illus.). 144p. 1996. reprint ed. pap. 8.95 (*0-916773-15-9*) Book Peddlers.

Trouble from the Past, Vol. 9. Hilda Stahl. (Elizabeth Gail Ser.: Vol. 9). 128p. (J). 1989. pap. 5.99 (*0-8423-0804-0*) Tyndale.

Trouble Hunter. large type ed. Alan Irwin. (Linford Western Library). 224p. 1996. pap. 15.99 (*0-7089-7827-4*, Linford) Ulverscroft.

Trouble in a Fur Coat. Janette Oke. (Illus.). 152p. (Orig.). (J). (gr. 3 up). pap. 4.99 (*0-934998-38-8*) Bethel Pub.

Trouble in Big Spur. large type ed. M. Duggan. (Linford Western Library). 272p. 1993. pap. 15.99 (*0-7089-7315-9*, Linford) Ulverscroft.

Trouble in Bugland: A Collection of Inspector Mantis Mysteries. William Kotzwinkle. LC 83-49338. (Illus.). 160p. (J). (gr. 4-7). 1996. reprint ed. pap. 14.95 (*1-56792-070-5*) Godine.

Trouble in Eden. Elise Title. (Superromance Ser.: No. 478). 1991. mass mkt. 3.29 (*0-373-70478-X*) Harlequin Bks.

Trouble in Eden: A Comparison of the British & Swedish Economies. Eli Schwartz. LC 80-17073. 160p. 1980. text ed. 45.00 (*0-275-90547-0*, C0547, Praeger Pubs) Greenwood.

Trouble in July. Erskine Caldwell. (Illus.). 160p. 1977. 25.00 (*0-88322-025-3*) Beehive GA.

Trouble in Paradise. Zuleyka Benitez. LC 78-17909. (Lost Roads Ser.: No. 19). (Illus.). 56p. (Orig.). 1980. pap. 9.00 (*0-918786-20-7*) Lost Roads.

Trouble in Paradise. Lisa Harris. 1994. mass mkt. 2.99 (*0-373-25595-0*, 1-25595-9) Harlequin Bks.

Trouble in Paradise. Marilyn Kaye. 224p. (Orig.). (YA). (gr. 5 up). 1996. pap. 3.95 (*0-8167-3972-2*) Troll Communs.

Trouble in Paradise: A Survivial Manual for Couples Who Are Parents. Dianne M. Aigaki. LC 86-72923. (Illus.). 304p. (Orig.). 1987. student ed., pap. 16.95 (*0-941941-01-9*) Dry Creek Pubns.

***Trouble in Paradise? Europe in the 21st Century.** 84p. 1996. pap. text ed. 35.00 (*1-57979-175-1*) BPI Info Servs.

***Trouble in Paradise: Europe in the 21st Century.** 1997. lib. bdg. 250.95 (*0-8490-7640-4*) Gordon Pr.

***Trouble in Paradise? Europe in the 21st Century.** Steven P. Kramer & Irene Kyriakopoulos. (Illus.). 77p. (Orig.). (C). 1997. pap. text ed. 30.00 (*0-7881-3169-9*) DIANE Pub.

Trouble in Paradise: New England Artists Address Topical Political & Social Issues Facing the United States. Dana Friis-Hansen. LC 89-13306. (Illus.). 44p. 1989. pap. 7.50 (*0-938437-27-5*) MIT List Visual Arts.

Trouble in Paradise: The Suburban Transformation & Its Challenges. Mark Baldassare. LC 85-19499. 267p. 1986. text ed. 45.00 (*0-231-06014-9*) Col U Pr.

Trouble in Paradise: The Suburban Transformation in America. Mark Baldassare. 251p. 1988. pap. text ed. 16.50 (*0-231-06015-7*) Col U Pr.

Trouble in Riddle City. Helena Mubarek. (J). (gr. 4-9). 1992. pap. text ed. 9.97 (*0-937659-49-5*) GCT.

Trouble in Space. Rose Greydanus. LC 81-5114. (Illus.). 32p. (J). (gr. k-2). 1997. pap. 3.95 (*0-89375-518-4*) Troll Communs.

Trouble in Surinam, 1975-1993. Edward M. Dew. LC 94-11301. 264p. 1994. text ed. 57.95 (*0-275-94834-X*, Praeger Pubs) Greenwood.

Trouble in Tahiti. Carolyn Keene. (Nancy Drew Ser.: No. 31). (YA). (gr. 6 up). 1991. pap. 3.50 (*0-671-73912-3*) PB.

Trouble in Tall Pine. John P. Legg. 1990. mass mkt. 2.95 (*0-8217-3047-9*, Zebra Kensgtn) Kensgtn Pub Corp.

Trouble in Tandem. Cathy Stanton. LC 94-77595. (Illus.). 108p. (Orig.). 1994. pap. 7.50 (*1-884540-07-4*) Haleys.

Trouble in Texas. Harris. 1995. pap. 3.75 (*0-373-07664-9*) Harlequin Bks.

Trouble in the Ark. Gerald Rose. (Illus.). 32p. (J). (ps-1). 1995. pap. 8.95 (*0-8192-1651-8*) Morehouse Pub.

Trouble in the Ark. Gerald Rose. (J). Date not set. 25.33 (*0-590-21010-6*); pap. 6.67 (*0-590-21012-2*); pap. 64.00 (*0-590-21118-8*) Scholastic Inc.

Trouble in the Bank. large type ed. Howard C. Davis. (Linford Mystery Library). 1991. pap. 15.99 (*0-7089-7082-6*) Ulverscroft.

Trouble in the Brasses. Alisa Craig, pseud. 224p. 1989. mass mkt. 4.50 (*0-380-75539-4*) Avon.

Trouble in the Caucasus. Avtandil Menteshashvili. (Illus.). 107p. (C). 1994. lib. bdg. 39.00 (*1-56072-177-4*) Nova Sci Pubs.

***Trouble in the Classroom: Managing Behavior Problems in Young Children.** W. George Scarlett. 1997. 26.95 (*0-7879-1067-8*) Jossey-Bass.

Trouble in the Deep End. Nancy S. Levene. LC 93-16602. (T. J. Ser.). 96p. (J). 1993. pap. 4.99 (*0-7814-0701-X*, Chariot Bks) Chariot Victor.

Trouble in the Men's Room. Mort McDonald. 1975. 5.00 (*0-685-79060-6*) Twowindows Pr.

Trouble in the Prostate? The New Short Guide to Intelligent Choices. (Illus.). 90p. (Orig.). 1996. pap. 10.95 (*0-9653110-0-7*) T H Coleman.

***Trouble in the Prostate? The New Short Guide to Intelligent Decisions.** 2nd rev. ed. (Illus.). 82p. (Orig.). 1996. pap. 11.95 (*0-9653110-1-5*) T H Coleman.

***Trouble in the Rainforest: British Columbia's Forest Economy in Transition.** Ed. by Trevor Barnes & Roger Hayter. 250p. 1997. pap. 24.95 (*0-919838-23-5*, Pub. by U BC Pr) U of Wash Pr.

Trouble in the Town Hall: A Dorothy Martin Mystery. Jeanne M. Dams. LC 96-26485. (Dorothy Martin Mystery Ser.). 256p. 1996. 20.95 (*0-8027-3285-2*) Walker & Co.

Trouble in Timberline. Max Brand. 192p. 1995. mass mkt., pap. text ed. 4.50 (*0-8439-3848-X*) Dorchester Pub Co.

Trouble in Tow. Cathy Stanton. LC 93-80125. (Illus.). 104p. (Orig.). 1993. pap. 7.50 (*0-9626308-2-9*) Haleys.

***Trouble in Toyland: The Brutal Business of Fun & Games.** G. Wayne Miller. 1998. write for info. (*0-8129-2984-5*, Times Bks) Random.

Trouble in Transylvania. Barbara Wilson. LC 93-25036. 288p. (Orig.). 1994. pap. 10.95 (*1-878067-49-4*) Seal Pr WA.

Trouble in Utopia: The Overburdened Polity of Israel. Dan Horowitz & Moshe Lissak. LC 88-37557. (SUNY Series in Israeli Studies). 357p. 1989. text ed. 74.50 (*0-7914-0112-X*); pap. text ed. 24.95 (*0-7914-0114-6*) State U NY Pr.

***Trouble in Ward J.** large type ed. William Neubauer. (Linford Romance Library). 240p. 1996. pap. 15.99 (*0-7089-7972-6*) Ulverscroft.

Trouble in Your Tank? Durney. 185p. 1988. 20.00 (*0-685-44516-X*) Am Electro Surface.

Trouble in Your Tank? 2nd ed. Lawrence J. Durney. 185p. (C). 1986. pap. 19.95 (*1-56990-013-2*) Hanser-Gardner.

Trouble in Your Tank? Handbook for Solving Plating Problems. 3rd ed. Lawrence J. Durney. 1996. write for info. (*1-56990-200-3*) Hanser-Gardner.

Trouble Is My Business. Raymond Chandler. LC 87-45924. (Crime Ser.). 1988. pap. 10.00 (*0-394-75764-5*, Vin) Random.

Trouble Is My Business. Raymond Chandler. 1992. pap. 9.00 (*0-394-23911-3*, Vin); pap. 9.00 (*0-679-74086-4*) Random.

Trouble Is Not in Your Set: A History of Television. 3rd ed. Mary A. Kelly. LC 90-93268. (Illus.). 359p. 1991. 25.00 (*0-9627159-0-5*) M A Kelly.

Trouble Is Their Business: Private Eyes in Fiction, Film & Television, 1927-1988. John Conquest. LC 89-33039. 552p. 1989. text ed. 69.00 (*0-8240-5947-6*, H1151) Garland.

Trouble Looking for a Place to Happen. Toni L. Kelner. 352p. 1996. mass mkt. 4.99 (*1-57566-007-5*) Kensgtn Pub Corp.

Trouble Making Toys. A. M. Pyle. LC 84-29162. 192p. 1985. 13.95 (*0-8027-5610-7*) Walker & Co.

Trouble No More. Anthony Grooms. 192p. (Orig.). 1995. pap. 11.00 (*0-9644348-0-6*) La Questa Pr.

Trouble of an Index see Byron's Letters & Journals

Trouble of Fools. Linda Barnes. 1988. mass mkt. 4.99 (*0-449-21640-3*) Fawcett.

Trouble of Fools. large type ed. Linda Barnes. (General Ser.). 370p. 1989. lib. bdg. 19.95 (*0-8161-4714-0*, GK Hall) Thorndike Pr.

Trouble on Board: The Plight of International Seafarers. Paul Chapman. 208p. 1992. 35.00 (*0-87546-180-8*, ILR Press); pap. 15.95 (*0-87546-181-6*, ILR Press) Cornell U Pr.

Trouble on His Trail. Bob Terrell. Ed. by Pat H. Roberts et al. LC 95-16882. (Illus.). 160p. (Orig.). 1995. pap. 9.95 (*1-57090-023-X*) Alexander Bks.

Trouble on Janus. Alfred Slote. LC 85-40099. (Illus.). 192p. (J). (gr. 3-6). 1985. lib. bdg. 14.89 (*0-397-32159-7*, Lipp Jr Bks) HarpC Child Bks.

Trouble on the Hill: And Other Stories. Michael Glenn. LC 79-88413. 156p. (Orig.). 1979. pap. 4.95 (*0-930720-61-X*) Lake View Pr.

***Trouble on the Job.** Jessie Schut. LC 96-32263. (Open Door Bks.). 64p. (Orig.). 1996. pap. 3.95 (*1-56212-219-3*, 1740-2180) CRC Pubns.

***Trouble on the Lordsburg Trail.** large type ed. Elliot Conway. (Dales Large Print Ser.). 200p. 1997. pap. 18.99 (*1-85389-710-8*) Ulverscroft.

Trouble on the Shoshone. Rosemary M. Laughlin. LC 88-50762. 94p. (J). (gr. 5-8). 1989. pap. 5.95 (*1-55523-154-3*) Winston-Derek.

Trouble on the T-Ball Team. Eve Bunting. LC 94-43699. (Illus.). (J). 1997. 13.95 (*0-395-66060-2*, Clarion Bks) HM.

Trouble on the Tracks. Donna J. Napoli. LC 96-27934. 1996. pap. write for info. (*0-590-13472-8*) Scholastic Inc.

Trouble on the Tracks. Donna J. Napoli. LC 96-27934. 1997. 14.95 (*0-590-13447-7*) Scholastic Inc.

Trouble on Triton: An Ambiguous Heterotopia. Samuel R. Delany. LC 95-46796. 326p. (C). 1996. reprint ed. pap. 14.95 (*0-8195-6298-X*, Wesleyan Univ Pr) U Pr of New Eng.

***Trouble on Tuesday.** Colleen L. Reece. (Juli Scott, Super Sleuth Ser.). 176p. 1997. pap. text ed. 6.95 (*1-55748-984-X*) Barbour & Co.

Trouble-Proofing Kids. Gary Hutchison. (Orig.). 1995. 32.50 incl. audio (*1-885631-11-1*) G F Hutchison.

Trouble-Proofing Kids. Gary Hutchison. 150p. (Orig.). 1996. pap. 20.00 (*1-885631-17-0*) G F Hutchison.

Trouble Rider. large type ed. Thomas Thompson. LC 92-41193. (Nightingale Ser.). 1993. pap. 15.95 (*0-8161-5480-5*) G K Hall.

Trouble Rides Tall. large type ed. Harry Whittington. (Linford Western Library). 1990. pap. 15.99 (*0-7089-6812-0*) Ulverscroft.

Trouble River. Betsy C. Byars. (Illus.). 160p. (J). (gr. 3-7). 1989. pap. 3.99 (*0-14-034243-5*, Puffin) Puffin Bks.

Trouble River: A Study Guide. Gloria Levine. (Novel-Ties Ser.). 1988. student ed., teacher ed., pap. text ed. 15.95 (*0-88122-065-5*) Lrn Links.

Trouble Shooter. Louis L'Amour. 240p. 1995. mass mkt. 4.99 (*0-553-57187-7*) Bantam.

***Trouble Shooter: A Hopalong Cassidy Novel.** Louis L'Amour. LC 96-36478. 1920. write for info. (*0-7862-0896-1*) Thorndike Pr.

Trouble Shooter for God in China. Arthur B. Coole. (Illus.). 1976. 20.00 (*0-912706-05-8*) M Akers.

Trouble-Shooter's Guide to Filing the ERISA Annual Reports. 104p. 1993. pap. 12.50 (*0-685-67048-1*, 4896) Commerce.

Trouble-Shooting. Severiano Ballesteros & Robert Green. LC 96-24648. (Golf Masters Ser.). 176p. 1996. 27.50 (*0-553-06164-X*) Broadway BDD.

Trouble Shooting Boundary Line Problems: Questions & Answers. John E. Keen. 225p. (C). 1995. pap. text ed. 45.00 (*1-56569-002-8*) Land Survey.

Trouble-Shooting SCR Motor Controls (Reference Card) Tel-A-Train, Inc. Staff. 1982. student ed. 0.15 (*1-56355-233-7*) Tel-A-Train.

Trouble Talking: A Guide for Parents of Children with Difficulties Communicating. James Law & Jane Elias. 200p. 1995. pap. text ed. 24.95 (*1-85302-253-5*) Taylor & Francis.

Trouble, the Horse Who Is Different. large type ed. William O. Beazley. (Illus.). 42p. (J). (gr. k-5). 1989. reprint ed. spiral bd., pap. 7.95 (*1-884758-04-5*) W O Beazley.

Trouble the Water. Melvin Dixon. 243p. 1989. 18.95 (*0-932511-23-6*); pap. 8.95 (*0-932511-24-4*) Fiction Coll.

Trouble the Waters: An Anthology of African American Poetry. Jerry W. Ward. 1997. pap. 6.99 (*0-451-62864-0*, Ment) NAL-Dutton.

Trouble They Seen: The Story of Reconstruction of the Words of African Americans. Ed. by Dorothy Sterling. (Illus.). 512p. reprint ed. pap. 15.95 (*0-306-80548-0*) Da Capo.

Trouble Times Two. Christine McDonnell. (J). 1998. pap. 12.99 (*0-670-83264-2*) Viking Penguin.

Trouble Times 2. Christine McDonnell. (J). Date not set. pap. 3.95 (*0-14-034393-8*, Viking) Viking Penguin.

Trouble Trail. large type ed. Max Brand. LC 90-38612. 373p. 1990. reprint ed. lib. bdg. 16.95 (*1-56054-036-2*) Thorndike Pr.

Trouble, Trust & Triumph. Spiros Zodhiates & Joan Zodhiates. (Zodhiates Commentary Ser.). 182p. 1995. pap. 6.99 (*0-89957-493-9*) AMG Pubs.

Trouble Valley. large type ed. Bret Rey. (Linford Western Library). 1991. pap. 15.99 (*0-7089-7010-9*) Ulverscroft.

Trouble Will Find You. Joan M. Lexau. LC 93-6813. (Illus.). (J). (ps-6). 1994. 14.95 (*0-395-64380-5*) HM.

Trouble Will Find You. Joan M. Lexau. (Illus.). 80p. (J). 1996. pap. 3.99 (*0-380-72565-7*, Camelot Young) Avon.

***Trouble with a Bad Fit.** Camilla Crespi. 320p. 1997. mass mkt. 4.99 (*0-06-109408-0*, Harp PBks) HarpC.

Trouble with a Bad Fit: A Novel of Food, Fashion, & Mystery. Camilla T. Crespi. 262p. 1996. 21.00 (*0-06-017661-X*) HarpC.

Trouble with a Capital T. Judy Baer. LC 88-71503. 144p. (Orig.). (YA). (gr. 7-10). 1988. mass mkt. 4.99 (*1-55661-021-1*) Bethany Hse.

Trouble with a Capital T. Mary Duplex. (Starburst Ser.). 96p. (J). 1992. pap. 2.97 (*0-8163-1057-2*) Pacific Pr Pub Assn.

***Trouble with a Hot Summer.** Camilla Crespi. mass mkt. write for info. (*0-06-109409-9*, Harp PBks) HarpC.

***Trouble with a Hot Summer: A Simona Griffo Mystery.** Camilla T. Crespi. LC 96-44460. 1997. write for info. (*0-06-017662-8*) HarpC.

Trouble with a Small Raise. Trella Crespi. 288p. 1991. mass mkt. 3.95 (*0-8217-3274-9*, Zebra Kensgtn) Kensgtn Pub Corp.

Trouble with Andrew. Heather G. Pozzessere. (Intimate Moments Ser.). 1993. mass mkt. 3.50 (*0-373-07525-1*, 5-07525-4) Silhouette.

Trouble with Angels. Debbie Macomber. 352p. 1994. mass mkt. 5.99 (*0-06-108308-9*, Harp PBks) HarpC.

Trouble with Babies. Madeline Harper. (Temptation Ser.). 1995. pap. 3.25 (*0-373-25627-2*, 1-25627-0) Harlequin Bks.

Trouble with Being Born. E. M. Cioran. Tr. by Richard Howard from FRE. LC 81-51526. Orig. Title: L' Inconvenient d'Etre Ne. 208p. 1981. reprint ed. pap. 8.95 (*0-8050-0001-1*) Seaver Bks.

Trouble with Ben. Barry L. Polisar. (Illus.). 34p. (J). (gr. k-5). 1992. 14.95 (*0-938663-13-5*) Rainbow Morn.

Trouble with Blame: Victims, Perpetrators, & Responsibility. Sharon Lamb. LC 95-47457. 256p. (C). 1996. 22.95 (*0-674-91010-9*) HUP.

Trouble with Boys: A Wise & Sympathetic Guide to the Risky Business of Raising Sons. Angela Phillips. 304p. 1995. pap. 14.00 (*0-465-08735-3*) Basic.

Trouble with Bubbles. Gregory Pickup. (Illus.). 64p. (Orig.). 1996. pap. 9.95 (*0-9641715-7-0*) Airplane Bks.

Trouble with Canada. William D. Gairdner. (Illus.). 470p. 1991. pap. 7.99 (*0-7736-7311-3*) Genl Dist Srvs.

Trouble with Canada: A Citizen Speaks Out. William D. Gairdner. 448p. 1990. 29.95 (*0-7737-2306-4*) Genl Dist Srvs.

Trouble With Christmas. Tom Flynn. (Illus.). 244p. 1993. pap. 15.95 (*0-87975-848-1*) Prometheus Bks.

Trouble with Cinderella: An Outline of Identity. Artie Shaw. LC 91-48190. (Illus.). 432p. 1992. reprint ed. pap. 12.95 (*1-56474-020-X*) Fithian Pr.

Trouble with Computers: Usefulness, Usability, & Productivity. Thomas K. Landauer. (Illus.). 440p. 1996. pap. 15.00 (*0-262-62108-8*) MIT Pr.

Trouble with Confucianism. W. Theodore De Bary. 152p. 1996. pap. text ed. 12.00 (*0-674-91016-8*) HUP.

Trouble with Confucianism. William T. De Bary. (Tanner Lectures on Human Values). 152p. (C). 1996. pap. (*0-674-91015-X*) HUP.

***Trouble with Dilbert: How Corporate Culture Gets the Last Laugh.** Norman Solomon. (Illus.). 160p. (Orig.). 1997. pap. 9.95 (*1-56751-132-5*); lib. bdg. 29.95 (*1-56751-133-3*) Common Courage.

Trouble with Dreams. Lee A. Lewis. LC 91-27503. 160p. (Orig.). (J). (gr. 4-7). 1991. pap. 5.99 (*0-8361-3571-7*) Herald Pr.

Trouble with Elephants. Chris Riddell. LC 87-24963. (Trophy Picture Bk.). (Illus.). 32p. (J). (ps-2). 1990. reprint ed. pap. 6.95 (*0-06-443170-3*, Trophy) HarpC Child Bks.

Trouble with Evil: Social Control at the Edge of Morality. Edwin M. Lemert. LC 96-30388. (SUNY Series in Deviance & Social Control). 185p. (C). 1997. text ed. 49.50 (*0-7914-3243-2*) State U NY Pr.

Trouble with Evil: Social Control at the Edge of Morality. Edwin M. Lemert. LC 96-30388. (SUNY Series in Deviance & Social Control). 185p. (C). 1997. pap. text ed. 16.95 (*0-7914-3244-0*) State U NY Pr.

Trouble with France. Alain Peyrefitte. Ed. by Tom Bishop & Nicholas Wahl. Tr. by William R. Byron. LC 85-31075. 356p. (C). 1986. pap. text ed. 13.20 (*0-8147-6596-3*) NYU Pr.

Trouble with Francis. Robert Francis. LC 75-150313. 256p. 1971. 30.00 (*0-87023-083-2*) U of Mass Pr.

Trouble with Friendship: Why Americans Can't Think Straight about Race. Benjamin DeMott. LC 95-4838. 224p. 1996. 22.00 (*0-87113-619-8*, Atlntc Mnthly) Grove-Atltic.

Trouble with Genius: Reading Pound, Joyce, Stein, & Zukofsky. Bob Perleman. LC 93-37181. 1994. 40.00 (*0-520-08583-3*); pap. 16.00 (*0-520-08755-0*) U CA Pr.

Trouble with Girls: Jungle Girls. Will Jacobs & Gerard Jones. Ed. by Chris Ulm. (Illus.). 72p. 1990. pap. 9.95 (*0-944735-72-X*) Malibu Comics Ent.

Trouble with Girls, Vol. 1: Graphic Novel. Will Jacobs & Gerard Jones. (Illus.). 89p. 1988. pap. 7.95 (*0-944735-08-8*) Malibu Comics Ent.

Trouble with God: God of the Third Millennium. Charles Turnbull. 176p. (Orig.). 1995. pap. 12.00 (*1-886676-00-3*) Longview Pr.

Trouble with Going Home. Camilla T. Crespi. 304p. 1996. mass mkt. 4.99 (*0-06-109153-7*) HarpC.

Trouble with Hairgrow. Margaret Watts. LC 93-26298. (Illus.). (J). 1994. 4.25 (*0-383-03782-4*) SRA McGraw.

Trouble with Henriette. Wende Devlin & Harry Devlin. (J). 1995. 15.00 (*0-02-729937-6*, S&S Bks Young Read) S&S Childrens.

Trouble with Herbert. Heather Eyles. LC 96-15047. (Illus.). (J). 1996. pap. write for info. (*1-57255-218-2*) Mondo Pubng.

Trouble with Horses. Ulrik Schramm. 110p. 1990. 60.00 (*0-85131-457-0*, Pub. by J A Allen & Co UK) St Mut.

Trouble with Jared. Kay Hooper. (Loveswept Ser.: No. 619). 1993. pap. 3.50 (*0-553-44339-9*, Loveswept) Bantam.

An Asterisk (*) at the beginning of an entry indicates that the title is appearing in BIP for the first time.

Trouble with Jenny's Ear. Oliver Butterworth. (J). (gr. 4-7). 1993. 4.95 (*0-316-11922-9*) Little.

***Trouble with Joe.** Emilie Richards. 1997. mass mkt. 5.50 (*1-55166-279-5*, 1-66279-0, Mira Bks) Harlequin Bks.

Trouble with Joe. Emilie Richards. 1994. mass mkt. 3.50 (*0-373-09873-1*, 5-09873-6) Silhouette.

Trouble with Lemons. Daniel Hayes. LC 89-46192. 128p. (YA). (gr. 6 up). 1991. 16.95 (*0-87923-825-9*) Godine.

Trouble with Lemons. Daniel Hayes. 192p. (YA). 1992. reprint ed. mass mkt. 4.50 (*0-449-70416-5*, Juniper) Fawcett.

Trouble with Lichens. John Wyndham. 1993. reprint ed. lib. bdg. 18.95 (*0-89968-388-6*, Lghtyr Pr) Buccaneer Bks.

***Trouble with Lucia.** E. F. Benson. 1997. pap. text ed. 20. 95 (*0-7862-0959-3*) Thorndike Pr.

Trouble with Men: A Wickedly Funny Analysis of Male Behavior, Vol. 1. Rina Piccolo. LC 95-79165. (Illus.). 136p. (Orig.). 1995. pap. 9.95 (*0-9648010-9-4*) Hypertext Pub.

Trouble with Mister. Debra Keller. LC 94-4048. (Illus.). 32p. (J). (ps-3). 1995. 13.95 (*0-8118-0358-9*) Chronicle Bks.

Trouble with Mom. Babette Cole. 32p. (J). (gr. 5-8). 1984. pap. 5.95 (*0-698-20681-9*, Putnam) Putnam Pub Group.

***Trouble with Mom.** Babette Cole. (Illus.). 32p. (J). (ps-3). 1997. pap. 5.95 (*0-698-11593-7*, Paperstar) Putnam Pub Group.

Trouble with Money. William Greider. Date not set. 14.95 (*0-393-03103-9*) Norton.

Trouble with Mothers. Margery Facklam. 144p. (J). (gr. 5). 1991. reprint ed. pap. 2.95 (*0-380-71139-7*, Camelot) Avon.

Trouble with Nigeria. Chinua Achebe. 68p. (C). 1984. pap. text ed. 8.50 (*0-435-90698-4*, 90698) Heinemann.

Trouble with Perfect. Ryan. (J). 15.00 (*0-671-86586-2*, S&S Bks Young Read) S&S Childrens.

Trouble with Perfect. Mary E. Ryan. 170p. (J). (gr. 5-9). 1995. 15.00 (*0-689-80276-5*, S&S Bks Young Read) S&S Childrens.

Trouble with Postmodernism. Stefan Morawski. LC 95-16085. 152p. (C). 1996. text ed. 65.00 (*0-415-09386-4*) Routledge.

Trouble with Prosperity. James Grant. 432p. 1996. 30.00 (*0-8129-2439-8*, Times Bks) Random.

***Trouble with Pteranodons.** Scott E. Sutton. (The Adventures of Dinosaur Dog Ser.: Vol. 3). (Illus.). 100p. (Orig.). (J). (gr. 3-6). 1996. pap. 6.95 (*1-883649-02-1*) Sutton Pubns.

Trouble with Rape: A Psychologist's Report on the Legal, Medical, Social, & Psychological Problems. Carolyn J. Hursch. LC 76-28757. (Illus.). 144p. 1977. 28.95 (*0-88229-323-0*) Nelson-Hall.

Trouble with Reporting Northern Ireland. David Butler. 176p. 1995. 59.95 (*1-85628-909-5*, Pub. by Avebury Pub UK) Ashgate Pub Co.

Trouble with Santa. Betsy Sachs. LC 89-24257. (Stepping Stone Bks.). (Illus.). 64p. (Orig.). (J). (gr. 2-4). 1990. pap. 2.50 (*0-679-80410-2*) Random Bks Yng Read.

Trouble with Sarah Gullion. Michael P. Harding. LC 88-7440. 116p. 1989. pap. 10.95 (*0-85640-410-1*, Pub. by Blackstaff Pr IE) Dufour.

Trouble with Sarah Gullion. Michael P. Harding. LC 88-7440. 116p. 8900. 23.00 (*0-85640-409-8*, Pub. by Blackstaff Pr IE) Dufour.

Trouble with School: A Family Story about Learning Disabilities. Kathryn B. Dunn & Allison B. Dunn. (Illus.). 32p. (Orig.). (J). (gr. 1-5). 1993. 9.95 (*0-933149-57-3*) Woodbine House.

Trouble with Science. Robin Dunbar. LC 96-17482. 224p. 1996. pap. 14.00 (*0-674-91019-2*) HUP.

Trouble with Secrets. Karen Johnsen. LC 85-51803. (Illus.). 32p. (Orig.). (J). (ps-3). 1986. pap. 5.95 (*0-943990-22-X*); lib. bdg. 15.95 (*0-943990-23-8*) Parenting Pr.

Trouble with Spitt. Vicki Blum. LC 96-73. 108p. (Orig.). (J). (gr. 4-8). 1996. pap. 5.95 (*1-57345-147-9*) Deseret Bk.

Trouble with Technology. Don Lamberton et al. LC 83-10961. 200p. 1983. text ed. 29.95 (*0-312-81985-4*) St Martin.

Trouble with Temik: An Historical-Environmental Look at Long Island Agriculture & Pesticide Usage. 15.00 (*0-936128-09-7*) De Young Pr.

***Trouble with Testosterone.** Sapolsky. LC 96-52357. 1997. 23.00 (*0-684-83409-X*, Scrbnr) Scribnrs Ref.

Trouble with Texans. Maggie Simpson. (Superromance Ser.). 1996. mass mkt. 3.99 (*0-373-70705-3*, 1-70705-8) Harlequin Bks.

Trouble with Thirteen. Betty Miles. LC 78-31678. (J). (gr. 4-7). 1979. lib. bdg. 12.99 (*0-394-93930-1*) Knopf Bks Yng Read.

Trouble with Thirteen. Betty Miles. LC 78-31678. 112p. (J). (gr. 3-7). 1989. reprint ed. pap. 2.95 (*0-394-82043-6*) Knopf Bks Yng Read.

***Trouble with Tonya.** Lorna Michaels. 1997. mass mkt. 3.50 (*0-373-25732-5*, 1-25732-8) Harlequin Bks.

Trouble with Too Much Sun. Camilla Crespi. (Simona Griffo Mystery Ser.). 1992. mass mkt. 3.99 (*0-8217-3776-7*, Zebra Kensgtn) Kensgtn Pub Corp.

Trouble with Trevor: The Good News Kids Learn about Goodness. Dorothy K. Mock. LC 92-27013. (Good News Kids Ser.). (Illus.). 32p. (Orig.). (J). (ps-2). 1993. pap. 4.99 (*0-570-04738-2*, 56-1695) Concordia.

Trouble with Trolls. Jan Brett. (Illus.). 32p. (J). (ps-3). 1992. 15.95 (*0-399-22336-3*, Putnam) Putnam Pub Group.

Trouble with Trucks. (Illus.). 24p. (J). 1996. 9.95 (*0-7894-1107-5*) DK Pub Inc.

Trouble with Trumpets. Veralee Wiggins. (Atarburst Ser.). 95p. 1990. pap. 0.97 (*0-8163-0860-8*) Pacific Pr Pub Assn.

Trouble with Tuck. Carol Klitzner. Ed. by J. Friedland & R. Kessler. (Novel-Ties Ser.). 1992. student ed., pap. text ed. 15.95 (*0-88122-727-7*) Lrn Links.

Trouble with Tuck. Theodore Taylor. LC 81-43139. 96p. (J). (gr. 4-6). 1989. 15.95 (*0-385-17774-7*) Doubleday.

Trouble with Tuck. Theodore Taylor. 120p. (J). (gr. 5 up). 1993. pap. 4.50 (*0-380-62711-6*, Camelot) Avon.

Trouble with Tyrannosaurus Rex. Lorinda B. Cauley. LC 86-33637. 32p. (J). (ps-3). 1988. pap. 5.00 (*0-15-290881-1*, Voyager Bks) HarBrace.

Trouble with Tyrannosaurus Rex. Lorinda B. Cauley. (Illus.). 32p. (J). (ps-3). 1988. 15.00 (*0-15-290880-3*) HarBrace.

Trouble with Voices. Francine L. Ringold-Johnson. 56p. 1996. pap. 9.95 (*1-57178-022-X*, Pub. by Green Bks UK) Coun Oak Bks.

Trouble with Weddings. Beverly Lewis. (Holly's Heart Ser.: Vol. 4). 160p. (J). (gr. 6-9). 1993. pap. 6.99 (*0-310-38081-2*) Zondervan.

Trouble with Wishes. Susan B. Pfeffer. LC 95-38200. (Illus.). 64p. (J). (gr. 2-4). 1996. 15.95 (*0-8050-3826-4*, Redfeather BYR) H Holt & Co.

Troubled Adolescent. White. (C). 1992. pap. text ed. 34.50 (*0-205-14503-5*, H4503) Allyn.

Troubled Adolescent: A Practical Guide. Ebrahim Amanat & Jean Beck. Ed. by Gregory Hacke. 432p. 1994. pap. text ed. 35.00 (*0-912791-93-4*) Ishiyaku Euro.

Troubled Adolescent: As He Emerges on Psychological Tests. Ernest A. Hirsch. LC 72-110262. 645p. 1970. 75. 00 (*0-8236-6650-6*) Intl Univs Pr.

Troubled Alliance: Atlantic Relations in the 1980s. Ed. by Lawrence Freedman. LC 83-40188. 224p. 1984. text ed. 29.95 (*0-312-81990-0*) St Martin.

***Troubled American Family: Which Way Out of the Storm?** Public Agenda Foundation Staff. 1996. pap. text ed. write for info. (*0-07-052212-X*) McGraw.

Troubled & Troubling Caribbean. Ed. by Roy A. Glasgow & Winston E. Langley. LC 88-13816. (Caribbean Studies: Vol. 1). 348p. 1989. lib. bdg. 99.95 (*0-88946-471-5*) E Mellen.

Troubled & Troubling Child. Nicholas Hobbs. LC 81-20875. (Jossey-Bass Social & Behavioral Science Ser.). 421p. reprint ed. pap. 120.00 (*0-7837-0173-X*, 2040470) Bks Demand.

Troubled Birth of Russian Democracy: Parties, Personalities, & Programs. Michael McFaul & Sergei Markov. (Hoover Press Publications: Vol. 415). 384p. (C). 1993. 39.95 (*0-8179-9231-6*); pap. 24.95 (*0-8179-9232-4*) Hoover Inst Pr.

Troubled Bodies: Critical Perspectives on Postmodernism, Medical Ethics & the Body. Ed. by Paul A. Komesaroff. LC 95-16274. 296p. 1995. text ed. 49.95 (*0-8223-1676-5*); pap. text ed. 16.95 (*0-8223-1688-9*) Duke.

Troubled Bodies: Medical Ethics in the Postmodern Era. Ed. by Paul A. Komesaroff. 224p. 1996. pap. 29.95 (*0-522-84684-X*, Pub. by Melbourne Univ Pr AT) Paul & Co Pubs.

***Troubled by an Angel.** Elizabeth Murawski. 30p. (Orig.). 1997. pap. 6.00 (*1-880834-37-5*) Cleveland St Univ Poetry Ctr.

Troubled by His Complexion. Lissa McLaughlin. (Prose Ser.). 120p. 1988. pap. 8.00 (*0-930901-52-5*) Burning Deck.

Troubled by His Complexion. limited ed. Lissa McLaughlin. (Prose Ser.). 120p. 1988. pap. 15.00 (*0-930901-53-3*) Burning Deck.

Troubled by Truth. Kenneth Cragg. 319p. (C). 1989. text ed. 60.00 (*1-872795-71-4*, Pub. by Pentland Pr UK) St Mut.

Troubled by Truth: Biographies in the Presence of Mystery. Kenneth Cragg. LC 94-6906. 320p. 1994. reprint ed. pap. 15.95 (*0-8298-1005-6*) Pilgrim OH.

Troubled Children in a Troubled World. Edith Buxbaum. LC 79-128623. 341p. (Orig.). 1970. 45.00 (*0-8236-6653-0*) Intl Univs Pr.

***Troubled Company Manual.** 132p. 1989. ring bd. 125.00 (*0-614-25937-1*, TRB-ZM) Nat Assn Insurance.

Troubled Construction Loans: Law & Practice. Stanley P. Sklar. LC 91-20262. (Construction Law Library: No. 1815). 504p. 1991. text ed. 130.00 (*0-471-52494-8*) Wiley.

Troubled Crusade: American Education 1945-1980. Diane Ravitch. 384p. 1985. pap. 19.00 (*0-465-08757-4*) Basic.

Troubled Days of Peace: Mountbatten & South East Asia Command, 1945-46. Peter Dennis. (War, Armed Forces & Society Ser.). 1991. 37.50 (*0-685-61135-3*, Pub. by Manchester Univ Pr UK); pap. 22.95 (*0-685-61136-1*, Pub. by Manchester Univ Pr UK) St Martin.

Troubled Debt Restructuring: An Alternative to Bankruptcy? John G. Hamer. LC 85-16503. (Research for Business Decisions Ser.: No. 81). (Illus.). 115p. reprint ed. pap. 32.80 (*0-8357-1716-X*, 2070386) Bks Demand.

Troubled Dream of Life: Living with Mortality. Daniel Callahan. LC 92-40448. 255p. 1993. 11.95 (*0-671-88721-1*) Georgetown U Pr.

Troubled Earth Acquires Lunar Perspective: A World History, 1961-1970. Franklin D. Parker. LC 82-45052. 922p. (Orig.). (C). 1982. pap. text ed. 64.00 (*0-8191-2478-8*) U Pr of Amer.

Troubled Eden: Nature & Society in the Works of George Meredith. Norman Kelvin. LC 60-15739. 111p. reprint ed. pap. 30.00 (*0-7837-1472-6*, 2057167) Bks Demand.

Troubled Encounter: The United States & Japan. Charles E. Neu. LC 79-4541. 272p. 1979. reprint ed. pap. 19.50 (*0-88275-951-5*) Krieger.

Troubled Eyes of Women & Other Stories. C. B. Christesen. 1990. pap. 14.95 (*0-7022-2271-2*, Pub. by Univ Queensland Pr AT) Intl Spec Bk.

Troubled Families: A Treatment Program. Matthew J. Fleischman et al. LC 82-62573. 284p. (Orig.). 1983. pap. text ed. 26.95 (*0-87822-271-5*, 2715) Res Press.

Troubled Families - Problem Children: Working with Parents: A Collaborative Process. Carolyn Webster-Stratton & Martin Herbert. LC 93-47493. 346p. 1994. text ed. 48.95 (*0-471-94251-0*) Wiley.

Troubled Families - Problem Children: Working with Parents: A Collaborative Process. Carolyn Webster-Stratton & Martin Herbert. LC 93-47493. 346p. 1994. pap. text ed. 42.95 (*0-471-94448-3*) Wiley.

Troubled Farmer: Rural Adjustment to Industrialism, 1850-1900. Earl W. Hayter. LC 67-26267. 349p. 1968. pap. 12.50 (*0-87580-515-9*) N Ill U Pr.

Troubled Friendships: Moscow's Third World Venture. Ed. by Margot Light. 288p. 1994. text ed. 59.50 (*1-85043-649-5*, Pub. by I B Tauris UK) St Martin.

Troubled Helix: Social & Psychological Implications of the New Human Genetics. Ed. by Theresa Marteau & Martin Richards. (Illus.). 371p. (C). 1996. text ed. 64.95 (*0-521-46288-6*) Cambridge U Pr.

Troubled House. Sheila O'Hagan. 64p. 9600. pap. 14.95 (*1-897648-16-2*, Pub. by Poolbeg Pr IE) Dufour.

Troubled in Mind: J. Saunders Redding's Early Years in Wilmington. J. Saunders Redding. LC 91-70169. (Illus.). 90p. (Orig.). 1991. pap. 4.00 (*0-924117-03-6*) Delaware HP.

Troubled Industries: Confronting Economic Change in Japan. Robert M. Uriu. (Cornell Studies in Political Economy & Studies of the East Asian Institute (Columbia)). (Illus.). 312p. 1996. 42.50 (*0-8014-3029-1*); pap. 17.95 (*0-8014-8329-8*) Cornell U Pr.

Troubled Journey: A Portrait of 6th-12th Grade Youth. Peter L. Benson. 92p. 1993. pap. 10.00 (*1-57482-308-6*) Search Inst.

***Troubled Journey: Coming to Terms with the Mental Illness of a Sibling or Parent.** Diane T. Marsh & Rex M. Dickens. 288p. 1997. 24.95 (*0-87477-875-1*, Tarcher Putnam) Putnam Pub Group.

Troubled Journey: Sermons for Pentecost, Middle Third - Gospel. John Lynch. LC 94-999. (Orig.). 1994. pap. 7.25 (*0-7880-0015-2*) CSS OH.

Troubled Lands: The Legacy of Soviet Environmental Destruction. D. J. Peterson. (Rand Corporation Research Study). 276p. (C). 1993. pap. text ed. 24.50 (*0-8133-1674-X*) Westview.

Troubled Lives: John & Sarah Austin. Lotte Hamburger & Joseph Hamburger. (Illus.). 288p. 1985. 30.00 (*0-8020-2521-8*) U of Toronto Pr.

Troubled Mind. large type ed. Miriam Sharman. (Linford Mystery Library). 432p. 1992. pap. 15.99 (*0-7089-7164-4*, Trailtree Bookshop) Ulverscroft.

Troubled Mirror: A Study of Yeats's "The Tower" David Young. LC 86-19126. (Illus.). 167p. (C). 1987. text ed. 24.95 (*0-87745-157-5*) U of Iowa Pr.

Troubled Neighbors: U. S.-Latin American Relations from FDR to Clinton & Beyond. Henry Raymont. (C). 1997. 35.00 (*0-8147-7474-1*) NYU Pr.

Troubled Origins of the Italian Catholic Labor Movement, 1878-1914. Sandor Agocs. LC 87-31961. 254p. 1988. 39.95 (*0-8143-1938-6*) Wayne St U Pr.

Troubled Paradise - Melbourne Village, Florida. Georgiana G. Kjerulff. LC 86-82011. (Local History Ser.: Vol. 13). (Illus.). 80p. (Orig.). 1987. pap. 8.95 (*0-9617352-0-1*) Kellersberger Fund.

Troubled Partnership: A History of U. S. - Japan Collaboration on the FS-X Fighter. Mark Lorell. LC 95-50670. 468p. 1996. pap. text ed. 24.95 (*1-56000-891-1*) Transaction Pubs.

Troubled Partnership: A Re-appraisal of the Atlantic Alliance. Henry A. Kissinger. LC 82-15533. xii, 266p. 1982. reprint ed. text ed. 38.50 (*0-313-23219-9*, KIPA, Greenwood Pr) Greenwood.

Troubled Partnership in Transition: Europe's Security Dilemmas & the Transatlantic Relationship. Intro. by John G. Halstead. (ISD Reports). (Illus.). 32p. (Orig.). 1992. pap. text ed. 3.00 (*0-934742-73-1*) Geo U Inst Dplmcy.

Troubled Pleasures: Writings on Politics, Gender & Hedonism. Kate Soper. 304p. (gr. 13). 1990. pap. 19.00 (*0-86091-536-0*, A5364, Pub. by Vrso UK) Norton.

Troubled Relationships. Ed. by Elam W. Nunnally et al. LC 88-6539. (Families in Trouble Ser.: No. 3). 288p. 1988. reprint ed. pap. 82.10 (*0-608-01511-3*, 2059555) Bks Demand.

Troubled Sleep. Jean-Paul Sartre. 1992. pap. 15.00 (*0-679-74079-1*, Vin) Random.

Troubled Society, 6 bks. Scott Hays et al. (Illus.). 384p. (YA). (gr. 7 up). 1990. Set. lib. bdg. 103.62 (*0-86593-068-6*); Set. lib. bdg. 77.70 (*0-685-36321-X*) Rourke Corp.

Troubled Society Series, 6 bks., Set II. (J). 1991. 77.70 (*0-86593-109-7*) Rourke Corp.

Troubled Tiger: Businessmen, Bureaucrats, & Generals in South Korea. Mark L. Clifford. LC 94-9867. 372p. (gr. 13). 1994. 67.95 (*1-56324-386-3*, East Gate Bk); pap. 24. 95 (*1-56324-387-3*, East Gate Bk) M E Sharpe.

***Troubled Tiger: Businessmen, Bureaucrats, & Generals in South Korea.** rev. ed. Mark L. Clifford. 400p. 1997. text ed. 65.00 (*0-7656-0140-0*, East Gate Bk); pap. text ed. 24.50 (*0-7656-0141-9*, East Gate Bk) M E Sharpe.

Troubled Times: A Survival Plan for the Future. Isao Horinouchi. (Orig.). 1978. pap. 4.95 (*0-89036-107-X*) Hawkes Pub Inc.

Troubled Times: Fortnight Magazine & the Troubles in Northern Ireland, 1970-1991. Ed. by Robert Bell et al. (Illus.). 221p. (Orig.). 1991. pap. 21.00 (*0-85640-462-4*, Pub. by Blackstaff Pr IE) Dufour.

Troubled Times for American Higher Education: The 1990s & Beyond. Clark Kerr. LC 92-47354. (SUNY Series, Frontiers in Education). 189p. (C). 1993. text ed. 59.50 (*0-7914-1705-0*); pap. text ed. 19.95 (*0-7914-1706-9*) State U NY Pr.

Troubled Transition: Poland's Struggle for Pluralism. Ed. by Tadeusz Jarski. (C). 1990. 45.00 (*0-907967-16-7*, Pub. by Inst Euro Def & Strat UK) St Mut.

Troubled Trinity: Godoy & the Spanish Monarchs. Douglas Hilt. LC 86-7017. (Illus.). 343p. 1987. reprint ed. pap. 97.80 (*0-608-01669-1*, 2062325) Bks Demand.

Troubled Triumphant Church: An Exposition of I Corinthians. 2nd ed. Paige Patterson. 326p. reprint ed. pap. 7.95 (*0-317-93397-3*) Criswell Pubns.

Troubled Village. Simon Henwood. (Illus.). 26p. (J). (ps-3). 1991. 13.95 (*0-374-37780-4*) FS&G.

Troubled Voices: Stories of Ethics & Illness. Richard M. Zaner. LC 93-3823. 192p. 1993. 19.95 (*0-8298-0964-3*) Pilgrim OH.

Troubled Water. Sally Gunning. Ed. by Jane Chelius. 240p. (Orig.). 1993. mass mkt. 5.50 (*0-671-76006-8*) PB.

Troubled Waters. Chris Carlson. (Harpoon Ser.). 80p. (Orig.). (YA). 1992. pap. 10.00 (*1-55878-098-X*) Game Designers.

Troubled Waters. Brian Kral. (Orig.). (YA). 1992. Playscript. pap. 5.00 (*0-87602-300-6*) Anchorage.

***Troubled Waters.** Carolyn Wheat. LC 96-53923. 240p. 1997. 21.95 (*0-425-15784-9*, Prime Crime) Berkley Pub.

Troubled Waters. large type ed. Jean Davidson. 1991. pap. 15.99 (*0-7089-6974-7*) Ulverscroft.

Troubled Waters: Champion International & the Pigeon River Controversy. Richard A. Bartlett. LC 94-18741. (Outdoor Tennessee Ser.). (Illus.). 376p. 1995. pap. 17. 95 (*0-87049-888-6*); text ed. 35.00 (*0-87049-887-8*) U of Tenn Pr.

Troubled Waters: Financing Water Investment in the West. Rodney T. Smith. Ed. by Barbara Dyer & Roger Vaughan. 201p. 1984. 16.95 (*0-934842-33-7*) CSPA.

Troubled Waters: New Policies for Managing Water in the American West. Mohamed T. El-Ashry & Diana C. Gibbons. LC 86-62910. 104p. (Orig.). 1986. pap. text ed. 10.00 (*0-915825-15-5*) World Resources Inst.

Troubled Waters: The Fight for the Boundary Waters Canoe Area. Kevin Proescholdt & Rip Rapson. LC 95-37239. (Illus.). 352p. (Orig.). 1995. pap. 19.95 (*0-87839-100-2*) North Star.

Troubled Waters: The Origins of the 1881 Anti-Jewish Pogroms in Russia. I. Michael Aronson. LC 90-33957. (Russian & East European Studies Ser.). 336p. 1990. 49. 95 (*0-8229-3656-9*) U of Pittsburgh Pr.

Troubled Year: Haitians in the Dominican Republic. Ed. by Human Rights Watch Staff. 54p. (Orig.). 1992. pap. 7.00 (*1-56432-082-0*) Hum Rts Watch.

Troubled Youth in Treatment Homes: A Handbook of Therapeutic Foster Care. Pamela Meadowcroft & Barbara A. Trout. (Trilogy Ser.: Bk. 2). 1990. pap. 22.95 (*0-87868-354-2*) Child Welfare.

Troubled Youth, Troubled Families. James Garbarino et al. Ed. by James K. Whittaker. LC 85-20154. (Modern Applications of Social Work Ser.). 369p. (Orig.). 1986. lib. bdg. 48.95 (*0-202-36039-3*) Aldine de Gruyter.

Troublemaker. Kenneth Copeland. 33p. 1978. pap. 2.95 (*0-938458-13-2*) K Copeland Pubns.

Troublemaker. Joseph Hansen. LC 81-4820. (David Brandstetter Mystery Ser.). 160p. 1988. reprint ed. pap. 5.95 (*0-8050-0812-8*, Owl) H Holt & Co.

***Troublemaker: One Man's Crusade.** Harry W. Wu & George Vecsey. 1998. write for info. (*0-345-41625-2*) Ballantine.

Troublemaker: One Man's Crusade Against China's Cruelty. Harry Wu & George Vecsey. (Illus.). 328p. 1996. 25.00 (*0-8129-6374-1*, Times Bks) Random.

***Troublemaker Bride.** Leanne Banks. (How to Catch a Princess Ser.). 1997. mass mkt. 3.50 (*0-373-76070-1*, 1-76070-1) Silhouette.

Troublemaker's Handbook: How to Fight Back Where You Work - & Win! Dan La Botz. (Illus.). 262p. (Orig.). 1991. pap. text ed. 17.00 (*0-914093-04-5*) Labor Notes.

Troubles. J. G. Farrell. 448p. 1986. 4.95 (*0-88184-269-9*) Carroll & Graf.

Troubles. Dale Jensen. (Mucho Somos Ser.: No. 14). 50p. (Orig.). (C). 1993. pap. text ed. 5.95 (*0-914370-60-X*) Mothers Hen.

Troubles: Ireland's Ordeal 1966-1995 & the Search for Peace. Tim P. Coogan. LC 96-67091. 500p. 1996. 29.95 (*1-57098-092-6*) R Rinehart.

***Troubles: Ireland's Ordeal 1966-1996 & the Search for Peace.** Tim P. Coogan. (Illus.). 488p. 1997. pap. 18.95 (*1-57098-144-2*) R Rinehart.

Troubles: The British Army in Northern Ireland, 1969-1970. Linda H. Flanagan & William Rosenau. (Pew Case Studies in International Affairs). 50p. (C). 1996. pap. text ed. 3.50 (*1-56927-369-3*, GU Schl Foreign) Geo U Inst Dplmcy.

Troubles dans les Andains. Boris Vian. 192p. (FRE.). 1984. pap. 13.95 (*0-7859-1476-5*, 2264001798) Fr & Eur.

Troubles de L'invention: Etude sur le doute poetique de Joe Bousquet. Joseph Brami. LC 87-62927. 168p. (FRE.). 1988. lib. bdg. 21.95 (*0-917786-58-0*) Summa Pubns.

Troubles of a Bibliophile or Outpourings from the Heart of a Bookloving Worldling. Martin Breslauer. 1970. 5.00 (*0-910330-16-6*) Grant Dahlstrom.

Troubles on the East Bank: Challenges to the Domestic Stability of Jordan. Robert B. Satloff. (Washington Papers: No. 123). 138p. 1986. pap. 9.95 (*0-317-63124-1*, B2618, Praeger Pubs); lib. bdg. 29.95 (*0-685-18952-X*, C2617, Praeger Pubs) Greenwood.

Troubles on the East Bank: Challenges to the Domestic Stability of the Middle East. Robert B. Satloff. LC 86-18675. (Washington Papers: No. 124). 151p. 1986. pap. text ed. 11.95 (0-275-92618-4, B2618, Praeger Pubs) Greenwood.

Troubles on the East Bank: Challenges to the Domestic Stability of the Middle East. Robert B. Satloff. LC 86-18675. (Washington Papers: No. 124). 151p. 1987. text ed. 49.95 (0-275-92617-6, C2617, Praeger Pubs) Greenwood.

***Troubles the Cat.** Richard Chevat. (Look-Look Bks.). (Illus.). (J). (ps-3). 1997. pap. 2.99 (0-614-28790-1, Golden Books) Western Pub.

***Troubles the Cat: It's Magic.** Richard Chevat. (Big Bag Bks.). (Illus.). 24p. (J). (ps-3). 1997. pap. 2.99 (0-307-12941-1, 12941, Golden Books) Western Pub.

***Troubleshoot on Boat.** Conrad M. Miller. Date not set. write for info. (0-688-05844-2) Hearst Bks.

Troubleshooter. Diana Hamilton. (Presents Ser.). 1993. mass mkt. 2.99 (0-373-11563-6, 1-11563-3) Harlequin Bks.

Troubleshooters Pre-Purchase Home Inspection System: Opens the Door to a Building's Hidden Secrets. Phil Barnard & Bill Quarton. 104p. (Orig.). 1990. pap. 19.95 (0-9626026-0-4) Troubleshooters Pub.

Troubleshooting. 5th ed. Herman. (C). 1994. suppl. ed., teacher ed., pap. text ed. 33.75 (0-15-501950-3) HB Coll Pubs.

***Troubleshooting, Vol. 2.** Marianne Hering. (Lights, Camera, Action! Mysteries Ser.). (J). 1997. pap. text ed. 4.99 (1-56476-563-6, Chariot Bks) Chariot Victor.

Troubleshooting: Basic Writing. 5th ed. Herman. (C). 1994. pap. text ed. 34.25 (0-15-501440-4) HB Coll Pubs.

Troubleshooting: Basic Writing Skills. 4th ed. William Herman & Jeffrey M. Young. 336p. (C). 1990. pap. text ed. 20.75 (0-03-023733-5) HB Coll Pubs.

Troubleshooting Analog Circuits. Robert A. Pease. (EDN Series for Design Engineers). 217p. 1993. pap. 28.95 (0-7506-9499-8) Buttrwrth-Heinemann.

***Troubleshooting & Configuring the Windows NT/95 Registry.** Clayton Johnson. 1600p. 1997. 49.99 (0-672-31066-X) Sams.

Troubleshooting & Configuring Your Linux Server. Mary Bennion & Geoff Galitz. 1996. pap. 39.95 (0-13-493099-1) P-H.

Troubleshooting & Human Factors in Automated Manufacturing Systems. Susan R. Bereiter & Steven M. Miller. LC 88-38248. (Illus.). 310p. 1989. 48.00 (0-8155-1187-6) Noyes.

***Troubleshooting & Repair of Color Television Systems.** Robert L. Goodman. LC 96-53482. (TAB Electronics Technician Library). (Illus.). 350p. 1997. text ed. 44.95 (0-07-024571-1); pap. text ed. 24.95 (0-07-024569-X) McGraw.

Troubleshooting & Repairing Audio & Video Cassette Players & Recorders. Homer L. Davidson. 1992. pap. text ed. 24.95 (0-07-157756-4) McGraw.

Troubleshooting & Repairing Audio & Video Cassette Players & Recorders. Homer L. Davidson. LC 92-9559. 432p. 1992. 29.95 (0-8306-4259-5, 3795); pap. 19.95 (0-8306-4258-7, 3795) McGraw-Hill Prof.

Troubleshooting & Repairing Audio Equipment. Homer L. Davidson. (Illus.). 336p. 1987. 25.95 (0-8306-7167-6, 2867) TAB Bks.

Troubleshooting & Repairing Audio Equipment. 2nd ed. Homer L. Davidson. LC 92-32380. 1993. write for info. (0-8306-3808-3); pap. 19.95 (0-8306-3807-5) McGraw-Hill Prof.

Troubleshooting & Repairing Audio Equipment. 3rd ed. Homer L. Davidson. (Illus.). 528p. 1996. text ed. 44.95 (0-07-015755-3); pap. text ed. 24.95 (0-07-015756-1) McGraw.

Troubleshooting & Repairing Camcorders. 2nd ed. Homer L. Davidson. (Illus.). 592p. 1996. text ed. 44.95 (0-07-015759-6); pap. text ed. 24.95 (0-07-015760-X) McGraw.

Troubleshooting & Repairing Cars. Homer L. Davidson. (Illus.). 576p. 1990. 35.95 (0-8306-8337-2); pap. 22.95 (0-8306-3337-5) McGraw-Hill Prof.

Troubleshooting & Repairing Compact Disc Players. Homer L. Davidson. (Illus.). 368p. 1989. 26.95 (0-8306-9107-3, 3107); pap. 18.95 (0-8306-3107-0, 3107) McGraw-Hill Prof.

Troubleshooting & Repairing Compact Disc Players. 2nd ed. Homer L. Davidson. LC 93-38578. 1994. pap. text ed. 24.95 (0-07-015670-0) McGraw-Hill Prof.

Troubleshooting & Repairing Compact Disc Players. 3rd ed. Homer L. Davidson. (Illus.). 560p. 1996. text ed. 44.95 (0-07-015761-8); pap. text ed. 24.95 (0-07-015762-6) McGraw.

Troubleshooting & Repairing Computer Monitors. Stephen J. Bigelow. LC 94-36797. 1995. text ed. 42.95 (0-07-005408-8) McGraw-Hill Prof.

Troubleshooting & Repairing Computer Monitors. 2nd ed. Stephen J. Bigelow. LC 96-34038. (Illus.). 352p. 1996. text ed. 44.95 (0-07-005733-8) McGraw.

Troubleshooting & Repairing Computer Monitors. 2nd ed. Stephen J. Bigelow. (Illus.). 352p. 1996. pap. text ed. 24.95 (0-07-005734-6) McGraw.

Troubleshooting & Repairing Computer Printers. Stephen J. Bigelow. 328p. 1992. 32.95 (0-8306-3935-7, 3923, Windcrest); pap. 22.95 (0-8306-3934-9, 3923, Windcrest) TAB Bks.

Troubleshooting & Repairing Computer Printers. 2nd ed. Stephen J. Bigelow. (Illus.). 368p. 1996. text ed. 44.95 (0-07-005731-1); pap. text ed. 24.95 (0-07-005732-X) McGraw.

Troubleshooting & Repairing Consumer Electronics Without a Schematic. Homer L. Davidson. LC 93-38577. 1994. text ed. 34.95 (0-07-015649-2); pap. text ed. 22.95 (0-07-015650-6) McGraw-Hill Prof.

***Troubleshooting & Repairing Consumer Electronics Without a Schematic.** 2nd ed. Homer L. Davidson. LC 96-37281. (Illus.). 1996. text ed. 44.95 (0-07-015764-2); pap. text ed. 24.95 (0-07-015765-0) McGraw.

Troubleshooting & Repairing Diesel Engines. 3rd ed. Paul Dempsey. 1995. pap. text ed. 24.95 (0-07-016348-0) McGraw.

Troubleshooting & Repairing Digital Video Systems. Robert L. Goodman. LC 94-48316. 1995. pap. text ed. 40.00 (0-07-024040-X) McGraw-Hill Prof.

Troubleshooting & Repairing Electronic Circuits. 2nd ed. Robert L. Goodman. (Illus.). 320p. 1989. 27.95 (0-8306-9258-4); pap. 18.95 (0-8306-3258-1) McGraw-Hill Prof.

Troubleshooting & Repairing Electronic Circuits. 2nd ed. Tobert L. Goodman. 1989. pap. text ed. 19.95 (0-07-157311-9) McGraw.

Troubleshooting & Repairing Electronic Music Synthesizers. Delton T. Horn. 216p. 1992. 26.95 (0-8306-3922-5); pap. 16.95 (0-8306-3921-7) McGraw-Hill Prof.

Troubleshooting & Repairing Fax Machines. Gordon McComb. (Illus.). 224p. 1991. 26.95 (0-8306-7778-X, 3778); pap. 16.95 (0-8306-3778-8) McGraw-Hill Prof.

Troubleshooting & Repairing Heat Pumps. R. Dodge Woodson. LC 94-29455. 1995. text ed. 44.95 (0-07-008612-5); pap. text ed. 24.95 (0-07-008613-3) McGraw-Hill Prof.

Troubleshooting & Repairing Major Appliances. Eric Kleinert. LC 94-34891. 1995. text ed. 44.95 (0-07-035078-7); pap. text ed. 29.95 (0-07-035079-5) McGraw-Hill Prof.

***Troubleshooting & Repairing Microwave Ovens.** 4th ed. Homer L. Davidson. (Illus.). 528p. 1996. text ed. 44.95 (0-07-015766-9); pap. text ed. 24.95 (0-07-015767-7) McGraw.

Troubleshooting & Repairing Notebook, Palmtop, & Pen Computers: A Technician's Guide. Stephen J. Bigelow. LC 93-32539. 1993. 36.95 (0-8306-4452-0, Windcrest); pap. 24.60 (0-8306-4453-9, Windcrest) TAB Bks.

Troubleshooting & Repairing PC & Memory Systems. Stephen J. Bigelow. 1994. pap. text ed. 24.95 (0-07-005314-6) McGraw.

Troubleshooting & Repairing PC Drives & Memory Systems. Stephen J. Bigelow. 1993. 34.95 (0-8306-4550-0, Windcrest); pap. 22.95 (0-8306-4551-9, Windcrest) TAB Bks.

Troubleshooting & Repairing PCs. 3rd ed. Michael F. Hordeski. LC 96-48864. (Illus.). 400p. 1997. text ed. 44.95 (0-07-030555-2); pap. text ed. 24.95 (0-07-030556-0) McGraw.

Troubleshooting & Repairing Personal Computers. 2nd ed. Margolis. pap. 23.95 (0-07-157666-5) McGraw.

Troubleshooting & Repairing Personal Computers. 2nd ed. Art Margolis. 544p. 1991. 34.95 (0-8306-2187-3, 3504, Windcrest); pap. 23.95 (0-8306-2186-5, Windcrest) TAB Bks.

Troubleshooting & Repairing Personal Computers. 3rd ed. Art Margolis. LC 93-39124. (Glencoe Tech Ser.). 1993. write for info. (0-02-802003-0) Macmillan.

Troubleshooting & Repairing Power Tools. Homer L. Davidson. (Illus.). 350p. 1990. pap. 17.95 (0-8306-3347-2) McGraw-Hill Prof.

Troubleshooting & Repairing Power Tools. Homer L. Davidson. (Illus.). 350p. 1990. 26.95 (0-8306-7347-4, 3347) TAB Bks.

Troubleshooting & Repairing Small Home Appliances. Bob Wood. (Illus.). 256p. 1988. 23.95 (0-8306-9912-0) McGraw-Hill Prof.

Troubleshooting & Repairing Solid-State TVs. Homer L. Davidson. (Illus.). 480p. 1986. pap. 18.95 (0-8306-2707-3, 2707P) McGraw-Hill Prof.

Troubleshooting & Repairing Solid-State TVs. 2nd ed. Homer L. Davidson. 624p. 1992. 36.95 (0-8306-3894-6); pap. 24.95 (0-8306-3893-8) McGraw-Hill Prof.

Troubleshooting & Repairing Solid-State TVs. 3rd ed. Homer L. Davidson. (Illus.). 592p. 1996. text ed. 44.95 (0-07-015753-7) McGraw.

Troubleshooting & Repairing Solid-State TVs. 3rd ed. Homer L. Davidson. (Illus.). 592p. 1996. pap. text ed. 24.95 (0-07-015754-5) McGraw.

Troubleshooting & Repairing the New Personal Computer. Art Margolis. (Illus.). 416p. (Orig.). 1987. 26.95 (0-8306-0209-7) McGraw-Hill Prof.

Troubleshooting & Repairing TVRO Systems. Stan Prentiss. (Illus.). 224p. 1988. 24.95 (0-8306-0592-4); pap. 16.95 (0-8306-2992-0) McGraw-Hill Prof.

Troubleshooting & Repairing VCRs. Gordon McComb. (Illus.). 432p. 1988. 26.95 (0-8306-0060-4, 2960) McGraw-Hill Prof.

Troubleshooting & Repairing VCRs. 2nd ed. Gordon McComb. (Illus.). 352p. 1991. 29.95 (0-8306-7777-1, 3777); pap. 19.95 (0-8306-3777-X) McGraw-Hill Prof.

Troubleshooting & Repairing VCRs. 3rd ed. Gordon McComb. LC 95-3221. 432p. 1995. pap. text ed. 22.95 (0-07-155017-8) McGraw.

Troubleshooting & Repairing VCRs. 3rd ed. Gordon McComb. LC 95-3221. 432p. 1995. text ed. 34.95 (0-07-155016-X) McGraw-Hill Prof.

Troubleshooting & Repairing Your Commodore 128. Art Margolis. (Illus.). 400p. 1988. 27.95 (0-8306-9099-9, 3099) McGraw-Hill Prof.

Troubleshooting & Repairing Your Commodore 64. Art Margolis. (Illus.). 288p. (Orig.). 1985. 22.95 (0-8306-0889-3, 1889) McGraw-Hill Prof.

Troubleshooting & Servicing Air Conditioning Equipment. S. Don Swenson. LC 90-2045. 383p. 1990. 29.95 (0-912524-56-1) Busn News.

Troubleshooting & Servicing Modern Air Conditioning & Refrigeration Systems. John Tomczyk. Ed. by Joanna Turpin. LC 94-26238. (Illus.). 296p. (C). 1995. text ed. 34.95 (0-912524-94-4) Busn News.

Troubleshooting & Supporting Networks: For Novell Test No. 50-602; NetWare Service & Support. 4th rev. ed. Muhammad Zafar. (CNE Training Manual Ser.). (Illus.). 300p. 1996. text ed. 75.00 (1-57739-006-7) PC Age.

Troubleshooting & Understanding Electrical & Motor Controls: Video Guide & Workbook. Luis A. Bryan & Eric A. Bryan. Ed. by Lou Thompson. (Illus.). 417p. (C). 1995. pap. text ed. 54.00 (0-944107-07-9, 661) Indust Text.

***Troubleshooting Anti-Lock Brakes.** Peter Bilotta. Ed. by Kelly Gorham. 27p. (YA). (gr. 10 up). 1995. wbk. ed., pap. write for info. (0-8064-0616-X, A45) Bergwall.

Troubleshooting Communications Facilities. Bertil C. Lindberg. LC 89-31891. 321p. 1990. text ed. 99.95 (0-471-61286-3) Wiley.

Troubleshooting Concrete Flatwork & Paving Problems. rev. ed. 44p. 1976. pap. 11.95 (0-924659-04-1, 4020) Aberdeen Group.

Troubleshooting Data Communications & Networks. Neil Hollingum. (Illus.). 350p. (C). 1991. pap. text ed. write for info. (0-201-54431-8) Addison-Wesley.

Troubleshooting DC-AC Circuits with Electronics Workbench. Richard Parker. 52p. 1994. pap. 27.50 (0-8273-6721-X) Delmar.

***Troubleshooting Digital Electronics & Microprocessor Systems.** Paul Cuthbertson. 1997. pap. text ed. 28.95 (0-7506-3098-1) Buttrwrth-Heinemann.

Troubleshooting Digital Systems Lab Manual. 6th ed. Deloach & Ambrosio. 1994. pap. text ed. 36.00 (0-13-303777-0) P-H.

***Troubleshooting Electric Motors.** 2nd ed. Thomas E. Proctor & G. A. Mazur. (Illus.). 299p. 1996. 28.96 (0-8269-1765-8) Am Technical.

Troubleshooting Electrical - Electronic Systems. Thomas E. Proctor & Glen A. Mazur. LC 94-10801. (Illus.). 476p. 1994. pap. text ed. 35.96 (0-8269-1775-5) Am Technical.

Troubleshooting Electrical Components. Peter Novellino. (Orig.). 1983. student ed. 5.00 (0-8064-0173-7, 461); audio, vhs 189.00 (0-8064-0174-5) Bergwall.

Troubleshooting Electronic Devices. Joel Goldberg. LC 92-40592. 242p. 1994. pap. 29.95 (0-8273-4889-4) Delmar.

Troubleshooting Electronic Devices: Instructor's Guide. Joel Goldberg. 22p. 1994. pap. 16.00 (0-8273-4890-8) Delmar.

Troubleshooting Electronic Devices with Electronics Workbench. Richard A. Parker. 57p. 1994. text ed. 26.95 (0-8273-6760-0) Delmar.

Troubleshooting Electronic Equipment the Right Way Without Using Expensive Test Instruments. John Douglas-Young. LC 92-28265. 240p. 1992. text ed. 47.00 (0-13-554114-X) P-H.

Troubleshooting Equipment in Combat Units. 1995. lib. bdg. 261.00 (0-8490-6666-2) Gordon Pr.

Troubleshooting for Electronics. Albert P. Malvino. (IBM PC Ser.). (Illus.). 82p. (C). 1990. student ed. 12.50 (1-56048-901-4, 904) Malvino Inc.

***Troubleshooting Game Guide.** Prima Publishing Staff. 1997. pap. 7.99 (0-7615-1218-7) Prima Pub.

Troubleshooting Grades K thru 6: A Handbook for Parents & Teachers. Lis Fleming. (Illus.). 72p. (Orig.). (C). 1983. pap. 9.95 (0-685-26802-0) Fleming Ltd.

Troubleshooting Grammar Problems in Writing. 2nd ed. Roach & Williams. 264p. 1995. per. 25.14 (0-8403-7337-6) Kendall-Hunt.

Troubleshooting Guide. rev. ed. 20p. 1982. pap. 7.00 (0-924659-13-0, 4040) Aberdeen Group.

***Troubleshooting Guide to Residential Construction.** Ed. by Steven Bliss & Josie Masterson-Glen. (Illus.). 304p. (Orig.). 1997. pap. 32.50 (0-9632268-4-3, Jrnl Lght) Builderburg Grp.

Troubleshooting Home Video Microprocessing. Bob Goodman. (Illus.). 384p. 1987. 24.95 (0-8306-0158-9) McGraw-Hill Prof.

Troubleshooting HVAC-R Systems. Jim Johnson. LC 95-35411. (Heating, Ventilation & Air Conditioning Ser.). 267p. 1996. pap. 27.95 (0-8273-6392-3) Delmar.

Troubleshooting Hydraulic Components Using Leakage Path Analysis Methods. Rory S. McLaren. 450p. (C). 1993. pap. text ed. 49.95 (0-9639619-1-8) R McLaren FPT.

Troubleshooting Hydraulic Systems. Tel-A-Train, Inc. Staff. 1986. student ed. 17.50 (1-56355-059-8) Tel-A-Train.

Troubleshooting Injection Molded Parts. William J. Tobin. (Illus.). 86p. (Orig.). (C). 1996. pap. text ed. 25.00 (0-936994-15-0) W J T Assocs.

Troubleshooting Internetworks: Tools, Techniques, & Protocols. Mark A. Miller. (Illus.). 350p. (Orig.). 1991. pap. 34.95 (1-55851-236-5, M&T Books) H Holt & Co.

Troubleshooting LC Systems: A Comprehensive Approach to Troubleshooting LC Equipment & Separations. John W. Dolan & Lloyd R. Snyder. LC 88-34722. (Illus.). 528p. 1989. 85.00 (0-89603-151-9) Humana.

Troubleshooting Local Area Networks. Othmar Kyas & Thomas Heim. 256p. 1995. pap. 37.95 (1-85032-122-1) ITCP.

Troubleshooting Macintosh Networks. Kurt Vandersluis. 1993. pap. 34.95 incl. disk (1-55851-315-9, M&T Books) H Holt & Co.

Troubleshooting, Maintaining, & Repairing Personal Computers: A Technician's Guide. Stephen J. Bigelow. LC 95-22071. 1995. pap. text ed. 44.95 (0-07-912099-7) McGraw.

Troubleshooting, Maintaining, & Repairing Personal Computers: A Technician's Guide. Stephen J. Bigelow. LC 95-22071. 1995. text ed. 70.00 (0-07-912098-9) McGraw-Hill Prof.

Troubleshooting Manufacturing Process. Ed. by Laroux K. Gillespie. LC 88-61825. 545p. 1988. 100.00 (0-87263-326-8) SME.

Troubleshooting Microprocessor Based Systems. G. B. Williams. 213p. 1984. pap. 34.95 (0-08-029988-1, Prgamon Press) Buttrwrth-Heinemann.

Troubleshooting Natural Gas Processing - Wellhead to Transmission. Norman P. Lieberman. 208p. 1987. 79.95 (0-87814-308-4) PennWell Bks.

Troubleshooting Netware Systems. 2nd ed. Logan Harbaugh. (Illus.). 496p. (Orig.). 1996. pap. 65.00 incl. cd-rom (0-7821-1904-2, Network Pr) Sybex.

Troubleshooting NetWare 3.12. Ken Neff & Michael Day. LC 94-42768. 1995. pap. text ed. 34.95 (1-55851-432-5, M&T Books) H Holt & Co.

Troubleshooting Netware 4.1. 2nd ed. Ken Neff & David Doering. 1995. pap. 34.95 (1-55851-285-3, M&T Books) H Holt & Co.

***Troubleshooting NT Networks.** 832p. 1997. 44.99 (0-7821-1981-6) Sybex.

Troubleshooting Process Operations. 3rd ed. Norman P. Lieberman. 576p. 1991. 94.95 (0-87814-348-3) PennWell Bks.

Troubleshooting Screens & Stencil Systems see Pocket Printer Series

Troubleshooting, Servicing, & Theory of AM, FM, & FM Stereo Receivers. 2nd ed. Clarence R. Green & Robert Bourque. (Illus.). 608p. 1986. text ed. 97.00 (0-13-931114-9) P-H.

Troubleshooting Solid State Circuits. George C. Loveday & Arthur H. Seidman. LC 80-21954. 110p. 1981. pap. text ed. 14.95 (0-471-08371-2) P-H.

Troubleshooting the Electrical System. Paul Tucker. Ed. by Dave Garman. (Automotive Ser.). student ed. 7.00 (0-8064-0007-2, A36); audio, vhs 439.00 (0-8064-0006-4, A42) Bergwall.

Troubleshooting the High School Band: How to Detect & Correct Common & Uncommon Performance Problems. Carrol M. Butts. LC 80-24776. 224p. 1981. 22.95 (0-13-931105-X, Parker Publishing Co) P-H.

Troubleshooting the Steel Casting Process. 1987. 45.00 (0-685-66218-7) Steel Founders.

Troubleshooting the Troubleshooting Course: Debug d'Bugs. Robert F. Mager. LC 82-81980. 1983. pap. 18.95 (1-56103-370-7) Ctr Effect Perf.

Troubleshooting Windows. Mark Minasi. LC 92-62324. 442p. 1992. 27.95 (0-7821-1115-7) Sybex.

Troubleshooting with the Vat Forty. John Primi. LC 80-730756. (Orig.). 1980. student ed. 5.00 (0-8064-0147-8, 441); audio, vhs 359.00 (0-8064-0148-6) Bergwall.

Troubleshooting with Your Triggered-Sweep Oscilloscope. Robert L. Goodman. 320p. 1991. 27.95 (0-8306-3892-X); pap. 18.95 (0-8306-3891-1) McGraw-Hill Prof.

Troubleshooting Your Multimedia PC. John Montgomery. LC 95-1577. 1995. pap. 19.95 (0-201-48347-5) Addison-Wesley.

Troubleshooting Your PC. Aspinwall et al. (Illus.). 496p. (Orig.). 1991. pap. 32.95 incl. disk (1-55851-244-6, M&T Books) H Holt & Co.

Troubleshooting Your PC. Jim Aspinwall. (Orig.). 1991. pap. 26.95 (1-55851-224-1) H Holt & Co.

Troubleshooting Your PC. 3rd ed. Jim Aspinwall. 1996. pap. 34.95 incl. cd-rom (1-55828-493-1) MIS Press.

Troubleshooting TCP/IP. 2nd ed. Mark Miller. 640p. 1996. pap. 49.95 incl. cd-rom (1-55851-450-3, M&T Books) H Holt & Co.

Troublesome Behaviour in the Classroom: Meeting Individual Needs. 2nd ed. Mick McManus. LC 94-34160. (Illus.). 224p. (C). 1995. pap. 17.95 (0-415-11360-1, C0070) Routledge.

Troublesome Bible Passages. David L. Watson & Douglas Wingeier. 112p. (Orig.). 1994. student ed., pap. 3.50 (0-687-78377-1); teacher ed., pap. 4.95 (0-687-78378-X) Abingdon.

***Troublesome Bible Passages, Vol. 2.** Randy Cross. 1997. pap. text ed. 3.95 (0-687-06173-3) Abingdon.

***Troublesome Board Member, Vol. 137.** Mark Bailey. (Illus.). 25p. (Orig.). 1996. pap. text ed. 17.00 (0-925299-55-3) Natl Ctr Nonprofit.

Troublesome Border. Oscar J. Martinez. LC 87-34294. (PROFMEX Ser.). 177p. 1989. reprint ed. pap. 12.50 (0-8165-1104-7) U of Ariz Pr.

***Troublesome Disguises.** Dinesh Bhugra & Alistair Munro. LC 97-4247. 1997. write for info. (0-86542-674-0) Blackwell Sci.

Troublesome English. Killian & Richard Firsten. 1994. wbk. ed., pap. text ed. 16.95 (0-13-328857-9) P-H.

Troublesome Presence: Democracy & the African-Americans. rev. ed. Eli Ginzberg & Alfred S. Eichner. LC 93-16163. 423p. (C). 1993. pap. text ed. 24.95 (1-56000-695-1) Transaction Pubs.

Troublesome Reign of King John. LC 75-133750. (Tudor Facsimile Texts. Old English Plays Ser.: No. 59). reprint ed. 49.50 (0-404-53359-0) AMS Pr.

Troublesome Snout. Jenny Hessell. LC 92-34274. (Voyages Ser.). (Illus.). (J). 1993. 14.00 (0-383-03662-3) SRA McGraw.

***Troublesome Teachings.** Henry R. Rust. 54p. 1993. pap. 8.45 (1-877871-52-4, 6445) Ed Ministries.

Troublesome Triangle: Sons, Wives & Mothers-in-Law. Emily C. Martinsen & Joyce Bolender. LC 95-72721. 93p. 1995. 9.95 (0-9651135-0-7) E C Martinsen.

Troubling a Star. Madeleine L'Engle. 304p. (YA). (gr. 5 up). 1995. mass mkt. 4.99 (0-440-21950-7, LLL BDD) BDD Bks Young Read.

An Asterisk (*) at the beginning of an entry indicates that the title is appearing in BIP for the first time.

Troubling a Star. Madeleine L'Engle. LC 93-50956. (J). 1994. 16.00 (*0-374-37783-9*) FS&G.

Troubling along the Border. Donald Aamodt. 288p. (Orig.). 1991. mass mkt. 4.50 (*0-380-75827-X*) Avon.

Troubling Children: Children & Social Problems. Ed. by Joel Best. (Social Problems & Social Issues Ser.). 259p. 1994. pap. text ed. 24.95 (*0-202-30492-2*); lib. bdg. 47.95 (*0-202-30491-4*) Aldine de Gruyter.

Troubling in My Soul: Womanist Perspectives on Evil & Suffering. Ed. by Emilie Townes. LC 93-23875. (Bishop Henry McNeal Turner Studies: Vol. 8). 300p. (Orig.). 1993. pap. 17.50 (*0-88344-783-5*) Orbis Bks.

***Troubling the Angels.** Patricia A. Lather. LC 97-3989. (C). 1997. pap. text ed. 15.00 (*0-8133-9016-8*) Westview.

Troublous Times in Canada: A History of the Fenian Raids of 1866 & 1870. John A. MacDonald. 255p. (C). 1987. 91.00 (*0-317-90438-8*, Pub. by Picton UK) St Mut.

Troublous Times in New Mexico, 1659-1670. France V. Scholes. LC 75-41242. (New Mexico Hist. Society. Publications in History: Vol. 11). reprint ed. 39.50 (*0-404-14701-1*) AMS Pr.

***Troupe de Marine.** Yves Debay. 1997. 49.95 (*2-908182-53-X*, Zenith Aviation) Motorbooks Intl.

Troupers & Tramps: One Person Plays. Rachael C. Burchard. Ed. by Arthur L. Zapel. LC 93-38914. 144p. (Orig.). 1994. pap. text ed. 10.95 (*1-56608-001-0*, B148) Meriwether Pub.

Troupers of the Gold Coast: or The Rise of Lotta Crabtree. Constance M. Rourke. 1992. reprint ed. lib. bdg. 75.00 (*0-7812-5082-X*) Rprt Serv.

Troupe's Re-Employment Resource Guide. Ed. by Brian Jud. (Illus.). 130p. (Orig.). (C). 1994. pap. text ed. 14.95 (*1-880218-15-1*) Mktg Dir Inc.

Trouping America. Bonnie Holt. (Illus.). 128p. (Orig.). 1992. pap. 12.95 (*0-939710-17-X*) Meridional Pubns.

Trouping in Oregon Country. Alice H. Ernst. LC 74-15552. (Illus.). 197p. 1974. reprint ed. text ed. 65.00 (*0-8371-7821-5*, EROC, Greenwood Pr) Greenwood.

Trouping Through Texas: Harley Sadler & His Tent Show. Clifford Ashby & Suzanne D. May. LC 81-82503. 194p. 1982. 15.95 (*0-87972-184-7*); pap. 9.95 (*0-87972-185-5*) Bowling Green Univ Popular Press.

***Trouser Press Guide to '90s Alternative Rock & Roll.** Robbins. 1997. pap. 24.95 (*0-684-81437-4*) S&S Trade.

Trouser Press Record Guide. 4th ed. Ira A. Robbins. 800p. 1991. pap. 20.00 (*0-02-036361-3*) Macmillan.

***Trouser-Wearing Character: The Life & Times of Nancy Spain.** Rose Collis. (Sexual Politics Ser.). (Illus.). 256p. 1997. 75.00 (*0-304-32879-0*); pap. 17.95 (*0-304-32877-4*) Cassell.

Trousseau. John Martone. 40p. (Orig.). 1991. pap. 3.00 (*0-926935-46-1*) Runaway Spoon.

***Trousseau of Blondinette Davranches: A Huret Doll & Her Wardrobe, 1862-1867.** Florence Theriault. (Illus.). 80p. 1996. 33.00 (*0-614-23815-3*, N5161) Hobby Hse.

Trousseau Wedding Organizer. Ed. & Illus. by C. R. Gibson. 68p. 1993. 20.00 (*0-8378-9916-8*) Gibson.

Trout. Ray Bergman. (Illus.). 608p. 1991. 14.99 (*0-517-05797-2*) Random Hse Value.

Trout. Dick Sternberg & Parker Bauer. LC 88-23684. (Hunting & Fishing Library). (Illus.). 160p. 1988. 19.95 (*0-86573-027-X*) Cowles Creative.

Trout. Ed. by Judith Stolz & Judith Schnell. LC 90-19751. (Wildlife Ser.). (Illus.). 384p. 1991. 59.95 (*0-8117-1652-X*) Stackpole.

***Trout.** Cherie Winner. LC 97-15497. (J). 1998. write for info. (*1-57505-245-8*, Carolrhoda) Lerner Group.

Trout: A Fisherman's Natural History. Rupert Watson. (Illus.). 208p. 1993. 42.95 (*1-85310-235-0*, Pub. by Swan Hill UK) Voyageur Pr.

Trout: An Illustrated History. James Prosek. 168p. 1996. 27.50 (*0-679-44453-X*) Knopf.

Trout: Fly Fishing; Fly Tying, 2 Vol. Set, Set. Philip White. LC 94-41900. (Illus.). 192p. 1995. 35.00 (*0-8478-1868-3*) Rizzoli Intl.

Trout: The Old Man & the Orphans. Don Schnake. 137p. 1992. pap. 11.95 (*0-9648738-0-X*) Richview Pr.

Trout & Salmon Culture (Hatchery Methods) Earl Leitritz & Robert C. Lewis. (Illus.). 197p. 1980. reprint ed. pap. 6.50 (*0-931876-36-2*, 4100) ANR Pubns CA.

Trout & Salmon Fishing in Northern New England: A Guide to Selected Waters in Maine, New Hampshire, Vermont & Massachusetts. Al Raychard. LC 82-5930. (Illus.). 206p. (Orig.). 1982. pap. 9.95 (*0-945980-42-6*) Nrth Country Pr.

Trout & Salmon Flies of Ireland. Peter O'Reilly. (Fly Fishing International Ser.). (Illus.). 176p. 1996. 34.95 (*0-8117-1610-4*) Stackpole.

Trout & Salmon Fly Index. Dick Surrette. LC 78-24196. (Illus.). 144p. 1979. pap. 18.95 (*0-8117-2093-4*) Stackpole.

Trout & Salmon of Pacific Coast. David S. Jordan. 16p. reprint ed. pap. 1.95 (*0-8466-0071-4*, S71) Shorey.

Trout & Salmon of the World. Silvio Calab. 1990. 34.98 (*1-55521-665-X*) Bk Sales Inc.

Trout & Salmon Rivers of Ireland: An Angler's Guide. Peter O'Reilly. (Fly Fishing International Ser.). (Illus.). 336p. 1995. 24.95 (*0-8117-1758-5*) Stackpole.

Trout & Sea Trout Rivers of Scotland. Roderick Wilkinson. (Illus.). 160p. 1992. 27.95 (*1-85310-094-3*, Pub. by Swan Hill UK) Voyageur Pr.

Trout & Terrestrials. Lou Stevens. (Illus.). 96p. (Orig.). 1996. pap. 19.95 (*1-85310-388-8*, Pub. by Swan Hill UK) Voyageur Pr.

Trout & the Fly. Brian Clarke & John Goddard. 192p. 1996. 40.00 (*1-55821-441-0*) Lyons & Burford.

Trout & Trouting. David Scholes. (Illus.). 80p. 1993. 19.95 (*0-86417-540-X*, Pub. by Kangaroo Pr AT) Seven Hills Bk.

Trout Biology: An Angler's Guide. William B. Willers. LC 81-50829. 224p. 1981. 22.50 (*0-299-08720-4*) U of Wis Pr.

Trout Book: A Complete Angler's Guide. Frank Sargeant. LC 92-71318. (Inshore Ser.). (Illus.). 160p. (Orig.). (YA). 1992. pap. 11.95 (*0-936513-21-7*) Larsens Outdoor.

Trout Bum. John Gierach. LC 86-4995. 227p. 1986. 25.00 (*0-87108-715-4*) Pruett.

Trout Bum: Essays on Fly-Fishing As a Way of Life. John Gierach. (Illus.). 224p. 1988. pap. 12.00 (*0-671-64413-0*, Fireside) S&S Trade.

Trout Cook: One Hundred Ways with Trout. Patricia A. Hayes. (Illus.). 141p. 1991. 29.95 (*1-85223-130-0*, Pub. by Crowood Pr UK) Trafalgar.

Trout Cookbook. A. D. Livingston. 160p. 1996. pap. 12.95 (*0-8117-2581-2*) Stackpole.

Trout Country. Michael Furtman. LC 95-15131. (Wildlife Country Ser.). (Illus.). 160p. 1995. 39.00 (*1-55971-472-7*) NorthWord.

Trout Farming Handbook. 5th ed. Stephen D. Sedgwick. (Illus.). 192p. 1990. pap. 39.95 (*0-85238-174-3*) Blackwell Sci.

Trout Farming Handbook. 6th ed. Stephen D. Sedgwick. 1995. pap. 34.95 (*0-85238-232-4*) Blackwell Sci.

Trout Fever. Bruce Cochran. (Fever Ser.). (Illus.). 96p. (Orig.). 1993. write for info. (*1-55971-148-5*); pap. 7.95 (*1-55971-149-3*) NorthWord.

***Trout Fishers Almanac: How to Catch & Comprehend America's Favorite Fish.** Ed. by Sid Evans. LC 97-13971. (Illus.). 320p. 1997. 25.00 (*0-87113-676-7*, Atlntc Mnthly) Grove-Atltic.

Trout Fishing: A Guide to New Zealand's South Island. Tony Busch. (Fly Fishing International Ser.). (Illus.). 232p. 1995. pap. 29.95 (*0-8117-2583-9*) Stackpole.

Trout Fishing: The Tactical Secrets of Lake Fishing. Ed A. Rychkun. 120p. 1994. pap. 11.95 (*0-88839-338-5*) Hancock House.

Trout Fishing in America, the Pill Versus the Spring Hill Mine Disaster & in Watermelon Sugar. Richard Brautigan. 1989. pap. 13.95 (*0-395-50076-1*) HM.

***Trout Fishing in California: 1997-1998 Edition.** 5th ed. Ron Kovach. (Illus.). 208p. (Orig.). 1997. pap. 14.95 (*0-934061-32-7*) Marketscope Bks.

Trout Fishing in North Georgia: A Comprehensive Guide to Public Streams & Rivers. 2nd rev. ed. Jimmy Jacobs. 224p. (Orig.). 1996. pap. 13.95 (*1-56145-128-2*) Peachtree Pubs.

Trout Fishing in Southeast Minnesota: A Selective Guide to the Streams & Rivers of Minnesota's Bluff Country. John Van Vliet. (Illus.). 52p. (Orig.). 1992. pap. 9.95 (*0-9632344-2-0*) Highweather.

Trout Fishing in the Shenandoah National Park. Harry W. Murray. (Illus.). 100p. (Orig.). 1989. pap. 10.95 (*0-9622555-0-5*) Shenandoah Edinburg.

Trout Fishing Sourcebook. Mark Williams. (Illus.). 320p. (Orig.). 1996. pap. 19.95 (*0-89732-189-8*) Menasha Ridge.

***Trout Fishing Wisconsin Spring Ponds.** unabridged ed. Christopher Deubler. LC 96-92605. (Illus.). viii, 128p. (Orig.). 1996. pap. 12.95 (*0-9654303-0-8*) Siskiwit Pr.

Trout Flies: Proven Patterns. Gary LaFontaine. (Illus.). 280p. 1993. 39.95 (*0-9626663-1-9*) Greycliff Pub.

Trout for Everyone. Thomas Gauthier. (Illus.). 287p. (Orig.). 1993. pap. text ed. 14.95 (*0-937866-46-6*) Atlantic Pub Co.

Trout for Everyone. Thomas Gauthier. (Illus.). 288p. (Orig.). 1994. pap. text ed. 14.95 (*0-937886-46-7*) Atlantic Pub Co.

Trout Madness. John Voelker. 178p. 1992. 21.95 (*1-878005-47-2*) Northmont Pub.

Trout Magic. Robert Traver. 1989. pap. 10.00 (*0-671-66194-9*, Fireside) S&S Trade.

Trout Magic. John Voelker. 216p. 1992. reprint ed. pap. 21.95 (*1-878005-50-2*) Northmont Pub.

Trout Maverick: Fly-Fishing Heresies & Tactics. Leonard M. Wright, Jr. LC 96-12461. (Illus.). 224p. 1996. 25.00 (*1-55821-476-3*) Lyons & Burford.

Trout on a Nymph. John Roberts. (Illus.). 192p. 1992. 45.00 (*1-85223-340-0*, Pub. by Crowood Pr UK) Trafalgar.

Trout on a Stick. John Wright. 144p. 1991. pap. 14.95 (*1-55971-111-6*, 0109) NorthWord.

Trout Reflections. David M. Carroll. 160p. 1996. pap. 11.95 (*0-312-14142-4*) St Martin.

Trout Stream Insects: An Orvis Streamside Guide. Dick Pobst. 96p. 1991. pap. 16.95 (*1-55821-067-9*) Lyons & Burford.

Trout Stream Therapy. Robert L. Hunt. LC 93-22106. (North Coast Bks.). (Illus.). 96p. (Orig.). 1993. 39.95 (*0-299-13890-9*); pap. 19.95 (*0-299-13894-1*) U of Wis Pr.

Trout Streams of Michigan. 1978. pap. 7.95 (*0-933112-03-3*) Mich United Conserv.

Trout Streams of Pennsylvania: An Angler's Guide. 2nd ed. Dwight Landis. LC 95-75138. (Illus.). 248p. (Orig.). 1995. pap. 18.95 (*1-879475-01-4*) Hempstead-Lyndell.

Trout Streams of Southern Appalachia: Fly-Casting in Georgia, Kentucky, North Carolina, South Carolina & Tennessee. Jimmy Jacobs. (Illus.). 320p. (Orig.). 1994. pap. 17.00 (*0-88150-303-7*, Backcountry) Countryman.

Trout Summer. Jane L. Conly. LC 95-16381. 208p. (J). (gr. 6-9). 1995. 15.95 (*0-8050-3933-3*) H Holt & Co.

Trout Tales & Other Angling Stories. Laurie Morrow. LC 95-61183. 1995. 29.00 (*1-885106-16-5*) Wild Adven Pr.

Trout the Size of Footballs. Richard Anderson. 150p. (Orig.). 1990. pap. 8.95 (*0-936608-90-0*) F Amato Pubns.

Trout Unlimited Book of Basic Trout Fishing. Bill Cairns. LC 82-50368. (Illus.). 128p. (Orig.). 1990. pap. 9.95 (*0-913276-37-5*) Stone Wall Pr.

Trout Unlimited's Guide to Pennsylvania Limestone Streams. A. Joseph Armstrong. LC 91-34271. (Illus.). 256p. 1992. 22.95 (*0-8117-1651-1*) Stackpole.

Trout Waters. William O. Foye. LC 91-65821. (Illus.). 152p. (Orig.). 1992. pap. 12.95 (*0-9626308-1-0*) Haleys.

Trout Waters in the Adirondack Mountains. 1984. pap. 3.00 (*0-939166-09-7*) Outdoor Pubns.

Trouts from London: William Trout Branch. Peter M. Rinaldo. LC 88-71508. (Illus.). 658p. (C). 1989. 45.00 (*0-9622123-1-8*) DorPete Pr.

Trouveres et Protecteurs De Trouveres Dans les Cours Seigneuriales De France. Holger N. Petersen-Dyggve. LC 80-2168. reprint ed. 41.50 (*0-404-19032-4*) AMS Pr.

Trouveres et Troubadours. 2nd ed. Pierre Aubrey. 223p. 1981. reprint ed. 50.00 (*3-487-07119-3*) G Olms Pubs.

***Trouvez-Moi un Coupable.** Margaret Yorke. 383p. 1997. pap. 25.99 (*2-84011-175-6*) Ulverscroft.

Trova. 2nd ed. Andrew Kagan. (Illus.). 390p. 1987. 125.00 (*1-55660-199-9*) A Wofsy Fine Arts.

Trova. 2nd ed. Andrew Kagan. (Illus.). 366p. 1988. 75.00 (*0-8109-1696-7*) Abrams.

Trovatore. Giuseppe Verdi. Ed. by Nicholas John. Tr. by T. Hammond from ITA. (English National Opera - Royal Opera House Guide Ser.: No. 20). (Illus.). 128p. (Orig.). 1983. pap. 9.95 (*0-7145-3877-9*) Riverrun NY.

Trovatore: Drama in Four Acts by Salvadore Cammarano, 2 vols. Giuseppe Verdi. Ed. by David Lawton. (Works of Giuseppe Verdi: No. I: Operas). 535p. 1993. Set incls. Score, lvi, 460p. & Commentary, 136p. lib. bdg. 275.00 (*0-226-85313-6*) U Ch Pr.

Trovatore: Libretto. Giuseppe Verdi. 44p. (ENG & ITA.). 1986. pap. 4.95 (*0-7935-2394-X*, 50340250) H Leonard.

Trow-Wife's Treasure. Olivier Dunrea. LC 96-24030. 1997. write for info. (*0-374-37792-8*) FS&G.

Trowbridge Family: Or, The Descendants of Thomas Trowbridge, One of the First Settlers of New Haven, Connecticut. F. W. Chapman. (Illus.). 461p. 1989. reprint ed. pap. 69.00 (*0-8328-1181-5*); reprint ed. lib. bdg. 77.00 (*0-8328-1180-7*) Higginson Bk Co.

Trowbridge Genealogy: History of the Trowbridge Family in America. F. B. Trowbridge. (Illus.). 848p. 1989. reprint ed. pap. 150.00 (*0-8328-1183-1*); reprint ed. lib. bdg. 158.00 (*0-8328-1182-3*) Higginson Bk Co.

Troxell - A Portrait of Our Ancestors Jury, Troxell, Shisler & Parrish Vol. II: Troxell. Irene P. Baker. (Illus.). 380p. 1995. pap. 59.50 (*0-8328-4588-4*); lib. bdg. 69.50 (*0-8328-4587-6*) Higginson Bk Co.

Troy. Mark Dunster. LC 74-437973. (Rin Ser.: Pt. 31). 1974. 4.00 (*0-89642-035-3*) Linden Pubs.

Troy: A Study in Homeric Geography. Walter Leaf. LC 70-150191. (Select Bibliographies Reprint Ser.). 1977. reprint ed. 39.95 (*0-8369-5704-0*) Ayer.

Troy: Excavations Conducted by the University of Cincinnati, 1932-1938, 3 vols., Vol. 2, Pt. 1. University of Cincinnati, Excavations in the Troad Staff. Ed. by Carl W. Blegen et al. reprint ed. pap. 86.80 (*0-317-10368-7*, 2001131) Bks Demand.

Troy: Excavations Conducted by the University of Cincinnati, 1932-1938, 3 vols., Vol. 2, Pt. 2. University of Cincinnati, Excavations in the Troad Staff. Ed. by Carl W. Blegen et al. reprint ed. pap. 52.30 (*0-317-10369-5*) Bks Demand.

Troy: Excavations Conducted by the University of Cincinnati, 1932-1938, 3 vols., Vol. 3, Pt. 1. University of Cincinnati, Excavations in the Troad Staff. Ed. by Carl W. Blegen et al. reprint ed. pap. 112.00 (*0-317-10370-9*) Bks Demand.

Troy: Excavations Conducted by the University of Cincinnati, 1932-1938, 3 vols., Vol. 3, Pt. 2. University of Cincinnati, Excavations in the Troad Staff. Ed. by Carl W. Blegen et al. reprint ed. pap. 75.00 (*0-317-10371-7*) Bks Demand.

Troy: Excavations Conducted by the University of Cincinnati, 1932-1938, 3 vols., Vol. 4, Pt. 1. University of Cincinnati, Excavations in the Troad Staff. Ed. by Carl W. Blegen et al. reprint ed. pap. 89.50 (*0-317-10372-5*) Bks Demand.

Troy: Excavations Conducted by the University of Cincinnati, 1932-1938, 3 vols., Vol. 4, Pt. 2. University of Cincinnati, Excavations in the Troad Staff. Ed. by Carl W. Blegen et al. reprint ed. pap. 58.80 (*0-317-10373-3*) Bks Demand.

Troy Aikman. James Beckett. (Beckett Great Sports Heroes Ser.). (Illus.). 128p. 1996. 15.00 (*0-676-60035-2*, House of Collect) Ballantine.

Troy Aikman. Carl R. Green. LC 93-17480. (Sports Headliners Ser.). (Illus.). 48p. (J). (gr. 5-6). 1994. pap. 7.95 (*0-382-24807-4*, Crstwood Hse); lib. bdg. 13.95 (*0-89686-833-8*, Crstwood Hse) Silver Burdett Pr.

Troy Aikman. Paul Joseph. LC 96-16088. (Awesome Athletes Ser.). (J). 1997. lib. bdg. 13.95 (*1-56239-643-9*) Abdo & Dghtrs.

Troy Aikman. Richard Rosenblatt. LC 95-18223. (Football Legends Ser.). (Illus.). 64p. (J). (gr. 3 up). 1996. lib. bdg. 15.95 (*0-7910-2457-1*) Chelsea Hse.

Troy Aikman: All-American Quarterback. R. Conrad Stein. LC 95-2496. (Sports Stars Ser.). 48p. (J). (gr. 2-8). 1995. lib. bdg. 17.50 (*0-516-04394-3*) Childrens.

Troy Aikman: All-American Quarterback. R. Conrad Stein. (Sports Stars Ser.). (Illus.). 48p. (J). (gr. 2-8). 1996. reprint ed. pap. 4.50 (*0-516-44394-1*) Childrens.

Troy Aikman: Super Quarterback. Bill Gutman. LC 95-8830. (The Millbrook Sports World Ser.). (Illus.). 48p. (J). (gr. 3-6). 1996. lib. bdg. 14.90 (*1-56294-570-X*) Millbrook Pr.

***Troy Aikman: Super Quarterback.** Bill Gutman. 1997. pap. 6.95 (*0-7613-0296-4*) Millbrook Pr.

Troy Aikman, Quick-Draw Quarterback. Joel Dippold. LC 93-47909. (Sports Achievers Biographies Ser.). (Illus.). 64p. (J). (gr. 4-9). 1994. lib. bdg. 19.95 (*0-8225-2880-0*, Lerner Publctns) Lerner Group.

Troy Aikman, Quick-Draw Quarterback. Joel Dippold. LC 93-47909. (Achievers Ser.). (Illus.). 64p. (YA). (gr. 4-9). 1994. pap. 5.95 (*0-8225-9663-6*, Lerner Publctns) Lerner Group.

***Troy Aikman, Star Quarterback.** Dean Spiros. LC 96-52840. (Sports Reports). (Illus.). 104p. (J). (gr. 4-10). 1997. lib. bdg. 18.95 (*0-89490-927-4*) Enslow Pubs.

Troy & Her Legend. Arthur M. Young. LC 76-141272. (Illus.). 194p. 1971. reprint ed. text ed. 35.00 (*0-8371-5862-1*, YOTR, Greenwood Pr) Greenwood.

Troy & Its Remains. Heinrich Schliemann. 1995. 23.50 (*0-8446-6862-1*) Peter Smith.

Troy & Its Remains. Heinrich Schliemann. Ed. by Philip Smith. LC 68-21228. (Illus.). 1972. reprint ed. 42.95 (*0-405-08934-1*, Pub. by Blom Pubns UK) Ayer.

Troy & Its Remains: A Narrative of Researches & Discoveries Made on the Site of Ilium, & in the Trojan Plain. Heinrich Schliemann. (Illus.). 428p. 1994. reprint ed. pap. 13.95 (*0-486-28079-9*) Dover.

Troy & Paeonia: With Glimpses of Ancient Balkan History & Religion. Grace H. Macurdy. xi, 259p. 1989. reprint ed. text ed. 50.00 (*0-89241-439-1*) Caratzas.

***Troy & Rensselaer County, a History.** Rutherford Hayner. (Illus.). 1242p. 1997. reprint ed. lib. bdg. 128.00 (*0-8328-6263-0*) Higginson Bk Co.

Troy & the Trojan War: A Symposium Held at Bryn Mawr College, October 1984. Ed. by Machteld J. Mellink. (Bryn Mawr Archaeological Monographs). (Illus.). xii, 101p. (Orig.). (C). 1986. pap. text ed. 10.00 (*0-929524-59-4*) Bryn Mawr Commentaries.

Troy Corner Poems. Carolyn Page. Ed. & Illus. by Roy Zarucchi. (Chapbook Ser.). 24p. (Orig.). 1994. pap. 5.00 (*1-879205-46-7*) Nightshade Pr.

Troy, NY. Historical Briefs, Inc. Staff. Ed. by Thomas Antonucci & Michael Antonucci. 176p. 1991. pap. 14.95 (*0-89677-042-7*) Hist Briefs.

***Troy, Piqua, & Miami County, & Representative Citizens.** Ed. by Thomas C. Harbaugh. (Illus.). 857p. 1997. reprint ed. lib. bdg. 87.50 (*0-8328-6345-9*) Higginson Bk Co.

***Troy Stone.** Rabley. 1990. pap. text ed. write for info. (*0-582-04598-3*, Pub. by Longman UK) Longman.

Troy the Coins. Alfred R. Bellinger. LC 81-50603. (Illus.). 1979. reprint ed. lib. bdg. 30.00 (*0-915262-32-0*) S J Durst.

Troy Township Cemeteries, Oakland County, Michigan. Ed. by Joan Pate. 105p. (Orig.). 1988. pap. 7.00 (*1-879766-10-8*) OCG Society.

Troyens Libretto Custom for Metropolitan Opera. H. Berlioz. 56p. 1993. pap. 2.46 (*0-7935-2978-6*) H Leonard.

Troy's One Hundred Years, 1789-1889 (New York) Arthur J. Weise. (Illus.). 453p. 1993. reprint ed. lib. bdg. 46.00 (*0-8328-3127-1*) Higginson Bk Co.

Troyville Mounds, Catahoula Parish, Louisiana. Winslow M. Walker. (Bureau of American Ethnology Bulletins Ser.). 73p. 1995. lib. bdg. 79.00 (*0-7812-4113-8*) Rprt Serv.

Trozas. B. Traven. Tr. by Hugh Young from GER. LC 93-33404. 272p. 1994. 22.50 (*1-56663-044-4*) I R Dee.

TRS-DOS 2.3 Decoded & Other Mysteries. James L. Farvour. (TRS-80 Information Ser.: Vol. 6). (Illus.). 298p. (Orig.). 1982. pap. 29.95 (*0-936200-07-3*) Blue Cat.

TRS-1 555 Timer Applications Source Book with Experiments. Howard M. Berlin. Ed. by David G. Larsen. (Bugbook Reference Ser.). 1976. pap. text ed. 8.00 (*0-89704-011-2*) E&L Instru.

TRS-80, Vol. 1. Henry A. Taitt & Kathy Taitt. (Thinking-Learning-Creating: TLC for Growing Minds Ser.). 53p. (J). (gr. 4-12). 1983. pap. text ed. 11.95 (*0-88193-011-3*) Create Learn.

TRS-80, Vol. 2. Henry A. Taitt & Kathy Taitt. (Thinking-Learning-Creating: TLC for Growing Minds Ser.). 56p. (J). (gr. 4-12). 1983. pap. text ed. 11.95 (*0-88193-012-1*) Create Learn.

TRS-80, Vol. 3. Henry A. Taitt & Jennifer Taitt. (Thinking-Learning-Creating: TLC for Growing Minds Ser.). 53p. (J). (gr. 5-12). 1983. pap. text ed. 11.95 (*0-88193-013-X*) Create Learn.

TRS-80, Vol. 4. Henry A. Taitt & Jennifer Taitt. (Thinking-Learning-Creating: TLC for Growing Minds Ser.). 56p. (J). (gr. 5-12). 1983. pap. text ed. 11.95 (*0-88193-014-8*) Create Learn.

TRS-80, Vol. 5. Henry A. Taitt & Jennifer Taitt. (Thinking-Learning-Creating: TLC for Growing Minds Ser.). 57p. (J). (gr. 6-12). 1983. pap. text ed. 11.95 (*0-88193-015-6*) Create Learn.

TRS-80, Vol. 6. Henry A. Taitt & Jennifer Taitt. (Thinking-Learning-Creating: TLC for Growing Minds Ser.). 54p. (J). (gr. 6-12). 1984. pap. text ed. 11.95 (*0-88193-016-4*) Create Learn.

TRS-80 Beginner's Guide to Games & Graphics. Tom Dempsey. 1984. 16.95 (*0-317-06048-1*); pap. 16.95 (*0-936200-10-3*) Blue Cat.

TRS-80 COBOL. Robert T. Grauer. (Illus.). 352p. 1983. text ed. 38.00 (*0-13-931212-9*) P-H.

TRS-80 Disk & Other Mysteries. Harvard C. Pennington. (TRS-80 Information Ser.: Vol. I). (Illus.). 128p. (Orig.). 1979. pap. 22.50 (*0-936200-00-6*) Blue Cat.

TRS-80 Disk BASIC for Business for the Model II & Model III. Alan J. Parker. 1982. pap. 14.95 (*0-8359-7872-9*, Reston) P-H.

TRS-80 Programming for Learning & Teaching: Forty Plus Application Programs. Frederick Bell. 1984. pap. text ed. 24.00 (*0-8359-7862-1*, Reston) P-H.

TRS-80 ROM Routines Documented. Jack Decker. 126p. 1983. pap. text ed. 19.95 (*0-915363-01-1*) Alter Source.

TRS-80 Teaching Aid: Ready-to-Run Programs for the Classroom & Home. Edward Burns. (Illus.). 1984. pap. 16.95 (*0-8359-7875-3*, Reston) P-H.

An Asterisk (*) at the beginning of an entry indicates that the title is appearing in BIP for the first time.

TRS-80 Word Processing Applications Using SuperScripsit. Carol M. Lehman et al. 1984. teacher ed. write for info. (0-8359-7880-X, Reston) P-H.

Truancy: The Politics of Compulsory Schooling. Pat Carlen et al. 176p. 1992. 90.00 (0-335-09615-8, Open Univ Pr); pap. 27.50 (0-335-09614-X, Open Univ Pr) Taylor & Francis.

Truancy & Non-Attendance in the Chicago Schools: A Study of the Social Aspects of the Compulsory Education & Child Labor Legislation of Illinois. Edith Abbott & Sophonisba P. Breckinridge. LC 74-12526. (Rise of Urban America Ser.). 1978. reprint ed. 29.95 (0-405-02432-0) Ayer.

Truancy, Chronic Absenteeism & Dropping Out. Charlotte G. Garman & Waln K. Brown. 20p. 1989. 2.95 (1-56456-006-6, 202) W Gladden Found.

Truancy in English Secondary Schools - a Report Prepared for the DFE. D. J. O'Keeffe. 134p. 1994. pap. 19.00 (0-11-270870-6, HM08706, Pub. by Stationery Ofc UK) Bernan Associates.

Truant Bather. Mark Taksa. 48p. 1986. pap. 5.95 (0-917658-24-8) BPW & P.

Truant Bride. large type ed. Sara Seale. 1978. 12.00 (0-7089-0237-5) Ulverscroft.

Truants from Life: The Rehabilitation of Emotionally Disturbed Children. Bruno Bettelheim. LC 55-7331. 516p. 1964. pap. 16.95 (0-02-903450-7, Free Press) Free Pr.

Truants from Life: Theory & Therapy. Ed. by Ved P. Varma. 224p. 1991. 77.00 (1-85346-156-3, Pub. by D Fulton UK) Taylor & Francis.

***Trubetzkoy's Orphan: Proceedings of the Montreal Round Table on Morphophonology, Contemporary Responses.** Ed. by Rajendra Singh. LC 96-44621. (Current Issues in Linguistic Theory Ser.: Vol. 144). 1996. lib. bdg. write for info. (1-55619-599-0) Benjamins North Am.

Trubner's Bibliographical Guide. Nikolaus Trubner. 1973. 35.00 (0-8490-1233-3) Gordon Pr.

Truce. Mark Dunster. (Drex Ser.: Pt. 2). 1979. pap. 4.00 (0-89642-050-7) Linden Pubs.

Truce: Ending the Sibling War. Janet Bode. 112p. (YA). (gr. 8-12). 1991. lib. bdg. 22.70 (0-531-10996-8) Watts.

***Truce at Bakura Sourcebook.** (Star Wars Ser.). 22.00 (0-87431-256-6, 40085) West End Games.

Trucial States. Donald Hawley. (Illus.). 379p. 1971. 39.50 (0-686-66022-6); pap. text ed. 14.95 (0-8290-0454-8) Irvington.

Truck. Donald Crews. LC 79-19031. (Illus.). 32p. (J). (ps-2). 1980. 16.00 (0-688-80244-3); lib. bdg. 15.93 (0-688-84244-5) Greenwillow.

***Truck.** Donald Crews. LC 79-19031. 1997. pap. 6.95 (0-688-15597-9) Hearst Bks.

Truck. Ed. by Dorling Kindersley Staff. (Mighty Machines Ser.). (Illus.). (J). 1995. 9.95 (0-7894-0299-8) DK Pub Inc.

Truck. Katherine Dunn. 1990. pap. 10.99 (0-446-39153-0) Warner Bks.

Truck. Claire Llewellyn. (Mighty Machines Ser.). (Illus.). 24p. (J). (ps-3). 1995. 9.95 (1-56458-516-6) DK Pub Inc.

Truck. Donald Crews. LC 79-19031. (Illus.). 32p. (J). (ps up). 1991. reprint ed. pap. 3.95 (0-688-10481-9, Mulberry) Morrow.

Truck: Big Book Edition. Donald Crews. (Illus.). 32p. (J). (ps up). 1993. reprint ed. pap. 18.95 (0-688-12611-1, Mulberry) Morrow.

Truck: On Rebuilding a Worn-Out Pickup & Other Post-Technological Adventures. John Jerome. LC 96-3911. (Illus.). 155p. 1996. reprint ed. pap. 10.95 (0-87451-755-9) U Pr of New Eng.

Truck Alternative Fuels & Exhaust Gas Emission. (International Truck & Bus Meeting & Exposition Ser.). 92p. 1993. pap. 19.00 (1-56091-440-8, SP-1001) Soc Auto Engineers.

Truck & Bus Accidents: Getting the Facts. Ralph Craft & Eric N. Dobson. 62p. (Orig.). 1992. pap. text ed. 15.00 (1-55877-132-8) Natl Governor.

Truck & Tractor Pullers. Jeff Savage. LC 95-35532. (Action Events Ser.). (J). 1996. pap. 4.95 (0-382-39296-5, Crstwood Hse) Silver Burdett Pr.

Truck & Tractor Pullers. Jeff Savage. LC 95-35532. (Action Events Ser.). (J). 1996. lib. bdg. 14.95 (0-89686-886-9, Crstwood Hse) Silver Burdett Pr.

Truck & Tractor Pulling. Jeff Savage. (MotorSports Ser.). 48p. (J). (gr. 3-9). 1995. lib. bdg. 17.80 (1-56065-260-8) Capstone Pr.

***Truck & Tractor Pulling.** Jeff Savage. (Motorsports Ser.). (Illus.). 48p. (J). (gr. 3-6). 1995. 18.40 (0-516-35260-1) Childrens.

Truck & Van Repair Manual 1990-94. Chilton Automotives Editorial Staff. 1664p. 1994. text ed. 26.95 (0-8019-7911-0) Chilton.

Truck & Van Service Manual 1988-92. 2112p. 1992. 97.00 (0-8019-8281-2) Chilton.

Truck & Van Service Manual 1990-94. Chilton Automotives Editorial Staff. 2112p. 1994. pap. 97.00 (0-8019-8547-1) Chilton.

Truck Book. Lawrence DiFiori. LC 83-83106. (Golden Sturdy Shape Bks.). (Illus.). 14p. (J). (ps). 1984. bds. 3.95 (0-307-12299-9, Golden Books) Western Pub.

Truck Book. Bill Gere. (Golden Super Shape Bks.). (Illus.). 24p. (J). (ps-3). 1987. pap. 1.95 (0-307-10051-0, Golden Books) Western Pub.

Truck Book. Harry McNaught. LC 77-79851. (Pictureback Ser.). (J). (ps-2). 1978. pap. 3.25 (0-394-83703-7) Random Bks Yng Read.

Truck Company Fireground Operations. 2nd ed. Harold Richman. (Illus.). 200p. 1986. 38.00 (0-87765-237-6, FSP-76A) Natl Fire Prot.

Truck Company Fireground Operations Study Guide. rev. ed. David Dunay. 81p. 1991. pap. 11.95 (0-945250-11-8) Davis Pub Co.

Truck Driver. Jack Rudman. (Career Examination Ser.: C-1161). 1994. pap. 23.95 (0-8373-1161-6) Nat Learn.

Truck Driver Handbook. 72p. 1994. pap. text ed. 2.90 (0-88711-223-4) Am Trucking Assns.

Truck Driver's Guide to Commercial Driver Licensing. Highway Users Federation for Safety & Mobility. (Illus.). 640p. 1990. pap. 24.95 (0-685-45028-7) P-H.

Truck Driver's Guide to Commercial Driver's License. Robert M. Calvin. Ed. by Marilyn M. Martin. 24.95 (0-89262-174-5) Career Pub.

***Truck Driver's Handbook.** 3rd ed. David P. Soye. (Driving Ser.). 1995. pap. 17.95 (0-7494-1489-8) Kogan Page Ltd.

Truck Fire Protection. National Fire Protection Association Staff. 1994. 16.75 (0-317-63483-6, 513-90) Natl Fire Prot.

Truck Games. Thomson C. Murray. 1993. pap. 3.95 (0-87131-748-6) M Evans.

Truck Guide, Set. Ed. by James E. Brumbaugh. Incl. Vol. 2. Transmissions, Steering & Brakes. 304p. 1984. 16.95 (0-672-23357-6); 1984. Set text ed. 50.95 (0-672-23392-4) Macmillan.

Truck License & Tax Manual. Keller, J. J. & Assocs., Inc. Staff. LC 90-70784. 400p. 1992. 99.00 (0-934674-85-X, 40M) J J Keller.

Truck Lubrication Guide, 1985. rev. ed. (Illus.). 100p. 1985. pap. 33.40 (0-88098-061-3, H M Gousha) P-H Gen Ref & Trav.

Truck Lubrication Guide, 1986. (Illus.). 96p. student ed. 34.75 (0-88098-083-4, H M Gousha) P-H Gen Ref & Trav.

Truck Lubrication Guide, 1987. rev. ed. Chek-Chart Staff. Ed. by Roger L. Fenneman. (Illus.). 96p. 1987. student ed. 35.80 (0-88098-091-5, H M Gousha) P-H Gen Ref & Trav.

Truck Lubrication Guide, 1990. 40p. 1990. 14.95 (0-13-130576-X, H M Gousha) P-H Gen Ref & Trav.

Truck Research Profiles - A Sample of Recent & Current U. S. & Canadian Projects. (Transportation Research Circular Ser.: No. 345). 50p. 1989. 6.00 (0-685-38594-9) Transport Res Bd.

Truck Safety: The Safety of Longer Combination Vehicles Is Unknown. (Illus.). 55p. (Orig.). (C). 1993. pap. text ed. 25.00 (1-56806-976-6) DIANE Pub.

Truck Song. Diane Siebert. LC 83-46173. (Illus.). 32p. (J). (ps-3). 1984. lib. bdg. 14.89 (0-690-04411-9, Crowell Jr Bks) HarpC Child Bks.

Truck Song. Diane Siebert. LC 83-46173. (Trophy Picture Bk.). (Illus.). 32p. (J). (ps-3). 1987. pap. 4.95 (0-06-443134-7, Trophy) HarpC Child Bks.

Truck Song. Diane Siebert. (J). (gr. k-3). 1988. pap. 15.95 incl. audio (0-87499-092-0) Live Oak Media.

Truck Song, 4 bks., Set. Diane Siebert. (J). (gr. k-3). 1988. pap. 31.95 incl. audio (0-87499-094-7) Live Oak Media.

Truck Stop. Bonnie Dobkin. (Rookie Readers Ser.). (Illus.). 32p. (J). (ps-2). 1994. pap. 3.50 (0-516-42027-5) Childrens.

Truck Stop. Bonnie Dobkin. (Rookie Readers Ser.). (Illus.). 32p. (J). (ps-2). 1994. lib. bdg. 15.00 (0-516-02027-7) Childrens.

Truck Stop. Photos by Marc F. Wise. LC 95-14949. (Illus.). 96p. 1995. 50.00 (0-87805-838-9) U Pr of Miss.

Truck Stop. Photos by Marc F. Wise. LC 95-14949. (Illus.). 96p. 1995. pap. 29.95 (0-87805-839-7) U Pr of Miss.

Truck Stop. limited ed. Photos by Marc F. Wise. LC 95-14949. (Illus.). 96p. 1995. 150.00 (0-87805-842-7) U Pr of Miss.

Truck Stop Rainbows. Iva Perkarkova. 1994. pap. 12.00 (0-679-74675-7, Vin) Random.

Truck Stop Rainbows: A Czech Road Novel. Iva Pekarkova. Tr. by David Powelstock. 1992. 22.00 (0-374-24065-5) FS&G.

Truck Systems Design Handbook. 762p. 1992. 29.00 (1-56091-285-5, PT-41) Soc Auto Engineers.

Truck Talk. Bobbi Katz. LC 96-21306. (J). 1997. 10.95 (0-590-69328-X) Scholastic Inc.

Truck-Tractor Identification. 2nd ed. Lee S. Cole. 96p. (Orig.). 1995. reprint ed. pap. 14.95 (0-939818-25-6) Lee Bks.

Truck Transportation. (Illus.). 32p. (J). (gr. 6-12). 1973. pap. 2.40 (0-8395-3371-3, 33371) BSA.

***Truck, Van & 4X4 Book 1997.** Jack Gills. (Illus.). 160p. (Orig.). 1997. pap. 12.95 (0-06-273449-0, Harper Ref) HarpC.

***Truck, Van & 4X4 Book 1998.** Jack Gillis. 160p. 1998. pap. 12.95 (0-06-273450-4, PL) HarpC.

***Truck, Van & 4X4 Book 1999.** Jack Gillis. 160p. Date not set. pap. 12.95 (0-06-273451-2, PL) HarpC.

Truck Weight Limits: Issues & Options. (Special Reports: No. 225). 307p. 1990. 25.00 (0-309-04955-5) Transport Res Bd.

Truck/Cement Mixer. (Things That Go Shaped Board Bks.). (Illus.). (J). 1996. 3.95 (0-7894-1136-9) DK Pub Inc.

Trucker. Ed. by John W. Dagion. (True Revelations & Strange Happenings Ser.: Vol. 2). (Illus.). 192p. (Orig.). 1986. pap. 10.95 (0-917342-22-4) Leyland Pubns.

Truckers. William Russell. LC 93-42484. (Careers Ser.). (J). 1994. write for info. (1-57103-058-1) Rourke Pr.

***Trucker's Atlas.** (Illus.). 1996. spiral bd. 19.95 (0-8416-9208-4) Creative Sales.

Trucker's Atlas, No. 162812. 1995. 19.95 (0-933162-81-2) Am Map.

Truckers Coverage Form Analysis. Ed. by Diana Kowatch. 92p. 1996. 12.50 (1-56461-178-7) Rough Notes.

***Trucker's Friend: National Truck Stop Directory.** 11th rev. ed. (Illus.). 288p. 1997. pap. 9.95 (1-890141-00-3, TF97) TR Info Pubs.

Truckers' Highway Safety Guide. Charles E. Hugenberger. 104p. 1994. pap. 12.95 (1-885057-09-1) C E Hugenberger.

***Trucker's Life.** Daren Flynn. LC 96-90374. (Orig.). 1996. pap. 8.95 (0-533-12019-5) Vantage.

Trucker's Night Before Christmas. Dawn V. Hadlock. (Little Night Before Christmas Bks.). (Illus.). 60p. 1996. 5.95 (0-87905-765-3, Peregrine Smith) Gibbs Smith Pub.

Trucker's Road Atlas. Will Balliett. 1990. pap. 16.95 (0-13-931104-1) P-H.

Trucker's Road Atlas. Will Balliett & F-Stop Fitzgerald. 208p. 1992. pap. 16.95 (0-13-948241-5, H M Gousha) P-H Gen Ref & Trav.

Trucker's Road Atlas, Nineteen Ninety Two. Gousha. 1991. pap. 16.95 (0-13-932211-6) P-H.

Trucker's Road Atlas 1995. Gousha. 1994. 16.95 (0-671-79985-1) S&S Trade.

Trucker's World: Risk, Safety, & Mobility. J. Peter Rothe. 240p. 1991. 44.95 (1-56000-023-6) Transaction Pubs.

Trucker's World: Risk, Safety, & Mobility. J. Peter Rothe. 240p. (C). 1991. pap. 24.95 (1-56000-551-3) Transaction Pubs.

Truckforms, Vol. 3: The Independent Driver. Lew Grill. (Independent Operator Training Ser.). 150p. 1992. pap. text ed. 16.95 (1-881912-03-5) Atlantic Pac Res.

Truckin' Eight Hundred: The Special Commodities Directory. 3rd ed. Dale Wilson. (Truckin' 800 Ser.: Vol. 1, No. 3). (Illus.). 400p. 1986. pap. text ed. write for info. (0-9610616-2-6) Cargo Serv Inc.

Truckin' Turtles. Jape Trostle & Kevin Siembieda. Ed. by Alex Marciniszyn. (Teenage Mutant Ninja Turtles RPG Adventures Ser.). (Illus.). 48p. (Orig.). (YA). (gr. 8 up). 1989. pap. 7.95 (0-916211-43-6, 509) Palladium Bks.

Trucking: Audit Technique Guides. (IRS Tax Audit Information Ser.). 112p. 1994. pap. 24.50 (1-57402-110-9) Athena Info Mgt.

Trucking: Tractor-Trailer Driver Handbook-Workbook. Professional Truck Driving Institute of America (PTDIA) Staff. Ed. by Marilyn M. Martin. 600p. 1993. pap. text ed. 39.95 (0-89262-426-4) Career Pub.

Trucking: Tractor-Trailer Driver Handbook-Workbook. Professional Truck Driving Institute of America (PTDIA) Staff. Ed. by Marilyn M. Martin. 600p. 1993. teacher ed. 99.95 (0-89262-428-0); 149.95 (0-89262-453-1) Career Pub.

***Trucking: Truths & Myths: Is This $35-50,000 Career for You?** Larry Evans. 80p. (Orig.). 1997. pap. 12.00 (0-9655027-0-8) Two Loons Pr.

Trucking & the Public Interest: The Emergence of Federal Regulation 1914-1940. William R. Childs. LC 85-5315. 260p. 1986. text ed. 28.00 (0-87049-473-2) U of Tenn Pr.

***Trucking & the Public Interest: The Emergence of Federal Regulation, 1914-1940.** William R. Childs. LC 85-5315. 269p. pap. 76.70 (0-608-05191-8, 2065728) Bks Demand.

Trucking & Truck Accident Handbook: 1995 Edition. Asa Ruhl. 250p. 1995. pap. text ed. write for info. (1-887257-01-2) Ruhl & Assocs.

Trucking-Audit Guide-Self-Study Course: Continuing Professional Education Credits-Self-Study Course-Worth 8 CPE Credits. 180p. 1995. pap. 50.00 (1-57402-310-1) Athena Info Mgt.

Trucking Hazardous Materials: Leader's Guide. Shirley Ayers. 52p. 1993. pap. write for info. (0-945790-06-6) Detrick Lawrence.

Trucking Illustrated, Vol. 1: The Interstate Driver. Lew Grill. (Independent Operator Training Ser.). 174p. 1992. pap. text ed. 16.95 (1-881912-01-9) Atlantic Pac Res.

Trucking in America: Moving the Goods. John Gunnell. LC 95-77304. (Illus.). 304p. 1995. pap. text ed. 16.95 (0-87341-371-7, ATR01) Krause Pubns.

Trucking Industry Valuation Guide. ATA National Accounting & Finance Council Staff & Deloitte & Touche Staff. 1995. pap. 60.00 (0-88711-271-4) Am Trucking Assns.

Trucking Issues 1990. (Transportation Research Record Ser.: No. 1256). 54p. 1990. 12.00 (0-309-05010-3) Transport Res Bd.

Trucking Permit Guide: Private, Contract, Common, Exempt 1G. rev. ed. Ed. by Keller, J. J. & Assocs., Inc. Staff. LC 75-16944. 725p. 1991. ring bd. 189.00 (0-934674-00-0, 1G) J J Keller.

Trucking Pioneers. (Illus.). 214p. (Orig.). 1996. pap. 13.95 (0-9645286-5-7, Bk. VI) Pionr Pr.

Trucking Pioneers, Bk. II. M. K. Terebecki. 210p. 1992. 13.95 (0-9645286-0-6) Pionr Pr.

Trucking Pioneers, Bk. III. M. K. Terebecki. 210p. 1993. 13.95 (0-9645286-1-4) Pionr Pr.

Trucking Pioneers, Bk. IV. M. K. Terebecki. 210p. 1994. 13.95 (0-9645286-2-2) Pionr Pr.

Trucking Pioneers, Bk. V. M. K. Terebecki. 210p. 1995. 13.95 (0-9645286-3-0) Pionr Pr.

Trucking Safety Guide. rev. ed. E. Betty Bartel-Weiland. Ed. by Keller, J. J. & Assocs., Inc. Staff. LC 78-71720. 1175p. 1991. ring bd. 189.00 (0-934674-24-8, 8G) J J Keller.

Trucking Terminal Impact & Community Response: Case Studies in the Philadelphia Region. Thomas A. Reiner. (Discussion Paper Ser.: No. 86). 1975. pap. 10.00 (1-55869-127-8) Regional Sci Res Inst.

Truckline Cafe. Maxwell Anderson. (Lost Play Ser.). 1986. pap. 3.95 (0-912262-86-9) Proscenium.

Trucks. LC 90-49260. (Eye Openers Ser.). (Illus.). 24p. (J). (ps-k). 1991. pap. 7.95 (0-689-71405-X, Aladdin Paperbacks) S&S Childrens.

Trucks. 1996. 4.99 (0-679-87820-3) Random.

***Trucks.** (Popular Mechanics for Kids Coloring & Activity Bks.). (Illus.). 32p. (J). (gr. k-2). 1997. pap. write for info. (1-56144-914-8, Honey Bear Bks) Modern Pub NYC.

***Trucks.** LC 97-24337. (Cutaway Ser.). (Illus.). 40p. (J). (gr. 1-3). 1997. lib. bdg. 17.40 (0-7613-0710-9, Copper Beech Bks) Millbrook Pr.

***Trucks.** Kay Barnham. (Pocket Gems Ser.). 1997. 3.95 (0-7641-5038-3) Barron.

Trucks. Byron Barton. LC 85-47901. (Illus.). 32p. (J). (ps). 1986. 6.95 (0-694-00062-0, Crowell Jr Bks); lib. bdg. 13.89 (0-690-04530-1, Crowell Jr Bks) HarpC Child Bks.

Trucks. J. Cooper. (Traveling Machines Ser.). (J). 1991. 8.95 (0-86592-491-0) Rourke Enter.

Trucks. Gail Gibbons. LC 81-43039. (Illus.). 32p. (J). (ps-2). 1981. lib. bdg. 14.89 (0-690-04119-5, Crowell Jr Bks) HarpC Child Bks.

Trucks. Claire Llewellyn. LC 95-10739. (Worldwise Ser.). (Illus.). 48p. (J). (gr. 4-6). 1995. lib. bdg. 22.70 (0-531-14378-3) Watts.

Trucks. Claire Llewellyn. LC 95-10739. (Worldwise Ser.). (Illus.). 48p. (J). (gr. 4-6). 1996. pap. 7.00 (0-531-15285-5) Watts.

Trucks. Mallory Loehr. LC 91-75344. (Chunky Shape Bks.). (Illus.). 22p. (J). (ps). 1992. 3.99 (0-679-83061-8) Random Bks Yng Read.

***Trucks.** Illus. by Edward Miller. (Sticker Stories Ser.). 16p. (Orig.). (J). (ps-1). 1997. pap. 4.95 (0-448-41581-X, G&D) Putnam Pub Group.

Trucks. Joyce Milton. (J). 1998. pap. 3.99 (0-679-88130-1) Random Bks Yng Read.

***Trucks.** Jan Pienkowski. 1997. pap. 7.99 (0-525-45853-0) Dutton Child Bks.

***Trucks.** Dee Ready. LC 97-12195. (J). 1998. write for info. (1-56065-613-1) Capstone Pr.

Trucks. Anne Rockwell. LC 84-1556. (Unicorn Paperbacks Ser.). (Illus.). 24p. (J). (ps-1). 1988. pap. 3.95 (0-525-44432-7) Dutton Child Bks.

Trucks. Anne Rockwell. (J). (ps-3). 1992. pap. 4.99 (0-14-054790-8) Viking Child Bks.

***Trucks.** Angela Royston. LC 97-19337. (Inside & Out Ser.). (J). 1997. write for info. (1-57572-181-3) Rigby Interact Libr.

Trucks. Andrew Salter. LC 93-49568. (Pointers Ser.). (Illus.). (J). 1994. lib. bdg. 22.83 (0-8114-6189-0) Raintree Steck-V.

Trucks. Andrew Salter. (Pointers Ser.). (J). 1996. pap. text ed. 4.95 (0-8114-9364-4) Raintree Steck-V.

***Trucks.** Gail Saunders-Smith. LC 97-23582. (J). 1997. write for info. (1-56065-496-1) Capstone Pr.

Trucks. Darlene R. Stille. LC 96-25727. (True Bk.). (J). 1997. lib. bdg. 19.00 (0-516-20343-6) Childrens.

Trucks. C. Young. (Young Machines Ser.). (Illus.). 32p. (J). (ps-2). pap. 6.95 (0-7460-0722-1, Usborne); lib. bdg. 14.95 (0-88110-556-2, Usborne) EDC.

Trucks. Gail Gibbons. LC 81-43039. (Trophy Picture Bk.). (Illus.). 32p. (J). (ps-1). 1985. reprint ed. pap. 4.95 (0-06-443069-3, Trophy) HarpC Child Bks.

Trucks. Harry McNaught. LC 75-36463. (Board Bks.). (Illus.). 14p. (J). (ps-1). 1976. reprint ed. 4.99 (0-394-83240-X) Random Bks Yng Read.

Trucks. Paul Stickland. LC 93-12593. (Illus.). 14p. (J). (ps). 1993. reprint ed. pap. 3.50 (0-525-67454-3, Lodestar Bks) Dutton Child Bks.

Trucks: A First Guide to the Wonders & Workings of Trucks. (What's Inside? Ser.). (Illus.). 24p. (J). (ps-3). 1993. 8.95 (1-56458-137-3) DK Pub Inc.

Trucks: An Educational Coloring Book. Spizzirri Publishing Co. Staff. Ed. by Linda Spizzirri. (Illus.). 32p. (J). 1979. pap. 1.25 (0-86545-051-X) Spizzirri.

Trucks: Truck Board Book. Harriet Castor. (Machines Board Bks.). (Illus.). 32p. (J). (ps). 1993. bds. 4.95 (0-7460-1098-2, Usborne) EDC.

Trucks All Around: A Foldout Book with Flaps to Lift. Playskool Staff. (Illus.). 22p. (J). 1996. pap. 7.99 (0-525-45698-8, Playskool Bks) Dutton Child Bks.

***Trucks at Work.** Frank Ansley. (J). 1997. 12.95 (0-689-81736-3) S&S Childrens.

Trucks in Your Neighborhood. Illus. by Joe Mathieu. (Wheel Bks.). 14p. (J). (ps). 1988. bds. 4.99 (0-394-89951-2) Random Bks Yng Read.

Trucks of the Eighties. Photos by Colin Wright. 64p. 1994. pap. 19.90 (1-873150-03-2) Taylor & Francis.

Trucks, Trouble & Triumph: The Norwalk Truck Line Company. Wayne G. Broehl, Jr. LC 75-41749. (Companies & Men: Business Enterprises in America Ser.). (Illus.). 1976. reprint ed. 31.95 (0-405-08066-2) Ayer.

Trucksource: Sources of Trucking Industry Information. American Trucking Association Staff. Ed. by Cathy M. Mahe & M. Sommers Pierce. 387p. 1996. pap. text ed. 50.00 (0-88711-278-1) Am Trucking Assns.

***Truckstops: A Complete Guide to over 5,000 Truck Stops in the U. S. & Canada.** 1997. pap. 12.95 (1-880477-13-0) Inter Am Pub.

Trucos de Clifford (Clifford's Tricks) Norman Bridwell. Tr. by Argentina Palacios. 32p. (SPA.). (J). (gr. k-3). 1986. pap. 2.99 (0-590-40123-8) Scholastic Inc.

Truculentus see Stichus

Trudging the Road: A Work-Study Journey Through the Twelve Steps of Alcoholics Anonymous. Chris F. Gladding. 170p. 1991. student ed. 16.00 (0-9629091-0-6) Glad Pubn.

***Trudging Through the Cement of Life: Without Getting Stuck.** Jan Knutson & Gregory J. Gerber. 144p. (Orig.). 1996. pap. 12.95 (0-9656986-0-2) PRplus Communs.

Trudi & the Minstrel. Alan Cullen. (J). (gr. 1-9). 1957. 5.00 (0-87602-214-X) Anchorage.

Trudi La Cane. Nicholas P. Georgiady & Louis G. Romano. Tr. by Patrice Thorne. (Look! I-Can-Read Bk.). (Illus.). 32p. (J). (gr. 1-4). 1982. reprint ed. pap. 5.00 (0-317-05572-0) Argee Pubs.

Trudy's Short Stories. Farideh Troudet. (J). 1993. pap. 8.95 (0-533-10451-3) Vantage.

***True.** Michael M. Melius. 112p. 1991. 15.00 (0-614-24796-9); per. 8.00 (0-614-24797-7) Tesseract SD.

An Asterisk (*) at the beginning of an entry indicates that the title is appearing in BIP for the first time.

True: Notes from Journeys in South Dakota. Michael M. Melius. LC 91-52925. (Illus.). 130p. 1991. 15.00 (0-937603-11-2, Tensleep Pubns); pap. 8.00 (0-937603-10-4, Tensleep Pubns) Melius Pub.

True Adventure of Daniel Hall. Diane Stanley. LC 94-29338. (J). 1995. pap. 15.99 (0-8037-1468-8); pap. 15.89 (0-8037-1469-6) Dial Bks Young.

True Adventures. Dan Greenburg. 256p. (Orig.). 1985. pap. 8.95 (0-88191-023-6) Freundlich.

True Adventures of Grizzly Adams. Robert M. McClung. LC 85-8886. (Illus.). 208p. (J). (gr. 5 up). 1985. 16.00 (0-688-05794-2, Morrow Junior) Morrow.

True Adventures of Huckleberry Finn. 2nd ed. As told by John Seelye. LC 87-8581. 368p. 1987. text ed. 29.95 (0-252-01446-4); pap. text ed. 11.95 (0-252-01432-4) U of Ill Pr.

True Adventures of John Steinbeck, Writer: A Biography. Jackson J. Benson. (Illus.). 1120p. 1990. reprint ed. pap. 19.95 (0-14-014417-X, Penguin Bks) Viking Penguin.

True Adventures of Prince Teentang. Kalpana Swaminathan. (Illus.). (C). 1993. 3.50 (81-7223-085-0, Pub. by Indus Pub II) S Asia.

True Adventures of the Rolling Stones. Stanley Booth. 600p. 1985. pap. 12.00 (0-394-74110-2, Vin) Random.

True Alchemy or the Quest for Perfection, Vol. 221. Omraam M. Aivanhov. (Izvor Collection). 191p. (Orig.). 1986. pap. 7.95 (2-85566-384-9) Prosveta USA.

True Americanism: Green Berets & War Resisters; a Study of Commitment. David M. Mantell. LC 74-2230. (Foresight Books in Psychology). (Illus.). 293p. 1974. reprint ed. pap. 83.60 (0-7837-8947-5, 2049658) Bks Demand.

True & Almost Incredible Report of an Englishman That Travelled by Land Through Many Kingdoms. Robert Coverte. LC 72-186. (English Experience Ser.: No. 302). 1971. reprint ed. 20.00 (90-221-0302-1) Walter J Johnson.

True & Authentic Register of Persons...Who in the Year 1709...Journeyed from Germany to America. Ulrich Simmendinger. LC 70-23539. 20p. 1991. reprint ed. pap. 4.00 (0-8063-0313-1) Genealog Pub.

*True & Exact History of Barbados. Ligon. 42.50 (0-7146-1941-8, Pub. by F Cass Pubs UK) Intl Spec Bk.

True & Faithful Account. Norman Murphy. (Illus.). 73p. 1995. 25.00 (0-87008-074-1) JAS Heineman.

True & Faithful Relation of Dr. John Dee & Some Spirits. John Dee. 592p. 1992. lib. bdg. 75.00 (0-685-55400-7) Magickal Childe.

True & False. David Mamet. 1996. pap. write for info. (0-679-77264-2) McKay.

True & False: Heresy & Common Sense for the Actor. David Mamet. 1997. 20.00 (0-679-44249-9) McKay.

True & False Allegations of Child Sexual Abuse: Assessment & Case Management. Ed. by Tara Ney. LC 94-47941. 400p. 1995. text ed. 45.95 (0-87630-758-6) Brunner-Mazel.

True & False Democracy. Nicholas M. Butler. LC 78-93323. (Essay Index Reprint Ser.). 1977. 17.95 (0-8369-1278-0) Ayer.

True & False Experience: The Human Element in Psychotherapy. Peter Lomas. 170p. (C). 1994. pap. 24.95 (1-56000-733-8) Transaction Pubs.

True & False Paths in Spiritual Investigation. Rudolf Steiner. Tr. by A. H. Parker from GER. 222p. 1986. 20.00 (0-88010-124-5); pap. 12.95 (0-88010-135-0) Anthroposophic.

True & False Repentance. Charles G. Finney. LC 66-10576. (Charles G. Finney Memorial Library). 122p. 1975. pap. 6.99 (0-8254-2617-0) Kregel.

True & False Romances. Ana L. Vega. Tr. by Andrew Hurley from SPA. (Masks Ser.). 192p. (Orig.). 1994. pap. 12.99 (1-85242-272-6) Serpents Tail.

True & False Tongues. Dale M. Yocum. 0.49 (0-88019-117-1) Schmul Pub Co.

True & Historical Narrative of the Colony of Georgia in America. Patrick Tailfer et al. LC 74-168522. (Black Heritage Library Collection). 1977. reprint ed. 15.95 (0-8369-8874-4) Ayer.

True & Invisible Rosicrucian Order: An Interpretation of the Rosicrucian Allegory & an Explanation of the Ten Rosicrucian Grades. Paul F. Case. LC 85-3185. 189p. (Orig.). 1989. pap. 22.50 (0-87728-709-0) Weiser.

True & Only Heaven: Progress & Its Critics. Christopher Lasch. 592p. 1991. pap. 15.95 (0-393-30795-6) Norton.

True & Perfect Description of Three Voyages. Gerrit De Veer. LC 93-7016. 1993. 100.00 (0-8201-1478-2) Schol Facsimiles.

True & Perfect Description of Three Voyages by the Ships of Holland & Zeland. Gerrit De Veer. Tr. by W. Phillip. LC 75-25746. (English Experience Ser.: No. 274). 164p. 1970. reprint ed. 30.00 (90-221-0274-2) Walter J Johnson.

True & Reasonable. Doug Jacoby. 110p. 1994. pap. 5.99 (1-884553-22-2) Discipleshp.

True & the False: The Domain of the Pragmatic. Charles Travis. (Pragmatics & Beyond Ser.: II: 2). vi, 165p. (Orig.). 1981. pap. 29.00 (90-272-2512-5) Benjamins North Am.

True & Tried Recipes. Shelly Lum. Ed. by Ethel Herr et al. (Illus.). 200p. (Orig.). pap. 14.95 (0-941201-06-6) INNPRO.

*True Animal Tales. large type ed. Rolf Harris. (Paperback Ser.). 224p. 1997. pap. 21.95 (0-7838-8253-X, GK Hall) Thorndike Pr.

True Artist & True Friend: A Biography of Hans Richter. Christopher Fifield. LC 92-37067. (Illus.). 552p. (C). 1993. 39.95 (0-19-816157-3, Old Oregon Bk Store) OUP.

True BASIC: A Tutorial. Larry J. Goldstein et al. 1985. 17.95 (0-89303-893-8) S&S Trade.

True BASIC: Programs & Subroutines. John C. Craig. (Illus.). 256p. (Orig.). 1985. 24.95 (0-8306-0990-3, 1990) McGraw-Hill Prof.

True Bear Stories. Joaquin Miller. LC 89-31044. 96p. (C). 1988. reprint ed. lib. bdg. 25.00 (0-8095-4051-7) Borgo Pr.

True Bear Tales: True Stories from Michigan's Upper Peninsula. 3rd ed. David E. Young. 140p. 1996. pap. 8.99 (0-9623664-4-7) Gold Oak Bks.

True Beauty: Positive Attitudes & Practical Tips for Women of Size. Emme & Daniel Paisner. LC 96-44351. 304p. 1997. 23.95 (0-399-14204-5, Putnam) Putnam Pub Group.

True Believer: Thoughts on the Nature of Mass Movements. Eric Hoffer. 190p. 1991. reprint ed. lib. bdg. 31.00 (0-8095-9111-1) Borgo Pr.

True Believers. Alyce Rohrer. LC 85-18521. 1987. 22.95 (0-87949-253-8) Ashley Bks.

True Believers Don't Ask Why. John Fischer. 194p. (Orig.). 1989. 13.99 (1-55661-055-6) Bethany Hse.

True Betrayals. Nora Roberts. 1996. mass mkt. 6.50 (0-515-11855-9) Jove Pubns.

True Betrayals. large type ed. Nora Roberts. 1995. 24.95 (0-7862-0505-9) Thorndike Pr.

True Bliss. Stella Cameron. 384p. 1996. mass mkt. 5.99 (0-8217-5369-X, Zebra Kensgtn) Kensgtn Pub Corp.

True Blue. David Milch & Bill Clark. 256p. 1997. mass mkt. 6.99 (0-380-72505-3) Avon.

True Blue. Ingrid Weaver. 1994. 3.50 (0-373-07570-7) Silhouette.

True Blue. Suzanne Weyn. LC 90-10830. (Sitting Pretty Ser.). 128p. (J). (gr. 4-8). 1997. pap. 2.95 (0-8167-2006-1) Troll Communs.

True Blue: Level 3. Joan Elste & DyAnne DiSalvo-Ryan. LC 96-1257. (All Aboard Reading Ser.: Level 3). (Illus.). 48p. (Orig.). (J). (gr. 2-4). 1996. pap. 3.95 (0-448-41264-0, G&D) Putnam Pub Group.

True Blue: Stories about Real Cops. Edward J. Nowicki. 1993. mass mkt. 4.99 (0-312-95061-6) St Martin.

True Blue: True Stories about Real Cops. Edward J. Nowicki. LC 91-66414. 280p. (Orig.). 1992. pap. 14.95 (1-879411-15-6) Perf Dimensions Pub.

*True Blue Dream of Sky. Meredy Maynard. 144p. (Orig.). (J). 1997. pap. 7.95 (1-896095-23-2, Pub. by Polestar Bk Pubs CN) Orca Bk Pubs.

*True Blue Hawaii. Reisfeld. (Clueless Ser.). (YA). 1997. mass mkt. 3.99 (0-671-01162-6) PB.

True Blue Hearts. Curtiss A. Matlock. 1993. mass mkt. 3.39 (0-373-09805-7, 5-09805-8) Silhouette.

True Blue Knight. Roseanne Williams. (Temptation Ser.). 1994. mass mkt. 2.99 (0-373-25604-3, 1-25604-9) Harlequin Bks.

True-Blue Laws of Connecticut & New Haven & the False Blue-Laws Invented by the Rev. Samuel Peters to Which Are Added Specimens of the Laws & Judicial Proceedings of Other Colonies & Some Blue-Laws of England in the Reign of James I. Ed. by J. Hammond Trumbull. 360p. 1987. reprint ed. 35.00 (0-8377-2632-8) Rothman.

True Blues: The Politics of Conservative Party Membership. Patrick Seyd et al. (Illus.). 320p. 1995. text ed. 65.00 (0-19-827785-7); pap. text ed. 23.00 (0-19-827786-5) OUP.

True Body. Miriam Sagan. 64p. 1991. pap. 8.00 (0-938077-46-5) Parallax Pr.

True Boundaries of the Holy Land: Described in Numbers XXIV: 1-12: Solving the Many Diversified Theories As to Their Location. Samuel H. Isaacs. Ed. by Moshe Davis. LC 77-70706. (America & the Holy Land Ser.). (Illus.). 1977. reprint ed. lib. bdg. 19.95 (0-405-10256-9) Ayer.

True Bounds of Christian Freedom. Samuel Bolton. (Puritan Paperbacks Ser.). 1978. pap. 8.50 (0-85151-083-3) Banner of Truth.

True Bugs of the World: (Hemiptera: Heteroptera) Classification & Natural History. Randall T. Schuh & James A. Slater. (Comstock Bk.). (Illus.). 416p. 1995. 87.50 (0-8014-2066-0) Cornell U Pr.

True Chameleons, Part II: Notes on Popular Species. Philippe De Vosjoli. 28p. 1990. pap. text ed. 6.00 (1-882770-05-6) Adv Vivarium.

True Champions: Great Athletes & Their Off-the-Field Heroics. Nathan Aaseng. LC 92-36942. (Illus.). 128p. (J). (gr. 5 up). 1993. 14.95 (0-8027-8246-9); lib. bdg. 15.85 (0-8027-8247-7) Walker & Co.

True Champions: The Good Guys in American Sports Speak Out. Mike Towle. LC 94-8917. (Illus.). 225p. 1994. 22.95 (1-56530-126-9) Summit TX.

*True Christian Religion. Emanual Swedenborg. Ed. by John C. Ager. 694p. 1997. pap. 11.95 (0-87785-292-8) Swedenborg.

True Christian Religion, 2 vols., Set. Emanuel Swedenborg. Tr. by John C. Ager from LAT. 1997. pap. 19.95 (0-87785-295-2) Swedenborg.

True Christian Religion, 2 vols., Set. Emanuel Swedenborg. Tr. by J. Ager. 1996. 30.00 (0-87785-296-0) Swedenborg.

True Christian Religion, Vol. 1. Emanuel Swedenborg. Tr. by J. Ager. LC 96-31792. 1996. 18.00 (0-87785-291-X) Swedenborg.

True Christian Religion, Vol. 2. Emanuel Swedenborg. Tr. by J. Ager. LC 96-31792. 522p. 1996. 18.00 (0-87785-293-6) Swedenborg.

*True Christian Religion Vol. 2: Containing The Universal Theology of the New Church Foretold by the Lord in Daniel 7:13, 14 & Revelation 21:1, 2. Emanuel Swedenborg & John C. Ager. LC 96-31792. 1997. pap. 11.95 (0-87785-294-4) Swedenborg.

True Christianity. Owen Weber. 86p. (Orig.). (C). 1988. pap. 3.95 (0-9618684-1-4) Christian Data.

True Christian's Love to the Unseen Christ. Thomas Vincent. Ed. by Don Kistler. 127p. 1993. 18.95 (1-877611-57-3) Soli Deo Gloria.

True Church, No. 29. pap. 0.15 (0-87377-154-0) GAM Pubns.

True Church & the Poor. Jon Sobrino. Tr. by Mathew J. O'Connell from SPA. LC 84-5661. Orig. Title: Resureccion de la Verdadera Iglesia, Los Pobres Lugar Teologica de la Eclesiologia. 384p. (Orig.). 1984. pap. 20.00 (0-88344-513-1) Orbis Bks.

True Church & the Poor. Jon Sobrino. Tr. by Matthew J. O'Connell from SPA. LC 84-5661. Orig. Title: Resureccion de la Verdadera Iglesia, Los Pobres Lugar Teologica de la Eclesiologia. 384p. (Orig.). 1984. reprint ed. pap. 109.50 (0-608-02149-0, 2062818) Bks Demand.

True Church Quizzes to a Street Preacher. Charles M. Carty & Leslie Rumble. (Radio Replies Quizzes to a Street Preacher Ser.). 32p. 1992. reprint ed. pap. 1.00 (0-89555-116-0) TAN Bks Pubs.

True Colors. Roger Birkman. LC 94-36196. 256p. 1995. pap. text ed. 14.99 (0-7852-7856-7) Nelson.

True Colors. Susan Kyle. 1991. mass mkt. 4.95 (0-446-36115-1) Warner Bks.

True Colors. Doris Mortman. 1996. mass mkt. 6.99 (0-8041-1111-1) Ivy Books.

*True Colors. Doris Mortman. 1997. 5.99 (0-517-17357-3) Random Hse Value.

*True Colors. Lynda Trent. 304p. 1997. mass mkt. 5.99 (0-8217-5568-4, Zebra Kensgtn) Kensgtn Pub Corp.

True Colors: A Novel. Doris Mortman. LC 94-13068. 1995. 24.00 (0-517-59262-2) Crown Pub Group.

True Colors: Adventures in the Art World. Anthony Haden-Guest. (Illus.). 320p. 1996. 27.50 (0-87113-660-0, Atlntc Mnthly) Grove-Atltic.

True Colors: An Artist's Journey from Beauty Queen to Feminist. Patricia H. Burnett. 183p. 1995. 29.95 (1-879094-48-7) Momentum Bks.

True Colors: One Thousand Four Days as a Prisoner of War. James Thompson. LC 88-39295. 1988. 22.95 (0-87949-282-1) Ashley Bks.

*True Colors: Real Voices, Communication Workbook 2. Jay Maurer. 1998. pap. text ed. write for info. (0-201-18636-5) Addison-Wesley.

*True Colors: Real Voices, Real Communication Workbook 1. Jay Maurer. 1998. pap. text ed. write for info. (0-201-18635-7) Addison-Wesley.

*True Colors Bk. 1: Real Voices Real Communication. Jay Maurer. 1996. student ed., pap. text ed. write for info. (0-201-87808-9) Addison-Wesley.

True Colors of Caitlynne Jackson. Carol L. Williams. LC 96-24835. 176p. (J). 1997. 14.95 (0-385-32249-6, Delacorte Pr Bks) BDD Bks Young Read.

True Confession of the Faith, Which Wee Falsley Called Brownists, Doo Hold. Henry Ainsworth. LC 78-26338. (English Experience Ser.: No. 158). 24p. 1969. reprint ed. 25.00 (90-221-0158-4) Walter J Johnson.

True Confessions. Kurt Hamilton. LC 95-90133. 120p. (Orig.). 1996. pap. 8.95 (1-56002-561-1, Univ Edtns) Aegina Pr.

*True Confessions... Liz Lochhead. 1987. 16.00 (0-7486-6156-5, Pub. by Polygon UK) Subterranean Co.

*True Confessions. Tashjian. LC 97-16098. 1997. 15.95 (0-8050-5254-2) H Holt & Co.

True Confessions: The Novel. Mary Bringle. LC 95-46856. 240p. 1996. pap. 21.95 (1-55611-488-5) D I Fine.

True Confessions & False Romances. William Hathaway. LC 72-182981. 64p. (gr. 4 up). 1972. 6.95 (0-87886-013-4, Greenfld Rev Pr) Greenfld Rev Lit.

True Confessions of an Albino Terrorist. Breyten Breytenbach. LC 94-12789. (Harvest Book Ser.). 1994. pap. 14.95 (0-15-600134-9) HarBrace.

True Confessions of Charlotte Doyle. Avi. 240p. (J). (gr. 6). 1992. mass mkt. 4.50 (0-380-71475-2, Flare) Avon.

True Confessions of Charlotte Doyle. Avi. LC 90-30624. (Illus.). 224p. (J). (gr. 6-8). 1990. 16.95 (0-531-05893-X); lib. bdg. 17.99 (0-531-08493-0) Orchard Bks Watts.

*True Confessions of Charlotte Doyle. Avi. 1997. pap. 4.50 (0-380-72885-0, Camelot) Avon.

True Confessions of Charlotte Doyle. Kathleen Fischer. Ed. by J. Friedland & R. Kessler. (Novel-Ties Ser.). 1993. student ed., pap. text ed. 15.95 (0-88122-900-8) Lrn Links.

True Confessions of Charlotte Doyle. large type ed. Avi. 1995. 64.50 (0-614-09613-8, L-81879-00) Am Printing Hse.

True Confessions of Charlotte Doyle. large type ed. Avi. LC 92-37075. 288p. (YA). 1993. reprint ed. lib. bdg. 15.95 (1-56054-592-5) Thorndike Pr.

True Copie of a Discourse Written by a Gentleman, Employed in the Late Voyage of Spaine & Portingale. Robert Devereux & Anthony Wingfield. LC 78-38172. (English Experience Ser.: No. 449). 1972. reprint ed. 15.00 (90-221-0449-4) Walter J Johnson.

True Copie of a Letter from the Queens Maiesty to the Lord Mayor of London. H. R. M. Queen Elizabeth I. LC 70-25636. (English Experience Ser.: No. 167). 8p. 1969. reprint ed. 25.00 (90-221-0167-3) Walter J Johnson.

*True Correspondence: A Phenomenology of Thomas Hardy's Novels. Bruce Johnson. LC 83-3456. 176p. reprint ed. pap. 50.20 (0-608-04508-X, 2065253) Bks Demand.

True Cost of Conflict: Seven Recent Wars & Their Effects on Society. Ed. by Michael Cranna. 240p. 1995. pap. 16.00 (1-56584-268-5) New Press NY.

True Costs of Road Transport. Olof Johansson et al. (Blueprint Ser.: Vol. 5). 176p. 1996. pap. 17.95 (1-85383-268-5, Pub. by Erthscan Pubns UK) Island Pr.

True Country: Themes in the Fiction of Flannery O'Connor. Carter W. Martin. LC 68-29047. 258p. 1994. reprint ed. pap. 16.95 (0-8265-1249-6) Vanderbilt U Pr.

True Crime. Andrew Klavan. 1995. 21.00 (0-517-70213-4, Crown) Crown Pub Group.

*True Crime. Andrew Klavan. 1997. mass mkt. 6.99 (0-440-22403-9) Dell.

True Crime. Andrew Klavan. 1996. mass mkt. 6.99 (0-449-22512-7) Fawcett.

True Crime. large type ed. Andrew Klavan. 522p. 1995. 24.95 (0-7838-1438-0, GK Hall) Thorndike Pr.

*True Crime Almanac. Judie Lewellen. (J). 1997. pap. write for info. (0-679-88429-7) Random Bks Yng Read.

True Crime Astrology: Famous Murders & Suicides. Edna Rowland. LC 96-19695. (Popular Astrology Ser.). (Illus.). 224p. (Orig.). 1996. pap. 14.95 (1-56718-588-6) Llewellyn Pubns.

True Crime Narratives: An Annotated Bibliography. Ben Harrison. LC 96-47525. 784p. 1997. 65.00 (0-8108-3260-7) Scarecrow.

*True Crime Stories. Terry Deary. 1997. pap. text ed. 3.99 (0-14-038588-6) Puffin Bks.

*True Crime Stories. Terry Deary. LC 96-44495. 1997. pap. 3.99 (0-14-038558-4) Viking Penguin.

True Crimes. Romulus Linney. 1996. pap. 5.25 (0-8222-1537-3) Dramatists Play.

True Crimes & How They Were Solved. Anita Larsen. 96p. (J). (gr. 7-9). 1993. pap. 2.99 (0-590-46856-1) Scholastic Inc.

True Cuban Bass. Carlos Del Puerto & Silvio Vergara. 63p. (Orig.). (ENG & SPA.). 1994. pap. text ed. 20.00 (1-883217-01-6) Sher Music.

True Declaration of the Troublesome Voyage of M. John Hawkins to the Parties of Guynea & the West Indies. John Hawkins. LC 73-6137. (English Experience Ser.: No. 602). 36p. 1973. reprint ed. 15.00 (90-221-0602-0) Walter J Johnson.

True Description of the Lake Superior Country. John R. St. John. LC 76-27042. (Institute of Church-State Studies). (Illus.). 1976. 17.50 (0-912382-20-1) Black Letter.

True Description of the Lake Superior Country. John R. St. John. LC 88-23876. 118p. 1988. reprint ed. 8.50 (0-933249-09-8) Mid-Peninsula Lib.

True Detective. Theodore Weesner. 400p. 1988. mass mkt. 4.50 (0-380-70499-4) Avon.

True Detectives: The Real World of Today's Private Investigators. William Parkhurst. 1988. 18.95 (0-517-56554-4); 4.99 (0-517-05608-9) Random Hse Value.

True Devotion to Mary. Louis De Montfort. Ed. by Company of Mary Fathers. LC 85-50571. 215p. 1994. pap. 7.00 (0-89555-279-5) TAN Bks Pubs.

True Devotion to Mary. Eddie Doherty. 1956. pap. 3.95 (0-910984-02-6) Montfort Pubns.

True Devotion to Mary. Mary Frederick. (Queen of Apostles Ser.: Vol. IV). 1989. 0.75 (0-911988-85-8, 49730) AMI Pr.

True Devotion to the Blessed Virgin. St. Louis M. De Montfort. 5.95 (0-910984-49-2); pap. 3.95 (0-910984-50-6) Montfort Pubns.

True Disbelievers: Is Elvis Really Alive? R. Serge Denisoff & George Plasketes. (Illus.). 319p. (C). 1995. 39.95 (1-56000-186-0) Transaction Pubs.

True Discipleship. William MacDonald. 1975. pap. 6.50 (0-937396-50-8) Walterick Pubs.

True Discipleship: Teaching the Process of a Relationship with God & Others. Glenn Egli. 85p. 1991. pap. 4.50 (0-88270-650-0) Bridge-Logos.

True Discourse Historical, of the Succeeding Governors in the Netherlands. Emanuel Van Meteren. Tr. by T. Churchyard & R. Robinson. LC 68-54653. (English Experience Ser.: No. 57). 154p. 1968. reprint ed. 25.00 (90-221-0057-X) Walter J Johnson.

True Discourse of the Present Estate of Virginia. Ralph Hamor. LC 72-25512. (English Experience Ser.: No. 320). 70p. 1971. reprint ed. 30.00 (90-221-0320-X) Walter J Johnson.

True Discourse of the Present State of Virginia. Ralph Hamor. LC 57-9000. (Publication Ser.: No. 3). xviii, 74p. 1957. pap. 4.95 (0-88490-044-4) Library of VA.

True Doctrine of Ultra Vires in the Law of Corporations, Being a Concise Presentation of the Doctrine in Its Application to the Powers & Liabilities of Private & Municipal Corporations. Reuben A. Reese. lxxi, 338p. 1981. reprint ed. lib. bdg. 30.00 (0-8377-1031-6) Rothman.

*"True Due" Lists: Things to Do Before You Die. Mae Mary. (Orig.). 1997. mass mkt. 4.95 (0-614-29779-6) Foxglove Found.

True Elixir: Healing the Shackled Eagle: The Emergence of Medical Autonomy vs. Therapeutic Fascism & Scienfific Dogma. annot. ed. Ed. & Intro. by Barbara J. Hertz. 276p. (Orig.). 1994. text ed. 25.00 (0-9640332-0-8) Noumenal Reality.

True Elixir: Healing the Shackled Eagle: The Emergence of Medical Autonomy vs. Therapeutic Fascism & Scienfific Dogma. annot. ed. Ed. & Intro. by Barbara J. Hertz. 276p. (Orig.). (C). 1994. pap. text ed. 12.95 (0-9640332-1-6, TXU 615795) Noumenal Reality.

True Enchanter. large type ed. Susan Napier. (Magna Large Print Ser.). 1994. 25.99 (0-7505-0745-4, Pub. by Magna Print Bks UK) Ulverscroft.

True Esoteric Traditions: A Search for Western Cultural Values. M. Dale Palmer. LC 94-66752. (Illus.). 350p. (C). 1994. 29.00 (0-9642633-0-0) Noetics Inst.

True Essentials of a Feast: A Collection of Recipes from the Staff of the Library of Congress. LC 87-17154. 161p. 1987. 17.95 (0-8444-0571-X) Lib Congress.

True Evangelism: Winning Souls by Prayer. Lewis Sperry Chafer. LC 92-44075. 112p. 1993. pap. 8.99 (0-8254-2345-7) Kregel.

True Exemplary & Remarkable History of the Earle of Tirone. Thomas Gainsford. LC 68-54644. (English Experience Ser.: No. 25). 1968. reprint ed. 15.00 (*90-221-0025-1*) Walter J Johnson.

True Experiences of Children Who Survived the Holocaust. 2nd ed. Ed. by Brana Gurewitsch & Yaffa Eliach. LC 88-70082. (Education Ser.). (Illus.). 36p. (Orig.). (YA). (gr. 6-12). 1988. pap. text ed. 4.95 (*0-9609970-5-9*) Mus Jew Heritage.

***True Facts, Tall Tales & Pure Fiction.** Larry L. King. LC 96-43867. (Southwestern Writers Collection). 232p. 1997. 34.95 (*0-292-74329-7*); pap. 15.95 (*0-292-74330-0*) U of Tex Pr.

True Faith & Allegiance: The Burden of Military Ethics. James H. Toner. LC 94-18472. 224p. 1995. lib. bdg. 25.00 (*0-8131-1881-6*) U Pr of Ky.

***True False Book of Cats.** Patricia Lauber. LC 97-11144. (Illus.). (J). 1998. write for info. (*0-7922-3440-5*) Natl Geog.

***True Flowers for Worship.** rev. ed. Sai B. Sathya. Date not set. pap. 1.75 (*0-614-19095-9*, BW-210) Sathya Sai Bk Ctr.

True France: The Wars over Cultural Identity, 1900-1945. Herman Lebovics. LC 91-44697. (Wilder House Series in Politics, History, & Culture). (Illus.). 248p. 1992. 39.95 (*0-8014-2687-1*) Cornell U Pr.

True France: The Wars over Cultural Identity, 1900-1945. Herman Lebovics. (Wilder House Series in Politics, History, & Culture). (Illus.). 248p. 1994. pap. 14.95 (*0-8014-8193-7*) Cornell U Pr.

True Francine. Marc T. Brown. (Illus.). 32p. (J). (ps-3). 1981. 15.95 (*0-316-11212-7*, Joy St Bks) Little.

***True, Free Spirit: The Biography of Chas. E. Morris, Historic Western Photographer.** William Morris. (Illus.). 170p. 1997. 49.95 (*0-9645626-3-4*) Dallywelter Pr.

***True, Free Spirit: The Biography of Chas. E. Morris, Historic Western Photographer.** William Morris. (Illus.). 170p. 1997. pap. 29.95 (*0-9645626-4-2*) Dallywelter Pr.

True Freedom. CRM Staff. 101p. (CHI.). 1985. pap. 3.50 (*1-56582-087-8*) Christ Renew Min.

***True Friend.** Alda Ellis. (Remembrance of Times Past). (Illus.). 16p. (Orig.). 1997. 6.99 (*1-56507-715-6*) Harvest Hse.

True Friends. Evelyn L. Beilenson. (Charming Petites Ser.). (Illus.). 80p. 1996. 4.95 (*0-88088-797-4*) Peter Pauper.

True Friends. Robin J. Gunn. LC 93-19978. (Christy Miller Ser.: Vol. 7). 1993. pap. 5.99 (*1-56179-131-8*) Focus Family.

***True Friends.** Amy Paulsen. 192p. 1996. mass mkt. 4.99 (*0-06-101190-8*, Harp PBks) HarpC.

True Friends. Bill Wallace. LC 94-6449. 160p. (J). (gr. 4-7). 1994. 14.95 (*0-8234-1141-9*) Holiday.

True Friends. Bill Wallace. (J). (gr. 3-6). 1996. pap. 3.99 (*0-671-53036-4*, Minstrel Bks) PB.

True Friends Always Remain in Each Other's Heart. Ed. by Susan P. Schutz. LC 89-90633. (Illus.). 64p. 1989. pap. 7.95 (*0-88396-277-2*) Blue Mtn Pr CO.

True Fright No. 1: Trapped under the Ice, No. 01. Ted Pederson. 128p. (J). (gr. 3). 1996. mass mkt., pap. 3.99 (*0-8125-4395-5*) Tor Bks.

True Game. Sheri S. Tepper. 1996. pap. 15.00 (*0-441-00331-1*) Ace Bks.

True Genius of Oliver Goldsmith. Robert H. Hopkins. LC 69-15760. (Illus.). 256p. reprint ed. pap. 73.00 (*0-317-41738-X*, 2025856) Bks Demand.

True George Washington. Paul L. Ford. LC 70-160973. (Select Bibliographies Reprint Ser.). 1977. reprint ed. 29.95 (*0-8369-5841-1*) Ayer.

True George Washington. Paul L. Ford. (Notable American Authors Ser.). 1992. reprint ed. lib. bdg. 75.00 (*0-7812-2880-8*) Rprt Serv.

True Ghost Stories. Terry Deary. LC 96-20241. (Illus.). 128p. (J). 1996. pap. 3.99 (*0-14-038224-0*) Viking Penguin.

True Ghost Stories. Hans Holzer. 1994. 9.98 (*0-88365-850-X*) Galahad Bks.

True Ghost Stories. Brad Steiger. 176p. 1990. pap. 9.95 (*0-914918-35-4*, Whitford Pr) Schiffer.

True Ghost Stories of Lancaster County, Pennsylvania. Dorothy B. Fiedel. (Illus.). 70p. (Orig.). 1995. pap. 6.99 (*0-9640254-1-8*) D B Fiedel.

***True Gifts of Leadership.** Depree. LC 97-21017. 1997. 20.00 (*0-7879-1063-5*) Jossey-Bass.

True Giver. Echo Heron. 22.00 (*0-685-71174-9*) Fawcett.

***True Glory: The Royal Navy 1914-1939.** Max Arthur. (Illus.). 292p. 1997. pap. 15.95 (*0-340-64733-7*, Pub. by H & S UK) Trafalgar.

True Glory: The Story of the Royal Navy. Warren Tute. 192p. 1982. 70.00 (*0-356-07915-5*) St Mut.

True Glory/Royal Navy: Jutland to Today. Max Arthur. (Illus.). 400p. 1995. 39.95 (*0-340-62301-2*, Pub. by H & S UK) Trafalgar.

True God. Betty Miller. (Overcoming Life Ser.). 46p. 1994. pap. 5.00 (*1-57149-002-7*) Christ Unltd.

True God Workbook. Betty Miller. (Overcoming Life Ser.). 1995. pap. 10.00 (*1-57149-003-5*) Christ Unltd.

True Gold. C. Rennie. 1995. 4.99 (*1-871676-90-8*, Pub. by Christian Focus UK) Spring Arbor Dist.

True Gospel. Jack Van Impe. 32p. 1974. pap. 2.00 (*0-685-57185-8*) J Van Impe.

True Gospel Revealed Anew by Jesus, Vol. III. James E. Padgett. 443p. 1989. 10.00 (*1-887621-03-2*) Found Ch Divine Truth.

True Government by Choice Men? Inspection, Education, & State Formation in Canada West. Bruce Curtis. (State & Economic Life Ser.: No. 17). 320p. (Orig.). 1992. 60.00 (*0-8020-5967-8*); pap. 19.95 (*0-8020-6894-4*) U of Toronto Pr.

True Grasses. Eduard Hackel. Tr. by F. Lamson-Scribner & E. A. Southworth from GER. (Illus.). 228p. 1982. reprint ed. text ed. 17.50 (*0-934454-98-1*) Lubrecht & Cramer.

True Grist. 3rd ed. Patricia B. Mitchell. 1992. pap. 4.00 (*0-925117-53-6*) Mitchells.

True Grit. Charles Portis. 304p. 1995. mass mkt. 5.50 (*0-451-18545-5*, Sig) NAL-Dutton.

True Grits. Junior League of Atlanta Staff. LC 95-60310. 1995. 26.95 (*0-87197-425-8*) Favorite Recipes.

True Grits: The Southern Foods Mail Order Catalog. Joni Miller. LC 88-51583. (Illus.). 384p. (Orig.). 1990. pap. 10.95 (*0-89480-344-1*, 1344) Workman Pub.

True Hallucinations: Being an Account of the Author's Extraordinary Adventures in the Devil's Paradise. Terence McKenna. LC 91-58904. 256p. 1994. pap. 14.00 (*0-06-250652-8*) Harper SF.

True Hauntings: Spirits with a Purpose. Hazel M. Denning. LC 96-24923. 240p. (Orig.). 1996. pap. 12.95 (*1-56718-218-6*) Llewellyn Pubns.

True Healing Art. R. T. Trall. 120p. 1993. reprint ed. spiral bd. 9.50 (*0-7873-0891-9*) Hlth Research.

True Healing Art or Hygienic vs. Drug Medication (1880) R. T. Trall. 109p. 1996. pap. 16.95 (*1-56459-808-X*) Kessinger Pub.

***True Heart.** Lamb. 1997. mass mkt. 5.99 (*0-671-88217-1*) PB.

True Heart. Marissa Moss. LC 95-50866. (Illus.). 1998. write for info. (*0-15-201344-X*) HarBrace.

***True Heart, Beguiled & Betrayed.** Arnette Lamb. (Clan Mackenzie Triology Ser.). 1997. mass mkt. write for info. (*0-671-85662-6*) PB.

True History of Chocolate. Sophie D. Coe & Michael D. Coe. LC 95-61824. (Illus.). 288p. 1996. 27.50 (*0-500-01693-3*) Thames Hudson.

***True History of Elijah Muhammad: Autobiographically Authoritative.** Elijah Muhammad. LC 96-80510. 324p. 1997. 21.95 (*1-884855-11-3*) Secretarius.

True History of Jesus. Elijah Muhammad. 37p. (Orig.). 1992. pap. 6.95 (*1-56411-047-8*) Coal Remb Elijah.

True History of Jesus: Religion. Elijah Muhammad. 37p. 1992. pap. text ed. 6.95 (*0-9632728-0-2*) Coal Remb Elijah.

***True History of Master Fard Muhammad: Allah (God) in Person.** Elijah Muhammad. 208p. 1996. 16.95 (*1-884855-10-5*) Secretarius.

True History of Mexico. C. Morris. 1976. lib. bdg. 59.95 (*0-8490-2772-1*) Gordon Pr.

True History of the Church of Scotland: From the Beginnings of the Reform to the End of the Reign of King James VI, 8 vols. David Calderwood. Ed. by Thomas Thomson. LC 83-45577. reprint ed. write for info. (*0-404-19894-5*) AMS Pr.

True History of the Land of Canaan. Jon P. Speller. 112p. 1989. pap. 4.00 (*0-9622881-1-X*) Morning NY.

True Holiness: The Wesleyan-Arminian Emphasis. Roy S. Nicholson. 1985. pap. 8.99 (*0-88019-195-3*) Schmul Pub Co.

True Horoscope of the U. S. Helen M. Boyd. LC 75-7188. 1975. 12.95 (*0-88231-007-0*) ASI Pubs Inc.

True Horror Stories. Terry Deary. (Illus.). 128p. (J). 1996. pap. 3.99 (*0-14-038225-9*) Viking Penguin.

True Humanism. Jacques Maritain. Tr. by M. R. Adamson. LC 71-114888. (Select Bibliographies Reprint Ser.). 1977. 30.95 (*0-8369-5292-8*) Ayer.

True Humanism. 3rd ed. Jacques Maritain. Tr. by Margot Adamson. LC 71-98781. 304p. 1970. reprint ed. text ed. 41.50 (*0-8371-2902-8*, MAHU, Greenwood Pr) Greenwood.

True Identity. Wendy Nentwig. (Palisades University Ser.: No. 4). 208p. (YA). (gr. 7-11). 1996. pap. 5.99 (*0-88070-949-9*, Palisades OR) Multnomah Pubs.

True Image: The Origin & Destiny of Man in Christ. fac. ed. Philip E. Hughes. LC 88-25843. 440p. 1989. reprint ed. pap. 125.40 (*0-7837-7958-5*, 2047714) Bks Demand.

True India. C. F. Andrews. 251p. 1985. 34.95 (*0-318-36983-4*) Asia Bk Corp.

True Intellectual System of the Universe: The First Part; Wherein All the Reason & Philosophy of Atheism Is Confuted, & Its Impossibility Demonstrated. Ralph Cudworth. (Collected Works: Vol. I). 899p. 1977. reprint ed. 305.00 (*3-487-06009-4*) G Olms Pubs.

***True Intellectual System of the Universe: 1845 Edition, 3 vols., Set.** Ralph Cudworth. (Cambridge Platonists Ser.). 2060p. 1996. reprint ed. write for info. (*1-85506-357-3*) Bks Intl VA.

True Interest & Political Maxims of the Republic of Holland. Pieter De La Court. LC 78-38278. (Evolution of Capitalism Ser.). 520p. 1972. reprint ed. 37.95 (*0-405-04117-9*) Ayer.

True Interest of Britain Set Forth in Regard to the Colonies & the Only Means of Living in Peace & Harmony with Them, Including Five Different Plans for Effecting This Desirable Event. Josiah Tucker. LC 76-141126. (Research Library of Colonial Americana). 1972. reprint ed. 20.95 (*0-405-03337-0*) Ayer.

True Intimacy: Fifty Two Devotions for Married Couples. Robert H. Lauer & Jeanette C. Lauer. LC 95-41091. 144p. (Orig.). 1996. pap. 9.00 (*0-687-00806-9*) Dimen for Liv.

True Irish Ghost Stories. John D. Seymour. 1993. 10.98 (*0-88365-812-7*) Galahad Bks.

True Israel: Uses of the Names Jew, Hebrew & Israel in Ancient Jewish & Early Christian Literature. Graham Harvey. LC 96-24692. (Arbeiten zur Geschichte des Antiken Judentums und des Urchristentums Ser.). 210p. 1996. 67.75 (*90-04-10617-0*) E J Brill.

***True Israel of God.** Russell Mercer. 112p. (Orig.). 1997. pap. 7.95 (*1-883928-21-4*) Longwood.

True Journal of the Sally Fleet, with the Proceedings of the Voyage. John Dunton. LC 71-25745. (English Experience Ser.: No. 242). 26p. 1970. reprint ed. 20.00 (*90-221-0242-4*) Walter J Johnson.

True Joy: The Wisdom of Francis & Clare. Tr. by Regis J. Armstrong & Ignatius C. Brady. LC 96-12041. (Spiritual Samplers Ser.). 96p. (Orig.). 1996. pap. 1.95 (*0-8091-3672-4*) Paulist Pr.

True Joy of Positive Living. Norman Vincent Peale. 288p. 1985. mass mkt. 4.95 (*0-449-20833-8*, Crest) Fawcett.

True Joy of Positive Living: An Autobiography. large type ed. Norman Vincent Peale. (Large Print Inspirational Ser.). 480p. 1985. pap. 16.95 (*0-8027-2503-1*) Walker & Co.

True Knight. Barrett Parker. (Illus.). 144p. (Orig.). (J). (gr. 6-8). 1995. pap. 10.00 (*1-879418-92-4*) Audenreed Pr.

True Knight Bk. 3: The Warhorse of Esdragon. Susan Dexter. 1996. mass mkt. 5.99 (*0-345-39345-7*, Del Rey Discovery) Ballantine.

True Lady. Edith Layton. 1995. mass mkt. 5.99 (*0-671-88301-1*) PB.

True Law of Kingship: Concepts of Monarchy in Early Modern Scotland. J. H. Burns. LC 95-17980. (Illus.). 340p. (C). 1996. 69.00 (*0-19-820384-5*, Clarendon Pr) OUP.

True Law of Population: Shown to Be Connected with the Food of the People. 2nd ed. Thomas Doubleday. LC 67-17492. (Reprints of Economic Classics Ser.). xxi, 278p. 1967. reprint ed. 45.00 (*0-678-00244-4*) Kelley.

True Legal Polymath: Essays on the Legal Career of Harold J. Berman. Howard O. Hunter. 164p. (C). 1996. text ed. 59.00 (*0-8133-2296-0*) Westview.

True Lies. Dewey Gram. 1994. pap. 4.99 (*0-451-18265-0*, Sig) NAL-Dutton.

True Lies. Dewey Gram. 1994. pap. write for info. (*0-451-18207-3*, Sig) NAL-Dutton.

True Lies. Philip Ross. 256p. 1994. mass mkt. 3.99 (*0-8125-1376-2*) Tor Bks.

True Lies. George Shannon. LC 96-7149. (Illus.). 48p. (J). (gr. 3 up). 1997. 15.00 (*0-688-14483-7*) Greenwillow.

True Lies. Ingrid Weaver. (Intimate Moments Ser.). 1995. mass mkt. 3.75 (*0-373-07660-6*, 1-07660-3) Silhouette.

True Lies: The Architecture of the Fantastic in the Plays of Sam Shepard. Jim McGhee. LC 93-9537. (American University Studies: Theatre Arts: Ser. XXVI, Vol. 18). 224p. (C). 1993. text ed. 42.95 (*0-8204-2052-2*) P Lang Pubng.

True-Life Adventures. Smith. 1993. pap. 4.99 (*0-446-77693-9*) Warner Bks.

True-Life Adventures of Nicky Ridge. Gary Bryant. 78p. (J). (gr. 4-8). 1992. pap. 6.95 (*1-881442-02-0*) New Legends Pub.

True Life in God. Vassula Ryden. (True Life in God Ser.: Vol. 8). 558p. 1995. pap. 12.00 (*1-883225-18-3*) Trinitas.

True Life in God. Vassula Ryden. (True Life in God Ser.: Vol. 7). 92p. 1994. pap. 8.50 (*1-883225-16-7*) Trinitas.

True Life in God. Vassula Ryden. (True Life in God Ser.: Vol. 6). 105p. 1993. pap. 8.50 (*0-9631193-9-7*) Trinitas.

True Life in God. Vassula Ryden. (True Life in God Ser.: Vol. 5). 80p. 1992. pap. 6.75 (*0-9631193-7-0*) Trinitas.

True Life in God. Vassula Ryden. (True Life in God Ser.: Vol. 4). 191p. 1991. pap. 9.95 (*0-9631193-6-2*) Trinitas.

True Life in God. Vassula Ryden. (True Life in God Ser.: Vol. 3). 208p. 1991. pap. 9.95 (*0-9631193-5-4*) Trinitas.

True Life in God. Vassula Ryden. (True Life in God Ser.: Vol. 2). 199p. 1991. pap. 9.95 (*0-9631193-4-6*) Trinitas.

True Life in God, Vol. 1. Vassula Ryden. 216p. (Orig.). 1991. pap. write for info. (*0-9631193-3-8*) Trinitas.

***True Life in God Vol. 9: Original Handwriting Edition.** Contrib. by Vassula Ryden. 547p. (Orig.). (YA). 1997. pap. 12.00 (*1-883225-20-5*) Trinitas.

True Life of Sir Richard F. Burton. G. M. Stisted. 436p. 1984. 250.00 (*1-85077-049-2*, Pub. by Darf Pubs Ltd UK) St Mut.

True Life Reader for Children & Parents. Philip Thody. 1977. 30.00 (*0-7045-0311-5*) St Mut.

True Life Stories. U. L. Prenn. (Illus.). 80p. (Orig.). 1991. 35.00 (*0-937041-97-1*); pap. 15.00 (*0-937041-98-X*) Systems Co.

True Life Story of Isabel Roundtree. Kathleen W. King. Ed. by Julie Rugenstein. 192p. 1995. pap. 10.00 (*0-671-89185-5*) PB.

True Life Story of Isobel Roundtree: A Novel. Kathleen Wallace. 178p. 1993. 19.00 (*0-87483-263-2*) August Hse.

True-Life Treasure Hunts. Judy Donnelly. (Step into Reading Bks.: Step 4). (Illus.). 48p. (J). (gr. 2-4). 1993. pap. 3.99 (*0-679-83980-1*) Random Bks Yng Read.

True Likeness: The Black South of Richard Samuel Roberts, 1920-1936. Thomas L. Johnson. Ed. by Philip Dunn. (Illus.). 188p. (Orig.). 1986. pap. 19.95 (*0-912697-50-4*) Algonquin Bks.

True Likeness: The Black South of Richard Samuel Roberts, 1920-1936. Ed. by Thomas L. Johnson & Phillip C. Dunn. (Illus.). 200p. 1994. 49.95 (*0-86316-176-6*); pap. 29.95 (*0-86316-175-8*) Writers & Readers.

True Likeness: The Black South of Richard Samuel Roberts, 1920-1936. limited ed. Thomas L. Johnson. Ed. by Philip Dunn. (Illus.). 188p. (Orig.). 1986. boxed 100.00 (*0-912697-47-4*) Algonquin Bks.

True Love. Evelyn L. Beilenson & Lois L. Kaufman. (Charming Petites Ser.). (Illus.). 80p. 1995. 4.95 (*0-88088-771-0*) Peter Pauper.

***True Love...** Ed. by Helen Exley. (Miniature Square Bks.). (Illus.). 64p. 1995. 6.00 (*1-85015-651-4*) Exley Giftbooks.

True Love. Jennifer Fulton. 240p. 1994. pap. 10.95 (*1-56280-035-3*) Naiad Pr.

***True Love.** Daphne R. Kingma. 1997. 6.98 (*1-56731-176-8*, MJF Bks) Fine Comms.

True Love. Sun M. Moon. 266p. 15.95 (*0-910621-53-5*); pap. 11.95 (*0-685-61698-3*) HSA Pubns.

True Love. Elise Title. (Temptation Ser.). 1992. mass mkt. 2.99 (*0-373-25520-9*, 1-25520-7) Harlequin Bks.

***True Love.** large type ed. Robert Fulghum. LC 97-9700. (Large Print Book Ser.). 1997. 24.95 (*1-56895-426-3*) Wheeler Pub.

True Love: A Comedy of the Affections. Edith Wyatt. LC 93-17968. (Prairie State Bks.). 321p. 1993. 14.95 (*0-252-06352-X*) U of Ill Pr.

True Love: How to Keep Your Relationship Sweeter, Deeper, & More Passionate. Daphne R. Kingma. 168p. 1991. reprint ed. lib. bdg. 29.00 (*0-8095-5852-1*) Borgo Pr.

True Love: How to Make Your Relationship Sweeter, Deeper & More Passionate. Daphne R. Kingma. LC 90-84636. 160p. (Orig.). 1991. pap. 9.95 (*0-943233-13-5*) Conari Press.

True Love: How to Make Your Relationship Sweeter, Deeper, & More Passionate. Daphne R. Kingma. 160p. 1994. reprint ed. 12.95 (*0-943233-58-5*) Conari Press.

***True Love: Real-Life Stories.** Robert Fulghum. 256p. 1997. 20.00 (*0-06-018784-0*) HarpC.

True Love & Bartholomew: Rebels on the Burmese Border. Jonathan Falla. (Illus.). 416p. (C). 1991. text ed. 52.95 (*0-521-39019-2*) Cambridge U Pr.

True Love & How to Get It. Gerald Lee. (Paperbacks Ser.). 204p. 1985. pap. 14.95 (*0-7022-1778-6*, Pub. by Univ Queensland Pr AT) Intl Spec Bk.

True Love & the Woolly Bugger. Dave Ames. 200p. 1996. 24.95 (*0-9626663-4-3*) Greycliff Pub.

True Love in a World of False Hope: Sex, Romance & Real People. Robbie Castleman. LC 96-16813. 178p. (Orig.). 1996. pap. 9.99 (*0-8308-1958-4*, 1958) InterVarsity.

***True Love Waits.** Mark Devries. LC 97-8903. (YA). 1997. pap. write for info. (*0-8054-6352-6*) Broadman.

***True Love Waits.** Kaminer. 1996. pap. 14.00 (*0-201-32793-7*) Addison-Wesley.

True Love Waits & Other Essays & Criticism. Wendy Kaminer. LC 95-43807. 256p. 1996. 22.00 (*0-201-48914-7*) Addison-Wesley.

True Magick: A Beginner's Guide. Amber K. LC 90-38260. (Practical Magick Ser.). (Illus.). 272p. (Orig.). 1990. mass mkt. 4.95 (*0-87542-003-6*) Llewellyn Pubns.

True Meaning of Christ's Teaching, Vol. 215. Omraam M. Aivanhov. (Izvor Collection: Vol. 215). (Illus.). 203p. (Orig.). 1989. pap. 7.95 (*2-85566-322-9*) Prosveta USA.

True Meaning of the Lord of Heaven. Matteo Ricci. Ed. by Edward J. Malatesta. LC 84-80944. (Jesuit Primary Sources in English Translation Series I: No. 6). (Illus.). xiv, 485p. (CHI & ENG.). 1985. 39.00 (*0-912422-78-5*); 34.00 (*0-912422-77-7*) Inst Jesuit.

***True Measure of a Woman: You Are More Than What You See.** Lisa Bevere. 1997. pap. 9.99 (*0-88419-487-6*) Creation House.

True Messiah. Phillip A. Malpas. 160p. 1989. pap. 12.95 (*0-913004-67-7*, 352) Point Loma Pub.

True Mexico: Tenochtitlan. A. Deverdun. 1976. lib. bdg. 59.95 (*0-8490-2773-X*) Gordon Pr.

True Mission of Jesus. Daniel G. Samuels. 1989. pap. 0.50 (*1-887621-09-1*) Found Ch Divine Truth.

True Mystic: Three Lectures on Mysticism (1914) Holden E. Sampson. 219p. 1996. reprint ed. pap. 17.95 (*1-56459-581-1*) Kessinger Pub.

***True Myths: The Life & Times of Arnold Schwarzenegger.** Nigel Andrews. 1996. 21.95 (*1-55972-364-5*, Birch Ln Pr) Carol Pub Group.

True Names: Vergil & the Alexandrian Tradition of Etymological Wordplay. James O'Hara. LC 96-4240. (C). 1995. 44.50 (*0-472-10660-0*) U of Mich Pr.

True Names & the Opening of the Cyberspace Frontier. Vernor Vinge. 1984. pap. 6.95 (*0-312-94444-6*) Tor Bks.

True Names & the Opening of the Cyberspace Frontier. Vernor Vinge. 384p. Date not set. pap. 14.95 (*0-312-86207-5*) St Martin.

True Native: The Afro American. Samuel Eastman. Ed. by Betty Allums & Rebecca H. Bezemek. 85p. (Orig.). 1993. pap. write for info. (*0-318-71700-X*) BA Cross Ctrl.

True Nebraskans. Paul Fell. 84p. 1994. pap. 5.95 (*0-934904-18-9*) J & L Lee.

True Newes from One of Sir F. Veres Companie. Francis Vere. LC 78-38227. (English Experience Ser.: No. 491). 24p. 1972. reprint ed. 15.00 (*90-221-0491-5*) Walter J Johnson.

***True Newfoundlanders: Early Home & Families of Newfoundland & Labrador.** Margaret McBurney. 1997. 28.00 (*1-55046-199-0*, Pub. by Boston Mills Pr CN) Genl Dist Srvs.

True North. Charles O. Hartman. LC 90-33137. 55p. (Orig.). 1990. pap. 7.95 (*0-914278-54-1*) Copper Beech.

***True North.** Stephanie Strickland. LC 96-27136. (Ernest Sandeen Prize for Poetry Ser.). 88p. (Orig.). 1996. pap. 12.00 (*0-268-01899-5*) U of Notre Dame Pr.

***True North.** Elliott Merrick. LC 88-38068. 375p. 1989. reprint ed. pap. 106.90 (*0-608-02783-9*, 2063850) Bks Demand.

True North: A Memoir. Jill Ker Conway. LC 93-45302. 1994. 23.00 (*0-679-42099-1*) Knopf.

True North: A Memoir. Jill Ker Conway. 1995. pap. 12.00 (*0-679-74461-4*) Random.

True North: A Memoir. large type ed. Jill Kerr Conway. LC 96-2652. 296p. 1996. lib. bdg. 22.95 (*1-57490-060-9*, Beeler LP Bks) T T Beeler.

True North: A Novel of the Underground Railroad. Kathryn Lasky. LC 95-2922. 208p. (YA). (gr. 7 up). 1996. 14.95 (*0-590-20523-4*, Blue Sky Press) Scholastic Inc.

True North: Diary of a North Country Year. Stephen J. Krasemann. 160p. 1992. 39.00 (*1-55971-176-0*) NorthWord.

True North Strong & Free? The Proceedings of a Public Inquiry into Canadian Defense Policy & Nuclear Arms. Intro. by Mel Hurtig. 280p. (Orig.). 1988. pap. 14.95 (*0-919574-83-1*) Gordon Soules Bk.

True Nutrition, True Fitness. Jerrold Winter. LC 90-5214. 408p. 1991. 19.95 (*0-89603-184-5*) Humana.

True Odds: How Risk Affects Your Everyday Life. James Walsh. 401p. 1996. 19.95 (*1-56343-114-9*) Merritt Pub.

True or False: The Westcott-Hort Textual Theory Examined. David O. Fuller. 317p. reprint ed. pap. 11.95 (*0-944355-12-9*) IBTS.

True or False? Judging Doctrine & Leadership. Guy Duininck. 509p. 1992. 15.95 (*0-929400-03-8*) Masters Touch Pub Co.

True Order & Method of Wryting & Reading Hystories. Thomas Blundeville. LC 79-84088. (English Experience Ser.: No. 908). 68p. 1979. reprint ed. lib. bdg. 20.00 (*90-221-0908-9*) Walter J Johnson.

True Organization of the New Church. Charles J. Hempel. LC 40-30032. reprint ed. 62.50 (*0-404-08464-8*) AMS Pr.

True Owners of the Soil. George A. Martin. LC 90-80408. (Illus.). 92p. (Orig.). 1990. pap. 11.00 (*1-878515-13-6*) W S Dawson.

True Partners: A Workbook for Building a Lasting Intimate Relationship. Tina B. Tessina & Riley K. Smith. 256p. (Orig.). 1993. pap. 13.95 (*0-87477-727-5*, Tarcher Putnam) Putnam Pub Group.

True Partnership. Patricia Lakin. LC 94-660. (My School Ser.). (J). (gr. 5 up). 1994. lib. bdg. 21.40 (*0-8114-3869-4*) Raintree Steck-V.

True Path To Peace & Joy. John R. Terry. (Illus.). 250p. 1982. pap. 7.50 (*0-933704-39-9*) Dawn Pr.

True Patriot. Henry Fielding. LC 72-10055. (English Literature Ser.: No. 33). 1972. reprint ed. lib. bdg. 75.00 (*0-8383-1597-6*) M S G Haskell Hse.

True Patriot: A Biography of Brooke Claxton. David J. Bercuson. (Illus.). 360p. 1993. 35.00 (*0-8020-2984-1*) U of Toronto Pr.

True Patriot & Related Writings. Henry Fielding. Ed. by W. B. Coley. LC 86-18463. (Works of Henry Fielding Ser.). (Illus.). 560p. 1987. text ed. 75.00 (*0-8195-5127-9*, Wesleyan Univ Pr) U Pr of New Eng.

True Picture of Emigration. Rebecca Burlend & Edward Burlend. 180p. 1974. reprint ed. pap. 2.95 (*0-8065-0457-9*, Citadel Pr) Carol Pub Group.

True Picture of Emigration. Rebecca Burlend & Edward Burlend. Ed. by Milo M. Quaife. LC 86-25114. (Illus.). xxxi, 167p. 1987. reprint ed. pap. text ed. 9.95 (*0-8032-6083-0*, Bison Books) U of Nebr Pr.

True Poems from the Heart. Genevia B. Beard. (Orig.). 1996. pap. write for info. (*1-57553-274-3*) Watermrk Pr.

True Poetry: Traditional & Popular Verse in Ontario. Pauline Greenhill. 248p. (C). 1989. text ed. 47.95 (*0-7735-0697-7*, Pub. by McGill CN) U of Toronto Pr.

*__True Power.__ John H. Dwiggins. LC 97-73126. 311p. 1997. 5.99 (*0-9658455-6-7*, BBSF1) Basswood.

True Prayer: An Invitation to Christian Spirituality. Kenneth Leech. LC 80-8358. 208p. 1986. pap. 13.00 (*0-06-065232-2*) Harper SF.

True Prayer: An Invitation to Christian Spirituality. Kenneth Leech. LC 95-9588. 208p. 1995. reprint ed. pap. 12.95 (*0-8192-1646-1*) Morehouse Pub.

True Priest: The Priesthood As Preached & Practiced by Saint Augustine. Michele Pellegrino. Ed. by John E. Rotelle. LC 87-71970. (Illus.). 144p. 1988. reprint ed. pap. 7.95 (*0-941491-08-0*) Augustinian Pr.

True Principles of Freemasonry. Melville R. Grant. 379p. 1992. reprint ed. pap. 35.50 (*1-56459-022-4*) Kessinger Pub.

True Professional Ideal in America: A History. Bruce A. Kimball. 444p. (C). 1996. reprint ed. pap. text ed. 23.95 (*0-8476-8143-2*) Rowman.

*__True Professionalism.__ David H. Maister. LC 96-51994. 1997. 24.00 (*0-684-83466-9*, Free Press) Free Pr.

*__True Professors & Mourners: Two Works by John Flavel (1630-1691)__ rev. unabridged ed. John Flavel. LC 96-61071. 176p. (Orig.). 1997. reprint ed. pap. 19.95 (*1-889298-17-4*) Wordspace.

True Promise. Abidullah Ghazi & Tasneema K. Ghazi. Ed. by Bushra Y. Ghazi & Suhaib Ghazi. (Illus.). 25p. (Orig.). (J). (gr. 1-5). 1992. pap. text ed. 6.00 (*1-56316-304-7*) Iqra Intl Ed Fdtn.

True Prosperity: Your Guide to a Cash-Based Lifestyle. K. C. Knouse. LC 96-83285. 224p. (Orig.). 1996. pap. 13.95 (*0-9650802-3-4*) Double-Dome.

True Relation of All the Remarkable Places Observed in the Travels of Thomas Lord Howard. William Crowne. LC 77-171742. (English Experience Ser.: No. 357). 1971. reprint ed. 30.00 (*90-221-0357-9*) Walter J Johnson.

True Relation of the Hardships Suffered by Governor Fernando De Soto & Certain Portuguese Gentlemen During the Discovery of the Province of Florida, Now Newly Set Forth by a Gentleman of Elvias: Volume 1: Facsimile of the Original Portuguese of 1557; Volume 2: Translation & Annotations. limited ed. Gentlemen of Elvias. Tr. by James A. Robertson. 1933. 500.00 (*0-317-27605-0*) Elliots Bks.

True Relation of the Late Battell Fought in New England. Philip Vincent. LC 74-80227. (English Experience Ser.: No. 700). 24p. 1974. reprint ed. 15.00 (*90-221-0700-0*) Walter J Johnson.

True Relation of the Lives & Deaths of the Two English Pyrats, Purser & Clinton. LC 77-171784. (English Experience Ser.: No. 408). 1971. reprint ed. 25.00 (*90-221-0408-7*) Walter J Johnson.

True Relation of the Unjust Proceedings Against the English of Amboyna. LC 72-228. (English Experience Ser.: No. 306). 38p. 1971. reprint ed. 20.00 (*90-221-0306-4*) Walter J Johnson.

*__True Relations: Essays on Autobiography & the Postmodern.__ Ed. by G. Thomas Couser & Joseph Fichtelberg. LC 97-9384. (Contributions to the Study of World Literature: Vol. 85). 1997. text ed. write for info. (*0-313-30509-9*, Greenwood Pr) Greenwood.

*__True Religion Delineated.__ Joseph Bellamy. 388p. 1997. 29.95 (*0-9641803-6-7*) Internat Outreach.

True Religion Explained & Defended. Hugo Grotius. Tr. by F. Coventry. LC 72-201. (English Experience Ser.: No. 318). 350p. 1971. reprint ed. 45.00 (*90-221-0318-8*) Walter J Johnson.

True Report of the Success Which God Gave Unto Our English Soldiers in Ireland, 1580. LC 72-6016. (English Experience Ser.: No. 541). 1973. reprint ed. 10.00 (*90-221-0541-5*) Walter J Johnson.

True Report on the Last Voyage into the West & Northwest Regions, & C. 1577: Worthily Atchieued by Capteine Frobisher of the Sayde Voyage the First Finder & Generall. Ed. by Dionyse Settle. 63p. pap. write for info. (*0-87770-073-7*) Ye Galleon.

True Reporte of the Laste Voyage by Capteine Frobisher. Dionyse Settle. LC 79-6343. (English Experience Ser.: No. 88). 48p. 1969. reprint ed. 45.00 (*90-221-0088-X*) Walter J Johnson.

True Reporte of the Late Discoueries of the Newfound Landes. George Peckham. LC 78-25630. (English Experience Ser.: No. 341). 1971. reprint ed. 20.00 (*90-221-0341-2*) Walter J Johnson.

True Republicanism: The Real & Ideal in Politics. Frank P. Stearns. 1977. text ed. 17.95 (*0-8369-9235-0*, 9089) Ayer.

True Resignation. Jacob Boehme. 57p. 1992. pap. 12.00 (*1-56459-217-0*) Kessinger Pub.

True Resurrection. H. A. Williams. 192p. 1983. pap. 9.95 (*0-87243-115-0*) Templegate.

True Riches. Joseph L. Palotta. 319p. (Orig.). 1985. pap. 8.95 (*0-9604852-2-8*) Revelation Hse.

True Rites & Maimed Rites: Ritual & Anti-Ritual in Shakespeare & His Age. Ed. by Linda Woodbridge & Edward Berry. 312p. (C). 1992. text ed. 44.95 (*0-252-01897-4*); pap. text ed. 15.95 (*0-252-06243-4*) U of Ill Pr.

True Saints. Charles G. Finney. LC 66-24880. (Charles G. Finney Memorial Library). 120p. 1975. pap. 6.99 (*0-8254-2622-7*) Kregel.

True Science of Living: The New Gospel of Health. Edward H. Dewey. 323p. 1972. reprint ed. spiral bd. 16.50 (*0-7873-0284-8*) Hlth Research.

*__True Scots.__ Walter Scot & Robert C. Wallace. (Illus.). 150p. (Orig.). (YA). (gr. 8 up). 1996. pap. 8.00 (*0-9634992-7-0*) R Clifton.

True Scotsman. Louise Kantenwein. (Illus.). (J). (gr. 2-4). 1996. 8.95 (*0-533-11643-0*) Vantage.

True Selves: Understanding Transsexualism: for Family, Friends, Coworkers & Helping Professionals. Mildred L. Brown & Chloe A. Rounsley. LC 96-10107. 1996. 25.00 (*0-7879-0271-3*) Jossey-Bass.

True Sentiments of America. Benjamin Franklin. (Notable American Authors Ser.). 1992. reprint ed. lib. bdg. 75.00 (*0-7812-2892-1*) Rprt Serv.

True Serenity: Based on Thomas a Kempis' the Imitation of Christ. John Kirvan. LC 95-77234. (30 Days with a Great Spiritual Teacher Ser.). 216p. (Orig.). 1995. pap. 6.95 (*0-87793-562-9*) Ave Maria.

True, Sincere & Modest Defense of English Catholics see Execution of Justice in England

True Sisterhood: Michigan Women & Their Kin, 1820-1920. Marilyn F. Motz. LC 82-19198. 199p. 1984. text ed. 64.50 (*0-87395-715-6*); pap. text ed. 21.95 (*0-87395-716-4*) State U NY Pr.

True Slime Molds. Marie L. Farr. (Pictured Key Nature Ser.). 200p. (C). 1981. spiral bd. write for info. (*0-697-04779-2*) Wm C Brown Pubs.

True Son of Heaven. 181p. (Orig.). 1996. pap. 9.00 (*1-883893-36-4*) WinePress Pub.

True South: Travels Through a Land of White Columns, Black-eyed Peas & Redneck Bars. Ed. by Jim Auchmutey et al. LC 93-81148. (Illus.). 192p. 1994. pap. 12.95 (*1-56352-136-9*) Longstreet Pr Inc.

True South Mullet Cook Book. George L. Griffin. (Illus.). 9.95 (*0-937759-00-7*) FL Mail Pr.

True Southern Family Recipes: The Joy of Home Cooking. rev. ed. Drew W. Weeks. Ed. by Diane Parker. LC 92-54173. (Illus.). 250p. 1994. pap. 14.95 (*1-56875-094-3*, 094-3) R & E Pubs.

*__True Spirit & Original Intent of Treaty 7.__ Treaty 7 Tribal Council Staff et al. 408p. 1996. pap. text ed. 18.95 (*0-7735-1522-4*, Pub. by McGill CN) U of Toronto Pr.

True Spirituality. Francis A. Schaeffer. 180p. 1972. pap. 8.99 (*0-8423-7351-9*) Tyndale.

True State of the Planet. Ed. by Ronald Bailey. LC 95-937. 1995. pap. 15.00 (*0-02-874010-6*) Free Pr.

True Stevenson. George S. Hellman. LC 72-1318. (English Literature Ser.: No. 33). 1972. reprint ed. lib. bdg. 75.00 (*0-8383-1443-0*) M S G Haskell Hse.

True Stories. Lev Razgon. Tr. by John Crowfoot from RUS. 1997. 27.95 (*0-87501-108-X*) Ardis Pubs.

*__True Stories: Fiction by Uncommon Women.__ Grace Cavalieri et al. LC 96-70943. (Illus.). 84p. (Orig.). 1997. pap. 11.95 (*0-9637704-6-2*) Red Dragon VA.

*__True Stories: Horror.__ Terrance Dicks. LC 96-50252. 352p. (J). 1997. pap. 7.95 (*0-8069-9655-2*) Sterling.

*__True Stories: Mystery.__ Anita Ganeri. LC 96-50253. 1997. write for info. (*0-8069-9659-5*) Sterling Pubng.

*__True Stories: Nonfiction Literacy in the Primary Classroom.__ Christine Duthie. LC 96-3417. (Illus.). 176p. 1996. pap. text ed. 16.00 (*1-57110-026-1*) Stenhse Pubs.

True Stories about Abraham Lincoln. Ruth B. Gross. 48p. (J). (gr. 4-7). 1991. pap. 2.50 (*0-590-43879-4*) Scholastic Inc.

True Stories by Three Men of the Sea. Joan Randolph. Ed. by Maureen Sappey. 192p. (Orig.). 1990. pap. 10.95 (*0-9627510-0-6*) Island Harbor Pr.

True Stories from History & Biography. Nathaniel Hawthorne. Ed. by William Charvat et al. LC 73-150220. (Centenary Edition of the Works of Nathaniel Hawthorne: Vol. 6). 380p. (J). (gr. 5 up). 1972. 55.00 (*0-8142-0157-1*) Ohio St U Pr.

True Stories from Nigeria. Helen C. Tullock. LC 91-66859. 65p. 1992. pap. 6.95 (*1-55523-474-7*) Winston-Derek.

True Stories from the American Past. William Graebner. LC 92-30973. 1992. pap. text ed. write for info. (*0-07-023915-0*) McGraw.

True Stories from the American Past. 2nd ed. Altina L. Waller & William Graebner. LC 96-9569. 1996. pap. text ed. write for info. (*0-07-067954-1*) McGraw.

True Stories from the American Past, Vol. 2. 2nd ed. Altina L. Waller & William Graebner. LC 96-9569. 1996. pap. text ed. write for info. (*0-07-023015-3*) McGraw.

*__True Stories in the News.__ 2nd ed. Sandra Heyer. Ed. by Allen Ascher. 1996. write for info. incl. audio (*0-614-19134-3*) Addison-Wesley.

True Stories in the News: A Beginning Reader. S. Meyer. 1987. pap. text ed. 15.95 (*0-582-90743-8*, 75252) Longman.

True Stories of False Memories. Eleanor C. Goldstein. Ed. by Kevin Farmer. 517p. (Orig.). (C). 1993. pap. 16.95 (*0-89777-145-1*, Upton Bks) Sirs Inc.

True Stories of Life on Earth. Richard Ferrie & Susan Schultz. (Illus.). 32p. (J). (gr. 4-8). pap. 9.95 (*1-882151-02-X*) Cinc Mus Nat Hist.

True Stories of Needed Justice: Biography of Judge Henry Smith. John I. Smith. (Illus.). 138p. 1979. 5.95 (*0-914546-14-7*) Rose Pub.

True Stories of New England Captives Carried to Canada During the Old French & Indian Wars. Alice C. Baker. (Illus.). 418p. 1991. pap. 27.50 (*1-55613-420-7*) Heritage Bk.

*__True Stories of the Barncastle.__ Leslie B. Parker. (Illus.). 80p. Date not set. pap. 8.95 (*0-934482-05-5*) Hathor House Bks.

*__True Stories of the Foreign Legion.__ Robin Hunter. (Illus.). (Orig.). 1997. mass mkt. 5.95 (*0-7535-0130-9*, Pub. by Virgin Pub UK) London Brdge.

True Stories of the Korean Comfort Women. Ed. by Keith Howard. 1996. pap. 16.95 (*0-304-33264-X*, Pub. by Cassell Pubng UK) LPC InBook.

True Stories of the SAS. Robin Hunter. 192p. (Orig.). 1996. mass mkt. 5.95 (*0-86369-912-X*, Pub. by Virgin Pub UK) London Brdge.

*__True Stories of the Wild West.__ Michel Lipman. 1997. pap. text ed. 8.95 (*0-912517-29-8*) Bluewood Bks.

True Stories of World War II. Ed. by Robin Cross. 246p. 1994. 39.50 (*1-85479-968-1*, Pub. by M OMara Books UK) Trans-Atl Phila.

True Story: A Comedy Novel. Bill Maher. 1994. pap. 12.00 (*0-679-75337-0*) Random.

True Story: Hope after Dope from a Drug Addict to a Doctor. Robert M. Gilmore, Sr. (Urban Ministry Ser.). 145p. (Orig.). 1991. 11.95 (*0-9630462-0-9*) Real Pub.

True Story Behind the Wilmington Ten. Larry R. Thomas. (Illus.). 62p. (Orig.). 1993. pap. 6.95 (*1-56411-052-4*) Untd Bros & Sis.

True Story of a Drunken Mother. Nancy L. Hall. 162p. (Orig.). (C). 1990. 25.00 (*0-89608-381-0*); pap. 8.00 (*0-89608-380-2*) South End Pr.

True Story of a Single Mother. Nancy L. Hall. LC 83-51283. 185p. (Orig.). 1984. pap. 8.00 (*0-89608-208-3*) South End Pr.

True Story of a Teenage Black Girl. Annie Ricks. 1995. 11.95 (*0-533-10822-5*) Vantage.

True Story of a Wimp. Susan Shreve. LC 94-44313. (Illus.). 128p. (YA). (gr. 3 up). 1995. 13.00 (*0-688-13551-X*, Tambourine Bks) Morrow.

True Story of Ah Q. 5th ed. Lu Hsun. Tr. by Yang Hsien-Yi & Gladys Yang from CHI. LC 89-81931. (C & T Asian Literature Ser.). 68p. (Orig.). (C). 1990. pap. 3.95 (*0-917056-93-0*) Cheng & Tsui.

True Story of Ah-Q: A Learning Guide. Jing-heng Ma. 230p. 1992. pap. text ed. 25.00 (*0-89264-105-3*) Ctr Chinese Studies.

True Story of Batman. (Golden Super Shape Bks.). (Illus.). 24p. (J). 1995. bds. 1.95 (*0-307-10007-3*, Golden Pr) Western Pub.

True Story of George Eliot. William Mottram. LC 72-3376. (English Literature Ser.: No. 33). 1972. reprint ed. lib. bdg. 65.95 (*0-8383-1508-9*) M S G Haskell Hse.

*__True Story of Guns N' Roses over the Top: Over the Top.__ Mark Putterford. (Illus.). 112p. pap. 19.95 (*0-7119-3338-3*, OP 47292) Omnibus NY.

True Story of J. Edgar Hoover & the FBI. Deneberg. (J). 1995. pap. 5.99 (*0-590-44157-4*) Scholastic Inc.

*__True Story of Johnny Appleseed.__ Margaret Hodges. LC 96-30939. (Illus.). 32p. (J). 1997. lib. bdg. 15.95 (*0-8234-1282-2*) Holiday.

True Story of Kaspar Hauser. Catherine Cleveland. 1976. lib. bdg. 59.95 (*0-8490-2774-8*) Gordon Pr.

True Story of Pocahontas: A Step 2 Book. Lucille R. Penner. LC 93-45709. (Step into Reading Bks.). (Illus.). 48p. (Orig.). (J). (gr. k-2). 1994. pap. 3.99 (*0-679-86166-1*); lib. bdg. 11.99 (*0-679-96166-6*) Random Bks Yng Read.

*__True Story of St. Nicholas.__ 2nd rev. ed. Rebecca B. Haskell. (Illus.). 24p. 1997. pap. 7.95 (*1-889833-01-0*) Memoirs Unltd.

True Story of Superman. Louise Simonson. (Golden Super Shape Bks.). (Illus.). (J). (ps-3). 1996. pap. write for info. (*0-307-10005-7*, Golden Books) Western Pub.

True Story of the Manger. Antonio Tarzia. Tr. by Edmund C. Lane. (Illus.). 48p. (ITA.). 1988. 9.95 (*0-8189-0541-7*) Alba.

True Story of the Novel. Margaret A. Doody. LC 94-39574. (Illus.). 553p. (C). 1997. 44.95 (*0-8135-2168-8*) Rutgers U Pr.

*__True Story of the Novel.__ Margaret A. Doody. (Illus.). 553p. 1997. pap. 25.00 (*0-8135-2453-9*) Rutgers U Pr.

True Story of the Three Little Pigs. (J). 1991. 22.50 incl. audio (*0-453-00768-6*) Viking Child Bks.

True Story of the Three Little Pigs. Jon Scieszka. (Illus.). 32p. (J). (ps up). 1989. pap. 15.99 (*0-670-82759-2*) Viking Child Bks.

True Story of the Three Little Pigs. Jon Scieszka. 1995. pap. write for info. (*0-14-054056-3*) NAL-Dutton.

True Story of the Three Little Pigs. A. Wolf. (Illus.). 32p. (J). 1996. pap. 4.99 (*0-14-054451-8*) Puffin Bks.

*__True Story of the 3 Little Pigs.__ Jon Scieszka. 1997. pap. text ed. 9.99 incl. audio (*0-14-095400-7*, Puffin) Puffin Bks.

True Story of Wonder Woman. Louise Simonson. (Golden Super Shape Bks.). (Illus.). (J). (ps-3). 1996. pap. write for info. (*0-307-10006-5*, Golden Books) Western Pub.

True Strength: Hercules & Amazon: Africa's Native Heroes, Yesterday, Today & Tomorrow. 2nd ed. Samuel D. Ewing. (Illus.). 216p. (Orig.). 1996. spiral bd. 45.00 (*0-9651572-7-X*) Natural Power. TRUE STRENGTH BY SAMUEL EWING. Samuel's TRUE STRENGTH is a detailed book that reveals the historical basis & origin of Hercules & Amazon in Africa. In addition, teenagers & adults are introduced to the importance of ethics, problem-solving, & team concepts. Customers have access to home-based businesses that offer opportunities to earn & increase their income. Some of the key features of this book are: A map of Africa. * Post test & goal setting quiz. * Questions in every chapter on human relations. * Emphasis on unity & team dynamics as opposed to the "gang mentality". * The origins of the idea of heroism in the continent of Africa. * Who were Hercules & Amazon? What does their example say to us today? * How the African concept of heroism became multi-cultural. * The relevance of heroism, education, & unity as we face the 21st Century. * The accomplishments of women from Africa to the United States who lived the Amazon ideal. * Numerous color photo inserts. Samuel Ewing has 24 years of experience in the fields of weight training, physique competitions, & fitness instruction. He also brings his 12 years of knowledge in physical therapy, meditation & historical studies in the writing of this informative text. This 8" by 11" Book is available for $18.00. To order copies send your money orders to: Samuel Ewing, 4131 Freepike Suite 2, Dayton, OH 45416. ***Publisher Provided Annotation.***

*__True Style: Pieced Jackets with Distinctive Applique.__ Peggy True. Ed. by Laura M. Reinstatler. LC 96-34443. (Illus.). 96p. (Orig.). 1997. pap. 21.95 (*1-56477-178-4*, B292) That Patchwork.

True Subject: Selected Poems of Faiz Ahmed Faiz. Naomi Lazard. 110p. 1987. pap. 13.95 (*0-691-01438-8*); text ed. 37.50 (*0-691-06704-X*) Princeton U Pr.

True Subject: Writers on Life & Craft. Ed. by Kurt Brown. 151p. 1993. pap. 12.00 (*1-55597-181-4*) Graywolf.

True Submission. Charles G. Finney. LC 66-24881. (Charles G. Finney Memorial Library). 128p. 1975. pap. 6.99 (*0-8254-2618-9*) Kregel.

True Success: A New Philosophy of Excellence. Tom Morris. 288p. (Orig.). 1995. pap. 14.00 (*0-425-14615-4*, Berkley Trade) Berkley Pub.

True Success: Ideas about Living & Loving in an Unbalanced World. James S. Wells, Jr. 152p. 1991. 11.95 (*0-9629461-1-7*) Ctr Crtve Bal.

*__True Survival Stories.__ Jack Monroe. LC 96-44496. 1997. pap. 3.99 (*0-14-038544-4*) Viking Penguin.

True Tales: 1882-1883, Vol. 2. Patti Unger. 200p. 1997. pap. 14.95 (*0-9631171-1-4*) SunDog Pub.

True Tales of American Violence. Chris Pfouts. 184p. 1993. text ed. 21.95 (*0-87364-742-4*) Paladin Pr.

True Tales of Birmingham. Larry Ragan. (Illus.). 64p. (Orig.). 1992. pap. 6.95 (*0-943994-19-5*) Birmingham Hist Soc.

*__True Tales of British India.__ Ed. by Michael Wise. LC 93-236844. (Illus.). 302p. 1997. pap. 16.95 (*1-873047-06-1*, Pub. by In Print Pub UK) Weatherhill.

True Tales of Hawaii & the South Seas. Ed. by A. Grove Day & Carl Stroven. 342p. 1993. mass mkt. 4.95 (*0-935180-22-2*) Mutual Pub HI.

True tales of La Crosse: Unusual Stories from Old Newspapers of La Crosse, Wisconsin. Ed. by Douglas Connell. LC 93-73807. (Illus.). 206p. (Orig.). 1995. pap. 19.95 (*0-9645549-0-9*) D Connell.

True Tales of Old St. Helena. Jarvis Finger. (C). 1990. pap. 30.00 (*0-86439-019-X*, Pub. by Boolarong Pubns AT) St Mut.

True Tales of Old-Time Kansas. David Dary. LC 84-40065. Orig. Title: True Tales of the Old-Time Plains. (Illus.). x, 326p. (Orig.). 1984. pap. 9.95 (*0-7006-0250-X*) U Pr of KS.

T

True Tales of Texas. Bertha M. Cox. LC 87-12091. (Illus.). 292p. (J). (gr. 3-8). 1987. reprint ed. 16.95 (0-937460-28-1); reprint ed. pap. 10.95 (0-937460-77-X) Hendrick-Long.

True Tales of the American Southwest. Howard Bryan. LC 96-30706. (Illus.). 256p. 1996. 24.95 (0-940666-95-2); pap. 14.95 (0-940666-96-0) Clear Light.

True Tales of the Everglades. Stuart McIver. (Illus.). 64p. 1989. pap. 4.95 (0-9613236-3-9) Florida Flair Bks.

True Tales of the Great Lakes. Dwight Boyer. (Illus.). 340p. 1960. reprint ed. pap. 12.75 (0-912514-48-5) Freshwater.

True Tales of the Old-Time Plains see True Tales of Old-Time Kansas

True Tales of the South at War: How Soldiers Fought & Families Lived, 1861-1865. Ed. by Clarence Poe & Betsy Seymour. LC 94-34997. 224p. 1995. pap. text ed. 5.95 (0-486-28451-4) Dover.

True Tales of the West. F. Oppel. 1994. 8.98 (0-89009-874-3) Bk Sales Inc.

True Tales-1882 & 1883, Vol. 1. Patti Unger. 193p. 1991. pap. 14.95 (0-9631171-0-6) SunDog Pub.

True Temperance Platform: or an Exposition of the Fallacy of Alcoholic Medication. R. T. Trall. 162p. 1977. reprint ed. spiral bd. 11.00 (0-7873-1298-3) Hlth Research.

True Temperance Platform or an Exposition of the Fallacy of Alcoholic Medication (1864) R. T. Trall. 162p. 1996. pap. 17.95 (1-56459-812-8) Kessinger Pub.

True Texas Tales. William F. Brown. LC 92-93887. (Illus.). 64p. (Orig.). (YA). (gr. 4 up). 1992. per. 8.75 (1-881936-14-7) WFB Ent.

***True Texas Tales Teacher's Guide to Student Activities.** William F. Brown. 24p. (YA). 1995. teacher ed., pap. text ed. 3.50 (1-881936-21-X) WFB Ent.

True Thai: The Modern Art of Thai Cuisine. Victor Sodsook et al. LC 94-40234. 1995. 25.00 (0-688-09917-3) Morrow.

***True the False & the Homosexual.** Samuel Waldron. 20p. (Orig.). 1993. pap. 0.80 (1-889520-07-1) Truth for Eternity.

True Thomas. Nigel Tranter. 432p. 1996. pap. 11.95 (0-340-32815-0, Pub. by H & S UK) Trafalgar.

True Thriller. Franklin W. Dixon. (Hardy Boys Case Files Ser.). (Illus.). (YA). (gr. 6 up). 1995. mass mkt. 3.99 (0-671-88211-2, Archway) PB.

True-to-Life Series from Hamilton High Teaching Guide. Marilyn Reynolds & David Doty. Ed. by Jeanne W. Lindsay. 1996. teacher ed., pap. 21.95 (1-885356-07-2) Morning Glory.

True to Temperament: Van Gogh & French Naturalist Literature. Judy Sund. (Illus.). 300p. (C). 1992. text ed. 110.00 (0-521-41080-0) Cambridge U Pr.

***True to the Faith: Charting the Course through the Acts of the Apostles.** 2nd ed. David Gooding. 413p. 1996. reprint ed. pap. 15.95 (1-882701-20-8) Uplook Min.

True to the Fire. Suzanne Carey. (Intimate Moments Ser.: No. 435). 1992. mass mkt. 3.39 (0-373-07435-2, 5-07435-6) Harlequin Bks.

***True to the Game.** Robert S. Jackson. 1997. pap. text ed. 13.95 (1-879360-47-0) Noble Pr.

True to This Earth: Global Challenges & Transforming Faith. Ed. by A. Race & R. Williamson. 200p. 1995. pap. 14.95 (1-85168-099-3) Onewrld Pubns.

True to Type. William C. Jeffries. 104p. 1991. pap. 12.95 (1-878901-08-7) Hampton Roads Pub Co.

True Tolerance: Liberalism & the Necessity of Judgment. J. Budziszewski. 240p. (C). 1992. 39.95 (1-56000-026-0) Transaction Pubs.

True Transcript of His Majesties Letters Patent for the Public Register for General Commerce. LC 74-80219. (English Experience Ser.: No. 655). 1974. reprint ed. 10.00 (90-221-0655-1) Walter J Johnson.

True Unity: Willing Communication Between Horse & Human. Tom Dorrance. Ed. by Milly H. Porter. LC 87-72039. (Illus.). 151p. 1994. reprint ed. 18.95 (1-884995-09-8) Word Dancer.

True Valor: Stories of Brave Men & Women in World War II. Phyllis R. Emert. LC 95-50392. (Illus.). 80p. (J). (gr. 3-7). 1996. pap. 5.95 (1-56565-458-7) Lowell Hse Juvenile.

***True Vine.** Andrew Murray. (Classics Ser.). 112p. 1997. mass mkt. 4.99 (0-8024-6397-5) Moody.

True Vine. Andrew Murray. 112p. 1983. mass mkt. 4.99 (0-88368-118-8) Whitaker Hse.

True Vine: On Visual Representation & the Western Tradition. Stephen Bann. (Cambridge New Art History & Criticism Ser.). (Illus.). 302p. (C). 1989. text ed. 90.00 (0-521-34144-2) Cambridge U Pr.

True Vipers: Biology & Toxinology. Mallow. Date not set. write for info. (0-89464-877-2) Krieger.

True Visual Magnitude Photographic Star Atlas: Southern Stars & Equatorial Stars. C. Papadopoulos. 1979. 865.00 (0-08-021622-6, Pergamon Pr) Elsevier.

True Voice of Feeling: Studies in English Romantic Poetry. Herbert E. Read. LC 75-30010. reprint ed. 34.50 (0-404-14016-5) AMS Pr.

True Wayfaring Christian: Studies in Milton's Puritanism. Nathaniel H. Henry. (American University Studies: English Language & Literature: Ser. IV, Vol. 53). 178p. (C). 1988. text ed. 28.50 (0-8204-0489-6) P Lang Pubng.

True Wealth. Paul Hwoschinsky. 224p. (Orig.). 1990. pap. 14.95 (0-89815-361-1) Ten Speed Pr.

True West. Christine Mather. 1992. 40.00 (0-517-58336-4, C P Pubs) Crown Pub Group.

***True Whigs & Honest Tories Vol. 1: A Green Interpretation of the Coming of the American Revolution: the Arc of Empire.** Thomas S. Martin. LC 96-46452. 424p. 1997. 69.95 (1-57309-131-6); pap. 49.95 (1-57309-130-8) Intl Scholars.

***True Whigs & Honest Tories Vol. 2: A Green Interpretation of the Coming of the American Revolution: The Unraveling of Empire.** Thomas S. Martin. 486p. 1997. 69.95 (1-57309-133-2); pap. 49.95 (1-57309-132-4) Intl Scholars.

True Wilderness. H. A. Williams. Ed. by Susan Howatch. (Library of Anglican Spirituality Ser.). 174p. 1994. reprint ed. pap. 9.95 (0-8192-1626-7) Morehouse Pub.

True Wilderness: A Selection of Addresses. Harry A. Williams. LC 68-4475. 168p. reprint ed. pap. 47.90 (0-317-55804-8, 2029386) Bks Demand.

True Wings: A Shared Personal Journey of Self Discovery. Julie Kerrigan. (Illus.). 96p. (Orig.). 1995. pap. 8.00 (0-9648613-0-5) J S Kerrigan. TRUE WINGS is an inspiring collection of poems & art filled with hope & new tools for life's challenges. This book is living proof that great power & creativity live inside each one of us, waiting to be born. Julie Kerrigan, author, wife & mother, shares her own journey of growth & self discovery, emphasizing that "Writing is a doorway to the soul." Through her poetry & illustration, she creates a safe starting place for the reader to begin their own journaling & writing process. She shows readers how journaling can successfully move them on their own path of self discovery, free of fear & inhibition. Following the author's example, readers can begin to unlock the wonders inside themselves & share in the joy of life. The book includes extra pages for the reader's own journaling discoveries. Omaha Printing Co., 1995. 96 pages, Pbk. ISBN 0-9648613-0-5. $8.00 plus $3.00 shipping & handling. Julie Kerrigan, Phone (402) 399-9700. ***Publisher Provided Annotation.***

***True Woman: The Beauty & Strength of a Godly Woman.** Susan Hunt. LC 96-36307. 240p. (Orig.). 1997. pap. 10.99 (0-89107-927-0) Crossway Bks.

True Women. Janice W. Windle. 1995. mass mkt. 6.99 (0-8041-1308-4) Ivy Books.

True Women. large type ed. Janice W. Windle. LC 94-920. 1994. lib. bdg. 24.95 (0-8161-7425-3, GK Hall) Thorndike Pr.

***True Women Cookbook: Original Antique Recipes, Photographs, & Family Folklore.** Janice W. Windle. 1997. pap. text ed. 22.95 (1-880092-41-7) Bright Bks TX.

True Work of Dying: A Practical & Compassionate Guide to Easing the Dying Process. Jan S. Bernard & Miriam Schneider. LC 96-33886. 256p. 1996. 22.00 (0-380-97329-4) Avon.

***True Work of Dying: A Practical & Compassionate Guide to Easing the Dying Process.** Jan S. Bernard. 1997. pap. text ed. 12.00 (0-380-78289-8) Avon.

True Worship: The Response of Love. H. David Edwards. (Illus.). 72p. (Orig.). 1987. pap. 2.95 (0-942203-00-3) Elim Bible Inst.

True Yoga. Zom. 4.95 (0-8065-0336-X, Citadel Pr) Carol Pub Group.

TrueBlood Professors' Seminar: Accounting & Auditing Case Studies, 2 vols. Deloitte et al. 91p. Student case bk., 91p. student ed. 5.00 (0-86539-046-0); Discussion leaders guide, 192p. teacher ed. 5.00 (0-86539-045-2) Am Accounting.

Truegate of Mogador. Sewell Ford. LC 76-142261. (Short Story Index Reprint Ser.). 1977. 23.95 (0-8369-3745-7) Ayer.

Truelove. Patrick O'Brian. 192p. 1992. 22.50 (0-393-03109-8) Norton.

Truelove. Patrick O'Brian. 256p. 1993. pap. 12.95 (0-393-31016-7) Norton.

Truelove. large type ed. Patrick O'Brian. 418p. 1992. reprint ed. lib. bdg. 17.95 (1-56054-522-4) Thorndike Pr.

Truely Tasteless Military Jokes. Blanche Knott. 1991. mass mkt. 3.99 (0-312-92726-6, Thomas Dunne Bks) St Martin.

***Trueno.** William H. Armstrong. 1996. pap. text ed. 9.95 (84-241-3187-8) Lectorum Pubns.

Trueno de la Justicia: La Advertencia, El Milagro, El Castigo, La Era de Paz. Ted Flynn & Maureen Flynn. Tr. by Renee Moore et al. from ENG. (Illus.). 499p. (SPA.). 1994. pap. 13.95 (0-9634307-3-4) MaxKol Communs.

Truer Liberty: Simone Weil & Marxism. Lawrence A. Blum & Victor J. Seidler. 200p. 1989. pap. 17.95 (0-415-90195-2, A3570, Routledge NY) Routledge.

Truer Liberty: Simone Weil & Marxism. Lawrence A. Blum & Victor J. Seidler. 200p. 1989. 49.50 (0-415-90046-8, Routledge NY) Routledge.

Truest Pleasure. Robert Morgan. LC 95-22740. 336p. 1995. 18.95 (1-56512-105-8, 72105) Algonquin Bks.

Truffle Beds. Katherine Pierpoint. 80p. (Orig.). 1995. pap. 10.95 (0-571-17360-8) Faber & Faber.

Truffle Hunter. Inga Moore. (Illus.). 32p. (J). (ps-3). 1987. 10.95 (0-916291-09-X) Kane-Miller Bk.

***Truffles.** Adams Media Staff. (Just Desserts Ser.). 1997. pap. text ed. 4.95 (1-55850-735-3) Adams Media.

Truffles, Candies, & Confections: Elegant Candy Making in the Home. Carole Bloom. 208p. (Orig.). 1996. pap. 14.95 (0-89594-833-8) Crossing Pr.

Truhe im Dachgeschoss. Mary M. Landis. (GER.). 1980. pap. 2.60 (0-686-32322-X) Rod & Staff.

Trujillo: The Death of the Dictator. Bernard Diederich. 264p. 1990. reprint ed. pap. 12.95 (0-943862-44-2) Wiener Pubs Inc.

Trukese-English Dictionary. Ward H. Goodenough & Hiroshi Sugita. LC 79-54277. (Memoirs Ser.: Vol. 141). 1980. pap. 15.00 (0-87169-141-8, M141-GOW) Am Philos.

Trullion: Alastor 2262 see Alastor

Truly. Mary Balogh. 352p. 1996. mass mkt. 5.99 (0-425-15329-0) Berkley Pub.

Truly Deviant Crime, Punishment & the Disadvantaged. Diiulio. 1994. 22.95 (0-02-907884-9) S&S Trade.

Truly Disadvantaged: The Inner City, the Underclass, & Public Policy. William J. Wilson. LC 87-10822. (Illus.). 266p. 1990. pap. 13.95 (0-226-90131-9) U Ch Pr.

Truly Fine Citizen: A Romantic Story of Past, Present & Future. Eckhard Gerdes. (Illus.). 96p. (Orig.). 1989. pap. 7.95 (0-913617-09-1) Highlander Pr.

Truly Grim Tales. Priscilla Galloway. LC 95-6037. 132p. (YA). (gr. 7 up). 1995. lib. bdg. 10.95 (0-385-32200-3, Delacorte Pr Bks) BDD Bks Young Read.

Truly Human-Truly Divine: Christological Language & the Gospel Form. W. Eugene Boring. LC 84-11382. 144p. 1984. pap. 11.99 (0-8272-3625-5) Chalice Pr.

***Truly Innocent.** Josephine Bozoukoff. (Illus.). 53p. 1997. pap. 8.00 (0-8059-4146-0) Dorrance.

Truly, Madly, Deeply. Anthony Minghella. (Illus.). 58p. (C). 1991. pap. 8.95 (0-413-64000-0, A0503, Pub. by Methuen UK) Heinemann.

Truly Married. Phyllis Halldorson. (Special Edition Ser.). 1995. pap. 3.75 (0-373-09958-4, 1-09958-9) Silhouette.

Truly Tasteless Blonde Jokes. Blanche Knott. 1992. mass mkt. 3.99 (0-312-92969-2) St Martin.

***Truly Tasteless Disadvantaged, Vol. 1.** Knott. 1997. mass mkt. 4.99 (0-312-96274-6) St Martin.

Truly Tasteless Insults. I. Q. Anonymous. (Illus.). 128p. 1987. 4.95 (1-55601-007-9) Great Sky.

Truly Tasteless Jokes. Blanche Knott. LC 81-22883. 128p. 1985. mass mkt. 4.95 (0-345-32920-1) Ballantine.

Truly Tasteless Jokes, No. 5. Blanche Knott. 1990. mass mkt. 4.50 (0-312-92556-5) St Martin.

Truly Tasteless Jokes, No. 7. Blanche Knott. 1991. mass mkt. 3.99 (0-312-92785-1) St Martin.

Truly Tasteless Jokes, No. 11. Blanche Knott. 128p. 1991. mass mkt. 4.50 (0-312-92619-7) St Martin.

Truly Tasteless Jokes, Vol. VIII. Blanche Knott. 1991. mass mkt. 3.99 (0-312-92557-3) Tor Bks.

Truly Tasteless Jokes, vol. IX. Blanche Knott. 1991. mass mkt. 3.99 (0-312-92611-1) Tor Bks.

Truly Tasteless Jokes Vol. XIV, Vol. 1. Blanche Knott. 1994. mass mkt. 4.50 (0-312-95351-8) St Martin.

Truly Tasteless Jokes Boxed Set. Knott. 1991. boxed 14.90 (0-312-92695-2) Tor Bks.

Truly Tasteless Jokes No. 4. Blanche Knott. 1991. mass mkt. 3.99 (0-312-92555-7) St Martin.

Truly Tasteless Jokes, No. 6. 1992. mass mkt. 3.99 (0-312-92869-6) St Martin.

Truly Tasteless Jokes, No. 7. Blanche Knott. 1992. mass mkt. 3.99 (0-312-92973-0) St Martin.

Truly Tasteless Jokes X. Blanche Knott. 1992. mass mkt. 4.50 (0-312-92839-4) Tor Bks.

Truly Tasteless Jokes XV, Vol. 1. Blanche Knott. 1995. mass mkt. 4.50 (0-312-95642-8) St Martin.

Truly Tasteless Jokes 2. Blanche Knott. 1985. mass mkt. 4.95 (0-345-32921-X) Ballantine.

Truly Tasteless Jokes 3. Blanche Knott. 1985. mass mkt. 5.99 (0-345-32922-8) Ballantine.

Truly Tasteless Kennedy Jokes. Blanche Knott. 1992. mass mkt. 3.99 (0-312-92910-2) St Martin.

Truly Tasteless Salesman Jokes. Blanche Knott. 1993. mass mkt. 3.99 (0-312-92978-1) St Martin.

Truly, the Tears Are Hard to Hide. Harry Wilson. 1994. 16.95 (0-533-11000-9) Vantage.

Truly Tiny Gardens. Thomasina Tarling. (Illus.). 96p. 1995. 22.95 (1-57076-024-1, Trafalgar Sq Pub) Trafalgar.

***Truly Wilde: Dolly Wilde & the Subversive Salon.** Joan Schenkar. 304p. Date not set. 25.00 (0-465-08772-8) Basic.

Trumai Indians of Central Brazil. Robert F. Murphy. LC 84-45523. (American Ethnological Society Monographs: No. 24). 1988. reprint ed. 22.00 (0-404-62923-7) AMS Pr.

Truman. David McCullough. (Illus.). 896p. 1992. 30.00 (0-671-45654-7) S&S Trade.

Truman. David McCullough. (Illus.). 1120p. 1993. pap. 16.00 (0-671-86920-5, Touchstone Bks) S&S Trade.

Truman Administration & the Growth of the Cold War, 1946-52, 7 yearbooks, Set 2. (Facts on File Yearbooks). 499.00 (0-87196-052-4) Facts on File.

Truman Administration & the Growth of the Cold War, 1946-52 see Facts on File Yearbooks

Truman Administration & the Problems of Postwar Labor 1945-1948. Arthur F. McClure. LC 68-57718. 267p. 1975. 35.00 (0-8386-6999-9) Fairleigh Dickinson.

Truman Administration, Its Principles & Practice. Harry S. Truman. Ed. by Louis W. Koenig. LC 78-12249. 394p. 1979. reprint ed. text ed. 99.75 (0-313-21186-8, TRTA, Greenwood Pr) Greenwood.

Truman, American Jewry, & Israel, 1945-1948. Zvi Ganin. LC 78-10221. 238p. (C). 1979. 37.95 (0-8419-0401-4) Holmes & Meier.

Truman, American Jewry, & Israel, 1945-1948. Zvi Ganin. LC 78-10221. 238p. (C). 1979. pap. text ed. 22.50 (0-8419-0497-9) Holmes & Meier.

Truman & Noyes: Story of a President's Alter Ego. Sidney O. Krasnoff. LC 96-93019. (Illus.). 250p. 1997. 38.95 (0-9656412-0-1) Jonathan Stuart Pr. The author has been a friend of the Noyes family since 1927. In 1943, Dr. Krasnoff first became aware of Noyes' involvement with the executive branch of the federal government. While visiting Noyes' mother in Chicago, he was shown several letters on White House stationery. It was not until 1987, six years after Noyes' death, that the author was able to begin a thorough research of David Noyes' anonymous role as adviser & associate of Harry S. Truman. Shortly after Truman's death, Noyes, in an interview, remarked that "every president needs an alter ego." When asked if he was Harry Truman's alter ego, he replies, "I was Truman's everything. I was Truman's total & complete confidant." This is the story of David M. Noyes, immigrant Jew, born in the Ukraine, with no formal education beyond the eighth grade & his thirty year relationship with President Harry S. Truman, Missouri born Baptist, with no formal education beyond high school, a relationship based on mutual trust & admiration. Edwin A. Locke, Jr., a member of the Roosevelt & Truman administrations, who worked closely with Noyes, "The author has undertaken one of the most difficult tasks in the world - to write about a rare & remarkable person." Benedict K. Zobrist, former director of the Harry S. Truman Library, "Noyes was totally dedicated to President Truman...here was a part of the Truman story that had to be told. Dr. Krasnoff tells the very moving tale with great feeling & care. I am pleased to see the story finally told." To order Jonathan Stuart Press, P.O. Box 2647, West Palm Beach, FL 33402. Phone: 561-659-3491, FAX: 561-659-9891, E-mail: jspress@aol.com.** ***Publisher Provided Annotation.

Truman & Taft-Hartley: A Question of Mandate. R. Alton Lee. LC 80-17251. viii, 254p. 1980. reprint ed. text ed. 45.00 (0-313-22618-0, LETT, Greenwood Pr) Greenwood.

***Truman & the Democratic Party.** Sean J. Savage. LC 96-49954. 1997. 34.95 (0-8131-2003-9) U Pr of Ky.

Truman & the Hiroshima Cult. Robert P. Newman. 260p. 1995. 34.95 (0-87013-403-5) Mich St U Pr.

Truman & the Russians. Herbert Druks. 1981. pap. 12.50 (0-8315-0183-9) Speller.

Truman & the Steel Seizure Case: The Limits of Presidential Power. Maeva Marcus. LC 93-43419. (Constitutional Conflicts Ser.). 424p. 1994. pap. text ed. 17.95 (0-8223-1417-7) Duke.

Truman Capote: A Bibliography. limited ed. Ed. by Kenneth Starosciak. 1973. 7.50 (0-686-05289-7) K Starosciak.

Truman Capote: Conversations. M. T. Inge. LC 86-19116. (Literary Conversations Ser.). 390p. 1987. 39.50 (0-87805-274-7) U Pr of Miss.

***Truman Capote: In Which Various Friends, Enemies, Acquaintances, & Detractors Recall His Turbulent Career.** George Plimpton. LC 97-14792. (Illus.). 512p. 1996. 35.00 (0-385-23249-7, N A Talese) Doubleday.

Truman Capote's Southern Years: Stories from a Monroeville Cousin. Marianne M. Moates. LC 95-23384. (Illus.). 240p. (C). 1996. reprint ed. pap. 19.95 (0-8173-0815-6) U of Ala Pr.

Truman Committee: A Study in Congressional Responsibility. Donald H. Riddle. LC 63-16306. 217p. reprint ed. pap. 61.90 (0-317-08280-9, 2050638) Bks Demand.

Truman Doctrine & the Origins of McCarthyism: Foreign Policy, Domestic Policy, & Internal Security, 1946-48. Richard M. Freeland. 448p. (C). 1985. text ed. 40.00 (0-8147-2575-9) NYU Pr.

Truman Doctrine & the Origins of McCarthyism: Foreign Policy, Domestic Policy, & Internal Security, 1946-48. Richard M. Freeland. 448p. (C). 1989. pap. text ed. 18.00 (0-8147-2576-7) NYU Pr.

Truman in Retirement. G. W. Sand. (Illus.). 1993. 19.95 (0-912083-63-8, NO. 63-8, Justice Bks) Diamond Communications.

Truman in the White House: The Diary of Eben A. Ayers. Comment by Robert H. Ferrell. (Illus.). 416p. 1991. text ed. 37.50 (0-8262-0790-1) U of Mo Pr.

Truman Nelson Reader. Ed. by William J. Schafer. LC 88-14701. 328p. (Orig.). (C). 1989. pap. text ed. 18.95 (0-87023-648-2); lib. bdg. 40.00 (0-87023-647-4) U of Mass Pr.

Truman of St. Helens: The Man & His Mountain. 4th ed. Shirley Rosen. (Illus.). 163p. reprint ed. pap. 9.95 (0-9623297-1-1) Rosebud Pub.

Truman, Palestine, & the Press: Shaping Conventional Wisdom at the Beginning of the Cold War. Bruce J. Evensen. LC 91-30604. (Contributions in American History Ser.: No. 144). 256p. 1992. text ed. 55.00 (0-313-27773-7, ETZ/, Greenwood Pr) Greenwood.

Truman Presidency. Ed. by Michael J. Lacey. (Woodrow Wilson Center Ser.). 480p. (C). 1989. text ed. 74.95 (0-521-37559-2) Cambridge U Pr.

Truman Presidency. Ed. by Michael J. Lacey. (Woodrow Wilson Center Ser.). 480p. (C). 1991. pap. text ed. 20.95 (0-521-40773-7) Cambridge U Pr.

Truman Presidency: Intimate Perspectives. Ed. by Kenneth W. Thompson. (Portraits of American Presidents Ser.). 200p. 1984. pap. text ed. 18.50 (0-8191-3699-9) U Pr of Amer.

Truman Presidency: The Origins of the Imperial Presidency & the National Security State. Ed. by Athan Theoharis. 1979. text ed. 39.50 (*0-930576-12-8*) E M Coleman Ent.

Truman Program. Harry S. Truman. Ed. by M. B. Schnapper. LC 75-152611. 261p. 1972. reprint ed. text ed. 35.00 (*0-8371-6046-4*, TRTP, Greenwood Pr) Greenwood.

Truman Program: Addresses & Messages. Harry S. Truman. (History - United States Ser.). 261p. 1993. reprint ed. lib. bdg. 79.00 (*0-7812-4810-8*) Rprt Serv.

Truman Scandals & the Politics of Morality. Andrew J. Dunar. LC 84-2205. 224p. 1997. 24.00 (*0-8262-0443-0*) U of Mo Pr.

***Truman Scandals & the Politics of Morality.** Andrew J. Dunar. 224p. 1997. pap. 16.95 (*0-8262-1118-6*) U of Mo Pr.

Truman Speaks: On the Presidency, the Constitution, & Statecraft. Harry S. Truman. LC 60-8389. 133p. 1975. text ed. 49.50 (*0-231-02384-7*); pap. text ed. 18.50 (*0-231-08339-4*) Col U Pr.

Truman Way. Jeffrey B. Morris. (Great Presidential Decisions Ser.). (Illus.). 128p. (YA). (gr. 5 up). 1994. lib. bdg. 22.95 (*0-8225-2927-0*, Lerner Publctns) Lerner Group.

Truman Years. Ed. by Eleanora W. Schoenebaum. (Political Profiles Ser.). 748p. 1982. 75.00 (*0-87196-453-8*) Facts on File.

***Truman Years.** Ed. by Eleanora W. Schoenebaum. LC 76-20897. (Political Profiles Ser.). 744p. 1978. reprint ed. pap. 180.00 (*0-608-02844-4*, 2063911) Bks Demand.

Truman's Aunt Farm. Jama K. Rattigan. LC 93-4860. (Illus.). 32p. (J). 1994. 14.95 (*0-395-65661-3*) HM.

***Truman's Aunt Farm.** Jama K. Rattigan. 32p. (J). (ps-3). 1996. pap. 5.95 (*0-395-81656-4*) HM.

Truman's Court: A Study in Judicial Restraint. Frances H. Rudko. LC 88-5664. (Contributions in Legal Studies: No. 45). 186p. 1988. text ed. 45.00 (*0-313-26316-7*, RTC/, Greenwood Pr) Greenwood.

Truman's Crises: A Political Biography of Harry S. Truman. Harold F. Gosnell. LC 79-7360. (Contributions in Political Science Ser.: No. 33). 656p. 1980. text ed. 36.95 (*0-313-21273-2*, GTC/, Greenwood Pr) Greenwood.

***Truman's Decision: The Bomb: Kamikazes the Unknown Factor.** William C. Sholin. (Illus.). 128p. 1997. 19.95 (*0-9641754-2-8*) Mtn View.

Truman's Memoirs Vol. 2: 1946-1950. Harry S. Truman. 1996. 14.98 (*0-8317-7319-7*) Smithmark.

***Truman's Scientific Guide to Pest Control Operations.** 5th rev. ed. Gary W. Bennett et al. LC 96-80199. (Illus.). 500p. 1997. 74.95 (*0-929870-45-X*) Advanstar Commns.

Truman's Scientific Guide to Pest Control Operations. Gary Bennett. LC 88-82584. (Illus.). 495p. 1988. reprint ed. text ed. 59.95 (*0-929870-00-X*) Advanstar Commns.

Trumans Spy. Noel Hynd. 448p. 1991. mass mkt. 4.95 (*0-8217-3309-5*, Zebra Kensgtn) Kensgtn Pub Corp.

Truman's Two-China Policy. June Grasso. LC 86-31344. 216p. (gr. 13). 1987. text ed. 59.95 (*0-87332-411-0*) M E Sharpe.

Trumbull: The Declaration of Independence. Irma B. Jaffe. (Art in Context Ser.). (Illus.). 124p. 1979. 24.95 (*0-8464-1199-7*) Beekman Pubs.

Trumbull Stickney. Amberys R. Whittle. LC 72-425. 164p. 1973. 15.00 (*0-8387-1154-5*) Bucknell U Pr.

Trumdeutung. Sigmund Freud. 672p. (GER.). 1991. pap. 22.50 (*3-596-10436-X*, Pub. by Fischer Taschbch Verlag GW) Intl Bk Import.

***Trumepets Sounding: Propaganda Plays of the American Revolution.** Ed. by Norman Philbrick. Date not set. write for info. (*0-405-09803-0*) Ayer.

Trump: Surviving at the Top. Donald J. Trump & Charles Leerhsen. (Illus.). 256p. 1990. 21.45 (*0-394-57597-0*) Random.

Trump: The Art of Survival. Donald J. Trump & Charles Leerhsen. 1991. mass mkt. 5.99 (*0-446-36209-3*) Warner Bks.

Trump: The Art of the Deal. Tony Schwartz & Donald J. Trump. 1989. mass mkt. 5.95 (*0-446-35325-6*) Warner Bks.

Trump: The Art of the Deal. Donald J. Trump & Tony Schwartz. LC 87-42663. (Illus.). 256p. 1987. 19.95 (*0-394-55528-7*) Random.

***Trump for Jericho.** Robert Kemp. 60p. (Orig.). 1996. pap. 6.00 (*0-88734-713-4*) Players Pr.

Trumpa, the Cheetah. Eduard Zingg. Ed. by Bob Italia. LC 93-10263. (African Animal Adventure Ser.). (J). (gr. 4 up). 1993. lib. bdg. 15.98 (*1-56239-214-X*) Abdo & Dghtrs.

Trumped! John R. O'Donnell. Ed. by Julie Rubenstein. (Illus.). 392p. 1992. reprint ed. mass mkt. 5.99 (*0-671-73818-6*) PB.

Trumpet. Bruce Pearson. (Standard of Excellence Ser.: Bk. 1). 1993. 6.45 (*0-8497-5935-8*, W21TP) Kjos.

Trumpet Bk. 1. (Breeze Easy Method Ser.). 32p. (Orig.). 1994. pap. 6.50 (*0-89724-374-9*, BE0019) Warner Brothers.

Trumpet Bk. 2. (Breeze Easy Method Ser.). 32p. (Orig.). 1994. pap. 6.50 (*0-89724-375-7*, BE0020) Warner Brothers.

Trumpet & Trombone in Graphic Arts, Fifteen Hundred to Eighteen Hundred. Tom L. Naylor. Ed. by Stephen L. Glover. LC 79-10044. (Brass Research Ser.: No. 9). (Illus.). 1979. lib. bdg. 30.00 (*0-914282-20-4*) Brass Pr.

Trumpet at Dawn. Robert D. Judy. (Orig.). 1991. pap. 8.95 (*0-9627383-1-X*) RDJ Assocs.

Trumpet Fingering Chart. Brenda Murphy. (Illus.). 1984. pap. 3.95 (*0-8256-2385-5*, AM35759) Music Sales.

Trumpet for a Walled City. Dolores Pala. 1979. pap. 1.75 (*0-449-23913-6*, Crest) Fawcett.

Trumpet for His People: Leopold Sedar Senghor of Senegal. Grace Collins. LC 95-7602. (Illus.). 32p. (J). 1996. 16.95 (*0-9629978-0-3*) Sights Prods.

Trumpet for His People: Leopold Sedar Senghor of Senegal. Grace Collins. LC 95-7602. (Illus.). (J). 1996. pap. 8.95 (*1-886366-04-7*) Sights Prods.

Trumpet for His People: Leopold Sedar Senghor of Senegal. Janet Vaillant & Brenda Randolph. LC 95-7602. (Illus.). (J). 1997. vhs write for info. (*1-886366-05-5*) Sights Prods.

Trumpet for His People: Leopold Sedar Senghor of Senegal. Janet Vaillant & Barbara Randolph. LC 95-7602. (Illus.). (J). 1997. cd-rom write for info. (*1-886366-06-3*) Sights Prods.

***Trumpet for Zion Year A: Black Church Worship Resources.** Linda H. Hollies. (C). 1997. pap. 19.99 (*1-880299-05-4*) Woman to Woman.

Trumpet from the Housetops: The Selected Writings of Lionel Forman. Lionel Forman. Ed. by Andre Odendaal & Sadie Forman. LC 92-1505. (UWC Mayibuye History Ser.: Vol. 6). (Illus.). 256p. (C). 1992. text ed. 29.95 (*0-8214-1041-5*); pap. text ed. 15.95 (*0-8214-1042-3*) Ohio U Pr.

Trumpet Handbook. William Bay. (Building Excellence Ser.). 1993. 4.95 (*0-87166-426-7*, 94113); audio 9.98 (*0-87166-427-5*, 94113C); audio 13.95 (*0-87166-428-3*, 94113P) Mel Bay.

Trumpet Hymn Variations. Contrib. by D. R. Heier. 1963. 9.99 (*0-685-68365-6*, MB-218) Lillenas.

Trumpet in the Twilight of Time. Raymond McCarty. LC 80-53734. (Illus.). 144p. (Orig.). 1981. 10.95 (*0-938310-00-3*); pap. 6.95 (*0-938310-01-1*) Volunteer Pubns.

***Trumpet in Zion.** Willa Tramble. 196p. (Orig.). 1994. pap. 7.95 (*1-56043-814-2*) Destiny Image.

Trumpet Judgments. pap. 0.95 (*0-937408-10-7*) GMI Pubns Inc.

Trumpet-Major. Thomas Hardy. (World's Classics Ser.). (Illus.). 416p. 1991. pap. 5.95 (*0-19-282718-9*) OUP.

Trumpet-Major. Thomas Hardy. (Nonfiction Ser.). 320p. 1985. mass mkt. 4.95 (*0-14-043142-X*, Penguin Classics) Viking Penguin.

Trumpet Major. Thomas Hardy. 320p. 1989. pap. 6.95 (*0-14-043273-6*, Penguin Classics) Viking Penguin.

Trumpet-Major. large type ed. Thomas Hardy. (Isis Clear Type Classic Ser.). 384p. 1992. 23.95 (*1-85089-387-X*, Pub. by ISIS UK) Transaction Pubs.

Trumpet Method. William Bay. 1993. 7.95 (*0-87166-915-3*, 93448) Mel Bay.

Trumpet Method, Bk. 1. Mitchell. 1990. 8.95 (*0-685-32178-9*, M304) Hansen Ed Mus.

Trumpet Method, Bk. 2. Mitchell. 1990. 8.95 (*0-685-32179-7*, M305) Hansen Ed Mus.

Trumpet Method, Bk. 3. Mitchell. 1990. 8.95 (*0-685-32180-0*, M306) Hansen Ed Mus.

Trumpet Method, Bk. 4. Mitchell. 1990. 8.95 (*0-685-32181-9*, M307) Hansen Ed Mus.

Trumpet of Conscience. Martin Luther King, Jr. LC 68-31061. 96p. 1989. pap. 8.95 (*0-685-22954-8*) Harper SF.

Trumpet of Gabriel. Michael H. Brown. LC 94-61406. 365p. (Orig.). 1994. pap. 11.00 (*1-880033-16-X*) Faith Pub OH.

***Trumpet of Reform: German Literature in New England of the Nineteenth Century.** Sigrid Bauschinger. Tr. by Thomas Hansen from GER. (GERM Ser.). 1997. 52.95 (*1-57113-176-0*) Camden Hse.

***Trumpet of Sedition.** Wood. 1998. pap. 17.50 (*0-8147-9321-5*) NYU Pr.

***Trumpet of Sedition: Political Theory & the Rise of Capitalism, 1509-1688.** Ellen M. Wood & Neal Wood. LC 96-34777. 1997. 30.00 (*0-8147-9317-7*) NYU Pr.

Trumpet of the Last Judgement Against the Athiest & Antichrist: An Ultimatum. Bruno Bauer. Tr. by Lawrence Stepelevich from GER. LC 88-1785. (Studies in German Thought & History: Vol. 5). 224p. 1989. lib. bdg. 89.95 (*0-88946-356-5*) E Mellen.

Trumpet of the Swan. Joseph Robinette. 1992. pap. 5.25 (*0-87129-206-8*, T85) Dramatic Pub.

Trumpet of the Swan. E. B. White. LC 72-112484. (Illus.). (J). (gr. 3-6). 1970. 13.00 (*0-06-026397-0*); lib. bdg. 12.89 (*0-06-026398-9*) HarpC Child Bks.

Trumpet of the Swan. E. B. White. LC 72-112484. (Trophy Bk.). (Illus.). 222p. (J). (gr. 3 up). 1973. reprint ed. pap. 3.95 (*0-06-440048-4*, Trophy) HarpC Child Bks.

Trumpet of the Swan: A Study Guide. Anne Spencer. Ed. by J. Friedland & R. Kessler. (Novel-Ties Ser.). 24p. (J). (gr. 4-6). 1992. pap. text ed. 15.95 (*0-88122-710-2*) Lrn Links.

Trumpet of the Swan see E. B. White Boxed Set: Charlotte's Web, Stuart Little, & The Trumpet of the Swan

Trumpet on the Land: The Aftermath of Custer's Massacre, 1876. Terry C. Johnston. 672p. 1995. mass mkt. 6.50 (*0-553-29975-1*) Bantam.

Trumpet Pocketbook. Bill Bay. pap. 0.95 (*0-87166-559-X*, 93743) Mel Bay.

***Trumpet Praise.** William Bay. 1993. pap. 16.95 incl. audio (*0-7866-0966-4*, 94054P) Mel Bay.

Trumpet Primer. William Bay. 1993. 4.95 (*0-87166-376-7*, 93405) Mel Bay.

Trumpet Records: An Illustrated History with Discography by Marc Ryan. 128p. 1992. pap. 25.00 (*0-936433-13-2*) Big Nickel.

***Trumpet Showstoppers.** rev. ed. Ed. by Carol Cuellar. 112p. (YA). 1997. pap. text ed. 12.95 (*0-89724-650-0*) Warner Brothers.

Trumpet Soundeth: William Jennings Bryan & His Democracy, 1896-1912. Paul W. Glad. LC 85-24695. (Illus.). x, 256p. 1986. reprint ed. text ed. 65.00 (*0-313-25049-9*, GLTS, Greenwood Pr) Greenwood.

Trumpet Story. Bill Coleman. (Illus.). 259p. 1991. text ed. 28.95 (*1-55553-091-5*) NE U Pr.

Trumpet Technic. expanded rev. ed. Clifford Lillya. 96p. 1995. pap. 12.60 (*0-9630856-3-8*) Balquhidder.

Trumpet to Arms: Alternative Media in America. David Armstrong. LC 79-66690. 359p. 1984. reprint ed. pap. 14.00 (*0-89608-193-1*) South End Pr.

Trumpet to the World. Mark Harris. LC 88-37847. (Landmark Edition Ser.). xiv, 242p. 1989. text ed. 30.00 (*0-8032-2353-6*) U of Nebr Pr.

***Trumpet Tune in C.** Michael Helman. Ed. by Dale Tucker. (St. Cecilia Ser.). 8p. (Orig.). (C). 1997. pap. text ed. 3.95 (*0-7692-0092-3*) Warner Brothers.

Trumpeter. Jeannine Savard. LC 92-71502. (Poetry Ser.). 1992. pap. 11.95 (*0-88748-153-1*) Carnegie-Mellon.

Trumpeter of Krakow. Eric P. Kelly. LC 66-16712. (Illus.). 224p. (YA). (gr. 7 up). 1968. reprint ed. lib. bdg. 17.00 (*0-02-750140-X*, Mac Bks Young Read) S&S Childrens.

Trumpeter of Krakow. Eric P. Kelly. LC 91-26879. (Illus.). 224p. (J). (gr. 3-7). 1992. reprint ed. pap. 4.50 (*0-689-71571-4*, Aladdin Paperbacks) S&S Childrens.

***Trumpeter Swan.** Jason Cooper. LC 96-52096. (Giants among Us Ser.). (J). 1997. write for info. (*1-55916-187-6*) Rourke Bk Co.

Trumpeter Swan: Its History, Habits, & Population in the United States. Winston E. Banko. LC 80-12533. (Illus.). 224p. reprint ed. pap. 63.90 (*0-7837-4651-2*, 2044375) Bks Demand.

Trumpeter Swan Bibliography. Ed. by James A. Cooper & David K. Weaver. 55p. (Orig.). 1986. pap. text ed. 10.00 (*0-9619936-3-4*); disk 25.00 (*0-9619936-5-0*) Trumpeter Swan Soc.

Trumpeter Swan Society Conference, 9th: Proceedings & Papers. Trumpeter Swan Society Staff. Ed. by Donna Compton. (Illus.). 132p. (Orig.). 1986. pap. 5.00 (*0-9619936-2-6*) Trumpeter Swan Soc.

Trumpeters' & Kettledrummers' Art (1795) J. Ernst Altenburg. Tr. by Edward H. Tarr from GER. LC 74-4026. (Illus.). 168p. 1974. 15.00 (*0-914282-01-8*) Brass Pr.

Trumpeter's Guide to Orchestral Excerpts. 2nd ed. Ed. by Anne Hardin. LC 86-70740. 70p. 1986. 18.00 (*0-938100-44-0*); 13.50 (*0-938100-46-7*) Camden Hse.

Trumpeter's Handbook: A Comprehensive Guide to Playing & Teaching the Trumpet. Roger C. Sherman. LC 78-73020. (Illus.). 1979. 29.50 (*0-918194-02-4*) Accura.

Trumpeter's Tunes. Wiggins. pap. 9.95 (*0-685-69169-1*, CH55982) Shawnee Pr.

Trumpets. Houghton Mifflin Company Staff. (Reading Ser.). (J). 1988. teacher ed., pap. 52.36 (*0-395-43693-1*) HM.

Trumpets. Houghton Mifflin Company Staff. (Reading Ser.). (J). 1988. teacher ed., wbk. ed., pap. 7.28 (*0-395-45561-8*) HM.

Trumpets. Houghton Mifflin Company Staff. (Reading Ser.). (J). 1988. wbk. ed., pap. 6.24 (*0-395-45546-4*) HM.

***Trumpets are Sounding.** Tim C. Ries. 1997. mass mkt. 4.99 (*1-55197-317-0*) Partners Pubs Grp.

Trumpets from the Islands of Their Eviction. Martin Espada. LC 87-71581. 96p. 1987. pap. 8.00 (*0-916950-72-7*) Biling Rev-Pr.

Trumpets from the Islands of Their Eviction. expanded ed. Martin Espada. LC 94-35250. (Illus.). 96p. 1994. pap. 9.00 (*0-927534-51-7*) Biling Rev-Pr.

Trumpets from the Tower: English Puritan Printing in the Netherlands, 1600-1640. Keith L. Sprunger. (Brill's Studies in Intellectual History: Vol. 46). 250p. 1994. 87.50 (*90-04-09935-2*) E J Brill.

Trumpets Sounding: Propanda Plays of the American Revolution. Ed. by Norman Philbrick. LC 77-184007. 1977. reprint ed. lib. bdg. 20.00 (*0-405-11192-4*, Pub. by Blom Pubns UK) Ayer.

Trumps. Harriot Curtis. (Works of Harriot Curtis Ser.). 1990. reprint ed. lib. bdg. 79.00 (*0-7812-2466-7*) Rprt Serv.

Trumps of Doom. Roger Zelazny. (Chronicles of Amber Ser.: Bk. 6). 192p. 1986. reprint ed. mass mkt. 5.99 (*0-380-89635-4*, AvoNova) Avon.

***Trumpy.** Robert Tolf. 1996. text ed. 49.95 (*0-07-049907-1*) McGraw.

Truncated & Censored Samples: Theory & Applications. A. Clifford Cohen. (Statistics: Textbooks & Monographs: Vol. 119). 328p. 1991. 150.00 (*0-8247-8447-2*) Dekker.

Truncated & Censored Samples from Normal Populations. Schneider. (Statistics: Textbooks & Monographs: Vol. 70). 288p. 1986. 115.00 (*0-8247-7591-0*) Dekker.

***Trunk: American Edition.** Brian Wildsmith. (Cat on the Mat Book). (Illus.). 16p. 1997. pap. 3.95 (*0-19-849007-0*) OUP.

Trunk & Vertebral Column see Physiology of the Joints

Trunk Full of Adventure. Carey Ostergard. 24p. (J). (gr. 4-12). 1992. pap. 5.00 (*1-886210-08-X*) Tyketoon Yng Author.

***Trunk Music.** Michael Connelly. 1997. 27.50 (*0-316-15391-5*) Little.

***Trunk Music.** Michael Connelly. LC 97-2945. 1997. 26.95 (*1-56895-440-9*, Compass) Wheeler Pub.

Trunk Music: A Harry Bosch Novel. Michael Connelly. LC 96-18988. 1997. 23.95 (*0-316-15244-7*) Little.

Trunk Show. Alison Glen. 1995. 20.00 (*0-671-79115-X*) S&S Trade.

TrunKalculator (Version 1.0) The Telecommunications Management Tool. John S. Craparo. 1989. 69.95 (*0-685-74155-9*); Incl. 3.5" diskette. 69.95 incl. disk (*0-685-74156-7*, CR1001) Wynnewood Rsch.

***Trupp: A Fuzzhead Tale.** Cannon. (J). 1998. pap. write for info. (*0-15-201695-3*, HB Juv Bks) HarBrace.

Trupp: A Fuzzhead Tale. Janell Cannon. LC 94-19765. 48p. (J). (ps-3). 1995. 15.00 (*0-15-200130-1*) HarBrace.

Truro-Cape Cod: Landmarks & Seamarks. Shebnah Rich. (Illus.). 580p. 1989. reprint ed. lib. bdg. 58.00 (*0-8328-0916-0*, MA0203) Higginson Bk Co.

Truro City Trail. Christine Oates. (C). 1989. 40.00 (*0-907566-16-2*, Pub. by Dyllansow Truran UK) St Mut.

***Truro, Massachusetts Marks of Cattle from the Original Records 1710-1768.** Ed. by Steven E. Sullivan & Debra Porter. (Illus.). 33p. (Orig.). 1996. pap. 13.50 (*0-89725-207-1*, 1638) Picton Pr.

Trussed Roof: Its History & Development. David Yeomans. 1992. 84.95 (*0-85967-874-1*, Pub. by Scolar Pr UK) Ashgate Pub Co.

Trust. Steven Dietz. 1995. pap. 5.25 (*0-8222-1405-9*) Dramatists Play.

Trust. Elaine Goley. (Learn the Value Ser.). (Illus.). 32p. (J). (gr. 1-4). 1987. lib. bdg. 15.94 (*0-86592-378-7*); lib. bdg. 11.95 (*0-685-67577-7*) Rourke Corp.

Trust. Muriel Jensen. (Historical Ser.). 1994. mass mkt. 3.99 (*0-373-28806-9*, 1-28806-7) Harlequin Bks.

Trust: Its Book. Ed. by James H. Bridge. LC 73-1995. (Big Business; Economic Power in a Free Society Ser.). 1973. reprint ed. 20.95 (*0-405-05077-1*) Ayer.

Trust: Representatives & Constitutents. William T. Bianco. 176p. 1994. text ed. 44.50 (*0-472-10510-8*); pap. text ed. 17.95 (*0-472-08267-1*) U of Mich Pr.

Trust: The Social Virtues & the Creation of Prosperity. Francis Fukuyama. 350p. 1995. 25.00 (*0-02-910976-0*, Free Press) Free Pr.

Trust: The Social Virtues & the Creation of Prosperity. Francis Fukuyama. 480p. 1996. pap. 15.00 (*0-684-82525-2*) Free Pr.

Trust - the Hand Book: A Guide to the Sensual & Spiritual Art of Handballing. Bert Herrman. LC 91-76792. (Illus.). 128p. (Orig.). 1991. pap. 12.00 (*0-9624751-5-7*) Alamo Sq Pr.

Trust Administration & Taxation, 4 vols. Walter L. Nossman & Joseph L. Wyatt. 1966. Updates. ring bd. write for info. (*0-8205-1470-5*) Bender.

Trust, AIDS & Your Dentist: Key Questions to Ask Your Dentist about Infection Control, HIV & Sterilization. Randall P. Westman. (Illus.). 114p. (Orig.). (YA). 1993. pap. text ed. 11.95 (*0-9637088-0-5*) Sweettooth.

Trust & Betrayal. Janet Bode. 176p. (J). 1997. mass mkt. 4.99 (*0-440-22035-1*) Dell.

Trust & Betrayal: Real Life Stories of Friends & Enemies. Janet Bode & Stan Mack. LC 94-21415. 176p. (J). 1995. 15.95 (*0-385-32105-8*) Delacorte.

Trust & Corporation Problems. Henry R. Seager & Charles A. Gulick, Jr. LC 73-2534. (Big Business; Economic Power in a Free Society Ser.). 1973. reprint ed. 48.95 (*0-405-05112-3*) Ayer.

***Trust & Economic Learning.** Ed. by Edward Lorenz & Nathalie Lazaric. 256p. 1997. 70.00 (*1-85898-460-2*) E Elgar.

Trust & Mercy: The Heart of the Good News. George W. Kosicki. 160p. 1993. pap. 7.95 (*0-940535-60-2*) Franciscan U Pr.

***Trust & Obey: Obedience & the Christian.** R. C. Sproul et al. Ed. by Don Kistler. 218p. (Orig.). 1996. pap. 15.95 (*1-57358-057-0*) Soli Deo Gloria.

Trust & Power: Two Works. Niklas Luhmann. Ed. by Tom Burns & Gianfranco Poggi. Tr. by Howard Davis et al. LC 79-40579. 228p. reprint ed. pap. 65.00 (*0-685-20594-0*, 2030528) Bks Demand.

Trust & Treachery. Joe Barnhart & Linda Kraeger. (Orig.). 1995. pap. text ed. 40.32 (*1-56870-210-8*) RonJon Pub.

Trust & Treachery: An Historical Novel of Early Seventeenth-Century England & New England. Linda Kraeger. LC 95-39255. 374p. 1996. text ed. 99.95 (*0-7734-4242-1*, Mellen Univ Pr) E Mellen.

Trust Assets: Investment of Trust Assets in Bank Proprietary Mutual Funds. (Illus.). 44p. (Orig.). (C). 1995. pap. text ed. 25.00 (*0-7881-2037-9*) DIANE Pub.

Trust Audit Manual: Fiduciary Audit Practices, Policies & Regulations. rev. ed. Kenneth J. Namjestnik. 250p. (C). 1995. per. 65.00 (*1-55738-782-6*) Irwin Prof Pubng.

Trust Betrayed? Munchausen Syndrome by Proxy Inter-agency Child Protection Work & Partnership with Families. Jan Howath & Brian Lawson. 150p. 1996. pap. 27.50 (*1-874579-62-8*, Pub. by Natl Childrens Bur UK) Paul & Co Pubs.

Trust Betrayed: What You Need to Know about the Country's Biggest Lobby. Dale Van Atta. 288p. Date not set. 24.95 (*0-89526-485-4*, Gateway Editions) Regnery Pub.

Trust Business. 2nd ed. John M. Clarke et al. (Illus.). 289p. (C). 1988. text ed. 43.00 (*0-89982-350-5*) Am Bankers.

Trust Compliance Handbook: 1994 Edition. 2nd ed. Price. 1994. per. 62.50 (*1-55738-707-9*) Irwin Prof Pubng.

Trust Compliance Handbook: 1995 Edition. 3rd ed. Price Waterhouse Staff. 158p. (C). 1995. per. 65.00 (*1-55738-764-8*) Irwin Prof Pubng.

Trust Connection: Mastering the Art of Relationships. Kerry L. Johnson. 1994. 18.95 (*0-9618535-1-4*) Louis & Ford.

Trust Department Administration & Operation, 2 vols. Victor P. Whitney. 1981. Updates. ring bd. write for info. (*0-8205-1754-2*) Bender.

***Trust Effect: Creating the High Trust, High Performance Organization.** Larry Reynolds. (People Skills for Professionals Ser.). (Illus.). 224p. 1997. 29.95 (*1-85788-187-7*); pap. 17.95 (*1-85788-186-9*) Nicholas Brealey.

Trust, Ethnicity, & Identity: Beyond the New Institutional Economics of Ethnic Trading Networks, Contract Law, & Gift-Changing. Janet T. Landa. LC 94-1727. 250p. 1994. text ed. 49.50 (*0-472-10361-X*) U of Mich Pr.

Trust Factor: Liberating Profits & Restoring Corporate Vitality. John O. Whitney. 1993. text ed. 22.95 (*0-07-070017-6*) McGraw.

Trust Factor: Liberating Profits & Restoring Corporate Vitality. John O. Whitney. 1996. pap. text ed. 14.95 (*0-07-070018-4*) McGraw.

***Trust Factor: The Art of Doing Business.** Cheryl A. Chatfield. LC 97-21295. 160p. (Orig.). 1997. pap. 16.95 (*0-86534-264-4*) Sunstone Pr.

Trust Fund Handling. Lynne A. Weinman. 50p. (Orig.). (C). Date not set. pap. text ed. 19.95 (*1-878025-80-5*) Western Schls.

Trust Fund Handling & Fair Housing Laws. Anthony Schools Corporation Staff. (Continuing Education in Real Estate Ser.). 196p. (Orig.). 1994. pap. text ed. 25.00 (*0-941833-49-6*) Anthony Schools.

Trust God for Your Finances. Jack Hartman. 175p. 1983. reprint ed. pap. 6.95 (*0-915445-00-X*) Lamplight FL.

Trust Handbook. 7th ed. Rounds. 1994. 110.00 (*0-316-35073-7*) Little.

Trust His Heart: Arrangements for Accompanied Piano. Des. by Bruce Greer. 1995. audio 10.99 (*0-614-01670-3*, TA-9186C) Lillenas.

Trust His Heart: Arrangements for Accompanied Piano, CD. Des. by Bruce Greer. 1995. 65.00 (*0-614-01672-X*, MU-9186T) Lillenas.

Trust in God: The Miracle of Healing. Gloria Gardner. 144p. (Orig.). 1996. pap. 9.95 (*1-878555-11-1*) Oakbridge Univ Pr.

Trust in Love. large type ed. Jeanne Bowman. (Linford Romance Library). 1991. pap. 15.99 (*0-7089-6969-0*) Ulverscroft.

Trust in Modern Societies: The Search for the Bases of Social Order. Barbara A. Misztal. LC 95-47706. 292p. (C). 1995. text ed. 57.95 (*0-7456-1248-2*, Pub. by Polity Pr UK); pap. text ed. 23.95 (*0-7456-1634-8*, Pub. by Polity Pr UK) Blackwell Pubs.

Trust in Numbers: The Pursuit of Objectivity in Science & Public Life. Theodore M. Porter. LC 94-21440. 312p. 1995. text ed. 35.00 (*0-691-03776-0*) Princeton U Pr.

***Trust in Numbers: The Pursuit of Objectivity in Science & Public Life.** Theodore M. Porter. 324p. 1995. pap. text ed. 16.95 (*0-691-02908-3*) Princeton U Pr.

Trust in Organizations. Ed. by Roderick M. Kramer & Tom R. Tyler. LC 95-20967. (Illus.). 400p. 1995. 52.00 (*0-8039-5739-4*); pap. 24.95 (*0-8039-5740-8*) Sage.

***Trust in the Balance: The Foundation for Business Success.** Robert B. Shaw. LC 96-52978. 1997. 25.00 (*0-7879-0286-1*) Jossey-Bass.

***Trust in the Lord: Letting the Spirit Be Your Guide.** Diane Bills. LC 96-30355. 1996. write for info. (*1-55503-983-9*) Covenant Comms.

***Trust in Yourself: Thoughts about Listening to Your Heart & Becoming the Person You Want to Be.** Donna Fargo. LC 97-10700. (Illus.). 48p. 1997. pap. 7.95 (*0-88396-450-3*) Blue Mtn Pr CO.

Trust Law: Texts & Materials. 2nd ed. Graham Moffat & Michael Chesterman. 1994. pap. text ed. 57.95 (*0-406-04537-2*, UK) MICHIE.

Trust Magic: The Ultimate Tax Shelter. Eagle Legal Services Staff. 1985. 19.95 (*0-685-10157-6*) Lifecraft.

Trust Marketing Handbook. Victor P. Whitney. LC 76-46444. 288p. reprint ed. pap. 82.10 (*0-685-20320-4*, 2052226) Bks Demand.

Trust Me. Judith Arnold. (American Romance Ser.: No. 431). 1992. mass mkt. 3.39 (*0-373-16431-9*, 1-16431-8) Harlequin Bks.

Trust Me. Malorie Blackman. (Livewire Ser.). (YA). (gr. 6-9). pap. 7.95 (*0-7043-4931-0*, Pub. by Womens Press UK) Trafalgar.

Trust Me. Jane M. Choate. LC 96-96380. 192p. 1996. 17.95 (*0-8034-9207-3*, Avalon Bks) Bouregy.

Trust Me. Paul Crispelli. 15p. 1993. pap. 2.00 (*1-884047-59-9*) Mass Extinct.

Trust Me. Jayne Ann Krentz. 22.00 (*0-615-00409-1*) PB.

Trust Me. Jayne Ann Krentz. 1995. mass mkt. 6.50 (*0-671-51692-2*, PB Trade Paper) PB.

***Trust Me.** Frank Kubic. LC 96-725051. 20p. (YA). (gr. 6 up). 1997. pap. text ed. 4.50 (*1-888958-01-4*) Nuggets Wisdom.

Trust Me. Charlotte Moore. (Shadows Ser.). 1996. mass mkt. 3.50 (*0-373-27062-3*, 1-27062-8) Silhouette.

Trust Me. William J. Morin. Ed. by Tim Lynch. 120p. 1995. pap. 9.95 (*1-880030-47-0*) DBM Pub.

Trust Me. Jon Ripslinger. 1997. write for info. (*0-15-201474-8*) HarBrace.

Trust Me. Jon Ripslinger. 1997. pap. write for info. (*0-15-201475-6*) HarBrace.

Trust Me. John Updike. 336p. 1988. mass mkt. 5.95 (*0-449-21498-2*, Crest) Fawcett.

***Trust Me.** John Updike. 1996. pap. 12.00 (*0-449-91217-5*) Fawcett.

Trust Me. large type ed. Jayne Ann Krentz. LC 95-3708. (Large Print Bks.). 1995. 25.95 (*1-56895-204-X*) Wheeler Pub.

Trust Me, I'm a Doctor: Humorous Second Opinions for Everyday Life. Mark DePaolis. LC 95-3180. 240p. 1995. pap. 10.95 (*0-925190-39-X*) Fairview Press.

***"Trust Me, I'm a Doctor" Understanding & Surviving Modern Health Care.** Thomas L. Minogue. 340p. (Orig.). 1996. pap. 16.95 (*0-9654891-0-8*) TLM Cnslting.

Trust Me On This. Donald E. Westlake. 304p. 1989. mass mkt. 5.99 (*0-445-40807-3*, Mysterious Paperbk) Warner Bks.

Trust Me on This. large type ed. Donald E. Westlake. (General Ser.). 436p. 1989. lib. bdg. 19.95 (*0-8161-4740-X*, GK Hall) Thorndike Pr.

***Trust Me on This, Vol. 843.** Jennifer Crusie. (Loveswept Ser.). 1997. mass mkt. 3.50 (*0-553-44558-8*) Bantam.

Trust Me! The Truth about Living Revocable Trusts: Use Living Trusts: Leave Nothing to Chance. Lee R. Phillips & Kristy S. Phillips. (Illus.). 337p. 1995. 24.95 (*0-9648965-0-8*) LegaLees.

Trust Me! Trust Me! Philip Ronzheimer. 1992. pap. 1.49 (*0-87509-498-8*) Chr Pubns.

Trust No One. Brian Lowry. (X-Files Ser.). 288p. 1996. pap. 15.00 (*0-06-105353-8*, HarperPrism) HarpC.

Trust No One: Reading the X-Files. Ed. by David Lavery et al. LC 96-28814. (Television Ser.). 288p. 1996. pap. 16.95 (*0-8156-0407-6*, LATNP) Syracuse U Pr.

Trust Operations. 419p. 1992. text ed. 120.00 (*0-685-62691-1*) Am Bankers.

Trust Practice Manual. 2nd ed. Coopers & Lybrand, Trust Department Staff. 250p. 1992. pap. text ed. 78.00 (*0-406-50361-3*, UK) MICHIE.

Trust Presentation. 94p. 1996. pap. text ed. 39.95 (*1-885661-06-1*) Estate Protection.

Trust Problem. Jeremiah W. Jenks & Walter E. Clark. Ed. by John J. Quigley. LC 73-2513. (Big Business; Economic Power in a Free Society Ser.). 1973. reprint ed. 37.95 (*0-405-05094-1*) Ayer.

***Trust Regulatory Handbook, 1996-1997.** 4th ed. 180p. (C). 1996. per. 65.00 (*0-7863-0952-0*) Irwin.

Trust Risk Management: Assessing & Controlling Fiduciary Risk. Kenneth J. Namjestnik. 250p. 1992. text ed. 62.50 (*1-55738-327-8*) Irwin Prof Pubng.

***Trust-T: Solving Problems Through Creativity.** Barbara N. Ekey. (Robert Ser.: Bk. 1). (Illus.). 48p. (J). (gr. 3-8). 1997. pap. 14.95 (*1-886755-25-6*) A D Clarke.

***Trust-T: Solving Problems Through Creativity.** Barbara N. Ekey. (Robert Ser.: Bk. 1). (Illus.). 48p. (J). (gr. 3-8). 1997. 21.95 (*1-886755-24-8*) A D Clarke.

***Trust-T: Solving Problems Through Creativity, Sheet Music.** Barbara N. Ekey. (Robert Ser.: Bk. 1). (J). (gr. 3-8). 1996. pap. 4.50 (*1-886755-26-4*) A D Clarke.

Trust, Taxes & Freedom. Karl Loren. 475p. 1991. 195.00 (*1-882537-00-9*) Bigelow Charter.

Trust Territory. Janet Morris & Chris Morris. 272p. 1993. pap. 4.99 (*0-451-45236-4*, ROC) NAL-Dutton.

Trust the Children: An Activity Manual for Homeschooling & Alternative Learning. Anna Kealoha. LC 95-15810. 274p. 1995. pap. 17.95 (*0-89087-748-3*) Celestial Arts.

Trust the Force: Change Your Life Through Attitudinal Healing. Todd Davison. LC 95-18420. 320p. 1995. 25.00 (*1-56821-594-0*) Aronson.

Trust the Liar. Susan Zannos. 1988. 16.95 (*0-8027-5697-2*) Walker & Co.

Trust the Process: How to Enhance Recovery & Prevent Relapse. Linda Free-Gardiner. (Orig.). 1996. pap. 15.95 (*1-879899-03-5*); student ed., teacher ed., pap. 15.95 (*1-879899-04-3*) Newjoy Pr.

Trust the Truth: A Symposium on Humanae Vitae. Ed. by Russell E. Smith. LC 91-20331. 381p. 1991. pap. text ed. 17.95 (*0-935372-30-X*) Pope John Ctr.

Trust to Good Versus: Herrick Tercentenary Essays, Dearborn, 1974. Robert Herrick Memorial Conference, University of Michigan Staff. Ed. by Roger B. Rollin & J. Max Patrick. LC 77-74547. 297p. reprint ed. pap. 84.70 (*0-7837-2147-1*, 2042433) Bks Demand.

***Trust Volition.** Michelle Pfeiffer. 256p. (Orig.). 1996. pap. 9.95 (*1-57502-333-4*, PO1115) Morris Pubng.

Trust Walk. Susan Ekberg. LC 94-92201. (Illus.). 32p. (J). (gr. k-5). 1995. 17.95 (*0-9630419-6-7*) Spiritseeker.

Trust with Your Life: (Dangerous Man) M. L. Gamble. (Intrigue Ser.). 1995. pap. 3.50 (*0-373-22321-8*, 1-22321-3) Harlequin Bks.

Trust Your Body! Trust Your Baby! Childbirth Wisdom & Cesarean Prevention. Ed. by Andrea F. Henkart. LC 94-30915. 200p. 1995. pap. text ed. 14.95 (*0-89789-294-1*, Bergin & Garvey) Greenwood.

Trust Your Children: Voices Against Censorship in Children's Literature. Mark I. West. 178p. 1988. pap. text ed. 24.95 (*1-55570-021-7*) Neal-Schuman.

Trust Your Children: Voices Against Censorship in Children's Literature. 2nd rev. ed. Mark I. West. LC 96-2648. 225p. 1997. pap. 24.95 (*1-55570-251-1*) Neal-Schuman.

Trust Your Feelings: A Protective Behaviours Resource Manual for Primary School Teachers. Ed. & Concept by Ingrid Lippett. (C). 1989. pap. text ed. 80.00 (*0-89771-037-1*, Pub. by Essence Pubns AT) St Mut.

Trust Your Gut! Practical Ways to Develop & Use Your Intuition for Business Success. Richard M. Contino. Ed. by Mary Glenn. LC 96-17190. 192p. (Orig.). 1996. pap. 16.95 (*0-8144-7877-8*) AMACOM.

Trust Your Mother But Cut the Cards. Sidney Zion. LC 92-35526. 320p. 15.95 (*0-942637-77-1*) Barricade Bks.

Trust Yourself to Life. Clara M. Codd. LC 75-4245. 116p. 1975. reprint ed. pap. 3.75 (*0-8356-0464-0*, Quest) Theos Pub Hse.

Trusted Criminals: White Collar Crime in Contemporary Society. David O. Friedrichs. LC 95-22353. 441p. (C). 1996. pap. 33.95 (*0-534-50517-1*) Wadsworth Pub.

Trusted Database Management System Interpretation of the Trusted Computer System Evaluation Criteria. (Illus.). 143p. (Orig.). (C). 1993. pap. text ed. 25.00 (*1-56806-487-X*) DIANE Pub.

Trusted Faces Violating Private Places: Teaching Your Children How to Protect Themselves from Sexual Assault. Roger O'Keefe. LC 95-18155. (Illus.). 150p. (Orig.). 1995. pap. 14.95 (*0-942963-56-3*) Distinctive Pub.

Trusted Network Interpretation Environments Guideline: Guidance for Applying the Trusted Network Interpretation. (Illus.). 68p. (C). 1994. pap. text ed. 35.00 (*0-7881-0549-3*) DIANE Pub.

Trusted Network Interpretation of the Trusted Computer System Evaluation Criteria. 278p. (Orig.). (C). 1994. pap. text ed. 50.00 (*0-7881-0550-7*) DIANE Pub.

Trusted Product Evaluation Questionnaire. 53p. (Orig.). (C). 1993. pap. text ed. 25.00 (*1-56806-485-3*) DIANE Pub.

Trusted Product Evaluations: A Guide for Vendors. (Illus.). 51p. (Orig.). (C). 1995. pap. text ed. 30.00 (*0-7881-1534-0*) DIANE Pub.

Trusted Steward: Moving Toward Total Stewardship. Calvin T. Partain. Ed. by Judith Edwards. 96p. (Orig.). 1996. pap. 7.95 (*1-56309-162-3*) Womans Mission Union.

Trusted UNIX Working Group (Trusix) Rationale for Selecting Access Control List Features for the UNIX System. (Illus.). 72p. (Orig.). (C). 1995. pap. text ed. 20.00 (*0-7881-2224-X*) DIANE Pub.

***Trustee Facts File.** 2nd ed. Ed. by Jane B. Shaw et al. LC 97-3444. 162p. 1997. pap. write for info. (*1-890249-00-9*) IL Lib Assn.

Trustee from the Toolroom. Nevil Shute. 311p. reprint ed. lib. bdg. 24.95 (*0-89244-016-3*, Queens House) Amereon Ltd.

Trustee Game: The Foundation of MacTitle-MacTrust; How to Be an Unlicensed, Undercapitalized, Inexperienced Success. United Entrepreneurs Association of America Staff & Al Rotola. (Illus.). xiii, 197p. write for info. (*0-318-60762-X*) Am Entrepreneurs.

Trustee Handbook. 6th ed. Barbara H. Stanton. 1989. pap. 16.00 (*0-934338-70-1*) NAIS.

Trustee Handbook 1995. Rounds. 1995. 75.00 (*0-316-35011-7*) Little.

Trustees & the Future of Foundations. John W. Nason. LC 77-76677. 112p. 1977. pap. 12.00 (*0-913892-00-9*) Coun Found.

***Trustees & Their Professional Advisors.** Ed. by Eugene B. Burroughs. 205p. (Orig.). 1996. pap. 30.00 (*0-89154-502-6*) Intl Found Employ.

***Trustees, Friends, & the Law.** Arlene Bielefield & Lawrence Cheeseman. (Libraries & the Law Ser.). 150p. 1998. pap. 39.95 (*1-55570-135-3*) Neal-Schuman.

Trustee's Guide to Board Duties, Responsibilities & Liabilities. Charles F. MacKelvie & Marcia S. Handler. LC 92-48301. 92p. 1993. per. 24.95 (*1-882198-15-8*) Hlthcare Fin Mgmt.

Trustee's Guide to Compensation for Healthcare Executives. Michael F. Doody. LC 93-257. (Hospital Trustee Guide Ser.). 96p. 1993. per. 24.95 (*1-882198-16-6*) Hlthcare Fin Mgmt.

Trustee's Guide to Understanding Healthcare Antitrust Law Issues. Jonathan P. Tomes. 76p. 1992. 24.95 (*0-930228-89-8*) Hlthcare Fin Mgmt.

Trustee's Guide to Understanding Healthcare Environmental Law. Jonathan P. Tomes. 75p. 1992. per. 24.95 (*0-930228-88-X*) Hlthcare Fin Mgmt.

Trustee's Guide to Understanding Hospital Business Fundamentals. James J. Unland. 92p. 1992. per. 24.95 (*0-930228-81-2*) Hlthcare Fin Mgmt.

Trustee's Guide to Understanding Medical Staff Privileges. Jonathan P. Tomes. 85p. 1992. per. 24.95 (*0-930228-90-1*) Hlthcare Fin Mgmt.

Trustees Handbook: A Basic Text on Labor-Management Employee Benefit Plans. 4th ed. Ed. by Marc Gertner. LC 90-83337. 479p. (Orig.). 1990. pap. 40.00 (*0-89154-411-9*) Intl Found Employ.

Trustee's Manual. Ted DeLong. 86p. 1996. pap. text ed. 35.00 (*1-885661-03-7*) Estate Protection.

Trustees, Trusteeship, & the Public Good: Issues of Accountability for Hospitals, Museums, Universities, & Libraries. James C. Baughman. LC 86-25574. 205p. 1987. text ed. 55.00 (*0-89930-195-9*, BLT/, Quorum Bks) Greenwood.

Trusteeship & the Management of Foundations. Donald R. Young & Wilbert E. Moore. LC 75-87819. 158p. 1969. 29.95 (*0-87154-970-0*) Russell Sage.

Trusteeship Council: 51st Session, 14 May-July 1984, Sessional Fascicle. (Official Records Ser.). 30p. 1986. 4.00 (*0-685-14640-5*) UN.

Trusteeship Council: 52nd Session, 13 May-11 July 1985, Sessional Fascicle. 23p. 1986. 4.00 (*0-685-14642-1*) UN.

Trusteeship Council, Sixteenth Special Session, 4-6 February 1986: 53rd Session, 12 May-30 June 1986, Resolution & Decisions, Official Records, Supplement No. 3. 1987. 4.00 (*0-317-63242-6*) UN.

Trusteeship in the Private College. Miriam M. Wood. LC 85-8051. 208p. 1986. text ed. 32.50 (*0-8018-3270-5*) Johns Hopkins.

Trusteeship Presidency: Jimmy Carter & the United States Congress. Charles O. Jones. LC 87-24379. (Miller Center Series on the American Presidency). (Illus.). 264p. 1988. 24.95 (*0-8071-1426-X*) La State U Pr.

Trusteeship System of the United Nations. Charmian E. Toussaint. LC 75-27689. 1976. reprint ed. text ed. 65.00 (*0-8371-8460-6*, TOTS, Greenwood Pr) Greenwood.

Trustful Surrender to Divine Providence: The Secret of Peace & Happiness. Jean B. Saint-Jure & Claude De La Colombiere. LC 83-50252. 139p. 1993. reprint ed. pap. 5.00 (*0-89555-216-7*) TAN Bks Pubs.

Trusting: Learning Who & How to Trust Again. Pat Springle. 230p. 1994. pap. 10.99 (*0-89283-844-2*, Vine Bks) Servant.

Trusting & the Maimed. James Plunkett. 12.50 (*0-8159-6909-0*) Devin.

Trusting Child Within, Pt. II. Gilbert Bowen. 1994. 5.00 (*0-614-13503-6*) CRIS.

Trusting Game. Penny Jordan. (Presents Ser.). 1996. mass mkt. 3.50 (*0-373-11839-2*, 1-11839-7) Harlequin Bks.

Trusting God: Even When Life Hurts. Jerry Bridges. LC 88-60825. 216p. 1988. pap. 12.00 (*0-89109-617-5*) NavPress.

Trusting God: Learning to Walk by Faith. 2nd rev. ed. David R. Reagan. LC 94-79447. 264p. (Orig.). 1995. pap. 9.95 (*0-945593-03-1*) Lamb Lion Minstrs.

Trusting God Again: Regaining Hope after Disappointment or Loss. Glandion Carney & William Long. LC 95-7840. 237p. (Orig.). 1995. pap. 10.99 (*0-8308-1609-7*, 1609) InterVarsity.

Trusting God in Times & Seasons of Change. Valerie S. DePastino. 128p. 1989. pap. 5.95 (*0-88144-138-4*) Christian Pub.

Trusting God (Study Guide) Even When Life Hurts. Jerry Bridges. 120p. (Orig.). 1990. pap. 7.00 (*0-89109-241-2*) NavPress.

Trusting God Through the Worst of Times. Joy P. Gage & Kenneth G. Gage. LC 92-42619. (Orig.). 1993. pap. 6.99 (*0-8054-1085-6*, 4210-85) Broadman.

Trusting More, Worrying Less. Max Lucado. 32p. 1995. pap. 2.99 (*0-8499-5148-8*) Word Pub.

Trusting Ourselves: The Complete Guide to Emotional Well-Being for Women. Karen Johnson. LC 89-38637. 477p. 1991. pap. 15.00 (*0-87113-447-0*, Atlntc Mnthly) Grove-Atltic.

Trusting Sarah. Cassandra Austin. (Historical Ser.). 1995. mass mkt. 4.50 (*0-373-28879-4*, 1-28879-4) Harlequin Bks.

***Trusting the Healer Within.** 2nd ed. Nick Bamforth. 176p. 1989. pap. 9.95 (*0-944256-26-0*, Pub. by Gateway Books UK) ACCESS Pubs Network.

***Trusting the People: The Dole-Kemp Plan to Free the Economy & Create a Better America.** Bob Dole & Jack Kemp. LC 96-35344. 1996. 15.00 (*0-06-101153-3*) HarpC.

Trusting the Song That Sings Within: Pioneer Woman Cantor. Dora B. Krakower. LC 94-78704. (Illus.). 230p. (Orig.). 1994. pap. 14.95 (*0-9643273-0-9*) Bloch.

Trusting the Tale. Hugh Hood. 140p. (C). 1983. pap. text ed. 8.95 (*0-920802-66-4*, Pub. by ECW Press CN) Genl Dist Srvs.

Trusting Your Life to Water & Eternity. Olav H. Hauge. Tr. by Robert Bly from NOR. LC 87-42897. 56p. 1987. 12.95 (*0-915943-23-9*); pap. 6.95 (*0-915943-28-X*) Milkweed Ed.

Trusting Yourself: How to Overcome the Psychological Barriers to Reaching Your Potential Selling Life Insurance, Investments & Financial Planning Services. Sidney C. Walker. LC 88-82621. (Illus.). 157p. 1988. pap. 29.95 (*0-9621177-0-6*) High Plns Pubns.

***Trustmate.** Holly Damalas. LC 97-93760. 311p. 1997. 21.95 (*0-9657959-0-X*) Bandit Book.

Trusts. George T. Bogert. (Hornbook Ser.). (C). 1987. Practitioner's ed., 950p. text ed. write for info. (*0-314-35140-X*) West Pub.

Trusts. 2nd ed. Howard K. Insall. (LBC Nutshell Ser.). xx, 98p. 1991. pap. 11.95 (*0-455-21037-3*, Pub. by Law Bk Co AT) Gaunt.

Trusts. 6th ed. George T. Bogert. (Hornbook Ser.). 794p. (C). 1987. Student ed., 794p. student ed. 33.00 (*0-314-35139-6*) West Pub.

Trusts: Adaptable to Courses Utilizing Bogert & Oak, Hansen & Hill's Casebook on Law of Trusts. Casenotes Publishing Co., Inc. Staff. Ed. by Peter Tenen. (Legal Briefs Ser.). 1991. pap. write for info. (*0-87457-140-5*, 1230) Casenotes Pub.

Trusts: Commentary & Materials. 6th ed. H. A. Ford & I. J. Hardingham. xxxix, 853p. 1990. 105.00 (*0-455-20962-6*, Pub. by Law Bk Co AT); pap. 85.00 (*0-455-20963-4*, Pub. by Law Bk Co AT) Gaunt.

Trusts: 1994. Fratcher. 1994. suppl. ed. 245.00 (*0-316-77692-0*) Little.

Trusts & Estates. Campbell. (American Casebook Ser.). Date not set. text ed. write for info. (*0-314-06780-9*) West Pub.

Trusts & Estates. Kurtz. (American Casebook Ser.). Date not set. text ed. write for info. (*0-314-06582-2*) West Pub.

Trusts & Powers. D. M. Maclean. xx, 139p. 1989. 43.00 (*0-455-20910-3*, Pub. by Law Bk Co AT) Gaunt.

Trusts & Trustees. Holmes F. Crouch. Ed. by Irma J. Crouch. LC 93-72405. (Series 300 Tax Guides: Vol. 305). (Illus.). 224p. 1994. pap. 16.95 (*0-944817-19-X*) Allyear Tax.

Trusts Law: Text & Materials. Graham Moffatt & Michael Chesterman. (Law in Context Ser.). xlii, 746p. 1988. 75.00 (*0-297-79402-7*) Rothman.

Trusts or Industrial Combinations & Coalitions in the United States. Ernst Von Halle. xvi, 350p. 1983. reprint ed. lib. bdg. 30.00 (*0-8377-1234-3*) Rothman.

Trustworthiness of Religious Experience. Elton Trueblood. LC 78-24656. 1979. reprint ed. pap. 4.95 (*0-944350-00-3*) Friends United.

Trustworthy Government. 30p. (Orig.). 1996. pap. 4.95 (*0-87510-306-5*) Christian Sci.

Trustworthy Government: Leadership & Management Strategies for Building Trust & High Performance. David G. Carnevale. LC 94-38540. (Public Administration Ser.). 255p. 27.95 (*0-7879-0062-1*) Jossey-Bass.

Trusty Sarcophagus Co. Rene Ricard. Ed. by Paola Igliori & Michele Zalopany. 98p. (Orig.). 1990. English with French translations. pap. 25.00 (*0-9625119-1-9*) Inanout Pr.

Trusty Sarcophagus Co. Rene Ricard. Ed. by Paola Igliori & Michele Zalopany. Tr. by Josef Ramaseder. 100p. (Orig.). 1990. English with German Translations. pap. 25.00 (*0-9625119-3-5*) Inanout Pr.

Trusty Sarcophagus Co. Rene Ricard. Ed. by Paola Igliori & Michele Zalopany. Tr. by Mario Diacono. 100p. (Orig.). 1990. English with Italian Translations. pap. 25.00 (*0-9625119-4-3*) Inanout Pr.

Trusty Sarcophagus Co. Rene Ricard. Ed. by Paola Igliori & Michele Zalopany. Tr. by Patricia Lhardy. 100p. (Orig.). 1990. English with French Translations. pap. 25.00 (*0-9625119-2-7*) Inanout Pr.

Trusty Sarcophagus Co. Rene Ricard. (Illus.). 100p. (Orig.). 1990. pap. 25.00 (*0-685-64744-7*) Petersburg Pr.

Truth, 3 vols. St. Thomas Aquinas. Tr. by R. W. Mulligan et al. from LAT. LC 94-29598. 1525p. (C). 1994. lib. bdg. 135.00 (*0-87220-270-4*) Hackett Pub.

T

An Asterisk (*) at the beginning of an entry indicates that the title is appearing in BIP for the first time.

Truth. Joe F. Watson. 1995. pap. 4.95 (*1-56794-073-0*) Star Bible.
Truth. Emile Zola. (Pocket Classics Ser.). 608p. 1994. pap. 9.00 (*0-7509-0660-X*, Pub. by Sutton Pubng UK) Bks Intl VA.
Truth, No. 4. pap. 0.15 (*0-87377-136-2*) GAM Pubns.
Truth: A Primer. Frederick F. Schmitt. (Focus Ser.). 251p. (C). 1994. pap. text ed. 19.95 (*0-8133-2001-1*) Westview.
***Truth: An Ashley Johnson Mystery.** Melanie McAllester. 288p. (Orig.). 1998. pap. 11.95 (*1-56280-179-1*) Naiad Pr.
Truth: Fruit of Wisdom & Love. Omraam M. Aivanhov. (Izvor Collection: Vol. 234). 227p. 1994. pap. 8.95 (*1-895978-03-3*) Prosveta USA.
Truth: The Universe Is a Growing God. Cyril J. Skidmore. LC 94-96705. (Orig.). 1995. pap. 12.95 (*0-9644449-4-1*) Adv Concepts Res.
Truth about Addiction & Recovery. Stanton Peele et al. 432p. 1992. pap. 12.00 (*0-671-75530-7*, Fireside) S&S Trade.
***Truth about Alien Abductions.** Peter Hough. 1997. pap. text ed. 14.95 (*0-7137-2601-6*, Pub. by Blandford Pr UK) Sterling.
Truth about an Author. Arnold Bennett. LC 74-17055. (Collected Works of Arnold Bennett: Vol. 84). 1977. reprint ed. 22.95 (*0-518-19165-6*) Ayer.
***Truth about Angels.** Elaine Cannon. 1996. 12.95 (*1-57008-289-8*) Bookcraft Inc.
Truth about Angels. Terry Law. 1994. pap. 10.99 (*0-88419-368-3*) Creation House.
Truth about Angels. Ellen G. White. LC 95-46980. 1996. 12.99 (*0-8163-1315-6*) Pacific Pr Pub Assn.
***Truth about Armageddon & the Middle East.** Thomas Ice & Tim Demy. (Pocket Prophecy Ser.). 48p. (Orig.). 1997. pap. 2.99 (*1-56507-683-4*) Harvest Hse.
Truth about Astral Projection. Keith Randolph. (Llewellyn's Truth about Ser.). 64p. (Orig.). 1983. mass mkt. 1.99 (*0-87542-350-7*) Llewellyn Pubns.
Truth about Astrology: What It Can Do for You. rev. ed. Llewellyn Publications Staff. (Llewellyn's Truth about Ser.). 32p. (Orig.). 1990. pap. 1.99 (*0-87542-375-2*) Llewellyn Pubns.
Truth about Automobiles. A. J. Smith. (Illus.). 165p. (Orig.). 1991. pap. 9.25 (*0-9647508-0-5*) Elect Car-Nation.
Truth about Bebe Donge. Georges Simenon. 1992. 18.95 (*0-15-191319-6*) HarBrace.
Truth about Black Biblical Hebrew-Israelites (Jews) The World's Best Kept Secret. Ella J. Hughley. (Orig.). 1982. pap. 13.95 (*0-9605150-1-1*) Hughley PubProdns.
Truth about Boulwarism: Trying to do Right Voluntarily. Lemuel R. Boulware. LC 77-91413. 192p. reprint ed. pap. 54.80 (*0-317-29423-7*, 2024305) Bks Demand.
***Truth about Boys.** Emily Costello. (Full House Stephanie Ser.). (YA). 1997. pap. 3.99 (*0-671-00361-5*, Minstrel Bks) PB.
***Truth about Breast Cancer.** Hay. LC 97-137478. 1996. pap. text ed. 12.95 (*0-7737-5794-5*, Pub. by Stoddart Pubng CN) Genl Dist Srvs.
Truth about Breast Cancer. Claire Hoy. 288p. Date not set. pap. 12.95 (*0-614-17727-8*, Pub. by Stoddart Pubng CN) Genl Dist Srvs.
Truth about Breast Implants. Randolph H. Guthrie. 145p. 1994. pap. text ed. 14.95 (*0-471-59418-0*) Wiley.
***Truth about Burnout: How Organizations Cause Personal Stress & What to Do about It.** Christina Maslach. 1997. 25.00 (*0-7879-0874-6*, Scrbnr) Scribnrs Ref.
Truth about Cabala. David Godwin. (Truth About Ser.). (Illus.). 64p. 1995. pap. 1.99 (*1-56718-325-5*) Llewellyn Pubns.
Truth about Castles. Gillian Clements. (Illus.). 40p. (J). (ps-3). 1990. lib. bdg. 14.96 (*0-87614-401-6*, Carolrhoda) Lerner Group.
Truth about Castles. Gillian Clements. (J). (ps-3). 1991. pap. 6.95 (*0-87614-552-7*, Carolrhoda) Lerner Group.
Truth about Catalogers. Will Manley. LC 95-14828. (Illus.). 142p. 1995. pap. 22.50 (*0-7864-0103-6*) McFarland & Co.
Truth about Cats. Alan Snow. (Illus.). 32p. (J). (ps-3). 1996. 14.95 (*0-316-80282-4*) Little.
Truth about CB Antennas. William I. Orr & Stuart Cowan. (Illus.). 240p. 1990. pap. 13.95 (*0-8230-8708-5*, RAC Bks) Watsn-Guptill.
Truth about CB Antennas. 2nd ed. William I. Orr & Stuart D. Cowan. LC 70-164932. (Illus.). 240p. 1971. 11.95 (*0-933616-08-2*) Radio Pubns.
Truth about Chain Letters. Dan Squier. 48p. 1990. pap. 12.00 (*0-915665-21-2*) Premier Publishers.
Truth about Chakras. Anodea Judith. (Vanguard Ser.). (Illus.). 32p. (Orig.). 1990. pap. 1.99 (*0-87542-362-0*) Llewellyn Pubns.
Truth about Chiropractic. Debra Levinson. (Illus.). 1993. 39.95 (*0-9633577-0-0*) Max Pubns.
Truth about Christmas. Ralph Becker. pap. 0.99 (*0-87377-012-9*) GAM Pubns.
***Truth about Christmas.** Santa Claus. LC 97-8902. 1997. pap. write for info. (*0-8245-1678-8*) Crossroad NY.
Truth about Cinderella - (Musical) June W. Rogers. 1974. 5.50 (*0-87129-235-1*, T03) Dramatic Pub.
Truth about College: How to Survive & Succeed As a Student in the Nineties. Scott Edelstein. 1991. pap. 9.95 (*0-8184-0546-5*) Carol Pub Group.
***Truth about College: 50 Lessons for Parents Before They Start Writing Checks.** Will S. Keim. LC 97-21803. 1997. pap. 11.99 (*0-8272-3633-6*) Chalice Pr.
Truth about Columbus: A Subversively True Poster Book for a Dubiously Celebration Occasion. James W. Loewen. 48p. 1992. pap. 12.95 (*1-56584-008-9*) New Press NY.
Truth about Cousin Ernie's Head. Matthew McElligott. LC 95-21743. (J). 1996. 15.00 (*0-689-80179-3*, S&S Bks Young Read) S&S Childrens.
***Truth about Cowboys.** Margot Early. (Home on the Ranch Ser.). 1997. mass mkt. 3.99 (*0-373-70743-6*, 1-70743-9) Harlequin Bks.
Truth about Creative Visualization. Llewellyn Publications Staff. (Llewellyn's Truth about Ser.). 32p. (Orig.). 1984. pap. 1.99 (*0-87542-353-1*) Llewellyn Pubns.
Truth about Crystal Healing. Phyllis Galde. (Vanguard Ser.). 64p. (Orig.). 1986. pap. 1.99 (*0-87542-360-4*) Llewellyn Pubns.
Truth about Dungeons & Dragons. Joan H. Robie. 1992. audio 7.95 (*0-914984-25-X*) Starburst.
Truth about Dungeons & Dragons. Joan H. Robie. 80p. 1992. pap. 5.95 (*0-914984-37-3*) Starburst.
Truth about Enochian Tarot. Betty Schueler & Gerald J. Schueler. (Vanguard Ser.). (Illus.). 30p. (Orig.). 1989. mass mkt. 1.99 (*0-87542-717-0*) Llewellyn Pubns.
Truth about Everything: An Irreverant History of Philosophy, with Illustrations. Matthew Stewart. LC 96-34427. (Illus.). 460p. 1996. 32.95 (*1-57392-110-6*) Prometheus Bks.
Truth about Evocation of Spirits. Donald M. Kraig. (Truth About Ser.). 64p. 1994. pap. 1.99 (*1-56718-393-X*) Llewellyn Pubns.
Truth about False Memory Syndrome. James G. Friesen. 208p. pap. 10.99 (*1-56384-111-8*) Huntington Hse.
Truth about Forecasting with Astrology. 2nd ed. Stan Barker. (Vanguard Ser.). 32p. 1989. pap. 1.99 (*0-87542-376-0*) Llewellyn Pubns.
Truth about Freud's Technique: The Encounter with the Real. M. Guy Thompson. LC 94-2933. (Psychoanalytic Crosscurrents Ser.). 296p. (C). 1994. 40.00 (*0-8147-8206-X*) NYU Pr.
Truth about Freud's Technique: The Encounter with the Real. M. Guy Thompson. (Psychoanalytic Crosscurrents Ser.). 296p. (C). 1995. pap. 19.50 (*0-8147-8219-1*) NYU Pr.
Truth about George. Nicholson. 1994. pap. 2.99 (*0-373-15568-9*) Harlequin Bks.
Truth about George. Peggy Nicholson. (Romance Ser.). 1994. mass mkt. 2.99 (*0-373-03322-2*, 1-03322-4) Harlequin Bks.
Truth about Geronimo. Britton Davis. Ed. by Milo M. Quaife. LC 75-37958. (Illus.). xxxii, 265p. 1976. reprint ed. pap. 10.95 (*0-8032-5840-2*, Bison Books) U of Nebr Pr.
Truth about Graphite Golf Shafts: Everything a Golfer Should Know about Graphite Shafted Golf Clubs! Eric Wichern. 128p. 1994. pap. 12.95 (*0-9640907-9-1*) A&E Pubng.
Truth about Graphology. Ruth Gardner. (Truth About Ser.). 1990. mass mkt. 1.99 (*0-87542-252-7*) Llewellyn Pubns.
***Truth about Heaven & Eternity.** Thomas Ice & Tim Demy. (Pocket Prophecy Ser.). 48p. (Orig.). 1997. pap. 2.99 (*1-56507-664-8*) Harvest Hse.
Truth about Helping: Strategies & Tactics for Helping Injured, Ill, & Disabled Persons Get Better & Go Back to Work & Life. Gene Dent. (Practical Management Ser.). 175p. 1995. pap. write for info. (*1-878403-05-2*) Martin-Dennison Pr.
Truth about Herb Magic. Scott Cunningham. (Truth About Ser.). 1993. mass mkt. 1.99 (*0-87542-132-6*) Llewellyn Pubns.
Truth about Herbs. C. F. Leyel. 106p. 1985. pap. 8.00 (*0-89540-145-2*, SB-145) Sun Pub.
Truth about Herbs. C. F. Leyel. 106p. 1966. reprint ed. spiral bd. 9.00 (*0-7873-0558-8*) Hlth Research.
Truth about Herpes. 3rd ed. Stephen L. Sacks. (Illus.). 216p. 1988. pap. 14.95 (*0-919574-58-0*) Gordon Soules Bk.
***Truth about Herpes.** 4th ed. Stephen L. Sacks. (Illus.). 316p. 1997. pap. 24.95 (*0-919574-66-1*) Gordon Soules Bk.
Truth about Hitler & the Roman Catholic Church. A. Ratcliffe. 1982. lib. bdg. 59.95 (*0-87700-362-9*) Revisionist Pr.
Truth about Homosexuality: The Cry of the Faithful. John Harvey. 412p. 1996. pap. text ed. 17.95 (*0-89870-583-5*) Ignatius Pr.
Truth about Hypnosis. William Hewitt. (Truth About Ser.). 64p. 1989. mass mkt. 1.99 (*0-87542-365-5*) Llewellyn Pubns.
Truth about Janice Henderson. large type ed. Joan Marsh. (Linford Romance Library). 240p. 1993. pap. 15.99 (*0-7089-7458-9*, Trailtree Bookshop) Ulverscroft.
Truth about Jerusalem in Bible Prophecy. Thomas Ice & Timothy Demy. (Pocket Prophecy Ser.: No. 6). 48p. (Orig.). 1996. pap. 2.99 (*1-56507-485-8*) Harvest Hse.
Truth about Jesus. Maneh Al-Johani. 24p. pap. write for info. (*1-882837-12-6*) W A M Y Intl.
Truth about Living Trusts. Nan L. Goodart. 157p. (Orig.). 1995. pap. 16.95 (*0-7931-1344-X*, 5680-1601) Dearborn Trade.
***Truth about Long-Term Care Insurance.** W. V. Montgomery, Jr. 52p. Date not set. pap. 4.50 (*0-9630975-4-7*) Mont Assocs.
Truth about Lorin Jones. Alison Lurie. 336p. 1990. pap. 11.00 (*0-380-70807-8*) Avon.
Truth about Marvin Kalish. Martin S. Cohen. LC 92-71041. 288p. 1992. pap. 13.95 (*0-914539-05-1*) Ben-Simon.
***Truth about Mary, Vol. I.** Bob Payesko. LC 96-70137. 190p. 1996. pap. text ed. 8.95 (*1-882972-82-1*) Queenship Pub.
***Truth about Mary, Vol. II.** Bob Payesko. LC 96-70137. 358p. 1996. pap. text ed. 9.95 (*1-882972-83-X*) Queenship Pub.
***Truth about Mary, Vol. III.** Bob Payesko. LC 96-70137. 422p. 1996. pap. text ed. 10.95 (*1-882972-84-8*) Queenship Pub.
Truth about Mary Rose. Marilyn Sachs. (J). (gr. 4-8). 1996. 17.50 (*0-8446-6899-0*) Peter Smith.
Truth About Mary Rose. Marilyn Sachs. LC 95-2959. (J). 1995. pap. 3.99 (*0-14-037083-8*) Puffin Bks.
Truth about Mind Power. William W. Hewitt. (Truth About Ser.). 64p. 1994. pap. 1.99 (*1-56718-350-6*) Llewellyn Pubns.
Truth about Money. (Money Reform Ser.). 1994. lib. bdg. 257.88 (*0-8490-9057-1*) Gordon Pr.
Truth about Money. Ric Edelman. LC 96-11853. (Illus.). 528p. (Orig.). (C). 1996. 45.00 (*0-87840-615-8*) Georgetown U Pr.
Truth about Money. Ric Edelman. LC 96-11853. (Illus.). 528p. (Orig.). (C). 1996. pap. 19.95 (*0-87840-616-6*) Georgetown U Pr.
Truth about Numerology. David A. Hulse. (Truth About Ser.). 1992. mass mkt. 1.99 (*0-87542-395-7*) Llewellyn Pubns.
Truth about Outsourcing. Brian Rothery & Ian Robertson. 200p. 1995. 54.95 (*0-566-07515-6*, Pub. by Gower UK) Ashgate Pub Co.
Truth about Past Life Regression. Florence W. McClain. (Truth About Ser.). (Illus.). 32p. (Orig.). 1986. mass mkt. 1.99 (*0-87542-359-0*) Llewellyn Pubns.
Truth about Pearl Harbor. John T. Flynn. 1984. lib. bdg. 79.95 (*0-87700-613-X*) Revisionist Pr.
Truth about Postmodernism. Christofer Norris. LC 92-33828. 1993. pap. 24.95 (*0-631-18718-9*) Blackwell Pubs.
Truth about Power Rangers. Phil Phillips. 96p. (Orig.). 1995. pap. 6.95 (*0-914984-67-5*) Starburst.
Truth about Psychic Powers. Donald M. King. (Llewellyn's Truth about Ser.). 32p. (Orig.). 1987. mass mkt. 1.99 (*0-87542-355-8*) Llewellyn Pubns.
Truth about Publishing. Stanley Unwin. 352p. 1995. pap. 17.95 (*1-55821-423-2*) Lyons & Burford.
Truth about Publishing. 8th ed. Stanley Unwin & Philip Unwin. 256p. 1982. reprint ed. pap. 9.00 (*0-89733-064-1*) Academy Chi Pubs.
Truth about Publishing. 8th ed. Stanley Unwin. 1976. 24.95 (*0-04-655014-3*) Routledge Chapman & Hall.
Truth about Radiation Accidents. Paul Zimmerman. 256p. (Orig.). 1993. pap. 20.00 (*0-685-70277-4*) Prof Pr NC.
Truth about Radiation Accidents. Paul Zimmerman. 249p. (Orig.). (C). pap. text ed. 20.00 (*0-9634857-0-9*) Wrld Life Inst.
Truth About Rainforest Destruction: Facts, False Progress & Future Directions. Russell G. Coffee. 125p. 1996. pap. 9.95 (*0-9641721-0-0*) Better Planet.
Truth about Reference Librarians. Will Manley. LC 96-1461. (Illus.). 164p. 1996. pap. 22.50 (*0-7864-0220-2*) McFarland & Co.
Truth about Ritual Magic. Donald Tyson. (Truth About Ser.). 64p. (Orig.). 1989. mass mkt. 1.99 (*0-87542-830-4*) Llewellyn Pubns.
Truth about Rockefeller. Emanuel M. Josephson. 1979. 250.00 (*0-685-96471-X*) Revisionist Pr.
Truth about Rockefeller "Public Enemy No. 1" Emanuel Josephson. LC 64-20630. (Blacked-Out History Ser.). 277p. 1964. 5.00 (*0-686-32439-0*); pap. 5.00 (*0-686-32440-4*) A-albionic Res.
Truth about Runes. Donald Tyson. (Truth About Ser.). 1990. mass mkt. 1.99 (*0-87542-829-0*) Llewellyn Pubns.
***Truth About Ryan.** Francine Pascal. (Sweet Valley University Ser.: No. 31). (YA). 1997. mass mkt. 3.99 (*0-553-57055-2*, Sweet Valley) BDD Bks Young Read.
***Truth about Sacajawea.** (Illus.). 96p. 1997. lib. bdg. 17.99 (*1-880114-16-X*) Grandview.
Truth about Sailing. J. E. Talley. (Illus.). 100p. (Orig.). 1989. pap. write for info. (*0-318-65068-1*) Cristal Globe.
Truth about Santa Claus. James C. Giblin. LC 85-47541. (Illus.). 96p. (J). (gr. 3-7). 1985. lib. bdg. 15.89 (*0-690-04484-4*, Crowell Jr Bks) HarpC Child Bks.
Truth about Self Protection. Massad F. Ayoob. (Illus.). 417p. 1983. 7.99 (*0-553-23664-4*) Police Bkshelf.
Truth about Shamanism. Amber Wolfe. (Truth About Ser.). (Illus.). 32p. (Orig.). 1988. mass mkt. 1.99 (*0-87542-889-4*) Llewellyn Pubns.
Truth about Sharks. Carol A. Amato. LC 95-13378. (Young Readers' Ser.). (Illus.). 48p. (J). (gr. 2-4). 1995. pap. 4.95 (*0-8120-9197-3*) Barron.
***Truth about Sharks.** Carol A. Amato. (Young Reader Ser.). (Illus.). 48p. (J). (gr. 3-6). 1996. lib. bdg. 12.95 (*1-56674-188-2*) Forest Hse.
Truth About Sinusitis. Charles P. Lebo. 1995. 12.95 (*1-880688-01-8*) New Life Opt.
Truth about Sixth Grade. Colleen O. McKenna. 192p. (J). (gr. 4-6). 1992. pap. 3.50 (*0-590-44392-5*, Apple Paperbacks) Scholastic Inc.
Truth about Spirit Communication. Ray Buckland. (Truth About Ser.). (Illus.). 64p. 1995. mass mkt. 1.99 (*1-56718-095-7*) Llewellyn Pubns.
Truth about Stacey. Ann M. Martin. (Orig.). (J). 1986. pap. 3.50 (*0-590-43511-6*) Scholastic Inc.
Truth about Stacey. Ann M. Martin. (Baby-Sitters Club Mystery Ser.: Vol. 3). 192p. (J). (gr. 4-6). 1995. pap. text ed. 3.99 (*0-590-25158-9*) Scholastic Inc.
Truth about Stacey. large type ed. Ann M. Martin. LC 95-21314. (Baby-Sitters Club Ser.: Vol. 3). 144p. (Orig.). (J). (gr. 4 up). 1995. lib. bdg. 15.93 (*0-8368-1316-2*) Gareth Stevens Inc.
Truth about Success & Motivation: Plain Advice on How to be One of Life's Real Winners. Bob Montgomery. 170p. (Orig.). 1995. pap. 12.95 (*0-85091-284-9*, Pub. by Lothian Pub AT) Seven Hills Bk.
Truth about Sugar in Cuba. Antonio Barro Y Segura. 1976. lib. bdg. 59.95 (*0-8490-2775-6*) Gordon Pr.
Truth about Sunday Laws. Susan Johnson. LC 91-65335. 72p. (Orig.). 1991. per. 1.95 (*0-945383-26-6*, 945-5821) Teach Servs.
Truth about Teutonic Magick. Edred Thorsson. (Llewellyn's Truth about Ser.). (Illus.). 32p. (Orig.). 1989. pap. 1.99 (*0-87542-779-0*) Llewellyn Pubns.
Truth about Texas: Who Needs to Brag? We've Got the Facts. rev. ed. Anne Dingus. LC 95-12594. 189p. 1995. pap. 9.95 (*0-87719-282-0*, 9282) Gulf Pub.
Truth about the American Flag. Robert Morris. LC 76-12730. (Illus.). 1976. 10.80 (*0-9601476-1-6*); pap. 7.65 (*0-9601476-2-4*) Wynnehaven.
Truth about the American Pit Bull Terrier. Richard F. Stratton. (TS Ser.). (Illus.). 320p. 1991. text ed. 69.95 (*0-86622-638-9*, TS-142) TFH Pubns.
Truth about the Antichrist & His Kingdom. Thomas Ice & Timothy Demy. (Pocket Prophecy Ser.: Vol. 4). 1996. pap. 2.99 (*1-56507-407-6*) Harvest Hse.
Truth about the Betsy Ross Story. Robert Morris. LC 82-70798. (Illus.). 1982. 15.95 (*0-9601476-3-2*); pap. 12.95 (*0-9601476-4-0*) Wynnehaven.
Truth about the Cajuns. Trent Angers. (Illus.). 120p. 1989. 11.95 (*0-925417-00-9*) Acadian Hse Pub.
Truth about the Cajuns. Trent Angers. (Illus.). 120p. 1991. 11.95 (*0-925417-04-1*) Acadian Hse Pub.
Truth about the Chase. Joseph D. Ossorio et al. (Life's Roadmap Ser.). (Illus.). 60p. (J). (gr. 4-6). 1994. pap. 6.95 (*1-56721-044-9*) Twnty-Fifth Cent Pr.
Truth about the Deficit: Hidden Dimensions of the Money Problem. 1994. lib. bdg. 250.95 (*0-8490-5701-9*) Gordon Pr.
Truth About "The God Makers" Gilbert W. Scharffs. 1994. pap. 7.95 (*0-88494-963-X*) Bookcraft Inc.
Truth about the Indian Press. J. N. Sahni. 154p. 1974. 13.95 (*0-318-37291-6*) Asia Bk Corp.
Truth about the Killing of Daniel Yock: Workers Inquiry Exposes Police Murder. Socialist Labour League Staff. (Illus.). 158p. (Orig.). 1994. pap. 14.95 (*1-875639-06-3*, Pub. by Labour Pr AT) Labor Pubns Inc.
Truth about the Last Days' Temple. Thomas Ice & Timothy Demy. (Pocket Prophecy Ser.: Vol. 2). 48p. 1996. pap. 2.99 (*1-56507-393-2*) Harvest Hse.
Truth about the Millennium. Thomas Ice & Timothy Demy. (Pocket Prophecy Ser.: No. 5). 48p. (Orig.). 1996. pap. 2.99 (*1-56507-486-6*) Harvest Hse.
Truth about the Moon. Clayton Bess. (Illus.). 48p. (J). (gr. k-3). 1983. 13.95 (*0-395-34551-0*) HM.
Truth about the Moon. Clayton Bess. (J). (ps-3). 1992. pap. 6.95 (*0-395-64371-6*) HM.
Truth about the Movies. L. Hughes. 1976. lib. bdg. 59.95 (*0-8490-2776-4*) Gordon Pr.
***Truth about the National Debt: Five Myths & One Reality.** Frances X. Cavanaugh. 1996. text ed. 22.95 (*0-07-103842-6*) McGraw.
Truth about the National Debt: Five Myths & One Reality. Francis X. Cavanaugh. LC 96-4074. 192p. 1996. 22.95 (*0-87584-734-X*) Harvard Busn.
Truth about the Power in Your Birth Chart. William Hewitt. (Truth About Ser.). 64p. 1994. mass mkt. 1.99 (*1-56718-351-4*) Llewellyn Pubns.
Truth about the Rapture. Thomas Ice & Timothy Demy. (Pocket Prophecy Ser.: Vol. 1). 48p. 1995. pap. 2.99 (*1-56507-392-4*) Harvest Hse.
Truth about the Rapture of the Church. Owen Pemberton. Ed. by M. L. Jones. LC 93-87080. 104p. (Orig.). 1994. pap. 8.95 (*1-882270-15-0*) Old Rugged Cross.
Truth about the Reign of Emperor Nicholas the Second. G. Knupffer. 1991. lib. bdg. 66.00 (*0-8490-4436-7*) Gordon Pr.
Truth about the Russian Church Abroad. M. Rodzianko. Tr. by Michael P. Hilko from RUS. LC 74-29321. (Illus.). 48p. (Orig.). 1975. pap. 1.50 (*0-88465-004-9*) Holy Trinity.
***Truth about the Signs of the Times.** Thomas Ice & Tim Demy. (Pocket Prophecy Ser.). 48p. (Orig.). 1997. pap. 2.99 (*1-56507-662-1*) Harvest Hse.
Truth about the Territory. Rich Ives. 530p. (Orig.). 1987. text ed. 21.00 (*0-937669-27-X*); pap. text ed. 14.00 (*0-937669-26-1*) Owl Creek Pr.
Truth about the Tribulation. Thomas Ice & Timothy Demy. (Pocket Prophecy Ser.: Vol. 3). 48p. 1996. pap. 2.99 (*1-56507-406-8*) Harvest Hse.
Truth about the Truth: De-Confusing & Re-Constructing the Postmodern World. Walter T. Anderson. LC 95-5537. 288p. (Orig.). 1995. pap. 14.95 (*0-87477-801-8*, Tarcher Putnam) Putnam Pub Group.
Truth about the UFO Crash at Roswell. Kevin D. Randle & Donald R. Schmitt. 336p. (Orig.). 1994. mass mkt. 6.99 (*0-380-77803-3*) Avon.
Truth About the Virgin: Sex, Ritual, & Myth in the Dead Scrolls, Vol. 1. Ita Sheres & Anne Kohn-Blau. 256p. 1995. 24.95 (*0-8264-0816-8*) Continuum.
Truth about the West African Land Question. J. E. Hayford. 208p. 1971. reprint ed. 39.50 (*0-7146-1755-5*, Pub. by F Cass Pubs UK) Intl Spec Bk.
Truth about the Yellow Pages: Making Them Work for You. Tom Davis. 175p. 1996. pap. text ed. 29.95 (*1-57444-078-0*) St Lucie Pr.
Truth about the 1980s. David R. Henderson. LC 94-11084. (Essays in Public Policy Ser.: No. 52). 1994. pap. 5.00 (*0-8179-5572-0*) Hoover Inst Pr.
Truth about Three Billy Goats Gruff. Steven Otfinoski. LC 93-42391. (Illus.). 32p. (J). (gr. k-3). 1994. pap. 3.95 (*0-8167-3013-X*) Troll Communs.
Truth about Three Billy Goats Gruff. Steven Otfinoski. LC 93-42391. (Illus.). 32p. (J). (gr. k-3). 1994. lib. bdg. 11.95 (*0-8167-3012-1*) Troll Communs.
Truth about TMJ: How to Help Yourself. Jennifer Hutchinson et al. (Illus.). 208p. 1994. pap. 14.95 (*0-9640485-0-7*) Reinhardt & Still.
***Truth about Toby.** Cheryl St. John. 1997. mass mkt. 3.99 (*0-373-07810-2*, 1-07810-4) Silhouette.
Truth about Tristrem Varick. Edgar E. Saltus. LC 74-95394. reprint ed. 37.50 (*0-404-05505-2*) AMS Pr.

Truth about Trouble. Michael Scanlan. 168p. (Orig.). (C). 1989. pap. 9.99 (*0-89283-621-0*, Charis) Servant.

Truth about Tubby & Slim. Stanford I. Polonsky. LC 92-60812. 50p. (J). (gr. k-3). 1993. 7.95 (*1-55523-543-3*) Winston-Derek.

Truth about Unicorns. James C. Giblin. LC 90-47233. (Illus.). 128p. (J). (gr. 3-7). 1991. lib. bdg. 14.89 (*0-06-022479-7*) HarpC Child Bks.

Truth about Unicorns. James C. Giblin. LC 90-47233. (Trophy Nonfiction Bk.). (Illus.). 128p. (J). (gr. 3-7). 1996. pap. 6.95 (*0-06-446147-5*, Trophy) HarpC Child Bks.

Truth about Uri Geller. rev. ed. James Randi. LC 82-60951. (Illus.). 234p. 1982. pap. 20.95 (*0-87975-199-1*) Prometheus Bks.

***Truth about Vasectomy & Reversal.** A. M. Durrani. Ed. by Pete Billac. LC 97-65578. (Illus.). 96p. (Orig.). 1997. pap. 9.95 (*0-943629-29-2*) Swan Pub.

Truth about Witchcraft. Scott Cunningham. (Truth about Ser.). Date not set. mass mkt. 1.99 (*0-87542-357-4*) Llewellyn Pubns.

Truth about Witchcraft. Keith Morgan. (Orig.). 1995. pap. 7.95 (*0-614-16789-2*, Pub. by Mandrake Pr UK) Holmes Pub.

Truth about Witchcraft Today. Scott Cunningham. LC 88-45197. (New Age Ser.). 208p. (Orig.). 1988. mass mkt. 4.99 (*0-87542-127-X*) Llewellyn Pubns.

Truth about Women: Fighting the Fourteen Outrageous Myths That Hold Women Back. Georgia Witkin. 192p. 1995. pap. 21.95 (*0-670-85060-8*, Viking) Viking Penguin.

***Truth about Work: How to Make a Life, Not a Living.** David Harder. 220p. 1997. pap. 11.95 (*1-55874-465-7*) Health Comm.

***Truth about Writing Fiction.** William Appel. 1997. pap. 14.95 (*0-8038-9390-6*) Hastings.

Truth about Wyatt Earp. 2nd ed. Richard E. Erwin. Ed. by Loren Nicholsen. (Illus.). 451p. (Orig.). 1994. pap. 19.50 (*0-9633930-3-0*) O K Pr CA.

Truth about You: Self-Image. Lori Carlson. (Inter Acta Ser.). (Illus.). 4p. (C). 1994. teacher ed., ring bd. 1.25 (*1-885702-81-7*, 741-059t, Inter Acta); student ed., ring bd. 3.25 (*1-885702-80-9*, 741-059s, Inter Acta) WSN Pr.

Truth about Your Height: Exploring the Myths & Realities of Human Size & Its Effects on Health, Performance, Pollution, & Survival. Thomas T. Samaras. (Illus.). 328p. (Orig.). (YA). 1994. pap. 24.95 (*0-938711-22-9*) Tecolote Pubns.

Truth about Yugoslavia: Why Working People Should Oppose Intervention. George Fyson et al. LC 93-84841. (Illus.). 89p. (Orig.). 1993. pap. 8.95 (*0-87348-776-1*); lib. bdg. 30.00 (*0-87348-777-X*) Pathfinder NY.

Truth about 2000 A. D. & Predicting Christ's Return. Thomas Ice & Timothy Demy. (Pocket Prophecy Ser.). 48p. (Orig.). 1996. pap. 2.99 (*1-56507-487-4*) Harvest Hse.

Truth Against the World: Frank Lloyd Wright Speaks for an Organic Architecture. Ed. by Patrick J. Meehan. LC 92-14034. (Illus.). 496p. 1995. pap. text ed. 24.95 (*0-471-14427-4*) Wiley.

Truth & Authority in Modernity. Lesslie Newbigin. LC 96-13846. (Christian Mission & Modern Culture Ser.). 96p. 1996. pap. 8.00 (*1-56338-168-0*) TPI PA.

Truth & Beauty. 1995. 3.98 (*0-7858-0302-5*) Bk Sales Inc.

Truth & Beauty: Aesthetics & Motivations in Science. S. Chandrasekhar. LC 87-13792. (Illus.). 180p. 1990. pap. text ed. 16.95 (*0-226-10087-1*) U Ch Pr.

Truth (& Beauty) in Radiation Measurement. John H. Harley. LC 85-15292. (Taylor Lectures: No. 9). 37p. (Orig.). 1985. pap. text ed. 25.00 (*0-913392-78-2*) NCRP Pubns.

Truth & Belief: Interpretation & Critique of the Analytical Theory of Religion. Heimo E. Hofmeister. (Studies in Philosophy & Religion). 256p. 1990. lib. bdg. 129.00 (*0-7923-0976-6*, Pub. by Klwr Acad Pubs NE) Kluwer Ac.

Truth & Consequence in Medieval Logic. Ernest A. Moody. LC 76-44307. (Studies in Logic & the Foundations of Mathematics). 113p. 1976. reprint ed. text ed. 38.50 (*0-8371-9053-3*, MOTC, Greenwood Pr) Greenwood.

Truth & Consequences. Tony Raskob. (Orig.). 1989. write for info. (*0-318-65039-8*) YNot Read.

***Truth & Consequences: How American Colleges & Universities Respond Publicly to Crises.** Jerrold K. Footlick. LC 97-24508. (American Council on Education/Oryx Press Series on Higher Education). 176p. (C). 1997. boxed 29.95 (*0-89774-970-7*) Oryx Pr.

Truth & Consequences: Relative Connections, Vol. III. Gyeorgos C. Hatonn. (The Phoenix Journals). 221p. 1993. pap. 6.00 (*1-56935-020-5*) Phoenix Source.

Truth & Consequences of Sexually Transmitted Diseases. Carole Marsh. (Smart Sex Stuff Ser.). (Orig.). 1994. pap. 29.95 (*1-55609-212-1*) Gallopade Pub Group.

Truth & Convention in the Middle Ages: Medieval Rhetoric & Representation. Ruth Morse. (Illus.). 304p. (C). 1990. text ed. 69.95 (*0-521-30211-0*) Cambridge U Pr.

Truth & Eros: Foucault, Lacan & the Question of Ethics. John Rajchman. 192p. (C). 1991. pap. 16.95 (*0-415-90380-7*, A2335, Routledge NY) Routledge.

Truth & Error: Or, the Science of Intellection. John W. Powell. LC 75-3322. reprint ed. 31.50 (*0-404-59318-6*) AMS Pr.

Truth & Existence. Michael Gelven. LC 90-31683. 200p. 1990. lib. bdg. 29.50 (*0-271-00707-9*) Pa St U Pr.

Truth & Existence. Jean-Paul Sartre. Tr. by Adrian Van Den Hoven. 143p. 1992. 22.50 (*0-226-73522-2*) U Ch Pr.

Truth & Existence. Jean-Paul Sartre. Ed. by Ronald Aronson. Tr. by Adrian Van Den Hoven. 145p. 1995. pap. 9.95 (*0-226-73523-0*) U Ch Pr.

Truth & Falsehood in Visual Images. Mark Roskill & David Carrier. LC 83-5123. (Illus.). 160p. 1983. lib. bdg. 22.50 (*0-87023-404-8*) U of Mass Pr.

Truth & Health. Fannie B. James. 1970. 8.95 (*0-686-24356-0*) Divine Sci Fed.

Truth & Historicity. Richard Campbell. 456p. 1992. 95.00 (*0-19-823927-0*) OUP.

Truth & Interpretation: An Essay in Thinking. Brayton Polka. 300p. 1990. text ed. 39.95 (*0-312-04218-3*) St Martin.

Truth & Its Magnificent Simplicity. Brown Landone. 62p. 1994. reprint ed. spiral bd. 7.00 (*0-7873-1086-7*) Hlth Research.

Truth & Knowledge: Introduction to "Philosophy of Spiritual Activity" 2nd ed. Rudolf Steiner. Ed. by Paul M. Allen. Tr. by Rita Stebbing from GER. 112p. 1981. reprint ed. pap. 8.75 (*0-89345-212-2*, Steinerbks) Garber Comm.

Truth & Knowledge: Introduction to "Philosophy of Spiritual Activity", Vol. 14. 2nd ed. Rudolf Steiner. Ed. by Paul M. Allen. Tr. by Rita Stebbing from GER. LC 81-51762. 112p. 1981. reprint ed. lib. bdg. 13.95 (*0-89345-008-1*, Spir Sci Lib) Garber Comm.

Truth & Knowledge: On Some Themes in Tractarian & Russellian Philosophy of Language. Eric H. Wefald. 204p. 1996. lib. bdg. 36.50 (*0-7618-0268-1*) U Pr of Amer.

Truth & Lamentation: Stories & Poems on the Holocaust. Ed. by Milton Teichman & Sharon Leder. 432p. 1993. 17.95 (*0-252-06335-X*); text ed. 39.95 (*0-252-02028-6*) U of Ill Pr.

Truth & Lies in Literature: Essays & Reviews. Stephen Vizinczey. 352p. 1988. pap. 15.95 (*0-226-85884-7*) U Ch Pr.

Truth & Lies That Press for Life: Sixty Los Angeles Poets. Ed. by Connie Hershey. 1991. pap. 12.95 (*0-9629097-0-X*) Artifact Pr.

Truth & Light: Brief Explanations. M. R. Bawa Muhaiyaddeen. LC 74-76219. (Illus.). 144p. 1974. pap. 6.00 (*0-914390-04-X*) Fellowship Pr PA.

***Truth & Meaning.** Kenneth Taylor. (C). Date not set. text ed. 64.95 (*1-57718-048-8*) Blackwell Pubs.

***Truth & Meaning.** Kenneth Taylor. (C). Date not set. pap. text ed. 27.95 (*1-57718-049-6*) Blackwell Pubs.

***Truth & Meaning of Human Sexuality: Guidelines for Education Within the Family.** Pontifical Council for the Family Staff. 112p. pap. 2.95 (*0-8198-7390-X*) Pauline Bks.

Truth & Meaning of Human Sexuality: Guidelines for Education Within the Family. Pontifical Council for the Family Staff. 60p. (C). 1996. pap. 4.95 (*1-57455-090-X*) US Catholic.

Truth & Method. rev. ed. Hans-Georg Gadamer. Ed. by Donald G. Marshall & Joel C. Weinsheimer. 600p. (C). 1993. pap. text ed. 24.95 (*0-8264-0585-1*) Continuum.

Truth & Modality for Knowledge Representation. Raymond Turner. (Artificial Intelligence - Bobrow, Brady & Davis Ser.). 136p. 1991. 25.00 (*0-262-20080-5*) MIT Pr.

Truth & Modality for Knowledge Representation. Raymond Turner. 128p. (C). 1990. text ed. 195.00 (*0-273-03186-4*, Pub. by Pitman Pubng UK) St Mut.

Truth & Objectivity. Crispin Wright. LC 92-15025. 247p. 1993. 34.50 (*0-674-91086-9*) HUP.

Truth & Objectivity. Crispin Wright. 247p. 1994. pap. 15.95 (*0-674-91087-7*) HUP.

Truth & Other Enigmas. Michael Dummett. LC 77-12777. 528p. 1978. 49.95 (*0-674-91075-3*) HUP.

Truth & Other Enigmas. Michael Dummett. LC 77-12777. 528p. 1981. pap. 21.00 (*0-674-91076-1*) HUP.

Truth & Poetry 101. unabridged ed. Warren B. Knox. LC 96-75346. (Illus.). 98p. (Orig.). 1996. pap. 7.95 (*0-9640165-1-6*) Minneola Pr.

Truth & Power: The Place of Scripture in the Christian Life. J. I. Packer. 250p. 1996. 14.99 (*0-87788-815-9*) Shaw Pubs.

***Truth & Progress in Economic Knowledge.** Roger E. Backhouse. (Advances in Economic Methodology Ser.). 256p. 1997. 70.00 (*1-85278-691-4*) E Elgar.

Truth & Rationality: Proceedings of a Conference Sponsored by Sociedad Filosofica Ibero-Americana. Ed. & Intro. by Enrique Villanueva. (Philosophical Issues Ser.: No. 5, 1994). (Orig.). 1994. pap. text ed. 25.00 (*0-924922-19-2*); lib. bdg. 42.00 (*0-924922-69-9*) Ridgeview.

Truth & Reality in Marx & Hegel: A Reassessment. Czeslaw Prokopczyk. LC 80-7976. 144p. 1980. lib. bdg. 22.50 (*0-87023-307-6*) U of Mass Pr.

Truth & Religious Belief: Conversations on Philosophy of Religion. Curtis L. Hancock et al. LC 97-23717. 224p. (C). (gr. 13). 1997. text ed. 54.95 (*1-56324-852-2*); pap. text ed. 19.95 (*1-56324-853-0*) M E Sharpe.

Truth & Rumor. large type ed. Jane Gillespie. (Linford Romance Library). 1995. pap. 15.99 (*0-7089-7719-7*, Linford) Ulverscroft.

Truth & Science: A Bibliography. 2nd ed. Norman Ansley et al. 1997. 15.00 (*0-317-01466-8*) Am Polygraph.

Truth & Scientific Knowledge in the Thought of Henry of Ghent. Steven P. Marrone. LC 84-62885. (Speculum Anniversary Monographs: No. 11). 164p. 1985. 20.00 (*0-910956-91-X*); pap. 12.00 (*0-910956-92-8*) Medieval Acad.

Truth & Symbol: The Apprehension & Consciousness of Being. Karl Jaspers. (Masterworks of Literature Ser.). (Orig.). 1959. pap. 11.95 (*0-8084-0303-6*) NCUP.

Truth & the End of Inquiry: A Peircean Account of Truth. C. J. Misak. (Oxford Philosophical Monographs). 200p. 1991. 65.00 (*0-19-824231-X*) OUP.

Truth & the Historicity of Man. Ed. by George F. McLean. (Proceedings of the American Catholic Philosophical Association Ser.: Vol. 43). 1969. pap. 20.00 (*0-918090-03-2*) Am Cath Philo.

Truth & Tradition: A Conversation about the Future of United Methodist Theological Education. Neal F. Fisher. LC 95-5894. 144p. 1995. 15.95 (*0-687-00810-7*) Abingdon.

Truth & Tradition in Chinese Buddhism. Karl L. Reichelt. 1972. 59.95 (*0-8490-1234-1*) Gordon Pr.

Truth & Tradition in Chinese Buddhism. Karl L. Reichelt. (Illus.). 415p. 1990. reprint ed. pap. 30.00 (*957-9482-17-9*) Oriental Bk Store.

Truth & Tragedy: A Tribute to Hans J. Morgenthau. Ed. by Kenneth Thompson & Robert J. Myers. 386p. (Orig.). 1983. pap. 21.95 (*0-87855-866-7*) Transaction Pubs.

Truth-Antidote for Error. Anthony D. Palma. LC 76-52177. (Radiant Life Ser.). 128p. 1977. pap. 3.95 (*0-88243-904-9*, 02-0904); teacher ed., pap. 5.50 (*0-88243-174-9*, 32-0174) Gospel Pub.

Truth, Beauty, & Design: Catalogue of an Exhibition of Victorian, Edwardian, & Later Decorative Art Held at Fischer Fine Art. Adrian J. Tilbrook. (Illus.). 92p. 1986. pap. 30.00 (*0-903685-47-7*, Pub. by R Dennis UK) Antique Collect.

Truth, Beauty & Goodness. Rudolf Steiner. 1986. pap. 2.50 (*0-916786-86-2*, Saint George Pubns) R Steiner Col Pubns.

Truth, Beauty, Goodness, Commitment: A Religious Examination of Philosophical Virtues. John M. Kettlewell. 1983. teacher ed. 25.00 (*1-881678-21-0*); student ed. 18.00 (*1-881678-22-9*) CRIS.

Truth Beyond Relativism: Karl Mannheim's Sociology of Knowledge. Gregory Baum. LC 77-76605. (Pere Marquette Lectures). 1977. 15.00 (*0-87462-509-2*) Marquette.

***Truth Can Get You Killed.** Mark R. Zubro. LC 97-2490. 1997. 21.95 (*0-312-15679-0*) St Martin.

Truth Concerning the Invention of Photography: Nicephore Niepce-His Life, Letters, & Works (1867) Victor Fouque. LC 72-9198. (Literature of Photography Ser.). 1978. reprint ed. 19.95 (*0-405-04907-2*) Ayer.

Truth Concerning The Trinity. Witness Lee. 37p. 1.50 (*0-87083-751-6*, 20101001) Living Stream Ministry.

Truth Cure. Firestone. 1981. 13.95 (*0-02-538380-9*) Macmillan.

Truth, Deduction, & Computation: Logic & Semantics for Computer Science. Ruth E. Davis. LC 89-34922. 220p. (C). 1995. text ed. write for info. (*0-7167-8201-4*) W H Freeman.

Truth Disguised: Allegorical Structure & Technique in Gracian's Criticon. T. L. Kassier. (Monografias A Ser.: No. 53). 150p. (C). 1976. 45.00 (*0-7293-0006-4*, Pub. by Tamesis Bks Ltd UK) Boydell & Brewer.

Truth Faith in the True God: An Introduction to Luther's Life & Thought. Hans Schwarz. LC 96-4127. 144p. 1996. pap. 11.99 (*0-8066-2821-9*, 9-2821) Augsburg Fortress.

Truth, Fiction & Literature: A Philosophical Perspective. Peter Lamarque & Stein H. Olsen. (Clarendon Library of Logic & Philosophy). 496p. 1997. reprint ed. pap. 26.00 (*0-19-823681-6*) OUP.

Truth for Germany. Udo Walendy. 1984. lib. bdg. 79.95 (*0-87700-607-5*) Revisionist Pr.

Truth for Life. John Blanchard. 1986. pap. 14.99 (*0-85234-225-X*, Pub. by Evangelical Pr) Presby & Reformed.

Truth for Life Bible Studies. Lela Birky. (J). (gr. 7-9). 1965. pap. 3.00 (*0-686-15481-9*) Rod & Staff.

***Truth for the Picking: Original Insights on Life from America's Heartland.** Peter Reese. (Home-Grown Wisdom Collection). 84p. (Orig.). 1997. spiral bd. 8.99 (*1-881830-50-0*, DS18475) Garborgs.

Truth from the "Zog Bog" Gyeorgos C. Hatonn. (Phoenix Journals). 224p. 1993. pap. 6.00 (*1-56935-025-6*) Phoenix Source.

Truth Functions & the Problem of Their Realization by Two Terminal Graphs. A. Adam. 206p. (C). 1968. 38.00 (*963-05-3333-2*, Pub. by Akad Kiado HU) St Mut.

***Truth Games: Lies, Money & Psychoanalysis.** John Forrester. LC 97-17559. 1997. 22.95 (*0-674-53962-1*) HUP.

Truth Has Been Thrown to the Bribed. Calvin Peterson. 64p. 1988. pap. 5.00 (*0-936978-06-6*) Pheasant Run.

***Truth Has Come to Earth: A True Disclosure from Messenger of the Way.** Mark E. Edwards. LC 97-65491. v, 111p. (Orig.). 1997. pap. 6.99 (*0-9656969-0-1*, Way Books) Davco Bk Pubs.

Truth Has No Alternative. Benny C. Watson. 96p. 1988. write for info. (*0-9620702-0-3*) Entrtnmnt Galore.

Truth, Hope, & Power: The Thought of Karl Popper. Douglas E. Williams. 304p. 1989. 37.50 (*0-8020-2643-5*) U of Toronto Pr.

Truth, Images & Distortions: A View of the Indian Press. Sunny Thomas. 1985. 17.50 (*0-8364-1372-5*, Pub. by Heritage IA) S Asia.

Truth in Accounting. Kenneth MacNeal. LC 74-75709. 1970. reprint ed. text ed. 20.00 (*0-914348-04-3*) Scholars Bk.

Truth in Advertising. Herbert W. Richardson et al. LC 72-7241. 45p. 1984. reprint ed. 59.95 (*0-88946-912-1*) E Mellen.

Truth in Advertising: An AMA Research Report. John T. Lucas & Richard Gurman. LC 72-79980. (AMA Research Report Ser.). 40p. reprint ed. pap. 25.00 (*0-317-28460-6*, 2051309) Bks Demand.

Truth in American Fiction: The Legacy of Rhetorical Idealism. Janet Gabler-Hover. LC 90-31609. 320p. 1990. 40.00 (*0-8203-1247-9*) U of Ga Pr.

Truth in Comedy: The Manual of Improvisation. Charna Halpern et al. Ed. by Arthur L. Zapel. LC 93-43701. 160p. (Orig.). (C). 1994. pap. 12.95 (*1-56608-003-7*, B164) Meriwether Pub.

Truth in Crisis, Vol. 2: The Controversy in the Southern Baptist Convention. James C. Hefley. 218p. 1987. pap. 7.95 (*0-929292-00-6*) Hannibal Bks.

Truth in Crisis, Vol. 3: The Controversy in the Southern Baptist Convention. James C. Hefley. 260p. 1988. pap. 7.95 (*0-929292-01-4*) Hannibal Bks.

Truth in Crisis, Vol. 4: The Controversy in the Southern Baptist Convention. James C. Hefley. 1991. pap. 8.95 (*0-929292-04-9*) Hannibal Bks.

Truth in Crisis, Vol. 6: The Conservative Resurgence in the Southern Baptist Convention. James C. Hefley. 1991. pap. 9.95 (*0-929292-18-9*) Hannibal Bks.

Truth in Ethics. Hooker. (C). Date not set. pap. text ed. 15.95 (*0-631-19701-X*) Blackwell Pubs.

Truth in Government: Restoring Pride & Prosperity in America. Jay H. Brown. 304p. 1996. pap. 12.95 (*0-9638152-3-7*) Freedom Pubng.

Truth in Hell & Other Essays on Politics & Culture, 1935-1987. Hans Speier. 384p. 1989. 49.95 (*0-19-505875-5*) OUP.

Truth in History. Oscar Handlin. LC 78-24157. 448p. 1979. 37.50 (*0-674-91025-7*) Belknap Pr.

Truth in History. Oscar Handlin. LC 78-24157. 448p. 1981. pap. 17.95 (*0-674-91026-5*) Belknap Pr.

***Truth in History.** Oscar Handlin. LC 96-29653. 1997. pap. 24.95 (*1-56000-951-9*) Transaction Pubs.

Truth in Jesus: Twelve Studies in John 1-11. annot. ed. Gracia Rinden. 116p. (Orig.). 1992. pap. 3.95 (*0-943167-09-4*) Faith & Fellowship Pr.

Truth in Lending. Roland E. Brandel et al. 1000p. 1985. write for info. (*0-318-65469-5*, H43724) P-H.

***Truth in Lending.** 3rd ed. National Consumer Law Center, Inc. Staff. LC 95-72046. (Consumer Credit & Sales Legal Practice Ser.). 798p. (Orig.). 1995. pap. 100.00 (*1-881793-37-0*) Nat Consumer Law.

Truth in Lending: A Comprehensive Guide. Roland E. Brandel et al. LC 84-22423. 850p. 1985. Supplements avail. suppl. ed. 85.00 (*0-15-004372-4*, #H43724) HarBrace.

Truth in Lending & Consumer Credit Agreements. J. Karpinski & S. Fielding. 288p. 1985. pap. 37.00 (*0-08-039200-8*, Pergamon Pr) Elsevier.

Truth-in-Lending & Regulation Z. Dennis Replansky. LC 84-71018. (Illus.). xvi, 297p. 1984. 95.00 (*0-8318-0242-1*, B242) Am Law Inst.

Truth in Lending Case Summaries. 3rd ed. National Consumer Law Center, Inc. Staff. 350p. (Orig.). 1983. pap. 15.00 (*0-941077-04-7*, 22,250) NCLS Inc.

Truth-in-Lending Manual, 2 vols. 6th rev. ed. Ralph C. Clontz, Jr. (Illus.). 1991. Set, updated semi-annually. pap. text ed. 175.00 (*0-7913-0546-5*) Warren Gorham & Lamont.

Truth in Money Book. rev. ed. Theodore R. Thoren & Richard F. Warner. Ed. by Margaret L. Thoren. LC 94-60088. (Illus.). 276p. 1994. pap. 14.95 (*0-9606938-7-4*) Truth in Money.

Truth in Money Book. 4th rev. ed. Theodore R. Thoren & Richard F. Warner. Ed. by Margaret L. Thoren. LC 94-60088. (Illus.). 276p. 1994. 25.00 (*0-9606938-8-2*) Truth in Money.

Truth in Negotiations Act (TINA) Handbook: U. S. Department of Defense. 150p. (Orig.). (C). 1996. pap. text ed. 40.00 (*0-7881-2828-0*) DIANE Pub.

Truth in Nursing Inquiry. June F. Kikuchi et al. (Illus.). 160p. 1996. 38.00 (*0-7619-0098-5*); pap. 17.95 (*0-7619-0099-3*) Sage.

Truth in Painting. Jacques Derrida. Tr. by Geoffrey Bennington & Ian McLeod. (Illus.). xvi, 408p. 1987. pap. text ed. 23.95 (*0-226-14324-4*) U Ch Pr.

Truth in Philosophy. Barry Allen. LC 92-35722. 244p. 1993. text ed. 32.00 (*0-674-91090-7*) HUP.

Truth in Philosophy. Barry Allen. 248p. 1995. pap. text ed. 15.95 (*0-674-91091-5*, ALLTRX) HUP.

Truth in Publishing: Federal Regulation of the Press's Business Practices, 1880-1920. Linda Lawson. LC 92-34828. 224p. (C). 1993. 29.95 (*0-8093-1829-6*) S Ill U Pr.

Truth in Religion: The Plurality of Religions & the Unity of Truth. Mortimer J. Adler. 176p. 1992. reprint ed. pap. 10.00 (*0-02-064140-0*) Macmillan.

Truth in Saving: Marketing Compliance Guide, the Final Regulations. Tom Thomas. 1993. pap. 59.00 (*0-942061-54-3*) Sourcebks.

Truth in Savings: A Guide to Compliance. 200p. 1992. pap. 25.00 (*0-685-67049-X*, 5493) Commerce.

Truth in Savings: Compliance Manual. James M. Mataya. 250p. (Orig.). 1993. pap. 69.95 (*1-882097-45-9*) Sav & Comm Bank.

Truth in Savings: Legal Analysis & Compliance Strategies. Barkley Clark et al. 1993. pap. 120.00 (*0-685-69619-7*, TISR) Warren Gorham & Lamont.

***Truth in Savings - Final Regs.** Sarah E. Hutchinson & Stacey Sawyer. 1992. text ed. 59.95 (*0-07-413201-6*) Irwin.

Truth in Savings Annual Percentage Yield Tables. 128p. (Orig.). 1993. pap. 59.95 (*1-882097-46-7*) Sav & Comm Bank.

Truth in Savings with Centsible Interest & Morse Rate Tables. Richard L. Morse. iv, 104p. (Orig.). 1992. pap. 11.95 (*1-881331-00-8*) Family Econ Trust.

***Truth in the Light: An Investigation of over 300 Near-Death Experiences.** Peter Fenwick & Elizabeth Fenwick. 288p. 1997. pap. 12.00 (*0-425-15608-7*, Berkley Trade) Berkley Pub.

Truth in the Night. Michael McLaverty. 255p. 1986. pap. 8.95 (*0-905169-72-7*, Pub. by Poolbeg Pr IE) Dufour.

An Asterisk (*) at the beginning of an entry indicates that the title is appearing in BIP for the first time.

Truth in Things: The Life & Career of Lamar Dodd. William U. Eiland. LC 95-47491. (C). 1996. text ed. 74.95 (*0-8203-1828-0*) U of Ga Pr.

Truth in Trial: Liberal Education Be Hanged. Robert K. Carlson. (Illus.). 213p. (Orig.). 1995. 22.00 (*1-883357-90-X*, Crisis Bks); pap. 13.95 (*1-883357-91-8*, Crisis Bks) Dumb Ox Bks.

Truth, Interpretation & Information: Selected Papers of the 3rd Amsterdam Colloquium. Ed. by Jeroen Groenendyk et al. (Groningen-Amsterdam Studies in Semantics). viii, 182p. (C). 1984. pap. 38.50 (*90-6765-001-3*) Mouton.

Truth Is a Bright Star: A Hopi Adventure. Joan Price. LC 82-1345. 120p. (J). 1995. pap. 8.95 (*0-89087-333-X*) Celestial Arts.

Truth Is Immortal: The Story of Baptists in Europe. Irwin Barnes. 127p. 1950. reprint ed. 4.50 (*0-87921-015-X*); reprint ed. pap. 2.50 (*0-87921-019-2*) Attic Pr.

Truth Is in Here: Conspiracies, Mysteries, Superstitions, Kooks & Cults on the Internet. Karl Mamer. (Go! Guides Ser.). (Illus.). 64p. (Orig.). 1996. pap. 10.95 (*1-57712-011-6*) Motion Works.

Truth Is Not Sober. Winifred Holtby. LC 77-121564. (Short Story Index Reprint Ser.). 1977. 20.95 (*0-8369-3521-7*) Ayer.

Truth Is Our Mask: An Essay on Theological Method. William L. Newell. LC 89-39428. 148p. (Orig.). (C). 1990. pap. text ed. 17.00 (*0-8191-7621-4*) U Pr of Amer.

Truth Is Out There: The Official Guide to the X-Files. Brian Lowry. 288p. 1995. pap. 15.00 (*0-06-105330-9*, HarperPrism) HarpC.

Truth Is Stranger Than It Used to Be: Biblical Faith in a Postmodern Age. Brian J. Walsh & J. Richard Middleton. 220p. (Orig.). 1995. pap. 14.99 (*0-8308-1856-1*, 1856) InterVarsity.

Truth Is Stranger Than Publicity. Alton Delmore. Ed. by Charles K. Wolfe. LC 95-69025. (Illus.). 333p. 1995. reprint ed. pap. 14.95 (*0-915608-15-4*) Country Music Found.

Truth Is Symphonic: Aspects of Christian Pluralism. Hans U. Von Balthasar. Tr. by Graham Harrison from GER. LC 86-83131. 192p. 1987. pap. 12.95 (*0-89870-141-4*) Ignatius Pr.

Truth Killers. Glen T. Brock. 240p. (Orig.). 1991. mass mkt. 3.50 (*0-87067-576-1*) Holloway.

Truth Lessons, Level 1, 1. Witness Lee. 158p. per. 6.00 (*0-87083-205-0*, 15032001) Living Stream Ministry.

Truth Lessons, Level 1, 2. Witness Lee. 213p. per. 8.00 (*0-87083-207-7*, 15033001) Living Stream Ministry.

Truth Lessons, Level 1, 3. Witness Lee. 134p. per. 5.00 (*0-87083-209-3*, 15034001) Living Stream Ministry.

Truth Lessons, Level 1, 4. Witness Lee. 135p. per. 5.25 (*0-87083-211-5*, 15035001) Living Stream Ministry.

Truth Lessons, Level 2, 1. Witness Lee. 164p. per. 6.25 (*0-87083-357-X*, 15036001) Living Stream Ministry.

Truth Lessons, Level 2, 2. Witness Lee. 116p. per. 4.50 (*0-87083-359-6*, 15041001) Living Stream Ministry.

Truth Lessons, Level 2, 3. Witness Lee. 125p. per. 4.75 (*0-87083-361-8*, 15057001) Living Stream Ministry.

Truth, Lie Detectors, & Other Problems in Labor Arbitration: Proceedings of the Thirty-First Annual Meeting, National Academy of Arbitrators, New Orleans, LA, April 4-7, 1978. National Academy of Arbitrators, Meeting (31st: 1978: New Orleans, LA) Staff. Ed. by James L. Stern & Barbara D. Dennis. LC 78-21950. 490p. 1979. reprint ed. pap. 139.70 (*0-608-00740-4*, 2061527) Bks Demand.

***Truth Machine.** James L. Halperin. 1996. 24.00 (*0-345-41056-4*) Ballantine.

***Truth Machine.** James L. Halperin. 1997. mass mkt. 6.99 (*0-345-41288-5*, Del Rey) Ballantine.

Truth Machine see Heinemann Guided Readers

Truth Maintenance Systems: ECAI-90 Workshop, Stockholm, Sweden, August 6, 1990 Proceedings. Ed. by Joerg H. Siekmann et al. (Lecture Notes in Artificial Intelligence Ser.: Vol. 515). vii, 177p. 1991. 25.95 (*0-387-54305-8*) Spr-Verlag.

Truth Matters: For You & Tomorrow's Generation. Josh McDowell. 208p. 1995. wbk. ed., pap. 13.95 (*0-8054-9834-6*, 7800-05) Broadman.

Truth Matters: For You & Tomorrow's Generation Leader's Guide. Josh McDowell. 64p. 1995. teacher ed., pap. 6.95 (*0-8054-9833-8*, 7800-06) Broadman.

Truth Messages. Witness Lee. 112p. per. 4.25 (*0-87083-658-7*, 08036001) Living Stream Ministry.

Truth More Than Man Can Bear. Charles E. Buchanan, Sr. LC 95-62084. 149p. 1997. 12.95 (*1-55523-774-6*) Winston-Derek.

Truth, Myth & Legend: Dragons. David Passes. LC 92-44745. (Illus.). 48p. (J). (ps-3). 1993. 12.95 (*0-307-17500-6*, Golden Books) Western Pub.

Truth Needs No Ally: Inside Photojournalism. Howard Chapnick. LC 94-6737. (Illus.). 384p. (C). 1994. pap. 24.95 (*0-8262-0955-6*) U of Mo Pr.

Truth Needs No Ally: Inside Photojournalism. Howard Chapnick. LC 94-6737. (Illus.). 384p. 1994. 49.95 (*0-8262-0954-8*) U of Mo Pr.

***Truth of a Madman: Memoirs of a Jewish Activist.** Jack N. Porter. (Illus.). 150p. 1997. pap. 10.95 (*0-614-29567-X*) Spencer Pr.

Truth of Authority: Ideology & Communication in the Soviet Union. Thomas F. Remington. LC 88-4745. (Russian & East European Studies). (Illus.). 270p. (Orig.). (C). 1988. 49.95 (*0-8229-3590-2*); pap. 19.95 (*0-8229-5408-7*) U of Pittsburgh Pr.

Truth of Broken Symbols. Robert C. Neville. LC 95-2363. (SUNY Series in Religious Studies). 320p. (C). 1995. text ed. 59.50 (*0-7914-2741-2*); pap. text ed. 19.95 (*0-7914-2742-0*) State U NY Pr.

Truth of Christmas Beyond the Myths: The Gospel of the Infancy of Christ. Rene Laurentin. LC 85-1402. (Studies in Scripture: Vol. III). 1986. pap. 21.95 (*0-932506-34-8*) St Bedes Pubns.

***Truth of History.** C. Behan McCullagh. LC 97-8185. 1997. write for info. (*0-415-17110-5*); pap. write for info. (*0-415-17111-3*) Routledge.

Truth of Imagination: An Introduction to Visionary Poetry. Andre J. Welburn. LC 89-10345. 192p. 1990. text ed. 45.00 (*0-312-03632-9*) St Martin.

Truth of Imagination: Essays & Reviews by Edwin Muir. Peter H. Butter. 274p. (C). 1988. text ed. 29.90 (*0-08-036392-X*, Pub. by Aberdeen U Pr) Macmillan.

***Truth of Poetry: Tensions in Modernist Poetry Since Baudelaire.** Michael Hamburger. 350p. 1996. pap. 17.95 (*0-85646-275-6*, Pub. by Anvil Press UK) Dufour.

***Truth of Science: Physical Theories & Reality.** Roger G. Newton. LC 97-9079. 1997. write for info. (*0-674-91092-3*) HUP.

Truth of the Resurrection. E. Maeve Vernon. 1995. pap. 5.95 (*0-7880-0610-X*, 610X) CSS OH.

Truth of the Stock Tape & Wall Street Stock Selector. W. D. Gann. (Illus.). (C). 1988. 49.00 (*0-939093-12-X*) Lambert Gann Pub.

***Truth of Things: Thoughts on the Impracticality of a Liberal Arts Education.** Marion Montgomery. 1998. write for info. (*0-9653208-7-1*) Spence Pub.

Truth on Fire. John Fleming & Bona Fleming. 1993. reprint ed. pap. 12.99 (*0-88019-309-3*) Schmul Pub Co.

Truth on Trial: The Ballad of Sojourner Truth. Douglas W. Larche. 1996. pap. write for info. (*0-87129-712-4*, TA6) Dramatic Pub.

Truth Option. Will Schutz. LC 83-40025. 224p. (Orig.). 1984. pap. 15.95 (*0-89815-107-4*) Ten Speed Pr.

***Truth or Consequences.** Sheila Black. (Code Blue Ser.: No. 3). 240p. (YA). 1997. mass mkt. 4.50 (*0-06-106424-6*, Harp PBks) HarpC.

Truth or Consequences. A. R. Plumb. (J). 1995. pap. 3.50 (*0-7868-4038-2*) Disney Pr.

Truth or Consequences: Essays in Honor of Nuel Belnap. Ed. by J. Michael Dunn & Anil Gupta. 392p. (C). 1990. lib. bdg. 167.00 (*0-7923-0920-0*, Pub. by Klwr Acad Pubs NE) Kluwer Ac.

Truth or Consequences: Putting Limits on Limits. Henry Louis Gates, Jr. (James Russell Wiggins Lectures in the History of the Book in American Culture). 37p. 1994. reprint ed. pap. 6.00 (*0-944026-49-4*) Am Antiquarian.

Truth or Dare. Caroline Cross. (Desire Ser.). 1995. mass mkt. 3.25 (*0-373-05910-8*, 1-05910-4) Silhouette.

Truth or Dare. Starhawk. LC 87-45197. 381p. 1989. pap. 17.00 (*0-06-250816-4*) Harper SF.

Truth or Dare. R. L. Stine. Ed. by Patricia MacDonald. (Fear Street Ser.). 176p. (Orig.). (YA). (gr. 7 up). 1995. mass mkt. 3.99 (*0-671-86836-5*, Archway) PB.

***Truth or Dare: A Sara Kingsley Mystery.** Anne Wilson. 210p. 1997. pap. 11.95 (*0-7043-4461-0*, Pub. by Womens Press UK) Trafalgar.

Truth or Dare Trap. Nancy J. Hopper. (YA). (gr. 7 up). 1988. mass mkt. 2.50 (*0-380-70269-X*, Flare) Avon.

Truth or Deception? Satan's Plan Exposed. Walter G. Squires, Jr. LC 96-90148. (Orig.). 1996. pap. 12.95 (*0-533-11914-6*) Vantage.

Truth or Die. Diane Hoh. (Nightmare Hall Ser.: No. 15). 176p. (YA). (gr. 7-9). 1994. pap. 3.50 (*0-590-48353-6*) Scholastic Inc.

Truth or Myth: Deception of the Ages. Jimmy Graham & G. Lamar Wilkie. LC 93-36423. 140p. (Orig.). 1993. pap. 8.95 (*1-882185-14-5*) Crnrstone Pub.

Truth or Tradition: What Is the Gospel? Maralene Wesner & Miles Wesner. LC 86-71139. 100p. 1986. pap. 4.95 (*0-936715-03-0*) Diversity Okla.

Truth Out of Africa: How the African Crisis Is Manipulated. I. Benson. 1986. 79.95 (*0-8490-3823-5*) Gordon Pr.

Truth, Peace, Love: 52 Words to Contemplate. Christine Tarantino. LC 96-90174. 128p. (Orig.). 1996. pap. 11.95 (*1-887480-11-0*) Wrds Lght Intl.

Truth, Possibility & Probability: New Logical Foundations of Probability & Statistical Inference. R. B. Chuaqui. 484p. 1991. 173.50 (*0-444-88840-3*, MSS 166) Elsevier.

***Truth Revealed: My Answer to the World.** Christopher A. Anderson. LC 96-90570. 124p. (Orig.). 1996. pap. 10.50 (*0-931353-42-4*) Andersons Pubns.

Truth Serum. Bernard Cooper. LC 95-38984. 225p. 1996. 21.95 (*0-395-74539-X*) HM.

***Truth Serum.** Bernard Cooper. 1997. pap. 11.00 (*0-395-85994-8*) HM.

Truth Shall Make You Free. David T. Demola. 24p. 1987. pap. 1.50 (*0-88144-092-2*) Christian Pub.

Truth Shall Make You Free: An Inquiry into the Legend of God. Robert A. Steiner. LC 80-80646. (Illus.). 47p. (Orig.). (J). (gr. 6 up). 1980. pap. 5.95 (*0-9604044-0-6*) Wide-Awake Bks.

Truth Shall Make You Free: Confrontations. Gustavo Gutierrez. LC 90-30553. 1990. pap. 17.50 (*0-88344-663-4*) Orbis Bks.

Truth Shall Set You Free. Victoria James. (7 American Daughters Ser.: Vol. 1). 250p. (Orig.). Date not set. pap. 9.99 (*1-889018-01-5*) Bay Shore Bks.

***Truth Shall Set You Free.** John Osteen. Date not set. mass mkt. 2.25 (*0-912631-13-9*) J O Pubns.

***Truth Shall Set You Free: A Memoir.** LC 96-6507. 1997. write for info. (*0-06-251393-1*) Harper SF.

Truth Shall Triumph. 9th ed. Ralph V. Reynolds. 111p. 1983. pap. 4.99 (*0-912315-07-5*) Word Aflame.

Truth Slayers: A Battle of Right from Wrong. Josh McDowell & Bob Hostetler. LC 94-47961. 192p. (J). 1995. pap. 10.99 (*0-8499-3662-4*) Word Pub.

Truth-Speaking & Power among Friends (Quakers) Ethical Alternatives & Consequences. Paul Barton-Kriese & Kenneth Ives. (Studies in Quakerism: No. 15). 52p. 1987. pap. 5.00 (*0-89670-018-6*) Progresiv Pub.

Truth Tales: Contemporary Stories by Women Writers of India. Ed. by Kali for Women Staff. LC 89-78155. 184p. 1990. 35.00 (*1-55861-011-1*); pap. 12.95 (*1-55861-012-X*) Feminist Pr.

Truth Tales: Contemporary Writings by Indian Women. Kali for Women Staff. 1987. 10.00 (*0-8364-2197-3*, Pub. by Manohar II) S Asia.

Truth Talk. William Backus. 1995. 9.98 (*0-88486-117-1*) Arrowood Pr.

Truth, Tall Tales, & Blatant Lies. William E. Gratwick. LC 81-65246. (Illus.). 192p. 1981. 20.00 (*0-89822-016-5*); pap. 10.95 (*0-89822-017-3*) Visual Studies.

Truth That Frees. Gerard Smith. LC 56-9140. (Aquinas Lectures). 1956. 15.00 (*0-87462-121-6*) Marquette.

Truth That Goes Unclaimed. rev. ed. Jean K. Foster. Ed. by Carl B. Foster. (God-Mind Bks.: Bk. 2). 214p. (Orig.). 1994. pap. 10.95 (*0-9626366-3-0*) TeamUp.

Truth That is Never Loud. Marjorie L. Turner. 64p. 1990. 8.50 (*0-8233-0469-8*) Golden Quill.

Truth That Kills. Ronald Levitsky. 352p. 1994. pap. 4.99 (*0-451-40401-7*, Onyx) NAL-Dutton.

***Truth That Matters: The Bible's Message to You.** Keavin Hayden. LC 97-11022. 1997. pap. write for info. (*0-8163-1393-8*) Pacific Pr Pub Assn.

Truth the Poet Sings. Illus. by Alan W. Peterson. LC 83-51133. 220p. 1984. 6.95 (*0-87159-160-X*) Unity Bks.

Truth, the Way, the Life: An Elementary Treatise on Theology: the Masterwork of B. H. Roberts. 2nd ed. B. H. Roberts. Ed. by Stan Larson. LC 94-14856. lxix, 730p. 1994. pap. 19.95 (*1-56085-077-9*, Smith Res) Signature Bks.

Truth, the Whole Truth & Nothing But... A Police Officer's Guide to Testifying in Court. D. W. Reynolds. 90p. (C). 1990. text ed. 23.95 (*0-398-05656-0*) C C Thomas.

Truth to Tell. Nancy Bond. LC 93-11248. 336p. (YA). (gr. 7 up). 1994. lib. bdg. 17.95 (*0-689-50601-5*, McElderry) S&S Childrens.

Truth to Tell. large type ed. Marigold West. (Linford Romance Library). 240p. 1993. pap. 15.99 (*0-7089-7466-X*, Trailtree Bookshop) Ulverscroft.

***Truth to Tell: Non-Fiction Anthology.** Woodhouse. 1993. pap. text ed. write for info. (*0-582-87677-X*, Pub. by Longman UK) Longman.

***Truth Trap.** Dubowski. (Secret World of Alex Mack Ser.: No. 21). (J). 1997. mass mkt. 3.99 (*0-671-01157-X*) PB.

Truth Trap. Frances A. Miller. 208p. (YA). 1986. reprint ed. mass mkt. 4.50 (*0-449-70247-2*, Juniper) Fawcett.

Truth Triumphant. fac. ed. Benjamin G. Wilkinson. LC 95-61346. 432p. 1995. reprint ed. per. 12.95 (*0-945383-85-1*) Teach Servs.

***Truth Triumphant.** unabridged ed. B. G. Wilkinson. 428p. 1996. reprint ed. pap. 14.95 (*0-923309-32-2*) Hartland Pubns.

Truth, Trust, & Relationships: Healing Interventions in Contextual Therapy. Barbara R. Krasner & Austin J. Joyce. LC 95-8927. 256p. 1995. text ed. 31.95 (*0-87630-755-1*) Brunner-Mazel.

Truth Twisters. Harold J. Berry. 1987. pap. 12.99 (*0-8474-1212-1*) Back to Bible.

Truth Unchanged, Unchanging. 2nd ed. D. Martyn Lloyd-Jones. LC 93-376. 128p. 1993. reprint ed. pap. 9.99 (*0-89107-706-5*) Crossway Bks.

***Truth under Attack: Cults & Contemporary Religions.** Eryl Davies. 1990. pap. 16.99 (*0-85234-341-8*, Pub. by Evangelical Pr) Presby & Reformed.

Truth Under Lock & Key: Jesus and The Dead Sea Scrolls. Klaus Berger. Tr. by James S. Currie from GER. LC 94-33665. 128p. (Orig.). 1995. pap. 13.00 (*0-664-25547-7*) Westminster John Knox.

Truth Until Paradox. Staley Krause. Ed. by Stewart Wieck. 400p. 1994. pap. 4.99 (*1-56504-088-0*, 04088/11004) White Wolf.

Truth, Vagueness, & Paradox: An Essay on the Logic of Truth. Vann McGee. LC 89-27742. 280p. (C). 1990. 39.95 (*0-87220-087-6*) Hackett Pub.

Truth, Value & Justification. Michael Fuller. 250p. 1991. 55.95 (*1-85628-151-5*, Pub. by Avebury Pub UK) Ashgate Pub Co.

Truth Versus Precision in Economics. Thomas Mayer. (Advances in Economic Methodology Ser.). 208p. 1992. 70.00 (*1-85278-546-2*); pap. 20.00 (*1-85278-552-7*) E Elgar.

Truth Vibrations: From TV Celebrity to World Visionary, Vol. 1. 2nd rev. ed. David Icke. 144p. 1993. reprint ed. pap. 9.95 (*1-85860-006-5*, Pub. by Gateway Books UK) ACCESS Pubs Network.

Truth, War, & the Dream-Game: Selected Prose Poems & Parables, 1966-1990. Lawrence Fixel. LC 91-35572. 166p. (Orig.). 1992. pap. 10.95 (*0-918273-88-9*) Coffee Hse.

Truth Well Told: McCann-Erickson & the Pioneering of Global Advertising. Stewart Alter. 320p. 1994. write for info. (*0-9642622-0-7*) McCann Erickson.

Truth Will Set You Free. Ann Gallagher et al. (Grade School Chastity - Project Genesis Ser.). (Illus.). 252p. (Orig.). (J). (gr. 8). 1996. teacher ed., pap. text ed. write for info. (*1-885845-20-0*); student ed., pap. text ed. write for info. (*1-885845-21-9*) Leaflet Missal.

Truth Will Set You Free. Purna. 160p. 1993. pap. 13.95 (*1-85230-015-9*) Element MA.

Truth Will Set You Free: A Presentation of the Catholic Faith for Young Adults Based on the Catechism of the Catholic Church. Michael J. Mazza. 85p. 1995. teacher ed. 20.00 (*0-9646214-1-X*) Veritas Pr SD.

Truth Will Set You Free: A Presentation of the Catholic Faith for Young Adults Based on the Catechism of the Catholic Church. Michael J. Mazza. (Illus.). 98p. (YA). (gr. 9-12). 1995. pap. 7.95 (*0-9646214-0-1*) Veritas Pr SD.

Truth with Her Boots On see Henry Cecil Reprint Series

Truth Without Facts: Selected Papers from the First Three International Conferences on Adult Education & the Arts. Ed. by Willem Elias et al. 421p. 1996. pap. 29.95 (*90-5487-114-8*, Pub. by VUB Univ Pr BE) Paul & Co Pubs.

***Truth Without Justice.** Date not set. pap. text ed. write for info. (*0-312-11205-X*) St Martin.

Truth Works - Making Right Choices: Leader's Guide. Josh McDowell. 128p. 1995. teacher ed., pap. 12.95 (*0-8054-9827-3*, 7800-13) Broadman.

Truth Works - Making Right Choices: Workbook for Children. Josh McDowell. 32p. (J). (gr. 4-6). 1995. wbk. ed., pap. 4.95 (*0-8054-9830-3*, 7800-11) Broadman.

Truth Works - Making Right Choices: Workbook for Children. Josh McDowell. 32p. (J). (gr. 1-3). 1995. wbk. ed., pap. 4.95 (*0-8054-9831-1*, 7800-12) Broadman.

Truth-Wrought-Words. Rudolf Steiner. 209p. 12.95 (*0-910142-82-3*) Anthroposophic.

***Truth Zone: Building the Truthful Organization from the Bottom Up!** Ward Flynn. (Illus.). 204p. (Orig.). 1996. pap. 20.00 (*1-889129-13-5*) Matrix CO.

Truthfeasting. Jahannes. per. 7.95 (*0-86543-192-2*) Africa World.

***Truthfeasting.** Ja Jahannes. 1996. 19.95 (*0-86543-191-4*) Africa World.

Truthful & the Good: Essays in Honor of Robert Sokolowski. Robert Sokolowski & James G. Hart. Ed. by John J. Drummond. LC 96-24927. (Contributions to Phanomenology Ser.). 230p. (C). 1996. lib. bdg. 125.00 (*0-7923-4134-1*) Kluwer Ac.

Truthful Living: What Christianity Really Teaches about Recovery. A. Boyd Luter & Kathy McReynolds. LC 94-29018. 200p. (Orig.). (C). 1994. pap. 10.99 (*0-8010-5692-6*) Baker Bks.

Truthful Woman in Southern California. Katherine A. Sanborn. (American Biography Ser.). 192p. 1991. reprint ed. lib. bdg. 59.00 (*0-7812-8336-1*) Rprt Serv.

Truthfulness & Tragedy: Further Investigations in Christian Ethics. Stanley Hauerwas et al. LC 76-30425. 1977. pap. text ed. 15.00 (*0-268-01832-4*) U of Notre Dame Pr.

Truthlikeness. I. Niiniluoto. (Synthese Library: Vol. 185). 528p. 1987. lib. bdg. 194.00 (*90-277-2354-0*, D Reidel) Kluwer Ac.

Truthlikeness for Multidemensional, Quantitative Cognitive Problems. I. A. Kieseppa. (Synthese Library SYLI: Vol. 254). 236p. (C). 1996. lib. bdg. 90.00 (*0-7923-4005-1*) Kluwer Ac.

***Truthquest.** 216p. (J). 1997. write for info. (*0-7814-0015-5*, Chariot Bks) Chariot Victor.

***Truthquest, No. 2.** 216p. (J). 1997. write for info. (*0-7814-0016-3*, Chariot Bks) Chariot Victor.

***Truthquest, No. 3.** 216p. (J). 1997. write for info. (*0-7814-0017-1*, Chariot Bks) Chariot Victor.

Truths & Fictions: A Journey from Documentary to Digital Photography. Pedro Meyer. LC 94-79645. (Illus.). 136p. 1995. 40.00 (*0-89381-608-6*) Aperture.

Truths & Half-Truths: Fictions & Memoirs by 13 Washington Writers. Shirley Cochrane et al. LC 95-61777. 225p. (Orig.). 1995. pap. 12.50 (*0-9609062-3-1*) WA Expatriates Pr.

Truths & Roses. Inglath Caulder. (Superromance Ser.). 1994. mass mkt. 3.50 (*0-373-70609-X*, 1-70609-2) Harlequin Bks.

***Truth's Bright Embrace: Essays & Poems in Honor of Arthur O. Roberts.** Ed. by Paul N. Anderson & Howard R. Macy. 375p. 1996. 25.00 (*0-9653474-0-0*); pap. 20.00 (*0-9653474-1-9*) G Fox Univ.

Truth's Debt to Value. David Weissman. LC 92-43608. 288p. (C). 1993. 40.00 (*0-300-05425-4*) Yale U Pr.

Truths from the West Indies. Studholme Hodgson. (Illus.). 1977. text ed. 22.95 (*0-8369-9224-5*, 9078) Ayer.

Truths, Half-Truths, & Outright Lies: Tales of the Deep South. Earle Ross. Ed. by Iris Ross. (Illus.). 230p. (Orig.). 1996. pap. 12.00 (*1-57502-144-7*) Morris Pubng.

Truths in Miniature. James E. Padgett. 1989. pap. 0.50 (*1-887621-23-7*) Found Ch Divine Truth.

Truths of Love: Sufi Poetry. Javad Nurbakhsh. Tr. by Leonard Lewisohn. 110p. (ENG & PER.). 1982. pap. 0.95 (*0-933546-08-4*) KNP.

Truths of Others: An Essay on Nativistic Intellectuals in Mexico. Alicja Iwanska. LC 76-40139. (Illus.). 124p. 1978. 34.95 (*0-87073-558-6*); pap. text ed. 18.95 (*0-87073-559-4*) Transaction Pubs.

Truths That Transform: Christian Doctrines for Your Life Today. 2nd ed. D. James Kennedy. LC 96-19548. 192p. (gr. 10). 1996. pap. 10.99 (*0-8007-5609-6*) Revell.

Truths the Hand Can Touch: The Theatre of Athol Fugard. Russell Vandenbroucke. LC 85-2760. 268p. 1985. pap. 12.50 (*0-930452-45-3*); lib. bdg. 22.50 (*0-930452-42-9*) Theatre Comm.

Truths to Live by. John E. Ross. LC 72-37834. (Essay Index Reprint Ser.). 1977. reprint ed. 21.95 (*0-8369-2622-6*) Ayer.

Trutine of Hermes: A Guide to Calculating & Interpreting the True Ascendant. Niek Scheps. 1993. pap. 19.95 (*1-85230-131-7*) Element MA.

***Trutor & the Balloonist.** Debbie L. Wesselmann. LC 96-46814. 288p. 1997. 22.95 (*1-878448-74-9*) MacMurray & Beck.

TRW: Pioneering Technology & Innovation 1900-1994. Davis Dyer. 1995. text ed. 35.00 (*0-07-103624-5*) McGraw.

TRW Inc. A Report on the Company's Environmental Policies & Practices. (Illus.). 38p. (C). 1994. reprint ed. pap. text ed. 250.00 (*0-7881-0910-3*, Coun on Econ) DIANE Pub.

Try. Dennis Cooper. 208p. 1994. 20.00 (*0-8021-1542-X*, Grove) Grove-Atltic.

Try. Dennis Cooper. LC 93-31364. 208p. 1995. pap. 11.00 (*0-8021-3338-X*, Grove) Grove-Atltic.

Try! A Survival Guide to Unemployment. Karen Okulicz. 70p. 1995. pap. 10.00 (*0-9644260-0-5*) K-Slaw.

Try a Little Shakespeare. Frumi Cohen. LC 93-32493. (J). 1993. pap. 10.00 (*0-88734-519-0*) Players Pr.

Try a Little Shakespeare: Music & Lyrics. Frumi Cohen. LC 93-32493. (J). 1993. pap. 15.00 (*0-88734-029-6*) Players Pr.

Try Again, Sally Jane. Mary Diestel-Feddersen. LC 86-42810. (Illus.). 30p. (J). (gr. 2-3). 1987. lib. bdg. 18.60 (*1-55532-150-X*) Gareth Stevens Inc.

Try Again, Trevor. Rob Lewis. (Illus.). 32p. (J). (ps-k). 1996. 17.95 (*0-370-31974-5*, Pub. by Bodley Head UK) Trafalgar.

***Try & Stop Me.** Bennett Cerf. Date not set. lib. bdg. 26.95 (*0-8488-1963-2*) Amereon Ltd.

Try & Trust. Horatio Alger, Jr. (Works of Horatio Alger Jr.). 1989. reprint ed. lib. bdg. 79.00 (*0-685-27540-X*) Rprt Serv.

Try Anything Twice. large type ed. Jan Struther. (Isis Reminiscence Ser.). 256p. 1992. 21.95 (*1-85089-534-1*, Pub. by ISIS UK) Transaction Pubs.

Try Being Healthy. Alec Forbes. 188p. 1976. pap. 11.95 (*0-8464-4305-8*) Beekman Pubs.

Try Being Healthy. Alec Forbes. 184p. (C). 1976. pap. 12.95 (*0-8464-1057-5*) Beekman Pubs.

Try God, You'll Like Him. Katie Tonn. (Uplook Ser.). 1975. pap. 0.99 (*0-8163-0178-6*, 20340-6) Pacific Pr Pub Assn.

Try It! Simple Vegetarian Recipes for the Non-Vegetarian. Sandra Bartiromo & Debbie Weir. (Illus.). (Orig.). 1984. spiral bd. 4.95 (*0-916005-02-X*) Silver Sea.

Try It Again. Phillip Auerbach. 121p. 1992. pap. 20.00 (*0-685-14676-6*) NJ Inst CLE.

Try It, You'll Like It! Eric Berg. LC 93-8907. (J). 1993. 10.00 (*1-56071-325-9*) ETR Assocs.

Try Thai. Sharon Wong Hoy. 100p. 1987. pap. 6.95 (*0-9607508-3-5*) Benshaw Pub.

***Try the Spirit...By the Spirit.** Mady Thomas, III. Date not set. pap. 7.95 (*1-890330-03-5*) Turning Pt Pub.

Try This Way. Clifford Fuller. 1961. pap. 1.00 (*0-87516-196-0*) DeVorss.

Try to Feel it My Way: New Help for Touch Dominant People & Those Who Care about Them. Suzette H. Elgin. LC 96-15553. 1996. text ed. 29.95 (*0-471-00669-6*) Wiley.

Try to Feel it My Way: New Help for Touch Dominant People & Those Who Care about Them. Suzette H. Elgin. LC 96-15553. 1996. pap. text ed. 14.95 (*0-471-00670-X*) Wiley.

Try to Live to See This! Kabir. Tr. by Robert Bly. 1976. pap. 3.00 (*0-915408-12-0*) Ally Pr.

Try to Remember. Carla Cassidy. (Intimate Moments Ser.). 1994. mass mkt. 3.50 (*0-373-07560-X*, 5-07560-1) Silhouette.

Try to Remember. Caroline L. Grinnell. 405p. (Orig.). 1992. pap. write for info. (*0-9631687-0-3*) Purple Star Pr.

Try to Remember. Zane Kotker. LC 96-24848. 1997. 23.00 (*0-679-44042-9*) Random.

***Try Try Again.** Brian Jones. LC 96-86542. (Illus.). 64p. (Orig.). (J). (ps-4). 1996. pap. 4.95 (*1-57733-007-2*) B Dolphin Pub.

***Try Us: '97 National Minority Business Directory.** LC 76-182148. 550p. 1997. 54.95 (*1-885786-06-9*) Try Us Res.

Try Your Luck. Peter Rosei. Tr. & Afterword by Kathleen E. Thorpe. LC 93-25580. (Studies in Austrian Literature, Culture, & Thought. Translation Ser.). 1994. pap. 10.50 (*0-929497-76-7*) Ariadne CA.

Tryall of Private Devotions. Henry Burton. LC 77-6863. (English Experience Ser.: No. 856). 1977. reprint ed. lib. bdg. 20.00 (*90-221-0856-2*) Walter J Johnson.

Trygve Lie & the Cold War: The UN Secretary-General Pursues Peace, 1946-1953. James Barros. 444p. 1989. text ed. 37.00 (*0-87580-148-X*) N Ill U Pr.

Trying Again. Laurie Rich. Date not set. write for info. (*0-393-03515-8*) Norton.

***Trying Cases: A Life in the Law.** Haliburton Fales. LC 96-51204. 1997. 30.00 (*0-8147-2671-2*) NYU Pr.

Trying Cases to Win. Herbert J. Stern. LC 91-20176. (Trial Practice Library: Trial Techniques). 656p. 1991. text ed. 110.00 (*0-471-55313-1*) Wiley.

Trying Cases to Win, Vol. 3. Herbert J. Stern. (Trial Practice Library Ser.). 477p. 1993. text ed. 110.00 (*0-471-57282-9*) Wiley.

Trying Cases to Win, 4 vols., Vol. 4. Herbert J. Stern. (Trial Practice Library). 2128p. 1995. text ed. 396.00 (*0-471-13318-3*) Wiley.

Trying Cases to Win: Summation, Vol. 4. Herbert J. Stern. (Trial Practice Library). 472p. 1995. text ed. 110.00 (*0-471-58577-7*) Wiley.

Trying Cases to Win, Vol. 2: Direct Examination, Vol. 2. Herbert J. Stern. 457p. 1992. text ed. 110.00 (*0-471-57128-8*) Wiley.

Trying Conclusions: New & Selected Poems, 1961-1991. Howard Nemerov. 174p. 1991. 18.95 (*0-226-57263-3*) U Ch Pr.

Trying Drug Cases in Massachusetts. Stephanie Page et al. LC 92-62586. 610p. 1992. ring bd. 75.00 (*0-944490-43-3*) Mass CLE.

Trying Hard to Hear You. Sandra Scoppettone. LC 96-1252. 256p. (YA). (gr. 8-12). 1996. reprint ed. pap. 9.95 (*1-55583-367-5*) Alyson Pubns.

***Trying on Great-Grandma's Boots.** Minerva Martinez-Zanca. Ed. by Gloria Chavez. (Illus.). (Orig.). 1997. pap. 14.95 (*0-9655516-2-8*) Obra Hispana.

Trying Out of Moby-Dick. Howard P. Vincent. (BCL1-PS American Literature Ser.). 400p. 1993. reprint ed. lib. bdg. 89.00 (*0-7812-6994-6*) Rprt Serv.

Trying Sociology. Kurt H. Wolff. LC 74-13165. (Illus.). 672p. reprint ed. pap. 180.00 (*0-317-08702-9*, 2017412) Bks Demand.

Trying Summary Ejectment & Other Landlord-Tenant Actions. Joan G. Brannon. (Special Ser.: Vol. 14). 31p. (Orig.). 1996. pap. text ed. 15.00 (*1-56011-291-3*) Institute Government.

Trying Times: Alabama Photographs, 1917-1945. Michael V. Thomason. LC 84-16329. (Illus.). 320p. 1985. 39.95 (*0-8173-0254-9*) U of Ala Pr.

Trying to Balance the Heart. Linda N. Foster. Ed. by Allen Berlinski. (Illus.). 28p. 1993. pap. 7.00 (*0-941543-04-8*) Sun Dog Pr.

Trying to Be an Honest Woman. Judith Barrington. LC 85-80278. 80p. 1985. pap. 6.95 (*0-933377-00-2*) Eighth Mount Pr.

Trying to Be Human: Zen Talks from Cheri Huber. Ed. by Sara Jenkins. LC 95-68525. 128p. (Orig.). 1995. pap. 9.95 (*0-9630784-1-0*) Present Perf.

Trying to Be Round. George Perreault. 64p. (Orig.). 1994. pap. 9.50 (*1-880286-20-3*) Singular Speech Pr.

Trying to Change the World. Peter M. Rinaldo. LC 91-90387. 172p. (C). 1992. 14.95 (*0-9622123-6-9*) DorPete Pr.

Trying to Cope with Continuing Disability Review Regulations. Edwin Lopez-Soto. 30p. 1986. pap. 3.25 (*0-685-44379-5*, 40,963) NCLS Inc.

Trying to Explain. Donald Davie. (Poets on Poetry Ser.). 1979. pap. 13.95 (*0-472-06310-3*) U of Mich Pr.

Trying to Find Chinatown & Bondage. David H. Hwang. 1996. pap. 5.25 (*0-8222-1552-7*) Dramatists Play.

Trying to Get Some Dignity: Stories of Triumph over Childhood Abuse. Richard Rhodes & Ginger Rhodes. 320p. 1996. 25.00 (*0-688-14096-3*) Morrow.

Trying to Get to Heaven. Dixie Carter. 1996. pap. 12.00 (*0-684-82699-2*, Fireside) S&S Trade.

Trying to Get to Heaven: Advice from a Tennessee Talker. Dixie Carter. LC 95-32059. (Illus.). 272p. 1996. 22.00 (*0-684-80101-9*) S&S Trade.

Trying to Get Toothpaste Back Into the Tube. Lorraine Peterson. 160p. (Orig.). (J). (gr. 7-10). 1993. pap. 7.99 (*1-55661-315-6*) Bethany Hse.

Trying to Grow: A Novel on India. Firclaus Kanga. (C). 1990. 17.50 (*0-685-39102-7*, Pub. by Ravi Dayal II) S Asia.

Trying to Make Law Matter: Legal Reform & Labor Law in the Soviet Union. Kathryn Hendley. LC 95-52805. (C). 1995. 39.50 (*0-472-10605-8*) U of Mich Pr.

Trying to Remember. Tom Hanson. 80p. (Orig.). 1995. pap. 7.95 (*0-945069-04-9*) Freedom Pr Assocs.

Trying to Save Piggy Sneed. John Irving. LC 95-17756. (Illus.). 432p. 1996. 21.95 (*1-55970-323-7*) Arcade Pub Inc.

***Trying to Save Piggy Sneed.** John Irving. 1997. pap. 12.00 (*0-345-40474-2*) Ballantine.

Trying to Say It: Outlook & Insights on How Poems Happen. Phillip Booth. LC 96-11039. 1995. 39.50 (*0-472-09586-2*); pap. 13.95 (*0-472-06586-6*) U of Mich Pr.

***Trying to Sleep in Bed You Made, Vol. 1.** Deberry. 1997. mass mkt. write for info. (*0-312-96313-0*) St Martin.

Trying to Smile: And Other Stories. Sara Lewis. 192p. 1996. pap. 13.00 (*0-15-600395-3*, Harvest Bks) HarBrace.

Trying to Take Root: Sustainable Agriculture in the U. S. Heartland. Patricia M. Morris et al. (Illus.). 94p. (Orig.). 1992. pap. 15.00 (*1-881360-00-8*) Public Voice.

Trying to Understand the Lunar Eclipse. Carol Dine. LC 91-78221. 72p. (Orig.). (C). 1992. pap. 8.95 (*0-942582-17-9*) Erie St Pr.

Trying to Understand What It Means to Be a Feminist: Essays on Women Writers. Rochelle Ratner. (Chapbook Ser.). 100p. (Orig.). (C). 1983. pap. 5.00 (*0-936556-10-2*) Contact Two.

***Trying Without Willing: An Essay in the Philosophy of Mind.** Timothy Cleveland. (Series in Philosophy). 208p. 1997. text ed. 55.95 (*1-85972-674-7*, Pub. by Avebury Pub UK) Ashgate Pub Co.

Trying Work: Gender, Youth & Work Experience. Ann Stafford. (Edinburgh Education & Society Ser.). 200p. 1991. 39.00 (*0-7486-0205-4*, Pub. by Edinburgh U Pr UK) Col U Pr.

Trying Work: Gender, Youth & Work Experience. Ann Stafford. (Edinburgh Education & Society Ser.). 176p. 1992. pap. text ed. 25.00 (*0-7486-0275-5*, Pub. by Edinburgh U Pr UK) Col U Pr.

Trylon & Perisphere: The 1939-40 World's Fair. Seymour Chwast et al. (Illus.). 196p. 1989. 24.95 (*0-318-32472-5*) Abrams.

Tryon County, North Carolina, Minutes of the Court of Pleas & Quarter Sessions, 1769-1779. Brent H. Holcomb. 234p. 1994. lib. bdg. 27.50 (*0-913363-15-4*) SCMAR.

Tryon Palace Mystery. Carole Marsh. (History Mystery Ser.). (Orig.). (J). (gr. 3-12). 1994. pap. 19.95 (*0-935326-58-8*) Gallopade Pub Group.

Tryon Palace Mystery. Carole Marsh. (History Mystery Ser.). (Orig.). (J). (gr. 3-12). 1997. 29.95 (*1-55609-193-1*) Gallopade Pub Group.

***Trypanosomiasis & Leishmaniasis.** Ed. by G. Hide et al. (A CAB International Publication). 384p. 1997. 100.00 (*0-85199-139-4*, Pub. by CAB Intntl UK) OUP.

Tryst. Grace L. Hill. reprint ed. lib. bdg. 25.95 (*0-89190-050-0*, Rivercity Pr) Amereon Ltd.

Tryst, Vol. 40. Grace L. Hill. (Grace Livingston Hill Ser.: Vol. 40). 1992. pap. 5.99 (*0-8423-7340-3*) Tyndale.

Tryst with Diplomacy. S. K. Upadhaya. 1991. 60.00 (*0-7855-0298-X*, Pub. by Ratna Pustak Bhandar) St Mut.

Tryst with Diplomacy. Shailendra K. Upadhyay. 124p. 1991. text ed. 17.95 (*0-7069-5810-1*) Advent Bks Div.

Tryst with Education in the Technetronic Society. V. R. Taneja. 98p. 1984. text ed. 10.95 (*0-86590-180-5*, Pub. by Sterling Pubs II) Apt Bks.

***Tryst with Terror.** V. N. Narayanan. (C). 1996. 20.00 (*81-202-0470-0*, Pub. by Ajanta II) S Asia.

***Trysting Tree.** Catherine Anderson. mass mkt. write for info. (*0-06-108062-4*, Harp PBks) HarpC.

T.S. Eliot & Hispanic Modernity, 1924-1993. 2nd ed. Ed. by Howard Young & K. M. Sibbald. LC 94-65605. 106p. 1994. pap. 25.00 (*0-89295-075-7*) Society Sp & Sp-Am.

T.S. Eliot & the Heritage of Africa: The Magus & the Moor as Metaphor. Robert F. Fleissner. LC 91-37697. (American University Studies: English Language & Literature: Ser. IV, Vol. 143). 255p. (C). 1992. text ed. 46.95 (*0-8204-1800-5*) P Lang Pubng.

***T.S. Eliot, Anti-Semitism & Literary Form: Anti-Semitism & Literary Form.** Anthony Julius. 322p. 1996. pap. text ed. 18.95 (*0-521-58673-9*) Cambridge U Pr.

T.S. Eliot As Editor. Shahid A. Agha. Ed. by A. Walton Litz. LC 86-1263. (Studies in Modern Literature: No. 60). 183p. reprint ed. 52.20 (*0-8357-1751-8*, 2070491) Bks Demand.

T.S. Eliot's Poems in French Translation: Pierre Leyris & Others. Joan F. Hooker. Ed. by A. Walton Litz. LC 83-9246. (Studies in Modern Literature: No. 26). 344p. reprint ed. 98.10 (*0-8357-1456-X*, 2070588) Bks Demand.

TSA Manual Release 1. J. D. Henstridge. 165p. (Orig.). 1982. pap. 13.72 (*0-317-52235-3*, Pub. by Numer Algo UK) Numer Algorithms.

***Tsaj Mo Ntuj (Hmong)** Tr. by Yer J. Thao. (J). (gr. k-3). 1995. write for info. (*1-57842-059-8*) Delmas Creat.

***Tsaj Nyob Tsua Huv Dlej Hav TXWV (Hmong)** Tr. by Yer J. Thao. (J). (gr. k-3). 1995. write for info. (*1-57842-063-6*) Delmas Creat.

***Tsaj Txhu Nyob Tsua Ntsua Dleg (Hmong)** Tr. by Yer J. Thao. (J). (gr. k-3). 1994. write for info. (*1-57842-012-1*) Delmas Creat.

Tsalagi. Carroll Arnett. 1976. pap. 5.00 (*0-685-79197-1*) Elizabeth Pr.

Tsali. Denton R. Bedford. LC 72-91136. (Illus.). 256p. 1972. pap. 15.00 (*0-913436-24-0*) Indian Hist Pr.

***Tsali's Hatchet.** Midge Shusta. 561p. (Orig.). 1997. mass mkt. 5.99 (*1-55197-828-8*, Pub. by Comnwlth Pub CN) Partners Pubs Grp.

Ts'ao Chung Weighs an Elephant. Lyndell Ludwig. LC 82-73197. (Illus.). 48p. (Orig.). (J). (ps-1). 1983. pap. 4.95 (*0-916870-52-9*) Star Dust Bks.

Ts'ao Yin & the K'Ang-Hsi Emperor: Bondservant & Master. Jonathan D. Spence. LC 87-51374. 352p. (C). 1988. 19.00 (*0-300-04278-7*); text ed. 45.00 (*0-300-04277-9*) Yale U Pr.

Ts'ao Yu, the Reluctant Disciple of Chekhov & O'Neill: A Study in Literary Influence. Joseph L. Siu-ming. 96p. (C). 1979. pap. text ed. 30.00 (*0-85656-005-7*, Pub. by Hong Kong U Pr HK) St Mut.

Tsar: The Lost World of Nicholas & Alexandra. Peter Kurth. LC 95-12820. (Illus.). 229p. 1995. 60.00 (*0-316-50787-3*) Bulfinch Pr.

Tsar Alexander I: Paternalistic Reformer. Allen McConnell. LC 70-101949. (Europe since 1500 Ser.). 240p. (C). 1970. pap. text ed. write for info. (*0-88295-745-7*) Harlan Davidson.

Tsar Alexis, His Reign & His Russia. Joseph T. Fuhrman. (Russian Ser.: No. 34). 1981. 25.00 (*0-87569-040-8*) Academic Intl.

Tsar Maksimilian. Aleksei M. Remizov. 128p. (RUS.). 1988. reprint ed. pap. 8.00 (*0-933884-55-9*) Berkeley Slavic.

Tsar Paul & the Question of Madness: An Essay in History & Psychology. Hugh Ragsdale. LC 88-24677. (Contributions to the Study of World History Ser.: No. 13). 284p. 1988. text ed. 59.95 (*0-313-26608-5*, RTS/, Greenwood Pr) Greenwood.

Tsardom of Moscow, Fifteen Forty-Seven to Sixteen Eighty-Two, Pt. 1. George Vernadsky. LC 43-1903. (History of Russia Ser.: Vol. 5). reprint ed. pap. 125.00 (*0-317-10883-2*, 2022048) Bks Demand.

Tsardom of Moscow, Fifteen Forty-Seven to Sixteen Eighty-Two, Pt. 2. George Vernadsky. LC 43-1903. (History of Russia Ser.: Vol. 5). reprint ed. pap. 102.50 (*0-317-10884-0*) Bks Demand.

Tsardom of Muscovy. Alexander E. Presniakov. Ed. & Tr. by R. F. Price. 1978. pap. 15.00 (*0-87569-090-4*) Academic Intl.

Tsarist Russia & Balkan Nationalism: Russian Influence in International Affairs of Bulgaria & Serbia, 1879-1886. Charles Jelavich. LC 77-26080. (Russian & East European Studies Ser.). (Illus.). 304p. 1978. reprint ed. 59.75 (*0-313-20085-8*, JETR) Greenwood.

Tsarist Secret Police & Russian Society, 1880-1917. Frederic S. Zuckerman. 400p. (C). 1996. 50.00 (*0-8147-9673-7*) NYU Pr.

Tsars & the Jews: Reform, Reaction, & Antisemitism in Imperial Russia, 1772-1917 (Antisemitismus und Reaktion Are Utopie. Heinz-Dietrich Lowe. LC 92-25147. 456p. (ENG & GER.). 1993. text ed. 75.00 (*3-7186-5289-7*) Gordon & Breach.

Tsar's Lieutenant: The Soviet Marshall. Thomas G. Butson. LC 84-47410. 224p. 1984. text ed. 29.95 (*0-275-91735-5*, C1735, Praeger Pubs) Greenwood.

Tsar's Loyal German: The Riga German Community, Social Change & the Nationality Question, 1855-1905. Anders Henriksson. 218p. 1983. text ed. 52.50 (*0-88033-020-1*) East Eur Monographs.

Tsar's Viceroys: Russian Provincial Governors in the Last Years of the Empire. Richard G. Robbins, Jr. LC 87-47700. 328p. 1987. 42.50 (*0-8014-2046-6*) Cornell U Pr.

Tsar's Window. Lucy H. Hooper. LC 74-164566. (American Fiction Reprint Ser.). 1977. reprint ed. 25.95 (*0-8369-7043-8*) Ayer.

Tsava't Ha-Rivash. 190p. 14.00 (*0-8266-5459-2*) Kehot Pubn Soc.

TSCA Compliance Handbook. Randolph L. Chrisman. (Environmental Compliance Handbook Ser.: Vol. 4). 1989. pap. 32.50 (*1-55840-108-3*) Exec Ent Pubns.

TSCA Compliance Handbook. 3rd ed. Ginger L. Griffin. LC 96-17529. (Environmental Compliance Handbook Ser.). 1996. pap. text ed. 54.95 (*0-471-16227-2*) Wiley.

***TSCA Handbook.** 3rd rev. ed. McKenna & Cuneo. 566p. 1997. pap. text ed. 95.00 (*0-86587-566-9*, 566) Gov Insts.

TSCA Inspection Guidance. Environmental Protection Agency Staff. 400p. 1993. pap. text ed. 89.00 (*0-86587-358-5*) Gov Insts.

TSCA's Impact on Society & Chemical Industry. Ed. by George W. Ingle. LC 83-2733. (Symposium Ser.: No. 213). 244p. 1983. lib. bdg. 38.95 (*0-8412-0766-6*) Am Chemical.

***TSCA's Impact on Society & Chemical Industry.** Ed. by George W. Ingle. LC 83-2733. (ACS Symposium Ser.: No. 213). (Illus.). 255p. 1983. reprint ed. pap. 72.70 (*0-608-03212-3*, 2063731) Bks Demand.

Tschiffely's Ride. A. F. Tschiffely. 1976. lib. bdg. 250.00 (*0-8490-2777-2*) Gordon Pr.

Tschudy: History & Genealogy of the Judy-Judah-Tschudy-Tschudin Family Who Have Lived in America, Switzerland & Other Countries of the World, Including Connected Families. M. P. Carlock. (Illus.). 576p. 1992. reprint ed. pap. 86.00 (*0-8328-2511-5*); reprint ed. lib. bdg. 96.00 (*0-8328-2510-7*) Higginson Bk Co.

Tse Ya Kin see Understanding the Anasazi of Mesa Verde & Hovenweep

Tseng Kuo-Fan's Private Bureaucracy. Jonathan Porter. LC 72-619560. (China Research Monographs: No. 9). 148p. 1972. pap. 2.50 (*0-912966-10-6*) IEAS.

Tsentral'nyi Gosudarstvennyi Arkhiv Sovetskii Armii Putevoditel'v Dvukh Tomakh, Tom I. Rossiiskii G. Arkhiv. Ed. by T. F. Kariaveva & M. V. Stegantsev. 422p. (RUS.). 1991. 59.95 (*1-879944-02-2*) East View Pubns.

Tsentral'nyi Gosudarstvennyi Arkhiv Sovetskii Armii, Putevoditel'v Dvukh Tomakh, Tom II. Rossiiskii G. Arkhiv. Ed. by T. F. Kariaveva & M. V. Stegantsev. 531p. (RUS.). 1993. 59.95 (*1-879944-03-0*) East View Pubns.

Tsereteli: A Democrat in the Russian Revolution. Roobol. (Studies in Social History: No. 1). 1977. lib. bdg. 123.50 (*90-247-1915-1*) Kluwer Ac.

Tserkov' Boga Ahivago, Stolp i Utverzhdjenije Istini. Archpriest Kyrill Zaits. 92p. 1956. pap. 2.00 (*0-317-29113-0*) Holy Trinity.

Tserkov', Rus' i Rim. N. N. Voieikvov. 512p. 1983. text ed. 25.00 (*0-88465-016-2*); pap. text ed. 20.00 (*0-88465-015-4*) Holy Trinity.

Tserkovno-Pjevcheskiji Sbornik, 5 Vols., Set. Incl. Vol. 1. Vsjenoshchnoje Bdjenije-All Night Vigil. 394p. 27.00 (*0-317-30454-2*); Pt. 1. Bozhestvjennaja Liturgija (Nachjalo)-Divine Liturgy (Beginning). 381p. 26.00 (*0-317-30455-0*); Pt. 2. Bozhestvjennaja Liturgija (Konjets)-Divine Liturgy (End). 621p. 33.00 (*0-317-30456-9*); Pt. 1. Triod' Postnaja-Lenten Triodion. 532p. 31.00 (*0-317-30457-7*); Pt. 2. Strastnaja Sedmitsa-Passion Week. 1059p. 40.00 (*0-317-30458-5*); Vol. 4. Triod' Tsvjetnaja-Pentacostarion. 680p. 33.00 (*0-317-30459-3*); Vol. 5. Oktojikh-Octoechos. 421p. 26.00 (*0-317-30460-7*); 216.00 (*0-317-30453-4*) Holy Trinity.

Tsewa's Gift: Magic & Meaning in an Amazonian Society. Michael F. Brown. LC 85-40401. (Series in Ethnographic Inquiry). (Illus.). 220p. 1986. text ed. 32.00 (*0-87474-294-3*, BRTG) Smithsonian.

Tsewa's Gift: Magic & Meaning in an Amazonian Society. Michael F. Brown. LC 85-40401. (Series in Ethnographic Inquiry). (Illus.). 220p. (C). 1993. reprint ed. pap. text ed. 14.95 (*1-56098-306-X*) Smithsonian.

TSFR: The Taoist Way to Total Sexual Fitness for Men. Bruce M. Wong. 80p. 1982. pap. 9.95 (*0-910295-00-X*) Golden Dragon Pub.

Tshi-Speaking Peoples of the Gold Coast of West Africa. Alfred B. Ellis. 1964. 25.00 (*0-910216-02-9*) Benin.

TSHR Universal Spinal Implementation. C. E. Johnston, II et al. 200p. 1993. text ed. write for info. (*0-9635430-1-6*) Hundley & Assocs.

T'shuva. Carolyn K. Paul. 240p. (Orig.). 1996. pap. 10.95 (*0-89407-115-7*) Strawberry Hill.

Tsimshian: Images of the Past, Views for the Present. Ed. by Margaret Seguin. LC 93-15996. 364p. 1993. reprint ed. Acid-free paper. 22.50 (*0-295-97311-0*) U of Wash Pr.

Tsimshian: Their Arts & Music. Viola E. Garfield et al. LC 84-4549. (American Ethnological Society Publications: No. 18). reprint ed. 45.00 (*0-404-58168-4*) AMS Pr.

Tsimshian & Their Neighbors of the North Pacific Coast. Ed. by Jay Miller & Carol M. Eastman. LC 83-28364. (Illus.). 366p. 1985. 40.00 (*0-295-96126-0*) U of Wash Pr.

***Tsimshian Culture: A Light Through the Ages.** Jay Miller. LC 96-35895. (Illus.). xvi, 204p. 1997. text ed. 45.00 (*0-8032-3192-X*) U of Nebr Pr.

Tsimshian Narratives No. 2: Trade & Warfare. Ed. by George F. MacDonald & John J. Cove. (Mercury Ser.: No. 3, Pt. 2). (Illus.). 244p. 1987. pap. 19.95 (*0-660-10770-8*, Pub. by Can Mus Civil CN) U of Wash Pr.

Tsimshian Texts. Franz Boas. (Bureau of American Ethnology Bulletins Ser.). 244p. 1995. lib. bdg. 89.00 (*0-7812-4027-1*) Rprt Serv.

Tsimshian Texts. Franz Boas. LC 90-44636. 244p. 1990. reprint ed. pap. 29.00 (*1-878592-16-5*); reprint ed. lib. bdg. 49.00 (*1-878592-15-7*) Native Amer Bk Pubs.

***Tsing Hua Lectures on Geometry & Analysis.** Ed. by Shing-Tung Yau. 300p. (C). 1997. 42.00 (*1-57146-042-X*) Intl Pr Boston.

Tsippi. Maurice Sendak. (J). 1994. 10.95 (*0-694-00615-7*, Festival) HarpC Child Bks.

Tsirelson's Space. P. G. Casazza & T. J. Shura. (Lecture Notes in Mathematics Ser.: Vol. 1363). 204p. 1989. pap. 21.10 (*0-318-41335-3*) Spr-Verlag.

TSO - E CLISTs: The Complete Tutorial & Desk Reference. Charles H. Rider. 1993. text ed. 45.00 (*0-471-58809-1*, GD4078) Wiley.

Tso Chuan: Selections from China's Oldest Narrative History. Tr. by Burton Watson from CHI. (Translations from the Asian Classics Ser.). 267p. (C). 1992. pap. 15.50 (*0-231-06715-1*) Col U Pr.

Tso Tsung T'ang: Soldier & Statesman of Old China. W. I. Bales. 1972. lib. bdg. 250.00 (*0-87968-475-5*) Krishna Pr.

***Tsoek: Earthy Writings by a Four-Paw.** Nelleke Nix & Tsoek. (Illus.). 50p. 1996. 95.00 (*1-881067-10-6*); pap. 95.00 (*1-881067-09-2*) N Nelleke Studio.

TSOHAR. Rabbi Nachman of Breslov. Tr. by Avraham Greenbaum from HEB. 64p. (Orig.). 1986. pap. text ed. 3.00 (*0-930213-26-2*) Breslov Res Inst.

Tsonakwa & Yolaikia: Legends in Stone, Bone, & Wood. Ed. by Jo West. (Illus.). 64p. (Orig.). 1986. pap. write for info. (*0-938541-03-X*) Origins Program.

Tsongkhapa's Six Yogas of Naropa. Tsongkhapa L. Drakpa. (Illus.). 30p. 1996. pap. 18.95 (*1-55939-058-1*) Snow Lion Pubns.

***TSOT. COM-Articles: Book of Articles, Ultimate Knowledge.** abr. ed. Harry S. Miller. (Illus.). 250p. (Orig.). Date not set. pap. 29.00 (*0-9657604-2-1*) Uniscience Educ.

TSQL2 Temporal Query Language. Richard T. Snodgrass. LC 95-30806. (International Series in Engineering & Computer Science: SECS 330). 704p. (C). 1995. lib. bdg. 205.00 (*0-7923-9614-6*) Kluwer Ac.

TSR Hotline. Lee R. Van Vechten. (Illus.). 200p. 1993. ring bd. 149.00 (*1-879644-04-5*) Direct Mktg.

T/S/R Towers, Inc. A General Office Assistant. Taylor & Ransbottom. (KM - Office Procedures Ser.). 1982. pap. 14.95 (*0-538-25500-5*) S-W Pub.

Tsubo: Vital Points for Oriental Therapy. Katsusuke Serizawa. (Illus.). 256p. 1976. 29.00 (*0-87040-350-8*) Japan Pubns USA.

Tsubu, the Little Snail. Carol Williams. LC 93-49344. (Illus.). (J). 1995. 15.00 (*0-671-87167-6*, S&S Bks Young Read) S&S Childrens.

Tsuda Umeko & Women's Education in Japan. Barbara Rose. (Illus.). 224p. 1992. text ed. 30.00 (*0-300-05177-8*) Yale U Pr.

Tsuen-Wan Township: Study Group Report on Its Development. Gerald Moore. 47p. reprint ed. pap. 25.00 (*0-317-11282-1*, 2017719) Bks Demand.

Tsuga Canadensis & Related Species. John C. Swartley. (Illus.). 1977. 15.00 (*0-913728-28-4*) Theophrastus.

Tsukemono: Japanese Pickled Vegetables. Kay Shimizu. (Illus.). 96p. 1993. bds. 27.00 (*0-87040-910-7*) Japan Pubns USA.

***Tsun & the Rats, Vol. 3.** John Vornholt. (Warriors of Virtue Ser.: No. 3). 112p. 1997. mass mkt. 3.99 (*1-57297-285-8*) Blvd Books.

Tsunami! Walter C. Dudley & Min Lee. LC 87-19070. (Illus.). 152p. 1988. pap. 12.95 (*0-8248-1125-9*, Kolowalu Bk) UH Pr.

Tsunami: Progress in Prediction, Disaster Prevention & Warning. Ed. by Yoshito Tsuchiya & Nobuo Shuto. LC 95-10782. (Advances in Natural & Technological Hazards Research Ser.: Vol. 4). 368p. (C). 1995. lib. bdg. 193.00 (*0-7923-3483-3*) Kluwer Ac.

Tsunami Hazard: A Practical Guide for Tsunami Hazard Reduction. Ed. by E. N. Bernard. (C). 1991. lib. bdg. 113.50 (*0-7923-1174-4*) Kluwer Ac.

Tsunami Years. Juliet S. Kono. LC 95-10306. (Bamboo Ridge Ser.: Nos. 65-66). 173p. 1995. pap. 10.00 (*0-910043-35-3*) Bamboo Ridge Pr.

Tsunamis: Their Science & Engineering. Ed. by T. Iwasaki & K. Iida. 1983. lib. bdg. 304.00 (*90-277-1611-0*) Kluwer Ac.

***Tsunamis Affecting Alaska 1737-1996.** James F. Lander. (Illus.). 195p. (Orig.). (C). 1997. pap. text ed. 40.00 (*0-7881-3933-9*) DIANE Pub.

***Tsunamis Affecting the West Coast of the United States 1806-1992.** James Lander et al. (Illus.). 242p. (C). 1997. reprint ed. pap. text ed. 50.00 (*0-7881-3934-7*) DIANE Pub.

Tsunamis in the World: Proceedings of the Fifteenth International Tsunami Symposium, Held in Vienna, Austria, 1991. Ed. by Stefano Tinti. LC 93-13341. (Advances in Natural & Technological Hazards Research Ser.: Vol. 1). 236p. (C). 1993. lib. bdg. 100.00 (*0-7923-2316-5*) Kluwer Ac.

Tsunamis: 1992-1994: Their Generation, Dynamics, & Hazards. Ed. by Kenji Satake & Fumihiko Imamura. LC 95-38183. 1995. reprint ed. 42.50 (*3-7643-5102-0*) Birkhauser.

Tsunamis: 1992-1994: Their Generation, Dynamics, & Hazards. Ed. by Kenji Satake & Fumihiko Imamura. LC 95-38183. 890p. 1995. reprint ed. pap. 42.50 (*0-8176-5102-0*, GC221) Birkhauser.

Tsung-Mi & the Sinification of Buddhism. Peter N. Gregory. (Illus.). 381p. 1991. text ed. 57.50 (*0-691-07373-2*) Princeton U Pr.

Tsungli Yamen: Its Organization & Functions. S. M. Meng. LC 62-53393. (East Asian Monographs: No. 13). 151p. 1962. pap. 11.00 (*0-674-91095-8*) HUP.

Tsuni-Ilgoam. Theophilus Hahn. LC 70-164388. (Black Heritage Library Collection). 1977. reprint ed. 20.95 (*0-8369-8847-7*) Ayer.

Tsuru-Nyobo see Crane Wife

Tsuruya Kokei: Kabuki Actor Prints. (Illus.). 104p. 1988. pap. 25.00 (*0-685-66769-3*) Pacific Asia.

***Tsuta: A Joy Forever.** Richard J. Walsh, Jr. 90p. (Orig.). 1996. pap. 15.95 (*1-882063-39-2*, Heritage Hse) Cottage Pr MA.

Tsutsugamushi Disease: An Overview. Ed. by Akiyoshi Kawamura, Jr. 361p. 1996. 120.00 (*0-86008-512-0*) Col U Pr.

Tsvet Vereska. Natalia Gorbanevskaia. LC 93-29452. 114p. (Orig.). (RUS.). 1993. pap. 9.00 (*1-55779-067-1*) Hermitage.

Tsvetaeva. Viktoria Schweitzer. 413p. 1995. pap. 14.00 (*0-374-52402-5*) FS&G.

Tsvetaeva. annot. ed. Viktoria Schweitzer. Ed. by Angela Livingstone. Tr. by Robert Chandler et al. from RUS. 1993. 35.00 (*0-374-27945-4*) FS&G.

Tswana. Isaac Schapera. 112p. 1985. pap. 19.95 (*0-7103-0096-4*) Routledge Chapman & Hall.

Tsymbaly Maker & His Craft: The Ukrainian Hammered Dulcimer in Alberta. Mark J. Bandera. 74p. pap. 14.95 (*0-920862-80-2*) Ukrainian Acad.

TTL & CMOS Circuits. Heath Company Staff. (Circuit Files Ser.). (Illus.). 124p. ring bd. 59.95 (*0-87119-001-X*, EH-702) Heathkit-Zenith Ed.

TTL Logic Data Book. Texas Instruments Engineering Staff. 1246p. 1988. 19.95 (*0-685-62489-7*, SDLD001A) Tex Instr Inc.

TTS Blue Book Quarterlies. Transportation Technical Services Staff. 102p. Date not set. pap. text ed. 150.00 (*1-880701-07-3*) Trans Tech Srvs.

TTS Contract Carrier & Routing Directory. Date not set. pap. text ed. 145.00 (*1-880701-17-0*) Trans Tech Srvs.

***TTT - God's Little Instruction.** 7.40 (*1-56292-199-1*); 7.40 (*1-56292-206-8*); 7.40 (*1-56292-200-9*) Honor Bks OK.

***TTT - God's Little Instruction, Vol. II.** 7.40 (*1-56292-207-6*) Honor Bks OK.

Tu. Cid Corman. LC 83-15814. 35p. (Orig.). 1983. pap. 12.50 (*0-915124-79-3*, Toothpaste) Coffee Hse.

Tu' A Moving Collection of Romantic Poetry. Armando De Peralta et al. Ed. by Marilyn A. Ward. LC 85-73610. (Illus.). 90p. 1986. 14.95 (*0-938727-00-1*) Scorpio Pr.

***Tu Andar Diario.** 446p. (SPA.). 1991. write for info. (*0-614-27148-7*) Editorial Unilit.

***Tu Andar Diario.** 446p. (SPA.). 1991. pap. write for info. (*0-614-27150-9*) Editorial Unilit.

Tu Andar Diario. Walk Through Staff. (SPA.). 1994. 14.99 (*1-56063-681-5*, 497550); pap. 9.99 (*1-56063-557-6*, 498550) Editorial Unilit.

Tu-Be or Not Tu-Be: Sit-Calm Spirituality. A. E. Amber. (Illus.). 100p. (Orig.). 1988. pap. write for info. (*0-9621282-0-1*) Jester Ink.

Tu Bishvat. Norma Simon. (Festival Series of Picture Storybooks). (Illus.). (J). (ps). 1961. spiral bd. 4.50 (*0-8381-0709-5*) USCJE.

Tu Cours Apres l'Ete, et l'Hiver... Charles M. Schulz. (Peanuts Ser.). (FRE.). (J). 1985. 9.95 (*0-8288-4535-2*) Fr & Eur.

Tu Cours apres l'Ete, et l'Hiver te Rattrape. Charles M. Schulz. LC 81-85099. 128p. (FRE.). 1982. pap. 5.95 (*0-03-061651-4*, Owl) H Holt & Co.

Tu Cuerpo: El Aprendizaje A Traves el Cuerpo y los Sentidos. Paula Kline. 160p. 1993. teacher ed. 24.00 incl. audio (*0-9637958-0-5*) Inst Promo Educ.

Tu Diras. John R. Gutierrez et al. (College Spanish Ser.). (ENG & SPA.). 1996. wbk. ed., pap. 36.95 (*0-8384-5788-6*) Heinle & Heinle.

Tu Diras. Harry L. Rosser. (College Spanish Ser.). (SPA.). 1995. student ed., wbk. ed. 15.95 incl. 3.5 hd, 5.25 hd, 3.5 ld (*0-8384-6007-0*); wbk. ed. 15.95 incl. mac hd, mac ld (*0-8384-5789-4*) Heinle & Heinle.

Tu Diras. Harry L. Rosser. (College Spanish Ser.). (SPA.). 1995. text ed. 55.95 incl. audio (*0-8384-6003-8*) Heinle & Heinle.

Tu Diras. Harry L. Rosser. (College Spanish Ser.). (SPA.). 1995. 55.95 incl. cd-rom (*0-8384-6004-6*) Heinle & Heinle.

Tu Diras. Harry L. Rosser. (College Spanish Ser.). (SPA.). 1996. suppl. ed., pap. 34.95 (*0-8384-5997-8*); pap. 0.95 (*0-8384-6001-1*) Heinle & Heinle.

Tu Diras. Harry L. Rosser. (College Spanish Ser.). (SPA.). 1996. pap. 13.95 (*0-8384-6152-2*) Heinle & Heinle.

Tu Diras. Harry L. Rosser. (College Spanish Ser.). (SPA.). 1995. suppl. ed., pap. 18.95 (*0-8384-5806-8*) Heinle & Heinle.

Tu Diras. annot. ed. Harry L. Rosser. (College Spanish Ser.). (SPA.). 1995. teacher ed., text ed. 56.95 (*0-8384-5787-8*) Heinle & Heinle.

Tu Diras! Introduction al la Lengua y Cultura Hispanicas. John R. Gutierrez et al. LC 94-28580. (ENG & SPA.). 1995. text ed. 57.95 (*0-8384-5786-X*) Heinle & Heinle.

Tu Diras: Practica Gramatical. Harry L. Rosser. (College Spanish Ser.). 1996. pap. 0.95 (*0-8384-7240-0*) Heinle & Heinle.

Tu Es dans le Vent, Charlie Brown. Charles M. Schulz. 128p. (FRE.). 1972. pap. 1.50 (*0-03-086657-X*, Owl) H Holt & Co.

Tu Es le Plus Beau, Charlie Brown. Charles M. Schulz. (FRE.). 1974. pap. 1.50 (*0-03-089255-4*, Owl) H Holt & Co.

Tu Estadia en el Hospital...Va a Ser Muy Buena. James M. Sorg. (Illus.). 36p. (Orig.). (SPA.). (J). (ps-5). 1988. pap. 4.95 (*0-9622172-2-0*) D Miller Fndtn.

Tu estais Si Gentil Quand Tu Etais Petit see Pieces Secretes

Tu Etais Si Gentil Quand Tu etais Petit. Jean Anouilh. 160p. 1973. pap. 9.95 (*0-7859-0354-2*, F81900) Fr & Eur.

Tu Hijo, Tu Amigo. V. Gilbert Beers. 176p. (Orig.). (SPA.). 1990. pap. 4.95 (*0-88113-249-7*) Edit Betania.

***Tu Hoc Trinh Bay Cac Trang Web: Build Your Own Web Pages.** Dung Q. Vu. (Illus.). xx, 180p. (VIE.). 1997. pap. 24.95 (*0-9654744-2-9*) VNI.

***Tu Lado.** B. J. James. (SPA.). 1997. mass mkt. 3.50 (*0-373-35190-9*, 1-35190-7) Harlequin Bks.

***Tu Mama Es una Llama?** Deborah Guarino. 1997. 6.99 (*0-590-38176-8*) Scholastic Inc.

Tu Mama es una Llama? Is Your Mama a Llama? Deborah Guarino. 32p. (SPA.). (J). (ps-3). 1993. pap. 4.99 (*0-590-46275-X*) Scholastic Inc.

Tu Ne T'Aimes Pas. Nathalie Sarraute. (FRE.). 1991. pap. 10.95 (*0-7859-2928-2*) Fr & Eur.

Tu Ne Tueras Point see Thou Shall Not Kill

Tu N'En Reviendras Pas, Charlie Brown. Charles M. Schulz. (FRE.). 1972. pap. 1.50 (*0-03-086658-8*, Owl) H Holt & Co.

Tu Nueva Vida. Ramon A. Madero. (Serie Realidades - Realities Ser.). 36p. (SPA.). 1989. pap. 1.79 (*1-56063-005-1*, 498109) Editorial Unilit.

Tu Parles Francais? Gillian Taylor. 1983. pap. text ed. 7.80 (*0-582-22324-5*, 70917); 22.61 (*0-582-22354-7*, 70919) Longman.

Tu Puedes! James D. Freeman. LC 82-70490. 256p. 1982. 6.95 (*0-87159-158-8*) Unity Bks.

***Tu Puedes Cambiar Al Mundo - You Can Change the World.** Johnstone. 126p. (SPA.). (J). write for info. (*1-56063-726-9*) Editorial Unilit.

Tu Puedes Dejar de Preocuparte. Jay E. Adams. 24p. (SPA.). 1992. pap. 1.50 (*1-56063-147-3*, 490481) Editorial Unilit.

Tu Puedes Dejar de Sentirte Culpable. William Caldwell. Orig. Title: You Can Stop Feeling Guilty. (SPA.). 1992. 1.50 (*1-56063-154-6*, 490488) Editorial Unilit.

***Tu Puedes Dejar de Sentirte Culpable.** William Caldwell. 24p. (SPA.). 1992. pap. write for info. (*0-614-27149-5*) Editorial Unilit.

Tu Puedes Derrotar la Ira. Jay E. Adams. (SPA.). 1982. 1.50 (*1-56063-148-1*, 490482) Editorial Unilit.

***Tu Puedes Derrotar la Ira.** Jay E. Adams. 24p. (SPA.). 1982. pap. write for info. (*0-614-27151-7*) Editorial Unilit.

Tu Puedes Endulzar Tu Amargo Matrimonio. Jay E. Adams. 24p. (SPA.). 1982. pap. 1.50 (*1-56063-149-X*, 490483) Editorial Unilit.

Tu Puedes Enfrentar el Sufrimiento. Luis Caldwell. 24p. (SPA.). 1982. pap. 1.50 (*1-56063-155-4*, 490489) Editorial Unilit.

Tu Puedes Evitar el Divorcio. Paul Meier. 24p. (SPA.). pap. 1.50 (*1-56063-156-2*, 490490) Editorial Unilit.

Tu Puedes Librarte del Habito de las Drogas. Jay E. Adams. 24p. (SPA.). 1982. pap. 1.50 (*1-56063-150-3*, 490484) Editorial Unilit.

Tu Puedes Recobrar el Gozo. Andres W. Blackwood. 24p. (SPA.). 1982. pap. 1.50 (*1-56063-153-8*, 490487) Editorial Unilit.

Tu Puedes Ser Biologa Marina. Florence McAlary & Judith L. Cohen. Tr. by Juan Yanez from ENG. (Illus.). 40p. (SPA.). (J). (gr. 4-7). 1992. pap. 6.00 (*1-880599-07-4*) Cascade Pass.

Tu Puedes Ser una Arquitecta. Judith L. Cohen & Margot Siegel. Tr. by Juan Yanez from ENG. (Illus.). 40p. (Orig.). (SPA.). (J). (gr. 4-7). 1992. pap. 7.00 (*1-880599-05-8*) Cascade Pass.

Tu Puedes Ser una Egiptologa. Betsy Bryan & Judith Cohen. Tr. by Juan Yanez from ENG. (Illus.). 40p. (SPA.). (J). (gr. 4-7). 1993. pap. 7.00 (*1-880599-11-2*) Cascade Pass.

Tu Puedes Ser una Ingeniera. Judith L. Cohen. Tr. by Juan Yanez from ENG. (Illus.). 40p. (Orig.). (SPA.). (J). (gr. 4-7). 1992. pap. 7.00 (*1-880599-03-1*) Cascade Pass.

Tu Puedes Ser una Zoologa. Judith L. Cohen & Valerie Thompson. Tr. by Juan Yanez. (Illus.). 40p. (SPA.). (J). (gr. 4-7). 1993. pap. 7.00 (*1-880599-09-0*) Cascade Pass.

Tu Puedes Superar el Temor. Jay E. Adams. 24p. (SPA.). 1982. pap. 1.50 (*1-56063-151-1*, 490485) Editorial Unilit.

Tu Puedes Vencer la Depresion. Jay E. Adams. 24p. (SPA.). 1982. pap. 1.50 (*1-56063-152-X*, 490486) Editorial Unilit.

Tu Puedos Ser una Oceanografa. Sharon Franks & Judith Cohen. Tr. by Juan Yanez. (Illus.). 40p. (SPA.). (J). (gr. 3-6). 1994. pap. 7.00 (*1-880599-15-5*) Cascade Pass.

Tu Te Crois Malin, Charlie Brown. Charles M. Schulz. (Peanuts Ser.). (FRE.). (J). 1985. 4.95 (*0-8288-4522-0*) Fr & Eur.

Tu Veux Rire, Charlie Brown. Charles M. Schulz. (Peanuts Ser.). (FRE.). (J). 1985. 4.95 (*0-8288-4524-7*) Fr & Eur.

Tu y Tu Dinero. Malcolm MacGregor & Stanley G. Baldwin. 160p. (SPA.). 1984. 3.95 (*0-88113-369-8*) Edit Betania.

Tu y Yo Para Siempre. Wally DeSmet. 144p. (Orig.). (SPA.). 1991. student ed. 5.95 (*0-88113-092-3*) Edit Betania.

Tu-16 Badger in Action. Richard Bock. (Aircraft in Action Ser.). (Illus.). 50p. 1990. pap. 7.95 (*0-89747-252-7*, 1108) Squad Sig Pubns.

Tuala Speaks. Tuala. Ed. by Jeanne Tamalelagi. LC 80-67870. 220p. (Orig.). 1980. pap. 8.95 (*0-87516-425-0*) DeVorss.

Tuamatuan Stone Structures. Kenneth P. Emory. (BMB Ser.). 1974. reprint ed. 25.00 (*0-527-02224-1*) Periodicals Srv.

Tuamotuan Legends (Island of Anaa), Pt. 1: The Demigods. J. F. Stimson. (BMB Ser.). 1974. reprint ed. 25.00 (*0-527-02256-X*) Periodicals Srv.

Tuamotuan Religion. J. F. Stimson. (BMB Ser.). 1974. reprint ed. 25.00 (*0-527-02209-8*) Periodicals Srv.

Tuamotuan Religious Structures & Ceremonies. Kenneth P. Emory. (BMB Ser.). 1974. reprint ed. 25.00 (*0-527-02299-3*) Periodicals Srv.

Tuan. Eva Boholm-Olsson. Tr. by Dianne Jonasson. (Illus.). 32p. (J). (ps up). 1988. 11.95 (*91-29-58766-2*, Pub. by R & S Bks) FS&G.

***Tuareg.** Victor Englebert. Date not set. write for info. (*0-688-13435-1*); lib. bdg. write for info. (*0-688-13436-X*) Lothrop.

Tuaregs: The Blue People. Karl G. Prasse. (Illus.). 136p. 1995. 34.00 (*87-7289-313-3*, Pub. by Mus Tusculanum DK) Paul & Co Pubs.

Tuatara. Jenny E. Tesar. LC 94-27857. (What on Earth Is...? Ser). 32p. (J). (gr. 2-5). 1994. lib. bdg. 14.95 (*1-56711-092-4*) Blackbirch.

Tub Grandfather. Pam Conrad. LC 92-31770. (Laura Geringer Bk.). (Illus.). 32p. (J). (ps-3). 1993. 15.00 (*0-06-022895-4*); lib. bdg. 14.89 (*0-06-022896-2*) HarpC Child Bks.

Tub Grandfather. Pam Conrad. LC 92-31770. (Laura Geringer Bk.). (Illus.). 32p. (J). (gr. k-3). 1996. pap. 5.95 (*0-06-443469-9*, Trophy) HarpC Child Bks.

Tub People. Pam Conrad. LC 88-32804. (Laura Geringer Bk.). (Illus.). 32p. (J). (ps-3). 1989. 15.00 (*0-06-021340-X*); lib. bdg. 14.89 (*0-06-021341-8*) HarpC Child Bks.

Tub People. Pam Conrad. LC 88-32804. (Laura Geringer Bk.). (Illus.). 32p. (J). (ps-3). 1995. pap. 4.95 (*0-06-443306-4*, Trophy) HarpC Child Bks.

***Tub People.** Pam Conrad. 32p. (J). 1996. pap. 7.95 incl. digital audio (*0-694-70058-4*) HarpC.

Tub Time see Homeplay: Joyful Learning for Children & Adults, Series I

Tub Time for Harry. Jesus Gaban. (Harry the Hippo Ser.). (Illus.). 16p. (J). (ps-1). 1992. lib. bdg. 17.27 (*0-8368-0718-9*) Gareth Stevens Inc.

Tuba. (Standard of Excellence Ser.: Bk. 1). 1993. 6.45 (*0-8497-5942-0*, W21BS) Kjos.

Tuba. (Standard of Excellence Ser.: Bk. 2). 1993. 6.45 (*0-8497-5967-6*, W22BS) Kjos.

Tuba. Bruce Pearson. (Standard of Excellence Ser.: Bk. 3). 1996. 6.45 (*0-8497-5990-0*, W23BS) Kjos.

***Tuba Lessons.** T. C. Bartlett. LC 96-44584. 1997. write for info. (*0-15-201643-0*) HarBrace.

Tuba Source Book. Ed. by R. Winston Morris & Edward R. Goldstein. LC 94-48097. 992p. 1995. 79.95 (*0-253-32889-6*) Ind U Pr.

Tubal Catheterization Procedures. Ed. by Norbert Gleicher. 1992. text ed. 199.95 (*0-471-58815-6*) Wiley.

Tubatulabal & Kawaiisu Kinship Terms. fac. ed. E. W. Gifford. (University of California Publications in American Archaeology & Ethnology: Vol. 12: 6). 29p. (C). 1917. reprint ed. pap. text ed. 2.75 (*1-55567-204-3*) Coyote Press.

Tubatulabal Ethnography. fac. ed. Erminie W. Voegelin. Ed. by Robert H. Lowie et al. (University of California Publications: No. 2:1). 96p. (C). 1937. reprint ed. pap. 8.70 (*1-55567-120-9*) Coyote Press.

Tubatulabal Grammer. fac. ed. Charles F. Voegelin. (University of California Publications in American Archaeology & Ethnology: Vol. 34: 2). 143p. (C). 1935. reprint ed. pap. text ed. 13.10 (*1-55567-293-0*) Coyote Press.

Tubatulabal Texts. fac. ed. Charles F. Voegelin. (University of California Publications in American Archaeology & Ethnology: Vol. 34: 3). 62p. (C). 1935. reprint ed. pap. text ed. 5.55 (*1-55567-294-9*) Coyote Press.

Tubby & the Lantern. Al Perkins. LC 70-158390. (Illus.). (J). (gr. k-2). 1971. lib. bdg. 4.99 (*0-394-92297-2*) Beginner.

***Tubby Time for Little Ernie.** Random House Staff. (Board Bks.). 1997. 2.50 (*0-679-88883-7*) Random Bks Yng Read.

Tube: The Invention of Television. David E. Fisher & Marshall J. Fisher. Ed. by Michael Bessie & Cornelia Bessie. (Illus.). 440p. 1996. 30.00 (*1-887178-17-1*) Counterpt DC.

***Tube: The Invention of Television.** David E. Fisher. LC 97-21765. 1997. pap. text ed. 15.00 (*0-15-600536-0*, Harvest Bks) HarBrace.

Tube Bundle Thermalhydraulics: Presented at 1982 AIAA-ASME Joint Fluids, Plasma, Thermophysics, & Heat Transfer Conference, St. Louis, Missouri, June 7-11, 1982. AIAA-ASME Joint Fluids, Plasma, Thermophysics, & Heat Transfer Conference Staff. Ed. by P. A. Pfund et al. LC 82-71169. 79p. reprint ed. pap. 25.00 (*0-8357-8771-0*, 2033634) Bks Demand.

Tube Domains & the Cauchy Problem. Simon Gindikin. LC 92-19406. (Translations of Mathematical Monographs: Vol. 111). 132p. 1992. 78.00 (*0-8218-4566-7*, MMONO/111) Am Math.

Tube Fabricating: Collected Articles & Technical Papers. 150p. 1992. pap. 24.95 (*1-881113-00-0*) Croydon Grp.

Tube Fabricating Vol. 2: Collected Articles & Technical Papers. Ed. by Amy J. Nickel. (Illus.). 270p. (Orig.). 1995. pap. 34.95 (*1-881113-09-4*) Croydon Grp.

Tube Flies: A Tying, Fishing & Historical Guide. Mark Mandell & Les Johnson. (Illus.). 95p. 1995. 45.00 (*1-57188-037-2*); pap. 29.95 (*1-57188-036-4*) F Amato Pubns.

***Tube Lore: A Reference for Users & Collectors.** Ludwell A. Sibley. (Illus.). ii, 184p. (Orig.). 1996. pap. 19.95 (*0-9654683-0-5*) L Sibley.

Tube of Plenty: The Evolution of American Television. rev. ed. Erik Barnouw. (Illus.). 624p. 1990. pap. 16.95 (*0-19-506484-4*) OUP.

Tube Producing: Collected Articles & Technical Papers. 190p. 1992. pap. 24.95 (*1-881113-01-9*) Croydon Grp.

An Asterisk (*) at the beginning of an entry indicates that the title is appearing in BIP for the first time.

Tube Strips. Bill Plympton. 1976. pap. 50.00 (*0-918266-04-1*) Smyrna.

Tube Strips. Bill Plympton. (Illus.). 35p. 1976. reprint ed. pap. 25.00 (*0-7837-9092-9*, 2049842) Bks Demand.

Tube Substitution Handbook: Complete Guide to Replacements for Vacuum Tubes & Picture Tubes. William Smith & Barry Buchanan. LC 92-. (Illus.). 149p. (Orig.). (C). 1992. pap. 16.95 (*0-7906-1036-1*) Prompt Publns.

Tube Type Dilatometers. Joseph H. Valentich. LC 80-82116. (Illus.). 233p. reprint ed. pap. 66.50 (*0-7837-5154-0*, 2044883) Bks Demand.

Tube-Wall Temperature Measurement in Fired Process Heaters. (MTI Publication: No. 24). (Illus.). 155p. 1986. 70.00 (*0-685-39505-7*) NACE Intl.

Tuber Crops. S. P. Ghosh et al. (C). 1988. 30.00 (*81-204-0366-5*, Pub. by Oxford IBH II) S Asia.

Tuberculosis. Elaine Landau. LC 94-39305. (Venture-Health & the Human Body Ser.). (Illus.). 112p. (YA). (gr. 7-12). 1995. lib. bdg. 22.00 (*0-531-12555-6*) Watts.

Tuberculosis. William N. Rom. LC 95-10766. 1002p. 1995. text ed. 179.95 (*0-316-75574-5*) Lppncott-Raven.

Tuberculosis. Ed. by Milton D. Rossman & Rob R. MacGregor. 352p. 1994. text ed. 65.00 (*0-07-053950-2*) McGraw-Hill HPD.

Tuberculosis. Ed. by David Schlossberg. (Clinical Topics in Infectious Disease Ser.). (Illus.). 225p. 1987. 106.00 (*0-387-96552-1*) Spr-Verlag.

Tuberculosis. Alvin Silverstein et al. LC 93-4686. (Diseases & People Ser.). (Illus.). 128p. (YA). (gr. 6 up). 1994. lib. bdg. 18.95 (*0-89490-462-0*) Enslow Pubs.

Tuberculosis. 3rd ed. Ed. by David Schlossberg. LC 93-12259. 1994. 122.00 (*0-387-94026-X*) Spr-Verlag.

***Tuberculosis.** 4th ed. David Schlossberg. Date not set. text ed. write for info. (*0-7216-7308-2*) Saunders.

Tuberculosis. William H. Hay et al. 37p. 1965. reprint ed. spiral bd. 6.50 (*0-7873-1020-4*) Hlth Research.

Tuberculosis: A Clinical Handbook. Ed. by Larry I. Lutwick. 378p. (gr. 13). 1994. pap. text ed. 36.95 (*0-412-60740-9*) Chapman & Hall.

Tuberculosis: A Comprehensive International Approach. Ed. by Lee Reichman & Earl Hershfield. LC 93-20307. (Lung Biology in Health & Disease Ser.: Vol. 66). 784p. 1993. 220.00 (*0-8247-8852-4*) Dekker.

Tuberculosis: A Comprehensive Update. Friedman. 384p. 1994. 99.95 (*0-8493-4825-0*) CRC Pr.

Tuberculosis: A Half-Century of Study & Conquest. Jay A. Myers. LC 75-96989. (Illus.). 378p. 1970. 14.80 (*0-87527-059-X*) Green.

Tuberculosis: A Sourcebook for Nursing Practice. Ed. by Felissa Cohen & Jerry Durham. LC 94-35452. (Illus.). 312p. 1995. 42.95 (*0-8261-8720-X*) Springer Pub.

Tuberculosis: Costly & Preventable Cases Continue in Five Cities. (Illus.). 55p. (Orig.). (C). 1995. pap. text ed. 25.00 (*0-7881-2048-4*) DIANE Pub.

Tuberculosis: Its Cause & Prevention. 1991. lib. bdg. 75.00 (*0-8490-4144-9*) Gordon Pr.

Tuberculosis: Pathogenesis, Protection & Control. Ed. by Barry R. Bloom. LC 94-2932. (Illus.). 500p. 1994. 72.00 (*1-55581-072-1*) Am Soc Microbio.

Tuberculosis among Certain Indian Tribes of the United States. Ales Hrdlicka. (Bureau of American Ethnology Bulletins Ser.). 99p. 1995. lib. bdg. 69.00 (*0-7812-4042-5*) Rprt Serv.

Tuberculosis among Certain Indian Tribes of the United States. Ales Hrdlicka. 1988. reprint ed. lib. bdg. 49.00 (*0-7812-0016-4*) Rprt Serv.

Tuberculosis among Certain Indian Tribes of the United States. Ales Hrdlicka. 96p. 1980. reprint ed. 49.00 (*0-403-02467-6*) Scholarly.

Tuberculosis & AIDS: The Relationship Between Mycrobacteria TB & the HIV Type 1. Linda K. Scharer. (Illus.). 160p. 1995. 33.95 (*0-8261-9000-6*) Springer Pub.

Tuberculosis & Its Prevention. Stefan Grzybowski. (Illus.). 124p. 1983. 19.75 (*0-87527-198-7*) Green.

Tuberculosis & Veterans' Medical Centers. (Illus.). 69p. (Orig.). (C). 1994. pap. text ed. 20.00 (*0-7881-0659-7*) DIANE Pub.

Tuberculosis As a Disease of the Masses & How to Combat It. S. Adolphus Knopf. Ed. by Barbara G. Rosenkrantz. LC 76-40633. (Public Health in America Ser.). 1977. reprint ed. lib. bdg. 19.95 (*0-405-09824-3*) Ayer.

***Tuberculosis Bacteriology: Organization & Practice.** 2nd ed. C. H. Collins et al. LC 97-3038. 1997. write for info. (*0-7506-2458-2*) Buttrwrth-Heinemann.

***Tuberculosis Case-Finding & Chemotherapy: Questions & Answers.** K. Toman. (Nonserial Publication). 239p. 1979. pap. text ed. 39.00 (*92-4-154136-9*, 1150155) World Health.

***Tuberculosis Control.** (Technical Report Ser.: No. 671). 26p. 1982. pap. text ed. 3.00 (*92-4-120671-3*) World Health.

***Tuberculosis Control: A Manual on Methods & Procedures for Integrated Programs.** (PAHO Scientific Publication Ser.: No. 498). 188p. 1986. pap. text ed. 20.00 (*92-75-11498-6*) World Health.

Tuberculosis Movement: A Public Health Campaign in the Progressive Era. LC 87-29432. (Contributions in Medical Studies: No. 22). 192p. 1988. text ed. 49.95 (*0-313-25748-5*, TCD/, Greenwood Pr) Greenwood.

Tuberculosis of the Bones & Joints. Ed. by M. Martini. (Illus.). 230p. 1988. 118.00 (*0-387-18166-0*) Spr-Verlag.

Tuberculosis Pearls. Ed. by Neil Schluger. (Pearls Ser.). 250p. (Orig.). 1995. pap. text ed. 39.00 (*1-56053-156-8*) Hanley & Belfus.

***Tuberculosis Resource Guide.** P. Heinsohn. 143p. (Orig.). 1996. pap. 35.00 (*0-7881-3337-3*) DIANE Pub.

Tuberculosis Resurgent. 2nd rev. ed. Ed. by Richard Westlund et al. 95p. (Orig.). 1995. pap. text ed. 33.00 (*1-879772-02-7*) Health Studies.

Tuberculosis Revival: Individual Rights & Societal Obligations in a Time of AIDS. LC 92-40474. (Special Reports). 1992. 10.00 (*1-881277-12-7*) United Hosp Fund.

Tuberculosis Statistics in the U. S. 1994. lib. bdg. 250.00 (*0-8490-8409-1*) Gordon Pr.

Tuberculous Meningitis: Tuberculomas & Spinal Tuberculosis: A Handbook for Clinicians. 2nd ed. Malcolm Parsons. (Illus.). 92p. 1988. 29.95 (*0-19-261721-4*) OUP.

Tuberoses & Nine-Patch. Ruth Dyer. Ed. by Sherri York. LC 87-42905. 65p. 1988. pap. 5.95 (*1-55523-112-8*) Winston-Derek.

Tuberous Begonias: Origin & Development. J. Haegeman. 1979. lib. bdg. 65.00 (*3-7682-1219-X*) Lubrecht & Cramer.

***Tuberous, Cormous & Bulbous Plants: Biology of an Adaptive Strategy in Western Australia.** John Pate & Kingsley Dixon. 39.95 (*0-85564-201-7*, Pub. by Univ of West Aust Pr AT) Intl Spec Bk.

Tuberous Sclerosis. 2nd ed. Ed. by Manuel R. Gomez. (Illus.). 288p. 1988. text ed. 105.00 (*0-88167-397-8*) Lppncott-Raven.

Tubes. Alfred Gray. (Illus.). 304p. (C). 1990. 44.95 (*0-201-15676-8*, Adv Bk Prog) Addison-Wesley.

Tubes in My Ears: My Trip to the Hospital. Virginia Dooley. (Illus.). 24p. (J). (gr. k-2). 1996. pap. 4.95 (*1-57255-118-6*) Mondo Pubng.

Tubingen Studies in Language & Literature, 1980. 1980. 7.00 (*0-936072-15-6*) Soc New Lang Study.

Tubinger Dichterhumanisten. Bebel, Frischlin, Flayder. Gustav Bebermeyer. vii, 108p. 1967. reprint ed. 25.00 (*0-318-71256-3*) G Olms Pubs.

Tubu: The Teda & the Daza. Catherine Baroin. (Heritage Library of African Peoples: Set 3). (Illus.). 64p. (YA). (gr. 7-12). 1997. lib. bdg. 15.95 (*0-8239-2000-3*, D2000-3) Rosen Group.

Tubular Cardwoven Neckpieces: Modern Adornment from an Ancient Weaving Technique. Linda Hendrickson. 39p. 1994. pap. text ed. 12.50 (*1-56659-076-0*) Robin & Russ.

Tubular Disease. Michael Michelis. Date not set. write for info. (*0-938607-33-2*) Field & Wood Inc Medical.

Tubular Heat Exchanger Operation & Repair. Andreone & Yokell. LC 97-26077. 1997. text ed. 80.00 (*0-07-001778-6*) McGraw.

Tubular Structures, No. 5. Ed. by M. G. Coutie & G. Davies. LC 93-33027. 1993. write for info. (*0-419-18770-7*, E & FN Spon) Routledge Chapman & Hall.

Tubular Structures: Proceedings of the 6th International Symposium, Melbourne, 14-16 December 1994. Ed. by P. Grundy et al. (Illus.). 550p. (C). 1994. text ed. 115.00 (*90-5410-520-8*, Pub. by A A Balkema NE) Ashgate Pub Co.

***Tubular Structures: Proceedings of the 7th International Symposium, Misolc, Hungary, 28-30 August 1996.** J. Farkas & K. Jarmai. 498p. 1996. 140.00 (*0-614-20214-0*, Pub. by A A Balkema NE) Ashgate Pub Co.

***Tubular Structures VII: Proceedings of the Seventh International Symposium, Miskolc, Hungary, 28-30 August 1996.** Ed. by J. Farkas & H. Jarmai. 540p. 1996. 140.00 (*90-5410-828-2*, Pub. by A A Balkema NE) Ashgate Pub Co.

Tubular Wire Welding. D. Widgery. 154p. 1994. 115.00 (*1-85573-088-X*, Pub. by Woodhead Pubng UK) Am Educ Systs.

***Tubulifera (Insecta: Thysanoptera)** L. A. Mound & A. K. Walker. (Fauna of New Zealand Ser.: Vol. 10). (Illus.). 140p. 1986. pap. 34.65 (*0-477-06784-0*, Pub. by Manaaki Whenua NZ) Balogh.

Tubulointerstitial & Cystic Disease of the Kidney. Ed. by S. M. Dodd et al. LC 95-3278. (Current Topics in Pathology Ser.: Vol. 88). (Illus.). 304p. 1995. 143.00 (*3-540-58842-6*) Spr-Verlag.

Tubulo-Interstitial Nephropathies. Ed. by Alberto Ameria et al. (Developments in Nephrology Ser.). (C). 1991. lib. bdg. 135.00 (*0-7923-1200-7*) Kluwer Ac.

Tuck. Mark Dunster. (Holiday Ser.: Pt. 2: Thanksgiving). 55p. (Orig.). 1981. pap. 4.00 (*0-89642-073-6*) Linden Pubs.

Tuck. Mamie Swallow. 264p. 1987. pap. 10.95 (*0-918292-14-X*) Griggs Print.

Tuck Everlasting. Natalie Babbitt. LC 75-33306. (Sunburst Ser.). 160p. (J). (gr. 3 up). 1975. 15.00 (*0-374-37848-7*) FS&G.

Tuck Everlasting. Natalie Babbitt. LC 75-33306. (Sunburst Ser.). 160p. (J). (gr. 3 up). 1985. pap. 3.95 (*0-374-48009-5*, Sunburst Bks) FS&G.

***Tuck Everlasting.** Natalie Babbitt. (J). (gr. 6). 1995. 9.00 (*0-395-73267-0*) HM.

***Tuck Everlasting.** Scholastic Staff. (Literature Guide Ser.). (J). 1997. pap. text ed. 3.95 (*0-590-37354-4*) Scholastic Inc.

***Tuck Everlasting.** large type ed. Natalie Babbitt. 160p. (J). (gr. 6). 41.00 (*0-614-20624-3*, L-38208-00 APHB) Am Printing Hse.

Tuck Everlasting: A Literature Unit. Caroline Nakajima. Ed. by Patricia Miriani. (Illus.). 48p. (Orig.). 1992. student ed., pap. 7.95 (*1-55734-408-6*) Tchr Create Mat.

Tuck Everlasting: A Study Guide. Joyce Friedland & Rikki Kessler. (Novel-Ties Ser.). 1982. student ed., teacher ed., pap. text ed. 15.95 (*0-88122-010-8*) Lrn Links.

Tuck in the Pool. Martha Weston. LC 94-7408. (J). (ps-1). 1995. 12.95 (*0-395-65479-3*, Clarion Bks) HM.

***Tuck Me in, Mummy.** Fred E. Katz. LC 97-11095. (SpineChillers Mysteries Ser.: Vol. 9). 144p. (Orig.). (J). (gr. 5-8). 1997. pap. 5.99 (*0-8499-4052-4*) Tommy Nelson.

Tuck-Me-in Tales: Bedtime Stories from Around the World. Margaret R. MacDonald. (Illus.). 64p. (J). 1996. 19.95 (*0-87483-461-9*, Aug Hse LittleFolk) August Hse.

Tuck 'n' Twist. Annie Tuley. (Illus.). 48p. (Orig.). 1993. pap. 22.00 (*0-9636715-0-2*) Clotilde.

Tuck Para Siempre: Tuck Everlasting. Natalie Babbitt. Tr. by Narcis Fradera. (Mirasol Ser.). 158p. (SPA.). (J). (gr. 5 up). 1991. 15.00 (*0-374-37849-5*) FS&G.

Tuck Para Siempre: Tuck Everlasting. Natalie Babbitt. (J). (gr. 4-7). 1993. pap. 4.95 (*0-374-48011-7*) FS&G.

Tuck Triumphant. Theodore Taylor. (J). (gr. 4-7). 1992. pap. 4.50 (*0-380-71323-3*, Camelot) Avon.

Tuck Triumphant. large type ed. Theodore Taylor. 1993. 42.50 (*0-614-09870-X*, L-04423-00) Am Printing Hse.

Tucker. Tom Birdseye. LC 89-46243. 120p. (J). (gr. 3-7). 1990. 15.95 (*0-8234-0813-2*) Holiday.

Tucker. Louis L'Amour. 192p. 1984. mass mkt. 3.99 (*0-553-25022-1*) Bantam.

Tucker Boone. Joan E. Pickart. (Loveswept Ser.: No. 285). 192p. 1988. pap. 2.50 (*0-318-32847-X*) Bantam.

Tucker Genealogy: A Record of Gilbert Ruggles & Evelina Christina (Snyder) Tucker, Their Ancestors & Descendants. T. S. Morris. (Illus.). 305p. 1989. reprint ed. pap. 45.50 (*0-8328-1187-4*); reprint ed. lib. bdg. 53.50 (*0-8328-1186-6*) Higginson Bk Co.

Tucker Knob Mountain: The Old Sorghum Sopper. Jay Boggs. 257p. (YA). (gr. 4-12). 1995. write for info. (*1-888423-00-5*); pap. write for info. (*1-888423-01-3*) Echoes Tucker Knob.

Tucker Pfeffercorn. Barry Moser. LC 92-34340. (J). 1994. 15.95 (*0-316-58542-4*) Little.

Tucker Talks. Fred C. Tucker, Jr. 125p. 1994. 18.95 (*1-878208-50-0*) Guild Pr IN.

Tucker's Countryside. George Selden. LC 69-14975. (Illus.). 176p. (J). (gr. 3 up). 1969. 16.00 (*0-374-37854-1*) FS&G.

Tucker's Countryside. George Seldon. 176p. (J). (gr. k-6). 1989. reprint ed. pap. 4.50 (*0-440-40248-4*, YB BDD) BDD Bks Young Read.

Tuckers Directory of the Surveyors 500: The Guide to U. K. Chartered Surveyors. Tuckers Directories Staff. 311p. 1993. pap. 125.00 (*1-872534-26-0*, Pub. by R-I-C-S Bks UK) St Mut.

Tucker's People. Ira Wolfert. LC 97-4100. 520p. 1997. 16.95 (*0-252-06598-0*) U of Ill Pr.

Tucker's Ridge. Peggy D. Katz. 42p. 1996. pap. 5.00 (*0-87129-664-0*, TA2) Dramatic Pub.

Tucker's Treasure. Robin Gibson. 1994. 17.95 (*0-8034-9079-8*, 094441) Bouregy.

***Tucket Teddy's Day at Work.** Bradley S. Cunningham. 7.95 (*0-9653674-0-1*) Nantucket Cblestns.

Tucket's Ride. Gary Paulsen. LC 96-21703. 112p. (J). 1997. 15.95 (*0-385-32199-6*, Delacorte Pr Bks) BDD Bks Young Read.

Tucking Mommy In. Morag Loh. LC 87-16740. (Illus.). 40p. (J). (ps-2). 1988. lib. bdg. 16.99 (*0-531-08340-3*) Orchard Bks Watts.

Tucking Mommy In. Morag Loh. LC 87-16740. (Illus.). 40p. (J). (ps-2). 1991. pap. 5.95 (*0-531-07025-5*) Orchard Bks Watts.

Tucson. Bernice Cosulich. (Illus.). (Orig.). 1987. reprint ed. pap. 12.00 (*0-918080-36-3*) Treas Chest Bks.

Tucson: A Short History. Charles W. Polzer et al. LC 85-63503. (Illus.). 160p. (Orig.). 1986. pap. 8.95 (*0-915076-11-X*) SW Mission.

Tucson: The Life & Times of an American City. Charles L. Sonnichsen. LC 82-40329. (Illus.). 400p. 1987. 45.00 (*0-8061-1823-7*); pap. 21.95 (*0-8061-2042-8*) U of Okla Pr.

Tucson: The Old Pueblo. Lisa S. Heidinger. LC 95-36761. (Illus.). 104p. (Orig.). 1995. pap. 12.95 (*1-56037-090-4*) Am Wrld Geog.

Tucson ABC Coloring & Activity Book. Betty Leavengood. (Illus.). 32p. (J). (gr. 1-3). 1995. pap. 4.95 (*0-9645487-0-4*) MP Pub AZ.

Tucson at the Turn of the Century: The Archaeology of a City Block. Jonathan B. Mabry et al. (Illus.). 198p. (Orig.). 1994. pap. 15.00 (*1-886398-14-3*) Desert Archaeol.

Tucson, AZ. (Streetfinder Ser.). (Illus.). 1995. pap. 14.95 (*0-528-91890-7*) Rand McNally.

Tucson Hiking Guide. 2nd ed. Betty Leavengood. LC 97-1805. (Orig.). 1997. pap. 14.95 (*0-87108-865-7*) Pruett.

***Tucson to Tombstone: A Guide to Southeastern Arizona.** 2nd ed. 1996. pap. text ed. 12.95 (*0-916179-61-3*) Ariz Hwy.

Tucson Uncovered. John Kamper & Donna Kamper. 304p. 1996. pap. 16.95 (*1-55622-393-5*, Seaside Pr) Wordware Pub.

Tucson 7: Harley Brown, Duane Bryers, Don Crowley, Tom Hill, Bob Kuhn, Ken Riley, Howard Terpning. Tisa R. Sherman & Robert A. Yassin. (Illus.). 64p. (Orig.). 1997. pap. 25.00 (*0-911611-10-X*) Tucson Mus Art.

Tucsonenses: The Mexican Community in Tucson, 1854-1941. Thomas E. Sheridan. LC 86-11404. (Illus.). 327p. 1992. reprint ed. pap. text ed. 18.95 (*0-8165-1298-1*) U of Ariz Pr.

Tucumcari Gal: Alice Evangeline Ramirez Herrera, a Biography. Jess R. Herrera. LC 94-96767. (Illus.). 224p. (Orig.). 1995. pap. write for info. (*1-881156-01-X*) J R Herrera.

Tudor Age. Jasper Ridley. LC 90-6884. (Illus.). 384p. 1990. 40.00 (*0-87951-405-1*) Overlook Pr.

Tudor Age. Jasper Ridley. (Illus.). 385p. 1996. pap. 24.95 (*0-87951-684-4*) Overlook Pr.

Tudor Age & Beyond: England from the Black Death to the End of the Age of Elizabeth. Arthur J. Slavin. LC 86-2723. 252p. (Orig.). (C). 1986. pap. text ed. 14.50 (*0-89874-945-X*) Krieger.

Tudor & Early Stuart Voyaging. B. Penrose. LC 79-65985. (Folger Guides to the Age of Shakespeare Ser.). 1979. pap. 4.95 (*0-918016-12-6*) Folger Bks.

Tudor & Jacobean Jewellery 1508-1625. Diana Scarisbrick. (Illus.). 104p. (C). 1996. pap. 19.95 (*1-85437-158-4*, Pub. by Tate Gallery UK) U of Wash Pr.

Tudor & Jacobean Portraits, 2 vol. Roy Strong. (Illus.). 700p. 1980. Set. 160.00 (*0-312-82220-0*) St Martin.

Tudor & Jacobean Tournaments. Alan Young. (Illus.). 230p. 1987. 34.95 (*0-911378-75-8*) Sheridan.

Tudor & Stuart Britain, 1471-1714. 2nd ed. Roger Lockyer. LC 84-10085. 494p. reprint ed. pap. 140.80 (*0-7837-1587-0*, 2041879) Bks Demand.

Tudor & Stuart Devon: The Common State & Government. Ed. by Gray et al. 208p. 1992. text ed. 60.00 (*0-85989-384-7*, Pub. by Univ Exeter Pr UK) Northwestern U Pr.

Tudor & Stuart Drama. 2nd ed. Irving Ribner & Clifford C. Huffman. LC 76-5215. (Goldentree Bibliographies Series in Language & Literature). (C). 1978. text ed. write for info. (*0-88295-572-1*); pap. text ed. write for info. (*0-88295-554-3*) Harlan Davidson.

***Tudor & Stuart Monarchy Pageantry, Painting, Iconography: Jacobean & Caroline.** Roy Strong. (Illus.). 352p. 1997. 108.00 (*0-85115-592-8*, Boydell Pr) Boydell & Brewer.

Tudor & Stuart Monarchy Vol. I: Pageantry, Painting, Iconography: Tudor. Roy Strong. (Illus.). 263p. 1995. text ed. 89.00 (*0-85115-400-X*) Boydell & Brewer.

Tudor & Stuart Monarchy Vol. II: Pageantry, Painting, Iconography: Elizabethan. Roy Strong. (Illus.). 494p. 1996. 108.00 (*0-85115-377-1*) Boydell & Brewer.

Tudor & Stuart Town: A Reader in English Urban History, 1530-1688. Ed. by Jonathan Barry. (Readers in Urban History Ser.). 272p. (C). 1990. pap. text ed. 22.75 (*0-685-72459-X*, 78601) Longman.

Tudor & Stuart Town 1530-1688: A Reader in English History. Jonathan Barry. (C). 1990. pap. text ed. 28.50 (*0-582-05130-4*, Pub. by Longman UK) Longman.

Tudor & Stuart Women Writers. Louise Schleiner. Tr. by Connie McQuillen & Lynn E. Roller from GRE. LC 93-44997. 320p. (C). 1994. 35.00 (*0-253-35098-0*); pap. 16.95 (*0-253-20886-6*) Ind U Pr.

Tudor Books of Private Devotion. Helen C. White. LC 78-21661. (Illus.). 284p. 1979. reprint ed. text ed. 55.00 (*0-313-21063-2*, WHTB, Greenwood Pr) Greenwood.

Tudor Books of Saints & Martyrs. Helen C. White. LC 63-13741. 292p. reprint ed. pap. 83.30 (*0-317-07866-6*, 2004164) Bks Demand.

Tudor Church Music. Denis Stevens. LC 73-4335. (Music Reprint Ser.). 144p. 1973. reprint ed. lib. bdg. 25.00 (*0-306-70579-6*) Da Capo.

Tudor Constitution: Documents & Commentary. 2nd ed. G. R. Elton. LC 81-15216. 522p. (C). 1982. 94.95 (*0-521-24506-0*); pap. text ed. 34.95 (*0-521-28757-X*) Cambridge U Pr.

Tudor Cornwall. A. L. Rowse. (C). 1989. 140.00 (*1-85022-058-1*, Pub. by Dyllansow Truran UK) St Mut.

***Tudor Costume & Fashion.** Herbert Norris. LC 97-19413. 1997. pap. write for info. (*0-486-29845-0*) Dover.

Tudor Drama & Politics: A Critical Approach to Topical Meaning. David M. Bevington. LC 68-17637. 360p. reprint ed. pap. 106.10 (*0-7837-1672-9*, 2057204) Bks Demand.

Tudor Drama & Religious Controversy. James C. Bryant, Jr. LC 84-10850. (Sesquicentennial Ser.). x, 168p. 1984. 14.50 (*0-86554-129-9*, MUP-H120) Mercer Univ Pr.

Tudor England. Roger Lockyer & Dan O'Sullivan. LC 93-23514. (Sources & Opinions Ser.). 1994. pap. text ed. 11.99 (*0-582-02202-9*, Pub. by Longman UK) Longman.

Tudor England. John S. Guy. (Illus.). 624p. 1990. reprint ed. pap. 19.95 (*0-19-285213-2*) OUP.

Tudor England, Vol. 5. S. T. Bindoff. 1950. mass mkt. 5.95 (*0-14-020212-9*, Penguin Bks) Viking Penguin.

Tudor England Through Venetian Eyes. Emma Gurney-Salter. 1977. lib. bdg. 59.95 (*0-8490-2778-0*) Gordon Pr.

Tudor England, 1485-1603. Mortimer Levine. LC 68-12060. (Conference on British Studies, Bibliographical Handbooks). 127p. reprint ed. pap. 36.20 (*0-685-16011-4*, 2027230) Bks Demand.

Tudor Facsimile Texts, 149 titles in 146 vols. Ed. by John S. Farmer. reprint ed. Set. 7,227.00 (*0-404-53300-0*) AMS Pr.

Tudor Farmhouse. Newbery. (J). 13.95 (*0-7136-3815-X*, 93340, Pub. by A&C Black UK) Talman.

Tudor Figures of Rhetoric. Warren Taylor. LC 75-186416. (C). 1972. text ed. 10.00 (*0-912386-03-7*) Language Pr.

Tudor Frontiers & Noble Power: The Making of the British State. Steven Ellis. (Illus.). 280p. 1995. 65.00 (*0-19-820133-8*) OUP.

***Tudor Government: Structures of Authority in the Sixteenth Century.** David Loades. 304p. (C). 1997. text ed. 64.95 (*0-631-19156-9*) Blackwell Pubs.

***Tudor Government: Structures of Authority in the Sixteenth Century.** David Loades. 304p. (C). 1997. pap. text ed. 24.95 (*0-631-19157-7*) Blackwell Pubs.

Tudor Homes & Other Popular Designs. Ed. by National Plan Service, Inc. Staff. (Illus.). 32p. (Orig.). 1987. pap. 3.95 (*0-934039-02-X*, A70) Natl Plan Serv.

***Tudor Housewife.** Alison Sim. (Illus.). 192p. 1996. 26.95 (*0-7735-1516-X*, Pub. by McGill CN) U of Toronto Pr.

Tudor Image. Maurice Howard. (Illus.). 80p. (C). 1996. pap. 18.95 (*1-85437-159-2*, Pub. by Tate Gallery UK) U of Wash Pr.

Tudor Law of Treason: An Introduction. John G. Bellamy. LC 79-303364. (Studies in Social History). 305p. reprint ed. pap. 87.00 (*0-685-16093-9*, 2056137) Bks Demand.

Tudor Mercenaries & Auxiliaries, 1485-1547. Gilbert J. Millar. LC 79-22164. (Illus.). 223p. 1980. text ed. 35.00 (*0-8139-0818-3*) U Pr of Va.

***Tudor Monarchy.** John Guy. LC 97-16440. 1997. write for info. (*0-340-65218-7*, Pub. by E Arnold UK) Routledge Chapman & Hall.

An Asterisk (*) at the beginning of an entry indicates that the title is appearing in BIP for the first time.

*Tudor Monarchy. LC 97-16440. 1997. pap. write for info. (0-340-65219-5, Pub. by E Arnold UK) Routledge Chapman & Hall.

Tudor Music. David Wulstan. LC 85-51090. (Illus.). 384p. reprint ed. pap. 109.50 (0-7837-1628-1, 2041921) Bks Demand.

Tudor Music: A Research & Information Guide, Vol. 18. Richard Turbet. LC 93-38771. (Music Research & Information Guides Ser.). (Illus.). 272p. 1994. text ed. 45.00 (0-8240-4296-4) Garland.

Tudor Navy: An Administrative Political & Military History. David Loades. (Studies in Naval History). 304p. 1992. 69.95 (0-85967-922-5, Pub. by Scolar Pr UK) Ashgate Pub Co.

Tudor Nobility. Ed. by G. W. Bernard. 320p. 1992. text ed. 69.95 (0-7190-3625-9, Pub. by Manchester Univ Pr UK) St Martin.

*Tudor Odours. Mary Dobson. (Smelly Old History). (Illus.). 32p. 1997. pap. 7.95 (0-19-910096-9) OUP.

Tudor Political Culture. Ed. by Dale E. Hoak. (Illus.). 272p. (C). 1995. text ed. 69.95 (0-521-40494-0) Cambridge U Pr.

Tudor Rebellions. 3rd rev. ed. Anthony Fletcher. (Seminar Studies in History). (Illus.). 176p. (C). 1981. pap. text ed. 13.50 (0-582-35255-X, 72158) Longman.

*Tudor Rebellions. 4th ed. Anthony Fletcher & Diarmaid MacCulloch. LC 96-38921. 1997. write for info. (0-582-28990-4) Longman.

*Tudor Royal Iconography: Literature & Art in an Age of Religious Crisis. John N. King. LC 88-18019. (Princeton Essays on the Arts Ser.). reprint ed. pap. 87.30 (0-608-04622-1, 2065309) Bks Demand.

Tudor Royal Proclamations, Vols. 2-3. Ed. by Paul L. Hughes & James F. Larkin. LC 63-13965. 1969. Set. 130.00 (0-300-00103-7) Yale U Pr.

Tudor School Boy Life. Juan L. Vives. 247p. 1970. 30.00 (0-7146-2279-6, Pub. by F Cass Pubs UK) Intl Spec Bk.

Tudor Secret. Carola Dunn. 1995. pap. 4.50 (0-8217-5172-7) NAL-Dutton.

Tudor Songs & Ballads from MS Cotton Vespasian A-25. Ed. by Peter J. Seng. LC 77-13165. (Illus.). 182p. reprint ed. pap. 51.90 (0-7837-5942-8, 2045741) Bks Demand.

Tudor Studies Presented to Albert Frederick Pollard. London University, Board of Studies in History Staff. Ed. by Robert W. Seton-Watson. LC 69-17582. (Essay Index Reprint Ser.). 1977. 20.95 (0-8369-0083-9) Ayer.

Tudor Tin Bounds: West Penwith. J. A. Buckley. (C). 1989. 40.00 (1-85022-028-X, Pub. by Dyllansow Truran UK) St Mut.

Tudor Translations, 56 vols., Set. Incl. Vols. 1-44. First Series. Ed. by William E. Henley. reprint ed. (0-318-50733-1); Vols. 1-12. Second Series. Ed. by Charles Whibley. reprint ed. (0-318-50734-X); 3,220.00 (0-404-51850-8) AMS Pr.

Tudor Translations of the Colloquies of Erasmus, 1536-1568., 7 vols. in one. Desiderius Erasmus. LC 74-161931. 384p. 1972. 60.00 (0-8201-1097-3) Schol Facsimiles.

Tudor Wales. Gareth E. Jones. (Illus.). 83p. (C). 1986. pap. 20.00 (0-86383-218-0, Pub. by Gomer Pr UK) St Mut.

Tudor Women: Commoners & Queens. Pearl Hogrefe. LC 75-20248. 192p. reprint ed. pap. 54.80 (0-685-17870-6, 2029470) Bks Demand.

Tudors. (History of Britain Ser.: No. F895-4). (Illus.). (YA). (gr. 5 up). 1990. pap. 3.95 (1-85543-009-6, Ladybrd) Penguin.

Tudors. Jennifer Ruby. (People in Costume Ser.). (YA). (gr. 7-12). 1995. 19.95 (0-7134-7214-6, Pub. by Batsford UK) Trafalgar.

Tudors: Personalities & Practical Politics in Sixteenth Century England. Conyers Read. LC 68-24854. (Essay Index Reprint Ser.). 1977. 20.95 (0-8369-0812-0) Ayer.

Tudors & Stuarts. Donna Cooper. (J). 1994. pap. 7.95 (0-563-35376-7, BBC-Parkwest) Parkwest Pubns.

Tudors Briefings Unit. David Birt & Ian Carstairs. (History Units Ser.). (Illus.). 1975. Incl. 10 briefings, tchr's. guide & ans. key. pap. text ed. 18.95 (0-582-39616-6) Longman.

Tudor's Soiree Musicale, Vol. 4. Ed. by Anne H. Guest. LC 92-37173. (Language of Dance Ser.: No. 4). 106p. 1993. text ed. 46.00 (2-88124-911-6); pap. text ed. 23.00 (2-88124-884-5) Gordon & Breach.

Tuerkisch - Arabisch - Perschishes - Handwoerterbuch: Dictionnaire Turc - Arabe - Persan, 2 vols., Set. Julius T. Zenker. xi, 980p. (FRE & GER.). 1994. reprint ed. lib. bdg. 275.00 (3-487-01753-9) G Olms Pubs.

Tuers sans Gages see Theatre

Tuesday. Edward Bond. 208p. 1994. pap. 11.95 (0-413-68220-X, A0693, Pub. by Methuen UK) Heinemann.

Tuesday. David Wiesner. Ed. by Dorothy Briley. (Illus.). 32p. (J). (gr. k up). 1991. 15.95 (0-395-55113-7, Clarion Bks) HM.

*Tuesday. David Wiesner. (J). 1997. pap. 5.95 (0-395-87082-8, Clarion Bks) HM.

Tuesday, Book & Doll Gift Box. David Wiesner. 1995. pap. 22.00 (0-395-73511-4, Clarion Bks) HM.

Tuesday Cafe. Don Trembath. 140p. (Orig.). (YA). 1996. pap. 6.95 (1-55143-074-6) Orca Bk Pubs.

Tuesday Club: A Shorter Edition of the History of the Ancient & Honorable Tuesday Club by Dr. Alexander Hamilton. Ed. by Robert Micklus. LC 94-20542. (Maryland Paperback Bookshelf Ser.). (Illus.). 360p. 1995. 48.50 (0-8018-5008-8); pap. text ed. 16.95 (0-8018-4968-3) Johns Hopkins.

Tuesday Club Murders. large type ed. Agatha Christie. 1992. lib. bdg. 19.95 (0-8161-4613-6, GK Hall) Thorndike Pr.

Tuesday Club of Annapolis (1745-1756) As Cultural Performance. Atwell W. Sommerville, Jr. LC 95-42671. (C). 1996. 45.00 (0-8203-1822-1) U of Ga Pr.

Tuesday Eight-Fifteen. Paterson Whyte. 55p. (Orig.). 1996. pap. 6.00 (0-88734-357-0) Players Pr.

*Tuesday in Arizona. Marian Harris. LC 97-5114. (Illus.). (J). Date not set. write for info. (1-56554-233-9) Pelican.

Tuesday Is Chicken, & Turkey & Cornish Hens & Chicken Salads & More. Time-Life Books Editors. LC 95-10415. (Everyday Cookbooks Ser.). (Illus.). 128p. 1995. 14.95 (0-8094-9187-7) Time-Life.

Tuesday Night Football. Alex Karras. Date not set. 3.98 (0-8317-4958-X) Smithmark.

Tuesday Night Football: A Comic Novel. Alex Karras. 1991. 17.95 (1-55972-081-6, Birch Ln Pr) Carol Pub Group.

Tuesday the Rabbi Saw Red. Harry Kemelman. (Rabbi Ser.). 1986. mass mkt. 4.95 (0-449-21321-8) Fawcett.

Tuesdays at Ten: A Garnering from the Talks of Thirty Years on Poets, Dramatists & Essayists. Cornelius Weygandt. LC 67-30235. (Essay Index Reprint Ser.). 1977. 20.95 (0-8369-0985-2) Ayer.

Tuesday's Child. Jenevy Michaels. 256p. 1996. mass mkt. 4.99 (0-7860-0339-1, Pinncle Kensgtn) Kensgtn Pub Corp.

*Tuesdays with Morrie: An Old Man, a Young Man & the Last. Mitch Albom. LC 96-52535. 192p. 1997. 19.95 (0-385-48451-8) Doubleday.

Tueur sans Gages. Eugene Ionesco. (Folio Ser.: No. 576). (FRE.). pap. 9.25 (2-07-036576-X) Schoenhof.

Tueur Sans Gages. Eugene Ionesco. (FRE.). 1974. pap. 10.95 (0-8288-3696-5, M3587) Fr & Eur.

Tueur Sous la Pluie. Raymond Chandler. 245p. (FRE.). 1988. pap. 10.95 (0-7859-2082-X, 2070379108) Fr & Eur.

*Tuff Stuff's Guide to Kenner's Starting Lineup Figures. Jim Warren, II. (Illus.). 208p. (Orig.). 1997. pap. 26.95 (0-930625-78-1, Antque Trdr Bks) Antique Trader Bks.

Tuffy, an Angel Hid in a Cloud. Allan Shields. LC 94-75781. (Illus.). 60p. (Orig.). (J). (gr. 3-7). 1994. pap. 8.95 (1-882803-07-8) Jerseydale Ranch.

Tuffy the Tiger. Tom LaFleur & Gale Brennan. (Illus.). 16p. (J). (gr. k-6). 1982. pap. 1.25 (0-685-05557-4) Brennan Bks.

Tuffy's Bike Race. Linda P. Silbert & Alvin J. Silbert. (Little Twirps Understanding People Bks.). (Illus.). (J). (gr. k-4). 1978. pap. 4.98 (0-89544-058-X) Silbert Bress.

*Tufro. John R. Whitman. (Illus.). vi, 52p. (Orig.). (J). (ps-6). 1996. pap. 24.99 incl. disk (0-9657074-0-7) Toothaccount.

Tuft of Primroses, with Other Late Poems for The Recluse. William Wordsworth. Ed. by Joseph S. Kishel. LC 84-27403. (Cornell Wordsworth Ser.). (Illus.). 408p. (C). 1986. 65.00 (0-8014-1819-4) Cornell U Pr.

*Tufted Titmouse. Thomas C. Grubb. LC 97-18000. (Wild Bird Guides Ser.). 1998. write for info. (0-8117-2967-2) Stackpole.

*Tuftonboro: An Historical Sketch. John W. Hayley. (Illus.). 111p. 1997. reprint ed. pap. 15.00 (0-8328-6028-X) Higginson Bk Co.

Tufts University Guide to Total Nutrition. 2nd rev. ed. Stanley Gershoff et al. LC 95-6386. (Illus.). 352p. (Orig.). 1996. pap. 16.00 (0-06-273316-8, Harper Ref) HarpC.

Tuftsin: Biochemistry, Immunology & Clinical Prospects. Nishioka. 1995. write for info. (0-8493-6701-8) CRC Pr.

TuFu - Kenneth Rexroth - Brice Marden. limited ed. TuFu. Tr. by Kenneth Rexroth from CHI. (Illus.). 114p. 1987. 170.00 (0-935875-04-2) P Blum Edit.

Tug. Stephen T. Booker. LC 94-1306. (Wesleyan Poetry Ser.). (Illus.). 62p. (C). 1994. pap. 11.95 (0-8195-1215-X, Wesleyan Univ Pr); text ed. 25.00 (0-8195-2212-0, Wesleyan Univ Pr) U Pr of New Eng.

Tug Hill Program: A Regional Planning Option for Rural Areas. Cynthia D. Dyballa et al. LC 81-8999. (New York State Study Ser.). (Illus.). 189p. reprint ed. pap. 53.90 (0-8357-3979-1, 2036677) Bks Demand.

*Tug of Home: Restful Words for Weary Families. Charles E. Poole. LC 97-6828. 1997. write for info. (1-57312-150-9, Peake Road) Smyth & Helwys.

Tug of Love. Penny Jordan & Sarah Holland. (Presents Ser.). 1995. mass mkt. 3.25 (0-373-11734-5, 1-11734-0) Harlequin Bks.

*Tug of War. Zachary Karabell. 256p. 1998. 24.00 (0-465-08770-1) Basic.

Tug of War. Carroll Kehne. (J). (gr. 4-7). 1994. 12.95 (0-86316-216-9) Writers & Readers.

Tug of War. J. C. Pearce. LC 93-15037. (Foul Play Ser.: No. 5). 144p. (J). (gr. 3-7). 1993. pap. 3.25 (0-14-036663-6, Puffin) Puffin Bks.

Tug of War. Barbara A. Scott. LC 93-70369. 218p. (YA). (gr. 8-12). 1993. pap. 7.95 (0-943864-70-4) Davenport.

Tug of War. Shelagh D. Whitaker. 470p. 1987. pap. 16.95 (0-7737-5103-3) Genl Dist Srvs.

Tug of War, No. 16. Francine Pascal. (Sweet Valley Twins Ser.). 112p. (Orig.). 1988. pap. 2.75 (0-685-18297-5, Skylark BDD) BDD Bks Young Read.

Tug of War: Peace Through Understanding Conflict. Terrence Webster-Doyle. (Education for Peace Ser.). (Illus.). 106p. (YA). (gr. 5-12). 1990. pap. 14.95 (0-942941-20-9) Atrium Soc Educ.

Tug of War: Today's Global Currency Crisis. Paul Erdman. LC 96-19401. 180p. 1996. 21.95 (0-312-15899-8) St Martin.

Tug of War: Today's Global Currency Crisis. Paul Erdman. 180p. 1996. 21.95 (0-614-96974-3) St Martin.

Tugboat. Arlene Blanchard. LC 94-25705. (Illus.). (J). (gr. 1-8). 1995. pap. 3.99 (1-56402-524-1) Candlewick Pr.

Tugboat Annie. Norman R. Raine. 17.95 (0-89387-010-2) Amereon Ltd.

Tugboats. Robert Maass. LC 96-17884. (J). 1997. 15.95 (0-8050-3116-2) H Holt & Co.

Tugboats in Action. Timothy Burke. LC 93-9131. (J). (gr. k-3). 1993. lib. bdg. 15.95 (0-8075-8112-7) A Whitman.

*Tugboats in Action. Timothy R. Burke. (Illus.). 32p. (J). (gr. k-3). 1997. reprint ed. pap. 6.95 (0-8075-8113-5) A Whitman.

Tugboats on the Piscataqua: A Brief History of Towing on One of America's Toughest Rivers. Woodward D. Openo. (Illus.). 184p. 1992. 25.00 (0-915819-17-1) Portsmouth Marine Soc.

Tugen Spyl: Nach der Ausgabe des Magister Johann Winckel von Strassburg. Hans-Gert Roloff. (Ausgaben Deutscher Literatur des XV bis XVIII Jahrhunderts Ser.). (C). 1968. 113.85 (3-11-000350-3) De Gruyter.

Tugford Wanted to Be Bad. Audrey Wood. LC 83-318. (Let Me Read Ser.). (Illus.). 32p. (J). (ps-3). 1983. 10.00 (0-15-291083-2, HB Juv Bks) HarBrace.

Tughlug Dynasty. Agha M. Husain. 718p. 1987. 150.00 (0-317-52161-6, Pub. by S Chand II) St Mut.

Tugman's Passage. Edward Hoagland. 1982. 12.50 (0-394-52268-0) Random.

Tugman's Passage. Edward Hoagland. 288p. 1995. pap. 14.95 (1-55821-369-4) Lyons & Burford.

Tugs & Towage. Michael K. Stammers. 1989. pap. 25.00 (0-7478-0039-1, Pub. by Shire UK) St Mut.

*Tugs Today: Vessels & Tech Towage Ind. M. J. Gaston. (Illus.). 200p. 1996. 29.95 (1-85260-521-9, Pub. by J H Haynes & Co UK) Motorbooks Intl.

Tugwell's Thoughts on Planning. Rexford G. Tugwell. Ed. by Salvador M. Padilla. 236p. 1974. 6.00 (0-8477-2428-X); pap. 5.00 (0-8477-2429-8) U of PR Pr.

Tuhami: Portrait of a Moroccan. Vincent Crapanzano. LC 79-24550. 204p. (C). 1986. reprint ed. pap. text ed. 10.95 (0-226-11871-1) U Ch Pr.

Tuition Dilemma. Arthur M. Hauptman. 1990. 26.95 (0-8157-3502-2); pap. 9.95 (0-8157-3501-4) Brookings.

Tuition Dilemma: State Policies & Practices for Pricing Public Higher Education. Charles L. Lenth. 1993. 15.00 (1-881543-02-1) SHEEO.

Tuition Discounting: The Impact of Institutionally Funded Financial Aid. Loren L. Hubbell. 60p. 1992. 35.00 (0-685-62920-1); 220.00 (0-915164-76-0); disk 199.00 (0-685-62921-X) NACUBO.

Tuition Discounting Executive Study (Annual) 54p. 1997. 34.95 (0-614-17595-X) NACUBO.

Tuition-Fees, Financial Aid Statistics: Private Colleges & Universities Awarding the Master's As the Highest Degree. Intro. by John Minter. (Institutional Research Reports). 50p. 1986. lib. bdg. write for info. (0-937767-15-8) Nat Data Service.

Tuition-Fees, Financial Aid Statistics: Private Colleges Awarding the Bachelor's As the Highest Degree. Intro. by John Minter. (Institutional Research Reports). 50p. 1986. lib. bdg. write for info. (0-937767-09-3) Nat Data Service.

Tuition-Fees, Financial Aid Statistics: Private Universities Awarding the Doctoral's As the Highest Degree. Intro. by John Minter. (Institutional Research Reports). 50p. 1987. lib. bdg. write for info. (0-937767-21-2) Nat Data Service.

Tuition-Fees, Financial Aid Statistics: Public Colleges & Universities Awarding the Comprehensive As the Highest Degree. Ed. & Intro. by John Minter. (Institutional Research Reports). 50p. 1987. lib. bdg. write for info. (0-937767-47-6) Nat Data Service.

Tuition-Fees, Financial Aid Statistics: Public Colleges Awarding the Bachelor's As the Highest Degree. Ed. & Intro. by John Minter. (Institutional Research Reports). 50p. 1987. lib. bdg. write for info. (0-937767-42-5) Nat Data Service.

Tuition Tax Credits for Private Education: An Economic Analysis. Donald E. Frey. LC 83-12676. (Illus.). 129p. 1983. reprint ed. pap. 36.80 (0-608-00031-0, 2060797) Bks Demand.

Tuition Tax Deductions & Parent School Choice: A Case Study of Minnesota. Linda Darling-Hammond et al. LC 85-16965. 1985. pap. 10.00 (0-8330-0670-3, R-3294-NIE) Rand Corp.

Tukama Tootles the Flute: A Tale from the Antilles. Illus. by Synthia Saint James. LC 93-2253. 32p. (J). (ps-2). 1994. 15.95 (0-531-06811-0); lib. bdg. 16.99 (0-531-08661-5) Orchard Bks Watts.

Tukaram. R. D. Ranade. 231p. (C). 1994. pap. 9.95 (0-7914-2092-2) State U NY Pr.

Tukes of York. William K. Sessions. (C). 1989. pap. 30.00 (1-85072-020-7, Pub. by W Sessions UK) St Mut.

Tukumba Pounding Songs: A Device for Resolving Familial Conflict. Enoch T. Mvula. (Graduate Student Term Paper Ser.). 19p. 1984. pap. text ed. 2.00 (0-941934-45-4) Indiana Africa.

Tukwila - Community at the Crossroads. Kay F. Reinartz. (Illus.). 264p. (Orig.). 1991. 35.00 (0-9629652-0-0); pap. 18.00 (0-9629652-1-9) City Tukwila.

Tul-Tok-A-Na: The Small One. Kathleen A. Meyer. (Illus.). 32p. (Orig.). (J). (gr. 1-5). 1992. pap. 6.95 (0-89992-105-1) Coun India Ed.

*Tula Oblast: Economy, Industry, Government, Business. 2nd rev. ed. Russian Information & Business Center, Inc. Staff. (Russian Regional Business Directories Ser.). (Illus.). 200p. 1997. pap. 99.00 (1-57751-419-X) Russ Info & Busn Ctr.

Tula of the Toltecs: Excavations & Survey. Ed. by Dan M. Healan. LC 88-18996. (Illus.). 313p. 1989. text ed. 49.95 (0-87745-209-1) U of Iowa Pr.

Tulane Law Review: 1916-1995/96, 70 vols. Bound set. 3,765.00 (0-8377-9165-0) Rothman.

Tulane Law School Annual Institute on Federal Taxation: 1994-95, Vol. 44. 1994. ring bd. 169.00 (0-614-06342-6) Claitors.

Tulane Maritime Law Journal: 1975-1995/96, 20 vols. Bound set. 700.00 (0-8377-9109-X) Rothman.

*Tulane Tax Institute, Vol. 23. 1982. 45.00 (0-87511-470-9) Claitors.

*Tulane Tax Institute, Vol. 24. 1982. pap. 45.00 (0-87511-471-7) Claitors.

*Tulane Tax Institute, Vol. 25. 1982. pap. 45.00 (0-87511-472-5) Claitors.

*Tulane Tax Institute, Vol. 26. 1982. 45.00 (0-87511-473-3) Claitors.

*Tulane Tax Institute, Vol. 27. 1982. 45.00 (0-87511-474-1) Claitors.

*Tulane Tax Institute, Vol. 28. 1982. 45.00 (0-87511-475-X) Claitors.

*Tulane Tax Institute, Vol. 29. 1982. 45.00 (0-87511-476-8) Claitors.

*Tulane Tax Institute, Vol. 30. 1982. 45.00 (0-87511-543-8) Claitors.

*Tulane Tax Institute, Vol. 31. 1982. 45.00 (0-87511-625-6) Claitors.

*Tulane Tax Institute, Vol. 32. 1982. 45.00 (0-87511-626-4) Claitors.

Tulane Tax Institute, Vol. 33. 1983. 45.00 (0-87511-627-2) Claitors.

Tulane University. Photos by Tommy Thompson. (Illus.). 112p. 1990. 39.00 (0-916509-60-5) Harmony Hse Pub.

Tulapai to Tokay: A Bibliography of Alcohol Use & Abuse Among Native Americans of North America. Patricia D. Mail & David R. McDonald. LC 80-81243. (Bibliographies Ser.). 372p. 1981. 25.00 (0-87536-253-2) HRAFP.

Tularemia Gambit. Steve Perry. 224p. (Orig.). 1981. pap. 2.25 (0-449-14411-9, GM) Fawcett.

*Tularosa. Michael McGarrity. 1997. mass mkt. 6.50 (0-671-00252-X) PB.

Tularosa. Michael McGarrity. LC 95-36128. 304p. 1996. 25.00 (0-393-03922-6) Norton.

*Tularosa. large type ed. Michael McGarrity. LC 96-3428. 1996. pap. 22.95 (1-56895-372-0, Compass) Wheeler Pub.

Tularosa: Last of the Frontier West. rev. ed. Charles L. Sonnichsen. LC 80-52286. (Illus.). 344p. 1980. reprint ed. pap. 14.95 (0-8263-0561-X) U of NM Pr.

Tule. Frederick A. Raborg, Jr. (Amelia Chapbooks Ser.). (Illus.). 24p. (Orig.). 1986. pap. 6.95 (0-936545-01-1) Amelia.

Tule Elk. Caroline Arnold. (Nature Watch Bks.). (Illus.). 48p. (J). (gr. 2-5). 1989. lib. bdg. 14.96 (0-87614-343-5, Carolrhoda) Lerner Group.

Tule Elk: Its History, Behavior, & Ecology. Dale R. McCullough. LC 75-626287. (University of California Publications in Social Welfare: No. 88). (Illus.). 219p. reprint ed. pap. 62.50 (0-685-23671-4, 2029053) Bks Demand.

Tule Lake. Edward T. Miyakawa. Ed. by Carol S. Van Strum. (Orig.). 1979. 12.95 (0-686-25250-0); pap. 7.95 (0-686-25251-9) Hse by the Sea.

Tule Lake: From Relocation to Segregation. Harold S. Jacoby. LC 95-43637. (Illus.). xvi, 121p. (Orig.). 1996. pap. 10.50 (0-933994-15-X) Comstock Bon.

Tule Springs, Nevada: With Other Evidences of Pleistocene Man in North America. M. R. Harrington & R. D. Simpson. 146p. 1961. pap. 5.00 (0-916561-65-8) Southwest Mus.

Tulidasa's Shriramacharitamanasa. Ed. by R. C. Prasad. (C). 1990. 42.00 (0-685-39090-X, Pub. by Motilal Banarsidass II) S Asia.

Tulip: The Five Points of Calvinism in the Light of Scripture. Duane E. Spencer. LC 78-73445. 80p. 1979. mass mkt. 5.99 (0-8010-8161-0) Baker Bks.

Tulip Elegies: An Alchemy of Writing. Denise Low. LC 92-85531. 70p. 1993. pap. 10.00 (0-9632475-0-6) Penthe Pub.

Tulip Parlour. (Paintability Ser.). (Illus.). 12p. 1995. pap. 12.95 (1-85410-135-8, Pub. by Aurum Pr UK) London Brdge.

Tulip Quilt. Eleanor Burns. (Illus.). 72p. 1991. 8.95 (0-922705-22-4) Quilt Day.

Tulip Sacrament. 'Annah Sobelman. LC 94-48729. (Wesleyan Poetry Ser.). 93p. 1995. pap. 11.95 (0-8195-1227-3, Wesleyan Univ Pr); text ed. 25.00 (0-8195-2223-6, Wesleyan Univ Pr) U Pr of New Eng.

*Tulip Sees America. Cynthia Rylant. LC 96-54267. (Illus.). (J). 1998. write for info. (0-590-84744-9, Blue Sky Press) Scholastic Inc.

*Tulip Touch: A Novel. LC 96-47185. (J). 1997. 15.95 (0-316-28325-8) Little.

Tulip Tree. Mary A. Gibbs. 1979. pap. 1.75 (0-449-50000-4, Coventry) Fawcett.

Tulipanes en Diciembre. Eddie Valencia. 96p. (Orig.). 1988. pap. 4.50 (0-311-37026-8, Edit Mundo) Casa Bautista.

Tulipe. Romain Gary. pap. 9.50 (0-685-34129-1) Fr & Eur.

Tulipe Noire. Alexandre Dumas. Ed. by Rene Simon. (Illus.). 188p. (FRE.). 1983. pap. 11.95 (0-7859-4670-5) Fr & Eur.

*Tulips. Peter Arnold. LC 97-7234. 1997. write for info. (1-57145-607-4) Thunder Bay CA.

Tulips. Jay O'Callahan. LC 96-14701. (Illus.). 32p. (J). (gr. 3-7). 1996. 15.95 (1-56145-134-7) Peachtree Pubs.

Tulips. John F. Prevost. (J). 1996. lib. bdg. 13.98 (1-56239-612-9) Abdo & Dghtrs.

*Tulips. Emelie Tolley. LC 97-20915. 1998. write for info. (0-609-60132-6, C P Pubs) Crown Pub Group.

Tulips: Taxonomy, Morphology, Cytology, Phytogeography & Physiology. Z. Botschantzeva. Ed. by H. Varekamp. 282p. (C). 1982. text ed. 150.00 (90-6191-029-3, Pub. by A A Balkema NE) Ashgate Pub Co.

Tulips: Ten Poems by Anna Rossetti. Ana Rossetti & Susan Suntree. Tr. by Nancy D. Nieman from SPA. (Illus.). 24p. (ENG & SPA.). 1990. 7.00 (1-882623-08-8) Exiled-Am Pr.

Tulips & Chimneys: Poems. rev. ed. e. e. Cummings. 1996. pap. 13.00 (0-87140-165-7) Liveright.

Tulips, Arabesques & Turbans: Decorative Arts from the Ottoman Empire. Ed. by Yanni Petsopoulos. LC 81-20534. (Illus.). 208p. 1982. 75.00 (*0-89659-279-0*) Abbeville Pr.

Tulips in the Prison Yard. Daniel Berrigan. 80p. pap. 9.95 (*1-873790-24-4*) Fortkamp.

Tulita la Patita. Nicholas P. Georgiady & Louis G. Romano. Tr. by Ida N. De Ninojosa. (Look! I-Can-Read Bk.). (Illus.). 32p. (J). (gr. 1-4). 1996. reprint ed. pap. 3.00 (*0-317-03352-2*) Argee Pubs.

Tulku. Peter Dickinson. 288p. (J). 1993. mass mkt. 3.99 (*0-440-21489-0*) Dell.

Tulku. Peter Dickinson. 1995. 17.75 (*0-8446-6830-3*) Peter Smith.

Tull: John Porter Tull & His Descendants. James P. Tull. Ed. by M. Tull-Boatner. (Illus.). xv, 170p. 1992. reprint ed. pap. 28.50 (*0-8328-2745-2*); reprint ed. lib. bdg. 38.50 (*0-8328-2744-4*) Higginson Bk Co.

Tullio Lombardo & Ideal Portait Sculpture in Renaissance Italy, 1490-1530. Alison Luchs. (Illus.). 336p. (C). 1995. text ed. 74.95 (*0-521-47075-7*) Cambridge U Pr.

Tullio Pericoli: Woody, Freud & Others. 156p. 1989. pap. 24.95 (*3-7913-1028-3*, Pub. by Prestel GW) te Neues.

Tullio's Orange Tree. Ted Gerstl. (Illus.). 40p. 1996. 12.95 (*1-888820-02-0*, Mllennium) Millennium Calif.

Tully. Paulina Simons. 1995. mass mkt. 6.99 (*0-312-95421-2*) St Martin.

Tully. Paullina Simons. 1994. 23.95 (*0-312-11083-9*) St Martin.

Tulo, the Cat Who Loved Zucchini. Laga Daemon. (Illus.). 52p. (Orig.). (J). (gr. 6-8). 1996. pap. 9.95 (*1-882427-15-7*, 315-7) Aspasia Inc.

Tulpehocken Church Records, 1730 to 1800: Christ (Little Tulpehocken) Church & the Altalaha Church at Rehrersburg. (Sources & Documents Ser.: No. 7). 1982. 15.00 (*0-911122-45-1*) Penn German Soc.

***Tulsa! Biography of the American City.** Danney Goble. (Illus.). 320p. (C). 1997. 29.95 (*1-57178-051-3*) Coun Oak Bks.

***Tulsa Education: George Washington Carver, an Inspired Scientist.** Peter D. Burchard. (Illus.). 110p. (Orig.). 1997. pap. 7.95 (*0-9658023-0-2*) Serpent Wise.

Tulsa Kid. Ron Padgett. Ed. by Kenward Elmslie. (Illus.). (Orig.). 1980. 10.00 (*0-915990-16-4*); pap. 5.00 (*0-915990-17-2*) Z Pr.

Tulsa Law Journal: 1964-1995/96, Vols. 1-31. Bound set. 1, 360.00 (*0-8377-9166-9*) Rothman.

Tulsa, OK. (Streetfinder Ser.). (Illus.). 1994. pap. 14.95 (*0-528-91322-0*) Rand McNally.

Tulsa-Tbilisi. Ed. by Francine Ringold. 168p. 1985. pap. 5.50 (*0-317-60730-8*) Art & Human Council Tulsa.

Tulu-English. A. Manner. 687p. 1983. 28.50 (*0-88431-263-1*) IBD Ltd.

Tulu English Dictionary. A. Manner. 696p. 1983. 79.95 (*0-8288-8466-8*) Fr & Eur.

Tulum: An Archaeological Study of the East Coast of Yucaton. Samuel K. Lothrop. 1976. lib. bdg. 69.95 (*0-8490-2779-9*) Gordon Pr.

Tumacacori: From Rancheria to National Monument. Nicholas J. Bleser. Ed. by T. J. Priehs. LC 89-61675. (Illus.). 48p. (Orig.). 1990. pap. 6.95 (*0-911408-84-3*) SW Pks Mnmts.

Tumacacori National Historical Park. Susan Lamb. Ed. by T. J. Priehs & Sandra Scott. LC 93-86297. (Illus.). 16p. (Orig.). 1993. pap. 3.95 (*1-877856-37-1*) SW Pks Mnmts.

Tumanov: Confessions of a KGB Agent. Oleg Tumanov. Tr. by David Floyd. LC 93-6427. 187p. 1993. 21.95 (*0-86715-269-9*) Edition Q.

Tumbas: The Tombs. Enrique Medina. LC 92-23401. (Library of World Literature in Translation: Vol. 4). 334p. 1992. text ed. 20.00 (*0-8240-7436-X*) Garland.

***Tumbas de Anac.** Frank E. Peretti. (Cooper Kids Adventure Ser.). (SPA.). (J). 1.50 (*0-8297-0293-8*) Life Pubs Intl.

Tumbas Reales de Sipan. Walter Alva & Christopher B. Donnan. LC 93-72310. (Illus.). 234p. 1993. 50.00 (*0-930741-31-5*); pap. 35.00 (*0-930741-32-3*) UCLA Fowler Mus.

Tumble Bumble. Felicia Bond. LC 96-14417. (Illus.). 32p. (J). (ps-3). 1996. 13.95 (*1-886910-15-4*, Front Street) Front Str.

Tumble-Down Tower. Michael Steinbaum & Jean Warmbold. (Ms. Stories Tell Tales Ser.). (Illus.). (J). (ps-4). 1993. pap. 9.95 (*0-8449-4254-5*) Good Morn Tchr.

***Tumble Home.** Amy Hempel. LC 97-9681. 1997. 21.00 (*0-684-83375-1*) S&S Trade.

Tumble of Reason: Alice Munro's Discourse of Absence. Ajay Heble. 210p. 1994. 35.00 (*0-8020-0617-5*) U of Toronto Pr.

Tumble Soup: Poems. Samuel H. Vasbinder. LC 95-19126. 60p. 1996. pap. 12.95 (*0-7734-2737-6*, Mellen Poetry Pr) E Mellen.

Tumble Tower. Anne Tyler. LC 92-44524. (Illus.). 32p. (J). (ps-2). 1993. 15.95 (*0-531-05497-7*); lib. bdg. 16.99 (*0-531-08647-X*) Orchard Bks Watts.

***Tumble Weed: A Kwanzaa Fairytale.** Paula D. Ferguson. (Illus.). 20p. (Orig.). (J). (gr. 1-3). 1997. pap. 8.99 (*1-55197-763-X*, Pub. by Comnwlth Pub CN) Partners Pubs Grp.

Tumblebugs & Hairy Bears: Exploring Insects with Children. Suzanne Samson. LC 96-67080. (Illus.). 32p. (Orig.). (J). (gr. 1-5). 1996. pap. 10.95 (*1-57098-088-8*) R Rinehart.

Tumbleweed. Janwillem Van de Wetering. LC 76-1865. (Soho Crime Ser.). 224p. 1994. pap. 10.00 (*1-56947-018-9*) Soho Press.

Tumbleweed & Gibraltar. Rita Rainville. (Desire Ser.). 1993. mass mkt. 2.99 (*0-373-05828-4*, 5-05828-4) Silhouette.

Tumbleweed Christmas. Alane Ferguson. LC 95-44058. (Illus.). (J). 1996. 15.00 (*0-689-80465-2*) S&S Childrens.

Tumbleweed Christmas. Shari A. Pence. LC 96-96223. (Illus.). 33p. (Orig.). 1997. pap. 6.95 (*0-9645771-2-7*) Funcastle Pubns.

Tumbleweed Gourmet: Cooking with Wild Southwestern Plants. Carolyn Niethammer. LC 87-5948. 229p. 1987. 12.95 (*0-8165-1021-0*) U of Ariz Pr.

Tumbleweed Heart. Tess Farraday. 1996. mass mkt. 5.99 (*0-515-11944-X*) Jove Pubns.

Tumbleweed Tom on the Texas Trail. Jackie Hopkins. LC 93-48614. (Illus.). 32p. (Orig.). (J). (ps-4). 1994. 14.95 (*0-88106-848-9*); pap. 6.95 (*0-88106-847-0*); lib. bdg. 15.88 (*0-88106-849-7*) Charlesbridge Pub.

Tumbleweeds. Marta Roberts. LC 74-22805. reprint ed. 37.50 (*0-404-58461-6*) AMS Pr.

Tumbleweeds: A Therapist's Guide to Treatment of ACOAs. Paul J. Curtin. 90p. (Orig.). 1985. pap. 6.95 (*0-934391-03-3*) Quotidian.

TumbleWords: Writers Reading the West. Ed. by William L. Fox. LC 95-17113. (Western Literature Ser.). 408p. (Orig.). 1995. pap. 20.00 (*0-87417-271-3*) U of Nev Pr.

***Tumbling.** Diane McKinney-Whetstone. LC 96-51546. 1997. pap. 12.00 (*0-684-83724-2*, Scribners PB Fict) S&S Trade.

Tumbling. Diane McKinney-Whetstone. LC 95-49146. 288p. 1996. 24.00 (*0-688-14487-X*) Morrow.

Tumbling Walls: A True Story of Ordinary People Bringing Reconciliation in Extraordinary Ways to an Alienated World. Walter E. James & Christy Zatkin. LC 90-82802. (Illus.). 221p. 1991. reprint ed. pap. 9.95 (*0-9627048-0-6*) Diaspora Found.

Tumescent Technique. Gerald H. Pitman. 19p. 1995. pap. 10.00 (*0-614-08700-7*); pap. 85.00 incl. vhs (*0-942219-95-3*); vhs 45.00 (*0-614-08701-5*) Quality Med Pub.

***Tumescent Technique: Local Anesthesia, Liposuction & Dermatologic Plastic Surgery.** Klein. 304p. (C). (gr. 13). 1998. text ed. 185.00 (*0-8151-5205-1*) Mosby Yr Bk.

Tummy: An Owner's Manual. Judson P. Cone. 63p. (Orig.). 1974. pap. 1.95 (*0-89074-008-9*) Charing Cross.

Tummy Trilogy. Calvin Trillin. LC 94-6651. 1994. 25.00 (*0-374-27950-0*); pap. 12.00 (*0-374-52417-3*) FS&G.

Tumor & Non-Tumor Aspects of Angiogenesis. Jacqueline B. Weiss & Barry McLaughlin. (Medical Intelligence Unit Ser.). 118p. 1994. 89.95 (*1-57059-038-9*, LN9038) CRC Pr.

Tumor & Tumor-Like Lesions of the Lung. Carter. LC 97-23526. 1998. text ed. write for info. (*0-7216-3312-9*) Saunders.

Tumor Aneuploidy. Ed. by T. Buchner et al. LC 85-9897. (Illus.). 140p. 1985. 42.95 (*0-387-15376-4*) Spr-Verlag.

Tumor-Associated Leukocytes: Pathophysiology & Therapeutic Applications. Alberto Mantovani. LC 93-50704. (Molecular Biology Intelligence Unit Ser.). 1994. 89.95 (*1-57059-013-3*) R G Landes.

***Tumor Biology: Regulation of Cell Growth, Differentiation & Genetics in Cancer.** NATO Scientific Affairs Organization Staff. Ed. by Asterios S. Tsiftoglou. LC 96-32244. (NATO ASI Ser.; Cell Biology). 331p. 1996. 149.50 (*3-540-61492-3*) Spr-Verlag.

Tumor Blood Circulation: Angiogenesis, Vascular Morphology & Blood Flow of Experimental & Human Tumors. Hans-Inge Peterson. 240p. 1979. 138.00 (*0-8493-5695-4*, RC255, CRC Reprint) Franklin.

Tumor Blood Supply & Metabolic Microenvironment: Characterization & Implications for Therapy. Ed. by Rakesh K. Jain & Peter W. Vaupel. (Illus.). 340p. (Orig.). 1991. pap. 96.00 (*1-56081-328-8*, Pub. by G Fischer Verlag GW) Lubrecht & Cramer.

Tumor Board: Cancer Diagnosis & Treatment. David Winchester et al. LC 96-23252. (Illus.). 800p. 1996. text ed. 99.50 (*0-397-51340-2*) Lppncott-Raven.

Tumor Cell Differentiation: Biology & Pharmacology. Ed. by Jarle Aarbakke et al. LC 87-17012. (Experimental Biology & Medicine Ser.: Vol. 17). (Illus.). 383p. (C). 1987. 109.50 (*0-89603-134-9*) Humana.

Tumor Diagnosis by Electron Microscope, Vol. 3. Jose Russo. Date not set. 75.00 (*0-938607-22-7*) Field & Wood Inc Medical.

Tumor Immunity in Prognosis: The Role of Mononuclear Cell Infiltration. Ed. by Stephen Haskill. LC 82-9991. (Immunolog Ser.: No. 18). (Illus.). 446p. reprint ed. pap. 127.20 (*0-7837-0662-6*, 2040998) Bks Demand.

Tumor Immunology. Ed. by A. G. Dalgleish & M. J. Browning. (Cancer: Clinical Science in Practice Ser.). (Illus.). 352p. (C). 1996. text ed. 74.95 (*0-521-47237-7*) Cambridge U Pr.

***Tumor Immunology: Symposium in Immunology IV.** Ed. by Martha Eibl & C. Huber. LC 96-35941. (Illus.). 130p. 1997. pap. 99.95 (*3-540-61755-8*) Spr-Verlag.

Tumor Immunology & Cancer Therapy. Ed. by Ronald H. Goldfarb & Theresa L. Whiteside. LC 93-39772. (Immunology Ser.: Vol. 61). 344p. 1993. 165.00 (*0-8247-9179-7*) Dekker.

Tumor Invasion & Metastasis. Lance A. Liotta & I. R. Hurt. 1982. lib. bdg. 304.00 (*90-247-2611-5*) Kluwer Ac.

***Tumor Marker Protocols.** Ed. by Margaret Hanausek & Zbigniew Walaszek. (Methods in Molecular Medicine Ser.: Vol. 14). (Illus.). 416p. 1997. 69.50 (*0-89603-380-5*) Humana.

Tumor Markers: Biology & Clinical Applications. Ed. by Nasser Javadpour. LC 85-30014. (Cancer Research Monographs: Vol. 4). 304p. 1987. text ed. 95.00 (*0-275-92145-X*, C2145, Praeger Pubs) Greenwood.

Tumor Matrix Biology. Ed. by Roza Adany. LC 94-44953. 272p. 1995. 205.00 (*0-8493-4882-X*, 4882) CRC Pr.

Tumor Necrosis Factor: Molecular & Celullar Biology & Clinical Relevance. International Conference on Tumor Necrosis Factor & Related Cytokines: Veldhoven, Netherlands (4th : 1992). Ed. by Walter Fiers & Wim A. Buurman. LC 92-48509. (Illus.). x, 256p. 1993. 258.50 (*3-8055-5676-4*) S Karger.

Tumor Necrosis Factor: Structure Function Relationship & Clinical Application. Ed. by T. Osawa & B. Bonavida. (Illus.). x, 292p. 1992. 242.75 (*3-8055-5458-3*) S Karger.

Tumor Necrosis Factor: Structure, Mechanism of Action, Role in Disease & Therapy. Ed. by B. Bonavida et al. (Illus.). x, 254p. 1990. 172.25 (*3-8055-4966-0*) S Karger.

Tumor Necrosis Factor-Cachectin & Related Cytokines. Ed. by B. Bonavida et al. (Illus.). viii, 276p. 1988. 158.50 (*3-8055-4755-2*) S Karger.

Tumor Necrosis Factors: Structure, Function & Mechanism of Action. Ed. by Bharat B. Aggarwal & J. Vilcek. (Immunology Ser.: Vol. 56). 624p. 1991. 225.00 (*0-8247-8554-1*) Dekker.

Tumor Necrosis Factors: The Molecules & Their Emerging Role in Medicine. Ed. by Bruce Beutler. 608p. 1991. text ed. 104.00 (*0-88167-852-X*) Lppncott-Raven.

Tumor Oxidation. Ed. by Peter W. Vaupel et al. (Funktions Analyse Biologischer Systeme Ser.: No. 24). (Illus.). 342p. (Orig.). 1995. pap. 65.00 (*3-437-30784-3*, Pub. by G Fischer Verlag GW) Lubrecht & Cramer.

Tumor Promoters: Biological Approaches for Mechanistic Studies & Assay Systems. Ed. by Robert Langenbach et al. LC 86-43223. (Progress in Cancer Research & Therapy Ser.: Vol. 34). 480p. 1988. reprint ed. pap. 136.80 (*0-608-00303-4*, 2061020) Bks Demand.

Tumor Response Monitoring & Treatment Planning. Ed. by A. Breit. (Illus.). 740p. 1992. 180.00 (*0-387-54783-5*) Spr-Verlag.

Tumor Stereotaxis. Kelly. (Illus.). 442p. 1990. text ed. 169.00 (*0-7216-5360-X*) Saunders.

Tumor Suppressor Genes. Klein. (Immunology Ser.: Vol. 51). 296p. 1990. 145.00 (*0-8247-8218-6*) Dekker.

Tumor Surgery of the Head & Neck. R. S. Pollack. (Illus.). x, 206p. 1975. 58.50 (*3-8055-2092-1*) S Karger.

Tumor Therapy with Tumor Cells & Neuraminidase: Cell Physiological, Immunological, & Oncological Aspects. H. H. Sedlacek. (Beitraege zur Onkologie, Contributions to Oncology Ser.: Vol. 27). (Illus.). viii, 96p. 1987. 40.00 (*3-8055-4549-5*) S Karger.

Tumorbiologie. J. G. Birkmayer. (Illus.). viii, 230p. 1984. 45.75 (*3-8055-3892-8*) S Karger.

Tumorchirurgie und Lebensqualitaet. Ed. by M. Duerig & U. Laffer. (Basler Beitraege zur Chirurgie Ser.: Vol. 2). (Illus.). x, 168p. 1989. 60.00 (*3-8055-5070-7*) S Karger.

Tumorigenic DNA Viruses. Ed. by George Klein. LC 87-42997. (Advances in Viral Oncology Ser.: Vol. 8). 283p. 1989. reprint ed. pap. 80.70 (*0-608-00295-X*, 2059323) Bks Demand.

Tumorimmunologie & Tumortherapie. H. H. Sedlacek. (Beitraege zur Onkologie, Contributions to Oncology Ser.: Vol. 25). (Illus.). x, 186p. 1986. 50.50 (*3-8055-4447-2*) S Karger.

Tumors. J. H. Tilden. 1996. pap. 9.95 (*1-56459-955-8*) Kessinger Pub.

Tumors: Structure & Diagnosis. R. C. Curran & E. L. Jones. (Harvey Miller Publication). (Illus.). 812p. 1991. 275.00 (*0-19-261840-7*) OUP.

Tumors - the Cause Combined with What Is Toxemia? J. H. Tilden. 29p. 1994. reprint ed. spiral bd. 6.50 (*0-7873-1134-0*) Hlth Research.

Tumors & Related Lesions of the Female Genital Tract: Proceedings of the Fifty Sixth Annual Anatomic Pathology Slide Seminar of the ASCP. Ed. by William R. Hart et al. 136p. 1991. 35.00 (*0-89189-337-7*) Am Soc Clinical.

Tumors & Tumor-Like Conditions of the Kidneys & Ureters. Ed. by John N. Eble. (Contemporary Issues in Surgical Pathology Ser.: Vol. 16). (Illus.). 268p. 1990. text ed. 72.00 (*0-443-08674-5*) Churchill.

Tumors & Tumor-Like Conditions of the Ovary. Ed. by Lawrence M. Roth & Bernard Czernobilsky. (Contemporary Issues in Surgical Pathology Ser.: Vol. 6). (Illus.). 296p. 1985. text ed. 72.00 (*0-443-08289-8*) Churchill.

Tumors & Tumor-Like Lesions of Soft Tissues. Ed. by Vito Ninfo & E. B. Chung. (Contemporary Issues in Surgical Pathology Ser.: Vol. 18). (Illus.). 295p. 1991. text ed. 95.00 (*0-443-08672-9*) Churchill.

Tumors & Tumor-Like Lesions of the Uterine Corpus & Cervix. Philip B. Clement & Robert H. Young. (Contemporary Issues in Surgical Pathology Ser.). (Illus.). 504p. 1993. text ed. 99.00 (*0-443-08801-2*) Churchill.

Tumors & Tumorlike Lesions of Bone: Pathology, Radiology, & Treatment. 2nd ed. Fritz Schajowicz. LC 92-49404. 1993. write for info. (*3-540-55366-5*) Spr-Verlag.

Tumors & Tumorlike Lesions of Bone: Pathology, Radiology, & Treatment. 2nd rev. ed. Fritz Schajowicz. (Illus.). 752p. 1995. 348.00 (*0-387-55366-5*) Spr-Verlag.

Tumors in Aquatic Animals. Ed. by F. Homburger. (Progress in Experimental Tumor Research Ser.: Vol. 20). 400p. 1976. 123.25 (*3-8055-2254-1*) S Karger.

Tumors in Domestic Animals. 3rd enl. rev. ed. Jack E. Moulton. 1990. 125.00 (*0-520-05818-6*) U CA Pr.

***Tumors in Urology.** D. E. Neal. (Illus.). 298p. 1995. 136.00 (*3-540-19867-9*) Spr-Verlag.

Tumors in Urology: Biology & Clinical Management. Ed. by David E. Neal. LC 94-14579. 1994. 149.00 (*0-387-19867-9*) Spr-Verlag.

Tumors of Connective Tissue Cells. Hashimoto. 1996. write for info. (*0-7506-9475-0*) Buttrwrth-Heinemann.

Tumors of Skin Appendages. Ken Hashimoto et al. (Practical Dermatopathology Ser.). (Illus.). 208p. 1987. 80.00 (*0-409-95159-5*) Buttrwrth-Heinemann.

Tumors of the Cardiovascular System. 1995. lib. bdg. 257.95 (*0-8490-6722-7*) Gordon Pr.

Tumors of the Central Nervous System, 2 vols., Set. 1995. lib. bdg. 600.99 (*0-8490-6726-X*) Gordon Pr.

Tumors of the Epidermis. Ken Hashimoto & Amir H. Mehregoan. (Practical Dermatopathology Ser.). (Illus.). 288p. 1990. 80.00 (*0-409-90163-6*) Buttrwrth-Heinemann.

Tumors of the Esophagus & Stomach, 2 vols. 1991. lib. bdg. 600.95 (*0-8490-4334-4*) Gordon Pr.

Tumors of the Exocrine Pancreas. 1995. lib. bdg. 251.99 (*0-8490-6715-4*) Gordon Pr.

Tumors of the Eye. Ed. by N. Bornfeld et al. LC 91-35368. (Illus.). 700p. 1991. lib. bdg. 219.00 (*90-6299-082-7*, Pub. by Kugler NE) Kugler Pubns.

Tumors of the Fetus & Newborn. Issacs. LC 96-38016. 1997. text ed. 85.00 (*0-7216-3813-9*) HarBrace.

Tumors of the Head & Neck. 3rd ed. John G. Batsakis. (Illus.). 776p. 1996. write for info. (*0-683-00477-8*) Williams & Wilkins.

Tumors of the Head & Neck in Children. Robert O. Greer et al. LC 82-19114. 430p. 1983. text ed. 95.00 (*0-275-91391-0*, C1391, Praeger Pubs) Greenwood.

Tumors of the Intestines, 2 vols., Set. 1995. lib. bdg. 605.75 (*0-8490-7565-3*) Gordon Pr.

Tumors of the Kidney. Michele Pavone-Macaluso & Jean B. DeKernion. (Surgery Ser.). (Illus.). 340p. 1986. 86.75 (*0-683-02426-4*) Williams & Wilkins.

Tumors of the Kidney & Urinary Tract. Steen Olsen. (Illus.). 291p. 1985. text ed. 135.00 (*0-7216-1588-0*) Saunders.

Tumors of the Liver & Extrahepatic Bile Ducts. 1995. lib. bdg. 252.99 (*0-8490-6718-9*) Gordon Pr.

Tumors of the Lung. Mackay et al. (Illus.). 432p. 1990. text ed. 87.50 (*0-7216-5807-5*) Saunders.

***Tumors of the Lung: Contemporary Issues.** B. Corrin. LC 97-7855. 1997. write for info. (*0-443-05367-7*) Churchill.

Tumors of the Male Genital System. 1995. lib. bdg. 257.99 (*0-8490-6720-0*) Gordon Pr.

Tumors of the Mediastinum. J. M. Verley & K. H. Hollmann. (Current Histopathology Ser.). (C). 1992. lib. bdg. 208.00 (*0-7923-8986-7*) Kluwer Ac.

Tumors of the Soft Tissues. 1995. lib. bdg. 275.95 (*0-8490-6725-1*) Gordon Pr.

***Tumors of the Soft Tissues.** 2nd ed. Dasgupta & Chaudhuri. 1997. text ed. 175.00 (*0-8385-9044-6*) P-H.

Tumors of the Spine: Diagnosis & Clinical Management. Sundaresan et al. (Illus.). 576p. 1990. text ed. 319.00 (*0-7216-2826-6*) Saunders.

Tumors of the Thymus. 1995. lib. bdg. 275.95 (*0-8490-6724-3*) Gordon Pr.

Tumors of the Upper Respiratory Tract & Ear. 1995. lib. bdg. 278.95 (*0-8490-6723-5*) Gordon Pr.

Tumors of the Urinary Bladder. 1995. lib. bdg. 263.95 (*0-8490-6716-2*) Gordon Pr.

Tumors of the Uterine Corpus & Gestational Trophoblastic Disease. Silverberg & Robert J. Kurman. (Illus.). 290p. 1992. 45.00 (*1-881041-01-8*) Am Registry Path.

***Tumour Angiogenesis.** Ed. by Roy Bicknell et al. (Illus.). 512p. 1997. 169.50 (*0-19-854937-7*) OUP.

Tumour Immunobiology: A Practical Approach. Ed. by G. Gallagher et al. LC 92-49322. (Practical Approach Ser.). (Illus.). 320p. (C). 1993. 95.00 (*0-19-963370-3*, IRL Pr); pap. 55.00 (*0-19-963369-X*, IRL Pr) OUP.

Tumour Localization with Radioactive Agents. LC 76-7616. (Panel Proceedings Ser.). (Illus.). 142p. 1976. pap. 35.00 (*92-0-111276-9*, ISP451, Pub. by IAEA AU) Bernan Associates.

Tumour Suppressor Genes, the Cell Cycle & Cancer. Ed. by Arnold J. Levine. (Cancer Surveys Ser.: Vol. 12). (Illus.). 300p. (C). 1992. text ed. 45.00 (*0-87969-369-X*) Cold Spring Harbor.

Tumours, Lymphomas & Selected Paraproteinaemias. Ed. by Julian L. Verbov. (New Clinical Applications Dermatology Ser.). (C). 1988. lib. bdg. 82.50 (*0-7462-0082-X*) Kluwer Ac.

***Tumours of the Brain & Skull, Pt. I.** Pierre J. Vinken & G. W. Bruyn. (Handbook of Clinical Neurology Ser.: Vol. 16). 748p. 1974. 492.00 (*0-7204-7216-4*) Elsevier.

***Tumours of the Brain & Skull, Pt. II.** Pierre J. Vinken & G. W. Bruyn. (Handbook of Clinical Neurology Ser.: Vol. 17). 748p. 1974. 492.00 (*0-7204-7217-2*) Elsevier.

***Tumours of the Brain & Skull, Pt. III.** Pierre J. Vinken & G. W. Bruyn. (Handbook of Clinical Neurology Ser.: Vol. 18). 582p. 1975. 343.75 (*0-7204-7218-0*) Elsevier.

Tumours of the Brain & Skull see Handbook of Clinical Neurology

***Tumours of the Epidermis & Ache.** Marks. (Illus.). 208p. (C). 1997. text ed. write for info. (*0-412-63530-5*, Chap & Hall NY) Chapman & Hall.

Tumours of the Eye. Hungerford. Date not set. write for info. (*0-7506-1436-6*) Buttrwrth-Heinemann.

Tumours of the Hand & Upper Limb. Ed. by George B. Bogumill & Earl J. Fleegler. (Hand & Upper Limb Ser.: No. 10). (Illus.). 256p. 1993. text ed. 150.00 (*0-443-04162-8*) Churchill.

Tumours of the Larynx. E. Meyer-Breiting. (Illus.). 240p. 1988. 224.00 (*0-387-16342-5*) Spr-Verlag.

***Tumours of the Spine & Spinal Cord, Pt. I.** Pierre J. Vinken & G. W. Bruyn. (Handbook of Clinical Neurology Ser.: Vol. 19). 394p. 1975. 232.00 (*0-7204-7219-9*) Elsevier.

***Tumours of the Spine & Spinal Cord, Pt. II.** Pierre J. Vinken & G. W. Bruyn. (Handbook of Clinical Neurology Ser.: Vol. 20). 860p. 1976. 526.00 (*0-7204-7220-2*) Elsevier.

Tumours of the Spine & Spinal Cord see Handbook of Clinical Neurology

Tumours of the Upper Jaw. Ed. by Donald Harrison & Valerie J. Lund. LC 92-49458. 360p. 1993. text ed. 150.00 (*0-443-04017-6*) Churchill.

Tumours That Secrete Catecholamines: Their Detection & Clinical Chemistry. Ronald Robinson. LC 79-41731. 144p. reprint ed. pap. 41.10 (*0-317-29342-7*, 2024034) Bks Demand.

Tumpisa (Panamint) Shoshone Grammar. Jon P. Dayley. (Publications in Linguistics: Vol. 115). (Illus.). 536p. 1990. pap. 55.00 (*0-520-09752-1*) U CA Pr.

Tumpline Economy: Production & Distribution Systems in Sixteenth-Century Eastern Guatemala. Lawrence H. Feldman. LC 85-50097. (Illus.). 152p. (Orig.). 1985. pap. 23.00 (*0-911437-16-9*) Labyrinthos.

Tumult & Silence at Second Creek: An Inquiry into a Civil War Slave Conspiracy. Winthrop D. Jordan. LC 92-22138. (Illus.). 408p. (C). 1993. 24.95 (*0-8071-1762-5*) La State U Pr.

Tumult & Silence at Second Creek: An Inquiry into a Civil War Slave Conspiracy. Winthrop D. Jordan. LC 92-22138. (Illus.). 416p. (C). 1996. pap. 16.95 (*0-8071-2039-1*) La State U Pr.

Tumult in the Clouds. James A. Goodson. 1986. mass mkt. 4.95 (*0-312-90477-0*) St Martin.

Tumult of Inner Voices. Douglas R. Hofstadter. (Grace A. Tanner Lecture in Human Values Ser.). 24p. 1982. text ed. 7.50 (*0-910153-01-9*) E T Woolf.

Tumult on the Mountains: Lumbering in West Virginia. 8th ed. Roy B. Clarkson. (Illus.). 416p. 1988. reprint ed. 25.00 (*0-87012-004-2*) McClain.

Tumulte des Flots. Yukio Mishima. (FRE.). 1978. pap. 10.95 (*0-7859-4095-2*) Fr & Eur.

Tumultuous Passage: American Society Approaching the Twenty-First Century. Frank E. Williams, Jr. 169p. (Orig.). 1994. pap. 9.00 (*0-87012-518-4*) McClain.

Tumultuous Years: The Presidency of Harry S. Truman, 1949-1953. Robert J. Donovan. (Illus.). 448p. (C). 1996. pap. 19.95 (*0-8262-1085-6*) U of Mo Pr.

Tumultuous Years - Schwenkfelder Chronicles Fifteen Eighty to Seventeen Fifty: The Reports of Martin John, Jr. & Balthazar Hoffmann. L. Allen Viehmeyer. 157p. (Orig.). 1980. pap. 3.00 (*0-935980-00-8*) Schwenkfelder Lib.

Tumultus de Asterige. Rene De Goscinny & A. Uderzo. (LAT.). 1992. 19.95 (*0-7859-1036-0*, 3770400690) Fr & Eur.

Tun Razak: His Life & Times. W. S. Shaw. (Illus.). 1976. text ed. 14.50 (*0-582-72414-7*) Longman.

Tun-Ta-Ca-Tun: More Stories & Poems in English & Spanish for Children. Ed. by Sylvia C. Pena. LC 84-72297. 80p. (Orig.). (ENG & SPA.). (J). (ps up). 1985. pap. 9.50 (*0-934770-43-3*) Arte Publico.

Tuna: Distribution & Migration. Hiroshi Nakamura. 1978. 125.00 (*0-685-63462-0*) St Mut.

Tuna: Status, Trends, & Alternative Management Arrangements. Saul B. Saila & Virgil J. Norton. LC 73-20846. (Resources for the Future, Program of International Studies of Fishery Arrangements, Paper: No. 6). 69p. reprint ed. pap. 25.00 (*0-317-26479-6*, 2023814) Bks Demand.

Tuna & Billfish: Fish Without a Country. 4th ed. James Joseph et al. LC 80-81889. (Illus.). 69p. (Orig.). (YA). (gr. 7-12). 1988. pap. 15.75 (*0-9603078-1-8*) Inter-Am Tropical.

Tuna & Billfish: Fish Without a Country. 4th ed. James Joseph et al. (Illus.). xi, 69p. (Orig.). 1988. pap. 15.75 (*0-9603078-2-6*) Inter-Am Tropical.

Tuna Baitfish in the Indo-Pacific Region. S. J. Blaber & J. W. Copland. 211p. (C). 1990. text ed. 215.00 (*1-86320-011-8*, Pub. by ACIAR) St Mut.

Tuna Fish Gourmet. Tracey Seaman. LC 93-40914. 1994. 12.00 (*0-679-41878-4*, Villard Bks) Random.

Tuna Fish Gourmet. Tracy Seaman. 1994. pap. 12.00 (*0-676-75439-3*, Vin) Random.

Tunable Laser Applications. Ed. by F. J. Duarte. LC 95-23394. (Optical Engineering Ser.: Vol. 50). 328p. 1995. 125.00 (*0-8247-8928-8*) Dekker.

Tunable Lasers. Ed. by L. F. Mollenauer & J. C. White. (Topics in Applied Physics Ser.: Vol. 59). (Illus.). 425p. 1987. 97.00 (*0-387-16921-0*) Spr-Verlag.

Tunable Lasers. 2nd ed. Ed. by J. C. White & C. R. Pollock. LC 92-19149. (Topics in Applied Physics Ser.: Vol. 59). (Illus.). 440p. 1992. 75.95 (*0-387-55571-4*) Spr-Verlag.

Tunable Lasers & Applications. Ed. by A. Mooradian et al. (Optical Sciences Ser: Vol. 3). 1976. 46.95 (*0-387-07968-8*) Spr-Verlag.

Tunable Lasers Handbook. F. J. Duarte. (Optics & Photonics Ser.). (Illus.). 477p. 1995. boxed 80.00 (*0-12-222695-X*) Acad Pr.

Tunable Solid State Lasers. Ed. by P. Hammerling et al. (Optical Sciences Ser.: Vol. 47). (Illus.). 210p. 1985. 72.95 (*0-387-15135-4*) Spr-Verlag.

Tunable Solid State Lasers. Ed. by Michael L. Shand & Hans P. Jenssen. LC 89-61045. (Proceedings Ser.: Vol. 5). 300p. (Orig.). 1989. lib. bdg. 82.00 (*1-55752-111-5*) Optical Soc.

Tunable Solid State Lasers for Remote Sensing. Ed. by R. L. Byer et al. (Optical Sciences Ser.: Vol. 51). (Illus.). 160p. 1986. 72.95 (*0-387-16168-6*) Spr-Verlag.

Tunable Solid-State Lasers II. Ed. by A. B. Budgor et al. (Optical Sciences Ser.: Vol. 52). (Illus.). 380p. 1987. 72.95 (*0-387-17320-X*) Spr-Verlag.

TUN..Ahhh: Smart Eating with Good Taste. Muriel G. Wagner & Irene H. Burchard. 114p. (Orig.). 1993. pap. write for info. (*0-9637175-0-2*) W & B Pr.

Tunbridge Ware. Margaret A. Gill. 1989. pap. 25.00 (*0-85263-712-8*, Pub. by Shire UK) St Mut.

Tunc. Lawrence Durrell. (FRE.). 1979. pap. 11.95 (*0-7859-1896-5*, 2070371220) Fr & Eur.

Tundish Metallurgy, Vol. I. LC 90-80226. 256p. 1990. 20.00 (*0-932897-49-5*) Iron & Steel.

Tundish Metallurgy, Vol. II. LC 90-80226. 316p. 1991. 20.00 (*0-932897-62-2*) Iron & Steel.

Tundra. Michael George. LC 93-18275. (Images Ser.). 40p. (J). (gr. 3 up). 1994. lib. bdg. 17.95 (*0-88682-601-2*) Creative Ed.

Tundra. Elizabeth Kaplan. LC 95-2192. (Biomes of the World Ser.). 64p. (J). (gr. 4-6). 1995. lib. bdg. 17.95 (*0-7614-0080-X*, Benchmark NY) Marshall Cavendish.

Tundra. April P. Sayre. (Exploring Earth's Biomes Ser.). (Illus.). 64p. (J). (gr. 5-8). 1994. lib. bdg. 15.98 (*0-8050-2829-3*) TFC Bks NY.

Tundra. Donna W. Shepherd. LC 96-33777. (First Books-Science). (Illus.). 64p. (J). 1996. lib. bdg. 21.00 (*0-531-20249-6*) Watts.

***Tundra.** Donna W. Shepherd. (First Bks.). 64p. (J). 1997. pap. 6.95 (*0-531-15819-5*) Watts.

Tundra. Philip Steele. LC 96-10914. (J). 1997. lib. bdg. write for info. (*1-57505-040-4*, Carolrhoda) Lerner Group.

Tundra: Cartoons from the Last Frontier. Chad Carpenter. (Illus.). 118p. (Orig.). 1993. pap. 10.00 (*1-878100-54-8*) Todd Commns.

Tundra II: More Cartoons from the Last Frontier. Chad Carpenter. (Illus.). 64p. (Orig.). 1994. pap. 10.00 (*1-878100-55-6*) Todd Commns.

Tundra III: Even More Cartoons of a Northerly Nature. Chad Carpenter. (Illus.). 128p. (Orig.). 1995. pap. 10.00 (*1-878100-67-X*) Todd Commns.

***Tundra Mouse: A Storyknife Book.** Megan McDonald. LC 96-53221. (Illus.). 32p. (J). (ps-2). 1997. 15.95 (*0-531-30047-1*); lib. bdg. 16.99 (*0-531-33047-8*) Orchard Bks Watts.

***Tundra Presents: And Now, a Break from Sanity.** Darin Carpenter. (Illus.). 136p. 1996. pap. 10.00 (*1-878100-35-1*) Todd Commns.

Tundra Swans. Bianca Lavies. (Illus.). 32p. (J). (gr. 2-5). 1994. pap. 15.99 (*0-525-45273-7*) Dutton Child Bks.

Tundra Tales. Nola M. Zobarskas. 1967. 5.00 (*0-87141-021-4*) Manyland.

***Tundra Trilogy.** Chad Carpenter. 25.00 (*1-878100-33-5*) Todd Commns.

Tune: The Structure of Melody. Imogen Holst. 1969. 9.50 (*0-8079-0126-1*); pap. 5.95 (*0-8079-0127-X*) October.

Tune Beyond the Clouds: Zen Teachings from Old China. Hsin-Yueh. Ed. & Tr. by J. C. Cleary from CHI. LC 91-70001. 135p. 1990. reprint ed. pap. 38.50 (*0-608-01780-9*, 2062438) Bks Demand.

Tune In! Music Listening Discovery Kit: Ready-to-Use Activities & Audiocassettes for Teaching Children How & Why to Listen. Marie Meachen. LC 93-44848. 1994. write for info. (*0-13-609009-5*, Parker Publishing Co) P-H.

Tune in, America. Daniel G. Mason. LC 72-90664. (Essay Index Reprint Ser.). 1977. 19.95 (*0-8369-1228-4*) Ayer.

Tune in America! A Study of Our Coming Musical Independence. Daniel G. Mason. LC 72-1720. reprint ed. 31.50 (*0-404-08328-5*) AMS Pr.

Tune in for Murder. Wendy Martin. 1993. 17.95 (*0-8034-9026-7*) Bouregy.

Tune in on Telephone Calls! 3rd ed. Tom Kneitel. (Illus.). 160p. (Orig.). 1996. pcr., pap. 16.95 (*0-939780-24-0*) CRB Res.

Tune in to English. Uwe Kind. (Illus.). 108p. (gr. 7-12). 1987. pap. text ed. 8.50 (*0-13-932807-6*, 18845); audio 25.00 (*0-13-932815-7*, 58846) Prentice ESL.

Tune In to Well-Being, Say No to Drugs: Substance Abuse. Girl Scouts of the U. S. A. Staff. (Contemporary Issues Ser.). 16p. 1985. pap. 1.50 (*0-88441-460-4*, 26-820) Girl Scouts USA.

Tune in Tomorrow. Mary Anderson. 192p. (J). (gr. 7 up). 1985. pap. 2.50 (*0-380-69870-6*, Flare) Avon.

Tune in Tomorrow. Tom Tomorrow. (Illus.). 128p. 1994. pap. 9.95 (*0-312-11344-7*) St Martin.

Tune in Tonight. Alexis Finger. 1985. pap. 22.95 (*0-8384-2983-1*, Newbury); audio 28.95 (*0-8384-2984-X*, Newbury) Heinle & Heinle.

Tune in Workbook. Nancy L. Tubesing & Donald A. Tubesing. 132p. 1973. student ed. 10.00 (*0-938586-14-9*) Whole Person.

Tune into Limericks. Elizabeth Nichols. 1983. 8.50 (*0-913650-05-6*, V092TMBX) Warner Brothers.

Tune into Terror. Marty Engle & Barnes. (Strange Matter Ser.: No. 17). 140p. (Orig.). (J). (gr. 4-7). 1996. pap. 3.99 (*1-56714-056-4*) Montage Bks.

***Tune My Heart to Sing: Devotions for Church Choirs Based on the Revised 3 Year Common Lectionary.** Wayne L. Wold. LC 97-15984. 1997. pap. text ed. 14.99 (*0-8066-3613-0*, Augsburg) Augsburg Fortress.

Tune Thy Musicke to Thy Harte: The Art of Eloquent Singing in England 1597-1622. Robert Toft. LC 92-955081. (Illus.). 176p. 1992. 50.00 (*0-8020-2848-9*) U of Toronto Pr.

Tune Time, 2 pts., Pt. A. rev. ed. Sarah L. Dittenhaver et al. Ed. by Louise Goss. (Frances Clark Library for Piano Students). 48p. (J). (gr. k-6). 1973. pap. text ed. 6.95 (*0-87487-194-8*) Summy-Birchard.

Tune Time, 2 pts., Pt. B. rev. ed. Sarah L. Dittenhaver et al. Ed. by Louise Goss. (Frances Clark Library for Piano Students). 48p. (J). (gr. k-6). 1973. pap. text ed. 6.95 (*0-87487-195-6*) Summy-Birchard.

Tune-up Ignition & Fuel Induction Systems. Bob Leigh et al. Ed. by Roger L. Fennema et al. (Automobile Mechanics Refresher Course Ser.: Bk. 1). (Illus.). 104p. 1981. student ed., pap. 9.95 (*0-88098-062-1*, H M Gousha) P-H Gen Ref & Trav.

Tune-up Ignition & Fuel Induction Systems. rev. ed. Bob Leigh et al. Ed. by Roger L. Fennema et al. (Automobile Mechanics Refresher Course Ser.: Bk. 1). (Illus.). 104p. 1981. audio 13.90 (*0-88098-068-0*, H M Gousha) P-H Gen Ref & Trav.

Tune-up Service. 3rd ed. Chek-Chart Staff. 1976. pap. 7.20 (*0-672-21449-0*, Bobbs) Macmillan.

Tune-up Service Manual. Michael Calkins. Ed. by Jo L. Phelps & Roger L. Fenneman. (Apprentice Mechanics Ser.). (Illus.). 192p. (C). 1985. teacher ed. 3.45 (*0-88098-003-6*, H M Gousha) P-H Gen Ref & Trav.

Tune-up Service Manual. rev. ed. Michael Calkins. Ed. by Jo L. Phelps & Roger L. Fenneman. (Apprentice Mechanics Ser.). (Illus.). 192p. (C). 1985. student ed., pap. 8.75 (*0-88098-002-8*, H M Gousha) P-H Gen Ref & Trav.

Tune-up Service Manual. rev. ed. Ed. by Michael Calkins et al. (Apprentice Mechanics Ser.). (Illus.). 208p. 1986. student ed. 9.19 (*0-88098-087-7*, H M Gousha) P-H Gen Ref & Trav.

Tune-up Service Manual, Nineteen Ninety. 240p. 1990. 15.95 (*0-13-130691-X*, H M Gousha) P-H Gen Ref & Trav.

Tune up Your PC for Windows 95: A Practical Guide. Michael H. Tooley. 250p. 1996. pap. 39.95 incl. disk (*0-7506-2224-5*, Digital DEC) Buttrwrth-Heinemann.

Tune up Your Tools. Sal Maccarone. (Illus.). 144p. (Orig.). 1996. pap. 22.99 (*1-55870-409-4*, Betrwy Bks) F & W Pubns Inc.

***Tune Your Brain.** Elizabeth Miles. 240p. 1997. pap. 12.00 (*0-425-16017-3*, Berkley Trade) Berkley Pub.

Tuned In: Television in American Life. Photos by Lloyd DeGrane. (Illus.). 96p. 1991. 24.95 (*0-252-01809-5*); 11.95 (*0-252-06222-1*) U of Ill Pr.

Tuned-In, Turned-On Book about Learning Problems. expanded rev. ed. Marnell L. Hayes. Ed. by Betty L. Kratoville. LC 94-3474. (Illus.). 132p. (YA). 1994. pap. text ed. 12.00 (*1-57128-090-1*) Acad Therapy.

Tuned up Parenting: Eight Studes (sic) to Invite Harmony in Your Home. Karen Dockrey. LC 94-4073. (Tapestry Collection). 96p. 1994. pap. 6.50 (*1-56476-211-4*, 6-3211, Victor Bks) Chariot Victor.

Tuneful Flame: Songs of Robert Burns As He Sang Them. Ed. by Robert D. Thorton. LC 57-6572. 87p. reprint ed. pap. 25.00 (*0-317-10087-4*, 2000774) Bks Demand.

Tuner Techniques. David Guptill. LC 85-12716. 72p. 1985. 18.50 incl. audio (*0-916715-01-9*) Guptill.

Tunes & Variations for Bluegrass Banjo. David Guptill. 32p. (Orig.). 1984. pap. 12.50 incl. audio (*0-916715-00-0*) Guptill.

Tunes for Bears to Dance To. Robert Cormier. 112p. (YA). 1994. mass mkt. 3.99 (*0-440-21903-5*) Dell.

Tunes for Bears to Dance To. R. O. Wallace. LC 82-23893. (Poetry Ser.). 64p. 1983. pap. 8.95 (*0-8229-5353-6*) U of Pittsburgh Pr.

Tunes for Bears to Dance To. Ronald Wallace. LC 82-23893. (Pitt Poetry Ser.). 79p. 1983. reprint ed. pap. 25.00 (*0-608-00910-5*, 2061704) Bks Demand.

***Tunes for Electric Keyboard, Bk. 1.** Haines. Date not set. pap. text ed. write for info. (*0-582-02664-4*) Addison-Wesley.

***Tunes for Electric Keyboard Bk. 2.** Haines. Date not set. pap. text ed. write for info. (*0-582-02663-6*, Pub. by Longman UK) Longman.

Tunes for Tots. Janice Andrews. (J). (ps). 1987. teacher ed. write for info. incl. audio (*1-878079-04-2*) Arts Pubns.

Tunes from a Tuscan Guitar: The Life & Times of an Italian Immigrant. Roland R. Bianchi. LC 93-37524. (Illus.). 160p. (Orig.). 1994. pap. 10.95 (*1-56474-085-4*) Fithian Pr.

Tunes on a Penny Whistle: A Derbyshire Childhood. Doris E. Coates. LC 93-5311. (Illus.). 1993. pap. 16.00 (*0-7509-0434-8*, Pub. by Sutton Pubng UK) Bks Intl VA.

Tunes, Tales, & Truths. Pam Campbell & Stan Campbell. (BibleLog Ser.). 180p. (Orig.). 1992. pap. 7.99 (*0-89693-873-5*, 6-1873, Victor Bks) Chariot Victor.

Tunes You Like: Favorite Songs Made Easy to Play for Piano, Vol. 3. rev. ed. 24p. 1986. pap. 4.95 (*0-7935-3750-9*) H Leonard.

Tunes You Like Vol. 1: Favorite Songs Made Easy Piano Solos. rev. ed. 24p. 1986. pap. 4.95 (*0-7935-0686-7*) H Leonard.

***Tunesische Spezialitaten: 3000 Jahre Esskultur.** 2nd ed. Hebara M. Lampert. (Illus.). 191p. (GER.). (C). 1993. 40.00 (*3-8170-0014-6*, Pub. by Knstvrlag Weingrtn GW) Intl Bk Import.

Tung Jen's Chinese Astrology. Ed. by England Foulsham. 192p. (Orig.). 1993. pap. 12.95 (*0-572-01893-2*, Pub. by W Foulsham UK) Trans-Atl Phila.

***Tung Jen's Chinese Love Signs.** Alan Butler. 1997. pap. text ed. 11.95 (*0-572-02266-2*, Pub. by W Foulsham UK) Trans-Atl Phila.

Tungaru Traditions: Writings on the Atoll Culture of the Gilbert Islands. Arthur F. Grimble. Ed. by H. E. Maude. LC 89-4714. (Pacific Islands Monographs: No. 7). (Illus.). 384p. 1989. text ed. 38.00 (*0-8248-1217-4*) UH Pr.

Tungo Zetu. Ibrahim N. Shariff. LC 88-90887. 265p. (Orig.). (C). 1988. 29.95 (*0-932415-32-6*); pap. 9.95 (*0-932415-33-4*) Red Sea Pr.

Tungsten. (Metals & Minerals Ser.). 1993. lib. bdg. 250.95 (*0-8490-8937-9*) Gordon Pr.

Tungsten: A Novel. Cesar Vallejo. 168p. 1988. 35.00 (*0-8156-0226-X*) Syracuse U Pr.

Tungsten: Sources, Metallurgy, Properties, & Applications. W. H. Yih & C. T. Wang. LC 78-10773. (Illus.). 516p. 1979. 125.00 (*0-306-31144-5*, Plenum Pr) Plenum.

Tungsten & Other Advanced Metals for ULSI Applications in 1990: Materials Research Society Conference Proceedings. Ed. by G. C. Smith & R. Blumenthal. 395p. 1991. text ed. 62.00 (*1-55899-112-3*, Vol. V-6) Materials Res.

Tungsten & Other Refractory Metals for VLSI Applications II. Ed. by Eliot K. Broadbent. 1987. text ed. 17.50 (*0-931837-66-9*, Vol. V-2) Materials Res.

Tungsten & Other Refractory Metals for VLSI Applications III. Ed. by Victor Wells. 1988. text ed. 17.50 (*0-931837-84-7*, Vol. V-3) Materials Res.

Tungsten & Other Refractory Metals for VLSI Applications IV. Ed. by Robert S. Blewer & Carol M. McConica. 1989. text ed. 17.50 (*0-931837-98-7*, Vol. V-4) Materials Res.

Tungsten & Refractory Metals, 1994: Proceedings of the Second International Conference on Tungsten & Refractory Metals. International Conference on Tungsten & Refractory Metals Staff. Ed. by Animesh Bose & Robert J. Dowding. LC 95-164912. 750p. 1995. reprint ed. pap. 180.00 (*0-608-01821-X*, 2062470) Bks Demand.

Tungsten & Refractory Metals 3. Ed. by Animesh Bose & Robert J. Dowding. (Illus.). 250p. (Orig.). 1995. pap. 150.00 (*1-878954-58-X*) Metal Powder.

***Tungsten & Tungsten Alloys: Recent Advances: Proceedings of a Symposium by the Refractory Metals Committee, Held at the 120th Annual Meeting of the Minerals, Metals & Materials Society in New Orleans, LA, February 17-22, 1991.** Ed. by Andrew Crowson & Edward S. Chen. LC 91-62467. 314p. 1991. reprint ed. pap. 89.50 (*0-608-03826-1*, 2062788) Bks Demand.

Tungsten & Tungsten Alloys, 1992: Proceedings of the First International Conference on Tungsten & Tungsten Alloys, Sponsored by the Metal Powder Industries Federation, Stouffer Concourse Hotel, Arlington, Virginia, November 15-18, 1992. International Conference on Tungsten & Tungsten Alloys Staff. Ed. by Animesh Bose & Robert J. Dowding. LC 92-43794. 570p. 1993. reprint ed. pap. 162.50 (*0-608-01818-X*, 2062467) Bks Demand.

Tungsten & Tungsten Alloys 2 - 1994: Proceedings of the 1994 Second International Conference. Ed. by Animesh Bose & Robert J. Dowding. (Illus.). 750p. 1995. pap. 170.00 (*1-878954-53-9*) Metal Powder.

Tungsten Arc Gas Shielded Welding. 1989. 60.00 (*0-85083-081-8*) St Mut.

***Tungsten Carbide Tools.** S. L. Hoyt. (Technical Papers: Vol. 99). 1929. pap. text ed. 30.00 (*1-55589-152-7*) AGMA.

Tungsten Statistics: 1992. 71p. 1993. 25.00 (*92-1-112326-7*) UN.

Tungsten Statistics 1993. (United Nations Conference on Trade & Development Ser.). 71p. 1994. pap. text ed. 25.00 (*92-1-112338-0*) UN.

Tunhuang Popular Narratives. Victor H. Mair. LC 83-1939. (Cambridge Studies in Chinese History, Literature & Institutions). 400p. 1984. text ed. 89.95 (*0-521-24761-6*) Cambridge U Pr.

Tunica. Mary R. Haas. pap. 15.00 (*0-685-71704-6*) J J Augustin.

***Tunica Sonada de Jose - Joseph's Dreamcoat.** D. Wilson. 20p. (SPA.). (J). 1994. write for info. (*1-56063-701-3*) Editorial Unilit.

Tuning. David Antin. LC 84-3446. 288p. (Orig.). 1984. pap. 12.00 (*0-8112-0894-X*, NDP570) New Directions.

Tuning. Jane Bailey. LC 78-11150. 1978. pap. 4.00 (*0-918366-09-7*) Slow Loris.

Tuning: The Perfection of Eighteenth-Century Temperament, the Lost Art of Nineteenth-Century Temperament, & the Science of Equal Temperament Complete with Instructions for Aural & Electronic Tuning. Owen Jorgensen. LC 90-50887. 800p. (C). 1991. 69.95 (*0-87013-290-3*) Mich St U Pr.

Tuning & Control Loop Performance: A Practitioners Guide. 3rd ed. G. K. McMillan. 432p. text ed. 76.00 (*1-55617-492-6*, A492-6) ISA.

Tuning & Temperament: A Historical Survey. James Murray Barbour. LC 74-37288. (Illus.). 228p. 1972. reprint ed. lib. bdg. 35.00 (*0-306-70422-6*) Da Capo.

Tuning BL's A-Series Engine. David Vizard. (Illus.). 39.95 (*0-85429-732-4*, F732, Pub. by G T Foulis Ltd) Haynes Pubns.

Tuning God's New Instrument. Denis Lane. 100p. (Orig.). (C). 1990. pap. text ed. 6.95 (*9971-972-97-2*) OMF Bks.

Tuning In. Robert Maidment. LC 84-5259. 86p. (Orig.). 1984. pap. 6.95 (*0-88289-439-0*) Pelican.

Tuning In. Scott Wilkinson. Ed. by Ronnie Schiff. (Illus.). 104p. (Orig.). 1988. pap. 14.95 (*0-88188-633-5*, HL 00183796) H Leonard.

Tuning In: A Layman's Guide to Youth Ministry. Phil Redding. 153p. 1990. pap. 5.95 (*1-882449-21-5*) Messenger Pub.

Tuning in & Turning on - Media Participation in the Arts: Research Division Report, No. 33. Charles M. Gray. LC 95-34806. (National Endowment for the Arts Research Division Report Ser.: No. 33). 96p. 1996. pap. 10.95 (*0-929765-39-7*) Seven Locks Pr.

***Tuning in Children Divorce: A Program for Divorcing & Divorced Parents.** Freyda Siegel & Frank A. Nelligan. LC 96-79861. 112p. (Orig.). (J). 1997. pap. 21.95 (*1-57543-022-3*) Mar Co Prods.

Tuning in the Sounds of the Radio: The Sounds of the Radio. Eve Stwertka & Albert Stwertka. LC 91-16058. (At Home with Science Ser.). (Illus.). 40p. (J). (gr. 2-5). 1993. pap. 5.95 (*0-671-69466-9*, Julian Messner) Silver Burdett Pr.

Tuning in to Grace the Quest for God. Andre Louf. Tr. by John Vriend. (Cistercian Studies). 300p. 1992. pap. 15.95 (*0-87907-929-0*) Cistercian Pubns.

Tuning in to RF Scanning: From Police to Satellite Bands. Bob Kay. LC 94-3088. 1994. text ed. 24.95 (*0-07-033963-5*); pap. text ed. 14.95 (*0-07-033964-3*) McGraw-Hill Prof.

Tuning in to Spoken Messages: Basic Listening Strategies. Lila Blum. 1990. audio 37.95 (*0-8013-0165-3*, 75827) Longman.

Tuning in to Spoken Messages: Basic Listening Strategies. Lila Blum. 1990. pap. text ed. 14.79 (*0-8013-0164-5*, 75826) Longman.

Tuning in to Young Viewers: Social Science Perspectives on Television. Ed. by Tannis M. MacBeth. LC 95-50231. 296p. (C). 1996. 45.00 (*0-8039-5825-0*); pap. 21.95 (*0-8039-5826-9*) Sage.

Tuning in Trouble: Talk TV's Destructive Impact on Mental Health. Jeanne A. Heaton & Nona L. Wilson. LC 95-14995. (Psychology Ser.). 298p. 22.00 (*0-7879-0106-7*) Jossey-Bass.

Tuning into My Future: A Middle School Career Guidance Program. Montgomery Co. Vocational Education Planning Dist, Center Career Development Program Staff. 36p. (YA). (gr. 7-10). 1992. student ed., pap. write for info. (*1-57515-038-7*) PPI Pubng.

Tuning into Nature. Philip S. Callahan. (Illus.). 240p. 1976. 24.95 (*0-8159-6309-2*) Devin.

Tuning of Industrial Control Systems. A. B. Corripio. 225p. 1990. 68.00 (*1-55617-253-2*, A253-2) ISA.

Tuning of My Harpsicord. Herbert A. Kellner. (Illus.). 55p. 1980. pap. 27.25 (*0-933224-35-4*, 1/45) Bold Strummer Ltd.

Tuning of the Word: The Musico-Literary Poetics of the Symbolist Movement. David M. Hertz. LC 86-3962. (Illus.). 256p. 1987. text ed. 29.95 (*0-8093-1312-X*) S Ill U Pr.

Tuning Oracle. Michael J. Corey et al. (Oracle Press Ser.). 544p. 1994. pap. text ed. 29.95 (*0-07-881181-3*) Osborne-McGraw.

Tuning Rover V-8 Engines: How to Get Best Performance for Road & Competition Use. David Hardcastle. (Illus.). 190p. 1994. 34.95 (*0-85429-933-5*) Haynes Pubns.

Tuning SAS Applications in the MVS Environment. Michael A. Raithel. 316p. (C). 1995. pap. 37.95 (*1-55544-278-1*, BR55231) SAS Inst.

Tuning-Shooting Your 3-D Bow. Larry Wise. Ed. by Glenn Helgeland. LC 92-83910. (On Target Ser.). (Illus.). 100p. 1994. pap. 10.95 (*0-913305-10-3*) Target Comm.

Tuning the Classic Mini. Clive Trickey. (Illus.). 112p. 1991. 21.95 (*0-947981-61-6*, Pub. by Motor Racing UK) Motorbooks Intl.

Tuning the Close Desk Top. Charles Fernandez. 1996. pap. text ed. 35.80 (*0-13-102724-7*) P-H.

Tuning the Heart: University Sermons. C. Welton Gaddy. LC 89-29749. 192p. (C). 1990. 14.95 (*0-86554-367-4*, MUP-H304) Mercer Univ Pr.

Tuning the Lily. Alexis K. Rotella. 20p. 1983. pap. 2.00 (*0-913719-61-7*) High-Coo Pr.

Tuning the Wood: Contemporary Illinois Stringed Instrument Builders. Kent J. Smith et al. Ed. by Joan Hemphill. (Illus.). 72p. (Orig.). (C). 1987. pap. 17.50 (*0-89792-113-5*) Ill St Museum.

***Tuning, Timbre, Spectrum, Scale.** William A. Sethares. LC 97-17623. 1997. write for info. (*3-540-76173-X*) Springer Pub.

Tuning to the Spiritual Frequencies. Greg Nielsen. LC 89-91602. (Illus.). 224p. (Orig.). 1990. pap. 12.95 (*0-9619917-1-2*) Conscious Bks.

Tuning Yachts & Small Keelboats. Lawrie Smith. 96p. (C). 1990. text ed. 59.00 (*0-906754-35-6*, Pub. by Fernhurst Bks UK) St Mut.

Tuning Your Broadheads. Larry Wise et al. (On Target Ser.). (Illus.). 100p. (Orig.). 1988. pap. 10.95 (*0-913305-08-1*) Target Comm.

Tuning Your Compound Bow. Larry Wise. Ed. by Glenn Helgeland. (On Target Ser.). (Illus.). 132p. (Orig.). 1985. pap. 10.95 (*0-913305-07-3*) Target Comm.

Tuning Your Dinghy. Laurie Smith. 64p. (C). 1990. text ed. 59.00 (*0-906754-18-6*, Pub. by Fernhurst Bks UK) St Mut.

Tuning Your Guitar. Donald Brosnac. (Illus.). 32p. pap. 4.95 (*0-8256-2180-1*, AM35858) Music Sales.

Tunis Hood Family: Its Lineage & Traditions. Dellmann O. Hood. (Illus.). 666p. 1960. 25.00 (*0-8323-0185-X*) Binford Mort.

Tunis-Kairous-an & Carthage. G. Petrie. 360p. 1985. 220.00 (*1-85077-067-0*, Pub. by Darf Pubs Ltd UK) St Mut.

Tunis Land & People. Chevalier De Hesse-Wartegg. (C). 1988. 145.00 (*1-85077-201-0*, Pub. by Darf Pubs Ltd UK) St Mut.

Tunisia. (Insight Guides Ser.). (Orig.). 1993. pap. 22.95 (*0-395-66319-9*) HM.

Tunisia. (Essential Guides Ser.). (Orig.). 1994. pap. 7.95 (*0-8442-8938-8*, Passport Bks) NTC Pub Grp.

Tunisia. (Orig.). 1992. write for info. (*0-318-69116-7*) P-H Gen Ref & Trav.

***Tunisia.** LC 97-15883. (Cultures of the World Ser.: Group 15). (Illus.). 128p. (YA). (gr. 5 up). 1997. lib. bdg. 23.95 (*0-7614-0690-5*) Marshall Cavendish.

Tunisia. Diana Darke. (Thomas Cook Illustrated Guides Ser.). (Illus.). 192p. (Orig.). 1996. pap. 12.95 (*0-8442-9003-3*, Passport Bks) NTC Pub Grp.

Tunisia. Allan M. Findlay et al. Ed. by Robert L. Collison. (World Bibliographical Ser.: No. 33). 251p. 1982. lib. bdg. 55.00 (*0-903450-63-1*) ABC-CLIO.

Tunisia. Kathleen Trayte. LC 95-22469. (Country Guide Series Report from the AACRAO-AID Project). 1996. 22.00 (*0-929851-61-7*) Am Assn Coll Registrars.

***Tunisia.** David Willett. (Illus.). 256p. (Orig.). 1998. pap. 14.95 (*0-86442-512-0*) Lonely Planet.

Tunisia. rev. ed. Mary V. Fox. LC 90-2199. (Enchantment of the World Ser.). (Illus.). 128p. (J). (gr. 5-9). 1994. lib. bdg. 30.00 (*0-516-02724-7*) Childrens.

Tunisia. 17th ed. Berlitz Editors. (Pocket Guides Ser.). 1995. pap. 7.95 (*2-8315-2502-0*) Berlitz.

Tunisia: A Country Study. 3rd ed. Ed. by Harold D. Nelson. LC 86-3351. (DA Pam Area Handbook Ser.: No. 550-89). Orig. Title: Area Handbook for the Republic of Tunisia. (Illus.). 407p. 1988. 17.00 (*0-16-001651-7*, S/N 008-020-01092-8) USGPO.

Tunisia: From Protectorate to Republic. Dwight L. Ling. LC 67-63013. (Indiana University International Studies). (Illus.). 284p. reprint ed. pap. 81.00 (*0-317-11307-0*, 2055232) Bks Demand.

Tunisia: Human Rights Crisis of 1987. MN. Advocates for Human Rights Staff. (MLIHRC Report Ser.). 70p. (Orig.). (C). 1988. pap. 7.00 (*0-929293-02-9*) MN Advocates.

Tunisia: Human Rights Report of 1989. John Borman & Inger Tangborn. Ed. by Barbara Frey. 74p. (Orig.). (C). 1990. pap. 7.00 (*0-929293-09-6*) MN Advocates.

***Tunisia: Recent Economic Developments.** Abdelali Jbill. (IMF Staff Country Report Ser.: Vol. 96/27). (Illus.). 100p. pap. 28.50 (*0-608-04851-8*, 2065510) Bks Demand.

Tunisia: Rural Labour & Structural Transformation. Samir Radwan et al. 128p. (C). (gr. 13). 1991. text ed. 74.95 (*0-415-04274-7*, A4710) Routledge.

Tunisia: The Political Economy of Reform. Ed. by I. William Zartman. LC 90-45574. (SAIS African Studies Library). 268p. 1991. lib. bdg. 46.00 (*1-55587-230-1*) Lynne Rienner.

***Tunisia Global Integration & Sustaining Development.** pap. 7.95 (*0-8213-3866-8*, 13866) World Bank.

***Tunisia Handbook with Libya.** Anne McLachlan. 1997. 18.95 (*0-8442-4867-3*) NTC Pub Grp.

Tunisia in Pictures. Ed. by Lerner Publications, Department of Geography Staff. (Visual Geography Ser.). (Illus.). 64p. (YA). (gr. 5 up). 1991. lib. bdg. 19.95 (*0-8225-1844-9*, Lerner Publctns) Lerner Group.

Tunisia of Ahmed Bey, 1837-1855. Leon C. Brown. LC 73-16770. (Princeton Studies on the Near East). 428p. 1974. reprint ed. pap. 122.00 (*0-7837-9306-5*, 2060046) Bks Demand.

Tunisian Peasants in the Eighteenth & Nineteenth Centuries. Lucette Valensi. Tr. by Beth Archer. (Studies in Modern Capitalism). 272p. 1985. 69.95 (*0-521-25558-9*) Cambridge U Pr.

***Tunisia's Global Integration & Sustainable Development: Strategic Choices for the 21st Century.** (Middle East & North Africa Economic Studies). 92p. 1996. 7.95 (*0-8213-3718-1*, 13718) World Bank.

Tunk Pond Episode. Carl C. Osgood. (Illus.). 203p. 1996. pap. 19.00 (*0-9638587-1-8*) Vista Hse.

Tunkashila: From the Birth of Turtle Island to the Blood of Wounded Knee. Gerald Hausman. (Illus.). 288p. 1994. pap. 13.95 (*0-312-11345-5*) St Martin.

Tunnel. William H. Gass. LC 94-12089. 652p. 1995. 30.00 (*0-679-43767-3*) Knopf.

Tunnel. William H. Gass. LC 95-42492. 672p. 1996. pap. 17.50 (*0-06-097686-1*) HarpC.

***Tunnel.** William Pearson. 139p. (Orig.). 1997. mass mkt. 4.99 (*0-614-28626-3*, Pub. by Comnwlth Pub CN) Partners Pubs Grp.

Tunnel. Ernesto Sabato. (Illus.). 272p. 1991. mass mkt. 5.99 (*0-345-37377-4*) Ballantine.

Tunnel. large type ed. Stanley Johnson. 608p. 1986. 27.99 (*0-7089-8307-3*, Charnwood) Ulverscroft.

Tunnel: Selected Poems of Russell Edson. Russell Edson. (Field Editions Ser.: No. 3). 225p. 1994. pap. 16.95 (*0-932440-65-7*) Oberlin Coll Pr.

Tunnel: Selected Poems of Russell Edson. Russell Edson. (Field Editions Ser.: No. 3). 225p. 1995. 31.95 (*0-932440-66-5*) Oberlin Coll Pr.

Tunnel: The Underground Homeless of New York City. Margaret Morton. (Architecture of Despair Ser.). (Illus.). 1996. 40.00 (*0-300-06538-8*); pap. 20.00 (*0-300-06559-0*) Yale U Pr.

Tunnel Beneath the Sea. Ruth Sargent. Ed. by Jane Weinberger. LC 93-60461. (Illus.). 120p. (J). (gr. 3-6). 1993. pap. 9.95 (*0-932433-11-1*) Windswept Hse.

Tunnel Boring Machines: Trends in Design & Construction of Mechanized Tunneling; Proceedings of the International Lecture Series, Hagenberg Castle, Linz, December 14-15, 1995. Harald Wagner & Alfred Schulter. (Illus.). 280p. 1996. 105.00 (*90-5410-811-8*, Pub. by A A Balkema NE) Ashgate Pub Co.

Tunnel Engineering Handbook. 2nd ed. Ed. by Thomas R. Kuesel & Elwyn H. King. LC 95-17571. 528p. (gr. 13). 1995. text ed. 119.95 (*0-412-99291-4*) Chapman & Hall.

Tunnel Engineering Handbook. John O. Bickel & Thomas R. Kuesel. LC 91-25911. 680p. (C). 1991. reprint ed. lib. bdg. 104.50 (*0-89464-655-9*) Krieger.

Tunnel in the Sky. Alan Garner. 192p. 1987. mass mkt. 5.99 (*0-345-35373-0*) Ballantine.

Tunnel King. Dave Sargent & Pat L. Sargent. (Animal Pride Ser.: No. 11). (Illus.). 33p. (Orig.). (J). (gr. 2-8). 1996. pap. 2.95 (*1-56763-033-2*); lib. bdg. 12.95 (*1-56763-032-4*) Ozark Pub.

Tunnel Maintainer. Jack Rudman. (Career Examination Ser.: C-824). 1994. pap. 23.95 (*0-8373-0824-0*) Nat Learn.

Tunnel of Hope. Sheri J. Vitolo. Ed. by Gwen Costa. LC 90-22321. 165p. 1990. 13.95 (*0-87949-348-8*) Ashley Bks.

Tunnel of Love. Hilma Wolitzer. 384p. 1995. pap. 12.00 (*0-06-118010-6*, PL) HarpC.

Tunnel Syndromes. Marko M. Pecina. (Illus.). 184p. 1991. 115.00 (*0-8493-6933-9*, RC422) CRC Pr.

Tunnel Syndromes: Peripheral Nerve Compression Syndromes. 2nd ed. Marko M. Pecina et al. LC 96-21241. 320p. 1996. 84.95 (*0-8493-2629-X*) CRC Pr.

Tunnel Thru the Air or Looking Back from 1940. W. D. Gann. 1987. 49.00 (*0-939093-05-7*) Lambert Gann Pub.

Tunnel Tigers. large type ed. Alexander Cordell. 480p. 1988. 25.99 (*0-7089-1818-2*) Ulverscroft.

Tunnel to Canto Grande. Claribel Alegria & Darwin J. Flakoll. LC 95-37983. 200p. 1996. pap. 12.95 (*1-880684-34-9*) Curbstone.

***Tunnel to Eternity: Beyond Near-Death.** Leon Rhodes. LC 97-24863. (Orig.). 1997. pap. 10.95 (*0-87785-378-9*, Chrysalis Books) Swedenborg.

Tunnel Vision. Sara Paretsky. 448p. 1994. 21.95 (*0-385-29932-X*) Delacorte.

Tunnel Vision. large type ed. Sara Paretsky. LC 94-40740. (Large Print Bks.). 1994. pap. text ed. 22.95 (*1-56895-084-5*) Wheeler Pub.

Tunnel Vision: A True Story of Multiple Murder & Justice in Chaos at America's Biggest Marine Base. N. P. Simpson. Ed. by Jerry Bledsoe. LC 93-71405. (Illus.). 225p. 1993. 21.95 (*1-878086-24-3*) Down Home NC.

Tunnel Vision: A V. I. Warshawski Novel. Sara Paretsky. 480p. 1995. mass mkt. 6.99 (*0-440-21752-0*) Dell.

***Tunnel Vision: The Failure of Political Imagination.** James Walter. 176p. 1997. pap. text ed. 19.95 (*1-86373-745-6*, Pub. by Allen Unwin AT) Paul & Co Pubs.

Tunnel Warfare, 4 vols., Set. Ed. by Bruce A. Hanesalo. (Illus.). 534p. 1996. vinyl bd. 60.00 (*1-886848-16-5*) Mil-Info.

Tunnel Warfare Vol. 1: A Treatise on Mines: A Reprinting of the 1815 Classic on Military Mining. I. Landmann. Ed. by Bruce A. Hanesalo. (Illus.). 102p. 1995. reprint ed. vinyl bd. 15.00 (*1-886848-12-2*) Mil-Info.

Tunnel Warfare Vol. 2: Early Military Mining: A Collection of Military Mining Instructions from 1800-1900. J. Williams. (Illus.). 122p. 1995. reprint ed. vinyl bd. 15.00 (*1-886848-13-0*) Mil-Info.

Tunnel Warfare Vol. 3: U. S. Army Manuals: A Collection. Ed. by Bruce A. Hanesalo. (Illus.). 168p. 1995. reprint ed. vinyl bd. 15.00 (*1-886848-14-9*) Mil-Info.

Tunnel Warfare Vol. 4: Asian Tunnel Warfare. Bruce A. Hanesalo. (Illus.). 142p. 1996. vinyl bd. 15.00 (*1-886848-15-7*) Mil-Info.

Tunneling. (Research Record Ser.: No. 1150). 48p. 1987. 7.50 (*0-309-04654-8*) Transport Res Bd.

Tunneling. Ed. by Joshua Jortner & Bernard Pullman. 1986. lib. bdg. 171.00 (*90-277-2334-6*) Kluwer Ac.

***Tunneling & Its Implications.** 550p. 1997. lib. bdg. 75.00 (*981-02-2905-4*) World Scientific Pub.

Tunneling in Soft & Water-Bearing Grounds: Proceedings of an International Symposium, Lyon, 27-29 November 1984. Ed. by M. Legrand. 286p. (C). 1985. text ed. 155.00 (*90-6191-590-2*, Pub. by A A Balkema NE) Ashgate Pub Co.

Tunneling Operations & Equipment: Proceedings of a Session Sponsored by the Construction Division. Ed. by D. D. Brennan. 37p. 1985. 10.00 (*0-87262-483-8*) Am Soc Civil Eng.

Tunneling Phenomena in Chemical Physics. V. I. Gol'danskii & V. N. Fleurov. 334p. 1988. text ed. 364.00 (*2-88124-655-9*) Gordon & Breach.

Tunneling Phenomena in High & Low Tc Superconductors. A. Di Chiara & M. Russo. 300p. 1993. text ed. 91.00 (*981-02-1030-2*) World Scientific Pub.

Tunneling Spectroscopy: Capabilities, Applications, & New Techniques. Ed. by Paul K. Hansma. LC 82-16161. 512p. 1982. 125.00 (*0-306-41070-2*, Plenum Pr) Plenum.

Tunnell, Genealogy of the Tunnell Family of Delaware. James M. Tunnell, Jr. 100p. 1993. reprint ed. pap. 19.50 (*0-8328-3599-4*); reprint ed. lib. bdg. 29.50 (*0-8328-3598-6*) Higginson Bk Co.

Tunnelling & Ground Conditions: Proceedings of the International Congress, Cairo, Egypt, April 1994. M. E. Salam. (Illus.). 690p. (C). 1994. text ed. 115.00 (*90-5410-363-9*, Pub. by A A Balkema NE) Ashgate Pub Co.

***Tunnelling Contracts & Site Investigation.** Attewell. (Illus.). 392p. 1995. text ed. 109.00 (*0-419-19140-2*, E & FN Spon) Routledge Chapman & Hall.

Tunnelling Research. G. Girnau & A. Haack. 1984. pap. 24.00 (*0-08-029952-0*, Pergamon Pr) Elsevier.

***Tunnelling Studies of High Temperature Superconductors.** Ed. by Anant Narlikar. (Studies of High Temperature Superconductors: Vol. 20). 239p. (C). 1996. lib. bdg. 89.00 (*1-56072-394-7*) Nova Sci Pubs.

Tunnelling under Difficult Conditions: Proceedings of the International Tunnel Symposium, Tokyo 1978. I. Kitamura. LC 79-40169. 1979. 190.00 (*0-08-024237-5*, Pub. by Pergamon Repr UK) Franklin.

Tunnels. Gail Gibbons. LC 83-18589. (Illus.). 32p. (J). (ps-3). 1987. pap. 5.95 (*0-8234-0670-9*) Holiday.

Tunnels. Joy Richardson. LC 93-30057. (Picture Science Ser.). (Illus.). 32p. (J). (gr. 2-4). 1994. lib. bdg. 20.00 (*0-531-14290-6*) Watts.

Tunnels. Philip Sauvain. Ed. by Rebecca Stefoff. LC 90-40248. (How We Build Ser.). (Illus.). 48p. (J). (gr. 4-7). 1990. lib. bdg. 17.26 (*0-944483-79-8*) Garrett Ed Corp.

Tunnels: Planning, Design, Construction, 2 vols., Set. T. M. Megaw & John Bartlett. LC 81-4111. (Engineering Science Ser.). 605p. 1982. text ed. 204.00 (*0-470-27217-1*) P-H.

Tunnels & Trolls. 5th ed. Ken St. Andre. Ed. & Illus. by Elizabeth Danforth. 1991. 9.95 (*0-940244-00-4*) Flying Buffalo.

Tunnels & Trolls Boxed Set. Ken St. Andre. Ed. & Illus. by Elizabeth Danforth. 1975. 15.95 (*0-940244-65-9*) Flying Buffalo.

Tunnels & Water: Proceedings of the International Congress, Madrid, 12-15 June 1988, 3 vols. Ed. by J. Manuel Serrano. 1500p. (C). 1988. text ed. 275.00 (*90-6191-821-9*, Pub. by A A Balkema NE) Ashgate Pub Co.

Tunnel's End. Marcia Whittley. 152p. 1995. mass mkt. 4.99 (*1-896329-12-8*, Pub. by Comnwlth Pub CN) Partners Pubs Grp.

***Tunnels for People/Tunnel Fuer Menschen World Tunnel Congress '97, Vienna, Austria: Proceedings/Sitzungsberichte 23rd World Assembly of the International Tunneling Association 12-17 April 1997, 2 vols.** Ed. by J. Golser et al. (Illus.). 880p. (C). 1997. text ed. 135.00 (*90-5410-868-1*, Pub. by A A Balkema NE) Ashgate Pub Co.

Tunnels of Cu Chi. Tom Mangold & John Penycate. 320p. 1986. mass mkt. 5.99 (*0-425-08951-7*) Berkley Pub.

Tunnels, Tracks, & Trains: Building A Subway. Joan Hewett. LC 94-9037. (J). (gr. 3-7). 1995. pap. 15.99 (*0-525-67466-7*, Lodestar Bks) Dutton Child Bks.

Tunnels with In-Situ Pressed Concrete Lining. Ryszard B. Zeidler. (Illus.). 256p. 1993. text ed. 80.00 (*90-5410-141-5*, Pub. by A A Balkema NE) Ashgate Pub Co.

Tunomas Honey. Jim Sagel. LC 83-71141. 141p. (ENG & SPA.). 1983. pap. 12.00 (*0-916950-40-9*) Biling Rev-Pr.

Tuntun de Pasa y Griferia. Luis Pales Matos. (Coleccion Puertorriquena Ser.). 226p. (SPA.). 1994. pap. 9.50 (*0-8477-0178-6*) U of PR Pr.

***Tuntun de Pasa y Griferia.** Luis Pales Matos. (Coleccion Puertorriquena Ser.). 226p. (SPA.). 1994. 11.50 (*0-8477-0217-0*) U of PR Pr.

Tuolumne River: From Lumsden Bridge to Ward's Ferry. Keith Robinson & Fred Lehman. (Whitewater Ser.). (Illus.). 1982. pap. 3.95 (*0-941838-02-1*) Lore Unlim.

Tuomen Domain Sourcebook. TSR Inc. Staff. (Advanced Dungeons & Dragons, 2nd Edition: Birthright Campaign World Ser.). 1995. 6.95 (*0-7869-0288-4*) TSR Inc.

***Tupac Shakur.** Ed. by Vibe Magazine Staff. LC 97-2175. 1997. 25.95 (*0-609-60072-9*) Random Hse Value.

Tupelo. John H. Aughey. LC 75-37300. (Black Heritage Library Collection). 1977. reprint ed. 37.95 (*0-8369-8937-6*) Ayer.

Tupelo, Mississippi: Outcome-Based Education. Thomas H. Saterfiel. xii, 34p. 1985. 8.00 (*0-87367-721-8*) Phi Delta Kappa.

***Tupolev: The Man & His Aircraft.** Andrei I. Kandalov & Paul Duffy. LC 96-45246. 232p. 1996. 29.00 (*1-56091-899-3*, R-173) Soc Auto Engineers.

Tupolev Aircraft since 1922. Bill Gunston. (Putnam Aviation Ser.). (Illus.). 288p. 1996. 56.95 (*1-55750-882-8*) Naval Inst Pr.

***Tupolev Tu-95/Tu-114/Tu-142 Bear: The History & Development of Russia's Extraordinary Intercontinental Range Heavy Bomber.** Yefim Gordon & Jay Miller. (Illus.). 80p. 1996. pap. 19.95 (*1-85780-046-X*) Specialty Pr.

Tupper. Thomas Tupper & His Descendants. F. W. Tupper. 71p. 1991. reprint ed. pap. 14.00 (*0-8328-1996-4*); reprint ed. lib. bdg. 24.00 (*0-8328-1995-6*) Higginson Bk Co.

***Tupsu: The Squirrel Who Was Afraid.** Melody Carlson. LC 96-49451. (Illus.). 48p. (J). (ps-3). 1997. 12.99 (*1-57673-052-2*, Gold & Honey) Multnomah Pubs.

Turandot. Marianna Mayer. LC 93-27033. (Illus.). 48p. (J). (ps up). 1995. 16.00 (*0-688-09073-7*, Morrow Junior); lib. bdg. 15.93 (*0-688-09074-5*, Morrow Junior) Morrow.

Turandot. Giacomo Puccini. Ed. by Nicholas John. (English National Opera - Royal Opera House Guide Ser.: No. 27). (Illus.). 1984. pap. 9.95 (*0-7145-4039-0*) Riverrun NY.

Turandot: Vocal Score. Giacomo Puccini. (ENG & ITA.). 1987. pap. 29.95 (*0-7935-5374-1*) H Leonard.

Turandot Libretto. Giacomo Puccini. (ENG & ITA.). 1987. pap. 8.95 (*0-7935-5362-8*) H Leonard.

Turandot Libretto. Giacomo Puccini. 1987. pap. 6.95 (*0-7935-5363-6*) H Leonard.

Turandot's Sisters: A Study of the Folktale at 851. Christine Goldberg. LC 93-8146. (Folklore Library: Vol. 7). 224p. 1993. text ed. 38.00 (*0-8153-1285-7*, H1694) Garland.

***Turane: The Hidden Village.** Patrick Deeley. 96p. 9500. 18.95 (*1-873790-70-8*); pap. 11.95 (*1-873790-69-4*) Dufour.

***Turas Troimh Alba: A Photographic Journey Through Scotland.** T. R. Gordon. (Illus.). VIII, 112p. 1996. 29.95 (*0-9655320-1-1*) Wanderings & Wonderings.

Turathuna al Fikri: (Our Intellectual Heritage - In the Balance of Religious Law & Reason) 2nd ed. Muhammad al Ghazali. LC 91-23711. (Silsilat Islamiyat al Ma'rifah Ser.: No. 8). 217p. 1991. pap. 8.00 (*0-912463-90-2*) IIIT VA.

Turba Philosophorum. Arthur E. Waite. 211p. 1992. reprint ed. pap. 14.50 (*0-922802-99-8*) Kessinger Pub.

***Turba Philosophorum; or, the Assembly of the Sages: An Ancient Alchemical Treatise.** Ed. by Troy Moncrief. Tr. by A. E. Waite from LAT. (Illus.). 1997. pap. 11.95 (*1-55818-389-2*, Alchemical) Holmes Pub.

Turban for the Crown: The Islamic Revolution in Iran. Said A. Arjomand. (Studies in Middle Eastern History). (Illus.). 302p. 1988. 35.00 (*0-19-504257-3*) OUP.

Turban for the Crown: The Islamic Revolution in Iran. Said A. Arjomand. (Studies in Middle Eastern History). 302p. 1989. pap. 11.95 (*0-19-504258-1*) OUP.

Turban Guerrilla: Practical & Religious Extremism in the Punjab. M. Aaron Talsky. (International Trends in Political Development Ser.). 200p. (Orig.). 1992. pap. 19.95 (*1-56543-014-X*) Mt SA Coll Philos.

Turbans & Traders: Hong Kong's Indian Community. Barbara-Sue White. (Asia Paperbacks Ser.). (Illus.). 256p. 1994. pap. 32.00 (*0-19-585287-7*) OUP.

Turbas Republicanas, 1900-1904. Mariano N. Porjtillo. LC 90-81370. 218p. 1990. pap. 9.50 (*0-929157-07-9*) Ediciones Huracan.

Turbellarian Biology. Ed. by Seth Tyler. (Developments in Hydrobiology Ser.). (C). 1992. lib. bdg. 255.00 (*0-7923-1373-9*) Kluwer Ac.

An Asterisk (*) at the beginning of an entry indicates that the title is appearing in BIP for the first time.

Turbidite-Hosted Gold Deposits. Ed. by J. Duncan Keppie et al. LC 87-166418. (Geological Association of Canada. Special Paper Ser.: No. 32). (Illus.). 192p. reprint ed. pap. 54.80 (*0-8357-7528-3*, 2036068) Bks Demand.

Turbidites & Associated Deep-Water Facies. Ed. by R. D. Winn & J. M. Armentrout. (SEPM Core Workshop Notes Ser.: No. 20). (Illus.). 184p. 1995. pap. text ed. 48.00 (*1-56576-018-2*) SEPM.

Turbidity Currents: Dynamics, Deposits, & Reversals. Deborah A. Edwards. LC 92-46171. (Lecture Notes in Earth Sciences Ser.: Vol. 44). 1993. 60.95 (*0-387-56123-4*) Spr-Verlag.

Turbidity Currents & the Transportation of Coarse Sediments to Deep Water: A Symposium. Ed. by Jack L. Hough. LC 52-2310. (Society of Economic Paleontologists & Mineralogists, Special Publication Ser.: No. 2). 111p. reprint ed. pap. 31.70 (*0-317-27102-4*, 2024731) Bks Demand.

Turbine Control. Center for Occupational Research & Development Staff. (EUTEC Power Plant Operator Curriculum Ser.). (Illus.). 44p. (C). 1984. pap. text ed. write for info. (*1-55502-245-6*) CORD Commns.

Turbine-Generators. (Principles of Steam Generation Ser.: Module 12). (Illus.). 135p. 1982. spiral bd. 49.50 (*0-87683-262-1*) GP Courseware.

Turbine Lube-Oil System. Center for Occupational Research & Development Staff. (EUTEC Power Plant Operator Curriculum Ser.). (Illus.). 20p. (C). 1986. pap. text ed. write for info. (*1-55502-240-5*) CORD Commns.

Turbine Lube Oil System Flushing & Cleaning. (Fossil Power Plant Startup Training Ser.: Module 8). (Illus.). 108p. 1982. spiral bd. 29.50 (*0-87683-365-2*) GP Courseware.

Turbine Lubrication. 92p. 1984. 15.00 (*0-318-17675-0*, SP-12) Soc Tribologists.

Turbine Oil Monitoring. Ed. by William C. Young & Reginald S. Roberton. LC 89-301. (Special Technical Publication Ser.: No. STP 1021). (Illus.). 81p. 1989. pap. text ed. 25.00 (*0-8031-1252-1*, 04-010210-12) ASTM.

Turbine Operation. Center for Occupational Research & Development Staff. (EUTEC Power Plant Operator Curriculum Ser.). (Illus.). 40p. (C). 1985. pap. text ed. write for info. (*1-55502-251-0*) CORD Commns.

Turbine Pilot's Flight Manual. Gregory N. Brown & Mark J. Holt. (Illus.). 160p. 1995. pap. 32.95 (*0-8138-2900-3*) Iowa St U Pr.

Turbine Protective System. Center for Occupational Research & Development Staff. (EUTEC Power Plant Operator Curriculum Ser.). (Illus.). 34p. (C). 1986. pap. text ed. write for info. (*1-55502-241-3*) CORD Commns.

Turbine Steam Path: Manufacturing Errors & Their Potential to Influence Blade System Performance. William P. Sanders. (Turbomachinery International Publications Monograph: No. S-3). 1987. 19.95 (*0-937506-19-2*) Turbo Intl Pubn.

Turbine Steam Path Components. William P. Sanders. (Turbomachinery International Publications Monograph: No. S-2). 1987. 19.95 (*0-937506-18-4*) Turbo Intl Pubn.

Turbine Steam Path Maintenance & Repair Methods. William P. Sanders. (Turbomachinery International Publications Monograph: No. S-5). 1985. 19.95 (*0-937506-21-4*) Turbo Intl Pubn.

Turbine Steam Path Performance. William P. Sanders. (Turbomachinery International Publications Monograph: No. S-1). 1987. 19.95 (*0-937506-17-6*) Turbo Intl Pubn.

Turbine Turning Gear Operation. Center for Occupational Research & Development Staff. (EUTEC Power Plant Operator Curriculum Ser.). (Illus.). 24p. (C). 1986. pap. text ed. write for info. (*1-55502-242-1*) CORD Commns.

Turbines. Center for Occupational Research & Development Staff. (EUTEC Power Plant Operator Curriculum Ser.). (Illus.). 28p. (C). 1986. pap. text ed. write for info. (*1-55502-239-1*) CORD Commns.

Turbines & Jet Nozzles with Two-Phase Flows. V. C. Venediktov. LC 70-130509. 253p. 1969. 22.00 (*0-403-04543-6*) Scholarly.

Turbines, Generators & Associated Plant see Modern Power Station Practice

Turbines Westward. Thomas R. Lee. 1975. 16.95 (*0-686-00363-2*) AG Pr.

Turbio Descubrimiento. Laura Marten. (Bianco Ser.). 1996. mass mkt. 3.50 (*0-373-33364-1*, 1-33364-0) Harlequin Bks.

Turbo Algorithms: Programmers Reference. Keith Weiskamp. 444p. 1989. pap. 26.95 (*0-471-61009-7*) Wiley.

Turbo C. Ira Pohl. (C). 1991. pap. text ed. 33.50 (*0-8053-6017-4*) Benjamin-Cummings.

Turbo C++ An Introduction to Computing. Joel Adams et al. LC 95-41348. 1248p. (C). 1995. pap. text ed. 54.00 (*0-13-439928-5*) P-H.

Turbo C: Memory Resident Utilities, Screen I-O & Programming Techniques. Alan Stevens. 315p. (Orig.). 1987. 44.95 incl. disk (*0-943518-76-8*) MIS Press.

Turbo C++ Step-by-Step. 2nd ed. Bryan Flamig. LC 92-33079. 416p. 1993. pap. text ed. 29.95 (*0-471-58056-2*) Wiley.

Turbo C: The Essentials of C Programming. Al Kelley & Ira Pohl. (Illus.). 450p. (C). 1988. pap. 38.75 (*0-8053-7880-4*) Benjamin-Cummings.

Turbo C at Any Speed. Richard S. Wiener. LC 87-30531. (Borland-Wiley Higher Education Ser.). 330p. reprint ed. pap. 94.10 (*0-7837-2374-1*, 2040060) Bks Demand.

Turbo C-C Plus Plus: The Complete Reference. 2nd ed. Herbert Schildt. 1056p. 1992. pap. text ed. 34.95 (*0-07-881776-5*) Osborne-McGraw.

Turbo C++ for Windows Program. 2nd ed. 1998. 39.95 (*0-672-30455-4*) Sams.

Turbo C Plus Plus: Programming & Problem Solving. Sanford Leestma. 1996. pap. 40.00 (*0-02-369725-3*, Macmillan Coll) P-H.

Turbo C Plus Plus Programming in 12 Easy Lessons. Greg M. Perry. (Illus.). 603p. (Orig.). 1994. 39.99 (*0-672-30523-2*) Sams.

Turbo C Plus Plus Trilogy. Eric P. Bloom. 1991. 29.95 incl. 3.5 hd (*0-8306-6759-8*) McGraw-Hill Prof.

Turbo C Plus Plus Trilogy, Version 2.0. Eric P. Bloom. 1991. 29.95 (*0-8306-6733-4*) McGraw-Hill Prof.

Turbo C Programmer's Resource Book. Frederick Holtz. (Illus.). 260p. 1987. pap. 17.95 (*0-8306-3030-9*, 3030) McGraw-Hill Prof.

Turbo C. Quickstart. Lance A. Leventhal. LC 91-53069. (Lance A. Leventhal Microtrend Ser.). 375p. (Orig.). 1992. pap. 29.95 (*0-915391-67-8*, Microtrend) Slawson Comm.

Turbo C Trilogy. Eric P. Bloom. 1991. 29.95 (*0-8306-6674-5*) McGraw-Hill Prof.

Turbo Genealogy: An Introduction to Research in the Information Age. John C. Cosgriff & Carolyn H. Cosgriff. LC 96-26239. 206p. 1997. pap. 17.95 (*0-916489-66-3*) Ancestry.

Turbo Genealogy: The Computer-Enhanced "How-to-Find-Your-Roots" Handbook. John C. Cosgriff & Carolyn H. Cosgriff. 128p. (Orig.). 1987. 27.95 (*0-917255-05-4*); pap. text ed. 17.95 (*0-917255-04-6*) Progenesys Pr.

Turbo Mac 3.5. Samuel L. Marateck. 862p. 1994. suppl. ed., text ed. write for info. incl. disk (*0-471-11050-7*) Wiley.

Turbo Pascal. Berlinger. Date not set. teacher ed., pap. text ed. write for info. (*0-314-70742-5*) West Pub.

Turbo Pascal. Eli Berlinger & Gene Zirkel. Ed. by Ricci. 490p. (C). 1990. pap. text ed. 50.75 (*0-314-66781-4*) West Pub.

Turbo Pascal. Samuel L. Marateck. LC 90-40176. 862p. 1991. Net. pap. text ed. 33.00 (*0-471-60547-6*) Wiley.

Turbo Pascal. Samuel L. Marateck. 862p. 1991. 1.00 (*0-471-55030-2*); 3.5 hd 1.00 (*0-471-55170-8*); 5.25 hd 1.00 (*0-471-53549-4*) Wiley.

Turbo Pascal. Samuel L. Marateck. 216p. 1991. teacher ed., pap. text ed. 24.50 (*0-471-53556-7*) Wiley.

Turbo Pascal. Samuel L. Marateck. 862p. 1991. disk 25.00 (*0-471-55574-6*) Wiley.

Turbo Pascal. Richard Mojena. 700p. (C). 1992. pap. 59.95 (*0-534-13050-X*) PWS Pubs.

Turbo Pascal. M. G. Settle. Date not set. lab manual ed., teacher ed., pap. text ed. 24.50 (*0-314-65242-6*) West Pub.

Turbo Pascal. Wilson. Date not set. lab manual ed., teacher ed., pap. text ed. write for info. (*0-314-01810-7*) West Pub.

Turbo Pascal. 2nd ed. Elliot B. Koffman. 1989. pap. text ed. 26.36 (*0-201-52737-5*) Addison-Wesley.

Turbo Pascal. 2nd ed. Carol Wilson. 155p. 1995. lab manual ed., spiral bd. 20.75 (*0-314-04681-X*) West Pub.

Turbo Pascal. 4th ed. Elliot B. Koffman. (Illus.). 900p. (C). 1993. pap. text ed. 44.25 (*0-201-55811-4*); pap. text ed. 47.50 incl. disk (*0-201-52442-2*) Addison-Wesley.

Turbo Pascal. 4th ed. Elliot B. Koffman & Bruce R. Maxim. LC 92-38717. (C). 1993. pap. text ed. 39.75 (*0-201-53920-9*) Addison-Wesley.

Turbo Pascal. 5th ed. Elliot B. Koffman. (C). 1995. pap. text ed. 45.25 (*0-201-51239-4*) Addison-Wesley.

Turbo Pascal: A Problem Solving Approach. Elliot B. Koffman. 600p. (C). 1986. pap. text ed. 29.25 (*0-201-11743-6*) Addison-Wesley.

Turbo Pascal: An Introduction to Computing. Fuori & Gioia. 1991. pap. text ed. 12.60 (*0-13-720145-1*) P-H.

Turbo Pascal: An Introduction to the Art & Science of Programming. 3rd ed. Walter J. Savitch. (C). 1992. pap. text ed. 45.25 (*0-8053-7021-8*) Benjamin-Cummings.

Turbo Pascal: Problem Solving & Program Design. 2nd ed. Elliot B. Koffman. (Illus.). (C). 1989. pap. text ed. write for info. (*0-201-14989-3*) Addison-Wesley.

Turbo Pascal: Problem Solving & Program Design. 3rd ed. Elliot B. Koffman & Bruce R. Maxim. (Illus.). 784p. (C). 1991. pap. text ed. 38.75 (*0-201-53466-5*) Addison-Wesley.

Turbo Pascal: Procedures & Functions for IBM PCs & Compatibles. Patrick Philippot. Ed. by David Beeson & Seth Keith. LC 87-18797. 204p. reprint ed. pap. 58.20 (*0-7837-0114-4*, 2040391) Bks Demand.

Turbo Pascal: Programmer's Guide. Paul M. Chirlian. 250p. 1986. pap. 21.95 (*0-938862-66-9*) Weber Systems.

Turbo Pascal: Programming & Problem Solving. 2nd ed. Sanford Leestma & Larry Nyhoff. (Illus.). 1008p. (C). 1993. pap. text ed. 59.00 (*0-02-388701-X*, Macmillan Coll) P-H.

Turbo Pascal: Programming & Problem Solving (HC) Mickey G. Settle. 535p. (C). 1988. text ed. 50.75 (*0-314-62309-4*) West Pub.

Turbo Pascal: Self-Teaching Guide. Keith Weiskamp. LC 91-18641. (Self-Teaching Guides Ser.: No. 1581). 344p. 1991. pap. text ed. 22.95 (*0-471-54492-2*) Wiley.

Turbo Pascal: Theory & Practice of Good Programming. Gary W. Martin. (Illus.). 1008p. (C). 1995. pap. text ed. 45.95 (*0-15-592375-7*) OUP.

Turbo Pascal & the Paradox Engine: Full-Powered Windows Applications. Robert Signore et al. LC 93-23113. 323p. 1993. pap. 39.95 incl. disk (*0-8306-4325-7*, Windcrest) TAB Bks.

Turbo Pascal for Chemists: A Problem Solving & Practical Approach. Gordon Filby & M. Klusmann. (Illus.). 400p. 1991. text ed. 68.00 incl. disk (*3-527-27830-3*, VCH) Wiley.

Turbo Pascal for Electronics. Edward J. Pasahow. 208p. (C). 1988. pap. text ed. 14.95 (*0-07-048732-4*) McGraw.

Turbo Pascal for Macintosh: Business. Leon A. Wortman. 1991. 24.95 (*0-8306-6246-4*) TAB Bks.

Turbo Pascal for the IBM PC. Radford & Haigh. (C). 1986. pap. 56.95 (*0-534-06426-4*) PWS Pubs.

Turbo Pascal for the MAC: Programming with Business Applications. Leon A. Wortman. 288p. 1987. pap. 17.95 (*0-8306-2927-0*) McGraw-Hill Prof.

Turbo Pascal for the Mac: Programming with Business Applications. Leon A. Wortman. 1987. pap. 24.95 (*0-07-156257-5*) McGraw.

Turbo Pascal for Windows Programming: The Complete Guide to Developing Windows Applications. William H. Murray. 1994. pap. write for info. (*0-201-58118-3*) Addison-Wesley.

Turbo Pascal for Windows 1.5. John DiElsi. 1994. pap. text ed. write for info. (*0-07-016910-1*) McGraw.

Turbo Pascal in the Lab: A Hands-On Approach 7.0 Edition. 4th ed. Louise C. Hewitt. 189p. (C). 1993. pap. text ed. 15.00 (*0-8053-7041-2*) Benjamin-Cummings.

Turbo Pascal Memory Management Techniques. Len Dorfman & Marc J. Neuberger. 1993. pap. text ed. 32.95 (*0-07-017807-0*) McGraw.

Turbo Pascal Memory Management Techniques. Len Dorfman & Marc J. Neuberger. (Illus.). 304p. 1993. pap. 32.95 (*0-8306-4059-2*, 4193, Windcrest) TAB Bks.

Turbo Pascal Object Oriented Utilities. Shammas. 1990. pap. 44.95 (*0-13-635418-1*) P-H.

Turbo Pascal Precisely. Judy Bishop. (C). 1992. pap. text ed. 27.95 (*0-201-54449-0*) Addison-Wesley.

***Turbo Pascal Programming High School Edition.** 11th ed. Steven L. Mandell. (DG - Computer Programming Ser.). (C). 1987. text ed. 36.95 (*0-314-34629-5*) West Pub.

Turbo Pascal Programming Today. Steven L. Mandell. (Illus.). 561p. (Orig.). (C). 1987. pap. text ed. 52.75 (*0-314-34628-7*); teacher ed., pap. text ed. 21.95 (*0-314-35260-0*) West Pub.

Turbo Pascal Programming Visual Masters. Donald D. Spencer. (Illus.). 96p. 1987. pap. 15.95 (*0-89218-108-7*, NO. 3003) Camelot Pub.

Turbo Pascal 7.0: An Introduction to the Art & Science of Programming. 4th ed. Walter J. Savitch. LC 92-42115. 700p. (C). 1993. pap. text ed. 46.25 (*0-8053-0418-5*) Benjamin-Cummings.

Turbo Pascal Trilogy. E. Bloom & Jeremy G. Soybel. 1991. 29.95 (*0-8306-6667-2*) McGraw-Hill Prof.

Turbo Pascal Trilogy: A Complete Library for Programmers, Featuring Version 5.0 & 5.5. Eric P. Bloom & Jeremy G. Soybel. (Illus.). 784p. 1989. pap. 29.95 (*0-8306-3310-3*, 3310, Windcrest) TAB Bks.

Turbo Pascal Trilogy: Version 5.0 & 5. E. Bloom & Jeremy G. Soybel. 1991. 24.95 (*0-8306-6737-7*); 24.95 (*0-8306-7738-0*) McGraw-Hill Prof.

Turbo Pascal with Turtle Graphics. James Slack. Ed. by Westby. 728p. (C). 1990. pap. text ed. 54.75 (*0-314-66782-2*) West Pub.

Turbo Pascal 4.0. Decker. (Computer Science Ser.). 1992. lab manual ed., pap. 21.95 (*0-534-16178-2*) PWS Pubs.

Turbo Pascal 4.0-5.0: An Introduction to the Art & Science of Programming. Walter J. Savitch. 880p. (C). 1989. teacher ed. 17.25 (*0-8053-0411-8*); pap. text ed. 40.95 (*0-8053-0410-X*); disk 10.75 (*0-8053-0413-4*) Benjamin-Cummings.

Turbo Pascal 4.0-5.0 an Introduction to Art & Science of Programming. Walter J. Savitch. 1989. pap. 40.75 (*0-8053-0415-0*) Benjamin-Cummings.

Turbo Pascal 6.0. 3rd ed. Louise Hewitt. (C). 1992. pap. text ed. 16.95 incl. disk (*0-8053-7029-3*) Benjamin-Cummings.

Turbo Pascal 6.0: The Nuts & Bolts of Program Construction. John DiElsi. 592p. 1991. pap. text ed. write for info. (*0-07-557790-9*) McGraw.

Turbo Prolog: An Introduction to Artificial Intelligence. Patrice Bihan. LC 87-16074. 180p. reprint ed. pap. 51.30 (*0-8357-2769-6*, 2039894) Bks Demand.

Turbo Prolog: Step by Step. Ralph Cafolla & Dan Kauffman. 496p. (C). 1990. pap. text ed. 49.00 (*0-675-20816-5*, Merrill Coll) P-H.

Turbo Prolog Advanced Programming. Safaa H. Hashim & Philip Seyer. 1988. pap. text ed. 29.95 (*0-8306-6664-8*) McGraw-Hill Prof.

Turbo Prolog Primer. Jean B. Rogers. LC 86-28707. (Illus.). 240p. (C). 1987. pap. text ed. 23.75 (*0-201-12198-0*) Addison-Wesley.

Turbo Prolog Programmer's Guide. Nathan Goldenthal. 300p. 1987. pap. 21.95 (*0-938862-83-9*) Weber Systems.

Turbo Success: How to Reprogram the Human Biocomputer. Ron G. Holland. 300p. (C). 1993. 100.00 (*1-85609-051-5*, Pub. by Witherby & Co UK) St Mut.

Turbo Tax for Windows for Dummies. Gail R. Perry. 384p. 1995. pap. 19.99 (*1-56884-228-7*) IDG Bks.

Turbo Tax for Windows for Dummies. 2nd ed. Gail Helsel. 1995. pap. 19.99 (*1-56884-948-6*) IDG Bks.

Turbo Tax Headstart 1994. Date not set. write for info. (*0-314-05912-1*) West Pub.

Turbo Turtle Graphs. Slack. Date not set. teacher ed., pap. text ed. write for info. (*0-314-73479-1*) West Pub.

Turbocharge Your MAC! Make Any Mac Faster & Smarter. Carla Rose. 1993. pap. text ed. 32.95 (*0-8306-4443-1*, Windcrest) TAB Bks.

Turbocharge Your Mac! Make Any Mac Faster & Smarter. Carla Rose. 1993. pap. text ed. 32.95 (*0-07-053660-0*) McGraw-Hill Prof.

Turbocharge Your Writing! The Vitale Instant Writing Method. Joe Vitale. 23p. (Orig.). (C). 1988. pap. 5.95 (*0-9617549-1-5*) Brockton Pubng.

Turbocharged Company: Igniting Your Business to Soar Ahead of the Competition. Larry Goddard & David Brown. LC 95-60619. (Illus.). 306p. 1995. 24.95 (*0-9634940-6-6*) York Pub.

TurboGrafx Secrets: The Power User's Guide. Rusel DeMaria & Andy Eddy. (Secrets of the Games Ser.). 272p. (Orig.). 1990. pap. 9.95 (*1-55958-064-X*) Prima Pub.

Turbografx 16 & Turboexpress Secrets, Vol. 2. Donn Navert. (Secrets of the Games Ser.). (Illus.). 256p. (Orig.). 1991. pap. 9.95 (*1-55958-126-3*) Prima Pub.

Turbomachine Blade Vibration. J. S. Rao. 445p. 1991. text ed. 59.95 (*0-470-21764-2*) Halsted Pr.

Turbomachine Unsteady Aerodynamics. J. S. Rao. 1994. write for info. (*81-224-0653-X*, Pub. by Wiley Estrn II) Franklin.

Turbomachinery: Basic Theory & Applications. 2nd rev. ed. Earl Logan. (Mechanical Engineering Ser.: Vol. 85). 280p. 1993. 75.00 (*0-8247-9138-X*) Dekker.

Turbomachinery Developments in Steam & Gas Turbines: Presented at the Winter Annual Meeting of the American Society of Mechanical Engineers, Atlanta, Georgia, November 27-December 2, 1977. American Society of Mechanical Engineers Staff. Ed. by W. G. Steltz. LC 77-88002. (Illus.). 104p. reprint ed. pap. 29.70 (*0-317-11146-9*, 2013321) Bks Demand.

Turbomachinery Diffuser Design Technology. David Japikse. LC 85-90311. (Design Technology Ser.: No. DTS 1). (Illus.). 400p. 1984. text ed. 1,450.00 (*0-933283-00-8*) Concepts ETI.

Turbomachinery Diffuser Design Technology. 2nd ed. David Japikse & Nicholas C. Baines. LC 95-68415. (Design Technology Ser.: No. DTS-1). (Illus.). 400p. 1997. write for info. (*0-933283-08-3*) Concepts ETI.

***Turbomachinery Performance Analysis.** write for info. (*0-340-63191-0*, Pub. by E Arnold UK) Routledge Chapman & Hall.

Turbomachinery Performance Analysis. R. I. Lewis. (Illus.). 352p. 1996. pap. 57.95 incl. disk (*0-470-23596-9*, Wiley-Interscience) Wiley.

Turbomachinery Rotordynamics: Phenomena, Modeling, & Analysis. Dara Childs. LC 92-35452. 496p. 1993. text ed. 95.00 (*0-471-53840-X*) Wiley.

***Turbomachinery Technology & Design, Vol. 110.** Ed. by Hah. LC 96-29979. (Mechanical Engineering Ser.: Vol. 110). 464p. 1997. 135.00 (*0-8247-9829-5*) Dekker.

Turbotax 94. Sanders. Date not set. student ed., pap. text ed. write for info. (*0-314-07089-3*) West Pub.

Turbotrains. Wolfgang Stoffels. 124p. 1983. 41.95 (*0-8176-1172-X*) Birkhauser.

Turbulence. Pierre Joris. 62p. 1991. pap. 8.00 (*1-880280-02-7*) St Lazaire.

***Turbulence.** Robert Walker. 1996. mass mkt. 6.99 (*0-8125-9051-1*) Forge NYC.

Turbulence. 2nd ed. J. O. Hinze. (C). 1975. text ed. write for info. (*0-07-029037-7*) McGraw.

Turbulence: A New Perspective for Pilots. Peter F. Lester. LC 93-13133. (Illus.). 280p. 1993. 19.95 (*0-88487-141-X*) Jeppesen Sanderson.

Turbulence: A Tentative Dictionary NATO Advanced Study Institute on Turbulence, Weak, & Strong (1993: Cargese, France) Ed. by P. Tabeling & O. Cardoso. LC 94-49720. (NATO ASI Ser.: Series B, Vol. 341). 149p. 1995. 65.00 (*0-306-44998-6*, Plenum Pr) Plenum.

Turbulence! Challenges & Opportunities in the World of Work; Are You Prepared? Roger E. Herman. Ed. by Karl E. Ziellenbach & Joyce L. Gioia. LC 95-5536. 276p. 1995. 22.95 (*1-886939-01-2*) Oak Hill Pr OH.

Turbulence: Perspectives on Flow & Sediment Transport. Ed. by N. J. Clifford et al. LC 93-3142. 360p. 1993. text ed. 125.00 (*0-471-93900-5*) Wiley.

Turbulence: The Legacy of A. N. Kolmogorov. Uriel Frisch. (Illus.). 300p. (C). write for info. (*0-614-07057-0*) Cambridge U Pr.

Turbulence & Coherent Structures. Ed. by O. Metais & Marcel Lesieur. (Fluid Mechanics & Its Applications Ser.). 640p. 1990. lib. bdg. 213.50 (*0-7923-0646-5*) Kluwer Ac.

Turbulence & Combustion. V. R. Kuznetsov & V. A. Sabelnikov. 290p. 1990. 142.00 (*0-89116-873-7*) Hemisp Pub.

Turbulence & Diffusion in Stable Environments. Ed. by J. C. Hunt. (Institute of Mathematics & Its Applications Conference Series, New Ser.: New Series 3). (Illus.). 336p. 1985. 59.00 (*0-19-853604-6*) OUP.

***Turbulence & Diffusion in the Atmosphere.** Alfred K. Blackadar. LC 96-35289. (Illus.). 187p. 1997. 59.95 (*3-540-61406-0*) Spr-Verlag.

Turbulence & Molecular Processes in Combustion: A Collection of Contributions Based on Lectures Presented at the Sixth Toyota Conference, Shizuoka, Japan, 11-14 October 1992. Sixth Toyota Conference, 1992 Staff. LC 93-13372. 462p. 1993. 228.50 (*0-444-89757-7*) Elsevier.

Turbulence & Nonlinear Dynamics in MHD Flows: Proceedings of the Workshop on Turbulence & Nonlinear Dynamics in MHD Flows, Cargese, France, July 4-8, 1988. Pierre-Louis Sulem. 300p. 1989. 140.75 (*0-444-87396-1*, North Holland) Elsevier.

Turbulence & Predictability in Geophysical Fluid Dynamics & Climate Dynamics: Proceedings of the International School of Physics, Enrico Fermi Course LXXXVIII, Varenna, Italy, 14 June-24 June, 1983. Ed. by Roberto Benzi et al. (Enrico Fermi International Summer School of Physics Ser.: Vol. 88). 454p. 1985. 199.00 (*0-444-86936-0*, North Holland) Elsevier.

Turbulence & Random Processes in Fluid Mechanics. 2nd ed. M. T. Landahl & E. Mollo-Christensen. (Illus.). 170p. (C). 1992. text ed. 69.95 (*0-521-41992-1*); pap. text ed. 22.95 (*0-521-42213-2*) Cambridge U Pr.

Turbulence & Transition Modelling: Lecture Notes from the ERCOTAC/IUJAM Summerschool Held in Stockholm, 12-20 June, 1995. Ed. by M. Hallback et al. LC 96-15902. (ERCOFTAC Ser.: Vol. 2). 384p. (C). 1996. lib. bdg. 148.00 (*0-7923-4060-4*) Kluwer Ac.

Turbulence, Coherent Structures, Symmetry & Dynamical Systems. Philip Holmes et al. (Cambridge Monographs on Mechanics & Applied Mathematics). (Illus.). 496p. (C). 1996. 69.95 (*0-521-55142-0*) Cambridge U Pr.

Turbulence Control. Ed. by D. E. Parekh. LC 94-71667. (Fluid Engineering Division Conference Ser.: Vol. 193). 63p. 1994. pap. 25.00 (*0-7918-1376-2*) ASME.

Turbulence Control by Passive Means. Ed. by E. Coustols. (C). 1990. lib. bdg. 124.50 (*0-7923-1020-9*) Kluwer Ac.

Turbulence, Current Sheets, & Shocks in Cosmic Plasma, Vol. 6. S. I. Vanshtein et al. Tr. by Oleg Pokhotelov from RUS. LC 93-25845. (Fluid Mechanics of Astrophysics & Geophysics Ser.: Vol. 6). 398p. 1993. text ed. 165.00 (*2-88124-877-2*) Gordon & Breach.

Turbulence, Heat & Mass Transfer. Ed. by K. Hanjalic & J. C. Pereira. 573p. 1995. 135.00 (*1-56700-040-1*) Begell Hse.

Turbulence in Complex Flows: 1994 International Mechanical Engineering Congress & Exposition, Chicago, Illinois - November 6-11, 1994. (FED Ser.: Vol. 203). 120p. 1994. 54.00 (*0-7918-1432-7*, G00927) ASME.

***Turbulence in Economics: An Evolutionary Appraisal of Cycles & Complexity in Historical Processes.** Francisco Louca. LC 97-13455. 416p. 1997. 85.00 (*1-85898-563-3*) E Elgar.

Turbulence in Fluid Flows: A Dynamical Systems Approach. Ed. by George R. Sell et al. LC 93-5272. (IMA Volumes in Mathematics & Its Applications Ser.: Vol. 55). 1993. 63.95 (*0-387-94113-4*) Spr-Verlag.

***Turbulence in Fluids.** Lesieur. 1997. pap. text ed. 70.00 (*0-7923-4416-2*) Kluwer Ac.

Turbulence in Fluids. 2nd rev. ed. Marcel Lesieur. (C). 1990. lib. bdg. 137.50 (*0-7923-0645-7*) Kluwer Ac.

***Turbulence in Fluids.** 3rd ed. LC 96-51041. 1997. lib. bdg. 225.00 (*0-7923-4415-4*) Kluwer Ac.

Turbulence in Lakes & Rivers. J. R. Smith. 1975. 35.00 (*0-900386-21-5*) St Mut.

Turbulence in Open-Channel Flows. Iehisa Nezu & Hiroji Nakagawa. (Monograph Ser.). (Illus.). 296p. (C). 1993. text ed. 85.00 (*90-5410-118-0*, Pub. by A A Balkema NE) Ashgate Pub Co.

Turbulence in Spatially Extended Systems. Ed. by R. Benzi et al. 315p. (C). 1993. lib. bdg. 125.00 (*1-56072-120-0*) Nova Sci Pubs.

Turbulence in the American Workplace. Peter B. Doeringer et al. (Illus.). 272p. 1991. 38.00 (*0-19-506461-5*) OUP.

Turbulence in the Ocean. A. S. Monin & R. V. Ozmidov. 1985. lib. bdg. 122.00 (*90-277-1735-4*) Kluwer Ac.

Turbulence in World Politics: A Theory of Change & Continuity. James N. Rosenau. (Illus.). 459p. (Orig.). 1990. pap. text ed. 18.95 (*0-691-02308-5*) Princeton U Pr.

Turbulence Management & Relaminarisation. Ed. by Hans W. Liepmann & R. Narashima. (Illus.). xxiii, 550p. 1987. 99.00 (*0-387-18574-7*) Spr-Verlag.

Turbulence Measurement & Flow Modeling. Ed. by Ching Jen Chen et al. 869p. 1987. 198.00 (*0-89116-558-4*) Hemisp Pub.

***Turbulence Modeling & Vortex Dynamics: Proceedings of a Workshop Held at Istanbul, Turkey, 2-6 September, 1996.** Olus Boratav et al. LC 97-20900. (Lecture Notes in Physics Ser.: Vol. 491). 1997. write for info. (*3-540-63051-1*) Spr-Verlag.

Turbulence Modeling for CFD. David C. Wilcox. 480p. (C). 1993. text ed. 75.00 (*0-9636051-0-0*) DCW Industries.

Turbulence Models & Their Application in Hydraulics: A State-of-the-Art Review. rev. ed. Wolfgang Rodi. (IAHR Monograph Ser.). (Illus.). 120p. (C). 1995. 35.00 (*90-5410-150-4*, Pub. by A A Balkema NE) Ashgate Pub Co.

Turbulence. Novel. Jia Pingwa. Tr. by Howard Goldblatt from CHI. LC 91-9890. 592p. 1991. 22.95 (*0-8071-1687-4*) La State U Pr.

Turbulence, Strange Attractors & Chaos. David Ruelle. 450p. 1995. text ed. 86.00 (*981-02-2310-2*); pap. text ed. 48.00 (*981-02-2311-0*) World Scientific Pub.

Turbulence Theory. Levich. Date not set. write for info. (*0-7506-9091-7*) Buttrwrth-Heinemann.

Turbulent & Reactive Flow Calculations: Special Issue - Combustion Science & Technology. Ronald M. So et al. 268p. 1988. pap. text ed. 128.00 (*0-677-22110-X*) Gordon & Breach.

Turbulent City: Paris 1783 to 1871. Andre Castelot. Tr. by Denise Folliot. LC 76-117867. (Select Bibliographies Reprint Ser.). 1977. 28.95 (*0-8369-5320-7*) Ayer.

Turbulent Decade: A History of the Cultural Revolution. Yan Jiaqi & Gao Gao. Ed. & Tr. by D. W. Kwok. LC 95-30358. (SHAPS Library of Translations). 1996. text ed. 48.00 (*0-8248-1695-1*) UH Pr.

Turbulent Enhanced Heat Transfer. Ed. by T. J. Rabas & R. L. Webb. (HTD Ser.: Vol. 239). 72p. 1993. 30.00 (*0-7918-1152-2*, G00796) ASME.

Turbulent Era: A Diplomatic Record of Forty Years, 1904-1945, 2 Vols, Set. Joseph C. Grew. Ed. by Walter Johnson. LC 72-114880. (Select Bibliographies Reprint Ser.). 1977. 96.95 (*0-8369-5284-7*) Ayer.

Turbulent Era: Riot & Disorder in Jacksonsian America. Michael Feldberg. 144p. 1980. pap. text ed. 14.95 (*0-19-502678-0*) OUP.

Turbulent Flow. R. J. Garde. 287p. 1994. text ed. 44.95 (*0-470-23340-0*) Halsted Pr.

Turbulent Flows - 1995. Ed. by B. F. Carroll et al. LC 87-71097. (1995 ASME/JSME Fluids Engineering Conference Ser.: FED-Vol. 208). 128p. 1995. 72.00 (*0-7918-1463-7*, G00958) ASME.

Turbulent Flows & Heat Transfer. Ed. by Chia-Ch'iao Lin. LC 58-50928. (High Speed Aerodynamics & Jet Propulsion Ser.: Vol. 5). 569p. reprint ed. pap. 162.20 (*0-317-09274-X*, 2001132) Bks Demand.

Turbulent Flows in Engineering. A. J. Reynolds. LC 73-8464. (Illus.). 478p. reprint ed. pap. 136.30 (*0-317-11132-9*, 2051617) Bks Demand.

Turbulent Flows of Gas Suspensions. Shraiber. 1990. 181.00 (*0-89116-905-9*) Hemisp Pub.

Turbulent Flows, 1993. Ed. by M. J. Morris & B. F. Carrol. LC 87-71097. (FED Ser.: Vol. 155). 189p. 1993. pap. 40.00 (*0-7918-0963-3*, H00795) ASME.

Turbulent Flows 1994. Ed. by M. J. Morris & B. F. Carroll. LC 87-71097. (Fluid Engineering Division Conference Ser.: Vol. 188). 83p. 1994. pap. 30.00 (*0-7918-1371-1*) ASME.

Turbulent Gulf: People, Politics & Power. Liesl Graz. 324p. 1993. text ed. 19.95 (*1-85043-557-X*, Pub. by I B Tauris UK) St Martin.

Turbulent Mirror: An Illustrated Guide to Chaos Theory & the Science of Wholeness. John Briggs & David Peat. LC 88-45567. (Illus.). 224p. 1990. reprint ed. pap. 15.00 (*0-06-091696-6*, PL) HarpC.

Turbulent Mixing 1993. Ed. by D. E. Parekh & M. J. Morris. LC 93-73259. 77p. pap. 35.00 (*0-7918-1023-2*) ASME.

Turbulent Motion & the Structure of Chaos: The New Approach to the Statistical Theory of Open Systems. Yu L. Klimontovich. 412p. (C). 1991. lib. bdg. 210.00 (*0-7923-1114-0*) Kluwer Ac.

Turbulent Passage: A Global History of the Twentieth Century. Peter N. Stearns et al. (C). 1994. text ed. 49.50 (*0-06-501039-6*) Addson-Wesley Educ.

Turbulent Passage: A Global History of the Twentieth Century. Peter N. Stearns et al. LC 93-32762. 1993. write for info. (*0-06-561037-7*, HarpT) HarpC.

Turbulent Passage: A Global History of the Twentieth Century. Peter N. Stearns et al. LC 93-32762. 320p. reprint ed. pap. 46.00 (*1-886746-49-4*, 93497) Talman.

Turbulent Reacting Flows. Ed. by Paul A. Libby & Forman A. Williams. (Combustion Treatise Ser.). (Illus.). 647p. 1994. text ed. 158.00 (*0-12-447945-6*) Acad Pr.

Turbulent Reacting Flows. Ed. by F. Williams & Paul A. Libby. (Topics in Applied Physics Ser.: Vol. 44). (Illus.). 260p. 1980. 86.95 (*0-387-10192-6*) Spr-Verlag.

Turbulent Reactive Flows. Ed. by R. P. Borghi & S. N. Murthy. (Lecture Notes in Engineering Ser.: Vol. 40). (Illus.). 940p. 1989. 175.95 (*0-387-96887-3*) Spr-Verlag.

Turbulent Shear Flows Eight: Selected Papers from the Eighth International Symposium on Turbulent Shear Flows, Munich, FRG, September 9-11, 1991. Ed. by F. Durst et al. LC 92-32190. 1992. 48.95 (*0-387-55740-7*) Spr-Verlag.

Turbulent Shear Flows Five. Ed. by F. Durst et al. (Illus.). 380p. 1987. 168.95 (*0-387-16885-0*) Spr-Verlag.

Turbulent Shear Flows Four. Ed. by L. J. Bradbury et al. (Illus.). 370p. 1985. 122.00 (*0-387-13744-0*) Spr-Verlag.

Turbulent Shear Flows One: Proceedings of the First International Symposium, Pennsylvania State University, University Park, Pennsylvania, April 18-20, 1977. Ed. by F. Durst et al. (Illus.). 1979. 72.95 (*0-387-09041-X*) Spr-Verlag.

Turbulent Shear Flows Seven: Selected Papers from the Seventh International Symposium on Turbulent Shear Flows, Stanford University, U. S. A., August 21-23, 1989. Ed. by F. Durst et al. (Illus.). 352p. 1991. 163.95 (*0-387-53177-7*) Spr-Verlag.

Turbulent Shear Flows Three: University of California, Selected Papers, 1981. L. J. Bradbury et al. (Illus.). 321p. 1983. 103.95 (*0-387-11817-9*) Spr-Verlag.

Turbulent Shear Flows Two. Ed. by J. S. Bradbury et al. (Illus.). 480p. 1980. 94.95 (*0-387-10067-9*) Spr-Verlag.

Turbulent Shear Flows 9. Ed. by F. Durst et al. 490p. 1995. 157.95 (*0-387-57704-1*) Spr-Verlag.

Turbulent Shear Layers in Supersonic Flow. Alexander J. Smits & Jan-Paul Dussauge. LC 96-20444. (Illus.). 366p. 1996. 80.00 (*1-56396-260-8*, AIP) Am Inst Physics.

Turbulent Skies: The History of Commercial Aviation. T. A. Heppenheimer. LC 95-21508. 400p. 1995. text ed. 30.00 (*0-471-10961-4*) Wiley.

Turbulent Spirit: Cleveland, Ohio, & Its Workers, 1877-1899. Leslie S. Hough. LC 90-27323. (Nineteenth Century American Political & Social History Ser.). 240p. 1991. 15.00 (*0-8240-8194-3*) Garland.

Turbulent Taos. rev. ed. Den Galbraith. LC 83-9290. (Illus.). 48p. 1983. pap. 4.95 (*0-86534-038-2*) Sunstone Pr.

Turbulent Teens: Understanding Helping, Surviving. James E. Gardner. 224p. 1991. pap. 8.95 (*0-913091-01-4*, JP-9101-4) Jalmar Pr.

***Turbulent Teens & Panicking Parents.** Jeenie Gordon. LC 96-49108. 1997. pap. 10.99 (*0-8007-5620-7*) Revell.

***Turbulent Time: The French Revolution & the Greater Caribbean.** David B. Gaspar & David P. Geggus. LC 96-33248. (Blacks in the Diaspora Ser.). 1997. write for info. (*0-253-33247-8*) Ind U Pr.

***Turbulent Time: The French Revolution & the Greater Caribbean.** David B. Gaspar & David. P. Geggus. LC 96-33248. (Blacks in the Diaspora Ser.). 1997. pap. write for info. (*0-253-21086-0*) Ind U Pr.

Turbulent Transfer in the Lower Atmosphere. Charles H. Priestley. LC 59-10427. 138p. reprint ed. pap. 39.40 (*0-317-08496-8*, 2011234) Bks Demand.

Turbulent Triangle. Susannah Bradley. (FunFax Ser.). (Illus.). 48p. (J). (gr. 3-6). 1992. pap. 2.95 (*1-56680-001-3*) Mad Hatter Pub.

Turbulent Voyage: Readings in African-American Studies. Floyd Hayes & Arlyne Lazerson. (Illus.). 425p. (C). 1992. pap. text ed. 30.90 (*0-939693-26-7*) Collegiate Pr.

Turbulent Years. Isaac F. Marcosson. LC 71-90661. (Essay Index Reprint Ser.). 1977. 30.95 (*0-8369-1305-1*) Ayer.

***Turbulent Years: F. D. Roosevelt to L. Johnson, 1933-1969.** Rose Blue & Corinne J. Naden. LC 97-19104. (Who's That in the White House? Ser.). (J). 1998. write for info. (*0-8172-4304-6*) Raintree Steck-V.

Turc Sans Peine: Turkish for French Speakers. Dominique Halbout & Assimil Staff. 529p. (FRE & TUR.). 1992. 31.95 (*0-7859-0999-0*, 2700501667) Fr & Eur.

Turc sans Peine - Turkish for French Speakers. Assimil Staff. (FRE & TUR.). 28.95 (*0-8288-8221-5*); audio 125.00 (*0-8288-8222-3*) Fr & Eur.

Turc sans Peine (Turkish for French Speakers) Denis Diderot. 476p. (FRE.). 1975. 99.50 incl. audio (*0-7859-1190-1*, 2705657932) Fr & Eur.

Turcaret. Alain-Rene Lesage. pap. 4.95 (*0-685-11607-7*) Fr & Eur.

Turco in Italia: Dramma Buffo in Two Acts. Gioachino Rossini. Ed. by Margaret Bent. 1374p. 1988. lib. bdg. 300.00 (*0-226-72842-0*) U Ch Pr.

Turek's Orthopaedics, Principles & Their Application. 5th ed. Ed. by Stuart L. Weinstein & Joseph A. Buckwalter. LC 93-39198. 736p. 1994. text ed. 129.00 (*0-397-50692-9*) Lppncott-Raven.

Turf: And Other Corporate Power Plays. Pamela Cuming. 1986. 19.95 (*0-13-933102-6*) S&S Trade.

Turf Accounts: A Prize Racing Anthology. Ed. by Gee Armytage & Mike Seabrook. 208p. 1996. pap. 19.95 (*0-85493-247-X*, Pub. by V Gollancz UK) Trafalgar.

Turf & Ornamental Chemicals Reference, 1994. 3rd ed. C & P Press, Inc. Staff. 1100p. 1993. 110.00 (*1-57009-001-7*) Chem & Pharmac.

Turf-cutter's Donkey. Patricia Lynch. 224p. 1984. 22.00 (*0-85105-900-7*, Pub. by Colin Smythe Ltd UK) Dufour.

Turf Cutter's Donkey. Patricia Lynch. 243p. (J). (ps-8). 1988. pap. 7.95 (*1-85371-016-4*, Pub. by Poolbeg Pr IE) Dufour.

***Turf Insects of Colorado & New Mexico.** Whitney Cranshaw & Charles R. Ward. Ed. by Debby Weitzel. (Illus.). 40p. (Orig.). 1996. pap. 8.00 (*1-889143-00-6*, 560A) CO St U Coop.

Turf Irrigation Manual: The Complete Guide to Turf & Landscape Irrigation Systems. rev. ed. Richard B. Choate. LC 93-50092. Orig. Title: Turf Irrigation Manual. 1994. 49.95 (*0-9635096-0-8*) Telsco Indust.

Turf Irrigation Manual see Turf Irrigation Manual: The Complete Guide to Turf & Landscape Irrigation Systems

***Turf Management Handbook.** Howard B. Sprague. 1996. 43.95 (*0-8134-3083-6*) Interstate.

Turf Management Handbook. 4th ed. Howard B. Sprague. LC 74-19656. 1994. 43.95 (*0-8134-2968-4*) Interstate.

Turf Management of a Golf Course. Beard. 1986. text ed. 100.00 (*0-02-307660-7*, Macmillan Coll) P-H.

Turf Management of Golf Courses. James B. Beard. 660p. 1982. 59.95 (*0-317-56418-8*) US Golf Assn.

***Turf Wars: How Congressional Committees Claim Jurisdiction.** David C. King. LC 96-53058. 1997. pap. text ed. 15.95 (*0-226-43624-1*); lib. bdg. 34.00 (*0-226-43623-3*) U Ch Pr.

Turf Weeds & Their Control. Ed. by Alfred J. Turgeon & Marian K. Viney. LC 94-4166. 259p. 1994. 60.00 (*0-89118-120-2*) Am Soc Agron.

Turfgrass: Nature's Constant Benediction: The History of the American Sod Producers Association 1967-1992. Ed. by Janice L. Betts & Wendell G. Mathews. 112p. (Orig.). 1992. pap. write for info. (*0-9633510-0-1*) Am Sod Prods.

Turfgrass: Science & Culture. J. Beard. (Illus.). 1972. text ed. 96.00 (*0-13-933002-X*) P-H.

***Turfgrass Biotechnology: Cell & Molecular Genetics Apprаches to Turfgrass Improvement.** Ed. by Miriam B. Sticklen & Michael P. Kenna. 250p. (C). 1997. 54.95 (*1-57504-074-3*, 074-3) Sleeping Bear Software.

Turfgrass Ecology & Management. T. Karl Danneberger. Ed. by Cindy Code. LC 93-78045. 201p. (C). 1993. 28.00 (*1-883751-00-4*) GIE Pub.

Turfgrass Insects of the United States & Canada. Haruo Tashiro. LC 86-6368. (Comstock Bk.). (Illus.). 448p. 1986. 49.95 (*0-8014-1814-3*) Cornell U Pr.

Turfgrass Management. rev. ed. Al J. Turgeon. (C). 1987. teacher ed. write for info. (*0-8359-7888-5*, Reston) P-H.

Turfgrass Management. 4th ed. A. J. Turgeon. LC 95-23407. (Illus.). 406p. 1995. text ed. 83.00 (*0-13-449257-9*) P-H.

Turfgrass Management Handbook: A Guide to Professional Lawn Care. Henry Decker & Jane Decker. (Illus.). 304p. 1988. text ed. 20.00 (*0-13-933128-X*) P-H.

***Turfgrass Management Information Directory.** Ed. by Keith Karnok. 115p. 1996. lab manual ed., spiral bd. 24.95 (*1-57504-058-1*) Ann Arbor Chelsea.

Turfgrass Patch Diseases Caused by Ectotrophic Root-Infecting Fungi. Ed. by Bruce B. Clarke & Ann B. Gould. LC 93-72095. (Illus.). 161p. 1993. pap. 28.00 (*0-89054-154-X*) Am Phytopathol Soc.

Turfgrass Pests. 2nd rev. ed. Ed. by Clyde L. Elmore. LC 88-83113. (Illus.). 128p. 1989. pap. 15.00 (*0-931876-86-9*, 4053) ANR Pubns CA.

Turfgrass Science. Ed. by A. A. Hanson & F. V. Juska. (Illus.). 715p. 1969. 12.50 (*0-89118-015-X*) Am Soc Agron.

Turfgrass Science & Management. R. Emmons. (Agriculture Ser.). 1984. teacher ed., pap. 12.00 (*0-8273-1342-X*) Delmar.

Turfgrass Science & Management. Robert D. Emmons. (Illus.). 384p. (C). 1984. teacher ed. 13.00 (*0-8273-1349-7*) Delmar.

Turfgrass Science & Management. 2nd ed. Emmons. 16p. 1996. teacher ed., pap. text ed. 12.75 (*0-8273-6848-8*) Delmar.

Turfgrass Science & Management. 2nd ed. Emmons. 224p. 1996. text ed. 29.00 (*0-8273-6847-X*) Delmar.

Turfgrass Science & Management. 2nd ed. Emmons. (Agriculture Ser.). 1995. teacher ed. 12.75 (*0-8273-6599-3*) Van Nos Reinhold.

Turfgrass Science & Management. 2nd ed. Robert D. Emmons. LC 94-30692. (Illus.). 480p. 1995. text ed. 51.95 (*0-8273-6598-5*) Delmar.

Turfgrass Sod Production. Stephen T. Cockerham. LC 88-71015. 88p. 1988. pap. 12.00 (*0-931876-85-0*, 21451) ANR Pubns CA.

Turfgrass Water Conservation. Victor A. Gibeault. LC 85-70730. (Illus.). 184p. 1985. pap. 12.00 (*0-931876-69-9*, 21405) ANR Pubns CA.

Turfgrasses: Their Management & Use in the Southern Zone. 2nd rev. ed. Richard L. Duble. LC 95-39690. (W. L. Moody, Jr., Natural History Ser.: No. 20). (Illus.). 356p. 1996. 49.95 (*0-89096-647-8*) Tex A&M Univ Pr.

Turfs-Fields-Pitches-Arenas. Richard Kostelanetz. 20p. 1980. pap. 2.00 (*0-913719-47-1*) High-Coo Pr.

Turgenev. Edward Garnett. LC 75-25925. (Studies in Russian Literature & Life: No. 100). 1974. lib. bdg. 75.00 (*0-8383-2011-2*) M S G Haskell Hse.

Turgenev: A Month in the Country (Mesyats V Derevne) Ed. by T. A. Greenan. (Bristol Russian Texts Ser.). 211p. (RUS.). 1992. pap. 19.95 (*1-85399-320-4*, Pub. by Brstl Class Pr UK) Focus Pub-R Pullins.

Turgenev: A Reading of His Fiction. Frank F. Seeley. (Studies in Russian Literature). 325p. (C). 1991. text ed. 80.00 (*0-521-36521-X*) Cambridge U Pr.

Turgenev: Asya. Ed. by F. Gregory & J. Andrew. (Bristol Russian Texts Ser.). 181p. (RUS.). 1992. pap. 17.95 (*1-85399-295-X*, Pub. by Brstl Class Pr UK) Focus Pub-R Pullins.

Turgenev: Fathers & Sons (Ottsy I Deti) Ed. by E. R. Sands. (Bristol Russian Texts Ser.). 253p. (RUS.). 1992. pap. 19.95 (*1-85399-319-0*, Pub. by Brstl Class Pr UK) Focus Pub-R Pullins.

Turgenev: First Love - Pervaya Lyubov. Ed. by F. Gregory & R. Lagerberg. (Russian Texts Ser.). 192p. (RUS.). 1996. pap. 16.95 (*1-85399-400-6*, Pub. by Brstl Class Pr UK) Focus Pub-R Pullins.

Turgenev: First Love (Pervaya Lyubov') Ed. by F. G. Gregory. (Bristol Russian Texts Ser.). 183p. (RUS.). 1991. pap. 17.95 (*1-85399-251-8*, Pub. by Brstl Class Pr UK) Focus Pub-R Pullins.

Turgenev: His Life & Times. Leonard B. Schapiro. 416p. 1990. pap. text ed. 15.95 (*0-674-91297-7*) HUP.

Turgenev: Mumu. Ed. by J. Muckle. (Bristol Russian Texts Ser.). 112p. (RUS.). 1992. pap. 15.95 (*1-85399-270-4*, Pub. by Brstl Class Pr UK) Focus Pub-R Pullins.

Turgenev: Rudin. Ivan S. Turgenev. Ed. by Patrick Waddington. (Bristol Russian Texts Ser.). 304p. (RUS.). 1994. pap. 20.95 (*1-85399-296-8*, Pub. by Brstl Class Pr UK) Focus Pub-R Pullins.

Turgenev's Early Works: From Character Sketches to a Novel. Walter Smyrniw. 212p. 1995. lib. bdg. 35.00 (*0-8095-4500-4*) Borgo Pr.

Turgenev's Early Works: From Character Sketches to a Novel. Walter Smyrniw. 212p. pap. 12.95 (*0-88962-115-2*) Mosaic.

Turgenev's Fathers & Sons: Critical Study. J. Woodward. (Critical Studies in Russian Literature). 128p. 1996. pap. 13.95 (*1-85399-391-3*, Pub. by Brstl Class Pr UK) Focus Pub-R Pullins.

Turgot & the Six Edicts. Robert P. Shepherd. LC 74-127488. (Columbia University Social Science Studies: No. 47). reprint ed. 31.50 (*0-404-51047-7*) AMS Pr.

Turgot on Progress, Sociology & Economics: A Philosophical Review of the Successive Advances of the Human Mind on Universal History & Reflections on the Distribution of Wealth. Ann R. Turgot. LC 72-83594. (Cambridge Studies in the History & Theory of Politics). 186p. reprint ed. pap. 53.10 (*0-317-27890-8*, 2025591) Bks Demand.

Turiana: Edicion Facsimil (Valencia, 1565) Juan de Timoneda. 134p. (SPA.). 1968. pap. 100.00 (*0-614-00237-0*) Elliots Bks.

***Turie Tales - Lost!** Debra S. DeVilbiss & Patricia A. Cockrell. (Illus.). 20p. (Orig.). (J). (gr. 1-2). 1997. pap. 8.99 (*1-55237-046-1*, Pub. by Comnwlth Pub CN) Partners Pubs Grp.

Turin, Biblioteca Nazionale Universitaria, MS Ris. Mus. I. 27 (Olim Qm III.59) Ed. by Brown et al. LC 87-750231. (Renaissance Music in Facsimile Ser.: Vol. 18). 232p. 1987. text ed. 30.00 (*0-8240-1467-7*) Garland.

***Turin, 1564-1680.** Pollak. 1991. pap. text ed. 14.95 (*0-226-67344-8*) U Ch Pr.

Turin Shroud: In Whose Image? The Truth Behind the Centuries-Long Conspiracy of Silence. Lynn Picknett & Clive Prince. 240p. 1995. pap. 12.00 (*0-06-092677-5*, PL) HarpC.

Turin 1564-1680: Urban Design, Military Culture, & the Creation of the Absolutist Capital. Martha D. Pollak. LC 90-44409. (Illus.). 414p. 1991. 55.00 (*0-226-67342-1*) U Ch Pr.

Turing Language: Formal & Informal Definitions. Richard C. Holt et al. (Illus.). 336p. 1988. pap. text ed. 32.00 (*0-13-933136-0*) P-H.

Turing Machines with Sublogarithmic Space. Andrzej Szepietowski. LC 94-30238. (Lecture Notes in Computer Science Ser.). 1994. 28.00 (*0-387-58355-6*) Spr-Verlag.

Turing Omnibus: Excursions in Computer Science. A. K. Dewdney. LC 87-37501. 341p. 1995. text ed. write for info. (*0-7167-8154-9*, Computer Sci Pr) W H Freeman.

Turing Option. Harry Harrison & Marvin Minsky. 416p. 1993. mass mkt. 5.99 (*0-446-36496-7*) Warner Bks.

Turing Test & the Frame Problem: AI's Mistaken Understanding of Intelligence. Larry J. Crocket. LC 93-9050. (Series in Artificial Intelligence). 224p. 1994. text ed. 78.50 (*0-89391-926-8*) Ablex Pub.

Turing Test & the Frame Problem: AI's Mistaken Understanding of Intelligence. Larry J. Crockett. LC 93-9050. (Series in Artificial Intelligence). 224p. 1994. pap. 39.50 (*1-56750-030-7*) Ablex Pub.

Turing's Man: Western Culture in the Computer Age. J. David Bolter. LC 83-6942. (Illus.). xii, 264p. 1984. pap. 14.95 (*0-8078-4108-0*) U of NC Pr.

Turing's World 3.0 Windows Version. Barwise. 1995. pap. 22.95 (*1-881526-88-7*) CSLI.

An Asterisk (*) at the beginning of an entry indicates that the title is appearing in BIP for the first time.

Turismo y Hosteleria: Tourism & Hotel Management. Conrad J. Schmitt. 1993. pap. text ed. 10.95 (*0-07-056816-2*) McGraw.

Turisticologia: Turismo-Fenomeno Social; Turismo-Ciencia Social. Jose J. Santa-Pinter. LC 77-11838. (Illus.). 141p. 1977. pap. 3.60 (*0-8477-2442-5*) U of PR Pr.

Turitella Zonation Across the Cretaceous-Tertiary Boundary, California. Louella R. Saul. LC 83-1317. (University of California Publications in Entomology: No. 125). 117p. 1983. pap. 33.40 (*0-7837-8425-2*, 2049227) Bks Demand.

Turk in French History, Thought & Literature, 1520-1660. Clarence D. Rouillard. LC 71-180375. reprint ed. 67.50 (*0-404-56321-X*) AMS Pr.

Turkana, 14 vols. Chieka Ifemesia. Ed. by George Bond. LC 95-13691. (Heritage Library of African Peoples: Set 1). (Illus.). 64p. (YA). (gr. 7-12). 1995. lib. bdg. 15.95 (*0-8239-1761-4*) Rosen Group.

***Turkana: Kenya's Nomads of the Jade Sea.** Nigel Pavitt. LC 97-7568. 1997. write for info. (*0-8109-3896-0*) Abrams.

Turkana Language. G. J. Dimmendaal. (Publications in African Languages & Linguistics). xviii, 496p. 1983. 152.35 (*90-70176-83-1*); pap. 134.65 (*90-70176-82-3*) Mouton.

Turkana Pastoralists. Dyson-Huds. (C). 1996. pap. text ed. write for info. (*0-15-502801-4*) HarBrace.

Turkenhirsch: A Study of Baron Maurice de Hirsch. Kurt Grunwald. 158p. 1966. boxed 34.95 (*0-87855-182-4*) Transaction Pubs.

Turkenkalender (1454) Attributed to Gutenberg & the Strasbourg Lunation Tracts. Eckehard Simon. LC 87-72032. 1988. 20.00 (*0-910956-98-7*, SAM 14); pap. 12.00 (*0-910956-99-5*, SAM 14) Medieval Acad.

Turkes Secretarie, Conteining His Sundrie Letters to Divers Emperours. Mohammed Second. LC 72-217. (English Experience Ser.: No. 263). 34p. 1970. reprint ed. 20.00 (*90-221-0263-7*) Walter J Johnson.

Turkestan Down to the Mongol Invasion. 3rd ed. W. Barthold. 1988. reprint ed. 40.00 (*0-89986-365-5*) Oriental Bk Store.

Turkestan Reunion. Eleanor H. Lattimore. LC 72-4440. reprint ed. 37.50 (*0-404-10636-6*) AMS Pr.

Turkestan Reunion. Eleanor H. Lattimore. (Illus.). 329p. 1994. reprint ed. pap. 14.00 (*1-56836-050-3*) Kodansha.

Turkey. 1993. pap. 21.95 (*0-395-66252-4*) HM.

Turkey. (Insider's Guides Ser.). (Illus.). 224p. 1991. pap. 17.95 (*1-55650-283-4*) Hunter NJ.

***Turkey.** 1997. lib. bdg. 255.99 (*0-8490-6130-X*) Gordon Pr.

***Turkey.** Luis A. Baralt. LC 96-49594. (Enchantment of the World Ser.). (J). 1997. lib. bdg. 30.00 (*0-516-20305-3*) Childrens.

Turkey. Thomas Cook. (Essential Guides Ser.). 1994. 7.95 (*0-8442-8939-6*, Passport Bks) NTC Pub Grp.

Turkey. Diane Darke. (Illustrated Travel Guides from Thomas Cook Ser.). (Illus.). 192p. 1994. pap. 12.95 (*0-8442-9066-1*, Passport Bks) NTC Pub Grp.

***Turkey.** Globe Pequot Press Staff. (Globetrotter Travel Guide Ser.). 1997. pap. text ed. 10.95 (*1-85368-635-2*, Pub. by New Holland UK) R Curtis Pubng.

***Turkey.** Grolier Educational Staff. LC 97-19803. (Fiesta! Ser.). (J). 1997. write for info. (*0-7172-9107-3*) Grolier Educ.

Turkey. Stanley Lane-Poole. 400p. 1986. 300.00 (*1-85077-130-8*, Pub. by Darf Pubs Ltd UK) St Mut.

Turkey. Frank Tachau. LC 84-3451. 204p. 1984. text ed. 85.00 (*0-275-91284-1*, C1284, Praeger Pubs) Greenwood.

***Turkey.** U. S. Government Staff. (Country Studies). 1996. 24.00 (*1-57980-055-6*, UTURKE) Claitors.

***Turkey.** U. S. Government Staff. (Country Studies). 1996. 24.00 (*0-614-30837-2*, UTURKE) Claitors.

***Turkey.** Zurcher. Date not set. text ed. 24.50 (*1-86064-222-5*, Pub. by I B Tauris UK) St Martin.

Turkey. rev. ed. Globe Pequot Press Staff. (Pocket Guides Ser.). 1996. pap. text ed. 11.95 (*2-8315-5991-X*) Berlitz.

Turkey. 3rd ed. Dana Facaros & Michael Pauls. LC 92-28241. (Cadogan Country Guides Ser.). (Illus.). 400p. 1993. pap. 18.95 (*1-56440-174-X*) Globe Pequot.

Turkey. 5th ed. Tom Brosnahan & Pat Yale. (Illus.). 752p. 1996. pap. 19.95 (*0-86442-364-0*) Lonely Planet.

Turkey. Anne O. Krueger. LC 74-77689. (Foreign Trade Regimes & Economic Development Ser.: No. 1). 365p. reprint ed. pap. 104.10 (*0-8357-7585-2*, 2056906) Bks Demand.

Turkey. Anne O. Krueger. (Special Conference Series on Foreign Trade Regimes & Economic Development: No. 1). 365p. 1974. reprint ed. 94.90 (*0-87014-501-0*) Natl Bur Econ Res.

Turkey. Arnold J. Toynbee & Kenneth P. Kirkwood. LC 75-18365. (Illus.). 329p. 1976. reprint ed. text ed. 35.00 (*0-8371-8323-5*, TOTU, Greenwood Pr) Greenwood.

Turkey, Vol. IV. Jo R. Leimenstoll. (Historic Preservation in Other Countries Ser.). (Illus.). 54p. (Orig.). (C). 1990. pap. text ed. 15.00 (*0-911697-06-3*) US ICOMOS.

Turkey: A Country Study. 4th ed. Ed. by Paul M. Pitman, III. LC 88-8844. (Area Handbook Ser.). (Illus.). 495p. 1996. text ed. 24.00 (*0-16-001710-6*, S/N008020013943) USGPO.

***Turkey: A Country Study.** Ed. by Helen C. Metz. (Illus.). 458p. 1996. reprint ed. pap. text ed. 60.00 (*0-7881-3546-5*) DIANE Pub.

***Turkey: A Short History.** Roderic H. Davison. 207p. 1997. pap. 25.00 (*0-906719-14-3*, Pub. by Eothen UK) Paul & Co Pubs.

Turkey: A Traveller's Historical & Architectural Guide. James Steele. (Illus.). 176p. 1990. pap. 24.95 (*0-905906-72-1*, Pub. by Scorpion Pub UK) Interlink Pub.

Turkey: America's Forgotten Ally. rev. ed. Dankwart A. Rustow. 174p. 1989. pap. 14.95 (*0-87609-065-X*) Coun Foreign.

Turkey: An Aerial Portrait. Photos by Guido A. Rossi. LC 93-31352. 1994. 55.00 (*0-8109-3866-9*) Abrams.

Turkey: Identity, Democracy, Politics. Ed. by Sylvia Kedourie. LC 96-11388. 260p. (C). 1996. 35.00 (*0-7146-4718-7*, Pub. by F Cass Pubs UK) Intl Spec Bk.

Turkey: Informatics & Economic Modernization. LC 93-16706. (Country Study Ser.). 270p. 1993. 15.95 (*0-8213-2376-8*, 12376) World Bank.

***Turkey: Perfect Food.** K. Aim. 1993. pap. 3.99 (*0-425-14093-8*) Berkley Pub.

Turkey: Political, Social & Economic Challenges in the 1990s. Ed. by Cigdem Balim et al. LC 95-12128. (Social, Economic & Political Studies of the Middle East: No. 53). 280p. 1995. 98.00 (*90-04-10283-3*) E J Brill.

Turkey: The Challenge of a New Role. Andrew Mango. LC 94-10581. (Washington Papers). 144p. 1994. text ed. 49.95 (*0-275-94985-0*, Praeger Pubs); pap. text ed. 14.95 (*0-275-94986-9*, Praeger Pubs) Greenwood.

Turkey: The Complete Guide with Ancient Ruins, Ottoman Sites & the Best Beach Resorts. 3rd ed. Fodor's Travel Staff. 1997. pap. 18.00 (*0-679-03292-4*) Fodors Travel.

Turkey: The Cradle of Europe. 2nd ed. Gilbert Horobin. (Illus.). 312p. 1995. pap. 16.95 (*0-8442-9955-3*, Passport Bks) NTC Pub Grp.

***Turkey: The Pendulum Swings Back.** Reza Shah-Kazemi. 174p. 1997. pap. 14.95 (*1-901230-02-3*, Pub. by Islamic Wrld Report UK) Intl Spec Bk.

Turkey: The Perfect Food for Every Occasion! Kristie Alm. 1993. pap. 3.99 (*0-425-14092-X*) Berkley Pub.

Turkey: Trade Reforms in the Nineteen Eighties. Anne O. Krueger & Okan H. Aktan. (Country Studies). 40p. 1992. pap. 5.00 (*1-55815-145-1*) ICS Pr.

Turkey: Weapons Transfers & Violations of the Laws of War in Turkey. Human Rights Watch Arms Project Staff. 184p. (Orig.). 1995. pap. 15.00 (*1-56432-161-4*) Hum Rts Watch.

Turkey: Women in Development. LC 93-14762. (Country Study Ser.). 230p. 1993. 11.95 (*0-8213-2375-X*, 12375) World Bank.

Turkey see Cultures of the World - Group 6

Turkey see Exploring Cultures of the World: Group 5

Turkey - The Greeks of Turkey: Denying Human Rights & Ethnic Identity. Helsinki Watch Staff. Ed. by Human Rights Watch Staff. 64p. (Orig.). 1992. pap. 7.00 (*1-56432-056-1*) Hum Rts Watch.

Turkey & Duck Menus. (Great Meals in Minutes Ser.). (Illus.). 104p. 1985. lib. bdg. 21.93 (*0-86706-257-6*) Time-Life.

Turkey & Europe. Ed. by Canan Balkir & Allan M. Williams. LC 92-41816. 224p. 1993. text ed. 59.00 (*1-85567-012-7*) St Martin.

***Turkey & Giant: Tazhii Doo Ye'iilbahi.** Nedra Emery. LC 96-41445. (Illus.). 36p. (J). (gr. k-3). 1996. 14.95 (*0-9644189-4-0*); pap. 9.95 (*0-9644189-5-9*) Salina Bkshelf.

Turkey & Its People. 2nd ed. Edwin Pears. LC 77-87634. reprint ed. 37.50 (*0-404-16459-5*) AMS Pr.

Turkey & the Dodecanese Cruising Pilot. Robin Petherbridge. (Illus.). 214p. 1985. pap. 29.95 (*0-229-11716-3*, Pub. by Adlard Coles UK) Sheridan.

Turkey & the Holocaust: Turkey's Role in Rescuing Turkish & European Jewry from Nazi Persecution, 1933-1945. Stanford J. Shaw. LC 92-354. (Illus.). 500p. (C). 1992. 55.00 (*0-8147-7960-3*) NYU Pr.

Turkey & the Holocaust: Turkey's Role in Rescuing Turkish & European Jewry from Nazi Persecution, 1933-1945. Stanford J. Shaw. LC 92-354. (Illus.). 500p. (C). 1995. pap. 23.00 (*0-8147-8015-6*) NYU Pr.

Turkey & the Turks. W. S. Monroe. 448p. 1985. 280.00 (*1-85077-061-1*, Pub. by Darf Pubs Ltd UK) St Mut.

Turkey & the Turks. Z. Duckett Ferriman. LC 77-87627. reprint ed. 37.50 (*0-404-16452-8*) AMS Pr.

Turkey & the United States: The Arms Embargo Period. Richard C. Campany, Jr. LC 86-9303. 154p. 1986. text ed. 45.00 (*0-275-92141-7*, C2141, Praeger Pubs) Greenwood.

Turkey & the West: Images of a New Political Culture. Ed. by Metin Heper et al. 288p. (C). 1993. text ed. 69.50 (*1-85043-611-8*, Pub. by I B Tauris UK) St Martin.

Turkey at the Straits: A Short History. James T. Shotwell & Francis Deak. LC 76-37354. (Select Bibliographies Reprint Ser.). 1977. reprint ed. 23.95 (*0-8369-6701-1*) Ayer.

***Turkey Between East & West: New Challenges for a Rising Regional Power.** Craig Nation. Ed. by Vojtech Mastny. LC 97-19972. (C). 1997. pap. text ed. 22.00 (*0-8133-3412-8*) Westview.

Turkey Beyond the Meander. George E. Bean. (Illus.). 256p. 1990. pap. 24.95 (*0-7195-4765-2*, Pub. by John Murray UK) Trafalgar.

Turkey, Brutal & Systematic Abuse of Human Rights. 73p. 1989. 6.00 (*0-939994-42-9*) Amnesty Intl USA.

Turkey Callmakers Past & Present Mick's Picks: Stories & History of Callmakers. Earl E. Mickel. LC 93-91846. (Illus.). 280p. (Orig.). 1994. pap. text ed. 23.00 (*0-9640164-0-0*) E E Mickel.

Turkey Drive & Other Tales. Barbara A. Porte. LC 91-48032. (Illus.). 64p. (J). (gr. k up). 1993. 14.00 (*0-688-11336-2*) Greenwillow.

Turkey Faces West. Halide Edib Adivar. LC 73-6266. (Middle East Ser.). 1973. reprint ed. 23.95 (*0-405-05320-7*) Ayer.

Turkey Foot Ridge Site: A Mogollon Village, Pine Lawn Valley, Western New Mexico. Paul S. Martin & John B. Rinaldo. LC 50-12533. (Chicago Natural History Museum. Fieldiana: Anthropology Ser.: Vol. 38, No. 2). 165p. reprint ed. pap. 47.10 (*0-317-42395-9*, 2056068) Bks Demand.

Turkey for Thanksgiving. Eve Bunting. (Illus.). 32p. (J). (ps-1). 1991. 13.95 (*0-89919-793-0*, Clarion Bks) HM.

Turkey for Thanksgiving. Eve Bunting. 1995. pap. 5.95 (*0-395-74212-9*) HM.

Turkey Girl: A Zuni Cinderella Story. Penny Pollock. LC 93-28947. (Illus.). 32p. (J). (ps-3). 1996. 16.95 (*0-316-71314-7*) Little.

***Turkey Guide.** Adam Peck. 1997. pap. text ed. 16.95 (*1-883323-48-7*) Open Rd Pub.

Turkey Hunter's Digest. rev. ed. Dwain Bland. 256p. (Orig.). 1994. pap. 17.95 (*0-87349-164-5*, THDR) DBI.

Turkey Hunting: Spring & Fall. Doug Camp. Ed. by Buck Taylor. (Illus.). 176p. (Orig.). 1983. pap. 12.95 (*0-940022-01-X*) Outdoor Skills.

Turkey Hunting (& Other Hunting) at Its Best. Rea W. Yarnall. Ed. by Gary Yarnall. (Illus.). 192p. 1989. 14.95 (*0-9621821-1-7*) Lil Jewel Enterp.

Turkey Hunting Tactics. John Phillips. LC 88-63557. (Hunter's Information Ser.). 183p. 1989. write for info. (*0-914697-19-6*) N Amer Outdoor Grp.

Turkey Hunting with Charlie Elliott. Charles Elliott. 288p. 1983. pap. 8.95 (*0-668-06072-7*, Arco) Macmillan Gen Ref.

Turkey Hunting with Gerry Blair. Gerry Blair. LC 90-63915. (Illus.). 280p. 1991. 19.95 (*0-87341-160-9*, TH01) Krause Pubns.

Turkey in Focus. Ed. by Hans Curvers & Jaap Hemelrijk. (Illus.). 158p. 1992. 29.95 (*0-7103-0441-2*, A7657) Routledge Chapman & Hall.

Turkey in Pictures. Department of Geography, Lerner Publications. (Visual Geography Ser.). (Illus.). 64p. (YA). (gr. 5 up). 1989. lib. bdg. 19.95 (*0-8225-1831-7*, Lerner Publctns) Lerner Group.

Turkey in Post-Soviet Central Asia. Gareth M. Winrow. (Former Soviet South Papers). 53p. (C). 1995. pap. 12.95 (*0-905031-99-7*) Brookings.

Turkey in the Straw. (J). (ps-1). pap. 7.50 (*0-932970-93-1*) Prinit Pr.

Turkey in the Straw. Barbara S. Hazen. LC 92-27516. (Illus.). 32p. (J). (ps-3). 1993. lib. bdg. 13.89 (*0-8037-1299-5*) Dial Bks Young.

Turkey in the World Capitalist System: A Study of Industrialisation, Power & Class. Ed. by Huseyin Ramazanoglu. 300p. 1985. text ed. 47.95 (*0-566-05049-8*, Pub. by Dartmth Pub UK) Ashgate Pub Co.

Turkey in Transition: New Perspectives, 1923 to the Present. Ed. by Irvin C. Schick & E. Ahmet Tonak. 324p. 1987. 59.00 (*0-19-504095-3*) OUP.

Turkey in Transition: The West's Neglected Ally. Kenneth Mackenzie. (C). 1984. 35.00 (*0-907967-20-5*, Pub. by Inst Euro Def & Strat UK) St Mut.

Turkey, Iran & the Middle East, 1918-1939 see British Documents on Foreign Affairs: Series B: Near & Middle East

Turkey John. Artie Whitworth. LC 96-33904. (Illus.). 175p. (J). 1996. 16.95 (*1-56763-190-8*); pap. 4.95 (*1-56763-191-6*) Ozark Pub.

Turkey of Ataturk: Social Process in the Turkish Reformation. Donald E. Webster. LC 71-180308. reprint ed. 39.50 (*0-404-56333-3*) AMS Pr.

Turkey Peace on Trial. Ed. by Jean Furtado. (C). 1983. pap. 7.50 (*0-85036-297-0*, Pub. by Merlin Pr UK) Humanities.

Turkey Pox. Laurie H. Anderson. LC 95-52931. (Illus.). 32p. (J). (gr. k-2). 1996. lib. bdg. 14.95 (*0-8075-8127-5*) A Whitman.

Turkey Red. Esther L. Vogt. (Junior-Teen Companion Ser.). 104p. 1987. pap. 4.95 (*0-919797-62-8*) Kindred Prods.

***Turkey Soup for the Inner Child: Or There's No Place Like Home for the Holidays.** Ed. by Sandra H. Martz. LC 97-15678. 160p. (Orig.). 1997. pap. 9.95 (*1-57601-053-8*) Egger Pub Inc.

Turkey Stearnes & the Detroit Stars: The Negro Leagues in Detroit, 1919-1933. Richard Bak. LC 93-34402. (Illus.). 302p. (C). 1994. text ed. 24.95 (*0-8143-2483-5*, Great Lks Bks) Wayne St U Pr.

Turkey Stearnes & the Detroit Stars: The Negro Leagues in Detroit, 1919-1933. Richard Bak. LC 93-34402. (Illus.). 302p. 1995. pap. 14.95 (*0-8143-2582-3*, Great Lks Bks) Wayne St U Pr.

Turkey That Ate My Father. Dean Marney. 96p. (J). 1995. pap. 2.99 (*0-590-47730-7*) Scholastic Inc.

Turkey, the Straits & U. S. Policy. Harry N. Howard. LC 74-6826. (Middle East Institute Sponsor Ser.). (Illus.). 352p. 1975. 45.00 (*0-8018-1590-8*) Johns Hopkins.

***Turkey to 2005.** 1997. write for info. (*0-614-25460-4*) Econ Intel.

Turkey Tracks. Lizbie Brown. LC 95-1733. 1995. 20.95 (*0-312-13193-3*) St Martin.

Turkey Tracks. Lizbie Brown. 240p. 1996. mass mkt. 4.99 (*0-440-22258-3*) Dell.

Turkey Travel Atlas. Contrib. by Tom Brosnahan. (Illus.). 112p. 1997. pap. 14.95 (*0-86442-272-5*) Lonely Planet.

Turkey Trouble. Patricia Hermes. (J). (gr. 4-7). 1996. pap. text ed. 2.99 (*0-590-50964-0*) Scholastic Inc.

Turkey Trouble: A Polk Street Special. Patricia R. Giff. 112p. (J). 1994. lib. bdg. 3.99 (*0-440-40955-1*) Dell.

Turkey Trouble: Adam Joshua's Thanksgiving. Janice L. Smith. (Trophy Chapter Bk.: No. 7). (Illus.). 64p. (J). (gr. 2-5). 1995. pap. 3.95 (*0-06-442024-8*, Trophy) HarpC Child Bks.

Turkeys. Jason Cooper. LC 94-39537. (Barn Yard Friends Ser.). (J). (gr. 2-6). 1995. write for info. (*1-55916-092-6*) Rourke Bk Co.

Turkeys: How to Sort Turkeys in Business. Ed. by O. Henry Garrett. LC 89-91098. (Illus.). 293p. (Orig.). 1989. pap. text ed. 8.95 (*0-9622687-0-4*) Publisher Group.

Turkeys & Eagles. Peter Lord. 104p. 1987. pap. 8.95 (*0-940232-40-5*) Seedsowers.

***Turkey's Kurdish Question.** Henri J. Barkey & Graham E. Fuller. (Carnegie Commission on Preventing Deadly Conflict Ser.). 256p. 1997. 65.00 (*0-8476-8552-7*) Rowman.

***Turkey's Kurdish Question.** Henri J. Barkey & Graham E. Fuller. (Carnegie Commission on Preventing Deadly Conflict Ser.). 256p. 1997. pap. 19.95 (*0-8476-8553-5*) Rowman.

Turkey's New Geopolitics: From the Balkans to Western China. Graham E. Fuller & Ian O. Lesser. LC 93-20402. 197p. (C). 1993. pap. text ed. 21.00 (*0-8133-8660-8*) Westview.

Turkeys, Pilgrims, & Indian Corn: The Story of the Thanksgiving Symbols. Edna Barth. LC 75-4703. (Illus.). 96p. (J). (gr. 3-6). 1981. pap. 6.95 (*0-89919-039-1*, Clarion Bks) HM.

***Turkey's Relations with a Changing Europe.** Meltem Muftuler-Bac. LC 96-3411. (Europe in Change Ser.). 1996. text ed. write for info. (*0-7190-4234-8*, Pub. by Manchester Univ Pr UK) St Martin.

***Turkey's Relations with a Changing Europe.** Meltem Muftuler-Bac. LC 96-3411. (Europe in Change Ser.). 1997. text ed. 59.95 (*0-7190-4233-X*, Pub. by Manchester Univ Pr UK) St Martin.

Turkey's Role in the Organization of Islamic Conference: 1960-1992. Mahmut B. Aykan. 1993. text ed. 14.95 (*0-533-10638-9*) Vantage.

Turkeys' Side of It: Adam Joshua's Thanksgiving. Janice L. Smith. LC 89-78419. (Illus.). 64p. (J). (gr. 1-4). 1990. lib. bdg. 12.89 (*0-06-025859-4*) HarpC Child Bks.

Turkeys That Fly & Turkeys That Don't. Allan Fowler. LC 94-14765. (Rookie Read-about Science Ser.). (Illus.). 32p. (J). (ps-2). 1994. pap. 3.95 (*0-516-46029-3*); lib. bdg. 17.30 (*0-516-06029-5*) Childrens.

Turkic Culture: Continuity & Change. Ed. by Sabri M. Akural & Ilhan Basgoz. (Turkish Studies Ser.: Vol. 6). 186p. (C). 1987. 11.95 (*0-685-29324-6*) IN Univ Turkish.

***Turkic Culture: Continuity & Change.** 2nd ed. Ed. by Sabri Akural. LC 87-80268. (Turkish Studies). (Illus.). 196p. (C). 1993. pap. text ed. 15.95 (*1-878318-06-3*) IN Univ Turkish.

***Turkic Languages.** Ed. by Lars Johanson & Eva Csato. (Language Family Descriptions Ser.). 544p. 1998. 130.00 (*0-415-08200-5*) Routledge.

Turkic Languages & Literature of Central Asia. Rudolph Loewenthal. (Central Asiatic Studies: No. 1). 1957. pap. text ed. 53.10 (*90-279-0014-0*) Mouton.

Turkic Oral Epic Poetry: Tradition, Forms, Poetic Structure. Karl Reichl. LC 92-16726. (Albert Bates Lord Studies in Oral Tradition: Vol. 7). 408p. 1992. text ed. 20.00 (*0-8240-7210-3*, H01247) Garland.

Turkic Peoples of the World. Ed. by Margaret Bainbridge. 350p. 1992. 75.00 (*0-7103-0409-9*, A5105) Routledge Chapman & Hall.

Turkic Protolanguage: A Computational Reconstruction. (Bibliotheca Nostratica Ser.: Vol. 11). 250p. 1997. 42.00 (*0-931922-42-9*) Eurolingua.

Turkisch-Deutsches Woerterbuch. 2nd ed. Karl Steuerwald. 1294p. (GER & TUR.). 1988. 395.00 (*0-7859-8367-8*, 3447028041) Fr & Eur.

Turkische Volkserzahlung und Die Erzahlerkunst, 2 vols. Pertev N. Boratav & Wolfram Eberhard. (Asian Folklore & Social Life Monographs: No. 73 & 74). (GER.). 1975. Set. 25.00 (*0-89986-069-9*) Oriental Bk Store.

***Turkish.** Jaklin Kornfilt. LC 97-2874. (Descriptive Grammars Ser.). 584p. (ENG & TUR.). (C). 1997. text ed. write for info. (*0-415-00010-6*) Routledge.

Turkish, Vol. I. Foreign Service Institute Staff. 385p. 1980. pap. text ed. 195.00 incl. audio (*0-88432-049-9*, AFT700) Audio-Forum.

***Turkish & Other Muslim Minorites of Bulgaria.** Ali Eminov. 219p. (C). 1997. text ed. 55.00 (*0-415-91976-2*, Routledge NY) Routledge.

Turkish Armenia. Henry F. Tozer. 470p. 1990. pap. 25.00 (*0-941567-09-5*) J C & A L Fawcett.

Turkish Armenia & Eastern Asia Minor. Henry F. Tozer. LC 77-87637. reprint ed. 35.00 (*0-404-16462-5*) AMS Pr.

Turkish Cassette Pack. Berlitz Editors. (Cassette Pack Ser.). (TUR.). 1995. pap. 16.95 incl. audio (*2-8315-1048-1*) Berlitz.

Turkish Coast. (Insight Guides Ser.). 1993. pap. 21.95 (*0-395-66274-5*) HM.

Turkish Code of Criminal Procedure. (American Series of Foreign Penal Codes: Vol. 5). x, 158p. 1962. 15.00 (*0-8377-0025-6*) Rothman.

Turkish Cooking. 2nd ed. Gulseren Ramazanoglu. Ed. by Anna G. Edmonds. (Illus.). 96p. (ENG & TUR.). 1992. reprint ed. pap. text ed. 15.95 (*975-7489-05-0*, Pub. by Ramazanoglu Yayinlari TU) Bosphorus Bks.

Turkish Cooking: A Culinary Journey Through Turkey. Carol Robertson. LC 95-18912. (Illus.). 225p. 1996. 24.95 (*1-883319-38-2*) Frog Ltd CA.

Turkish Course, Vol. II. Foreign Service Institute Staff. 358p. 1968. pap. text ed. 195.00 incl. audio (*0-88432-105-3*, AFT750) Audio-Forum.

Turkish Criminal Code. (American Series of Foreign Penal Codes: Vol. 9). xvii, 190p. 1965. 15.00 (*0-8377-0029-9*) Rothman.

Turkish Culture for Americans. Hasan Dindi et al. LC 88-83130. 180p. 1989. pap. 19.95 (*0-924602-44-9*) Intl Concepts.

T

An Asterisk (*) at the beginning of an entry indicates that the title is appearing in BIP for the first time.

Turkish Culture in German Society Today. Ed. by David Horrocks & Eva Kolinsky. LC 96-12385. (Culture & Society in Germany Ser.: Vol. 1). (Illus.). 160p. 1996. 39.95 (1-57181-899-5); pap. 15.00 (1-57181-047-1) Berghahn Bks.

Turkish Delight. Jan Wolkers. Tr. by Greta Kilburn from DUT. 160p. 1983. reprint ed. pap. 7.50 (0-7145-2787-4) M Boyars Pubs.

Turkish Delights. 160p. (Orig.). 1991. mass mkt. 4.95 (1-878320-40-8) Masquerade.

Turkish Delights. Novel. David R. Slavitt. LC 92-37640. vi, 184p. 1993. 19.95 (0-8071-1813-3) La State U Pr.

Turkish Dictionary. (Handy Dictionaries Ser.). 120p. (Orig.). (TUR.). 1991. pap. 8.95 (0-87052-982-X) Hippocrene Bks.

Turkish Diplomacy, Nineteen Eighteen to Nineteen Twenty-Three: Mustafa Kemal & the Turkish National Movement. Salahi R. Sonyel. LC 74-83960. (Sage Studies in 20th Century History: Vol. 3). 284p. reprint ed. pap. 81.00 (0-317-08770-3, 2021960) Bks Demand.

Turkish Embassy Letters: Lady Mary Wortley Montagu. Mary W. Montagu. LC 93-928. 200p. (C). 1993. 35.00 (0-8203-1580-X) U of Ga Pr.

Turkish Embroidery. 2nd ed. Gulseren Ramazanoglu. (Illus.). 104p. 1987. reprint ed. pap. 13.95 (0-442-26799-1, Pub. by Ramazanoglu Yayinlari TU) Bosphorus Bks.

Turkish-English - English-Turkish Dictionary. Ziya Sak. (ENG & TUR.). 39.50 (0-87557-085-2) Saphrograph.

Turkish-English - English-Turkish Standard Dictionary. Hippocrene Staff. 793p. 1995. pap. 24.95 (0-7818-0380-2) Hippocrene Bks.

Turkish-English-Arabic-Persian Dictionary. M. Sari. 923p. 125.00 (0-88431-028-0) IBD Ltd.

Turkish-English Comprehensive Dictionary. Ali Bayram. 650p. (ENG & TUR.). 1996. 60.00 (0-7818-0468-X) Hippocrene Bks.

Turkish-English Dictionary. Berlitz Editors. (Bilingual Pocket Dictionaries Ser.). 360p. 1990. 6.95 (2-8315-0981-5) Berlitz.

Turkish-English Dictionary, 3 pts. James W. Redhouse. (ENG & TUR.). 1977. reprint ed. Set. 297.95 (0-518-19005-6) Ayer.

Turkish-English Dictionary of Technical Terminology. Nuri Ozbalkan. 1152p. (ENG & TUR.). 1984. 150.00 (0-8288-0672-1, M1980) Fr & Eur.

Turkish-English Dictionary of Technical Terms. 2nd rev. ed. Nuri Ozbalkan. 1152p. 1989. 123.00 (975-7368-19-9) IBD Ltd.

Turkish-English, English-Turkish Dictionary: New Red House. 12th ed. 1292p. 1991. Turkish-English, 12th ed., 1991, 1292p. 103.00 (975-413-022-1) IBD Ltd.

Turkish-English, English-Turkish Dictionary: New Red House. 18th ed. 1152p. 1991. English-Turkish, 18th ed., 1991, 1152p. 98.75 (975-413-021-3) IBD Ltd.

Turkish-English, English-Turkish Dictionary (The Redhouse Portable Dictionary) 11th ed. Ed. by Robert Avery et al. 503p. (ENG & TUR.). 1988. 35.75 (975-413-037-X) IBD Ltd.

Turkish-English, English-Turkish Science Dictionary. K. Ulukoy & A. Mitcheson. 300p. (ENG & TUR.). 24.95 (0-7859-7159-9) Fr & Eur.

Turkish Folktale: The Art of Behcet Mahir. Ed. by Warren S. Walker & Carl Lindahl. LC 96-5793. (World Folktale Library: Vol. 4). (Illus.). 168p. 1996. text ed. 30.00 (0-8153-2366-2, H1994) Garland.

***Turkish Foreign Policy: Recent Developments.** Ed. by Kemal H. Karpat. 214p. (Orig.). 1996. pap. 27.00 (0-299-15234-0) U of Wis Pr.

Turkish Foreign Policy During the Second World War: An Active Neutrality. Selim Deringil. (London School of Economics Monographs in International Studies). (Illus.). 248p. 1989. text ed. 69.95 (0-521-34466-2) Cambridge U Pr.

Turkish Grammar. Geoffrey L. Lewis. 328p. 1985. pap. 49.95 (0-19-815838-6) OUP.

Turkish Grammar. Robert Underhill. LC 75-46535. (C). 1976. 47.50 (0-262-21006-1) MIT Pr.

Turkish History, 3 Vols, Set. 6th ed. Richard Knolles. LC 72-153621. reprint ed. lib. bdg. 200.00 (0-404-09510-0) AMS Pr.

Turkish in Three Months. (Hugo's Language Courses Ser.). 160p. (Orig.). 1989. pap. 9.95 (1-55650-176-5) Hunter NJ.

Turkish in Three Months. (Hugo's Language Courses Ser.). 160p. 1989. audio 49.95 (0-85285-137-5) Hunter NJ.

Turkish in 7 Days. Tayfun Caga & Gillian Caga. (Language in 7 Days Ser.). 96p. (TUR.). 1995. pap. 12.95 incl. audio (0-8442-9144-7, Natl Textbk) NTC Pub Grp.

Turkish Intonation: An Instrumental Study. Rose Nash. LC 71-120351. (Janua Linguarum, Series Practica: No. 114). (Illus.). 190p. (Orig.). 1973. pap. text ed. 55.40 (90-279-2369-8) Mouton.

Turkish Labor Law. Ed. by Michael N. Schmitt & Mehmet N. Tanisik. LC 96-23687. 300p. 1996. lib. bdg. 115.00 (1-57105-034-5) Transnatl Pubs.

Turkish Life in Town & Country. Lucy M. Garnett. LC 77-87629. reprint ed. 52.50 (0-404-16454-4) AMS Pr.

Turkish Linguistics Today. Ed. by Hendrik Boeschoten & Ludo T. Verhoeven. LC 90-28654. (Illus.). ix, 194p. 1991. 68.00 (90-04-09375-3) E J Brill.

Turkish Literature. LC 77-111117. (Play Anthology Reprint Ser.). 1977. 25.95 (0-8369-8210-X) Ayer.

Turkish Literature. Epiphanus Wilson. 1972. 69.95 (0-8490-1235-X) Gordon Pr.

***Turkish Meat: An Erotic Novel.** Tom Kvaale. LC 97-9993. 1997. pap. write for info. (0-943595-66-5) Leyland Pubns.

Turkish Minstrel Tale Tradition. Natalie Moyle. LC 90-3620. (Harvard Dissertations in Folklore & Oral Literature Ser.). 244p. 1990. reprint ed. text ed. 20.00 (0-8240-2673-X) Garland.

Turkish Nationalism & Western Civilization: Selected Essays of Ziya Gokalp. Ziya Gokalp. Ed. & Tr. by Niyazi Berkes from TUR. LC 81-13235. 336p. 1981. reprint ed. text ed. 59.75 (0-313-23196-6, GOTN, Greenwood Pr) Greenwood.

Turkish Newspaper Reader. John D. Murphy & Metin Somay. LC 88-70934. 328p. 1988. text ed. 49.00 (0-931745-35-7) Dunwoody Pr.

Turkish Newspaper Reader. Contrib. by Metin Somay. 1988. audio 15.00 (0-931745-44-6) Dunwoody Pr.

Turkish People: Their Social Life, Religious Beliefs & Institutions & Domestic Life. Lucy M. Garnett. LC 77-87630. (Illus.). 352p. reprint ed. 49.50 (0-404-16455-2) AMS Pr.

Turkish Phrase Book. Berlitz Editors. (Phrase Bk.). 192p. 1993. pap. 6.95 (2-8315-0913-0) Berlitz.

Turkish Phrasebook. (Hugo's Phrasebks.). 128p. (Orig.). 1988. pap. 4.95 (0-85285-105-7) Hunter NJ.

Turkish Phrasebook. Tom Brosnahan. (Illus.). 160p. (Orig.). 1990. pap. 3.95 (0-86442-069-2) Lonely Planet.

Turkish Politics & the Military. William Hale. LC 93-4192. 248p. (C). (gr. 13). 1993. text ed. 85.00 (0-415-02455-2, B2440) Routledge.

Turkish Reflections: A Biography of a Place. Mary Lee Settle. (Illus.). 256p. 1992. pap. 11.00 (0-671-77997-4, Touchstone Bks) S&S Trade.

Turkish Revolution, 1960-1961: Aspects of Military Politics. Walter F. Weiker. LC 79-27852. (Illus.). viii, 172p. 1980. reprint ed. text ed. 65.00 (0-313-22303-3, WETR, Greenwood Pr) Greenwood.

Turkish Sampler. (Turkish Studies Book Ser.). 20.00 (0-614-04310-7) IN Univ Turkish.

Turkish State & History: Clio Meets the Gray Wolf. Speros Vryonis, Jr. 160p. (C). 1993. text ed. 25.00 (0-89241-532-0) Caratzas.

Turkish State, Turkish Society. Andrew Finkel & Nukhet Sirman. 288p. 1990. 52.50 (0-415-00106-4, A4357) Routledge.

Turkish State, Turkish Society. Ed. by Andrew Finkle & Nukhet Sirman. 336p. (C). (gr. 13 up). 1990. text ed. 85.00 (0-415-04685-8, Routledge NY) Routledge.

Turkish Stories from Four Decades. Aziz Nesin. Tr. & Intro. by Louis Mitler. 160p. (Orig.). 1991. pap. 13.00 (0-89410-688-0, Three Contnts); text ed. 25.00 (0-89410-687-2, Three Contnts) Lynne Rienner.

Turkish Straits. Christos L. Rozakis & Petros N. Stagos. LC 86-28581. (International Straits of the World Ser.: Vol. 9). 1987. lib. bdg. 100.00 (90-247-3464-9) Kluwer Ac.

Turkish Tapestry: A Traveller's Portrait of Turkey. Holly Chase. LC 92-74019. 300p. (Orig.). 1992. pap. 12.95 (1-881443-00-4) Bosphorus Bks.

Turkish Theatre. Nicholas N. Martinovitch. LC 68-20241. (Illus.). 125p. 1972. reprint ed. 21.95 (0-405-08761-6, Pub. by Blom Pubns UK) Ayer.

Turkish Traditional Art Today. Henry Glassie. LC 91-70795. (Indiana University Turkish Studies: No. 11). 962p. 1993. 89.95 (0-253-32555-2) Ind U Pr.

Turkish Traditional Art Today. rev. ed. Timothy Corrigan. LC 93-4971. (Indiana University Turkish Studies: No. 11). (Illus.). 248p. 1994. pap. 14.95 (0-253-20841-6) Ind U Pr.

Turkish Transformation: A Study in Social & Religious Development. Henry E. Allen. LC 68-57588. (Illus.). 251p. 1969. reprint ed. text ed. 35.00 (0-8371-0284-7, ALTT, Greenwood Pr) Greenwood.

Turkish Travel Pack. (Hugo's Travel Packs Ser.). 128p. (Orig.). 1990. Includes audio cassette. pap. 14.95 (0-85285-124-3) Hunter NJ.

Turkish Waters Pilot. Rod Heikell. 256p. 1984. 170.00 (0-85288-094-4, Pub. by Imray Laurie Norie & Wilson UK) St Mut.

Turkish Waters Pilot. Rod Heikell. 256p. (C). 1986. 170.00 (0-85288-105-3, Pub. by Imray Laurie Norie & Wilson UK) St Mut.

Turkish Waters Pilot. Rod Heikell. 256p. (C). 1989. 130.00 (0-85288-138-X, Pub. by Imray Laurie Norie & Wilson UK) St Mut.

***Turkish Waters Pilot.** 5th ed. Rod Heikell. (Illus.). 320p. 1997. 67.95 (0-85288-363-3, Pub. by Imray Laurie Norie & Wilson UK) Bluewater Bks.

Turkish Workers in Europe: An Interdisciplinary Study. Ed. by Ilhan Basgoz & Norman Furniss. (Turkish Studies Ser.: Vol. 5). 191p. (C). 1985. 11.95 (0-685-29323-8) IN Univ Turkish.

***Turkish/English Dictionary.** Berlitz Editors. 368p. 1998. pap. 7.95 (2-8315-6386-0) Berlitz.

Turkmen: Tribal Carpets & Traditions. Ed. by Louise W. Mackie & Jon Thompson. LC 80-53159. (Illus.). 240p. 1980. 75.00 (0-87405-014-6) Textile Mus.

Turkmen English Dictionary. Allen Frank. LC 95-83381. 1997. write for info. (1-881265-29-3) Dunwoody Pr.

Turkmen Reader. Allen Frank. LC 96-83013. 1996. 54.00 (1-881265-41-2) Dunwoody Pr.

Turkmenistan. Ed. by Lerner Geography Department Staff. (Then & Now Ser.). (Illus.). 64p. (YA). (gr. 5 up). 1993. lib. bdg. 22.95 (0-8225-2813-4, Lerner Publctns) Lerner Group.

Turkmenistan. World Bank Staff. (Country Study Ser.). 196p. 1994. 15.95 (0-8213-2832-8, 12832) World Bank.

Turkmenistan: Economic Review. International Monetary Fund Staff. 88p. 1992. pap. 10.00 (1-55775-262-1) Intl Monetary.

***Turkmenistan: Recent Economic Developments.** Emine Gurgen. (IMF Staff Country Report Ser.: Vol. 96/30). (Illus.). 102p. pap. 29.10 (0-608-04854-2, 2065513) Bks Demand.

Turkmenistan: Russian Edition. 279p. 1994. 15.95 (0-8213-2967-7, 12967) World Bank.

Turko-Persia in Historical Perspective. Ed. by Robert L. Canfield. (School of American Research Advanced Seminar Ser.). (Illus.). 248p. (C). 1991. text ed. 85.00 (0-521-39094-X) Cambridge U Pr.

Turkoman Carpet. George W. O'Bannon. 1986. 65.95 (0-7156-0740-5, Pub. by Duckworth UK) Focus Pub-R Pullins.

Turkoman Figural Bronze Coins & Their Iconography Vol. II: The Zengids. William F. Spengler & Wayne G. Sayles. (Illus.). 160p. (C). 1996. 35.00 (1-879080-04-4) Clios Cabinet.

***Turks & Caicos Islands: Lands of Discovery.** Amelia Smithers. 1996. pap. text ed. 11.95 (0-333-63195-1, Pub. by Macmillan UK) Humanities.

Turks & Caicos Islands Land of Discovery. Amelia Smithers. 1991. pap. 11.95 (0-333-53968-0, Pub. by Macmillan UK) Humanities.

***Turks & Greeks: Neighbors in Conflict.** Vamik D. Volkan & Norman Itzkowitz. 233p. 1997. reprint ed. pap. 27.95 (0-906719-30-5, Pub. by Eothen UK) Paul & Co Pubs.

Turks & the Caicos Islands. Paul G. Boultebee. (World Bibliographical Ser.). 1992. lib. bdg. 59.00 (1-85109-162-9) ABC-CLIO.

Turks of Central Asia. Charles W. Hostler. LC 92-37525. 256p. 1993. text ed. 59.95 (0-275-93931-6, C3931, Praeger Pubs) Greenwood.

Turks of Greece. Helsinki Watch Staff. LC 90-84212. (Destroying Ethnic Identity Ser.). 58p. 1990. pap. 7.00 (0-929692-70-5, Helsinki Watch) Hum Rts Watch.

***Turmeric & the Healing Curcuminoids.** Muhammad Majeed et al. (Good Health Guides Ser.). 48p. (Orig.). 1997. pap. 3.95 (0-87983-768-3) Keats.

Turmoil. Booth Tarkington. 27.95 (0-8488-0321-3) Amereon Ltd.

Turmoil & Triumph: My Years as Secretary of State. George P. Shultz. (Robert Stewart Book Ser.). (Illus.). 1184p. 1993. 30.00 (0-684-19325-6) S&S Trade.

Turmoil & Triumph: My Years as Secretary of State. George P. Shultz. 1995. pap. 20.00 (0-684-80332-1, Touchstone Bks) S&S Trade.

Turmoil & Triumph: The Controversial Railway to Hudson Bay. Ian Bickle. (Illus.). 224p. 1995. 29.95 (1-55059-107-X, Pub. by Detselig CN) Temeron Bks.

Turmoil in Hong Kong on the Eve of Communist Rule: The Fate of the Territory & Its Anglican Church. Deborah A. Brown. LC 93-23579. 472p. 1993. 109.95 (0-7734-2242-0, Mellen Univ Pr) E Mellen.

Turmoil in Hungary: An Anthology of Twentieth Century Hungarian Poetry. Ed. by Nicholas Kolumban. LC 82-81365. (Illus.). 186p. 1982. pap. 6.00 (0-89823-039-X) New Rivers Pr.

Turmoil in the Box. Phil Phillips. 208p. 1986. pap. 9.95 (0-914984-04-7) Starburst.

Turmoil in the Peacable Kingdom: The Quebec Sovereignty Movement & Its Implications for Canada & the U. S. Jonathan Lemco. (Illus.). 266p. 1994. 50.00 (0-8020-0532-2); pap. 17.95 (0-8020-6970-3) U of Toronto Pr.

Turmoil in the Toy Box II. Joan H. Robie. 1989. audio 7.95 (0-914984-26-8) Starburst.

Turmoil in the Toy Box II. Joan H. Robie. 224p. 1989. pap. 9.95 (0-914984-20-9) Starburst.

Turmoil to Triumph: The Odyssey of Captain Harris O. Machus Through Six War Devastated Countries in Search of Survival. Angus D. McKellar. LC 86-72281. (Illus.). 257p. 1987. 18.95 (0-939528-00-2) Brookside Pub.

Turmoil to Turning Points: Building Hope for Children in Crisis Placements. Richard Kagan. 256p. 1996. 30.00 (0-393-70218-9) Norton.

Turn: The Journal of an Artist. Anne Truitt. 224p. 1987. pap. 12.95 (0-14-009249-8, Penguin Bks) Viking Penguin.

Turn again to Life. Abraham Schmitt. LC 86-33581. 136p. (Orig.). 1987. pap. 9.99 (0-8361-3436-2) Herald Pr.

Turn again to Me. Helen Adam. 1977. 7.00 (0-686-22908-8); pap. 3.50 (0-686-22909-6) Kulchur Foun.

Turn & Learn. Illus. by Fiona Redmond. (Brimax Interactive Ser.). 12p. (J). (ps-k). 1996. bds. 6.98 (1-85854-492-0) Brimax Bks.

***Turn Around: Acting Edition.** Don Kukla. 48p. 1996. pap. 4.00 (0-614-18958-6) Bakers Plays.

Turn Around: Strategies for Successful Restructuring. Friedrich Reutner. Tr. by Stephen E. Corsi. LC 93-4618. 272p. 1993. 66.95 (0-631-19143-7) Blackwell Pubs.

Turn Around Once, & Keep Running. Alfredo Lopez. 180p. (Orig.). 1990. pap. 8.00 (0-685-26446-7) Atabex Collection.

Turn Around One Hundred Times. Ian Hickingbotham. 1988. pap. 30.00 (0-7223-1917-7, Pub. by A H S Ltd UK) St Mut.

Turn Aside from Evil & Do Good: An Introduction & a Way to the Tree of Life. Zevi H. Eichenstein. Tr. & Intro. by Louis Jacobs. 198p. 1995. 45.00 (1-874774-10-2); pap. 21.95 (1-874774-11-0) Bnai Brith Bk.

Turn Back the Night. Jennifer Drew. 1994. pap. 2.75 (0-373-19040-9, 1-19040-4) Harlequin Bks.

Turn Ever Northward see My Cousin Justin

Turn for Noah: A Hanukkah Story. Susan R. Topek. LC 92-22958. (Illus.). 24p. (J). 1992. 12.95 (0-929371-37-2); pap. 4.95 (0-929371-38-0) Kar-Ben.

Turn from Games & Lies to the Truth & from the Power of Satan unto God Acts 26: 18. deluxe ed. Stefani O. Chamness. write for info. (0-9631276-1-6) Church Liv God.

Turn-from Poverty to Prosperity. Samarjit Ghosh. 140p. 1986. 21.95 (0-318-37221-5) Asia Bk Corp.

Turn Here for the Big Hole. Mary P. Berthold. 1970. 3.95 (0-8187-0025-4) Harlo Press.

Turn Homeward, Hannalee. Patricia Beatty. 193p. (J). (gr. 5-9). 1990. pap. 3.95 (0-8167-2260-9) Troll Communs.

Turn Homeward, Hannalee. Patricia Beatty. LC 84-8960. 208p. (J). (gr. 5-9). 1984. 16.00 (0-688-03871-9, Morrow Junior) Morrow.

Turn in the South. V. S. Naipaul. 1990. pap. 13.00 (0-679-72488-5, Vin) Random.

Turn in the Trail. Walt Sandberg. 215p. 1980. 15.95 (0-932558-14-3) Willow Creek Pr.

Turn It into Glory. Meg Woodson. 226p. 1991. 13.99 (1-55661-178-1) Bethany Hse.

Turn It UP! Fifty All-New, Fiery Recipes for Cooking with Chiles, Peppercorns, Mustards, Horseradish & Ginger. Janet Hazen. LC 94-13095. 120p. 1995. pap. 12.95 (0-8118-0633-2) Chronicle Bks.

Turn It Up (I Can't Hear the Words) The Best of the Singer - Songwriters. Bob Sarlin. (Illus.). 224p. 1992. pap. 9.95 (0-8065-1315-2, Citadel Pr) Carol Pub Group.

Turn Left at Orion: One Hundred Night Sky Objects to See in a Small Telescope & How to Find Them. 2nd ed. Guy J. Consolmagno & Daniel M. Davis. (Illus.). 206p. (C). 1995. text ed. 24.95 (0-521-48211-9) Cambridge U Pr.

Turn Left at the Pub: 22 Walking Tours Through the British Countryside. George W. Oakes. 1996. pap. 14.95 (0-8050-3860-4) H Holt & Co.

Turn Left in Order to Go Right. Norman Fischer. LC 89-61548. 104p. 1989. 9.00 (1-882022-00-9) O Bks.

***Turn Loose of Your 'But' & Go with God.** Eastman Curtis. 80p. 1996. mass mkt. 4.99 (0-89274-989-X, HH989) Harrison Hse.

Turn Me on, Dead Man: The Complete Story of the Paul McCartney Death Hoax. Andru J. Reeve. (Rock & Roll Remembrances Ser.: No. 12). (Illus.). 224p. 1994. lib. bdg. 40.00 (1-56075-035-9) Popular Culture.

Turn Me over - I'm Reversible: Quick & Easy Reversible Quilts. Kaye Wood. (Illus.). 60p. (Orig.). 1988. reprint ed. pap. 9.95 (0-944588-03-4) K Wood.

***Turn Northward, Love.** Ruth E. Glover. LC 96-39247. (Wildrose Ser.: Vol. 4). 216p. (Orig.). 1996. per., pap. 9.99 (0-8341-1590-5) Beacon Hill.

***Turn of Glory.** Al Lacy. (Battles of Destiny Ser.: No. 8). 1998. pap. 9.99 (1-57673-217-7) Multnomah Pubs.

Turn of the Cards. Georgina Grey. (Regency Romance Ser.). 1979. pap. 1.75 (0-449-23969-1, Crest) Fawcett.

***Turn of the Century.** Ellen B. Jackson. LC 97-14264. (Illus.). 1998. write for info. (0-88106-369-X) Charlesbridge Pub.

Turn of the Century: Our Nation One Hundred Years Ago. Nancy S. Levinson. LC 93-4604. (Illus.). 144p. (J). (gr. 5-9). 1994. pap. 16.99 (0-525-67433-0, Lodestar Bks) Dutton Child Bks.

Turn of the Century: The First Futurists. William B. Schafer. LC 93-41679. (American University Studies, Series XX: Vol. 23). 232p. (C). 1995. text ed. 42.95 (0-8204-2438-2) P Lang Pubng.

Turn of the Century - Le Tournant du Siecle: Modernism & Modernity in Literature & the Arts - Le Modernisme et la Modernite dans la Litterature et les Arts, No. 3. Ed. by Christian Berg et al. LC 94-13181. (European Cultures Ser.). 670p. (FRE.). (C). 1994. lib. bdg. 164.60 (3-11-014018-7) De Gruyter.

Turn of the Century American Dinnerware 1880s to 1920s: Identification & Value Guide. Joanne Jasper. 256p. 1996. 24.95 (0-89145-684-8, 4629) Collector Bks.

Turn-of-the-Century Cabaret: Paris, Barcelona, Berlin, Munich, Vienna, Cracow, Moscow, St. Petersburg, Zurich. Harold B. Segel. LC 86-31699. (Illus.). 418p. 1987. text ed. 45.00 (0-231-05128-X) Col U Pr.

***Turn-of-the-Century Decorative Millwork: Doors, Windows, Stained Glass, Etc.** unabridged ed. Wholesale Sash, Door & Blind Manufacturers' Association Staff. (Illus.). 416p. 1996. reprint ed. pap. text ed. 17.95 (0-486-29280-0) Dover.

Turn-of-the-Century Dolls, Toys & Games. Carl P. Stirn. 1990. pap. 7.95 (0-486-26365-7) Dover.

Turn-of-the-Century Doors, Windows & Decorative Millwork: The Mulliner Catalog of 1893. Mulliner Box & Planing Co. Staff. LC 94-23833. Orig. Title: Combined Book of Sash, Doors, Blinds, Mouldings, Stair Work, Mantels & All Kinds of Interior & Exterior Finish. (Illus.). 336p. 1995. pap. text ed. 13.95 (0-486-28514-6) Dover.

Turn-of-the-Century House Designs: With Floor Plans, Elevations & Interior Details of 24 Residences. unabridged ed. William T. Comstock. LC 94-12113. Orig. Title: Suburban & Country Homes. (Illus.). 96p. 1994. reprint ed. pap. text ed. 7.95 (0-486-28186-8) Dover.

Turn of the Century Houses, Cottages & Villas: Floor Plans & Illustrations of 120 Homes from Shoppell's Catalogs. R. W. Shoppell. (Architecture Ser.). 128p. (Orig.). 1984. pap. 8.95 (0-486-24567-5) Dover.

***Turn-of-the-Century Poster Designs.** Ed Sibbett. (Illus.). pap. 3.95 (0-486-23705-2) Dover.

Turn-of-the-Century Posters. (Shorewood Art Programs for Education Ser.). 12p. 1983. teacher ed. 107.00 (0-88185-073-X); 143.00 (0-685-09214-3) Shorewood Fine Art.

Turn-of-the-Century Protestantism. Henry R. Rust. (Worship Through the Centuries Ser.). 1990. pap. 5.95 (0-940754-85-1, 3514) Ed Ministries.

Turn-of-the-Century Vienna & Its Legacy: Essays in Honor of Donald G. Daviau. Ed. by Jeffrey B. Berlin et al. 546p. 1993. text ed. 49.50 (0-929497-74-0) Ariadne CA.

Turn of the Millennium: An Agenda for Christian Religion in an Age of Science. Jeffrey S. Sobosan. LC 95-50971. 264p. 1996. pap. 16.95 (0-8298-1083-8) Pilgrim OH.

An Asterisk (*) at the beginning of an entry indicates that the title is appearing in BIP for the first time.

***Turn of the Mind: Constituting Consciousness in Henry James.** Adr E. Marshall. LC 97-18972. 1997. write for info. (*0-8386-3695-0*) Fairleigh Dickinson.

Turn of the Screw. Jeffrey Hatcher. 1996. pap. 5.25 (*0-8222-1554-3*) Dramatists Play.

Turn of the Screw. Henry James & Guido Crepax. 64p. (Orig.). 1995. pap. 9.95 (*1-56163-139-6*, Eurotica) NBM.

Turn of the Screw. Henry James. (Orig.). 1995. pap. 10.95 (*0-312-13833-4*) St Martin.

Turn of the Screw. Henry James. (Airmont Classics Ser.). (J). (gr. 9 up). 1967. mass mkt. 1.75 (*0-8049-0155-4*, CL-155) Airmont.

Turn of the Screw. Henry James. 1991. pap. 1.00 (*0-486-26684-2*) Dover.

Turn of the Screw. Henry James. (C). 1966. pap. text ed. 9.95 (*0-393-09669-6*) Norton.

Turn of the Screw. Henry James. Ed. by Alan Lloyd-Smith. 173p. 1993. pap. 3.95 (*0-460-87299-0*, Everyman's Classic Lib) C E Tuttle.

Turn of the Screw. Henry James. (Now Age Illustrated V Ser.). (Illus.). 64p. (J). (gr. 4-12). 1979. student ed. 1.25 (*0-88301-420-3*); pap. text ed. 2.95 (*0-88301-396-7*) Pendulum Pr.

Turn of the Screw. Henry James. 160p. (YA). 1993. pap. 2.50 (*0-8125-3341-0*) Tor Bks.

Turn of the Screw. Henry James. Bd. with Daisy Miller. 192p. 1978. Set mass mkt. 5.50 (*0-440-39154-7*, LE) Dell.

Turn of the Screw. Henry James. 320p. (Orig.). 1994. pap. text ed. 6.50 (*0-312-08083-2*) St Martin.

Turn of the Screw. Meyer. (Bedford Introduction to Literature Ser.). Date not set. pap. text ed. 36.90 (*0-312-13893-8*) St Martin.

Turn of the Screw. Stewart. LC 81-5217. (Short Classics Ser.). (Illus.). 48p. (YA). (gr. 4 up). 1981. lib. bdg. 22.83 (*0-8172-1672-3*) Raintree Steck-V.

Turn of the Screw. large type ed. Henry James. LC 95-13852. 187p. 1995. lib. bdg. 20.95 (*0-7838-1354-6*, GK Hall) Thorndike Pr.

Turn of the Screw. large type ed. Henry James. LC 96-14571. 182p. 1996. text ed. 21.95 (*1-56000-547-5*) Transaction Pubs.

Turn of the Screw. 2nd ed. Henry James. Ed. by Robert Kimbrough. (Critical Editions Ser.). (C). 1990. pap. text ed. write for info. (*0-393-95904-X*) Norton.

Turn of the Screw. Henry James. Date not set. reprint ed. lib. bdg. 20.95 (*0-89190-315-1*, Am Repr) Amereon Ltd.

Turn of the Screw. Henry James. 1992. reprint ed. lib. bdg. 17.95 (*0-89968-268-5*, Lghtyr Pr) Buccaneer Bks.

Turn of the Screw. Henry James. 1977. reprint ed. lib. bdg. 21.95 (*0-89244-046-5*) Queens Hse-Focus Serv.

Turn of the Screw: A Case Study in Contemporary Criticism. Henry James. Ed. by Peter G. Beidler. 320p. 1995. pap. 8.65 (*0-312-53341-1*) St Martin.

Turn of the Screw: A Semiotic Reading. Sigrid Renaux. LC 92-26035. (American University Studies: American Literature: Ser. XXIV, Vol. 46). 290p. 1992. 46.95 (*0-8204-2017-4*) P Lang Pubng.

Turn of the Screw: And Other Short Novels. Henry James. 456p. 1995. pap. 4.95 (*0-451-52606-6*, Sig Classics) NAL-Dutton.

Turn of the Screw Vol. 1. Peter G. Beidler. 1994. text ed. 39.95 (*0-312-12260-8*) St Martin.

***Turn of the Screw & Daisy Miller.** unabridged ed. Henry James. 230p. 1997. reprint ed. pap. 14.95 (*1-57002-057-4*) Univ Publng Hse.

Turn of the Screw & Other Short Fiction. Henry James. 416p. (Orig.). (YA). (gr. 9-12). 1981. mass mkt. 3.95 (*0-553-21059-9*, Bantam Classics) Bantam.

Turn of the Screw & Other Short Novels. Henry James. 456p. (Orig.). 1962. pap. 2.25 (*0-451-52331-8*, Sig Classics) NAL-Dutton.

Turn of the Screw & Other Stories. Henry James. 1970. pap. 1.95 (*0-14-003026-3*, Penguin Bks) Viking Penguin.

Turn of the Screw & Other Stories. Henry James. Ed. by Tim Lustig. (World's Classics Ser.). 256p. 1992. pap. 6.95 (*0-19-282927-0*) OUP.

Turn of the Screw & the Lesson of the Master. Henry James. (Literary Classics Ser.). 215p. 1996. pap. 6.95 (*1-57392-099-1*) Prometheus Bks.

***Turn of the Screw Readalong.** Henry James. (Illustrated Classics Collection 5). 64p. 1994. pap. 14.95 incl. audio (*0-7854-0802-9*, 40576) Am Guidance.

Turn of the Seasons. Fox Outreach Poets Staff. Ed. by Peter Sherrill. (Illus.). 37p. (Orig.). 1996. pap. 5.95 (*1-889216-00-3*) Meadowcroft.

***Turn of the Tide.** W. Vernon Higham. LC 95-78315. 124p. (Orig.). 1995. pap. 7.95 (*0-926474-15-4*) Intl Awakening Pr.

Turn of the Tide: Computerization in Dutch Society, 1900-1965. J. Van Den Ende. 270p. 1994. pap. 57.50 (*90-407-1005-8*, Pub. by Delft U Pr NE) Coronet Bks.

***Turn of the Tide: When God Floods His Church with True Revival Blessing.** W. Vernon Higham. LC 95-78315. 124p. 1995. pap. 7.95 (*0-940033-52-6*) R O Roberts.

Turn of the Verse. John J. Obrien. 1991. 2.00 (*0-9628932-0-X*) J Obrien.

Turn of the Wheel. Oliver Friggieri. Tr. & Intro. by Grazio Falzon. LC 87-70813. (Unesco Collection of Representative Works, Series of Translations from the Literature of the Union of Soviet Socialist Republics). 77p. 8700. pap. 13.95 (*0-905075-25-0*, Pub. by Wilfion Bks UK) Dufour.

Turn of the Year, for Four Viols. Freda Burford. (Charney Manor Ser.: No. 2). i, 16p. 1991. pap. text ed. 9.00 (*1-56571-037-1*) PRB Prods.

Turn of Traitors. large type ed. Palma Harcourt. 368p. 1982. 25.99 (*0-7089-0781-4*) Ulverscroft.

Turn of Zero. Sung-won Ko. (Poetry Ser.). (Illus.). 1974. pap. 7.50 (*0-89304-003-7*) Cross-Cultrl NY.

Turn of Zero. deluxe ed. Sung-won Ko. (Poetry Ser.). (Illus.). 1974. 15.00 (*0-89304-021-5*, CCC102) Cross-Cultrl NY.

Turn Off the Tap: How to Cut Your Water Usage by 50 Percent. Randall D. Schultz. (Illus.). 64p. 1991. write for info. (*1-880047-00-4*) Creative Des.

Turn off the TV & Anne Rogovin. 224p. (Orig.). 1995. pap. 14.95 (*0-687-00233-8*) Abingdon.

Turn Off Your Age see Think Young-Be Young!

***Turn on the Light.** pap. 5.00 (*0-614-18214-X*, TOTL1) Let Us Tch Kids.

Turn on the Light. John C. Hagee. Ed. by Lucretia Hobbs & Connie Reece. (Illus.). 18p. (Orig.). 1993. 3.00 (*1-56908-026-7*) Global Evang.

Turn on the Light at Christmas. Earl Paulk. 32p. 1987. mass mkt. 1.50 (*0-917595-23-8*) Kingdom Pubs.

Turn on the Lights - From Bed! Electronic Inventions, Contraptions, & Gadgets Kids Can Build. Robert Carrow. LC 96-49657. (Illus.). 160p. (YA). (gr. 5 up). 1996. text ed. 24.95 (*0-07-011656-3*, Lrng Triangle); pap. text ed. 14.95 (*0-07-011659-8*, Lrng Triangle) McGraw-Hill Prof.

Turn on to Reading (All Night Long) Sylvia Blake & Sy Kaufman. 1984. student ed. 1.00 (*0-910307-04-0*) Comp Pr.

Turn-Ons! One Hundred Eighty-Five Strategies for the Secondary Classroom. Stephen K. Smuin. LC 77-92903. (J). (gr. 7-12). 1978. pap. 11.99 (*0-8224-7051-9*) Fearon Teach Aids.

Turn Right at Death Valley. John Merrill. 1986. 40.00 (*0-907496-26-1*, Pub. by JNM Pubns UK) St Mut.

Turn Right at Land's End. John N. Merrill. 208p. (C). 1989. 39.00 (*0-907496-74-1*, Pub. by JNM Pubns UK) St Mut.

Turn Right at the Fountain. George W. Oakes. 1981. pap. 11.95 (*0-8050-1234-6*) H Holt & Co.

Turn Right at the Fountain. rev. ed. George W. Oakes & Alexandra Chapman. LC 80-17568. (Illus.). 352p. 1981. pap. 9.95 (*0-03-059189-9*) H Holt & Co.

Turn Right at the Fountain: Fifty-Three Walking Tours Through Europe's Most Enchanting Cities. rev. ed. Alexandra Chapman. 1996. pap. 15.95 (*0-8050-2356-9*) H Holt & Co.

Turn Screw - Taming Screw. James. Date not set. pap. text ed. 11.25 (*0-312-15013-X*) St Martin.

Turn Signals Are the Facial Expressions of Automobiles. Donald A. Norman. (Illus.). 224p. 1993. pap. 14.00 (*0-201-62236-X*) Addison-Wesley.

Turn Signals Are the Facial Expressions of Automobiles: Notes of a Technology Watcher. Donald A. Norman. (Illus.). 1992. 21.95 (*0-201-58124-8*) Addison-Wesley.

Turn the Battle to the Gate. Betsey Frye. 48p. 1988. pap. 2.95 (*0-88144-099-X*) Christian Pub.

***Turn the Cup Around.** Barbara Mariconda. LC 96-38631. (J). 1997. mass mkt. 15.95 (*0-385-32292-5*) Delacorte.

Turn the Gas Back On: A Musical. Max Goughtly. 54p. (Orig.). 1992. pap. 5.00 (*1-57514-237-6*, 0032) Encore Perform Pub.

***Turn the Hall Light On.** Elizabeth Kontoyiannaki. (Illus.). 17p. (J). (gr. k-3). 1997. pap. 14.95 (*1-56606-044-3*) Bradley Mann.

Turn the Key on Emerson: Larry & Stretch. large type ed. Marshall Grover. (Linford Western Library). 1991. pap. 15.99 (*0-7089-6966-6*) Ulverscroft.

Turn the Tables on Turnover: 52 Ways to Find, Hire & Keep the Best Hospitality Employees. Jim Sullivan et al. (Illus.). 123p. (Orig.). 1995. pap. 19.95 (*1-879239-05-1*) Pencom.

***Turn to Applied Ethics: Practical Consequences for Research, Education, & the Role of Ethicists in Public Debate.** Ed. by F. Robert Heeger & Theodoor Van Willigenburg. 117p. 1993. pap. 23.25 (*90-390-0048-4*, Pub. by KOK Pharos NE) Eisenbrauns.

Turn to Experience In Contemporary Theology. Donald L. Gelpi. LC 93-38868. 176p. (Orig.). 1994. pap. 9.95 (*0-8091-3452-7*) Paulist Pr.

***Turn to Learn.** Virginia Dooley. (J). 1997. pap. 9.95 (*0-590-70134-7*) Scholastic Inc.

Turn to the Native: Studies in Criticism & Culture. Arnold Krupat. LC 96-15152. xiv, 151p. 1996. text ed. 30.00 (*0-8032-2735-3*) U of Nebr Pr.

Turn to the South: Essays on Southern Jewry. Ed. by Nathan M. Kaganoff & Melvin I. Urofsky. LC 78-9306. 221p. reprint ed. pap. 63.00 (*0-8357-3275-4*, 2039497) Bks Demand.

Turn Toward the Wind: Embracing Change in Your Life. Dale H. Bourke. 240p. 1995. 14.99 (*0-310-41170-X*) Zondervan.

Turn-Up. large type ed. Alan Sewart. (Linford Mystery Library). 368p. 1996. pap. 15.99 (*0-7089-7855-X*, Linford) Ulverscroft.

Turn West, Turn East: Mark Twain & Henry James. Henry S. Canby. LC 65-23485. 1951. pap. 23.00 (*0-8196-0154-3*) Biblo.

Turn Your Business Around! Hands-on Strategies for Long-Term Survival. Suzanne Caplan. 1994. 22.95 (*0-13-302068-1*) P-H.

Turn Your City Upside Down. Holt Vaughn. 70p. (Orig.). 1995. pap. 5.00 (*0-9647914-1-2*) Vaughn Minist.

Turn Your Eyes Toward Texas: Pioneers Sam & Mary Maverick. Paula M. Marks. LC 88-27573. (Centennial Series of the Association of Former Students: No. 30). (Illus.). 344p. 1989. 29.50 (*0-89096-380-0*) Tex A&M Univ Pr.

Turn Your Good Idea into a Profitable Home Video. Matthew White. (Illus.). 288p. 1987. pap. 12.95 (*0-312-01043-5*) St Martin.

Turn Your Ideas into Millions: Selling & Marketing Your Idea or Product. Kate Masters. LC 93-44225. 1994. 8.95 (*0-8065-1525-2*, Citadel Pr) Carol Pub Group.

Turn Your Little Ones into Book of Mormon Whiz Kids. Christine Melonakos. LC 90-85979. 167p. (Orig.). 1991. pap. 15.98 (*0-88290-407-8*) Horizon Utah.

Turn Your Pressure Valve Down. Richard Flint. 100p. 1982. pap. 10.00 (*0-937851-15-9*) Pendelton Lane.

***Turnabout.** Ann Jonas. (J). Date not set. write for info. (*0-688-14174-9*); lib. bdg. write for info. (*0-688-14173-0*) Greenwillow.

Turnabout: Help for a New Life. Jean Kirkpatrick. 1978. 8.95 (*0-686-30132-3*) WFS.

Turnabout: Megilas Esther According to the Malbim. Mendel Weinbach. 1990. 15.95 (*0-685-32886-4*) Feldheim.

Turnabout: The Malbim on Megillas Esther. Mendel Weinbach. 190p. 1990. 14.95 (*0-944070-24-8*) Targum Pr.

Turnabout Paul Storybook. Michael Williams. 48p. (Orig.). (J). (gr. 3 up). 1995. pap. 7.95 (*0-687-00793-3*) Abingdon.

Turnabout Songs Program Complete Set: A Shortcut to Knowledge. Kaboblin Theo Carus Harter. Ed. by Betty N. Smith & Catherine Anderson. (Illus.). 262p. (J). 1993. ring bd. 150.00 incl. audio (*0-944528-41-4*) Child Mus Wkshop.

Turnabout Years: American Cultural Life, 1900-1950. John Chamberlain. 254p. (Orig.). 1992. pap. 12.95 (*0-915463-61-X*) Jameson Bks.

***Turnaround. Gene Elmore. vi, 260p. 1997. pap. 16.95 (*0-9656908-0-6*) A-Genda Pub.**

Speaking to Mike, "I see--you're all alike." Samir lays the picture aside, turns, & walks half the distance toward where the women were tied. Pointing to Mike's wife, Joyce, the order is given in Farsi. "Let's start with her." When Mike Tolson learns about the things Samir Heric is doing to his wife, & to Jane Baxter -- while holding the country hostage -- the ultimate test & confrontation between these two men is put in place. THE TURNAROUND is a tale of intrigue, murder, & revenge that draws upon the most terrifying aspects of our modern world, insurrection & multi-faceted characters. Samir Heric, an Iranian terrorist with intense purpose, will do whatever is required to complete an assignment. Jane Baxter, the beautiful journalist with the strongest reason of all to hate & seek revenge is caught in the turmoil. Mike Tolson, the Managing Editor for a national news network, has a faith which holds steady, never shaken except for one slip years earlier for which his wife faces the retaliation. The plot twists & turns with increasing intensity to a startling conclusion, offering an inspiring message in the face of adversity. Order from A-GENDA Publishing, 7920 Blue Lake Drive, San Diego, CA 92119-3325. (619) 460-5740, FAX: (619) 460-5727. ***Publisher Provided Annotation.***

Turnaround: Avoid Bankruptcy & Revitalize Your Company. Edmond P. Freiermuth. 184p. (Orig.). 1989. pap. 14.95 (*0-8306-3043-0*, Liberty Hse) TAB Bks.

Turnaround: The Political Economy of Development & Liberalization in Ecuador, 1984-1988. Francisco X. Swett. LC 89-35515. 30p. 1989. pap. 6.95 (*1-55815-034-X*, NO. 20) ICS Pr.

***Turnaround: The Untold Story of Bear Bryant's First Year As Head Coach at Alabama.** Tom Stoddard. 1996. 22.00 (*1-881320-70-7*, Black Belt) Black Belt Comm.

Turnaround Experience: Real-World Lessons in Revitalizing Corporations. Frederick M. Zimmerman. 336p. 1991. text ed. 24.95 (*0-07-072899-2*) McGraw.

Turnaround Experience: Saving Troubled Companies. T. F. Schopflocher. (Life Line Ser.). 175p. (Orig.). 1995. pap. 14.95 (*1-55059-101-0*, Pub. by Detselig CN) Temeron Bks.

Turnaround Imperative: A Leader's Guide for Survival in a Turbulent Health Care Environment. Victor A. Cocowitch & Kevin M. Fickenscher. LC 95-79896. 117p. (Orig.). (C). 1996. pap. text ed. 44.00 (*0-924674-37-7*) Am Coll Phys Execs.

Turnaround Prescription: Repositioning Troubled Companies. Mark R. Goldston. LC 92-10752. 224p. 1992. 27.95 (*0-02-912395-X*, Free Press) Free Pr.

Turnaround Selling: How to Cash in on Hidden Big-Money Opportunities in Everyday Sales Situation. Richard F. Gabriel. 1977. 49.50 (*0-13-933176-X*) Exec Reports.

Turnaround Strategies for the Small Church. Ronald Crandall. (Effective Church Ser.). 176p. (Orig.). 1995. pap. 12.95 (*0-687-00467-5*) Abingdon.

Turnaround Tactics. Joe E. McBride, Jr. 76p. (Orig.). 1990. pap. 7.95 (*0-9625668-0-2*) First Renaissance.

Turnaround Time: The Best of Computerworld's Q & A's. Larry Long. 192p. 1987. 17.50 (*0-13-933029-1*) P-H.

Turnaround Wind. Arnold Lobel. LC 87-45293. (Illus.). 32p. (J). (ps-3). 1988. lib. bdg. 14.89 (*0-06-023988-3*) HarpC Child Bks.

Turnaway. Jesse Browner. 288p. 1996. 23.00 (*0-679-44788-1*, Villard Bks) Random.

Turnbo's Tales of the Ozarks: Bear Stories. Silas C. Turnbo. Ed. by Desmond W. Allen. 148p. 1988. pap. 18.00 (*0-941765-33-4*) Arkansas Res.

Turnbo's Tales of the Ozarks: Biographical Stories. rev. ed. Silas C. Turnbo. Ed. by Desmond W. Allen. 180p. 1989. pap. 20.00 (*0-941765-45-8*) Arkansas Res.

Turnbo's Tales of the Ozarks: Deer Hunting Stories. Silas C. Turnbo. Ed. by Desmond W. Allen. 101p. 1989. pap. 15.00 (*0-941765-40-7*) Arkansas Res.

Turnbo's Tales of the Ozarks: Incidents, Mean Tricks & Fictitious Stories. rev. ed. Silas C. Turnbo. Ed. by Desmond W. Allen. 99p. 1990. pap. 15.00 (*0-941765-49-0*) Arkansas Res.

Turnbo's Tales of the Ozarks: Panther Stories. Silas C. Turnbo. Ed. by Desmond W. Allen. 142p. 1989. pap. 18.00 (*0-941765-43-1*) Arkansas Res.

Turnbo's Tales of the Ozarks: Schools, Indians, Hard Times & More Stories. rev. ed. Silas C. Turnbo. Ed. by Desmond W. Allen. 138p. 1989. pap. 18.00 (*0-941765-47-4*) Arkansas Res.

Turnbo's Tales of the Ozarks: Snakes, Birds & Insect Stories. Silas C. Turnbo. Ed. by Desmond W. Allen. 96p. 1989. pap. 15.00 (*0-941765-44-X*) Arkansas Res.

Turnbo's Tales of the Ozarks: War & Guerrilla Stories. rev. ed. Silas C. Turnbo. Ed. by Desmond W. Allen. 165p. 1989. pap. 18.00 (*0-941765-46-6*) Arkansas Res.

Turnbo's Tales of the Ozarks: Wolf Stories. Silas C. Turnbo. Ed. by Desmond W. Allen. 141p. 1989. pap. 18.00 (*0-941765-42-3*) Arkansas Res.

Turnbull: A Library & Its World. Rachel Barrowman. 240p. 1996. pap. 29.95 (*1-86940-137-9*, Pub. by Auckland Univ NZ) Paul & Co Pubs.

Turnbulls. Taylor Caldwell. 1993. reprint ed. lib. bdg. 27.95 (*1-56849-154-9*) Buccaneer Bks.

Turncoat. Sean Dalton. 192p. (Orig.). 1994. mass mkt. 4.99 (*0-441-00117-3*) Ace Bks.

Turncoats: Changing Party Allegiance by British Politicians. Robert Leach. (Illus.). 304p. 1995. text ed. 59.95 (*1-85521-617-5*, Pub. by Dartmth Pub UK) Ashgate Pub Co.

Turncoats & True Believers: The Dynamics of Political Belief & Disillusionment. Ted Goertzel. 428p. (C). 1992. 30.95 (*0-87975-755-8*) Prometheus Bks.

Turned-Bowl Design. Richard Raffan. LC 87-72008. (Illus.). 176p. 1987. pap. 21.95 (*0-918804-82-5*) Taunton.

Turned Card: Christianity Before & after the Wall. Desmond O'Grady. (Illus.). 178p. (Orig.). 1995. pap. 15.95 (*0-85244-303-X*, Pub. by Gracewing UK) Morehouse Pub.

***Turned Card: Christianity Before & after the Wall.** 2nd ed. Desmond O'Grady. LC 96-52196. 200p. (Orig.). 1997. 22.95 (*0-8294-0938-6*) Loyola Pr.

***Turned Inside Out: Recollections of a Private Soldier in the Army of the Potomac.** Frank Wilkeson. 1997. pap. text ed. 10.95 (*0-8032-9799-8*) U of Nebr Pr.

Turned On: American Decorative Lamps of the '50s. Leland Payton & Crystal Payton. (Illus.). 96p. 1989. 27.50 (*0-89659-916-7*) Abbeville Pr.

***Turned On: Eight Vital Insights to Energize Your People, Customers & Profits.** Roger Dow. 336p. 1997. pap. 13.50 (*0-88730-861-9*) Harper Busn.

Turned-On Advising: Computer & Video Resources for Educational Advising. Edward A. Reidinger. 96p. 1995. pap. text ed. 18.00 (*0-912207-73-6*) NAFSA Washington.

***Turned on by Electricity.** Elise Richards. (J). 1997. pap. 7.95 (*0-8167-4254-5*) Troll Communs.

Turned to Account: The Forms & Functions of English Criminal Biography in the Late 17th & Early 18th Century England. Lincoln B. Faller. (Illus.). 368p. 1987. text ed. 69.95 (*0-521-32672-9*) Cambridge U Pr.

Turner. A. Bailey. 560p. 1997. 35.00 (*0-06-118002-5*, HarpT) HarpC.

***Turner.** M. Bockemuhl. 1994. pap. text ed. 9.99 (*3-8228-0554-8*) Taschen Amer.

Turner. Ed. by Michael Lloyd. LC 95-61908. (Illus.). 250p. (Orig.). 1996. pap. 24.95 (*0-500-97437-3*) Thames Hudson.

Turner. Camille Mauclair. Tr. by E. B. Shaw. (Illus.). 168p. 1939. lib. bdg. 35.00 (*0-8288-3930-1*) Fr & Eur.

Turner. Graham Reynolds. (World of Art Ser.). (Illus.). 216p. 1985. pap. 14.95 (*0-500-20083-1*) Thames Hudson.

Turner. John Walker. (Masters of Art Ser.). 1983. 22.95 (*0-8109-1679-7*) Abrams.

Turner. William Gaunt. (Color Library). (Illus.). 128p. (C). 1994. reprint ed. pap. 14.95 (*0-7148-2759-2*, Pub. by Phaidon Press UK) Chronicle Bks.

Turner: His Life & Work. Jack Lindsay. (Illus.). 379p. 1980. reprint ed. pap. 8.95 (*0-586-03852-3*) Academy Chi Pubs.

Turner: New & Selected Poems. David Dabydeen. 74p. 1995. pap. 15.95 (*0-224-03895-8*, Pub. by Jonathan Cape UK) Trafalgar.

Turner: Paintings, Watercolors, Prints & Drawings. Luke Herrmann. 1986. 22.95 (*0-306-80270-8*) Da Capo.

Turner & George IV In Edinburgh, 1822. Gerald Finley. 250p. 1982. 30.00 (*0-85224-432-0*, Pub. by Edinburgh U Pr UK) Col U Pr.

Turner & the Sublime. Andrew J. Wilton. LC 80-28398. (Illus.). 192p. 1981. pap. 21.95 (*0-226-06189-2*) U Ch Pr.

Turner at Petworth: Painter & Patron. Martin Butlin et al. (Illus.). 300p. 1990. 75.00 (*0-295-96951-2*) U of Wash Pr.

Turner, Bolton, & Webb: Three Historians of the American Frontier. Wilbur R. Jacobs et al. (Illus.). 127p. (Orig.). 1979. reprint ed. pap. 5.95 (*0-295-95677-1*) U of Wash Pr.

Turner Brooks: Work. Turner Brooks et al. (Illus.). 152p. 1995. pap. 27.95 (*1-56898-031-0*) Princeton Arch.

Turner Collection in the Clore Gallery: An Illustrated Guide. Andrew J. Wilton. (Illus.). 128p. 1987. 40.00 (*0-295-96770-6*); pap. 19.95 (*0-295-96771-4*) U of Wash Pr.

Turner Diaries. 2nd ed. Andrew Macdonald. LC 80-82692. 216p. (Orig.). 1980. pap. 12.95 (0-937944-02-5) Natl Vanguard.

Turner Diaries: A Novel. Andrew Macdonald. LC 80-82692. 224p. 1996. reprint ed. pap. 12.00 (1-56980-086-3) Barricade Bks.

Turner Family Magazine: Genealogical, Historical & Biographical, Set, Vols. 1 & 2. Ed. by Wm. M. Clemens. 95p. 1994. reprint ed. lib. bdg. 28.00 (0-8328-4386-5) Higginson Bk Co.

Turner Family Magazine: Genealogical, Historical & Biographical, Set, Vols. 1 & 2. Ed. by Wm. M. Clemens. 95p. 1994. reprint ed. pap. 18.00 (0-8328-4387-3) Higginson Bk Co.

Turner Group of Earthworks, Hamilton County, Ohio. C. C. Willoughby. (HU PMP Ser.). 1922. 25.00 (0-527-01214-9) Periodicals Srv.

Turner in Dorset: Images from the Picturesque Views on the Southern Coast of England. Howard J. Hanley. (Illus.). 1992. pap. 9.00 (0-9633015-9-4) H Hanley.

***Turner in Indianapolis: The Pantzer Collection of Drawings & Watercolors by J. M. W. Turner & by His Contemporaries at the Indianapolis Museum of Art.** Martin F. Krause. LC 97-10107. (Illus.). 272p. 1997. write for info. (0-936260-66-1) Ind Mus Art.

Turner in the North. David Hill. (Illus.). 208p. 1996. 50.00 (0-300-06942-1) Yale U Pr.

Turner in the North: A Tour Through Derbyshire, Yorkshire, Durham, Northumberland, the Scottish Borders, the Lake District, Lancashire & Lincolnshire in the Year 1797. David Hill. LC 96-21635. 1996. pap. write for info. (0-300-06944-8) Yale U Pr.

Turner in the South. Cecilia Powell. LC 86-26673. 216p. 1987. 45.00 (0-300-03870-4) Yale U Pr.

Turner Journals. Robert Leigh. 288p. 1996. 22.95 (0-8027-3260-7) Walker & Co.

***Turner on the Loire.** Ian Warrell. (Illus.). 240p. 1997. pap. 50.00 (1-85437-218-1, Pub. by Tate Gallery UK) U of Wash Pr.

Turner on the Thames: River Journeys in the Year 1805. David Hill. (Illus.). 208p. (C). 1993. text ed. 55.00 (0-300-05389-4) Yale U Pr.

Turner Prints: The Engraved Work of J. M. W. Turner. Luke Herrmann. 296p. (C). 1990. text ed. 108.00 (0-8147-3472-3) NYU Pr.

***Turner Prize.** Virginia Button & Adrian Searle. (Illus.). 104p. 1997. pap. 35.00 (1-85437-221-1, Pub. by Tate Gallery UK) U of Wash Pr.

***Turner Reunion.** Lionel L. Tipton. 214p. (Orig.). 1997. mass mkt. 4.99 (1-55237-030-5, Pub. by Comnwlth Pub CN) Partners Pubs Grp.

Turner Soldat: A Turner Soldier in the Civil War; Germany to Antietam. C. Eugene Miller & Forrest F. Steinlage. LC 88-70880. (Illus.). 135p. 1988. 13.95 (0-9620368-0-3) Calmar Pubns.

Turner Syndrome. Rosenfeld et al. 647p. 1989. 225.00 (0-8247-8108-2) Dekker.

***Turner Syndrome: Growth Promoting Therapies.** M. B. Ranke & R. G. Rosenfeld. x, 278p. 1991. 141.25 (0-444-81380-2, Excerpta Medica) Elsevier.

Turner Syndrome in a Life Span Perspective: Research & Clinical Aspects : Proceedings of the 4th International Symposium, Gothenburg, 12-21 May, 1995. Ed. by K. Albertsson-Wikland & M. B. Ranke. (International Congress Ser.: Vol. 1089). 340p. 1995. 217.50 (0-444-82188-0) Elsevier.

Turner, the Fighting Temeraire. Judy Egerton. 1995. 25.00 (0-300-06224-9) Yale U Pr.

Turner Thesis: Concerning the Role of the Frontier in American History. 3rd ed. Ed. by George R. Taylor. (Problems in American Civilization Ser.). 208p. (C). 1972. pap. text ed. 16.76 (0-669-81059-2) HM College Div.

***Turner Watercolors from Manchester.** Charles Nugent & Melva Croal. (Illus.). 128p. (Orig.). 1996. pap. 24.95 (1-882507-05-3) Trust Mus Exhib.

Turner Watercolours in the Clore Gallery. Andrew J. Wilton. (Illus.). 152p. 1987. 55.00 (0-295-96778-1); pap. 27.50 (0-295-96779-X) U of Wash Pr.

Turners. Jerome McDonough. 40p. (Orig.). (YA). (gr. 7-12). 1989. pap. 4.00 (0-88680-320-9) I E Clark.

Turners & Burners: The Folk Potters of North Carolina. Charles G. Zug, III. LC 86-1456. (Fred W. Morrison Series in Southern Studies). (Illus.). xxii, 451p. 1989. reprint ed. 49.95 (0-8078-1704-X); reprint ed. pap. 29.95 (0-8078-4276-1) U of NC Pr.

Turner's Angels. Douglas Graham. (Illus.). 52p. (Orig.). 1992. pap. 5.95 (0-317-04269-6) Turner Mus.

Turner's Classical Landscapes: Myth & Meaning. Kathleen Nicholson. (Illus.). 360p. 1990. text ed. 65.00 (0-691-04080-X) Princeton U Pr.

Turner's Cosmic Optimism. Douglas Graham. (Illus.). 52p. (Orig.). 1991. pap. 9.95 (0-317-04094-4) Turner Mus.

Turner's "Drawing Book" The Liber Studiorum. Gillian Forrester. (Illus.). 152p. (C). 1996. pap. 40.00 (1-85437-182-7, Pub. by Tate Gallery UK) U of Wash Pr.

Turner's Holland. Fred G. Bachrach. (Illus.). 72p. 1995. pap. 30.00 (1-85437-140-1, Pub. by Tate Gallery UK) U of Wash Pr.

Turner's Latest Milwaukee & Nearby Cities Street Guide. 128p. (Orig.). 1982. pap. text ed. 3.50 (0-936537-00-0) Metro WI.

Turner's Liber Studiorum: History & Catalogue Raisonne. Alexander J. Finberg. 472p. 1988. reprint ed. 95.00 (1-55660-022-4) A Wofsy Fine Arts.

Turner's Painting Techniques. Joyce Townsend. (Illus.). 84p. 1996. pap. 27.95 (1-85437-202-5, Pub. by Tate Gallery UK) U of Wash Pr.

Turner's Third Book of Atari ST Topics. Ralph C. Turner. LC 91-9413. (Illus.). 158p. (Orig.). 1991. pap. 16.95 (0-945959-02-8) Index Legalis Pub Co.

Turner's Vignettes. Jan Piggot. (Illus.). 128p. 1994. pap. 40.00 (1-85437-132-0) U of Wash Pr.

***Turner's Watercolour Explorations 1818-1842.** Eric Shanes. (Illus.). 112p. 1997. pap. 30.00 (1-85437-222-X, Pub. by Tate Gallery UK) U of Wash Pr.

Turning. LC 94-3368. 1994. 9.95 (0-88010-384-1) Anthroposophic.

***Turning.** Hilda Morley. LC 96-44931. 190p. (Orig.). 1997. 16.95 (1-55921-202-0, Asphodel Pr) Moyer Bell.

***Turning.** Terry M. West. (Confessions of a Teenage Vampire Ser.). (Illus.). (J). (gr. 4-7). 1997. mass mkt. 4.99 (0-590-10466-7) Scholastic Inc.

Turning: A Sequence. Greg Kuzma. 48p. (Orig.). 1988. pap. 5.95 (0-935153-06-3) Stormline Pr.

Turning: From Persuasion to Philosophy. Michael Naas. LC 93-20211. (Philosophy & Literary Theory Ser.). 344p. (C). 1995. text ed. 55.00 (0-391-03821-4) Humanities.

Turning & Boring: Angles & Applications. Ed. by Donald O. Wood. LC 85-50271. (Illus.). 254p. reprint ed. pap. 72.40 (0-8357-6473-7, 2035844) Bks Demand.

Turning Around: Keys to Motivation & Productivity. Beverly A. Potter. (Illus.). 292p. 1989. pap. 9.95 (0-914171-16-X) Ronin Pub.

Turning Around the Upside-Down Kids: Helping Dyslexic Kids Overcome Their Disorder. Harold N. Levinson & Addie Sanders. LC 92-13440. 180p. 1992. 17.95 (0-87131-700-1) M Evans.

Turning Assets into Prosperity: How to Trade Your Way to Financial Success. Neil Burnett. 206p. 1982. pap. 7.95 (0-940986-03-5) ValuWrite.

Turning Awareness into Action: What Your Community Can Do about Drug Abuse in America. 1994. lib. bdg. 250.95 (0-8490-8946-8) Gordon Pr.

Turning Awareness into Action: What Your Community Can Do about Drug Use in America. rev. ed. 148p. (ENG & SPA.). (C). 1993. pap. 20.00 (0-7881-0208-7) DIANE Pub.

***Turning away from Technology.** Stephanie Mills. 1997. pap. 16.00 (0-87156-953-1) Sierra.

Turning Back: The Retreat from Racial Justice in American Thought & Policy. Stephen Steinberg. 304p. (C). 1995. 25.00 (0-8070-4110-6) Beacon Pr.

Turning Back: The Retreat from Racial Justice in American Thought & Policy. Stephen Steinberg. 288p. 1996. pap. 15.00 (0-8070-4111-4) Beacon Pr.

Turning Back the Aging Clock: Dr. Lee-Benners' Scientifically Designed & Medically Based Longevity Program. Lee-Benner. (Illus.). 230p. (Orig.). 1991. pap. 25.00 (0-944213-05-7) World Hlth Found.

Turning Back the Clock: The Reagan-Bush Retreat for Civil Rights in Higher Education. Gary Orfield. 150p. (C). 1992. pap. text ed. 14.50 (0-941410-85-4); lib. bdg. 42.00 (0-941410-86-2) Jt Ctr Pol Studies.

***Turning Back the Tide of Illiteracy.** Marguerite F. Hoerl. LC 96-45820. 1996. pap. write for info. (0-89420-298-7) Eductnl Resch Assocs.

Turning Blade. large type ed. Clare F. Holmes. (Nightingale Ser.). 1996. pap. 17.95 (0-7838-1624-3, GK Hall) Thorndike Pr.

Turning Bowls: Step-By-Step. David Regester. (Illus.). 112p. 1996. 29.95 (0-7134-7239-1, Pub. by Batsford UK) Trafalgar.

***Turning Boxes.** Richard Raffan. (Illus.). 176p. 1998. pap. 24.95 (1-56158-224-7, 070358) Taunton.

Turning Boxes & Spindles: Step-by-Step. David Regester. (Illus.). 110p. 1995. 29.95 (0-7134-7240-5, Pub. by Batsford UK) Trafalgar.

Turning Committees into Communities. Roberta Hestenes. 32p. 1991. pap. 4.00 (0-89109-302-8) NavPress.

Turning Continuous Quality Improvement into Institutional Practice: The Tools & Techniques. Robert Cornesky. (Illus.). 154p. (C). 1995. text ed. 24.50 (1-881807-09-6) Cornesky & Assocs.

Turning Disadvantaged Youth into an Economic Development Resource: Education & Training Linkages. James Breagy. Ed. by Jenny Murphy. 62p. (Orig.). 1991. pap. 22.50 (0-317-04802-3) Natl Coun Econ Dev.

***Turning Electricity On.** Bernie Zubrowski. (J). Date not set. lib. bdg. write for info. (0-688-09427-9, Morrow Junior) Morrow.

Turning Every Stone: Autism with Love - Reality Therapy. Phyllis H. Lambert. (Illus.). 1990. per., pap. 15.00 (0-9624737-4-X) S P-Persephone Pr.

***Turning Feedback into Change: 31 Principles for Personal Development.** Joe Folkman. 128p. 1996. pap. 10.00 (0-9634917-2-5) Exec Excell.

Turning Fifty. William K. Klingaman. 144p. (Orig.). 1994. pap. 7.95 (0-452-27033-2, Plume) NAL-Dutton.

Turning Fifty. Photos & Text by Bea Nettles. (Illus.). 64p. (Orig.). 1995. pap. 10.00 (0-930810-11-2) Inky Pr.

Turning for Furniture - Creating Furniture Parts on Your Lathe. Ernie Conover. (Illus.). 144p. 1996. pap. 19.95 (1-56158-117-8, 070245) Taunton.

Turning Forty: Wit, Wisdom, & Whining. William K. Klingaman. 1992. pap. 8.95 (0-452-26821-4, Plume) NAL-Dutton.

Turning Global Competition into Local Economic Development. Jenny Murphy & Wayne Welch. Ed. by Kenneth Poole. 30p. (Orig.). 1990. pap. 19.00 (0-317-04870-8) Natl Coun Econ Dev.

Turning Goblets. Michael Cripps. LC 96-15554. (Illus.). 64p. 1996. pap. 12.95 (0-7643-0033-4) Schiffer.

Turning Health Care Leadership Around: Cultivating Inspired, Empowered, & Loyal Followers. Thomas A. Atchison. LC 90-5192. (Health-Management Ser.). 183p. text ed. 40.00 (1-55542-295-0) Jossey-Bass.

Turning Hearts. Orson Scott Card & David Dollahite. 1994. pap. 10.95 (0-88494-948-6) Bookcraft Inc.

Turning Hobbies into Cash. C. Andrew Beck. LC 94-70101. (Illus.). 128p. (Orig.). 1994. pap. 8.95 (0-9640401-0-7) Four Crnrs Grp.

Turning Hobbies into Cash. C. Andrew Beck. LC 91-77197. (Illus.). 144p. (Orig.). 1991. pap. 11.95 (0-9631520-0-9) Monterey Prods.

Turning Hopeless Situations Around. Kenneth E. Hagin. 1981. pap. 1.95 (0-89276-022-2) Hagin Ministries.

Turning Horse Power Into Marketing Power: How to Use the Racing Industry As a Marketing Tool. Thomas Amshay & Christina Clement. Ed. by Anne Gottlieb. LC 93-83684. 215p. (Orig.). 1993. pap. 50.00 (0-939401-15-0) RFTS Prod.

Turning in. Rajneesh Osho Staff. Ed. by Yoga Sudha & Veet Shabda. (Zen Ser.). (Illus.). 288p. 1989. 12.95 (3-89338-059-0, Pub. by Rebel Hse GW) Osho America.

Turning Information into Profits: How to Manage Information Technology to Increase Your Bottom Line. Gerald M. Hoffman. 288p. 1994. text ed. 25.00 (1-55623-838-X) Irwin Prof Pubng.

Turning It On: A Reader in Women & the Media. Ed. by Helen Baehr & Ann Gray. LC 95-37773. 1995. text ed. 59.95 (0-340-63220-8); text ed. 14.95 (0-340-61396-3) St Martin.

Turning It Over: How to Find Tranquility When You Never Thought You Could. HTP, pseud. 135p. (Orig.). 1992. pap. 7.95 (1-55874-216-6) Health Comm.

***Turning Japanese.** David Galet. LC 97-23546. 1998. write for info. (1-57962-010-8) Permanent Pr.

Turning Japanese. David Mura. 384p. 1992. pap. 12.00 (0-385-42344-6, Anchor NY) Doubleday.

Turning Japanese? Britain with a Permanent Party of Government. Ed. by Helen Margetts & Gareth Smyth. 224p. (C). 1994. pap. 29.95 (0-85315-785-5, Pub. by Lawrence & Wishart UK) NYU Pr.

Turning Key: Autobiography & the Subjective Impulse Since 1800. Jerome H. Buckley. 208p. 1984. 23.50 (0-674-91330-2) HUP.

Turning Kids on to Science in the Home: Forces & Motion, Vol. 3. Tik L. Liem. (Illus.). 122p. 1992. pap. text ed. 17.50 (1-878106-06-6) Sci Inquiry.

Turning Kids on to Science in the Home: Living Things, Vol. 4. Tik L. Liem. (Illus.). 67p. 1992. pap. text ed. 12.50 (1-878106-07-4) Sci Inquiry.

Turning Kids on to Science in the Home, Vol. 2: Energy, Vol. 2. Tik L. Liem. (Illus.). 168p. 1992. pap. text ed. 20.00 (1-878106-05-8) Sci Inquiry.

Turning Lathes: A Guide to Turning, Screw Cutting, Metal Spinning & Ornamental Turning. Ed. by James Lukin. (Illus.). 432p. 1994. reprint ed. pap. 24.95 (1-879335-49-2) Astragal Pr.

Turning Lead into Gold: The Modern Alchemist's Manual for Improving Health, Neurological, & Motor Function in Children. Nancy Hallaway & Zigurts Strauts. 224p. 1995. 12.00 (0-921586-52-3) LPC InBook.

Turning Lead into Gold: The Modern Alchemist's Manual for Improving Health, Neurological, & Motor Function in Children. Nancy Hallaway & Zigurts Strauts. 1996. pap. 14.00 (0-921586-51-5) LPC InBook.

Turning Learning Inside Out: A Guide for Using Any Subject to Enrich Life & Creativity. Ann I. Nevin & Herb Leff. LC 94-11062. 1994. pap. 29.00 (1-56976-000-4) Zephyr Pr AZ.

***Turning Leaves: The Photograph Collections of Two Japanese American Families.** Richard Chalfen. LC 90-43793. (Illus.). 288p. 1991. reprint ed. pap. 82.10 (0-608-04146-7, 2064879) Bks Demand.

Turning Life into Fiction. Robin Hemley. 208p. 1994. 17.99 (1-884910-00-9, Story Press) F & W Pubns Inc.

***Turning Life into Fiction.** Robin Hemley. 1997. pap. text ed. 14.99 (1-884910-37-8, Story Press) F & W Pubns Inc.

Turning Lost Customers into Gold: ...And the Art of Achieving Zero Defections. Joan K. Cannie. 208p. 1993. 19.95 (0-8144-5110-1) AMACOM.

Turning Memories into Memoirs: A Handbook for Writing Lifestories. Denis Ledoux. (Illus.). 208p. (Orig.). (C). 1993. pap. 17.95 (0-9619373-2-7) Soleil Pr.

Turning Notes into Music: An Introduction to Musical Interpretation. Hans Lampl. LC 96-7833. 152p. 1996. 44.00 (0-8108-3164-3); pap. 26.00 (0-8108-3165-1) Scarecrow.

Turning Obstacles into Opportunities: Sermons for Lent & Easter - First Lesson. Rodney T. Smothers. LC 94-2647. (Orig.). 1994. pap. 7.75 (0-7880-0030-6) CSS OH.

Turning of the Key: Meher Baba in Australia. Bill Le Page. (Illus.). 460p. (Orig.). 1993. pap. 12.00 (0-913078-70-0) Sheriar Pr.

Turning of the Tide. Samuel Lewin. Tr. by Joseph Leftwich. 8.95 (0-8453-2087-4, Cornwall Bks) Assoc Univ Prs.

Turning of the Tide: Religion in China Today. Ed. by Julian F. Pas. (Illus.). 392p. 1990. pap. 15.95 (0-19-585117-X) OUP.

Turning of the Wheel. Siva P. Ray. Ed. by A. Ghosh. (Illus.). 132p. (Orig.). 1987. pap. 6.95 (0-9611614-2-6) A Ghosh.

Turning of the Wheel: A Wiccan Book of Shadows for Moons & Festivals. Stanley J. Modrzyk. LC 92-45558. (Illus.). 196p. (Orig.). 1993. pap. 12.95 (0-87728-767-8) Weiser.

***Turning of the Year.** Bill Martin. LC 96-53078. (Illus.). (J). 1997. write for info. (0-15-201085-8) HarBrace.

Turning on Learning. Grant & Christine E. Sleeter. 288p. (C). 1990. pap. text ed. 40.00 (0-675-20805-X, Merrill Coll) P-H.

***Turning on Learning: Five Approaches for Multicultural Teaching Plans for Race, Class, Gender, & Disability.** 2nd ed. Carl A. Grant & Christine E. Sleeter. LC 97-1574. 1997. pap. 34.00 (0-13-651134-1) P-H.

Turning on the Light: A Plan for Self-Empowerment & Fullness of Life. Bob Earll. LC 92-81368. 178p. (Orig.). 1992. pap. 10.95 (0-922641-64-1) Stem Pubns.

Turning One. 1989. 75.00 (0-85083-010-9) St Mut.

Turning Our Kids on to Science in the Home: Our Environment, 4 vols. Tik L. Liem. (Illus.). 185p. 1992. Set. pap. text ed. 25.00 (1-878106-08-2) Sci Inquiry.

Turning Our Kids on to Science in the Home: Our Environment, 4 vols., 1. Tik L. Liem. (Illus.). 185p. 1992. write for info. (1-878106-04-X) Sci Inquiry.

Turning Our School Around. Phyllis A. Wilken. 1996. pap. text ed. 19.95 (0-9647738-0-5) Scherer Communs.

Turning out the Lights. Sigrid Bergie. 1988. pap. 6.00 (0-89823-111-6) New Rivers Pr.

Turning Pages. Archer M. Huntington. 1950. 5.00 (0-87535-065-8) Hispanic Soc.

Turning Pens & Other Desk Accessories. Mike Cripps. (Illus.). 64p. 1996. pap. 12.95 (0-7643-0051-2) Schiffer.

Turning People On: The Motivation Challenge. Andrew Sargent. 128p. (C). 1990. pap. text ed. 65.00 (0-85292-444-5, Pub. by IPM Hse UK) St Mut.

***Turning Point.** 32p. (Orig.). 1995. pap. write for info. (0-614-21762-8) M Hickey Min.

***Turning Point.** 32p. (Orig.). 1995. pap. write for info. (0-614-21765-2) M Hickey Min.

Turning Point. Fritjof Capra. 468p. 1984. pap. 16.95 (0-553-34572-9, New Age Bks) Bantam.

Turning Point. Irene Johnson. 115p. 1984. 30.00 (0-7212-0651-4, Pub. by Regency Press UK) St Mut.

***Turning Point.** Martha J. McHenry. LC 96-90012. 1997. 11.95 (0-533-12266-X) Vantage.

Turning Point. Lisanne Norman. 256p. (Orig.). 1993. mass mkt. 3.99 (0-88677-575-2) DAW Bks.

Turning Point. Shannon O'Cork. 384p. 1988. mass mkt. 4.50 (0-373-97062-5) Harlequin Bks.

Turning Point. Friend Stuart. 38p. 1982. pap. 2.95 (0-912132-01-9) Dominion Pr.

Turning Point. Joyce D. Weinsheimer. 128p. 1993. pap. 18.95 (0-534-19422-2) Wadsworth Pub.

Turning Point. large type ed. Jan Tempest. 432p. 1988. 25.99 (0-7089-1843-3) Ulverscroft.

Turning Point: A Candidate, a State, & a Nation Come of Age. large type ed. Jimmy Carter. LC 93-13564. 1993. lib. bdg. 18.95 (1-56054-772-3) Thorndike Pr.

Turning Point: A Christian Worldview Declaration. Herbert Schlossberg & Marvin N. Olasky. LC 87-70458. (Turning Point Christian Worldview Ser.). 160p. (Orig.). 1987. pap. 12.99 (0-89107-449-X) Crossway Bks.

Turning Point: A History of Early A. A.'s Spiritual Roots & Successes. Dick B. LC 96-92645. (Illus.). 776p. (Orig.). 1997. pap. 29.95 (1-885803-07-9, 971) Paradise Res Inc. The first & only comprehensive reference book that brings together & details the spiritual ideas early AAs took from the Bible, Oxford Group, teachings of Rev. Sam Shoemaker, journal of Dr. Bob's wife (Anne Smith), Christian literature of the 1930s, & daily meditation materials such as THE UPPER ROOM. If you are in a Twelve Step program & want to know its roots, or if you are a therapist & want to understand A.A. spirituality, or if you are a church or clergy & want to know A.A.'s roots in the Bible, Christianity & religion, this is the book for you. Other historical book titles by Dick B.: DR. BOB'S LIBRARY, ANNE SMITH'S JOURNAL, THE AKRON GENESIS OF ALCOHOLICS ANONYMOUS, DESIGN FOR LIVING: THE OXFORD GROUP'S CONTRIBUTION TO EARLY A.A., NEW LIGHT ON ALCOHOLISM: THE A.A. LEGACY FROM SAM SHOEMAKER, THE BOOKS EARLY AAS READ FOR SPIRITUAL GROWTH, THE GOOD BOOK & THE BIG BOOK: A.A.'S ROOTS IN THE BIBLE, THAT AMAZING GRACE: THE ROLE OF CLARENCE & GRACE S. IN ALCOHOLICS ANONYMOUS, GOOD MORNING!: QUIET TIME, MORNING WATCH, MEDITATION, & EARLY A.A. Dick B. is a recovered alcoholic, retired attorney, & Bible student who has sponsored seventy AAs in their recovery. ***Publisher Provided Annotation.***

***Turning Point: A Novel about Growth & Suspense in an English Seminary.** Devorah Reich. 15.99 (0-89906-528-7, TURH); pap. 12.99 (0-89906-529-5, TURP) Mesorah Pubns.

***Turning Point: Breaking Free from the Deadly Power of Drug Addiction.** Lee Savage. 1997. pap. text ed. 6.95 (0-87148-871-X) Pathway Pr.

Turning Point: Convictions. Keith Davy. (Inter Acta Ser.). (Illus.). 6p. (C). 1994. teacher ed., ring bd. 1.25 (1-885702-97-3, 741-070t, Inter Acta); student ed., ring bd. 3.25 (1-885702-96-5, 741-070s, Inter Acta) WSN Pr.

Turning Point: Getting Started in Your New Life with Jesus. Ed Gungor. 83p. 1991. pap. 5.99 (0-9624161-1-8) Mini Res Fndt.

Turning Point: Getting Started in Your New Life with Jesus. rev. ed. Ed Gungor. 87p. 1994. pap. 5.99 (0-9624161-4-2) Mini Res Fndt.

Turning Point: How Men of Conscience Brought about Major Change in the Care of America's Mentally Ill. Alex Sareyan. LC 93-9227. (Illus.). 314p. 1993. text ed. 45.00 (0-88048-560-4, 8560) Am Psychiatric.

Turning Point: How Persons of Conscience Brought about Major Change in the Care of America's Mentally Ill. Alex Sareyan. LC 94-26396. 314p. 1994. pap. 16.95 (*0-8361-3596-2*) Herald Pr.

Turning Point: Pivotal Moments in the Lives of Celebrities. Glenn Plaskin. (Illus.). 208p. 1992. 18.95 (*1-55972-138-3*, Birch Ln Pr) Carol Pub Group.

Turning Point: The Autobiography of Klaus Mann. Klaus Mann. LC 83-27414. 420p. 1984. reprint ed. 18.95 (*0-910129-13-4*); reprint ed. pap. 9.95 (*0-910129-14-2*) Wiener Pubs Inc.

Turning Point: The Deichmann Pottery, 1935-1963. Stephen Inglis. (Illus.). 73p. (ENG & FRE.). 1991. pap. 17.95 (*0-660-50298-4*, Pub. by Can Mus Civil CN) U of Wash Pr.

Turning Point: The Inside Story of the Papal Birth Control Commission, & How Humanae Vitae Changed the Life of Patty Crowley & the Future of the Church. Robert McClory. (Illus.). 192p. 1995. 19.95 (*0-8245-1458-0*) Crossroad NY.

***Turning Point: The Inside Story of the Papal Birth Control Commission, & How "Humane Vitae" Changed the Life of Patty Crowley & the Future of the Church.** Robert McClory. 224p. 1997. pap. 15.95 (*0-8245-1613-3*) Crossroad NY.

***Turning Point: The Myths & Realities of Menopause.** C. Sue Furman. 224p. 1997. reprint ed. pap. text ed. 12.95 (*0-19-511384-5*) OUP.

Turning Point: The Other Side of Menopause. C. Sue Hudson-Ferman. 192p. 1995. 25.00 (*0-19-508773-9*) OUP.

Turning Point: Zionism & Reform Judaism. Howard Greenstein. LC 81-8996. (Brown Judaic Studies). 186p. (C). 1981. pap. 13.00 (*0-89130-512-2*, 140012) Scholars Pr GA.

Turning Point for Europe. Joseph C. Ratzinger. LC 93-78528. 177p. pap. 12.95 (*0-89870-461-8*) Ignatius Pr.

Turning Point in Africa: British Colonial Policy, 1938-48. R. D. Pearce. 234p. 1982. text ed. 42.50 (*0-7146-3160-4*, Pub. by F Cass Pubs UK) Intl Spec Bk.

Turning Point in China: An Essay on the Cultural Revolution. William Hinton. LC 76-178715. 112p. 1972. pap. 10.00 (*0-85345-215-6*) Monthly Rev.

Turning Point in Mamluk History: The Third Reign of Al-Nasir Muhammad ibn Qalawun (1310-1341) Amalia Levanoni. (Islamic History & Civilization, Studies & Texts Ser.). 1995. 92.00 (*90-04-10182-9*) E J Brill.

Turning Point in World War II: August 23, 1944 in Rumania. Ilie Ceaucescu et al. 235p. 1985. 48.50 (*0-88033-084-8*) East Eur Monographs.

Turning Point to Shakedown. Reid Angus. 352p. 1996. 29.95 (*0-385-25610-8*) Doubleday.

Turning Points. (Dialog Ser.). 104p. 1992. student ed., pap. 6.25 (*0-8341-1401-1*) Beacon Hill.

Turning Points. 40p. 1992. teacher ed., pap. 5.25 (*0-8341-1400-3*) Beacon Hill.

Turning Points. 96p. 1995. pap. 5.95 (*1-56138-643-X*) Courage Bks.

Turning Points. Sol Landau. 1986. 13.95 (*0-88282-017-6*) New Horizon NJ.

Turning Points. Marshall. 1996. 28.00 (*0-02-376451-1*, Macmillan Coll) P-H.

***Turning Points.** Sarah H. Pierce. (Illus.). 128p. (Orig.). 1996. pap. 11.95 (*0-9645451-6-0*, Swann Pubns) F Swann Pubns.

Turning Points. Martha Smock. LC 75-41954. 1976. 6.95 (*0-87159-156-1*) Unity Bks.

Turning Points. 2nd ed. Papa Iantorno. 1144p. 1994. pap. text ed. 12.72 (*0-201-53818-0*) Addison-Wesley.

Turning Points. 2nd ed. Papa Iantorno. 80p. 1994. pap. text ed. 6.36 (*0-201-76532-2*); student ed., ring bd. 4.24 (*0-201-76534-9*) Addison-Wesley.

Turning Points. 2nd ed. Mario Papa & Giuliano Iantorno. (ESL Ser.). (Illus.). (C). 1994. pap. text ed. 12.72 (*0-201-53814-8*); ring bd. 8.40 (*0-201-53815-6*) Addison-Wesley.

Turning Points, Level 1. Mario Papa. 1989. wbk. ed. 7.26 (*0-201-06316-6*) Addison-Wesley.

***Turning Points: Decisive Moments in the History of Christianity.** Mark A. Noll. 320p. Date not set. 24.99 (*0-8010-1159-0*); pap. 17.99 (*0-8010-5778-7*) Baker Bks.

***Turning Points: Essays in the History of Cultural Expressions.** Marshall Brown. 1997. pap. text ed. 16.95 (*0-8047-2923-9*) Stanford U Pr.

Turning Points: Essays in the History of Cultural Expressions. Marshall Brown. 1997. write for info. (*0-8047-2708-2*) Stanford U Pr.

***Turning Points: Moments of Grace, Steps Toward Wholeness.** Marlene L. Hamilton. LC 96-39623. 128p. (Orig.). 1997. pap. 12.00 (*0-8170-1259-1*) Judson.

Turning Points: Preparing American Youth for the 21st Century. 2nd ed. Carnegie Council on Adolescent Development's Task Force on Education of Young Adolescents Staff. (Illus.). 108p. 1989. reprint ed. pap. 6.00 (*0-9623154-1-9*) CCAD DC.

Turning Points: Self-Renewal at Mid-Life. Sol Landau. 1992. pap. 11.95 (*0-88282-109-1*) New Horizon NJ.

Turning Points: Sermons for Lent & Easter. Robert A. Beringer. LC 94-33074. 86p. (Orig.). 1995. pap. 8.00 (*0-7880-0283-X*) CSS OH.

Turning Points: Stories of People Who Made a Difference. Max L. Christensen. LC 92-17831. 128p. (Orig.). 1993. pap. 10.00 (*0-664-25357-1*) Westminster John Knox.

Turning Points: Treating Families in Transition & Crisis. Frank S. Pittman, III. (Professional Bks.). 1987. 34.95 (*0-393-70040-2*) Norton.

***Turning Points: When Everything Changes.** Walter D. Myers et al. (Target Ser.). 160p. (Orig.). (J). (ps-1). 1996. pap. text ed. 11.95 (*0-8167-4275-8*) Troll Communs.

Turning Points see Leading Corporate Change: How the World's Foremost Companies Are Launching Revolutionary Change

Turning Points Four. Giuliano Iantorno & Mario Papa. (Illus.). 128p. 1989. pap. text ed. 14.24 (*0-201-52160-1*) Addison-Wesley.

Turning Points Four. Iantorno Papa. (Turning Points Ser.). 128p. (YA). (gr. 7-12). 1989. pap. text ed. 11.32 (*0-201-06324-7*) Addison-Wesley.

Turning Points Four: Teachers Edition. Iantorno Papa. (Secondary ESOL Ser.). 208p. 1987. teacher ed. 12.60 (*0-201-06326-3*) Addison-Wesley.

Turning Points in American Educational History. Ed. by David B. Tyack. 502p. reprint ed. pap. 143.10 (*0-317-28112-7*, 2055735) Bks Demand.

Turning Points in American History, 17 vols. (Illus.). 1472p. (YA). (gr. 5 up). 1990. Set. pap. 135.15 (*0-382-09628-2*); Set. lib. bdg. 313.95 (*0-382-09627-4*) Silver Burdett Pr.

Turning Points in Analytic Therapy: From Winnicott to Kernberg. Gerald Schoenewolf. LC 89-17949. 256p. 1990. 32.00 (*0-87668-809-1*) Aronson.

Turning Points in Analytic Therapy: The Classic Cases. Gerald Schoenewolf. LC 89-17949. 256p. 1990. 35.00 (*0-87668-819-9*) Aronson.

Turning Points in Business Cycles. Leonard P. Ayres. LC 68-20527. (Reprints of Economic Classics Ser.). xii, 170p. 1969. reprint ed. 35.00 (*0-678-00453-6*) Kelley.

Turning Points in Cataract Formation, Syndromes & Retinoblastoma. Ed. by W. Straub. (Developments in Ophthalmology Ser.: Vol. 7). (Illus.). viii, 100p. 1982. 75.25 (*3-8055-3564-3*) S Karger.

Turning Points in El Paso, Texas. Leon C. Metz. LC 85-60638. (Illus.). 128p. 1985. 19.95 (*0-930208-18-8*) Mangan Books TX.

Turning Points in History. Frederick E. Birkenhead. LC 78-86730. (Essay Index Reprint Ser.). 1977. 26.95 (*0-8369-1246-2*) Ayer.

***Turning Points in History, 4 bks.** Illus. by Robert R. Ingpen. (Turning Points in History Ser.). 96p. (YA). (gr. 5 up). 79.80 (*0-7910-2760-0*) Chelsea Hse.

Turning Points in History. Frederick E. Smith. (Essay Index Reprint Ser.). (Illus.). 285p. 1982. reprint ed. lib. bdg. 23.50 (*0-8290-0805-5*) Irvington.

Turning Points in Life. Frederick Arnold. LC 72-4480. (Essay Index Reprint Ser.). 1977. reprint ed. 24.95 (*0-8369-2934-9*) Ayer.

Turning Points in Middle School: Strategic Transitions for Educators. Mary Gallagher-Polite et al. (Illus.). 144p. 1996. 44.00 (*0-8039-6295-9*) Corwin Pr.

Turning Points in Middle School: Strategic Transitions for Educators. Mary Gallagher-Polite et al. (Illus.). 144p. 1996. pap. 20.00 (*0-8039-6296-7*) Corwin Pr.

Turning Points in Modern Times: Essays on German & European History. Karl D. Bracher. Tr. by Thomas Dunlap. LC 94-34988. 352p. 1995. text ed. 49.95 (*0-674-91353-1*, BRATUX); pap. text ed. 24.95 (*0-674-91354-X*, BRATUX) HUP.

Turning Points in Religious Studies. Ursula King. 1996. 44.95 (*0-567-09564-9*) Bks Intl VA.

***Turning Points in Religious Studies.** Ursula King. 272p. 1996. pap. 25.95 (*0-567-08534-1*, Pub. by T & T Clark UK) Bks Intl VA.

Turning Points in Retinal Surgery: Proceedings of the Jules Gorin Club Meeting, Lausanne, June 1976. Gorin, Jules, Club Staff. Ed. by E. W. Norton et al. (Modern Problems in Ophthalmology Ser.: Vol. 18). (Illus.). 1977. 196.00 (*3-8055-2425-0*) S Karger.

Turning Points in Social Security: From "Cruel Hoax" to "Sacred Entitlement" Sheryl R. Tynes. LC 95-18238. 284p. 1996. 39.50 (*0-8047-2579-9*) Stanford U Pr.

***Turning Points in Western Technology.** Cardwell. 256p. 1972. pap. text ed. 8.95 (*0-614-18188-7*, Sci Hist) Watson Pub Intl.

Turning Points in World History, 5 bks. 1991. pap. 39.75 (*0-382-24134-7*); Set. lib. bdg. 74.75 (*0-382-24128-2*) Silver Burdett Pr.

Turning Points Management Guide High School. Addison-Wesley Staff. (Turning Points Ser.). (Illus.). 40p. 1989. pap. text ed. 12.95 (*0-201-19718-9*) Addison-Wesley.

Turning Points Management Guide Middle School. Addison-Wesley Staff. (Illus.). 32p. 1989. pap. text ed. 12.95 (*0-201-19717-0*) Addison-Wesley.

Turning Points of the Civil War. James A. Rawley. LC 89-4873. xvi, 230p. 1989. pap. 9.95 (*0-8032-8935-9*, Bison Books) U of Nebr Pr.

Turning Points of the New Phenomenological Era: Husserl Research Drawing upon the Full Extent of His Development. Ed. by Anna-Teresa Tymieniecka. 584p. (C). 1991. lib. bdg. 213.50 (*0-7923-1134-5*, Pub. by Klwr Acad Pubs NE) Kluwer Ac.

Turning Points One. Giuliano Iantorno & Mario Papa. (Illus.). 128p. 1989. pap. text ed. 14.24 (*0-201-52151-2*) Addison-Wesley.

Turning Points Placement Test Package. J. Michael O'Malley & Anna U. Chamot. (Turning Points Ser.). (Illus.). 80p. 1989. pap. text ed. 34.50 (*0-201-52169-5*) Addison-Wesley.

Turning Points Placement Tests. Mario Papa. 80p. 1995. pap. write for info. (*0-201-53804-0*) Addison-Wesley.

Turning Points Three. Giuliano Iantorno & Mario Papa. (Illus.). 128p. 1989. pap. text ed. 14.24 (*0-201-52157-1*) Addison-Wesley.

Turning Points Two. Giuliano Iantorno & Mario Papa. (Illus.). 128p. 1989. pap. text ed. 14.24 (*0-201-52154-7*) Addison-Wesley.

***Turning Points 1A.** Mario Papa. 1988. pap. text ed. 6.31 (*0-201-19012-5*) Addison-Wesley.

***Turning Points 1A.** 2nd ed. Mario Papa. 1994. wbk. ed., ring bd. 4.24 (*0-201-76521-7*) Addison-Wesley.

***Turning Points 1B.** 2nd ed. Mario Papa. 1994. wbk. ed., ring bd. 4.24 (*0-201-76522-5*) Addison-Wesley.

***Turning Points 2.** 2nd ed. Mario Papa. 1994. wbk. ed., ring bd. 8.40 (*0-201-53819-9*) Addison-Wesley.

***Turning Points 2A.** Mario Papa. 1986. wbk. ed., ring bd. 3.72 (*0-201-19024-9*) Addison-Wesley.

***Turning Points 2A.** 2nd ed. Mario Papa. 1994. student ed., pap. text ed. 6.36 (*0-201-76523-3*); wbk. ed., ring bd. 4.24 (*0-201-76525-X*) Addison-Wesley.

***Turning Points 2B.** Mario Papa. 1986. wbk. ed., ring bd. 3.72 (*0-201-19025-7*) Addison-Wesley.

***Turning Points 2B.** Mario Papa. 1988. pap. text ed. 6.31 (*0-201-19015-X*) Addison-Wesley.

***Turning Points 2B.** 2nd ed. Mario Papa. 1994. student ed., pap. text ed. 6.36 (*0-201-76524-1*); wbk. ed., ring bd. 4.24 (*0-201-76526-8*) Addison-Wesley.

***Turning Points 3.** 2nd ed. Mario Papa. 1994. student ed., pap. text ed. 12.72 (*0-201-53822-9*); wbk. ed., ring bd. 8.40 (*0-201-53823-7*) Addison-Wesley.

***Turning Points 3A.** 2nd ed. Mario Papa. 1994. student ed., pap. text ed. 6.36 (*0-201-76527-6*); ring bd. 4.24 (*0-201-76529-2*) Addison-Wesley.

***Turning Points 3B.** 2nd ed. Mario Papa. 1994. student ed., pap. text ed. 6.36 (*0-201-76528-4*); wbk. ed., ring bd. 4.24 (*0-201-76530-6*) Addison-Wesley.

***Turning Points 4.** rev. ed. Mario Papa. 1989. wbk. ed., ring bd. 7.10 (*0-201-52680-8*) Addison-Wesley.

***Turning Points 4.** 2nd ed. Mario Papa. 1994. student ed., pap. text ed. 12.72 (*0-201-53826-1*); wbk. ed., ring bd. 8.40 (*0-201-53827-X*) Addison-Wesley.

***Turning Points 4A.** 2nd ed. Mario Papa. 1994. pap. text ed. 6.36 (*0-201-76531-4*); wbk. ed., ring bd. 4.24 (*0-201-76533-0*) Addison-Wesley Educ.

Turning Problem Employees into Successes. Carol C. Smith. 80p. 1992. pap. 10.95 (*1-56246-029-3*, P184) Johnsn Inst.

***Turning Problems into Praise.** Marshall L. Hoffman. LC 96-61786. 128p. (Orig.). 1997. pap. 8.99 (*1-883893-85-2*) WinePress Pub.

Turning Professors into Teachers: A New Approach to Faculty Development & Student Learning. Joseph Katz & Mildred Henry. LC 92-45049. (American Council on Education-Oryx Press Series on Higher Education). 192p. 1988. boxed 27.95 (*0-89774-803-4*) Oryx Pr.

Turning Projects. Richard Raffan. (Illus.). 176p. 1991. pap. text ed. 21.95 (*0-942391-38-1*) Taunton.

Turning Promises into Performance: The Management Challenge of Implementing Workfare. Richard P. Nathan. LC 92-42821. 160p. (C). 1993. pap. 15.50 (*0-231-07963-X*); text ed. 49.50 (*0-231-07962-1*) Col U Pr.

Turning Research & Development into Profits: A Systematic Approach. Attilio Bisio & Lawrence Gastwirt. LC 78-10239. 287p. reprint ed. pap. 81.80 (*0-317-27063-X*, 2023541) Bks Demand.

Turning Right: The Making of the Rehnquist Supreme Court. David G. Savage. LC 91-43263. 480p. 1992. text ed. 22.95 (*0-471-53660-1*) Wiley.

Turning Right: The Making of the Rehnquist Supreme Court. David G. Savage. 480p. 1993. pap. text ed. 14.95 (*0-471-59553-5*) Wiley.

Turning Right in the Sixties: The Conservative Capture of the GOP. Mary C. Brennan. LC 95-11799. 224p. 1995. 29.95 (*0-8078-2230-2*) U of NC Pr.

Turning Sales over to the Pros: Fourteen CPA Firms Share Their Experiences. Colette P. Nassutti. LC 96-14161. 1996. write for info. (*0-87051-178-5*) Am Inst CPA.

Turning Senility Misery into Victory. Leonard D. Orr. 1990. 10.00 (*0-945793-17-0*) Inspir Univ.

Turning Setbacks into Comebacks. John Nicols. 75p. (Orig.). (C). pap. text ed. 4.99 (*0-940487-15-2*) Omega Pubns OR.

Turning Sights in a Circular Driveway. Stacey Sollfrey. (Illus.). 32p. (Orig.). 1989. pap. 3.00 (*0-926935-24-0*) Runaway Spoon.

Turning Snow & Company. John Casti. 25.00 (*0-06-016887-0*, HarpT) HarpC.

***Turning Stones: My Days & Nights.** Marc Parent. 1998. pap. write for info. (*0-449-91235-3*) Fawcett.

Turning Stones: My Days & Nights with Children at Risk. Marc Parent. 366p. 1996. 25.00 (*0-15-100204-5*) HarBrace.

Turning Strategy into Action. Ed. by Ken Irons. (Best of Long Range Planning Ser.: No. 9). 144p. 1991. pap. text ed. 47.00 (*0-08-040667-X*, Pergamon Pr) Elsevier.

Turning Students on to Science: High-Interest, Hands-on Activities for Grades 4-8. Dorothea Allen. 308p. 1991. 24.95 (*0-87628-906-5*) P-H.

Turning Sweden Around. Assar Lindbeck et al. (Illus.). 180p. 1994. 32.50 (*0-262-12181-6*) MIT Pr.

Turning Swords into Plowshares: Defense Conversion. Michael Ryan et al. (Pew Case Studies in International Affairs). 50p. (C). 1995. pap. text ed. 3.50 (*1-56927-713-3*, GU Schl Foreign) Geo U Inst Dplmcy.

Turning Teaching into Learning: The Role of Student Responsibility in the Collegiate Experience. Todd M. Davis & Patricia H. Murrell. Ed. & Frwd. by Jonathan D. Fife. (ASHE-ERIC Higher Education Reports: No. 8). 97p. (Orig.). 1994. pap. 18.00 (*1-878380-29-X*) GWU Grad Schl E&HD.

Turning Technology: Engine & Turret Lathes. Stephen F. Krar & J. William Oswald. LC 78-153723. (C). 1971. pap. 25.95 (*0-8273-0206-1*) Delmar.

Turning the Century: Feminist Theory in the 1990s. Ed. by Glynis Carr. LC 92-8980. (Review Ser.: Vol. 36, No. 2). 200p. (C). 1992. 22.00 (*0-8387-5241-1*) Bucknell U Pr.

Turning the Gorgon: A Meditation on Shame. Sandra Edelman. 184p. (Orig.). 1996. pap. 18.50 (*0-88214-514-2*) Spring Jrnl.

***Turning the Legislative Thumbscrew: Minority Rights & Procedural Change in Legislative Politics.** Douglas Dion. LC 97-22819. (C). 1997. 49.50 (*0-472-10820-4*) U of Mich Pr.

Turning the Map: Images from the Americas. Camerawork Ltd. Staff. 90p. (C). 1990. 75.00 (*1-871103-04-5*, Pub. by Camerawork UK) St Mut.

***Turning the Mask.** Kerry S. Keys. 36p. 1997. pap. 6.00 (*0-930502-32-9*) Pine Pr.

***Turning the Page Without Closing the Book: The Right to Truth in the Irish Conflict.** Ed. by Bill Rolston. 48p. (Orig.). 1996. pap. 7.95 (*0-614-18873-3*, Pub. by Beyond the Pale IE); pap. 7.95 (*0-614-24336-X*, Pub. by Beyond the Pale IE) Irish Bks Media.

Turning the Sod: How a Pioneer Family Established a Homestead on the Prairie. Lawrence Kruger. (Illus.). 8p. (Orig.). 1993. pap. text ed. 12.95 (*1-878853-20-1*) Venture Pr FL.

Turning the Soul: Teaching Through Conversation in the High School. Sophie Haroutunian-Gordon. LC 90-43533. 224p. 1991. pap. text ed. 17.95 (*0-226-31676-9*) U Ch Pr.

Turning the Soul: Teaching Through Conversation in the High School. Sophie Haroutunian-Gordon. LC 90-43533. 224p. 1991. lib. bdg. 52.00 (*0-226-31675-0*) U Ch Pr.

***Turning the Stones.** Rufus Collinson. (Chapbook Ser.: No. 5). 40p. (Orig.). 1997. pap. 8.95 (*0-9649463-4-3*) Folly Cove.

Turning the Tables. Barbara Cameron. LC 84-71622. 128p. 1984. 13.00 (*0-86690-282-1*, C2559-014) Am Fed Astrologers.

Turning the Tables: A Machiavellian Strategy for Dealing with Japan. Daniel Burstein. 256p. 1993. 22.00 (*0-671-78953-8*) S&S Trade.

Turning the Tables: Using Japanese Techniques for Implementing A.I. in the U. S. A. Richard T. Greene. 1987. 19.95 (*0-317-65779-8*) McGraw.

Turning the Tables on Las Vegas. Ian Andersen. 1978. pap. 8.00 (*0-394-72509-3*, Vin) Random.

Turning the Thing Around: An NCAA Championship & Two Super Bowl Wins-Now Will You Leave Me Alone? Jimmy Johnson. (Illus.). 336p. 1994. pap. 14.95 (*0-7868-8077-5*) Hyperion.

Turning the Thing Around: Pulling America's Team Out of the Dumps - & Myself Out of the Doghouse. Jimmy Johnson. LC 93-24918. 304p. 1993. 22.95 (*1-56282-725-1*) Hyperion.

Turning the Tide. Noam Chomsky. 330p. 36.95 (*0-920057-90-X*, Pub. by Black Rose Bks CN); pap. 16.95 (*0-920057-91-8*, Pub. by Black Rose Bks CN) Consort Bk Sales.

***Turning the Tide.** Noam Chomsky. 1996. 48.99 (*0-920057-78-0*, Pub. by Black Rose Bks CN) Consort Bk Sales.

Turning the Tide. Bartie Jones. (Illus.). 60p. (Orig.). 1983. pap. 3.00 (*0-9618702-2-2*) Barth Pub.

Turning the Tide. Malcom Smith. 1995. pap. text ed. 4.99 (*1-880089-25-4*) Albury Pub.

Turning the Tide: Early Los Angeles Modernists, 1920-1956. Paul Karlstrom. 168p. 1990. 24.95 (*0-89951-076-0*) Santa Barb Mus Art.

Turning the Tide: Saving the Chesapeake Bay. Tom Horton & William Eichbaum. LC 91-8586. (Illus.). 321p. (Orig.). 1991. 22.95 (*1-55963-101-5*); pap. 16.95 (*1-55963-100-7*) Island Pr.

Turning the Tide: Strategic Planning for Labor Unions. David Weil. LC 93-36649. (Emerging Issues in Employee Relations Ser.). 319p. 45.00 (*0-02-934065-9*, Free Press) Free Pr.

Turning the Tide: U. S. Intervention in Central America & the Struggle for Peace. Noam Chomsky. LC 85-27940. 298p. (Orig.). 1985. 35.00 (*0-89608-267-9*); pap. 16.00 (*0-89608-266-0*) South End Pr.

Turning the Tide on Trash: A Learning Guide on Marine Debris. (Illus.). 78p. (Orig.). (YA). (gr. 7-12). 1994. pap. text ed. 25.00 (*0-7881-0392-X*) DIANE Pub.

Turning the Tide on Trash: A Learning Guide on Marine Debris. 1996. lib. bdg. 250.95 (*0-8490-5968-2*) Gordon Pr.

Turning the Wheel: American Women Creating the New Buddhism. Sandy Boucher. LC 93-16630. (Illus.). 400p. 1993. pap. 16.00 (*0-8070-7305-9*) Beacon Pr.

Turning the World Inside Out & 174 Other Simple Physics Demonstrations. Robert Ehrlich. (Illus.). 242p. (Orig.). 1990. pap. text ed. 16.95 (*0-691-02395-6*) Princeton U Pr.

Turning the World Upside Down: The Anti-Slavery Convention of American Women Held in New York City, May 9-12, 1837. Ed. by Dorothy Sterling. LC 87-1. (Illus.). 32p. (Orig.). 1987. pap. 2.95 (*0-935312-78-1*) Feminist Pr.

Turning Them Around: Developing Motivation, Responsibility, & Self-Discipline in At-Risk Youth. Vicki Phillips. (Illus.). 296p. (Orig.). 1996. pap. 49.95 (*0-9628482-8-X*) Prsnl Dev.

Turning Things Around: A Women's Occupational & Environmental Health Resource Guide. Lin Nelson et al. (Illus.). 162p. (Orig.). 1990. pap. 12.95 (*0-939522-01-2*) Nat Womens Hlth Netwk.

Turning Things over. Edward V. Lucas. LC 72-107723. (Essay Index Reprint Ser.). 1977. 19.95 (*0-8369-1524-0*) Ayer.

Turning Tide. Pat Robertson. 334p. 1995. mass mkt. 5.99 (*0-8499-3694-2*) Word Pub.

Turning Tide: From the Desegregation of the Armed Forces to the Montgomery Bus Boycott (1948-1956) Ed. by Darlene C. Hine et al. (Milestones in Black American History Ser.). (Illus.). 144p. (YA). (gr. 5 up). 1995. lib. bdg. 19.95 (*0-7910-2255-2*) Chelsea Hse.

T

*Turning Tide: From the Desegregation of the Armed Forces to the Montgomery Bus Boycott (1948-1956) Ed. by Darlene C. Hine et al. (Milestones in Black American History Ser.). (Illus.). 144p. (YA). (gr. 5 up). 1995. pap. 8.95 (0-7910-2681-7) Chelsea Hse.

Turning Tides: Translations of Twentieth Century Dutch Poetry: A Bilingual Anthology. Peter Van De Kamp. 424p. pap. 17.95 (0-934257-70-1) Story Line.

Turning to Christ: A Theology of Evangelization & Renewal. Urban T. Holmes. LC 94-31671. 250p. 1994. pap. 13.95 (1-56101-098-7) Cowley Pubns.

Turning to Technology: A Strategic Plan for the Nineties. Southern Technology Council Staff. Ed. by Robert Donnan. 78p. 1989. pap. text ed. 10.00 (0-927364-00-X) Southern Growth.

Turning to the Source: An Eastern View of Western Mind - Using Insight Meditation & Psychotherapy for Personal Growth, Health & Wholeness. V. Dhiravamsa. LC 90-47087. 256p. (Orig.). 1990. 19.95 (0-931892-20-1) B Dolphin Pub.

Turning to Torah: The Emerging Noachide Movement. Kimberly E. Hanke. LC 95-18664. 272p. 1995. pap. 25.00 (1-56821-500-2) Aronson.

Turning to Wheels: An Integrated Activity Unit. Ed Catherall & Bev McKay. (Illus.). 32p. 1993. pap. text ed. 4.95 (0-86530-237-5) Incentive Pubns.

Turning Toward Freedom. David Jeremiah. (Turning Point Ser.). 240p. (Orig.). 1997. pap. 9.99 (1-56476-124-X, Victor Bks) Chariot Victor.

Turning Toward Happiness: Conversations with a Zen Teacher & Her Students. Ed. by Sara Jenkins. 168p. 1991. pap. 8.95 (0-9630784-0-2) Present Perf.

Turning Toward Home: Reflections on the Family from Harper's Magazine. Ed. by Katharine Whittemore & Ilena Silverman. (American Retrospective Ser.: Vol. 2). 1993. Acid-free paper. 21.95 (1-879957-09-4, Franklin Sq Pr); Acid-free paper. pap. 14.95 (1-879957-08-6, Franklin Sq Pr) Harpers Mag Found.

Turning Toward Integrity. David Jeremiah. (Turning Point Ser.). 192p. (Orig.). 1993. pap. 9.99 (1-56476-070-7, 6-3070, Victor Bks) Chariot Victor.

Turning Toward Jesus: A Video & Study Resource for New Believers. Jerry L. Holsopple. 120p. 149.95 incl. vdisk (1-877736-16-3) MB Missions.

Turning Toward Joy. David Jeremiah. (Turning Point Ser.). 240p. (Orig.). 1992. pap. 9.99 (1-56476-009-X, 6-3009, Victor Bks) Chariot Victor.

Turning Toward Morning. Joe Cardillo. 64p. 1986. reprint ed. 19.95 (0-89002-237-2); reprint ed. pap. 6.95 (0-89002-236-4) Northwoods Pr.

Turning Toward the World: The Pivotal Years. Thomas Merton & Victor A. Kramer. LC 96-16561. (Journals of Thomas Merton). 469p. 1996. 30.00 (0-06-065480-5); pap. 14.00 (0-06-065481-3) Harper SF.

Turning Troubled Kids Around: The Complete Student Assistance Program for Secondary Schools: An Easy to Use Manual for Busy Educators. Johnson Institute Staff. LC 93-20033. 250p. 1993. pap. 39.95 (1-56246-062-5, P237) Johnsn Inst.

Turning Troubles into Triumphs. J. K. Patterson. LC 88-62641. 144p. (Orig.). 1988. pap. 7.95 (1-55725-003-0) Paraclete MA.

Turning Two. 1982. 60.00 (0-685-05805-0) St Mut.

Turning up the Heat: MI5 after the Cold War. Larry O'Hara. 96p. (Orig.). 1994. pap. 10.95 (0-948984-29-5, Pub. by Phoenix Pr UK) AK Pr Dist.

Turning up the Volume on International Radio. Ed. by Michael O. Garcia. 261p. (Orig.). 1991. pap. text ed. 10.00 (0-89206-197-9) CSI Studies.

Turning Vision into Action. George Barna. LC 96-8076. 1996. pap. 11.99 (0-8307-1866-4, 5422895) Regal.

Turning Wheel: A Study of Contracts & Oaths in Wagner's Ring. David A. White. LC 87-42795. 136p. 1988. 24.50 (0-941664-89-9) Susquehanna.

Turning Wood with Richard Raffan. Richard Raffan. LC 84-52130. (Illus.). 176p. 1985. pap. 19.95 (0-918804-24-8) Taunton.

Turning Wooden Jewelry. Judith A. Ditmer. Ed. by Douglas Congdon-Martin. LC 94-65631. (Illus.). 64p. (Orig.). 1994. pap. 12.95 (0-88740-611-4) Schiffer.

Turning Wool into a Cottage Industry. rev. ed. Paula Simmons. Ed. by Gwen Steege. LC 91-50000. (Illus.). 192p. (Orig.). 1991. pap. 14.95 (0-88266-685-1, Storey Pub) Storey Comm Inc.

Turning Word: American Literary Modernism & Continental Theory. Joseph N. Riddel. 192p. 1996. text ed. 36.50 (0-8122-3378-6); pap. text ed. 16.50 (0-8122-1600-8) U of Pa Pr.

Turning Yellow Pages to Gold: Secrets to More Business at Lower Cost from Yellow Pages Advertising. Thomas G. Foster. Ed. by Edward T. Foster. (Illus.). 197p. (Orig.). 1995. pap. text ed. 39.95 (0-9648915-0-6) T & E Pubng.

Turning Your Adversity into Victory. Jerry Savelle. 128p. 1994. pap. 6.99 (0-89274-909-1, HH-909) Harrison Hse.

Turning Your Great Idea into a Great Success: How to Develop, License, Protect, & Promote Your Product Idea. Judy Ryder. LC 94-45493. 256p. (Orig.). 1995. pap. 14.95 (1-56079-462-3, Petersons Pacesetter) Petersons.

Turning Your Human Resources Department into a Profit Center. Michael W. Mercer. LC 88-48024. 265p. 1989. 59.95 (0-8144-5841-6) AMACOM.

Turning Your Teen Around: How a Couple Helped Their Troubled Son While Keeping Their Marriage... Betsy T. White. 30p. 1996. pap. text ed. 11.95 (0-9615995-5-3) Recover Comns.

*Turning Your Trauma into Triumph - Eight Practical Steps: Personal Insights from a Near Death Experience. Jerry Brecheisen. (Illus.). 127p. 1996. 12.95 (0-89827-162-2, BK938) Wesleyan Pub Hse.

Turning Your Vision to Success. David A. Fitch. Ed. by Grace Lessner. 80p. 1986. pap. 7.98 (0-9616406-0-X) Visions Success.

Turning Your World Right Side Up. Jim Smoke. 1995. pap. 10.99 (1-56179-404-X) Focus Family.

Turning Yourself Around: Self-Help for Troubled Teens. Kendall Johnson. LC 92-4477. 224p. (YA). (gr. 7-12). 1992. pap. 11.95 (0-89793-092-4) Hunter Hse.

Turning Yourself Around: Self-Help for Troubled Teens. Kendall Johnson. 224p. 1991. reprint ed. lib. bdg. 29.00 (0-8095-6327-4) Borgo Pr.

Turnings of Darkness & Light: Essays in Philosophical & Systematic Theology. Kenneth Surin. 352p. 1989. text ed. 85.00 (0-521-34159-0) Cambridge U Pr.

Turnip. Walter J. De La Mare. LC 92-6191. (Illus.). (J). 1992. 18.95 (0-87923-934-4) Godine.

Turnip. Illus. & Retold by Pierr Morgan. 32p. (J). (ps-1). 1996. pap. 5.95 (0-698-11426-4, Paperstar) Putnam Pub Group.

Turnip. Illus. by Laura Radar. (Easy-to-Read Classics Ser.). 32p. (J). (ps-3). 1996. pap. 11.99 (0-670-86053-0, Viking) Viking Child Bks.

Turnip. Harriet Ziefert. (Easy-to-Read Ser.: Level 1). (Illus.). 32p. (J). (ps-2). 1996. pap. 3.50 (0-14-038082-5, Puffin) Puffin Bks.

Turnip. Harriet Ziefert. Date not set. pap. 3.99 (0-14-055545-5) NAL-Dutton.

*Turnip-Head. Frances M. Hendry. LC 94-79401. (Ten-Minute Mysteries Ser.). 32p. (YA). (gr. 6-12). 1994. pap. 2.95 (0-7854-0849-5, 40778) Am Guidance.

*Turnip-Head Readalong. Frances M. Hendry. LC 94-79401. (Ten-Minute Mysteries Ser.). 32p. 1994. pap. 12.95 incl. audio (0-7854-1058-9, 40780) Am Guidance.

Turnip Soup. Lynne B. Myers & Christopher A. Myers. LC 93-11744. (Illus.). 32p. (J). (ps-2). 1994. 13.95 (1-56282-445-7); lib. bdg. 13.89 (1-56282-446-5) Hyprn Child.

Turnip's Blood. Cassin Maxine. Ed. by Everette Maddox et al. (Illus.). 112p. (Orig.). 1985. pap. 15.00 (0-9614371-0-3) Sisters Grim Pr.

Turnley, the Turnleys: A Brief Record, Biographic & Narrative, of Some Turnleys in the U. S. & Europe. P. T. Turnley. (Illus.). 298p. 1991. reprint ed. pap. 46.50 (0-8328-1739-2); reprint ed. lib. bdg. 56.50 (0-8328-1738-4) Higginson Bk Co.

Turnover & Recruitment in the Maquila Industry: Causes & Solutions. Edward J. Williams & John T. Passe-Smith. 59p. (Orig.). (C). 1989. pap. text ed. 10.00 (0-937795-10-0) Border Res Inst.

Turnpike Roads. Geoffrey Wright. 1989. pap. 25.00 (0-7478-0155-X, Pub. by Shire UK) St Mut.

Turnpikes of New England. abr. ed. Frederic J. Wood. (Illus.). 432p. 1997. pap. write for info. (0-942147-05-7) Branch Line Pr.

Turnpikes of New England, & the Evolution of the Same Throughout England, Virginia & Maryland. Frederick J. Wood. (Illus.). 461p. 1995. reprint ed. lib. bdg. 49.00 (0-8328-4600-7) Higginson Bk Co.

*Turns. John Matthias. Date not set. pap. 14.95 (0-85646-023-0, Pub. by Anvil Press UK) Dufour.

*Turns of Thought: Teaching Composition As Reflexive Inquiry. Donna Qualley. LC 97-2906. (Orig.). (C). 1997. pap. text ed. write for info. (0-86709-418-4, 0418) Boynton Cook Pubs.

Turnspeak. Thomas E. Steele. Ed. by M. B. Steele. 36p. (Orig.). 1988. pap. 1.95 (0-939497-13-1) Promise Pub.

Turnspit Dog. Pamela Gillilan. (Illus.). 64p. 9300. pap. 16.95 (1-85224-144-6, Pub. by Bloodaxe Bks UK) Dufour.

*Turnstile Justice. Alleman & Gido. 1997. pap. text ed. 38.00 (0-13-301227-1) P-H.

Turnstile Maintainer. Jack Rudman. (Career Examination Ser.: C-825). 1994. pap. 23.95 (0-8373-0825-9) Nat Learn.

Turntable Illusions: Kinetic Optical Illusions for Your Record Turntable. John Kremer. (Illus.). 96p. (Orig.). 1992. pap. 9.95 (0-912411-37-6) Open Horizons.

*Turok: Acclaim Adventure Zone. Evan Skolnick. (Acclaim Adventure Zone Ser.). 1997. pap. text ed. 4.50 (1-57840-081-3) Acclaim Bks.

*Turok: Dinosaur Hunter: The Official Strategy Guide. Bart Farkas. 144p. 1997. per. 12.99 (0-7615-1060-5) Prima Pub.

Turolian Fauna from the Island of Samos, Greece. N. Solounias. (Contributions to Vertebrate Evolution Ser.: Vol. 6). (Illus.). xvi, 232p. 1981. pap. 39.25 (3-8055-2692-X) S Karger.

Turover Aid Society of Detroit. Jeffrey N. Borin. 144p. per. write for info. (0-318-68936-7) Harlo Pr.

Turpin Francais, dit le Turpin I: Edition Critique. Ed. by Ronald N. Walpole. (Medieval Texts & Translations Ser.: No. 3). 276p. (FRE.). 1985. 50.00 (0-8020-2536-6) U of Toronto Pr.

Turquoise. Anya Seton. 1995. reprint ed. lib. bdg. 36.95 (1-56849-652-4) Buccaneer Bks.

Turquoise: The Gem of the Centuries. Oscar T. Branson. LC 77-358470. (Illus.). 64p. 1975. pap. 11.95 (0-918080-01-0) Treas Chest Bks.

Turquoise & Six-Guns: The Story of Cerrillos, New Mexico. 3rd ed. Marc Simmons. LC 85-30350. (Illus.). 64p. 1993. pap. 6.95 (0-86534-082-X) Sunstone Pr.

Turquoise Boy. Terri Cohlene. (Native American Legends Ser.). (Illus.). 48p. (J). (gr. 4-8). 1990. lib. bdg. 19.93 (0-86593-003-1); lib. bdg. 14.95 (0-685-36335-X) Rourke Corp.

Turquoise Boy: A Navajo Legend. Terri Cohlene. 48p. (J). (gr. 4-7). 1996. pap. 4.95 (0-8167-2360-5) Troll Communs.

Turquoise Brooch. large type ed. Joan Terry. 1995. 25.99 (0-7089-3357-2) Ulverscroft.

Turquoise Day. 1990. pap. 4.50 (0-8216-5081-5, Univ Books) Carol Pub Group.

Turquoise Jewelry. Nancy Schiffer. LC 90-61801. (Illus.). 64p. (Orig.). 1990. pap. 9.95 (0-88740-262-3) Schiffer.

Turquoise Jewelry of the Indians of the Southwest. Edna M. Bennett & John F. Bennett. (Illus.). 1973. 21.00 (0-917834-01-1) Turquoise Bks.

Turquoise Lament. John D. MacDonald. 256p. 1987. mass mkt. 5.99 (0-449-13249-8) Fawcett.

Turquoise Lament. John D. Macdonald. 1996. mass mkt. 5.99 (0-449-22478-3, Crest) Fawcett.

Turquoise Mask. Phyllis A. Whitney. 1981. mass mkt. 5.99 (0-449-23470-3, Crest) Fawcett.

Turquoise Ridge & Late Prehistoric Residential Mobility in the Desert Mogollon Region. Michael E. Whalen. LC 93-35601. (Anthropological Papers: No. 118). (Illus.). 176p. (C). 1994. pap. text ed. 27.50 (0-87480-436-1) U of Utah Pr.

Turquoise Sun. Linda P. Sandifer. 384p. 1997. mass mkt. 4.99 (0-8217-5541-2, Zebra Kensgtn) Kensgtn Pub Corp.

Turquoise Tattoo. Nancy B. Jacobs. 1992. reprint ed. mass mkt. 4.99 (0-671-75535-8) PB.

Turquoise Trail. Shirley Seifert. 1976. reprint ed. lib. bdg. 27.95 (0-89190-140-X, Rivercity Pr) Amereon Ltd.

Turquoise Trail: Native American Jewelry of the Southwest. Photos by Jeffrey J. Foxx. LC 93-20114. (Illus.). 1993. 49.50 (0-8109-3869-3) Abrams.

Turra Coo: A Legal Episode in the Popular Culture of North-East Scotland. Alexander Fenton. (Illus.). 80p. 1989. pap. 8.00 (0-08-037729-7, 3507, Pub. by Aberdeen U Pr) Macmillan.

*Turret Lathe Methods Applied to Small Lot Gear Production. J. R. Longstreet. (Technical Papers). 1939. pap. text ed. 30.00 (1-55589-447-X) AGMA.

Turrid Illustrations, Mainly Claibornian, No. 7 see Palaeontographica Americana: Vol. 2

*Turtle. Lenny Flank. LC 96-46119. (Owner's Guide to a Happy, Healthy Pet Ser.). 1997. 12.95 (0-87605-499-8) Howell Bk.

Turtle. David Hawcock. (Egg Pop-ups Ser.). (Illus.). 12p. (J). (ps-3). 1994. 3.95 (0-307-17305-4, Golden Books) Western Pub.

Turtle, Reading Level 3-4. Propper. (World Animal Library). (Illus.). 28p. (J). (gr. 2-5). 1983. lib. bdg. 16.67 (0-86592-856-8); lib. bdg. 12.50 (0-685-58828-9) Rourke Corp.

Turtle & Rabbit. (Illus.). (J). (ps-2). 1991. pap. 5.10 (0-8136-5586-2); lib. bdg. 7.95 (0-8136-5086-0) Modern Curr.

Turtle & the Monkey. Paul Galdone. (Illus.). 32p. (J). (ps-3). 1990. pap. 6.95 (0-395-54425-4, Clarion Bks) HM.

Turtle & the Moon. Charles Turner. LC 90-43841. (Illus.). 32p. (J). (ps-2). 1991. pap. 14.99 (0-525-44659-1) Dutton Child Bks.

Turtle & the Moon. Charles Turner. (Illus.). 32p. (J). 1996. pap. 4.99 (0-14-055812-8) Puffin Bks.

Turtle & the Oak. Ewart A. Autry & Lola M. Autry. 104p. 1992. pap. 7.95 (0-9602806-2-6) Whippoorwill.

*Turtle & the Stork. abr. large type ed. Kambiz-Azordegan. (Tootee's Magical Stories Ser.: Vol. 9). (Illus.). 34p. (J). (gr. 1-3). 1997. write for info. (1-890571-33-4) Parrot Prod.

Turtle & Tortoise. Vincent Serventy. LC 84-15881. (Animals in the Wild Ser.). (Illus.). 24p. (J). (gr. k-5). 1985. pap. 3.95 (0-8114-6891-7) Raintree Steck-V.

Turtle Baby. Abigail Padgett. 256p. 1996. mass mkt. 5.99 (0-446-40478-0, Mysterious Paperbk) Warner Bks.

*Turtle Baby. large type ed. Abigail Padgett. (Large Print Ser.). 496p. 1996. 25.99 (0-7089-3560-5) Ulverscroft.

*Turtle Bay. Saviour Pirotta. LC 96-31676. (Illus.). (J). 1997. write for info. (0-374-37888-6) FS&G.

Turtle Blessing: Poems. Penny Harter. 64p. (Orig.). 1996. pap. 11.00 (1-888809-01-9) La Alameda Pr.

Turtle Bogue: Afro-Caribbean Life & Culture in a Costa Rican Village. Harry G. Lefever. LC 90-50792. (Illus.). 256p. 1992. 39.50 (0-945636-23-7) Susquehanna U Pr.

Turtle Count. Illus. by Norman Gorbaty. 12p. (J). (ps). 1991. pap. 3.95 (0-671-74434-8, Litl Simon S&S) S&S Childrens.

*Turtle Creek Residence. Antoine Predock. 1997. pap. 19.95 (1-885254-48-2) Monacelli Pr.

Turtle Day. Douglas Florian. LC 88-30321. (Illus.). 32p. (J). (ps-2). 1989. lib. bdg. 14.89 (0-690-04745-2, Crowell Jr Bks) HarpC Child Bks.

Turtle Dream. Gerald Hausman. (Illus.). 128p. 1989. pap. 9.95 (0-933553-06-4) Mariposa Print Pub.

*Turtle Dreams: A Holiday Reader. Marion D. Bauer. LC 97-2213. (Illus.). 48p. (J). (gr. k-3). 1997. lib. bdg. 14.95 (0-8234-1322-5) Holiday.

Turtle Geometry: The Computer As a Medium for Exploring Mathematics. Harold Abelson & Andrea DiSessa. (Artificial Intelligence Ser.). (Illus.). 477p. 1986. 37.50 (0-262-01063-1); pap. 19.95 (0-262-51037-5) MIT Pr.

*Turtle Going Nowhere in the Plenty of Time: Native American Tales from the South- & Midwest/& Maria Posa (Healing Wings) Davis Many Voices Staff. (Illus.). 48p. (Orig.). (J). (gr. 4 up). 1996. pap. 7.95 (0-87961-244-4) Naturegraph.

Turtle in July. Marilyn Singer. LC 89-2745. (Illus.). 32p. (J). (gr. k-3). 1989. lib. bdg. 14.95 (0-02-782881-6, Mac Bks Young Read) S&S Childrens.

Turtle in July. 93th ed. 1993. pap. text ed. 10.00 (0-15-300340-5) HarBrace.

Turtle in July. Marilyn Singer. LC 93-14430. (Illus.). 32p. (J). (gr. k-3). 1994. reprint ed. pap. 4.95 (0-689-71805-5, Aladdin Paperbacks) S&S Childrens.

Turtle Island. Gary Snyder. LC 74-8542. (Illus.). 128p. 1974. pap. 8.95 (0-8112-0546-0, NDP381) New Directions.

Turtle Island. Gary Snyder. LC 93-20167. (Pocket Classics Ser.). 240p. 1993. reprint ed. pap. 6.00 (0-87773-952-8) Shambhala Pubns.

Turtle Island ABC: A Gathering of Native American Symbols. Gerald Hausman. LC 92-14982. (Illus.). 32p. (J). (gr. 1 up). 1994. 15.00 (0-06-021307-8) HarpC Child Bks.

Turtle Island Alphabet: A Lexicon of Native American Symbols & Culture. Gerald Hausman. (Illus.). 224p. 1992. 19.95 (0-312-07103-5) St Martin.

Turtle Island Alphabet: A Lexicon of Native American Symbols & Culture. Gerald Hausman. (Illus.). 204p. 1993. pap. 13.95 (0-312-09406-X) St Martin.

Turtle Islands: Balinese Ritual & the Green Turtle. Charles Lindsay. LC 94-60220. (Illus.). 124p. 1995. 39.50 (1-883489-10-5) Takarajima.

Turtle Knows Your Name. Ashley Bryan. LC 89-2. (Illus.). 32p. (J). (ps-2). 1989. lib. bdg. 14.95 (0-689-31578-3, Atheneum Bks Young) S&S Childrens.

Turtle Knows Your Name. Illus. & Retold by Ashley Bryan. LC 92-33553. 32p. (J). (ps-3). 1993. reprint ed. pap. 4.95 (0-689-71728-8, Aladdin Paperbacks) S&S Childrens.

Turtle Magic. Illus. by Ruth Young & Mitchell Rose. LC 89-61634. (Rhyme-Fingerplay-Puppet Bk.). 12p. (J). (ps-1). 1990. bds. 5.95 (1-877779-01-6) Schneider Educational.

Turtle Mazes: Educational Activity-Coloring Book. Peter M. Spizzirri. Ed. by Linda Spizzirri. (Illus.). 32p. (J). (gr. k-5). 1984. pap. 1.25 (0-86545-059-5) Spizzirri.

Turtle Meat & Other Stories. Joseph Bruchac. LC 92-54182. 144p. (Orig.). 1992. 18.95 (0-930100-48-4); pap. 10.95 (0-930100-49-2) Holy Cow.

Turtle Moon. Alice Hoffman. 304p. 1993. mass mkt. 6.99 (0-425-13699-X) Berkley Pub.

Turtle Moon. large type ed. Alice Hoffman. 344p. 1992. reprint ed. lib. bdg. 21.95 (1-56054-477-5) Thorndike Pr.

Turtle Moon. large type ed. Alice Hoffman. 344p. 1993. lib. bdg. 14.95 (1-56054-926-2) Thorndike Pr.

*Turtle Moon. Alice Hoffman. 288p. 1997. reprint ed. pap. 13.00 (0-425-16128-5, Berkley Trade) Berkley Pub.

Turtle Nest. Lola Schaefer. (Books for Young Learners). (Illus.). 16p. (Orig.). (J). (gr. k-2). 1996. pap. 5.00 (1-57274-026-4) R Owen Pubs.

*Turtle on a Fence Post. June R. Wood. 256p. (J). (gr. 4-8). 1997. 16.95 (0-399-23184-6, Putnam) Putnam Pub Group.

Turtle on a Post. Warren M. Hoffman. 165p. 1990. pap. 8.95 (0-940916-01-0) Daybreak Pr.

Turtle on a Summer Day. Frances Gilbert. LC 94-75988. (Illus.). 32p. (J). (ps-2). 1994. 14.95 (1-880851-15-6) Greene Bark Pr.

Turtle Paradise-Gahirmatha: (An Ecological Analysis & Conservation Strategy) Ed. by M. C. Dash & C. S. Kar. 300p. (C). 1990. 500.00 (81-85017-48-4, Pub. by Interprint II) St Mut.

Turtle Paths: 2-D Geometry. Douglas H. Clements et al. Ed. by Priscilla C. Samii et al. (Investigations in Number, Data, & Space Ser.). (Illus.). 171p. (Orig.). 1994. teacher ed., pap. 32.95 (0-86651-806-1, DS21244) Seymour Pubns.

*Turtle Paths: 2-D Geometry. rev. ed. Douglas H. Clements et al. Ed. by Catherine Anderson & Beverly Cory. (Investigations in Number, Data, & Space Ser.). (Illus.). 172p. (YA). (gr. 3 up). 1997. pap. text ed. 32.95 (1-57232-701-4, 43848) Seymour Pubns.

Turtle Quest. Piers Harper. LC 96-16136. (Illus.). 32p. (J). (gr. 3-6). 1997. 14.99 (1-56402-959-X) Candlewick Pr.

*Turtle Sky. Diane Averill. 26p. 1995. 5.00 (0-614-30117-3) Skydog OR.

Turtle Soup. Elizabeth Greene. LC 91-67766. (Illus.). 64p. (J). 1993. pap. 7.00 (1-56002-166-7, Univ Edtns) Aegina Pr.

*Turtle Spring. Deborah T. Zagwyn. LC 97-15608. 1998. write for info. (1-883672-53-8) Tricycle Pr.

Turtle Stickers. Christopher Santoro. (Illus.). (J). (gr. k-3). 1994. pap. 1.00 (0-486-27997-9) Dover.

Turtle Talk: Voices for a Sustainable Future. Judith Plant & Christopher Plant. (New Catalyst Bioregional Ser.). (Illus.). 144p. (Orig.). 1990. pap. 9.95 (0-86571-186-0); lib. bdg. 34.95 (0-86571-185-2) New Soc Pubs.

Turtle Tattoo: Timeless Tales for Finding & Fulfilling Your Dreams. Margaret O. Wolfson. 1996. 14.95 (1-882591-28-3) Nataraj Pub.

Turtle Teasers: Puzzles. Mike Bryce. 128p. (J). (gr. k up). 1991. pap. 4.95 (0-924771-34-8, Covered Brdge Pr) D C Press.

Turtle That Lost His Shell. Paul Levy. LC 95-75420. (Illus.). 24p. (J). (ps up). 1995. 5.95 (1-57064-048-3) Lyrick Pub.

Turtle, the Orphan see Hewitt Early Readers: Level II

Turtle Time. Jeanne Betancourt. 112p. 1985. pap. 2.50 (0-380-89675-3, Camelot) Avon.

*Turtle Time. Sandal Stoddard. 1997. pap. 4.95 (0-395-85157-2) HM.

Turtle Time. Sandol Stoddard. LC 93-39192. (Illus.). 32p. (J). (gr. k-3). 1995. 13.95 (0-395-56754-8) HM.

*Turtle Was Gone a Long Time: Crossing the Kedron. John Moriarty. 242p. 9700. 34.95 (1-874675-63-5) Dufour.

*Turtle Was Gone a Long Time: The Horeshead Nebula Neighing. John Moriarty. 288p. 1997. 39.95 (1-874675-90-2) Dufour.

Turtle Watchers. Pamela Powell. 128p. (J). (gr. 3-7). 1994. pap. 3.99 (0-14-037077-3) Puffin Bks.

Turtle Watchers. Pamela Powell. LC 92-5822. 160p. (J). (gr. 3-7). 1992. pap. 13.00 (0-670-84294-X) Viking Child Bks.

Turtle Who Lost His Shell. Paul Levy. Ed. by Margie Larsen. LC 95-75420. (Barney Book & Tape Ser.). (Illus.). 24p. (J). (ps-3). 1996. pap. 6.95 incl. audio (1-57064-096-3) Lyrick Pub.

An Asterisk (*) at the beginning of an entry indicates that the title is appearing in BIP for the first time.

Turtle Who Wanted to Run. J. Grey. LC 68-56813. (Illus.). 32p. (J). (gr. 1-3). 1968. lib. bdg. 9.95 (*0-87783-045-2*) Oddo.

Turtleons Are Coming. Jean-Pierre Maury. (I Love to Read Collection). (Illus.). 46p. (J). (gr. 2-4). 1990. lib. bdg. 12.79 (*0-89565-810-0*) Childs World.

Turtles. Timothy L. Biel. (Zoobooks Ser.). (J). 1991. lib. bdg. 14.95 (*0-88682-411-7*) Creative Ed.

***Turtles.** John Coborn. (Illus.). 64p. 1997. 6.95 (*0-7938-2023-5*, RE-167) TFH Pubns.

Turtles. Janet Craig. LC 81-11448. (Now I Know Ser.). (Illus.). 32p. (J). (gr. k-2). 1982. lib. bdg. 12.95 (*0-89375-664-4*) Troll Communs.

Turtles. Janet Craig. LC 81-11448. (Now I Know Ser.). (Illus.). 32p. (J). (gr. k-2). 1997. pap. 2.95 (*0-89375-665-2*) Troll Communs.

Turtles. Frisch. (Responsible Pet Care Ser.: Set II). (J). 1991. 11.95 (*0-86625-194-4*) Rourke Pubns.

Turtles. James E. Gerholdt. LC 94-10696. (Remarkable Reptiles Ser.). (J). 1994. lib. bdg. 14.98 (*1-56239-308-1*) Abdo & Dghtrs.

***Turtles.** Ann L. Hansen. LC 97-6054. (Popular Pet Care Ser.). (J). 1997. write for info. (*1-56239-784-2*) Abdo & Dghtrs.

Turtles. L. Martin. (Reptile Discovery Library). (Illus.). 24p. (J). (gr. k-5). 1989. lib. bdg. 11.94 (*0-86592-578-X*); lib. bdg. 8.95 (*0-685-58607-3*) Rourke Corp.

Turtles. John M. Mehrtens. (Illus.). 80p. 1984. pap. text ed. 6.95 (*0-86622-512-9*, PB-129) TFH Pubns.

Turtles. Anne T. Perkins. (Big Books - Mini Bks.). (Illus.). 8p. (J). (ps). 1993. 12.00 (*1-884204-00-7*) Teach Nxt Door.

Turtles. Mirvin F. Roberts. 1989. 9.95 (*0-86622-834-9*, KW-051) TFH Pubns.

Turtles. Anita Salzberg-Baskin & Allen Salzberg. LC 95-45362. (First Bks.). (Illus.). 64p. (J). (gr. 4-6). 1996. lib. bdg. 21.00 (*0-531-20220-8*) Watts.

Turtles. Wildlife Education, Ltd. Staff. (Zoobooks Ser.). (Illus.). 20p. (Orig.). (J). (gr. 5 up). 1985. pap. 2.75 (*0-937934-41-0*) Wildlife Educ.

Turtles. Wildlife Education, Ltd. Staff. (Zoobooks Ser.). (Illus.). 24p. (Orig.). (J). (gr. 5 up). 1992. 13.95 (*0-937934-89-5*) Wildlife Educ.

Turtles: A Complete Pet Owners Manual. Hartmut Wilke. (Barron's Pet Owner's Manuals Ser.). (Illus.). 64p. 1991. pap. 6.95 (*0-8120-4702-8*) Barron.

Turtles: Perspectives & Research. Marion Harless & Henry Morlock. LC 88-12933. 712p. 1989. reprint ed. 84.50 (*0-89464-319-3*) Krieger.

Turtle's Adventure in Alphabet Town. Janet McDonnell. LC 92-2984. (Read Around Alphabet Town Ser.). (Illus.). 32p. (J). (ps-2). 1992. lib. bdg. 17.50 (*0-516-05420-1*) Childrens.

Turtles All the Way Down. John Grinder & Judith DeLozier. LC 87-80282. 392p. (C). 1987. 24.95 (*0-929514-01-7*) Grinder Delozier.

Turtles All the Way Down: Prerequisites to Personal Genius. rev. ed. John Grinder & Judith DeLozier. 416p. 1995. pap. 22.95 (*1-55552-022-7*) Metamorphous Pr.

Turtles & Tortoises. R. D. Bartlett & Patricia P. Bartlett. LC 96-11156. (Complete Pet Owner's Manuals Ser.). (Illus.). 1996. pap. 6.95 (*0-8120-9712-2*) Barron.

Turtles & Tortoises of the World. David Alderton. (Of the World Ser.). (Illus.). 191p. 1988. 25.95 (*0-8160-1733-6*) Facts on File.

Turtles As a Hobby. William P. Mara. (Illus.). 96p. 1993. 8.95 (*0-86622-324-X*, TT013) TFH Pubns.

Turtles As a New Pet. Al David. (Illus.). 64p. (Orig.). 1990. pap. 6.95 (*0-86622-621-4*, TU-013) TFH Pubns.

Turtle's Darshan for All the Animals. Bob Brown. (Illus.). 32p. (J). (gr. 2 up). 1973. pap. 5.00 (*0-913078-17-4*) Sheriar Pr.

Turtle's Day. Photos by Dwight R. Kuhn. LC 93-9006. (J). 1994. pap. 12.99 (*0-525-65172-1*, Cobblehill Bks) NAL-Dutton.

Turtles for Home & Garden. Willy Jocher. (Illus.). 1973. 8.95 (*0-87666-777-9*, PS-307) TFH Pubns.

Turtles Go Hollywood. Daniel Greenberg & Kevin Siembieda. Ed. by Alex Marciniszyn. (Teenage Mutant Ninja Turtles RPG Adventures Ser.). (Illus.). 48p. (Orig.). (YA). (gr. 8 up). 1990. pap. 7.95 (*0-916211-46-0*, 510) Palladium Bks.

Turtles in Kansas. Janalee P. Caldwell & Joseph T. Collins. LC 81-66138. pap. text ed. 5.25 (*0-685-19241-5*) Meseraule Prnting.

Turtles of the United States. Carl H. Ernst & Roger W. Barbour. LC 72-81315. 383p. reprint ed. pap. 109.20 (*0-8357-8593-9*, 2034967) Bks Demand.

Turtles of the United States & Canada. 2nd ed. Carl H. Ernst et al. LC 93-34939. (Illus.). 682p. 1994. text ed. 60.00 (*1-56098-346-9*) Smithsonian.

Turtles of the World. Carl H. Ernst & Roger W. Barbour. LC 88-29727. (Illus.). 313p. 1992. pap. 24.95 (*1-56098-212-8*) Smithsonian.

Turtles of Venezuela. Pritchard & Trebbau. LC 83-51450. 1984. Regular ed. write for info. (*0-916984-11-7*) SSAR.

***Turtles, Orphans at Birth.** Arthur Morton. (Illus.). (J). (gr. k-3). 1994. write for info. (*1-57842-089-X*) Delmas Creat.

Turtles Take Their Time. Allan Fowler. LC 92-7403. (Rookie Read-about Science Ser.). (Illus.). 32p. (J). (ps-2). 1992. lib. bdg. 17.30 (*0-516-06005-8*) Childrens.

Turtles Take Their Time. Allan Fowler. LC 92-7403. (Rookie Read-about Science Ser.). (Illus.). 32p. (J). (ps-2). 1993. pap. 3.95 (*0-516-46005-6*) Childrens.

Turtles Take Their Time Big Book. Allan Fowler. LC 92-7403. (Rookie Read-about Science Big Bks.). (Illus.). 32p. (J). (ps-2). 1992. pap. 32.40 (*0-516-49632-8*) Childrens.

Turtles, Termites, & Traffic Jam: Explorations in Massively Parallel Microworlds. Michael Resnick. (Bradford Series in Complex Adaptive Systems). (Illus.). 192p. 1994. 24.95 (*0-262-18162-2*, Bradford Bks) MIT Pr.

***Turtles, Termites, & Traffic Jams: Explorations in Massively Parallel Microworlds.** Mitchel Resnick. (Complex Adaptive Systems Ser.). (Illus.). 184p. 1997. reprint ed. pap. 12.50 (*0-262-68093-9*, Bradford Bks) MIT Pr.

Turtles, Toads, & Frogs. George S. Fichter. (Junior Guides Ser.). (Illus.). 36p. (J). (ps-3). 1993. 5.50 (*0-307-11433-3*, 11433, Golden Books) Western Pub.

Turtles Today. John Coborn. (Illus.). 64p. 1996. 12.95 (*0-7938-0109-5*, WW-011) TFH Pubns.

***Turtles Today: A Complete & Up-to-Date Guide.** John Coborn & American Society for the Prevention of Cruelty to Animals Staff. LC 97-3623. (Basic Domestic Pet Library). 1997. 19.95 (*0-7910-4618-4*) Chelsea Hse.

***Turtles, Wolves, & Bears: A Mohawk Family History.** Barbara J. Sivertsen. 344p. (Orig.). 1996. pap. 29.00 (*0-7884-0484-9*, S388) Heritage Bk.

Turturado por Cristo. Richard Wurmbrand. 1986. pap. 2.95 (*0-88264-134-4*) Living Sacrifice Bks.

***Turvey.** Earle Birney. 1996. pap. text ed. 6.95 (*0-7710-9953-3*) McCland & Stewart.

Tus Cinco Sentidos (Your Five Senses) Ray Broekel. LC 84-7603. (Spanish New True Bks.). 48p. (SPA.). (J). (gr. k-4). 1987. lib. bdg. 18.30 (*0-516-31932-9*) Childrens.

Tus Ojos Cuba, Sosiego, Viento y Ola. Jose Sanchez-Boudy. LC 88-82315. (Coleccion Espejo de Paciencia). 68p. (Orig.). (SPA.). 1989. pap. 6.95 (*0-89729-372-X*) Ediciones.

Tus Ojos y Yo. Uva A. Clavijo. (Coleccion Espejo de Paciencia). 14p. (Orig.). (SPA.). 1985. pap. 4.50 (*0-89729-373-8*) Ediciones.

Tusayan Katcinas & Hopi Altars. Jesse W. Fewkes. LC 90-20077. (Illus.). 134p. 1991. reprint ed. pap. 17.95 (*0-936755-15-6*) Avanyu Pub.

Tuscaloosa: City Business Profiles. James E. Turner et al. LC 94-30112. 165p. 1994. reprint ed. pap. 19.95 (*1-885352-05-0*) Community Comm.

Tuscaloosa: Portrait of An Alabama County, An Illustrated History. G. Ward Hubbs. LC 87-8307. 128p. 1987. 22.95 (*0-89781-202-6*) Am Historical Pr.

Tuscaloosa: The Tradition, the Spirit, the Vision. James E. Turner. LC 94-30112. (Illus.). 192p. 1994. pap. 24.95 (*1-885352-04-2*) Community Comm.

Tuscaloosa's Own: A Short History & Muster Roll of Confederate Units from Tuskaloosa County, Alabama. Beasy Hendrix. (War Between the States Ser.). (Illus.). 152p. 1989. pap. 15.95 (*0-938991-43-4*) Colonial Pr AL.

Tuscan & le Messie. (Illus.). 53p. 1990. reprint ed. 19.95 (*0-614-06910-6*, TUSC, Woodstocker Bks) A Schwartz & Co.

Tuscan & Umbrian Schools. Michael Jaffe. (Devonshire Collection of Italian Drawings). (Illus.). 208p. (C). 1994. 95.00 (*0-7148-2933-1*, Pub. by Phaidon Press UK) Chronicle Bks.

Tuscan in the Kitchen: Recipes & Tales from My Home. Pino Luongo et al. (Illus.). 1988. 24.95 (*0-517-56916-7*, C P Pubs) Crown Pub Group.

***Tuscan Landscapes of Richard Lipton: Richard Lipton's Cortona Landscapes.** Stanley I. Grand & Fred Licht. (Illus.). 50p. 1997. pap. 25.00 (*0-942945-09-3*) Sordoni Gal.

***Tuscan Marble Sculpture, 1250-1350: Sculpture & Civic Pride.** Francis Ames-Lewis. 224p. 1997. text ed. 68.95 (*1-85928-376-4*, NB619.T9A47, Pub. by Scolar Pr UK) Ashgate Pub Co.

Tuscan Poetry of the Duecento: An Anthology. Ed. & Tr. by Frede Jensen. LC 94-3346. (Garland Library of Medieval Literature: No. 99A). 392p. 1994. text ed. 20.00 (*0-8153-1625-9*) Garland.

Tuscan Year: Life & Food in an Italian Valley. Elizabeth Romer. LC 88-37226. 182p. 1989. pap. 11.00 (*0-86547-387-0*, North Pt Pr) FS&G.

Tuscan Year: Life & Food in an Italian Valley. Elizabeth Romer. 1994. 20.00 (*0-86547-478-8*, North Pt Pr) FS&G.

Tuscans & Their Families: A Study of the Florentine Catasto of 1427. David Herlihy. (C). 1989. pap. 23.00 (*0-300-04611-1*) Yale U Pr.

Tuscans & Their Families: A Study of the Florentine Catasto to 1427. David Herlihy & Christiane Klapisch-Zuber. LC 84-40195. (Economic History Ser.). 416p. 1985. text ed. 47.00 (*0-300-03056-8*) Yale U Pr.

Tuscany. (Insight Guides Ser.). 1993. pap. 22.95 (*0-395-66275-3*) HM.

Tuscany. 1996. pap. 24.00 (*0-614-12836-6*) Macmillan.

Tuscany. Photos by Sonja Bullaty & Angelo Lomeo. (Illus.). 180p. 1995. 45.00 (*1-55859-895-2*) Abbeville Pr.

***Tuscany.** Oz Clarke. (Oz Clarke's Companions Ser.). (Illus.). 1997. 19.95 (*0-614-28084-2*, Pub. by DeAgostini Edits UK) Stewart Tabori & Chang.

Tuscany. Chiara Libero. (Illus.). 160p. 1995. 17.98 (*0-8317-8018-5*) Smithmark.

***Tuscany.** Marc Millon. (Oz Clarke's Wine Companions Ser.). 1997. pap. text ed. 19.95 (*1-86212-038-2*, Pub. by DeAgostini Edits UK) Stewart Tabori & Chang.

***Tuscany.** Costanza Poli. (Places & History Ser.). (Illus.). 136p. 1997. 24.95 (*1-55670-533-6*) Stewart Tabori & Chang.

Tuscany. 2nd ed. Baedeker Staff. (Baedeker's Travel Guides Ser.). 258p. 1996. 24.00 (*0-02-860084-3*) Macmillan.

Tuscany. 2nd ed. Alta Macadam. (Blue Guides Ser.). (Illus.). 448p. 1996. pap. 24.95 (*0-393-31401-4*, Norton Paperbks) Norton.

Tuscany: Nelles Guide. (Nelles Guides Ser.). (Illus.). 256p. (Orig.). 1995. pap. 14.95 (*3-88618-407-2*, Pub. by Nelles Verlag GW) Seven Hills Bk.

***Tuscany: Places, History & Art.** Francesca Brandes. 1997. pap. text ed. 19.95 (*1-56886-047-1*) Marsilio Pubs.

Tuscany & Umbria. Passport Books Editors. 120p. 1994. pap. 17.95 (*0-8442-9971-5*, Passport Bks) NTC Pub Grp.

***Tuscany & Umbria: The Rough Guide.** 3rd ed. Tim Jepson et al. 1997. pap. 18.95 (*1-85828-243-8*) Viking Penguin.

Tuscany & Umbria Charming Small Hotels. (Charming Small Hotel Guides Ser.). (Illus.). 176p. (Orig.). 1996. pap. 12.95 (*1-55650-742-9*) Hunter NJ.

***Tuscany, Family Style.** Lynne R. Kasper. Date not set. write for info. (*0-688-13444-0*) Morrow.

Tuscany Green Guide. Ed. by Michelin Travel Publications, Staff. (Orig.). 1996. per. 20.00 (*2-06-159701-7*, 1597) Michelin.

Tuscany in Your Pocket Guide. Michelin Travel Publications, Staff. (In Your Pocket Guides Ser.). (Orig.). 1996. per. 9.95 (*2-06-650801-2*, 6508) Michelin.

***Tuscany-Italian Regional Cooking.** Nancy H. Jenkins. Date not set. write for info. (*0-688-14703-8*) Morrow.

Tuscany the Beautiful Cookbook. Lorenza De'Medici. (Illus.). 256p. 1992. 45.00 (*0-00-255032-6*) Collins SF.

Tuscany, Umbria & the Marches. Dana Facaros & Michael Pauls. LC 93-48978. (Cadogan Country Guides Ser.). (Illus.). 544p. 1994. pap. 19.95 (*1-56440-464-1*) Globe Pequot.

Tuscarawas & Muskingum Valley, Ohio: History 1775-1840. Ed. by C. H. Mitchener. 392p. 17.00 (*1-885463-27-8*) Ohio Genealogy.

Tuscarawas Valley in Indian Days, 1750-1797: Original Journals & Old Maps. Russell H. Booth, Jr. LC 94-75795. (Illus.). 424p. 1994. 27.50 (*0-9640634-6-8*) Gomber Hse.

Tuscarora. Jill D. Duvall. LC 91-3037. (New True Bks.). 48p. (J). (gr. k-4). 1991. pap. 5.50 (*0-516-41128-4*); lib. bdg. 19.00 (*0-516-01128-6*) Childrens.

Tusculan Disputations. Marcus Tullius Cicero. (Loeb Classical Library: No. 141). 630p. 1927. 18.95 (*0-674-99156-7*) HUP.

Tusculan Disputations, Bk. I. Marcus Tullius Cicero. Ed. by Douglas. (Classical Texts Ser.). 1985. 49.95 (*0-85668-250-0*, Pub. by Aris & Phillips UK); pap. 19.95 (*0-85668-251-9*, Pub. by Aris & Phillips UK) David Brown.

Tusculan Disputations, Vol. II & V: With a Summary of II & IV, Vol. II & V. Marcus Tullius Cicero. Ed. by Douglas. (Classical Texts Ser.). 1989. 49.95 (*0-85668-432-5*, Pub. by Aris & Phillips UK); pap. 19.95 (*0-85668-433-3*, Pub. by Aris & Phillips UK) David Brown.

***Tusk.** Robert Watson. LC 95-90569. 216p. (Orig.). 1997. pap. 9.00 (*1-56002-591-3*, Univ Edtns) Aegina Pr.

Tusk & Stone. Malcolm Bosse. LC 95-23448. 240p. (YA). (gr. 5 up). 1995. 15.95 (*1-886910-01-4*) Front Str.

Tusk & Stone. Malcolm Bosse. LC 96-23201. 256p. (J). 1996. pap. 4.99 (*0-14-038217-8*) Viking Penguin.

Tusk Fairy. Nicola Smee. LC 93-28444. (Illus.). 32p. (J). (ps-2). 1995. pap. 3.95 (*0-8167-3312-0*) BrdgeWater.

Tusk Fairy. Nicola Smee. LC 93-28444. (Illus.). 32p. (J). (ps-2). 1997. pap. 14.95 (*0-8167-3311-2*) BrdgeWater.

Tusk Tusk. David McKee. (Illus.). 32p. (J). (ps-3). 1990. reprint ed. pap. 6.95 (*0-916291-28-6*) Kane-Miller Bk.

Tuskegee: Its Story & Its Work. Max B. Thrasher. LC 77-161274. (Black Heritage Library Collection). 1977. reprint ed. 27.95 (*0-8369-8833-7*) Ayer.

Tuskegee Airmen: Black Heroes of World War II. Jacqueline L. Harris. LC 95-14366. 128p. (J). (gr. 6). 1995. 13.95 (*0-382-39215-9*, Dillon Silver Burdett) Silver Burdett Pr.

Tuskegee Airmen: Black Heroes of World War II. Jacqueline L. Harris. LC 95-14366. 128p. (YA). (gr. 6 up). 1995. pap. 7.95 (*0-382-39217-5*, Dillon Silver Burdett) Silver Burdett Pr.

Tuskegee Airmen: Heroes in Flight for Dignity Inclusion & Citizenship Rights. Ann C. Howell. Ed. by Alton H. Chandler. (Illus.). 24p. (Orig.). (J). (gr. 3-8). 1994. pap. text ed. 1.50 (*0-685-71995-2*) Chandler White.

Tuskegee Airmen: The Men Who Change a Nation. Charles Francis. Ed. by A. Caso. (Illus.). 1993. 24.95 (*0-8283-1955-3*) Branden Pub Co.

Tuskegee Airmen: The Men Who Change a Nation. limited ed. Ed. by A. Caso. 1995. 39.95 (*0-8283-2011-X*) Branden Pub Co.

***Tuskegee Airmen: The Men Who Changed a Nation.** 4th enl. rev. ed. Charles E. Francis & Adolph Caso. LC 97-5027. (Illus.). 486p. 1987. 29.95 (*0-8283-2029-2*) Branden Pub Co.

Tuskegee & Its People: Their Ideals & Achievements. Ed. by Booker T. Washington. LC 74-161276. (Black Heritage Library Collection). 1977. reprint ed. 32.95 (*0-8369-8835-3*) Ayer.

***Tuskegee University Custom Pub.** Douglass et al. (C). (gr. 13 up). 1996. 34.95 (*0-8151-3667-6*, 31284) Mosby Yr Bk.

Tuskegee University - Then & Now. Photos by Bud E. Smith & Tommy Thompson. (Illus.). 112p. 1993. 39.95 (*1-56469-010-5*) Harmony Hse Pub.

Tuskegee's Heroes: As Depicted in the Aviation Art of Roy E. La Grone. Charlie Cooper & Ann Cooper. LC 96-2735. (Illus.). 156p. 1996. pap. 29.95 (*0-7603-0254-5*) Motorbooks Intl.

***Tuskey's Big Decision.** Kenneth R. Greenberg. (Illus.). 75p. (Orig.). (J). (gr. 1-5). 1997. pap. 8.99 (*1-55197-743-5*, Pub. by Comnwlth Pub CN) Partners Pubs Grp.

Tussie Mussies. Geraldine A. Laufer. LC 92-50927. 1993. 22.95 (*1-56305-106-0*, 3106) Workman Pub.

Tustiw: The City of Trees. Carol Jordan. Ed. by Lori Parks. 200p. 1996. 39.95 (*1-886483-08-6*) Heritge Pubng.

***Tut-Ankh-Amen: The Living Image of the Lord.** Moustafa Gadalla. LC 97-92976. (Illus.). 144p. (Orig.). 1997. pap. 9.50 (*0-9652509-9-7*, SAN 299-0016) Bastet Pubng.

Tut-Ankh-Amun-& His Friends. Cyril Aldred. (J). (gr. 6-8). 1977. pap. 4.95 (*0-88388-043-1*) Bellerophon Bks.

TUT-D. Margaret L. Lial & E. John Hornsby. (C). 1996. 21.50 (*0-673-99789-8*) Addson-Wesley Educ.

TUT-M. Charles D. Miller et al. (C). 1996. 21.50 (*0-673-99788-X*) Addson-Wesley Educ.

Tut, Tut. Jon Scieszka. (Time Warp Trio Ser.). (Illus.). 80p. (J). (gr. 2-6). 1996. pap. 11.99 (*0-670-84832-8*) Viking Child Bks.

Tutankhamen. E. A. Budge. 165p. 1995. pap. 18.00 (*0-8196-2484-5*) Biblo.

Tutankhamen. E. A. Budge. (Amenism, Atenism & Egyptian Monotheism - with Hieroglyphic Texts of Hymns to Amen & Aten Ser.). (Illus.). 192p. 1992. reprint ed. pap. 5.95 (*0-486-26950-7*) Dover.

Tutankhamen: Amenism, Atenism & Egyptian Monotheism. Ernest A. Budge. LC 79-160615. (Illus.). 1972. reprint ed. 23.95 (*0-405-08323-8*, Pub. by Blom Pubns UK) Ayer.

Tutankhamen: Life & Death of a Pharaoh. Christiane Desroches-Noblecourt. 312p. 1990. pap. 17.95 (*0-14-011665-6*, Penguin Bks) Viking Penguin.

Tutankhamen's Egypt. Frances Welsh. (Shire Egyptology Ser.). (Illus.). 80p. 1989. pap. 25.00 (*0-7478-0196-7*, Pub. by Shire UK) St Mut.

Tutankhamen's Gift. Robert Sabuda. LC 93-5401. (Illus.). 32p. (J). (gr. 1-4). 1994. lib. bdg. 17.00 (*0-689-31818-9*, Atheneum Bks Young) S&S Childrens.

Tutankhamon. Edward L. Jones. 1978. pap. 18.00 (*0-9602458-2-0*) Ed-Lynne Jones.

Tutankhamun. Robert Green. LC 95-46150. (First Bks.). (Illus.). 64p. (J). (gr. 4-6). 1996. lib. bdg. 21.00 (*0-531-20233-X*) Watts.

Tutankhamun. Robert Green. LC 95-46150. (First Bks.). (Illus.). 64p. (J). (gr. 4-6). 1996. pap. 6.95 (*0-531-15802-0*) Watts.

***Tutankhamun & Ancient Egypt: An Interactive Guide to the Mystery of Tutankhamun.** (Illus.). (YA). (gr. 3 up). 1996. pap. 17.95 (*0-7894-1005-2*) DK Pub Inc.

Tutankhamun & the Discovery of the Tomb. Magnus Magnusson. (Jackdaws Ser.). 1992. 24.95 (*1-56696-002-9*); 32.00 (*0-614-07317-0*) Golden Owl NY.

Tutankhamun & the Sporting Tradition. Zaki I. El Habashi. LC 91-34357. (American University Studies: History: Ser. IX, Vols. 124). 200p. (C). 1992. text ed. 43.95 (*0-8204-1782-3*) P Lang Pubng.

Tutankhamun Variations. John Greening. 96p. 9100. pap. 14.95 (*1-85224-104-7*) Dufour.

Tutankhmun. Cyril Aldred. (Illus.). (J). (gr. 5). 1978. pap. 3.50 (*0-88388-059-8*) Bellerophon Bks.

Tutelary Pluralism: A Critical Approach to Venezuelan Democracy. Luis J. Oropeza. (Harvard Studies in International Affairs: No. 46). 144p. 1984. reprint ed. pap. text ed. 18.00 (*0-8191-4120-8*) U Pr of Amer.

Tutelary Tales - Formynderfortaellinger. Sven H. Rossel. LC 87-25624. (Modern Scandinavian Literature in Translation Ser.). 250p. 1988. reprint ed. pap. 71.30 (*0-7837-8916-5*, 2049627) Bks Demand.

Tutelo Rituals on Six Nations Reserve, Ontario. Gertrude P. Kurath. 184p. 10.00 (*0-318-16571-6*) Soc Ethnomusicology.

Tutor. Bertolt Brecht. Tr. by Pip Broughton from GER. (Old Vic Theatre Collection Ser.: Vol. 2). 86p. (Orig.). 1988. pap. 7.95 (*1-55783-022-3*) Applause Theatre Bk Pubs.

Tutor. Portia Da Costa. (Black Lace Ser.). 1995. pap. 5.95 (*0-352-32946-7*, Pub. by Virgin Pub UK) London Brdge.

Tutor. 6th ed. Ruth J. Colvin & Jane Root. Ed. by V. K. Lawson. 106p. 1987. pap. text ed. 9.50 (*0-318-41220-9*) Lit Vol Am.

***Tutor: A Collaborative Approach to Literacy Instruction.** Cheatham et al. 198p. 1993. pap. 12.50 (*0-930713-81-8*) Lit Vol Am.

Tutor: A Personal Computer Analysis of Spark Gap Tesla Coils. James F. Corum et al. Ed. & Illus. by Corum & Associates, Inc. Staff. LC 88-92703. 96p. (C). 1988. pap. 75.00 (*0-924758-01-5*) Corum & Assocs.

Tutor Clients Module, Competency-Based Career Guidance (CBCG) - Category C: Implementing. National Center for Research in Vocational Education Staff. 1985. 7.95 (*0-317-03921-0*, CG100C02) Ctr Educ Trng Employ.

Tutor-Notetaker. Russell T. Osguthorpe. 98p. (Orig.). (C). 1980. pap. text ed. 8.00 (*0-88200-131-0*, N6680) Alexander Graham.

Tutor to Tachygraphy: or Short-Writing: And Tachygraphy, the Most Exact & Compendious Methode of Short & Swift Writing that Hath Ever Yet Been Published by Any. Thomas Shelton. LC 92-22976. (Augustan Reprints Ser.: No. 145-146). 1970. reprint ed. 21.50 (*0-404-70145-0*) AMS Pr.

Tutoraids. Sivasailam Thiagarajan. Ed. by Danny G. Langdon. LC 77-25137. (Instructional Design Library). (Illus.). 88p. 1978. 27.95 (*0-87778-124-9*) Educ Tech Pubns.

***Tutor'd Mind: Indian Missionary-Writers in Antebellum America.** Bernd C. Peyer. LC 96-51956. (Native Americans of the Northeast Ser.). 408p. 1997. pap. 19.95 (*1-55849-099-X*); text ed. 70.00 (*1-55849-098-1*) U of Mass Pr.

***Tutored in Lust.** 3rd ed. Paul Little. 1997. reprint ed. mass mkt. 6.95 (*1-56333-547-6*) Masquerade.

Tutorial: Analysis of Particulate Contaminants: Microscopical Methods. 43p. pap. text ed. 60.00 (*0-685-14380-5*) Inst Environ Sci.

Tutorial: Bridging the Gap Between MIL-STD-810 & MIL-STD-781. Michelle L. Lindsley. LC 62-38584. 221p. 1990. pap. text ed. 100.00 (*0-915414-32-5*) Inst Environ Sci.

Tutorial: Development of a Test-Verified Finite-Element Model. Richard C. Stroud & Robert Coppolino. LC 62-38584. 126p. (Orig.). 1987. pap. 80.00 (*0-915414-95-3*) Inst Environ Sci.

Tutorial: Environmental Stress Screening. rev. ed. C. E. Mandel, Jr. 125p. 1991. pap. 100.00 (*1-877862-09-6*) Inst Environ Sci.

Tutorial: Mil-Std-810D Dynamic Environments - Guidelines to Implementation. Ed. by Edward A. Szymkowiak. 160p. 1985. 75.00 (*0-915414-80-5*) Inst Environ Sci.

Tutorial: Pyrotechnic Shock. 300p. 1985. pap. 80.00 (*0-915414-90-2*) Inst Environ Sci.

Tutorial: Specifying Environments, a Generalized Primer. Howard C. Schafer. 201p. 1991. pap. 75.00 (*1-877862-11-8*) Inst Environ Sci.

Tutorial: Test Tailoring & Environmental Engineering. Henry Caruso. LC 62-38584. 182p. (Orig.). 1988. pap. text ed. 100.00 (*0-915414-97-X*) Inst Environ Sci.

Tutorial: The Environmental Engineering Specialist's Role in Procurement: A Systems Acquisition Primer. Michelle L. Lindsley. LC 62-38584. 93p. (Orig.). 1988. pap. text ed. 75.00 (*0-915414-39-2*) Inst Environ Sci.

Tutorial Digital Resolution Requirements for Replacing Test-Based Material: Methods for Benchmarking Image Quality. 22p. 1995. pap. 10.00 (*1-887334-38-6*) Comm Preserv & Access.

Tutorial Essays in Psychology, Vol. 1. Ed. by Norman S. Sutherland. 182p. 1977. 36.00 (*0-89859-148-1*) L Erlbaum Assocs.

Tutorial Essays in Psychology, Vol. 2. Ed. by N. S. Sutherland. 160p. 1979. 36.00 (*0-89859-199-6*) L Erlbaum Assocs.

Tutorial for AMPLE & STAMP. Alan Buseman. 150p. (Orig.). 1991. pap. text ed. 5.00 (*1-878606-01-8*) JAARS Inc.

Tutorial Guide to Aldus PageMaker: 4.0 Mac. Isaac V. Kerlow. 1991. 24.75 (*0-201-50627-0*) Addison-Wesley.

Tutorial Guide to AutoCAD Release 13 for Windows: Includes Coverage of AutoVision & AutoCAD Designer. Shawna D. Lockhart. LC 95-39483. (C). 1996. pap. text ed. 36.95 (*0-201-82373-X*) Addison-Wesley.

Tutorial Guide to CAD-CAM, CAE Systems, 3 pts. Incl. Pt. 1. Contemporary Technology. (Illus.). 252p. 1984. 107.00 (*0-444-86861-5*); Pt. 2. Evaluating Today's Systems. (Illus.). 120p. 1984. 89.00 (*0-444-86862-3*); Pt. 3. Survey, Review & Buyers' Guide. (Illus.). 458p. 1984. 168.00 (*0-444-86863-1*); 1984. write for info. (*0-318-57883-2*) Elsevier.

Tutorial Guide to dBase IV. James A. Senn. 1991. 24.50 incl. disk (*0-201-50626-2*) Addison-Wesley.

Tutorial Guide to dbase IV. James A. Senn. 1991. pap. 21.75 (*0-201-56872-1*) Addison-Wesley.

Tutorial Guide to Lotus 1-2-3: Release 2.2. Timothy J. O'Leary. 1991. 24.75 incl. disk (*0-201-50625-4*) Addison-Wesley.

Tutorial Guide to Lotus 1-2-3 Release 2.3: An Introduction to Problem-Solving with Spreadsheets. Diane Zak. 1992. pap. 26.95 (*0-201-60509-0*) Addison-Wesley.

Tutorial Guide to Solving Classic Business Problems: An Introduction to Lotus 1-2-3 Release 2.3. Jane P. Laudon. (C). 1992. 28.95 (*0-201-60572-4*) Addison-Wesley.

Tutorial Guide to Solving Classic Business Problems: An Introduction to Lotus 1-2-3, Release 2.3. Kenneth C. Laudon. 1992. pap. 23.75 (*0-201-50695-5*) Addison-Wesley.

Tutorial Guide to the Student Edition of Lotus 1-2-3, Release 2.3. Timothy J. O'Leary. (C). 1992. pap. 27.95 (*0-201-50694-7*) Addison-Wesley.

Tutorial Horizons: Microsoft Works 4.0 Mac. Andelora. (DA - Computer Education Ser.). (J). (gr. k-8). 1996. pap. 30.95 (*0-538-64585-7*) S-W Pub.

Tutorial Introduction to Derive. Ellis, Jr. & Lodi. 106p. (C). 1991. pap. 22.95 (*0-534-15522-7*) Brooks-Cole.

Tutorial Introduction to Mathematica. Wade Ellis, Jr. & Lodi. 94p. (C). 1991. pap. 21.95 (*0-534-15588-X*) Brooks-Cole.

Tutorial Lecture Series: Proceedings. Annual Meeting Education Sessions Staff. 1969. pap. text ed. 10.00 (*0-915414-48-1*) Inst Environ Sci.

Tutorial Notes for Trainee General Practitioners. W. E. Warren. 192p. 1995. pap. 32.50 (*0-7506-2164-8*) Buttrwrth-Heinemann.

Tutorial on Data-Base Organization see Annual Review in Automatic Programming

Tutorial on Gatewaying Between X.400 & Internet Mail. Jeroen Houttuin. 53p. (Orig.). (C). 1993. pap. text ed. 25.00 (*0-7881-0040-8*) DIANE Pub.

Tutorial on Manufacturing Yield Evaluation of VLSI - WSI Systems. Ed. by Bruno Ciciani. LC 94-20185. 1994. pap. write for info. (*0-8186-6290-5*); Microfiche. fiche write for info. (*0-8186-6291-3*) IEEE Comp Soc.

Tutorial on Precision Signal Handling & Converter-Microprocessor Interface Techniques. Donald Travers. LC 84-142871. 92p. reprint ed. pap. 26.30 (*0-7837-5134-6*, 2044862) Bks Demand.

Tutorial Process. rev. ed. Howard S. Barrows. 75p. (C). 1992. pap. 12.95 (*0-931369-25-8*) Southern IL Univ Sch.

Tutorial System & Its Future. W. G. Moore. LC 67-30293. (C). 1968. 40.00 (*0-08-012659-6*, Pub. by Pergamon Repr UK) Franklin.

***Tutorial Topics.** Robottom & Leake. 1993. pap. text ed. write for info. (*0-582-33119-6*, Pub. by Longman UK) Longman.

Tutorials. Ed. by C. J. McDonald. (M.D. Computing: Benchmark Papers). 1987. 49.00 (*0-387-96505-X*) Spr-Verlag.

Tutorials for Junior Students of Surgery. Graham D. Hill & Andrew G. Hill. 124p. 1990. pap. text ed. 17.00 (*0-443-04449-X*) Churchill.

Tutorials for the Biomedical Sciences: Animations, Simulations, & Calculations Using Mathematica. Ed. by Charles Pidgeon. LC 95-25624. (Illus.). xxviii, 300p. 1996. pap. 79.95 incl. disk (*1-56081-928-6*, VCH) Wiley.

***Tutorials in Bilingualism: Psycholinguistic Perspectives.** Ed. by Annette M. De Groot & Judith F. Kroll. LC 96-47320. 368p. 1997. text ed. 79.95 (*0-8058-1950-9*); pap. text ed. 37.50 (*0-8058-1951-7*) L Erlbaum Assocs.

Tutorials in Clinical Surgery in General. F. G. Smiddy. 256p. (Orig.). 1991. pap. text ed. 48.00 (*0-443-04577-1*) Churchill.

Tutorials in Clinical Surgery in General - Two. F. G. Smiddy. 292p. (Orig.). 1993. pap. text ed. 54.00 (*0-443-04796-0*) Churchill.

Tutorials in Differential Diagnosis. 3rd ed. Eric R. Beck et al. (Illus.). 236p. (Orig.). 1992. pap. text ed. 29.95 (*0-443-04472-4*) Churchill.

Tutorials in General Practice. 2nd ed. Michael Mead & Henry Patterson. (Illus.). 206p. (Orig.). 1992. pap. text ed. 36.00 (*0-443-04332-9*) Churchill.

Tutorials in Motor Behavior. George E. Stelmach & Jean Requin. (Advances in Psychology Ser.: Vol. 1). 680p. 1987. 187.25 (*0-444-85466-5*, North Holland) Elsevier.

***Tutorials in Motor Behavior II.** Jean Requin & G. E. Stelmach. (Advances in Psychology Ser.: Vol. 87). 960p. 1992. 203.25 (*0-444-88801-2*, North Holland) Elsevier.

Tutorials in Motor Neuroscience: Proceedings of the NATO Advanced Study Institute. Jean Requin & George E. Stelmach. 696p. (C). 1991. lib. bdg. 270.50 (*0-7923-1385-2*) Kluwer Ac.

Tutorials in Optics. Ed. by Duncan T. Moore. LC 92-80124. 151p. (Orig.). 1992. pap. 61.00 (*1-55752-038-0*) Optical Soc.

Tutorials in Paediatric Differential Diagnosis. D. Field et al. (Illus.). 204p. 1989. pap. text ed. 32.00 (*0-443-03677-2*) Churchill.

***Tutorials in Physics.** Lillian C. McDermott. (C). 1997. pap. text ed. 7.50 (*0-13-954637-5*) P-H.

Tutorials in Surgery. F. G. Smiddy. 1977. 39.00 (*0-8464-0938-0*) Beekman Pubs.

Tutorials in Surgery, Vol. 2. 2nd ed. F. G. Smiddy. LC 83-19302. (Illus.). 319p. (C). 1986. pap. 50.00 (*0-443-03603-9*) Churchill.

Tutoring: Learning by Helping: A Student Handbook for Training Peer & Cross Age Tutors. rev. ed. Elizabeth S. Foster. LC 92-71011. (Illus.). 140p. (YA). (gr. 8-12). 1992. pap. text ed. 12.95 (*0-932796-44-3*) Ed Media Corp.

Tutoring & Mentoring: Starting a Peer-Helping Program in Your Elementary School. Nancy Keim & Cindy Tolliver. LC 93-8. 152p. (Orig.). 1993. pap. 14.95 (*0-89390-259-4*) Resource Pubns.

Tutoring Basic Skills in Reading with an Adult Newspaper: A Practical Guide to One-on-One Tutoring with Newspaper Learning Modules. Clarice C. Isaac. 79p. 1988. teacher ed., pap. 12.95 (*0-685-28897-8*) Tel Read Skills.

Tutoring for Pay: Earn While You Help Others Learn. Betty O. Carpenter. 214p. 1991. pap. 29.95 (*0-398-06041-X*) C C Thomas.

Tutoring for Pay: Earn While You Help Others Learn. Betty O. Carpenter. 214p. (C). 1991. text ed. 45.95 (*0-398-05714-1*) C C Thomas.

Tutoring Handbook: A Student's Guide to Profitable Tutoring. Marilyn Jones. (Careers in Depth Ser.). (Illus.). 128p. (YA). (gr. 7-12). 1984. lib. bdg. 7.97 (*0-8239-0599-3*) Rosen Group.

Tutoring Is Caring: You Can Help Someone to Read. Aline D. Wolf. (Illus.). 1981. reprint ed. 19.95 (*0-9601016-1-6*) Parent-Child Pr.

Tutoring Reading in Schools Training Module. 25p. (Orig.). 1980. teacher ed. 95.00 incl. audio, sl. (*0-930713-49-4*) Lit Vol Am.

Tutoring Tricks & Tips. 55p. 1970. pap. 2.90 (*0-912041-04-8*) Natl Comm Res Youth.

Tutoring with Students: A Handbook for Establishing Tutorial Programs in Schools. Ralph J. Melaragno. LC 75-40045. 172p. 1976. pap. 34.95 (*0-87778-090-0*) Educ Tech Pubns.

Tutor's Bride. Martin Pyx. 224p. 1996. mass mkt. 7.95 (*0-929654-44-7*, 30) Blue Moon Bks.

Tutor's First Love. George MacDonald. Ed. by Mike Phillips. LC 84-6481. 240p. 1984. reprint ed. pap. 7.99 (*0-87123-596-X*) Bethany Hse.

Tutor's Guide to the Ecology Game. Michael A. Tribe & Derek Peacock. (Basic Biology Course; Tutor's Guide Ser.). 161p. reprint ed. pap. 45.90 (*0-685-16369-5*, 2027291) Bks Demand.

Tut's Mummy: Lost & Found. Judy Donnelly. LC 87-20790. (Step into Reading Bks.). (Illus.). (Orig.). (J). (gr. 2-3). 1988. pap. 3.99 (*0-394-89189-9*) Random Bks Yng Read.

Tut's Mummy: Lost & Found. Judy Donnelly. LC 87-20790. (Step into Reading Bks.). (Illus.). (Orig.). (J). (gr. 2-3). 1988. lib. bdg. 7.99 (*0-394-99189-3*) Random Bks Yng Read.

Tutsi. Aimable Twagilimana. (Heritage Library of African Peoples: Set 3). (Illus.). 64p. (YA). (gr. 7-12). 1997. lib. bdg. 15.95 (*0-8239-1999-4*, D1999-4) Rosen Group.

TUTT: An Annotated Bibliography of Arthur Train's Tutt Short Stories. Compiled by Philip DeTurk. (Tarlton Law Library Legal Bibliography Ser.: No. 39). 33p. (C). 1994. 16.00 (*0-935630-44-9*) U of Tex Tarlton Law Lib.

Tutt & Mr. Tutt. Arthur Train. reprint ed. lib. bdg. 25.95 (*0-89190-585-5*, Rivercity Pr) Amereon Ltd.

Tutti - Beethoven: Beethoven No. Five, Issue No. 5. (Illus.). 176p. 1995. 16.95 incl. disk (*1-57301-012-X*) TuTTi USA.

Tutti - Bernstein, Issue No. 2. (Illus.). 176p. 1995. 16.95 incl. disk (*1-57301-001-4*) TuTTi USA.

Tutti - Gershwin: Gershwin No. Four, Issue No. 4. (Illus.). 176p. 1995. 16.95 incl. disk (*1-57301-016-2*) TuTTi USA.

Tutti - Mozart, Issue No. 1. (Illus.). 176p. 1994. 16.95 incl. disk (*1-57301-000-6*) TuTTi USA.

Tutti-Frutti Town: Blinky Blueberry Finds a Friend. Melina P. Costello. (Illus.). 32p. (Orig.). (J). (gr. k-3). 1991. pap. 6.50 (*1-878130-01-3*) Bang A Drum.

Tutti-Tchaikovsky: Tchaikovsky No. Three, Issue No. 3. (Illus.). 176p. 1995. 16.95 incl. disk (*1-57301-008-1*) TuTTi USA.

Tuttle - Tuthill: One Branch of the Eli Tuthill Family of Liberty Township of Michigan, Descendants of the Tuthill Family of Southold & Orient, Long Island, 1640, & of Tharston, England. Jean L. LaPorte. (Illus.). 107p. 1992. pap. 15.00 (*0-8328-2358-9*); lib. bdg. 25.00 (*0-8328-2357-0*) Higginson Bk Co.

Tuttle Dictionary of Antiques & Collectibles Terms. Don Bingham & Joan Bingham. LC 91-67337. 272p. (Orig.). 1992. pap. 19.95 (*0-8048-1756-1*) C E Tuttle.

Tuttle Dictionary of Legal Terms. Richard S. Keirstead. 1995. pap. 18.95 (*0-8048-2039-2*) C E Tuttle.

Tuttle Dictionary of the Martial Arts of Korea, China, & Japan. Daniel Kogan. 1995. pap. 12.95 (*0-8048-2016-3*) C E Tuttle.

Tuttle Kanji Cards, Set. Alexander Kask. 1994. boxed 14.95 (*0-8048-1945-9*) C E Tuttle.

Tuttle Practical Cambodian Dictionary. David Smyth & Tran Kien. (Tuttle Langauge Library). 336p. (Orig.). (CAM & ENG.). 1995. pap. 14.95 (*0-8048-1954-8*) C E Tuttle.

Tuttle's Concise Indonesian Dictionary. A. L. Kramer. 400p. 1993. pap. 16.95 (*0-8048-1864-9*) C E Tuttle.

Tuttle's Dictionary of Legal & Business Terms: English-Japanese - Japanese-English. Richard S. Keirstead. 600p. (ENG & JPN.). 1994. pap. 18.95 (*0-8048-1907-6*) C E Tuttle.

Tuttle's Dictionary of Loan Words in Japanese. Taeko Kamiya. 408p. 1993. pap. 14.95 (*0-8048-1888-6*) C E Tuttle.

Tutu: The True Story of a Budgie. Alix Weill. (Illus.). 1979. pap. 3.95 (*0-89127-056-6*) Peyton's.

Tutu: Voice of the Voiceless. Shirley Du Boulay. LC 88-11037. (Illus.). 294p. 1988. reprint ed. pap. 83.80 (*0-7837-5564-3*, 2045339) Bks Demand.

Tutu & the Ti Plant. Sandra Goforth. (Illus.). 40p. 1993. 12.95 (*1-56647-044-7*) Mutual Pub HI.

Tutu & the Ulu Tree. Sandra Goforth. (Illus.). 40p. 1994. 12.95 (*1-56647-043-9*) Mutual Pub HI.

Tutu for Mimi. Tynia Thomassie. LC 94-33022. (Illus.). 32p. (J). (gr. k-3). 1996. 14.95 (*0-590-44020-9*) Scholastic Inc.

Tutu Kane & Granpa. Nancy A. Mower. (Illus.). 32p. (J). (ps). 1989. 8.95 (*0-916630-66-8*) Pr Pacifica.

Tutu Much Ballet. Gabrielle Charbonnet. (Illus.). 80p. (J). (gr. 2-4). 1996. pap. 5.95 (*0-8050-4643-7*) H Holt & Co.

Tuva or Bust! Richard Feynman's Last Journey. Ralph Leighton. (Illus.). 256p. 1992. pap. 11.95 (*0-14-015614-3*, Penguin Bks) Viking Penguin.

Tuvan Manual. 1977. write for info. (*0-87750-214-5*) Mongolia.

Tuvia & the Tiny Teacher. Clara Lebowitz. (Illus.). 100p. (J). (gr. 3-4). 1991. 8.95 (*1-56062-105-2*) CIS Comm.

Tuvia's Train That Had No End. Michael Muchnik. (Illus.). 48p. (J). 1984. reprint ed. 7.00 (*0-8266-0353-X*, Merkos LInyonei Chinuch) Kehot Pubn Soc.

TUXEDO: An Open Approach to OLTP. Fulvio Primatesta. LC 95-8367. (C). 1995. pap. text ed. 50.00 (*0-13-101833-7*) P-H.

***Tuxedo Administrator's Guide.** David M. Indeck. (Illus.). 450p. 1997. pap. 49.95 (*0-12-370770-6*, AP Prof) Acad Pr.

Tuxedo Junction: Essays on American Culture. Gerald Early. 1994. pap. 13.00 (*0-88001-233-1*) Ecco Pr.

Tuxedo Park. large type ed. Basil Copper. (Linford Mystery Library). 1990. pap. 15.99 (*0-7089-6845-7*) Ulverscroft.

Tuxedo Park: A Journal of Recollections. Albert F. Winslow. (Illus.). 253p. 1992. 30.00 (*0-9634696-0-6*) Tuxedo Hist Soc.

Tuxedo System: A Guide to Constructing Distributed Business Applications. Juan Andrade et al. 444p. (C). 1996. text ed. 45.95 (*0-201-63493-7*) Addison-Wesley.

Tuxedo System Vol. 1: Application Development & Administration. Unix Staff. (Tuxedo System Ser.). (Illus.). (C). write for info. (*1-884173-01-2*) Decision Support.

Tuxedo System Vol. 2: Application Programming. Unix Staff. (Tuxedo System Ser.). (Illus.). (C). write for info. (*1-884173-02-0*) Decision Support.

Tuxedo System Vol. 3: Reference Manual. Unix Staff. (Tuxedo System Ser.). (Illus.). (C). write for info. (*1-884173-03-9*) Decision Support.

Tuxedo System Vol. 4: Client-Server Extensions. Unix Staff. (Tuxedo System Ser.). (Illus.). (C). write for info. (*1-884173-04-7*) Decision Support.

Tuxedo System Vol. 5: Cobol Guide. Unix Staff. (Tuxedo System Ser.). (Illus.). (C). write for info. (*1-884173-05-5*) Decision Support.

Tuxedo System Vol. 6: Installation Guide. Unix Staff. (Tuxedo System Ser.). (Illus.). (C). write for info. (*1-884173-06-3*) Decision Support.

Tuxedo System Vol. 7: Documentation Updates for Release 4.2.2. Unix Staff. (Tuxedo System Ser.). (Illus.). (C). write for info. (*1-884173-07-1*) Decision Support.

Tuxedo System Vol. 8: Domains Guide. Unix Staff. (Tuxedo System Ser.). (Illus.). (C). write for info. (*1-884173-08-X*) Decision Support.

Tuxedo System Vol. 9: System Message Manual. Unix Staff. (Tuxedo System Ser.). (Illus.). (C). write for info. (*1-884173-09-8*) Decision Support.

Tuxedo System Documentation Series, Vols. 1-9. Unix Staff. (Illus.). write for info. (*1-884173-00-4*) Decision Support.

Tuxedo Tatting. JoAnn Stearns. 8p. 1995. pap. 3.95 (*1-888837-08-X*) Silver Shuttle.

***Tuxedo's Adventure.** large type ed. Kathleen Hayes. (Illus.). 36p. (J). (gr. 2-4). 1997. lib. bdg. 12.95 (*0-9657252-0-0*) Tuxedo Enter.

Tuyau-Zwingli see Grande Encyclopedie

Tuzigoot National Monument. Rose Houk. Ed. by Sandra Scott. LC 95-71326. (Illus.). 16p. 1995. pap. 3.95 (*1-877856-55-X*) SW Pks Mnmts.

Tuzuk-I-Jahangiri, or Memoirs of Jahangir. Jahangir. Ed. by Henry Beveridge. Tr. by Alexander Roberts. reprint ed. Set. text ed. 52.50 (*0-685-13404-0*) Coronet Bks.

Tuzuk-I-Jahangirl Or Memoirs of Jahangir. Henry Beveridge. Tr. by A. Rogers. 1989. reprint ed. 22.50 (*81-85395-13-6*, Pub. by BR Pub II) S Asia.

TV - Becoming Unglued: A Guide to Help Children Develop Positive TV Habits. Addie Jurs. LC 92-9315. (Illus.). 120p. (Orig.). 1992. pap. 7.95 (*0-9628463-0-9*) Clarendon Hills.

TV - Becoming Unglued: A Guide to Help Children Develop Positive TV Habits. Addie Jurs. (Orig.). 1992. pap. 7.95 (*0-945339-25-9*) Columbine Communs.

TV Almanac. Louis Phillips & Burnham Holmes. LC 94-14094. (Illus.). 256p. 1994. pap. 10.00 (*0-671-88798-X*) Macmillan.

TV American Presidency. Plissner. 1996. 24.95 (*0-02-874033-5*) Free Pr.

TV & Films: Behind the Scenes. Odile Limousin & Daniele Neumann. (Young Discovery Library). (Illus.). 40p. (J). (gr. k-5). 1993. lib. bdg. 9.95 (*1-56674-073-8*, HTS Bks) Forest Hse.

TV & Films: Behind the Scenes. Odile Limousin & Daniele Neumann. Tr. by Vicki Bogard from FRE. LC 92-966. (Illus.). (J). (gr. k-5). 1992. 5.95 (*0-944589-36-7*) Young Discovery Lib.

***TV & Radio Announcing, 8 Vols.** Hyde. (C). Date not set. pap. 59.96 (*0-395-87540-4*) HM.

TV & Radio Announcing, 7 Vols. Hyde. (C). 1994. text ed. 60.76 (*0-395-70880-X*) HM.

TV & Radio Announcing, 7 Vols. Hyde. (C). 1994. teacher ed., pap. 11.96 (*0-395-70881-8*) HM.

TV & Radio Production, Techknowledge Reference Series. Brad Thode. (TP - Technology Education Ser.). 176p. (J). (gr. k-12). 1996. pap. 21.95 (*0-538-64479-6*) S-W Pub.

TV & Studio Cast Musicals on Record: A Discography of Television Musicals & Studio Recordings of Stage & Film Musicals. Ed. by Richard C. Lynch. LC 90-40205. (Discographies Ser.: No. 38). 352p. 1990. text ed. 59.95 (*0-313-27324-3*, LTV, Greenwood Pr) Greenwood.

TV & Video. Ingrid Geser. Ed. by Rebecca Stefoff. LC 90-13868. (Media Story Ser.). (Illus.). 32p. (J). (gr. 4-8). 1991. lib. bdg. 17.26 (*0-944483-99-2*) Garrett Ed Corp.

TV & Video Projects. Maplin Staff. (Maplin Ser.). 208p. 1996. pap. 19.95 (*0-7506-2297-0*) Buttrwrth-Heinemann.

TV Arab. Jack G. Shaheen. LC 84-71627. 146p. 1984. pap. 11.95 (*0-87972-310-6*) Bowling Green Univ Popular Press.

TV Babylon. Jeff Rovin. 304p. 1987. pap. 4.99 (*0-451-16633-7*, Sig) NAL-Dutton.

TV Babylon Two. Jeff Rovin. (Illus.). 304p. (Orig.). 1991. pap. 4.99 (*0-451-17015-6*, Sig) NAL-Dutton.

TV Book: The Kids' Guide to Talking Back. Shelagh Wallace. (Illus.). 96p. (Orig.). (YA). (gr. 4 up). 1996. pap. 12.95 (*1-55037-480-X*, Pub. by Annick CN) Firefly Bks Ltd.

TV Dimensions '97. 500p. 1997. pap. 245.00 (*0-9621947-3-5*) Media Dynamics.

***TV Dinner.** Everitt. (J). 1997. pap. write for info. (*0-15-201565-5*, HB Juv Bks) HarBrace.

T.V. Dinner Culture Poem. Ken Dimaggio. 6p. 1994. per., pap. 3.00 (*1-886206-09-0*) Venom Pr.

TV Director - Interpreter. rev. ed. Lewis Colby & Tom Greer. Ed. by Joanne Dolinar. 288p. (C). 1990. pap. text ed. 24.00 (*0-8038-9318-3*) Hastings.

***TV Drama in Transition: Forms, Values, & Cultural Change.** LC 96-47005. 1997. text ed. 55.00 (*0-312-17276-1*) St Martin.

TV Establishment: Programming for Power & Profit. Gaye Tuchman. 1974. pap. 3.45 (*0-13-902395-X*, Spectrum IN) Macmillan Gen Ref.

TV Favorites. 96p. 1993. otabind 9.95 (*0-7935-2407-5*, 00110016) H Leonard.

TV Financial Report 1993. National Association of Broadcasters Staff. 235p. (Orig.). 1993. pap. 225.00 (*0-89324-148-2*) Natl Assn Broadcasters.

TV Game Show Almanac. Ernie Wood & John P. Holms. (Illus.). 288p. 1995. pap. 8.95 (*0-8019-8740-7*) Chilton.

TV Generations. Ed. by Meg Cranston & Jeff Mann. (Illus.). 71p. (Orig.). (C). 1986. pap. 10.00 (*0-937335-00-2*) LA Contemp Exhib.

TV Genres: A Handbook & Reference Guide. Ed. by Brian G. Rose & Robert S. Alley. LC 84-22460. ix, 453p. 1985. text ed. 69.50 (*0-313-23724-7*, RHG/, Greenwood Pr) Greenwood.

TV Guidance Counselor. A. C. LeMieux. 192p. (YA). 1994. mass mkt. 3.99 (*0-380-72050-7*, Flare) Avon.

TV Guidance Counselor. A. C. LeMieux. LC 92-33664. 240p. (YA). (gr. 7 up). 1993. 13.00 (*0-688-12402-X*, Tambourine Bks) Morrow.

TV Guide Crossword Companion, Vol. 1. 1995. pap. 25.00 (*1-57495-023-1*) Herbko Intl.

TV Guide Crossword Companion, Vol. 2. 1995. pap. 12.00 (*1-57495-024-X*) Herbko Intl.

TV Guide Crossword Companion, Vol. 3. 1995. pap. 12.00 (*1-57495-025-8*) Herbko Intl.

TV Guide Crossword Companion, Vol. 4. 1995. pap. 12.00 (*1-57495-026-6*) Herbko Intl.

An Asterisk (*) at the beginning of an entry indicates that the title is appearing in BIP for the first time.

TV Guide Crossword Companion, Vol. 5. 1995. pap. 12.00 (1-57495-027-4) Herbko Intl.

TV Guide Crossword Companion, Vol. 6. 1995. pap. 12.00 (1-57495-028-2) Herbko Intl.

TV Guide Crossword Companion, Vol. 7. 1995. pap. 12.00 (1-57495-029-0) Herbko Intl.

TV Guide Crossword Companion, Vol. 8. 1995. pap. 12.00 (1-57495-030-4) Herbko Intl.

TV Guide Crossword Companion, Vol. 9. 1995. pap. 12.00 (1-57495-031-2) Herbko Intl.

TV Guide Index Cumulative Supplement, 1983-1987. Catherine E. Johnson. 299p. 1988. pap. text ed. 80.00 (0-9603684-8-5) TV Guide.

TV Guide Index, 1978 to 1980 Supplement. Catherine E. Johnson. LC 82-80797. 113p. (C). 1982. pap. text ed. 30.00 (0-9603684-1-8) TV Guide.

TV Guide Index 1978-1982 Cumulative Supplement. Catherine E. Johnson. LC 83-51316. 176p. 1983. pap. text ed. 40.00 (0-9603684-3-4) TV Guide.

TV Guide Index 1981 Supplement. Catherine E. Johnson. LC 82-74385. 41p. 1983. pap. text ed. 12.00 (0-9603684-2-6) TV Guide.

TV Guide Index 1983 Supplement. Catherine E. Johnson. LC 84-52336. 64p. 1984. pap. 12.00 (0-9603684-4-2) TV Guide.

TV Guide Index 1984 Supplement. Catherine E. Johnson. LC 85-51243. 68p. 1985. pap. text ed. 12.00 (0-9603684-5-0) TV Guide.

TV Guide Index 1985 Supplement. Catherine E. Johnson. LC 86-50728. 70p. 1986. pap. 15.00 (0-9603684-6-9) TV Guide.

TV Guide Index 1986 Supplement. Catherine E. Johnson. 78p. 1987. pap. 22.00 (0-9603684-7-7) TV Guide.

TV Guide Supplement, 1988. Catherine E. Johnson. 81p. 1989. pap. text ed. 35.00 (0-9603684-9-3) TV Guide.

TV Guide Twenty-Five Year Index: 1953-1977. Catherine E. Johnson. LC 79-67725. 506p. 1979. text ed. 60.00 (0-9603684-0-X) TV Guide.

TV Hits. 80p. 1993. pap. 9.95 (0-7935-2409-1, 00221805) H Leonard.

TV Interactive Toys: The New High-Tech Threat to Children. Pamela Tuchscherer. 1988. pap. 9.95 (0-939705-02-8) Pinnaroo.

TV Kid. Betsy C. Byars. (Novels Ser.). (Illus.). (J). (gr. 2-7). 1987. pap. 3.99 (0-14-032308-2, Puffin) Puffin Bks.

TV Land: A Guide to America's Television Shrines, Sets & Sites. Robin Keats. LC 95-9894. 1995. pap. 12.95 (0-312-13194-1) St Martin.

TV Market Analysis 1990. National Association of Broadcasters Staff. 135p. (Orig.). 1990. pap. 400.00 (0-89324-096-6) Natl Assn Broadcasters.

*TV Nation. M. Moore & K. Glynn. 1997. pap. 15.00 (0-609-80092-2) Random Hse Value.

TV News: Building a Career in Broadcast Journalism. Ray White. (Illus.). 151p. 1989. pap. 29.95 (0-240-80036-2, Focal) Buttrwrth-Heinemann.

TV News Ethics. Marilyn J. Matelski. (Electronic Media Guide Ser.). (Illus.). 96p. 1991. pap. 19.95 (0-240-80089-3) Buttrwrth-Heinemann.

TV News Studio. Marilyn Miller. LC 95-19525. (Behind the Scenes Ser.). (Illus.). (J). 1996. lib. bdg. 21.40 (0-8172-4089-6) Raintree Steck-V.

TV News, Urban Conflict & the Inner City. Simon Cottle. (Studies in Communication & Society). 266p. 1993. pap. 22.50 (0-7185-1462-9, Pub. by Leicester Univ Pr) Bks Intl VA.

TV News, Urban Conflict & the Inner City. Simon Cottle. (Leicester University Press Book). 266p. 1993. 69.00 (0-7185-1447-5, Pub. by Leicester Univ Pr) Bks Intl VA.

TV Newscast Processes & Procedures. Robert J. Schihl. (Multiple Camera Video Ser.). 176p. 1991. pap. 32.95 (0-240-80094-X, Focal) Buttrwrth-Heinemann.

*TV or No TV. (Spanish Golden Look Look Bks.). (J). write for info. (0-307-72652-5, P12652-10, Golden Books) Western Pub.

T.V. Production Workbook. 6th ed. Herbert Zettl. (Radio/TV/Film Ser.). 1997. pap. 18.95 (0-534-26061-6) Wadsworth Pub.

*TV-Proof Your Kids: A Parent's Guide to Safe & Healthy Viewing. Lauryn Axelrod. 256p. 1997. 17.95 (1-55972-408-0, Birch Ln Pr) Carol Pub Group.

TV Repair for Beginners. 4th ed. George Zwick & Homer L. Davidson. 1991. pap. text ed. 21.95 (0-07-073092-X) McGraw.

TV Repair for Beginners. 4th ed. George Zwick. 1991. pap. 19.95 (0-8306-2180-6) McGraw-Hill Prof.

*TV Repair for Beginners. 5th ed. Homer L. Davidson & George Zwick. LC 97-25446. 1997. write for info. (0-07-015805-3); pap. write for info. (0-07-015806-1) McGraw.

*TV Scenic Desgin Handbook. 2nd ed. Gerald Millerson. 1997. pap. text ed. 39.95 (0-240-51493-9) Buttrwrth-Heinemann.

TV Scenic Design Handbook. 3rd ed. Gerald Millerson. 249p. 1989. pap. 59.95 (0-240-51285-5, Focal) Buttrwrth-Heinemann.

TV Scriptwriter's Handbook: Dramatic Writing for Television & Film. Alfred Brenner. 325p. 1992. pap. 15.95 (1-879505-10-X) Silman James Pr.

TV Sets. Mark Bennett. 1997. pap. 19.95 (1-57500-017-2, Viewer Bks) TV Bks.

TV Theme Song Sing-Along Songbook. John Javna. 128p. 1984. pap. 6.95 (0-312-78215-2) St Martin.

TV Theme Song Trivia Book: Mind-Boggling Questions about Those Songs & Themes You Can't Get Out of Your Head. Vincent Terrace. 176p. 1996. pap. 9.95 (0-8065-1786-7, Citadel Pr) Carol Pub Group.

TV Theme Soundtrack Directory & Discography with Cover Versions. Craig W. Pattillo. 287p. 1990. pap. 14.50 (0-9612044-2-7) Braemar OR.

TV Themes. 1990. pap. 5.95 (0-7935-0126-1, 00001286) H Leonard.

TV Themes ABC, Vol. 306. 1990. pap. 4.95 (0-7935-0167-9, 00001375) H Leonard.

TV Themes Piano Solos. 96p. 1994. pap. 9.95 (0-7935-2408-3, 00292030) H Leonard.

*TV Tie-Ins: A Bibliography of American TV Tie-In Paperbacks. Kurt Peer. LC 96-92907. (Illus.). 384p. 1997. pap. 24.95 (0-9654536-3-4) Neptune Pub.

*TV Tie-Ins: A Bibliography of American TV Tie-In Paperbacks. Kurt Peer. LC 96-92907. (Illus.). 384p. 1997. 55.00 (0-9654536-4-2) Neptune Pub.

TV Time for Five Finger Piano. 32p. 1994. pap. 5.95 (0-7935-3573-5, 00292069) H Leonard.

TV Time for Five Finger Piano. 32p. 1994. pap. 5.95 (0-7935-3574-3, 00292070) H Leonard.

TV Toys & the Shows That Inspired Them. Cynthia B. Liljebald. LC 95-82426. (Illus.). 224p. 1996. pap. 19.95 (0-87341-440-3, TTT) Krause Pubns.

TV Trivia Teasers. W. Wilson Casey. (Illus.). 260p. 1984. pap. 29.50 (0-87650-164-1) Popular Culture.

TV Tunes. 144p. 1994. otabind 14.95 (0-7935-3045-8, 00311643) H Leonard.

TV Tunes: Easy Guitar. pap. 12.95 (0-7935-4378-9, 00702007) H Leonard.

TV Tunes for Guitar. pap. 12.95 (0-7935-5587-6, 00698985) H Leonard.

TV Tutor. 1993. 15.00 (0-88336-043-8); student ed. 4.95 (0-88336-143-4); student ed. 4.95 (0-88336-141-8); student ed. 4.95 (0-88336-145-0); student ed. 4.95 (0-88336-147-7); audio 69.95 (0-88336-142-6); audio 69.95 (0-88336-140-X); audio 69.95 (0-88336-144-2); audio 69.95 (0-88336-146-9) New Readers.

T.V. Vet Book for Stock Farmers No. 2: Calving the Cow & Care of the Calf. Ed Straiton. (T.V. Vet Ser.). (Illus.). 312p. 1994. 34.95 (0-85236-184-X, Pub. by Farming Pr UK) Diamond Farm Bk.

*TV Video Systems for the Hobbyist & Technician: The How-To Guide to Installation, Operation & Troubleshooting. rev. ed. L. W. Pena & Bert A. Pena. (Illus.). 128p. (C). 1996. reprint ed. pap. 14.95 (0-7906-1082-5) Prompt Publns.

TV Violence & the Child: The Evolution & Fate of the Surgeon General's Report. Douglass Cater & Stephen P. Strickland. LC 74-83207. 168p. 1975. 25.00 (0-87154-203-X) Russell Sage.

TVA: Fifty Years of Grass-Roots Bureaucracy. Ed. by Erwin C. Hargrove & Paul K. Conkin. LC 83-6475. 368p. 1983. text ed. 34.95 (0-252-01086-8) U of Ill Pr.

TVA & Black Americans: Planning for the Status Quo. Nancy L. Grant. 240p. (C). 1990. 39.95 (0-87722-626-1) Temple U Pr.

TVA & the Dispossessed: The Resettlement of Population in the Norris Dam Area. Michael J. McDonald & John Muldowny. LC 81-16333. (Illus.). 352p. 1982. 38.00 (0-87049-345-0) U of Tenn Pr.

TVA & the Grass Roots: A Study of Politics & Organization. Philip Salznick. (California Library Reprint). 288p. reprint ed. pap. 82.10 (0-7837-4682-2, 2044429) Bks Demand.

TVA & the Tellico Dam, 1936 - 1979: A Bureaucratic Crisis in Post-Industrial America. William B. Wheeler & Michael J. McDonald. LC 85-22224. (Illus.). 304p. 1986. text ed. 34.50 (0-87049-492-9) U of Tenn Pr.

TVA & the Tellico Dam, 1936-1979: A Bureaucratic Crisis in Post-Industrial America. William B. Wheeler & Michael J. McDonald. LC 85-22224. 303p. 1986. reprint ed. pap. 86.40 (0-608-01600-4, AU00456) Bks Demand.

TVacations: A Fun Guide to the Sites, the Stars, & the Inside Stories Behind Your Favorite TV Shows. Fran W. Golden. LC 95-42987. 368p. 1996. pap. 12.00 (0-671-89024-7) PB.

TVA's Public Planning: The Vision, the Reality. Walter L. Creese. LC 89-28129. 304p. 1990. text ed. 40.00 (0-87049-638-7) U of Tenn Pr.

TVEI: The Organisation of the Early Years. Ed. by Colin McCabe. 68p. 1984. pap. 19.95 (0-905028-62-7, Pub. by Multilingual Matters UK) Taylor & Francis.

TVEI & Secondary Education: A Critical Appraisal. Ed. by Dennis Gleeson. 224p. 1987. 85.00 (0-335-15539-1, Open Univ Pr); pap. 32.00 (0-335-15538-3, Open Univ Pr) Taylor & Francis.

TVEI at the Change of Life. Ed. by David Hopkins. 130p. 1990. 69.00 (1-85359-075-4); pap. 24.95 (1-85359-074-6) Taylor & Francis.

TVEI Story: Policy, Practice & Preparation for the Workforce. Roger Dale et al. 192p. 1990. 90.00 (0-335-09563-1, Open Univ Pr); pap. 32.00 (0-335-09562-3, Open Univ Pr) Taylor & Francis.

*Tver Oblast: Economy, Industry, Government, Business. 2nd rev. ed. Russian Information & Business Center, Inc. Staff. (Russian Regional Business Directories Ser.). (Illus.). 200p. 1997. pap. 99.00 (1-57751-420-3) Russ Info & Busn Ctr.

Tvorcheskaia Sud'ba Panteleimona Romanova. Valerii Petrochenkov. Ed. by Elena Krashoshchekova. LC 88-10990. (Russian Ser.). 208p. (Orig.). 1988. pap. 14.50 (1-55779-002-7) Hermitage.

Tvoreniia 1906-1908 Godov. Velimir Khlebnikov. (Illus.). xii, 106p. (RUS.). (C). 1989. reprint ed. pap. 12.00 (0-933884-75-3) Berkeley Slavic.

TVP Cookbook: Using the Quick-Cooking Meat Substitute. Dorothy R. Bates. LC 91-27400. (Illus.). 96p. 1991. pap. 6.95 (0-913990-79-5) Book Pub Co.

TV/PR: How to Promote Yourself, Your Product, Your Service or Your Organization on Television. Wicke Chambers & Spring Asher. LC 85-73428. 1986. 14.95 (0-9615565-9-5) Chase Comns.

TVR: The Complete Story. John Tipler. (Illus.). 216p. 1994. 35.95 (1-85223-796-1, Pub. by Crowood UK) Motorbooks Intl.

TVRs, Vol. 1: Grantura to Taimar Collector's Guide. Graham Robson. (Collector's Guide Ser.). (Illus.). 128p. 1994. 27.95 (0-947981-80-2, Pub. by Motor Racing UK) Motorbooks Intl.

TVR's, Vol. 2: Tasmin to Chimaera Collector's Guide. Graham Robson. (Collector's Guide Ser.). (Illus.). 128p. 1994. 27.95 (0-947981-81-0, Pub. by Motor Racing UK) Motorbooks Intl.

TV's Biggest Hits. Jon Burlingame. 400p. 1996. 25.00 (0-02-870324-3) Schirmer Bks.

TV's Forgotten Hero: The Story of Philo Farnsworth. Stephanie S. McPherson. LC 95-26383. (J). 1996. lib. bdg. 16.13 (1-57505-017-X, Carolrhoda) Lerner Group.

TV's On! Featuring Themes from Star Trek & Cheers. 48p. 1994. pap. 9.95 (0-7935-3061-X, 00290452) H Leonard.

TV's Sheena Irish McCalla. Bill Black & Bill Feret. 100p. 1992. pap. 19.95 (0-685-60576-0) A C Comics.

*TWA Flight 800: The Mystery Solved. Catherine B. White. Orig. Title: TWA Flight 800 - An Analysis of the Crash. (Illus.). 20p. 1997. pap. 9.95 (1-885592-00-0, Shining Str Pubns) ScanFan Pubns.

TWA Flight 800 - An Analysis of the Crash see TWA Flight 800: The Mystery Solved

Twachtman Monograph. write for info. (0-87413-228-2) U Delaware Pr.

Twain: Wit & Wisecracks. Mark Twain. 1961. 7.99 (0-88088-546-7) Peter Pauper.

Twain, Mark, Short Stories Of. Mark Twain. (Airmont Classics Ser.). (J). (gr. 8 up). 1968. mass mkt. 3.95 (0-8049-0171-6, CL-171) Airmont.

Twain Meet: The Physical Sciences & Poetry. Noojin Walker & Martha F. Walker. (American University Studies: General Literature: Ser. IXX, Vol. 23). 306p. (C). 1989. text ed. 51.00 (0-8204-0953-7) P Lang Pubng.

Twain, Plains & Automobiles: Driving Tours Through the Historical Midwest. Joanne Y. Cleaver. LC 93-49329. (Illus.). 288p. (Orig.). 1994. pap. 11.95 (1-55652-210-X) Chicago Review.

Twain Plus Twain. Bernard Sabath. 1984. pap. 5.25 (0-8222-1175-0) Dramatists Play.

Twain Shall Meet. large type ed. Hilda Durman. (Linford Romance Library). 304p. 1993. pap. 15.99 (0-7089-7331-0, Linford) Ulverscroft.

Twain's Library of Humor. Mark Twain. Ed. by E. N. Fetskog. (Masterworks of Literature Ser.). 1995. pap. 12.95 (0-8084-0477-6) NCUP.

Twain's Tales. David T. London. 38p. (Orig.). (J). 1994. pap. 4.00 (1-57514-125-6, 1165) Encore Perform Pub.

Twana, Chemakum, & Klallam Indians of Washington Territory. Myron Eells. LC 96-16552. 87p. 1996. pap. 9.95 (0-87770-585-2) Ye Galleon.

Twana Narratives: Native Historical Accounts of a Coast Salish Culture. William W. Elmendorf. LC 92-43842. 376p. (C). 1993. 40.00 (0-295-97238-6) U of Wash Pr.

Twana Twined Basketry. D. L. Nordquist & G. E. Nordquist. (Illus.). 100p. (Orig.). (C). 1983. pap. 19.95 (0-916552-27-6) Acoma Bks.

Twang! Raymond Obstfeld. LC 97-5464. 1997. pap. 12.95 (0-8050-4888-X) H Holt & Co.

Twanged. Carol H. Clark. 1997. 22.00 (0-446-51763-1) Warner Bks.

*Twanged. Carol H. Clark. 1998. mass mkt. write for info. (0-446-60536-0, Warner Vision) Warner Bks.

*T'was a Dark & Dreary Night. McManus. 1992. 14.95 (0-8050-1905-7) W H Freeman.

Twas a Twig. Petrie R. Booser. (Illus.). 80p. 1990. lib. bdg. 19.00 (0-685-35753-8) Inniea Pub Co.

'Twas Only an Irishman's Dream: The Image of Ireland & the Irish in American Popular Song Lyrics, 1800-1920. William H. Williams. 1996. text ed. 42.50 (0-252-02246-7); pap. text ed. 17.95 (0-252-06551-4) U of Ill Pr.

T'was the Fight before Christmas. (McGee & Me! Ser: Vol. 9). (J). 1990. pap. 5.99 (0-8423-4114-5) Tyndale.

'Twas the Night. Lass Small. (Desire Ser.: No. 684). 1991. pap. 2.79 (0-373-05684-2) Harlequin Bks.

'Twas the Night after Christmas. Jean Schick-Jacobowitz et al. (Petites Ser.). (Illus.). 60p. 1994. 4.95 (0-88088-782-6) Peter Pauper.

'Twas the Night Before: A Picture-Story of the Nativity. Rachel Olson. Ed. by Rhonda Wray. LC 93-26740. (Illus.). 24p. (Orig.). (J). (gr. k-3). 1993. 14.95 (0-916260-85-2, B143) Meriwether Pub.

'Twas the Night before Christmas. (Favorite Christmas Tales Ser.). (Illus.). 24p. (J). 1993. 4.98 (1-56173-724-0) Pubns Intl Ltd.

Twas the Night Before Christmas. Illus. by Moore Clement Clarke. LC 93-37281. 32p. (J). (ps-1). 1994. pap. 10.95 (0-689-71801-2, Aladdin Paperbacks) S&S Childrens.

'Twas the Night before Christmas. Clement C. Moore. (Christmas Fun-to-Read Fairy Tales Ser.). (Illus.). 24p. (J). (gr. k-3). 1992. pap. 2.50 (1-56144-163-5, Honey Bear Bks) Modern Pub NYC.

*Twas the Night Before Christmas. Clement C. Moore. (J). Date not set. write for info. (0-688-12039-3); lib. bdg. write for info. (0-688-12040-7) Lothrop.

'Twas the Night before Christmas. Carolyn Quattrocki. (Favorite Christmas Tales Ser.). (Illus.). 24p. (J). (ps-4). 1992. lib. bdg. 10.95 (1-56674-027-4, HTS Bks) Forest Hse.

'Twas the Night before Christmas. anniversary ed. Clement C. Moore. LC 93-40243. (Illus.). 48p. (J). 1992. pap. 4.95 (0-395-64374-0) HM.

'Twas the Night before Christmas: A Visit from St. Nicholas. Clement C. Moore. (Illus.). (J). (ps-2). 1912. 14.95 (0-395-06952-1) HM.

'Twas the Night before Jesus. Robert F. Heise. (Illus.). 28p. (J). (gr. 3-6). 1990. 12.95 (0-9627049-0-3) Dogwood Pr NC.

T'was the Night Before MacChristmas: A Christmas Tale for Macintosh Users. Carole Marsh. (Lifewrite Ser.). (Illus.). 1994. pap. 19.95 (0-7933-0006-1) Gallopade Pub Group.

'Twas the Night Before Thanksgiving. Dave Pilkey. LC 89-48941. (Illus.). 32p. (J). (ps-2). 1990. 15.95 (0-531-05905-7); lib. bdg. 16.99 (0-531-08505-8) Orchard Bks Watts.

'Twas the Night before the Orange Bowl. Clair Gilliland. 40p. 1989. 11.95 (0-912081-05-8) Delmar Co.

'Twas the Night B'fore Christmas: An African-American Version. Illus. & Retold by Melodye Rosales. LC 95-53236. 32p. (J). (ps-3). 1996. 12.95 (0-590-73944-1, Cartwheel) Scholastic Inc.

'Twas the Week Before Christmas Coloring Book. Illus. by Geoffrey H. Brittingham. 32p. (Orig.). (J). (ps-3). 1996. pap. 2.49 (1-57102-093-4, Ideals Child) Hambleton-Hill.

*Twas the Week Before Christmas. Connie Hall. LC 96-94764. (Illus.). 30p. (J). (gr. k up). 1996. 12.95 (0-9654869-0-7) Bks by Connie.

Tweak & the Absolutely Right Whale. Patricia B. Dubin. (Illus.). 48p. (Orig.). (J). (gr. k-3). 1993. pap. 9.95 (1-880812-06-1) S Ink WA.

Tweaking the Nose of the Russians. J. Harrington & B. Courtney. 1991. text ed. 54.50 (0-88033-193-3) Col U Pr.

Tweed: Man of the Month. Lass Small. (Desire Ser.). 1993. mass mkt. 2.99 (0-373-05817-9, 5-05817-7) Silhouette.

Tweed Ring. Alexander B. Callow, Jr. LC 81-6528. (Illus.). xi, 351p. 1981. reprint ed. text ed. 35.00 (0-313-22761-6, CATR, Greenwood Pr) Greenwood.

Tweedles & Foodles for Young Noodles. Malvina Reynolds. LC 73-80670. (Illus.). 42p. (J). (gr. k-4). 1961. pap. 5.75 (0-915620-08-1) Schroder Music.

Tweedlioop. Stanley Schmidt. 240p. 1988. pap. 3.95 (0-8125-3155-8) Tor Bks.

'Tween Me 'n God: (But I'll Let You Peek!) Nancy A. Benn. 70p. (Orig.). 1995. pap. 7.95 (1-57502-084-X) Morris Pubng.

Tweens at Deep Lake: An Original American Fantasy. Douglas A. Ploss. LC 79-90996. (Illus.). 88p. (J). (gr. 3 up). 1979. pap. 8.50 (0-9603632-1-1) OPC.

Tweet, Tweet, Tweet. Stewart Cowley. (Hear! Hear! Ser.). (Illus.). 20p. (J). (ps-3). 1994. 3.95 (0-307-17350-X, Golden Books) Western Pub.

Tweetsie: The Blue Ridge Stemwinder. Julian Scheer & Elizabeth M. Black. (Illus.). 80p. 1991. reprint ed. 12.95 (0-932807-60-7) Overmountain Pr.

Tweetsie Adventure. Alice B. Lentz. (Illus.). 32p. (J). (gr. k-3). 1995. 9.95 (1-57072-025-8) Overmountain Pr.

Tweetsie Country: The East Tennessee & Western North Carolina Railroad. Mallory H. Ferrell. (Illus.). 232p. 1997. reprint ed. 44.95 (0-932807-58-5) Overmountain Pr.

Tweety. Golden Western Staff. (Illus.). (J). (ps-3). pap. 1.95 (0-307-08239-3, Golden Books) Western Pub.

Tweety Trap. Golden Books Staff. (First Little Golden Bks.). (Illus.). 24p. (J). 1995. 1.09 (0-307-10248-3, Golden Pr) Western Pub.

Tweety's Knock, Knock Jokes. Illus. by Steve Smallwood. (Looney Tunes Joke Bks.). 96p. (J). (ps-3). 1995. pap. 3.50 (0-307-13176-9, Golden Books) Western Pub.

Twelfe Night: or What You Will. M.H. Publications Staff. 191p. 1990. 110.00 (1-872680-02-X, Pub. by M H Pubns UK) St Mut.

Twelfth Aerospace Seminar Proceedings. 248p. 1990. pap. 100.00 (1-877862-01-0) Inst Environ Sci.

Twelfth Air Force Story. Kenn Rust. (Illus.). 72p. 1993. pap. text ed. 15.95 (0-911852-77-8) Aviation Heritage.

Twelfth & After. J. K. Stanford. (Illus.). 127p. 1989. 19.95 (0-948253-00-2, Pub. by Sportmans Pr UK) Trafalgar.

Twelfth Angel. Og Mandino. 160p. 1994. mass mkt. 5.99 (0-449-22303-5) Fawcett.

*Twelfth Angel. Og Mandino. 1996. pap. 10.00 (0-449-91150-0) Fawcett.

Twelfth Annual Computer Law Institute. (Commercial Law & Practice Course Handbook Ser.). 1990. 17.50 (0-685-69366-X) PLI.

Twelfth Annual Exhibition: National Academy of Western Art, 1984. Ed. by Sara Dobberteen. (Illus.). 100p. (Orig.). 1984. pap. 15.00 (0-932154-14-X) Natl Cowboy Hall of Fame.

12th Annual Insurance, Excess & Reinsurance Coverage Disputes, 2 vols., Set. (Litigation & Administrative Practice Course Handbook, 1983-84 Ser.). 1376p. 1994. pap. 149.00 (0-614-17259-4, H4-5211) PLI.

Twelfth Armored Division, Vol. II. Turner Publishing Company Staff. LC 86-51588. 128p. 1990. 48.00 (0-938021-92-3) Turner Pub KY.

Twelfth Armored Division Association History. Twelfth Armored Division Association Staff. LC 86-51588. 264p. 1987. 48.00 (0-938021-09-5) Turner Pub KY.

Twelfth Assembling Annual. Ed. by Charles Dorta et al. (Illus.). 100p. (Orig.). 1986. pap. 100.00 (0-915066-59-9); suppl. ed., pap. 200.00 (0-915066-60-2) Assembling Pr.

Twelfth Biennial Color Aerial Photography & Videography Workshop in the Plant Science & Related Fields. 312p. 1990. pap. 15.00 (0-944426-67-0) ASP & RS.

Twelfth-Century Cistercian Manuscripts from Sitticum. Natasa Golob. (Illus.). 340p. 1996. text ed. 140.00 (1-872501-86-9, ECU117, Harwood Acad Pubs) Gordon & Breach.

Twelfth-Century Homilies in Ms. Bodley 343, Pt. I: Text. Ed. by A. O. Belfour. (EETS, OS Ser.: Vol. 137). 1974. reprint ed. pap. 36.00 (0-8115-3369-7) Periodicals Srv.

Twelfth Century Studies. Josiah C. Russell. LC 77-83792. (Studies in the Middle Ages: No. 1). 34.50 (0-404-16022-0) AMS Pr.

An Asterisk (*) at the beginning of an entry indicates that the title is appearing in BIP for the first time.

Twelfth House: The Hidden Power in the Horoscope. Karen Hamaker-Zondag. LC 91-28354. 189p. (Orig.). 1992. pap. 12.95 (*0-87728-727-9*) Weiser.

***12th International Conference on Computers & Their Applications.** 285p. 1997. write for info. (*1-880843-19-6*) Int Soc Comp App.

12th International Conference on NDE in the Nuclear & Pressure Vessel Industries. 514p. 1994. 100.00 (*0-87170-506-0*, 6530) ASM.

***Twelfth International Conference on Raman Spectroscopy: Proceedings of the Twelfth International Conference on Raman Spectroscopy, 13-17 August 1990, Columbia, South Carolina.** Ed. by J. R. Durig & J. F. Sullivan. LC 90-12450. (Illus.). 961p. pap. 180.00 (*0-608-05258-2*, 2065796) Bks Demand.

Twelfth International Conference on Raman Spectroscopy: Proceedings of 12th International Conference. Ed. by James R. Durig & J. F. Sullivan. 919p. 1990. text ed. 356.00 (*0-471-92785-6*) Wiley.

Twelfth International Diatom Symposium: Proceedings of the Twelfth International Diatom Symposium, Renesse, Held at Renesse, The Netherlands - 30th August-5th September 1992. Ed. by Herman Van Dam. LC 93-30682. (Developments in Hydrobiology Ser.). 560p. (C). 1993. lib. bdg. 333.50 (*0-7923-2484-6*) Kluwer Ac.

Twelfth Man. Iftikhar Arif. LC 89-80342. 91p. 8900. pap. 16.95 (*0-948259-49-3*) Dufour.

Twelfth Man. John Parker. (Illus.). 208p. 1992. 23.95 (*0-233-98769-X*, Pub. by A Deutsch UK) Trafalgar.

Twelfth Meeting of the French Colonial Historical Society Ste. Genevieve, May 1986: Proceedings. Ed. by Philip P. Boucher & Serge Courville. (Illus.). 168p. (Orig.). (C). 1989. lib. bdg. 40.50 (*0-8191-7205-7*) U Pr of Amer.

12th Mental Measurements Yearbook. Ed. by Jane C. Conoley & James C. Impara. (Mental Measurements Yearbook Ser.). 1200p. (C). 1995. text ed. 150.00 (*0-910674-40-X*) Buros Inst Mental.

***Twelfth Night.** (Longman Critical Essays Ser.). Date not set. pap. text ed. write for info. (*0-582-06050-8*, Pub. by Longman UK) Longman.

Twelfth Night. Ed. by Alan Durband. (Shakespeare Made Easy Ser.). 288p. 1985. pap. 6.95 (*0-8120-3604-2*) Barron.

***Twelfth Night.** Ed. by Roma Gill. (Oxford School Shakespeare Ser.). (C). 1994. text ed. 10.72 (*0-669-40348-2*) HM College Div.

***Twelfth Night.** Michael Llewellyn. 480p. 1998. mass mkt. 5.99 (*1-57566-253-1*, Knsington) Knsgtn Pub Corp.

Twelfth Night. Michael Llwellyn. 384p. 1997. 21.95 (*1-57566-082-2*, Knsington) Knsgtn Pub Corp.

Twelfth Night. Ed. by A. L. Rowse. LC 84-15387. (Contemporary Shakespeare Ser.: Vol. II). 112p. 1985. pap. text ed. 3.45 (*0-8191-3912-2*) U Pr of Amer.

***Twelfth Night.** William Shakespeare. (Illustrated Classics Shakespeare Collection). 64p. 1994. pap. 4.95 (*0-7854-0814-2*, 40624) Am Guidance.

Twelfth Night. William Shakespeare. (Classics Ser.). 160p. 1988. pap. 3.95 (*0-553-21308-3*, Bantam Classics) Bantam.

Twelfth Night. William Shakespeare. (Book Notes Ser.). 1985. pap. 2.95 (*0-8120-3548-8*) Barron.

Twelfth Night. William Shakespeare. Ed. by Elizabeth S. Donno. (New Cambridge Shakespeare Ser.). 200p. 1985. text ed. 39.95 (*0-521-22752-6*); pap. text ed. 10.95 (*0-521-29633-1*) Cambridge U Pr.

Twelfth Night. William Shakespeare. Ed. by Rex Gibson. (School Shakespeare Ser.). (Illus.). 172p. (C). 1993. pap. text ed. 7.95 (*0-521-43536-6*) Cambridge U Pr.

Twelfth Night. William Shakespeare. Ed. by John Andrews. 224p. 3.95 (*0-460-87518-3*, Everyman's Classic Lib) C E Tuttle.

Twelfth Night. William Shakespeare. Ed. by John Hort & Leela Hort. 46p. 1992. pap. 6.00 (*0-948662-00-X*, Pub. by Kabet Pr UK) Empire Pub Srvs.

Twelfth Night. William Shakespeare. Ed. by Richard Adams. (J). 1989. pap. text ed. 4.29 (*0-582-01346-1*, 78433) Longman.

Twelfth Night. William Shakespeare. Ed. by Roy Blatchford. (Literature Ser.). 1993. pap. 5.95 (*0-582-08834-8*, TG7666) Longman.

Twelfth Night. William Shakespeare. 1965. pap. 3.95 (*0-451-52129-3*, Sig Classics) NAL-Dutton.

Twelfth Night. William Shakespeare. (BBC Television Plays Ser.). 1979. pap. 4.95 (*0-563-17778-0*, Pub. by BBC UK) Parkwest Pubns.

***Twelfth Night.** William Shakespeare. 1996. pap. 5.95 (*0-14-026399-3*) Penguin.

***Twelfth Night.** William Shakespeare. (English Text Ser.). 1975. pap. 9.95 (*0-415-02708-X*) Routledge.

Twelfth Night. William Shakespeare. Ed. by J. M. Lothian & T. W. Craik. (Arden Shakespeare Ser.). 1975. 49.95 (*0-416-17950-9*, NO. 2496); pap. 8.95 (*0-416-17960-6*, NO. 2497) Routledge Chapman & Hall.

Twelfth Night. William Shakespeare. Ed. by Charles T. Prouty. (Pelican Shakespeare Ser.). 120p. 1958. pap. 3.95 (*0-14-071411-1*, Pelican Bks) Viking Penguin.

Twelfth Night. William Shakespeare. Ed. by M. M. Mahood. (New Penguin Shakespeare Ser.). 208p. 1981. pap. 5.95 (*0-14-070711-5*, Penguin Classics) Viking Penguin.

***Twelfth Night.** William Shakespeare. (English Ser.). (C). Date not set. pap. 9.95 (*0-17-443538-X*) Wadsworth Pub.

Twelfth Night. William Shakespeare. Date not set. write for info. (*0-517-15122-7*) Random Hse Value.

Twelfth Night. White. 1996. text ed. 39.95 (*0-312-16027-5*) St Martin.

Twelfth Night. abr. ed. William Shakespeare. (Illus.). 36p. (YA). (gr. 7 up). 1984. pap. 3.25 (*0-88680-213-X*) I E Clark.

Twelfth Night. large type ed. William Shakespeare. 1991. pap. 24.95 (*0-7089-4505-8*, Trail West Pubs) Ulverscroft.

***Twelfth Night.** 3rd ed. William Shakespeare. (English Ser.). (C). Date not set. text ed. 45.00 (*0-17-443571-1*) Wadsworth Pub.

Twelfth Night: A Play Packet to Accompany Elementary, My Dear Shakespeare. Barbara Engen & Joy Campbell. (Illus.). 44p. 1992. 8.95 (*0-922947-08-2*) Mkt Masters.

Twelfth Night: Complete Study Guide. Sidney Lamb. 1965. pap. 6.95 (*0-8220-1444-0*) Cliffs.

Twelfth Night: HBJ Shakespeare 1989. William Shakespeare. Ed. by Maitman. 1990. student ed., pap. 12.00 (*0-7747-1356-9*) HB Schl Dept.

***Twelfth Night: Shakespeare Made Easy.** (Shakespeare Made Easy Ser.). 1985. pap. 14.95 (*0-7487-0351-9*) Dufour.

Twelfth Night for Kids. Lois Burdett & Christine Coburn. (Illus.). 40p. (Orig.). 1995. pap. 7.95 (*0-88753-233-0*, Pub. by Black Moss Pr CN) Firefly Bks Ltd.

Twelfth Night for Young People. William Shakespeare. Ed. & Illus. by Diane Davidson. LC 96-19754. (Shakespeare for Young People Ser.: No. 9). 64p. (Orig.). (J). (gr. 5-8). 1996. pap. text ed. 5.95 (*0-934048-26-6*) Swan Books.

Twelfth Night Notes. Marilynn Harper. (Cliffs Notes Ser.). 1982. pap. 4.25 (*0-8220-0094-6*) Cliffs.

Twelfth Night: or What You Will. William Shakespeare. Ed. by Stanley Wells. (Shakespeare Ser.). (Illus.). 256p. 1995. 55.00 (*0-19-812366-3*) Dover.

Twelfth Night, or What You Will. William Shakespeare. Ed. by Roger Warren & Stanley Wells. (World's Classics Ser.). (Illus.). 256p. 1995. pap. 6.95 (*0-19-283140-2*) OUP.

Twelfth Night, or, What You Will. William Shakespeare. Ed. by Paul Werstine & Barbara A. Mowat. (New Folger Library). (Illus.). 288p. 1993. mass mkt. 3.99 (*0-671-72294-8*, Folger Lib) PB.

Twelfth Night, or, What You Will. William Shakespeare. Ed. & Intro. by Laurie E. Osborne. LC 95-1817. (Shakespearean Originals--First Editions Ser.). 1995. pap. 12.95 (*0-13-355504-6*) P-H.

***Twelfth Night: or What You Will.** unabridged ed. William Shakespeare. 80p. 1996. reprint ed. pap. text ed. 1.00 (*0-486-29290-8*) Dover.

Twelfth Night, or What You Will: A Bibliography to Supplement the New Variorum Edition of 1901. Compiled by William C. McAvoy. LC 84-6546. (New Variorum Edition of Shakespeare Ser.). vi, 57p. 1984. pap. text ed. 10.00 (*0-87352-285-0*, Z125P) Modern Lang.

***Twelfth Night Readalong.** William Shakespeare. (Illustrated Classics Shakespeare Collection). 64p. 1994. pap. 14.95 incl. audio (*0-7854-0830-4*, 40626) Am Guidance.

Twelfth of August: Biography of "Walking Tall" Sheriff Buford Pusser. expanded ed. W. R. Morris. 1994. 19.95 (*0-9634779-9-4*) Cherokee Pr.

Twelfth of June. Marilyn Gould. LC 85-45173. 183p. (J). (gr. 4 up). 1994. lib. bdg. 12.95 (*0-9632305-4-9*) Allied Crafts.

Twelfth Penguin Book of the Times Crosswords. Ed. by John Grant. 144p. (Orig.). 1991. pap. 6.50 (*0-14-012112-9*) Viking Penguin.

Twelfth Planet. Zecharia Sitchin. 448p. 1978. mass mkt. 6.99 (*0-380-39362-X*) Avon.

Twelfth Planet: The First Book of the Earth Chronicles. Zecharia Sitchin. LC 91-7904. (Earth Chronicles Ser.: Bk. 1). (Illus.). 384p. 1991. reprint ed. 22.95 (*0-939680-88-2*) Bear & Co.

Twelfth Process Technology Conference: Environmental Concerns in the Iron & Steel Industry, Vol. XII. LC 82-197229. 392p. 1994. 90.00 (*0-932897-88-6*) Iron & Steel.

Twelfth Rose of Spring. Doris E. Fell. LC 95-10375. (Seasons of Intrigue Ser.: Bk. 4). 352p. (Orig.). 1995. pap. 9.99 (*0-89107-861-4*) Crossway Bks.

Twelfth S. S. Panzer Armored Division. Herbert Walther. Tr. by Edward Force from GER. LC 88-64000. (Illus.). 120p. 1989. 24.95 (*0-88740-166-X*) Schiffer.

Twelfth Symposium on Nucleic Acids Chemistry. Ed. by Tozo Fujii. (Nucleic Acids Symposium Ser.: No. 15). 208p. 1984. pap. 65.00 (*0-904147-94-0*, IRL Pr) OUP.

Twelfth Texas Symposium on Relativistic Astrophysics, Vol. 470. Ed. by Mario Livio & Giora Shaviv. 100.00 (*0-89766-335-7*); 100.00 (*0-89766-336-5*) NY Acad Sci.

Twelfth Virginia Cavalry. Dennis E. Frye. (Illus.). 188p. 1988. 19.95 (*0-930919-52-1*) H E Howard.

Twelfth Virginia Infantry. William D. Henderson. (Virginia Regimental Histories Ser.). (Illus.). 174p. 1985. 19.95 (*0-930919-12-2*) H E Howard.

12th International Corrosion Congress Preceedings Vol. 1: Coatings. 493p. 1993. 85.00 (*1-877914-65-7*) NACE Intl.

12th International Corrosion Congress Preceedings Vol. 2: Process Industries Plant Operations. 608p. 1993. 85.00 (*0-614-02599-0*) NACE Intl.

12th International Corrosion Congress Preceedings Vol. 4: Oil-Gas-Pipeline. 738p. 1993. 85.00 (*0-614-02600-8*) NACE Intl.

Twelve. Leslie Flynn. 156p. 1982. pap. 9.99 (*0-88207-310-9*, 6-2310, Victor Bks); pap. 1.30 (*0-88207-425-3*, Victor Bks) Chariot Victor.

Twelve. Carlos Franqui. Tr. by Albert Teicher. LC 68-10011. 1968. 4.50 (*0-8184-0089-7*) Carol Pub Group.

Twelve. Elaine Kittredge. (Illus.). 84p. (J). 1989. pap. 9.95 (*0-9611266-1-2*) Optext.

Twelve. Read by Jason Liss. 84p. (J). 1989. audio 9.95 (*0-9611266-2-0*) Optext.

XII Abusivis, De. Ed. & Intro. by Aidan Breen. 330p. 1997. boxed 55.00 (*1-85182-192-9*, Pub. by Four Cts Pr IE) Intl Spec Bk.

Twelve Across. Barbara Delinsky. 1994. mass mkt. 4.50 (*0-373-83290-7*, 1-83290-6) Harlequin Bks.

Twelve Against the Empire: The Anti-Imperialists, 1898-1900. Robert L. Beisner. 336p. 1992. reprint ed. pap. 15.95 (*1-879176-10-6*) Imprint Pubns.

***Twelve American Crime Stories.** Ed. by Rosemary Herbert. (Oxford Twelves). 256p. 1998. pap. 11.95 (*0-19-288047-0*) OUP.

Twelve American Plays. Ed. by Richard Corbin & Miriam Belf. LC 69-11437. 480p. (C). 1969. pap. text ed. 37.00 (*0-02-325180-8*, Macmillan Coll) P-H.

Twelve American Poets Before Nineteen Hundred. Rica Brenner. LC 68-22092. (Essay Index Reprint Ser.). 1977. 20.95 (*0-8369-0250-5*) Ayer.

Twelve Americans: Their Lives & Times. Howard Carroll. LC 70-37154. (Essay Index Reprint Ser.). 1977. reprint ed. 33.95 (*0-8369-2489-4*) Ayer.

Twelve & One-Half Keys. Edward Hays. LC 81-50505. (Illus.). 152p. (Orig.). 1981. pap. 8.95 (*0-939516-00-4*) Forest Peace.

Twelve Angry Men. rev. ed. Reginald Rose. 1983. 5.95 (*0-87129-327-7*, T42) Dramatic Pub.

Twelve Angry Men: A Screen Adaptation, Directed by Sidney Lumet. Reginald Rose. Ed. by George P. Garrett et al. LC 71-135273. (Film Scripts Ser.). 1989. reprint ed. pap. text ed. 19.95 (*0-89197-970-0*) Irvington.

Twelve Angry Women. rev. ed. Reginald Rose. 1983. Women. 5.95 (*0-87129-401-X*, T43) Dramatic Pub.

Twelve Apostles. William J. Coughlin. 1994. lib. bdg. 24.95 (*1-56849-407-6*) Buccaneer Bks.

Twelve Artists From the German Democratic Republic. Peter H. Selz et al. (Illus.). 171p. 1995. pap. 4.95 (*0-916724-71-9*, 4719) Harvard Art Mus.

Twelve Aspects of a Complete System of Spiritual Health & Nutrition: The Example of Ancient Egypt. Manu Ampim. (Illus.). 1994. pap. write for info. (*0-9636447-2-6*) Advan The Res.

Twelve Bad Men. Sidney Dark. LC 68-54343. (Essay Index Reprint Ser.). 1977. 23.95 (*0-8369-0361-7*) Ayer.

Twelve-Bar Blues James Trax for Guitar. Ralph Agresta. 1994. pap. 9.95 (*0-8256-1415-5*, AM91476) Music Sales.

***12-Bar Blues Piano.** Jack Long. 64p. pap. 9.95 incl. cd-rom (*0-7119-4521-7*) Omnibus NY.

12 Basic Skills of Fly Fishing. Ted Peck & Ed A. Rychkun. (Illus.). 48p. (Orig.). (C). 1996. pap. 6.95 (*0-88839-392-X*) Hancock House.

Twelve Baskets Full. Ed. by E. Catherwood. 16.99 (*1-85792-008-2*, Pub. by Christian Focus UK) Spring Arbor Dist.

Twelve Baskets Full, Vol. 1. Watchman Nee. 168p. per. 6.50 (*0-87083-086-4*, 07019001) Living Stream Ministry.

Twelve Baskets Full, Vol. 2. Watchman Nee. 155p. per. 6.00 (*0-87083-049-X*, 07020001) Living Stream Ministry.

Twelve Baskets Full, Vol. 3. Watchman Nee. 91p. per. 4.50 (*0-87083-050-3*, 07021001) Living Stream Ministry.

Twelve Baskets Full, Vol. 4. Watchman Nee. 154p. per. 5.75 (*0-87083-087-2*, 07022001) Living Stream Ministry.

Twelve Bindings. Michael Wilcox. 42p. 1985. 150.00 (*0-614-16151-7*) Oak Knoll.

Twelve Bindings. Michael Wilcox. 1986. 275.00 (*0-935072-07-1*) W T Taylor.

Twelve Blessings. Ed. by George King. LC 86-204674. 63p. 1958. 12.95 (*0-937249-02-5*) Aetherius Soc.

Twelve Bowls of Glass. Bucky Sinister. 20p. (Orig.). 1990. pap. 3.00 (*0-916397-06-8*) Manic D Pr.

***12 x 12 Mexican Contemporary Textile.** 48p. 1990. 5.00 (*0-614-24042-5*) Mexican Museum.

Twelve Caesars. Suetonius. Tr. & Rev. by Robert Graves. (Classics Ser.). 320p. (Orig.). 1957. pap. 11.95 (*0-14-044072-0*, Penguin Classics) Viking Penguin.

Twelve Caesars. Graves R. Suetonius. 1993. 16.00 (*0-453-00834-8*, NAL Bks) NAL-Dutton.

Twelve Candles, 4 vols. Elaine L. Schulte. (J). 1993. Set. 23.99 (*1-55661-781-X*) Bethany Hse.

***12 Cats of Christmas.** Wendy Darling & Evelyn Loeb. (Pocket Gift Editions Ser.). (Illus.). 64p. 1997. 4.95 (*0-88088-063-5*) Peter Pauper.

Twelve Cats of Christmas. Illus. by Kandy Radzinski. 26p. (J). 1992. 9.95 (*0-8118-0102-0*) Chronicle Bks.

Twelve Cell Salts of the Zodiac. George W. Carey. 31p. 1994. reprint ed. spiral bd. 7.00 (*0-7873-1224-X*) Hlth Research.

***Twelve Chairs.** Arnold Dovich et al. LC 96-29783. (European Classics Ser.). 1997. write for info. (*0-8101-1484-4*, Hydra Bks) Northwestern U Pr.

Twelve Children's Bookmarks. Jill Dubin. (Illus.). (J). (gr. 4-7). 1993. pap. 1.00 (*0-486-27705-4*) Dover.

Twelve Choral Preludes on Gregorian. Jeanne Demessieux. 32p. 1995. pap. text ed. 6.95 (*0-87487-603-6*) Summy-Birchard.

Twelve "Christian" Beliefs That Can Drive You Crazy: Relief from False Assumptions. Henry Cloud & John Townsend. 128p. 1995. pap. 8.99 (*0-310-49491-5*) Zondervan.

12 Christmas Sermons. Charles H. Spurgeon. 144p. (C). 1995. reprint ed. pap. 6.99 (*0-8010-8391-5*) Baker Bks.

Twelve Circus Rings. Seymour Chwast. LC 92-13576. (Illus.). 32p. (J). (ps-3). 1993. 15.00 (*0-15-200627-3*, Gulliver Bks) HarBrace.

Twelve Circus Rings. Seymour Chwast. (J). 1996. pap. 6.00 (*0-15-201361-X*) HarBrace.

Twelve Classics. Joshua Baer. (Illus.). 32p. 1989. 12.95 (*0-685-28861-7*) J Baer & Co.

Twelve Contemporary Russian Stories. Ed. & Tr. by Vytas Dukas from RUS. LC 74-4969. 130p. 1977. 25.00 (*0-8386-1491-4*) Fairleigh Dickinson.

Twelve Core Functions of a Counselor. 4th rev. ed. Stanley F. Kulewicz. (Orig.). (C). 1996. pap. text ed. 19.95 (*0-9624963-1-6*) Counselor Pubns.

THE TWELVE CORE FUNCTIONS OF A COUNSELOR provides the foundation for the development of SUBSTANCE ABUSE COUNSELOR education programs. As the most prominent textbook dealing exclusively with the TREATMENT PROCESS of the victim of addiction, it provides a thorough description & explanation of the functions of the counselor. Illustrative forms needed in the treatment process are provided & are used as a guide for the counselor in his working with the client. The twelve integrated functions, interdependent & mutually supportive, provide the blueprint for the complete treatment of the addicted client. Written in simple, understandable terms, it has wide appeal with students as well as practicing counselors & TREATMENT FACILITY MANAGERS. It is used as the training manual for the education of candidates for COUNSELOR CERTIFICATION OR LICENSURE in many colleges, universities & prison systems, as well as by the individual candidate. Schools in the ALLIED HEALTH fields such as nursing, physicians' assistants, medical assisting & police science have integrated the textbook into their curriculum. It is readily adaptable for use in the treatment of compulsive & dysfunctional behaviors such as gambling & physical abuse. To order contact: Counselor Publications, P.O. Box 515, Marlborough CT 06447. Phone/FAX (860) 295-9185. ***Publisher Provided Annotation.***

Twelve Counseling Programs for Children at Risk. Susan T. Dennison. (Illus.). 430p. 1989. pap. 44.95 (*0-398-06090-8*) C C Thomas.

Twelve Counseling Programs for Children at Risk. Susan T. Dennison. (Illus.). 430p. (C). 1989. text ed. 79.95 (*0-398-05626-9*) C C Thomas.

Twelve Crimes of Christmas. Ed. by Carol-Lynn R. Waugh et al. 256p. (Orig.). 1981. pap. 2.95 (*0-380-78931-0*) Avon.

Twelve Dancing Princesses. Marianna Mayer. LC 83-1034. (Illus.). 40p. (J). (ps up). 1989. 16.00 (*0-688-08051-0*, Morrow Junior) Morrow.

Twelve Dancing Princesses. Marianna Mayer. LC 83-1034. (Illus.). 40p. (J). (ps up). 1989. lib. bdg. 15.93 (*0-688-02026-7*, Morrow Junior) Morrow.

Twelve Dancing Princesses. I. E. Clark. 40p. (J). (ps up). 1969. pap. 4.00 (*0-88680-197-4*); Director's Production Script. pap. 15.00 (*0-88680-198-2*) I E Clark.

Twelve Dancing Princesses. Golden Books Staff. (Little Golden Bks.). (Illus.). 24p. (J). (ps-2). 1995. 1.49 (*0-307-30265-2*, Golden Pr) Western Pub.

Twelve Dancing Princesses. Jacob W. Grimm & Wilhelm K. Grimm. LC 78-18077. (Illus.). 32p. (J). (gr. k-4). 1979. lib. bdg. 11.89 (*0-89375-139-1*) Troll Communs.

Twelve Dancing Princesses. Jacob W. Grimm & Wilhelm K. Grimm. LC 78-18077. (Illus.). 32p. (J). (gr. k-4). 1997. pap. 3.95 (*0-89375-117-0*) Troll Communs.

Twelve Dancing Princesses. Jacob W. Grimm & Wilhelm K. Grimm. (Illus.). 32p. (J). (ps-3). 1996. pap. 15.99 (*0-525-45595-7*) NAL-Dutton.

Twelve Dancing Princesses. Jacob W. Grimm & Wilhelm K. Grimm. 32p. 1996. pap. 19.95 (*0-385-25591-8*) Doubleday.

***Twelve Dancing Princesses.** Marianna Mayer. (J). Date not set. pap. write for info. (*0-688-14392-X*, Mulberry) Morrow.

Twelve Dancing Princesses. Retold by Ruth Sanderson. (J). (gr. 2-4). 1990. 15.95 (*0-316-77017-5*) Little.

Twelve Dancing Princesses. Retold by Ruth Sanderson. (Illus.). (J). (gr. 4-8). 1993. mass mkt. 5.95 (*0-316-77062-0*, Joy St Bks) Little.

Twelve Dancing Princesses. Sucie Stevenson. LC 94-32512. (Illus.). 48p. (J). (gr. 1-3). 1995. pap. 3.99 (*0-440-41088-6*, YB BDD) BDD Bks Young Read.

Twelve Dancing Princesses. Illus. & Retold by Sucie Stevenson. LC 94-32512. 1995. write for info. (*0-440-41091-6*) Dell.

Twelve Dancing Princesses: A Fairy Tale by Jacob & Wilhelm Grimm. Jacob W. Grimm & Wilhelm K. Grimm. Tr. by Anthea Bell from GER. LC 95-2267. Orig. Title: Zertanzten Schuhe. (Illus.). 32p. (J). (gr. k-3). Date not set. 16.95 (*1-55858-216-9*) North-South Bks NYC.

***Twelve Dancing Princesses: A Fairy Tale by Jacob & Wilhelm Grimm.** Jacob W. Grimm & Wilhelm K. Grimm. Tr. by Anthea Bell from GER. LC 95-2267. Orig. Title: Zertanzten Schuhe. (Illus.). 32p. (J). (gr. k-3). Date not set. lib. bdg. 16.88 (*1-55858-217-7*) North-South Bks NYC.

Twelve Dancing Princesses - Musical. June W. Rogers et al. 1976. 5.00 (*0-87129-516-4*, T04) Dramatic Pub.

Twelve Dancing Princesses & Other Fairy Tales. Alfred David & Mary E. Meek. LC 73-16517. (Illus.). 320p. (J). (gr. 1-6). 1974. pap. 13.95 (*0-253-20173-X*, MB-173) Ind U Pr.

Twelve Daughters of Democracy. Eleanor M. Sickels. LC 68-55858. (Essay Index Reprint Ser.). 1977. 18.95 (*0-8369-0879-1*) Ayer.

Twelve Days. Ed. by Blair G. Meeks. (Liturgy Ser.). (Illus.). 72p. 1995. pap. 10.95 (*0-918208-70-X*) Liturgical Conf.

Twelve Days. Sidney Rogerson. 172p. 1988. 65.00 (*0-947893-10-5*, Pub. by Gliddon Bks UK) St Mut.

An Asterisk (*) at the beginning of an entry indicates that the title is appearing in BIP for the first time.

Twelve Days in August. Liza K. Murrow. 192p. (YA). 1995. reprint ed. mass mkt. 3.99 (0-380-72353-0, Flare) Avon.

Twelve Days in August: A Novel. Liza K. Murrow. LC 92-54489. 160p. (J). (gr. 7 up). 1993. 15.95 (0-8234-1012-9) Holiday.

Twelve Days in May: The Air Battle for France & the Low Countries, 10-21 May 1940, As Told by the Allied & German Pilots Themselves. Brian Cull & Bruce Lander. (Illus.). 256p. 1995. 29.95 (1-898697-20-5, Pub. by Grub St Pubns UK) Seven Hills Bk.

Twelve Days in Texas. Donna D. Cooner. (Illus.). 32p. (J). (gr. k up). 1994. pap. 7.95 (0-937460-85-0) Hendrick-Long.

***12 Days in Walleye Heaven.** M. Doug Burns. Ed. & Pref. by Bernie R. Barringer. (Illus.). 180p. (Orig.). Date not set. pap. 14.95 (1-885149-02-6) Moving Mtn.

Twelve Days of...? Thoughts on Being Alone, Yet Loved During the Holidays. Robert E. Steinkamp. 101p. (Orig.). 1992. pap. 5.95 (1-886045-07-0) Covenant Marriages.

Twelve Days of Christmas. (Christmas Fun-to-Read Fairy Tales Ser.). (Illus.). 24p. (J). (gr. k-3). 1992. pap. 2.50 (1-56144-164-3, Honey Bear Bks) Modern Pub NYC.

Twelve Days of Christmas. (Christmas Titles Ser.: No. S808-15). (Illus.). (J). 3.95 (0-7214-5078-4, Ladybrd) Penguin.

Twelve Days of Christmas. (Favorite Christmas Tales Ser.). (Illus.). 24p. (J). 1993. 4.98 (0-7853-0270-0) Pubns Intl Ltd.

Twelve Days of Christmas. (Silver Elm Classic Ser.). (Illus.). 24p. (J). (gr. k-3). 1991. pap. 3.99 (0-87406-576-3) Willowisp Pr.

Twelve Days of Christmas. (Christmas Stickers Ser.). (Illus.). 12p. (J). 1996. pap. 3.95 (0-7894-1126-1) DK Pub Inc.

Twelve Days of Christmas. (Christmas Classic Holiday Ser.). 24p. (J). (ps-3). Date not set. text ed. 3.50 (1-56987-240-6) Landoll.

Twelve Days of Christmas. (Little Landoll Christmas Ser.). 32p. (J). (ps-6). Date not set. text ed. 1.29 (1-56987-279-1) Landoll.

Twelve Days of Christmas. (My Favorite Beanstalk Bks.). 24p. (J). 1996. write for info. (1-57719-079-3) GT Pubng Corp.

Twelve Days of Christmas. Bolam. LC 96-25147. (J). 1997. 16.00 (0-689-81101-2) S&S Childrens.

Twelve Days of Christmas. Jan Brett. (Illus.). 32p. (J). 1990. 15.95 (0-399-22037-2, Putnam) Putnam Pub Group.

***Twelve Days of Christmas.** Jan Brett. (Illus.). 32p. (Orig.). (J). 1997. pap. 5.95 (0-698-11569-4, Paperstar) Putnam Pub Group.

Twelve Days of Christmas. Illus. by Diane DeGroat. 20p. 1990. pap. 2.95 (0-8167-1891-1) Troll Communs.

Twelve Days of Christmas. Dorothee Duntze. 1996. pap. text ed. 6.95 (1-55858-608-3) North-South Bks NYC.

***Twelve Days of Christmas.** Illus. by Vladimir V. Evich. (J). 1998. lib. bdg. write for info. (0-06-027653-3) HarpC.

Twelve Days of Christmas. Anne Geddes. (Anne Geddes Line Ser.). (Illus.). (J). (gr. k-3). 1995. 19.95 (1-55912-003-7) CEDCO Pub.

***Twelve Days of Christmas.** Anne Geddes. (Illus.). 32p. 1997. 19.95 (0-7683-2004-6) CEDCO Pub.

Twelve Days of Christmas. Benjamin Hanby. (Illus.). 24p. (J). (ps-3). 1989. pap. 2.95 (0-8249-8391-2, Ideals Child) Hambleton-Hill.

Twelve Days of Christmas. Woodleigh M. Hubbard. LC 96-1215. 32p. (J). 1996. 15.95 (0-8118-1264-2) Chronicle Bks.

Twelve Days of Christmas. Jonathan Lambert. (J). (ps-3). 1992. pap. 12.00 (0-671-78396-3, S&S Bks Young Read) S&S Childrens.

Twelve Days of Christmas. Illus. by John Lawrence. (Miniature Editions Ser.). 88p. 1994. 4.95 (1-56138-420-8) Running Pr.

Twelve Days of Christmas. Martin Marix-Evans. (Charming Petites Ser.). (Illus.). 80p. 1993. 5.95 (0-88088-780-X) Peter Pauper.

Twelve Days of Christmas. Darcy May. 12p. (J). 1993. 5.00 (1-55670-336-8) Stewart Tabori & Chang.

Twelve Days of Christmas. McClanahan Staff. (Christmas Storytime Bks.). (Illus.). 24p. (J). (ps-2). 1994. bds. 1.29 (1-56293-495-3) McClanahan Bk.

Twelve Days of Christmas. John O'Brien. LC 92-73990. (Illus.). 32p. (J). 1993. 14.95 (1-56397-142-9) Boyds Mills Pr.

Twelve Days of Christmas. Riley. (J). 1996. 15.00 (0-671-89202-9, S&S Bks Young Read) S&S Childrens.

Twelve Days of Christmas. Illus. by Linnea A. Riley. LC 95-14362. (J). 1995. 15.00 (0-689-80275-7, S&S Bks Young Read) S&S Childrens.

Twelve Days of Christmas. Illus. by Susan E. Swan. LC 80-28097. 32p. (J). (gr. k-4). 1981. pap. 3.95 (0-89375-475-7) Troll Communs.

***Twelve Days of Christmas.** Illus. by Vladimir V. Vagin. LC 97-11749. (J). 1998. write for info. (0-06-027652-5) HarpC.

Twelve Days of Christmas. Brian Wildsmith. LC 95-14420. (Illus.). 32p. (J). (ps-3). 1995. pap. 5.95 (1-56294-907-1) Millbrook Pr.

Twelve Days of Christmas. rev. ed. Benjamin R. Hanby. (Illus.). 24p. (J). (ps-3). 1995. pap. 2.49 (1-57102-078-0, Ideals Child) Hambleton-Hill.

Twelve Days of Christmas. 2nd ed. Louise Brierley. LC 94-19705. (Illus.). (J). (ps up). 1995. pap. 5.99 (1-56402-525-X) Candlewick Pr.

Twelve Days of Christmas. Suzy-Jane Tanner. (Bunnies & Bears Ser.). (Illus.). 31p. (J). (ps up). 1993. reprint ed. 4.95 (1-882607-11-2) Merrybooks VA.

Twelve Days of Christmas: A Celebration & History. Leigh Grant. (Illus.). 40p. 1995. 14.95 (0-8109-3881-2) Abrams.

Twelve Days of Christmas: A Christmas Carol. (Little Golden Books Holiday Favorites Ser.). (Illus.). 24p. (J). (ps-2). 1995. bds. 1.49 (0-307-00149-0, Golden Pr) Western Pub.

Twelve Days of Christmas: A Revolving Picture Book. Illus. by Maggie Kneen. 12p. (J). (ps-6). 1992. pap. 13.95 (0-525-44654-0) Dutton Child Bks.

Twelve Days of Christmas: Easy Piano. (Easy Play Ser.). 72p. 1994. otabind 14.95 (0-7935-3531-X, 00222584) H Leonard.

***Twelve Days of Christmas: Miniature Editions Gift Set.** (Illus.). 88p. 1997. 7.95 (0-7624-0205-9) Running Pr.

Twelve Days of Christmas: The Twelve Stages of a Soul (The Creation of a Universe) John D. Rea & Alayna Rea. 40p. (Orig.). 1987. pap. 4.95 (0-938183-04-4) Two Trees Pub.

Twelve Days of Christmas: 14 Delightful Ornament Designs. Annette Bradshaw & Gwyn Franson. 48p. (Orig.). 1981. pap. 5.98 (0-88290-151-6, 2803) Horizon Utah.

Twelve Days of Christmas Cookbook. Ruth Moorman & Lalla Williams. (Cookbook Ser.: No. 1). (Illus.). 80p. 1978. pap. 5.95 (0-937552-00-3) Quail Ridge.

***Twelve Days of Christmas (Mini)** Anne Geddes. (Illus.). 32p. 1997. 9.95 (0-7683-2003-8) CEDCO Pub.

12 Days of Christmas Pop-Up Book: A Pop-Up Celebration. Robert Sabuda. 12p. (J). 1996. 19.95 (0-689-80865-8) S&S Childrens.

Twelve Days of Summer. Elizabeth L. O'Donnell. LC 89-35161. (Illus.). 32p. (J). (ps up). 1991. 16.00 (0-688-08202-5, Morrow Junior); lib. bdg. 15.93 (0-688-08203-3, Morrow Junior) Morrow.

Twelve Days on the Road: The Sex Pistols & America. Noel E. Monk & Jimmy Guterman. LC 92-11416. 1992. pap. 10.00 (0-688-11274-9, Quill) Morrow.

Twelve Dazes of Christmas: And One Holy Night. Charlene A. Baumbich. LC 96-16489. 141p. (Orig.). 1996. pap. 9.99 (0-8308-1961-4, 1961, Saltshaker Bk) InterVarsity.

***Twelve Deaths of Christmas.** Marian Babson. 1996. mass mkt. 4.99 (0-614-20526-3) St Martin.

***12 Deaths of Christmas, Vol. 1.** Marian Babson. 1996. mass mkt. 4.99 (0-312-96039-5) St Martin.

Twelve Decisive Battles of the Mind: The Story of Propaganda During the Christian Era, with Abridged Versions of Texts That Have Shaped History. Gorham B. Munson. LC 72-167388. (Essay Index Reprint Ser.). 1977. reprint ed. 20.95 (0-8369-2705-2) Ayer.

Twelve Doors to the Soul. Jane Evans. LC 78-64907. (Illus.). (Orig.). 1979. pap. 8.95 (0-8356-0521-3, Quest) Theos Pub Hse.

Twelve Dreams. rev. ed. James Lapine. 1996. pap. 5.25 (0-8222-1506-3) Dramatists Play.

Twelve Duets for Flutes. Kaplan. 1990. 5.95 (0-685-32127-4, 77-53) Hansen Ed Mus.

Twelve Easy Scarlatti Sonatas. D. Scarlatti. 24p. 1984. pap. 4.95 (0-7935-2913-1, 00009222) H Leonard.

12 Easy Steps to Successful Research Papers. Nell W. Meriwether. LC 96-858. (Illus.). 176p. (C). 1996. pap. 7.95 (0-8442-5891-1) NTC Pub Grp.

Twelve English Authoresses. Ed. by Lucy B. Walford. LC 72-1314. (Essay Index Reprint Ser.). 1977. reprint ed. 18.95 (0-8369-2871-7) Ayer.

Twelve Englishmen of Mystery. Ed. by Earl F. Bargainnier. LC 83-72499. 1984. 23.95 (0-87972-249-5); pap. 12.95 (0-87972-250-9) Bowling Green Univ Popular Press.

Twelve Entry Points to Legal Research: A User Friendly System. Berton E. Ballard. LC 86-26611. (Illus.). 375p. (Orig.). (C). 1986. pap. 19.95 (0-940199-00-9) B E Ballard.

***12 Essential Laws for Getting a Job & Becoming Indispensable.** Tony Zeiss. 1997. pap. text ed. 5.99 (0-7852-7564-9) Nelson.

12 Essential Skills for Great Preaching. Wayne McDill. LC 93-38953. (Professional Development Bks.). 304p. 1994. 17.99 (0-8054-2012-6, 4220-12) Broadman.

Twelve Etudes for Clarinet. P. L. Polatschek. 24p. 1984. pap. 4.95 (0-7935-5271-0, 00008300) H Leonard.

Twelve Etudes for the Piano: Centennial Edition. Claude Debussy. 64p. 1994. pap. 7.95 (0-7935-3158-6) H Leonard.

***Twelve Faces of Saturn: Your Guardian Angel Planet.** Bil Tierney. 360p. (Orig.). 1998. pap. 16.95 (1-56718-711-0) Llewellyn Pubns.

Twelve Famous Plays of the Restoration & Eighteenth Century, 3 vols. reprint ed. 150.00 (0-403-03071-4) Somerset Pub.

Twelve Fantasias: For Flute & Piano. G. Telemann. 28p. 1986. pap. 7.95 (0-7935-4861-6, 50335080) H Leonard.

Twelve Farm Drawings. limited ed. Carl Schaefer. (Illus.). 1980. 65.00 (0-920806-12-0, Pub. by Penumbra Pr CN) U of Toronto Pr.

Twelve Frets to One Octave. Larry Coryell. 5.95 (1-56222-830-7, 95013); audio 10.98 (1-56222-869-2, 95013C); audio compact disk 15.98 (1-56222-872-2, 95013CD) Mel Bay.

***Twelve Frets to One Octave.** Larry Coryell. 20.95 incl. audio compact disk (0-7866-1173-1, 95013CDP); 15.95 incl. audio (0-7866-1174-X, 95013P) Mel Bay.

Twelve Friends: A Counting Book about Jesus. Joy Hutchinson. LC 91-71037. 32p. (J). (gr. 2 up). 1991. pap. 5.99 (0-8066-2559-7, 9-2559) Augsburg Fortress.

Twelve Frights of Christmas. Ed. by Isaac Asimov et al. 272p. 1986. mass mkt. 3.50 (0-380-75098-8) Avon.

***12 from R-H-Y-M-M-S: 4 Color Visual Works.** Robert Grenier. (Illus.). 16p. 1996. pap. 20.00 (1-886350-78-7) Pavement Saw.

Twelve from the Sixties. Ed. by Richard Kostelanetz. (C). 1978. reprint ed. pap. 10.00 (0-932360-03-3) Archae Edns.

Twelve Gates to the City: Spiritual Views on the Journey from 30 Authors. Ed. by Carol S. Lawson. (Chrysalis Reader Ser.: Vol. 2). (Illus.). 160p. (Orig.). 1996. pap. 12.95 (0-87785-226-X) Swedenborg.

***12 Gauge Paddle: And Other True Tales of the Outdoors.** R. Blair Savage. LC 96-86544. (Illus.). 160p. (Orig.). 1997. pap. 13.95 (0-9649239-6-3) Buffalo Run.

Twelve Geometric Essays. H. S. Coxeter. LC 68-13859. 288p. (C). 1968. text ed. 14.95 (0-8093-0303-5) S Ill U Pr.

Twelve German Novellas. Ed. & Tr. by Harry Steinhauer from GER. 648p. 1977. pap. 16.00 (0-520-03002-8) U CA Pr.

Twelve Gifts of Christmas. Rita C. Estrada. (Temptation Ser.). 1994. mass mkt. 2.99 (0-373-25618-3, 1-25618-9) Harlequin Bks.

12 Going on 13: An Autobiographical Novel. Jan Myrdal. Tr. by Christine Swanson from SWE. LC 95-35488. 200p. 1995. 19.95 (1-884468-01-2, 01-2) Ravenswood Bks.

***Twelve Golden Threads.** Aliske Webb. 224p. mass mkt. 5.99 (0-06-101199-1, Harp PBks) HarpC.

Twelve Golden Threads. Aliske Webb. 1996. 18.00 (0-614-95802-4) HarpC.

***Twelve Golden Threads: Lessons for Successful Living from Grama's Guilt.** Aliske Webb. 1997. pap. text ed. 10.00 (0-06-092845-X, PL) HarpC.

Twelve Golden Threads: Lessons for Successful Living from Grama's Quilt. Aliske Webb. 176p. 1996. 18.00 (0-06-017463-3) HarpC.

***Twelve Golden Threads: Lessons for Successful Living from Grama's Quilt.** large type ed. Aliske Webb. LC 96-34750. (Wheeler Large Print Book Ser.). 1996. 23.95 (1-56895-376-3, Compass) Wheeler Pub.

Twelve Good Men & True: The Criminal Trial Jury in England, 1200-1800. Ed. by J. S. Cockburn & Thomas A. Green. (Illus.). 375p. 1988. text ed. 70.00 (0-691-05511-4) Princeton U Pr.

Twelve Great Chess Players & Their Best Games. Irving Chernev. LC 95-5916. (Illus.). 256p. 1995. pap. text ed. 11.95 (0-486-28674-6) Dover.

Twelve Great Diamonds. Jane G. Austin. (Works of Jane (Goodin) Austin). 1989. reprint ed. lib. bdg. 79.00 (0-7812-1837-3) Rprt Serv.

Twelve Great Modernists. Lawrence F. Abbott. LC 76-84292. (Essay Index Reprint Ser.). 1977. 22.95 (0-8369-1118-0) Ayer.

Twelve Great Philosophers for Introductory Students: Historical Perspectives on Human Nature. Wayne P. Pomerleau. (Illus.). 477p. (C). 1997. text ed. write for info. (1-880157-54-3); teacher ed., text ed. write for info. (1-880157-57-8) Ardsley.

Twelve Great Questions about Christ. Clarence E. Macartney. LC 92-23990. 160p. 1993. pap. 9.99 (0-8254-3267-7) Kregel.

Twelve Great Western Philosophers. Howard A. Ozmon. LC 68-16403. (Illus.). 48p. (J). (gr. 4 up). 1967. lib. bdg. 9.95 (0-87783-046-0) Oddo.

Twelve Great Western Philosophers. deluxe ed. Howard A. Ozmon. LC 68-16403. (Illus.). 48p. (J). (gr. 4 up). 1967. pap. 3.94 (0-87783-115-7) Oddo.

Twelve Guiding Energy Sitting Mediations of Yin Style Ba Gua. Xie Peiqi. Tr. by Andrew Nugent-Head. 108p. 1995. pap. 13.50 (1-888179-51-1) Assn For Tradit.

Twelve Harmonies. Rudolf Steiner. Tr. by Daisy Aldan. 1986. pap. 4.95 (0-913152-21-8) Folder Edns.

Twelve Healers. Bach. 111p. 1941. pap. 2.50 (0-85207-041-1, Pub. by C W Daniel UK) Natl Bk Netwk.

Twelve Healers. 23th ed. Edward Bach. 32p. pap. 3.95 (0-8464-4306-6) Beekman Pubs.

Twelve Healers & Other Remedies. Edward Bach. 50p. 1988. pap. 3.50 (0-89540-174-6, SB-174) Sun Pub.

Twelve Healers of the Zodiac. Peter Damian. LC 86-1652. (Illus.). 96p. 1986. pap. 5.95 (0-87728-653-1) Weiser.

Twelve Health Center Districts in Need: A Birth Atlas. Constance T. Gager et al. LC 89-170901. 161p. 1988. 13.00 (0-88156-065-0) Comm Serv Soc NY.

***Twelve Holy Nights & the Spiritual Hierarchies.** 2nd ed. Sergei O. Prokofieff. Tr. by Simon B. De Lange from RUS. 208p. 1993. write for info. (0-904693-54-6, Pub. by Temple Ldge Pub UK) Anthroposophic.

***1,201 Toughest TV Trivia Questions of All Time.** Vincent Terrace. 360p. 1997. pap. 12.95 (0-8065-1886-3, Citadel Pr) Carol Pub Group.

1200 Art Appreciation SG. R. William McCarter. 176p. (C). 1995. per., pap. text ed. 20.94 (0-7872-1099-4) Kendall-Hunt.

Twelve Hundred Calorie a Day Menu Cookbook: Quick & Easy Recipes for Delicious Low-Fat Breakfasts, Lunches, Dinners & Desserts. Nancy S. Hughes. 416p. 1994. pap. 10.95 (0-8092-3633-8) Contemp Bks.

Twelve Hundred MCQ's in Medicine. 2nd ed. Michael J. Ford. (Illus.). 196p. 1991. pap. text ed. 24.00 (0-443-04252-7) Churchill.

***1200 Paint Effects for the Home Decorator.** Ray Bradshaw. (Illus.). 1997. pap. text ed. 29.99 (0-89134-816-6, North Lght Bks) F & W Pubns Inc.

Twelve Hundred Pilze in Farbfotos. Rose M. Daehncke. (Illus.). 1179p. (GER.). 1993. lib. bdg. 102.95 (3-85502-503-7) Lubrecht & Cramer.

***Twelve Impossible Things Before Breakfast: Stories.** Jane Yolen. LC 97-667. (J). 1997. write for info. (0-15-201524-8) HarBrace.

Twelve in Arcady. E. L. Kennedy. 1986. pap. 9.95 (0-85640-338-5, Pub. by Blackstaff Pr IE) Dufour.

12 Inch Baby That Fried an Omlet: And Other Crazy Dreams. Richard P. Cadway. 160p. 1996. pap. 7.95 (0-9644434-1-4) RPC Intl.

Twelve Is Too Old. Peggy Mann. 140p. (YA). (gr. 6-9). 1987. pap. 6.95 (0-942493-00-1) Woodmere Press.

Twelve Jewish Steps to Recovery: A Personal Guide to Turning from Alcoholism & Other Addictions. Kerry M. Olitzky et al. LC 91-25346. (Illus.). 136p. (Orig.). 1992. 19.95 (1-879045-08-7); pap. 13.95 (1-879045-09-5) Jewish Lights.

Twelve Jews. Ed. by Hector Bolitho. LC 67-23179. (Essay Index Reprint Ser.). 1977. 23.95 (0-8369-0223-8) Ayer.

Twelve Journeys in Maine. Wesley McNair. (Illus.). 48p. 1992. 195.00 (0-913341-16-9); pap. 9.95 (0-913341-15-0) Coyote Love.

Twelve Key Strategies to Improve Cash Flow in Medical Groups. 2nd ed. David Zimmerman. Ed. by Janice Pramik. (C). 1992. pap. text ed. 42.50 (0-933948-43-3, 3264) Ctr Res Ambulatory.

***Twelve Keys Effective Living.** Callahan. 20.00 (0-06-061262-2) HarpC.

***Twelve Keys to an Effective Church.** LC 97-24748. 1997. write for info. (0-7879-3873-4) Jossey-Bass.

Twelve Keys to an Effective Church. Kennon L. Callahan. LC 83-47718. 1983. 18.00 (0-06-061297-5) Harper SF.

Twelve Keys to an Effective Church. Kennon L. Callahan. LC 86-45802. 1987. teacher ed. 15.00 (0-06-061295-9) Harper SF.

***Twelve Keys to an Effective Church.** Kennon L. Callahan. LC 97-24760. 1997. 19.95 (0-7879-3871-8) Jossey-Bass.

Twelve Keys to an Effective Church: The Planning Workbook. rev. ed. Kennon L. Callahan. 1991. pap. 9.95 (0-06-061304-1) Harper SF.

***Twelve Labors of Hercules.** Marc Ceracini. LC 97-10010. 1997. lib. bdg. 11.99 (0-679-98393-7) Random Bks Yng Read.

***Twelve Labors of Hercules.** James Riordan. LC 97-10182. (J). 1997. 16.90 (0-7613-0315-4) Millbrook Pr.

***12 Labors of Hercules Coloring Book.** Susan Blackaby. (J). 1997. pap. text ed. 1.95 (1-57719-135-8) GT Pubng Corp.

12-Lead ECG Interpretation. Mullholland. 1995. 26.95 (0-683-17208-5) Williams & Wilkins.

Twelve Lead ECG Interpretation: A Self-Teaching Manual. Ann E. Norman. (Illus.). 300p. 1992. pap. text ed. 24.00 (0-07-105396-4) McGraw-Hill HPD.

Twelve Lead Egg Interpretation: The Self-Assessment Approach. Abedin & Conner. 336p. 1989. pap. text ed. 32.50 (0-7216-2846-X) Saunders.

Twelve Lead EKG. rev. ed. Carolyn G. Smith-Marker. 53p. 1984. pap. text ed. 7.00 (0-932491-01-4); wbk. ed. 17.50 incl. audio (0-932491-00-6); vhs 297.00 (0-932491-14-6) Res Appl Inc.

Twelve Lead EKG Stat: A Light-Hearted Approach. Donna M. Koenig et al. 1991. pap. 19.95 (0-9631206-0-3) CEU Access.

12 Lead EKG Stat! A Light Hearted Approach. Donna M. Koenig. 175p. 1995. per. 19.95 (0-9627246-8-8) Power NY.

Twelve-Lead Electrocardiography for ACLS Providers. Bruce Foster. (Illus.). 144p. 1995. pap. text ed. 21.00 (0-7216-5873-3) Saunders.

Twelve-Lead Vectorcardiography. Peter W. Macfarlane et al. (Illus.). 117p. 1995. pap. 45.00 (0-7506-0778-5) Buttrwrth-Heinemann.

12-Lead Workbook for the Medical Practitioner. Vernon R. Stanley. (Illus.). 93p. (Orig.). 1996. pap. 15.00 (0-9651073-1-0) Kopy Xpress.

Twelve Lessons for Confirmation in Secondary Schools. Anne Burke. (C). 1988. 30.00 (0-85439-091-X, Pub. by St Paul Pubns UK) St Mut.

***Twelve Lessons in Personal Spirituality: An Overview of the Edgar Cayce Readings on Personal Transformation.** Kevin J. Todeschi. LC 96-28324. 168p. (Orig.). 1997. pap. 12.95 (0-87604-369-4, 492) ARE Pr.

Twelve Lessons in the Astro Biochemic System of Body Building. Inez E. Perry & George W. Carey. 80p. 1973. reprint ed. spiral bd. 15.00 (0-7873-0668-1) Hlth Research.

***12 Lessons on Life I Learned from My Garden: Spiritual Wisdom from the Vegetable Patch.** Vivian E. Glyck. LC 96-36844. 128p. 1997. 14.95 (0-87596-426-5) Rodale Pr Inc.

***Twelve Lies That Enslave Humanity.** unabridged ed. Thomas A. Vogel. Ed. by Mondra Rose & Gayle Caldwell. LC 96-97161. (Illus.). 106p. (Orig.). 1996. pap. 8.95 (0-9655030-0-3) T A Vogel.

Twelve Little Duets Opus 38 Bk. 1: For 2 Violins. J. F. Mazas. 16p. 1986. pap. 7.95 (0-7935-5450-0) H Leonard.

Twelve Little Housemates. Karl Von Frisch. Tr. by A. T. Sugar. LC 78-40341. 1979. 80.00 (0-08-021959-4, Pub. by Pergamon Repr UK) Franklin.

Twelve Madrigals to Five Voices, 1597 see Old English Edition

Twelve Marvellous Men. Esther E. Enoch. 1993. reprint ed. pap. 4.99 (0-88019-305-0) Schmul Pub Co.

Twelve Mayors of Boston: 1900-1970. Ed. by Philip J. McNiff. (Illus.). 1970. 2.00 (0-89073-033-4) Boston Public Lib.

Twelve Men. Theodore Dreiser. 1988. reprint ed. lib. bdg. 49.00 (0-7812-0371-6) Rprt Serv.

Twelve Men. Theodore Dreiser. LC 74-144985. 1971. reprint ed. 69.00 (0-403-00914-6) Scholarly.

Twelve Men of Action in Graeco-Roman History. Arnold J. Toynbee. LC 69-17592. (Essay Index Reprint Ser.). 1977. 17.95 (0-8369-0095-2) Ayer.

Twelve Miles from a Lemon. Mary A. Dodge. LC 76-37512. (Essay Index Reprint Ser.). 1977. reprint ed. 23.95 (0-8369-2544-0) Ayer.

Twelve Million Black Voices. Photos by Edwin Rosskam. (Classic Reprint Ser.). 160p. 1988. reprint ed. pap. 15.95 (0-938410-44-X) Thunders Mouth.

Twelve-Minute Total-Body Workout. Joyce L. Vedral. 192p. (Orig.). 1993. pap. 12.95 (0-446-77816-8) Warner Bks.

12-Minute Total-Body Workout. Joyce L. Vedral. 192p. 1989. pap. 13.99 (*0-446-38961-7*) Warner Bks.

Twelve Modern Apostles & Their Creeds. Gilbert K. Chesterton et al. LC 68-16982. (Essay Index Reprint Ser.). 1977. 19.95 (*0-8369-0955-0*) Ayer.

Twelve Monkeys. Elizabeth Hand. 224p. 1995. mass mkt. 5.99 (*0-06-105658-8*, Harp PBks) HarpC.

***Twelve-Month Marriage.** Kathryn Jensen. (Intimate Moments Ser.: No. 797). 1997. mass mkt. 3.99 (*0-373-07797-1*, 1-07797-3) Silhouette.

Twelve-Month Pregnancy: What You Need to Know Before You Conceive to Ensure a Healthy Beginning for You & Your Baby. Barry Herman & Susan K. Perry. 240p. 1992. pap. 12.95 (*0-929923-51-0*) Lowell Hse.

Twelve-Month Pregnancy: What You Need to Know Before You Conceive to Ensure a Healthy Beginning for You & Your Baby. Barry Herman & Susan K. Perry. 228p. 1996. pap. 16.00 (*1-56565-480-3*) Lowell Hse.

Twelve Months. Llewelyn Powys. 96p. (C). 1987. 50.00 (*0-948265-90-6*, Pub. by Redcliffe Pr Ltd) St Mut.

Twelve Months of Monastery Soups: International Favorites. Victor-Antoine D'Avila-Latourrette. LC 96-10865. 208p. 1996. 25.00 (*0-89243-931-9*, Triumph Books) Liguori Pubns.

Twelve Moons. Mary Oliver. LC 79-10428. 1979. pap. 12.95 (*0-316-65000-5*) Little.

Twelve More Ladies. Sidney Dark. LC 70-86744. (Essay Index Reprint Ser.). 1977. 20.95 (*0-8369-1177-6*) Ayer.

Twelve More Mormon Temples, Bk. B: The Personal Touch. Annette Bradshaw & Gwyn Franson. 1980. 7.98 (*0-88290-150-8*) Horizon Utah.

Twelve More Weeks of Summer. Mona Kerby. Date not set. pap. 12.95 (*0-670-83216-2*) Viking Penguin.

Twelve More Weeks of Summer. Mona Kerby. 1999. pap. 3.95 (*0-14-034384-9*) Viking Penguin.

Twelve Mormon Temples, Bk. A: The Personal Touch. Annette Bradshaw & Gwyn Franson. 1980. 7.98 (*0-88290-149-4*) Horizon Utah.

Twelve Muscle Tones. L. C. Phillips. 104p. 1980. 19.95 (*0-912282-08-8*) Pulse-Finger.

Twelve Myths Americans Believe. Erwin W. Lutzer. (Orig.). 1993. pap. 10.99 (*0-8024-9017-4*) Moody.

***Twelve N. C. Christmas Stories: And Twelve Poems, Too.** Ed. by Ruth Moose. (Illus.). 120p. 1997. 14.95 (*1-878086-61-8*) Down Home NC.

Twelve Negro Americans. Mary Jenness. LC 74-86764. 190p. 1977. reprint ed. 24.95 (*0-8369-1143-1*) Ayer.

12 New Etudes for Piano, Vol. 2. Weins Bolcom. 64p. 1988. pap. 12.95 (*0-7935-2801-1*, 00009221) H Leonard.

Twelve Northern Drawings. limited ed. Carl Schaefer. (Illus.). 1979. 59.00 (*0-920806-02-3*, Pub. by Penumbra Pr CN) U of Toronto Pr.

Twelve-Note Music of Anton Webern. Kathryn Bailey. (Music in the Twentieth Century Ser.: No. 2). (Illus.). 300p. (C). 1991. 85.00 (*0-521-39088-5*) Cambridge U Pr.

Twelve O'clock High. Sy Bartlett & Lay. (Illus.). 274p. 1989. pap. 16.95 (*0-942397-16-9*) Buckeye Aviat Bk.

Twelve O'Clock High! Beirne Lay, Jr. & Sy Bartlett. Ed. by James B. Gilbert. LC 79-7278. (Flight: Its First Seventy-Five Years Ser.). (Illus.). 1980. reprint ed. lib. bdg. 25.95 (*0-405-12187-3*) Ayer.

12 O'Clock House. Rosean Krueger. (Illus.). 56p. (Orig.). (J). (gr. 7-9). 1995. pap. 12.00 (*0-938041-59-2*) Arc Pr AR.

Twelve Olympians. Joanne H. Stroud et al. (Entities Trilogy Ser.). 160p. (Orig.). 1995. pap. 20.00 (*0-911005-28-5*) Dallas Inst Pubns.

Twelve on the River St. John. Charles Bennett. 1989. pap. 19.95 (*0-8130-0948-0*); lib. bdg. 29.95 (*0-8130-0913-8*) U Press Fla.

Twelve Original Essays on Great American Novels. Charles Shapiro. LC 57-13316. 303p. (Orig.). reprint ed. pap. 86.40 (*0-685-23369-3*, 2032480) Bks Demand.

Twelve Original Essays on Great English Novels. Ed. by Charles Shapiro. LC 60-6374. 294p. reprint ed. pap. 83.80 (*0-7837-3608-8*, 2043473) Bks Demand.

Twelve Papers in Algebra. Ed. by Lev J. Leifman. LC 82-24434. (Translations Ser.: Series 2, Vol. 119). 139p. 1983. 45.00 (*0-8218-3074-0*, TRANS2/119) Am Math.

Twelve Papers in Analysis. LC 80-20715. (Translations Ser.: Series 2, Vol. 115). 202p. 1980. 57.00 (*0-8218-3065-1*, TRANS2/115) Am Math.

Twelve Papers in Logic & Algebra. M. I. Semenenko et al. Ed. by Ben Silver. LC 79-9994. (American Mathematical Society Translations Ser. 2: Vol. 113). 250p. 1979. 49.00 (*0-8218-3063-5*, TRANS2/113) Am Math.

Twelve Papers on Algebra, Algebraic Geometry & Topology. S. N. Cernikov et al. LC 51-5559. (Translations Ser.: Series 2, Vol. 84). 275p. 1969. 50.00 (*0-8218-1784-1*, TRANS2/84) Am Math.

Twelve Papers on Algebra & Real Functions. S. N. Cernikov et al. (Translations Ser.: Series 2, Vol. 17). 373p. 1960. 42.00 (*0-8218-1717-5*, TRANS2/17) Am Math.

Twelve Papers on Algebra, Number Theory & Topology. M. S. Calenko et al. (Translations Ser.: Series 2, Vol. 58). 260p. 1967. 47.00 (*0-8218-1758-2*, TRANS2/58) Am Math.

Twelve Papers on Analysis & Applied Mathematics. Ju. M. Berezanskii et al. (Translations Ser.: Series 2, Vol. 35). 363p. 1964. 42.00 (*0-8218-1735-3*, TRANS2/35) Am Math.

Twelve Papers on Analysis, Applied Mathematics & Algebraic Topology. E. A. Barbasin et al. (Translations Ser.: Series 2, Vol. 25). 334p. 1963. 38.00 (*0-8218-1725-6*, TRANS2/25) Am Math.

Twelve Papers on Approximations & Integrals. K. I. Babenko et al. (Translations Ser.: Series 2, Vol. 44). 268p. 1965. reprint ed. 35.00 (*0-8218-1744-2*, TRANS2/44) Am Math.

Twelve Papers on Function Theory, Probability, & Differential Equations. A. E. Andreev et al. (Translations Ser.: Series 2, Vol. 8). 356p. 1957. 59.00 (*0-8218-1708-6*, TRANS2/8) Am Math.

Twelve Papers on Functional Analysis & Geometry. V. T. Fomenko et al. (Translations Ser.: Series 2, Vol. 85). 258p. 1970. 47.00 (*0-8218-1785-X*, TRANS2/85) Am Math.

Twelve Papers on Logic & Algebra. N. I. Feldman et al. (Translations Ser.: Series 2, Vol. 59). 284p. 1967. 50.00 (*0-8218-1759-0*, TRANS2/59) Am Math.

Twelve Papers on Logic & Differential Equations. M. S. Gel'fand et al. (Translations Ser.: Series 2, Vol. 29). 381p. 1963. 42.00 (*0-8218-1729-9*, TRANS2/29) Am Math.

Twelve Papers on Number Theory & Function Theory. A. O. Gel'fond et al. (Translations Ser.: Series 2, Vol. 19). 321p. 1962. 38.00 (*0-8218-1719-1*, TRANS2/19) Am Math.

Twelve Papers on Real & Complex Function Theory. I. I. Eremin et al. (Translations Ser.: Series 2, Vol. 88). 325p. 1970. 51.00 (*0-8218-1788-4*, TRANS2/88) Am Math.

Twelve Papers on Topology, Algebra & Number Theory. V. A. Andrunakievic et al. (Translations Ser.: Series 2, Vol. 52). 275p. 1966. 50.00 (*0-8218-1752-3*, TRANS2/52) Am Math.

Twelve Parts of Her. Jena Osman. (Burning Deck Poetry Chapbooks Ser.). 24p. 1989. pap. 4.00 (*0-930901-63-0*) Burning Deck.

Twelve Pathways to Feeling Better about Yourself. Dov P. Elkins. LC 79-88299. 1980. pap. 7.50 (*0-918834-08-2*) Growth Assoc.

12 Philipine Women Writers. Ed. by Amelia Lapena-Bonifacio. 136p. (Orig.). 1995. pap. text ed. 12.00 (*971-542-040-0*, Pub. by U of Philippines Pr PH) UH Pr.

Twelve Photographers of the American Social Landscape. Ed. by Thomas H. Garver. (Illus.). 1968. 15.00 (*0-8079-0128-8*) October.

Twelve Photographs of Yellowstone. Ronald Koertge. 1976. pap. 2.50 (*0-88031-030-8*) Invisible-Red Hill.

***12 Pillars of Business Success.** Ron Sewell. 1997. 19.95 (*0-7494-2005-7*, Kogan Pg Educ) Stylus Pub VA.

Twelve Plays. Anton P. Chekhov. Ed. by Ronald Hingley. (World's Classics Ser.). 196p. 1992. pap. 5.95 (*0-19-282813-4*) OUP.

Twelve Plays. Joyce Carol Oates. 288p. (Orig.). 1991. pap. 24.95 (*0-525-93376-X*, Plume) NAL-Dutton.

Twelve Plays for the Theatre. Ed. by Robert Cohen. LC 93-2608. 626p. 1993. pap. text ed. 29.95 (*1-55934-144-0*, 1144) Mayfield Pub.

Twelve Plays of the Noh & Kyogen Theaters. Ed. by Karen Brazell. (Cornell East Asia Ser.: No. 50). 272p. 1988. pap. 12.00 (*0-939657-00-7*) Cornell East Asia Pgm.

Twelve Plus Me. Pat D. Likes. (Illus.). 160p. 1991. reprint ed. pap. 5.95 (*0-929292-09-X*) Hannibal Bks.

Twelve Poems: With Preludes & Postludes. Joseph Langland. 40p. (Orig.). 1988. pap. 6.00 (*0-938566-37-7*) Adastra Pr.

Twelve Portraits of the French Revolution. Henri Beraud. Tr. by M. Boyd. LC 68-16909. (Essay Index Reprint Ser.). 1977. 20.95 (*0-8369-0197-5*) Ayer.

Twelve Pound Cigarette. Ann Darr. LC 90-52932. (SCOP Ser.: No. XV). 64p. 1990. pap. 9.95 (*0-930526-14-7*) SCOP Pubns.

Twelve Pound Look (Playscript) James M. Barrie. LC 93-13403. 1993. pap. 5.00 (*0-88734-330-9*) Players Pr.

Twelve Power Meditation Exercise. Charles Roth. LC 89-50837. 90p. 1989. 6.95 (*0-87159-161-8*) Unity Bks.

Twelve Powers of Animals. Eloise Dikis. Ed. by Mary Wortman. (Illus.). 44p. (J). (ps-5). 1989. spiral bd. 7.95 (*0-939339-06-4*) AFCOM Pub.

Twelve Powers of Man. Charles Fillmore. LC 89-50843. 1995. reprint ed. 11.95 (*0-87159-186-3*, 121) Unity Bks.

Twelve Powers of Man Instructors' Course Guide. 1998. ring bd. 17.95 (*0-87159-997-X*, 2102, Unity Schl Relgs Studies) Unity Bks.

Twelve Powers of Man Learners' Workbook. (Orig.). 1998. pap. text ed. 14.95 (*0-87159-996-1*, 2103, Unity Schl Relgs Studies) Unity Bks.

Twelve Problems in Health Care Ethics. Thomas A. Shannon. LC 84-22654. (Studies in Health & Human Services: Vol. 2). 320p. 1984. lib. bdg. 99.95 (*0-88946-127-9*) E Mellen.

Twelve Prophets. Ed. by K. Elliger. (Biblia Hebraica Stuttgartensia Ser.). x, 96p. 1970. pap. 10.50 (*3-438-05210-5*, 104088, Pub. by United Bible GW) Am Bible.

Twelve Prophets, Vol. 1. Peter C. Craigie. LC 84-2372. 256p. 1993. pap. text ed. 22.00 (*0-7152-0534-X*, Pub. by St Andrew UK) St Mut.

Twelve Prophets, Vol. 2. Peter C. Craigie. LC 84-2372. 260p. 1993. pap. text ed. 22.00 (*0-7152-0538-2*) St Mut.

Twelve Prophets: Hebrew Text & English Translation. Comment & Intro. by A. Cohen. LC 93-23901. (Books of the Bible Ser.). 368p. 1994. 14.95 (*1-871055-80-6*) Soncino Pr.

Twelve Prophets see Daily Study Bible - Old Testament

Twelve Prophets see Daily Study Bible for the Old Testament

Twelve Questions for Theologians. Ian McCrimmon. (C). 1992. text ed. 59.95 (*0-9514698-1-9*, Pub. by Cosmatom UK) St Mut.

Twelve Ravens. Howard Rose. 405p. 1990. reprint ed. 20.00 (*1-878352-02-4*); reprint ed. pap. 10.00 (*1-878352-03-2*) R Saroff Pub.

Twelve Readers Reading: Responding to College Student Writing. Richard O. Straub. LC 95-8716. (Written Language Ser.). 464p. 1995. pap. text ed. 29.95 (*1-881303-40-3*) Hampton Pr NJ.

Twelve Red Herrings. Jeffrey Archer. 384p. 1995. mass mkt. 6.50 (*0-06-109365-3*, Harp PBks) HarpC.

Twelve Red Herrings. large type ed. Jeffrey Archer. LC 94-33996. 25.95 (*1-56895-150-7*) Wheeler Pub.

Twelve Religions of the Bible. Rolland E. Wolfe. LC 82-20401. (Studies in the Bible & Early Christianity: Vol. 2). (Illus.). 416p. 1983. lib. bdg. 109.95 (*0-88946-600-9*) E Mellen.

***Twelve Reproducible Attendance Charts.** Edna Zimmerly. 48p. 1996. pap. 5.99 (*0-7847-0481-3*, 03311) Standard Pub.

Twelve Reproducible Charts for All Seasons. Edna Zimmerly. 1996. pap. text ed. 5.99 (*0-7847-0480-5*, 03310) Standard Pub.

***Twelve Roles of Facilitators for School Change.** R. Bruce Williams. (Orig.). 1997. pap. 29.95 (*1-57517-027-2*, 1490) IRI-SkyLght.

Twelve Royal Ladies. Sidney Dark. LC 73-99689. (Essay Index Reprint Ser.). 1977. 26.95 (*0-8369-1459-7*) Ayer.

Twelve Seasons. Joseph W. Krutch. LC 72-134106. (Essay Index Reprint Ser.). 1977. 18.95 (*0-8369-1970-X*) Ayer.

Twelve Seconds to the Moon. rev. ed. Rosamond Young & Catharine Fitzgerald. LC 78-71073. (Illus.). 208p. 1983. 13.95 (*0-9611634-0-2*) US Air Force Mus.

Twelve Secrets for Cashing Out: How to Sell Your Company for the Most Profit. R. Bergeth. 1994. text ed. 39.95 (*0-13-176454-3*); pap. text ed. 18.95 (*0-13-176462-4*) P-H.

Twelve Secrets to Finding Love & Commitment. Jeffrey Ullman. 1995. pap. 11.00 (*0-671-89207-X*, Fireside) S&S Trade.

Twelve Senses. Albert Soesman. Tr. by Jakob Cornelis. (Social Ecology Ser.). (Illus.). 162p. 1989. pap. text ed. 19.95 (*1-869890-22-1*, 1478, Pub. by Hawthorn Press UK) Anthroposophic.

12 Sermons of Comfort & Cheer. Charles H. Spurgeon. 150p. (C). 1994. reprint ed. pap. 7.99 (*0-8010-8082-7*) Baker Bks.

12 Sermons on Commitment. Charles H. Spurgeon. 144p. (C). 1994. reprint ed. pap. 7.99 (*0-8010-8137-8*) Baker Bks.

Twelve Sermons on Holiness. Charles H. Spurgeon. pap. 4.99 (*0-87377-083-8*) GAM Pubns.

12 Sermons on Praise. Charles H. Spurgeon. 144p. (C). 1994. reprint ed. pap. 7.99 (*0-8010-8218-8*) Baker Bks.

12 Sermons on Prayer. Charles H. Spurgeon. 152p. 1971. reprint ed. pap. 7.99 (*0-8010-7923-3*) Baker Bks.

12 Sermons on Thanksgiving. Charles H. Spurgeon. 144p. (C). 1995. reprint ed. pap. 6.99 (*0-8010-8390-7*) Baker Bks.

12 Sermons on the "Cries from the Cross" Charles H. Spurgeon. 144p. (C). 1995. pap. 6.99 (*0-8010-8392-3*) Baker Bks.

12 Sermons on the Holy Spirit. Charles H. Spurgeon. 152p. (C). 1994. reprint ed. pap. 7.99 (*0-8010-7983-7*) Baker Bks.

12 Sermons on the Love of Christ. Charles H. Spurgeon. 128p. (C). 1994. reprint ed. pap. 7.99 (*0-8010-8096-7*) Baker Bks.

12 Sermons on the Passion & Death of Christ. Charles H. Spurgeon. 152p. (C). 1995. reprint ed. pap. 6.99 (*0-8010-8396-6*) Baker Bks.

12 Sermons on the Resurrection. Charles H. Spurgeon. 152p. (C). 1995. reprint ed. pap. 6.99 (*0-8010-8395-8*) Baker Bks.

12 Sermons on the Second Coming of Christ. Charles H. Spurgeon. 144p. (C). 1994. reprint ed. pap. 7.99 (*0-8010-8066-5*) Baker Bks.

12 Short Hikes: Aspen. Tracy Salcedo. (Twelve Short Hikes Ser.). (Illus.). 32p. (Orig.). 1995. pap. 4.95 (*0-934641-53-6*) Chockstone Pr.

***12 Short Hikes: Rocky Mountain National Park, Estes Park.** (Illus.). (Orig.). 1997. pap. 4.95 (*1-57540-084-7*) Chockstone Pr.

***12 Short Hikes: Rocky Mountain National Park, Grand Lake.** (Orig.). 1997. pap. 4.95 (*1-57540-085-5*) Chockstone Pr.

Twelve Shot. Abbott. 1990. pap. 5.00 (*0-915990-04-0*) Z Pr.

***Twelve Shots: Stories About Guns.** Harry Mazer. LC 96-37838. (J). 1997. mass mkt. 15.95 (*0-385-32238-0*) Doubleday.

***Twelve Shots: Stories about Guns.** Harry Mazer. 1997. mass mkt. 15.95 (*0-385-44698-5*) Doubleday.

Twelve Simple Steps to a Winning Marketing Plan. Geraldine A. Larkin. 210p. 1992. per. 17.95 (*1-55738-297-2*) Irwin Prof Pubng.

Twelve Simple Words. Jack McArdle. 134p. (Orig.). 1994. pap. 7.95 (*1-85607-119-7*, Pub. by Columba Pr IE) Twenty-Third.

Twelve Sisters. Leslie B. Hedley. LC 93-24540. vi, 201p. 1993. pap. 9.95 (*0-87579-779-2*) Deseret Bk.

Twelve Sixteen to Twelve Thirty-Five see Royal & Other Historical Letters Illustrative of the Reign of Henry III, from the Originals in the Public Record Office

Twelve Snails to the Lizard. Monaco. LC 96-2403. (J). 1997. 13.00 (*0-689-80452-0*) S&S Childrens.

Twelve Solos for Soprano Recorder: With Keyboard Accompaniment. Selected by Maurice C. Whitney. 1977. 4.00 (*0-913334-38-3*, CM1044) Consort Music.

Twelve Sonatinas Opus 36, Opus 37, Opus 38 for the Piano. M. Clementi. 72p. 1986. pap. 5.95 (*0-7935-5173-0*) H Leonard.

12 Song by Jacques Brel. Ed. by Michael Lefferts. (Illus.). 64p. (Orig.). (C). 1997. pap. text ed. 25.95 (*0-8256-1291-8*, 01020681) Warner Brothers.

Twelve Songs of the Soul. Ruth L. Eichler. (Illus.). 272p. (Orig.). 1995. pap. 16.95 (*0-929915-15-1*) Headline Bks.

Twelve Sons of Israel. Compiled by Norman L. Heap. 196p. 1988. 12.50 (*0-945905-04-1*) Family Hstory Pubns.

12 Spiritual Stones. Jarman Esperance. LC 95-90287. 125p. (Orig.). 1995. pap. 8.95 (*0-9647001-0-7*) Branch & Vine.

12 Stages of Healing. Donald M. Epstein. (Illus.). 256p. 1995. bds. 12.95 (*1-56865-141-4*, GuildAmerica) Dblday Direct.

12 Stages of Healing: A Network Approach to Wholeness. Donald M. Epstein & Nathaniel Altman. (Illus.). 256p. 1994. pap. 12.95 (*1-878424-08-4*) Amber-Allen Pub.

12 Step Approach to Healing in Nursing. Mikiuscak. (Professional Reference - Nursing Ser.). 1998. pap. 20.95 (*0-8273-6604-3*) Delmar.

Twelve-Step Facilitation Handbook: A Systematic Approach to Early Recovery from Alcoholism & Addiction. Joseph Nowinski & Stuart Baker. LC 92-17693. 214p. 32.95 (*0-02-923225-2*, Free Press) Free Pr.

***Twelve Step Facilitation Therapy Manual.** (Illus.). 134p. 1994. pap. text ed. 35.00 (*1-57979-139-5*) BPI Info Servs.

Twelve Step Facilitation Therapy Manual: A Clinical Research Guide for Therapists Treating Individuals with Alcohol Abuse & Dependence. Joseph Nowinski et al. 123p. (Orig.). (C). 1995. pap. text ed. 35.00 (*0-7881-2463-3*) DIANE Pub.

Twelve-Step Journal. Claudette Wassil-Grimm. 260p. 1995. 19.95 (*0-87951-618-6*) Overlook Pr.

Twelve Step Life Recovery Devotional. S. Arterburn & D. Stoop. 384p. 1991. pap. 9.99 (*0-8423-4753-4*) Tyndale.

Twelve Step Prayer Book. Bill Pittman. 128p. (Orig.). 1990. pap. 7.95 (*0-934125-11-2*) Hazelden.

Twelve Step Prayers for a Way Out: A Companion to the Twelve Steps - a Way Out. Friends in Recovery. LC 93-11016. (Illus.). 125p. (Orig.). 1993. pap. 8.95 (*0-941405-29-X*) RPI Pubng.

***Twelve Step Programs: A Contemporary American Quest for Meaning & Spiritual Renewal.** Ann M. Minnick. LC 97-9178. 1997. text ed. write for info. (*0-275-95850-7*, Praeger Pubs) Greenwood.

Twelve Step Sponsorship: Sponsor's Guide to How It Works. Hamilton B. 400p. 1996. pap. text ed. 11.95 (*1-56838-122-0*) Hazelden.

Twelve-Step Workbook of Overeaters Anonymous. Overeaters Anonymous, Inc. Staff. LC 93-83640. 1993. pap. 7.99 (*0-9609898-5-4*) Overeaters Anym.

Twelve Steps. (TUR.). 1993. write for info. (*0-916856-62-3*) AAWS.

Twelve Steps: A Key to Living with Attention Deficit Disorder. Friends in Recovery. (Illus.). 252p. (Orig.). 1996. wbk. ed., pap. 16.95 (*0-941405-34-6*) RPI Pubng.

Twelve Steps: A Recovery Program (Explained & Revised) R. Winn Henderson & Marvin Overman. 54p. (Orig.). 1995. pap. text ed. 11.95 (*0-9634173-4-7*) Hugos Pr.

Twelve Steps: A Way Out: A Spiritual Process for Healing Damaged Emotions. Friends in Recovery Staff. 1995. pap. 15.95 (*0-941405-11-7*) RPI Pubng.

Twelve Steps: The Church's Challenge & Opportunity. Charles T. Knippel. LC 94-8327. 1994. pap. 9.99 (*0-570-04653-X*, 12-3234) Concordia.

Twelve Steps - a Spiritual Journey: A Working Guide for Healing Damaged Emotions Based on Biblical Teachings. rev. ed. Friends in Recovery. (Illus.). 258p. (Orig.). 1994. pap. 15.95 (*0-941405-44-3*) RPI Pubng.

Twelve Steps a Guide for Adults with Attention Deficit Disorder: A Guide. Friends in Recovery. (Illus.). 220p. (Orig.). 1996. pap. 11.95 (*0-941405-35-4*) RPI Pubng.

Twelve Steps & Dual Disorders: A Framework of Recovery for Those of Us with Addiction & an Emotional or Psychiatric Illness. Tim Hamilton & Pat Samples. LC 94-8240. 96p. (Orig.). 1994. pap. 6.95 (*1-56838-018-6*) Hazelden.

Twelve Steps & Twelve Traditions. LC 53-5454. 192p. 1953. 2.70 (*0-916856-01-1*) AAWS.

Twelve Steps & Twelve Traditions. 213p. (RUS.). 1989. 2.75 (*0-916856-26-7*) AAWS.

Twelve Steps & Twelve Traditions. (UKR.). 1993. 7.95 (*0-916856-51-8*) AAWS.

Twelve Steps & Twelve Traditions. (TUR.). 1994. pap. write for info. (*0-916856-30-5*) AAWS.

Twelve Steps & Twelve Traditions. (RUM.). 1994. write for info. (*0-916856-64-X*) AAWS.

Twelve Steps & Twelve Traditions. Alcoholics Anonymous World Serv., Inc. Staff. 192p. (LIT.). 1953. pap. 5.25 (*0-916856-48-8*) AAWS.

Twelve Steps & Twelve Traditions. deluxe ed. LC 53-5454. 192p. 1988. reprint ed. 2.90 (*0-916856-06-2*) AAWS.

Twelve Steps & Twelve Traditions. large type ed. 1991. 5.65 (*0-916856-45-3*) AAWS.

Twelve Steps & Twelve Traditions. LC 53-5454. 192p. 1988. reprint ed. pap. 2.50 (*0-916856-29-1*) AAWS.

Twelve Steps & Twelve Traditions of Overeaters Anonymous. Overeaters Anonymous, Inc. Staff. LC 93-85052. 1993. 10.99 (*0-9609898-6-2*) Overeaters Anym.

Twelve Steps for Adult Children. rev. ed. Friends in Recovery. 1996. pap. 9.95 (*0-941405-12-5*) RPI Pubng.

Twelve Steps for Christian Living: Growth in a New Way of Living. rev. ed. Vernon J. Bittner. 138p. 1994. pap. 10.00 (*0-9643105-0-3*) ICL Renewed.

Twelve Steps for Christians. rev. ed. Friends in Recovery. (Illus.). 239p. 1994. pap. 10.95 (*0-941405-57-5*) RPI Pubng.

Twelve Steps for Everyone. 1985. pap. 10.00 (*1-56838-047-X*) Hazelden.

Twelve Steps for Tobacco Users. Jeanne E. 25p. (Orig.). 1984. pap. 2.50 (*0-89486-229-4*, 1419) Hazelden.

***12 Steps from a Biblical Perspective.** Mady Thomas, III. Ed. by Elsie Clark. 240p. (Orig.). 1997. pap. 19.95 (*1-890330-00-0*) Turning Pt Pub.

Twelve Steps from the East. Ralph L. Brockway. LC 92-13156. 156p. 1992. reprint ed. pap. 44.50 (*0-608-01774-4*, 2062432) Bks Demand.

***Twelve Steps Illustrated.** Karen Greene. 1997. 9.95 (*0-943545-10-2*) New Hope Pr.

An Asterisk (*) at the beginning of an entry indicates that the title is appearing in BIP for the first time.

Twelve Steps of Alcoholics Anonymous. Deborah Thornton. 52p. 1995. student ed. 16.99 (*0-9636638-4-4*) Inspirat Prayer.

Twelve Steps of Forgiveness. Paul Ferrini. (Illus.). 128p. (Orig.). 1991. pap. 10.00 (*1-879159-10-4*) Heartways Pr.

Twelve Steps of Overeaters Anonymous. 1996. pap. text ed. 10.00 (*0-89486-905-1*) Hazelden.

Twelve Steps of Phobics Anonymous. Contrib. by Marilyn Gellis & Rosemary Muat. 156p. (Orig.). 1989. pap. 9.95 (*0-9627373-0-5*) Inst Phobic Awareness.

Twelve Steps ot Holiness & Salvation. St. Alphonsus De Liguori. LC 86-50419. Orig. Title: The School of Christian Rejections. 246p. 1993. reprint ed. pap. 7.50 (*0-89555-298-1*) TAN Bks Pubs.

12 Steps to a Better Memory. Carol A. Turkington. LC 95-37513. 208p. 1995. 9.95 (*0-02-860579-9*) Macmillan Info.

***12 Steps to a Better Memory.** Carol Turkinton. 1996. 9.95 (*0-02-861368-6*) Macmillan.

***12 Steps to a Flawless Notarization.** National Notary Association Editors. 48p. 1996. pap. 9.95 (*0-933134-78-9*) Natl Notary.

Twelve Steps to a Never Union Company. Robert Riggs. 74p. (Orig.). 1995. pap. 19.95 (*0-9645296-0-2*) Fam Busn Bks.

Twelve Steps to a New Day: An Interactive Recovery Workbook for Spiritual Growth. Ron Keller. LC 92-28038. 1993. 14.99 (*0-8407-3460-3*) Nelson.

Twelve Steps to a New Day for Teens. Ron Keller. LC 92-21046. 1993. 14.99 (*0-8407-7797-3*) Nelson.

12 Steps to a Worry-Free Retirement. Daniel M. Kehrer. 1995. pap. 14.95 (*0-8129-2713-3*, Times Bks) Random.

12 Steps to a Worry-Free Retirement. rev. ed. Rev. by Daniel M. Kehrer. 1995. pap. 15.00 (*0-8129-2644-7*) Kiplinger Bks.

Twelve Steps to Clear Writing: A Concise Guide for Writers & Editors. 2nd ed. Leigh F. Stephens. 100p. 1990. pap. 15.95 (*0-9634803-0-8*) Creat Comm.

12 Steps to Destruction: Codependency - Recovery Heresies. Martin Bobgan & Deidre N. Bobgan. LC 91-72638. 256p. (Orig.). 1991. pap. 10.99 (*0-941717-05-4*) EastGate Pubs.

***12 Steps to Effective Meetings: Tips, Traps & Terrible Truths.** 3rd rev. ed. Joe Caruso. (Illus.). 104p. (Orig.). 1997. write for info. (*1-885671-10-5*) Caruso Leader Inst.

Twelve Steps to Happiness. Joe Klaas. 128p. 1990. mass mkt. 5.99 (*0-345-36787-1*) Ballantine.

Twelve Steps to Heaven: My First Impression of Sex. Bernice Lum. (Illus.). 78p. (Orig.). 1995. 6.00 (*1-872819-00-1*, Pub. by Tuppy Owens UK) AK Pr Dist.

Twelve Steps to Loving Yourself: Loving Your Enemy & Liking It. Dorothy M. England. 112p. (Orig.). 1991. pap. 3.95 (*0-88028-116-2*, 1106) Forward Movement.

Twelve Steps to Personal & Professional Development. Darlene B. Bordeaux. Ed. by Beth Morgan. (Illus.). 243p. 1993. 21.95 (*0-9637703-0-6*) Wld Flower Pr.

Twelve Steps to Self-Improvement. Elwood N. Chapman. Ed. by Michael G. Crisp. LC 90-85867. (Fifty-Minute Ser.). (Illus.). 107p. (Orig.). 1991. pap. 10.95 (*1-56052-102-3*) Crisp Pubns.

Twelve Steps to Self Parenting for Adult Children. Patricia O'Gormand & Philip Oliver-Diaz. 1988. pap. 7.95 (*0-932194-68-0*) Health Comm.

Twelve Steps to Spiritual Wholeness: A Christian Pathway. Philip St. Romain. LC 91-77986. 96p. (Orig.). 1992. pap. text ed. 4.95 (*0-89243-429-5*) Liguori Pubns.

***Twelve Steps to Success in Selling.** Doug Wyman & Tim Spacek. 91p. 55.00 (*0-614-25572-4*, 00SM4421) Print Indus Am.

***12 Steps Toward Spiritual Growth: A 12-Lesson Study for One-to-One Discipling.** 3rd rev. ed. David D. Durey. (Illus.). 82p. 1996. pap. 5.00 (*0-9656237-0-X*) Fnd of Hope.

Twelve Steps, Twelve Traditions, 5 vols. Alcoholics Anonymous World Services, Inc. Staff. (HUN.). 1993. 8.45 (*0-916856-52-6*) AAWS.

***Twelve Stories.** Guy Davenport. 1997. pap. 14.00 (*1-887178-44-9*) Counterpt DC.

Twelve Stories: Selected & Annotated for English-Speaking Students. Mikhail Zoshchenko. Ed. by Lesli LaRocco & Slava Paperno. 114p. (Orig.). (ENG & RUS.). (C). 1990. pap. text ed. 11.95 (*0-89357-206-3*) Slavica.

Twelve Stories & a Dream. H. G. Wells. LC 72-152963. (Short Story Index Reprint Ser.). 1977. reprint ed. 20.95 (*0-8369-3878-X*) Ayer.

Twelve Stories for Late at Night. Ed. by Alfred Hitchcock. 1976. 21.95 (*0-8488-0530-5*) Amereon Ltd.

***Twelve Stories You & Your Children Need to Know: Finding Hope for a New Generation in the Biblical Story.** William Hockin. 96p. 8.95 (*1-55126-110-3*) Forward Movement.

Twelve-String Guitar Guide. Mark Hanson. (Illus.). 48p. 1992. pap. 4.95 (*0-8256-1244-6*, AM80235) Music Sales.

Twelve String Guitar Styles. Roger Holtman & Roger Erb. 1993. 5.95 (*0-87166-516-6*, 93216) Mel Bay.

Twelve String Quartets: Opus 55, 64 & 71 Complete. Joseph Haydn. 288p. 1980. reprint ed. pap. 11.95 (*0-486-23933-0*) Dover.

Twelve Sunday Mornings with Pastor Hagee. John C. Hagee. Ed. by Lucretia Hobbs & Connie Reece. (Sermon Digest Ser.: Vol. 1). 146p. (Orig.). 1992. per. 12.00 (*1-56908-010-0*) Global Evang.

Twelve Sunday Mornings with Pastor Hagee, Vol. 2. John C. Hagee. Ed. by Lucretia Hobbs & Connie Reece. (Sermon Digest Ser.: Vol. 2). (Orig.). 1994. per. 12.00 (*1-56908-015-1*) Global Evang.

Twelve Sunday Mornings with Pastor Hagee, Vol. 3. John C. Hagee. Ed. by Lucretia Hobbs & Connie Reece. (Sermon Digest Ser.: Vol. 3). (Orig.). 1994. per. 12.00 (*1-56908-016-X*) Global Evang.

Twelve Sunday Mornings with Pastor Hagee, Vol. 4. John C. Hagee. Ed. by Connie Reece. (Sermon Digest Ser.: Vol. 4). 188p. (Orig.). 1995. per., pap. 12.00 (*1-56908-019-4*) Global Evang.

12 Take Home Thematic. 1994. pap. 15.95 (*0-590-49649-2*) Scholastic Inc.

Twelve Tales. Hans Christian Andersen. Tr. & Illus. by Erik Blegvad. LC 93-6927. 96p. (J). 1994. lib. bdg. 19.95 (*0-689-50584-1*, McElderry) S&S Childrens.

Twelve Tales of Christmas. Richard M. Siddoway. 1992. pap. 4.95 (*0-88494-845-5*) Bookcraft Inc.

Twelve Tales of Suspense & Supernatural. Davis Grubb. 1993. reprint ed. lib. bdg. 18.95 (*0-89968-432-7*, Lghtyr Pr) Buccaneer Bks.

***Twelve Tales of the Supernatural.** Michael Cox. (Oxford Twelves). 208p. 1997. pap. 9.95 (*0-19-288027-6*) OUP.

Twelve Tales Untold: A Study Guide for Ecumenical Reception. Ed. by John T. Ford & Darlis J. Swan. 176p. (Orig.). 1993. pap. text ed. 13.00 (*0-8028-0553-1*) Eerdmans.

Twelve Tattoos. Ed. by Daric Beil. LC 93-37371. (Illus.). 176p. 1994. 16.95 (*0-913720-89-5*) Beil.

Twelve Teaching Methods to Enhance Student Learning. David Bartz & Laura Miller. (What Research Says to the Teacher Ser.). 32p. 1991. pap. 3.95 (*0-8106-1093-0*) NEA.

Twelve Theological Dilemmas. Gregory C. Higgins. 1991. pap. 7.95 (*0-8091-3232-X*) Paulist Pr.

Twelve Therapists: How They Live & Actualize Themselves. Arthur Burton. LC 72-83966. (Jossey-Bass Behavioral Science Ser.). 342p. reprint ed. pap. 97.50 (*0-685-16339-3*, 2027747) Bks Demand.

Twelve Things I Want My Kids to Remember Forever. Jerry B. Jenkins. 1991. text ed. 14.99 (*0-8024-8756-4*) Moody.

Twelve Thirty-Six to Twelve Seventy-One see Royal & Other Historical Letters Illustrative of the Reign of Henry III, from the Originals in the Public Record Office

12,000 Religious Quotations. Ed. & Compiled by Frank S. Mead. 534p. (Orig.). 1989. pap. 24.99 (*0-8010-6253-5*) Baker Bks.

Twelve Thrones. Jim Lewis. LC 83-91008. 85p. (Orig.). 1983. pap. 5.95 (*0-942482-06-9*) Unity Church Denver.

12 Tiger Steps Out of Nicotine Addiction: A Step Study Guide for Nicotine Addiction Recovery. Paul Lagergren. LC 95-90081. (Illus.). 256p. 1995. pap. 19.95 (*0-9645492-4-7*) Tigerworks Pub.

Twelve Tissue Remedies of Schuessler. William Boericke & Willis Dewey. 9.95 (*0-89378-065-0*) Formur Intl.

Twelve Tissue Remedies of Schuessler: Comprising Theory, Therapeutical Application, Materia Medica & a Complete Repertory. Ed. by W. Boericke & W. A. Dewey. 1991. lib. bdg. 250.00 (*0-8490-4102-3*) Gordon Pr.

Twelve Tissue Remedies of Schussler. William Boericke & Willis A. Dewey. 303p. 1994. reprint ed. spiral bd. 15.00 (*0-7873-1220-7*) Hlth Research.

Twelve to Sixteen: Early Adolescence. Ed. by Jerome Kagan et al. (Illus.). (C). 1972. pap. text ed. 11.95 (*0-393-09621-1*) Norton.

Twelve-Tone Tonality. 2nd ed. George Perle. LC 94-40067. 1995. 45.00 (*0-520-20142-6*) U CA Pr.

Twelve Tools for Improving Mobility & Managing Congestion. Robert T. Dunphy. 1991. pap. text ed. 24.95 (*0-87420-718-5*, T11) Urban Land.

Twelve Top Hits for Easy Piano. (Easy Piano Ser.). 72p. 1994. pap. 7.95 (*0-7935-3249-3*, 00311669) H Leonard.

12 Totally Terrific Theme Units. 1993. pap. 12.95 (*0-590-49413-9*) Scholastic Inc.

Twelve Tough Issues: What the Church Teaches & Why. Daniel E. Pilarczyk. 83p. (Orig.). 1989. pap. 4.95 (*0-86716-104-3*) St Anthony Mess Pr.

Twelve Traps in Today's Marriage: And How to Avoid Them. Brent A. Barlow. LC 86-13429. 1994. pap. 7.95 (*0-87579-947-7*) Deseret Bk.

Twelve-Tribe Nations & the Science of Enchanting the Landscape. John Michell & Christine Rhone. LC 91-26915. (Illus.). 192p. (Orig.). 1991. 25.00 (*0-933999-48-8*); pap. 17.95 (*0-933999-49-6*) Phanes Pr.

Twelve-Tribe Nations & the Science of Enchanting the Landscape. deluxe ed. John Michell & Christine Rhone. LC 91-26915. (Illus.). 192p. (Orig.). 1991. 35.00 (*0-933999-47-X*) Phanes Pr.

Twelve Tribes: From Jacob Until Joseph see Torah Anthology: Meam Lo'ez

Twelve Tribes of Israel. Elizabeth R. Hunter. (Illus.). 250p. (Orig.). 1990. pap. text ed. 8.00 (*0-9625252-0-0*) E Hunter.

Twelve Tribes of Israel & Their Enemies. (Walk with Jesus Ser.). 28p. 1987. pap. 10.00 (*1-57277-501-7*) Script Rsch.

***12 Truths, about Surviving & Succeeding in the Office, & Some of Them Aren't Very Nice: And Some of Them Aren't Very Nice.** Karen Randall. 192p. 1997. pap. 12.00 (*0-425-15621-4*, Berkley Trade) Berkley Pub.

Twelve Types. Gilbert K. Chesterton. LC 75-30017. reprint ed. 32.50 (*0-404-14022-X*) AMS Pr.

***12 Universal Laws.** Leia Stinnett. 1996. pap. text ed. 18.95 (*0-929385-81-0*) Light Tech Comns Servs.

***Twelve Universal Laws of Success.** Herbert Harris. LC 96-95348. 160p. (Orig.). 1997. pap. 12.95 (*1-890199-00-1*, 1944) Lifeskills Inst.

Twelve Universal Laws, Principles & Applications: A Workbook for Children of All Ages. Leia G. Stinnett. (Little Angel Books Ser.). (Illus.). 138p. 1993. student ed., pap. text ed. 18.95 (*1-880737-14-0*) Crystal Jrns.

***Twelve Victorian Ghost Stories.** Ed. by Michael Cox. (Oxford Twelves). 224p. 1997. pap. 9.95 (*0-19-288026-8*) OUP.

***12 Views: From Women's Eyes: Managing the New Majority.** Laura Ricci & George Wilkerson. LC 97-91622. (Illus.). 220p. (Orig.). 1997. pap. 14.95 (*0-9657399-0-2*) RThree.

12 Views of Manet's Bar. Ed. by Bradford R. Collins. LC 95-38924. (Series in Nineteenth-Century Art, Culture, & Society). 384p. 1996. text ed. 55.00 (*0-691-03690-X*); pap. text ed. 19.95 (*0-691-03691-8*) Princeton U Pr.

Twelve Voices for Truth. Jack W. Hayford. (Spirit-Filled Life Study Guide Ser.). 1995. pap. 6.99 (*0-8407-2093-9*) Nelson.

12 Voices of Christmas. Woodrow M. Kroll. 1993. pap. 8.99 (*0-8474-1456-6*) Back to Bible.

Twelve-Volt Bible. Miner Brotherton. (Illus.). 174p. 1987. pap. text ed. 14.95 (*0-915160-81-1*) Seven Seas.

Twelve-Volt Bible for Boats. Miner Brotherton. 1987. pap. text ed. 14.95 (*0-07-156091-2*) Intl Marine.

Twelve Volt Doctor's Alternator Book. rev. ed. Edgar J. Beyn. (Twelve Volt Doctor's Bks.). (Illus.). 182p. 1989. reprint ed. pap. 21.00 (*1-878797-02-6*) C Plath North Amer.

Twelve Volt Doctor's Practical Handbook: For the Boat's Electric System. rev. ed. Edgar J. Beyn. (Twelve Volt Doctor's Bks.). (Illus.). 233p. 1989. reprint ed. pap. 26.50 (*1-878797-00-X*) C Plath North Amer.

Twelve Volt Doctor's Project Book. Edgar J. Beyn. (Twelve Volt Doctor's Bks.). (Illus.). 57p. (Orig.). 1990. pap. 16.00 (*1-878797-01-8*) C Plath North Amer.

Twelve Volt Doctor's Troubleshooting Book. Edgar J. Beyn. (Twelve Volt Doctor's Bks.). (Illus.). 58p. (Orig.). 1990. pap. 16.00 (*1-878797-03-4*) C Plath North Amer.

Twelve Walks Around Olympia: Enjoying Washington's Capital City. Rosana Hart. LC 95-94996. (Illus.). 128p. (Orig.). 1995. pap. 12.00 (*0-916289-20-6*) Hartworks.

Twelve Ways to Develop a Positive Attitude. Galloway. 59p. 1975. mass mkt. 3.99 (*0-8423-7550-3*) Tyndale.

Twelve Ways to Get to Eleven. Eve Merriam. LC 92-25810. (Illus.). 40p. (J). (ps-1). 1993. pap. 15.00 (*0-671-75544-7*, S&S Bks Young Read) S&S Childrens.

Twelve Ways to Get to Eleven. Eve Merriam. (J). (ps-1). 1996. 5.99 (*0-689-80892-5*, S&S Bks Young Read) S&S Childrens.

Twelve Wedding Songs: Medium Voice & Guitar. 48p. 1995. pap. 12.95 (*0-7935-4073-9*, 00740007) H Leonard.

12 Week Diet. Blackburn. 1999. 18.95 (*0-446-51547-7*) Warner Bks.

Twelve Weeks to a Better Body for Men. Ronald S. Laura. 144p. 1994. pap. 9.95 (*1-86373-482-1*) IPG Chicago.

Twelve Weeks to a Better Body for Women. Ronald S. Laura. 144p. 1994. pap. 9.95 (*1-86373-483-X*) IPG Chicago.

***Twelve Weeks to a Successful Data Dictionary.** Maida R. Herbst. (Illus.). 125p. (Orig.). 1997. pap. text ed. 77.00 (*1-57839-000-1*) Opus Communs.

Twelve Who Made It Big. Jason Marks. LC 81-68767. (Illus.). 112p. (Orig.). 1981. pap. write for info. (*0-9606858-0-4*) Alumni Assn.

Twelve Who Ruled. Robert R. Palmer. 432p. 1941. pap. text ed. 17.95 (*0-691-00761-6*) Princeton U Pr.

Twelve Who Survive: Strengthening Programmes of Early Childhood Development in the Third World. 2nd ed. Robert Myers. 496p. 1995. 14.95 (*0-929816-99-4*) High-Scope.

Twelve Who Survive: Strenthening Programmes of Early Childhood Development in the Third World. Robert Myers. LC 91-32497. (Illus.). 496p. (C). (gr. 13 up). 1992. text ed. 110.00 (*0-415-07307-3*) Routledge.

***Twelve Wild Ducks.** Jim Lamarche. (J). Date not set. write for info. (*0-688-12047-4*); lib. bdg. write for info. (*0-688-12048-2*) Lothrop.

Twelve Wild Geese. Matt Faulkner. LC 92-9708. (Illus.). 32p. (J). (gr. k-4). 1995. 14.95 (*0-590-45684-9*) Scholastic Inc.

Twelve Wings of the Eagle: Our Spiritual Evolution Through the Ages of the Zodiac. Maria K. Simms. (Illus.). 304p. (Orig.). 1996. pap. 12.95 (*0-917086-95-3*) ACS Pubns.

***Twelve Woman Detective Stories.** Ed. by Laura Marcus. (Oxford Twelves). 240p. 1998. pap. 11.95 (*0-19-288036-5*) OUP.

Twelve Women Apostles, Bk. 1. Virgil Armstrong. Ed. by Beth Whitman. 300p. (Orig.). 1990. pap. 9.99 (*0-925390-15-1*) Armstrong Assocs.

Twelve Words of the Gypsy. Keostees Palamas. Tr. & Intro. by Frederic Will. LC 64-17223. 229p. reprint ed. pap. 65.30 (*0-7837-6175-9*, 2045897) Bks Demand.

Twelve World Teachers. Manly P. Hall. pap. 14.95 (*0-89314-816-4*) Philos Res.

12-Year Reich: A Social History of Nazi Germany, 1933-1945. Richard Grunberger. (Illus.). 560p. 1995. reprint ed. pap. 17.95 (*0-306-80660-6*) Da Capo.

Twelve Years - First & Last. Jack Petersen & Ruby Petersen. LC 87-81107. (Illus.). 100p. 1987. lib. bdg. 50.00 (*0-87208-203-2*) Shoeless Pub.

Twelve Years a Slave. Solomon Northup. Ed. by Sue Eakin & Joseph Logsdon. LC 68-13454. (Library of Southern Civilization). (Illus.). xxxviii, 274p. 1968. pap. text ed. 12.95 (*0-8071-0150-8*) La State U Pr.

Twelve Years a Slave: Excerpts from the Narrative of Solomon Northup. Alice Lucas. Ed. by Geoffrey Link. (Illus.). 43p. (Orig.). (J). (gr. 5-12). 1992. teacher ed., pap. text ed. 5.00 (*0-936434-59-7*, Pub. by Zellerbach Fam Fund) SF Study Ctr.

Twelve Years a Slave: Excerpts from the Narrative of Solomon Northup. abr. ed. Solomon Northup. Ed. by Alice Lucas. (Illus.). 48p. (Orig.). (J). (gr. 5-12). 1991. pap. text ed. 7.00 (*0-936434-39-2*, Pub. by Zellerbach Fam Fund) SF Study Ctr.

Twelve Years in America Being Observations on the Country, the People, Institutions, & Religion. James Shaw. 1977. text ed. 28.95 (*0-8369-9234-2*, 9088) Ayer.

Twelve Years in China: The People, the Rebels, & the Mandarins. John Scarth. LC 72-79838. (China Library). (Illus.). 1972. reprint ed. lib. bdg. 35.00 (*0-8420-1365-2*) Scholarly Res Inc.

Twelve Years in the Saddle. John L. Sullivan. LC 67-6749. (Concordance Ser., No. 37). 1970. lib. bdg. 61.95 (*0-8383-1106-7*) M S G Haskell Hse.

Twelve Years in the Saddle for Law & Order on the Frontiers of Texas. W. John Sullivan. (American Biography Ser.). 284p. 1991. reprint ed. lib. bdg. 69.00 (*0-7812-8375-2*) Rprt Serv.

Twelve Years of Commonwealth Diplomatic History: Commonwealth Summit Meetings, 1979-1991. Stephen Chan. LC 91-6856. 168p. 1992. lib. bdg. 79.95 (*0-7734-9498-7*) E Mellen.

***Twelve Years with Mary Baker Eddy: Recollections & Experiences.** Irving C. Tomlinson. LC 96-83621. 300p. 1996. 25.00 (*0-87510-311-1*) Christian Sci.

Twelve Youthful Martyrs. Esther E. Enock. pap. 3.99 (*0-88019-114-7*) Schmul Pub Co.

Twelvemonth & a Day. Christopher Rush. 196p. 1985. text ed. 25.00 (*0-08-032428-2*, Pergamon Pr) Elsevier.

Twelvemonth & a Day. Christopher Rush. 296p. 1986. pap. text ed. 11.95 (*0-08-032469-X*, R145, R150, K150, P110, Pergamon Pr) Elsevier.

12th International Corrosion Congress Preceedings Vol. 6: Electric Power Industry Workshop. (Illus.). 243p. 1993. 85.00 (*0-614-02601-6*) NACE Intl.

12th International Corrosion Congress Preceedings Vols. 1-6, 6 vols., Set. 1993. 400.00 (*0-614-02604-0*) NACE Intl.

12th International Corrosion Congress Preceedings Vols. 3A & 3B: Corrosion: Specific Issues, 2 vols., Set. 1993. 142.00 (*0-614-02602-4*) NACE Intl.

12th International Corrosion Congress Preceedings Vols. 5A & 5B: Corrosion: General Issues, 2 vols., Set. 1993. 142.00 (*0-614-02603-2*) NACE Intl.

Twende! A Practical Swahili Course. Joan E. Maw. (Illus.). 352p. 1985. 42.00 (*0-19-713605-2*) OUP.

***20th Century Novel.** Kershner. 1997. pap. text ed. 8.00 (*0-312-10244-5*) St Martin.

Twenties. Jackson MacLow. (Roof Bks.). 112p. 1991. pap. text ed. 8.95 (*0-937804-42-8*) Segue NYC.

Twenties: American Writing in the Postwar Decade. Frederick J. Hoffman. 1965. pap. 17.95 (*0-02-914780-8*, Free Press) Free Pr.

Twenties: The Lawless Decade. Paul Sann. (Quality Paperbacks Ser.). (Illus.). 240p. 1984. reprint ed. pap. 12.95 (*0-306-80216-3*) Da Capo.

20's & 30's Style. Michael Horsham. (Illus.). 128p. 1996. 21.95 (*1-57215-171-4*) World Pubns.

Twenties in America. 2nd ed. Paul A. Carter. Ed. by John H. Franklin & A. S. Eisenstadt. LC 74-26538. (American History Ser.). 144p. (C). 1975. pap. text ed. write for info. (*0-88295-717-1*) Harlan Davidson.

***Twenties in the Nineties.** Beller. 1998. pap. write for info. (*0-395-85796-1*) HM.

Twenties in the Sixties. Richard Kostelanetz. LC 77-90708. (C). 1978. 75.00 (*0-915066-57-2*); pap. 10.00 (*0-915066-58-0*) Assembling Pr.

Twentieth Air Force Story. Kenn Rust. (Illus.). 72p. 1993. pap. text ed. 15.95 (*0-911852-85-9*) Aviation Heritage.

Twentieth Anniversary Edition Math Their Way Package. anniversary ed. Mary Baratta-Lorton. 1994. pap. 59.00 (*0-201-86153-4*) Addison-Wesley.

Twentieth Anniversary Exhibition of the Vogel Collection. Georgia Coopersmith. (Illus.). 94p. 1982. pap. 12.50 (*0-942746-03-1*) SUNYP R Gibson.

20th Anniversary Journal United Brethren for Christ, Inc. African American Inner City - Community Ministry. Ed. by Diane Johnson. (Illus.). 50p. (Orig.). Date not set. pap. 5.00 (*1-877971-15-4*) Mid Atl Reg Pr.

20th Anniversary Journal United Outreach for Christ Mission Team: Prison Ministry. Ed. by Evelyn M. Taylor. LC 95-13323. (Illus.). 80p. (Orig.). 1995. pap. 10.00 (*1-877971-16-2*) Mid Atl Reg Pr.

Twentieth Anniversary of Fluidics Symposium: Presented at the Winter Annual Meeting of the American Society of Mechanical Engineers, Chicago, Illinois, November 16-21, 1980. Fluidics Symposium Staff. Ed. by Tadusz M. Drzewiecki & M. E. Franke. LC 80-69185. (Illus.). 231p. reprint ed. pap. 65.90 (*0-8357-2855-2*, 2039090) Bks Demand.

Twentieth Anniversary Symposium -- PCMR: Maximizing the Quality of Life for Individuals with Mental Retardation & Other Developmental Disabilities. 194p. 1988. write for info. (*1-55672-008-4*) US HHS.

Twentieth Annual Institute on Employment Law. John J. Ross. (Litigation & Administrative Practice Ser.). 1018p. 1991. 70.00 (*0-685-59336-3*, H4-5112) PLI.

Twentieth Annual Institute on International Taxation. (Tax Law & Estate Planning Ser.). 435p. 1989. 70.00 (*0-317-99762-9*, J4-3637) PLI.

Twentieth Annual Middle Atlantic Regional Gospel Music Festival Journal, 1992. E. Myron Noble. 25p. (Orig.). 1993. pap. 5.00 (*1-877971-06-5*) Mid Atl Reg Pr.

Twentieth Annual Northeast Bioengineering Conference, 1994. IEEE, Engineering in Medicine & Biology Society Staff. Ed. by Institute of Electrical & Electronics Engineers, Inc. Staff. LC 88-646567. 110p. 1994. pap. text ed. write for info. (*0-7803-1930-3*); lib. bdg. write for info. (*0-7803-1931-1*, 94CH3439-7); fiche write for info. (*0-7803-1932-X*) Inst Electrical.

***Twentieth Army Science Conference: Award-Winning Papers, Norfolk, Virginia, 24-27 June 1996.** Ed. by Richard Chait et al. 150p. 1997. 38.00 (*981-02-3178-4*) World Scientific Pub.

***Twentieth Century, 7 bks.** 219.65 (*0-7910-3569-7*) Chelsea Hse.

An Asterisk (*) at the beginning of an entry indicates that the title is appearing in BIP for the first time.

Twentieth Century. C. Hopkinson. (History of the Modern World Ser.). 96p. (J). (gr. 5 up). 1994. lib. bdg. 18.95 (*0-88110-674-7*, Usborne) EDC.

Twentieth Century. C. Hopkinson. (History of the Modern World Ser.). 96p. (J). (gr. 5 up). 1994. pap. 10.95 (*0-7460-0701-9*, Usborne) EDC.

Twentieth Century. Rosemary Lambert. (Cambridge Introduction to Art Ser.). 96p. (C). 1981. pap. text ed. 13.95 (*0-521-29622-6*) Cambridge U Pr.

Twentieth Century, 6 vols., Set. Visual Education Corporation Staff. 784p. 1992. 275.00 (*0-02-897442-5*) Macmillan.

Twentieth Century, Vol. 7. Ed. by Martin Dodsworth. (Penguin History of Literature Ser.). 432p. 1994. pap. 12.95 (*0-14-017757-4*, Penguin Bks) Viking Penguin.

Twentieth Century: A Global History. 4th ed. Richard Goff et al. LC 93-37280. 1993. pap. text ed. write for info. (*0-07-023566-X*) McGraw.

Twentieth Century: A People's History. Howard Zinn. LC 83-48397. 336p. 1984. pap. 12.00 (*0-06-091103-4*, CN 1103, PL) HarpC.

Twentieth Century: An Epic of American History. Robert K. Garrity. 208p. (Orig.). (YA). (gr. 9-12). 1991. pap. write for info. (*0-9628375-0-4*) R K Garrity.

Twentieth Century: Great Athletes, 23 vols., Set. Salem Press Editors. LC 91-32301. (Illus.). 3562p. (YA). (gr. 6 up). 1992. lib. bdg. 400.00 (*0-89356-775-2*) Salem Pr.

Twentieth Century: Great Events, 10 vols. Salem Press Editors. LC 92-28671. (Illus.). 1431p. (YA). (gr. 6 up). 1992. Set. lib. bdg. 250.00 (*0-89356-796-5*) Salem Pr.

Twentieth Century: Great Scientific Achievements, 10 vols. Ed. by Salem Press Editors. LC 94-1829. (Illus.). 1114p. (YA). (gr. 6 up). 1994. Set. lib. bdg. 250.00 (*0-89356-860-0*) Salem Pr.

Twentieth Century: Major Composers of Our Time. Denes Agay. (Anthology of Piano Music Ser.: Vol. 4). 238p. 1971. pap. 17.95 (*0-8256-8044-1*, YK20246, Yorktown Mus) Music Sales.

Twentieth Century: Mirrors of Mind - A Study in Commitment & Creativity. 2nd ed. Roberts & Schlegel. 315p. 3991. pap. 31.95 (*0-88725-158-7*) Hunter Textbks.

Twentieth Century: The Definitive Compendium of Astonishing Events, Amazing People, & Strange-But-True Facts. David Wallechinsky. 1995. 24.95 (*0-614-15511-8*) Little.

***Twentieth-Century Pt. 1.** (Spanish American Literature Ser.). 350p. 1997. text ed. 75.00 (*0-8153-2680-7*) Garland.

***Twentieth-Century Pt. 2.** (Spanish American Literature Ser.). 350p. 1997. text ed. 75.00 (*0-8153-2681-5*) Garland.

Twentieth Century see American Painting

Twentieth-Century African-American Writers & Artists. Chester M. Hedgepeth, Jr. LC 90-301. 336p. (C). 1991. text ed. 50.00 (*0-8389-0534-X*, 0534-X) ALA.

***Twentieth Century America.** Foster R. Dulles. 582p. 1972. 28.95 (*0-8369-2898-9*) Bks for Libraries.

Twentieth-Century America. Irwin Unger & Debi Unger. LC 89-63078. 576p. 1989. text ed. 45.00 (*0-312-03590-X*) St Martin.

Twentieth-Century America: A Primary Source Collection from the Associated Press, 10 vols., Set. LC 95-12550. (Illus.). 272p. (YA). (gr. 7 up). 1995. lib. bdg. 349.00 (*0-7172-7494-2*) Grolier Educ.

Twentieth Century America: Key Events in History. Ed. by Bob Baron. (Millennium 2000 Ser.). 144p. 1995. 12.95 (*1-55591-276-1*) Fulcrum Pub.

Twentieth Century America: One-Hundred Influential People. Ed. by Bob Baron. (Millennium 2000 Ser.). 128p. 1995. 12.95 (*1-55591-277-X*) Fulcrum Pub.

Twentieth-Century America: Recent Interpretations. 2nd ed. Ed. by Barton J. Bernstein & Allen J. Matusow. 582p. (Orig.). (C). 1972. pap. text ed. 20.00 (*0-15-592391-9*) HB Coll Pubs.

Twentieth Century America: The Intellectual & Cultural Context. Douglas Tallack. (Literature in English Ser.). (Illus.). 480p. (C). 1991. pap. text ed. 32.50 (*0-582-49455-9*) Longman.

***Twentieth-Century America: The Intellectual & Cultural Context.** Douglas Tallack. LC 90-41577. (Longman Literature in English Ser.). 466p. 1991. reprint ed. pap. 132.90 (*0-608-03608-0*, 2064431) Bks Demand.

***20th Century American & Jewish Writers.** 1984. 140.00 (*0-8103-1706-0*, 00006760, Gale Res Intl) Gale.

Twentieth-Century American City. 2nd ed. Jon C. Teaford. LC 92-23198. (American Moment Ser.). 200p. 1993. text ed. 38.95 (*0-8018-4550-5*); pap. text ed. 13.95 (*0-8018-4551-3*) Johns Hopkins.

Twentieth-Century American Composers. 2nd ed. Harold Gleason & Warren Becker. LC 80-53732. (Music Literature Outlines Ser.: No. IV). 250p. 1988. pap. text ed. 13.95 (*0-88284-382-6*, 2894) Alfred Pub.

Twentieth-Century American Dramatists, 2 vols., Set. Ed. by John MacNicholas. (Dictionary of Literary Biography Ser.: Vol. 7). (Illus.). 848p. 1981. 260.00 (*0-8103-0928-9*) Gale.

Twentieth-Century American Folk, Self-Taught, & Outsider Art. Betty-Carol Sellen & Cynthia J. Johanson. LC 93-3146. (Illus.). 475p. 1993. 90.00 (*1-55570-142-6*) Neal-Schuman.

Twentieth-Century American Heroes: A Thematic Approach to Cultural Awareness. Shirley Cook. Ed. by Jan Keeling. (Illus.). 80p. (Orig.). 1993. pap. text ed. 9.95 (*0-86530-259-6*) Incentive Pubns.

Twentieth-Century American Historians, Vol. 17. Ed. by Clyde N. Wilson. (Dictionary of Literary Biography Ser.: Vol. 17). 536p. 1983. 140.00 (*0-8103-1144-5*) Gale.

Twentieth-Century American Literary Naturalism: An Interpretation. Donald Pizer. LC 81-5606. (Crosscurrents-Modern Critiques, New Ser.). 187p. 1982. 19.95 (*0-8093-1027-9*) S Ill U Pr.

***Twentieth-Century American Literature, 15 bks.** (Modern Critical Interpretations Ser.). 469.25 (*0-7910-3576-X*) Chelsea Hse.

***Twentieth-Century American Literature, 8 bks.** (Library of Literary Criticism). 575.00 (*0-87754-800-5*) Chelsea Hse.

Twentieth-Century American Literature Biographical Supplement & Index see Library of Literary Criticism

Twentieth-Century American Masterpieces from the Whitney Museum of American Art: Thirty-Two Postcards in Full Color. Whitney Museum of American Art Staff. (Illus.). 16p. 1989. pap. 6.00 (*0-486-26012-7*) Dover.

Twentieth-Century American Masters: Barber, Berstein, Cage, Carter, Copland, Cowell, Gershwin, Ives, Sessions, & Thomson. William W. Austin et al. Ed. by Stanley Sadie. (New Grove Composer Biography Ser.). (Orig.). 1988. pap. 12.95 (*0-393-30353-5*) Norton.

Twentieth-Century American Music for the Dance: A Bibliography. Ed. by Isabelle Emerson. LC 96-6829. (Music Reference Collection: Vol. 53). 256p. 1996. text ed. 69.50 (*0-313-29350-3*, Greenwood Pr) Greenwood.

Twentieth-Century American Newspapers. William R. Lindley. (Illus.). 116p. 1993. pap. 14.95 (*0-89745-160-0*) Sunflower U Pr.

Twentieth-Century American Nicknames. Ed. by Laurence Urdang. LC 79-23390. 398p. 1979. 42.00 (*0-8242-0642-8*) Wilson.

Twentieth-Century American Painting: The Thyssen-Bornemisza Collection. Gail Levin. LC 87-61728. (Illus.). 408p. 1988. 95.00 (*0-85667-332-3*, Pub. by P Wilson Pubs) Sothebys Pubns.

Twentieth Century American Paintings from the Metropolitan Museum of Art. Intro. by Henry Geldzahler. (Illus.). 44p. (Orig.). 1977. pap. 3.00 (*0-943526-41-8*) Parrish Art.

Twentieth-Century American Playwrights: Views of a Changing Culture. Compiled by Cathy Henderson. (Illus.). 169p. 1994. pap. 15.00 (*0-87959-133-1*) U of Tex H Ransom Ctr.

Twentieth-Century American Science Fiction Writers, 2 vols., Set. Ed. by David Cowart. (Dictionary of Literary Biography Ser.: Vol. 8). 688p. 1981. 270.00 (*0-8103-0918-1*) Gale.

Twentieth Century American Short Stories. Jean A. McConochie. 1975. pap. 17.95 (*0-8384-3233-6*) Heinle & Heinle.

Twentieth Century American Short Stories. Jean A. McConochie. 1986. 9.95 (*0-02-971270-X*, Free Press) Free Pr.

Twentieth-Century American Short Stories, Vol. 1. 2nd rev. ed. Jean A. McConochie. 160p. 1995. pap. 21.95 (*0-8384-4850-X*) Heinle & Heinle.

Twentieth-Century American Short Stories Vol. 1. 2nd rev. ed. Jean A. McConochie. 160p. 1995. pap. 21.95 (*0-8384-4851-8*) Heinle & Heinle.

Twentieth Century American Watercolor. Janice C. Oresman. (Illus.). 56p. 1983. 15.00 (*0-934483-03-5*) Gal Assn NY.

***Twentieth-Century American Writers - Novelists, 13 bks.** (Modern Critical Views Ser.). 394.35 (*0-7910-3585-9*) Chelsea Hse.

***Twentieth-Century American Writers - Poets & Dramatists, 9 bks.** (Modern Critical Views Ser.). 279.55 (*0-7910-3586-7*) Chelsea Hse.

20th Century Architecture: A Reader's Guide. M. Pawlay. 160p. 1995. 34.50 (*0-419-19740-0*, Blackie & Son-Chapman NY) Routledge Chapman & Hall.

Twentieth Century Architecture: A Visual History. rev. ed. Dennis Sharp. (Illus.). 424p. 1991. 65.00 (*0-8160-2438-3*) Facts on File.

Twentieth Century Architecture & Urbanism: Milano. (Architecture & Urbanism Extra Edition Ser.). (Illus.). 280p. (Orig.). (ENG & JPN.). (C). pap. text ed. 82.50 (*4-900211-35-4*, Pub. by Japan Architect JA) Gingko Press.

Twentieth Century Architecture & Urbanism: Paris. (Architecture & Urbanism Extra Edition Ser.). (Illus.). 268p. (Orig.). (ENG & JPN.). (C). pap. text ed. 82.50 (*4-900211-31-1*, Pub. by Japan Architect JA) Gingko Press.

20th-Century Architecture in Ireland. Ed. by Annette Becker et al. LC 97-3740. (Illus.). 240p. 1997. 65.00 (*3-7913-1719-9*, Pub. by Prestel GW) te Neues.

***20th-Century Architecture in Ireland.** Annette Becker et al. LC 97-3740. 1997. write for info. (*3-7913-1706-7*, Pub. by Prestel GW) te Neues.

20th Century Architecture in the Netherlands. Hans Ibelings. 192p. Date not set. pap. 50.00 (*90-72469-96-8*, Pub. by NAi Uitgevers NE) Dist Art Pubs.

20th Century Arms & Armor. Stephen Bull. LC 95-12020. (Illus.). 224p. 1995. 35.00 (*0-8160-3349-8*) Facts on File.

Twentieth Century Art: Panorama '76 Total Art Pt. 1, No. 47. Ed. by Alain Jouffroy. 1976. 30.00 (*0-8148-0688-0*) L Amiel Pub.

Twentieth Century Art: 1950's-1990's Prints. (Illus.). 12p. 1993. 29.95 (*1-56290-088-9*, 6035) Crystal.

20th Century Art Book. (Illus.). 512p. 1996. 39.95 (*0-7148-3542-0*, Pub. by Phaidon Press UK) Chronicle Bks.

Twentieth Century Art, No. 38: Panorama '72. Ed. by G. Di San Lazzaro. (Illus.). (FRE.). 1972. 19.95 (*0-8148-0539-6*) L Amiel Pub.

Twentieth Century Art, No. 39. Ed. by G. Di San Lazzaro. (Illus.). (ENG & FRE.). 19.95 (*0-8148-0566-3*) L Amiel Pub.

Twentieth Century Art, No. 42: Surrealism, Pt. 1. Ed. by G. Di San Lazzaro. (Illus.). 1975. 30.00 (*0-8148-0683-X*) L Amiel Pub.

Twentieth Century Art, No. 43: Surrealism, Pt.2. Ed. by G. Di San Lazzaro. (Illus.). 1975. 30.00 (*0-8148-0684-8*) L Amiel Pub.

Twentieth Century Art, No. 44: The Imaginary Reality, Pt. 1. Ed. by Alain Jouffroy. (Illus.). (FRE.). 1975. 30.00 (*0-8148-0685-6*) L Amiel Pub.

Twentieth Century Art, No. 45: The Imaginary Reality, Pt. 2. Ed. by Alain Jouffroy. (Illus.). (FRE.). 1975. 30.00 (*0-8148-0686-4*) L Amiel Pub.

Twentieth Century Art Songs: Medium Voice for Recital & Study. 116p. 1986. per. 18.95 (*0-7935-0685-9*, 50331200) H Leonard.

Twentieth-Century Artists on Art. Ed. by Dore Ashton. (Illus.). 1986. 24.95 (*0-394-52276-1*) Pantheon.

Twentieth Century Artists on Art: An Index to Artists' Writings, Statements, & Interviews. 2nd ed. Jack S. Robertson. LC 95-33700. 1996. 95.00 (*0-8161-9059-3*, GK Hall) Thorndike Pr.

Twentieth Century Atheist. Justin Van Auden. 1995. pap. 42.25 (*0-942004-62-0*) Throwkoff Pr.

Twentieth-Century Author Biographies Master Index. Ed. by Barbara McNeil. 539p. 1984. 69.00 (*0-8103-2095-9*); 39.00 (*0-8103-2096-7*) Gale.

Twentieth Century Authors: A Biographical Dictionary of Modern Literature. Ed. by Stanley J. Kunitz & Howard Haycraft. LC 43-51003. (Wilson Authors Ser.). (Illus.). 1123p. 1942. P. 1123. suppl. ed. 85.00 (*0-8242-0050-0*) Wilson.

Twentieth Century Baseball Chronicle. (Illus.). 608p. 1993. 29.95 (*0-7853-0335-9*, 3512502) Pubns Intl Ltd.

Twentieth Century Biographical Dictionary of Notable Americans, 10 vols., Set. Rossiter Johnson. 1972. 100. 00 (*0-8490-1237-6*) Gordon Pr.

Twentieth Century Black American Women in Print: Essays by Ralph Reckley, Sr. Ed. by Lola E. Jones. 128p. 1991. pap. 16.35 (*0-87411-406-3*) Copley Pub.

Twentieth Century Brass Musical Instruments in the United States. Richard J. Dundas. LC 86-90264. (Illus.). 74p. (Orig.). 1989. reprint ed. pap. 10.00 (*0-9617093-1-6*) R J Dundas Pubns.

Twentieth-Century Brass Soloists: Bio-Critical Source Books on Musical Performance. Michael Meckna. LC 93-23943. 344p. 1994. text ed. 79.50 (*0-313-26468-6*, MTC/, Greenwood Pr) Greenwood.

Twentieth-Century Britain: An Encyclopedia. Ed. by F. M. Leventhal. LC 95-30749. (Illus.). 944p. 1995. text ed. 95.00 (*0-8240-7205-7*, H1378) Garland.

Twentieth-Century Britain: Economic, Social, & Cultural Change. Ed. by Paul Johnson. LC 93-44674. (C). 1995. pap. text ed. 33.95 (*0-582-22817-4*, Pub. by Longman UK) Longman.

Twentieth Century British Art. (Art & Design Profiles Ser.). (Illus.). 80p. 1987. pap. 21.95 (*0-312-00844-9*) St Martin.

20th Century British Art. John R. Taylor. Ed. by Andreas Papadakis. (Art & Design Ser.: No. 1). (Illus.). 104p. (Orig.). 1987. pap. 21.95 (*0-85670-912-3*) Academy Ed UK.

***Twentieth-Century British Literature, 11 bks.** (Modern Critical Interpretations Ser.). 359.45 (*0-7910-3574-3*) Chelsea Hse.

Twentieth Century British Music: A Collector's Guide. Peter J. Pirie. (Front Music Publications: No. 2). 20p. (Orig.). 1980. pap. 6.50 (*0-934082-02-2*) Theodore Front.

***Twentieth-Century British Writers, 9 bks.** (Modern Critical Views Ser.). 289.55 (*0-7910-3583-2*) Chelsea Hse.

Twentieth-Century Building Materials: History & Conservation. Ed. by Thomas C. Jester. 1996. text ed. 55.00 (*0-07-032573-1*) McGraw.

Twentieth Century Capitalism. Erugen Varga. Tr. by George H. Hanna from RUS. LC 74-38269. (Evolution of Capitalism Ser.). 162p. 1978. reprint ed. 19.95 (*0-405-04141-1*) Ayer.

Twentieth-Century Caribbean & Black African Writers. Ed. by Bernth Lindfors & Reinhard W. Sander. (Dictionary of Literary Biography Ser.: Vol. 157). 1995. 140.00 (*0-8103-9352-2*) Gale.

Twentieth-Century Caribbean & Black African Writers, Vol. 117. Ed. by Reinhard W. Sander & Bernth Linffors. LC 92-8972. (Dictionary of Literary Biography Ser.: Vol. 117). 406p. 1992. 140.00 (*0-8103-7594-X*, 006585) Gale.

Twentieth-Century Children's Writers. 3rd ed. Ed. by Tracy Chevalier. 1288p. 1989. 132.00 (*0-912289-95-3*, 200015-M99019) St James Pr.

Twentieth-Century Children's Writers, Vol. 1. 4th ed. Ed. by Laura S. Berger. (Twentieth Century Writers Ser.). 1272p. 1994. 140.00 (*1-55862-177-6*, PN1009) St James Pr.

Twentieth Century China. 3rd ed. O. Edmund Clubb. LC 77-18991. 559p. 1978. pap. text ed. 24.50 (*0-231-04519-0*) Col U Pr.

Twentieth-Century Chinese Stories. Ed. by Chih-Tsing Hsia. LC 72-173986. (Companions to Asian Studies). 256p. reprint ed. pap. 73.00 (*0-685-20796-X*, 2030110) Bks Demand.

Twentieth Century Chinese Writers & Their Pen Names, 2 vols. 2nd ed. Ed. by Pao-liang Chu. 913p. (Orig.). 1989. pap. 75.00 (*0-88727-151-0*) Cheng & Tsui.

Twentieth-Century Choral Music: An Annotated Bibliography of Music Suitable for Use by High School Choirs. 2nd ed. J. Perry White. LC 90-20005. 226p. 1990. 25.00 (*0-8108-2394-2*) Scarecrow.

Twentieth Century City. Josiah Strong. LC 77-112575. (Rise of Urban America Ser.). 1974. reprint ed. 17.95 (*0-405-02477-0*) Ayer.

20th Century Collectible Ceramics: Collectible Pottery & Porcelain Wares Produced since the Turn of the Century. Ed. by Susan N. Cox. LC 95-76097. (Illus.). 248p. (Orig.). 1996. pap. 14.95 (*0-930625-42-0*, Antque Trdr Bks) Antique Trader Bks.

Twentieth Century Collection at the National Portrait Gallery. Honor Clerk & Robin Gibson. (Illus.). 64p. 1993. pap. 9.95 (*1-85514-025-X*, Pub. by Natl Port Gall UK) Antique Collect.

Twentieth Century Colorado see Story of Colorado

Twentieth-Century Composer Speaks: An Index of Interviews. Mari Nishimura. LC 93-29548. (Reference Books in Music: No. 28). xxxii, 189p. 1993. 39.50 (*0-914913-29-8*) Fallen Leaf.

Twentieth Century Composers. David Ewen. LC 68-16930. (Essay Index Reprint Ser.). 1977. 24.95 (*0-8369-0434-6*) Ayer.

Twentieth-Century Conceptions of Language: Mastering the Metaphysics Market. Rudolf P. Botha. 336p. 1993. 64. 95 (*0-631-18198-9*) Blackwell Pubs.

Twentieth Century Construction of "Judaism" Essays on the Religion of Torah in the History of Religion. Jacob Neusner. (USF Studies in the History of Judaism). 392p. (C). 1991. 74.95 (*1-55540-645-9*, 240032) Scholars Pr GA.

Twentieth Century Continental Philosophy, Vol. 8. Ed. by Richard Kearney. LC 93-15763. (History of Philosophy Ser.: Vol. 8). 440p. (C). (gr. 13). 1994. 89.95 (*0-415-05629-2*) Routledge.

Twentieth Century Continental Philosophy: A Reader. Ed. & Intro. by Todd May. LC 96-6794. 1996. pap. text ed. 41.00 (*0-13-450826-2*) P-H.

Twentieth Century Crime & Mystery Writers. 3rd ed. Ed. by Lesley Henderson. 1294p. 1991. 132.00 (*1-55862-031-1*, 200109-M99019) St James Pr.

***Twentieth Century Criticism, Vol. 72.** 1998. 134.00 (*0-7876-1174-3*, 00156299, Gale Res Intl) Gale.

***Twentieth Century Criticism, Vol. 73.** 1998. 134.00 (*0-7876-1175-1*, 00156300, Gale Res Intl) Gale.

Twentieth Century Criticism Vol. 55 & Index: Excerpts from Criticism of the Works of Novelists, Poets, Playwrights, Short Story Writers & Other Creative Writers who Lived Between 1900 & 1960, from the First Published Critical Appraisals to Current Evaluations. Ed. by Marie Lazzari. 532p. 1994. 134.00 (*0-8103-2435-0*) Gale.

***Twentieth Century Criticism & Topics, Vol. 66.** 1996. 134. 00 (*0-7876-1164-6*, 00156288, Gale Res Intl) Gale.

***Twentieth Century Criticism & Topics, Vol. 69.** 1997. 134. 00 (*0-7876-1169-7*, 00156297, Gale Res Intl) Gale.

***Twentieth Century Criticism & Topics, Vol. 70.** 1997. 134. 00 (*0-7876-1170-0*, 00156298, Gale Res Intl) Gale.

***Twentieth Century Critics, Vol. 65.** 1996. 134.00 (*0-7876-0779-7*, 00153454, Gale Res Intl) Gale.

***Twentieth Century Critisism, Vol. 68.** 1997. 134.00 (*0-7876-1168-9*, 00156296, Gale Res Intl) Gale.

Twentieth Century Cultural Life in Texas. Ronald L. Davis. (Texas History Ser.). (Illus.). 50p. 1981. pap. text ed. 8.95 (*0-89641-072-2*) American Pr.

Twentieth Century Czechoslovakia: The Meanings of Its History. Josef Korbel. LC 76-54250. 346p. 1977. text ed. 49.50 (*0-231-03724-4*) Col U Pr.

***Twentieth-Century Design.** Jonathan M. Woodham. (Oxford History of Art). (Illus.). 288p. 1997. 39.95 (*0-19-284247-1*); pap. 15.95 (*0-19-284204-8*) OUP.

Twentieth-Century Dictatorships: The Ideological One-Party States. Paul Brooker. 311p. (C). 1994. 45.00 (*0-8147-1233-9*) NYU Pr.

Twentieth-Century Dictatorships: The Ideological One-Party States. Paul Brooker. 311p. (C). 1995. pap. 18.95 (*0-8147-1251-7*) NYU Pr.

Twentieth-Century Dictionary of Christian Biography. Ed. by J. D. Douglas. LC 95-91. 439p. (C). 1995. 24.99 (*0-8010-3031-5*) Baker Bks.

Twentieth-Century Drawings from the Whitney Museum of American Art. Whitney Museum of American Art Staff. (Illus.). 144p. (Orig.). 1982. pap. 8.95 (*0-486-24143-2*) Dover.

Twentieth Century Economic Thought. Ed. by Glenn E. Hoover. LC 78-128261. (Essay Index Reprint Ser.). 1977. 44.95 (*0-8369-1957-2*) Ayer.

Twentieth Century, Eighteen Eighty to Nineteen Thirty-Nine. Paul M. Hayes. LC 77-93695. (Modern British Foreign Policy Ser.). 1978. text ed. 29.95 (*0-312-82409-2*) St Martin.

Twentieth Century Embroidery in Great Britain from 1978, Vol. IV. Constance Howard. (Illus.). 1986. 42.50 (*0-7134-4658-7*) Branford.

Twentieth Century English. Ed. by William Knickerbocker. LC 75-107721. (Essay Index Reprint Ser.). 1977. 30.95 (*0-8369-1668-9*) Ayer.

Twentieth Century English History Plays: From Shaw to Bond. Niloufer Harben. LC 87-1024. (Illus.). 240p. 1987. 56.50 (*0-389-20734-9*) B&N Imports.

***Twentieth Century English Short Stories.** Pierce & Cochrane. 1992. pap. text ed. write for info. (*0-17-555850-7*) Addison-Wesley.

Twentieth-Century Essays & Addresses. Ed. by William A. Archbold. LC 78-128202. (Essay Index Reprint Ser.). 1977. 20.95 (*0-8369-1861-4*) Ayer.

Twentieth Century Ethical Theory. Steven M. Cahn & Jeram G. Haber. 650p. (C). 1994. pap. text ed. 46.00 (*0-02-318031-5*, Macmillan Coll) P-H.

***Twentieth-Century Europe.** pap. write for info. (*0-340-58018-6*, Pub. by E Arnold UK) Routledge Chapman & Hall.

***Twentieth-Century Europe.** write for info. (*0-340-66189-5*, Pub. by E Arnold UK) Routledge Chapman & Hall.

***Twentieth-Century Europe.** Smyth. (C). Date not set. pap. write for info. (*0-669-34431-1*) HM.

Twentieth Century Europe: Paths to Unity. Richard Vaughan. LC 78-13007. 261p. 1979. text ed. 42.00 (*0-06-497172-4*, N6719) B&N Imports.

Twentieth-Century European Drama. Ed. by Brian Docherty. LC 92-43732. (Insights Ser.). 256p. 1993. text ed. 39.95 (*0-312-09526-0*) St Martin.

An Asterisk (*) at the beginning of an entry indicates that the title is appearing in BIP for the first time.

Twentieth Century Literature Criticism, Vol. 30: Archives, Vol. 30. Ed. by Paula Kepos & Dennis Poupard. 1988. 134.00 (*0-8103-2412-1*) Gale.

Twentieth Century Literature in Retrospect. Ed. by Reuben A. Brower. LC 76-168430. (English Studies: No. 2). 371p. 1971. pap. 8.95 (*0-674-91424-4*) HUP.

Twentieth-Century Los Angeles: Power, Promotion & Social Conflict. Ed. by Norman Klein & Martin Schiesl. 240p. (C). 1990. 29.95 (*0-941690-38-5*); pap. text ed. 14.95 (*0-941690-39-3*) Regina Bks.

Twentieth Century Masters of Erotic Art. Bradley Smith. LC 80-36666. (Illus.). 1985. 30.00 (*0-517-54236-6*) Gemini Smith.

20th Century Masters of Finger-Style Guitar. John Stropes & Peter J. Lang. LC 82-90413. (Illus.). 96p. (Orig.). 1982. spiral bd. 16.95 (*0-9608512-0-8*) Stropes Editions.

Twentieth-Century Memoirs. Aurel Kolnai. 300p. 1994. 36.00 (*1-870626-63-X*, Pub. by Claridge Pr UK) Paul & Co Pubs.

Twentieth-Century Mexico. Ed. by W. Dirk Raat & William H. Beezley. LC 85-14109. (Illus.). xviii, 318p. 1986. pap. text ed. 12.95 (*0-8032-8914-6*, Bison Books) U of Nebr Pr.

Twentieth-Century Microtonal Notation. Gardner Read. LC 90-2782. (Contributions to the Study of Music & Dance Ser.: No. 18). 216p. 1990. text ed. 49.95 (*0-313-27398-7*, RCD/, Greenwood Pr) Greenwood.

Twentieth Century Mind: Essays on Contemporary Thought. Donald A. Zoll. LC 67-13892. 160p. reprint ed. 45.60 (*0-8357-9393-1*, 2051674) Bks Demand.

Twentieth-Century Modern Masters: The Jacques & Natasha Gelman Collection. William S. Lieberman & Sabine Rewald. (Illus.). 336p. 1990. 60.00 (*0-8109-1037-3*) Abrams.

Twentieth-Century Modern Masters: The Jacques & Natasha Gelman Collection. Ed. by William S. Lieberman. (Illus.). 368p. 1989. 95.00 (*0-87099-568-5*, 0-8109-1037-3) Metro Mus Art.

Twentieth-Century Montana: A State of Extremes. K. Ross Toole. LC 75-177348. (Illus.). 278p. (Orig.). 1983. pap. 12.95 (*0-8061-1826-1*) U of Okla Pr.

Twentieth Century Music. Elliott Antokoletz. 512p. 1991. text ed. 48.00 (*0-13-934126-9*) P-H.

Twentieth Century Music. Richard Burbank & Nicholas Slonimsky. (Illus.). 500p. 1984. 50.00 (*0-87196-464-3*) Facts on File.

Twentieth Century Music. James McCalla. 1996. 45.00 (*0-02-871348-6*) Macmillan.

Twentieth-Century Music. Norton Staff & Robert P. Morgan. (Introduction to Music History Ser.). (C). 1991. text ed. 35.95 (*0-393-95272-X*) Norton.

***Twentieth Century Music.** Richard D. Burbank. LC 80-25040. 509p. 1984. reprint ed. pap. 145.10 (*0-608-02845-2*, 2063912) Bks Demand.

Twentieth Century Music: An Introduction. 2nd ed. Lloyd S. Kaplan & Nancy Carroll. (Illus.). 112p. 1991. pap. text ed. 14.95 (*0-940139-21-9*) Consortium RI.

Twentieth Century Music: An Introduction. 2nd ed. E. Solzman. 1974. pap. 23.00 (*0-13-935007-1*) P-H.

Twentieth Century Music: An Introduction. 3rd ed. Eric Salzman. (Illus.). 352p. (C). 1987. pap. text ed. 37.33 (*0-13-935057-8*) P-H.

Twentieth Century Music: How It Developed, How to Listen to It. Marion Bauer. (Music Ser.). 354p. 1978. reprint ed. lib. bdg. 37.50 (*0-306-79503-5*) Da Capo.

Twentieth Century Music: How It Developed, How to Listen to It: Music Book Index. Marion Bauer. 463p. 1993. reprint ed. lib. bdg. 99.00 (*0-7812-9563-7*) Rprt Serv.

Twentieth Century Music: Its Evolution from the End of the Harmonic Era into the Present Era of Sound. Peter Yates. LC 80-23310. xv, 367p. 1981. reprint ed. text ed. 38.50 (*0-313-22516-8*, YATC, Greenwood Pr) Greenwood.

Twentieth Century Music for Piano. Compiled by Joseph Castle. 1993. 5.95 (*1-56222-579-0*, 94772) Mel Bay.

Twentieth-Century Music for Trumpet & Organ: An Annotated Bibliography. Philip T. Cansler. LC 84-20422. (Research Ser.: No. 11). 1984. pap. 10.00 (*0-914282-30-1*) Brass Pr.

Twentieth-Century Music Idioms. G. Welton Marquis. LC 81-4197. xvi, 269p. 1981. reprint ed. text ed. 38.50 (*0-313-22624-5*, MATC, Greenwood Pr) Greenwood.

Twentieth-Century Musical Chronicle: Events, 1900-1988. Compiled by Charles J. Hall. LC 89-2138. 358p. 1989. text ed. 59.95 (*0-313-26577-1*, HTC, Greenwood Pr) Greenwood.

Twentieth Century Negro Literature. Ed. by Daniel W. Culp. LC 73-89416. (Black Heritage Library Collection). 1977. 26.95 (*0-8369-8551-6*) Ayer.

Twentieth Century Negro Literature. Ed. by Daniel W. Culp. LC 69-18586. (American Negro: His History & Literature. Series 2). 1969. reprint ed. 25.95 (*0-405-01856-8*) Ayer.

Twentieth Century Newfoundland: Explorations. Ed. by Peter Neary & James Hiller. 384p. 1995. pap. 19.95 (*1-55081-072-3*, Pub. by Breakwater Bks CN) Paul & Co Pubs.

Twentieth-Century Newspaper Press in Britain: An Annotated Bibliography. David Linton & Ray Boston. 416p. 1995. 120.00 (*0-7201-2159-0*, Mansell Pub) Cassell.

Twentieth Century (Nineteen Hundred to Present) Ed. by Neil McEwan. LC 89-70174. (St. Martin's Anthologies of English Literature Ser.: Vol. No. 5). 646p. 1990. text ed. 20.00 (*0-312-04475-5*) St Martin.

Twentieth Century Novel. Kershner. 1997. text ed. 35.00 (*0-312-16376-2*) St Martin.

Twentieth-Century Novel in English: A Checklist. 2nd ed. E. C. Bufkin. LC 83-6598. 192p. 1983. 35.00 (*0-8203-0685-1*) U of Ga Pr.

Twentieth Century Odyssey - a Study of Heimito von Doderer's "Die Daemonen" A Study of Heimito Von Doderer's "Die Damonen" Elizabeth C. Hesson. LC 81-69885. (GERM Ser.: Vol. 9). (Illus.). x, 158p. 1983. 34.00 (*0-938100-07-6*) Camden Hse.

20th Century Painting. Sam Hunter. (Illus.). 1996. pap. 4.95 (*0-89659-123-9*) Abbeville Pr.

Twentieth-Century Painting & Sculpture: Selections from the Tenth Anniversary of the East Building. Jeremy Strick. LC 88-38481. (Illus.). 155p. 1989. pap. 19.95 (*0-89468-125-7*) Natl Gallery Art.

Twentieth-Century Peace Movements: Successes & Failures. Ed. by Guido Grunewald & Peter Van Den Dungen. LC 94-17928. 272p. 1994. text ed. 89.95 (*0-7734-9065-5*) E Mellen.

Twentieth Century Performance Reader. Compiled by Michael Huxley & Noel Witts. LC 95-21772. 328p. (C). 1996. pap. 22.95 (*0-415-11628-7*); text ed. 69.95 (*0-415-11627-9*) Routledge.

Twentieth-Century Pessimism & the American Dream. Ed. by Raymond C. Miller. LC 79-26081. (Franklin Memorial Lectures: No. 8). 118p. reprint ed. pap. 33.70 (*0-7837-3802-1*, 2043622) Bks Demand.

Twentieth-Century Pessimism & the American Dream. Ed. by Raymond C. Miller. LC 79-26081. (Franklin Memorial Lectures Ser.: Vol. VIII). (Illus.). ix, 104p. 1980. reprint ed. text ed. 38.50 (*0-313-22122-7*, MITW, Greenwood Pr) Greenwood.

Twentieth-Century Philosophy: The Analytic Tradition. Morris Weitz. LC 66-10366. 1966. pap. 16.95 (*0-02-934990-7*, Free Press) Free Pr.

Twentieth Century Physics. American. 1995. 375.00 (*1-56396-314-0*) Am Inst Physics.

Twentieth Century Physics, 3 vols., Set. Laurie Brown et al. (Illus.). 2576p. 1995. 375.00 (*0-7503-0310-7*) IOP Pub.

Twentieth Century Physics, Vol. 1. Ed. by Laurie M. Brown et al. 1995. write for info. (*1-56396-047-8*) Am Inst Physics.

Twentieth Century Physics, Vol. 1. Ed. by Laurie M. Brown et al. 1995. write for info. (*0-7503-0353-0*) Am Inst Physics.

Twentieth Century Physics, Vol. 2. Ed. by Laurie M. Brown et al. 1995. write for info. (*1-56396-048-6*) Am Inst Physics.

Twentieth Century Physics, Vol. 2. Ed. by Laurie M. Brown et al. 1995. write for info. (*0-7503-0354-9*) Am Inst Physics.

Twentieth Century Physics, Vol. 3. Ed. by Laurie M. Brown et al. 1995. write for info. (*1-56396-049-4*) Am Inst Physics.

Twentieth Century Physics, Vol. 3. Ed. by Laurie M. Brown et al. 1995. write for info. (*0-7503-0355-7*) Am Inst Physics.

Twentieth Century Piano Music. David Burge. 284p. 1990. 46.00 (*0-02-870321-9*) Schirmer Bks.

Twentieth Century Pilgrimage: Walter Lippman & the Public Philosophy. Charles Wellborn. LC 69-17624. 208p. 1969. reprint ed. pap. 59.30 (*0-7837-9881-4*, 2060607) Bks Demand.

Twentieth Century Pioneer. Edna W. Shannon. 1987. pap. write for info. (*0-9602284-5-4*) Long Haul.

Twentieth Century Pioneer: Still Exploring. Evelyn Messmore & Milli B. Whitworth. 60p. (Orig.). Date not set. pap. text ed. 12.95 (*0-9643885-5-3*) Personal Profiles.

Twentieth-Century Pirate. large type ed. Lorna McKenzie. (Linford Romance Library). 272p. 1994. pap. 15.99 (*0-7089-7545-3*, Linford) Ulverscroft.

Twentieth Century Pittsburgh: Government, Business & Change. rev. ed. Roy Lubove. (Illus.). 208p. (C). 1994. pap. 19.95 (*0-8229-5551-2*) U of Pittsburgh Pr.

Twentieth-Century Pittsburgh: The Post-Steel Era, Vol. 2. Roy Lubove. LC 85-40854. (Illus.). 426p. (C). 1996. 44.95 (*0-8229-3892-8*); pap. 19.95 (*0-8229-5566-0*) U of Pittsburgh Pr.

***Twentieth Century Pleasures: Prose on Poetry.** Robert Hass. 1997. pap. text ed. 15.00 (*0-88001-539-X*) Ecco Pr.

Twentieth Century Poetry, an Anthology. Ed. by Harold Monro. reprint ed. 29.00 (*0-403-03062-5*) Somerset Pub.

Twentieth-Century Poetry, Fiction, Theory. Ed. by Harry R. Garvin & John D. Kirkland, Jr. (Bucknell Review Ser.: Vol. 22, No. 2). 231p. 22.00 (*0-8387-1934-1*) Bucknell U Pr.

***Twentieth Century Poets, 8 vols.** (Collected Critical Heritage Ser.). 3681p. (C). 1997. text ed. 70.00 (*0-415-15946-6*) Routledge.

Twentieth-Century Polish Theatre. Ed. by Bohdan Drozdowsky. 256p. 1983. 14.95 (*0-7145-3738-1*) Riverrun NY.

Twentieth-Century Popular Culture in Museums & Libraries. Ed. by Fred E. Schroeder. LC 80-85197. 1981. 31.00 (*0-87972-162-6*) Bowling Green Univ Popular Press.

20th-Century Poster: Design of the Avant-Garde. rev. ed. Dawn Ades et al. Ed. by Mildred Friedman. (Illus.). 220p. 1990. reprint ed. pap. 29.95 (*1-55859-130-3*) Abbeville Pr.

Twentieth-Century Presidential Quotations. LC 95-14081. 1996. write for info. (*1-880875-07-1*) National Archives & Recs.

Twentieth Century Prophet: Being the Life & Thought of William Alexander Guerry, Eighth Bishop of South Carolina. William A. Guerry. Ed. by Edward B. Guerry. (Illus.). 212p. 1976. 5.00 (*0-918769-26-4*) Univ South Pr.

Twentieth-Century Psalms: Reflections on This Life. 2nd rev. ed. Justin F. Stone. 71p. 1989. pap. 6.95 (*0-9620812-3-X*) Good Karma.

Twentieth Century Psychiatry: Its Contribution to Man's Knowledge of Himself. William A. White. LC 73-2428. (Mental Illness & Social Policy; the American Experience Ser.). 1973. reprint ed. 19.95 (*0-405-05236-7*) Ayer.

Twentieth Century Psychology: Recent Developments. Ed. by Philip Harriman et al. LC 75-128255. (Essay Index Reprint Ser.). 1977. 41.95 (*0-8369-1948-3*) Ayer.

***Twentieth Century Reader.** Dock. Date not set. pap. text ed. write for info. (*0-312-16734-2*); pap. text ed. write for info. (*0-312-16735-0*); pap. text ed. write for info. (*0-312-16736-9*) St Martin.

Twentieth Century Religious Thought. John Macquarrie. LC 81-9349. (C). 1981. pap. text ed. write for info. (*0-684-17334-4*) S&S Trade.

Twentieth-Century Religious Thought. rev. ed. John Macquarrie. LC 89-5026. 472p. 1989. pap. 19.95 (*0-334-01709-2*) TPI PA.

***20th Century Revolutions in Technology.** Edward N. Singer. (Illus.). 270p. 1997. 39.00 (*1-56072-432-3*) Nova Sci Pubs.

Twentieth-Century Richmond: Planning, Politics, & Race. Christopher Silver. LC 83-16848. (Twentieth-Century America Ser.). (Illus.). 352p. 1984. 41.00 (*0-87049-421-X*); pap. 19.95 (*0-87049-422-8*) U of Tenn Pr.

***Twentieth Century Romance & Gothic Writers.** 1982. 95.00 (*0-8103-0226-8*, 00005468) Gale.

Twentieth-Century Romance & Historical Writers. 2nd ed. Ed. by Lesley Henderson. 856p. 1990. 132.00 (*0-912289-97-X*, 200013-M99019) St James Pr.

Twentieth-Century Romance & Historical Writers. 3rd ed. Ed. by Aruna Vasudevan & Lesley Henderson. LC 94-16924. 890p. 1994. 140.00 (*1-55862-180-6*) St James Pr.

Twentieth Century Rumania. 2nd ed. Stephen Fischer-Galati. 312p. 1992. text ed. 65.00 (*0-231-07462-X*) Col U Pr.

Twentieth Century Rumania. Stephen Fischer-Galati. LC 77-108838. (Illus.). 274p. reprint ed. pap. 78.10 (*0-8357-3577-X*, 2034633) Bks Demand.

Twentieth Century Russia. 8th ed. Donald W. Treadgold. LC 94-25860. (C). 1994. pap. text ed. 28.00 (*0-8133-1811-4*) Westview.

Twentieth-Century Russian & East European Painting: The Thyssen-Bornemisza Collection. Irene Martin. (Illus.). 1993. 250.00 (*0-302-00619-2*, Pub. by Zwemmer Bks UK) Sothebys Pubns.

Twentieth-Century Russian Drama: From Gorky to the Present. rev. ed. Harold B. Segel. LC 93-10350. (PAJ Bks.). (Illus.). 544p. (C). 1993. text ed. 65.00 (*0-8018-4690-0*); pap. text ed. 19.95 (*0-8018-4691-9*) Johns Hopkins.

Twentieth-Century Russian Drama: From Gorky to the Present. Harold B. Segel. LC 79-11673. (Illus.). 520p. reprint ed. pap. 148.20 (*0-685-20375-1*, 2029830) Bks Demand.

Twentieth-Century Russian Literary Criticism. Ed. by Victor Erlich. LC 74-29720. 329p. reprint ed. pap. 93.80 (*0-8357-8356-1*, 2033719) Bks Demand.

Twentieth-Century Russian Literature. Harry T. Moore. LC 74-13812. (Crosscurrents-Modern Critiques Ser.). 208p. 1974. 12.95 (*0-8093-0703-0*) S Ill U Pr.

Twentieth-Century Russian Novel: An Introduction. David Gillespie. 224p. 1996. 38.95 (*1-85973-078-7*); pap. 16.95 (*1-85973-083-3*) Berg Pubs.

Twentieth Century Russian Poetry. Yevgeny Yevtushenko. 1168p. 1994. pap. 19.95 (*0-385-05264-2*, Anchor NY) Doubleday.

Twentieth-Century Russian Poetry. 2nd ed. Ed. by John Glad & Daniel Weissbort. LC 92-3786. 422p. 1992. pap. 19.95 (*0-87745-365-9*); text ed. 42.95 (*0-87745-373-X*) U of Iowa Pr.

Twentieth-Century Schwenkfelders: A Narrative History. W. Kyrel Meschter. 1984. pap. 7.50 (*0-935980-03-2*) Schwenkfelder Lib.

***Twentieth Century Science.** Lisa Yount. LC 96-49420. (World History Ser.). (Illus.). (YA). (gr. 4-12). 1997. lib. bdg. 17.96 (*1-56006-304-1*) Lucent Bks.

20th Century Science Fiction Writers 4, Vol. 1. 4th rev. ed. Jay P. Pederson. LC 95-36171. (St. James Guide Ser.). 1175p. 1995. 140.00 (*1-55862-179-2*) Gale.

Twentieth Century Science Fiction Writers. Ed. by Curtis S. Smith. LC 81-8944. (Twentieth Century Writers Ser.). 649p. 1981. 75.00 (*0-312-82420-3*) St Martin.

Twentieth-Century Science-Fiction Writers. 2nd ed. Ed. by Curtis C. Smith. 1986. 95.00 (*0-912289-27-9*) St James Pr.

Twentieth Century Sculptors. Stanley Casson. LC 67-23189. (Essay Index Reprint Ser.). 1977. 15.95 (*0-8369-0283-1*) Ayer.

Twentieth-Century Shapers of American Popular Religion. Ed. by Charles H. Lippy. LC 88-15487. 519p. 1989. text ed. 89.50 (*0-313-25356-0*, LTW/, Greenwood Pr) Greenwood.

Twentieth Century Short Stories Explication: Supplement III to Third Edition. Compiled by Warren S. Walker. LC 80-16175. (Short Story Explication Ser.). 486p. (C). 1987. lib. bdg. 47.50 (*0-208-02122-1*) Shoe String.

Twentieth-Century Short Story Explication: An Index to 1961-1991, 5 suppls. 3rd ed. Ed. by Barbara K. Walker. LC 91-9856. (Short Story Explication Ser.). 280p. (C). 1991. lib. bdg. 47.50 (*0-208-02320-8*) Shoe String.

Twentieth-Century Short Story Explication: Interpretations, 1900-1975, of Short Fiction since 1800. 3rd ed. Compiled by Warren S. Walker. LC 76-30666. (Short Story Explication Ser.). vii, 880p. (C). 1977. lib. bdg. 69.50 (*0-208-01570-1*) Shoe String.

Twentieth-Century Short Story Explication: Supplement Five to the Third Edition, Suppl. V. Compiled by Warren S. Walker. (Short Story Explication Ser.). viii, 401p. (C). 1991. lib. bdg. 49.50 (*0-208-02299-6*) Shoe String.

Twentieth-Century Short Story Explication: Supplement One to Third Edition. Compiled by Warren S. Walker. LC 80-16175. (Short Story Explication Ser.). v, 257p. (C). 1980. lib. bdg. 39.50 (*0-208-01813-1*) Shoe String.

Twentieth Century Short Story Explication: Supplement Two to the Third Edition. Compiled by Warren S. Walker. LC 80-16175. (Short Story Explication Ser.). 348p. (C). 1984. lib. bdg. 45.00 (*0-208-02005-5*) Shoe String.

Twentieth Century Short Story Explication New Series, 1989-1990, Vol. 1. Compiled by Warren S. Walker. LC 92-22790. (Short Story Explication Ser.). vi, 366p. (C). 1993. lib. bdg. 49.50 (*0-208-02340-2*) Shoe String.

Twentieth-Century Short Story Explication, New Series, 1991-1993, Vol. II: 1991-1993. Ed. by Wendell M. Aycock. LC 92-22790. (Short Story Explication Ser.). viii, 295p. (C). 1995. lib. bdg. 49.50 (*0-208-02370-4*) Shoe String.

***Twentieth-Century Short Story Explication, New Series, 1993-1994, Vol. III.** Ed. by Wendell M. Aycock. (Short Story Explication Ser.: Vol. III). viii, 347p. (C). 1997. lib. bdg. 49.50 (*0-208-02419-0*) Shoe String.

Twentieth-Century Short Story Explication, Supplement IV to the Third Edition. Compiled by Warren S. Walker. (Short Story Explication Ser.). viii, 335p. (C). 1989. lib. bdg. 45.00 (*0-208-02188-4*) Shoe String.

Twentieth Century Social Thought. 4th ed. Robert P. Cuzzort & Edith King. 390p. (C). 1989. pap. text ed. 33.25 (*0-03-023763-7*) HB Coll Pubs.

Twentieth-Century Social Thought. 5th ed. R. P. Cuzzort & Edith W. King. (Illus.). 512p. (C). pap. text ed. write for info. (*0-15-501750-0*) HB Coll Pubs.

Twentieth Century Sociology. Ed. by Georgy D. Gurvich & Wilbert E. Moore. LC 78-134090. (Essay Index Reprint Ser.). 1977. 42.95 (*0-8369-2110-0*) Ayer.

Twentieth-Century South Africa. William Beinart. LC 93-50619. 192p. 1994. pap. 15.95 (*0-19-289239-8*) OUP.

***Twentieth Century Southern Literature.** J. A. Bryant, Jr. LC 97-10495. (New Perspectives on the South Ser.). 288p. (C). 1997. 29.95 (*0-8131-2040-3*); pap. 16.95 (*0-8131-0937-X*) U Pr of Ky.

Twentieth-Century Spanish American Fiction. Naomi Lindstrom. LC 93-42557. (Texas Pan American Ser.). 256p. (C). 1994. pap. 15.95 (*0-292-74682-2*); text ed. 37.50 (*0-292-78119-9*) U of Tex Pr.

Twentieth-Century Spanish Poets. Ed. by Jerry P. Winfield. Vol. 134. 1993. write for info. (*0-318-72154-6*) Gale.

Twentieth Century Stage Decoration, 2 vols. in 1. Ed. by Rene Fuerst & Samuel J. Hume. LC 67-28846. (Illus.). 428p. 1972. 46.95 (*0-405-08540-0*, Pub. by Blom Pubns UK) Ayer.

***Twentieth-Century Still-Life Paintings from the Phillips Collection.** Stephen B. Phillips. Ed. by Ellen Hirzy. LC 97-14554. (Illus.). 128p. 1997. pap. 18.95 (*0-943044-22-7*) Phillips Coll.

***Twentieth-Century Stone Age Medicine.** Stan Mahon. LC 96-90311. 70p. (Orig.). 1997. pap. 8.95 (*0-533-11991-X*) Vantage.

Twentieth-Century Surgeon: My Life in the Massachusetts General Hospital. Claude E. Welch. (Illus.). xx, 392p. 1992. 24.95 (*0-88135-181-4*) Watson Pub Intl.

Twentieth-Century Surgeon: My Life in the Massachusetts General Hospital. rev. ed. Claude E. Welch. (Illus.). xviii, 394p. 1993. 24.95 (*0-88135-182-2*) Watson Pub Intl.

Twentieth-Century Suspense: The Thriller Comes of Age. Ed. by Clive Bloom. (Insights Ser.). 300p. 1990. text ed. 39.95 (*0-312-03708-2*) St Martin.

Twentieth Century System of Ladies' Garment Cutting see Edwardian Ladies Tailoring: The Twentieth Century System of Ladies Garment Cutting (1910)

Twentieth Century Table of Houses. A. LeRoi Simmons. 202p. 1972. text ed. 6.00 (*0-9605126-2-4*) Aquarian Bk Pubs.

Twentieth-Century Texas: A High School Texas Studies Curriculum Guide. William C. Hardt et al. 167p. 1990. pap. text ed. 10.00 (*0-87611-092-8*) Tex St Hist Assn.

Twentieth Century Theatre: Observations on the Contemporary English & American Stage. William L. Phelps. LC 67-28764. (Essay Index Reprint Ser.). 1977. 18.95 (*0-8369-0787-6*) Ayer.

20th-Century Theology: God & the World in a Transitional Age. Stanley J. Grenz & Roger E. Olson. LC 92-8184. 424p. (C). 1992. 27.99 (*0-8308-1761-1*, 1761) InterVarsity.

20th-Century Theology: God & the World in a Transitional Age. Stanley J. Grenz & Roger E. Olson. LC 92-8184. 393p. 1997. pap. 19.99 (*0-8308-1525-2*, 1525) InterVarsity.

Twentieth Century Thinkers in Adult Education. Ed. by Peter Jarvis. (International Perspectives on Adult & Continuing Education Ser.). 256p. 1987. 30.00 (*0-7099-1482-2*, Pub. by Croom Helm UK) Routledge Chapman & Hall.

Twentieth Century to Quine & Derrida. 3rd ed. W. T. Jones & Robert J. Fogelin. (History of Western Philosophy Ser.: Vol. 5). 608p. (C). 1997. pap. text ed. write for info. (*0-15-500379-8*) HB Coll Pubs.

Twentieth Century to Wittgenstein & Sartre see History of Western Philosophy

Twentieth-Century Type Designers. rev. ed. Sebastian Carter. (Illus.). 192p. 1995. 35.00 (*0-393-70199-9*) Norton.

Twentieth Century U. S. History. Schaller. (C). Date not set. pap. 34.76 (*0-395-67309-7*) HM.

An Asterisk (*) at the beginning of an entry indicates that the title is appearing in BIP for the first time.

Twentieth Century, Vol. 1: The Progressive Era & the First World War (1900-1918) Visual Education Corporation Staff. 1992. 50.00 (*0-02-897443-3*) Macmillan.

Twentieth Century, Vol. 2: The Roaring Twenties & an Unsettled Peace (1919-1929) Visual Education Corporation Staff. 1992. 50.00 (*0-02-897444-1*) Macmillan.

Twentieth Century, Vol. 3: The Great Depression & World War II (1930-1945) Visual Education Corporation Staff. 1992. 50.00 (*0-02-897446-8*) Macmillan.

Twentieth Century, Vol. 4: Post War Prosperity & the Cold War (1946-1963) Visual Education Corporation Staff. 1992. 50.00 (*0-02-897447-6*) Macmillan.

Twentieth Century, Vol. 5: The Civil Rights Movement & the Vietnam Era (1964-1975) Visual Education Corporation Staff. 1992. 50.00 (*0-02-897448-4*) Macmillan.

Twentieth Century, Vol. 6: Baby Boomers & the New Conservatism (1976-1991) Visual Education Corporation Staff. 1992. 50.00 (*0-02-897449-2*) Macmillan.

Twentieth Century War & Politics: An Annotated Bibliography. Robert Cole. LC 96-27825. (Magill Bibliographies Ser.). 416p. 1996. 48.50 (*0-8108-3196-1*) Scarecrow.

Twentieth Century Warrior: The Life & Service of Major General Edwin D. Patrick. Wilson A. Heefner. LC 95-12915. 216p. (C). 1995. 24.95 (*0-942597-81-8*) White Mane Pub.

Twentieth Century Wars: Their Causes & Their Effects on American Life. Wilbur H. Morrison. LC 93-5305. 436p. 1993. 29.50 (*0-7818-0120-6*) Hippocrene Bks.

Twentieth-Century Watercolors: Master of the Oil Sketch. Christopher Finch. (Illus.). 312p. 1988. 95.00 (*0-89659-811-X*) Abbeville Pr.

Twentieth Century Welsh Poems. Ed. by Gomer Press Staff. 253p. (C). 1982. text ed. 65.00 (*0-85088-406-3*, Pub. by Gomer Pr UK) St Mut.

***Twentieth Century Western Writers.** 1983. 95.00 (*0-8103-0227-6*, 00008305) Gale.

Twentieth-Century Western Writers. 2nd ed. Ed. by Geoff Sadler. 848p. 1991. lib. bdg. 132.00 (*0-912289-98-8*, 200014) St James Pr.

Twentieth Century Women. Arthur Vogelsand. LC 87-19200. (Contemporary Poetry Ser.). 80p. 1988. pap. 14.95 (*0-8203-0996-6*) U of Ga Pr.

Twentieth-Century Women Scientists. Lisa Yount. LC 95-10888. (Global Profiles Ser.). (Illus.). 128p. (YA). (gr. 9 up). 1995. 16.95 (*0-8160-3173-8*) Facts on File.

Twentieth Century Wordsworth. Margaret G. Barnes. 60p. 1996. pap. 12.95 (*1-85756-236-4*, Pub. by Janus Pubng UK) Paul & Co Pubs.

***Twentieth Century World.** Brooman. 1995. pap. text ed. write for info. (*0-582-24975-9*, Pub. by Longman UK) Longman.

Twentieth-Century World. Carter V. Findley et al. LC 87-71109. 526p. (C). 1986. teacher ed. 2.36 (*0-685-18703-9*) HM.

20th Century World, 3 Vols. Carter V. Findley. (C). 1994. teacher ed., pap. 5.96 (*0-395-66864-6*) HM.

20th Century World. Carter V. Findley. (C). 1995. pap. 23.96 (*0-395-72179-2*) HM.

20th Century World, 3 Vols. Carter V. Findley. (C). 1993. 41.56 (*0-395-66863-8*) HM.

Twentieth Century World: An International History. 3rd ed. William R. Keylor. (Illus.). 624p. 1996. 52.00 (*0-19-509769-6*); pap. 24.00 (*0-19-509770-X*) OUP.

***Twentieth Century World: War, Revolution & Technology.** Sean Lang. (Illus.). 112p. (C). 1997. pap. text ed. 9.95 (*0-521-48324-7*) Cambridge U Pr.

Twentieth Century World History: A Select Bibliography. Freda Harcourt & Francis Robinson. LC 79-10154. 154p. 1979. text ed. 42.00 (*0-06-492680-X*, N6506) B&N Imports.

Twentieth-Century World Religious Movements in Neo-Weberian Perspective. Ed. by William H. Swatos, Jr. LC 92-10797. 356p. 1992. lib. bdg. 99.95 (*0-7734-9550-9*) E Mellen.

Twentieth Century Worship Services, Vol. III. Ralph E. Dessem. 1991. pap. 9.25 (*1-55673-402-6*, 9215) CSS OH.

Twentieth-Century Writers: 1900-1950. Tom Verde. (American Profiles Ser.). 144p. (J). (gr. 5-12). 1993. 17.95 (*0-8160-2573-8*) Facts on File.

Twentieth-Century Writers, 1950-1990. (American Profiles Ser.). (Illus.). 144p. (YA). 1995. 17.95 (*0-8160-2967-9*) Facts on File.

Twentieth-Century Young Adult Writers. Ed. by Laura S. Berger. LC 93-42870. (Twentieth-Century Writers Ser.). 800p. 1993. 140.00 (*1-55862-202-0*) St James Pr.

***Twentieth Century's Fox: Darryl F. Zanuck & the Culture of Hollywood.** George F. Custen. (Illus.). 384p. 1997. 27.50 (*0-465-07619-X*) Basic.

20th Division in France & Flanders: A History. Kincaid-Smith & Picton Publishing (Chippenham) Ltd. Staff. (Illus.). 429p. (C). 1990. 75.00 (*0-948251-36-0*, Pub. by Picton UK) St Mut.

Twentieth-Eighth Amendment: The People's Voting Network. John Citizen. 32p. 1992. 5.00 (*1-882350-00-6*) Whte Horse Pub.

***20th Fighter Group.** Ron MacKay. (Illus.). 80p. (Orig.). 1996. pap. 12.95 (*0-89747-368-X*, 6176) Squad Sig Pubns.

Twentieth Maine. John Pullen. 388p. 1980. 24.95 (*0-89029-055-5*); pap. 14.95 (*0-89029-755-X*) Morningside Bkshop.

20th Maine at Fredericksburg & Other Writings by General Ellis Spear. Ellis Spear & Abbott Spear. 130p. 1995. pap. text ed. 11.95 (*0-9642029-3-X*) Union Pubng.

Twentieth March, a Day Like Any Other. K. A. Abbas. 134p. (C). 1978. 11.95 (*0-7069-0610-1*, Pub. by Vikas II) Asia Bk Corp.

***XX Munich 1972 & Innsbruck 1976.** LC 96-48959. (Olympic Century Ser.). (Illus.). 1996. 21.95 (*1-888383-18-6*, Wrld Spt) Wld Sport Resch.

Twentieth Oil Shale Symposium Proceedings. Frwd. by James H. Gary. (Illus.). 238p. 1987. pap. text ed. 25.00 (*0-918062-76-4*) Colo Sch Mines.

***20th Princeton Conference: On Cerebrovascular Disease.** Ed. by James T. Robertson. (American Heart Association Monograph Ser.). 1997. write for info. (*0-87993-674-6*) Futura Pub.

Twentieth Reunion & Other Poems. limited ed. Gladys Merrifield. LC 84-70671. (Living Poets' Library: No. 31). 1984. 5.00 (*0-934218-31-5*) Dragons Teeth.

20th Century American Short Stories: Anthology. 2nd ed. Jean A. McConochie. LC 94-43027. 1995. pap. 26.95 (*0-8384-6146-8*) Heinle & Heinle.

Twenty - Twenty: A Total Guide to Improving Your Vision & Preventing Eye Disease. Mitchell H. Friedlaender & Stef Donev. LC 94-7719. 1994. 3.99 (*0-517-12195-6*) Random Hse Value.

Twenty Active Training Programs. Melvin L. Silberman. LC 91-24858. 428p. 1992. ring bd. 149.00 (*0-88390-301-6*, Pfffr & Co) Jossey-Bass.

Twenty Active Training Programs, Vol. II. Melvin L. Silberman. LC 91-24858. 452p. 1993. ring bd. 149.00 (*0-88390-415-2*, Pfffr & Co) Jossey-Bass.

***20 Active Training Programs, Vol. 3.** Mel Silberman. 1997. 149.00 (*0-7879-0903-3*) Jossey-Bass.

Twenty Activities for Developing Sales Effectiveness. Patrick Forsyth & Marek Gitlin. 300p. 1988. text ed. 169.95 (*0-566-02707-0*, Pub. by Gower UK) Ashgate Pub Co.

***20 Advanced Communication Tips for Couples.** Doyle Barnett. 1997. pap. 8.00 (*0-609-80031-0*) Crown Pub Group.

***Twenty Adventures in the Beyond.** Erich Stirnemann. LC 96-34943. 96p. 1997. 9.95 (*1-880090-39-2*) Galde Pr.

20 All-Time Favorite Piano Solos. 72p. 1986. pap. 8.95 (*0-7935-3166-7*, 00361382) H Leonard.

Twenty & Ten. Claire H. Bishop. (Illus.). (J). (gr. 5-9). 1984. 18.00 (*0-8446-6168-6*) Peter Smith.

Twenty & Ten. Claire H. Bishop. (Illus.). (J). (gr. 3-7). 1978. pap. 3.99 (*0-14-031076-2*, Puffin) Puffin Bks.

Twenty Artists: Yale School of Art, 1950-1970. Irving Sandler. LC 80-54616. (Illus.). 64p. 1981. pap. 8.00 (*0-89467-016-6*) Yale Art Gallery.

Twenty Artists-Los Angeles. Denis Wood. (Illus.). 32p. (Orig.). (C). 1988. pap. 7.50 (*0-317-91388-3*) City Gallery Cntmprry Art.

***20 Best Garden Designs.** Tim Newbury. 1997. pap. text ed. 14.95 (*0-7063-7642-0*, Pub. by Ward Lock UK) Sterling.

Twenty Best Walks in Australia. Tyrone Thomas. (Hill of Content Walking Guides Ser.). (Illus.). 178p. (Orig.). 1994. pap. 15.95 (*0-85572-180-4*, Pub. by Hill Content Pubng AT) Seven Hills Bk.

Twenty Blue Devils. Aaron J. Elkins. 288p. 1997. 22.00 (*0-89296-467-7*) Warner Bks.

***Twenty Blue Devils.** Aaron J. Elkins. 288p. 1997. pap. 5.99 (*0-446-40526-4*, Mysterious Paperbk) Warner Bks.

***Twenty Blue Devils.** large type ed. Aaron J. Elkins. LC 97-6331. (Cloak & Dagger Ser.). 421p. 1997. 24.95 (*0-7862-1091-5*, Thorndike Lrg Prnt) Thorndike Pr.

Twenty Cases Suggestive of Reincarnation. 2nd enl. rev. ed. Ian Stevenson. LC 79-93627. 396p. 1980. pap. 14.95 (*0-8139-0872-8*) U Pr of Va.

Twenty Centuries in Sedlescombe. Beryl Lucey. 523p. 1984. 40.00 (*0-7212-0548-8*, Pub. by Regency Press UK) St Mut.

Twenty Centuries of Catholic Church Music. Erwin E. Nemmers. LC 78-17248. 213p. 1978. reprint ed. text ed. 35.00 (*0-313-20542-6*, NETW, Greenwood Pr) Greenwood.

Twenty Centuries of Education. Edgar W. Knight. LC 83-45904. reprint ed. 47.50 (*0-404-20147-4*) AMS Pr.

Twenty Centuries of Mexican Art: Viento Siglos de Arte Mexicano. New York City Museum of Modern Art Staff. LC 79-169322. (Museum of Modern Art Publications in Reprint). (Illus.). 200p. 1972. reprint ed. 25.95 (*0-405-01580-1*) Ayer.

Twenty-cm Schmidt-Cassegrain Telescope. Peter L. Manly. LC 93-42045. (Illus.). 256p. (C). 1994. text ed. 30.95 (*0-521-43360-6*) Cambridge U Pr.

Twenty Colors. Elizabeth Kirschner. (Poetry Ser.). 88p. (Orig.). 1992. pap. 11.95 (*0-88748-129-9*); lib. bdg. 20.95 (*0-88748-128-0*) Carnegie-Mellon.

20 Communication Tips for Couples: A 30-Minute Guide to a Better Relationship. Doyle Barnett. LC 95-2938. 96p. (Orig.). 1995. pap. 7.95 (*1-880032-68-6*) New Wrld Lib.

Twenty Copy Prepack for PGW Use. 80p. 1988. 3.00 (*0-9620519-1-8*) Iris Bks.

Twenty Count: Secret Mathematical System of the Aztec-Maya. Roger Montgomery. (Illus.). 276p. 1995. pap. 15.00 (*1-879181-26-6*) Bear & Co.

20 Custom Designed Track Plans: Model Railroad Handbook. John Armstrong. Ed. by George Drury. (Illus.). 96p. 1994. per. 15.95 (*0-89024-191-0*, 12133) Kalmbach.

20-Day Rejuvenation Diet Program. Jeffrey S. Bland. 240p. (Orig.). 1996. bds. 24.95 (*0-87983-760-8*) Keats.

Twenty Days. Dorothy M. Kunhardt. 1993. 19.98 (*1-55521-975-6*) Bk Sales Inc.

Twenty Days. Dorothy M. Kunhardt & Philip Kunhardt. 320p. 1985. reprint ed. pap. 19.95 (*0-87877-079-8*) Newcastle Pub.

Twenty Days to Better Spelling. Norman Lewis. (Orig.). 1989. pap. 3.95 (*0-317-02802-2*) NAL-Dutton.

Twenty Decoding Games. Marla Love. (J). (gr. 2-6). 1982. pap. 13.99 (*0-8224-5801-2*) Fearon Teach Aids.

***Twenty Demonstrations Guaranteed to Knock Your Socks Off, Vol. II.** Bob Becker. (Illus.). 104p. (Orig.). 1997. pap. text ed. 14.95 (*1-877991-42-2*) Flinn Scientific.

***Twenty Dollar Christmas. Robie L. Eccleston. (Illus.). 101p. (Orig.). 1996. per. 8.95 (*0-9654908-0-7*) L G L G Pub.**
Emmy Lou lives in the slums of Chicago with her dysfunctional mother Clara. She dreams of having her first Christmas tree, & Clara realizes they must change their environment. They drive to a small town in Missouri & rent a ramshackle cabin in the woods, where Emmy Lou discovers the "Perfect Christmas Tree" growing outside her front door. Surviving on welfare, Emmy Lou supplements their food & decorations by visits to the local dumpsters. Her mother is ill so they exchange roles. In school, the children's cruelty surfaces as they judge her shabby clothing, but her forgiving nature & sunny disposition, reinforced by her chats with "her tree" changes them. She wins $20.00 with her class essay & gives it unselfishly to all around her. She is rewarded by the North Star which sits on top of "her tree" & when her mother dies the day after Christmas, she is removed & placed for adoption. It takes place in six weeks. Twenty years later, Emmy returns as a government social worker & town benefactor. The North Star crowns "her tree" every Christmas Eve, & becomes a legendary Christmas gift to the town. To order contact: LGLG Publishing, P.O. Box 158, Fillmore, CA 93016-0158. 805-524-3232. ***Publisher Provided Annotation.***

Twenty Easy Machine-Made Rugs. Jackie Dodson. LC 90-55323. (Illus.). 176p. 1990. pap. 17.95 (*0-8019-8019-4*) Chilton.

28 Biggest Writing Blunders. William Noble. 120p. 1992. 12.95 (*0-89879-504-4*, Wrtrs Digest Bks) F & W Pubns Inc.

Twenty-Eight - Six. Adrian Wisnicki. Tr. by Adam Lizakowski from POL. (Poetry Group Ser.: Vol. 4). 69p. (Orig.). 1993. pap. 6.95 (*0-9639011-0-9*) Unpaid Rent.

Twenty-Eight Barbary Lane: The Tales of the City Omnibus. Armistead Maupin. 1990. 27.50 (*0-06-016466-2*, HarpT) HarpC.

***28 Bible Learning Activities for Kids.** Carol Greene. 32p. (J). (gr. 5-7). 3.99 (*0-570-04023-X*, 61-1020) Concordia.

Twenty-Eight Black Styles for Student Practice. Kenneth Young. 62p. 1992. pap. 16.95 (*1-56253-042-9*) Milady Pub.

Twenty-Eight Compensation Plans for Executive Search Professionals. James H. Kennedy. 1987. ring bd. 50.00 (*0-916654-51-6*) Kennedy Info.

Twenty-Eight Days. Kathleen Elgin & John F. Osterritter. LC 73-77779. (Illus.). 64p. (J). (gr. 5 up). 1973. pap. 5.95 (*0-679-51382-5*) McKay.

28 Days to a Better Body. Janet Thomson. LC 96-13214. (Illus.). 192p. (Orig.). 1996. pap. 12.95 (*1-882606-64-7*) Peoples Med Soc.

28 Days to Better Business Writing. Heidi Thorne. 110p. (Orig.). (C). 1994. 18.95 (*0-9642664-1-5*) Tech Seminars.

28 Hyde Park Gate: Churchill's London Home. Frank Knight & Rutley Estate Agents Ltd. Staff. (Educational Ser.: No. 5). (Illus.). 20p. 1992. pap. 10.00 (*0-614-04947-4*) Intl Churchill Soc.

28 Melodious Pieces Opus 149: Piano 4 Hands: Centennial Edition. 14.95 (*0-7935-4514-5*, 50482388) H Leonard.

Twenty-Eight Piano Pieces. D. Kabalevsky. 112p. 1993. otabind 12.95 (*0-7935-1779-6*, 00290391) H Leonard.

Twenty-Eight Questions: Anton Christian Paintings for Erich Fried. Peter Frank & Krista Hauser. (Illus.). 98p. (Orig.). (ENG & GER.). (C). 1991. pap. 29.00 (*0-685-59683-4*) SDSU Univ Art.

Twenty-Eight Songs. Mary C. Moore. (Women Composers Ser.). 1988. 27.50 (*0-306-79716-X*) Da Capo.

Twenty Eight Styles for Student Practice. Salvatore J. Manfredonia. (SPA.). 1984. 10.95 (*0-87350-149-7*) Milady Pub.

Twenty-Eight Styles for Student Practice. Salvatore J. Manfredonia. Ed. by Mary Healy. (Illus.). 62p. 1984. pap. 15.95 (*0-87350-400-3*) Milady Pub.

Twenty-Eight Styles for Student Practice. 2nd ed. Kenneth Young. LC 90-24207. (Illus.). 64p. (C). 1991. pap. 16.95 (*1-56253-070-4*) Milady Pub.

28 Top Hits: Alto Sax. 32p. 1991. pap. 4.95 (*0-7935-1234-4*, 00843799) H Leonard.

28 Top Hits: Flute. 32p. 1991. pap. 4.95 (*0-7935-1232-8*, 00843797) H Leonard.

28 Top Hits: Trombone. 1991. pap. 4.95 (*0-7935-1236-0*, 00843801) H Leonard.

28 Top Hits: Trumpet. 32p. 1991. pap. 4.95 (*0-7935-1235-2*, 00843800) H Leonard.

28th Annual Immigration & Naturalization Institute. (Litigation & Administrative Practice Course Handbook, 1983-84 Ser.). Date not set. pap. 99.00 (*0-614-17264-0*, H4-5217) PLI.

Twenty-Eighth Ceramic National: Clay, Color, Content. Barbara Perry et al. Ed. by Thomas E. Piche. LC 90-81161. (Illus.). 88p. (Orig.). 1990. pap. text ed. write for info. (*0-914407-13-9*) Everson Mus.

28th Light Cavalry in Persia, & Russian Turkestan 1915-1920. Picton Publishing (Chippenham) Ltd. Staff. Ed. by G. Vloth & R. A. Kreger. 203p. (C). 1990. 105.00 (*0-948251-35-2*, Pub. by Picton UK) St Mut.

Twenty-Eighth Star: Texas During the Period of Early Statehood, 1846-1861. Frank H. Smyrl. (Texas History Ser.). (Illus.). 51p. (Orig.). (C). 1983. pap. text ed. 8.95 (*0-89641-132-X*) American Pr.

Twenty-Eighth Virginia Infantry. Frank E. Fields. (Virginia Regimental Histories Ser.). (Illus.). 89p. 1985. 19.95 (*0-930919-15-7*) H E Howard.

Twenty-Fifth Amendment: Its Complete History & Earliest Applications. rev. ed. John D. Feerick. LC 92-26911. xxxvi, 275p. 1992. pap. 19.95 (*0-8232-1373-0*) Fordham.

Twenty-Fifth Amendment: Its Complete History & Earliest Applications. 2nd rev. ed. John D. Feerick. LC 92-26911. xxxvi, 275p. 1992. 30.00 (*0-8232-1372-2*) Fordham.

Twenty-Fifth Anniversary of Vatican II, a Look Back & a Look Ahead: Human Person & Exceptionless Moral Norms. Ed. by Russell E. Smith. LC 90-20863. (Proceedings of the Ninth Bishop's Workshop Ser.). 315p. 1990. pap. text ed. 17.95 (*0-935372-29-6*) Pope John Ctr.

Twenty-Fifth Anniversary Symposium-Polymer Institute. Ed. by Kurt C. Frisch. LC 94-61173. 131p. 1994. text ed. 49.95 (*1-56676-251-0*) Technomic.

25th Annual Advanced Antitrust Workshop. (Corporate Law & Practice Course Handbook, 1985-86 Ser.). 384p. 1994. pap. 99.00 (*0-614-17181-4*, B4-7091) PLI.

25th Annual Estate Planning Institute. (Tax Law & Estate Planning Course Handbook Ser.). 1008p. 1994. pap. 99.00 (*0-614-17276-4*, D4-5253) PLI.

Twenty-Fifth Annual Immigration & Naturalization Institute. (Litigation & Administrative Practice Course Handbook, 1983-84 Ser.: Vol. 452). 420p. 1992. 70.00 (*0-685-65528-8*, H4-5140) PLI.

25th Division & World War II. Ed. by Robert F. Karolevitz. (Divisional Ser.: No. 45). (Illus.). 202p. 1995. reprint ed. 49.95 (*0-89839-213-6*) Battery Pr.

Twenty-Fifth Hour. Lawrence Russell. (Illus.). 48p. (Orig.). 1981. pap. 2.95 (*0-914580-11-6*) Angst World.

Twenty-Fifth Infantry Division History. Twenty-Fifth Infantry Division Association. LC 87-71199. 144p. 1987. 48.00 (*0-938021-19-2*) Turner Pub KY.

Twenty-Fifth Infantry Division 50th Anniversary Tropic Lightning. Turner Publishing Company Staff. LC 91-67159. 204p. 1992. 45.00 (*1-56311-043-1*) Turner Pub KY.

***XXV Olympiad, Barcelona 1992 & Lillihammer 1994.** (Olympic Century Ser.). (Illus.). 1996. 21.95 (*1-888383-23-2*, Wrld Spt) Wld Sport Resch.

Twenty-Fifth Virginia Infantry & Ninth Battalion Virginia Infantry. Richard L. Armstrong. (Virginia Regimental Histories Ser.). (Illus.). 263p. 1990. 19.95 (*1-56190-007-9*) H E Howard.

Twenty-Fifth Zakopane School on Physics: Proceedings, 2 vols., 1. A. T. Pedziwiatv. Ed. by J. Stanek. 852p. (C). 1990. text ed. write for info. (*981-02-0340-3*) World Scientific Pub.

Twenty-Fifth Zakopane School on Physics: Proceedings, 2 vols., Set. A. T. Pedziwiatv. Ed. by J. Stanek. 852p. (C). 1990. text ed. 189.00 (*981-02-0339-X*) World Scientific Pub.

Twenty-First Annual Institute on Employment Law, 2 vols. (Litigation & Administrative Practice Course Handbook, 1983-84 Ser.: Vols. 441-442). 1215p. 1992. Set. 80.00 (*0-685-65521-0*, H4-5137) PLI.

Twenty-First Application of Computers & Operations Research in the Mineral Industry. International Symposium on the Application of Computers & Operations Research in the Mineral Industry, Twenty-First, Las Vegas, NV Staff. Ed. by Alfred Weiss. LC 89-207403. (Illus.). 1139p. reprint ed. pap. 180.00 (*0-7837-1805-5*, 2042005) Bks Demand.

21st Century: A Philosophical View on the Millennium. Jack Dawsey. Orig. Title: Israel: The 21st Century. 328p. (Orig.). (C). 1995. pap. 13.95 (*0-9640579-0-5*) J H Dawsey.

Twenty-First Century: Technology's Impact on Academic Research & Law Libraries (HC) Betty Taylor et al. (Professional Librarian Ser.). 248p. (C). 1988. 40.00 (*0-8161-1882-5*, Hall Reference) Macmillan.

Twenty-First Century Africa: Towards a New Vision of Self-Sustainable Development. Ed. by Ann Seidman & Frederick Anang. LC 91-76982. 342p. 1992. 49.95 (*0-86543-329-1*); pap. 16.95 (*0-86543-330-5*) Africa World.

Twenty-First-Century Africa: Towards a New Vision of Self-Sustainable Development. Ed. by Ann Seidman & Frederick Anang. 1992. pap. 16.95 (*0-918456-67-3*) African Studies Assn.

Twenty-First Century African-American Legacies: A Bibliography of Biographies for Children about Notable African-Americans. Jeanette Lambert. 25p. (Orig.). (J). (gr. k-8). 1994. pap. 5.95 (*0-9632736-1-2*) Edit Cetera.

Twenty-First Century American. Theodore W. Keller. 124p. (C). 1991. pap. 10.95 (*0-9614150-1-0*) Prismatique.

***21st Century American English Compendium: A Guidebook for Translators, Interpreters, Writers, Editors & Students.** Marv Rubinstein. 350p. (Orig.). 1997. pap. 29.95 (*1-887563-38-5*) Schreiber Pub.

***Twenty-First Century Anarchism: Unorthodox Ideas for the New Millennium.** Jon Purkis & James Bowen. LC 96-43321. (Global Issues Ser.). (Illus.). 224p. 1997. 75.00 (*0-304-33742-0*); pap. 21.95 (*0-304-33743-9*) Cassell.

Twenty-First Century Art: Rene Robles Assertionism. Palmer Poroner. (Illus.). 204p. 1994. 75.00 (*0-9638583-0-0*) P J Sweeney.

An Asterisk (*) at the beginning of an entry indicates that the title is appearing in BIP for the first time.

Twenty First Century Blueprint. Thomas B. Albright. LC 93-85850. 254p. 1994. pap. 12.95 (0-933451-21-0) Twty-Frst Ctry.

Twenty-First Century Board of Education: Planning, Leading, Transforming. Robert Flinchbaugh. LC 92-64421. 515p. 1992. text ed. 49.95 (0-87762-952-8) Technomic.

Twenty First Century Capitalism. Robert Heilbroner. 176p. 1994. pap. 11.00 (0-393-31228-3) Norton.

***21st Century Careers: 101 Hot New Jobs & How to Prepare for Them.** James V. Smith. 1997. pap. text ed. 12.95 (0-8065-1936-3, Citadel Pr) Carol Pub Group.

21st Century Ceramics. Ed. by D. P. Thompson & H. Mandal. 331p. 1996. text ed. 150.00 (0-901716-85-5, Pub. by Inst Materials UK) Ashgate Pub Co.

Twenty-First Century Challenge: Lesbians & Gays in Education: Bridging the Gap. Ed. by Sue McConnell-Celi. LC 93-78393. (Illus.). 200p. (Orig.). 1993. pap. text ed. 17.95 (0-9636909-0-6) Lavender Crystal.

***Twenty-First Century City.** Stephen Goldsmith. 250p. 1997. 24.95 (0-89526-435-8) Regnery Pub.

21st Century Corporate Board. Ralph D. Ward. LC 96-21408. 1996. text ed. 39.95 (0-471-15679-5) Wiley.

Twenty-First Century Dictionary of Computer Terms. Princeton Language Institute Staff. 416p. 1994. mass mkt. 6.99 (0-440-21557-9) Dell.

Twenty-First Century Dictionary of Quotations. Princeton Language Institute Staff. 624p. 1993. mass mkt. 5.99 (0-440-21447-5) Dell.

Twenty-First Century Dictionary of Slang. Princeton Language Institute Staff. 352p. 1994. mass mkt. 5.99 (0-440-21551-X) Dell.

21st Century Disciples with a 1st Century Faith. Waldo Werning. 1995. pap. 12.95 (0-7880-0605-3, 6053); wbk. ed., pap. 6.95 (0-7880-0607-X, 607X); student ed., pap. 4.95 (0-7880-0608-8, 6088) CSS OH.

21st Century Earth: Opposing Viewpoints. Ed. by Oliver W. Markley & Walter R. McCuan. (Opposing Viewpoints Ser.). (Illus.). 312p. (J). (gr. 5-12). 1996. pap. 12.95 (1-56510-414-5); lib. bdg. 20.96 (1-56510-415-3) Greenhaven.

Twenty-First Century Electronic Projects for a New Age. Delton T. Horn. 1992. text ed. 27.95 (0-07-030388-6); pap. text ed. 16.95 (0-07-030389-4) McGraw.

Twenty-First Century Electronic Projects for a New Age. Delton T. Horn. 200p. 1992. 27.95 (0-8306-3806-7, 4111); pap. 16.95 (0-8306-3805-9, 4111) McGraw-Hill Prof.

Twenty-First Century Family Legal Guide. Joseph W. Mierzwa. 448p. 1994. pap. 19.95 (0-9637285-0-4) Prose Assocs.

Twenty-First Century Fox. Scott Eller. (Illus.). (YA). (gr. 12 up). 1989. pap. 12.95 (0-590-41939-0) Scholastic Inc.

Twenty First Century German-English English-German Dictionary. Philip Lief. 320p. (ENG & GER.). 1996. mass mkt. 5.99 (0-440-22089-0) Dell.

Twenty-First Century Grammar Handbook. Barbara A. Kipfer. Ed. by Princeton Language Institute Staff. 336p. 1993. mass mkt. 5.99 (0-440-21508-0) Dell.

Twenty-First Century Guide to Building Your Vocabulary. Elizabeth Read. Ed. by Princeton Language Institute Staff. 224p. 1995. mass mkt. 5.99 (0-440-21721-0) Dell.

Twenty-First Century Guide to Improving Your Writing. Princeton Language Institute Staff. 272p. 1995. mass mkt. 5.99 (0-440-21727-X) Dell.

Twenty-First Century Guide to Increasing Your Reading Speed. Princeton Language Institute Staff. 240p. 1995. mass mkt. 5.99 (0-440-21724-5) Dell.

Twenty-First Century in Space. Ed. by George V. Butler. LC 57-43769. (Advances in the Astronautical Sciences Ser.: Vol. 70). (Illus.). 446p. 1990. pap. text ed. 75.00 (0-87703-315-3); lib. bdg. 90.00 (0-87703-314-5) Univelt Inc.

21st Century in Space. rev. ed. Isaac Asimov et al. (Asimov's New Library of the Universe). 32p. (J). (gr. 3 up). lib. bdg. 18.60 (0-8368-1294-8) Gareth Stevens Inc.

Twenty-First Century in Space, Vol. 58: AAS. Ed. by George V. Butler. LC 57-43769. (Advances in the Astronautical Sciences Ser.: Vol. 70). (Illus.). 446p. 1990. Vol. 58 AAS. fiche 10.00 (0-87703-316-1) Univelt Inc.

21st Century Jet: Making & Marketing the Boeing 777. Karl Sabbagh. (Illus.). 416p. 1996. 25.00 (0-684-80721-1) S&S Trade.

21st Century Leadership: Dialogues with One-Hundred Top Leaders. Lynne J. McFarland et al. 336p. 1993. 21.95 (0-9636018-0-6); pap. 15.95 (0-9636018-1-4) Ldrship Pr.

Twenty-First Century Management: Keeping Ahead of the Japanese. Dan Waters. 127p. 1992. boxed 17.95 (0-13-932344-9, Busn) P-H.

Twenty-First-Century Management: The Revolutionary Strategies That Have Made Computer Associates a Multibillion-Dollar Software Giant. Hesh Kestin. LC 92-4089. (Illus.). 224p. 1992. pap. 10.00 (0-87113-539-6, Atlntc Mnthly) Grove-Atltic.

21st Century Manager: Meeting the Challenge & Opportunities of the New Corporate Age. Gareth S. Gardiner. LC 95-18934. 216p. 1995. 22.95 (1-56079-455-0, Petersons Pacesetter) Petersons.

Twenty-First Century Manual of Style. Princeton Language Institute Staff. 368p. 1995. mass mkt. 5.99 (0-440-22074-2) Dell.

21st Century Manufacturing: Creating Winning Business Performance. Thomas G. Gunn. 300p. 1995. pap. text ed. 19.95 (0-471-13214-4) Wiley.

Twenty-First Century Manufacturing: The National Initiative for Product Data Exchange: Product Data Exchange Baseline Activities, Vol. 1. (Illus.). 430p. (Orig.). (C). 1994. pap. text ed. 95.00 (0-7881-0201-X) DIANE Pub.

Twenty-First Century Manufacturing: The National Initiative for Product Data Exchange: Product Data Exchange Baseline Activities, Vol. 2. (Illus.). 225p. (Orig.). (C). 1994. pap. text ed. 80.00 (0-7881-0202-8) DIANE Pub.

Twenty-First Century Manufacturing Enterprise Strategy, 2 vols., Vol. 1: An Industry-Led View. Twenty-First Century Manufacturing Enterprise Strategy Staff. Ed. by Steve Goldman & Kenneth Preiss. (Illus.). 58p. (C). 1991. reprint ed. Vol. 1, An Industry-Led View, 58p. 25.00 (0-9624866-3-9) Lehigh U PA.

Twenty-First Century Manufacturing Enterprise Strategy, 2 vols., Vol. 2: Infrastructure. Twenty-First Century Manufacturing Enterprise Strategy Staff. Ed. by Steve Goldman & Kenneth Preiss. (Illus.). 126p. (C). 1991. reprint ed. Vol. 2, Infrastructure, 126p. 25.00 (0-9624866-4-7) Lehigh U PA.

***21st-Century Miracle Medicine: Robosurgery, Wonder Cures, & the Quest for Immortality.** Alexandra Wyke. (Illus.). 342p. (C). 26.95 (0-306-45565-X, Plenum Pr) Plenum.

Twenty-First Century Musical Instruments: Hardware & Software. Jon Appleton. LC 89-82244. (I.S.A.M. Monographs: No. 29). (Illus.). 44p. (Orig.). 1990. pap. 12.00 (0-914678-32-9) Inst Am Music.

***21st Century New Public Series.** Alan C. Walter. Ed. by Beverly Miles. 110p. 1996. pap. text ed. 29.97 (1-57569-028-4) Wisdom Pubng.

Twenty-First Century Nonprofit: Remaking the Organization for a New Era. Paul B. Firstenberg. LC 96-3764. 320p. 1996. pap. 34.95 (0-87954-672-7) Foundation Ctr.

Twenty-First Century Not-For-Profit: Remaking the Organization for a New Era. Paul B. Firstenberg. LC 96-3764. 1996. 39.95 (0-87954-652-2) Foundation Ctr.

Twenty-First Century Obstetrics Now!, 2 vols. 2nd ed. David Stewart & Lee Stewart. LC 77-72854. (Illus.). 1978. pap. 12.25 (0-917314-09-3) NAPSAC.

Twenty-First Century Obstetrics Now!, 2 vols., 1. 2nd ed. David Stewart & Lee Stewart. LC 77-72854. (Illus.). 1978. pap. 7.50 (0-917314-07-7) NAPSAC.

Twenty-First Century Obstetrics Now!, 2 vols., 2. 2nd ed. David Stewart & Lee Stewart. LC 77-72854. (Illus.). 1978. pap. 7.50 (0-917314-08-5) NAPSAC.

21st Century Office Assistant's Manual. Philip L. Group. 320p. 1996. mass mkt. 5.99 (0-440-21725-3) Dell.

***21st Century Organization.** Bennis & Mische. 1997. pap. 15.00 (0-7879-0939-4) Jossey-Bass.

Twenty-First Century Organization: Analyzing Current Trends, Imagining the Future. Guy Benveniste. LC 93-35549. (Public Administration Series, Nonprofit Sector Series, & Management Ser.). 336p. 29.95 (1-55542-626-3) Jossey-Bass.

21st Century Organization: Reinventing Through Reengineering. Warren Bennis & Michael Mische. LC 95-16196. (Warren Bennis Executive Briefing Ser.). (Illus.). 128p. 1995. 19.95 (0-89384-273-7, Pfffr & Co) Jossey-Bass.

21st Century Pastor: A Vision Based on the Ministry of Paul. David Fisher. 192p. 1996. pap. 12.99 (0-310-20154-3) Zondervan.

Twenty-First Century Physics. Jacob Gorbulsky. Ed. by Maria Teleshova. (Illus.). 96p. 1990. 19.95 (0-685-48968-X); lib. bdg. 24.95 (0-685-48969-8) ATS NY.

Twenty-First Century Physics. Jacob Gorbulsky. Ed. by Maria Teleshova. (Illus.). 96p. (C). 1990. 19.95 (1-878361-00-7); lib. bdg. 24.95 (1-878361-01-5) ATS NY.

Twenty-First Century Pioneering: A Scrapbook of the Future. David P. Young. (Illus.). (Orig.). 1986. pap. 5.95 (0-377-00160-0) Friendship Pr.

21st Century Principal. Ed. by Jeffrey S. Kaiser. (Illus.). 421p. (C). 1995. text ed. 58.95 incl. disk (1-878016-10-5) Stylex Pub.

Twenty-First Century Roberts Rules of Order. Princeton Institute Staff. 272p. 1995. mass mkt. 5.99 (0-440-21722-9) Dell.

Twenty-First Century Synonym & Antonym Finder. Barbara A. Kipfer. Ed. by Princeton Language Institute Staff. 528p. 1993. mass mkt. 5.99 (0-440-21323-1) Dell.

Twenty-First Century Timber Engineering: Proceedings of the ASCE Convention in Dallas, Texas, October 24-28, 1993. Ed. by Kevin C. Cheung. LC 93-35386. 1993. 14.00 (0-87262-985-6) Am Soc Civil Eng.

***21st Century Trucking, Vol. II.** Date not set. pap. text ed. 195.00 (0-88711-357-5) Am Trucking Assns.

21st Century Turfs, Powers, Solutions. unabridged ed. Thomas B. Albright. LC 96-90450. 265p. (Orig.). 1996. 21.95 (1-888264-00-4); pap. 12.95 (1-888264-04-7) Twty-Frst Ctry.

Twenty-First Century Watchmaking Vol. 2: The Joy of Making Parts with Ease. William O. Smith, Jr. (Illus.). 211p. 1996. write for info. (0-918845-18-1) Am Watchmakers.

***21st Century Wicca: A Young Witch's Guide to Living the Magical Life.** Jennifer Hunter. LC 97-8640. (Illus.). 256p. 1997. pap. 14.95 (0-8065-1887-1, Citadel Pr) Carol Pub Group.

Twenty-First Century Will Be American. Alfredo Valladao. Tr. by John Howe. 224p. 1996. 25.00 (1-85984-939-3, Pub. by Vrso UK) Norton.

***Twenty-First Century Will Be American.** Alfredo Valladao. 1997. pap. text ed. 17.00 (1-85984-074-4, Pub. by Verso UK) Routledge Chapman & Hall.

Twenty-First Journees Nationales de Neonatologie, 1991. Ed. by J. P. Relier. (Progres en Neonatologie Ser.: Vol. 11). (Illus.). vi, 370p. 1991. pap. 161.00 (3-8055-5446-X) S Karger.

Twenty-First Missouri: From Home Guard to Union Regiment. Leslie Anders. LC 75-64. (Contributions in Military History Ser.: No. 11). (Illus.). 298p. 1975. text ed. 55.00 (0-8371-7962-9, AVI/, Greenwood Pr) Greenwood.

21st National Passive Solar Conference Proceedings. Ed. by Rebecca Campbell-Howe. (Illus.). 400p. (Orig.). 1996. pap. 100.00 (0-614-11336-9) Am Solar Energy.

***XXI Olympiad, Montreal 1976 & Lake Placid 1980.** (Olympic Century Ser.). (Illus.). 1996. 21.95 (1-888383-19-4, Wrld Spt) Wld Sport Resch.

Twenty-First Virginia Cavalry. John E. Olson. (Virginia Regimental Histories Ser.). (Illus.). 91p. 1989. 19.95 (0-930919-81-5) H E Howard.

Twenty-First Virginia Infantry. Susan A. Riggs. (Virginia Regimental Histories Ser.). (Illus.). 105p. 1991. 19.95 (1-56190-013-3) H E Howard.

25 Giao Phan Vietnam: 20 Nam Qua, 5 Vols., Vol. 1. Tran Phuc Long. LC 95-68005. (Illus.). 400p. (Orig.). (VIE.). 1995. pap. 39.99 (1-887163-00-X) St John the Bap Chur.

***25 Activities Connecting Writing & Math.** Scholastic Inc. Staff. 1997. pap. text ed. 9.95 (0-590-25109-0) Scholastic Inc.

Twenty-Five Activities for Teams. Intro. by Fran Rees. LC 92-85291. 108p. (Orig.). 1993. pap. text ed. 34.95 (0-88390-362-8, Pfffr & Co) Jossey-Bass.

Twenty-Five American Folksongs: High. pap. 12.95 (0-7935-4640-0, 00740025) H Leonard.

Twenty-Five American Folksongs: Low. pap. 12.95 (0-7935-4641-9, 00740026) H Leonard.

25 & Under. Alice George. 176p. 1996. pap. 25.00 (0-393-31576-2) Norton.

***25 & Under: Fiction.** Ed. by Susan Ketchin & Neil Giordano. LC 96-45017. 240p. 1997. 25.00 (0-393-04120-4); pap. 12.00 (0-393-31610-6) Norton.

Twenty-Five Artists. Hans Namuth. Ed. by Arlene Bujese. 108p. 1982. text ed. 75.00 (0-313-27081-3, U7081, Greenwood Pr) Greenwood.

Twenty-Five Best Proposals by Management Consulting Firms. Ed. by James H. Kennedy. ring bd. 119.00 (0-916654-32-X) Kennedy Info.

Twenty-Five Best Tax-Saving Ideas of the '90s. Irving L. Blackman. (Special Report Ser.). 1992. pap. 21.00 (0-916181-30-8) Blackman Kallick Bartelstein.

Twenty-Five Bible Studies: Including Two Contents, Two Realities. Francis A. Schaeffer. LC 95-49080. 144p. 1996. pap. 8.99 (0-89107-893-2) Crossway Bks.

25 Bicycle Tours in & Around Washington, D. C. From the Capitol Steps to Country Roads. Anne H. Oman. LC 90-26986. (Bicycle Tours Ser.). 144p. 1991. pap. 12.00 (0-88150-190-5, Backcountry) Countryman.

25 Bicycle Tours in Eastern Pennsylvania: Day Trips & Overnights from Philadelphia to the Highlands. 2nd ed. Dale Adams & Dale Speicher. LC 94-23347. (Bicycle Tours Ser.). (Illus.). 168p. pap. 12.00 (0-88150-317-7, Backcountry) Countryman.

25 Bicycle Tours in Maine: Coastal & Inland Rides from Kittery to Caribou. 2nd ed. Howard Stone. LC 89-78407. (Bicycle Tours Ser.). (Illus.). 176p. pap. 12.00 (0-88150-170-0, Backcountry) Countryman.

25 Bicycle Tours in Maryland: From The Allegheny Mountains to the Atlantic Ocean. Anne H. Oman. LC 93-45462. (Bicycle Tours Ser.). (Illus.). 200p. (Orig.). 1994. pap. 12.00 (0-88150-287-1, Backcountry) Countryman.

25 Bicycle Tours in New Jersey: Over 900 Miles of Scenic Pleasures & Historic Treasures. Joel L. Zatz. LC 87-34922. (Bicycle Tours Ser.). (Illus.). 176p. (Orig.). 1988. pap. 12.00 (0-942440-42-0, Backcountry) Countryman.

25 Bicycle Tours in Ohio's Western Reserve: Historic Northeast Ohio from the Lake Erie Islands to the Pennsylvania Border. Sally Walters. (Bicycle Tours Ser.). (Illus.). 240p. 1991. pap. 12.00 (0-88150-166-2, Backcountry) Countryman.

25 Bicycle Tours in the Adirondacks: Road Adventures in the East's Largest Wilderness. Bill McKibben et al. (Bicycle Tours Ser.). (Illus.). 192p. (Orig.). 1995. pap. 13.00 (0-88150-318-5, Backcountry) Countryman.

25 Bicycle Tours in the Hudson Valley: Scenic Rides from Saratoga to Northern Westchester County. 2nd ed. Howard Stone. LC 89-31143. (Bicycle Tours Ser.). (Illus.). 208p. (Orig.). 1996. pap. 15.00 (0-88150-366-5, Backcountry) Countryman.

25 Bicycle Tours in the Texas Hill Country & West Texas: Adventure Rides for Road & Mountain Bikes. Norman D. Ford. (Bicycle Tours Ser.). (Illus.). 256p. (Orig.). 1995. pap. 14.00 (0-88150-324-X, Backcountry) Countryman.

25 Bicycle Tours in Vermont. 3rd ed. John Freidin. (Bicycle Tours Ser.). (Illus.). 224p. 1996. pap. 15.00 (0-88150-330-4, Backcountry) Countryman.

25 Bicycle Tours on Cape Cod & the Islands. Kevin Jeffrey et al. (Bicycle Tours Ser.). (Illus.). 208p. (Orig.). 1996. pap. 15.00 (0-88150-343-6, Backcountry) Countryman.

25 Bicycle Tours on Delmarva: Cycling the Chesapeake Bay County. 2nd ed. John R. Wennersten. (Bicycle Tour Ser.). (Illus.). 204p. 1995. pap. 14.00 (0-88150-338-X, Backcountry) Countryman.

25 Bilingual Mini-Books. Helen H. Moore. (ENG & SPA.). (J). 1994. pap. text ed. 9.95 (0-590-49802-9) Scholastic Inc.

Twenty-Five Black African Filmmakers: A Critical Study, with Fimography & Bio-Bibliography. Francoise Pfaff. LC 87-15024. 352p. 1988. text ed. 52.95 (0-313-24695-5, PBA/, Greenwood Pr) Greenwood.

Twenty-Five Centuries of Technological Change: An Historical Survey, Vol. 35. Hugo Sonnenschein & Joel Mokyr. (Fundamentals of Pure & Applied Economics Ser.: 35). 148, viiip. 1990. pap. text ed. 56.00 (3-7186-4936-5) Gordon & Breach.

Twenty-Five Christmas Favorites: With Notes & Tablature. 64p. 1991. pap. 8.95 (0-7935-0964-5, 00702075) H Leonard.

***25 Common Sales Objections & How to Overcome Them.** Bob Taylor. 1991. pap. text ed. 6.95 (0-85013-192-8) Dartnell Corp.

25 Days of Christmas. Rebecca H. Bauer. (Illus.). 144p. 1994. 17.99 (1-56476-417-6, 6-3417, Victor Bks) Chariot Victor.

***$25 & Under: A Guide to the Best Inexpensive Restaurants in New York.** Eric Asimov. 1997. pap. 10.95 (0-06-273402-4, Harper Ref) HarpC.

25 Dollars & under, 1997: A Guide to the Best Inexpensive Restaurants in New York. Eric Asimov. 256p. 1996. pap. text ed. 10.95 (0-06-273401-6) HarpC.

25 Dore Romantic Engravings: 11x15 Detachable Parchment Prints, Suitable for Framing Ser. Gustave Dore. (Illus.). 52p. 1996. per. 19.95 (1-888957-01-8) MCE Publ Co.

Twenty-Five Easy & Progressive Studies for Piano, Op. 100. F. Burgmueller. Ed. by Carl Hoffman. (Carl Fischer Music Library: No. 324). 1909. pap. 5.25 (0-8258-0107-9, L324) Fischer Inc NY.

Twenty-Five Easy & Progressive Studies for the Piano Opus 100 Complete. F. Burgmuller. 36p. 1986. pap. 4.95 (0-7935-2556-X) H Leonard.

Twenty-Five Engineers & Inventors. Charles Susskind. (Illus.). 1977. 7.50 (0-911302-29-8) San Francisco Pr.

***Twenty-Five Essays, Vol. 1.** Skom. Date not set. pap. text ed. write for info. (0-312-02785-0) St Martin.

Twenty-Five Etudes for Bass Viol with Optional Second Bass Viol. Carol Herman. (Educational Ser.: No. 4). 55p. 1995. pap. text ed. 19.00 (1-56571-107-6) PRB Prods.

Twenty-Five Favourite Classics Everybody Loves to Hear. Selected by Kenneth Baker. (Illus.). 160p. 1975. pap. 14.95 (0-8256-2688-9, AM21569) Music Sales.

Twenty-Five Favourite Classics Everybody Loves to Hear, Vol. 2. Selected by Kenneth Baker. (Illus.). 160p. 1975. pap. 14.95 (0-8256-2689-7, AM21577) Music Sales.

Twenty Five First Grade Piano Pieces. A. Diller. 24p. 1986. pap. 7.95 (0-7935-5175-7, 50327710) H Leonard.

***Twenty-Five Gold-Tooled Bookbindings: An International Tribute to Bernard C. Middleton's "Recollections"** (Illus.). 76p. 1997. pap. 45.00 (1-884718-35-3) Oak Knoll.

***Twenty-Five Gold-Tooled Bookbindings: An International Tribute to Bernard C. Middleton's "Recollections"** (Illus.). 76p. 1997. 95.00 (1-884718-36-1) Oak Knoll.

Twenty-Five Good Reasons Why Men Should Marry: With a Marriage Manual for Husbands on How to Treat a Wife. Ira Lunan-Ferguson. LC 76-2990. 1976. 9.95 (0-685-03132-2) Lunan-Ferguson.

25 Guided Prayer Services for Middle Graders. Pat E. Dexter. LC 95-62342. 88p. (Orig.). (J). 1996. teacher ed., pap. 12.95 (0-89622-688-3) Twenty-Third.

25 Gunfighter Patterns for Carvers: With Step-by-Step Carving Instructions. Al Streetman. LC 95-10801. (Woodcarvers Bks.). (Illus.). 64p. (Orig.). 1995. pap. 12.95 (0-88740-783-8) Schiffer.

25 Hikes along the Pacific Crest Trail. Don Skillman & Lolly Skillman. (Illus.). 320p. 1994. pap. 17.95 (0-8117-3093-X) Stackpole.

Twenty-Five Human Rights Documents. rev. ed. Intro. by J. Paul Martin. 228p. 1994. pap. 10.00 (1-881482-01-4) Columbia Ctr Stu Human Rts.

Twenty-Five Hundred Dollars a Year: From Scarcity to Abundance. Mordecai Ezekiel. LC 72-2369. (FDR & the Era of the New Deal Ser.). 348p. 1973. reprint ed. lib. bdg. 39.50 (0-306-70468-4) Da Capo.

Twenty-Five Hundred Historical Woodwind Instruments: An Inventory of the Major Collections. Phillip T. Young. LC 81-17724. (Illus.). 1982. lib. bdg. 78.00 (0-918728-17-7) Pendragon NY.

Twenty-Five Hundred Jokes to Start 'em Laughing. Robert Orben. 1987. 10.00 (0-87980-387-8) Wilshire.

Twenty-Five Impressionist Masterpieces. Frank Getlein. 1995. pap. 14.95 (0-8109-2607-5) Abrams.

25 Interventions for Improving Team Performance. Dave Francis & Mike Woodcock. 250p. 1996. ring bd. 149.95 (0-566-07636-5, Pub. by Gower UK) Ashgate Pub Co.

Twenty-Five Kites That Fly. Leslie L. Hunt. (Illus.). (YA). (gr. 5 up). 1990. 17.50 (0-8446-0151-9) Peter Smith.

Twenty-Five Kites That Fly. Leslie L. Hunt. (Illus.). 1971. reprint ed. pap. 2.95 (0-486-22550-X) Dover.

***25 Legal Luminaries from Vanity Fair'** Rupret Collens. (Illus.). 126p. 1990. 36.00 (1-872708-04-8) Gaunt.

Twenty Five Leprechaun Patterns for Carvers. Al Streetman. LC 95-42135. (Illus.). 64p. (YA). (gr. 10-13). 1996. pap. 12.95 (0-88740-957-1) Schiffer.

Twenty Five Lessons in Citizenship. D. L. Hennessey. (SPA.). 1991. pap. 4.50 (1-879773-01-5) D L Hennessey.

Twenty-Five Lessons in Citizenship. 96th rev. ed. D. L. Hennessey. Ed. by Lenore H. Richardson. 1991. reprint ed. pap. 4.50 (1-879773-00-7) D L Hennessey.

Twenty-Five Lessons in Citizenship. 97th ed. D. L. Hennessey. 1993. pap. 4.95 (1-879773-02-3) D L Hennessey.

Twenty-Five Lessons in Citizenship. 98th ed. D. L. Hennessey. 95p. 1995. pap. 5.25 (1-879773-04-X) D L Hennessey.

***Twenty-Five Lessons in Citizenship.** 99th ed. D. L. Hennessey. 95p. 1997. pap. 5.50 (1-879773-05-8) D L Hennessey.

***Twenty-Five Lessons in Citizenship: Chinese.** D. L. Hennessey. 94p. 1997. pap. 3.50 (0-9602958-3-6) D L Hennessey.

Twenty-Five Little Known Money Making Secrets. Allan H. Smith. LC 86-90659. 50p. (Orig.). 1986. pap. 4.00 (0-931113-07-5) Success Publ.

An Asterisk (*) at the beginning of an entry indicates that the title is appearing in BIP for the first time.

25 Management Lessons from the Customer's Side of the Counter. James H. Donnelly, Jr. 1996. per. 16.95 (0-7863-1004-9) Irwin Prof Pubng.

Twenty Five Miles to Nowhere: The Story of the Walhonding Canal with Canal Guide. Terry K. Woods. (Illus.). 47p. (Orig.). 1991. reprint ed. pap. 2.00 (1-880443-01-5) Roscoe Village.

Twenty-Five Mixtec Cats. Matthew Gollub. LC 92-13585. (Illus.). 32p. (J). (gr. 1 up). 1993. 15.00 (0-688-11639-6, Tambourine Bks); lib. bdg. 14.93 (0-688-11640-X, Tambourine Bks) Morrow.

25 Most Common Problems in Business. Jim Zabloski. LC 96-22552. 272p. 1996. pap. 12.99 (0-8054-6079-9, 4260-79) Broadman.

Twenty-Five Most Common Sales Mistakes: And How to Avoid Them. 2nd ed. Stephan Schiffman. 132p. 1995. pap. 6.95 (1-55850-511-3) Adams Media.

25 Most Difficult Nursing Situations. Sutton. (Nursing Education Ser.). 1998. pap. 20.95 (0-8273-5680-3) Delmar.

***25 Most Remarkable People.** Mike Wallace. 256p. Date not set. 25.00 (0-06-018759-X) HarpC.

25 Mother Goose Peak-a-Books: Reproducible, Easy-to-Make, Easy-to-Read. Helen H. Moore. 1993. pap. text ed. 9.95 (0-590-49729-4) Scholastic Inc.

25 Mountain Bike Tours in Massachusetts: From the Connecticut River to the Atlantic Coast. Robert S. Morse. LC 91-15374. (Bicycle Tours Ser.). 176p. 1991. pap. 12.00 (0-88150-191-3, Backcountry) Countryman.

***25 Mountain Bike Tours in New Jersey.** Peter Kick. LC 97-12812. (25 Mountain Bike Tour Ser.). (Illus.). 212p. (Orig.). 1997. pap. 14.95 (0-88150-386-X, Backcountry) Countryman.

25 Mountain Bike Tours in the Hudson Valley. Peter Kick. (Bicycle Tours Ser.). (Illus.). 208p. (Orig.). 1996. pap. 15.00 (0-88150-360-6, Backcountry) Countryman.

25 Mountain Bike Tours in Vermont: Scenic Tours Along Dirt Roads, Forest Trails, & Forgotten Byways. William J. Busha. LC 89-32132. (Twenty-Five Bike Tour Ser.). (Illus.). 176p. (Orig.). 1989. pap. 12.00 (0-88150-130-1, Backcountry) Countryman.

Twenty-Five Objections to Divine Healing & the Bible Answers. Gordon Lindsay. 1971. 1.95 (0-89985-030-8) Christ for the Nations.

Twenty-Five Papers on Statistics & Probability. I. V. Culanovski et al. LC 61-9803. (Selected Translations in Mathematical Statistics & Probability Ser.: Vol. 1). 306p. 1961. 51.00 (0-8218-1451-6, STAPRO/1) Am Math.

Twenty-Five Planets Speak to Planet Earth. Ruth E. Norman. (Tesla Speaks Ser.: Vol. V). (Illus.). 298p. 1975. 12.00 (0-932642-26-8); pap. 8.00 (0-932642-45-4) Unarius Acad Sci.

***25 Poems to Christmas.** Paul V. Nee. (Orig.). 1997. write for info. (1-57553-477-0) Watermrk Pr.

Twenty-Five Questions God Asks. Dick Bernal. 96p. (Orig.). 1993. 7.99 (1-56043-780-4) Destiny Image.

Twenty-Five Role Plays for Counselling Skills Training. David Couper & Jacqueline Stewart. 216p. 1993. ring bd. 125.95 (0-566-07341-2, Pub. by Gower UK) Ashgate Pub Co.

Twenty-Five Role Plays for Developing Management Skills. Dianne Kamp. 220p. 1993. ring bd. 125.95 (1-85904-027-6, Pub. by Gower UK) Ashgate Pub Co.

Twenty-Five Role Plays for Interview Training. Geof Cox & Chuck Dufault. 1993. ring bd. 125.00 (0-87425-213-X) HRD Press.

Twenty-Five Role Plays for Interview Training. Geoff Cox & Chuck Dufault. 218p. 1992. lib. bdg. 189.95 (0-566-07315-3, Pub. by Gower UK) Ashgate Pub Co.

25 Role Plays for Negotiation Skills. Ira G. Asherman & Sandra V. Asherman. 181p. (Orig.). 1996. pap. 39.95 (0-87425-997-5) HRD Press.

Twenty-Five Roleplays for Developing Management Skills. Dianne Kamp. 276p. 1994. ring bd. 125.00 (0-87425-961-4) HRD Press.

Twenty-Five Roleplays for Interpersonal Skills. Teresa Williams. 350p. 1993. ring bd. 125.00 (0-87425-240-7) HRD Press.

***25 Roleplays for Interview Training.** Geof Cox & Chuch Dufault. 216p. 1997. pap. 79.95 (0-566-07903-8, Pub. by Gower UK) Ashgate Pub Co.

Twenty-Five Romantic Lines to Say to Your Lover in Spanish. Ruben Leos. 28p. (Orig.). 1987. pap. 1.50 (0-945228-00-7) Chico Bks.

Twenty-Five Sales Habits of Highly Successful Salespeople. 2nd ed. Stephan Schiffman. 1994. pap. 5.95 (1-55850-391-9) Adams Media.

25 Scariest Hauntings in the World. Mary Batten. LC 96-35884. (Illus.). 64p. (J). (gr. 3-7). 1996. pap. 6.95 (1-56565-486-2) Lowell Hse Juvenile.

25 Scariest Places in the World. Phyllis Emert. LC 95-494. (Illus.). 64p. (J). (gr. 5-7). 1995. pap. 5.95 (1-56565-277-0) Lowell Hse.

Twenty-Five Science Mini-Books. Esther Weiner. 72p. (J). 1999. pap. 9.95 (0-590-49507-0) Scholastic Inc.

25 Scores. Arthur Bull. 25p. (Orig.). 1994. pap. 3.00 (1-57141-006-6) Runaway Spoon.

25 Selected Songs Low Voice: Piano. G. Faure. 116p. (ENG & FRE.). 1986. per. 12.95 (0-7935-4868-3, 50261070) H Leonard.

Twenty-Five Selections American Art: Charles H. MacNider Museum. Richard E. Leet. LC 91-70433. (Illus.). 72p. (Orig.). 1991. pap. 12.50 (0-9628930-0-5) C H MacNider Mus.

Twenty-Five Stages of My Spine. Margaret Randall. 1967. 3.00 (0-685-01011-2) Elizabeth Pr.

Twenty-Five Steps to Power & Mastery Over People. James K. Van Fleet. 260p. 1983. pap. text ed. 10.95 (0-13-934802-6, Parker Publishing Co) P-H.

Twenty-Five Steps to Power & Mastery Over People. James K. Van Fleet. 260p. 1986. 18.95 (0-13-934810-7, Parker Publishing Co) P-H.

25 Steps to Safe Computing. Don Sellers. 72p. (C). 1995. pap. text ed. 5.95 (0-201-88366-X) Peachpit Pr.

25 Stupid Things Nurses Do to Self Destruct. Teresa Allen et al. LC 94-92408. 157p. (Orig.). 1995. pap. 19.95 (0-9627246-3-7) Power NY.

***25 Surprising Marriages: Faith-Building Stories from the Lives of Famous Christians.** 2nd ed. William J. Petersen. LC 96-45565. 480p. (Orig.). 1997. pap. 19.99 (0-8010-5753-1) Baker Bks.

Twenty-five Suttas from Uparipannasa: Suttanta Pitaka. Majjhima Nikaya Medium Length Discourses of the Buddha. Ed. by Myanmar Pitaka Associates Staff. (C). 1991. 23.00 (81-7030-294-3) S Asia.

Twenty-Five Team Management Training Sessions. John Allan. 664p. 1994. 255.95 (0-566-07513-X, Pub. by Gower UK) Ashgate Pub Co.

Twenty-Five Thematic Mini Books. Scholastic Books Staff. 1992. pap. 9.95 (0-590-49215-2) Scholastic Inc.

Twenty-Five Things Every New Mother Should Know. Martha Sears & William Sears. Ed. by Linda Ziedrich. LC 94-47976. 128p. 1995. 14.95 (1-55832-068-7); pap. 7.95 (1-55832-069-5) Harvard Common Pr.

Twenty-Five Things You Can Do to Beat the Recession in the 1990's. Alan Weintraub. 1991. pap. 3.95 (0-312-92646-4) St Martin.

Twenty-Five Things You Can Do to Feel Better Right Now. Bill Chandler. 156p. 1993. pap. 10.95 (0-9639167-0-X) Andante Pubng.

Twenty-Five Top Christmas Songs. 80p. 1989. pap. 8.95 (0-7935-2729-5, 00290064) H Leonard.

Twenty-Five Top Christmas Songs. (Easy Piano Ser.). 80p. 1989. pap. 9.95 (0-7935-2737-6, 00490058) H Leonard.

Twenty-Five Top Christmas Songs. 80p. 1989. pap. 9.95 (0-7935-2738-4, 00490059) H Leonard.

Twenty-Five Top Christmas Songs, No. 238. 64p. 1989. pap. 7.95 (0-7935-2149-1, 00290059) H Leonard.

Twenty-Five Top Christmas Songs for Alto Saxophone. 32p. 1989. pap. 5.95 (0-7935-2948-4, 00660019) H Leonard.

Twenty-Five Top Christmas Songs for Clarinet. 32p. 1989. pap. 5.95 (0-7935-2949-2, 00660017) H Leonard.

Twenty-Five Top Christmas Songs for Flute. 32p. 1989. pap. 5.95 (0-7935-2724-4, 00660016) H Leonard.

Twenty-Five Top Christmas Songs for Guitar. 64p. 1989. pap. 8.95 (0-7935-3114-4, 00660015) H Leonard.

Twenty-Five Top Christmas Songs for Trombone. 32p. 1989. pap. 5.95 (0-7935-2725-2, 00660020) H Leonard.

Twenty-Five Top Christmas Songs for Trumpet. 32p. 1989. pap. 5.95 (0-7935-3115-2, 00660018) H Leonard.

Twenty-Five Top Christmas Songs for Violin. 32p. 1989. pap. 5.95 (0-7935-3783-5, 00660021) H Leonard.

25 Top Rhythm & Blues Hits. 152p. 1992. otabind 14.95 (0-7935-1594-7, 00120867) H Leonard.

Twenty-Five Training Activities for Creating & Managing Change. Mike Woodcock & Dave Francis. 1992. ring bd. 125.00 (0-87425-198-2) HRD Press.

25 Uncle Sam Patterns for Carvers. Al Streetman. LC 94-23250. (Book for Woodcarvers). (Illus.). 64p. (Orig.). 1995. pap. 12.95 (0-88740-717-X) Schiffer.

Twenty-Five Vegetables Anyone Can Grow. Ann R. Robbins. 1974. pap. 5.95 (0-486-23029-5) Dover.

Twenty-Five Ways to Cook a Mouse: Whisker-Licking Recipes for Your Gourmet Cat. Orson Bean. (Illus.). 1993. 9.95 (1-55972-199-5, Birch Ln Pr) Carol Pub Group.

***25 Ways to Get Your Child to Read.** Jalynn S. Venis. Ed. by James S. Venis. LC 96-94899. (Illus.). 84p. (Orig.). 1996. pap. 10.95 (0-9654743-0-5, 9611-01) Haven Pub CO.

***25 Ways to Keep Your Cat Happy.** Raymond Webster. (Illus.). 101p. (Orig.). 1994. pap. 5.50 (0-9657252-5-1) Tuxedo Enter.

Twenty-Five Ways to Make & Save Money. 1980. pap. 0.95 (0-686-30853-0) Crusade Pubs.

25 Ways to Make Your Business More Profitable. R. Dodge Woodson. 196p. 1995. 74.95 (1-56842-054-4) Marshall & Swift.

Twenty-Five Ways to Tell Someone off in Spanish. Ruben Leos. 28p. (Orig.). 1987. pap. 1.50 (0-945228-01-5) Chico Bks.

Twenty-Five-Year War: America's Military Role in Vietnam. Bruce Palmer, Jr. LC 84-5091. (Illus.). 248p. 1984. 27.00 (0-8131-1513-2) U Pr of Ky.

Twenty-Five Year War: America's Military Role in Vietnam. Bruce Palmer, Jr. (Quality Paperbacks Ser.). (Illus.). 264p. 1990. pap. 13.95 (0-306-80383-6) Da Capo.

Twenty-Five-Year Wheel Alignment Specifications Guide. 48p. 1986. write for info. (0-318-67326-6, H M Gousha) P-H Gen Ref & Trav.

Twenty-Five Years: A Retrospective. Ellen Landau et al. (Illus.). 78p. 1993. pap. text ed. 20.00 (1-880353-04-0) Cleveland Ctr.

Twenty-Five Years: Judah L. Magnes Museum. Ruth Eis. Ed. by Nelda Cassuto. (Illus.). 136p. (Orig.). 1987. pap. 20.00 (0-943376-38-6) Magnes Mus.

Twenty-Five Years: Nineteen Forty-five to Nineteen Seventy. Ed. by G. Kerry Smith. LC 73-110640. (Jossey-Bass Higher Education Ser.). 350p. reprint ed. 99.80 (0-8357-9352-4, 2013899) Bks Demand.

Twenty-Five Years: Special Collections at Kent State University. Ed. by Dean H. Keller & Alex Gildzen. LC 93-31427. (Illus.). 112p. (Orig.). 1994. pap. 14.00 (0-87338-500-4) Kent St U Pr.

Twenty-Five Years at Brooklands Track with the "Railton Era" R. H. Beauchamp. 108p. 1984. 39.00 (0-7212-0619-0, Pub. by Regency Press UK) St Mut.

Twenty-Five Years European Social Charter. C. M. Jaspers & L. Betten. 190p. 1988. pap. 57.00 (90-6544-345-2) Kluwer Law Tax Pubs.

Twenty-Five Years in the Black Belt. William J. Edwards et al. LC 93-19789. (Library of Alabama Classics). 192p. 1993. pap. 16.95 (0-8173-0716-8) U of Ala Pr.

Twenty-Five Years in the Rifle Brigade. William Surtees. 480p. 1996. 40.00 (1-85367-230-0, Pub. by Greenhill Bks UK) Stackpole.

Twenty-Five Years of Accounting Responsibility 1911-1936, Vols. I & II. George O. May. Ed. by Carleton Hunt. 1971. reprint ed. text ed. 25.00 (0-914348-03-5) Scholars Bk.

Twenty-Five Years of American Education. Ed. by Isaac L. Kandel. LC 79-89191. (American Education: Its Men, Institutions, & Ideas. Series 1). 1970. reprint ed. 23.95 (0-405-01429-5) Ayer.

Twenty-Five Years of American Education: Collected Essays Written by a Group of His Former Students As a Tribute to Paul Monroe on His Completion of Twenty-Five Years of Service to American Education. Ed. by Isaac L. Kandel. LC 67-22124. (Essay Index Reprint Ser.). 1977. 23.95 (0-8369-0956-9) Ayer.

Twenty-Five Years of American Painting. Max Kozloff & James T. Demetrion. LC 73-75776. (Illus.). 72p. 1973. pap. 12.00 (0-614-06999-8) Edmundson.

***Twenty-Five Years of Anselm Studies, 1969-1994: Review & Critique of Recent Scholarly Views.** Ed. by Frederick Van Fleteren & Joseph C. Schnaubelt. 356p. 1996. text ed. 99.95 (0-7734-8957-6) E Mellen.

Twenty-Five Years of Building the Future: Doctors Hospital, Pinole, CA. Margaret Finnerty. Ed. by John Myers & Robert Gryder. 100p. (C). 1992. 39.95 (0-929690-15-X) Herit Pubs AZ.

Twenty-Five Years of Chemical Engineering Progress. American Institute of Chemical Engineers Annual Meeting, San Francisco, November 25-29, 1979. Ed. by S. D. Kirkpatrick. LC 68-55837. (Essay Index Reprint Ser.). 1977. 23.95 (0-8369-0149-5) Ayer.

Twenty-Five Years of Economic Development, 1950 to 1975. David Morawetz. LC 77-17243. 139p. reprint ed. pap. 39.70 (0-7837-4257-6, 2043947) Bks Demand.

Twenty-Five Years of Educational Practice & Theory. Ed. by Leo Fernig & James Bowen. vi, 353p. 1980. lib. bdg. 70.50 (90-247-2284-5) Kluwer Ac.

Twenty-Five Years of Excellence: A History of the Texas Heart Institute. Ed. by Marianne Mallia. (Illus.). 300p. (C). 1989. 35.00 (0-317-91336-0) TX Heart Inst Found.

***25 Years of Innovation: The Story of Pfizer Central Research.** Ogden Tanner. LC 95-82399. (Illus.). 216p. 1996. write for info. (0-944641-17-2) Greenwich Pub Group.

Twenty-Five Years of Logical Methodology in Poland. Ed. by Marian Przezecki & Ryszard Wojcicki. LC 76-7064. (Synthese Library: No. 87). 743p. 1977. lib. bdg. 182.50 (90-277-0601-8, D Reidel) Kluwer Ac.

Twenty-Five Years of Marxist-Humanism in the U. S. A History of Worldwide Revolutionary Developments. Raya Dunayevskaya. (Illus.). 30p. (Orig.). 1980. pap. 1.50 (0-914441-20-5) News & Letters.

Twenty-Five Years of Mustang Advertising. Jerry Heasley. LC 89-81364. (Illus.). 136p. (Orig.). 1989. pap. 8.95 (0-9624908-0-6) CA Mustang Sales.

25 Years of Non-Equilibrium Statistical Mechanics: Proceedings of the XIII Sitges Conference, Sitges, Barcelona, Spain, 13-17 June 1994. Thirteenth Sitges Conference Staff. Ed. by Joaquin Marro et al. (Lecture Notes in Physics Ser.: Vol. 445). 450p. 1995. 101.95 (3-540-59158-3) Spr-Verlag.

Twenty-Five Years of Service: One Day at a Time. Nancy B. Kincheloe. Ed. by Claudia Wilson. LC 84-63043. 105p. 1985. write for info. (0-9614550-0-4); pap. write for info. (0-9614550-1-2) Radiation Med Found SW.

Twenty-Five Years of the American Astronautical Society, Historical Reflections & Projections, 1954-1979. Ed. by Eugene M. Emme. (AAS History Ser.: Vol. 2). (Illus.). 248p. 1980. pap. 15.00 (0-87703-118-5); lib. bdg. 25.00 (0-87703-117-7) Univelt Inc.

Twenty-Five Years of the Life Review: Theoretical & Practical Considerations. Intro. & Pref. by Robert Disch. LC 88-14203. (Journal of Gerontological Social Work: Vol. 12, Nos. 3-4). (Illus.). 148p. 1989. text ed. 39.95 (0-86656-836-0) Haworth Pr.

Twenty-Five Years of the Peachtree Road Race. Karen Rosen. LC 93-81144. (Illus.). 144p. 1994. 25.00 (1-56352-127-X) Longstreet Pr Inc.

Twenty-Five Years of the Philadelphia Orchestra, 1900-1925. Frances A. Wister. LC 70-126265. (Select Bibliographies Reprint Ser.). 1977. 20.95 (0-8369-5492-0) Ayer.

Twenty-Five Years of the Sun at Work: Proceedings of the Annual Meeting of the American Section of the International Solar Energy Society, Phoenix 1980, 2 vols., Set. Ed. by Gregory E. Franta & Barbara H. Glenn. 1980. pap. 100.00 (0-89553-021-X) Am Solar Energy.

Twenty Florida Pirates. Kevin M. McCarthy. LC 93-48310. (Illus.). 96p. 1994. pap. 17.95 (1-56164-050-6) Pineapple Pr.

Twenty for Teens. Ed. by Evelyn Stenbock. (YA). 1980. 5.50 (0-8341-9090-7, MP-611) Lillenas.

Twenty Four. Joanie Whitebird. LC 78-1142. 1978. pap. 5.00 (0-915016-21-4) Second Coming.

Twenty-Four British Potters: Exhibition Catalogue. William Hull. (Illus.). 48p. 1976. pap. 3.00 (0-911209-08-5) Palmer Mus Art.

Twenty-Four Caprices: Studies - Violin. Pierre Rode. 56p. 1986. pap. 8.95 (0-7935-5133-1) H Leonard.

Twenty-Four Caprices in the Form of Etudes for Violin. Pierre Rode. Ed. by Gustav Saenger. (Carl Fischer Music Library: No.583). 52p. 1910. pap. 9.00 (0-8258-0076-5, L583) Fischer Inc NY.

Twenty-Four Classics in Puzzle Form. Rich Latta. 280p. (J). (gr. 4-8). 1993. pap. 7.50 (0-913853-28-3, 32542, Alleyside) Highsmith Pr.

Twenty-Four Cuentos Favorites de Ninos. (SPA.). 1985. pap. 1.50 (0-317-02031-5) Rod & Staff.

Twenty-Four Days Before Christmas. Madeleine L'Engle. 80p. (J). (gr. k-6). 1987. pap. 3.99 (0-440-40105-4, YB BDD) BDD Bks Young Read.

Twenty-Four Days Before Christmas: An Austin Family Story. Madeleine L'Engle. LC 84-5540. (Illus.). 48p. 1984. 11.99 (0-87788-843-4) Shaw Pubs.

***24 de Febrero de 1895: Un Programa Vigente.** Jorge Castellanos. (SPA.). pap. 18.00 (0-89729-752-0) Ediciones.

Twenty-Four Early American Country Dances: Cotillions & Reels for the Year 1976. James E. Morrison. LC 76-3969. (Illus.). 72p. 1976. spiral bd. 14.00 (0-917024-04-4) Country Dance & Song.

Twenty Four Etudes: Opus 15 Flute. J. Andersen. 72p. 1986. pap. 9.95 (0-7935-5266-4, 50335090) H Leonard.

Twenty-Four Etudes & Caprices for the Violin Opus 35. J. Dont. 48p. 1986. pap. 7.95 (0-7935-5221-4) H Leonard.

Twenty-Four Eyes. Sakae Tsuboi. Tr. by Akira Miura from JPN. LC 82-51098. 256p. 1983. reprint ed. pap. 12.95 (0-8048-1462-7) C E Tuttle.

Twenty-Four Favorite One-Act Plays. Ed. by Van H. Cartmell & Bennett Cerf. LC 58-13274. 560p. 1963. pap. 12.95 (0-385-06617-1, C423, Dolp) Doubleday.

24 Flower Arrangement Recipes. Rachel Carr. (Illus.). 65p. (Orig.). 1995. pap. 12.00 (0-9634021-1-0) Pennington CA.

24 Food Programs: In Good Taste. Lynne M. Erickson. (Illus.). 104p. 1995. ring bd. 24.00 (0-9649414-0-6, BK324) Bi-Folkal.

Twenty Four Haiku After the Japanese. Tom Weigel. Ed. by Maureen Owen. (Summer Ser.). 1982. pap. 4.00 (0-916382-29-X) Telephone Bks.

Twenty-Four Hour ACE Inhibition: Current & Future Perspectives: Journal: Cardiology, Vol. 79, Suppl. 1, 1991. Ed. by C. Johnston. (Illus.). 84p. 1991. pap. 52.25 (3-8055-5461-3) S Karger.

24-Hour Business: Maximizing Productivity Through Round-the-Clock Operations. Richard M. Coleman. 208p. 1995. 24.95 (0-8144-0240-2) AMACOM.

Twenty-Four-Hour Coverage. Ed. by Richard A. Victor. LC 91-21114. 1991. 25.00 (0-935149-28-7, WC-91-2) Workers Comp Res Inst.

24-Hour Coverage: An Analysis & Report about Current Developments. Keith T. Bateman & Cynthia J. Veldman. 57p. 1991. pap. text ed. 20.00 (1-887271-07-4) Alliance Am Insurers.

Twenty-Four Hour Drink Book. Ralph Maloney. (Illus.). 1962. 10.95 (0-8392-1121-X) Astor-Honor.

***Twenty Four Hour Net News.** Que Development Group Staff. 96p. 1996. pap. text ed. 9.99 incl. cd-rom (0-7897-0997-X) Que.

Twenty-Four-Hour Society: Understanding Human Limits in a World That Never Stops. Martin C. Moore-Ede. 1993. pap. 12.00 (0-201-62611-X) Addison-Wesley.

Twenty-Four Hour Trading: Network of Futures & Options Markets. Diamond. 304p. 1989. text ed. 29.95 (0-471-60072-5) Wiley.

24 Hour Turn-Around: Discovering the Power to Change. Jim Hartness & Neil Eskelin. LC 93-1764. 176p. (Orig.). (YA). (gr. 10). 1994. pap. 9.99 (0-8007-1680-9) Revell.

Twenty-Four Hour Wake. Carmen M. Pursifull. Ed. by Karen K. Singer. (Chapbook Ser.: No. 16). (Illus.). 57p. (Orig.). 1989. pap. 4.95 (0-932884-16-4) Red Herring.

24 Hour War. Nick Pollotta. LC 94-68158. (Endless Quest Ser.). (Orig.). 1995. pap. 3.99 (0-7869-0198-5) TSR Inc.

Twenty-Four Hours a Day. large type ed. Faith Baldwin. LC 91-34433. 345p. 1992. reprint ed. lib. bdg. 18.95 (1-56054-273-X) Thorndike Pr.

Twenty-Four Hours a Day. rev. ed. 365p. 1975. 10.00 (0-89486-012-7, 1050A) Hazelden.

Twenty-Four Hours a Day. 384p. 1992. reprint ed. pap. 9.00 (0-89486-834-9) Hazelden.

Twenty-Four Hours AM. Ed. by Oliver Hailey. 1983. pap. 5.25 (0-8222-1177-7) Dramatists Play.

Twenty-Four Hours Hardcover. 12.00 (0-685-53509-6) Harper SF.

Twenty-Four Hours in a Montana Jail: Jail: What's It Really Like? 75p. 1993. 35.00 (1-881417-01-8) D F Curran Prods.

24 Hours in Cyberspace: Painting on the Walls of the Digital Cave. Rick Smolan. (Illus.). 224p. 1996. 49.99 (0-7897-0925-2) Mac Comp Pub.

Twenty-Four Hours PM. Ed. by Oliver Hailey. 1983. pap. 5.25 (0-8222-1178-5) Dramatists Play.

Twenty-Four Hundred Tennessee Pensioners: Revolution & War of 1812. Zella Armstrong. LC 75-971. 121p. 1996. reprint ed. pap. 9.00 (0-8063-0665-3) Genealog Pub.

Twenty-Four Italian Songs & Arias Vol. 1722A: For Medium High Voice. 1987. pap. 12.95 incl. audio (0-7935-5320-2, 50480073) H Leonard.

Twenty-Four Italian Songs & Arias Vol. 1723A: For Medium Low Voice. 1987. pap. 12.95 incl. audio (0-7935-5328-8, 50480074) H Leonard.

Twenty-Four Italian Songs & Arias of the 17th & 18th Century: Medium High Voice. 104p. 1986. otabind 5.95 (0-7935-1006-6, 50261140) H Leonard.

Twenty-Four Italian Songs & Arias of the 17th & 18th Century: Medium Low Voice. 104p. 1986. otabind 5.95 (0-7935-2554-3, 50261150) H Leonard.

Twenty-Four Karat. 1987. pap. 5.00 (0-911479-30-9) Dial Pub.

An Asterisk (*) at the beginning of an entry indicates that the title is appearing in BIP for the first time.

Twenty-Four Metalworking Projects. Percy W. Blandford. pap. 9.95 (*0-8306-2784-7*, 2784) McGraw-Hill Prof.

***Twenty-Four Motets, Vol. 14/1.** Francisco Penalosa. (Gesamtausgaben - Collected Works). Date not set. write for info. (*0-931902-84-3*) Inst Mediaeval Mus.

Twenty-Four Papers on Statistics & Probability. A. Aleskjavicene et al. LC 61-9803. (Selected Translations in Mathematical Statistics & Probability Ser.: Vol. 7). 302p. 1968. 51.00 (*0-8218-1457-5*, STAPRO/7) Am Math.

Twenty-Four Papers on Statistics & Probability. D. V. Anosov et al. LC 61-9803. (Selected Translations in Mathematical Statistics & Probability Ser.: Vol. 14). 296p. 1978. 80.00 (*0-8218-1464-8*, STAPRO/14) Am Math.

Twenty-Four Pieces for Children Opus 39 Piano. D. Kabalevsky. 20p. (J). 1986. pap. text ed. 7.95 (*0-7935-3582-4*, 50330040) H Leonard.

24 Preludes, Opus 11. Alexander Scriabin. 1984. 7.95 (*0-7935-1187-9*, 00009229) H Leonard.

Twenty-Four Preludes, Opus 38: For Piano. D. Kabalevsky. 72p. 1985. pap. 9.95 (*0-7935-3977-3*, 00123070) H Leonard.

Twenty-Four Robbers. Audrey Wood. LC 90-46182. (Illus.). 32p. (J). (ps-2). 1989. 7.99 (*0-85953-100-7*); pap. 3.99 (*0-85953-324-7*) Childs Play.

***24 Robbers.** Audrey Wood. (J). 1996. lib. bdg. 11.95 (*0-85953-896-6*) Childs Play.

Twenty-Four Router Projects. Percy W. Blandford. (Illus.). 120p. 1988. pap. 6.95 (*0-8306-9062-X*, 9062P) McGraw-Hill Prof.

Twenty-Four Router Projects. 2nd ed. Percy W. Blandford. 1993. pap. 12.95 (*0-8306-4546-2*) TAB Bks.

Twenty-Four Seven. Betty Burston. 256p. 1994. mass mkt. 4.95 (*0-87067-951-1*) Holloway.

Twenty-Four Songs of Early Americans - For Church: A Thanksgiving Celebration. Gordon Myers. (Orig.). (C). 1994. pap. 12.95 (*1-878617-06-0*) Leyerle Pubns.

24 Strange Little Animals: The Haunted House. Graham Percy. LC 96-5208. (Illus.). 40p. (J). (ps-3). 1996. 12.95 (*0-8118-1035-6*) Chronicle Bks.

Twenty-Four Studies in All Major & Minor Keys: For the Flute Opus 21. J. Andersen. 28p. 1986. pap. 5.95 (*0-7935-5417-9*, 50260890) H Leonard.

Twenty-Four Table Saw Projects. Percy W. Blandford. (Illus.). 128p. 1987. pap. 6.95 (*0-8306-2964-5*) McGraw-Hill Prof.

Twenty-Four Table Saw Projects. Percy W. Blandford. 1991. 6.95 (*0-8306-5309-0*) McGraw-Hill Prof.

Twenty-Four Top Country Hits of the 90's. (Decade Ser.). 136p. 1992. per. 10.95 (*0-7935-1910-1*, 00311598) H Leonard.

Twenty-Four Ways of Looking at Mary McCarthy: The Writer & Her Work. Ed. by Eve Stwertka & Margo Viscusi. LC 96-5801. (Contributions to the Study of World Literature Ser.: Vol. 70). 240p. 1996. text ed. 55.00 (*0-313-29776-2*, Greenwood Pr) Greenwood.

Twenty-Four Ways to Greater Business Productivity: Master Checklists for Marketing, Advertising, Sales, Distribution & Customer Service. Charles R. MacDonald. LC 81-7096. 446p. 1981. text ed. 49.50 (*0-87624-203-4*, Inst Busn Plan) P-H.

***24 Ways to Improve Your Self-Serve.** Patrick Crowe. 115p. 1997. ring bd. 39.00 (*0-9642640-6-4*) Power Inc.

Twenty-Four Ways to Improve Your Teaching. Kenneth O. Gangel. LC 74-77453. 131p. 1986. pap. 9.99 (*0-89693-235-4*, 6-2235, Victor Bks) Chariot Victor.

Twenty-Four Woodturning Projects. Percy W. Blandford. 1990. 18.95 (*0-07-155629-X*) McGraw.

Twenty-Four Woodturning Projects. Percy W. Blandford. (Illus.). 140p. 1990. 18.95 (*0-8306-8334-8*, 3334); pap. 9.95 (*0-8306-3334-0*) McGraw-Hill Prof.

Twenty-Four Years in the Argentine Republic. J. Anthony King. LC 71-161042. reprint ed. 57.50 (*0-404-03691-0*) AMS Pr.

***24/7.** Amy S. Wilensky. (Love Stories Ser.: No. 18). 192p. (YA). 1997. mass mkt. 3.99 (*0-553-57074-9*) BDD Bks Young Read.

Twenty-Fourth Annual Immigration & Naturalization Institute. 1006p. 1991. 70.00 (*0-685-51880-9*, H4-5111) PLI.

24th Annual Institute on Employment Law. (Litigation & Administrative Practice Course Handbook, 1983-84 Ser.). Date not set. pap. 99.00 (*0-614-17265-9*, H4-5219) PLI.

Twenty-Fourth Annual Institute on Securities Regulation, 2 vols. (Corporate Law & Practice Course Handbook, 1985-86 Ser.: Vols. 792-793). 1742p. 1992. Set. 80.00 (*0-685-65495-8*, B4-7017) PLI.

Twenty-Fourth Michigan of the Iron Brigade. Donald L. Smith. 312p. 1984. reprint ed. 30.00 (*0-942211-56-1*) Olde Soldier Bks.

Twenty-Fourth Virginia Infantry. Ralph W. Gunn. (Virginia Regimental Histories Ser.). (Illus.). 112p. 1987. 19.95 (*0-930919-43-2*) H E Howard.

Twenty-Fourth Zakopane School on Physics: Proceedings, 2 vols., 1. J. Styczen et al. 790p. (C). 1989. text ed. 104.00 (*981-02-0051-X*) World Scientific Pub.

Twenty-Fourth Zakopane School on Physics: Proceedings, 2 vols., 2. J. Styczen et al. 790p. (C). 1989. text ed. 104.00 (*981-02-0052-8*) World Scientific Pub.

***Twenty Generations.** Walter Kendrick. Date not set. write for info. (*0-688-15404-2*) Morrow.

20 Golden Rules of New Home Marketing. Rick Golden. 152p. (Orig.). 1994. pap. 15.95 (*0-9623646-3-0*) Wales Pub.

20 Gram Diet: Fat Counter. Gabe Mirkin. LC 94-77443. 96p. (Orig.). 1994. pap. text ed. 4.99 (*0-9642386-0-8*) Linx Corp.

Twenty Gram Diet Seven-Day Jump Start. Gabe Mirkin. 1996. pap. text ed. 6.99 (*0-9642386-4-0*) Linx Corp.

***Twenty Holy Hours.** Mateo C. Boevey. 1978. pap. 5.95 (*0-8198-7328-4*) Pauline Bks.

Twenty Hot Potatoes Christians Are Afraid to Touch. Tony Campolo. 1993. pap. 10.99 (*0-8499-3505-9*) Word Pub.

20 Hottest Investments for the 21st Century. Andrew Leckey. LC 95-32764. 288p. 1994. 19.95 (*0-8092-3558-7*) Contemp Bks.

20 Hottest Investments for the 21st Century. Andrew Leckey. LC 95-32764. 320p. 1995. pap. 14.95 (*0-8092-3339-8*) Contemp Bks.

Twenty Hours Forty Minutes: Our Flight in the Friendship. Amelia Earhart. Ed. by James B. Gilbert. LC 79-7249. (Flight: Its First Seventy-Five Years Ser.). (Illus.). 1980. reprint ed. lib. bdg. 28.95 (*0-405-12161-X*) Ayer.

20 Ideas for Teaching Gifted Kids in the Middle School & High School. Ed. by Joel McIntosh. 132p. 1991. pap. 19.95 (*1-882664-05-1*) Prufrock Pr.

Twenty Innovative Electronics Projects for Your Home. Joseph O'Connell. (Illus.). 256p. 1988. 21.95 (*0-8306-0947-4*); pap. 13.95 (*0-8306-2947-5*) McGraw-Hill Prof.

Twenty International Short Stories: For ESL Students. Raja T. Nasr. LC 94-48839. (Illus.). 114p. (C). 1995. reprint ed. pap. text ed. 15.00 (*0-8191-9866-8*) U Pr of Amer.

***Twenty Israeli Composers: Voices of a Culture.** Robert J. Fleisher. LC 96-52284. 340p. 1997. 39.95 (*0-8143-2648-X*) Wayne St U Pr.

Twenty Jataka Tales. Noor I. Khan. (Orig.). 1991. pap. 9.95 (*0-89281-323-7*) Inner Tradit.

20 Keys to Workplace Improvement. rev. ed. Iwao Kobayashi. LC 95-23802. (Illus.). 302p. (JPN.). 1995. 50.00 (*1-56327-109-5*) Prod Press.

Twenty Lectures: Sociological Theory since World War II. Jeffrey C. Alexander. LC 86-17106. 432p. 1987. text ed. 50.00 (*0-231-06210-9*) Col U Pr.

Twenty Lectures: Sociological Theory since World War II. Jeffrey C. Alexander. LC 86-17106. 432p. 1988. pap. text ed. 18.50 (*0-231-06211-7*) Col U Pr.

Twenty Lectures Delivered at the International Congress of Mathematicians in Vancouver, 1974. Ed. by D. V. Anosov. LC 77-9042. (Translations Ser.: Series 2, Vol. 109). 129p. 1977. reprint ed. pap. 38.00 (*0-8218-3059-7*, TRANS2/109) Am Math.

Twenty Lectures on Chinese Culture: An Intermediary Chinese Textbook. Parker P. Huang et al. 1967. pap. text ed. 19.00 (*0-300-00127-4*) Yale U Pr.

Twenty Lectures on Chinese Culture: Exercise Book. Parker P. Huang. LC 66-21520. 1967. pap. text ed. 19.00 (*0-300-00128-2*) Yale U Pr.

Twenty Legal Pitfalls for Nurses to Avoid. Janine Fiesta. LC 93-34184. (Real Nursing Ser.). 192p. 1994. pap. 20.95 (*0-8273-6152-1*) Delmar.

Twenty Lessons in Keyboard Choreography. S. Bernstein. 200p. 1991. pap. 18.95 (*0-7935-0372-8*) H Leonard.

Twenty Lines a Day. Harry Mathews. LC 87-73070. 134p. 1989. reprint ed. pap. 8.95 (*0-916583-41-4*) Dalkey Arch.

Twenty Little Amish Quilts: With Full-Size Templates. Gwen Marston. LC 93-9357. (Needlework Ser.). (Illus.). 1993. pap. 3.95 (*0-486-27582-5*) Dover.

Twenty Little Four-Patch Quilts: With Full-Size Templates. Gwen Marston. (Illus.). 56p. (Orig.). Date not set. pap. 5.95 (*0-486-29184-7*) Dover.

Twenty Little Log Cabin Quilts: With Full-Size Templates. Gwen Marston. LC 95-17401. (Needlework Ser.). (Illus.). 56p. (Orig.). 1995. pap. text ed. 4.95 (*0-486-28809-9*) Dover.

Twenty Little Patchwork Quilts. Gwen Marston. 1990. pap. 3.95 (*0-486-26131-X*) Dover.

Twenty Little Pinwheel Quilts: With Full-Size Templates. Gwen Marston. (Illus.). 56p. (Orig.). 1994. pap. text ed. 4.95 (*0-486-28216-3*) Dover.

***Twenty Little Triangle Quilts: With Full-Size Templates.** Gwen Marston. LC 97-7959. (Illus.). 56p. (Orig.). 1997. pap. text ed. 5.95 (*0-486-29700-4*) Dover.

Twenty Love Poems. Pablo Neruda. Date not set. pap. 8.95 (*0-14-086293-5*) Viking Penguin.

Twenty Love Poems & a Song of Despair. Pablo Neruda. (Illus.). 80p. 1993. 12.95 (*0-8118-0320-1*) Chronicle Bks.

Twenty Love Poems & a Song of Despair. Pablo Neruda. LC 70-481699. (Cape Editions Ser.). 1976. mass mkt. 4.95 (*0-14-042205-6*, Penguin Bks) Viking Penguin.

Twenty Love Poems & a Song of Despair. Pablo Neruda. Tr. by W. S. Merwin. 88p. 1993. pap. 8.95 (*0-14-018648-4*, Penguin Classics) Viking Penguin.

20 Master Plots: (And How to Build Them) Ronald B. Tobias. 240p. 1993. 17.99 (*0-89879-595-8*, Wrtrs Digest Bks) F & W Pubns Inc.

Twenty Memorable Horse Races. Rick Snider. LC 93-11576. 1994. 50.00 (*1-56554-028-X*) Pelican.

Twenty Miles from a Match: Homesteading in Western Nevada. Sarah E. Olds. LC 78-13766. (Illus.). 200p. 1990. reprint ed. pap. 12.95 (*0-87417-052-4*) U of Nev Pr.

Twenty Million Walking Dead. Leo Lindenbauer. (Health Ser.). 145p. 1992. pap. 11.95 (*1-879331-30-6*) L Lindenbauer.

Twenty Million Yankees. (Civil War Ser.). (Illus.). 176p. 1985. 18.95 (*0-8094-4752-5*); lib. bdg. 25.93 (*0-8094-4753-3*) Time-Life.

20 Minute Break: Using the New Science of Ultradian Rhythms. Ernest L. Rossi & David Nimmons. 210p. 1996. 17.95 (*0-9651985-1-0*) Palisades Gateway.

Twenty-Minute Chicken Dishes: Delicious, Easy-to-Prepare Meals Everyone Will Love! Karen A. Levin & Kevin Morrissey. 128p. 1991. pap. 9.95 (*0-8092-4033-5*) Contemp Bks.

Twenty-Minute Chords & Harmony Workout. Stuart Isacoff. 1990. pap. 14.95 (*0-943748-41-0*) Ekay Music.

Twenty Minute Cookbook. Steven Wheeler. (Step by Step Ser.). 96p. 1995. 9.98 (*0-8317-8054-1*) Smithmark.

Twenty-Minute Counselor: Transforming Brief Conversations into Effective Helping Experiences. Charles H. Huber & Barbara A. Backlund. 144p. 1995. reprint ed. pap. 12.95 (*0-8245-1447-5*) Crossroad NY.

***20 Minute Gardener.** M. Asher & T. Christopher. 1997. 19.95 (*0-679-44814-4*) Random.

***20 Minute Gardener: The Garden of Your Dreams without Giving up Your Life, Job, or Your Sanity.** 1997. audio 14.00 (*0-679-45820-4*) Random.

***20-Minute Gardener: How to Plant & Maintain the Garden of Your Dreams Without Giving up Your Life, Your Job, or Your Sanity.** Marty Asher & Tom Christopher. 1997. 22.00 (*0-614-27247-5*) Random.

Twenty Minute Hour: A Guide to Brief Psychotherapy for the Physican. Pietro Castelnuovo-Tedesco. LC 86-7890. 173p. 1986. pap. text ed. 13.00 (*0-88048-238-9*, 8238) Am Psychiatric.

Twenty-Minute Intermediate Piano Workout. Cimino Publishing Staff. 1992. pap. 19.95 (*0-943748-44-5*) Ekay Music.

Twenty-Minute Low-Fat Gourmet: Mouth-Watering Recipes for Delicious Low-Fat Meals in a Flash. Karen A. Levin. 160p. 1994. pap. 9.95 (*0-8092-3809-8*) Contemp Bks.

20-Minute Menus: Time-Wise Recipes & Strategic Plans for Freshly Cooked Meals Every Day. Marian Burros. 1995. pap. 12.00 (*0-684-80135-3*, Fireside) S&S Trade.

Twenty-Minute One-Dish Gourmet: Delicious, Easy-to-Make Meals That Everyone Will Love. Karen A. Levin. 160p. 1996. pap. 10.95 (*0-8092-3198-0*) Contemp Bks.

20 Minute Piano Workout. Douglas Riva. 1990. pap. 14.95 (*0-943748-30-5*) Ekay Music.

Twenty-Minute Workshops. rev. ed. John F. Parker. (Illus.). (Orig.). 1992. pap. 150.00 incl. disk (*0-9694762-1-3*); disk write for info. (*0-9694762-2-1*) JFP Prodns.

20 Minute Yoga Workouts. American Yoga Association Staff & Alice Christensen. 160p. 1995. pap. 12.95 (*0-345-38845-3*) Ballantine.

20 Minutes to Dinner: Quick, Low-Fat, Low-Calorie Vegetarian Meals. Bryanna C. Grogan. LC 96-40101. (Illus.). 192p. (Orig.). 1997. pap. 12.95 (*1-57067-027-7*) Book Pub Co.

Twenty Months a Prisoner of War. Bernhard Domschke. LC 85-46015. 1987. 33.50 (*0-8386-3286-6*) Fairleigh Dickinson.

Twenty Months in Auschwitz. Pelagia Lewinska. Tr. by Albert Teichner. 1968. 4.95 (*0-8184-0090-0*) Carol Pub Group.

Twenty Months in Captivity: Memoirs of a Union Officer in Confederate Prisons. Bernhard Domschcke. Ed. by Frederic Trautmann. LC 85-46015. 176p. 1987. 26.50 (*0-317-64558-7*) Fairleigh Dickinson.

Twenty More Ideas for Teaching Gifted Kids in the Middle School & High School. Ed. by Joel McIntosh. 115p. 1994. pap. 19.95 (*1-882664-15-9*) Prufrock Pr.

Twenty More Teen Prayer Services. Kevin Regan. LC 94-60339. 112p. (Orig.). 1994. pap. 9.95 (*0-89622-605-0*) Twenty-Third.

Twenty Most Asked Questions about the Amish & Mennonites. rev. ed. Merle Good & Phyllis Good. LC 95-37851. (People's Place Book Ser.: Vol. 1). (Illus.). 96p. 1995. pap. 6.95 (*1-56148-185-8*) Good Bks PA.

Twenty-Mule Team & a Sketch of Its Famous Driver - Borax Bill. (Illus.). 1981. 1.95 (*0-930704-05-3*) Sagebrush Pr.

Twenty Mule Team Days in Death Valley. 7th ed. Harold O. Weight. 1985. pap. 2.95 (*0-912714-00-X*) Calico Pr.

Twenty Myths about National Health Insurance. John C. Goodman & Gerald L. Musgrove. (Illus.). 87p. (C). 1991. pap. 10.00 (*0-943802-69-5*, 166) Natl Ctr Pol.

20 Nam Van Hoc Viet Nam Hai Ngoai 1975-1995, 2 vols., Vol. 1. 800p. (VIE.). 1995. 30.00 (*1-888652-00-4*) Dainam.

20 Nam Van Hoc Viet Nam Hai Ngoai 1975-1995, Vol. 1 & 2. 1585p. (VIE.). 1995. 60.00 (*1-888652-02-0*) Dainam.

20 Nam Van Hoc Viet Nam Hai Ngoai 1975-1995, 2 vols., Vol. 2. 785p. (VIE.). 1995. 30.00 (*1-888652-01-2*) Dainam.

Twenty New Ways to Get the Minister Out of Moneyraising. E. F. Brose. 1976. pap. 2.50 (*0-941500-18-7*) Sharing Co.

29 Bump Street. Alain Vaes. LC 96-3524. (Illus.). 48p. (J). 1996. 16.95 (*1-57036-292-0*) Turner Pub GA.

Twenty-Nine Compensation Plans for Executive Search Professionals, 1994. Ed. by James H. Kennedy. 200p. 1994. ring bd. 149.00 (*0-916654-88-5*) Kennedy Info.

Twenty Nine Fifty Nine Deluxe Prayer Plan. 1976. 10.95 (*0-918403-01-4*) Agape Ministries.

Twenty Nine Fifty Nine Regular Prayer Plan. 1976. 9.95 (*0-918403-00-6*) Agape Ministries.

Twenty-Nine Let's Go: A History of the 29th Infantry Division in World War II. Joseph E. Ewing. (Divisional Ser.: No. 6). (Illus.). 315p. 1979. reprint ed. 49.95 (*0-89839-018-4*) Battery Pr.

Twenty-Nine Mini-Essays. Brainard. 1990. pap. 5.00 (*0-915990-14-8*) Z Pr.

29 Most Common Writing Mistakes & How to Avoid Them. Judy Delton. 96p. (Orig.). 1991. pap. 10.99 (*0-89879-453-6*, Wrtrs Digest Bks) F & W Pubns Inc.

***Twenty-Nine New Lionel Layouts You Can Build.** Peter H. Riddle. (Illus.). 80p. (Orig.). 1997. pap. write for info. (*0-89778-408-1*, 10-8030, Kalmbach Books) Kalmbach.

Twenty-Nine Papers on Statistics & Probability. A. Aksomaitis et al. (Selected Translations in Mathematical Statistics & Probability Ser.: Vol. 9). 315p. 1971. 51.00 (*0-8218-1459-1*, STAPRO/9) Am Math.

Twenty-Nine Questions That Will Energize Your Team & Positively Astonish Your Customers. Darby V. Checketts. (Illus.). 40p. (Orig.). 1993. student ed., pap. 9.95 (*0-9618170-4-6*) Corner Pro-Dev Pr.

Twenty-Nine Reasons Not to Go to Law School. 4th ed. Ralph Warner & Toni Ihara. LC 94-350. 160p. 1996. pap. 9.95 (*0-87337-243-3*) Nolo Pr.

29 Stepping Stones: A Wisewoman Journal. Jacqueline M. Brown & Dixie Connelly. 128p. 1996. pap. 9.95 (*0-9651782-0-X*) Upstream Pr.

Twenty-Nine Tales from the French. Ed. by Alys E. Macklin. Tr. & Intro. by Robert Herrick. LC 72-157785. (Short Story Index Reprint Ser.). 1977. reprint ed. 21.95 (*0-8369-3897-6*) Ayer.

Twenty-Nine Top Hits Flute. 32p. 1994. pap. 4.95 (*0-7935-3257-4*, 00849927) H Leonard.

Twenty-Nine Top Hits for Alto Saxophone. 32p. 1994. pap. 4.95 (*0-7935-3259-0*, 00849929) H Leonard.

Twenty-Nine Top Hits for Clarinet. 32p. 1994. pap. 4.95 (*0-7935-3258-2*, 00849928) H Leonard.

Twenty-Nine Top Hits for Trombone. 32p. 1994. pap. 4.95 (*0-7935-3261-2*, 00849931) H Leonard.

Twenty-Nine Top Hits for Trumpet. 32p. 1994. pap. 4.95 (*0-7935-3260-4*, 00849930) H Leonard.

Twenty-Nine Years in the West Indies & Central Africa. 2nd rev. ed. H. M. Waddell. 1970. reprint ed. 55.00 (*0-7146-1881-0*, BHA-01881, Pub. by F Cass Pubs UK) Intl Spec Bk.

29th Asilomar Conference on Signals, Systems & Computers, 2-vol.set. LC 10-586393. 1600p. 1996. pap. 220.00 (*0-8186-7370-2*, PRO7370) IEEE Comp Soc.

29th Annual Simulation Symposium. Ed. by Taieb F. Znati & Philip A. Wilsey. 276p. 1996. pap. 90.00 (*0-8186-7432-6*, ANSS-29) Soc Computer Sim.

Twenty-Ninth Congress of the European Society for Surgical Research (ESSR), Abstracts, Montpellier, France, May 1994. Ed. by L. Teot. (Journal: European Surgical Research: Vol. 26, Suppl. 1, 1994). xii, 118p. 1994. pap. 36.75 (*3-8055-6002-8*) S Karger.

Twenty-Ninth Infantry Division. Turner Publishing Company Staff. LC 90-71720. 128p. 1991. 48.00 (*1-56311-010-5*) Turner Pub KY.

Twenty-Ninth Intersociety Energy Conversion Engineering Conference, 1994. 2400p. 1994. lib. bdg. write for info. (*0-7803-2060-3*, 94CH3478-5) Inst Electrical.

Twenty-Ninth Virginia Infantry. John P. Alderman. (Virginia Regimental Histories Ser.). (Illus.). 143p. 1989. 19.95 (*0-930919-66-1*) H E Howard.

Twenty of the Plays, 4 Vols. William Shakespeare. Ed. by George Steevens. LC 68-55094. reprint ed. Set. lib. bdg. 195.00 (*0-404-05820-5*) AMS Pr.

21. Len Wein & Billy Tan. (Illus.). 80p. (Orig.). (YA). 1996. pap. 9.95 (*1-887279-29-6*) Image Comics.

Twenty-One Afternoons of Biology: A Laboratory Manual. Stefan O. Schiff. 208p. (C). 1996. pap. text ed., spiral bd. write for info. (*0-8403-9680-5*) Kendall-Hunt.

Twenty-One Americans. Niven Busch. LC 72-99686. (Essay Index Reprint Ser.). 1977. 26.95 (*0-8369-1552-6*) Ayer.

Twenty-One, & Over. William L. Fox. Ed. by Kirk Robertson. (Illus.). 36p. 1982. pap. 3.00 (*0-916918-18-1*); pap. 10.00 (*0-916918-19-X*) Duck Down.

Twenty-One Balloons. William P. Du Bois. (Newbery Library). (Illus.). 184p. (J). (gr. 5-9). 1986. pap. 4.99 (*0-14-032097-0*, Puffin) Puffin Bks.

Twenty-One Balloons. William Pene Du Bois. (Illus.). (J). (gr. 5-9). 1947. pap. 15.99 (*0-670-73441-1*) Viking Child Bks.

Twenty-One Balloons: A Study Guide. Linda Stewart. (Novel-Ties Ser.). 1989. teacher ed., wbk. ed., pap. text ed. 15.95 (*0-88122-053-1*) Lrn Links.

Twenty-One Balloons see Newbery Library Award

Twenty-One Bottles of Beer on the Wall: If One Should Happen to Fall. Joseph P. McCarthy, Sr. (Illus.). 24p. (Orig.). 1989. pap. text ed. write for info. (*0-318-66434-8*) J P McCarthy.

Twenty-One Bridges to the Twenty-First Century: The Future of Pastoral Ministry. Lyle E. Schaller. LC 93-8278. (Ministry for the Third Millennium Ser.). 176p. (Orig.). 1994. pap. 12.95 (*0-687-42664-2*) Abingdon.

21 Carvings for the Day after Christmas. Al Chapman & Trinka Chapman. LC 95-2552. (Books for Woodworkers). (Illus.). 64p. (Orig.). 1995. pap. 12.95 (*0-88740-730-7*) Schiffer.

21st Century Positioning: Proven Selling Precepts. Jack Kinder, Jr. & Garry D. Kinder. 230p. 1996. 25.00 (*0-9652791-9-7*) Kinder Bros.

Twenty-One Cookbook: Recipes & Lore from New York's Fabled Restaurant. Michael Lomonaco & Donna Forsman. LC 95-5983. (Illus.). 320p. 1995. 35.00 (*0-385-47570-5*) Doubleday.

***Twenty-One Days: Another Life Lost to HIV.** Richard A. Krebs. 232p. 1996. 18.00 (*0-8059-3979-2*) Dorrance.

Twenty-One Days to a Trained Dog. Dick Maller & Jeffrey Feinman. 144p. 1979. pap. 8.00 (*0-671-25193-7*, Fireside) S&S Trade.

Twenty-One Days to Unlimited Power with People. James K. Van Fleet. 1992. pap. text ed. 12.95 (*0-13-927724-2*) P-H.

Twenty-One Days to Unlimited Power with People. James K. Van Fleet. 1992. 24.95 (*0-13-948365-9*) P-H.

21 Divorcees: Personal Stories of Divorced Women. A. L. Tarvin. Ed. by C. J. Holzman. 220p. 1995. pap. 12.95 (*0-9643250-2-0*) CJH Ent.

2150 A. D. Thea Alexander. 288p. 1989. mass mkt. 6.50 (*0-446-35649-2*) Warner Bks.

2150 A. D. rev. ed. Thea Alexander. 352p. 1976. pap. 6.95 (*0-913080-04-7*) Macro Bks.

2150 A. D. The Macro Love Story. Thea Alexander. 281p. (Orig.). 1971. pap. 6.95 (*0-913080-03-9*) Macro Bks.

Twenty-One Figures by Robert Graham. (Illus.). 34p. 1990. pap. 25.00 (*0-944680-09-7*) R Miller Gal.

An Asterisk (*) at the beginning of an entry indicates that the title is appearing in BIP for the first time.

21 Great New Zealand Trout Waters. Tony Orman. (Illus.). 136p. 1994. pap. 24.95 (*0-8117-2567-7*) Stackpole.

Twenty-One Great Stories. Ed. by Abraham H. Lass & Norma L. Tasman. (Orig.). 1969. pap. 5.99 (*0-451-62785-7*, Sig) NAL-Dutton.

Twenty One Lessons in Acting: A Workbook for Young Actors. Donald W. Keyes & Dorothy Sands. 112p. 1980. 19.95 (*0-318-16876-6*) World Modeling.

Twenty-One Lessons of Merlyn: Adventures in Druid Magic & Lore. Douglas Monroe. LC 92-20033. (Illus.). 420p. 1992. pap. 12.95 (*0-87542-496-1*) Llewellyn Pubns.

Twenty-One Letters of Ambrose Bierce. Ambrose Bierce. (American Biography Ser.). 33p. 1991. reprint ed. lib. bdg. 59.00 (*0-7812-8019-2*) Rprt Serv.

Twenty-One Magically Successful Attitudes & Insiders Secrets Utilized Daily by America's Most Successful & Wealthy People! Full of Hot Air or Amazing Reality. Richard A. Starr. (Illus.). 200p. (Orig.). 1993. pap. 39.00 (*0-9640217-5-7*) Results Now.

21 New Testament Revelations by Jesus. Daniel G. Samuels. 64p. 1989. pap. 7.50 (*1-887621-07-5*) Found Ch Divine Truth.

***21 Pages/21 Seiten.** Robert Lax. Tr. by Alfred Kuoni from GER. 84p. (Orig.). 1984. pap. text ed. 15.00 (*3-85842-090-5*) Franciscan Inst.

Twenty One Pieces for Violin with Guitar. Heck. 38p. 1989. pap. text ed. 6.95 (*0-87487-295-2*) Summy-Birchard.

Twenty-One Plays for Children. Pelham Moffat. 224p. 1990. 29.50 (*0-86315-094-2*, 1287, Pub. by Floris Books UK) Anthroposophic.

Twenty-One Poems. Jack Lindeman. 1963. pap. 6.00 (*0-685-62609-1*) Atlantis Edns.

Twenty-One Poems. Marco A. Montes De Oca. Ed. by Yvette E. Miller. Tr. by Laura Villasenor. LC 82-20833. (Discoveries Ser.). 74p. (ENG & SPA.). 1982. pap. 9.00 (*0-935480-09-9*) Lat Am Lit Rev Pr.

Twenty-One Poems: Old & New. Naomi Replansky. (Orig.). 1988. pap. 5.95 (*0-9619869-0-5*) Gingko Pr.

21 Reasons Why Christians Should Speak in Other Tongues. Gordon Lindsay. 1971. 1.95 (*0-89985-269-6*) Christ for the Nations.

Twenty-One Rules of This House. rev. ed. Gregg Harris. 52p. (J). 1993. pap. text ed. 12.95 (*0-923463-88-7*) Noble Pub Assocs.

21 Secrets for Irrigation Contractors: How to Turn Your Company Into a Marketing Powerhouse. Robin Tulleners. 146p. (Orig.). 1996. pap. 24.95 (*0-9635096-1-6*) Telsco Indust.

Twenty-One Stories. Graham Greene. 200p. 1981. mass mkt. 5.95 (*0-14-003093-X*, Penguin Bks) Viking Penguin.

Twenty One Stories. Graham Greene. 208p. 1993. pap. 8.95 (*0-14-018534-8*) Viking Penguin.

Twenty-One Sugar Street. Lynn Lauber. 240p. 1994. pap. 10.00 (*0-393-31235-6*) Norton.

Twenty-One Techniques of Silent Killing. Master Hei Long. (Illus.). 104p. 1989. pap. 12.00 (*0-87364-508-1*) Paladin Pr.

Twenty-One Things Shortly to Come to Pass in Israel. Gordon Lindsay. 1964. 1.95 (*0-89985-192-4*) Christ for the Nations.

Twenty-One Unbreakable Laws of Life. Max Anders. 240p. 1996. 16.99 (*0-7852-7611-4*) Nelson.

Twenty One Voices: The Art of Presenting the Performing Arts. Naomi Rhodes. Ed. by Melinda Robins. (Illus.). 324p. (Orig.). 1990. pap. 27.00 (*0-926517-09-0*) Assn Perf Arts Presenters.

Twenty-One Waking Dreams. Roger Weaver. 60p. (Orig.). 1985. pap. 4.95 (*0-916155-01-3*) Trout Creek.

Twenty-One Ways to Create Candy. Jodi Hughey. (Illus.). 50p. (Orig.). 1994. pap. 3.50 (*1-885419-01-5*) Mtn-top Kip.

Twenty-One Who Speak: Powerful Voices of Christianity from the First Through the Twentieth Centuries. Jeffrey J. Richards. 123p. (Orig.). (C). 1992. pap. text ed. 18.65 (*0-88252-154-3*) Paladin Hse.

21 Words for Nurses. Jeanine Young-Mason. 50p. 1995. 12.95 (*0-912083-85-9*); pap. 5.95 (*0-912083-88-3*) Diamond Communications.

***21 Workplace Personalities: How to Say the Right Things to the Right People.** Communication Briefings Editors. 46p. 1996. pap. 12.50 (*1-878604-23-6*) Comn Pubns & Resources.

20 Pageants. Caroline Cooney. 192p. (J). 1995. mass mkt. 3.99 (*0-440-21962-0*) Dell.

Twenty Papers on Analytic Functions & Ordinary Differential Equations. V. G. Boltyanskii et al. (Translations Ser.: Series 2, Vol. 18). 382p. 1961. 42.00 (*0-8218-1718-3*, TRANS2/18) Am Math.

Twenty Papers on Statistics & Probability. M. Arato et al. LC 61-9803. (Selected Translations in Mathematical Statistics & Probability Ser.: Vol. 13). 298p. 1973. 75.00 (*0-8218-1463-X*, STAPRO/13) Am Math.

Twenty Papers on Statistics & Probability. Ch'En Hsi-Ju et al. LC 61-9803. (Selected Translations in Mathematical Statistics & Probability Ser.: Vol. 12). 312p. 1973. 62.00 (*0-8218-1462-1*, STAPRO/12) Am Math.

***20 Party Tricks to Amuse & Amaze Your Friends.** Sophie Blackall & Leith Hillard. LC 96-33497. 1996. 8.95 (*0-8118-1659-1*) Chronicle Bks.

20% Solution: Using Rapid Redesign to Create Tomorrow's Organization Today. John J. Cotter. LC 95-36689. 288p. 1995. text ed. 24.95 (*0-471-13278-0*) Wiley.

Twenty-Percent Solution: Using Rapid Redesign to Create Tomorrow's Organizations - Today. John J. Cotter. 288p. 1995. 25.00 (*0-939246-80-5*) Wiley.

Twenty Piano's Greatest Hits. 1992. pap. 8.95 (*0-943748-52-6*) Ekay Music.

Twenty Plays of the No Theatre. Ed. by Donald Keene. Tr. by Royall Tyler et al. from JPN. LC 74-121556. (Records of Civilizatio: Sources & Studies). 336p. 1970. pap. text ed. 22.50 (*0-231-03455-5*) Col U Pr.

Twenty Plus Two. large type ed. Frank Gruber. 1991. 25.99 (*0-7089-2501-4*) Ulverscroft.

***Twenty Poems.** Scott King. 34p. 1996. 6.00 (*1-890193-00-3*) Red Dragonfly.

Twenty Poems. 3rd ed. John Haines. LC 78-134756. 48p. 1982. pap. 7.50 (*0-87775-045-9*) Unicorn Pr.

Twenty Poems of Anna Akhmatova. Anna Akhmatova. Tr. by Jane Kenyon & Vera S. Dunham from RUS. 54p. 1985. pap. 6.95 (*0-915408-30-9*) Ally Pr.

Twenty Poems of Rolf Jacobsen. Rolf Jacosen. Ed. by Robert Bly. LC 76-50338. 1977. pap. 3.50 (*0-685-88845-2*) Eighties Pr.

Twenty Poems of Viktor Bokov: Bilingual Edition. Edward Jamosky. (Illus.). 67p. (Orig.). (C). 1992. pap. text ed. 10.00 (*0-9632404-0-4*) Rosetta Pr.

20 Poetry Writing Exercises: Getting the Knack. Stephen Dunning & William Stafford. LC 92-36710. 203p. (YA). 1992. 15.95 (*0-8141-1848-8*) NCTE.

20 Prayer Lessons for Children. Phyllis Wezeman & Jude D. Fournier. LC 95-62294. 64p. (Orig.). 1996. pap. 9.95 (*0-89622-689-1*) Twenty-Third.

Twenty Principles for Teaching Excellence: The Teacher's Workbook. M. Walker Buckalew. 155p. 1992. reprint ed. pap. 15.00 (*1-883627-02-8*) Indep Schl Mgmt.

Twenty Problems--Twenty Solutions: The Basic Design Workbook. Raymond Dorn. (Illus.). 88p. (C). 1980. pap. 12.95 (*0-931368-03-0*) Ragan Comm.

Twenty Prose Poems. rev. ed. Charles P. Baudelaire. Tr. & Intro. by Michael Hamburger. 64p. 1988. reprint ed. pap. 6.95 (*0-87286-216-X*) City Lights.

Twenty Questions. Dennis Phillips. 48p. (Orig.). 1992. pap. 5.95 (*0-9629903-0-2*) Jahbone Pr.

Twenty Questions. 3rd ed. Bowie. (C). 1995. pap. text ed. 49.00 (*0-15-502660-7*) HB Coll Pubs.

***Twenty Questions: A Collection of Short & Very Short Stories.** Paul McComas. LC 97-22225. 176p. (Orig.). 1998. pap. 12.95 (*1-56474-238-5*) Fithian Pr.

Twenty Questions: An Introduction to Philosophy. G. Lee Bowie et al. 782p. (C). 1988. pap. text ed. 26.75 (*0-15-592388-9*) HB Coll Pubs.

Twenty Questions: An Introduction to Philosophy. 2nd ed. G. Lee Bowie et al. 750p. (C). 1992. pap. text ed. 26.75 (*0-15-592389-7*) HB Coll Pubs.

Twenty Questions: Answers for the Inquiring Writer. Clay Reynolds. 115p. (Orig.). 1997. pap. 12.95 (*0-9651359-2-6*) Browder Springs. American novelist Clay Reynolds, author of RAGE & FRANKLIN'S CROSSING. Answers the twenty most commonly asked questions from his fiction workshops. By necessity TWENTY QUESTIONS goes beyond quick & easy replies. Reynolds explains: "In many cases, the only short answer is 'it depends.'" In chapter-length depth, Clay Reynolds addresses such tricky questions as "How should I prepare a manuscript?" & "How long should I wait for an editor or agent to respond?" along with "Should I think about self-publishing?" Blending West Texas common sense with national publishing experience, Clay Reynolds gives his insider's knowledge on the big picture as well as the nuts & bolts of this difficult-to-break-into industry. Although the very honest Dr. Reynolds hardly promises that this book will transform you into a best-selling author, the savvy information in TWENTY QUESTIONS will position you, the inquiring writer, to make the most of your luck, ability & ambition. Browder Springs Publishing Company, 214-368-4360, P.O. Box 823521, Dallas, TX 75382. *Publisher Provided Annotation.

Twenty Questions for Scientists. Ian McCrimmon. (C). 1992. text ed. 30.00 (*0-9514698-2-7*, Pub. by Cosmatom UK) St Mut.

Twenty Questions for the Writer. 6th ed. Berke. (C). 1994. pap. text ed. 33.75 (*0-15-500857-9*) HB Coll Pubs.

Twenty Questions for the Writer. 6th ed. Berke. (C). 1994. teacher ed., pap. text ed. 33.75 (*0-15-500858-7*) HB Coll Pubs.

Twenty Questions for the Writer: A Rhetoric with Readings. 5th ed. Jacqueline Berke. 722p. (C). 1990. pap. text ed. 22.75 (*0-15-592405-2*); pap. text ed. 3.00 (*0-15-592406-0*) HB Coll Pubs.

Twenty Reading Comprehension Games. Marla Love. (Makemaster Bk.). (J). (gr. 4-6). 1977. pap. 9.99 (*0-8224-5800-4*) Fearon Teach Aids.

Twenty Reproducible Assessment Instruments. Philip R. Harris. 80p. 1995. ring bd. 99.95 (*0-87425-989-4*) HRD Press.

Twenty Rules for Fasting: An Excerpt from the Philosophy of Fasting. Edward E. Purinton & Chet Day. 26p. 1993. pap. 8.50 (*1-885194-02-1*) Hlth & Beyond.

Twenty Second Annual Estate Planning Institute. (Tax Law & Estate Planning Ser.). 950p. 1991. pap. text ed. 65.00 (*0-685-56938-1*, D4-5222) PLI.

Twenty-Second Annual Institute on Securities Regulation. 340p. 1991. text ed. 85.00 (*0-685-51879-5*, B2-1335) PLI.

Twenty-Second Gear. Mike Sirota. 208p. (Orig.). 1993. mass mkt. 4.99 (*0-441-83242-3*) Ace Bks.

Twenty-Second Man. David L. Hammer. (Illus.). 125p. 1989. 15.95 (*0-938501-08-9*) Wessex.

***XXII Olympiad, Moscow 1980 & Sarajevo 1984.** (Olympic Century Ser.). (Illus.). 1997. 21.95 (*1-888383-20-8*, Wrld Spt) Wld Sport Resch.

Twenty-Second Virginia Cavalry. Jeffrey C. Weaver. (Virginia Regimental Histories Ser.). (Illus.). 116p. 1992. 19.95 (*1-56190-029-X*) H E Howard.

Twenty-Second Virginia Infantry. Terry D. Lowry. (Virginia Regimental Histories Ser.). (Illus.). 216p. 1988. 19.95 (*0-930919-55-6*) H E Howard.

Twenty Sensing (Instruction) Compositions. Kenneth Gaburo. (Illus.). 40p. 1977. 7.25 (*0-939044-11-0*) Lingua Pr.

***Twenty-Seven & a Half Missions in the Fifteenth Air Force.** Douglas Ackley. LC 96-90353. (Orig.). 1996. pap. 8.95 (*0-533-12011-X*) Vantage.

***Twenty-Seven Dollars: Memories of a German Immigrant.** Edwin K. Mahlo. (Memories...Ser.: Vol. 3). (Illus.). 1997. 24.95 (*0-9655013-4-5*) Condor Literary.

***2700 Words of Wisdom.** Random House Value Publishing, Inc. Staff. 1998. 7.99 (*0-517-18837-6*) Random Hse Value.

Twenty-Seven Ingredient Chili Con Carne Murders: A Eugenia Potter Mystery. Nancy Pickard. 288p. 1994. mass mkt. 4.99 (*0-440-21641-9*) Dell.

Twenty Seven Ingredient Chili Con Carne Murders: Based on Characters & a Story Created by Virginia Rich. large type ed. Nancy Pickard. LC 92-46346. 399p. 1993. reprint ed. lib. bdg. 21.95 (*1-56054-636-0*) Thorndike Pr.

Twenty-Seven Masters of Politics, in a Personal Perspective. Raymond Moley. (History - United States Ser.). 276p. 1993. reprint ed. lib. bdg. 79.00 (*0-7812-4812-4*) Rprt Serv.

***27 Star Patchwork Patterns with Plastic Templates.** Rita Weiss. (Illus.). pap. 4.95 (*0-486-25844-0*) Dover.

Twenty-Seven Things the Church Must Go Through Before the Great Tribulation. Peter Popoff. Ed. by Don Tanner. LC 81-68675. (Illus.). 50p. 1981. pap. 1.00 (*0-938544-08-X*) Faith Messenger.

Twenty Seven Wagons Full of Cotton. 3rd ed. Tennessee Williams. LC 53-12488. 1966. pap. 10.95 (*0-8112-0225-9*, NDP217) New Directions.

27th & 4th. Robert Lax. 1994. pap. 9.95 (*1-873012-66-7*, Pub. by Stride Publns UK) New Earth Pr.

27th Annual Immigration & Naturalization Institute. (Litigation & Administrative Practice Course Handbook, 1983-84 Ser.). 576p. 1994. 99.00 (*0-614-17251-9*, H4-5198) PLI.

27th Annual Institute on Securities Regulation, 3 vols., Set. (Corporate Law & Practice Course Handbook, 1985-86 Ser.). Date not set. pap. 249.00 (*0-614-17192-X*, B4-7086) PLI.

Twenty-Seventh Arkansas Confederate Infantry. Desmond W. Allen. LC 87-70001. 101p. 1987. pap. 14.00 (*0-941765-10-5*) Arkansas Res.

27th Asilomar Conference on Signals, Systems, & Computers, 2 vols. LC 89-640232. 1728p. 1994. pap. text ed. 140.00 (*0-8186-4120-7*, 4120) IEEE Comp Soc.

Twenty-Seventh City. Jonathan Franzen. 1990. pap. 8.95 (*0-380-70840-X*) Avon.

Twenty-Seventh City. Jonathan Franzen. 544p. 1988. 19.95 (*0-374-27972-1*) FS&G.

***Twenty-Seventh City.** Jonathan Franzen. 1997. pap. text ed. 14.00 (*0-374-52505-6*, Noonday) FS&G.

***Twenty-Seventh City.** Jonathan Franzen. 1997. pap. 14.00 (*0-614-27277-7*, Noonday) FS&G.

Twenty-Seventh Indiana Volunteer Infantry. E. R. Brown. 1988. 47.00 (*0-934085-04-8*) Amereon Ltd.

Twenty-Seventh Indiana Volunteer Infantry. Edmund R. Brown. 640p. 1985. reprint ed. 40.00 (*0-942211-43-X*) Olde Soldier Bks.

Twenty-Seventh Street Storefronts. Ed. by Douglas Ryhn & David Reed. (Publications in Architecture & Urban Planning: No. R89-5). (Illus.). iii, 52p. (C). 1989. 2.50 (*0-938744-68-2*) U of Wis Ctr Arch-Urban.

Twenty-Seventh Virginia Infantry. Lowell Reidenbaugh. (Virginia Regimental Histories Ser.). (Illus.). 191p. 1993. 19.95 (*1-56190-044-3*) H E Howard.

Twenty-Seventh Wife. Irving Wallace. 1985. pap. 4.50 (*0-451-13761-2*, Sig) NAL-Dutton.

Twenty-Seventh Wife. Irving Wallace. 386p. 1986. reprint ed. lib. bdg. 24.95 (*0-89966-562-4*) Buccaneer Bks.

Twenty Shadows. Stephen Knauth. LC 94-71639. 62p. 1995. pap. 11.95 (*1-884800-01-7*) Four Way Bks.

Twenty Short Pieces For Piano: Sports et Divertissments. Erik Satie. (Illus.). 48p. 1982. reprint ed. pap. 4.95 (*0-486-24365-6*) Dover.

Twenty-Six & One: And Other Stories. Maxim Gorky. LC 72-11935. (Short Story Index Reprint Ser.). 1977. reprint ed. 18.95 (*0-8369-4233-7*) Ayer.

Twenty-six Bars. Kenward Elmslie. LC 85-52100. (Illus.). 165p. (Orig.). 1987. pap. 28.00 (*0-915990-28-8*) Z Pr.

Twenty-Six Composers Teach the Violinist. William Starr. 62p. 1980. pap. text ed. 6.95 (*0-87487-607-9*) Summy-Birchard.

Twenty-Six Contemporary Hits. 160p. 1992. otabind 12.95 (*0-7935-1933-0*, 00311599) H Leonard.

26 Easy Piano Hits of the 90's. (Easy Play Ser.). 136p. 1992. per. 12.95 (*0-7935-1504-1*, 00222550) H Leonard.

Twenty-Six Friends: The Shape of the Alphabet Letters. 2nd ed. Robert F. Blankholm. LC 90-71355. (Illus.). 64p. (J). 1990. reprint ed. pap. 7.95 (*0-933499-02-7*) Stagecoach Rd Pr.

***26 Great Tales of Terror & the Supernatural, 6 vols., Set.** Dover Staff. boxed, pap. 6.00 (*0-486-27891-3*) Dover.

Twenty-Six Italian Songs & Arias: For Medium High Voice. John G. Paton. 152p. (Orig.). (C). 1991. pap. 8.50 (*0-88284-489-X*, 3402) Alfred Pub.

Twenty-Six Italian Songs & Arias: For Medium Low Voice. John G. Paton. 152p. (Orig.). (C). 1991. pap. 8.50 (*0-88284-490-3*, 3403) Alfred Pub.

Twenty-Six Keys to Living with Greater Awareness. J. Donald Walters. 18p. 1989. pap. 1.95 (*0-916124-62-2*) Crystal Clarity.

Twenty-Six Lessons on First Corinthians. Wallace Wartick. (Bible Student Study Guides Ser.). 174p. (Orig.). (C). 1980. pap. 4.99 (*0-89900-168-8*) College Pr Pub.

Twenty-Six Lessons on Revelation, Pt. 1. Paul T. Butler. LC 82-71688. (Bible Student Study Guides Ser.). 134p. 1982. pap. 4.99 (*0-89900-173-4*) College Pr Pub.

Twenty-Six Lessons on Revelation, Pt. 2. Paul T. Butler. LC 82-71688. (Bible Student Study Guides Ser.). 284p. 1982. pap. 6.99 (*0-89900-176-9*) College Pr Pub.

Twenty-Six Lessons on...Acts, Vol. II. Wallace Wartick. (Bible Student Study Guides Ser.). 130p. (C). 1978. pap. 4.99 (*0-89900-154-8*) College Pr Pub.

Twenty-Six Letters & Ninety-Nine Cents. Tana Hoban. LC 86-11993. (Illus.). 32p. (J). (ps-3). 1987. 16.00 (*0-688-06361-6*); lib. bdg. 15.93 (*0-688-06362-4*) Greenwillow.

26 Letters & 99 Cents. Tana Hoban. LC 86-11993. (Illus.). 32p. (J). (ps up). 1995. pap. 4.95 (*0-688-14389-X*, Mulberry) Morrow.

Twenty Six Men & a Girl & Other Stories. Maxim Gorky. LC 74-103510. (Short Story Index Reprint Ser.). 1977. 23.95 (*0-8369-3252-8*) Ayer.

26 Minnesota Writers. Ed. by Monica D. DeGrazia & Emilio DeGrazia. 367p. 1995. pap. 13.95 (*0-931714-67-2*) Nodin Pr.

Twenty-Six Minutes. Robert Hawks. 190p. (Orig.). (YA). (gr. 8-12). 1988. pap. 4.95 (*0-938961-03-9*, Stamp Out Sheep Pr) Sq One Pubs.

Twenty-Six Paintings. Robin Tewes. 1982. pap. 7.00 (*0-914610-32-5*) Hanging Loose.

Twenty-Six Political & Other Poems from the Oxford Ms. Ed. by J. Kail. (EETS, OS Ser.: No. 124). 1974. reprint ed. 45.00 (*0-527-00120-1*) Periodicals Srv.

Twenty-Six Selected Studies for Flute. H. Altes. 100p. 1986. per. 11.95 (*0-7935-5422-5*) H Leonard.

Twenty-Six Species of Oncaeidae (Copepoda: Cyclopoida) from the Southwest Pacific-Antarctic Area: Paper 2 in Biology of the Antarctic Seas IV. Gayle A. Heron. Ed. by David L. Pawson. LC 77-2302. (Antarctic Research Ser.: Vol. 26). 1977. 28.25 (*0-87590-130-1*) Am Geophysical.

Twenty-Six Steps: Controlled Composition for Intermediate & Advanced Language Development. rev. ed. Linda A. Kunz & Helen Munch. 64p. (YA). (gr. 7-12). teacher ed. 4.64 (*0-13-904129-X*) Alemany Pr.

Twenty-Six Steps: Controlled Composition for Intermediate & Advanced Language Development. 2nd rev. ed. Linda A. Kunz & Helen Munch. 64p. (gr. 7-12). pap. text ed. 4.65 (*0-13-933722-9*) Alemany Pr.

Twenty-Six Steps: Controlled Composition for Language Development. 3rd ed. Linda A. Kunz. 64p. 1995. pap. 8.75 (*0-13-458787-1*) P-H.

Twenty-Six Ways to Better Days: A Guide for Improving Your Life from A to Z. Marilyn Kremen. 117p. 1994. pap. 9.95 (*0-9638774-0-2*) Maldaver Pubng.

Twenty-Six Ways to Use Drama in Teaching the Bible. Judy G. Smith. LC 87-33688. (Griggs Educational Resources Ser.). 112p. 1988. pap. 11.95 (*0-687-42745-2*) Abingdon.

26th Annual Advanced Antitrust Workshop. (Corporate Law & Practice Course Handbook, 1985-86 Ser.). Date not set. pap. 99.00 (*0-614-17210-1*, B4-7129) PLI.

26th Annual Child Language Research Forum: Proceedings. Ed. by Eve V. Clark. (CSLI Lecture Notes Ser.). 1995. pap. 22.95 (*0-521-52657-4*) Cambridge U Pr.

26th Annual Estate Planning Institute. (Tax Law & Estate Planning Course Handbook Ser.). Date not set. pap. 99.00 (*0-614-17280-2*, D4-5258) PLI.

26th Annual Institute on Securities Regulation, 3 vols., Set. (Corporate Law & Practice Course Handook, 1994-95 Ser.). 2664p. 1994. pap. 198.00 (*0-614-17172-5*, B4-7068) PLI.

Twenty-Sixth Annual SMPTE Advanced Television & Electronic Imaging Conference: Proceedings. Ed. by Jeffrey Friedman. 248p. 1992. pap. 25.00 (*0-940690-20-9*) Soc Motion Pic & TV Engrs.

Twenty-Sixth Battalion Virginia Infantry. Terry Lowry. (Virginia Regimental Histories Ser.). (Illus.). 167p. 1992. 19.95 (*1-56190-028-1*) H E Howard.

26th Man: One Minor League Pitcher's Pursuit of a Dream. Steve Fireovid & Mark Winegardner. LC 96-18147. (Illus.). xxv, 236p. 1996. pap. 12.95 (*0-8032-6891-2*, Bison Books) U of Nebr Pr.

***XXVI Olympiad, Atlanta 1996.** LC 97-1144. (Olympic Century Ser.). (Illus.). 1997. 21.95 (*1-888383-25-9*, Wrld Spt) Wld Sport Resch.

Twenty-Sixth Virginia Cavalry. Richard L. Armstrong. (Virginia Regimental Histories Ser.). (Illus.). 151p. 1995. 19.95 (*1-56190-074-5*) H E Howard.

Twenty-Sixth Virginia Infantry. Alex L. Wiatt. (Virginia Regimental Histories Ser.). (Illus.). 90p. 1984. 19.95 (*0-930919-08-4*) H E Howard.

Twenty Something & Breast Cancer: Images in Healing. Linda P. McCoy. Ed. by Tomi Keitlen & Marsha Swearenger. LC 95-76050. (Illus.). 160p. (Orig.). 1995. pap. 13.95 (*1-886966-02-8*) In Print.

Twenty Sonatas Bk. 2: Piano Numbers 11-20. F. J. Hayden. 92p. 1986. pap. 9.95 (*0-7935-0770-7*) H Leonard.

Twenty Stories by Turkish Women Writers. (Turkish Studies Book Ser.). 14.95 (*0-614-04311-5*) IN Univ Turkish.

Twenty Studies for the Guitar. Ferdinand Sor. 32p. 1984. pap. 6.95 (*0-7935-0436-8*, 00006363) H Leonard.

***20 Tales of California: A Rare Collection of Western Stories.** Hector Lee. (Illus.). 160p. 1997. 16.95 (*1-877810-63-0*); pap. 9.95 (*1-877810-62-2*) Rayve Prodns.

An Asterisk (*) at the beginning of an entry indicates that the title is appearing in BIP for the first time.

20 Teachable Virtues: Practical Ways to Pass on Lessons of Virtue & Character to Your Children. Ed. by Jerry L. Wyckoff. LC 94-41671. 256p. 1995. pap. 12.00 (0-399-51959-9, Perigee Bks) Berkley Pub.

Twenty Teachers. Ken Macrorie. (Illus.). 272p. 1987. pap. 10.95 (0-19-504982-9) OUP.

Twenty Tellable Tales: Audience Participation for the Beginning Storyteller. Ed. by Margaret R. MacDonald. LC 85-26565. 220p. 1986. 35.00 (0-8242-0719-X); pap. 20.00 (0-8242-0822-6) Wilson.

Twenty Texans, Historic Lives for Young Readers. Betsy Warren. LC 85-13926. (Illus.). 120p. (J). (gr. 3-7). 1985. pap. 8.95 (1-885777-08-6) Hendrick-Long.

Twenty Things I Want My Kids to Know. Hal Urban. LC 92-15389. 1992. pap. 9.99 (0-8407-9153-4) Nelson.

Twenty-Third Annual Advanced Antitrust Workshop. (Corporate Law & Practice Course Handbook, 1985-86 Ser.: Vol. 809). 464p. 1993. 70.00 (0-685-65499-0, B4-7021) PLI.

Twenty-Third Annual Estate Planning Institute. (Tax Law & Estate Planning Course Handbook Ser.: Vol. 216). 1027p. 1992. 70.00 (0-685-65540-7, D4-5234) PLI.

23rd Annual Institute on Employment Law. (Litigation & Administrative Practice Course Handbook, 1983-84 Ser.). 1064p. 1994. pap. 99.00 (0-614-17252-7, H4-5199) PLI.

Twenty-Third Annual Institute on Securities Regulation, 2 vols. (Corporate Law & Practice Ser.). 1511p. 1991. Set. pap. text ed. 30.00 (0-685-56883-0, B4-6978) PLI.

Twenty-Third Annual Institute on Securities Regulation Transcript - The SEC in a New Environment - Securitization - Troubled Companies - Sharehold Activism Enforcement. Ed. by Harvey L. Pitt et al. 350p. 1992. 105.00 (0-685-69368-6) PLI.

Twenty-Third Battalion Virginia Infantry. Johnny L. Scott. (Virginia Regimental Histories Ser.). (Illus.). 94p. 1991. 19.95 (1-56190-024-9) H E Howard.

Twenty-Third Dream. Kathlyn W. Egbert. LC 93-13796. (Southwest Life & Letters Ser.). 216p. (Orig.). 1993. 22.50 (0-87074-352-X); pap. 10.95 (0-87074-360-0) SMU Press.

***Twenty-Third Man.** Peggy Nicholson. 1997. mass mkt. 3.99 (0-373-70740-1, 1-70740-5) Harlequin Bks.

***XXIV Olympiad, Seoul 1988 & Albertville 1992.** (Olympic Century Ser.). (Illus.). 1997. 21.95 (1-888383-22-4, Wrld Spt) Wld Sport Resch.

23rd Psalm. Helen Caswell. 24p. (Orig.). (J). 1995. pap. 5.95 (0-687-01588-X) Abingdon.

Twenty-Third Psalm. Helen Caswell. 1995. pap. 5.95 (0-687-01172-8) Abingdon.

Twenty-Third Psalm. Donald Curtis. 64p. 1992. pap. 5.95 (0-87516-644-X) DeVorss.

***23rd Psalm.** Michael Hague. LC 96-44905. (J). 1997. 19.95 (0-8050-3820-5) H Holt & Co.

23rd Psalm, As Amended by Jesus. Daniel G. Samuels. 1989. pap. 3.50 (1-887621-13-X) Found Ch Divine Truth.

Twenty-Third Psalm for Today. Ed. by Royal V. Carley. LC 73-101450. (Illus.). (J). (gr. 3 up). 1971. 6.95 (0-8378-2001-4) Gibson.

Twenty Third Virginia Infantry. Thomas M. Rankin. (Virginia Regimental Histories Ser.). (Illus.). 141p. 1985. 19.95 (0-930919-14-9) H E Howard.

20,000 Leagues Under the Sea. 1993. pap. 5.25 (0-19-585469-1) OUP.

Twenty Thousand A.D. Ed Sanders. 80p. 1975. pap. 3.50 (0-913028-38-X) North Atlantic.

Twenty-Thousand Baseball Cards under the Sea. Jon Buller & Susan Schade. LC 90-40704. (Step into Reading Bks.). (Illus.). 48p. (Orig.). (J). (gr. 2-3). 1991. pap. 3.99 (0-679-81569-4) Random Bks Yng Read.

Twenty-Thousand Baseball Cards under the Sea. Jon Buller & Susan Schade. LC 90-40704. (Step into Reading Bks.). (Illus.). 48p. (Orig.). (J). (gr. 2-3). 1991. lib. bdg. 11.99 (0-679-91569-9) Random Bks Yng Read.

Twenty Thousand Homeless Men: A Study of Unemployed Men in the Chicago Shelters. Edwin H. Sutherland & Harvey J. Locke. LC 74-137189. (Poverty U. S. A. Historical Record Ser.). 1975. reprint ed. 19.95 (0-405-03127-0) Ayer.

***20,000 Jobs under the Sea: A History of Diving & Underwater Engineering.** Torrance R. Parker. Ed. by Don Walsh. LC 97-92206. (Illus.). 368p. 1997. write for info. (0-9657823-3-6) Sub Sea.

***20,000 Leagues under the Sea.** 1997. mass mkt. write for info. (1-57840-032-5) Acclaim Bks.

20,000 Leagues under the Sea. (J). 9.95 (1-56156-307-2) Kidsbks.

Twenty-Thousand Leagues under the Sea. Illus. by Gino D'Achille. (Step-up Adventures Ser.: No. 6). 96p. (J). (gr. 2-5). 1983. lib. bdg. 4.99 (0-394-95333-9) Random Bks Yng Read.

Twenty-Thousand Leagues under the Sea. Illus. by Gino D'Achille. (Step-up Adventures Ser.: No. 6). 96p. (J). (gr. 2-5). 1983. pap. 3.99 (0-394-85333-4) Random Bks Yng Read.

***20,000 Leagues under the Sea.** Peter Glassman. (J). Date not set. write for info. (0-688-10535-1, Morrow Junior); lib. bdg. write for info. (0-688-10536-X, Morrow Junior) Morrow.

Twenty Thousand Leagues under the Sea. Jules Verne. (Airmont Classics Ser.). (YA). (gr. 8 up). 1964. mass mkt. 3.25 (0-8049-0012-4, CL-12) Airmont.

***Twenty Thousand Leagues under the Sea.** Jules Verne. (Illustrated Classics Collection 1). 64p. 1994. pap. 4.95 (0-7854-0673-5, 40364) Am Guidance.

Twenty Thousand Leagues under the Sea. Jules Verne. 384p. 1985. mass mkt. 3.95 (0-553-21252-4, Bantam Classics) Bantam.

Twenty Thousand Leagues under the Sea. Jules Verne. Ed. by Peter Costello. 294p. 1993. pap. 2.95 (0-460-87354-7, Everyman's Classic Lib) C E Tuttle.

***Twenty Thousand Leagues under the Sea.** Jules Verne. LC 97-25055. 1997. 23.95 (0-7838-8260-2) G K Hall.

Twenty Thousand Leagues under the Sea. Jules Verne. Tr. by Mendor T. Brunetti. 384p. 1969. pap. 2.50 (0-451-51849-7, CE1849, Sig Classics) NAL-Dutton.

Twenty Thousand Leagues under the Sea. Jules Verne. Ed. by Otto Binder. LC 73-75466. (Now Age Illustrated Ser.). (Illus.). 64p. (J). (gr. 5-10). 1973. student ed. 1.25 (0-88301-180-8); pap. 2.95 (0-88301-104-2) Pendulum Pr.

Twenty Thousand Leagues under the Sea. Jules Verne. 1981. pap. 2.50 (0-685-03982-X) PB.

Twenty Thousand Leagues under the Sea. Jules Verne. (Classics Ser.). 1987. pap. 3.99 (0-14-035053-5, Puffin) Puffin Bks.

Twenty Thousand Leagues under the Sea. Jules Verne. LC 79-23887. (Short Classics Ser.). (Illus.). 48p. (J). (gr. 4 up). 1983. lib. bdg. 24.26 (0-8172-1652-9) Raintree Steck-V.

Twenty Thousand Leagues under the Sea. Jules Verne. (American Short Classics Ser.). (J). (gr. 4-7). 1993. pap. 4.95 (0-8114-6846-1) Raintree Steck-V.

Twenty Thousand Leagues under the Sea. Jules Verne. Ed. by Raymond James. LC 89-34248. (Illustrated Classics Ser.). (Illus.). 48p. (J). (gr. 3-6). 1990. pap. 5.95 (0-8167-1880-6); lib. bdg. 14.95 (0-8167-1879-2) Troll Communs.

Twenty Thousand Leagues under the Sea. Jules Verne. 1997. pap. 3.95 (0-89375-412-9) Troll Communs.

Twenty Thousand Leagues under the Sea. Jules Verne. 272p. 1995. pap. 3.99 (0-14-036721-7) Viking Penguin.

Twenty-Thousand Leagues under the Sea. Jules Verne. 24.95 (0-8488-0773-1) Amereon Ltd.

20,000 Leagues under the Sea. Jules Verne. (Illustrated Junior Library). (Illus.). 432p. (YA). 1996. 16.95 (0-448-41307-8, G&D) Putnam Pub Group.

***20,000 Leagues under the Sea.** Jules Verne. 1998. 16.50 (0-679-60253-4, Modern Lib) Random.

20,000 Leagues under the Sea. Jules Verne. 320p. (YA). (gr. 10 up). 1995. mass mkt. 2.99 (0-8125-5092-7) Tor Bks.

20,000 Leagues Under the Sea. Jules Verne. (Signet Classics Ser.). (YA). 1969. mass mkt. 5.95 (0-451-52453-5, Sig Classics) NAL-Dutton.

20,000 Leagues Under the Sea. Jules Verne. 320p. 1995. 2.99 (0-614-09358-9) Tor Bks.

***20,000 Leagues under the Sea.** Jules Verne. Ed. by Malvina Vogel. (Great Illustrated Classics Ser.: Vol. 18). (Illus.). 240p. (J). (gr. 3-6). 1992. 9.95 (0-86611-969-8) Playmore Inc.

Twenty-Thousand Leagues under the Sea. adapted ed. Jules Verne. (Bullseye Step into Classics Ser.). (Illus.). 96p. (J). (gr. 2-6). 1994. pap. 2.99 (0-679-85363-4, Bullseye Bks) Random Bks Yng Read.

Twenty Thousand Leagues under the Sea. rev. ed. Jules Verne. Ed. by Diane F. Grund. (Illustrated Classics Ser.). (Illus.). 128p. (J). 1990. pap. 2.95 (0-942025-85-7) Kidsbks.

***20,000 Leagues under the Sea.** unabridged ed. Jules Verne. 1997. reprint ed. pap. 14.95 (1-57002-053-1) Univ Publng Hse.

Twenty Thousand Leagues under the Sea: The Definitive, Unabridged Edition. Jules Verne. Tr. by Walter J. Miller & Fredrick P. Walter. LC 93-13835. 392p. 1993. pap. 24.95 (0-87021-678-3) Naval Inst Pr.

***Twenty Thousand Leagues under the Sea Readalong.** Jules Verne. (Illustrated Classics Collection 1). 64p. 1994. pap. 14.95 incl. audio (0-7854-0714-6, 40366) Am Guidance.

Twenty Thousand Medical Words. Robert W. Prichard & Robert E. Robinson. 288p. (gr. 13). 1972. pap. text ed. 11.95 (0-07-050874-7) Mosby Yr Bk.

20,001 Names for Baby. Carol M. Wallace. 432p. 1995. reprint ed. pap. 10.00 (0-380-78047-X) Avon.

20,001 Names for Baby: The Best, Most Complete Baby Name Book. Carol M. Wallace. 432p. 1992. reprint ed. mass mkt. 4.99 (0-380-76227-7) Avon.

Twenty Thousand Phrases et Expressions De la Correspondance Commerciale et Privee. rev. ed. C. I. Duttweiler & G. Duttweiler. 422p. (ENG, FRE & GER.). 1987. 70.00 (3-7225-6191-4) IBD Ltd.

***Twenty Thousand Plus Words.** Charles E. Zoubek & G. A. Condon. 288p. 1985. spiral bd. 7.88 (0-07-037463-5) McGraw.

Twenty Thousand Plus Words. 8th ed. Charles E. Zoubek et al. 288p. 1993. text ed. 7.88 (0-07-037462-7) McGraw.

20,000+ Words: Spelled & Divided for Quick Reference. 10th ed. Mary M. Hosler. LC 95-36011. 1995. write for info. (0-02-802158-4); spiral bd. write for info. (0-02-802159-2) Glencoe.

***20,000 Spanish American Pseudonyms.** Daniel C. Scroggins. LC 97-18959. 1997. write for info. (0-8108-3364-6) Scarecrow.

Twenty Thousand Words. 7th large type ed. Louis A. Leslie. 300p. (YA). (gr. 7 up). 1981. reprint ed. 75.50 (0-317-01950-3, J-26190-00) Am Printing Hse.

20000 Thousand Words. 9th ed. Charles E. Zoubek. Date not set. pap. text ed. 10.95 (0-02-820050-0) Macmillan.

Twenty Thousand Words in Spanish, in Twenty Minutes! Charles Mazal-Cami. LC 91-91298. 198p. (Orig.). (C). 1991. pap. 14.95 (0-9630572-2-7) Palabra Pr.

20,000 Words in Spanish, in 20 Minutes! 2nd ed. Ed. by Charles Mazal-Cami. 198p. (Orig.). (C). 1995. pap. 14.95 (0-9630572-3-5) Palabra Pr.

Twenty Thousand Years in Sing Sing. Lewis E. Lawes. LC 74-3830. (Criminal Justice in America Ser.). 1974. reprint ed. 37.95 (0-405-06150-1) Ayer.

Twenty Thousand Years of Fashion: The History of Costume & Personal Adornment. Francois Boucher. (Illus.). 356p. 1987. 49.50 (0-8109-1693-2) Abrams.

Twenty Thousand Years of History: A New Mexico Bibliography. Frances L. Swadesh. 1973. pap. 4.95 (0-913270-14-8) Sunstone Pr.

23 Toughest Letters to Write. Ed. by P-H Editorial Staff. 1990. pap. text ed. 5.95 (0-13-933656-7) P-H.

***23.** Mark Sonnenfeld. 36p. Date not set. pap. 3.00 (1-887379-12-6) M Sonnenfeld.

23 Below. Gerry LaFemina. 56p. (Orig.). 1994. pap. 6.95 (0-9642273-2-0) Back Porch Pr.

Twenty-Three Best Proposals by Executive Search Firms. Ed. by James H. Kennedy. 1985. ring bd. 79.00 (0-916654-35-4) Kennedy Info.

Twenty Three Letters see Selected Works

23 Lithographs 1978-1980. David Hockney. (Illus.). 64p. pap. 8.00 (0-614-13071-9) Tyler Graphics Ltd.

Twenty-Three Principles to Being a Successful Entrepreneur: The Block Buster. Anthony Bragdon. 85p. 1989. pap. 9.95 (0-9622538-1-2) Multi Concepts.

Twenty Three Skidoo. Barbara J. Hughes. Ed. by Philip Sharples. LC 95-95001. (Illus.). 196p. 1995. 9.95 (0-9649846-0-1) Twnty Three Skiddoo.

Twenty-Three Songs. Amy Beach. (Women Composers Ser.). 102p. 1992. reprint ed. lib. bdg. 29.50 (0-306-79717-8) Da Capo.

Twenty Three Strategies to Build Your Empire. Peter Devine. 40p. 1993. 5.95 (0-9645804-0-3) Devine Prod.

***Twenty-Three Wood Engravings.** Alyson MacNeill. 1993. boxed 70.00 (0-907664-16-4, Pub. by Old Stiles UK) St Mut.

Twenty Three Wood Engravings from the Song of the Forest by Colin Mackay. Alyson MacNeill. 1993. 180.00 (0-907664-15-6, Pub. by Old Stiles UK) St Mut.

Twenty-Three Words: A Biography of Francis Bellamy, Author of the Pledge of Allegiance. Margarette S. Miller. LC 79-9478. (Illus.). 400p. 1976. 15.00 (0-686-15626-9) Natl Bellamy.

Twenty Three Years: A Study of the Prophetic Career of Mohammad. Ali Dashti. Tr. by F. R. Bagley from PER. 224p. (Orig.). 1985. 29.95 (0-04-297048-2) Routledge Chapman & Hall.

Twenty Three Years: A Study of the Prophetic Career of Mohammad. Ali Dashti. Tr. by F. R. Bagley from PER. (Bibliotheca Iranica Ser.: No. 2). 246p. (Orig.). (C). 1994. reprint ed. pap. 15.95 (1-56859-029-6) Mazda Pubs.

Twenty-Three Years under a Skylight: or Life & Experiences of a Photographer. H. J. Rodgers. LC 72-9233. (Literature of Photography Ser.). (Illus.). 1973. reprint ed. 21.95 (0-405-04938-2) Ayer.

Twenty Tips for a Stress Free, Pain Free Life. Robert Hochstein. (Illus.). 28p. (Orig.). 1994. pap. 6.95 (1-884667-08-2) Gage Res & Develop.

Twenty Towns: Their Histories, Town Plans, & Architecture. Marian M. Ohman. (Illus.). 260p. 1985. pap. 6.00 (0-933842-04-X) Extension Div.

Twenty Training Workshops for Customer Service, Vol. 1. Terry Gillen. 1992. ring bd. 139.95 (0-87425-193-1) HRD Press.

Twenty Training Workshops for Customer Service, Vol. 2. Sarah Cook. 1993. ring bd. 139.95 (0-87425-226-1) HRD Press.

Twenty Training Workshops for Developing Customer Care. Terry Gillen. 300p. 1990. ring bd. 179.95 (0-566-02897-2, Pub. by Gower UK) Ashgate Pub Co.

Twenty Training Workshops for Developing Managerial Effectiveness, Vol. 1. Mike Lewis & Graham Kelly. 288p. 1986. text ed. 154.95 (0-566-02515-9, Pub. by Gower UK) Ashgate Pub Co.

Twenty Training Workshops for Developing Managerial Effectiveness, Vol. 1. Mike Lewis & Graham Kelly. 1992. ring bd. 139.95 (0-87425-186-9) HRD Press.

Twenty Training Workshops for Developing Managerial Effectiveness, Vol. 2. Graham Kelly & Roger Armstrong. 450p. 1991. ring bd. 179.95 (0-566-02800-X, Pub. by Gower UK) Ashgate Pub Co.

Twenty Training Workshops for Developing Managerial Effectiveness, Vol. 2. Graham Kelly & Roger Armstrong. 1992. ring bd. 139.95 (0-87425-199-0) HRD Press.

Twenty Training Workshops for Developing Sales Effectiveness. Patrick Forsyth & Mark Giflin. 1992. ring bd. 139.95 (0-87425-210-5) HRD Press.

Twenty Training Workshops for Improving Management Performance. Grant Davies. 386p. 1992. 139.95 (0-566-07279-3, Pub. by Gower UK) Ashgate Pub Co.

Twenty Training Workshops for Improving Management Performance. Grant Davies. 1993. ring bd. 139.95 (0-87425-237-7) HRD Press.

Twenty Training Workshops for Listening Skills. Clare Sproston & Glenna E. Sutcliffe. (Illus.). 384p. 1989. ring bd. 169.95 (0-566-02789-5, Pub. by Gower UK) Ashgate Pub Co.

Twenty Training Workshops for Listening Skills. Clare Sproston & Glenna E. Sutcliffe. 1992. ring bd. 139.95 (0-87425-204-0) HRD Press.

Twentieth Century Jews. S. J. Goldsmith. LC 70-101827. (Biography Index Reprint Ser.). 1977. 23.95 (0-8369-8000-X) Ayer.

Twenty-Twenty Business Thinking: A Dictionary of Business Acumen Seed Thoughts. Caldwell Van Roden. 100p. (Orig.). 1987. spiral bd. 6.00 (0-940844-60-5) Wellspring.

Twenty-Twenty Career Planning: How to Get a Job & Keep It. Elizabeth L. Stockton. 32p. 1987. 2.95 (0-89262-056-0) Career Pub.

Twenty-Twenty Is Not Enough. Arthur S. Seiderman & Steven E. Marcus. 256p. 1991. mass mkt. 5.99 (0-449-21991-7, Crest) Fawcett.

Twenty-Twenty Statistics Tutorial Workbook. George W. Bergeman & James P. Scott. 208p. (C). 1986. pap. text ed. 17.50 (0-03-002867-1) SCP.

Twenty-Twenty Vision. Earl Paulk. 1988. pap. 2.50 (0-917595-24-6) Kingdom Pubs.

Twenty-Twenty Vision. Jerry Pournelle. 1976. mass mkt. 0.95 (0-380-01632-X) Avon.

Twenty-Twenty Vision. Jerry Pournelle. 256p. 1980. pap. 2.25 (0-449-24302-8, Crest) Fawcett.

2020 Vision: Biological Diversity: Saving All the Pieces. George D. Davis. (Twenty Twenty Vision: Fulfilling the Promise of the Adirondack Park Ser: Vol. 1). (Illus.). 64p. (Orig.). 1988. pap. 10.00 (0-9621202-0-0) Adirondack Council.

2020 Vision: Fulfilling the Promise of the Adirondack Park, 6 vols., Set. George D. Davis et al. (Illus.). (Orig.). 1988. pap. write for info. (0-9621202-6-X) Adirondack Council.

2020 Vision: Realizing the Recreational Potential of Adirondack Wild Forests. Barbara McMartin. (Twenty Twenty Vision: Fulfilling the Promise of the Adirondack Park Ser: Vol. III). 52p. 1990. pap. 10.00 (0-9621202-2-7) Adirondack Council.

2020 Vision: Transform Your Business Today to Succeed in Tomorrow's Economy. Stan M. Davis & Bill Davidson. (Illus.). 224p. 1992. pap. 12.00 (0-671-77815-3, Fireside) S&S Trade.

Twenty-Twenty Vision in Materials for 2000: National SAMPE Technical Conference, 15th, Marriott Inn, Cincinnati, Ohio, October 4-6, 1983. National SAMPE Technical Conference Staff. LC 83-231242. (National SAMPE Technical Conference Ser.: No. 15). 795p. reprint ed. pap. 180.00 (0-7837-1291-X, 2041432) Bks Demand.

2020 Visions: Health Care Information, Standards, & Technologies. 225p. 1993. 24.95 (0-913595-72-1, 932234) US Pharmacopeia.

Twenty Twenty Visions: Long View of a Changing World. Richard Carlson & Bruce Goldman. (Portable Stanford Bks.). 246p. (Orig.). 1991. pap. 12.95 (0-916318-44-3) Stanford Alumni Assn.

Twenty-Two Biggest Mistakes Managers Make & How to Correct Them. James K. Van Fleet. 1986. 8.95 (0-13-934869-7, Reward) P-H.

Twenty-Two Biggest Mistakes Managers Make & How to Correct Them. James K. Van Fleet. 32p. 1990. wbk. ed., pap. 59.95 incl. audio (0-13-934993-6) P-H.

Twenty-Two Caliber Varmint Rifles. Charles S. Landis. 1991. 32.00 (0-935632-60-3) Wolfe Pub Co.

Twenty-Two Europeans in Japan & Much More. William Corr. 208p. 1991. pap. 9.50 (0-933704-90-9) Dawn Pr.

Twenty-Two Europeans in Japan & Much More. 2nd ed. William Corr. 208p. 1992. pap. 9.50 (0-933704-96-8) Dawn Pr.

Twenty-Two Foreigners In Funny Shorts: The Intelligent Fan's Guide to Soccer & World Cup '94. Pete Davies. LC 93-41274. 1994. pap. 10.00 (0-679-77493-9) Random.

Twenty-Two Gates to the Garden. Steven M. Rosman. LC 93-35944. 224p. (J). 1994. pap. 24.95 (1-56821-124-4) Aronson.

Twenty-Two Gathering Prayers: Praying in Inclusive Language. Joseph J. Arackal. 120p. (Orig.). 1992. pap. 8.95 (1-55612-560-7) Sheed & Ward MO.

Twenty-Two Immutable Laws of Marketing: Violate Them at Your Own Risk! Al Ries & Jack Trout. LC 92-53334. (Illus.). 160p. 1994. reprint ed. pap. 13.00 (0-88730-666-7) Harper Busn.

Twenty-Two Indigo Place. Sandra Brown. 224p. (Orig.). 1991. 5.99 (0-553-29085-1) Bantam.

22 Indigo Place. large type ed. Sandra Brown. 234p. (Orig.). 1992. reprint ed. lib. bdg. 22.95 (1-56054-406-6) Thorndike Pr.

Twenty-Two Leadership Principles. Rulon D. Skinner. LC 92-47123. 1992. 15.98 (0-88290-437-X) Horizon Utah.

***22 Management Secrets to Achieve More with Less.** John H. Zenger. 1997. pap. text ed. 14.95 (0-07-072717-1) McGraw.

Twenty-Two Microcomputer Projects to Build, Use & Learn. Daniel L. Metzger. (Illus.). 272p. 1985. pap. 20.50 (0-13-934712-7) P-H.

Twenty-Two Mistakes the Beginner Always Makes in Mail Order. Jerry Buchanan. 32p. (Orig.). 1984. pap. 12.95 (0-930668-01-4) Towers Club.

22 Non-Negotiable Laws of Wellness: Take Your Health into Your Own Hands to Feel, Think & Live Better Than You Ever Thought Possible. Greg Anderson. LC 94-42770. 176p. 1995. 17.00 (0-06-251235-8) Harper SF.

22 Non-Negotiable Laws of Wellness: Take Your Health into Your Own Hands to Feel, Think & Live Better Than You Ever Thought Possible. Greg Anderson. LC 94-42770. 256p. 1996. pap. 12.00 (0-06-251238-2) Harper SF.

Twenty-Two Papers on Algebra, Number Theory, & Differential Geometry. M. S. Calenko et al. LC 51-5559. (Translations Ser.: Series 2, Vol. 37). 429p. 1964. 47.00 (0-8218-1737-X, TRANS2/37) Am Math.

Twenty-Two Papers on Statistics & Probability. S. A. Aivazjan et al. LC 61-9803. (Selected Translations in Mathematical Statistics & Probability Ser.: Vol. 6). 274p. 1966. 49.00 (0-8218-1456-7, STAPRO/6) Am Math.

Twenty-Two Papers on Statistics & Probability. A. Aleskjavicene et al. LC 61-9803. (Selected Translations in Mathematical Statistics & Probability Ser.: Vol. 11). 279p. 1973. 45.00 (0-8218-1461-3, STAPRO/11) Am Math.

Twenty-Two Quaint Cases in South African Law. G. Colman. 114p. 1980. pap. 15.00 (0-7021-1085-X, Pub. by Juta SA) Gaunt.

An Asterisk (*) at the beginning of an entry indicates that the title is appearing in BIP for the first time.

22 Questions Most Frequently Asked by the Unsaved. Gordon Lindsay. 1970. 2.95 (*0-89985-118-5*) Christ for the Nations.

***22 Ready-to-Use Programs for Women's Groups.** Dorothy MacNeill. 136p. 1996. pap. 9.95 (*0-687-05089-8*) Abingdon.

Twenty-Two Sonnets. Ira Rosenstein. LC 87-102639. 44p. (Orig.). 1986. pap. 4.00 (*0-9605438-3-X*) Starlight Pr.

Twenty-Two Splendid Tales, Vol. I. Pleasant DeSpain. 128p. (J). 1993. pap. 11.95 (*0-87483-340-X*) August Hse.

Twenty-Two Splendid Tales, Vol. II. Pleasant DeSpain. 128p. (J). 1994. pap. 11.95 (*0-87483-341-8*) August Hse.

Twenty-Two Texas Women: Strong, Tough & Independent. Michele Bennett & Barbara Bennett. LC 95-37373. (Illus.). 120p. (J). (gr. 6-9). 1996. 14.95 (*1-57168-062-4*, Eakin Pr) Sunbelt Media.

Twenty-Two Unpublished Letters of Elizabeth Barrett Browning & Robert Browning. Elizabeth Barrett Browning. LC 75-163206. (Studies in Browning: No. 4). 1971. reprint ed. lib. bdg. 75.00 (*0-8383-1313-2*) M S G Haskell Hse.

Twenty-Two Year Cumulative Index to Journal of APCA. 192p. 1973. 35.00 (*0-318-12282-0*) Air & Waste.

Twenty-Two Years: Causes & Consequences of Mental Retardation. Stephen A. Richardson & Helene Koller. (Illus.). 416p. 1996. 45.00 (*0-674-21297-5*) HUP.

20 Under 30: Best Stories by America's New Young Writers. Debra Spark. 288p. 1996. pap. 11.00 (*0-684-81514-1*, Scribners PB Fict) S&S Trade.

Twenty Vision Steps to Wisdom. Jennifer James. 128p. 1997. 14.95 (*1-55704-302-7*) Newmarket.

Twenty Voices: A Pentecost Celebration. James Bowser. 20p. 1991. pap. 5.95 (*1-877871-13-3*, 3520) Ed Ministries.

***Twenty Volume Author Index of Mathematical Reviews, 1940-59, 2 pts.** American Mathematical Society Staff. LC 42-4221. 2201p. 1980. 466.00 (*0-8218-0024-8*, MREVIN 40/59) Am Math.

20 Ways to Calm a Crying Baby. Rebecca B. Barns. (Illus.). 48p. 1994. 5.95 (*1-56566-060-9*) Lickle Pubng.

Twenty Ways to Improve Customer Service. Lloyd Finch. Ed. by Follin Armfield. LC 93-73184. (Quick Read Ser.). (Illus.). 107p. (Orig.). 1994. pap. 13.95 (*1-56052-246-1*) Crisp Pubns.

Twenty Ways to Manage Better. Ed. by Andrew Leigh. 192p. (C). 1984. 60.00 (*0-85292-334-1*) St Mut.

20 Ways to Manage Better. 2nd ed. Andrew Leigh. 192p. 1995. pap. 35.00 (*0-85292-591-3*, Pub. by IPM UK) St Mut.

20 Ways You Lose Money on Your Way to the Stock Market. Scott S. Fraser. 192p. 1996. 19.95 (*0-7931-1789-5*, 5680-3101) Dearborn Trade.

Twenty Word Funny Farm Series, 6 bks., Set. Wendy Kanno. (Illus.). (J). (gr. k-2). 1984. 59.70 (*0-89868-235-5*); pap. 23.70 (*0-89868-154-5*) ARO Pub.

Twenty Word Structure Games. Marla Love. (J). (gr. 2-6). 1983. pap. 13.99 (*0-8224-5802-0*) Fearon Teach Aids.

Twenty-Year Update. FASA Staff. (Illus.). 1989. pap. 12.00 (*1-55560-104-9*, 1639) FASA Corp.

Twenty Years. John C. Harrell. Ed. by Lee Mallory. LC 93-2996. (Illus.). 55p. (Orig.). 1992. pap. 12.95 (*0-9632702-2-2*) Lightning.

***Twenty Years.** John C. Harrell. Ed. by Lee Mallory. (Illus.). 55p. (Orig.). 1992. 19.95 (*0-614-28560-7*) Lightning.

Twenty Years: Harriet FeBland. Georgia Coopersmith. (Illus.). 17p. 1986. pap. 0.75 (*0-942746-12-0*) SUNYP R Gibson.

Twenty Years After. Alexandre Dumas. 1976. 28.95 (*0-8488-1296-4*) Amereon Ltd.

Twenty Years After. Alexandre Dumas. LC 92-38573. 880p. (C). 1993. 13.95 (*0-19-283074-0*) OUP.

Twenty Years After. Alexandre Dumas. 467p. 1981. reprint ed. lib. bdg. 27.95 (*0-89968-229-4*, Lghtyr Pr) Buccaneer Bks.

Twenty Years after the Embargo: The Costs of U. S. Oil Import Dependence & How They Can Be Reduced. Critical Mass Energy Project Staff. (Illus.). 44p. (C). 1993. pap. text ed. 30.00 (*0-937188-43-3*) Pub Citizen Inc.

Twenty Years among Primitive Papuans. William E. Bromilow. LC 75-32800. reprint ed. 41.50 (*0-404-14103-X*) AMS Pr.

Twenty Years among the Twenty Year Olds. James A. Hawes. LC 76-130550. (Select Bibliographies Reprint Ser.). 1977. 20.95 (*0-8369-5523-4*) Ayer.

Twenty Years & Forty Days: Life in a Cuban Prison. Jorge Valls. 125p. 1986. 8.00 (*0-938579-18-5*, Fund Free Exp) Hum Rts Watch.

Twenty Years as Military Attache. Thomas B. Mott. Ed. by Richard H. Kohn. LC 78-22390. (American Military Experience Ser.). 1980. reprint ed. lib. bdg. 25.95 (*0-405-11867-8*) Ayer.

Twenty Years at Hull-House. Jane Addams. pap. 4.50 (*0-451-51955-8*, Sig Classics) NAL-Dutton.

Twenty Years at Hull-House. Jane Addams. (Prairie State Bks.). (Illus.). 328p. 1990. 14.95 (*0-252-06107-1*) U of Ill Pr.

Twenty Years at Hull House. Jane Addams. 1992. reprint ed. lib. bdg. 27.95 (*0-89968-259-6*, Lghtyr Pr) Buccaneer Bks.

***Twenty Years at Pemaquid: Sketches of Its History & Its Remains, Ancient & Modern.** J. Henry Cartland. (Illus.). 224p. 1997. reprint ed. lib. bdg. 29.50 (*0-8328-5890-0*) Higginson Bk Co.

***Twenty Years at Play: A New Play Centre Anthology.** Ed. by Jerry Wasserman. 24.95 (*0-88922-275-4*, Pub. by Talonbooks CN) Genl Dist Srvs.

Twenty Years Before the Mast: With the More Thrilling Scenes & Incidents While Circumnavigating the Globe under the Command of the Late Admiral Charles Wilkes, 1838-1842. Charles Erskine. LC 82-2271. (Illus.). 322p. 1985. reprint ed. pap. 15.95 (*0-87474-415-6*, ERTYP) Smithsonian.

Twenty Years' Crisis, Nineteen Nineteen to Nineteen Thirty Nine: An Introduction to the Study of International Relations. Edward H. Carr. 1964. pap. text ed. 14.00 (*0-06-131122-7*, TB1122, Torch) HarpC.

Twenty Years in Bed with the Same Man: Marriage Poems. Joan Logghe. 118p. (Orig.). 1995. pap. 12.00 (*0-9631909-7-0*) La Alameda Pr.

Twenty Years in Khama Country & Pioneering among the Batuana of Lake Ngami. J. D. Hepburn. (Illus.). 398p. 1970. 47.50 (*0-7146-1870-5*, Pub. by F Cass Pubs UK) Intl Spec Bk.

Twenty Years in Paris: Being Some Recollections of a Literary Life. 2nd ed. Robert H. Sherard. LC 79-8077. (Illus.). reprint ed. 44.50 (*0-404-18386-7*) AMS Pr.

Twenty Years in Review: A Look at Early Childhood Education 1971-1990. James L. Hymes, Jr. LC 91-60160. 438p. (Orig.). 1991. pap. text ed. 10.00 (*0-935989-41-2*, NAEYC #291) Natl Assn Child Ed.

Twenty Years in Tibet. David MacDonald. (C). 1991. reprint ed. 36.00 (*81-85326-50-9*, Pub. by Vintage II) S Asia.

Twenty Years of British Film: 1925-1945. Michael Balcon et al. LC 73-169326. (National Cinema Ser.). (Illus.). 120p. 1975. reprint ed. 16.95 (*0-405-03890-9*) Ayer.

***Twenty Years of Censored News.** Carl Jensen & Project Censored Staff. LC 97-24373. (Illus.). 352p. 1997. 24.95 (*1-888363-51-7*) Seven Stories.

***Twenty Years of Censored News: The News That Didn't Make the News & Why, 1976-1995.** Carl Jensen & Project Censored Staff. (Illus.). 352p. 1997. pap. 16.95 (*1-888363-52-5*) Seven Stories.

Twenty Years of Community Medicine: A Hunterdon Medical Center Symposium. Henderson et al. LC 74-80237. (Illus.). 192p. 1974. 15.00 (*0-914366-01-7*) Columbia Pub.

Twenty Years of French Literary Criticism: FLS, Vingt Ans Apres - A Memorial Volume for Philip A. Wadsworth (1913-1992) Intro. by Freeman G. Henry. 338p. 1994. lib. bdg. 44.95 (*1-883479-02-9*) Summa Pubns.

Twenty Years of Hands. Simon Perchik. 1966. 3.00 (*0-685-01008-2*) Elizabeth Pr.

Twenty Years of I Predict. Lester Sumrall. 64p. (Orig.). 1986. pap. text ed. 1.95 (*0-937580-97-X*) LeSEA Pub Co.

Twenty Years of Jewish-Catholic Relations. James Rudin et al. 336p. (Orig.). 1986. pap. 11.95 (*0-8091-2762-8*) Paulist Pr.

Twenty Years of Nationalization: British Experience. R. Kelf-Cohen. LC 69-13689. 1969. text ed. 29.95 (*0-312-82460-2*) St Martin.

Twenty Years of OSHA (Occupational Safety & Health Administration) Federal Enforcement Data: A Review & Explanation of the Major Trends. Frederic B. Siskind. (Illus.). 50p. (Orig.). (C). 1993. pap. text ed. 30.00 (*0-7881-0003-3*) DIANE Pub.

Twenty Years of Papers on the Presidency. Ed. by Kenneth W. Thompson. (In Commemoration of the Miller Center's 20th Anniversary Ser.: Vol. 1). 1995. pap. text ed. 26.50 (*0-7618-0071-9*); lib. bdg. 54.00 (*0-7618-0070-0*) U Pr of Amer.

Twenty Years of Plasma Physics: Proceedings of the Workshop on Twenty Years of Plasma Physics (1964-1984), Trieste, Italy, September 1984. Ed. by B. McNamara. 376p. 1985. 70.00 (*9971-978-31-8*) World Scientific Pub.

Twenty Years of Psychoanalysis. Ed. by Franz Alexander & Helen Ross. LC 77-93312. (Essay Index Reprint Ser.). 1977. 28.95 (*0-8369-1541-0*) Ayer.

Twenty Years of Public Housing. Robert M. Fisher. LC 75-29075. (Illus.). 303p. 1975. reprint ed. text ed. 69.50 (*0-8371-8411-8*, FIPH, Greenwood Pr) Greenwood.

Twenty Years of Science in the Public Interest: A History of the Congressional Science & Engineering Fellowship Program. Jeffrey K. Stine. LC 94-24801. 1994. write for info. (*0-87168-532-9*) AAAS.

Twenty Years of Stanford Short Stories. Ed. by Wallace Stegner & Richard Scowcroft. xx, 416p. 1966. 49.50 (*0-8047-0394-9*) Stanford U Pr.

Twenty Years of Statutory Reduncdancy Payments in Great Britain. Paul Lewis. (C). 1988. text ed. 39.00 (*0-685-22130-X*, Pub. by Univ Nottingham UK) St Mut.

Twenty Years of Statutory Redundancy Payments in Great Britain... Paul Lewis. (Leeds-Nottingham Occasional Papers in Industrial Relations: No. 8). (C). 1985. 35.00 (*0-900572-63-9*) St Mut.

Twenty Years of the Problem Page, Vol. I. Roy H. Lanier, Sr. 1985. pap. 7.50 (*0-89137-549-X*) Quality Pubns.

Twenty Years of the Problem Page, Vol. II. Roy H. Lanier, Sr. 1985. pap. 7.50 (*0-89137-555-4*) Quality Pubns.

Twenty Years of Tidings. Friend Stuart. 180p. 1986. vinyl bd. 29.95 (*0-912132-10-8*) Dominion Pr.

Twenty Years of Toxicology. Conning. (Food & Chemical Toxicology Ser.). 1982. pap. 48.00 (*0-08-028856-1*, Pergamon Pr) Elsevier.

***Twenty Years On.** John Swannell. (Illus.). 232p. 1997. 65.00 (*1-85793-917-4*, Pub. by Pavilion UK) Trafalgar.

Twenty Years On: New Federal & State Roles to Achieve Equity in Education. Cynthia Brown & Jill Reid. 130p. 1987. 14.95 (*0-89788-099-4*) CPA Washington.

Twenty Years on Broadway, & the Years It Took to Get There. George M. Cohan. (American Biography Ser.). 264p. 1991. reprint ed. lib. bdg. 69.00 (*0-7812-8086-9*) Rprt Serv.

Twenty Years on Broadway & the Years It Took to Get There: The True Story of a Trouper's Life from the Cradle to the Closed Shop. George M. Cohan. LC 76-138106. (Illus.). 264p. 1971. reprint ed. text ed. 38.50 (*0-8371-5682-3*, COTY) Greenwood.

Twenty Years on Wheels. Andy Kirk. 156p. 1989. 24.95 (*0-472-10134-X*) U of Mich Pr.

Twenty Years Too Soon: Prelude to Major-League Integrated Baseball. Quincy Trouppe. LC 95-7522. 158p. 1995. pap. 14.95 (*1-883982-07-3*) MO Hist Soc.

Twentysomething. 1993. 12.95 (*0-942361-62-8*) MasterMedia Pub.

Twentysomething: A Self-Help Guide to Making It Through Your Twenties. Steven Gibb. LC 91-50625. 176p. (Orig.). 1991. pap. 10.95 (*1-879360-03-9*) Noble Pr.

Twentysomething: Managing & Motivating Today's New Work Force. Lawrence J. Bradford & Claire Raines. LC 91-60814. 240p. 1992. 22.95 (*0-942361-35-0*) MasterMedia Pub.

Twentysomething American Dream: A Cross-Country Quest for a Generation. Michael L. Cohen. 320p. 1994. pap. 10.95 (*0-452-27230-0*) NAL-Dutton.

Twentysomething Guide to Creative Self-Employment: Making Money While Keeping Your Freedom. Jeff Porten. 288p. 1996. per. 14.95 (*0-7615-0445-1*) Prima Pub.

20/20 Vision: How to Create a Successful Church with Lay Pastors & Cell Groups. Dale E. Galloway. 160p. 1986. 13.95 (*1-885605-00-5*) Scott-Twnty-Twnty.

TWI Basic Course. (Hippocrene Basic Course Guides Ser.). 225p. 1995. pap. 16.95 (*0-7818-0394-2*) Hippocrene Bks.

Twi Basic Course. Foreign Service Institute Staff. 240p. 1963. pap. text ed. 185.00 incl. audio (*0-88432-111-8*, AFTW01) Audio-Forum.

TWI English, English TWI Concise Dictionary. Paul F. Kotey. 250p. (Orig.). (ENG & TWI.). 1998. pap. 12.95 (*0-7818-0264-4*) Hippocrene Bks.

***Twice Vol. I: Feet.** Laura Jacobs et al. Ed. by J. Abbott Miller. (Illus.). 90p. (Orig.). 1997. pap. 18.00 (*0-9657481-0-3*) Dance Ink.

Twice a Champion: The Toney Lineberry Story. 2nd ed. Tommy Lineberry. Ed. by Frederick Talbolt. 200p. 1988. 14.95 (*0-685-23257-3*); pap. 8.95 (*0-685-23258-1*) T Lineberry.

Twice a Father. Moyra Tarling. (Romance Ser.). 1996. mass mkt. 3.25 (*0-373-19156-1*, 1-19156-8) Silhouette.

Twice a Hero. Harold L. Crist. 112p. (Orig.). (YA). 1990. pap. 5.95 (*0-9621743-1-9*) H L Crist.

***Twice a Hero.** Susan Krinard. 1997. mass mkt. 5.99 (*0-553-56918-X*, Fanfare) Bantam.

Twice a Victim. large type ed. Cyril A. Joyce. (Linford Mystery Library). 288p. 1992. pap. 15.99 (*0-7089-7228-4*) Ulverscroft.

Twice Across the Plains to California 1849-1856. William J. Pleasants. 74p. 1981. 14.95 (*0-87770-259-4*) Ye Galleon.

***Twice As Far.** Kevin Henkes. (J). Date not set. write for info. (*0-688-05195-2*) Greenwillow.

***Twice As Far.** Kevin Henkes. (J). Date not set. lib. bdg. write for info. (*0-688-05196-0*) Morrow.

***Twice As Funny...Twins: A Book of Cartoons.** David Lochner. (Illus.). (Orig.). 1996. pap. 10.95 (*0-9655442-1-4*) Busn Word.

***Twice As Less.** Eleanor Orr. Date not set. pap. 12.95 (*0-393-31741-2*) Norton.

Twice As Less: Black English & the Performance of Black Students in Mathematics & Science. Eleanor W. Orr. LC 87-5758. 1987. 15.95 (*0-393-02392-3*) Norton.

Twice As Less: Black English & the Performance of Black Students in Mathematics & Science. Eleanor W. Orr. LC 87-5758. 1989. pap. 8.95 (*0-393-30585-6*) Norton.

Twice Blessed. Kathryn T. Windham. 160p. 1995. 20.00 (*1-881320-47-2*, Black Belt) Black Belt Comm.

Twice Blessed: On Being Lesbian or Gay & Jewish. Ed. by Christie Balka & Andy Rose. LC 89-42598. 320p. 1991. pap. 16.00 (*0-8070-7909-X*) Beacon Pr.

Twice-Born Heretic: MN Roy & Comintern. Samaren Roy. 1986. 27.50 (*0-8364-1576-0*, KL Mukhopadhyay) S Asia.

Twice-Born Men: A Clinic in Regeneration. Harold Begbie. LC 94-79790. 280p. 1995. 14.95 (*0-9605642-9-2*) Messengers Hope.

***Twice Burned.** Pamela Burford. (Double Dare Ser.). 1997. mass mkt. 3.75 (*0-373-22420-6*, 1-22420-3) Harlequin Bks.

Twice Burned. Kit Craig. 352p. 1995. pap. text ed. 5.99 (*0-425-14877-7*) Berkley Pub.

***Twice Burned.** Kit Craig. 286p. 3.98 (*0-8317-7063-5*) Smithmark.

Twice Burned No. 4: Freddy Krueger's Tales of Terror, 6. David Bergantino & Bruce Richards. (New Elm Street Novel Ser.: No. 4). (Orig.). (YA). (gr. 6 up). 1995. 3.99 (*0-8125-5192-3*) Tor Bks.

Twice Chosen. Charles Hoffman. LC 95-68114. 148p. (Orig.). 1995. pap. 6.95 (*1-882972-56-2*) Queenship Pub.

Twice Christmas. Christopher Coast. LC 90-83942. 52p. (Orig.). 1990. pap. 2.95 (*0-9627067-0-1*) Bear Flag CA.

Twice Dead. Paul Bishop. 336p. (Orig.). 1996. mass mkt. 5.50 (*0-380-77862-9*) Avon.

***Twice Golden: The Story of Michael Johnson & His Triumphs in Atlanta.** Mark Ribowsky. LC 97-22321. 1997. 19.95 (*1-55972-425-0*, Birch Ln Pr) Carol Pub Group.

Twice in a Blue Moon. Karen Morrell. 1993. 17.95 (*0-8034-9021-6*) Bouregy.

Twice in a Blue Moon. large type ed. Patricia Moyes. LC 93-47393. 1994. lib. bdg. 20.95 (*0-7862-0168-1*) Thorndike Pr.

Twice in a Lifetime. M. I. Hudson. (C). 1989. pap. 30.00 (*0-7223-1583-X*, Pub. by A H S Ltd UK) St Mut.

Twice in a Lifetime. Bonnie J. Perry. 320p. 1996. mass mkt. 4.99 (*0-7860-0213-1*, Pinncle Kensgtn) Kensgtn Pub Corp.

Twice in a Lifetime. large type ed. Pat Dalton. LC 96-5902. 1996. pap. 20.00 (*0-7838-1729-0*, GK Hall) Thorndike Pr.

Twice in a Lifetime. large type ed. Rebecca Flanders. 368p. 1984. 25.99 (*0-7089-1158-7*) Ulverscroft.

***Twice in a Lifetime, Bk. 33.** B. J. James. (Born in the U. S. A. Ser.). 1997. 4.50 (*0-373-47183-1*, 1-47183-8) Harlequin Bks.

Twice Loved. Rita C. Estrada. (Temptation Ser.: No. 361). 1991. mass mkt. 2.99 (*0-373-25461-X*) Harlequin Bks.

Twice Loved. LaVyrle Spencer. 416p. 1986. mass mkt. 6.50 (*0-515-09065-4*) Jove Pubns.

Twice Loved. large type ed. LaVyrle Spencer. LC 92-27194. (General Ser.). 513p. 1993. 23.95 (*0-8161-5299-3*) G K Hall.

Twice Migrants: East African Sikh Settlers in Britain. Parminder Bhachu. 256p. 1986. text ed. 35.00 (*0-422-78910-0*, 9773, Pub. by Tavistock UK) Routledge Chapman & Hall.

Twice Neokoros: Ephesus, Asia, & the Cult of the Flavian Imperial Family. Steven J. Friesen. LC 92-31027. (Religions in the Graeco-Roman World Ser.: No. 116). (Illus.). 237p. 1993. 96.50 (*90-04-09689-2*) E J Brill.

Twice Out of Sight. Roscoe E. Plowman. 122p. (Orig.). 1982. pap. 5.00 (*0-935680-11-X*) Kentucke Imprints.

Twice Raped. Audrey Savage. Ed. by Pat Sexton et al. LC 89-91663. (Illus.). 264p. (Orig.). 1989. pap. 11.95 (*0-929698-01-0*) Bk Weaver Pub.

Twice Real. Silvia Sanza. (Ninety's Title Ser.). 176p. (Orig.). 1993. pap. 12.99 (*1-85242-264-5*) Serpents Tail.

Twice Removed: The Experience of German-American Women Writers in the 19th Century. Dorothea D. Stuecher. LC 89-13753. (New German-American Studies - Neue Deutsch-Amerikanische Studien: Vol. 1). 230p. (C). 1990. text ed. 56.95 (*0-8204-1162-0*) P Lang Pubng.

***Twice Shy.** 1997. mass mkt. 1.78 (*0-8217-5777-6*) Viking Penguin.

Twice Shy. Dick Francis. 352p. 1987. mass mkt. 5.95 (*0-449-21314-5*, Crest) Fawcett.

Twice Sold, Twice Ransomed. L. P. Ray. LC 76-173613. (Black Heritage Library Collection). 1977. reprint ed. 28.95 (*0-8369-8905-8*) Ayer.

Twice Taken. Susan B. Pfeffer. 176p. (YA). (gr. 7 up). 1996. mass mkt. 3.99 (*0-440-22004-1*, LLL BDD) BDD Bks Young Read.

Twice Taken. Susan B. Pfeffer. LC 93-39010. 208p. (J). 1994. 14.95 (*0-385-32033-7*) Delacorte.

***Twice Tempted.** Bill Manchee. LC 96-90135. 1996. 17.95 (*0-533-11898-0*) Vantage.

***Twice the Spice.** Patricia Ryan. 1997. mass mkt. 3.50 (*0-373-25731-7*, 1-25731-0) Harlequin Bks.

Twice the Work of Free Labor: The Political Economy of Convict Labor in the New South. Lichtenstein. 240p. (C). 1995. text ed. 65.00 (*1-85984-991-1*, C0513, Pub. by Vrso UK); pap. text ed. 19.00 (*1-85984-086-8*, C0514, Pub. by Vrso UK) Norton.

Twice-Told Proverbs & the Composition of the Book of Proverbs. Daniel C. Snell. LC 92-46623. xiv, 146p. 1993. 39.50 (*0-931464-66-8*) Eisenbrauns.

Twice Told Tales. Nathaniel Hawthorne. (Airmont Classics Ser.). (J). (gr. 9 up). 1965. mass mkt. 2.50 (*0-8049-0066-3*, CL-66) Airmont.

Twice-Told Tales. Nathaniel Hawthorne. Ed. by William Charvat et al. LC 73-5363. (Centenary Edition of the Works of Nathaniel Hawthorne: Vol. 9). 649p. 1974. 75.00 (*0-8142-0202-0*) Ohio St U Pr.

Twice Told Tales. Daniel Stern. Ed. by Jay McCulloch. 160p. 1989. 17.95 (*0-945167-13-X*) British Amer Pub.

Twice Told Tales. Nathaniel Hawthorne. 225p. 1990. reprint ed. lib. bdg. 21.95 (*0-89966-738-4*) Buccaneer Bks.

Twice Told Tales. Nathaniel Hawthorne. (Notable American Authors Ser.). 1992. reprint ed. lib. bdg. 75.00 (*0-7812-3042-X*) Rprt Serv.

Twice Told Tales: A Masonic Reader. L. C. Helms. LC 85-61083. (Illus.). viii, 111p. 1985. pap. 7.95 (*0-88053-081-2*, M-082) Macoy Pub.

Twice-Told Tales: Brunetto Latino & Dante Alighieri. Julia B. Holloway. LC 92-18571. 550p. 1992. 59.95 (*0-8204-1954-0*) P Lang Pubng.

Twice Told Tales: Stories. Daniel Stern. LC 95-7872. (Rice Modern Masters Ser.). 1995. pap. 11.95 (*0-89263-336-0*) Tex A&M Univ Pr.

Twice Told Tales: The Families of Irvine Hockaday Dunham & Martin Baskett Dunham in Callaway 1870-1930. John H. Dunham. (Illus.). 132p. 1991. lib. bdg. 10.00 (*0-9627098-8-3*) B Wyman.

***Twice-Told Tales of the Blue Ridge & Great Smokies, Vol. 1.** Mead Parce. Ed. by Alice Lawson. (Illus.). 114p. 1995. reprint ed. pap. 7.95 (*0-9657461-0-0*) Harmon Den.

Twice Twenty-Two. Ray Bradbury. 1994. lib. bdg. 19.95 (*1-56849-430-0*) Buccaneer Bks.

Twice upon a Time. Philip Bernardi & Diane Havens. LC 95-15994. (Illus.). 24p. (J). 1995. pap. 6.00 (*0-88734-425-9*) Players Pr.

Twice upon a Time. Judy Sierra & Robert Kaminski. 242p. 1989. 35.00 (*0-8242-0775-0*) Wilson.

Twice upon a Time: Stories. Daniel Stern. LC 95-32712. (Rice Modern Masters Ser.). (C). 1996. reprint ed. pap. 11.95 (*0-89263-337-9*) Tex A&M Univ Pr.

Twice upon Time. Nina Beaumont. (Historical Ser.). 1996. mass mkt. 4.50 (*0-373-28903-0*, 1-28903-2) Harlequin Bks.

Twick or Tweet. Patricia Lakin. (J). 1996. 3.25 (*0-679-87258-2*) Random.

Twickenham Edition of the Poems of Alexander Pope, 12 vols., Set. Ed. by John Butt. 5796p. (C). (gr. 13). 1993. boxed, text ed. 1,395.00 (*0-415-10500-5*, B3761) Routledge.

Twiddle Twins' Haunted House. Howard Goldsmith. LC 96-15258. (Illus.). (J). 1996. pap. write for info. (*1-57255-222-0*) Mondo Pubng.

***Twiddle Twins' Music Box Mystery.** Howard Goldsmith. LC 96-38005. 1997. pap. write for info. (*1-57255-475-4*) Mondo Pubng.

Twiddledum Twaddledum. Peter Spielberg. LC 74-77779. 196p. 1974. 15.95 (*0-914590-04-9*); pap. 5.95 (*0-914590-05-7*) Fiction Coll.

Twiddy House. Dorothy P. Hoover. 160p. 1994. 12.95 (*1-57087-063-2*) Prof Pr NC.

Twig & the Mouse, Bk. 2. Ralph F. Parkison. Ed. by Marion O. Withrow. (Illus.). 17p. (Orig.). (J). (gr. 2-6). 1988. pap. 4.25 (*0-929949-01-3*) Little Wood Bks.

Twig from the Calvert Tree. Margaret Jamieson. LC 91-65118. (Illus.). 304p. 1991. text ed. 40.00 (*0-936029-26-9*) Western Bk Journ.

Twig Is Bent. Troy W. Parsons. (Illus.). 230p. (Orig.). 1994. pap. 13.95 (*0-9637109-1-5*) Fayette Pub.

***Twig of Revelation.** Colle H. Van. 1997. pap. text ed. 10. 95 (*1-85398-101-X*, Pub. by Ashgrove UK) Words Distrib.

Twiggs & Cinnamon: Little People of the Ozark Mountains. Gary Hutchison. 148p. (Orig.). 1996. pap. 8.95 (*1-885631-18-9*) G F Hutchison.

Twiggs County Georgia Abstracts: Records of a Burned County. Bess V. Clark. 1988. 25.00 (*0-9619864-0-9*) B V Clark.

Twiggy: Story of a Greyhound. Ginny A. Folkman. 40p. (J). (gr. 4-6). 1995. pap. 10.95 (*0-9644470-0-2*) Emerald Press.

Twiggy: The Abandoned, Diabetic Dog. Intro. by Henrietta Howard-Moineau. (Illus.). 73p. (Orig.). (J). (gr. 4 up). 1982. pap. 5.00 (*0-318-01113-1*) Hampshire Pr.

Twigs: Poems by Mildred P. Richards. Mildred P. Richards. (Illus.). 53p. (Orig.). 1992. pap. 5.00 (*0-9637521-0-3*) Arlington Pl.

Twigs: The Absorbing World of Church Education. Gaylord Noyce. 1991. pap. 9.50 (*1-877871-28-1*, 4228) Ed Ministries.

***Twigs Bent under God: New & Selected Poems.** Illus. by John C. Ransom. 120p. 1996. 8.95 (*0-9636373-2-0*) OverBoard Pr.

***Twigs Bent under God: New & Selected Poems.** Illus. by John C. Ransom. 120p. 1996. pap. 19.95 (*0-9636373-3-9*) OverBoard Pr.

Twigs for an Eagle's Nest see In Great Decades

Twigs from My Tree. Edith N. Chase. LC 83-22408. (Illus.). 79p. (Orig.). 1984. pap. 8.95 (*0-87233-074-5*) Bauhan.

Twigs to Flowers: Carving Flowers from Twigs & Shavings for Fun & Profit. Orville Stickney. LC 88-50016. (Illus.). 48p. (Orig.). 1988. pap. 8.95 (*0-945129-05-X*) Wilderness Creations.

Twilight. Kit Gardner. (Historical Ser.). 1995. mass mkt. 4.50 (*0-373-28874-3*, 1-28874-5) Harlequin Bks.

Twilight. Avner Gold. Ed. by Y. Y. Reinman. LC 85-72404. (Ruach Ami Ser.: No. 4). (Illus.). 128p. (J). (gr. 7-11). 1985. 9.95 (*0-935063-11-0*); pap. 7.95 (*0-935063-03-X*) CIS Comm.

Twilight. Timothy McNeal. (Orig.). 1996. pap. write for info. (*1-57553-136-4*) Watermrk Pr.

Twilight. Moni Moulik. 1976. text ed. 6.75 (*0-89253-830-9*) Ind-US Inc.

Twilight. Nancy Pickard. Ed. by Linda Marrow. LC 95-30614. 320p. 1995. 22.00 (*0-671-78271-1*, PB Hardcover) PB.

Twilight. Nancy Pickard. 1996. mass mkt. 5.99 (*0-671-78290-8*) PB.

Twilight. Don L. Richards. 289p. (Orig.). 1992. pap. 10.95 (*0-9632478-0-8*) R T Partners.

Twilight. Elie Wiesel. Tr. by Marion Wiesel from FRE. LC 95-22710. 1995. pap. 12.00 (*0-8052-1058-X*) Schocken.

Twilight. Elie Wiesel. 224p. 1989. pap. 9.95 (*0-446-39066-6*) Warner Bks.

***Twilight.** Sherryl Woods. 304p. 1997. mass mkt. 5.50 (*0-8217-5805-5*, Zebra Kensgtn) Kensgtn Pub Corp.

Twilight. large type ed. Nancy Pickard. (Americana Ser.). 522p. 1996. 24.95 (*0-7862-0552-0*) Thorndike Pr.

Twilight: A Study in Atmospheric Optics. Georgii V. Rozenberg. LC 65-11345. 368p. reprint ed. pap. 104.90 (*0-317-27113-X*, 2024702) Bks Demand.

Twilight: Daily Reading with the Bible. Andrew Kuyvenhoven. LC 94-33505. 372p. 1994. pap. 13.75 (*1-56212-071-9*, 1700-9010) CRC Pubns.

Twilight: Two Thousand. Frank A. Chadwick. (Illus.). 280p. (Orig.). (YA). 1990. pap. 20.00 (*1-55878-070-X*) Game Designers.

Twilight - Los Angeles, 1992: On the Road, a Search for American Character. Anna D. Smith. LC 93-38298. 320p. 1994. pap. 14.00 (*0-385-47376-1*, Anchor NY) Doubleday.

Twilight & Dawn. Kathryn Kuhlman. 94p. (Orig.). 1994. pap. 3.45 (*0-88270-682-9*) Bridge-Logos.

Twilight & Other Stories. Shulamith Hareven. Tr. by Hillel Halkin et al. from HEB. LC 91-9959. 144p. (Orig.). 1992. pap. 10.95 (*1-56279-012-9*) Mercury Hse Inc.

Twilight at Mac's Place. Ross Thomas. 352p. 1990. 75.00 (*0-89296-434-0*) Mysterious Pr.

Twilight at Mac's Place. Ross Thomas. 352p. 1991. mass mkt. 5.99 (*0-446-40059-9*, Mysterious Paperbk) Warner Bks.

Twilight at Mac's Place. large type ed. Ross Thomas. 547p. 1991. lib. bdg. 14.95 (*1-56054-986-6*) Thorndike Pr.

***Twilight at the Equator: A Novel.** Jaime Manrique. LC 96-43422. 1997. 23.95 (*0-571-19901-1*) Faber & Faber.

Twilight at the Well of Souls: The Legacy of Nathan Brazil. Jack L. Chalker. (Saga of the Well World Ser.: Vol. 5). 320p. 1986. mass mkt. 5.99 (*0-345-34408-1*, Del Rey) Ballantine.

***Twilight Beach.** Terry Dowling. (Greatwinter Ser.). 270p. (Orig.). pap. 10.00 (*1-875346-08-2*, Pub. by Aphelion AT) Firebird Dist.

Twilight Child. Warren Adler. 1989. pap. 3.95 (*0-317-02803-0*) NAL-Dutton.

Twilight Children. James Axler. 1994. mass mkt. 4.99 (*0-373-62521-9*, 1-62521-9) Harlequin Bks.

***Twilight Comes Twice.** Ralph J. Fletcher. LC 96-50888. (Illus.). (J). 1997. 15.00 (*0-395-84826-1*, Clarion Bks) HM.

Twilight Country. Knut Faldbakken. Tr. by Joan Tate from NOR. (UNESCO Collection of Representative Works, Series of Translations from the Literature of the Union of Soviet Socialist Republics). 224p. 1993. 29.00 (*0-7026-0855-6*, Pub. by P Owen Ltd UK) Dufour.

Twilight Country. Knut Faldbakken. Tr. by Joan Tate from NOR. 216p. 9300. 29.00 (*0-7206-0885-6*, Pub. by P Owen Ltd UK) Dufour.

***Twilight Country.** Knut Faldbakken. 240p. 1993. 11.95 (*1-55082-077-X*, Pub. by Quarry Pr CN) LPC InBook.

Twilight Dwellers: Ghosts, Ghouls & Goblins of Colorado. MaryJoy Martin. LC 85-16716. (Illus.). 167p. (Orig.). 1985. pap. 13.95 (*0-87108-686-7*) Pruett.

Twilight Eyes. Dean R. Koontz. 464p. 1987. mass mkt. 7.50 (*0-425-10065-0*) Berkley Pub.

***Twilight for Sabers.** William West. 1997. mass mkt. 4.99 (*1-55197-298-0*, Pub. by Comnwlth Pub CN) Partners Pubs Grp.

Twilight for the Gods. Ernest K. Gann. 1976. 23.95 (*0-8488-0497-X*) Amereon Ltd.

Twilight for the Gods. large type ed. Ernest K. Gann. 1977. 25.99 (*0-7089-0071-2*) Ulverscroft.

Twilight Gallery. Karen S. Powell. (Illus.). 72p. (Orig.). 1996. pap. 12.95 (*0-9651406-0-1*) Silverhawke.

Twilight Gate. Rhondi V. Salsitz. LC 92-22040. (Illus.). 192p. (YA). (gr. 7 up). 1993. 16.95 (*0-8027-8213-2*) Walker & Co.

***Twilight Glow.** Jimmye Hill. 124p. (Orig.). 1997. mass mkt. 4.99 (*1-55237-166-2*, Pub. by Comnwlth Pub CN) Partners Pubs Grp.

Twilight Hunters: Wolves, Coyotes, & Foxes. Gary Turbak. LC 87-42821. (Western Horizons Bks.). (Illus.). 112p. (Orig.). 1987. pap. 15.95 (*0-87358-453-8*) Northland AZ.

Twilight in Dehli. Ahmed Ali. LC 93-45363. 224p. (Orig.). 1994. pap. 12.95 (*0-8112-1267-X*, NDP782) New Directions.

Twilight in Delhi. 2nd ed. Ahmed Ali. 290p. 1974. pap. 3.50 (*0-88253-281-2*) Ind-US Inc.

***Twilight in Grace Falls.** Natalie Honeycutt. LC 96-42388. 192p. (J). (gr. 6-9). 1997. 16.95 (*0-531-30007-2*); lib. bdg. 17.99 (*0-531-33007-9*) Orchard Bks Watts.

***Twilight in Italy.** D. H. Lawrence. 1997. pap. 12.95 (*0-14-018994-7*) Viking Penguin.

Twilight in Italy & Other Essays. D. H. Lawrence. Ed. by Paul Eggert. LC 93-31879. (Cambridge Edition of the Works of D. H. Lawrence). 1988. pap. 6.95 (*0-521-36888-X*) Cambridge U Pr.

Twilight in Italy & Other Essays. D. H. Lawrence. Ed. by Paul Eggert. (Cambridge Edition of the Works of D. H. Lawrence). (Illus.). 400p. (C). 1994. text ed. 95.00 (*0-521-26888-5*) Cambridge U Pr.

Twilight in the Forbidden City. Reginald F. Johnston. 1976. 34.95 (*0-8488-1390-1*) Amereon Ltd.

Twilight in the Forbidden City. Reginald F. Johnston. 486p. 1990. reprint ed. lib. bdg. 45.95 (*0-89966-686-8*) Buccaneer Bks.

***Twilight Labyrinth: Why Does Spiritual Darkness Linger Where It Does?** George Otis. LC 97-15171. 448p. 1997. pap. 16.99 (*0-8007-9255-6*) Chosen Bks.

Twilight Language: Explorations in Buddhist Meditation & Symbolism. R. S. Bucknell & Martin Stuart-Fox. 248p. (C). 1992. pap. text ed. 20.00 (*0-7007-0234-2*, Pub. by Curzon Press UK) UH Pr.

Twilight Magic. Saranne Dawson. (American Romance Ser.). 1993. mass mkt. 3.50 (*0-373-16504-8*, 1-16504-2) Harlequin Bks.

Twilight Man. Karen Leabo. (Desire Ser.). 1994. mass mkt. 2.99 (*0-373-05838-1*, 5-05838-3) Silhouette.

Twilight Man. large type ed. Frank Gruber. 1990. 25.99 (*0-7089-2284-8*) Ulverscroft.

Twilight Marsh: And Other Wilderness Adventures. Todd Lee. (Illus.). 96p. (Orig.). (J). 1995. pap. 8.95 (*1-896095-07-0*, Pub. by Polestar Bk Pubs CN) Orca Bk Pubs.

Twilight Memories. Maggie B. Shayne. (Shadows Ser.). 1994. mass mkt. 3.50 (*0-373-27030-5*, 5-27030-1) Silhouette.

Twilight Memories: Marking Time in a Culture of Amnesia. Andreas Huyssen. (Illus.). 280p. (C). 1994. pap. 17.95 (*0-415-90935-X*, B3862) Routledge.

Twilight Memories: Marking Time in a Culture of Amnesia. Andreas Huyssen. 280p. (C). (gr. 13). 1995. text ed. 59. 95 (*0-415-90934-1*, B3858) Routledge.

Twilight Nightmares. Loren K. Wiseman. (Twilight: Two Thousand Ser.). 104p. (Orig.). (YA). 1991. pap. 12.00 (*1-55878-095-5*) Game Designers.

Twilight of a Great Civilization. Carl F. Henry. LC 88-70393. 192p. 1988. 12.99 (*0-89107-491-0*) Crossway Bks.

Twilight of Amateur Diplomacy: The American Foreign Service & Its Senior Officers in the 1890s. Henry E. Mattox. LC 88-29022. (American Diplomatic History Ser.: No. 2). (Illus.). 228p. 1989. 21.00 (*0-87338-375-3*) Kent St U Pr.

Twilight of an Empire. Sayed Z. Ahmed. 1996. 16.95 (*1-57097-108-0*) Dawn Horse Pr.

Twilight of an Empire. Syed Z. Ahmed. 128p. 1995. pap. 22.00 (*1-57087-108-6*) Prof Pr NC.

Twilight of Arcadia: American Landscape Painters in Rome, 1830-1880. John W. Coffey. LC 87-70111. (Illus.). 89p. (Orig.). 1987. pap. 15.00 (*0-916606-14-7*) Bowdoin Coll.

Twilight of British Ascendancy in the Middle East: A Case Study of Iraq, 1941-1950. Daniel Silverfarb. LC 93-49550. 1994. text ed. 55.00 (*0-312-12090-7*) St Martin.

Twilight of British Rule in Revolutionary America: The New York Letter Book of General James Robertson, 1780-1783. Ed. by Milton M. Klein & Ronald W. Howard. LC 83-62896. 1983. 17.50 (*0-917334-12-4*) Fenimore Hse Mus.

Twilight of Common Dreams: Why America Is Wracked by Culture Wars. Todd Gitlin. LC 95-22321. 1995. 25.00 (*0-8050-4090-0*) H Holt & Co.

Twilight of Common Dreams: Why America Is Wracked by Culture Wars. Todd Gitlin. 288p. 1996. pap. 14.95 (*0-8050-4091-9*) H Holt & Co.

Twilight of Corporate Strategy: A Comparative Ethical Critique. Daniel R. Gilbert, Jr. (Ruffin Series in Business Ethics). (Illus.). 288p. 1992. 38.00 (*0-19-506514-X*) OUP.

Twilight of Courage. Bodie Thoene & Brock Thoene. 528p. 1995. pap. 12.99 (*0-7852-7596-7*) Nelson.

Twilight of Empire: Memoirs of Prime Minister Clement Attlee. Francis E. Williams. LC 78-5918. 264p. 1978. reprint ed. text ed. 59.75 (*0-313-20450-0*, WITE, Greenwood Pr) Greenwood.

Twilight of Empire, No. 6. Allan W. Eckert. 752p. 1989. mass mkt. 7.50 (*0-553-28059-7*) Bantam.

Twilight of Evolution. Henry M. Morris. LC 63-21471. 104p. (C). 1964. pap. 6.99 (*0-8010-5862-7*) Baker Bks.

Twilight of Federalism: The Disintegration of the Federalist Party - 1815-1830. Shaw Livermore. LC 73-150413. 302p. 1972. reprint ed. 75.00 (*0-87752-137-9*) Gordian.

Twilight of Federalism: The Disintegration of the Federalist Party, 1815-1830. Shaw Livermore. LC 62-7410. 305p. reprint ed. pap. 87.00 (*0-317-09983-3*, 2000593) Bks Demand.

***Twilight of French Eastern Alliances, 1926-1936: French - Czechoslovak - Polish Relations from Locarno to the Remilitarization of the Rhineland.** Piotr S. Wandycz. LC 88-5789. 555p. 1988. reprint ed. pap. 158.20 (*0-608-03299-9*, 2063817) Bks Demand.

***Twilight of Heroes.** Ralph Peters. 464p. 1997. mass mkt. 6.50 (*0-380-78898-5*) Avon.

Twilight of Imperial Russia. Richard Charques. (Illus.). 258p. 1974. pap. 15.95 (*0-19-519787-9*) OUP.

Twilight of Individual Liberty. Hamilton Vreeland, Jr. LC 75-172238. (Right Wing Individualist Tradition in America Ser.). 1972. reprint ed. 17.95 (*0-405-00446-X*) Ayer.

Twilight of International Morality. Nans J. Morgenthau. (Reprint Series in Social Sciences). (C). 1993. reprint ed. pap. text ed. 1.00 (*0-8290-2765-3*, PS-211) Irvington.

Twilight of Liberty: The Legacy of the ACLU. William A. Donohue. 310p. (C). 1994. text ed. 39.95 (*1-56000-049-X*) Transaction Pubs.

Twilight of Magic. Hugh Lofting. LC 92-15766. (Illus.). (J). 1993. pap. 15.00 (*0-671-78358-0*, S&S Bks Young Read) S&S Childrens.

Twilight of Majesty: The Regions of the Mamluk Sultans al-Ashraf Qaytbay & Qansuh al-Ghawri in Egypt. Carl F. Petry. LC 93-4632. (Occasional Papers, Middle East Center Ser.: No. 4). 264p. 1993. 20.00 (*0-295-97307-2*) U of Wash Pr.

Twilight of Painting. R. H. Gammell. (Illus.). 208p. 1990. reprint ed. pap. 19.95 (*0-940160-45-5*) Parnassus Imprints.

Twilight of Progressivism: The Western Republican Senators & the New Deal. fac. ed. Ronald L. Feinman. LC 80-20124. (Johns Hopkins Studies in Historical & Political Science: No. 1). (Illus.). 280p. 1981. pap. 79.80 (*0-7837-7637-3*, 2047390) Bks Demand.

Twilight of Sovereignty: How the Information Revolution Is Transforming Our World. Walter B. Wriston. 256p. 1992. 25.00 (*0-684-19454-6*) S&S Trade.

Twilight of Subjectivity: Contributions to a Post-Individualist Theory of Politics. Fred R. Dallmayr. LC 80-23433. 376p. 1981. lib. bdg. 37.50 (*0-87023-314-9*) U of Mass Pr.

Twilight of the Ascendancy: The Land-Owning Families of Ireland. Mark Bence-Jones. (Illus.). 327p. 1993. pap. 36.50 (*0-09-472350-8*, Pub. by Constable Pubs UK) Trans-Atl Phila.

Twilight of the Celtic Gods: An Exploration of Britain's Hidden Pagan Traditions. David Clarke & Andy Roberts. (Illus.). 176p. 1996. 24.95 (*0-7137-2522-2*, Pub. by Blandford Pr UK) Sterling.

***Twilight of the Empire.** Simon R. Green. 1997. mass mkt. 6.99 (*0-451-45649-1*, ROC) NAL-Dutton.

Twilight of the Goddesses: Representations of Women in the French Revolutionary Era. Madelyn Gutwirth. LC 91-30118. (Illus.). 400p. (C). 1992. text ed. 50.00 (*0-8135-1787-7*) Rutgers U Pr.

Twilight of the Goddesses: Representations of Women in the French Revolutionary Era. Madelyn Gutwirth. (Illus.). 440p. (C). 1994. reprint ed. pap. text ed. 22.95 (*0-8135-1799-0*) Rutgers U Pr.

Twilight of the Gods. Michael Baran. LC 93-79455. (Illus.). 220p. (C). 1993. spiral bd. 18.00 (*1-883147-24-7*) Intern Guild ASRS.

***Twilight of the Gods.** Christopher Bulis. (Dr. Who Missing Adventures Ser.). 280p. 1996. mass mkt. 5.95 (*0-426-20480-8*, Pub. by Virgin Pub UK) London Brdge.

Twilight of the Gods (Gotterdammerung) Richard Wagner. Ed. by Nicholas John. Tr. by Andrew Porter from GER. LC 85-790. (English National Opera - Royal Opera House Guide Ser.: No. 31). (Illus.). (Orig.). 1985. pap. 9.95 (*0-7145-4063-3*) Riverrun NY.

***Twilight of the Habsburgs: The Life & Times of Emperor Francis Joseph.** Alan Palmer. 400p. 1997. reprint ed. pap. 14.00 (*0-87113-665-1*, Atlntc Mnthly) Grove-Atltic.

Twilight of the Hapsburgs: The Life & Times of Emperor Franz Josef. Alan Palmer. LC 94-40982. (Illus.). 384p. 1995. 27.50 (*0-8021-1560-8*, Grove) Grove-Atltic.

***Twilight of the Idols.** Friedrich Nietzsche. Tr. by Richard Polt from GER. LC 96-40331. (Classics Ser.). 192p. 1997. pap. text ed. 7.95 (*0-87220-354-9*); lib. bdg. 29.95 (*0-87220-355-7*) Hackett Pub.

Twilight of the Idols: The Tragedy of Yugoslavia. Ales Debelijak. Tr. by Michael Biggins. (Illus.). 86p. (Orig.). 1994. pap. 10.00 (*1-877727-51-2*) White Pine.

Twilight of the Idols & the Anti-Christ. Friedrich W. Nietzche. (Classics Ser.). 208p. (Orig.). 1990. pap. 10.95 (*0-14-044514-5*, Penguin Classics) Viking Penguin.

Twilight of the Jackass Prospector: Death Valley Area Portraits of the 1930's. George R. Cartter. LC 82-62025. (Illus.). (Orig.). 1982. 9.95 (*0-930704-13-4*) Sagebrush Pr.

Twilight of the Monongahela. Harry Stegmaier & Jim Mollison. (Illus.). 88p. (Orig.). 1994. pap. text ed. 32.95 (*1-882608-09-7*) H & M Prods.

Twilight of the Mughals. Percival Spear. (C). 1991. reprint ed. 22.50 (*0-685-50020-9*, Pub. by Munshiram Manoharial II) S Asia.

Twilight of the Mughuls: Studies in the Late Mughal Delhi. Thomas G. Spear. 279p. 1991. reprint ed. text ed. 27.50 (*82-215-0517-X*) Coronet Bks.

Twilight of the Panther: Biology, Bureaucracy & Failure in an Endangered Species Program. Kenneth C. Alvarez. 502p. 1993. pap. 19.95 (*0-9635656-0-5*) Myakka River.

Twilight of the Pepper Empire: Portuguese Trade in Southwest India in the Early Seventeenth Century. A. R. Disney. LC 77-17376. (Historical Studies: No. 95). 272p. 1978. 18.50 (*0-674-91429-5*) HUP.

Twilight of the Presidency: From Johnson to Reagan. rev. ed. George E. Reedy. 208p. 1971. pap. 4.50 (*0-451-62510-2*, Sig) NAL-Dutton.

Twilight of the Sea Gods. Thaddeus V. Tuleja. LC 75-32533. (Illus.). 284p. 1976. reprint ed. text ed. 65.00 (*0-8371-8367-7*, TUTS, Greenwood Pr) Greenwood.

Twilight of the Sioux. John G. Neihardt. LC 74-134771. xiv, 292p. 1971. reprint ed. pap. 10.95 (*0-8032-5734-1*, Bison Books) U of Nebr Pr.

Twilight of the U. S. Cavalry: Life in the Old Army, 1917-1942. Lucian K. Truscott, Jr. Ed. by Lucian K. Truscott, III. LC 88-27152. (Modern War Studies). (Illus.). xxii, 202p. 1989. 22.50 (*0-7006-0403-0*) U Pr of KS.

Twilight of the Universities. F. X. Foulke-ffeinberg. 320p. (C). 19.50 (*1-880177-01-3*) Cui Bono Bks.

***Twilight of the West.** Christopher Coker. 1997. text ed. 22.00 (*0-8133-3368-7*) Westview.

Twilight of the White Races. M. Muret. 1976. lib. bdg. 59. 95 (*0-8490-2780-2*) Gordon Pr.

***Twilight of World Steam.** Ron Ziel. Date not set. reprint ed. lib. bdg. 29.95 (*0-614-25290-3*, Am Repr) Amereon Ltd.

***Twilight on the Caucasus: Triumph & Tragedy of Imam Shayml Lion of Daghestan.** Syed Ahmed. 232p. 1997. pap. 22.00 (*1-57087-317-8*) Prof Pr NC.

Twilight on the Lighthouses. Jim Gibbs. (Illus.). 192p. (YA). (gr. 10-13). 1996. 39.95 (*0-88740-930-X*) Schiffer.

Twilight on the Narrow Gauge. Frederick Kramer. 1976. pap. 8.50 (*0-915276-14-3*) Quadrant Pr.

***Twilight on the Silk Road.** S. Z. Ahmed. 1997. pap. text ed. 22.00 (*1-57087-281-3*) Prof Pr NC.

Twilight Over Burma: My Life As a Shan Princess. Inge Sargent. LC 94-17047. (Illus.). 256p. (C). 1994. 24.95 (*0-8248-1623-4*, Kolowalu Bk); pap. 14.95 (*0-8248-1628-5*, Kolowalu Bk) UH Pr.

Twilight Rebels. Keith Wilkerson. LC 91-60940. 288p. 1991. reprint ed. pap. 8.95 (*0-89221-206-3*) New Leaf.

Twilight Secrets. Marylyle Rogers. Ed. by Caroline Tolley. 336p. (Orig.). 1994. mass mkt. 5.50 (*0-671-87186-2*, Pocket Star Bks) PB.

***Twilight Sleep.** Edith Wharton. 1997. pap. 11.00 (*0-684-83964-4*, Scribners PB Fict) S&S Trade.

Twilight Stations. Charles Hinton. (Orig.). 1995. pap. 14.95 (*0-9639934-5-3*) C Hinton.

Twilight Struggle: American Power & Nicaragua, 1977-1990. Robert Kagan. 903p. 1996. 37.50 (*0-02-874057-2*) Free Pr.

Twilight Struggle: The Life of John Fitzgerald Kennedy. Barbara Harrison & Daniel Terris. LC 91-1492. (Illus.). 224p. (J). (gr. 5 up). 1992. 18.00 (*0-688-08830-9*) Lothrop.

Twilight Time. Rick Hautala. 480p. 1994. mass mkt. 4.99 (*0-8217-4713-4*, Zebra Kensgtn) Kensgtn Pub Corp.

Twilight Visitors: Ghost Tales! Sharon A. Gill & David R. Oester. 179p. (Orig.). 1995. pap. write for info. (*1-885591-84-5*) Morris Pubng.

Twilight Walk. A. B. Shiffrin. 1951. pap. 13.00 (*0-8222-1179-3*) Dramatists Play.

Twilight War. Michael H. Morgan. 464p. 1992. pap. 5.99 (*0-451-17228-0*, Sig) NAL-Dutton.

***Twilight Warriors: Inside the World's Special Forces.** Martin C. Arostegui. LC 96-37352. 1997. 24.95 (*0-312-15234-5*) St Martin.

Twilight Whispers. Barbara Delinsky. 416p. (Orig.). 1994. mass mkt. 5.99 (*0-446-60079-2*) Warner Bks.

Twilight Whispers. Morgan Hayes. (Superromance Ser.). 1994. mass mkt. 3.50 (*0-373-70591-3*, 1-70591-2) Harlequin Bks.

Twilight Whispers. large type ed. Barbara Delinsky. LC 96-2653. 496p. (Orig.). 1996. lib. bdg. 24.95 (*1-57490-061-7*, Beeler LP Bks) T T Beeler.

Twilight with Halfmoon Rising: Selected Poems by Peter Gimpel. Peter Gimpel. 71p. 1991. pap. 7.95 (*0-9631478-0-3*) Red Heifer Pr.

An Asterisk (*) at the beginning of an entry indicates that the title is appearing in BIP for the first time.

Twilight Years. Sawako Ariyoshi. Tr. by Mildred Tahara from JPN. LC 84-47687. 216p. 1988. pap. 10.00 (0-87011-852-8) Kodansha.
Twilight Years of Lady Osler: Letters of a Doctor's Wife. Frederick B. Wagner, Jr. LC 85-10722. (Illus.). 144p. 1985. 20.00 (0-88135-002-8, Sci Hist) Watson Pub Intl.
Twilight Zone. Bloch. 1983. 2.95 (0-446-32200-8) Warner Bks.
Twilight Zone. Rod Serling. 1993. reprint ed. lib. bdg. 25.95 (1-56849-219-7) Buccaneer Bks.
***Twilight Zone: Scripts & Stories.** George C. Johnson. (Streamline Pictures Book Ser.). xiii, 206p. (Orig.). (C). 1996. pap. 12.95 (1-57300-055-8, 93024) Streamline Ent.
Twilight Zone: The Original Stories. Ed. by Martin Greenberg et al. 1994. 9.98 (1-56731-065-6, MJF Bks) Fine Comms.
Twilight Zone: The Original Stories. Ed. by Richard Matheson et al. 576p. 1985. pap. 8.95 (0-380-89601-X) Avon.
Twilight Zone Companion. 2nd ed. Marc S. Zicree. LC 92-23881. (Illus.). 466p. 1992. pap. 15.95 (1-879505-09-6) Silman James Pr.
Twilight Zone Omnibus. Rod Serling. 25.95 (0-89190-114-0) Amereon Ltd.
Twilight Zone Programme Guide. Jean-Marc Lofficier & Randy Lifficier. 1995. pap. 5.95 (0-86369-844-1, Pub. by Virgin Pub UK) London Brdge.
***Twilight Zones: The Hidden Life of Cultural Images from Plato to O. J.** Susan Bordo. LC 97-2223. 1997. write for info. (0-520-21101-4) U CA Pr.
***Twilightcycle: 2000.** (Paranoia Ser.). 6.00 (0-87431-155-1, 12018) West End Games.
Twilights & Chants. Ray Gonzalez. Ed. by Nancy Andrews. LC 87-71098. 112p. (Orig.). 1987. pap. 8.95 (0-9614643-1-3) James Andrews Co.
Twilight's Child. V. C. Andrews. Ed. by Linda Marrow. 448p. 1992. pap. 6.99 (0-671-69514-2) PB.
Twilight's Child. large type ed. V. C. Andrews. LC 92-19028. (General Ser.). 555p. 1993. pap. 17.95 (0-8161-5525-9); lib. bdg. 20.95 (0-8161-5524-0) G K Hall.
Twilight's End. Jerry Oltion. (Star Trek Ser.: Vol. 77). 1996. mass mkt. 5.99 (0-671-53873-X, Pocket Books) PB.
Twilight's Last Gleaming: The Price of Happiness in America. James R. Cooper. 372p. (C). 1992. 30.95 (0-87975-719-1) Prometheus Bks.
Twilights of Anthony Wayne Drive. Hernan Castellano-Giron. Tr. by Emil Efthimides from SPA. (Illus.). 60p. (Orig.). 1984. pap. 6.00 (0-931081-00-9) Operation DOME.
Twill Basketry: A Handbook of Designs, Techniques, & Styles. Shereen LaPlantz. LC 92-29051. (Illus.). 144p. 1992. 19.95 (0-937274-64-X) Lark Books.
Twilley. Bruce E. Fleming. 288p. (Orig.). 1997. pap. 13.95 (1-885983-20-4) Turtle Point Pr.
Twin. Anne Schraff. Ed. by Carol Newell. (Standing Tall Mystery Ser.). 49p. (Orig.). (J). (gr. 5-9). 1995. pap. 4.95 (1-56254-158-7, SP1587) Saddleback Pubns.
Twin Again. Linda J. Singleton. (My Sister, the Ghost Ser.: No. 1). 122p. (Orig.). (J). (gr. 4-6). 1995. pap. 3.50 (0-380-77893-9, Camelot) Avon.
Twin Beds. Regan Forest. (Temptation Ser.). 1996. mass mkt. 3.50 (0-373-25691-4, 1-25691-6) Harlequin Bks.
***Twin Buildings & Applications to S-Arithmetic Groups.** LC 96-48283. (Lecture Notes in Mathematics Ser.: Vol. 1641). 123p. 1996. pap. 29.00 (3-540-61973-9) Spr-Verlag.
***Twin Chariot.** Spiro. 1992. pap. text ed. write for info. (0-340-52419-7) Addison-Wesley.
***Twin Cheeks.** Anne Tilby. (Illus.). 48p. (Orig.). 1997. pap. 9.99 (1-85410-446-2, Pub. by Aurum Pr UK) London Brdge.
Twin Cities Area Fishing Map Guide. James F. Billig. 1994. spiral bd. 18.95 (1-885010-02-8) Sptsmans Connect.
Twin Cities' Best Seats. Laurel Lindahl. 80p. (Orig.). 1994. pap. text ed. 14.95 (0-9643511-2-9) MN Monthly.
Twin Cities Bicycling: Fred's Best Guide to Twin Cities Bicycling. Richard Arey. (Illus.). 128p. (Orig.). 1995. pap. 14.50 (0-9620918-1-2) MN Outdoors Pr.
Twin Cities' Birding Map. Vicky L. Vogels. (Illus.). 1p. 1995. 7.95 (0-9641238-3-5) Little Transport.
Twin Cities Brunches. Lynn D. Soli et al. (Illus.). 80p. (Orig.). 1986. pap. 4.95 (0-935201-12-2) Affordable Adven.
***Twin Cities Creative Sourcebook 1997.** (Illus.). 300p. 1997. pap. 50.00 (1-886295-10-7) Everest Pubng.
Twin Cities Family Fun Sports. Victor M. Spadaccini. 304p. (Orig.). 1995. pap. 12.95 (0-911493-16-6) Blue Sky.
Twin Cities Fishing Guide: Where the Experts Fish & How! 2nd rev. ed. Sybil C. Smith. 224p. 1993. pap. 12.95 (0-9615221-3-5, Fins) Smith Hse Pr.
Twin Cities Gold Book, 1985-86. Ed. by Duffy Busch. 600p. (Orig.). 1985. pap. 13.50 (0-932053-00-9) Prime Pubns.
Twin Cities, Naturally! A Pictorial Tour of the Minneapolis-St. Paul Metropolitan Area. Greg Ryan & Sally Beyer. LC 93-34642. (Illus.). 96p. 1994. pap. 16.95 (0-89658-232-9) Voyageur Pr.
Twin Cities One to One Mobilization Feasibility Study. Dale A. Blyth & Rebecca N. Saito. 58p. 1993. pap. 8.00 (1-57482-323-X) Search Inst.
Twin Cities Perceived: A Study in Words & Drawings. Jean Ervin. LC 76-7338. (Illus.). 143p. reprint ed. pap. 40.80 (0-317-41717-7, 2055861) Bks Demand.
Twin Cities Summer Recreation. Richard F. Arey. (Illus.). 1997. pap. 14.50 (0-9620918-3-9) MN Outdoors Pr.
Twin Cities Then & Now. Larry Millett. LC 96-5746. (Illus.). x, 203p. 1996. 40.00 (0-87351-326-6); pap. 24.95 (0-87351-327-4) Minn Hist.
Twin Cities Uncovered: The Arthur Family. Lindsay G. Arthur & Jean Arthur. LC 94-48650. 296p. 1995. pap. 16.95 (1-55622-388-9, Seaside Pr) Wordware Pub.
Twin Cities Winter Recreation. Richard F. Arey. (Illus.). 128p. (Orig.). 1996. pap. 14.95 (0-9620918-2-0) MN Outdoors Pr.
Twin City Scenic Collection: Popular Entertainment 1896-1929. University Art Museum Staff & University of Minnesota Staff. (Illus.). 112p. (Orig.). 1987. pap. write for info. (0-938713-01-9) Univ MN Art Mus.
Twin City Slickers. rev. ed. Norm Rockwell. 104p. (Orig.). 1983. pap. 3.95 (0-9612002-1-9) Moonlight Press.
Twin City Tales: A Hermeneutical Reassessment of Tula & Chichen Itza. Lindsay Jones. (Illus.). 736p. 1995. 49.95 (0-87081-403-6) Univ Pr Colo.
Twin City Tractor Photo Archive. Ed. by P. A. Letourneau. LC 93-79372. (Photo Archive Ser.). (Illus.). 144p. 1993. pap. 29.95 (1-882256-06-9) Iconografix.
Twin Dilemma. Carolyn Keene. (Nancy Drew Mystery Stories Ser.: No. 63). (J). (gr. 3-7). 1988. mass mkt. 3.99 (0-671-67301-7, Minstrel Bks) PB.
Twin Earth Chronicles: Twenty Years of Reflection on Hilary Putnam's "The Meaning of Meaning" Ed. by Andrew Pessin & Sanford Goldberg. LC 95-10001. 448p. 1995. 49.95 (1-55778-720-4); pap. 19.95 (1-55778-721-2) M E Sharpe.
Twin Earth Chronicles: Twenty Years of Reflection on Hilary Putnam's the Meaning of Meaning' Ed. by Andrew Pessin & Sanford Goldberg. LC 95-10001. 432p. (gr. 13). 1996. text ed. 64.95 (1-56324-873-5) M E Sharpe.
Twin Earth Chronicles: Twenty Years of Reflection on Hilary Putnam's the Meaning of Meaning' Ed. by Andrew Pessin & Sanford Goldberg. LC 95-10001. 432p. (gr. 13). 1996. pap. text ed. 24.95 (1-56324-874-3) M E Sharpe.
Twin Educational Version. Mosaic Software Inc. Staff. (Illus.). 208p. (C). 1987. pap. text ed. 22.60 (0-13-935370-4) P-H.
***Twin Galaxies Official Video Game & Pinball Book of World Records: The Official Book of Records Listing the High Scores on Arcade Video Game, Pinball, Home Video Games, & Network Games.** Walter A. Day. LC 96-72617. (Illus.). 250p. (Orig.). 1997. pap. 14.95 (1-887472-25-8) Sunstar Pubng.
Twin Hearts No. 2: Sweet Valley High TV Novelization. Francine Pascal. 144p. (YA). (gr. 7 up). 1996. mass mkt. 4.50 (0-553-57012-9, Sweet Valley) BDD Bks Young Read.
Twin Holy Days - Birthday of Baha'u'llah, Birthday of the Bab: A Compilation. 1995. 14.95 (0-933770-90-1) Kalimat.
Twin in the Tavern. Barbara B. Wallace. LC 92-36429. 192p. (J). (gr. 3-7). 1993. lib. bdg. 15.00 (0-689-31846-4, Atheneum Bks Young) S&S Childrens.
Twin in the Tavern. Barbara B. Wallace. (J). 1995. 3.95 (0-689-80167-X, Aladdin Paperbacks) S&S Childrens.
Twin Justice...Shattered Dreams: A Mother Tells of the Heartbreaking Events That Preceded the Death of Her Twin Sons. Ann Mullen. Ed. by Kathleen Smith. 128p. (Orig.). 1992. pap. 9.95 (0-943135-14-1, Grn Briar Patch) Gallagher Jordan.
Twin Killing: The Bill Mazeroski Story. John T. Bird. 316p. 1995. 24.95 (0-9649011-0-2) Esmerelda AL.
Twin Menaechmi see Anthology of Roman Drama
Twin Oaks. Anne Logan. (Superromance Ser.). 1993. mass mkt. 3.50 (0-373-70550-6, 1-70550-8) Harlequin Bks.
Twin of Fire. Jude Deveraux. Ed. by Linda Marrow. 1991. pap. 6.99 (0-671-73979-4) PB.
Twin of Fire. large type ed. Jude Deveraux. 432p. 1992. pap. 17.95 (0-8161-5340-X, GK Hall) Thorndike Pr.
Twin of Ice. Jude Deveraux. Ed. by Linda Marrow. 1991. pap. 6.99 (0-671-73971-9) PB.
Twin of Ice. large type ed. Jude Deveraux. (General Ser.). 406p. 1992. pap. 17.95 (0-8161-5333-7) G K Hall.
***Twin of Trust.** Barbara Wilkins. mass mkt. write for info. (0-06-109159-6, Harp PBks) HarpC.
Twin Peaks. Ed. by Milton Okun. pap. 12.95 (0-89524-613-9) Cherry Lane.
Twin Pickle. Ann Doro. LC 95-38430. (Illus.). 32p. (J). (ps-2). 1996. 14.95 (0-8050-3802-7, B Martin BYR) H Holt & Co.
Twin Powers: Politics & the Sacred. Thomas S. Molnar. LC 88-10204. 157p. reprint ed. pap. 44.80 (0-7837-0520-4, 2040844) Bks Demand.
***Twin Princes.** Tedd Arnold. LC 97-2216. (J). 1998. write for info. (0-8037-1417-3); write for info. (0-8037-1418-1) Dial Bks Young.
Twin Rivers. John D. Nesbitt. 192p. 1995. 19.95 (0-8027-4152-5) Walker & Co.
***Twin Rivers.** John D. Nesbitt. 1997. mass mkt. 4.50 (0-06-101160-6, Harp PBks) HarpC.
Twin Rivers. large type ed. John D. Nesbitt. LC 96-10454. 293p. 1996. 20.95 (0-7862-0703-5) Thorndike Pr.
Twin Rivers Bibliography: Assyrian, Chaldian, & Syrians Past & Present. Francis K. Khosho. 390p. (Orig.). (C). 1987. pap. 20.00 (0-9619310-1-9) Khosho.
Twin Screw Extruders: A Basic Understanding. Fabrizio G. Martelli. 128p. (gr. 13). 1982. text ed. 82.95 (0-442-26363-5) Chapman & Hall.
Twin Screw Extrusion: Technology & Principles. James L. White. 295p. (C). 1991. text ed. 79.95 (1-56990-109-0) Hanser-Gardner.
Twin Sisters. Janice Harrell. (YA). (gr. 5 up). 1995. pap. 3.95 (0-8167-3793-2) Troll Communs.
Twin Sombreros. Zane Grey. 336p. 1990. mass mkt. 3.99 (0-06-100101-5, Harp PBks) HarpC.
Twin Sombreros. large type ed. Zane Grey. 355p. 1995. lib. bdg. 20.95 (0-8161-5973-4, GK Hall) Thorndike Pr.
Twin Sombreros. large type ed. Zane Grey. 1983. 15.95 (0-7089-0986-8) Ulverscroft.
Twin Sons of Different Mirrors: Poems in Dialogue. Bill Meissner & Jack Driscoll. LC 89-3106. 64p. (Orig.). 1989. pap. 6.95 (0-915943-35-2) Milkweed Ed.
Twin Souls: A Guide to Finding Your True Spiritual Partner. Patricia Joudry. 208p. 1995. 21.00 (0-517-70059-X, C P Pubs) Crown Pub Group.
Twin Spirits: The Novels of Emily & Anne Bronte. Robert Liddell. LC 90-80795. 144p. 9000. 32.00 (0-7206-0776-0, Pub. by P Owen Ltd UK) Dufour.
***Twin Star Jacket.** Kaye Wood & Jane Hill. (Illus.). 16p. (Orig.). 1996. pap. 8.00 (0-944588-30-1) K Wood.
***Twin Stars of Kira.** (Star Wars Adventures Ser.). 15.00 (0-87431-191-8, 40060) West End Games.
Twin Talk: Vocabulary Study Writing Book, Bk. 1. Jim DeWitt. (Vocabulary Studies). (Illus.). 78p. (Orig.). (YA). (gr. 4-12). 1987. student ed., pap. 6.00 (0-915199-25-4) Pen-Dec.
Twin Terror. Janice Harrell. 224p. (Orig.). (YA). (gr. 5 up). 1996. pap. 3.95 (0-8167-3911-0, WestWind) Troll Communs.
Twin Thomasons: Perfumed Bed - Eye Feast. Edwin Thomason. 90p. 1993. 22.50 (1-56591-051-6) Hollym Intl.
Twin 'Toons: Cartoons about Twins. Nancy B. Miller. (Illus.). 64p. (Orig.). 1996. pap. 7.95 (0-9632526-8-2) Laugh Lines.
Twin Tragedy. large type ed. Margaret A. Carr. (Linford Mystery Library). 272p. 1987. pap. 15.99 (0-7089-6453-2, Linford) Ulverscroft.
Twin Trailer Trucks. (Special Reports: No. 211). 388p. 1986. 25.00 (0-309-04050-7) Transport Res Bd.
***Twin Trouble, Vol. 4.** Mary C. Reid. (Bakcpack Mysteries Ser.). (J). (gr. 2-5). 1997. pap. text ed. 3.99 (1-55661-718-6) Bethany Hse.
***Twin Trouble, Vol. 6.** Ann M. Martin. (Kids in Ms. Coleman's Class Ser.). 1997. pap. 3.50 (0-590-69202-X, Little Apple) Scholastic Inc.
Twin Troubles. Pfeffer. (J). 1994. pap. 4.95 (0-8050-3272-X) H Holt & Co.
Twin Troubles. Mary Wright. Ed. by Lisa Clancy. (Full House: Stephanie Ser.: No. 3). 128p. (Orig.). (J). (gr. 3-6). mass mkt. 3.99 (0-671-88290-2, Minstrel Bks) PB.
Twin Willows. Kay Cornelius. 1996. pap. 7.99 (0-345-40356-8) Ballantine Trade.
Twin-Wire Seminar, 1985: Notes of TAPPI, Denver Marriott, Denver, CO, April 17-19. Technical Association of the Pulp & Paper Industry Staff. 96p. pap. 27.40 (0-317-26852-X, 2025287) Bks Demand.
Twin-Wire Seminar, 1986: Notes of TAPPI, Marriott Hotel, New Orleans, LA, April 16-18. Technical Association of the Pulp & Paper Industry. pap. 31.30 (0-317-55391-7, 202918) Bks Demand.
Twin-Wire Seminar, 1987: Notes of TAPPI, Hyatt Regency, Atlanta, GA, April 8-10. Technical Association of the Pulp & Paper Industry Staff. 187p. pap. 53.30 (0-685-20517-7, 2029977) Bks Demand.
Twin-Wire Seminar, 1989: Washington Hilton, Washington, DC, April 12-14. Technical Association of the Pulp & Paper Industry Staff. (TAPPI Notes Ser.). (Illus.). 151p. reprint ed. pap. 43.10 (0-8357-6344-7, 2035617) Bks Demand.
***Twinderella: En Espanol, Gemelarela.** Jerome McDonough. Tr. by Betty Alderette. (Illus.). 39p. (Orig.). (ENG & SPA.). 1996. pap. write for info. (0-88680-433-7) I E Clark.
Twined Knitting. Birgitta Dandamell & Ulla Danielsson. Tr. by Robin O. Hansen from SWE. LC 89-83442. (Illus.). 120p. 1994. pap. 16.95 (1-883010-02-0) Interweave.
Twining, Genealogy of the Twining Family: Descendants of William Twining, Sr., Who Came from Wales & Died at Eastham, Mass., 1659. T. J. Twining. x, 172p. 1992. reprint ed. pap. 27.00 (0-8328-2747-9); reprint ed. lib. bdg. 37.00 (0-8328-2746-0) Higginson Bk Co.
Twinkie Squad. Gordon Korman. 208p. (J). 1992. 13.95 (0-590-45249-5, Scholastic Hardcover) Scholastic Inc.
Twinkle. James Eldridge, pseud. (Illus.). 64p. (Orig.). 1980. pap. 3.25 (0-938900-00-5) Creations Unltd.
Twinkle & the All-Star Angel Band. Ed. by David Huntsinger et al. (J). 1992. 9.99 (0-685-68511-X, MC-78A) Lillenas.
Twinkle & the All-Star Angel Band. Ed. by David Huntsinger et al. (J). 1992. student ed. 3.99 (0-685-68510-1, MC-78); audio 10.99 (0-685-68512-8, TA-9142C) Lillenas.
Twinkle-Dust. rev. ed. Alice W. Bowman. LC 95-78256. 24p. (J). (gr. k-6). 1996. pap. 5.95 (0-9645870-4-1) Big Ft Pub.
Twinkle-Dust: A Dazzling Adventure. Alice W. Bowman. LC 96-83952. (Illus.). 32p. (J). (gr. k-6). 1996. pap. 6.95 (0-9645870-3-3) Big Ft Pub.
Twinkle Dust - His Awesome Adventure. Alice W. Bowman. LC 95-78257. (Twinkle Dust Ser.: No. 2). (Illus.). 24p. (Orig.). (J). (ps-6). 1995. pap. 5.95 (0-9645870-2-5) Big Ft Pub.
***Twinkle.. Little Suns.** Thomas-Cochran. (What a Wonderful World Intro Ser.). 1993. pap. text ed. write for info. (0-582-91079-X, Pub. by Longman UK) Longman.
Twinkle Squad. Gordon Kormann. 208p. (J). (gr. 4-7). 1994. pap. 3.99 (0-590-45250-9) Scholastic Inc.
Twinkle, Twinkle. (Little Golden Sound Story Bks.). (Illus.). 24p. (J). 1995. bds. 6.95 (0-307-74833-2, Golden Pr) Western Pub.
***Twinkle Twinkle.** Katrina Allen. 1997. pap. 14.99 (0-525-45906-5) NAL-Dutton.
***Twinkle, Twinkle.** Annalisa McMorrow. (Super-Duper Science Ser.). (Illus.). 80p. (Orig.). (J). (ps-k). 1996. pap. 9.95 (1-878279-87-4, MM2016) Monday Morning Bks.
Twinkle, Twinkle, Little Bug. Katharine Ross. LC 94-48341. (Step into Reading: Step 1 Bks.). (Illus.). (J). (ps-4). 1996. pap. 3.99 (0-679-87666-9); lib. bdg. 11.99 (0-679-97666-3) Random.
Twinkle, Twinkle Little SK. Shirley Backels. (Feelings & Communication Unit Ser.). 22p. 1992. pap. text ed. 4.99 (1-57156-022-X) Wild Goose UT.
Twinkle, Twinkle, Little Star. (J). 1994. write for info. (0-7853-0770-2) Pubns Intl Ltd.
Twinkle Twinkle Little Star. (J). (ps). 1996. 3.99 (0-88705-917-1, Wshng Well Bks) Joshua Morris.
Twinkle, Twinkle, Little Star. Illus. by Isobel Bushell. (Musical Board Bk.). 12p. (J). (ps). 1994. 5.95 (0-694-00575-4, Festival) HarpC Child Bks.
Twinkle, Twinkle, Little Star. Ed. by Kathleen Cubley. (Cut & Tell Cutout Ser.). (Illus.). 8p. (J). (ps). 1994. pap. 2.95 (1-57029-005-9, WPH 2212, Totline Bks) Warren Pub Hse.
Twinkle, Twinkle, Little Star. Illus. by Tracey Moroney. (My First Nursery Rhyme Books Ser.). (J). (ps). 1995. 3.99 (0-88705-777-2, Wshng Well Bks) Joshua Morris.
Twinkle, Twinkle, Little Star. Jane Taylor. 32p. (J). 1992. 10.95 (0-590-45566-4, Cartwheel) Scholastic Inc.
Twinkle, Twinkle, Little Star. Jane Taylor. LC 92-421. (J). (ps-3). 1992. lib. bdg. 14.93 (0-688-11169-6, Morrow Junior) Morrow.
Twinkle Twinkle Little Star. Iza Trapani. LC 93-33635. 32p. (J). 1994. 15.95 (1-879085-87-9) Whsprng Coyote Pr.
Twinkle, Twinkle Little Star. Iza Trapani. (Extended Nursery Rhymes Ser.). (Illus.). 32p. (J). (ps up). 1996. lib. bdg. 18.60 (0-8368-1552-1) Gareth Stevens Inc.
***Twinkle, Twinkle, Little Star.** Iza Trapani. (Illus.). 32p. (J). 1997. pap. 6.95 (1-879085-70-4) Whsprng Coyote Pr.
***Twinkle, Twinkle Little Star.** Amanda Wallwork. (J). 1997. 8.95 (0-7641-5001-4) Barron.
***Twinkle, Twinkle Little Star: A Lullaby Book with Twinkling Light & Musical Sound Chip.** Jannat Messenger. 1997. 9.95 (1-888443-29-4, Piggytoes Pr) Intervisual Bks.
Twinkles: The Story of a Christmas Star. large type ed. Illus. by Linda Pollok. 18p. (Orig.). (J). (gr. k-3). 1995. per., pap. 9.95 (0-943487-47-1) Sevgo Pr.
Twinkling Decatur Celebration. Decatur Celebration Writers. (Wee Write Bks.: No. 27). (Illus.). 40p. (J). (ps-3). 1995. pap. 8.95 (1-884987-91-5) WeWrite.
Twinky & Friends. Orpha N. Wilson. (Illus.). (J). 1995. 7.95 (0-533-11420-9) Vantage.
Twinnies. Eve Bunting. LC 96-7645. (Illus.). (J). 1997. write for info. (0-15-291592-3) HarBrace.
Twinning & Twins. fac. ed. Ed. by Ian MacGillivray. LC 88-14385. (Wiley Medical Publications). 331p. 1988. reprint ed. pap. 94.40 (0-7837-8268-3, 2049049) Bks Demand.
Twinning in Advanced Materials: Proceedings: Symposium Sponsored by the Chemistry & Physics of Materials Committee & the Alloy Phases Committee of the TMS Technical Divisions. Ed. by Man H. Yoo & Manfred Wittig. LC 94-77253. 460p. 1994. 40.00 (0-87339-236-1, 2361) Minerals Metals.
Twins. Monica Colli. LC 91-36606. (J). 1992. 6.99 (0-85953-394-8) Childs Play.
Twins. Caroline B. Cooney. 176p. (YA). (gr. 7-9). 1994. pap. 3.50 (0-590-47478-2) Scholastic Inc.
***Twins.** Hans G. Daellenbach. 448p. (Orig.). 1997. mass mkt. 5.99 (1-55237-364-9, Pub. by Comnwlth Pub CN) Partners Pubs Grp.
Twins. Mark Dunster. LC 75-192367. (Rin Ser.: Pt. 35). 1975. 4.00 (0-89642-036-1) Linden Pubs.
Twins. Benzion Firer. Tr. by Bracha Scae from HEB. 230p. (J). (gr. 4-8). 1983. 10.95 (0-87306-279-5); pap. 7.95 (0-87306-340-6) Feldheim.
Twins. Roxanne Pulitzer. 304p. 1990. 18.95 (0-394-57919-4, Villard Bks) Random.
Twins. Scott. LC 97-5049. (J). 1998. 15.00 (0-689-80347-8, S&S Bks Young Read) S&S Childrens.
Twins. Katherine Stone. 1989. mass mkt. 4.50 (0-8217-2646-3, Zebra Kensgtn) Kensgtn Pub Corp.
***Twins.** Katherine Stone. LC 97-9214. 1997. 25.95 (1-56895-428-X) Wheeler Pub.
Twins. Katherine Stone. 480p. 1996. mass mkt. 6.99 (0-8217-5207-3, Zebra Kensgtn) Kensgtn Pub Corp.
Twins. Katherine Stone. 1989. pap. 4.95 (0-8217-3492-X) NAL-Dutton.
Twins. Alan Swenson. LC 89-50187. 141p. (Orig.). 1990. pap. 7.95 (0-916383-88-1) Aegina Pr.
***Twins.** William Wallis. LC 96-70204. (Illus.). 80p. (Orig.). 1996. pap. 8.00 (0-614-30317-6) Stone & Scott Pubs.
Twins. Bari Wood & Jack Geasland. 1978. pap. 3.95 (0-451-13654-3, Sig) NAL-Dutton.
***Twins.** large type ed. Katherine Stone. LC 96-42513. (Star-Romance Ser.). 464p. 1997. 23.95 (0-7862-0904-6, Five Star) Mac Lib Ref.
***Twins.** large type ed. Anna-Teresa Tymieniecka & World Institute for Advanced Phenomenological Research & Learning Staff. LC 97-2276. (Analecta Husserliana Ser.). 1997. lib. bdg. write for info. (0-7923-4462-6) Kluwer Ac.
Twins: A Study of Three Pairs of Twins (with 30 Charts) Dorothy Burlingham. LC 53-6599. 230p. reprint ed. pap. 65.60 (0-317-10374-1, 2010702) Bks Demand.
Twins: A Tribute. C. Gangi. 17.00 (0-517-20059-7) Random Hse Value.
Twins: A Unique World Scenario. Jorgen Lyngbye. 1995. 10.95 (0-533-11247-8) Vantage.
Twins: From Conception to Five Years. Averil Clegg & Anne Woolett. (Illus.). 128p. 1988. pap. 11.00 (0-345-35661-6, Ballantine Trade) Ballantine.

T

*Twins! Pregnancy, Birth & the First Year of Life with Twins. Connie Agnew & Alan Klein. LC 97-14657. 300p. 1997. pap. 16.00 (0-06-273460-1, PL) HarpC.

Twins & Homosexuality: A Casebook. Geoff Puterbaugh. LC 90-31756. (Gay & Lesbian Studies: Vol. 2). 164p. 1990. text ed. 30.00 (0-8240-6149-7, 627) Garland.

Twins & the Double. John Lash. LC 93-60203. (Art & Imagination Ser.). (Illus.). 96p. 1993. pap. 15.95 (0-500-81042-7) Thames Hudson.

Twins & the Wild West. Francine Pascal. (Sweet Valley Kids Ser.: No. 10). 80p. (J). (gr. 3-6). 1990. pap. 3.50 (0-553-15811-2) Bantam.

Twins & Twin Relations. Helen L. Koch. (Midway Reprint Ser.). 318p. reprint ed. pap. 90.10 (0-685-23858-X, 2056643) Bks Demand.

Twins as a Tool of Behavior Genetics: Report of the Dahlem Worshop on What Are the Mechanisms Mediating the Genetic & Environmental Determinants of Behavior? Ed. by Thomas J. Bouchard, Jr. & Peter Propping. LC 93-8773. (Dahlem Workshop Reports, Life Sciences Research Report: Vol. 53). 310p. 1993. text ed. 152.00 (0-471-94174-3) Wiley.

Twin's Big Pow-Wow. Francine Pascal. (Sweet Valley Kids Ser.: No. 44). 80p. (J). (ps-3). 1993. pap. 2.99 (0-553-48098-7) Bantam.

*Twins Book. Stewart C. Cohen. Ed. & Des. by Ana Bohanan. (Illus.). 32p. (Orig.). 1997. pap. write for info. (1-888457-01-5) Photo Do Not Bend.

Twins' First Bike. Mary Rogers. (Cityscapes Ser.). 34p. (J). (gr. 1). 1992. pap. text ed. 4.50 (1-56843-069-8) BGR Pub.

Twins' First Bike: Big Book. Mary Rogers. (Cityscapes Ser.). 34p. (J). (gr. 1). 1992. pap. text ed. 23.00 (1-56843-019-1) BGR Pub.

Twins Get Caught. Francine Pascal. (Sweet Valley Twins Ser.: No. 41). 144p. (J). (gr. 4 up). 1990. pap. 3.50 (0-553-15810-4) Bantam.

*Twins Go to College. Francine Pascal. (Sweet Valley Twins Ser.). (J). 1997. pap. 3.99 (0-553-48347-1, Sweet Valley) BDD Bks Young Read.

Twins Go to the Hospital. Francine Pascal. (Sweet Valley Kids Ser.: No. 20). 80p. (J). (gr. 4-7). 1991. pap. 3.50 (0-553-15912-7) Bantam.

*Twins Hit Hollywood. Francine Pascal. (Sweet Valley Twins Ser.: No. 107). (J). 1997. pap. 3.50 (0-553-48438-9, Sweet Valley) BDD Bks Young Read.

Twins in Children's & Adolescent Literature: An Annotated Bibliography. Dee Storey. 410p. 1992. 42.50 (0-8108-2641-0) Scarecrow.

Twins in Love. Francine Pascal. (Sweet Valley Teens Ser.: No. 101). 144p. (J). 1996. pap. 3.50 (0-553-48346-3) BDD Bks Young Read.

Twins in Trouble. Amu Djoleto. (Junior African Writers Ser.). (Illus.). (J). (gr. 3-4). 1992. pap. 3.88 (0-7910-2905-0) Chelsea Hse.

Twins' Little Sister. Francine Pascal. (Sweet Valley Twins Ser.: No. 49). 144p. (J). (gr. 4-7). 1991. pap. 3.50 (0-553-15899-6) Bantam.

Twins of Ceylon. Harry Williams. LC 65-12044. (Twins Ser.). (Illus.). (J). (gr. 6-9). 6500. 12.95 (0-8023-1108-3) Dufour.

Twins on Toes: A Ballet Debut. Joan Anderson. LC 92-35104. (Illus.). 32p. (J). (gr. 3-7). 1993. pap. 14.99 (0-525-67415-2, Lodestar Bks) Dutton Child Bks.

Twins Stories: Participant Coding in Yagua Narrative. Thomas E. Payne. LC 92-23632. (Publications in Linguistics: Vol. 120). 236p. 1992. pap. 30.00 (0-520-09774-2) U CA Pr.

Twins Strike Back. Valerie Flournoy. (Illus.). 32p. (J). (gr. 2 up). 1994. 13.00 (0-940975-51-3); pap. 5.00 (0-940975-52-1) Just Us Bks.

Twins Take Paris. Francine Pascal. 192p. (J). 1996. pap. 3.99 (0-553-48390-0) Bantam.

Twins, the Dream - Las Gemelas, el Sueno: Two Voices - Dos Voces. Diana Bellessi & Ursula K. Le Guin. LC 96-16944. (ENG & SPA.). 1996. 16.95 (1-55885-170-4); pap. 11.95 (1-55885-179-8) Arte Publico.

Twins, the Pirates & the Battle of New Orleans. Robinet. LC 96-22028. (J). 1997. 15.00 (0-689-81208-6) S&S Childrens.

Twins Together. Illus. by Jim Pallas. LC 95-76651. 32p. (J). (ps-1). 1995. 13.95 (1-887403-23-X) Good Growing Bks.

Twins, Triplets, & More: From Pre-Birth Through High School - What Every Parent Needs to Know When Raising Two or More. Elizabeth Bryan. 160p. 1992. 17.95 (0-312-07876-5) St Martin.

Twins, Two by Two. Catherine Anholt & Laurence Anholt. LC 91-71820. (Illus.). 32p. (J). (ps). 1992. 13.95 (1-56402-041-X) Candlewick Pr.

Twins, Two by Two. Catherine Anholt & Laurence Anholt. LC 91-71820. 32p. (J). (ps-3). 1994. pap. 4.99 (1-56402-397-4) Candlewick Pr.

*Twinsburg, 1817-1917: Part I, History; Part II, Genealogies. (Illus.). 533p. 1997. reprint ed. lib. bdg. 56.00 (0-8328-6367-X) Higginson Bk Co.

*Twinsen's Odyssey: The Official Strategy Guide. Prima Publishing Staff. 240p. 1997. per. 19.99 (0-7615-1228-4) Prima Pub.

Twinship Sourcebook: Your Guide to Understanding Multiples. TWINS Magazine Editors. Ed. by Barbara C. Unell. LC 93-60586. 270p. (Orig.). 1993. pap. 18.25 (0-9636745-4-4) TWINS Mag.

Twirling & Jet Lag. Da Avabhasa. Ed. by Bill Gottlieb. 48p. 1994. pap. 2.95 (0-614-07282-4) Dawn Horse Pr.

Twist: The Story of the Song & Dance That Changed the World. Jim Dawson. LC 94-12766. 200p. (Orig.). 1995. pap. 14.95 (0-571-19852-X) Faber & Faber.

Twist & Shout: A Decade of Feminist Writing in "This Magazine". Ed. by Susan Crean. 1991. pap. 14.95 (0-929005-27-9, Pub. by Second Story Pr CN) LPC InBook.

Twist in the Silk. large type ed. Zoe Cass. 320p. 1983. 25.99 (0-7089-0969-8) Ulverscroft.

*Twist in the Tale. Archer. 1991. pap. text ed. write for info. (0-582-06022-2, Pub. by Longman UK) Longman.

Twist in the Tale. Jeffrey Archer. 256p. 1994. mass mkt. 5.99 (0-06-100717-X, Harp PBks) HarpC.

Twist in Time: Spellbound. Karr. 1995. pap. 3.75 (0-373-07662-2) Harlequin Bks.

Twist Mappings & Their Applications. Ed. by A. Friedman et al. LC 92-14149. (IMA Volumes in Mathematics & Its Applications Ser.: Vol. 44). (Illus.). xiii, 199p. 1992. 57.95 (0-387-97858-5) Spr-Verlag.

Twist 'n Turn: A Fun Way to Frame Quilt Blocks. Sharyn S. Craig. Ed. by Nancy Roberts. LC 96-23733. (Illus.). 32p. (Orig.). 1996. pap. 11.95 (1-885588-10-0, 800-628-8244) Chitra Pubns.

Twist O' Smoke. Mildred Bowers. LC 77-144731. (Yale Series of Younger Poets: No. 24). reprint ed. 37.50 (0-404-53824-X) AMS Pr.

Twist of Cain. Frank Rich. (Jake Strait Ser.). 1994. mass mkt. 4.99 (0-373-63610-5, 1-63610-9) Harlequin Bks.

*Twist of Faith. Berit Kjos. 250p. 1997. pap. 11.95 (0-89221-358-2) New Leaf.

Twist of Faith: Scriptural Insights from the Poetry of Annelle Warren. Annelle Warren. 88p. 1995. pap. 14.29 (1-887404-04-X) A Griffin Pr.

Twist of Fate. Diane L. Carey. (Distress Call 911 Ser.: No. 1). (J). (gr. k-7). 1996. mass mkt. 3.99 (0-671-55306-2) PB.

Twist of Fate. Jayne Ann Krentz. 1993. mass mkt. 4.50 (0-373-83268-0, 1-83268-2) Harlequin Bks.

Twist of Fate. Suzanne Weyn. LC 89-30585. (No Way Ballet Ser.). (Illus.). 96p. (J). (gr. 3-5). 1996. pap. 2.95 (0-8167-1622-6) Troll Communs.

Twist of Fate. Linda R. Wisdom. (American Romance Ser.). 1996. mass mkt. 3.75 (0-373-16627-3, 1-16627-1) Harlequin Bks.

*Twist of Fate: The Locket. John Saul. (Blackstone Chronicles Ser.: Pt. 2). 1997. mass mkt. 2.99 (0-449-22784-7) Fawcett.

Twist of Hate. large type ed. Cyril A. Joyce. (Linford Mystery Library). 304p. 1993. pap. 15.99 (0-7089-7383-3, Linford) Ulverscroft.

*Twist of Lime. Claudia McKay. LC 97-19531. (Lynn Evans Mystery Ser.). 1997. pap. 10.95 (0-934678-88-X) New Victoria Pubs.

Twist of Sand. large type ed. Geoffrey Jenkins. 1974. 25.99 (0-85456-250-8) Ulverscroft.

*Twist of the Knife. T. Deary. Date not set. pap. text ed. write for info. (0-582-39098-2, Pub. by Longman UK) Longman.

Twist of the Knife. Stephen Solomita. 336p. 1990. mass mkt. 4.95 (0-380-70997-X) Avon.

Twist of the Wrist: The Motorcycle Road Racers Handbook. Keith Code. LC 82-73771. (Illus.). 120p. 1983. 14.95 (0-918226-08-2) Acrobat.

*Twist of the Wrist: The Motorcycle Roadracers Handbook. Keith Code. (Illus.). 144p. 1983. reprint ed. pap. 19.95 (0-9650450-1-3) Code Break.

Twist of the Wrist, Vol. II: The Basics of High-Performance Rider Improvement. Keith Code. LC 82-73771. (Illus.). (Orig.). 1993. pap. 17.95 (0-918226-31-7) Acrobat.

Twist with a Burger, Jitter with a Bug. Linda Lowery. LC 93-38236. (Illus.). 32p. (J). (ps-2). 1995. 14.95 (0-395-67022-5) Ticknor & Fields.

Twisted. R. L. Stine. 176p. (Orig.). (YA). (gr. 7-9). 1987. pap. 3.99 (0-590-43139-0) Scholastic Inc.

*Twisted: Inside the Mind of a Drug Addict. Carl A. Richmond. LC 97-8851. (Master Work Ser.). 306p. 1997. pap. text ed. 19.95 (0-7657-0089-1) Aronson.

Twisted: One Drug Addict's Desperate Struggle for Recovery. Carl Richmond. LC 91-50641. 290p. 1991. pap. 11.95 (1-879360-08-X) Noble Pr.

*Twisted Cadillac: A Spoken Word Odyssey. Doug Knott et al. LC 96-68464. (Illus.). 136p. (Orig.). 1996. pap. 12.00 (0-9652048-0-4) Sacred Beverage.

Twisted Claw. rev. ed. Franklin W. Dixon. LC 77-86667. (Hardy Boys Ser.: Vol. 18). (Illus.). 180p. (J). (gr. 5-9). 1939. 5.95 (0-448-08918-1, G&D) Putnam Pub Group.

Twisted Cross. Mack Maloney. (Wingman Ser.: No. 5). 400p. 1989. mass mkt. 3.95 (0-8217-2553-X, Zebra Kensgtn) Kensgtn Pub Corp.

Twisted Cross: The German Christian Movement in the Third Reich. Doris L. Bergen. LC 95-17954. (Illus.). 370p. (C). 1996. pap. text ed. 16.95 (0-8078-4560-4); lib. bdg. 39.95 (0-8078-2253-1) U of NC Pr.

Twisted Cross: The Occultic Religion of Hitler & the New Age Nazism of the Third Reich. Joseph Carr. LC 84-62776. 316p. 1985. pap. 12.99 (0-910311-22-6) Huntington Hse.

Twisted Cross & Dietrich Bonhoeffer. Thomas E. Patten. 1992. pap. 5.75 (1-55673-475-1, 7925) CSS OH.

Twisted Earth: Reflections on Patterns People & Places. Howard F. De Kalb. (Illus.). 160p. 1990. pap. 19.95 (0-9623271-0-7) Lytel Eorthe.

Twisted Genius: Confessions of a 10 Million Dollar Scam Man. Phil Berger & Craig Jacob. (Illus.). 208p. 1995. 19.95 (1-56858-044-4) FWEW.

Twisted Histories, Altered Contexts: Representing the Chambri in a World System. Deborah B. Gewertz & Frederick K. Errington. (Illus.). 272p. (C). 1991. pap. text ed. 18.95 (0-521-39587-9) Cambridge U Pr.

Twisted Honeycombs. H. S. Coxeter. LC 75-145638. (CBMS Regional Conference Series in Mathematics: Vol. 4). 47p. 1971. 16.00 (0-8218-1653-5, CBMS/4C) Am Math.

Twisted Image. Ace Backwords. LC 90-63506. 120p. (Orig.). 1990. pap. 12.95 (1-55950-056-5, 85120) Loompanics.

*Twisted Justice. Blane Cade. Ed. by Doug Martin. (Greyhorse Ser.: Vol. 1). 123p. 1997. pap. 2.99 (0-9658418-0-4, G-1) CTN-WILDCO.

Twisted Justice. large type ed. Jeffrey Ashford. LC 94-18221. 1994. lib. bdg. 17.95 (0-8161-7409-1, GK Hall) Thorndike Pr.

Twisted Kicks. Tom Carson. LC 81-22901. 260p. 1982. pap. 5.95 (0-915904-62-4) And-Or Bks.

Twisted Kicks. Tom Carson. LC 81-67560. 264p. 1981. 12.95 (0-934558-03-5) Entwhistle Bks.

*Twisted Lights. Susan M. Hoskins. Ed. by Roderick Townley. 270p. (Orig.). 1997. pap. 12.00 (0-9656581-0-4) Integrity Pr.

*Twisted Mazes for Twisted Minds. Illus. by Charles Duncan. (Troubador Ser.). Orig. Title: MazeCraze 4. 32p. (J). (ps up). 1997. reprint ed. pap. 3.50 (0-8431-7960-0) Price Stern Sloan.

Twisted Memories: Collected Poetry of Kinoshita (Surname) Yuji. Kinoshita Yuji. Tr. & Intro. by Robert Epp. 280p. (C). 1993. text ed. 30.00 (1-880276-25-9) Yakusha.

Twisted Menorah & Other Devora Doresh Mysteries. Carol K. Hubner. 1981. 7.95 (0-910818-41-X); pap. 6.95 (0-910818-42-8) Judaica Pr.

*Twisted Metal 2: Unauthorized Game Secrets. Anthony Lynch. 96p. 1997. per. 12.99 (0-7615-1081-8) Prima Pub.

"The Twisted Mind" Madness in Herman Melville's Fiction. Paul McCarthy. LC 90-10754. 192p. (C). 1990. text ed. 26.95 (0-87745-284-9) U of Iowa Pr.

*Twisted Muse: Musicians & Their Music in the Third Reich. Michael H. Kater. 336p. 1997. 35.00 (0-19-509620-7) OUP.

Twisted Polynomial Hyperalgebras. Edward Halpern. LC 52-42839. (Memoirs Ser.: No. 1/29). 61p. 1972. reprint ed. pap. 19.00 (0-8218-1229-7, MEMO/1/29) Am Math.

Twisted Road to Auschwitz: Nazi Policy Toward German Jews, 1933-1939. Karl A. Schleunes. 304p. 1990. pap. text ed. 13.95 (0-252-06147-0) U of Ill Pr.

Twisted Road to Auschwitz: Nazi Policy Toward German Jews, 1933-1939. Karl A. Schleunes. LC 74-102024. 288p. reprint ed. pap. 82.10 (0-317-11169-8, 2011134) Bks Demand.

Twisted Road to Freedom: America's Granting of Independence to the Philippines. Keith T. Carlson. 176p. (C). 1996. pap. text ed. 16.00 (971-542-051-6, Pub. by U of Philippines Pr PH) UH Pr.

Twisted Scriptures: A Path to Freedom from Abusive Churches. Mary A. Chrnalogar. Ed. by Stephen D. Martin et al. LC 96-84980. (Illus.). 273p. (Orig.). 1997. pap. 15.95 (0-9649588-0-5) Control Technques.

Twisted Sisters Vol. 2: Drawing the Line. Carol Lay & M. K. Brown. Ed. by Diane Noomin. (Illus.). 176p. 1995. 24.95 (0-87816-344-1) Kitchen Sink.

Twisted Sisters Vol. 2: Drawing the Line. Ed. by Diane Noomin. (Illus.). 176p. 1995. pap. 15.95 (0-87816-339-5) Kitchen Sink.

Twisted Sisters Vol. 2: Drawing the Line. limited ed. Carol Lay & M. K. Brown. Ed. by Diane Noomin. (Illus.). 176p. 1995. 39.95 (0-87816-345-X) Kitchen Sink.

Twisted Summer. Roberts. (J). 1998. mass mkt. 3.99 (0-689-80600-0, Aladdin Paperbacks) S&S Childrens.

Twisted Summer. Willo D. Roberts. LC 95-585. 160p. (YA). (gr. 7 up). 1996. 15.00 (0-689-80459-8, Atheneum Bks Young) S&S Childrens.

Twisted Sword, Oart 1. large type ed. Winston Graham. (Charnwood Large Print Ser.). 1995. 27.99 (0-7089-8822-9, Charnwood) Ulverscroft.

Twisted Sword Part 2. large type ed. Winston Graham. (Charnwood Large Print Ser.). 1995. 27.99 (0-7089-8828-8, Charnwood) Ulverscroft.

Twisted Tails: Sifted Fact, Fantasy & Fiction from U. S. Coin History. Robert R. Van Ryzin. LC 95-79729. (Illus.). 240p. 1995. pap. text ed. 9.95 (0-87341-393-8, HGR01) Krause Pubns.

*Twisted Tale of Tiki Island, Vol. 21. R. L. Stine. (Give Yourself Goosebumps Ser.). (J). 1997. pap. text ed. 3.99 (0-590-93500-3) Scholastic Inc.

Twisted Tales: The Dripping Head & Other Gruesome Stories. R. C. Welch. (Illus.). 128p. (Orig.). (J). (gr. 3-7). 1992. pap. 4.95 (1-56288-314-3) Checkerboard.

Twisted Tales: The Slithering Corpse & Other Sinister Stories. R. C. Welch. (Illus.). 128p. (Orig.). (J). (gr. 3-7). 1992. pap. 4.95 (1-56288-315-1) Checkerboard.

Twisted Taurus. Ellen Steiber. (Zodiac Chillers Ser.: No. 4). 176p. (J). 1995. pap. 3.99 (0-679-87307-4) Random Bks Yng Read.

Twisted Thing. large type ed. Mickey Spillane. LC 93-38622. 1994. lib. bdg. 21.95 (0-8161-5556-9, GK Hall) Thorndike Pr.

Twisted Thing. large type ed. Mickey Spillane. LC 93-38622. 1994. lib. bdg. 17.95 (0-8161-5557-7, GK Hall) Thorndike Pr.

Twisted Tours. B. J. Specter. Ed. by Ruth Ashby. (Beetlejuice Ser.: No. 4). 128p. (Orig.). (J). 1992. pap. 2.99 (0-671-75558-7, Minstrel Bks) PB.

Twisted Tree. large type ed. Palma Harcourt. 384p. 1983. 25.99 (0-7089-0902-7) Ulverscroft.

Twisted Whiskers: Solving Your Cat's Behavior Problems. Pam Johnson. 1994. pap. 12.95 (0-89594-710-2) Crossing Pr.

Twisted Window. Lois Duncan. 192p. (J). (gr. k-12). 1988. mass mkt. 3.99 (0-440-20184-5, LLL BDD) BDD Bks Young Read.

Twister! Darleen B. Beard. LC 95-13862. (Illus.). (J). (gr. 3-7). write for info. (0-374-37977-7) FS&G.

Twister. Barbara Block. 304p. 1996. mass mkt. 4.99 (1-57566-062-8, Knsington) Kensgtn Pub Corp.

Twister. Michael Crichton. 1996. pap. 10.00 (0-345-40833-0) Ballantine.

*Twister. Michael Crichton & A. Martin. 1996. mass mkt. 4.99 (0-345-40970-1) Ballantine.

Twister. Keay Davidson. (Illus.). 224p. 1996. pap. 14.00 (0-671-00029-2) PB.

Twister. Lucille R. Penner. LC 96-19352. 1996. pap. 3.99 (0-679-88271-5) McKay.

Twister. Lucille R. Penner. LC 96-19352. 1996. lib. bdg. 11.99 (0-679-98271-X) McKay.

*Twister: Music from the Motion Picture Soundtrack. Ed. by Jeannette DeLisa & Sy Feldman. 52p. (Orig.). (YA). 1996. pap. text ed. 16.95 (1-57623-494-0, PF9628) Warner Brothers.

Twister: The Science of Tornadoes & the Making of Adventure Movie. Keay Davidson. (J). 1996. mass mkt. 3.99 (0-671-00396-8) PB.

Twister & Shout, Vol. 5. Focus on the Family Staff et al. (McGee & Me! Ser: Vol. 5). (J). 1989. pap. 5.99 (0-8423-4166-8) Tyndale.

Twister Country: A Novel. Don Monkerud. 232p. (Orig.). 1996. pap. 11.95 (1-886312-03-6) Buying Best.

*Twister Theory III. Mason. 1996. pap. write for info. (0-582-20992-7, Pub. by Longman UK) Longman.

*Twisters, Bronc Riders & Cherry Pie. Herb Marlow. LC 96-32100. (Illus.). (J). 1997. write for info. (1-56763-273-4); pap. write for info. (1-56763-274-2) Ozark Pub.

*Twisters, Stories from Other Centuries. (Longman Literature Ser.). 1992. pap. text ed. write for info. (0-582-07807-5, Pub. by Longman UK) Longman.

Twisting History: Lessons in Balloon Sculpting. Larry Moss. LC TT926.M67 1995. (Illus.). 110p. 1995. pap. text ed. 14.95 (0-9648497-3-9) Fooled Ya.

Twisting of the Rope see Three Irish Plays

Twisting Paths. large type ed. D. Y. Cameron. 1990. pap. 15.99 (0-7089-6873-2, Trailtree Bookshop) Ulverscroft.

Twistor. John Cramer. 352p. 1991. mass mkt. 5.99 (0-380-71027-7) Avon.

Twistor Geometry & Field Theory. R. S. Ward & R. O. Wells, Jr. (Monographs on Mathematical Physics). 350p. 1990. 110.00 (0-521-26890-7) Cambridge U Pr.

Twistor Geometry & Field Theory. R. S. Ward & R. O. Wells, Jr. (Monographs on Mathematical Physics). (Illus.). 532p. (C). 1991. pap. text ed. 42.95 (0-521-42268-X) Cambridge U Pr.

Twistor Theory. Ed. by Stephen Huggett. LC 94-37775. (Lecture Notes in Pure & Applied Mathematics Ser.: Vol. 169). 288p. 1994. 125.00 (0-8247-9321-8) Dekker.

Twistor Theory for Riemannian Symmetric Spaces. F. E. Burstall & J. H. Rawnsley. Ed. by A. Dold et al. (Lecture Notes in Mathematics Ser.: Vol. 1424). iii, 112p. 1990. 30.95 (0-387-52602-1) Spr-Verlag.

Twistors in Mathematics & Physics. Ed. by T. N. Bailey & R. J. Baston. (London Mathematical Society Lecture Note Ser.: No. 156). (Illus.). 350p. (C). 1990. pap. text ed. 44.95 (0-521-39783-9) Cambridge U Pr.

Twists & Braids. Consumer Guide Staff. 1996. pap. 7.99 (0-451-82309-5) NAL-Dutton.

Twists & Turns: A Mother's Caring Journey: Two Children with Schizophrenia. Ruth C. Ackerman. LC 93-94015. (Illus.). 164p. (Orig.). 1993. pap. 12.00 (0-9637493-0-7) Paths of Life.

Twists & Turns & Tangles in Math & Physics: Instructional Material for Developing Scientific & Logical Thinking. Samuel Katzoff. (Illus.). 428p. (Orig.). (YA). (gr. 5-12). 1994. pap. text ed. 40.00 (1-881622-15-0) JHU IAAY.

Twists of Fate. Francis D. Lyon. 256p. (Orig.). 1993. pap. 14.95 (1-879260-10-7) Evanston Pub.

Twists of the Tale. Ellen Datlow. 352p. 1996. mass mkt. 5.50 (0-440-21771-7) Dell.

*Twitch & Shout. Lowell Handler. 1998. pap. 23.95 (0-525-94216-5) NAL-Dutton.

Twits. Roald Dahl & Mary Tannen. LC 80-18410. (Illus.). (J). (ps-5). 1981. 12.00 (0-394-84599-4); lib. bdg. 12.99 (0-394-94599-9) Knopf Bks Yng Read.

Twits. Roald Dahl. (Illus.). 96p. (J). (gr. 2-6). 1991. pap. 3.99 (0-14-034640-6, Puffin) Puffin Bks.

Twitter Machine, or The Necessity for Theory: Essays on Language & Linguistics. N. V. Smith. (Illus.). 288p. 1989. pap. text ed. 24.95 (0-631-16926-1) Blackwell Pubs.

Twixt Land & Sea: Three Tales. Joseph Conrad. Ed. & Intro. by Boris Ford. 240p. (J). 1991. pap. 8.95 (0-14-018392-2, Penguin Classics) Viking Penguin.

Twixt Sand & Sea. C. F. Grant & L. Grant. 622p. 1986. 350.00 (1-85077-094-8, Pub. by Darf Pubs Ltd UK) St Mut.

TWO. Shelby C. Laney. LC 91-67929. 96p. (J). 1993. pap. 8.00 (1-56002-188-8, Univ Edtns) Aegina Pr.

2. Romulus Linney. 1993. pap. 5.25 (0-8222-1486-5) Dramatists Play.

Two. John D. MacDonald. 104p. 1983. pap. 2.50 (0-88184-011-4) Carroll & Graf.

Two: Gertrude Stein & Her Brother & Other Early Portraits, Vol. One Of Unpublished Works Of Gertrude Stein In. Gertrude Stein. LC 74-103667. (Select Bibliographies Reprint Ser.). 1977. 30.95 (0-8369-5167-0) Ayer.

Two: Learning to Drown - Addy, Laura & Old Jack Butler. Sebastian Beaumont. 1994. pap. 13.95 (1-873741-17-0, Pub. by Millvres Bks UK) LPC InBook.

Two - Wheeler Technology, Dictionary of German, French, & English. B. Couzereau. 432p. 1990. 75.00 (3-87073-054-4) IBD Ltd.

Two Academic Lives: George Herbert Palmer & Alice Freeman Palmer a Compilation. Arthur J. Linenthal. LC 94-96814. (Illus.). 630p. 1995. 25.00 (0-9626606-1-2) A J Linenthal.

Two Addresses. James W. Nesmith. 56p. 1978. pap. 9.95 (0-87770-202-0) Ye Galleon.

An Asterisk (*) at the beginning of an entry indicates that the title is appearing in BIP for the first time.

Two Admirals. James Fenimore Cooper. (Works of James Fenimore Cooper Ser.). 1990. reprint ed. lib. bdg. 79.00 (*0-7812-2388-1*) Rprt Serv.

Two Admirals: A Tale. James Fenimore Cooper. LC 88-12190. 511p. (Orig.). (YA). (gr. 9-12). 1990. text ed. 59.50 (*0-88706-905-3*); pap. text ed. 19.95 (*0-88706-907-X*) State U NY Pr.

Two Aesthetic Realism Papers: Opposites in the Drama; Opposites in Myself. Martha Baird. LC 79-268159. 59p. (Orig.). 1971. pap. 5.50 (*0-910492-15-8*) Definition.

Two Against Hitler: Stealing the Nazis' Best-Kept Secrets. John V. Dippel. LC 91-25248. 272p. 1992. text ed. 49.95 (*0-275-93745-3*, C3745, Praeger Pubs) Greenwood.

Two Against One. Frederick Barthelme. 272p. 1996. reprint ed. pap. 12.00 (*0-8021-3460-2*, Grove) Grove-Atltic.

Two Against the Tide. Bruce Clements. (Sunburst Ser.). 224p. (J). (gr. 4 up). 1987. pap. 3.50 (*0-374-48016-8*) FS&G.

Two Against the Tide: A Conscientious Objector in World War II. Adrian Wilson. 212p. 1990. 25.00 (*0-614-16149-5*) Oak Knoll.

Two Against the Tide, A Conscientious Objector in World War II: Selected Letters, 1941-1948. Adrian Wilson. Ed. & Comment by Joyce L. Wilson. (Illus.). 200p. 1990. 25.00 (*0-935072-19-5*) W T Taylor.

Two Against the World. large type ed. Mary A. Wilson. (Romance Ser.). 1996. 19.95 (*0-373-59667-7*) Silhouette.

Two Ages. Ed. by Robert L. Perkins. LC 83-25106. (International Kierkegaard Commentary Ser.: No. 14). xxiv, 266p. 1984. 18.95 (*0-86554-081-0*, MUP-H059) Mercer Univ Pr.

Two Alberts: Fountain & Fall. Gordon R. Owen. (Illus.). 576p. 1996. 28.95 (*1-881325-20-2*) Yucca Tree Pr.

Two Alone. Sandra Brown. (Mira Bks.). 1995. mass mkt. 4.99 (*1-55166-049-0*, 1-66049-7, Mira Bks) Harlequin Bks.

Two Americans Within the Gates: The Story of Levi Parsons & Pliny Fisk in Jerusalem. Eli Mizrachi. (Illus.). 394p. 1995. 19.95 (*1-884369-23-5*) McDougal Pubng.

Two Amish Folk Artists: The Story of Henry Lapp & Barbara Ebersol. Louise Stoltzfus. LC 93-35424. (Illus.). 128p. (Orig.). 1995. pap. 19.95 (*1-56148-078-9*) Good Bks PA.

Two Ancient Christologies: A Study in the Christological Thought of the Schools of Alexandria & Antioch in the Early History of Christian Doctrine. Robert V. Sellers. LC 82-45824. (Orthodoxies & Heresies in the Early Church Ser.). reprint ed. 39.50 (*0-404-62394-8*) AMS Pr.

Two & a Half Men in a Boat. large type ed. Nigel Williams. 1995. 25.99 (*0-7089-3286-X*) Ulverscroft.

Two & Bed. Jim Cartwright. 180p. 1994. pap. 13.95 (*0-413-68330-3*, A0697, Pub. by Methuen UK) Heinemann.

Two & Company. rev. ed. Ed. by W. P. Baxter & McRae Williams. (Illus.). 410p. reprint ed. 16.95 (*0-9627326-0-5*) St Thomas Garrison.

Two & Three Part Inventions (Fifteen Inventions & Fifteen Symphonies) Johann Sebastian Bach. Ed. by Eric Simon. LC 68-11918. (Facsimile Series of Musical Manuscripts). (Orig.). 1969. pap. 8.95 (*0-486-21982-8*) Dover.

Two & Three-Part Inventions for Piano. Johann Sebastian Bach. Ed. by Carl Czerny. (Carl Fischer Music Library: No. 304). 63p. (ENG & GER.). 1903. pap. 7.95 (*0-8258-0102-8*, L 304) Fischer Inc NY.

Two & Two Are Four. Carolyn Haywood. LC 86-4619. (Illus.). 180p. (J). (gr. 1-5). 1986. pap. 5.00 (*0-15-291771-3*, Voyager Bks) HarBrace.

***Two Anglo-Saxon Buildings & Associated Finds.** G. Milne & J. Richards. (Wharram Ser.: Vol. VII). 114p. 1992. 14.00 (*0-946722-09-9*, Pub. by U York Dept Archaeol UK) David Brown.

Two Anglo-Saxon Pontificals. Ed. by H. M. Banting. (Henry Bradshaw Society Ser.: No. CIV). 240p. 1989. 55.00 (*0-9501009-6-X*) Boydell & Brewer.

Two Angry Women of Abingdon. Henry Porter. LC 70-133722. (Tudor Facsimile Texts. Old English Plays Ser.: No. 87). reprint ed. 49.50 (*0-404-53387-6*) AMS Pr.

Two Are Better Than One: A Guide to Prayer Partnerships That Work. David R. Mains & Steve Bell. 144p. (Orig.). 1995. reprint ed. pap. 4.99 (*1-879050-78-1*) Chapel of Air.

Two Are Twins. June Albertsen. LC 86-70195. (Illus.). 31p. (J). (ps-3). 1987. pap. 5.95 (*0-9615839-0-8*) Double Talk.

Two Armies & One Fatherland: The End of the Nationale Volksarmee. Jorg Schonbohm. Tr. by Peter Johnson & Elfi Johnson from GER. LC 95-38478. (Modern German Studies). 256p. 1996. 49.95 (*1-57181-069-2*) Berghahn Bks.

Two Arrows Meeting in Mid-Air: The Zen Koan. John D. Loori. LC 94-7737. (Library of Enlightenment). 288p. (Orig.). 1994. pap. 16.95 (*0-8048-3012-6*) C E Tuttle.

Two Asian Democracies: Comparative Study of the Single Predominant Party Systems of India & Japan. Takako Hirose. (C). 1994. 24.00 (*81-220-0339-7*, Pub. by Konark Pubs II) S Asia.

Two Aspirations of Humanity. Nassif Isaac. 168p. (C). 1988. 35.00 (*0-7212-0773-1*, Pub. by Regency Press UK) St Mut.

Two Aspirin - First Dose. John N. Withers. LC 89-81186. 100p. 1989. pap. 9.95 (*0-9624722-0-4*) IPO Pub.

Two Aspirin, Second Dose. John N. Withers. 125p. (Orig.). 1990. pap. 9.95 (*0-9624722-1-2*) IPO Pub.

Two at One Piano, Bk. 1. Jon George. (Frances Clark Library for Piano Students). 16p. 1969. pap. text ed. 5.95 (*0-87487-141-7*) Summy-Birchard.

Two at One Piano, Bk. 2. Jon George. (Frances Clark Library for Piano Students). 16p. 1972. pap. text ed. 5.95 (*0-87487-142-5*) Summy-Birchard.

***Two at One Piano, Bk. 3.** Jon George. (Frances Clark Library for Piano Students). 16p. 1976. pap. text ed. 5.95 (*0-87487-143-3*) Summy-Birchard.

Two Augustans: John Locke, Jonathan Swift. Ricardo Quintana. LC 77-91059. 157p. 1978. reprint ed. pap. 44.80 (*0-608-01909-7*, 2062561) Bks Demand.

Two Aztec Wood Idols: Iconographic & Chronologic Analysis. H. B. Nicholson & Rainer Berger. LC 68-58701. (Studies in Pre-Columbian Art & Archaeology: No. 5). (Illus.). 28p. 1968. pap. 6.00 (*0-88402-026-6*) Dumbarton Oaks.

Two-B & the Rock 'n' Roll Band. Sherry Paul. (See How I Read Ser.). (Illus.). 32p. (Orig.). (J). (ps-2). 16.20 (*0-685-01197-6*) CPI Pub.

Two-B & the Rock 'n' Roll Band, Set. Sherry Paul. (See How I Read Ser.). (Illus.). 32p. (Orig.). (J). (ps-2). pap. 14.10 (*0-675-01082-9*) CPI Pub.

Two-B & the Space Visitor. Sherry Paul. (See How I Read Ser.). (Illus.). 32p. (Orig.). (J). (ps-2). pap. 14.10 (*0-685-01198-4*); pap. 16.20 (*0-685-01199-2*) CPI Pub.

Two Babylons. Alexander Hislop. 330p. 1943. 18.99 (*0-87213-330-3*) Loizeaux.

Two Babylons. Gordon Lindsay. (Revelation Ser.: Vol. 13). 1962. 1.95 (*0-89985-046-4*) Christ for the Nations.

Two Bacchises see Amphitryon

Two Bad Ants. Chris Van Allsburg. (Illus.). 32p. (J). (ps up). 1988. 17.95 (*0-395-48668-8*) HM.

Two Bad Boys: A Very Old Cherokee Tale. Illus. & Retold by Gail E. Haley. LC 95-21415. 32p. (J). (gr. k-3). 1996. pap. 14.99 (*0-525-45311-3*) Dutton Child Bks.

Two Bad Mice. (Beatrix Potter Coloring Bks.: No. S884-5). (J). 1991. pap. 1.95 (*0-7214-5285-X*, Ladybrd) Penguin.

Two Bad Mice. (Classic Tales Ser.). (Illus.). 24p. (J). 1993. 4.98 (*1-56173-478-0*) Pubns Intl Ltd.

Two Bad Mice. Illus. by T. F. Marsh et al. (Classic Tales Ser.). 24p. (J). (gr. 2-4). 1992. lib. bdg. 10.95 (*1-56674-011-8*, HTS Bks) Forest Hse.

Two Bad Mice Deluxe. Beatrix Potter. 1997. pap. 16.00 (*0-7232-4184-8*) Warne.

***Two Bad Mice Hide n' Seek.** Beatrix Potter. (J). 1997. pap. 3.99 (*0-7232-4358-1*) Warne.

Two Badd Babies. Jeffie R. Gordon. LC 91-72869. (Illus.). 32p. (J). (ps-3). 1992. 14.95 (*1-878093-85-1*) Boyds Mills Pr.

Two Battles of Little Big Horn. Carroll. 1976. pap. 15.95 (*0-685-71831-X*, J M C & Co) Amereon Ltd.

Two Battles of the Little Horn. Ed. by John M. Carroll. (Illus.). 1985. pap. 23.95 (*0-8488-0029-X*, J M C & Co) Amereon Ltd.

***Two Bear Cubs.** LC 97-17226. 1997. write for info. (*0-939666-87-1*) Yosemite Assn.

Two Bear Cubs. Houghton Mifflin Company Staff. (Literature Experience 1991 Ser.). (J). (gr. 2). 1990. pap. 5.44 (*0-395-53430-5*) HM.

Two Bear Cubs. Ann Jonas. LC 82-2860. (Illus.). 24p. (J). (gr. k-3). 1982. lib. bdg. 14.93 (*0-688-01408-9*) Greenwillow.

Two-Bear Mambo. Joe R. Lansdale. 288p. 1996. mass mkt. 5.99 (*0-446-40188-9*, Mysterious Paperbk) Warner Bks.

Two Bedrooms in San Francisco. David Reed & Carlos Basualdo. Tr. by Roberto Echavarren. (Illus.). 12p. (Orig.). (ENG & SPA.). 1992. pap. 5.00 (*0-930495-17-9*) San Fran Art Inst.

Two Best Friends. Elizabeth Koda-Callan. LC 94-25767. (Illus.). 40p. (J). (ps-3). 1994. 12.95 (*1-56305-730-1*, 3730) Workman Pub.

Two Best Job Search Methods. J. Michael Farr & Susan Christophersen. Ed. by Sara Hall. (Living Skills Ser.). (Illus.). 64p. 1992. pap. 5.95 (*1-56370-040-9*, TBJS) JIST Works.

Two Billion Dollar Cookbook. EFFC, Inc. Staff. 312p. 1990. 19.95 (*0-9630440-0-1*) Beans Cafe.

Two Biographies by African-American Women. Intro. by William L. Andrews. (Schomburg Library of Nineteenth-Century Black Women Writers). 512p. 1991. 32.50 (*0-685-47937-4*) OUP.

Two Birds Flying. Phyllis S. Prokop. Ed. by Frances B. Goodman. (Illus.). 1984. 12.95 (*0-89896-150-5*) Larksdale.

Two Birthdays for Beth. Gay L. Cronin. LC 94-39797. (Illus.). 32p. (J). (ps-3). 1995. 14.00 (*0-944934-13-7*) Perspect Indiana.

Two-Bit Heroes. Doris Egan. 320p. (Orig.). 1992. mass mkt. 4.99 (*0-88677-500-0*) DAW Bks.

Two-Bit Tango. Elizabeth Pincus. LC 92-17511. (Neil Fury Ser.). (Illus.). 193p. (Orig.). 1992. pap. 9.95 (*0-933216-88-2*) Spinsters Ink.

Two Bites at a Cherry, with Other Tales. Thomas B. Aldrich. 1972. reprint ed. lib. bdg. 27.00 (*0-8422-8002-2*) Irvington.

Two Bites at a Cherry, with Other Tales. Thomas B. Aldrich. (C). 1986. reprint ed. pap. text ed. 6.95 (*0-8290-2044-6*) Irvington.

Two Bites at a Cherry, with Other Tales. Thomas B. Aldrich. (Works of Thomas Bailey Aldrich). 1989. reprint ed. lib. bdg. 79.00 (*0-7812-1676-1*) Rprt Serv.

***2-Bits Worth of Tennis Tips: For Just a Few Bucks.** Jerry Cooper. 24p. (Orig.). 1996. pap. 3.95 (*1-889419-06-0*) J Cooper.

Two Black Folk Artists: Clementine Hunter & Nellie Mae Rowe. Sterling Cook. LC 86-62956. 16p. 1986. pap. 5.00 (*0-940784-09-2*) Miami Univ Art.

Two Black Teachers During the Civil War: Mary S. Peake: The Colored Teacher at Fortress Monroa. Lewis C. Lockwood & Charlotte L. Forten. 1970. 12.95 (*0-405-01931-9*, 16381) Ayer.

Two Black Views of Liberia: Four Months in Liberia, or African Colonization Exposed Four Years in Liberia, a Sketch of the Life of Rev. Samuel Williams. William Nesbit & Samuel W. Williams. LC 70-92234. (American Negro: His History & Literature. Series 3). 1970. reprint ed. 16.95 (*0-405-01936-X*) Ayer.

Two Blades of Grass: A History of Scientific Development in the U. S. Department of Agriculture. T. Swann Harding. Ed. by I. Bernard Cohen. LC 79-7966. (Three Centuries of Science in America Ser.). (Illus.). 1980. reprint ed. lib. bdg. 35.95 (*0-405-12547-X*) Ayer.

Two Blind Mice. Samuel Spewack. 1949. pap. 13.00 (*0-8222-1180-7*) Dramatists Play.

Two Blocks East of Vine. Iris Berry. (Illus.). 108p. (Orig.). 1994. pap. 11.00 (*1-884615-00-7*) Incommcdo San Diego.

Two Bohemians in Paris: Selected Works of Ignaz Moscheles (1794-1870) & Alexander Dreyschock (1818-1869) Ed. by Jeffrey Kallberg. LC 92-42777. (Piano Music of the Parisian Virtuosos, 1810-1860 Ser.: Vol. 5). 328p. 1993. text ed. 110.00 (*0-8153-0851-5*) Garland.

***Two Bookes of Francis Bacon: Of Proficience & Advancement of Learning (1605 Edition)** Francis Bacon. Ed. & Intro. by Jeffrey Stern. (Classics in Education Ser.). 120p. 1996. reprint ed. write for info. (*1-85506-267-4*) Bks Intl VA.

Two Books of the Duty of Man & Citizen According to Natural Law, Vol. 2. Samuel Von Pufendorf. LC 95-77089. (Classics in International Law Reprint Ser.: No. 10). 1995. reprint ed. 85.00 (*1-57588-255-8*, 310200) W S Hein.

Two Books of the Pleas of a Spanish Advocate, No. 9, Vol. 2. Albercio Gentili. LC 95-77185. 1995. reprint ed. 100.00 (*1-57588-254-X*, 310180) W S Hein.

Two Books on Stanzas of Dzyan. H. P. Blavatsky. 1986. 8.75 (*81-7059-006-X*) Theos Pub Hse.

Two Books on Verbal Music. Gaspar Stoquerus. Ed. & Tr. by Albert C. Rotola from LAT. LC 88-25045. (Greek & Latin Music Theory Ser.). xii, 298p. 1988. text ed. 35.00 (*0-8032-4163-1*) U of Nebr Pr.

Two Books...of the Proficience & Advancement of Learning. Francis Bacon. LC 70-25525. (English Experience Ser.: No. 218). 236p. 1970. reprint ed. 45.00 (*90-221-0218-1*) Walter J Johnson.

Two Boxes of Gold. 1993. 5.25 (*0-19-585396-2*) OUP.

Two-Boy Weekend. Francine Pascal. (Sweet Valley High Ser.: No. 54). 160p. (YA). 1989. pap. 2.99 (*0-553-27856-8*) Bantam.

Two-Boy Weekend. large type ed. Francine Pascal. (Sweet Valley High Ser.: No. 54). 150p. (J). (gr. 5-8). 1989. reprint ed. 9.50 (*1-55905-009-8*, Gareth Stevens Inc); reprint ed. lib. bdg. 10.50 (*1-55905-019-5*, Gareth Stevens Inc) Grey Castle.

Two Brahman Sources of Emerson & Thoreau, 1822-1832. Ed. by William B. Stein. LC 67-10340. 1967. 50.00 (*0-8201-1043-4*) Schol Facsimiles.

Two Brahmanical Institutions-Gotra & Charana. Govind S. Ghurye. 312p. 1972. 15.95 (*0-318-37173-1*) Asia Bk Corp.

Two Brazilian Capitals: Architecture & Urbanism in Rio De Janeiro & Brasilia. Norma Evenson. LC 72-91293. 343p. reprint ed. pap. 97.80 (*0-8357-8357-X*, 2033720) Bks Demand.

Two-Bridge Knots Have Property P. Moto-O Takahashi. LC 80-26113. (Memoirs Ser.: No. 29/239). 104p. 1981. pap. 16.00 (*0-8218-2239-X*, MEMO/29/239) Am Math.

Two Brothers. 1982. pap. 2.95 (*0-87306-242-6*) Feldheim.

Two Brothers. Chen Li. (Asian Folk Tales Ser.). (Illus.). 24p. (J). 1995. 9.95 (*983-9808-70-2*, Pub. by Delta Edits MY) Weatherhill.

Two Brothers. Tr. by Saphan Ros. LC 94-14516. (Illus.). 32p. (J). (gr. k up). 1995. 15.00 (*0-688-12550-6*); lib. bdg. 14.93 (*0-688-12551-4*) Lothrop.

Two Brothers. Waldman. (J). 1997. 17.00 (*0-689-31936-3*, Atheneum Bks Young) S&S Childrens.

Two Brothers - Lili & Li Zheng: Contemporary Painting from the People's Republic of China. Terry Sohre et al. (Illus.). 40p. 1992. pap. text ed. 12.00 (*1-881756-00-9*) C J Smith Gallery.

Two Brothers - Paths West & East: 1800s America. Mary S. Heimburger. Ed. by Roberta Debono. (Illus.). 186p. (Orig.). 1992. pap. 10.00 (*0-9613901-3-1*) Ankh Pr CA.

Two Brothers & Their Magic Gourds. Ed. by Edward B. Adams. (Korean Folk Story for Children Ser.). (Illus.). 32p. (J). (gr. 3). 1981. 10.95 (*0-8048-1474-0*, Pub. by Seoul Intl Tourist KO) C E Tuttle.

***Two Brothers That Aren't the Same.** Christopher P. Roland, Jr. Ed. by Malik R. Bey. (Illus.). (Orig.). (J). (gr. k-4). 1997. pap. 1.99 (*0-9656137-8-X*) M Bey.

Two Bullies Meet. Dorothy I. Murray. 12p. 1994. pap. 5.99 (*0-925037-20-6*) Great Lks Poetry.

Two Burner Gourmet: Cooking. Terry Searfoss. 192p. 1994. reprint ed. pap. text ed. 14.95 (*0-9643733-0-0*) The Two Burner.

Two Bushy Badgers. Patience Brewster. LC 92-40696. (Illus.). (J). 1995. 14.95 (*0-316-10862-6*) Little.

***Two, But Not Two: Inspired Poems.** Mary Robinson. 24p. 1996. pap. 7.00 (*0-8059-3860-5*) Dorrance.

***Two Butterflies.** Corazon S. Vigilia. Ed. by Ceres S. Alabado. (English-Philipino Bilingual Ser.: No. 1). (Illus.). 20p. (Orig.). (J). (gr. k-3). 1997. pap. 5.99 (*1-890903-00-0*) SB Intl Corp.

Two Butterflies on My Head: Psychoanalysis in the Interdisciplinary Scientific Dialogue. Ed. by M. Leuzinger-Bohleber et al. (Illus.). 280p. 1992. pap. 40.00 (*0-387-53899-2*) Spr-Verlag.

Two by Four Furniture: Simple, Inexpensive & Great-Looking Projects You Can Make. Stevie Henderson. (Illus.). 128p. 1994. pap. 14.95 (*0-8069-0294-9*) Sterling.

Two by Ralph Waldo Trine. Ralph W. Trine. LC 86-10294. (Pivot Family Reader Ser.). 306p. (Orig.). pap. 4.50 (*0-87983-382-3*) Keats.

Two by Two. (Vocal Score Ser.). 160p. 1981. pap. 40.00 (*0-88188-054-X*, 00312461) H Leonard.

***Two by Two.** Frank Schaffer Publications Staff. 1997. pap. text ed. 2.49 (*0-7647-0239-4*) Schaffer Pubns.

Two by Two. Godwin. (J). 1998. 13.00 (*0-671-75354-1*, S&S Bks Young Read) S&S Childrens.

Two by Two. Barbara Reid. 1996. pap. text ed. 4.95 (*0-590-64942-6*) Scholastic Inc.

***Two by Two.** Capper Sample. 128p. (Orig.). 1997. mass mkt. 4.99 (*1-55197-879-2*, Pub. by Comnwlth Pub CN) Partners Pubs Grp.

Two by Two: A Cartoonist's Look at Missionary Life. Darold L. Westover. (Illus.). 96p. 1992. pap. 7.98 (*0-88290-453-1*) Horizon Utah.

Two by Two: Favorite Bible Stories. Harry Araten. LC 90-46841. (Illus.). 32p. (J). (gr. k-3). 1991. pap. 7.95 (*0-929371-54-2*) Kar-Ben.

Two-by-Two: Statistical Methods: Games & Songs. Turkan Kumbaraci & George H. Gardenier. LC 89-90944. (Gardenier Math-Stat Ser.). (Illus.). 19p. (J). (gr. 1-8). 1989. 20.00 (*0-685-29042-5*, 0006) Teka Trends.

***Two by Two: The Story of Noah's Faith.** Marilyn Lashbrook. (Me Too Bks.). (Illus.). 30p. (J). 1996. 7.95 (*0-87973-842-1*) Our Sunday Visitor.

Two by Two: The Story of Noah's Faith. Marilyn Lashbrook. LC 87-60263. (Me Too! Bks.). (Illus.). 32p. (J). (ps). 1987. 5.95 (*0-86606-427-3*, 842) Treasure Pub.

Two by Two: The Untold Story. Kathryn Hewitt. LC 84-4579. (Illus.). 32p. (J). (ps-3). 1984. 13.00 (*0-15-291801-9*, HB Juv Bks) HarBrace.

Two by Two: The Untold Story. Kathryn Hewitt. LC 84-4579. (Illus.). 32p. (J). (ps-3). 1989. pap. 4.00 (*0-15-291802-7*, Voyager Bks) HarBrace.

Two by Two: Twenty-Two Pairs of Maps from the Newberry Library Illustrating 500 Years of Western Cartographic History. J. Akerman et al. (Illus.). 48p. 1993. pap. 12.00 (*0-911028-52-8*) Newberry.

Two by Two: Vocal Selections. (Illus.). 040p. 1981. pap. 8.95 (*0-88188-120-1*, 00312460) H Leonard.

***Two by Two: With Cassette.** Frank Schaffer Publications Staff. 1997. pap. text ed. 12.95 incl. audio (*0-7647-0271-8*) Schaffer Pubns.

Two by Two see De Dos en Dos (Noe)

Two-by-Two-by-Two. Jonathan Allen. LC 94-25900. (Illus.). 40p. (J). 1995. pap. 14.99 (*0-8037-1838-1*) Dial Bks Young.

***Two Caddoan Farmsteads in the Red River Valley: The Archeology of the McLelland & Joe Clark Sites.** Ed. by David B. Kelley. LC 97-16922. (Research Ser.: No. 51). (Illus.). 1997. write for info. (*1-56349-082-X*) AR Archaeol.

Two Californias: The Truth about the Split-State Movement. Michael DiLeo & Eleanor Smith. LC 83-307. (Illus.). 248p. (Orig.). 1985. pap. 14.95 (*0-933280-16-5*) Island Pr.

Two Called Together. George Gerl & George Lane. 1978. teacher ed. 4.00 (*0-8294-0277-2*); pap. text ed. 4.00 (*0-8294-0274-8*) Loyola Pr.

Two Can Toucan. David McKee. (Illus.). 32p. (J). (gr. k-3). 1987. 15.95 (*0-86264-094-6*, Pub. by Andersen Pr UK) Trafalgar.

***Two Cantatas for Soprano & Chamber Ensemble.** Louis-Nicolas Clerambault. Ed. by Donald H. Foster. (Recent Researches in Music of the Baroque Era Ser.: Vol. RRB27). (Illus.). xxiv, 89p. 1979. pap. 38.40 (*0-89579-104-8*) A-R Eds.

Two Careers, One Family: The Promise of Gender Equality. Lucia A. Gilbert. (Series on Close Relationships: Vol. 4). (Illus.). 154p. (C). 1993. text ed. 38.00 (*0-8039-5072-1*); pap. text ed. 16.95 (*0-8039-5073-X*) Sage.

Two Carlyles. O. Burdett. LC 71-130269. (English Biography Ser.: No. 31). 1970. reprint ed. lib. bdg. 62.95 (*0-8383-1176-8*) M S G Haskell Hse.

Two Carlyles. Osbert Burdett. LC 78-164591. (Select Bibliographies Reprint Ser.). 1977. reprint ed. 23.95 (*0-8369-5875-6*) Ayer.

Two Cartographers: Gudbrandur Thorlaksson & Thordur Thorlaksson. Haandor Hermannsson. LC 27-13445. (Islandica Ser.: Vol. 17). 1926. 25.00 (*0-527-00347-6*) Periodicals Srv.

***Two Cases on Institutionalizing Service Learning: How Campus Climate Affects the Change Process.** 64p. 1996. pap. 10.00 (*0-614-30597-7*) Ed Comm States.

Two Cats for Puerto Rico & A Sailor's Yarns & Observations. Dean Nichols. LC 93-71481. (Illus.). 1993. pap. 14.95 (*0-8323-0502-2*) Binford Mort.

Two-Center Effects in Ion-Atom Collisions: A Symposium in Honor of M. Eugene Rudd upon His Retirement: Lincoln, Nebraska, May 13-14, 1994. Ed. by Timothy J. Gay & Anthony F. Starace. (CP Ser.: No. 362). (Illus.). 288p. 1996. 145.00 (*1-56396-342-6*) Am Inst Physics.

***Two Cents & a Milk Bottle.** Lee C. Batterman. LC 97-12092. (Illus.). 272p. (J). (gr. 3-5). 1997. 18.95 (*1-881283-17-8*) Alef Design.

Two Cents Pieces. 2nd ed. M. Kliman. LC 82-70831. (Illus.). 1983. pap. 10.00 (*0-915262-84-3*) S J Durst.

***Two Centuries of American Planning.** Ed. by Daniel Schaffer. LC 86-31293. 335p. 1988. reprint ed. pap. 95.50 (*0-608-03707-9*, 2064532) Bks Demand.

Two Centuries of Art & Life in America. Howard E. Wooden. LC 87-51156. (Illus.). 80p. 1987. pap. 5.00 (*0-939324-31-8*) Wichita Art Mus.

Two Centuries of Costume in America, 2 vols. Alice Earle. 824p. 1974. reprint ed. Set. 75.00 (*0-87928-054-9*) Corner Hse.

Two Centuries of Costume in America, 2 Vols. Alice M. Earle. LC 68-56468. (Illus.). 1972. reprint ed. Set. 44.95 (*0-405-08477-3*, Pub. by Blom Pubns UK) Ayer.

Two Centuries of Costume in America, 2 Vols, 1. Alice M. Earle. LC 68-56468. (Illus.). 1972. reprint ed. 23.95 (*0-405-08478-1*, Pub. by Blom Pubns UK) Ayer.

Two Centuries of Costume in America, 2 Vols, 2. Alice M. Earle. LC 68-56468. (Illus.). 1972. reprint ed. 23.95 (*0-405-08479-X*, Pub. by Blom Pubns UK) Ayer.

Two Centuries of Ecumenism. Georges H. Tavard. LC 78-6449. 239p. 1978. reprint ed. text ed. 55.00 (*0-313-20490-X*, TATC, Greenwood Pr) Greenwood.

Two Centuries of Education in New South Wales. Alan Barcan. 1988. pap. 29.95 (*0-86840-322-9*, Pub. by New South Wales Univ Pr AT) Intl Spec Bk.

Two Centuries of Hispanic Theatre in the Southwest. Nicolas Kanellos. (Illus.). 1982. pap. 3.00 (*0-88734-614-6*) Arte Publico.

Two Centuries of New Milford, Connecticut, 1707-1907. (Illus.). 307p. 1994. reprint ed. lib. bdg. 32.50 (*0-8328-3902-7*) Higginson Bk Co.

Two Centuries of Prints in America, 1680-1880: A Selective Catalogue of the Winterthur Collection. E. McSherry Fowble. LC 87-611. (Illus.). 543p. 1987. text ed. 75.00 (*0-8139-1124-9*) U Pr of Va.

Two Centuries of Roman Poetry. Eberhard C. Kennedy & A. Davis. (Latin Texts Ser.). 1992. 21.95 (*0-17-438516-1*) Focus Pub-R Pullins.

Two Centuries of Roman Prose. Eberhard C. Kennedy & A. Davis. (Latin Texts Ser.). 21.95 (*0-17-438519-6*) Focus Pub-R Pullins.

Two Centuries of Spanish & English Bilingual Lexicography, 1590-1800. Roger J. Steiner. LC 74-110958. (Janua Linguarum, Ser. Practica: No. 108). (Orig.). 1970. pap. text ed. 26.15 (*90-279-0743-9*) Mouton.

Two Centuries of Spenserian Scholarship. Jewel Wurtsbaugh. LC 77-126682. reprint ed. 21.50 (*0-404-07058-2*) AMS Pr.

Two Centuries of U. S. Foreign Policy: The Documentary Record. Ed. by Stephen J. Valone. LC 95-13433. 208p. 1995. text ed. 59.95 (*0-275-95324-6*, Praeger Pubs); pap. text ed. 17.95 (*0-275-95325-4*, Praeger Pubs) Greenwood.

***Two Centuries Plus.** Hageman. 1984. pap. 12.00 (*0-8028-0039-4*) Eerdmans.

***Two Chains.** Paul Buxton. 1992. pap. 3.00 (*1-57514-293-7*) Encore Perform Pub.

Two Chapbooks. David Steingass & Joseph Hutchison. (Juniper Bk. Ser.: No. 54). 1990. pap. 6.00 (*1-55780-125-8*) Juniper Pr WI.

Two-Character Play. rev. ed. Tennessee Williams. LC 73-78789. 1979. pap. 8.95 (*0-8112-0729-3*, NDP483) New Directions.

Two-Character Plays for Student Actors: A Collection of 15 One-Act Plays. Robert Mauro. Ed. by Arthur L. Zapel. LC 88-60078. 192p. (Orig.). 1988. pap. text ed. 14.95 (*0-916260-53-4*, B174) Meriwether Pub.

Two Cheers for Democracy. E. M. Forster. LC 51-13652. 363p. 1962. pap. 14.00 (*0-15-692025-5*, Harvest Bks) HarBrace.

***Two Cheers for GATT.** James Bovard. 21p. 1994. pap. 5.00 (*1-56808-052-2*, BG135) Natl Ctr Pol.

Two Cheers for Industrial Policy: A Critical Look at Some Urban & Distributional Issues. Norman J. Glickman & Marcia Van Wagner. (Working Paper Ser.: No. 32). 46p. 1985. pap. 5.00 (*0-89940-513-4*) LBJ Sch Pub Aff.

Two Chiefs of Dunboy: or An Irish Romance of the Last Century. James A. Froude. LC 79-8421. reprint ed. 44.50 (*0-404-61853-7*) AMS Pr.

Two Children Who Knew Jesus: The Apple of Her Father's Eye & The Boy with the Picnic Lunch. Eileen Lomasney. (Illus.). 32p. (Orig.). (J). (gr. k-4). 1994. pap. 6.95 (*0-9641725-0-X*) Canticle Press.

Two Chimneys. Geri K. Strigenz. LC 91-35817. (History's Children Ser.). (Illus.). 48p. (J). (gr. 4-5). 1992. lib. bdg. 21.36 (*0-8114-3506-7*) Raintree Steck-V.

Two Chinese Philosophers: The Metaphysics of the Brothers Ch'eng. A. C. Graham. LC 92-22626. 230p. 1992. 44.95 (*0-8126-9214-4*); pap. 18.95 (*0-8126-9215-2*) Open Court.

Two Chinese Poets: Vignettes of Han Life & Thought. Ernest R. Hughes. LC 77-4821. 266p. 1977. reprint ed. text ed. 55.00 (*0-8371-9648-5*, HUTC, Greenwood Pr) Greenwood.

Two Chinese Treatises on Calligraphy. Tr. by Chang Chung-ho & Hans H. Frankel. LC 95-2684. 176p. 1995. 25.00 (*0-300-06118-8*) Yale U Pr.

Two Choose to Continue. 2nd rev. ed. Bobbie G. Custer. 106p. 1991. reprint ed. pap. text ed. 9.95 (*0-9620061-0-6*) BGC Pub Co.

Two Christmas Plays. Nancy Funk. 1984. 4.75 (*0-89536-695-9*, 4872) CSS OH.

Two Christmas Stories. C. Rush. (Illus.). 54p. 1988. pap. 8.00 (*0-08-036586-8*, Pergamon Pr) Elsevier.

Two Churches: Catholicism & Capitalism in the World System. Michael L. Budde. LC 91-42023. 182p. 1992. text ed. 34.95 (*0-8223-1229-8*) Duke.

Two Churches: England & Italy in the 13th Century (with an Additional Essay by the Author) Robert Brentano. (C). 1988. pap. 18.00 (*0-520-06098-9*) U CA Pr.

Two Cities. Adam Zagejewski. Tr. by Lillian Vallee. 1995. 24.00 (*0-374-28016-9*) FS&G.

Two Cities: Medieval Europe 1050-1320. Malcolm C. Barber. (Illus.). 612p. (gr. 13). 1993. pap. 19.95 (*0-415-09682-0*, B2556) Routledge.

***Two Cities of God: The Church's Responsibility for the Earthly City.** Ed. by Carl E. Braaten & Robert W. Jenson. LC 97-8589. 152p. (Orig.). 1997. pap. 18.00 (*0-8028-4304-2*) Eerdmans.

Two Cities, Two Loves: Christian Responsibility in a Crumbling Culture. James M. Boice. LC 96-8115. 280p. 1996. 19.99 (*0-8308-1987-8*, 1987) InterVarsity.

Two Citizens. James Wright. 1987. pap. 7.00 (*0-934834-09-1*) White Pine.

Two Collars. Jeri Massi. Ed. by Mark Sidwell. (Light Line Ser.). (Illus.). 164p. (Orig.). 1988. pap. 6.49 (*0-89084-441-0*, 033175) Bob Jones Univ Pr.

Two Collections of Derbicisms Containing Words & Phrases in a Great Measure... Derby. S. Pegge. Ed. by T. Hallum & Walter W. Skeat. (English Dialect Society Publications: No. 78). 1974. reprint ed. pap. 30.00 (*0-8115-0496-4*) Periodicals Srv.

Two Colonial Empires. Ed. by C. A. Bayly & Dirk H. Kolff. 1986. lib. bdg. 115.50 (*90-247-3274-3*) Kluwer Ac.

Two-Colored Brocade: The Imagery of Persian Poetry. Annemarie Schimmel. LC 92-2642. xxvi, 532p. (C). 1992. text ed. 75.00 (*0-8078-2050-4*) U of NC Pr.

Two Colored Women with American Expeditionary Forces: African-American Women Writers 1910-1940 by Hunton. Gates. LC 96-36682. 1996. 30.00 (*0-7838-1434-8*, Hall Reference) Macmillan.

Two Colored Women with the American Expeditionary Forces. Addie Hunton & Kathryn Johnson. LC 75-155624. (Illus.). reprint ed. 36.50 (*0-404-00174-2*) AMS Pr.

Two Commentaries on the Samdhinirmocana-Sutra by Asanga & Jnanagarbha. Asanga & Jnanagarbha. Tr. by John Powers. LC 92-520. (Studies in Asian Thought & Religion: Vol. 13). 156p. 1992. lib. bdg. 69.95 (*0-7734-9477-4*) E Mellen.

Two Communities in Stitches: A History of Dale & McLoud, OK. Leah H. Bird. 323p. 1977. 20.00 (*0-9601364-0-1*); text ed. 20.00 (*0-685-60798-4*); pap. text ed. 15.00 (*0-9601364-1-X*) Henrys Postscript.

Two Community Protective Service Systems: Comparative Evaluation of Systems Operations, 2 Vols., Vol. 1. Clara L. Johnson. 51p. 1976. 5.00 (*0-318-16359-4*, B5) Regional Inst Social Welfare.

Two Community Protective Service Systems: Comparative Evaluation of Systems Operations, 2 Vols., Vol. 2. Clara L. Johnson. 182p. 1977. 5.00 (*0-318-16360-8*) Regional Inst Social Welfare.

Two Complete Books: The Bonfire of the Vanities; The Right Stuff. Tom Wolfe. LC 94-11788. 1994. 13.99 (*0-517-11998-6*) Random.

Two Complete Novels: Red Storm Rising; The Cardinal of the Kremlin. Tom Clancy. LC 92-39237. 880p. 1993. 11.98 (*0-399-13841-2*, Putnam) Putnam Pub Group.

Two Component High Explosive Mixtures. 1986. lib. bdg. 175.00 (*0-8490-3574-0*) Gordon Pr.

Two-Component Signal Transduction. Ed. by James A. Hoch & Thomas J. Silhavy. LC 95-6254. 1995. write for info. (*1-55581-089-6*) Am Soc Microbio.

Two Computer Programs for the Analysis of Simple Markov Chains. Duane F. Marble. (Discussion Paper Ser.: No. 6). 1964. pap. 10.00 (*1-55869-128-6*) Regional Sci Res Inst.

Two Concepts of Rules. John Rawls. (Reprints in Philosophy Ser.). (C). 1991. reprint ed. pap. text ed. 1.00 (*0-8290-2601-0*) Irvington.

Two Concordances to Ripa's Inconologia. Compiled by Mason Tung. LC 91-57967. (Studies in the Emblem: No. 9). (Illus.). 170p. 1993. 59.50 (*0-404-63709-4*) AMS Pr.

Two Connecticut Composers: The Collected Works of Asahel Benham & Merit Woodruff. Ed. by Karl Kroeger. LC 95-32689. (Music of the New American Nation Ser.: Vol. 8). 192p. 1995. text ed. 77.00 (*0-8153-2171-6*) Garland.

Two Connecticut Yankees Teaching in Appalachia see Case for Socially Functional Art Culture & Education

Two Contrariant Schools, Concerning the Establishment of a Christian University. Apostolos Makrakis. Ed. by Orthodox Christian Educational Society Staff. Tr. by Denver Cummings. 87p. (Orig.). 1949. pap. 2.95 (*0-938366-27-0*) Orthodox Chr.

Two Cool Cows. Toby Speed. LC 93-34258. (Illus.). 32p. (J). 1995. 15.95 (*0-399-22647-8*, Putnam) Putnam Pub Group.

***Two Cool Cows.** Toby Speed. (Illus.). 32p. (J). (ps-3). 1997. pap. 5.95 (*0-698-11599-6*, Paperstar) Putnam Pub Group.

Two Corinthians. Carola Dunn. 224p. 1989. 19.95 (*0-8027-1087-5*) Walker & Co.

Two Corinthians. large type ed. Carola Dunn. LC 90-44227. 340p. 1990. reprint ed. lib. bdg. 18.95 (*1-56054-049-4*) Thorndike Pr.

***2 Corinthians, Vol. 10.** V. George Shillington. (Believers Church Bible Commentary Ser.). 336p. (Orig.). 1997. pap. 19.99 (*0-8361-9073-4*) Herald Pr.

***2 Corporate Design Systems.** Moto Nakanishi. 1987. 35.00 (*0-688-07443-X*) Morrow.

Two Covenants. Andrew Murray. 1992. pap. 4.95 (*0-87508-396-X*) Chr Lit.

Two Coventry Corpus Christi Plays. Ed. by H. Craig. (EETS Extra Ser.: Vol. 87). 1966. reprint ed. 20.00 (*0-19-722577-2*, Pub. by EETS UK) Boydell & Brewer.

Two Crazy Pigs. Karen B. Nagel. (Illus.). 32p. (J). (gr. k-2). 1992. pap. 3.50 (*0-590-44972-9*, Cartwheel) Scholastic Inc.

Two Creative Traditions in English Poetry. Ed. by Seymour M. Pitcher et al. LC 72-450. (Granger Index Reprint Ser.). 1977. reprint ed. 23.95 (*0-8369-6367-9*) Ayer.

Two Crimes. Jorge Ibarguengoitia. Tr. by Asa Zatz. 208p. 1985. mass mkt. 3.95 (*0-380-89616-8*, Bard) Avon.

Two Crosses. Elizabeth Musser. 425p. 1996. 11.99 (*1-56476-577-6*, 6-3577, Victor Bks) Chariot Victor.

***Two Crowns for America.** Katherine Kurtz. 1997. mass mkt. 6.50 (*0-553-57287-3*) Bantam.

Two Crows Counting. Doris Orgel. LC 94-32240. (Ready-to-Read Ser.). (Illus.). 32p. (J). (ps-1). 1995. 13.95 (*0-553-09741-5*); pap. 3.99 (*0-553-37573-3*, Bank St) BDD Bks Young Read.

Two Crows Counting. Doris Orgel. LC 96-11067. (Bank Street Ready-to-Read Ser.). (Illus.). (J). 1996. lib. bdg. 17.27 (*0-8368-1617-X*) Gareth Stevens Inc.

Two Crows Denies It: A History of Controversy in Omaha Sociology. R. H. Barnes. LC 84-2276. (Illus.). xiv, 272p. 1984. text ed. 35.00 (*0-8032-1182-1*) U of Nebr Pr.

Two Cuban Poets, 2 vols. in 1. Juan F. Manzano & Gabriel De La Concepcion Valdes. (B. E. Ser.: No. 54). 1937. Two works in one unit. 45.00 (*0-8115-3005-1*) Periodicals Srv.

Two Cultures. C. P. Snow. (Canto Book Ser.). 150p. (C). 1993. pap. text ed. 10.95 (*0-521-45730-0*) Cambridge U Pr.

***Two Cultures - One Marriage: Premarital Counseling for Mixed Marriages.** Reger C. Smith. LC 96-83149. 145p. 1996. pap. 12.95 (*1-883925-07-X*) Andrews Univ Pr.

Two Cultures of Belief: The Fallacy of Christian Certitude. Ronald Quillo. LC 95-12690. 176p. (Orig.). 1995. pap. 14.95 (*0-89243-819-3*, Triumph Books) Liguori Pubns.

Two Cultures of Policing: Street Cops & Management Cops. Elizabeth Reuss-Ianni. 145p. (C). 1993. pap. text ed. 21.95 (*1-56000-654-4*) Transaction Pubs.

Two Currents in the Thought Stream of Europe. Elmer G. Suhr. LC 78-19299. 1979. 37.95 (*0-405-10631-9*) Ayer.

Two-Cylinder Collector's Series, Vol. 3. Jack D. Cherry. (Illus.). 148p. 1995. 24.95 (*1-887446-00-1*) Two-Cylinder.

2D Basics: Autocad Visual Approach. Steven Foster. LC 96-20290. (Illus.). 240p. 1996. spiral bd. 14.95 incl. disk (*0-8273-6899-2*) Delmar.

Two-D Echo Book. Gura. 1989. 325.00 incl. audio (*0-316-33207-0*) Little.

Two D-Gravity in Non-Critical Strings: Discrete & Contiuum Approaches. E. Abdalla. LC 94-7928. (Lecture Notes in Physics Ser.: Vol. 20). 1994. write for info. (*3-540-57805-6*) Spr-Verlag.

Two D-Gravity in Non-Critical Strings: Discrete & Contiuum Approaches. E. Abdalla. LC 94-7928. (Lecture Notes in Physics Ser.: Vol. 20). 1994. 59.95 (*0-387-57805-6*) Spr-Verlag.

Two Dates for the Prom. Steve Swanson. LC 93-6965. 96p. (YA). 1993. pap. 4.99 (*1-55513-937-X*, Chariot Bks) Chariot Victor.

Two-Day Diet. Glenn Cooper. 1990. mass mkt. 5.99 (*0-449-21848-1*) Fawcett.

Two-Day Diet: A Metabolic & Motivational Approach to Quick Weight Loss. Glenn Cooper & Tessa Cooper. LC 88-42673. (Illus.). 256p. 1988. 16.95 (*0-394-56577-0*) Random.

Two Deaths of Christopher Martin see Pincher Martin

Two Deaths of George Wallace: The Question of Forgiveness. Thomas J. Healey. LC 95-49435. 1996. 21.00 (*1-881320-65-0*, Black Belt) Black Belt Comm.

Two Deaths of Quincas Wateryell: A Tall Tale. Jorge Amado. 112p. 1988. pap. 5.95 (*0-380-75476-2*) Avon.

Two Decades of Excellence: A Foundation for the Future. Douglas Watson et al. (Monograph Ser.: No. 14). 271p. (Orig.). 1988. pap. 12.00 (*0-914494-16-3*) ADARA.

Two Decades of Hamady & the Perishable Press Limited: An Anecdotally Annotated Check List with an Anthology of Articles by & about the Press for an Exhibition at Gallery 210, University of Missouri October 3 to November 4 1984 Entitled: Hamady's Perishable Press: A Twentieth Anniversary Sampling of Hand Crafted Books. Walter S. Hamady. (Illus.). 100p. (Orig.). 1984. pap. 15.00 (*0-318-03765-3*) Perishable Pr.

Two Decades of Indian Banking: The Service Sector Scenario. Sushila Thakur. (C). 1990. text ed. 32.00 (*81-7001-082-9*, Pub. by Chanakya II) S Asia.

Two Deer. Ben Howard. (Broadside Ser.: No. 15). 1991. 20.00 (*0-937035-21-1*) Stone Hse NY.

Two Democratic Traditions. George H. Sabine. (Reprint Series in Social Sciences). (C). 1993. reprint ed. pap. text ed. 1.90 (*0-8290-3666-0*, P-249) Irvington.

Two Dialogues: Containing a Comparative View of the Lives, Characters, & Writings of Philip, the Late Earl of Chesterfield, & Dr. Samuel Johnson. William Hayley. LC 71-122486. 1970. reprint ed. 50.00 (*0-8201-1080-9*) Schol Facsimiles.

Two Dialogues: Of the Want of Respect Due to Age & Concerning Education: From "the Miscellaneous Works of the Right Honourable Edward, Earl of Clarendon, Lord High Chancellor of England. 2nd ed. Edward Hyde. LC 92-22975. (Augustan Reprints Ser.: Nos. 227-228). 1984. reprint ed. 21.50 (*0-404-70227-9*) AMS Pr.

Two Diaries of the Long Parliament. Maija Jansson. LC 84-15132. 192p. 1985. text ed. 29.95 (*0-312-82681-8*) St Martin.

Two Different Girls. Eve Bunting. (Author's Signature Collection). (Illus.). 64p. (J). (gr. 3-8). 1992. lib. bdg. 12.79 (*0-89565-772-4*) Childs World.

Two Different Worlds: Christian Absolutes & the Relativism of Social Science. Charles E. Garrison. LC 87-40119. 176p. 1988. 29.50 (*0-87413-330-0*) U Delaware Pr.

Two Dilemmas of Equal Educational Opportunity. (DeGarmo Lectures: No. 13). 1990. 3.00 (*0-685-37904-3*) Soc Profs Ed.

***Two Dimension Riemann.** Zhang. 1996. write for info. (*0-582-24408-0*, Pub. by Longman UK) Longman.

Two Dimensional Analysis of Geological Maps: Techniques of Interpretation. Clive A Boulter. LC 88-33369. 1989. write for info. (*0-471-92161-0*) Wiley.

2-Dimensional Attractor of X T Equals - Mu X T Plus F X T-1. Hans-Otto Walther. LC 94-36555. (Memoirs Ser.: Vol. 544). 1995. pap. text ed. 33.00 (*0-8218-2602-6*, MEMO/113/544) Am Math.

***Two-Dimensional Conformal Geometry & Vertex Operator Algebras.** Y. Z. Huang. LC 96-48469. (Progress in Mathematics Ser.: Vol. 148). 280p. 49.50 (*0-8176-3829-6*) Birkhauser.

Two-Dimensional Crystals. Igor Lyuksyutov et al. (Illus.). 423p. 1992. text ed. 117.00 (*0-12-460590-7*) Acad Pr.

Two-Dimensional Digital Filters. Lu & Andreas Antoniou. LC 92-18745. (Electrical Engineering & Electronics Ser.: Vol. 80). 416p. 1992. 140.00 (*0-8247-8434-0*) Dekker.

Two-Dimensional Echocardiographic Atlas: Congenital Heart Disease, Vol. 1. James B. Seward et al. (Illus.). 615p. 1987. 321.00 (*0-387-96473-8*) Spr-Verlag.

Two-Dimensional Echocardiography. Joseph A. Kisslo. (Clinics in Diagnostic Ultrasound Ser.: Vol. 4). (Illus.). 224p. 1980. text ed. 38.95 (*0-443-08076-3*) Churchill.

Two-Dimensional Echocardiography. Ed. by Joseph A. Kisslo. LC 80-36826. (Clinics in Diagnostic Ultrasound Ser.: No. 4). 222p. reprint ed. pap. 63.30 (*0-7837-6819-2*, 2046651) Bks Demand.

Two-Dimensional Echocardiography: Clinical Pathological Correlations in Adult & Congenital Heart Disease. Arthur D. Hagan et al. 1983. text ed. 82.50 (*0-316-33781-1*) Little.

Two-Dimensional Echocardiography & Cardiac Doppler. 2nd ed. Jay N. Schapira et al. (Illus.). 696p. 1989. 109.00 (*0-683-07522-5*) Williams & Wilkins.

Two-Dimensional Echocardiography in Infants & Children. J. P. Lintermans. 1986. lib. bdg. 232.50 (*0-89838-778-7*) Kluwer Ac.

Two-Dimensional Elastostatic Analysis Using Boundary Elements. J. C. Telles. 1987. ring bd. 395.00 incl. disk (*0-931215-14-5*) Computational Mech MA.

Two-Dimensional Electron Systems of Dielectric Material. Ed. by K. Kajita. 250p. (C). 1994. text ed. 73.00 (*9971-5-0851-6*) World Scientific Pub.

Two-Dimensional Electrophoresis: Operation of the ISO-DALTR System. Leigh Anderson. (Illus.). 174p. (C). 1988. teacher ed. 35.00 (*0-945532-00-8*) Large Scale Biol.

***Two-Dimensional Electrophoresis: Proceedings of the International Two-Dimensional Electrophoresis Conference.** Ed. by A. T. Endler & S. Hanash. (Illus.). x, 343p. 1989. 120.00 (*3-527-27831-1*, VCH) Wiley.

Two-Dimensional Electrophoresis & Immunological Techniques. Bonnie S. Dunbar. LC 86-30393. (Illus.). 388p. (C). 1988. 79.50 (*0-306-42439-8*, Plenum Pr); spiral bd. 39.50 (*0-306-42839-3*, Plenum Pr) Plenum.

Two-Dimensional Electrophoresis Protein Mapping, Vol. 30, No. 12. Ed. by J. Stanton King. 211p. 1984. 10.00 (*0-317-47296-8*) Am Assn Clinical Chem.

Two-Dimensional Gel Electrophoresis: A Special Issue of Clinical Chemistry, Vol. 28, No. 4. Ed. by J. Stanton King. 355p. 1982. 10.00 (*0-686-91956-4*) Am Assn Clinical Chem.

Two-Dimensional Geometric Variational Problems. Jurgen P. Jost. LC 90-12622. (Pure & Applied Mathematics Ser.). 236p. 1991. text ed. 170.00 (*0-471-92839-9*) Wiley.

***Two Dimensional Heaven & Earth.** Myungkark Park. 100p. (Orig.). 1993. pap. write for info. (*1-877974-23-4*) Prompter Pubns.

Two-Dimensional Homotopy & Combinatorial Group Theory. Ed. by Cynthia Hog-Angeloni et al. (London Mathematical Society Lecture Note Ser.: No. 197). (Illus.). 424p. (C). 1994. pap. text ed. 44.95 (*0-521-44700-3*) Cambridge U Pr.

Two Dimensional Imaging. Ronald N. Bracewell. 640p. 1994. text ed. 89.33 (*0-13-062621-X*) P-H.

Two-Dimensional Ising Model. Barry McCoy & Tai T. Wu. LC 72-188972. (Illus.). 438p. 1973. 38.50 (*0-674-91440-6*) HUP.

Two-Dimensional Linear Systems. Tadeusz Kaczorek. (Lecture Notes in Control & Information Sciences Ser.: Vol. 68). x, 398p. 1985. 50.95 (*0-387-15086-2*) Spr-Verlag.

Two-Dimensional Man: An Essay on the Anthropology of Power & Symbolism in Complex Society. Abner Cohen. LC 72-93525. 1974. pap. 14.00 (*0-520-03241-1*) U CA Pr.

Two-Dimensional Manifolds of Bounded Curvature: Proceedings. Ed. by A. D. Aleksandrov & V. A. Zalgaller. (Proceedings of the Steklov Institute of Mathematics Ser.: No. 76). 183p. 1967. pap. 58.00 (*0-8218-1876-7*, STEKLO/76) Am Math.

Two Dimensional Models & String Theories. Ed. by Maria C. Abdalla & Elcio Abdalla. 228p. (C). 1988. text ed. 77.00 (*9971-5-0580-0*) World Scientific Pub.

Two-Dimensional NMR Methods for Establishing Molecular Connectivity: A Chemist's Guide to Experiment Selection, Performance & Interpretation. Gary E. Martin & Andrew S. Zektzer. LC 88-27705. (Methods in Stereochemical Analysis Ser.). (Illus.). xviii, 508p. 1988. 80.00 (*0-89573-703-5*, VCH) Wiley.

***Two-Dimensional NMR Methods for Establishing Molecular Connectivity: A Chemist's Guide to Experiment Selection, Performance & Interpretation.** Andrew S. Zektzer. (Methods in Stereochemical Analysis Ser.). 1988. text ed. 95.00 (*0-471-18707-0*) Wiley.

Two-Dimensional NMR Spectroscopy. Jan Schraml & Jon M. Bellama. LC 87-33315. (Chemical Analysis Ser.). 220p. 1988. text ed. 115.00 (*0-471-60178-0*) Wiley.

***Two-Dimensional NMR Spectroscopy: Applications for Chemists & Biochemists.** 2nd ed. Ed. by W. R. Croasmun & R. M. Carlson. (Methods in Stereochemical Analysis Ser.). 1994. text ed. 135.00 (*0-471-18593-0*) Wiley.

An Asterisk (*) at the beginning of an entry indicates that the title is appearing in BIP for the first time.

Two-Dimensional NMR Spectroscopy: Applications for Chemists & Biochemists. 2nd rev. ed. Ed. by William R. Croasmun & Robert M. K. Carlson. LC 94-358. (Methods in Stereochemical Analysis Ser.). 1994. 125.00 (*1-56081-664-3*, VCH) Wiley.

Two-Dimensional Potential Analysis Using Boundary Elements. L. C. Wrobel. 1987. ring bd. 395.00 incl. disk (*0-931215-13-7*) Computational Mech MA.

Two Dimensional Quantum Gravity & Random Surfaces. Ed. by D. J. Gross et al. 350p. (C). 1991. text ed. 93.00 (*981-02-0642-9*); pap. text ed. 43.00 (*981-02-0643-7*) World Scientific Pub.

Two-Dimensional Real-Time Ultrasonic Imaging of the Heart. Ed. by Emilio R. Giuliana. 1985. lib. bdg. 204.50 (*0-89838-671-3*) Kluwer Ac.

Two-Dimensional Riemann Problems for Systems of Conservation Laws. Tong Zhang & Shuli Yang. LC 95-12928. (Pitman Monographs & Surveys in Pure & Applied Mathematics). 1995. write for info. (*0-615-00694-9*) Longman.

Two-Dimensional Signal & Image Processing. Joe S. Lim. 880p. 1989. text ed. 86.00 (*0-13-935322-4*) P-H.

Two Dimensional Spline Interpolation Algorithms. Helmuth Spath. LC 93-38858. (Illus.). 312p. (C). 1995. text ed. 65.00 (*1-56881-017-2*) AK Peters.

Two-Dimensional Strongly Correlated Electronic Systems, Vol. 3. Ed. by Zi-Zhao Gan. (China Center of Advanced Science & Technology (World Laboratory) Symposium - Workshop Proceedings Ser.). 314p. 1989. 35.00 (*2-88124-695-8*) Gordon & Breach.

Two-Dimensional Systems: Physics & New Devices. Ed. by G. Bauer et al. (Solid-State Sciences Ser.: Vol. 67). (Illus.). 335p. 1986. 78.95 (*0-387-16748-X*) Spr-Verlag.

Two-Dimensional Tame & Maximal Orders of Finite Representation Type. I. Reiten & M. Van Den Bergh. LC 89-15024. (Memoirs Ser.: Vol. 80/408). 72p. 1989. pap. 18.00 (*0-8218-2469-4*, MEMO/80/408) Am Math.

Two Discourses Concerning the Soul of Brutes, Which Is That of the Sensations of Man. Thomas Willis. Tr. by S. Pordage from LAT. LC 72-161936. (History of Psychology Ser.). 1971. 50.00 (*0-8201-1096-5*) Schol Facsimiles.

Two Dissertations. Jonathan Edwards. (Notable American Authors Ser.). 1992. reprint ed. lib. bdg. 75.00 (*0-7812-2773-9*) Rprt Serv.

Two Dissertations on the Hamlet of Saxo Grammaticus & of Shakespear. R. G. Latham. LC 71-171658. reprint ed. 39.50 (*0-404-03883-2*) AMS Pr.

Two Divine Promises. Roman Hoppe. LC 83-50588. 52p. 1993. reprint ed. pap. 1.50 (*0-89555-219-1*) TAN Bks Pubs.

Two Dog Biscuits. Beverly Cleary. (J). 1996. pap. 4.95 (*0-688-14735-6*, Mulberry) Morrow.

Two Dog Biscuits. rev. ed. Beverly Cleary. LC 85-18816. (Illus.). 32p. (J). (ps-1). 1986. lib. bdg. 15.93 (*0-688-05848-5*, Morrow Junior) Morrow.

Two Dogmas of Philosophy & Other Essays in the Philosophy of Philosophy. Dennis A. Rohatyn. LC 75-63. 199p. (C). 1976. 29.50 (*0-8386-1673-9*) Fairleigh Dickinson.

Two Dogs & Freedom: The Open School in Soweto. (J). 1987. pap. 4.95 (*0-8050-0637-0*, North Star Line) Blue Moon Bks.

Two Dogs Plus. John C. Campbell. (Illus.). 95p. (Orig.). (J). (gr. 8 up). 1984. pap. 7.95 (*0-685-09160-0*); pap. text ed. 9.95 (*0-9613596-0-9*) Deer Creek Pr.

Two-Dollar Bet Means Murder. Fred J. Cook. LC 72-854. 248p. 1972. reprint ed. lib. bdg. 22.50 (*0-8371-5927-X*, COTD, Greenwood Pr) Greenwood.

Two Dollar Bill: One Man's Year in Viet Nam. Roger H. Soiset. 249p. 1993. pap. 9.50 (*0-9623065-3-3*) Palmetto Bookworks.

Two-Dollar Bill: One Man's Year in Vietnam. Roger H. Soiset. Ed. by Jennifer Teunon. 249p. (Orig.). 1993. pap. 9.50 (*0-9640018-0-2*) R H Soiset.

Two-Dollar Boat: Boat Stories & Other Lies. Dudley B. Magruder, Jr. LC 91-24247. (Illus.). 208p. 1992. 18.95 (*1-56474-000-5*) Fithian Pr.

Two Dozen Dinosaurs: A First Book of Dinosaur Facts & Mysteries, Games & Fun. Catherine Ripley. (Illus.). 32p. (J). (gr. k up). 1992. pap. 5.95 (*0-920775-55-1*, Pub. by Owl Bks CN) Firefly Bks Ltd.

Two Dozen in Two Parts: Arrangements for Choir or Ensemble. 1993. 6.25 (*0-8341-9000-1*, MB-677) Lillenas.

Two Dozen Red Roses. Kenneth Horne. 1953. pap. 5.25 (*0-8222-1181-5*) Dramatists Play.

Two Dreams: New & Selected Stories. Shirley G. Lim. LC 96-52523. 240p. (Orig.). 1997. 24.00 (*1-55861-164-9*) Feminist Pr.

Two Dutch Houses: Tradition & Change in Early New York: The Schenck Houses at the Brooklyn Museum. Brooklyn Museum Staff. LC 129.B7B748 1990. Date not set. write for info. (*0-87273-123-5*) Bklyn Mus.

Two Eagles - Dos Aguilas: The Natural World of the United States-Mexico Borderlands. Photos by Tupper A. Blake. LC 93-32431. 1994. 55.00 (*0-520-08482-9*) U CA Pr.

Two Eagles in the Sun: Your Questions Answered about Mexican Hispanics in the Border Southwest & Other Hispanics in the United States. Richard C. Campbell. Ed. by Paul E. Huntsberger. LC 94-61432. (Illus.). (Orig.). 1995. pap. 19.95 (*1-884512-74-7*) Two Eagles.

Two Early Chinese Bronze Weapons with Meteoritic Iron Blades. Rutherford J. Gettens et al. (Occasional Papers: Vol. 4, No. 1). (Illus.). 1971. pap. 5.00 (*0-934686-08-4*) Freer.

Two Early Historic Iroquoian Sites in Western New York. Michael Gramly. (Persimmon Press Monographs in Archaeology). 1996. pap. 12.95 (*1-882903-03-X*) Persimmon NY.

Two Early Histories of Haverhill, Massachusetts: The 1816 Saltonstall History & 1832 Mirick History. Leverett Saltonstall & Benjamin L. Mirick. (Illus.). 300p. 1990. pap. 15.00 (*1-878651-11-0*) HPL Pr.

Two Early Renaissance Bird Poems: The Harmony of Birds & the Parliament Birds. Ed. by Malcolm Andrew. LC 83-48646. 120p. 1985. 24.50 (*0-918016-73-8*) Folger Bks.

Two Early Tudor Lives. Incl. Life & Death of Cardinal Wolsey. George Cavendish. 1962. (*0-318-56530-7*); Life of Sir Thomas More. William Roper. (*0-318-56531-5*); xxi, 260p. 1963. pap. 15.00 (*0-300-00239-4*, Y81) Yale U Pr.

Two Ears of Corn: A Guide to People-Centered Agricultural Improvement. 2nd ed. Roland Bunder. (Illus.). 250p. (Orig.). (ENG, FRE & SPA.). 1985. pap. 8.00 (*0-942716-03-5*) World Neigh.

Two East Anglian Diaries 1641-1729: Isaac Archer & William Coe. Ed. by Matthew Storey. (Suffolk Records Society Ser.: Vol. XXXVI). (Illus.). 296p. 1994. 35.00 (*0-85115-564-2*) Boydell & Brewer.

Two-Edged Sword. Thomas K. Martin. 272p. (Orig.). 1994. mass mkt. 4.99 (*0-441-83344-6*) Ace Bks.

Two-Edged Sword: A Study of the Paranoid Personality in Action. William H. Hampton & Virginia S. Burnham. Ed. by James C. Smith, Jr. LC 90-37097. (Illus.). 160p. (Orig.). 1990. pap. 14.95 (*0-86534-147-8*) Sunstone Pr.

Two Eleven Book: Armed Robbery Investigation. Burt Rapp. 184p. 1989. pap. text ed. 15.95 (*1-55950-019-0*) Loompanics.

Two Elizabethan Puritan Diaries. Richard Rogers & Samuel Ward. Ed. by Marshall M. Knappen. 1933. 14.50 (*0-8446-1387-8*) Peter Smith.

***Two Ends of Sleep.** Lizard Jones. 1997. pap. 12.95 (*0-88974-072-0*, Pub. by Press Gang CN) LPC InBook.

Two Enormous Elephants: God's Wonderful World of Numbers. Glenda Palmer. LC 92-34714. (Almost on My Own Ser.). (Illus.). 32p. (J). 1993. pap. 4.99 (*0-7814-0709-5*, Chariot Bks) Chariot Victor.

***Two Epics from the Plains.** Elizabeth B. Lewis. 14p. 1990. pap. 3.50 (*0-614-24771-3*) Tesseract SD.

Two Erotic Tales by Pierre Louys: Aphrodite & The Songs of Bilitis. Pierre Louys. Ed. by Dorothy Kavka. Tr. by Mary H. Harrison from FRE. 320p. (Orig.). 1994. pap. 18.00 (*1-879260-24-7*) Evanston Pub.

Two Essays: On the Foundation of Civil Government & On the Constitution of the United States. Thomas Cooper. LC 72-99477. (American Constitutional & Legal History Ser). 1970. reprint ed. lib. bdg. 19.50 (*0-306-71852-9*) Da Capo.

Two Essays: Relation of the State to Industrial Action & Economics & Jurisprudence. Henry C. Adams. Ed. by Joseph Dorfman. LC 75-76510. (Reprints of Economic Classics Ser.). xi, 211p. 1969. reprint ed. 35.00 (*0-678-00494-3*) Kelley.

Two Essays see Works of Robert Whytt

Two Essays by Wilhelm Roepke: The Problem of Economic Order, Welfare, Freedom & Inflation. Intro. by Johannes Overbeek. LC 86-33982. 114p. (Orig.). (C). 1987. pap. text ed. 14.00 (*0-8191-6126-8*) U Pr of Amer.

Two Essays on Colin Wilson: World Rejection & Criminal Romantics; From Outsider to Post-Tragic Man. Gary Lachman. (Colin Wilson Studies: No. 6). 64p. 1994. pap. 17.00 (*0-946650-52-7*); lib. bdg. 27.00 (*0-8095-6776-8*) Borgo Pr.

Two Essays on Dai Viet in the Fourteenth Century. O. W. Wolters. LC 88-63030. (Lac-Viet Ser.: No. 9). xl, 180p. 1988. pap. 15.00 (*0-938692-38-0*) Yale U SE Asia.

Two Essays on the Liberty of the Press. George Hay. LC 75-112703. (Civil Liberties in American History Ser.). 1970. reprint ed. lib. bdg. 19.50 (*0-306-71918-5*) Da Capo.

Two Evenings in Saramaka: Afro-American Tale-Telling in the Suriname Rain Forest. Richard Price & Sally Price. LC 90-35941. (Illus.). 432p. 1991. pap. text ed. 23.95 (*0-226-68062-2*) U Ch Pr.

Two Evenings in Saramaka: Afro-American Tale-Telling in the Suriname Rain Forest. Richard Price & Sally Price. LC 90-35941. (Illus.). 432p. 1991. lib. bdg. 66.00 (*0-226-68061-4*) U Ch Pr.

Two Explanations of Motion, Space & Time. James P. Fitzgerald. LC 86-71835. 128p. 1990. 17.50 (*0-8158-0437-7*) Chris Mass.

Two Eyes, a Nose & a Mouth: A Book of Many Faces, Many Races. Roberta G. Intrater. LC 94-18390. (Illus.). 32p. (J). (ps-2). 1995. 12.95 (*0-590-48247-5*, Cartwheel) Scholastic Inc.

Two Eyes for Seeing. Angus Hudson. ("Two" Bks.). (Illus.). 8p. (J). (ps). 1993. bds. 2.99 (*1-56476-180-0*, 6-3180, Victor Bks) Chariot Victor.

Two Fables. Roald Dahl. (Illus.). 63p. 1987. 12.95 (*0-374-28018-5*) FS&G.

Two-Faced Press? A Twentieth Century Fund Paper. Tom Goldstein. 54p. (Orig.). (C). 1986. pap. text ed. 7.50 (*0-87078-204-5*) TCFP-PPP.

Two Faced Woman. Gordon. 1995. pap. 3.25 (*0-373-05953-1*) Harlequin Bks.

Two-Faced Woman. Roberta Leigh. (Presents Ser.). 1993. pap. 2.89 (*0-373-11541-5*, 1-11541-9) Harlequin Bks.

***Two Faces: Walking in Two Worlds.** George McMullen. 168p. (Orig.). Date not set. pap. 11.95 (*1-57174-071-6*) Hampton Roads Pub Co.

Two Faces in the Shadows: A Dramatic Dialogue for Tenebrae. Paul Duke & Jeff Allee. 16p. 1992. pap. 3.25 (*0-687-42665-0*) Abingdon.

Two Faces of Chemistry. Luciano Caglioti & Mirella Giacconi. LC 82-12706. 240p. (C). 1983. 25.00 (*0-262-03088-8*) MIT Pr.

Two Faces of Civil Society: NGOs & Politics in Africa. Stephen N. Ndegwa. LC 95-38747. (Books on International Development). (Illus.). 160p. 1996. pap. 21.95 (*1-56549-055-X*); text ed. 35.00 (*1-56549-056-8*) Kumarian Pr.

Two Faces of Co-Existence. Alfreds Berzins. 1967. 10.95 (*0-8315-0018-2*) Speller.

Two Faces of Economics. Anthony Dawson. 280p. (C). 1996. pap. text ed. 22.50 (*0-582-27451-6*, Pub. by Longman UK) Longman.

Two Faces of Ionesco. Ed. by Rosette C. Lamont & Melvin J. Friedman. LC 76-51038. 285p. 1978. 15.00 (*0-87875-110-6*) Whitston Pub.

Two Faces of January. Patricia Highsmith. 288p. 1988. pap. 7.95 (*0-87113-209-5*, Atlntc Mnthly) Grove-Atltic.

Two Faces of Man: Two Studies on the Sense of Time & on Ambivalence. Joost A. Meerloo. LC 54-12141. (Illus.). 251p. reprint ed. pap. 71.60 (*0-317-10297-4*, 2010703) Bks Demand.

***Two Faces of Management.** Sven-Erik Sjostrand. 232p. 1997. pap. 29.95 (*0-415-11322-9*, Pub. by Intl Thomson Busn UK) Inter Thomson.

Two Faces of National Interest. W. David Clinton. LC 93-24206. (Political Traditions in Foreign Policy Ser.). 280p. (C). 1994. text ed. 35.00 (*0-8071-1841-9*); pap. text ed. 16.95 (*0-8071-1895-8*) La State U Pr.

Two Faces of Political Apathy. Tom DeLuca. 288p. (Orig.). (C). 1995. text ed. 59.95 (*1-56639-314-0*); pap. text ed. 19.95 (*1-56639-315-9*) Temple U Pr.

Two Faces of Protest: Contrasting Modes of Women's Activism in India. Amrita Basu. 1992. pap. 15.00 (*0-520-08919-7*) U CA Pr.

Two Faces of Reality. Morris Jastrow. 14.95 (*0-393-02400-8*) Norton.

Two Faces of Time. Lawrence W. Fagg. LC 85-40412. (Illus.). 210p. (Orig.). 1985. pap. 7.75 (*0-8356-0599-X*, Quest) Theos Pub Hse.

***Two Faces of Tomorrow.** James P. Hogan. 464p. 1997. mass mkt. 6.99 (*0-671-87848-4*) Baen Bks.

***Two Faiths, One God: Study Guide to the World of Islam.** Sarah Klos. 45p. 1996. pap. 15.95 (*0-614-21688-5*, 1266) Kazi Pubns.

Two Families in Colonial Chile. Della M. Flusche. LC 88-39147. (Latin American Studies: Vol. 2). 264p. 1989. lib. bdg. 89.95 (*0-88946-491-X*) E Mellen.

Two Fantasia Suites for Treble Viol (Violin), Bass Viol & Organ. John Jenkins. Ed. by Andrew Ashbee. (Viol Consort Ser.: No. 10). iv, 30p. 1991. pap. text ed. 25.00 (*1-56571-029-0*) PRB Prods.

Two Fantasias for Three Viols. Martha Bishop. (Contemporary Consort Ser.: No. 6). i, 21p. 1990. pap. text ed. 10.00 (*1-56571-010-X*) PRB Prods.

Two Farms. Pearce. mass mkt. write for info. (*0-312-90334-0*) Tor Bks.

Two Feet from the Third Rail: Being a Compendium of Thoughts, Ideas, Advice, Castigations, & Memoirs on 50 Years in Public Relations. Wade Atkinson. 305p. 1994. per. write for info. (*0-9640851-1-9*) W Atkinson.

Two Feet-Small Book. David Kenneth. 8p. (J). 1987. 3.95 (*0-88679-537-0*) Educ Insights.

Two Feet-Tall Book. David Kenneth. 8p. (J). 1987. 19.95 (*0-88679-536-2*) Educ Insights.

Two Fifteenth-Century Cookery-Books. Ed. by T. Austin. (EETS, OS Ser.: Vol. 91). 1974. reprint ed. 45.00 (*0-8115-0148-5*) Periodicals Srv.

Two Films by Ang Lee. Ed. by James Schamus. LC 94-27236. 1994. 13.95 (*0-87951-568-6*) Overlook Pr.

Two Fine Swine. Gina C. Erickson & Kelli C. Foster. (Get Ready...Get Set...Read! Ser.). (Illus.). 24p. (J). (ps-3). 1994. pap. 3.50 (*0-8120-1838-9*) Barron.

Two Fine Swine. Kelli C. Foster & Gina C. Erickson. (Get Ready, Get Set, Read! Ser.). (Illus.). 24p. (J). 1995. lib. bdg. 11.95 (*1-56674-114-9*) Forest Hse.

Two First Centuries of Florentine History. Pasquale Villari. LC 77-153609. reprint ed. 62.50 (*0-404-09294-2*) AMS Pr.

Two First Languages - Early Grammatical Development in Bilingual Children. Ed. by J. M. Meisel. (Studies on Language Acquisition: No. 10). iv, 318p. 1990. pap. 83.10 (*3-11-013133-1*) Mouton.

***Two Fish, Four Fish, My Fish, Your Fish: A Rebus Sticker Storybook to Color.** 1997. pap. 2.75 (*0-679-88516-1*) Random Bks Yng Read.

Two Fluid Flows - With or Without Phase Change: 1994 International Mechanical Engineering Congress & Exposition, Chicago, Illinois - November 6-11, 1994. (AMD Ser.: Vol. 184). 116p. 1994. 54.00 (*0-7918-1405-X*, G00900) ASME.

***Two Flutes Playing: A Spiritual Journey Book for Gay Men.** Andrew Ramer. LC 97-71665. 160p. (Orig.). 1997. pap. 12.95 (*1-886360-05-7*) Alamo Sq Pr.

***Two-Fold Vibration, Vol. 158.** Raymond Federman. (Sun & Moon Classics Ser.). 1997. pap. text ed. 12.95 (*1-55713-319-0*) Sun & Moon CA.

Two Fools Who Gained a Measure of Wisdom (Checkhov) Tim Kelly. 1968. pap. 3.25 (*0-8222-1182-3*) Dramatists Play.

Two for America: The True Story of a Swiss Immigrant. Gloria Jacobson. (Illus.). 36p. (J). (gr. 4). 1989. pap. 8.50 (*0-9618399-1-0*) G Jacobson.

Two for Jack Spicer. Stephen Jonas. 1988. 1.50 (*0-318-41314-0*) Man-Root.

Two for One. Jana Ellis. LC 88-12384. (Merivale Mall Ser.). 160p. (YA). (gr. 7 up). 1988. pap. text ed. 2.50 (*0-8167-1354-5*) Troll Communs.

Two for One Christmas Fun. Peter Landesman. (Full House Stephanie Ser.: No. 13). (J). (gr. 3-6). 1995. mass mkt. 3.99 (*0-671-53546-3*) PB.

Two for Stew. Barney Saltzberg & Laura J. Numeroff. (J). 1996. 15.00 (*0-689-80571-3*) S&S Childrens.

***Two for Tea.** Jan McDaniel. LC 96-97023. 192p. 1996. 17.95 (*0-8034-9179-4*, Avalon Bks) Bouregy.

Two for Tea Book No. 7. Muldrow. 1996. 3.25 (*0-689-80823-2*) S&S Childrens.

***Two for Texas.** James L. Burke. Date not set. lib. bdg. 18.95 (*0-8488-1777-X*) Amereon Ltd.

Two for Texas. James Lee Burke. LC 94-32465. 148p. 1995. pap. 10.95 (*0-7868-8011-2*) Hyperion.

Two for the Dough. Janet Evanovich. 1996. mass mkt. 5.50 (*0-671-00179-5*) PB.

Two for the Dough. Janet Evanovich. 1996. 22.00 (*0-684-82592-9*) S&S Trade.

Two for the Dough: A Stephanie Plum Novel. Janet Evanovich. 304p. 1996. 22.00 (*0-684-19638-7*) S&S Trade.

Two for the Heart. Betty A. Neels & Ellen James. (Romance Ser.). 1994. mass mkt. 2.99 (*0-373-03299-4*, 1-03299-4) Harlequin Bks.

Two for the Heart. Betty A. Neels. 1994. pap. 2.99 (*0-373-15545-X*) Harlequin Bks.

Two for the Heart. large type ed. Betty A. Neels & Ellen James. LC 94-43668. 240p. 1995. pap. 17.95 (*0-7838-1213-2*, GK Hall) Thorndike Pr.

Two for the Money. Penny D. Paradise. (Illus.). 240p. (YA). (gr. 6 up). 1996. text ed. 30.00 (*0-9649395-0-9*) Pen Line.

Two for the Road. (Leisure Reading Ser.). 32p. 1979. 3.60 (*0-88336-319-4*) New Readers.

Two for the Road. Wright Morris. LC 94-38984. 304p. (Orig.). (C). 1994. 25.00 (*0-87685-945-7*); pap. 15.00 (*0-87685-944-9*) Black Sparrow.

Two for the Road. J. Nichels. 1988. 39.00 (*0-317-43671-6*, Pub. by Regency Press UK) St Mut.

Two for the Road. large type ed. Mary A. Wilson. (Silhouette Romance Ser.). 1996. 18.95 (*0-373-59661-8*) Harlequin Bks.

Two for the Road, signed ed. deluxe ed. Wright Morris. LC 94-38984. 304p. (Orig.). (C). 1994. 40.00 (*0-87685-946-5*) Black Sparrow.

***Two for Your Money.** Jo Parrott. (Illus.). 104p. pap. text ed. 8.95 (*0-486-29474-9*) Dover.

Two Foraminiferal Assemblages from the Duplin Marl in Georgia & South Carolina, No. 293 see Bulletins of American Paleontology: Vol. 70

***Two Forgers.** limited ed. John Collins. 1996. 270.00 (*0-85967-754-0*, 34885) Oak Knoll.

Two Forgers: A Biography of Harry Buxton Forman & Thomas James Wise. John Collins. (Illus.). 280p. 1992. 55.00 (*0-938768-29-8*) Oak Knoll.

2, 4, 8... Destiny of the Human Species. Don Hansler. LC 95-90811. 365p. (Orig.). 1996. pap. 11.95 (*1-886839-10-7*) Fun Ed Prods.

Two, Four, Six, Eight, When You Gonna Integrate? Frank A. Petroni et al. 1971. reprint ed. pap. 2.75 (*0-87140-241-6*) Liveright.

Two Franklins. Bernard Fay. LC 70-93277. reprint ed. 31.50 (*0-404-02372-X*) AMS Pr.

Two Franklins: Fathers of American Democracy. Bernard Fay. 1993. reprint ed. lib. bdg. 89.00 (*0-7812-5452-3*) Rprt Serv.

Two Fremont Sites & Their Position in Southwestern Perehistory. Dee C. Taylor. (Utah Anthropological Papers: No. 29). reprint ed. 37.50 (*0-404-60629-6*) AMS Pr.

Two French Moralists. Odette De Mourgues. LC 77-82506. (Major European Authors Ser.). 1978. 49.95 (*0-521-21823-3*) Cambridge U Pr.

Two French Precursors of Marxism: Rousseau & Fourier. Naaman Kessous. 128p. 1996. 55.95 (*1-85972-253-9*, Pub. by Avebury Pub UK) Ashgate Pub Co.

Two Frenchmen. David Thomson. LC 75-8806. 255p. 1975. reprint ed. text ed. 38.50 (*0-8371-8115-1*, THTWF, Greenwood Pr) Greenwood.

Two Friends. Guy De Maupassant. Ed. by Ann A. Redpath. (Creative's Classic Short Stories Ser.). (Illus.). 32p. (J). (gr. 4 up). 1985. lib. bdg. 13.95 (*0-88682-003-0*) Creative Ed.

Two Friends: And Other Nineteenth-Century Lesbian Stories by American Women Writers. Intro. by Susan Koppelman. 288p. 1994. pap. 10.95 (*0-452-01119-1*, Mer) NAL-Dutton.

Two Friends II. Menke Katz & Harry Smith. (Illus.). 112p. (Orig.). 1988. Letterpress edition. 20.00 (*0-913559-09-1*); pap. 11.95 (*0-913559-10-5*) Birch Brook Pr.

Two from Galilee. Marjorie Holmes. 224p. 1982. mass mkt. 5.50 (*0-553-28100-3*) Bantam.

***Two from Galilee.** Marjorie Holmes. 224p. (gr. 10). 1996. 14.99 (*0-8007-1733-3*) Revell.

Two Fronts, a Small Town at War. Paul Fridlund. 200p. 1985. 19.95 (*0-87770-326-4*) Ye Galleon.

Two Galilees. Khalil Nakhleh. (Occasional Papers: No. 7). 27p. 1982. pap. text ed. 1.00 (*0-937694-57-6*) Assn Arab-Amer U Grads.

Two-Generation Programs for Families in Poverty: A New Intervention Strategy. Ed. by Sheila Smith & Foundation for Child Development Staff. (Advances in Applied Developmental Psychology Ser.: Vol. 9). (Illus.). 300p. 1996. pap. 39.50 (*1-56750-100-1*) Ablex Pub.

Two-Generation Programs for Families in Poverty: A New Intervention Strategy, Vol. 9. Ed. by Foundation for Child Development Staff & Sheila Smith. (Advances in Applied Developmental Psychology Ser.: Vol. 9). (Illus.). 300p. 1996. text ed. 73.25 (*1-56750-204-0*) Ablex Pub.

Two Generations of Soviet Man. John Kosa. 1962. pap. 16.95 (*0-8084-0304-4*) NCUP.

Two Generations of Soviet Man: A Study in the Psychology of Communism. John Kosa. 1962. 20.00 (*0-8078-0860-1*) U of NC Pr.

Two Generations of Zionism. Bernard A. Rosenblatt. LC 67-18134. 1967. 18.95 (*0-88400-017-6*) Shengold.

T

An Asterisk (*) at the beginning of an entry indicates that the title is appearing in BIP for the first time.

Two-Generator Discrete Subgroups of PSL (2, R) Jane Gilman. (Memoirs of the American Mathematical Society Ser.: No. 561). 1995. pap. 41.00 (0-8218-0361-1, MEMO/117/561) Am Math.

Two Gentlemen & a Lady. Alexander Woollcott. LC 79-134984. (Short Story Index Reprint Ser.). (Illus.). 1977. 15.95 (0-8369-3714-7) Ayer.

Two Gentlemen from Texas: Larry & Stretch. large type ed. Marshall Grover. (Linford Western Library). 1991. pap. 15.99 (0-7089-6959-3) Ulverscroft.

Two Gentlemen of Kentucky. James L. Allen. (Principle Works of James Lane Allen). 1989. reprint ed. lib. bdg. 79.00 (0-7812-1733-4) Rprt Serv.

Two Gentlemen of Rome: Keats & Shelley. Ernest Raymond. 1972. 69.95 (0-8490-1238-4) Gordon Pr.

Two Gentlemen of Verona. William Shakespeare. Ed. by Kurt Schlueter. (New Cambridge Shakespeare Ser.). (Illus.). 180p. (C). 1990. text ed. 39.95 (0-521-22222-2); pap. text ed. 10.95 (0-521-29406-1) Cambridge U Pr.

Two Gentlemen of Verona. William Shakespeare. Ed. by Susan Leach & Rex Gibson. (Shakespeare Ser.). (Illus.). 160p. (C). 1994. pap. text ed. 9.95 (0-521-44603-1) Cambridge U Pr.

Two Gentlemen of Verona. William Shakespeare. Ed. by Louis B. Wright & Virginia A. La Mar. (Folger Library). 224p. (YA). (gr. 10 up). mass mkt. 4.99 (0-671-74395-3, WSP) PB.

Two Gentlemen of Verona. William Shakespeare. Ed. by Norman Sanders. (New Penguin Shakespeare Ser.). 222p. 1981. pap. 5.95 (0-14-070717-4, Penguin Classics) Viking Penguin.

Two Gentlemen of Verona. William Shakespeare. (BBC Television Plays Ser.). 1984. pap. 5.95 (0-563-20277-7, Pub. by BBC UK) Parkwest Pubns.

***Two Gentlemen of Verona.** William Shakespeare. (English Ser.). (C). Date not set. pap. 9.95 (0-17-443539-8) Wadsworth Pub.

Two Gentlemen of Verona. large type ed. William Shakespeare. 1994. pap. 24.95 (0-7089-4517-1, Charnwood) Ulverscroft.

Two Gentlemen of Verona. 2nd ed. William Shakespeare. Ed. by Clifford Leech. (Arden Shakespeare Ser.). 1969. text ed. 45.00 (0-416-47490-X, NO. 2498) Routledge Chapman & Hall.

Two Gentlemen of Verona. 2nd ed. William Shakespeare. Ed. by Clifford Leech. (Arden Shakespeare Ser.). 1969. pap. 8.95 (0-416-70080-2, NO. 2499) Routledge Chapman & Hall.

***Two Gentlemen of Verona.** 2nd ed. William Shakespeare. (English). 1969. pap. 9.95 (0-415-02709-8) Routledge.

***Two Gentlemen of Verona.** 3rd ed. William Shakespeare. (English Ser.). (C). Date not set. text ed. 45.00 (0-17-443572-X) Wadsworth Pub.

Two Gentlemen of Verona: Critical Essays. Ed. by June Schlueter. LC 95-45741. (Shakespeare Criticism Ser.: Vol. 15). (Illus.). 320p. 1995. reprint ed. text ed. 60.00 (0-8153-1020-X, H1645) Garland.

Two Gentlemen of Verona: Modern Text with Introduction. Ed. by A. L. Rowse. LC 86-11026. (Contemporary Shakespeare Ser.). 106p. (Orig.). (C). 1986. pap. text ed. 3.45 (0-8191-3933-5) U Pr of Amer.

Two Georges. Richard Dreyfuss & Harry Turtledove. 384p. 1996. 23.95 (0-312-85969-4) Tor Bks.

Two German States & European Security. Ed. by F. Stephen Larrabee. 286p. 1989. text ed. 45.00 (0-312-02683-8) St Martin.

Two Germanies. Peter Lust. LC 66-23304. 237p. reprint ed. pap. 67.60 (0-8357-6441-9, 2035812) Bks Demand.

Two Germanies since 1945 see Germany from Partition to Reunification

Two Germanies 1945-1990. Fulbrook. 1996. text ed. 10.95 (0-333-54341-6, Pub. by Macm UK) St Martin.

Two Germans of Genius. Oswald Mosley. 44p. 1987. 30.00 (0-930126-22-X) Typographeum.

Two Girls in Sister Dresses. Jean Van Leeuwen. LC 91-23633. (Illus.). 56p. (J). (gr. 1-5). 1994. pap. 12.99 (0-8037-1230-8); lib. bdg. 12.89 (0-8037-1231-6) Dial Bks Young.

***Two Girls in Sister Dresses.** Jean Van Leeuwen. (J). (gr. 1-5). 1997. pap. 3.99 (0-14-037600-3) Viking Penguin.

Two Girls on a Raft. Charlotte Gordon. (Chapbook Ser.: No. 1). 40p. 1995. pap. 8.95 (0-9649463-0-0) Folly Cove.

Two Gods of Leriathan: Thomas Hobbes on Religion & Politics. A. P. Martinich. 432p. (C). 1992. text ed. 80.00 (0-521-41849-6) Cambridge U Pr.

Two Gothic Classics by Women: The Italian by Ann Radcliffe & Northanger Abbey by Jane Austen. Ed. by Deborah Rogers. 688p. 1995. pap. 6.95 (0-451-52607-4, Sig Classics) NAL-Dutton.

Two Grammatical Models of Modern English: The Old & the New from A to Z. Frits Stuurman. (Germanic Linguistics Ser.). 272p. (C). 1993. pap. text ed. 24.95 (0-415-09344-9, B0330) Routledge.

Two Grandpas Are Better. Catherine K. Hooper. LC 92-31383. 128p. (Orig.). 1993. pap. 8.95 (1-56474-037-4) Fithian Pr.

Two Great Mysteries In God's Economy. Witness Lee. 48p. 2.00 (0-87083-492-4, 04009001) Living Stream Ministry.

***Two Great Prophets.** Elkan V. Kemp. 1996. mass mkt. 4.99 (1-55197-030-9, Pub. by Comnwlth Pub CN) Partners Pubs Grp.

Two Great Rebel Armies: An Essay in Confederate Military History. Richard M. McMurry. LC 88-14374. (Illus.). xviii, 204p. (C). 1989. 22.50 (0-8078-1819-4) U of NC Pr.

Two Great Rebel Armies: An Essay in Confederate Military History. Richard M. McMurry. LC 88-14374. 222p. (C). 1996. pap. 14.95 (0-8078-4569-8) U of NC Pr.

Two Great Scientists of the Nineteenth Century: Correspondence of Emil Du Bois-Reymond & Carl Ludwig. Emil H. Du Bois-Reymond. Tr. by Sabine L. Ayes & Paul F. Cranefield. LC 79-24140. (Illus.). 203p. reprint ed. pap. 57.90 (0-8357-6609-8, 2035254) Bks Demand.

Two Great Scouts & Their Pawnee Battalion: The Experiences of Frank J. North & Luther H. North. George Grinnell. LC 29-2718. vii, 299p. 1996. pap. 12.00 (0-8032-5775-9, Bison Books) U of Nebr Pr.

Two Greatest Prayers Of The Apostle Paul. Witness Lee. 47p. 1.75 (0-87083-430-4, 08026001) Living Stream Ministry.

***Two Greek Historical Treatises from the Roman Empire: Introduction, Text & Translation of the Arts of Rhetoric, Attributed to Anonymous Seguerianus & to Apsines of Gadara.** Mervin R. Dilts & George A. Kennedy. LC 96-50247. (Memosyne, Bibliotheca Classica Batava Ser.). 1997. write for info. (90-04-10728-2) E J Brill.

Two Group Reactor Theory. J. L. Meem. xiv, 417p. 1964. text ed. 321.00 (0-677-00520-2) Gordon & Breach.

Two Groups of Thessalian Gold. Stella G. Miller. LC 77-80473. (University of California Publications in Social Welfare: No. 18). (Illus.). 126p. reprint ed. pap. 36.00 (0-685-23997-7, 2031581) Bks Demand.

Two Guadalupes: Hispanic Legends & Magic Tales from Northern New Mexico. Ed. by Marta Weigle. LC 86-71416. (New Deal & Folk Culture Ser.). (Illus.). 176p. (Orig.). 1987. pap. 12.95 (0-941270-32-7) Ancient City Pr.

Two Gulls, One Hawk: Two Long Poems. James Hoggard. 1983. pap. 7.95 (0-933384-08-4); lib. bdg. 11.95 (0-933384-10-6) Prickly Pear.

***Two Gun Cohen.** Levy. Date not set. 27.95 (0-312-15681-2) St Martin.

Two Gun Reel. Richard Reel. LC 91-67925. 194p. 1993. pap. 12.95 (1-56002-185-3, Univ Edtns) Aegina Pr.

Two Guns from Harlem: The Detective Fiction of Chester Himes. Robert E. Skinner. LC 89-60980. 200p. (C). 1989. 33.95 (0-87972-453-6); pap. 15.95 (0-87972-454-4) Bowling Green Univ Popular Press.

Two Guns from Texas. Erle Adkins. 1990. mass mkt. 2.95 (0-8217-2925-X, Zebra Kensgtn) Kensgtn Pub Corp.

Two Guns North. large type ed. Lee Floren. (Linford Western Library). 1991. pap. 15.99 (0-7089-6965-8) Ulverscroft.

Two Guys Fooling Around With the Moon & Other Drawings. B. Kliban. LC 81-43780. (Illus.). 144p. 1982. pap. 5.95 (0-89480-198-8, 474) Workman Pub.

***Two Guys, Four Corners: Great Photographs, Great Times & a Million Laughs.** Don Imus & Fred Imus. LC 96-29851. (Illus.). 1997. 29.95 (0-679-45307-5, Villard Bks) Random.

Two Guys on Holy Land. Walid Bitar. LC 92-25033. (Wesleyan Poetry Ser.). 68p. 1993. pap. 11.95 (0-8195-1209-5, Wesleyan Univ Pr); text ed. 25.00 (0-8195-2206-6, Wesleyan Univ Pr) U Pr of New Eng.

Two Halves. Lass Small. (Desire Ser.). 1992. pap. 2.89 (0-373-05743-1, 5-05743-5) Silhouette.

Two Halves of a Whole: Torah Guidelines for Marriage. Tehilla Abramov & Yirmiyohu Abramov. 210p. 1994. 16.95 (1-56871-068-2) Targum Pr.

Two Halves of the Same Silence. Susan A. Katz. LC 84-71176. 76p. 1985. pap. 6.95 (0-917652-46-0) Confluence Pr.

***Two Hander.** Sara Kestelman & Susan Penhaligon. 110p. 9600. pap. 13.95 (1-899344-08-X) Dufour.

Two Harmonies: Poetry & Prose in the Seventeenth Century. Kenneth G. Hamilton. LC 77-18929. 218p. 1978. reprint ed. text ed. 55.00 (0-313-20180-3, HATH, Greenwood Pr) Greenwood.

Two Harness Textiles, the Loom Controlled Weaves, the Open Work Weaves, Brocade. Harriet Tidball. LC 87-80655. (Guild Monographs: No. 20, 21, 22). (Illus.). 118p. 1987. pap. 14.95 (0-916658-44-9) Shuttle Craft.

***Two-Head Bird: One Life.** Mitsuko Ando. Tr. by Ken'ichi Yokogawa from JPN. Orig. Title: Gumyo No Tori. 171p. (Orig.). 1996. pap. 14.95 (0-9651914-0-0) Daishinkai Pr.

Two-Headed Deer: Illustrations of the Ramayana in Orissa. Joanna Williams. LC 95-4978. (California Studies in the History of Art: Vol. 34). (Illus.). 330p. (C). 1996. 65.00 (0-520-08065-3) U CA Pr.

Two-Headed Eagle. John Biggins. LC 96-8482. 368p. 1996. 24.95 (0-312-14751-1) St Martin.

Two Headed God. Adams. LC 94-69726. 96p. (Orig.). 1995. pap. 9.95 (1-879384-26-4) Cypress Hse.

Two Headed Tale. Steven Leske. 16p. (J). (gr. k-6). 1992. pap. text ed. 5.99 (1-881617-02-5) Teapot Tales.

Two Heads Are Better Than One. Peter Warnock. (Illus.). 72p. (Orig.). 1985. pap. 8.50 (0-943456-09-6) Bearly Ltd.

Two Hearts. Mel Gilden. (Beverly Hills 90210 Ser.: No. 07). 192p. (YA). 1993. mass mkt. 3.99 (0-06-106144-1, Harp PBks) HarpC.

***Two Hearts Desire: Gay Couples on Their Love.** Michael Lassell. 1997. 12.00 (0-312-15239-6, Stonewall Inn) St Martin.

Two Hearts in a Melting Pot. Paul Kolesar. 104p. 1983. 8.95 (0-87141-074-5) Manyland.

Two Hearts, One Fire: A Glimpse Behind the Mask of Leprosy. Howard E. Crouch & Sr. Mary Augustine. LC 89-50271. (Illus.). 240p. (Orig.). 1989. pap. 6.95 (0-9606330-1-4) Damien-Dutton Soc.

Two Hearts, Slightly Used. Dixie Browning. 1994. mass mkt. 2.99 (0-373-05890-X, 1-05890-8) Harlequin Bks.

Two Hearts, Slightly Used. large type ed. Dixie Browning. (Silhouette Romance Ser.). 1996. 18.95 (0-373-59662-6) Harlequin Bks.

Two Hearts Too Late. Christie Clark. 1994. pap. 2.75 (0-373-19041-7, 1-19041-2) Harlequin Bks.

Two Histories of Ireland. James Ware. LC 71-171796. (English Experience Ser.: No. 421). 500p. 1971. reprint ed. 80.00 (90-221-0421-4) Walter J Johnson.

***Two Holiday Folktales from Mexico.** Anthony Ramirez. Ed. by Bernard H. Hamel. (Illus.). 36p. (ENG & SPA.). (YA). 1996. 8.95 (1-886835-04-7) Bilingual Bk Pr.

Two Homes for Dainty Dinosaur. (Illus.). (J). (ps-2). 1991. pap. 5.10 (0-8136-5716-4); lib. bdg. 7.95 (0-8136-5216-2) Modern Curr.

Two Horse Power. John Hewitt. 144p. 1994. pap. 30.00 (0-86138-084-3, Pub. by T Dalton UK) St Mut.

Two Hot Girls on a Hot Summer Night. Terry Hooper & Art Wetherell. (Eros Graphic Novel Ser.: No. 4). 88p. 1992. pap. 10.95 (1-56097-203-3) Fantagraph Bks.

Two-Hour Applique: Over 200 Original Designs. Leslie Allen. LC 95-49198. 128p. 1996. 24.95 (0-8069-4277-0) Sterling.

Two-Hour Beaded Projects: More Than 200 Designs. Ann Benson. LC 95-37042. 128p. 1996. 24.95 (0-8069-4270-3) Sterling.

***Two-Hour Beaded Projects: More Than 200 Designs.** Ann Benson. 1997. pap. text ed. 14.95 (0-8069-4271-1, Chapelle) Sterling.

Two-Hour Country Cross-Stitch: Over 500 Designs. Susie Steadman. LC 96-25871. (Illus.). 128p. 1996. 24.95 (0-8069-6124-4, Chapelle) Sterling.

Two-Hour Cross-Stitch: 515 Fabulous Designs. Patrice Boerens. LC 94-30301. (Illus.). 144p. 1995. 24.95 (0-8069-0952-8, Chapelle) Sterling.

***Two Hour Cross-Stitch: 515 Fabulous Designs.** Patrice Boerens. 1997. pap. text ed. 14.95 (0-8069-0953-6, Chapelle) Sterling.

***Two-Hour Mini Quilt Projects: Over 111 Appliqued & Pieced Designs.** McKenzie Kate. 128p. 1997. 24.95 (0-8069-8643-3) Sterling.

***Two-Hour Nature Crafts.** Kate Mckenzie. LC 96-38702. 1997. 24.95 (0-8069-4293-2) Sterling.

Two-Hour Painted Wood Projects. Linda Durbano. LC 95-23016. 144p. 1996. 24.95 (0-8069-1399-1) Sterling.

***Two-Hour Quilted Christmas Projects.** Cheri Saffiote. LC 97-13978. 1997. write for info. (0-8069-9771-0) Sterling.

***Two-Hour Silk Ribbon Embroidery: Over 200 Designs.** Malissa Williams. LC 96-9926. 1997. 24.95 (0-8069-8613-1) Sterling.

***2 Hours & 47 Years Ago.** (Orig.). 1997. pap. 10.95 (1-57532-041-X) Press-Tige Pub.

Two Hours Beyond Atlanta: Day Trips from the Capital of the South, 3. Lincoln S. Bates. (Adventure Roads Travel Ser.). 144p. 1996. pap. 12.95 (0-943734-27-4) Ocean Tree Bks.

Two Houses: New Tarbat House, Easter Ross; Royston House, Edinburgh, & the Family of Mackenzie, Earls of Cromartie 1656-1784. Monica Clough. 1990. pap. text ed. 19.95 (0-08-040909-1, Pub. by Aberdeen U Pr) Macmillan.

Two Hundred All-American Home Plans: Popular Home Styles from Across America. Home Planners, Inc. Staff. 1994. pap. 8.95 (1-881955-17-6) Home Planners.

Two Hundred & Eighty Titles & Symbols of Christ. James Large. (Bible Study Ser: Pulpit Legends Collection: Vol. 578). 578p. 1995. 19.99 (0-89957-201-4) AMG Pubs.

Two Hundred & Fifty Years of the British Novel 1740-1989. William R. Cagle & Dorian Gossy. (Illus.). 1990. pap. 10.00 (1-879598-07-8) IN Univ Lilly Library.

Two Hundred & One Awesome, Magical, Bizarre, & Incredible Experiments. Janice P. VanCleave. 128p. (J). 1994. pap. text ed. 12.95 (0-471-31011-5) Wiley.

Two-Hundred-&-One Great Questions. LC 88-63708. 160p. (Orig.). 1988. pap. 6.00 (0-89109-284-6) NavPress.

201 Principles of Software Development. Alan M. Davis. LC 94-47075. 1995. text ed. 24.95 (0-07-015840-1) McGraw.

Two Hundred & One Things You Should Know about AIDS & Other Sexually Transmitted Diseases. Jeffrey S. Nevid. (Illus.). 1993. pap. 13.95 (0-205-14873-5) Allyn.

Two Hundred & One Ways to Get Even with Your Boss. Linda Higgins. LC 94-20518. 1994. 8.95 (0-8065-1570-8, Citadel Pr) Carol Pub Group.

Two Hundred & Three Ways to Drive a Man Wild in Bed. Olivia St. Clair. LC 93-14791. 1993. 16.00 (0-517-59533-8, Harmony) Crown Pub Group.

Two Hundred & Twenty Easy-to-Do Science Experiments for Young People: Three Complete Books. Muriel Mandell. (Juveniles Ser.). 287p. (J). (gr. 3 up). 1985. pap. 10.50 (0-486-24874-7) Dover.

Two Hundred Anecdotes & Illustrations see Doscientas Anecdotas e Ilustraciones

Two Hundred Budget-Smart Home Plans: Affordable Home Plans from 902 to 2540 Square Feet. (Illus.). 224p. 1992. pap. 8.95 (0-918894-97-2) Home Planners.

200 Challenging Chess Puzzles. Martin Grief. LC 94-43421. (Illus.). 200p. 1995. pap. 6.95 (0-8069-0894-7, Sterling-Main St) Sterling.

Two Hundred Classic Chess Puzzles. Martin Greif. LC 93-14610. (Illus.). 144p. 1993. pap. 6.95 (0-8069-0462-3) Sterling.

200 Classic Sauces: Guaranteed Recipes for Every Occasion. Tom Bridge. LC 96-29684. 1996. text ed. 29.95 (0-470-23679-5) Wiley.

Two Hundred Conspicuous, Unusual, Or Economically Important Tropical Plants of the Caribbean. John M. Kingsbury. LC 88-30161. (Illus.). 225p. 1988. pap. 20.00 (0-9612610-2-1) Bullbrier Pr.

200 Creative & Thought-Provoking Questions: Conversation Piece. rev. ed. Paul Lowrie & Bret Nicholaus. LC 94-65462. 64p. 1995. pap. 3.95 (0-9634251-1-0) Questmarc Pub.

Two Hundred Decorative Title Pages. Alexander Nesbitt. (Illus.). (Orig.). 1964. pap. 8.95 (0-486-21264-5) Dover.

200 Demanding Chess Puzzles. Ed. by Martin Greif. LC 95-43167. (Illus.). 1p. 1996. 6.95 (0-8069-5977-0) Sterling.

Two Hundred Dollar Look. F. E. Peters. 1987. 14.95 (0-8184-0434-5) Carol Pub Group.

***200 Drum Machine Patterns.** 80p. 9.95 (0-614-20116-0, 00657370) H Leonard.

Two Hundred Drum Machine Patterns: A Beginning Guide to Programming Your Drum Machine. 80p. 1986. pap. 9.95 (0-88188-632-7, 00657370) H Leonard.

Two Hundred Easy Recorder Tunes. P. Hawthorn. (First Music Ser.). (J). (gr. 4-7). 1993. pap. 17.95 (0-7460-1397-3, Usborne) EDC.

208 Ways to Annoy People: French Fries up Your Nose. Alden Nusser. LC 95-6192. 96p. (Orig.). (J). (gr. 3-7). 1995. pap. 3.50 (0-380-77913-7, Camelot) Avon.

Two Hundred Eighty Eight Chronological Events in the Personal Life of the Lord Jesus Christ. (Walk with Jesus Ser.). 24p. 1992. pap. 5.00 (1-57277-405-3) Script Rsch.

Two Hundred Eighty-Nine Most Asked Questions on Condominiums Answered. Jake Aronson. 224p. 1984. pap. 4.95 (0-913428-39-6) Landfall Pr.

Two Hundred Eighty Paradoxes or Wondrous Sayings. Sebastian Franck. Tr. by E. J. Furcha. LC 86-662. (Texts & Studies in Religion: Vol. 26). 562p. 1986. lib. bdg. 119.95 (0-88946-814-1) E Mellen.

Two Hundred Examples of Letters: Deux Cents Modeles de Lettres. Pierre Maury. 285p. (FRE.). 1986. pap. 17.95 (0-8288-1557-7, F113580) Fr & Eur.

200 Expandable Home Plans: Stylish Designs with Bonus, Flexible or Finish-Later Space. Home Planners, Inc. Staff. (Illus.). 160p. 1995. pap. 8.95 (1-881955-21-4) Home Planners.

Two Hundred Family Favored Home Plans. (Illus.). 224p. (Orig.). 1993. pap. 8.95 (1-881955-07-9) Home Planners.

Two Hundred Farmhouse & Country Home Plans: Classic & Modern Farmhouses from 1299 to 4890 Square Feet. (Illus.). 224p. 1992. pap. 8.95 (0-918894-96-4) Home Planners.

Two Hundred Fifteen African-American Women You Should Know about: Trivia Facts. Gloria Gaymon. 91p. (Orig.). 1992. pap. text ed. 13.00 (0-9633393-2-X) Nationtime Pubs.

Two Hundred Fifteen Days in the Life of an American Ambassador. Martin F. Herz. LC 90-4258. 277p. 1990. reprint ed. pap. text ed. 10.00 (0-934742-60-X) Geo U Inst Dplmcy.

***250 Authentic Art Nouveau Borders.** M. P. Verneuil. (Illus.). pap. 9.95 (0-486-26461-0) Dover.

258 Great Dates While You Wait. Susie Shellenberger & Greg Johnson. LC 94-34346. 160p. (J). 1995. pap. 8.99 (0-8054-6177-9, 4261-77) Broadman.

Two Hundred Fifty Essential Kanji for Everyday Use. Ed. by Akiyo Nishimo. (Illus.). 232p. 1993. pap. 17.95 (0-8048-1911-4) C E Tuttle.

250 Everyday Science Activities. (Illus.). 240p. 1996. pap. text ed. write for info. (0-9652679-0-3) Early Years.

250 Funniest Office Jokes, Memos & Cartoon Pinups. Adam Warlock. LC 94-75550. (Two Hundred Fifty Funniest Ser.: Vol. 1). (Illus.). 250p. (Orig.). 1993. pap. 12.95 (0-9638942-0-X) Knightraven.

250 Funniest Office Jokes, Memos & Cartoon Pinups. 2nd ed. Adam Warlock. LC 95-77126. (Two Hundred Fifty Funniest Ser.: Vol. 2). (Illus.). 250p. (Orig.). 1995. pap. 12.95 (0-9638942-1-8) Knightraven.

250 Great R/C Marine Tips. Jim Newman. (Illus.). 46p. (Orig.). 1996. pap. 12.95 (0-911295-16-X) Air Age.

***250 GT: Tour de France.** John Starkey. (Illus.). 144p. 1997. 39.95 (1-874105-75-8, Pub. by Veloce Pub UK) Motorbooks Intl.

250 Management Success Stories: From Child Care Center Directors. Ed. by Roger Neugebauer. 48p. (Orig.). 1995. pap. 10.00 (0-942702-16-6) Child Care.

Two Hundred Fifty Reasons to Quit Smoking. Molli E. Nagel. Ed. by Andrea Bacci. 78p. (Orig.). (C). 1994. pap. 8.95 (1-56550-021-0) Vis Bks Intl.

***250 Short Cases in Clinical Medicine.** Baliga. 1997. pap. text ed. write for info. (0-7020-2205-5, Bailliere-Tindall) Saunders.

250 Stencil Designs from India. K. Prakash. (Design Library). (Illus.). pap. 5.95 (0-486-29026-3) Dover.

***250 Tips for Making Life with Arthritis Easier.** Arthritis Foundation Staff. 1997. pap. 9.95 (1-56352-381-7) Longstreet Pr Inc.

250 Ways to Be Romantic: The King of Romance. Barry Rosen. 189p. 1990. pap. 9.95 (0-9625593-0-X) B R Pub Co TN.

Two Hundred Fifty Years of Afro-American Art: An Annotated Bibliography. Lyn Igoe & James Igoe. LC 81-12226. 1291p. reprint ed. pap. 180.00 (0-8357-8673-0, 2056829) Bks Demand.

***249 at War: The Authorized History of the RAF's Top Claiming Squadron of WWII.** Brian Cull. (Illus.). 384p. 1997. 44.95 (1-898697-49-3, Pub. by Grub St Pubns UK) Seven Hills Bk.

247 Best Movie Scenes in Film History: A Filmgoer's Guide to Cigar Scenes, Car Chase Scenes, Haircut Scenes, Whistling Scenes, Dentist Scenes, Fluttering Drapes, Funny Walks, Mirrors, Name Mispronunciations, Parking Meters, Sagging Shoulders, Steambaths, & Numerous Other Scenes Long Noted... Sanford Levine. LC 91-50953. (Illus.). 192p. 1992. lib. bdg. 29.95 (0-89950-671-2) McFarland & Co.

Two Hundred Forty-Six Solved Structural Engineering Problems. C. Dale Buckner. (Engineering Reference Manual Ser.). (Illus.). 440p. 1991. pap. 52.95 (0-912045-32-9) Prof Pubns CA.

214 Ways to Say I Love You. Julian Biddle. 96p. 1996. mass mkt. 4.99 (0-7860-0234-4, Pinncle Kensgtn) Kensgtn Pub Corp.

An Asterisk (*) at the beginning of an entry indicates that the title is appearing in BIP for the first time.

200 Funniest Sports. Greg MacNeil. 1995. mass mkt. 6.99 (*0-7704-2720-0*) Bantam.

*__200 Great Painting Ideas for Artists.__ Carole Katchen. LC 97-23677. 1997. write for info. (*0-89134-799-2*, North Lght Bks) F & W Pubns Inc.

Two Hundred Hadith. Ed. by Abdul Rahim AlFahim. 250p. 1993. pap. text ed. 14.95 (*1-56744-483-0*) Kazi Pubns.

Two Hundred Illustrated Science Experiments for Children. Robert J. Brown. (Orig.). 1987. pap. text ed. 12.95 (*0-07-157390-9*) McGraw.

Two Hundred Illustrated Science Experiments for Children. Robert J. Brown. (Illus.). 196p. (Orig.). 1987. pap. 9.95 (*0-8306-2825-8*) McGraw-Hill Prof.

200 Intriguing Chess Puzzles. Martin Greif. LC 96-8987. (Illus.). 144p. 1996. pap. 6.95 (*0-8069-8152-0*) Sterling.

Two Hundred Kid-Tested Ways to Lower the Fat in Your Child's Favorite Foods: How to Make the Brand-Name & Homemade Foods Your Kids Love More Healthful - & Delicious. Elaine Moquette-Magee. 297p. 1994. pap. 12.95 (*1-56561-034-2*, 004231) Chronimed.

Two Hundred Letters for Job Hunters. William S. Frank. 320p. (Orig.). 1990. pap. 17.95 (*0-89815-363-8*) Ten Speed Pr.

Two Hundred Letters for Job Hunters. rev. ed. William S. Frank. LC 93-26780. 352p. (Orig.). 1993. pap. 19.95 (*0-89815-558-4*) Ten Speed Pr.

Two Hundred Level-Headed Ideas for School Library Media Centers: A Plan Book. June S. Level. 86p. 1988. pap. text ed. 13.50 (*0-87287-668-3*) Libs Unl.

*__200 Magic Tricks Anyone Can Do.__ (Magical Library). (Illus.). (YA). (gr. 5 up). 14.95 (*0-614-21964-7*) Random.

Two Hundred Meters & Down. Clinton DeSoto. 1985. pap. 8.00 (*0-87259-001-1*) Am Radio.

Two Hundred Mile Exclusive Economic Zone in the New Law of the Sea. Barbara Kwiatkowska. (C). 1989. lib. bdg. 148.50 (*0-7923-0074-2*) Kluwer Ac.

*__200 Minute Marketing System: Tools, Tips & Techniques for the Occasional Marketer.__ Rob Fey. (Illus.). 300p. 1997. 34.95 (*0-9654105-0-1*) Fey Mktg.

Two Hundred Move-Up Home Plans. Home Planners, Inc. Staff. 224p. 1996. pap. text ed. 8.95 (*1-881955-30-3*) Home Planners.

Two Hundred Narrow-Lot Home Plans. (Illus.). 224p. (Orig.). 1993. pap. 8.95 (*1-881955-06-0*) Home Planners.

200 New Food Combining Recipes: Tasty Dishes from Around the World. Inge Dries. 1995. pap. 9.95 (*1-85230-579-7*) Element MA.

Two Hundred Ninety-One, Nos. 1-12. LC 75-138694. (Contemporary Art Ser.). (Illus.). 1972. reprint ed. 99.95 (*0-405-00774-4*) Ayer.

Two Hundred Ninety-Three Renaissance Woodcuts for Artists & Illustrators: Jost Amman's Kunstbuchlein. Alfred Werner. LC 68-14561. 300p. 1968. reprint ed. pap. 7.95 (*0-486-21987-9*) Dover.

Two Hundred Nuzi Texts from the Oriental Institute of the University of Chicago, Pt. I. M. P. Maidman. (Studies on the Civilization & Culture of Nuzi & the Hurrians: Vol. 6). 449p. (C). 1994. 50.00 (*1-883053-05-6*) CDL Pr.

201 Answers to the Toughest Interview Questions. Mathew J. DeLuca. (Illus.). 160p. 1996. pap. text ed. 10.95 (*0-07-016357-X*) McGraw.

201 Arabic Verbs. R. Scheindlin. 1978. pap. 12.95 (*0-8120-0547-3*) Barron.

201 Best Things Ever Said. Michael Ryan. 168p. (Orig.). 1993. pap. 5.95 (*1-56245-079-4*) Great Quotations.

201 Chinese Verbs: Compounds & Phrases for Everyday Usage. Eugene Ching & Nora Ching. LC 77-8811. 1977. pap. text ed. 14.95 (*0-8120-0674-7*) Barron.

Two Hundred One Christmas Ornaments. Ed. by Phyllis Hoffman & Barbara Cockerham. (Illus.). 128p. 1992. 19. 95 (*0-932437-01-X*) Symbol Exc Pubs.

201 Dutch Verbs: Fully Conjugated in All the Tenses. A. Z. Stern. LC 78-18844. 1979. pap. text ed. 11.95 (*0-8120-0738-7*) Barron.

*__201 Dynamite Job Search Letters.__ 3rd ed. Ronald L. Krannich & Caryl R. Krannich. LC 97-5199. 284p. (Orig.). 1997. pap. 19.95 (*1-57023-072-2*) Impact VA.

201 Group Games. Linda Magee. (Game & Party Bks.). 72p. (gr. 10). 1984. pap. 5.99 (*0-8010-6154-7*) Baker Bks.

201 Hebrew Verbs. A. S. Halkin. 1977. pap. 12.95 (*0-8120-0331-4*) Barron.

201 Icebreakers: Group Mixers, Warm-Ups, Energizers, & Playful Activities. Edie West. 400p. 1996. text ed. 99. 95 (*0-07-069599-7*); pap. text ed. 39.95 (*0-07-069600-4*) McGraw.

201 Killer Cover Letters. Sandra Podesta & Andrea Paxton. 1995. 16.95 (*0-614-15512-6*) McGraw.

201 Korean Verbs. Seok C. Song. 1988. pap. 8.95 (*0-8120-2567-9*) Barron.

201 Latin Verbs. J. Wohlberg. 1977. pap. 9.95 (*0-8120-0211-3*) Barron.

201 Modern Greek Verbs. Constantine N. Tsirpanlis. LC 80-13900. 1980. pap. 10.95 (*0-8120-0475-2*) Barron.

201 Polish Verbs. C. Kaipio. 1977. pap. 11.95 (*0-8120-0577-5*) Barron.

201 Questions Every Homebuyer & Homeseller Must Ask. Edith Lank. LC 95-9131. 250p. (Orig.). 1995. pap. 15.95 (*0-7931-1434-9*, 1913-3501, Real Estate Ed) Dearborn Finan.

Two Hundred One Ready-to-Use Word Games for the English Classroom. Jack Umstatter. LC 94-18901. 1994. spiral bd. 27.95 (*0-87628-911-1*) Ctr Appl Res.

201 Swedish Verbs. Richard Auletta. LC 74-9748. 1975. pap. 11.95 (*0-8120-0528-7*) Barron.

201 Things for Which to Be Grateful. Slightly Off Center Writers Group Staff. (Orig.). 1995. pap. 8.95 (*1-56721-097-X*) Twnty-Fifth Cent Pr.

Two Hundred One Things to Do While You're Getting Better (at Home or in the Hospital) How to Successfully Cope with Boredom & Pain Without Losing Your Sanity. Erica L. Klein. 273p. 1993. pap. 10.95 (*1-56561-033-4*, 004230) Chronimed.

201 Turkish Verbs. Talat S. Halman. LC 80-27006. 1981. pap. text ed. 12.95 (*0-8120-2034-0*) Barron.

*__201 Unique Ways to Make Your Wedding Special.__ 2nd expanded rev. ed. Don Altman. Ed. by Maryanne Hammers. LC 97-15175. (Illus.). 144p. 1997. pap. 9.95 (*0-9639161-4-9*) Moon Lake Media.

201 Vietnamese Verbs. Nguyen Dinh-Hoa. LC 79-14200. (YA). (gr. 10-12). 1979. pap. text ed. 11.95 (*0-8120-2019-7*) Barron.

*__201 Ways to Deal with Difficult People.__ (Quick-Tip Survival Guides Ser.). 160p. 1997. pap. text ed. 10.95 (*0-07-006218-8*) McGraw.

Two Hundred One Ways to Enjoy Your Dog. Ellie Milon. LC 89-18403. (Illus.). 292p. 1990. pap. 18.95 (*0-931866-33-2*) Alpine Pubns.

*__201 Ways to Manage Your Time Better.__ (Quick Tip Survival Guides Ser.). 160p. 1997. pap. text ed. 10.95 (*0-07-006217-X*) McGraw.

*__201 Ways to Say No Effectively & Gracefully.__ (Quick-Tip Survival Guides Ser.). 160p. 1997. pap. text ed. 10.95 (*0-07-006219-6*) McGraw.

*__201 Winning Cover Letters for $100,000+ Jobs.__ Wendy Enelow. 200p. 1997. pap. 24.95 (*1-57023-088-9*) Impact VA.

Two Hundred Open Games. David Bronstein. 1991. pap. 7.95 (*0-486-26857-8*) Dover.

Two Hundred Original Shop Aids & Jigs for Woodworking. Rosario Capotosto. LC 87-10144. (Illus.). 362p. 1987. pap. 17.95 (*0-8069-6582-7*) Sterling.

Two Hundred Patterns for Multiple Harness Looms. Russell E. Groff. (Illus.). 1980. pap. 12.95 (*1-56659-021-3*) Robin & Russ.

*__200% Cracked Wheat.__ Ed. by Gary Hyland et al. 8.95 (*1-55050-038-4*, Pub. by Coteau CN) Genl Dist Srvs.

Two Hundred Percent of Nothing: An Eye-Opening Tour Through the Twists & Turns of Math Abuse & Innumeracy. A. K. Dewdney. Ed. by S. Ross. LC 92-42173. 192p. 1993. text ed. 22.95 (*0-471-57776-6*) Wiley.

200 Percent of Nothing: An Eye-Opening Tour Through the Twists & Turns of Math Abuse & Innumeracy. A. K. Dewdney. LC 92-42173. 1996. pap. text ed. 12.95 (*0-471-14574-2*) Wiley.

*__200% Wife.__ Jennifer Greene. (Special Edition Ser.: No. 1111). 1997. mass mkt. 3.99 (*0-373-24111-9*, 1-24111-6) Silhouette.

Two Hundred Pilze: One Hundred Eighty Pilze fuer die Kueche und ihre giftigen Dopplegaenger. Rose M. Daehncke. (Illus.). 246p. (GER.). 1982. lib. bdg. 25.00 (*3-85502-145-7*) Lubrecht & Cramer.

Two Hundred Plus: History of Bradford, New Hampshire. Ed. by Bradford Town History Committee. LC 76-26494. (Illus.). 1976. 20.00 (*0-914016-31-8*) Phoenix Pub.

Two Hundred Plus Games & Fun Activities for Teaching Preschoolers. Kathryn Kizer. (Illus.). 72p. (Orig.). (J). (ps). 1989. pap. text ed. 4.95 (*0-936625-70-8*, New Hope AL) Womans Mission Union.

Two Hundred Plus Ideas for Drama. Anna Scher & Charles Verrall. LC 91-29021. 246p. 1992. pap. 15.95 (*0-435-08606-5*, 08606) Heinemann.

Two Hundred Plus Ideas for Teaching Preschoolers. Kathryn Kizer & Ethel McIndoo. 72p. (Orig.). 1986. pap. 4.95 (*0-936625-06-6*, New Hope AL) Womans Mission Union.

Two Hundred Plus Things to Make for Teaching Preschoolers. Kathryn Kizer & Ethel McIndoo. Ed. by Karen Gross. 64p. (Orig.). 1991. pap. text ed. 4.95 (*1-56309-019-8*, New Hope AL) Womans Mission Union.

Two Hundred Poems. Ed. by Ricardo Quintana. LC 74-80377. (Granger Index Reprint Ser.). 1977. 23.95 (*0-8369-6058-0*) Ayer.

Two Hundred Rooms in the Inn: The Story of Providence Mission Homes. Mercedes Gribble. LC 83-15367. (Illus.). 99p. (Orig.). 1983. pap. 4.95 (*0-87808-195-X*) William Carey Lib.

Two Hundred Selections from the Permanent Collection. Columbus Museum of Art Staff. LC 78-74706. (Illus.). 130p. (Orig.). 1978. pap. 2.50 (*0-918881-03-X*) Columbus Mus Art.

200 Sermon Outlines. Jabez Burns. LC 75-92502. (Sermon Outline Ser.). 424p. 1969. reprint ed. pap. 12.99 (*0-8254-2264-7*) Kregel.

*__277 Secrets Your Cat Wants You to Know.__ Paulette Cooper. 208p. (Orig.). 1997. pap. 8.95 (*0-89815-952-0*) Ten Speed Pr.

277 Secrets Your Dog Wants You to Know: A Doggie Bag of Unusual & Useful Information. Paulette Cooper. 208p. (Orig.). 1995. pap. 8.95 (*0-89815-682-3*) Ten Speed Pr.

277 Secrets Your Dog Wants You to Know: A Doggie Bag of Unusual & Useful Information. Paulette Cooper & Paul Noble. 204p. (Orig.). 1995. 14.95 (*0-89815-737-4*) Ten Speed Pr.

*__272 Artistic Silhouettes.__ Floyd Mooris. (Illus.). 96p. 1996. 12.40 (*1-56637-313-1*) Goodheart.

*__200 Short Cases in Clincal Medicine.__ R. R. Baliga. 416p. 1993. pap. write for info. (*0-7020-1684-5*, Pub. by W B Saunders UK) Saunders.

Two Hundred Sixty Drum Machine Patterns. 96p. 1987. pap. 9.95 (*0-88188-887-7*, 00657371) H Leonard.

*__260 Drum Machine Patterns.__ 96p. 9.95 (*0-614-20117-9*, 00657371) H Leonard.

Two Hundred Sixty-One North American Indian Designs. Madeleine Orban-Szontagh. LC 93-11145. 1993. pap. write for info. (*0-486-27718-6*) Dover.

Two-Hundred Sixty Plates Illustrate Ten Gold Bullae: Two Bulloteria, Four Thousand Fifty Lead Seals & Eight Hundred Eighty-Four Monograms see Byzantine Lead Seals

Two Hundred Sixty-Three Brain Busters: Just How Smart Are You, Anyway? Louis Phillips. LC 85-40446. (Novels Ser.). (Illus.). 87p. (J). (gr. 4-7). 1985. pap. 3.99 (*0-14-031875-5*, Puffin) Puffin Bks.

*__200 Small House Plans: Selected Designs Under 2,500 Square Feet.__ (Illus.). 224p. 1997. pap. 8.95 (*1-881955-34-6*) Home Planners.

210 Killer Cover Letters. Sandra Podesta & Andrea Paxton. LC 95-37325. 1995. pap. text ed. 16.95 (*0-07-050456-3*) McGraw.

Two Hundred Thirteen Valentines. Barbara Cohen. LC 91-7151. (Illus.). 64p. (J). (gr. 2-4). 1993. pap. 4.95 (*0-8050-2627-4*, Redfeather BYR) H Holt & Co.

Two Hundred Thirty Four Welsh Verbs: Standard Literary Forms. Kathryn Klingebiel. LC 93-41684. 1994. pap. 18.95 (*0-926689-04-5*) Ford & Bailie Pubs.

Two Hundred Thirty-Seven Intimate Questions Every Woman Should Ask a Man. Laura Corn. 256p. (Orig.). 1995. pap. 9.95 (*0-9629628-0-5*) Park Ave Pubs.

236 Killer Voice Processing Applications. Edwin Margulies. 34.95 (*0-936648-70-8*) Flatiron Pubng.

Two Hundred Thousand: A Proven Program You Can Use to Get 200,000 Miles of Reliable Transportation from Your Automobile. James T. Powell. 200p. (Orig.). 1989. pap. 8.95 (*0-911168-85-0*) Prakken.

203 Ways to Be Supremely Successful in the New World of Selling. John R. Graham. 1996. 15.95 (*0-02-861177-2*) Macmillan.

*__200 Tips for Growing Beautiful Perennials.__ Barbara Ashman. LC 97-15712. (Two Hundred Tips for Growing...Ser.). 128p. 1998. pap. 7.95 (*1-55652-278-9*) Chicago Review.

*__200 Tips for Growing Beautiful Perennials.__ Barbara Ashmun. 1998. pap. text ed. 79.50 (*1-55652-283-5*) Chicago Review.

*__200 Tips for Growing Beautiful Roses.__ Barbara Ashman. LC 97-15721. (Two Hundred Tips for Growing...Ser.). 128p. 1998. pap. 7.95 (*1-55652-277-0*) Chicago Review.

*__200 Tips for Growing Beautiful Roses.__ Barbara Ashmun. 1998. pap. text ed. 79.50 (*1-55652-282-7*) Chicago Review.

200 Tips for Growing Flowers in the Northeast. Miranda Smith. LC 95-37096. 120p. (Orig.). 1996. pap. 7.95 (*1-55652-251-7*) Chicago Review.

200 Tips for Growing Flowers in the Pacific Northwest. Barbara Ashmun. LC 95-37094. 128p. (Orig.). 1996. pap. 7.95 (*1-55652-253-3*) Chicago Review.

Two Hundred Tips for Growing Flowers in the Midwest. Pamela Wolfe. LC 92-44584. (Illus.). 144p. (Orig.). 1993. pap. 6.95 (*1-55652-177-4*) Chicago Review.

200 Tips for Growing Vegetables in the Pacific Northwest. Maggie Stuckey. LC 95-43278. 128p. (Orig.). 1996. pap. 7.95 (*1-55652-254-1*) Chicago Review.

Two Hundred Tips for Growing Vegetables in the Midwest. Pamela Wolfe. LC 92-43359. (Illus.). 128p. (Orig.). 1993. pap. 6.95 (*1-55652-175-8*) Chicago Review.

Two Hundred Tips for Growing Vegetables in the Northeast. Miranda Smith. LC 95-37096. 116p. 1996. pap. 7.95 (*1-55652-252-5*) Chicago Review.

*__200 Tips for Passing the ABPN Oral Exam.__ Ed. by Donald R. Hall. LC 96-33251. 125p. (Orig.). 1996. pap. text ed. 9.95 (*1-56053-202-5*) Hanley & Belfus.

Two Hundred Tips to Students on How to Study. 2nd ed. Berlie J. Fallon. 48p. 1982. Discounts 10-49 copies $1.80 ea., 50-99 copies $1.60 ea., 100-499 copies $1.40 ea., 500-999 or more. pap. 2.00 (*0-8134-2213-2*) Interstate.

Two Hundred Twelve Ideas for Making Low-Cost Physical Education Equipment. Ed. by A. Bruce Frederick. LC 79-187903. 219p. 1972. 7.95 (*0-685-24216-1*) Sch Aid.

Two Hundred Twenty Best Franchises to Buy. rev. ed. Constance Jones & Philip Lief Group Inc. Staff. LC 92-28438. 496p. 1993. pap. 13.95 (*0-553-35155-9*) Bantam.

223 Remington Cartridges. David R. Hughes. (Illus.). 200p. 1991. pap. 20.95 (*0-9626096-1-7*) Far West Pubns.

Two Hundred Twenty-two BASIC Computer Programs for Home, School & Office. Don Roberts. 288p. 1984. 18. 95 (*0-86668-039-X*) ARCsoft.

*__222 More Ways to Make Love with Life: How to Love, Laugh & Live in the Moment.__ Ken Vegotsky. Ed. by Dave Christie. (Love Living & Live Loving Ser.). 101p. (Orig.). 1997. pap. 7.95 (*1-886508-03-8*) Adi Gaia Esalen.

222 Terrific Tips for Two: Ideas for a Happy & Lasting Marriage. Caryl W. Krueger. 288p. (Orig.). 1995. pap. 8.37 (*0-687-00776-3*) Dimen for Liv.

222 Tips for Building Model Railroad Structures. Dave Frary. Ed. by Michael Emmerich. LC 92-22782. (Illus.). 64p. (Orig.). 1992. per. 9.95 (*0-89024-145-7*, 12115) Kalmbach.

222 Ways to Make Love with Life: How to Love, Laugh & Live in the Moment. Ken Vegotsky. Ed. by D. Christie. LC 96-50333. (Love Living & Live Loving Ser.). 96p. 1997. pap. 9.95 (*1-886508-24-0*) Adi Gaia Esalen.

Two Hundred Two Plus Microcomputer Software Packages to Use in Your Library: Descriptions, Evaluations & Practical Advice. Patrick R. Dewey. LC 91-42688. (One Hundred One Micro Ser.). 190p. (C). 1992. pap. 6.00 (*0-8389-0582-X*) ALA.

202 Science Investigations: Exciting Adventures in Earth, Life, & Physical Sciences. Marjorie Frank. (Illus.). 240p. (Orig.). 1990. pap. text ed. 16.95 (*0-86530-173-5*, IP 190-8) Incentive Pubns.

202 Tips Even the Best Business Travelers May Not Know: MCI Special Edition. Christopher McGinnis. 1994. per. 11.00 (*0-7863-0339-5*) Irwin Prof Pubng.

Two Hundred Two Tips Even the Best Business Travelers May Not Know. Christopher J. McGinnis. LC 94-2846. 160p. 1994. per. 12.95 (*1-55623-966-1*) Irwin Prof Pubng.

Two Hundred Ways of Using Imagery in the Classroom: A Guide for Developing Imagination & Creativity in Elementary Students. Michael T. Bagley et al. (gr. 1-8). 1987. pap. 15.00 (*0-89824-084-0*) Trillium Pr.

Two Hundred Ways to Help Children Learn While You're at It. Nassau County, Board of Cooperative Education Services Staff. 1976. text ed. 30.00 (*0-87909-845-7*, Reston) P-H.

Two Hundred Ways to Praise a Child. Frederick Sion. Ed. by Tim Beauchemin et al. (Illus.). 224p. (Orig.). 1992. pap. text ed. 8.50 (*1-884332-04-8*) Netwrk Pr TX.

Two Hundred Years: Stories of the Nation's Capital. Jeanne M. Fogle. LC 90-71876. (Illus.). 184p. 1990. 14. 95 (*0-918339-16-2*) Vandamere.

Two Hundred Years Astray: The Epistle to the Creationists. Neil B. Christianson. LC 96-92371. (Illus.). (Orig.). 1996. pap. text ed. 12.00 (*0-9627240-1-7*) Ne-Do-Pr.

Two Hundred Years at the Falls of the Ohio: A History of Louisville & Jefferson County. George H. Yates. (Illus.). 261p. 1987. reprint ed. 19.00 (*0-9601072-3-1*) Filson Club.

Two Hundred Years of American Communes. Yaacov Oved. Tr. by Hannah Lash. 419p. 1988. 49.95 (*0-88738-113-8*) Transaction Pubs.

Two Hundred Years of American Communes. Yaacov Oved. 516p. (C). 1992. pap. 24.95 (*1-56000-647-1*) Transaction Pubs.

Two Hundred Years of American Educational Thought. Henry J. Perkinson. 342p. 1987. reprint ed. pap. text ed. 27.00 (*0-8191-6124-1*) U Pr of Amer.

Two Hundred Years of Black Culture in Knoxville, Tennessee: 1791 to 1991. Robert J. Booker. LC 93-45411. 1994. write for info. (*0-89865-890-X*) Donning Co.

Two Hundred Years of Chairs & Chairmaking: An Exhibition of Chairs from the Chester County Historical Society. Margaret B. Blades. LC 87-11676. (Illus.). 32p. (Orig.). 1987. pap. 6.50 (*0-685-21897-X*) Chester Co Hist Soc.

Two Hundred Years of Charleston Cooking. 3rd ed. Blanche S. Rhett. Ed. by Lettie Gay. 311p. 1982. reprint ed. pap. 14.95 (*0-87249-348-2*) U of SC Pr.

200 Years of Dolls: Identification & Price Guide. Dawn T. Herlocher. (Illus.). 280p. (Orig.). 1996. pap. 17.95 (*0-930625-29-3*, Antique Trdr Bks) Antique Trader Bks.

Two Hundred Years of English Naive Art 1700-1900. James Ayres. LC 96-18681. 1996. pap. write for info. (*0-88397-120-8*) Art Srvc Intl.

Two Hundred Years of Flight in America. Ed. by Eugene M. Emme. (AAS History Ser.: Vol. 1). (Illus.). 1979. pap. 25.00 (*0-87703-101-0*); text ed. 35.00 (*0-87703-091-X*) Univelt Inc.

Two Hundred Years of Geology in America: Proceedings of the New Hampshire Bicentennial Conference on the History of Geology. New Hampshire Bicentennial Conference on the History of Geology (1976: University of New Hampshire) Staff. Ed. by Cecil J. Schneer. LC 78-63149. (Illus.). 399p. reprint ed. pap. 113.80 (*0-8357-7522-4*, 2036029) Bks Demand.

Two Hundred Years of Gringos. Carlos A. Montaner. Tr. by Gaston Fernandez de la Torriente & James F. Horton. 142p. (Orig.). (C). 1983. pap. text ed. 19.50 (*0-8191-3375-2*); lib. bdg. 45.00 (*0-8191-3374-4*) U Pr of Amer.

Two Hundred Years of Historic Pueblo Pottery: The Gallegos Collection. Francis H. Harlow. LC 90-62273. (Illus.). 96p. 1990. 48.00 (*0-9617085-1-4*) Morning Star Gal.

Two-Hundred Years of Hydrogeology in the United States. 80p. 1987. 12.50 (*1-56034-047-9*, T409) Natl Grnd Water.

200 Years of Rochester Architecture & Gardens. Richard O. Reisem. (Illus.). 144p. 1994. 39.95 (*0-9641706-1-2*) Landmark Soc.

Two Hundred Years of the American Circus. Tom Ogden. LC 92-31880. (Illus.). 416p. 1993. 50.00 (*0-8160-2611-4*) Facts on File.

Two Hundred Years of the Chakri Dynasty. Ed. by Ronald Provencher. (Crossroads Ser.: Ser. 2.2). 145p. (Orig.). 1985. pap. 6.00 (*1-877979-84-8*) SE Asia.

Two Hundred Years of the New York State Legislature. David Zdunczyk. LC 78-74182. (Illus.). 85p. 1978. 4.00 (*0-686-32420-X*) Albany Hist & Art.

Two Hundred Years of Theology: Report of a Personal Journey. fac. ed. Hendrikus Berkhof. Tr. by John Vriend. LC 89-11786. 336p. 1989. reprint ed. pap. 95.80 (*0-7837-7945-3*, 2047701) Bks Demand.

*__200 Years Through 200 Stories: A Tennessee Bicentennial Collection.__ Anne Klebenow. Ed. by Suzanne Ivester. LC 96-47663. (Illus.). 416p. (Orig.). (C). 1996. pap. 25. 00 (*0-9642219-6-9*) U TN Ofc U Relations.

Two Hungry Giants: The United States & Japan in the Quest for Oil & Ores. Raymond Vernon. (Center for International Affairs Ser.). (Illus.). 176p. 1983. 25.95 (*0-674-91470-8*) HUP.

Two If by Sea. Edward M. Holmes. Ed. by Roy Zarucchi & Carolyn Page. (Novel-Fiction Ser.). (Illus.). 264p. (Orig.). 1994. pap. 14.95 (*1-879205-50-5*) Nightshade Pr.

Two If by Sea: The Development of American Coastal Defense Policy. Robert S. Browning, III. LC 83-1638. (Contributions in Military History Ser.: No. 33). (Illus.). xii, 210p. 1983. text ed. 49.95 (*0-313-23688-7*, BRT/, Greenwood Pr) Greenwood.

Two in a Trap: A One-Act Play. Allean L. Hale. 32p. reprint ed. pap. 25.00 (0-7837-1958-2, 2042175) Bks Demand.

Two in Nomines for Six Viols. Richard Dering. Ed. by Virginia Brookes. ii, 23p. 1992. pap. text ed. 12.00 (1-56571-051-7, VC12) PRB Prods.

Two in One Books, Bk. 1. (J). 1991. pap. 1.97 (1-56297-078-X) Lee Pubns KY.

Two in One Books, Bk. 2. (J). 1991. pap. 1.97 (1-56297-079-8) Lee Pubns KY.

Two-in-One Herb Book. Alyson Huxley & Philippa Back. LC 81-82166. (Illus.). 1982. pap. 8.95 (0-87983-225-8) Keats.

Two in the Bush. Peter Farrow. LC 89-9266. (Illus.). 64p. (Orig.). 1989. pap. 4.50 (0-945980-10-8) Nrth Country Pr.

Two in the Bush. large type ed. Gerald Durrell. 1980. 12.00 (0-7089-0516-1) Ulverscroft.

Two in the Far North. 2nd ed. Margaret E. Murie. LC 78-16407. (Illus.). 398p. 1978. reprint ed. pap. 14.95 (0-88240-111-4) Alaska Northwest.

***Two in the Far North.** 5th ed. Margaret E. Murie. LC 97-12760. (Illus.). 376p. 1997. pap. 15.95 (0-88240-495-4) Alaska Northwest.

***Two in the Far North: 35th Anniversary Edition.** Margaret E. Murie. 1997. pap. 15.95 (0-88240-489-X) Alaska Northwest.

Two in the Game. Stanley D. Beck. Ed. by Renais J. Hill. LC 92-55008. 270p. (Orig.). 1993. pap. 10.95 (1-55666-086-3) Pubs Grp Toluca.

Two Incomes & Still Broke: It's Not How Much You Make, but How Much You Keep. Linda Kelley. 224p. 1996. 20.00 (0-8129-2569-6, Times Business) Random.

2-Ingredient Cookbook. Adeline Rosemire. LC 95-37458. 110p. (Orig.). 1996. pap. 9.95 (0-9640044-8-8) Meridian Calif.

Two Ingredient Cookbook: A Recipe Collection Appealing to the Palate. Ruthie Wornall. 1994. pap. 6.95 (0-9624467-6-9) Wornall Pub.

***Two-Ingredient Cookbook: The Easy Way to Make Delicious Meals Fast.** Adeline Rosemire. 1996. pap. text ed. 9.95 (0-07-053996-0) McGraw.

Two Interpretations from Central Park. Graeme Merry. 1994. 8.95 (0-533-10809-8) Vantage.

Two-Inverse & Their Statistical Application. A. J. Getson & F. C. Hsuan. (Lecture Notes in Statistics Ser.: Vol. 47). x, 110p. 1988. 34.95 (0-387-96849-0) Spr-Verlag.

Two is for Dancing: A One, Two, Three of Actions. Woodleigh Hubbard. (Illus.). 32p. (J). (ps-1). 1991. 13.95 (0-87701-895-2) Chronicle Bks.

Two Issues in Public Key Cryptography: RSA BIT Security & a New Knapsack Type System. Ben-Zion Chor. (Association of Computer Machinery Distinguished Dissertation Award Ser.). (Illus.). 71p. 1986. 24.00 (0-262-03121-3) MIT Pr.

Two Jamaicas: The Role of Ideas in a Tropical Colony, 1830-1865. Philip D. Curtin. LC 69-10082. (Illus.). 270p. 1968. reprint ed. text ed. 49.75 (0-8371-0055-0, CUTJ, Greenwood Pr) Greenwood.

Two Japanese Novelists: Soseki & Toson. Edwin McClellan. LC 76-81223. 180p. reprint ed. pap. 51.30 (0-317-10055-6, 2007276) Bks Demand.

Two Jewish Justices: Outcasts in the Promised Land. Robert A. Burt. 200p. 1988. pap. 10.00 (0-520-06749-5) U CA Pr.

***Two Journals.** James Schuyler & Darragh Park. 62p. 1995. 9.95 (0-9639033-4-9) Tibor de Nagy.

Two Jungle Books, 2 Vols. Rudyard Kipling. LC 71-150477. (Short Story Index Reprint Ser.). (J). 1977. reprint ed. 30.95 (0-8369-3818-6) Ayer.

Two Kids & the Three Bears. John D. Brown. LC 75-40538. (Lucky Heart Book Ser.). 32p. 1976. reprint ed. pap. 25.00 (0-7837-9165-8, 2049866) Bks Demand.

Two Kinds of Faith. E. W. Kenyon. 116p. (Orig.). (C). 1942. pap. 6.75 (1-57770-008-2) Kenyons Gospel.

Two Kinds of Knowledge. E. W. Kenyon. 72p. (Orig.). (C). 1938. pap. 3.75 (1-57770-012-0) Kenyons Gospel.

Two Kinds of Life. E. W. Kenyon. 151p. (Orig.). (C). 1943. pap. 9.25 (1-57770-002-3) Kenyons Gospel.

Two Kinds of Rationality: Kibbutz Democracy & Generational Conflict. T. M. Evans. LC 94-41350. (Contradictions on Modernity Ser.: Vol. 2). 1995. text ed. 49.95 (0-8166-2642-1); pap. text ed. 19.95 (0-8166-2643-X) U of Minn Pr.

Two Kinds of Righteousness. E. W. Kenyon. 71p. (Orig.). (C). 1972. pap. 6.75 (1-57770-009-0) Kenyons Gospel.

Two Kinds of Time. Graham Peck. LC 83-45833. (Illus.). reprint ed. 67.50 (0-404-20198-9) AMS Pr.

Two Kingdoms: The Church & Culture Through the Ages. Robert G. Clouse et al. 689p. 1993. text ed. 35.99 (0-8024-8590-1) Moody.

***Two Kings.** Scharff. 1997. 14.95 (1-85744-159-1, Pub. by Cadogan Books UK) Macmillan.

Two Kings of Uganda: or Life by the Shores of Victoria Nyanza. Robert P. Ashe. (Illus.). 354p. 1970. reprint ed. 40.00 (0-7146-1862-4, BHA-01862, Pub. by F Cass Pubs UK) Intl Spec Bk.

Two-Knots & Their Groups. J. A. Hillman. (Australian Mathematical Society Lecture Ser.: No. 4). 200p. (C). 1989. pap. text ed. 28.95 (0-521-37812-5) Cambridge U Pr.

Two Korean Brothers: The Story of Hungbu & Nolbu. Grace S. Yoo. LC 73-18023. (Oriental Stories: No. 7). (J). (gr. k-3). 1970. 7.95 (0-912580-01-1) Far Eastern Res.

Two Koreas in Development: A Comparative Study of Principles & Strategies of Capitalist & Communist Third World Development. Byoung-Lo Philo Kim. 240p. (C). 1991. text ed. 39.95 (0-88738-437-4) Transaction Pubs.

Two Koreas in East Asian Affairs. Ed. by William J. Barnds. LC 75-27379. 216p. (C). 1976. text ed. 40.00 (0-8147-0988-5) NYU Pr.

***Two Ladies of Colonial Algeria: The Lives & Times of Aurelie Picard & Isabelle Eberhardt.** Ursula K. Hart. LC 87-11094. (Monographs in International Studies: No. 49). (Illus.). 161p. 1987. reprint ed. pap. 45.90 (0-608-04101-7, 2064833) Bks Demand.

Two Lads & a Dad: The Prodigal Son. Marilyn Lashbrook. LC 90-63769. (Me Too! Readers Ser.). (Illus.). (J). (gr. k-3). 1991. 5.95 (0-86606-446-X, 877) Treasure Pub.

***Two Lambs.** George A. McCabe. 136p. 1996. pap. 14.95 (0-929529-08-1) Vision Ministry Pr.

Two Lamentable Tragedies. Robert Yarington. (Tudor Facsimile Texts. Old English Plays Ser.: No. 96). reprint ed. 59.50 (0-404-53396-5) AMS Pr.

Two Lands on One Soil. Frank Wright. 608p. 1996. text ed. 45.00 (0-312-15924-2) St Martin.

Two Lands, One Heart: An American Boy's Journey to His Mother's Vietnam. Jeremy C. Schmidt. LC 94-33648. (Illus.). 48p. (J). (gr. 3-6). 1995. 15.95 (0-8027-8357-0); lib. bdg. 16.85 (0-8027-8358-9) Walker & Co.

Two-Lane Highway Traffic Operations: Theory & Practice, Vol. 11. J. R. McLean. (Transportation Studies). 408p. 1989. text ed. 150.00 (2-88124-725-3) Gordon & Breach.

***Two Languages at Work: Bilingual Life on the Production Floor.** Tara Goldstein. LC 96-36176. (Contributions to the Sociology of Language: Vol. 74). xv, 276p. (C). 1997. lib. bdg. 141.45 (3-11-015058-1) Mouton.

Two Laws: Studies in Medieval Legal History Dedicated to Stephan Kuttner. Ed. by Laurent Mayali & Stephanie J. Tibbetts. LC 90-1686. (Studies in Medieval & Early Modern Canon Law). 248p. 1990. 39.95 (0-8132-0725-8) Cath U Pr.

Two Leaps Across Chasm: A Russian Mystery. Nikolai Aleksandrov. 256p. 1992. text ed. 20.00 (0-684-19415-5) S&S Trade.

Two Lectures on Population: Delivered Before the University of Oxford. Nassau W. Senior. LC 75-38143. (Demography Ser.). 1976. reprint ed. 17.95 (0-405-07996-6) Ayer.

Two Lectures on the Subjects of Slavery & Abolition. Compiled by Charles Olcott. LC 71-164391. (Black Heritage Library Collection). 1977. reprint ed. 17.95 (0-8369-8850-7) Ayer.

Two Lectures on the Work of Allen Ginsberg. Barry Miles. LC 93-36395. (Turret Papers). 1993. 20.00 (0-935061-54-1) Contemp Res.

***Two Lectures on Theism: 1897 Edition.** Andrew Seth. 80p. 1996. reprint ed. write for info. (1-85506-198-8) Bks Intl VA.

***Two Lectures; Stalin's Great Terror: Origins & Consequences: Leon Trotsky & the Fate of Marxism in the U. S. S. R.** Vadim Z. Rogovin. (Illus.). 46p. (Orig.). 1996. pap. 9.95 (1-875639-13-6, Pub. by Labour Pr AT) Labor Pubns Inc.

Two Left Brains: Public Radio Commentaries from KCMU-Seattle, Washington. Irv Pollack & George Howland, Jr. 40p. (Orig.). 1993. 6.00 (0-940880-44-X, Littlebook) Open Hand.

Two Leftist Parties of India, 1982. Shiv Lal. 200p. 1986. 165.00 (0-317-61987-X, Pub. by Archives Pubs II) St Mut.

Two-Legged Creature: An Otoe Story. Illus. by Carol Bowles. LC 92-56510. 32p. (J). (gr. k up). 1993. lib. bdg. 14.95 (0-87358-553-4) Northland AZ.

Two Leggings: The Making of a Crow Warrior. Peter Nabokov. LC 82-6979. (Illus.). xxx, 242p. 1982. reprint ed. pap. 9.95 (0-8032-8351-2, Bison Books) U of Nebr Pr.

Two Lenses. Aron Lankin. Ed. & Tr. by Dmitriy Koronkevich. (Illus.). 80p. 1995. pap. 15.99 (0-9643971-3-7) Isometry.

Two Letters & Short Rules of a Good Life. Robert Southwell. Ed. by Nancy P. Brown. (Documents Ser.). 1978. 25.00 (0-918016-53-3) Folger Bks.

Two-Level Functional Languages. Flemming Nielson & Hanne R. Nielson. (Tracts in Theoretical Computer Science Ser.: No. 34). (Illus.). 300p. (C). 1992. text ed. 47.95 (0-521-40384-7) Cambridge U Pr.

Two Liberation Plays. Mig A. Enriquez. 95p. (Orig.). (C). 1991. pap. 8.75 (971-10-0427-5, Pub. by New Day Pub PH) Cellar.

Two Lions of Lyons: The Tale of Two Surgeons, Alexis Carrel & Rene Leriche. rev. ed. Angelo M. May & Alice G. May. (Illus.). 323p. (C). 1994. 39.50 (0-930329-45-7) Kabel Pubs.

Two Literary Riddles in the Exeter Book: Riddle 1 & the Easter Riddle. James E. Anderson. LC 85-40471. (Illus.). 288p. 1986. 37.95 (0-8061-1947-0) U of Okla Pr.

Two Little Christmas Classics. Clement C. Moore. (Illus.). 32p. (J). (ps up). 1989. 4.95 (0-394-84629-X) Random Bks Yng Read.

Two Little Devils. 2nd rev. ed. Ed. by Robert E. Holt. LC 79-50193. (Illus.). 113p. 1989. reprint ed. pap. 6.95 (0-9611596-9-3) Wilderness Adventure Bks.

Two Little Knights of Kentucky. Annie F. Johnson. LC 96-9808. (Little Colonel Ser.). (Illus.). 192p. (J). (gr. 3-8). 1997. reprint ed. pap. 9.95 (1-55709-316-4) Applewood.

Two Little Ladies. Michel & Company Staff. (Illus.). 32p. 1994. 6.95 (0-8362-4715-9) Andrews & McMeel.

Two Little Monkeys. Laura Magni. LC 92-70226. (Illus.). 18p. (J). (ps-k). 1992. bds. 3.95 (1-56397-154-2) Boyds Mills Pr.

Two Little Rich Girls. large type ed. Mignon G. Eberhart. LC 93-1777. 1993. lib. bdg. 22.95 (1-56054-558-5) Thorndike Pr.

Two Little Savages. Ernest T. Seton. (Illus.). 286p. (J). (gr. 4-8). 1903. pap. 6.95 (0-486-20985-7) Dover.

Two Little Savages. Ernest T. Seton. (Illus.). 1990. 20.50 (0-8446-2909-X) Peter Smith.

Two Little Savages: Being the Adventures of Two Boys Who Lived As Indians & What They Learned. Ernest T. Seton. (Illus.). 550p. (YA). 1994. pap. 29.95 (1-885529-16-3) Stevens Pub.

***Two Little Shoes.** Razvan. (Illus.). 28p. (J). 3.98 (0-7651-0028-2) Smithmark.

Two Little Trains. Margaret Wise Brown. LC 84-43138. 40p. (J). 1986. lib. bdg. 12.89 (0-06-020768-X) HarpC Child Bks.

Two Little Witches: A Halloween Counting Story. Harriet Ziefert. LC 96-83551. (Illus.). 32p. (J). (ps-k). 1996. 9.99 (1-56402-621-3) Candlewick Pr.

Two Lives. Lucille MacDonald. LC 95-62162. (Illus.). 272p. 1996. pap. 16.95 (0-936029-43-9) Western Bk Journ.

Two Lives. Joyce Pope. LC 91-17460. (Curious Creatures Ser.). (Illus.). 48p. (J). (gr. 4-8). 1992. pap. 4.95 (0-8114-6257-9); lib. bdg. 24.26 (0-8114-3153-3) Raintree Steck-V.

Two Lives. William Trevor. 1992. pap. 11.95 (0-14-017263-7, Viking) Viking Penguin.

Two Lives. limited ed. Ken Wainio. 28p. 1992. pap. 4.50 (0-685-64795-1) New Native Pr.

Two Lives: Two Novels: Reading Turgenev - My House in Umbria. William Trevor. 384p. 1992. pap. 11.95 (0-14-015372-1, Penguin Bks) Viking Penguin.

Two Lives - Georgia O'Keeffe & Alfred Stieglitz: A Conversation in Paintings & Photographs. Ed. by Belinda Rathbone et al. LC 92-36411. (Illus.). 144p. 1992. pap. 28.00 (0-943044-17-0) Phillips Coll.

Two Lives & a Dream. Marguerite Yourcenar. Tr. by Walter Kaiser from FRE. 250p. 1987. 16.95 (0-374-28019-3) FS&G.

Two Lives & a Dream. Marguerite Yourcenar. Tr. by Walter Kaiser. 246p. 1994. pap. 14.95 (0-226-96529-5) U Ch Pr.

***Two Lives for Onate.** Miguel Encinias. LC 96-35687. (Paso por Aqui Ser.). 1997. 45.00 (0-8263-1777-4); pap. 19.95 (0-8263-1782-0) U of NM Pr.

Two Lives Had I - One Was a Drag! An Autobiography. Tom Devlin. LC 95-90778. 1996. 16.95 (0-533-11705-4) Vantage.

Two Lives of Charlemagne. Einhard & Notker. Tr. by Lewis Thorpe. (Classics Ser.). 240p. 1969. pap. 9.95 (0-14-044213-8, Penguin Classics) Viking Penguin.

Two Lives of Errol Flynn. Michael Freedland. 1993. reprint ed. lib. bdg. 24.95 (1-56849-246-4) Buccaneer Bks.

Two Lives of Saint Cuthbert. Ed. by Bertram Colgrave. LC 69-13862. 375p. 1968. reprint ed. text ed. 70.00 (0-8371-0355-X, COST, Greenwood Pr) Greenwood.

Two Lives, One Russia. Nicholas Daniloff. 368p. 1990. mass mkt. 4.95 (0-380-70841-8) Avon.

Two Lives to Lead: Bisexuality in Men & Women. Ed. by Fritz Klein & Timothy J. Wolf. LC 85-5868. (Journal of Homosexuality Ser.: Vol. 11, Nos. 1 & 2). 255p. 1985. reprint ed. pap. 14.95 (0-918393-22-1) Harrington Pk.

Two Living & One Dead. Sigurd Christiansen. Tr. by Edwin A. Bjorkman from NOR. LC 73-22751. 288p. 1975. reprint ed. text ed. 59.75 (0-8371-7348-5, CHTL, Greenwood Pr) Greenwood.

Two Living Traditions: Essays on Religion & the Bible. Samuel Sandmel. LC 72-173919. 367p. reprint ed. pap. 104.60 (0-7837-3622-3, 2043488) Bks Demand.

***Two Lockets.** Donald C. Wellington. 144p. (Orig.). 1998. mass mkt. 4.99 (1-55237-425-4, Pub. by Comnwlth Pub CN) Partners Pubs Grp.

Two Long Poems. Judson Jerome & Bruce Cutler. (Juniper Bk. Ser.: No. 55). 1991. pap. 6.00 (1-55780-115-0) Juniper Pr WI.

Two Long Poems. Gerald Stern. (Classic Contemporaries Ser.). 71p. (Orig.). (C). 1990. pap. 12.95 (0-88748-100-0) Carnegie-Mellon.

Two Loves. large type ed. David Farrell. (Linford Romance Library). 1990. pap. 15.99 (0-7089-6815-5, Trailtree Bookshop) Ulverscroft.

Two Loves & Other Poems: A Selection. Alfred Douglas. LC 89-81154. 63p. 1990. 20.00 (0-9624631-1-6) Bennett & Kitchel.

Two Loves for Selena: Explaining Adoption to Children. Laurie Tanner. Ed. by Joy Johnson. (Illus.). 24p. (J). (gr. k-5). 1993. pap. 2.95 (1-56123-061-8) Centering Corp.

***Two LSATs Explained.** Kaplan Staff. LC 97-16781. 1997. 34.95 (0-684-84168-1) S&S Trade.

***Two M. D.'s & a Pharmacist Ask: Are You Getting It 5 Times a Day? Fruits & Vegetables.** Sydney H. Crackower et al. LC 96-76768. 75p. 1996. pap. 6.95 (0-934252-35-1) Hohm Pr.

Two Madonnas: The Politics of Festival in a Sardinian Community. Sabina Magliocco. LC 92-16538. (American University Studies: Anthropology & Science: Ser. XI, Vol. 61). 158p. (Orig.). (C). 1993. pap. text ed. 22.95 (0-8204-1896-X) P Lang Pubng.

Two Maids of Moreclacke. Robert Armin. LC 77-133634. (Tudor Facsimile Texts. Old English Plays Ser.: No. 127). reprint ed. 49.50 (0-404-53427-9) AMS Pr.

Two Major Francophone Women Writers: Assia Djebar & Leila Sebbar. Rafika Merini. LC 94-30420. (Francophone Cultures & Literatures Ser.: Vol. 5). 1995. write for info. (0-8204-2635-0) P Lang Pubng.

Two Major New Methods of Creative Problem-Solving: Incentive-Equilibrium Analysis, & Post-Einsteinian Discovery Technique. 2nd rev. ed. Win Wenger. 70p. (C). 1990. pap. text ed. 12.95 (0-931865-16-6) Psychegenics.

Two Majorities: The Issue Context of Modern American Politics. Byron E. Shafer & William J. Claggett. LC 94-43426. (Interpreting American Politics Ser.). 256p. 1995. text ed. 45.00 (0-8018-5018-5); pap. text ed. 14.95 (0-8018-5019-3) Johns Hopkins.

Two Margarets. C. MacKenzie. 5.99 (0-906731-43-7, Pub. by Christian Focus UK) Spring Arbor Dist.

Two Marine Quaternary Localities see Palaeontographica Americana: Vol. 3

Two Masters: Prior Engagements. Frank Manley. LC 87-24619. (Illus.). 176p. (Orig.). 1987. pap. 8.95 (0-932419-14-3) Cherokee.

Two Masters of Irony: Oscar Wilde & Lytton Strachey. Margaret M. Yu. LC 79-8090. reprint ed. 27.50 (0-404-18398-0) AMS Pr.

Two Mather Biographies: Life & Death & Parentator. Ed. by William J. Scheick. LC 88-45761. 248p. 1989. 38.50 (0-934223-06-8) Lehigh Univ Pr.

Two Maya Monuments in Yucatan: The Palace of the Stuccoes at Acanceh & the Temple of the Owls at Chichen Itza. Hasso Von Winning. LC 85-62288. (Frederick Webb Hodge Publications: No. 12). (Illus.). 104p. (Orig.). 1985. pap. 14.95 (0-916561-68-2) Southwest Mus.

Two Measures of Rice. T. S. Pillai. Tr. by M. A. Shakoor from MAL. 118p. 1975. pap. 2.50 (0-88253-169-7) Ind-US Inc.

Two Medieval Merchant Guilds of South India. Meera Abraham. (C). 1988. 34.00 (81-85054-48-7, Pub. by Manohar II) S Asia.

***Two Medieval Outlaws: The Romances of Eustace the Monk & Fouke Fitz Waryn.** Glyn S. Burgess. LC 96-45609. 196p. 1997. 53.00 (0-85991-438-0, DS Brewer) Boydell & Brewer.

Two Memoirs of Renaissance Florence: The Diaries of Buonaccorso Pitti & Gregorio Dati. Ed. by Gene A. Brucker. Tr. by Julia Martines from ITA. 141p. (C). 1991. reprint ed. pap. text ed. 9.50 (0-88133-622-X) Waveland Pr.

Two Men. Mark Dunster. 18p. 1983. pap. 4.00 (0-89642-102-3) Linden Pubs.

Two Men & a Kangaroo Go into a Bar. Eric Felderman. (Illus.). 102p. 1990. pap. 9.95 (0-945942-05-2, 89-39845) Portmanteau Editions.

Two Men Called Adam: A Fresh Look at the Creation-Evolution Controversy. Arthur C. Custance. 273p. 1983. pap. 14.95 (0-919857-02-7, Pub. by Doorway Pubns CN) Doorway USA.

Two Men for Modern Music. Vivian Perlis. (I.S.A.M. Monographs: No. 9). (Illus.). 35p. 1978. pap. 10.00 (0-914678-09-4) Inst Am Music.

Two Men in Me. Henry Daniel-Rops. Tr. by Gil Meynier from FRE. LC 76-163024. (Short Story Index Reprint Ser.). 1977. reprint ed. 19.95 (0-8369-3938-7) Ayer.

Two Menaechmuses see Casina

Two Merry Milkmaids. LC 79-133751. (Tudor Facsimile Texts. Old English Plays Ser.: No. 137). reprint ed. 49.50 (0-404-53437-6) AMS Pr.

2-Methoxyethanol, 2-Ethoxyethanol, & Their Acetates. (Environmental Health Criteria Ser.: No. 115). 126p. 1990. pap. text ed. 24.00 (92-4-157115-2, 1160115) World Health.

Two Mice in Three Fables. Lynn W. Reiser. LC 93-35935. (Illus.). 32p. (J). (ps up). 1995. 15.00 (0-688-13389-4); lib. bdg. 14.93 (0-688-13390-8) Greenwillow.

Two Mighty Rivers: Son of Pocahontas. Mari Hanes. (Illus.). 152p. (J). (gr. 3-7). 1996. pap. 5.99 (0-88070-999-5, Gold & Honey) Multnomah Pubs.

Two Millimeter Wave Band Spectroscopy of Condensed Systems. Victor I. Krinichnyi. LC 94-15896. 236p. 1994. 179.95 (0-8493-4776-9) CRC Pr.

***Two Million Heartbeats.** H. C. Wolford. 240p. 1997. 16.95 (0-9654563-1-5) Easy Money.

Two Million Unnecessary Arrests: Removing a Social Service Concern from the Criminal Justice System. Raymond T. Nimmer. LC 70-160799. (American Bar Foundation Publications). ix, 202p. 1970. 25.00 (1-57588-369-4, 305060); pap. 20.00 (0-614-96713-9, 305060) W S Hein.

Two Million-Year-Old Self. Anthony Stevens. LC 92-48861. (Carolyn & Ernest Fay Series in Analytical Psychology: No. 3). (Illus.). 162p. 1993. 24.50 (0-89096-536-6) Tex A&M Univ Pr.

Two Million-Year-Old Self. Anthony Stevens. LC 96-9215. (Carolyn & Ernest Fay Series in Analytical Psychology). 160p. 1996. reprint ed. pap. 14.95 (0-88064-214-9) Fromm Intl Pub.

Two Milpas of Chan Kom: Scenarios of a Maya Village Life. Alicia Re Cruz. LC 95-15375. (SUNY Series in the Anthropology of Work). 203p. 1996. text ed. 74.50 (0-7914-2829-X); pap. text ed. 24.95 (0-7914-2830-3) State U NY Pr.

Two Minus One. Lynn Buck. (C). 1994. pap. text ed. 5.00 (1-878173-40-5) Birnham Wood.

Two Minute Awesomely Awful Manager. W. L. Kelsall. LC 92-91115. (Illus.). 89p. 1993. pap. 10.00 (1-56002-266-3, Univ Edtns) Aegina Pr.

Two Minute Bunny Tales. Nicola Baxter. (Illus.). 32p. (J). 1994. 2.99 (0-7214-5444-5, Ladybrd) Penguin.

Two-Minute Christmas Stories. (Golden Two-Minute Stories Ser.). (Illus.). 36p. (J). (ps-1). 1989. write for info. (0-307-12188-7) Western Pub.

Two-Minute Crosswords, No. 5. David King. 224p. 1996. pap. 5.95 (0-684-81341-6, Fireside) S&S Trade.

***Two Minute Histories of Houston.** Betty Chapman & Garvin Berry. (Illus.). 120p. 1996. pap. 9.95 (0-9650400-2-X) Houston Busin Jrnl.

Two Minute Kitten Tales. Joan Stimson. (Illus.). 32p. (J). 1994. 2.99 (0-7214-5443-7, Ladybrd) Penguin.

Two-Minute Lover: Building Successful Relationships in a Fast Paced World. Asa H. Sparks. Ed. by Bradley L. Winch. LC 88-83565. (Creative Loving Ser.). (Illus.). 112p. (Orig.). 1989. pap. 9.95 (0-915190-52-4, JP9052-4) Jalmar Pr.

2 Minute Motivation: How to Inspire Superior Performance. Robert W. Wendover. LC 94-29647. 160p. 1994. 14.95 (*1-57071-019-8*) Sourcebks.

Two Minute Motivator: How to Inspire Superior Performance. Robert W. Wendover. LC 92-80076. (Illus.). 136p. 1992. 16.95 (*0-9623289-1-X*) Leadership Res.

Two-Minute Mysteries. Donald J. Sobol. 160p. (Orig.). (J). (gr. 5-8). 1986. pap. 2.50 (*0-590-41292-2*, Apple Paperbacks) Scholastic Inc.

Two-Minute Mysteries. Donald J. Sobol. 160p. (Orig.). (J). (gr. 4-6). 1991. pap. 3.99 (*0-590-44787-4*, Apple Paperbacks) Scholastic Inc.

Two Minute Philosopher. Lindy H. Lumbert. 19.00 (*0-943280-01-X*); pap. 8.50 (*0-943280-02-8*) Blossom Bks.

Two Minute Puppy Tales. Tony Bradman. (Illus.). 32p. (J). 1994. 2.99 (*0-317-06156-9*, Ladybrd) Penguin.

Two Minute Teddy Bear Tales. Joan Stimson. (Illus.). 32p. (J). 1994. 2.99 (*0-7214-5442-9*, Ladybrd) Penguin.

Two Minutes a Day for a Life of Love. Daniel G. Amen. 1996. mass mkt. 5.99 (*0-312-95869-2*) St Martin.

2 Minutes & Under: Character Monologues for Actors. Glenn Alterman. (Monologue Audition Ser.). 100p. 1993. pap. 9.95 (*1-880399-49-0*) Smith & Kraus.

Two Minutes for Roughing. Joseph Romain. (J). (gr. 3-8). 1995. pap. 8.95 (*1-55028-458-4*); bds. 16.95 (*1-55028-459-2*) Formac Dist Ltd.

Two Minutes of Silence: Selected Short Stories. Hans C. Branner. LC 66-22865. (Nordic Translation Ser.). 243p. reprint ed. pap. 69.30 (*0-8357-6776-0*, 2035452) Bks Demand.

Two Minutes to Shine, Bk. 3. Pamela Sackett. 48p. (Orig.). (YA). 1993. pap. text ed. 8.95 (*0-573-69384-6*) French.

Two Minutes with God: One Minute to Listen, One Minute to Pray. Leslie F. Brandt. LC 88-6326. 128p. 1988. pap. 9.99 (*0-8066-2350-0*, 10-6724, Augsburg) Augsburg Fortress.

Two Mr. Gladstones: A Study in Psychology & History. Travis L. Crosby. LC 96-26547. 1997. write for info. (*0-300-06827-1*) Yale U Pr.

Two Mr. Smiths: The Life & Work of Sir Matthew Smith 1879-1959. Alice Keene. (Illus.). 240p. 1995. pap. 40.00 (*0-85331-669-4*, Pub. by Lund Humphries UK) Antique Collect.

Two Moms, the Zark, & Me. Johnny Valentine. (Illus.). 48p. (J). (gr. k-3). 1993. 12.95 (*1-55583-236-9*) Alyson Pubns.

Two Monographs on Japanese Canadians. Ed. by Roger Daniels. LC 78-3222. (Asian Experience in North America Ser.). 1979. lib. bdg. 17.95 (*0-405-11304-8*) Ayer.

***Two Monsters.** McKee. (J). Date not set. pap. text ed. write for info. (*0-05-004546-6*) Addison-Wesley.

Two Monsters: A Fable. Lucretia Fisher. LC 76-21684. (Illus.). 48p. (J). (ps up). 1976. pap. 3.95 (*0-916144-08-9*) Stemmer Hse.

Two Months in the Confederate States: An Englishman's Travels Through the South. W. C. Corsan. LC 96-20861. (Illus.). 216p. (C). 1996. 26.95 (*0-8071-2037-5*) La State U Pr.

Two Moons in August. Martha Brooks. (YA). (gr. 7 up). 1992. 15.95 (*0-316-10979-7*) Little.

Two Moral Essays: Human Personality & on Human Obligations. Simone Weil. LC 81-84860. 1981. reprint ed. 3.00 (*0-87574-240-8*) Pendle Hill.

Two More. David Drew. LC 92-31957. (Voyages Ser.). (Illus.). (J). 1993. 3.75 (*0-383-03600-3*) SRA McGraw.

Two Morrow's Legacy. Arthur E. Morrow & Edith M. Morrow. (Illus.). 1988. 10.95 (*0-9620550-0-X*) Dodson Assocs.

Two Mothers: One Daughter. Sherie R. Balk. Ed. by David A. Russell. 312p. (Orig.). 1996. pap. 12.95 (*1-884559-07-7*) Allen Pubng.

Two Mothers Speak. Judith McKenzie. LC 90-71367. 138p. 1990. pap. 7.95 (*1-55523-390-2*) Winston-Derek.

Two Mountains & a River. Harold W. Tilman. LC 50-196. 277p. reprint ed. pap. 79.00 (*0-317-11324-0*, 2050720) Bks Demand.

Two Moves to Better Golf. rev. ed. Dudley Wolford. LC 88-70792. (Illus.). 146p. (Orig.). 1992. pap. 9.95 (*1-882091-01-9*); text ed. 16.95 (*1-882091-02-7*) Brentwood Productions.

Two Mrs. Gibsons. Toyomi Igus. LC 95-37572. (Illus.). 32p. (J). (gr. 1-6). 1996. 14.95 (*0-89239-135-9*) Childrens Book Pr.

***Two Mrs. Gibsons.** Toyomi Igus. (Illus.). 32p. (J). (gr. 2-4). 1996. 19.90 (*0-516-20001-1*) Childrens.

Two Mrs. Grenvilles. Dominick Dunne. 384p. 1986. mass mkt. 6.99 (*0-553-25891-5*) Bantam.

Two Much! Donald E. Westlake. 288p. 1989. mass mkt. 4.99 (*0-445-40719-0*, Mysterious Paperbk) Warner Bks.

Two Mujeres. Sara L. Calderon. Tr. by Gina Kaufer from SPA. LC 91-21444. 204p. (Orig.). 1991. pap. 9.95 (*1-879960-00-1*) Aunt Lute Bks.

Two Nations. Andrew Hacker. 1995. pap. 12.00 (*0-345-40537-4*) Ballantine.

Two Nations. Christopher Hollis. 1973. 250.00 (*0-87968-230-2*) Gordon Pr.

Two Nations: Black & White, Separate, Hostile, Unequal. Andrew Hacker. 272p. 1995. pap. 12.00 (*0-345-39338-4*) Ballantine.

Two Nations: Black & White, Separate, Hostile, Unequal. Andrew Hacker. (Illus.). 320p. 1992. text ed. 24.95 (*0-684-19148-2*) S&S Trade.

Two Nations & Educational Structure. Simon. (C). 1960. pap. 18.50 (*0-85315-348-5*, Pub. by Lawrence & Wishart UK) NYU Pr.

Two Nations Over Time: Spain & the United States, 1776-1977. James W. Cortada. LC 77-94752. (Contributions in American History Ser.: No. 74). 305p. 1978. text ed. 59.95 (*0-313-20319-9*, CTN/, Greenwood Pr) Greenwood.

Two Nations under God Vol. 1: The Deuteronomist History of Solomon & the Dual Monarchies: The Reign of Solomon & the Rise of Jeroboam. Gary N. Knoppers. LC 93-37963. (Harvard Semitic Monographs). 316p. 1993. 39.95 (*1-55540-913-X*, 040052) Scholars Pr GA.

Two Nations under God Vol. 2: The Deuteronomistic History of Solomon & the Dual Monarchies: The Reign of Jeroboam, the Fall of Israel, & the Reign of Josiah. Gary N. Knoppers. LC 93-37963. (Harvard Semitic Monographs). 366p. 1994. 39.95 (*1-55540-914-8*, 040053) Scholars Pr GA.

Two Nationwide Surveys: Pilot Assessment of the Unmet Legal Needs of the Poor & the Public Generally, 1989. LC 89-81239. 97p. 1989. pap. 10.95 (*0-89707-496-3*, 429-0009) Amer Bar Assn.

Two Nativity Dramas. Edward S. Long. 1984. 5.00 (*0-89536-697-5*, 4874) CSS OH.

Two NATO Allies at the Threshold of War: Cyprus, a Firsthand Account of Crisis Management, 1965-1968. Parker T. Hart. LC 89-16941. (Illus.). 248p. 1990. text ed. 42.95 (*0-8223-0977-7*) Duke.

Two Natures. Watchman Nee. 19p. 1.00 (*0-87083-608-0*, 07035001) Living Stream Ministry.

Two Natures in Christ. Martin Chemnitz. Tr. by J. A. Preus. LC 74-115465. Orig. Title: De Duabus Naturis in Christo. 608p. 1970. 26.95 (*0-570-03210-5*, 15-2109) Concordia.

Two Naval Journals: 1864-Battle of Mobile Bay. Ed. by C. Carter Smith. (Illus.). 1964. pap. 5.95 (*0-87651-210-4*) Southern U Pr.

Two New Genera & Species of Oligocene Spikefishes: Tetraodontiformes: Triacanthodidae, the First Fossils of the Hollardiinae & Triacanthodinae. James C. Tyler et al. LC 93-672. (Smithsonian Contributions to Paleobiology Ser.: No. 75). (Illus.). 31p. reprint ed. pap. 25.00 (*0-7837-5898-7*, 2045689) Bks Demand.

Two New Sciences, Including Centers of Gravity & Force of Percussion. Galileo Galilei & Stillman Drake. LC 73-2043. 365p. reprint ed. pap. 104.10 (*0-317-55783-1*, 2029307) Bks Demand.

Two New Tools & a Working Method for Crisis Management of Accidental Spills at Sea. Wierd Koops. 400p. (Orig.). 1992. pap. 72.50 (*90-6275-804-5*, Pub. by Delft U Pr NE) Coronet Bks.

Two New Yorks: State-City Relations in the Changing Federal System. Ed. by Gerald Benjamin & Charles Brecher. LC 88-15778. 560p. 1989. 55.00 (*0-87154-107-6*) Russell Sage.

Two Nineteen Ninety-One Individual Tax Return Practice Problems. 6th ed. Marguerite R. Hutton & Thomas Dalton. 216p. (C). 1992. pap. text ed. 20.95 (*0-256-11268-1*, 34-2650-06) Irwin.

Two Nineteenth Century Versions of the New Testament: Translated by JNO & by Wk, with Comments on Text & Translation from the Works of William Kelly of Blackheath. Dennis Ryan. 766p. 1995. 45.00 (*0-9640037-9-1*) Pres Truth.

2-Nitropropane. (Environmental Health Criteria Ser.: No. 138). 108p. (ENG, FRE & SPA.). 1992. pap. text ed. 26.00 (*92-4-157138-1*, 1160138) World Health.

Two Nixon Shocks & Japan-U. S. Relations. Atsushi Kusano. (Research Monograph: No. 50). 46p. 1987. 8.00 (*0-318-22897-1*) Princeton CIS.

Two Nixon Shocks & Japan-U. S. Relations. Atsushi Kusano. LC 87-176256. (Center of International Studies, Woodrow Wilson School of Public & International Affairs - Research Monograph Ser.: No. 50). 52p. reprint ed. pap. 25.00 (*0-8357-3070-0*, 2039327) Bks Demand.

Two Noble Kinsmen. John Fletcher & William Shakespeare. Ed. by Eugene M. Waith. (Oxford Shakespeare Series & Oxford English Texts Ser.). (Illus.). 248p. 1989. pap. 6.95 (*0-19-281498-2*) OUP.

Two Noble Kinsmen. John Fletcher & William Shakespeare. Ed. by Lois Potter. LC 95-36174. (Arden Shakespeare Ser.: Ser. 3). 300p. 1997. pap. 9.95 (*0-415-01667-3*); text ed. 45.00 (*0-415-01666-5*) Routledge.

***Two Noble Kinsmen.** Lois Potter. 1996. pap. text ed. 9.95 (*0-17-443462-6*) Nelson Aus.

Two Noble Kinsmen. William Shakespeare. Ed. by N. W. Bawcutt. (New Penguin Shakespeare Ser.). 256p. 1981. pap. 5.50 (*0-14-070730-1*, Penguin Classics) Viking Penguin.

***Two Noble Kinsmen.** William Shakespeare. (English Ser.). (C). 1997. text ed. 45.00 (*0-17-443463-4*) Wadsworth Pub.

Two Noble Kinsmen. John Fletcher & William Shakespeare. LC 72-133736. (Tudor Facsimile Texts. Old English Plays Ser.: No. 141). reprint ed. 59.50 (*0-404-53441-4*) AMS Pr.

Two Noble Kinsmen. 71. John Fletcher. Bd. with Quarto of 1634, Pt. 1. rev. ed. (New Shakespeare Society, London, Ser. 2: Nos. 7, 8 & 15). 1974. reprint ed. Set pap. 80.00 (*0-8115-0235-X*) Periodicals Srv.

Two Nonsense Stories. Edward Lear. (Illus.). 64p. 1993. 130.00 (*0-907664-19-9*, Pub. by Old Stiles UK) St Mut.

Two Nonsense Stories. limited ed. Edward Lear. (Illus.). 64p. 1993. 500.00 (*0-907664-18-0*, Pub. by Old Stiles UK) St Mut.

Two Notebooks of Thomas Carlyle: From 23rd March 1822 to 16th May 1832. Ed. by Charles E. Norton. 317p. 1972. reprint ed. 15.00 (*0-911858-21-0*) Appel.

Two Novels: Ironic Tales: A New Brautigan & Comrades. Marne Marcus. 64p. 1995. pap. 9.95 (*4-88117-419-3*) Lowell Print.

***Two Novels: The Stony Heart & Boondocks/Moondocks.** Arno Schmidt. Tr. by John E. Woods from GER. LC 97-23296. (Collected Early Fiction of Arno Schmidt Ser.). 420p. 1997. reprint ed. 49.95 (*1-56478-170-4*) Dalkey Arch.

Two Novels: You Didn't Even Try & Imaginary Speeches for a Brazen Head. Philip Whalen. LC 85-51335. 272p. 1985. pap. 9.95 (*0-939010-06-2*) Zephyr Pr.

Two Novels: You Didn't Even Try & Imaginary Speeches for a Brazen Head. deluxe ed. Philip Whalen. LC 85-51335. 272p. 1985. 25.00 (*0-939010-07-0*) Zephyr Pr.

Two Novels by Edith Wharton: Ethan Frome, & Summer. large type ed. Edith Wharton. (Large Print Ser.). 449p. 1993. reprint ed. lib. bdg. 24.00 (*0-939495-27-9*) North Bks.

Two Novels of Mexico: The Flies & The Bosses. Mariano Azuela. Tr. by Lesley B. Simpson. 1956. pap. 12.00 (*0-520-00053-6*) U CA Pr.

Two Ocean War, Vol. 1. Samuel E. Morison. 1989. pap. 22.95 (*0-316-58352-9*) Little.

***Two-Ocean War: A Short History of the United States Navy in the Second World War.** Samuel E. Morison. 1997. pap. text ed. 14.99 (*1-57866-003-3*) Galahad Bks.

***Two of a Kind.** Cullinan. 1994. 11.00 (*0-15-302382-1*) HarBrace.

Two of a Kind. Ann Gabhart. (J). (gr. 4-7). 1992. pap. 3.50 (*0-380-76153-X*, Camelot) Avon.

Two of a Kind. large type ed. Beatriz Doumerc & Ricardo Alcantara. Tr. by Laura M. Perez & Kathryn Corbett. (Illus.). 1994. 13.50 (*0-614-09811-4*, L-34101-00) Am Printing Hse.

Two of a Kind. Lori Copeland. 288p. 1993. reprint ed. mass mkt., pap. text ed. 4.99 (*0-505-51903-8*, Love Spell) Dorchester Pub Co.

Two of a Kind: The Dick & Tom Vanarsdale Story. Kerry Marshall. (Illus.). 224p. 1992. 18.95 (*0-9630362-2-X*) Scott IN.

Two of a Kind: The Hillside Stranglers. Darcy O'Brien. (Illus.). 384p. 1994. 12.99 (*1-56865-077-9*, GuildAmerica) Dblday Direct.

***Two of Everything.** Babette Cole. LC 97-13854. (J). 1998. 17.00 (*0-679-88898-5*) Knopf Bks Yng Read.

Two of Everything. Ed. by Judith Mathews. LC 92-29880. (Illus.). 32p. (J). (gr. k-3). 1993. lib. bdg. 15.95 (*0-8075-8157-7*) A Whitman.

Two of Everything. 95th ed. HB Staff. (J). (gr. 2). 1995. text ed., lib. bdg. 40.00 (*0-15-305200-7*) HB Coll Pubs.

Two of Them. Aliki. LC 79-10161. 32p. (J). (ps up). 1987. pap. 4.95 (*0-688-07337-9*, Mulberry) Morrow.

Two of Us. Charles Gallagher. (Celebrate Love Ser.). 86p. (Orig.). 1990. pap. text ed. 3.95 (*0-911905-40-5*) Past & Mat Rene Ctr.

Two of Us Make a World: The Single Mother's Guide to Pregnancy, Childbirth & the First Year. Sherrill Tippins & Prudence Tippins. LC 95-4468. 256p. 1996. pap. 14.95 (*0-8050-3780-2*, Owl) H Holt & Co.

Two Offices for St. Elizabeth of Hungary. Ed. by Barbara Haagh. (Wissen-schaftliche Abhnadlungen-Musicological Studies: Vol. 65/1). xxvi, 48p. (ENG & LAT.). 1995. lib. bdg. 48.00 (*0-931902-97-5*) Inst Mediaeval Mus.

Two Ohio Tractions: Miamisburg & Germantown and Lebanon & Franklin. Richard Wagner & Birdella Wagner. LC 74-84714. 1974. pap. 2.50 (*0-914196-15-4*) JAS Pubng.

Two Oilfield Water Systems. Bryant W. Bradley. LC 86-3004. 272p. (C). 1987. text ed. 48.50 (*0-89874-918-2*) Krieger.

Two Old Women. Velma Wallis. LC 94-9704. 160p. 1994. pap. 10.00 (*0-06-097584-9*) HarpC.

Two Old Women: An Alaska Legend of Betrayal, Courage & Survival. Velma Wallis. LC 93-25044. (Illus.). 160p. (Orig.). 1993. 16.95 (*0-945397-18-6*) Epicenter Pr.

***Two on a Big Ocean.** Hal Roth. LC 97-15416. 288p. 1997. reprint ed. pap. 15.95 (*0-9639566-4-7*, SW-HROTH1) Seaworthy WI.

Two on a Tower. Thomas Hardy. LC 92-29053. (World's Classics Ser.). 352p. 1993. 9.95 (*0-19-282919-X*) OUP.

Two on a Tower. Thomas Hardy. (New Wessex Edition Ser.). 264p. 1990. 42.50 (*0-333-17763-0*, Pub. by Macmlln UK) Trans-Atl Phila.

Two on the Aisle: How to Get Tickets to Any Event, Anytime, Anywhere. Dale Ratermann & Mark A. Zwartynski. 128p. (Orig.). 1996. pap. 12.95 (*1-57028-074-6*) Masters Pr IN.

Two on the Square. Bill Moore. LC 86-20781. (Illus.). 208p. 1986. 14.95 (*0-914875-13-2*) Bright Mtn Bks.

Two One Act Plays by Gabriel Marcel: Dot the I & the Double Expertise. Tr. by Katharine R. Hanley. 80p. (Orig.). (C). 1986. pap. text ed. 14.00 (*0-8191-5077-0*) U Pr of Amer.

Two or Three Degrees off Plumb. Sam Venable. 1991. pap. 7.95 (*0-9615656-3-2*) Knoxville News-Sentinel.

Two or Three Things I Know about Her: Analysis of a Film by Godard. Alfred Guzzetti. LC 80-15832. (Harvard Film Studies). (Illus.). 376p. 1981. 44.50 (*0-674-91500-3*) HUP.

Two or Three Things I Know for Sure. Dorothy Allison. LC 95-17752. (Illus.). 96p. 1995. pap. 14.95 (*0-525-93921-0*) NAL-Dutton.

Two or Three Things I Know for Sure. Dorothy Allison. 96p. 1996. pap. 8.95 (*0-452-27340-4*, Plume) NAL-Dutton.

Two Orations of the Emperor Julian: One to the Sun & the Other to the Mother of the Gods. Thomas Taylor. 145p. 1992. pap. 18.95 (*1-56459-127-1*) Kessinger Pub.

Two Orphan Cubs. Barbara Brenner & May Garelick. (J). (ps-1). 1989. 12.95 (*0-8027-6868-7*); lib. bdg. 13.85 (*0-8027-6869-5*) Walker & Co.

Two Orthodox Ukrainian Churchmen of the Early Eighteenth Century: Teofan Prokopovych & Stefan Iavors'kyi. George Y. Shevelov. 40p. 1994. write for info. (*0-9609822-8-0*) Ukrainian Studies Fund.

Two Ounce Backpacker. A Problem Solving Manual for Use in the Wilds. R. S. Wood. LC 82-80236. 128p. 1982. pap. 4.95 (*0-89815-070-1*) Ten Speed Pr.

Two over One - Game Force "Simplified" 150p. (Orig.). (C). 1994. pap. text ed. 12.95 (*0-9642384-0-3*) Kara Jarman.

Two Over One Game Force. rev. ed. Max Hardy. LC 90-159367. 303p. 1989. 14.95 (*0-939460-36-X*) Devyn Pr.

Two-over-One Game Force: An Introduction. Bruno-Hardy. 9.95 (*0-939460-01-7*, 4750) Devyn Pr.

Two-over-One Game Force Quiz Book. Hardy. 11.95 (*0-939460-74-2*, 0770) Devyn Pr.

Two-Over-One Same Force Bidding Problems No. 1: Responses When Responder Has Fit with Opener's Major Suit. J. N. Larone. 88p. (Orig.). 1996. pap. 9.95 (*0-89412-255-X*, B-1) Aegean Park Pr.

***Two Oxfordshire Anglo-Saxon Cemeteries: Berinsfield & Didcot.** A. Boyle et al. (Thames Valley Ser.: Vol. 8). (Illus.). 274p. 1995. pap. 50.00 (*0-947816-86-0*, Pub. by Oxford Univ Comm Arch UK) David Brown.

Two Ozark Rivers: The Current & the Jacks Fork. Photos by Oliver Schuchard. (Illus.). 144p. (Orig.). (C). 1996. pap. 19.95 (*0-8262-0925-4*) U of Mo Pr.

Two Pages from Roman History. 3rd ed. Daniel De Leon & National Executive Committee - Socialist Labor Party Staff. LC 87-61305. 104p. (Orig.). 1988. pap. 2.50 (*0-935534-45-8*) NY Labor News.

Two Pails of Water. Aad Greidanus. (J). (gr. 1-7). 1965. 5.00 (*0-87602-215-8*) Anchorage.

Two Paiute Autobiographies. fac. ed. Julian H. Steward. (University of California Publications in American Archaeology & Ethnology: Vol. 33: 5). 17p. (C). 1934. reprint ed. pap. text ed. 1.80 (*1-55567-292-2*) Coyote Press.

Two Pan Galley: A Cookbook for Boaters. Deborah A. Hoy. (Illus.). 1984. 7.95 (*0-9614129-0-9*) Rainshadow Pubns.

Two Papers: Eta-Coextensions of Monoids & the Structure of a Band of Groups. J. Leech. (Memoirs Ser.: No. 2/157). 95p. 1975. pap. 18.00 (*0-8218-1857-0*, MEMO/2/157) Am Math.

Two Papers on Extremal Problems in Complex Analysis. S. Ya Khavinson. LC 86-3545. (AMS Translations Ser.: Series 2, Vol. 129). 114p. 1986. text ed. 64.00 (*0-8218-3098-8*, TRANS2/129) Am Math.

Two Papers on Homotopy Theory of Continuous Mappings. V. G. Boltyanskii & M. M. Postnikov. LC 51-5559. (Translations Ser.: Series 2, Vol. 7). 321p. 1957. reprint ed. 38.00 (*0-8218-1707-8*, TRANS2/7) Am Math.

Two Papers on Similarity of Certain Volterra Integral Operators. S. J. Osher. (Memoirs of the American Mathematical Society Ser.: No. 73). 47p. 1967. pap. 16.00 (*0-8218-1273-4*, MEMO/1/73C) Am Math.

Two Papers on Special Functions. Ja L. Geronimus & Gabor Szego. LC 76-30843. (Translations Ser. 2: Vol. 108). 130p. 1977. 47.00 (*0-8218-3058-9*, TRANS2/108) Am Math.

Two Papers on the Aboriginal Ethnography of California. fac. ed. A. L. Kroeber. (Reports of the University of California Archaeological Survey: No. 56). 64p. 1962. reprint ed. pap. 5.90 (*1-55567-371-6*) Coyote Press.

Two Papers on the Predicate Calculus. Stephen C. Kleene. LC 52-42839. (Memoirs Ser.: No. 1/10). 68p. 1985. reprint ed. pap. 18.00 (*0-8218-1210-6*, MEMO/1/10) Am Math.

Two-Parameter Martingales & Their Quadratic Variation. P. Imkeller. (Lecture Notes in Mathematics Ser.: Vol. 1308). iv, 177p. 1988. 35.95 (*0-387-19233-6*) Spr-Verlag.

Two-Parent Family. Patricia Knoll. 1997. mass mkt. 3.25 (*0-373-03442-3*, 1-03442-0) Silhouette.

***Two-Parent Family.** large type ed. Patricia Knoll. (Baby Boom Ser.). 1997. mass mkt. 3.25 (*0-373-15688-X*) Harlequin Bks.

Two-Parent Family Is Not the Best. June Stephenson. 454p. (Orig.). 1991. pap. 18.00 (*0-941138-10-0*) Diemer-Smith.

Two Park Street. Paul Brooks. 1986. 12.95 (*0-317-52344-9*) HM.

Two Park Street: A Publishing Memoir. Paul Brooks. 1986. 12.95 (*0-395-37774-9*) HM.

Two Part Conductus in Two Central Sources. Ed. by Gordon A. Anderson. (Gesamtausgaben - Collected Works Ser.: Vol. X, Pt. 4). 148p. 1986. lib. bdg. 94.00 (*0-931902-22-3*) Inst Mediaeval Mus.

Two-Part Invention. Madeleine L'Engle. 64p. 1993. pap. 5.00 (*0-06-250638-2*) Harper SF.

***Two-Part Invention: The Crosswicks Journal.** Madeleine L'Engle. 240p. 1996. 35.00 (*0-8095-9226-6*) Borgo Pr.

Two-Part Invention: The Story of a Marriage. Madeleine L'Engle. 224p. 1988. 18.95 (*0-374-28020-7*) FS&G.

Two-Part Invention: The Story of a Marriage. Madeleine L'Engle. 240p. 1996. pap. 13.00 (*0-06-250501-7*) Harper SF.

Two Part Inventions, 3 bks., Bk. I. I. S. Bach. (Quality Edition Classics Ser.). 32p. 1983. Bk . I. pap. text ed. 2.95 (*0-935474-12-9*) Carousel Pubns Ltd.

Two Part Inventions, 3 bks., Bk. II. I. S. Bach. (Quality Edition Classics Ser.). 32p. 1983. Bk.II. pap. text ed. 4.95 (*0-935474-11-0*) Carousel Pubns Ltd.

Two Part Inventions, 3 bks., Bk. III. I. S. Bach. (Quality Edition Classics Ser.). 32p. 1983. Bk.III. pap. 2.95 (*0-935474-13-7*) Carousel Pubns Ltd.

Two-Party Line: Conversations in the Field. Jane C. Goodale & Ann Chowning. LC 96-15066. 240p. 1996. pap. text ed. 22.95 (*0-8476-8264-1*); lib. bdg. 57.50 (*0-8476-8263-3*) Rowman.

***Two-Party Politics in the One-Party South: Alabama's Hill Country, 1874-1920.** Samuel L. Webb. LC 97-20596. 1997. write for info. (*0-8173-0895-4*) U of Ala Pr.

Two-Party South. 2nd enl. ed. Alexander P. Lamis. 464p. 1990. reprint ed. pap. 21.00 (*0-19-506579-4*) OUP.

Two-Party Texas: The John Tower Era, 1961-1984. John R. Knaggs. (Illus.). 300p. 1985. 17.95 (*0-89015-529-1*) Sunbelt Media.

Two Passengers for Chelsea & Other Plays. Oscar W. Firkins. LC 77-94340. (One-Act Plays in Reprint Ser.). 1978. reprint ed. 28.00 (*0-8486-2038-0*) Roth Pub Inc.

Two Paths to Equality. Janet Z. Giele. (Social Movements Past & Present Ser.). (Illus.). 256p. 1995. 28.95 (*0-8057-9700-9*, Twayne) Scribnrs Ref.

Two Paths to Equality. Janet Z. Giele. (Social Movements Past & Present Ser.). (Illus.). 256p. 1995. pap. 16.95 (*0-8057-4523-8*, Twayne) Scribnrs Ref.

Two Paths to the New South: The Virginia Debt Controversy, 1870-1883. James T. Moore. LC 73-86404. 181p. reprint ed. pap. 51.60 (*0-8357-4296-2*, 2037095) Bks Demand.

Two Paths Toward Peace. Donald Scherer & James E. Child. (C). 1992. 49.95 (*0-87722-882-5*) Temple U Pr.

Two Patterns of Rationality in Freud's Writings. Steven E. Goldberg. LC 87-5821. 222p. 1988. reprint ed. pap. 63.30 (*0-608-01667-5*, 2062322) Bks Demand.

Two Paychecks: Life in Dual-Earner Families. Ed. by Joan Aldous. LC 82-10538. (Sage Focus Editions Ser.: No. 56). 247p. reprint ed. pap. 70.40 (*0-8357-4739-5*, 2037659) Bks Demand.

Two Peach Baskets: The Little Basketball Man: Phog Allen, Doc Naismith & I: Reminiscences of a Kansas Boy, 2 bks. in 1. Bernice L. Webb. LC 91-67300. xi, 166p. 1991. pap. 14.95 (*0-9631384-0-5*) Spider Pr.

Two Peninsulas Called Michigan. Jean Shafer & Lynne Deur. (Michigan Themes Ser.). (Illus.). 32p. (Orig.). 1995. teacher ed., pap. 14.95 (*0-938682-31-8*) River Rd Pubns.

Two-Penny Wedding. Karen T. Whittenburg. (American Romance Ser.). 1996. mass mkt. 3.75 (*0-373-16648-6*, 1-16648-7) Harlequin Bks.

Two Peoples . . . One Land: Federal Solutions for Israel, the Palestinians, & Jordan. Daniel J. Elazar. 216p. (C). 1991. pap. 14.95 (*0-8191-8265-6*); lib. bdg. 46.50 (*0-8191-8096-3*) U Pr of Amer.

***Two Perfectly Marvellous Cats.** Rosamond M. Young. (Illus.). 1997. pap. 15.00 (*1-880158-16-7*) J N Townsend.

Two Perfectly Marvellous Cats: A True Story. Rosamond M. Young. LC 96-8039. (Illus.). 176p. 1996. 20.00 (*1-880158-12-4*) J N Townsend.

Two-Person Bargaining Experiments with Incomplete Information. Bettina Kuon. LC 94-9061. (Lecture Notes in Economics & Mathematical Systems Ser.: Vol. 412). 1994. write for info. (*3-540-57920-6*) Spr-Verlag.

Two-Person Bargaining Experiments with Incomplete Information. Bettina Kuon. LC 94-9061. (Lecture Notes in Economics & Mathematical Systems Ser.: Vol. 412). 1994. 62.95 (*0-387-57920-6*) Spr-Verlag.

Two-Person Zero-Sum Games. Alan R. Washburn. (Topics in Operations Research Ser.). vii, 118p. 1991. 15.00 (*1-877640-09-3*) INFORMS.

Two Phase Annular & Dispersed Flow: Proceedings of the International Symposium, University of Pisa, Italy, 24-29 June 1984. Ed. by T. J. Hanratty et al. 200p. 1985. pap. 50.00 (*0-08-031653-0*, Pergamon Pr) Elsevier.

Two-Phase Cooling & Corrosion in Nuclear Power Plant. M. A. Styrikovich et al. Tr. by Dov B. Lederman from RUS. 415p. 1987. 170.00 (*0-89116-424-3*) Hemisp Pub.

Two-Phase Flow & Heat Transfer. P. B. Whalley. (Oxford Chemistry Primers Ser.: No. 42). (Illus.). 96p. (C). 1996. pap. text ed. 11.95 (*0-19-856444-9*) OUP.

Two-Phase Flow & Heat Transfer in Rod Bundles: Presented at the Winter Annual Meeting of the American Society of Mechanical Engineers, Los Angeles, November, 18, 1969. Ed. by V. F. Schrock. LC 73-28391. 100p. reprint ed. pap. 28.50 (*0-317-08165-9*, 2013315) Bks Demand.

Two Phase Flow Dynamics & Reactor Safety. Arthur E. Bergles & Seiken Ishigai. 1981. text ed. 110.00 (*0-07-004904-1*) McGraw.

Two-Phase Flow in Energy Exchange Systems. Ed. by M. S. Sohal & T. J. Rabas. (HTD Ser.: Vol. 220). 116p. 1992. 37.50 (*0-7918-1063-1*, G00707) ASME.

Two Phase Flow Measurements: Principles, Designs, & Applications: The Technical Report of an International Colloquium on Two-Phase Flow Instrumentation. International Colloquium on Two-Phase Flow Instrumentation Staff. Ed. by EG & G Idaho, Inc., Staff. LC 82-227454. (Illus.). 583p. reprint ed. pap. 166.20 (*0-8357-4429-9*, 2037260) Bks Demand.

Two-Phase Flows. Shih-I Pai. (Vieweg Tracts in Pure & Applied Physics Ser.: Vol. 3). xii, 360p. 1977. 70.00 (*3-528-08340-9*, Pub. by Vieweg & Sohn GW) Informatica.

Two Phase Flows & Waves. Ed. by D. D. Joseph & D. G. Schaeffer. (IMA Volumes in Mathematics & Its Applications Ser.: Vol. 26). (Illus.). xi, 164p. 1990. 41.95 (*0-387-97293-5*) Spr-Verlag.

Two Phase Flows in Chemical Engineering. David Azbel. LC 80-20936. (Illus.). 400p. 1981. 140.00 (*0-521-23772-6*) Cambridge U Pr.

Two-Phase Industrial Thermosyphons. L. S. Pioro & I. L. Pioro. 200p. 1991. 75.00 (*0-89116-765-X*) CRC Pr.

Two-Phase Momentum, Heat & Mass Transfer in Chemical, Process & Energy Engineering Systems. F. Durst et al. 1979. Set. text ed. 92.00 (*0-07-079166-X*) McGraw.

Two-Phase Polymer Systems. Leszek A. Utracki. 412p. (C). 1991. text ed. 84.50 (*1-56990-105-8*) Hanser-Gardner.

Two-Phase Thermosyphons & Their Industrial Applications. I. L. Pioro et al. LC 96-39875. 300p. 1996. 97.50 (*1-56700-064-9*) Begell Hse.

Two-Phased Approach to Model Validation for the Susceptibility Model Assessment & Range Test (SMART) Project. Gregory Born. LC 94-19233. 1994. pap. text ed. 9.00 (*0-8330-1554-0*, MR-399-AF) Rand Corp.

Two-Photon Physics: From DAPHNE to LEP200 & Beyond. Ed. by F. Kapusta & J. Urgen Parisi. LC 94-35622. 356p. 1994. text ed. 83.00 (*981-02-1890-7*) World Scientific Pub.

Two Piano Sonatas by Young Soviet Composers: One by Gubaidulina & Mansurian. 44p. pap. 15.00 (*0-7935-3820-3*) H Leonard.

Two Pianos. M. Gould. 36p. 1994. pap. 15.00 (*0-7935-3062-8*) H Leonard.

Two Pictures. Maria J. McIntosh. LC 72-39094. (Black Heritage Library Collection). 1977. reprint ed. 28.95 (*0-8369-9032-3*) Ayer.

Two Pigs in Wigs. Joe Larke. (J). (ps-3). 1991. 11.95 (*0-9620112-2-3*) Grin A Bit.

Two Pioneers of Cliometrics: Robert W. Fogel & Douglass C. North. Cliometric Society Staff. (Illus.). 104p. (C). 1993. 17.50 (*0-9640068-0-4*); pap. 7.50 (*0-9640068-1-2*) Cliometric Soc.

Two Pioneers of Color Photography: Cros & Du Hauron. Ed. by Robert A. Sobieszek. LC 76-24667. (Sources of Modern Photography Ser.). (FRE.). 1979. lib. bdg. 12.95 (*0-405-09644-5*) Ayer.

***Two Pioneers of Young Adult Library Services.** Patty Campbell. (VOYA Occasional Papers Ser.). 48p. 1997. pap. 14.00 (*0-8108-3423-5*) Scarecrow.

Two Plays. Arnold Colbath. 1980. pap. text ed. 5.95 (*0-913006-17-3*) Puckerbrush.

Two Plays. May Davenport. LC 75-55603. (J). (gr. 5-12). 1977. pap. 2.50 (*0-9603118-0-7*) Davenport.

Two Plays. Wendell Metzger. Ed. by Joyce Carbone. (Illus.). 44p. (Orig.). 1995. pap. 4.95 (*1-878116-44-4*) JVC Bks.

Two Plays. Marco Micone. 1988. pap. 10.00 (*0-919349-72-2*) Guernica Editions.

Two Plays. Douglas T. Ward. 80p. 1971. 15.95 (*0-89388-006-X*); pap. 9.95 (*0-89388-007-8*) Okpaku Communications.

***Two Plays.** George Woodcock. 13.95 (*0-88922-123-5*, Pub. by Talonbooks CN) Genl Dist Srvs.

Two Plays: A Murder of Crows & The Hyacinth Macaw. Mac Wellman. (Sun & Moon Classics/American Theater in Literature Ser.: No. 62). 168p. (Orig.). 1994. pap. 11.95 (*1-55713-197-X*) Sun & Moon CA.

Two Plays: Christopher Columbus & Don Juan. Charles Bertin. Tr. by William J. Smith. LC 78-109941. (Minnesota Drama Editions Ser.: No. 6). 148p. reprint ed. pap. 42.20 (*0-317-29397-4*, 2055843) Bks Demand.

Two Plays: Dr. Harmer's Holidays & Child Man. Arthur W. Pinero. (BCL1-PR English Literature Ser.). 245p. 1992. reprint ed. lib. bdg. 79.00 (*0-7812-7619-5*) Rprt Serv.

Two Plays - Sodom & Gomorrah & Comedy: A Tragedy in One Act. Nikos Kazantzakis. Ed. by Theofanis G. Stavrou. Tr. by Kimon Friar & Peter Bien from GRE. (Modern Greek History & Culture Ser.). 120p. 1982. 20.00 (*0-935476-12-1*) Nostos Bks.

Two Plays by Bertolt. Bertolt Brecht. 1983. pap. 11.95 (*0-452-01055-1*, Mer) NAL-Dutton.

Two Plays by Bertolt Brecht. Bertolt Brecht. 1983. mass mkt. 4.95 (*0-452-00857-3*, Mer) NAL-Dutton.

Two Plays by Dominique Hippolyte, 2 vols. in 1. Dominique Hippolyte. (B. E. Ser.: No. 13). 1933. Two works in one unit. 40.00 (*0-8115-2964-9*) Periodicals Srv.

Two Plays by Eugene Labiche: Ninety Degrees in the Shade, & Dust in Your Eyes. Eugene Labiche. 1962. pap. 5.25 (*0-8222-0343-X*) Dramatists Play.

Two Plays by Gabriel Marcel: The Lantern & The Torch of Peace, Plus "From Comic Theater to Musical Creation" a Previously Unpublished Essay by Gabriel Marcel. Ed. by Katharine R. Hanley. (Illus.). 164p. (C). 1988. lib. bdg. 34.00 (*0-8191-7086-0*) U Pr of Amer.

***Two Plays by Oscar Wilde: An Ideal Husband & a Woman of No Importance.** Oscar Wilde. (Signet Classic Ser.). 320p. 1997. mass mkt. 4.95 (*0-451-52663-5*, Sig Classics) NAL-Dutton.

Two Plays for the Right: Birth on a Hard Shoulder & Loud Boy. Howard Barker. 150p. (Orig.). 1984. pap. 11.95 (*0-7145-3896-5*) Riverrun NY.

Two Plays from the New Russia. Ed. & Tr. by John Freedman. (Russian Theatre Archive Ser.). 1996. text ed. 46.00 (*3-7186-5780-5*); pap. text ed. 23.00 (*3-7186-5781-3*) Gordon & Breach.

***Two Plays, One Day & a Third.** limited ed. Joyce Carbone. (Illus.). 100p. (Orig.). 1997. pap. 9.95 (*1-878116-68-1*) JVC Bks.

Two Plus Two Equals Reality. William Samuel. 57p. 1989. pap. 2.00 (*1-877999-00-8*) W Samuel Fndtn.

Two Poems Against Pope. Intro. by Joseph V. Guerinot. LC 92-2370. (Augustan Reprints Ser.: No. 114). 1965. reprint ed. 14.50 (*0-404-70114-0*, PR3763) AMS Pr.

Two Poems by Theodore Metochites. Ihor Sevcenko & Jeffrey Featherstone. 46p. 1981. pap. 1.00 (*0-916586-83-9*) Hellenic Coll Pr.

***Two Poets of "Paradise Lost"** Robert McMahon. LC 97-24426. 224p. 1998. text ed. 32.50 (*0-8071-2188-6*) La State U Pr.

Two Poets of the Oxford Movement: John Keble & John Henry Newman. Rodney S. Edgecombe. LC 95-21769. 296p. 1995. 42.50 (*0-8386-3669-1*) Fairleigh Dickinson.

Two Point Eight Angstroms: The Unifying Force of G & c. Kenneth G. Salem. (Illus.). 136p. (Orig.). 1990. pap. 8.95 (*0-9625398-0-5*) Salem Bks.

Two Points. Jane Kennedy & Audrey Eaton. (Illus.). 8p. (Orig.). (J). (gr. k-1). 1995. pap. 3.50 (*1-880612-48-8*) Seedling Pubns.

Two Points for Murder: After Marriage, Motherhood, & Middle Age, Cat's Going Back to High. D. B. Borton. 1993. mass mkt. 4.99 (*0-425-13947-6*) Berkley Pub.

Two Points to Murder. Carolyn Keene. (Nancy Drew Files Ser.: No. 8). (YA). (gr. 7 up). 1991. pap. 3.50 (*0-671-73663-9*, Archway) PB.

Two Points to Murder: The Nancy Drew Files, Case 8. large type ed. Carolyn Keene. 151p. (J). (gr. 5-10). 1988. reprint ed. 9.50 (*0-942545-39-7*); reprint ed. lib. bdg. 10.50 (*0-942545-34-6*) Grey Castle.

Two Portuguese Communities in New England. Donald R. Taft. LC 23-17483. (Columbia University. Studies in the Social Sciences: No. 241). reprint ed. 21.00 (*0-404-51241-0*) AMS Pr.

Two Portuguese Communities in New England. Donald R. Taft. LC 69-18792. (American Immigration Collection. Series 1). 1969. reprint ed. 18.95 (*0-405-00541-5*) Ayer.

Two Post-Modern Plays: Jackets & In the Company of Men. Edward Bond. (Methuen Modern Plays Ser.). 244p. (Orig.). (C). 1990. pap. 13.95 (*0-413-62650-4*, A0464, Pub. by Methuen UK) Heinemann.

Two Pragmatisms: From Peirce to Rorty. H. O. Mounce. LC 96-21878. 256p. (C). 1997. pap. write for info. (*0-415-15283-6*) Routledge.

***Two Pragmatisms: From Peirce to Rorty.** Howard Mounce. 256p. (C). 1997. text ed. 69.95 (*0-415-15282-8*) Routledge.

Two Prayers for Patches. Diane M. Stortz. LC 94-1122. (Little Deer Bks.). (Illus.). 28p. (J). (ps). 1994. 5.49 (*0-7847-0201-2*, 03887) Standard Pub.

Two Presidencies: A Quarter Century Assessment. Steven A. Shull. (Political Science Ser.). 300p. (Orig.). (C). 1991. pap. text ed. 21.95 (*0-8304-1249-2*) Nelson-Hall.

Two Primary Sources for a Study of the Life of Jonas Swensson. Evald R. Lawson. (Augustana Historical Society Publications: Vol. 17). 39p. 1957. pap. 3.00 (*0-910184-17-8*) Augustana.

***Two Princesses: Sleeping Beauty & Beauty & the Beast.** abr. large type ed. Jennifer Roth. (Illus.). 32p. (Orig.). (J). (gr. k up). 1995. pap. 14.95 (*1-886201-00-5*) Nana Banana.

Two Private Banking Partnerships: An Original Anthology. Ed. by Vincent P. Carosso. LC 75-2676. (Wall Street & the Security Market Ser.). (Illus.). 1975. 50.95 (*0-405-07238-4*) Ayer.

2-Propanol. (Environmental Health Criteria Ser.: No. 103). 132p. 1990. pap. text ed. 26.00 (*92-4-157103-9*, 1160103) World Health.

Two-Putt Greens in Eighteen Days: A How-to Guide for the Weekend Golfer. Walter Ostroske & John Devaney. (Illus.). 128p. (Orig.). 1992. pap. 10.00 (*0-399-51747-2*, Perigee Bks) Berkley Pub.

Two Quartets: Party of Four & Melodie for Recorders. Ann McKinley. (Contemporary Consort Ser.: No. 14). i, 18p. 1991. pap. text ed. 8.00 (*1-56571-032-0*) PRB Prods.

Two Queens of Baghdad, Mother & Wife of Harun Al-Rashid. Nabia Abbott. LC 46-3799. 295p. reprint ed. pap. 84.10 (*0-317-11341-0*, 2011225) Bks Demand.

Two Quiet Lives: Dorothy Osborne & Thomas Gray. David Cecil. (Illus.). 194p. 1989. reprint ed. pap. 22.50 (*0-09-469420-6*, Pub. by Constable Pubs UK) Trans-Atl Phila.

Two Races Beyond the Altar. Patrick Huber. LC 75-30268. 1976. pap. 11.95 (*0-8283-1646-5*) Branden Pub Co.

Two Races One Face Two Faces One Race. Tom Gayton & John Peterson. (Illus.). 131p. 1993. pap. 12.00 (*0-9638412-0-3*) Drury Ln.

Two Radicals: Unpublished Essays on Jean Genet & Ezra Pound Plus Selected Reviews on Sundry Subjects. Richard W. Nason. LC 92-75617. 112p. 1993. pap. 25.00 (*0-9635297-5-7*) Black Spruce.

Two Ramesside Tombs at El Mashayikh, Vol. 1: The Tomb of Anhurmose The Outer Room. Ed. by Ockinga. 1988. pap. 75.00 (*0-85668-453-8*, Pub. by Aris & Phillips UK) David Brown.

Two Ramesside Tombs at Mashayakh, No. II. Ockinga. pap. 75.00 (*0-85668-566-6*, Pub. by Aris & Phillips UK) David Brown.

Two Ravens: The Life & Teachings of a Spiritual Warrior. Louis Two Ravens Irwin & Robert Liebert. (Illus.). 144p. 1996. pap. 12.95 (*0-89281-571-X*, Destiny Bks) Inner Tradit.

Two Reels & a Crank. Albert E. Smith & Phil A. Koury. LC 82-49235. (Cinema Classics Ser.). 285p. 1985. lib. bdg. 11.00 (*0-8240-5778-3*) Garland.

***Two Renaissance Book Collectors: Jean Grolier & Diego Hurtado de Mendoza.** Anthony Hobson. (Lyell Lectures in Bibliography). (Illus.). 220p. 1997. 110.00 (*0-19-818418-2*) OUP.

Two Renaissance Book Hunters. Phyllis Walter & Goodhart Gordan. (Records of Western Civilization Ser.). 393p. 1991. text ed. 75.00 (*0-231-03777-5*); pap. text ed. 17.50 (*0-231-09633-X*) Col U Pr.

Two Renaissance Plays: Ariosto, 'Il Negromante', & Trissino, 'Sofonisba' Ed. by B. Corrigan. (Italian Texts Ser.). 184p. (ITA.). (C). 1975. pap. 11.00 (*0-685-07670-9*, Pub. by Manchester Univ Pr UK) St Martin.

Two Reports on Harmonic Maps. James Eells & Luc Lemaire. 228p. 1995. text ed. 61.00 (*981-02-1466-9*) World Scientific Pub.

Two Reports on Japanese Canadians in World War II, 2 Vols. Canada Department of Labour Staff. Ed. by Roger Daniels. LC 78-7079. (Asian Experience in North America Ser.). (Illus.). 1979. reprint ed. lib. bdg. 15.95 (*0-405-11266-1*) Ayer.

Two Revolutions: An Eye-Witness Account of Russia, 1917. R. H. Lockhart. LC 67-24887. 144p. 6700. 18.95 (*0-8023-1124-5*) Dufour.

Two Revolutions: Antonio Gramsci & the Dilemmas of Marxism. Carl Boggs. LC 84-50943. 311p. (Orig.). 1984. 35.00 (*0-89608-226-1*); pap. 9.50 (*0-89608-225-3*) South End Pr.

***Two Revolutions: Village Reconstruction & the Cooperation Movement in Northern Shaaxi, 1934-1945.** Pauline B. Keating. LC 97-5041. 1997. write for info. (*0-8047-2825-9*) Stanford U Pr.

Two Roads. Chris Crowe. 1994. pap. 7.95 (*0-88494-920-6*) Bookcraft Inc.

Two Roads & This Spring. Hugh Ogden. (Red Hill Ser.). 88p. (Orig.). 1993. pap. 9.95 (*1-879969-03-3*) Catskill Reading.

***Two Roman Stories.** Nelson U. K. Staff. 1991. pap. text ed. write for info. (*0-17-556646-1*) Addison-Wesley.

***Two Roman Villas at Wharram Street.** P. Rahtz et al. (Wharram Ser.: Vol. IV). 88p. 1986. 10.00 (*0-614-21850-0*, Pub. by U York Dept Archaeol UK) David Brown.

Two Romances: A Study & Edition of Two Medieval Spanish Romances. Benaim De Lasry. Ed. by Thomas Lathrop et al. 234p. 1982. 17.50 (*0-936388-09-9*); pap. 12.50 (*0-936388-13-7*) Juan de la Cuesta.

Two Romantic Plays: The Spaniards in Denmark by Prosper Merimee & the Rebels of Nantucket by Oscar Mandel. unabridged ed. Prosper Merimee & Oscar Mandel. LC 96-68760. (Illus.). 175p. (Orig.). 1996. pap. 15.95 (*0-914502-11-5*) Spectrum Prods.

Two Romantic Trios: A Sextet of Extraordinary Musicians. Sheryl Macy. 250p. 1991. per. 12.95 (*0-9627040-0-8*) Allegro OR.

Two Rooms. Lee Blessing. 1990. pap. 5.25 (*0-8222-1183-1*) Dramatists Play.

Two Rosetos. Carla Bianco. LC 73-16523. (Illus.). 254p. reprint ed. pap. 72.40 (*0-8357-9249-8*, 2055234) Bks Demand.

Two Royall Entertainments, Lately Given to Charles, Prince of Great Britaine, by Philip the Fourth of Spaine. Andres De Almansa & Andres De Mendoza. LC 77-6847. (English Experience Ser.: No. 842). 1977. reprint ed. lib. bdg. 15.00 (*90-221-0842-2*) Walter J Johnson.

***Two Rulers in One Reign: Dorgon & Shun-Chih, 1644-1660.** Adam Lui. (Faculty of Asian Studies Monographs: Vol. 13). (Illus.). 170p. 1997. pap. text ed. 25.00 (*0-7315-0654-5*, Pub. by Aust Nat Univ AT) UH Pr.

Two Runaways & Other Stories. Harry S. Edwards. 1972. reprint ed. lib. bdg. 24.00 (*0-8422-8042-1*) Irvington.

Two Russian Thinkers: An Essay in Berdyaev & Shestov. James C. Wernham. LC 68-85112. 132p. reprint ed. pap. 37.70 (*0-317-08859-9*, 2014455) Bks Demand.

***Two Sabbaths.** George A. McCabe. 112p. 1996. pap. 12.95 (*0-929529-06-5*) Vision Ministry Pr.

Two Saunters: Summer & Winter 1978. 1986. 20.00 (*0-9615665-0-7*) Pencil Pr.

Two Scars Against One. LaJoyce Martin. LC 94-3763. 192p. (Orig.). 1995. pap. 7.99 (*1-56722-025-8*) Word Aflame.

Two Scenes Antony & Cleopatra: Soprano Piano: Scene 1. Give Me Some Music; Scene 2. Death of Cleopatra. S. Barber. 64p. 1986. pap. 10.00 (*0-7935-1796-6*, 50339660) H Leonard.

Two Scholarly Friends: Yates Snowden-John Bennett Correspondence, 1902-1932. Ed. by Mary C. Anderson. LC 93-14054. 421p. 1993. text ed. 29.95 (*0-87249-961-8*) U of SC Pr.

Two Schools of Thought: Some Tales of Learning and Romance. Carolyn See & John Espey. LC 90-46324. 128p. (Orig.). 1991. pap. 8.95 (*0-936784-88-1*) J Daniel.

***Two Sciences of Mind: Readings in Cognitive Science & Consciousness.** Ed. by Sean O'Nuallain et al. LC 96-52164. (Advances in Consciousness Research Ser.: Vol. 9). 450p. 1997. pap. 59.95 (*1-55619-189-8*) Benjamins North Am.

Two Screenplays: The Blood of a Poet, The Testament of Orpheus. Jean Cocteau. Tr. by Carol Martin-Sperry from FRE. LC 63-30778. (Illus.). 144p. 1968. 16.95 (*0-910278-07-5*) Boulevard.

Two-Sector General Equilibrium Model: A New Approach. C. L. Dinwiddy & F. J. Teal. LC 87-36935. 160p. 1988. text ed. 49.95 (*0-312-01877-0*) St Martin.

Two-Sector Model of Economic Growth with Technological Progress. Frederick O. Goddard. LC 75-625421. (University of Florida Monographs: Social Sciences: No. 36). 70p. reprint ed. pap. 25.00 (*0-7837-4987-2*, 2044654) Bks Demand.

Two Self-Portraits: Liang Chi'i-ch'ao & Hu Shih. Liang Ch'i-ch'ao & Hu Shih. Tr. by Li Yu-ning & William A. Wycoff from CHI. (C). 1992. 30.00 (*0-9622934-0-7*) Outer Sky.

Two Selves of Jessica Throckmorton: An Aesthetic Realism Lesson. Eli Siegel. 27p. 1971. pap. 3.00 (*0-911492-10-0*) Aesthetic Realism.

***Two Serious Ladies.** Jane Bowles. 200p. 1996. pap. 18.95 (*0-7206-1006-0*, Pub. by P Owen Ltd UK) Dufour.

Two Sermons. John Cotton. LC 79-141108. (Research Library of Colonial Americana). 1972. reprint ed. 24.95 (*0-405-03322-2*) Ayer.

Two Sets of Footprints. Pamela Toth. (Special Edition Ser.: No. 729). 1992. mass mkt. 3.39 (*0-373-09729-8*, 5-09729-0) Harlequin Bks.

***Two Settings of Palestrina's Missa Papae Marcelli.** Pierluigi D. Palestrina et al. Ed. by Hermann J. Busch. (Recent Researches in Music of the Baroque Era Ser.: Vol. RRB16). 106p. 1973. pap. 33.60 (*0-89579-048-3*) A-R Eds.

An Asterisk (*) at the beginning of an entry indicates that the title is appearing in BIP for the first time.

Two Shakespearean Actors. Richard Nelson. 103p. (Orig.). 1990. pap. 8.95 (*0-571-16103-0*) Faber & Faber.

Two Shall Be One. C. M. Ward. 148p. 1986. mass mkt. 3.99 (*0-88368-184-6*) Whitaker Hse.

Two Shall Be One: Preparing Your Church Wedding - A Workbook for Engaged Couples. Peter Schavitz & Kathleen McAnany. LC 94-77056. 96p. (Orig.). 1994. pap. 2.95 (*0-89243-676-X*) Liguori Pubns.

Two Shoes, New Shoes. Shirley Hughes. LC 86-2733. (Illus.). 24p. (J). (ps). 1986. pap. 4.95 (*0-688-04207-4*) Lothrop.

Two Short Novels. R. V. Cassill & James White. 180p. 1991. 25.00 (*0-685-40747-0*); pap. 9.95 (*0-685-40748-9*) Soft Teach Inc.

Two Short Novels: The Unknown Soldier & Clara's Call. R. V. Cassill & James P. White. 161p. (Orig.). (C). 1991. text ed. 19.95 (*0-916092-14-3*) Tex Ctr Writers.

Two Short Novels: Unknown Soldier by R. V. Cassill - Clara's Call by James White. R. V. Cassill & James White. 154p. (Orig.). 1993. pap. 9.95 (*0-916092-12-7*) Tex Ctr Writers.

Two Short Plays by Lewis John Carlino: Mr. Flannery's Ocean & Objective Case. Lewis J. Carlino. 1962. pap. 5.25 (*0-8222-0781-8*) Dramatists Play.

Two Short Plays by Owen G. Arno. Owen G. Arno. 1964. pap. 5.25 (*0-8222-0867-9*) Dramatists Play.

***Two Short Stories.** (Young Dragon Readers 1 Ser.). (J). 1995. pap. text ed. write for info. (*962-359-531-X*) Addison-Wesley.

Two Siblings & Other Stories. Luisa M. Levinson. Ed. by Yvette E. Miller. Tr. by Sylvia E. Lipp from SPA. LC 96-17097. (Discoveries Ser.). 128p. 1996. pap. 14.95 (*0-935480-74-9*) Lat Am Lit Rev Pr.

Two-Sided Matching: A Study in Game-Theoretic Modeling & Analysis. Alvin E. Roth & Marilda A. Sotomayor. (Econometric Society Monographs: No. 18). (Illus.). 300p. (C). 1990. text ed. 80.00 (*0-521-39015-X*) Cambridge U Pr.

Two-Sided Matching: A Study in Game-Theoretic Modeling & Analysis. Alvin E. Roth & Marilda A. Sotomayor. (Econometric Society Monographs: No. 18). (Illus.). 288p. (C). 1992. pap. text ed. 21.95 (*0-521-43788-1*) Cambridge U Pr.

Two Sides of a Coin. Miriam Elias. 160p. (J). (gr. 6-9). 1994. 9.95 (*1-56871-053-4*) Targum Pr.

Two Sides of a Coin. Charles Hunter & Frances Hunter. 1973. pap. 6.95 (*0-917726-36-7*) Hunter Bks.

Two Sides of a Coin. rev. ed. 167p. (SPA.). 1986. pap. 4.00 (*0-917726-77-4*) Hunter Bks.

Two Sides of Love. Gary Smalley & John Trent. 1990. pap. 10.99 (*0-929608-46-1*) Focus Family.

Two Sides of Love. Gary Smalley & John Trent. 1992. student ed., pap. 10.99 (*1-56179-071-0*) Focus Family.

Two Sides of Love. Gary Smalley & John Trent. 256p. 1993. reprint ed. mass mkt. 5.99 (*0-671-75053-4*) PB.

***Two Sides of Perception.** Richard B. Ivry & Lynn C. Robertson. LC 96-50975. (Cognitive Neuroscience Ser.). 1997. write for info. (*0-262-09034-1*) MIT Pr.

Two Sides of the Sunbelt: The Growing Divergence Between the Rural & Urban South. Thomas A. Lyson. LC 88-31928. 163p. 1989. text ed. 49.95 (*0-275-93201-X*, C3201, Praeger Pubs) Greenwood.

Two Sides, the Best of Personal Opinion, 1964-1984. John H. Redekop. 306p. (Orig.). 1984. 15.95 (*0-919797-47-4*); pap. 2.00 (*0-919797-13-X*) Kindred Prods.

Two Sides to Everything: The Cultural Construction of Class Consciousness in Harlan County, Kentucky. Shaunna L. Scott. LC 94-13464. (SUNY Series in Oral & Public History). 259p. (C). 1995. text ed. 57.50 (*0-7914-2343-3*); pap. text ed. 19.95 (*0-7914-2344-1*) State U NY Pr.

Two Silly Trolls. Nancy Jewell. LC 90-4387. (Trophy I Can Read Bk.). (Illus.). 64p. (J). (ps-3). 1994. pap. 3.75 (*0-06-444173-3*) HarpC Child Bks.

Two Sisters. (Red Stripe Ser.). 1989. pap. 4.50 (*0-8216-5067-X*, Univ Books) Carol Pub Group.

Two Sisters. Nancy Wagner. 384p. (Orig.). 1993. mass mkt. 4.99 (*0-380-76456-3*) Avon.

Two Sisters. large type ed. H. E. Bates. (General Fiction Ser.). 416p. 1993. 25.99 (*0-7089-2963-X*) Ulverscroft.

Two Sisters. Gore Vidal. 1987. reprint ed. mass mkt. 4.95 (*0-345-33117-6*) Ballantine.

***Two Sisters: Story of the Planet.** large type unabridged ed. David Pinto. Ed. by Carol Kaminsky. LC 96-94640. (Illus.). 104p. 1997. 14.95 (*0-9657390-0-7*) Indigo Pubns TX.

Two Sisters for Social Justice: A Biography of Grace & Edith Abbott. Lela B. Costin. LC 82-21790. (Illus.). 336p. 1983. text ed. 29.95 (*0-252-01013-2*) U of Ill Pr.

Two Sisters in Spirit: Therese of Lisieux & Elizabeth of the Trinity. Hans U. Von Balthasar. Tr. by Donald Nicholl et al. from GER. LC 92-70556. (Illus.). 499p. (Orig.). 1992. pap. 19.95 (*0-89870-148-1*) Ignatius Pr.

Two Sites on Martha's Vineyard, Vol. 1 No. 1. D. Byers & F. Johnson. LC 40-3078. 1940. pap. 35.00 (*0-939312-00-X*) Peabody Found.

***Two Sixes: A Western Trio.** large type ed. Max Brand. LC 97-24398. (Circle V Western Ser.). 1997. write for info. (*1-57490-088-9*) T T Beeler.

Two Small Bodies. Neal Bell. 1980. pap. 5.25 (*0-8222-1185-8*) Dramatists Play.

Two Social Psychologies. 2nd ed. Cookie W. Stephan & Walter G. Stephan. 521p. (C). 1990. text ed. 59.95 (*0-534-11706-6*) Wadsworth Pub.

Two Societies in Opposition: The Republic of China & the People's Republic of China after Forty Years, No. P 401. Ed. by Ramon H. Myers. 370p. (C). 1991. text ed. 38.95 (*0-8179-9091-7*); pap. text ed. 25.95 (*0-8179-9092-5*) Hoover Inst Pr.

***Two Solitudes.** large type ed. Hugh MacLennan. 1997. pap. 21.95 (*1-55041-308-2*, Pub. by Fitzhenry & Whiteside CN) Iowa St U Pr.

Two Sonatas: 2 Pianos 4 Hands. M. Clementi. 48p. 1986. pap. 9.95 (*0-7935-5206-0*, 50259880) H Leonard.

Two Sonatas for Two Bass Viols. Johann Schenck. Ed. by Francois-Pierre Goy. (Baroque Ser.: No. 4). iv, 24p. 1994. pap. text ed. 18.00 (*1-56571-093-2*, B004) PRB Prods.

Two Sons of Heaven: Studies in Sung-Liao Relations. Jing-shen Tao. LC 88-1330. 173p. 1988. 32.50 (*0-8165-1051-2*) U of Ariz Pr.

Two Sons of Satan. large type ed. Brett Austin. (Linford Western Library). 304p. 1994. pap. 15.99 (*0-7089-7572-0*, Linford) Ulverscroft.

Two Sought Adventure. Fritz Leiber. 1993. reprint ed. lib. bdg. 18.95 (*0-89968-405-X*, Lghtyr Pr) Buccaneer Bks.

Two Souls. David Davila. LC 95-70722. 183p. 1996. 17.95 (*1-887750-02-9*) Rutledge Bks.

Two Sources of Morality & Religion. Henri Bergson. Tr. by R. Ashley Audra et al. from FRE. LC 77-89762. 1977. pap. text ed. 16.50 (*0-268-01835-9*) U of Notre Dame Pr.

Two Sources of Morality & Religion. Henri L. Bergson. LC 74-10373. 308p. 1975. reprint ed. text ed. 38.50 (*0-8371-7679-4*, BETS, Greenwood Pr) Greenwood.

Two Sovereigns: Social Contradictions of European Modernity. Keith Tester. LC 92-17765. 250p. (C). (gr. 13). 1992. text ed. 62.95 (*0-415-06191-1*, A7115) Routledge.

Two Space Six. Peter Ganick. 36p. (Orig.). 1982. pap. 5.50 (*0-937013-08-0*) Potes Poets.

Two Spanish Picaresque Novels. Incl. Lazarillo De Tormes. Tr. by Michael Alpert. 1969. pap. (*0-318-55113-6*); Swindler. Francisco Quevedo. 1969. (*0-318-55114-4*); (Classics Ser.). 216p. (Orig.). 1969. pap. 11.95 (*0-14-044211-1*, Penguin Classics) Viking Penguin.

Two Spanish-Quiche Dance Dramas of Rabinal, Vol. 3. Carroll E. Mace. 221p. 1970. pap. 7.00 (*0-912788-02-X*) Tulane Romance Lang.

Two Special Valentines. Janet McDonnell. LC 93-37097. (Circle the Year with Holidays Ser.). (Illus.). 32p. (J). (ps-2). 1994. lib. bdg. 17.50 (*0-516-00692-4*) Childrens.

Two Special Valentines. Janet McDonnell. (Circle the Year with Holidays Ser.). 1994. pap. 3.95 (*0-516-40692-2*) Childrens.

Two Speeches by Malcolm X. 3rd ed. Malcolm X. 46p. (Orig.). 1990. reprint ed. pap. 3.50 (*0-87348-591-2*) Pathfinder NY.

Two Speeches of the Mayor: Martin T. Krueger. Martin T. Krueger. (Little Bit of History Ser.: Bk. 3). 44p. (Orig.). (YA). (gr. 8 up). 1989. pap. text ed. 2.00 (*0-935549-13-7*) MI City Hist.

***Two Spirit People: American Indian Lesbian Women & Gay Men.** Ed. by Lester B. Brown. LC 97-3475. 116p. 1997. pap. 12.95 (*1-56023-089-4*) Haworth Pr.

***Two Spirit People: American Indian Lesbian Women & Gay Men.** Ed. by Lester B. Brown. LC 97-3475. 116p. 1997. 29.95 (*0-7890-0003-2*) Haworth Pr.

***Two-Spirit People: Native American Gender Identity, Sexuality, & Spirituality.** Date not set. 19.95 (*0-252-06645-6*) U of Ill Pr.

***Two-Spirit People: Perspectives on the Intersection of Native American Gender Identity, Sexuality & Spirituality.** Sue-Ellen Jacobs et al. LC 96-51214. 1997. text ed. 44.95 (*0-252-02344-7*) U of Ill Pr.

Two States - One Nation? Gunter Grass et al. 1990. 18.95 (*0-15-192270-5*) HarBrace.

Two Statesmen of Mediaeval Islam: Vizir Ibn Hubayra (499-560 A. H., 1105-1165 A. D.) & Califh an-Nasir Li Din Allah (553-622 A. H., 1158-1225 A. D.) Herbert Mason. 146p. 1972. text ed. 44.65 (*90-279-6979-5*) Mouton.

Two Stein Talks. Lyn Hejinian. (Illus.). 48p. 1995. write for info. (*1-878460-02-1*) Weaselsleeves Pr.

Two-Step: Dancing Toward Intimacy. Eileen McCann. LC 85-14764. (Illus.). 160p. 1985. pap. 12.95 (*0-8021-3032-1*, Grove) Grove-Atltic.

Two Steps Ahead of the Thought Police. John Leo. 320p. 1994. 22.00 (*0-671-88698-3*) S&S Trade.

Two Stories. Giambattista Basile. Tr. & Intro. by Felix Stefanile. (Poverty Pamphlets Ser.: No. 50). 28p. (Orig.). 1986. pap. text ed. 2.50 (*0-935552-21-9*) Sparrow Pr.

Two Stories. limited ed. Brian Moore. (Santa Susana Press Ser.). 1979. 35.00 (*0-937048-22-4*); 60.00 (*0-937048-29-1*) Santa Susana.

Two Stories: Los Gabrieles - Carnal. limited ed. Jessica Hagedorn. (Illus.). 32p. 1993. 50.00 (*1-56689-022-5*) Coffee Hse.

***Two Stories by Fielding Dawson.** Fielding Dawson. (Illus.). 16p. 1996. pap. 3.00 (*1-885710-18-6*) Geekspeak Unique.

Two Stories of Prague: King Bohush & The Siblings. Rainer M. Rilke. Tr. & Intro. by Angela Esterhammer. LC 93-35912. (Illus.). 151p. (C). 1994. text ed. 25.00 (*0-87451-661-7*) U Pr of New Eng.

Two Stories of Prague: King Bohush & The Siblings. Rainer M. Rilke. LC 93-35912. (Illus.). 151p. 1994. reprint ed. pap. 12.95 (*0-87451-789-3*) U Pr of New Eng.

Two Story Farmhouse. Elva Schultz. (Illus.). (J). (ps-3). 1986. write for info. (*0-9616431-0-2*) E Schultz.

***Two-Story Frame.** Tierney McClellan. 1997. pap. 5.99 (*0-451-19197-8*, Sig) NAL-Dutton.

***Two Story Home Plans.** 224p. 1997. pap. 9.95 (*0-696-20721-4*) Meredith Bks.

***Two Story Home Plans.** 2nd ed. Garlinghouse, L. F., Co. Staff. (Illus.). 256p. 1997. pap. 6.95 (*0-938708-73-2*) L F Garlinghouse Co.

Two-Story Homes. (Illus.). 384p. 1996. pap. 9.95 (*1-881955-31-1*) Home Planners.

Two-Story Homes: Four Hundred Seventy-Eight Designs for One & One-Half & Two Stories. (Illus.). 416p. 1991. pap. 8.95 (*0-918894-86-7*) Home Planners.

Two-Story Outhouse. Norman D. Weis. LC 87-35425. (Illus.). (Orig.). 1988. pap. 12.95 (*0-87004-326-9*) Caxton.

Two Strand River. Keith Maillard. 320p. 1996. pap. 14.00 (*0-00-648143-4*) HarpC.

Two-Stroke Engine Design & Emissions. 136p. 1994. pap. 30.00 (*1-56091-546-3*, SP1049) Soc Auto Engineers.

Two Stroke Engine Diagnostics & Design. 268p. 1992. pap. 19.00 (*1-56091-218-9*, SP-901) Soc Auto Engineers.

Two-Stroke Engines: Theoretical & Experimental Investigation: SAE International Congress & Exposition 1994, 12 papers. (Special Publications). 196p. 1994. pap. 36.00 (*1-56091-471-8*, SP-1019) Soc Auto Engineers.

Two Stroke Engines: 2 Stroke Exam. Schuster. (Automotive Technology Ser.). 64p. 1994. pap. 10.00 (*0-8273-6621-3*) Delmar.

Two Stroke Engines, Small Engines & Emissions Reduction. 180p. 1991. pap. 19.00 (*1-56091-175-1*, SP-883) Soc Auto Engineers.

2-Stroke Glow Engines for R/C Aircraft. C. David Gierke. Ed. by Chris Chianelli & Tom Atwood. (Illus.). 178p. (Orig.). 1994. pap. 19.95 (*0-911295-30-5*) Air Age.

2 Stroke Motorcycles Dating from the Early 1960s to the Mid 70s. Intertec Publishing Staff. (Intertecs Vintage Collection Ser.). 1990. pap. 29.95 (*0-87288-386-8*, VCS-2) Intertec Pub.

Two Studies in Attic Particle Usage: Lysias & Plato. C. M. Sicking & J. M. Van Ophuijsen. LC 93-15296. (Mnemosyne, Bibliotheca Classica Batava Ser.: Vol. 129). xii, 175p. 1993. 64.50 (*90-04-09867-4*) E J Brill.

Two Studies in Chinese Literature. Li Chi & Dale Johnson. (Michigan Monographs in Chinese Studies: No. 3). (Illus.). 98p. 1968. pap. text ed. 15.00 (*0-89264-003-0*) Ctr Chinese Studies.

Two Studies in Latin Phonology. Andrew M. Devine & Laurence D. Stephens. (Studia Linguistica et Philological Ser.: No. 3). 1978. pap. 46.50 (*0-915838-42-7*) Anma Libri.

Two Studies in Mental Tests. Carl Brigham. Bd. with Radiometric Apparatus for Use in Psychological Optics. C. E. Ferree. ; Transfer of Training & Retroaction. L. E. Webb. ; Reliability of Mental Tests in the Division of an Academic Group. B. Ruml. (Psychology Monographs General & Applied: Vol. 24). 1974. reprint ed. Set pap. 55.00 (*0-8115-1423-4*) Periodicals Srv.

Two Studies in Middle American Comparative Linguistics. David Oltrogge & Calvin R. Rensch. (Publications in Linguistics: No. 55). 108p. 1977. fiche 8.00 (*0-88312-474-2*) Summer Instit Ling.

***Two Studies in Roman Nomenclature.** D. R. Bailey. (APA American Classical Studies). 114p. 1976. pap. 29.95 (*1-55540-666-1*) Scholars Pr GA.

Two Studies in Soviet Terms of Trade, (1918-1970) Michael Dohan & Edward Hewett. (Studies in East European & Soviet Planning, Development, & Trade: No. 21). 1973. pap. text ed. 3.00 (*0-89249-001-2*) Intl Development.

Two Studies in the Early Academy. R. M. Dancy. LC 90-40610. (SUNY Series in Ancient Greek Philosophy). 231p. (C). 1991. text ed. 64.50 (*0-7914-0632-6*); pap. text ed. 21.95 (*0-7914-0633-4*) State U NY Pr.

Two Studies in the Semantics of the Verb in Classical Greek. C. M. Sicking & Peter Stork. LC 96-18306. (Mnemosyne, Bibliotheca Classica Batava: Supplementum Ser.). 180p. 1996. 66.50 (*90-04-10460-7*) E J Brill.

Two Studies on Israel. Ayad Al-Qazzaz & Ibrahim M. Oweiss. (Information Papers: No. 13). 29p. (Orig.). 1974. pap. text ed. 1.00 (*0-937694-29-0*) Assn Arab-Amer U Grads.

Two Studies on Roman Expansion: An Original Anthology. A. Afzelius. LC 75-7301. (Roman History Ser.). (GER.). 1975. reprint ed. 31.95 (*0-405-07178-7*) Ayer.

Two Studies on the Palestinians Today & American Policy. Ibrahim Abu-Lughod & Edward W. Said. (Information Papers: No. 17). 22p. (Orig.). (C). 1976. pap. 1.00 (*0-937694-33-9*) Assn Arab-Amer U Grads.

Two Studies on the Roman Lower Classes: An Original Anthology. M. E. Park & M. Maxey. LC 75-7347. (Roman History Ser.). 1977. reprint ed. 33.95 (*0-405-07069-1*) Ayer.

Two Studies on the Roman Pontifices. P. Preibisch. LC 75-10647. (Ancient Religion & Mythology Ser.). 1976. 23.95 (*0-405-07271-6*) Ayer.

Two Studies on Women in Antiquity: Vassal Queens & Some Contemporary Women in the Roman Empire - Portraits of Royal Ladies on Greek Coins. L. Forrer & Grace H. Macurdy. (Illus.). 1993. pap. 25.00 (*0-89005-543-2*) Ares.

Two Summer Sequences. Gerald Locklin. 1979. 4.00 (*0-917554-10-8*) Maelstrom.

Two Suns & a Green Sky: Twenty Wacky Weather Models. Thomas R. Baker. 1997. pap. text ed. 12.95 (*0-07-005143-7*) McGraw.

***Two Suns Rising: A Collection of Sacred Writings.** J. Star. 1996. 7.98 (*0-7858-0723-3*) Bk Sales Inc.

Two Surf Stories for Children. Fred Van Dyke. 64p. (J). 1995. pap. 5.95 (*1-56647-049-8*) Mutual Pub HI.

Two Surprises. Lucy Conley. (Jewel Bks.). 1986. pap. 2.15 (*0-317-01350-5*) Rod & Staff.

Two Tablets a Day: God's Prescription for Happiness. William R. Van Der Zee. Tr. by Gerard M. Verschuuren from DUT. LC 96-40130. 144p. 1997. pap. 16.95 (*1-886670-04-8*) Genesis Publ.

Two Tactics of Social Democracy in the Democratic Revolution. Vladimir I. Lenin. Tr. by Alexander Trachtenberg from RUS. xxx, 128p. 1989. reprint ed. pap. text ed. 3.25 (*0-7178-0206-X*) Intl Pubs Co.

Two Tales: Man Who Would Be King & Without Benefit of Clergy. Rudyard Kipling. pap. 4.95 (*0-8283-1460-8*, 2, Intl Pocket Lib) Branden Pub Co.

Two Tales of Christmas: The Best Christmas Ever - An Angels Song. Larry Forkner. 211p. 1995. write for info. (*1-887856-01-3*) Badger Mtn.

***Two Tales of Crow & Sparrow: A Freudian Folkloristic Essay on Caste & Untouchability.** Alan Dundes. LC 97-25277. 1997. write for info. (*0-8476-8456-3*); pap. write for info. (*0-8476-8457-1*) Rowman.

Two Tales of the East Indies: The Last House in the World & The Counselor. Beb Vuyk & H. J. Friedericy. Tr. by Andre Lefevere & Hans Koning from DUT. LC 83-4812. (Library of the Indies). 216p. 1983. lib. bdg. 27.50 (*0-87023-403-X*) U of Mass Pr.

***Two Tales to Skin a Cat: Secrets Between a Husband & Wife & Real Men Don't Cry.** Ruth James. 132p. (Orig.). 1996. pap. 14.00 (*1-889570-00-1*) ISSA Inc.

Two Talmuds Compared Vol. IA: Tractate Berakhot & the Division of Appointed Times in the Talmud of the Land of Israel & the Talmud of Babylonia: Tractate Berakhot. Jacob Neusner. LC 96-3363. (South Florida Academic Commentary Ser.). 288p. (C). 1996. 89.95 (*0-7885-0255-7*, 243060) Scholars Pr GA.

Two Talmuds Compared Vol. IB: Tractate Berakhot & the Division of Appointed Times in the Talmud of the Land of Israel & the Talmud of Babylonia: Tractate Shabbat. Jacob Neusner. LC 96-3363. (South Florida Academic Commentary Ser.). 473p. (C). 1996. 114.95 (*0-7885-0241-7*, 243059) Scholars Pr GA.

Two Talmuds Compared Vol. IC: Tractate Berakhot & the Division of Appointed Times in the Talmud of the Land of Israel & the Talmud of Babylonia: Tractate Erubin. Jacob Neusner. LC 96-3363. (South Florida Academic Commentary Ser.). 292p. (C). 1996. 89.95 (*0-7885-0263-8*, 243062) Scholars Pr GA.

Two Talmuds Compared Vol. ID: Tractate Berakhot & the Division of Appointed Times in the Talmud of the Land of Israel & the Talmud of Babylonia: Tractates Yoma & Sukkah. Jacob Neusner. LC 96-3363. (South Florida Academic Commentary Ser.). 322p. (C). 1996. 94.95 (*0-7885-0264-6*, 243063) Scholars Pr GA.

Two Talmuds Compared Vol. IIA: The Division of Women in the Talmud of the Land of Israel & the Talmud of Babylonia: Tractates Yebamot & Ketubot. Jacob Neusner. LC 96-3363. (South Florida Academic Commentary Ser.: No. 53). 494p. (C). 1996. 119.95 (*0-7885-0233-6*, 243053) Scholars Pr GA.

Two Talmuds Compared Vol. IIB: The Division of Women in the Talmud of the Land of Israel & the Talmud of Babylonia: Tractates Nedarim, Nazir & Sotah. Jacob Neusner. LC 96-3363. (South Florida Academic Commentary Ser.). 494p. (C). 1996. 119.95 (*0-7885-0234-4*, 243054) Scholars Pr GA.

Two Talmuds Compared Vol. IIC: The Division of Women in the Talmud of the Land of Israel & the Talmud of Babylonia: Tractates Qiddushin & Gittin. Jacob Neusner. LC 96-3363. (South Florida Academic Commentary Ser.). 522p. (C). 1996. 129.95 (*0-7885-0235-2*, 243055) Scholars Pr GA.

Two Talmuds Compared Vol. IIIA: The Division of Damages in the Talmud of the Land of Israel & the Talmud of Babylonia: Tractates Baba Qamma & Baba Mesia. Jacob Neusner. LC 96-3363. (South Florida Academic Commentary Ser.). 548p. (C). 1996. 129.95 (*0-7885-0236-0*, 243056) Scholars Pr GA.

Two Talmuds Compared Vol. IIIB: The Division of Damages in the Talmud of the Land of Israel & the Talmud of Babylonia: Tractates Baba Batra & Niddah. Jacob Neusner. LC 96-3363. (South Florida Academic Commentary Ser.). 476p. (C). 1996. 114.95 (*0-7885-0237-9*, 243057) Scholars Pr GA.

Two Talmuds Compared Vol. IIIC: The Division of Damages in the Talmud of the Land of Israel & the Talmud of Babylonia: Tractates Sanhedrin & Makkot. Jacob Neusner. LC 96-3363. (South Florida Academic Commentary Ser.). 424p. (C). 1996. 109.95 (*0-7885-0238-7*, 243058) Scholars Pr GA.

Two Talmuds Compared Vol. IIID: The Division of Damages in the Talmud of the Land of Israel & the Talmud of Babylonia: Tractates Shebuot, Abodah Zarah & Horayot. Jacob Neusner. LC 96-3363. (South Florida Academic Commentary Ser.). 392p. (C). 1996. 104.95 (*0-7885-0256-5*, 243061) Scholars Pr GA.

***Two Talmuds Compared, I. Tractate Berakhot & the Division of Appointed Times in the Talmud of the Land of Israel & the Talmud of Babylonia Pt. I, Vol. E: E. Tractate Pesahim.** Jacob Neusner. (University of South Florida Academic Commentary Ser.). 363p. 1996. 99.95 (*0-7885-0265-4*, 243064) Scholars Pr GA.

***Two Talmuds Compared, I. Tractate Berakhot & the Division of Appointed Times in the Talmud of the Land of Israel & the Talmud of Babylonia Pt. I, Vol. F: F. Tractates, Taanit, Magilah.** Jacob Neusner. (University of South Florida Academic Commentary Ser.). 414p. 1996. 104.95 (*0-7885-0266-2*, 243065) Scholars Pr GA.

***Two Talmuds Compared, I. Tractate Berakhot & the Division of Appointed Times in the Talmud of the Land of Israel & the Talmud of Babylonia Pt. I, Vol. G: G. Rosh Hashanah, Hagigah & Moed Qatan.** Jacob Neusner. (University of South Florida Academic Commentary Ser.). 310p. 1996. 89.95 (*0-7885-0267-0*, 243066) Scholars Pr GA.

Two Tamil Folk Tales: The Story of King Matanakama, the Story of Peacock Ravana. Tr. by Kamil V. Zvelebil. (C). 1987. 21.50 (*81-208-0212-8*, Pub. by Motilal Banarsidass II) S Asia.

Two Targums of Esther. Tr. by Bernard Grossfeld from ARC. (Aramaic Bible Ser.: No. 18). 225p. 1991. text ed. 65.00 (0-8146-5454-1) Liturgical Pr.

Two Teenagers in Twenty: Writings by Gay & Lesbian Youth. Ed. by Ann Heron. LC 94-9761. 186p. (YA). (gr. 8-12). 1995. pap. 9.95 (1-55583-282-2) Alyson Pubns.

***Two Tenebrae Readings & Services.** Richard A. Dinges. 24p. (Orig.). 1997. pap. 4.50 (0-7880-0757-2) CSS OH.

Two Terminal Archaic/Early Woodland Sites in Central Michigan. Scott G. Beld. (Technical Reports: No. 22). xii, 140p. (Orig.). (C). 1992. pap. 12.00 (0-915703-27-0) U Mich Mus Anthro.

***Two Testaments.** 1997. write for info. (1-56476-610-1, Victor Bks) Chariot Victor.

Two Testaments, One Bible: A Study of the Theological Relationship Between the Old & New Testaments. rev. ed. David L. Baker. LC 91-31817. 304p. 1992. pap. 19.99 (0-8308-1765-4, 1765) InterVarsity.

***Two Texas Hearts.** Jodi Thomas. 352p. 1997. mass mkt. 5.99 (0-515-12099-5) Jove Pubns.

Two Thackerays: Anne Thackeray Richie's Centenary Biographical Introductions to the Works of William Makepeace Thackeray, 2 vols. Peter L. Shillingburg & Julia Maxey. LC 85-48065. (Studies in the Nineteenth Century: No. 5). 1988. Set. 165.00 (0-404-61483-3) AMS Pr.

Two Theban Monuments from the Reign of Amenhotep II. Charles C. Van Siclen, III. (Illus.). 46p. 1982. pap. text ed. 10.00 (0-933175-01-9) Van Siclen Bks.

Two Theological Languages & Other Essays by George Grant et Al. George Grant et al. Ed. by Wayne Whillier. LC 90-31387. (Toronto Studies in Theology: Vol. 43). 176p. 1990. lib. bdg. 79.95 (0-88946-882-6) E Mellen.

Two Thieves. Theodore F. Powys. LC 79-167466. (Short Story Index Reprint Ser.). 1977. reprint ed. 20.95 (0-8369-3992-1) Ayer.

***2000.** Joan MacLeod. 128p. 1997. pap. 10.95 (0-88922-373-4, Pub. by Talonbooks CN) Genl Dist Srvs.

***Two Thousand.** Betsy C. Maestro. Date not set. write for info. (0-688-14548-5); lib. bdg. write for info. (0-688-14549-3) Lothrop.

Two Thousand. Pablo Neruda. Tr. by Richard Schaaf from SPA. LC 92-70941. 88p. (Orig.). 1992. pap. 10.95 (0-9632363-0-X) Azul Edits.

***2000.** Pablo Neruda. 1997. pap. 10.95 (1-885214-11-1) Azul Edits.

***2000 A. D. Are You Ready?** Peter Lalonde & Paul Lalonde. 192p. 1997. pap. 12.99 (0-7852-7188-0) Nelson.

***2000 & Beyond.** Mark Finley. LC 96-31274. 1996. pap. 1.99 (0-8163-1361-X) Pacific Pr Pub Assn.

***2000 & Beyond.** Larry King. 304p. 1997. 23.00 (0-06-017457-9) HarpC.

Two Thousand & One: A Space Odyssey. Arthur C. Clarke. 1968. pap. 3.95 (0-451-15580-7, Sig) NAL-Dutton.

Two Thousand & One: A Space Odyssey. large type ed. Arthur C. Clarke. LC 94-29899. 1994. lib. bdg. 22.95 (0-8161-7486-5, GK Hall) Thorndike Pr.

Two Thousand & One Nights, Vol. 1. Yukinobu Hoshino. Ed. by Seiji Horibuchi. Tr. by Fred Burke from JPN. (Illus.). 72p. (Orig.). 1990. pap. 3.75 (0-929279-69-7) Viz Commns Inc.

Two Thousand & One Nights, Vol. 2. Yukinobu Hoshino. Ed. by Seiji Horibuchi. Tr. by Fred Burke from JPN. (Illus.). 80p. (Orig.). 1990. pap. 3.95 (0-929279-70-0) Viz Commns Inc.

Two Thousand & One Nights, Vol. 3. Yukinobu Hoshino. Ed. by Seiji Horibuchi. Tr. by Fred Burke from JPN. (Illus.). 80p. (Orig.). 1990. pap. 3.95 (0-929279-71-9) Viz Commns Inc.

Two Thousand & One Nights, Vol. 4. Yukinobu Hoshino. Ed. by Seiji Horibuchi. Tr. by Fred Burke from JPN. (Illus.). 72p. (Orig.). 1990. pap. 3.75 (0-929279-72-7) Viz Commns Inc.

Two Thousand & One Nights, Vol. 5. Yukinobu Hoshino. Ed. by Seiji Horibuchi. Tr. by Fred Burke from JPN. (Illus.). 72p. (Orig.). 1990. pap. 3.75 (0-929279-73-5) Viz Commns Inc.

Two Thousand & One Nights, Vol. 6. Yukinobu Hoshino. Ed. by Seiji Horibuchi. Tr. by Fred Burke from JPN. (Illus.). 80p. (Orig.). 1990. pap. 4.25 (0-929279-74-3) Viz Commns Inc.

Two Thousand & One Nights, Vol. 7. Yukinobu Hoshino. Ed. by Seiji Horibuchi. Tr. by Fred Burke from JPN. (Illus.). 80p. (Orig.). 1991. pap. 4.25 (0-929279-26-3) Viz Commns Inc.

Two Thousand & One Nights, Vol. 8. Yukinobu Hoshino. Ed. by Seiji Horibuchi. Tr. by Fred Burke from JPN. (Illus.). 72p. (Orig.). 1991. pap. 4.25 (0-929279-11-5) Viz Commns Inc.

Two Thousand & One Nights, Vol. 9. Yukinobu Hoshino. Ed. by Seiji Horibuchi. Tr. by Fred Burke from JPN. (Illus.). 72p. (Orig.). 1991. pap. 4.25 (0-929279-12-3) Viz Commns Inc.

Two Thousand & One Nights, Vol. 10. Yukinobu Hoshino. Ed. by Seiji Horibuchi. Tr. by Fred Burke from JPN. (Illus.). 72p. (Orig.). 1991. pap. 4.25 (0-929279-13-1) Viz Commns Inc.

Two Thousand & One the Church in Crisis. Leonidas C. Contos. 60p. (C). 1981. pap. 2.95 (0-916586-46-4) Holy Cross Orthodox.

Two Thousand & One Winning Strategies for Interpersonal Effectiveness. Kenneth R Schock. 1991. pap. 33.44 (0-685-50188-4) Sales Focus.

Two Thousand & Two Things to Do on a Date. Cyndi Haynes & Dale Edwards. 128p. 1992. pap. 5.95 (1-55850-131-2) Adams Media.

Two Thousand & Two Ways to Say "I Love You" Cyndi Haynes & Dale Edwards. 1995. pap. 5.95 (1-55850-437-0) Adams Media.

Two Thousand Baby Names. Nahda Salah. (Dual Language Ser.). 202p. 1990. 6.00 (1-887584-02-1) Intl Prom Art.

2000 Early Advertising Cuts. 4th ed. Clarence P. Hornung. LC 95-6701. (Pictorial Archive Ser.). 1995. write for info. (0-486-28843-9) Dover.

Two Thousand Eight Hundred & Fifty House & Garden Plants. Rob Herwig. 1987. 19.99 (0-517-48688-1) Random Hse Value.

***2011: The Evacuation of Planet Earth.** G. Cope Schellhorn. 260p. (Orig.). 1997. pap. 14.95 (1-881852-16-4) Horus Hse Pr.

Two Thousand Five Hundred Anecdotes for All Occasions. Edmund Fuller. 1990. 10.99 (0-517-05576-7) Random Hse Value.

2548 Best Things Anybody Ever Said. Robert Byrne. 1996. 12.98 (0-88365-960-3) Galahad Bks.

Two Thousand Five Hundred Palabras Mas Usadas en Ingles: Cortina Method: 2500 Most Common English Words. Cortina Staff. (Cortina Language Ser.). 145p. (SPA.). 1991. pap. 4.95 (0-8050-1890-5) H Holt & Co.

Two Thousand Five Hundred Solved Problems in Fluid Mechanics & Hydraulics. rev. ed. Jack B. Evett & Cheng Liu. (Schaum's Solved Problems Ser.). 1992. pap. text ed. 24.95 (0-07-019784-9) McGraw.

***2040.** Erica Jong. Date not set. mass mkt. write for info. (0-06-109180-4, Harp PBks) HarpC.

***2048: The Future of Privacy.** Simson Garfinkel. 336p. 1997. 22.95 (1-888869-23-2) HardWired.

Two Thousand Forty-One: Twelve Stories about the Future by Top Science Fiction Writers. Jane Yolen. 240p. (YA). 1994. mass mkt. 4.50 (0-440-21898-5) Dell.

Two Thousand Four Hundred Jokes to Brighten Your Speeches. Robert Orben. 1989. pap. 10.00 (0-87980-425-4) Wilshire.

Two Thousand Hard to Locate Latin Forms. Stanford M. Miller. 18p. (Orig.). (LAT.). 1992. spiral bd. 2.20 (0-939507-21-8, B104) Amer Classical.

Two Thousand Maniacs. 2nd rev. ed. Herschell G. Lewis. (Illus.). 144p. 1988. pap. 9.95 (0-938782-08-8) Fantaco.

Two Thousand Miles on the Appalachian Trail. Donald J. Fortunato. (Illus.). 160p. (Orig.). 1991. reprint ed. pap. 8.95 (0-9613494-0-9) Fortunato Bks.

Two Thousand Miles' Ride Through the Argentine Provinces, 2 Vols. William MacCann. LC 70-128433. reprint ed. Set. 97.00 (0-404-04102-7) AMS Pr.

2000 More Insults. Louis A. Safian. 1984. mass mkt. 4.50 (0-671-64552-8) PB.

Two Thousand Most Challenging & Obscure Words. Norman W. Schur. 1994. 11.98 (0-88365-848-8) Galahad Bks.

2,000 Movies of the 1940s. Cross. 1986. (0-517-47274-0) Random Hse Value.

Two Thousand New Laughs for Speakers. Robert Orben. 1980. pap. 7.00 (0-87980-382-7) Wilshire.

2095. Jon Scieszka. (Time Warp Trio Ser.). (Illus.). 80p. (J). (gr. 2-6). 1995. pap. 11.99 (0-670-85795-5) Viking Child Bks.

2095. Jon Scieszka. 1997. pap. 3.50 (0-14-037191-5) Viking Penguin.

***2095.** Jon Scieszka. 1997. pap. 42.00 (0-14-774411-3) Viking Penguin.

2000 Notable American Men. Ed. by J. M. Evans. 381p. 1992. 125.00 (0-934544-62-X); 125.00 (0-934544-71-9) Am Biog Inst.

Two Thousand Notable American Women. Ed. by J. M. Evans. (Illus.). 500p. 1989. 135.00 (0-934544-45-X) Am Biog Inst.

2000 Notable American Women. 2nd ed. Ed. by J. M. Evans. (Illus.). 511p. 1990. 125.00 (0-934544-58-1) Am Biog Inst.

2000 Notable American Women. 3rd ed. Ed. by J. M. Evans. (Illus.). 479p. 1991. 125.00 (0-934544-60-3) Am Biog Inst.

2000 Notable American Women. 4th ed. Ed. by J. M. Evans. (Illus.). 503p. 1992. 125.00 (0-934544-61-1) Am Biog Inst.

2000 Notable American Women. 5th ed. Ed. by J. M. Evans. (Illus.). 429p. 1992. 125.00 (0-934544-69-7) Am Biog Inst.

2000 Notable American Women. 6th ed. Ed. by J. M. Evans. (Illus.). 380p. 1994. 125.00 (0-614-14548-1) Am Biog Inst.

2000 Notable American Women. 7th ed. Ed. by J. M. Evans. 382p. 1995. 125.00 (0-614-14549-X) Am Biog Inst.

Two Thousand Notable Americans. 3rd ed. Ed. by J. M. Evans. LC 83-73395. (Illus.). 500p. 1989. 135.00 (0-934544-39-5) Am Biog Inst.

Two Thousand One: A Space Odyssey. Arthur C. Clarke & Stanley Kubrick. 1994. lib. bdg. 24.95 (1-56849-417-3) Buccaneer Bks.

Two Thousand One: A Space Odyssey. Arthur C. Clarke. 240p. 1968. pap. 4.99 (0-451-45063-9, ROC) NAL-Dutton.

Two Thousand One: A Space Odyssey. 25th anniversary ed. Arthur C. Clarke. 240p. 1993. pap. 12.95 (0-451-45273-9, ROC) NAL-Dutton.

Two Thousand One: A Sports Odyssey Hypnosis Cybernetics Conditioning Biofeedback. Judd Biasiotto. 160p. (Orig.). 1984. pap. 8.00 (0-933079-04-4) World Class Enterprises.

2001: Preparing Families for the Future: NCFR Presidential Report. Ed. by David H. Olson & Meredith K. Hanson. (Illus.). 40p. (Orig.). (C). 1990. pap. text ed. 13.00 (0-916174-26-3) Natl Coun Family.

Two Thousand One: The Next Generation in Victim Assistance. Nova. 152p. 1994. per. 24.95 (0-8403-9540-X) Kendall-Hunt.

2001: Filming the Future. Piers Bizony. (Illus.). 168p. 1995. pap. 19.95 (1-85410-365-2, Pub. by Aurum Pr UK) London Brdge.

2001 French & English Idioms: Idiotismes Francais et Anglais 2001. 2nd ed. Francois Denoeu & Frances Sices. (ENG & FRE.). 1996. pap. text ed. 13.95 (0-8120-9024-1) Barron.

2001 German & English Idioms. Henry Strutz. (2001 Idioms Ser.). 670p. 1995. pap. 12.95 (0-8120-9009-8) Barron.

Two Thousand One Hundred Laughs for All Occasions. Robert Orben. LC 82-45448. 240p. 1986. pap. 9.95 (0-385-23488-0) Doubleday.

Two Thousand One Hundred-Seven Curious Word Origins, Sayings & Expressions. Charles E. Funk. 1993. 14.98 (0-88365-845-3) Galahad Bks.

Two Thousand One Hundred Victorian Monograms. Karl Klimsch. LC 94-13694. (Pictorial Archive Ser.). Orig. Title: Monogramme Entworfen & Ausgef Uhrt. 1994. pap. write for info. (0-486-28301-1) Dover.

2001 Italian & English Idioms (2001 Locuzione Italiane e Inglese) 2nd ed. D. Gobetti et al. LC 81-66403. (ENG & ITA.). 1996. pap. 13.95 (0-8120-9030-6) Barron.

2001 Japanese/English Idioms. Carol Akiyama. 1996. pap. text ed. 13.95 (0-8120-9433-6) Barron.

Two Thousand One Nights. Yokinobu Hoshino. 1996. pap. 16.95 (1-56931-056-4) Viz Commns Inc.

2001 on the Edge of Eternity. Jack Van Impe. 204p. 1996. pap. 12.99 (0-8499-3891-0) Word Pub.

***2001 Questions & Answers about the Year 2000 Problem.** William N. Franklin. (Illus.). 750p. 1997. pap. 94.95 (1-884051-20-0) Metro Info Systs.

***2001 Russian & English Idioms.** Agnes Arany-Makkai. (Two Thousand One Idioms Ser.). 608p. 1997. pap. text ed. 14.95 (0-8120-9532-4) Barron.

Two Thousand One Southern Superstitions. 2.95 (0-936672-34-X) Aerial Photo.

2001 Spanish & English Idioms: 2001 Modismos Espanoles y Ingleses. 2nd ed. Eugen Saviano & Lynn W. Winget. LC 75-11955. (2001 Idioms Ser.). 670p. (ENG & SPA.). 1995. pap. text ed. 12.95 (0-8120-9028-4) Barron.

***2,001 Things to Do Before You Die.** Dane Sherwood. LC 96-39971. 1997. 9.95 (0-06-273490-3, PL) HarpC.

2,001 Winning Ads for Real Estate. 3rd ed. Steve Kennedy & Deborah Johnson. LC 95-25929. (Illus.). 320p. 1996. reprint ed. pap. 29.95 (1-887145-04-4) Argyle Pr NV.

Two Thousand One Winning Sales Strategies. 2nd ed. Kenneth R. Schock. Ed. by Kenneth Hanford. (Illus.). 368p. (C). 1991. reprint ed. pap. text ed. 33.44 (0-923168-00-1) Sales Focus.

Two Thousand Plus Creative Dates: Dating Ideas & Activities. David Olsen. Ed. by Jean Akens et al. (Illus.). 52p. (Orig.). 1991. pap. 5.95 (0-925685-99-2) Canyon Country Pubns.

Two-Thousand-Pound Goldfish. Betsy C. Byars. LC 81-48652. 160p. (YA). (gr. 5 up). 1982. lib. bdg. 14.89 (0-06-020890-2) HarpC Child Bks.

***Two Thousand Seasons.** Armah. 1980. pap. 8.95 (0-435-90218-0) Third World.

Two Thousand Seven Hundred Fifteen One-Line Quotations for Speakers, Writers & Raconteurs. Edward F. Murphy. 1996. 8.99 (0-517-68236-2) Random Hse Value.

***2605 Decorative Letters & Initials, 3 vols., Set.** Grafton. (Illus.). pap. 14.85 (0-486-26572-2) Dover.

2069: A Science Fiction Trilogy. Larry Townsend. 1995. reprint ed. mass mkt. 6.95 (1-56333-244-2, Badboy) Masquerade.

Two Thousand Sixty-One: Odyssey Three. Arthur C. Clarke. 288p. 1989. mass mkt. 5.95 (0-345-35879-1, Del Rey) Ballantine.

***2061: Odyssey Three.** Arthur C. Clarke. 1997. pap. 10.00 (0-345-41398-9) Ballantine.

Two Thousand Solved Problems in Discrete Mathematics. Seymour Lipschutz. (Schaum's Solved Problems Ser.). 544p. 1992. pap. text ed. 16.95 (0-07-038031-7) McGraw.

Two Thousand Solved Problems in Statistics: A Workbook for Writers, Form C. Stephen Bernstein. (Schaum's Solved Problems Ser.). 1992. pap. text ed. write for info. (0-07-005023-6) McGraw.

Two Thousand Sure Fire Jokes for Speakers & Writers. Robert Orben. LC 86-24240. 240p. 1986. pap. 9.95 (0-385-23465-1) Doubleday.

Two Thousand Ten: Odyssey Two. Arthur C. Clarke. 352p. 1984. mass mkt. 5.95 (0-345-30306-7, Del Rey) Ballantine.

***2010: Odyssey Two.** Arthur C. Clarke. 1997. pap. 10.00 (0-345-41397-0) Ballantine.

Two-Thousand Ten The America System: Resurrection or Revolution? Louis F. Bush. LC 92-96824. 69p. (Orig.). (C). 1992. pap. text ed. 6.00 (0-9633936-0-X) Scorpio OR.

***2036 A. D. the Return.** 267p. (Orig.). 1996. pap. 10.00 (0-9655952-0-X) W L Sharon.

***2000 True Type Fonts.** 64p. pap. 39.95 incl. cd-rom (1-57176-053-9) Walnut Creek.

2025 Scenarios of U. S. & Global Society Reshaped by Science & Technology. Joseph F. Contes et al. LC 96-18376. (Illus.). 540p. 1996. 27.95 (1-886939-09-8) Oak Hill Pr OH.

2020 Vision - Health in the 21st Century. Institute of Medicine Staff. 136p. (Orig.). 1996. pap. text ed. 32.00 (0-309-05488-5) Natl Acad Pr.

Two Thousand Two Gems of Educational Wit & Humor. P. Susan Mamchak & Steven R. Mamchak. LC 93-47894. 1994. write for info. (0-13-489683-1, Parker Publishing Co) P-H.

Two Thousand Two Hundred & One Fascinating Facts, 2 vols. in 1. David Louis. 1988. 11.99 (0-517-39574-6) Random Hse Value.

Two Thousand Two Hundred Eighty-Six Traditional Stencil Designs. H. Roessing. (Illus.). 128p. reprint ed. pap. 6.95 (0-486-26845-4) Dover.

2,200 Quotations from the Writings of Charles H. Spurgeon: Arranged Topically or Textually & Indexed by Subject, Scripture & People. Charles H. Spurgeon. LC 95-31421. 400p. (Orig.). (YA). (gr. 10). 1996. reprint ed. pap. 19.99 (0-8010-5365-X) Baker Bks.

***2002 Romantic Ideas.** Cyndi Haynes & Dale Edwards. Date not set. pap. 5.95 (1-55850-819-8) Adams Media.

Two Thousand Two Things to Do on a Date: The Dater's Handbook. Cyndi Haynes & Dale Edwards. LC 91-65299. 116p. 1991. pap. 4.95 (0-9629118-0-1) Todd & Tweedwrth.

2002 Ways to Find, Attract, & Keep a Mate. Cyndi Haynes & Dale Edwards. 1996. pap. 5.95 (1-55850-555-5) Adams Media.

***2,000 Voices: Young Adolescents' Perceptions & Curriculum Implications.** Cynthia S. Mee. LC 97-5315. 1997. pap. write for info. (1-56090-116-0) Natl Middle Schl.

2000-Year History of the Haga-Helgoy & Krick-Keller Families: Ancestors & Descendants. Enoch J. Haga. LC 94-72562. (Illus.). xviii, 296p. (Orig.). 1994. pap. 50.00 (1-885794-01-0) E Haga Pub.

2000 Years: Germany, Vol. 3. enl. rev. ed. Gerhart Hoffmeister & Frederic C. Tubach. LC 60-53139. (German Library). (Illus.). 312p. (C). 1992. pap. text ed. 19.95 (0-8264-0601-7) Continuum.

2000 Years of Disbelief: Famous People with the Courage to Doubt. James A. Haught. (Illus.). 325p. 1996. 26.95 (1-57392-067-3) Prometheus Bks.

Two Thousand Years of Tapestry Weaving: A Loan Exhibition. (Illus.). 86p. 1952. pap. 2.50 (0-317-13607-0) Wadsworth Atheneum.

Two Tickets for Tangier. Mason. 1976. 23.95 (0-89190-354-2) Amereon Ltd.

Two Tickets to Freedom: The True Story of Ellen & William Craft, Fugitive Slaves. Florence B. Freedman. (Illus.). 96p. (J). (gr. 4 up). 1989. 12.95 (0-87226-330-4); pap. 5.95 (0-87226-221-9) P Bedrick Bks.

Two Tickets to the Revolution, Please. J. W. Leach. 105p. (Orig.). Date not set. pap. write for info. (0-9641752-4-X) J L Loving.

Two-Tier Compensation Structures: Their Impact on Unions, Employers, & Employees. James E. Martin. LC 89-48881. 280p. 1990. text ed. 25.00 (0-88099-087-2); pap. text ed. 15.00 (0-88099-088-0) W E Upjohn.

Two Times in the Stream. Charles Lupia. 100p. 1993. pap. 5.00 (0-9637558-0-3) Celnote Pr.

2 x 2 = Boo! Loreen Leedy. (Illus.). (J). (ps-3). 1996. pap. 6.95 (0-8234-1272-5) Holiday.

2 x 2 = BOO! A Set of Spooky Multiplication Stories. Loreen Leedy. LC 94-46711. (Illus.). 32p. (J). (gr. k-3). 1995. lib. bdg. 15.95 (0-8234-1190-7) Holiday.

Two Times Two Equals Four. Anatolii Shteiger. LC 80-54026. (Russica Poetry Ser.: No. 1). 104p. (Orig.). (RUS.). 1982. pap. 6.95 (0-89830-029-0) Russica Pubs.

Two-Timing Man. Roberta Leigh. 1993. mass mkt. 2.99 (0-373-11609-8, 1-11609-4) Harlequin Bks.

Two-Timing Man. large type ed. Roberta Leigh. (Harlequin Ser.). 1993. lib. bdg. 18.95 (0-263-13423-7) Thorndike Pr.

Two Tipperarys: The National & Local Politics - Devolution & Determination - of the Unique 1838 Division into Two Ridings, & the Aftermath. Donal A. Murphy. (Illus.). 342p. 1994. pap. 29.95 (0-946327-14-9, Pub. by Relay Pubns IE) Irish Bks Media.

Two Titans: Mardersteig & Tschichold: a Study in Contrasts, No. 59. Hans Schmoller. Ed. by Abe Lerner. (Typophile Chap Bks.). (Illus.). 78p. 1990. 27.50 (0-945074-01-8) Dawsons.

Two to Begin With: The True Story of Identical Twins. Helen Campbell. (Illus.). 64p. 1995. text ed. 11.00 (0-8059-3713-7) Dorrance.

Two to Conquer. Marion Zimmer Bradley. (Darkover Ser.). (Orig.). 1980. mass mkt. 4.99 (0-88677-174-9) DAW Bks.

Two to Tangle: Two One Act Plays. Forrest Kleinman. 45p. (Orig.). 1994. pap. 4.00 (1-57514-238-4, 1155) Encore Perform Pub.

Two to Tango. Kristina Logan. (Romance Ser.: No. 852). 1992. pap. 2.69 (0-373-08852-3, 5-08852-1) Silhouette.

Two to Tango. large type ed. Kristina Logan. 240p. 1992. reprint ed. lib. bdg. 13.95 (1-56054-461-9) Thorndike Pr.

***Two to Tango: Bibliography - Discography with an Introduction.** Oscar De Buenosaires. 133p. (Orig.). 1997. lib. bdg. 16.00 (0-929928-20-2) Fog Pubns.

Two to Twenty-Two Days in Great Britain: The Itinerary Planner, 1991 Edition. Rick Steves. LC 91-7563. (Two to Twenty-Two Days Ser.). (Illus.). 192p. 1991. 9.95 (0-945465-85-8) John Muir.

Two to Twenty-Two Days in Norway, Sweden, & Denmark: The Itinerary Planner, 1991 Edition. Rick Steves. LC 90-28566. (Two to Twenty-Two Days Ser.). (Illus.). 184p. 1991. pap. 9.95 (0-945465-87-4) John Muir.

Two Tocquevilles, Father & Son: Herve & Alexis de Tocqueville on the Coming of the French Revolution. Ed. by Robert R. Palmer. (Illus.). 264p. 1987. text ed. 39.50 (0-691-05495-9) Princeton U Pr.

Two-ton Secret. Gail Jarrow. 144p. (J). (gr. 5). 1989. pap. 2.95 (0-380-75904-7, Camelot) Avon.

Two-Tone Set-Bells of Marquis Yi: Hubei Provincial Museum, Wuhan, China - University of California, San Diego, U. S. A., August 1988. Ed. by C. Y. Chen et al. 500p. (C). 1994. text ed. 130.00 (981-02-0740-9) World Scientific Pub.

Two Tone Story. George Marshall. (Illus.). 128p. (Orig.). 1997. pap. 16.95 (0-9518497-3-5, Pub. by S T Pubng UK) AK Pr Dist.

An Asterisk (*) at the beginning of an entry indicates that the title is appearing in BIP for the first time.

Two Towers. J. R. R. Tolkien. (Illus.). 368p. 1992. 30.00 (0-395-64739-8) HM.

Two Towers. anniversary ed. J. R. R. Tolkien. Date not set. write for info. (0-395-31266-3) HM.

Two Towers. large type ed. J. R. R. Tolkien. (Lord of the Rings Ser.: Pt. 2). (Illus.). 448p. 24.95 (1-85089-419-1, Pub. by ISIS UK) Transaction Pubs.

Two Towers, Vol. 2. J. R. R. Tolkien. 447p. 1986. mass mkt. 5.99 (0-345-33971-1, Del Rey) Ballantine.

Two Towers: Being the Second Part of the Lord of the Rings. J. R. R. Tolkien. (Illus.). 356p. 1988. 21.95 (0-395-48933-4); pap. 11.95 (0-395-27222-X) HM.

Two Town in Provence. M. F. K. Fisher. 1994. 24.00 (0-8446-6746-3) Peter Smith.

Two Towns in Germany: Commerce & the Urban Transformation. Norbert Dannhaeuser. LC 95-40690. (Contemporary Urban Studies). 328p. 1996. text ed. 65.00 (0-89789-458-8, Bergin & Garvey) Greenwood.

Two Towns in Provence: Map of Another Town & a Considerable Town. M. F. K. Fisher. LC 83-6901. (Illus.). 512p. 1983. pap. 16.00 (0-394-71631-0, Vin) Random.

Two Tracts on Cartomancy. Austin O. Spare. Ed. by Gavin Semple. 1997. pap. 39.95 (1-55818-344-2) Holmes Pub.

Two Traditions of Meditation in Ancient India. Johannes Bronkhorst. (Orig.). (C). 1993. text ed. 14.00 (81-208-1114-3, Pub. by Motilal Banarsidass II) S Asia.

Two Tragedies: Hippolyte & Marc Antoine. Robert Garnier. Ed. by Christine M. Hill & Mary G. Morrison. (Renaissance Library). 181p. (FRE.). (C). 1975. pap. 16.95 (0-485-12809-8, Pub. by Athlone Pr UK); text ed. 36.50 (0-485-13809-3, Pub. by Athlone Pr UK) Humanities.

***Two Trails: A Treasure Free Adventure.** John T. Trent. LC 97-11118. (Illus.). 96p. (J). (gr. 1-5). 1998. 15.99 (0-8499-1450-7) Tommy Nelson.

Two Trains Running. August Wilson. 128p. (Orig.). 1993. pap. 8.95 (0-452-26929-6, Plume) NAL-Dutton.

Two Travel Stories. Wendell Metzger. Ed. by Joyce Carbone. 48p. (Orig.). 1995. pap. 4.95 (1-878116-47-9) JVC Bks.

Two Travellers & Other Korean Short Stories. So Ki-won et al. Ed. by Korean National Commission for UNESCO. Tr. by Mun Sang-duk et al. from KOR. (Modern Korean Short Stories Ser.: No. 7). viii, 144p. 1983. 20.00 (0-89209-208-4) Pace Intl Res.

Two Treatises Concerning the Perservation of Eye-Sight. Walter Bailey. LC 74-28827. (English Experience Ser.: No. 709). 1975. reprint ed. 20.00 (90-221-0709-4) Walter J Johnson.

Two Treatises of Government. John Locke. Ed. by Mark Goldie. 298p. 1993. pap. 6.95 (0-460-87356-3, Everyman's Classic Lib) C E Tuttle.

Two Treatises of Government. John Locke. Ed. & Intro. by Thomas I. Cook. Bd. with Patriarcha. (Library of Classics: No. 2). 352p. 1970. Set pap. 17.95 (0-02-848500-9) Hafner.

Two Treatises of Government. rev. ed. John Locke. Ed. by Peter Laslett. (Cambridge Texts in the History of Political Thought Ser.). 200p. 1988. pap. text ed. 10.95 (0-521-35730-6) Cambridge U Pr.

Two Treatises of Government. 3rd rev. ed. John Locke. Ed. by Peter Laslett. (Cambridge Texts in the History of Political Thought Ser.). 200p. 1988. 27.95 (0-521-35448-X) Cambridge U Pr.

Two Treatises of Philo of Alexandria: A Commentary on De Gigantibus & Quod Deus Sit Immutabilis. David Winston & John Dillon. LC 82-786. (Brown Judaic Studies). 416p. (C). 1983. pap. 16.00 (0-89130-563-7, 14 00 25) Scholars Pr GA.

Two Treatises on the Accentuation of the Old Testament. rev. ed. William Wickes. 1970. 39.50 (0-87068-004-8) Ktav.

Two Treatises on the Christian Priesthood, 3 Vols. George Hickes. (Library of Anglo-Catholic Theology: No. 9). reprint ed. Set. 87.50 (0-404-52100-2) AMS Pr.

Two Trees. Arlene B. Petrosky. (Illus.). 62p. 1989. 16.95 (0-9623965-0-8) ABR Petrosky.

Two Trees. Ellen B. Voigt. 64p. 1994. pap. 8.95 (0-393-31100-7) Norton.

Two Trends in Modern Quaker Thought. Albert Fowler. LC 61-9979. (C). 1961. pap. 3.00 (0-87574-112-6) Pendle Hill.

Two Truths in the Madhyamika Philosophy of the Ge-luk-ba Order of Tibetan Buddhism. Guy Newland. 312p. 1992. 39.95 (0-937938-80-7); pap. 19.95 (0-937938-79-3) Snow Lion Pubns.

Two Tudor Interludes: The Interlude of Youth, Hick Scorner. Ed. by Ian Lancashire. LC 79-3123. (Revels Plays Ser.). 303p. reprint ed. pap. 86.40 (0-7837-0337-6, 2040656) Bks Demand.

Two Tudor Tragedies. Ed. & Intro. by Willaim Tydeman. 368p. 1992. pap. 12.95 (0-14-044531-5, Penguin Classics) Viking Penguin.

Two Twenty-One B: Studies in Sherlock Holmes. Ed. by Vincent Starrett. LC 93-4650. (Illus.). 272p. 1994. reprint ed. pap. 7.95 (1-883402-07-7) S&S Trade.

Two Twisted Topological Tales: Of Snakes & Their Attraction for the Double- Breasted Mattress Thrasher - an X-Rated Synopsis of the Volume Closed Strings in Closed Space-Time. Sean Sheeter. (Projective - Elliptic Geometry & Unified Space-Time Ser.: Vol. IIB). (Illus.). 180p. (Orig.). pap. 12.50 (0-9605378-3-X) Process Pr.

Two under Par. Kevin Henkes. LC 86-7556. (Illus.). 128p. (J). (gr. 2-6). 1987. 16.00 (0-688-06708-5) Greenwillow.

***Two Under Par.** Kevin Henkes. 1997. pap. 3.99 (0-14-038426-X) Viking Penguin.

Two under the Covers. Jean MacCready & Vicki Quade. (Illus.). (Orig.). 1981. pap. 2.95 (0-9602604-1-2) V Quade.

Two-Valued Iterative Systems of Mathematical Logic. Emil L. Post. (Annals of Mathematics Studies). 1941. pap. 25.00 (0-527-02721-9) Periodicals Srv.

Two Vanrevels. Booth Tarkington. 1975. lib. bdg. 15.80 (0-89966-175-0) Buccaneer Bks.

Two Vanrevels. Booth Tarkington. 16.95 (0-8488-1482-7) Amereon Ltd.

***Two Vermont Composers: The Collected Works of Elisha West & Justin Morgan.** Karl Kroeger. LC 56-5. (Music of the New American Nation Ser.: Vol. 7). 196p. 1997. text ed. 75.00 (0-8153-2405-7) Garland.

Two Verse Anthems for Six Voices & Six Viols (or Organ) "Almighty Lord" & "Bend down, O Lord, Thy Gracious Eyes" William White. Ed. by Patrice Connelly. (Baroque Ser.: No. 8). ii, 12p. 1994. pap. text ed. 16.00 (1-56571-098-3) PRB Prods.

Two Versions of Malory's Morte D'Arthur: Multiple Negation & the Editing of the Text. Ingrid Tieken-Boon Van Ostade. (Arthurian Studies: Vol. 35). 182p. (C). 1995. 53.00 (0-85991-437-2) Boydell & Brewer.

Two Versions of Mariano Azuela's "Los De Abajo" A Comparative Study. Thomas W. Renaldi. 1978. lib. bdg. 250.00 (0-8490-1396-8) Gordon Pr.

Two Versions of Waerferth's Translation of Gregory's Dialogues: An Old English Thesaurus. David Yerkes. LC 79-10546. (Old English Ser.). 1979. 32.50 (0-8020-5464-1) U of Toronto Pr.

Two Very Notable Commentaries, of the Originall of Turcks, Etc. Andrea Cambini. Tr. by J. Shute. LC 75-25772. (English Experience Ser.: No. 235). 1970. reprint ed. 45.00 (90-221-0235-1) Walter J Johnson.

Two Views of Freedom in Process Thought. George R. Lucas. LC 79-12287. (American Academy of Religion. Dissertation Ser.: No. 28). 186p. reprint ed. pap. 53.10 (0-7837-5415-9, 2045179) Bks Demand.

Two Views of Italy: Master Prints by Canaletto & Piranesi. Timothy Rub et al. (Illus.). 1995. pap. 14.00 (0-614-12958-3) Hood Mus Art.

Two Views of Siam: On the Eve of the Chakri Reformation. Nigel Brailey. (Illus.). 164p. (Orig.). (C). 1995. pap. 27.00 (1-870838-25-4, Pub. by Kiscadale UK) Weatherhill.

Two Villages: Story of Chelsea & Kensington. Mary C. Borer. (Illus.). 288p. 1974. 18.00 (0-491-01061-3) Transatl Arts.

Two Visions of the Way: A Study of the Wang Pi & the Ho-shang Kung Commentaries on the Lao-Tzu. Alan K. Chan. LC 89-78198. (SUNY Series in Chinese Philosophy & Culture). 314p. (C). 1991. text ed. 64.50 (0-7914-0455-2); pap. text ed. 21.95 (0-7914-0456-0) State U NY Pr.

Two Voices: A Father & Son Discuss Family & Faith. Jim Doyle & Brian Doyle. LC 96-11396. 192p. (Orig.). 1996. pap. 11.00 (0-89243-934-3) Liguori Pubns.

Two Voices of Indo-Anglian Poetry: A Stylistic Study. C. P. Sivadasan. (C). 1995. 15.00 (81-207-1619-1, Pub. by Sterling Plns Pvt II) S Asia.

Two Volume Brockhaus: Der Brockhaus in 2 Banden, 2 vols. Brockhaus. 1440p. (GER.). 1984. Set. 295.00 (0-8288-4412-7, M7327) Fr & Eur.

Two Voyagers at the Court of King Alfred. Christine E. Fell et al. (C). 1989. pap. 21.00 (0-900657-86-3, Pub. by W Sessions UK) St Mut.

Two Voyages to the South Seas. Helen Rosenman. 340p. 1992. pap. 29.95 (0-522-84432-4, Pub. by Melbourne Univ Pr AT) Paul & Co Pubs.

***Two Voyages to the South Seas.** Jules-Sebastien-Cesar Dumont d'Urville. Tr. & Retold by Helen Rosenman. LC 92-22735. (Illus.). 340p. 1992. reprint ed. pap. 96.90 (0-608-04395-8, 2065176) Bks Demand.

Two Voyages to the South Seas, 2 vols., Set. Dumont D'Urville. Ed. & Tr. by Helen Rosenman. LC 92-22735. 702p. 1987. boxed 110.00 (0-522-84338-7, Pub. by Melbourne Univ Pr AT) Paul & Co Pubs.

Two Way Bilingual Songs for Elementary School. Ursula O. Ronnholm. 41p. (J). (gr. k-12). 1987. Incl. cass. 8.00 incl. audio (0-941911-06-3) Two Way Bilingual.

Two-Way Cable Television: Experiences with Pilot Projects in North America, Japan, & Europe. Proceedings of a Symposium Held in Munich, Germany, April 27-29, 1977. Ed. by W. A. Kaiser et al. LC 77-13725. (Illus.). 1977. pap. 35.00 (0-387-08498-3) Spr-Verlag.

Two Way Cut. large type ed. Peter Turnbull. 1990. 25.99 (0-7089-2262-7) Ulverscroft.

Two-Way Mirror. David Meltzer. 1977. 6.95 (0-685-80005-9); 2.95 (0-685-80006-7) Oyez.

Two-Way Pitcher. Bonner. (YA). (gr. 7 up). lib. bdg. 7.19 (0-8313-0008-6) Lantern.

Two-Way Prayer. Clifton King. 91p. (Orig.). 1987. pap. 4.95 (0-87516-590-7) DeVorss.

Two-Way Street: The Klepsch Report on U. S. A. - Europe Arms Procurement. E. Klepsch & T. Normantoe. 95p. 1979. pap. 16.85 (0-08-027011-5, Pergamon Pr) Elsevier.

Two Way Stretch. Robert Maxwell. (Polemics Ser.). 96p. (Orig.). 1996. pap. 15.95 (1-85490-438-8) Academy Ed UK.

Two Way Toll. Zachery Klein. (Boston Mysteries Ser.). 1993. mass mkt. 4.99 (0-8041-1005-0) Ivy Books.

Two Ways - Commentary on the Gauri Vavs of Guru Ram Das. Ajaib Singh. Ed. by Russell Perkins & Judith Perkins. LC 85-50963. (Illus.). 232p. (Orig.). 1985. pap. 10.00 (0-89142-045-2) Sant Bani Ash.

Two Ways of Life & Death. Virginia B. Phelan. LC 90-3497. (Studies in Comparative Literature). 272p. 1990. reprint ed. 15.00 (0-8240-0050-1) Garland.

Two Ways of Praying. Paul Bradshaw. 160p. (Orig.). 1995. pap. 13.95 (0-687-42667-7) Abingdon.

Two Ways of the First Century Church. 2nd ed. David A. Anderson. LC 91-93081. 248p. 1989. 9.95 (0-9630958-0-3) D A Anderson.

Two Ways to Count to Ten. Ruby Dee. LC 86-33513. (Illus.). 32p. (J). (ps-2). 1990. pap. 5.95 (0-8050-1314-8, Owlet BYR) H Holt & Co.

***Two Ways to God.** Borchsenius. Date not set. 18.00 (0-85303-011-1, Pub. by Vallentine Mitchell UK) Intl Spec Bk.

Two Ways to Murder. large type ed. E. Radford & M. A. Radford. (Linford Mystery Library). 320p. 1995. pap. 15.99 (0-7089-7711-1, Linford) Ulverscroft.

Two Wedding & a Feud. Jenna McKnight. (American Romance Ser.). 1996. mass mkt. 3.75 (0-373-16628-1, 1-16628-9) Harlequin Bks.

Two Weddings & a Bride (Debut Author) Anne Eames. (Desire Ser.). 1996. mass mkt. 3.50 (0-373-05996-5) Silhouette.

Two Weeks in the Midday Sun: A Cannes Notebook. Roger Ebert. LC 87-25183. (Illus.). 192p. (Orig.). 1987. pap. 8.95 (0-8362-7942-5) Andrews & McMeel.

Two Weeks in the Yosemite & Vicinity. J. M. Buckley. (Illus.). 36p. reprint ed. pap. 3.95 (0-8466-0153-2, S153) Shorey.

Two Weeks Off. Kirk Robertson. (Illus.). 48p. (Orig.). 1984. pap. 5.00 (0-912449-11-X) Floating Island.

Two Weeks to a Tighter Tummy. Ellington Darden. LC 91-46775. 128p. 1992. pap. 9.95 (0-87833-790-3) Taylor Pub.

Two Weeks with the Psychic Surgeons. Marti Sladek. LC 76-45732. (Illus.). 1977. 12.95 (0-917816-01-3) Doma.

Two Were Prisoners. G. J. Parle. 493p. 1986. 35.00 (0-7223-1941-X, Pub. by A H S Ltd UK) St Mut.

Two Wheels: A Cycling Murder Mystery. Greg Moody. 256p. 1996. pap. 12.95 (1-884737-11-0) VeloPress.

Two Wheels & a Pair of Nuts. Harold Rainwater. LC 95-60238. 304p. (Orig.). 1995. pap. 10.95 (0-9645385-0-4) Wiregrass Pubs.

Two Wheels & a Taxi: A Slightly Daft Adventure in the Andes. Virginia Urrutia. (Illus.). 256p. 1987. 14.95 (0-89886-141-1) Mountaineers.

Two Wheels Around New Zealand: A Bicycle Journey on Friendly Roads. Scott Bischke. LC 89-35041. (Illus.). 286p. 1996. reprint ed. pap. 12.95 (0-9639705-1-8) Ecopress.

Two Wheels for Grover. Dan Elliott. LC 84-4732. (Sesame Street Start-to-Read Bks.). (Illus.). 40p. (J). (ps-3). 1984. lib. bdg. 6.99 (0-394-96586-8) Random Bks Yng Read.

Two Wheels to Florida: An East Coast Bicycling Adventure. Richard A. Sanford. Ed. by Janet Frick. LC 95-92037. (Illus.). 214p. (Orig.). 1995. pap. 14.95 (0-9645232-0-5) Next Experience.

Two Wheels to Panama. William Carroll. (Illus.). 144p. (Orig.). 1995. pap. 20.00 (0-910390-40-1) Auto Bk.

***2 Wheels, 2 Years, & 3 Continents.** Ralph W. Galen. (Illus.). 560p. (Orig.). 1997. pap. 15.95 (0-9612050-7-5) Spring Garden Pubns.

Two White Pebbles. Retold by Robert D. San Souci. LC 93-43952. (J). 1995. write for info. (0-8037-1640-0); lib. bdg. write for info. (0-8037-1641-9) Dial Bks Young.

Two Who Were There: A Biography of Stanley Nowak. Margaret C. Nowak. LC 88-39057. (Illus.). 276p. 1989. 39.95 (0-8143-1883-5); pap. 18.95 (0-8143-1878-9) Wayne St U Pr.

Two Willow Chairs. Jess Wells. 192p. (Orig.). 1987. pap. 8.95 (0-940721-01-5) Libr B Bks.

Two Willow Chairs. Jess Wells. 126p. (Orig.). 1991. reprint ed. pap. 8.95 (1-879427-05-2) Third Side Pr.

Two Wings to Veil My Face. Leon Forrest. LC 88-70789. 298p. 1988. pap. 8.95 (0-9614644-4-5) Another Chicago Pr.

Two Wings to Veil My Face. Leon Forrest. 296p. 1997. pap. 11.95 (1-55921-192-X, Asphodel Pr) Moyer Bell.

Two Wise Men & All the Rest Fools. LC 72-133752. (Tudor Facsimile Texts. Old English Plays Ser.: No. 135). reprint ed. 49.50 (0-404-53435-X) AMS Pr.

Two Witnesses. pap. 0.95 (0-937408-12-3) GMI Pubns Inc.

Two Witnesses. Gordon Lindsay. (Revelation Ser.: Vol. 6). 1962. 1.95 (0-89985-039-1) Christ for the Nations.

Two Witnesses. rev. ed. Lance B. Johnson. LC 91-93097. 386p. 1991. pap. write for info. (0-9631328-0-6) Come & See Minist.

Two Witnesses. 2nd rev. ed. Lance B. Johnson. 386p. 1994. 18.00 (0-9631328-1-4) Come & See Minist.

***Two Witnesses: The Holy-GRAM of Biblical Physics.** Dwayne Sheffield. 244p. 1996. pap. 12.95 (1-882330-29-3) Magni Co.

Two Witnesses at Gettysburg. Ed. by Gary W. Gallagher. (Illus.). 192p. (Orig.). (C). 1994. pap. text ed. 9.96 (1-881089-23-1) Brandywine Press.

Two Women Dancing: New & Selected Poems. Elizabeth Bartlett. Ed. by Carol Rumens. 224p. 9600. pap. 19.95 (1-85224-297-3, Pub. by Bloodaxe Bks UK) Dufour.

Two Women in a Birth. Daphne Marlatt & Betsy Warland. 170p. 1994. pap. 13.00 (1-55071-003-6) Guernica Editions.

Two Women in One. Nawal El-Saadawi. Tr. by Osman Nusairi & Jana Gough from ARA. 124p. 1991. reprint ed. pap. 9.95 (1-879679-01-9) Women Translation.

Two Women, Two Shores. M. McGuckian & Nuala Archer. (New Poets Ser.: Vol. 16). 64p. 1989. pap. 5.95 (0-932616-19-4) Brick Hse Bks.

***Two Women under Water.** Peggy Phillips, pseud. (Illus.). 224p. (Orig.). 1998. pap. 12.95 (1-56474-239-3) Fithian Pr.

Two-Word Sentence in Child Language Development: A Study Based on Evidence Provided by Dutch-Speaking Triplets. A. M. Schaerlaekens. 1973. text ed. 67.70 (90-279-2541-0) Mouton.

Two-Word Verbs in English. J. N. Hook. 198p. (Orig.). (C). 1981. pap. text ed. 12.00 (0-15-592506-7) HB Coll Pubs.

Two Works of Grace. H. M. Riggle. 56p. pap. 0.40 (0-686-29168-9); pap. 1.00 (0-686-29169-7) Faith Pub Hse.

Two Worlds. Marietta Barron. 93p. (Orig.). (J). (gr. 4-6). pap. 5.00 (0-88092-120-X) Royal Fireworks.

Two Worlds: First Meetings Between Maori & Europeans, 1642- 1772. Anne Salmond. (Illus.). 478p. 1992. text ed. 39.00 (0-8248-1467-3); pap. text ed. 24.95 (0-8248-1765-6) UH Pr.

Two Worlds: Literary Essays. Hakob Karapents. LC 92-9679. 400p. (ARM.). 1992. pap. 20.00 (0-9628715-2-4) Blue Crane Bks.

Two Worlds: Notes on the Death of Modernity in America & Russia. Thomas C. Oden. LC 91-37117. 168p. (Orig.). 1992. pap. 9.99 (0-8308-1763-8, 1763) InterVarsity.

***Two Worlds: Short Stories.** Theano Papazoglou-Margari. LC 93-86372. 184p. (Orig.). (GRE.). 1993. pap. text ed. 10.00 (0-918618-59-2) Pella Pub.

Two Worlds: The Protestant Culture of Nineteenth-Century Ontario. William Westfall. (McGill-Queen's Studies in the History of Religion). 288p. (C). 1990. reprint ed. pap. text ed. 18.95 (0-7735-0797-3, Pub. by McGill CN) U of Toronto Pr.

Two Worlds for Our Children. 2nd ed. Myron E. Gruenwald. (Illus.). 36p. 1985. pap. 3.50 (0-9601536-3-2) M E Gruenwald.

***Two Worlds in the Tennessee Mountains: Exploring the Origins of Appalachian Stereotypes.** David C. Hsiung. LC 96-42954. 224p. 1997. text ed. 32.95 (0-8131-2001-2) U Pr of Ky.

Two Worlds of Cotton: Colonialism & the Regional Economy in the French Soudan, 1800-1946. Richard Roberts. 1996. write for info. (0-8047-2652-3) Stanford U Pr.

Two Worlds of Helen Duncan. Ed. by Gena Brealey & Kay Hunter. 194p. (C). 1988. 35.00 (0-7212-0730-8, Pub. by Regency Press UK) St Mut.

Two Worlds of International Relations: Academics, Practitioners & the Trade in Ideas. Ed. by Christopher Hill & Pamela Beshoff. LC 94-6424. 240p. (C). 1994. pap. 17.95 (0-415-11323-7, B4703) Routledge.

Two Worlds of International Relations: Academics, Practitioners & the Trade in Ideas. Ed. by Christopher Hill & Pamela Beshoff. LC 94-6424. 256p. (C). (gr. 13). 1994. text ed. 62.95 (0-415-06970-X, A7693) Routledge.

Two Worlds of Islam: Interaction Between Southeast Asia & the Middle East. Fred R. Von der Mehden. LC 92-44707. 144p. 1993. pap. text ed. 14.95 (0-8130-1209-0); lib. bdg. 34.95 (0-8130-1208-2) U Press Fla.

Two Worlds of Joseph Race. large type ed. Steve Race. 1990. 25.99 (0-7089-2143-4) Ulverscroft.

Two Worlds of Judaism: The Israeli & American Experiences. Charles S. Liebman & Steven M. Cohen. LC 89-28455. 224p. (C). 1990. 35.00 (0-300-04726-6) Yale U Pr.

Two Worlds of Judaism: The Israeli & American Experiences. Charles S. Liebman & Steven M. Cohen. 213p. (C). 1992. reprint ed. pap. text ed. 15.00 (0-300-05231-6) Yale U Pr.

Two Worlds of Music. Berta Geissmar. LC 74-28326. Orig. Title: The Baton & the Jackboot. (Illus.). 327p. 1975. reprint ed. lib. bdg. 39.50 (0-306-70664-4) Da Capo.

Two Worlds of the Poet: New Perspectives on Vergil. Ed. by Robert M. Wilhelm & Howard Jones. LC 92-30789. (Classical Studies: Pedagogy Ser.). (Illus.). 524p. (ENG, FRE, GER, ITA & LAT.). (C). 1992. text ed. 49.95 (0-8143-2450-9) Wayne St U Pr.

Two Worlds of the Washo: An Indian Tribe of California & Nevada. Downs. 104p. (C). 1966. pap. text ed. 13.50 (0-03-056610-X) HB Coll Pubs.

Two Worlds of William March. Roy S. Simmonds. LC 83-1100. 387p. 1984. reprint ed. pap. 110.30 (0-608-01680-2, 2062336) Bks Demand.

Two Worlds, One Art: Literary Translation in Russia & America. Lauren G. Leighton. LC 90-28531. 292p. 1991. lib. bdg. 35.00 (0-87580-160-9) N Ill U Pr.

Two Worlds One Heart. Tom Butler. (Orig.). 1996. mass mkt. 5.99 (1-55197-053-8, Pub. by Comnwlth Pub CN) Partners Pubs Grp.

Two Worlds Walking: Short Stories, Essays, & Poetry by Writers with Mixed Heritages. Ed. by C. W. Truesdale. LC 93-83972. 256p. (Orig.). 1994. pap. 17.95 (0-89823-149-3) New Rivers Pr.

Two Writings of Martin Luther. Intro. by Marion R. Winkler. LC 90-90200. 56p. 1990. 6.95 (0-9610344-3-2) M R Winkler.

Two Wycliffite Texts. Ed. by Anne Hudson. (Early English Text Society Original Ser.: No. 301). (Illus.). 250p. (C). 1993. 55.00 (0-19-722303-6, 14301) OUP.

Two Yachts, Two Voyages. Eric C. Hiscock. 1985. 15.95 (0-393-03307-4) Norton.

Two-Year College English: Essays for A New Century. Ed. by Mark Reynolds. LC 93-46898. 241p. 1994. text ed. 19.95 (0-8141-5541-3) NCTE.

Two-Year College Mathematics Library Recommendations. Ed. by Lynn A. Steen. 92p. 1992. pap. 18.00 (0-88385-077-X, TYR) Math Assn.

Two-Year Colleges, Doing Business with Business: A Handbook for Colleges Planning to Serve Commerce & Industry. fac. ed. Russell L. Hamm & Lynn T. Burger. LC 88-144641. (Keeping America Working Ser.: No. 5). 158p. 1988. pap. 45.10 (0-7837-7642-X, 2047395) Bks Demand.

***Two Years.** unabridged ed. Richard H. Dana. 230p. 1997. reprint ed. pap. 14.95 (1-57002-047-7) Univ Publng Hse.

Two Years: A Teacher's Memoir. Mary K. Glover. LC 92-27090. (Teacher-to-Teacher Ser.). 110p. 1992. pap. text ed. 17.50 (0-435-08738-X, 08738) Heinemann.

Two Years After. John Kiang. LC 86-63770. 96p. (Orig.). 1987. pap. 4.95 (0-916301-02-8) One World Pub.

Two Years after Tiananmen: Political Prisoners in China. Ed. by Human Rights Watch Staff. 158p. (Orig.). 1991. pap. 15.00 (1-56432-030-8) Hum Rts Watch.

T

An Asterisk (*) at the beginning of an entry indicates that the title is appearing in BIP for the first time.

Two Years Before the Mast. Charles H. Dana. (Regents Illustrated Classics Ser.). (gr. 7-12). 1987. pap. text ed. 3.75 (0-13-935123-X, 20571) Prentice ESL.

Two Years Before the Mast. Richard H. Dana. (Airmont Classics Ser.). (J). (gr. 8 up). 1965. mass mkt. 2.25 (0-8049-0085-X, CL-85) Airmont.

***Two Years Before the Mast.** Richard H. Dana. (Illustrated Classics Collection 3). 64p. 1994. pap. 4.95 (0-7854-0727-8, 40468) Am Guidance.

Two Years Before the Mast. Richard H. Dana, Jr. 383p. 1964. mass mkt. 5.95 (0-451-52369-5, CE1764, Sig Classics) NAL-Dutton.

Two Years Before the Mast. Richard H. Dana, Jr. Ed. by Thomas Philbrick. (American Library). 576p. 1981. pap. 11.95 (0-14-039008-1, Penguin Classics) Viking Penguin.

Two Years Before the Mast. abr. ed. Richard H. Dana. Ed. by John N. Fago. (Now Age Illustrated III Ser.). (Illus.). (J). (gr. 4-12). 1977. pap. text ed. 2.95 (0-88301-270-7) Pendulum Pr.

Two Years Before the Mast. Richard Dana. 1981. reprint ed. lib. bdg. 21.95 (0-89966-426-1) Buccaneer Bks.

Two Years Before the Mast. Richard H. Dana, Jr. (Notable American Authors Ser.). 1992. reprint ed. lib. bdg. 75.00 (0-7812-2613-9) Rprt Serv.

Two Years Before the Mast: Student Activity Book. Marcia Sohl & Gerald Dackerman. (Now Age Illustrated Ser.). (Illus.). (gr. 4-12). student ed. 1.25 (0-88301-294-4) Pendulum Pr.

***Two Years Before the Mast Readalong.** Richard H. Dana. (Illustrated Classics Collection 3). 64p. 1994. pap. 14.95 (0-7854-0743-X, 40470) Am Guidance.

Two Years Behind the Mast: An American Landlubber at Sea in World War Two. Harold J. McCormick. (Illus.). 147p. (Orig.). 1991. pap. 16.00 (0-89745-138-4) Sunflower U Pr.

Two Years Experience Among the Shakers. David R. Lamson. LC 71-134418. reprint ed. 40.00 (0-404-08477-X) AMS Pr.

Two Years in Limbo. Robert H. Stone. (Illus.). 85p. 1981. text ed. 7.50 (0-9609192-1-X) R H Stone.

Two Years in Revolutionary China, 1925-27. Vera V. Vishnyakova-Akimova. Tr. by Steven I. Levine from RUS. LC 78-148942. (East Asian Monographs: No. 40). 370p. 1971. pap. 14.00 (0-674-91601-8) HUP.

Two Years in the French West Indies. Lafcadio Hearn. LC 73-104479. (Illus.). 431p. reprint ed. lib. bdg. 39.50 (0-8398-0775-9) Irvington.

Two Years in the French West Indies. Lafcadio Hearn. (Notable American Authors Ser.). 1992. reprint ed. lib. bdg. 75.00 (0-7812-3066-7) Rprt Serv.

Two Years in the Melting Pot. rev. ed. Liu Zongren. 1988. reprint ed. 16.95 (0-8351-2048-1); reprint ed. pap. 9.95 (0-8351-2035-X) China Bks.

Two Years in the Pacific & Arctic Oceans & China, Being a Journal of Events Peculiar to a Whaling Voyage. James Munger. 82p. 1987. 14.95 (0-87770-401-5) Ye Galleon.

Two Years of French Foreign Policy: Vichy, 1940-1942. Adrienne D. Hytier. LC 74-7448. (Etudes D'histoire Economique Politique et Sociale: No. 25). 402p. 1974. reprint ed. text ed. 35.00 (0-8371-7551-8, HYFP, Greenwood Pr) Greenwood.

Two Years on the Alabama. Arthur Sinclair. Ed. by Jack Sweetman. LC 88-19953. (Classics of Naval Literature Ser.). (Illus.). 336p. 1989. reprint ed. 32.95 (0-87021-698-8) Naval Inst Pr.

Two Years' Service on the Reorganized State Board of Insanity in Massachusetts, August, 1914 to August, 1916. Lloyd V. Briggs. Ed. by Gerald N. Grob. LC 78-22551. (Historical Issues in Mental Health Ser.). (Illus.). 1980. reprint ed. lib. bdg. 50.95 (0-405-11905-4) Ayer.

Two Years under the Crescent. H. C. Wright. 360p. 1990. 125.00 (1-85077-056-5, Pub. by Darf Pubs Ltd UK) St Mut.

Two Years Without Sleep: Working Moms Talk about Having a Baby & a Job. Ed. by Cathy Feldman. (Working Women Ser.). (Illus.). 110p. (Orig.). 1994. pap. 9.95 (1-883423-01-5) Blue Pt Bks.

Two Young Two Go Four Boys. Linda Lewis. (J). (gr. 2-5). 1990. pap. 2.75 (0-671-69560-6, Archway) PB.

Two Youths & Other Stories. Peter Cox. (C). 1990. 29.00 (0-7223-2500-2, Pub. by A H S Ltd UK) St Mut.

Twofold Vibration. Raymond Federman. LC 81-47831. 175p. reprint ed. pap. 49.90 (0-7837-3701-7, 2057879) Bks Demand.

Twopence to Cross the Mersey see Minerva's Stepchild

Tworzenie Zespolu: Rozwijanie Umiejetnosci Zarzadzania. Robert B. Maddux. Ed. by Czeslaw J. Grycz & Andrzej Salski. Tr. by Andrzej Salski from ENG. (Illus.). iv, 74p. (Orig.). (POL.). (C). 1991. pap. 7.95 (1-56513-002-2) W Poniecki Charit.

Two's a Crowd. Diana Gregory. (Sweet Dreams Ser.: No. 90). 144p. (Orig.). (J). (gr. 6 up). 1995. pap. 3.50 (0-553-24992-4) Bantam.

Two's a Crowd. Willard Simms. 1970. pap. 3.25 (0-8222-1186-6) Dramatists Play.

Two's Company. Amanda Benjamin. LC 94-39223. 32p. 1995. pap. 13.99 (0-670-84876-X, Viking) Viking Penguin.

Two's Company. Amanda Cohen. 1999. pap. 4.99 (0-14-054901-3) NAL-Dutton.

Two's Company... Shirley Greenway. LC 96-23968. (Illus.). 32p. (J). (ps-3). 1997. 15.95 (0-88106-963-9); pap. 6.95 (0-88106-962-0) Charlesbridge Pub.

Two's Company. Carole Mortimer. (Harlequin Presents Ser.: No. 1823). 1996. mass mkt. 3.50 (0-373-11823-6, 1-11823-1) Harlequin Bks.

Two's Company. large type ed. Carole Mortimer. (Harlequin Romance Ser.). 1996. lib. bdg. 19.95 (0-263-14552-2, Pub. by Mills & Boon UK) Thorndike Pr.

2's Experience - Art. Liz Wilmes & Dick Wilmes. (Illus.). 214p. (Orig.). 1995. pap. 16.95 (0-943452-21-X) Building Blocks.

2's Experience - Dramatic Play. Liz Wilmes & Dick Wilmes. (Illus.). 120p. (Orig.). 1995. pap. 12.95 (0-943452-20-1) Building Blocks.

2's Experience - Felt Board Fun. Liz Wilmes & Dick Wilmes. (Illus.). 204p. (Orig.). 1994. pap. 14.95 (0-943452-19-8) Building Blocks.

2's Experience - Fingerplays. Liz Wilmes & Dick Wilmes. (Illus.). 144p. (Orig.). 1994. pap. 12.95 (0-943452-18-X) Building Blocks.

2's Experience - Sensory Play. Liz Wilmes & Dick Wilmes. (Illus.). (Orig.). 1996. pap. 14.95 (0-943452-22-8) Building Blocks.

Twospot. Bill Pronzini & Collin Wilcox. 272p. 1993. 4.95 (0-7867-0042-4) Carroll & Graf.

2000andWhat? Short Stories about the Turn of the Millennium. Harry Mathews et al. Ed. by Karl Roeseler & David Gilbert. 238p. (Orig.). 1996. pap. 12.00 (0-9639192-2-9) Trip St Pr.

***2U Black Children.** Royce Whittle. (Illus.). 32p. (J). (gr. k-5). 1996. pap. 8.00 (0-8059-3845-1) Dorrance.

2V & 3Fs= A Diet for Life. Michael Ritota. 72p. 1996. pap. 11.00 (0-8059-3910-5) Dorrance.

***Twyford Down: Roads, Campaigning & Environmental Law.** Bryant & Anderson. (Illus.). 352p. (Orig.). 1995. pap. text ed. 25.95 (0-419-20270-6, E & FN Spon) Routledge Chapman & Hall.

Twyllyp. Peter Farrow & Diane Lampert. (Illus.). (J). (gr. 3-7). 1963. 10.95 (0-8392-3040-0) Astor-Honor.

TX Advanced Diemaking. D. Eugene Ostergaard. (Diemaking Ser.). 166p. 1967. 43.95 (0-07-046093-0) McGraw.

Ty: Night People, Part 1. Mark Dunster. (Rin Ser.: Pt. 19). 34p. (Orig.). 1987. pap. 5.00 (0-89642-149-X) Linden Pubs.

Ty: The Ty Detmer Story. Frank Herbert et al. 1992. 11.95 (0-88494-834-X) Bookcraft Inc.

Ty Animation in 21 Days. 1998. 35.00 (0-672-30742-1) Sams.

Ty Cobb. Charles C. Alexander. LC 83-17409. (Illus.). 272p. 1985. pap. 12.95 (0-19-503598-4) OUP.

Ty Cobb. Norman L. Macht. (Baseball Legends Ser.). (Illus.). 64p. (J). (gr. 3 up). 1992. lib. bdg. 15.95 (0-7910-1172-0) Chelsea Hse.

Ty Cobb: Bad Boy of Baseball. S. A. Kramer. LC 94-39675. (Step into Reading: Step 4 Bks.). (J). 1995. pap. 3.99 (0-679-87283-3) Random.

***Ty Detmer: The Making of a Legend.** Dick Harmon. 1992. 19.95 (1-55517-085-4) CFI Dist.

TY Dutch Dictionary. Peter King & Margaret King. (Teach Yourself Ser.). 1974. pap. 9.95 (0-679-10251-5) McKay.

TY French Dictionary. (Teach Yourself Ser.). (FRE.). 1977. pap. 8.95 (0-679-10245-0) McKay.

Ty Hits the Mat. Randy Simpson. 64p. 1993. pap. 6.95 (0-9635215-2-7) Cylinder Pub.

Ty Loves Flowers: A Toddlers' Environmental Awareness Book. Elizabeth Bramhall. (Illus.). 16p. (J). (ps). 1993. pap. write for info. (0-9636038-0-9) E Bramhall.

Ty More Visual Basic in 21 Days. 1998. 29.99 (0-672-30781-2) Sams.

Ty Ole Programming in 21 Days. 2nd ed. 1998. 39.99 (0-672-30806-1) Sams.

Tyagaraja: Life & Lyrics. William J. Jackson. (Illus.). 418p. 1993. pap. 14.95 (0-19-563222-2) OUP.

Tyagaraja & the Renewal of Tradition: Translation & Reflections. William Jackson. (C). 1995. 24.00 (81-208-1146-1, Pub. by Motilal Banarsidass II) S Asia.

Tyagu. Sivasankari. 1991. pap. 12.00 (81-85336-37-7, Three Contnts) Lynne Rienner.

Tyche. Eugen Taubler. iv, 240p. 1979. write for info. (3-487-06729-3) G Olms Pubs.

Tychonic & Semi-Tychonic World Systems. Christine J. Schofield. Ed. by I. Bernard Cohen. LC 80-2094. (Development of Science Ser.). (Illus.). 1981. lib. bdg. 38.95 (0-405-13859-8) Ayer.

Tyconius: The Book of Rules. William S. Babcock. LC 89-10389. (Texts & Translations Ser.). 153p. 1989. 20.95 (1-55540-366-2, 06 02 31); pap. 15.95 (1-55540-367-0, 06 02 31) Scholars Pr GA.

***Tycoon.** Harold Robbins. LC 96-48523. 1997. 23.50 (0-684-81068-9) S&S Trade.

Tycoon. large type ed. Mary Wells. 1990. 25.99 (0-7089-2229-5) Ulverscroft.

***Tycoon & the Townie.** Elizabeth Lane. 1997. mass mkt. 3.25 (0-373-19250-9, 1-19250-9) Silhouette.

***Tycoon's Tots.** Stella Bagwell. (Romance Ser.: No. 1228). 1997. mass mkt. 3.25 (0-373-19228-2, 1-19228-5) Silhouette.

Tye May & the Magic Brush. Molly G. Bang. LC 80-16488. (Illus.). 56p. (J). (gr. 1 up). 1992. pap. 4.95 (0-688-11504-7, Mulberry) Morrow.

Tye May & the Magic Brush. Garrett Christopher. Ed. by J. Friedland & R. Kessler. (Novel-Ties Ser.). 1994. student ed., pap. text ed. 15.95 (1-56982-055-4) Lrn Links.

Tyendinaga Tales. Compiled & Intro. by Rona Rustige. (Illus.). 96p. (C). 1988. 24.95 (0-7735-0650-0, Pub. by McGill CN) U of Toronto Pr.

Tyger. William Blake. LC 92-23378. (Illus.). 36p. (J). (ps-3). 1993. 16.00 (0-15-292375-6) HarBrace.

Tyger: Wild Stallion of the Badlands. Les Sellnow. LC 94-90841. 344p. (YA). 1995. 23.95 (0-9644400-8-3) Wind Riv Pub.

Tyger, the Lamb, the Desart. write for info. (0-8386-3566-0) Fairleigh Dickinson.

Tyger Tyger. Richard Hoyt. 256p. 1996. 21.95 (0-312-85804-3) St Martin.

Tying & Fishing the Fuzzy Nymphs. 4th rev. ed. E. H. Rosborough. LC 88-2190. (Illus.). 192p. 1988. 21.95 (0-8117-1818-2) Stackpole.

Tying & Fishing the Nymph. Taff Price. (Illus.). 256p. 1996. pap. 19.95 (0-7137-2595-8, Pub. by Blandford Pr UK) Sterling.

Tying Arrangements. William A. Montgomery. (Corporate Practice Ser.: No. 39). 1984. 92.00 (1-55871-248-8) BNA.

***Tying Arrangements: Practice under Federal Antitrust, Patent, & Banking Law.** William M. Hannay & William A. Montgomery. 1997. 95.00 (1-55871-350-6) BNA.

Tying Bass Flies: 12 of the Best. Deke Meyer. (Illus.). 32p. 1995. pap. 9.95 (1-57188-041-0) F Amato Pubns.

Tying Cameras to Deer Tails. Janice L. Tucker. (Orig.). 1990. pap. 14.95 (0-9622061-1-3) El Rancho Pr.

Tying Dry Flies. Randall Kaufmann. (Illus.). 204p. (Orig.). 1990. 39.95 (0-9617059-3-0); pap. 26.95 (0-9617059-2-2) West Fishermans.

***Tying Dry Flies: Learn to Tie the World's Most Popular Dry Flies.** rev. ed. Randall Kaufmann. (Illus.). 144p. 1995. 42.95 (1-885212-06-2); spiral bd. 42.95 (1-885212-07-0); pap. 32.95 (1-885212-05-4) West Fishermans.

***Tying Flies.** Brian Grossenbacher. (Workstations Ser.). (Illus.). 48p. (YA). (gr. 3 up). 1997. 21.95 (0-8431-7679-0) Price Stern Sloan.

Tying Flies with Jack Dennis. Jack Dennis. 1993. spiral bd. 29.95 (0-937556-01-7) Snake River Bk.

Tying Foam Flies. Skip Morris. (Illus.). 48p. 1994. 29.95 (1-878175-90-4); pap. 16.95 (1-878175-89-0) F Amato Pubns.

***Tying Nymphs: Collectors Editon.** Randall Kaufmann. (Illus.). 144p. (Orig.). 1994. 42.95 (1-885212-01-1); pap. 32.95 (1-885212-00-3); spiral bd. 42.95 (1-885212-02-X) West Fishermans.

Tying of Aid. OECD Staff & Catrinus J. Jepma. 80p. (Orig.). 1991. pap. 12.00 (92-64-13459-X) OECD.

Tying Rocks to Clouds: Meetings and Conversations with Wise and Spiritual People. William Elliott. 288p. 1996. pap. 12.95 (0-385-48191-8, Image Bks) Doubleday.

Tying Rocks to Clouds: Meetings & Conversations with Wise & Spiritual People. William J. Elliott. 276p. 1995. 22.00 (0-8356-0708-9, Quest) Theos Pub Hse.

Tying Saltwater Flies: 12 of the Best. Deke Myer. (Illus.). 32p. 1996. 9.95 (1-57188-066-6) F Amato Pubns.

Tying Shoelaces. Jill Block. (California Master Ser.: No. 8). (Illus.). 16p. 1989. text ed. 96.00 (0-937048-44-5); pap. text ed. 37.50 (0-685-27865-4) Santa Susana.

Tying Strong Fishing Knots. Bill Herzog. (Illus.). 48p. 1995. pap. 6.95 (1-57188-022-4) F Amato Pubns.

***Tying the Classic Salmon Fly: A Modern Approach to Traditional Techniques.** Michael D. Radencich. LC 96-54306. (Illus.). 256p. 1997. 59.95 (0-8117-0331-2) Stackpole.

***Tying the Knot: The Sharp Dresser's Guide to Ties & Handkerchiefs.** Andrew G. Cochran. (Illus.). 48p. (Orig.). 1996. pap. 5.95 (0-9630152-6-5) Five Star AZ.

Tying Trout Flies: Twelve of the Best. Deke Meyer. (Illus.). 32p. 1993. pap. 9.95 (1-878175-40-8) F Amato Pubns.

Tying Trout Nymphs: Twelve of the Best. Deke Meyer. (Illus.). 32p. 1994. pap. 9.95 (1-878175-87-4) F Amato Pubns.

Tying up Strings. John P. Schumake et al. 125p. (Orig.). 1987. teacher ed. 7.95 (0-9616789-2-5, A3); pap. text ed. 7.95 (0-9616789-1-7, A2) Earnest Pubns.

Tyinya Farzhi. Esther Jost. 30p. (J). (gr. 1-4). 1990. pap. 4.50 (0-921788-07-X) Kindred Prods.

TykeOsaurs. Photos by Tom Arma. 18p. (J). (ps). 1995. bds. 4.95 (0-448-40092-8, G&D) Putnam Pub Group.

Tyler County, West Virginia, Marriage Records: 1815-1852. Mary D. Atkinson. LC 80-67521. 73p. 1980. pap. text ed. 10.00 (0-937436-01-1) Atkinson.

Tyler Davidson Fountain Given by Mr. Henry Probasco to the City of Cincinnati. deluxe ed. William F. Poole. (Illus.). 117p. 1988. reprint ed. boxed 39.95 (0-911497-06-4) Cinc Hist Soc.

Tyler Davidson Fountain Given by Mr. Henry Probasco to the City of Cincinnati. William F. Poole. (Illus.). 117p. 1988. reprint ed. pap. 19.95 (0-911497-07-2) Cinc Hist Soc.

Tyler Genealogy: The Descendants of Job Tyler of Andover, Massachusetts, 1619-1700, 2 vols. in 1. W. I. Brigham. 891p. 1989. reprint ed. pap. 153.50 (0-8328-1191-2); reprint ed. lib. bdg. 161.50 (0-8328-1190-4) Higginson Bk Co.

Tyler Graphics: The Extended Image. Elizabeth Armstrong et al. (Illus.). 256p. 1987. 19.98 (0-89659-750-4) Abbeville Pr.

Tyler Graphics: The Extended Image. Elizabeth Armstrong et al. (Illus.). 256p. 1996. 19.98 (0-89659-772-5) Abbeville Pr.

***Tyler, Texas.** Randy Mallory & Donna Lastage. (Illus.). 150p. 1997. 34.95 (1-890291-01-3) Platinum Pubng.

Tyler Texas C.S.A. William A. Albaugh, III. (William Albaugh Collection Ser.). (Illus.). 235p. 1993. reprint ed. 25.00 (1-56837-263-9) Broadfoot.

Tyler Toad & the Thunder. Robert L. Crowe. LC 80-347. (Unicorn Paperbacks Ser.). (Illus.). 32p. (J). (ps-1). 1986. pap. 4.95 (0-525-44243-X) Dutton Child Bks.

Tyler Turkle: Plastic Criteria. J. Jacobs et al. (Illus.). 8p. 1992. 5.00 (1-879293-03-X) Contemp Art Mus.

Tyler, Wilkin & Skee. Robert Burch. LC 89-28245. (Brown Thrasher Bks.). 160p. (J). (gr. 4-6). 1990. reprint ed. 19.95 (0-8203-1194-4) U of Ga Pr.

Tyler's Family Provision. 2nd ed. R. D. Oughton & E. L. Tyler. 1984. 90.00 (0-86205-075-8) MICHIE.

Tyler's Quarterly Historical & Genealogical Magazine: Genealogies of Virginia Families from Tyler's Quarterly Historical & Genealogical Magazine, 4 vols. LC 81-82083. (Illus.). 3621p. 1981. 180.00 (0-8063-0947-4) Genealog Pub.

Tylers Row. Miss Read. (Illus.). 240p. 1990. pap. 9.00 (0-89733-339-X) Academy Chi Pubs.

***Tyler's Row.** Read. Date not set. lib. bdg. 21.95 (0-8488-1702-8) Amereon Ltd.

Tyler's Row. large type ed. Miss Read. LC 92-30416. (General Ser.). 312p. 1993. lib. bdg. 20.95 (0-8161-5509-7) G K Hall.

Tylman's Theory & Practice of Fixed Prosthodontics. 8th ed. William F. Malone & David L. Koth. 461p. 1989. 59.50 (0-912791-48-9) Ishiyaku Euro.

Tylo. Mark Dunster. 25p. (Orig.). 1995. pap. 5.00 (0-89642-279-8) Linden Pubs.

***Tymora's Luck.** 1997. pap. 5.99 (0-7869-0726-6) TSR Inc.

Tympano-Ossicular, Allograft Tympanoplasty: A Manual of Techniques. Bernard Ars & Nicole Ars-Piret. (Illus.). 55p. 1993. pap. text ed. 28.50 (90-6299-093-2, Pub. by Kugler NE) Kugler Pubns.

Tympanoplasty: Osteoplastic Epitympanotomy. Horst Wullstein & Sabina Wullstein. Tr. by P. M. Stell from GER. (Illus.). 210p. 1990. text ed. 135.00 (0-86577-301-7) Thieme Med Pubs.

***Tympanoplasty, Mastoidectomy & Stapes Surgery.** Ugo Fisch. (Illus.). 304p. 1994. 115.00 (0-86577-559-1) Thieme Med Pubs.

***Tyndale Crossword Puzzles.** Terry Hall & Randy Petersen. 1994. pap. 7.99 (0-8423-7393-4, No. 4) Tyndale.

Tyndale Crossword Puzzles, No. 1. Terry Hall. 91p. 1993. pap. 7.99 (0-8423-7390-X) Tyndale.

Tyndale Crossword Puzzles, No. 2. Terry Hall. 91p. 1993. pap. 7.99 (0-8423-7391-8) Tyndale.

Tyndale Crossword Puzzles, No. 3. Terry Hall & Randy Petersen. 96p. 1994. pap. 7.99 (0-8423-7392-6) Tyndale.

Tyndale New Testament Comentary, 20 vols. 1982. pap. 250.00 (0-8028-1399-2) Eerdmans.

Tyndale Old Testament Commentaries, 26 bks., Set. 1981. 469.06 (0-87784-880-7, 880); pap. 296.16 (0-87784-280-9, 280) InterVarsity.

***Tyndale Old Testament Commentaries, 26 vols., Set.** 1996. 487.10 (0-8308-8584-6) InterVarsity.

***Tyndale Old Testament Commentaries, 26 vols., Set.** 1996. pap. 307.55 (0-8308-8585-4) InterVarsity.

Tyndale's New Testament. Ed. by David Daniell. Tr. by William Tyndale. 1996. pap. 15.00 (0-300-06580-9) Yale U Pr.

Tyndale's Old Testament. William Tyndale. 688p. (C). 1992. text ed. 45.00 (0-300-05211-1) Yale U Pr.

Tyner McCoy. 120p. 1992. per. 14.95 (0-7935-0747-2, 00673215) H Leonard.

Tyngsborough, MA. H. Morton. (Images of America Ser.). 128p. 1996. pap. 16.99 (0-7524-0295-1, Arcdia) Chalford.

Tyomarkkinasanatso. 140p. (FIN.). 1980. 39.95 (0-8288-2271-9, F22242) Fr & Eur.

Type A Behavior. Ed. by Michael J. Strube. (Illus.). 464p. 1991. 48.00 (0-8039-4089-0); pap. 24.00 (0-8039-4090-4) Sage.

Type A Behavior: Its Diagnosis & Treatment. Meyer Friedman. LC 96-44150. (Prevention in Practice Library). (Illus.). 150p. (C). 1996. pap. 19.50 (0-306-45357-6, Plenum Pr) Plenum.

Type A Behavior: Its Diagnosis & Treatment. Meyer Friedman. (Prevention in Practice Library). (Illus.). 150p. (C). 1996. 37.50 (0-306-45356-8, Plenum Pr) Plenum.

Type A Behavior & Your Heart. Meyer Friedman & Ray H. Rosenman. 1974. 16.95 (0-394-48011-2) Knopf.

Type A Behavior & Your Heart. Meyer Friedman. (Heart Care Titles Ser.). 1982. mass mkt. 5.99 (0-449-20073-6) Fawcett.

Type A Personality: Index of Authors & Subjects with Guide for Rapid Research. rev. ed. D. J. Randall. 1994. 44.50 (0-7883-0182-9); pap. 39.50 (0-7883-0183-7) ABBE Pubs Assn.

***Type & Archetype.** Carol S. Pearson. (Orig.). pap. write for info. (1-878287-44-3) Type & Temperament.

Type & Color: A Handbook of Creative Combinations. Ed. by Alton Cook. (Design Sourcebook Ser.). (Illus.). 160p. 1989. 39.99 (0-935603-19-0, 30166) Rockport Pubs.

Type & Color 2: How to Choose & Specify Color Fades & Type & Color Combinations. Richard Emery. (Illus.). 144p. 1994. 24.99 (1-56496-065-X, 30603) Rockport Pubs.

Type & Figured Specimens of Fossil Vertebrates in the Collection of the University of Kansas Museum of Natural History: Part I. Fossil Fishes. Hans-Peter Schultze et al. (Miscellaneous Publications: No. 73). 53p. 1982. 3.25 (0-317-04815-5) U KS Nat Hist Mus.

Type & Image: The Language of Graphic Design. Philip B. Meggs. (Illus.). 208p. 1992. pap. 39.95 (0-442-01165-2) Van Nos Reinhold.

Type & Layout: How Typography & Design Can Get Your Message Across, or Get in the Way. Colin Wheildon. Ed. & Intro. by Mal Warwick. LC 94-48089. 264p. 1996. pap. 24.95 (0-9624891-5-8) Strathmoor Pr.

Type & Learn C. Tom Swan. 416p. 1994. pap. 34.95 (1-56884-073-X) IDG Bks.

Type & Learn Windows Programming. Tom Swan. 520p. 1994. pap. 34.95 (1-56884-071-3) IDG Bks.

Type & Team Development Seminar Kit: Using Type to Unleash the Power of Your Team. William D. Murray & Peter Walsh. (Type & Temperament Seminar Kits Ser.). 160p. 1990. 159.95 (1-878287-14-1, KTAE) Type & Temperament.

T

An Asterisk (*) at the beginning of an entry indicates that the title is appearing in BIP for the first time.

Type & Your Career Seminar Kit: Using Type in Career Selection. William D. Murray & Rosalie R. Murray. 1991. 159.95 (*1-878287-15-X*, KTAD) Type & Temperament.

Type Communications Seminar Kit: Using Type to Enhance Organizational & Interpersonal Communication. William D. Murray & Rosalie R. Murray. 130p. 1988. 139.95 (*1-878287-11-7*, KTAB) Type & Temperament.

Type Composition in the Private Press. H. W. Larken. 128p. 1983. 35.00 (*0-946095-11-6*, Pub. by Gresham Bks UK) St Mut.

Type Crossings: Sentential Meaninglessness in the Border Area of Linguistics & Philosophy. Theodore Drange. (Janua Linguarum, Ser. Minor: No. 44). (Orig.). 1966. pap. text ed. 36.95 (*90-279-0578-9*) Mouton.

Type Design in the Digital Realm. Bigelow. (Design & Graphic Design Ser.). 1995. text ed. 49.95 (*0-442-02218-2*) Van Nos Reinhold.

Type Designations, Areas of Use, Maintenance & Operation of Powered Industrial Trucks. (Five Hundred Ser.). 1992. pap. 16.75 (*0-685-58223-X*, 505-92) Natl Fire Prot.

Type du Valet chez Moliere et Ses Successeurs: Regnard, Dufresny, Dancourt, et Lesage. Caracteres et Evolution. Gerard R. Gouvernet. LC 84-47806. (American University Studies: Romance Languages & Literature: Ser. II, Vol. 15). 260p. (FRE.). (C). 1985. text ed. 29.00 (*0-8204-0141-2*) P Lang Pubng.

Type Evidence: A Thesaurus for Use in Rare Book & Special Collection Cataloguing. 19p. 1990. pap. 8.95 (*0-8389-7428-7*) Assn Coll & Res Libs.

Type Faces. Gerry Rosentswieg. (Illus.). 224p. 1996. 37.50 (*0-942604-46-6*) Madison Square.

Type Foundries of American & Their Catalogues. Maurice Annenberg. LC 94-29933. 304p. 1994. 49.95 (*1-884718-06-X*) Oak Knoll.

Type Hype: How Hot Designers Are Creating Cool Fonts. Allan Haley. 144p. 1997. 29.99 (*1-56496-317-9*) Rockport Pubs.

Type II Diabetes: Your Healthy Living Guide. American Diabetes Association Staff. LC 92-17906. (Illus.). 248p. 1996. pap. 24.95 (*0-945448-27-9*) Am Diabetes.

***Type II Diabetes: Your Healthy Living Guide.** 2nd ed. American Diabetes Association Staff. LC 96-54838. 1997. pap. text ed. 16.95 (*0-945448-79-1*) Am Diabetes.

***Type II Diabetes Cookbook.** Lois Soneral. LC 97-3177. 1997. 25.00 (*1-56565-700-4*) Contemp Bks.

***Type II Diabetes Diet Book.** 2nd rev. ed. Cal Ezrin & Robert E. Kowalski. 304p. 1997. pap. 16.00 (*1-56565-807-8*, Anodyne) Lowell Hse.

***Type II Diabetes Sourcebook.** David Drum & Terry Zierenberg. LC 97-651. 1997. 25.00 (*1-56565-646-6*) Contemp Bks.

Type II Diabetic's Diet Book: The Doctor's Weight Loss Program for Diabetics & Others. Calvin Ezrin & Robert E. Kowalski. 264p. 1995. pap. 16.00 (*1-56565-334-3*) Lowell Hse.

Type in Place: A Thumbnail Approach to Creative Type Placement. Richard Emery. (Illus.). 160p. 1991. 34.95 (*0-935603-87-5*, 30389) Rockport Pubs.

Type in Use. Alex White. 192p. 1992. 34.95 (*0-8306-3796-6*, 3543, Design Pr) TAB Bks.

Type It Right! The Little Black Book for Your Computer. Anita Stumbo. (Little Black Bks.: No. 1). 128p. (Orig.). 1996. pap. 5.95 (*1-886110-07-7*) Addax Pubng.

Type Logical Grammar: Categorical Logic of Signs. Glyn V. Morrill. LC 94-33169. 332p. 1994. lib. bdg. 116.00 (*0-7923-3095-1*, Pub. by Klwr Acad Pubs NE) Kluwer Ac.

***Type-Logical Semantics.** Bob Carpenter. LC 97-863. 1997. write for info. (*0-262-53149-6*); pap. write for info. (*0-262-03248-1*) MIT Pr.

Type-Material of Diptera (Insecta) Described by G. H. Verrall & J. E. Collin. Adrian C. Pont. (Illus.). 240p. 1995. 200.00 (*0-19-854919-9*) OUP.

Type O Negative: Bloody Kisses. 92p. 1995. pap. 19.95 (*0-89524-902-2*) Cherry Lane.

Type I Diabetes: Molecular, Cellular & Clinical Immunology. Ed. by George S. Eisenbarth & Kevin J. Lafferty. (Illus.). 320p. 1996. 69.50 (*0-19-509126-4*) OUP.

Type One Supernovae: Proceedings of the Workshop, Austin, March 17-19, 1980. Texas Workshop on Type I Supernovae Staff. Ed. by J. C. Wheeler. LC 80-52944. (Illus.). 1980. pap. 10.00 (*0-9603796-1-4*) U of Tex Dept Astron.

Type Right! A Complete Program for Business Typewriting. Delores Cotton & Vito Metta. LC 78-73160. 1986. text ed. 25.32 (*0-02-830550-7*); teacher ed., ring bd. 18.64 (*0-02-830560-4*); 13.32 (*0-02-830570-1*) Glencoe.

Type Specimen Book. Van Nostrand Reinhold Staff. 648p. 1974. pap. 34.95 (*0-442-27915-9*) Van Nos Reinhold.

Type Specimens of Recent Mammals in the Museum of Vertebrate Zoology, University of California, Berkeley. Blair A. Csuti. LC 80-13264. (University of California Publications in Social Welfare: No. 114). 83p. reprint ed. pap. 25.00 (*0-8357-6860-0*, 2035558) Bks Demand.

Type Studies of North American & Other Related Taxa of Stipitate Hydnums: Genera Hydnellum, Phellodon, Sarcodon. Richard E. Baird. (Bibliotheca Micologica Ser.: No. 103). 90p. 1986. 50.00 (*3-443-59004-7*) Lubrecht & Cramer.

Type Study of American Banking. Stuart Bruchey. Ed. by Russell A. Stevenson. LC 80-1169. (Rise of Commercial Banking Ser.). (Illus.). 1981. reprint ed. lib. bdg. 24.95 (*0-405-13679-X*) Ayer.

Type Tales: Teaching Type to Children. 48p. 1991. pap. 9.95 (*0-89106-047-2*, 7339) Davies-Black.

Type Talk. Otto Kroeger & Janet M. Thuesen. 320p. 1989. pap. 13.95 (*0-440-50704-9*) Dell.

Type Talk at Work. Otto Kroeger & Janet M. Thuesen. 416p. 1993. pap. 13.95 (*0-440-50699-9*) Dell.

Type Terminology on the Desktop. Katharine Green & Claudia Buisson. 14p. 1991. pap. 1.95 (*1-881231-00-3*) Altsys.

Type-Theoretical Grammar. Aarne Ranta. (Indices Ser.: No. 1). (Illus.). 240p. 1995. 59.00 (*0-19-853857-X*) OUP.

Type Theory & Functional Programming. Simon Thompson. (C). 1991. text ed. 35.50 (*0-201-41667-0*) Addison-Wesley.

Type VII U-Boats. Robert Stern. (Illus.). 160p. 1991. 38.95 (*1-55750-828-3*) Naval Inst Pr.

Type with One Hand. 2nd ed. Richardson. (TA - Typing/Keyboarding Ser.). 1959. text ed. 10.95 (*0-538-20090-1*) S-W Pub.

***Type with One Hand.** 3rd ed. Richardson. (Typing/Keyboarding Ser.). 1998. pap. 13.95 (*0-538-68275-2*) S-W Pub.

Type with the Left or Right Hand on the Typewriter or Computer Keyboard. Charles W. Ruetten. (Illus.). 95p. (Orig.). (YA). (gr. 5 up). 1993. pap. text ed. 10.95 (*1-881842-03-7*) Sundial Pub.

Typed Lambda: Calculus. Jean Krivine. 176p. (C). 1993. text ed. 50.00 (*0-13-062407-1*) P-H.

Typed Lambda Calculi & Applications: International Conference on Typed Lambda Calculi & Applications, March 16-18, 1993, Utrecht, The Netherlands, Proceedings. Ed. by M. Bezem & J. F. Groote. LC 93-21883. (Lecture Notes in Computer Science Ser.: Vol. 664). 1993. 61.95 (*0-387-56517-5*) Spr-Verlag.

Typed Lambda Calculi & Applications: Second International Conference on Typed Lambda Calculi & Applications, TLCA '95, Edinburgh, United Kingdom, April 1995: Proceedings. Ed. by Mariangiola Dezani-Ciancaglini & Gordon Plotkin. LC 95-5969. (Lecture Notes in Computer Science Ser.: No. 902). 443p. 1995. pap. 68.00 (*0-387-59048-X*) Spr-Verlag.

Typed Lambda Calculus. J. Y. Girard et al. (Cambridge Tracts in Theoretical Computer Science Ser.: No.7). 250p. (C). 1989. text ed. 47.95 (*0-521-37181-3*) Cambridge U Pr.

***Typee.** Herman Melville. (Classics Illustrated Ser.). (Illus.). 1997. pap. text ed. 4.99 (*1-57840-061-9*) Acclaim Bks.

Typee. Herman Melville. (Airmont Classics Ser.). (J). (gr. 10 up). 1965. mass mkt. 1.50 (*0-8049-0053-1*, CL-53) Airmont.

Typee. Herman Melville. 293p. 1993. pap. 3.95 (*0-460-87276-1*, Everyman's Classic Lib) C E Tuttle.

Typee. Herman Melville. Ed. by Harrison Hayford et al. LC 67-11990. (Northwestern-Newberry Edition of the Writings of Herman Melville: Vol. 1). (Illus.). 374p. (C). 1968. 59.95 (*0-8101-0161-0*); pap. 59.95 (*0-8101-0159-9*) Northwestern U Pr.

Typee. Herman Melville. Ed. by Ruth Blair. (The World's Classics Ser.). (Illus.). 392p. 1996. pap. 8.95 (*0-19-282307-8*) OUP.

Typee. Herman Melville. Ed. by George Woodcock. (English Library). 368p. 1972. pap. 9.95 (*0-14-043070-9*, Penguin Classics) Viking Penguin.

***Typee.** unabridged ed. Herman Melville. 175p. 1997. reprint ed. pap. 14.95 (*1-57002-020-5*) Univ Pubing Hse.

Typee. Herman Melville. 300p. 1990. reprint ed. lib. bdg. 25.95 (*0-89966-715-5*) Buccaneer Bks.

Typee: A Peep at Polynesian Life. Hermann Melville. 1976. 26.95 (*0-8488-0581-X*) Amereon Ltd.

Typee: A Peep at Polynesian Life. Herman Melville. LC 95-32699. 320p. 1996. pap. 12.95 (*0-14-043488-7*, Penguin Bks) Viking Penguin.

Typee: Four Months Residence in the Marquesas Islands. Herman Melville. (Pacific Basin Bks.). 300p. (Orig.). 1985. pap. 14.95 (*0-7103-0132-4*) Routledge Chapman & Hall.

Typee, Omoo, Mardi. Herman Melville. Ed. by G. Thomas Tanselle. LC 81-18600. 1333p. 1982. 37.50 (*0-940450-00-3*) Library of America.

Typeface Design Standards. Ed. by Cynthia Hollandsworth & Elizabeth Nelson. (Illus.). 356p. 1992. pap. 49.95 (*0-8306-4063-0*, 4195, Design Pr) TAB Bks.

***Typeface Sourcebook.** Rockport Staff. Date not set. 42.50 (*0-688-09785-5*) Morrow.

Typeface Sourcebook: Homage to the Alphabet. rev. ed. Ed. by Phil's Photo Staff. 565p. 1990. pap. 39.99 (*0-935603-47-6*, 30254) Rockport Pubs.

***Typefaces.** Madison Square Press Staff. 1996. 32.50 (*0-688-14532-9*) Morrow.

Typefaces for Books. James Sutton & Alan Bartram. (Illus.). 288p. (C). 1990. 65.00 (*1-56131-016-6*); pap. 45.00 (*1-56131-017-4*) New Amsterdam Bks.

Typefounding in America, 1787-1825. Rollo G. Silver. LC 65-19396. 200p. reprint ed. pap. 57.00 (*0-317-10827-1*, 2007195) Bks Demand.

Typen und Strukturen Plausibler Folgerung see Mathematik und Plausibles Schliessen

TypEncyclopedia: A User's Guide to Better Typography. Frank Romano. 224p. 1984. pap. 34.95 (*0-8352-1925-9*) Bowker.

***Typeplay.** PBC International Staff. 1994. 47.50 (*0-688-13825-X*) Morrow.

***Typeplay.** PBC International Staff. 1999. pap. 29.95 (*0-688-15049-7*) Morrow.

Types: Essays in Metaphysics. Eddy M. Zemach. LC 91-35669. (Philosophy of History & Culture Ser.: Vol. 9). 341p. 1992. 114.00 (*90-04-09500-4*) E J Brill.

Types & Motifs of Judeo-Spanish Folktales. Reginetta Haboucha. LC 92-8897. (Folklore Library: Vol. 6). 1000p. 1992. text ed. 145.00 (*0-8240-9727-0*, H1397) Garland.

Types & Problems of Philosophy. 3rd ed. Hunter Mead. LC 59-6277. 1959. text ed. 37.95 (*0-03-006240-3*) Irvington.

Types & Special Collections (Flowering Plants & Ferns) of the Herbarium of the Academy of Natural Sciences of Philadelphia: Indices to the Microfiche. Compiled by James A. Mears. 274p. 1984. 370.00 (*0-930466-87-X*) Chadwyck-Healey.

Types Best Remembered--Types Best Forgotten. Ed. by Robert Norton. (Illus.). 176p. 1994. 16.00 (*1-884606-00-8*) Parsimony Pr.

Types for Proofs & Programs: International Workshop TYPES '93, Nijmegen, the Netherlands, May 1993: Selected Papers. Ed. by Hank Barendregt & Tobias Nipkow. LC 94-12368. (Lecture Notes in Computer Science Ser.: Vol. 806). 1994. 55.95 (*0-387-58085-9*) Spr-Verlag.

Types for Proofs & Programs: International Workshop TYPES '94, Bastad, Sweden, June 6-10, 1994 Proceedings. Ed. by Peter Dybjer et al. LC 95-44954. (Lecture Notes in Computer Science Ser.: Vol. 996). 202p. 1995. 43.00 (*3-540-60579-7*) Spr-Verlag.

***Types for Proofs & Programs: International Workshop Types '95, Torino, Italy, June 5-8, 1995 Selected Papers, Vol. 115.** Stefano Berardi & Mario Coppo. LC 96-43300. (Lecture Notes on Computer Science Ser.). 1996. 56.00 (*3-540-61780-9*) Spr-Verlag.

Types in Genesis. Andrew Jukes. LC 92-23987. 460p. 1993. 14.99 (*0-8254-2959-5*, Kregel Class) Kregel.

Types in Hebrews. Robert Anderson. LC 78-9545. (Sir Robert Anderson Library). 192p. 1978. reprint ed. pap. 7.99 (*0-8254-2129-2*, Kregel Class) Kregel.

Types in Logic Programming. Ed. by Frank Pfenning. (Logic Programming Ser.). (Illus.). 325p. 1992. 42.50 (*0-262-16131-1*) MIT Pr.

Types, Levels-Irregularities of Response to a Nursery School Situation of 40 Children Observed with Special Reference to the Home Environment. E. C. Slater. (SRCD M Ser.: Vol. 4, No. 2). 1939. 25.00 (*0-527-01509-1*) Periodicals Srv.

Types of A' Dependencies. Guglielmo Cinque. (Illus.). 200p. 1990. 32.50 (*0-262-03154-X*) MIT Pr.

Types of Alcoholics: Evidence from Clinical, Experimental & Genetic Research. Ed. by Thomas F. Babor et al. LC 94-3082. (Annals Ser.: Vol. 708). 1994. write for info. (*0-89766-799-9*); pap. 75.00 (*0-89766-800-6*) NY Acad Sci.

Types of Building Construction. 1992. pap. 16.75 (*0-685-58207-8*, 220-92) Natl Fire Prot.

Types of Children's Literature. Walter Barnes. 1972. 59.95 (*0-8490-1239-2*) Gordon Pr.

Types of Christian Theology. Hans W. Frei. Ed. by George Hunsinger & William C. Placher. (Illus.). 192p. 1994. pap. 14.00 (*0-300-05945-0*) Yale U Pr.

Types of Drama. 6th ed. Sylvan Barnet. (C). 1992. 40.00 (*0-673-52181-8*) Addson-Wesley Educ.

Types of Drama: Plays & Contexts. 7th ed. Sylvan Barnet. LC 96-23983. (C). 1997. text ed. 45.50 (*0-673-52514-7*) Longman.

Types of Drama: Plays & Essays. 6th ed. Sylvan Barnet et al. 806p. 1994. pap. text ed. 35.00 (*0-8230-4953-1*, Back Stage Bks) Watsn-Guptill.

Types of Drama: Plays & Essays. 17th ed. Sylvan Barnet. 1996. pap. text ed. 46.00 (*0-8230-4989-2*) Watsn-Guptill.

Types of Economic Theory: From Mercantilism to Institutionalism, Vol. 2. Ed. by Wesley C. Mitchell & J. Dorfman. LC 67-16418. xii, 875p. 1969. 49.50 (*0-678-04027-3*) Kelley.

Types of English Drama. Ed. by John W. Ashton. reprint ed. 79.00 (*0-403-07209-3*) Somerset Pub.

Types of Folktale: A Classification & Bibliography. Antti Arne. 1995. 49.95 (*0-253-32959-0*) Ind U Pr.

Types of Formalization in Small-Group Research. Joseph Berger et al. LC 79-27703. (Illus.). x, 159p. 1980. reprint ed. text ed. 49.75 (*0-313-22328-9*, BETF, Greenwood Pr) Greenwood.

Types of Generalization in Instruction: Logical & Psychological Problems in the Structuring of School Curricula. Joan W. Teller. LC 90-5542. (Soviet Studies in Mathematics Education). 438p. 1990. pap. 25.00 (*0-87353-291-0*) NCTM.

Types of Injuries by Selected Characteristics: United States, 1985-87 PHS 91-1503. (Vital & Health Statistics Ser. 10: Data from the National Health Interview Survey: No. 175). 86p. 1991. 3.75 (*0-685-61566-9*, 017-022-01126-3) Natl Ctr Health Stats.

Types of Mankind: Or, Ethnological Researches. J. C. Nott & George R. Gliddon. LC 76-89386. (Black Heritage Library Collection). (Illus.). 1977. 54.95 (*0-8369-8639-3*) Ayer.

Types of Modern & Ancient Chinese Love-Songs. Ch'I-Ch'Ao Liang. (Asian Folklore & Social Life Monographs: No. 8). (CHI.). 1970. 14.00 (*0-89986-011-7*) Oriental Bk Store.

Types of Musical Form & Composition: Fifty Ready-to-Use Activities. Audrey J. Adair. (Music Curriculum Activities Library). 112p. 1987. text ed. 12.95 (*0-13-934985-5*) P-H.

Types of Naval Officers: Drawn from the History of the British Navy. Alfred T. Mahan. LC 77-84323. (Essay Index Reprint Ser.). 500p. reprint ed. lib. bdg. 21.75 (*0-8290-0473-4*) Irvington.

Types of Naval Officers, Drawn from the History of the British Navy. Alfred T. Mahan. LC 77-84323. (Essay Index Reprint Ser.). 1977. 25.95 (*0-8369-1093-1*) Ayer.

Types of Schedules Training Aid. Spencer B. Smith. LC 82-73447. 31p. 1983. 35.00 (*0-935406-22-0*) Am Prod & Inventory.

Types of Shape. enl. ed. John Hollander. 96p. (Orig.). (C). 1991. pap. 14.00 (*0-300-04925-0*); text ed. 30.00 (*0-300-04974-9*) Yale U Pr.

Types of Society in Medieval Literature. Frederick Tupper. LC 67-29555. 1968. reprint ed. 22.00 (*0-8196-0212-4*) Biblo.

Typesense. Wheeler. (Computer Science Ser.). 1996. pap. 27.95 (*0-442-02096-1*) Van Nos Reinhold.

Typesense: Making Sense of Type on the Computer. Susan G. Wheeler & Gary S. Wheeler. 176p. 1996. pap. 32.95 (*1-85032-818-8*) ITCP.

Typesetting & Composition. 2nd ed. Geoff Barlow & S. Eccles. 288p. 1992. 39.95 (*0-948905-72-7*) Chapman & Hall.

Typesetting & Printing: How to Recognize Superior Typesetting, Choose the Right Paper & Avoid Printing Propblems. Cook Communications Ministries International Staff. (Interlit Imprint Ser.: Vol. 14). (Illus.). 40p. (Orig.). 1996. pap. 5.95 (*1-884752-23-3*, 44297) Cook Min Intl.

Typesetting by Microcomputer. Michael L. Kleper. (Illus.). 1982. pap. 10.00 (*0-930904-04-4*) Graphic Dimensions.

Typetronics II: Applied Professional Typewriting. Carolyn H. Butler et al. LC 88-83269. xvi, 185p. 1989. write for info. (*0-02-830561-2*) Glencoe.

Typewriter & the Men Who Made It. Richard N. Current. (Illus.). 176p. 1988. 17.95 (*0-911160-88-4*) Post Group.

Typewriter Battalion: Dramatic Front-Line Dispatches from World War II. Jack Stenbuck. 416p. 1996. reprint ed. pap. 14.00 (*0-688-14946-4*, Quill) Morrow.

Typewriter in the Sky. L. Ron Hubbard. 208p. Date not set. 16.95 (*0-88404-933-7*) Bridge Pubns Inc.

Typewriter Poems. Peter Finch. 1971. pap. 15.00 (*0-87110-078-9*) Ultramarine Pub.

Typewriter Profits. 1987. lib. bdg. 75.00 (*0-8490-3869-3*) Gordon Pr.

Typewriter Repairman (Electric) Jack Rudman. (Career Examination Ser.: C-1646). 1994. pap. 27.95 (*0-8373-1646-4*) Nat Learn.

Typewriter Repairman (Manual) Jack Rudman. (Career Examination Ser.: C-1645). 1994. reprint ed. pap. 27.95 (*0-8373-1645-6*) Nat Learn.

***Typewriter Ribbon: A Collection of Poetry.** Kristin N. Hinga. LC 96-96870. (Illus.). 100p. (Orig.). 1996. pap. 10.00 (*0-9654472-0-0*) Brown Booth.

***Typewriter Ribbon: A Collection of Poetry.** 2nd rev. ed. Kristin N. Hinga. 101p. (Orig.). 1996. reprint ed. pap. 10.00 (*0-9654472-1-9*) Brown Booth.

Typewriting: Intermediate. 5th ed. Duncan & Susie H. Vanhuss. (TE - Keyboarding Ser.). 1991. pap. 33.95 (*0-538-14850-0*) S-W Pub.

Typewriting: Theory & Practice. R. C. Bhatia. 1991. pap. 15.95 (*81-207-1237-4*, Pub. by Sterling Pubs II) Apt Bks.

Typewriting Behavior: Psychology Applied to Teaching & Learning Typewriting. August Dvorak et al. (Illus.). 521p. 1936. 30.00 (*0-935309-12-8*) Freelance Comm.

Typewriting Drills for Speed & Accuracy. 4th ed. John L. Rowe & A. Faborn Etier. LC 76-50096. 1977. text ed. 12.96 (*0-07-054151-5*) McGraw.

Typewriting in a Swimming Pool. John A. Bennett. (Illus.). 23p. (Orig.). (J). (gr. 2 up). 1995. pap. 2.00 (*0-935350-52-7*) Luna Bisonte.

Typewriting, Jr. H. S. Jack Rudman. (Teachers License Examination Ser.: T-63). 1994. pap. 27.95 (*0-8373-8063-4*) Nat Learn.

Typhoid & the Politics of Public Health in Nineteenth Century Philadelphia. Michael P. McCarthy. LC 86-72881. (Memoirs Ser.: Vol. 179). (Illus.). 150p. (Orig.). (C). 1988. pap. 10.00 (*0-87169-179-5*, M179-MCM) Am Philos.

Typhoid Fever: Its Nature, Mode of Spreading & Prevention. William Budd. Ed. by Barbara G. Rosenkrantz. LC 76-25656. (Public Health in America Ser.). (Illus.). 1977. reprint ed. lib. bdg. 21.95 (*0-405-09809-X*) Ayer.

Typhoid Fever: Strategies for the Nineties. T. Pang. 300p. 1992. text ed. 95.00 (*981-02-0953-3*) World Scientific Pub.

Typhoid Mary: Captive to the Public's Health. Judith W. Leavitt. LC 95-43486. 352p. 1996. 25.00 (*0-8070-2102-4*) Beacon Pr.

***Typhoid Mary: Captive to the Public's Health.** Judith W. Leavitt. 352p. 1997. pap. 14.00 (*0-8070-2103-2*) Beacon Pr.

Typhon. Joseph Conrad. 160p. (FRE.). 1973. pap. 10.95 (*0-7859-2203-2*, 207036416X) Fr & Eur.

Typhoon. Edward Packard. (Choose Your Own Adventure Ser.: No. 162). 128p. (J). (gr. 4-7). 1995. pap. 3.50 (*0-553-56624-5*) Bantam.

Typhoon. Mark Joseph. Ed. by Paul McCarthy. 320p. 1992. reprint ed. mass mkt. 5.99 (*0-671-70866-X*, Pocket Star Bks) PB.

Typhoon: And Other Tales. 448p. 1963. mass mkt. 4.50 (*0-452-00936-7*, Mer) NAL-Dutton.

Typhoon - The Other Enemy: The Third Fleet & the Pacific Storm of December 1944. C. Raymond Calhoun. LC 81-38384. (Illus.). 247p. 1993. reprint ed. pap. 14.95 (*1-55750-107-6*) Naval Inst Pr.

Typhoon & Other Stories. Joseph Conrad. 336p. 1991. 17.00 (*0-679-40547-X*, Everymans Lib) Knopf.

Typhoon & Other Stories. Joseph Conrad. Ed. & Intro. by Cedric P. Watts. (World's Classics Ser.). 336p. 1987. pap. 4.95 (*0-19-281711-6*) OUP.

Typhoon & Other Stories. Joseph Conrad. Ed. & Intro. by Paul Kirschner. 320p. 1991. pap. 6.95 (*0-14-018257-8*, Penguin Classics) Viking Penguin.

Typhoon Pilot. John S. Slaney. Ed. by Richard D. Wissolik & Gary E. Smith. LC 95-18863. 1995. write for info. (*1-885851-06-5*) St Vincent Coll.

Typhoon Shipments. Kevin Klose & Philip A. McCombs. 280p. 1974. 6.95 (*0-393-08693-3*) Norton.

Typhoon Tale. James Kyle. LC 93-27193. 1993. reprint ed. 16.00 (*0-7509-0458-5*, Pub. by Sutton Pubng UK) Bks Intl VA.

Typhus & Doughboys: The American Polish Typhus Relief Expedition, Nineteen Nineteen to Nineteen Twenty-One. Alfred E. Cornebise. LC 81-70530. (Illus.). 240p. 1983. 29.50 (*0-87413-216-9*) U Delaware Pr.

Typical: Short Stories. Padgett Powell. 176p. 1991. 19.00 (*0-374-28022-3*) FS&G.

Typical American. Gish Jen. 304p. 1992. reprint ed. pap. 11.95 (*0-452-26774-9*, Plume) NAL-Dutton.

Typical American Town. large type ed. John M. Roberts. 480p. 1996. 25.99 (*0-7089-3507-9*) Ulverscroft.

Typical & Atypical Antidepressants: Molecular Mechanisms. fac. ed. Ed. by E. Costa & Giorgio Racagni. LC 81-23409. (Advances in Biochemical Psychopharmacology Ser.: No. 31). 415p. pap. 118.30 (*0-7837-7202-5*, 2047097) Bks Demand.

Typical & the Topical. Andrew Watson. 1993. 10.00 (*0-533-10585-4*) Vantage.

Typical Costs for Seismic Rehabilitation of Existing Buildings, Vol. I: Summary. Thomas A. Sabol et al. (Illus.). 76p. (Orig.). (C). 1993. pap. text ed. 20.00 (*1-56806-574-4*) DIANE Pub.

Typical Costs for Seismic Rehabilitation of Existing Buildings, Vol. II: Supporting Documentation. (Illus.). 200p. (Orig.). (C). 1993. pap. text ed. 35.00 (*1-56806-995-2*) DIANE Pub.

Typical Elizabethan Plays. Ed. by Felix E. Schelling & Matthew W. Black. LC 78-132140. (Play Anthology Reprint Ser.). 1977. 40.95 (*0-8369-8219-3*) Ayer.

Typical Girls: Young Women from School to the Full-Time Job Market. Christine Griffin. 1985. pap. 13.95 (*0-7100-9881-2*, RKP) Routledge.

Typical Land Surveyor's Exam Questions with Answers. John E. Keen. 298p. (C). 1995. pap. text ed. 35.00 (*1-56569-000-1*) Land Survey.

Typical Residential, Commercial & Industry Bills: Investor-Owned Utilities. 41p. Winter Issue. 12.50 (*0-685-73754-3*, 04048004); Summer Issue. write for info. (*0-318-59922-8*, 04048011) Edison Electric.

Typical Singularities of Differential 1-Forms & Pfaffian Equations. Michael Zhitomirskii. LC 92-24410. (Translations of Mathematical Monographs: Vol. 113). 176p. 1992. 116.00 (*0-8218-4567-5*, MMONO/113) Am Math.

Typical Stories. Padgett Powell. 192p. 1992. pap. 9.95 (*0-8050-2111-6*, Owl) H Holt & Co.

Typically Atypical Day. Richard Norquist. 1985. pap. 3.00 (*0-87129-184-3*, T60) Dramatic Pub.

Typically English. Sharon J. Beard. (Illus.). 144p. 1994. pap. 12.00 (*0-8059-3603-3*) Dorrance.

Typing. Verleigh Ernest. LC 72-142516. 1971. pap. write for info. (*0-672-96002-8*) Macmillan.

Typing. Pitman. 224p. 1995. pap. 7.95 (*0-8442-3944-5*, Teach Yourslf) NTC Pub Grp.

Typing & Keyboard for Everyone. 10th ed. Nathan Levine. 160p. 1996. 14.95 (*0-02-860597-7*) Macmillan.

Typing by Design. Herbert L. Becker. 1982. pap. 6.96 (*0-02-830760-7*) Glencoe.

Typing, First Course see First Course: Keyboarding & Document Processing

Typing for Beginners. Speedwriting Institute Staff. 1976. 6.00 (*0-671-18138-6*, Arco) Macmillan Gen Ref.

Typing for Beginners. rev. ed. Betty Owen. (Practical Handbook Ser.). 80p. 1985. pap. 8.95 (*0-399-51147-4*, Perigee Bks) Berkley Pub.

Typing for Everyone. 9th ed. Nathan Levine. Ed. by Sheryl Lindsell-Roberts. LC 93-31880. (Illus.). 1994. pap. 13.00 (*0-671-87285-0*) P-H Gen Ref & Trav.

***Typing for Everyone.** 11th ed. Nathan Levine. 1998. pap. 12.95 (*0-02-862194-8*) Macmillan.

Typing for Individual Achievement. Jack Heller. Ed. by Audrey S. Rubin. LC 80-26244. (Illus.). 192p. 1981. text ed. 26.96 (*0-07-027921-7*) McGraw.

***Typing for Kids! Learning to Type on Typewriters & Computer Keyboards.** L. S. McClaine. (Illus.). 32p. (Orig.). (J). (gr. 2-8). 1996. pap. text ed. 5.95 (*1-890537-01-2*) Nutmeg Pubns.

Typing for the Physically Handicapped: Methods & Keyboard Presentation Charts. Jack Heller. (gr. 10-12). 1978. text ed. 250.00 (*0-07-028079-7*) McGraw.

Typing from Handwritten Copy. A. E. Klein. 1978. 10.00 (*0-936862-01-7*, HC-33) DDC Pub.

Typing Improvement Practice for Manual Typists. Robert L. Grubbs & David H. Weaver. 1984. write for info. (*0-07-025065-0*) McGraw.

Typing in Ten Minutes: On Any Keyboard - At Any Age. Carole Marsh. (Quantum Leap Ser.). (Illus.). (J). (gr. k-12). 1994. 29.95 (*1-55609-194-X*); pap. 19.95 (*0-935326-12-X*) Gallopade Pub Group.

Typing in the Dark. Saundra Sharp. 96p. (Orig.). 1991. 19.95 (*0-86316-300-9*); pap. 9.95 (*0-86316-305-X*) Writers & Readers.

Typing Made Easy: Featuring the "See It, Say It, Strike It" Method. Elza Dinwiddie-Boyd. (Practical Handbook Ser.). 96p. 1991. pap. 8.95 (*0-399-51671-9*, Perigee Bks) Berkley Pub.

Typing Made Easy: Includes Computer Usage. 7th ed. Diane Bellavance. (Illus.). 20p. (Orig.). 1994. pap. 3.95 (*0-9605276-6-4*) DBA Bks.

***Typing Made Easy: Includes Computer Usage.** 8th rev. ed. Diane Bellavance. (Illus.). 20p. (Orig.). (J). (ps-10). 1997. pap. 4.25 (*0-9605276-8-0*, SAN:281-5877) DBA Bks.

Typing Mailable Letters. 3rd ed. Parker Liles et al. Ed. by Audrey S. Rubin. (Illus.). (J). (gr. 9-12). 1978. text ed. 11.24 (*0-07-037855-X*) McGraw.

Typing One: General Course Gregg Typing. Alan C. Lloyd et al. LC 81-15629. (Gregg Typing Ser.: No. 7). (Illus.). 288p. 1982. text ed. 21.96 (*0-07-038281-6*) McGraw.

Typing Power - Spelling Power, Vol. I. Norman W. Elliott et al. LC 75-8458. 1975. teacher ed. write for info. (*0-672-96791-X*); pap. write for info. (*0-672-96415-5*) Macmillan.

Typing Power Drills. 3rd ed. Alan C. Lloyd et al. LC 83-8592. (Illus.). 96p. 1984. text ed. 12.96 (*0-07-038176-3*) McGraw.

Typing Seventy-Five. Ed. by Alan C. Lloyd et al. Incl. Professional. 1971. text ed. 25.95 (*0-07-038168-2*); 1971. write for info. (*0-318-54189-0*) McGraw.

Typing Seventy Five: Advanced. Ed. by Alan C. Lloyd et al. (Gregg College Typing Ser.: No. 4). 1979. text ed. 24.50 (*0-07-038257-3*) McGraw.

Typing Seventy Five: Expert. 4th ed. Ed. by Alan C. Lloyd et al. (Gregg College Typing Ser.: No. 4). 1978. text ed. 24.50 (*0-07-038258-1*) McGraw.

Typing Seventy-Five: Intermediate. Alan C. Lloyd et al. (Gregg College Typing Ser.: No. 5). 1984. text ed. 26.90 (*0-07-038323-5*) McGraw.

Typing Skill Drills. E. C. Archer & LeRoy A. Pemberton. 1973. pap. text ed. 6.95 (*0-89420-103-4*, 143000) Natl Book.

Typing Skill Drives. 2nd ed. Alan C. Lloyd et al. 1974. text ed. 13.96 (*0-07-038161-5*) McGraw.

Typing Skills, Book I. Stanley Thornes. (C). 1984. 60.00 (*0-85950-127-2*, Pub. by S Thornes Pubs UK) St Mut.

Typing Skills, Book II. Stanley Thornes. (C). 1985. 55.00 (*0-85950-160-4*, Pub. by S Thornes Pubs UK) St Mut.

Typing Sourcebook. Jordan Hale. LC 77-25064. 1978. teacher ed. write for info. (*0-672-97184-4*); pap. write for info. (*0-672-97324-3*) Macmillan.

Typing the Easy Way. 3rd ed. Warren T. Schimmel & S. A. Lieberman. LC 95-44495. (Easy Way Ser.). 152p. 1996. pap. 14.95 (*0-8120-9147-7*) Barron.

Typing Three Hundred, 2 vols., Vol. 1: General Course. John L. Rowe et al. (Illus.). 288p. (gr. 9-12). 1972. Vol. 1 General Course. text ed. 24.24 (*0-07-054090-X*) McGraw.

Typing Tutor IV IBM PC, PC-XT, PC AT, PC JR 5 1-4" S & S Software Staff. 1991. write for info. (*0-318-68270-2*) P-H.

Typing Tutor 5 DOS. 1994. 49.95 (*1-56686-161-6*) Brady Pub.

Typing Tutor 5 for Mac. 1994. 49.95 (*1-56686-160-8*) Brady Pub.

Typing Tutor 5 for Windows. 1994. 49.95 (*1-56686-159-4*) Brady Pub.

Typing Two: Advanced Course Gregg Typing. Alan C. Lloyd et al. LC 81-15629. (Gregg Typing Ser.: No. 7). (Illus.). 288p. 1982. text ed. 21.96 (*0-07-038282-4*) McGraw.

***Typing: Two-in-One: Keyboarding & Document Processing.** 3rd ed. Archie Drummond & Anne Coles-Mogford. 208p. (Orig.). 1996. pap. 32.50 (*0-7487-2437-0*, Pub. by Stanley Thornes UK) Trans-Atl Phila.

Typings. Christopher Knowles. 112p. 1979. 12.50 (*0-931428-36-X*); pap. 7.50 (*0-931428-09-2*) Vehicle Edns.

Typisch Deutsch. Behal-Thomsen et al. 144p. 1993. 24.50 (*3-468-49446-7*) Langenscheidt.

Typist. Jack Rudman. (Career Examination Ser.: C-826). 1994. pap. 19.95 (*0-8373-0826-7*) Nat Learn.

Typist see Gregg Office Job Training Program, Classroom Installation

Typists & The Tiger: Two Plays. Murray Schisgal. 1963. pap. 5.25 (*0-8222-1150-5*) Dramatists Play.

TYPIX Standardized Data & Crystal Chemical Characterization of Inorganic Structure Types, Vol. I. 2nd ed. Ed. by Gmelin Institute for Inorganic Chemistry of the Max-Planck-Society Staff. (Gmelin Handbook of Inorganic & Organometallic Chemistry Ser.). xv, 260p. 1993. 875.00 (*0-387-93682-3*) Spr-Verlag.

TYPIX Standardized Data & Crystal Chemical Characterization of Inorganic Structure Types, Vol. 3. (Gmelin Handbook of Inorganic & Organometallic Chemistry Ser.). xi, 512p. 1994. 835.00 (*0-387-93684-X*) Spr-Verlag.

TYPIX Standardized Data & Crystal Chemical Characterization of Inorganic Structure Types, Vol. 4. (Gmelin Handbook of Inorganic & Organometallic Chemistry Ser.). xiii, 416p. 1994. 835.00 (*0-387-93685-8*) Spr-Verlag.

TYPIX Standardized Data & Crystal Chemical Characterization of Inorganic Structure Types, Vol. II, Vol. II. 2nd ed. Ed. by Gmelin Institute for Inorganic Chemistry of the Max-Planck-Society Staff. (Gmelin Handbook of Inorganic & Organometallic Chemistry Ser.). xi, 408p. 1993. 945.00 (*0-387-93683-1*) Spr-Verlag.

Typodirection in Japan, Vol. 6. P.I.E. Books Editorial Staff & Tokyo Typodirecturs Club Staff. (Illus.). 250p. 1996. pap. 69.95 (*4-938586-83-5*, Pub. by PIE Bks JA) Bks Nippan.

Typodirection Japan, No. 5. Tokyo Typodirectors Club Staff. (Illus.). 250p. 1994. 69.95 (*4-938586-54-1*, Pub. by PIE Bks JA) Bks Nippan.

Typographia Universitatis Hungaricae Budae 1777-1848. P. Kiraly. 504p. (ENG, FRE & GER.). (C). 1983. pap. 100.00 (*963-05-2960-2*, Pub. by Akad Kiado HU) St Mut.

Typographers on Type: An Illustrated Anthology. Ed. by Ruari McLean. (Illus.). 180p. 1995. 27.00 (*0-393-70201-4*) Norton.

***Typographers on Type: An Illustrated Anthology from William Morris to the Present Day.** Ruari McLean. (Illus.). 200p. Date not set. write for info. (*0-85331-657-0*, Pub. by Lund Humphries UK) Antique Collect.

***Typographic.** Clairk. (Design & Graphic Design Ser.). 1997. wbk. ed., pap. 34.95 (*0-442-02520-3*) Van Nos Reinhold.

Typographic Bookplates of Ward Ritchie. limited ed. Compiled by Melissa Beck. (Illus.). 108p. 1990. 45.00 (*0-931043-03-4*) K Karmiole.

Typographic Communications Today. Edward M. Gottschall. (Illus.). 256p. 1989. 85.00 (*0-262-07114-2*) MIT Pr.

***Typographic Design.** 1992. 49.95 (*0-688-11106-8*) Morrow.

Typographic Design. Ed. by David Brier. 256p. 1992. 49.95 (*0-942604-23-7*) Madison Square.

Typographic Design. 2nd ed. Ronald A. Carter. 1993. pap. 39.95 (*0-442-00759-0*) Van Nos Reinhold.

Typographic Design: Promotion. David Brier. 192p. 1993. 45.00 (*0-942604-25-3*) Madison Square.

Typographic Milestones. Allan Haley. (Illus.). 144p. 1992. pap. 34.95 (*0-442-23642-5*) Van Nos Reinhold.

Typographic Scene. Walter Tracy. 96p. 1990. 19.95 (*0-86902-112-5*, Pub. by Scolar Pr UK) Ashgate Pub Co.

Typographic Specimens. Philip B. Meggs. 415p. 1994. pap. 44.95 (*0-442-00758-2*) Van Nos Reinhold.

Typographic Years: A Printer's Journey Through a Half Century. Joseph Blumenthal. LC 82-71904. (Illus.). 153p. 1982. 26.50 (*0-913720-38-0*) Beil.

Typographical & Ornamental see Handbook of Early Advertising Art

Typographical Antiquities or the History of Printing in England, Scotland & Ireland, 4 vols. Joseph Ames. 2337p. 1969. reprint ed. Set. lib. bdg. 785.00 (*0-685-43586-5*, 05102047) G Olms Pubs.

Typographical Gazetteer. Henry Cotton. 1975. reprint ed. 40.00 (*1-55888-238-3*) Omnigraphics Inc.

Typographical Journey Through the Inland Printer 1883-1900. Intro. by Maurice Annenberg. LC 77-89269. (C). boxed 45.00 (*0-916526-04-6*) Maran Pub.

Typographics: Magazines, No. 2. Roger Walton. (Illus.). 244p. 1996. 49.95 (*0-688-15043-8*) Hearst Bks.

Typographics 1. Roger Walton. (Illus.). 224p. 1995. 49.95 (*0-688-14253-2*, North Lght Bks) F & W Pubns Inc.

***Typographics 1.** Roger Walton. (Illus.). 224p. 1997. pap. 34.95 (*0-688-15066-7*) Hearst Bks.

Typography: Its History & Use. Day. 3.00 (*0-318-19216-0*) Quill & Scroll.

Typography: Mimesis, Philosophy, Politics. Phillipe Lacoue-Labarthe. Ed. by Christopher Fynsk. LC 88-36989. 312p. 1989. 42.50 (*0-674-91700-6*) HUP.

Typography & Design. Boston Public Library Staff. 10.00 (*0-685-60072-6*) Boston Public Lib.

Typography & Typesetting. Ronald A. Labuz. (Illus.). 375p. 1988. text ed. 44.95 (*0-442-25966-2*) Van Nos Reinhold.

***Typography Design.** 2nd ed. Madison Square Press Staff. 1995. 47.50 (*0-688-13848-9*) Morrow.

Typography for Desktop Publishers. Mark Hengesbaugh. 1990. per. 30.00 (*1-55623-428-7*) Irwin Prof Pubng.

Typography for Desktop Publishers. Grant Shipcott. (Graphic Design in the Computer Age Ser.). (Illus.). 96p. 1996. 39.95 (*0-7134-7212-X*, Pub. by Batsford UK) Trafalgar.

***Typography Now!** 1992. 49.50 (*0-688-10773-7*) Morrow.

Typography Now, No. 2. Ed. by Rick Poynor. (Illus.). 240p. 1996. 55.00 (*0-688-14515-9*, Quill) Hearst Bks.

Typography 13: The Annual of the Type Directors Club. Type Directors Club Staff. (Illus.). 272p. 1992. 50.00 (*0-8230-5547-7*, Watsn-Guptill) Watsn-Guptill.

Typography 14: The Annual of the Type Directors Club. (Illus.). 232p. 1993. 50.00 (*0-8230-5548-5*, Watsn-Guptill) Watsn-Guptill.

Typography 17. Annual of the Type Directors Club Staff. 1996. 59.95 (*0-8230-5552-3*) Watsn-Guptill.

Typologia: Studies in Type Design & Type Making with Comments on the Invention of Typography, the First Types, Legibility & Fine Printing. Frederic W. Goudy. 1978. reprint ed. pap. 14.00 (*0-520-03278-0*) U CA Pr.

Typological Discourse Analysis: Quantitative Approaches to the Study of Linguistic Function. John Myhill. 1992. text ed. 60.95 (*0-631-17614-4*) Blackwell Pubs.

Typological Studies in Negation. Ed. by Peter Kahrel & Rene Van den Berg. LC 93-5763. (Typological Studies in Language (TSL): No. 29). x, 385p. 1993. 85.00 (*1-55619-422-6*); pap. 29.95 (*1-55619-423-4*) Benjamins North Am.

Typological Vocabulary of Forestry Stations: Vocabulaire Typologie Des Stations Forestieres. R. Delpech et al. 246p. (FRE.). 1986. 39.95 (*0-8288-1430-9*, M15565) Fr & Eur.

Typologie der Testaufgaben fur den Dt. Unterricht. Peter Doye. 223p. 1988. 26.25 (*3-468-49437-8*) Langenscheidt.

Typologies: Nine Contemporary Photographers. Marc Freidus et al. LC 90-2445. (Illus.). 138p. 1991. pap. 24.95 (*0-917493-18-4*) Newport Harbor.

Typologies & Taxonomies: An Introduction to Classification Techniques. Kenneth D. Bailey. (Quantitative Applications in the Social Sciences Ser.: Vol. 102). (Illus.). 96p. 1994. pap. 9.95 (*0-8039-5259-7*) Sage.

***Typologies in England, 1650-1820.** Paul J. Korshin. LC 81-47139. 488p. 1982. reprint ed. pap. 139.10 (*0-608-02888-6*, 2063952) Bks Demand.

Typology & English Medieval Literature. Ed. by Hugh T. Keenan. LC 89-45872. (Georgia State Literary Studies: No. 7). 1992. 55.00 (*0-404-63207-6*) AMS Pr.

***Typology & Nomenclature for New York Projectile Points.** William A. Ritchie. (Illus.). 119p. 1971. reprint ed. pap. 7.00 (*0-614-26370-0*) Purple Mnt Pr.

Typology & Seventeenth-Century Literature. Joseph A. Galdon. (De Proprietatibus Litterarum, Ser. Major: No. 28). 164p. 1975. text ed. 64.65 (*90-279-3366-9*) Mouton.

Typology & Structure of Roman Historical Reliefs. Mario Torelli. (Thomas Spence Jerome Lecture Ser.: No. 14). (Illus.). 208p. (C). 1992. pap. text ed. 32.50 (*0-472-08171-3*) U of Mich Pr.

Typology & Universals. William Croft. (Cambridge Textbooks in Linguistics Ser.). 324p. (C). 1991. 55.00 (*0-521-36583-X*); pap. text ed. 21.95 (*0-521-36765-4*) Cambridge U Pr.

Typology in Scripture: A Study of Hermeneutical Tupos Structures. Richard M. Davidson. (Andrews University Seminary Doctoral Dissertation Ser.: Vol. 2). 510p. (Orig.). 1981. pap. 19.99 (*0-943872-34-0*) Andrews Univ Pr.

***Typology of Adjectival Predication.** Harrie Wetzer. (Empirical Approaches to Language Topology Ser.: Vol. 17). xiv, 398p. (C). 1996. lib. bdg. 120.00 (*0-614-30645-0*) Mouton.

Typology of Community Residential Services: Report. American Psychiatric Association Staff, Task Force on Psychosocial Aspects of Nuclear Developments. LC 82-24467. (American Psychiatric Association Task Force Report Ser.: No. 21). 97p. reprint ed. pap. 27.70 (*0-8357-7803-7*, 2036172) Bks Demand.

Typology of Industrialization Processes in the Nineteenth Century, Vol. 39. Hugo Sonnenschein. (Fundamentals of Pure & Applied Economics Ser.: 39). 106, viiip. 1990. pap. text ed. 40.00 (*3-7186-5007-X*) Gordon & Breach.

Typology of Reflexives. Emma Geniusiene. (Empirical Approaches to Language Typology Ser.: No. 2). 435p. 1987. lib. bdg. 153.85 (*0-89925-084-X*) Mouton.

Typology of Resultative Constructions. Ed. by Vladimir P. Nedjalkov & Bernard Comrie. LC 88-2598. (Typological Studies in Language: Vol. 12). xx, 573p. (C). 1988. reprint ed. 144.00 (*0-915027-78-X*); reprint ed. pap. 42.95 (*0-915027-79-8*) Benjamins North Am.

Typology of Scripture, 2 vols. in 1. Patrick Fairbairn. LC 89-2574. 918p. 1989. pap. 26.99 (*0-8254-2628-6*, Kregel Class); lib. bdg. 32.99 (*0-8254-2631-6*, Kregel Class) Kregel.

Typology of Subordination in Georgian & Abkhaz. Brian G. Hewitt. (Empirical Approaches to Language Typology Ser.: No. 5). 292p. 1987. lib. bdg. 110.00 (*3-11-010709-0*) Mouton.

Typology of the Early Codex. Eric G. Turner. LC 75-10125. (Haney Foundation Ser.). 212p. reprint ed. pap. 60.50 (*0-8357-9750-3*, 2055282) Bks Demand.

Typology of the Racehorse. Franco Varola. (Illus.). 1977. 35.00 (*0-87556-270-1*) Saifer.

Typology of the Racehorse. Franco Varola. 242p. 1990. 65.00 (*0-85131-196-2*, Pub. by J A Allen & Co UK) St Mut.

Typology of Urban & Regional Planners: Why Plan? John M. Udy. LC 91-31507. (Illus.). 164p. 1991. lib. bdg. 79.95 (*0-7734-9652-1*) E Mellen.

Typology Relationship & Time. Ed. by Vitalij V. Shevoroshkin & T. L. Markey. xxxii, 129p. 1986. pap. 14.50 (*0-89720-072-1*) Karoma.

Typomania. Kraus. 1995. 49.00 (*0-387-58182-0*) Spr-Verlag.

Typomania: Selected Essays on Typesetting. L. W. Wallis. (Illus.). 176p. (C). 1993. 49.95 (*1-874084-01-7*, Pub. by Lund Humphries UK) Antique Collect.

Typophily. H. Jackson. 1972. 59.95 (*0-8490-1240-6*) Gordon Pr.

Tyranena. Craig Froelich. LC 92-91106. 280p. 1994. pap. 12.95 (*1-56002-275-2*, Univ Edtns) Aegina Pr.

Tyrannies of Virtue: The Cultural Criticism of John P. Sisk. John P. Sisk. LC 89-48726. 304p. 1990. 28.95 (*0-8061-2267-6*) U of Okla Pr.

Tyrannius Rufinus: Historia Monachorum Sive de Vita Sanctorum Patrum. Ed. by Eva Schulz-Flugel. (Patristische Texte und Studien: Band 34). xxv, 423p. (C). 1990. lib. bdg. 166.15 (*3-11-012040-2*) De Gruyter.

Tyrannosaur. David Drake. 224p. (Orig.). 1994. mass mkt. 4.99 (*0-8125-3530-8*) Tor Bks.

Tyrannosaurus. William Lindsay. LC 92-52820. (American Museum of Natural History Ser.). (Illus.). 32p. (J). (gr. 3 up). 1993. 12.95 (*1-56458-124-1*) DK Pub Inc.

Tyrannosaurus. Janet Riehecky. LC 88-1692. (Dinosaur Bks.). (Illus.). 32p. (J). (gr. k-4). 1988. lib. bdg. 21.36 (*0-89565-424-5*) Childs World.

Tyrannosaurus. Sheehan. (Dinosaur Library: Set I). (Illus.). 24p. (J). 1981. lib. bdg. 14.00 (*0-86592-114-8*) Rourke Enter.

Tyrannosaurus. Glenn Storrs. LC 93-45531. (Dinoworld Ser.). 40p. (J). (gr. 3-7). 1994. pap. 5.95 (*1-85697-993-8*, Kingfisher LKC) LKC.

***Tyrannosaurus: The Tyrant Lizard.** Janet Riehecky. LC 96-48540. (Dinosaur Days Ser.: Group 1). (Illus.). (J). (ps up). 1997. lib. bdg. 14.95 (*0-7614-0601-8*, Benchmark NY) Marshall Cavendish.

Tyrannosaurus & Other Wrecks: Fossil Trivia for Kids. Carole Marsh. (Quantum Leap Ser.). (Illus.). (Orig.). (J). (gr. 2 up). 1994. 29.95 (*1-55609-166-4*); pap. 19.95 (*0-935326-56-1*) Gallopade Pub Group.

Tyrannosaurus Forest. (Adventures of Dinosaur Dog Ser.: No. 1). (J). (gr. 3-7). 1993. pap. 6.95 (*1-883649-00-5*) Sutton Pubns.

Tyrannosaurus Game. Steven Kroll. LC 75-37078. (Illus.). 40p. (J). (ps-3). 1976. lib. bdg. 15.95 (*0-8234-0275-4*) Holiday.

Tyrannosaurus Game. Steven Kroll. LC 75-37078. (Illus.). 40p. (J). (ps-3). 1986. pap. 5.95 (*0-8234-0620-2*) Holiday.

Tyrannosaurus Game. Steven Kroll. (Illus.). (J). 1988. 22.95 incl. audio (*0-87499-096-3*); pap. 15.95 incl. audio (*0-87499-095-5*) Live Oak Media.

Tyrannosaurus Game, 4 bks., Set. Steven Kroll. (Illus.). (J). 1988. pap. 33.95 incl. audio (*0-87499-097-1*) Live Oak Media.

Tyrannosaurus Prescription: And One Hundred Other Essays. Isaac Asimov. 323p. 1989. 26.95 (*0-87975-540-7*) Prometheus Bks.

Tyrannosaurus Rex. Betty G. Birney. (Illus.). 32p. (J). (ps-3). 1996. pap. 5.95 (*0-395-81654-8*) HM.

An Asterisk (*) at the beginning of an entry indicates that the title is appearing in BIP for the first time.

Tyrannosaurus Rex. David Petersen. LC 88-38054. (New True Bks.). (Illus.). 48p. (J). (gr. k-4). 1989. pap. 5.50 (0-516-41167-5); lib. bdg. 19.00 (0-516-01167-7) Childrens.

***Tyrannosaurus Rex.** Dale A. Russell & John Acorn. (Illus.). 32p. Date not set. pap. 12.95 (0-8362-4216-5) Andrews & McMeel.

Tyrannosaurus Rex & Its Kin: The Mesozoic Monsters. Helen R. Sattler. LC 88-1577. (Illus.). 48p. (J). (gr. 3 up). 1989. 16.00 (0-688-07747-1); lib. bdg. 15.93 (0-688-07748-X) Lothrop.

Tyrannosaurus Rex & Other Cretaceous Meat-Eaters. Daniel Cohen. (Dinosaurs of North America Ser.). (Illus.). 48p. (J). (gr. 3-9). 1996. 17.80 (1-56065-288-8) Capstone Pr.

Tyrannosaurus Rex & Other Cretaceous Meat-Eaters. Daniel Cohen. (Illus.). 48p. (J). (gr. 3-7). 1995. 13.35 (0-516-35288-1) Childrens.

Tyrannosaurus Rex & Other Dinosaur Wonders. Querida L. Pearce. (Amazing Science Ser.). (Illus.). 64p. (J). (gr. 4-6). 1990. pap. 5.95 (0-671-70688-8, Julian Messner) Silver Burdett Pr.

Tyrannosaurus Rex Book & Diorama. Christine Economos. (Illus.). 64p. (J). (gr. 1-4). 1996. pap. 10.95 (0-7611-0539-5, 10539) Workman Pub.

***Tyrannosaurus Rex Book & Diorama.** Christine Economos. (Illus.). (J). (gr. 6-9). 1996. pap. 10.95 (0-614-19278-1) Workman Pub.

Tyrannosaurus Tex. Betty G. Birney. LC 93-30727. (Illus.). (J). 1994. 14.95 (0-395-67648-7) HM.

Tyrannosaurus Tex. Robert B. Greenberg. LC 89-4225. (Tyrannosaurus Tex Ser.: Vol. 1). (Illus.). 64p. (J). (gr. k-4). 1989. pap. 6.95 (0-938349-38-4) State House Pr.

Tyrannosaurus Tex: First Grade. Robert B. Greenberg. LC 90-9749. (Tyrannosaurus Tex Ser.: Vol. 2). (Illus.). 64p. (J). (gr. k-4). 1991. pap. 5.95 (0-938349-56-2) State House Pr.

Tyrannosaurus Tex in the Timeless Town. Robert B. Greenberg. LC 94-7864. (Tyrannosaurus Tex Ser.: Vol. 3). (Illus.). 64p. (J). (gr. k-4). 1994. pap. 6.95 (1-880510-14-6) State House Pr.

***Tyrannosaurus Therapy: How to Avoid Becoming Emotionally Extinct.** Ray Dean. (Illus.). 288p. 1997. 29.00 (0-614-29606-4) Blue Note Pubns.

Tyrannosaurus Was a Beast. Jack Prelutsky. LC 87-25131. (Illus.). 32p. (J). (ps-6). 1988. 16.00 (0-688-06442-6) Greenwillow.

Tyrannosaurus Was a Beast. Jack Prelutsky. LC 87-25131. (Illus.). 32p. (J). (ps up). 1992. pap. 4.95 (0-688-11569-1, Mulberry) Morrow.

Tyrannosaurus Was a Beast: Big Book Edition. Jack Prelutsky. (Illus.). 32p. (J). (ps up). 1993. reprint ed. pap. 18.95 (0-688-12613-8, Mulberry) Morrow.

Tyrannous Reign of Mary Stewart. George Buchanan. Tr. by W. A. Gatherer from LAT. LC 78-3556. (Edinburgh University Publication: History, Philosophy, & Economics: No. 10). 228p. 1978. reprint ed. text ed. 59.75 (0-313-20343-1, BUTR) Greenwood.

Tyrannsasaurus Rex: The Fierce Dinosaur. Elizabeth Sandell. Ed. by Marjorie Oelerich & Howard Schroeder. LC 88-958. (Dinosaur Discovery Era Ser.). (Illus.). 32p. (J). (gr. k-5). 1988. pap. 5.95 (0-944280-06-4); lib. bdg. 12.95 (0-944280-00-5) Bancroft-Sage.

Tyranny: The First Seal. Mitchell J. Gross. (Illus.). (Orig.). 1995. pap. 10.00 (0-9648726-2-5) Quintessential Mercy.

Tyranny & Legitimacy: A Critique of Political Theories. James S. Fishkin. LC 79-11177. 176p. 1979. text ed. 28.00 (0-8018-2206-8); pap. text ed. 13.95 (0-8018-2256-4) Johns Hopkins.

Tyranny & Political Culture in Ancient Greece. James F. McGlew. LC 93-15653. 232p. 1993. 35.00 (0-8014-2787-8) Cornell U Pr.

Tyranny & Political Culture in Ancient Greece. James F. McGlew. 248p. 1996. pap. 14.95 (0-8014-8387-5) Cornell U Pr.

***Tyranny of Change.** 3rd ed. Chambers. Date not set. pap. text ed. write for info. (0-312-11209-2) St Martin.

***Tyranny of Corporations & Foundations.** Max. 50p. (Orig.). 1997. pap. 30.00 (0-922070-78-4) M Tecton Pub.

Tyranny of Experts: Blowing the Whistle on the Cult of Expertise. Morris E. Chafetz. 173p. 1996. 19.95 (1-56833-064-2) Madison Bks UPA.

***Tyranny of Gun Control.** Ed. by Jacob G. Hornberger. 115p. 1997. pap. 9.95 (0-9640447-7-3) Future of Freedom.

Tyranny of Hate: The Roots of Antisemitism. abr. ed. Constantin Brunner. Tr. by Graham Harrison. LC 92-13724. 208p. 1992. lib. bdg. 89.95 (0-7734-9562-2) E Mellen.

Tyranny of Kindness: Dismantling the Welfare System to End Poverty in America. Theresa Funiciello. 368p. 1994. pap. 12.00 (0-87113-578-7, Atlntc Mnthly) Grove-Atltic.

Tyranny of Love. Kenneth G. Mills. Ed. by Mary J. Leaper & Megan MacQueen. (Illus.). 264p. (Orig.). 1995. pap. 21.95 (0-919842-17-8, KGOB12) Sun-Scape Ent.

Tyranny of Numbers: Mismeasurement & Misrule. Nicholas Eberstadt. 327p. 1995. pap. 16.95 (0-8447-3764-X) Am Enterprise.

Tyranny of Numbers: Mismeasurement & Misrule. Nicholas Eberstadt. 327p. (C). 1995. 39.75 (0-8447-3763-1) Am Enterprise.

***Tyranny of Relativism: Culture & Politics in Contemporary English Society.** Richard Hoggart. LC 97-2268. 1997. pap. 21.95 (1-56000-953-5) Transaction Pubs.

***Tyranny of Roses.** Anatasia Cleaver. Date not set. write for info. (0-688-04471-9) Morrow.

Tyranny of Survival: And Other Pathologies of Civilized Life. Daniel Callahan. LC 85-5316. (Illus.). 300p. 1985. reprint ed. pap. text ed. 24.50 (0-8191-4636-6) U Pr of Amer.

Tyranny of Taste: A Study of British Public Policy on Design Architecture & Town Planning Since 1550. Jules Lubbock. LC 94-26853. 1995. 55.00 (0-300-05889-6) Yale U Pr.

Tyranny of Testing. Banesh Hoffman. LC 77-26028. 223p. 1978. reprint ed. text ed. 55.00 (0-313-20097-1, HOTT, Greenwood Pr) Greenwood.

Tyranny of the Bottom Line: Why Corporations Make Good People Do Bad Things. Ralph Estes. LC 95-25473. 288p. 1996. 27.95 (1-881052-75-3) Berrett-Koehler.

Tyranny of the Dark. Hamlin Garland. (Collected Works of Hamlin Garland). 1988. reprint ed. lib. bdg. 59.00 (0-7812-1234-0) Rprt Serv.

Tyranny of the Dark see Collected Works of Hamlin Garland

***Tyranny of the Discrete: A Discussion of the Problems of Local History in England.** John D. Marshall. LC 96-33160. 164p. 1997. text ed. 68.95 (1-85928-290-3, Pub. by Scolar Pr UK) Ashgate Pub Co.

Tyranny of the Group. Andrew Malcolm. (Quality Paperback Ser.: No. 294). 190p. (Orig.). 1975. reprint ed. pap. 8.00 (0-8226-0294-6) Littlefield.

Tyranny of the Majority: Fundamental Fairness & Representative Democracy. Lani Guinier. 1995. pap. 13.00 (0-02-913169-3, Free Press) Free Pr.

Tyranny of the Market: A Critique of Theoretical Foundations. Douglas Vickers. LC 95-11181. 1995. text ed. 52.50 (0-472-10618-X) U of Mich Pr.

Tyranny of the Normal: An Anthology. Ed. by Carol Donley & Sheryl Buckley. LC 95-36898. (Literature & Medicine Ser.: No. 2). 389p. (Orig.). (C). 1995. pap. 29.00 (0-87338-535-7) Kent St U Pr.

Tyranny of the Normal: Essays on Bioethics, Theology, & Myth. Leslie Fiedler. LC 95-34579. 192p. 1996. 22.95 (1-56792-003-9) Godine.

Tyranny of the Spirit: Domination & Submission in Adolescent Relationships. David K. Curran. LC 96-11820. 1996. 40.00 (1-56821-833-8) Aronson.

Tyranny of the Status Quo. Milton Friedman & Rose Friedman. LC 83-22637. 192p. 1984. 13.95 (0-15-192379-5) HarBrace.

Tyranny of the Urgent. Charles E. Hummel. (Orig.). 1984. pap. text ed. 0.99 (0-87784-128-4) InterVarsity.

Tyranny of the Urgent. Charles E. Hummel. (Christian Classics Ser.). 1995. pap. 2.99 (1-56570-012-0) Meridian MI.

Tyranny of the Urgent see IVP Booklets

Tyranny of Values. unabridged ed. Carl Schmitt. Ed. & Tr. by Simona Draghici from GER. LC 96-50191. 44p. (Orig.). 1996. pap. text ed. 3.95 (0-943045-11-8) Plutarch Pr DC.

Tyranny of Words. Stuart Chase. LC 38-27108. 420p. 1959. pap. 8.00 (0-15-692394-7, Harvest Bks) HarBrace.

Tyranny on Trial: The Evidence at Nuremberg. Whitney R. Harris. LC 54-11298. 672p. reprint ed. pap. 180.00 (0-8357-7061-3, 2033421) Bks Demand.

Tyranny Unmasked. John Taylor. Ed. by F. Thornton Miller. LC 92-26255. 314p. 1992. 16.00 (0-86597-104-8); pap. 6.50 (0-86597-105-6) Liberty Fund.

Tyranny 2000: The Justice Conflict. William Hester. LC 87-90616. 372p. (Orig.). 1988. 9.00 (0-945665-02-4) Cole & Sherwood.

Tyranosaurus Rex. Stuart A. Kallen. Ed. by Julie Berg. LC 94-4533. (If the Dinosaurs Could Talk Ser.). (J). 1994. 14.98 (1-56239-284-0) Abdo & Dghtrs.

Tyrant: The Story of John Barber - Jacobite Lord Mayor of London, Printer & Friend to Dr. Swift. Sessions, William, Ltd. Staff & Charles A. Rivington. (C). 1989. pap. 54.00 (1-85072-039-8, Pub. by W Sessions UK) St Mut.

Tyrant & Victim in Dostoevsky. Gary Cox. 119p. 1984. pap. 15.95 (0-89357-125-?) Slavica.

Tyrant from Illinois. Blair Bolles. LC 73-16641. 248p. 1974. reprint ed. text ed. 35.00 (0-8371-7205-5, BOTI, Greenwood Pr) Greenwood.

Tyrant in Cap & Gown. Carl W. Salser, Jr. LC 73-91074. 1974. 18.95 (0-89420-100-X, 110055, Halcyon) Natl Book.

***Tyrant of the Badlands.** Sigmund Brouwer. (Accidental Detective Ser.: Vol. 13). 132p. (J). (gr. 3-7). 1996. mass mkt. 5.99 (1-56476-160-6, Victor Bks) Chariot Victor.

Tyrant of the Past & the Slave of the Future. Christopher Davis. LC 89-4996. (Orig.). (C). 1989. 15.00 (0-89672-199-X); pap. 8.50 (0-89672-200-7) Tex Tech Univ Pr.

Tyrant of Time. Lloyd A. Eshbach. 1991. 10.00 (1-880418-15-0) D M Grant.

Tyrant Slayers. rev. ed. Michael W. Taylor. Ed. by W. R. Connnor. LC 80-2671. (Monographs in Classical Studies). (Illus.). 1981. lib. bdg. 25.00 (0-405-14054-1) Ayer.

Tyrant Slayers: The Heroic Image in Fifth Century B.C. Athenian Art & Politics. 2nd ed. Michael W. Taylor. (Illus.). 192p. (C). 1990. 38.95 (0-88143-113-3) Ayer.

Tyrants. Charles E. Jarvis. LC 77-78167. (Illus.). (C). 1977. pap. text ed. 4.95 (0-915940-02-7) Ithaca Pr MA.

Tyrants & Mountains: A Reckless Life. Denis Hills. (Illus.). 320p. 1992. 39.95 (0-7195-4640-0, Pub. by John Murray UK) Trafalgar.

Tyrants, Knaves, & Citizens: The Liberal Foundations of American Citizenship. Richard Sinopoli. 224p. 1992. 45.00 (0-19-507067-4) OUP.

Tyrant's Test: Star Wars. Michael P. Kube-McDowell. (Black Fleet Crisis Ser.: Vol. 3). 352p. (YA). 1997. mass mkt. 5.99 (0-553-57275-X, Spectra) Bantam.

Tyrantula! David Jacobs. (Bug Files Ser.: No. 3). 1996. mass mkt. 4.50 (0-425-15321-5) Berkley Pub.

Tyre Models for Vehicle Dynamic Analysis: Proceedings of the First International Colloquium on Tyre Models for Vehicle Dynamics Analysis, Held in Delft, The Netherlands, Oct. 21-22, 1991. Ed. by Hans B. Pacejka. LC 92-46188. viii, 192p. 1993. 117.50 (90-265-1332-1) Swets.

***Tyre Models for Vehicle Dynamic Analysis: Proceedings of the 2nd International Colloquium, Held at the Technical University of Berlin, Germany, February 20-21, 1997, Germany.** Ed. by F. Bohm & H. P. Willumeit. (Supplement Vehicle System Dynamics (VSD) Ser.: Vol. 27). 356p. 1997. 89.00 (90-265-1488-3) Swets.

Tyre Technology. Tom French. (Illus.). 180p. 1989. 44.00 (0-85274-360-2) IOP Pub.

Tyrell County, North Carolina Marriage Bonds & Certificates, 1761-1862. Francis T. Ingmire. 96p. 1994. pap. 15.00 (0-8095-8704-1); lib. bdg. 39.00 (0-8095-8134-5) Borgo Pr.

Tyres, Suspension & Handling. J. C. Dixon. (Illus.). 400p. (C). 1992. 125.00 (0-521-40194-1) Cambridge U Pr.

Tyrian Influence in the Upper Galilee. Richard S. Hanson. LC 79-11775. (Meiron Excavation Project Ser.: Vol. 2). (Illus.). 89p. 1980. pap. text ed. 8.00 (0-89757-505-9) Am Sch Orient Res.

Tyro: A Review of the Arts of Painting, Sculpture & Design, Nos. 1 & 2: 1921-22. Ed. by Wyndham Lewis. (Illus.). 120p. 1970. 65.00 (0-7146-2116-1, Pub. by F Cass Pubs UK) Intl Spec Bk.

Tyrone & the Swamp Gang. Hans Wilhelm. (J). 1995. pap. 3.95 (0-590-25474-X) Scholastic Inc.

Tyrone Geter: Images of Africa & Recent Works. Catherine L. O'Hara & Ruth K. Meyer. (Illus.). 20p. (Orig.). 1989. pap. 5.00 (0-915577-18-6) Taft Museum.

Tyrone Goes Camping. Linda P. Silbert & Alvin J. Silbert. (Little Twirps Understanding People Bks.). (Illus.). (J). (gr. k-4). 1978. pap. 4.98 (0-89544-055-5) Silbert Bress.

Tyrone Mitchell. Beryl J. Wright. LC 90-49647. 1990. pap. 5.00 (0-932828-24-8) Newark Mus.

Tyrone the Double Dirty Rotten Cheater. Hans Wilhelm. (Illus.). 32p. (J). 1992. pap. 3.95 (0-590-44080-2) Scholastic Inc.

***Tyrone the Double Dirty Rotten Cheater.** Hans Wilhelm. (FRE.). (J). pap. 6.99 (0-590-74141-1) Scholastic Inc.

Tyrone the Horrible. Hans Wilhelm. 32p. (J). (ps). 1992. pap. 4.99 (0-590-41472-0) Scholastic Inc.

Tyrone's Rebellion: The Outbreak of the Nine Years War in Tudor Ireland. Hiram Morgan. (Royal Historical Society: Studies in History: Vol. 67). (Illus.). 264p. (C). 1993. 63.00 (0-86193-224-2) Boydell & Brewer.

Tyrosine Hydroxylase: A Tribute to Toshiharu Nagatsu. Ed. by M. Naoi & S. H. Parvez. x, 312p. 1993. 163.50 (90-6764-154-5) Coronet Bks.

Tyrosine Kinases & Neoplastic Transformation. S. Kellie. (Molecular Biology Intelligence Unit Ser.). 100p. 1994. 89.95 (1-57059-075-3) R G Landes.

Tyrosine Phosphorylation-Dephosphorylation & Downstream Signalling. Ed. by Ludwig M. Heilmeyer, Jr. LC 93-15958. (NATO ASI Series H: Cell Biology: Vol. 76). (Illus.). xii, 376p. 1993. 227.95 (0-387-56745-3) Spr-Verlag.

Tyrrell Cemetaries (North Carolina) 1732-1984. rev. ed. Camille B. Everton. 238p. 1995. pap. text ed. 33.00 (0-7884-0165-3) Heritage Bk.

Tyrrell County North Carolina Minutes Court of Pleas & Quarter Sessions: 1755-1761, Bk. 2. LC 81-120466. (Illus.). 154p. 1983. pap. 15.50 (0-911619-03-8) B F Burr.

Tyrrell County North Carolina Minutes Court of Pleas & Quarter Sessions, 1735-1754, Bk. 1. Prod. by Betty Fagan Burr. 137p. (Orig.). 1981. pap. 14.50 (0-911619-01-1) B F Burr.

Tyrus. Patrick Creevy. 1995. write for info. (0-312-85664-4) Tor Bks.

Ty's One Man Band. Houghton Mifflin Company Staff. (Literature Experience 1993 Ser.). (J). (gr. 4). 1992. pap. 9.16 (0-395-61801-0) HM.

Ty's One-Man Band. Mildred P. Walter. 40p. (J). (gr. k-3). 1984. pap. 5.99 (0-590-40178-5) Scholastic Inc.

Ty's One-Man Band. Mildred P. Walter. LC 80-11224. (Illus.). 32p. (J). (gr. k-3). 1987. reprint ed. lib. bdg. 14.95 (0-02-792300-2, Four Winds Pr) S&S Childrens.

Tysiacha I Odin Izbrannyi Sovetskii Politicheskii Anekdot. Yulius Telesin. LC 85-30588. 220p. (RUS.). 1986. pap. 10.00 (0-938920-65-0) Hermitage.

Tysk-Dansk: Dansk-Tysk Ordbog. F. Albertus. 532p. (DAN & GER.). 1982. 39.95 (0-8288-4424-0, M1293) Fr & Eur.

Tysk-Dansk Dansk-Tysk Special Ordbog: German - Danish, Danish - German Dictionary. E. Fryd. 175p. (DAN & GER.). 1974. 49.95 (0-8288-6216-8, M-1274) Fr & Eur.

Tysk-Dansk Rode Ordboger. 12th ed. Egon Bork & E. Kaper. 604p. 1986. 49.95 (0-7859-3724-2) Fr & Eur.

Tysk-Dansk Teknisk Ordbog: German - Danish Technical Dictionary. A. Warrern. 275p. (DAN & GER.). 1974. 75.00 (0-8288-6217-6, M-1291) Fr & Eur.

Tysk-Norsk Ordbog. Ed. by J. Haukoy & W. Zickfedt. 360p. (GER & NOR.). 1978. 39.95 (0-8288-5274-X, M9465) Fr & Eur.

Tysk-Svensk Ordbok: German-Swedish Dictionary. Esselte Studium. 896p. (GER & SWE.). 1980. 59.95 (0-8288-1691-3, F29001) Fr & Eur.

Tyson: From Farm to Market. Marvin Schwartz. 170p. 1991. 24.00 (1-55728-189-0) U of Ark Pr.

Tyssot de Patot & His Work (1655-1738) Aubrey Rosenberg. (International Archives of the History of Ideas Ser.: No. 47). 243p. 1972. lib. bdg. 88.00 (90-247-1199-1) Kluwer Ac.

***Tyumen Oblast: Economy, Industry, Government, Business.** 2nd rev. ed. Russian Information & Business Center, Inc. Staff. (Russian Regional Business Directories Ser.). (Illus.). 200p. 1997. pap. 99.00 (1-57751-421-1) Russ Info & Busn Ctr.

***Tyva Republic: Economy, Industry, Government, Business.** 2nd rev. ed. Russian Information & Business Center, Inc. Staff. (Russian Regional Business Directories Ser.). (Illus.). 200p. 1997. pap. 99.00 (1-57751-369-X) Russ Info & Busn Ctr.

Tzacones. Stam C. Caratzas. (Supplementa Byzantina Ser.: Vol. 4). (C). 1976. 392.35 (3-11-004799-3) De Gruyter.

***T'zaddhi.** Phoenix Hilson. 410p. (Orig.). 1998. mass mkt. 9.99 (1-58006-004-8, Stargate Pr) Sovereign.

Tzaddik. Rabbi Nathan. Tr. by Avraham Greenbaum from HEB. Orig. Title: Chayey Moharan. 1988. 17.00 (0-930213-17-3) Breslov Res Inst.

Tzaddik in Our Time. Simcha Raz. Tr. by Charles V. Wengrov from HEB. (Illus.). 1976. 20.95 (0-87306-130-6) Feldheim.

Tzadik Yesod Olam. Isaac Luria. 124p. 1960. write for info. (0-943688-21-3) Res Ctr Kabbalah.

Tzbrannaya Proza v Dvuch Tomach T L Beey Koriolor: The White Corridor - Selected Prose, Vol. I. 2nd ed. Vladislav F. Khodasevich. Ed. by Gregory Poliak & Joceph Prodsky. 320p. (Orig.). (RUS.). pap. 17.50 (0-940294-10-9) Silver Age Pub.

Tzedakah. Amye Rosenberg. (Jewish Awareness Ser.). (Illus.). (J). (gr. k-1). 1979. pap. text ed. 4.95 (0-87441-279-X) Behrman.

Tzedakah: Can Jewish Philanthropy Buy Jewish Survival? Jacob Neusner. (Brown Judaic Studies). 126p. 1990. 44.95 (1-55540-475-8) Scholars Pr GA.

***Tzedakah: Can Jewish Philanthropy Buy Jewish Survival?** Jacob Neusner. LC 97-2339. 1997. pap. 10.00 (0-8074-0637-6, 383807) UAHC.

Tzedakah see Mitzvah of the Month

Tzedakah Workbook. Jan Rabinowitz. (Illus.). 32p. (Orig.). (J). (gr. 4-5). 1986. pap. text ed. 4.95 (0-933873-07-7) Torah Aura.

Tzeltal Numerical Classifiers: A Study in Ethnographic Semantics. Brent Berlin. (Janua Linguarum, Ser. Practica: No. 70). (Orig.). 1968. pap. text ed. 73.85 (3-11-000011-3) Mouton.

Tzeltal Tales of Demons & Monsters: Modern Folk Tales from the Tzeltal Maya Town of Tenejapa, Chiapas, Pt. 2. Ed. by Richard Diehl et al. Tr. by Brian Stross. LC 78-622530. (Museum Briefs Ser.: No. 24). iv, 40p. 1978. pap. 2.00 (0-913134-24-4) Mus Anthro MO.

***Tzemach Tzedek, 7 vols.** Menachem M. Schneerson. Incl. Vol. 7. Chidushim Al Hashas. LC 82-81722. (HEB.). 568p. 1994. Not sold separately (0-8266-5607-2); Vol. 6. Sha'alot V'Teshuvot Chelek Khoy'Shen Mish Pat. LC 82-81722. (HEB.). 100p. 1994. Not sold separately (0-8266-5606-4); Vol. 5. Sha'Alot V'Tes Huvot Chekel Even Hoezer, Part 2. LC 82-81722. (HEB.). 636p. 1994. Not sold separately (0-8266-5605-6); Vol. 4. Sha'alot V'Teshuvot Chelek Even Hoezer, Part 1. LC 82-81722. (HEB.). 480p. 1994. Not sold separately (0-8266-5604-8); Vol. 3. Sha'alot V'Teshuvot Chelek Yoreh De'ah. LC 82-81722. (HEB.). 728p. 1994. Not sold separately (0-8266-5603-X); Vol. 2. Sha'alot V'Teshuvot Chelek Orach Chayim. LC 82-81722. (HEB.). 216p. 1994. Not sold separately (0-8266-5602-1); LC 82-81727. 300.00 (0-8266-5600-5) Kehot Pubn Soc.

Tzili. Aharon Appelfeld. Tr. by Dalya Bilu from HEB. 204p. 1996. reprint ed. pap. 11.00 (0-8021-3455-6, Grove) Grove-Atltic.

Tzintzuntzan: Mexican Peasants in a Changing World. George M. Foster. 404p. 1988. reprint ed. pap. text ed. 14.95 (0-88133-315-8) Waveland Pr.

Tzipisa Leyeshua. Tr. by Moshe Miller. 1993. 19.95 (0-944070-97-3) Feldheim.

Tzitzit - Halacha Lema'aseh. Eliyahu Y. Gurary. (Illus.). 280p. (HEB.). 1995. 17.00 (1-887601-00-7) Machon Ohelei.

Tzorchei Tzibbur: Community & Responsibility in the Jewish Tradition. 6.00 (0-686-96047-5); teacher ed. 8.50 (0-686-99687-9) USCJE.

Tzutujil Grammar. Jon P. Dayley. LC 84-28118. (Publications in Linguistics: Vol. 107). 1985. pap. 40.00 (0-520-09962-1) U CA Pr.

Tzutujil Mayas: Continuity & Change, 1250-1630. Sandra L. Orellana. LC 83-47837. (Civilization of the American Indian Ser.: Vol. 162). (Illus.). 320p. 1984. 34.95 (0-8061-1739-7) U of Okla Pr.

Tzvi Tells the Truth. Aurohom Finkelstien. 64p. (J). 1991. 10.95 (1-56062-094-3) CIS Comm.

1067-1216 see Matthaei Parisiensis, Monachi Sancti Albani: Chronica Majora

***T183 or T182 Mini Labs: Algebraic Investigations.** Phil DeMarois. 200p. (Orig.). (C). 1996. pap. text ed. 16.95 (0-9623629-9-9) MathWare.

U

U. A. R. in Africa: Egypt's Policy Under Nasser. Tareq Y. Ismael. LC 73-126902. 272p. reprint ed. 77.60 (0-8357-9475-X, 2015299) Bks Demand.

U & I. Illus. & Intro. by Ann B. Moody. 200p. 1994. pap. 9.95 (0-9639366-0-3) A B Moody.

U & I: A True Story. Nicholson Baker. 1992. pap. 10.00 (0-679-73575-5, Vin) Random.

U. B. Phillips: A Southern Mind. John H. Roper. LC 84-682. vi, 204p. 1984. 16.95 (0-86554-112-4, MUP-H103) Mercer Univ Pr.

An Asterisk (*) at the beginning of an entry indicates that the title is appearing in BIP for the first time.

***U-Bet: A Greenhorn in Old Montana.** Ed. by John R. Barrows. LC 89-24970. 292p. 1990. reprint ed. pap. 83.30 (*0-608-03466-5*, 2064173) Bks Demand.

***U-Boat: 1939-1945.** Jean-Philippe Dallies. 1996. pap. text ed. 37.95 (*2-908182-42-4*, Zenith Aviation) Motorbooks Intl.

U-Boat Ace: The Story of Wolfgang Luth. Jordan Vause. LC 90-6280. (Illus.). 256p. 1990. 26.95 (*0-87021-666-X*) Naval Inst Pr.

U-Boat Commander: A Periscope View of the Battle of the Atlantic. Peter Cremer. LC 84-61243. 244p. 1984. 25.95 (*0-87021-969-3*) Naval Inst Pr.

U-Boat Commander's Handbook. High Command of German Navy Staff. Tr. by U. S. Navy Staff from GER. (Illus.). 120p. (C). 1989. pap. text ed. 8.95 (*0-939631-21-0*) Thomas Publications.

U-Boat Hunters: The Royal Canadian Navy & the Offensive Against Germany's Submarines. Marc Milner. LC 94-66600. (Illus.). 280p. 1994. 31.95 (*1-55750-854-2*) Naval Inst Pr.

U-Boat Hunters: The Royal Canadian Navy & the Offensive Against Germany's Submarines. Marc Milner. 1994. 35.00 (*0-8020-0588-8*) U of Toronto Pr.

U-Boat Offensive, 1914-1945. V. E. Tarrant. 192p. 1989. 33.95 (*0-87021-764-X*) Naval Inst Pr.

U-Boat Type VII - Grey Ghosts of the Sea. Heinz J. Nowarra. Tr. by Edward Force from GER. (Illus.). 48p. 1992. pap. 7.95 (*0-88740-409-X*) Schiffer.

U-Boat War in the Caribbeann. Gaylord T. Kelshall. LC 94-3130. (Illus.). 528p. 1994. 32.95 (*1-55750-452-0*) Naval Inst Pr.

U-Boat War, 1914-1918. Edwyn A. Gray. (Illus.). 280p. 1994. 39.50 (*0-85052-405-9*, Pub. by L Cooper Bks UK) Trans-Atl Phila.

U-Boats: General Electric's Diesel Locomotives. Greg McDonnell. (Illus.). 192p. 1996. 50.00 (*1-55046-112-5*, Pub. by Boston Mills Pr CN) Genl Dist Srvs.

U-Boats Against Canada: German Submarines in Canadian Waters. Michael L. Hadley. 416p. (C). 1990. reprint ed. pap. text ed. 24.95 (*0-7735-0801-5*, Pub. by McGill CN) U of Toronto Pr.

***U-Boats Destroyed: German Submarine Losses in the World Wars.** Paul Kemp. 256p. 1997. 32.95 (*1-55750-859-3*) Naval Inst Pr.

U-Boats in Action. Robert Stern. (Warships in Action Ser.: No. 1). (Illus.). 50p. 1996. reprint ed. pap. 7.95 (*0-89747-054-0*, 4001) Squad Sig Pubns.

U-Boats under the Swastika. rev. ed. Jak P. Showell. (Illus.). 144p. 1987. 26.95 (*0-87021-970-7*) Naval Inst Pr.

U. C. Davis Law Review: 1969-1994/95, 28 vols. Set. 1,210.00 (*0-8377-9168-5*) Rothman.

U. C. L. A. Photos by Phil Schermeister. (Illus.). 112p. 1989. 39.00 (*0-916509-62-1*) Harmony Hse Pub.

U. C. System for Producing Healthy Container-Grown Plants. Kenneth Baker. 332p. (C). 1985. text ed. 80.00 (*0-7855-0034-0*, Pub. by Surrey Beatty & Sons AT) St Mut.

***U Can Cartoon! Drawing Kit.** Jack Keeley. (Walter Foster Kit Ser.). (Illus.). 32p. 1997. 14.95 (*1-56010-247-0*, K09) W Foster Pub.

U. D. I. The International Politics of the Rhodesian Rebellion. Robert C. Good. LC 73-14082. 368p. reprint ed. pap. 104.90 (*0-7837-0248-5*, 2040557) Bks Demand.

U. F. O. of Bethlehem. Frank R. Zindler. 15p. (Orig.). 1991. 4.00 (*0-910309-63-9*, 5568) Am Atheist.

U. F. O.'s: The Greatest Stories. Ed. by Martin H. Greenberg. 1996. 8.98 (*1-56731-086-9*, MJF Bks) Fine Comms.

U Geminorum Light Curves, 1985-1990. Janet A. Mattei et al. (AAVSO Monograph: No. 2, Supplement 1). (Illus.). 36p. 1991. pap. text ed. 7.50 (*1-878174-06-1*) Am Assn Var Star.

U Geminorum Light Curves 1991-1995: AAVSO Monograph 2, Supplement 2. Janet A. Mattei et al. (Illus.). 20p. 1996. pap. text ed. 10.00 (*1-878174-15-0*) Am Assn Var Star.

U. K. Nineteen Ninety-Two & Beyond. Euromonitor Staff. (C). 1990. 1,800.00 (*0-86338-415-3*, Pub. by Euromonitor Pubns UK) Gale.

U. K. Activity Holidays: Over Two Hundred Fifty Ideas Inside. Rosters Ltd. Staff & S. Struthers. 374p. (C). 1989. pap. text ed. 40.00 (*0-948032-93-6*, Pub. by Rosters Ltd) St Mut.

U. K. Banking after Deregulation. Andy Mullineux. 192p. 1987. lib. bdg. 55.00 (*0-7099-4689-9*, Pub. by Croom Helm UK) Routledge Chapman & Hall.

U. K. Before the European Court of Human Rights: Case Law & Commentary. Sue Farran. 403p. 1996. pap. 56.00 (*1-85431-455-6*, Pub. by Blackstone Pr UK) Gaunt.

U. K. Brokers Yearbook 1994/1995. (DYP Textbook Ser.). 400p. 250.00 (*1-870255-32-1*) LLP.

U. K. Brokers, 1988. I. R. R. G. Staff. (C). 1988. 850.00 (*0-685-32685-3*, Pub. by Witherby & Co UK) St Mut.

U. K. Business Finance Directory, 1990. Ed. by J. Carr & P. Isbell. (C). 1991. lib. bdg. 289.50 (*1-85333-362-X*, Pub. by Graham & Trotman UK) Kluwer Ac.

U. K. Cinema Today: 1991. 1991. 325.00 (*0-686-71958-1*, Pub. by Euromonitor Pubns UK) St Mut.

U. K. Commodities Yearbook. Ed. by A. Buckley. 1990. 175.00 (*0-85941-050-1*) St Mut.

U. K. Consumer Packaging Report. Euromonitor Staff. (C). 1990. 1,800.00 (*0-86338-388-2*, Pub. by Euromonitor Pubns UK) Gale.

U. K. Cosmetics & Toiletries Report Nineteen Ninety. Euromonitor Staff. (C). 1990. 1,800.00 (*0-685-37365-7*, Pub. by Euromonitor Pubns UK) Gale.

U. K. Cycling Guide 1994. Les Lumsdon. (Illus.). 250p. (Orig.). 1994. pap. 27.50 (*1-85058-386-2*, Pub. by Sigma Press UK) Coronet Bks.

U. K. Economy. 14th ed. Ed. by Michael Artis. (Illus.). 400p. 1996. 90.00 (*0-19-877512-1*); pap. 32.00 (*0-19-877511-3*) OUP.

U. K. Economy: Manual of Applied Economics. 6th ed. Ed. by A. R. Prest & D. J. Coppock. 1977. 24.95 (*0-8464-0942-9*) Beekman Pubs.

U. K. Electricals Report Nineteen Ninety. Euromonitor Staff. (C). 1990. 1,800.00 (*0-86338-425-0*, Pub. by Euromonitor Pubns UK) Gale.

***U. K. Energy Experience: A Model or a Warning? Proceedings of the British Institute of Energy Economics.** 524p. 1996. lib. bdg. 61.00 (*1-86094-022-6*) World Scientific Pub.

***U. K. Equity Gap: The Failure of Government Policy since 1945.** Chris Lonsdale. LC 97-23058. (Illus.). 248p. 1997. text ed. 63.95 (*1-85521-865-8*, HC256.5L63, Pub. by Dartmth Pub UK) Ashgate Pub Co.

U. K. Fast Food Industry, 1993: A Market Analysis. Stuart Price. (Illus.). 96p. 1994. spiral bd. 390.00 (*0-304-32728-X*) Cassell.

U. K. Finance Directory: A Directory of Sources of U. K. Corporate Finance. Ed. by M. Morgano. 600p. 1990. 695.00 (*0-86010-342-0*, Pub. by Graham & Trotman UK); pap. 395.00 (*0-86010-341-2*, Pub. by Graham & Trotman UK) St Mut.

U. K. Financial Markets. Ed. by Michael Hughes. 192p. 1996. 145.00 (*1-85573-249-1*, Pub. by Woodhead Pubng UK) Am Educ Systs.

U. K. Financial System. Buckle. 1995. text ed. 79.95 (*0-7190-4815-X*, Pub. by Manchester Univ Pr UK) St Martin.

U. K. GAAP. 5th ed. Mike Davies et al. 1500p. 1996. 100.00 (*1-56159-189-0*, Stockton Pr) Groves Dictionaries.

U. K. GAAP: Generally Accepted Accounting Practice in the United Kingdom. 4th ed. Mike Davies et al. Ed. by Ernst & Young Staff. 1610p. 1994. 137.50 (*0-333-61619-7*) Trans-Atl Phila.

U. K. Health Economics Report Nineteen Eighty-Nine. Euromonitor Staff. (C). 1989. 1,500.00 (*0-86338-356-4*, Pub. by Euromonitor Pubns UK) Gale.

U. K. Health Markets. 100p. 1987. 170.00 (*0-686-71959-X*, Pub. by Euromonitor Pubns UK) St Mut.

U. K. Holiday & Tourism: 1992. 150p. 1992. 595.00 (*0-686-71960-3*, Pub. by Euromonitor Pubns UK) St Mut.

U. K. Hotel Groups Directory, 1992-93. Linda Harrison & Keith Johnson. 316p. 1992. pap. text ed. 350.00 (*0-304-32541-4*) Cassell.

U. K. Household Chemical Markets. 1986. 225.00 (*0-686-71961-1*, Pub. by Euromonitor Pubns UK) St Mut.

U. K. Labour Market: Comparative Aspects & Institutional Developments. Ed. by Ray Barrell. LC 93-36552. (Illus.). 280p. (C). 1994. text ed. 59.95 (*0-521-46160-X*) Cambridge U Pr.

U. K. Labour Market: Comparative Aspects & Institutional Developments. Ed. by Ray Barrell. LC 93-36552. (Illus.). 280p. (C). 1994. pap. text ed. 22.95 (*0-521-46825-6*) Cambridge U Pr.

U. K. Maintenance Market Contract Maintenance for Building Engineering Services. S. Whittome. 1990. 1,280.00 (*0-86022-276-4*, Pub. by Build Servs Info Assn UK) St Mut.

U. K. Market for Clean Rooms. A. Giles & S. Whittome. 1993. 1,580.00 (*0-86022-349-3*, Pub. by Build Servs Info Assn UK) St Mut.

U. K. Market for Commercial Boilers. P. Crampton & S. Whittome. 1991. 1,280.00 (*0-86022-277-2*, Pub. by Build Servs Info Assn UK) St Mut.

U. K. Market for Fans & Ventilation. S. French & S. Whittome. 1992. 1,280.00 (*0-86022-390-6*, Pub. by Build Servs Info Assn UK) St Mut.

U. K. Market for Industrial Heating. S. Whittome & A. Milledge. 1991. 1,280.00 (*0-86022-305-1*, Pub. by Build Servs Info Assn UK) St Mut.

U. K. Market for Packaged Air Conditioning. A. King & S. Whittome. 1992. 1,400.00 (*0-86022-348-5*, Pub. by Build Servs Info Assn UK) St Mut.

U. K. Market for Replacement Car Parts No. R310: 1994 Edition. 1993. 985.00 (*0-85058-723-9*) Economist Intell.

U. K. Market for Toys & Games. 1986. 190.00 (*0-686-71962-X*, Pub. by Euromonitor Pubns UK) St Mut.

U. K. Market for Water Heating. A. Giles & S. Whittome. 1992. 1,580.00 (*0-86022-309-4*, Pub. by Build Servs Info Assn UK) St Mut.

U. K. Materials Information Sources. 2nd ed. Ed. by Keith W. Reynard. 432p. (C). 1992. pap. 42.95 (*0-85072-293-4*, Pub. by Design Council Bks UK) Ashgate Pub Co.

U. K. Menswear Markets. 1986. 256.00 (*0-686-71963-8*, Pub. by Euromonitor Pubns UK) St Mut.

U. K. Monetary & Financial System: An Introduction. J. H. Gilbody. 256p. 1988. lib. bdg. 55.00 (*0-415-00435-7*) Routledge.

U. K. Monetary Policy: The Challenge for the 1990s. Paul Temperton. LC 90-44810. 208p. 1991. text ed. 65.00 (*0-312-05569-2*) St Martin.

U. K. Non-Life Insurance Yearbook 1994/1995. (DYP Directory Ser.). 250.00 (*1-870255-37-2*) LLP.

U. K. OTC Healthcare Markets Nineteen Ninety. Euromonitor Staff. (C). 1990. 1,800.00 (*0-86338-381-5*, Pub. by Euromonitor Pubns UK) Gale.

U. K. Parallel '96: Proceedings of the BCS PPSG Annual Conference, 3-5 July 1996. British Computer Society Staff. Ed. by C. R. Jesshope & A. V. Shafarenko. LC 96-24166. 205p. 1996. pap. 69.95 (*3-540-76068-7*) Spr-Verlag.

U. K. Pesticide Guide 1995. R. Whitehead. 596p. 1995. pap. 35.00 (*0-85198-953-5*) CAB Intl.

U. K. Recreation & Resources: Leisure Patterns & Leisure Places. J. Allan Patmore. (Illus.). 288p. Date not set. 55.00 (*0-631-17229-7*); pap. 55.00 (*0-631-19249-2*) Blackwell Pubs.

U. K. Security Report Nineteen Eighty-Nine. Euromonitor Staff. (C). 1989. 1,500.00 (*0-86338-361-0*, Pub. by Euromonitor Pubns UK) Gale.

U. K. Smoking Statistics. 2nd ed. Ed. by Nicholas J. Wald & Ans Nicolaides-Bouman. (Illus.). 280p. 1991. pap. 75.00 (*0-19-261680-3*) OUP.

U. K. Snack Foods Report Nineteen Ninety. Euromonitor Staff. (C). 1989. 1,500.00 (*0-86338-359-9*, Pub. by Euromonitor Pubns UK) Gale.

U. K. Stationery Report Nineteen Eighty-Nine. Euromonitor Staff. (C). 1989. 1,500.00 (*0-86338-366-1*, Pub. by Euromonitor Pubns UK) Gale.

U. K. Taxation of Modern Financial Instruments & Transactions. D. Ross. 64p. 1989. text ed. 60.00 (*0-304-31831-0*) Cassell.

U. K. Taxation of Trusts. Ed. by Tony Sherring & Ian Ferrier. 235p. 1995. pap. 195.00 (*0-86012-054-6*, Pub. by Tolley Pubng UK) St Mut.

U. K. to U. S. A. Dictionary. Claudine Dervaes & John Hunter. 112p. (Orig.). 1994. pap. 3.95 (*0-933143-18-4*) Solitaire Pub.

U. K. Travel & Tourism. Euromonitor Staff. (C). 1989. 1,500.00 (*0-86338-372-6*, Pub. by Euromonitor Pubns UK) Gale.

***U. K./U. S. GAAP Comparison: A Comparison Between U. K. & U. S. Accounting Principles.** 3rd ed. Vivian Pereira. 1997. pap. text ed. 69.00 (*0-7494-1472-3*, Kogan Pg Educ) Stylus Pub VA.

U. L. & Wire-Cable Industry. 15.00 (*0-318-03189-2*, 7518) Wire Assn Intl.

U Mikrofona Aleksandr Galich: Izbrannye Teksty I Zapisi. Aleksandr Galich. LC 90-4701. 172p. (Orig.). (RUS.). 1990. pap. 12.00 (*1-55779-034-5*) Hermitage.

U-Musik und Osterreich: Max Schonherr in Seinen Schriften und Erinnerungen - Light Music from Austria: Writings & Reminiscences of Max Schonherr. Andrew Lamb. LC 91-29172. (Austrian Culture Ser.: Vol. 6). 262p. (ENG & GER.). (C). 1992. text ed. 62.95 (*0-8204-1671-1*) P Lang Pubng.

U. N. Assessing Soviet Abuses. Juliana G. Pilon & Ralph K. Bennett. (C). 1990. 45.00 (*0-907967-90-6*, Pub. by Inst Euro Def & Strat UK) St Mut.

U. N. - In or Out? A Debate. Ernest Van den Haag & John P. Conrad. 350p. 1987. 19.95 (*0-306-42524-6*, Plenum Pr) Plenum.

U. N. Adventure. Ramsey Montgomery. (Choose Your Own Adventure Ser.: No. 157). 128p. (J). (gr. 4-7). 1995. pap. 3.50 (*0-553-56396-3*) Bantam.

***U. N. after the Cold War.** Joseph P. Lorenz. 1997. 35.00 (*0-8133-8061-8*) Westview.

U. N. Ambassador: A Behind-the-Scenes Look at Madeleine Albright's World. Robert Maass. (Illus.). 48p. (J). (gr. 3-7). 1995. 16.95 (*0-8027-8355-4*); lib. bdg. 17.85 (*0-8027-8356-2*) Walker & Co.

***U. N. & Global Issues.** Mason. 1994. pap. text ed. write for info. (*0-582-22668-6*, Pub. by Longman UK) Longman.

U. N. & the Palestinian Refugees: A Study in Nonterritorial Administration. Edward H. Buehrio. LC 71-160124. (Indiana University International Development Research Center Studies in Development: No. 3). 231p. reprint ed. pap. 65.90 (*0-317-09059-3*, 2055235) Bks Demand.

U. N. Commission on Human Rights Orientation Manual for Nongovernmental Organizations: An Orientation Manual. Minnesota Advocates for Human Rights, International Service for Human Rights Staff. 100p. 1993. pap. 7.50 (*0-929293-14-2*) MN Advocates.

U. N. Convention on Contracts for the International Sale of Goods Annotated. Ed. by Grant R. Ackerman. 1992. ring bd. 425.00 (*0-685-69647-2*, CISG) Warren Gorham & Lamont.

U. N. Convention on the Law of the Sea: Impact & Implementation, 19th Annual Conference Proceedings. Ed. by E. D. Brown & Robin Churchill. 654p. 1988. 38.50 (*0-911189-16-5*) Law Sea Inst.

U. N. Declaration on Friendly Relations & the System of Sources of International Law. G. Arangio-Ruiz. 354p. 1979. lib. bdg. 65.50 (*90-286-0149-X*) Kluwer Ac.

U. N. Declaration on the Elimination of Religious Intolerance & Discrimination. Sidney Liskofsky. 20p. 1982. pap. 2.00 (*0-87495-041-4*) Am Jewish Comm.

U. N. Development Aid: Criteria & Methods of Evaluation. William R. Leonard et al. LC 75-140126. (UNITAR Studies). 1971. 23.95 (*0-405-02235-2*) Ayer.

U. N. Disarmament Studies. United Nations Staff. 200p. 1989. 52.00 (*0-8448-1617-5*, Crane Russak) Taylor & Francis.

U. N. Draft Model Taxation Convention: Trends in Income Tax Treaties Involving Developing Countries (with Special Reference to the U. N. Group of Experts on Tax Treaties Between Developed & Developing Countries) United Nations Experts on Tax Treaties Staff & International Fiscal Association Staff. LC 82-106896. (IFA Congress Seminar Ser.: No. 4). (Illus.). 76p. 1979. 16.50 (*90-200-0600-2*) Kluwer Ac.

U. N. for Beginners. Ian Williams. 160p. 1995. pap. 11.00 (*0-86316-185-5*) Writers & Readers.

U. N. Forces, 1948-1994. Robert Pitta. (Elite Ser.). (Illus.). 64p. 1994. pap. 12.95 (*1-85532-454-7*, 9469, Pub. by Osprey UK) Stackpole.

U. N. General Assembly Resolutions: A Selection of the Most Important Resolutions During the Period 1949 Through 1974, Sessions I-XXVII. Knud Krakau et al. xiii, 442p. 1975. text ed. 33.00 (*0-685-04379-7*) Rothman.

U. N. International Court of Justice, 1947-1990: Reports of Judgements, Advisory Opinions & Orders, 24 bks., Set. 1992. 2,570.00 (*0-89941-780-9*, 307450) W S Hein.

U. N. Law-Fundamental Rights: Two Topics in International Law. Ed. by Antonio Cassese. 268p. 1979. lib. bdg. 88.50 (*90-286-0828-1*) Kluwer Ac.

***U. N., Peace, & Force.** Ed. by Michael C. Pugh. LC 97-9826. (Cass Series in Peacekeeping: No. 2). 208p. 1997. 42.50 (*0-7146-4759-4*, Pub. by F Cass Pubs UK); pap. 19.50 (*0-7146-4320-3*, Pub. by F Cass Pubs UK) Intl Spec Bk.

U. N. Peace Imperative. John S. Applegate. 1992. 16.95 (*0-533-10113-1*) Vantage.

U. N. Peacekeepers: Soldiers with a Difference. Augustus R. Norton & Thomas G. Weiss. LC 90-82248. (Headline Ser.: No. 292). 64p. 1990. pap. 5.95 (*0-87124-133-1*) Foreign Policy.

U. N. Peacekeeping: Japanese & American Perspectives. Ed. by Selig S. Harrison & Masashi Nishihara. 178p. (C). 1995. pap. 12.95 (*0-87003-066-3*) Carnegie Endow.

***U. N. Peacekeeping, American Policy, & the Uncivil Wars of the 1990s.** Ed. by William J. Durch. 416p. (Orig.). 1996. text ed. 19.95 (*0-312-16075-5*) St Martin.

U. N. Peacekeeping in Cambodia: UNTAC's Civil Mandate. Michael W. Doyle. LC 94-43542. (IPA Occasional Paper Ser.). 64p. 1995. pap. text ed. 9.95 (*1-55587-497-5*) Lynne Rienner.

U. N. Protection of Civil & Political Rights, Vol. 1. John Carey. LC 71-104674. (Procedural Aspects of International Law Ser.). xiii, 205p. 1970. 45.00 (*0-8156-2146-9*, 306480) W S Hein.

U. N. Role in the Persian Gulf & Iraqi Compliance with U. N. Resolutions. (Illus.). 400p. (Orig.). (C). 1994. pap. text ed. 50.00 (*0-7881-0737-2*) DIANE Pub.

U. N. Security Council & Human Rights. Sydney D. Bailey. LC 94-19511. 1994. text ed. 69.95 (*0-312-12324-8*) St Martin.

U. N. Security Council Resolution 242: The Building Block of Peacemaking, Proceedings from the Washington Institute's Harris Symposium. LC 93-18860. 1993. pap. 16.95 (*0-944029-51-5*) Wash Inst NEP.

U. N., South Africa, & the Middle East: Power Games, Hot Air & Dirty Tricks. Albert Zarka. (Illus.). 224p. 1996. pap. 17.00 (*0-8059-3971-7*) Dorrance.

U. N. Spacy. John Zeleznik. (Macross II RPG Sourcebook Ser.: No. 1). (Illus.). 64p. (Orig.). (YA). (gr. 8 up). 1993. pap. 9.95 (*0-916211-63-0*, 591) Palladium Bks.

U. N., UNESCO & the Politics of Knowledge. Clare Wells. LC 86-6567. 300p. 1987. text ed. 39.95 (*0-312-83277-X*) St Martin.

U. N. Veto in World Affairs, 1946-1990: A Complete Record & Case Histories of the Security Council's Veto. Anjali V. Patil. 574p. 1992. write for info. (*0-7201-2115-9*, Mansell Pub) Cassell.

U Nas Byla Velikaia Epokha. Eduard Limonov. 150p. (Orig.). (RUS.). 1989. pap. 15.50 (*0-89830-124-6*) Russica Pubs.

U-ni-ty. Michael Schmidt. 316p. 1996. 60.00 (*1-881616-64-9*, Pub. by Scalo Pubs) Dist Art Pubs.

U Nikh V Michigane. Pavel Leonidov. LC 85-61782. 120p. (Orig.). 1987. pap. 12.50 (*0-89830-100-9*) Russica Pubs.

U No Es Ningu. Joan Brossa. (Illus.). 100p. (CAT.). 1993. pap. 475.00 (*0-614-00140-4*) Elliots Bks.

U No Es Ningu. Joan Brossa. (Ediciones Especiales y de Bibliofilo Ser.). (Illus.). 100p. (CAT.). 1993. 750.00 (*84-343-0302-7*) Elliots Bks.

U Nu of Burma. 2nd rev. ed. Richard Butwell. (Illus.). viii, 327p. 1969. 45.00 (*0-8047-0155-5*) Stanford U Pr.

U-One Hundred Sixty-Eight Incident. Steve Reynolds & H. E. Carver. LC 84-51393. (Mercenary Adventures Ser.). 260p. (Orig.). 1985. 14.95 (*0-918379-01-6*); pap. 6.95 (*0-317-14780-3*) Wild Geese.

U. P. Agricultural Credit Act, 1973. Ed. by B. C. Shukla. (C). 1988. 110.00 (*0-685-39803-X*) St Mut.

U. P. Agricultural Credit Act, 1973. 4th ed. B. C. Shukla. 1985. reprint ed. 90.00 (*0-317-54766-6*) St Mut.

U. P. Co-Operative Societies Act, 1965. 4th ed. Mahavir Singh. (C). 1992. 275.00 (*0-89771-769-4*, Pub. by Eastern Book II) St Mut.

U. P. Ccnsolidation of Holdings Act. Surendra Malik. 250p. 1980. 82.50 (*0-317-54837-9*) St Mut.

U. P. Consolidation of Holdings Act, 1953: Together with Exhaustive Commentaries, Notifications & Rules. Surendra Malik. (C). 1991. 95.00 (*0-685-39776-9*) St Mut.

U. P. Excise Act, 1910: Together with Rules & Notifications. 4th ed. P. L. Malik. (C). 1991. 95.00 (*0-685-39707-6*) St Mut.

U. P. Government Servants Conduct Rules, 1956. B. N. Upadhyaya. (C). 1991. 60.00 (*0-89771-685-X*) St Mut.

U. P. Industrial Disputes Act, 1947: With Rules & Notifications. Ed. by P. L. Malik. (C). 1991. 95.00 (*0-685-39651-7*) St Mut.

U. P. Land Records Manual. Vijay Malik. 138p. 1975. 50.00 (*0-317-54592-2*) St Mut.

U. P. Police Regulations. 4th ed. P. L. Malik. (C). 1991. 95.00 (*0-685-39586-3*) St Mut.

U. P. Public Premises (Eviction of Unauthorised Occupants) Act, 1972. S. P. Gupta. (C). 1988. 60.00 (*0-685-22629-8*) St Mut.

U. P. (Regulation of Building Operations) Act: Rules & Regulations, 1958, & Urban Planning & Development Act, 1973. Uma Shanker. (C). 1990. text ed. 225.00 (*0-89771-516-0*) St Mut.

U. P. (Regulation of Building Operations) Act, 1958: With Rules & Regulations & Urban Planning & Development Act, 1973. 5th ed. Ed. by Uma Shanker. (C). 1990. 225.00 (*0-685-39524-3*) St Mut.

An Asterisk (*) at the beginning of an entry indicates that the title is appearing in BIP for the first time.

U. P. Regulation of Building Operations, 1958: With Rules & Regulations & Urban Planning & Development Act, 1973. 5th ed. Uma Shanker. (C). 1990. 225.00 (*0-685-39572-3*) St Mut.

U. P. Sales Tax Act, Nineteen Forty-Eight: Together with Rules & Notifications. P. L. Malik. 220p. 1985. 108.00 (*0-317-54852-2*) St Mut.

U. P. Sales Tax Act, 1948: Together with Rules & Notifications with Supplement. 8th ed. P. L. Malik. (C). 1990. 65.00 (*0-685-39565-0*) St Mut.

U. P. Trail. Zane Grey. 1976. 23.95 (*0-8488-0278-0*) Amereon Ltd.

U. P. Trail. Zane Grey. 496p. 1991. mass mkt. 3.99 (*0-06-100176-7*, Harp PBks) HarpC.

U. P. Trail. Zane Grey. 1995. mass mkt. 4.99 (*0-671-50672-2*) PB.

U. P. Urban Building Regulation of Letting, Rent & Eviction Act, 1972, 1987 with Supplement. 3rd ed. V. K. Sircar. (C). 1992. 137.50 (*81-7012-350-X*, Pub. by Eastern Book II) St Mut.

U. P. Urban Buildings Act, 1972 (Regulation of Letting, Rent & Eviction in English) 3rd ed. V. K. Sircar. (C). 1987. 225.00 (*0-685-39571-5*) St Mut.

U. P. Urban Buildings (Regulation of Letting, Rent & Eviction) Act, 1972. V. K. Sircar. 833p. 1983. 315.00 (*0-317-57704-2*) St Mut.

U. P. Urban Buildings (Regulation of Letting, Rent & Eviction) Act, 1972. V. K. Sircar. (C). 1992. 275.00 (*0-89771-791-0*, Pub. by Eastern Book II) St Mut.

U. R. S. S. un Portrait en Couleurs. Jean Marabin. (Illus.). 276p. (FRE.). 1960. lib. bdg. 19.95 (*0-8288-3980-8*) Fr & Eur.

U. S A Cultural Mosaic. 380p. (J). (gr. 6-8). 17.00 (*0-686-74871-9*) ADL.

U. S. - Arab Economic Relations: A Time of Transition. Ed. by Michael R. Czinkota & Scot Marciel. LC 85-3614. 368p. 1985. text ed. 46.95 (*0-275-90081-9*, C0081, Praeger Pubs) Greenwood.

U. S. - Arab Relations: Security in the Arabian Peninsula & Gulf States, 1974-84, No. 7. J. E. Peterson. 154p. (Orig.). 1985. pap. 8.00 (*0-916729-12-5*) Natl Coun Arab.

U. S. - Arab Relations: The Economic Dimension, No. 6. Joseph Story. 28p. (Orig.). 1985. pap. 4.00 (*0-916729-07-9*) Natl Coun Arab.

U. S. - Arab Relations: The Iran-Iraq War & the Gulf Cooperation Council, No. 12. John D. Anthony. (Orig.). 1984. pap. 2.00 (*0-916729-10-9*) Natl Coun Arab.

U. S. - Arab Relations: The Iran-Iraq War & U. S.-Iraq Relations: An Iraqi Perspective, No. 11. Anthony H. Cordesman. 40p. (Orig.). pap. 4.00 (*0-685-10615-2*) Natl Coun Arab.

U. S. - Arab Relations: The Iraq Dimension, No. 5. Fred Axelgard. 45p. (Orig.). 1985. pap. 4.00 (*0-916729-05-2*) Natl Coun Arab.

U. S. - Arab Relations: The Literary Dimension, No. 2. Gregory Orfalea. 44p. (Orig.). 1984. pap. 4.00 (*0-916729-01-X*) Natl Coun Arab.

U. S. - Arab Relations: The Syrian Dimension, No. 4. Talcott Seelye. 40p. (Orig.). 1985. pap. 4.00 (*0-916729-02-8*) Natl Coun Arab.

U. S. - Bangladesh Relations: A Study of the Political & Economic Developments During 1971-1981. Jayasee Biswas. 1985. 12.50 (*0-8364-1309-1*) S Asia.

U. S. - Brazilian Informatics Dispute. Ellene A. Felder & Andrew Hurrell. LC 88-21771. (FPI Case Studies: No. 13). (Orig.). (C). 1989. pap. text ed. 10.00 (*0-941700-39-9*); lib. bdg. 24.25 (*0-941700-38-0*) JH FPI SAIS.

***U. S. - Canada Free Trade Agreement: Factors Contributing to Controversy in Appeals of Trade Remedy Cases to Binational Panels.** (Illus.). 104p. (C). 1996. reprint ed. pap. 30.00 (*0-7881-3659-3*) DIANE Pub.

U. S. - Canada Free Trade Agreement: The Complete Resource Guide, 3 vols. 1988. Set. ring bd. 260.00 (*1-55871-000-0*); Vol. I, Industry Guide. write for info. (*1-55871-001-9*); Vol. II, Legal Guide. write for info. (*1-55871-002-7*); Vol. III, Tariff Schedules. write for info. (*1-55871-003-5*) BNA Plus.

U. S. - Canadian Economic Relations: Next Steps? Ed. by Edward R. Fried & Philip H. Trezise. LC 84-72025. (Dialogues on Public Policy Ser.). 141p. 1984. pap. 10. 95 (*0-8157-2925-1*) Brookings.

U. S. - Canadian Softwood Lumber: Trade Dispute Negotiations. Charles F. Doran & Timothy J. Naftali. 62p. (Orig.). (C). 1987. pap. text ed. 11.75 (*0-941700-11-9*) JH FPI SAIS.

U. S. - Caribbean Relations into the Twenty-First Century. Ed. by Georges A. Fauriol. (CSIS Report Ser.). (C). 1995. pap. text ed. 14.95 (*0-89206-235-5*) CSI Studies.

U. S. - Chilean Trade: Pesticide Standards & Concerns Regarding Chilean Sanitary Rules. (Illus.). 50p. (Orig.). (C). 1995. pap. text ed. 25.00 (*0-7881-1241-4*) DIANE Pub.

U. S. - China Economic Relations: Present & Future. Ed. by Richard Holton & Wang Xi. (Research Papers & Policy Studies: No. 29). 460p. (Orig.). (C). 1990. pap. 20.00 (*1-55729-012-1*) IEAS.

U. S. - China Normalization: An Evaluation of Foreign Policy. Joanne Chang. (World Affairs Ser.: Vol. 22, Bk. 4). (Orig.). 1986. pap. 9.95 (*0-87940-083-8*) Monograph Series.

U. S. - China Relations. Laurence W. Levine. 7.95 (*0-8315-0136-7*) Speller.

***U. S. - China Relations, 1784-1992.** Ta J. Liu. LC 96-46100. 480p. 1996. 68.50 (*0-7618-0598-2*); pap. 46.50 (*0-7618-0599-0*) U Pr of Amer.

U. S. - China Trade: Problems & Prospects. Ed. by Eugene K. Lawson. LC 88-3214. 352p. 1988. text ed. 69.50 (*0-275-92494-7*, C2494, Praeger Pubs) Greenwood.

U. S. - Dutch Legal Concepts on Business & Tax Law: A Glossary. M. J. Sinke. 192p. 1990. 72.00 (*90-6544-450-5*) Kluwer Law Tax Pubs.

U. S. - Eastern European Trade Sourcebook. Ed. by William S. Loiry. 250p. 1991. 59.95 (*1-55862-156-3*) St James Pr.

U. S. - Iana. 2nd ed. Ed. by Wright Howes. 652p. 1978. reprint ed. 49.95 (*0-8352-0103-1*) Bowker.

U. S. - Iran Relations: Areas of Tension & Mutual Interest. Ed. by Hooshang Amirahmadi & Eric Hooglund. 127p. 1994. pap. 15.00 (*0-916808-41-6*) Mid East Inst.

U. S. - Japan Economic Relations: A Symposium on Critical Issues. James C. Abegglen et al. LC 80-620017. (Research Papers & Policy Studies: No. 1). 57p. 1980. pap. 2.50 (*0-912966-25-4*) IEAS.

U. S. - Japan Relations: Towards Burden Sharing. Ed. by Richard B. Finn. 243p. 1986. pap. 21.95 (*0-88738-661-X*) Transaction Pubs.

U. S. - Japan Seminar of Piezoelectric Polymers: Proceedings: Honolulu, Hawaii, July 1983: Special Issue of Journal Ferroelectrics. Ed. by K. D. Pae. (Ferroelectricity & Related Materials Ser.). 354p. 1984. text ed. 149.00 (*0-677-16555-2*) Gordon & Breach.

U. S. - Japan Strategic Reciprocity: A Neo-Internationalist View. Edward A. Olsen. (Publication Ser.: No. 307). xiii, 194p. 1985. 24.95 (*0-8179-8071-7*); pap. 10.95 (*0-8179-8072-5*) Hoover Inst Pr.

U. S. - Japan Technology Linkages in Biotechnology: Challenges for the 1990's. National Research Council, Office of International Affairs Staff. 106p. (C). 1992. pap. text ed. 19.00 (*0-309-04699-8*) Natl Acad Pr.

U. S. - Japan Trade Friction: Its Impact on Security Cooperation in the Pacific Basin. Ed. by T. David Mason & Abdul M. Turay. 208p. 1991. text ed. 49.95 (*0-312-05328-2*) St Martin.

U. S. - Korea Economic Partnership: Policy Directions for Trade & Economic Cooperation. Ed. by Kim Youn-Suk & Oh Kap-Soo. 324p. 1995. text ed. 68.95 (*1-85972-022-6*, Pub. by Avebury Pub UK) Ashgate Pub Co.

U. S. - Mexican Border Literature: Short Stories. Ed. by Jose M. Di Bella et al. (Binational Press Ser.: No. 2). 144p. (ENG & SPA.). 1989. pap. 10.00 (*0-916304-97-3*) SDSU Press.

U. S. - Mexican Free Trade: The Effect on Petrochemicals, Textiles, & Banking in Texas. Sidney Weintraub et al. (Policy Reports: No. 5). 128p. 1993. 15.00 (*0-89940-320-4*) LBJ Sch Pub Aff.

U. S. - Mexican Trade Relations: From the Generalized System of Preferences to a Formal Bilateral Trade Treaty. Gustavo Del Castillo. (Research Reports: No. 14). 27p. (Orig.). (C). 1985. pap. 5.00 (*0-935391-13-4*) UCSD Ctr US-Mex.

U. S. - Mexican Treaties, 11 vols. Compiled by Richard A. Westin. LC 95-37157. 1996. 1,250.00 (*0-89941-985-2*, 308780) W S Hein.

U. S. - Mexico - Canada Free-Trade Agreement: Do We Just Say No? William McGaughey, Jr. 230p. (Orig.). 1992. pap. 11.95 (*0-9605630-2-4*) Thistlerose.

U. S. - Mexico Free Trade Agreement: Economic Impact on Texas. Sidney Weintraub & Leigh Boske. (Special Project Report). 136p. 1992. pap. 11.00 (*0-89940-871-0*) LBJ Sch Pub Aff.

U. S. - Mexico Relations: Labor Market Interdependence. Ed. by Jorge A. Bustamante et al. LC 91-42423. (U. S. - Mexican Relations Ser.). 516p. (C). 1992. 55.00 (*0-8047-2020-7*) Stanford U Pr.

U. S. - Mexico Tax Convention: Text & Analysis. Phillips & Washick. 80p. 1993. pap. 39.00 (*0-685-67054-6*, 5404) Commerce.

U. S. - Mexico Trade: The Work Environment at Eight U. S.-Owned Maquiladora Auto Parts Plants. (Illus.). 52p. (Orig.). (C). 1994. pap. text ed. 25.00 (*0-7881-0558-2*) DIANE Pub.

U. S. - Mexico Trade & Transportation: Corridors, Logistics Practices, & Multimodal Partnerships. Contrib. by Leigh B. Boske & Robert Harrison. (Policy Research Project Report: No. 113). 195p. 1995. pap. 15.00 (*0-89940-721-8*) LBJ Sch Pub Aff.

U. S. - NATO Burden Sharing: Allies' Contributions to Common Defense During the 1980s. (Illus.). 70p. (Orig.). (C). 1994. pap. text ed. 25.00 (*0-7881-0312-1*) DIANE Pub.

U. S. - Pakistan & India Strategic Relations. Rajvir Singh. 1986. 28.50 (*0-8364-1631-7*, Pub. by Chugh Pubns II) S Asia.

U. S. - PLO Dialogue: Secret Diplomacy & Conflict Resolution. Mohamed Rabie. LC 94-5294. 224p. 1995. lib. bdg. 34.95 (*0-8130-1326-7*) U Press Fla.

U. S. - Republic of China (Taiwan) Fisheries Negotiations, 1989, No. 4. Mark Mon-Chang Hsieh. 84p. 1991. 6.00 (*0-925153-16-8*, 105) Occasional Papers.

U. S. - Russian Naval Cooperation. Charles A. Meconis & Boris N. Makeeev. LC 95-30655. 192p. 1995. text ed. 57.95 (*0-275-95387-4*, Praeger Pubs) Greenwood.

U. S. - South Asian Relations. Iftikhar H. Malik. LC 90-34611. 290p. 1991. text ed. 65.00 (*0-312-04892-0*) St Martin.

U. S. - Soviet Relations. Simon Serfaty. 84p. (Orig.). (C). 1985. pap. text ed. 15.75 (*0-941700-30-5*) JH FPI SAIS.

U. S. - Soviet Summits: An Account of East-West Diplomacy at the Top, 1955-1985. Gordon R. Weihmiller & Dusko Doder. LC 86-11023. 230p. (Orig.). 1986. pap. text ed. 5.00 (*0-934742-36-7*) Geo U Inst Dplmcy.

U. S. - Soviet Summits: An Account of East-West Diplomacy at the Top, 1955-1985. Gordon R. Weihmiller. 230p. (Orig.). 1986. pap. text ed. 16.00 (*0-8191-5443-1*, Inst Study Diplomacy); lib. bdg. 40.00 (*0-8191-5442-3*, Inst Study Diplomacy) U Pr of Amer.

U. S. - Soviet Trade Sourcebook. Ed. by William S. Loiry. 283p. 1990. 59.95 (*1-55862-142-3*) St James Pr.

U. S. - Thailand Relations in a New International Era, No. 33. Ed. by Wiwat Mungkandi & Clark D. Neher. (Research Papers & Policy Studies). 350p. (Orig.). 1990. pap. 20.00 (*1-55729-018-0*) IEAS.

U. S. - U. S. S. R. Agenda for Communication: Proceedings. Ed. by Marvin E. Wolfgang & Richard D. Lambert. LC 74-80143. (Annals Ser.: No. 414). 300p. (Orig.). 1974. pap. 18.00 (*0-87761-179-3*) Am Acad Pol Soc Sci.

***U. S. - Vietnam Relations: Issues & Implications.** (Illus.). 34p. 1995. pap. text ed. 25.00 (*1-57979-132-8*) BPI Info Servs.

U. S. - West European Cooperation in Out-of-Area Military Operations: Problems & Prospects. Richard L. Kugler. LC 93-39288. 1994. pap. 15.00 (*0-8330-1476-5*, MR-349-USDP) Rand Corp.

U. S.- Japan Relations: Technology, Economics, & Security. Harold Brown. 48p. 1987. 4.00 (*0-87641-228-2*) Carnegie Ethics & Intl Affairs.

U. S. A. (Your School Reports). 1995. boxed 19.95 (*1-884618-10-3*) Unique Information.

U. S. A. Baedeker. (Baedeker's Travel Guides Ser.). 1995. 24.00 (*0-02-860069-X*) Macmillan.

U. S. A. Berlitz Editors. (Pocket Guides Ser.). 256p. 1994. 10.95 (*2-8315-2379-6*) Berlitz.

U. S. A. Daphne Butler. LC 92-13647. (On the Map Ser.). (Illus.). 32p. (J). (gr. 3-4). 1992. lib. bdg. 22.83 (*0-8114-3676-4*) Raintree Steck-V.

***U. S. A.** St. Martin's Press Staff. (Let's Go Ser.). 1997. pap. 19.99 (*0-312-16903-5*) St Martin.

U. S. A., No. 3. 3rd ed. Jamie Jensen et al. (Rough Guide Ser.). (Illus.). 1120p. 1996. pap. 19.95 (*1-85828-161-X*, Penguin Bks) Viking Penguin.

U. S. A. A Picture Memory. 1990. 8.99 (*0-517-01747-4*) Random Hse Value.

U. S. A. Aspects of Political & Social Life, Vol. XV. Ed. & Intro. by Richard E. Hattwick. 75p. pap. 4.00 (*0-931497-27-2*) WIU CBER.

U. S. A. Customs & Institutions, Vol. 4. Tiersky. (gr. 7 up). 1987. pap. text ed. write for info. (*0-13-939828-7*, 18438) Prentice ESL.

U. S. A. Men & Machines, Vol. 3. Crymes et al. (gr. 7 up). 1987. pap. text ed. 7.50 (*0-13-939810-4*, 18437) Prentice ESL.

U. S. A. The Land & the People. rev. ed. Robert J. Dixson. (Illus.). 169p. (gr. 7 up). 1987. pap. text ed. 7.50 (*0-13-939373-0*, 18435) Prentice ESL.

U. S. A. The 42nd Parallel; 1919; The Big Money. John R. Dos Passos. Ed. by Townsend Ludington & Daniel Aaron. LC 95-49282. 1996. 40.00 (*1-883011-14-0*) Library of America.

U. S. A. Vol. 2, Men & History. rev. ed. Herbert Fox. (Illus.). 179p. 1987. pap. text ed. 7.50 (*0-13-939422-2*, 18436) Prentice ESL.

U. S. A. - Spanish America: Challenge & Response. Solomon Lipp. (Monografías A Ser.: No. 154). 166p. (C). 1994. 53.00 (*1-85566-033-4*, Pub. by Tamesis Bks Ltd UK) Boydell & Brewer.

U. S. A. - the East, Midwest & South: Nelles Guide. (Nelles Guides Ser.). (Illus.). 256p. (Orig.). 1996. pap. 14.95 (*3-88618-414-5*, Pub. by Nelles Verlag GW) Seven Hills Bk.

U. S. A. - the West, Rockies & Texas: Nelles Guide. (Nelles Guides Ser.). (Illus.). 256p. (Orig.). 1996. pap. 14.95 (*3-88618-416-1*, Pub. by Nelles Verlag GW) Seven Hills Bk.

U. S. A. - U. S. S. R. Facts & Figures. (Illus.). 90p. (Orig.). (C). 1992. pap. text ed. 20.00 (*1-56806-013-0*) DIANE Pub.

U. S. A., Canada, Mexico - Delicious Recipes: Collected from the Finest Award-Winning Restaurants & Inns. Marilyn S. Howard. 104p. (Orig.). 1985. pap. text ed. 8.95 (*0-9616125-0-9*) M Serrett Howard.

***U. S. A. A. A Tradition of Service, 1922-1997.** Paul T. Ringenbach. LC 97-11162. 1997. write for info. (*0-89865-993-0*) Donning Co.

U. S. A. Airborne 50th Anniversary. Turner Publishing Company Staff. LC 90-70635. 500p. 1990. 49.95 (*0-938021-90-7*) Turner Pub KY.

U. S. A., an Outline of the Country, Its People & Institutions. Denis W. Brogan. (History - United States Ser.). 143p. 1993. reprint ed. lib. bdg. 69.00 (*0-7812-4850-7*) Rprt Serv.

***U. S. A. & Canada Travellers Survival Kit.** Simon Calder. (Travellers Survival Kit Guides Ser.). 480p. (Orig.). 1997. pap. 17.95 (*1-85458-089-2*, Pub. by Vac Wrk Pubns UK) Seven Hills Bk.

***U. S. A. & Canada TSK.** 4th ed. Simon Calder. (Travellers Survival Kit Ser.). 480p. 1997. pap. 17.95 (*1-85458-179-1*, Pub. by Vac Wrk Pubns UK) Seven Hills Bk.

U. S. A. & Canada 1994. 2nd ed. 565p. 1993. 375.00 (*0-946653-93-3*) Intl Pubns Serv.

U. S. A. & Russia. P. J. Larkin. (World History in 20th Century Ser.). (Illus.). 158p. 7700. pap. 11.95 (*0-7175-0063-2*) Dufour.

U. S. A. & the Middle East since World War 2. T. G. Fraser. LC 88-37028. 260p. 1989. text ed. 39.95 (*0-312-03018-5*) St Martin.

U. S. A. & the Soviet Myth. Lev E. Dobriansky. 9.50 (*0-8159-7005-6*) Devin.

***U. S. A. at Risk.** Nathaniel I. Korman. 20p. (Orig.). 1996. pap. 0.95 (*0-9654300-1-4*) Runamiro Bks.

U. S. A. Atlas, 1991. Richard S. Wurman. 1990. pap. 9.95 (*0-13-946831-5*) P-H.

U. S. A. Business: The Portable Encyclopedia for Doing Business with the United States. James Nolan et al. LC 95-7680. (Country Business Guide Ser.). 507p. (Orig.). 1995. pap. 24.95 (*1-885073-01-1*) Wrld Trade Pr.

U. S. A. by Rail. 2nd ed. John Pitt. LC 96-15662. (Rail Guides Ser.). 1996. pap. 16.95 (*1-56440-949-X*) Globe Pequot.

***U. S. A. Cookbook.** Sheila Lukins. LC 97-9411. 1997. pap. text ed. 18.95 (*1-56305-807-3*) Workman Pub.

***U. S. A. Cookbook.** Sheila Lukins. LC 97-9411. 1997. 28. 95 (*0-7611-0775-4*) Workman Pub.

U. S. A. Crosswords, No. 20. Charles Preston. 80p. (Orig.). 1996. pap. 7.95 (*0-399-52219-0*, Perigee Bks) Berkley Pub.

***U. S. A. Crosswords #21.** Charles Preston. 80p. (Orig.). 1997. pap. 7.95 (*0-399-52275-1*, Perigee Bks) Berkley Pub.

***U. S. A. Divided Nation.** Demarco. 1994. pap. text ed. write for info. (*0-582-22674-0*, Pub. by Longman UK) Longman.

U. S. A. F. Fighter Interceptor Squadrons. Peter R. Foster. (Osprey Colour Library). (Illus.). 128p. 1994. pap. 15.95 (*1-85532-435-0*, Pub. by Osprey Pubng Ltd UK) Motorbooks Intl.

U. S. A. F. Flotation Equipment. 1995. lib. bdg. 261.95 (*0-8490-6603-4*) Gordon Pr.

***U. S. A. from Space: Maps Come Alive for Kids.** Anne-Catherine Fallen. 1997. 19.95 (*1-55209-159-7*) Firefly Bks Ltd.

***U. S. A. from Space: Maps Come Alive for Kids.** Anne-Catherine Fallen. (J). 1997. pap. text ed. 7.95 (*1-55209-157-0*) Firefly Bks Ltd.

U. S. A. Guide to the Underground Railroad. Charles Blockson. (Illus.). 380p. 1995. pap. 16.95 (*0-7818-0429-9*) Hippocrene Bks.

U. S. A. Gymnastics Safety Handbook (1994 Edition) For Gymnastics & Other Sport Activities. U. S. A. Gymnastics Department of Educational Services & Safety Staff. 137p. 1994. pap. 19.95 (*1-885250-00-2*) USA Gymnastics.

***U. S. A. Hockey: The Celebration of a Great Tradition.** Kevin Allen. 256p. 1997. 35.00 (*1-57243-236-5*) Triumph Bks.

***U. S. A. Immigration & Orientation.** unabridged ed. Bob McLaughlin & Mary McLaughlin. LC 97-90370. x, 400p. (Orig.). 1997. pap. 35.00 (*0-9657571-2-9*) Wellesworth Pub.

U. S. A. Immigration Guide. 2nd ed. Ramon Carrion. LC 94-68893. 144p. (Orig.). 1994. pap. 19.95 (*1-57248-000-9*, Leg Surv Guides) Sourcebks.

***U. S. A. in Space.** Ed. by Russell R. Tobias. (Illus.). 1100p. 1996. lib. bdg. 210.00 (*0-89356-924-0*) Salem Pr.

U. S. A. Jography: A Fun Run Thru the United States, Vol. II. Carole Marsh. (Jography Ser.). (Illus.). 60p. (J). (gr. k-12). 1994. pap. 19.95 (*1-55609-300-4*); lib. bdg. 29.95 (*1-55609-301-2*); disk 29.95 (*1-55609-302-0*) Gallopade Pub Group.

U. S. A. Junior Hockey Coaches Manual. 100p. 1990. 12. 00 (*0-318-49984-3*) US Field Hockey.

U. S. A. Mathematical Olympiads, 1972-1986: Problems & Solutions. Compiled by Murray S. Klamkin. LC 88-62611. (New Mathematical Library). 180p. (Orig.). 1988. pap. 17.50 (*0-88385-634-4*, NML-33) Math Assn.

U. S. A. Medical Directories: Dallas - Fort Worth 1995-96 Issue. rev. ed. American Medical Sales School, Inc. Staff. Ed. & Intro. by Diane Huggins. (Illus.). 410p. 1995. 42.50 (*1-882328-03-5*) Am Med Sales.

U. S. A. Photography Guide 2. Nazraeli Press Staff. 208p. 1996. pap. 29.00 (*3-923922-36-1*, 610402, Pub. by Nazraeli Pr GW) Dist Art Pubs.

U. S. A. Phrasebook. Ed. by Sally Steward. (Illus.). 240p. 1995. pap. 5.95 (*0-86442-257-1*) Lonely Planet.

***U. S. A. Road Map.** 1996. 8.95 (*2-06-700930-3*, 930) Michelin.

U. S. A. since 1945: After Hiroshima. 3rd ed. Albert C. Ganley et al. 384p. 1993. pap. 23.25 (*0-8013-0934-4*, 79216) Longman.

***U. S. A. Sourcebook.** Black Book Marketing Group Staff. 1994. 55.00 (*0-688-13525-0*) Morrow.

U. S. A. Sports Golf Tournament Guide. Will Balliett. 1996. 19.95 (*0-02-860475-X*) Macmillan.

***U. S. A. Tax: A Progressive Consumption Tax.** Lawrence S. Seidman. LC 96-41990. 1997. 20.00 (*0-262-19383-3*) MIT Pr.

U. S. A. Tennis Course: 500 Visual Ways to Better Tennis. Victor Tantalo. Ed. by Jacqueline Hartt. LC 86-50302. (Illus.). 208p. (Orig.). 1986. 17.95 (*0-936577-01-0*) USA Pubs.

U. S. A. the Hard Way: An Autobiography of a B-17 Crew Member. Roger W. Armstrong. Ed. by Ken Stone. LC 90-64463. (Illus.). 350p. 1991. reprint ed. pap. 15.95 (*0-9629161-1-0*) Quail Hse.

U. S. A., the Permanent Revolution. Fortune Magazine Editors & Russell W. Davenport. LC 80-15776. 267p. 1980. reprint ed. text ed. 59.75 (*0-313-22500-1*, FMUS, Greenwood Pr) Greenwood.

U. S. A. Today. Scott Nearing & Helen K. Nearing. LC 55-12158. 254p. 1955. 15.00 (*0-685-83846-3*); pap. 10.00 (*0-685-83847-1*) Good Life Ctr.

***U. S. A. Today.** Scott Nearing & Helen Nearing. 15.00 (*0-614-30477-6*) Good Life Ctr.

***U. S. A. Today.** Scott Nearing & Helen Nearing. pap. 10. 00 (*0-614-30478-4*) Good Life Ctr.

U. S. A. Today Baseball Weekly 1995 Almanac. USA Today Staff. (Illus.). 400p. 1995. pap. 12.95 (*0-7868-8048-1*) Hyperion.

***U. S. A. Today Baseball Weekly 1997 Almanac.** Ed. by Paul White et al. (Orig.). 1997. pap. 12.95 (*0-614-27668-3*, Owl) H Holt & Co.

***U. S. A. Today Baseball Weekly, 1998 Almanac.** Paul White. 1998. pap. text ed. 12.95 (*0-8050-5148-1*) H Holt & Co.

UV

U. S. A. Today Crossword Puzzle Dictionary: The Newest, Most Comprehensive & Authoritative Crossword Reference Book. Charles Preston & Barbara A. Kipfer. 928p. 1996. pap. 12.95 (*0-7868-8060-0*) Hyperion.

U. S. A. Today Financial Aid for College: A Quick Guide to Everything You Need to Know, with the New 1996 Forms! rev. ed. Pat Ordovensky. LC 95-26614. 160p. 1995. pap. 8.95 (*1-56079-568-9*) Petersons.

U. S. A. Today Getting into College: A Quick Guide to Everything You Need to Know. Pat Ordovensky. LC 95-12443. 160p. (Orig.). 1995. pap. 8.95 (*1-56079-463-1*) Petersons.

U. S. A. Today Golf Atlas. 2nd ed. Gousha. H. M., Editors. 1995. pap. text ed. 16.95 (*0-671-53457-2*, H M Gousha) P-H Gen Ref & Trav.

U. S. A. Today North American Ski Atlas: The Complete Guide to Alpine & Nordic Ski Areas. Will K. Balliett. 1994. pap. 12.95 (*0-671-89138-3*) S&S Trade.

U. S. A. Today Way: A Candid Look at the National Newspaper's First Decade, 1982-1992. John K. Hartman. LC 92-90447. 224p. (Orig.). 1992. pap. 30.00 (*0-9633729-0-4*) J K Hartman.

U. S. A. Today 1995 Golf Almanac. Ed. by Steve Hershey et al. (Illus.). 384p. 1995. pap. 12.95 (*0-7868-8058-9*) Hyperion.

U. S. A. Trampoline & Tumbling Level One Coaching Manual. U. S. A. Trampoline & Tumbling Staff. 128p. (Orig.). 1996. pap. 15.00 (*1-884125-53-0*) Cooper Pubng.

U. S. A. Travel Phone Book: A Quick-Help Guide to Essential Addresses & Telephone Numbers for Business & Vacation Travellers. Conrad Persson. 192p. 1991. pap. 8.95 (*1-878446-03-7*) Bon A Tirer Pub.

U. S. A. up Close: From the Atlantic Pact to Bush. Guilio Andreotti. Tr. by Peter Farrell from ITA. 240p. (C). 1991. text ed. 32.00 (*0-8147-0604-5*) NYU Pr.

U. S. A. up Close: From the Atlantic Pact to Bush. Guilio Andreotti. Tr. by Peter Farrell from ITA. 240p. (C). 1993. pap. 18.50 (*0-8147-0627-4*) NYU Pr.

U. S. A. 2012: After the Middle-Class Revolution. Kenneth M. Dolbeare & Janette K. Hubbell. 208p. (C). 1996. 25.00 (*1-56643-036-4*); pap. text ed. 17.95 (*1-56643-035-6*) Chatham Hse Pubs.

***U S A '98.** Fodors Travel Staff. 1997. pap. 21.00 (*0-679-03542-7*) Fodors Travel.

U. S. Absorbable & Erodible Biomaterial Product Markets: Emerging Technologies Create Multi-Billion Dollar Industry. Market Intelligence Staff. 333p. 1995. 1,995.00 (*0-7889-0206-7*, S239S4) Frost & Sullivan.

U. S. Accounting Profession in the 1890s & Early 1900s. Ed. by Stephen A. Zeff. (Foundations in Accounting Ser.: No. 23). 579p. 1989. reprint ed. text ed. 15.00 (*0-8240-6135-7*) Garland.

U. S. Acquires the Philippines: Consensus vs. Reality. Louis J. Halle. LC 85-9233. (Credibility of Institutions, Policies & Leadership Ser.: Vol. 15). 72p. (Orig.). 1985. pap. 11.00 (*0-8191-4760-5*); lib. bdg. 26.50 (*0-8191-4759-1*, Pub. by White Miller Center) U Pr of Amer.

U. S. Ad Review, Vol. 3, No. 1. Ed. by Jamie Scott. (Illus.). 256p. (C). 1993. pap. 39.95 (*0-934590-23-0*) Retail Report.

U. S. Ad Review: The Best American Print Advertising. Ed. by Telefashion Group Staff. (Illus.). 336p. (Orig.). 1991. pap. 39.95 (*0-935603-99-9*) Rockport Pubs.

U. S. Ad Review: The Best American Print Advertising, No. 11. 320p. 1994. write for info. (*1-56496-122-2*) Rockport Pubs.

U. S. Ad Review: The Best American Print Advertising, Vol. 2. 320p. 1991. pap. 39.99 (*1-56496-017-X*) Rockport Pubs.

U. S. Ad Review: The Best American Print Advertising, Vol. 3. 320p. 1992. pap. 39.99 (*1-56496-020-X*) Rockport Pubs.

U. S. Ad Review: The Best American Print Advertising, Vol. 4. 320p. 1992. pap. 39.99 (*1-56496-022-6*) Rockport Pubs.

U. S. Ad Review No. 12. Jamie Scott. 256p. 1994. 49.95 (*0-934590-05-2*) Retail Report.

U. S. Ad Review No. 13. Jamie Scott. 256p. 1994. 49.95 (*0-934590-65-6*) Retail Report.

U. S. Ad Review No. 14. Jamie Scott. 256p. 1994. 49.95 (*0-934590-32-X*) Retail Report.

U. S. Ad Review No. 15. Jamie Scott. 256p. 1994. 49.95 (*0-934590-10-9*) Retail Report.

U. S. Adhesives & Sealants Industry. 310p. 1995. 1,095.00 (*0-685-10301-3*) Busn Trend.

U. S. Advanced Ceramics Industry-Markets, Players & New Developments, No. GB-058N. 321p. 1993. 2,250.00 (*0-89336-978-0*) BCC.

U. S. Aging Policy Interest Groups: Institutional Profiles. Ed. by David D. Van Tassel & Jimmy E. Meyer. LC 91-29198. 288p. 1992. text ed. 65.00 (*0-313-26543-7*, VTA/, Greenwood Pr) Greenwood.

U. S. Agricultural Chemicals Industry. (Illus.). 280p. (Orig.). 1991. spiral bd. 1,095.00 (*0-685-21990-9*) Busn Trend.

U. S. Agricultural Groups: Institutional Profiles. Ed. by William P. Browne & Allan J. Cigler. LC 89-25786. 312p. 1990. text ed. 69.50 (*0-313-25088-X*, CGR/, Greenwood Pr) Greenwood.

U. S. Agricultural Outlook (1994) 111p. (Orig.). (C). 1995. pap. text ed. 35.00 (*0-7881-2108-1*) DIANE Pub.

U. S. Agricultural Research: Strategic Challenges & Options. Ed. by Robert Weaver. 350p. (Orig.). (C). 1993. pap. text ed. 30.00 (*0-944919-04-9*) Agri Research Inst.

***U. S. Agricultural Response to Income Taxation.** Hoy F. Carman. LC 97-10763. 1997. write for info. (*0-8138-2175-4*) Iowa St U Pr.

U. S. Agriculture: Status of the Farm Sector. (Illus.). 43p. (Orig.). (C). 1995. pap. text ed. 25.00 incl. 5.25 hd (*0-7881-2036-0*) DIANE Pub.

U. S. Agriculture & Third World Development: The Critical Linkage. Ed. by Randall B. Purcell & Elizabeth Morrison. LC 86-29860. 240p. 1987. lib. bdg. 36.50 (*1-55587-011-2*) Lynne Rienner.

U. S. Agriculture in a Global Setting, an Agenda for the Future. Ed. by M. Ann Tutwiler. LC 88-12468. 234p. 1988. pap. 20.00 (*0-915707-45-4*) Resources Future.

U. S. Aid to Israel & Its Reflection in the New York Times & the Washington Post 1948-1973: The Pen, the Sword, & the Middle East. Bat-Ami Zucker. LC 91-46531. (Jewish Studies: Vol. 11). 188p. 1992. lib. bdg. 79.95 (*0-7734-9435-9*) E Mellen.

U. S. Aid to Sub-Saharan Africa: Challenges, Constraints, & Choices. Carol Lancaster. (Significant Issues Ser.: Vol. 10, No. 16). 1988. pap. 6.95 (*0-89206-128-6*) CSI Studies.

U. S. Air Emissions Monitor & Analyzer Markets: Multiple Environmental Regulations Continue to Drive Growth. Market Intelligence Staff. 400p. (Orig.). 1994. 1,895.00 (*1-56753-892-4*) Frost & Sullivan.

U. S. Air Force. Rose Blue & Corinne J. Naden. LC 92-13431. (Defending Our Country Ser.). (Illus.). 64p. (J). (gr. 3-6). 1993. pap. 5.95 (*1-56294-754-0*); lib. bdg. 16.40 (*1-56294-217-4*) Millbrook Pr.

U. S. Air Force. Nancy W. Ferrell. (Armed Services Ser.). (Illus.). 72p. (YA). (gr. 5 up). 1990. lib. bdg. 22.95 (*0-8225-1433-8*, Lerner Publctns) Lerner Group.

U. S. Air Force Air Power Directory. Ed. by David Donald. (Illus.). 232p. Date not set. reprint ed. pap. 21.95 (*1-880588-16-1*) AIRtime Pub.

U. S. Air Force Air Power Directory: World Air Power. Aerospace Publishing Ltd. Staff. Ed. by David Donald & Jon Lake. (Illus.). 224p. 1992. 29.95 (*1-880588-01-3*) AIRtime Pub.

U. S. Air Pollution Control Markets. Market Intelligence Staff. 410p. 1994. 2,395.00 (*0-7889-0149-4*) Frost & Sullivan.

U. S. Air Service in the Great War: An International Exploration. James J. Cooke. LC 95-34093. 264p. 1996. text ed. 59.95 (*0-275-94862-5*, Praeger Pubs) Greenwood.

U. S. Airborne in Action. Leroy Thompson. (Combat Troops in Action Ser.). (Illus.). 50p. 1992. pap. 7.95 (*0-89747-283-7*, 3010) Squad Sig Pubns.

U. S. Aircraft & Armament of Operation Desert Storm. Bert Kinzey. (Detail & Scale Ser.: Vol. 40). 64p. 1991. pap. 10.95 (*0-8306-3093-7*, 25056) McGraw-Hill Prof.

U. S. Aircraft Carriers: An Illustrated Design History. Norman Friedman. LC 82-14357. (Illus.). 427p. 1983. 59.95 (*0-87021-739-9*) Naval Inst Pr.

***U. S. Aircraft Carriers in Action, Pt. 2.** Michael Smith. (Warships in Action Ser.: No. 10). (Illus.). 50p. (Orig.). 1997. pap. 7.95 (*0-89747-373-6*, 4010) Squad Sig Pubns.

U. S. Aircraft Carriers, Pt. 1: In Action. Robert Stern. (Warships in Action Ser.). (Illus.). 50p. 1991. pap. 7.95 (*0-89747-265-9*, 4005) Squad Sig Pubns.

U. S. Aircrew Combat Flight & Survival Gear. Hans Halberstadt & Mike Halberstadt. (Illus.). 128p. 1996. pap. 24.95 (*0-7603-0267-7*) Motorbooks Intl.

U. S. Airline Industry: End of an Era. Paul Biederman. LC 81-17845. 222p. 1982. text ed. 38.50 (*0-275-90763-5*, C0763, Praeger Pubs) Greenwood.

U. S. Airpower. Ed. by Consumer Guide Staff. (Illus.). 320p. 1991. 14.99 (*0-517-67591-9*) Random Hse Value.

***U. S. All Media E-Mail Directory.** Paul J. Krupin. 115p. 1997. pap. 39.95 (*1-885035-03-9*) Direct Contact.

U. S. Allergy & Asthma Markets. Market Intelligence Staff. 300p. 1994. 3,295.00 (*0-7889-0158-3*) Frost & Sullivan.

U. S. Allergy & Asthma Treatment Markets: New Approaches in Therapy Promise Major Breakthroughs. Market Intelligence Staff. 240p. 1993. 2,295.00 (*1-56753-544-5*) Frost & Sullivan.

U. S. Alternative Care Respiratory Therapy Product Markets. Frost & Sullivan Staff. 384p. 1996. write for info. (*0-7889-0466-3*, 5414) Frost & Sullivan.

U. S. Analytical Instruments in Process Control. Market Intelligence Staff. 1994. 1,995.00 (*0-7889-0147-8*) Frost & Sullivan.

U. S. Analytical Laboratory Instrumentation Markets: Industry Markets & Software Enhancements Reshape Competitive Strategies. Date not set. write for info. (*0-7889-0376-4*) Frost & Sullivan.

U. S. & Canadian Businesses, 1955 to 1987: A Bibliography. Priscilla C. Geahigan. LC 88-30538. 601p. 1989. 52.50 (*0-8108-2186-9*) Scarecrow.

U. S. & Canadian Electrical & Electronic Wire & Cable Manufacturers, 1993: Competitive Analysis. Kimberly McGowan. 600p. 1993. pap. text ed. 2,400.00 (*1-878218-39-5*) World Info Tech.

U. S. & Canadian Electronic Wire & Cable Manufacturers: 1990 Competitive Analysis. Amadee Bender. (Illus.). 200p. (Orig.). 1990. pap. 1,800.00 (*1-878218-11-5*) World Info Tech.

U. S. & Canadian Electronic Wire & Cable Manufacturers: 1995 Competitive Analysis. Kimberly O'Brien. 220p. 1995. pap. text ed. 2,900.00 (*1-878218-63-8*) World Info Tech.

U. S. & China Relations at a Crossroads. Ed. by David M. Lampton & Alfred D. Wilhelm, Jr. 306p. (Orig.). (C). 1995. lib. bdg. 62.50 (*0-8191-9888-9*) U Pr of Amer.

U. S. & China since 1949: A Troubled Affair. Robert Garson. 256p. 1995. write for info. (*0-86187-160-X*, Pub. by Pntr Pubs UK) Bks Intl VA.

U. S. & East Europe in the 1990s. Intro. by Richard F. Staar. 250p. (C). 1989. text ed. 65.00 (*0-8448-1612-4*, Crane Russak); pap. text ed. 36.00 (*0-8448-1613-2*, Crane Russak) Taylor & Francis.

U. S. & European Automotive Emissions Technology: Twenty-four Papers. 1993. 29.00 (*1-56091-342-8*, SP-957) Soc Auto Engineers.

U. S. & Global Capital Shortages: The Problem & Possible Solutions. Sara L. Gordon. LC 95-3264. 240p. 1995. text ed. 59.95 (*0-89930-772-8*, Quorum Bks) Greenwood.

U. S. & International Production Market for T. V. & New Video Technologies (U. S.), 2 vols., Set. Market Intelligence Staff. 1992. 2,450.00 (*1-56753-840-1*, A2258) Frost & Sullivan.

U. S. & Israel, 1945-1986: A Diplomatic History. Herbert J. Druks. 1997. 15.00 (*0-8315-0193-6*) Speller.

U. S. & Japan Foreign Trade: An Annotated Bibliography of Socioeconomic Perspectives. Ed. by Rita Neri. LC 87-34805. 332p. 1988. text ed. 55.00 (*0-8240-8471-3*) Garland.

U. S. & Japan in Figures IV. 120p. 1996. pap. text ed. 22.00 (*4-8224-0703-9*, Pub. by JETRO JA) Taylor & Francis.

U. S. & Japanese Nonproliferation Export Controls: Theory, Description & Analysis. Ed. by Gary K. Bertsch et al. 388p. (Orig.). (C). 1995. pap. text ed. 38.50 (*0-7618-0192-8*); lib. bdg. 49.00 (*0-7618-0191-X*) U Pr of Amer.

U. S. & Latin America in the 1980s: Contending Perspectives on a Decade of Crisis. Ed. by Kevin J. Middlebrook & Carlos Rico. LC 85-40359. (Latin American Ser.). (Illus.). 640p. (Orig.). 1986. 75.00 (*0-8229-3518-X*); pap. 19.95 (*0-8229-6087-7*) U of Pittsburgh Pr.

U. S. & Mexico: Face to Face with New Technology. Cathryn L. Thorup et al. 224p. 1987. 32.95 (*0-685-11983-1*); pap. 17.95 (*0-88738-663-6*) Transaction Pubs.

U. S. & NATO Force Structure & Military Operations in the Mediterranean. 53p. (Orig.). (C). 1994. pap. text ed. 25.00 (*0-7881-1195-7*) DIANE Pub.

***U. S. & Russian Policymaking with Respect to the Use of Force.** Ed. by Jeremy R. Azrael & Emil A. Payin. 225p. (Orig.). 1996. pap. 15.00 (*0-8330-2468-X*, CF-129-CRES) Rand Corp.

U. S. & South Africa, Nineteen Sixty-Eight to Nineteen Eighty-Five: Constructive Engagement & Its Critics. Christopher Coker. LC 86-2203. xv, 328p. 1986. text ed. 52.50 (*0-8223-0665-4*) Duke.

U. S. & Soviet Agriculture: The Shifting Balance of Power. Lester R. Brown. 1982. pap. write for info. (*0-916468-51-8*) Worldwatch Inst.

***U. S. & the British Virgin Islands '98.** Fodors Travel Staff. 1997. pap. 14.00 (*0-679-03541-9*) Fodors Travel.

U. S. & the Problem of Recovery after 1893. Gerald T. White. LC 80-39558. 172p. 1982. pap. 49.10 (*0-7837-8415-5*, 2059226) Bks Demand.

U. S. & the Rise of East Asia, 1945-1990: Dilemmas of the Postwar International Political Economy. Jacques Hersh. LC 92-36150. (International Political Economy Ser.). 250p. 1993. text ed. 69.95 (*0-312-09487-6*) St Martin.

U. S. & the Use of Force in the Post-Cold War Era. Aspen Strategy Group Report Staff. 291p. 1995. pap. 10.95 (*0-89843-163-8*) Aspen Inst Human.

U. S. & U. K. Unemployment Between the Wars: Doleful Story. Dan Benjamin & Kent Matthews. 174p. (C). 1992. text ed. 59.95 (*0-255-36305-2*, Pub. by Inst Economic Affairs UK) St Mut.

U. S. & Vietnam, 1787-1941. Robert H. Miller. (Illus.). 323p. (Orig.). (C). 1994. pap. text ed. 50.00 (*0-7881-0810-7*) DIANE Pub.

U. S. & World Blood Pressure Equipment Markets. Black Forest Group Staff. (Illus.). 142p. 1995. 995.00 (*0-614-09908-0*) Theta Corp.

U. S. & World Energy Resources: Prospects & Priorities. Ragaei E. Mallakh. LC 77-88785. (Illus.). 1977. 12.50 (*0-918714-03-6*) Intl Res Ctr Energy.

U. S. & World Filtration Markets. (Market Research Reports: No. 461). (Illus.). 119p. 1994. 795.00 (*0-614-01244-9*) Theta Corp.

U. S. & World Wide Guide to Retreat Center Guest Houses. John Jensen & Mary Jensen. LC 92-71162. (Illus.). 180p. (Orig.). 1995. pap. 15.95 (*0-9640313-0-2*) CTS Pubns.

U. S. Anesthesia & Gas Monitoring Equipment Markets Continuing Development of Integrated & Compact Products. Market Intelligence Staff. 210p. 1994. 1,995.00 (*0-7889-0027-7*) Frost & Sullivan.

***U. S. Animal Stamps.** Ariel Books Staff. 1996. 3.95 (*0-8362-0989-3*, Arie Bks) Andrews & McMeel.

U. S. Antibiotic Markets: Loss of Patient Protection among Blockbuster Drugs, Will Result in the Infusion of Generics. Frost & Sullivan Staff. 364p. 1996. write for info. (*0-7889-0458-2*, 5400) Frost & Sullivan.

U. S. Antifungal Markets: High Growth Era for Systemic & OTC Products. Market Intelligence Staff. 340p. (Orig.). 1994. 2,495.00 (*1-56753-899-1*) Frost & Sullivan.

U. S. Apparel Industry: International Challenge - Domestic Response. Jeffrey S. Arpan et al. LC 88-6647. (Research Monograph: No. 88). 328p. 1982. pap. 24.95 (*0-88406-141-8*) GA St U Busn Pr.

U. S. Approach to the Latin American Debt Crisis. Michael T. Clark et al. 92p. (Orig.). (C). 1988. pap. text ed. 15.75 (*0-941700-32-1*) JH FPI SAIS.

U. S. Armour Camouflage & Markings 1917-45. Steven J. Zaloga. (Vanguard Ser.: No. 39). (Illus.). 48p. pap. 10.95 (*0-85045-515-4*, 9328, Pub. by Osprey UK) Stackpole.

U. S. Arms to Pakistan: A Study in Alliance Relationship. (C). 1991. 22.50 (*81-7024-383-1*, Pub. by Ashish II) S Asia.

U. S. Army. Henry I. Kurtz. LC 92-12660. (Defending Our Country Ser.). (Illus.). 64p. (J). (gr. 3-6). 1993. pap. 5.95 (*1-56294-752-4*); lib. bdg. 16.40 (*1-56294-242-5*) Millbrook Pr.

U. S. Army. Tom Moran. (Armed Services Ser.). (Illus.). 88p. (YA). (gr. 5 up). 1990. lib. bdg. 22.95 (*0-8225-1434-6*, Lerner Publctns) Lerner Group.

U. S. Army Air Arm, April 1861 to April 1917. Juliette A. Hennessy. (USAF General Histories Ser.). (Illus.). 258p. 1986. reprint ed. pap. 13.00 (*0-912799-34-X*) Off Air Force.

U. S. Army Air Force One. Gordon L. Rottman. (Elite Ser.: No. 46). (Illus.). 64p. pap. 12.95 (*1-85532-294-3*, 9461, Pub. by Osprey UK) Stackpole.

U. S. Army Air Force (2) Gordon L. Rottman. (Elite Ser.). (Illus.). 64p. 1994. pap. 12.95 (*1-85532-339-7*, 9466, Pub. by Osprey UK) Stackpole.

U. S. Army Airborne 1940-1990: The First Fifty Years. Gordon L. Rottman. (Elite Ser.: No. 31). (Illus.). 64p. 1990. pap. 12.95 (*0-85045-948-6*, 9431, Pub. by Osprey Pubng Ltd UK) Stackpole.

***U. S. Army Aircraft since 1947: An Illustrated Reference.** Stephen Harding. (Illus.). 264p. 1997. 45.00 (*0-7643-0190-X*) Schiffer.

U. S. Army Chemical Warfare Service: Chemicals in Combat. Brooks E. Kleber & Dale Birdsell. Ed. by Stetson Conn. (Illus.). 697p. (Orig.). (C). 1995. 50.00 (*0-7881-1847-1*) DIANE Pub.

U. S. Army Combat Equipments. Gordon L. Rottman. (Men-at-Arms Ser.: No. 205). (Illus.). 48p. 1989. pap. 11.95 (*0-85045-842-0*, 9138) Stackpole.

U. S. Army Command & General Staff Colllege: A Centennial History. Boyd L. Dastrup. (Illus.). 157p. 1982. 40.00 (*0-89745-033-7*) Sunflower U Pr.

U. S. Army Counterterrorism Handbook. 1986. lib. bdg. 250.00 (*0-8490-3493-0*) Gordon Pr.

U. S. Army Field Manual 100-5: Fighting Future Wars - New Edition. Department of the Army Staff. 172p. 1994. pap. 21.95 (*0-02-881103-8*) Brasseys Inc.

U. S. Army Guard & Reserve: Rhetoric, Realities, Risks. Martin Binkin & William W. Kaufmann. (Studies in Defense Policy). 160p. 1989. pap. 12.95 (*0-8157-0979-X*) Brookings.

U. S. Army Handbook 1939-1945. G. Forty. (Illus.). 192p. 1995. 24.95 (*0-7509-1078-X*, Pub. by Sutton Pubng UK) Bks Intl VA.

U. S. Army Heraldic Crests: A Complete Illustrated History of Authorized Distinctive Unit Insignia. Barry J. Stein. (Illus.). 607p. (C). 1993. text ed. 59.95 (*0-87249-963-4*) U of SC Pr.

U. S. Army in a New Security Era. Ed. by Sam C. Sarkesian & John A. Williams. LC 90-8052. 325p. 1990. lib. bdg. 45.00 (*1-55587-191-7*) Lynne Rienner.

U. S. Army in the Occupation of Germany 1944-1946 2 vols., Set. 1995. lib. bdg. 599.75 (*0-8490-6584-4*) Gordon Pr.

U. S. Army in the West, 1870-1880: Uniforms, Weapons, & Equipment. Douglas C. McChristian. LC 94-48216. (Illus.). 384p. 1995. 36.95 (*0-8061-2705-8*) U of Okla Pr.

U. S. Army in Transition II: Landpower in the Information Age. Frederic J. Brown. LC 92-12999. (AUSA Book Ser.). 205p. 1993. 24.00 (*0-02-881034-1*) Brasseys Inc.

U. S. Army in World War II: A Reader's Guide. (Military History Ser.). 1995. lib. bdg. 251.75 (*0-8490-7420-7*) Gordon Pr.

U. S. Army in World War II: Three Battles: Arnaville, Altuzzo & Schmidt. 1994. lib. bdg. 250.00 (*0-8490-5803-1*) Gordon Pr.

U. S. Army in World War II: War in the Pacific. 1994. lib. bdg. 250.00 (*0-8490-5798-1*) Gordon Pr.

U. S. Army in World War II, Mediterranean Theater of Operations, Sicily & the Surrender of Italy, 2 vols., Set. 1994. lib. bdg. 600.00 (*0-8490-5713-2*) Gordon Pr.

U. S. Army in World War 2, Technical Services, The Corps of Engineers: The War Against Germany. Alfred M. Beck. LC 84-11376. (Center for Military History Publication German Report Series, DA Pam: No. 10-22). (Illus.). 626p. 1985. 40.00 (*0-16-001938-9*, S/N 008-029-00131-4) USGPO.

U. S. Army Military Vehicles, W.W. 2. (Illus.). 588p. 1995. pap. 39.95 (*0-938242-21-0*) Portrayal.

U. S. Army Mobilization & Logistics in the Korean War: A Research Approach. (Illus.). 134p. (Orig.). (C). 1994. pap. text ed. 40.00 (*0-7881-1210-4*) DIANE Pub.

U. S. Army Officer & Enlisted Rank Insignia, 1924-1989. D. V. Olson. (Illus.). 50p. (Orig.). 1988. pap. 12.00 (*0-929757-15-7*) Regt QM.

U. S. Army Order of Battle: Europe (Companies & Regiments) LC 83-81812. 200p. 1993. 14.00 (*0-941052-71-0*) Valor Pub.

U. S. Army Order of Battle: Mediterranean & Europe 1942-1945. Ed. by W. Victor Madeja. 190p. 1984. 14.00 (*0-941052-70-2*); pap. 14.00 (*0-941052-26-5*) Valor Pub.

U. S. Army Order of Battle: Pacific Divisions. W. Victor Madeja. (U. S. Army Units Ser.). pap. 14.00 (*0-941052-19-2*) Valor Pub.

U. S. Army Order of Battle: Pacific Divisions. W. Victor Madeja. 1984. 14.00 (*0-941052-72-9*) Valor Pub.

U. S. Army Order of Battle: Pacific Theater Command. LC 83-81812. (U. S. Army Units Ser.). 176p. pap. 14.00 (*0-941052-16-8*) Valor Pub.

U. S. Army Order of Battle: Pacific Theater Command. LC 83-81812. 176p. 1984. 14.00 (*0-941052-73-7*) Valor Pub.

U. S. Army Ordnance Research & Development in World War II: A Review. Ed. by Ray Merriam. (World War II Historical Society Monograph Ser.). 56p. 1995. 7.00 (*1-57638-026-2*) Merriam Pr.

***U. S. Army Patches: An Illustrated Encyclopedia of Cloth Unit Insignia.** Barry J. Stein. LC 96-35684. (Illus.). 260p. 1997. 39.95 (*1-57003-179-7*) U of SC Pr.

An Asterisk (*) at the beginning of an entry indicates that the title is appearing in BIP for the first time.

***U. S. Army Photo Album: Shooting the War in Color, 1941-45 U. S. A. to E. T. O.** Jonathan Gawne. 1996. 37.95 (*2-908182-40-8*, Zenith Aviation) Motorbooks Intl.

U. S. Army Privates, Sergeants, Fire & Smoke. Arthur R. Killingbeck. 1991. 13.95 (*0-533-09407-0*) Vantage.

U. S. Army Rangers. James Koons. (Serving Your Country Ser.). (Illus.). 48p. (J). (gr. 3-9). 1995. lib. bdg. 17.80 (*1-56065-284-5*) Capstone Pr.

U. S. Army Rangers. James Koons. (Illus.). 48p. (J). (gr. 3-7). 1995. 13.35 (*0-516-35284-9*) Childrens.

U. S. Army Rangers & LRRP Units 1942-87. Gordon L. Rottman. (Elite Ser.: No. 13). (Illus.). 64p. pap. 12.95 (*0-85045-795-5*, 9412, Pub. by Osprey UK) Stackpole.

U. S. Army Signals Intelligence in World War II: A Documentary History. (Military History Ser.). 1995. lib. bdg. 265.75 (*0-8490-7418-5*) Gordon Pr.

U. S. Army Signals Intelligence in World War II: A Documentary History. James L. Gilbert & John P. Finnegan. (Illus.). 268p. (C). 1994. 50.00 (*0-7881-0502-7*) DIANE Pub.

U. S. Army Soldiers' Promotion Board Study Guide. Roy Bowen & Robert K. Spear. 150p. (Orig.). 1990. pap. 8.95 (*0-9622627-3-0*) U Force Dynamics.

U. S. Army Special Forces A-Team Vietnam Combat Manual. Pref. by SHelby L. Stanton. (Illus.). 304p. 1988. pap. 25.00 (*0-87364-481-6*) Paladin Pr.

U. S. Army Special Forces Medical Handbook. Glen K. Craig. (Illus.). 608p. 1988. pap. 22.95 (*0-87364-454-9*) Paladin Pr.

U. S. Army Special Forces Medical Handbook. U. S. Military Institute for Military Assistance Staff. (Illus.). 424p. 1987. reprint ed. pap. 9.95 (*0-8065-1045-5*, Citadel Pr) Carol Pub Group.

U. S. Army Special Forces 1952-84. Gordon L. Rottman. (Elite Ser.: No. 4). (Illus.). 64p. pap. 12.95 (*0-85045-610-X*, 9403, Pub. by Osprey Pubng Ltd UK) Stackpole.

***U. S. Army Survival Manual.** Platinum Press Staff. 416p. 1997. 29.95 (*1-879582-00-7*) Platinum Pr.

***U. S. Army Today: From the End of the Cold War to the Present Day.** Christopher J. Anderson. LC 96-39716. (GI: The Illustrated History of the American Soldier, His Uniform, & His Equipment Ser.). 1997. write for info. (*1-85367-269-6*) Stackpole.

U. S. Army Uniforms & Equipment, 1889: Specifications for Clothing, Camp & Garrison Equipage, & Clothing & Equipage Materials. Quartermaster General of the Army Staff. LC 86-6972. (Illus.). x, 375p. 1986. reprint ed. pap. 14.95 (*0-8032-9552-9*, Bison Books) U of Nebr Pr.

U. S. Army Uniforms of the Cold War, 1948-1973. Shelby L. Stanton. LC 93-13745. (Illus.). 273p. 1994. 29.95 (*0-8117-1821-2*) Stackpole.

U. S. Army Uniforms of the Korean War. Shelby L. Stanton. LC 92-4007. (Illus.). 256p. 1992. 29.95 (*0-8117-1819-0*) Stackpole.

U. S. Army Uniforms of the Vietnam War. Shelby L. Stanton. 1992. pap. 19.95 (*0-8117-2584-7*) Stackpole.

U. S. Army Uniforms of World War Two. Shelby L. Stanton. LC 94-13066. (Illus.). 288p. 1995. 19.95 (*0-8117-2595-2*) Stackpole.

U. S. Army Vehicles of World War II. Jean-Michael Boniface & Jean-Gabriel Jeudy. (Illus.). 264p. 1991. 59.95 (*0-85429-811-8*, Pub. by G T Foulis Ltd) Haynes Pubns.

U. S. Army War College Guide to the Battle of Chickamauga. Ed. by Matt Spruill. LC 92-46288. (U. S. Army War College Guides to Civil War Battles Ser.). (Illus.). 208p. 1993. 27.50 (*0-7006-0595-9*); pap. 12.95 (*0-7006-0596-7*) U Pr of KS.

U. S. Army War College Guide to the Battle of Gettysburg. Jay Luvaas & Harold W. Nelson. (Illus.). 240p. 1994. pap. 12.95 (*0-7006-0686-6*) U Pr of KS.

U. S. Army War College Guide to the Battle of Shiloh. Ed. by Jay Luvaas et al. LC 96-24199. (Illus.). 232p. 1996. 29.95 (*0-7006-0782-X*) U Pr of KS.

U. S. Army War College Guide to the Battle of Shiloh. Ed. by Jay Luvaas et al. LC 96-24199. (U. S. Army War College Guides to Civil War Battles). (Illus.). 253p. 1996. pap. 12.95 (*0-7006-0783-8*) U Pr of KS.

U. S. Army War College Guide to the Battles of Chancellorsville & Fredericksburg. Jay Luvaas. (U. S. Army War College Guides to Civil War Battles Ser.). 364p. 1996. pap. text ed. 14.95 (*0-7006-0785-4*) U Pr of KS.

U. S. Army 1890-1920. Philip R. Katcher. (Men-at-Arms Ser.: No. 230). (Illus.). 48p. 1991. pap. 11.95 (*1-85532-103-3*, 9188, Pub. by Osprey UK) Stackpole.

U. S. Army 1941-45. Philip R. Katcher. (Men-at-Arms Ser.: No. 70). (Illus.). 48p. pap. 11.95 (*0-85045-522-7*, 9016) Stackpole.

***U. S. Arthritis Therapeutic Product Markets.** Frost & Sullivan Staff. 370p. 1996. write for info. (*0-7889-0598-8*, 5483) Frost & Sullivan.

U. S. As a World Power. Archibald C. Coolidge, Jr. 1988. reprint ed. lib. bdg. 59.00 (*0-7812-0460-7*) Rprt Serv.

U. S. As a World Power. Archibald C. Coolidge, Jr. 1981. reprint ed. lib. bdg. 69.00 (*0-403-00907-3*) Scholarly.

U. S. Asian Relations: The National Security Paradox. Ed. by James C. Hsiung. LC 83-13930. 220p. 1983. text ed. 49.95 (*0-275-91013-X*, C1013, Praeger Pubs) Greenwood.

U. S. Atlas. (Giant Step Picture Library). (Illus.). 14p. (J). (gr. 3 up). 1992. 9.95 (*0-88679-903-1*) Educ Insights.

U. S. ATM WAN Equipment & Service Markets: Laying the Network Infrastructure for High-Speed Applications. Frost & Sullivan Staff. 334p. 1996. write for info. (*0-7889-0421-3*, 5271-61) Frost & Sullivan.

***U. S. Attorneys: More Accountability for Implementing Priority Programs Is Desirable.** (Illus.). 73p. (Orig.). 1996. pap. 25.00 (*0-7881-3447-7*) DIANE Pub.

U. S. Audioconferencing & Audiographics System & Services Markets. Frost & Sullivan Staff. 284p. 1995. write for info. (*0-7889-0300-4*) Frost & Sullivan.

U. S. Autoimmune Disease Markets. Market Intelligence Staff. 370p. 1994. 2,395.00 (*0-7889-0138-9*) Frost & Sullivan.

***U. S. Autoimmune Disease Therapeutic Markets.** Frost & Sullivan Staff. Date not set. write for info. (*0-7889-0524-4*, 5484) Frost & Sullivan.

U. S. Autoimmune Disease Therapeutic Markets: Betaseron & Other New Compounds Advance Through Clinical Trials. Market Intelligence Staff. 450p. 1993. 1,995.00 (*1-56753-545-3*) Frost & Sullivan.

U. S. Automotive Hard Parts Markets. Market Intelligence Staff. 460p. 1994. 2,395.00 (*0-7889-0063-3*) Frost & Sullivan.

U. S. Ballistic Missile Subs. Al Adcock. (Warships in Action Ser.). (Illus.). 50p. 1993. pap. 7.95 (*0-89747-293-4*, 4006) Squad Sig Pubns.

***U. S. Banking & Its Regulation in the Political Context.** Sarkis J. Khoury. 320p. 1997. 54.50 (*0-7618-0732-2*) U Pr of Amer.

***U. S. Banking & Its Regulation in the Political Context.** Sarkis J. Khoury. 320p. 1997. pap. 34.50 (*0-7618-0733-0*) U Pr of Amer.

U. S. Bankruptcy Court Speaks. LC 94-78711. 1994. pap. text ed. 55.00 (*0-944490-75-1*) Mass CLE.

U. S. Basic Writings of George Washington. George Washington. (History - United States Ser.). 697p. 1993. reprint ed. lib. bdg. 109.00 (*0-7812-4829-9*) Rprt Serv.

U. S. Battery Industry, No. GB-086N. enl. ed. 387p. 1994. 2,750.00 (*1-56965-207-4*) BCC.

U. S. Battery Market. 180p. 1997. 1,495.00 (*0-318-00531-X*) Busn Trend.

U. S. Battleships: An Illustrated Design History. Norman Friedman. LC 85-13769. (Illus.). 463p. 1985. 59.95 (*0-87021-715-1*) Naval Inst Pr.

U. S. Battleships in Action, Pt. 1. (Illus.). 50p. 1980. pap. 7.95 (*0-89747-107-5*) Squad Sig Pubns.

U. S. Battleships in Action, Pt. 2. Robert Stern. (Warships in Action Ser.). (Illus.). 50p. 1995. reprint ed. pap. 7.95 (*0-89747-157-1*, 4004) Squad Sig Pubns.

U. S. Bearing Markets: Path to Prosperity Dependent to Tangible Cost Savings. Frost & Sullivan Staff. 304p. 1995. write for info. (*0-7889-0276-8*) Frost & Sullivan.

U. S. Beer Market: Impact Databank Review & Forecast, 1996. Marvin R. Shanken. (Illus.). 304p. (Orig.). 1992. pap. 795.00 (*1-881659-02-X*) M Shanken Comm.

U. S. Bicentennial Mural Souvenir Sheets, 1976. George W. Brett & James T. DeVoss. (Illus.). 22p. 1988. reprint ed. pap. 8.75 (*0-318-40120-7*) Am Philatelic Society.

U. S. Bicentennial Music I. Richard Jackson. LC 77-66. (I. S.A.M. Special Publications: No. 1). 20p. (Orig.). 1977. pap. 4.00 (*0-914678-06-X*) Inst Am Music.

***U. S. Bingo Guide: California/Nevada Edition.** Bennett Roche. (Illus.). 256p. (Orig.). 1996. pap. 11.95 (*1-57885-101-7*) Rock Bridge Pub.

***U. S. Biographical Dictionary & Portrait Gallery of Eminent & Self-Made Men, Illinois Volume, 2 vols.** (Illus.). 798p. 1997. reprint ed. lib. bdg. 85.00 (*0-8328-5707-6*) Higginson Bk Co.

U. S. Biographies, Bk. 1: Beginning to 1800. Center for Learning Network Staff. (U. S. Biography Ser.). 48p. 1992. student ed. 3.95 (*1-56077-200-X*); teacher ed., spiral bd. 19.95 (*1-56077-160-7*) Ctr Learning.

U. S. Biographies, Bk. 2: 1800-1830. Center for Learning Network Staff. (U. S. Biography Ser.). 56p. 1992. student ed. 3.95 (*1-56077-201-8*); teacher ed., spiral bd. 19.95 (*1-56077-161-5*) Ctr Learning.

U. S. Biographies, Bk. 3: 1830-1850. Center for Learning Network Staff. (U. S. Biography Ser.). 56p. 1992. student ed. 3.95 (*1-56077-202-6*); teacher ed., spiral bd. 19.95 (*1-56077-162-3*) Ctr Learning.

U. S. Biographies, Bk. 4: 1850-1890. Center for Learning Network Staff. (U. S. Biography Ser.). 56p. 1992. student ed. 3.95 (*1-56077-203-4*); teacher ed., spiral bd. 19.95 (*1-56077-163-1*) Ctr Learning.

U. S. Biographies, Bk. 5: 1890-1930. Center for Learning Network Staff. (U. S. Biography Ser.). 54p. 1992. student ed. 3.95 (*1-56077-204-2*); teacher ed., spiral bd. 19.95 (*1-56077-164-X*) Ctr Learning.

U. S. Biographies, Bk. 6: 1930-1960. Center for Learning Network Staff. (U. S. Biography Ser.). 54p. 1992. student ed. 3.95 (*1-56077-205-0*); teacher ed., spiral bd. 19.95 (*1-56077-165-8*) Ctr Learning.

U. S. Biographies, Bk. 7: 1960-1990. Center for Learning Network Staff. (U. S. Biography Ser.). 139p. 1992. teacher ed., spiral bd. 19.95 (*1-56077-166-6*) Ctr Learning.

U. S. Biographies, Bk. 7: 1960-1990. Center for Learning Network Staff. (U. S. Biography Ser.). 56p. (J). (gr. 4-8). 1992. student ed. 3.95 (*1-56077-206-9*) Ctr Learning.

U. S. Biopharmaceutical Markets: Wall Street Dries Up: Growth Through Alliances. Market Intelligence Staff. 345p. 1994. 1,995.00 (*0-7889-0088-9*) Frost & Sullivan.

U. S. Biotech Company Profiles: An In-Depth Look at 100 Leading Industry Innovators. Market Intelligence Staff. 1995. 1,695.00 (*0-7889-0169-9*, 5085-80) Frost & Sullivan.

U. S. Biotechnology: A Legislative & Regulatory Roadmap. LC 89-23897. (Special Report Series on Biotechnology: No. 2). 1989. 95.00 (*1-55871-139-2*, BSP 153) BNA.

U. S. Biotechnology & Pharmaceutical Instrument Markets. Frost & Sullivan Staff. 506p. Date not set. write for info. (*0-7889-0415-9*, 5310-55) Frost & Sullivan.

U. S. Blowers & Fans Industry: A Product-by-Product Marketing Analysis & Competitor Profile. 355p. 1992. 950.00 (*0-317-55212-0*) Busn Trend.

U. S.-BNA Postage Stamp Catalog, 1995. rev. ed. H. E. Harris & Co. Staff. (Illus.). 1994. pap. 7.95 (*0-937458-59-7*) Harris & Co.

U. S. Bomber Force Modernization. Mike Synar et al. LC 86-21401. (National Security Papers: No. 7). 1986. 7.50 (*0-89549-078-1*) Inst Foreign Policy Anal.

U. S. Book: Stories. August C. Varga. LC 95-90008. 102p. (Orig.). 1995. pap. write for info. (*0-9645382-3-7*) A C Varga.

U. S. Book Publishing Industry. 195p. 1997. pap. 1,195.00 (*0-318-04399-8*) Busn Trend.

U. S. Bottled Water Market. 3rd ed. Ed. by Peter Allen. 300p. 1986. pap. 1,250.00 (*0-931634-31-8*) FIND-SVP.

U. S. Breast Cancer Diagnostics, Therapeutics & Prosthetics Markets. Frost & Sullivan Staff. 255p. 1996. write for info. (*0-7889-0499-X*, 5345) Frost & Sullivan.

U. S. Bureau of Land Management Cadastral Survey. Mark Smirnov & Marlin Livermore. (Surveying & Land Information Systems Journal Ser.: Vol. 51, No. 4). 91p. 1991. 20.00 (*0-614-06106-7*, SM514) Am Congrs Survey.

U. S. Business Access to Foreign State-of-the-Art Technology in Semiconductors, Semiconductor Materials & Equipment, & Computers. (Illus.). 52p. (Orig.). (C). 1994. pap. text ed. 25.00 (*0-7881-0573-6*) DIANE Pub.

U. S. Business & Today's Germany: A Guide for Corporate Executives & Attorneys. James A. Hart & Dieter Schultze-Zeu. LC 94-46179. 256p. 1995. text ed. 59.95 (*0-89930-839-2*, Quorum Bks) Greenwood.

U. S. Business in Post Sanctions South Africa: The Road Ahead. Jennifer D. Kibbe. 48p. 1991. pap. 15.00 (*0-931035-90-2*) IRRC Inc DC.

U. S. Business in South Africa: The Economic, Political, & Moral Issues. Desaix B. Myers et al. LC 79-3638. 389p. reprint ed. pap. 111.50 (*0-685-44452-X*, 2056713) Bks Demand.

U. S. Business in South Africa 1993. 9th ed. Alison Cooper. 237p. (Orig.). 1993. pap. text ed. 50.00 (*1-879775-05-0*) IRRC Inc DC.

***U. S. Business in South Africa 1995.** 11th rev. ed. Peter DeSimone et al. Ed. by Meg Voorhes. 224p. (Orig.). 1995. pap. 250.00 (*1-879775-24-7*) IRRC Inc DC.

U. S. Business Investments in Foreign Countries: A Supplement to the Survey of Current Business. U. S. Department of Commerce Staff. Ed. by Stuart Bruchey & Eleanor Bruchey. LC 76-5038. (American Business Abroad Ser.). (Illus.). 1976. reprint ed. 19.95 (*0-405-09304-7*) Ayer.

U. S. Buyers' Relationships with Pacific Rim Suppliers. Robert E. Spekman. Ed. by Carol L. Ketchum. LC 89-61095. 28p. (Orig.). (C). 1989. pap. text ed. 20.00 (*0-945968-04-3*) Ctr Advanced Purchasing.

U. S. Cable Television & Associated Technology Product Markets. Market Intelligence Staff. (Orig.). 1994. 2,295.00 (*0-614-00722-4*) Frost & Sullivan.

U. S. Call Center Hardware & Software Markets. Frost & Sullivan Staff. 1996. write for info. (*0-7889-0411-6*, 2878-62) Frost & Sullivan.

U. S. Call Processing Equipment Markets: Popularity of Call Centers & Computer Integration Creates a Dramatic Revolution. Market Intelligence Staff. 401p. 1993. 2,895.00 (*1-56753-703-0*) Frost & Sullivan.

U. S. Canadian Automotive Products Agreement of 1965: An Evaluation for Its Twentieth Year. Sidney Weintraub. LC 85-50653. (Policy Research Project Report: No. 68). 169p. 1985. pap. 8.50 (*0-89940-670-X*) LBJ Sch Pub Aff.

U. S.-Canadian Free Trade Negotiations: Gaining Approval to Proceed. Glenn Tobin. (Pew Case Studies in International Affairs). 50p. (C). 1989. pap. text ed. 3.50 (*1-56927-143-7*) Geo U Inst Dplmcy.

U. S.-Canadian Free Trade Negotiations: The Canadian Dilemma. Vlad S. Jenkins. (Pew Case Studies in International Affairs). 50p. (C). 1988. pap. text ed. 3.50 (*1-56927-142-9*) Geo U Inst Dplmcy.

U. S.-Canadian Negotiations for Acid Rain Controls. Vicki Golich & Terry F. Young. (Pew Case Studies in International Affairs). 50p. (C). 1993. pap. text ed. 3.50 (*1-56927-452-5*) Geo U Inst Dplmcy.

U. S.-Canadian Softwood Lumber: Trade Dispute Negotiations. Cahrles F. Doran & Timothy J. Naftali. (Pew Case Studies in International Affairs). 50p. 1988. pap. text ed. 3.50 (*1-56927-141-0*) Geo U Inst Dplmcy.

U. S. Capitalist Development since 1976: Of, By, & For Which People? Douglas F. Dowd. LC 93-16219. 592p. (C). (gr. 13). 1993. text ed. 72.95 (*1-56324-166-8*); pap. text ed. 29.95 (*1-56324-167-6*) M E Sharpe.

U. S. Capitol. Henry Reed. Date not set. write for info. (*0-393-03831-9*) Norton.

U. S.-Caribbean-Grenada Relations: Before & After Bishop. Linus A. Hoskins. (International Affairs Ser.). 130p. (Orig.). (C). 1984. pap. text ed. 6.00 (*0-9613067-0-X*) Imhotep.

***U. S.-Caribbean Relations: Their Impact on Peoples & Culture.** Ed. by Ransford W. Palmer. LC 96-53610. 1997. text ed. write for info. (*0-275-95859-0*, Praeger Pubs) Greenwood.

***U. S. Carriers at War.** Peter Kilduff. (Illus.). 128p. 1997. 31.95 (*1-55750-858-5*) Naval Inst Pr.

U. S. Catholic Elementary & Secondary Schools, 1986-1987. Frank H. Bredeweg. 1987. 7.30 (*0-317-60173-3*) Natl Cath Educ.

U. S. Catholic Elementary & Secondary Schools, 1981-1982. 64p. 1982. 9.55 (*0-318-12105-0*) Natl Cath Educ.

U. S. Catholic Elementary & Secondary Schools, 1982-1983. pap. 3.55 (*0-318-12106-9*) Natl Cath Educ.

U. S. Catholic Elementary & Secondary Schools, 1983-1984. pap. 6.00 (*0-318-12107-7*) Natl Cath Educ.

U. S. Catholic Elementary & Secondary Schools, 1985-1986. Frank H. Bredweg. 21p. 1986. 7.30 (*0-318-20578-5*) Natl Cath Educ.

U. S. Catholic Elementary & Secondary Schools, 1989-1990: Annual Statistical Report on Schools, Enrollment & Staffing. Frederick H. Brigham. (Illus.). 1990. pap. 9.00 (*1-55833-050-X*) Natl Cath Educ.

U. S. Catholic Elementary & Secondary Schools, 1984-85. Frank H. Bredeweg. 1985. 6.60 (*0-685-11857-6*) Natl Cath Educ.

U. S. Catholic Elementary & Secondary Schools, 1987-88. Frank H. Bredeweg. 21p. (Orig.). 1988. pap. 7.30 (*1-55833-002-X*) Natl Cath Educ.

***U. S. Catholic Elementary & Secondary Schools 1995-96.** Frank X. Savage & Mary J. Milks. (Data Bank Ser.). (Illus.). 41p. (Orig.). 1996. pap. 10.00 (*1-55833-170-0*) Natl Cath Educ.

U. S. Catholic Elementary Schools & Their Finances, 1987. Frank H. Bredeweg. 1987. 6.75 (*0-317-60174-1*) Natl Cath Educ.

U. S. Catholic Schools: Nineteen Seventy-Three to Nineteen Seventy-Four. 92p. 1974. 2.40 (*0-685-06885-4*) Natl Cath Educ.

U. S. Catholic Sources: A Diocesan Research Guide. Virginia Humling. LC 95-25259. 105p. (Orig.). 1995. pap. 14.95 (*0-916489-60-4*, 760) Ancestry.

U. S. Cavalry on the Plains. Philip R. Katcher. (Men-at-Arms Ser.: No. 168). (Illus.). 48p. pap. 11.95 (*0-85045-609-6*, 9100) Stackpole.

U. S. Cavalryman 1865-90. Martin Pegler. (Warrior Ser.). (Illus.). 64p. 1993. pap. 12.95 (*1-85532-319-2*, 9603, Pub. by Osprey UK) Stackpole.

U. S. Cell & Tissue Culture Products. Frost & Sullivan Staff. 1996. write for info. (*0-7889-0455-8*, 5354) Frost & Sullivan.

U. S. Cell & Tissue Culture Products. Frost & Sullivan Staff. 1996. write for info. (*0-614-14185-0*, 5354-52) Frost & Sullivan.

U. S. Cellular & PCS Telephone, Pager & Accessory Markets: Time to Focus on Applications. Market Intelligence Staff. 546p. 1993. 2,295.00 (*1-56753-705-7*) Frost & Sullivan.

***U. S. Cellular Equipment Markets.** Frost & Sullivan Staff. 500p. Date not set. write for info. (*0-7889-0521-X*, 5269) Frost & Sullivan.

***U. S. Cellular Service Markets.** Frost & Sullivan. 402p. 1997. write for info. (*0-7889-0635-6*, 5268) Frost & Sullivan.

U. S. Cemetery Address Book. Elizabeth G. Kot & James D. Kot. LC 94-76039. 890p. 1994. pap. 50.00 (*0-9641213-2-8*) Indices Pubng.

U. S. Census of Eighteen Fifty, Barbour County, Ala. Helen S. Foley. 178p. 1976. 15.00 (*0-89308-178-7*) Southern Hist Pr.

U. S. Centers for Disease Control: Index of Modern Activities. Ellis W. Watkins. LC 88-47795. 150p. (Orig.). 1988. 37.50 (*0-88164-886-8*); pap. 39.50 (*0-88164-887-6*) ABBE Pubs Assn.

U. S. Centrifugal & Turbine Pump Markets. 329p. Date not set. write for info. (*0-7889-0359-4*) Frost & Sullivan.

U. S. Championship, 1983. Larry Christiansen. (U. S. Tournament Ser.). (Illus.). 135p. (Orig.). 1984. pap. 6.50 (*0-931462-28-2*) Chess Ent.

U. S. Cheese Market. (Illus.). 200p. 1997. reprint ed. spiral bd. 1,150.00 (*0-685-21991-7*) Busn Trend.

U. S. Chemotherapy Market. Leading Edge Group Staff. 325p. 1987. 1,950.00 (*0-317-63102-0*) Busn Trend.

U. S. Chess Federation's (U. S. C. F.) Official Rules of Chess. 1987. pap. 7.95 (*0-679-14154-5*) McKay.

***U. S. Chicanas & Latinas Within a Global Context: Women of Color at the Fourth World Women's Conference.** Irene I. Blea. LC 97-12806. 1997. text ed. write for info. (*0-275-95623-7*, Praeger Pubs); pap. text ed. write for info. (*0-275-95624-5*, Praeger Pubs) Greenwood.

U. S. Chief of Counsel for the Prosecution of Axis Criminality: Nazi Conspiracy & Aggression, 11 vols. reprint ed. Set. 620.00 (*0-404-56180-2*) AMS Pr.

U. S. Children in Confinement in Louisiana. Human Rights Watch Children's Rights Project Staff. 141p. (Orig.). 1995. pap. 10.00 (*1-56432-159-2*) Hum Rts Watch.

U. S. China Policy & the Problem of Taiwan. William M. Bueler. LC 79-25371. 143p. 1980. reprint ed. text ed. 49.75 (*0-313-22153-7*, BUUS, Greenwood Pr) Greenwood.

U. S.-Chinese Trade Negotiations. John W. DePauw. LC 80-27254. 252p. 1981. text ed. 59.95 (*0-275-90603-5*, C0603, Praeger Pubs) Greenwood.

U. S.-Chippewa Treaty at La Pointe, 1854. 12.50 (*0-317-66462-X*) Inst Dev Indian Law.

***U. S. Christian Church Directory & Resource Handbook.** Randy W. Vaughan. LC 96-79977. 304p. (Orig.). 1997. pap. 24.95 (*0-9656157-7-4*) Inspirit Pr.

U. S. Chromatography Reagents Markets. BCC Staff. 338p. 1993. 2,250.00 (*0-89336-738-9*, C114) BCC.

U. S. Cities & Towns: Source of Water Supply. NWWA Staff. 26p. 1989. 6.25 (*1-56034-055-X*, K500) Natl Grnd Water.

***U. S. Citizens Package.** Ronna Magy. (Illus.). 110p. 1996. pap. 17.95 incl. audio (*0-8384-6750-4*) Heinle & Heinle.

***U. S. Citizenship Handbook.** 2nd rev. ed. Simon Vladovich. LC 96-61630. (Illus.). 202p. 1997. pap. text ed. 19.95 (*0-9623753-3-0*) Vladovich Intl Pub.

U. S. Citizenship-Yes! Ronna Magy. (Global ESL/ELT Ser.). (Illus.). 108p. 1996. pap. 11.95 (*0-8384-6714-8*) Heinle & Heinle.

U. S. Civil Aircraft, Vol. 4. Joseph Juptner. 1994. 29.95 (*0-8306-4369-9*) McGraw-Hill Prof.

U. S. Civil Aircraft, Vol. 6. Joseph Juptner. 1994. 29.95 (*0-8306-4371-0*) McGraw-Hill Prof.

U
V

U. S. Civil Aircraft: ATCs 601-700, Vol. 7. Joseph P. Juptner. 1994. 29.95 (*0-8306-4372-9*) McGraw-Hill Prof.

U. S. Civil Aircraft: ATCs 701-800, Vol. 8. Joseph P. Juptner. 1994. 29.95 (*0-8306-4373-7*) McGraw-Hill Prof.

U. S. Civil Aircraft: ATCs 801-817, Vol. 9. Joseph P. Juptner. 1994. 29.95 (*0-8306-4374-5*) McGraw-Hill Prof.

U. S. Civil Aircraft Series, Vol. 8. Joseph P. Juptner. 1994. text ed. 29.95 (*0-07-032987-7*) McGraw-Hill Prof.

U. S. Civil Aircraft Series, Vol. 9. Joseph P. Juptner. 1994. text ed. 29.95 (*0-07-032988-5*) McGraw-Hill Prof.

U. S. Civil Aircraft Series: ATCs 1-100, Vol. 1. Joseph P. Juptner. 256p. 1993. pap. 29.95 (*0-8306-4366-4*, TAB-Aero) TAB Bks.

U. S. Civil Aircraft Series: ATCs 101-200, Vol. 2. Joseph P. Juptner. 304p. 1993. pap. 29.95 (*0-8306-4367-2*, TAB-Aero) TAB Bks.

U. S. Civil Aircraft Series: ATCs 201-300, Vol. 3. Joseph P. Juptner. (Illus.). 304p. 1993. pap. 29.95 (*0-8306-4368-0*, 4372, TAB-Aero) TAB Bks.

U. S. Civil Aircraft Series: ATCs 401-500, Vol. 5. Joseph Juptner. 1993. 29.95 (*0-8306-4370-2*) McGraw-Hill Prof.

U. S. Civil Liberties in Times of War: A History. 1991. lib. bdg. 250.00 (*0-8490-4769-2*) Gordon Pr.

U. S. Civil-Military Relations: In Crisis or Transition? Ed. by Don M. Snider & Miranda A. Carlton-Carew. LC 95-261. (Significant Issues Ser.: Vol. 17, No. 5). 240p. (C). 1995. pap. 18.95 (*0-89206-305-X*) CSI Studies.

U. S. Civil War Store Cards. rev. ed. George Fuld & Melvin Fuld. LC 75-1785. (Illus.). 704p. 1975. 75.00 (*0-88000-135-6*) Quarterman.

U. S. Coal & the Electric Power Industry. Richard L. Gordon. LC 74-24403. (Resources for the Future Ser.). 232p. 1975. 17.50 (*0-8018-1697-1*) Johns Hopkins.

U. S. Coal Goes Abroad: A Social Action Perspective in Interorganizational Networks. Kathryn S. Rogers. LC 85-12467. 272p. 1985. text ed. 55.00 (*0-275-90036-3*, C0036, Praeger Pubs) Greenwood.

U. S. Coal Industry, 1970-1990: Two Decades of Change. (Illus.). 105p. (Orig.). (C). 1994. pap. text ed. 35.00 (*0-7881-0231-1*) DIANE Pub.

U. S. Coal Plant Statistics. 7th ed. Utility Data Institute Staff. 300p. 1995. pap. 225.00 (*1-56760-025-5*) Utility Data Inst.

U. S. Coal Reserves: An Update by Heat & Sulfur Content. (Illus.). 96p. (Orig.). (C). 1994. pap. text ed. 30.00 (*0-7881-0498-5*) DIANE Pub.

U. S. Coast Guard. Nancy W. Ferrell. (Armed Services Ser.). (Illus.). 72p. (J). (gr. 5 up). 1989. lib. bdg. 22.95 (*0-8225-1431-1*, Lerner Publctns) Lerner Group.

U. S. Coast Guard. Corinne J. Naden & Rose Blue. LC 92-31042. (Defending Our Country Ser.). (Illus.). 64p. (J). (gr. 3-6). 1993. lib. bdg. 16.40 (*1-56294-321-9*) Millbrook Pr.

U. S. Coast Guard Aircraft since 1916. Arthur Pearcy. LC 91-62723. (Illus.). 330p. 1992. 39.95 (*1-55750-852-6*) Naval Inst Pr.

U. S. Coast Guard & Revenue Cutters, 1790-1935. Donald L. Canney. LC 94-33326. (Illus.). 192p. 1995. 49.95 (*1-55750-101-7*, Diciple Jour) Naval Inst Pr.

U. S. Coast Guard Cutters & Craft 1946 to 1990. Robert L. Scheina. LC 89-60039. 352p. 1990. 55.00 (*0-87021-719-4*) Naval Inst Pr.

U. S. Coast Guard in World War II. Malcolm F. Willoughby. LC 79-6163. (Navies & Men Ser.). (Illus.). 1980. reprint ed. lib. bdg. 44.95 (*0-405-13081-3*) Ayer.

U. S. Coast Survey vs. Naval Hydrographic Office: A 19th-Century Rivalry in Science & Politics. Thomas G. Manning. LC 87-25524. (History of American Science & Technology Ser.). 216p. 1988. text ed. 24.50 (*0-8173-0390-1*) U of Ala Pr.

U. S. Coin Price Trends. Ken Bressett. 1993. pap. 14.95 (*0-307-09360-3*) Western Pub.

U. S. Colonial History: Readings & Documents. Ed. by David Hawke. LC 66-27854. (C). 1966. pap. write for info. (*0-672-60707-7*, Bobbs) Macmillan.

U. S. Combat: America's Land Based Weaponry. Consumer Guide Staff. 1990. 9.99 (*0-517-68763-1*) Random Hse Value.

***U. S. Combat Air Power: Aging Refueling Aircraft Are Costly to Maintain & Operate.** (Illus.). 45p. (Orig.). (C). 1996. pap. 25.00 (*0-7881-3641-0*) DIANE Pub.

***U. S. Combat Helmets of the 20th Century.** Mark A. Reynosa. 160p. 1997. 39.95 (*0-7643-0357-0*) Schiffer.

U. S. Commercial & Industrial Security Equipment. 485p. 1995. write for info. (*0-7889-0347-0*) Frost & Sullivan.

U. S. Commercial Opportunities in the Soviet Union: Marketing, Production, & Strategic Planning Perspectives. Chris C. Carvounis & Brinda Z. Carvounis. LC 88-23666. 204p. 1989. text ed. 55.00 (*0-89930-351-X*, CAV/, Quorum Bks) Greenwood.

U. S. Communications Test Equipment Markets. Market Intelligence Staff. 260p. 1994. 1,895.00 (*0-614-00344-X*) Frost & Sullivan.

U. S. Companies & Support for the South African Government: The Legal Requirements. David Hauck. 41p. 1985. 10.00 (*0-931035-66-X*) IRRC Inc DC.

U. S. Companies in Russia & Nis. 2nd rev. ed. (Russian Business Library). (Illus.). 200p. 1996. pap. 59.00 (*1-57751-019-4*) Russ Info & Busn Ctr.

***U. S. Companies in Russia & NIS.** 2nd rev. ed. Russian Information & Business Center, Inc. Staff. (Russian Business Library). 400p. 1997. pap. 99.00 (*0-614-30775-9*) Russ Info & Busn Ctr.

***U. S. Companion Animal Health Product Markets: Market Forecast to Exceed $2 Billion by 2002.** Frost & Sullivan Staff. 317p. 1996. write for info. (*0-7889-0511-2*, 5068) Frost & Sullivan.

U. S. Competitiveness & the Aging American Workforce. Ed. by James A. Auerbach & Joyce C. Welsh. 257p. (Orig.). 1994. pap. text ed. 17.50 (*0-89068-128-7*) Natl Planning.

U. S. Competitiveness in the World Economy. Bruce R. Scott & George C. Lodge. 1985. text ed. 35.00 (*0-07-103266-5*) McGraw.

U. S. Complex Carbohydrate Therapeutics Markets. Market Intelligence Staff. 1994. 2,195.00 (*0-7889-0135-4*) Frost & Sullivan.

U. S. Computer Facsimile Hardware & Software Equipment Markets. 330p. Date not set. write for info. (*0-7889-0386-1*) Frost & Sullivan.

U. S. Computer Outlet to Laser Disk (Cold) Markets. Market Intelligence Staff. 256p. 1994. 2,495.00 (*0-7889-0095-1*) Frost & Sullivan.

U. S. Computers in the Banking Industry Markets. Market Intelligence Staff. (Orig.). 1994. 1,995.00 (*0-7889-0137-0*) Frost & Sullivan.

U. S. Concerns Regarding Mexico's Oil & Gas: Evolution of the Debate, 1977-1980. D. Olga Pellicer. (Research Reports: No. 10). 21p. (Orig.). (C). 1981. pap. 5.00 (*0-935391-09-6*, RR-10) UCSD Ctr US-Mex.

U. S. Congress. Don Nardo. LC 93-41137. (Overview Ser.). (J). (gr. 5-8). 1994. lib. bdg. 17.96 (*1-56006-155-3*) Lucent Bks.

U. S. Congress, Constitution of the United States. 1993. pap. 3.50 (*0-575-11561-0*) Claitors.

U. S. Congressional Districts & Data, 1843-1883. Stanley B. Parsons et al. LC 85-67582. (Illus.). 254p. 1986. text ed. 79.50 (*0-313-22045-X*, PUN/, Greenwood Pr) Greenwood.

U. S. Constitution: Locating the Author's Main Idea. William Dudley. LC 90-42328. (Opposing Viewpoints Juniors Ser.). (Illus.). 36p. (J). (gr. 3-6). 1990. lib. bdg. 12.96 (*0-89908-601-2*) Greenhaven.

U. S. Constitution: Two Hundred Years of Anti-Federalist, Abolitionist, Feminist, Muckraking, Progressive, & Especially Socialist Criticism. Ed. by Bertell Ollman & Jonathan Birnbaum. 416p. (C). 1990. 50.00 (*0-8147-6169-0*); pap. 18.50 (*0-8147-6170-4*) NYU Pr.

U. S. Constitution - a Thematic Unit. Mary E. Sterling. (Thematic Units Ser.). (Illus.). 80p. (Orig.). 1994. student ed., pap. 9.95 (*1-55734-582-1*) Tchr Create Mat.

U. S. Constitution & Constitutionalism in Africa. Ed. by Kenneth W. Thompson. LC 89-24758. (Miller Center Bicentennial Series on Constitutionalism: Vol. V). 160p. (C). 1990. lib. bdg. 41.00 (*0-8191-7630-3*) U Pr of Amer.

***U. S. Constitution & Fascinating Facts about It.** Robert F. Tedeschi. 1996. pap. text ed. 2.95 (*1-881473-21-X*) Oak Hill Pub Co.

***U. S. Constitution & Fascinating Facts about It.** Robert F. Tedeschi. 1996. pap. 73.75 (*1-881473-22-8*) Oak Hill Pub Co.

U. S. Constitution & Foreign Policy: Terminating the Taiwan Treaty. Victoria M. Kraft. LC 90-45323. (Contributions in Political Science Ser.: No. 270). 200p. 1991. text ed. 49.95 (*0-313-27531-9*, KSF, Greenwood Pr) Greenwood.

U. S. Constitution & International Influences. Ed. by Donald P. Kommers & Sotirios A. Barber. LC 94-15940. 1994. write for info. (*0-268-01901-0*) U of Notre Dame Pr.

U. S. Constitution & the Constitutions of Asia. Ed. by Kenneth W. Thompson. LC 88-27720. (Miller Center Bicentennial Series on Constitutionalism: Vol. IV). 96p. (Orig.). (C). 1989. pap. text ed. 13.00 (*0-8191-7220-0*, Pub. by White Miller Center) U Pr of Amer.

U. S. Constitution & the Constitutions of Latin America. Ed. by Kenneth Thompson. (Miller Center Bicentennial Series on Constitutionalism: Vol. VII). 200p. (C). 1991. pap. text ed. 23.50 (*0-8191-8238-9*) U Pr of Amer.

U. S. Constitution & the Constitutions of Latin America. Ed. by Kenneth W. Thompson. (Miller Center Bicentennial Series on Constitutionalism: Vol. VII). 200p. (C). 1991. lib. bdg. 45.00 (*0-8191-8237-0*) U Pr of Amer.

U. S. Constitution & the Power to Go to War: Historical & Current Perspectives. Ed. by Gary M. Stern & Morton H. Halperin. LC 93-15840. 208p. 1993. text ed. 55.00 (*0-313-28958-1*, Greenwood Pr) Greenwood.

U. S. Constitution for Beginners. Steven Bachmann. (Documentary Comic Bks.). (Illus.). 192p. (Orig.). (C). 1987. pap. 7.95 (*0-86316-126-X*) Writers & Readers.

U. S. Constitution for Everyone: A Guide to the Most Important Document Written by & for the People of the United States. Mort Gerberg. (Illus.). 64p. 1991. pap. 6.50 (*0-399-51305-1*, Perigee Bks) Berkley Pub.

U. S. Constitution for the Year 2000. Chester J. Antineau. LC 94-13209. (Values & Ethics Ser.: Vol. 10). 283p. 1994. 23.95 (*0-8294-0809-6*) Loyola Pr.

U. S. Constitution Text. rev. ed. Ellen M. Glisan. (Illus.). 41p. (YA). (gr. 7-12). 1989. pap. text ed. write for info. (*0-944791-92-1*, SS505) Peekan Pubns.

U. S. Constitutional History & Law. Albert H. Putney. 599p. 1985. reprint ed. lib. bdg. 45.00 (*0-8377-1021-9*) Rothman.

U. S. Constitutional Law. Hall. (Paralegal Ser.). 1997. teacher ed. 12.00 (*0-8273-7188-8*) Delmar.

U. S. Consul at Work. William D. Morgan & Charles S. Kennedy. LC 90-19910. (Contributions in Political Science Ser.: No. 275). 272p. 1991. text ed. 59.95 (*0-313-27796-6*, MUW/, Greenwood Pr) Greenwood.

U. S. Consumer Interest Groups: Institutional Profiles. Ardith L. Maney & Loree Bykerk. LC 94-27949. 296p. 1995. text ed. 69.50 (*0-313-26429-5*, Greenwood Pr) Greenwood.

***U. S. Consumer Markets for Interactive Television - Services & Advertising.** Frost & Sullivan Staff. 1996. write for info. (*0-614-18870-9*, 2881) Frost & Sullivan.

***U. S. Consumer Photography Equipment & Accessory Markets.** Frost & Sullivan. 535p. 1997. write for info. (*0-7889-0636-4*, 2614) Frost & Sullivan.

U. S. Consumer Telephone Equipment Product Markets: New Technologies Rejuvenate a Mature Market. Frost & Sullivan Staff. 1995. write for info. (*0-7889-0405-1*, 2831-62) Frost & Sullivan.

U. S. Consumer Video Cameras, Players, & Recorders: Digital Technology Promises Market Revival. Frost & Sullivan Staff. 509p. 1996. write for info. (*0-7889-0483-3*, 2786) Frost & Sullivan.

U. S. Containment Policy & the Conflict in Indochina. William J. Duiker. LC 93-41544. xii, 453p. 1994. 52.50 (*0-8047-2283-8*) Stanford U Pr.

U. S. Contract Manufacturing Services Market: E. M. S. I. Building upon a Strong Foundation. 260p. Date not set. write for info. (*0-7889-0393-4*) Frost & Sullivan.

U. S. Corporate Profitability & Capital Formation: Are Rates of Return Sufficient? Herman I. Liebling. (Policy Studies). 1980. 58.00 (*0-08-024622-2*, Pergamon Pr) Elsevier.

U. S. Corporate Withdrawal from South Africa: The Likely Impact on Political Change. David Hauck. 22p. 1986. 10.00 (*0-931035-67-8*) IRRC Inc DC.

U. S. Counterintelligence Today. Francis J. McNamara. Ed. by Nathan Hale Institute Staff. 88p. (Orig.). 1985. 9.95 (*0-935067-06-X*) Nathan Hale Inst.

U. S. Court Directory. 397p. (Orig.). 1996. pap. text ed. 50. 00 (*0-7881-2831-0*) DIANE Pub.

U. S. Credit Card Industry: An Assessment of Its Competetiveness. (Illus.). 64p. (Orig.). (C). 1994. pap. text ed. 40.00 (*0-7881-1019-5*) DIANE Pub.

U. S. Criminal Justice Interest Groups: Institutional Profiles. Michael A. Hallett & Dennis J. Palumbo. LC 92-45070. 152p. 1993. text ed. 65.00 (*0-313-28452-0*, PCB, Greenwood Pr) Greenwood.

U. S. Crude Oil, Natural Gas & Natural Gas Liquids Reserves. 1994. lib. bdg. 250.00 (*0-8490-8601-9*) Gordon Pr.

U. S. Cruise Missile Programs: Development, Deployment & Implications for Military Balance. C. A. Sorrels. (Brassey Bks.). 300p. 1983. 47.50 (*0-08-030527-X*, Pergamon Pr) Elsevier.

U. S. Cruisers: An Illustrated Design History. Norman Friedman. LC 84-14767. (Illus.). 488p. 1984. 65.00 (*0-87021-718-6*) Naval Inst Pr.

U. S. Crystal Oscillator Markets, Technologies, & Opportunities: 1991-1996 Analysis. Tim Archdeacon. (Illus.). 175p. 1991. pap. text ed. 1,800.00 (*1-878218-21-2*) World Info Tech.

U. S. Cuba Relations: The Reagan Years. Antonio De La Cova. Ed. by Robert Kvederas. 250p. 1991. write for info. (*0-944273-08-4*) U S Cuba Inst.

U. S. Custom House Guide. rev. ed. Ed. by Tery Moran-Lever. 1600p. 1990. 349.00 (*0-912920-56-4*) North Am Pub Co.

U. S. Custom House Guide. rev. ed. Ed. by Tery Moran-Lever. 1800p. 1991. 369.00 (*0-912920-58-0*) North Am Pub Co.

***U. S. Custom House Guide: 1996 Edition.** Ed. by Terese Moran-Lever. (Illus.). 2912p. 1996. text ed. 399.00 (*0-9649630-2-7*) K-III Dirctry.

***U. S. Custom House Guide: 1997 Edition.** Terese Moran-Lever. (Illus.). 2892p. Date not set. text ed. 425.00 (*0-9649630-5-1*) K-III Dirctry.

U. S. Customer Receptions of Diagnostic Imaging Equipment: Users Evaluate Manufacturers. Market Intelligence Staff. 250p. 1993. 1,195.00 (*1-56753-573-9*) Frost & Sullivan.

U. S. Customs & the Madero Revolution. Michael D. Carman. (Southwestern Studies: No. 48). 1976. pap. 5.00 (*0-87404-105-8*) Tex Western.

U. S. Customs Service: A Bicentennial History. Carl E. Prince & Mollie Keller. LC 89-600730. (Illus.). 320p. (C). 1989. pap. text ed. 12.00 (*0-317-93799-5*) DT US Customs.

***U. S. Customs Service Guide for Private Flyers.** (Illus.). 119p. 1996. reprint ed. pap. text ed. 30.00 (*0-7881-3718-2*) DIANE Pub.

U. S. Dairy Product Markets. 500p. 1995. write for info. (*0-614-09482-8*) Frost & Sullivan.

U. S. Data Compression Markets: Established Standards Set Stage for Rhenomenal Growth Quarterly. Market Intelligence Staff. 1995. 2,995.00 (*0-7889-0214-8*) Frost & Sullivan.

U. S. Data Compression Product Markets: Video Compression Leads Growth Through the 1990s. Market Intelligence Staff. 207p. (Orig.). 1994. 1,895.00 (*1-56753-926-2*) Frost & Sullivan.

***U. S. Debit Terminal Markets.** Frost & Sullivan. 406p. 1997. write for info. (*0-7889-0606-2*, 2864) Frost & Sullivan.

***U. S. Defense: The Way Forward.** Dick Cheqey. 1997. pap. text ed. 9.95 (*0-8447-4017-9*) Am Enterprise.

U. S. Defense & Military Fact Book. C. W. Borklund. LC 90-23756. 250p. 1991. lib. bdg. 55.00 (*0-87436-593-7*) ABC-CLIO.

U. S. Defense Bases in the United Kingdom: A Matter for Joint Decision? Simon W. Duke. LC 87-4318. 260p. 1987. text ed. 49.95 (*0-312-00769-8*) St Martin.

U. S. Defense Posture. Walter Laqueur. (Task Force on the Eighties Ser.). 24p. 1981. pap. 2.50 (*0-87495-036-8*) Am Jewish Comm.

U. S. Dental Equipment & Supplies Market. (Market Research Reports). 1995. write for info. (*0-614-96229-3*) Theta Corp.

***U. S. Department of Energy Reports to Congress on the Status of the Electric & Hybrid Vehicles Program for Fiscal Year 1976-1995.** U. S. Department of Energy Staff. (Illus.). 1250p. 1997. lib. bdg. 1,750.00 (*0-89934-336-8*, BT978) Bus Tech Bks.

U. S. Department of Justice: A History & Analysis. 1991. lib. bdg. 245.95 (*0-8490-5093-6*) Gordon Pr.

U. S. Department of Justice Current Documents, 1988. Ed. by Congressional Information Service, Inc., Staff. 1989. write for info. (*0-88692-175-9*) Cong Info.

U. S. Department of Justice Current Documents, 1989. Ed. by Congressional Information Service, Inc., Staff. 1990. write for info. (*0-88692-197-X*) Cong Info.

U. S. Department of Justice Current Documents, 1990. Ed. by Congressional Information Service, Inc., Staff. 1991. write for info. (*0-88692-222-4*) Cong Info.

U. S. Department of Justice Current Documents, 1991. Ed. by Congressional Information Service, Inc., Staff. 1992. write for info. (*0-88692-240-2*) Cong Info.

U. S. Department of Justice Current Documents, 1992. Ed. by Congressional Information Service, Inc., Staff. 1993. write for info. (*0-88692-266-6*) Cong Info.

U. S. Department of Justice Current Documents, 1993. Ed. by Congressional Information Service, Inc., Staff. 1994. write for info. (*0-88692-299-2*) Cong Info.

U. S. Department of Justice Simplified Risk Analysis Guidelines (SRAG) 53p. (Orig.). (C). 1995. pap. text ed. 25.00 (*0-7881-2576-1*) DIANE Pub.

U. S. Dependence on Strategic Materials from Southern African Nations. Patrick D. Allen & Peter C. Noehrenberg. LC 92-15871. 1992. pap. 7.50 (*0-8330-1252-5*, R-4165-OSD) Rand Corp.

U. S. Dept. of the Interior. Paul Metcalf. LC 80-66485. (Illus.). 88p. (Orig.). 1980. pap. 10.50 (*0-917788-23-0*) Gnomon Pr.

***U. S. Desktop & Portable Modem Markets.** Frost & Sullivan. 355p. 1997. write for info. (*0-7889-0641-0*, 5430) Frost & Sullivan.

U. S. Desktop Publishing Equipment Markets. Frost & Sullivan Staff. 469p. 1995. write for info. (*0-7889-0304-7*) Frost & Sullivan.

U. S. Desktop Video Markets: The First Definitive Business & Technology Assessment. Market Intelligence Staff. 450p. 1993. 1,895.00 (*1-56753-841-X*) Frost & Sullivan.

U. S. Destroyers. LC 94-60015. 144p. 1994. 48.00 (*1-56311-134-9*) Turner Pub KY.

U. S. Destroyers: An Illustrated Design History. Norman Friedman. LC 81-85444. (Illus.). 489p. 1982. 59.95 (*0-87021-733-X*) Naval Inst Pr.

***U. S. Detergent & Cleaning Chemical Market: Multifunctionality & Biodegradibility Drive the Market.** Frost & Sullivan Staff. 335p. 1996. write for info. (*0-7889-0557-0*, 2739) Frost & Sullivan.

U. S. Diplomats in Europe, Nineteen Nineteen to Nineteen Forty-One. Ed. by Kenneth P. Jones. LC 82-24402. (Topics in Diplomatic History Ser.). 240p. 1983. 19.95 (*0-87436-349-7*) Regina Bks.

U. S. Diplomats in Europe, 1919-1941. Ed. by Kenneth P. Jones. LC 82-24402. (Topics in Diplomatic History Ser.). 240p. 1983. pap. 12.95 (*0-87436-351-9*) Regina Bks.

U. S. Direct Investment in the Latin American-Caribbean Region: Trends & Issues. Ramesh F. Ramsaran. LC 84-18364. 224p. 1985. text ed. 39.95 (*0-312-83317-2*) St Martin.

U. S. Direct Marketing Law: The Complete Handbook for Managers. Richard J. Leighton & Alfred S. Regnery. LC 93-26620. 302p. 1993. 70.00 (*1-882222-02-4*) Libey Pub.

***U. S. Direct-to-Home Satellite Television Market.** 328p. 1996. write for info. (*0-7889-0564-3*, 5415) Frost & Sullivan.

U. S. Directory of Entertainment Employers: 1996 Edition. 160p. 1996. pap. 95.00 (*0-9644353-3-0*) Monumental Comm.

***U. S. Directory of Entertainment Employers: 1997 Edition.** 3rd ed. LC 95-652889. 185p. 1997. pap. 55.00 (*0-9644353-4-9*) Monumental Comm.

***U. S. Directory of Entertainment Employers: 1998 Edition.** 4th ed. LC 95-652889. Date not set. pap. 55.00 (*0-9644353-5-7*) Monumental Comm.

U. S. Directory of Entertainment Employers 1995. 150p. 1995. pap. 95.00 (*0-9644353-2-2*) Monumental Comm.

U. S. Directory of Vendors see CAD-CAM, CAE: Survey, Review & Buyers' Guide

U. S. Disposable Medical Gloves & Condom Markets: Gloves & Condoms. Frost Sullivan Staff. 364p. 1996. write for info. (*0-7889-0498-1*, 5480) Frost & Sullivan.

***U. S. Disposable Needles, Syringes, & Related Product Markets.** Frost & Sullivan Staff. 341p. 1996. write for info. (*0-7889-0596-1*, 5341) Frost & Sullivan.

U. S. Distilled Spirits Market: Impact Databank Review & Forecast, 1996. Marvin R. Shanken. (Illus.). 256p. (Orig.). 1992. pap. 795.00 (*1-881659-04-6*) M Shanken Comm.

U. S. Distribution Channels for Electronic Wire & Cable. Amadee Bender. 150p. 1989. pap. text ed. 1,800.00 (*1-878218-04-2*) World Info Tech.

U. S. Distribution Channels for Electronic Wire & Cable: 1992-1996 Analysis. Amadee Bender. 220p. 1993. pap. text ed. 2,400.00 (*1-878218-34-4*) World Info Tech.

U. S. Distribution Channels for Electronic Wire & Cable: 1995-2000 Analysis & Forecasts. Kimberly O'Brien. 253p. 1995. pap. text ed. 2,700.00 (*1-878218-57-3*) World Info Tech.

U. S. District Court for the District of Puerto Rico: Local Rules. Ed. by Butterworth Staff. 115p. 1994. pap. 25.00 (*0-250-44817-3*) MICHIE.

U. S. District Court of Puerto Rico: Local Rules. Ed. by Butterworths Staff. 157p. 1994. pap. 25.00 (*0-614-03768-9*) MICHIE.

U. S. District Court Speaks. rev. ed. Joseph L. Tauro et al. LC 91-68117. 522p. 1992. pap. text ed. 55.00 (*0-944490-44-1*) Mass CLE.

U. S. District Court Speaks. rev. ed. Joseph L. Tauro et al. LC 94-78713. 522p. 1994. pap. text ed. 55.00 (*0-944490-73-5*) Mass CLE.

***U. S. DNA Probe Markets.** Frost & Sullivan. 345p. 1996. write for info. (0-7889-0620-8, 5066) Frost & Sullivan.

U. S. Documents in the Prop. Fide Archives: A Calendar, Vol. 11. Ed. by Mathias C. Kiemen & James Manamon. 339p. 1988. 55.00 (0-88382-237-7) AAFH.

U. S. Domestic & National Security Agendas: Into the 21st Century. Ed. by Sam C. Sarkesian & John M. Flanagin. LC 93-21499. (Contributions in Military Studies). 272p. 1994. text ed. 62.95 (0-313-28870-4, Greenwood Pr) Greenwood.

U. S. Dragoons 1833-55. John P. Langellier. (Men-at-Arms Ser.). (Illus.). 48p. 1995. pap. 11.95 (1-85532-389-3, Pub. by Osprey UK) Stackpole.

U. S. Driver's Manual. (GRE.). pap. 10.00 (0-685-25478-X) Divry.

U. S. Drug Approval System: Preparation & Processing of INDS & NDAS. Albert Ghignone. 535p. 1994. ring bd. 129.95 (1-56676-188-3) Technomic.

***U. S. Dual-Use Exports to Iraq & Their Impact on the Health of the Persian Gulf War Veterans.** (Illus.). 551p. 1997. reprint ed. pap. text ed. 50.00 (0-7881-3825-1) DIANE Pub.

U. S. E-Mail & Voice Mail Markets. Market Intelligence Staff. 266p. (Orig.). 1992. 2,900.00 (1-56753-656-5) Frost & Sullivan.

U. S. Earth Moving Equipment Markets. Market Intelligence Staff. 313p. 1994. 1,995.00 (0-7889-0143-5) Frost & Sullivan.

U. S. Economic Assistance to Russia & Nis. (Russian Business Library). (Illus.). 300p. (Orig.). 1996. pap. write for info. (1-57751-004-6) Russ Info & Busn Ctr.

***U. S. Economic Assistance to Russia & NIS: U. S. Aid Contractors, U. S. Non-Profits, Investment Funds.** 2nd rev. ed. Russian Information & Business Center, Inc. Staff. (Russian Business Library). 400p. 1997. pap. 99.00 (1-57751-304-5) Russ Info & Busn Ctr.

U. S. Economic Foreign Aid: A Case Study of the U. S. Agency for International Development. David Porter. LC 90-3612. (Foreign Economic Policy of the United States Ser.). 292p. 1990. reprint ed. text ed. 25.00 (0-8240-7466-1) Garland.

U. S. Economic History. 2nd ed. Albert W. Niemi, Jr. LC 87-10730. (Illus.). 492p. 1987. reprint ed. pap. text ed. 32.00 (0-8191-6335-X) U Pr of Amer.

***U. S. Economic History since 1945.** LC 96-46267. 1997. text ed. 79.95 (0-7190-4185-6, Pub. by Manchester Univ Pr UK) St Martin.

U. S. Economic Policies Affecting Industrial Trade: A Quantitative Assessment. Peter Morici & Laura L. Megna. LC 83-60013. (Committee on Changing International Realities Ser.). 140p. (Orig.). 1983. pap. 12.00 (0-89068-068-X, CIR-13) Natl Planning.

U. S. Economic Policy Toward the Association of Southeast Asian Nations: Meeting the Japanese Challenge. Lawrence B. Krause. LC 82-9656. 98p. 1982. 26.95 (0-8157-5026-9) Brookings.

U. S. Economy Demystified: The Meaning of U. S. Business Statistics & What They Portend about the Future. 3rd ed. Albert T. Sommers & Lucie R. Blau. LC 92-34701. 1993. pap. 19.95 (0-02-930116-5, Free Press) Free Pr.

U. S. Economy in Crisis: Adjusting to the New Realities. Pearl M. Kamer. LC 88-9959. 215p. 1988. text ed. 55.00 (0-275-93072-6, C3072, Praeger Pubs) Greenwood.

U. S. Economy in the Light of Justice, Solidarity, & Complementarity: An Interdisciplinary Perspective. Jacob J. Krabbe et al. (Studies in Social Science). 212p. (Orig.). 1994. per. write for info. (1-883199-04-2) W GA College.

U. S. Economy in the Nineteen Fifties: An Economic History. Harold G. Vatter. LC 84-6727. xii, 308p. 1984. reprint ed. text ed. 65.00 (0-313-24531-2, VAUS, Greenwood Pr) Greenwood.

U. S. Economy in World War II. Harold G. Vatter. LC 85-7789. (Columbia Studies in Business, Government & Society). 224p. 1985. text ed. 42.00 (0-231-05768-7) Col U Pr.

U. S. Economy in World War Two. Harold G. Vatter. (Columbia Studies in Business, Government & Society). (Illus.). 198p. 1988. pap. text ed. 16.00 (0-231-05769-5) Col U Pr.

U. S. Educational Policy Interest Groups: Institutional Profiles. Gregory S. Butler & James D. Slack. LC 93-44516. 256p. 1994. text ed. 69.50 (0-313-27292-1, Greenwood Pr) Greenwood.

U. S.-E.E.C. Trade Negotiations on the Acession of Spain & Portugal. Bradley B. Billings. (Pew Case Studies in Internatioanl Affairs). 50p. (C). 1993. pap. text ed. 3.50 (1-56927-147-X) Geo U Inst Dplmcy.

U. S. EFT - POS Debit Terminal Market. Market Intelligence Staff. 279p. 1993. 2,900.00 (1-56753-527-5) Frost & Sullivan.

U. S. Electoral Assistance & Democratic Development: Chile, Nicaragua & Panama. Washington Office on Latin America Staff. 33p. 1990. pap. 4.00 (0-929513-14-2) WOLA.

U. S. Electric District Operation & Maintenance Expense Comparisons 1990. James R. Schetter. 89p. 1991. pap. 345.00 (1-57016-225-5) TECC Grp.

U. S. Electric IOU Administrative & General Benchmark & Expense Comparisons 1993. James R. Schetter. 166p. 1994. pap. 645.00 (1-57016-925-X) TECC Grp.

U. S. Electric IOU Administrative & General Expense Comparisons 1993. James R. Schetter. 133p. 1994. pap. 345.00 (1-57016-900-4) TECC Grp.

U. S. Electric IOU Administrative & General Expense Trends 1989-98. James R. Schetter. 126p. 1994. pap. 495.00 (1-57016-950-0) TECC Grp.

U. S. Electric IOU Customer & Sales Benchmark & Expense Comparisons 1991. James R. Schetter. 166p. 1992. pap. 645.00 (1-57016-375-8) TECC Grp.

U. S. Electric IOU Customer & Sales Benchmark & Expense Comparisons 1992. James R. Schetter. 166p. 1993. pap. 645.00 (1-57016-376-6) TECC Grp.

U. S. Electric IOU Customer & Sales Benchmark & Expense Comparisons, 1993. James R. Schetter. 166p. 1994. pap. 645.00 (1-57016-377-4) TECC Grp.

U. S. Electric IOU Customer & Sales Expense Comparisons 1990. James R. Schetter. 133p. 1991. pap. 345.00 (1-57016-125-9) TECC Grp.

U. S. Electric IOU Customer & Sales Expense Comparisons 1991. James R. Schetter. 133p. 1992. pap. 345.00 (1-57016-126-7) TECC Grp.

U. S. Electric IOU Customer & Sales Expense Comparisons 1992. James R. Schetter. 133p. 1993. pap. 345.00 (1-57016-127-5) TECC Grp.

U. S. Electric IOU Customer & Sales Expense Comparisons, 1993. James R. Schetter. 133p. 1994. pap. 345.00 (1-57016-128-3) TECC Grp.

U. S. Electric IOU Customer & Sales Expense Trends 1988-97. James R. Schetter. 126p. 1993. pap. 495.00 (1-57016-550-5) TECC Grp.

U. S. Electric IOU Customer & Sales Expense Trends, 1989-98. James R. Schetter. 126p. 1994. pap. 495.00 (1-57016-551-3) TECC Grp.

U. S. Electric IOU Distribution Benchmark & Expense Comparisons 1991. James R. Schetter. 166p. 1992. pap. 645.00 (1-57016-350-2) TECC Grp.

U. S. Electric IOU Distribution Benchmark & Expense Comparisons 1992. James R. Schetter. 166p. 1993. pap. 645.00 (1-57016-351-0) TECC Grp.

U. S. Electric IOU Distribution Benchmark & Expense Comparisons, 1993. James R. Schetter. 166p. 1994. pap. 645.00 (1-57016-352-9) TECC Grp.

U. S. Electric IOU Distribution Expense Comparisons 1990. James R. Schetter. 133p. 1991. pap. 345.00 (1-57016-100-3) TECC Grp.

U. S. Electric IOU Distribution Expense Comparisons 1991. James R. Schetter. 133p. 1992. pap. 345.00 (1-57016-101-1) TECC Grp.

U. S. Electric IOU Distribution Expense Comparisons 1992. James R. Schetter. 133p. 1993. pap. 345.00 (1-57016-102-X) TECC Grp.

U. S. Electric IOU Distribution Expense Comparisons, 1993. James R. Schetter. 133p. 1994. pap. 345.00 (1-57016-103-8) TECC Grp.

U. S. Electric IOU Distribution Expense Trends 1988-97. James R. Schetter. 126p. 1993. pap. 495.00 (1-57016-525-4) TECC Grp.

U. S. Electric IOU Distribution Expense Trends, 1989-98. James R. Schetter. 126p. 1994. pap. 495.00 (1-57016-526-2) TECC Grp.

U. S. Electric IOU Operation & Maintenance Benchmark & Expense Comparisons 1991. James R. Schetter. 166p. 1992. pap. 645.00 (1-57016-250-6) TECC Grp.

U. S. Electric IOU Operation & Maintenance Benchmark & Expense Comparisons 1992. James R. Schetter. 166p. 1993. pap. 645.00 (1-57016-251-4) TECC Grp.

U. S. Electric IOU Operation & Maintenance Benchmark & Expense Comparisons, 1993. James R. Schetter. 166p. 1994. pap. 645.00 (1-57016-252-2) TECC Grp.

U. S. Electric IOU Operation & Maintenance Expense Comparisons 1988. James R. Schetter. 133p. 1989. pap. 345.00 (1-57016-000-7) TECC Grp.

U. S. Electric IOU Operation & Maintenance Expense Comparisons 1989. James R. Schetter. 133p. 1990. pap. 345.00 (1-57016-001-5) TECC Grp.

U. S. Electric IOU Operation & Maintenance Expense Comparisons 1990. James R. Schetter. 133p. 1991. pap. 345.00 (1-57016-002-3) TECC Grp.

U. S. Electric IOU Operation & Maintenance Expense Comparisons 1991. James R. Schetter. 133p. 1992. pap. 345.00 (1-57016-003-1) TECC Grp.

U. S. Electric IOU Operation & Maintenance Expense Comparisons 1992. James R. Schetter. 133p. 1993. pap. 345.00 (1-57016-004-X) TECC Grp.

U. S. Electric IOU Operation & Maintenance Expense Comparisons, 1993. James R. Schetter. 133p. 1994. pap. 345.00 (1-57016-005-8) TECC Grp.

U. S. Electric IOU Operation & Maintenance Expense Trends 1988-97. James R. Schetter. 126p. 1993. pap. 495.00 (1-57016-425-8) TECC Grp.

U. S. Electric IOU Operation & Maintenance Expense Trends, 1989-98. James R. Schetter. 126p. 1994. pap. 495.00 (1-57016-426-6) TECC Grp.

U. S. Electric IOU Power Marketing Expense Comparisons 1989. James R. Schetter. 144p. 1990. pap. 345.00 (1-57016-175-5) TECC Grp.

U. S. Electric IOU Power Marketing Expense Comparisons 1991. James R. Schetter. 144p. 1992. pap. 345.00 (1-57016-176-3) TECC Grp.

U. S. Electric IOU Power Production Benchmark & Expense Comparisons 1991. James R. Schetter. 166p. 1992. pap. 645.00 (1-57016-275-1) TECC Grp.

U. S. Electric IOU Power Production Benchmark & Expense Comparisons 1992. James R. Schetter. 166p. 1993. pap. 645.00 (1-57016-276-X) TECC Grp.

U. S. Electric IOU Power Production Benchmark & Expense Comparisons, 1993. James R. Schetter. 166p. 1994. pap. 645.00 (1-57016-277-8) TECC Grp.

U. S. Electric IOU Power Production Expense Comparisons 1991. James R. Schetter. 133p. 1992. pap. 345.00 (1-57016-025-2) TECC Grp.

U. S. Electric IOU Power Production Expense Comparisons 1992. James R. Schetter. 133p. 1993. pap. 345.00 (1-57016-026-0) TECC Grp.

U. S. Electric IOU Power Production Expense Comparisons, 1993. James R. Schetter. 133p. 1994. pap. 345.00 (1-57016-027-9) TECC Grp.

U. S. Electric IOU Power Production Expense Trends 1988-97. James R. Schetter. 126p. 1993. pap. 495.00 (1-57016-450-9) TECC Grp.

U. S. Electric IOU Power Production Expense Trends, 1989-98. James R. Schetter. 126p. 1994. pap. 495.00 (1-57016-451-7) TECC Grp.

U. S. Electric IOU Research, Development & Demonstration Expense Comparisons 1986. James R. Schetter. 124p. 1987. pap. 345.00 (1-57016-150-X) TECC Grp.

U. S. Electric IOU Research, Development & Demonstration Expense Comparisons 1987. James R. Schetter. 124p. 1988. pap. 345.00 (1-57016-151-8) TECC Grp.

U. S. Electric IOU Research, Development & Demonstration Expense Comparisons 1988. James R. Schetter. 124p. 1989. pap. 345.00 (1-57016-152-6) TECC Grp.

U. S. Electric IOU Research, Development & Demonstration Expense Comparisons 1989. James R. Schetter. 124p. 1990. pap. 345.00 (1-57016-153-4) TECC Grp.

U. S. Electric IOU Research, Development & Demonstration Expense Comparisons 1990. James R. Schetter. 124p. 1991. pap. 345.00 (1-57016-154-2) TECC Grp.

U. S. Electric IOU Research, Development & Demonstration Expense Comparisons 1991. James R. Schetter. 124p. 1992. pap. 345.00 (1-57016-155-0) TECC Grp.

U. S. Electric IOU Research, Development & Demonstration Expense Comparisons 1992. James R. Schetter. 124p. 1993. pap. 345.00 (1-57016-156-9) TECC Grp.

U. S. Electric IOU Research, Development & Demonstration Expense Comparisons, 1993. James R. Schetter. 124p. 1994. pap. 345.00 (1-57016-157-7) TECC Grp.

U. S. Electric IOU Research, Development & Demonstration Expense Trends 1983-87. James R. Schetter. 158p. 1988. pap. 445.00 (1-57016-575-0) TECC Grp.

U. S. Electric IOU Research, Development & Demonstration Expense Trends 1984-88. James R. Schetter. 158p. 1989. pap. 445.00 (1-57016-576-9) TECC Grp.

U. S. Electric IOU Research, Development & Demonstration Expense Trends 1985-89. James R. Schetter. 158p. 1990. pap. 445.00 (1-57016-577-7) TECC Grp.

U. S. Electric IOU Research, Development & Demonstration Expense Trends 1986-90. James R. Schetter. 158p. 1991. pap. 445.00 (1-57016-578-5) TECC Grp.

U. S. Electric IOU Research, Development & Demonstration Expense Trends 1987-91. James R. Schetter. 158p. 1992. pap. 445.00 (1-57016-579-3) TECC Grp.

U. S. Electric IOU Research, Development & Demonstration Expense Trends 1988-92. James R. Schetter. 158p. 1993. pap. 445.00 (1-57016-580-7) TECC Grp.

U. S. Electric IOU Research, Development & Demonstration Expense Trends, 1989-93. James R. Schetter. 158p. 1994. pap. 445.00 (1-57016-581-5) TECC Grp.

U. S. Electric IOU Salary & Wage Benchmark & Expense Comparisons 1991. James R. Schetter. 166p. 1992. pap. 645.00 (1-57016-300-6) TECC Grp.

U. S. Electric IOU Salary & Wage Benchmark & Expense Comparisons 1992. James R. Schetter. 166p. 1993. pap. 645.00 (1-57016-301-4) TECC Grp.

U. S. Electric IOU Salary & Wage Benchmark & Expense Comparisons, 1993. James R. Schetter. 166p. 1994. pap. 645.00 (1-57016-302-2) TECC Grp.

U. S. Electric IOU Salary & Wage Expense Comparisons 1989. James R. Schetter. 133p. 1990. pap. 345.00 (1-57016-050-3) TECC Grp.

U. S. Electric IOU Salary & Wage Expense Comparisons 1990. James R. Schetter. 133p. 1991. pap. 345.00 (1-57016-051-1) TECC Grp.

U. S. Electric IOU Salary & Wage Expense Comparisons 1991. James R. Schetter. 133p. 1992. pap. 345.00 (1-57016-052-X) TECC Grp.

U. S. Electric IOU Salary & Wage Expense Comparisons 1992. James R. Schetter. 133p. 1993. pap. 345.00 (1-57016-053-8) TECC Grp.

U. S. Electric IOU Salary & Wage Expense Comparisons, 1993. James R. Schetter. 133p. 1994. pap. 345.00 (1-57016-054-6) TECC Grp.

U. S. Electric IOU Salary & Wage Expense Trends 1988-97. James R. Schetter. 126p. 1993. pap. 495.00 (1-57016-475-4) TECC Grp.

U. S. Electric IOU Salary & Wage Expense Trends, 1989-98. James R. Schetter. 126p. 1994. pap. 495.00 (1-57016-476-2) TECC Grp.

U. S. Electric IOU Transmission Benchmark & Expense Comparisons 1991. James R. Schetter. 166p. 1992. pap. 645.00 (1-57016-325-1) TECC Grp.

U. S. Electric IOU Transmission Benchmark & Expense Comparisons 1992. James R. Schetter. 166p. 1993. pap. 645.00 (1-57016-326-X) TECC Grp.

U. S. Electric IOU Transmission Benchmark & Expense Comparisons, 1993. James R. Schetter. 166p. 1994. pap. 645.00 (1-57016-327-8) TECC Grp.

U. S. Electric IOU Transmission Expense Comparisons 1990. James R. Schetter. 133p. 1991. pap. 345.00 (1-57016-075-9) TECC Grp.

U. S. Electric IOU Transmission Expense Comparisons 1991. James R. Schetter. 133p. 1992. pap. 345.00 (1-57016-076-7) TECC Grp.

U. S. Electric IOU Transmission Expense Comparisons 1992. James R. Schetter. 133p. 1993. pap. 345.00 (1-57016-077-5) TECC Grp.

U. S. Electric IOU Transmission Expense Comparisons, 1993. James R. Schetter. 133p. 1994. pap. 345.00 (1-57016-078-3) TECC Grp.

U. S. Electric IOU Transmission Expense Trends 1988-97. James R. Schetter. 126p. 1993. pap. 495.00 (1-57016-500-9) TECC Grp.

U. S. Electric IOU Transmission Expense Trends, 1989-98. James R. Schetter. 126p. 1994. pap. 495.00 (1-57016-501-7) TECC Grp.

U. S. Electric Municipal Operation & Maintenance Benchmark & Expense Comparisons 1991. James R. Schetter. 136p. 1992. pap. 645.00 (1-57016-400-2) TECC Grp.

U. S. Electric Municipal Operation & Maintenance Expense Comparisons 1990. James R. Schetter. 112p. 1991. pap. 345.00 (1-57016-200-X) TECC Grp.

U. S. Electric Municipal Operation & Maintenance Expense Comparisons 1991. James R. Schetter. 112p. 1992. pap. 345.00 (1-57016-201-8) TECC Grp.

U. S. Electrical & Electric Film Capacitor Markets, Technologies & Opportunities. Dennis M. Zogbi. 156p. (Orig.). 1993. pap. 995.00 (0-929717-17-1) Paumanok Pubns.

U. S. Electrical & Electronic Circuit Breaker & Fuse Markets. Amadee Bender. (Illus.). 200p. 1989. pap. text ed. 1,800.00 (1-878218-03-4) World Info Tech.

U. S. Electrical & Electronic Surge Protection Markets. Amadee Bender. (Illus.). 225p. 1989. pap. text ed. 1,800.00 (1-878218-05-0) World Info Tech.

U. S. Electrical & Electronic Surge Protector, Suppressor, & Arrester Markets: 1991-1996 Analysis. Dennis M. Zogbi. (Illus.). 400p. 1991. pap. text ed. 2,400.00 (1-878218-19-0) World Info Tech.

***U. S. Electricity Deregulation: Impacts on Gas & Commodity Markets.** Peter C. Fusaro. 20p. 1997. pap. 10.00 (0-918714-51-6) Intl Res Ctr Energy.

U. S. Electro-Optical Instrument & Inspection System Markets. Market Intelligence Staff. 336p. 1994. 2,195.00 (0-7889-0144-3) Frost & Sullivan.

***U. S. Electro-Optical Instrument & Microscope Markets.** Frost & Sullivan. 279p. 1997. write for info. (0-7889-0631-3, 5372) Frost & Sullivan.

***U. S. Electronic Access Control System Markets.** Frost & Sullivan Staff. 382p. 1996. write for info. (0-7889-0591-0, 5517) Frost & Sullivan.

U. S. Electronic Access Control System Markets Requirements: High Security Promote Biometric Identification. Market Intelligence Staff. 250p. 1994. 1,895.00 (1-56753-998-X) Frost & Sullivan.

U. S. Electronic & Electrical Capacitor Markets: U. S. Markets, Technologies, & Opportunities: 1994-1999 Analysis & Forecasts. Lane Gorton. 150p. 1994. pap. text ed. 2,400.00 (1-878218-55-7) World Info Tech.

U. S. Electronic Data Storage & Retrieval Equipment Markets: Electronic Data Automation Propelled by Expanded User Base, New Applications, & Price/Performance Improvements. Frost & Sullivan Staff. 472p. 1995. write for info. (0-7889-0266-0) Frost & Sullivan.

U. S. Electronic-Electrical Adhesive, Sealant & Coating Markets: Growth Applications Swing Toward Polyimide. Market Intelligence Staff. 250p. 1993. 2,895.00 (1-56753-574-7) Frost & Sullivan.

U. S. Electronic Warfare Markets: Opportunities Emerge As Parochialism Dies. Frost & Sullivan Staff. 334p. 1995. write for info. (0-7889-0397-7) Frost & Sullivan.

***U. S. Electronic Wire & Cable Companies: 1996 Competitive Analysis.** Kimberly O'Brien. 146p. 1996. pap. text ed. 2,700.00 (1-878218-72-7) World Info Tech.

***U. S. Elite Counterterrorist Forces.** S. F. Tomaiczyk. LC 97-15637. (Power Ser.). (Illus.). 128p. 1997. pap. 16.95 (0-7603-0220-0) Motorbooks Intl.

U. S. Emergency & Trauma Care Device Markets: New Technologies Focus on Safety & Ease of Use. Market Intelligence Staff. 410p. (Orig.). 1994. 1,895.00 (0-7889-0119-2) Frost & Sullivan.

U. S. Employer's Guide: A Handbook of Employment Laws & Regulations. Amy L. Greenspan. 596p. 1996. ring bd. 119.50 (1-56759-012-8) Summers Pr.

U. S. Enclosed Geardrive & Gearmotor Markets: Another Traditional Domestic Market under International Pressure. Market Intelligence Staff. 298p. 1993. 2,395.00 (1-56753-546-1) Frost & Sullivan.

U. S. Endoscope Markets: Intracranial & Spinal Markets Emerge. Frost & Sullivan Staff. 363p. Date not set. write for info. (0-7889-0400-0, 5231-57) Frost & Sullivan.

U. S. Ends & Means in Central America: A Debate. Ernest Van den Haag & Tom J. Farer. 275p. 1988. 19.95 (0-306-42857-1, Plenum Pr) Plenum.

U. S. Energy & Environmental Interest Groups: Institutional Profiles. Lettie M. Wenner. LC 90-2705. 372p. 1990. text ed. 65.00 (0-313-25362-5, Greenwood Pr) Greenwood.

U. S. Energy Future: Environmental/Social Costs, No. E-007U. Business Communications Co., Inc. Staff. 1992. 2,450.00 (0-89336-805-9) BCC.

U. S. Energy Imperatives for the 1990s: Leadership, Efficiency, Environmental Responsibility, & Sustained Economic Growth. Ed. by Donald L. Guertin et al. 300p. (C). 1991. lib. bdg. 54.50 (0-8191-8336-9) U Pr of Amer.

U. S. Energy Imperatives for the 1990s: Leadership, Efficiency, Environmental Responsibility, & Sustained Economic Growth. Ed. by Donald L. Guertin et al. 280p. (C). 1992. pap. 28.50 (0-8191-8337-7) U Pr of Amer.

U. S. Energy Policy: Alternatives for Security. Douglas R. Bohi & Milton Russell. LC 75-4209. 141p. reprint ed. pap. 40.20 (0-685-44466-X, 2032988) Bks Demand.

UV

U. S. Energy Policy: Crisis & Complacency. Don E. Kash & Robert W. Rycroft. LC 83-17093. (Illus.). 352p. 1984. 24.95 (*0-8061-1869-5*) U of Okla Pr.

U. S. English for French Phrase Book. Berlitz Editors. (Phrase Bk.). 192p. 1993. pap. 6.95 (*2-8315-0860-6*) Berlitz.

U. S. Environmental Imperatives & the Accelerated Export Capacity. Peter C. Fusaro. 20p. 1992. pap. 10.00 (*0-918714-34-6*) Intl Res Ctr Energy.

U. S. Environmental Laws: 1994 Edition. Wallis E. McClain, Jr. LC 90-36685. 1292p. 1994. pap. text ed. 60.00 (*0-87179-836-0*) BNA Books.

***U. S. Environmental Markets: 1997-2000.** 8th ed. Richard K. Miller et al. 414p. 1996. 485.00 (*0-614-29510-6*) R K Miller Assocs.

***U. S. Environmental Markets, 1997-2000.** 8th rev. ed. Richard K. Miller et al. 481p. 1997. 485.00 (*1-881503-74-7*) R K Miller Assocs.

U. S. EPA Manual of Chemical Methods for Pesticides & Devices. 2nd ed. Charles J. Stafford et al. 790p. 1992. ring bd. 153.00 (*0-935584-47-1*) AOAC Intl.

U. S. Equities on Floppy 1995-96 Edition User's Manual. 3rd ed. Morningstar. 120p. (C). 1995. 37.95 (*0-256-18734-7*) Irwin.

U. S. Errors: Inverts, Imperfrates & Colors Omitted on U. S. Postage Stamps see Errors on U. S. Postage Stamps 1996-97

U. S. Essay, Proof & Specimen Notes. Gene Hessler. LC 79-7481. 256p. 1979. 27.50 (*0-931960-04-5*) BNR Pr.

***U. S. Ethical Nutrition Markets: Contract Pricing Forces Greater Competition.** Frost & Sullivan Staff. Date not set. write for info. (*0-7889-0522-8*, 5301) Frost & Sullivan.

U. S. Ethical Nutrition Markets: Manufacturers Target Home Healthcare for Growth. Market Intelligence Staff. 1994. 1,895.00 (*0-7889-0061-7*) Frost & Sullivan.

U. S.-European Negotiations to Clarify the GATT Aircraft Agreement. John Schriefer. (Pew Case Studies in International Affairs). 50p. (C). 1993. pap. text ed. 3.50 (*1-56927-121-6*) Geo U Inst Dplmcy.

U. S. Excise Tax Guide, 1991. 264p. 1991. pap. 17.00 (*0-317-44559-6*, 5901) Commerce.

U. S. Expansionism & Cuban Annexationism in the 1850s. Josef Opatrny. LC 93-15343. 324p. 1993. text ed. 99.95 (*0-7734-2308-7*) E Mellen.

U. S. Experience in Evaluation Urban Regeneration. (Reviews of Urban Research Ser.). 75p. 1990. pap. 16.50 (*0-11-752280-5*, HM2805, Pub. by Stationery Ofc UK) Bernan Associates.

U. S. Experiment in Social Medicine: The Community Health Center Program, 1965-1986. Alice Sardell. LC 87-35847. (Series in Policy & Institutional Studies). (Illus.). 288p. (Orig.). (C). 1988. pap. 19.95 (*0-8229-5803-1*) U of Pittsburgh Pr.

U. S. Export Directory, 1995. Ed. by Bowker, R. R., Staff. 1994. 239.00 (*0-8352-3605-6*) Bowker.

***U. S. Exports & Imports by Harmonized Commodities, 2 vols.** 1997. lib. bdg. 600.95 (*0-8490-6073-7*) Gordon Pr.

U. S. Exports & Imports by Harmonized Commodity, 2 vols., Set. 1994. lib. bdg. 595.00 (*0-8490-8535-7*) Gordon Pr.

U. S. Exports of High-Value Agricultural Products: Background, Analysis, Economic Issues & Export Assistance. (Illus.). 53p. (Orig.). (C). 1994. pap. text ed. 40.00 (*0-7881-0210-9*) DIANE Pub.

U. S. Exports to Mexico: A State-by-State Overview. 1994. lib. bdg. 250.00 (*0-8490-8536-5*) Gordon Pr.

U. S. F. Constellation: Yankee Racehorse. Sanford Sternlicht & Edwin M. Jameson. LC 81-84998. (Illus.). 192p. 1981. pap. 4.95 (*0-89709-030-6*) Liberty Pub.

U. S. Farm Machinery & Equipment Market. 340p. 1989. 995.00 (*0-318-03906-0*) Busn Trend.

***U. S. FDA Methods for the Microbiological Analysis of Selected Nutrients.** Ed. by Gerald Angyal. 86p. 1996. pap. 42.00 (*0-935584-61-7*) AOAC Intl.

U. S. FDC Catalogue, 1994: Mass Market Pocket Catalogue for First Day Covers. 1993. pap. 6.95 (*0-89487-197-8*) Scott Pub Co.

U. S. Federal Budget Process: An Overview & Glossary of Terms. Ed. by G. I. Maltese. 137p. (C). 1995. lib. bdg. 49.00 (*1-56072-192-8*) Nova Sci Pubs.

U. S. Federal Income Tax Guide for International Students & Scholars. rev. ed. Deborah L. Vance & Deborah Ahlstedt. 96p. 1995. pap. 20.00 (*0-685-74780-8*) NAFSA Washington.

U. S. Federal Non-DOD Physical Security Equipment Markets: Government Market Still Provides Lucrative Growth. Market Intelligence Staff. 325p. (Orig.). 1994. 1,995.00 (*0-7889-0113-3*) Frost & Sullivan.

U. S. Fertilizer Market. (Illus.). 245p. 1987. spiral bd. 750.00 (*0-317-65736-4*) Busn Trend.

U. S. Fibre-Optic Test Equipment Markets: New Product Development & Telecommunications Bill of '96 Revolutionize FTE Industry. Frost Sullivan Staff. 416p. 1996. write for info. (*0-7889-0488-4*, 5371) Frost & Sullivan.

U. S. Field & On-Site Waste Water Analytical Instrument Markets. Market Intelligence Staff. 360p. 1995. 1,995.00 (*0-7889-0150-8*) Frost & Sullivan.

U. S. Filtration Product Markets: A Comprehensive Overview of Four Filtration Types: Macro, Micro, Ultra, & Reverse Osmosis. Market Intelligence Staff. 1994. 1,995.00 (*1-56753-996-3*) Frost & Sullivan.

U. S. Financial Institutions in Crisis: Overview of the 50 Largest Banks & 50 Largest S&Ls. 4th ed. Kenneth Coleman. Ed. by Catherine Chambers & David Lewis. 24p. 1986. pap. 14.95 (*0-942632-01-X*) Seraphim Pr.

U. S. Financial System: Money, Markets, & Institutions. 4th ed. George G. Kaufman. 720p. (C). 1989. Casebound. boxed write for info. (*0-13-936031-X*) P-H.

U. S. Financial System: Money, Markets, & Institutions. 6th ed. George G. Kaufman. LC 94-9691. 680p. 1994. text ed. 78.00 (*0-13-122912-5*) P-H.

U. S. Financing of East-West Trade: The Political Economy of Government Credits & the National Interest. Paul Marer. (Studies in East European & Soviet Planning, Development, & Trade: No. 22). (Illus.). 1975. pap. text ed. 5.00 (*0-89249-030-6*) Intl Development.

U. S. Fine & Ultrafine Filtration Product Markets: Capturing Smaller Particles Generates Larger Dollars. Market Intelligence Staff. 470p. 1994. 1,995.00 (*1-56753-966-1*) Frost & Sullivan.

***U. S. Firms in Germany 1995.** Ed. by Sven C. Dehme. 140p. 1995. 100.00 (*0-86640-055-9*) German Am Chamber.

U. S. Fish Industry. Ed. by Peter Allen. 299p. (Orig.). 1982. pap. 1,095.00 (*0-931634-22-9*) FIND-SVP.

U. S. Fishing Rod Patents & Other Tackle. Mary K. Kelly. Ed. by Brian J. McGrath. LC 90-60460. (Illus.). 120p. 1990. text ed. 30.00 (*0-9620155-2-0*) T B Reel.

U. S. Fitness & Exercise Equipment Markets: How Is the Industry Shaping Up? Market Intelligence Staff. 520p. (Orig.). 1994. 1,895.00 (*0-685-71179-X*) Frost & Sullivan.

U. S. Flat Panel Display Markets. Frost & Sullivan Staff. Date not set. write for info. (*0-7889-0487-6*, 5286) Frost & Sullivan.

U. S. Flea Market Directory. 2nd ed. Albert LaFarge. 496p. (Orig.). 1996. pap. 6.99 (*0-380-78494-7*, Confident Collect) Avon.

U. S. Floor Coverings Industry. 310p. 1996. 1,095.00 (*0-318-00536-0*) Busn Trend.

U. S. Fluid & Drug Delivery System Markets. Market Intelligence Staff. (Orig.). 1994. 2,295.00 (*0-7889-0097-8*) Frost & Sullivan.

U. S. Foamed Plastics Markets & Directory. Ed. by James P. Harrington. 293p. 1994. pap. 49.95 (*1-56676-020-8*, 760208) Technomic.

U. S. Food Additive Markets. Date not set. write for info. (*0-7889-0384-5*) Frost & Sullivan.

U. S. Food & Drug Administration: Index of Progress & Activities. Gilbert K. Yamano. LC 88-47630. 150p. 1988. 44.50 (*0-88164-732-2*); pap. 39.50 (*0-88164-733-0*) ABBE Pubs Assn.

U. S. Food Processing & Packaging Equipment Industry. 260p. 1990. 950.00 (*0-318-04396-3*) Busn Trend.

U. S. Footwear Market. 360p. 1995. 995.00 (*0-318-01958-2*) Busn Trend.

***U. S. Forces in the Middle East: Resources & Capabilities.** LC 96-46615. (CSIS Middle East Dynamic Net Assessment Ser.). 1997. text ed. 62.00 (*0-8133-3245-1*) Westview.

***U. S. Forces in the Middle East: Resources & Capabilities.** LC 96-46615. (CSIS Middle East Dynamic Net Assessment Ser.). (C). 1997. pap. text ed. 26.00 (*0-8133-3246-X*) Westview.

U. S. Forces Travel & Transfer Guide: U. S. A. & Caribbean Areas. L. Ann Crawford & William R. Crawford, Sr. Ed. by Leon G. Russ & Donna L. Russell. LC 95-51192. 1996. write for info. (*0-914862-60-X*) Military Living Pubns.

***U. S. Forces Travel & Transfer Guide: U. S. A. & Caribbean Areas.** L. Ann Crawford & William R. Crawford, Sr. Ed. by Leon G. Russ & Donna L. Russell. LC 95-51192. 1996. write for info. (*0-914862-63-4*) Military Living Pubns.

U. S. Foreign Aid & the National Interest. Gordon Donald, Jr. (Committee on Changing International Realities Ser.). 32p. (Orig.). 1983. pap. 4.00 (*0-89068-067-1*) Natl Planning.

U. S. Foreign Aid Policy - a Critique. Nicholas Eberstadt. Ed. by Nancy L. Hoepli. LC 90-80874. (Headline Ser.: No. 293). 64p. (Orig.). 1990. pap. 5.95 (*0-87124-134-X*) Foreign Policy.

U. S. Foreign & Strategic Policy in the Post-Cold War Era: A Geopolitical Perspective. Howard J. Wiarda. LC 95-33973. (Contributions in Political Science Ser.: Vol. 366). 272p. 1995. text ed. 59.95 (*0-313-29360-0*, Greenwood Pr) Greenwood.

U. S. Foreign Assistance: Investment or Folly. Ed. by John Wilhelm & Gerry Feinstein. LC 84-15896. 412p. 1984. text ed. 45.95 (*0-275-91292-2*, C1292, Praeger Pubs) Greenwood.

U. S. Foreign Economic & Military Aid: The Reagan & Bush Administrations. Simon Payaslian. 190p. (Orig.). (C). 1995. pap. text ed. 29.00 (*0-7618-0240-1*); lib. bdg. 44.00 (*0-7618-0239-8*) U Pr of Amer.

U. S. Foreign Economic Policy & the Latin American Debt Issue. C. Roe Goddard. LC 92-32355. (Foreign Economic Policy of the United States Ser.). 176p. 1993. text ed. 15.00 (*0-8153-1104-4*) Garland.

U. S. Foreign Policy: An African Agenda. Ed. by William Minter. 28p. (Orig.). 1994. pap. 6.50 (*0-9634238-1-9*) Africa Policy Info.

U. S. Foreign Policy: The Search for a New Role. Ed. by Robert J. Art & Seyom Brown. LC 92-14606. 416p. (C). 1992. pap. text ed. 40.00 (*0-02-303941-8*, Macmillan Coll) P-H.

U. S. Foreign Policy: Toward the Nineteen Nineties. Ed. by Greg Schmergel. LC 90-43367. 260p. 1991. text ed. 49.95 (*0-312-05366-5*) St Martin.

U. S. Foreign Policy after the Cold War. Ed. by Brad Roberts. (Illus.). 310p. 1992. 31.50 (*0-262-18148-7*); pap. 18.00 (*0-262-68074-2*) MIT Pr.

U. S. Foreign Policy after the Cold War: Superpower Without a Mission? Michael Cox. (Chatham House Papers). 160p. 1995. pap. 15.95 (*1-85567-221-9*, Pub. by Cassell Pubng UK) LPC InBook.

U. S. Foreign Policy after the Cold War: Superpower Without a Mission? Michael Cox. (Chatham House Papers). 160p. 1995. 50.00 (*1-85567-220-0*, Pub. by Pntr Pubs UK) Bks Intl VA.

U. S. Foreign Policy & Developing Countries: Discourse & Data 1991. Stuart K. Tucker & Rosemarie Philips. 48p. (Orig.). 1991. pap. 12.95 (*1-56517-003-2*) Overseas Dev Council.

U. S. Foreign Policy & Economic Reform in Three Giants: The U. S. S. R., China, & India. Richard E. Feinberg et al. Ed. by Valeriana Kallab. (U. S. Third World Policy Perspectives Ser.: No. 14). 256p. 1989. 39.95 (*0-88738-316-5*); pap. 21.95 (*0-88738-820-5*) Transaction Pubs.

U. S. Foreign Policy & European Security. Arthur Cyr. LC 86-20379. 250p. 1987. text ed. 39.95 (*0-312-00221-1*) St Martin.

***U. S. Foreign Policy & Intellectual Property Rights in Latin America.** Edgardo Buscaglia & Clarisa Long. LC 97-2576. (Essays in Public Policy Ser.). 1997. write for info. (*0-8179-5822-3*) Hoover Inst Pr.

***U. S. Foreign Policy & the Four Horsemen of the Apocalypse: Humanitarian Relief in Complex Emergencies.** Andrew S. Natsios. LC 96-52721. 216p. 1997. text ed. 55.00 (*0-275-95920-1*); pap. text ed. 15.95 (*0-275-95921-X*) Greenwood.

U. S. Foreign Policy & the Shah: Building a Client State in Iran. Mark Gasiorowski. LC 90-55919. 296p. 1990. 39.95 (*0-8014-2412-7*) Cornell U Pr.

U. S. Foreign Policy & the Third World: Agenda 1982. 268p. 1982. text ed. 49.95 (*0-275-90813-5*, C0813, Praeger Pubs) Greenwood.

U. S. Foreign Policy & the Third World: Agenda 1983. Ed. by John P. Lewis & Valeriana Kallab. LC 83-3373. 304p. 1983. text ed. 65.00 (*0-275-91034-2*, C1034, Praeger Pubs) Greenwood.

U. S. Foreign Policy & the Third World: Agenda 1985-1986. Ed. by John W. Sewell et al. (U. S. Third World Policy Perspectives Ser.). 256p. 1985. 39.95 (*0-88738-042-5*); pap. 21.95 (*0-87855-990-6*) Transaction Pubs.

U. S. Foreign Policy & Water Resources in the Middle East: Instrument for Peace & Development. Joyce R. Starr & Daniel C. Stoll. (CSIS Panel Report). (C). 1987. pap. 14.95 (*0-89206-110-3*) CSI Studies.

***U. S. Foreign Policy & World Order.** 5th ed. Ed. by Nathan. (C). 1998. text ed. write for info. (*0-321-01107-4*) Addison-Wesley.

U. S. Foreign Policy in Sub-Saharan Africa: National Interest & Global Strategy. Robert M. Price. LC 78-65499. (Policy Papers in International Affairs: No. 8). 1978. pap. text ed. 4.50 (*0-87725-508-3*) U of Cal IAS.

U. S. Foreign Policy in Transition. Ed. by James E. Winkates et al. LC 93-9173. 350p. 1993. pap. text ed. 21.95 (*0-8304-1343-X*) Nelson-Hall.

U. S. Foreign Relations: A Guide to Information Sources. Ed. by Elmer Plischke. LC 74-11516. (American Government & History Information Guide Ser.: Vol. 6). 736p. 1980. 68.00 (*0-8103-1204-2*) Gale.

U. S. Foreign Relations Law: Documents & Sources, 5 vols. Michael J. Glennon & Thomas M. Franck. 1984. Set. lib. bdg. 200.00 (*0-379-20355-3*) Oceana.

U. S. Foreign Relations with the Middle East & North Africa: A Bibliography. Sanford R. Silverburg. Ed. by Bernard Reich. LC 93-11103. (Area Bibliographies Ser.: No. 3). 607p. 1994. 59.50 (*0-8108-2699-2*) Scarecrow.

U. S. Foreign Tax Credit. 165.00 (*1-85271-326-7*, Pub. by IBC Finan Pubng UK) IBC Pubns.

U. S. Foreign Tax Policy: America's Berlin Wall. 83p. 1991. pap. 14.95 (*0-614-04371-9*) IRET.

U. S. Foreign Tax Policy: America's Berlin Wall. Ed. by Institute for Research on the Economics of Taxation Staff. 120p. (C). 1991. pap. text ed. 18.50 (*0-8191-8340-7*); lib. bdg. 39.50 (*0-8191-8339-3*) U Pr of Amer.

U. S. Foreign Taxation. Joseph Isenbergh. write for info. (*0-318-59312-2*) Little.

U. S. Foreign Trade, Vol. 2. Bruce E. Clubb. 1991. 165.00 (*0-316-14766-4*) Little.

U. S. Foreign Trade Law. Bruce E. Clubb. 1991. 165.00 (*0-316-14748-6*) Little.

U. S. Forest Service Grazing & Rangelands: A History. William D. Rowley. LC 85-40048. (Environmental History Ser.: No. 8). (Illus.). 288p. 1985. 31.95 (*0-89096-218-9*) Tex A&M Univ Pr.

U. S. Forty: Cross Section of the United States of America. George R. Stewart. LC 72-11338. (Illus.). 311p. 1973. reprint ed. text ed. 65.00 (*0-8371-6655-1*, STUS, Greenwood Pr) Greenwood.

U. S. Forty Today: Thirty Years of Landscape Change in America. Thomas R. Vale & Geraldine R. Vale. LC 83-50081. (Illus.). 208p. 1983. 27.50 (*0-299-09480-4*); pap. 14.95 (*0-299-09484-7*) U of Wis Pr.

***U. S. Fractional Horsepower Motor Markets.** 333p. 1996. write for info. (*0-7889-0577-5*, 5323) Frost & Sullivan.

U. S. Freight Transportation Forecast...to 2004. Contrib. by DRI/McGraw-Hill Staff. 1996. pap. 50.00 (*0-88711-334-6*) Am Trucking Assns.

U. S. Gas LDC Administrative & General Benchmark & Expense Comparisons, 1992. James R. Schetter. 149p. 1993. pap. text ed. 645.00 (*1-57016-725-7*) TECC Grp.

U. S. Gas LDC Administrative & General Expense Comparisons, 1992. James R. Schetter. 116p. 1993. pap. text ed. 345.00 (*1-57016-875-X*) TECC Grp.

U. S. Gas LDC Customer & Sales Benchmark & Expense Comparisons, 1992. James R. Schetter. 149p. 1993. pap. text ed. 645.00 (*1-57016-700-1*) TECC Grp.

U. S. Gas LDC Customer & Sales Expense Comparisons, 1992. James R. Schetter. 116p. 1993. pap. text ed. 345.00 (*1-57016-850-4*) TECC Grp.

U. S. Gas LDC Distribution Benchmark & Expense Comparisons, 1992. James R. Schetter. 149p. 1993. pap. text ed. 645.00 (*1-57016-675-7*) TECC Grp.

U. S. Gas LDC Distribution Expense Comparisons, 1992. James R. Schetter. 116p. 1993. pap. text ed. 345.00 (*1-57016-825-3*) TECC Grp.

U. S. Gas LDC Operation & Maintenance Benchmark & Expense Comparisons, 1992. James R. Schetter. 149p. 1993. pap. text ed. 645.00 (*1-57016-600-5*) TECC Grp.

U. S. Gas LDC Operation & Maintenance Expense Comparisons, 1992. James R. Schetter. 116p. 1993. pap. 345.00 (*1-57016-750-8*) TECC Grp.

U. S. Gas LDC Production & Storage Benchmark & Expense Comparisons, 1992. James R. Schetter. 149p. 1993. pap. text ed. 645.00 (*1-57016-625-0*) TECC Grp.

U. S. Gas LDC Production & Storage Expense Comparisons, 1992. James R. Schetter. 116p. 1993. pap. 345.00 (*1-57016-775-3*) TECC Grp.

U. S. Gas LDC Transmission Benchmark & Expense Comparisons, 1992. James R. Schetter. 149p. 1993. pap. text ed. 645.00 (*1-57016-650-1*) TECC Grp.

U. S. Gas LDC Transmission Expense Comparisons, 1992. James R. Schetter. 116p. 1993. pap. text ed. 345.00 (*1-57016-800-8*) TECC Grp.

U. S. Gasket Packaging & Mechanical Sealing Device Markets. Market Intelligence Staff. 246p. 1993. 2,895.00 (*1-56753-577-1*) Frost & Sullivan.

U. S. Genitourological Pharmaceutical & Diagnostic Markets: Competitors Focus on Quality of Life for an Aging Population. Market Intelligence Staff. 1995. 2,495.00 (*0-7889-0202-4*, 5080-52) Frost & Sullivan.

U. S. Geography. Randy L. Womack. (Illus.). 80p. (gr. 4 up). 1996. student ed. 9.95 (*1-56500-020-X*) Gldn Educ.

U. S. Geography Jingo. Gary Grimm & Phoebe Wear. 32p. (J). (gr. k-6). 1995. 12.00 (*1-56490-009-6*) G Grimm Assocs.

U. S. Geography Journey. rev. ed. L. Schwartz. 48p. (J). (gr. 4-8). 1992. reprint ed. 6.95 (*0-88160-181-0*, LW287) Learning Wks.

U. S. Geological Survey: Its History, Activities & Organization. Brookings Institution Staff. LC 72-3014. (Service Monographs of the U. S. Government: No. 1). reprint ed. 21.50 (*0-404-57101-8*) AMS Pr.

U. S. Geological Survey Toxic Substances Hydrology Program: Proceedings of the Technical Meeting, 1991. Ed. by G. E. Mallard & D. E. Aronson. (Illus.). 730p. (Orig.). (C). 1994. pap. text ed. 195.00 (*0-7881-0438-1*) DIANE Pub.

***U. S. GL TR Outlook/IND Outlook 95.** U. S. Department of Commerce Staff. 1996. pap. 19.00 (*0-614-30822-4*, UUSGLP) Claitors.

U. S. Global Change Research Program: An Assessment in the FY 1991 Plans. National Research Council Staff. 128p. 1990. pap. text ed. 15.00 (*0-309-04328-X*) Natl Acad Pr.

U. S. Global Trade Outlook 1995-2000: Toward the 21st Century. (Illus.). 222p. (Orig.). (C). 1995. pap. text ed. 35.00 (*0-7881-1960-5*) DIANE Pub.

U. S. Government: Executive Branch: Syllabus. Robert E. Adam. (U. S. Government Ser.). (gr. 7-12). 1979. pap. text ed. 8.35 (*0-89420-089-5*, 194030); audio 150.05 (*0-89420-189-1*, 194000) Natl Book.

U. S. Government: How It Functions: Syllabus. Carl W. Salser. (U. S. Government Ser.). 1976. pap. text ed. 6.45 (*0-89420-090-9*, 196051); audio 36.05 (*0-89420-190-5*, 196040) Natl Book.

U. S. Government: How Our Laws Are Made: Syllabus. Carl W. Salser. 1976. pap. text ed. 6.45 (*0-89420-091-7*, 196033); audio 36.05 (*0-89420-191-3*, 196000) Natl Book.

***U. S. Government Agency Checklists.** Ed. by Seymour Rothstein. 68p. 1995. pap. 50.00 (*0-939190-17-6*) Intl Trademark.

***U. S. Government & International Officials Working with Russia & NIS.** Russian Info & Business Center, U. S. A. Staff. Ed. by Igor S. Oleynik & Natalia Alexeyeva. (Illus.). 105p. 1996. lib. bdg. 49.00 (*1-57751-148-4*) Russ Info & Busn Ctr.

U. S. Government & IRS Tax Cheating. Gordon Leitch, Jr. 7p. 1992. pap. 1.00 (*0-9605734-2-9*) Bicent Era.

U. S. Government & the Vietnam War: Executive & Legislative Roles & Relationships. William C. Gibbons. 992p. (C). 1995. 79.50 (*0-691-00636-9*) Princeton U Pr.

U. S. Government & the Vietnam War: Executive & Legislative Roles & Relationships, Pt. IV. William C. Gibbons. 992p. (C). 1995. pap. text ed. 24.95 (*0-691-00635-0*) Princeton U Pr.

U. S. Government & the Vietnam War: Executive & Legislative Roles & Relationships, 1965-66, Part III. William C. Gibbons. 489p. 1989. pap. text ed. 19.95 (*0-691-02263-1*) Princeton U Pr.

U. S. Government Computer Software for Mainframes & Microcomputers. (Illus.). 152p. (Orig.). (C). 1993. pap. text ed. 95.00 (*1-56806-349-0*) DIANE Pub.

U. S. Government Correspondence Manual. 84p. (Orig.). (C). 1995. pap. text ed. 25.00 (*0-7881-2111-1*) DIANE Pub.

***U. S. Government Directories 1982-1995.** Joyce A. Pearson & Pamela Tull. 200p. 1997. lib. bdg. 45.00 (*1-56308-290-X*) Libs Unl.

U. S. Government Home Give Away: How to Save Thousands of Dollars & Hundreds More on Fees. Ted Thomas. 221p. 1993. pap. 29.95 (*0-9623701-1-8*) New Growth Fin.

U. S. Government I. Laurel Williamson. 72p. (C). 1996. per., pap. 11.49 (*0-7872-1392-6*) Kendall-Hunt.

government leaders are profiled in individual biographies in this 3 volume reference work. Among those included are all U.S. Presidents, historical figures such as Benjamin Franklin & Sam Houston, current news makers such as Madeleine Albright & Jesse Jackson, Jr. In addition to discussion of their lives & works, bibliographies accompany these biographical essays. Other leaders that appear include: George Bush, Bill Clinton, Robert Dole, Alan Greenspan, Thomas "Tip" O'Neill, H. Ross Perot, Colin Powell, William Marcy Tweed & George Wallace. For more information call Salem Press at 800-221-1592 or FAX: 201-871-8668. ***Publisher Provided Annotation.***

U. S. Government Manual, 2 vols. 1994. lib. bdg. 600.00 (*0-8490-8943-3*) Gordon Pr.

U. S. Government Manual 1991-92. 1996. pap. 36.00 (*0-87511-945-X*) Claitors.

***U. S. Government Manual 1996-97.** Federal Register Staff. 1996. pap. 36.00 (*0-614-30821-6*, FUS96P) Claitors.

***U. S. Government Manual 1996/1997.** (Illus.). 925p. 1996. pap. text ed. 110.00 (*1-57979-052-6*) BPI Info Servs.

***U. S. Government Manual 96-97.** USGPO Staff. 1996. pap. 36.00 (*0-16-048675-0*, 009-000-00069-0) USGPO.

U. S. Government Offices in California: A Directory. 3rd ed. (California Information Guides Ser.). 40p. (Orig.). 1987. pap. 16.50 (*0-912102-81-0*) Cal Inst Public.

***U. S. Government Officials Working with Russia & NIS.** 2nd rev. ed. Russian Information & Business Center, Inc. Staff. (Russian Business Library). 400p. 1997. pap. 99.00 (*1-57751-307-X*) Russ Info & Busn Ctr.

U. S. Government Overviews of International Electric Vehicle Activities. Vicki L. Bruch. (Electric Vehicle Information Ser.: Vol. 4, Pts. A-B). (Illus.). 172p. 1996. pap. 75.00 (*0-89934-247-7*, BT031) Bus Tech Bks.

U. S. Government Overviews of International Electric Vehicle Activities. Vicki L. Bruch. (Electric Vehicle Information Ser.: Vol. 4, Pts. A-C). (Illus.). 172p. 1996. lib. bdg. 125.00 (*0-89934-248-5*, BT931) Bus Tech Bks.

U. S. Government Planning & Related Program Documents for Electric & Hybrid Electric Vehicles (Compilation of 6 Key Documents) U. S. Department of Energy Staff. (Electric Vehicle Information Ser.: Vol. 6, Pts. A-F). (Illus.). 262p. 1996. lib. bdg. 245.00 (*0-89934-252-3*, BT933) Bus Tech Bks.

U. S. Government Planning & Related Program Documents for Electric & Hybrid Electric Vehicles (Compilation of 6 Key Documents), Vol. VI, Pts. A-F. U. S. Department of Energy Staff. (Electric Vehicle Information Ser.: Vol. 6, Pts. A-F). (Illus.). 262p. 1996. pap. 195.00 (*0-89934-251-5*, BT033) Bus Tech Bks.

U. S. Government Publications for the School Library Media Center. 2nd ed. Leticia T. Ekhaml & Alice J. Wittig. xii, 156p. 1991. lib. bdg. 24.50 (*0-87287-822-8*) Libs Unl.

U. S. Government Securities Accrued Interest. Financial Publishing Company Staff. 94p. 1997. pap. 204.00 (*0-87600-152-5*) Finan Pub.

U. S. Government Structure Level I: A Federal Immigration & Naturalization Text. 111p. (Orig.). 1996. pap. text ed. 20.00 (*0-7881-2896-5*) DIANE Pub.

U. S. Government Structure Level II: A Federal Citizenship & Naturalization Text. (Illus.). 103p. (Orig.). (C). 1994. pap. text ed. 20.00 (*0-7881-0609-0*) DIANE Pub.

U. S. Government Surplus: A Complete Buyer's Manual. 6th ed. James J. Senay. LC 80-18466. 120p. (Orig.). 1981. pap. 7.95 (*0-936218-01-0*) Rainbow Pub Co.

U. S. Grain: The Political Commodity. Joseph Halow. LC 89-37173. 266p. (C). 1989. lib. bdg. 56.00 (*0-8191-7562-5*) U Pr of Amer.

U. S. Grain Exports, Russian Buyers & Short Supplies 1971-1975. Joseph G. Gavin. LC 90-3473. (Foreign Economic Policy of the United States Ser.). 432p. 1990. reprint ed. text ed. 30.00 (*0-8240-7468-8*) Garland.

U. S. Grant & the American Military Tradition. Bruce Catton. 1985. 20.95 (*0-8488-0279-9*, J M C & Co) Amereon Ltd.

U. S. Greeting Cards Market. 200p. 1995. 1,195.00 (*0-318-00525-5*) Busn Trend.

U. S. Ground Based & Ship Based Electronic Warfare Markets. Market Intelligence Staff. 400p. 1992. 2,700.00 (*1-56753-692-1*, A2377) Frost & Sullivan.

U. S. Ground Forces & the Defense of Central Europe. William P. Mako. LC 83-2817. (Studies in Defense Policy). 137p. 1983. 26.95 (*0-8157-5444-2*); pap. 9.95 (*0-8157-5443-4*) Brookings.

U. S. Guerrilla Warfare. 1987. lib. bdg. 175.00 (*0-8490-3932-0*) Gordon Pr.

U. S. Gunboat Carondolet, 1861-1865. Myron J. Smith, Jr. 195p. 1982. pap. 34.95 (*0-89126-104-4*) MA-AH Pub.

U. S. Hand Tool Market. 255p. 1997. 15.00 (*0-686-32754-3*) Busn Trend.

U. S. Hands off the Mideast! Cuba Speaks Out at the United Nations. 2nd ed. Fidel Castro & Ricardo Alarcon. LC 90-63931. (Illus.). 126p. (Orig.). (C). 1990. pap. 10.95 (*0-87348-629-3*); lib. bdg. 35.00 (*0-87348-630-7*) Pathfinder NY.

U. S. Health Care At the Cross-Roads. 80p. (Orig.). 1992. pap. 15.00 (*92-64-13780-7*) OECD.

U. S. Health Care Crisis: The Fight over Access, Quality, & Cost. Victoria Sherrow. LC 93-51508. (Issue & Debate Ser.). 128p. (gr. 7 up). 1994. lib. bdg. 17.90 (*1-56294-364-2*) Millbrook Pr.

U. S. Health Policy Groups: Institutional Profiles. Ed. by Craig Ramsay. LC 94-27942. 488p. 1995. text ed. 79.50 (*0-313-28618-3*) Greenwood.

U. S. Health Politics: Public Policy & Political Theory. C. R. Paton. 240p. 1990. text ed. 63.95 (*0-566-07101-0*, Pub. by Avebury Pub UK) Ashgate Pub Co.

U. S. Health System: Origins & Function. 3rd ed. Marshal W. Raffel & Norma K. Raffel. 1989. pap. text ed. 41.95 (*0-8273-4336-1*) Delmar.

U. S. Health System: Origins & Functions. 4th ed. Marshall W. Raffel & Norma K. Raffel. LC 93-11931. 302p. 1994. pap. 41.95 (*0-8273-5408-8*) Delmar.

U. S. Health Workforce: Power, Politics & Policy. Marian Osterweis et al. 300p. 1996. pap. 25.00 (*1-879694-11-5*) AAH Ctrs.

U. S. Healthcare Compendium Vol. I: A Demographic & Statistical Analysis. Market Intelligence Staff. 221p. (Orig.). 1994. 795.00 (*0-7889-0127-3*) Frost & Sullivan.

U. S. Healthcare Delivery System in the Year 2000: Opportunities for Suppliers, Goods & Services. 120p. 1993. 2,450.00 (*0-89336-965-9*, B-101) BCC.

U. S. Hegemony & the Project of Universal Human Rights. Tony Evans. (Southampton Studies in International Policy). 256p. 1996. text ed. 59.95 (*0-312-15921-8*) St Martin.

U. S. Hegemony under Siege: Class Politics & Development in Latin America. James Petras & Morris Morley. 224p. (C). 1990. pap. text ed. 19.00 (*0-86091-995-1*, A4503, Pub. by Vrso UK) Norton.

***U. S. High Speed LAN Markets.** Frost & Sullivan. 500p. 1996. write for info. (*0-7889-0616-X*, 5174) Frost & Sullivan.

U. S. Higher Education: A Guide to Information Sources. Ed. by Franklin Parker & Betty J. Parker. (Education Information Guide Ser.: Vol. 9). 688p. 1980. 68.00 (*0-8103-1476-2*) Gale.

U. S. Hispanic Market. Ed. by Peter Allen. 260p. 1984. pap. 295.00 (*0-931634-48-2*) FIND-SVP.

U. S. Historical Fiction: A Whole Language Approach. Nancy Polette. (Illus.). 48p. (J). (gr. 5-8). 1990. pap. 5.95 (*0-913839-85-X*) Pieces of Lrning.

U. S. History. (National Teacher Examination Ser.: NT-62). 1996. pap. 23.95 (*0-8373-8482-6*) Nat Learn.

U. S. History. Burns & Dunfey. 1996. lib. bdg. write for info. (*0-679-92752-2*) Random.

U. S. History. Downey. Date not set. teacher ed. write for info. (*0-314-09865-8*) West Pub.

***U. S. History: Discipline Analysis, Vol. 7P.** Nancy Hewitt. (Women in the Curriculum Ser.). 30p. (Orig.). 1997. pap. 7.00 (*1-885303-30-0*) Towson St Univ.

U. S. History: The Nineteenth Century. rev. ed. Gaeel Beaham. (Learning Packets - History Ser.). (Illus.). 86p. (J). (gr. k-8). 1992. pap. text ed. 19.95 (*0-913705-15-2*) Zephyr Pr AZ.

U. S. History - One, 4 vols. Incl. Vol. 1. America - Its Discovery, Independence & Early Problems. Richard G. Allen. 290p. 1981. 10.95 (*0-86624-001-2*, UT1); Vol. 2. Strengthening the New Nation. Richard G. Allen. 270p. 1981. 10.95 (*0-86624-002-0*, UT2); Vol. 3. Republic Expands. Richard G. Allen. 192p. 1981. 10.95 (*0-86624-003-9*, UT3); Vol. 4. Expansion, Destruction & Reconstruction. Richard G. Allen. 156p. 1981. 10.95 (*0-86624-004-7*, UT4); Teacher's Guide. 5.95 (*0-685-00759-6*, UT5); End of Unit Test. Ed. by Richard G. Allen. 1981. 5.95 (*0-685-73189-8*, UT6); (Illus.). 1981. Set pap. text ed. write for info. (*0-318-51083-9*) Bilingual Ed Serv.

U. S. History - Two, 5 vols. Incl. Vol. 1. Modern America Takes Shape. Richard G. Allan. 242p. 1981. 10.95 (*0-86624-005-5*, UU4); Vol. 2. Imperialism to Progressivism. Richard G. Allan. 192p. 1981. 10.95 (*0-86624-006-3*, UU5); Vol. 3. War, Prosperity & Depression. Richard G. Allan. 180p. 1981. 10.95 (*0-86624-007-1*, UU6); Vol. 4. Roosevelt Years of Depression & War. Richard G. Allan. 184p. 1981. 10.95 (*0-86624-008-X*, UU7); Vol. 5. Cold War Years. Richard G. Allan. 244p. 1981. 10.95 (*0-86624-009-8*, UU8); Teacher's Guide. text ed. 5.95 (*0-685-00761-8*, UV9); End of Unit Test. 5.95 (*0-685-00762-6*, UV0); (Illus.). 1981. Set pap. text ed. write for info. (*0-685-00760-X*) Bilingual Ed Serv.

U. S. History & Geography, Bk. 1: Beginnings to 1877. Center for Learning Network Staff. (Intermediate Social Studies Activities). 192p. (J). (gr. 5-8). 1992. spiral bd. 24.95 (*1-56077-119-4*) Ctr Learning.

U. S. History & Geography, Bk. 2: 1878 to the Present. Center for Learning Network Staff. (Intermediate Social Studies Activities Ser.). 194p. (J). (gr. 5-8). 1992. spiral bd. 24.95 (*1-56077-120-8*) Ctr Learning.

U. S. History & Government, Cornerstone Documents. Louis Reichman et al. 360p. (C). 1992. pap. text ed. 31.19 (*1-56226-094-4*) CT Pub.

U. S. History as Women's History: Knowledge, Power, & State Formation. Ed. by Linda K. Kerber et al. LC 94-27192. (Gender & American Culture Ser.). (Illus.). 460p. (C). 1995. pap. 15.95 (*0-8078-4495-0*); text ed. 37.50 (*0-8078-2185-3*) U of NC Pr.

U. S. History Builder. Research & Education Association Staff. 640p. 1995. pap. text ed. 14.95 (*0-87891-961-9*) Res & Educ.

***U. S. History Crossword Puzzle Bk. 1: Pre-Exploration to the 1990s.** John H. Thompson. 1997. pap. text ed. 7.95 (*0-13-624883-7*) P-H.

***U. S. History Crossword Puzzle Bk. 2: Presidents Washington to Clinton.** John H. Thompson. 1997. pap. text ed. 7.95 (*0-13-624891-8*) P-H.

U. S. History Documented: Liberty & Equality, Vol. II. Murrin. (C). 1995. pap. text ed. 7.00 (*0-15-503677-7*) HB Coll Pubs.

U. S. History Domestic Liberty & Equality. Murrin. (C). 1995. pap. text ed. 7.00 (*0-15-502200-8*) HB Coll Pubs.

U. S. History Plan Guide. Downey. Date not set. write for info. (*0-314-09860-7*) West Pub.

U. S. History Readers Theatre. Nancy Polette. 48p. 1994. pap. text ed. 5.95 (*1-879287-30-7*) Pieces of Lrning.

U. S. History Readings. Michael White. 512p. (C). 1995. per., pap. text ed. 31.44 (*0-7872-1333-0*) Kendall-Hunt.

***U. S. History Through Children's Literature: From the Colonial Period to World War II.** Wanda J. Miller. 240p. 1997. pap. text ed. 25.00 (*1-56308-440-6*) Teacher Ideas Pr.

U. S. History, 1600-1987: A Federal Citizenship & Naturalization Text. (Illus.). 199p. (Orig.). (C). 1994. pap. text ed. 25.00 (*0-7881-0808-5*) DIANE Pub.

U. S. History 1787 to 1865. (Regional Map Packages Ser.). (Illus.). 1989. Incl. 57 maps. ring bd. 50.00 (*0-8160-1339-X*) Facts on File.

U. S. History 1865 to 1980. (Regional Map Packages Ser.). (Illus.). 1989. Incl. 37 maps. 35.00 (*0-8160-1340-3*) Facts on File.

U. S. Hockey Team, 1980: Miracle on Ice. Wayne Coffey. LC 92-21231. (Olympic Gold! Ser.). (Illus.). 64p. (J). (gr. 3-7). 1993. lib. bdg. 15.95 (*1-56711-007-X*) Blackbirch.

U. S. Holocaust Memorial Museum. Eleanor H. Ayer. 72p. (J). 1995. pap. 7.95 (*0-382-24728-0*) Silver Burdett Pr.

***U. S. Holocaust Memorial Museum.** Philip Brooks. LC 95-18633. (Cornerstones of Freedom Ser.). 32p. (J). 1996. lib. bdg. 18.00 (*0-516-20007-0*) Childrens.

U. S. Home Diagnostic & Monitoring Product Markets: An Evolution in Self-Help Spawns a Revolution in Preventive Care. Frost & Sullivan Staff. 333p. 1996. write for info. (*0-7889-0460-4*, 5315) Frost & Sullivan.

U. S. Home Diagnostic & Monitoring Product Markets: Cost Containment Pressures Motivate Self-Testing. Market Intelligence Staff. 289p. 1994. 1,995.00 (*0-7889-0018-8*) Frost & Sullivan.

U. S. Home Healthcare Register, 1994. 1994. write for info. (*1-56363-113-X*) Med Econ.

U. S. Home Improvement Product Markets: DIY: A Bright Spot in a Mature Construction Industry. Market Intelligence Staff. 290p. (Orig.). 1993. 2,595.00 (*1-56753-629-8*) Frost & Sullivan.

U. S. Hood Ornaments & More! Lynn Huntsburger. (Illus.). 217p. 1995. pap. 26.95 (*0-9644110-0-8*) Huntsburger Pub.

U. S. Hospital Infection Control Equipment & Supply Markets: New Product Development Substantially Alters Market Share. Market Intelligence Staff. 360p. 1994. 2,295.00 (*1-56753-961-0*) Frost & Sullivan.

U. S. Hospital Infection Control Equipment & Supply Markets: New Sterilization Systems Lead Industry Growth. Frost & Sullivan Staff. 389p. 1995. write for info. (*0-7889-0267-9*) Frost & Sullivan.

U. S. Hospital Information Systems Market. Market Intelligence Staff. 388p. 1992. 2,600.00 (*1-56753-683-2*, A2546) Frost & Sullivan.

U. S. Hospital Kit & Tray Markets: Manufacturers Meet User Demands with Customization & Safety Features. Market Intelligence Staff. 358p. 1994. 1,895.00 (*0-7889-0107-9*) Frost & Sullivan.

U. S. Hospital Respiratory Therapy Markets: Vendors Strategize in the Face of Economic Pressures. Market Intelligence Staff. 290p. 1994. 1,995.00 (*1-56753-945-9*) Frost & Sullivan.

***U. S. Hospital Respiratory Therapy Product Markets.** Frost & Sullivan Staff. 270p. 1996. write for info. (*0-7889-0555-4*, 5482) Frost & Sullivan.

U. S. Hot Beverage Market. 1994. 995.00 (*0-686-38412-1*, 126) Busn Trend.

U. S. Hot Melt Markets: Technology Is Geared for Fast Packaging Applications. Market Intelligence Staff. 271p. (Orig.). 1994. 2,995.00 (*1-56753-895-9*) Frost & Sullivan.

***U. S. Household Cleaning Products Market.** 436p. 1996. write for info. (*0-7889-0565-1*, 2802) Frost & Sullivan.

U. S. Hurricanes & Windstorms. D. G. Friedman. (DYP Textbook Ser.). 272p. 1990. pap. 180.00 (*1-870255-70-4*) LLP.

U. S. Hydraulic Power Component Markets: Applications Open Opportunities As Industry Experiences Resurgance. Market Intelligence Staff. 1995. 2,495.00 (*0-7889-0250-4*) Frost & Sullivan.

***U. S. Iana (1650-1950)** Compiled by Wright Howes. 652p. 1995. reprint ed. 55.00 (*1-888262-47-8*) Martino Pubng.

U. S. Identification Manual 1986. Drivers License Guide Co. Staff. (Illus.). 700p. 1986. text ed. 103.50 (*0-938964-10-0*) Drivers License Guide.

U. S. Identification Manual, 1993. D. R. Myers Distributing Company Incorporated Staff. (Illus.). 700p. 1993. 149.00 (*0-938964-25-9*) Drivers License Guide.

***U. S. Imaging Software & Scanner Markets: Resolution Revolution.** Frost & Sullivan Staff. 356p. Date not set. write for info. (*0-7889-0510-4*, 5381) Frost & Sullivan.

U. S. Immigration: A Reference Handbook. E. Willard Miller & Ruby M. Miller. LC 96-19542. (Contemporary World Issues Ser.). 304p. 1996. lib. bdg. 39.50 (*0-87436-845-6*) ABC-CLIO.

U. S. Immigration & Citizenship - Your Complete Guide: Everything You Need to Know about Visiting, Working, & Staying in the United States. Allan Wernick. LC 96-51760. 304p. 1997. per., pap. 22.00 (*0-7615-0450-8*) Prima Pub.

U. S. Immigration & Refugee Policy: The Federal Policy & Its Impact on States. (State-Federal Issue Brief Ser.: Vol. 3, No. 2). 17p. 1990. 6.50 (*1-55516-884-1*, 8500-0302) Natl Conf State Legis.

U. S. Immigration Laws: How to Apply. K. Tausif Kamal. 101p. (Orig.). 1993. pap. 14.95 (*1-880365-88-X*) Prof Pr NC.

U. S. Immigration Made Easy. 5th ed. Laurence A. Canter & Martha S. Siegel. (Illus.). 500p. 1996. pap. 39.95 (*0-87337-303-0*) Nolo Pr.

***U. S. Immigration Made Easy.** 6th ed. Laurence A. Canter. 1997. pap. text ed. 39.95 (*0-87337-404-5*) Nolo Pr.

U. S. Immigration Made Easy: An Action Guide. Laurence A. Canter & Martha S. Siegel. LC 88-93057. 620p. (Orig.). 1989. pap. 79.00 (*0-9621876-4-X*) Sheridan Chandler.

U. S. Immigration Made Easy: The Insiders' Guide. Martha S. Siegel & Laurence A. Canter. 636p. 1990. 79.00 (*0-9621876-5-8*) Sheridan Chandler.

U. S. Immigration Policy. Ed. by Richard R. Hofstetter. LC 83-20815. (Duke Press Policy Studies). vii, 310p. 1984. text ed. 43.95 (*0-8223-0476-7*) Duke.

***U. S. Immigration Policy: Restoring Credibility.** 1997. lib. bdg. 253.75 (*0-8490-6177-6*) Gordon Pr.

U. S. Immigration Policy Reform in the 1980s: A Preliminary Assessment. Ed. by Francisco L. Rivera-Batiz et al. LC 90-7377. 160p. 1991. text ed. 42.95 (*0-275-93620-1*, C3620, Praeger Pubs) Greenwood.

U. S. Immunodiagnostic Markets: Industry Leader Aggressively Pursues Market Share Through New Instrumentation. Market Intelligence Staff. 350p. 1994. 2,295.00 (*0-7889-0087-0*) Frost & Sullivan.

***U. S. Immunotherapeutic Markets.** 530p. 1996. write for info. (*0-7889-0558-9*, 5481) Frost & Sullivan.

U. S. Implantable & Interventional Cardiovascular Device Markets. Market Intelligence Staff. (Orig.). 1994. 2,295.00 (*0-7889-0130-3*) Frost & Sullivan.

***U. S. Implantable Cardiovascular Device Markets.** Frost & Sullivan. 305p. 1996. write for info. (*0-7889-0617-8*, 5348) Frost & Sullivan.

U. S. Import Statistics for Agricultural Commodities (1981-1986) Kevin M. Yokoyama et al. 620p. 1988. 89.95 (*0-88738-236-3*) Transaction Pubs.

U. S. Import Statistics for Animal Related Commodities: (1981-1986) Kevin M. Yokoyama et al. 310p. 1989. 69.95 (*0-88738-277-0*) Transaction Pubs.

U. S. Import Statistics for Fisher & Marine-Related Commodities (1981-1986) Kevin M. Yokoyama et al. 280p. 1989. 64.95 (*0-88738-266-5*) Transaction Pubs.

U. S. Import Trade Law, 2 vols. Eugene T. Rossides & Alexandra Maravel. 1350p. 1992. spiral bd. 200.00 (*0-88063-803-6*) MICHIE.

***U. S. Importers Product Guide.** Ed. by C. DePaula. 500p. 1997. pap. 195.00 (*0-915344-77-7*) Todd Pubns.

U. S. Imports: Unit Values Vary Widely for Identically Classified Commodities. (Illus.). 82p. (Orig.). (C). 1995. pap. text ed. 30.00 (*0-7881-1811-0*) DIANE Pub.

U. S. in Norwegian History. Sigmund Skard. LC 76-5263. (Contributions in American Studies: No. 26). 216p. (Orig.). 1976. text ed. 49.95 (*0-8371-8909-8*, SKU/, Greenwood Pr) Greenwood.

U. S. in Prophetic Events. Hilton Sutton. (Mini-Bks.). 32p. 1984. pap. 0.99 (*0-89274-333-6*, HH-333) Harrison Hse.

U. S. in Space: Issues & Policy Choices for a New Era. Ed. by Edmund S. Muskie. 94p. 1988. 19.75 (*0-944237-23-1*); pap. 8.50 (*0-944237-24-X*) Ctr National Policy.

U. S. in the War, 1917-18 see Naval History of the World War

U. S. in the World Economy. rev. ed. (Private Enterprise Market System Program Ser.). (Illus.). 1993. reprint ed. student ed. 4.00 (*0-614-13405-6*) Free Ent Partner.

U. S. in the World Economy. rev. ed. (Private Enterprise Market System Program Ser.). (Illus.). 1993. reprint ed. teacher ed. 14.00 (*0-943447-15-1*) Free Ent Partner.

U. S. in the 20th Century: America since 1945, 2 vols., Vol. 2. James S. Olsen et al. 430p. 1995. pap. text ed. 19.00 (*0-312-08437-4*) St Martin.

U. S. in the 20th Century: America, 1900-1945, 2 vols., Vol. 1. James S. Olson et al. 430p. 1995. pap. text ed. 19.00 (*0-312-10104-X*) St Martin.

U. S. Indian Policy: A Critical Bibliography. Francis P. Prucha. LC 77-6920. (Bibliographical Ser.). 64p. reprint ed. pap. 25.00 (*0-685-44453-8*, 2056714) Bks Demand.

U. S. Industrial Air Filtration Markets. Market Intelligence Staff. (Orig.). 1994. 1,995.00 (*0-7889-0129-X*) Frost & Sullivan.

***U. S. Industrial & Global Trade Outlook.** (Illus.). 800p. 1997. pap. text ed. 69.95 (*0-07-032931-1*) McGraw.

U. S. Industrial & Scientific Laser System Markets Expanding Industrial Sales Lead Resurgence. Market Intelligence Staff. (Orig.). 1994. 1,895.00 (*0-7889-0132-X*) Frost & Sullivan.

U. S. Industrial Battery Markets. Market Intelligence Staff. 289p. 1995. 2,495.00 (*0-7889-0163-X*) Frost & Sullivan.

U. S. Industrial Competitiveness: A Comparison of Steel, Electronics & Automobiles. 1992. lib. bdg. 189.00 (*0-8490-8788-0*) Gordon Pr.

U. S. Industrial Directory, 1995. Ed. by Bowker, R. R., Staff. 1994. 195.00 (*0-8352-3606-4*) Bowker.

U. S. Industrial Fastener Industry: Past Performance, Current Trends & Opportunities for Growth. 260p. 1997. 1,150.00 (*0-317-55203-1*) Busn Trend.

U. S. Industrial Gas Sensor Markets: Migration from Traditional to More Innovative Technologies. Market Intelligence Staff. 237p. 1994. 1,895.00 (*0-7889-0037-4*) Frost & Sullivan.

***U. S. Industrial Gas Sensor Markets: Technological Enhancements Reshape Demand.** Frost & Sullivan Staff. 400p. 1996. write for info. (*0-7889-0550-3*, 5100) Frost & Sullivan.

U. S. Industrial Outlook. 1991. lib. bdg. 250.00 (*0-8490-5022-7*) Gordon Pr.

U. S. Industrial Outlook. U. S. Dept. of Commerce Staff. 700p. 1994. reprint ed. pap. 29.95 (*1-56370-159-6*, USIND) JIST Works.

UV

U. S. Industrial Outlook, 1992: Business Forecasts for 350 Industries. U. S. Department of Commerce Staff. (Illus.). 672p. 1993. pap. 37.00 (*0-89059-015-X*) Bernan Pr.

U. S. Industrial Outlook, 1994: An Almanac of Industry, Technology & Services. annuals 35th ed. International Trade Administration U. S. Dept. of Commerce Staff. 680p. 1994. lib. bdg. 27.95 (*1-878753-54-1*) Hoovers TX.

U. S. Industrial Outlook, 1994: An Almanac of Industry, Technology & Services. U. S. Department of Commerce Staff. (Illus.). 675p. 1994. reprint ed. lib. bdg. 39.00 (*0-89059-022-2*) Bernan Pr.

U. S. Industrial Outlook, 1994: Business Forecasts for 350 Industries. (Illus.). 660p. (Orig.). (C). 1994. pap. text ed. 75.00 (*0-7881-0432-2*) DIANE Pub.

U. S. Industrial Outlook '94. 1994. pap. 37.00 (*0-87511-920-4*) Claitors.

***U. S. Industrial Outlook 97.** Miller & Fairmont Press Staff. 1997. pap. text ed. 135.00 (*0-13-647231-1*) P-H.

U. S. Industrial Personal Protection Equipment Markets: Fashion, Comfort, & Style Replace Regulatory Driven Market. Frost & Sullivan Staff. write for info. (*0-7889-0440-X*, 5281) Frost & Sullivan.

U. S. Industrial Sales & Purchasing Directory. 1360p. 1992. pap. 125.00 (*1-56868-003-1*) Gov Data Pubns.

U. S. Industrial Scale & Weighing Equipment Markets: Systems Approach Tilts the Balance. Market Intelligence Staff. 350p. 1993. 2,395.00 (*1-56753-515-1*) Frost & Sullivan.

U. S. Industrial Solvent Markets: New Environmental Legislation Changes Market Dynamics. Market Intelligence Staff. 260p. 1994. 2,295.00 (*0-7889-0078-1*) Frost & Sullivan.

U. S. Industry Profiles. Diane M. Sawinski. 1995. 99.00 (*0-7876-0533-6*) Gale.

***U. S. Industry Profiles.** 2nd ed. 1997. 99.00 (*0-7876-0856-4*, 00155756, Gale Res Intl) Gale.

U. S. Infantry & Rifle Tactics: The School of the Soldier. (Illustrated Reprint Ser.). (C). 1994. pap. text ed. 17.95 (*0-9638823-1-7*) Stone Eagle.

U. S. Infantry & Rifle Tactics (1861) The Manual of Arms for the Rifle & Rifle Musket. James R. Gunn. (Illustrated Reprint Ser.). (Illus.). 67p. (Orig.). (C). 1993. pap. text ed. 10.25 (*0-9638823-0-9*) Stone Eagle.

U. S. Infantry Equipments 1775-1910. Philip R. Katcher. (Men-at-Arms Ser.: No. 214). (Illus.). 48p. pap. 11.95 (*0-85045-936-2*, 9147) Stackpole.

U. S. Infantry Tactics, 3 vols. in 1. Silas Casey. (Illus.). 810p. 1991. 50.00 (*0-89029-085-7*) Morningside Bkshop.

U. S. Infantry Weapons of World War II. 2nd ed. Bruce N. Canfield. LC 94-78247. (Illus.). 417p. 1996. 35.00 (*0-917218-67-1*) A Mowbray.

***U. S. Information Agency: Options for Addressing Possible Budget Reductions.** (Illus.). 72p. (Orig.). (C). 1996. pap. 25.00 (*0-7881-3573-2*) DIANE Pub.

U. S. Information Policy & Cultural Diplomacy. Frank A. Ninkovich. LC 95-83910. (Headline Ser.: No. 308). (Illus.). 64p. (Orig.). (YA). (gr. 9-12). 1996. pap. text ed. 5.95 (*0-87124-168-4*) Foreign Policy.

U. S. Information Systems for Physician Markets: From the Doctor's Office to the Clinics Without Walls. Frost & Sullivan Staff. 1996. write for info. (*0-7889-0424-8*, 5334-74) Frost & Sullivan.

***U. S. Infrastructure Report: A Recent NTIA Report.** 125.00 (*0-614-18424-X*) Info Gatekeepers.

U. S. Insulated Wire & Cable Industry. 400p. 1996. 1,450.00 (*0-317-55170-1*, L330) Busn Trend.

U. S. Insulated Wire & Cable Markets. 143p. 1992. 1,750.00 (*0-945235-62-3*) Lead Edge Reports.

***U. S. Integral Electrical Motor Markets.** Frost & Sullivan. 454p. 1996. write for info. (*0-7889-0621-6*, 5317) Frost & Sullivan.

U. S. Intelligence: Evolution & Anatomy. 2nd ed. Mark M. Lowenthal. Ed. by Walter Laqueur & Donna R. Spitler. LC 92-15913. (Washington Papers: No. 157). 178p. 1992. text ed. 47.95 (*0-275-94435-2*, C4435); pap. text ed. 16.95 (*0-275-94434-4*, B4434) Greenwood.

U. S. Intelligence & the Soviet Strategic Threat. Lawrence Freedman. LC 85-43345. 236p. 1986. pap. text ed. 13.95 (*0-691-02242-9*) Princeton U Pr.

U. S. Intelligence at the Crossroads: Agendas for Reform. Ed. by Roy Godson et al. (Intelligence & National Security Library). 325p. 1995. 25.95 (*1-57488-036-5*) Brasseys Inc.

U. S. Intelligence Community. Stafford T. Thomas. LC 83-1246. 134p. (Orig.). 1983. pap. text ed. 14.50 (*0-8191-3099-0*); lib. bdg. 45.00 (*0-8191-3098-2*) U Pr of Amer.

U. S. Intelligence Community. 3rd ed. Jeffrey T. Richelson. (C). 1995. pap. text ed. 29.00 (*0-8133-2376-2*) Westview.

U. S. Intelligence Community: An Annotated Bibliography. Mark M. Lowenthal. LC 94-10298. (Organizations & Interest Groups Ser.: Vol. 11). 224p. 1994. text ed. 39.00 (*0-8153-1423-X*, H1765) Garland.

U. S. Intelligence Community: Organizations, Operations & Management, 1947-1989, Guide & Index. National Security Archive Staff & Chadwyck-Healey Staff. Ed. by Jeffrey T. Richelson. (Making of U. S. Policy Ser.). 1990. 900.00 (*0-89887-083-6*) Chadwyck-Healey.

U. S. Intelligence Requirements for the Late 1980s. Leo Cherne. 1986. write for info. (*0-935067-10-8*) Nathan Hale Inst.

***U. S. Intelligent Transportation Systems Market.** Frost & Sullivan. 381p. 1996. write for info. (*0-7889-0618-6*, 5575) Frost & Sullivan.

U. S. Interactive Television Equipment & Software Markets: Energy Market with Unlimited Growth Potential. Date not set. write for info. (*0-7889-0362-4*) Frost & Sullivan.

U. S. Interest Rates & the Interest Rate Dilemma for the Developing World. J. Pierre Benoit. LC 85-12348. (Illus.). 248p. 1986. text ed. 55.00 (*0-89930-131-2*, BIR/, Quorum Bks) Greenwood.

U. S. Interests & Global Natural Resources: Energy, Minerals, Food. Ed. by Emery N. Castle & Kent A. Price. LC 83-42905. 147p. 1983. 20.00 (*0-8018-3099-0*); pap. 12.95 (*0-8018-3106-7*) Resources Future.

U. S. Interests in Africa: Diversity of Decision Making. Helen Kitchen. LC 83-2408. 119p. 1983. pap. text ed. 11.95 (*0-275-91575-1*, B1575, Praeger Pubs) Greenwood.

U. S. International Antitrust Enforcement: A Practical Guide to the Justice Department Guidelines. Joseph P. Griffin. (Corporate Practice Ser.: No. 53). 1990. ring bd. 95.00 (*1-55871-108-2*, BSP-128) BNA Plus.

U. S. International Broadcasting & National Security. James L. Tyson. 151p. (Orig.). 1983. pap. text ed. 7.95 (*0-915071-00-2*) Ramapo Pr.

U. S. International Competitiveness: Evolution or Revolution? John C. Hilke & Philip B. Nelson. LC 88-1137. (Illus.). 246p. 1988. text ed. 55.00 (*0-275-92964-7*, C2964, Praeger Pubs) Greenwood.

U. S. International Estate Planning. William P. Streng. 1168p. 1996. 235.00 (*0-7913-2601-2*) Warren Gorham & Lamont.

U. S. International Tax Forms Manual. Stuart R. Singer. 1992. ring bd. 220.00 (*0-685-69556-5*, FMIT) Warren Gorham & Lamont.

U. S. International Taxation. Joel D. Kuntz & Robert J. Peroni. 1992. ring bd. 355.00 (*0-685-69555-7*, FTFT) Warren Gorham & Lamont.

U. S. International Trade Regulation: A Primer. William H. Lash, 3rd & Robert P. Parker. 200p. 1998. 29.95 (*0-8447-3930-8*) Am Enterprise.

***U. S. International Trade Regulation: A Primer.** William H. Lash & Robert P. Parker, 3rd. 200p. 1998. pap. 16.95 (*0-8447-3931-6*) Am Enterprise.

U. S. Internet Equipment Markets. Frost & Sullivan Staff. 1996. write for info. (*0-7889-0447-7*, 2879-60) Frost & Sullivan.

***U. S. Internet Service Markets.** 304p. 1996. write for info. (*0-7889-0578-3*, 2880) Frost & Sullivan.

U. S. Intervention in Lebanon, 1958 & 1982: Presidential Decision Making. Agnes C. Korbani. LC 90-24275. 160p. 1991. text ed. 47.95 (*0-275-93682-1*, C3682, Praeger Pubs) Greenwood.

U. S. Intervention in the Exchange Market for DM, 1977-80. Paul Wonnacott. LC 82-21263. (Studies in International Finance: No. 51). 38p. 1982. pap. text ed. 11.00 (*0-88165-222-9*) Princeton U Int Finan Econ.

U. S. Intervention in the Post-Cold War World: New Challenges & New Responses. Ed. by Arnold L. Kanter & Linton F. Brooks. 288p. 1994. 25.00 (*0-393-03698-7*) Norton.

U. S. Intervention Policy for the Post-Cold War World: New Challenges & New Responses. Ed. by Arnold L. Kanter & Linton F. Brooks. LC 94-27932. 256p. (C). 1995. pap. text ed. 9.95 (*0-393-96636-4*) Norton.

U. S. Interventionism in South America: The OAS & the Dominican Crisis. Shiv Kumar. LC 86-73078. 250p. 1987. text ed. 22.50 (*0-89891-012-9*) Advent Bks Div.

U. S. Intravenous Customer Equipment & Supply Markets, Vol. Three: Infusion Devices. Market Intelligence Staff. 155p. 1993. 1,295.00 (*1-56753-534-8*) Frost & Sullivan.

U. S. Intravenous Equipment & Supply Markets, Vol. One: Intravenous Solutions. Market Intelligence Staff. 101p. 1993. 1,295.00 (*1-56753-532-1*) Frost & Sullivan.

U. S. Intravenous Equipment & Supply Markets, Vol. Two: Vascular Access Devices. Market Intelligence Staff. 182p. 1993. 1,295.00 (*1-56753-533-X*) Frost & Sullivan.

U. S. Invasion of Panama: The Truth Behind Operation "Just Cause" Independent Commission of Inquiry on the U. S. Invasion of Panama Staff. 150p. (Orig.). 1990. 25.00 (*0-89608-408-6*); pap. 10.00 (*0-89608-407-8*) South End Pr.

U. S. Investment Strategies for Quality Assurance. (Illus.). 223p. (Orig.). (C). 1994. pap. text ed. 50.00 (*0-7881-0300-8*) DIANE Pub.

U. S. Investments in the Latin American Economy. U. S. Department of Commerce Staff. Ed. by Stuart Bruchey & Eleanor Bruchey. LC 76-5039. (American Business Abroad Ser.). (Illus.). 1976. reprint ed. 23.95 (*0-405-09305-5*) Ayer.

U. S. IRS International Tax Compliance Information, 3 vols. Internal Revenue Service Staff. 1992. ring bd. 300.00 (*90-6544-924-8*) Kluwer Law Tax Pubs.

U. S. ISDN Customer Premise Equipment (CPE) Markets. Market Intelligence Staff. 294p. 1994. 3,300.00 (*1-56753-927-0*) Frost & Sullivan.

***U. S.-Israeli Relations at the Crossroads.** Ed. by Gabriel Sheffer. LC 96-19072. 248p. 1997. text ed. 45.00 (*0-7146-4747-0*, Pub. by F Cass Pubs UK); pap. text ed. 22.50 (*0-7146-4305-X*, Pub. by F Cass Pubs UK) Intl Spec Bk.

U. S. IV Therapy Device Markets. 450p. 1995. write for info. (*0-7889-0323-3*) Frost & Sullivan.

U. S. IV Therapy Device Markets. 550p. 1995. write for info. (*0-7889-0338-1*) Frost & Sullivan.

U. S. IV Vein Access Markets: Mini-Series. Date not set. write for info. (*0-7889-0377-2*) Frost & Sullivan.

U. S.-Japan Alliance Diplomacy, 1945-1990. Roger Buckley. (Studies in International Relations: No. 21). (Illus.). 256p. (C). 1992. text ed. 59.95 (*0-521-35141-3*) Cambridge U Pr.

U. S.-Japan Alliance Diplomacy 1945-1990. Roger Buckley. (Studies in International Relations: No. 21). (Illus.). 239p. (C). 1995. pap. text ed. 18.95 (*0-521-55865-4*) Cambridge U Pr.

U. S.-Japan Codevelopment: Update of the FS-X Program. (Illus.). 40p. (Orig.). (C). 1993. pap. text ed. 30.00 (*1-56806-933-2*) DIANE Pub.

U. S.-Japan Cooperative Development: Progress on the FS-X Program Enhances Japanese Aerospace Capabilities. (Illus.). 112p. (Orig.). (C). 1996. pap. text ed. 40.00 (*0-7881-2883-3*) DIANE Pub.

U. S.-Japan Economic Relationship in East & Southeast Asia: A Policy Framework for Asia-Pacific Economic Cooperation. Ed. by Kaori Okuizumi et al. (Significant Issues Ser.: Vol. XIV, No. 1). 295p. (Orig.). 1992. pap. text ed. 16.95 (*0-89206-184-7*) CSI Studies.

U. S.-Japan Energy Policy Considerations for the 1990s. Ed. by John E. Gray & Yoshihiro Nakayama. LC 88-17335. (Illus.). 120p. (Orig.). (C). 1988. pap. text ed. 14.00 (*0-8191-7095-X*) Atl Coun US.

U. S.-Japan Macroeconomic Relations: Interactions & Interdependence in the 1980s. Ed. by Yukio Noguchi & Kozo Yamamura. 320p. 1996. text ed. 50.00 (*0-295-97551-2*) U of Wash Pr.

U. S.-Japan Partnership in Conflict Management: The Case of Korea. Ed. by Chae-Jin Lee & Hideo Sato. LC 93-34391. (Keck Center for International & Strategic Studies: No. 5). viii, 174p. 1993. pap. 10.95 (*0-930607-16-3*) Keck Ctr.

U. S.-Japan Relations: An Agenda for the Future. Ed. by Ronald A. Morse. LC 88-36667. 80p. (Orig.). (C). 1989. pap. text ed. 15.00 (*0-8191-7349-5*); lib. bdg. 29.00 (*0-8191-7348-7*) U Pr of Amer.

U. S.-Japan Relations: New Attitudes for a New Era. Ed. by Richard B. Finn. 221p. 1984. pap. 21.95 (*0-88738-666-0*) Transaction Pubs.

U. S.-Japan Relations: Toward a New Equilibrium. Ed. by Richard B. Finn. 185p. 1983. pap. 21.95 (*0-88738-667-9*) Transaction Pubs.

U. S.-Japan Relations: Towards Burden Sharing. Ed. by Richard B. Finn. 182p. 1982. pap. 21.95 (*0-88738-668-7*) Transaction Pubs.

U. S.-Japan Security Relationship after the Cold War. Francis Fukuyama & Kongdan Oh. LC 93-26325. 125p. 1993. pap. 15.00 (*0-8330-1438-2*, MR-283-USDP) Rand Corp.

U. S.-Japan Strategic Alliances in the Semiconductor Industry: Technology Transfer, Competition, & Public Policy. (Illus.). 118p. (Orig.). (C). 1993. pap. text ed. 40.00 (*1-56806-682-1*) DIANE Pub.

U. S.-Japan Strategic Alliances in the Semiconductor Industry: Technology Transfer, Competition, & Public Policy. Office of International Affairs, National Research Council Staff. 126p. (C). 1992. pap. text ed. 19.00 (*0-309-04779-X*) Natl Acad Pr.

U. S.-Japan Technology Linkages in Biotechnology: Challenges for the 1990's. 98p. (Orig.). (C). 1993. pap. text ed. 40.00 (*1-56806-681-3*) DIANE Pub.

U. S.-Japan Workshop on Ion Temperature Gradient-Driven Turbulent Transport. Horton. (AIP Conference Proceedings Ser.: No. 284). (Illus.). 448p. 1993. text ed. 125.00 (*1-56396-221-7*, AIP) Am Inst Physics.

U. S.-Japanese Agricultural Trade Relations. Emery N. Castle et al. LC 82-7832. 463p. 1982. 35.00 (*0-8018-2815-5*); pap. 21.95 (*0-8018-2814-7*) Resources Future.

U. S.-Japanese Competition in International Markets: A Study of the Trade - Investment Cycle in Modern Capitalism. John E. Roemer. LC 75-620086. (Research Ser.: No. 22). (Illus.). 225p. 1975. pap. text ed. 3.95 (*0-87725-122-3*) U of Cal IAS.

U. S.-Japanese Competition in the Semiconductor Industry: A Study in International Trade & Technological Development. Michael Borrus et al. LC 82-81106. (Policy Papers in International Affairs: No. 17). (Illus.). x, 155p. 1982. pap. text ed. 8.50 (*0-87725-517-2*) U of Cal IAS.

U. S.-Japanese FSX Fighter Agreement. Louis L. Ortmayer. (Pew Case Studies in International Affairs). 50p. (C). 1992. pap. text ed. 3.50 (*1-56927-350-2*) Geo U Inst Dplmcy.

U. S.-Japanese Semiconductor Problem. Timothy J. O'Shea. (Pew Case Studies in International Affairs). 86p. (C). 1995. pap. text ed. 3.50 (*1-56927-139-9*) Geo U Inst Dplmcy.

U. S.-Korean Relations. Donald Clark et al. (Keck Center for International & Strategic Studies: No. 8). viii, 117p. 1995. pap. 10.95 (*0-930607-19-8*) Regina Bks.

U. S. Labor & the Vietnam War. Philip S. Foner. Ed. by Betty Smith. LC 88-23136. 192p. (Orig.). 1989. pap. 7.95 (*0-7178-0672-3*) Intl Pubs Co.

***U. S. Labor in the Twentieth Century: Studies in Working Class Fragmentation & Insurgency.** Paul Le Blanc. (C). Date not set. pap. write for info. (*0-391-04040-5*); text ed. write for info. (*0-391-04039-1*) Humanities.

U. S. Labor Movement & Latin America: A History of Workers' Response to Intervention. Philip S. Foner. LC 87-38134. 228p. 1988. text ed. 55.00 (*0-89789-131-7*, Bergin & Garvey) Greenwood.

U. S. Labor Relations Law: Historical Development. Benjamin J. Taylor & Fred Witney. 256p. 1991. pap. text ed. 30.40 (*0-13-928573-3*) P-H.

U. S. Labour Unions Today: Basic Problems & Trends - A Soviet View. A. Mkrtchian. 203p. 1975. 15.95 (*0-8464-0949-6*) Beekman Pubs.

U. S. LAN Systems Integration Markets. Market Intelligence Staff. 240p. 1994. 1,995.00 (*0-7889-0014-5*) Frost & Sullivan.

U. S. Large Cogeneration Equipment Markets: Competition Intensifies As Industry Matures. Market Intelligence Staff. 1995. 2,395.00 (*0-7889-0213-X*, 5008-10) Frost & Sullivan.

U. S. Latin American Policymaking: A Reference Handbook. David W. Dent. LC 94-27947. 592p. 1995. text ed. 99.50 (*0-313-27951-9*, Greenwood Pr) Greenwood.

U. S.-Latin American Relations. 3rd ed. Michael J. Kryzanek. LC 95-31399. 296p. 1996. text ed. 65.00 (*0-275-95083-2*, Praeger Pubs); pap. text ed. 19.95 (*0-275-95084-0*, Praeger Pubs) Greenwood.

U. S.-Latin American Trade Relations: Issues & Concerns. Juan Luis Colaiacovo et al. Ed. by Michael R. Czinkota. LC 83-2311. 316p. 1983. text ed. 55.00 (*0-275-90966-2*, C0966, Praeger Pubs) Greenwood.

U. S. Latino Literature: An Essay & Annotated Bibliography. Marc Zimmerman. 158p. 1992. pap. 10.95 (*1-877636-01-0*) March Abrazo.

U. S. Law Schools: A Directory of Courses & Other Special Programs Available at the American Law Schools. Abayomi Moses. LC 81-52882. 180p. 1981. 14.00 (*0-9606958-0-X*); pap. 11.00 (*0-9606958-1-8*) Sekoni Pubs.

U. S. Leadership & Postwar Progress. Allan H. Meltzer. LC 93-24884. (Occasional Papers: No. 42). 1993. pap. 9.95 (*1-55815-254-7*) ICS Pr.

U. S. Leadership in Asia & the Middle East: The Credibility of Institutions, Policies & Leadership, Vol. 18. Ed. by Kenneth W. Thompson. LC 85-670. 156p. (Orig.). 1985. pap. text ed. 15.00 (*0-8191-4427-4*); lib. bdg. 45.00 (*0-8191-4426-6*) U Pr of Amer.

U. S. Legislation Relating Human Rights to U. S. Foreign Policy. 4th ed. Ed. by International Human Rights Law Group Staff. xiii, 186p. 1991. ring bd. 35.00 (*0-89941-779-5*, 307370) W S Hein.

U. S. Life-Saving Service: Heroes, Rescues & Architecture of the Early Coast Guard. Lisa W. Shanks & Ralph C. Shanks. LC 95-92424. (Illus.). 262p. 1996. 34.95 (*0-930268-15-6*); pap. 21.95 (*0-930268-16-4*) Costano.

U. S. Life-Saving Service 1889-1915, U. S. Coast Guard Service 1915-1989. Dennis L. Noble & Mike O'Brien. (Illus.). 24p. (Orig.). (YA). (gr. 8 up). 1989. reprint ed. pap. text ed. 2.00 (*0-935549-12-9*) MI City Hist.

U. S. Lifestyles & Mainline Churches: A Key to Researching People in the 90's. Tex Sample. 192p. (Orig.). 1990. pap. 15.00 (*0-664-25099-8*) Westminster John Knox.

U. S. Lighting Fixtures Industry: A Product-by-Product Marketing Analysis & Competitor Profile. 375p. 1997. 1,150.00 (*0-317-55198-1*) Busn Trend.

U. S. Liquid & Solid Separation Equipment Markets. Market Intelligence Staff. (Orig.). 1994. 1,895.00 (*0-7889-0128-1*) Frost & Sullivan.

***U. S. Livestock Market for Veterinary Medical Services & Products.** 2nd ed. Center for Info. Management Staff. Orig. Title: The U. S. Market for Food Animal Veterinary Medical Services. (Illus.). 103p. (Orig.). 1995. pap. 74.50 (*1-882691-08-3*) Am Veterinary Med Assn.

U. S. Long Distance & Reseller Service Markets. Market Intelligence Staff. 755p. 1994. 1,995.00 (*0-7889-0157-5*) Frost & Sullivan.

***U. S. Long Distance Fiber Optic Networks: Technology, Evolution & Advanced Concepts, 3 vols., Set.** (Fiber Optics User's Manual & Design Ser.: Vol. XIII). 1985. 475.00 (*0-614-18469-X*, 152U13) Info Gatekeepers.

***U. S. Long Distance Service & Reseller Markets.** Frost & Sullivan Staff. 472p. 1996. write for info. (*0-7889-0551-1*, 2426) Frost & Sullivan.

U. S. Low End Workstations for the Commercial Marketplace. Market Intelligence Staff. 261p. 1994. 1,995.00 (*0-7889-0177-X*, 2610-70) Frost & Sullivan.

U. S. Lubricant Additive Markets. Market Intelligence Staff. 215p. 1993. 2,900.00 (*1-56753-599-2*) Frost & Sullivan.

U. S. M. C. Sniping: FMFM 1-3B. Orig. Title: USMC Field Manual. (Illus.). 200p. 1991. reprint ed. 14.95 (*0-685-51063-8*) Lancer.

U. S. Machine Tool Industry: Past Performance, Current Trends, & Strategies for the Future. Business Trend Analysts, Inc. Staff. 200p. 1995. ring bd. 1,995.00 (*0-685-24424-5*) Busn Trend.

U. S. Macro Filter Markets: Strategic Analysis of Macro Filter Industry. Frost & Sullivan Staff. 364p. 1996. write for info. (*0-614-15988-1*, 5374) Frost & Sullivan.

***U. S. Macro Filtration Markets: Strategic Analysers of Macro Filter Industry.** Frost & Sullivan Staff. 364p. 1996. write for info. (*0-614-18867-9*, 5374) Frost & Sullivan.

U. S. Macroeconomic Statistics: A Set of Figures & Data Tables. Pingle. (Illus.). 1994. pap. text ed. write for info. (*0-07-066663-6*) McGraw.

U. S. Mail Service Pharmacy Markets: Distribution Channel Comes of Age in the Face of Economic Pressures. Market Intelligence Staff. 450p. 1994. 2,995.00 (*1-56753-936-X*) Frost & Sullivan.

U. S. Man-Made Fiber Industry: Its Structure & Organization Since 1948. David I. Goldenberg. LC 90-14557. 304p. 1992. text ed. 55.00 (*0-275-93360-1*, C3360, Praeger Pubs) Greenwood.

U. S. Manufactured Blasting & Tumbling Abrasive Markets, Materials, & Manufacturers. Dennis M. Zogbi. 84p. (Orig.). 1993. pap. 995.00 (*0-929717-18-X*) Paumanok Pubns.

U. S. Manufacturing Systems Integration. Market Intelligence Staff. 283p. 1994. 2,495.00 (*0-7889-0062-5*) Frost & Sullivan.

U. S. Map & Sticker Book. V. Nichols. (Illus.). 32p. (J). (gr. k-6). 1993. reprint ed. pap. 3.95 (*1-879424-10-X*) Nickel Pr.

U. S. Marine Corp Technical Manual. 1991. lib. bdg. 79.00 (*0-8490-4565-7*) Gordon Pr.

U. S. Marine Corps. Hans Halberstadt. LC 93-13163. (Power Ser.). (Illus.). 128p. 1993. pap. 16.95 (*0-87938-769-6*) Motorbooks Intl.

UV

An Asterisk (*) at the beginning of an entry indicates that the title is appearing in BIP for the first time.

U. S. Marine Corps. J. F. Warner. (Armed Services Ser.). (Illus.). 80p. (YA). (gr. 5 up). 1991. lib. bdg. 22.95 (*0-8225-1432-X*, Lerner Publctns) Lerner Group.

***U. S. Marine Corps & Defense Unification, 1944-47: The Politics of Survival.** Gordon W. Keiser. LC 96-31456. 1996. write for info. (*1-877853-48-8*) Nautical & Aviation.

U. S. Marine Corps Essential Subjects. 1995. lib. bdg. 257.99 (*0-8490-6663-8*) Gordon Pr.

U. S. Marine Corps in Crisis: Ribbon Creek & Recruit Training. Keith Fleming, Jr. LC 89-38175. (Illus.). 165p. (C). 1990. text ed. 29.95 (*0-87249-635-X*) U of SC Pr.

U. S. Marine Corps Scout-Sniper. Peter R. Senich. (Illus.). 230p. 1993. text ed. 39.95 (*0-87364-710-6*) Paladin Pr.

U. S. Marine Corps Scout-Sniper Training Manual. USMC Development-Education Command Staff. 178p. 1989. pap. 14.94 (*0-935856-04-8*) Lancer.

U. S. Marine Corps since 1945. Lee Russell. (Elite Ser.: No. 2). (Illus.). 64p. pap. 12.95 (*0-85045-574-X*, 9401, Pub. by Osprey Pubng Ltd UK) Stackpole.

U. S. Marine Corps Story. J. Robert Moskin. 1992. pap. 27.50 (*0-316-58558-0*) Little.

U. S. Marine Corps 1941-45. Gordon Rottmann. (Elite Ser.). (Illus.). 64p. 1995. pap. 12.95 (*1-85532-497-0*, Pub. by Osprey UK) Stackpole.

U. S. Marine in Vietnam 1965-1974. Charles D. Melson. (Illus.). 64p. 1996. pap. 12.95 (*1-85532-542-X*, Pub. by Osprey UK) Stackpole.

U. S. Marine Insigna. Turner Publishing Company Staff. LC 95-60546. 112p. 1995. 48.00 (*1-56311-211-6*) Turner Pub KY.

U. S. Marine Operations in Korea, 4 vols. U. S. Marine Corps Staff. 1968. reprint ed. Set. 250.00 (*0-403-03719-0*) Scholarly.

U. S. Marine Operations in Korea, 4 vols., Ea. U. S. Marine Corps Staff. 1968. reprint ed. 75.00 (*0-318-68146-3*) Scholarly.

U. S. Marine Operations in Korea Vol. V: Operations in West Korea. Volker Meid. (Illus.). 643p. (C). 1992. reprint ed. lib. bdg. 25.00 (*0-944495-05-2*) R J Speights.

U. S. Marine Operations in Korea, Vol. I: The Pusan Perimeter. C. Montross & Canzona. (Illus.). 271p. (C). 1992. reprint ed. lib. bdg. 25.00 (*0-944495-01-X*) R J Speights.

U. S. Marine Operations in Korea, Vol. II: The Inchon-Seoul Operation. C. Montross & Canzona. (Illus.). 361p. (C). 1992. reprint ed. lib. bdg. 25.00 (*0-944495-02-8*) R J Speights.

U. S. Marine Operations in Korea, Vol. III: The Chosin Reservoir Campaign. C. Montross & Canzona. (Illus.). 432p. (C). 1992. reprint ed. lib. bdg. 25.00 (*0-944495-03-6*) R J Speights.

U. S. Marine Operations in Korea, Vol. IV: The East Central Front. C. Montross & Hicks Kuokku. (Illus.). 342p. (C). 1992. reprint ed. lib. bdg. 25.00 (*0-944495-04-4*) R J Speights.

U. S. Marine Operations in Korea, 1950-53, 4 vols. Lynn Montross & Ca Montross. 1988. reprint ed. Set. lib. bdg. 295.00 (*0-7812-0421-6*) Rprt Serv.

U. S. Marine Operations in Korea, 1950-53, 4 vols. Lynn Montross & Nicholas A. Canzona. 1971. reprint ed. Set. 250.00 (*0-403-00030-0*) Scholarly.

U. S. Marine Operations in Korea, 1950-53, 4 vols., Ea. Lynn Montross & Nicholas A. Canzona. 1971. reprint ed. 50.00 (*0-318-68145-5*) Scholarly.

***U. S. Marines: A Short History.** Henry Berry. Date not set. write for info. (*0-688-11253-6*) Morrow.

U. S. Marines & Amphibious War. Duane Isely & Crowl. (Illus.). 636p. 1988. reprint ed. 15.95 (*0-686-31000-4*) Marine Corps.

U. S. Marines in Action. LC 85-40981. (Villard Military Ser.: The Elite Forces). (Illus.). 96p. 1986. 4.95 (*0-394-74402-0*, Villard Bks) Random.

***U. S. Marines in the Persian Gulf.** 1997. lib. bdg. 251.95 (*0-8490-6072-9*) Gordon Pr.

U. S. Marines in the Persian Gulf, 1990-1991: With the 2D Marine Division in Desert Shield & Desert Storm. 1994. lib. bdg. 250.00 (*0-8490-8529-2*) Gordon Pr.

***U. S. Marines in the Persian Gulf, 1990-1991: With the 2D Marine Division in Desert Shield & Desert Storm.** Dennis P. Mroczkowski. (Illus.). 107p. 1996. reprint ed. pap. 30.00 (*0-7881-3356-X*) DIANE Pub.

U. S. Marines in Vietnam: The Bitter End, 1973-1975. George R. Dunham & David A. Quinlan. (Illus.). 315p. (Orig.). (C). 1995. 45.00 (*0-7881-1877-3*) DIANE Pub.

***U. S. Marines in Vietnam, 1965: The Landing & the Buildup.** Jack Shulimson & Charles M. Johnson. (Vietnam War Ser.: Vol. 9). (Illus.). 274p. 1996. reprint ed. 39.95 (*0-89839-259-4*) Battery Pr.

U. S. Marines on Iwo Jima. 6th ed. Raymond Henri et al. (Elite Unit Ser.). 294p. 1987. reprint ed. 27.95 (*0-89839-095-8*) Battery Pr.

U. S. Maritime Policy: History & Prospects. H. David Bess & Martin T. Farris. LC 81-1503. 238p. 1981. text ed. 55.00 (*0-275-90584-5*, C0584, Praeger Pubs) Greenwood.

U. S. Market for Air Emission Monitors & Analyzers: Market Matures, Competitive Landscape Changing. Frost & Sullivan Staff. write for info. (*0-7889-0439-6*, 5254) Frost & Sullivan.

U. S. Market for Animal Health Products: Past Performance, Current Trends & Strategies for the Future. 280p. 1991. 995.00 (*0-317-55211-2*) Busn Trend.

U. S. Market for Centrifugal & Turbine Pumps. Market Intelligence Staff. 210p. 1993. 2,200.00 (*1-56753-487-2*) Frost & Sullivan.

U. S. Market for Dental Equipment & Supplies. Business Trend Analysts, Inc. Staff. (Illus.). 160p. 1988. spiral bd. 795.00 (*0-685-24421-0*) Busn Trend.

***U. S. Market for Diagnostic & Interventional Catheters & Allied Vascular Devices.** 300p. 1994. spiral bd. 1,475.00 (*1-57936-054-8*, 902) IBC USA.

U. S. Market for Electronic Games, Radio Controlled Hobby Models & Video Games. Frost & Sullivan Staff. 460p. 1996. write for info. (*0-7889-0459-0*, 2850-87) Frost & Sullivan.

U. S. Market for Firearms & Accessories: 1992-1997 Analysis of Markets, Manufacturers. Dennis M. Zogbi. 120p. (Orig.). 1992. pap. text ed. 295.00 (*0-929717-16-3*) Paumanok Pubns.

U. S. Market for Firearms & Ammunitiion: 1995-1996 Economic-Analysis of Markets, Manufacturers & Importers. Dennis M. Zogbi. 175p. (Orig.). 1995. pap. 295.00 (*0-929717-28-7*) Paumanok Pubns.

U. S. Market for Fishing Tackle: A Research & Marketing Guide for the 90's. Dennis M. Zogbi. 141p. 1992. pap. text ed. 295.00 (*0-929717-13-9*) Paumanok Pubns.

U. S. Market for Flat Panel Display: Readout Types. Market Intelligence Staff. 1993. 1,650.00 (*1-56753-497-X*) Frost & Sullivan.

U. S. Market for Flat Panel Displays: Display Systems. Market Intelligence Staff. 1993. 1,650.00 (*1-56753-498-8*) Frost & Sullivan.

U. S. Market for Flat Panel Displays: Panel Types. Market Intelligence Staff. 1993. 1,650.00 (*1-56753-499-6*) Frost & Sullivan.

U. S. Market for Food Animal Veterinary Medical Services see **U. S. Livestock Market for Veterinary Medical Services & Products**

U. S. Market for Household Paper Products: A Strategic Marketing Analysis & Biennial Review. 270p. 1995. 995.00 (*0-317-55202-3*) Busn Trend.

U. S. Market for Integral Horsepower Adjustable Speed Drives. Market Intelligence Staff. 147p. 1993. 2,800.00 (*1-56753-486-4*) Frost & Sullivan.

U. S. Market for Leisure & Recreational Vehicles. 350p. 1995. 895.00 (*0-318-03909-5*) Busn Trend.

U. S. Market for Prepared Animal Feeds & Ingredients: A Product by Product Marketing Analysis & Competitor Profile. (Illus.). 270p. 1996. 1,195.00 (*0-317-63095-4*) Busn Trend.

U. S. Market for Private Satellige Networks. Market Intelligence Staff. 212p. 1993. 2,900.00 (*1-56753-549-6*) Frost & Sullivan.

U. S. Market for Riflescopes & Electronic Weapon Sights: A Technical-Economic Analysis of U. S. Markets, Technologies & Domestic Suppliers. Dennis M. Zogbi. 118p. (Orig.). 1993. pap. text ed. 995.00 (*0-929717-14-7*) Paumanok Pubns.

U. S. Market for Small Household Appliances. 178p. 1992. 1,750.00 (*0-945235-58-5*) Lead Edge Reports.

U. S. Market for Video & Audio Post-Production Software & Hardware: Technology Advances & Changes in the Market Environment Challenge Post Production Manufacturers. 462p. 1995. write for info. (*0-7889-0278-4*) Frost & Sullivan.

U. S. Market for Writing Instruments. 200p. 1996. 995.00 (*0-318-00529-8*) Busn Trend.

U. S. Markets for Incontinence Devices. Richard Bradley. 420p. 1994. spiral bd. 4,200.00 (*0-945510-23-3*) Intl Info Assocs.

U. S. Markets for Infant Products: Past Performance, Current Trends & Opportunities for Growth. 305p. 1988. 795.00 (*0-317-55181-7*) Busn Trend.

U. S. Markets for Wound Care. Richard Bradley. 350p. 1994. spiral bd. 3,500.00 (*0-945510-24-1*) Intl Info Assocs.

U. S. Martial. Tony Harrison. 8900. pap. 6.95 (*0-906427-29-0*, Pub. by Bloodaxe Bks UK) Dufour.

U. S. Martial Web Belts & Bandoliers, 1903-1981. R. Stephen Dorsey. LC 92-74358. (Illus.). 143p. (Orig.). 1993. pap. 20.00 (*0-9631208-1-6*) Collect Lib.

***U. S. Master Accounting Guide, 1996.** 400p. 1996. pap. 29.50 (*0-8080-0084-5*, 11095BLS01) Commerce.

***U. S. Master Employee Benefits Guide, 1997.** 640p. 1996. pap. 39.00 (*0-614-26845-1*, 17797BLS01) Commerce.

***U. S. Master Pension Guide, 1997.** 900p. 1996. pap. 39.00 (*0-614-26846-X*, 15896BLS01) Commerce.

***U. S. Master Tax Guide, FTS Edition, 1997.** 672p. 1996. 32.50 (*0-614-26828-1*, 12396BLS01) Commerce.

U. S. Master Tax Guide, 1994. 660p. 1993. pap. 29.50 (*0-685-67052-X*, 5954) Commerce.

U. S. Master Tax Guide, 1994. rev. ed. 600p. 1992. 29.50 (*0-318-35097-1*, 5884); pap. 28.50 (*0-685-20973-3*, 5954) Commerce.

U. S. Master Tax Guide, 1994: Permanent Edition. 600p. 1993. pap. 45.00 (*0-685-67053-8*, 5884) Commerce.

***U. S. Master Tax Guide, 1997.** 672p. 1996. 49.00 (*0-614-26829-X*, 13196BLS01) Commerce.

***U. S. Master Tax Guide, 1997.** 80th ed. 672p. 1996. pap. 32.50 (*0-614-26827-3*, 12196BLS01) Commerce.

U. S. Mechanical Testing Equipment Markets: Quality Insurance Standardization & Product Liability Are Key Growth Factors. 364p. 1995. write for info. (*0-7889-0289-X*) Frost & Sullivan.

U. S. Media & the Middle East: Image & Perception. Yahya R. Kamalipour. LC 94-33136. (Contributions to the Study of Media & Communications: Vol. 46). 264p. 1995. text ed. 59.95 (*0-313-29279-5*, Greenwood Pr) Greenwood.

***U. S. Media & the Middle East: Image & Perception.** Ed. by Yahya R. Kamalipour. LC 94-33136. 264p. 1997. pap. text ed. 22.95 (*0-275-95914-7*, Praeger Pubs) Greenwood.

***U. S. Media & Yugoslavia, 1991-1995.** James J. Sadkovich. 1998. text ed. write for info. (*0-275-95046-8*, Praeger Pubs) Greenwood.

U. S. Medical & Dental Suction & Irrigation Equipment Markets: Manufacturer's Focus on Portability & Product Integration. Date not set. write for info. (*0-7889-0382-9*) Frost & Sullivan.

U. S. Medical & Pharmaceutical Packaging Markets: Blister Packaging & Roll Stock Lead Industry Growth. Frost & Sullivan Staff. 334p. 1996. write for info. (*0-7889-0410-8*, 5076-54) Frost & Sullivan.

U. S. Medical & Pharmaceutical Packaging Markets: Manufacturers Focus on Cost Containment & Waste Reduction. Market Intelligence Staff. 300p. (Orig.). 1993. 1,695.00 (*1-56753-628-X*) Frost & Sullivan.

U. S. Medical Directory. 8th ed. LC 72-92344. 1989. 150.00 (*0-916524-30-2*, 604/8) US Direct Serv.

U. S. Medical Disposable Product Markets: Specialized Products Show Greatest Growth. Market Intelligence Staff. 316p. 1995. 1,895.00 (*0-7889-0191-5*) Frost & Sullivan.

U. S. Medical Disposable Product Markets, Vol. 3: Needles, Syringes & Related Products. Market Intelligence Staff. 370p. (Orig.). 1994. 1,895.00 (*1-56753-924-6*) Frost & Sullivan.

***U. S. Medical Glove End-User Study.** 80p. 1996. write for info. (*0-7889-0563-5*, 5525) Frost & Sullivan.

U. S. Medical License Examination (USMLE), 3 vols. in 1. (Admission Test Ser.: ATS-104). 1994. pap. 89.95 (*0-8373-5804-3*) Nat Learn.

U. S. Medical License Examination (USMLE) Step I: Basic Medical Sciences. Jack Rudman. (Admission Test Ser.: ATS-104A). 1994. pap. 49.95 (*0-8373-6967-3*) Nat Learn.

U. S. Medical License Examination (USMLE) Step II: Clinical Sciences. Jack Rudman. (Admission Test Ser.: ATS-104B). 1994. pap. 49.95 (*0-8373-6968-1*) Nat Learn.

U. S. Medical Licensing Exam (USMLE) Step III: Patient Management. (Admission Test Ser.: ATS-104C). 1996. pap. 49.95 (*0-8373-6969-X*) Nat Learn.

U. S. Medical Licensure Statistics & Current Licensure Requirements, 1993. 1993. 70.00 (*0-89970-544-8*, OP399093) AMA.

***U. S. Medical Licensure Statistics & Current Licensure Requirements, 1996 Edition.** American Medical Association Staff. 79.95 (*0-614-19695-7*, OP399096WE) AMA.

U. S. Medical Waste Management & Disposal Markets: Huge Impact on Alternate Cites Due to Stringent Regulation Enforcement. Market Intelligence Staff. 560p. 1994. 1,995.00 (*0-7889-0012-9*) Frost & Sullivan.

U. S. Men's Personal Care Product Markets: Manufacturers Shift Focus in Response to Changing Attitudes. Market Intelligence Staff. 371p. 1994. 1,895.00 (*0-7889-0019-6*) Frost & Sullivan.

U. S. Merchant Marine Academy. Photos by Mike Yamashita. (First Edition Ser.). (Illus.). 112p. 1988. 39.00 (*0-916509-45-1*) Harmony Hse Pub.

U. S. Merchant Marines. Turner Publishing Company Staff. LC 93-61016. 128p. 1993. 48.00 (*1-56311-084-9*) Turner Pub KY.

U. S. Merchant Tokens. 3rd ed. Russell Rulau. LC 82-80394. (Illus.). 192p. 1990. pap. 16.95 (*0-87341-137-4*, MT03) Krause Pubns.

U. S. Merchant Vessel War Casualties of World II. Robert M. Browning, Jr. LC 95-10711. (Illus.). 600p. 1996. 49.95 (*1-55750-087-8*) Naval Inst Pr.

U. S.-Mexican Economic Relations: Prospects & Problems. Ed. by Khosrow Fatemi. LC 88-311. (Illus.). 239p. 1988. text ed. 55.00 (*0-275-92955-8*, C2955, Praeger Pubs) Greenwood.

U. S.-Mexico Border Region: Anticipating Resource Needs & Issues to the Year 2000. Cesar Sepulvada & Albert E. Utton. LC 64-63319. 452p. 1982. pap. 15.00 (*0-87404-091-4*) Tex Western.

U. S.-Mexico Borderlands: Historical & Contemporary Perspectives, Vol. 11. Ed. by Oscar J. Martinez. LC 95-21781. (Jaguar Books on Latin America: No. 11). 264p. 1995. pap. 16.95 (*0-8420-2447-6*); text ed. 40.00 (*0-8420-2446-8*) Scholarly Res Inc.

U. S.-Mexico Relations: Agriculture & Rural Development. Ed. by Bruce F. Johnston et al. LC 86-23103. 416p. 1987. 52.50 (*0-8047-1319-7*) Stanford U Pr.

U. S.-Mexico Relations: Economic & Social Aspects. Ed. by Clark W. Reynolds & Carlos Tello. LC 81-86450. xvi, 373p. 1983. reprint ed. 55.00 (*0-8047-1163-1*); reprint ed. pap. 17.95 (*0-8047-1286-7*) Stanford U Pr.

U. S. Microelectronics Industry: Technical Change, Industry Growth, & Social Impact. Nico Hazewindus & N. V. Phillips. LC 82-12191. (Technology Policy & Economic Growth Ser.). (Illus.). 165p. 1982. 99.00 (*0-08-029376-X*, Pergamon Pr) Elsevier.

U. S. Microfiltration Markets: End-Users Define Market Parameters. Frost & Sullivan Staff. 299p. 1996. write for info. (*0-614-15987-3*, 5289) Frost & Sullivan.

U. S. Military: Ready for the New World Order? John E. Peters. LC 92-25627. (Contributions in Military Studies: No. 133). 192p. 1993. text ed. 52.95 (*0-313-28591-8*, PUM, Greenwood Pr) Greenwood.

U. S. Military & Commercial Infrared System Markets: Emerging Materials, Price Reduction Offer Excellent Opportunities. Market Intelligence Staff. 1995. 2,495.00 (*0-7889-0204-0*) Frost & Sullivan.

U. S. Military Combat Aircrew Individual Survival Equipment: WW II to Present, a Reference Guide for the Collector. Michael S. Breuninger. Ed. by Alan R. Wise. LC 93-90752. (Illus.). 201p. 1994. pap. 29.95 (*0-9638400-0-2*) M Breuninger.

U. S. Military Command Control, Communications, & Intelligence, C3I: Service Markets. Market Intelligence Staff. 510p. 1993. 2,495.00 (*1-56753-590-9*) Frost & Sullivan.

U. S. Military Command Control, Communications, & Intelligence (C3I) Services & Equipment Markets: Industry Consolidation Continues, Focus on Tactical Applications. Frost & Sullivan Staff. 1995. write for info. (*0-7889-0273-3*) Frost & Sullivan.

***U. S. Military Communications Equipment Markets.** Frost & Sullivan Staff. 283p. 1996. write for info. (*0-7889-0506-6*, 5211) Frost & Sullivan.

U. S. Military Datalink Markets. 240p. 1995. write for info. (*0-7889-0330-6*) Frost & Sullivan.

U. S. Military Datalink Markets. 240p. 1995. write for info. (*0-7889-0333-0*) Frost & Sullivan.

U. S. Military Display Markets. Market Intelligence Staff. 343p. 1995. 2,195.00 (*0-7889-0156-7*, S207-16) Frost & Sullivan.

U. S. Military Electro-Optic Application Markets: Special Requirements Lead to Dynamic Growth. Frost & Sullivan Staff. Date not set. write for info. (*0-614-97067-9*, 5217-16) Frost & Sullivan.

U. S. Military Electronic Warfare Markets. Market Intelligence Staff. 600p. 1994. 2,950.00 (*0-7889-0022-6*) Frost & Sullivan.

U. S. Military Holsters & Pistol Cartridge Boxes. Edward S. Meadows. (Illus.). 432p. 1987. 45.00 (*0-9618191-0-3*) Ordnance Pubns.

U. S. Military Logistics, 1607-1991: A Research Guide. Charles R. Shrader. LC 92-9263. (Research Guides in Military Studies: No. 4). 384p. 1992. text ed. 69.50 (*0-313-27246-8*, SUK, Greenwood Pr) Greenwood.

U. S. Military Museums, Historic Sites & Exhibits. 2nd ed. Bryce D. Thompson. LC 91-46788. 1992. 13.95 (*0-914862-34-0*) Military Living Pubns.

U. S. Military Non-Mission Avionics Equipment Markets: Aircraft Upgrades, New Technologies Offset Declining Defense Budget. Market Intelligence Staff. 600p. 1994. 2,195.00 (*1-56753-976-9*) Frost & Sullivan.

***U. S. Military Online: A Directory for Internet Access to the Department of Defense.** William M. Arkin. LC 97-11163. 256p. (Orig.). 1997. pap. 29.95 (*1-57488-143-4*) Brasseys Inc.

U. S. Military Policy & the Cold War Endgame. S. J. Cimbala. LC 94-17487. 280p. 1995. 47.50 (*0-7146-4556-7*, Pub. by F Cass Pubs UK); pap. 24.50 (*0-7146-4117-0*, Pub. by F Cass Pubs UK) Intl Spec Bk.

U. S. Military Presence in the Middle East: Problems & Prospects. Robert J. Hanks. LC 82-84308. (Foreign Policy Reports). 77p. 1982. 11.95 (*0-89549-047-1*) Inst Foreign Policy Anal.

U. S. Military Records. James C. Neagles. LC 94-3848. (Illus.). 455p. 1994. 39.95 (*0-916489-55-8*) Ancestry.

U. S. Military Satellite Communications Equipment Markets: Budget Constraints Bring Spending Down to Earth. Market Intelligence Staff. 364p. 1993. 2,295.00 (*1-56753-601-8*) Frost & Sullivan.

U. S. Military Selective Service Act. Roger A. Kessinger. 81p. (Orig.). 1991. pap. 14.95 (*0-922802-16-5*) Kessinger Pub.

U. S. Military Strategy & Force Posture for the 21st Century: Capabilities & Requirements. Richard L. Kugler. LC 93-41904. 1994. pap. 15.00 (*0-8330-1481-1*, MR-328-JS) Rand Corp.

U. S. Military Tracked Vehicles. Fred W. Crismon. LC 92-70681. (Crestline Ser.). (Illus.). 416p. 1992. 29.98 (*0-87938-672-X*, Crestline Pub) Motorbooks Intl.

U. S. Military Trainer Markets. Market Intelligence Staff. (Orig.). 1994. 2,900.00 (*0-7889-0126-5*) Frost & Sullivan.

U. S. Military Trainers & Simulator Markets, Vols. I & II. Market Intelligence Staff. 806p. 1993. 2,900.00 (*1-56753-622-0*) Frost & Sullivan.

***U. S. Military Training & Simulation Markets: Technical Advances, Emphasis on Readiness, Provides Opportunity.** Frost & Sullivan Staff. Date not set. write for info. (*0-7889-0527-9*, 2809) Frost & Sullivan.

U. S. Military Unmanned Vehicle & Robotics Markets. Market Intelligence Staff. 200p. 1994. 1,995.00 (*0-7889-0000-5*) Frost & Sullivan.

U. S. Military Vehicles, Nineteen Forty-One to Nineteen Forty-Five. Compiled by Arthur Bryson. 100p. 1987. pap. 12.95 (*0-938242-16-4*) Portrayal.

U. S. Military Wheeled Vehicles. Fred Crismon. LC 93-49704. (Crestline Ser.). (Illus.). 472p. 1994. 44.95 (*0-87938-907-9*, Crestline Pub) Motorbooks Intl.

U. S. Military's Policy on Homosexuality. (Illus.). 142p. (Orig.). (C). 1992. pap. text ed. 40.00 (*1-56806-026-2*) DIANE Pub.

U. S. Militiaman's Handbook. 1996. lib. bdg. 250.95 (*0-8490-6913-0*) Gordon Pr.

U. S. Millwork Industry: A Product-by-Product Marketing Analysis & Biennial Review. 400p. 1995. 995.00 (*0-317-55196-5*) Busn Trend.

U. S. Mining Machinery & Equipment Industry. 170p. 1991. 1,950.00 (*0-318-00500-X*) Busn Trend.

***U. S. Mint: Commemorative Coins Could Be More Profitable.** (Illus.). 66p. (Orig.). (C). 1996. pap. 25.00 (*0-7881-3606-2*) DIANE Pub.

U. S. Mint & Coinage. Don Taxay. LC 66-18413. 1983. reprint ed. lib. bdg. 40.00 (*0-915262-68-1*); reprint ed. suppl. ed. (*0-318-55576-X*) S J Durst.

U. S. Misc. Vets & Widows Index, 1890. 1983. 45.00 (*0-89593-648-8*) Accelerated Index.

U. S. Mkt. for Nonprescription Drugs. 255p. 1997. 1,450.00 (*0-318-00516-6*) Busn Trend.

U. S. Mobil Communications Service Markets. 554p. 1995. write for info. (*0-7889-0307-1*) Frost & Sullivan.

U S Modem Markets: Wireless Saves the Day. Market Intelligence Staff. 350p. 1994. 1,995.00 (*1-56753-986-6*) Frost & Sullivan.

UV

U. S. Monetary Policy. rev. ed. American Assembly Staff. Ed. by Neil H. Jacoby. LC 79-164586. (Select Bibliographies Reprint Ser.). 1977. reprint ed. 20.95 (*0-8369-5702-4*) Ayer.

U. S. Monoclonal Antibody Markets: Introduction of New Applications Will Result in a Shift in Revenue Application. Frost & Sullivan Staff. 554p. 1996. write for info. (*0-7889-0450-7*, 5405) Frost & Sullivan.

U. S. Motion Picture Theatre Industry: A Strategic Marketing Analysis & Biennial Review. 200p. 1995. 995.00 (*0-317-55186-8*) Busn Trend.

***U. S. Motor Drives, Feedback, Elements & Variables Speed Drive Markets: New Technologies Offer Additional Opportunities.** Frost & Sullivan Staff. 270p. 1996. write for info. (*0-7889-0508-2*, 5455) Frost & Sullivan.

U. S. Multinationals & Worker Participation in Management: The American Experience in the European Community. Ton Devos. LC 80-23597. xv, 229p. 1981. text ed. 49.95 (*0-89930-004-9*, DUM/, Quorum Bks) Greenwood.

U. S. Multivendor & Third-Party Maintenance Markets: Break-Fax: Out, Full Service: In. Frost & Sullivan Staff. 331p. 1996. write for info. (*0-7889-0413-2*, 5376-71) Frost & Sullivan.

U. S. M1 Carbines: Wartime Production. 2nd ed. Craig Riesch. (For Collectors Only Ser.). (Illus.). 131p. (Orig.). 1994. pap. 16.95 (*1-882391-12-8*) N Cape Pubns.

U. S. N. Seal Combat Manual. 240p. 1985. pap. 19.95 (*0-318-36165-5*) Lancer.

U. S. National Bibliography & the Copyright Law: An Historical Study. Joseph W. Rogers. LC 60-15545. 119p. reprint ed. pap. 34.00 (*0-317-10597-3*, 2050963) Bks Demand.

U. S. National Economic Policy, 1917-1985. Anthony S. Campagna. LC 86-30316. 640p. 1987. text ed. 55.00 (*0-275-92426-2*, C2426, Praeger Pubs) Greenwood.

U. S. National Economic Policy, 1917-1985. Anthony S. Campagna. LC 86-30316. (Illus.). 662p. 1988. pap. text ed. 21.95 (*0-275-92907-8*, B2907, Praeger Pubs) Greenwood.

U. S. National Health Policy: An Analysis of the Federal Role. Jennie J. Kronenfeld & Marcia L. Whicker. LC 84-2169. 304p. 1984. text ed. 65.00 (*0-275-91207-8*, C1207, Praeger Pubs) Greenwood.

U. S. National Income & Product Accounts: Selected Topics. Murray F. Foss. LC 82-11081. (National Bureau of Economic Research Studies in Income & Wealth: No. 47). (Illus.). 448p. (C). 1983. lib. bdg. 60.00 (*0-226-25728-2*) U Ch Pr.

U. S. National Labor Relations Board: Annual Report, 1936-1965, Vols. 1-30. Bound set. 405.00 (*0-686-90076-6*) Rothman.

U. S. National Plant Germplasm System. National Research Council Staff. 196p. 1990. text ed. 19.95 (*0-309-04390-5*) Natl Acad Pr.

U. S. National Quadrennial Report 1987-1990 to the International Union of Geodesy & Geophysics. Ed. by M. A. Shea et al. (Special Publications). 1186p. 1991. 28.00 (*0-87590-787-3*) Am Geophysical.

U. S. National Report to FIG, 1990. Ed. by James R. Plasker. (Surveying & Land Information Systems Journal Ser.: Vol. 50, No. 2). 124p. 1990. 20.00 (*0-614-06107-5*, SM502) Am Congrs Survey.

***U. S. National Report to International Union of Geodesy & Geophysics, 1991-1994, 2 vols.** Ed. by Roger A. Pielke. 1432p. 1995. text ed. 75.00 (*0-87590-863-2*) Am Geophysical.

U. S. National Report to the International Union of Geodesy & Geophysics 1967-1970. 504p. reprint ed. pap. 5.00 (*0-317-66486-7*) Am Geophysical.

U. S. National Report to the International Union of Geodesy & Geophysics, 1983-1986, Vol. 3. 1108p. 1975. reprint ed. pap. 28.00 (*0-87590-750-4*) Am Geophysical.

U. S. National Security: Policymakers, Processes & Politics. 2nd ed. Sam C. Sarkesian. LC 94-91657. 273p. 1994. pap. text ed. 19.95 (*1-55587-411-8*) Lynne Rienner.

U. S. National Security Policy & Strategy: Documents & Policy Proposals. Sam C. Sarkesian & Robert A. Vitas. LC 88-10244. (Documentary Reference Collections). 466p. 1988. text ed. 65.00 (*0-313-25482-6*, SML/, Greenwood Pr) Greenwood.

U. S. National Security Policy & Strategy, 1987-1994: Documents & Policy Proposals. Robert A. Vitas & John A. Williams. LC 95-47147. (Documentary Reference Collections). 352p. 1996. text ed. 75.00 (*0-313-29635-9*, Greenwood Pr) Greenwood.

U. S. National Security Policy & the Soviet Union: Persistent Regularities & Extreme Contingencies. Richard J. Stoll. 279p. 1990. text ed. 39.95 (*0-87249-678-3*); pap. text ed. 21.95 (*0-87249-698-8*) U of SC Pr.

U. S. National Security Policy Groups: Institutional Profiles. Cynthia Watson. LC 89-23381. 320p. 1990. text ed. 69.50 (*0-313-25733-7*, WMY/, Greenwood Pr) Greenwood.

U. S. National Security Strategy for the 1990s. Ed. by Daniel J. Kaufman et al. LC 90-2763. 304p. 1991. text ed. 42.50 (*0-8018-4163-1*); pap. text ed. 15.95 (*0-8018-4164-X*) Johns Hopkins.

U. S. National Wage Stabilization Board, Jan. 1, 1946-Feb. 24, 1947: A Documentary History with Brief Explanations of Its Formation, Organization & Activities. viii, 594p. 1973. reprint ed. text ed. 25.00 (*0-8377-0901-6*) Rothman.

U. S. Natural Gas Market in the 1990s. Gerald Pollio. 20p. 1991. pap. 10.00 (*0-918714-27-3*) Intl Res Ctr Energy.

U. S. Naval Academy: An Illustrated History. 2nd ed. Jack Sweetman. (Illus.). 328p. 1995. 37.95 (*1-55750-143-2*) Naval Inst Pr.

***U. S. Naval Academy: An Illustrated History.** 2nd limited ed. Jack Sweetman. (Illus.). 328p. 1995. boxed 100.00 (*1-55750-147-5*) Naval Inst Pr.

U. S. Naval & Marine Corps Reserve Aviation, Vol. I: 1916-1942 Chronology. Wayne H. Heiser. 189p. 1991. pap. 38.95 (*0-89126-168-0*) MA-AH Pub.

U. S. Naval Aviation Patches: Aircraft Carriers, Carrier Air Wings, Support Establishment. Roberts. LC 95-67278. (Illus.). 160p. 1995. 29.95 (*0-88740-753-6*) Schiffer.

U. S. Naval Communications Intelligence Activities. Laurance Safford & J. N. Wenger. 91p. 1993. pap. 18.80 (*0-89412-229-0*) Aegean Park Pr.

U. S. Naval Cryptographic Activities in the Philippines Prior to World War II. Ed. by Sheila Carlisle. 108p. 1994. pap. 20.80 (*0-89412-222-3*) Aegean Park Pr.

***U. S. Naval Experiences in the North Pacific During World War II: Selected Documents.** Ed. by Ronald H. Spector. (Illus.). 98p. 1996. reprint ed. pap. 25.00 (*0-7881-3422-1*) DIANE Pub.

U. S. Naval Handguns, 1808-1911. Fredrick R. Winter. LC 90-60327. (Illus.). 128p. 1990. 26.00 (*0-917218-42-6*) A Mowbray.

U. S. Naval History: A Bibliography, 2 vols., Set. 1994. lib. bdg. 600.00 (*0-8490-5714-0*) Gordon Pr.

U. S. Naval Railway Batteries in France. Frwd. by Joseph Metcalf, 3rd. (Illus.). 97p. (C). 1995. reprint ed. pap. text ed. 25.00 (*0-7881-2306-8*) DIANE Pub.

U. S. Naval Vessels, 1943. Prod. by U. S. Navy Department Staff. (Illus.). 288p. 1986. 26.95 (*0-87021-724-0*) Naval Inst Pr.

U. S. Navy. Corinne J. Naden & Rose Blue. LC 92-13430. (Defending Our Country Ser.). (Illus.). 64p. (J). (gr. 3-6). 1993. pap. 5.95 (*1-56294-753-2*); lib. bdg. 16.40 (*1-56294-216-6*) Millbrook Pr.

U. S. Navy. Kathy Pelta. (Armed Services Ser.). (Illus.). 88p. (YA). (gr. 5 up). 1990. lib. bdg. 22.95 (*0-8225-1435-4*, Lerner Publctns) Lerner Group.

***U. S. Navy: A History.** Nathan Miller. (Illus.). 312p. 1997. pap. 22.95 (*1-55750-595-0*) Naval Inst Pr.

U. S. Navy Aircraft 1921-1941, U. S. Marine Corps Aircraft 1914-1959: Two Classics in One Volume. William T. Larkins. LC 88-17753. (Illus.). 203p. 1995. 39.95 (*0-88740-742-0*) Schiffer.

U. S. Navy & Marine Corps Air Power Directory: World Air Power. Ed. by David Donald & Jon Lake. (Illus.). 224p. 1992. 29.95 (*1-880588-02-1*) AIRtime Pub.

U. S. Navy Cag Aircraft, Part 2: Attack Aircraft. Bert Kinzey & Ray Leader. (Colors & Markings Ser.: Vol. 16). (Illus.). 64p. 1990. pap. 12.95 (*0-8306-7540-X*, 24540) TAB Bks.

U. S. Navy Camouflage, Pt. 1: Of the World War Two Era. rev. ed. Thomas F. Walkowiak. LC 89-80590. (Illus.). 52p. 1989. reprint ed. pap. 9.95 (*0-944055-01-X*) Floating Drydock.

U. S. Navy Diver's Handbook. Ed. by Best Publishing Co. Staff. (Illus.). 212p. (C). 1995. text ed. 27.50 (*0-941332-16-0*, D005) Best Pub Co.

U. S. Navy Diving Manual, Vol. I. Ed. by Best Publishing Co. Staff. (Illus.). 500p. (C). 1996. ring bd. 57.00 (*0-941332-18-7*, D002) Best Pub Co.

U. S. Navy Diving Manual, Vol. 2: Mixed-Gas Diving. U. S. Navy Staff. (Illus.). 225p. (C). 1997. ring bd. 37.00 (*0-941332-22-5*, D003) Best Pub Co.

U. S. Navy F-4 Phantoms, Pt. 1: Atlantic Coast Markings. Bert Kinzey & Ray Leader. (Colors & Markings Ser.: Vol. 17). (Illus.). 64p. 1991. pap. 12.95 (*0-8306-4541-1*, 24541) TAB Bks.

***U. S. Navy Fighter Squadrons in World War II.** Barrett Tillman. 1997. 22.95 (*0-933424-74-4*) Specialty Pr.

U. S. Navy Fights. Walter A. Roberts. (Essay Index Reprint Ser.). 1977. 23.95 (*0-8369-2068-6*) Ayer.

U S Navy in Pensacola: From Sailing Ships to Naval Aviation, 1825-1930. George F. Pearce. LC 80-12167. (Illus.). vii, 207p. 1980. 29.95 (*0-8130-0665-1*) U Press Fla.

U. S. Navy Seabees: Since Pearl Harbor. Jay Kimmel. (Illus.). 220p. (Orig.). 1995. pap. 25.00 (*0-942893-03-4*) CoryStevens Pub.

U. S. Navy Seals. Robert Genat. (Europa Militaria Ser.: No. 16). (Illus.). 64p. 1994. pap. 15.95 (*1-85915-000-4*, Pub. by Windrow & Green UK) Motorbooks Intl.

U. S. Navy SEALs. Hans Halberstadt. (Power Ser.). (Illus.). 128p. 1993. pap. 16.95 (*0-87938-781-5*) Motorbooks Intl.

U. S. Navy SEALs. Thomas Streissguth. (Serving Your Country Ser.). (Illus.). 48p. (J). (gr. 3-9). 1995. lib. bdg. 13.35 (*1-56065-282-9*) Capstone Pr.

U. S. Navy SEALs in Action. Hans Halberstadt. (Illus.). 144p. 1995. 17.95 (*0-87938-993-1*) Motorbooks Intl.

U. S. Navy Ships & Coast Guard Cutters: A Naval Institute Book for Young Readers. M. D. Van Orden. LC 89-13539. (Illus.). 96p. (J). (gr. 5-11). 1990. lib. bdg. 18.95 (*0-87021-212-5*) Naval Inst Pr.

U. S. Navy, the Mediterranean, & the Cold War, 1945-1947. Edward J. Sheehy. LC 91-33479. (Contributions in Military Studies: No. 126). 208p. 1992. text ed. 49.95 (*0-313-27615-3*, SYR, Greenwood Pr) Greenwood.

U. S. Negotiation of Voluntary Restraint Agreements in Steel, 1984: Domestic Sources of International Economic Diplomacy. Robert S. Walters. (Pew Case Studies in International Affairs). 69p. (C). 1994. pap. text ed. 3.50 (*1-56927-107-0*) Geo U Inst Dplmcy.

U. S. Negotiations with the Republic of South Vietnam, 1961. Roger Hilsman & Stewart Lawrence. (Pew Case Studies in International Affairs). 67p. (C). 1988. pap. text ed. 3.50 (*1-56927-338-3*) Geo U Inst Dplmcy.

U. S. Neocolonialism in Africa. Stuart J. Seborer. LC 73-87863. 270p. reprint ed. pap. 77.00 (*0-317-28062-7*, 2025548) Bks Demand.

U. S. Network Management System & Service Markets. Market Intelligence Staff. 272p. 1994. 2,800.00 (*1-56753-988-2*) Frost & Sullivan.

***U. S. Network Systems Integration Markets.** Frost & Sullivan Staff. 323p. 1996. write for info. (*0-7889-0595-3*, 2695) Frost & Sullivan.

U. S. Network Systems Integration Markets: New Revenue Growth Offers Great Potential to New Entrants. Market Intelligence Staff. 180p. 1993. 3,150.00 (*1-56753-610-7*) Frost & Sullivan.

U. S. Neurodiagnostic & Neurosurgical Equipment Markets. Market Intelligence Staff. 1995. 1,995.00 (*0-7889-0198-2*, 5197-57) Frost & Sullivan.

U. S. Neurodiagnostic & Neurosurgical Product Markets. Market Intelligence Staff. 414p. 1995. 1,995.00 (*0-7889-0151-6*) Frost & Sullivan.

U. S. News & World Report Stylebook for Writers & Editors. 7th ed. Ed. by Robert O. Grover. LC 93-31050. (Illus.). 198p. 1994. 10.55 (*0-89193-353-0*) U S News & Wrld.

***U. S. News Coverage of Racial Minorities: A Sourcebook, 1934-1996.** Ed. by Beverly A. Keever et al. LC 96-53850. 392p. 1997. text ed. 85.00 (*0-313-29671-5*, Greenwood Pr) Greenwood.

U. S. Newspaper Program: National Union List. 3rd ed. Online Computer Library Center, Inc. Staff. 1989. fiche 275.00 (*0-685-25894-7*) OCLC Online Comp.

U. S. NGOs (Non-Governmental Organizations) Viet Nam Programs: A Directory. Ed. by Dao N. Spencer. 126p. (Orig.). (C). 1994. pap. text ed. 25.00 (*0-7881-0399-7*) DIANE Pub.

U. S. Nonproliferation Policy in Action: South Asia. Shrikant Paranjpe. LC 87-80662. 192p. 1988. text ed. 22.50 (*0-938719-18-1*, Envoy Pr) Apt Bks.

U. S., Norway & the Cold War 1954-1960. Berdal. 1997. text ed. 49.95 (*0-312-16281-2*) St Martin.

U. S. Nuclear Engineering Education: Status & Prospects. National Research Council Staff. 180p. (C). 1990. pap. text ed. 19.00 (*0-309-04280-1*) Natl Acad Pr.

U. S. Nuclear Strategy for the Post-Cold War Era. Glenn C. Buchan. LC 94-11713. 1994. pap. 15.00 (*0-8330-1531-1*, MR-420-RC) Rand Corp.

U. S. Nuclear Strategy in the New World. Cimbala. 1994. 46.95 (*1-56924-986-5*) Marlowe & Co.

U. S. Nuclear Weapons in Europe: Issues & Alternatives. Jeffrey Record. LC 74-23433. (Studies in Defense Policy). 70p. 1974. pap. 8.95 (*0-8157-7365-X*) Brookings.

U. S. Numbered Highways. 1989. 49.25 (*1-56051-039-0*, US-4) AASHTO.

U. S. Nursing Home Industry. 170p. 1989. 750.00 (*0-318-00523-9*) Busn Trend.

U. S. Nutritionals Markets. (Market Research Reports: No. 422). (Illus.). 155p. 1994. 795.00 (*0-614-09921-8*) Theta Corp.

U. S. Occupational Outlook Handbook. 1991. 22.00 (*0-87511-926-3*); pap. 17.00 (*0-87511-925-5*) Claitors.

U. S. OEM Coating Markets. Market Intelligence Staff. 256p. 1994. 2,395.00 (*0-7889-0145-1*) Frost & Sullivan.

U. S. of A. the Republic: How You Lost It, How You Get It Back. Lee Brobst & A. F. Beddoe. (Illus.). 96p. (Orig.). 1992. pap. 15.00 (*1-881201-03-1*) S & J Unltd.

U. S. Office Equipment Market. 275p. 1987. 750.00 (*0-318-02833-6*) Busn Trend.

U. S. Officers of the Continental Army, 1775-1783. (Illus.). lib. bdg. 60.00 (*0-89593-452-3*) Accelerated Index.

U. S. Official Propaganda During the Vietnam War, 1965-1973: The Limits of Persuasion. Caroline Page. LC 95-41263. 1996. pap. 18.95 (*0-7185-1999-X*, Pub. by Leicester Univ Pr) Bks Intl VA.

U. S. Official Propaganda During the Vietnam War, 1965-1973: The Limits of Persuasion. Caroline Page. LC 95-41263. 240p. 1996. pap. 18.95 (*0-7185-1376-2*, Pub. by Cassell Pubng UK) LPC InBook.

U. S. Official Statements Regarding Israeli Settlements & the Fourth Geneva Convention. Ed. by Jody Boudreault et al. (U. S. Official Statements Ser.). 180p. (Orig.). (C). 1992. pap. text ed. 19.95 (*0-88728-244-X*) Inst Palestine.

U. S. Official Statements Regarding the Status of Jerusalem. Ed. by Jody Boudreault et al. (U. S. Official Statements Ser.). 180p. (Orig.). (C). 1992. pap. text ed. 19.95 (*0-88728-245-8*) Inst Palestine.

U. S. Official Statements Regarding U. N. Resolution 242. Ed. by Jody Boudreault et al. (U. S. Official Statements Ser.). 184p. (Orig.). (C). 1992. pap. text ed. 19.95 (*0-88728-239-3*) Inst Palestine.

***U. S. Oil & Gas Companies Interested in Russia & NIS.** Russian Information & Business Center, Inc. Staff. 250p. 1997. pap. 99.00 (*1-57751-232-4*) Russ Info & Busn Ctr.

U. S. Oil Import Vulnerability: The Technical Replacement Capability. (Illus.). 135p. (Orig.). (C). 1993. pap. text ed. 35.00 (*1-56806-684-8*) DIANE Pub.

U. S. Oil Production: The Effect of Low Oil Prices. 1990. lib. bdg. 79.95 (*0-8490-4059-0*) Gordon Pr.

U. S. Olympians. Zachary Kent. LC 92-4812. (Cornerstones of Freedom Ser.). (Illus.). 32p. (J). (gr. 3-6). 1992. lib. bdg. 18.00 (*0-516-06659-5*) Childrens.

U. S. On-Premises Telecommunications Equipment Markets. Market Intelligence Staff. 217p. 1994. 2,595.00 (*1-56753-946-7*) Frost & Sullivan.

U. S. One: Maine to Florida. Federal Writers' Project. 344p. 1938. reprint ed. 49.00 (*0-403-02208-8*) Somerset Pub.

U. S. One, Maine to Florida. Federal Writers' Project Staff & Writers Program-WPA Staff. (American Guide Ser.). 1989. reprint ed. lib. bdg. 59.00 (*0-7812-1064-X*, 1064) Rprt Serv.

***U. S. Open: America's Grand Slam.** Ed. by Time-Life Books Editors. LC 97-13592. (Illus.). 192p. 1997. write for info. (*0-7835-5260-2*) Time-Life.

U. S. Open: Ft. Worth 1984. Jim Marfia. (Illus.). 98p. (Orig.). 1985. pap. 5.00 (*0-931462-40-1*) Chess Ent.

U. S. Open: Golf's Ultimate Challenge. 2nd ed. Robert Sommers. (Illus.). 357p. 1989. reprint ed. 28.00 (*0-940889-23-4*) Classics Golf.

U. S. Open: Golf's Ultimate Challenge. 2nd ed. Robert Sommers. (Illus.). 432p. 1996. 30.00 (*0-19-510049-2*) OUP.

U. S. Open: St. Paul 1982. Jim Marfia & John Watson. (Illus.). 83p. (Orig.). 1982. pap. 5.00 (*0-931462-21-5*) Chess Ent.

U. S. Open: 1983. Jim Marfia. (U. S. Tournament Ser.). (Illus.). 100p. (Orig.). 1984. pap. 6.00 (*0-931462-29-0*) Chess Ent.

U. S. Operator Services & Calling Card Markets: Deregulation & Dial-Around Impact Markets. Frost & Sullivan Staff. 675p. 1996. write for info. (*0-7889-0465-5*, 2882) Frost & Sullivan.

U. S. Operator Services & Card Calling Markets. Market Intelligence Staff. 334p. (Orig.). 1994. 1,895.00 (*0-7889-0030-7*) Frost & Sullivan.

U. S. Ophthalmic Diagnostic Equipment Markets: Manufacturers Visualize High Growth from Emerging Technologies. Market Intelligence Staff. 320p. 1994. 1,895.00 (*0-7889-0050-1*) Frost & Sullivan.

U. S. Ophthalmic Surgical Device Markets. Market Intelligence Staff. 288p. (Orig.). 1994. 1,895.00 (*0-7889-0103-6*) Frost & Sullivan.

U. S. Options in Central America. Eduardo Ulibarri. 1982. write for info. (*0-318-63149-0*) Cuban Amer Natl Fndtn.

U. S. Oral OTC Markets: Line Extensions & Rx to OTC Switches Support Self Medication Trends. Market Intelligence Staff. 360p. 1994. 1,995.00 (*1-56753-930-0*) Frost & Sullivan.

***U. S. Organ Transplant & Related Product Markets.** Frost & Sullivan. 322p. 1996. write for info. (*0-7889-0609-7*, 5404) Frost & Sullivan.

U. S. Organ Transplantation Products & Artificial Organs. Market Intelligence Staff. 310p. 1994. 1,995.00 (*0-7889-0165-6*) Frost & Sullivan.

***U. S. Orientalisms: Race, Nation, & Gender in Literature, 1790-1890.** Malini J. Schueller. (C). 1997. 42.50 (*0-472-10885-9*) U of Mich Pr.

U. S. Orthopedic Prosthetic Device & Ins. Market Intelligence Staff. 367p. 1994. 2,295.00 (*0-7889-0081-1*) Frost & Sullivan.

U. S. Orthopedic Soft Goods & Cast Room Product Markets. Market Intelligence Staff. 453p. 1994. 1,995.00 (*0-7889-0079-X*) Frost & Sullivan.

U. S. Orthopedic Soft Goods Company Profiles: Manufacturers Expand Beyond Classic Markets. Frost & Sullivan Staff. 421p. 1995. write for info. (*0-7889-0298-9*) Frost & Sullivan.

***U. S. Orthopedic Soft Goods Product Markets.** Frost & Sullivan. 475p. 1996. write for info. (*0-7889-0607-0*, 5314) Frost & Sullivan.

U. S. Osteoporosis Markets. Market Intelligence Staff. 412p. 1994. 2,295.00 (*0-7889-0122-2*) Frost & Sullivan.

U. S. Outdoor Atlas & Recreation Guide: A State by State Guide to over 5,000 Wildlife & Outdoor Recreation Areas. rev. ed. John O. Jones. LC 93-46935. 1994. pap. 19.95 (*0-395-66329-6*) HM.

U. S. Outline Maps. Randy L. Womack. (Illus.). 112p. (gr. 4 up). 1996. student ed. 10.95 (*1-56500-019-6*) Gldn Educ.

U. S. Ownership of Firms in Canada: Issues & Policy Approaches. Steven Globerman. LC 79-51649. (Canadian-U. S. Prospect Ser.). 104p. 1979. 5.00 (*0-88806-052-1*, CUSP3) Natl Planning.

U. S. P. A. Annual Conference Proceedings, 1985. Ed. by U.S.P.A. Staff. (Illus.). 268p. (Orig.). (C). 1986. 25.00 (*0-317-89790-X*) US Psychotronics Assn.

U. S.-Pakistan Relations. Ed. by Leo E. Rose & Noor A. Husain. LC 85-80563. (Research Papers & Policy Studies: No. 13). 245p. 1985. pap. 8.50 (*0-912966-78-5*) IEAS.

U. S. Paper Industry & Sustainable Production: An Argument for Restructuring. Maureen Smith. LC 96-41991. (Urban & Industrial Environment Ser.). (Illus.). 300p. (C). 1997. 30.00 (*0-262-19377-9*) MIT Pr.

U. S. Paper Money. House of Collectibles Staff. Date not set. pap. write for info. (*0-676-60000-X*) Random.

U. S. Paper Money: Comprehensive Catalog Of. Gene Hessler. (Illus.). 544p. 1997. 40.00 (*0-931960-51-7*) BNR Pr.

***U. S. Paper Money: Comprehensive Catalog Of.** 6th ed. Gene Hessler. (Illus.). 544p. 1997. pap. 29.95 (*0-931960-50-9*) BNR Pr.

***U. S. Participation in Special-Purpose International Organizations.** (Illus.). 82p. 1997. pap. text ed. 30.00 (*1-57979-224-3*) BPI Info Servs.

U. S. Pasta Market. 250p. 1997. 1,195.00 (*0-318-00493-3*) Busn Trend.

U. S. Patient & Mobility Aid Markets. Market Intelligence Staff. 345p. 1994. 1,895.00 (*0-7889-0155-9*) Frost & Sullivan.

U. S. Patient & Mobility Aid Markets: Niche Markets on the Move. Market Intelligence Staff. (Orig.). 1994. 1,895.00 (*0-7889-0123-0*) Frost & Sullivan.

U. S. Patient Monitoring Company Profiles. 585p. 1995. write for info. (*0-7889-0343-8*) Frost & Sullivan.

U. S. Patient Monitoring Markets. Market Intelligence Staff. 368p. 1995. 2,195.00 (*0-7889-0161-3*) Frost & Sullivan.

U. S. Patriots as Victims. 1992. lib. bdg. 79.95 (*0-8490-5407-9*) Gordon Pr.

U. S. Patriots, Victims of the ZOG (Zionist Occupation Government) 240p. 1991. 17.45 (*0-685-49446-2*); pap. 10.95 (*0-685-49447-0*) Ichthys Bks.

An Asterisk (*) at the beginning of an entry indicates that the title is appearing in BIP for the first time.

U. S. Patterns & Related Issues. Andrew W. Pollock, 3rd. (Illus.). 524p. 1994. text ed. 79.00 (*0-943161-58-4*) Bowers & Merena.

U. S. Payment System: Efficiency, Risk & the Role of the Federal Reserve. Ed. by David B. Humphrey. (C). 1989. lib. bdg. 75.00 (*0-7923-9020-2*) Kluwer Ac.

U. S. PC - Workstation Storage Strategies: Technology Tradeoffs: How Big? How Much? Market Intelligence Staff. 320p. 1994. 1,695.00 (*1-56753-991-2*) Frost & Sullivan.

U. S. Pensioneers Census 1840, Vol. 2. Ronald V. Jackson. (Illus.). lib. bdg. 50.00 (*0-89593-785-9*) Accelerated Index.

U. S. Pensioners List Index, 1840. 1983. 50.00 (*0-89593-649-6*) Accelerated Index.

U. S. Personal Care Product Markets: Manufacturers Identify New Niches to Sustain Sales. 627p. Date not set. write for info. (*0-7889-0349-7*) Frost & Sullivan.

U. S. Pet Food Market. 335p. 1995. 1,295.00 (*0-318-04173-1*) Busn Trend.

***U. S. Pet Ownership & Demographics Sourcebook.** 2nd ed. Center for Info. Management Staff. (Illus.). (Orig.). 1997. pap. 79.50 (*1-882691-02-4*) Am Veterinary Med Assn.

U. S. Petroleum Industry: Past As Prologue. 1994. lib. bdg. 250.00 (*0-8490-8602-7*) Gordon Pr.

U. S. Petroleum Industry: Past As Prologue, 1970-1992. (Illus.). 70p. (Orig.). (C). 1994. pap. text ed. 40.00 (*0-7881-0885-9*) DIANE Pub.

U. S. Petroleum Strategies in the Decade of the Environment. Bob Williams. 352p. 1991. 25.00 (*0-87814-365-3*) PennWell Bks.

U. S. Pharmaceutical Products for Food-Animals: Consolidation of End-Users Spurs Biotech Development. 262p. 1995. write for info. (*0-614-09483-6*) Frost & Sullivan.

U. S. Pizza Market. 200p. 1995. 1,295.00 (*0-614-09707-X*) Busn Trend.

U. S. Plastic Compounding Industry: Sophisticated Blends & Alloys Replace Engineered Resins. Market Intelligence Staff. 270p. 1993. 3,295.00 (*1-56753-615-8*) Frost & Sullivan.

U. S. Plumbing Fixtures & Fittings Industry. 400p. 1995. 1,095.00 (*0-318-04397-1*) Busn Trend.

U. S. Pocket Catalogue, 1994: Mass Market Pocket Catalogue for U. S. Stamps. 1993. pap. 6.95 (*0-89487-196-X*) Scott Pub Co.

U. S. Policy & Regional Security in Central America. Edward Best. 240p. 1987. text ed. 39.95 (*0-312-00212-2*) St Martin.

U. S. Policy & the Global Environment. Robert C. Rowland. 160p. 1992. pap. 22.60 (*0-8442-5163-1*, NTC Busn Bks) NTC Pub Grp.

U. S. Policy & the Security of Asia. Fred Greene. LC 68-11606. (United States & China in World Affairs Ser.). 447p. reprint ed. pap. 127.40 (*0-317-09320-7*, 2002943) Bks Demand.

U. S. Policy in Central America: The Endless Debate. Dario Moreno. 208p. (C). 1990. pap. text ed. 19.95 (*0-8130-1020-9*); lib. bdg. 39.95 (*0-8130-1005-5*) U Press Fla.

***U. S. Policy in the Third World.** Ed. by Harold Isaacs. (Journal of Third World Studies: Vol. II, No. 1). (Orig.). pap. 7.00 (*0-614-30654-X*) Assn Third Wld.

U. S. Policy on Jerusalem. Yossi Feintuch. LC 87-13407. (Contributions in Political Science Ser.: No. 191). 184p. 1987. text ed. 55.00 (*0-313-25700-0*, FHP/, Greenwood Pr) Greenwood.

U. S. Policy on Palestine: From Wilson to Clinton. Ed. by Michael W. Suleiman. 1994. write for info. (*0-614-00532-9*) Assn Arab-Amer U Grads.

U. S. Policy on Palestine: From Wilson to Clinton. Ed. by Michael W. Suleiman. LC 94-36125. (Orig.). 1994. pap. 15.95 (*0-937694-88-6*, AAUG Pr) Assn Arab-Amer U Grads.

U. S. Policy Toward China. Ed. by Charles P. Cozic. (At Issue Ser.). 96p. (YA). (gr. 10 up). 1996. pap. text ed. 8.96 (*1-56510-388-2*); lib. bdg. 14.96 (*1-56510-389-0*) Greenhaven.

***U. S. Policy Toward China: The Role of Interest Groups.** Robert Sutter. 156p. 1998. 53.00 (*0-8476-8724-4*) Rowman.

***U. S. Policy Toward China: The Role of Interest Groups.** Robert Sutter. 156p. 1998. pap. 21.95 (*0-8476-8725-2*) Rowman.

U. S. Policy Toward Economic Nationalism in Latin America, 1917-1929. Michael L. Krenn. LC 89-24122. (America in the Modern World: Studies in International History). 169p. 1990. 40.00 (*0-8420-2346-1*) Scholarly Res Inc.

U. S. Policy Toward the Bretton Woods Institutions. Ed. by Alvin P. Drischler & M. P. Benjenk. 60p. (Orig.). (C). 1988. pap. text ed. 14.25 (*0-941700-31-3*) JH FPI SAIS.

U. S. Policy Toward the Middle East & Persian Gulf. 159p. (Orig.). (C). 1994. pap. text ed. 35.00 (*0-7881-0735-6*) DIANE Pub.

U. S. Policy Towards Radical Middle East States. Barry Rubin. LC 92-44064. 1992. pap. 16.95 (*0-944029-22-1*) Wash Inst NEP.

U. S. Pony Club Manual of Horsemanship. Susan E. Harris. 480p. 1996. pap. 22.95 (*0-87605-981-7*) S&S Trade.

U. S. Population Estimates, by Age, Sex, Race, & Hispanic Origin, 1980 to 1991. (Illus.). 52p. (Orig.). (C). 1993. pap. text ed. 20.00 (*1-56806-408-X*) DIANE Pub.

U. S. Population of States & Counties - 1790 Through 1990. Ed. by Richard L. Forstall. 210p. (Orig.). 1995. pap. text ed. 35.00 (*0-934213-48-8*, PB96) Natl Tech Info.

U. S. Portable Power Tool Consumable Markets. Market Intelligence Staff. 380p. 1994. 2,295.00 (*0-7889-0159-1*) Frost & Sullivan.

U. S. Postage Stamps. House of Collectibles Staff. Date not set. pap. write for info. (*0-676-60001-8*) Random.

U. S. Postal Service: Labor-Management Problems Persist on the Workroom Floor, 2 vols., Set. (Illus.). 175p. (Orig.). (C). 1995. pap. text ed. 40.00 (*0-7881-1735-1*) DIANE Pub.

U. S. Postal Service: New Focus on Improving Service Quality & Customer Satisfaction. (Illus.). 90p. (Orig.). (C). 1996. pap. text ed. 30.00 (*0-7881-2929-5*) DIANE Pub.

U. S. Postal Service: Status & Prospects of a Public Enterprise. John T. Tierney. LC 88-6274. 210p. 1988. text ed. 49.95 (*0-86569-181-9*, Auburn Hse) Greenwood.

***U. S. Postal Service: Stronger Mail Acceptance Controls Could Help Prevent Revenue Losses.** (Illus.). 35p. (Orig.). (C). 1996. pap. 25.00 (*0-7881-3456-6*) DIANE Pub.

U. S. Postal Service: Unresolved Issues in the International Mail Market. 48p. (Orig.). (C). 1996. pap. text ed. 20.00 (*0-7881-2875-2*) DIANE Pub.

U. S. Postal Service Bicentennial Postmarks, 1972-1984. Bertram Rothenberg. 42p. 1986. pap. text ed. 5.00 (*0-935991-01-8*) Am Topical Assn.

U. S. Postal Service 470 Battery Exam. Ed. by Jim Gish. LC 97-22384. (Law Enforcement Library). 256p. (Orig.). 1997. pap. 12.95 (*1-57685-045-5*) LrningExprss.

U. S. Postmarks & Cancellations. Ed. by Scott R. Trepel. (Seminar Textbook Ser.). (Illus.). vii, 164p. (Orig.). 1992. pap. 24.95 (*0-911989-26-9*) Philatelic Found.

U. S. Power Supply Manufactures Profiles. Market Intelligence Staff. 310p. 1994. 975.00 (*0-7889-0112-5*) Frost & Sullivan.

U. S. Prescription Anti-Imflammatory Pharmaceutical Markets: Aggressive R&D Enhances New Compounds & Treatments. Date not set. write for info. (*0-7889-0395-0*) Frost & Sullivan.

U. S. Prescription Gastrointestinal Pharmaceutical Markets in a Period of Transition. Market Intelligence Staff. 1994. 2,495.00 (*0-7889-0064-1*) Frost & Sullivan.

U. S. Prescription Generic Pharmaceutical Markets. Market Intelligence Staff. (Quarterly Business Planning Ser.). 260p. 1993. 3,295.00 (*0-7889-0099-4*) Frost & Sullivan.

U. S. Prescription Generic Pharmaceutical Markets: Quarterly. Frost & Sullivan Staff. 507p. Date not set. write for info. (*0-7889-0422-1*, 5353-52) Frost & Sullivan.

U. S. Prescription Neurological - Psychotherapeutic Pharmaceuticals: R & D Efforts Paying Off. Market Intelligence Staff. 300p. 1993. 2,295.00 (*1-56753-617-4*) Frost & Sullivan.

U. S. Prescription Respiratory Pharmaceutical Markets: New Asthma Treatment Guidelines Breathe Life into Industry. Market Intelligence Staff. 300p. 1994. 2,295.00 (*1-56753-962-9*) Frost & Sullivan.

U. S. Presidency. Don Nardo. (Lucent Overview Ser.). (Illus.). (J). (gr. 5-8). 1995. lib. bdg. 17.96 (*1-56006-157-X*) Lucent Bks.

***U. S. Presidency in Crisis: A Comparative Perspective.** Collin Campbell. 272p. (C). 1997. pap. text ed. 18.95 (*0-19-509144-2*) OUP.

***U. S. Presidency in Crisis: A Comparative Perspective.** Collin Campbell. 272p. (C). 1997. text ed. 45.00 (*0-19-509143-4*) OUP.

U. S. Presidential Elections & Candidates Vol. 1: Biographical & Historical Guide. Havel. 1996. 90.00 (*0-02-864622-3*, Free Press) Free Pr.

U. S. Presidential Elections & Candidates Vol. 2: Biographical & Historical Guide, Elections 1789-1992, No. 2. Havel. 1996. 90.00 (*0-02-864623-1*, Free Press) Free Pr.

***U. S. Presidential Primaries & the Caucus-Convention System: A Sourcebook.** James W. Davis. LC 96-32980. 312p. 1997. text ed. 75.00 (*0-313-29629-4*, Greenwood Pr) Greenwood.

U. S. Presidents: Crossword Challenge. Timothy Beatty. (Illus.). 120p. (Orig.). 1996. pap. 10.95 (*1-886661-16-2*, 61162) Ryan Place Pub.

U. S. Presidents As Orators: A Bio-Critical Sourcebook. Ed. by Halford R. Ryan. LC 94-43039. 408p. 1995. text ed. 89.50 (*0-313-29059-8*, Greenwood Pr) Greenwood.

U. S. Press & Iran: Foreign Policy & the Journalism of Deference. William A. Dorman & Mansour Farhang. LC 86-25032. 300p. 1987. pap. 14.00 (*0-520-06472-0*) U CA Pr.

U. S. Pressure Sensitive Adhesive Markets: Recycling Technology & Label Applications Lead the Way. Market Intelligence Staff. 233p. 1993. 3,295.00 (*1-56753-614-X*) Frost & Sullivan.

U. S. Processed Meat Industry. 400p. 1995. pap. 1,095.00 (*0-318-00494-1*) Busn Trend.

U. S. Profiles of Cable TV Manufacturers. 632p. Date not set. write for info. (*0-7889-0358-6*) Frost & Sullivan.

U. S. Programmable Logic Controller Markets. Market Intelligence Staff. 370p. 1994. 2,995.00 (*0-7889-0148-6*) Frost & Sullivan.

U. S. Prop. During Vietnam War. write for info. (*0-8386-3611-X*) Fairleigh Dickinson.

***U. S. Prosthetic Joint Implants Market.** 230p. 1996. write for info. (*0-7889-0559-7*, 5279) Frost & Sullivan.

U. S. Protectionism & the World Debt Crisis. Edward J. Ray. LC 89-3774. 259p. 1989. text ed. 59.95 (*0-89930-367-6*, RUP/, Quorum Bks) Greenwood.

U. S. Protein Ingredients Markets. Market Intelligence Staff. 281p. 1993. 2,900.00 (*1-56753-516-X*) Frost & Sullivan.

U. S. Public Data Service Markets: LAN Interconnection, High Bandwidth Applications Fuel Fast-Packet Surge. Market Intelligence Staff. 340p. 1994. 2,495.00 (*1-56753-964-5*) Frost & Sullivan.

U. S. Pump & Compressor Industry: An Analysis of Current Markets & Prospects for Future Growth. 430p. 0994. 1,150.00 (*0-685-17771-8*) Busn Trend.

U. S. Radio Broadcasting to Cuba: Policy Implications. 1982. write for info. (*0-318-63148-2*) Cuban Amer Natl Fndtn.

***U. S. Radio Frequency Identification Equipment Markets.** 265p. 1996. write for info. (*0-7889-0579-1*, 5512) Frost & Sullivan.

U. S. Radio Frequency Identification Equipment Markets: Demand Fueled by Transportation Industry. Market Intelligence Staff. 1995. 2,195.00 (*0-7889-0241-5*) Frost & Sullivan.

U. S. Radio Paging Equipment & Service Markets: An Economical & Efficient Option for Everyone. Market Intelligence Staff. 425p. 1994. 2,395.00 (*0-7889-0186-9*, 2748-62) Frost & Sullivan.

U. S. Railroad Industry in the Post-World War II Period: A Profile. John R. Meyer & Alexander L. Morton. (Explorations in Economic Research Two Ser.: No. 4). 52p. 1975. reprint ed. 35.00 (*0-685-61387-9*) Natl Bur Econ Res.

U. S. Rangers: The Law of the Land. Paul Berkowitz. 484p. 1994. pap. text ed. 24.08 (*1-56226-203-3*) CT Pub.

U. S. Ratification of the International & Covenants on Human Rights. Hurst Hannum & Dana D. Fischer. LC 92-33196. 343p. 1993. lib. bdg. 85.00 (*0-941320-79-0*) Transnatl Pubs.

U. S. Reactions to the British Mandate. Ed. by Aaron Klieman & Adrian L. Klieman. LC 90-45363. (American Zionism Ser.: Vol. 7). 352p. 1991. text ed. 40.00 (*0-8240-7355-X*) Garland.

U. S. Reclamation Service: Its History, Activities & Organization. Brookings Institution Staff. LC 72-3015. (Service Monographs of the U. S. Government: No. 2). reprint ed. 24.50 (*0-404-57102-6*) AMS Pr.

***U. S. Recoilless Rifle 105mm.** rev. ed. Ed. by Bruce A. Hanesalo. (Antiarmor Ser.). (Illus.). 70p. 1995. reprint ed. vinyl bd. 10.00 (*1-886848-08-4*) Mil-Info.

U. S. Recoilless Rifle 106mm M40A2. Ed. by Bruce A. Hanesalo. (Antiarmor Ser.). (Illus.). 123p. 1994. reprint ed. vinyl bd. 10.00 (*1-886848-09-2*) Mil-Info.

U. S. Recoilless Rifle 57mm. Ed. by Bruce A. Hanesalo. (Antiarmor Ser.). (Illus.). 63p. 1995. reprint ed. vinyl bd. 10.00 (*1-886848-05-X*) Mil-Info.

U. S. Recoilless Rifle 75 MM M20. Ed. by Bruce A. Hanesalo. (Antiarmor Ser.). (Illus.). 68p. 1996. vinyl bd. 10.00 (*1-886848-06-8*) Mil-Info.

U. S. Recoilless Rifle 90mm M67. Ed. by Bruce A. Hanesalo. (Antiarmor Ser.). (Illus.). 66p. 1994. reprint ed. vinyl bd. 10.00 (*1-886848-07-6*) Mil-Info.

U. S. Recycled: A Transcontinental Bicycling Adventure. Bill Hullfish & Sue Hullfish. LC 95-78210. (Illus.). 313p. (Orig.). 1995. pap. 12.00 (*0-9647620-0-5*) Bravoprods.

U. S. Recycling Equipment & Services Markets: Lanfill Legislation Drives Growth. Frost & Sullivan Staff. 275p. 1995. write for info. (*0-7889-0295-4*) Frost & Sullivan.

***U. S. Reference Lab Testing Markets.** Frost & Sullivan. 405p. 1996. write for info. (*0-7889-0624-0*, 5537) Frost & Sullivan.

U. S. Refugee Policy. 1985. write for info. (*0-318-60433-7*) US Comm Refugees.

***U. S. Refugee Policy: Dilemmas & Directions.** Kathleen Newland. (International Migration Policy Issues Ser.). 60p. 1995. pap. 5.95 (*0-87003-071-X*) Carnegie Endow.

U. S. Regional Deterrence Strategies. Kenneth H. Watman et al. LC 94-24372. xv, 121p. 1995. pap. text ed. 15.00 (*0-8330-1595-8*, MR-490-A/AF) Rand Corp.

U. S. Regional Outlook for Cement & Ready Mix Concrete Markets. 369p. 1990. 2,150.00 (*0-945235-35-6*) Lead Edge Reports.

U. S. Regional Publications Directory. William T. Harrison. 288p. 1986. pap. 43.95 (*0-936045-00-0*) Bradley Comm.

U. S. Registry's Who's Who in Leading American Executives. 352p. 1991. write for info. (*0-9630708-0-0*) Whos Who Lead Am.

U. S. Regulation of Ocean Transportation under the Shipping Act of 1984. Gerald H. Ullman. LC 95-14074. 304p. 1995. text ed. 45.00 (*0-87033-470-0*) Cornell Maritime.

U. S. Rehabilitation Product Markets. Market Intelligence Staff. 300p. 1994. 1,895.00 (*0-7889-0048-X*) Frost & Sullivan.

U. S. Relation with China, 2 vols. U. S. Department of State Staff. 1988. reprint ed. Set. lib. bdg. 52.00 (*0-7812-0538-7*) Rprt Serv.

U. S. Relations with China, 2 vols. U. S. Department of State Staff. LC 76-145342. xli, 1054p. 1972. reprint ed. Set. 49.00 (*0-403-01293-7*) Scholarly.

U. S. Relations with the World Bank, 1945-92. Cathrine Gwin. 100p. (C). 1994. pap. 9.95 (*0-8157-3349-6*) Brookings.

U. S. Relay Markets: Shift from Conventional to Solid State Technology. Market Intelligence Staff. 363p. 1994. 1,895.00 (*1-56753-967-X*) Frost & Sullivan.

U. S. Religious Interest Groups: Institutional Profiles. Paul J. Weber & W. Landis Jones. LC 93-37502. (Reference Volumes on American Public Policy Formation Ser.). 240p. 1994. text ed. 69.50 (*0-313-26695-6*, Greenwood Pr) Greenwood.

U. S. Repeater Mapbook 1995-1996. William V. Smith & John P. Mitchell. 1995. pap. 9.95 (*0-917963-05-9*) Artsci Inc.

***U. S. Repeater Mapbook 1997-1998.** William V. Smith. 1997. pap. text ed. 9.95 (*0-917963-29-6*) Artsci Inc.

U. S. Repeater Mapbook 96/97. William V. Smith. 176p. 1996. pap. 9.95 (*0-917963-19-9*) Artsci Inc.

U. S. Research Biochemical Markets: Cross-Discipline Applications Multiply Commercial Value of Products. Market Intelligence Staff. 350p. (Orig.). 1994. 2,995.00 (*1-56753-898-3*) Frost & Sullivan.

U. S. Research Reactors. AEC Technical Information Center Staff, Jr. Ed. by Joel W. Chastain. 76p. 1957. pap. 19.50 (*0-87079-380-2*, TID-7013); fiche 9.00 (*0-87079-483-3*, TID-7013) DOE.

U. S. Reserve Forces: The Problem of the Weekend Warrior. Martin Binkin. LC 73-23109. (Studies in Defense Policy). 63p. 1974. pap. 8.95 (*0-8157-0959-5*) Brookings.

U. S. Residential Security Markets. Market Intelligence Staff. 214p. 1994. 2,495.00 (*1-56753-938-6*) Frost & Sullivan.

U. S. Residential Security Product & Service Markets: Increase in Homeowner Investment Promotes Industry Growth. Market Intelligence Staff. (Orig.). 1993. 2,450.00 (*1-56753-640-9*) Frost & Sullivan.

U. S. Response: The Making of U. S. Foreign Policy. rev. ed. Close Up Foundation Staff. (YA). (gr. 7-12). 1990. pap. text ed. 21.95 (*0-932765-25-4*) Close Up Fnd.

U. S. Rifle: A Manual. 1989. lib. bdg. 79.95 (*0-8490-3970-3*) Gordon Pr.

U. S. Rifle Caliber .30 Model 1903. 1979. 4.95 (*0-913150-16-9*) Pioneer Pr.

U. S. Rifle Model 1866 Springfield. reprint ed. 2.25 (*0-913150-14-2*) Pioneer Pr.

U. S. Rifle Model 1870 Remington. reprint ed. 2.25 (*0-913150-15-0*) Pioneer Pr.

***U. S. Road Atlas - 1998.** large type ed. 1997. pap. text ed. 8.95 (*0-7625-0577-X*) Universal Map Enterprises Inc.

***U. S. Road Atlas, 1997.** (Illus.). 1996. per. 7.95 (*0-8416-9207-6*) Creative Sales.

U. S. Robotic Markets: Diversification & Integration Lead to Market Expansion. Date not set. write for info. (*0-7889-0389-6*) Frost & Sullivan.

***U. S. Rocket Launcher M72 (LAW)** Ed. by Bruce A. Hanesalo. (Antiarmor Ser.). (Illus.). 97p. 1994. reprint ed. vinyl bd. 10.00 (*1-886848-04-1*) Mil-Info.

U. S. Rocket Launcher 2.36 Inch M1A1 & M9. Ed. by Bruce A. Hanesalo. (Antiarmor Ser.). (Illus.). 52p. 1994. reprint ed. vinyl bd. 10.00 (*1-886848-02-5*) Mil-Info.

U. S. Rocket Launcher 3.5 Inch. Ed. by Bruce A. Hanesalo. (Antiarmor Ser.). (Illus.). 57p. 1994. reprint ed. vinyl bd. 10.00 (*1-886848-03-3*) Mil-Info.

U. S. Rockets Hypersonic Mach Busters Guide. Jerry Irvine. 60p. 1985. 25.00 (*0-912468-26-2*, USRHMB6) CA Rocketry.

U. S. Rockets Multi-Stage Flight Sheet Guide. Jerry Irvine. 26p. 1985. 9.95 (*0-912468-25-4*, FSG-2) CA Rocketry.

U. S. Rockets Single Stage Flight Sheet Guide, No. 1. Jerry Irvine. 26p. 1984. 9.95 (*0-912468-10-6*, FSG-1) CA Rocketry.

***U. S. Role in the Asian Century: A Panel of Experts Looks at National Interest in the New Environment.** Ed. by Sol Sanders. LC 96-47346. 602p. 1997. 74.50 (*0-7618-0618-0*) U Pr of Amer.

***U. S. Role in the Asian Century: A Panel of Experts Looks at National Interest in the New Environment.** Ed. by Sol Sanders. LC 96-47346. 602p. 1997. pap. 52.50 (*0-7618-0619-9*) U Pr of Amer.

U. S. S. Alabama. Turner Publishing Company Staff. LC 93-60211. 128p. 1993. 48.00 (*1-56311-063-6*) Turner Pub KY.

U. S. S. Arizona Ship's Data: A Photographic History. Norman Friedman et al. (Illus.). 52p. 1989. reprint ed. pap. 3.95 (*0-9631388-2-0*) AZ Mem Mus.

U. S. S. Cassin Young (DD-793) A Fletcher Class Destroyer. J. Scott Harmon. LC 84-63014. (Illus.). 1985. pap. 5.95 (*0-933126-58-1*) Pictorial Hist.

U. S. S. Chandeleur. Turner Publishing Company Staff. LC 94-60148. 112p. 1994. 48.00 (*1-56311-103-9*) Turner Pub KY.

***U. S. S. Enterprise.** Ruth Wickings. (Star Trek Make Your Own Starship Ser.). (J). 1997. 5.99 (*0-689-81589-1*) S&S Childrens.

***U. S. S. Excelsior/Ingram Class Blueprints.** rev. ed. Todd Guenther. 1996. 11.95 (*0-9656016-2-5*) Mstrcom Data.

U. S. S. Franklin (CV-13) The Ship That Wouldn't Die. Turner Publishing Company Staff. LC 89-51931. 152p. 1990. 48.00 (*0-938021-78-8*) Turner Pub KY.

U. S. S. Intrepid. Turner Publishing Company Staff. LC 93-60655. 304p. 1993. 48.00 (*1-56311-107-1*) Turner Pub KY.

U. S. S. Liberty. 1992. lib. bdg. 75.00 (*0-8490-5436-2*) Gordon Pr.

U. S. S. Monitor: The Ship that Launched a Modern Navy. Edward M. Miller. 1978. 24.95 (*0-915268-10-8*) Ayer.

***U. S. S. Oriskany: A Fact Book.** Joe Kelly. LC 96-78290. 64p. 1997. pap. 8.95 (*0-9639290-9-7*) Good Times.

U. S. S. R. Ed. by Susan Taylor-Boyd et al. LC 88-42891. (Children of the World Ser.). (Illus.). 64p. (J). (gr. 5-6). 1989. lib. bdg. 23.93 (*1-55532-215-8*) Gareth Stevens Inc.

U. S. S. R. From an Idea by Karl Marx. Marc Polonsky & Russell Taylor. 176p. (Orig.). 1986. pap. 8.95 (*0-571-13842-X*) Faber & Faber.

U. S. S. R. Its People, Its Society, Its Culture. Thomas Fitzsimmons et al. LC 74-12074. (Illus.). 590p. 1974. reprint ed. text ed. 95.00 (*0-8371-7667-0*, FIUS, Greenwood Pr) Greenwood.

U. S. S. R. Languages & Realities: Nations, Leaders, & Scholars. Michael Bruchis. (East European Monographs: No. 250). 393p. 1988. text ed. 91.50 (*0-88033-147-X*) East Eur Monographs.

U. S. S. R. New Management Mechanism in Foreign Economic Relations. 22p. (ENG, FRE & SPA.). 1988. pap. 12.00 (*92-1-112245-7*, 88.II.D.5); French. pap. 12. 00 (*92-1-212189-6*, 88.II.D.5); Spanish. pap. 12.00 (*92-1-312199-7*, 88.II.D.5) UN.

U. S. S. R. - Decorations, Orders & Medals. Martin M. Kozlowski. (Illus.). 108p. (Orig.). 1988. pap. 12.00 (*0-929757-19-X*, Pub. by Militaria Hse CN) Regt QM.

U. S. S. R. - U. S. A. Bering Sea Experiment: Proceedings of the Final Symposium on the Results of the Joint Soviet-American Expedition, Leningrad, May 12-17, 1974. Ed. by K. Ya. Kodrat'ev et al. Tr. by P. Datta from RUS. 316p. (C). 1986. text ed. 110.00 (*90-6191-403-5*, Pub. by A A Balkema NE) Ashgate Pub Co.

U. S. S. R. after Brezhnev. Seweryn Bialer. LC 83-83061. (Headline Ser.: No. 265). (Illus.). 64p. (Orig.). (YA). (gr. 11-12). 1983. pap. 5.95 (*0-87124-086-9*) Foreign Policy.

U. S. S. R. & Africa: Foreign Policy under Khrushchev. Dan C. Heldman. LC 81-4975. 204p. 1981. text ed. 49. 95 (*0-275-90642-6*, C0642, Praeger Pubs) Greenwood.

U. S. S. R. & Eastern Europe: The Shattered Heartland. John C. Kimball. Ed. by Nancy L. Hoepli. LC 91-58110. (Headline Ser.: No. 295). (Illus.). 104p. (Orig.). 1991. pap. 11.25 (*0-87124-141-2*) Foreign Policy.

U. S. S. R. & Iraq: The Soviet Quest for Influence. Oles M. Smolansky & Bettie M. Smolansky. LC 90-48597. 358p. 1991. text ed. 59.95 (*0-8223-1103-8*); pap. text ed. 29.95 (*0-8223-1116-X*) Duke.

U. S. S. R. & Latin America: A Developing Relationship. Ed. by Eusebio Mujal-Leon. 288p. 1989. text ed. 39.95 (*0-04-445165-2*) Routledge Chapman & Hall.

U. S. S. R. & Marxist Revolutions in the Third World. Ed. by Mark N. Katz. (Woodrow Wilson Center Ser.). 150p. (C). 1991. text ed. 57.95 (*0-521-39265-9*) Cambridge U Pr.

U. S. S. R. & Socialism: The Trotskyist Perspective. David North. 41p. 1989. pap. 3.00 (*0-929087-45-3*) Labor Pubns Inc.

U. S. S. R. & the Middle East. Ed. by M. Confino & Shimon Shamir. 441p. 1973. 44.95 (*0-87855-160-3*) Transaction Pubs.

U. S. S. R. & the U. N.'s Economic & Social Activities. Harold K. Jacobson. LC 63-19327. (Notre Dame University, Committee on International Relations, International Studies). 327p. reprint ed. pap. 93.20 (*0-317-42107-7*, 2025947) Bks Demand.

U. S. S. R. & the Western Alliance. Robbin F. Laird & Susan L. Clark. 288p. 1989. 55.00 (*0-04-445392-2*) Routledge Chapman & Hall.

U. S. S. R. & the World Economy: Challenges for the Global Integration of Soviet Markets under Perestroika. Ed. by Deborah A. Palmieri. LC 91-44452. 208p. 1992. text ed. 55.00 (*0-275-94015-2*, C4015, Praeger Pubs) Greenwood.

U. S. S. R. & World Peace. Andrei Vyshinsky. Ed. by Jessica Smith. LC 70-76919. (Essay Index Reprint Ser.). 1977. 17.95 (*0-8369-1071-0*) Ayer.

U. S. S. R. Calendar of Events Annual, 1987-1991. Joseph P. Mastro. 72.00 (*0-685-27034-3*) Academic Intl.

U. S. S. R. Calendar of Events Annual, 1987-1991, 5 vols., Set. Joseph P. Mastro. 375.00 (*0-87569-113-7*) Academic Intl.

U. S. S. R. Country Notes. Ed. by World Eagle Staff. (Country Notes Ser.). (Illus.). 40p. 1991. teacher ed., pap. 14.95 (*0-930141-41-5*) World Eagle.

U. S. S. R. Crime Statistics & Summaries: 1989 & 1990. Tr. by Joseph Serio from RUS. LC 92-50141. (Illus.). 100p. 16.00 (*0-942511-53-0*) OICJ.

U. S. S. R. Documents Annual, 1987-1991. Ed. by J. L. Black. Non-subscription. 92.00 (*0-87569-110-2*) Academic Intl.

U. S. S. R. Economic Handbook. (Economic Handbook Ser.). 250p. 1986. 80.00 (*0-86338-156-1*, Pub. by Euromonitor Pubns UK) Gale.

U. S. S. R. Facts & Figures Annual, Vol. 16 Index Vols. 1-10. 1992. 77.00 (*0-87569-154-4*) Academic Intl.

U. S. S. R. Facts & Figures Annual, Vol. 17. Ed. by Krasniak. 1992. 75.95 (*0-87569-158-7*) Academic Intl.

U. S. S. R. Facts & Figures Annual see Russia-Eurasia Facts & Figures Annual (REFFA)

U. S. S. R. Facts & Figures Annual, Vol. 12-14: 1988-1990, Vol. 12-14. Ed. by Alan P. Pollard. 1988. 95.00 (*0-87569-103-X*); 95.00 (*0-685-44198-9*) Academic Intl.

U. S. S. R. Facts & Figures Annual, 1977-1987, Vols. 1-3, 7, 11. Ed. by John L. Scherer. (UFFA Ser.). 96.00 (*0-685-00095-8*); 72.00 (*0-685-00096-6*) Academic Intl.

U. S. S. R.-German Aggression Against Lithuania: 1918-1945. Bronis J. Kaslas. 17.95 (*0-8315-0135-9*) Speller.

U. S. S. R. in Third World Conflicts: Soviet Arms & Diplomacy in Local Wars, 1945-1980. Bruce D. Porter. LC 83-26265. (Illus.). 256p. 1984. text ed. 54.95 (*0-521-26308-5*) Cambridge U Pr.

U. S. S. R. in Third World Conflicts: Soviet Arms & Diplomacy in Local Wars, 1945-1980. Bruce D. Porter. LC 83-26265. (Illus.). 256p. 1986. pap. text ed. 17.95 (*0-521-31064-4*) Cambridge U Pr.

U. S. S. R.-India: The Path to the Stars. Vladimir Shatalov. (Illus.). 188p. 1986. text ed. 35.00 (*0-7069-2733-8*, Pub. by Vikas II) S Asia.

U. S. S. R. Labor Camps. Avraham Shifrin. 282p. 1987. pap. 4.95 (*0-88264-159-X*) Living Sacrifice Bks.

U. S. S. R. Legislative Documents Series, 2 vols. in 1, Ea. Ed. by Patrick J. Rollins. 1993. 170.00 (*0-87569-166-8*) Academic Intl.

U. S. S. R. Olympiad Problem Book: Selected Problems & Theorems of Elementary Mathematics. D. O. Shklarsky et al. LC 93-11553. (Illus.). xvi, 452p. 1993. reprint ed. pap. 10.95 (*0-486-27709-7*) Dover.

U. S. S. R. Sub-Saharan Africa in the 1980s. David E. Albright. (Washington Papers: No. 101). 144p. 1983. pap. text ed. 9.95 (*0-275-91558-1*, B1558, Praeger Pubs) Greenwood.

U. S. S. R. Today: Perspectives from the Soviet Press, the Gorbachev Era, 1986-1988. 7th ed. Ed. by Robert Ehlers et al. 190p. 1988. pap. 10.00 (*0-913601-77-2*) Current Digest.

U. S. S. R. Today: Perspectives from the Soviet Press, 1977-1981. 5th ed. Ed. by Fred Schulze & Gordon Livermore. 242p. 1981. pap. 10.00 (*0-913601-75-6*) Current Digest.

U. S. S. R. Today: Perspectives from the Soviet Press, 1989-1991. 8th ed. Ed. by Gordon Livermore et al. 180p. 1991. pap. 18.00 (*0-913601-78-0*) Current Digest.

U. S. S. R., 1987-1991: Marxist Perspectives. Ed. by Marilyn Vogt-Downey. LC 92-17792. (Revolutionary Studies). (Illus.). 552p. (C). 1993. text ed. 65.00 (*0-391-03772-2*) Humanities.

U. S. S. Ralph Talbot & Her Gallant Men. Alfred Samuels. 256p. 1991. lib. bdg. write for info. (*0-9622415-1-2*) Pubs Syndication.

U. S. S. R.'s Emerging Multiparty System. Vera Tolz. LC 90-45046. (Washington Papers: No. 148). 144p. 1990. text ed. 45.00 (*0-275-93838-7*, C3838, Praeger Pubs); pap. text ed. 13.95 (*0-275-93839-5*, B3839, Praeger Pubs) Greenwood.

U. S. S. Solace Was There: The History of a Hospital Ship During World War II. H. C. Daly. LC 90-84769. (Illus.). 735p. (Orig.). 1991. 39.95 (*0-935902-17-1*); text ed. 39.95 (*0-685-48505-6*) Balboa Pub.

U. S. S. Spadefish (SS-411) in World War II. Val Scanlon, Jr. (World War II Historical Society Monograph Ser.). 46p. 1995. pap. 6.00 (*1-57638-022-X*) Merriam Pr.

U. S. S. Yorktown. Turner Publishing Company Staff. LC 93-60160. 152p. 1993. 48.00 (*1-56311-064-4*) Turner Pub KY.

U. S. Sailing & Yachting First Aid. John Bergan & Vincent Guzzetta. 485p. 1992. pap. 15.00 (*1-882502-04-3*) US Sail Assn.

U. S. Sailing Appeals & IYRU Cases. 1994. ring bd. 45.00 (*1-882502-10-8*) US Sail Assn.

U. S. Sailing Official Logbook of Sailing. rev. ed. Date not set. pap. text ed. 8.95 (*1-882502-31-0*) US Sail Assn.

U. S. Sales Automation Software Markets: Customizing, Implementation, Training & Services Explode. Market Intelligence Staff. 300p. 1994. 1,795.00 (*1-56753-992-0*) Frost & Sullivan.

U. S.-Sandinista Diplomatic Relations: Voice of Intolerance. David Ryan. LC 95-14923. 250p. 1995. text ed. 49.95 (*0-312-12821-5*) St Martin.

U. S. Satellite Network Markets. Frost & Sullivan Staff. 1996. write for info. (*0-7889-0425-6*, 2856-61) Frost & Sullivan.

***U. S. Savings Bonds: A Comprehensive Guide for Bond Owners & Financial Professionals.** 3rd rev. ed. Daniel J. Pederson. LC 96-61980. (Illus.). 264p. (Orig.). 1997. pap. 24.95 (*0-9643020-2-0*) TSBI.

U. S. Secondary Telecom Industry - Markets & Opportunities: 1989-1995 Analysis. Frank Murawski. (Illus.). 320p. 1989. pap. text ed. 2,400.00 (*1-878218-24-7*) World Info Tech.

U. S. Securities & Exchange Commission: A Research & Information Guide. John W. Graham. LC 92-28409. (Research & Information Guides in Business, Industry & Economic Institutions Ser.: Vol. 8). 376p. 1993. text ed. 61.00 (*0-8153-0071-9*, SS755) Garland.

U. S. Securities & Exchange Commission: Annual Report, 1935-1967, Vols. 1-33. Bound set. 346.00 (*0-686-90077-4*) Rothman.

U. S. Securities & Investment Regulation Handbook. Ed. by Peter Farmery. 480p. (C). 1992. lib. bdg. 158.00 (*1-85333-631-9*, Pub. by Graham & Trotman UK) Kluwer Ac.

***U. S. Securities Regulation.** Afterman. 1997. lib. bdg. write for info. (*90-411-0610-3*) Kluwer Law Tax Pubs.

***U. S. Securities Regulation of Foreign Issuers.** Afterman. 1996. 275.00 (*1-56706-297-0*) Aspen Pub.

U. S. Security & Surveillance Markets. Stotter. 138p. 1995. 2,450.00 (*0-614-10909-4*, G-143) BCC.

U. S. Security in an Uncertain Era. Ed. by Brad Roberts. (Illus.). 350p. 1993. 30.00 (*0-262-18155-X*); pap. 17.00 (*0-262-68080-7*) MIT Pr.

U. S. Security Interests in Asia. James C. Hsiung. write for info. (*0-275-90013-4*, C0013, Praeger Pubs) Greenwood.

U. S. Senate Decision-Making: The Trade Agreement Act of 1979. Robert W. Jerome. LC 89-23300. (Contributions in Political Science Ser.: No. 249). 192p. 1990. text ed. 55.00 (*0-313-26614-X*, JUS/, Greenwood Pr) Greenwood.

U. S. Senators & Their World. Donald R. Matthews. LC 80-17163. (Illus.). xvi, 303p. 1980. reprint ed. text ed. 59.75 (*0-313-22664-4*, MASE, Greenwood Pr) Greenwood.

U. S.-Seneca Treaty, 1842. 5.00 (*0-317-66465-4*) Inst Dev Indian Law.

U. S. Sentencing Commission Guidelines Manual, 2 vols., Set. 790p. (Orig.). (C). 1995. pap. text ed. 60.00 (*0-7881-1928-1*) DIANE Pub.

U. S. Sentencing Guidelines: Implications for Criminal Justice. Ed. by Dean J. Champion. LC 89-16092. 301p. 1989. text ed. 55.00 (*0-275-93324-5*, C3324, Praeger Pubs) Greenwood.

U. S. Sentencing Guidelines Manual, 2 vols., Set. 1994. pap. 42.00 (*0-16-045243-0*) Claitors.

U. S. Septecemia & Septic Shock Markets: The Search for Therapy Continues: New Agents & Their Potential. Market Intelligence Staff. 250p. 1994. 2,895.00 (*1-56753-935-1*) Frost & Sullivan.

U. S. Sexually Transmitted Disease, Diagnostic & Therapeutic Markets. Market Intelligence Staff. (Orig.). 1994. 2,295.00 (*0-7889-0136-2*) Frost & Sullivan.

U. S. Shotguns: Identification, Operation & Care. 1991. lib. bdg. 69.95 (*0-8490-4564-9*) Gordon Pr.

U. S. Small Combatants: An Illustrated Design History Including PT-Boats, Subchasers, & the Brown-Water Navy. Norman Friedman. LC 87-15893. (Illus.). 500p. 1987. 59.95 (*0-87021-713-5*) Naval Inst Pr.

U. S. Small Compressor & Vacuum Pump Markets. Market Intelligence Staff. 342p. 1995. 2,295.00 (*0-7889-0160-5*) Frost & Sullivan.

U. S. Snack Food Market. 420p. 0994. 1,250.00 (*0-318-03902-8*) Busn Trend.

U. S. Social Policy Shareholder Resolutions: Including Voting Practices of Institutional Investors. 71p. (Orig.). 1996. pap. 50.00 (*1-879775-37-9*) IRRC Inc DC.

U. S. Social Studies Yellow Pages for Students & Teachers. Kathy LaMorte & Sharen Lewis. Ed. by Jan Keeling. (Illus.). 64p. (Orig.). (J). 1993. pap. text ed. 8.95 (*0-86530-267-7*) Incentive Pubns.

U. S. Soft Drink Market: Past Performance, Current Trends & Opportunities for Growth. 345p. 1995. 1,095. 00 (*0-317-55175-2*) Busn Trend.

U. S. Solvents Markets & Ancillary Solvent Substitute & Recycling Phenomena. Innes. 108p. 1994. 2,450.00 (*0-614-10875-6*, C-154R) BCC.

U. S. Sourcebook of Advertisers. 175p. 1992. pap. text ed. 325.00 (*1-878339-17-6*) Schonfeld & Assocs.

U. S. Sourcebook of Advertisers. 175p. 1993. pap. text ed. 325.00 (*1-878339-24-9*) Schonfeld & Assocs.

U. S. Sourcebook of Advertisers. 175p. 1994. pap. text ed. 325.00 (*1-878339-32-X*) Schonfeld & Assocs.

U. S. Sourcebook of Advertisers. 190p. 1995. pap. text ed. 325.00 (*1-878339-39-7*) Schonfeld & Assocs.

U. S. Sourcebook of Advertisers: 1990 Edition. Schonfeld & Associates Staff. 175p. (C). 1990. pap. text ed. 295.00 (*1-878339-07-9*) Schonfeld & Assocs.

U. S. Sourcebook of Advertisers: 1996 Edition. 190p. 1996. pap. text ed. 325.00 (*1-878339-46-X*) Schonfeld & Assocs.

***U. S. Sourcebook of Advertisers: 1997 Edition.** 190p. 1997. pap. text ed. 345.00 (*1-878339-55-9*) Schonfeld & Assocs.

U. S. Sourcebook of Advertisers, 1989. Schonfeld & Associates Staff. 176p. (C). 1989. pap. text ed. 295.00 (*1-878339-02-8*) Schonfeld & Assocs.

U. S. Sourcebook of Advertisers, 1991. Schonfeld & Associates Staff. 175p. (C). 1991. pap. text ed. 295.00 (*1-878339-12-5*) Schonfeld & Assocs.

U. S. Sourcebook of R & D Spenders. 135p. 1992. pap. text ed. 325.00 (*1-878339-18-4*) Schonfeld & Assocs.

U. S. Sourcebook of R & D Spenders. 135p. 1993. pap. text ed. 325.00 (*1-878339-25-7*) Schonfeld & Assocs.

U. S. Sourcebook of R & D Spenders. 150p. 1995. pap. text ed. 325.00 (*1-878339-40-0*) Schonfeld & Assocs.

U. S. Sourcebook of R & D Spenders: 1990 Edition. Schonfeld & Associates Staff. 135p. (C). 1990. pap. text ed. 295.00 (*1-878339-08-7*) Schonfeld & Assocs.

U. S. Sourcebook of R & D Spenders: 1996 Edition. 150p. 1996. pap. text ed. 325.00 (*1-878339-47-8*) Schonfeld & Assocs.

***U. S. Sourcebook of R & D Spenders: 1997 Edition.** 150p. 1997. pap. text ed. 345.00 (*1-878339-56-7*) Schonfeld & Assocs.

U. S. Sourcebook of R & D Spenders, 1989. Schonfeld & Associates Staff. 136p. (C). 1989. pap. text ed. 295.00 (*1-878339-03-6*) Schonfeld & Assocs.

U. S. Sourcebook of R & D Spenders, 1991. Schonfeld & Associates Staff. 135p. (C). 1991. pap. text ed. 295.00 (*1-878339-13-3*) Schonfeld & Assocs.

U. S. Sourcebook of R&D Spenders. 135p. 1994. pap. text ed. 325.00 (*1-878339-33-8*) Schonfeld & Assocs.

U. S. South Korean Alliance: Time for a Change. Ed. by Doug Bandow & Ted G. Carpenter. 206p. (C). 1992. 39. 95 (*1-56000-018-X*); pap. 24.95 (*1-56000-583-1*) Transaction Pubs.

U. S.-Soviet Conventional Arms Transfer Negotiations. Barry M. Blechman & Janne E. Nolan. (Pew Case Studies in International Affairs). 50p. (C). 1993. pap. text ed. 3.50 (*1-56927-302-2*) Geo U Inst Dplmcy.

U. S. Soviet Conventional Arms Transfer Negotiations. Barry M. Blechman & Janne E. Nolan. (Orig.). (C). 1987. pap. text ed. 11.75 (*0-941700-06-2*) JH FPI SAIS.

U. S.-Soviet Cooperation: A New Future. Ed. by Nish Jamgotch, Jr. LC 88-27504. 243p. 1989. text ed. 55.00 (*0-275-93082-3*, C3082, Praeger Pubs) Greenwood.

U. S.-Soviet Relations. Close Up Foundation Staff. 128p. (YA). (gr. 7-12). 1990. pap. 9.95 (*0-932765-33-5*, 833-910) Close Up Fnd.

U. S.-Soviet Relations: From Confrontation to Cooperation Through Verificational Deterrence. Vitalii I. Goldanskii & Michael D. Intriligator. (CISA Working Papers: No. 64). 14p. (Orig.). 1989. pap. 15.00 (*0-86682-083-3*) Ctr Intl Relations.

U. S.-Soviet Relations: The Next Phase. Ed. by Arnold L. Horelick. LC 85-48274. 304p. 1986. 49.95 (*0-8014-1912-3*); pap. 17.95 (*0-8014-9383-8*) Cornell U Pr.

U. S.-Soviet Trade Policy. Carol R. Hansen. (FPI Policy Briefs Ser.). 64p. (C). 1988. pap. text ed. 12.75 (*0-941700-41-0*) JH FPI SAIS.

U. S. Space Camp Book of Astronauts. Anne Baird. 48p. (J). (gr. 4-6). 1996. 16.00 (*0-688-12226-4*, Morrow Junior); lib. bdg. 15.93 (*0-688-12227-2*, Morrow Junior) Morrow.

U. S. Space Camp Book of Rockets. Anne Baird. LC 93-26148. (Official U. S. & Space Camp Book). (Illus.). (J). (gr. 3 up). 1994. 15.00 (*0-688-12228-0*, Morrow Junior); lib. bdg. 14.93 (*0-688-12229-9*, Morrow Junior) Morrow.

U. S. Space Directory - 1994. Ed. by Scott Sacknoff. 222p. (C). 1994. pap. 79.00 (*1-887022-01-5*) Space Pubns.

U. S. Space Directory, 1995-96. Ed. by Scott Sacknoff. 213p. (C). 1995. pap. 79.95 (*1-887022-02-3*) Space Pubns.

U. S. Special Forces Recon Manual. 1986. lib. bdg. 79.95 (*0-8490-3578-3*) Gordon Pr.

U. S. Special Forces Recon Manual. 120p. 1983. pap. 14.95 (*0-318-36167-1*) Lancer.

U. S. Special Forces Shoulder & Pocket Insignia. Harry F. Pugh. LC 93-72379. (Elite Insignia Guides Ser.). (Illus.). 320p. (Orig.). 1993. pap. 24.00 (*0-9633231-2-1*) C&D Ent.

U. S. Special Operations Forces: Posture Statement. (Illus.). 64p. (Orig.). (C). 1993. pap. text ed. 25.00 (*1-56806-780-1*) DIANE Pub.

U. S. Specialty Biocide Markets: EPA Regulations Redefine Industry Focus. Market Intelligence Staff. 510p. 1994. 1,995.00 (*1-56753-997-1*) Frost & Sullivan.

U. S. Spectrum Management Policy: Agenda for the Future. 233p. (Orig.). (C). 1994. pap. text ed. 50.00 (*0-7881-0604-X*) DIANE Pub.

U. S. Spinal Implants & Surgical Product Markets: Implant Market Rebounds. Frost & Sullivan Staff. 338p. 1995. write for info. (*0-7889-0401-9*, 5347-54) Frost & Sullivan.

U. S. State Quilt Blocks: The Classic Collection. Workbasket Magazine Staff. LC 87-34844. (Illus.). 96p. 1995. pap. 9.95 (*0-86675-300-1*) KC Pub.

U. S. Statistical Abstract. 111th ed. 1991. 34.00 (*0-87511-943-3*); pap. 28.00 (*0-87511-944-1*) Claitors.

U. S. Steel Industry in Recurrent Crisis: Policy Options in a Competitive World. Robert W. Crandall. LC 81-4642. 184p. 1981. 26.95 (*0-8157-1602-8*); pap. 9.95 (*0-8157-1601-X*) Brookings.

U. S. Strategic Airlift: Requirements & Capabilities. Jeffrey Record. LC 85-23927. (National Security Papers: No. 2). 43p. 1986. 7.50 (*0-89549-068-4*) Inst Foreign Policy Anal.

U. S. Strategic Airlift Choices. William S. Cohen et al. LC 86-21425. (National Security Papers: No. 8). 1986. 7.50 (*0-89549-079-X*) Inst Foreign Policy Anal.

U. S. Strategic Interests & the India Pakistan Military Balance. Anthony H. Cordesman. (C). 1988. pap. 45.00 (*81-7002-035-2*, Pub. by Himalayan Bks II) St Mut.

U. S. Strategic Interests in Southwest Asia. Shirin Tahir-Kheli. Ed. by Mack Lipkin. LC 82-5305. 236p. 1982. text ed. 49.95 (*0-275-90915-8*, C0915, Praeger Pubs) Greenwood.

U. S. Strategy at the Crossroads: Two Views. Jeffrey Record & Robert J. Hanks. LC 82-82774. (Foreign Policy Reports). 69p. 1982. 11.95 (*0-89549-044-7*) Inst Foreign Policy Anal.

U. S. Strategy for the Asia-Pacific. Douglas T. Stuart & William T. Tow. (Adelphi Papers: No. 299). 76p. 1996. pap. 24.95 (*0-19-829073-X*) OUP.

U. S. Strategy in the Gulf. Leila Meo. (Monographs: No. 14). 130p. (Orig.). 1981. pap. 6.00 (*0-937694-50-9*) Assn Arab-Amer U Grads.

U. S. Strategy to Counter Domestic Political Terrorism. 55p. (Orig.). (C). 1993. pap. text ed. 25.00 (*1-56806-847-6*) DIANE Pub.

U. S. Submarine Attacks during World War II. John D. Alden. LC 89-30878. (Illus.). 320p. 1989. 26.95 (*0-87021-767-4*) Naval Inst Pr.

U. S. Submarine Production Base: An Analysis of Cost, Schedule & Risk for Selected Force Structures. John Birkler & J. Schank. LC 94-28415. 230p. 1994. pap. 15. 00 (*0-8330-1548-6*, MR-456-OSD) Rand Corp.

U. S. Submarine Production Base: An Analysis of Cost, Schedule & Risk for Selected Force Structures, Executive Summary. John Birkler et al. LC 94-32570. 1994. pap. 7.50 (*0-8330-1587-7*, MR-456/1-OSD) Rand Corp.

U. S. Submarines in World War II: An Illustrated History. Larry Kimmett & Margaret Regis. (Illus.). 160p. (Orig.). 1996. 39.95 (*1-879932-03-2*); pap. 19.95 (*1-879932-01-6*) Navigator Pub.

U. S. Submarines since Nineteen Forty-Five: An Illustrated Design History. Norman Friedman. LC 93-42132. (Illus.). 352p. 1994. 59.95 (*1-55750-260-9*) Naval Inst Pr.

U. S. Submarines Through 1945: An Illustrated Design History. Norman Friedman. (Illus.). 352p. 1995. 59.95 (*1-55750-263-3*) Naval Inst Pr.

U. S. Sugar Program: Its Impact on Sweetener Users & Producers & How Domestic & International Conditions Will Affect Its Future. (Illus.). 70p. (Orig.). (C). 1994. pap. text ed. 30.00 (*0-7881-0262-1*) DIANE Pub.

U. S. Supreme Court & the Uses of Social Science Data. Ed. by Abraham L. Davis. LC 73-8983. 150p. (C). 1975. pap. text ed. 7.95 (*0-8422-0338-9*) Irvington.

U. S. Supreme Court Digest: Annotated, 22 vols. in 46 bks. 1992. Suppl. 1992. suppl. ed. write for info. (*0-318-57184-6*) Lawyers Cooperative.

***U. S. Supreme Court Education Cases.** 4th ed. 1990. pap. 69.75 (*0-939675-54-4*) Data Res MN.

***U. S. Supreme Court Employment Cases.** 2nd ed. 1993. pap. 64.70 (*0-939675-51-X*) Data Res MN.

U. S. Supreme Court Reports: Lawyers Edition, 108 vols. 1992. Set; Suppl. 1992. suppl. ed. write for info. (*0-318-57183-8*) Lawyers Cooperative.

***U. S. Synthetically Derived Therapeutic Peptides.** Frost & Sullivan Staff. 401p. 1996. write for info. (*0-7889-0512-0*, 5030) Frost & Sullivan.

U. S. Tactical Air Power: Missions, Forces, & Costs. William D. White. LC 74-20695. (Studies in Defense Policy). 121p. 1974. pap. 8.95 (*0-8157-9371-5*) Brookings.

UV

An Asterisk (*) at the beginning of an entry indicates that the title is appearing in BIP for the first time.

U. S. Tax Aspects of Doing Business Abroad. 4th rev. ed. Michael L. Moore & Edmund Outslay. LC 95-5646. 1995. 66.00 (*0-87051-164-5*) Am Inst CPA.

*__U. S. Tax Law Dictionary.__ Jacques Melek. (Tax Law Dictionary Ser.). (Illus.). 638p. (Orig.). 1996. pap. 24.95 (*0-942330-00-5*) J Melek.

U. S. Taxation of Foreign Controlled Businesses. Marc M. Levey. Ed. by D Davis. 1200p. 1995. 195.00 (*0-7913-2293-9*) Warren Gorham & Lamont.

U. S. Taxation of International Income: Blueprint for Reform. Gary C. Hufbauer. LC 92-9256. (Policy Analyses in International Economics Ser.). 276p. 1992. pap. 22.95 (*0-88132-134-6*) Inst Intl Eco.

U. S. Taxation of International Mergers, Acquisitions, & Joint Ventures, 2 vols., Set. Kevin Dolan. 2000p. 1995. 345.00 (*0-7913-2569-5*) Warren Gorham & Lamont.

U. S. Taxation of International Mergers, Acquisitions, & Joint Ventures, Vol. 1. Kevin Dolan. 1995. write for info. (*0-7913-2586-5*) Warren Gorham & Lamont.

U. S. Taxation of International Mergers, Acquisitions, & Joint Ventures, Vol. 2. Kevin Dolan. 1995. write for info. (*0-7913-2587-3*) Warren Gorham & Lamont.

U. S. Taxation of International Operations. ring bd. write for info. (*0-318-57365-2*) P-H.

U. S. Taxation of International Transactions, Teacher's Manual to Accompany. Samuel C. Thompson, Jr. (American Casebook Ser.). 65p. (C). 1995. pap. text ed. write for info. (*0-314-06990-9*) West Pub.

U. S. Taxes & Tax Policy. David G. Davies. LC 85-31414. 336p. 1986. pap. text ed. 18.95 (*0-521-31769-X*) Cambridge U Pr.

U. S. Telecommunications Multimedia Markets. Market Intelligence Staff. 189p. 1994. 2,295.00 (*0-7889-0073-0*) Frost & Sullivan.

U. S. Telecommunications Network Security & Reliability Equipment & Service Markets. Market Intelligence Staff. 221p. 1995. 2,495.00 (*0-7889-0178-8*, 2821-60) Frost & Sullivan.

U. S. Telecommunications Services in Europe. (Illus.). 220p. (Orig.). (C). 1993. pap. text ed. 125.00 (*0-7881-0047-5*) DIANE Pub.

U. S. Telecommunications Services in European Markets. 1994. lib. bdg. 250.00 (*0-8490-8537-3*) Gordon Pr.

U. S. Telecommunications Voice Processing Market: Computer Telephony Integration Makes Voice Processing. Frost & Sullivan Staff. 590p. 1996. write for info. (*0-7889-0476-0*, 2897) Frost & Sullivan.

U. S. Teleconferencing & Document Conferencing Services, Systems & Software Markets: T.120 Spurs Growth in Market. Frost & Sullivan Staff. 387p. 1996. write for info. (*0-7889-0464-7*, 2787) Frost & Sullivan.

*__U. S. Telemedicine Market: Issues, Forecasts, & Trends 1995-2000.__ Fran Fields. (Illus.). 207p. (Orig.). 1996. spiral bd., pap. write for info. (*1-889713-01-5*) Feedback Rsch.

U. S. Ten Cent Stamps of 1855-59. Mortimer L. Neinken. (Illus.). 252p. 1960. 30.00 (*0-912574-07-0*) Collectors.

U. S. Territories Freely Associated States. Terry Dunnahoo. Ed. by Jennie Rakos. LC 88-16982. (Venture Bks.). (Illus.). 128p. (J). 1988. lib. bdg. 22.00 (*0-531-10605-5*) Watts.

U. S., the U. N., & the Management of Global Change. Ed. by Toby T. Gati. (UNA-USA Book Ser.). 392p. (C). 1983. text ed. 36.00 (*0-8147-2986-X*); pap. text ed. 18.00 (*0-8147-2987-8*) NYU Pr.

U. S. Thermistor, Thyristor & Varistor Markets: 1994-1999 Analysis & Forecasts. Frank Kuzler. 100p. 1994. pap. text ed. 2,400.00 (*1-878218-54-9*) World Info Tech.

U. S. Thrombosis Markets: Anticoagulants, Antithrombotics & Thrombolytics: New Drugs, New Indications Expand Market. Market Intelligence Staff. 290p. 1994. 2,495.00 (*1-56753-957-2*) Frost & Sullivan.

U. S. Timber Resources in a World Economy. John A. Zivnuska. LC 67-21585. (Resources for the Future Ser.). 137p. reprint ed. 39.10 (*0-8357-9290-0*, 2016069) Bks Demand.

*__U. S. Top Oil & Gas Company Benchmark Report, 1991-1995.__ 750p. 1996. 995.00 incl. disk (*0-614-26639-4*, E1031-96) PennWell Bks.

*__U. S. Top Oil & Gas Company Benchmark Report, 1991-1995.__ 750p. 1996. 995.00 incl. cd-rom (*0-614-26640-8*, E1033-96) PennWell Bks.

*__U. S. Top Oil & Gas Company Benchmark Report, 1991-1995.__ 750p. 1996. 295.00 (*0-87814-510-9*) PennWell Bks.

U. S. Topics: Understanding Contemporary America. 2nd ed. Charles Cooper. 114p. 1995. pap. 31.00 (*82-00-22686-7*) Scandnvan Univ Pr.

U. S. Trade Barriers: A Legal Analysis. Eberhard Grabitz & Armin Von Bogdandy. LC 91-50826. 700p. 1992. lib. bdg. 92.50 (*0-379-20151-8*) Oceana.

U. S. Trade Deficit - Causes, Consequences & Cures: Proceedings of the Twelfth Annual Economic Policy Conference of the Federal Reserve Bank of St. Louis. Ed. by Albert E. Burger. (C). 1989. lib. bdg. 79.00 (*0-89838-292-0*) Kluwer Ac.

U. S. Trade Dollar. J. Willem. (Illus.). 1983. reprint ed. lib. bdg. 20.00 (*0-915262-98-3*) S J Durst.

*__U. S. Trade Dress Law.__ 1996. pap. 83.95 (*0-939190-22-2*) Intl Trademark.

U. S. Trade, Foreign Direct Investment & Global Competitiveness. Rolf Hackmann. LC 96-14338. (Illus.). 490p. (C). 1997. 129.95 (*0-7890-0085-7*, Intl Busn Pr) Haworth Pr.

*__U. S. Trade, Foreign Direct Investment & Global Competitiveness.__ Rolf Hackmann. LC 96-14338. (Illus.). 490p. (C). 1997. pap. 39.95 (*0-7890-0187-X*, Intl Busn Pr) Haworth Pr.

U. S. Trade Policies in a Changing World Economy. Ed. by Robert M. Stern. 448p. 1987. reprint ed. 35.00 (*0-262-19253-5*) MIT Pr.

U. S. Trade Policies in a Changing World Economy. Ed. by Robert M. Stern. 448p. 1989. reprint ed. pap. 13.95 (*0-262-69132-9*) MIT Pr.

U. S. Trade Policy & Global Growth: New Directions in the International Economy. Ed. by Robert A. Blecker. LC 95-9028. (Economic Policy Institute Ser.). 336p. (C). (gr. 13). 1995. text ed. 62.95 (*1-56324-530-2*) M E Sharpe.

U. S. Trade Policy & Global Growth: New Directions in the International Economy. Ed. by Robert A. Blecker. LC 95-9028. (Economic Policy Institute Ser.). 336p. (C). (gr. 13). 1995. pap. text ed. 25.95 (*1-56324-531-0*) M E Sharpe.

U. S. Trade Policy Beyond the Uraguay Round: A Statement. Research & Policy Committee of the Committee for Economic Development. LC 94-14783. 1994. 10.00 (*0-87186-098-8*) Comm Econ Dev.

U. S. Trade Policy Toward Mexico: Are There Reasons to Expect Special Treatment? D. Olga Pellicer. (Research Reports: No. 9). 24p. (Orig.). (C). 1981. pap. 5.00 (*0-935391-08-8*, RR-09) UCSD Ctr US-Mex.

U. S. Trade Problems in Steel: Japan, West Germany & Italy. Albert W. Harris. LC 83-6266. (Illus.). 288p. 1983. text ed. 65.00 (*0-275-90998-0*, C0998, Praeger Pubs) Greenwood.

U. S. Trade Shifts in Selected Industries. 1995. lib. bdg. 250.00 (*0-8490-7408-8*) Gordon Pr.

U. S. Trademark Law: Rules of Practice, Forms & Federal Statutes, DOS. annuals LC 84-50807. 342p. 1996. ring bd. 125.00 incl. disk (*0-939190-02-8*) Intl Trademark.

*__U. S. Trademark Law: Rules of Practice, Forms & Federal Statutes, Windows.__ annuals 342p. 1996. ring bd. 165.95 incl. disk (*0-614-29588-2*) Intl Trademark.

*__U. S. Trademark Law Revision Act of 1988.__ 492p. 1989. pap. 49.95 (*0-939190-03-6*) Intl Trademark.

U. S. Transformer Industry. 250p. 1995. ring bd. 1,995.00 (*0-317-55172-8*) Busn Trend.

U. S. Treasury Securities Market: The Scholars' Assesment. Catalyst Institute Staff. LC 94-26475. 1994. write for info. (*0-7863-0355-7*) Irwin.

U. S. Treaties in Force. 1994. pap. 29.00 (*0-16-045091-8*) Claitors.

U. S. Treaties...Digests... Bevans: U. S. Treaties & Other International Agreements of the United States of America, General Index. Charles I. Bevans. LC 70-600742. 75.00 (*1-57588-371-6*, 201220) W S Hein.

U. S. Treaties...Digests... Bevans: U. S. Treaties & Other International Agreements of the United States of America, 1776-1949, 13 vols., Set. Charles I. Bevans. LC 70-600742. 1979. 780.00 (*1-57588-370-8*, 201220) W S Hein.

U. S. Treaties...Digests... Digest of United States Practice in International Law, 10 vols., Set. Arthur W. Rovine et al. 1979. 995.00 (*1-57588-372-4*, 201250) W S Hein.

U. S. Treaties...Digests...Miller: Treaties & Other International Acts of the United States of America, 8 vols., Set. Ed. by Hunter Miller. LC 31-28952. 1977. reprint ed. 415.00 (*1-57588-373-2*, 201240) W S Hein.

U. S. Treaties...Digests...Wharton: Digest of International Law of the United States, 3 vols., Set. 2nd ed. Ed. by Francis Wharton. LC 10-6949. 1977. reprint ed. 150.00 (*1-57588-374-0*, 201260) W S Hein.

U. S. Treaties...Digests...Whiteman: Digest of International Law, 15 vols., Set. Ed. by Marjorie M. Whiteman. LC 63-62002. 1975. reprint ed. 1,250.00 (*1-57588-375-9*, 201280) W S Hein.

U. S. Treaty with the Sioux-Brule, Oglala, Miniconjou, Yanktoni, Hunkpapa, Blackfeet, Cuthead, Two Kettle, Sans Arcs, & Santee & Arapaho, 1868. Lynn Kickingbird. (Treaty Manuscripts Ser.: No. 28). 30p. 10.00 (*0-944253-50-4*) Inst Dev Indian Law.

U. S. Treaty with the Walla Walla, Cayuse, Wascoes, etc., 1855. 5.00 (*0-944253-27-X*) Inst Dev Indian Law.

*__U. S. Trends in Eating Away from Home 1982-89: A Survey by Eating Occasion, Type of Foodservice Establishment, & Kind of Food.__ Jesus C. Dumagan & John W. Hackett. (Illus.). 70p. (C). 1997. reprint ed. pap. 25.00 (*0-7881-3701-8*) DIANE Pub.

U. S. Turkish NATO Middle East Connection: How the Truman Doctrine & Turkey's NATO Entry Contained the Soviets in the Middle East. George McGhee. 1990. text ed. 39.95 (*0-312-03540-3*) St Martin.

U. S. Two Way Land Mobile Radio Markets: Traditional Markets Being Affected by Evolving Technologies & Regulatory Conditions. Market Intelligence Staff. 276p. 1993. 2,900.00 (*1-56753-568-2*) Frost & Sullivan.

U. S., U. N. & British Commonwealth see Scott Standard Postage Stamp Catalog

U. S.-U. S. S. R. Report on Climate & Climate Change. MacCracken. 288p. 1990. 82.00 (*0-87371-440-7*, L440) Lewis Pubs.

*__U. S. Ultra, NANO & Reverse Osmosis Filter Element Markets: Crossflow Membrane Technology Gains Greater Acceptance among a Wider Range of End Users.__ Frost & Sullivan Staff. Date not set. write for info. (*0-7889-0513-9*, 5293) Frost & Sullivan.

U. S. Unilateral Arms Control Initiatives: When Do They Work? William Rose. LC 88-17774. (Contributions in Military Studies: No. 82). 209p. 1988. text ed. 55.00 (*0-313-25787-6*, RUR/, Greenwood Pr) Greenwood.

U. S. Uninterruptible Power Supply Markets. Market Intelligence Staff. 217p. 1993. 2,900.00 (*1-56753-575-5*) Frost & Sullivan.

U. S. Urology Product Markets: Infection Control in an Aging Population Stimulates Growth. Market Intelligence Staff. 250p. 1993. 1,995.00 (*1-56753-619-0*) Frost & Sullivan.

U. S. Vaccines Markets. Black Forest Group Staff. (Market Research Reports: No. 501). (Illus.). 91p. 1995. 995.00 (*0-614-09906-4*) Theta Corp.

U. S. Valve & Pipe Fittings Industry. 275p. 1997. 1,150.00 (*0-686-31541-3*) Busn Trend.

U. S. Vessel & Navy Vets Index, 1890. 1983. 45.00 (*0-89593-650-X*) Accelerated Index.

U. S. Veterans on U. S. Vessels Union Veterans. Ronald V. Jackson. (Illus.). lib. bdg. 45.00 (*0-89593-786-7*) Accelerated Index.

U. S. Video & Audio Production Equipment Markets: Advances in Digital Technology Improve Sound & Picture Quality. Frost & Sullivan Staff. Date not set. write for info. (*0-7889-0435-3*, 2840) Frost & Sullivan.

*__U. S. Videoconferencing Systems & Services Markets: Market Expands Through Merging Multimedia Technologies & Services.__ Frost & Sullivan Staff. Date not set. write for info. (*0-7889-0529-5*, 2675) Frost & Sullivan.

U. S. Videodisc Market: Forecasts & Analysis to 1990. John H. Sayers. (Monitor Reports). (Illus.). 300p. (Orig.). 1985. 795.00 (*0-938907-01-8*) Future Syst.

U. S. Vietnam Relations: Issues & Implications. (Illus.). 33p. (Orig.). (C). 1995. pap. text ed. 20.00 (*0-7881-1810-2*) DIANE Pub.

U. S. Virgin Islands: Caribbean Sunseekers. Don Philpott. (Caribbean Sunseekers Ser.). (Illus.). 160p. 1996. pap. 10.95 (*0-8442-4943-2*) NTC Pub Grp.

U. S. Virgin Islands: Jewels of the Caribbean--St. Croix, St. Thomas, St. John. Katharine R. Bailey & Gloria Bourne. LC 86-82891. (Illus.). 48p. (Orig.). (YA). (gr. 7-12). 1986. pap. 7.95 (*0-88714-012-2*) KC Pubns.

U. S. Virgin Islands Souvenir Book. (Orig.). pap. text ed. write for info. (*1-56944-024-7*) Terrell Missouri.

U. S. Virgins Swimsuit Calendar, 1990. Illus. by Lausch, David, Graphics Staff. 8p. 1989. 9.95 (*0-927400-00-6*) Deaner Pub.

U. S. Virtual Reality Hardware, Software, System & Service Markets: Current Applications Show Great Promise. Market Intelligence Staff. 320p. 1993. 2,795.00 (*1-56753-563-1*) Frost & Sullivan.

U. S. Voc Recovery & Destruction Equipment Markets: Regulations Spark New Acquisition Activity. Market Intelligence Staff. 210p. 1993. 1,895.00 (*1-56753-600-X*) Frost & Sullivan.

U. S. Voice Messaging Service Markets. Market Intelligence Staff. 349p. 1994. 1,995.00 (*0-7889-0168-0*) Frost & Sullivan.

U. S. vs. Downing: Opinion of U. S. Court of Appeals, Third Circuit, Reversing Due to Exclusion of Expert Opinion on Eyewitness Identification, 753 Fed. 2nd, 1224. (Monographs: No. CR-51). 1985. 4.00 (*1-55524-052-6*) Ctr Respon Psych.

U. S. vs. Schubert. (Monographs: No. CR-49). 1985. 8.00 (*1-55524-050-X*) Ctr Respon Psych.

U. S. vs. Steven F. Soliah. S. Otis. (Monographs: No. CR-6). 1975. 4.00 (*1-55524-006-2*) Ctr Respon Psych.

U. S. Vxlbus Instrumentation Markets. Market Intelligence Staff. 207p. 1993. 2,900.00 (*1-56753-576-3*) Frost & Sullivan.

U. S. War Crimes Trial Program in Germany, 1946-1955. Frank M. Buscher. LC 88-24706. (Contributions in Military Studies: No. 86). 197p. 1989. text ed. 45.00 (*0-313-26471-6*, BUW, Greenwood Pr) Greenwood.

U. S. War Drive & the World Economic Crisis. Fidel Castro. 31p. 1982. pap. 2.50 (*0-87348-447-9*) Pathfinder NY.

U. S. War in Somalia: The New Face of Colonialism. Workers World Staff. 26p. 1993. pap. 2.50 (*0-614-02750-0*) World View Forum.

U. S. War Relocation Authority, 11 vols., Set. Incl. 1. Administrative Highlights of the WRA Program. Ed. by U. S. War Relocation Authority. 1946. (*0-404-58001-7*); 2. Community Government in War Relocation Centers. Ed. by U. S. War Relocation Authority. 1946. (*0-404-58002-5*); 3. Evacuated People, a Quantitative Description. U. S. War Relocation Authority. 1946. (*0-404-58003-3*); 4. Legal & Constitutional Phases of the WRA Program. U. S. War Relocation Authority. 1946. (*0-404-58004-1*); 5. People in Motion: The Postwar Adjustment of the Evacuated Japanese Americans. U. S. War Relocation Authority. 1947. (*0-404-58005-X*); 6. Relocation Program: A Guidebook for the Residents of Relocation Centers. U. S. War Relocation Authority. 1943. (*0-404-58006-8*); 7. Relocation Program. U. S. War Relocation Authority. 1946. (*0-404-58007-6*); 8. Token Shipment: The Story of America's War Refugee Shelter. U. S. War Relocation Authority. 1946. (*0-404-58008-4*); 9. WRA, a Story of Human Conservation. U. S. War Relocation Authority. 1946. (*0-404-58009-2*); 10. Wartime Exile, the Exclusion of the Japanese Americans from the West Coast. U. S. War Relocation Authority. 1946. (*0-404-58010-6*); 11. Wartime Handling of Evacuee Property. U. S. War Relocation Authority. 1946. (*0-404-58011-4*); 1946. 372.50 (*0-404-58000-9*) AMS Pr.

U. S. Warships since Nineteen Forty-Five. Paul H. Silverstone. 240p. 1987. 29.95 (*0-87021-769-0*) Naval Inst Pr.

U. S. Wartime Aid to Britain, 1940-1946. Alan P. Dobson. LC 85-27920. 240p. 1986. text ed. 39.95 (*0-312-83519-9*) St Martin.

U. S. Waste-to-Energy Plant Markets: Increasing MSW Capacity Creates Opportunities for Capital Investment. 230p. 1996. write for info. (*0-7889-0236-9*) Frost & Sullivan.

U. S. Wastewater Treatment Equipment Markets: Market Grows Despite Regulatory, Funding Uncertainties. Frost & Sullivan Staff. 418p. 1996. write for info. (*0-7889-0433-7*, 5333-15) Frost & Sullivan.

U. S. Water & Wastewater Treatment Chemicals Market: Manufacturers Develop New Products & Technologies in Response to Performance & Regulatory Requirements. Frost & Sullivan Staff. 442p. 1996. write for info. (*0-7889-0448-5*, 2849-82) Frost & Sullivan.

U. S. Water Purification Equipment Markets: Growing Concerns over Health Issues Impact Market Trends. Date not set. write for info. (*0-7889-0388-8*) Frost & Sullivan.

U. S. Water Soluble Polymers: Green Thinking Means Growth Despite Overcapacity. Market Intelligence Staff. 300p. 1993. 2,950.00 (*1-56753-616-6*) Frost & Sullivan.

U. S. Water Treatment Equipment Markets. 422p. Date not set. write for info. (*0-7889-0373-X*) Frost & Sullivan.

U. S. Weapons at War: Arms Deliveries to Regions of Conflict. William D. Hartung. (World Policy Papers). 53p. 1995. pap. 7.50 (*0-911646-61-2*) World Policy.

U. S. Welding Apparatus Industry. (Illus.). 155p. (Orig.). 1992. spiral bd. 1,950.00 (*0-685-44202-0*) Busn Trend.

U. S. Welding Apparatus Market. 167p. 1992. 1,950.00 (*0-945235-59-3*) Lead Edge Reports.

U. S. West European Relations During the Reagan Years: The Perspective of West European Publics. Steven K. Smith. 1992. text ed. 65.00 (*0-312-06838-7*) St Martin.

U. S. Winchester Trench & Riot Guns & Other U. S. Combat Shotguns. Joe Poyer. (For Collectors Only Ser.). (Illus.). 122p. (Orig.). 1992. pap. 15.95 (*1-882391-02-0*) N Cape Pubns.

U. S. Wine Industry. 290p. 1989. 995.00 (*0-686-38415-6*, 131) Busn Trend.

U. S. Wine Market: Impact Databank Review & Forecast, 1996. Marvin R. Shanken. (Illus.). 298p. (Orig.). 1992. pap. 795.00 (*1-881659-03-8*) M Shanken Comm.

U. S. Wire & Cable Markets: Ten Applications & Eight Industries Led by Telecommunications & Consumer Electronics. Market Intelligence Staff. 488p. 1993. 3,900.00 (*1-56753-611-5*) Frost & Sullivan.

U. S. Wireless Office Equipment Markets: Anytime, Anywhere Communications. Market Intelligence Staff. 360p. 1994. 2,295.00 (*0-7889-0094-3*) Frost & Sullivan.

U. S. Women in Struggle: A Feminist Studies Anthology. Ed. by Claire G. Moses & Heidi Hartmann. (Women in American History Ser.). 464p. 1995. text ed. 49.95 (*0-252-02166-5*); pap. text ed. 19.95 (*0-252-06462-3*) U of Ill Pr.

*__U. S. Women's Gymnastics Team.__ Richard Rambeck. LC 97-9040. (J). 1997. write for info. (*1-56766-410-5*) Childs World.

U. S. Women's History. 2nd ed. Linda Gordon. (New American History Essays Ser.). 30p. 1997. reprint ed. pap. 5.00 (*0-87229-059-X*) Am Hist Assn.

U. S. Women's Interest Groups. Ed. by Sarah Slavin. LC 94-38500. (Reference Volumes on American Public Policy Formation Ser.). 704p. 1995. text ed. 99.50 (*0-313-25073-1*, Greenwood Pr) Greenwood.

U. S. Wood-Based Industry: Industrial Organization & Performance. Paul V. Ellefson & Robert N. Stone. LC 84-8278. 508p. 1984. text ed. 75.00 (*0-275-91150-0*, C1150, Praeger Pubs) Greenwood.

U. S. Wound Management Markets: The Quest for Less Damaging, More Active Products. Market Intelligence Staff. 300p. (Orig.). 1994. 2,295.00 (*1-56753-887-8*) Frost & Sullivan.

U. S. Wound Management Product Markets: Newest Dressings Setting the Pace. Frost & Sullivan Staff. Date not set. write for info. (*0-7889-0432-9*, 5344-54) Frost & Sullivan.

U. S. Z. Kush. (Voices in the Wind Ser.: No. 1). (Illus.). 108p. 1983. pap. 5.00 (*0-938392-03-4*) Homeward Pr.

*__U. S. Zinc Industry.__ James Jolly. LC 96-80084. 328p. (Orig.). 1997. pap. write for info. (*1-56167-356-0*) Am Literary Pr.

U. S. Zip Codes Atlas. American Map Corp. Staff. 1994. pap. 29.95 (*0-8416-9607-1*, 696071) Am Map.

U. S. 395 Between Reno & Los Angeles: History, Geology & Points of Interest. Len Ettinger. (Ride along with Me Adventure Ser.). (Illus.). 32p. (Orig.). 1989. pap. 3.95 (*0-9614840-3-9*) Ettinger.

U Samago Moria. Anna Akhmatova. 36p. (RUS.). (C). 1994. reprint ed. pap. text ed. 4.00 (*0-933884-62-1*) Berkeley Slavic.

*__U-Shaped Shoes.__ Melba C. Ellmore. LC 97-6153. (Illus.). (J). 1998. 14.95 (*1-57102-116-7*, Ideals Child) Hambleton-Hill.

*__U. S./Mexico Tax Convention.__ Phillips & Washlick. 80p. 1993. pap. 39.00 (*0-8080-0000-4*, BLS-3188) Commerce.

*__U. S.Naval & Marine Corps Reserve Aviation Vol. 2: Aircraft 1916-1942.__ Wayne H. Heiser. 209p. 1996. pap. 39.95 (*0-89126-192-3*) MA-AH Pub.

U-Statistics: Theory & Practice. Lee. (Statistics: Textbooks & Monographs: Vol. 110). 320p. 1990. 115.00 (*0-8247-8253-4*) Dekker.

U-Statistics in Banach Spaces. Yu V. Borovskikh. 432p. 1996. 237.50 (*90-6764-200-2*, Pub. by VSP NE) Coronet Bks.

*__U Sviti Mystets'kykh Chariv - Fascinating Corners in the World of Art.__ George Moschinsky. (Illus.). 323p. (UKR.). 1963. 23.95 (*0-938103-09-1*) ZZYZX Pub.

U Thant in New York. Ramses Nassit. 180p. 1988. 24.95 (*0-685-20013-2*) St Martin.

U-Turn, U. S. A. LC 93-72329. (Wendells Family - Fiction Ser.). write for info. (*0-614-04114-7*) ASDA Pub.

U-Turn, U. S. A. The Wendells Family. Carl Bradfield. (Illus.). 150p. (Orig.). 1992. pap. 6.95 (*0-9632319-1-X*) ASDA Pub.

U2 Live: A Concert Documentary. Pimm J. De La Parra. (Illus.). 176p. pap. 22.95 (*0-7119-3666-8*, OP 47526) Omnibus NY.

U-Uran, Uranium. 1980. 670.00 (*0-387-93423-5*) Spr-Verlag.

*__U Uranium: Chemistry in Nonaqueous Solutions, Vol. XII.__ K. Zdenekk. Ed. by R. Keim. (Formation of Complexes & Redox Reactions Ser.: Supplement Vol. D6). (Illus.). 237p. 1996. 1,020.00 (*3-540-93735-8*) Spr-Verlag.

UV

U Uranium, Suppl Vol. B, Pt. 3, Alloys of Uranium with Transition Metals of Groups 1B to IVB see Gmelin: Handbook of Inorganic & Organometallic Chemistry

U Uranium, Supplement Volume B 4, Alloys of Uranium with Transition Metals of Groups V B to VIII B see Gmelin: Handbook of Inorganic & Organometallic Chemistry

U-2 Spyplane. Larry Davis. (Aircraft in Action Ser.). (Illus.). 50p. 1988. pap. 7.95 (*0-89747-202-0*, 1086) Squad Sig Pubns.

UAB Marcel Proust Symposium: In Celebration of the 75th Anniversary of "Swann's Way" (1913-1988) Intro. by William C. Carter. LC 89-62847. 154p. 1989. lib. bdg. 25.95 (*0-917786-75-0*) Summa Pubns.

***UAE: Internal Boundaries & the Boundary with Oman, 8 vols.** Ed. by J. F. Walker. (Illus.). 4000p. 1994. reprint ed. lib. bdg. 2,795.00 (*1-85207-575-9*, Pub. by Archive Editions UK) N Ross.

UAHC Kids Catalog of Jewish Living. Chaya M. Burstein. LC 91-42815. (J). (gr. 4-6). 1992. pap. 8.95 (*0-8074-0464-0*, 123934) UAHC.

'Uala: Sweet Potato. Lisa L. Adams. (Illus.). 24p. (Orig.). (ENG & HAW.). 1994. pap. 5.50 (*0-9641577-2-1*) Spiral Triangle.

Uanga--Fetico: Romance Folclorico Angolano. 2nd ed. Oscar B. Ribas. (B. E. Ser.: No. 69). (POR.). 1969. 30.00 (*0-8115-3019-1*) Periodicals Srv.

UATS Pilot Training Program Instructor Guide. Des. by Curtis Hughes. 19.95 (*0-614-13162-6*, 21-13028) EAA Aviation.

UAV - Unmanned Aerial Vehicle; RPV - Remotely Piloted Vehicles. Louis Gerken. Ed. & Illus. by ASTA Corp Staff. LC 91-5. 300p. 1991. 40.00 (*0-9617163-4-7*) Amer Scientific.

UAW & the Heyday of American Liberalism, 1945-1968. Kevin Boyle. 360p. 1995. 35.00 (*0-8014-3064-X*) Cornell U Pr.

UAW & Walter Reuther. I. Howe & B. J. Widick. LC 72-2375. (FDR & the Era of the New Deal Ser.). 324p. 1973. reprint ed. lib. bdg. 39.50 (*0-306-70485-4*) Da Capo.

UAW Politics in the Cold War Era. Martin Halpern. LC 87-13890. (SUNY Series in American Labor History). 361p. 1988. text ed. 74.50 (*0-88706-671-2*) State U NY Pr.

Uaxactun: Extincion de una Cultura. Paul Schmidt. 120p. 1983. pap. 1.25 (*1-877812-45-5*, UN023) UPLAAP.

Uaxactun, Guatemala: Excavations of 1931-1937. Augustus L. Smith. LC 77-11523. (Carnegie Institution of Washington. Publications: No. 588). reprint ed. 42.50 (*0-404-16288-6*) AMS Pr.

U.B.C. Field Inspection Workbook, 1994. 400p. 1994. pap. text ed. 37.95 (*1-884590-70-5*) Intl Conf Bldg Off.

Ubel Velez: Lawyer. Jennifer Bryant. (Working Moms: A Portrait of Their Lives Ser.). (Illus.). 40p. (J). (gr. 2-4). 1991. lib. bdg. 15.98 (*0-941477-52-5*) TFC Bks NY.

Ubena of the Rivers. Arthur T. Culwick & G. M. Culwick. LC 76-44707. reprint ed. 69.50 (*0-404-15883-8*) AMS Pr.

Uber Arabische Pferde. Rochus Kameke & Furst Puckler. (Documenta Hippologica Ser.). (Illus.). 223p. 1987. reprint ed. write for info. (*3-487-08246-2*) G Olms Pubs.

Uber das Conjugationssystem der Sanskritsprache. Franz Bopp. (Documenta Semiotica, Ser. 1). xlvi, 312p. 1975. reprint ed. 80.00 (*3-487-05354-3*) G Olms Pubs.

Uber das Lachen und Studien: Uber den Platonischen Sokrates. F. Neumann. 177p. 1971. pap. text ed. 47.00 (*90-247-5118-7*) Kluwer Ac.

Uber Den Satz des Widerspruchs Bei Aristoteles, Band V. Jan Lukasiewicz. (Zur Modernendeutung der Aristotelischen Logik Ser.). (GER.). 1910. 80.00 (*3-487-09761-3*) G Olms Pubs.

Uber den Umgang mit der deutschen Sprache: Stilistische Beobachtungen zum Sprachgebrauch der Gegenwart. Peter Wapnewski. 32p. (Orig.). (GER.). (C). 1991. pap. text ed. 4.00 (*0-942017-01-3*) Amer Assn Teach German.

Uber die Arzneiwissensschaft (De Medicina, Deutscsh) Cornelius Celsus. xlii, 862p. 1967. reprint ed. 190.00 (*0-318-71087-0*) G Olms Pubs.

Uber die Dorfer see Walk about the Villages: A Dramatic Poem

Uber Die Epochen der Neueren Geschichte & das Politische Gesprach und Andere Schdriften Zur Wissenschaftslehre, 2 Vols. Leopold Von Ranke. LC 78-67376. (European Political Thought Ser.). 1980. reprint ed. lib. bdg. 19.95 (*0-405-11726-4*) Ayer.

Uber die Gedichte, Funftes Buch. Philodemos of Garada. xi, 178p. 1973. write for info. (*3-296-14930-9*) G Olms Pubs.

Uber die Geheimlehren (De Mysteriis) Jamblichus. (Quellenschriften der Griechischen Mystik Ser.: Bd. 1). xxiv, 278p. 1988. reprint ed. write for info. (*3-487-07947-X*) G Olms Pubs.

Uber die Leibnizsche Logik Mit Besonderer Berucksicitigung des Problems der Intension und der Extension. Raili Kauppi. Ed. by R. C. Sleigh, Jr. LC 84-48421. (Philosophy of Leibniz Ser.). 279p. 1985. text ed. 15.00 (*0-8240-6534-4*) Garland.

Uber die Musik der Nordamerikanischen Wilden. Theodore Baker. LC 71-38496. reprint ed. 31.50 (*0-404-08337-4*) AMS Pr.

***Uber die Pflicht Eine Analyse des Werks Von Siegfried Lenz.** Claus Nordbruch. (Germanistische Texte und Studien: Vol. 53). 250p. (GER.). 1996. write for info. (*3-487-10078-9*) G Olms Pubs.

***Uber die Ruinen des Museums das Museum, die Photographie und die Postmoderne.** Douglas Crimp. 1996. text ed. 51.00 (*3-364-00328-9*) Gordon & Breach.

Uber Existenz: Die Ontologie Romans Ingardens. Gregor Haefliger. (Phaenomenologica Ser.). 500p. (GER.). (C). 1994. lib. bdg. 186.50 (*0-7923-2227-4*, Pub. by Klwr Acad Pubs NE) Kluwer Ac.

Uber Finanzen und Monopole Im Alten Griechenland: Zur Theorie und Geschichte der antiken Stadtwirtschaft. Kurt Riezler. Ed. by Moses Finley. LC 79-5002. (Ancient Economic History Ser.). (GER.). 1979. reprint ed. lib. bdg. 15.95 (*0-405-12391-4*) Ayer.

Uber Malerei, Vermeer - La Tour - Turner. Michel Serres. 126p. 1995. text ed. 14.00 (*3-364-00311-4*) Gordon & Breach.

Uberall Blicke Ich Nach Einem Heimatlichen Boden Aus: Exil Im Werk Else Lasker-Sch Ulers. Sonja M. Hedgepeth. LC 93-29663. (Exilstudien Ser.: Vol. 1). 256p. (GER.). (C). 1994. text ed. 44.95 (*0-8204-2219-3*) P Lang Pubng.

Ubergang Vom Feudalen Zum Burgerlichen Weltbild. Franz Borkenau. LC 74-25740. (European Sociology Ser.). 574p. 1975. reprint ed. 47.95 (*0-405-06496-9*) Ayer.

***Ubergang von Den Metaphysischen Anfangsgrunden der Naturwissenschaft Zur Physik.** Immanuel Kant. viii, 108p. (GER.). 1996. write for info. (*3-487-10137-8*) G Olms Pubs.

Ubergange. Corl & Jurasek. (College German Ser.). (GER.). 1994. teacher ed., pap. 13.95 (*0-8384-4640-X*); teacher ed., pap. 13.95 (*0-8384-5372-4*) Heinle & Heinle.

Ubergange: Sprechen, Berichten, Diskutieren. Clausing. (Bridging the Gap Ser.). 1994. pap. 36.95 (*0-8384-4632-9*) Heinle & Heinle.

Ubergange: Texte Erfassen. Corl et al. (Bridging the Gap Ser.). 1994. pap. 36.95 (*0-8384-5370-8*) Heinle & Heinle.

Ubergange: Texte Verfassen. Corl et al. (Bridging the Gap Ser.). 1994. pap. 36.95 (*0-8384-4638-8*) Heinle & Heinle.

***Uberleben Multinationaler Unternehmungen: Generierung & Transfer von Wissen im Internationalen Wettbewerb.** Ulrich Becker. (Illus.). xliv, 373p. (GER.). 1996. 63.95 (*3-631-49633-8*) P Lang Pubng.

***Ubersetzerische Kompetenz: Beitrage Zur Universitaren Ubersetzerausbildung in Deutschland und Skandinavien.** Andreas F. Kelletat. (Publikationen des Fachbereichs Angewandte Sprach- und Kulturwissenschaft der Johannes Gutenberg-Universitat Mainz in Germersheim Ser.: Bd. 22). (Illus.). 288p. (GER.). 1996. 54.95 (*3-631-49773-3*) P Lang Pubng.

Ubersetzung und Leser: Untersuchungen Zur Ubersetzungsaquivalenz Dargestellt an Der Rezeption von Multatulis Max Havelaar und Seinen Deutschen Ubersetzungen. Jelle Stegemann. (Studia Linguistica Germanica: Bd. 30). xvi, 555p. (GER.). (C). 1991. lib. bdg. 178.50 (*3-11-012470-X*) De Gruyter.

***Ubersetzungsprobleme Im Fruhen Mittelalter.** Phillip Heck. xv, 303p. (GER.). 1977. reprint ed. write for info. (*3-487-06442-1*) G Olms Pubs.

***Ubersicht des Russischen Reichs Nach Seiner Gegenwartigen Neu Eingerichteten Verfassung Aufgesetzt Von Sergei Pleschtschejew, Seekapitan und Ritter des Heiligen Georgen-Ordens.** S. Pleschtschejew. iv, 220p. (GER.). 1992. write for info. (*3-487-09614-5*) G Olms Pubs.

Ubi Sumus? The State of Naval & Maritime History, 11. Ed. by John B. Hattendorf. LC 94-34667. (Historical Monographs: No. 11). (Illus.). 430p. (Orig.). 1994. pap. 10.00 (*1-884733-04-2*) Naval War Coll.

Ubijaj Boljsevicke Lazi i Zlocine - Kill Bolshevik Lies & Crimes. Ivo Omrcanin. 104p. (CRO.). 1993. pap. 10.00 (*1-878716-11-5*) Ivor Pr.

Ubik. Philip K. Dick. LC 91-50097. 224p. 1991. pap. 11.00 (*0-679-73664-6*, Vin) Random.

Ubiquitin. Ed. by M. Rechsteiner. LC 88-9809. (Illus.). 364p. 1988. 85.00 (*0-306-42850-4*, Plenum Pr) Plenum.

Ubiquitin System. Milton J. Schlesinger. (Current Communications in Molecular Biology Ser.). (Illus.). 200p. (C). 1988. pap. text ed. 25.00 (*0-87969-318-5*) Cold Spring Harbor.

Ubiquitous Markets for Blister Packaging & Competing Technologies. 154p. 1993. 2,650.00 (*0-89336-991-8*, P-213) BCC.

Ubiquitous Photon: Helicity Methods for QED & QCD. R. Gastmans & Tai Tsun Wu. (International Series of Monographs on Physics: No. 80). (Illus.). 664p. 1990. 98.00 (*0-19-852043-3*) OUP.

Ubiquitous Pig. Marilyn Nissenson & Susan Jonas. (Illus.). 136p. 1996. pap. 17.98 (*0-8109-8155-6*) Abrams.

Ubiquitous Urbanism - Total Architecture: The Tokyo Experiment. Ed. by Tony Wong & Lois Nesbitt. (Studio Work Ser.: No. 2). (Illus.). 75p. (Orig.). 1994. pap. 12.95 (*1-883584-03-5*) CUGSA.

Ubiquity of Chaos. Ed. by Saul Krasner. LC 90-31235. (AAAS Miscellaneous Publications: No. 89-15S). 255p. reprint ed. pap. 72.70 (*0-7837-6738-2*, 2046366) Bks Demand.

Ubiquity of the Finite: Hegel, Heidegger, & the Entitlements of Philosophy. Dennis J. Schmidt. (Studies in Contemporary German Social Thought). 264p. 1990. reprint ed. pap. 9.95 (*0-262-69139-6*) MIT Pr.

***Ublasaun - First Light: Inupiaq Hunters & Herders in the Early Twentieth Century, Northern Seward Peninsula, Alaska.** Ed. by Jeanne Schaaf & Thetus H. Smith. (Illus.). 150p. (Orig.). 1996. write for info. (*0-941555-03-8*); pap. write for info. (*0-941555-02-X*) Natl Pk AK.

***Ubu.** Alfred Jarry. (Nick Hern Books, Drama Classics). 1997. pap. text ed. 6.95 (*1-85459-189-4*, Pub. by N Hern Bks UK) Theatre Comm.

Ubu. unabridged ed. Alfred Jarry. (FRE.). pap. 5.95 (*2-87714-211-6*, Pub. by Bookking Intl FR) Distribks Inc.

Ubu: The Witch Who Would Be Rich. Mary Melfi. 160p. 1994. pap. 10.95 (*0-385-25448-2*) Doubleday.

Ubu: Ubu Roi, Ubu Cocu, Ubu Enchaine, Ubu sur la Butte. Alfred Jarry. Ed. by Noel Arnaud & Henri Bordillon. 533p. (FRE.). 1978. 7.95 (*0-7859-0104-3*, M3598) Fr & Eur.

Ubu: Ubu Roi; Ubu Cocu; Ubu Enchaine; Ubu sur la Butte. Alfred Jarry. (Folio Ser.: No. 980). (FRE.). pap. 12.50 (*2-07-036980-3*) Schoenhof.

Ubu Cocu see Tout Ubu

Ubu Enchaine see Tout Ubu

UBU Guide to New French-Language Plays in English Translations. UBU Repertory Theater Staff. 64p. (Orig.). (C). 1986. pap. 8.95 (*0-913745-22-7*) Ubu Repertory.

Ubu Plays: Ubu Rex; Ubu Cuckolded; Ubu Enchained, 3 vols. Alfred Jarry. Tr. by Simon W. Taylor & Cyrill Connolly from FRE. LC 69-19439. 148p. 1968. reprint ed. pap. 10.95 (*0-8021-5010-1*, E496, Grove) Grove-Atltic.

Ubu Repertory Theater, 1982-1992. Ed. by Francoise Kourilsky. 116p. (ENG & FRE.). 1992. pap. 14.95 (*0-913745-38-3*) Ubu Repertory.

Ubu Roi. Alfred Jarry. Tr. by Barbara Wright from FRE. LC 61-10124. (Illus.). 196p. 1961. pap. 8.95 (*0-8112-0072-8*, 105) New Directions.

Ubu Roi: An Analytical Study, Vol. 6. Judith Cooper. 120p. 1974. pap. 7.00 (*0-912788-05-4*) Tulane Romance Lang.

Ubu Roi see Tout Ubu

Ubu sur la Butte see Tout Ubu

Ubungen Dt. Rechtschr. One: Der Schreibungder Worter. Jakob Ebner. (Schulerduden-Ubungsbucher Ser.). 300p. 1992. 16.90 (*3-411-05242-2*, Pub. by Bibliogr Inst Brockhaus GW) Langenscheidt.

Ubungen Dt. Rechtschr. Three: Die Zeichensetzrng. Heinrich Wolff. (Schulerduden-Ubungsbucher Ser.). 205p. 1980. 16.95 (*3-411-01781-3*, Pub. by Bibliogr Inst Brockhaus GW) Langenscheidt.

Ubungen Z. Dt. Rechtschr. Two: Gross-und Kleinschreibung. Jakob Ebner & Helga Ebner. (Schulerduden-Ubungsbucher Ser.). 256p. 1973. 16.95 (*3-411-01332-X*, Pub. by Bibliogr Inst Brockhaus GW) Langenscheidt.

***Ubungen zu den Wichtigsten Kapiteln der Englischen Grammatik: Schlusselheft.** Wilhelm Dittrich. 32p. (GER.). 1968. 5.90 (*3-296-50401-X*, Pub. by Weidmann GW) Lubrecht & Cramer.

***Ubungen zu den Wichtigsten Kapiteln der Franzosischen Grammatik.** Friedrich Lange & Otto Geertz. 60p. (GER.). 1974. 5.90 (*3-296-60300-X*, Pub. by Weidmann GW) Lubrecht & Cramer.

***Ubungen Zu Den Wichtigsten Kapiteln der Franzosischen Grammatik.** Friedrich Lange & Otto Geertz. 29p. (GER.). 1974. 5.90 (*3-296-60301-8*, Pub. by Weidmann GW) Lubrecht & Cramer.

Ubungen Zu Schwerpunkten der Dt. Grammatik. 1992. 17.50 (*3-324-00002-5*) Langenscheidt.

Ubungen Zur Dt. Sprache One: Grammatische Ubungen. Stefanie Kufmann & Gerhard Kaufmann. (Schulerduden-Ubungsbucher Ser.). 239p. 1975. 16.95 (*3-411-01336-2*, Pub. by Bibliogr Inst Brockhaus GW) Langenscheidt.

Ubungen Zur Dt. Sprache Two: Ubungen Zum Wortschatz. Heindrun Muller. (Schulerduden-Ubungsbucher Ser.). 295p. 1988. 16.95 (*3-411-01363-X*, Pub. by Bibliogr Inst Brockhaus GW) Langenscheidt.

Ubungen zur Projektiven Geometrie. H. Herrmann. (Mathematische Reihe Ser.: No. 18). (Illus.). 168p. (GER.). 1980. 28.50 (*0-8176-0170-8*) Birkhauser.

Ubungsgrammatik Deutsch. Gerhard Helbig & Joachim Buscha. 379p. 1991. 23.50 (*3-324-00379-2*) Langenscheidt.

***Ubungssatze zur Einpragung der Franzosischen Unregelmabigen Verban Teil 1: Deutscher Text.** Wilhelm S. Dittrich. 34p. (GER.). 1959. 3.90 (*3-296-60201-1*, Pub. by Weidmann GW) Lubrecht & Cramer.

***Ubungssatze zur Einpragung der Franzosischen Unregelmabigen Verban Teil 2: Franzosischer Text.** Wilhelm S. Dittrich. 26p. (GER.). 1967. 3.90 (*3-296-60202-X*, Pub. by Weidmann GW) Lubrecht & Cramer.

UC Davis Book of Horses. University of California, Davis, School of Veterinary Medicine Staff. Ed. by Mordecai Siegal. 1996. 30.00 (*0-614-96840-2*, Harper Ref); 30.00 (*0-614-96963-8*, Harper Ref) HarpC.

UC Davis Book of Horses: Complete Medical Reference Guide for Horses & Colts. Members of the Faculty & Staff, University of California, Davis School of Veterinary Medicine. Ed. by Mordecai Siegal. (Animal & Pet Care Ser.). (Illus.). 464p. 1996. 30.00 (*0-06-270139-8*, Harper Ref) HarpC.

UC Integrated Pest Management Guidelines. Barbara Ohlendorf & Mary L. Flint. 737p. 1990. ring bd. 80.00 (*0-931876-92-3*, 3339) ANR Pubns CA.

UC Irvine. Melinda Wortz. LC 75-37097. (Illus.). 96p. 1975. 7.00 (*0-686-99815-4*) Mus Contemp Art.

***Ucalendar.** Dan Youra. (Illus.). 128p. 1994. pap. 5.00 (*0-940828-22-7*) D Youra Studios.

UCC: Reporter Digest, 12 vols. Frederick M. Hart. 1965. Set. Updates. ring bd. write for info. (*0-8205-1747-X*) Bender.

UCC - Real Estate Telephone Directory: Real Property, Too. 2nd ed. Carl R. Ernst. 196p. 1992. write for info. (*1-881627-06-3*) UCC Guide.

U.C.C. Adaptable to Courses Utilizing Epstein, Martin, Henning & Nickle's Casebook on Basic Uniform Commercial Code: Adaptable to Courses Utilizing Epstein & Martin's Casebook on Basic Uniform Commercial Code. Casenotes Publishing Co., Inc. Staff. Ed. by Norman S. Goldenberg & Peter Tenen. (Legal Briefs Ser.). 1988. pap. write for info. (*0-87457-142-1*, 1410) Casenotes Pub.

U.C.C. Amendments to Article Eight, 1977: Official Text with Comments. 1978. pap. 3.95 (*0-685-91310-4*) West Pub.

U.C.C. Amendments to Article Nine, 1972: Official Text with Comments. 1978. pap. 3.95 (*0-685-91309-0*) West Pub.

UCC Article 4A: A Practical Guide for Bankers & Bank Counsel. 130p. 1991. pap. 195.00 (*0-89982-349-1*, 242200) Am Bankers.

UCC Law. Crandall. 1993. 135.00 (*0-316-16010-5*); 595.00 (*0-316-16026-1*) Little.

UCC Law, Vol. 2. Crandall. 1993. 135.00 (*0-316-16022-9*) Little.

UCC Law, Vol. 3. Crandall. 1993. 135.00 (*0-316-16023-7*) Little.

UCC Law, Vol. 4. Crandall. 1993. 135.00 (*0-316-16024-5*) Little.

UCC Law, Vol. 5. Crandall. 1993. 135.00 (*0-316-16025-3*) Little.

UCC Revised Articles Three & Four: The Banker's Guide to Checks, Drafts & Other Negotiable Instruments. Paul A. Carrubba. 250p. 1993. text ed. 60.00 (*1-55738-351-0*) Irwin Prof Pubng.

UCC/EAN-128 Application Identifier Standard. 1995. 30.00 (*0-614-15095-7*) Uniform Code.

UCH Handbook of Psychiatry. Ed. by R. Tredgold & H. Wolff. 240p. 1984. pap. 18.95 (*0-7156-0937-8*, Pub. by Duckworth UK) Focus Pub-R Pullins.

Uch Tepe I, Tell Razuk, Tell Ahmed al-Mughir, Tell Ajamat. Ingolf Thuesen et al. Ed. by McGuire Gibson et al. (Chicago-Copenhagen Expedition to the Hamrin Ser.: No. 10). (Illus.). xi, 198p. 1981. pap. 25.00 (*0-918986-34-6*) Orient Inst.

Uch Tepe Two: Technical Reports. Ed. & Intro. by McGuire Gibson. (Chicago-Copenhagen Expedition to the Hamrin Ser.: No. 11). (Illus.). 140p. (Orig.). 1990. pap. 25.00 (*0-918986-61-3*) Orientl Inst Pr IT.

UCH Textbook of Psychiatry: An Integrated Approach. D. Wolff. pap. 37.95 (*0-7156-2289-7*, Pub. by Duckworth UK) Focus Pub-R Pullins.

Uchenije o Pravoslavnom Bogosluzhenii. V. Mikhailovsky. 146p. reprint ed. pap. text ed. 6.00 (*0-317-30287-6*) Holy Trinity.

Uchinanchu: A History of Okinawans in Hawaii. Ed. by University of Hawaii, Ethnic Studies Oral History Project Staff. 696p. 1982. text ed. 25.00 (*0-8248-0749-9*) UH Pr.

Uchjebnik Tserkovnago Penija. A. Ryazhsky. 105p. 1966. reprint ed. pap. 5.00 (*0-317-30382-1*) Holy Trinity.

UCI: The First Twenty-Five Years. Frank McGee. Ed. by Barbara Cronin. (Illus.). 155p. 1992. text ed. 24.95 (*0-9634697-0-3*) U CA Alumni.

UCLA-Alaska Law Review: 1971-1983, Vols. 1-12. Bound set. 420.00 (*0-686-90065-0*) Rothman.

UCLA Football: Touchdown UCLA. rev. ed. Hendrick Van Leuven. LC 81-85248. (College Sports Bks.). 1988. 16.95 (*0-87397-310-0*, Strode Pubs) Circle Bk Service.

***UCLA International Conference on Imaging Detectors in High Energy, Astroparticle & Medical Physics.** 200p. 1996. lib. bdg. 33.00 (*981-02-2895-3*) World Scientific Pub.

UCLA-Intramural Law Review: 1952-1953, 1 Vol. Bound set. 37.50 (*0-8377-9217-7*) Rothman.

UCLA Law Review: 1953-1995/96, 43 vols. Bound set. 2,427.50 (*0-686-90071-5*) Rothman.

UConn - 35-0 the Championship Season: Year of the UConn Women. Hartford Courant Staff et al. Ed. by Mark Leary & John Scanlan. LC 95-76791. (Illus.). 144p. (Orig.). 1995. pap. 13.95 (*0-9646638-0-5*) Hartford Courant.

UCP Five Hundred & Standby Letters of Credit: Special Report. Brooke Wunnicke & Diane B. Wunnicke. 79p. 1994. pap. text ed. 70.00 (*0-471-05346-5*) Wiley.

Ucrainica at the University of Toronto Library: A Catalogue of Holdings. Ed. by Nadia O. Diakun. 1845p. 1985. text ed. 90.00 (*0-8020-3430-6*) U of Toronto Pr.

UCS Architecture Guide. 1995. 115.00 (*0-614-15372-7*) Uniform Code.

UCS Standards Manual: Version 3030. 1993. 400.00 (*0-614-15363-8*) Uniform Code.

UCS Standards Manual: Version 3040. 1994. 440.00 (*0-614-15364-6*) Uniform Code.

UCS Standards Manual: Version 3050. 1995. 475.00 (*0-614-15365-4*) Uniform Code.

UCS Standards Manual: Version 3060. 1996. 475.00 (*0-614-15366-2*) Uniform Code.

UCSD Healthy Diet for Diabetes: A Comprehensive Nutritional Guide & Cookbook. University of California, San Diego, School of Medicine Staff et al. 352p. 1991. pap. 15.95 (*0-395-57225-8*) HM.

UCSD Pascal: A Beginner's Guide to Programming Microcomputers. Richard C. Holt & J. N. Hume. 368p. 1982. 30.00 (*0-8359-7915-6*, Reston) P-H.

UCSD Pascal Examples & Exercises. David V. Moffat. (Illus.). 224p. 1986. pap. text ed. 16.00 (*0-13-935396-8*) P-H.

UCSD Pascal for the IBM PC. Iain MacCallum. write for info. (*0-318-59632-6*) S&S Trade.

UCSD Pascal Handbook. Randy Clark & Stephen Koehler. (Software Ser.). (Illus.). 384p. 1982. 24.95 (*0-13-935536-7*); text ed. 32.00 (*0-13-935544-8*) P-H.

An Asterisk (*) at the beginning of an entry indicates that the title is appearing in BIP for the first time.

UCS/DSD Implementation & User Guide (Version 3050) 1995. 200.00 (*0-318-50033-7*) Uniform Code.

uction, Probability, & Skepticism. Debiprasad Chattopadhyaya. LC 90-42945. (SUNY Series in Philosophy). 480p. 1991. text ed. 74.50 (*0-7914-0681-4*) State U NY Pr.

Uda: Japan's First County. John R. Terry. (Illus.). 200p. 1988. pap. 9.95 (*0-933704-67-4*) Dawn Pr.

Udana. Tr. by Peter Masefield from PLI. 218p. (C). 1994. 35.90 (*0-86013-311-7*) Wisdom MA.

Udana - Verses of Uplift & Itivuttaka - As It Was Said. Tr. by F. L. Woodward from PLI. (Minor Anthologies Ser.: Vol. 2). (C). 1935. 23.00 (*0-86013-036-3*, Pub. by Pali Text) Wisdom MA.

Udana Commentary, Vol. I. Dhammapala. Tr. by Peter Masefield from PLI. 582p. (C). 1994. 49.50 (*0-86013-316-8*) Wisdom MA.

Udana, or the Solemn Utterances of the Buddha. Tr. by D. M. Strong from PLI. LC 78-70131. reprint ed. 31.50 (*0-404-17399-3*) AMS Pr.

Uddat Al-Jalis of Ibn Bishi (Gi) Jones. 1992. 75.00 (*0-906094-40-2*, Pub. by Aris & Phillips UK) David Brown.

***Udder Confusion: An Alaskan Homesteader True Life Adventure.** Elverda Lincoln. (Illus.). 194p. 1992. pap. 12.95 (*1-888125-18-7*) Publ Consult.

Udderly Inviting. Ruth Seeley-Scheel. (Illus.). 1987. pap. 6.95 (*0-9619815-1-2*) Laugh Goose.

Udderwise. Emil Van Beest. (Illus.). 96p. 1987. pap. 8.95 (*0-85236-176-9*, Pub. by Farming Pr UK) Diamond Farm Bk.

Uddhava Gita: The Last Message of Sri Krishna. Tr. by Swami Madhavananda from SAN. 425p. pap. 6.95 (*0-87481-211-9*, Pub. by Advaita Ashrama II) Vedanta Pr.

Uderzo de Flamberge a Asterix. Rene De Goscinny & A. Uderzo. 64p. (FRE.). 1993. 19.95 (*0-7859-3653-X*, 2865030077) Fr & Eur.

***Udmurt Republic Economy, Industry, Government, Business.** 2nd rev. ed. Russian Information & Business Center, Inc. Staff. (Russian Regional Business Directories Ser.). (Illus.). 200p. 1997. pap. 99.00 (*1-57751-370-3*) Russ Info & Busn Ctr.

Ueber den Eintrag Anorganischer Naehrstoffe in Ombrogene Moore als Indikator der Ehemaligen Aerosolbelastung. Marcel Goerres. (Dissertationes Botanicae Ser.: Vol. 181). (Illus.). 196p. (GER.). 1991. pap. text ed. 59.00 (*3-443-64093-1*) Lubrecht & Cramer.

Ueber Den Umlaut: Zwei Abhandlungen (1843), & Ueber Den Ablaut (1844) Adolf Holtzmann. (Amsterdam Classics in Linguistics Ser.: No. 12). xxix, 129p. 1977. 46.00 (*90-272-0937-5*) Benjamins North Am.

Ueber die Aelteste Irische Dichtung. Kuno Meyer. LC 78-72641. (Celtic Language & Literature Ser.: Goidelic & Brythonic). reprint ed. 57.50 (*0-404-17574-0*) AMS Pr.

Ueber die Auferstehung des Fleisches: Studien zur Fruenchristlichen Eschatologie. Horacio E. Lona. (Beihefte zur Zeitschrift fuer die Neuetestamentliche Wissenschaft Ser.: Bd. 66). xiv, 304p. (GER.). (C). 1993. lib. bdg. 98.50 (*3-11-013828-X*) De Gruyter.

Ueber die Beeinflussbarkeit psychiatrischer Krankheitsverlaeufe, 1980, Vol. 13, No. 3-4. Ed. by E. Gabriel. (Illus.). iv, 136p. 1981. pap. 26.50 (*3-8055-2336-X*) S Karger.

Ueber die Spaet- & Postglaziale Vegetationsgeschichte des Donaumoores & Seiner Umgebung. Christine Kortfunke. (Dissertationes Botanicae Ser.: Vol. 184). (Illus.). 178p. (GER.). pap. text ed. 71.50 (*3-443-64096-6*, Pub. by Cramer-Borntraeger GW) Lubrecht & Cramer.

Ueber Die Sprache und Weisheit der Indier: Ein Beitrag Zur Begrundung der Altertumskunde. Friedrich Schlegel. (Amsterdam Classics in Linguistics Ser.: No. 1). lvii, 194p. 1977. 65.00 (*90-272-0872-7*) Benjamins North Am.

Ueber die Wirksamkeit der Daseinanalytischen Therapie Bei Psychosomatischen Stoerungen. B. Weber. (Journal: Daseinsanalyse: Vol. 11, No. 1, 1994). (Illus.). 98p. 1994. pap. 26.25 (*3-8055-5952-6*) S Karger.

Ueber Michael Kohlhaas: Damals und Heute. Horst Sendler. (Schriftenreihe der Juristischen Gesellschaft zu Berlin Ser.: Heft 92). 48p. (GER.). 1985. pap. 18.50 (*3-11-010454-7*) De Gruyter.

Ueberblick ueber die Ackerunkrautvegetation Oesterreichs und Ihre Entwicklung in Neuerer Zeit. C. Ries. (Dissertationes Botanicae Ser.: Vol. 187). (Illus.). 188p. (GER.). 1992. pap. text ed. 84.00 (*3-443-64099-0*, Pub. by Cramer-Borntraeger GW) Lubrecht & Cramer.

Ueberlebenszeiten beim Mammakarzinom. H. E. Wander. (Illus.). viii, 24p. 1991. pap. 42.75 (*3-8055-5248-3*) S Karger.

Ueberredung in der Presse: Texte, Strategien, Analysen. Ed. by Markku Moilanen & Liisa Tiittula. (Sprache, Politik, Oeffentlichkeit Ser.: Bd. 3). 249p. (GER.). (C). 1994. lib. bdg. 103.10 (*3-11-014346-1*) De Gruyter.

Uebersetzung Als Vollendung der Auslegung: Studien Zur Genesis-Septuaginta. Martin Roesel. (Beiheft zur Zeitschrift fuer die Alttestamentliche Wissenschaft Ser.: Bd. 223). viii, 290p. (GER.). (C). 1994. lib. bdg. 106.15 (*3-11-014234-1*, 8-94) De Gruyter.

Uebersetzung und Kommentar Zu Den Altaegyptischen Pyramidentexten. Kurt Sethe. Incl. . 65.00 (*0-685-71715-1*); . 65.00 (*0-685-71716-X*); . 65.00 (*0-685-71717-8*); . 65.00 (*0-685-71718-6*); . 80.00 (*0-685-71719-4*); . 50.00 (*0-685-71720-8*); write for info. (*0-685-71714-3*) J J Augustin.

Ueberwindung des Mathematischen Erkenntnisideals: Kants Grenzbestimmung von Mathematik & Philosophie. Brigitta-Sophie Von Wolff-Metternich. (Quellen & Studien zur Philosophie Ser.: Bd 39). x, 225p. (GER.). (C). 1995. lib. bdg. 98.50 (*3-11-014511-1*) De Gruyter.

Uebungstypologie zum Kommunikativen Deutschunterricht. Gerd Neuner et al. 184p. 1981. pap. 26.25 (*3-468-49430-0*) Langenscheidt.

UEC Woerterbuch des Rechnungswesens. Union Europeenne Comptable Staff. 194p. 1980. 39.95 (*0-8288-0156-8*, M 15231) Fr & Eur.

Uechiryu Karate Do. George E. Mattson. LC 75-5978. (Illus.). 492p. (Orig.). 1974. 40.00 (*0-686-10569-9*); pap. 25.00 (*0-685-03984-6*) Peabody Pub.

Ueda Theory: Theorems & Problems. A. Neeman. LC 89-15176. (Memoirs Ser.: Vol. 81/415). 123p. 1989. pap. 21.00 (*0-8218-2478-3*, MEMO/81/415) Am Math.

Uelsmann: Process & Perception. Jerry N. Uelsmann. LC 85-6035. (Illus.). 134p. (Orig.). 1985. pap. 24.95 (*0-8130-0830-1*) U Press Fla.

Uelsmann - Yosemite. Jerry N. Uelsmann. LC 95-50346. (Illus.). 80p. (C). 1996. 39.95 (*0-8130-1444-1*); pap. 24.95 (*0-8130-1445-X*) U Press Fla.

UFA Film. Ed. by R. Gordon. 1976. lib. bdg. 100.95 (*0-8490-2781-0*) Gordon Pr.

UFA Story: A History of German's Greatest Film Company, 1918-1945. Klaus Kreimeier. Tr. by Robert Kimber & Rita Kimber. LC 96-7201. 544p. 1996. 35.00 (*0-8090-9483-5*) Hill & Wang.

UFAS Retrofitting Guide: Accessibility Modifications for Existing Buildings: Designed to be Used in Conjunction with the Uniform Federal Accessibility Standards for Compliance with Title II of the Americans with Disabilities Act, Section 50-4 of the Rehabilitation Act of 1973, the Architectural Barriers Acts of 1968. Des. by Barrier Free Environments, Inc. Staff. LC 92-42361. 1993. text ed. 52.95 (*0-442-01567-4*) Van Nos Reinhold.

***UFAW Handbook on the Care & Management of Cephalopods in the Laboratory.** P. R. Boyle. 1991. pap. 100.00 (*0-900767-72-3*, Pub. by Univs Fed Animal Welfare UK) St Mut.

***UFAW Handbook on the Care & Management of Decapod Crustaceans in Captivity.** R. Ingle. 119p. 1995. pap. 150.00 (*0-900767-86-3*, Pub. by Univs Fed Animal Welfare UK) St Mut.

UFAW Handbook on the Care & Management of Laboratory Animals. 5th ed. Ed. by Universities Federation for Animal Welfare Staff. 1940. 195.00 (*0-317-43832-8*) St Mut.

UFAW Handbook on the Care & Management of Laboratory Animals. 6th ed. Universities Federation for Animal Welfare Staff. Ed. by T. B. Poole. (Illus.). 933p. 1987. pap. 195.00 (*0-582-40911-X*, Pub. by Univs Fed Animal Welfare UK) St Mut.

UFF DA Jokes. E. C. Stangland. (Mitzi's Office Jokes Ser.). (Illus.). (Orig.). 1979. pap. 2.50 (*0-9602692-4-X*) Norse Pr.

Uffda Trial. Gerald Anderson. 202p. 1995. pap. 9.95 (*0-9613437-3-7*) Redbird Prods.

Uffizi. Luciano Berti & Anna M. Tofani. (Illus.). 264p. 1993. 40.00 (*1-870248-81-3*) Scala Books.

Uffizi: Guide to the Collections & Catalogue of All Paintings. Caterina Caneva et al. (Illus.). 192p. 1992. 24.95 (*0-8161-0607-X*) G K Hall.

UFMCC Mission Statement. Virginia G. Miles & R. Adam DeBaugh. 30p. 1990. pap. 2.50 (*1-888493-07-0*) Chi Rho Pr.

***UFO.** Charles E. Sellier & Joe Meier. 1997. 18.95 (*0-614-28010-9*) Contemp Bks.

UFO: End-Time Delusion. David Lewis & Robert Shreckhise. LC 91-61713. 256p. (Orig.). 1991. pap. 9.95 (*0-89221-213-6*) New Leaf.

UFO: The Definitive Guide to Unidentified Flying Objects & Related Phenomena. David Ritchie. LC 93-31037. (Illus.). 272p. 1994. 40.00 (*0-8160-2894-X*) Facts on File.

UFO a Deadly Concealment: The Official Cover-Up? Derek Sheffield. (Illus.). 288p. 1996. pap. 12.95 (*0-7137-2620-2*, Pub. by Blandford Pr UK) Sterling.

UFO Abductions. Neal Bernards. LC 94-2123. (Exploring the Unknown Ser.). (J). 1995. lib. bdg. 17.96 (*1-56006-161-8*) Lucent Bks.

UFO-Abductions: A Dangerous Game. Philip J. Klass. LC 87-43249. (Illus.). 222p. 1989. pap. 20.95 (*0-87975-509-1*) Prometheus Bks.

UFO Abductions in Gulf Breeze. Ed Walters & Frances Walters. 320p. (Orig.). 1994. mass mkt. 4.99 (*0-380-77333-3*) Avon.

***UFO Book: Encyclopedia of the Extraterrestrial.** 1997. 19.95 (*1-57859-029-9*, 00157411) Visible Ink Pr.

UFO Casebook. Kevin D. Randle. 256p. (Orig.). 1989. mass mkt. 5.99 (*0-446-35715-4*) Warner Bks.

UFO Conspiracy. 2nd ed. Frank E. Stranges. (Illus.). 122p. 1985. pap. 8.95 (*0-933470-02-9*) Intl Evang.

UFO Controversy in America. David M. Jacobs. LC 74-11886. (Illus.). 378p. reprint ed. pap. 109.50 (*0-8357-3962-7*, 2057058) Bks Demand.

UFO Cover-up: What the Government Won't Say. Lawrence Fawcett & Barry J. Greenwood. 266p. 1990. pap. 10.00 (*0-671-76555-8*) S&S Trade.

UFO Crash at Roswell. Donald R. Schmitt. 352p. (Orig.). 1991. mass mkt. 5.99 (*0-380-76196-3*) Avon.

***UFO Cults & the New Millennium.** William M. Alnor. 160p. Date not set. pap. 12.99 (*0-8010-5791-4*) Baker Bks.

UFO Cults & Urantia. Kevin Lewis & Kenneth B. Samples. (Zondervan Guide to Cults & Religious Movements Ser.). 96p. pap. 5.99 (*0-310-48941-5*) Zondervan.

UFO Danger Zone: Terror & Death in Brazil. Bob Pratt. (Illus.). 349p. (Orig.). 1996. pap. 16.95 (*1-881852-14-8*) Horus Hse Pr.

***UFO Diaries.** Sellier. LC 97-401. 1997. write for info. (*0-8092-3137-9*) Contemp Bks.

UFO Diary. Satoshi Kitamura. (J). (ps up). pap. 4.95 (*0-374-48041-9*) FS&G.

UFO Diary. Satoshi Kitamura. (J). (ps up). 1989. 14.00 (*0-374-38026-0*) FS&G.

***UFO Directory: A Guide to Organizations, Research Collections, Museums, Publications, Periodicals, Web Sites, & Other Resources Concerning UFO Phenomena.** Jerome C. Clark. 300p. 1997. lib. bdg. 48.00 (*0-7808-0289-6*) Omnigraphics Inc.

UFO-Dynamics: Psychiatric & Psychic Aspects of the UFO Syndrome. rev. ed. Berthold E. Schwarz. LC 87-28384. (Illus.). 564p. (Orig.). 1988. pap. 29.95 (*0-935834-64-8*) Rainbow Books.

UFO Encounters: Sightings, Visitations, & Investigations. (Illus.). 128p. 1993. 14.98 (*1-56173-605-8*, 3312200) Pubns Intl Ltd.

UFO Encounters & Beyond: Sightings, Visitations, & Investigations. Consumer Guide Editors. (Illus.). 256p. (Orig.). 1993. pap. 4.50 (*0-451-17900-5*, Sig) NAL-Dutton.

UFO Encyclopedia. Compiled by John Spencer. (Illus.). 392p. (Orig.). 1993. pap. 15.00 (*0-380-76887-9*) Avon.

UFO Exist! Paris Flammonde. 1987. mass mkt. 5.95 (*0-345-33951-7*) Ballantine.

***UFO Files.** Martin H. Greenberg. 1998. pap. 5.99 (*0-88677-772-0*) DAW Bks.

***UFO Files: Out of This World...But True?** Sean Plottner. LC 97-65681. (Disney Adventures Ser.). (J). 1997. pap. text ed. 3.95 (*0-7868-4146-X*) Disney Pr.

***UFO Files: The Canadian Connection Exposed.** Palmiro Campagna. (Illus.). 8p. 1997. pap. 21.95 (*0-7737-3015-X*, Pub. by Stoddart Pubng CN) Genl Dist Srvs.

UFO Guidebook. Norman J. Briazack & Simon Mennick. 1978. pap. 4.95 (*0-8065-0763-2*, Citadel Pr) Carol Pub Group.

***UFO Healings: True Accounts of People Healed by Extraterrestrials.** Preston E. Dennett. Ed. by Amy Demmon. LC 96-31331. (Illus.). 188p. (Orig.). 1997. pap. 13.95 (*0-926524-33-X*, Wild Flower Pr) Blue Wtr Pubng.

***UFO Invasion: The Roswell Incident, Alien Abductions & Government Coverups.** Kendrick Frazier. LC 96-53067. 1997. 25.95 (*1-57392-131-9*) Prometheus Bks.

UFO Kids. Allan Zullo. LC 94-27528. (Illus.). 128p. (J). (gr. 3-6). 1994. pap. text ed. 2.95 (*0-8167-3566-2*, Rainbow NJ) Troll Communs.

UFO Mystery. Mary B. Christian. Ed. by Janet L. Bolinske. LC 88-60632. (Sherlock Street Detectives Ser.). (Illus.). 32p. (Orig.). (J). (gr. 1-3). 1989. pap. text ed. 4.95 (*0-88335-598-1*) Milliken Pub Co.

UFO Mystery. Susan Saunders. (Double Detectives Ser.: No. 2). 80p. (J). 1995. mass mkt. 3.50 (*0-06-106071-2*, Harp PBks) HarpC.

UFO Occupants & Critters. John B. Musgrave. 64p. 1979. reprint ed. spiral bd. 9.50 (*0-7873-1266-5*) Hlth Research.

***UFO Phenomena: A Scientific Look at the Evidence for Extraterrestrial Contacts.** Edward Ashpole. (Illus.). 304p. 1997. pap. 13.95 (*0-7472-4745-5*, Pub. by Headline UK) Trafalgar.

UFO Phenomenon. (Mysteries of the Unknown Ser.). (Illus.). 144p. 1987. 14.95 (*0-8094-6324-5*); lib. bdg. 23.27 (*0-8094-6325-3*) Time-Life.

***UFO Photo Album, Vol. 1.** Susan A. Farnsworth. (Illus.). 100p. 1997. spiral bd. 24.95 (*1-881260-17-8*) Southwest Pubns.

UFO Primer. Virginia Bennett. Ed. by Sara Glaser. (Fringe Ser.: Vol. 2). (Illus.). 32p. (Orig.). 1993. pap. 3.95 (*0-916147-37-1*) Regent Pr.

UFO Quest: In Search of the Mystery Machines. Alan Watts. (Illus.). 200p. 1994. pap. 12.95 (*0-7137-2449-8*, Pub. by Blandford Pr UK) Sterling.

UFO Question: Not Yet Answered. P. J. Willcox. LC 75-393401. 1976. 12.95 (*0-87212-054-6*) Libra.

UFO Report. Ed. by Timothy Good. 264p. (Orig.). 1991. mass mkt. 4.99 (*0-380-71324-1*) Avon.

UFO Reports Involving Vehicle Interference: A Catalogue & Data Analysis. Mark Rodeghier. 156p. (C). 1981. pap. 8.00 (*0-929343-55-7*) J A Hynek Ctr UFO.

UFO Retrievals: The Recovery of Alien Spacecraft. Jenny Randles. (Illus.). 200p. 1995. pap. 10.95 (*0-7137-2493-5*, Pub. by Blandford Pr UK) Sterling.

UFO Verdict - Examining the Evidence. Robert Sheaffer. LC 80-84406. (Illus.). 242p. (Orig.). 1986. pap. 19.95 (*0-87975-338-2*) Prometheus Bks.

UFO Visitation: Preparing for the Twenty-First Century. Alan Watts. (Illus.). 224p. 1996. pap. 12.95 (*0-7137-2600-8*, Pub. by Blandford Pr UK) Sterling.

UFOs. Elaine Landau. (Mysteries of Science Ser.). (Illus.). 48p. (J). (gr. 3-6). 1995. lib. bdg. 15.40 (*1-56294-542-4*) Millbrook Pr.

UFO's. Ted Wilding-White. (World ofthe Unknown Ser.). 32p. (J). (gr. k-6). 1977. pap. 6.95 (*0-86020-150-3*) EDC.

***UFOs: A Great New Dawn for Humankind.** Enrique Castillo. LC 97-11568. (Illus.). 256p. (Orig.). 1997. pap. 19.95 (*1-57733-000-5*, Pelican Pond) B Dolphin Pub.

***UFOs: Amazing Stories of the Unexplained.** Rowan Wilson. (Strange but True Ser.). 1997. pap. text ed. 5.95 (*0-8069-0577-8*) Sterling.

UFOs: An Insider's View of the Official Quest for Evidence. Roy Craig. LC 95-10882. (Illus.). 276p. 1995. pap. 18.95 (*0-929398-94-7*) UNTX Pr.

UFO's: From Earth or Outer Space?: An Investigation into UFO's & Their Occupants Concerning Their Possible Interdimensional, Earthly Origins. Paul Tice. (Illus.). 30p. (Orig.). 1996. pap. 3.50 (*1-885395-14-0*) Book Tree.

UFOs: Key to the New Age. Arthur Shuttlewood. 216p. 1984. 45.00 (*0-317-43654-6*, Pub. by Regency Press UK) St Mut.

***UFO's: The Definitive Guide to UFO's.** David Ritchie. (Illus.). 1997. 9.98 (*1-56731-200-4*, MJF Bks) Fine Comms.

UFOs: The Public Deceived. Philip J. Klass. LC 83-60202. (Illus.). 310p. 1986. pap. 19.95 (*0-87975-322-6*) Prometheus Bks.

UFOs: True Mysteries or Hoaxes. rev. ed. Greg Walz-Chojnacki et al. (Library of the Universe). (Illus.). (J). (gr. 3 up). 1995. lib. bdg. 18.60 (*0-8368-1198-4*) Gareth Stevens Inc.

UFO's, Aliens or Demons? Doris Pottenger. Ed. by Don Smith. 128p. (Orig.). 1990. pap. 5.50 (*0-927022-02-8*) CHJ Pub.

***UFOs; Aliens or...Alienation?** 545p. (Orig.). 1997. pap. 18.00 (*0-9656098-0-4*) B D Belfry.

UFOs & Abductions in Brazil. Irene Granchi. LC 95-75447. (Illus.). 243p. (Orig.). 1995. reprint ed. pap. 14.95 (*1-881852-09-1*) Horus Hse Pr.

***UFOs & Anti-Gravity: Piece for a Jig-Saw.** Leonard G. Cramp. 1997. pap. text ed. 16.95 (*0-932813-43-7*) Adventures Unltd.

UFOs & ETs: The Truth about the Conspiracies. Clifford Williams. (Illus.). 2550p. 1996. pap. 9.95 (*0-934274-39-8*) Consumertronics.

UFOs & How to See Them. Jenny Randles. (Illus.). 144p. 1993. pap. 14.95 (*0-8069-0297-3*) Sterling.

***UFO's & Related Subjects.** 1979. 80.00 (*0-8103-2021-5*, 00009689, Gale Res Intl) Gale.

***UFOs & the Alien Agenda: Uncovering the Mystery Behind UFOs & the Paranormal.** Bob Larson. LC 97-20782. 228p. (Orig.). 1997. pap. 12.99 (*0-7852-7182-1*, J Thoma Bks) Nelson.

UFOs & the Alien Presence. M. Lindeman. 234p. 1995. pap. 12.95 (*0-926524-08-9*) Blue Wtr Pubng.

UFOs & the Alien Presence: Six Viewpoints. Michael Lindemann. 240p. (Orig.). 1991. pap. 12.95 (*0-9630104-0-9*) Twenty Twenty Grp.

UFO's & the Complete Evidence from Space: The Truth about Venus, Mars, & the Moon. Daniel Ross. (Illus.). 242p. (Orig.). (C). 1987. pap. 9.95 (*0-944255-00-0*) Pintado Pub.

UFOs & the Nature of Reality: Understanding Alien Consciousness & Interdimensional Mind. Ramtha-Jz Knight. Ed. by Judi P. Koteen. LC 90-83741. 120p. (Orig.). 1990. pap. 11.00 (*0-9627267-4-5*) Indelible Inc.

UFOs & the Psychic Factor: How to Understand Encounters with UFOs & ETs. Ida Kannenberg. Ed. by Brian Crissey. (UFO Chronicles Ser.). (Illus.). 168p. (Orig.). 1992. pap. 12.95 (*0-926524-13-5*, Wild Flower Pr) Blue Wtr Pubng.

***UFOs Are Real: Extraterrestrial Encounters Documented by the U. S. Government.** Clifford E. Stone. 1997. pap. 19.95 (*1-56171-972-2*) Spi Bks.

***UFOs Are Real... Here's the Proof.** Ed Walters. 1997. mass mkt. 5.99 (*0-380-78599-4*) Avon.

UFOs, Crop Circles, & Mars Structures: Their Common Origin. Steve Canada. 59p. 1993. pap. 6.95 (*1-883424-24-0*) S Canada.

UFOs from the Volcanoes. Egon W. Bach. LC 93-1903. (Illus.). 400p. (Orig.). 1994. pap. 21.95 (*1-55779-062-0*) Hermitage.

UFOs in the New Age: Extraterrestrial Messages & the Truth of Scripture. William M. Alnor. LC 92-482. 296p. (gr. 10). 1992. pap. 12.99 (*0-8010-0226-5*) Baker Bks.

UFOs in the 1980s. Jerome Clark. (UFO Encyclopedia Ser.: Vol. 1). 234p. 1990. lib. bdg. 95.00 (*1-55888-301-0*) Omnigraphics Inc.

UFOs' Origin Identified: The Mystery of Their Source Solved. Steve Canada. 64p. 1993. pap. 6.95 (*0-88342-414-2*) S Canada.

UFOs over Africa. Cynthia Hind. (Illus.). 250p. (Orig.). 1997. pap. 15.95 (*1-881852-15-6*) Horus Hse Pr.

UFOs over Hampshire & the Low. Ed. by Robert Price. (C). 1989. 39.00 (*1-85455-037-3*, Pub. by Ensign Pubns & Print UK) St Mut.

***UFOs over Israel: Strong Delusion in the End-Times.** Texe Marrs. 216p. 1997. pap. 13.95 (*1-884302-03-3*) Living Truth Pubs.

UFOs Psychic Close Encounters: The Electromagnetic Indictment. Albert Budden. (Illus.). 264p. 1995. pap. 10.95 (*0-7137-2421-8*, Pub. by Blandford Pr UK) Sterling.

UFO's, the Third Wave. Daniel Cohen. LC 88-16558. 172p. (YA). (gr. 7 up). 1988. 12.95 (*0-87131-541-6*) M Evans.

***Uganda.** Ettagale Blauer & Jason Laure. LC 96-51469. (Enchantment of the World Ser.). (J). 1997. lib. bdg. 30.00 (*0-516-20306-1*) Childrens.

Uganda. Trudy Hanmer. LC 89-31171. (Venture Bks.). (Illus.). 128p. (YA). (gr. 6 up). 1989. lib. bdg. 22.00 (*0-531-10816-3*) Watts.

Uganda. Paul Lisicky. (Let's Visit Places & Peoples of the World Ser.). (Illus.). 96p. (J). (gr. 5 up). 1988. lib. bdg. 19.95 (*1-55546-189-1*) Chelsea Hse.

Uganda. rev. ed. Balam Nyeko. (World Bibliographical Ser.). 1996. lib. bdg. 102.00 (*1-85109-243-9*) ABC-CLIO.

Uganda: A Country Study. 2nd ed. Library of Congress, Federal Research Div. Staff. Ed. by Rita M. Byrnes. LC 92-513. (Area Handbook Ser.: No. 550-74). 1992. write for info. (*0-8444-0749-6*) Lib Congress.

Uganda: A Pre-Election Assessment Report. Laurie Cooper & Jerry Henderson. LC 96-16751. 1996. write for info. (*1-879720-10-8*) Intl Fndt Elect.

Uganda: Adjustment with Growth, 1987-94. Robert L. Sharer et al. LC 95-7670. (Occasional Paper Ser.: No. 121). 52p. 1995. pap. 15.00 (*1-55775-461-6*) Intl Monetary.

Uganda: Agriculture. LC 93-1591. (Country Study Ser.). 238p. 1993. 13.95 (*0-8213-2461-6*, 12461) World Bank.

Uganda: An Annotated Bibliography of Source Materials. Cherry J. Gertzel. 244p. 1991. lib. bdg. 75.00 (*0-905450-83-3*, Pub. by H Zell Pubs UK) Bowker-Saur.

Uganda: An Historical Accident? Class, Nation, State Formation. Ramkrishna MukherJee. LC 85-71370. 290p. 1985. 35.00 (*0-86543-015-2*); pap. 14.95 (*0-86543-016-0*) Africa World.

Uganda: Growing Out of Poverty. World Bank Staff. LC 93-17518. (Country Study Ser.). 226p. 1993. 12.95 (*0-8213-2460-8*, 12460) World Bank.

Uganda: Social Sectors. LC 93-43863. (Country Study Ser.). 222p. 1994. 11.95 (*0-8213-2713-5*, 12713) World Bank.

Uganda: Tarnished Pearl of Africa. Thomas P. Ofcansky. LC 95-13468. (Nations of the Modern World: Africa Ser.). 166p. 1995. text ed. 59.95 (*0-8133-1059-8*) Westview.

Uganda: The Asian Exiles. Thomas P. Melady & Margaret B. Melady. LC 76-10321. 96p. reprint ed. pap. 27.40 (*0-8357-7062-1*, 2033550) Bks Demand.

Uganda: The Challenge of Growth & Poverty Reduction. LC 95-52496. (Country Study Ser.). 204p. 1996. 11.95 (*0-8213-3552-9*, 13552) World Bank.

Uganda: The Dilemma of Nationhood. G. N. Uzoigwe. LC 74-81845. 376p. 1982. 21.95 (*0-88357-037-8*); pap. 9.95 (*0-88357-038-6*) NOK Pubs.

***Uganda Asian Expulsion: 90 Days & Beyond Through the Eyes of the International Press.** Contrib. by Zane Lalani. (Illus.). v, 416p. 1997. 30.00 (*0-9658740-0-1*) Expulsion Pubns.

Uganda Controversy, Vol 2. Ed. by Michael Heymann. 390p. 1977. 39.95 (*0-87855-271-5*) Transaction Pubs.

Uganda Controversy: Minutes of the Zionist General Council, Vol. 1. Intro. by Michael Heymann. 136p. 1970. 34.95 (*0-87855-185-9*) Transaction Pubs.

Uganda, Death in the Countryside: Killings of Civilians by the Army in 1990. 5p. 1990. 2.00 (*0-685-50865-X*, 59-15-90) Amnesty Intl USA.

Uganda Now: Between Decay & Development. Ed. by Holger B. Hansen & Michael Twaddle. LC 88-5370. 384p. 1988. pap. text ed. 19.95 (*0-8214-0897-6*); lib. bdg. 34.95 (*0-8214-0896-8*) Ohio U Pr.

Uganda since Independence. Phares Mutibwa. LC 92-53941. 150p. 1992. 49.95 (*0-86543-356-9*); pap. 16.95 (*0-86543-357-7*) Africa World.

Uganda, The Human Rights Record 1986-1989. 52p. 1989. 5.00 (*0-939994-44-5*) Amnesty Intl USA.

Uganda's AIDS Crisis: Its Implications for Development. Jill Armstrong. LC 95-37063. (Discussion Papers: No. 298). 108p. 1995. 8.95 (*0-8213-3437-9*) World Bank.

Uganda's Katikiro in England. Ham Mukasa. Tr. by Ernest Millar. LC 74-152926. (Black Heritage Library Collection). 1977. 22.95 (*0-8369-8770-5*) Ayer.

Ugarit: Religion & Culture: Proceedings of the Edinburgh University International Colloquium 20-23 July 1994. Ed. by N. Wyatt et al. 1996. write for info. (*3-927120-37-5*, Pub. by UGARIT GW) Eisenbrauns.

Ugarit - Ein Ostmediterranes Kulturzentrum im Alten Orient. Ergebnisse und Perspektiven der Forschung Band 2: Ugarit und Seine Beziehungen zur Agais. Ed. by H. G. Buchholz et al. (Abhandlvorgen zur Literatur Alt-Syrien-Palastinas und Mesopatamieus Ser.: No. 7/2). Date not set. write for info. (*3-927120-38-3*, Pub. by UGARIT GW) Eisenbrauns.

Ugarit - ein Ostmediterranes Kulturzentrum Im Alten Orient: Ergebnisse und Perspektiven der Forschung, Band 1: Ugarit und Seine Altorientalioche Umwelt. Ed. by Manfried Dietrich & Oswald Loretz. (Abhandlungen Zur Literatur Alt-Syrien-Palastinas Ser.: Vol. 7/1). xii, 298p. (GER.). 1995. text ed. 86.00 (*3-927120-17-0*, Pub. by UGARIT GW) Eisenbrauns.

Ugarit & the Bible: Proceedings of the Internatinoal Symposium on Ugarit & the Bible, Manchester, September 1992. Ed. by George J. Brooke et al. (Ugaritisch-Biblische Literatur Ser.). ix, 470p. 1994. text ed. 78.00 (*3-927120-22-7*, Pub. by UGARIT GW) Eisenbrauns.

Ugarit in Retrospect: Fifty Years of Ugarit & Ugaritic. Ed. by Gordon D. Young. LC 81-12664. xv, 238p. 1981. text ed. 32.50 (*0-931464-07-2*) Eisenbrauns.

Ugarit (Ras Shamra) Adrian Curtis. LC 86-102759. (Cities of the Biblical World Ser.). (Illus.). 125p. reprint ed. pap. 35.70 (*0-7837-5555-4*, 2045330) Bks Demand.

Ugarit-Texte und Thronbesteigungspsalmen: Die Metamorphose des Regenspenders Baal-Jahwe (Ps. 24: 7-10; 29; 47; 93; 95-100; Sowie Ps. 77: 17-20; 114) Oswald Loretz. (Ugaritisch-Biblische Literatur Ser.: Vol. 7). xiv, 550p. (GER.). 1988. text ed. 63.00 (*3-927120-04-9*, Pub. by UGARIT GW) Eisenbrauns.

Ugaritic Baal Cycle. Ed. by Mark S. Smith. (Supplements to Vetus Testamentum Ser.: 55). 1994. 141.50 (*90-04-09995-6*) E J Brill.

Ugaritic Hippiatric Texts: A Critical Edition. C. Cohen & D. Sivan. (American Oriental Ser.: No. 9). x, 72p. 1983. pap. 12.50 (*0-940490-99-4*) Am Orient Soc.

***Ugaritic Narrative Poems.** Mark S. Smith. (Writings from the Ancient World Ser.). 1997. write for info. (*0-7885-0336-7*); pap. write for info. (*0-7885-0337-5*) Scholars Pr GA.

Ugaritic Poem of AQHT: Text - Translation - Commentary. Baruch Margalit. xviii, 534p. (C). 1989. lib. bdg. 161.55 (*3-11-011632-4*) De Gruyter.

Ugaritic Vocabulary in Syllabic Transcription. John Huehnergard. (Harvard Semitic Studies). 371p. 1989. 23.95 (*1-55540-201-1*, 04 04 32) Scholars Pr GA.

Ugaritische Kausativstamm und die Kausativbildungen des Semitischen: Eine Morphologisch-Semantische Untersuchung Zum S-Stamm und Zu Den Umstrittenen Nichtsibilantischen Kausativstammen Des Ugaritischen. Josef Tropper. (Abhandlungen Zur Literatur Alt-Syrien-Palastinas Ser.: Vol. 2). x, 229p. (GER.). 1990. text ed. 50.00 (*3-927120-06-5*, Pub. by UGARIT GW) Eisenbrauns.

U
V

UGC & the Management of British Universities. Michael Shattock. LC 93-5622. (C). 1994. 95.00 (*0-335-19161-4*, Open Univ Pr) Taylor & Francis.

Ugetsu. Ed. by Keiko McDonald. LC 92-8419. (Films in Print Ser.: Vol. 17). (Illus.). 200p. (C). 1992. 37.00 (*0-8135-1861-X*); pap. 17.00 (*0-8135-1862-8*) Rutgers U Pr.

UGF-Twenty-Six. Manning Spencer, pseud. 314p. (Orig.). 1988. pap. text ed. 14.95 (*0-9621710-3-4*) C R Hayes.

Ugh. Arthur Yorinks. 32p. (J). (ps-3). 1990. 13.95 (*0-374-38028-7*) FS&G.

Ugh. Arthur Yorinks. (J). (ps-3). 1993. pap. 4.95 (*0-374-48050-8*) FS&G.

Ugh! Bugs! An Integrated Unit. Kathy Rogers. (Primary Thematic Units Ser.). (Illus.). 96p. (Orig.). 1994. pap. 12.95 (*0-944459-87-0*) ECS Lrn Systs.

Uglerodnye Zvezdy see Carbon Stars

Ugliest Dog in the World. Bruce Whatley. (Illus.). 32p. (J). (ps-1). 1995. 7.00 (*0-207-18768-1*) HarperColl Wrld.

***Ugliest House in the World: Stories.** Peter H. Davies. LC 97-12873. 1997. 20.00 (*0-395-78629-0*) HM.

Ugly American. William J. Lederer. 240p. 1987. mass mkt. 5.95 (*0-449-21526-1*) Fawcett.

Ugly American. William J. Lederer & Eugene Burdick. (J). (gr. 9 up). 1965. pap. 11.95 (*0-393-00305-1*) Norton.

Ugly Beautiful People: Essays on Liberal Culture. Leopold Tyrmand. LC 84-20972. 130p. (Orig.). 1985. pap. text ed. 15.00 (*0-8191-4143-7*); lib. bdg. 47.50 (*0-8191-4086-4*) U Pr of Amer.

***Ugly Bug.** Donald Charles. (Illus.). 32p. (J). 3.98 (*0-8317-4468-5*) Smithmark.

Ugly Chinaman & the Crisis of Chinese Culture. Tr. by Don Cohn from CHI. 224p. reprint ed. pap. 19.95 (*1-86373-116-4*, Pub. by Allen Unwin AT) Paul & Co Pubs.

Ugly Christmas Tree. Bob Scott. LC 92-93614. (Illus.). 24p. (Orig.). (J). (gr. 3-8). 1993. 7.95 (*0-9621201-1-1*); pap. 4.95 (*0-9621201-2-X*) B Scott Bks.

***Ugly Dachshund.** G. B. Stern. (Illus.). 156p. 1997. reprint ed. pap. 15.00 (*1-880158-15-9*) J N Townsend.

Ugly Duck. James Still. 56p. (J). (gr. 1-6). 1996. 5.00 (*0-87602-339-1*) Anchorage.

Ugly Duckling. (Fun-to-Read Fairy Tales Series III). (Illus.). 24p. (J). (gr. k-3). 1993. pap. 2.50 (*1-56144-299-2*, Honey Bear Bks) Modern Pub NYC.

Ugly Duckling. (First Fairy Tales Ser.: No. S852-6). (Illus.). (J). (ps-2). 3.95 (*0-7214-5099-7*, Ladybrd) Penguin.

Ugly Duckling. (Square Format Fairy Tales Ser.: No. S874-5). (Illus.). 28p. (J). (ps up). 1987. boxed 3.95 (*0-7214-5032-6*, Ladybrd) Penguin.

Ugly Duckling. (Favorite Fairy Tales Ser.). (Illus.). 24p. (J). 1993. 4.98 (*1-56173-912-X*) Pubns Intl Ltd.

Ugly Duckling. (Read Along With Me Ser.). (Illus.). (J). (ps-1). 1985. 1.98 (*0-517-47900-1*) Random Hse Value.

Ugly Duckling. (J). 1988. write for info. (*0-671-10038-6*) S&S Trade.

Ugly Duckling. (Story Activity Bks.: No. S909-3). (J). 1991. pap. 1.95 (*0-7214-5280-9*, Ladybrd) Penguin.

Ugly Duckling. (Favorite Fairy Tales Ser.). (J). 1989. 5.99 (*0-517-69315-1*) Random Hse Value.

Ugly Duckling. (Fairy Tale Fun Ser.). (J). 3.95 (*0-7214-5432-1*, Ladybrd) Penguin.

Ugly Duckling. (J). pap. 1.25 (*0-8167-1347-2*) Troll Communs.

Ugly Duckling. (Illus.). 32p. (J). (ps-2). 1996. pap. 2.50 (*0-7214-5616-2*, Ladybrd) Penguin.

Ugly Duckling. (Timeless Tales from Hallmark Fairy Tale Classics Ser.). 24p. (J). Date not set. text ed. 4.95 (*1-56987-217-1*) Landoll.

Ugly Duckling. Hans Christian Andersen. LC 78-18059. (Illus.). 32p. (J). (ps-3). 1992. 6.95 (*0-8362-4911-9*) Andrews & McMeel.

Ugly Duckling. Hans Christian Andersen. LC 86-185. (Knopf Book & Cassette Classics Ser.). (Illus.). 48p. (J). (gr. k up). 1986. 12.95 (*0-394-88403-5*); 15.95 incl. audio (*0-394-88298-9*) Knopf Bks Yng Read.

Ugly Duckling. Hans Christian Andersen. (Oxford Graded Readers Ser.). (J). (gr. k-6). 1983. pap. 3.50 (*0-19-421704-3*) OUP.

Ugly Duckling. Hans Christian Andersen. (Illus.). 48p. (J). (ps-2). 1988. pap. 4.99 (*0-590-43794-1*) Scholastic Inc.

Ugly Duckling. Hans Christian Andersen. LC 75-145207. (Illus.). 32p. (J). (ps-3). 9.95 (*0-87592-055-1*) Scroll Pr.

Ugly Duckling. Hans Christian Andersen. (Golden Storytime Bks.). (Illus.). 24p. (J). (ps-3). 1990. 3.50 (*0-307-12106-2*, Golden Books) Western Pub.

Ugly Duckling. Hans Christian Andersen. (Illus.). 32p. (J). (gr. k-3). 1993. pap. 2.99 (*0-87406-656-5*) Willowisp Pr.

Ugly Duckling. Hans Christian Andersen. LC 90-61004. (Illus.). 24p. (J). (gr. k-2). 1995. 3.99 (*0-517-10196-3*) Andrews & McMeel.

Ugly Duckling. Hans Christian Andersen. LC 90-61004. (Pictureback Ser.). (Illus.). (J). (ps-2). 1991. pap. 3.25 (*0-679-81039-0*) Random Bks Yng Read.

Ugly Duckling. Hans Christian Andersen. LC 78-18059. (Illus.). 32p. (J). (gr. k-2). 1997. pap. 3.95 (*0-89375-106-5*) Troll Communs.

Ugly Duckling. Ed. by Janet L. Bolinske. LC 87-61671. (Children's Classics Ser.). (Illus.). 32p. (Orig.). (J). (gr. 1-3). 1987. pap. text ed. 4.95 (*0-88335-574-4*); spiral bd. 14.95 (*0-88335-544-2*) Milliken Pub Co.

Ugly Duckling. Harry Bornstein et al. (Signed English Ser.). (Illus.). 48p. (J). (ps-2). 1974. pap. 6.50 (*0-913580-29-5*, Pub. by K Green Pubns) Gallaudet Univ Pr.

Ugly Duckling. Margaret Wise Brown. LC 93-73578. (Illus.). 32p. (J). 1994. 13.95 (*0-7868-3007-7*); lib. bdg. 13.89 (*0-7868-5001-9*) Disney Pr.

Ugly Duckling. Illus. by Lynne Byrnes. (Happytime Storybks.). 24p. (J). (ps-1). 1991. pap. 1.25 (*0-7214-5304-X*, S9016-5, Ladybrd) Penguin.

***Ugly Duckling.** Richard Caudle & Brad Caudle. (Rock 'N Learn Ser.). (Illus.). 20p. (J). (gr. 1 up). 1996. pap. 7.95 (*1-878489-68-2*) Rock n Learn.

Ugly Duckling. Lorinda B. Cauley. LC 79-12340. (Illus.). 48p. (J). (gr. k up). 1979. pap. 5.00 (*0-15-692528-1*, Voyager Bks) HarBrace.

Ugly Duckling. Marc Cerasini. (Storyshapes Ser.). (Illus.). 24p. (Orig.). (J). (ps-1). 1996. pap. 2.25 (*1-56293-906-8*) McClanahan Bk.

Ugly Duckling. Gail Erwin. 23p. (Orig.). (J). (gr. 3-9). 1992. pap. 3.50 (*1-57514-159-0*, 0068) Encore Perform Pub.

Ugly Duckling. Golden Books Staff. (Little Golden Bks.). (Illus.). 24p. (J). (ps-2). 1995. 1.49 (*0-307-30264-4*, Golden Pr) Western Pub.

Ugly Duckling. Illus. by Gill Guile. (Once Upon a Time Ser.). 24p. (J). (ps-1). 1996. 3.98 (*1-85854-416-5*) Brimax Bks.

***Ugly Duckling.** Illus. by Margitta Hanff. (Froggy's Country Storybook Ser.: Vol. 3). 16p. (J). (gr. k-3). 1997. pap. write for info. (*1-890818-28-3*) Virginia Recs.

Ugly Duckling. Iris Johansen. LC 95-36175. 323p. 1996. 19.95 (*0-553-09714-8*, Bantam Trade Bks); audio 16.99 (*0-553-47672-6*) Bantam.

Ugly Duckling. Iris Johansen. 448p. 1997. mass mkt. 6.99 (*0-553-56991-0*) Bantam.

Ugly Duckling. Carrie Mapes & Judith Gold. (Folktale Theme Ser.: Vol. 6). (Illus.). 64p. (J). (gr. k-2). 1995. teacher ed., pap. text ed. 6.95 (*1-55799-377-7*, EMC 529) Evan-Moor Corp.

Ugly Duckling. Adrian Mitchell. LC 93-39962. (Illus.). 32p. (J). (ps-3). 1994. 14.95 (*1-56458-557-3*) DK Pub Inc.

Ugly Duckling. Illus. by Gerda Muller. 48p. (J). (gr. 2-6). 1991. 2.99 (*0-517-02422-5*) Random Hse Value.

Ugly Duckling. Illus. by Betina Ogden. (Pudgy Pal Board Bks.). 18p. (J). (ps). 1994. bds. 3.95 (*0-448-40184-3*, G&D) Putnam Pub Group.

Ugly Duckling. Illus. by David Pace. (Fairy Tale Pop-ups Ser.). 16p. (J). 1994. 3.95 (*0-7214-9420-X*, Ladybrd) Penguin.

Ugly Duckling. Illus. by Susan Spellman & Sam Thiewes. (Favorite Fairy Tales Ser.). 24p. (J). (gr. k-4). 1993. lib. bdg. 10.95 (*1-56674-066-5*, HTS Bks) Forest Hse.

Ugly Duckling. Illus. by Van Gool Studio Staff. (Classic Ser.). 64p. (J). (ps-1). 1994. 4.98 (*0-8317-1668-1*) Smithmark.

Ugly Duckling. Harriet Ziefert. LC 96-40056. 1997. pap. 11.99 (*0-670-86780-2*) Viking Penguin.

***Ugly Duckling.** Harriet Ziefert. (J). 1997. pap. 3.99 (*0-14-038352-2*) Viking Penguin.

Ugly Duckling. large type ed. Iris Johansen. LC 96-5478. 1996. lib. bdg. 20.00 (*0-7838-1708-8*, GK Hall) Thorndike Pr.

Ugly Duckling: A Pop-up Classic Storybook. Clare Segnit & Jack Segnit. (Illus.). 12p. (J). (ps-3). 1993. bds. 14.95 (*0-689-71722-9*, Mac Bks Young Read) S&S Childrens.

***Ugly Duckling: Based on the Tale by Hans Christian Andersen.** Hans Christian Andersen. (Illus.). 30p. (J). (ps up). 1995. pap. 3.25 (*0-88680-408-6*, 408-6) I E Clark.

Ugly Duckling: Fairy Tales. Hans Christian Andersen. Ed. by Tony Tallarico. (Tuffy Story Bks.). (Illus.). 32p. (J). (ps-3). 1987. pap. text ed. 1.95 (*0-89828-333-7*, 83337, Tuffy) Putnam Pub Group.

Ugly Duckling: Musical. Willard Simms & Jan Powell. 34p. 1990. pap. 5.00 (*0-87129-002-2*, U20) Dramatic Pub.

Ugly Duckling & Other Fairy Tales. Hans Christian Andersen. (Illus.). 96p. (Orig.). (J). 1992. pap. 1.00 (*0-486-27081-5*) Dover.

Ugly Duckling Literature Mini-Unit. Janet Lovelady. (Illus.). 32p. (J). (gr. 3-5). 1990. student ed. 4.95 (*1-56096-015-9*) Mari.

***Ugly Duckling Sticker Storybook.** Marty Noble. (Illus.). 16p. (Orig.). (J). 1997. pap. text ed. 1.00 (*0-486-29728-4*) Dover.

Ugly Face of Power: And Masks of Deception. Robert M. Watkins. LC 92-62000. 184p. 1994. pap. 10.95 (*1-56002-222-1*, Univ Edtns) Aegina Pr.

Ugly Kid Joe - America's Least Wanted: Play-It-Like-It-Is-Guitar. pap. 19.95 (*0-89524-732-1*) Cherry Lane.

Ugly Little Boy & The Widget, the Wadget, & Boff. Isaac Asimov & Theodore Sturgeon. (Double Ser.: No. 9). (J). 1989. 3.50 (*0-8125-5966-5*) Tor Bks.

Ugly Menorah. Marissa Moss. (Illus.). 32p. (J). (gr. k-3). 1996. 14.00 (*0-374-38027-9*) FS&G.

Ugly Stepsisters. Walt Disney Productions Staff. (Walt Disney's Fun-to-Read Library Ser.: Vol. 6). (Illus.). 44p. (J). (gr. 1-6). 1986. reprint ed. 3.49 (*1-885222-18-1*) Advance Pubs.

Ugly Truth about Men: A Guide to the Weaker Sex. Tom Carey. Ed. by Cliff Carle. 1992. pap. 5.95 (*0-918259-46-0*) CCC Pubns.

Ugly Truth about Rush Limbaugh: And the Attempted Hijacking of the 1992 Election. Mark A. Crouch. 96p. (Orig.). 1996. pap. 10.00 (*1-887934-96-0*) Delmax.

Ugly Truth about the Anti-Defamation League. Executive Intelligence Review Editors. (Illus.). 152p. (Orig.). 1992. pap. 7.00 (*0-943235-07-3*) Exec Intel Review.

Ugly Ways. Tina M. Ansa. LC 93-16395. 1993. 19.95 (*0-15-192553-4*) HarBrace.

Ugly Ways: A Novel. Tina M. Ansa. LC 94-33938. 1995. pap. 12.00 (*0-15-600077-6*, Harvest Bks) HarBrace.

UglyPuss. Caroline Gregorie. (J). 1994. 14.95 (*0-8050-3300-9*) H Holt & Co.

Ugly's Electrical References. rev. ed. George V. Hart. (Illus.). 144p. 1996. pap. 9.50 (*0-9623229-4-6*) Burleson Dist. An invaluable pocket size electrical reference book. George V. Hart has condensed a lifetime of electrical industry experience into a one volume toolbox library. This book is currently used worldwide by contractors, engineers, military, colleges & vocational training courses. Includes mathematics review, electrical formulas, wiring diagrams, charts, tables, & first aid information. Quantity discounts. For further information contact: Burleson Distributing Corporation, 3501 Oak Forest Dr., Houston, TX 77018. 1-800-531-1660. *Publisher Provided Annotation.*

Ugo La Pietra. Pierre Restany & Vitra. Date not set. pap. 28.95 (*84-252-1482-3*) St Martin.

***Ugo Rondinone: Heyday.** Michelle Nicol. 1996. 40.00 (*3-9520497-5-1*, Pub. by Memory-Cage SZ) Dist Art Pubs.

***Ugs & Lee Skits.** (J). pap. 6.95 (*0-614-18221-2*, PS03) Let Us Tch Kids.

Uh Oh. (J). 1993. pap. 8.98 (*1-879496-38-0*) Lightyear Entrtnmnt.

***Uh-Oh.** Robert Fulghum. 1997. pap. 11.00 (*0-449-00098-2*) Fawcett.

Uh-Oh. Robert Fulghum. 1991. 19.00 (*0-679-40103-2*, Villard Bks) Random.

Uh-Oh: Some Observations from Both Sides of the Refrigerator Door. Robert Fulghum. 256p. 1993. mass mkt. 5.99 (*0-8041-1189-8*) Ivy Books.

Uh-Oh: Some Observations from Both Sides of the Refrigerator Door. large type ed. Robert Fulghum. 272p. 1991. 21.00 (*0-679-40286-1*) Random Hse Lrg Prnt.

Uh-oh, Baby. Wendy C. Lewison. 16p. (J). (ps). 1992. 4.95 (*0-590-45171-5*, Cartwheel) Scholastic Inc.

Uh-oh! Cawed the Crow. Joanne F. Oppenheim. LC 92-1629. (Bank Street Ready-to-Read Ser.). (Illus.). 32p. (J). 1993. pap. 3.99 (*0-553-37186-X*, Litl Rooster) BDD Bks Young Read.

Uh Oh, Dopey. (Squeeze Me Ser.). (J). 1996. 6.98 (*1-57082-392-8*) Mouse Works.

Uh Oh! Gotta Go! Potty Tales from Toddlers. Bob McGrath. LC 96-1527. (Illus.). 32p. (J). 1996. 5.95 (*0-8120-6564-6*) Barron.

Uh! Oh! Hanukkah. Illus. by Don Channen. (Uh! Oh! Hidden Objects Ser.: Vol. 1). 32p. (J). (gr. 3-7). 1993. 12.95 (*0-943706-15-7*) Pitspopany.

Uh-Oh! It's Mama's Birthday! Naturi Thomas. LC 96-10168. (Illus.). 24p. (J). 1997. lib. bdg. 12.95 (*0-8075-8268-9*) A Whitman.

Uh! Oh! Jewish Holidays. Illus. by Janet Zwebner. (Uh! Oh! Hidden Objects Ser.: Vol. 2). 32p. (J). (gr. 3-6). 1993. 12.95 (*0-943706-14-9*) Pitspopany.

Uh-Oh Not Me. Darleen Carter. LC 90-71360. (Illus.). 44p. (J). (gr. k-3). 1991. 5.95 (*1-55523-398-8*) Winston-Derek.

Uh! Oh! Passover. Illus. by Janet Zwebner. 48p. (J). (gr. 3-7). 1994. 12.95 (*965-465-003-7*) Pitspopany.

***"Uh-Oh!" Said the Crow.** Joanne Oppenheim. LC 97-1629. (Bank Street Ready-To-Read Ser.). (Illus.). (J). 1997. lib. bdg. write for info. (*0-8368-1753-2*) Gareth Stevens Inc.

Uh-Uh, Not Now Said the Cow. Yaffa L. Gottleib. Ed. by Ruth Zakutinsky. (E-Z Reader Ser.). (Illus.). 32p. (J). (gr. k-1). 1995. 7.95 (*0-911643-18-4*) Aura Bklyn.

UH-1 Huey in Color. Wayne Mutza. (Fighting Colors Ser.). (Illus.). 32p. 1992. pap. 9.95 (*0-89747-279-9*, 6564) Squad Sig Pubns.

UH-1C Huey. Peter W. Harlem. LC 85-70918. (Crewchief Ser.: No. 1). (Illus.). 56p. (Orig.). 1985. pap. 6.50 (*0-933907-00-1*, CE-1) Cobra Co.

UH-1H/V Flight Handbook for U. S. Army Aviators. Bruce W. Dawson. Ed. by Michael E. Jose & Denise C. Dawson. LC 90-64133. (Illus.). 310p. 1995. 80.00 (*1-878595-00-8*) Silver Wngs Pubs.

UHC Special Edition, 11 vols. AT&T UNIX System Staff. Set. pap. 425.00 (*0-13-587734-2*) P-H.

UHF - Microwave Projects Manual. 1994. pap. 20.00 (*0-87259-449-1*) Am Radio.

UHF-Microwave Experimenter's Manual. 1990. pap. 20.00 (*0-87259-312-6*) Am Radio.

Uhibbu al-Madrasah, 12 vols., Set. Abd-al-Wahid Ulwani. 192p. 1992. pap. 13.95 (*1-57547-148-5*) Dar Al-Fikr.

Uhibbu al-Madrasah, Vol. 1. Abd-al-Wahid Ulwani. 1992. pap. write for info. (*1-57547-149-3*) Dar Al-Fikr.

Uhibbu al-Madrasah, Vol. 2. Abd-al-Wahid Ulwani. (J). 1992. pap. write for info. (*1-57547-150-7*) Dar Al-Fikr.

Uhibbu al-Madrasah, Vol. 3. Abd-al-Wahid Ulwani. (J). 1992. pap. write for info. (*1-57547-151-5*) Dar Al-Fikr.

Uhibbu al-Madrasah, Vol. 4. Abd-al-Wahid Ulwani. (J). 1992. pap. write for info. (*1-57547-152-3*) Dar Al-Fikr.

Uhibbu al-Madrasah, Vol. 5. Abd-al-Wahid Ulwani. (J). 1992. pap. write for info. (*1-57547-153-1*) Dar Al-Fikr.

Uhibbu al-Madrasah, Vol. 6. Abd-al-Wahid Ulwani. (J). 1992. pap. write for info. (*1-57547-154-X*) Dar Al-Fikr.

Uhibbu al-Madrasah, Vol. 7. Abd-al-Wahid Ulwani. (J). 1992. pap. write for info. (*1-57547-155-8*) Dar Al-Fikr.

Uhibbu al-Madrasah, Vol. 8. Abd-al-Wahid Ulwani. (J). 1992. pap. write for info. (*1-57547-156-6*) Dar Al-Fikr.

Uhibbu al-Madrasah, Vol. 9. Abd-al-Wahid Ulwani. (J). 1992. pap. write for info. (*1-57547-157-4*) Dar Al-Fikr.

Uhibbu al-Madrasah, Vol. 10. Abd-al-Wahid Ulwani. (J). 1992. pap. write for info. (*1-57547-158-2*) Dar Al-Fikr.

Uhibbu al-Madrasah, Vol. 11. Abd-al-Wahid Ulwani. (J). 1992. pap. write for info. (*1-57547-159-0*) Dar Al-Fikr.

Uhibbu al-Madrasah, Vol. 12. Abd-al-Wahid Ulwani. (J). 1992. pap. 13.95 (*1-57547-160-4*) Dar Al-Fikr.

Uhibbu an Akun: Silsilat Qisas Il-Atfal, 20 vols., Set. Shawqi Abu-Khalil. 640p. 1991. pap. 35.90 (*1-57547-120-5*) Dar Al-Fikr.

An Asterisk (*) at the beginning of an entry indicates that the title is appearing in BIP for the first time.

Uhibbu an Akun: Silsilat Qisas Il-Atfal, Vol. 1. Shawqi Abu-Khalil. (J). 1991. pap. write for info. (1-57547-121-3) Dar Al-Fikr.

Uhibbu an Akun: Silsilat Qisas Il-Atfal, Vol. 2. Shawqi Abu-Khalil. 1991. pap. write for info. (1-57547-122-1) Dar Al-Fikr.

Uhibbu an Akun: Silsilat Qisas Il-Atfal, Vol. 3. Shawqi Abu-Khalil. (J). 1991. pap. write for info. (1-57547-123-X) Dar Al-Fikr.

Uhibbu an Akun: Silsilat Qisas Il-Atfal, Vol. 4. Shawqi Abu-Khalil. (J). 1991. pap. write for info. (1-57547-124-8) Dar Al-Fikr.

Uhibbu an Akun: Silsilat Qisas Il-Atfal, Vol. 5. Shawqi Abu-Khalil. (J). 1991. pap. write for info. (1-57547-125-6) Dar Al-Fikr.

Uhibbu an Akun: Silsilat Qisas Il-Atfal, Vol. 6. Shawqi Abu-Khalil. 1991. pap. write for info. (1-57547-126-4) Dar Al-Fikr.

Uhibbu an Akun: Silsilat Qisas Il-Atfal, Vol. 7. Shawqi Abu-Khalil. 1991. pap. write for info. (1-57547-127-2) Dar Al-Fikr.

Uhibbu an Akun: Silsilat Qisas Il-Atfal, Vol. 8. Shawqi Abu-Khalil. 1991. pap. write for info. (1-57547-128-0) Dar Al-Fikr.

Uhibbu an Akun: Silsilat Qisas Il-Atfal, Vol. 9. Shawqi Abu-Khalil. 1991. pap. write for info. (1-57547-129-9) Dar Al-Fikr.

Uhibbu an Akun: Silsilat Qisas Il-Atfal, Vol. 10. Shawqi Abu-Khalil. 1991. pap. write for info. (1-57547-130-2) Dar Al-Fikr.

Uhibbu an Akun: Silsilat Qisas Il-Atfal, Vol. 11. Shawqi Abu-Khalil. 1991. pap. write for info. (1-57547-131-0) Dar Al-Fikr.

Uhibbu an Akun: Silsilat Qisas Il-Atfal, Vol. 12. Shawqi Abu-Khalil. 1991. pap. write for info. (1-57547-132-9) Dar Al-Fikr.

Uhibbu an Akun: Silsilat Qisas Il-Atfal, Vol. 13. Shawqi Abu-Khalil. 1991. pap. write for info. (1-57547-133-7) Dar Al-Fikr.

Uhibbu an Akun: Silsilat Qisas Il-Atfal, Vol. 14. Shawqi Abu-Khalil. 1991. pap. write for info. (1-57547-134-5) Dar Al-Fikr.

Uhibbu an Akun: Silsilat Qisas Il-Atfal, Vol. 15. Shawqi Abu-Khalil. 1991. pap. write for info. (1-57547-135-3) Dar Al-Fikr.

Uhibbu an Akun: Silsilat Qisas Il-Atfal, Vol. 16. Shawqi Abu-Khalil. 1991. pap. write for info. (1-57547-136-1) Dar Al-Fikr.

Uhibbu an Akun: Silsilat Qisas Il-Atfal, Vol. 17. Shawqi Abu-Khalil. 1991. pap. write for info. (1-57547-137-X) Dar Al-Fikr.

Uhibbu an Akun: Silsilat Qisas Il-Atfal, Vol. 18. Shawqi Abu-Khalil. 1991. pap. write for info. (1-57547-138-8) Dar Al-Fikr.

Uhibbu an Akun: Silsilat Qisas Il-Atfal, Vol. 19. Shawqi Abu-Khalil. 1991. pap. write for info. (1-57547-139-6) Dar Al-Fikr.

Uhibbu an Akun: Silsilat Qisas Il-Atfal, Vol. 20. Shawqi Abu-Khalil. 1991. pap. write for info. (1-57547-140-X) Dar Al-Fikr.

Uhibbu an A'rif A'lam Ummati: Sirat Rijal Sanau al-Tarikh, 6 vols., Set. Hani Al-Mubarak. 96p. (J). 1993. pap. 7.95 (1-57547-141-8) Dar Al-Fikr.

Uhibbu an A'rif A'lam Ummati: Sirat Rijal Sanau al-Tarikh, Vol. 1. Hani Al-Mubarak. (J). 1993. pap. write for info. (1-57547-142-6) Dar Al-Fikr.

Uhibbu an A'rif A'lam Ummati: Sirat Rijal Sanau al-Tarikh, Vol. 2. Hani Al-Mubarak. (J). 1993. pap. write for info. (1-57547-143-4) Dar Al-Fikr.

Uhibbu an A'rif A'lam Ummati: Sirat Rijal Sanau al-Tarikh, Vol. 3. Hani Al-Mubarak. (J). 1993. pap. write for info. (1-57547-144-2) Dar Al-Fikr.

Uhibbu an A'rif A'lam Ummati: Sirat Rijal Sanau al-Tarikh, Vol. 4. Hani Al-Mubarak. (J). 1993. pap. write for info. (1-57547-145-0) Dar Al-Fikr.

Uhibbu an A'rif A'lam Ummati: Sirat Rijal Sanau al-Tarikh, Vol. 5. Hani Al-Mubarak. (J). 1993. pap. write for info. (1-57547-146-9) Dar Al-Fikr.

Uhibbu an A'rif A'lam Ummati: Sirat Rijal Sanau al-Tarikh, Vol. 6. Hani Al-Mubarak. (J). 1993. pap. write for info. (1-57547-147-7) Dar Al-Fikr.

Uhibbu an A'rif Tarikh Ummati, 6 vols., Set. Shawqi Abu-Khalil. (Safhat min Tarikhina Ser.). 1993. pap. 7.95 (1-57547-113-2) Dar Al-Fikr.

Uhibbu an A'rif Tarikh Ummati, Vol. 1. Shawqi Abu-Khalil. (Safhat min Tarikhina Ser.). 1993. pap. write for info. (1-57547-114-0) Dar Al-Fikr.

Uhibbu an A'rif Tarikh Ummati, Vol. 2. Shawqi Abu-Khalil. (Safhat min Tarikhina Ser.). 1993. pap. write for info. (1-57547-115-9) Dar Al-Fikr.

Uhibbu an A'rif Tarikh Ummati, Vol. 3. Shawqi Abu-Khalil. (Safhat min Tarikhina Ser.). 1993. pap. write for info. (1-57547-116-7) Dar Al-Fikr.

Uhibbu an A'rif Tarikh Ummati, Vol. 4. Shawqi Abu-Khalil. (Safhat min Tarikhina Ser.). 1993. pap. write for info. (1-57547-117-5) Dar Al-Fikr.

Uhibbu an A'rif Tarikh Ummati, Vol. 5. Shawqi Abu-Khalil. (Safhat min Tarikhina Ser.). 1993. pap. write for info. (1-57547-118-3) Dar Al-Fikr.

Uhibbu an A'rif Tarikh Ummati, Vol. 6. Shawqi Abu-Khalil. (Safhat min Tarikhina Ser.). 1993. pap. write for info. (1-57547-119-1) Dar Al-Fikr.

Uhura's Song. (Star Trek Ser.: No. 21). 1987. mass mkt. 5.50 (0-671-65227-3, Pocket Star Bks) PB.

Uhuru. Robert Ruark. 1993. reprint ed. lib. bdg. 39.95 (1-56849-025-9) Buccaneer Bks.

Uhuru Street. M. G. Vassanji. (African Writers Ser.). 144p. (C). 1991. pap. 8.95 (0-435-90585-6, 90585) Heinemann.

UI Design Book for the Applications Programmer. Alexander Martin. 300p. 1996. pap. text ed. 50.00 (0-471-95371-7) Wiley.

UIA International Exhibition of Architecture, Cairo 1985. Ed. by Jorge Glusberg. (Academy Architecture Ser.). (Illus.). 88p. 1985. pap. 14.95 (0-312-82780-6) St Martin.

Uintah Railway: The Gilsonite Route. Henry E. Bender, Jr. LC 75-135999. (Illus.). 252p. 1995. 39.95 (0-911581-36-7) Heimburger Hse Pub.

Uirsgeul. Gairm Publications Staff. (C). 1991. 45.00 (1-871901-06-5, Pub. by Gairm Pubns UK) St Mut.

Uitleg van Wette. L. C. Steyn. 389p. 1981. write for info. (0-7021-1216-X, Pub. by Juta SA); pap. write for info. (0-7021-1218-6, Pub. by Juta SA) Gaunt.

Uj Egtajak. Ed. by Gyorgy Gomori & Vilmos Juhasz. LC 71-94112. 1969. pap. 6.00 (0-911050-35-3) Occidental.

Ujamaa Villages in Tanzania: Analysis of a Social Experiment. Michaela Von Freyhold. LC 79-13401. 201p. 1981. 14.50 (0-85345-512-0); pap. 10.00 (0-85345-513-9) Monthly Rev.

UK Consumer Market Factfile. 350p. 1988. 450.00 (0-86338-322-X, Pub. by Euromonitor Pubns UK) Gale.

UK Consumer Spending Trends & Forecasts. Euromonitor Staff. 135p. (C). 1989. 1,125.00 (0-86338-344-0, Pub. by Euromonitor Pubns UK) Gale.

UK Cosmetics & Toiletries Report 1988. Euromonitor Staff. 230p. (C). 1991. 1,125.00 (0-685-30322-5, Pub. by Euromonitor Pubns UK) Gale.

UK Economy & Europe. Bruce Jewell. 320p. (Orig.). 1993. pap. 39.50 (0-273-60084-2, Pub. by Pitman Pub Ltd UK) Trans-Atl Phila.

UK Food Report. Euromonitor Staff. 500p. (C). 1992. 1,575.00 (0-86338-347-5, Pub. by Euromonitor Pubns UK) Gale.

UK GAAP. 4th ed. Mike Davies et al. 1610p. 1995. 100.00 (1-56159-165-3, Stockton Pr) Groves Dictionaries.

UK Home Hygiene Report. Euromonitor Staff. 144p. (C). 1988. 975.00 (0-86338-293-2, Pub. by Euromonitor Pubns UK) Gale.

UK Hotels in the Nineteen Hundred Eighties. Euromonitor Staff. 100p. 1987. 825.00 (0-86338-205-3, Pub. by Euromonitor Pubns UK) Gale.

UK Import Market Reports, No. 1: Knitwear. (C). 1987. 125.00 (0-317-89784-5, Pub. by Trade Rsch Pubns UK) St Mut.

UK Import Market Reports, No. 2: Furniture. Trade Research Publications Staff. (C). 1987. 95.00 (0-904783-17-0, Pub. by Trade Rsch Pubns UK) St Mut.

UK Market for Contact Lenses: Trends, Opportunities & Prospects to 1991. Euromonitor Staff. 105p. (C). 1988. 2,250.00 (0-685-30318-7, Pub. by Euromonitor Pubns UK) Gale.

UK Military R & D. Council for Science & Society Staff. (Illus.). 90p. 1986. pap. 9.95 (0-19-859930-7) OUP.

UK Nuclear Fuel Waste Management Program: Special Issue of the Journal Radioactive Waste Management & the Nuclear Fuel Cycle. J. R. Grover. 308p. 1987. pap. text ed. 287.00 (3-7186-0471-X) Gordon & Breach.

UK OTC Healthcare Report. Euromonitor Staff. 150p. (C). 1987. 975.00 (0-86338-268-1, Pub. by Euromonitor Pubns UK) Gale.

UK Own Brands 1989. Euromonitor Staff. 80p. (C). 1989. 1,125.00 (0-86338-349-1, Pub. by Euromonitor Pubns UK) Gale.

UK Personal Financial Services. Euromonitor Staff. 200p. (C). 1987. 975.00 (0-86338-210-X, Pub. by Euromonitor Pubns UK) Gale.

***UK Pesticide Guide 1997.** Ed. by R. Whitehead. (CAB International Publication). 664p. 1997. pap. 31.00 (0-85199-205-6) CAB Intl.

UK Pub: Prospects into the 1990's. Euromonitor Staff. 130p. (C). 1989. 1,125.00 (0-86338-346-7, Pub. by Euromonitor Pubns UK) Gale.

U.K. Statistics: A Guide for Business Users. David Mort. 300p. 1992. 72.95 (0-566-02971-5, Pub. by Gower UK) Ashgate Pub Co.

UK Telecommunications Policy Review. David Gillick & Sandy Skinner. 168p. (C). 1991. 495.00 (1-85271-181-7, Pub. by IBC Tech Srvs UK) St Mut.

Ukandoit. Alma Burnette. Ed. by Lafe Miller. (Illus.). 28p. (Orig.). (J). (gr. 1-8). 1994. 2.95 (1-886452-00-8) Amer Recycling.

Ukazatel' k sovetskim dissertatsionnym issledovaniiam: Iuzhnye i Zapadnye Slaviane: Guide to Slavic Dissertations. Ed. by Leonid Gorizontov. LC 94-10711. xiii, 170p. (RUS.). 1994. lib. bdg. 60.00 (0-88354-357-5) N Ross.

Ukazatel' Skazochnykh Siuzhetov Po Sisteme Aarne. Nikolai P. Andreev. 118p. (RUS.). (C). 1993. reprint ed. pap. 12.00 (0-933884-90-7) Berkeley Slavic.

Ukiah Valley Pomo Religious Life, Supernatural Doctoring, & Beliefs Observations of 1939-1941. fac. ed. Birbeck Wilson. Ed. by Caroline L. Hills. (Reports of the University of California Archaeological Survey: No. 72). 98p. 1968. reprint ed. pap. 8.70 (1-55567-388-0) Coyote Press.

Ukifune: Love in the Tale of Genji. Ed. by Andrew J. Pekarik. LC 82-1157. 264p. 1983. text ed. 49.50 (0-231-04598-0) Col U Pr.

Ukimwi Road: From Kenya to Zimbabwe. Dervla Murphy. 290p. 1995. 22.95 (0-87951-556-2) Overlook Pr.

Ukimwi Road: From Kenya to Zimbabwe. Dervla Murphy. 290p. 1996. pap. 13.95 (0-87951-671-2) Overlook Pr.

Ukimwi Road: From Kenya to Zimbabwe. Dervla Murphy. 426p. 1995. 24.95 (1-85695-235-5, Pub. by ISIS UK) Transaction Pubs.

Ukiyo: Stories of the "Floating World" of Postwar Japan. Jay Gluck. 288p. 1993. pap. 10.95 (4-89360-037-0, Pub. by Personally Oriented JA) Weatherhill.

Ukiyo-E. Amy R. Newland & Christianus C. Uhlenbeck. 112p. 1994. 14.98 (0-8317-6116-4) Smithmark.

Ukiyo-E: A Kodansha Postcard Book. Kodansha International Staff. Ed. by Ogawa. (Illus.). 56p. (Orig.). 1992. pap. 9.95 (4-7700-1678-6) Kodansha.

Ukiyo-E: An Introduction to Japanese Woodblock Prints. Tadashi Kobayashi. Tr. by Mark A. Harbison from JPN. (Illus.). 96p. 1992. 35.00 (4-7700-1657-3) Kodansha.

Ukiyo-E Cats: A Kodansha Postcard Book. Kodansha International Staff. Ed. by Ogawa & Pockell. (Illus.). 56p. 1993. 9.00 (4-7700-1782-0) Kodansha.

Ukiyo-E from the Museum of Fine Arts, Springfield, MA. Text by Tadashi Kobayashi. (Illus.). 160p. (JPN.). 1994. 29.95 (0-916746-56-9) Springfield Lib & Mus.

Ukiyo-E Masterpieces in Europe Collections: The British Museum, Vol. 2. Muneshige Narazaki. LC 87-81680. (Illus.). 278p. 1988. 300.00 (0-87011-869-2) Kodansha.

Ukiyo-E Masterpieces in European Collections: Museum fur Ostasiatische Kunst, Berlin, Vol. 12. Contrib. by Muneshige Narazaki. LC 87-81680. 260p. 1988. 300.00 (0-87011-882-X) Kodansha.

Ukiyo-E Masterpieces in European Collections: Victor & Albert Museum, I, Vol. 4. Contrib. by Muneshige Narazaki. LC 87-81680. 280p. 1989. 300.00 (0-87011-875-7) Kodansha.

Ukiyo-E Masterpieces in European Collections: Vol. 1: British Museum I. LC 87-81680. (Ukiyo-E Masterpieces Ser.). (Illus.). 268p. 1988. 300.00 (0-87011-855-2) Kodansha.

Ukiyo-E Masterpieces in European Collections Vol. 3: British Museum III. Ed. by Muneshige Narazaki. LC 87-81680. 278p. 1989. 300.00 (0-87011-874-9) Kodansha.

Ukiyo-E Masterpieces in European Collections Vol. 6: Musee Guimet 1, Paris. Muneshige Narazaki. (UKIYO-E Ser.). (Illus.). 280p. 1990. 300.00 (0-87011-877-3) Kodansha.

Ukiyo-E Masterpieces in European Collections Vol. 7: Musee Guimet II, Paris. LC 87-81680. 286p. 1991. 300.00 (0-87011-878-1) Kodansha.

Ukiyo-E Masterpieces in European Collections Vol. 8: Bibliotheque Nationale, Paris. Muneshige Narazaki. (UKIYO-E Ser.). (Illus.). 284p. 1990. 300.00 (0-87011-879-X) Kodansha.

Ukiyo-E Masterpieces in European Collections Vol. 9: Musees Royaux d'Art et D'Histoire. Contrib. by Muneshige Narazaki. (Illus.). 272p. 1989. 300.00 (0-87011-880-3) Kodansha.

Ukiyo-e Masterpieces in European Collections Vol. 11: Museo d'Arte Orientale, Genoa II. Ed. by Muneshige Narazaki. 260p. 1989. 300.00 (0-87011-881-1) Kodansha.

Ukiyo-E Masterpieces in European Collections Appendix Vol. 13: Collectors' Guide to Ukiyo-E Prints in Europe. LC 87-81680. 1991. 300.00 (0-87011-883-8) Kodansha.

Ukiyo-E Masterpieces in European Collections, Vol. 5: Victoria & Albert Museum II. Muneshige Nazaraki & Guiliano Frabetti. (Illus.). 272p. 1989. 300.00 (0-87011-876-5) Kodansha.

Ukiyo-E Masterpieces in European Collections, Vol. 10: Museo d'Arte Orientale, Genoa I, Vol. 10. Muneshige Narazaki. LC 87-81680. (Ukiyo-E Masterpieces Ser.). (Illus.). 232p. 1988. 300.00 (0-87011-856-0) Kodansha.

Ukiyo-E Paintings: In the British Museum. Timothy Clark. LC 92-64231. (Illus.). 256p. (Orig.). 1993. pap. 39.95 (1-56098-243-8) Smithsonian.

Ukiyoe: Images of Unknown Japan. Lawrence Smith. 1989. pap. 21.95 (0-486-26006-2) Dover.

Ukrain Hearld, Issue 7, 8-9, 10. Ed. by Vyacheslav Chornovil. LC 88-90879. 624p. 1988. 24.50 (0-914834-60-6) Smoloskyp.

Ukraina na Peremoli, 1657-1659: Zamitky do Istorii Ukrains'koho Derzhavnoho Budivnyctva v XVII-im Stolittiu. Viacheslav Lypyns'kyi. (Viacheslav Lypyns'kyi, Tvory Ser.: Vol. 3). 400p. 1992. text ed. 39.95 (0-9631165-0-9) WKL East Europ.

***Ukraine.** Volodymyr Bassis. LC 96-40207. (Cultures of the World Ser.: Group 14). (Illus.). 128p. (YA). (gr. 5 up). 1997. lib. bdg. 23.95 (0-7614-0684-0) Marshall Cavendish.

Ukraine. Bohdan Krawchenko. (World Bibliographical Ser.). 1996. lib. bdg. 80.00 (1-85109-163-7) ABC-CLIO.

Ukraine. Compiled by Lerner Publications, Department of Geography Staff. LC 92-10284. (Then & Now Ser.). (Illus.). 64p. (YA). (gr. 5 up). 1993. lib. bdg. 22.95 (0-8225-2808-8, Lerner Publctns) Lerner Group.

Ukraine. Michael M. Lustig. LC 95-38611. (Nations in Transition Ser.). (J). 1996. write for info. (0-614-08633-7) Facts on File.

Ukraine: A Bibliographic Guide to English-Language Publications. Bohdan S. Wynar. xiii, 406p. 1990. lib. bdg. 65.00 (0-87287-761-2) Libs Unl.

Ukraine: A Historical Atlas. Paul R. Magocsi. 64p. 1985. 50.00 (0-8020-3428-4) U of Toronto Pr.

Ukraine: A Historical Atlas. Paul R. Magocsi. 64p. 1986. pap. 27.50 (0-8020-3429-2) U of Toronto Pr.

Ukraine: A History. Orest Subtelny. (Illus.). 678p. 1988. 50.00 (0-8020-5808-6); pap. 29.95 (0-8020-6775-1) U of Toronto Pr.

Ukraine: A History. 2nd ed. Orest Subtelny. (Illus.). 700p. 1993. 60.00 (0-8020-0591-8); pap. 35.00 (0-8020-7191-0) U of Toronto Pr.

Ukraine: A Study in Revolution. Ed. by Taras Hunczak. (Series in Ukrainian). 389p. 1978. 7.50 (0-674-92009-0) HUP.

Ukraine: A Tourist Guide. Osyp Zinkewych & Volodymyr Hula. Tr. by M. Olynyk. LC 93-84208. 432p. 1993. 27.75 (0-914834-93-2) Smoloskyp.

Ukraine: From Perestroika to Independence. Taras Kuzio & Andrew Wilson. LC 92-20998. 1994. text ed. 39.95 (0-312-08652-0) St Martin.

Ukraine: IMF Economic Review. International Monetary Fund Staff. v, 69p. 1992. pap. 10.00 (1-55775-283-4) Intl Monetary.

***Ukraine: Sasha Kotyenko's Painting "Embroidery Time"** Jacquiline Touba. (Young Artists of the World Ser.). (J). 1997. write for info. (0-8239-5105-7) Rosen Group.

***Ukraine: Stability & Instability.** 88p. 1995. pap. text ed. 30.00 (1-57979-164-6) BPI Info Servs.

Ukraine: Stability & Instability. John Jaworsky. (Illus.). 87p. (Orig.). (C). 1996. pap. text ed. 30.00 (0-7881-2715-2) DIANE Pub.

Ukraine: The Agriculture Sector in Transition. LC 94-35367. (Country Study). 1994. 10.95 (0-8213-3076-4, 13076) World Bank.

Ukraine: The Legacy of Intolerance. David Little. LC 91-20695. 1991. pap. text ed. 14.95 (1-878379-12-7) US Inst Peace.

Ukraine: The Social Sectors During Transition. LC 93-21580. (Country Study Ser.). 330p. 1993. 19.95 (0-8213-2584-1, 12584) World Bank.

Ukraine: A New Independence see Exploring Cultures of the World

***Ukraine & European Security.** Tor Bukkvoll. (Chatham House Papers). 128p. 1997. 39.95 (1-85567-464-5, Pub. by Pntr Pubs UK) Bks Intl VA.

***Ukraine & European Security.** Tor Bukkvoll. (Chatham House Papers). 128p. 1997. pap. 15.95 (1-85567-465-3, Pub. by Pntr Pubs UK) Bks Intl VA.

Ukraine & Ukrainians Throughout the World: A Demographic & Sociological Guide to the Homeland & Its Diaspora. Ed. by Ann L. Pawliczko. (Illus.). 464p. (C). 1994. 75.00 (0-8020-0595-0); pap. 35.00 (0-8020-7200-3) U of Toronto Pr.

Ukraine During World War II: History & Its Aftermath. Ed. by Yury Boshyk et al. xix, 291p. 19.95 (0-920862-37-3) Ukrainian Acad.

Ukraine During World War II: History & Its Aftermath. Ed. by Yury Boshyk et al. xix, 291p. 1986. pap. 9.95 (0-920862-36-5) Ukrainian Acad.

Ukraine in the Seventies. Peter J. Potichnyj. 360p. 1995. lib. bdg. 29.00 (0-8095-4945-X) Borgo Pr.

Ukraine in the Seventies. Peter J. Potichnyj. 360p. pap. 9.95 (0-88962-000-8) Mosaic.

Ukraine in the United Nations: A Study in Soviet Foreign Policy, 1944-1950. Konstantin Sawczuk. LC 74-83055. (East European Monographs: No. 9). 158p. 1975. text ed. 52.00 (0-914710-02-8) East Eur Monographs.

***Ukraine Seminar Proceedings.** LC 97-775. 1997. write for info. (1-55775-619-8) Intl Monetary.

Ukraine Today: Perspectives for the Future. Ed. by Halyna Koscharsky. 137p. 1995. lib. bdg. 49.00 (1-56072-229-0) Nova Sci Pubs.

***Ukraine under Kuchma: Political Reform, Economic Transformation & Security in Independent Ukraine.** Taras Kuzio. LC 97-15184. (Studies in Russian & East European History & Society). 1997. write for info. (0-312-17625-2) St Martin.

Ukraine under Perestroika: Ecology, Economics & the Workers' Revolt. David R. Marples. LC 91-8110. 255p. 1991. text ed. 49.95 (0-312-06196-X); text ed. 16.95 (0-312-06197-8) St Martin.

Ukraine's Economic Reform: Obstacles, Errors, Lessons. Raphael Shen. LC 95-50468. 152p. 1996. text ed. 59.95 (0-275-95240-1, Praeger Pubs) Greenwood.

Ukraine's Non-Nuclear Option. (UNDIR Research Papers: No. 14). 34p. Date not set. pap. 12.00 (92-9045-071-1, E.GV.92.0.28) UN.

Ukrainian - English English - Ukrainian Dictionary. W. Niniowskyi. 1991. lib. bdg. 29.95 (0-8288-2634-X) Fr & Eur.

Ukrainian Americans: Roots & Aspirations 1884-1954. Myron B. Kuropas. 624p. 1991. 50.00 (0-8020-2749-0) U of Toronto Pr.

Ukrainian Americans: Roots & Aspirations 1884-1954. Myron B. Kuropas. (Illus.). 600p. 1994. pap. 25.00 (0-8020-7471-5) U of Toronto Pr.

Ukrainian Catholic Church: 1945-1975. Ed. by Miroslav Labunka & Leonid Rudnytzky. LC 76-26753. 1976. 7.50 (0-686-28475-5) St Sophia Religious.

Ukrainian Catholics & Orthodox in Poland & Czechoslovakia. Andrew Sorokowski. 33p. 1994. write for info. (0-940465-04-3) Ukrainian Studies Fund.

Ukrainian Challenge: Reforming Labour Market & Social Policy. International Labour Organization-Central & Eastern European Team Staff. (Central European University Press Bks.). (Illus.). 304p. 1995. 59.00 (1-85866-044-0); pap. 23.00 (1-85866-045-9) OUP.

Ukrainian Churches in New Jersey. Bohdan S. Polanskyi. (Illus.). 107p. 1993. 85.00 (0-9635415-0-1) B S P Pub.

Ukrainian Churches in New Jersey. deluxe ed. Bohdan S. Polanskyi. (Illus.). 107p. 1993. 125.00 (0-9635415-1-X) B S P Pub.

Ukrainian Churches under Soviet Rule: Two Case Studies. Bohdan R. Bociurkiw. 63p. 1994. write for info. (0-9609822-3-X) Ukrainian Studies Fund.

Ukrainian Citadel: The First Hundred Years of the Ukrainian National Association. Myron B. Kuropas. 420p. 1995. 59.00 (0-88033-313-8, E European Monographs) Col U Pr.

Ukrainian Corporate Legislation: A Foreign Investor's Practical Guide. Alex Frishberg et al. 1994. write for info. (90-6544-870-5) Kluwer Law Tax Pubs.

Ukrainian Culinary Glossary. Natalia Chaplenko. LC 80-54687. 113p. 1980. pap. 6.00 (0-317-36114-7) UNWLA.

Ukrainian Dumy: Editio Minor. Tr. by George Tarnawsky & Patricia Kilina. LC 79-94350. 219p. (UKR.). pap. 5.95 (0-920862-02-0) Ukrainian Acad.

Ukrainian Economic History: Interpretive Essays. Ed. by Iwan S. Koropeckyj. LC 90-50460. (Harvard Series in Ukrainian Studies). 392p. (C). 1991. 27.00 (*0-916458-35-0*); pap. 17.00 (*0-916458-63-6*) Harvard Ukrainian.

Ukrainian Economy: Achievements, Problems, Challenges. Intro. by Iwan S. Koropeckyj. (Harvard Series in Ukrainian Studies). 471p. (C). 1993. text ed. 32.95 (*0-916458-51-2*); pap. text ed. 17.00 (*0-916458-57-1*) Harvard Ukrainian.

Ukrainian Egg Mystery. George E. Stanley. 112p. 1986. pap. 2.50 (*0-380-89962-0*, Camelot) Avon.

Ukrainian-English - English-Ukrainian. 2nd rev. ed. W. Niniowski. 679p. 1990. pap. 31.50 (*0-88431-319-0*) IBD Ltd.

Ukrainian-English & English-Ukrainian Dictionary. W. Niniowskyi. 680p. 1992. pap. 21.00 (*0-317-05517-8*) Szwede Slavic.

Ukrainian-English Dictionary. Zhlutenko. 432p. (ENG & UKR.). 1982. 14.95 (*0-7859-1088-3*, F65550) Fr & Eur.

Ukrainian-English Dictionary. 2nd ed. Ed. by M. L. Podvesko. 42.50 (*0-87557-088-7*) Saphrograph.

Ukrainian-English, English-Ukrainian Compact Dictionary. 448p. (Orig.). (ENG & UKR.). 1996. pap. 8.95 (*0-7818-0498-1*) Hippocrene Bks.

Ukrainian English, English Ukrainian Practical Dictionary: Including Menu Terms. rev. ed. L. Hrabovsky. (Practical Dictionaries Ser.). 406p. 1994. reprint ed. pap. 14.95 (*0-7818-0306-3*) Hippocrene Bks.

Ukrainian-English, English-Ukrainian Standard Dictionary. Oleg Benyuch. (Hippocrene Standard Dictionaries Ser.). 590p. (Orig.). (ENG & UKR.). 1995. pap. 24.95 (*0-7818-0374-8*) Hippocrene Bks.

Ukrainian-English Phrasebook. 2nd ed. Levchuk. 190p. (ENG & UKR.). 1980. 7.95 (*0-8288-1730-8*, F65560) Fr & Eur.

Ukrainian-English Standard Dictionary (with Complete Phonetics) Oleg Benyuch. (Standard Dictionaries Ser.). 286p. (Orig.). 1994. pap. 14.95 (*0-7818-0189-3*) Hippocrene Bks.

Ukrainian, Everyday. Zirka Derlycia. 342p. 1993. pap. text ed. 195.00 incl. audio (*0-88432-491-5*, AFUK10) Audio-Forum.

Ukrainian Experience in the United States: A Symposium. Ed. by Paul R. Magocsi. LC 78-59968. (Sources & Documents Ser.). (Orig.). 1979. pap. 7.50 (*0-916458-04-0*) Harvard Ukrainian.

Ukrainian Folk Ballad in Canada. Robert B. Klymasz. LC 89-45444. (Immigrant Communities & Ethnic Minorities in the U. S. & Canada Ser.: No. 65). 1989. 59.50 (*0-404-19475-3*) AMS Pr.

Ukrainian Folk-Tales. Retold by Christina Oparenko. (Oxford Myths & Legends Ser.). (Illus.). 160p. (J). (gr. 7 up). 1996. pap. 12.95 (*0-19-274168-3*) OUP.

Ukrainian Folklore in Canada: An Immigrant Complex in Transition. Robert B. Klymasz. Ed. by Richard M. Dorson. LC 80-731. (Folklore of the World Ser.). 1981. lib. bdg. 35.95 (*0-405-13318-9*) Ayer.

Ukrainian for Beginners. Y. Slavutych. 60p. 1987. reprint ed. pap. 10.50 (*0-88431-025-6*) IBD Ltd.

Ukrainian for Undergraduates. Danylo H. Struk. xxxii, 350p. 1978. pap. 19.95 (*0-88962-079-2*) Ukrainian Acad.

Ukrainian Futurism, 1914-1930: A Historical & Critical Study. Oleh S. Ilnytzkyj. (Harvard Series in Ukrainian Studies). (Illus.). 320p. 1994. 35.00 (*0-916458-56-3*); pap. 17.00 (*0-916458-59-8*) Harvard Ukrainian.

Ukrainian-German Dictionary: Ukrainisch-Deutsches Woerterbuch. 2nd ed. Kuzela. 1500p. (GER & UKR.). 1983. 175.00 (*0-8288-4418-6*, F65570) Fr & Eur.

Ukrainian Helsinki Group, 1978-1982: A Collection of Documents & Materials. Osyp Zinkewych. LC 83-60960. 998p. (UKR.). 1983. 29.75 (*0-914834-50-9*) Smoloskyp.

Ukrainian Herald, Issue 6: Dissent in Ukraine. Ed. by Lesya Jones & Bohdan Yasen. LC 75-39367. 1977. 6.95 (*0-914834-05-3*); pap. 3.95 (*0-914834-06-1*) Smoloskyp.

Ukrainian Herald, Issue 7-8: Ethnocide of Ukrainians in the U. S. S. R. 2nd ed. Tr. by Bohdan Yasem & Olena Saciuk. LC 75-38397. 209p. 1981. 8.95 (*0-914834-45-2*) Smoloskyp.

***Ukrainian Icon from 11th-18th Centuries: From Byzantine Sources to the Baroque.** Liudmilla Miliaeva. (Temporis Ser.). 1996. 55.00 (*1-85995-241-0*) Parkstone Pr.

Ukrainian Impact on Russian Culture, 1750-1850. David Saunders. x, 415p. pap. 14.95 (*0-920862-34-9*) Ukrainian Acad.

Ukrainian-Jewish Relations in Historical Perspective. 2nd ed. Ed. by Peter J. Potichnyj & Howard Aster. xii, 531p. 1988. 34.95 (*0-920862-53-5*) Ukrainian Acad.

Ukrainian Language in the First Half of the Twentieth Century (1900-1941) Its State & Status. George Y. Shevelov. LC 88-81195. (Monograph Ser.). 240p. (C). 1990. 17.00 (*0-916458-30-X*) Harvard Ukrainian.

***Ukrainian Listening Comprehension.** A. Humesky. (C). 1996. pap. 47.00 incl. audio (*0-87415-279-8*, 121A) Christian Light.

***Ukrainian Listening Comprehension No. 121, Vol. I: Foreign Language Publications.** Ruth Shamraj. 480p. (Orig.). (UKR.). (C). 1996. student ed., pap. text ed. 31.00 (*0-87415-278-X*, UKR-121) OSU Foreign Lang.

Ukrainian Literature: Studies of the Leading Authors. Clarence A. Manning. LC 70-86771. (Essay Index Reprint Ser.). 1977. reprint ed. 20.95 (*0-8369-2244-1*) Ayer.

Ukrainian Literature in the Twentieth Century: A Reader's Guide. George S. Luckyj. 136p. (Orig.). 1992. 40.00 (*0-8020-5019-0*); pap. 18.95 (*0-8020-6003-X*) U of Toronto Pr.

***Ukrainian Minstrels: And the Blind Shall Sing.** Natalie Kononenko. (Folklores & Folk Cultures of Eastern Europe Ser.). 320p. (C). (gr. 13). 1997. text ed. 62.95 (*0-7656-0144-3*) M E Sharpe.

Ukrainian Nationalism. 3rd ed. John A. Armstrong. xviii, 271p. 1990. lib. bdg. 45.00 (*0-87287-755-8*) Libs Unl.

Ukrainian Nationalism in the Post-Stalin Era: Myth, Symbols & Ideology in Soviet Nationalities Policy. Kenneth C. Farmer. (Studies in Contemporary History: Vol. 4). 253p. 1980. lib. bdg. 88.00 (*90-247-2401-5*) Kluwer Ac.

***Ukrainian Nationalism in the 1990s: A Minority Faith.** Andrew Wilson. 320p. (C). 1996. text ed. 59.95 (*0-521-48285-2*); pap. text ed. 19.95 (*0-521-57457-9*) Cambridge U Pr.

Ukrainian Olympic Champions. Osyp Zinkewych. LC 84-51196. 158p. 1984. 9.75 (*0-914834-54-1*); pap. 7.50 (*0-914834-56-8*) Smoloskyp.

Ukrainian Orthodox Question in the U. S. S. R. Frank E. Sysyn. 28p. 1994. write for info. (*0-940465-02-7*) Ukrainian Studies Fund.

Ukrainian Past, Ukrainian Present. Ed. by Bohdan Krawchenko. LC 92-25188. 1993. text ed. 39.95 (*0-312-08671-7*) St Martin.

Ukrainian Phrasebook: Language Survival Kit. Olena Bekh & Jim Dingley. (Illus.). 176p. 1996. pap. 5.95 (*0-86442-339-X*) Lonely Planet.

Ukrainian Phrasebook & Dictionary. Oleg Benyuch. 205p. (Orig.). 1993. pap. 11.95 (*0-7818-0188-5*); audio 12.95 (*0-7818-0191-5*) Hippocrene Bks.

Ukrainian-Polish Defensive Alliance 1919-1921. Michael Palij. 44.95 (*0-614-14385-3*) Ukrainian Acad.

Ukrainian Primer. E. Shkanka. 125p. 1986. pap. 13.75 (*0-88431-031-0*) IBD Ltd.

Ukrainian Prose Manual: A Text for Intermediate Language Studies. Walter Smyrniw. 192p. 1995. lib. bdg. 29.00 (*0-8095-4883-6*) Borgo Pr.

Ukrainian Recipes. 140p. 1996. 5.95 (*1-57216-019-5*) Penfield.

***Ukrainian Resurgence: From Dependence to Independence.** Bohdan Nahaylo. 1997. pap. text ed. 24.95 (*0-8020-7977-6*) U of Toronto Pr.

Ukrainian Revolution: The Nineteen Nineteen to Nineteen Twenty-One Documents: Editor's Text in English, Documents in French, Polish, Russian & Ukrainian. Taras Hunczak. (Sources of Modern History of the Ukraine Ser.). (Illus.). 464p. 1984. 25.00 (*0-916381-00-5*) Ukrainian Arts Sci.

Ukrainian Revolution, 1917-1920: A Study in Nationalism. John S. Reshetar, Jr. LC 72-4292. (World Affairs Ser.: National & International Viewpoints). 376p. 1980. reprint ed. 31.95 (*0-405-04584-0*) Ayer.

Ukrainian Security Policy. Taras Kuzio. LC 95-19071. (Washington Papers: Vol. 167). 168p. 1995. pap. text ed. 14.95 (*0-275-95385-8*, Praeger Pubs) Greenwood.

Ukrainian Security Policy. Taras Kuzio. LC 95-19071. (Washington Papers: Vol. 167). 168p. (C). 1995. text ed. 52.95 (*0-275-95384-X*, Praeger Pubs) Greenwood.

Ukrainian Women's Bibliography Beyond the Borders of Ukraine. Natalia Chaplenko. 54p. 1974. pap. 2.00 (*0-317-36115-5*) UNWLA.

Ukrainians in America. Myron B. Kuropas. LC 94-14807. (In America Ser.). (Illus.). 80p. (YA). (gr. 5 up). 1995. lib. bdg. 18.95 (*0-8225-1955-0*, Lerner Publctns) Lerner Group.

Ukrainians in America. Myron B. Kuropas. 80p. (YA). (gr. 6 up). 1995. lib. bdg. 14.21 (*0-8225-1043-X*) Lerner Group.

Ukrainians in Canada & the United States: A Guide to Information Sources. Ed. by Aleksander Sokolyszyn & Vladimir Wertsman. (Ethnic Studies Information Guide Ser.: Vol. 7). 256p. 1981. 68.00 (*0-8103-1494-0*) Gale.

Ukrainians in North America: An Illustrated History. Orest Subtelny. 280p. 1991. 45.00 (*0-8020-5920-1*) U of Toronto Pr.

Ukrainians in North America: An Illustrated History. Orest Subtelny. (Illus.). 284p. 1994. pap. 19.95 (*0-8020-7619-X*) U of Toronto Pr.

Ukrainians in Rhode Island: Faith & Determination. Ed. by John J. Mowatt. (Rhode Island Ethnic Heritage Pamphlet Ser.). (Illus.). (Orig.). 1988. pap. 4.75 (*0-917012-90-9*) RI Pubns Soc.

Ukrainians in the Making: Their Kingston Story. Lubomyr Y. Luciuk. (Builders of Canada Ser.: No. 1). (Illus.). 1980. 16.50 (*0-919642-91-8*) Limestone Pr.

Ukrainians in the United States. Wasyl Halich. LC 78-129399. (American Immigration Collection, Ser. 2). (Illus.). 1977. reprint ed. 16.95 (*0-405-00552-0*) Ayer.

Ukranian see Spohady Memoirs

Ukrayina: Putivnyk. Osyp Zinkewych & Volodymyr Hula. LC 93-84207. 432p. (UKR.). 1993. 27.75 (*0-914834-92-4*) Smoloskyp.

Ukrayinsky Pravozakhysny Rukh: Ukrainian Movement in Defense of Rights: Documents of Kiev Ukrainian Helsinki Group. (UKR.). pap. 9.75 (*0-914834-17-7*) Smoloskyp.

UK's First Report to the UN Committee on the Rights of the Child. Department of Health Staff. 136p. 1994. pap. 25.00 (*0-11-321715-3*, HM17153, Pub. by Stationery Ofc UK) Bernan Associates.

Ukulele: A Portuguese Gift to Hawaii. John H. Felix et al. LC 80-66299. (Illus.). 75p. (Orig.). (gr. 4-12). 1980. pap. 5.95 (*0-9604190-0-4*) Nunes.

***Ukulele: A Visual History.** Jim Beloff. (Illus.). 112p. 1997. pap. 24.95 (*0-87930-454-5*) Miller Freeman.

Ukulele Chords: In Picture & Diagram Form. Bay, Mel, Publications, Inc. Staff. (Illus.). 1993. 4.95 (*0-87166-865-3*, 93269) Mel Bay.

Ukulele Method. Roy Smeck. 1993. 6.95 (*0-87166-483-6*, 93461) Mel Bay.

Ukulele Music - Perduta Gente. Peter Reading. (TriQuarterly Bks.). 112p. (Orig.). 1994. 26.95 (*0-8101-5030-1*); pap. 11.95 (*0-8101-5005-0*) Northwestern U Pr.

Ukulele Pocketbook. pap. 0.95 (*0-87166-560-3*, 93707) Mel Bay.

Ula Li'i & the Magic Shark. Donivee M. Laird. LC 86-3390. (Illus.). 42p. (J). (gr. k-3). 1985. 8.95 (*0-940350-23-8*) Barnaby Bks.

Ulam Problem of Optimal Motion of Line Segments. V. A. Dubovitskij. Ed. by A. V. Balakrishnan. LC 84-19035. (Translations Series in Mathematics & Engineering). 128p. 1985. text ed. 58.00 (*0-911575-04-9*) Optimization Soft.

Ulam Problem of Optimal Motion of Line Segments. V. A. Dubovitskij. Tr. by J. T. Ellis from RUS. LC 84-19035. xiii, 113p. 1985. 59.95 (*0-387-90946-X*) Spr-Verlag.

Ulama' Dimashq wa-Ayanuha fi al-Qarn al-Thalith Ashar al-Hijri, 2 vols., Set. M. Muti Al-Hafiz. 1991. 23.95 (*1-57547-181-7*) Dar Al-Fikr.

Ulama' Dimashq wa-Ayanuha fi al-Qarn al-Thalith Ashar al-Hijri, Vol. 1. M. Muti Al-Hafiz. 1991. write for info. (*1-57547-182-5*) Dar Al-Fikr.

Ulama' Dimashq wa-Ayanuha fi al-Qarn al-Thalith Ashar al-Hijri, Vol. 2. M. Muti Al-Hafiz. 1991. write for info. (*1-57547-183-3*) Dar Al-Fikr.

***Ulaq & the Northern Lights.** Harriet P. Taylor. LC 97-12427. (J). 1998. write for info. (*0-374-38063-5*) FS&G.

Ulas, Oscar, & the Buzzard. Dave Sargent. Ed. by Debbie Bowen. (Illus.). 120p. (J). (gr. k-6). pap. text ed. 3.95 (*1-56763-109-6*); lib. bdg. 16.95 (*1-56763-108-8*) Ozark Pub.

Ulcer & Non-Ulcer Dyspepsias. Ed. by M. J. Smith. (Practical Clinical Medicine Ser.). 1987. lib. bdg. 101.50 (*0-85200-970-4*) Kluwer Ac.

Ulcer Disease: New Aspects of Pathogenesis & Pharmacology. Ed. by Sandor Szabo & Carl J. Pfeiffer. 448p. 1989. 248.00 (*0-8493-6216-4*, RC822) CRC Pr.

Ulcer Story: The Authoritative Guide to Ulcers, Dyspepsia, & Heartburn. W. Grant Thompson. (Illus.). 390p. (C). 1996. 29.95 (*0-306-45275-8*, Plenum Pr) Plenum.

Ulcerative Colitis. O'Morain. 208p. 1991. 127.00 (*0-8493-5498-6*, RC862) CRC Pr.

***Ulcers: What Are They & How Can You Treat Them?** Rikki Ostrov. 1996. pap. 9.00 (*0-7225-3252-0*) Thorsons SF.

Ulendo: Travels of a Naturalist in & Out of Africa. George B. Schaller. LC 92-34453. 344p. 1993. reprint ed. pap. 16.95 (*0-8130-1179-5*) U Press Fla.

***Ulex Auction Sale Catalog.** Adolph H. Nachfolger. 173p. 1981. reprint ed. 5.00 (*1-889172-10-3*) Numismatic Intl.

ULF Pulsations in the Magnetosphere. D. J. Southwood. 1981. lib. bdg. 97.00 (*90-277-1232-8*) Kluwer Ac.

ULI - UMTA Policy Forum on Joint Development of Rail Transit Facilities: June 11-12, 1986. Uli & Umta Policy Forum on Joint Development Staff. LC 87-82098. (Illus.). 113p. 1987. reprint ed. pap. 32.30 (*0-7837-8928-9*, 2049638) Bks Demand.

***ULI Market Forecast: 1997.** ELI-The Urban Land Institute Staff. 1997. pap. write for info. (*0-87420-811-4*) Urban Land.

***ULI Market Profiles: Europe, 3 vols.** Urban Land Institute Staff. 150p. 1997. pap. 99.95 (*0-87420-805-X*, M67) Urban Land.

***ULI Market Profiles: North America, 3 vols.** Urban Land Institute Staff. (Illus.). 400p. (Orig.). 1997. pap. 299.95 (*0-87420-804-1*, M66) Urban Land.

***ULI Market Profiles: Pacific Rim, 3 vols.** Urban Land Institute Staff. (Illus.). 80p. (Orig.). 1997. pap. 49.95 (*0-87420-806-8*, M68) Urban Land.

ULI Market Profiles 1989. Urban Land Institute Staff. (Illus.). 229p. 1989. reprint ed. pap. 65.30 (*0-7837-8920-3*, 2049632) Bks Demand.

ULI Market Profiles 1991. Urban Land Institute Staff. (Illus.). 404p. 1991. reprint ed. pap. 115.20 (*0-7837-8922-X*, 2049634) Bks Demand.

ULI Market Profiles 1992. Urban Land Institute Staff. 464p. 1992. reprint ed. pap. 132.30 (*0-7837-8921-1*, 2049633) Bks Demand.

ULI Market Profiles 1993, Vol. 1. Urban Land Institute Staff. 270p. 1993. reprint ed. pap. 77.00 (*0-7837-8923-8*, 2049635) Bks Demand.

ULI Market Profiles 1993, Vol. 2. Urban Land Institute Staff. 235p. 1993. reprint ed. pap. 67.00 (*0-7837-8924-6*, 2049635) Bks Demand.

ULI Market Profiles 1994, Vol. 1. Urban Land Institute Staff. 284p. 1994. reprint ed. pap. 81.00 (*0-7837-8925-4*, 2049636) Bks Demand.

ULI Market Profiles 1994, Vol. 2. Urban Land Institute Staff. 286p. 1994. reprint ed. pap. 81.60 (*0-7837-8926-2*, 2049636) Bks Demand.

***ULI Market Profiles 1996: Europe.** Urban Land Institute Staff. 131p. 1996. pap. text ed. 74.95 (*0-87420-790-8*, M53) Urban Land.

***ULI Market Profiles 1996: North America.** Urban Land Institute Staff. 401p. 1996. pap. text ed. 224.95 (*0-87420-789-4*, M52) Urban Land.

***ULI Market Profiles 1996: Pacific Rim.** Urban Land Institute Staff. 401p. 1996. pap. text ed. 36.95 (*0-87420-791-6*, M54) Urban Land.

***ULI on the Future: Creating Tomorrow's Competitive Advantage.** Urban Land Institute Staff. 51p. 1996. pap. text ed. 49.95 (*0-87420-793-2*, U06) Urban Land.

***ULI on the Future: 1997.** Uli & Urban Land Institute Staff. 1997. pap. write for info. (*0-87420-810-6*) Urban Land.

ULI Sourcebook. ULI Staff. 630p. 1994. pap. text ed. 220.00 (*0-87420-760-6*, S44) Urban Land.

ULI-UMTA Policy Forum on Joint Development of Rail Transit Facilities. Uli & Urban Land Institute Staff. LC 87-82098. 107p. 1987. pap. 22.95 (*0-87420-671-5*, I01) Urban Land.

***ULI 1996 Real Estate Forecast: Outlook by Sector, Area & Enterprise.** Urban Land Institute Staff. 51p. 1996. pap. text ed. 24.95 (*0-87420-794-0*, U07) Urban Land.

Ulithi: A Micronesian Design for Living. William A. Lessa. (Illus.). 118p. (C). 1986. reprint ed. pap. text ed. 9.50 (*0-88133-212-7*) Waveland Pr.

***Ulitmate Chinese Cooking.** Christine McFadden. 1996. 16.98 (*0-7651-9684-0*) Smithmark.

***Ultimate Patient Satisfaction: Designing & Implementing an Effective Patient Satisfaction Program.** John F. O'Malley. 1997. 55.00 (*0-7863-1219-X*) Irwin Prof Pubng.

***Ulitmate Vegetarian Cooking.** Christine McFadden. 1996. 16.98 (*0-7651-9687-5*) Smithmark.

***Ulla-Maija Grace's Aromatherapy for Practitioners.** Date not set. 17.95 (*0-8464-4572-7*) Beekman Pubs.

***Ulla-Maija Grace's Aromatherapy for Practitioners.** Ulla-Maija Grace. 1996. 17.95 (*0-85207-293-7*, Pub. by C W Daniel UK) Natl Bk Netwk.

Ullin Macbeth. Christine M. Fraser. 224p. 1996. 22.00 (*0-7278-4976-X*) Severn Hse.

***Ullmann's Encyclopedia of Industrial Chemistry, 36 vols.** 5th ed. Incl. Vol. A1 Abrasives to Aluminium Oxide. 5th ed. LC 84-25829. 594p. 1985. lib. bdg. 410.00 (*3-527-20101-7*, VCH); Vol. A2 Amines, Aliphatics to Antibiotics. 5th ed. 557p. 1985. lib. bdg. 410.00 (*3-527-20102-5*, VCH); Vol. A3 Antidiabetic Drugs to Benzoquinone & Naphthoquinone Dyes. 5th ed. W. Gerhartz. LC 84-25829. (Illus.). 578p. 1985. lib. bdg. 410.00 (*3-527-20103-3*, VCH); Vol. A4 Benzyl Alcohol to Calcium Sulfate. 5th ed. Ed. by W. Gerhartz. 584p. 1985. lib. bdg. 410.00 (*3-527-20104-1*, VCH); Vol. A5 Cancer Chemotherapy to Ceramics Colorants. 5th ed. Ed. by W. Gerhartz. LC 84-25829. 556p. 1986. lib. bdg. 410.00 (*3-527-20105-X*, VCH); Vol. A6 Ceramics, General Survey to Chlorohydrins. 5th ed. Ed. by W. Gerhartz. 593p. 1986. lib. bdg. 410.00 (*3-527-20106-8*, VCH); Vol. A7 Chlorophenols to Copper Compounds. 5th ed. Ed. by W. Gerhartz. 593p. 1986. lib. bdg. 410.00 (*3-527-20107-6*, VCH); Vol. A8 Coronary Therapeutics to Display Technology. 5th ed. Ed. by W. Gerhartz. 624p. 1987. lib. bdg. 410.00 (*3-527-20108-4*, VCH); Vol. A9 Dithiocarbamic Acid & Derivatives to Ethanol. 5th ed. Ed. by W. Gerhartz. (Illus.). 653p. 1987. lib. bdg. 410.00 (*3-527-20109-2*, VCH); Vol. A10 Ethanolamines to Fibers, 4, Synthetic Organic. Ed. by W. Gerhartz. LC 84-25829. 655p. 1987. lib. bdg. 410.00 (*3-527-20110-6*, VCH); Vol. A11 All Fibers 5. Synthetic Inorganic to Formaldehyde. LC 84-25829. 651p. 1988. lib. bdg. 410.00 (*3-527-20111-4*, VCH); Vol. A12 Formamides to Hexamethylenediamine. LC 84-25829. 624p. 1989. lib. bdg. 410.00 (*3-527-20112-2*, VCH); Vol. A13 High-Performance Fibers to Imidazole & Derivatives. LC 84-25829. 668p. 1989. lib. bdg. 410.00 (*3-527-20113-0*, VCH); Vol. A14 Immobilized Biocatalysts to Isoprene. LC 84-25829. 656p. 1989. lib. bdg. 410.00 (*3-527-20114-9*, VCH); Vol. A15 Isotopes, Natural to Magnesium Compounds. 5th ed. 628p. 1990. lib. bdg. 410.00 (*3-527-20115-7*, VCH); Vol. A16 Magnetic Materials to Mutagenic Agents. 5th ed. 758p. 1990. lib. bdg. 410.00 (*3-527-20116-5*, VCH); Vol. A17 Naphthalene to Nuclear Technology. 5th ed. 813p. 1991. lib. bdg. 410.00 (*3-527-20117-3*, VCH); Vol. A18 Nucleic Acids to Parasympatholytics & Parasympathomimetics. 5th ed. 693p. 1991. lib. bdg. 410.00 (*3-527-20118-1*, VCH); Vol. A19 Parkinsonism Treatment to Photoelectricity. 5th ed. 608p. 1991. text ed. 410.00 (*3-527-20119-X*, VCH); Vol. B1 Fundamentals of Chemical Engineering. 5th ed. 775p. 1990. lib. bdg. 410.00 (*3-527-20131-9*, VCH); Vol. A28 Wood, Treatment & Preservation to Zirconimum & Zirconium Compounds. 5th rev. ed. Ed. by Barbara Elvers et al. (Illus.). 600p. 1996. 450.00 (*3-527-20128-9*, VCH); Vol. A20 Photography to Plastics, Processing. 774p. 1992. lib. bdg. 410.00 (*3-527-20120-3*, VCH); Vol. A21 Plastics, Properties & Testing to Polyvinyl Compounds, Others. 758p. 1992. lib. bdg. 410.00 (*3-527-20121-1*, VCH); Vol. A22 Polyvinyl Esters to Reduction. iv, 716p. 1993. lib. bdg. 410.00 (*3-527-20122-X*, VCH); Vol. A23 Refractory Ceramics to Silicon Carbide. xv, 759p. 1993. lib. bdg. 410.00 (*3-527-20123-8*, VCH); Vol. A24 Silicon Compounds, Inorganic to Starch & Other Polysaccharides. xv, 580p. 1993. lib. bdg. 410.00 (*3-527-20124-6*, VCH); Vol. A25 Starch & Other Polysaccharides to Surfactants. xv, 818p. 1994. lib. bdg. 410.00 (*3-527-20125-4*, VCH); Surgical Materials to Thiourea. xv, 816p. 1995. lib. bdg. 410.00 (*3-527-20126-2*, VCH); Vol. A27 Thorium & Thorium Compounds to Vitamins. Ed. by Barbara Elvers et al. (Illus.). 600p. 1996. lib. bdg. 410.00 (*3-527-20127-0*, VCH); Cumulative Index to Vols. A1-A25, B1-B6 on CD-ROM. 1995. cd-rom 165.00 (*3-527-20153-X*, VCH); Cumulative Index to Vols. A1-A25, B1-B6. xvii, 626p. 1995. pap. 195.00 (*3-527-20149-1*, VCH); Vol. B6 Analytical Methods II & Process Control Engineering. 5th ed. Ed. by Barbara Elvers et al. 760p. 1994. lib. bdg. 410.00 (*3-527-20136-X*, VCH); Vol. B2 Unit Operations I. xvii, 630p. 1988. lib. bdg. 410.00 (*3-527-20132-7*, VCH); Vol. B3 Unit Operations II. xv, 685p. 1988. lib. bdg. 410.00 (*3-527-20133-5*, VCH); Vol. B4 Principles of Chemical Reaction Engineering & Plant Design. xvii, 625p. 1992. lib. bdg. 410.00 (*3-527-20134-3*, VCH); Vol. B5 Analytical Methods I. xv, 742p. 1994. lib. bdg. 410.00 (*3-527-20135-1*, VCH); Vol. B7 Environmental Protection & Industrial Safety I. xvii, 788p. 1995. lib. bdg. 410.00 (*3-527-20137-8*, VCH); Vol. B8 Environmental Protection & Industrial Safety II.

U
V

An Asterisk (*) at the beginning of an entry indicates that the title is appearing in BIP for the first time.

600p. 1995. lib. bdg. 410.00 (*3-527-20138-6*, VCH); LC 84-25829. 12,600.00 (*0-685-09701-3*, VCH) Wiley.

Ullstein Lexikon der Medizin. (GER.). 1970. 49.95 (*0-8288-6557-4*, M-7674) Fr & Eur.

Ullstein Lexikon der Pflanzenwelt: Ullstein Lexicon of the Plant World. Hartmut Bastian. (GER.). 1973. 49.95 (*0-8288-6333-4*, M7675) Fr & Eur.

Ullstein Lexikon der Tierwelt. Hartmut Bastian. (GER.). 1967. 49.95 (*0-8288-6694-5*, M7676) Fr & Eur.

Ullstein Lexikon des Rechts. Otto Gritschneder. (GER.). 1971. 75.00 (*0-8288-6483-7*, M-7677) Fr & Eur.

Ullstein Synonymen-Lexikon. Bernhard Bauer. (GER.). 19. 95 (*0-7859-8424-0*, 3548346332) Fr & Eur.

Ulm Design: The Morality of Objects. Herbert Lindinger. Tr. by David Britt from GER. (Illus.). 288p. 1990. 50.00 (*0-262-12147-6*) MIT Pr.

Ulpan: How to Learn Hebrew in a Hurry! Theodor Schuchat. 510p. 1992. pap. 24.95 (*965-229-062-9*, Pub. by Gefen Pub Hse IS) Gefen Bks.

Ulrich Becher: A Computer-Assisted Case Study of the Reception of an Exile. Nancy A. Zeller. LC 82-84614. (American University Studies: Germanic Languages & Literature: Ser. I, Vol. 7). 426p. 1983. pap. text ed. 46.85 (*0-8204-0006-8*) P Lang Pubng.

Ulrich Bonnell Phillips: A Southern Historian & His Critics. Ed. by John D. Smith & John C. Inscoe. LC 93-4160. (Brown Thrasher Bks.). 296p. 1993. reprint ed. pap. 25.00 (*0-8203-1589-3*) U of Ga Pr.

Ulrich Bonnell Phillips: Historian of the Old South. Merton L. Dillon. LC 85-10229. (Southern Biography Ser.). (Illus.). 190p. 1985. text ed. 29.95 (*0-8071-1206-2*) La State U Pr.

Ulrich Fuetrer's Parzival: Material & Sources. James Boyd. 1977. lib. bdg. 59.95 (*0-8490-2782-9*) Gordon Pr.

Ulrich Von Hutten. David F. Strauss. Tr. by G. Sturge from GER. LC 77-130624. reprint ed. 52.50 (*0-404-06296-2*) AMS Pr.

Ulrich Von Hutten & the German Reformation. Hajo Holborn. Tr. by Roland H. Bainton. LC 77-25067. (Yale Historical Publications: No. XI). (Illus.). 214p. 1978. reprint ed. text ed. 55.00 (*0-313-20125-0*, HOUV, Greenwood Pr) Greenwood.

***Ulrich von Turheim.** Deutschen Akademie der Wissenschaften Staff & Alfred Hubner. (Deutsche Texte des Mittelalters Ser.: Band XXXIX). li, 614p. (GER.). 1966. write for info. (*3-296-17239-4*, Pub. by Weidmann GW) Lubrecht & Cramer.

***Ulrich von Wilamowitz-Moellendorff: Further Letters of Ulrich von Wilamowitz-Moellendorff (1869-1930)** Ed. by William M. Calder, III. xii, 262p. (GER.). 1994. 68. 00 (*3-615-00099-4*, Pub. by Weidmann GW) Lubrecht & Cramer.

***Ulrich Zwingli: Early Writings, 1510-1522.** Ulrich Zwingli. Ed. by Samuel M. Jackson. 320p. (C). 1995. pap. 17.99 (*0-8010-2028-X*, Labyrinth) Baker Bks.

Ulrich's International Periodicals Directory 1996, 5 vols. 34th ed. Ed. by Bowker, R. R., Staff. 9992p. 1995. 425. 00 (*0-8352-3676-5*) Bowker.

Ulrich's International Periodicals Directory 1996, 5 vols., Vol. 1. 34th ed. Ed. by Bowker, R. R., Staff. 2084p. 1995. write for info. (*0-8352-3677-3*) Bowker.

Ulrich's International Periodicals Directory 1996, 5 vols., Vol. 2. 34th ed. Ed. by Bowker, R. R., Staff. 2006p. 1995. write for info. (*0-8352-3678-1*) Bowker.

Ulrich's International Periodicals Directory 1996, 5 vols., Vol. 3. 34th ed. Ed. by Bowker, R. R., Staff. 2512p. 1995. write for info. (*0-8352-3680-3*) Bowker.

Ulrich's International Periodicals Directory 1996, 5 vols., Vol. 4. 34th ed. Ed. by Bowker, R. R., Staff. 2306p. 1995. write for info. (*0-8352-3681-1*) Bowker.

Ulrich's International Periodicals Directory 1996, 5 vols., Vol. 5. 34th ed. Ed. by Bowker, R. R., Staff. 1084p. 1995. write for info. (*0-8352-3683-8*) Bowker.

Ulrich's International Periodicals Directory 1997, 5 vols. 35th ed. Ed. by Bowker, R. R., Staff. 1996. 449.95 (*0-8352-3806-7*) Bowker.

Ulrich's International Periodicals Directory 1997, 5 vols., Vol. 1. 35th ed. Ed. by Bowker, R. R., Staff. 1996. write for info. (*0-8352-3807-5*) Bowker.

Ulrich's International Periodicals Directory 1997, 5 vols., Vol. 2. 35th ed. Ed. by Bowker, R. R., Staff. 1996. write for info. (*0-8352-3808-3*) Bowker.

Ulrich's International Periodicals Directory 1997, 5 vols., Vol. 3. 35th ed. Ed. by Bowker, R. R., Staff. 1996. write for info. (*0-8352-3809-1*) Bowker.

Ulrich's International Periodicals Directory 1997, 5 vols., Vol. 4. 35th ed. Ed. by Bowker, R. R., Staff. 1996. write for info. (*0-8352-3810-5*) Bowker.

Ulrich's International Periodicals Directory 1997, 5 vols., Vol. 5. 35th ed. Ed. by Bowker, R. R., Staff. 1996. write for info. (*0-8352-3811-3*) Bowker.

***Ulrich's International Periodicals Directory 1998. 36th ed. Ed. by Bowker, R. R., Staff. 11200p. 1997. 459.95 (*0-8352-3967-5*) Bowker.**
"This attractively bound, easy-to-use reference source is without peer in the quantity & quality of the material contained," --AMERICAN REFERENCE BOOKS JOURNAL. "...the principal listing of serial titles...[an] excellent value."--REFERENCE REVIEW. "One of the core library reference tools."--REFERENCE & RESEARCH BOOK NEWS. Featuring comprehensiveness & usefulness that have been its hallmark for 65 years, this latest edition of ULRICH'S provides more serials data -- & more ways to access it -- than any other directory. ULRICH'S 1998 is extensively indexed to make every serials reference or collection task a breeze. You'll use it to: * find ordering rates, frequency, addresses, phone & fax numbers, e-mail & Web site addresses, & up to 45 other important data elements for each publication * locate specific serials to build a collection or to satisfy research needs * track down serials publishers from around the globe * determine if a serial has ceased or changed its name * find online & CD-ROM serials to develop electronic collections * offer patrons a one-stop guide to research sources, subscription information, & opportunities to publish worldwide * & much more! In five convenient volumes, ULRICH'S 1998 keeps you up to date with thousands of new titles & over 112,000 entry revisions among the 165,000 regularly & irregularly issued serials profiled -- & alerts you to nearly 10,000 cessations. You'll easily find: * addresses & phone numbers for some 80,000 publishers from 200 countries, as well as 25,000 e-mail addresses, 98,000 fax numbers, & 21,000 telex numbers * 7, 000 serials available online, with over 3,400 vendor names, file names, &/or numbers -- as well as 2,300 serials available on CD-ROM * 7, 400 daily & weekly U.S. newspapers in the newspaper volume & some 3,500 non-U.S. papers in the main volumes * 13,800 refereed serials * 13,500 Rights & Permissions contact names * micropublisher, reprint service, & A&I service notations...document delivery notations (including CISTI & Library KNAW)...Copyright Clearance center notations for registered titles...& much more. You also receive ULRICH'S UPDATE -- a free, bound supplement sent to you twice a year -- plus unlimited use of our toll-free subscriber hotline for help with any serials question. With its accuracy, comprehensiveness, & currency, ULRICH'S is the only serials guide you'll ever need. ***Publisher Provided Annotation.***

***ULRO: Paintings by Adam.** unabridged ed. Jo Dereske et al. Ed. by Jason Stoneking. (Illus.). 24p. (Orig.). 1997. pap. 8.95 (*0-9658336-0-7*) Adam Studio.

ULSI Science & Technology: Fifth International Symposium. E. M. Middlesworth & H. Massoud. 1995. 59.00 (*1-56677-099-8*, PV 95-5) Electrochem Soc.

ULSI Technology. C. Y. Chang & Simon M. Sze. (Illus.). 726p. 1996. text ed. 62.50 (*0-07-063062-3*) McGraw.

Ulster. Stephen Gwynn. 1972. 59.95 (*0-8490-1241-4*) Gordon Pr.

Ulster: A Case Study in Conflict Theory. R. S. Elliot & John Ickie. LC 78-182186. 180p. 1971. 29.50 (*0-8290-0213-8*); pap. text ed. 14.95 (*0-8290-0683-4*) Irvington.

Ulster & North America: Transatlantic Perspectives on the Scotch-Irish. Ed. by Tyler Blethen & Curtis Wood. LC 96-25002. 320p. 1997. text ed. 39.95 (*0-8173-0823-7*) U of Ala Pr.

Ulster Arts Directory. Ulster Arts Alliance Staff. 96p. (Orig.). 1994. pap. 10.00 (*0-9644310-0-9*) Ulster Arts.

Ulster County in the Revolution. Ed. by Ruth P. Heidgerd. 297p. 1976. 9.50 (*0-685-14022-9*) Huguenot Hist.

Ulster County, New York Atlas. Orange County Genealogical Society Staff et al. 130p. 1984. reprint ed. lib. bdg. 30.00 (*0-9604116-8-2*) Orange County Genealog.

Ulster County, New York Probate Records: In the Office of the Surrogate, & in the County Clerk's Office At Kingston, NY, Vol. I. Gustave Anjou. (Illus.). 248p. (Orig.). 1992. reprint ed. pap. text ed. 20.00 (*1-55613-704-4*) Heritage Bk.

Ulster County, New York Probate Records (from 1665) In the Office of the Surrogate, & in the County Clerk's Office in Kingston, N. Y., 2 vols. in 1, Set. Gustave Anjou. 528p. 1996. reprint ed. pap. 40.00 (*0-614-16588-1*) Clearfield Co.

Ulster County, New York Probate Records, in the Office of the Surrogate at Hingston, New York, in the Surrogate's Office, New York, & in the Library of Long Island Historical Society: A Careful Abstract & Translation of Dutch & English Wills, Letters of Administration after Intestates & Inventories with Genealogical & Historical Notes, Vol. 2. Gustave Anjou. 280p. 1993. reprint ed. pap. text ed. 20.00 (*1-55613-698-6*) Heritage Bk.

Ulster County, NY, Probate Records in the Office of the Surrogate & in the County Clerk's Office at Kingston NY: Careful Abstract & Translation of the Dutch & English Wills, Letters of Administration after Intestates & Inventories from 1665 with Genealogical & Historical Notes, & List of Dutch & Frisian Baptismal Names with Their English Equivalents. Gustave Anjou & Arthur C. Kelly. 280p. 1981. reprint ed. lib. bdg. 40. 00 (*1-56012-052-5*, 51) Kinship Rhinebeck.

***Ulster Crisis: Resistance to Home Rule, 1912-1914.** A. T. Stewart. 284p. 1997. pap. 19.95 (*0-85640-599-X*, Pub. by Blackstaff Pr IE) Dufour.

Ulster Crisis: Resistance to Home Rule, 1912-1914. Anthony Stewart. (Modern Revivals in History Ser.). 300p. 1993. 59.95 (*0-7512-0183-9*, Pub. by Gregg Revivals UK) Ashgate Pub Co.

Ulster Folkstories for Children. Patrick Tunney. 96p. 1990. pap. 10.95 (*0-85342-930-8*, Pub. by Poolbeg Pr IE) Dufour.

Ulster Migration to America: Letters from Three Irish Families. Ronald A. Wells. LC 91-7337. (Irish Studies: Vol. 2). 192p. (C). 1991. text ed. 42.95 (*0-8204-1635-5*) P Lang Pubng.

Ulster Presbyterianism: The Historical Perpective. Peter Brooke. LC 87-16705. 256p. 1987. text ed. 39.95 (*0-312-01271-3*) St Martin.

Ulster Reciter. Ed. by Joe McPartland. 90p. 8400. pap. 8.95 (*0-85640-321-0*) Dufour.

Ulster Reciter: Ballads, Poems & Recitations for Every Occasion. Ed. by Joe McPartland. 90p. 1984. pap. 7.95 (*0-685-25949-8*, Pub. by Blackstaff Pr IE) Dufour.

Ulster Sails West: The Story of the Great Emigration from Ulster to North America in the 18th Century... William F. Marshall. LC 76-56641. 79p. 1996. reprint ed. pap. 7.50 (*0-8063-0754-4*) Genealog Pub.

***Ulster Scots & Blandford (MA) Scouts.** Sumner G. Wood. (Illus.). 436p. 1997. pap. 31.50 (*0-7884-0632-9*, W553) Heritage Bk.

Ulster Scots Speech: A Sociolinguistic Study. Rona K. Kingsmore. Ed. by Michael B. Montgomery. LC 94-27839. 272p. (Orig.). 1995. pap. 26.95 (*0-8173-0711-7*) U of Ala Pr.

Ulster Snapshot. Neville Hughes. 170p. (C). 1989. 30.00 (*0-7223-2387-5*, Pub. by A H S Ltd UK) St Mut.

Ulster Trivia Quiz Book. Robert Kirk. 72p. (Orig.). 1986. pap. 7.95 (*0-86281-172-4*, Pub. by Appletree Pr IE) Irish Bks Media.

Ulster under Home Rule: A Study of the Political & Economic Problems of Northern Ireland. Ed. by Thomas Wilson. LC 86-2291. 253p. 1986. reprint ed. text ed. 65.00 (*0-313-25169-X*, WIUL, Greenwood Pr) Greenwood.

Ulster Unionism & British National Identity Since 1885. James Loughlin. LC 95-3881. 257p. 1995. 80.00 (*0-86187-845-0*, Pub. by Pntr Pubs UK) Bks Intl VA.

***Ulster Wean's A to Z.** Illus. by Philip McIvor. 56p. (J). 9600. pap. 8.95 (*0-85640-581-7*, Pub. by Blackstaff Pr IE) Dufour.

Ulsterheart: An Ancient Irish Habitation. Cecil B. Ingram. LC 88-72366. (Illus.). 350p. (YA). (gr. 12). 1988. 60.00 (*0-9621544-0-7*) All Ireland Inc.

***Ulster's Office, 1552-1800: A History of the Irish Office of Arms from the Tudor Plantations to the Act of Union.** MacCarthy Mor. (Illus.). 280p. 1996. 35.00 (*0-9654220-0-3*) Gryfons Pubs & Dist.

Ulster's Uncertain Defenders: Protestant Political, Paramilitary, & Community Groups & the Northern Ireland Conflict. Sarah Nelson. (Irish Studies). 206p. 1987. pap. text ed. 16.95 (*0-8156-2418-2*) Syracuse U Pr.

Ulster's White Negroes. Fionnbarra O'Dochartaigh. 136p. (Orig.). 1994. pap. 8.95 (*1-873176-67-8*, AK Pr San Fran) AK Pr Dist.

Ulterior Motives, No. 3. Terri Blackstock. (Sun Coast Chronicles Ser.: Bk. 3). 304p. 1996. pap. 9.99 (*0-310-20017-2*) Zondervan.

Ulterior Motives: The Killing & Dark Legacy. Suzanne Finstad. 1988. mass mkt. 4.50 (*0-312-91185-8*) St Martin.

Ultima: The Avatar Adventures. Rusel DeMaria & Caroline Spector. (Secrets of the Games Ser.). (Illus.). 416p. (Orig.). 1992. pap. 18.95 (*1-55958-130-1*) Prima Pub.

Ultima Batalla - The Last Battle. C. S. Lewis. 1995. pap. text ed. 11.95 (*84-204-4698-X*) Santillana.

Ultima Llamada. Jack T. Chick. (Illus.). 64p. (Orig.). (SPA.). 1972. pap. 3.50 (*0-937958-02-6*) Chick Pubns.

***Ultima Lucha de Lenin.** V. I. Lenin. 325p. (SPA.). 1997. pap. 21.95 (*0-87348-843-1*) Pathfinder NY.

Ultima Niebla. Maria L. Bombal. (SPA.). 8.50 (*0-8288-2554-8*, S655) Fr & Eur.

***Ultima Online: The Official Strategy Guide.** Prima Development Staff. 240p. 1997. per., pap. 19.99 (*0-7615-0926-7*) Prima Pub.

***Ultima Parada: Matrimonio.** Emma Darcy. (SPA.). 1997. mass mkt. 3.50 (*0-373-33403-6*, 1-33403-6) Harlequin Bks.

Ultima Seven & Underworld: More Avatar Adventures. Caroline Spector. (Illus.). 384p. (Orig.). 1993. pap. 19.95 (*1-55958-251-0*) Prima Pub.

ULTIMA Underworld Clue Book: Mysteries of the Abyss. Aaron Allston. (Illus.). 64p. (Orig.). 1992. pap. 14.95 (*0-929373-08-1*) Origin Syst.

Ultima Underworld II Clue Book: Gems of Enlightenment. Austin Grossman. (Illus.). 80p. (Orig.). 1993. pap. 14.95 (*0-929373-12-X*) Origin Syst.

ULTIMA VII Clue Book: Key to the Black Gate. Andrew Morris. (Illus.). 64p. (Orig.). 1992. pap. 14.95 (*0-929373-09-X*) Origin Syst.

Ultima VII, Pt. 2 Clue Book: Balancing the Scales. Sheri Hobbs & Andrew Morris. (Illus.). 80p. (Orig.). 1993. pap. 14.95 (*0-929373-13-8*) Origin Syst.

Ultima VIII Clue Book: Pentology. Melissa Mead. (Illus.). 96p. (Orig.). 1994. pap. 14.95 (*0-929373-18-9*) Origin Syst.

***Ultima 9: The Official Strategy Guide.** Prima Development Staff. 240p. 1998. per., pap. 19.99 (*0-7615-0040-5*) Prima Pub.

Ultimas Preguntas. John Blanchard. 32p. (SPA.). 1987. pap. 1.95 (*0-85234-237-3*) Editorial Unilit.

Ultimate. Michael Bates. (Bloodlust Ser.: No. 6). 192p. (YA). 1995. mass mkt. 3.99 (*0-553-56739-X*) Bantam.

Ultimate: Fundamentals of the Sport. Irv Kalb & Tom Kennedy. LC 81-90610. (Illus.). 104p. (Orig.). 1982. pap. 7.95 (*0-942156-00-5*) Rev Pubns.

Ultimate Advantage: Creating the High-Involvement Organization. Edward E. Lawler, III. LC 91-41095. (Management Ser.). 392p. text ed. 29.95 (*1-55542-414-7*) Jossey-Bass.

Ultimate Adventure - Chinese Edition. Moody Institute of Science Staff. Tr. by CRM Staff. 15p. (CHI.). 1986. 0.40 (*1-56582-055-X*) Christ Renew Min.

Ultimate Adventure Sourcebook. Paul McMenamin. Ed. by Susan Watrous. (Illus.). 432p. 1992. pap. 29.95 (*1-878685-18-X*); text ed. 39.95 (*1-878685-19-8*) Turner Pub GA.

***Ultimate Adventure Sourcebook: The Complete Resource for Adventure, Sports & Travel.** Paul McMenamin. LC 97-361. 1997. 29.95 (*1-57036-280-7*) Turner Pub GA.

Ultimate Aikido: Secrets of Self-Defense & Inner Power. Yoshimitsu Yamada & Steven Pimsler. LC 94-20352. 224p. 1994. write for info. (*0-8065-1566-X*, Citadel Pr) Carol Pub Group.

Ultimate Air Travel Guide. Loren Lynch. 1996. pap. 16.95 (*0-930030-99-0*) ProStar Pubns.

***Ultimate Alphabet.** M. Wilks. (J). 1986. wbk. ed. 2.50 (*0-8050-0159-X*) H Holt & Co.

Ultimate Alphabet. Mike Wilks. (Illus.). 64p. (J). 1986. Set, shrink-wrapped. 21.95 (*0-8050-0160-3*) H Holt & Co.

Ultimate Amazing X-Men. Fabian Nicieza. (Illus.). 96p. 1995. pap. 8.95 (*0-7851-0126-8*) Marvel Entmnt.

***Ultimate America: Unlimited Power & Total Control - Building Our Perfect World.** v, 240p. 1997. pap. 9.95 (*0-9658323-0-9*) R M Mitchell.

Ultimate Angel Book: More Than 600 Clip Art Images. Ed. by Jim Harter. LC 95-30421. (Illus.). 224p. 1995. 19.99 (*0-517-14806-4*) Random Hse Value.

***Ultimate Answering Machine Message Book.** Marnie Winston-Macauley. 128p. (Orig.). 1997. pap. 7.95 (*0-8362-3225-9*) Andrews & McMeel.

***Ultimate Aphrodisiac.** John Hole. 320p. 1997. 27.00 (*0-340-65398-1*, Pub. by H & S UK); pap. 10.95 (*0-340-65399-X*, Pub. by H & S UK) Trafalgar.

Ultimate Aquarium: A Definitive Guide to Identifying & Keeping Freshwater & Marine Fishes. Mary Bailey. 1995. 19.98 (*0-8317-1037-3*) Smithmark.

Ultimate Art: Essays Around & about Opera. David Littlejohn. 1992. 30.00 (*0-520-07608-7*) U CA Pr.

Ultimate Art: Essays Around & about Opera. David Littlejohn. (Illus.). 320p. (C). 1994. pap. 15.00 (*0-520-07609-5*) U CA Pr.

Ultimate Asteroid Book. J. Lee Lehman. LC 88-50479. (Illus.). 351p. (Orig.). 1988. pap. 18.95 (*0-914918-78-8*) Schiffer.

Ultimate Astonishing X-Men. Scott Lobdell. (Illus.). 96p. 1995. pap. 8.95 (*0-7851-0127-6*) Marvel Entmnt.

Ultimate Athlete: Revisioning Sports, Physical Education & the Body. George Leonard. 280p. 1990. reprint ed. pap. 12.95 (*1-55643-076-0*) North Atlantic.

Ultimate Atlanta Guidebook. Atlanta Journal & Constitution Staff. LC 93-81140. (Illus.). 144p. 1994. pap. 8.95 (*1-56352-135-0*) Longstreet Pr Inc.

***Ultimate Audition Book: 200 Monologues, 2 Minutes & Under.** Ed. by Jocelyn A. Beard. (Audition Bks.). 256p. (Orig.). 1996. 30.00 (*0-614-21798-9*) Smith & Kraus.

***Ultimate Audition Book: 200 Monologues, 2 Minutes & Under.** Ed. by Jocelyn A. Beard. LC 97-10471. (Audition Bks.). 256p. (Orig.). 1997. pap. 19.95 (*1-57525-066-7*) Smith & Kraus.

Ultimate Auto Detailing. 2nd ed. David H. Jacobs, Jr. (Illus.). 208p. 1995. pap. 19.95 (*0-87938-941-9*) Motorbooks Intl.

Ultimate Auto Sound: Your Guide to Heaven on Wheels. Daniel L. Ferguson. (Illus.). Date not set. pap. text ed. 29.95 (*0-614-10197-2*) Audio Amateur.

Ultimate Automobile Book. Eisenberg. Date not set. write for info. (*0-395-32200-6*) HM.

Ultimate Baby Name Book. Consumer Guide Editors & Kelsey Harder. 256p. (Orig.). 1989. pap. 13.00 (*0-452-26275-5*, Plume) NAL-Dutton.

Ultimate Baby Name Book. Consumer Guide Editors & Cleveland K. Evans. 544p. (Orig.). 1994. pap. 13.00 (*0-452-27285-8*) NAL-Dutton.

***Ultimate Baby-Sitter's Handbook.** Debra M. Zakarin. LC 96-42997. (Illus.). (J). 1997. 4.95 (*0-8431-7936-8*) Price Stern Sloan.

***Ultimate Babysitter's Handbook.** Debra M. Zakarin. (Illus.). (J). 1997. write for info. (*0-614-29286-7*) Price Stern Sloan.

Ultimate Babysitter's Survival Guide. Mary Guileserian & Therese Furey. LC 96-22915. 1996. pap. text ed. 8.99 (*1-56179-476-7*) Focus Family.

***Ultimate Back Book: Understand, Manage & Conquer Your Back Pain.** Judylaine Fine. (Illus.). 368p. 1997. pap. 19.95 (*0-7737-5863-1*, Pub. by Stoddart Pubng CN) Genl Dist Srvs.

Ultimate Barbecue Sauce Cookbook: Your Guide to the Best Sauce, Rubs, Sops, Mops, & Marinades. Jim Auchmutey & Susan Puckett. 1995. 14.95 (*1-56352-201-2*) Longstreet Pr Inc.

Ultimate Barbie Doll Book. Marcie Melillo. 256p. 1996. 39.95 (*0-87341-397-0*) Krause Pubns.

Ultimate Baseball Book. rev. ed. Ed. by Daniel Okrent & Harris Lewine. (Illus.). 384p. 1991. pap. 25.00 (*0-395-59697-1*) HM.

Ultimate Baseball Players Yearbook. Joe Newberger & Elrod Hendricks. (Illus.). 96p. (J). (gr. 3-9). 1991. student ed. 12.95 (*0-9629307-0-9*) Batboy Pr.

Ultimate Baseball Quiz Book. Dom Forker. 400p. (Orig.). 1990. pap. 4.99 (*0-451-15236-0*, Sig) NAL-Dutton.

Ultimate Baseball Quiz Book. rev. ed. Dom Forker. 1996. mass mkt. 5.99 (*0-451-18821-7*, Sig) NAL-Dutton.

Ultimate Baseball Trivia Encyclopedia. Ed. by Bert R. Sugar. 1989. pap. 16.95 (*0-318-41608-5*) St Martin.

Ultimate Basketball Trivia Challenge: It's a Basketball Game & Trivia Game in One! Cort D. Reynolds. 84p. (Orig.). 1995. pap. 10.00 (*0-9648665-1-X*) Corts Ct.

Ultimate Batch File Book! Ronny Richardson. 1995. text ed. 49.95 (*0-07-912050-4*) McGraw.

U V

Ultimate Beatles Encyclopedia. Bill Harry. (Illus.). 736p. 1993. 35.00 (*1-56282-814-2*) Hyperion.

Ultimate Beatles Encyclopedia. Bill Harry. (Illus.). 736p. 1994. pap. 19.95 (*0-7868-8071-6*) Hyperion.

Ultimate Beatles Quiz Book. Michael J. Hockinson. (Illus.). 448p. 1992. pap. 14.95 (*0-312-07104-3*) St Martin.

***Ultimate Beauty Book: The Complete Professional Guide to Haircare, Make-Up, Fitness & Health.** Sally Norton. 1996. 19.98 (*0-7651-9780-4*) Smithmark.

Ultimate Benefit Book: How to Raise $50,000-Plus for Your Favorite Organization. Marilyn E. Brentlinger & Judith M. Weiss. LC 87-12171. (Illus.). 232p. 1987. 35.00 (*0-940601-01-X*) Octavia Ohio.

Ultimate Betrayal. large type ed. Michelle Reid. (Harlequin Romance Ser.). 1996. 20.95 (*0-263-14360-0*) Thorndike Pr.

Ultimate Betrayal (Wedlocked!) Michelle Reid. 1996. 3.50 (*0-373-11799-X*, 1-11799-3) Harlequin Bks.

***Ultimate Birdhouse Book: 40 Functional, Fantastic & Fanciful Homes to Make for Our Own.** Deborah Morgenthal. 1997. 24.95 (*0-8069-9934-9*) Sterling.

***Ultimate Black Book: The Only 400 Telephone or Fax Numbers You'll Ever Need to Find Most of the Information You'll Ever Want.** 2nd rev. ed. Godfrey Harris & Kenneth L. Harris. LC 96-43001. 80p. 1996. pap. 7.95 (*0-935047-22-0*) Americas Group.

Ultimate Blackjack Book. Edward Early. LC 94-25590. 144p. 1995. pap. 12.00 (*1-56980-024-3*) Barricade Bks.

Ultimate Blackjack Book. Walter F. Thomason. 240p. (Orig.). 1997. pap. write for info. (*0-9641989-2-4*) W & C Thomason.

***Ultimate Blackjack Book: Basic Strategies, Money Management, & More.** Walter Thomason. LC 96-51712. 192p. 1997. pap. 14.95 (*0-8184-0589-9*, L Stuart) Carol Pub Group.

Ultimate Book of Beer Trivia. Tom Debolski & Bill Yenne. (Illus.). 112p. (Orig.). 1994. pap. 8.95 (*0-912517-07-7*) Bluewood Bks.

***Ultimate Book of Bible Trivia.** J. Stephen Lang. LC 97-8874. 1997. pap. 11.99 (*0-8423-7949-5*) Tyndale.

Ultimate Book of Cross-Sections. (Illus.). 304p. (J). 1996. 29.95 (*0-7894-1195-4*) DK Pub Inc.

***Ultimate Book of Cross Sections.** (J). (gr. 1-3). 29.95 (*0-614-19298-6*) DK Pub Inc.

Ultimate Book of Excuses: Fresh, Exciting, Scintillating Excuses. John W. Thompson & Damon M. Hunzeker. (Illus.). (Orig.). 1995. pap. 9.95 (*0-9647896-0-4*) Fountnhead Pubng.

***Ultimate Book of Freshwater Fishing.** Ken Schultz. LC 97-17865. (Illus.). 192p. 1997. pap. 29.95 (*1-57028-154-8*) Masters Pr IN.

Ultimate Book of Puzzles: Mathematical Diversions, & Brainteasers. Erwin Brecher. 352p. 1996. pap. 14.95 (*0-312-14143-2*, Griffin) St Martin.

***Ultimate Book of Sports Lists.** Mike Meserole. LC 97-20800. 224p. 1997. 24.95 (*0-7894-2279-4*) DK Pub Inc.

***Ultimate Book of Sports Lists 1998.** Mike Meserole. LC 97-20800. 224p. 1997. pap. 17.95 (*0-7894-2134-8*) DK Pub Inc.

Ultimate Book Report Book. Nancy Polette. (Illus.). 48p. 1991. pap. 5.95 (*0-913839-95-7*) Pieces of Lrning.

***Ultimate Border Collie.** 1998. 34.95 (*0-87605-375-4*) Macmillan.

Ultimate Bowl: We the People vs. the Capitol Royalty. Dinesh Shah. (Save the Democracy Ser.: Vol. I). 192p. (Orig.). 1995. pap. 12.00 (*0-9634764-3-2*) TwentyTwenty Bks.

Ultimate Bread Machine Cookbook: An Insider's Guide to Automatic Bread Making. Tom Lacalamita. LC 93-1513. 1993. 25.00 (*0-671-88023-3*) S&S Trade.

***Ultimate Broadway Fake Book.** Stanley Green. 1997. pap. 39.95 (*0-7935-8259-8*) H Leonard.

Ultimate Bug Book: A Unique Introduction to the World of Insects in Fabulous, Full-Color Pop-Ups. Luise Woelflein. (Illus.). 12p. (J). (ps-3). 1993. pap. 19.95 (*0-307-17600-2*, Golden Books) Western Pub.

***Ultimate Business Library: 50 Business Books That Shaped Management Thinking.** Stuart Crainer. 352p. 1997. 24.95 (*0-8144-0395-6*) AMACOM.

Ultimate Cake: The New Illustrated Guide to Baking Luscious Cakes. Barbara Maher. 160p. 1996. 29.95 (*0-7894-0441-9*) DK Pub Inc.

***Ultimate Camp Counsellor Manual: How to Survive & Succeed Magnificently at Summer Camp.** Mark S. Richman. (Illus.). 150p. 1997. lib. bdg. 24.95 (*0-9649007-2-6*) M Richman.

***Ultimate Camp-Out Party Book.** Douglas Love. LC 96-41806. (Illus.). (J). 1997. pap. 6.95 (*0-688-15258-9*) Morrow.

Ultimate Canon of Knowledge. Alvin B. Kuhn. 174p. (Orig.). 1985. reprint ed. spiral bd. 21.00 (*0-7873-1089-1*) Hlth Research.

Ultimate Card Trick Book. Devereaux. 1995. 19.95 (*0-7858-0323-8*) Bk Sales Inc.

Ultimate Cat Book: A Unique Photographic Guide to More than One-Hundred International Breeds and Variations-with Practical Information on Cat Care and Behavior. David Taylor. 750p. 1989. 29.95 (*0-671-68649-6*) S&S Trade.

Ultimate Cause & Preventive Cure for the Common Cold: How to Prevent Yourself from Catching the Common Cold or the Flu. Lloyd R. Stark. LC 93-80126. (Illus.). 161p. (Orig.). 1994. pap. 12.95 (*0-9639123-0-5*) Mojave Pubns.

Ultimate Challenge. Michael Eng. 1996. pap. 3.25 (*0-679-88209-X*) McKay.

Ultimate Challenge. Maralene Wesner & Miles Wesner. 115p. 1992. pap. 4.95 (*0-936715-43-X*) Diversity Okla.

***Ultimate Cherokee Cookbook.** Oukah. (Illus.). 72p. (Orig.). 1996. pap. 10.00 (*1-890174-03-3*) Triskelion Pr.

***Ultimate Chicken.** Christian Teubner. (J). 1997. pap. 27.95 (*0-670-87370-5*) Viking Penguin.

***Ultimate Chocolate.** Patricia Lousada. LC 97-13144. 144p. 1997. 29.95 (*0-7894-2084-8*) DK Pub Inc.

Ultimate Chocolate Cake Cookbook. Pamella Z. Asquith. 1995. 9.98 (*0-88365-916-6*) Galahad Bks.

Ultimate Christmas. Jane Newdick. 192p. 1996. 29.95 (*0-7894-1084-2*) DK Pub Inc.

Ultimate Christmas: 100 Seasonal Favorites - Easy Piano. (Easy Play Ser.). 248p. 1984. otabind 19.95 (*0-7935-0944-0*, 00241003) H Leonard.

Ultimate Cigar Book. 2nd rev. ed. Richard C. Hacker. (Illus.). 320p. 1996. 34.95 (*0-931253-05-5*) Autumngold Pub.

Ultimate Claris Works Solutions! for Education. Ronnie Peters. Ed. by Barry Peters. (Illus.). 270p. (C). 1994. spiral bd. 36.95 (*0-9643120-0-X*); ring bd. 425.00 (*0-9643120-1-8*) EduPress Pubng.

Ultimate ClarisWorks Solutions 4.0. Ronnie Peters. Ed. by Barry Peters. (Illus.). 352p. 1995. spiral bd. 49.95 incl. disk (*0-9643120-9-3*, 2001) EduPress Pubng.

Ultimate Classic Car Book: The Definitive Guide to the World's Most Wanted Classic Cars. Quentin Willson. LC 95-11903. (Illus.). 224p. (YA). 1995. 29.95 (*0-7894-0159-2*, 6-70489) DK Pub Inc.

Ultimate Clint Eastwood Trivia Book. Lee Pfeiffer & Michael Lewis. (Illus.). 128p. 1996. pap. 8.95 (*0-8065-1789-1*, Citadel Pr) Carol Pub Group.

Ultimate Cocktail Book. Raymond P. Foley. Ed. by Jaclyn W. Foley. 320p. (Orig.). 1991. pap. 8.95 (*0-9617655-1-8*) Foley Pub.

Ultimate Coercive Sanction: A Cross-Cultural Study of Capital Punishment. Keith F. Otterbein. LC 86-80163. 164p. (C). 1987. pap. 16.00 (*0-87536-346-6*) HRAFP.

***Ultimate Collector Car Price Guide 1900-1990.** (Illus.). 1000p. 1997. pap. 15.95 (*1-880524-24-4*) Cars & Parts.

Ultimate Collector Car Price Guide 1900-1990. 1,997th ed. Cars & Parts Magazine Editors. (Illus.). 800p. 1996. pap. 15.95 (*1-880524-23-6*) Cars & Parts.

Ultimate College Shopper's Guide. Heather Evans & Deidre Sullivan. LC 92-450. 1992. pap. 12.45 (*0-201-60894-4*) Addison-Wesley.

Ultimate College Student Handbook. rev. ed. Alice Lawhead & Steve Lawhead. (Illus.). 228p. (C). 1989. reprint ed. pap. 9.99 (*0-87788-864-7*) Shaw Pubs.

Ultimate College Survival Guide. Janet F. Worthington & Ronald Farrar. LC 94-42142. 250p. (C). 1995. pap. 11.95 (*1-56079-396-1*) Petersons.

Ultimate Combination. Jason Winters. 100p. 1985. pap. 6.00 (*1-885026-08-0*) Vinton Pubng.

***Ultimate Communion of Mankind.** Karen Swassjan. Tr. by J. Collis. 112p. 1996. write for info. (*0-904693-82-1*, Pub. by Temple Ldge Pub UK) Anthroposophic.

Ultimate Computer Buyer's Guide. Greg M. Thomas, Jr. 172p. (Orig.). 1995. pap. 21.95 (*1-55622-446-X*) Wordware Pub.

Ultimate Computer Security Survey. James L. Schaub & Ken D. Biery, Jr. LC 95-24149. 200p. 1995. pap. 59.95 incl. 3.5 hd (*0-7506-9692-3*) Buttrwrth-Heinemann.

Ultimate Computing: Biomolecular Consciousness & Nano Technology. S. R. Hameroff. 358p. 1987. 153.25 (*0-444-70283-0*) Elsevier.

Ultimate Con Man. Steve Wexler. 300p. (Orig.). 1987. pap. write for info. (*0-89894-038-9*) Advocate Pub Group.

***Ultimate Consignment & Thrift Store Guide (TM)** Carolyn M. Schneider. LC 97-91451. (Illus.). 200p. (Orig.). 1997. pap. 14.95 (*0-9656571-0-8*) Consignment & Thrift.

Ultimate Conspiracy: Poems. Jacqueline Lapidus. 84p. (Orig.). 1987. pap. 7.95 (*0-9619598-0-0*) Lynx Pubns.

Ultimate Consumer: A Study in Economic Illiteracy. Ed. by J. Grist Brainerd. LC 75-39236. (Getting & Spending: The Consumer's Dilemma Ser.). 1976. reprint ed. 23.95 (*0-405-08012-3*) Ayer.

***Ultimate Consumer's Guide to Diets & Nutrition.** James Marti. 1997. pap. 16.00 (*0-395-72860-6*) HM.

Ultimate Country Fake Book Update. (Fake Bks.). 95p. 1987. spiral bd. 40.00 (*0-88188-389-1*, HL00240047) H Leonard.

Ultimate Coven. Robert A. Powell. (Illus.). 224p. 1996. 19.95 (*0-9651406-1-X*) Silverhawke.

Ultimate Crappie Techniques. Samuel L. Calvin. 1994. pap. 12.95 (*1-878175-84-X*) F Amato Pubns.

***Ultimate Credit Handbook.** rev. ed. Gerri Detweiler. 1997. pap. 12.95 (*0-452-27712-4*, Plume) NAL-Dutton.

Ultimate Credit Handbook: How to Double Your Credit, Cut Your Debt, & Have a Lifetime of Financial Health. Gerri Detweiler. LC 92-26083. 1993. pap. 11.95 (*0-452-26946-6*, Plume) NAL-Dutton.

***Ultimate Cross Stitch Companion: An Encyclopedia of Techniques & Ideas with over 150 Step-by-Step.** Dorothy Wood. 1996. 19.98 (*0-7651-9781-2*) Smithmark.

Ultimate Cure: The Healing Energy Within You. Jim Dreaver. LC 95-45883. 312p. 1996. pap. 14.95 (*1-56718-244-5*) Llewellyn Pubns.

Ultimate Death. Warren Murphy & Richard Sapir. (Destroyer Ser.: No. 88). 256p. (Orig.). 1992. pap. 4.50 (*0-451-17115-2*, Sig) NAL-Dutton.

Ultimate Deception. Ray Comfort. 268p. (Orig.). 1993. pap. 5.95 (*0-88270-715-9*) Bridge-Logos.

***Ultimate Deception.** Edgar Posey. 1997. pap. 9.99 (*1-56043-279-9*) Destiny Image.

Ultimate Desktop Publishing Starter Kit. Anne F. Lent. LC 95-891. 1995. pap. 29.95 (*0-201-41032-X*) Addison-Wesley.

Ultimate Dessert Book. Linda Lewis. (Illus.). 12.95 (*0-394-41276-1*) Random.

Ultimate Destination. W. Norman Cooper. 95p. 1980. 7.50 (*0-87516-413-7*); pap. 4.50 (*0-87516-381-5*) DeVorss.

Ultimate Deterrent: Foundations of U. S.-U. S. S. R. Security under Stable Competition. William G. Shepherd. LC 86-20486. 147p. 1986. text ed. 45.00 (*0-275-92368-1*, C2368, Praeger Pubs) Greenwood.

Ultimate Diet: The Simple & Inexpensive Way to Beat Hospital, Drug & Physicians' Bills. 1992. lib. bdg. 79.95 (*0-8490-8811-9*) Gordon Pr.

Ultimate Diet Tool Kit: Ohio Distinctive Software Guide to Diet & Nutrition. Stanford Apseloff & Glen Apseloff. 250p. (Orig.). 1994. pap. 8.95 (*0-9647934-0-7*) OH Distinct Pub.

Ultimate Dim-Mak. Erle Montaigue. (Illus.). 248p. 1996. pap. 35.00 (*0-87364-878-1*) Paladin Pr.

Ultimate Dinosaur Book. David Lambert. LC 93-21885. (Illus.). 192p. 1993. 29.95 (*1-56458-304-X*) DK Pub Inc.

Ultimate Directory of the Silent Screen Performers: A Necrology of Births & Deaths & Essays on 50 Lost Players. Billy Doyle. Ed. by Anthony Slide. LC 94-36832. (Illus.). 368p. 1995. 49.50 (*0-8108-2958-4*) Scarecrow.

Ultimate Disney Joke Book. Chip Lovitt. LC 94-71693. (Illus.). 64p. (J). (gr. 1-4). 1995. pap. 3.50 (*0-7868-4022-6*) Disney Pr.

Ultimate Disney Trivia Book. Dave Smith & Kevin Neary. (Illus.). 192p. 1993. pap. 9.95 (*1-56282-925-4*) Hyperion.

Ultimate Disney Trivia Book, Bk. 2. Kevin Neary & Dave Smith. LC 94-2207. (Illus.). 208p. (J). 1994. pap. 9.95 (*0-7868-8024-4*) Hyperion.

***Ultimate Disney Trivia Book, No. 3.** Kevin Neary & Dave Smith. (Illus.). 224p. 1997. pap. 9.95 (*0-7868-8253-0*) Hyperion.

Ultimate Do-It-Yourself Survival Shelter Construction Manual. rev. ed. Michael A. Pugliese. (Illus.). 126p. (Orig.). 1994. pap. 19.95 (*1-886774-02-1*) M & M Engr.

Ultimate Dog Book. David Taylor. Ed. by Connie Vanacore. 240p. 1990. 29.95 (*0-671-70988-7*) S&S Trade.

Ultimate Dog Quiz Book. Theresa Slomick. 192p. (Orig.). 1996. 7.95 (*0-87605-762-8*) Howell Bk.

Ultimate Doll Book. Caroline Goodfellow. LC 92-30516. (Illus.). 160p. 1993. 24.95 (*1-56458-273-6*) DK Pub Inc.

Ultimate Dolls' House Book. Faith Eaton. LC 94-6325. (Illus.). 160p. 1994. 24.95 (*1-56458-616-2*) DK Pub Inc.

Ultimate DOS Programmer's Manual. John Mueller & Wallace Wang. (Illus.). 800p. 1990. 36.95 (*0-8306-7534-5*, 3534, Windcrest); pap. 29.95 (*0-8306-3534-3*, Windcrest) TAB Bks.

Ultimate DOS Programmers Manual. John Mueller & Wallace Wang. 1991. 29.95 (*0-8306-6752-0*); 29.95 (*0-8306-6753-9*) McGraw-Hill Prof.

Ultimate DOS Programmer's Manual. 2nd ed. John Mueller. 1993. text ed. 40.00 (*0-07-043965-6*) McGraw.

Ultimate DOS Programmer's Manual. 2nd ed. John Mueller. (Illus.). 880p. 1993. text ed. 39.95 (*0-8306-4114-9*, 4221, Windcrest); pap. text ed. 29.95 (*0-8306-4115-7*, 4221, Windcrest) TAB Bks.

Ultimate Dracula. Leonard Wolf. 358p. 1991. pap. 13.95 (*0-440-50353-1*, Dell Trade Pbks) Dell.

Ultimate Dragon. Ed. by Byron Preiss. (Ultimate Ser.). 313p. (Orig.). 1995. pap. 13.95 (*0-440-50630-1*, Dial Pr) Dell.

Ultimate Dumb Blonde Joke Book. Eva R. Stuart. LC 92-80467. (Illus.). 78p. (Orig.). 1992. pap. 6.95 (*0-929957-05-9*) JSA Pubns.

Ultimate Educator's Handbook. Sandy McMaster & Teddi L. Baird. Ed. by DSMV Publishing Staff. 378p. (Orig.). 1995. pap. 42.00 (*0-9642852-1-5*) DSMV Pubng.

***Ultimate Einstein.** Goldsmith. 1997. 21.99 (*0-671-01171-5*) S&S Trade.

Ultimate Elvis: Elvis Presley Day by Day. Patricia J. Pierce. LC 94-4612. (Illus.). 560p. 1994. 30.00 (*0-671-87022-X*) S&S Trade.

Ultimate Elvis: Elvis Presley Day by Day. Patricia J. Pierce. 1995. pap. 14.00 (*0-684-80328-3*, Fireside) S&S Trade.

Ultimate Encyclopedia of Beer: The Complete Guide to the World's Great Brews. Roger Protz. 1995. 19.98 (*0-8317-1899-4*) Smithmark.

***Ultimate Encyclopedia of Boxing.** P. Arnold. 1996. 19.98 (*0-7858-0641-5*) Bk Sales Inc.

***Ultimate Encyclopedia of Chocolate: With Over 200 Recipes.** Christine McFadden. 1997. 19.98 (*0-7651-9476-7*) Smithmark.

Ultimate Encyclopedia of Classical Music. Robert Ainsley. 1995. 24.98 (*0-8317-1454-9*) Smithmark.

***Ultimate Encyclopedia of Extreme Sports: The Illustrated Guide to Maximum Adrenalin Thrills.** Joe Tomlinson. 1996. 22.98 (*0-7651-9881-9*) Smithmark.

***Ultimate Encyclopedia of Formula One.** Frwd. by Damon Hill. 256p. 19.98 (*0-8317-5496-6*) Smithmark.

Ultimate Encyclopedia of Formula One: The Definitive Illustrated Guide to Grand Prix Motor... Bruce Jones. (Illus.). 256p. 1996. pap. 29.95 (*0-7603-0313-4*) Motorbooks Intl.

***Ultimate Encyclopedia of Science Fiction.** David Pringle. 1996. 24.99 (*1-57215-212-5*, JG1212) World Pubns.

Ultimate Encyclopedia of Soccer: The Definitive Illustrated Guide to World Soccer. Keir Radnedge. LC 94-34097. (Illus.). 1994. 29.95 (*1-55958-702-4*) Prima Pub.

Ultimate Enemy: British Intelligence & Nazi Germany, 1933-1939. Wesley K. Wark. LC 85-4685. (Cornell Studies in Security Affairs). 304p. 1985. reprint ed. pap. 86.70 (*0-608-01693-4*, 2062348) Bks Demand.

Ultimate Espresso Machine Cookbook. Tom Lacalamita. 192p. 1995. 27.50 (*0-684-81336-X*, S&S) S&S Trade.

Ultimate Evangelism, the Church in the Harvest Age. 1986. write for info. (*0-9618197-0-7*) Crushed Grapes.

Ultimate Factor X. John Francis Moore. (Illus.). 96p. 1995. pap. 8.95 (*0-7851-0128-4*) Marvel Entmnt.

Ultimate Fake Book. 688p. 1981. spiral bd. 39.95 (*0-9607350-0-3*, 00240050) H Leonard.

Ultimate Fantasy Football Notebook. Kurt Charon. 200p. 1993. 19.95 (*0-9637224-0-9*) Turn The Pg.

Ultimate Fantasy Football Notebook. Kurt Cliacon & Grant S. Julian. 175p. 1992. 19.92 (*0-9634280-0-4*) Going Deep.

***Ultimate Fat-Free Cookbook: The Best Ever Step-by-Step Collection of No-Fat & Low-Fat Recipes for Tempting Delicious & Healthy Eating.** Anne Sheasby. (Illus.). 256p. 1997. 24.95 (*1-85967-355-4*, Lorenz Bks) Anness Pub.

Ultimate Fate of the Universe. Jumal N. Islam. LC 82-14558. 150p. 1983. 18.95 (*0-521-24814-0*) Cambridge U Pr.

Ultimate Field Trip: Crow Canyon. Goodman & Doolittle. 1998. 16.00 (*0-689-81121-7*) S&S Childrens.

Ultimate Financial Security Survey. James L. Schaub & Ken D. Biery, Jr. LC 95-17613. 107p. 1995. pap. 59.95 incl. 3.5 hd (*0-7506-9693-1*) Buttrwrth-Heinemann.

Ultimate First Guitar Book. B. Aslanian. (Ultimate Guitar Ser.). 48p. 1993. pap. 5.95 (*0-7935-2252-8*, 00697274) H Leonard.

Ultimate Fishing Book. Lee Eisenberg. 1991. 19.98 (*0-88365-778-3*) Galahad Bks.

Ultimate Fishing Guide: Where to Go, When to Leave, What to Take, What to Wear, What to Know, How to Find Out, & Other Indispensable Information for the Angler. Steven D. Price. LC 95-19028. (Illus.). 304p. (Orig.). 1996. pap. 20.00 (*0-06-273290-0*, Harper Ref) HarpC.

Ultimate Fitness. David Luna. LC 88-61234. (Illus.). 152p. (Orig.). 1989. pap. 16.95 (*0-915677-38-5*) Roundtable Pub.

***Ultimate Fitness Book: Physical Fitness Forever.** Charles B. Corbin & Ruth Lindsey. LC 84-47519. (Illus.). 272p. 1984. reprint ed. pap. 77.60 (*0-608-04285-4*, 2065064) Bks Demand.

Ultimate Fitness Through Martial Arts. Sang H. Kim. LC 93-13327. (Illus.). 235p. 1993. pap. 16.95 (*1-880336-02-2*) Turtle CT.

Ultimate Football Quiz Book. R. Etheredge & Warren Etheredge. 1988. pap. 3.99 (*0-451-15774-5*, Sig) NAL-Dutton.

Ultimate Freedom. John H. Wyndham. 120p. (Orig.). 1994. pap. 7.95 (*0-9642628-0-0*) Mtntop Pubng.

***Ultimate Freedom.** John H. Wyndham. Tr. by Fainna Solasko. 128p. (ENG & RUS.). 1997. pap. 7.95 (*0-9642628-5-1*) Mtntop Pubng.

***Ultimate French Basic.** Crown Publishing Group Staff. 1998. write for info. (*0-609-60175-X*, Living Language) Crown Pub Group.

Ultimate Frontier. rev. ed. Eklal Kueshana. (Illus.). 1984. reprint ed. pap. 6.95 (*0-9600308-1-6*) Stelle.

Ultimate Frontier. rev. ed. Eklal Kueshana. 285p. 1992. reprint ed. pap. 4.95 (*0-9632252-0-0*) Adelphi Org.

Ultimate Gambit & The X-Ternals. Fabian Nicieza. (Illus.). 96p. 1995. pap. 8.95 (*0-7851-0129-2*) Marvel Entmnt.

Ultimate Game. Terrance Dicks. LC 94-33293. (Chronicles of a Computer Game Addict Ser.). (Illus.). 80p. 1995. pap. 3.50 (*0-8120-9184-1*) Barron.

Ultimate Game. Jesse Jones. 256p. 1992. mass mkt. 3.95 (*0-87067-381-5*) Holloway.

Ultimate Game Developers Sourcebook. Coriolis Staff. 1995. pap. 44.99 incl. cd-rom (*1-883577-59-4*) Coriolis Grp.

Ultimate Game of Golf: Mental & Strategic Tips for Your Best Game. Bob Cisco. Ed. by Andre Makovsky. (Illus.). 200p. (Orig.). 1993. pap. 19.95 (*1-882180-38-0*) Griffin CA.

Ultimate Garden Book for North America. David Stevens & Ursula Buchan. LC 95-79049. (Illus.). 352p. 1996. 49.50 (*0-8478-1870-5*) Rizzoli Intl.

Ultimate Garden Designer. Tim Newbury. (Illus.). 256p. (Orig.). 1995. 35.00 (*0-7063-7335-9*, Pub. by Ward Lock UK) Sterling.

Ultimate Garden Designer. Tim Newbury. (Illus.). 256p. (Orig.). 1996. pap. 19.95 (*0-7063-7486-X*, Pub. by Ward Lock UK) Sterling.

Ultimate Gardening Book. 528p. 1996. 50.00 (*0-517-70189-8*) Random Hse Value.

Ultimate Generation Next. Scott Lobdell. (Illus.). 96p. 1995. pap. 8.95 (*0-7851-0130-6*) Marvel Entmnt.

***Ultimate German Basic.** Crown Publishing Group Staff. 1998. pap. write for info. (*0-609-80250-X*, Living Language) Crown Pub Group.

Ultimate Gift: As the Artist Sees It. Walt Crawford. (Illus.). 176p. (Orig.). 1989. pap. 7.95 (*0-927277-00-X*) HEPC Inc.

***Ultimate Giles: An Illustrated Tribute to the Legendary Cartoonist.** Peter Tory. (Illus.). 320p. 1997. 45.00 (*0-7472-1592-8*, Pub. by Headline UK) Trafalgar.

Ultimate Gnatrat. Mark Martin. (Illus.). 120p. 1990. pap. 11.95 (*1-56097-027-8*) Fantagraph Bks.

***Ultimate Golden Retriever.** Valerie Foss. 1997. 34.95 (*0-87605-196-4*) Howell Bk.

Ultimate Golf. Malcolm Campbell. (Illus.). 240p. 1996. (*0-7894-0442-7*) DK Pub Inc.

***Ultimate Golf Book: The Essential Guide to Playing Better Golf.** Steve Newell. 1997. 24.98 (*0-7624-0116-8*) Courage Bks.

Ultimate Good Clean Jokes for Kids. Bob Phillips. (J). 1993. mass mkt. 3.99 (*1-56507-085-2*) Harvest Hse.

Ultimate Good Luck. Richard Ford. (Vintage Contemporaries Ser.). 1987. pap. 12.00 (*0-394-75089-6*, Vin) Random.

Ultimate Good Luck. Richard Ford. 1996. pap. 12.00 (*0-676-51110-4*, Vin) Random.

Ultimate Gospel Series: 100 Songs of Devotion. 288p. 1983. otabind 19.95 (*0-7935-4594-3*, 00241009) H Leonard.

Ultimate Grad School Survival Guide. Lesli Mitchell. 256p. (Orig.). 1996. pap. 14.95 (*1-56079-580-8*) Petersons.

U V

***Ultimate Grammar Book.** Phillips. Date not set. pap. text ed. write for info. (*0-312-15775-4*) St Martin.
***Ultimate Grammar Book, Vol. 1.** Phillips. Date not set. pap. text ed. write for info. (*0-312-13347-2*) St Martin.
Ultimate Guide: To Forms for Early Childhood Programs. Wendy Biasetto. LC 95-78356. 238p. 1995. 29.95 (*0-9625907-1-1*) Learning Expo.
***Ultimate Guide to Anal Sex for Women.** Tristan Taormino. 1997. pap. 14.95 (*1-57344-028-0*) Cleis Pr.
Ultimate Guide to Fractal Design Painter. Seth Greenberg & Adele Greenberg. LC 95-68272. 437p. 1995. 27.99 (*0-7821-1700-7*) Sybex.
***Ultimate Guide to Homeschooling.** Debra Bell. LC 96-38912. 1997. pap. 19.99 (*0-8499-3988-7*) Tommy Nelson.
Ultimate Guide to Lesbian & Gay Film & Video. Ed. by Jenni Olson. (Illus.). 288p. (Orig.). 1996. pap. 25.00 (*1-85242-339-0*) Serpents Tail.
***Ultimate Guide to Marathons.** Dennis Craythorn & Rich Hanna. (Illus.). 344p. (Orig.). 1997. pap. 19.95 (*0-9655187-0-1*) Marathon Pubs Inc.
Ultimate Guide to Pampering Your Horse: All Sorts of Tips & Recipes for Pampering Horses, Dedicated to Horses. June V. Evers. Ed. by James E. Kersbergen. (Illus.). 168p. 1996. 24.95 (*0-9638814-2-6*) Horse Hollow.
Ultimate Guide to Planting. Noel Kingsbury. (Illus.). 224p. 1996. 35.00 (*0-7063-7370-7*, Pub. by Ward Lock UK) Sterling.
Ultimate Guide to Raising Money for Growing Companies. Michael C. Thomsett. 275p. 1990. 45.00 (*1-55623-240-3*) Irwin Prof Pubng.
Ultimate Guide to Scales. 2nd ed. Anthony Parello. LC 92-93279. 96p. (Orig.). 1992. 14.95 (*0-9632995-0-6*); pap. 9.95 (*0-9632995-3-0*); text ed. 12.95 (*0-9632995-2-2*); pap. text ed. 10.95 (*0-9632995-4-9*); lib. bdg. 13.95 (*0-9632995-1-4*) Theory Guides.
Ultimate Guide to Science Fiction: An A-Z of Science Fiction Books by Title. 2nd ed. David Pringle. 480p. 1995. 59.95 (*1-85928-071-4*, Pub. by Scolar Pr UK) Ashgate Pub Co.
Ultimate Guide to Sport Event Management & Marketing. Stedman Graham et al. LC 94-33952. 320p. 1995. text ed. 32.50 (*0-7863-0244-5*) Irwin Prof Pubng.
***Ultimate Guide to Student Contests, Grades K-6.** Scott Pendleton. (Illus.). 288p. (Orig.). 1997. pap. 14.95 (*0-8027-7513-6*) Walker & Co.
***Ultimate Guide to Student Contests, Grades 7-12.** Scott Pendleton. LC 97-19244. 280p. (YA). (gr. 7 up). 1997. pap. 14.95 (*0-8027-7512-8*) Walker & Co.
***Ultimate Guide to the Sky.** John Mosley. Date not set. pap. 5.95 (*1-56565-596-6*) Contemp Bks.
Ultimate Guide to the VI & EX. Hewlett-Packard Company Staff. 400p. (C). 1990. pap. text ed. 34.50 (*0-8053-4460-8*) Benjamin-Cummings.
Ultimate Guide to Toronto. Margaret MacKenzie & Roderick MacKenzie. (Illus.). 240p. 1992. pap. 11.95 (*0-8118-0151-9*) Chronicle Bks.
Ultimate Guitar Book. Bacon. Date not set. pap. write for info. (*0-679-76545-X*) Random.
Ultimate Guitar Book. Tony Bacon. LC 91-52714. (Illus.). 192p. 1991. 40.00 (*0-394-58955-6*) Knopf.
***Ultimate Guitar Book.** Tony Bacon. 1997. pap. 25.00 (*0-375-70090-0*, Vin) Random.
***Ultimate Guitar Play-Along, Vol. 1.** Ed. by Aaron Stang. 64p. (Orig.). (YA). 1996. pap. text ed. 19.95 (*1-57623-487-8*, CPM0004CD) Warner Brothers.
***Ultimate Guitar Play-Along, Vol. 2.** Ed. by Aaron Stang. 64p. (Orig.). (YA). 1996. pap. text ed. 19.95 (*1-57623-497-5*, CPM0005CD) Warner Brothers.
Ultimate Healing System. Donald Lepore. 402p. 1987. pap. 19.95 (*0-913923-63-X*) Woodland UT.
Ultimate Healing System. Donald Lepore. 1996. 19.95 (*1-885670-08-7*) Woodland UT.
Ultimate Hitchhiker's Guide. Douglas Adams. LC 95-37384. 1996. 14.99 (*0-517-14925-7*) Random.
Ultimate HMO Handbook: How to Make the Most of the Revolution in Managed Care. Rhys W. Jones. 140p. (Orig.). 1994. pap. 7.95 (*0-9635819-1-0*) TTM Pub.
***Ultimate Hockety Drill Book Vol. 1: Beginning Skills.** Richard M. Trimble. (Illus.). 256p. (Orig.). 1997. pap. 14.95 (*1-57028-133-5*) Masters Pr IN.
***Ultimate Hockey Drill Book Vol. 2: Advanced Skills.** Richard M. Trimble. (Illus.). 245p. (Orig.). 1997. pap. 14.95 (*1-57028-143-2*) Masters Pr IN.
Ultimate Hockey Trivia: Games - Puzzles - Quizzes. Don Weekes & Kerry Banks. 128p. 1996. pap. 6.95 (*1-55054-507-8*, Pub. by Greystone Bks) Sterling.
***Ultimate Hollywood Tour Book: The Incomparable Guide to Movie Stars' Homes, Movie & TV Locations, Scandals, Murders, Suicides & All the Famous Tourist Sites.** 2nd rev. ed. William A. Gordon. LC 97-65351. (Illus.). 272p. 1997. pap. 15.95 (*0-937813-06-0*) North Ridge Bks.
***Ultimate Home Office: Designing, Planning, & Creating the Perfect Workspace for Your Home or Apartment.** Time-Life Books Staff. LC 97-16864. 1997. write for info. (*0-7835-4948-2*) Time-Life.
Ultimate Homemaking Handbook, Vol. 1. Delayne Winmill. LC 92-72488. 1992. pap. 6.95 (*1-55503-404-7*, 01111108) Covenant Comms.
Ultimate Hoosier Hoops Trivia Challenge: It's a Basketball Game & Trivia Game in One! Cort D. Reynolds. 68p. (Orig.). 1995. pap. 9.00 (*0-9648665-0-1*) Corts Ct.
Ultimate Hope Without God: The Atheistic Eschatology of Ernst Bloch. Thomas H. West. LC 91-3825. (American University Studies: Theology & Religion: Ser. VII, Vol. 97). 368p. 1992. 56.95 (*0-8204-1488-3*) P Lang Pubng.
Ultimate Horse Book. Elwyn H. Edwards. LC 91-60138. (Illus.). 240p. 1991. 34.95 (*1-879431-03-3*) DK Pub Inc.
***Ultimate Hot & Spicy Cookbook: 200 of the Most Fiery, Mouth-Searing & Palate-Pleasing Recipes Ever.** Lorenz Books Staff. (Illus.). 256p. 1997. 24.95 (*1-85967-367-8*, Lorenz Bks) Anness Pub.
Ultimate Household Help. Cassandra Kent. 1996. 22.95 (*0-614-96929-8*) DK Pub Inc.
Ultimate Images. Terra Parma. (Illus.). 52p. 1995. 11.95 (*0-936459-28-X*) Stained Glass.
Ultimate in Rifle Accuracy. Glenn Newick. (Illus.). 210p. (Orig.). 1990. pap. 11.95 (*0-88317-159-7*) Stoeger Pub Co.
Ultimate in Rifle Precision. Whelen. (Library Classics Ser.). 1990. 42.00 (*0-935632-92-1*) Wolfe Pub Co.
***Ultimate Indian Cooking.** Christine McFadden. 1996. write for info. (*0-7651-9685-9*) Smithmark.
***Ultimate Ingles Basic.** Crown Publishing Group Staff. 1998. write for info. (*0-609-60173-3*, Living Language); write for info. (*0-609-60174-1*, Living Language) Crown Pub Group.
Ultimate Insiders: U. S. Senators in the National Media. Stephen Hess. LC 85-48177. 151p. 1986. 29.95 (*0-8157-3598-7*); pap. 12.95 (*0-8157-3597-9*) Brookings.
***Ultimate Insult.** Compiled by Maria Leach. 256p. 1997. pap. 11.95 (*0-7867-0487-X*) Carroll & Graf.
***Ultimate Interior Designer.** Ruth Pretty. (Illus.). 256p. 1997. 35.00 (*0-7063-7463-0*, Pub. by Ward Lock UK) Sterling.
Ultimate Interview: How to Get It, Get Ready & Get the Job You Want. John Caple. 192p. 1991. pap. 11.95 (*0-385-26583-2*) Doubleday.
Ultimate Intimacy: The Psychodynamics of Jewish Mysticism. Ed. by Mortimer Ostow. 432p. 1996. 62.50 (*0-8236-6686-7*, BN 06686) Intl Univs Pr.
Ultimate Intimacy: The Psychodynamics of Jewish Mysticism. Mortimer Ostow. 432p. 1996. pap. text ed. 53.95 (*1-85575-105-4*, Pub. by Karnac Bks UK) Brunner-Mazel.
Ultimate Investments. Ferleger. Date not set. 25.00 (*0-684-82728-X*) Free Pr.
Ultimate Investments. Ferleger. 1996. 25.00 (*0-02-874030-0*) Free Pr.
***Ultimate Irony.** Mabel W. Martin. LC 97-71101. 233p. (Orig.). 1997. mass mkt. 15.00 (*0-9629142-1-5*) Janze Pubns.
Ultimate Island: On the Nature of British Science Fiction. Nicholas Ruddick. LC 92-24136. (Contributions to the Study of Science Fiction & Fantasy Ser.: No. 55). 216p. 1993. text ed. 49.95 (*0-313-27373-1*, RUC, Greenwood Pr) Greenwood.
Ultimate Issues. R. C. Sproul. 88p. (YA). (gr. 10). 1996. pap. 7.99 (*0-8010-5736-1*) Baker Bks.
***Ultimate Italian Basic.** Crown Publishing Group Staff. 1998. write for info. (*0-609-60182-2*, Living Language) Crown Pub Group.
Ultimate Italian Cookbook. Carla Capalbo. 256p. 1994. 19.98 (*0-8317-9068-7*) Smithmark.
***Ultimate Italian Cooking.** Christine McFadden. 1996. 16.98 (*0-7651-9686-7*) Smithmark.
Ultimate Italian Pastries. Virginia Defendorf. Ed. by Susan L. Carr. LC 94-20104. 36p. (Orig.). 1994. pap. 9.95 (*1-56790-103-4*) Cool Hand Comms.
***Ultimate Italian Pastries: Old World Recipes from an Italian American Family.** 2nd ed. Virginia Defendorf. (Illus.). 144p. (Orig.). 1997. pap. 12.95 (*1-884962-13-0*) Bkwrld Press.
Ultimate Italian Sausage Cookbook. Papa Cantella. Ed. by Tom Cantella. (Illus.). 108p. 1995. pap. 12.95 (*0-9649632-0-5*) Papa Cantellas.
Ultimate James Bond Trivia Book. Michael Lewis & Lee Pfeiffer. (Illus.). 128p. 1996. pap. 8.95 (*0-8065-1793-X*, Citadel Pr) Carol Pub Group.
Ultimate Jazz Fake Book: E Flat Edition. 448p. 1988. spiral bd. 39.95 (*0-88188-981-4*, 00240081) H Leonard.
***Ultimate Job Search Kit: Featuring Interview Preparation, Flash Cards & Job Search Handbook.** Damir J. Stimac. 1997. pap. 29.99 (*1-886989-42-7*) Seaton Corp.
Ultimate Journey. Robert A. Monroe. 320p. 1996. pap. 12.95 (*0-385-47208-0*, Anchor NY) Doubleday.
Ultimate Juggling. Richard Dingman. (Illus.). 80p. 1996. 15.98 (*1-56138-774-6*) Courage Bks.
Ultimate Kansas City Baseball Trivia Quiz Book: Royals, Monarchs, Blues, Athletics & More. Phil S. Dixon. (Illus.). 224p. (Orig.). 1992. pap. 10.95 (*1-878446-07-X*) Bon A Tirer Pub.
Ultimate Kauai Guidebook. 2nd rev. ed. Andrew Doughty & Harriett Friedman. LC 95-78819. (Illus.). 200p. (Orig.). 1997. pap. 12.95 (*0-9639429-1-3*) Wizard Pubns.
Ultimate Keyboard Chord Book. pap. 12.95 (*0-7935-5144-7*, 00290045) H Leonard.
Ultimate Kick. Bill Wallace. LC 86-51504. 230p. (Orig.). 1987. pap. 12.95 (*0-86568-088-4*, 406) Unique Pubns.
Ultimate Kid. Jeff Goelitz. (Illus.). 150p. 1986. pap. 9.95 (*0-916438-61-9*) Planetary Pubns.
Ultimate Kid: Levels of Learning That Make a Difference. Jeffrey Goelitz. 144p. 1991. reprint ed. lib. bdg. 29.00 (*0-8095-5805-X*) Borgo Pr.
Ultimate Kids' Club Book: How to Organize, Find Members, Run Meetings, Raise Money, Handle Problems, & Much More! Melissa Maupin. Ed. by Rosemary Wallner. LC 96-13095. (Illus.). 120p. (Orig.). (J). (gr. 5-9). 1996. pap. 11.95 (*1-57542-007-4*) Free Spirit Pub.
Ultimate Kingdom. 2nd ed. Earl Paulk. 264p. (Orig.). 1987. reprint ed. pap. 7.95 (*0-917595-13-0*) Kingdom Pubs.
Ultimate Kingdom see Ultimo Reino
***Ultimate Kitten Sticker Book.** (Illus.). (J). (ps-7). 1996. 6.95 (*0-7894-1347-7*) DK Pub Inc.
***Ultimate Labrador Retriever.** Michael Hingley. 1997. 14.95 (*0-87605-697-4*) Howell Bk.
***Ultimate Labrador Retriever.** Heather Wiles-Fone. 1997. 34.95 (*0-87605-204-9*) Howell Bk.
***Ultimate Labrador Retriever.** Heather Wiles-Fone. 1997. 34.95 (*0-614-27821-X*) Mac Pub USA.
Ultimate Lark: An Epicurean Adventure. Jim Lark. LC 96-41204. (Illus.). 320p. 1996. 29.95 (*1-879094-49-5*) Momentum Bks.
Ultimate Las Vegas & Beyond. 2nd ed. David Stratton. Ed. by Zippy & Joanna Pearlman. LC 94-60467. (Ultimate Guidebook Ser.). (Illus.). 240p. 1994. pap. 11.95 (*1-56975-016-5*) Ulysses Pr.
Ultimate Lean Routine: 12 Week Cross Training & Fat Loss Program. Greg Isaacs. 1996. pap. text ed. 17.95 (*1-56530-203-6*) Summit TX.
Ultimate Learning States Vol. 1: Exploring Intellectual Performance with Brainwave Technology. Brian Morrissey. (Illus.). 102p. 1996. 27.95 (*0-9651721-4-7*) Self Study Systs.
***Ultimate Legacy: How Owners of Family & Closely Held Businesses Can Achieve Their Real Purpose.** Donald J. Jonovic. LC 96-37761. 1997. write for info. (*0-915607-13-1*) Jamieson Pr.
Ultimate Lesson: 10 Point Guide on How to Teach Yourself Anything. Art Niemann. LC 96-92211. iix, 177p. (Orig.). 1996. pap. 14.95 (*0-9651335-5-9*, SLI Pr) Niemann Ent.
***Ultimate Lifestyle: Simple Steps to Feeling Good & Enjoying Life.** Hans Diehl & Aileen Ludington. LC 90-27774. 1991. write for info. (*0-8163-1026-2*) Pacific Pr Pub Assn.
Ultimate Limit State of Concrete Girders Prestressed with Unbonded Tendons. Douglas P. Gauvreau. LC 93-9971. 1993. 32.00 (*0-8176-2873-8*, Pub. by Birkhauser Vlg SZ) Birkhauser.
Ultimate Limits of Fabrication & Measurement: Proceedings of the NATO Advanced Research Workshop on "Ultimate Limits of Fabrication & Measurement," Cambridge, U. K., April 1-3, 1994. Ed. by M. E. Welland & J. K. Gimzewski. LC 95-14998. (NATO ASI Series E: Vol. 292). 1995. lib. bdg. 132.00 (*0-7923-3504-X*) Kluwer Ac.
Ultimate Little Shooter Book. Raymond P. Foley. Ed. by Jaclyn W. Foley & Loretta Natiello. 336p. 1995. pap. 7.95 (*0-9617655-2-6*) Foley Pub.
Ultimate Load Design of Continuous Concrete Beams. Derrick Beckett. LC 67-31269. 126p. reprint ed. pap. 36.00 (*0-317-08608-1*, 2020707) Bks Demand.
Ultimate Load Test of a Segmentally Constructed Prestressed Concrete I-Beam. (PCI Journal Reprints Ser.). 16p. 1974. pap. 12.00 (*0-686-40065-8*, JR146) P-PCI.
Ultimate Loss: Coping with the Death of a Child. Joan W. Bordow. LC 81-18182. 192p. 1982. 12.95 (*0-8253-0091-6*) Beaufort Bks NY.
Ultimate Love. Kris Mackay. 1994. 10.95 (*0-88494-926-5*) Bookcraft Inc.
Ultimate Love: The Real Thing. Neil T. Anderson & Dave Park. LC 96-17396. (Freedom in Christ for Teens Ser.: No. 4). 200p. (Orig.). (YA). 1996. pap. 7.99 (*1-56507-410-6*) Harvest Hse.
Ultimate Lovemaking Guide: Lessons from the Deaths of Relationships & How to Unlock Your Mind-Body-Soul Potential at Play & in Bed. Ken Vegotsky. (Love Living & Live Loving Ser.). 1998. audio write for info. (*1-886508-20-8*, Ages Pubns) Adi Gaia Esalen.
Ultimate Lovemaking Guide: Lessons from the Deaths of Relationships & How to Unlock Your Mind-Body-Soul Potential at Play & in Bed. Ken Vegotsky. (Love Living & Live Loving Ser.). 1999. pap. write for info. (*1-886508-16-X*, Ages Pubns) Adi Gaia Esalen.
Ultimate Low Cholesterol, Low Fat Cookbook: Over 220 Delicious, Healthy Recipes for All. Christine France. 1996. 19.98 (*0-8317-7291-3*) Smithmark.
Ultimate Low-Fat Mexican Cookbook. Anne L. Greer. LC 94-35995. 144p. 1995. 21.95 (*0-87719-258-8*, 9258) Gulf Pub.
Ultimate Lunchbox Book: The Best Recipes & Ideas from the Pack-a-Lively Lunchbox Contest. Larry Zisman & Honey Zisman. LC 95-17148. 1995. pap. 8.95 (*0-312-13196-8*) St Martin.
Ultimate Marketing Plan. Daniel S. Kennedy. 192p. 1991. pap. 10.95 (*1-55850-017-0*) Adams Media.
Ultimate Marriage Builder: A Do-It-Yourself Encounter Weekend for You & Your Mate. Dave Arp. 1994. pap. 14.99 (*0-7852-8250-5*) Nelson.
Ultimate Martial Art: Renbukai, Vol. II. Ronald L. Marchini. 144p. 1982. pap. 7.95 (*0-940522-01-2*) ROMARC Inc.
Ultimate Martial Art: Renbukai, Vol. III. Ronald L. Marchini. 152p. 1982. pap. 7.95 (*0-940522-02-0*) ROMARC Inc.
Ultimate Martial Art: Renbukai, Vol. 1. Ronald L. Marchini. 128p. (Orig.). (C). 1981. pap. 6.95 (*0-940522-00-4*) ROMARC Inc.
Ultimate Medicine: As Prescribed by Sri Nisargadatta Maharaj. 2nd ed. Sri Nisargadatta Maharaj. Ed. by Robert Powell. LC 94-34676. 214p. (Orig.). 1995. pap. 14.00 (*1-884997-09-0*) Blue Dove Pr.
Ultimate Memory Book: Remember Anything - Quickly & Easily. Robert Sandstrom. LC 90-70923. (Illus.). 160p. (Orig.). 1990. pap. 12.95 (*0-9626918-5-2*) Stepping CA.
Ultimate Michigan Adventures: Ninety-Eight One-of-a-Kind Destinations & Diversions. rev. ed. Gary W. Barfknecht. (Illus.). 288p. 1994. pap. 14.95 (*0-923756-10-8*) Friede Pubns.
***Ultimate Mickey Mantle Trivia Book.** Tom Burkhard. LC 97-12712. (Illus.). 128p. 1997. pap. 9.95 (*0-8065-1893-6*, Citadel Pr) Carol Pub Group.
Ultimate Missionary Cookbook. Ralph Thomas & Sherry Thomas. (Illus.). 60p. (C). 1995. spiral bd. 9.00 (*0-9650266-8-X*) Repent.
Ultimate Mortal Kombat 3. Bradygames Staff. 121p. 1996. 9.99 (*1-56686-521-2*) Brady Pub.
Ultimate Mortal Kombat 3 Official Arcade Secrets. PCS Staff. 1996. pap. text ed. 9.99 (*0-7615-0586-5*) Prima Pub.
Ultimate Motorcycle Book. Hugo Wilson. LC 93-21884. (Illus.). 192p. 1993. 29.95 (*1-56458-303-1*) DK Pub Inc.
Ultimate Motorcycle Detailing: The Secrets for Making Any Bike Look Better. David H. Jacobs. (Illus.). 160p. 1989. pap. 16.95 (*0-87938-360-7*) Motorbooks Intl.
***Ultimate Mountain Bike Book.** Nicky Crowther. LC 97-3909. (Illus.). 192p. 1997. 15.98 (*0-7603-0333-9*) Motorbooks Intl.
Ultimate Movie Thesaurus: The Only Book You'll Ever Need to Find the Movie You Want. Christopher Case. LC 96-36427. 704p. 1996. pap. 22.50 (*0-8050-3496-X*, Owl) H Holt & Co.
Ultimate Multimedia Handbook. 2nd ed. Ed. by Jessica Keyes. LC 96-47090. (Illus.). 1,024p. 1996. pap. text ed. 69.95 (*0-07-034530-9*) McGraw.
Ultimate Mushroom Book: The Complete Guide to Identifying, Picking, & Using Mushrooms. Peter Jordan. 1995. 19.98 (*0-8317-3080-3*) Smithmark.
Ultimate Musician's Reference Handbook: The Most Complete Guide to Who's Who in Popular Music. Brent E. Kick. (Illus.). 256p. (Orig.). (C). 1996. pap. 24.95 (*1-57424-023-4*, 00000190) Centerstream Pub.
Ultimate Mutual Fund Guide: Seventeen Experts Pick the 46 Top Funds You Should Own. Warren Boroson. 250p. 1993. per. 18.95 (*1-55738-425-8*) Irwin Prof Pubng.
Ultimate Mutual Fund Guide: 17 Experts Pick the 46 Top Funds You Should Own. rev. ed. Warren Boroson. 250p. 1995. 16.95 (*1-55738-864-4*) Irwin Prof Pubng.
***Ultimate Mutual Fund Guide: 20 Experts Pick the 46 Top Funds You Should Own.** 2nd rev. ed. Warren Boroson. 288p. 1996. per. 18.95 (*0-7863-1130-4*) Irwin Prof Pubng.
Ultimate Nashville Blackbook: A Guide to the Nashville Music Business (Contact Guide) unabridged ed. Rob English. 280p. (Orig.). 1996. pap. 39.95 (*0-9651453-6-0*) English Ent.
***Ultimate Natural Health & Healing Book: The Complete Guide to Achieving & Maintaining Health & Well-Being Through Natural Remedies & Therapies.** Mark Evans. (Illus.). 256p. 1997. 30.00 (*1-85967-332-5*, Lorenz Bks) Anness Pub.
***Ultimate New York City Trivia Book.** Hy Brett. 224p. (Orig.). 1997. pap. 6.95 (*1-55853-499-7*) Rutledge Hill Pr.
Ultimate No B. S. Business Success Package. Dan Kennedy. (Audio Ser.). 1993. boxed 19.95 incl. audio (*0-88908-766-0*) Self-Counsel Pr.
Ultimate No B.S., No Holds Barred, Kick Butt, Take No Prisoners, & Make Lots of Money Business Success Book. Dan Kennedy. (Business Ser.). 168p. 1993. pap. 8.95 (*0-88908-278-2*) Self-Counsel Pr.
Ultimate Nutrient: Glutamine, the Essential Nonessential Amino Acid. Judy Shabert & Nancy Ehrlich. LC 93-45656. 160p. pap. 9.95 (*0-89529-588-1*) Avery Pub.
Ultimate Ocean Book: A Unique Introduction to the Amazing World under Water in Fabulous, Full-Color Pop-Ups. Maria Mudd-Ruth. (Illus.). 5p. (J). (ps-3). 1995. pap. 19.95 (*0-307-17628-2*, Golden Books) Western Pub.
Ultimate On-Line Homework Helper. Marian Salzman & Robert Pondiscio. LC 96-23296. (Orig.). (J). (gr. 3-7). 1996. pap. 5.99 (*0-380-78662-1*, Camelot) Avon.
Ultimate Opera Quiz. Kenn Harris. LC 96-39323. 1997. pap. 15.95 (*0-14-025390-4*) Viking Penguin.
***Ultimate Origami Kit: A Step-by-Step Guide to the Art of Paper Folding.** John Morin. (Illus.). 80p. 1997. 15.98 (*0-7624-0017-X*) Courage Bks.
Ultimate Ornament Book. (Memories in the Making Ser.: No. 21). (Illus.). 128p. 1996. 19.95 (*1-57486-007-0*) Oxmoor Hse.
Ultimate OS-2 Programmer's Manual. John Mueller. LC 93-43685. 1994. text ed. 50.00 (*0-07-043971-0*); pap. text ed. 36.95 (*0-07-043972-9*) McGraw-Hill Prof.
Ultimate Overseas Business Guide for Growing Companies. Henry H. Rodkin. 300p. 1990. pap. 50.00 (*1-55623-300-0*) Irwin Prof Pubng.
Ultimate Paper Airplane. Richard Kline & Floyd Fogelmann. 128p. 1985. pap. 11.00 (*0-671-55551-0*) S&S Trade.
***Ultimate Pasta.** Julia Della Croce. 168p. 1997. 29.95 (*0-7894-2086-4*) DK Pub Inc.
***Ultimate Pasta Cookbook.** Pasquale Bruno. LC 96-33493. 1997. pap. write for info. (*0-8092-3169-7*) Contemp Bks.
Ultimate Pasta Machine Cookbook. Tom LaCalamita. 1994. 25.00 (*0-671-50102-X*) S&S Trade.
***Ultimate Peacekeeper: Economic Intervention & U. S. Foreign Policy.** David J. Rothkopf. 1997. pap. text ed. 10.95 (*0-87003-150-3*) Carnegie Endow.
Ultimate Penalties: Capital Punishment, Life Imprisonment, Physical Torture. Leon S. Sheleff. LC 87-5553. 492p. 1987. 49.50 (*0-8142-0436-8*) Ohio St U Pr.
Ultimate Penalties: Capital Punishment, Life Imprisonment, Physical Torture. Leon S. Sheleff. 1991. pap. 24.50 (*0-8142-0531-3*) Ohio St U Pr.
Ultimate Performance System. Ashley Reece-Podgorski. LC 94-90309. 270p. 1993. 49.95 (*0-9644303-0-4*) Ultimate Perf.
Ultimate Performance System, II. Ashley Reece-Podgorski. LC 94-90308. 344p. (C). 1994. 89.95 (*0-9644303-1-2*) Ultimate Perf.
Ultimate Phillies Trivia Quiz. Lou Orlando. 80p. (Orig.). 1994. write for info. (*0-9641936-0-4*) Rockford Assocs.
***Ultimate Phillies Trivia Quiz 1997 Update.** Lou Orlando. (Illus.). 80p. (Orig.). 1997. pap. write for info. (*0-614-30168-8*) Rockford Assocs.
Ultimate Pit Bull Terrier. Jacqueline Fraser. LC 95-12141. (Illus.). 256p. 1995. 19.95 (*0-87605-248-0*) Howell Bk.

U
V

Ultimate Pizza: The World's Favorite Pizza Recipes--from Deep Dish to Dessert. Pasquale Bruno, Jr. LC 95-31565. 176p. 1995. pap. 11.95 (*0-8092-3349-5*) Contemp Bks.

***Ultimate Plant & Garden Book.** Ed. by R. J. Turner. 1996. 50.00 (*0-614-20662-6*) Crown Pub Group.

***Ultimate Play Along.** Dave Wechl. Ed. by Dan Thress. (Illus.). 56p. (Orig.). 1996. pap. text ed. 24.95 (*1-57623-402-9*, MMBK0063CD) Warner Brothers.

Ultimate Pocket Atlas. Ed. by Dorling Kindersley Staff. 192p. 1995. 12.95 (*0-7894-0192-4*) DK Pub Inc.

***Ultimate Pocket Flags of the World.** 240p. 1997. pap. 12.95 (*0-7894-2085-6*) DK Pub Inc.

***Ultimate Pocket World Atlas, 2 vols.** Dk Pub Inc., Staff. 1997. 24.95 (*0-7894-1826-6*) DK Pub Inc.

Ultimate Pocket World Factfile. 248p. 1996. pap. 12.95 (*0-7894-0439-7*) DK Pub Inc.

***Ultimate Pop Rock Fake Book.** Joel Whitburn. 1997. pap. 35.00 (*0-7935-7000-X*) H Leonard.

Ultimate Porno. PierNico Solinas. LC 80-69871. (C). 1981. 15.95 (*0-938112-00-7*) Eyecontact.

Ultimate Potato Bazooka: Hair Spray Powered Vegetable Gun. Michael A. Pugliese. 36p. 1994. pap. write for info. (*1-886774-05-6*) M & M Engr.

Ultimate Power. Joanne Bunce. 64p. 1990. pap. 2.95 (*0-88144-150-3*) Christian Pub.

Ultimate Power: Lessons from a Near-Death Experience & How to Unlock Your Mind-Body-Soul Potential. Ken Vogotsky. (Love Living & Live Loving Ser.). 232p. 1995. pap. 14.95 (*1-886508-15-1*, Ages Pubns) Adi Gaia Esalen.

Ultimate Power: Lessons from a Near-Death Experience & How to Unlock Your Mind-Body-Soul Potential. Ken Vogotsky. LC 94-24030. (Love Living & Live Loving Ser.). 1996. audio write for info. (*1-886508-17-8*, Ages Pubns) Adi Gaia Esalen.

Ultimate Power Revisited: More Lessons from a Near-Death Experience & How to Apply the Laws of Success. Ken Vegotsky. Ed. by Liba Berry. (Love Living & Live Loving Ser.). audio write for info. (*1-886508-22-4*) Adi Gaia Esalen.

Ultimate Power Revisited: More Lessons from a Near-Death Experience & How to Apply the Laws of Success. Ken Vegotsky. Ed. by Liba Berry. (Love Living & Live Loving Ser.). 224p. 1999. pap. write for info. (*1-886508-21-6*) Adi Gaia Esalen.

Ultimate Pressure Cooker Cookbook. Tom Lacalamita. LC 96-40229. 1997. 25.00 (*0-684-82496-5*) S&S Trade.

Ultimate Pressure Cooker Cookbook: Home-Cooked Flavors for Today's Easy-to-Use Pressure Cookers. Maureen B. Keane & Daniella Chace. LC 95-5286. 1995. pap. 16.95 (*0-7615-0026-X*) Prima Pub.

Ultimate Priority. John J. MacArthur, Jr. 1983. pap. 10.99 (*0-8024-0186-4*) Moody.

Ultimate Prizes. Susan Howatch. 448p. 1990. mass mkt. 6.99 (*0-449-21811-2*, Crest) Fawcett.

Ultimate Prophecy Bk. 1: The Initiation. Moshe Zwang. LC 95-80574. (Illus.). 288p. (Orig.). pap. 16.95 (*0-9645519-0-X*) Ult Mind Pub.

Ultimate Prophecy Bk. 1: The Initiation. Moshe Zwang. LC 95-80574. (Illus.). 288p. (Orig.). 1996. 24.95 (*0-9645519-1-8*) Ult Mind Pub.

Ultimate Psychopolitics, Mass Mind Control & the Global Control System. Ceres. (Phoenix Journals). 248p. 1993. pap. 7.95 (*1-56935-005-1*) Phoenix Source.

***Ultimate Puppy Sticker Book.** (Illus.). 16p. (J). (ps-7). 1996. 6.95 (*0-7894-1348-5*) DK Pub Inc.

Ultimate Purpose & Fundamental Principles of Life. Josef G. Lowder. LC 85-701. (What in the World Are You Doing with Your Life Ser.: No. 1). 72p. 9.95 (*0-935597-00-X*); pap. 3.95 (*0-935597-01-8*); disk 9.95 (*0-935597-04-2*) Comm Architects.

Ultimate Questions: A Theological Primer. Clyde R. Crews. 176p. 1986. pap. 11.95 (*0-8091-2774-1*) Paulist Pr.

Ultimate Questions: An Anthology of Modern Russian Religious Thought. Ed. by Alexander Schmemann. 310p. 1977. reprint ed. pap. 11.95 (*0-913836-46-X*) St Vladimirs.

***Ultimate Quilting & Patchwork Book.** Smithmark Staff. 1996. 19.98 (*0-7651-9786-3*) Smithmark.

Ultimate Raw Diet: How to Live on a 100 Percent Raw Diet Healthfully. 2nd rev. ed. Stanley S. Bass. Ed. by Chet Day. 18p. 1996. pap. 10.00 (*1-885194-07-2*) Hlth & Beyond.

Ultimate Recipe for Fitness. Sheila Cluff & Eleanor Brown. (Illus.). 192p. 1990. pap. 14.95 (*0-9618805-3-8*) Fitness Ojai.

Ultimate Recipe for Fitness. Sheila Cluff & Eleanor Brown. (Illus.). 192p. 1990. pap. 14.95 (*0-9618805-4-6*) Fitness Ojai.

***Ultimate Recording Guide to the Rolling Stones.** James Karnbach & Carol Bernson. LC 97-1056. 1997. write for info. (*0-8160-3035-9*) Facts on File.

Ultimate Recruitment Guide & Notebook. David L. Kaplan. 1996. pap. text ed. 24.95 (*1-882180-54-2*) Griffin CA.

Ultimate Reference Book: The Wit's Thesaurus. Lance Davidson. 688p. (Orig.). 1994. pap. 15.00 (*0-380-76957-3*) Avon.

Ultimate Resource, Vol. II. Julian L. Simon. LC 95-39586. 656p. (C). 1996. 35.00 (*0-691-04269-1*) Princeton U Pr.

Ultimate Revolution. Walter J. Starcke. LC 88-72196. 180p. (C). 1988. reprint ed. pap. 8.95 (*0-929845-01-3*) Guadalupe Pr.

Ultimate Revolution: Introducing the New Age. rev. ed. Walter J. Starcke. LC 88-72196. 176p. (C). 1991. reprint ed. pap. 8.95 (*0-929845-05-6*) Guadalupe Pr.

***Ultimate Rewards: What Really Motivates People to Achieve.** Harvard Business School Press Staff. 1997. text ed. 29.95 (*0-07-105058-2*) McGraw.

***Ultimate Rewards: What Really Motivates People to Achieve.** Ed. by Steven Kerr. LC 97-19265. (Review Book Ser.). 288p. 1997. 29.95 (*0-87584-808-7*, HBS Pr) Harvard Busn.

Ultimate Ribbon Book. Annabel Lewis. (Illus.). 128p. 1995. 29.95 (*1-57076-030-6*, Trafalgar Sq Pub) Trafalgar.

Ultimate Rice Cooker Cookbook: Delicious Flavors for Today's Easy-to-Use Rice Cookers. Betty L. Torre. LC 95-23437. 1995. pap. text ed. 14.95 (*0-7615-0193-2*) Prima Pub.

Ultimate Rip-Off: A Taxing Tale. rev. ed. Iris W. Collett. LC 87-83032. 1991. pap. text ed. 9.95 (*0-913878-50-2*) T Horton & Dghts.

Ultimate Ripoff. Bill Stringfellow. LC 81-49329. 176p. 1981. pap. 3.95 (*0-939286-00-9*) Concerned Pubns.

Ultimate Risk. Adam Raphael. 1995. pap. 8.99 (*0-552-13935-1*) Bantam.

Ultimate Risk: The Inside Story of the Lloyd's Catastrophe. Adam Raphael. LC 95-11797. (Illus.). 316p. 1995. 24.95 (*1-56858-056-8*) FWEW.

***Ultimate Road Atlas & Vacation Guide 1997.** Rand McNally Staff. 1996. pap. text ed. 19.95 (*0-528-81574-1*) Rand McNally.

Ultimate Rock Bass Guitar Chord Finder. pap. 4.95 (*0-7935-1672-2*, 00697232) H Leonard.

Ultimate Rock Bass Guitar Scale Finder. pap. 4.95 (*0-7935-1671-4*, 00697234) H Leonard.

Ultimate Rose Book: One Thousand Five Hundred Roses--Antique, Modern (Including Miniature), & Wild--All Shown in Color & Selected for Their Beauty, Fragrance, & Enduring Popularity. Stirling Macoboy. LC 93-10419. (Illus.). 472p. 1993. 49.50 (*0-8109-3920-7*) Abrams.

***Ultimate Rose Book: The Complete Book for Rose Lovers - Growing, Arranging & Creative Crafts with Fresh & Dried Flowers.** Sarah Whittington. (Illus.). 256p. 1997. 34.95 (*1-85967-452-6*, Lorenz Bks) Anness Pub.

Ultimate Rottweiler. Ed. by Andrew Brace. LC 95-7586. (Illus.). 288p. 1995. 34.95 (*0-87605-293-6*) Howell Bk.

Ultimate Rubber Stamp Kit: Art Action Book. Alicia Newman. (Illus.). 18p. (J). (gr. 1 up). 1995. bds. 19.95 (*1-56138-570-0*) Running Pr.

***Ultimate Rush.** Joe Quirk. Date not set. write for info. (*0-688-15270-8*, R Weisbach Bks) Morrow.

Ultimate Sales Letter. Daniel S. Kennedy. 204p. 1990. pap. 9.95 (*1-55850-948-8*) Adams Media.

Ultimate Sales Professional. Dale Ledbetter. Ed. by Randy Gaye. (Sales Mastery Ser.). (Orig.). 1994. pap. 11.95 (*1-884667-02-3*) Gage Res & Develop.

Ultimate Scanner: Cheek 3. Bill Cheek. LC 95-75846. (Illus.). 244p. (Orig.). 1995. pap. 29.95 (*1-56866-058-8*) Index Pub Grp.

Ultimate Scene & Monologue Sourcebook: An Actor's Guide to over 1000 Monologues & Dialogues from More Than 300 Contemporary Plays. Ed Hooks. LC 93-43030. 272p. 1994. pap. 18.95 (*0-8230-7771-3*, Back Stage Bks) Watsn-Guptill.

Ultimate School Yearbook: For Your Cool School Memories. Sharon McCoy. (Illus.). 64p. (J). (gr. 2-7). 1996. pap. 8.95 (*1-56565-526-5*) Lowell Hse Juvenile.

Ultimate Science Quiz Book, Vol. I. Bill G. Aldridge. (Illus.). 144p. (YA). (gr. 9-12). 1995. pap. 8.00 (*0-531-15754-7*) Watts.

Ultimate Science Quiz Book Vol. I. Bill G. Aldridge. LC 94-15518. (Science Literacy Ser.). (Illus.). 128p. (YA). (gr. 9-12). 1994. lib. bdg. 22.70 (*0-531-11198-9*) Watts.

***Ultimate Scrap Quilt.** Joyce Mori. (Illus.). 128p. (Orig.). 1997. pap. 21.95 (*0-8019-8925-6*, USQ) Krause Pubns.

***Ultimate Season.** Steve Kerr. (Illus.). 84p. 1996. pap. text ed. 12.95 (*1-56625-072-2*) Bonus Books.

Ultimate Secret to Getting Absolutely Everything You Want. Mike Hernacki. Ed. by Sallye Levanthal. 112p. 1988. mass mkt. 4.99 (*0-425-10686-1*) Berkley Pub.

Ultimate Secret to Permanent Prosperity. Mike Hernacki. 128p. (Orig.). 1994. pap. 4.99 (*0-425-14463-1*) Berkley Pub.

Ultimate Secrets of Knowing God, Vol. 1. Michael L. McCann. Ed. by Irene Cotton. 95p. (Orig.). (C). 1993. pap. text ed. 6.00 (*0-9638195-0-X*) M L McCann.

Ultimate Secrets of Total Self-Confidence. Robert Anthony. 1986. mass mkt. 5.99 (*0-425-10170-3*) Berkley Pub.

Ultimate Security: The Environmental Basis of Political Instability. Norman Myers. 319p. (C). 1996. reprint ed. pap. text ed. 14.95 (*1-55963-499-5*) Island Pr.

Ultimate Security Survey. James L. Schaub & Ken D. Biery, Jr. LC 94-11989. 256p. 1994. pap. 120.00 incl. 3.5 hd (*0-7506-9577-3*) Buttrwrth-Heinemann.

Ultimate Sega Genesis Game Strategies. Corey Sandler. (J). 1990. pap. 9.95 (*0-679-79062-4*) Random.

Ultimate Serger Answer Guide. Naomi Baker et al. (Creative Machine Arts Ser.). 96p. 1996. pap. 16.95 (*0-8019-8645-1*) Chilton.

Ultimate Series Love & Wedding. (Piano-Vocal-Guitar Ser.). 295p. 1988. per. 17.95 (*0-88188-785-4*, HL 00361445) H Leonard.

Ultimate Service: Complete Handbook to the World of the concierge. Holly Stiel & Delta Collins. LC 93-25093. 208p. (C). 1993. text ed. 41.00 (*0-13-175357-6*) P-H.

Ultimate Sex Book. Anne Hooper. LC 92-6542. (Illus.). 192p. 1992. 29.95 (*1-56458-063-6*) DK Pub Inc.

Ultimate Sex, Love, & Romance Quiz Book. Marnie Winston-Macauley. 128p. (Orig.). 1995. pap. 5.95 (*0-8362-0559-6*) Andrews & McMeel.

Ultimate Sex, Love, & Romance Quiz Book, No. 2. Marnie Winston-Macauley. 128p. (Orig.). 1996. pap. 5.95 (*0-8362-1323-8*) Andrews & McMeel.

Ultimate Sherlock Holmes Encyclopedia. 1987. 9.99 (*0-517-65444-X*) Random Hse Value.

***Ultimate Show-Me-How Activity Book.** Smithmark Staff. (J). 1997. 14.98 (*0-7651-9419-8*) Smithmark.

Ultimate Silver Surfer. Ed. by Stan Lee. 352p. (Orig.). 1995. pap. 12.00 (*1-57297-029-4*) Blvd Books.

***Ultimate Silver Surfer.** Ed. by Stan Lee. 1997. mass mkt. 5.99 (*1-57297-299-8*) Blvd Books.

***Ultimate Skate Guide: To the San Francisco Bay Area.** Todd Ray. LC 95-61280. 224p. (Orig.). 1995. pap. 17.95 (*1-56550-053-9*) Vis Bks Intl.

Ultimate SKS Full Auto Plans. Michael A. Pugliese. (Illus.). 28p. (Orig.). pap. text ed. write for info. (*1-886774-01-3*) M & M Engr.

Ultimate Sleep-Over Book. Kayte Kuch. LC 95-51383. (Illus.). 64p. (J). (gr. 3-7). 1996. pap. 4.95 (*1-56565-325-4*) Lowell Hse Juvenile.

***Ultimate Slumber Party Book.** Douglas Love. LC 96-41807. (Illus.). (J). 1997. pap. 6.95 (*0-688-15259-7*) Morrow.

Ultimate Sniper. John L. Plaster. (Illus.). 464p. 1993. pap. 39.95 (*0-87364-704-1*) Paladin Pr.

Ultimate Soap Opera Guide: The Inside Scoop on Your Favorite Daytime Soaps. Seli Groves. (Illus.). 448p. 1995. 14.95 (*0-7876-0508-5*, 089557) Gale.

Ultimate Solution. Alistair M. Stephen. 1994. 17.95 (*0-533-10865-9*) Vantage.

Ultimate Solution of the American Negro Problem. Edward Eggleston. LC 78-144604. reprint ed. 37.50 (*0-404-00155-6*) AMS Pr.

***Ultimate Soul Music Trivia Book: 501 Questions & Answers about Motown, Rhythm & Blues & More.** Bobby Bennett. 1997. pap. text ed. 9.95 (*0-8065-1923-1*, Citadel Pr) Carol Pub Group.

Ultimate Soup Book: Two Hundred Fifty Soups for Appetizers, Entrees, & Desserts. Julia Older & Steve Sherman. (Illus.). 224p. (Orig.). 1991. pap. 11.95 (*0-452-26609-2*, Plume) NAL-Dutton.

Ultimate Spa Book. Sarnoff P. Martin. 1989. 24.95 (*0-446-51520-5*) Warner Bks.

***Ultimate Spanish Basic.** Crown Publishing Group Staff. 1998. pap. write for info. (*0-609-80247-X*, Living Language) Crown Pub Group.

Ultimate Spider-Man. Stan Lee. 352p. (Orig.). 1996. mass mkt. 5.99 (*1-57297-103-7*) Blvd Books.

Ultimate Spiderman. Stan Lee. 352p. (Orig.). 1994. pap. 12.00 (*0-425-14610-3*, Berkley Trade) Berkley Pub.

Ultimate Sports: Short Stories by Outstanding Writers for Young Adults. Ed. by Donald R. Gallo. LC 94-49610. 320p. (YA). (gr. 7 up). 1995. 15.95 (*0-385-32152-X*, Delacorte Pr Bks) BDD Bks Young Read.

***Ultimate Sports: Short Stories by Outstanding Writers for Young Adults.** Ed. by Donald R. Gallo. 352p. (YA). (gr. 7 up). 1997. mass mkt. 5.99 (*0-440-22707-0*) BDD Bks Young Read.

Ultimate Sports Nutrition: A Scientific Approach to Peak Athletic Performance. Frederick C. Hatfield. (Illus.). 192p. (Orig.). 1987. pap. 15.95 (*0-8092-4887-5*) Contemp Bks.

Ultimate Sports Nutrition Handbook. Ellen Coleman & Suzanne N. Steen. (Illus.). 240p. (Orig.). 1996. pap. 14.95 (*0-923521-34-8*) Bull Pub.

Ultimate Sports Trivia Book: The Official Bar Book of Runyon's Saloon. Jim Benagh. 1991. pap. 8.95 (*0-8065-1273-3*, Citadel Pr) Carol Pub Group.

Ultimate Spy Book. H. Keith Melton. LC 95-44054. 176p. 1996. 29.95 (*0-7894-0443-5*) DK Pub Inc.

Ultimate Stand, Vol. I: Poetic Tales of Deer Hunting from the Pearly Swamp Camp. Mert Cowley. LC 90-84001. (Illus.). 157p. (Orig.). 1990. pap. text ed. 9.95 (*0-9627867-0-5*) Banksiana.

Ultimate Star Trek Quiz Book. Robert Bly. 192p. 1994. pap. 10.00 (*0-06-273321-4*, HarpT) HarpC.

***Ultimate Star Wars Trivia Challenge.** James Hatfield & George D. Burt. 320p. 1997. pap. 14.00 (*1-57566-185-3*, Knsington) Kensgtn Pub Corp.

Ultimate Stock Pickers Guide: 20 Top Experts Pick the Hot Stocks of Tomorrow. Warren Boroson. 228p. 1995. per. 17.95 (*1-55738-823-7*) Irwin Prof Pubng.

Ultimate Stranger: The Autistic Child. rev. ed. Carl H. Delacato. 240p. 1984. reprint ed. pap. 10.00 (*0-87879-446-8*, 446-8) Acad Therapy.

***Ultimate Stress Handbook for Women.** Ursula Markham. LC 96-51515. 160p. 1997. pap. 10.95 (*1-85230-857-5*) Element MA.

Ultimate Success: Laying up Your Treasures in Heaven. David Shibley. LC 93-87258. 176p. 1994. reprint ed. pap. 8.95 (*0-89221-252-7*) New Leaf.

Ultimate Success Manual: How to Lie, Cheat, & Steal Your Way to the Top. Clifford Williams. 3052p. 1997. pap. 15.00 (*0-934274-26-6*) Consumertronics.

***Ultimate Sunflower Book.** Lucy Peel. 1997. write for info. (*0-06-270212-2*) HarpC.

Ultimate Super-Villains. Ed. by Stan Lee. 352p. 1996. pap. 14.00 (*1-57297-113-4*) Blvd Books.

***Ultimate Surrender.** Jill Shalvis. (Loveswept Ser.: Vol. 861). 1997. mass mkt. 3.50 (*0-553-44619-3*, Loveswept) Bantam.

Ultimate Surrender. large type ed. Theresa Charles. 1991. 25.99 (*0-7089-2385-2*) Ulverscroft.

Ultimate Teddy Bear Book. Pauline Cockrill. LC 91-60148. (Illus.). 128p. 1991. 19.95 (*1-879431-06-8*) DK Pub Inc.

Ultimate Teddy Bear Large Blank Journal. Pauline Cockrill. 1992. 6.95 (*1-56458-164-0*) DK Pub Inc.

Ultimate Teddy Bear Sticker Album. Pauline Cockrill. 1992. pap. 6.95 (*1-56458-193-4*) DK Pub Inc.

Ultimate Telecommunications Security Survey. James L. Schaub & Toni Ames. LC 95-18090. 172p. 1995. pap. 44.95 (*0-7506-9691-5*) Buttrwrth-Heinemann.

Ultimate Tennis: A Unique Instructional Guide for All Levels of Play. Al Secunda. (Illus.). 256p. 1993. reprint ed. pap. 19.95 (*0-940279-53-3*) Masters Pr IN.

Ultimate Things: An Orthodox Christian Perspective on the End Times. Dennis Engleman. 302p. (Orig.). 1995. pap. 14.95 (*0-9622713-9-X*) Conciliar Pr.

Ultimate Tiny Book. Jay Cutler & David Field. 1991. ring bd. 89.95 (*0-9629742-0-X*) Separacolor.

Ultimate Training: Gary's Null's Complete Guide to Eating Right, Exercising & Living Longer. Gary Null. LC 92-44033. 1993. pap. 10.95 (*0-312-08796-9*) St Martin.

Ultimate Transformation. 2nd ed. R. P. Kaushik. LC 77-85215. 1977. pap. 8.95 (*0-918038-04-9*) Journey Pubns.

Ultimate Travel Journal. F. Michael & Irene Sisavic. LC 87-81868. 128p. (Orig.). 1987. 19.95 (*0-9619093-1-5*); 44.95 (*0-9619093-2-3*); pap. 9.95 (*0-9619093-0-7*) Florian Group.

Ultimate Treasure Hunt: Finding the Child Inside. Adair N. Renning. (Illus.). 281p. 1996. pap. 19.95 (*0-9648773-0-9*) A Renning.

Ultimate Treasury Child. (J). 1995. pap. 19.95 (*0-7871-0255-5*, Dove Bks) Dove Audio.

Ultimate Trek Trivia Challenge for the Next Generation. James Hatfield & George Burt. 1996. pap. 9.95 (*0-614-97732-0*, Knsington) Kensgtn Pub Corp.

Ultimate Trek Trivia Challenge for the Next Generation. James Hatfield & George Burt. 384p. 1996. pap. 14.00 (*1-57566-063-6*, Knsington) Kensgtn Pub Corp.

***Ultimate Truth: How to Get Out of Dysfunction Instead of in to Recovery.** Geoffrey Hamilton. LC 96-78426. xv, 300p. (Orig.). 1997. pap. 21.95 (*0-9654915-7-9*) Northwoods Cnslting.

***Ultimate Truth: The Light at the End of the Tunnel.** 224p. (Orig.). 1998. pap. 12.95 (*1-56718-322-0*) Llewellyn Pubns.

Ultimate Turkey Hunting. Wade L. Bourne. LC 94-70372. (Illus.). 182p. 1993. pap. text ed. 11.95 (*1-887180-00-1*) Knight & Hale.

Ultimate TV Trivia Book. Vincent Terrace. 207p. (Orig.). 1991. pap. 13.95 (*0-571-12913-7*) Faber & Faber.

Ultimate Unauthorized Game Boy Nintendo. Corey Sandler. 1990. pap. 9.95 (*0-679-79035-7*) Random.

Ultimate Unauthorized Nintendo. Corey Sandler. (J). 1991. pap. 9.95 (*0-679-79090-X*) Random.

Ultimate Unauthorized Nintendo, Vol. 3. Corey Sandler. (J). 1990. pap. 9.95 (*0-679-79051-9*) Random.

Ultimate Unauthorized Nintendo Super NES Game Strategies. Corey Sandler. 1993. pap. 6.99 (*0-679-79001-2*) Random.

***Ultimate Unauthorized Star Wars Trilogy Trivia Challenge.** James Hatfield & George D. Burt. 1997. pap. 14.00 (*0-614-27459-1*, Knsington) Kensgtn Pub Corp.

***Ultimate Unauthorized Stephen King Trivia Challenge.** Robert W. Bly. 304p. 1997. pap. 14.00 (*1-57566-228-0*, Knsington) Kensgtn Pub Corp.

Ultimate USP Is You. Jim Cowden. 192p. 1994. pap. 45.00 (*0-273-60617-4*, Pub. by Pitman Pubng UK) St Mut.

Ultimate Vegetarian Cookbook. Roz Denny. 256p. 1994. 19.98 (*0-8317-9064-4*) Smithmark.

Ultimate Victory: An Exposition of the Book of Revelation. Stanley M. Horton. LC 90-25581. 368p. 1991. kivar 9.95 (*0-88243-710-0*, 02-0710) Gospel Pub.

Ultimate View: The Himalayan Journeys of Samuel Bourne (1863-1866) Clark Worswick. (Illus.). 152p. (Orig.). 1983. 55.00 (*0-940492-05-9*) Asian Conserv Lab.

Ultimate Visions. Martin Forward. 1995. pap. 14.95 (*1-85168-100-0*) Onewrld Pubns.

Ultimate Visual Basic Controls Sourcebook with CD-ROM. Don Kiely. 1995. pap. text ed. 39.99 incl. audio compact disk (*1-883577-49-7*) IDG Bks.

Ultimate Visual Dictionary. LC 94-11173. (Illus.). 640p. 1994. 39.95 (*1-56458-648-0*) DK Pub Inc.

Ultimate Warriors: Dare to Share Your World for Christ. Tom Sirotnak & Kenneth Walker. 192p. 1996. pap. 10.99 (*0-8054-6081-0*, 4260-81) Broadman.

Ultimate Water Garden Book. Jean-Claude Arnoux. (Illus.). 216p. 1996. 39.95 (*1-56158-159-3*, 070288) Taunton.

Ultimate Weapon. Marco Lala. (Illus.). 70p. (Orig.). 1987. pap. 16.95 (*0-939427-82-6*, 05052) Alpha Pubns OH.

Ultimate Weapon. Ben Sloane. (Horn Ser.: No. 4). 1991. mass mkt. 4.50 (*0-373-64004-8*) Harlequin Bks.

Ultimate Weapon X. Larry Hama. (Illus.). 96p. 1995. pap. 8.95 (*0-7851-0131-4*) Marvel Entmnt.

Ultimate Web Developers Sourcebook. Ben Sawyer. 1996. pap. text ed. 49.99 incl. cd-rom (*1-57610-000-6*) Coriolis Grp.

Ultimate Wheel Book. Jack Wiley. (Illus.). 29p. (gr. 7 up). 1988. pap. 6.95 (*0-913999-21-0*) Solipaz Pub Co.

Ultimate Will. Irvin J. Keeys, Jr. 80p. 1994. pap. 7.95 (*0-8059-3509-6*) Dorrance.

Ultimate Wine Book: Everything You Need to Know about Wine Appreciation, Wine with Food & the Latest Health Findings. Bob Shocklely & Robert Mondavi. Ed. by Don W. Martin & Betty W. Martin. (Illus.). 160p. (Orig.). 1993. pap. 8.95 (*0-942053-15-X*) Pine Cone Pr CA.

Ultimate Woman. rev. ed. Bea Basansky. 160p. 1992. reprint ed. pap. 8.95 (*0-9632190-8-1*) Longwood.

***Ultimate Woman Study Guide.** Bea Basansky. pap. 4.00 (*0-9632190-2-2*) Longwood.

Ultimate Word Challenges. J. G. Barton. LC 93-74243. (Illus.). 176p. 1994. pap. 7.95 (*0-940685-48-5*) Cardoza Pub.

Ultimate Workout Journal (for Nautilus Enthusiasts) A Personal Workout Guide. 2nd ed. Joseph Mullen. 150p. 1986. 29.95 (*0-935783-03-2*) Fitness Ctr Info.

Ultimate Workout Log. Suzanne Schlosberg. 1994. pap. 11.95 (*0-395-66599-X*) HM.

Ultimate World. Robert Whitelaw. pap. 1.49 (*0-87377-116-8*) GAM Pubns.

Ultimate Wreath Book: Hundreds of Beautiful Wreaths to Make from Natural Materials. Ellen S. Platt. 246p. 1995. 27.95 (*0-87596-720-5*, Educ Pub Div) Rand McNally.

Ultimate Wreck-Diving Guide. Gary Gentile. (Illus.). 152p. 1992. pap. 20.00 (*0-9621453-4-3*) GGP.

Ultimate X-Calibre. Warren Ellis. (Illus.). 96p. 1995. pap. 8.95 (*0-7851-0132-2*) Marvel Entmnt.
Ultimate X-Man. Jeph Loeb. (Illus.). 96p. 1995. pap. 8.95 (*0-7851-0133-0*) Marvel Entmnt.
Ultimate X-Men. Ed. by Stan Lee. 352p. (YA). 1996. pap. 14.00 (*1-57297-217-3*) Blvd Books.
Ultimate You: With the Personal Magna Carta. George Celia. LC 88-92579. (Illus.). 120p. (Orig.). 1989. 13.95 (*0-9621057-0-8*); pap. 7.95 (*0-9621057-2-4*); lib. bdg. 12.95 (*0-9621057-1-6*) G Celia.
Ultimate 7.62 X 39 mm SKS-AK-47-MAX 90 Muffler Pipe Silencer Plans. Michael A. Pugliese. (Illus.). 28p. (Orig.). pap. text ed. write for info. (*1-886774-00-5*) M & M Engr.
Ultimately Fiction: Design in Modern American Literary Biography. Dennis W. Petrie. LC 80-84578. 250p. 1981. 18.00 (*0-911198-62-8*) Purdue U Pr.
Ultimatum. R. J. Pineiro. 416p. 1995. 5.99 (*0-8125-2400-4*) Tor Bks.
Ultimatum. large type ed. Sally Wentworth. (Magna Large Print Ser.). 1994. 25.99 (*0-7505-0738-1*) Ulverscroft.
***Ultimatum to Mankind: An Unprecedented Social Revolution or Extinction.** Zeev Dickmann. LC 96-95143. 150p. (Orig.). 1997. pap. 15.95 (*0-9655244-1-8*) AIT-ORN Pr.
Ultimaze Book. Rolf Heimann. (Illus.). 32p. (Orig.). (J). (gr. 3-7). 1995. pap. 4.95 (*0-8167-3699-5*, Watermill Pr) Troll Communs.
***Ultimo de la Brigada.** Eugenio Cuevas. (SPA.). pap. 16.00 (*0-89729-568-4*) Ediciones.
Ultimo Desembarco. Vente a Sinapia. Fernando Savater. (Nueva Austral Ser.: Vol. 68). (SPA.). 1991. pap. text ed. 24.95 (*84-239-1868-8*) Elliots Bks.
Ultimo en Tirarse es un Miedoso: Spanish Edition of Last One in Is a Rotten Egg. Leonard Kessler. Tr. by Tomas Gonzales. LC 94-39089. (Ya Se Leer Ser.). (Illus.). 64p. (SPA.). (J). (gr. 1-3). 1995. 14.95 (*0-06-025448-3*, HpArco Iris); pap. 3.75 (*0-06-444194-6*, HpArco Iris) HarpC Child Bks.
Ultimo Giorno di Pomoei & Excerpts from Niobe, Vol. 32. Giovanni Pacini. (Italian Opera II Ser.). 315p. 1987. text ed. 30.00 (*0-8240-6581-6*) Garland.
Ultimo Godo' & the Dynamics of the Urdrama. Susan N. McCrary. 116p. 1990. 27.50 (*0-916379-36-1*) Scripta.
Ultimo Reino. Earl Paulk. Orig. Title: The Ultimate Kingdom. 268p. (Orig.). (SPA.). 1987. pap. 3.50 (*0-917595-19-X*) Kingdom Pubs.
Ultimo Trovador. Carmelo Gariano. LC 91-71262. (Coleccion Teatro). 80p. (Orig.). (SPA.). 1991. pap. 9.95 (*0-89729-601-X*) Ediciones.
Ultimo Vals de los Tiranos Vol. 1: La Profecia. Ed. by Judi Pope. Tr. by Juan M. Castro. x, 139p. (Orig.). (SPA.). pap. 12.00 (*0-9632573-1-5*) Sin Limites.
Ultimo Viaje del Buque Fantasma. deluxe limited ed. Gabriel Garcia Marquez. (Ediciones Especiales y de Bibliofilo Ser.). (Illus.). (SPA.). 1993. 7,500.00 (*84-343-0174-1*) Elliots Bks.
Ultra & the History of the United States. LC 80-52057. 224p. 1980. text ed. 55.00 (*0-313-27072-4*, U7072, Greenwood Pr) Greenwood.
Ultra Black Hair Growth II: Another Six Inches Longer One Year from Now. rev. ed. Cathy Howse. LC 90-90326. 125p. (Orig.). (YA). (gr. 8 up). 1994. pap. 12.95 (*0-9628330-1-0*) UBH Pubns.
Ultra-Clean Technology Handbook Vol. 1: Ultra-Pure Water. T. Ohmi. 944p. 1993. 235.00 (*0-8247-8753-6*) Dekker.
Ultra-Cold Neutrons. R. Golub et al. (Illus.). 320p. 1991. 132.00 (*0-7503-0115-5*) IOP Pub.
Ultra Deep. William H. Lovejoy. 1992. mass mkt. 4.50 (*0-8217-3694-9*, Zebra Kensgtn) Kensgtn Pub Corp.
Ultra-Fashionable Peerage of America. Charlie W. Nichols. LC 75-1864. (Leisure Class in America Ser.). 1975. reprint ed. 16.95 (*0-405-06930-8*) Ayer.
Ultra-Fast Silicon Bipolar Technology. Ed. by L. Treitinger & M. Miura-Mattausch. (Electronics & Photonics Ser.: Vol. 27). (Illus.). ix, 167p. 1989. 53.95 (*0-387-50638-1*) Spr-Verlag.
Ultra-Fast, Ultra-Parallel Optoelectronics. Takanori Okoshi & T. Sueta. 450p. 1996. text ed. 89.95 (*0-471-95665-1*) Wiley.
Ultra Fiche. write for info. (*0-318-57486-1*) West Pub.
Ultra-Fine Particles: Exploratory Science & Technology. Ed. by Chikara Hayashi et al. 650p. 1996. 76.00 (*0-8155-1404-2*) Noyes.
***Ultra Fine Pitch Gears.** T. Macnew. (Technical Papers). (Illus.). (Orig.). 1956. pap. text ed. 30.00 incl. audio compact disk (*1-55589-394-5*) AGMA.
Ultra Guitar Method: Arpeggios, Vol. 4. Michael E. Fletcher. (Illus.). 65p. (Orig.). (C). 1988. pap. text ed. 19.95 (*0-943355-03-6*) Ultra Guitar Pubns.
Ultra Guitar Method: Minor Key Signatures, Vol. 5. Michael E. Fletcher. (Illus.). 65p. (Orig.). (C). 1988. pap. text ed. 19.95 (*0-943355-04-4*) Ultra Guitar Pubns.
Ultra Guitar Method: Progressions, Vol. 2. Michael E. Fletcher. (Illus.). 65p. (Orig.). (C). 1988. pap. text ed. 19.95 (*0-943355-01-X*) Ultra Guitar Pubns.
Ultra Guitar Method: The Power of Pentatonics & Substitution Principles, Vol. 3. Ed. by Michael E. Fletcher. (Illus.). 65p. (Orig.). (C). 1988. pap. text ed. 19.95 (*0-943355-02-8*) Ultra Guitar Pubns.
Ultra Guitar Method: Unlocking the Fingerboard, Vol. 1. Michael E. Fletcher. (Illus.). 63p. (Orig.). (C). 1986. pap. text ed. 19.95 (*0-943355-00-1*) Ultra Guitar Pubns.
Ultra High Dilution: Physiology & Physics. Ed. by P. C. Endler & J. Schulte. LC 93-48594. 280p. (C). 1994. lib. bdg. 130.00 (*0-7923-2676-8*) Kluwer Ac.
Ultra-High Molecular Weight Polyethylene as a Biomaterial in Orthopedic Surgery. Ed. by H. Willert et al. LC 89-24609. 350p. 1991. text ed. 94.00 (*0-920887-60-0*) Hogrefe & Huber Pubs.
Ultra-High Purity Fluid. BCC Staff. 138p. 1989. 2,250.00 (*0-89336-590-4*, C098) BCC.
***Ultra High-Sensitivity Mass Spectrometry with Accelerators.** 178p. 1988. text ed. 80.00 (*0-521-36346-2*) Cambridge U Pr.
Ultra High Temperature Mechanical Testing. Ed. by R. D. Lohr & M. Steen. 234p. 1995. 139.95 (*1-85573-155-X*, 73155X, Pub. by Woodhead Pubng UK) Technomic.
***Ultra-High Temperature Processing of Milk & Milk Products.** H. Burton. (Illus.). 354p. 1988. text ed. 142.95 (*0-7514-0276-1*, Pub. by Blackie Acad & Prof UK) Routledge Chapman & Hall.
Ultra in the Atlantic: The German Naval Grid & Its Cipher, Vol. V. Jeffrey K. Bray. 91p. 1994. pap. 16.80 (*0-89412-240-1*) Aegean Park Pr.
Ultra in the Atlantic Vol. I: Allied Communications Intelligence & Battle of the Atlantic. Jeffrey K. Bray. 99p. 1994. pap. 16.80 (*0-89412-235-5*) Aegean Park Pr.
Ultra in the Atlantic Vol. II: U-Boat Operations. Jeffrey K. Bray. 267p. 1994. pap. 24.80 (*0-89412-236-3*) Aegean Park Pr.
Ultra in the Atlantic Vol. III: German Naval Communications Intelligence. Jeffrey K. Bray. 117p. 1994. pap. 16.80 (*0-89412-237-1*) Aegean Park Pr.
Ultra in the Atlantic Vol. IV: Technical Intelligence from Allied Communications Intelligence. Jeffrey K. Bray. 95p. 1994. pap. 16.80 (*0-89412-238-X*) Aegean Park Pr.
Ultra in the Atlantic Vol. VI: Appendices. Jeffrey K. Bray. 293p. 1994. pap. 24.80 (*0-89412-241-X*) Aegean Park Pr.
Ultra in the Pacific: How Breaking Japanese Codes & Ciphers Affected Naval Operations Against Japan, 1941-45. John Winton. 247p. 1994. 28.95 (*1-55750-856-9*) Naval Inst Pr.
Ultra Klutz, Bk. 1. Jeff Nicholson. (Illus.). 520p. (Orig.). 1996. pap. 29.95 (*1-885047-02-9*) Bad Habit.
***Ultra Large Scale Integration Science & Technology: 6th International Symposium.** Ed. by H. Z. Massoud et al. (Illus.). 678p. 1997. 72.00 (*1-56677-130-7*, PV97-3) Electrochem Soc.
Ultra Light Cookbook: Cooking the No Fat Way for Health & Fitness. Edward A. Wiegleb. 210p. (Orig.). 1997. pap. 14.95 (*0-9643471-1-3*) Faunus Pr.
***Ultra Lounge: The Lexicon of Easy Listening.** Dylan Jones. (Illus.). 160p. 1997. pap. 19.95 (*0-7893-0095-8*) Universe.
***Ultra-Lounge: The Lexicon of Easy Listening.** Dylan Jones. 1997. pap. 20.00 (*0-614-27467-2*) Universe.
Ultra Low Doses. Ed. by Christian Doutremepuich. 180p. 1991. 65.00 (*0-7484-0021-4*, Pub. by Tay Francis Ltd UK) Taylor & Francis.
Ultra Marathoning. Osier. 1984. 14.95 (*0-02-499840-0*, Macmillan Coll) P-H.
Ultra Narrow Row Corn: Squeezing the Most Out of Your Crop. Darrell Bruggink. (Illus.). 48p. (Orig.). 1996. pap. 11.95 (*0-944079-04-0*) Lessiter Pubns.
Ultra Rich: How Much Is too Much? Vance Packard. 1989. 22.95 (*0-316-68752-9*) Little.
Ultra-Ripped Abs. Robert Kennedy. LC 87-10124. (Body Parts Ser.). (Illus.). 128p. (Orig.). 1987. pap. 9.95 (*0-8069-6416-2*) Sterling.
Ultra Secrets of Game Boy Games. Seth Godin. 1991. pap. 3.50 (*0-446-36220-4*) Warner Bks.
Ultra-Solutions: How to Fail Most Successfully. Paul Watzlawick. 1987. 12.95 (*0-393-02514-4*) Norton.
Ultra Teams: Unlocking the Secrets of the New Teamwork Quality Connection. Dartnell Corporation Staff. (High Performance Teams Ser.). 250p. 1995. pap. 13.95 (*0-85013-236-3*) Dartnell Corp.
Ultra Video Incorporated. Wisdom. (MB - Business/Vocational Math Ser.). 1992. pap. 13.95 (*0-538-61164-2*) S-W Pub.
Ultra Violet Spectrometry: Practical Techniques, Instrumentation & Data Handling. T. Frost. (Illus.). 208p. (C). (gr. 13). 1993. text ed. 66.95 (*0-412-40530-X*, A7129) Chapman & Hall.
Ultra-Wideband Coherent Optical LANs. Ed. by S. Forcesi. (Research Reports ESPRIT: Vol. 1). viii, 97p. 1993. 29.95 (*0-387-56885-9*) Spr-Verlag.
Ultra-Wideband Radar: Proceedings First Los Alamos Symposium. 576p. 1991. 148.00 (*0-8493-0198-X*, TK6573) CRC Pr.
Ultra-Wideband Sar Forest Experiment Near Raco, Michigan: April 4-12, 1992. M. Craig Dobson. (University of Michigan Reports: No. TR-029312-1). 70p. reprint ed. pap. 25.00 (*0-7837-4624-5*, 2044347) Bks Demand.
Ultra-Wideband SAR Forest Experiment Near Raco, Michigan: July 1992 Data & Radiative Transfer Model Results. M. Craig Dobson. (University of Michigan Reports: No. 029312-2-F). 62p. reprint ed. pap. 25.00 (*0-7837-6289-5*, 2046004) Bks Demand.
Ultra-Wideband, Short-Pulse Electromagnetics. Ed. by H. L. Bertoni et al. 1993. 115.00 (*0-306-44530-1*, Plenum Pr) Plenum.
***Ultra-Wideband, Short-Pulse Electromagnetics No. 3: Proceedings of the Third International Conference Held in Albuquerque, New Mexico, May 27-31, 1996.** Ed. by Carl E. Baum et al. LC 97-11193. (Illus.). 500p. (C). 1997. 129.50 (*0-306-45593-5*, Plenum Pr) Plenum.
Ultra-Wideband, Short-Pulse Electromagnetics 2: Proceedings of the Second International Conference Held at Weber Research Institute, Polytechnic University, Brooklyn, New York, April 7-9, 1994, Vol. 2. Ed. by Lawrence Carin & Leopold B. Felsen. LC 95-17339. 610p. 1995. 139.50 (*0-306-45002-X*, Plenum Pr) Plenum.
Ultra 3-D Book. W. Mark. 1994. 9.98 (*1-56714-025-4*) Montage Bks.
Ultracapacitors: A Technology That Meets Tomorrow's Portable Power Needs in Autos, Electronics, Communications. (Illus.). 115p. 1996. spiral bd. 850.00 (*1-56217-019-8*) Tech Insights.
Ultracentrifugation, 94. M. D. Lechner. Ed. by F. Kremer et al. (Progress in Colloid & Polymer Science Ser.). 120p. 1994. 68.95 (*0-387-91483-8*) Spr-Verlag.
Ultraclean Semiconductor Processing Technology & Surface Chemical Cleaning & Passivation. Ed. by M. Liehr et al. (Symposium Proceedings Ser.: Vol. 386). 411p. 1995. text ed. 68.00 (*1-55899-289-8*) Materials Res.
***Ultracold Atoms & Bose-Einstein-Condensation: Trends in Optics & Photonics.** Ed. by Keith Burnett. LC 96-69617. (TOPS Ser.: Vol. 7, 1996). 300p. (Orig.). 1996. pap. 55.00 (*1-55752-465-3*) Optical Soc.
Ultradian Rhythms in Life Processes: An Inquiry into Fundamental Principles of Chronobiology & Psychobiology. Ed. by David Lloyd & Ernest L. Rossi. LC 92-2298. xiii, 419p. 1992. 227.95 (*0-387-19746-X*) Spr-Verlag.
Ultrafast Diode Lasers: Fundamentals & Applications. Peter Vasil'ev. LC 95-6095. 271p. 1995. 89.00 (*0-89006-736-8*) Artech Hse.
Ultrafast Dynamics of Chemical Systems. Ed. by John D. Simon. (Understanding Chemical Reactivity Ser.). 392p. (C). 1994. lib. bdg. 208.00 (*0-7923-2489-7*) Kluwer Ac.
Ultrafast Electronics & Optoelectronics. LC 95-67797. (1995 Technical Digest Ser.: Vol. 13). 222p. (Orig.). 1995. pap. 75.00 (*1-55752-398-3*) Optical Soc.
Ultrafast Electronics & Optoelectronics. Ed. by Jagdeep Shah & Umesh Mishra. (Proceedings Ser.: Vol. 14). 300p. (Orig.). 1993. lib. bdg. 75.00 (*1-55752-275-8*) Optical Soc.
Ultrafast Fiber Switching Devices & Systems. Mohammed N. Islam. LC 92-5531. (Cambridge Studies in Modern Optics: No. 12). (Illus.). 200p. (C). 1992. text ed. 59.95 (*0-521-43191-3*) Cambridge U Pr.
***Ultrafast Magnetic Resonance Imaging.** Matthijs Oedkerk et al. 400p. (Orig.). 1997. pap. text ed. 125.00 (*0-632-04179-X*) Blackwell Sci.
Ultrafast Phenomena. LC 89-64033. (Technical Digest Series, 1990: Vol. 6). 350p. 1990. lib. bdg. 75.00 (*1-55752-130-1*) Optical Soc.
Ultrafast Phenomena. LC 94-65351. (Nineteen Ninety-Four Technical Digest Ser.: Vol. 7). 300p. 1994. pap. 75.00 (*1-55752-339-8*) Optical Soc.
***Ultrafast Phenomena.** LC 95-72762. (Technical Digest Ser.: No. 8). 464p. (Orig.). 1996. pap. 75.00 (*1-55752-441-6*) Optical Soc.
Ultrafast Phenomena Eight: Proceedings of the Eight International Conference, Antibes Juan-les-Pins, France, June 8-12, 1992. Ed. by J. L. Martin et al. LC 93-12330. (Chemical Physics Ser.: Vol. 55). 1993. Alk. paper. 99.00 (*0-387-56475-6*) Spr-Verlag.
Ultrafast Phenomena in Spectroscopy: Proceedings of the Sixth International Symposium, Neubrandenburg, German Democratic Republic, August 23-27, 1989. Ed. by E. Klose & B. Wilhelmi. (Proceedings in Physics Ser.: Vol. 49). (Illus.). 304p. 1990. 81.00 (*0-387-52781-8*) Spr-Verlag.
Ultrafast Phenomena in Spectroscopy: Proceedings of the 5th International Symposium. Ed. by Z. Rudzikas et al. 536p. (C). 1988. text ed. 138.00 (*9971-5-0616-5*) World Scientific Pub.
Ultrafast Phenomena IV. Ed. by D. H. Auston & Kenneth B. Eisenthal. (Chemical Physics Ser.: Vol. 38). (Illus.). xvi, 509p. 1984. 71.00 (*0-387-13834-X*) Spr-Verlag.
Ultrafast Phenomena IX: Proceedings of the 9th International Conference, Dana Point, CA, May 1-5, 1994. Paul F. Barbara. LC 94-39999. (Series in Chemical Physics: Vol. 60). 1994. 119.95 (*3-540-58455-2*) Spr-Verlag.
Ultrafast Phenomena V, Vol. 46. Ed. by G. R. Fleming & A. E. Siegman. (Chemical Physics Ser.). (Illus.). 575p. 1986. 79.95 (*0-387-17077-4*) Spr-Verlag.
Ultrafast Phenomena VI. Ed. by T. Yajima et al. (Chemical Physics Ser.: Vol. 48). (Illus.). 640p. 1988. 93.95 (*0-387-50469-9*) Spr-Verlag.
Ultrafast Phenomena VII: Proceedings of the International Conference, 7th, Monterey, CA, Held May 14-17, 1990, Vol. 53. Ed. by C. B. Harris et al. (Chemical Physics Ser.). (Illus.). 576p. 1990. 86.95 (*0-387-53049-5*) Spr-Verlag.
***Ultrafast Phenomena X: Proceedings of the 10th International Conference, Del Coronado, CA, May 28-June 1, 1996.** Paul F. Barbara & J. G. Fujimoto. LC 96-35229. (Springer Series in Chemical Physics: Vol. 62). (Illus.). 473p. 1996. 109.00 (*3-540-61704-3*) Spr-Verlag.
Ultrafast Processes in Chemistry & Photobiology. Ed. by I. Tanaka et al. LC 94-30827. (Chemistry in the 21st Century Monograph). (Illus.). 300p. 1995. 79.50 (*0-86542-893-X*) Blackwell Sci.
***Ultrafast Processes in Spectroscopy: Proceedings of the Ninth International Conference Held in Trieste, Italy, October 30-November 3, 1995.** Ed. by Orazio Svelto et al. LC 96-43801. 666p. 1997. 149.50 (*0-306-45481-5*) Plenum.
Ultrafast Processes in Spectroscopy 1991: Proceedings of the Seventh International Symposium, Bayreuth, 1991. Ed. by A. Laubereau & A. Seilmeier. (Illus.). 688p. 1992. 284.00 (*0-7503-0198-8*) IOP Pub.
Ultrafast Reaction Dynamics & Solvent Effects. Yann Goudel & Peter J. Rossley. (AIP Conference Proceedings Ser.: No. 298). 500p. 1994. text ed. 571.00 (*1-56396-280-2*) Am Inst Physics.
Ultrafiltration Handbook. Munir Cheryan. LC 86-50330. 369p. 1986. 69.95 (*0-87762-456-9*) Technomic.
Ultrafine Particles: Proceedings of the Symposium, Indianapolis, 1961. Electrochemical Society, Ultrafine Particles Symposium Staff. Ed. by W. E. Kuhn. LC 63-20239. (Electrochemical Society Ser.). 574p. reprint ed. pap. 163.60 (*0-317-11065-9*, 2007076) Bks Demand.
***Ultrafit Older Cat.** Claire Bessant & Bradley Viner. LC 96-43186. 1997. 10.95 (*0-8120-9856-0*) Barron.
Ultrahigh-Pressure Metamorphic Rocks in the Dabieshan-Sulu Region of China. Po-Lin Tsung. Ed. by Cong Bolin. LC 96-28668. (Petrology & Structural Geology Ser.). 240p. (C). 1997. lib. bdg. 110.00 (*0-7923-4163-5*) Kluwer Ac.
Ultrahigh Pressure Metamorphism. Ed. by Robert G. Coleman & Xiaomin Wang. (Cambridge Topics in Petrology Ser.: No. 1). (Illus.). 500p. (C). 1995. text ed. 85.00 (*0-521-43214-6*) Cambridge U Pr.
Ultrahigh Resolution Chromatography. Ed. by Satinder Ahuja. LC 84-2792. (ACS Symposium Ser.: No. 250). 237p. 1984. lib. bdg. 49.95 (*0-8412-0835-2*) Am Chemical.
***Ultrahigh Resolution Chromatography.** Ed. by Satinder Ahuja. LC 84-2792. (ACS Symposium Ser.: No. 250). (Illus.). 240p. 1984. reprint ed. pap. 68.40 (*0-608-03134-8*, 2063587) Bks Demand.
Ultraje, un Crimen Que No Cometi. Roberto A. Aviles & Gloria Velazquez. 137p. (Orig.). (SPA.). 1991. pap. 6.99 (*0-9630423-0-0*) R A Aviles.
Ultralight Aircraft Log. deluxe ed. 1981. pap. 5.95 (*0-317-01150-2*, A-1) Markowski Intl.
Ultralight Airmanship: How to Master the Air in an Ultralight. Jack Lambie. Ed. by Michael A. Markowski. LC 81-71888. (Ultralight Aviation Ser.: No. 2). (Illus.). 144p. (Orig.). 1984. pap. 11.95 (*0-938716-02-6*) Markowski Intl.
Ultralight Boatbuilding. Thomas J. Hill. (Illus.). 134p. 1987. pap. text ed. 19.95 (*0-87742-244-3*) Intl Marine.
Ultralight Boatbuilding. Thomas J. Hill. 1987. pap. text ed. 19.95 (*0-07-156703-8*) McGraw.
Ultralight Flight: The Pilot's Handbook of Ultralight Knowledge. Michael A. Markowski. LC 81-71889. (Ultralight Aviation Ser.: No. 3). (Illus.). 206p. (Orig.). 1984. 20.95 (*0-938716-07-7*); pap. 14.95 (*0-938716-06-9*) Markowski Intl.
Ultralight Pilot Flight Log. deluxe ed. 1981. pap. 5.95 (*0-317-01149-9*, P-1) Markowski Intl.
Ultralight Pilot's Flight Training Manual. Curtis Hughs. (Illus.). 260p. (Orig.). (C). 1995. pap. text ed. 24.95 (*1-885703-00-7*) A-I Prods.
Ultralight Spin-Fishing: A Practical Guide for Freshwater & Saltwater Anglers. Peter F. Cammann. (Illus.). 160p. (Orig.). 1994. pap. 12.00 (*0-88150-301-0*) Countryman.
Ultralight Training Manual. 24.95 (*0-614-13161-8*, 21-51248) EAA Aviation.
UltraMacros Primer. Ed. by Warren Williams & Cathleen Merritt. 250p. 1989. pap. 19.95 (*0-9620807-3-X*) Natl AppleWrks.
Ultramafic & Related Rocks. Ed. by Peter J. Wyllie. LC 78-12080. 484p. (Orig.). 1979. reprint ed. 52.50 (*0-88275-755-5*) Krieger.
Ultramafic Rocks of the Appalachian Piedmont. Ed. by S. K. Mittwede & E. F. Stoddard. (Special Papers: No. 231). 110p. 1989. pap. 7.00 (*0-8137-2231-4*) Geol Soc.
Ultramarine. Raymond Carver. LC 86-10221. 128p. 1986. 14.95 (*0-394-55379-9*) Random.
Ultramarine. Raymond Carver. LC 87-40081. 160p. 1987. pap. 12.00 (*0-394-75535-9*, Publishers Media) Random.
Ultramicroelectrodes. Martin Fleischmann et al. (Illus.). 363p. (C). 1987. 44.95 (*0-9618927-0-6*) Datatech Systems.
Ultramicroelectrodes. Martin Fleischmann et al. (Illus.). 363p. (C). 1988. lib. bdg. 44.95 (*0-9618927-1-4*) Datatech Systems.
Ultramicroelectrodes. Debra R. Rolison. 363p. 1987. 75.00 (*0-614-04931-8*) Electrosyn Co.
UltraModern: The Art of Contemporary Brazil. Aracy A. Amaral & Paulo Herkenhoff. (Illus.). 128p. 1993. 34.95 (*0-318-70269-X*); pap. text ed. 21.95 (*0-940979-24-1*) Natl Museum Women.
Ultramodern Firearms. Charles Ryan. (Illus.). 176p. (Orig.). 1993. pap. 20.00 (*0-9628748-4-1*) Chameleon Eclectic.
***Ultramoderne Organisationstheorien: Management im Kontext des Sozial- & Naturwissenschaftlichen Paradigmenwechsels.** Martin Heinl. (Illus.). 518p. (GER.). 1996. 82.95 (*3-631-50059-9*) P Lang Pubng.
Ultrapure Chemicals & Water for the Semiconductor Industry. 1992. 1,950.00 (*0-89336-873-3*, C-152) BCC.
***Ultrapure Materials for the Semiconductor Industry.** (Report Ser.: No. C-152R). 166p. 1996. 2,650.00 (*1-56965-049-7*) BCC.
Ultrapurity: Methods & Techniques. Ed. by Morris Zief et al. LC 72-179387. (Illus.). 719p. reprint ed. pap. 180.00 (*0-317-07978-6*, 2055009) Bks Demand.
Ultrarelativistic Heavy Ion Collisions. Gordon Baym & McLerran. 352p. 1988. 43.25 (*0-201-15670-9*) Addison-Wesley.
Ultrashort Laser Pulse Phenomena: Fundamentals, Techniques, & Applications on a Femtosecond Time Scale. Jean-Claude Diels & Wolfgang Rudolph. (Optics & Photonics Ser.). (Illus.). 581p. 1996. text ed. 95.00 (*0-12-215492-4*) Acad Pr.
Ultrashort Laser Pulses: Generation & Applications. 2nd ed. Ed. by W. A. Kaiser. LC 92-37219. (Topics in Applied Physics Ser.: Vol. 60). 1993. 75.95 (*0-387-55877-2*) Spr-Verlag.
Ultrashort Laser Pulses & Applications. Ed. by W. A. Kaiser. (Topics in Applied Physics Ser.: Vol. 60). (Illus.). 440p. 1988. 99.00 (*0-387-18605-0*) Spr-Verlag.
Ultrashort Processes in Condensed Matter. Ed. by W. E. Bron. (NATO ASI Series B, Physics: Vol. 314). (Illus.). 400p. (C). 1992. 115.00 (*0-306-44574-3*, Plenum Pr) Plenum.

UV

Ultrasoft X-Ray Microscopy: Its Application to Biological & Physical Sciences. Ed. by Donald F. Parsons. (Annals Ser.: Vol. 342). 402p. 1980. 72.00 (*0-89766-066-8*); pap. 72.00 (*0-89766-067-6*) NY Acad Sci.

Ultrasonic Absorption: An Introduction to the Theory of Sound Absorption & Dispersion in Gases, Liquids & Solids. A. B. Bhatia. 440p. 1985. reprint ed. pap. 11.95 (*0-486-64917-2*) Dover.

Ultrasonic Bioinstrumentation. Douglas Christenson. LC 87-34066. 256p. 1988. text ed. 57.50 (*0-471-60496-8*) Wiley.

Ultrasonic Diagnosis of Cerebrovascular Disease. Ed. by Merrill P. Spencer. (Developments in Cardiovascular Medicine Ser.). 1987. lib. bdg. 171.00 (*0-89838-836-8*) Kluwer Ac.

Ultrasonic Diagnosis of Digestive Diseases. 4th rev. ed. Francis S. Weill. LC 95-39184. 760p. 1996. 198.00 (*3-540-60412-X*) Spr-Verlag.

Ultrasonic Energy: Biological Investigations & Medical Applications. Ed. by Elizabeth Kelly. LC 65-10078. (Illus.). 396p. reprint ed. 112.90 (*0-8357-9701-5*, 2019048) Bks Demand.

Ultrasonic Examination of the Breast. International Congress on the Ultrasonic Examination of the Breast (3rd: 1983: Tokyo, Japan) Staff. LC 83-17092. (Illus.). 397p. reprint ed. pap. 113.20 (*0-8357-3826-4*, 2036550) Bks Demand.

Ultrasonic Exposimetry. Ed. by Marvin C. Ziskin & Peter A. Lewin. 480p. 1992. 243.00 (*0-8493-6436-1*, RC78) CRC Pr.

Ultrasonic Fatigue: Proceedings of the First International Conference on Fatigue & Corrosion Fatigue up to Ultrasonic Frequencies Held October 25-30, 1981, at Seven Springs Resort, Champion, PA. International Conference on Fatigue & Corrosion Fatigue up to Ultrasonic Frequencies Staff. Ed. by Joseph M. Wells et al. LC 82-61407. 679p. reprint ed. pap. 180.00 (*0-8357-2527-8*, 2052404) Bks Demand.

Ultrasonic Imaging & Animal Reproduction, Bk. 1, Fundamentals. O. J. Ginther. (Illus.). 225p. (C). 1995. 45.00 (*0-9640072-3-1*) Equisrvs Pubng.

Ultrasonic Imaging & Animal Reproduction, Bk. 2, Horses. O. J. Ginther. 375p. 1995. 75.00 (*0-9640072-4-X*) Equisrvs Pubng.

Ultrasonic Inspection & Failure Analysis of Expansion Bellows Pub. No. 28. MTI Staff. (Illus.). 36p. 1987. 24.00 (*0-614-02634-2*) NACE Intl.

Ultrasonic Measurement of Weld Flaw Size. (National Cooperative Highway Research Program Report Ser.: No. 242). 76p. 1981. 8.00 (*0-309-03302-0*) Transport Res Bd.

Ultrasonic Measurements for Process Control: Theory, Techniques, Applications. Lawrence C. Lynnworth. 694p. 1989. text ed. 146.00 (*0-12-460585-0*) Acad Pr.

Ultrasonic Methods in Evaluation of Inhomogeneous Materials. Ed. by Adriano Alippi & Walter G. Mayer. (C). 1987. lib. bdg. 208.50 (*90-247-3490-8*) Kluwer Ac.

***Ultrasonic Methods of Non-Destructive Testing.** J. Blitz & G. Simpson. (Engineering NDE Ser.). (Illus.). 280p. 1996. text ed. 90.00 (*0-412-60470-1*, Chap & Hall NY) Chapman & Hall.

Ultrasonic Motors: Theory & Applications. S. Ueha & Y. Tomikawa. (Monographs in Electrical & Electronic Engineering: No. 29). (Illus.). 352p. 1994. 110.00 (*0-19-859376-7*) OUP.

Ultrasonic Physics & Instrumentation. Beth Anderhub & O'Brien Anderhub. (Illus.). 304p. 1988. pap. text ed. write for info. (*0-316-03918-7*, Little Med Div) Little.

Ultrasonic Scattering in Biological Tissues. Shung & Thieme. 512p. 1992. 224.95 (*0-8493-6568-6*, QP82) CRC Pr.

Ultrasonic Sensors for Chemical & Process Plant. R. C. Asher. (Illus.). 350p. 1997. 127.50 (*0-7503-0361-1*) IOP Pub.

Ultrasonic Signal Processing. Ed. by A. Alippi. 594p. (C). 1989. text ed. 151.00 (*9971-5-0864-8*) World Scientific Pub.

Ultrasonic Spectral Analysis for Nondestructive Evaluation. Dale Fitting & Laszlo Adler. LC 80-14991. 364p. 1981. 105.00 (*0-306-40484-2*, Plenum Pr) Plenum.

Ultrasonic Surgical Techniques for the Pelvic Surgeon. Ed. by Janet S. Rader & Neil B. Rosenhein. LC 94-21216. (Illus.). 112p. 1994. 76.00 (*0-387-94244-0*) Spr-Verlag.

***Ultrasonic Techniques for Fluids Characterization.** M. J. W. Povey. LC 97-9788. 1997. write for info. (*0-12-563730-6*) Acad Pr.

Ultrasonic Testing Classroom Training Book. (Classroom Training Handbook Ser.). 207p. 1980. 17.50 (*0-318-17237-2*, 1610) Am Soc Nondestructive.

Ultrasonic Testing of Materials. 4th rev. ed. J. Krautkramer & H. Krautkramer. (Illus.). 688p. 1990. 219.95 (*0-387-51231-4*) Spr-Verlag.

Ultrasonic Testing of Steel Castings. 1976. 20.00 (*0-686-44985-1*) Steel Founders.

Ultrasonic Tissue Characterization. Ed. by F. Dunn et al. (Illus.). 250p. 1996. 139.00 (*4-431-70162-1*) Spr-Verlag.

Ultrasonic Tissue Characterization. Ed. by J. M. Thijsen & D. Nicholas. 1982. lib. bdg. 93.00 (*90-247-2757-X*) Kluwer Ac.

Ultrasonic Tomography in Obstetrics & Gynaecology. E. G. Loch. (Advances in Obstetrics & Gynaecology Ser.: Vol. 51). (Illus.). 1973. 39.25 (*3-8055-1585-5*) S Karger.

Ultrasonic Transducer Materials. Ed. by Oskar E. Mattiat. LC 71-131885. 186p. 1971. 69.50 (*0-306-30501-1*, Plenum Pr) Plenum.

***Ultrasonic Transducers: August 82 - November 87.** Engineering Index Staff. 85.00 (*0-614-18504-1*, 135P31) Info Gatekeepers.

***Ultrasonic Transducers: December 87 - December 89.** Engineering Index Staff. 85.00 (*0-614-18505-X*, 135P32) Info Gatekeepers.

***Ultrasonic Transducers: January 70 - February 90.** NTIS Staff. 85.00 (*0-614-18506-8*, 135P43) Info Gatekeepers.

Ultrasonics. Arthur P. Cracknell. 200p. 1980. pap. 29.00 (*0-85109-770-7*) Taylor & Francis.

Ultrasonics. Arthur P. Cracknell & J. L. Clark. LC 79-26250. (Wykeham Science Ser.: No. 55). 200p. (C). 1980. pap. 18.00 (*0-8448-1330-3*, Crane Russak) Taylor & Francis.

Ultrasonics: The Low & High-Intensity Applications. 2nd rev. ed. Ensminger. (Mechanical Engineering Ser.: Vol. 65). 600p. 1988. 155.00 (*0-8247-7659-3*) Dekker.

Ultrasonics: The Low & High-Intensity Applications. Dale Ensminger. LC 72-90963. (Illus.). 587p. reprint ed. pap. 167.30 (*0-317-07982-4*, 2055005) Bks Demand.

Ultrasonics as a Medical Diagnostic Tool. Ed. by J. I. DiStasio. LC 79-26029. (Radiology Review Ser.: No. 1). (Illus.). 330p. 1980. 32.00 (*0-8155-0785-2*) Noyes.

Ultrasonics Business, What's It All about? Where Are the Opportunities. Miller & Nicholson. (Illus.). 182p. 1995. 2,650.00 (*0-614-03440-X*, GB123) BCC.

***Ultrasonics for Engineering NDE.** Ludwig. (Engineering NDE Ser.). (C). (gr. 13 up). 1997. text ed. write for info. (*0-412-46310-5*) Chapman & Hall.

Ultrasonics in Early Pregnancy: Diagnostic Scanning & Fetal Motor Activity. E. Reinold. Ed. by P. J. Keller. (Contributions to Gynecology & Obstetrics Ser.: Vol. 1). 1976. 47.25 (*3-8055-2332-7*) S Karger.

Ultrasonics in the Chemical Industry. Vladimir A. Nosov. LC 64-23248. (Soviet Progress in Applied Ultrasonics Ser.: Vol. 2). 171p. reprint ed. pap. 48.80 (*0-317-10629-5*, 2020692) Bks Demand.

Ultrasonics of Snow. Isobel Thrilling. 72p. (C). 1988. pap. 30.00 (*0-947612-09-2*, Pub. by Rivelin Grapheme Pr) St Mut.

Ultrasonography: An Introduction to Normal Structure & Functional Anatomy. Ed. by Reva A. Curry & Betty B. Tempkin. LC 93-26475. (Illus.). 800p. 1995. text ed. 68.00 (*0-7216-4585-2*) Saunders.

***Ultrasonography: An Introduction to Normal Structure & Functional Anatomy.** Ed. by Reva A. Curry & Betty B. Tempkin. (Illus.). 1995. teacher ed. write for info. (*0-7216-4748-0*) Saunders.

***Ultrasonography for Surgeons.** Meyers. Date not set. text ed. write for info. (*0-7216-7236-1*) Saunders.

Ultrasonography in Infants & Children. Teele & Share. (Illus.). 528p. 1991. text ed. 135.00 (*0-7216-8775-X*) Saunders.

Ultrasonography in Obstetrics & Gynecology. 3rd ed. Ed. by Peter W. Callen. LC 93-6621. (Illus.). 736p. 1993. text ed. 87.00 (*0-7216-6712-0*) Saunders.

Ultrasonography in Ophthalmology. Ed. by J. M. Thijssen & A. M. Verbeek. 1981. lib. bdg. 275.00 (*90-6193-724-8*) Kluwer Ac.

Ultrasonography in Ophthalmology II: Proceedings of the 11th SIDUO Congress, Capri 1986. Ed. by J. M. Thijssen et al. (Documenta Ophthalmologica Proceedings Ser.). (C). 1988. lib. bdg. 197.00 (*0-89838-378-1*) Kluwer Ac.

Ultrasonography in Ophthalmology 12. Ed. by R. Sampaolesi. (Documenta Ophthalmologica Proceedings Ser.). (C). 1990. lib. bdg. 252.00 (*0-7923-0765-8*) Kluwer Ac.

Ultrasonography in Ophthalmology 14: Proceedings of the 14th SIDUO Congress, Tokyo, Japan 1992. Ed. by J. M. Thijssen et al. LC 95-14247. (Documenta Ophthalmologica Proceedings Ser.: Vol. 58). 324p. (C). 1995. lib. bdg. 125.00 (*0-7923-3475-2*) Kluwer Ac.

***Ultrasonography in Ophthalmology 15.** G. Cennamo. LC 97-231. (Documenta Ophthalmologicia Proceedings Ser.). 1997. text ed. write for info. (*0-7923-4464-2*) Kluwer Ac.

Ultrasonography of the Spleen. J. N. Bruneton et al. (Illus.). 120p. 1988. 86.95 (*0-387-18595-X*) Spr-Verlag.

Ultrasonography on Ophthalmology, Siduo 5: Proceedings of the International Society for Ultrasonic Diagnosis in Ophthalmology, Ghent, May, 1973. International Society for Ultrasonic Diagnosis in Ophthalmology Staff. Ed. by J. Francois & F. Goes. (Bibliotheca Ophthalmologica Ser.: Vol. 83). (Illus.). 450p. 1975. 141.00 (*3-8055-1777-7*) S Karger.

Ultrasonography Quick Reference. Hagen & Ansert. 64p. (gr. 13). 1994. pap. text ed. 11.95 (*0-8016-7949-4*) Mosby Yr Bk.

***Ultrasound.** (Environmental Health Criteria Ser.: No. 22). 199p. 1982. pap. text ed. 26.00 (*92-4-154082-6*, 1160022) World Health.

Ultrasound. Alfred B. Kurtz & William D. Middleton. (Requisites Ser.). 1995. write for info. (*0-8016-8096-4*) Taylor & Francis.

Ultrasound: A Pattern Approach. Patricia L. Abbitt. (Illus.). 472p. 1994. text ed. 125.00 (*0-07-000031-X*) McGraw-Hill HPD.

Ultrasound: Biological Effects & Potential Hazards. A. R. Williams. (Medical Physics Ser.). 1983. text ed. 128.00 (*0-12-756960-X*) Acad Pr.

Ultrasound: Its Chemical, Physical, & Biological Effects. Kenneth S. Suslick. LC 87-28050. 336p. 1988. 75.00 (*0-89573-328-5*, VCH) Wiley.

Ultrasound: Medical Applications, Biological Effects, & Hazard Potential. Ed. by M. H. Repacholi et al. 386p. 1987. 89.50 (*0-306-42411-8*, Plenum Pr) Plenum.

Ultrasound: Physical, Chemical, & Biological Effects (Authorized Translation from the Russian) by F. L. Sinclair. Isaak E Imovich El Piner. LC 64-7760. 381p. reprint ed. pap. 108.60 (*0-317-08454-2*, 2003361) Bks Demand.

Ultrasound - Medical Sonography: Clinical Manual. Lynn Ross & Robert J. Parelli. 124p. (C). 1991. text ed. 35.00 (*1-880359-03-0*) Par Rad.

Ultrasound & Ballistocardiography in Cardiovascular Research: Proceedings of the Ballistocardiography & Cardiovascular Dynamics Congress, 3rd World, 9th European, Sofia, 1973. Ballistocardiographic Research Society Staff. Ed. by Jan Baan. (Bibliotheca Cardiologica Ser.: No. 34). (Illus.). 120p. 1974. 43.25 (*3-8055-1763-7*) S Karger.

Ultrasound & Doppler Imaging of the Acutely Ill Patient: Course Syllabus. Date not set. 57.00 (*0-614-14619-4*) Am Inst Ultrasound.

Ultrasound & Early Pregnancy. Ed. by D. Jurkovic & E. Juaniaux. LC 95-33638. (Progress in Obstetric & Gynecological Sonography Ser.). (Illus.). 150p. 1996. text ed. 78.00 (*1-85070-615-8*) Prthnon Pub.

***Ultrasound & the Endometrium.** S. Granberg. Ed. by A. C. Fleischer & Asim Kurjak. LC 97-2669. (Progress in Obstetric & Gynecological Sonography Ser.). (Illus.). 200p. 1997. 78.00 (*1-85070-906-8*) Prthnon Pub.

Ultrasound & the Fallopian Tube. Ed. by Ilan E. Timor-Tritsch & Asim Kurjak. (Progress in Obstetric & Gynecological Sonography Ser.). (Illus.). 140p. 1996. text ed. 78.00 (*1-85070-616-6*) Prthnon Pub.

Ultrasound & the Fetal Brain. Ed. by Frank A. Chervenak et al. LC 95-23988. (Progress in Obstetric & Gynecological Sonography Ser.). (Illus.). 150p. 1995. text ed. 78.00 (*1-85070-612-3*) Prthnon Pub.

***Ultrasound & the Fetal Heart.** Ed. by Juri W. Wladimiroff & G. Pilu. LC 96-3059. (Progress in Obstetric & Gynecological Sonography Ser.). (Illus.). 150p. 1996. text ed. 78.00 (*1-85070-617-4*) Prthnon Pub.

Ultrasound & the Ovary. Ed. by Asim Kurjak. LC 94-2029. (Progress in Obstetric & Gynecological Sonography Ser.: Vol. 1). 1994. 78.00 (*1-85070-508-9*) Prthnon Pub.

Ultrasound & the Uterus. R. Osmers & Asim Kurjak. (Progress in Obstetric & Gynecological Sonography Ser.). (Illus.). 150p. (C). 1995. text ed. 78.00 (*1-85070-613-1*) Prthnon Pub.

Ultrasound Angioplasty. Ed. by Robert J. Siegel. (Developments in Cardiovascular Medicine Ser.: Vol. 178). 304p. 1996. lib. bdg. 205.00 (*0-7923-3722-0*) Kluwer Ac.

Ultrasound Annual, 1982. fac. ed. Ed. by Roger C. Sanders. LC 84-10324. (Illus.). 363p. 1982. pap. 103.50 (*0-7837-7502-4*, 2047004) Bks Demand.

Ultrasound Annual 1983. Ed. by Roger C. Sanders & Michael C. Hill. (Illus.). 332p. 1983. reprint ed. pap. 94.70 (*0-7837-7124-X*, 2046953) Bks Demand.

Ultrasound Annual, 1984. fac. ed. Ultrasound Annual Staff. Ed. by Roger C. Sanders & Michael C. Hill. LC 84-10324. (Illus.). 302p. 1984. pap. 86.10 (*0-7837-7184-3*, 2047115) Bks Demand.

***Ultrasound Annual, 1985.** Ed. by Roger C. Sanders & Michael C. Hill. LC 84-10324. 381p. 1985. reprint ed. pap. 108.60 (*0-608-03446-0*, 2064147) Bks Demand.

Ultrasound Annual, 1986. Ed. by Roger C. Sanders & Michael C. Hill. LC 84-10324. 280p. 1986. reprint ed. pap. 79.80 (*0-608-00393-X*, 2061107) Bks Demand.

Ultrasound Atlas of Disease Processes. Carol A. Krebs. (Illus.). 432p. (C). 1993. text ed. 170.00 (*0-8385-9245-7*, A9245-0) Appleton & Lange.

Ultrasound Atlas of Fetal Malformations. Nyberg. 792p. (C). (gr. 13). 1989. text ed. 210.00 (*0-8151-6439-4*, Yr Bk Med Pubs) Mosby Yr Bk.

Ultrasound Biomicroscopy of the Eye. Charles J. Pavlin & F. Stuart Foster. LC 93-40948. (Illus.). 164p. 1994. 110.00 (*0-387-94206-8*) Spr-Verlag.

Ultrasound Diagnosis in Obstetrics & Gynecology. M. Hansmann et al. Ed. by B. K. Wittman. Tr. by Terry C. Telger from GER. (Illus.). 480p. 1986. 352.00 (*0-387-15348-9*) Spr-Verlag.

Ultrasound Diagnosis of Breast Disease. Eriko Tohno et al. (Illus.). 160p. 1994. text ed. 99.00 (*0-443-04387-6*) Churchill.

Ultrasound Diagnosis of Cerebrovascular Disease: Doppler Sonography of the Extra- & Intracranial Arteries Duplex Scanning. Gerhard-Michael Von Reutern & Hans J. Von Budingen. Tr. by T. C. Telger. LC 93-28853. 397p. 1993. 165.00 (*0-86577-457-9*) Thieme Med Pubs.

Ultrasound Eighty-two. Lerski & Morley. (Ultrasound in Medicine & Biology). 1983. pap. 8.65 (*0-08-030769-8*, Pergamon Pr) Elsevier.

Ultrasound Exam Review: Sonographer's Self-Assessment Guide. 2nd ed. Marveen Craig et al. LC 93-41354. (Illus.). 400p. 1994. pap. text ed. 35.95 (*0-397-55021-9*) Lppncott-Raven.

Ultrasound for Midwifery. Proud. 1994. 22.50 (*1-898507-03-1*) Buttrwrth-Heinemann.

Ultrasound for Surgeons. Ed. by Junji Machi & Bernard Sigel. LC 96-9300. (Illus.). 368p. 1996. 98.50 (*0-89640-321-1*) Igaku-Shoin.

Ultrasound for the Surgeon. Ed. by Edgar D. Staren & Maurice E. Arregui. 352p. 1996. text ed. 99.00 (*0-397-51587-1*) Lppncott-Raven.

Ultrasound Handbook: Clinical, Etiologic, Pathologic Implications of Sonographic Findings. 2nd ed. Rebecca Hall. LC 92-49534. 320p. 1993. spiral bd. 28.95 (*0-397-55029-4*) Lppncott-Raven.

Ultrasound Imaging: Liver, Spleen, Pancreas. David O. Cosgrove & V. Ralph McCready. 377p. 1982. text ed. 515.00 (*0-471-10068-4*) Wiley.

Ultrasound Imaging: The Kidney. David O. Cosgrove & Andrew M. Fried. 350p. text ed. write for info. (*0-471-91639-0*, Wiley-Interscience) Wiley.

Ultrasound in Ambulatory Medicine. Simon & Snoey. 300p. (C). (gr. 13). 1996. text ed. 64.95 (*0-8151-8519-7*) Mosby Yr Bk.

Ultrasound in Breast & Endocrine Disease. Ed. by George Leopold. (Clinics in Diagnostic Ultrasound Ser.: Vol. 12). (Illus.). 198p. 1984. text ed. 37.00 (*0-443-08234-0*) Churchill.

Ultrasound in Breast & Endocrine Disease. fac. ed. George R. Leopold. LC 83-21054. (Clinics in Diagnostic Ultrasound Ser.: No. 12). (Illus.). 210p. 1984. reprint ed. pap. 59.90 (*0-7837-7878-3*, 2047635) Bks Demand.

Ultrasound in Cancer. Ed. by Barry B. Goldberg. LC 80-23399. (Clinics in Diagnostic Ultrasound Ser.: No. 6). (Illus.). 235p. reprint ed. pap. 67.00 (*0-7837-2570-1*, 2042729) Bks Demand.

Ultrasound in Cardiology. Kurt Schmailzl & Oliver Ormerod. (Illus.). 450p. 1994. 175.00 (*0-86542-802-6*) Blackwell Sci.

Ultrasound in Coronary Artery Disease. Ed. by Sabino Iliceto et al. (Developments in Cardiovascular Medicine Ser.). (C). 1990. lib. bdg. 222.50 (*0-7923-0784-4*) Kluwer Ac.

Ultrasound in Dermatology. Ed. by P. Altmeyer et al. (Illus.). 544p. 1992. 272.00 (*0-387-53750-3*) Spr-Verlag.

Ultrasound in Emergency Medicine. Michael Heller. LC 94-13906. (Illus.). 240p. 1995. text ed. 55.00 (*0-7216-4506-2*) Saunders.

Ultrasound in Emergency Medicine. Ed. by Kenneth J. Taylor & Gregory N. Viscomi. LC 81-3800. (Clinics in Diagnostic Ultrasound Ser.: No. 7). 322p. reprint ed. pap. 91.80 (*0-7837-3151-5*, 2042834) Bks Demand.

Ultrasound in Gastroenterology. Paul A. Dubbins & A. E. Joseph. LC 94-16246. (Clinics in Diagnostic Ultrasound Ser.: Vol. 29). 1994. 85.00 (*0-443-08905-1*) Churchill.

***Ultrasound in Gynaecology.** Ed. by Jane Bates. (Greenwich Medical Media Ser.). (Illus.). 208p. 1997. pap. 69.50 (*1-900151-51-0*) OUP.

Ultrasound in Gynecology. Steven R. Goldstein & Ilan E. Timor-Tritsch. LC 95-4803. 321p. 1995. 95.00 (*0-443-08957-4*) Churchill.

Ultrasound in High-Risk Obstetrics. Rudy E. Sabbagha. LC 79-15161. (Current Concepts in Obstetrics & Gynecology Ser.). (Illus.). 122p. 1979. reprint ed. pap. 34.80 (*0-8357-7656-5*, 2056982) Bks Demand.

Ultrasound in Industrial Processing & Control. LC 63-17637. (Soviet Progress in Applied Ultrasonics Ser.: Vol. 1). 210p. reprint ed. pap. 59.90 (*0-317-08430-5*, 2020691) Bks Demand.

Ultrasound in Infertility. A. Kurjak. 224p. 1989. 153.00 (*0-8493-4766-1*, RC889) CRC Pr.

Ultrasound in Liquid & Solid Metals. O. V. ABramov. LC 93-25193. 512p. 1994. 191.95 (*0-8493-9355-8*, TA369) CRC Pr.

***Ultrasound in Neurosurgery.** Jonathan M. Rubin & William F. Chandler. LC 88-43078. 223p. 1990. reprint ed. pap. 63.60 (*0-608-03443-6*, 2064144) Bks Demand.

Ultrasound in Obstetrics & Gynecology. Ed. by Frank A. Chervenak et al. (Illus.). 1919p. 1993. text ed. 229.95 (*0-316-13865-7*) Lppncott-Raven.

Ultrasound in Obstetrics & Gynecology. E. Merz. (Illus.). 343p. 1990. text ed. 145.00 (*0-86577-376-9*) Thieme Med Pubs.

Ultrasound in Obstetrics & Gynecology. E. Albert Reece et al. (Illus.). 272p. (C). 1993. text ed. 75.00 (*0-8385-9247-3*, A9247-6) Appleton & Lange.

Ultrasound in Ophthalmologic Diagnosis. R. Guthoff. (Illus.). 174p. 1991. text ed. 67.00 (*0-86577-378-5*) Thieme Med Pubs.

Ultrasound in Orthopedics. 1988. 209.00 (*0-387-91327-0*) Spr-Verlag.

Ultrasound in Othopedics. 1988. 209.00 (*0-387-91328-9*) Spr-Verlag.

Ultrasound in Pediatrics. Ed. by Jack O. Haller & Arnold Shkolnik. LC 81-6184. (Clinics in Diagnostic Ultrasound Ser.: No. 8). (Illus.). 320p. reprint ed. pap. 91.20 (*0-7837-2571-X*, 2042730) Bks Demand.

Ultrasound in Perinatal Care. Ed. by Michael J. Bennett. LC 83-21632. (Wiley Series on Perinatal Practice: No. 1). (Illus.). 199p. reprint ed. pap. 56.80 (*0-8357-4546-5*, 2037445) Bks Demand.

Ultrasound in Perinatology. Ed. by Nabil F. Maklad. (Clinics in Diagnostic Ultrasound Ser.: Vol. 19). (Illus.). 222p. 1986. text ed. 35.95 (*0-443-08365-7*) Churchill.

Ultrasound in Perinatology. fac. ed. Ed. by Nabil F. Maklad. LC 85-29139. (Clinics in Diagnostic Ultrasound Ser.: No. 19). (Illus.). 238p. 1986. reprint ed. pap. 67.90 (*0-7837-7892-9*, 2047648) Bks Demand.

Ultrasound in Synthesis. S. V. Ley & C. M. Low. (Reactivity & Structure Ser.: Vol. 27). (Illus.). 185p. 1989. 119.95 (*0-387-51023-0*) Spr-Verlag.

Ultrasound in Urology: Journal: Urologia Internationalis, Vol. 45, No. 4, 1990. Ed. by D. Hauri. (Illus.). 76p. 1990. pap. 55.00 (*3-8055-5226-2*) S Karger.

Ultrasound Mammography: Methods, Results, Diagnostic Strategies. B. J. Hackeloer et al. (Illus.). 145p. 1988. 133.00 (*0-387-96494-0*) Spr-Verlag.

Ultrasound Markers for Fetal Chromosomal Defects. Ed. by R. J. Snijders & K. H. Nicolaides. (Frontiers in Fetal Medicine Ser.). (Illus.). 192p. 1995. text ed. 65.00 (*1-85070-610-7*) Prthnon Pub.

Ultrasound of Fetal Anomalies. David A. Nyberg. 1994. vdisk 700.00 (*1-56815-017-2*, 10027) Mosby Yr Bk.

Ultrasound of Human Diseases. Jones. 1998. text ed. write for info. (*0-7216-4929-7*) Saunders.

Ultrasound of Superficial Structures: High Frequencies, Doppler, & Interventional Procedures. Ed. by Luigi Salbiati et al. 416p. 1995. 175.00 (*0-443-05131-3*) Churchill.

Ultrasound of the Eye & Orbit. Green & Byrne. (Illus.). 505p. (C). (gr. 13). 1992. text ed. 110.00 (*0-8016-1968-8*) Mosby Yr Bk.

Ultrasound of the Fetal & Neonatal Brain. Timor. 1996. text ed. 135.00 (*0-8385-9074-8*) Appleton & Lange.

UV

An Asterisk (*) at the beginning of an entry indicates that the title is appearing in BIP for the first time.

Ultrasound of the Head & Neck. Ed. by C. D. Verwoerd. (Journal: Oto-Rhino-Laryngology: Vol. 55, No. 5, 1993). (Illus.). 68p. 1993. pap. 58.50 (*3-8055-5836-8*) S Karger.

Ultrasound of the Infant Brain. Malcolm I. Levene et al. (Clinics in Developmental Medicine Ser.: No. 92). (Illus.). 148p. (C). 1991. text ed. 39.95 (*0-521-41212-9*, Pub. by Mc Keith Pr UK) Cambridge U Pr.

Ultrasound of the Pediatric Abdomen & Pelvis: A Correlative Imaging Approach. Hooshang Kangarloo & W. Fred Sample. LC 79-25906. (Illus.). 391p. reprint ed. pap. 111.50 (*0-8357-3578-8*, 2034264) Bks Demand.

Ultrasound of the Prostate. Bruno D. Fornage. 344p. 1989. text ed. 350.00 (*0-471-91257-3*) Wiley.

Ultrasound of the Prostate. 2nd ed. Matthew D. Rifkin. LC 96-23896. 400p. 1996. text ed. 135.00 (*0-397-51769-6*) Lppncott-Raven.

Ultrasound Physics & Instrumentation. 3rd ed. Wayne R. Hendrick & David L. Hykes. 382p. (C). (gr. 13). 1994. text ed. 48.00 (*0-8151-4246-3*) Mosby Yr Bk.

Ultrasound Physics & Instrumentation. David L. Hykes et al. LC 85-420. (Illus.). 261p. reprint ed. pap. 74.40 (*0-8357-6576-8*, 2035962) Bks Demand.

Ultrasound Renal Stone Surgery. 1982. 545.00 (*0-387-91211-8*) Spr-Verlag.

Ultrasound Review of Obstetrics & Gynecology. Janice Hickey & Franklin Goldberg. 180p. 1996. pap. text ed. 42.95 (*0-397-51654-1*) Lppncott-Raven.

Ultrasound Scanning. 2nd ed. Betty B. Tempkin. 1998. text ed. write for info. (*0-7216-6879-8*) HarBrace.

Ultrasound Scanning: Principles & Protocols. Betty B. Tempkin. (Illus.). 347p. 1992. pap. text ed. 58.00 (*0-7216-3706-X*) Saunders.

***Ultrasound Scanning Guide.** Lisa Bachan. (Orig.). 1996. pap. write for info. (*0-9651644-0-3*) Chrlston Ultrasnd.

Ultrasound Teaching Cases Vol. 2: 1988. Ultrasound Teaching Cases Staff et al. (Wiley Medical Publication Ser.). (Illus.). 203p. 1988. reprint ed. pap. 57.90 (*0-608-01630-6*, 2062215) Bks Demand.

***Ultrasound Teaching Manual.** M. Hifer. (Illus.). 364p. 1997. pap. 19.95 (*0-86577-725-X*) Thieme Med Pubs.

Ultrastructural Appearances of Tumours. 2nd ed. Douglas W. Henderson et al. (Illus.). 456p. 1986. text ed. 215.00 (*0-443-03111-8*) Churchill.

Ultrastructural Cytochemistry of Blood-Brain Barrier Endothelia. Andrzej W. Vorbrodt. LC 88-20469. (Progress in Histochemistry & Cytochemistry Ser.: Vol. 18, No. 3). 99p. 1989. pap. 75.00 (*0-89574-273-X*) G F Verlag.

Ultrastructural Distribution of NADPase Within the Golgi Apparatus & Lysosomes of Mammalian Cells. Charles E. Smith et al. (Progress in Histochemistry & Cytochemistry Ser.: Vol. 21-3). 124p. (Orig.). 1990. pap. 90.00 (*0-89574-322-1*, Pub. by G Fischer Verlag GW) Lubrecht & Cramer.

Ultrastructural Effects of Radiation on Tissues & Cells. Ed. by K. E. Carr & T. M. Seed. (Illus.). 172p. (Orig.). 1983. pap. text ed. 18.00 (*0-931288-29-0*) Scanning Microscopy.

Ultrastructural Immunocytochemistry of the Hypothalamic Corticotropin Releasing Hormone Synthesizing System: Anatomical Basis of Neuronal & Humoral Regulatory Mechanisms. Zsolt Liposits. (Progress in Histochemistry & Cytochemistry Ser.: Vol. 21/2). (Illus.). 98p. (Orig.). 1990. pap. 80.00 (*0-89574-317-5*, Pub. by G Fischer Verlag GW) Lubrecht & Cramer.

Ultrastructural Kidney Pathology. Ed. by V. Marinozzi. (Journal: Applied Pathology: Vol. 2, No. 4, 1984). (Illus.). 52p. 1985. pap. 38.50 (*3-8055-4251-8*) S Karger.

Ultrastructural Pathology: An Introduction to Interpretation. Norman F. Cheville. LC 93-37657. (Illus.). 954p. (C). 1994. text ed. 189.95 (*0-8138-2398-6*) Iowa St U Pr.

Ultrastructural Pathology of the Cell & Matrix. 4th ed. Feroze N. Ghadially. LC 96-18218. 1996. write for info. (*0-7506-9855-1*); write for info. (*0-7506-9856-X*); pap. 299.00 (*0-7506-9635-4*) Buttrwrth-Heinemann.

Ultrastructural Pathology of the Kidney. Ed. by C. L. Pirani. (Journal: Applied Pathology: Vol. 5, No. 2, 1987). (Illus.). 68p. 1987. pap. 36.00 (*3-8055-4634-3*) S Karger.

Ultrastructural Study of the Human Diseased Peripheral Nerve. C. Vital. 1987. text ed. 89.50 (*0-8385-9243-0*) Appleton & Lange.

Ultrastructure de la Paroi Cellulaire des Desmidiacees au Microscope Electronique a Balayage. Guillermo Tell. (Nova Hedwigia Beiheft Ser.: No. 68). (Illus.). 228p. (FRE.). 1982. lib. bdg. 96.00 (*3-7682-5468-2*) Lubrecht & Cramer.

Ultrastructure, Macromolecules, & Evolution. Lawrence S. Dillon. LC 80-20550. 716p. 1981. 120.00 (*0-306-40528-8*, Plenum Pr) Plenum.

Ultrastructure, Membrane & Cell Interactions. Horst Robenek. Ed. by Nicholas J. Severs. 336p. 1992. 225.00 (*0-8493-5505-2*, RC692) CRC Pr.

Ultrastructure of Bacterial Viruses. Anna S. Tikhonenko. Tr. by Basil Haigh. LC 69-17902. 304p. (RUS.). reprint ed. pap. 86.70 (*0-685-15930-2*, 2026311) Bks Demand.

Ultrastructure of Brain Tumors & Biopsies: A Diagnostic Atlas. C. L. Dolman. LC 84-3469. (Methods in Laboratory Medicine Ser.: Vol. 5). 272p. 1984. text ed. 59.95 (*0-275-91426-7*, C1426, Praeger Pubs) Greenwood.

Ultrastructure of Endocrine Cells & Tissues: Electron Microscopy in Biology & Medicine. Ed. by P. M. Motta. 1983. lib. bdg. 198.00 (*0-89838-568-7*) Kluwer Ac.

***Ultrastructure of Fossil Spores & Pollen.** Ed. by M. H. Kurmann & J. A. Doyle. (Illus.). vi, 221p. 1994. pap. 36.00 (*0-947643-60-5*, Pub. by Royal Botnic Grdns UK) Balogh.

Ultrastructure of Human Gametogenesis & Early Embryogenesis. Ed. by Jonathan Van Blerkom & Pietro M. Motta. (Electron Microscopy in Biology & Medicine Ser.). (C). 1989. lib. bdg. 132.00 (*0-89838-383-8*) Kluwer Ac.

Ultrastructure of Male Urogenital Glands: Prostrate, Semial Vesicles, Urethral, & Bulbourethral Glands. Ed. by Alessandro Riva et al. LC 94-11636. (Electron Microscopy in Biology & Medicine Ser.: EMBM 11). 224p. (C). 1994. lib. bdg. 204.00 (*0-7923-2800-0*) Kluwer Ac.

Ultrastructure of Microalgae. Berner. 320p. 1993. 226.95 (*0-8493-6323-3*, QK568) CRC Pr.

Ultrastructure of Reproduction Gametogenesis, Fertilization & Embryogenesis. Ed. by Jonathan Van Blerkom & Pietro M. Motta. (Electron Microscopy in Biology & Medicine Ser.). 1983. lib. bdg. 163.00 (*0-89838-572-5*) Kluwer Ac.

Ultrastructure of Skeletal Tissue. Ed. by E. Bonucci & P. M. Motta. (Electron Microscopy in Biology & Medicine Ser.). (C). 1990. lib. bdg. 264.50 (*0-7923-0373-3*) Kluwer Ac.

Ultrastructure of Smooth Muscle. Ed. by Pietro M. Motta. (Electron Microscopy in Biology & Medicine Ser.). (C). 1990. lib. bdg. 200.00 (*0-7923-0480-2*) Kluwer Ac.

Ultrastructure of the Animal Cell. 2nd ed. L. T. Threadgold. Ed. by G. A. Kerkut. 472p. 1976. 234.00 (*0-08-018958-X*, Pub. by Pergamon Repr UK) Franklin.

Ultrastructure of the Conjunctival Epithelium. K. P. Steuhl. (Developments in Ophthalmology Ser.: Vol. 19). (Illus.). x, 106p. 1989. 77.00 (*3-8055-4943-1*) S Karger.

Ultrastructure of the Connective Tissue Matrix. Ed. by A. Ruggeri & P. M. Motta. 228p. 1984. lib. bdg. 131.50 (*0-89838-600-4*) Kluwer Ac.

Ultrastructure of the Digestive Tract. Ed. by P. M. Motta & Hisao Fujita. (Electron Microscopy in Biology & Medicine Ser.). (C). 1988. lib. bdg. 162.50 (*0-89838-893-7*) Kluwer Ac.

Ultrastructure of the Ovary. Ed. by G. Familiari et al. (Electron Microscopy in Biology & Medicine Ser.). (C). 1991. lib. bdg. 256.50 (*0-7923-1003-9*) Kluwer Ac.

Ultrastructure of the Root-Soil Interface. R. C. Foster et al. 157p. 1983. text ed. 42.00 (*0-89054-051-9*) Am Phytopathol Soc.

Ultrastructure of the Small Intestinal Mucosa: Normal & Disease-Related Appearances. Margot Shiner. (Illus.). 175p. 1983. 170.00 (*0-387-11732-6*) Spr-Verlag.

Ultrastructure Processing of Advanced Materials. Donald R. Uhlmann et al. LC 91-23612. 752p. 1992. pap. text ed. 134.00 (*0-471-52986-9*) Wiley.

Ultrastructure Processing of Advanced Structural & Electronic Materials. Ed. by L. L. Hench. LC 84-14835. (Illus.). 324p. 1985. 36.00 (*0-8155-1004-7*) Noyes.

Ultrastructure Techniques for Microorganisms. Ed. by Henry C. Aldrich & William J. Todd. 530p. 1986. 115.00 (*0-306-42251-4*, Plenum Pr) Plenum.

Ultrathin Magnetic Structures I: Introduction to the Electronic, Magnetic, & Structural Properties. Ed. by J. A. Bland & Heinrich Bretislav. LC 93-38679. (Illus.). 350p. 1994. 75.95 (*0-387-57407-7*) Spr-Verlag.

Ultrathin Magnetic Structures II: Measurement Techniques & Novel Magnetic Properties. J. A. Bland & B. Heinrich. 368p. 1994. 86.95 (*0-387-57687-8*) Spr-Verlag.

Ultratrace Analysis of Pharmaceuticals & Other Compounds of Interests. Ed. by Satinder Ahuja. LC 85-29407. (Chemical Analysus Ser.). 384p. 1986. text ed. 159.00 (*0-471-82673-1*) Wiley.

Ultratrace Metal Analysis in Biological Sciences. Ed. by Terence H. Risby. LC 78-31903. (Advances in Chemistry Ser.: No. 172). 1979. 43.95 (*0-8412-0416-0*) Am Chemical.

***Ultratrace Metal Analysis in Biological Sciences & Environment.** Ed. by Terence H. Risby. LC 78-31903. (Advances in Chemistry Ser.: Vol. 172). 272p. 1979. reprint ed. pap. 77.60 (*0-608-03868-7*, 2064315) Bks Demand.

Ultraviolent Movies: From Sam Peckinpah to Quentin Tarantino. Laurent Bouzereau. (Illus.). 256p. 1996. pap. 17.95 (*0-8065-1787-5*, Citadel Pr) Carol Pub Group.

Ultraviolet & Visible Spectroscopy. Michael J. Thomas. Ed. by David J. Ando. (Analytical Chemistry by Open Learning Ser.). 1996. write for info. (*0-471-96742-4*) Wiley.

Ultraviolet & Visible Spectroscopy. 2nd ed. Michael J. Thomas. Ed. by David J. Ando. (Analytical Chemistry by Open Learning Ser.). 1996. pap. text ed. 39.95 (*0-471-96743-2*) Wiley.

***Ultraviolet Disinfection in Municipal Water & Wastewater.** Richard K. Miller et al. (Market Research Survey Ser.: No. 280). 50p. 1996. 200.00 (*1-55865-307-4*) Future Tech Surveys.

Ultraviolet Laser Technology & Applications. David Elliott. (Illus.). 328p. 1995. boxed 49.95 (*0-12-237070-8*) Acad Pr.

***Ultraviolet Light & Fluorescent Minerals: Understanding, Collecting & Displaying Fluorescent Minerals.** (Illus.). 200p. (Orig.). 1995. pap. text ed. 24.95 (*0-614-29836-9*) T S Warren.

Ultraviolet Light & Fluorescent Minerals: Understanding, Collecting & Displaying Fluorescent Minerals. Thomas S. Warren et al. 150p. 1992. pap. 19.75 (*0-9635098-0-2*) T S Warren.

***Ultraviolet Light Induced Reactions in Polymers: An International Symposium.** Santokh S. Labana. LC 76-3421. (ACS Symposium Ser.: Vol. 25). (Illus.). 503p. pap. 143.40 (*0-608-04804-6*, 2052581) Bks Demand.

Ultraviolet Radiation. 1995. lib. bdg. 250.95 (*0-8490-7529-7*) Gordon Pr.

***Ultraviolet Radiation.** (Environmental Health Criteria Ser.: No. 14). 110p. 1979. pap. text ed. 16.00 (*92-4-154074-5*, 1160014) World Health.

Ultraviolet Radiation: An Authoritative Scientific Review of Environmental & Health Effects of Ultraviolet Radiation, with Reference to Global Ozone Layer Depletion. (Environmental Health Criteria Ser.: No. 160). 352p. 1994. pap. text ed. 67.00 (*92-4-157160-8*, 1160160) World Health.

Ultraviolet Radiation in Antarctica: Measurements & Biological Effects. Ed. by C. Susan Weiler & Polly A. Penhale. LC 94-1422. (Antarctic Research Ser.: Vol. 62). 257p. 1994. 70.00 (*0-87590-841-1*) Am Geophysical.

Ultraviolet Radiation in Medicine. B. L. Diffey. (Medical Physics Handbooks Ser.: No. 11). (Illus.). 172p. 1982. 19.00 (*0-85274-535-4*) IOP Pub.

Ultraviolet Rays, Factors & Adverse Effects: Medical Analysis Index with Research Bibliography. John C. Bartone, II. LC 85-47862. 150p. 1987. 44.50 (*0-88164-398-X*); pap. 39.50 (*0-88164-399-8*) ABBE Pubs Assn.

Ultraviolet Reflectance of Paint (ULR) 94p. 1976. 39.00 (*0-686-95641-9*) Am Welding.

Ultraviolet Reflections: Life under a Thinning Ozone Layer. Annika Nilsson. LC 96-11463. 1996. pap. text ed. 40.00 (*0-471-95843-3*) Wiley.

Ultraviolet Sky. Alma L. Villanueva. LC 88-70522. 379p. 1988. 28.00 (*0-916950-85-9*); pap. 18.00 (*0-916950-86-7*) Biling Rev-Pr.

Ultraviolet Spectroscopy of Proteins. A. P. Demchenko. (Illus.). 340p. 1986. 139.00 (*0-387-16013-2*) Spr-Verlag.

Ultrawide Radar Technology: Applications & Systems. Ed. by James D. Taylor. 688p. 1994. 135.00 (*0-8493-4440-9*) CRC Pr.

Ultrawide Technology Handbook. Taylor. 1995. write for info. (*0-8493-4267-8*) CRC Pr.

Ultrawideband Radar. Ed. by I. J. LaHaie. 1992. 20.00 (*0-8194-0777-1*, 1631) SPIE.

Ultrfast Spectroscopy of Semiconductors & Semiconductor Nanostructures, Vol. 115. Jagdeep Shah. LC 96-11374. (Springer Series in Solid-State Sciences: Vol. 115). 360p. 1996. 79.95 (*3-540-60912-1*) Spr-Verlag.

'Ulu: Breadfruit. Lisa L. Adams. (Illus.). 24p. (Orig.). 1994. pap. 5.50 (*0-9641577-3-X*) Spiral Triangle.

***Ulum al-Quran.** Ahmad Von Denffer. 200p. 1996. pap. 10.50 (*0-614-21075-5*, 1268) Kazi Pubns.

***Uluru Journey: An Exploration into Narrative Theology.** Denham Grierson. 166p. (Orig.). 1997. pap. 22.95 (*1-86407-122-2*, Pub. by JBCE AT) Morehouse Pub.

Uluru-Kata Tjuta & Watarrka National Parks: Ayers Rock, the Olgas & Kings Canyon. Anne Kerle. (Illus.). 208p. 1995. pap. 24.95 (*0-86840-055-6*, Pub. by New South Wales Univ Pr AT) Intl Spec Bk.

Ulverscroft Large Print Song Book: Singing for Pleasure. large type ed. 1964. pap. 7.95 (*0-85456-288-5*) Ulverscroft.

Ulverton. Adam Thorpe. 1993. 23.00 (*0-374-28031-2*) FS&G.

Ulverton. Adam Thorpe. 396p. 1994. pap. 13.00 (*0-374-52394-0*, Noonday) FS&G.

***Ulyanovsk Oblast: Economy, Industry, Government, Business.** 2nd rev. ed. Russian Information & Business Center, Inc. Staff. (Russian Regional Business Directories Ser.). (Illus.). 200p. 1997. pap. 99.00 (*1-57751-422-X*) Russ Info & Busn Ctr.

Ulysse Nardin Chronometers, Pocket Watches & Wrist Watches with 1988 Price Guide. Tran D. Ly. (Illus.). 20p. 1988. pap. 4.95 (*0-930163-66-4*) Arlington Bk.

Ulysse, Tome I. James Joyce. (FRE.). 1979. pap. 11.95 (*0-7859-2368-3*, 2070367711) Fr & Eur.

Ulysse, Tome II. rev. ed. James Joyce. 544p. (FRE.). 1982. pap. 12.95 (*0-7859-2636-4*, 207036772X) Fr & Eur.

***Ulysses.** James Joyce. 1997. 25.00 (*0-679-45513-2*, Everymans Lib) Knopf.

Ulysses. James Joyce. LC 44-679. 1979. 17.95 (*0-394-60486-5*, Modern Lib) Random.

Ulysses. James Joyce. LC 89-40555. 816p. 1990. pap. 17.00 (*0-679-72276-9*, Vin) Random.

Ulysses. James Joyce. LC 92-50221. 816p. 1992. 21.00 (*0-679-60011-6*, Modern Lib) Random.

Ulysses. James Joyce. Date not set. 35.00 (*0-393-03390-2*) Norton.

***Ulysses.** James Joyce. Ed. & Intro. by Jeri Johnson. (The World's Classics Ser.). (Illus.). 1000p. 1997. pap. text ed. 15.95 (*0-19-282866-5*) OUP.

Ulysses. rev. ed. Hugh Kenner. LC 86-27773. 192p. 1987. pap. text ed. 11.95 (*0-8018-3384-1*) Johns Hopkins.

Ulysses. James Joyce. 1992. reprint ed. lib. bdg. 27.95 (*0-89968-284-7*, Lghtyr Pr) Buccaneer Bks.

Ulysses, Vol. 1. Pichard & Lob. Tr. by Michael Koch from FRE. 64p. 1991. pap. 9.95 (*1-56163-033-0*, Eurotica) NBM.

Ulysses, Vol. 2. Lob Pichard. Tr. by M. Koch from FRE. 64p. 1992. pap. 9.95 (*1-56163-043-8*, Eurotica) NBM.

Ulysses: A Critical & Synoptic Edition, 3 vols. Ed. by Hans W. Gable. (James Joyce Archive Ser.). 1930p. 1990. pap. text ed. 58.00 (*0-8240-4748-6*) Garland.

Ulysses: A Facsimile of the Manuscript, 3 Vols. limited ed. James Joyce. (Octagon Bk.). 1016p. 1976. 200.00 (*0-374-28033-9*) FS&G.

Ulysses: A Monologue. Carl G. Jung. LC 76-30789. (Studies in Joyce: No. 96). 1976. lib. bdg. 75.00 (*0-8383-2117-8*) M S G Haskell Hse.

Ulysses: His Story. Robert J. Hing. LC 95-81079. (Illus.). 176p. (Orig.). 1996. pap. 12.95 (*0-9631460-1-7*) Anchor Watch.

Ulysses: Notes & "Telemachus" - "Scylla" & "Charybdis": A Facsimile of Notes for the Book & Mauscripts for Episodes 1-9. James Joyce. Ed. by Michael Groden. LC 78-16032. (James Joyce Archive Ser.). 1978. text ed. 30.00 (*0-8240-2822-8*) Garland.

Ulysses: The Corrected Text. James Joyce. LC 85-28279. 608p. 1986. 29.95 (*0-394-55373-X*, Vin) Random.

Ulysses: The Corrected Text. James Joyce. LC 85-28279. 608p. 1986. pap. 19.00 (*0-394-74312-1*, Vin) Random.

Ulysses: The Mechanics of Meaning. 2nd ed. David Hayman. LC 81-70007. 192p. 1982. reprint ed. pap. 14.95 (*0-299-09024-8*) U of Wis Pr.

Ulysses & Justice. James McMichael. 198p. 1991. text ed. 39.50 (*0-691-06547-0*) Princeton U Pr.

Ulysses & the Irish God. Frederick King. LC 88-47648. 320p. 1993. 48.50 (*0-8387-5150-4*) Bucknell U Pr.

Ulysses & the Sirens: Studies in Rationality & Irrationality. Jon Elster. 330p. 1985. pap. text ed. 22.95 (*0-521-26984-9*) Cambridge U Pr.

Ulysses Annotated. Don Gifford. 1989. 85.00 (*0-520-05639-6*); pap. 21.95 (*0-520-06745-2*) U CA Pr.

Ulysses As a Comic Novel. Zack Bowen. LC 89-32238. 168p. 1989. 34.95 (*0-8156-2471-9*) Syracuse U Pr.

Ulysses Due South Guide: Saint Barts. Pascale Couture. 1995. pap. text ed. 7.95 (*2-89464-002-1*) Ulysses Travel.

Ulysses Factor: Evaluating Visitors in Tourist Settings. P. L. Pearce. (Recent Research in Psychology Ser.). (Illus.). 275p. 1990. 64.95 (*0-387-96834-2*) Spr-Verlag.

Ulysses Guide: Tours Through Joyce's Dublin. Robert Nicholson. 150p. 1989. pap. 9.95 (*0-415-90144-8*, A3315, Routledge NY) Routledge.

Ulysses in Progress. Michael Groden. LC 77-1217. 251p. reprint ed. pap. 71.60 (*0-8357-2787-4*, 2039913) Bks Demand.

Ulysses in Traction. Albert Innaurato. 1978. pap. 5.25 (*0-8222-1187-4*) Dramatists Play.

Ulysses Kay: A Bio-Bibliography. Constance T. Hobson & Deborra A. Richardson. LC 93-45940. (Bio-Bibliographies in Music Ser.: No. 53). 210p. 1994. text ed. 65.00 (*0-313-25546-6*, Greenwood Pr) Greenwood.

Ulysses Notes. Edward A. Kopper, Jr. 1981. pap. 3.95 (*0-8220-1315-0*) Cliffs.

Ulysses on the Liffey. Richard Ellmann. 256p. 1986. pap. 16.95 (*0-19-501663-7*) OUP.

Ulysses S. Grant. Bill Bentley. LC 93-416. (First Bks.). (Illus.). 64p. (J). (gr. 4-6). 1993. lib. bdg. 21.00 (*0-531-20162-7*) Watts.

Ulysses S. Grant. Zachary Kent. LC 88-38056. (Encyclopedia of Presidents Ser.). (Illus.). 100p. (J). (gr. 3 up). 1989. lib. bdg. 22.00 (*0-516-01364-5*) Childrens.

Ulysses S. Grant. Steven O'Brian. (World Leaders - Past & Present Ser.). (Illus.). 112p. (J). (gr. 5 up). 1991. lib. bdg. 19.95 (*1-55546-809-8*) Chelsea Hse.

Ulysses S. Grant. rev. ed. Dan Zadra. (We the People Ser.). (J). (gr. 2-4). 1988. lib. bdg. 14.95 (*0-88682-188-6*) Creative Ed.

Ulysses S. Grant. Louis A. Coolidge. Ed. by John T. Morse, Jr. LC 75-128953. (American Statesmen Ser.: No. 32). reprint ed. 49.50 (*0-404-50894-4*) AMS Pr.

Ulysses S. Grant. Hamlin Garland. (Collected Works of Hamlin Garland). 1988. reprint ed. lib. bdg. 59.00 (*0-7812-1225-1*) Rprt Serv.

***Ulysses S. Grant: Soldier & President.** Geoffrey Perret. LC 97-9171. 576p. 1997. 35.00 (*0-679-44766-0*) Random.

Ulysses S. Grant: 18th President of the United States. Lucille Falkof. Ed. by Richard G. Young. LC 87-32817. (Presidents of the United States Ser.). (Illus.). (J). (gr. 5-9). 1988. lib. bdg. 17.26 (*0-944483-02-X*) Garrett Ed Corp.

Ulysses S. Grant see Collected Works of Hamlin Garland

Ulysses S. Grant & the Period of National Preservation & Reconstruction. William C. Church. LC 73-14437. (Heroes of the Nations Ser.). reprint ed. 64.50 (*0-404-58255-9*) AMS Pr.

Ulysses S. Grant & the Strategy of Victory. Laura Rickerby. (History of the Civil War Ser.). (Illus.). 160p. (YA). (gr. 5 up). 1990. pap. 7.95 (*0-382-24053-7*) Silver Burdett Pr.

Ulysses S. Grant, Politician. William B. Hesseltine. (History - United States Ser.). 480p. 1993. reprint ed. lib. bdg. 99.00 (*0-7812-4912-0*) Rprt Serv.

Ulysses' Sail: An Ethnographic Odyssey of Power, Knowledge, & Geographical Distance. Mary W. Helms. (Illus.). 312p. 1988. pap. text ed. 16.95 (*0-691-02840-0*) Princeton U Pr.

***Ulysses' Sail: An Ethnographic Odyssey of Power, Knowledge, & Geographical Distance.** Mary W. Helms. LC 87-14038. 310p. 1988. reprint ed. pap. 88.40 (*0-608-03310-3*, 2064022) Bks Demand.

Ulysses Smiled. Charles E. Ziavras. LC 87-81798. (Illus.). 1986. 15.95 (*0-915940-08-6*); pap. 4.95 (*0-915940-09-4*) Ithaca Pr MA.

Ulysses Theme: A Study in the Adaptability of a Traditional Hero. W. Bedell Stanford. LC 92-32876. xvii, 340p. (Orig.). 1992. reprint ed. pap. 24.00 (*0-88214-355-7*) Spring Pubns.

***Ulysses Travel Guide: Vancouver.** Paul-Eric Dumontier. (Ulysses Travel Guides Ser.). 1996. pap. text ed. 10.95 (*2-89464-014-5*) Ulysses Travel.

Ulysses, "Wandering Rocks," & the Reader: Multiple Pleasures in Reading. Kathleen A. McCormick. LC 90-21975. (Studies in British Literature: Vol. 12). 196p. 1991. lib. bdg. 79.95 (*0-88946-493-6*) E Mellen.

Um Corso Em Milagres. LC 94-61357. (POR.). 1994. 35.00 (*1-883360-00-5*) Found Inner Peace.

***Um die Wahre Kirche: Ekklesiologische Studien.** Klaus Schwarzwaller. (Kontexte Ser.: Bd. 20). 321p. (GER.). 1996. 57.95 (*3-631-30059-X*) P Lang Pubng.

***Uma Introducao Basica a Um Curso em Milagres.** Kenneth Wapnick. 172p. (Orig.). (POR.). 1996. pap. write for info. (*0-933291-27-2*) Foun Miracles.

Umami: A Basic Taste: Physiology, Biochemistry, Nutrition Food Science. Ed. by Yojiro Kawamura & Morley R. Kare. LC 86-19891. (Food Science & Technology Ser.: Vol. 20). 670p. 1987. reprint ed. pap. 180.00 (*0-608-00554-1*, 2061437) Bks Demand.

Uman, Uman, Rosh HaShanah: A Guide to Rebbe Nachmans Rosh HaShanah in Uman. Yonatan Lifshits & Tanya Lifshits. Ed. by Avraham Greenbaum. (Illus.). 96p. 1992. pap. 2.00 (*0-930213-43-2*) Breslov Res Inst.

UMAP Modules: Tools for Teaching 1977-1979. Compiled by UMAP Central Staff. 727p. (C). 1982. text ed. 54.95 (*0-8176-3049-X*) Birkhauser.

UMAP Modules: Tools for Teaching 1981. 746p. (C). 1982. text ed. 54.95 (*0-8176-3085-6*) Birkhauser.

UMAP Modules: Tools for Teaching 1982. Ed. by COMAP, Inc. Staff. 544p. (Orig.). 1983. pap. 35.00 (*0-912843-03-9*) COMAP Inc.

UMAP Modules: Tools for Teaching 1984. Ed. by Philip D. Straffin, Jr. & Paul J. Campbell. 360p. (Orig.). (C). 1985. pap. 35.00 (*0-912843-07-1*) COMAP Inc.

UMAP Modules: Tools for Teaching 1985. Ed. by Philip D. Straffin, Jr. & Paul J. Campbell. 336p. (Orig.). 1986. pap. 35.00 (*0-912843-08-X*) COMAP Inc.

UMAP Modules: Tools for Teaching 1986. COMAP, Inc. Staff. Ed. by Paul J. Campbell. (Illus.). 350p. 1987. pap. text ed. 35.00 (*0-912843-11-X*) COMAP Inc.

UMAP Modules: Tools for Teaching 1987. COMAP, Inc. Staff. Ed. by Paul J. Campbell. (Illus.). 320p. (Orig.). 1988. pap. text ed. 35.00 (*0-912843-12-8*) COMAP Inc.

UMAP Modules: Tools for Teaching 1988. COMAP, Inc. Staff. Ed. by Paul J. Campbell. (Illus.). 314p. (Orig.). 1989. pap. text ed. 35.00 (*0-912843-14-4*) COMAP Inc.

UMAP Modules: Tools for Teaching 1990. Ed. by Paul J. Campbell. (Illus.). 184p. 1991. pap. text ed. 35.00 (*0-912843-19-5*) COMAP Inc.

UMAP Modules: Tools for Teaching, 1991. COMAP Inc. Staff. Ed. by Paul J. Campbell. (Illus.). 208p. 1992. pap. text ed. 35.00 (*0-912843-22-5*) COMAP Inc.

Umap Modules: Tools for Teaching: 1992. Ed. by Paul J. Campbell. (Illus.). 230p. 1993. pap. text ed. 35.00 (*0-912843-28-4*) COMAP Inc.

UMAP Modules Tools for Teaching, 1989. COMAP, Inc. Staff. Ed. by Paul J. Campbell. (Illus.). 250p. (Orig.). (C). 1990. pap. text ed. 35.00 (*0-912843-18-7*) COMAP Inc.

Umap Modules 1993: Tools for Teaching. Ed. by Paul J. Campbell. (Illus.). 208p. 1994. pap. text ed. 35.00 (*0-912843-37-3*) COMAP Inc.

Umar bin Abd al-Aziz. Abd al-Salam Nadvi. 200p. (YA). (gr. 7-12). 1985. pap. 9.95 (*1-56744-406-7*) Kazi Pubns.

Umar the Great, 2. Shibli Naumani. 14.50 (*0-933511-80-9*) Kazi Pubns.

Umar the Great, Vol. II. Shibli Numani. Tr. by M. Saleem. 200p. (YA). (gr. 7-12). 1985. 14.50 (*1-56744-407-5*) Kazi Pubns.

Umayyad, Abbasid & Tulunid Glass Weights & Vessel Stamps. Paul Balog. (Numismatic Studies: No. 13). (Illus.). 377p. 1976. 60.00 (*0-89722-066-8*) Am Numismatic.

Umayyads & Abbasids: Islamic Civilisation. G. Zaydan. 332p. 1987. 250.00 (*1-85077-171-5*, Pub. by Darf Pubs Ltd UK) St Mut.

Umbanda: Religion & Politics in Urban Brazil. Diana DeG Brown. LC 94-17210. 1994. reprint ed. pap. 16.00 (*0-231-10005-1*) Col U Pr.

Umbertina. Helen Barolini. LC 89-6973. 432p. (C). 1989. reprint ed. pap. 12.95 (*0-88143-107-9*) Ayer.

*__Umberto Eco & the Open Text: Semiotics, Fiction, Popular Culture.__ Peter Bondanella. 212p. (C). 1997. text ed. 44.95 (*0-521-44200-1*) Cambridge U Pr.

Umberto Menghi Cookbook. Umberto Menghi. (NFS Canada Ser.). 192p. 1993. spiral bd. 14.95 (*0-88922-197-9*) Genl Dist Srvs.

Umberto Menghi Seafood Cookbook. Umberto Menghi. (Illus.). 196p. (Orig.). 1987. pap. 12.95 (*1-55013-039-0*, Pub. by Key Porter Bks CN) Firefly Bks Ltd.

Umberto Saba: Thirty-One Poems. Tr. by Felix Stephanile from ITA. 1978. 20.00 (*0-686-59679-X*); pap. 8.00 (*0-686-59680-3*) Elizabeth Pr.

*__Umberto's Kitchen: The Flavours of Tuscany.__ Umberto Menghi. (Illus.). 172p. 1997. 35.00 (*1-55054-422-5*) Orca Bk Pubs.

*__Umbo: Otto Umbehr 1902-1980.__ Photos by Otto Umbehr. (Illus.). 384p. 1996. 140.00 (*3-928762-43-5*, 620402, Pub. by Richter Verlag GW) Dist Art Pubs.

Umbra: The Velvet Shadow. Daniel Greenberg & Harry Heckel. (Werewolf Ser.). 1993. 15.00 (*1-56504-076-7*, 3204) White Wolf.

Umbral Anthology of Science Fiction Poetry. Ed. by Steve R. Tem. 230p. (Orig.). 1982. pap. 14.95 (*0-938075-56-X*) Ocean View Bks.

Umbral Calculus & Hopf Algebras. Ed. by Robert Morris. LC 81-22756. (Contemporary Mathematics Ser.: Vol. 6). 84p. 1982. pap. 17.00 (*0-8218-5003-2*, CONM/6) Am Math.

Umbrella. Garrett Christopher. Ed. by J. Friedland & R. Kessler. (Novel-Ties Ser.). 1992. student ed., pap. text ed. 14.95 (*0-88122-736-6*) Lrn Links.

Umbrella. Ferdinand Mount. 224p. 1995. pap. 7.99 (*0-7493-2193-8*, Reed Trade) Buttrwrth-Heinemann.

Umbrella. Taro Yashima. (Illus.). (J). (ps-1). 1977. pap. 4.99 (*0-14-050240-8*, Puffin) Puffin Bks.

Umbrella. Illus. by Taro Yashima. (J). (ps-1). 1958. pap. 15.99 (*0-670-73858-1*) Viking Child Bks.

*__Umbrella: A Pacific Tale.__ Ferdinand Mount. LC 97-7283. 1997. 19.95 (*0-8112-1363-3*) New Directions.

Umbrella Book, 3 vols., Set. rev. ed. Ed. by Warren, McVeigh & Griffin, Inc. Staff. LC 81-216095. (Illus.). 1500p. 1979. ring bd. 269.00 (*0-941360-00-8*) Griffin Comns.

*__Umbrella Day.__ Nancy E. Cooney. (Illus.). 32p. (Orig.). (J). (ps-1). 1997. pap. 5.95 (*0-698-11562-7*, Paperstar) Putnam Pub Group.

Umbrella Guide to Bicycling the Oregon Coast. Robin Cody. (Illus.). 128p. 1991. pap. 10.95 (*0-914143-25-5*, Umbrella Bks) Epicenter Pr.

Umbrella Guide to California Lighthouses. Sharlene P. Nelson & Ted Nelson. Ed. by B. G. Olson. (Umbrella Guides Ser.). (Illus.). 192p. (Orig.). 1993. pap. 12.95 (*0-945397-21-6*, Umbrella Bks) Epicenter Pr.

*__Umbrella Guide to Exploring the Columbia-Snake River Inland Waterway: By River & by Road.__ Sharlene P. Nelson & Ted Nelson. (Umbrella Guides Ser.). (Illus.). 160p. (Orig.). (C). 1997. pap. 12.95 (*0-945397-58-5*) Epicenter Pr.

Umbrella Guide to Oregon Lighthouses. Sharlene P. Nelson & Ted Nelson. (Illus.). 128p. 1994. pap. 10.95 (*0-945397-27-5*, Umbrella Bks) Epicenter Pr.

Umbrella Guide to Ports of Call of Southeast Alaska. Sherry Simpson. Ed. by B. G. Olson. (Umbrella Guides Ser.). (Illus.). 160p. 1993. pap. 12.95 (*0-945397-19-4*, Umbrella Bks) Epicenter Pr.

*__Umbrella Guide to Skiing in Alaska: Downhill & Cross-Country.__ Elizabeth Tower. Ed. by Christine Ummel. (Illus.). 160p. (Orig.). 1997. pap. 12.95 (*0-945397-45-3*, Umbrella Bks) Epicenter Pr.

Umbrella Guide to the Inland Empire. Bill London. (Illus.). 192p. 1990. pap. 10.95 (*0-914143-26-3*, Umbrella Bks) Epicenter Pr.

Umbrella Guide to Washington Lighthouses. Sharlene P. Nelson & Ted Nelson. (Illus.). 160p. 1990. pap. 10.95 (*0-914143-24-7*, Umbrella Bks) Epicenter Pr.

Umbrella-Maker's Daughter. large type ed. Janet Caird. 464p. 1983. 25.99 (*0-7089-0943-4*) Ulverscroft.

*__Umbrella Man.__ Michael P. Sapourn. 343p. (Orig.). 1997. mass mkt. 4.99 (*1-55197-970-5*, Pub. by Comnwlth Pub CN) Partners Pubs Grp.

Umbrella of Glass. Henry Alley. LC 88-11729. 170p. 1988. 14.95 (*0-932576-61-3*) Breitenbush Bks.

Umbrella Parade. Kathy Feczko. LC 84-8650. (Giant First Start Reader Ser.). (Illus.). 32p. (J). (gr. k-2). 1985. lib. bdg. 12.95 (*0-8167-0356-6*) Troll Communs.

Umbrella Parade. Kathy Feczko. LC 84-8650. (Giant First Start Reader Ser.). (Illus.). 32p. (J). (gr. k-2). 1997. pap. 3.95 (*0-8167-0436-8*) Troll Communs.

Umbrella Thief. Sybil Wettasinghe. (Illus.). 32p. (J). (ps-3). 1987. 11.95 (*0-916291-12-X*) Kane-Miller Bk.

Umbria. (Insight Guides Ser.). 1993. pap. 22.95 (*0-395-66443-8*) HM.

Umbria. 2nd ed. Alta Macadam. (Blue Guides Ser.). (Illus.). 224p. 1996. pap. 19.95 (*0-393-31402-2*, Norton Paperbks) Norton.

Umbria, the Marches & San Marino. Christopher Catling. (Regional Guides of Italy Ser.). (Illus.). 192p. 1994. pap. 16.95 (*0-8442-9964-2*, Passport Bks) NTC Pub Grp.

Umbundu Kinship & Character: Being a Description of Social Structure & Individual Development of the Ovimbundu of Angola, with Observations Concerning the Bearing on the Enterprise of Christian Missions of Certain Phases of the Life & Culture Described. Gladwyn M. Childs. LC 50-2385. 264p. reprint ed. pap. 75.30 (*0-8357-3227-4*, 2057122) Bks Demand.

UMD Comes of Age: The First One Hundred Years. Ken Moran & Neil Storch. LC 96-18263. 1996. write for info. (*0-89865-970-1*) Donning Co.

Ume Plum's Secrets. Ushio Moriyasu. 1992. per. 4.75 (*0-916508-40-4*) Happiness Pr.

*__Umfundalai: An African Dance Technique.__ Kariamu Welsh-Asante. LC 97-17412. 1997. write for info. (*0-86543-490-5*) Africa Wrld Bks.

Umfundalai: An African Dance Technique. Kariamu Welsh-Asante. LC 97-17412. 1995. pap. text ed. 16.95 (*0-86543-491-3*) Africa World.

Umgang mit schwierigen Kindern und Jugendlichen. H. J. Von Schumann. (Psychologische Praxis Ser.: No. 48). 80p. 1973. 15.75 (*3-8055-1561-8*) S Karger.

Umile Italia in Dante Alighieri. Vincenzo Tripodi. 360p. (ITA.). 1995. 69.50 (*1-882528-13-1*) Scripta.

Umkehr und Suende im Hebraeerbrief. Hermut Loehr. (Beihefte zur Zeitschrift fuer die Neuetestamentliche Wissenschaft Ser.: Bd. 73). 375p. (GER.). (C). 1994. lib. bdg. 129.25 (*3-11-014202-3*) De Gruyter.

*__UML & C++ A Practical Guide to Object-Oriented Development.__ Richard C. Lee. 512p. (C). 1997. pap. text ed. 36.00 (*0-13-619719-1*) P-H.

*__UML in a Nutshell.__ Martin Fowler. (C). 1997. pap. text ed. 26.95 (*0-201-32563-2*) Addison-Wesley.

*__UML Reference Guide.__ James Rumbaugh. (C). 1998. pap. text ed. write for info. (*0-201-30998-X*) Addison-Wesley.

Umma in the Sargonic Period. Benjamin R. Foster. (Connecticut Academy of Arts & Sciences Ser., Trans.: Vol. 20). 1981. 75.00 (*0-685-22851-7*) Elliots Bks.

Umma-Texte aus den Archaologischen Museen zu Istanbul, Band III. Fatma Yildiz & Gomi Tohru. 291p. (GER.). 1993. 48.00 (*1-883053-01-3*) CDL Pr.

Umnutzen-Umbauen. 1995. 65.00 (*0-8176-5228-0*) Birkhauser.

*__Umpires: Classic Baseball Stories from the Men Who Made the Calls.__ John C. Skipper. LC 97-7447. (Illus.). 168p. 1997. pap. 24.50 (*0-7864-0364-0*) McFarland & Co.

Umpire's Adventure in Alphabet Town. Laura Alden. LC 92-12668. (Read Around Alphabet Town Ser.). (Illus.). 32p. (J). (ps-2). 1992. lib. bdg. 17.50 (*0-516-05421-X*) Childrens.

Umpiring Made Easy: How to Command Respect! Glen D. Eley. (Illus.). 24p. (Orig.). 1983. pap. 4.95 (*0-940934-03-5*) GDE Pubns OH.

Umpoled Synthons: A Survey of Sources & Uses in Synthesis. Ed. by Tapio A. Hase. LC 86-26702. 387p. 1987. text ed. 139.00 (*0-471-80667-6*) Wiley.

*__Umrao Jan Ada.__ Mirza M. Rusva. Tr. by David Matthews. (C). 1996. 9.00 (*81-7167-311-2*, Pub. by Rupa II) S Asia.

Umrib Einer Fachkunde fur Buchersammler. Gustav A. Bogeng et al. (Buchkunliche Arbeiten Ser.: Vol. IV). 436p. 1978. reprint ed. 75.00 (*3-487-06479-0*) G Olms Pubs.

*__Umwelt-Lesebuch: Green Issues in Contemporary German Writing.__ Axel Goodbody. (German Texts Ser.). 1997. 49.95 (*0-7190-5147-9*, Pub. by Manchester Univ Pr UK); pap. text ed. 19.95 (*0-7190-4178-3*, Pub. by Manchester Univ Pr UK) St Martin.

Umwelt-Lexikon. Bruno Streit. 384p. (GER.). 1992. 85.00 (*0-7859-8377-5*, 3451226790) Fr & Eur.

Umweltbelastung der Nahrung, Gefahr fuer den Menschen? Environmental Contamination of Foods: Danger to Man? Ed. by J. C. Somogyi & D. Hotzel. (Bibliotheca Nutritio et Dieta Ser.: No. 41). (Illus.). vi, 114p. 1987. 88.00 (*3-8055-4661-0*) S Karger.

*__Umweltinformatik im Atlastenbereich.__ H. L. Jessberger. 1996. 70.00 (*90-5410-808-8*, Pub. by A A Balkema NE) Ashgate Pub Co.

Umweltstandards: Grundlagen, Tatsachen und Bewertungen Am Beispiel Des Strahlenrisikos. Ed. by K. Pinkau & Sprecher. (Akademie der Wissenschaften zu Berlin, Forschungsbericht Ser.: No. 2). xv, 494p. (GER.). (C). 1992. lib. bdg. 75.40 (*3-11-013450-0*) De Gruyter.

Umwertung aller Werte? Deutsche Literatur im Urteil Nietzsches. Matthias Politycki. (Monographien und Texte zur Nietzscge-Forschung Ser.: Vol. 21). x, 447p. (C). 1989. lib. bdg. 161.55 (*3-11-011709-6*) De Gruyter.

Un-American. Emanuel Fried. 518p. 1992. pap. 14.95 (*0-9603888-6-9*) Labor Arts.

Un-American: An Autobiographical Novel. Emanuel Fried. (Illus.). 1992. pap. 14.95 (*1-877800-02-3*) Springhse Editions.

Un-American Activities. Sally Belfrage. 272p. 1995. pap. 13.00 (*0-06-092626-0*, PL) HarpC.

Un-American Activities: The Trials of William Remington. Gary May. LC 93-25321. (Illus.). 416p. (C). 1994. 30.00 (*0-19-504980-2*) OUP.

Un-American Childhood. Ann Kimmage. LC 95-13229. 320p. 1996. 29.95 (*0-8203-1768-3*) U of Ga Pr.

Un-Civil War. Sheila S. Klass. LC 95-15548. (J). 1996. write for info. (*0-590-22632-0*) Scholastic Inc.

Un-Common Ground: Virginia Artists 1996. Julia W. Boyd. (Illus.). 64p. 1996. pap. write for info. (*0-917046-42-0*) Va Mus Arts.

Un, Deux, Trois: My First French Rhymes. Opal Dunn. (Illus.). 24p. (J). (ps up). 1995. 18.95 incl. audio (*0-8120-8402-0*); 12.95 incl. audio (*0-8120-8153-6*) Barron.

Un-Divine Comedy. Zygmunt Krasinski. Tr. by Harriette Kennedy & Zofia Uminska. LC 74-5774. 111p. 1976. reprint ed. text ed. 45.00 (*0-8371-7513-5*, KRUD, Greenwood Pr) Greenwood.

Un-Due West. Roland Sodowsky. LC 89-82343. (Illus.). 152p. 1990. pap. 8.95 (*0-931722-77-2*) Corona Pub.

UN-ECE Standard for Eggs in Shell & Explanatory Brochure. 32p. 1990. 14.00 (*92-1-116475-3*, 90-II.E.10) UN.

UN-ECE Standard for Poultry Meat & Explanatory Brochure. 35p. 1990. 15.00 (*92-1-116476-1*, 90.II.E.11) UN.

UN-ECE Standards for Fresh Fruit & Vegetables. 405p. 1988. 45.00 (*92-1-116436-2*, E.88.II.E.31) UN.

Un-Friendly Persuasion: A Quaker Mystery. Chuck Fager. 176p. (Orig.). 1995. pap. 9.95 (*0-945177-12-7*) Kimo Pr.

Un-Health Can Be Changed to a State of Health Thru Natural Methods. George S. White. 173p. 1963. reprint ed. spiral bd. 13.50 (*0-7873-0961-3*) Hlth Research.

U'n I Read a Note. Alta C. Grasmick. (Illus.). 68p. (J). (gr. k-1). 1989. pap. 15.95 (*0-9621909-0-X*) A C Grasmick.

Un Jardin a Hammamet see Garden at Hammamet

*__Un-Jobbing: The Adult Liberation Handbook.__ LC 96-86570. 118p. (Orig.). 1997. pap. 9.95 (*0-9654834-0-1*) Free Choice.

Un-Peeling Tradition: Contemporary Policing. Ed. by Keith Bryett & Colleen Lewis. 224p. 1995. pap. 39.95 (*0-7329-2786-2*, Pub. by Macmill Educ AT) Paul & Co Pubs.

*__Un Popular Culture: Lesbian Writing after the Sex Wars.__ Kathleen Martindale. LC 96-47153. (Series, Identities in the Classroom). 224p. 1997. text ed. 59.50 (*0-7914-3289-0*); pap. text ed. 19.95 (*0-7914-3290-4*) State U NY Pr.

Un Regalo del Papa a Diego see Gift from Pap a Diego

Un-Risky Business: Your Ratings Guide to Choosing a Small Business That Makes Sense. Glenn Desmond. Ed. by Monica Faulkner. 300p. (Orig.). 1994. pap. 14.95 (*0-935853-01-4*) Camden Harbor Pub.

Un-Sheltered. Eva Liljendahl. 63p. 1996. pap. write for info. (*0-9637979-3-X*) T Y Okosun.

Un teilbare Geist: Modularismus und Holismus in der Kognitionsforschung. Ralph A. Mueller. (Foundations of Communication & Cognition Ser.). xix, 443p. (GER.). (C). 1991. lib. bdg. 152.35 (*3-11-012916-7*, 250-91) De Gruyter.

Un-Terrible Tiger. Miroslav Zahradka. LC 78-155815. (Illus.). 32p. (J). (ps-3). 7.95 (*0-87592-056-X*) Scroll Pr.

Un-TV & the Ten MPH Car: Experiments in Personal Freedom & Everyday Life. Bernard McGrane. LC 93-87106. (Illus.). 350p. (Orig.). 1994. pap. 17.50 (*1-878020-05-6*) Small Pr CA.

Una: A Novel. Bernice Speight. 112p. (Orig.). 1993. pap. 8.95 (*1-56474-053-6*) Fithian Pr.

Una de Dos. Daniel Sada. (SPA.). 1995. pap. 10.50 (*0-679-76522-0*) Random.

Una, Dos, Tres, Por Bambi. (Illus.). (SPA.). (J). (ps-3). 1993. pap. 3.95 (*0-307-72392-5*, Golden Books) Western Pub.

*__Una Paso Del Infierno.__ D. Wilkerson. (SPA.). 7.95 (*0-8297-1987-3*) Life Pubs Intl.

Una Vez Mas. James H. Couch et al. 240p. 1993. student ed. 17.33 (*0-8013-0973-5*, 79254) Longman.

Una Vez Mas. 2nd ed. James H. Couch et al. 240p. 1993. student ed., pap. 25.33 (*0-8013-0971-9*, 79252); student ed., text ed. 32.00 (*0-8013-0972-7*, 79253) Longman.

Unabandoned Abstraction: Past & Present Works by Judy Cooke, Melkatz, Linda Parker, Margaret Shirley, Paul Sutinen. Terri M. Hopkins. (Illus.). 1991. pap. 2.00 (*0-914435-17-5*) Marylhurst Art.

*__Unabashed Garlic & Onion Lover's International Cookbook: A Robust Collection of Classic & Contemporary Onion & Garlic Recipes from Around the World.__ Sunny Baker & Michelle Sbraga. LC 97-6063. 204p. 1997. pap. 13.95 (*0-89529-785-X*) Avery Pub.

Unabashed Self-Promoter's Guide: What Every Man, Woman, Child & Organization in America Needs to Know About Getting Ahead by Exploiting the Media. 2nd ed. Jeffrey Lant. (Enterprise Ser.: Vol. 2). 366p. (Orig.). 1992. pap. 35.00 (*0-940374-18-8*) JLA Pubns.

*__Unabhangigkeit und Zinspolitik der Deutschen Bundesbank im Prozeb der Deutschen Vereinigung (1989-1992)__ Thilo Busching. (Europaische Hochschulschriften: Reihe 5: Bd. 2023). 235p. (GER.). 1997. pap. 44.95 (*3-631-30671-7*) P Lang Pubng.

Unabomber: On the Trail of America's Most-Wanted Serial Killer. John Douglas & Olshaker. 1996. mass mkt. 6.50 (*0-671-00411-5*) PB.

*__Unabomber Manifesto.__ 1997. lib. bdg. 251.99 (*0-8490-6068-0*) Gordon Pr.

Unabomber Manifesto: Industrial Society & Its Future. FC. 100p. 1995. pap. 9.95 (*0-9634205-2-6*) J Roger Pr.

Unaborted Socrates. Peter Kreeft. LC 83-8430. 155p. (Orig.). 1983. pap. 10.99 (*0-87784-810-6*, 810) InterVarsity.

Unabridged Edgar Allan Poe. Edgar Allan Poe. LC 83-16023. (Illus.). 1280p. (Orig.). 1983. pap. 16.95 (*0-89471-233-0*) Running Pr.

*__Unabridged Edgar Allan Poe.__ unabridged ed. (Orig.). 1997. pap. write for info. (*0-614-29860-1*) Sweetwtr Pr AL.

*__Unabridged Edgar Allan Poe.__ unabridged ed. Edgar Allan Poe. (Orig.). 1997. write for info. (*1-889372-34-X*) Sweetwtr Pr AL.

*__Unabridged Edgar Allan Poe: The Conqueror Worm/The Fall of the House of Usher/The Murders in the Rue Morgue.__ Edgar Allan Poe. (Unabridged Classics Ser.). 1186p. 1997. 18.98 (*0-7624-0178-8*) Courage Bks.

Unabridged Jack London. Jack London. 1986. 12.98 (*0-89471-156-3*) Courage Bks.

Unabridged Jack London. Richard E. Nicholls. LC 81-4383. (Illus.). 1150p. (Orig.). 1981. pap. 16.95 (*0-89471-124-5*) Running Pr.

*__Unabridged Jack London.__ unabridged ed. (Orig.). 1997. pap. write for info. (*0-614-29859-8*) Sweetwtr Pr AL.

*__Unabridged Jack London.__ unabridged ed. Jack London. LC 97-333. (Orig.). (J). 1997. write for info. (*1-889372-35-8*) Sweetwtr Pr AL.

*__Unabridged Jack London: The Call of the Wild/White Fang/The Sea-Wolf.__ Jack London. (Unabridged Classics Ser.). 1152p. 1997. 18.98 (*0-7624-0179-6*) Courage Bks.

Unabridged Marilyn: Her Life. Randall Riese. 1990. 7.99 (*0-517-69619-3*) Random Hse Value.

Unabridged Mark Twain. Mark Twain, pseud. LC 76-43094. (Illus.). 1250p. (Orig.). 1976. pap. 16.95 (*0-914294-54-7*) Running Pr.

*__Unabridged Mark Twain.__ unabridged ed. (Orig.). 1997. pap. write for info. (*0-614-29858-X*) Sweetwtr Pr AL.

*__Unabridged Mark Twain, Vol. 2.__ unabridged ed. (Orig.). 1997. pap. write for info. (*0-614-29857-1*) Sweetwtr Pr AL.

*__Unabridged Mark Twain: The Celebrated Jumping Frog of Calaveras County/The Adventures of Tom Sawyer, No. 1.__ Mark Twain, pseud. (Unabridged Classics Ser.). 1312p. 1997. 18.98 (*0-7624-0180-X*) Courage Bks.

*__Unabridged Mark Twain: The Tragedy of Pudd'nhead Wilson/Curing a Cold, No. 2.__ Mark Twain, pseud. (Unabridged Classics Ser.). 1120p. 1997. 18.98 (*0-7624-0181-8*) Courage Bks.

Unabridged Shakespeare. William Shakespeare. LC 88-43386. 1420p. (Orig.). 1989. pap. 17.95 (*0-89471-699-9*) Running Pr.

*__Unabridged Shakespeare.__ unabridged ed. (Orig.). 1997. pap. write for info. (*0-614-29861-X*) Sweetwtr Pr AL.

*__Unabridged William Shakespeare.__ William Shakespeare. (Unabridged Classics Ser.). 1440p. 1997. 18.98 (*0-7624-0177-X*) Courage Bks.

*__Unabridged William Shakespeare.__ unabridged ed. William Shakespeare et al. LC 97-334. 1997. write for info. (*1-889372-33-1*) Sweetwtr Pr AL.

Unacceptable Offer. Mary Balogh. 1988. mass mkt. 4.99 (*0-451-15314-6*, Sig) NAL-Dutton.

*__Unaccompanied Children Retained by the U. S. Immigration & Naturalization Service (INS) Slipping Through the Cracks.__ Children's Rights Project Staff. 120p. (Orig.). 1997. pap. 10.00 (*1-56432-209-2*) Hum Rts Watch.

Unaccountable. Eric Duncan. (Illus.). 500p. 1997. pap. text ed. 5.99 (*1-888347-14-7*, Enigma); cd-rom 24.00 (*1-888347-13-9*, Enigma) Donnchad.

Unaccusativity: At the Syntax-Lexical Semantics Interface. Beth Levin & Malka R. Hovav. LC 94-17439. (Linguistic Inquiry Monographs: Vol. 26). 1994. 39.95 (*0-262-12185-9*); pap. 19.95 (*0-262-62094-4*) MIT Pr.

An Asterisk (*) at the beginning of an entry indicates that the title is appearing in BIP for the first time.

Unaccustomed Mercy: Soldier-Poets of the Vietnam War. Ed. by W. D. Ehrhart. LC 88-38693. (Illus.). xx, 147p. (Orig.). (C). 1989. 16.95 (0-89672-189-2); pap. 9.95 (0-89672-190-6) Tex Tech Univ Pr.

Unaccustomed to Fear: Biography of Gen. Roy S. Geiger. 2nd ed. Roger Willock. 333p. reprint ed. 9.95 (0-940328-05-4) Marine Corps.

Unacknowledged Harmony: Philo-Semitism & the Survival of European Jewry. Alan Edelstein. LC 81-1563. (Contributions in Ethnic Studies: No. 4). xii, 235p. 1982. text ed. 55.00 (0-313-22754-3, EDP/, Greenwood Pr) Greenwood.

Unadjusted Girl, with Cases & Standpoint for Behavior Analysis. William I. Thomas. LC 69-14951. (Criminology, Law Enforcement, & Social Problems Ser.: No. 26). 1969. reprint ed. 22.00 (0-87585-026-X) Patterson Smith.

Unadjusted Man: A New Hero for Americans. Peter R. Viereck. LC 74-178795. 339p. 1973. reprint ed. text ed. 59.75 (0-8371-6285-8, VUMA, Greenwood Pr) Greenwood.

Unafraid. Winnifred K. Rugg. LC 73-114891. (Select Bibliographies Reprint Ser.). 1977. 19.95 (0-8369-5295-2) Ayer.

Unafraid: A Life of Anne Hutchinson see Anne Hutchinson: Unsung Heroine of History 1591-1643

***Unafraid of the Dark.** Rosemary Bray. 1998. 24.00 (0-679-42555-1) Random.

Unamericans in Paris: A Novel. Jack Grant. LC 88-7320. 204p. (Orig.). 1988. pap. 7.95 (0-89087-525-1) Celestial Arts.

Unamonos en la Adoracion: Una Guia Administrativa. Tr. by Daniel Zamora from ENG. 96p. (Orig.). (SPA.). 1993. pap. 3.99 (0-311-32436-3) Casa Bautista.

Unamuno: Afinidades y Coincidencias Kierkegaardianas. Gemma Roberts. LC 86-60967. 144p. 1986. pap. 30.00 (0-89295-041-2) Society Sp & Sp-Am.

Unamuno: An Existential View of Self & Society. Paul Ilie. LC 67-25944. 311p. reprint ed. pap. 88.70 (0-317-08975-7, 2004654) Bks Demand.

Unamuno & the Novel as Expressionistic Conceit. David W. Foster. LC 73-75405. 52p. (Orig.). 1973. pap. 2.50 (0-913480-15-0) Inter Am U Pr.

Unamuno in English Literature. Peter G. Earle. 160p. 1960. 5.50 (0-318-22352-X) Hispanic Inst.

Unamuno Multiple: Antologia. Amelia Agostino De Del Rio. LC 81-10347. (Coleccion Mente y Palabra). 297p. 1982. 8.00 (0-8477-0582-X); pap. 7.00 (0-8477-0583-8) U of PR Pr.

Unamuno's Webs of Fatality. David G. Turner. (Monografias A Ser.: Vol. XLV). 170p. (Orig.). (C). 1974. pap. 36.00 (0-900411-90-2, Pub. by Tamesis Bks Ltd UK) Boydell & Brewer.

Unancestral Voice. Owen Barfield. LC 65-19854. 163p. 1986. pap. 12.95 (0-8195-6151-7, Wesleyan Univ Pr) U Pr of New Eng.

Unangam Ungiikangin Kayux Tunusangin: Aleut Tales & Narratives, 1909-1910. Ed. by Knut Bergsland & Moses Dirks. (Illus.). 715p. (Orig.). 1990. pap. text ed. 25.00 (1-55500-036-3) Alaska Native.

Unanimistic Imagery in Twentieth Century French Literature. Kathryn D. Wyatt. LC 74-75723. (Romance Monographs: No. 7). 1974. 26.00 (84-399-2159-4); pap. 21.00 (0-686-31731-9) Romance.

Unanimity Role & the League of Nations. Cromwell A. Riches. LC 70-174318. reprint ed. 39.50 (0-404-05330-0) AMS Pr.

Unanimous Tradition: Essays on the Essential Unity of all Religions. Ed. by Ranjit Fernando. (Illus.). 241p. 1995. 75.00 (955-9028-01-4) Paul & Co Pubs.

Unanswered Cries. Thomas French. 1992. mass mkt. 5.99 (0-312-92645-6) St Martin.

Unanswered Prayers. Penny Richards. 1994. mass mkt. 3.99 (0-373-82533-1, 1-82533-0) Harlequin Bks.

***Unanswered Prayers.** Penny Richards. 1997. mass mkt. 4.50 (0-373-87006-X, 1-87006-2) Harlequin Bks.

Unanswered Question: Six Talks at Harvard. Leonard Bernstein. (Charles Eliot Norton Lectures). 438p. 1976. boxed 30.00 incl. lp (0-674-81065-1) HUP.

Unanswered Question: Six Talks at Harvard. Leonard Bernstein. (Charles Eliot Norton Lectures). 438p. 1981. pap. text ed. 18.95 (0-674-92001-5) HUP.

***Unanswered Questions.** Rebecca L. Varady. (Orig.). 1997. pap. 8.95 (0-533-12331-3) Vantage.

Unanswered Questions: Theological Views of Jewish-Catholic Relations. Ed. by Roger Brooks. LC 87-40353. (C). 1995. reprint ed. pap. text ed. 14.95 (0-268-01902-9) U of Notre Dame Pr.

Unante: The Secrets of Karate. Sells. 1995. pap. 49.95 (0-910704-89-9) Hawley.

Unanticipated City: Loft Conversions in Lower Manhattan. James R. Hudson. LC 87-6003. (Illus.). 176p. (C). 1987. lib. bdg. 25.00 (0-87023-579-6) U of Mass Pr.

Unapologetic Theology: A Christian Voice in a Pluralistic Conversation. William C. Placher. LC 88-27706. 178p. 1989. pap. 16.00 (0-664-25064-5) Westminster John Knox.

***Unappropriated People: Freedmen in the Slave Society of Barbados.** Jerome S. Handler. LC 73-18489. 240p. 1974. reprint ed. pap. 68.40 (0-608-03732-X, 2064557) Bks Demand.

Unapproved Pension Schemes. Aidan Langley & Richard Mulcahy. 140p. 1994. boxed 143.00 (0-406-02982-2, UK) MICHIE.

Unarius a Biographical History, Vol. 1. Ruth E. Norman. (Illus.). 406p. 1985. 17.00 (0-932642-57-8) Unarius Acad Sci.

Unarius a Biographical History, Vol. 2. Ruth Norman. (Illus.). 387p. 1985. 17.00 (0-932642-58-6) Unarius Acad Sci.

Unarius Publications Catalogue. Unarius Educational Foundation Staff. (Illus.). 36p. 1995. pap. 2.00 (0-935097-01-5) Unarius Acad Sci.

Unarmed Against Hitler: Civilian Resistance in Europe, 1939-1943. Jacques Semelin. LC 92-32669. 216p. 1993. text ed. 55.00 (0-275-93960-X, C3960, Praeger Pubs); pap. text ed. 19.95 (0-275-93961-8, B3961, Praeger Pubs) Greenwood.

***Unarmed Bodyguards: International Accompaniment for the Protection of Human Rights.** Liam Mahony & Luis E. Eguren. LC 96-37848. (Illus.). xii, 290p. 1997. 46.00 (1-56549-069-X); pap. 21.95 (1-56549-068-1) Kumarian Pr.

Unarmed but Dangerous: Withering Attacks on All Things Phony, Foolish, & Fundamentally Wrong with America Today. Hal Crowther. 240p. 1995. 19.95 (1-56352-193-8) Longstreet Pr Inc.

Unarmed into Battle: The Story of the Air Observation Post. H. J. Parham & E. M. Belfield. 1987. reprint ed. 91.00 (0-317-90385-3, Pub. by Picton UK) St Mut.

Unarmed into Battle: The Story of the Air Observation Post by Major General H. J. Parham CB, CBE, DSO, & E.M.G. Belfield, MA. Ed. by Picton Publishing (Chippenham) Ltd. Staff. 1990. reprint ed. pap. 39.00 (0-948251-14-X, Pub. by Picton UK) St Mut.

Unarmed Urban Combat: A Realistic Self-Defense System. 1991. lib. bdg. 79.95 (0-8490-4752-8) Gordon Pr.

Unarmed Urban Combat: How to Survive in the Streets of America's Dangerous Cities. 1992. lib. bdg. 79.95 (0-8490-5249-1) Gordon Pr.

Unashamed Anglicanism: Authority & Ecclesiology. Stephen W. Sykes. 192p. (Orig.). 1995. pap. 17.95 (0-687-01460-3) Dimen for Liv.

Unassimilated Greeks of Denver. George J. Patterson, Jr. LC 88-36704. (Immigrant Communities & Ethnic Minorities in the U. S. & Canada Ser.: No. 41). 1989. 49.50 (0-404-19451-6) AMS Pr.

Unassisted Childbirth. Laura K. Shanley. LC 93-5268. 176p. 1993. text ed. 49.95 (0-89789-370-0, Bergin & Garvey); pap. text ed. 14.95 (0-89789-377-8, Bergin & Garvey) Greenwood.

Unassuming Agent. M. R. Foot. 405p. (C). 1993. 49.00 (1-85634-066-X, Pub. by Excalibur UK) St Mut.

Unattainable Earth. Czeslaw Milosz & Robert Hass. 140p. 1986. 17.95 (0-88001-098-3) Ecco Pr.

Unattainable Earth. Czeslaw Milosz & Robert Hass. 1987. pap. 10.95 (0-88001-102-5) Ecco Pr.

Unauthorised Flat Rate Schedule for Harley Davidson Motorcycles 1984. Mike Arman & John Bolender. 1986. ring bd. 8.00 (0-933078-13-7, H-D FLATRATE BO) M Arman.

Unauthorized Access. Diane Dean. 192p. 1992. 17.95 (0-8034-8977-3) Bouregy.

Unauthorized Action: Mountbatten & the Dieppe Raid. Brian L. Villa. (Illus.). 328p. 1989. 27.50 (0-19-540679-6) OUP.

Unauthorized Anne Rice Companion. Ed. by George W. Beahm. LC 95-4507. 264p. (Orig.). 1996. pap. 12.95 (0-8362-1036-0) Andrews & McMeel.

Unauthorized Broadcast: An Adventure Resource for Over the Edge. Robin D. Laws. (Over the Edge Ser.). 16p. 1993. pap. 4.95 (1-887801-06-5, Atlas Games) Trident MN.

***Unauthorized Guide to Snoopy Collectibles.** Jan Lindenberger. (Illus.). 160p. 1997. pap. 29.95 (0-7643-0200-0) Schiffer.

Unauthorized Guide to the X-Files. Hal J. Schuster. LC 97-8798. 240p. 1997. per., pap. 16.00 (0-7615-0845-7) Prima Pub.

Unauthorized History: Robbie Conal's Portraits of Power. Ed. by Deborah Irmas. 1990. pap. 19.50 (0-685-56970-5) Pasadena Art.

Unauthorized History of Dallas. Rose-Mary Rumbley. (Illus.). 192p. 1991. pap. 9.95 (0-89015-833-9) Sunbelt Media.

Unauthorized History Portraits. Robbie Conal. 1991. pap. 19.50 (0-932499-46-5) Lapis Pr.

***Unauthorized Insider's Guide to Nintendo 64.** Scott McCall. 96p. 1996. pap. text ed. 12.99 (0-7615-0523-7) Prima Pub.

Unauthorized Practice Handbook. Ed. by Justine Fischer & Dorothy H. Lackmann. LC 73-189569. xvi, 368p. 1990. reprint ed. 47.50 (0-89941-734-5, 306720) W S Hein.

Unauthorized Practice News: 1934-1976, Vols. 1-40. Bound set. 1,200.00 (0-8377-9171-5) Rothman.

***Unauthorized Starfleet Daily Meditation Manual: Going Boldly on Your Inner Voyage.** Mark S. Haskett. iv, 386p. (Orig.). 1996. pap. 11.95 (0-9655894-0-4, IF Books) Inner-Faith.

Unauthorized Strategy Guide to the Magic: The Gathering Card Game. Greg Williams. 1995. pap. text ed. 14.95 (0-7615-0260-2) Prima Pub.

Unauthorized Teacher Survival Guide. Jack Warner et al. LC 94-25315. 178p. (Orig.). 1995. pap. 12.95 (1-57112-068-8, P0688, Park Avenue) JIST Works.

Unauthorized Teenage Mutant Ninja Turtles Quiz Book. Jeff Rovin. 1990. pap. 3.50 (0-312-92469-0) St Martin.

Unauthorized Version: Truth & Fiction in the Bible. Robin L. Fox. LC 92-50601. 1993. pap. 16.00 (0-679-74406-1, Vin) Random.

Unauthorized Windows: Develop Res Kit. Andrew Schulman. 608p. 1994. pap. 39.99 (1-56884-305-4) IDG Bks.

Unauthorized Windows 95: A Programmer's Guide to Exploring the Foundations of Chicago with Disk. Andrew Schulman. 608p. 1994. pap. 29.99 (1-56884-169-8) IDG Bks.

Unauthorized X-Files Challenge. James Hatfield & George Burt. 256p. 1996. pap. 14.00 (1-57566-096-2, Knsington) Kensgtn Pub Corp.

***Unavoidable Germans: Art vs. Politics & the Consequences.** John Mosher. 402p. 1997. 49.50 (0-7618-0647-4) U Pr of Amer.

Unavoidable Industrial Restructuring in Latin America. Fernando Fajnzylber. LC 90-36418. 224p. (C). 1990. pap. text ed. 19.95 (0-8223-1095-3) Duke.

Unavoidable Industrial Restructuring in Latin America. Fernando Fajnzylber. LC 90-36418. 224p. (C). 1990. text ed. 49.95 (0-8223-1077-5) Duke.

***Unavoidable Man.** Barry Dempster. 80p. 1990. pap. 12.95 (0-919627-97-8, Pub. by Quarry Pr CN) LPC InBook.

Unavowable Community. Maurice Blanchot. Tr. by Pierre Joris. LC 87-15996. 96p. 1988. 13.95 (0-88268-043-9) Station Hill Pr.

Unaweep to Uravan: Time Travel Through 1.7 Billion Years into the Atomic Age. James Keener & Christine B. Keener. (Illus.). 46p. (Orig.). 1988. pap. 5.55 (0-929290-00-3) Grand Rivr CO.

***Unbabbling.** Reyoung. 256p. 1997. pap. 13.95 (1-56478-164-X) Dalkey Arch.

Unbaited Trap. rev. ed. Catherine Cookson. 336p. 1995. mass mkt. 7.99 (0-552-14076-7) Bantam.

***Unbaked Urns of Rudely Shape: Essays on British & Irish Pottery.** Ed. by Ian Kinnes & Gillian Varndell. (Oxbow Monographs in Archaeology: No. 55, 1995). (Illus.). 218p. 1995. pap. 48.00 (0-946897-94-8, Pub. by Oxbow Bks UK) David Brown.

Unbalance Response & Balancing of Flexible Rotors in Bearings. N. F. Rieger. LC 72-92595. (Flexible Rotor-Bearing System Dynamics Ser.: Vol. 2). (Illus.). 33p. reprint ed. pap. 25.00 (0-317-11118-3, 2012305) Bks Demand.

Unbalanced Acts. Jeff Raines. 272p. 1990. mass mkt. 4.50 (0-380-76008-8) Avon.

Unbalanced Mind: Alexander Pope & the Rule of Passion. Rebecca Ferguson. LC 86-7940. 222p. 1986. text ed. 42.95 (0-8122-8027-X) U of Pa Pr.

Unbalancing Acts: Foundations for a Theater. Richard Foreman. 368p. 1992. reprint ed. pap. 15.95 (1-55936-076-3) Theatre Comm.

Unbank the Fire: Visions for the Education of African American Children. Janice E. Hale. LC 94-2864. 1994. 29.95 (0-8018-4821-0); pap. 14.95 (0-8018-4822-9) Johns Hopkins.

***Unbearable.** Paul Jennings. 1998. pap. 4.99 (0-14-038595-9) Viking Penguin.

Unbearable! More Bizarre Stories. Paul Jennings. LC 94-45198. (J). 1995. pap. 14.99 (0-670-86262-2, Viking) Viking Penguin.

Unbearable Affect: A Guide to the Psychotherapy of Psychosis. David A. Garfield. LC 94-44789. (Series in General & Clinical Psychiatry). 177p. 1995. text ed. 32.50 (0-471-02536-4) Wiley.

Unbearable Bassington. Saki. 18.95 (0-8488-0843-6) Amereon Ltd.

Unbearable Heart. Kimiko Hahn. LC 94-75769. 80p. (Orig.). 1996. 22.00 (1-885030-00-2); pap. 11.95 (1-885030-01-0) Kaya Prod.

Unbearable Lightness of Being. Milan Kundera. LC 83-48383. 320p. 1988. reprint ed. pap. 13.00 (0-06-091465-3, PL/1465, PL) HarpC.

Unbearable Weight: Feminism, Western Culture, & the Body. Susan Bordo. LC 92-41582. 362p. 1993. 30.00 (0-520-07979-5) U CA Pr.

Unbearable Weight: Feminism, Western Culture, & the Body. Susan Bordo. 1995. pap. 15.00 (0-520-08883-2) U CA Pr.

Unbearables. Ed. by Ron Kolm et al. 288p. Date not set. 12.00 (1-57027-053-8) Autonomedia.

Unbearably Gross Jokes, Vol. XXII. Julius Alvin. 160p. 1996. mass mkt. 4.99 (0-8217-5264-2, Zebra Kensgtn) Kensgtn Pub Corp.

Unbeatable Bessie: A Biography of Bessie Kidd Best. Elinor C. Kyte. LC 87-71714. 256p. (Orig.). 1988. pap. 10.00 (0-916383-31-8) Aegina Pr.

Unbeatable Bread. Lyn L. Hoopes. LC 94-17043. (Illus.). 32p. (J). (ps-3). 1996. pap. 14.99 (0-8037-1611-7); pap. 14.89 (0-8037-1612-5) Dial Bks Young.

***Unbeatable Chicken Recipes.** Lou S. Pappas. (Illus.). 176p. (Orig.). 1997. pap. 8.95 (1-55867-189-7, Nitty Gritty Ckbks) Bristol Pub Ent CA.

Unbeatable Spirit of Faith. Gloria Copeland. 20p. 1995. pap. 1.00 (1-57562-014-6) K Copeland Pubns.

Unbeaten Tracks in Japan. Isabella L. Bird. LC 75-172002. (Illus.). 352p. 1971. pap. 12.95 (0-8048-1000-1) C E Tuttle.

***Unbecoming.** Eric Michaels. LC 97-7920. 152p. 1997. text ed. 39.95 (0-8223-2005-3); pap. text ed. 13.95 (0-8223-2014-2) Duke.

Unbecoming Conduct. Berneice Bell. Ed. by Renais J. Hill. LC 92-54778. (Illus.). 188p. (Orig.). 1993. pap. 10.95 (1-55666-084-7) Pubs Grp Toluca.

Unbecoming Men: A Men's Consciousness-Raising Group Writes on Oppression & Themselves. LC 87-176689. (Illus.). 64p. (Orig.). (C). 1971. pap. 4.25 (0-87810-015-6) Times Change.

Unbecoming Women: British Women Writing & the Novel of Development. Susan Fraiman. (Gender & Culture Ser.). 189p. 1994. pap. 15.50 (0-231-08001-8) Col U Pr.

Unbehagen in der Kultur. Sigmund Freud. 192p. (GER.). 1994. pap. 15.25 (3-596-10453-X, Pub. by Fischer Taschbch Verlag GW) Intl Bk Import.

Unbeholden Bk. 3: Vampire: The Masquerade of the Red Death Trilogy. Robert Weinberg. (Illus.). (Orig.). (YA). 1996. pap. 5.99 (1-56504-842-3, 12402, Wrld of Darkness) White Wolf.

***Unbekannte Judische Sekte.** Louis Ginzberg. x, 384p. (GER.). 1972. reprint ed. write for info. (3-487-04502-8) G Olms Pubs.

Unbelievable! More Surprising Stories. Paul Jennings. (J). 1995. pap. 3.99 (0-14-037635-6) Puffin Bks.

Unbelievable Bubble Book. John Cassidy. 138p. (Orig.). 1987. pap. 12.95 (0-932592-15-5) Klutz Pr.

***Unbelievable Good Deals.** 9th ed. Rattner & Heilman. LC 97-3773. 1997. pap. write for info. (0-8092-3101-8) Contemp Bks.

Unbelievable Truth! Jeff Rovin. 176p. (Orig.). 1994. pap. 3.99 (0-451-17761-4, Sig) NAL-Dutton.

Unbelievably Good Deals & Great Adventures That You Absolutely Can't Get Unless You're over 50. Joan R. Heilman. (Illus.). 320p. 1995. pap. 8.95 (0-8092-3426-2) Contemp Bks.

Unbelievably Good Deals & Great Adventures That You Absolutely Can't Get Unless You're over 50. 6th rev. ed. Joan R. Heilman. 304p. 1994. pap. 8.95 (0-8092-3637-0) Contemp Bks.

Unbelievably Good Deals & Great Adventures That You Absolutely Can't Get Unless You're Over 50. 8th ed. Joan R. Heilman. (Illus.). 320p. (Orig.). 1996. pap. 9.95 (0-8092-3233-2) Contemp Bks.

***Unbelievably Good Deals That You Absolutely Can't Get Unless You're a Parent.** (Orig.). 1997. pap. 12.95 (0-614-28120-2) Contemp Bks.

***Unbelievably Good Deals That You Absolutely Can't Get Unless You're a Parent.** Cary O. Yager. LC 97-19561. 1997. pap. 12.95 (0-8092-3205-7) Contemp Bks.

Unbelievably Good Deals That You Absolutely Can't Get Unless You're a Teacher. Barry Harrington & Beth Christensen. LC 95-37269. 320p. 1995. pap. 12.95 (0-8092-3510-2) Contemp Bks.

Unbeliever. Lisa Lewis. LC 94-10661. (Brittingham Prize in Poetry Ser.). 72p. (C). 1994. pap. 10.95 (0-299-14404-6); text ed. 17.95 (0-299-14400-3) U of Wis Pr.

Unbeliever: The Poetry of Elizabeth Bishop. Robert D. Parker. LC 87-34285. 184p. 1988. text ed. 24.95 (0-252-01509-6) U of Ill Pr.

Unbelieving Husbands & the Wives Who Love Them. Michael J. Fanstone. LC 95-44472. 156p. 1996. pap. 9.99 (0-89283-940-6, Vine Bks) Servant.

Unbelonging. rev. ed. Joan Riley. 144p. 1997. pap. 11.95 (0-7043-3959-5, Pub. by Womens Press UK) Trafalgar.

***Unbending Intent.** Rodger Moody. 26p. 1997. 5.00 (0-614-30125-4) Skydog OR.

***Unbescheidene Charakterologie: Geistige Differenz von Jedentum und Christentum, Otto Weiningers Lehre von Bestimmten Charakter.** Waltraud Hirsch. (Tubinger Beitrage Zur Religionswissenschaft Ser.: Bd. 3). (Illus.). 414p. (GER.). 1997. 63.95 (3-631-31129-X) P Lang Pubng.

Unbiased Estimators & Their Applications Vol. 2: Multivariate Case. Vasilii G. Voinov. (Mathematics & Its Applications Ser.). 272p. (C). 1996. lib. bdg. 135.00 (0-7923-3939-8) Kluwer Ac.

Unbiased Estimators & Their Applications, Vol. 1: Univariate Case. Vasilii G. Voinov & M. S. Nikulin. LC 93-22145. (Mathematics & Its Applications Ser.: Vol. 263). 532p. (ENG.). (C). 1993. lib. bdg. 269.50 (0-7923-2382-3) Kluwer Ac.

***Unbiased Stereology: A Practical Guide.** M. Reed & V. Howard. (Microscopy Handbooks Ser.). 144p. 1997. pap. 16.95 (1-85996-071-5, Pub. by Bios Scientific UK) Coronet Bks.

***Unbiased Stereology: A Practical Guide.** M. Reed & V. Howard. (Microscopy Handbooks Ser.). (Illus.). 144p. 1997. pap. 32.95 (0-387-91516-8) Spr-Verlag.

Unbidden Guest. Silvio Villa. LC 77-142280. (Short Story Index Reprint Ser.). (Illus.). 1977. 20.95 (0-8369-3764-3) Ayer.

Unbinding of Prometheus. Howard P. Kainz. LC 76-4231. 1976. 10.95 (0-87212-055-4) Libra.

Unbinding Prometheus: Education for the Coming Age. Donald Cowan. 223p. 1988. 17.00 (0-911005-12-9); pap. 15.00 (0-911005-33-1) Dallas Inst Pubns.

UNBIS Thesaurus. 557p. 1986. 25.00 (92-1-100279-6, E. 85.I.20) UN.

UNBIS (United Nations Bibliographic Information System) Thesaurus. 2nd ed. United Nations Staff. 557p. (ENG, FRE & SPA.). 1992. 49.95 (0-8288-7360-7, 9211002796) Fr & Eur.

Unblocking Organizational Communication. Dave Francis. 200p. 1987. text ed. 54.95 (0-566-02572-8, Pub. by Gower UK) Ashgate Pub Co.

Unblocking Your Organization. Mike Woodcock & Dave Francis. Orig. Title: People at Work. 256p. 1990. text ed. 56.95 (0-566-02854-9, Pub. by Gower UK) Ashgate Pub Co.

Unbodied Hope: Narcissism & the Modern Novel. Lawrence Thornton. LC 83-43104. 224p. 1984. 34.50 (0-8387-5065-6) Bucknell U Pr.

Unbonded Tendons in Post-Tensioned Construction. Arthur E. Andrew. 48p. 1987. 30.00 (0-7277-0379-X, Pub. by T Telford UK) Am Soc Civil Eng.

Unborn: The Life & Teachings of Zen Master Bankei (1622-1693) Bankei Yotaku. Tr. by Norman Waddell from JPN. LC 83-63133. 192p. 1982. pap. 11.95 (0-86547-153-3, North Pt Pr) FS&G.

Unborn Baby Book. Jack H. McCubbin & Marjorie V. Fuqua. (Illus.). 128p. (Orig.). 1985. pap. 7.95 (0-9615085-7-4) Tex Med Pr.

Unborn Baby Book. 2nd ed. Jack H. McCubbin & Marjorie F. McCubbin. LC 85-51698. (Illus.). 144p. (Orig.). 1986. pap. 7.95 (0-9615085-8-2) Tex Med Pr.

Unborn Child: How to Recognize & Overcome Pre-Natal Trauma. Roy Ridgway. 160p. 1987. text ed. 36.95 (0-7045-3089-9, Pub. by Avebury Pub UK) Ashgate Pub Co.

Unborn Patient: Prenatal Diagnosis & Treatment. 2nd ed. Harrison & Roy A. Filly. (Illus.). 674p. 1990. text ed. 199.00 (0-7216-4538-0) Saunders.

Unborn Revolution. Guy Sorman. vi, 327p. 1991. text ed. 37.50 (0-7069-5799-7) Advent Bks Div.

U V

Unbottled Scotch. Nonie Rienow. 1987. pap. 10.95 (*0-940168-06-5*) Boxwood.

***Unbought Grace of Life: Essays in Honor of Russell Kirk.** Ed. by James E. Person. Date not set. pap. 19.95 (*0-89385-043-8*) Sugden.

Unbound. Marcus Van Heller. 368p. 1994. pap. 5.95 (*0-7867-0112-9*) Carroll & Graf.

Unbound: A Book of Aids. Aaron Shurin. 89p. 1997. 17.95 (*1-55713-112-0*) Sun & Moon CA.

Unbound: A Spiritual Guide to Mastery of the Material World. Dorien Israel. 188p. (Orig.). 1986. pap. 15.00 (*1-879473-00-3*) Willow Way.

Unbound Feet: A Social History of Chinese Women in San Francisco. Judy Yung. LC 94-40397. 374p. 1995. 45.00 (*0-520-08866-2*); pap. 15.95 (*0-520-08867-0*) U CA Pr.

Unbound Prometheus: Technological Change & Industrial Development in Western Europe from 1750 to the Present. David S. Landes. 576p. (C). 1969. pap. text ed. 22.95 (*0-521-09418-6*) Cambridge U Pr.

Unbounded Community: Neighborhood Life & Social Structure in New York City, 1830-1875. Kenneth A. Scherzer. LC 91-40452. 375p. 1992. text ed. 39.95 (*0-8223-1228-X*) Duke.

Unbounded Community: Papers in Christian Ecumenism in Honor of Jaroslav Pelikan. Ed. by William Caferro & Duncan G. Fisher. LC 95-19418. (Garland Reference Library of the Humanities: Vol. 1822). 264p. 1996. text ed. 39.00 (*0-8153-1596-1*, H1822) Garland.

Unbounded Frame: Freedom & Community in Nineteenth Century American Utopianism. Michael Fellman. LC 72-797. 203p. 1973. text ed. 49.95 (*0-8371-6369-2*, FUF/, Greenwood Pr) Greenwood.

Unbounded Light: The Inward Journey. William E. Williams. LC 92-1759. 256p. (Orig.). 1992. pap. 14.95 (*0-89254-023-0*) Nicolas-Hays.

Unbounded Linear Operations: Theory & Applications. Seymour Goldberg. (Mathematics Ser.). 199p. 1985. reprint ed. pap. 7.95 (*0-486-64830-3*) Dover.

Unbounded Love: A Good News Theology for the 21st Century. Clark H. Pinnock & Robert C. Brow. LC 94-26381. 192p. (Orig.). 1994. pap. 12.99 (*0-8308-1853-7*, 1853) InterVarsity.

Unbounded Mind: Breaking the Chains of Traditional Business Thinking. Ian I. Mitroff & Harold A. Linstone. (Illus.). 192p. 1995. pap. 10.95 (*0-19-510288-6*) OUP.

Unbounded Non-Commutative Integration. J. P. Jurzak. 1985. lib. bdg. 122.00 (*90-277-1815-6*) Kluwer Ac.

Unbounded Operator Algebras & Representation Theory. Konrad Schmudgen. (Operator Theory Ser.: No. 37). 290p. 1990. 146.50 (*0-8176-2321-3*) Birkhauser.

Unbreakable Code. Sara H. Hunter. LC 95-26589. (Illus.). 32p. (YA). (gr. 3 up). 1996. lib. bdg. 14.95 (*0-87358-638-7*) Northland AZ.

Unbreakable Promises: How to Know & Receive all that God Has Given You. R. Russell Bixler. 192p. (Orig.). 1987. pap. 5.95 (*0-9617094-1-3*) Baldwin Manor Pr.

Unbreakable Thread: Non-Racialism in South Africa. Julie Frederikse. (Illus.). 304p. 1991. 39.95 (*0-253-32473-4*); pap. 7.95 (*0-253-20619-7*, MB-619) Ind U Pr.

Unbribed Soul. D. W. Lambert. 1979. pap. 4.95 (*0-87508-305-6*) Chr Lit.

Unbridgeable Gulf. Michael R. Warren. Ed. by William Smith. (Illus.). 298p. (Orig.). 1995. pap. 13.95 (*0-9618862-3-4*) Bay Limited.

Unbridled. Mark Daniel. 256p. 1992. mass mkt. 4.99 (*0-380-71443-4*) Avon.

Unbridled Ego. James L. Henderson. 157p. 1988. 10.95 (*0-318-36923-0*) Asia Bk Corp.

Unbridled Love. large type ed. Jessica Porter. (Linford Romance Library). 288p. 1992. pap. 15.99 (*0-7089-7289-6*, Trailtree Bookshop) Ulverscroft.

***Unbridled Power: Inside the Secret Culture of the IRS.** Shelley L. Davis. 288p. 1997. 25.00 (*0-88730-829-5*) Harper Busn.

Unbridled Spirits: Short Fiction about Women in the Old West. Ed. by Judy Alter et al. LC 93-14335. 392p. (C). 1994. pap. 17.95 (*0-87565-124-0*) Tex Christian.

***Unbroken Bread: Healing Worship Wounds.** Mike Root. LC 97-11028. 270p. (Orig.). (C). 1997. pap. 8.99 (*0-89900-779-1*) College Pr Pub.

Unbroken Chain. Neil Rosenstein. (C). 1990. 69.95 (*1-56062-023-4*) CIS Comm.

Unbroken Circle: Ecotheology, Theodicy, & Ethics. J. Michael Clark. LC 95-51980. 220p. 1996. pap. 20.00 (*0-930383-47-8*) Monument Pr.

***Unbroken Circle: How to Take Your Family Through the End Time.** John Youngberg & Millie Youngberg. LC 97-12840. 1997. pap. write for info. (*0-8163-1344-X*) Pacific Pr Pub Assn.

***Unbroken Circle: Talks from the African American & Ancient Christianity Conferences.** Ed. by Paisius Altschul. (Illus.). 250p. Date not set. pap. 12.95 (*0-916700-51-8*) Christ Saviour.

***Unbroken Circles: Traditional Arts of Contemporary Woodland Peoples.** Ed. by Jose Barreiro. (Illus.). 96p. (Orig.). 1990. pap. 10.00 (*0-614-29680-3*) Akwe Kon Pr.

Unbroken Curses. Rebecca Brown. 175p. (SPA.). 1996. pap. 9.99 (*0-88368-399-7*) Whitaker Hse.

Unbroken Curses: Hidden Source of Trouble in the Christian's Life. Rebecca Brown. 175p. 1995. pap. 9.99 (*0-88368-372-5*) Whitaker Hse.

Unbroken Force of Abraham's Blessings, Vol. 3. Jay S. Snell. (Orig.). 1990. pap. 9.00 (*0-685-67690-0*) J Snell Evangelistic.

Unbroken Landscape: Commodity, Category, Sign & Identity: Their Production as Myth & Knowledge from 1500. Frank Perlin. (Collected Studies). 376p. 1994. 94.95 (*0-86078-431-2*, Pub. by Variorum UK) Ashgate Pub Co.

Unbroken Poetry II, Poesie ininterrompue II. Paul Eluard. Tr. by Gilbert Bowen from FRE. LC 96-164135. 160p. 9600. pap. 18.95 (*1-85224-134-9*, Pub. by Bloodaxe Bks UK) Dufour.

Unbroken Promises: A True Story of Courage & Belief. Vance A. Davis & Brian Blashaw. Ed. & Intro. by Brian Blashaw. 280p. 1995. 22.95 (*1-887266-00-3*) White Mesa Pubs.

Unbroken Thread: A History of Quiltmaking in the Catskills. Steve Hoare. (Illus.). 248p. (Orig.). 1996. pap. 21.95 (*1-883789-07-9*) Blk Dome Pr.

Unbroken Thread: An Anthology of Plays by Asian American Women. Ed. by Roberta Uno. LC 93-21858. 336p. (C). 1993. pap. 19.95 (*0-87023-856-6*) U of Mass Pr.

***Unbroken Thread : Conserving the Textile Traditions of Oaxaca.** Kathryn Klein & Getty Conservation Institute Staff. LC 97-15961. 1997. pap. write for info. (*0-89236-381-9*, J P Getty Museum) J P Getty Trust.

***Unbroken Thread: Conserving the Textile Traditions of Oaxaca.** Kathryn Klein & Getty Conservation Institute Staff. LC 97-15961. 1997. write for info. (*0-89236-380-0*, J P Getty Museum) J P Getty Trust.

Unbroken Ties: Lesbian Ex-Lovers. Carol Becker. 230p. (Orig.). 1988. pap. 9.95 (*1-55583-106-0*) Alyson Pubns.

Unbroken Vows. Ralph V. Reynolds. 132p. (Orig.). (C). 1986. pap. 6.95 (*0-685-27253-2*) Alpha Bible Pubns.

Unbroken Vows. Frances Williams. (Intimate Moments Ser.: No. 724). 1996. mass mkt. 3.99 (*0-373-07724-6*, 1-07724-7) Silhouette.

Unbuilding. David Macaulay. (Illus.). (J). (gr. 3 up). 1980. 16.95 (*0-395-29457-6*) HM.

Unbuilding. David Macaulay. (J). (gr. k-3). 1987. pap. 7.95 (*0-395-45425-5*) HM.

Unbuilding. David Macaulay. LC 80-15491. (Sandpipers Ser.). (Illus.). 128p. (J). (gr. 5 up). 1987. pap. 6.95 (*0-395-45360-7*) HM.

Unbuilding Jerusalem: Apocalypse & Romantic Representation. Steven Goldsmith. LC 92-27066. (Illus.). 344p. 1993. 49.95 (*0-8014-2717-7*); pap. 18.95 (*0-8014-9999-2*) Cornell U Pr.

UnBuilt. Raimund Abraham. (Illus.). 315p. 1996. 104.00 (*3-211-82671-8*) Spr-Verlag.

Unbuilt Oxford. Howard Colvin. LC 83-42870. (Illus.). 208p. 1983. pap. 26.00 (*0-300-03126-2*, Y-481) Yale U Pr.

Unbundling Credit Department Costs. William G. Dearhammer. LC 84-16618. (Illus.). 76p. (Orig.). 1984. pap. text ed. 36.00 (*0-936742-19-4*) Robt Morris Assocs.

***UNC Coloring Book.** unabridged ed. John V. Allcott. (Illus.). 16p. (Orig.). (J). (gr. 1-3). 1993. pap. 2.00 (*0-940715-07-4*) Chapel Hill Hist.

Uncaged. Lucy Gordon. 1994. mass mkt. 2.99 (*0-373-05864-0*, 5-05864-9) Harlequin Bks.

Uncaged. TSR Hobbies Staff. 1996. 20.00 (*0-7869-0385-6*) TSR Inc.

Uncaging Animal Spirits: Essays on Engineering, Entrepreneurship, & Economics. Ralph Landau. Ed. by Martha V. Gottron. (Illus.). 380p. 1994. 42.50 (*0-262-12183-2*) MIT Pr.

Uncalled. Paul L. Dunbar. 15.00 (*1-56675-010-5*) Mnemosyne.

Uncalled. Paul L. Dunbar. LC 78-164804. reprint ed. 19.50 (*0-404-00042-8*) AMS Pr.

Uncalled. Paul L. Dunbar. LC 71-81116. (Black Heritage Library Collection). (C). 1977. reprint ed. 38.95 (*0-8369-8567-2*) Ayer.

Uncalled. Paul L. Dunbar. LC 71-81116. (Black Heritage Library Collection). (C). 1991. reprint ed. pap. 26.95 (*0-88143-130-3*) Ayer.

Uncalled. Paul L. Dunbar. LC 70-104443. reprint ed. lib. bdg. 9.50 (*0-8398-0374-5*) Irvington.

Uncalled. Paul L. Dunbar. (Notable American Authors Ser.). 1992. reprint ed. lib. bdg. 75.00 (*0-7812-2711-9*) Rprt Serv.

Uncancelled Challenge: The Work of Raymond Williams. Nicolas Tredell. 96p. 1990. reprint ed. pap. 17.00 (*0-946650-16-0*); reprint ed. lib. bdg. 27.00 (*0-8095-6763-6*) Borgo Pr.

***Uncanny.** Andrew Klavan. LC 97-16764. 1998. write for info. (*0-609-60112-1*) Crown Pub Group.

Uncanny! Even More Surprising Stories. Paul Jennings. 144p. (J). 1995. pap. 3.99 (*0-14-037576-7*) Puffin Bks.

Uncanny! Even More Surprising Stories. Paul Jennings. (J). (gr. 5-7). 1991. pap. 13.95 (*0-670-84174-9*) Viking Child Bks.

***Uncanny Quarry: The Shadow of Cheops.** unabridged ed. Stephen Wagshel. LC 97-71222. (Illus.). 100p. (Orig.). 1997. pap. 10.95 (*1-879629-56-9*) Galaxy Pub CO.

***Uncanny Spectacle: The Public Career of the Young John Singer Sargent.** Marc Simpson et al. LC 97-5781. 1997. pap. write for info. (*0-931102-38-3*) Yale U Pr.

***Uncanny Spectacle: The Public Career of the Young John Singer Sargent.** Marc Simpson. LC 97-5781. (Illus.). 240p. 1997. 40.00 (*0-300-07177-9*) Yale U Pr.

Uncanny Tales. Douglas A. Menville. LC 75-46294. (Supernatural & Occult Fiction Ser.). 1976. reprint ed. lib. bdg. 23.95 (*0-405-08155-3*) Ayer.

Uncanny X-Men. Marvel Entertainment Staff. 128p. 1990. pap. 3.99 (*0-8125-1021-6*) Tor Bks.

Uncanny X-Men Masterworks. Stan Lee. (Illus.). 1993. pap. 12.95 (*0-87135-964-2*) Marvel Entmnt.

Uncaring Eyes Can Never See. Genevieve Mancini. 1979. 2.95 (*0-9604328-0-9*) G Mancini.

Uncas Slattery: A Two Act Play. Robert F. Morgan. 90p. 1994. pap. 34.00 (*1-885679-07-6*) Morgan Fnd Pubs.

Unceasing Abuses: Human Rights in Mexico One Year after the Introduction of Reform. Ed. by Human Rights Watch Staff. 38p. (Orig.). 1991. pap. 5.00 (*1-56432-040-5*) Hum Rts Watch.

Unceasing Memory of God. Theophan the Recluse. 1996. pap. 0.50 (*0-89981-160-4*) Eastern Orthodox.

Uncegila's Seventh Spot: A Lakota Legend. Illus. by Irving Toddy. LC 93-33350. 28p. (J). (gr. 3-6). 1995. 14.95 (*0-395-68970-8*, Clarion Bks) HM.

Uncensored Celebrities. Edward R. Thompson. LC 71-117855. (Essay Index Reprint Ser.). 1977. 20.95 (*0-8369-1687-5*) Ayer.

***Uncensored Fantasies.** Danielle Engle. (Orig.). 1997. mass mkt. 6.95 (*1-56333-572-7*, Rosebud) Masquerade.

Uncensored Paper Mill: Excerpts from the Man on the Moon. Tom Fallon. 56p. (Orig.). 1986. pap. 5.00 (*0-9616146-2-5*) Small-Small Pr.

Uncensored Thoughts: Pot Shots from a Public Librarian. Will Manley. LC 94-20155. (Illus.). 173p. 1994. lib. bdg. 23.95 (*0-89950-992-4*) McFarland & Co.

Uncensored War: The Media & Vietnam. Daniel C. Hallin. 1989. pap. 14.95 (*0-520-06543-3*) U CA Pr.

Uncertain Angels. Kim Cates. (Intimate Moments Ser.). 1994. mass mkt. 3.50 (*0-373-07550-2*, 5-07550-2) Silhouette.

Uncertain April. Betty P. Nelson. 336p. 1994. 20.95 (*0-312-11084-7*) St Martin.

Uncertain Balance: Federal Regulators in a Changing Political Economy. Glenn Davis & Gary Helfand. LC 84-12329. (Illus.). 208p. (Orig.). 1985. pap. text ed. 9.95 (*0-89529-185-1*) Avery Pub.

Uncertain Belief: Is It Rational to Be a Christian? David J. Bartholomew. LC 95-24826. 304p. 1996. 29.95 (*0-19-826378-3*, Clarendon Pr) OUP.

Uncertain Boundaries: The Social & Political Construction of European Economies. Marino Regini. (Cambridge Studies in Comparative Politics). (Illus.). 192p. (C). 1995. 57.95 (*0-521-47371-3*) Cambridge U Pr.

Uncertain Certainty: Interviews, Essays, & Notes on Poetry. Charles Simic. 280p. 1986. pap. 13.95 (*0-472-06359-6*) U of Mich Pr.

Uncertain Companions. Robbi Sommers. 224p. 1992. pap. 9.95 (*1-56280-017-5*) Naiad Pr.

Uncertain Crusade: America & the Russian Revolution of 1905. Arthur W. Thompson & Robert A. Hart. LC 73-96707. 192p. 1970. 27.50 (*0-87023-056-5*) U of Mass Pr.

Uncertain Death. Laura Coburn. 1996. pap. 5.99 (*0-451-40640-0*, Onyx) NAL-Dutton.

Uncertain Detente. Frans A. Alting Von Geusau. 310p. 1979. lib. bdg. 107.00 (*90-286-0818-4*) Kluwer Ac.

Uncertain Earth. Kay Cornelius. Date not set. pap. write for info. (*0-345-40357-6*) Ballantine Trade.

Uncertain Friendship: American-French Diplomatic Relations Through the Cold War. Marvin R. Zahniser. LC 75-23047. (America & the World Ser.). 328p. (C). reprint ed. 93.50 (*0-8357-9997-2*, 2012526) Bks Demand.

Uncertain Friendship: Theodore Roosevelt & Japan, 1906-1909. Charles E. Neu. LC 67-27091. 359p. 1967. reprint ed. pap. 102.40 (*0-7837-4172-3*, 2059021) Bks Demand.

Uncertain Future: Commercial Banks in the Third World. Ed. by Richard E. Feinberg & Valeriana Kallab. (U. S. Third World Policy Perspectives Ser.). 146p. 1984. 39.95 (*0-88738-041-7*); pap. 21.95 (*0-87855-989-2*) Transaction Pubs.

Uncertain Future: Thought Control & Repression During the Reagan-Bush Era. Richard O. Curry. LC 92-82816. (Illus.). 100p. 1993. pap. 12.00 (*0-9627705-1-5*) Frst Amendment.

Uncertain Future of China. H. J. Hsia. (East-West Communication Ser.). 300p. 1994. 29.95 (*1-881673-12-X*); pap. 9.95 (*1-881673-13-8*) Amer Assoc Pub.

Uncertain Future of the Urban Core. Ed. by E. K. Grime et al. 272p. 1988. lib. bdg. 55.00 (*0-415-00464-0*) Routledge.

Uncertain Futures: Occupied City-Owned Housing in East Harlem. Luis F. Sierra. 72p. 1992. 9.00 (*0-88156-124-X*) Comm Serv Soc NY.

Uncertain Glory: Folklore & the American Revolution. Tristram P. Coffin. LC 77-147812. 284p. 1971. 40.00 (*0-8103-5040-8*) Gale.

Uncertain Glory: Letters of Cautious but Sound Advice. Frederic W. Ness. LC 74-152812. (Jossey-Bass Higher Education Ser.). 168p. reprint ed. 47.90 (*0-8357-9353-2*, 2013820) Bks Demand.

Uncertain Glory: Robert E. Lee at War. John D. McKenzie. (Illus.). 400p. 1996. 29.95 (*0-7818-0502-3*) Hippocrene Bks.

Uncertain Grace: Essays by Eduardo Galeano & Fred Ritchin. Eduardo Galeano & Fred Ritchin. (Illus.). 154p. 60.00 (*0-89381-421-0*) Aperture.

Uncertain Grace: Essays by Eduardo Galeano & Fred Ritchin. Eduardo Galeano & Fred Ritchin. (Illus.). 154p. pap. 39.95 (*0-89381-460-1*) Aperture.

Uncertain Haven: Refugee Protection on the 40th Anniversary of the 1951 United Nations Refugee Convention. Lawyers Committee for Human Rights Staff. 243p. (Orig.). 1991. pap. 12.00 (*0-934143-45-5*) Lawyers Comm Human.

Uncertain Health. Stuart Friebert. LC 78-68473. 1979. 7.95 (*0-913506-08-7*) Woolmer-Brotherson.

Uncertain Hour. Nicholas A. Patricca. 1995. 5.25 (*0-87129-534-2*, U17) Dramatic Pub.

Uncertain Information Processing in Expert Systems. Peter Hajek & Tomas Havranek. 232p. 1992. 165.95 (*0-8493-6368-3*, QA76) CRC Pr.

Uncertain Knowledge: An Image of Science for a Changing World. R. G. Dolby. (Illus.). 340p. (C). 1996. text ed. 59.95 (*0-521-56004-7*) Cambridge U Pr.

Uncertain Legacies: Federal Budget Policy from Roosevelt Through Reagan. Dennis S. Ippolito. 352p. 1990. text ed. 37.50 (*0-8139-1287-3*) U Pr of Va.

Uncertain Light. Anson Crane. 320p. (Orig.). 1994. pap. 7.85 (*0-9639069-5-X*) Desert Low.

***Uncertain Lives, Untimely Deaths: Experiences & Psychological Needs of the Young Adult with Serious Chronic Illness.** Suzanne Quin. (Developments in Nursing & Health Care Ser.). 176p. 1996. text ed. 55.95 (*1-85972-497-3*, Pub. by Avebury Pub UK) Ashgate Pub Co.

Uncertain Magic. Laura Kinsale. 384p. 1987. mass mkt. 5.99 (*0-380-75140-2*) Avon.

Uncertain Mandate: Politics of the U. N. Congo Operation. Ernest W. Lefever. LC 67-22890. 270p. reprint ed. pap. 77.00 (*0-317-28789-3*, 2020540) Bks Demand.

Uncertain Models & Robust Control. A. Weinmann. (Illus.). xxix, 693p. 1991. 158.95 (*0-387-82299-2*) Spr-Verlag.

Uncertain Motherhood. Ed. by Peggy A. Field & Patricia Marck. 256p. 1994. 46.00 (*0-8039-5564-2*); pap. 22.50 (*0-8039-5565-0*) Sage.

Uncertain Outcome: The Politics of the Portuguese Transition to Democracy. Paul C. Manuel. 214p. (C). 1994. lib. bdg. 39.00 (*0-8191-9651-7*) U Pr of Amer.

Uncertain Partners: Stalin, Mao, & the Korean War. Sergei N. Goncharov et al. LC 93-23971. (Studies in International Security & Arms Control). (Illus.). 432p. (C). 1993. 55.00 (*0-8047-2115-7*) Stanford U Pr.

Uncertain Partners: Stalin, Mao, & the Korean War. Sergei N. Goncharov et al. (Illus.). 424p. 1995. pap. 17.95 (*0-8047-2521-7*) Stanford U Pr.

Uncertain Passage: China's Transition to the Post-Mao Era. A. Doak Barnett. LC 73-22482. 405p. reprint ed. pap. 115.50 (*0-317-30179-9*, 2025361) Bks Demand.

Uncertain Perceptions: U. S. Cold War Crisis Decision Making. Robert B. McCalla. 250p. (C). 1992. text ed. 44.50 (*0-472-10228-1*) U of Mich Pr.

***Uncertain Pilgrim: All That Life Has to Offer.** 3rd ed. J. Patrick Ware. 219p. (Orig.). 1997. spiral bd. 20.00 (*0-9658224-2-7*) J P Ware.

Uncertain Profession: Harvard & the Search for Educational Authority. Arthur G. Powell. LC 79-26096. 361p. 1980. reprint ed. pap. 102.90 (*0-7837-4180-4*, 2059029) Bks Demand.

Uncertain Promise: Value Conflicts in Technology Transfer. Denis Goulet. LC 88-34485. 364p. 1989. reprint ed. pap. 17.50 (*0-945257-04-X*) Apex Pr.

Uncertain Promise of Law: Lessons from Bhopal. Jamie Cassels. 364p. 1993. 45.00 (*0-8020-2841-1*); pap. 19.95 (*0-8020-7722-6*) U of Toronto Pr.

Uncertain Reasoner's Companion: A Mathematical Perspective. J. B. Paris. (Tracts in Theoretical Computer Science Ser.: No. 39). 180p. (C). 1995. text ed. 42.95 (*0-521-46089-1*) Cambridge U Pr.

Uncertain Refuge: Italy & the Jews During the Holocaust. Nicola Caracciolo. Ed. by Florette R. Koffler & Richard Koffler. Tr. by Richard Koffler. LC 94-16156. (Illus.). 224p. 1995. 16.95 (*0-252-06424-0*); text ed. 39.50 (*0-252-01923-7*) U of Ill Pr.

Uncertain Retirement: Securing Pension Promises in a World at Risk. James H. Smalhout. 366p. (C). 1996. per. 32.50 (*0-7863-0799-4*) Irwin Prof Pubng.

Uncertain Return: Refugees & Reconciliation in Guatemala. Washington Office on Latin America Staff. (Illus.). 52p. (Orig.). (C). 1989. pap. text ed. 6.00 (*0-929513-07-X*) WOLA.

Uncertain Roads: Searching for the Gypsies. Yale Strom. LC 93-21962. (Illus.). 112p. (J). (gr. 5-11). 1993. lib. bdg. 19.95 (*0-02-788531-3*, Mac Bks Young Read) S&S Childrens.

Uncertain Saints. Alan Graebner. LC 75-1573. (Contributions in American History Ser.: No. 42). 320p. 1975. text ed. 59.95 (*0-8371-7963-7*, GUS/, Greenwood Pr) Greenwood.

Uncertain Science. Ahmed Gurnah & Alan Scott. 224p. (C). 1992. pap. text ed. 18.95 (*0-415-08023-1*, Routledge NY) Routledge.

Uncertain Science; Criticism of Sociological Formalism. Ahmed Gurnah & Alan Scott. LC 91-34727. 209p. (C). (gr. 13). 1992. text ed. 85.00 (*0-415-04136-8*) Routledge.

***Uncertain Seasons.** Elizabeth S. Morgan. 168p. 1996. pap. text ed. 15.95 (*0-8173-0865-2*) U of Ala Pr.

Uncertain Terms: Negotiating Gender in American Culture. Ed. by Fay Ginsburg & Anna L. Tsing. 352p. 1992. reprint ed. pap. 17.00 (*0-8070-4613-2*) Beacon Pr.

Uncertain the Final Run to Winter. William Kloefkorn. 1977. pap. 5.95 (*0-931534-01-1*) Windflower Pr.

Uncertain Tradition: American Secretaries of State in the Twentieth Century. Ed. by Norman A. Graebner. LC 79-26791. (McGraw-Hill Series in American History). 341p. 1980. reprint ed. text ed. 38.50 (*0-313-22317-3*, GRUT, Greenwood Pr) Greenwood.

Uncertain Tradition: Constitutionalism & the History of the South. Ed. by Kermit L. Hall & James W. Ely, Jr. LC 88-5579. 416p. 1989. pap. 25.00 (*0-8203-1075-1*) U of Ga Pr.

Uncertain Triumph: Federal Education Policy in the Kennedy & Johnson Years. Hugh D. Graham. LC 83-23424. xxiv, 280p. 1984. 34.95 (*0-8078-1599-3*) U of NC Pr.

Uncertain Truth. Frederick Sontag. LC 94-46769. 172p. (Orig.). (C). 1995. pap. text ed. 24.50 (*0-8191-9851-X*); lib. bdg. 36.50 (*0-8191-9850-1*) U Pr of Amer.

***Uncertain Union: British & Norwegian Social Democrats in an Integrating Europe.** Robert Geyer. (Perspectives on Europe Ser.). 240p. 1997. text ed. 59.95 (*1-85972-504-X*, Pub. by Avebury Pub UK) Ashgate Pub Co.

Uncertain Unions & Broken Lives. Lawrence Stone. 672p. 1995. pap. 21.00 (*0-19-285308-2*) OUP.

An Asterisk (*) at the beginning of an entry indicates that the title is appearing in BIP for the first time.

Uncertain Verdict: A Study of the 1969 Elections in Four Indian States. rev. ed. Ramashray Roy. LC 75-328407. (Illus.). 313p. reprint ed. pap. 89.30 (*0-685-44496-1*, 2031513) Bks Demand.
Uncertain Victory: Social Democracy & Progressivism in European & American Thought, 1870-1920. James T. Kloppenberg. 556p. 1988. pap. text ed. 20.95 (*0-19-505304-4*) OUP.
*__Uncertain Vision.__ R. A. Washbrook. 250p. 1997. pap. 16.95 (*1-85756-293-3*, Pub. by Janus Pubng UK) Paul & Co Pubs.
Uncertain Voyage. Dorothy Gilman. 1988. mass mkt. 5.99 (*0-449-21628-4*) Fawcett.
Uncertain Warriors: Lyndon Johnson & His Vietnam Advisers. David M. Barrett. LC 93-15654. 284p. 1994. pap. 12.95 (*0-7006-0631-9*) U Pr of KS.
Uncertain Years: Chinese-American Relations, 1947-1950. Ed. by Dorothy Borg & Waldo H. Heinrichs. LC 79-28297. (Studies of the East Asian Institute). 1980. text ed. 52.00 (*0-231-04738-X*) Col U Pr.
Uncertainity Analysis. Yigal Ronen. 272p. 1988. 166.00 (*0-8493-6714-X*, Q375, CRC Reprint) Franklin.
Uncertainity & Control: Future Soviet & American Strategy. Stephen J. Cimbala. LC 90-8061. 191p. 1990. text ed. 45.00 (*0-312-04226-4*) St Martin.
Uncertainties. H. Lloyd Van Brunt. LC 68-22413. (Illus.). 94p. 10.00 (*0-912292-00-8*) Smith.
Uncertainties & Rest: Poems. fac. ed. Timothy Steele. LC 78-15063. 61p. 1979. reprint ed. pap. 25.00 (*0-7837-7756-6*, 2047512) Bks Demand.
Uncertainties in French Grammar. Lewis Harmer. Ed. by Peter Rickard & G. S. Combe. LC 78-58793. 1980. 99.95 (*0-521-22233-8*) Cambridge U Pr.
Uncertainties of Empire: Essays in Iberian & Ibero-American Intellectual History. Anthony Padgen. (Collected Studies: No. CS468). 320p. 1994. 89.95 (*0-86078-461-4*, Pub. by Variorum UK) Ashgate Pub Co.
*__Uncertainty.__ Michael Larsen. 1998. pap. write for info. (*0-449-91236-1*) Fawcett.
Uncertainty: A Guide to Dealing with Uncertainty in Quantitative Risk & Policy Analysis. M. Granger Morgan & Max Henrion. (Illus.). 250p. (C). 1990. text ed. 59.95 (*0-521-36542-2*) Cambridge U Pr.
Uncertainty: A Guide to Dealing with Uncertainty in Quantitative Risk & Policy Analysis. M. Granger Morgan & Max Henrion. 344p. (C). 1992. pap. text ed. 19.95 (*0-521-42744-4*) Cambridge U Pr.
Uncertainty: A Novel. Michael Larsen. Tr. by Lone T. Blecher & George Blecher from DAN. LC 96-7256. 272p. 1996. 22.00 (*0-15-100202-9*) HarBrace.
Uncertainty: Behavioral & Social Dimensions. Ed. by Seymour Fiddle. LC 80-82073. 410p. 1980. text ed. 65.00 (*0-275-90480-6*, C0480, Praeger Pubs) Greenwood.
Uncertainty: Studies in Philosophy, Economics & Socio-Political Theory. Luigi Bonatti. (Bochumer Studien zur Philosophie Ser.: Vol. 2). xii, 132p. 1984. 35.00 (*90-6032-230-4*, Pub. by B R Gruener NE) Benjamins North Am.
Uncertainty: The Life & Science of Werner Heisenberg. David C. Cassidy. (Illus.). 544p. 1995. text ed. write for info. (*0-7167-2243-7*) W H Freeman.
Uncertainty: The Life & Science of Werner Heisenberg. David C. Cassidy. LC 91-13818. 1995. pap. text ed. write for info. (*0-7167-2503-7*) W H Freeman.
Uncertainty & Conservatism in the Seismic Analysis & Design of Nuclear Facilities: Working Group on Quantification of Uncertainties. 302p. 1986. 25.00 (*0-87262-547-8*) Am Soc Civil Eng.
*__Uncertainty & Economic Evolution: Essays in Honour of Armen Alchian.__ John L. Lott. 224p. (C). 1997. text ed. 69.95 (*0-415-15166-X*, Routledge NY) Routledge.
Uncertainty & Expectations in Economics: Essays in Honour of G. L. S. Shackle. Ed. by C. F. Carter & J. L. Ford. LC 72-184239. ix, 299p. 1972. lib. bdg. 45.00 (*0-678-06277-3*) Kelley.
*__Uncertainty & Plenitude: Five Contemporary Poets.__ Peter Stitt. LC 97-8756. 224p. 1997. text ed. 27.95 (*0-87745-599-6*) U of Iowa Pr.
Uncertainty & Quality in Science for Policy. Silvio O. Funtowicz & Jerome R. Ravetz. (Theory & Decision Library). 232p. 1990. lib. bdg. 129.00 (*0-7923-0799-2*, Pub. by Klwr Acad Pubs NE) Kluwer Ac.
Uncertainty & Relativity of Knowledge & Survival. James Constant. 300p. (Orig.). 1996. pap. 29.95 (*0-930293-01-0*) RCS Assocs.
Uncertainty & the Theory of International Trade, Vol. 15. Earl L. Grinols. (Fundamentals of Pure & Applied Economics Ser.: Vol. 15). 94, viiip. 1987. pap. text ed. 36.00 (*3-7186-0356-X*) Gordon & Breach.
*__Uncertainty & the Whole Language Teacher: The Messy Reality of Classroom Practice.__ Curt Dudley-Marling. LC 96-53389. 1995. pap. text ed. write for info. (*0-435-07234-X*, 07234) Heinemann.
Uncertainty & Vagueness in Knowledge Based Systems: Numerical Methods. Robert Kruse et al. Ed. by D. W. Loveland. (Artificial Intelligence Ser.). (Illus.). xi, 491p. 1991. 87.95 (*0-387-54165-9*) Spr-Verlag.
Uncertainty Business. W. John Maunder. 1987. 55.00 (*0-416-36100-5*) Routledge Chapman & Hall.
Uncertainty, Calibration & Probability: The Statistics of Scientific & Industrial Measurement. 2nd rev. ed. C. F. Dietrich. (Measurement Science & Technology Ser.). (Illus.). 556p. 1991. 226.00 (*0-7503-0060-4*) IOP Pub.
Uncertainty Concepts in Hydrology & Water Resources. Ed. by Zbigniew W. Kundzewicz. (International Hydrology Ser.). (Illus.). 416p. (C). 1995. text ed. 130.00 (*0-521-46118-9*) Cambridge U Pr.
Uncertainty in Artificial Intelligence. Ed. by L. N. Kanal et al. (Machine Intelligence & Pattern Recognition Ser.: No. 8). 416p. 1989. 100.00 (*0-318-43150-5*, North Holland) Elsevier.
Uncertainty in Artificial Intelligence. Ed. by L. N. Kanal & J. F. Lemmer. (Machine Intelligence & Pattern Recognition Ser.: No. 4). 510p. 1990. pap. 79.75 (*0-444-88745-8*, North Holland) Elsevier.
Uncertainty in Artificial Intelligence, No. 4. Ed. by R. D. Shachter et al. (Machine Intelligence & Pattern Recognition Ser.: No. 9). 422p. 1990. 133.75 (*0-444-88650-8*, North Holland); pap. 79.75 (*0-444-88737-7*, North Holland) Elsevier.
Uncertainty in Artificial Intelligence, No. 5. Ed. by Max Henrion et al. (Machine Intelligence & Pattern Recognition Ser.: No. 10). 460p. 1990. 133.75 (*0-444-88738-5*, North Holland); pap. 76.00 (*0-444-88739-3*, North Holland) Elsevier.
Uncertainty in Artificial Intelligence, Vol. 5. Ed. by J. F. Lemmer & L. N. Kanal. (Machine Intelligence & Pattern Recognition Ser.: No. 2). 484p. 1988. 157.00 (*0-444-70396-9*, North Holland) Elsevier.
Uncertainty in Artificial Intelligence: Proceedings of the 12th Annual Conference. Ed. by Eric Horvitz & Finn Jensen. 600p. (Orig.). 1996. pap. 49.95 (*1-55860-412-X*) Morgan Kaufmann.
*__Uncertainty in Artificial Intelligence 3.__ L. N. Kanal et al. (Machine Intelligence & Pattern Recognition Ser.: Vol. 8). xiv, 424p. 1989. 157.00 (*0-444-87417-8*, North Holland) Elsevier.
*__Uncertainty in Artificial Intelligence 6.__ P. P. Bonissone et al. (Machine Intelligence & Pattern Recognition Ser.: Vol. 12). 530p. 1991. 185.25 (*0-444-89264-8*, North Holland) Elsevier.
Uncertainty in Economic Thought. Ed. by Christian Schmidt. LC 95-19500. 256p. 1996. 80.00 (*1-85898-318-5*) E Elgar.
Uncertainty in Economics: Readings & Exercises. 2nd rev. ed. Ed. by Peter Diamond & Michael Rothschild. (Economic Theory, Econometrics & Mathematical Economics Ser.). 586p. 1989. text ed. 42.00 (*0-12-214851-7*) Acad Pr.
Uncertainty in Environmental Health Risk Assessment. Kenneth T. Bogen. LC 90-3766. (Environment: Problems & Solutions Ser.). 219p. 1990. text ed. 15.00 (*0-8240-0407-8*) Garland.
Uncertainty in Information Systems: An Introduction to Techniques & Applications. Anthony Hunter. LC 96-11370. 1996. pap. write for info. (*0-07-709326-7*) McGraw.
Uncertainty in Intelligent Systems. Ed. by Bernadette Bouchon-Meunier et al. LC 93-5532. 480p. 1993. 190.75 (*0-444-81508-2*, North Holland) Elsevier.
Uncertainty in Knowledge-Based Systems. Bernadette Bouchon-Meunier & Ronald R. Yager. (Lecture Notes in Computer Science Ser.: Vol. 286). vii, 405p. 1987. 45.00 (*0-387-18579-8*) Spr-Verlag.
Uncertainty in Knowledge Bases: Third International Conference on Information Processing & Management of Uncertainty in Knowledge-Based Systems, IPMU '90, Paris, France, July, 1990 Proceedings. Bernadette Bouchom-Meunier et al. Ed. by G. Goos et al. (Lecture Notes in Computer Science Ser.: Vol. 521). x, 609p. 1991. 63.95 (*0-387-54346-5*) Spr-Verlag.
Uncertainty in National Population Forecasting: Issues, Backgrounds, Analyses & Recommendations. Nico W. Keilman. (NIDI-CBGS Publications, Population & Family Study Center Ser.). x, 218p. 1990. pap. 29.95 (*90-265-1141-8*) Swets.
Uncertainty in NCRP Screening Models Relating to Atmosphere Transport, Deposition & Uptake by Humans. Intro. by Charles B. Meinhold. LC 92-36388. (Commentary Ser.: No. 8). (Illus.). 56p. 1993. pap. text ed. 30.00 (*0-929600-28-2*) NCRP Pubns.
Uncertainty in Risk Assessment, Risk Management & Decision Making. Ed. by Lester B. Lave & Vincent T. Covello. (Advances in Risk Analysis Ser.: Vol. 4). 538p. 1987. 130.00 (*0-306-42557-2*, Plenum Pr) Plenum.
Uncertainty in the Geologic Environment: From Theory to Practice, Proceedings of Uncertainty '96, July 31-August 3, 1996, Madison, Wisconsin. Charles D. Shackelford et al. LC 96-23902. (Geotechnical Special Publications). 1488p. 1996. 125.00 (*0-7844-0188-8*) Am Soc Civil Eng.
*__Uncertainty Management in Information Systems: From Needs to Solutions.__ Ed. by Amihai Motro. 480p. (C). 1996. lib. bdg. 135.00 (*0-7923-9803-3*) Kluwer Ac.
Uncertainty Modeling & Analysis, 3rd International Symposium on (ISUMA '95) LC 10-682228. 832p. 1995. pap. 120.00 (*0-8186-7126-2*, PR07126) IEEE Comp Soc.
*__Uncertainty Modeling in Finite Element, Fatigue & Stability of Systems.__ (Stability Ser.: No. 9). 400p. 1997. text ed. 53.00 (*981-02-3128-8*) World Scientific Pub.
*__Uncertainty Modeling in Vibration, Control & Fuzzy Analysis of Structural Systems, 10.__ 350p. 1997. text ed. 40.00 (*981-02-3134-2*) World Scientific Pub.
Uncertainty Modelling & Analysis: Theory & Applications. Ed. by Bilal M. Ayyub & Madan M. Gupta. LC 94-36567. (Machine Intelligence & Pattern Recognition Ser.: 17). 558p. 1994. 191.50 (*0-444-81954-1*) Elsevier.
Uncertainty of Analysis: Problems in Truth, Meaning, & Culture. Timothy J. Reiss. LC 88-47741. 312p. 1988. 39.95 (*0-8014-2162-4*) Cornell U Pr.
Uncertainty of Law & Constitutional Government: Government 30,000-Inventors 0. limited ed. James N. Constant. 260p. (Orig.). 1993. pap. 29.95 (*0-930293-00-2*) RCS Assocs.
Uncertainty of Strangers & Other Stories. Patrick Franklin. LC 85-7653. 152p. 1985. pap. 7.95 (*0-912516-91-7*) Grey Fox.
Uncertainty of the International Coffee Agreement. Richard E. Mshomba. (Pew Case Studies in International Affairs). 50p. (C). 1994. pap. 3.50 (*1-56927-159-3*) Geo U Inst Dplmcy.
*__Uncertainty Principle.__ Ruth Brandon. 306p. 1997. 26.00 (*0-224-04454-0*, Pub. by Jonathan Cape UK) Trafalgar.
*__Uncertainty Principle.__ Steven J. Frank. 230p. 1997. pap. 12.00 (*1-882633-26-1*) Permeable.
Uncertainty Principle & Foundations of Quantum Mechanics: A Fifty Years' Survey. Ed. by William C. Price & Seymour S. Chissick. LC 76-18213. 590p. reprint ed. pap. 168.20 (*0-685-20688-2*, 2030478) Bks Demand.
Uncertainty Principle in Harmonic Analysis. Victor Havin & Burglind Joricke. LC 93-40608. (Ergebnisse der Mathematik und Ihrer Grenzgebiete Ser.: Vol. 3, Folge, Bd. 28). ix, 535p. 1994. 158.95 (*0-387-56991-X*) Spr-Verlag.
*__Uncertainty, Risk & Transient Pollution Events: Selected Proceedings of the IAWQ Interdisciplinary International Symposium on Uncertainty, Risk & Transient Pollution Events, Held in Exeter, UK, 26-28 July 1995.__ Ed. by M. B. Beck & W. Schilling. (Water Science & Technology 33 Ser.). 236p. 1996. pap. text ed. 207.00 (*0-08-042893-2*, Pergamon Pr) Elsevier.
Unchain My Heart. Howard. 1993. pap. 2.99 (*0-373-17160-9*) Harlequin Bks.
*__Unchained.__ Mac Gober. 1996. pap. text ed. 8.95 (*1-57562-041-3*) K Copeland Pubns.
Unchained Destinies. Sara Wood. (Presents Ser.). 1996. mass mkt. 3.50 (*0-373-11796-5*, 1-11796-9) Harlequin Bks.
Unchained Lightning. Potter. 1996. mass mkt. 5.99 (*0-312-95928-1*) St Martin.
Unchained Melody - Someday: And Other Top Hits. (Easy Piano Ser.). 64p. 1991. pap. 7.95 (*0-7935-0767-7*, 00222531) H Leonard.
Unchained Memories: True Stories of Traumatic Memories, Lost & Found. Lenore Terr. 304p. 1995. pap. 13.00 (*0-465-09539-9*) Basic.
Unchained Memories: True Stories of Traumatic Memory Loss. Lenore Terr. 288p. 1994. 22.00 (*0-465-08823-6*) Basic.
Unchained Reactions: Chernobyl, Glasnost & Nuclear Deterrence. 1994. lib. bdg. 256.00 (*0-8490-5812-0*) Gordon Pr.
*__Unchained Reactions: Chernobyl, Glasnost, & Nuclear Deterrence.__ (Illus.). 154p. 1993. pap. text ed. 45.00 (*1-57979-165-4*) BPI Info Servs.
Unchained Reactions: Chernobyl, Glasnost, & Nuclear Deterrence. Arthur T. Hopkins. (Illus.). 153p. (Orig.). (C). 1994. pap. text ed. 35.00 (*0-7881-1257-0*) DIANE Pub.
Unchained Voices: An Anthology of Black Authors in the English-Speaking World of the Eighteenth Century. Ed. by Vincent Caretta. LC 96-1019. (Illus.). 416p. 1996. pap. 19.95 (*0-8131-0884-5*); text ed. 42.95 (*0-8131-1976-6*) U Pr of Ky.
Unchained Worker: Principles of Ownership in the Workplace. Jeffrey C. Petkeuicius. Ed. by Dwain Smart. (Illus.). 154p. (Orig.). 1995. pap. 11.95 (*0-9645204-3-5*) Cybernetix.
Unchallenged Violence: An American Ordeal. Robert B. Toplin. LC 75-72. 332p. 1975. text ed. 55.00 (*0-8371-7748-0*, TLV/, Greenwood Pr) Greenwood.
Unchanging American Voter. Eric R. Smith. 1989. pap. 15.00 (*0-520-06830-0*) U CA Pr.
Unchanging Love. Romulus Linney. 1991. pap. 5.25 (*0-8222-1188-2*) Dramatists Play.
*__Unchanging You in a Changing World.__ Melvin Rubenstein & Jayne Burks. (Illus.). 128p. (Orig.). 1996. pap. 12.95 (*0-9655143-0-7*) Blick & Staff.
Uncharged Battery. Edra D. Blixseth. Ed. by Cheryl Hodgson. 256p. 1988. text ed. 16.95 (*0-945033-00-1*) PEP Pr.
Uncharged Battery. Edra D. Blixseth. 256p. 1990. pap. 9.95 (*0-446-39059-3*) Warner Bks.
Uncharged Misconduct Evidence. Edward J. Imwinkelried. LC 84-7619. 1990. 130.00 (*0-317-06219-0*) Clark Boardman Callaghan.
Uncharged Misconduct Evidence. annuals Edward J. Imwinkelried. 1990. suppl. ed. write for info. (*0-318-57918-9*) Clark Boardman Callaghan.
Uncharted Journey. Reynolds. 5.00 (*0-8065-0337-8*, Citadel Pr) Carol Pub Group.
Uncharted Journey: Fifty Years in Social Work by One of Its Great Teachers. Bertha C. Reynolds. LC 90-28265. 352p. 1991. reprint ed. 21.95 (*0-87101-193-X*) Natl Assn Soc Wkrs.
Uncharted Lives: Understanding the Life Passages of Gay Men. Stanley Siegel & Ed Lowe. 1995. pap. 10.95 (*0-452-27448-6*, Plume) NAL-Dutton.
Uncharted Seas. Fuller Albright & Read Ellsworth. 124p. 1990. 24.95 (*0-318-50058-2*) JBK Pub.
Uncharted Seas. deluxe ed. Fuller Albright & Read Ellsworth. 124p. 1990. ring bd. 59.95 (*0-945892-02-0*) JBK Pub.
Uncharted Territory. Connie Willis. 176p. 1994. mass mkt. 3.99 (*0-553-56294-0*) Bantam.
Unchaste. Thakazhi S. Pillai. Tr. by M. K. Bhaskaran. 112p. 1971. pap. 2.10 (*0-88253-067-4*) Ind-US Inc.
Uncheese Cookbook. Joanne Stepaniak. LC 93-42489. 192p. 1994. pap. 11.95 (*0-913990-42-6*) Book Pub Co.
Unchosen Presidents: The Vice-President & Other Frustrations of Presidential Succession. Allan P. Sindler. LC 75-46041. (Quantum Bks.: No. 7). 1976. pap. 9.00 (*0-520-03493-7*) U CA Pr.
Uncion. Benny Hinn. 167p. (SPA.). 1992. pap. 7.99 (*1-56063-253-4*, 498422) Editorial Unilit.
Uncitral: Arbitration Rules. 32p. 1996. 10.00 (*92-1-133443-8*, E.93.V.6) UN.
Uncitral: Legal Guide on International Countertrade Transactions. 192p. 1993. 30.00 (*92-1-133444-6*, E.93.V.7) UN.
Uncitral: United Nations Commission on International Trade Law. 288p. 1992. 60.00 (*92-1-133434-9*, E.92.V.11) UN.
UNCITRAL Arbitration Rules in Practice: The Experience of the Iran-United States Claims Tribunal. Stewart A. Baker & Mark D. Davis. LC 92-17357. 1992. 80.00 (*90-6544-628-1*) Kluwer Law Tax Pubs.
UNCITRAL Framework for Arbitration in Contemporary Perspective. Isaak I. Dore. LC 93-987. (International Arbitration Law Library). 1993. lib. bdg. 118.50 (*1-85333-573-8*, Pub. by Graham & Trotman UK) Kluwer Ac.
Uncitral Model Law on International Commercial Arbitration. 24p. 1995. 7.50 (*92-1-133498-5*, E.95.V.18) UN.
Uncitral Model Law on International Credit Transfers. 24p. 1995. 7.50 (*92-1-133497-7*) UN.
Uncitral, Proceedings New York, 18-22 May 1922. 1995. 280.00 (*92-1-133476-4*, E.94.V.14) UN.
UNCITRAL, United Nations Commission on International Trade Law Yearbook Vol. 24: 1993. 440p. 1994. 60.00 (*92-1-133478-0*) UN.
UNCITRAL's Model Law on International Commercial Arbitration. Ed. by P. Sanders. 1984. pap. text ed. 63.00 (*90-6544-183-2*) Kluwer Law Tax Pubs.
Uncivil Liberty: An Essay to Show the Injustice & Impolicy of Ruling Woman Without Her Consent. Ezra H. Heywood. (Libertarian Broadsides Ser.: No. 8). (Illus.). 1978. pap. 1.00 (*0-87926-023-8*) R Myles.
Uncivil Religion: Interreligious Hostility in America. Robert N. Bellah & Frederick Greenspahn. 500p. 1986. 49.50 (*0-8245-0756-8*) Crossroad NY.
Uncivil Rites: American Fiction, Religion, & the Public Sphere. Robert Detweiler. (Public Expressions of Religion in America Ser.). 250p. 1996. text ed. 29.95 (*0-252-01932-6*) U of Ill Pr.
Uncivil Rites: American Fiction, Religion & the Public Sphere. Robert Detweiler. (Public Expressions of Religion in America Ser.). 250p. 1996. 17.95 (*0-252-06580-8*) U of Ill Pr.
Uncivil Seasons. Michael Malone. Ed. by Jane Rosenman. 320p. 1993. pap. 12.00 (*0-671-87528-0*, WSP) PB.
Uncivil War. Franklin W. Dixon. Ed. by Anne Greenberg. (Hardy Boys Casefiles Ser.: No. 52). 160p. (Orig.). (J). (gr. 6 up). 1991. pap. 3.50 (*0-671-70049-9*, Archway) PB.
*__Uncivil War.__ Sheila S. Klass. 160p. (J). (gr. 3-7). 1997. 15.95 (*0-8234-1329-2*) Holiday.
UnCivil War. Dusty Rumsey. (Illus.). 64p. (Orig.). 1992. pap. 8.95 (*0-941711-19-6*) Wyrick & Co.
Uncivil War: Alabama vs. Auburn. Scott Brown & Will Collier. LC 95-31628. (Illus.). 256p. (Orig.). 1995. pap. 12.95 (*1-55853-354-0*) Rutledge Hill Pr.
*__Uncivil War: Korea, 1945-1953.__ James I. Matray. 240p. Date not set. text ed. 56.95 (*0-7656-0219-9*); pap. text ed. 22.95 (*0-7656-0220-2*) M E Sharpe.
Uncivil War: The Southern Backcountry During the American Revolution. Ed. by Ronald Hoffman et al. LC 84-19632. (Perspectives on the American Revolution Ser.). 362p. reprint ed. pap. 103.20 (*0-7837-2680-5*, 2043057) Bks Demand.
Uncivil War: The Struggle Between Black Men & Women. Elsie B. Washington. LC 92-51079. 1994. 24.95 (*1-879360-25-X*) Noble Pr.
UnCivil Wars: International Security & the New Internal Conflicts. Donald M. Snow. 177p. (Orig.). 1996. 42.00 (*1-55587-648-X*); pap. 18.95 (*1-55587-655-2*) Lynne Rienner.
Uncivil Wars: Ireland Today. 3rd ed. Padraig O'Malley. 560p. 1997. pap. 18.00 (*0-8070-0223-2*) Beacon Pr.
Uncivil Wars: Men & Women in the Office of the 90's. Beverly H. Patrick. 144p. 1994. boxed 24.95 (*0-8403-9261-3*) Kendall-Hunt.
Uncivil Wars: Political Camp. Thomas. Date not set. pap. text ed. write for info. (*0-312-15026-1*) St Martin.
Uncivil Wars Pathology of Terrorism in India. Ved Marwah. (C). 1995. 34.00 (*81-7223-221-7*, Pub. by Indus Pub II) S Asia.
*__Unclaimed Assets: Money the Government Owes You! A Guide to the Recovery of over $300 Billion Held by State & Federal Agencies.__ 2nd ed. Mark Tofal. 160p. 1997. pap. 29.95 (*0-9656900-0-8*) NUPA.
Unclaimed Experience: Trauma, Narrative, & History. Cathy Caruth. 152p. (C). 1996. text ed. 33.50 (*0-8018-5246-3*); pap. text ed. 14.95 (*0-8018-5247-1*) Johns Hopkins.
Unclaimed Fortunes: How to Discover Your Share. Truedie L. Ross & Richard G. Ross. LC 91-78132. 68p. 1992. pap. 9.95 (*0-9631885-0-X*) Kalia Pubns.
Unclaimed Fortunes: How to Get Your Share. Loren J. Bialik. 176p. 1994. pap. 150.00 (*0-9639772-0-2*) Mazel Pubng.
Unclaimed Property Law & Reporting Forms, 5 vols. David J. Epstein & Andrew W. McThenia. 1984. Updates. ring bd. write for info. (*0-8205-1136-6*) Bender.
Unclaimed Treasures. Patricia MacLachlan. LC 83-47714. (Trophy Bk.). 128p. (J). (gr. 5-7). 1987. pap. 3.95 (*0-06-440189-8*, Trophy) HarpC Child Bks.
Unclaimed Treasures. Baruch Silverstein. 1983. 20.00 (*0-88125-029-5*) Ktav.
Unclassed. 24.50 (*0-8386-1885-5*) Fairleigh Dickinson.
Unclassed. George R. Gissing. Ed. by Jacob Korg. 327p. 24.50 (*0-685-16474-8*) Fairleigh Dickinson.
Unclassed. George Gissing. LC 68-54269. reprint ed. 15.00 (*0-404-02811-X*) AMS Pr.
Unclassed. George R. Gissing. (BCL1-PR English Literature Ser.). 312p. 1992. reprint ed. lib. bdg. 89.00 (*0-7812-7536-9*) Rprt Serv.
Unclassed see Works of George Gissing
Unclay. Theodore F. Powys. (Literature Ser.). 328p. 1972. reprint ed. 39.00 (*0-403-01162-0*) Scholarly.

U V

Uncle Alfredo's Zoo. Judith Vigna. (J). (gr. 4-7). 1994. 14. 95 (*0-8075-8292-1*) A Whitman.

Uncle Alphonso & the Frosty, Fibbing Dinosaurs. Jack Pearson. LC 92-39373. (On My Own Bks.). (Illus.). 32p. (J). 1993. pap. 4.99 (*0-7814-0100-3*, Chariot Bks) Chariot Victor.

Uncle Alphonso & the Greedy Green Dinosuar. Pearson. LC 90-20340. 32p. (J). 1992. pap. 4.99 (*1-55513-424-6*, Chariot Bks) Chariot Victor.

Uncle Alphonso & the Puffy Proud Dinosaur. Pearson. LC 90-32442. 32p. (J). 1992. pap. 4.99 (*1-55513-562-5*, Chariot Bks) Chariot Victor.

Uncle Al's Catalog from Hell. Steve Jackson Games Staff. (Illus.). 208p. 1992. suppl. ed., pap. 19.95 (*1-55634-220-9*, 7150) S Jackson Games.

Uncle Alton. Lannie Hill. (European & American Playwright Ser.). 72p. (Orig.). 1995. pap. 8.95 (*0-9649753-9-4*) Dagenham Hse.

Uncle & Other Stories. Joan Shaw. Ed. by Angela Jaffray. LC 82-70936. 101p. 1983. pap. 6.00 (*0-932274-31-5*) Cadmus Eds.

Uncle Arthur's Bedtime Story Book. Arthur Maxwell. (YA). Date not set. 29.99 (*0-8280-0163-4*) Review & Herald.

***Uncle Arthur's Bedtime Storybook.** Review & Herald Staff. 1994. 29.99 (*0-8280-0897-3*) Review & Herald.

Uncle Arthur's Bible Book. Arthur Maxwell. 512p. (J). (gr. 1-3). 1968. 29.99 (*0-8280-0997-X*) Review & Herald.

Uncle Arthur's Storytime. Arthur S. Maxwell & Cheryl W. Holloway. (Children's True Adventures Classic Edition Ser.: Vol. 3). (Illus.). 128p. (J). 1989. 29.90 (*1-877773-03-4*) Fam Media.

Uncle Arthur's Storytime, Vol. 1. Arthur S. Maxwell & Cheryl W. Holloway. (Children's True Adventures Classic Edition Ser.). (Illus.). 128p. (J). 1989. lib. bdg. 29.90 (*1-877773-01-8*) Fam Media.

Uncle Arthur's Storytime, Vol. 2. Arthur S. Maxwell & Cheryl W. Holloway. (Children's True Adventures Classic Edition Ser.). (Illus.). 128p. (YA). 1989. lib. bdg. 29.90 (*1-877773-02-6*) Fam Media.

Uncle Bill. Will James. 1976. 22.95 (*0-8488-1061-9*) Amereon Ltd.

Uncle Billy: The Ancestors & Descendants of William B. Shoemaker of Jasper County. Mattie S. Holliday. 257p. 1987. pap. 30.00 (*0-9619875-0-2*) M S Holliday.

Uncle Billy's Downeast Barbeque Book. Jonathan St. Laurent & Charles Neave. Ed. by Kerry Leichtman & Caron Leichtman. LC 91-70126. 208p. (Orig.). 1991. pap. 12.95 (*0-9622518-0-1*) Dancing West.

Uncle Bob. Austin Pendleton. 1995. pap. 5.25 (*0-8222-1476-8*) Dramatists Play.

Uncle Bob, Aplomb Magnificent: The Story of Kansas Senator Bob George. Bob George. Ed. by Patricia Humphrey. LC 93-79103. (Illus.). 192p. (Orig.). 1993. pap. 12.95 (*1-882420-04-7*) Hearth KS.

Uncle Bobby's Finally Sober. Bob Lang. 77p. (Orig.). 1987. pap. 2.95 (*0-9618264-0-1*) Psalm Thirty Pubs.

Uncle Bob's Animal Stories see Historias de Animales Para Toda la Familia

Uncle Bob's Bible Stories. Bob Wolf. (Illus.). 108p. (Orig.). (J). (gr. 4-8). 1982. pap. 1.50 (*0-89323-028-6*) Bible Memory.

***Uncle Bob's Guide to the Colorado High Country.** Robert R. Walden. 90p. 1996. ring bd. 9.95 (*1-888554-12-6*) Lamplighter Bks.

Uncle Cam. James C. Hefley & Marti Hefley. Tr. by James C. Yu from ENG. 288p. (Orig.). (CHI.). 1987. pap. text ed. 5.50 (*0-940043-29-7*) Evangel Lit.

Uncle Carmello. David Zucker. LC 91-15258. (Illus.). 32p. (J). (gr. k-4). 1993. lib. bdg. 14.95 (*0-02-793760-7*, Mac Bks Young Read) S&S Childrens.

***Uncle Carmello.** David Zucker. (Illus.). 32p. (J). 4.98 (*0-7651-0029-0*) Smithmark.

Uncle Charles. large type ed. Georges Simenon. (Keating's Choice Ser.). 202p. 1991. 22.95 (*1-85089-418-3*, Pub. by ISIS UK) Transaction Pubs.

Uncle Charles Has Locked Himself In. Georges Simenon. Tr. by Howard Curtis. 1987. 19.95 (*0-15-192685-9*) HarBrace.

Uncle Charlie's Hunting Shack. Bruce Cochran. (Illus.). 96p. 1994. 12.50 (*1-57223-018-5*); pap. 7.95 (*1-57223-019-3*) Idyll Arbor.

Uncle Chuck's Truck. Hope N. Coulter. LC 91-42638. (Illus.). 32p. (J). (ps-1). 1993. lib. bdg. 13.95 (*0-02-724825-9*, Bradbury S&S) S&S Childrens.

***Uncle Chuck's Truck.** Hope N. Coutler. (Illus.). 32p. (J). 3.98 (*0-7651-0030-4*) Smithmark.

Uncle Comanche. J. A. Benner. LC 95-36530. (Chaparral Books for Young Readers). 169p. (Orig.). (J). (gr. 5-9). 1996. pap. 12.95 (*0-87565-152-6*) Tex Christian.

Uncle Daddy. Kasey Michaels. (Romance Ser.). 1993. pap. 2.69 (*0-373-08916-3*, 5-08916-4) Silhouette.

Uncle Dan Drumheller Tells Thrills of Western Trails in 1854. Dan Drumheller. 123p. 1985. 14.95 (*0-87770-366-3*) Ye Galleon.

Uncle Dan Drumheller Tells Thrills of Western Trails in 1854. Dan Drumheller. (Illus.). 131p. reprint ed. pap. 4.95 (*0-8466-0234-2*, S234) Shorey.

Uncle Daney's Way. Jessie Haas. LC 93-22192. (J). (gr. 4 up). 1994. 15.00 (*0-688-12794-0*) Greenwillow.

***Uncle Daney's Way.** Jessie Haas. (J). Date not set. pap. 4.95 (*0-688-15491-3*, Beech Tree Bks) Morrow.

Uncle Dick Wootton: The Pioneer Frontiersman of the Rocky Mountain Region. Richens L. Wootton. (American Biography Ser.). 465p. 1991. reprint ed. lib. bdg. 89.00 (*0-7812-8429-5*) Rprt Serv.

Uncle Don's Adventure down East Cookbook. Donald B. Drew. (Illus.). 217p. 1987. pap. 8.95 (*0-9617940-0-3*) D B Drew.

Uncle Dudley's Odd Hours: Western Sketches, Indian Trail Echoes. Morris C. Russell. LC 73-104558. (Illus.). 255p. reprint ed. lib. bdg. 22.00 (*0-8398-1768-1*) Irvington.

Uncle Dynamite. P. G. Wodehouse. 252p. 1991. pap. 8.95 (*0-14-012449-7*, Arkana) Viking Penguin.

Uncle Earl Deserved Better. Jack B. McGuire. (Illus.). 329p. (Orig.). 1995. pap. text ed. 20.00 (*1-888042-00-1*) Good Readng.

Uncle Ebeneezer's Book for Creative Children. Uncle Ebeneezer. (Illus.). 54p. (Orig.). 1988. pap. 2.50 (*1-880596-02-4*) Allegan Educ.

Uncle Elephant. Arnold Lobel. LC 80-8944. (Harper I Can Read Bk.). (Illus.). 64p. (J). (gr. k-3). 1981. 14.95 (*0-06-023979-4*); lib. bdg. 14.89 (*0-06-023980-8*) HarpC Child Bks.

Uncle Elephant. Arnold Lobel. LC 80-8944. (Trophy I Can Read Bk.). (Illus.). 64p. (J). (gr. k-3). 1986. pap. 3.75 (*0-06-444104-0*, Trophy) HarpC Child Bks.

Uncle Elephant. Arnold Lobel. (J). Date not set. pap. 1.95 (*0-590-32764-X*) Scholastic Inc.

Uncle Elephant - Tio Elefante. Arnold Lobel. (SPA.). (J). 9.95 (*84-204-3716-6*) Santillana.

Uncle Eric Talks about Personal, Career & Financial Security. Richard J. Maybury. LC 94-11733. (Uncle Eric Book Ser.). 46p. (YA). (gr. 7 up). 1994. 7.95 (*0-942617-20-7*) Blstckng Pr.

Uncle Ernie's African Stories. Ernest L. Green. (Illus.). 81p. (J). (gr. 1-4). 1982. 4.50 (*0-89814-057-9*) Grace Publns.

Uncle Ernie's Minions of Doom: The Battlelord's Guide to Pain. Doug Nelson et al. (Illus.). 96p. (Orig.). (YA). 1994. pap. 11.95 (*1-889155-03-9*, ODS501A) Optimus Design.

Uncle Ezra's Short Stories for Children. Ezra Meeker. 100p. reprint ed. pap. 4.95 (*0-8466-0242-3*, S242) Shorey.

Uncle Foster's Hat Tree Level 2, Red. Doug Cushman. (Easy-to-Read Ser.). (Illus.). 48p. (J). (gr. k-4). 1996. pap. 3.50 (*0-14-037995-9*) Puffin Bks.

Uncle Fred in the Springtime. P. G. Wodehouse. 1976. pap. 8.95 (*0-14-000971-X*, Penguin Bks) Viking Penguin.

Uncle Fred in the Springtime. P. G. Wodehouse. 1994. reprint ed. lib. bdg. 32.95 (*1-56849-362-2*) Buccaneer Bks.

Uncle Gene's Breadbook for Kids! Eugene Bove. (Illus.). 64p. (J). (gr. 5-12). 1986. pap. 11.95 (*0-937395-00-5*) Happibook Pr.

Uncle George: Poems from a Maine Boyhood. 2nd rev. ed. Robert M. Chute. (Illus.). 54p. (Orig.). 1990. reprint ed. per. 10.00 (*0-9624912-0-9*) Ciderpress.

Uncle Giorgio. Marie-Aude Murail. (I Love to Read Collection). (Illus.). 46p. (J). (gr. 2-4). 1990. lib. bdg. 12. 79 (*0-89565-809-7*) Childs World.

Uncle Gust & the Temple of Healing. Julie H. White. (Indiana Short Fiction Contest Ser.: No. 2). 77p. 1991. pap. 5.95 (*1-880649-25-X*) Writ Ctr Pr.

Uncle Henry: A Documentary Profile of the First Henry Wallace. Richard S. Kirkendall. LC 93-24343. (Henry A. Wallace Series on Agricultural History & Rural Studies). (Illus.). 276p. (C). 1993. text ed. 46.95 (*0-8138-0424-8*) Iowa St U Pr.

Uncle Henry's Dinner Guests. Benedicte Froissart. (Illus.). 32p. (J). (ps-2). 1990. 15.95 (*1-55037-141-X*, Pub. by Annick CN); pap. 4.95 (*1-55037-140-1*, Pub. by Annick CN) Firefly Bks Ltd.

Uncle Homer's Outdoor Chuckle Book. Homer Circle. LC 93-79797. (Illus.). 128p. (Orig.). 1993. pap. text ed. 7.95 (*0-936513-37-3*) Larsens Outdoor.

Uncle in the Purple Lighted Basement, Vol. 1. Gwendolyn L. Evans. Ed. by Sandra Pasqua. LC 95-67426. (Illus.). 72p. (YA). (gr. 6 up). 1997. pap. 9.00 (*1-886580-30-8*) Pinnacle-Syatt.

Uncle Isaac. William D. Powers. LC 74-170703. (Black Heritage Library Collection). 1977. reprint ed. 22.95 (*0-8369-8893-0*) Ayer.

***Uncle Isaaco.** Patricia Polacco. LC 96-43892. (J). 1997. write for info. (*0-399-23164-1*, Philomel Bks) Putnam Pub Group.

Uncle Jack among the English. John W. Loughary. (Illus.). 60p. (Orig.). 1984. pap. 3.95 (*0-915671-00-X*) United Learn.

Uncle Jack's Fiddlin Around. Gordon A. Tracy. 1992. pap. 15.00 (*0-9634372-0-8*) Tracy Mgmt.

Uncle Jake. Ellen Kort. (Fox Sense Collection). (Illus.). 20p. (Orig.). 1994. pap. 24.95 (*1-885520-01-8*) Fox Print.

***Uncle Jake Blows the Shofar.** Leslie Kimmelman. LC 96-45027. (Illus.). (J). 1998. write for info. (*0-06-027501-4*); lib. bdg. write for info. (*0-06-027498-0*) HarpC.

***Uncle Jeb & the Spirit.** Thomas Benton. 1997. 15.95 (*1-57980-000-9*, BUNCLE) Claitors.

***Uncle Jed's Barbershop.** Margaree K. Mitchell. (Illus.). (J). (gr. 4). 1995. 7.56 (*0-395-73246-8*) HM.

Uncle Jed's Barbershop. Margaree K. Mitchell. 40p. (J). (ps-6). 1993. pap. 15.00 (*0-671-76969-3*, S&S Bks Young Read) S&S Childrens.

***Uncle Jed's Barbershop.** large type ed. Margaree K. Mitchell. (Illus.). 46p. (J). (gr. 4). 11.50 (*0-614-20625-1*, L-38182-00 APHB) Am Printing Hse.

Uncle Jerry Has AIDS. Jim Boulden. (Illus.). 32p. (Orig.). (J). (gr. 3-7). 1992. pap. 3.95 (*1-878076-18-3*) Boulden Pub.

Uncle Jimmy. Illana Katz. (Illus.). 40p. (J). (gr. k-6). 1994. 16.95 (*1-882388-03-8*) Real Life Strybks.

Uncle Jimmy: AIDS. Illana Katz. (J). (gr. k-6). 1994. pap. 9.95 (*1-882388-09-7*) Real Life Strybks.

Uncle Jim's Book of Pancakes. 2nd ed. James E. Banks. (Wild & Woolly West Ser.: No. 3). (Illus.). (Orig.). 1977. pap. 3.00 (*0-910584-44-3*) Filter.

Uncle Jim's Dairy Farm: A Summer Visit with Aunt Helen & Uncle Jim. National Dairy Council Staff. (Illus.). 4p. (J). (gr. 3-6). 1980. Set incls. 12 user's guides & 1 tchr's. guide. write for info. (*1-55647-611-6*); vhs write for info. (*1-55647-634-5*) Natl Dairy Coun.

Uncle Joe Cannon: The Story of a Pioneer American. L. White Busbey. (History - United States Ser.). 362p. 1992. reprint ed. lib. bdg. 89.00 (*0-7812-6194-5*) Rprt Serv.

Uncle Joe Cannon: The Story of a Pioneer American. Joseph G. Cannon. (American Biography Ser.). 362p. 1991. reprint ed. lib. bdg. 79.00 (*0-7812-8058-3*) Rprt Serv.

Uncle Joe's Record Guide: Eric Clapton, Jimi Hendrix, The Who. Joe Benson. 288p. 1988. pap. 9.95 (*0-943031-03-6*) J Benson Unlimit.

Uncle Joe's Record Guide: Hard Rock, the First Two Generations. Joe Benson. 320p. 1988. pap. 9.95 (*0-943031-04-4*) J Benson Unlimit.

Uncle Joe's Record Guide: Progressive Rock. Joe Benson. (Illus.). 320p. (Orig.). 1989. pap. 9.95 (*0-943031-11-7*) J Benson Unlimit.

Uncle Joe's Record Guide: The Beatles. Joe Benson. 124p. 1990. pap. 9.95 (*0-943031-13-3*) J Benson Unlimit.

Uncle Joe's Record Guide: The Rolling Stones. Joe Benson. 124p. 1987. pap. 9.95 (*0-943031-02-8*) J Benson Unlimit.

Uncle John's Bathroom Reader. Bathroom Readers' Institute Staff. 224p. (Orig.). 1988. pap. 9.95 (*0-312-02663-3*) St Martin.

Uncle John's Fifth Bathroom Reader. Bathroom Readers' Institute Staff. 224p. 1992. pap. 9.95 (*1-879682-28-1*) Earth Works.

Uncle John's Fourth Bathroom Reader. Bathroom Readers' Institute Staff. 224p. (Orig.). 1991. pap. 9.95 (*0-312-06484-5*) St Martin.

***Uncle John's Giant 10th Anniversary Bathroom Reader.** Bathroom Readers' Institute Staff. 1997. pap. text ed. 16. 95 (*1-879682-68-0*) Earth Works.

Uncle John's Second Bathroom Reader. Bathroom Readers' Institute Staff. 224p. (Orig.). 1989. pap. 9.95 (*0-312-03446-6*) St Martin.

Uncle John's Seventh Bathroom Reader. Bathroom Readers' Institute Staff. 228p. 1994. pap. 9.95 (*1-879682-58-3*) Earth Works.

Uncle John's Sixth Bathroom Reader. Bathroom Readers' Institute Staff. 228p. 1993. pap. 9.95 (*1-879682-45-1*) Earth Works.

***Uncle John's Stories for Good California Children - The First Story Book for the Holidays.** 64p. 1988. pap. 4.95 (*0-935089-11-X*) CA History Ctr.

Uncle John's Third Bathroom Reader: The Bathroom Readers' Institute. 224p. (Orig.). 1990. pap. 9.95 (*0-312-04586-7*) St Martin.

Uncle John's Ultimate Bathroom Reader. 8th ed. 400p. 1996. pap. 14.95 (*1-879682-65-6*) Publishers Group.

Uncle Lester's Lemonade Lure. Susan Ginny. (Illus.). 15p. (Orig.). (J). (gr. 2-3). 1988. pap. 4.95 (*0-9621556-0-8*) SYF Enter.

Uncle Lisha's Shop: Life in A Corner of Yankeeland. Rowland E. Robinson. LC 79-96892. 187p. reprint ed. lib. bdg. 19.00 (*0-8398-1761-4*) Irvington.

Uncle Lisha's Shop: Life in a Corner of Yankeeland. Rowland E. Robinson. 187p. (C). 1986. reprint ed. pap. text ed. 6.95 (*0-8290-2045-4*) Irvington.

Uncle Lumpy Comes to Visit & No Time: Two Short Plays. Laurence Klavan. 36p. 1986. pap. 5.25 (*0-8222-1189-0*) Dramatists Play.

Uncle Mike's Totally Cool Way Excellent Tasty Sweet & Real Fattening Heirloom Dessert Recipes in No Particular Order & Some Candy Recipes Too, Cookbook. Michael G. Michaud. LC 93-80824. (Illus.). 165p. (Orig.). (C). 1993. spiral bd. 25.00 (*1-882585-00-3*) MGM Pr.

***Uncle Moishy Visits Torah Island.** Faigy Safran. (Illus.). (J). pap. 5.99 (*0-89906-806-5*, UM1P) Mesorah Pubns.

Uncle Nacho's Hat: El sombrero del Tio Nacho. Tr. by Alma F. Ada & Rosalma Zubizarreta. (Illus.). 32p. (ENG & SPA.). (J). (ps-5). 1993. pap. 6.95 (*0-89239-112-X*) Childrens Book Pr.

Uncle Nacho's Hat (El Sombrero de Tio Nacho) Tr. by Alma Flor Ada & Rosalma Zubizarreta. LC 88-37090. (Illus.). 32p. (ENG & SPA.). (J). (ps-5). 1989. 14.95 (*0-89239-043-3*) Childrens Book Pr.

Uncle Nacho's Hat Read-Along. Ed. by Anna Olivarez. (ENG & SPA.). (J). (ps-7). 1990. 22.95 incl. audio (*0-89239-061-1*) Childrens Book Pr.

Uncle Noel's Fun Fables Program. S. Noel Rideau. (Illus.). 80p. 1991. student ed. 8.95 (*0-9630734-0-0*) Aesop Systs.

Uncle Noruz (Uncle New Year) Farideh Farjam & Meyer Azaad. Ed. & Tr. by Ahmad Jabbari from PER. LC 83-60450. (Illus.). 24p. (Orig.). (J). (gr. k up). 1983. reprint ed. pap. 4.95 (*0-939214-14-8*) Mazda Pubs.

***Uncle Obadiah & the Alien.** Geoffrey Philp. 160p. 1997. pap. 12.95 (*1-900715-01-5*, Pub. by Peepal Tree Pr UK) Paul & Co Pubs.

Uncle of an Angel, & Other Stories. Thomas A. Janvier. LC 73-98578. (Short Story Index Reprint Ser.). 1977. 21.95 (*0-8369-3152-1*) Ayer.

Uncle Ovid's Exercise Book. Don Webb. LC 88-18060. 224p. (Orig.). 1988. 18.95 (*0-932511-17-1*); pap. text ed. 8.95 (*0-932511-18-X*) Fiction Coll.

Uncle Pete the Pirate. S. Leigh. (Young Puzzle Adventure Ser.). (Illus.). 32p. (J). (ps). 1994. pap. 4.95 (*0-7460-1529-1*, Usborne); lib. bdg. 12.95 (*0-88110-713-1*, Usborne) EDC.

***Uncle Pete's Pirate Adventure.** Susannah Leigh. (Young Puzzle Adventures Ser.). (Illus.). 32p. (J). (ps-1). 1997. pap. 4.95 (*0-7460-2298-0*, Usborne); lib. bdg. 12.95 (*0-88110-918-5*, Usborne) EDC.

Uncle Philip's Fickle Formula. Norman B. Howard. LC 94-60125. (Illus.). 44p. (J). (gr. 1-4). 1994. pap. 5.95 (*1-55523-682-0*) Winston-Derek.

***Uncle Phil's Diner.** Helena C. Pittman. LC 96-44326. (J). 1997. write for info. (*1-57505-083-8*, Carolrhoda) Lerner Group.

Uncle Pink & Other Central Missouri Fiddle Tunes from Lyman Enloe. Ed. by Bill Shull. 34p. 1993. pap. 12.00 (*0-9637812-2-7*) MO St Old Time.

Uncle Rebus: Alabama Picture Stories for Computer Kids. Carole Marsh. (Carole Marsh Alabama Bks.). (Illus.). (J). (gr. k-3). 1994. pap. 19.95 (*0-7933-4505-7*); lib. bdg. 29. 95 (*0-7933-4504-9*); disk 29.95 (*0-7933-4506-5*) Gallopade Pub Group.

Uncle Rebus: Alaska Picture Stories for Computer Kids. Carole Marsh. (Carole Marsh Alaska Bks.). (Illus.). (J). (gr. k-3). 1994. pap. 19.95 (*0-7933-4508-1*); lib. bdg. 29. 95 (*0-7933-4507-3*); disk 29.95 (*0-7933-4509-X*) Gallopade Pub Group.

Uncle Rebus: Arizona Picture Stories for Computer Kids. Carole Marsh. (Carole Marsh Arizona Bks.). (Illus.). (J). (gr. k-3). 1994. pap. 19.95 (*0-7933-4511-1*); lib. bdg. 29. 95 (*0-7933-4510-3*); disk 29.95 (*0-7933-4512-X*) Gallopade Pub Group.

Uncle Rebus: Arkansas Picture Stories for Computer Kids. Carole Marsh. (Carole Marsh Arkansas Bks.). (Illus.). (J). (gr. k-3). 1994. pap. 19.95 (*0-7933-4514-6*); lib. bdg. 29.95 (*0-7933-4513-8*); disk 29.95 (*0-7933-4515-4*) Gallopade Pub Group.

Uncle Rebus: California Picture Stories for Computer Kids. Carole Marsh. (Carole Marsh California Bks.). (Illus.). (J). (gr. k-3). 1994. pap. 19.95 (*0-7933-4517-0*); lib. bdg. 29.95 (*0-7933-4516-2*); disk 29.95 (*0-7933-4518-9*) Gallopade Pub Group.

Uncle Rebus: Colorado Picture Stories for Computer Kids. Carole Marsh. (Carole Marsh Colorado Bks.). (Illus.). (J). (gr. k-3). 1994. pap. 19.95 (*0-7933-4520-0*); lib. bdg. 29.95 (*0-7933-4519-7*); disk 29.95 (*0-7933-4521-9*) Gallopade Pub Group.

Uncle Rebus: Connecticut Picture Stories for Computer Kids. Carole Marsh. (Carole Marsh Connecticut Bks.). (Illus.). (J). (gr. k-3). 1994. pap. 19.95 (*0-7933-4523-5*); lib. bdg. 29.95 (*0-7933-4522-7*); disk 29.95 (*0-7933-4524-3*) Gallopade Pub Group.

Uncle Rebus: Delaware Picture Stories for Computer Kids. Carole Marsh. (Carole Marsh Delaware Bks.). (Illus.). (J). (gr. k-3). 1994. pap. 19.95 (*0-7933-4526-X*); lib. bdg. 29.95 (*0-7933-4525-1*); disk 29.95 (*0-7933-4527-8*) Gallopade Pub Group.

Uncle Rebus: Florida Picture Stories for Computer Kids. Carole Marsh. (Carole Marsh Florida Bks.). (Illus.). (J). (gr. k-3). 1994. pap. 19.95 (*0-7933-4529-4*); lib. bdg. 29. 95 (*0-7933-4528-6*); disk 29.95 (*0-7933-4530-8*) Gallopade Pub Group.

Uncle Rebus: Georgia Picture Stories for Computer Kids. Carole Marsh. (Carole Marsh Georgia Bks.). (Illus.). (J). (gr. k-3). 1994. pap. 19.95 (*0-7933-4532-4*); lib. bdg. 29. 95 (*0-7933-4531-6*); disk 29.95 (*0-7933-4533-2*) Gallopade Pub Group.

Uncle Rebus: Hawaii Picture Stories for Computer Kids. Carole Marsh. (Carole Marsh Hawaii Bks.). (Illus.). (J). (gr. k-3). 1994. pap. 19.95 (*0-7933-4535-9*); lib. bdg. 29. 95 (*0-7933-4534-0*); disk 29.95 (*0-7933-4536-7*) Gallopade Pub Group.

Uncle Rebus: Idaho Picture Stories for Computer Kids. Carole Marsh. (Carole Marsh Idaho Bks.). (Illus.). (J). (gr. k-3). 1994. pap. 19.95 (*0-7933-4538-3*); lib. bdg. 29. 95 (*0-7933-4537-5*); disk 29.95 (*0-7933-4539-1*) Gallopade Pub Group.

Uncle Rebus: Illinois Picture Stories for Computer Kids. Carole Marsh. (Carole Marsh Illinois Bks.). (Illus.). (J). (gr. k-3). 1994. pap. 19.95 (*0-7933-4541-3*); lib. bdg. 29. 95 (*0-7933-4540-5*); disk 29.95 (*0-7933-4542-1*) Gallopade Pub Group.

Uncle Rebus: Indiana Picture Stories for Computer Kids. Carole Marsh. (Carole Marsh Indiana Bks.). (Illus.). (J). (gr. k-3). 1994. pap. 19.95 (*0-7933-4544-8*); lib. bdg. 29. 95 (*0-7933-4543-X*); disk 29.95 (*0-7933-4545-6*) Gallopade Pub Group.

Uncle Rebus: Iowa Picture Stories for Computer Kids. Carole Marsh. (Carole Marsh Iowa Bks.). (Illus.). (J). (gr. k-3). 1994. pap. 19.95 (*0-7933-4547-2*); lib. bdg. 29. 95 (*0-7933-4546-4*); disk 29.95 (*0-7933-4548-0*) Gallopade Pub Group.

Uncle Rebus: Kansas Picture Stories for Computer Kids. Carole Marsh. (Carole Marsh Kansas Bks.). (Illus.). (J). (gr. k-3). 1994. pap. 19.95 (*0-7933-4550-2*); lib. bdg. 29. 95 (*0-7933-4549-9*); disk 29.95 (*0-7933-4551-0*) Gallopade Pub Group.

Uncle Rebus: Kentucky Picture Stories for Computer Kids. Carole Marsh. (Carole Marsh Kentucky Bks.). (Illus.). (J). (gr. k-3). 1994. pap. 19.95 (*0-7933-4553-7*); lib. bdg. 29.95 (*0-7933-4552-9*); disk 29.95 (*0-7933-4554-5*) Gallopade Pub Group.

Uncle Rebus: Louisiana Picture Stories for Computer Kids. Carole Marsh. (Carole Marsh Louisiana Bks.). (Illus.). (J). (gr. k-3). 1994. pap. 19.95 (*0-7933-4556-1*); lib. bdg. 29.95 (*0-7933-4555-3*); disk 29.95 (*0-7933-4557-X*) Gallopade Pub Group.

Uncle Rebus: Maine Picture Stories for Computer Kids. Carole Marsh. (Carole Marsh Maine Bks.). (Illus.). (J). (gr. k-3). 1994. pap. 19.95 (*0-7933-4559-6*); lib. bdg. 29. 95 (*0-7933-4558-8*); disk 29.95 (*0-7933-4560-X*) Gallopade Pub Group.

Uncle Rebus: Maryland Picture Stories for Computer Kids. Carole Marsh. (Carole Marsh Maryland Bks.). (Illus.). (J). (gr. k-3). 1994. pap. 19.95 (*0-7933-4562-6*); lib. bdg. 29.95 (*0-7933-4561-8*); disk 29.95 (*0-7933-4563-4*) Gallopade Pub Group.

An Asterisk (*) at the beginning of an entry indicates that the title is appearing in BIP for the first time.

Uncle Rebus: Massachusetts Picture Stories for Computer Kids. Carole Marsh. (Massachuseets Bks.). (Illus.). (J). (gr. k-3). 1994. pap. 19.95 (*0-7933-4565-0*); lib. bdg. 29.95 (*0-7933-4564-2*); disk 29.95 (*0-7933-4566-9*) Gallopade Pub Group.

Uncle Rebus: Michigan Picture Stories for Computer Kids. Carole Marsh. (Carole Marsh Michigan Bks.). (Illus.). (J). (gr. k-3). 1994. pap. 19.95 (*0-7933-4568-5*); lib. bdg. 29.95 (*0-7933-4567-7*); disk 29.95 (*0-7933-4569-3*) Gallopade Pub Group.

Uncle Rebus: Minnesota Picture Stories for Computer Kids. Carole Marsh. (Carole Marsh Minnesota Bks.). (Illus.). (J). (gr. k-3). 1994. pap. 19.95 (*0-7933-4571-5*); lib. bdg. 29.95 (*0-7933-4570-7*); disk 29.95 (*0-7933-4572-3*) Gallopade Pub Group.

Uncle Rebus: Mississippi Picture Stories for Computer Kids. Carole Marsh. (Carole Marsh Mississippi Bks.). (Illus.). (J). (gr. k-3). 1994. pap. 19.95 (*0-7933-4574-X*); lib. bdg. 29.95 (*0-7933-4573-1*); disk 29.95 (*0-7933-4575-8*) Gallopade Pub Group.

Uncle Rebus: Missouri Picture Stories for Computer Kids. Carole Marsh. (Carole Marsh Missouri Bks.). (Illus.). (J). (gr. k-3). 1994. pap. 19.95 (*0-7933-4577-4*); lib. bdg. 29.95 (*0-7933-4576-6*); disk 29.95 (*0-7933-4578-2*) Gallopade Pub Group.

Uncle Rebus: Montana Picture Stories for Computer Kids. Carole Marsh. (Carole Marsh Montana Bks.). (Illus.). (J). (gr. k-3). 1994. pap. 19.95 (*0-7933-4580-4*); lib. bdg. 29.95 (*0-7933-4579-0*); disk 29.95 (*0-7933-4581-2*) Gallopade Pub Group.

Uncle Rebus: Nebraska Picture Stories for Computer Kids. Carole Marsh. (Carole Marsh Nebraska Bks.). (Illus.). (J). (gr. k-3). 1994. pap. 19.95 (*0-7933-4583-9*); lib. bdg. 29.95 (*0-7933-4582-0*); disk 29.95 (*0-7933-4584-7*) Gallopade Pub Group.

Uncle Rebus: Nevada Picture Stories for Computer Kids. Carole Marsh. (Carole Marsh Nevada Bks.). (Illus.). (J). (gr. k-3). 1994. pap. 19.95 (*0-7933-4586-3*); lib. bdg. 29.95 (*0-7933-4585-5*); disk 29.95 (*0-7933-4587-1*) Gallopade Pub Group.

Uncle Rebus: New Hampshire Picture Stories for Computer Kids. Carole Marsh. (Carole Marsh New Hampshire Bks.). (Illus.). (J). (gr. k-3). 1994. pap. 19.95 (*0-7933-4589-8*); lib. bdg. 29.95 (*0-7933-4588-X*); disk 29.95 (*0-7933-4590-1*) Gallopade Pub Group.

Uncle Rebus: New Jersey Picture Stories for Computer Kids. Carole Marsh. (Carole Marsh New Jersey Bks.). (Illus.). (J). (gr. k-3). 1994. pap. 19.95 (*0-7933-4592-8*); lib. bdg. 29.95 (*0-7933-4591-X*); disk 29.95 (*0-7933-4593-6*) Gallopade Pub Group.

Uncle Rebus: New Mexico Picture Stories for Computer Kids. Carole Marsh. (Carole Marsh New Mexico Bks.). (Illus.). (J). (gr. k-3). 1994. pap. 19.95 (*0-7933-4595-2*); lib. bdg. 29.95 (*0-7933-4594-4*); disk 29.95 (*0-7933-4596-0*) Gallopade Pub Group.

Uncle Rebus: New York Picture Stories for Computer Kids. Carole Marsh. (Carole Marsh New York Bks.). (Illus.). (J). (gr. k-3). 1994. pap. 19.95 (*0-7933-4598-7*); lib. bdg. 29.95 (*0-7933-4597-9*); disk 29.95 (*0-7933-4599-5*) Gallopade Pub Group.

Uncle Rebus: North Carolina Picture Stories for Computer Kids. Carole Marsh. (Carole Marsh North Carolina Bks.). (Illus.). (J). (gr. k-3). 1994. pap. 19.95 (*0-7933-4601-0*); lib. bdg. 29.95 (*0-7933-4600-2*); disk 29.95 (*0-7933-4602-9*) Gallopade Pub Group.

Uncle Rebus: North Dakota Picture Stories for Computer Kids. Carole Marsh. (Carole Marsh North Dakota Bks.). (Illus.). (J). (gr. k-3). 1994. pap. 19.95 (*0-7933-4604-5*); lib. bdg. 29.95 (*0-7933-4603-7*); disk 29.95 (*0-7933-4605-3*) Gallopade Pub Group.

Uncle Rebus: Ohio Picture Stories for Computer Kids. Carole Marsh. (Carole Marsh Ohio Bks.). (Illus.). (J). (gr. k-3). 1994. pap. 19.95 (*0-7933-4607-X*); lib. bdg. 29.95 (*0-7933-4606-1*); disk 29.95 (*0-7933-4608-8*) Gallopade Pub Group.

Uncle Rebus: Oklahoma Picture Stories for Computer Kids. Carole Marsh. (Oklahoma Bks.). (Illus.). (J). (gr. k-3). 1994. pap. 19.95 (*0-7933-4610-X*); lib. bdg. 29.95 (*0-7933-4609-6*); disk 29.95 (*0-7933-4611-8*) Gallopade Pub Group.

Uncle Rebus: Oregon Picture Stories for Computer Kids. Carole Marsh. (Oregon Bks.). (Illus.). (J). (gr. k-3). 1994. pap. 19.95 (*0-7933-4613-4*); lib. bdg. 29.95 (*0-7933-4612-6*); disk 29.95 (*0-7933-4614-2*) Gallopade Pub Group.

Uncle Rebus: Pennsylvania Picture Stories for Computer Kids. Carole Marsh. (Pennsylvania Bks.). (Illus.). (J). (gr. k-3). 1994. pap. 19.95 (*0-7933-4616-9*); lib. bdg. 29.95 (*0-7933-4615-0*); disk 29.95 (*0-7933-4617-7*) Gallopade Pub Group.

Uncle Rebus: Rhode Island Picture Stories for Computer Kids. Carole Marsh. (Rhode Island Bks.). (Illus.). (J). (gr. k-3). 1994. pap. 19.95 (*0-7933-4619-3*); lib. bdg. 29.95 (*0-7933-4618-5*); disk 29.95 (*0-7933-4620-7*) Gallopade Pub Group.

Uncle Rebus: South Carolina Picture Stories for Computer Kids. Carole Marsh. (South Carolina Bks.). (Illus.). (J). (gr. k-3). 1994. pap. 19.95 (*0-7933-4622-3*); lib. bdg. 29.95 (*0-7933-4621-5*); disk 29.95 (*0-7933-4623-1*) Gallopade Pub Group.

Uncle Rebus: South Dakota Picture Stories for Computer Kids. Carole Marsh. (South Dakota Bks.). (Illus.). (J). (gr. k-3). 1994. pap. 19.95 (*0-7933-4625-8*); lib. bdg. 29.95 (*0-7933-4624-X*); disk 29.95 (*0-7933-4626-6*) Gallopade Pub Group.

Uncle Rebus: Tennessee Picture Stories for Computer Kids. Carole Marsh. (Tennessee Bks.). (Illus.). (J). (gr. k-3). 1994. pap. 19.95 (*0-7933-4628-2*); lib. bdg. 29.95 (*0-7933-4627-4*); disk 29.95 (*0-7933-4629-0*) Gallopade Pub Group.

Uncle Rebus: Texas Picture Stories for Computer Kids. Carole Marsh. (Texas Bks.). (Illus.). (J). (gr. k-3). 1994. pap. 19.95 (*0-7933-4631-2*); lib. bdg. 29.95 (*0-7933-4630-4*); disk 29.95 (*0-7933-4632-0*) Gallopade Pub Group.

Uncle Rebus: Utah Picture Stories for Computer Kids. Carole Marsh. (Utah Bks.). (Illus.). (J). (gr. k-3). 1994. pap. 19.95 (*0-7933-4634-7*); lib. bdg. 29.95 (*0-7933-4633-9*); disk 29.95 (*0-7933-4635-5*) Gallopade Pub Group.

Uncle Rebus: Vermont Picture Stories for Computer Kids. Carole Marsh. (Vermont Bks.). (Illus.). (J). (gr. k-3). 1994. pap. 19.95 (*0-7933-4637-1*); lib. bdg. 29.95 (*0-7933-4636-3*); disk 29.95 (*0-7933-4638-X*) Gallopade Pub Group.

Uncle Rebus: Virginia Picture Stories for Computer Kids. Carole Marsh. (Virginia Bks.). (Illus.). (J). (gr. k-3). 1994. pap. 19.95 (*0-7933-4640-1*); lib. bdg. 29.95 (*0-7933-4639-8*); disk 29.95 (*0-7933-4641-X*) Gallopade Pub Group.

Uncle Rebus: Washington, DC Picture Stories for Computer Kids. Carole Marsh. (Washington, D.C. Bks.). (Illus.). (J). (gr. k-3). 1994. pap. 19.95 (*0-7933-4646-0*); lib. bdg. 29.95 (*0-7933-4645-2*); disk 29.95 (*0-7933-4647-9*) Gallopade Pub Group.

Uncle Rebus: Washington Picture Stories for Computer Kids. Carole Marsh. (Washington Bks.). (Illus.). (J). (gr. k-3). 1994. pap. 19.95 (*0-7933-4643-6*); lib. bdg. 29.95 (*0-7933-4642-8*); disk 29.95 (*0-7933-4644-4*) Gallopade Pub Group.

Uncle Rebus: West Virginia Picture Stories for Computer Kids. Carole Marsh. (West Virginia Bks.). (Illus.). (J). (gr. k-3). 1994. pap. 19.95 (*0-7933-4649-5*); lib. bdg. 29.95 (*0-7933-4648-7*); disk 29.95 (*0-7933-4650-9*) Gallopade Pub Group.

Uncle Rebus: Wisconsin Picture Stories for Computer Kids. Carole Marsh. (Wisconsin Bks.). (Illus.). (J). (gr. k-3). 1994. pap. 19.95 (*0-7933-4652-5*); lib. bdg. 29.95 (*0-7933-4651-7*); disk 29.95 (*0-7933-4653-3*) Gallopade Pub Group.

Uncle Rebus: Wyoming Picture Stories for Computer Kids. Carole Marsh. (Wyoming Bks.). (Illus.). (J). (gr. k-3). 1994. pap. 19.95 (*0-7933-4655-X*); lib. bdg. 29.95 (*0-7933-4654-1*); disk 29.95 (*0-7933-4656-8*) Gallopade Pub Group.

Uncle Remus: His Songs & His Sayings. Joel C. Harris. 265p. 18.00 (*0-9645990-0-7*) Historic Pr-S.

Uncle Remus: His Songs & His Sayings. Joel C. Harris. Ed. & Intro. by Robert Hemenway. LC 81-69529. (American Library). 288p. 1982. pap. 9.95 (*0-14-039014-6*, Penguin Classics) Viking Penguin.

Uncle Remus: His Songs & His Sayings. Joel C. Harris. LC 81-69529. (Illus.). 242p. 1981. reprint ed. 16.95 (*0-87797-060-2*); reprint ed. pap. 9.95 (*0-87797-230-3*) Cherokee.

Uncle Remus: His Songs & Sayings. Joel C. Harris. Date not set. lib. bdg. 24.95 (*0-8488-0711-1*) Amereon Ltd.

Uncle Remus: Tales. Joel C. Harris. (Illus.). 207p. 1992. 20.00 (*0-88322-011-3*) Beehive GA.

Uncle Remus & Br'er Rabbit. Joel C. Harris. (J). 1986. reprint ed. lib. bdg. 17.95 (*0-89966-540-3*) Buccaneer Bks.

Uncle Remus Con Chile. Compiled by Americo Paredes. LC 92-14986. 200p. 1992. pap. 12.00 (*1-55885-053-8*) Arte Publico.

Uncle Rhythm's Cosmic Riff & Gig Guide: The First How-Not-to Book for a Career in Music. Chuck McCabe. LC 93-60729. 164p. 1993. pap. 12.95 (*0-9636869-6-8*) Woodshed Prods.

***Uncle Ronald.** Brian Doyle. LC 96-34401. (J). 1997. write for info. (*0-88899-266-1*) Douglas & McIntyre Canada.

***Uncle Ronald.** Brian Doyle. LC 96-34401. 144p. (J). 1997. mass mkt. write for info. (*0-88899-267-X*, Pub. by Groundwood-Douglas & McIntyre CN) Firefly Bks Ltd.

Uncle Russ's Way. Russ Chittenden. 200p. 1995. 16.95 (*0-9649228-0-0*) Good Ole Boys.

Uncle Sam & the Flag. Lee Mountain. LC 77-83633. (Illus.). 32p. (J). (gr. 2-3). 1978. lib. bdg. 9.95 (*0-87783-145-9*) Oddo.

Uncle Sam & the Flag. deluxe ed. Lee Mountain. LC 77-83633. (Illus.). 32p. (J). (gr. 2-3). 1978. pap. 3.94 (*0-87783-148-3*) Oddo.

Uncle Sam at Home. James H. Bridge. LC 73-13153. (Foreign Travelers in America, 1810-1935 Ser.). (Illus.). 248p. 1974. reprint ed. 20.95 (*0-405-05446-7*) Ayer.

Uncle Sam at Home: Civilian Mobilization, Wartime Federalism, & the Council of National Defense, 1917-1919. William J. Breen. LC 83-12576. (Contributions in American Studies: No. 70). 240p. 1984. text ed. 59.95 (*0-313-24112-0*, BRU/) Greenwood.

Uncle Sam in Nicaragua: A History. K. C. Tessendorf. LC 86-17340. 144p. (YA). (gr. 7 up). 1987. lib. bdg. 14.95 (*0-689-31286-5*, Atheneum Bks Young) S&S Childrens.

Uncle Sam Must Be... Losing the War: Black Marines of the 51st. Bill Downey. LC 82-5879. (Illus.). 224p. (Orig.). 1982. pap. 7.95 (*0-89407-050-9*) Strawberry Hill.

***Uncle Sam Presents: A Memoir of the Federal Theatre, 1935-1939.** Tony Buttitta & Barry B. Witham. LC 81-43517. (Illus.). 265p. 1982. reprint ed. pap. 75.60 (*0-608-03632-3*, 2064459) Bks Demand.

Uncle Sam Wants You: Military Men & Women of World War II. Sylvia Whitman. LC 92-14832. (YA). (gr. 5 up). 1993. lib. bdg. 19.95 (*0-8225-1728-0*, Lerner Publctns) Lerner Group.

Uncle Sam Ward & His Circle. Maud H. Elliott. LC 75-1844. (Leisure Class in America Ser.). (Illus.). 1975. reprint ed. 52.95 (*0-405-06912-X*) Ayer.

Uncle Sam's Acres. Marion Clawson. LC 74-106685. 414p. 1970. reprint ed. text ed. 65.00 (*0-8371-3356-4*, CLSA, Greenwood Pr) Greenwood.

Uncle Sam's Architects: Builders of the Capitol. William Bushong. LC 94-60547. (Illus.). 64p. (Orig.). (YA). 1994. pap. 7.95 (*0-614-00693-7*) US Capitol Hist.

Uncle Sam's Assassination Conspiracy. Gerald R. Duke. LC 92-93913. 100p. (Orig.). 1993. pap. write for info. (*0-9635221-0-8*) G R Duke.

Uncle Sam's Cabins: A Visitor's Guide to Historic U. S. Forest Service Ranger Stations of the West. Les Joslin. LC 95-90370. (Illus.). 272p. (Orig.). 1995. pap. 16.95 (*0-9647167-1-2*) Wilderness Assocs.

Uncle Sam's Emancipation. Harriet Beecher Stowe. LC 74-133163. (Black Heritage Library Collection). 1977. 24.95 (*0-8369-8719-5*) Ayer.

Uncle Sam's Family: Issues & Perspectives on American Demographic History. Robert Wells. LC 84-8733. 184p. 1985. 59.50 (*0-87395-962-0*); pap. text ed. 19.95 (*0-87395-963-9*) State U NY Pr.

Uncle Sam's Farmers: The New Deal Communities in the Lower Mississippi Valley. Donald Holley. LC 75-20091. 328p. reprint ed. pap. 93.50 (*0-8357-3579-6*, 2034444) Bks Demand.

Uncle Sam's Little Helpers Paper Dolls in Full Color. Wenham Museum Staff. (Illus.). (J). (gr. k-3). 1992. pap. 3.95 (*0-486-27090-4*) Dover.

Uncle Scrooge: Blast to the Past. (Illus.). 48p. (J). (gr. 3-7). 1992. pap. 2.95 (*1-56115-270-6*, 21811, Golden Pr) Western Pub.

Uncle Scrooge & Huey, Dewey & Louie. (Disney Learn to Draw Ser.). (Illus.). 28p. (J). 1991. pap. 6.95 (*1-56010-092-3*, DS06) W Foster Pub.

Uncle Scrooge Comes Home see Walt Disney's Read & Grow Library

Uncle Scrooge McDuck: His Life & Times. Carl Barks. Ed. by Edward Summer. LC 81-66953. (Illus.). 376p. (J). (ps-3). 1995. pap. 59.95 (*0-89087-511-1*) Celestial Arts.

Uncle Shamus. James Duffy. LC 91-19217. 144p. (J). (gr. 4-6). 1992. lib. bdg. 13.95 (*0-684-19434-1*, C Scribner Sons Young) S&S Childrens.

Uncle Shelby's ABZ Book. Shel Silverstein. 80p. 1985. pap. 11.00 (*0-671-21148-X*, Fireside) S&S Trade.

Uncle Silas. Joseph S. Le Fanu. Ed. by W. J. McCormack. (World's Classics Ser.). 432p. 1982. pap. 9.95 (*0-19-281541-5*) OUP.

Uncle Silas. large type ed. Sheridan Le Fanu. (Large-Print Ser.). 655p. 1992. reprint ed. lib. bdg. 25.00 (*0-939495-37-6*) North Bks.

Uncle Silas. J. Sheridan Le Fanu. 1966. reprint ed. pap. 8.95 (*0-486-21715-9*) Dover.

Uncle Silas. J. Sheridan LeFanu. 400p. 1992. reprint ed. lib. bdg. 34.95 (*0-89968-311-8*, Lghtyr Pr) Buccaneer Bks.

Uncle Silas: A Tale of Bartram-Haugh, 3 vols. Joseph S. Le Fanu. Ed. by Devendra P. Varma. LC 76-5278. (Collected Works). 1977. reprint ed. Set. 90.95 (*0-405-09237-7*) Ayer.

Uncle Silas: A Tale of Bartram-Haugh, 3 vols, 1. Joseph S. Le Fanu. Ed. by Devendra P. Varma. LC 76-5278. (Collected Works). 1977. reprint ed. 30.95 (*0-405-09238-5*) Ayer.

Uncle Silas: A Tale of Bartram-Haugh, 3 vols, Vol. 2. Joseph S. Le Fanu. Ed. by Devendra P. Varma. LC 76-5278. (Collected Works). 1977. reprint ed. 30.95 (*0-405-09239-3*) Ayer.

Uncle Silas: A Tale of Bartram-Haugh, 3 vols, Vol. 3. Joseph S. Le Fanu. Ed. by Devendra P. Varma. LC 76-5278. (Collected Works). 1977. reprint ed. 30.95 (*0-405-09240-7*) Ayer.

Uncle Smoke Stories: Four Fires in the Big Belly Lodge of the Nehawka. Roger Welsch. LC 93-48309. (Illus.). 96p. (J). (gr. 3-7). 1994. lib. bdg. write for info. (*0-679-95450-3*) Knopf.

Uncle Snake. Matthew Gollub. LC 95-612. (J). 1996. 16.00 (*0-688-13944-2*, Tambourine Bks) Morrow.

Uncle Snake. Israel Horovitz. 1976. pap. 5.25 (*0-8222-1190-4*) Dramatists Play.

Uncle Snake. limited ed. Matthew Gollub. LC 95-612. (J). 1996. lib. bdg. 15.93 (*0-688-13945-0*, Tambourine Bks) Morrow.

Uncle Stephen. Reid. 1995. per. 9.95 (*0-85449-083-3*, Pub. by Gay Mens Pr UK) LPC InBook.

Uncle Switch: Loony Limericks. X. J. Kennedy. LC 96-888. 1997. 15.00 (*0-689-80967-0*, S&S Bks Young Read) S&S Childrens.

Uncle Target. large type ed. Gavin Lyall. 487p. 1989. 25.99 (*0-7089-1945-6*) Ulverscroft.

Uncle Terrible: More Adventures of Anatole. Nancy Willard. LC 82-47940. (Illus.). 120p. (J). (gr. 3-7). 1985. pap. 6.00 (*0-15-292794-8*, HB Juv Bks) HarBrace.

***Uncle Theodor.** James Ringo. LC 97-65967. 96p. 1997. 16.95 (*1-57197-058-4*) Pentland Pr.

Uncle Tim's Book of Chords Vol. 2: Chord Construction for the Guitar. Timothy D. Gillespie. LC 96-94301. (Uncle Tim's Series for the Guitar). (Illus.). 106p. (Orig.). 1996. pap. 14.95 (*0-9647059-9-0*, UTBC) MTN STUDIOS.

Uncle Tim's Building Blocks: A Visual Way to Completely Understand the Guitar. 3rd rev. ed. Timothy O. Gillespie. LC 95-77468. (Uncle Tim's Series for the Guitar). (Illus.). 96p. (Orig.). 1995. pap. 14.95 (*0-9647059-7-4*) MTN STUDIOS.

Uncle Tom Andy Bill. Charles Major. 350p. 1992. reprint ed. lib. bdg. 26.95 (*0-89966-914-X*) Buccaneer Bks.

Uncle Tom Andy Bill: A Story of Bears & Indian Treasure. Charles Major. LC 93-22086. (Library of Indiana Classics). 352p. (C). 1993. 17.95 (*0-253-33653-8*); pap. 10.95 (*0-253-33654-6*) Ind U Pr.

Uncle Tom at Home: A Review of the Reviewers & Repudiators of Uncle Tom's Cabin by Mrs. Stowe. F. C. Adams. LC 78-107789. (Select Bibliographies Reprint Ser.). 1977. 20.95 (*0-8369-5210-3*) Ayer.

Uncle Tom of the Old South: A Story of the South in Reconstruction Days. M. F. Surghnor. LC 72-3108. (Black Heritage Library Collection). 1977. reprint ed. 36.95 (*0-8369-9082-X*) Ayer.

Uncle Tom's Cabin. George L. Aiken & George C. Howard. Ed. by Thomas L. Riis. LC 94-1962. (Nineteenth-Century American Musical Theater Ser.: No. 5). (Illus.). 128p. 1994. text ed. 72.00 (*0-8153-1366-7*) Garland.

***Uncle Tom's Cabin.** Harriet Beecher Stowe. (Classics Illustrated Ser.). (Illus.). 1997. pap. text ed. 4.99 (*1-57840-060-0*) Acclaim Bks.

Uncle Tom's Cabin. Harriet Beecher Stowe. 1996. 18.50 (*0-679-60200-3*, Modern Lib) Random.

***Uncle Tom's Cabin.** Harriet Beecher Stowe. 1998. mass mkt. 5.95 (*0-451-52670-8*, Penguin Classics) Viking Penguin.

Uncle Tom's Cabin. Harriet Beecher Stowe. (Airmont Classics Ser.). (J). (gr. 9 up). 1967. mass mkt. 5.95 (*0-8049-0143-0*, CL-143) Airmont.

Uncle Tom's Cabin. Harriet Beecher Stowe. 29.95 (*0-8488-0637-9*) Amereon Ltd.

Uncle Tom's Cabin. Harriet Beecher Stowe. 480p. 1983. mass mkt. 4.95 (*0-553-21218-4*, Bantam Classics) Bantam.

Uncle Tom's Cabin. Harriet Beecher Stowe. (Book Notes Ser.). 1985. pap. 3.95 (*0-8120-3600-X*) Barron.

Uncle Tom's Cabin. Harriet Beecher Stowe. Ed. by Christopher Bigsby. 480p. 1993. pap. 4.95 (*0-460-87139-0*, Everyman's Classic Lib) C E Tuttle.

Uncle Tom's Cabin. Harriet Beecher Stowe. 1970. mass mkt. 5.00 (*0-06-080618-4*, PL) HarpC.

Uncle Tom's Cabin. Harriet Beecher Stowe. 496p. (YA). 1966. pap. 5.95 (*0-451-52302-4*, Sig Classics) NAL-Dutton.

Uncle Tom's Cabin. Harriet Beecher Stowe. LC 85-4992. 552p. 17.50 (*0-394-60527-6*, Modern Lib) Random.

Uncle Tom's Cabin. Harriet Beecher Stowe. Ed. by Elizabeth Ammons. (Critical Editions Ser.). (C). 1993. pap. text ed. 11.95 (*0-393-96303-9*) Norton.

Uncle Tom's Cabin. Harriet Beecher Stowe. 1995. 20.00 (*0-679-44365-7*) Knopf.

Uncle Toms Cabin. George L. Aiken. (Works of George Aiken (1830-1876)). 1989. reprint ed. lib. bdg. 79.00 (*0-7812-1590-0*) Rprt Serv.

Uncle Tom's Cabin. Harriet Beecher Stowe. 1982. reprint ed. lib. bdg. 27.95 (*0-89966-378-8*) Buccaneer Bks.

Uncle Tom's Cabin: Or, Life among the Lowly. Harriet Beecher Stowe. Ed. & Intro. by Ann Douglas. (American Library). 640p. 1981. pap. 8.95 (*0-14-039003-0*, Penguin Classics) Viking Penguin.

Uncle Tom's Cabin: With an Introduction Setting Forth the History of the Novel & a Key (The Writings-Riverside Edition), 2 vols. Harriet Beecher Stowe. (Anglistica & Americana Ser.: No. 156). 1975. reprint ed. Set. 88.40 (*3-487-05691-7*) G Olms Pubs.

Uncle Tom's Cabin & American Culture. Thomas F. Gossett. LC 83-17245. (Illus.). 496p. 1985. 29.95 (*0-87074-189-6*) SMU Press.

Uncle Tom's Cabin Contrasted with Buckingham Hall, the Planter's Home. Robert Criswell. LC 72-950. reprint ed. 32.50 (*0-404-00254-4*) AMS Pr.

Uncle Tom's Cabin Notes. J. M. Lybyer. 70p. 1984. pap. text ed. 3.75 (*0-8220-1313-4*) Cliffs.

Uncle Tom's Cabin of To-Day. Andasia K. Bruce. LC 72-6488. (Black Heritage Library Collection). 1977. reprint ed. 18.95 (*0-8369-9161-3*) Ayer.

Uncle Tom's Cabin, or, Life Among the Lowly. large type ed. Harriet Beecher Stowe. LC 93-9844. 1993. lib. bdg. 21.95 (*0-8161-5714-6*, GK Hall) Thorndike Pr.

Uncle Tom's Cabin, or, Life Among the Lowly. large type ed. Harriet Beecher Stowe. LC 93-9844. 1994. pap. 15.95 (*0-8161-5893-2*, GK Hall) Thorndike Pr.

Uncle Tom's Children. Richard Wright. 215p. 1991. reprint ed. lib. bdg. 25.00 (*0-8095-9070-0*) Borgo Pr.

Uncle Tom's Children. Richard Wright. LC 88-45968. 256p. 1993. reprint ed. pap. 7.00 (*0-06-081251-6*, P 988, PL) HarpC.

***Uncle Tom's Story of His Life from 1789 to 1877.** Josiah Henson. Ed. by John Lobb. LC 96-62041. 240p. 1997. reprint ed. 12.95 (*1-55523-856-4*) Winston-Derek.

Uncle Valentine & Other Stories: Willa Cather's Uncollected Short Fiction, 1915-1929. Willa Cather. Ed. by Bernice Slote. LC 72-83755. xxx, 183p. 1973. reprint ed. pap. 11.95 (*0-8032-6317-1*, Bison Books) U of Nebr Pr.

Uncle Vampire. Cynthia D. Grant. (YA). (gr. 9-12). 1996. 18.00 (*0-8446-6889-3*) Peter Smith.

Uncle Vampire. Cynthia D. Grant. LC 92-44455. 160p. (YA). (gr. 8 up). 1993. lib. bdg. 14.00 (*0-689-31852-9*, Atheneum Bks Young) S&S Childrens.

Uncle Vampire. Cynthia D. Grant. 1995. pap. 4.99 (*0-679-86726-0*) Random.

Uncle Vanya. Anton P. Chekhov. Tr. by Tyrone Guthrie & Leonid Kipnis from RUS. LC 75-75974. 86p. 1969. 16.95 (*0-910278-94-6*) Boulevard.

Uncle Vanya. Anton P. Chekhov. Tr. by Jean-Claude Van Itallie. 1980. pap. 5.25 (*0-8222-1191-2*) Dramatists Play.

Uncle Vanya. Anton P. Chekhov. (Five Major Plays). write for info. (*0-318-56842-X*) OUP.

***Uncle Vanya.** Anton P. Chekhov. 55p. 1996. pap. 7.00 (*0-88734-707-X*) Players Pr.

Uncle Vanya. Anton P. Chekhov. Tr. by Pam Gems. 80p. Date not set. pap. 12.95 (*1-85459-176-2*, Pub. by N Hern Bks UK) Theatre Comm.

Uncle Vanya. Anton P. Chekhov. (Plays). write for info. (*0-318-55068-7*) Viking Penguin.

***Uncle Vanya.** rev. ed. Jean-Claude Van Itallie. 1997. pap. 5.25 (*0-8222-1587-X*) Dramatists Play.

Uncle Vanya. Anton P. Chekhov. LC 88-21455. 82p. 1988. reprint ed. pap. 8.95 (*0-8021-3151-4*, Grove) Grove-Atltic.

U V

Uncle Vanya: A New Version. Tr. by John Murrell from RUS. 57p. (Orig.). 1990. 7.95 (*0-317-91358-1*) Playsmith.

Uncle Vanya: Scenes from Country Life in Four Acts. Anton Chekhov. LC 75-75974. (Minnesota Drama Editions Ser.: 5). 92p. reprint ed. pap. 26.30 (*0-317-27952-1*, 2055849) Bks Demand.

Uncle Vanya see Plays

Uncle Vova's Tree. Patricia Polacco. LC 88-22522. (Illus.). 32p. (Orig.). (J). (ps-3). 1989. 15.95 (*0-399-21617-0*, Philomel Bks) Putnam Pub Group.

Uncle Vova's Tree. Patricia Polacco. (Illus.). 32p. (Orig.). (J). (gr. k-3). 1995. pap. 5.95 (*0-399-22838-1*, Sandcastle Bks) Putnam Pub Group.

Uncle What-Is-It Is Coming to Visit!!! Michael Willhoite. (Illus.). 32p. (J). (ps-5). 1993. 12.95 (*1-55583-205-9*) Alyson Pubns.

***Uncle Wiggily Bedtime Stories.** unabridged ed. Howard R. Garis. LC 96-28386. (Children's Thrift Editions Ser.). (Illus.). 80p. (J). 1996. pap. text ed. 1.00 (*0-486-29372-6*) Dover.

Uncle Wiggily to the Rescue. Howard R. Garis. (Illus.). 32p. (J). (ps-2). 1989. pap. 5.95 (*0-448-19119-9*, Platt & Munk Pubs) Putnam Pub Group.

Uncle Wiggily's Story Book. Howard R. Garis. (Illus.). 260p. (J). (ps-4). 1987. 12.95 (*0-448-40090-1*, G&D) Putnam Pub Group.

Uncle Willie & the Soup Kitchen. Dyanne DiSalvo-Ryan. LC 90-6375. (Illus.). 32p. (J). (gr. 1 up). 1991. 16.00 (*0-688-09165-2*, Morrow Junior) Morrow.

***Uncle Willie & the Soup Kitchen.** Dyanne Disalvo-Ryan. 1997. pap. 4.95 (*0-688-15285-6*, Mulberry) Morrow.

Uncle Willy's Tickles. Marcie Aboff & Jill Neimark. (Illus.). 32p. (J). (ps-3). 1996. 11.95 (*0-945354-64-9*) Magination Pr.

***Uncle Willy's Tickles.** Marcie Aboff. (Illus.). 32p. (J). 1996. pap. 11.95 (*0-945354-67-3*) Magination Pr.

Uncle Wizzmo's New Used Car. Rodney A. Greenblat. LC 89-36577. (Illus.). 32p. (J). (ps-3). 1990. 13.95 (*0-06-022097-X*); lib. bdg. 13.89 (*0-06-022098-8*) HarpC Child Bks.

Uncle Wooley. August Keating. LC 87-82084. 55p. (Orig.). (YA). (gr. 9 up). 1988. pap. 5.00 (*0-916383-47-4*) Aegina Pr.

Unclean Bird. Madge Reinhardt. LC 85-72901. 135p. 1986. pap. 8.00 (*0-917162-10-2*) Back Row Pr.

Unclear Family. Damian Lopes. 24p. (Orig.). 1992. pap. 3.00 (*0-926935-65-8*) Runaway Spoon.

Uncle's Dream & Other Stories. Fyodor Dostoyevsky. Tr. & Intro. by David McDuff. 304p. 1989. pap. 10.95 (*0-14-044518-8*, Penguin Classics) Viking Penguin.

Uncle's Handbook (& Aunt's Too) One Hundred One Things to Do with Kids. Andy Newman. 160p. (Orig.). 1993. pap. 8.00 (*0-380-77192-6*) Avon.

Uncle's South China Sea Blue Nightmare. Lamont B. Steptoe. (Illus.). 60p. (Orig.). (C). 1988. 7.00 (*0-685-23084-8*) Whirlwind Pr.

Uncle's South China Sea Blue Nightmare. Lamont B. Steptoe. LC 94-18354. (Orig.). 1994. 20.00 (*1-882611-06-3*); pap. 11.95 (*1-882611-07-1*) Yardbird Bks.

Uncloistered Virtue: English Political Literature, 1640-1660. Thomas N. Corns. 345p. 1992. 85.00 (*0-19-812883-5*) OUP.

Unclutter Your Personal Life: A Learning Annex Book. Susan Wright. 1993. pap. 8.95 (*0-8065-1466-3*, Citadel Pr) Carol Pub Group.

***Uncluttered: Storage Room by Room.** Candace Manroe. LC 97-24986. 1997. 27.50 (*1-56799-428-8*, Friedman-Fairfax) M Friedman Pub Grp Inc.

Uncola. Paul Bates et al. (Illus.). 99p. (Orig.). 1989. pap. 8.00 (*1-56046-129-2*) Interact Pubs.

Uncollected Early Prose of Katherine Anne Porter. Katherine Anne Porter. Ed. by Ruth M. Alvarez & Thomas F. Walsh. LC 93-3361. (Illus.). 288p. 1994. 35.00 (*0-292-76544-4*) U of Tex Pr.

***Uncollected Oscar Wilde.** Ed. by John W. Jackson. 215p. 1997. pap. 13.95 (*1-85702-334-X*, Pub. by Fourth Estate UK) Trafalgar.

Uncollected Poems. Basil Bunting. Ed. by Richard Caddel. 80p. 1991. pap. 11.95 (*0-19-282870-3*) OUP.

Uncollected Poems. W. S. Graham. (C). 1990. 35.00 (*0-906887-39-9*, Pub. by Greville Pr UK) St Mut.

Uncollected Poems. Rainer M. Rilke. Tr. by Edward Snow from GER. LC 94-24438. 266p. 1995. 22.00 (*0-86547-482-6*, North Pt Pr) FS&G.

***Uncollected Poems.** Rainer M. Rilke. 1997. pap. 12.00 (*0-86547-513-X*, North Pt Pr) FS&G.

Uncollected Poems of Irving Layton. limited ed. Irving Layton. 153p. 150.00 (*0-88962-042-3*) Mosaic.

Uncollected Poems, 1604-1617. Samuel Rowlands. LC 78-119867. 210p. 1970. 50.00 (*0-8201-1074-4*) Schol Facsimiles.

Uncollected Prose of James Stephens, 1907-1948, I. Ed. by Patricia McFate. LC 82-10560. 170p. 1983. text ed. 29.95 (*0-312-82859-4*) St Martin.

Uncollected Stories of Mary Wilkins Freeman. Ed. by Mary R. Reichardt. LC 91-48011. 350p. 1992. 40.00 (*0-87805-564-9*); pap. 16.95 (*0-87805-565-7*) U Pr of Miss.

Uncollected Stories of William Faulkner. William Faulkner & Joseph Blotner. LC 80-6120. 732p. (C). 1981. 17.95 (*0-394-40044-5*, V-656, Vin) Random.

Uncollected Stories of William Faulkner. William Faulkner. Ed. by Joseph L. Blotner. LC 80-6120. 732p. (C). 1981. pap. 20.00 (*0-394-74656-2*, Vin) Random.

***Uncollected Stories of William Faulkner.** William Faulkner. 1997. pap. 19.00 (*0-375-70109-5*, Vin) Random.

Uncollected Works of Karl Polanyi. Karl Polanyi. Date not set. text ed. write for info. (*0-312-04803-3*) St Martin.

Uncollected Writings, 2 vols. Thomas De Quincey. LC 72-6781. (Essay Index Reprint Ser.). 1977. reprint ed. Set. 38.95 (*0-8369-7270-8*) Ayer.

Uncollected Writings, 2 vols. in 1. Thomas De Quincey. (Anglistica & Americana Ser.: No. 144). xx, 714p. 1974. reprint ed. 115.70 (*3-487-04887-6*) G Olms Pubs.

Uncollected Writings. Ralph Waldo Emerson. (Notable American Authors Ser.). 1992. reprint ed. lib. bdg. 75.00 (*0-7812-2818-2*) Rprt Serv.

Uncollected Writings on Russian Literature. Dimitry S. Mirsky. (Modern Russian Literature & Culture, Studies & Texts: Vol. 13). (Illus.). 406p. (Orig.). (ENG & RUS.). (C). 1989. pap. 24.00 (*0-933884-68-0*) Berkeley Slavic.

Uncollected Writings 1785-1822. William Godwin. LC 68-24208. (Illus.). 1968. 75.00 (*0-8201-1023-X*) Schol Facsimiles.

Uncollectible Accounts: Allowances & Writeoffs. 9p. 1986. 40.00 (*0-939050-50-1*) Credit Res NYS.

Uncomfortable Learning. R. L. Gaudino. 244p. 1974. 15.95 (*0-318-36828-5*) Asia Bk Corp.

Uncommercial Traveller, & Reprinted Pieces see Oxford Illustrated Dickens

Uncommitted. Gracianus R. Reyes. 90p. (Orig.). 1986. pap. 6.50 (*971-10-0249-3*, Pub. by New Day Pub PH) Cellar.

Uncommon Adventures: A Travel Guide to the Journey of Faith. Mark Tabb. (Orig.). 1996. pap. 9.99 (*0-8024-0727-7*) Moody.

Uncommon Affair. Leigh Michaels. (Romance Ser.: No. 3119). 1991. pap. 2.75 (*0-373-03119-X*) Harlequin Bks.

Uncommon Book of Christmas. Elsa Bailey. (Illus.). 80p. (Orig.). 1987. pap. 6.95 (*0-9618943-1-8*) Lord & Bilder.

Uncommon Book of Prayer. Elsa Bailey. LC 87-17119. (Illus.). 80p. (Orig.). 1987. pap. 6.95 (*0-9618943-0-X*) Lord & Bilder.

Uncommon Boston: A Guide to Hidden Spaces & Special Places. Susan Berk & Jill Bloom. LC 86-20684. 224p. 1987. pap. 7.95 (*0-201-10662-0*) Addison-Wesley.

Uncommon Calling: A Gay Christian's Struggle to Serve the Church. expanded rev. ed. Chris Glaser. LC 87-46207. 272p. (Orig.). 1996. pap. 20.00 (*0-664-25659-7*) Westminster John Knox.

***Uncommon Care for Common Animals: 1995 IWRC Conference Proceedings.** Ed. by Mary D. Reynolds. (Illus.). 223p. (Orig.). 1996. pap. 20.00 (*1-884196-05-5*) IWRC.

Uncommon Casebook. William H. O'Hanlon. 1990. 34.95 (*0-393-70101-8*) Norton.

Uncommon Cats: The Who's Who of Cats. John R. Guevin. LC 93-90382. (Illus.). 224p. 1993. 23.95 (*0-9637240-4-5*) Biograph Pub.

Uncommon Child. Ed. by Michael Lewis & Leonard A. Rosenblum. LC 80-20601. (Genesis of Behavior Ser.: Vol. 3). 354p. 1981. 65.00 (*0-306-40499-0*, Plenum Pr) Plenum.

Uncommon Clay: The Life & Works of Augustus Saint Gaudens see Life & Works of Augustus Saint Gaudens

Uncommon Common Sense: A Guide for Engaged & Married Couples. Lynn H. Poulson. LC 92-46167. (Illus.). 336p. 1993. pap. 15.95 (*0-935834-98-2*) Rainbow Books.

Uncommon Common Sense: Between Mathematics & Logic I. J. Fang. 1996. pap. write for info. (*0-318-72904-0*) PAIDEIA & PM.

Uncommon Common Women: Ordinary Lives of the West. Anne M. Butler & Ona Siporin. LC 96-10025. (Illus.). 144p. 1996. 34.95 (*0-87421-209-X*); pap. 21.95 (*0-87421-210-3*) Utah St U Pr.

Uncommon Courtesy for Kids Kit. Gregg Harris & Josh Harris. 56p. (J). 1990. pap. text ed. 13.95 (*0-923463-72-0*) Noble Pub Assocs.

Uncommon Cultures: Popular Culture & Post-Modernism. Jim Collins. 224p. 1989. 35.00 (*0-415-90016-6*, Routledge NY) Routledge.

Uncommon Cultures: Popular Culture & Post-Modernism. Jim Collins. 224p. (C). 1989. pap. 13.95 (*0-415-90137-5*, Routledge NY) Routledge.

Uncommon Decency: Christian Civility in an Uncivil World. Richard J. Mouw. LC 92-5680. 192p. (Orig.). 1992. 16.99 (*0-8308-1826-X*); pap. 9.99 (*0-8308-1825-1*) InterVarsity.

Uncommon Eloquence: A Biography of Angna Enters. Dorothy Mandel. LC 86-17386. (Illus.). 368p. (Orig.). 1986. 24.50 (*0-912869-07-0*) Arden Pr.

Uncommon Farm Animals. Ann L. Hansen. LC 96-12464. (Farm Animals Ser.). (Illus.). (J). 1997. lib. bdg. 12.95 (*1-56239-607-2*) Abdo & Dghtrs.

Uncommon Fathers: Reflections on Raising a Child with a Disability. Ed. by Donald Meyer. 206p. (Orig.). (C). 1995. pap. 14.95 (*0-933149-68-9*) Woodbine House.

Uncommon Freedom: The Amway Experience & Why It Grows. Charles P. Conn. 208p. 1985. mass mkt. 5.99 (*0-425-08896-0*) Berkley Pub.

Uncommon Friends. James Newton. 1989. pap. 13.00 (*0-15-692620-2*) HarBrace.

Uncommon Fruits Worthy of Attention: A Gardener's Guide. Lee Reich. LC 90-45118. (Illus.). 1991. 18.95 (*0-201-52381-7*) Addison-Wesley.

Uncommon Fruits Worthy of Attention: A Gardener's Guide. Lee Reich. 1992. pap. 10.00 (*0-201-60820-0*) Addison-Wesley.

Uncommon Genius: How Great Ideas Are Born. Denise Shekerjian. 272p. 1991. pap. 11.00 (*0-14-010986-2*) Viking Penguin.

Uncommon Gourmet. Ellen Helman. LC 92-32082. 416p. (Orig.). 1993. pap. 16.95 (*0-89815-519-3*) Ten Speed Pr.

Uncommon Gourmet's All-Occasion Cookbook. Ellen Helman. 512p. 1996. pap. text ed. 18.95 (*1-883280-08-7*) Font & Ctr Pr.

Uncommon Grace: Reminiscences & Photographs of Jacqueline Bouvier Kennedy Onassis. J. C. Suares. LC 94-32337. (Illus.). 128p. 1994. 24.95 (*1-56566-077-3*) Thomasson-Grant.

***Uncommon Ground.** Berg. 1997. 47.50 (*1-85973-946-6*); pap. 19.50 (*1-85973-951-2*, Pub. by Berg Pubs UK) NYU Pr.

Uncommon Ground. Paradigm Poets Staff. 190p. (Orig.). 1995. pap. 9.95 (*1-881168-41-7*) Red Danceflr.

***Uncommon Ground.** Susan Prest. Date not set. write for info. (*1-55710-039-X*) Morrow.

Uncommon Ground: Archaeology & Early African America, 1650-1800. Leland Ferguson. LC 91-52833. (Illus.). 252p. (C). 1992. pap. text ed. 14.95 (*1-56098-059-1*) Smithsonian.

Uncommon Ground: Rethinking the Human Place in Nature. William Cronon. 562p. 1996. pap. 15.95 (*0-393-31511-8*) Norton.

Uncommon Ground: Toward Reinventing Nature. Ed. by William Cronon. LC 95-2147. (Illus.). 544p. 1995. 29.95 (*0-393-03872-6*) Norton.

Uncommon Guide to Carmel, Monterey & Big Sur. Lachlan P. MacDonald. (Illus.). 1990. pap. 8.95 (*0-939919-03-6*) Bear Flag Bks.

Uncommon Guide to Easter Island: Exploring Archaeological Mysteries of Rapa Nui. Georgia Lee. (Illus.). 128p. 1989. 18.95 (*0-937480-17-7*) Intl Resources.

***Uncommon Guide to Florida: A Resident's Guide to the Real Florida.** 2nd ed. Nina McGuire. 232p. 1997. pap. 16.95 (*0-9631241-9-6*) Tail Tours.

Uncommon Guide to San Luis Obispo County California. 2nd rev. ed. Lachlan P. MacDonald. LC 75-2794. (Illus.). 1990. pap. 8.95 (*0-939919-00-1*) Bear Flag Bks.

Uncommon Hero. S. Curwood. 1999. 19.45 (*0-446-51448-9*) Warner Bks.

Uncommon Heroes. Intro. by Phillip Sherman. (Illus.). 272p. (Orig.). 1994. pap. 25.00 (*0-9641779-0-0*) Fletcher Pr.

Uncommon Infections & Special Topics. Ed. by Louis G. Keith. 1985. lib. bdg. 205.00 (*0-85200-861-9*) Kluwer Ac.

Uncommon Influence. Terry G. Dodd. 1994. pap. 14.95 (*0-9641600-0-5*) DCG Pubng.

Uncommon Knowledge. Hawkins. (C). 1995. pap. 25.96 (*0-395-70958-X*) HM.

Uncommon Knowledge. Judy Lewis. 1995. pap. 6.50 (*0-671-70020-0*) PB.

***Uncommon Knowledge: An Introduction to Past Life & Health Readings.** Ed. by Barbara Condron. 208p. (Orig.). 1996. pap. 13.00 (*0-944386-19-9*) SOM Pub.

***Uncommon Knowledge: Exploring Ideas Through Reading & Writing.** Rose Hawkins & Robert Isaacson. (C). 1995. teacher ed., text ed. 11.96 (*0-395-76579-X*) HM.

Uncommon Law. A. P. Herbert. 500p. pap. 10.95 (*1-55882-107-4*) Intl Polygonics.

Uncommon Lives: Eighteen Extraordinary New Jersey Jews. Ruth M. Patt. 1994. 17.95 (*0-533-10970-1*) Vantage.

***Uncommon Love.** Beverly A. Rushin. 303p. (Orig.). 1997. mass mkt. 4.99 (*1-55237-275-8*, Pub. by Comnwlth Pub CN) Partners Pubs Grp.

***Uncommon Love: How to Survive a Love Affair.** Lydia Edelhaus. 168p. (Orig.). 1997. pap. 12.95 (*0-9653286-0-0*) Prism Pub & Seminars.

Uncommon Man: The Triumph of Herbert Hoover. Richard N. Smith. LC 89-82766. (Illus.). 488p. 1990. reprint ed. pap. 15.00 (*0-9623333-1-X*) High Plns WY.

Uncommon Man in American Business. Wallace J. Johnson. 1966. 6.95 (*0-8159-7001-3*) Devin.

***Uncommon Marketing Techniques: Practical Real-Life Lessons in Marketing & Direct Marketing.** Jeffrey Dobkin. Ed. by Michelle Axelrod. 224p. (Orig.). 1997. pap. 17.95 (*0-9642879-3-5*) Danielle Adams.

Uncommon Martyrs: How the Berrigans & Others Are Turning Swords into Plowshares. Fred A. Wilcox. (Illus.). 272p. 1992. pap. 9.95 (*0-201-60814-6*) Addison-Wesley.

Uncommon Men: The Sergeants Major of the Marine Corps. John C. Chapin. LC 92-32620. (Illus.). 366p. (C). 1993. 35.00 (*0-942597-45-1*) White Mane Pub.

Uncommon Miss. Melissa L. Jones. 304p. 1993. mass mkt. 3.99 (*0-8217-4074-1*, Zebra Kensgtn) Kensgtn Pub Corp.

Uncommon Numbers Vol. I: A Source Book for Artists. Ed. by Brenda Casey. (Illus.). vi, 58p. (Orig.). 1996. pap. 13.95 (*0-9651382-0-8*) PenUltimates.

Uncommon Opportunities: An Agenda for Peace & Equitable Development. International Commission on Peace & Food Staff. LC 94-41474. (C). 1994. pap. 19.95 (*1-85649-306-7*, Pub. by Zed Bks Ltd UK); text ed. 55.00 (*1-85649-305-9*, Pub. by Zed Bks Ltd UK) Humanities.

Uncommon Places. David Muench. LC 91-65. (Illus.). 168p. 1991. 39.95 (*0-917953-40-1*) Appalachian Trail.

Uncommon Plant Drugs of Ayurveda. Gyanendra Pandey. (C). 1995. 34.00 (*81-7030-404-0*, Pub. by Sri Satguru Pubns II) S Asia.

Uncommon Poet for the Common Man: A Study of the Poetry of Philip Larkin. Lolette Kuby. (De Proprietatibus Litterarum, Ser. Practica: No. 60). 190p. 1974. pap. text ed. 32.35 (*90-279-2720-0*) Mouton.

***Uncommon Prayer: Approaching Intimacy with God.** Kenneth Swanson. 1997. pap. text ed. 9.95 (*1-885478-31-3*) Genesis Press.

Uncommon Psychiatric Syndromes. 3rd ed. M. D. Enoch & William H. Trethowan. 256p. 1991. pap. 50.00 (*0-7506-1400-5*) Buttrwrth-Heinemann.

Uncommon Quotes, Vol. 1. William S. Burroughs. Ed. by Kathelin Hoffman. (C). 1989. 12.50 (*0-929856-00-7*); audio write for info. (*0-318-63927-0*) Caravan Dreams Prodns.

Uncommon Quotes: Dr. Timothy Leary. Ed. by Kathelin Hoffman. (Uncommom Quotes Ser.: Vol. III). 1989. 12.50 (*0-929856-01-5*) Caravan Dreams Prodns.

Uncommon Quotes: The Dream & Drink of Freedom. Johnny Dolphin. Ed. & Intro. by Kathelin Hoffman. (Uncommon Quotes Ser.: Vol. II). (C). 1989. 12.50 (*0-929856-03-1*); audio write for info. (*0-318-63725-1*) Caravan Dreams Prodns.

Uncommon Reader. George Steiner. (Chapbooks in Literature Ser.). (Illus.). 22p. (Orig.). 1978. pap. text ed. 5.00 (*0-9614940-2-6*) Bennington Coll.

***Uncommon Remedies for America's Ills: Futuring for the New Millennium. John F. McGrew. LC 96-92648. 160p. (Orig.). 1997. pap. 13.50 (*0-936544-08-2*) New Vista.**

UNCOMMON REMEDIES FOR AMERICA'S ILLS: FUTURING FOR THE NEW MILLENNIUM by Dr. John F. McGrew, a professional educator & historian, examines America's current sociological & economic concerns with minimal regard for political correctness. His solutions to our nation's woes vary from creative & logical to "off the wall". In all cases McGrew's tongue-in-cheek style should hold the reader's interest through an analysis of perplexing current issues. The author's controversial projection of a baby licensing plan along with "solution Y" could eliminate or reduce abortion, poverty, homelessness, welfare & crime. McGrew, a U.S. Naval Academy graduate, projects a lean, mean military machine with which to face peace time international challenges. He conjectures that a national "sue a lawyer month" might encourage adoption of the English system of law to minimize spurious law suits. Chapters also cover education (the problem may be apathetic clients--the students), medicine, special interests, media, religion, sex, minorities, international relations & futuring. The book challenges readers to become activists. $13.50 (plus $2.50 s&h). New Vista Press, Box 3554, Ashland, OR 97520. ***Publisher Provided Annotation.***

***Uncommon Scents: Growing Herbs & Spices in Florida.** Hank Bruce. Ed. by Erv Lampert. (Illus.). 224p. (Orig.). 1996. pap. 13.95 (*0-932855-50-4*) Winner Enter.

Uncommon Scold. Abby Adams. 272p. 1994. 8.00 (*0-671-88526-X*, Fireside) S&S Trade.

***Uncommon Sense.** Louis O. Bruneau. 272p. 1995. pap. 11.95 (*1-57087-169-8*) Prof Pr NC.

Uncommon Sense, Vol. 1. Ed. by Russell Ferguson. (Illus.). 164p. 1997. 30.00 (*0-914357-43-3*) Los Angeles Mus Contemp.

Uncommon Sense: Certain Values for Uncertain Times. Maryann G. Hedaa. (Industrial Engineering Ser.). 280p. 1997. text ed. 24.95 (*0-442-02053-8*) Van Nos Reinhold.

Uncommon Sense: The Heretical Nature of Science. Alan Cromer. (Illus.). 256p. 1995. pap. 12.95 (*0-19-509636-3*) OUP.

Uncommon Sense: The Heretical Nature of Science. Alan H. Cromer. (Illus.). 224p. (C). 1993. 27.50 (*0-19-508213-3*, 11091) OUP.

Uncommon Sense: The Real American Manifesto. William J. Murray. LC 94-27822. 383p. (Orig.). 1994. pap. text ed. 6.95 (*0-922356-95-5*) Amer West Pubs.

Uncommon Sense: The World's Fullest Compendium of Wisdom. Joseph Telushkin. 238p. 1987. 14.95 (*0-933503-48-2*) Sure Seller.

Uncommon Sense: Theoretical Practice in Language Education. John S. Mayher. LC 89-31482. 302p. (Orig.). 1989. pap. text ed. 25.00 (*0-86709-247-5*, 0247) Boynton Cook Pubs.

Uncommon Sense: What Separates the Winners from the Losers in the Manufacturing Game. Stephen George. LC 96-42474. 1997. text ed. 29.95 (*0-471-15377-X*) Wiley.

Uncommon Sense about Organizations: Cases, Studies, & Field Observations. Geert Hofstede. LC 93-46435. 312p. (C). 1994. text ed. 55.00 (*0-8039-5366-6*); pap. text ed. 26.00 (*0-8039-5367-4*) Sage.

Uncommon Sense for Parents with Teenagers. Michael Riera. 250p. 1995. pap. 12.95 (*0-89087-749-1*) Celestial Arts.

Uncommon Sense Leadership: Leadership Principles to Grow Your Business Profitably. Thomas W. Faranda. 120p. (Orig.). 1991. pap. 15.00 (*1-877629-02-2*) Knowledge AZ.

Uncommon Soldier: The Civil War Letters of Sarah Rosetta Wakeman, Alias Private Lyons Wakeman, 153rd Regiment, New York State Volunteers. Lauren C. Burgess. LC 94-76283. (Illus.). 120p. 1994. 25.00 (*0-9634895-1-8*) Minerva Ctr.

Uncommon Soldier: The Civil War Letters of Sarah Rosetta Wakeman, alias Pvt. Lyons Wakeman, 153rd Regiment, New York State Volunteers, 1862-1864. Sarah Wakeman. Ed. by Lauren C. Burgess. 128p. 1996. pap. 9.95 (*0-19-510243-6*) OUP.

Uncommon Spring. William D. Pease. Date not set. pap. write for info. (*0-14-013990-7*, Viking) Viking Penguin.

Uncommon Stock. Terri Lynn. (Supermromance Ser.). 1993. mass mkt. 3.39 (*0-373-70534-4*, 1-70534-2) Harlequin Bks.

Uncommon Subject: Drawings & Prints by Sharon Ellis. Georgia Coopersmith & Sharon Ellis. 1986. pap. 0.75 (*0-942746-11-2*) SUNYP R Gibson.

An Asterisk (*) at the beginning of an entry indicates that the title is appearing in BIP for the first time.

Uncommon Therapy: The Psychiatric Techniques of Milton H. Erickson, M. D. Jay Haley. 320p. 1993. pap. 9.95 (*0-393-31031-0*) Norton.

***Uncommon Threads: Threads That Wove the Fabric of Baltimore Jewish Life.** Philip Kahn, Jr. Ed. by Elizabeth R. Kahn. LC 96-95005. (Illus.). 370p. (Orig.). 1996. per. 19.95 (*0-9655057-0-7*) P Kahn Jr.

Uncommon Tongue: The Poetry & Criticism of Geoffrey Hill. Vincent Sherry. 272p. (C). 1987. 42.50 (*0-472-10084-X*) U of Mich Pr.

Uncommon Tongue: The Uses & Resources of English. Walter Nash. LC 91-30397. 192p. (Orig.). (C). 1992. pap. 17.95 (*0-415-06361-2*, A6697) Routledge.

Uncommon Tongue: The Uses & Resources of English. Walter Nash. LC 91-30397. 192p. (Orig.). (C). (gr. 13). 1992. text ed. 59.95 (*0-415-06360-4*, A6693) Routledge.

Uncommon Touch: An Investigation of Spiritual Healing. Tom Harpur. 1994. 24.95 (*0-7710-3944-1*) McCland & Stewart.

Uncommon Touch: An Investigation of Spiritual Healing. Tom Harpur. 275p. 1995. pap. 14.95 (*0-7710-3946-8*) McCland & Stewart.

Uncommon Valor: Marine Divisions in Action. George McMillan et al. (Elite Unit Ser.: 5th). (Illus.). 272p. 1986. reprint ed. 27.95 (*0-89839-094-X*) Battery Pr.

Uncommon Valour. A. G. Goulding. (C). 1989. 39.00 (*0-86303-274-5*) St Mut.

Uncommon Values: A Rare Book Dealer's World. F. J. Manasek. 148p. 1995. 20.00 (*1-883817-02-1*) Anglers & Scholars.

Uncommon Vows. Mary J. Putney. 384p. (Orig.). 1991. pap. 4.99 (*0-451-40244-8*, Onyx) NAL-Dutton.

Uncommon Voyage: Parenting a Special Needs Child in the World of Alternative Medicine. Laura S. Kramer. 224p. 1996. 24.95 (*0-571-19887-2*) Faber & Faber.

Uncommon Waters: Women Write about Fishing. Ed. by Holly Morris. LC 91-21455. (Women in Sports Ser.). (Illus.). 320p. (Orig.). 1991. pap. 14.95 (*1-878067-10-9*) Seal Pr WA.

Uncommon Wisdom of Jacqueline Kennedy Onassis. Bill Adler. 1994. 12.95 (*0-8065-1592-9*, Citadel Pr) Carol Pub Group.

***Uncommon Wisdom of Oprah Winfrey: A Portrait in Her Own Words.** Ed. by Bill Adler. LC 96-37404. 334p. 1997. 14.95 (*1-55972-419-6*, Birch Ln Pr) Carol Pub Group.

Uncommon Wisdom of Oprah Winfrey: A Portrait in Her Own Words. Oprah Winfrey. LC 96-20295. 1999. 15.00 (*0-688-14382-2*) Morrow.

Uncommon Wisdom of Ronald Reagan: A Portrait in His Own Words. Bill Adler. LC 96-575. 160p. 1996. 14.95 (*0-316-05600-6*) Little.

Uncommon Woman. Julie Ellis. 448p. 1997. mass mkt. 5.99 (*1-57566-122-5*, Knsington) Kensgtn Pub Corp.

***Uncommon Woman.** Pakula. 1997. pap. 17.00 (*0-684-84216-5*) S&S Trade.

Uncommon Woman: Empress Frederick, Daughter of Queen Victoria, Wife of the Crown Prince of Prussia, Mother of Kaiser Wilhelm. Hannah Pakula. LC 95-36848. (Illus.). 710p. 1995. 35.00 (*0-684-80818-8*, S&S) S&S Trade.

Uncommon Women & Others. Wendy Wasserstein. 1978. pap. 5.25 (*0-8222-1192-0*) Dramatists Play.

***Uncommon Word Puzzles for the Creative Thinker.** Rita Norr & Audrey Tumbarello. (Illus.). 96p. 1997. pap. 5.95 (*0-8069-8118-0*) Sterling.

***UncommonSense Selling, Vol. 1.** Thomas W. Faranda. Ed. by Cheryl K. Lee. 125p. (Orig.). (C). 1997. pap. 15.00 (*1-877629-03-0*) Knowledge AZ.

Uncompahgre. Muriel Marshall. LC 80-11666. (Illus.). 214p. (Orig.). 1981. reprint ed. pap. 61.00 (*0-8357-7939-4*, 2057012) Bks Demand.

Uncompensated Hospital Care: Rights & Responsibilities. Ed. by Frank A. Sloan et al. LC 85-45045. (Johns Hopkins Series in Contemporary Medicine & Public Health). (Illus.). 222p. reprint ed. pap. 63.30 (*0-8357-8358-8*, 2034114) Bks Demand.

Uncompleted Mission: Christianity & Exclusivism. Kwesi A. Dickson. LC 91-11351. 150p. (Orig.). 1991. pap. 19.50 (*0-88344-751-7*) Orbis Bks.

Uncompleted Past: Postwar German Novels & the Third Reich. Judith Ryan. LC 83-6744. 184p. reprint ed. pap. 52.50 (*0-318-39791-9*, 2033194) Bks Demand.

***Uncompromising Vol. 1: Family Style.** Elizabeth L. Bodner. LC 97-90128. 235p. (Orig.). 1997. pap. 14.95 (*0-9657162-0-1*) EBW Assocs.

Uncompromising Chess: The Games of Viktor Kupreichik. Gene H. McCormick. 66p. (Orig.). 1986. pap. 6.00 (*0-931462-58-4*) Chess Ent.

Uncompromising Faith: One Man's Notes from Prison. Jaroslav J. Vajda. 128p. (Orig.). 1992. pap. 8.99 (*0-570-04575-4*, 12-3175) Concordia.

Uncompromising Fictions of Cynthia Ozick. Sanford Pinsker. LC 86-30788. 128p. 1987. pap. 12.95 (*0-8262-0635-2*) U of Mo Pr.

***Unconditional Demand for Health Care in Cote d'Ivoire: Does Selection on Health Status Matter?** William H. Dow. (Living Standards Measurement Study Working Paper Ser.: No. 127). 62p. 1996. pap. 7.95 (*0-8213-3757-2*, 13757) World Bank.

Unconditional Eternal Security Fact or Fable. J. E. Gray. 22p. reprint ed. pap. 1.00 (*1-56722-044-4*) Word Aflame.

Unconditional Freedom: Social Revolution Through Individual Empowerment. William J. Murray. LC 93-78631. 260p. (Orig.). (C). 1993. pap. 16.95 (*1-55950-103-0*, 94222) Loompanics.

Unconditional Good News: Toward an Understanding of Biblical Universalism. Neal Punt. LC 80-10458. 179p. reprint ed. pap. 51.10 (*0-317-39671-4*, 2023222) Bks Demand.

Unconditional Hatred: German War Guilt Post W.W.II. Russell Grenfell. 1953. 9.95 (*0-8159-7002-1*) Devin.

Unconditional in Human Knowledge: Four Early Essays (1794-1796) by F. W. J. Schelling. Fritz Marti. Tr. by F. W. Schelling. LC 77-74407. 272p. 1980. 37.50 (*0-8387-2020-X*) Bucknell U Pr.

Unconditional Life: Discovering the Power to Fulfill Your Dreams. Deepak Chopra. 288p. 1992. pap. 13.95 (*0-553-37050-2*) Bantam.

Unconditional Love. Gene Steiner. 124p. (Orig.). 1994. pap. 5.95 (*1-886045-12-7*) Covenant Marriages.

Unconditional Love. John Powell. (Illus.). 124p. 1995. reprint ed. pap. 9.50 (*0-88347-312-7*) Res Christian Liv.

Unconditional Love: A Course of Multidimensional Transformation. Betty J. Hudson. 133p. 1995. pap. text ed. 12.95 (*0-9648317-1-6*) Patterson CA.

Unconditional Love: Mom! Dad! Love Me! Please! Sylvia Goldstaub. (Illus.). 180p. 1991. 14.95 (*0-9629414-1-7*) S Goldstaub.

Unconditional Love & Forgiveness. Edith R. Stauffer. (Illus.). 224p. (Orig.). 1987. pap. 9.95 (*0-940111-03-9*) Triangle.

Unconditional Money: A Magical Journey into the Heart of Abundance. David Cates. 256p. (Orig.). 1996. pap. 14.95 (*0-9647578-7-7*) Buffalo Pr OR.

Unconditional Quality. Harvard Business Review Staff. (Strategy in Action Ser.). 115p. 1991. pap. 19.95 (*0-87584-274-7*) Harvard Busn.

Unconditional Quality. Harvard Business School Press Staff. 1991. pap. text ed. 19.95 (*0-07-103334-3*) McGraw.

Unconditional Surrender. Emyr Humphreys. 180p. 1996. 24.95 (*1-85411-164-7*, Pub. by Seren Bks UK) Dufour.

Unconditional Surrender. Anne Armstrong. LC 73-22633. 304p. (C). 1974. reprint ed. text ed. 35.00 (*0-8371-7042-7*, ARUS, Greenwood Pr) Greenwood.

Unconditional Surrender: God's Program for Victory. Gary North. 417p. 1988. pap. 5.95 (*0-930464-12-5*) Inst Christian.

Unconditional Surrender: U.S. Grant and the Civil War. Albert Marrin. LC 93-20041. (Illus.). 208p. (J). (gr. 5-9). 1994. 21.00 (*0-689-31837-5*, Atheneum Bks Young) S&S Childrens.

***Unconfined Vapor Cloud Explosions.** Keith Gugan. LC 78-74101. (Illus.). 184p. 1979. reprint ed. pap. 52.50 (*0-608-04207-2*, 2064942) Bks Demand.

Unconformities & Porosity in Carbonate Strata. Ed. by David A. Budd et al. (AAPG Memoir Ser.: No. 63). (Illus.). xii, 313p. 1995. 119.00 (*0-89181-342-X*, 558-28) AAPG.

Unconformities in Shakespeare's Later Comedies. Kristian Smidt. LC 92-37355. 1993. text ed. 39.95 (*0-312-09099-4*) St Martin.

Unconformities in Shakespeare's Tragedies. Kristian Smidt. LC 89-36480. 250p. 1989. text ed. 45.00 (*0-312-03664-7*) St Martin.

Unconjugated Pterins & Related Biogenic Amines. Ed. by H. C. Curtius et al. 398p. (C). 1987. lib. bdg. 161.55 (*3-11-011341-4*) De Gruyter.

Unconjugated Pterins in Neurobiology: Basic & Clinical Aspects. Ed. by Walter Lovenberg & R. A. Levine. LC 86-23177. (Topics in Neurochemistry & Neuropharmacology Ser.: Vol. 1). 250p. 1987. 99.00 (*0-85066-370-9*) Taylor & Francis.

Unconquerable, No. II. Created by Keith Laumer. (BOLOS Ser.). 336p. (Orig.). 1994. mass mkt. 5.99 (*0-671-87629-5*) Baen Bks.

Unconquerable Rebel: Robert W. Wilcox & Hawaiian Politics, 1880-1903. Ernest Andrade, Jr. (Illus.). 376p. 1996. text ed. 39.95 (*0-87081-417-6*) Univ Pr Colo.

Unconquerable Spirit: Vignettes of the Jewish Religious Spirit the Nazis Could Not Destroy. Simon Zuker. Ed. by Gertrude Hirschler. (ArtScroll History Ser.). (Illus.). 160p. 1981. 16.99 (*0-89906-202-4*) Mesorah Pubns.

***Unconquerable World.** Schell. Date not set. pap. write for info. (*0-8050-4457-4*) St Martin.

***Unconquerable World.** Schell. 1997. write for info. (*0-8050-4456-6*) St Martin.

Unconquered. Hannah Howell. 352p. 1996. mass mkt. 5.99 (*0-8217-5417-3*, Zebra Kensgtn) Kensgtn Pub Corp.

Unconquered. Bertrice Small. 1984. mass mkt. 4.99 (*0-345-31401-8*, Del Rey) Ballantine.

Unconquered: Journal of a Year's Adventure Among the Fighting Peasants of North China. James M. Bertram. (China in the 20th Century Ser.). (Illus.). ix, 340p. 1975. reprint ed. lib. bdg. 39.50 (*0-306-70688-1*) Da Capo.

Unconquered Knight: A Chronicle of the Deeds of Don Pero Nino. Diaz De Gamez. Tr. by Joan Evans. LC 78-63494. reprint ed. 34.50 (*0-404-17143-5*) AMS Pr.

***Unconquered Spirits.** Josefina Lopez. 80p. 1997. pap. 5.25 (*0-87129-724-8*, U22) Dramatic Pub.

Unconquered Uncontrolled: The Klamath Indian Reservation. Carrol B. Howe. (Illus.). 156p. (J). 1991. pap. 9.95 (*0-9624860-1-9*); lib. bdg. 15.95 (*0-9624860-0-0*) C B Howe.

Unconscionable Bargains. Mindy Chen-Wishart. 184p. 1989. pap. 27.00 (*0-409-78881-3*, NZ) MICHIE.

Unconscious. Robert C. Murphy. 1996. pap. 3.00 (*0-87574-325-0*) Pendle Hill.

***Unconscious: A Conceptual Analysis.** Alasdair MacIntyre. (Key Texts Ser.). 109p. 1997. reprint ed. pap. 19.99 (*1-85506-520-7*) Thoemmes Pr.

Unconscious: A Guide to the Sources. Natalino Caputi. LC 85-1979. (American Theological Library Association Monograph: No. 16). 161p. 1985. 22.50 (*0-8108-1798-5*) Scarecrow.

Unconscious: The Fundamentals of Human Personality Normal & Abnormal. 2nd ed. Morton Prince. LC 73-2411. (Mental Illness & Social Policy; the American Experience Ser.). 1973. reprint ed. 44.95 (*0-405-05221-9*) Ayer.

Unconscious, a Symposium. Charles M. Child et al. LC 67-22125. (Essay Index Reprint Ser.). 1977. 19.95 (*0-8369-0957-7*) Ayer.

***Unconscious & Its Narratives.** Zvi Giora. 266p. 1997. pap. text ed. 27.50 (*0-7657-0100-6*) Aronson.

Unconscious & the Theory of Psychoneuroses. Zvi Giora. (Psychoanalytic Crosscurrents Ser.). 256p. (C). 1989. text ed. 36.00 (*0-8147-3021-3*) NYU Pr.

Unconscious & the Theory of Psychoneuroses. Zvi Giora. (Psychoanalytic Crosscurrents Ser.). 256p. (C). 1992. pap. 18.50 (*963-7977-06-6*) NYU Pr.

Unconscious As Infinite Sets. C. Matte Bianco & T. Woodhouse. pap. 39.95 (*0-7156-1230-1*, Pub. by Duckworth UK) Focus Pub-R Pullins.

Unconscious at Work: Individual & Organizational Stress in the Human Services. Anton Obholzer et al. LC 93-44323. 240p. (C). (gr. 13). 1994. text ed. 62.95 (*0-415-10205-7*, B4440, Routledge NY) Routledge.

Unconscious at Work: Individual & Organizational Stress in the Human Services. 256th ed. Anton Obholzer et al. LC 93-44323. 240p. (C). 1994. pap. 18.95 (*0-415-10206-5*, B4444, Routledge NY) Routledge.

Unconscious Beethoven: An Essay in Musical Psychology. Ernest Newman. 154p. 1990. reprint ed. lib. bdg. 59.00 (*0-7812-9045-7*) Rprt Serv.

Unconscious Christian: Images of God in Dreams. James A. Hall. Ed. by Daniel J. Meckel. LC 92-26395. (Jung & Spirituality Ser.). 128p. 1993. pap. 7.95 (*0-8091-3353-9*) Paulist Pr.

Unconscious Civilization. John R. Saul. LC 96-41910. 160p. 1997. 22.00 (*0-684-83257-7*) S&S Trade.

Unconscious Communication in Everyday Life. Robert J. Langs. LC 82-1669. 224p. 1993. pap. 27.50 (*1-56821-106-6*) Aronson.

Unconscious Conspiracy: Why Leaders Can't Lead. Bennis G. Warren. LC 75-37851. 185p. reprint ed. pap. 52.80 (*0-317-42056-9*, 2056091) Bks Demand.

Unconscious Contracts: A Psychoanalytic Theory of Society. Michael Allingham. 176p. 1988. text ed. 45.00 (*0-7102-0996-7*, RKP) Routledge.

Unconscious Fantasy in Psychotherapy: Its Meaning & Mastery in Psychotherapy. Kenneth Levin. LC 92-49153. 320p. 1994. 40.00 (*0-87668-260-3*) Aronson.

Unconscious for Sale: Advertising, Psychoanalysis, & the Public. Doris-Louise Haineault & Jean-Yves Roy. Tr. by Kimball Lockhart & Barbara Kerslake. LC 92-32340. (Theory & History of Literature Ser.: Vol. 86). (Illus.). 240p. (C). 1993. text ed. 49.95 (*0-8166-2185-3*); pap. text ed. 19.95 (*0-8166-2186-1*) U of Minn Pr.

Unconscious Humourist: And Other Essays. E. Lacon Watson. LC 72-13313. (Essay Index Reprint Ser.). 1977. reprint ed. 19.95 (*0-8369-8177-4*) Ayer.

Unconscious Life of Organizations: Interpreting Organizational Identity. Michael A. Diamond. LC 93-6766. 272p. 1993. text ed. 65.00 (*0-89930-833-3*, Q833, Quorum Bks) Greenwood.

Unconscious Logic: An Introduction to Matte Blanco's Bi-Logic & Its Uses. Eric Rayner. LC 94-45146. (New Library of Psychoanalysis). 192p. (C). 1995. pap. 18.95 (*0-415-12726-2*, C0566); text ed. 59.95 (*0-415-12725-4*, C0565) Routledge.

Unconscious Quantum: Metaphysics in Modern Physics & Cosmology. Victor J. Stenger. 322p. 1995. 32.95 (*1-57392-022-3*) Prometheus Bks.

Unconscious Today: Essays in Honor of Max Schur. Ed. by Mark Kanzer. LC 74-14337. 544p. 1971. 70.00 (*0-8236-6680-8*) Intl Univs Pr.

Unconscious Victorious & Other Stories. Stanley Berne. LC 69-20442. (Archives of Post-Modern Literature Ser.). (Illus.). 1969. pap. 15.00 (*0-913844-04-7*) Am Canadian.

Unconsciously Freeing the Body: (A Course of 16 Lessons) Brown Landone. 36p. 1966. reprint ed. spiral bd. 7.00 (*0-7873-0525-1*) Hlth Research.

Unconsoled. Kazuo Ishiguro. LC 95-15829. 535p. 1995. 25.00 (*0-679-40425-2*) Knopf.

Unconsoled. Kazuo Ishiguro. 554p. 1996. pap. 13.00 (*0-679-73587-9*) Knopf.

Unconsolidated Mineral Deposits in the Exclusive Economic Zone. 80p. 1985. 9.50 (*92-1-104235-6*) UN.

***Unconstitutional Essays.** Pacifico A. Agabin. 276p. 1996. pap. text ed. 25.00 (*971-542-077-X*, Pub. by U of Philippines Pr PH) UH Pr.

Unconstitutional Family. Anne Dunne. pap. text ed. write for info. (*1-85475-136-0*, IE) MICHIE.

Unconstitutionality of Slavery. Lysander Spooner. LC 77-97843. 304p. reprint ed. 20.50 (*0-8337-3353-2*) Ayer.

Uncontainable Romanticism: Shelley, Bronte, Kleist. Carol Jacobs. LC 88-7852. 240p. 1989. text ed. 38.50 (*0-8018-3786-3*) Johns Hopkins.

Uncontrollable Bodies: Testimonies of Identity & Culture. Ed. by Rodney Sappington & Tyler Stallings. LC 94-17123. (Illus.). 288p. (Orig.). 1994. pap. 16.95 (*0-941920-27-5*) Bay Pr.

Uncontrollable Fields. Steve Griffiths. (Illus.). 72p. (Orig.). 1990. pap. 14.95 (*1-85411-042-X*, Pub. by Seren Bks UK) Dufour.

Uncontrollable Spending for Social Services Grants. Martha Derthick. LC 75-5155. 149p. reprint ed. pap. 42.50 (*0-8357-7063-X*, 2033592) Bks Demand.

Uncontrolled Chancellor: Charles Townshend & His American Policy. Cornelius P. Forster. LC 78-63017. 155p. 1978. 14.95 (*0-917012-16-X*) RI Pubns Soc.

Unconventional Agents & Unclassified Viruses: Recent Advances in Biology & Epidemiology. Ed. by O. R. Kaaden et al. 340p. 1996. pap. 185.00 (*0-387-82480-4*) Spr-Verlag.

Unconventional Aircraft. Peter M. Bowers. (Illus.). 288p. (Orig.). 1984. pap. 17.95 (*0-8306-2384-1*, 2384) McGraw-Hill Prof.

Unconventional Aircraft Concepts. Ed. by F. Sterk & E. Torenbeek. 172p. (Orig.). 1987. pap. 42.50 (*90-6275-331-0*, Pub. by Delft U Pr NE) Coronet Bks.

Unconventional & Community Transport in the U. K., Vol. 14. Nutley. (Transportation Studies). 430p. 1990. text ed. 145.00 (*2-88124-764-4*) Gordon & Breach.

Unconventional Approaches to Conventional Arms Control Verification: An Exploratory Assessment. Ed. by John Grin & Henry J. Van Der Graaf. 256p. 1990. 49.95 (*0-685-38698-8*) St Martin.

Unconventional Cancer Treatments. 1991. lib. bdg. 250.00 (*0-8490-4956-3*) Gordon Pr.

Unconventional Conflicts in a New Security Era: Lessons from Malaya & Vietnam. Sam C. Sarkesian. LC 92-25634. (Contributions in Military Studies: No. 134). 240p. 1993. text ed. 55.00 (*0-313-27763-X*, SNQ, Greenwood Pr) Greenwood.

***Unconventional Diplomacy.** Robin Renwick. LC 96-32086. 1997. text ed. 45.00 (*0-312-16533-1*) St Martin.

Unconventional Flying Objects: A Scientific Analysis. Paul R. Hill. 432p. (Orig.). 1995. pap. 15.95 (*1-57174-027-9*) Hampton Roads Pub Co.

Unconventional Imaging, Science & Technology: Advanced Printing of Paper Summaries, the 22nd Fall Symposium, Key Bridge Marriott Hotel, Arlington, Virginia, November 15-18, 1982. Society of Photographic Scientists & Engineers Staff. 86p. reprint ed. pap. 25.00 (*0-317-29897-6*, 2019357) Bks Demand.

Unconventional Invention Book. Bob Stanish. (J). (gr. 3-12). 1981. 12.99 (*0-86653-035-5*, GA 263) Good Apple.

***Unconventional Miss.** Alice Holden. 224p. 1997. mass mkt. 4.99 (*0-8217-5622-2*, Zebra Kensgtn) Kensgtn Pub Corp.

Unconventional Natural Gas: Resources, Potential & Technology. M. J. Satriana. LC 80-15215. (Energy Technology Review Ser.: No. 56). 358p. (Orig.). 1980. 42.00 (*0-8155-0808-5*) Noyes.

Unconventional Partners: Religion & Liberal Culture in the United States. Robert B. Fowler. LC 88-11251. 195p. reprint ed. pap. 55.60 (*0-7837-0514-X*, 2040838) Bks Demand.

Unconventional Perceptions of Yugoslavia. Ed. by Steven K. Pavlowitch. 166p. 1985. 52.50 (*0-88033-081-3*) East Eur Monographs.

Unconventional Photoactive Solids. Ed. by H. Scher. (Institute for Amorphous Studies). (Illus.). 262p. 1988. 69.50 (*0-306-43025-8*, Plenum Pr) Plenum.

Unconventional Sources of Dietary Fiber. Ed. by Ivan Furda. LC 83-2691. (Symposium Ser.: No. 214). 315p. 1983. lib. bdg. 64.95 (*0-8412-0768-2*) Am Chemical.

***Unconventional Sources of Dietary Fiber: Physiological & in Vitro Functional Properties.** Ed. by Ivan Furda. LC 83-2691. (ACS Symposium Ser.: No. 214). (Illus.). 324p. 1983. reprint ed. pap. 92.40 (*0-608-03211-5*, 2063730) Bks Demand.

***Unconventional Warfare: Rebuilding U. S. Special Operations Forces.** Susan L. Marquis. LC 96-53963. 385p. 1997. pap. 19.95 (*0-8157-5475-2*) Brookings.

***Unconventional Warfare: Rebuilding U. S. Special Operations Forces.** Susan L. Marquis. LC 96-53963. 385p. 1997. 49.95 (*0-8157-5476-0*) Brookings.

Unconventional Warfare: Selective Assassination As an Instrument of National Policy. 56p. 1990. pap. 8.00 (*0-87364-556-1*) Paladin Pr.

Unconventional Warfare Devices & Techniques: Incendiaries. 1982. lib. bdg. 250.00 (*0-87700-325-4*) Revisionist Pr.

Unconventional Wisdom. Michael R. Milken. (Illus.). 1996. audio 15.00 (*1-888232-13-7*) Knowldge Exchange.

Unconventional Wisdom. Michael R. Milken. (Illus.). 300p. 1996. 25.00 (*1-888232-12-9*) Knowldge Exchange.

Unconventional Wisdom: Irreverent Solutions for Tough Problems at Work. Thomas L. Quick. LC 89-45594. (Management Ser.). 202p. text ed. 28.95 (*1-55542-177-6*) Jossey-Bass.

***Unconventional Wisdoms: The Best of Warren Brookes.** Warren T. Brookes. Ed. by Thomas J. Bray. LC 97-13938. 1997. pap. text ed. 16.95 (*0-936488-83-2*) PRIPP.

***UnCook Book: Raw Food Adventure to a New Health High.** Elizabeth Baker. 230p. (Orig.). 1996. pap. 12.95 (*1-57901-009-1*) Intl Promotions.

Uncook Book: Raw Food Adventures to a New Health High. Elizabeth Baker & Elton Baker. (Illus.). 208p. 1980. pap. 11.95 (*0-937766-05-4*) Drelwood Comns.

Uncooked Foods & How to Use Them. Eugene Christian. 246p. 1993. reprint ed. spiral bd. 16.00 (*0-7873-0171-X*) Hlth Research.

Uncooked Foods & How to Use Them: To Get the Highest Form of Energy from Food. E. Christian & M. G. Christian. 1991. lib. bdg. 79.95 (*0-8490-4970-9*) Gordon Pr.

Uncork It!!! How to be a Wine Expert Overnight. Cathleen Michaels. (Illus.). 88p. (Orig.). 1996. pap. 8.95 (*0-9652389-0-3*) Core Pubng.

Uncorking Wine, Vol. 1. Doug Frost. (Illus.). (Orig.). 1996. pap. 10.00 (*0-9653177-0-6*) Writers Co.

Uncorrected World. Kenneth O. Hanson. LC 73-6012. (Wesleyan Poetry Program Ser.: Vol. 67). 59p. 1973. pap. 11.95 (*0-8195-1067-X*, Wesleyan Univ Pr) U Pr of New Eng.

Uncorrupted Heart: Journal & Letters of Frederick Julius Gustorf 1800-1845. Frederick Gustorf & Gisela Gustorf. LC 70-93049. 192p. 1969. text ed. 27.50 (*0-8262-0079-6*) U of Mo Pr.

Uncounselled King: Charles I & the Scottish Troubles, 1637-1641. P. H. Donald. (Studies in Early Modern British History). 361p. (C). 1990. text ed. 69.95 (*0-521-37235-6*) Cambridge U Pr.

U V

An Asterisk (*) at the beginning of an entry indicates that the title is appearing in BIP for the first time.

Uncountably Categorical Theories. Boris I. Zilber. LC 92-31151. (Translations of Mathematical Monographs: Vol. 117). 122p. 1993. 97.00 (*0-8218-4586-1*, MMONO/117) Am Math.

Uncounted Irish in Canada & the United States. Margaret E. Fitzgerald & Joseph A. King. (Illus.). 391p. 1990. 23.95 (*0-88835-024-4*) P D Meany.

Uncoupling: How & Why Relationships Come Apart. Diane Vaughan. LC 89-40709. 1990. pap. 13.00 (*0-679-73002-8*, Vin) Random.

Uncoupling: Turning Points in Intimate Relationships. Diane Vaughan. LC 86-5401. 272p. 1986. 25.00 (*0-19-503910-6*) OUP.

***Uncover the Truth.** 2nd rev. ed. Barry Zalma. Orig. Title: The Art of Information Gathering. 152p. (Orig.). 1997. pap. 38.95 (*1-884770-14-2*) Claimschool.

***Uncover the Truth: The Investigative Interviewing Book.** Barry Zalma. 152p. (Orig.). (C). 1997. pap. 45.00 (*0-918487-07-2*) Thomas Pubns TX.

Uncovered! Weird, Weird, Stories. Paul Jennings. LC 95-46464. 134p. (YA). (gr. 5 up). 1996. pap. 14.99 (*0-670-86856-6*, Viking) Viking Child Bks.

***Uncovering & Investigating Insurance Healthcare Claims Fraud.** Robert P. Campbell. 103p. (Orig.). (C). 1997. pap. 45.00 (*0-918487-97-8*) Thomas Pubns TX.

***Uncovering Lives: The Uneasy Alliance of Biography & Psychology.** Alan C. Elms. 328p. 1997. reprint ed. pap. 16.95 (*0-19-511379-9*) OUP.

Uncovering Shame: An Approach Integrating Individuals & Their Family Systems. James M. Harper & Margaret H. Hoopes. 350p. 1990. 34.95 (*0-393-70100-X*) Norton.

Uncovering Soviet Disasters. James E. Oberg. LC 87-42658. (Illus.). 336p. 1988. 19.95 (*0-394-56095-7*) Random.

Uncovering Sydney: Walks into Sydney's Unexpected & Endangered Places. Graham Spindler. (Illus.). 192p. 1991. pap. 12.95 (*0-86417-362-8*, Pub. by Kangaroo Pr AT) Seven Hills Bk.

Uncovering the Curriculum: Whole Language in Secondary & Postsecondary Classrooms. Kathleen Strickland & James Strickland. LC 93-5801. (Illus.). 225p. (Orig.). (J). 1993. pap. text ed. 25.00 (*0-86709-332-3*, 0332) Boynton Cook Pubs.

Uncovering the Dome. Amy Klobuchar. (Illus.). 174p. (C). 1986. reprint ed. pap. text ed. 10.95 (*0-88133-218-6*) Waveland Pr.

Uncovering the Forces for War. Conrad Grieb. 115p. reprint ed. pap. 4.00 (*0-89562-096-0*) Sons Lib.

Uncovering the Mystery of MPD: Its Shocking Origins...Its Surprising Cure. James G. Friesen. 400p. (Orig.). 1991. pap. 12.99 (*0-8407-4385-8*) Nelson.

Uncovering the Past: A History of Archaeology. William Steibing, Jr. (Illus.). 315p. (C). 1993. 28.95 (*0-87975-764-7*) Prometheus Bks.

Uncovering the Past: A History of Archaeology. William H. Stiebing, Jr. (Illus.). 318p. 1994. reprint ed. pap. 12.95 (*0-19-508921-9*) OUP.

Uncovering the Past at College of Marin. Ed. by Betty Goerke. (Mapom Occasional Papers: No. 7). (Illus.). 100p. (Orig.). 1994. pap. 10.00 (*0-9629718-1-2*) Miwok Archaeol Preserve.

Uncovering the Real Columbus. John Wolcott. LC 92-91047. 165p. (Orig.). 1993. pap. 9.00 (*1-56002-243-4*) Aegina Pr.

***Uncovering the Secrets of Successful Digital Printing: A How-to Guide for File Planning, Preparation & Preflight.** Loida Alvarez-Thamm. Ed. by Jennifer Hostetter. (Illus.). 50p. 1997. pap. 28.00 (*0-9656560-1-2*) BPI Info Servs.

Uncovering the Sixties: The Life & Times of the Underground Press. Abe Peck. 1991. pap. 12.95 (*0-8065-1225-3*, Citadel Pr) Carol Pub Group.

Uncovering the Sources of Love & Hate. Colter Rule. LC 95-1450. 288p. (Orig.). 1995. 26.95 (*0-86534-102-8*); pap. 18.95 (*0-86534-229-6*) Sunstone Pr.

Uncoverings 1980. Ed. by Sally Garoutte. LC 81-649486. (Research Papers of the American Quilt Study Group: Vol. 1). (Illus.). 76p. 1993. reprint ed. pap. 18.00 (*1-877859-03-6*) Am Quilt.

Uncoverings 1981. Ed. by Sally Garoutte. LC 81-649486. (Research Papers of the American Quilt Study Group: Vol. 2). (Illus.). 112p. (Orig.). 1993. reprint ed. pap. 18.00 (*0-9606590-1-3*) Am Quilt.

Uncoverings 1982. Ed. by Sally Garoutte. LC 81-649486. (Research Papers of the American Quilt Study Group: Vol. 3). (Illus.). 136p. 1993. reprint ed. pap. 18.00 (*1-877859-05-2*) Am Quilt.

Uncoverings 1984. Ed. by Sally Garoutte. LC 81-649486. (American Quilt Study Group Research Papers: No. 5). (Illus.). 170p. (Orig.). 1997. pap. 18.00 (*0-9606590-4-8*) Am Quilt.

Uncoverings 1985. Ed. by Sally Garoutte. LC 81-649486. (Research Papers of the American Quilt Study Group: Vol. 6). (Illus.). 170p. (Orig.). 1987. pap. 18.00 (*0-9606590-5-6*) Am Quilt.

Uncoverings 1986. Ed. by Sally Garoutte. LC 81-649486. (Research Papers of the American Quilt Study Group: Vol. 7). (Illus.). (Orig.). 1987. pap. 18.00 (*0-9606590-6-4*) Am Quilt.

Uncoverings 1987: Research Papers of the American Quilt Study Group, Vol. 8. Ed. by Laurel Horton & Sally Garoutte. LC 81-649486. (Illus.). 176p. (Orig.). 1989. pap. 18.00 (*0-9606590-8-0*) Am Quilt.

Uncoverings 1988: Research Papers of the American Quilt Study Group, Vol. 9. Ed. by Laurel Horton. LC 81-649486. (Illus.). 202p. (Orig.). 1989. pap. 18.00 (*0-9606590-7-2*) Am Quilt.

Uncoverings 1989: Research Papers of the American Quilt Study Group, Vol. 10. Ed. by Laurel Horton. LC 81-649486. (Illus.). 166p. (Orig.). 1990. pap. 18.00 (*1-877859-00-1*) Am Quilt.

Uncoverings 1990: Research Papers of the American Quilt Study Group, Vol. 11. Ed. by Laurel Horton. LC 81-649486. (Illus.). 176p. (Orig.). 1991. pap. 18.00 (*1-877859-01-X*) Am Quilt.

Uncoverings 1991: Research Papers of the American Quilty Study Group, Vol. 12. Ed. by Laurel Horton. (Illus.). 176p. (Orig.). 1992. pap. 18.00 (*1-877859-02-8*) Am Quilt.

Uncoverings 1992. Ed. by Laurel Horton. LC 81-649486. (Research Papers of the American Quilt Study Group: Vol. 13). (Illus.). 200p. (Orig.). 1993. pap. 18.00 (*1-877859-06-0*) Am Quilt.

Uncoverings 1993. Ed. by Laurel Horton. LC 81-64986. (Research Papers of the American Quilt Study Group: Vol. 14). (Illus.). 200p. (Orig.). 1994. pap. 18.00 (*1-877859-07-9*) Am Quilt.

Uncoverings 1994. Ed. by Virginia Gunn. (Research Papers of the American Quilt Study Group: Vol. 15). (Illus.). (Orig.). 1995. pap. 18.00 (*1-877859-08-7*) Am Quilt.

Uncoverings 1995. Ed. by Virginia Gunn. (Research Papers of the American Quilt Study Group: Vol. 16). (Illus.). 1995. pap. 18.00 (*1-877859-11-7*) Am Quilt.

Uncoverings 1996. Ed. by Virginia Gunn. (Research Papers of the American Quilt Study Group: Vol. 17). (Illus.). (Orig.). 1996. pap. 18.00 (*1-877859-12-5*) Am Quilt.

***Uncoverings 1997.** Ed. by Virginia Gunn. (Research Papers: Vol. 18). (Illus.). (Orig.). 1997. pap. 18.00 (*1-877859-13-3*) Am Quilt.

Uncreated Light. John D. Richards. 32p. (Orig.). 1993. pap. 3.95 (*1-881692-05-1*) Trillium WV.

Uncreating Word: Romanticism & the Object. Irving J. Massey. LC 77-126213. 144p. reprint ed. pap. 41.10 (*0-8357-9250-1*, 2013020) Bks Demand.

Uncritical Theory: Postmodernism, Intellectuals, & the Gulf War. Christopher Norris. LC 92-12147. 224p. 1992. 30.00 (*0-87023-817-5*); pap. 14.95 (*0-87023-818-3*) U of Mass Pr.

Uncrowned King. Harold B. Wright. 1.00 (*1-56723-112-8*) Yestermorrow.

Uncrowned King. H. B. Wright. 1982. reprint ed. lib. bdg. 17.95 (*0-89966-439-3*) Buccaneer Bks.

***Uncrowned King: Prince Albert.** Stanley Weintraub. LC 96-37752. 1997. 27.50 (*0-684-83486-3*) Free Pr.

Uncrystallized Philippine Society: A Social Anthropological Analysis. Yasuchi Kikuchi. 64p. (Orig.). (C). 1992. pap. 7.50 (*971-10-0466-6*, Pub. by New Day Pub PH) Cellar.

UNCTAD: Statistical Pocket Book. 102p. 1994. 15.00 (*92-1-012035-3*, E.94.II.D.32) UN.

UNCTAD: Tungsten Statistics. 74p. 1990. 25.00 (*92-1-112298-8*) UN.

UNCTAD & the South-North Dialogue: The First Twenty Years. Ed. by M. Zammit Cutajar. LC 84-6484. 338p. 1985. 147.00 (*0-08-028144-3*, Pub. by Aberdeen U Pr) Macmillan.

UNCTAD Commodity Yearbook. 402p. 1991. 68.00 (*92-1-112304-6*, B.91.II.D.9) UN.

UNCTAD Commodity Yearbook: 1992. 410p. 1992. 70.00 (*92-1-012030-2*) UN.

UNCTAD Commodity Yearbook: 1993. 412p. 1993. 70.00 (*92-1-012031-0*) UN.

Unctad Commodity Yearbook Nineteen Ninety. 1990. 65.00 (*92-1-112294-5*, E 90.II.D.9) UN.

UNCTAD Commodity Yearbook 1986. 584p. 1987. 60.00 (*92-1-112228-7*, E.86.II.D.8) UN.

UNCTAD Commodity Yearbook, 1987. 377p. (ENG, FRE & SPA.). 1987. pap. 60.00 (*92-1-112239-2*, E.87.II.D.13) UN.

UNCTAD Commodity Yearbook, 1988. 375p. 60.00 (*92-1-112265-1*) UN.

UNCTAD Commodity Yearbook, 1989. 390p. 1989. 65.00 (*92-1-112285-6*, 89.II.D.18) UN.

UNCTAD Commodity Yearbook 1994: United Nations Conference on Trade & Development, New York & Geneva, 1994. 422p. 1994. pap. 70.00 (*92-1-012033-7*) UN.

***UNCTAD Commodity Yearbook, 1995.** United Nations Conference on Trade & Development Staff. 428p. Date not set. pap. 70.00 (*92-1-012038-8*, HF10) UN.

UNCTAD Model Clauses on Marine Hull & Cargo Insurance. 66p. 1989. 15.00 (*92-1-112267-8*, 89.II.D.2) UN.

***UNCTAD Review.** 1997. 95.00 (*1-57588-196-9*, 310860) W S Hein.

UNCTAD Review No. 5: 1994. 170p. 1994. 28.00 (*92-1-112355-0*) UN.

UNCTAD Review, 1989, Vol. 1, No. 1. 89p. 6.00 (*92-1-112269-4*) UN.

UNCTAD Review, 1989, Vol. 1, No. 2. 83p. 1989. 20.00 (*92-1-112286-4*, 89.II.D.20) UN.

***UNCTAD Review, 1995.** United Nations Conference on Trade & Development Staff. 222p. Date not set. pap. 30.00 (*92-1-112391-7*, TN10) UN.

UNCTAD Reviews No. 4: 1993. 142p. 1993. 20.00 (*92-1-112328-3*) UN.

Uncursing the Dark: Treasures from the Underworld. Betty D. Meador. LC 92-23029. 192p. (Orig.). 1992. pap. 15.95 (*0-933029-65-9*) Chiron Pubns.

Uncut Jewel: A Divine Communication to Mankind. Ed. by Gerda Johst. 184p. (C). 1989. pap. 32.00 (*0-7212-0779-0*, Pub. by Regency Press UK) St Mut.

Uncut Leaves, Vol. I: Quests (1920) & Sea Level (1933) Sylvia H. Bliss. LC 89-14854. 212p. 1989. 15.00 (*0-912362-07-3*) Adamant Pr.

Uncut Leaves, Vol. II: Prose Writings. Sylvia H. Bliss. LC 89-14854. 367p. 1990. lib. bdg. 40.00 (*0-912362-08-1*) Adamant Pr.

Und Sagte Kein Einziges Wort. Heinrich Boll. Ed. by William Hanson. 190p. (C). 1990. pap. text ed. 16.95 (*0-423-51640-X*, A3852) Routledge Chapman & Hall.

Undaunted Courage: Meriwether Lewis, Thomas Jefferson & the Opening of the American West. Stephen E. Ambrose. LC 95-37146. (Illus.). 511p. 1996. 27.50 (*0-684-81107-3*) S&S Trade.

***Undaunted Courage: Meriwether Lewis, Thomas Jefferson, & the Opening of the American West.** Stephen E. Ambrose. 1997. pap. 16.00 (*0-684-82697-6*) S&S Trade.

Undaunted Faith - Memorial Edition: The Life Story of Jennie Dean. Stephen J. Lewis et al. 149p. 1995. 18.00 (*1-886826-04-8*) Manassas Mus.

Undaunted Garden: Planting for Weather-Resilient Beauty. Lauren Springer. (Illus.). 256p. 1994. 32.95 (*1-55591-115-3*) Fulcrum Pub.

Undaunted Heroes: A Soviet Vietnam Diary. Sergei Vysotsky & Ilya Glazunov. (Illus.). 177p. 1975. 22.00 (*0-8464-0944-5*) Beekman Pubs.

Undaunted Psychologist: Adventures in Research. Ed. by Gary G. Brannigan & Matthew R. Merrens. LC 92-16328. 1992. pap. text ed. write for info. (*0-07-041531-5*) McGraw.

Undaunted Psychologist: Adventures in Research. Ed. by Gary G. Brannigan & Matthew R. Merrens. LC 92-16793. 320p. (C). 1992. 49.95 (*1-56639-015-X*) Temple U Pr.

Undaunted Spirits: Portraits of Recovery from Trauma. Mary Baures. LC 93-37931. 192p. 1994. pap. 16.95 (*0-914783-71-8*) Charles.

Undead. Roxanne Longstreet. 320p. 1993. mass mkt. 4.50 (*0-8217-4068-7*, Zebra Kensgtn) Kensgtn Pub Corp.

***Undead: Army of Night.** Mayfair Games Staff. Date not set. 25.00 (*0-923763-92-9*) Mayfair Games.

***Undead & Buried.** 1992. 9.00 (*0-923763-53-8*) Mayfair Games.

Undead Express. J. R. Black. (Shadow Zone Ser.). 132p. (Orig.). (J). (gr. 3-7). 1994. pap. 4.50 (*0-679-85408-8*, Bullseye Bks) Random Bks Yng Read.

Undecidability of the Domino Problem. Robert Berger. (Memoirs Ser.: No. 1/66). 72p. 1966. pap. 16.00 (*0-8218-1266-1*, MEMO/1/66) Am Math.

Undecidable: Basic Papers on Undecidable Propositions, Unsolvable Problems & Computable Functions. Ed. by Martin Davis. LC 65-3996. 446p. 1965. text ed. 61.00 (*0-911216-01-4*) Lppncott-Raven.

Undecided? A Workbook for Career Decision Making & Life Planning. Randall D. Wilson. (C). pap. text ed. write for info. (*1-884155-01-4*) Day & Nite Pub.

Undecided College Student: An Academic & Career Advising Challenge. 2nd ed. Virginia N. Gordon. LC 95-18738. (Illus.). 160p. (C). 1995. text ed. 39.95 (*0-398-06539-X*); pap. text ed. 24.95 (*0-398-06540-3*) C C Thomas.

Undeclared War: Twilight Zone of Constitutional Power. Edward Keynes. LC 82-9854. 236p. 1991. 30.00 (*0-271-00327-8*); pap. 14.95 (*0-271-00779-6*) Pa St U Pr.

Undefeated. Abraham S. Hyman. 1992. 19.95 (*965-229-087-4*, Pub. by Gefen Pub Hse IS) Gefen Bks.

Undefeated Nation. Adolfs Blodnieks. 1959. 9.95 (*0-8315-0019-0*) Speller.

Undefeated Rhumba Champ: One Act. Charles Leipart. 1982. pap. 3.25 (*0-8222-1193-9*) Dramatists Play.

Undefended Borders. Charles Long. 256p. 1995. pap. 14.95 (*1-895629-46-2*, Pub. by Warwick Pub CN) Firefly Bks Ltd.

Undefended City. large type ed. Sophie Weston. 336p. 1984. 25.99 (*0-7089-1108-0*) Ulverscroft.

Undefended Self: Living the Pathwork of Spiritual Wholeness. 2nd ed. Susan Thesenga. LC 94-68275. (Pathwork Ser.). 290p. (Orig.). 1994. pap. 17.95 (*0-9614777-4-1*) Pathwork Pr.

Undefined Familiarities. William Kluback. (American University Studies: Romance Languages & Literature: Ser. II, Vol. 84). 232p. (C). 1989. text ed. 35.00 (*0-8204-0660-0*) P Lang Pubng.

Undeniable. Francis Ray. 256p. 1995. mass mkt. 4.99 (*0-8217-0125-8*, Zebra Kensgtn); mass mkt. 4.99 (*0-7860-0125-9*, Pinncle Kensgtn) Kensgtn Pub Corp.

Under. David Meltzer. (Orig.). 1995. mass mkt. 6.95 (*1-56333-290-6*, R Kasak Bks) Masquerade.

Under a Crescent Moon. Daniel De Souza. (Masks Ser.). 144p. (Orig.). 1990. pap. 10.95 (*1-85242-142-8*) Serpents Tail.

Under a Cruel Star: A Life in Prague 1941-1968. Heda M. Kovaly. Tr. by Helen Epstein & Franci Epstein from CZE. LC 96-54710. 192p. (Orig.). 1997. reprint ed. pap. 15.00 (*0-8419-1377-3*) Holmes & Meier.

Under a Different Sky. Savage. 1997. 15.95 (*0-395-77395-4*) HM.

Under a Far Away Star. Howard L. Norskog. 40p. (Orig.). 1994. pap. 6.00 (*0-9625171-4-3*) H L Norskog.

***Under a Gibbous Moon: The Adventures of Mr. Funky.** Larry Beresford. LC 96-78883. 82p. 1996. per. 10.00 (*0-9636156-1-0*) Broken Shadow.

Under a Glass Bell. Anais Nin. LC 94-32163. 101p. (Orig.). 1995. pap. 8.95 (*0-8040-0302-5*) Swallow.

Under a Gull's Wing: Poems & Photographs of the Jersey Shore. Ed. by Rich Youmans & Frank Finale. LC 96-21310. (Illus.). 220p. 1996. 25.00 (*0-945582-36-6*) Down the Shore Pub.

Under a Hoodoo Moon: The Life of the Night Tripper. John Mac Rebennack & Jack Rummel. LC 95-2219. 1995. pap. 12.00 (*0-312-13197-6*) St Martin.

Under a Killing Moon: A Tex Murphy Novel. Aaron Conners. 1996. mass mkt., per. 5.99 (*0-7615-0420-6*) Prima Pub.

Under a Killing Moon: Official Strategy Guide. Rick Barba. 1994. pap. 19.95 (*1-55958-679-6*) Prima Pub.

Under a Lemon Moon: A Metaphysical Mystery. David N. Martin. 288p. (Orig.). 1995. pap. 14.95 (*0-9646601-7-2*) Oaklea Pr.

Under a Lucky Star: The Story of Frederick A. Hauck. Priscilla H. Petty. LC 86-72173. (Illus.). 180p. 1987. 22.95 (*0-9617747-0-3*) Cin Oral Hist Foun.

Under a Mantle of Stars. rev. ed. Manuel Puig. Tr. by Ronald Christ. (Orig.). 1993. pap. 10.00 (*0-930829-32-8*) Lumen Inc.

Under a Maui Sun: A Celebration of the Island of Maui. Penny Pence-Smith. (Illus.). 188p. (JPN.). 1989. 24.95 (*0-89610-181-9*) Island Heritage.

Under a Melting Sky. Jabiya Dragonson. Ed. by Zulma Gonzalez-Parker. (Orig.). 1989. pap. write for info. (*0-318-65769-4*) Heartfelt Pr.

Under a New Sky: A Reunion with Russia. Olga A. Carlisle. 1993. 21.95 (*0-685-63199-0*) HM.

Under a Silent Sun: A Selection of Oriya Women's Poems. Ed. by J. P. Das & A. Zide. 80p. (C). 1992. text ed. 12.95 (*0-7069-5968-X*, Pub. by Vikas II) S Asia.

Under a Soprano Sky. Sonia Sanchez. LC 87-70962. 110p. (C). 1987. 16.95 (*0-86543-052-7*); pap. 8.95 (*0-86543-053-5*) Africa World.

Under a Texas Moon. Faye Adams. 1996. mass mkt. 5.99 (*0-671-52727-4*) PB.

Under a Thatched Roof. James N. Hall. LC 75-107705. (Essay Index Reprint Ser.). 1977. 21.95 (*0-8369-1655-7*) Ayer.

Under a Turquoise Sky: Stories from Three Cultures. Raymond J. Stovich. LC 91-51147. 104p. (Orig.). 1992. pap. 9.95 (*0-87358-540-2*, Entrada Bks) Northland AZ.

Under a Tyler Moon. Patience McClendon. (Illus.). 50p. (Orig.). 1988. pap. write for info. (*0-941402-06-1*) Devon Pub.

***Under African Skies: Modern African Short Stories.** Charles R. Larson. LC 96-48601. 1997. write for info. (*0-374-17659-0*) FS&G.

***Under African Skies: Modern African Stories.** Charles R. Larson. 1997. 25.00 (*0-374-21178-7*) FS&G.

Under African Sun. Marianne Alverson. LC 86-16474. (Illus.). 256p. (C). 1989. pap. 12.95 (*0-226-01624-2*) U Ch Pr.

Under-Age Drinking. Waln K. Brown. 20p. 1989. 2.95 (*1-56456-000-7*, 217) W Gladden Found.

***Under an Apple Tree, Vol. 1.** (Illus.). xv, 102p. 1996. 12.00 (*0-9654363-0-6*) C R S Publishing.

Under an Open Sky: Rethinking America's Western Past. Ed. by William Cronon et al. 368p. 1993. pap. 12.95 (*0-393-31063-9*) Norton.

Under Attack!! Electromagnetic Health Hazards. Clifford Williams. (Illus.). 35p. 1997. pap. 19.00 (*0-934274-36-3*) Consumertronics.

***Under Attack: The Case Against Bilingual Education.** Stephen D. Krashen. LC 96-77012. 108p. (Orig.). (C). 1996. pap. text ed. 16.00 (*0-9652808-2-9*) Lang Educ.

Under Attack, Fighting Back: Women & Welfare in the United States. Mimi Abramovitz. (Cornerstone Bks.). 1996. 26.00 (*0-85345-962-2*) Monthly Rev.

Under Attack, Fighting Back: Women & Welfare in the United States. Mimi Abramovitz. (Cornerstone Bks.). (Illus.). 160p. 1996. pap. 13.00 (*0-85345-963-0*) Monthly Rev.

Under Berlin: New Poems 1988. John Tranter. (Poetry Ser.). 119p. (Orig.). 1989. pap. text ed. 16.95 (*0-7022-2137-6*, Pub. by Univ Queensland Pr AT) Intl Spec Bk.

Under Bondage to the Law of Christ - the Only Real Freedom. Thomas B. Warren. 318p. 1989. pap. 13.00 (*0-934916-02-0*) Natl Christian Pr.

Under Briggflatts: A History of Poetry in Great Britain, 1960-1988. Donald Davie. LC 89-5111. 262p. 1989. 29.95 (*0-226-13756-2*) U Ch Pr.

Under Brinkie's Brae. George M. Brown. 152p. (C). 1989. 39.00 (*0-903065-29-0*, Pub. by G Wright Pub Ltd) St Mut.

Under Capricorn: A History of Southern Hemisphere Astronomy. D. S. Evans. (Illus.). 408p. 1988. 60.00 (*0-85274-384-X*) IOP Pub.

Under Changing Skies: Landscapes by Frederic E. Church, Oil Sketches & Drawings from the Cooper-Hewitt Museum. Elaine E. Dee. (Illus.). 80p. (Orig.). (C). 1992. pap. 16.95 (*0-8122-1413-7*, Arthur Ross Gallery) U of Pa Pr.

Under Clouded Skies & Beauregard: Pensees sous les nuages & Beauregard. Philippe Jaccottet. Tr. by Mark Treharne & David Constantine from FRE. 160p. (ENG & FRE.). 9500. pap. 18.95 (*1-85224-259-0*, Pub. by Bloodaxe Bks UK) Dufour.

Under Construction: Exploring Technology: Materials, Tools, & Design. Carol Gossett. Ed. by Betty Cordel. (Illus.). 136p. (Orig.). (J). (gr. k-2). 1996. teacher ed., wbk. ed., pap. 16.95 (*1-881431-64-9*, 1110) AIMS Educ Fnd.

Under Construction: The Body in Spanish Novels. Elizabeth A. Scarlett. 256p. (C). 1995. text ed. 37.50 (*0-8139-1532-5*) U Pr of Va.

Under Construction: Work & Alienation in the Building Trades. Marc L. Silver. LC 85-30447. (SUNY Series in the Sociology of Work). 251p. (Orig.). (C). 1986. pap. text ed. 21.95 (*0-88706-309-8*) State U NY Pr.

Under Construction: Work & Alienation in the Building Trades. Marc L. Silver. LC 85-30447. (SUNY Series in the Sociology of Work). 251p. (Orig.). (C). 1986. text ed. 64.50 (*0-88706-308-X*) State U NY Pr.

Under Construction (Ephesians) (New Horizons Bible Study Ser.). 48p. 1981. teacher ed. 2.35 (*0-89367-056-1*) Light & Life Comm.

Under Construction, Round I: U.S.-Japanese Negotiations to Open Japan's Constructiona Markets to American Firms, 1985-1988. Ellis S. Krauss. 52p. (C). 1994. pap. text ed. 3.50 (*1-56927-145-3*) Geo U Inst Dplmcy.

An Asterisk (*) at the beginning of an entry indicates that the title is appearing in BIP for the first time.

Under Construction, Round II: U.S.-Japanese Negotiations to Open Japan's Construction Markets to American Firms, 1988-1992. Todd Cloud & David Wilsford. (Pew Case Studies in International Affairs). 50p. (C). 1993. pap. text ed. 3.50 (*1-56927-158-5*) Geo U Inst Dplmcy.

Under Control: Life in a Nineteenth Century Silk Factory. Carol Adams et al. LC 83-7500. (Women in History Ser.). 48p. 1984. pap. text ed. 11.95 (*0-521-27481-8*) Cambridge U Pr.

Under Cover: An Anthology of Contemporary Scottish Writing. Ed. by Colin Nicholson. 224p. 1994. pap. 15.95 (*1-85158-548-6*, Pub. by Mnstream UK) Trafalgar.

***Under Cover of Daylight.** James W. Hall. 352p. 1997. pap. 9.95 (*0-385-31867-7*, Delta) Dell.

***Under Cover of Law: More on the Legality of Surreptitious Recording.** Ed. by Thomas E. Murray & Carmin O. Ross-Murray. LC 96-7062. (Publications of the American Dialect Society: No. 79). 80p. 1996. pap. text ed. 12.00 (*0-8173-0825-3*) U of Ala Pr.

Under Cover of Night: A Peter Ellsworth Mystery. Paul Schiele. 235p. (Orig.). 1995. pap. 19.95 (*1-884690-16-5*) Owl Press.

Under Cover of the Night. Roberta Tobeck. (Intimate Moments Ser.). 1996. mass mkt. 3.99 (*0-373-07744-0*, 1-07744-5) Silhouette.

Under Crescent & Cross: The Jews in the Middle Ages. Mark R. Cohen. LC 93-42865. 304p. 1994. text ed. 39.50 (*0-691-03378-1*) Princeton U Pr.

Under Crescent & Cross: The Jews in the Middle Ages. Mark R. Cohen. 304p. (C). 1994. pap. text ed. 15.95 (*0-691-01082-X*) Princeton U Pr.

***Under Cultures Inflate Behavior V.** Brislin. (C). 1993. pap. write for info. (*0-03-075897-1*) HB Coll Pubs.

***Under Damaris' Dress.** Bart Edelman. Ed. by Lee Mallory. LC 95-81463. 61p. 1996. pap. 9.95 (*0-9632702-6-5*) Lightning.

Under de Taman Tree. Richard A. Schrader, Sr. (Illus.). 142p. (YA). 1996. pap. write for info. (*0-9622987-5-1*) R A Schrader.

Under-Development of Africa: Colonialism, Neo-Colonialism & Socialism. Alfred A. Jarrett. 192p. (Orig.). (C). Date not set. pap. text ed. 26.50 (*0-7618-0106-5*); lib. bdg. 51.00 (*0-7618-0105-7*) U Pr of Amer.

Under Dispute. Agnes Repplier. LC 75-167406. (Essay Index Reprint Ser.). 1977. reprint ed. 23.95 (*0-8369-2668-4*) Ayer.

Under Eastern Eyes: A Critical Reading of Maritime Fiction. Janice K. Keefer. 299p. 1987. 35.00 (*0-8020-5747-0*); pap. 18.95 (*0-8020-6656-9*) U of Toronto Pr.

Under Eastern Eyes: The West As Reflected in Recent Russian Emigre Writing. Arnold McMillin. 1992. text ed. 55.00 (*0-312-06809-3*) St Martin.

Under Egypt: A Novel. Douglas A. Menville. LC 88-34592. 300p. (C). pap. write for info. (*0-89370-938-7*); lib. bdg. write for info. (*0-89370-838-0*) Borgo Pr.

Under Ephemeral Light: Vignettes de Lumiere. Juan Collignon Hoff et al. LC 96-96244. (Illus.). 110p. 1997. 49.95 incl. cd-rom (*0-9651824-7-9*) Calif Pubng.

Under Every Green Tree: Popular Religion in Sixth Century Judah. Susan Ackerman. (Harvard Semitic Monographs). 272p. 1992. 35.95 (*1-55540-273-9*, 040046) Scholars Pr GA.

Under Every Roof: A Kid's Sytle & Field Guide to the Architecture of American Houses. Patricia B. Glenn. LC 95-50574. (Illus.). 112p. (YA). (gr. 5 up). 1995. text ed. 17.95 (*0-471-14428-2*) Wiley.

Under Fire: Gun Buy-Backs, Exchanges & Amnesty Programs. LC 96-68370. 234p. (Orig.). (C). 1996. pap. text ed. 21.00 (*1-878734-47-4*) Police Exec Res.

Under Fire: U. S. Military Restrictions on the Media from Grenada to the Persian Gulf. Jacqueline Sharkey. 320p. 1995. pap. 15.00 (*0-9629012-3-7*) U Pr of Amer.

Under Fire with the Tenth U. S. Cavalry. Herschel V. Cashin. 1993. 29.95 (*0-87081-280-7*); pap. 19.95 (*0-87081-270-X*) Univ Pr Colo.

Under Fire with the Tenth U. S. Cavalry. Herschel V. Cashin et al. LC 69-18550. (American Negro: His History & Literature. Series 2). 378p. 1969. reprint ed. 32.95 (*0-405-01854-1*) Ayer.

Under Five, under Educated? Tricia David. 1990. 80.00 (*0-335-09263-2*, Open Univ Pr); pap. 27.00 (*0-335-09262-4*, Open Univ Pr) Taylor & Francis.

Under Flag. Myung Mi Kim. Ed. by Patricia Dienstfrey & Rena Rosenwasser. LC 91-23726. (Illus.). 56p. (Orig.). 1991. pap. 9.00 (*0-932716-27-X*) Kelsey St Pr.

***Under Gemini.** Rosamunde Pilcher. 1996. mass mkt. 5.99 (*0-312-96124-3*) St Martin.

Under Gemini: The Selected Poems of Miklos Radnoti with a Prose Memoir. Miklos Radnoti. Tr. by Jascha Kessler et al. from HUN. LC 83-23751. (Illus.). 108p. 1985. pap. text ed. 11.95 (*0-8214-0764-3*) Ohio U Pr.

Under God: Religion & American Politics. Garry Wills. 1990. write for info. (*0-671-65701-1*) S&S Trade.

Under God with Liberty: The Religious Dimension of American Liberty. Peter A. Lawler. LC 93-38666. 300p. 1994. text ed. 35.00 (*0-89341-686-X*, Longwood Academic) Hollowbrook.

Under Ground. Michael Daly. 1997. pap. 5.99 (*0-451-19154-4*, Sig) NAL-Dutton.

Under Ground: A Novel. Michael Daly. LC 94-48453. 1995. 21.95 (*0-316-21709-3*) Little.

Under Heaven. large type ed. Brenda Clarke. 1989. 25.99 (*0-7089-2084-5*) Ulverscroft.

Under Her Influence. Kelly Street. (Temptation Ser.: No. 388). 1992. mass mkt. 2.99 (*0-373-25488-1*, 1-25488-7) Harlequin Bks.

Under His Spell. 384p. 1995. mass mkt. 4.99 (*0-8217-5115-8*, Zebra Kensgtn) Kensgtn Pub Corp.

Under His Spell. Carolyn Keene. (Nancy Drew Files Ser.: No. 116). (YA). 1996. mass mkt. 3.99 (*0-671-50372-3*) PB.

Under His Wings. Patsy Clairmont. 1994. audio 15.99 (*1-56179-285-3*) Focus Family.

Under His Wings. Patricia J. Laperle. LC 86-63915. (Illus.). 52p. (Orig.). 1987. pap. 7.75 (*0-910147-41-8*) World Poetry Pr.

Under His Wings. Ruth Strang. 64p. (Orig.). 1987. pap. 1.95 (*0-937580-01-5*) LeSEA Pub Co.

Under His Wings: And Other Places of Refuge. Patsy Clairmont. 1994. 14.99 (*1-56179-279-9*) Focus Family.

Under His Wings: Meeting the Spiritual Needs of the Mentally Disabled. Robert Bittner. LC 94-31611. 192p. (Orig.). 1994. pap. 11.99 (*0-89107-805-3*) Crossway Bks.

Under Hitler's Banner: Serving the Third Reich. Edmund Blandford. (Illus.). 248p. 1996. 24.95 (*0-7603-0268-5*) Motorbooks Intl.

***Under House Arrest.** Yevgeny Kharitonov. 1998. pap. text ed. 14.99 (*1-85242-355-2*) Serpents Tail.

Under Its Generous Dome: Collections & Programs of the American Antiquarium Society. 2nd rev. ed. Ed. by Nancy H. Burkett & John B. Hench. LC 92-26828. (Illus.). 190p. 1992. pap. 12.95 (*0-944026-38-9*, 42174) Am Antiquarian.

Under Lock & Key: A Story, 3 vol. in 1. Thomas W. Speight. LC 75-32785. (Literature of Mystery & Detection Ser.). 1976. reprint ed. 68.95 (*0-405-07900-1*) Ayer.

Under Mad Anthony's Banner. James B. Naylor. 1993. reprint ed. lib. bdg. 89.00 (*0-7812-5393-4*) Rprt Serv.

Under Milk Wood: A Play for Voices. Dylan Thomas. LC 54-9641. 1957. pap. 7.95 (*0-8112-0209-7*, NDP73) New Directions.

Under Milk Wood - a Play for Voices: A Reproduction of the Illuminated Manuscript. Dylan Thomas. (Illus.). 88p. 1989. text ed. 90.00 (*0-9623131-0-6*) Intl Letter Arts.

***Under Milwaukee Wires.** Bill Marvel. (Illus.). 1996. 49.95 (*1-878887-69-6*) Morning NJ.

Under My Elm. David Grayson, pseud. LC 86-24819. (Illus.). 288p. 1986. reprint ed. pap. 14.95 (*0-939650-23-1*) R H Pub.

Under My Eyelids. Olly Komenda-Soentgerath. Tr. by Tom Beck from GER. 90p. 1994. pap. 14.95 (*1-85610-037-5*, Pub. by Forest Bks UK) Dufour.

Under My Nose. Lois Ehlert. LC 96-15441. (Meet the Author Ser.). (Illus.). 32p. (J). (gr. 2-5). 1996. 13.95 (*1-57274-027-2*) R Owen Pubs.

Under My Own Roof. Stanislaw Baranczak. Tr. by Frank Kujawinski. (Poetry Chapbook Ser.). 1980. Bilingual edition. 3.95 (*0-932191-03-7*) Mr Cogito Pr.

Under My Skin. Michele M. Di. 1994. pap. 12.95 (*1-55082-099-0*, Pub. by Quarry Pr CN) LPC InBook.

Under My Skin. Jaye Maiman. (Robin Miller Mystery Ser.: No. 3). 336p. 1993. pap. 10.95 (*1-56280-049-3*) Naiad Pr.

Under My Skin. large type ed. Sarah Dunant. 382p. 1996. pap. 20.95 (*0-7862-0621-7*, Thorndike Lrg Prnt) Thorndike Pr.

Under My Skin: A Hannah Wolfe Novel. Sarah Dunant. LC 95-13115. 288p. 1995. 20.00 (*0-684-81521-4*) S&S Trade.

***Under My Skin: My Autobiography, to 1949, Vol. 1.** Doris Lessing. 416p. 1994. 100.00 (*0-06-017164-2*) HarpC.

Under My Skin: Volume One of My Autobiography, to 1949. Doris Lessing. 1995. lib. bdg. 35.00 (*0-8095-9174-X*) Borgo Pr.

Under My Skin Vol. 1: Of My Autobiography, to 1949. Doris Lessing. 432p. 1995. pap. 14.00 (*0-06-092664-3*, PL) HarpC.

Under My Wings. Basil Rowe. (Airlines History Project Ser.). reprint ed. 30.00 (*0-404-19333-1*) AMS Pr.

Under New Management: Essential Tips for Turning Managers into Leaders. Mike Whitty & Irene M. McDonald. Ed. by Kim Faulkner. (C). 1994. 19.95 (*0-9625079-5-4*) Michael Pub.

Under New Management: Organized Common Sense: A Powerful Guide to Help You Solve Today's Management Puzzle. Michael R. Hagy & Mary L. Hagy. LC 94-94226. (Illus.). 368p. 1994. pap. 29.95 (*1-885004-00-1*) Atlantic Alliance.

Under Northern Eyes: Latin American Studies & U. S. Hegemony in the Americas, 1898-1990. Mark T. Berger. LC 94-44645. (Caribbean & Latin American Studies). 1995. text ed. 31.50 (*0-253-31172-1*) Ind U Pr.

Under Oath. Shelby Yastrow. 352p. (Orig.). 1994. mass mkt. 5.50 (*0-7865-0005-0*) Diamond.

Under Observation. Amalie Skram. Tr. by Katherine Hanson & Judith Messick from NOR. LC 92-14129. 369p. (Orig.). 1992. pap. 15.95 (*1-879679-03-5*) Women Translation.

Under Observation: Life Inside a Psychiatric Hospital. Lisa Berger & Alexander Vuckovic. 288p. 1994. 22.95 (*0-395-63413-X*) Ticknor & Fields.

Under Observation: Life Inside McLean Psychiatric Hospital. Lisa Berger & Alexander Vuckovic. 288p. 1995. pap. 12.95 (*0-14-025147-2*, Penguin Bks) Viking Penguin.

Under One Roof. Shannon Waverly. (Superromance Ser.). 1996. mass mkt. 3.99 (*0-373-70703-7*, 1-70703-3) Harlequin Bks.

Under One Roof: A Gathering of Poems. R. Wilbur et al. Ed. by Maureen Sternlieb & Barry Sternlieb. (Illus.). 28p. 1992. pap. 20.00 (*0-944156-06-1*) Mad River MA.

Under One Roof: A Gathering of Poems. deluxe limited ed. R. Wilbur et al. Ed. by Maureen Sternlieb & Barry Sternlieb. (Illus.). 28p. 1992. 100.00 (*0-944156-07-X*) Mad River MA.

Under One Roof: Issues & Innovations in Shared Housing. Ed. by George C. Hemmens et al. LC 95-18576. (SUNY Series in Urban Public Policy). 192p. 1996. text ed. 49.50 (*0-7914-2905-9*); pap. text ed. 16.95 (*0-7914-2906-7*) State U NY Pr.

Under One Roof: Retail Banking & the International Mortgage Finance Revolution. Michael Ball. 240p. 1990. text ed. 39.95 (*0-312-05566-8*) St Martin.

Under Open Sky: Poets on William Cullen Bryant. Ed. by Norbert Krapf. LC 86-61717. xvi, 111p. 1986. 35.00 (*0-8232-1167-3*); pap. 19.95 (*0-8232-1168-1*) Fordham.

Under Orion. K. N. Daruwalla. (Writers Workshop Redbird Ser.). 93p. 1975. 8.00 (*0-88253-728-8*); 4.80 (*0-89253-597-0*) Ind-US Inc.

***Under Our Skin: Kids Talk about Race.** Debbie H. Birdseye & Tom Birdseye. LC 97-9395. (Illus.). 32p. (J). (gr. 4-7). 1997. lib. bdg. 15.95 (*0-8234-1325-X*) Holiday.

Under Our Wing: 1992 IWRC Conference Proceedings. Ed. by William Marshall. 148p. 1993. pap. 15.00 (*1-884196-00-4*) IWRC.

Under Peace Rising. Merilene M. Murphy. (Series 1A). (Illus.). 64p. 1996. pap. 15.00 (*0-934172-38-2*) WIM Pubns.

***Under Pegasus: A Novel.** David Beckman. LC 96-52223. 200p. 1997. 19.95 (*0-9651244-1-X*, Gldengrove Bks) Derrynane Pr.

Under Plowman's Floor: A Novel. Richard Watson. LC 78-16386. 244p. (Orig.). 1978. 7.95 (*0-914264-25-7*) Cave Bks MO.

Under Prairie Skies. Margot Dalton. (Superromance Ser.: No. 401). 1990. pap. 2.95 (*0-373-70401-1*) Harlequin Bks.

Under Pressure: Some Crack Contenders. William Burns. Ed. by Don D. Wilson. 48p. 1989. pap. 7.00 (*0-9607756-9-2*) Singular Speech Pr.

Under Raps: Toward Grassroots Ecological Democracy in the Great Lakes Basin. Ed. by John H. Hartig & Michael A. Zarull. LC 91-41479. (Illus.). 260p. (C). 1992. text ed. 49.50 (*0-472-10258-3*); pap. text ed. 27.50 (*0-472-08175-6*) U of Mich Pr.

Under Review: Further Writings on Writers, 1946-1990. Anthony Powell. LC 93-41020. 480p. 1994. 34.95 (*0-226-67712-5*) U Ch Pr.

Under Sail in the Last of the Clippers. F. W. Wallace. (C). 1987. 138.00 (*0-85174-508-3*, Pub. by Brwn Son Ferg) St Mut.

Under Saturn's Shadow: The Wounding & Healing of Men. James Hollis. 144p. 1993. pap. 16.00 (*0-919123-64-3*, Pub. by Inner City CN) BookWorld Dist.

Under Scorpio. Thomas G. Bergin. LC 82-19377. 39p. 1982. pap. 2.95 (*0-933760-02-7*) Solaris Pr.

Under Scrutiny: The Educational Administration Professoriate. Martha M. McCarthy et al. 1988. 13.95 (*0-922971-01-3*) Univ Council Educ Admin.

***Under Sentence of Death: Lynching in the South.** W. Fitzhugh Brundage. LC 96-30204. 400p. (C). (gr. 13). 1997. 49.95 (*0-8078-2326-0*); pap. 17.95 (*0-8078-4636-8*) U of NC Pr.

Under Side of Snow. LoVerne Brown. LC 96-60890. 60p. (Orig.). 1996. pap. 8.95 (*0-938711-41-5*) Tecolote Pubns.

Under Siege. Arthur Aughey. 222p. 1989. text ed. 39.95 (*0-312-03709-0*) St Martin.

Under Siege. Stephen Coonts. Ed. by Paul McCarthy. (Orig.). 1991. pap. 6.99 (*0-671-74294-9*) PB.

Under Siege. Josh McDowell. (Powerlink Chronicle Ser.: No. 1). 192p. (J). 1992. pap. 8.99 (*0-8499-3363-3*) Word Pub.

Under Siege. large type ed. Stephen Coonts. LC 90-28432. 847p. (Orig.). 1991. pap. 16.95 (*1-56054-991-2*) Thorndike Pr.

Under Siege: Literary Life in London Nineteen Thirty-Nine - Nineteen Forty-Five. Robert Hewison. 5.95 (*0-7043-3283-3*, Pub. by Quartet UK) Charles River Bks.

***Under Siege: Moving Outside the Walls to Victory.** J. D. Fuller, III. 160p. (Orig.). 1997. pap. write for info. (*0-9657827-0-0*) Under Siege.

Under Siege: P. L. O. Decisionmaking During the 1982 War. Rashid Khalidi. 224p. 1985. text ed. 42.50 (*0-231-06186-2*) Col U Pr.

Under Six Reigns. G. P. Gooch. vii, 344p. (C). 1971. reprint ed. 38.50 (*0-208-01263-X*, Archon Bks) Shoe String.

Under-Standing of Eclipses. Guy Ottewell. (Illus.). 93p. (Orig.). 1991. pap. 12.95 (*0-934546-24-X*) Univ Wrkshop.

Under Stars. Tess Gallagher. LC 77-95331. 53p. (C). 1978. pap. 7.50 (*0-915308-20-7*) Graywolf.

Under-Studied Relationships: Off the Beaten Track. Julia T. Wood & Steve Duck. LC 95-5097. (Understanding Relationship Processes Ser.: Vol. 6). (Illus.). 264p. 1995. 36.00 (*0-8039-5650-9*); pap. 16.95 (*0-8039-5651-7*) Sage.

Under Sunny Skies. Pat Warren. (Special Edition Ser.: No. 731). 1992. mass mkt. 3.39 (*0-373-09731-X*, 5-09731-6) Harlequin Bks.

Under Suspicion of Sisters. 2nd ed. Susan H. Sibbet. (Illus.). 27p. 1990. reprint ed. pap. 2.00 (*0-9625104-2-4*) White Mtn Pr.

Under Technology's Thumb. William Leiss. 184p. (C). 1990. pap. text ed. 12.95 (*0-7735-0748-5*, Pub. by McGill CN) U of Toronto Pr.

Under the Ancestors' Shadow: Kinship, Personality, & Social Mobility in China. 2nd rev. ed. Francis L. Hsu. xxi, 370p. 1967. reprint ed. 49.50 (*0-8047-0767-7*) Stanford U Pr.

Under the Andes. Rex T. Stout. 290p. 1994. 4.95 (*0-7867-0179-X*) Carroll & Graf.

Under the Apple. Mark Wallace. 30p. 1994. pap. 10.00 (*0-614-04110-4*) Hozomeen Pr.

***Under the Apple Tree.** Elsie A. Schmied. 260p. (Orig.). 1998. mass mkt. 7.99 (*1-58006-009-9*, Flirtation) Sovereign.

Under the Apple Tree: Marrying - Birthing - Parenting. Helen Wessel. LC 79-52050. 319p. (Orig.). 1981. pap. 8.95 (*0-933082-02-9*) Bookmates Intl.

Under the Apple Trees. John Burroughs. (Works of John Burroughs). 1989. reprint ed. lib. bdg. 79.00 (*0-7812-2199-4*) Rprt Serv.

Under the Aruban Sun. Chi Sun Rhee. LC 96-69279. (Illus.). 208p. 1996. 19.95 (*1-884570-51-8*) Research Triangle.

Under The Backyard Sky. Neil B. Shulman. (Illus.). 32p. (J). (gr. 1-4). 1995. 13.95 (*1-56145-093-6*) Peachtree Pubs.

Under the Banner of Science: Erasmus Darwin & His Age. Maureen McNeil. (History of Science Ser.). 340p. 1988. text ed. 59.95 (*0-7190-1492-1*, Pub. by Manchester Univ Pr UK) St Martin.

Under the Banyan Tree. R. K. Narayan. 256p. 1987. mass mkt. 6.95 (*0-14-008012-0*, Penguin Bks) Viking Penguin.

Under the Banyan Tree. R. K. Narayan. 208p. 1993. pap. 8.95 (*0-14-018544-5*, Penguin Classics) Viking Penguin.

Under the Banyan Tree: The Communist Movement in India, 1920-1964. Sada N. Talwar. 450p. 1986. 27.50 (*0-8364-1822-0*, Pub. by Allied II) S Asia.

Under the Beetle's Cellar. large type ed. Mary W. Walker. LC 96-2292. 1996. pap. 22.95 (*1-56895-313-5*) Wheeler Pub.

Under the Beetle's Cellar. Mary W. Walker. 384p. 1996. reprint ed. mass mkt. 5.99 (*0-553-57173-7*, Crimeline) Bantam.

Under the Big Sky. Trevor Romain. (Illus.). 64p. (YA). (gr. 5-12). 1994. 13.95 (*1-880092-13-1*) Bright Bks TX.

Under the Big Stick: Nicaragua & the United States since 1848. Karl Berman. LC 86-1767. 339p. (Orig.). 1986. pap. 12.00 (*0-89608-323-3*); boxed 35.00 (*0-89608-324-1*) Compita Pub.

Under the Big Top: A Season with the Circus. Bruce Feiler. LC 94-43120. 1995. 23.00 (*0-684-19758-8*) S&S Trade.

***Under the Bigtop.** Contrib. by Larry Lukas. 24p. (Orig.). 1996. pap. text ed. 6.95 (*1-889416-01-0*, LS40002) Lukasound.

Under the Black Flag. Erik C. Haugaard. LC 93-85476. 170p. (J). (gr. 6 up). 1993. pap. 8.95 (*1-879373-63-7*) R Rinehart.

Under the Black Flag. Kit Dalton. (Illus.). 236p. 1995. reprint ed. 24.95 (*0-9649732-6-X*) L J Tolbert.

***Under the Black Flag: The Romance & Reality of Life.** Cordingly. LC 97-15048. (J). 1997. pap. write for info. (*0-15-600549-2*) HarBrace.

Under the Black Flag: The Romance & the Reality of Life Among the Pirates. David Cordingly. LC 95-41414. 320p. 1996. 25.00 (*0-679-42560-8*) Random.

Under the Black Sun. Eric Woro. 392p. (Orig.). 1995. pap. 8.95 (*1-887096-00-0*) Axiom Publ.

Under the Blood Red Sun. Graham Salisbury. LC 94-444. 256p. (J). (gr. 6 up). 1994. 15.95 (*0-385-32099-X*) Delacorte.

Under the Blood-Red Sun. Graham Salisbury. 256p. (YA). (gr. 5 up). 1995. pap. 4.50 (*0-440-41139-4*, YB BDD) BDD Bks Young Read.

Under the Blood-Red Sun. Graham Salisbury. 256p. (YA). (gr. 7 up). 1995. reprint ed. pap. 3.99 (*0-614-97639-1*, YB BDD) BDD Bks Young Read.

Under the Bo Tree: Studies in Caste, Kinship & Marriage in the Interior of Ceylon. Nur Yalman. 1967. pap. 13.95 (*0-520-02054-5*) U CA Pr.

Under the Boardwalk. Carla Cassidy. (Desire Ser.). 1994. mass mkt. 2.99 (*0-373-05882-9*, 1-05882-5) Silhouette.

Under the Bombs: The German Home Front, 1942-1945. Earl R. Beck. LC 85-24681. (Illus.). 280p. 1986. 30.00 (*0-8131-1567-1*) U Pr of Ky.

Under the Bone. Anne-Christine D'Adesky. LC 93-11962. 1994. 23.00 (*0-374-28066-5*) FS&G.

Under the Bridge. Ellen K. McKenzie. (J). (gr. 4-7). 1995. 14.95 (*0-8050-3398-X*, Bks Young Read) H Holt & Co.

Under the Bridge. Ellen K. McKenzie. LC 94-3415. 144p. (J). (gr. 3-7). 1996. pap. 4.50 (*0-06-440629-6*, Trophy) HarpC Child Bks.

Under the Bridge: A Study Guide for the Film. Vivian Ling. 325p. 1994. pap. text ed. 25.00 (*0-89264-113-4*) Ctr Chinese Studies.

Under the Bridge: Notes from a ME Generation Dropout. Randy L. Viscio. 200p. 1992. pap. text ed. 10.95 (*0-9634494-6-X*) Cowpasture Prods.

Under the Bright Lights. Daniel Woodrell. 192p. 1988. pap. 3.50 (*0-380-70456-0*) Avon.

***Under the Brilliant Emperor: Imperial Authority in Tang China As Seen in the Writings of Chang Chiu-Ling.** P. A. Herbert. (Oriental Monograph Ser.: Vol. 21). 164p. 1997. pap. text ed. 25.00 (*0-7081-1348-6*, Pub. by Aust Nat Univ AT) UH Pr.

Under the Burning Sun. H. A. DeRosso. Ed. by Bill Pronzini. (Five Star Ser.). 263p. 1997. 17.95 (*0-7862-0737-X*, Five Star) Mac Lib Ref.

Under the Canopy. Tallahassee Junior Womens Club Staff. 1995. 16.95 (*0-9644244-0-1*) GFWC TJWC.

***Under the Capitol Dome.** George M. White. LC 97-19677. 1997. write for info. (*1-55835-154-X*) American Institute of Industrial Engineers.

Under the Carambola Tree Independent Reader 5-Pack, Unit 7. (Networks Ser.). 1991. 15.00 (*0-88106-760-1*, N238) Charlesbridge Pub.

***Under the Cherry Blossom Tree.** Allen Say. LC 96-36278. (J). 1997. 13.95 (*0-395-84546-7*) HM.

***Under the Cherry Blossom Tree.** Allen Say. (J). 1997. 13.95 (*0-395-84506-8*) HM.

Under the Chinook Arch: Tales of a Montana Veterinarian. R. W. Gustafson. LC 93-90729. 108p. (Orig.). 1993. pap. 9.95 (*1-56044-248-4*) Falcon Pr MT.

Under the Cloak of Justice: The Work of Ned Cartledge. Joan Muller. Ed. by Steven High. (Illus.). 24p. 1994. 9.00 (*0-935519-19-X*) Anderson Gal.

UV

Under the Clock: The True Story of the First Godfather. William Balsamo & George Carpozi, Jr. 400p. 1988. 22.95 (*0-88282-044-3*) New Horizon NJ.

Under the Clock see Crime, Inc.: The Inside Story of the Mafia's First 100 Years

Under the Cope of Heaven: Religion, Society, & Politics in Colonial America. Patricia U. Bonomi. (Illus.). 304p. 1988. pap. 17.95 (*0-19-505417-2*) OUP.

***Under the Cover of Kindness: The Invention of Social Work.** Leslie Margolin. LC 96-47986. (Knowledge: Disciplinarity & Beyond Ser.). 219p. 1997. 29.95 (*0-8139-1713-1*) U Pr of Va.

Under the Covers. David C. Aston. 40p. 1987. 20.00 (*0-7223-2158-9*, Pub. by A H S Ltd UK) St Mut.

***Under the Covers.** Roseanne Williams. 1998. mass mkt. 4.50 (*0-373-81037-7*, 1-81037-3) Harlequin Bks.

Under the Covers - Between the Sheets: Cartoons by Kurt Erichsen & Bruce Billings. Kurt Erichsen & Bruce Billings. (Illus.). 96p. (Orig.). 1989. pap. 10.95 (*0-943595-19-3*) Leyland Pubns.

Under the Desert Moon. Marsha Canham. 512p. 1992. mass mkt. 5.50 (*0-440-20612-X*) Dell.

***Under the Distant Sky.** Al Lacy et al. LC 96-40158. (Hannah of Fort Bridger Ser.: No. 1). 274p. 1997. pap. 9.99 (*1-57673-033-6*, Multnomah Bks) Multnomah Pubs.

Under the Domim Tree. Gila Almagor. Tr. by Hillel Schenker. LC 95-3356. (J). 1995. 15.00 (*0-671-89020-4*, S&S Bks Young Read) S&S Childrens.

Under the Double Cross. Anne Marshall & James Huston. 295p. 1984. 10.95 (*0-89697-214-3*) Intl Univ Pr.

Under the Dove, the Reign of Peace see Egregor of the Dove or the Reign of Peace

Under the Eagle's Wings: The Army on the Eve of Civil War, 2 vols. George T. Ness, Jr. 650p. 1983. Set. 87.95 (*0-89126-112-5*) MA-AH Pub.

Under the Eastern Stars. Linda L. Chaikin. LC 93-25160. (Heart of India Ser.: Bk. 2). 1993. pap. 9.99 (*1-55661-366-0*) Bethany Hse.

Under the Eaves of Shanghai: Shanghai Wuyansya, an Annotated Chinese Play. Ed. by Richard F. Chang. 1974. 13.95 (*0-88710-122-4*) Yale Far Eastern Pubns.

Under the Ether Dome: A Physician's Apprenticeship. Stephen Hoffman. 1990. pap. 9.95 (*0-8065-1207-5*, Citadel Pr) Carol Pub Group.

Under the Evening Sky. Finn Carling. Tr. by L. A. Muinzer from NOR. 120p. 9300. 30.00 (*0-7206-0783-3*, Pub. by P Owen Ltd UK) Dufour.

Under the Exchange: The Unprofitable Business of Michael Perry, a Seventeenth-Century Boston Bookseller. Hugh Amory. 29p. (Orig.). 1993. pap. 9.00 (*0-944026-45-1*) Am Antiquarian.

Under the Fairy Tale Tree. (J). (gr. 1-2). 1993. 12.95 (*1-56644-957-X*) Educ Impress.

Under the Fang. Sally Peters. 352p. (Orig.). 1991. pap. 6.50 (*0-671-69573-8*, Pocket Star Bks) PB.

Under the Feet of Jesus. Helena M. Viramontes. 192p. 1996. pap. 9.95 (*0-452-27387-0*, Plume) NAL-Dutton.

Under the Fifth Sun. Earl Shorris. 624p. 1993. pap. 11.95 (*0-393-31083-3*) Norton.

Under the Fig Tree. William Breault. (Illus.). 95p. (Orig.). 1989. pap. 9.00 (*0-910845-37-9*) Landmark Ent.

Under the Flame. Ed. by Evelyn G. Klapp. 1978. pap. 6.00 (*0-685-60197-8*) Aegis Pub Co.

***Under the Frog.** Tibor Fischer. LC 97-2029. 1997. pap. 12.00 (*0-8050-5245-3*, Owl) H Holt & Co.

***Under the Frog.** Tibor Fischer. 1992. 18.00 (*0-7486-6133-6*, Pub. by Polygon UK) Subterranean Co.

Under the Frog: A Black Comedy. Tibor Fischer. LC 93-46679. 256p. 1994. 17.00 (*1-56584-148-4*) New Press NY.

Under the Frog: A Black Comedy. Tibor Fischer. 256p. 1995. pap. 11.00 (*1-56584-149-2*) New Press NY.

***Under the Gaslight.** Augustin Daly. Ed. & Intro. by Walter J. Meserve. (On Stage, America! Ser.). 54p. 1996. spiral bd. 3.95 (*0-937657-29-8*) Feedbk Theabks & Prospero.

Under the Gaslight. Augustin Daly. LC 76-108468. 1971. reprint ed. 19.00 (*0-403-00428-4*) Scholarly.

Under the Gaslight: A Totally Original & Picturesque Drama of Life & Love in These Times, in Five Acts. Augustin Daly. (BCL1-PS American Literature Ser.). 47p. 1992. reprint ed. lib. bdg. 59.00 (*0-7812-6699-8*) Rprt Serv.

***Under the Glacier.** Donald R. Thompson. 1997. mass mkt. 4.99 (*1-55197-273-5*, Pub. by Comnwlth Pub CN) Partners Pubs Grp.

Under the Golden Cod: A Shared History of the Old North Church & the Town of Marblehead, Massachusetts. Three Hundred & Fiftieth Anniversary Book Committee of Old North Church. LC 84-7821. (Illus.). 160p. 1984. 17.95 (*0-914659-05-7*) Phoenix Pub.

Under the Golden Pagoda: The Best of Burma's Cuisine. Aung A. Taik. LC 92-18405. 1993. pap. 11.95 (*0-87701-833-2*) Chronicle Bks.

Under the Golden Roof: A Swedish Intermezzo. F. J. Ostfeld. (Illus.). 80p. (Orig.). 1989. pap. 9.95 (*0-9620757-0-1*) Belvedere WA.

Under the Golden Throne. Ralph Batten. (Illus.). 96p. (Orig.). (J). (gr. 3-6). 1989. pap. text ed. 3.95 (*0-85648-780-5*) Lion USA.

***Under the Grammar Hammer.** Douglas Cazort. Date not set. pap. 12.00 (*1-56565-647-4*) Contemp Bks.

Under the Grammar Hammer: The Twenty-Five Most Common Mistakes & How to Avoid Them. Douglas Cazort. 128p. 1992. pap. 12.00 (*0-929923-75-8*) Lowell Hse.

Under the Green Tree Hotel. Dick Stahl. (Illus.). 96p. (Orig.). 1996. pap. 10.95 (*1-878326-06-6*) East Hall Pr.

Under the Green Willow. Elizabeth Coatsworth. LC 84-1471. (Illus.). 24p. (J). (gr. k-3). 1984. 9.25 (*0-688-03845-X*); lib. bdg. 8.59 (*0-688-03846-8*) Greenwillow.

Under the Greenwood Tree. Thomas Hardy. 1976. 22.95 (*0-8488-0517-8*) Amereon Ltd.

Under the Greenwood Tree. Thomas Hardy. Ed. & Intro. by Simon Gatrell. (World's Classics Ser.). (Illus.). 224p. 1985. pap. 4.95 (*0-19-281706-X*) OUP.

Under the Greenwood Tree. Thomas Hardy. Ed. by David Wright. (English Library). 256p. 1978. pap. 5.95 (*0-14-043123-3*, Penguin Classics) Viking Penguin.

Under the Greenwood Tree. William Shakespeare. Ed. by Barbara Holdridge. (Stemmer House Poetry for Young People Ser.). (Illus.). 80p. (J). (gr. 4 up). 1986. 21.95 (*0-88045-028-2*); pap. 14.95 (*0-88045-029-0*); audio 23.90 (*0-88045-103-3*); audio 8.95 (*0-88045-100-9*) Stemmer Hse.

***Under the Ground.** (Sense of History Ser.). Date not set. pap. text ed. write for info. (*0-582-04025-6*, Pub. by Longman UK) Longman.

Under the Ground. Gallimard Jeunesse. LC 94-25421. (First Discovery Bks.). (Illus.). 24p. (J). (ps-2). 1995. 11.95 (*0-590-20302-9*, Cartwheel) Scholastic Inc.

Under the Ground. Henry Pluckrose. LC 93-45659. (Walkabout Ser.). 32p. (J). 1994. lib. bdg. 17.60 (*0-516-08122-5*) Childrens.

Under the Ground. Henry Pluckrose. (Walkabout Ser.). (J). (ps-2). 1994. pap. 4.95 (*0-516-40122-X*) Childrens.

***Under the Guardianship of the Nation: The Freedmen's Bureau & the Reconstruction of Georgia, 1865-1870.** Paul A. Cimbala. LC 96-31225. 1997. 50.00 (*0-8203-1891-4*) U of Ga Pr.

***Under the Gun.** Helen Forelle. Ed. by Janet Leih. 40p. (Orig.). 1997. pap. text ed. 3.00 (*1-877649-31-7*) Tesseract SD.

Under the Gun. large type ed. Theodore V. Olsen. LC 94-1037. 1994. lib. bdg. 19.95 (*0-8161-5862-2*) G K Hall.

Under the Gun: Weapons, Crime, & Violence in America. James D. Wright et al. LC 83-2615. 360p. (C). 1983. pap. text ed. 28.95 (*0-202-30306-3*); lib. bdg. 49.95 (*0-202-30303-9*) Aldine de Gruyter.

***Under the Guns of the German Aces: Immelmann, Voss, Goring, Lothar, Von Richthofen - Complete Record of Their Victories & Victims.** Norman Franks & Hal Giblin. (Illus.). 224p. 1997. 35.00 (*1-898697-72-8*, Pub. by Grub St Pubns UK) Seven Hills Bk.

Under the Guns of the Red Baron: Complete Record of Von Richthofen's Victories & Victims in Graphic Detail. Norman Franks et al. (Illus.). 256p. 1995. 35.00 (*1-898697-27-2*, Pub. by Grub St Pubns UK) Seven Hills Bk.

Under the Hawthorn Tree. Marita Conlon-McKenna. LC 90-55097. 160p. (J). (gr. 3-7). 1990. 13.95 (*0-8234-0838-8*) Holiday.

Under the Hawthorn Tree: Children of the Famine. Marita Conlon-McKenna. LC 92-18955. 160p. (J). (gr. 5 up). 1992. pap. 4.99 (*0-14-036031-X*) Puffin Bks.

Under the Haystack. P. A. Engebrecht. (J). (gr. 5-12). 1991. 20.25 (*0-8446-6473-1*) Peter Smith.

Under the Healing Sun. Nick O'Donohoe. 352p. (Orig.). 1995. mass mkt. 4.99 (*0-441-00180-7*) Ace Bks.

Under the Heel of Mary. Nicholas Perry & Loreto Echeverria. 336p. 1989. 39.95 (*0-415-01296-1*) Routledge.

Under the Hermes, & Other Stories. Clotilde I. Graves. LC 70-121554. (Short Story Index Reprint Ser.). 1977. 23.95 (*0-8369-3510-1*) Ayer.

Under the House. Leslie H. Pinder. LC 87-43217. 184p. 1988. 15.95 (*0-394-56932-6*) Random.

Under the Hula Moon: Living in Hawai'i. Jocelyn K. Fujii. (Illus.). 180p. 1992. 40.00 (*0-517-58131-0*, Crown) Crown Pub Group.

Under the Ice. Richard P. Henrick. 1989. mass mkt. 4.50 (*0-8217-2808-3*, Zebra Kensgtn) Kensgtn Pub Corp.

Under the Indian Sun: British Landscape Artists. Ed. by Pauline Rohatgi & Pheroza Godrej. (C). 1995. 105.00 (*81-85026-29-7*, Pub. by Marg) S Asia.

***Under the Influence.** Ron Parker. (Illus.). 42p. (Orig.). 1993. pap. 4.25 (*0-88680-378-0*) I E Clark.

Under the Influence. Elizabeth Travis. (Worldwide Library Mystery: No. 92). 1992. mass mkt. 3.99 (*0-373-26092-X*, 1-26092-6) Harlequin Bks.

Under the Influence: Alcohol & Human Behavior. John Jung. LC 92-43587. 336p. 1994. pap. 41.95 (*0-534-20448-1*) Brooks-Cole.

Under the Influence? Drugs & the American Workforce. National Research Council, Institute of Medicine. Ed. by Jacques Normand et al. 336p. (C). 1993. text ed. 39.95 (*0-309-04885-0*) Natl Acad Pr.

Under the Influence: Presidential Candidates & Their Campaign Advisers. Center for Public Integrity Staff. 80p. 1995. pap. 10.00 (*0-9629012-5-3*) U Pr of Amer.

Under the Influence: Spirit Power. rev. ed. Keith Davy. (Inter Acta Ser.). (Illus.). 6p. (C). 1996. teacher ed., ring bd. 1.25 (*0-614-14269-5*, 741-012t, Inter Acta); student ed., ring bd. 3.25 (*1-57334-015-4*, 741-012s, Inter Acta) WSN Pr.

Under the Influence: The Destructive Effects of Group Dynamics. John D. Goldhammer. 320p. 1996. 25.95 (*1-57392-006-1*) Prometheus Bks.

Under the Influence: The Students of Thomas Hart Benton. Marianne Berardi. (Illus.). 150p. (Orig.). 1993. pap. write for info. (*0-9615372-2-1*) Albrecht Art Mus.

Under the Influence: The Unauthorized Story of the Anheuser-Busch Dynasty. Peter Hernon & Terry Ganey. 496p. 1992. pap. 12.50 (*0-380-71847-2*) Avon.

Under the Influence - Myths-Realities-Alcoholism. James R. Milam & Katherine Ketcham. 256p. 1984. mass mkt. 5.99 (*0-553-27487-2*) Bantam.

Under the Influence of Blackbirds: A Collection of Poems. Sharon Van Sluys. LC 92-64705. (Minnesota Voices Project Ser.: Vol. 59). 72p. (Orig.). 1993. pap. 7.95 (*0-89823-148-5*) New Rivers Pr.

Under the Influence of Water: Poems, Essays, & Stories. Michael Delp. LC 92-10989. (Great Lakes Bks.). (Illus.). 98p. 1992. pap. 13.95 (*0-8143-2391-X*) Wayne St U Pr.

***Under the Inquisition: An Experience Relived.** Linda Tarazi. 600p. (Orig.). 1997. pap. 14.95 (*1-57174-058-9*) Hampton Roads Pub Co.

Under the Jaguar Sun. Italo Calvino. Tr. by William Weaver. 1990. pap. 9.00 (*0-15-692794-2*) HarBrace.

Under the Juniper Tree. Margaret Deming. (Orig.). 1995. pap. write for info. (*1-57553-086-4*) Watermrk Pr.

Under the Kapok Tree. S. T. Garne. LC 92-36810. (Illus.). 1994. 14.00 (*0-671-86495-5*, Green Tiger S&S) S&S Childrens.

Under the Kapok Tree: Identity & Difference in Beng Thought. Alma Gottlieb. LC 91-25926. (African Systems of Thought Ser.). (Illus.). 212p. 1992. text ed. 27.50 (*0-253-32607-9*) Ind U Pr.

Under the Kapok Tree: Identity & Difference in Beng Thought. Alma Gottlieb. LC 96-26356. (Illus.). xvii, 184p. 1996. pap. text ed. 14.95 (*0-226-30507-4*) U Ch Pr.

***Under the Knife.** Francis Roe. 1998. mass mkt. 5.99 (*0-451-40702-4*, Onyx) NAL-Dutton.

Under the Lake. Stuart Woods. 288p. 1988. mass mkt. 6.50 (*0-380-70519-2*) Avon.

***Under the Lens: A Look at the American Media.** Carol K. Bishop. LC 96-61724. (Orig.). 1997. pap. 16.95 (*0-472-08403-8*) U of Mich Pr.

***Under the Lens: A Look at the American Media.** Carol K. Bishop. LC 96-61724. (Orig.). 1997. teacher ed., pap. 15.95 (*0-472-08429-1*) U of Mich Pr.

Under the Lilacs. Louisa May Alcott. (Illus.). (YA). (gr. 5 up). 1996. 17.95 (*0-316-03774-5*) Little.

Under the Lilacs. Louisa May Alcott. (Illus.). (YA). (gr. 5 up). 1996. 8.95 (*0-316-03087-2*) Little.

Under the Lilacs. Louisa May Alcott. (J). 1997. pap. 2.95 (*0-8167-1472-X*) Troll Communs.

Under the Lilacs. Louisa May Alcott. 1996. 8.99 (*0-517-14828-5*) Random.

Under the Lilacs. Louisa May Alcott. (Works of Louisa May Alcott). 1989. reprint ed. lib. bdg. 79.00 (*0-7812-1637-0*) Rprt Serv.

Under the Limerick Tree: One Hundred Forty-Four Original Limericks. Vassar W. Smith. (Illus.). 100p. (Orig.). 1991. pap. 6.95 (*1-880964-01-5*) Zapizdat Pubns.

Under the Lion. Steve Jacobs. 240p. (C). 1993. pap. 10.95 (*0-435-90588-0*, 90588) Heinemann.

***Under the Lizard Trees.** Sue Storm. 44p. 1996. pap. 4.95 (*0-9640168-8-5*) Pirate Writings.

***Under the Lone Star Flagstick.** Hauser. 1997. 25.00 (*0-684-84011-1*) S&S Trade.

***Under the Lucky Bean Tree.** 56p. 1991. 3.00 (*0-8341-1374-0*) Nazarene.

Under the Man-Fig. Mollie E. Davis. 1993. lib. bdg. 75.00 (*0-7812-5873-1*) Rprt Serv.

Under the Management of Mr. Charles Dickens: His Production of "The Frozen Deep" Ed. by Robert L. Brannan. LC 66-22927. (Illus.). 173p. 1966. 18.95 (*0-910278-91-1*) Boulevard.

Under the Map of Germany: Nationalism & Propaganda 1918-1945. G. Henrik Herb. LC 96-7437. 256p. (C). 1996. text ed. 65.00 (*0-415-12749-1*) Routledge.

Under the Mask of William Shakespeare. Abel Lefranc. Tr. by Cecil Cragg. (C). 1989. 45.00 (*0-86303-352-0*, Pub. by Merlin Bks UK) St Mut.

Under the Mercy: A Sequel to A Severe Mercy. Sheldon Vanauken. LC 88-81090. 263p. 1988. pap. 10.95 (*0-89870-213-5*) Ignatius Pr.

Under the Mermaid Angel. Martha A. Moore. LC 95-1991. 192p. (J). (gr. 7 up). 1995. 14.95 (*0-385-32160-0*, Delacorte Pr Bks) BDD Bks Young Read.

***Under the Mermaid Angel.** Martha A. Moore. 176p. (YA). 1997. mass mkt. 3.99 (*0-440-22682-1*, LLL BDD) BDD Bks Young Read.

Under the Mexican Flag: The Mexican Struggle Outlined. C. J. Velarde. 1976. lib. bdg. 250.00 (*0-8490-2783-7*) Gordon Pr.

***Under the Microscope: The Report of the Twentieth Century Fund Task Force on Presidential Appointments; with Background Papers.** G. Calvin Mackenzie et al. LC 96-27236. 1996. write for info. (*0-87078-401-3*) TCFP-PPP.

Under the Moon. 1992. pap. 5.25 (*0-19-422691-3*) OUP.

Under the Moon. Vivian French. LC 93-877. (Illus.). 96p. (J). (gr. 1-4). 1994. 14.95 (*1-56402-330-3*) Candlewick Pr.

Under the Moon. Dyan Sheldon. LC 93-11711. (Illus.). 32p. (J). (ps-3). 1994. pap. 15.99 (*0-8037-1670-2*) Dial Bks Young.

Under the Moon: The Early Unpublished Poetry. William Butler Yeats. Ed. by George Bornstein. 112p. 1995. 22.00 (*0-684-80254-6*) S&S Trade.

Under the Moon & Stars. Scott Emerson. LC 93-50707. (Illus.). 32p. (J). 1995. pap. 14.95 (*0-87905-633-9*) Gibbs Smith Pub.

Under the Mountain. Molly F. Knudtsen. LC 82-8552. (Illus.). 144p. 1982. 14.95 (*0-87417-072-9*) U of Nev Pr.

Under the Mountain Wall: A Chronicle of Two Seasons in Stone Age New Guinea. Peter Matthiessen. Ed. by Edward Hoagland. (Illus.). 320p. 1987. pap. 12.95 (*0-14-025270-3*, Penguin Bks) Viking Penguin.

Under the Mummy's Spell. Kate McMullan. 176p. (J). (gr. 5 up). 1992. 16.00 (*0-374-38033-3*) FS&G.

Under the Neem Tree. Susan Lowerre. LC 90-53323. 256p. 1991. 22.00 (*1-877946-03-6*) Permanent Pr.

Under the Neem Tree. Susan Lowerre. LC 92-43188. 264p. (C). 1993. pap. 12.95 (*0-295-97273-4*) U of Wash Pr.

Under the Net. Iris Murdoch. 1977. pap. 11.95 (*0-14-001445-4*, Penguin Bks) Viking Penguin.

Under the Northern Lights: My Memories of Life in the Finnish Community of Northern Ontario. Nelma Sillanpaa. Ed. by Edward W. Laine. (Mercury Ser.: No. 45). (Illus.). 160p. 1994. pap. 17.95 (*0-660-14020-9*, Pub. by Can Mus Civil CN) U of Wash Pr.

Under the Olive. Annie Fields. (Notable American Authors Ser.). 1992. reprint ed. lib. bdg. 75.00 (*0-7812-2820-4*) Rprt Serv.

Under the Orange Umbrella Independent Reader 5-Pack, Unit 1. (Networks Ser.). 1991. 15.00 (*0-88106-707-5*, N118) Charlesbridge Pub.

Under the Pear Tree. Brenda Seabrooke. (J). 1997. pap. 13.99 (*0-525-65213-2*, Cobblehill Bks) Dutton Child Bks.

Under the Pomegranate Tree: The Best New Latino Erotica. Ray Gonzalez. 253p. 1996. pap. 12.00 (*0-671-89823-X*, PB Trade Paper) PB.

Under the Portico. large type ed. Olivia K. Lab. 260p. (Orig.). 1995. 12.95 (*1-881542-24-6*) Book World Inc.

***Under the Radar: Talking to Today's Cynical Consumer.** Jonathan Bond & Richard Kirshenbaum. (Adweek Magazine Ser.). 256p. 1997. 27.95 (*0-471-17469-6*) Wiley.

Under the Rainbow. Arnie Kantrowitz. 240p. 1996. pap. 12.95 (*0-312-14439-3*) St Martin.

Under the Rainbow. Randall Silvis. LC 92-34300. 1993. 22.00 (*1-877946-28-1*) Permanent Pr.

Under the Rainbow: The Real Liza Minnelli. George Mair. LC 95-19243. 360p. 1995. 22.50 (*1-55972-312-2*, Birch Ln Pr) Carol Pub Group.

***Under the Red Flag: Stories by Ha Jin.** Ha Jin. LC 97-12235. (Falnnery O'Conner Award for Short Fiction Ser.). 224p. 1997. 22.95 (*0-8203-1939-2*) U of Ga Pr.

***Under the Red Patch: Story of the 63rd Regiment, Penna. Volunteers, 181-1864.** Compiled by Gilbert A. Hays. 479p. 1996. reprint ed. lib. bdg. 52.00 (*0-8328-5217-1*) Higginson Bk Co.

Under the Redwoods. Bret Harte. LC 72-113674. (Short Story Index Reprint Ser.). 1977. 21.95 (*0-8369-3403-2*) Ayer.

***Under the Ribs of Death.** John Marlyn. 1996. pap. text ed. 6.95 (*0-7710-9866-9*) McCland & Stewart.

Under the Rising Sun: Memories of a Japanese Prisoner of War. Mario Machi. (Illus.). 176p. (Orig.). 1995. pap. 12.95 (*0-9642521-0-4*) Wolfenden.

Under the Rising Sun: War, Captivity & Survival 1941-1945. rev. ed. Edward W. Weiss. LC 92-96896. (Illus.). 300p. 1995. pap. 12.00 (*0-9646024-0-7*) E W Weiss.

Under the Roofs of Paris. Henry Miller. LC 84-73204. Orig. Title: Opus Pistorum. 272p. 1985. pap. 10.00 (*0-8021-3183-2*, Grove) Grove-Atltic.

***Under the Safety Net.** Charles Baxter. 1998. pap. write for info. (*0-679-77649-4*, Vin) Random.

Under the Safety Net: The Health & Social Welfare of the Homeless in the United States. Philip W. Brickner. 1990. 27.95 (*0-393-02885-2*) Norton.

Under the Safety Net: The Health & Social Welfare of the Homeless in the United States. Ed. by Philip W. Brickner et al. 464p. 1992. pap. 14.95 (*0-393-30875-8*) Norton.

***Under the Scott-Light: British Government Seen Through the Scott Report.** Ed. by Brian Thompson & F. F. Ridley. (Hansard Society Series in Government & Politics: No. 5). (Illus.). 180p. 1997. pap. text ed. 24.95 (*0-19-922278-9*) OUP.

Under the Scuds: Gulf War in Israel. Zigmund Hahn. 112p. 1992. pap. 9.95 (*965-229-075-0*, Pub. by Gefen Pub Hse IS) Gefen Bks.

Under the Sea. (Glow in the Dark Bks.). (Illus.). 24p. (J). (ps). 1991. 6.50 (*0-307-06255-4*, Golden Pr) Western Pub.

***Under the Sea.** Booth. (J). (gr. 3). 1989. pap. text ed. 35.50 (*0-03-926818-7*); student ed., pap. text ed. 13.00 (*0-03-926819-5*) HR&W Schl Div.

Under the Sea. Jennifer Dussling. (Books & Stuff). (Illus.). 24p. (J). (gr. k-5). 1995. pap. 7.95 (*0-448-40078-2*, G&D) Putnam Pub Group.

Under the Sea. Judith Mullican. (HRL Little Bks.). 8p. (J). (ps-k). 1995. pap. text ed. 10.95 (*1-57332-012-9*) HighReach Lrning.

Under the Sea. Kate Petty. (Around & About Ser.). (Illus.). 32p. (J). (gr. 2-4). 1993. pap. 5.95 (*0-8120-1759-5*) Barron.

Under the Sea. Cynthia Rothman. Ed. by Janet Reed. (Early Learning Program Ser.). (Illus.). 16p. (Orig.). (J). (ps-2). 1994. pap. 14.95 (*1-56784-302-6*) Newbridge Comms.

***Under the Sea.** Angela Royston. LC 97-19333. (Inside & Out Ser.). (J). 1997. write for info. (*1-57572-178-3*) Rigby Interact Libr.

Under the Sea. Ed. by Frank H. Talbot. LC 95-12948. (Discoveries Ser.). (Illus.). 64p. (J). (gr. 3 up). 1995. lib. bdg. 15.00 (*0-7835-4760-9*) Time-Life.

***Under the Sea: Color Surprise.** Golden Books Staff. (Little Mermaid Ser.). (Illus.). (J). 1997. pap. text ed. 2.99 (*0-307-15282-0*, Golden Books) Western Pub.

***Under the Sea: Dot-to-Dot.** Evan Kimble. 1997. pap. text ed. 5.95 (*0-8069-6152-X*) Sterling.

Under the Sea: Mini-Book. Cynthia Rothman. Ed. by Janet Reed. (Early Learning Program Ser.). (Illus.). 16p. (Orig.). (J). (ps-1). 1996. pap. 2.95 (*1-56784-327-1*) Newbridge Comms.

Under the Sea: One Book Makes Hundreds of Pictures of Undersea Life. Time-Life Books Editors. LC 95-49039. (EcoSystems Xplorer Ser.). (Illus.). 16p. (J). (gr. k-3). 1996. 11.95 (*0-7835-4786-2*) Time-Life.

Under the Sea: Weird & Wonderful Creatures from the Deep. Leiguron Taylor. LC 92-40517. (Illus.). 96p. 1993. pap. 12.95 (*0-8118-0263-9*) Chronicle Bks.

U V

An Asterisk (*) at the beginning of an entry indicates that the title is appearing in BIP for the first time.

***Under-the-Sea ABC's.** Golden Books Staff. (Little Mermaid Ser.). (Illus.). (J). 1997. pap. text ed. 2.99 (*0-307-05664-3*, Golden Books) Western Pub.

Under the Sea Activity Book. Jennifer Riggs. 32p. (J). (ps-3). 1993. pap. 1.95 (*0-590-46297-0*) Scholastic Inc.

Under the Sea from A to Z. Anne Doubilet. LC 90-1355. (Illus.). 32p. (J). (gr. k-6). 1991. 16.00 (*0-517-57836-0*) Crown Bks Yng Read.

Under the Sea in 3-D! Rick Sammon & Susan Sammon. (3-D Photography Children's Ser.). (Illus.). 28p. 1995. 9.95 (*1-57359-005-3*, Elliott Clark) Black Belt Comm.

Under the Sea Wind. Rachel L. Carson. (Illus.). 320p. 1996. pap. 11.95 (*0-14-025380-7*, Penguin Bks) Viking Penguin.

Under the Shadow. Gilbert Sorrentino. LC 91-15014. 137p. 1993. reprint ed. pap. 9.95 (*0-916583-93-7*) Dalkey Arch.

Under the Shadow of Apartheid: Agrarian Transformation in Swaziland. D. C. Funnell. 311p. 1991. text ed. 72.95 (*1-85628-112-4*, Pub. by Avebury Pub UK) Ashgate Pub Co.

Under the Shadow of War: Fascism, Anti-Fascism, & Marxists, 1918-1939. Larry Ceplair. LC 86-32652. 272p. 1987. text ed. 49.50 (*0-231-06532-9*) Col U Pr.

Under the Shadow of Weimar: Democracy, Law & Racial Incitement in Six Countries. Ed. by Louis Greenspan & Cyril Levitt. LC 92-23062. 248p. 1993. text ed. 57.95 (*0-275-94055-1*, C4055, Praeger Pubs) Greenwood.

Under the Shadow of Wings. Banks. LC 96-21180. (J). 1997. 15.00 (*0-689-81207-8*) S&S Childrens.

Under the Shadow of Your Wings. Craig D. Erickson. Ed. by Michael L. Sherer. LC 86-28348. (Orig.). 1987. pap. 7.25 (*0-89536-844-7*, 7803) CSS OH.

Under the Shadows of Mt. Fanny: Life Was to Change. Dorothy G. Dryden. (Illus.). 83p. (Orig.). 1996. pap. 6.95 (*0-9644370-4-X*) Dryden Publ.

Under the Sidewalks of New York: The Story of the Greatest Subway System in the World. 2nd rev. ed. Brian J. Cudahy. LC 95-18861. 1995. pap. 19.95 (*0-8232-1618-7*) Fordham.

Under the Sign: John Bargrave As Collector, Traveller, & Witness. Stephen Bann. (Body in Theory: Histories of Cultural Materialism Ser.). (Illus.). 178p. (C). 1994. text ed. 34.50 (*0-472-10436-5*) U of Mich Pr.

Under the Sign of Ambiguity: Saint John Perse - Alexis Leger. Erika Ostrovsky. LC 85-8946. 280p. (C). 1987. pap. text ed. 12.00 (*0-8147-6166-6*) NYU Pr.

Under the Sign of Saturn. 224p. 1991. pap. 12.95 (*0-385-26712-6*, Anchor NY) Doubleday.

Under the Sign of the Waterbearer: A Life of Thomas Merton. James T. Baker. 1976. pap. 2.95 (*0-915216-15-9*) Marathon Intl Bk.

Under the Silk Cotton Tree. Jean Buffong. LC 93-1663. (Emerging Voices: New International Fiction Ser.). 144p. 1993. 22.95 (*1-56656-126-4*); pap. 9.95 (*1-56656-122-1*) Interlink Pub.

Under the Skin. Ken Norris. 24p. 1976. pap. 1.00 (*0-916696-00-6*) Cross Country.

Under the Skin of the Road. Walter F. Nash. 1993. pap. 9.00 (*0-9639407-0-8*) W F Nash.

Under the Sky. Rozanne L. Williams. (Emergent Reader Bks.). 8p. 1994. 1.59 (*0-916119-58-0*) Creat Teach Pr.

Under the Sky. Rozanne L. Williams. (Emergent Reader Big Bks.). (Illus.). 8p. (Orig.). (J). (gr. k-2). 1995. pap. 7.98 (*1-57471-070-2*) Creat Teach Pr.

Under the Skylights. Henry B. Fuller. 1972. reprint ed. lib. bdg. 34.00 (*0-8422-8056-1*) Irvington.

Under the Skylights. Henry B. Fuller. (Collected Works of Henry B. Fuller). 1988. reprint ed. lib. bdg. 79.00 (*0-7812-1206-5*) Rprt Serv.

Under the Skylights. Henry B. Fuller. 1984. reprint ed. 59.00 (*0-403-04590-8*) Scholarly.

***Under the Snow.** Kerstin Ekman. 224p. 1997. 22.95 (*0-385-48866-1*, Anchor NY) Doubleday.

Under the Snowball Tree. Ellie Kirby. (Illus.). 36p. 1986. 14.95 (*0-9626737-0-6*) Fox Creek Pr.

Under the Southern Cross. Claire McNab. 224p. 1992. pap. 10.95 (*1-56280-011-6*) Naiad Pr.

Under the Southern Cross: A Brief History of Astronomy in Australia. Ragbir Bhathal & Graeme White. (Illus.). 96p. 24.95 (*0-86417-376-8*, Pub. by Kangaroo Pr AT) Seven Hills Bk.

Under the Southern Cross: A Petty Officer's Chronicle of the U.S.S. Octans, Banana Boat Become World War II Supply Ship for the Southern Pacific Fleet. Kenneth G. Oliver. LC 94-31153. (Illus.). 312p. 1995. pap. 25.95 (*0-89950-999-1*) McFarland & Co.

Under the Southern Cross: South America, Australia, Africa. G. B. Redmore. (Life & Livelihood Geographies Ser.: Bk. 2). (Illus.). pap. 8.95 (*0-685-20646-7*) Transatl Arts.

Under the Southern Moon. Virginia Gaffney. (Richmond Chronicles Ser.: Vol. 1). 375p. (Orig.). 1996. pap. 9.99 (*1-56507-507-2*) Harvest Hse.

Under the Spell of God: Poems for the Lord's Pleasure. Robin M. Cannon. LC 95-16896. 128p. 1995. pap. 8.95 (*1-887089-02-0*) Torchlght Pub.

Under the Spell of Mother Earth. Berit Kjos. 180p. 1992. pap. 9.99 (*0-89693-850-6*, 6-1850, Victor Bks) Chariot Victor.

Under the Spell of Orpheus: The Persistence of a Myth in Twentieth-Century Art. Judith E. Bernstock. (Illus.). 272p. (C). 1991. 34.95 (*0-8093-1659-5*) S Ill U Pr.

Under the Spell of the Gauge Principle. G. T. Hooft. 696p. 1994. text ed. 109.00 (*981-02-1308-5*); pap. text ed. 61.00 (*981-02-1309-3*) World Scientific Pub.

Under the Starfruit Tree: Folktales from Vietnam. Alice M. Terada. LC 89-5123. (Illus.). (J). (gr. 4-8). 1989. pap. 12.95 (*0-8248-1553-X*, Kolowalu Bk) UH Pr.

Under the Starry Cross: Our Family Veterans of the American Civil War. 2nd ed. 1995. pap. 29.00 (*0-9643418-1-6*) R L Witt.

***Under the Starry Night: A Wayfarer's Guide Through an Uncertain World.** Dennis J. Billy. LC 96-44076. 160p. 1997. pap. 8.95 (*0-87793-614-5*) Ave Maria.

Under the Stars: Essays on Labor Relations in the Arts & Entertainment. Ed. by Lois S. Gray & Ronald L. Seeber. (ILR Press Book). 224p. 1996. 38.00 (*0-87546-350-9*); pap. 16.95 (*0-87546-349-5*) Cornell U Pr.

Under the Still Standing Sun. Dora Dueck. 279p. (Orig.). 1989. pap. 10.95 (*0-919797-93-8*) Kindred Prods.

Under the Streets of Nice: The Bank Heist of the Century. Ken Follett & Rene L. Maurice. (Zenith Edition Ser.). Orig. Title: The Gentlemen of 16 July. 165p. 1991. reprint ed. 17.95 (*0-915765-76-4*) Natl Pr Bks.

***Under the Sufe's Cloak: Stories of Abu Said & His Mystical Teachings.** Mohammad A. Jamnia & Mojdeh Bayat. 130p. 1996. pap. 10.00 (*0-614-21374-6*, 1269) Kazi Pubns.

Under the Sufi's Cloak: Stories of Abu Sa'id & His Mystical Teachings. Mohammad A. Jamnia & Mojdeh Bayat. LC 94-39424. 144p. 1995. pap. 10.00 (*0-9627854-6-6*) Writers Inc.

***Under the Sun.** Date not set. 35.00 (*1-881997-01-4*) Fraenkel Gal.

Under the Sun. Erik Jay. LC 87-61377. 152p. 8700. 21.00 (*0-7206-0654-3*, Pub. by P Owen Ltd UK) Dufour.

Under the Sun. George Junghanns. 1969. 4.50 (*0-686-05524-1*); 10.00 (*1-881946-02-9*); pap. 2.45 (*0-686-05525-X*); pap. 5.00 (*1-881946-03-7*) Gauntlet Bks.

***Under the Sun.** Ellen Kandoian. (J). Date not set. write for info. (*0-688-06359-4*); lib. bdg. write for info. (*0-688-06360-8*) Greenwillow.

Under the Sun. large type ed. Dane Coolidge. LC 94-33480. (Nightingale Ser.). 312p. 1995. pap. 16.95 (*0-7838-1147-0*, GK Hall) Thorndike Pr.

Under the Sun: Desert Architecture & Style. Photos by Terrence Moore. LC 95-11432. (Illus.). 248p. 1995. 45.00 (*0-8212-2226-0*) Bulfinch Pr.

Under the Sun: Myth & Realism in Western American Literature. Ed. by Barbara H. Meldrum. LC 85-50609. (Illus.). vi, 231p. 1986. 22.50 (*0-87875-303-6*) Whitston Pub.

***Under the Sun: Occasional Essays.** Alexander Scala. 160p. 1988. pap. 12.95 (*0-919627-90-0*, Pub. by Quarry Pr CN) LPC InBook.

***Under the Sun: Photographs by Christopher Bucklow, Susan Derges, Garry Fabian Miller, Adam Fuss.** Ed. & Intro. by Jeffrey Fraenkel. (Illus.). 104p. Date not set. pap. 35.00 (*1-881337-01-4*) Fraenkel Gal.

Under the Sun & in the Heavenlies: Youth & Adult Teacher. Carol E. Miller. 1985. pap. 2.25 (*0-915374-49-8*) Rapids Christian.

Under the Sun & the Moon & Other Poems. Margaret Wise Brown. LC 92-72031. (Illus.). 40p. (J). (ps-2). 1993. 14.95 (*1-56282-354-X*); lib. bdg. 14.89 (*1-56282-355-8*) Hyprn Child.

Under the Sun & the Moon & Other Poems. Margaret Wise Brown. LC 92-72031. (Illus.). 40p. (J). (ps-2). 1995. pap. 4.95 (*0-7868-1035-1*) Hyprn Child.

Under the Sunday Tree. Eloise Greenfield. LC 87-29373. (Trophy Picture Bk.). (Illus.). 48p. (J). (gr. 1 up). 1991. pap. 6.95 (*0-06-443257-2*, Trophy) HarpC Child Bks.

Under the Sweetwater Rim. Louis L'Amour. 181p. 1984. mass mkt. 3.99 (*0-553-24760-3*) Bantam.

Under the Sycamore Tree. Samuel Spewack. 1960. pap. 5.25 (*0-8222-1194-7*) Dramatists Play.

***Under the Tabachin Tree: A New Home in Mexico.** Celia Wakefield. LC 96-71032. (Illus.). 128p. 1997. pap. 13.50 (*0-88739-121-4*) Creat Arts Bk.

Under the Table. Marisabina Russo. LC 96-7145. (Illus.). 32p. (J). (ps up). 1997. 15.00 (*0-688-14602-3*); lib. bdg. 14.93 (*0-688-14603-1*) Greenwillow.

Under the Table (And How to Get Up) Jewish Pathways of Spiritual Growth. Avraham Greenbaum. 320p. 1991. pap. 12.00 (*0-930213-41-6*) Breslov Res Inst.

Under the Tarnished Dome: How Notre Dame Betrayed its Ideal for Football Glory. Don Yaeger & Doulas S. Looney. 304p. 1994. pap. 12.00 (*0-671-89938-4*, Fireside) S&S Trade.

Under the Texas Sun: Adventures of a Young Cowpuncher. Anna M. Dana. LC 86-14401. (Wardlaw Bk.). 112p. 1986. 15.95 (*0-89096-284-7*) Tex A&M Univ Pr.

Under the Thin Brittle of Every Situation. Karin Falcone. 36p. (Orig.). 1995. pap. 5.00 (*1-887289-02-X*) Rodent Pr.

Under the Tongue. Larry Zirlin. 1992. 16.00 (*0-914610-82-1*); pap. 9.00 (*0-914610-81-3*) Hanging Loose.

Under the Torrent of His Love: His Love Grew Within Me. Marie-Eugene L. Jesus. Tr. by Mary Thomas from FRE. LC 94-43124. (Orig.). 1995. pap. 5.95 (*0-8189-0720-7*) Alba.

Under the Tower of Babel. Dean Isaacson. 145p. 1995. pap. text ed. 7.00 (*1-887008-00-4*) Cominus Bks.

Under the Trapeze: Being the True & Unembellished Account of the Last Original Old-Fashioned All-American Independently Owned & Operated Family Circus. Robert F. McKay. 500p. 1989. 20.00 (*0-317-93517-8*) Brass Ring.

Under the Trees Planted. Elizabeth. LC 96-54636. 1997. text ed. write for info. (*0-312-12860-6*) St Martin.

Under the Tumtum Tree: From Nonsense to Sense, a Study in Non-Automatic Comprehension. Marlene Dolitsky. LC 84-28471. (Pragmatics & Beyond Ser.: Series V: 1). vii, 118p. (Orig.). 1984. pap. 41.00 (*0-915027-39-9*) Benjamins North Am.

Under the Tuscan Sun: At Home in Italy. Frances Mayes. 288p. 1996. 22.95 (*0-8118-0842-4*) Chronicle Bks.

***Under the Tuscan Sun: At Home in Italy.** Frances Mayes. LC 97-20218. 288p. 1997. reprint ed. pap. 13.00 (*0-7679-0038-3*) Broadway BDD.

Under the Unpredictable Plant: An Exploration in Vocational Holiness. Eugene H. Peterson. 206p. 1994. pap. text ed. 14.00 (*0-8028-0848-4*) Eerdmans.

***Under the Veil.** Doris J. Shahrokhimanesh. LC 96-90333. 282p. (Orig.). (YA). (gr. 10-12). 1996. pap. 19.95 (*0-9653158-0-0*) Under The Veil.

Under the Volcano. Malcolm Lowry. 1984. pap. 12.95 (*0-452-25595-3*, Plume) NAL-Dutton.

Under the Voodoo Moon. Laura Leone. (Desire Ser.). 1994. mass mkt. 2.99 (*0-373-05834-9*, 5-05834-2) Silhouette.

Under the Watchful Eye: Managing Presidential Campaigns in the Television Era. Ed. by Mathew D. McCubbins. LC 92-24570. 193p. 1992. 21.95 (*0-87187-752-X*) Congr Quarterly.

Under the Water. (Animal Pictures Ser.). (Illus.). 24p. (J). (ps-3). Date not set. text ed. 3.50 (*1-56987-335-6*) Landoll.

Under the Water. Harriet Ziefert. (Hello Reading! Ser.). (Illus.). 32p. (J). (ps-3). 1990. pap. 3.50 (*0-14-054221-3*, Puffin) Puffin Bks.

Under the Water Level 2, Red. Harriet Ziefert. (Easy-to-Read Ser.). (Illus.). (J). (gr. k-3). 1993. pap. 3.50 (*0-14-036535-4*, Puffin) Puffin Bks.

Under the Wedding Canopy: Love & Marriage in Judaism. David Gross & Esther Gross. 200p. 1996. 22.50 (*0-7818-0481-7*) Hippocrene Bks.

Under the Wheat. Rick DeMarinis. 157p. 1987. pap. 7.50 (*0-88001-149-1*) Ecco Pr.

Under the Wheat. Rick DeMarinis. LC 86-7007. (Drue Heinz Literature Prize Ser.). 168p. 1986. 22.50 (*0-8229-3544-9*) U of Pittsburgh Pr.

Under the Wheel. Hamlin Garland. (Collected Works of Hamlin Garland). 1988. reprint ed. lib. bdg. 79.00 (*0-7812-1214-6*) Rprt Serv.

Under the Wheel see Collected Works of Hamlin Garland

Under the White Boar. Mary D. Few. LC 70-161090. (Illus.). 219p. 1973. 9.95 (*0-87667-069-9*) Carolina Edns.

Under the Winds of Yaquina. E. Wayne Courtney. Orig. Title: Dunlins & Sanderlings: Under the Winds of Yaquina. (Illus.). 66p. (Orig.). 1988. pap. text ed. 3.95 (*0-9616063-5-5*) Sanderling Pr.

Under the X in Texas: Little Stories from the Big Country. Mike Renfro. LC 95-32155. (C). 1995. 21.95 (*0-89672-355-0*) Tex Tech Univ Pr.

Under the Yoke. S. M. Stirling. 512p. 1991. mass mkt. 4.95 (*0-671-72077-5*) Baen Bks.

Under the Yum Yum Tree. Lawrence Roman. 1961. pap. 5.25 (*0-8222-1195-5*) Dramatists Play.

Under the 82nd Airborne: Stories. Deborah Eisenberg. 225p. 1992. 20.00 (*0-374-28068-1*) FS&G.

Under Their Own Vine & Fig Tree: The African-American Church in the South, 1865-1900. William E. Montgomery. LC 92-21041. 358p. (C). 1994. pap. 14.95 (*0-8071-1965-2*) La State U Pr.

Under This Blazing Light. Amos Oz. Tr. by Nicholas De Lange. 224p. (C). 1995. text ed. 22.95 (*0-521-44367-9*) Cambridge U Pr.

Under This Blazing Light. Amos Oz. Tr. by Nicholas De Lange. (Canto Book Ser.). 224p. (C). 1996. pap. text ed. 9.95 (*0-521-57622-9*) Cambridge U Pr.

Under This Roof. Nancy King. 24p. (Orig.). 1983. pap. text ed. write for info. (*0-932460-03-8*) Summer Stream.

Under Three Flags: A History Coloring Book of the Erie Area. Linda Steiner. 1989. pap. 3.95 (*0-910042-55-1*) Allegheny.

Under Timpanogos Green. Clyde E. Weeks, Jr. 243p. 1993. pap. 14.95 (*0-9643423-1-6*) Magnif Mormon.

Under Tropic Skies. Louis Becke. LC 73-113650. (Short Story Index Reprint Ser.). 1977. 19.95 (*0-8369-3379-6*) Ayer.

Under Twelve Not Allowed. Page McBrier. (Treehouse Times Ser.: No. 1). 128p. (J). (gr. 4). 1989. pap. 2.50 (*0-380-75780-X*, Camelot) Avon.

Under Twenty-Five: Duke Narrative & Verse, 1945-1962. William M. Blackburn. LC 63-9005. 250p. reprint ed. pap. 71.30 (*0-317-42244-8*, 2026187) Bks Demand.

Under Twenty-Five: Duke Narrative & Verse, 1945-1962: A Collection of Short Stories & Verse by Sixteen Duke Authors. Ed. by William M. Blackburn. LC 63-9005. xi, 240p. 1963. pap. text ed. 19.00 (*0-8223-0349-3*) Duke.

Under Two Flags. Ouida. Ed. by John Sutherland & David Trotter. (Oxford Popular Fiction Ser.). 560p. 1995. pap. 12.95 (*0-19-282328-0*) OUP.

Under Two Flags, 3 vols. in 2. Ouida, pseud. LC 79-8187. reprint ed. Set. 84.50 (*0-404-62088-4*) AMS Pr.

Under Two Flags: The American Navy in the Civil War. William M. Fowler, Jr. 352p. 1991. pap. 10.95 (*0-380-71551-1*) Avon.

Under Two Flags: The American Navy in the Civil War. William M. Fowler, Jr. 1990. 22.50 (*0-393-02859-3*) Norton.

Under Two Heavens. Wes Dakota. 1991. pap. 14.95 (*0-933025-22-X*) Blue Bird Pub.

Under Water. Sally Gunning. Ed. by Jane Chelius. 256p. (Orig.). 1992. mass mkt. 4.50 (*0-671-72805-9*) PB.

***Under Water with Ogden Nash.** Ogden Nash. LC 96-51448. 1997. 16.95 (*0-8212-2404-2*) Little.

Under Western Eyes. Joseph Conrad. 512p. 1991. 20.00 (*0-679-40554-2*, Everymans Lib) Knopf.

Under Western Eyes. Joseph Conrad. 1976. 17.95 (*0-8488-0749-9*) Amereon Ltd.

Under Western Eyes. Joseph Conrad. 1979. pap. 3.95 (*0-14-001254-0*, Penguin Bks) Viking Penguin.

Under Western Eyes. Joseph Conrad. Ed. & Intro. by Boris Ford. 352p. 1990. pap. 9.95 (*0-14-018287-X*, 158, Penguin Classics) Viking Penguin.

***Under Western Eyes.** Joseph Conrad. 1997. pap. 9.95 (*0-14-018849-5*) Viking Penguin.

Under Western Eyes. Joseph Conrad. Ed. by Jeremy Hawthorn. (World's Classics Ser.). 416p. (C). 1996. pap. 7.95 (*0-19-281619-5*) OUP.

Under Western Skies: Nature & History in the American West. Donald Worster. 304p. 1992. 30.00 (*0-19-505820-8*) OUP.

Under Western Skies: Nature & History in the American West. Donald Worster. 304p. 1994. reprint ed. pap. 13.95 (*0-19-508671-6*) OUP.

Under Whose Influence? Rebekah J. Strecker. LC 93-86233. (Decision Is Yours Ser.). (Illus.). 64p. (J). (gr. 5-7). 1994. pap. 5.95 (*0-943990-97-1*); lib. bdg. 16.95 (*0-943990-98-X*) Parenting Pr.

***Under Wing & Sky: Birds of the Badlands & Black Hills.** Michael M. Melius. (Illus.). 88p. 1995. per. 12.00 (*0-912410-13-2*) Tesseract SD.

Under Words. Robert Kelly. LC 83-12325. 164p. (Orig.). 1983. 25.00 (*0-87685-595-8*); pap. 10.00 (*0-87685-594-X*) Black Sparrow.

Under World. Subhas C. Saha. (Redbird Ser.). 1975. 8.00 (*0-88253-666-4*); pap. text ed. 4.00 (*0-88253-665-6*) Ind-US Inc.

Under World Arrest. Clayton Eshleman. LC 94-16085. 195p. (Orig.). (C). 1994. 25.00 (*0-87685-936-8*); pap. 13.00 (*0-87685-935-X*) Black Sparrow.

Under World Arrest, signed ed. deluxe ed. Clayton Eshleman. LC 94-16085. 195p. (Orig.). (C). 1994. 30.00 (*0-87685-937-6*) Black Sparrow.

Under Wraps. Engle & Barnes. (Strange Matter Ser.: Vol. 21). 140p. (Orig.). (J). (gr. 4 up). 1996. pap. 3.99 (*1-56714-064-5*) Montage Bks.

Under Your Feet: The Story of the American Mound Builders. Blanche B. King. LC 73-152990. (Select Bibliographies Reprint Ser.). 1977. reprint ed. 24.95 (*0-8369-5742-3*) Ayer.

Under 35 Guide to Starting & Running Your Business. Lisa Shaw. 224p. 1996. pap. 14.95 (*1-57410-029-7*, 5614-4501) Upstart Pub.

Under 40 Financial Planning Guide: From Graduation to Your First House. Cornelius McCarthy. 398p. 1996. pap. 19.95 (*1-56343-134-3*) Merritt Pub.

Underachievement: Reversing the Process: A Parents Guide for Assisting Your Underachiever to Success. Carolyn Warnemuende & John H. Samson. LC 91-70386. 201p. (Orig.). 1991. pap. 13.95 (*0-9628925-1-3*) Fam Life Pubns.

Underachievers: New York City Elementary Education Through the Eyes of a Teacher. Paul Friedman. LC 79-84194. 1980. 12.95 (*0-87212-110-0*) Libra.

Underachievers among the Gifted/Talented Students see Reaching for the Stars Series: A Minicourse for Education of Gifted Students

Underachievers in School: Issues & Intervention. fac. ed. Nava Butler-Por. LC 87-8295. (Illus.). 205p. 1987. reprint ed. pap. 58.50 (*0-608-00963-6*, 2061811) Bks Demand.

Underachievers in School: Issues & Interventions. Nava Butler-Por. LC 87-8295. 187p. 1987. text ed. 140.00 (*0-471-91109-7*) Wiley.

Underachievers in Secondary School: Education off the Mark. Robert Griffin. 360p. 1988. text ed. 69.95 (*0-8058-0181-2*) L Erlbaum Assocs.

Underachieving Curriculum: Assessing U. S. School Mathematics from an International Perspective. C. McNight. Ed. by Kenneth J. Travers. 140p. 1987. pap. text ed. 8.00 (*0-87563-298-X*) Stipes.

Underage Angel. James E. Richardson. (Illus.). 224p. (Orig.). 1996. pap. write for info. (*0-942495-56-X*) Amherst Pr.

Underbed. Cathryn Hoellwarth. LC 89-28884. 32p. (J). (ps-3). 1990. 12.95 (*0-934672-79-2*) Good Bks PA.

Underbed. Cathryn C. Hoellwarth. (Illus.). 32p. (J). (ps-3). 1995. pap. 6.95 (*1-56148-151-3*) Good Bks PA.

***Underbelly of the U. S. Economy: Joblessness & the Paupereization of Work in America.** rev. ed. David Dembo & Ward Morehouse. (Illus.). 44p. 1996. pap. 5.00 (*0-945257-78-3*) Apex Pr.

Underbelly Poems. James A. Costello. 1981. pap. 2.95 (*0-9605098-0-1*) En Passant Poet.

***Underboss: Sammy the Bull Gravano's Story of Life in the Mafia.** Peter Maas. (Illus.). 308p. 1997. 25.00 (*0-06-018256-3*) HarpC.

Underbrush. James T. Fields. (Notable American Authors Ser.). 1992. reprint ed. lib. bdg. 75.00 (*0-7812-2834-4*) Rprt Serv.

Undercar. Jana. (EZ Auto Ser.). (C). 1996. text ed. 39.00 (*0-8273-8056-9*) Delmar.

Undercar. Jana. (EZ Auto Ser.). (C). 1996. wbk. ed., pap. text ed. 13.50 (*0-8273-8057-7*) Delmar.

Underclass. Ken Auletta. LC 82-40433. 368p. 1983. pap. 7.95 (*0-394-71388-5*, Vin) Random.

Underclass Debate: Views from History. Ed. by Michael B. Katz. LC 92-24994. (Illus.). 496p. (C). 1993. text ed. 75.00 (*0-691-04810-X*); pap. text ed. 18.95 (*0-691-00628-8*) Princeton U Pr.

Underclass Question. Ed. by Bill E. Lawson. 350p. (C). 1992. 49.95 (*0-87722-922-8*) Temple U Pr.

Underclass Question. Intro. by Bill E. Lawson & William J. Wilson. 232p. 1992. pap. 19.95 (*1-56639-062-1*) Temple U Pr.

Underclassified. Julia Vinograd. (Illus.). 60p. (Orig.). 1990. pap. 4.95 (*0-929730-14-3*) Zeitgeist Pr.

Underconstrained Structural Systems. E. N. Kuznetsov. Ed. by Frederick F. Ling. (Mechanical Engineering Ser.). (Illus.). xiii, 312p. 1991. 87.95 (*0-387-97594-2*) Spr-Verlag.

Undercooled Alloy Phases: Proceedings of the 1986 Hume-Rothery Memorial Symposium Which Was Organized by the TMS Committee on Alloy Phases, & Was Held in New Orleans, Louisiana, March 2-6, 1986 at the 115th Annual Meeting of TMS-AIME. Hume-Rothery Memorial Symposium Staff. Ed. by E. W. Collings & C. C. Koch. LC 86-33243. 513p. reprint ed. pap. 146.30 (0-7837-4078-6, 2052475) Bks Demand.

***Undercover.** Jasmine Cresswell. 1998. mass mkt. 4.50 (0-373-81022-9, 1-81022-5) Harlequin Bks.

Undercover. Hilda Stahl. (Amber Ainslie Detective Ser.: Bk. 3). 176p. (Orig.). pap. 5.99 (0-934998-37-X) Bethel Pub.

Undercover: Police Surveillance in America. Gary T. Marx. (Twentieth Century Fund Bk.: No. 1). (Illus.). 280p. 1988. 35.00 (0-520-06286-8); pap. 14.00 (0-520-06969-2) U CA Pr.

Undercover Affair. Lilian Peake. (Presents Ser.). 1993. pap. 2.89 (0-373-11532-6, 1-11532-8) Harlequin Bks.

***Undercover Agents.** Paul Thomas. LC 96-40440. (Rebels with a Cause Ser.). (J). 1998. write for info. (0-8172-4659-2) Raintree Steck-V.

Undercover Agents in the Russian Revolutionary Movement: The SR Party, 1902-14. Nurit Scheifman. LC 86-21888. 250p. 1988. text ed. 35.00 (0-312-00077-4) St Martin.

***Undercover Angels.** Created by Francine Pascal. (Sweet Valley University Ser.: No. 35). 240p. (Orig.). (YA). (gr. 9 up). 1997. mass mkt. 3.99 (0-553-57059-5) BDD Bks Young Read.

Undercover Artists. Judy Baer. (Live from Brentwood High Ser.: Vol. 5). 144p. (YA). (gr. 7-10). 1996. pap. 4.99 (1-55661-390-3) Bethany Hse.

Undercover Baby. Gina F. Wilkins. (Temptation Ser.: No. 524). 1995. mass mkt. 2.99 (0-373-25621-3, 1-25621-3) Harlequin Bks.

Undercover Cat. Gordon Gordon & Mildred Gordon. 167p. 1994. 17.00 (0-9643324-0-X) Dover Hill Pr.

Undercover Cat. abr. ed. Gordon Gordon & Mildred Gordon. 1995. audio 17.00 (0-9643324-1-8) Dover Hill Pr.

***Undercover Christmas.** Daniels. 1997. mass mkt. 3.75 (0-373-22446-X) Harlequin Bks.

Undercover Cleo. Anne Scott. 256p. (Orig.). (YA). 1995. mass mkt. 4.50 (0-425-14967-6) Berkley Pub.

Undercover Cleo: The Canine Caper. Anne Scott. (J). 1996. mass mkt. 4.50 (0-425-15293-6) Berkley Pub.

Undercover Cop. Jose L. Guzman & Carl Fick. (Orig.). 1979. mass mkt. 2.25 (0-89083-488-1, Zebra Kensgtn) Kensgtn Pub Corp.

Undercover Cowboy. Beverly Bird. (Intimate Moments Ser.). 1996. mass mkt. 3.99 (0-373-07711-4, 1-07711-4) Silhouette.

Undercover Daddy. Lindsay Longford. (Romance Ser.). 1996. mass mkt. 3.25 (0-373-19168-5, 1-19168-3) Silhouette.

***Undercover FBI.** Robert J. Nash. Date not set. write for info. (0-688-05361-0) Morrow.

Undercover Fighters: The British 22nd SAS Regiment. LC 85-40983. (Villard Military Ser.: The Elite Forces). (Illus.). 96p. 1986. 4.95 (0-394-74405-5, Villard Bks) Random.

Undercover Honeymoon. Laura Anthony. (Romance Ser.: No. 1166). 1996. mass mkt. 3.25 (0-373-19166-9, 1-19166-7) Silhouette.

Undercover Husband. Leann Harris. (Intimate Moments Ser.). 1996. mass mkt. 3.99 (0-373-07719-X, 1-07719-7) Silhouette.

Undercover Investigation. 3rd ed. J. Kirk Barefoot. LC 95-38. 132p. 1995. 29.95 (0-7506-9645-1) Buttrwrth-Heinemann.

***Undercover Lover.** Sally Steward. 400p. 1996. mass mkt. 3.99 (1-85487-499-3, Pub. by Scarlet Bks UK) London Bridge.

***Undercover Lover.** large type ed. Sally Steward. 359p. 1997. 25.99 (1-86110-045-0) Ulverscroft.

Undercover Lover: (The Prayer Substitute) David Grote. (Illus.). 39p. 1978. pap. 10.00 (0-88680-200-8); pap. 3.25 (0-88680-199-0) I E Clark.

Undercover Lover (Sealed with a Kiss) Heather Allison. 1995. mass mkt. 2.99 (0-373-03386-9) Harlequin Bks.

***Undercover Man.** Gerald Astor. Date not set. write for info. (0-688-08360-9) Morrow.

Undercover Man. Merline Lovelace. 1995. mass mkt. 3.75 (0-373-07669-X, 1-07669-4) Silhouette.

***Undercover Mom.** Muriel Jensen. 1997. mass mkt. 4.50 (0-373-82557-9, 1-82557-9) Harlequin Bks.

Undercover Operations. Kingdon P. Anderson. 1990. pap. 5.95 (0-8065-1166-4, Citadel Pr) Carol Pub Group.

Undercover Operations: A Manual for the Private Investigator. Kingdon P. Anderson. 88p. 1988. pap. 10.00 (0-87364-486-7) Paladin Pr.

Undercover Operations Survival in Narcotics Investigations. Tony Alvarez. LC 93-13542. 130p. 1993. pap. 21.95 (0-398-06005-3) C C Thomas.

Undercover Operations Survival in Narcotics Investigations. Tony Alvarez. LC 93-13542. 130p. (C). 1993. text ed. 32.95 (0-398-05871-7) C C Thomas.

Undercover or Overexposed. Phavia Kujichagulia. Ed. by Odie Hawkins & Frank Lowney. (Illus.). 99p. (Orig.). 1989. 10.00 (1-886856-00-1) Wisdom Co CA.

Undercover-Police Surveillance in Comparative Perspective. Ed. by Cyrille Fijnaut & Gary T. Marx. LC 95-18010. 1995. write for info. (90-411-0015-6) Kluwer Law Tax Pubs.

Undercover Tailback. Matt Christopher. LC 92-19770. (Illus.). (J). 1992. 15.95 (0-316-14251-4) Little.

Undercover Tailback. Matt Christopher. (Illus.). (J). (gr. 3-6). 1994. pap. text ed. 3.95 (0-316-14254-9) Little.

Undercover Vows. Judi Lind. (Intrigue Ser.). 1996. mass mkt. 3.50 (0-373-22355-2, 1-22355-1) Harlequin Bks.

Undercover War. (Black OPS Ser.). 1996. mass mkt. 4.99 (0-373-63810-8, 1-63810-5, Wrldwide Lib) Harlequin Bks.

Undercover Washington: Touring the Sites Where Famous Spies Lived, Worked, & Loved. Pamela Kessler. LC 91-47883. (Illus.). 159p. 1992. pap. 9.95 (0-939009-60-9) EPM Pubns.

Undercover Work: A Complete Handbook. Burt Rapp. LC 85-82011. 152p. (Orig.). 1985. pap. 14.95 (0-915179-32-6) Loompanics.

Undercurrent. Lisa Harris. (Temptation Ser.). 1994. mass mkt. 2.99 (0-373-25585-3, 1-25585-0) Harlequin Bks.

Undercurrent of Suspicion: Anti-Communism in America During World War II. George Sirgiovanni. 288p. 1989. 44.95 (0-88738-122-7) Transaction Pubs.

Undercurrents. Ridley Pearson. 1992. mass mkt. 6.50 (0-312-92958-7) Tor Bks.

Undercurrents: A Therapist's Reckoning with Depression. Martha Manning. LC 94-33043. 208p. 1995. pap. 12.00 (0-06-251184-X) Harper SF.

Undercurrents in the Floating World: Censorship & Japanese Prints. Sarah E. Thompson & H. D. Harootunian. LC 91-58105. (Illus.). 112p. 1992. pap. 25.00 (0-87848-074-9, U of Wash Pr) Asia Soc.

Undercurrents of Influence in English Romantic Poetry. Margaret P. Sherwood. LC 68-26474. (Essay Index Reprint Ser.). 1977. 23.95 (0-8369-0875-9) Ayer.

Undercurrents of Influence in English Romantic Poetry. Margaret P. Sherwood. LC 70-155612. reprint ed. 24.50 (0-404-05959-7) AMS Pr.

***Undercutting in Worms & Worm-Gears.** John R. Colbourne. (1993 Fall Technical Meeting). 1993. pap. text ed. 30.00 (1-55589-594-8) AGMA.

Underdeveloped Areas Within the Common Market. Sergio Barzanti. LC 65-10822. 447p. reprint ed. pap. 127.40 (0-8357-7064-8, 2052289) Bks Demand.

Underdeveloping the Amazon: Extraction, Unequal Exchange, & the Failure of the Modern State. Stephen G. Bunker. (Illus.). xvi, 294p. 1988. pap. text ed. 17.95 (0-226-08032-3) U Ch Pr.

Underdeveloping the Amazon: Extraction, Unequal Exchange, & the Failure of the Modern State. Stephen G. Bunker. LC 83-18197. 296p. 1985. text ed. 29.95 (0-252-01121-X) U of Ill Pr.

Underdevelopment & Economic Growth: Studies in Hungarian Social & Economic History. T. I. Berend & Gyorgy Ranki. 300p. 1979. 75.00 (0-614-11814-X, Pub. by Akad Kiado HU) St Mut.

Underdevelopment & Economic Growth Studies in Hungarian Social & Economic History. T. I. Berend & Gyorgy Ranki. 300p. (C). 1979. 75.00 (963-05-1754-X, Pub. by Akad Kiado HU) St Mut.

Underdevelopment & Health Care in Africa: The Ghanaian Experience. Randolph Quaye. LC 95-687. 188p. 1996. text ed. 79.95 (0-7734-2254-4, Mellen Univ Pr) E Mellen.

Underdevelopment & Spatial Inequality: Approaches to the Problems of Regional Planning in the Third World see Progress in Planning

Underdevelopment & the Development of Law: Corporations & Corporation Law in Nineteenth Century Colombia. Robert C. Means. LC 79-23936. (Studies in Legal History). 350p. reprint ed. pap. 99.80 (0-8357-3894-9, 2036626) Bks Demand.

Underdevelopment in Kenya: The Political Economy of Neo-Colonialism, 1964-1971. Colin T. Leys. LC 74-76387. 1975. pap. 17.00 (0-520-02770-1) U CA Pr.

Underdevelopment Is a State of Mind: The Latin American Case. Lawrence E. Harrison. 210p. (Orig.). (C). 1988. 31.00 (0-8191-4685-4) U Pr of Amer.

Underdevelopment of Development: For Andre Gunder Frank & Beyond. Ed. by Sing C. Chew & Robert A. Denemark. 427p. 1996. 58.00 (0-8039-7260-1); pap. 27.95 (0-8039-7261-X) Sage.

Underdevelopment of Political Economy. Martin Staniland. (CISA Working Papers: No. 32). 54p. (Orig.). 1981. pap. 15.00 (0-86682-031-0) Ctr Intl Relations.

Underdevelopment State & Mode of Production in Bangladesh: A Sociological Outline. Hasanuzzaman Chowdhury. 120p. 1986. 12.50 (0-8364-1561-2, Pub. by Minerva II) S Asia.

Underdog. Laurien Berenson. 320p. 1996. 18.95 (1-57566-011-3) Kensgtn Pub Corp.

Underdog. Laurien Berenson. 1996. pap. 16.95 (0-8217-5224-3) NAL-Dutton.

Underdog. Laurien Berenson. 336p. 1996. mass mkt. 4.99 (1-57566-108-X, Knsington) Kensgtn Pub Corp.

Underdog. Michael Z. Lewin. 272p. 1993. 18.95 (0-89296-440-5) Mysterious Pr.

Underdog. Michael Z. Lewin. 256p. 1995. mass mkt. 5.50 (0-446-40436-5, Mysterious Paperbk) Warner Bks.

Underdog & Other Stories. Agatha Christie. 224p. 1984. pap. text ed. 5.50 (0-425-06808-0) Berkley Pub.

Underdog Appeal. Vladimir Volkoff. 229p. 1984. 14.95 (0-914707-02-7) Ren Pr GA.

Underdog Marketing: Successful Strategies for Out Marketing the Leader. Edmund O. Lawler. 1995. 19.95 (1-57101-053-X) MasterMedia Pub.

Underdoggerels. Eric Felderman. LC 90-42600. (Illus.). 101p. (Orig.). 1991. pap. 15.95 (0-945942-08-7) Portmanteau Editions.

Underdogs. Mariano Azuela. Tr. by Frederick H. Fornoff. LC 92-10582. (Latin American Ser.). 184p. (ENG & SPA.). (C). 1992. 49.95 (0-8229-3728-X); pap. text ed. 14.95 (0-8229-5484-2) U of Pittsburgh Pr.

Underdogs. Mariano Azuela. 1996. pap. 4.95 (0-451-52625-2, Sig Classics) NAL-Dutton.

Underdogs. Mariano Azuelo. Tr. by E. Munguia, Jr. (Orig.). pap. 3.50 (0-451-52102-1, CE1741, Sig Classics) NAL-Dutton.

Underdogs. Mariano Azuela. 160p. 1986. reprint ed. lib. bdg. 18.95 (0-89966-515-2) Buccaneer Bks.

Underdraining of Farmland in England During the Nineteenth Century. A. D. Phillips. (Cambridge Studies in Historical Geography: No. 15). (Illus.). 334p. (C). 1989. text ed. 69.95 (0-521-36444-2) Cambridge U Pr.

Undereducation in America: The Demography of High School Dropouts. Dorothy Waggoner. LC 91-3980. 256p. 1991. text ed. 49.95 (0-86569-043-X, T043, Auburn Hse) Greenwood.

Undereducation of American Youth. Jose A. Cardenas et al. (Illus.). 24p. (Orig.). 1988. pap. text ed. 6.00 (1-878550-02-0) Inter Dev Res Assn.

Underemployment Equilibria: Essays in Theory, Econometrics & Policy. Jacques H. Dreze. (Illus.). 583p. (C). 1991. text ed. 80.00 (0-521-39318-3) Cambridge U Pr.

Underemployment Equilibria: Essays in Theory, Econometrics & Policy. Jacques H. Dreze. (Illus.). 583p. (C). 1993. pap. text ed. 30.95 (0-521-43524-2) Cambridge U Pr.

Underemployment from a Human Perspective. David P. Meyer. 63p. 1985. 6.25 (0-317-01303-3, IN303) Ctr Educ Trng Employ.

***Underfoot.** Jocasta Innes. (Around the House Ser.). 1997. 12.95 (0-8212-2452-2) Bulfinch Pr.

Underfoot. David Kopaska-Merkel. (Illus.). 44p. (Orig.). 1992. pap. 3.00 (0-926935-60-7) Runaway Spoon.

***Underfoot.** David M. Schwartz. (Look Once, Look Again! Ser.: Vol. 2). (Illus.). 16p. (Orig.). 1997. pap. 2.99 (1-57471-210-1, 3002) Creat Teach Pr.

Underfoot: A Geologic Guide to the Appalachian Trail. 2nd ed. V. Collins Chew. LC 93-4652. (Illus.). 272p. 1993. 12.95 (0-917953-59-2) Appalachian Trail.

Underfoot in Show Business. Helene Hanff. 192p. 1996. reprint ed. pap. 11.95 (1-55921-017-6) Moyer Bell.

Underglaze Soft Sculpture. Jean Kristofer. LC 86-63579. 52p. 1986. pap. text ed. 8.95 (0-916809-15-3) Scott Pubns MI.

Undergraduate Algebra. Serge A. Lang. (Undergraduate Texts in Mathematics Ser.). (Illus.). 250p. 1986. 36.00 (0-387-96404-5) Spr-Verlag.

Undergraduate Algebra. 2nd ed. Serge A. Lang. Ed. by J. H. Ewing et al. (Undergraduate Texts in Mathematics Ser.). (Illus.). xi, 367p. 1994. 43.95 (0-387-97279-X) Spr-Verlag.

Undergraduate Algebra: A First Course. C. W. Norman. 400p. 1986. 39.95 (0-19-853249-0) OUP.

Undergraduate Algebraic Geometry. M. Reid. (London Mathematical Society Student Texts Ser.: No. 12). (Illus.). 120p. 1989. pap. text ed. 19.95 (0-521-35662-8) Cambridge U Pr.

Undergraduate Almanac: A Low Life Guide to Higher Education. Jon Sbar. (Illus.). 200p. (Orig.). 1992. pap. 9.95 (0-9631672-7-8) Crazed Rodent.

Undergraduate Analysis. 2nd ed. Serge A. Lang. LC 96-26339. (Undergraduate Texts in Mathematics Ser.). 656p. 1996. 54.95 (0-387-94841-4) Spr-Verlag.

Undergraduate Analysis, Vol. XIII. rev. ed. Serge A. Lang. Ed. by J. H. Ewing et al. (Undergraduate Texts in Mathematics Ser.). (Illus.). 545p. (C). 1996. 45.00 (0-387-90800-5) Spr-Verlag.

Undergraduate Career Decisions: Correlates of Occupational Choice. James A. Davis. LC 64-15604. (Monographs in Social Research: No. 2). (Illus.). 1965. 9.95 (0-202-09007-8) Natl Opinion Res.

Undergraduate Commutative Algebra. Miles Reid. (London Mathematical Society Student Texts Ser.: No. 29). (Illus.). 128p. (C). 1996. text ed. 59.95 (0-521-45255-4) Cambridge U Pr.

Undergraduate Commutative Algebra. Miles Reid. (London Mathematical Society Student Texts Ser.: No. 29). (Illus.). 128p. (C). 1996. pap. text ed. 19.95 (0-521-45889-7) Cambridge U Pr.

***Undergraduate Econometrics.** R. Carter Hill et al. LC 96-44704. 400p. 1997. text ed. write for info. (0-471-13993-9) Wiley.

Undergraduate Education. Rudolph H. Weingartner. 1991. lib. bdg. 27.95 (0-02-897455-7) Macmillan.

Undergraduate Education: Goals & Means. Rudolph H. Weingartner. LC 92-42399. (American Council on Education-Oryx Press Series on Higher Education). 176p. 1991. reprint ed. boxed 27.95 (0-89774-807-7) Oryx Pr.

***Undergraduate Education in Cancer in the European Region: Report on a UICC/WHO Meeting.** (Euro Reports & Studies Ser.: No. 49). 30p. 1981. pap. text ed. 4.00 (92-890-1215-3) World Health.

Undergraduate Engineering Laboratory. Ed. by Edward W. Ernst. LC 83-82477. 226p. (Orig.). 1983. pap. 40.00 (0-939204-21-5, 83-14) Eng Found.

Undergraduate Instrumental Analysis. 5th expanded rev. ed. James W. Robinson. LC 94-21455. 888p. 1994. 65.00 (0-8247-9215-7) Dekker.

Undergraduate Medical Education & the Elective System: Experience with the Duke Curriculum, 1966-75. Ed. by James F. Gifford. LC 77-84615. 257p. reprint ed. pap. 73.30 (0-317-26746-9, 2023383) Bks Demand.

Undergraduate Obstetrics & Gynecology. 2nd ed. M. G. R. Hull et al. 336p. 1986. pap. text ed. 25.00 (0-7506-0398-4) Buttrwrth-Heinemann.

Undergraduate Obstetrics & Gynecology. 3rd ed. Michael Hull et al. LC 96-24741. 467p. 1996. pap. 50.00 (0-7506-1351-3) Buttrwrth-Heinemann.

Undergraduate Origins of Recent Science & Engineering Doctorate Recipients. Susan T. Hill. (Illus.). 51p. (Orig.). (C). 1993. pap. text ed. 25.00 (1-56806-473-X) DIANE Pub.

Undergraduate Papers (Eighteen Fifty-Seven to Eighteen Fifty-Eight) An Oxford Journal Conducted by A. C. Swinburne. LC 74-12387. 220p. 1974. lib. bdg. 50.00 (0-8201-1134-1) Schol Facsimiles.

Undergraduate Physical Education Programs: Issues & Approaches. Ed. by Hal A. Lawson. 112p. reprint ed. pap. 32.00 (0-685-15769-5, 2026622) Bks Demand.

Undergraduate Program Field Test Series. Jack Rudman. 1994. pap. write for info. (0-8373-6000-5) Nat Learn.

Undergraduate Reasearcher's Handbook: Creative Experimentation in Social Psychology. Ralph J. McKenna. LC 94-32870. 1995. pap. text ed. 36.00 (0-205-15537-5) Allyn.

Undergraduate Social Work Education: Today & Tomorrow. 1972. 3.10 (0-318-35379-2) Coun Soc Wk Ed.

Undergraduate Tuition & Fees: Trends 1977 to 1986. Ed. & Intro. by John Minter. 250p. 1987. lib. bdg. 95.00 (0-937767-31-X) Nat Data Service.

Undergraduate Urology. Tolley. Date not set. pap. write for info. (0-7506-1387-4) Buttrwrth-Heinemann.

Underground. Mary M. Douglas. LC 96-998. 124p. (Orig.). 1996. spiral bd., pap. 26.50 (0-9643764-4-X) Wildot Pr.

Underground. David Macaulay. (Illus.). (J). (gr. 1 up). 1976. 16.95 (0-395-24739-X) HM.

Underground. David Macaulay. (Illus.). (J). (gr. 1 up). 1983. pap. 8.95 (0-395-34065-9) HM.

Underground. Moore. 1995. 24.95 (0-8057-9113-2, Twayne) Scribnrs Ref.

Underground. large type ed. Russell James. (Mystery Ser.). 416p. 1992. 25.99 (0-7089-2641-X) Ulverscroft.

Underground. 2nd ed. Corrinne Hales. Ed. by Dale K. Boyer. LC 85-72151. (Ahsahta Press Modern & Contemporary Poets of the West Ser.). 60p. (Orig.). 1986. pap. 6.95 (0-916272-30-3) Ahsahta Pr.

Underground! A Novel. Emil Hoffman. 10.95 (957-586-110-8, Pub. by Bookman Bks CC) Bookman Bks.

Underground: The London Alternative Press, 1966-74. Nigel Fountain. (Comedia Bk.). 350p. 1988. pap. text ed. 13.95 (0-415-00728-3) Routledge.

***Underground: The Shanghai Communist Party & the Politics of Survival, 1927-1937.** Patricia Stranahan. 240p. 1998. 62.00 (0-8476-8722-8) Rowman.

***Underground: The Shanghai Communist Party & the Politics of Survival, 1927-1937.** Patricia Stranahan. 240p. 1998. pap. 22.95 (0-8476-8723-6) Rowman.

***Underground & Other Upstate Tales: Freedom's Road.** Arch Merrill. (Illus.). 182p. Date not set. reprint ed. pap. 12.95 (0-932771-50-5) Creek.

Underground Architecture: How to Build an Underground House at Low Cost. 1991. lib. bdg. 76.95 (0-8490-4668-8) Gordon Pr.

Underground Armoured Cable Protected Against Solvent Penetration & Corrosive Attack. (C). 1988. 150.00 (0-685-54763-9, Pub. by EEMUA UK) St Mut.

Underground Armoured Cable Protected Against Solvent Penetration & Corrosive Attack. EEMUA Staff. 1988. 125.00 (0-85931-142-2, Pub. by EEMUA UK) St Mut.

Underground Army. Chaika Grossman. 1988. 18.95 (0-89604-053-4, Holocaust Library) US Holocaust.

Underground Army: Fighters of the Bialystok Ghetto. Grossman. 1988. pap. 10.95 (0-89604-054-2, Holocaust Library) US Holocaust.

Underground Bases & Tunnels: What Is the Government Trying to Hide? (Illus.). 218p. (Orig.). 1996. pap. 15.95 (0-932813-37-2) Adventures Unltd.

Underground Blue Book: A Guide to Buying & Selling New & Used Cars, Trucks & R. V.'s. Lee. 136p. (Orig.). 1987. pap. 9.95 (0-9617946-0-7) Diamond S Pub.

Underground Businesses. 1992. lib. bdg. 255.95 (0-8490-8891-7) Gordon Pr.

Underground Cable Thermal Backfill: Proceedings. Symposium on Underground Cable Thermal Backfill, Toronto, Ont., Canada, Sept. 1981. Ed. by S. A. Boggs et al. (Illus.). 248p. 1982. 33.00 (0-08-025393-8, Pergamon Pr) Elsevier.

Underground Cannabis Library. Adam Gottlieb. (Orig.). 1995. pap. 17.95 (0-914171-71-2) Ronin Pub.

Underground Collective. Lawrence R. Sims. (Illus.). 96p. (Orig.). (YA). 1996. pap. 11.95 (1-889155-12-8, ODS3100) Optimus Design.

Underground Communion Rail. Susan Firer. 58p. (Orig.). 1992. pap. 8.95 (0-931122-72-4) West End.

***Underground Companion.** Mayfair Games Staff. 1994. 18.00 (1-56905-065-1) Mayfair Games.

Underground Construction in Soft Ground: Proceedings of the International Symposium, New Delhi, 3 January 1994. Osamu Kusakabe. Ed. by K. Fujita. (Illus.). 384p. (C). 1995. text ed. 125.00 (90-5410-536-4, Pub. by A A Balkema NE) Ashgate Pub Co.

Underground Corrosion. LC 89-63212. (Illus.). 227p. 1989. 66.00 (0-915567-47-4) NACE Intl.

Underground Corrosion - STP 741. Ed. by E. Escalante. 210p. 1990. 26.00 (0-8031-0703-X, 04-741000-27) ASTM.

Underground Corrosion Control. Ed. by B. Lewis et al. (Illus.). 1993. 78.00 (1-877914-48-7) NACE Intl.

Underground Crossing for Europe: Proceedings of an International Conference, Lille, 16 - 18 October 1990. Ed. by M. Legrand. (Illus.). 372p. (C). 1990. text ed. 125.00 (90-6191-157-5, Pub. by A A Balkema NE) Ashgate Pub Co.

Underground Database. Index Pub Group Staff. LC 10-690654. (Electronic Underground Ser.: Vol. 1). 102p. (Orig.). 1993. pap. 23.75 (1-56866-043-X) Index Pub Grp.

Underground Economics: A Decade of Institutionalist Dissent. William M. Dugger. LC 90-19792. (Studies in Institutional Economics). 404p. (gr. 13). 1991. text ed. 75.95 (0-87332-799-3) M E Sharpe.

U V

An Asterisk (*) at the beginning of an entry indicates that the title is appearing in BIP for the first time.

Underground Economies. Ed. by Edgar L. Feige. (Illus.). 400p. 1989. text ed. 74.95 (0-521-26230-5) Cambridge U Pr.

Underground Economy: An Annotated Bibliography. Nancy K. Humphreys. (CompuBibs Ser.: No. 9). 75p. 1985. pap. 15.00 (0-914791-08-7) Vantage Info.

*Underground Education: The Unauthorized & Outrageous Supplement to Everything You Thought You Knew about Art, Business, Crime, Science, Medicine & Other Fields of Human Knowledge. Richard Zacks. LC 97-10892. 1997. write for info. (0-385-47994-8) Doubleday.

Underground Engineering: Proceedings of an International Symposium, New Delhi, April, 1988, 2 vols. 1000p. (C). 1988. Set. text ed. 175.00 (90-6191-926-6, Pub. by A A Balkema NE) Ashgate Pub Co.

*Underground Excavations in Rock: Published for the Institution of Mining & Metallurgy by Elsevier Applied Science. E. Hoek & Brown. (Illus.). 532p. (Orig.). 1980. pap. text ed. 64.00 (0-419-16030-2, E & FN Spon) Routledge Chapman & Hall.

Underground Film: A Critical History. Parker Tyler. (Illus.). 287p. 1995. reprint ed. pap. 13.95 (0-306-80632-0) Da Capo.

Underground Frequency Guide: A Directory of Unusual, Illegal, & Covert Radio Communications. Donald W. Schimmel. 200p. 1994. pap. 14.95 (1-878707-17-5) HighText.

Underground Gas Storage Facilities: Design & Implementation. Orin Flanigan. 180p. 1995. 85.00 (0-88415-204-9, 5204) Gulf Pub.

*Underground Gourmet: European. Joseph Raff. Date not set. write for info. (0-688-05389-0) Morrow.

Underground Government: The Off-Budget Public Sector. James T. Bennett & Thomas J. DiLorenzo. 184p. 1983. pap. 3.00 (0-932790-37-2) Cato Inst.

Underground Guide to Color Printing. M. David Stone. (C). 1996. pap. text ed. 24.95 (0-201-48378-5) Addison-Wesley.

Underground Guide to Communcations & Modems. M. David Stone. 1996. pap. write for info. (0-201-40891-0) Addison-Wesley.

Underground Guide to Computer Security: Slightly Askew Advice on Protecting Your PC & What Is on It. Michael Alexander. LC 95-40661. (Underground Guide Ser.). 239p. (C). 1996. pap. text ed. 19.95 (0-201-48918-X) Addison-Wesley.

Underground Guide to Excel 5.0 for Windows: Slightly Askew Advice from Two Excel Wizards. Lee Hudspeth & Timothy-James Lee. LC 94-34330. 1994. pap. 19.95 (0-201-40651-9) Addison-Wesley.

Underground Guide to Laser Printers. Flash Magazine Editorial Staff. (Illus.). 176p. (Orig.). 1993. pap. 12.00 (1-56609-045-8) Peachpit Pr.

Underground Guide to Microsoft Internet Assistant: Master the Web with WinWord. Eileen Wharmby. LC 95-45781. 1996. pap. 16.95 incl. cd-rom (0-201-48944-9) Addison-Wesley.

Underground Guide to Microsoft Office, OLE & VBA: Slightly Askew Advice from Two Integration Wizards. Lee Hudspeth & Timothy-James Lee. LC 95-11546. (Underground Guide Ser.). 352p. 1995. pap. 24.95 (0-201-41035-4) Addison-Wesley.

Underground Guide to PC Hardware. Alfred Poor. 1996. pap. 19.95 (0-201-48997-X) Addison-Wesley.

Underground Guide to San Francisco. Ed. by Jennifer Joseph. 195p. (Orig.). 1995. pap. 10.95 (0-916397-39-4) Manic D Pr.

*Underground Guide to Teenage Sexuality. 2nd rev. ed. Michael J. Basso. LC 96-48166. (Illus.). 256p. (Orig.). (YA). 1997. reprint ed. pap. 14.95 (1-57749-034-7) Fairview Press.

Underground Guide to Telecommuting: Slightly Askew Advice on Leaving the Rat Race Behind. Woody Leonhard. LC 95-9089. (Underground Guide Ser.). 1995. pap. 24.95 (0-201-48343-2) Addison-Wesley.

Underground Guide to University Study in Britain & Ireland. Bill Griesar. LC 91-45425. 240p. (Orig.). 1992. pap. 7.95 (1-877864-03-X) Intercult Pr.

Underground Guide to UNIX: Slightly Askew Advice from a UNIX Guru. John Montgomery. 368p. (C). 1995. pap. text ed. 24.95 (0-201-40653-5) Addison-Wesley.

Underground Guide to Windows 95: Slighlty Askew Advice from a Windows Wizard. Finnie Scot. 448p. (C). 1996. pap. text ed. 24.95 (0-201-40652-7) Addison-Wesley.

Underground Guide to Word for Windows: Slightly Askew Advice from a Winword Wizard. Woody Leonhard. 1994. pap. 19.95 (0-201-40650-0) Addison-Wesley.

Underground Harmonies: Music & Politics in the Subways of New York. Susie J. Tanenbaum. (Anthropology of Contemporary Issues Ser.). (Illus.). 256p. 1995. 37.50 (0-8014-3051-8); pap. 14.95 (0-8014-8222-4) Cornell U Pr.

Underground Hero. Elaine K. McEwan. LC 92-27104. 96p. (J). (gr. 3-6). 1993. pap. 4.99 (0-7814-0113-5, Chariot Bks) Chariot Victor.

Underground Homes. 1991. lib. bdg. 250.00 (0-8490-4735-8) Gordon Pr.

Underground Homes. rev. ed. Louis Wampler. LC 80-18701. (Illus.). 121p. 1980. pap. 9.95 (0-88289-273-8) Pelican.

Underground Humour in Nazi Germany, 1933-1945. F. K. Hillenbrand. LC 94-6069. (Illus.). 240p. (C). 1995. 49.95 (0-415-09785-1, B3431) Routledge.

Underground Kids. Shusterman. (J). 1998. 17.00 (0-689-80375-3) S&S Childrens.

Underground Lawyer. Michael L. Minns. Ed. by L. R. Robertson & Gene Nail. (Illus.). 625p. (C). 1989. 29.95 (0-929801-00-8) Gopher Pubns.

Underground Leakage of Flammable & Combustible Liquids. (Thirty Ser.). 26p. 1992. pap. 20.25 (0-685-46064-9, 329-92) Natl Fire Prot.

Underground Literature During the Emergency, India. Sajal Bose. 1978. 10.00 (0-8364-0034-8) S Asia.

Underground Man. J. P. Hailey. (C). 1994. pap. 4.99 (0-8125-5011-0) Tor Bks.

Underground Man. Ross MacDonald. 1996. pap. 11.00 (0-679-76808-4, Vin) Random.

Underground Man. Milton Meltzer. LC 90-36277. 224p. (J). (gr. 3-7). 1990. pap. 5.00 (0-15-292846-4, Gulliver Bks) HarBrace.

*Underground Man. unabridged ed. Mick Jackson. LC 97-12456. 272p. 1997. 22.00 (0-688-15449-2) Morrow.

Underground Man. Edward F. Abood. LC 72-97331. 189p. 1973. reprint ed. pap. 11.95 (0-88316-048-X) Chandler & Sharp.

Underground Man & Raskolnikov: A Comparative Study. Preben Villadsen. (Odense Slavic Studies: No. 3). 159p. (Orig.). 1981. pap. 24.00 (87-7492-326-9, Pub. by Odense Universitets Forlag DK) Coronet Bks.

Underground Military Command Bunkers of Zossen, Germany: History of Their Construction & Use by the Wehrmacht & Soviet Army 1937-1994. Hans G. Kampe. (Illus.). 48p. 1996. pap. 9.95 (0-7643-0164-0) Schiffer.

Underground Missouri. Bruce Carlson. (Illus.). 172p. (Orig.). 1991. pap. 9.95 (1-878488-47-3) Quixote Pr IA.

*Underground Notebook. Mayfair Games Staff. 1993. 30.00 (0-923763-91-0) Mayfair Games.

Underground Notes. 2nd ed. Mihajlo Mihajlov et al. Tr. by Maria M. Ivusic & Christopher Ivusic from CRO. LC 80-65723. 208p. 1982. reprint ed. pap. 6.95 (0-89241-131-7); reprint ed. lib. bdg. 20.00 (0-89241-132-5) Caratzas.

Underground Office Humor: Real Memos, Rude Faxes, Tasteless Jokes & Eye-Popping True Stories from the Workplace. Compiled by S. E. Mills. LC 94-20043. 1994. 9.95 (0-8065-1567-8, Citadel Pr) Carol Pub Group.

Underground Piping Handbook. L. A. Peggs. LC 83-19906. 296p. 1985. lib. bdg. 32.50 (0-89874-616-7) Krieger.

Underground Plastic Pipe. ASCE Pipeline Division, New Orleans, March, 1981. Ed. by B. J. Schrock. LC 81-65630. 553p. 1981. pap. 41.00 (0-87262-265-7) Am Soc Civil Eng.

Underground Power Cables. S. Y. King & N. A. Halfter. LC 81-15657. (Illus.). 427p. reprint ed. pap. 121.70 (0-8357-2990-7, 2039253) Bks Demand.

Underground Power Cables: Some Aspects of Their Thermal Environment. S. Y. King & N. A. Halfter. LC 77-377295. (Illus.). 197p. reprint ed. pap. 56.20 (0-8357-6665-9, 2035333) Bks Demand.

Underground Press in America. Robert J. Glessing. LC 84-6521. (Illus.). xvi, 207p. 1984. reprint ed. text ed. 55.00 (0-313-24450-2, GLUP, Greenwood Pr) Greenwood.

Underground Railroad. Raymond Bial. LC 94-19614. (Illus.). 48p. (J). (gr. 3-7). 1995. 16.00 (0-395-69937-1) HM.

Underground Railroad. R. Conrad Stein. LC 96-24122. (Cornerstones of Freedom Bks.). (J). 1997. lib. bdg. 18.00 (0-516-20298-7) Childrens.

*Underground Railroad. R. Conrad Stein. 1997. pap. 4.95 (0-516-26140-1) Childrens.

Underground Railroad. William Still. LC 74-102982. (Ebony Classics Ser.). (Illus.). 812p. 1970. 10.50 (0-87485-033-9) Johnson Chi.

Underground Railroad. Doug Wilhelm. (Choose Your Own Adventure Ser.: No. 175). 128p. (YA). (gr. 5 up). 1996. pap. 3.50 (0-553-56744-6, Choose) BDD Bks Young Read.

Underground Railroad. William Still. LC 68-29019. (American Negro: His History & Literature. Series 1). (Illus.). 1977. reprint ed. 63.95 (0-405-01838-X) Ayer.

Underground Railroad, Vol. 3. Sally Marcey. (Choice Adventures Ser.: Vol. 3). (J). (gr. 3-7). 1991. pap. 4.99 (0-8423-5027-6) Tyndale.

Underground Railroad: A Play in Three Acts. Karin L. Badt. 20p. (Orig.). (J). (gr. 5-9). 1995. wbk. ed., pap. 10.00 (1-878668-58-7) Disc Enter Ltd.

Underground Railroad: Dramatic Firsthand Accounts of Daring Escapes to Freedom. Charles L. Blockson. 304p. 1994. pap. 10.00 (0-425-14136-5, Berkley Trade) Berkley Pub.

Underground Railroad: Life on the Road to Freedom. Intro. by Ellen Hansen. LC 93-72239. (Perspectives on History Ser.). (Illus.). 64p. (Orig.). (YA). (gr. 5-12). 1993. pap. 5.95 (1-878668-27-7) Disc Enter Ltd.

*Underground Railroad Back to America: A True Story. Phyllis Christian-Omoyale. LC 96-90479. (Orig.). 1997. pap. 8.95 (0-533-12063-2) Vantage.

Underground Railroad from Slavery to Freedom. Wilbur H. Siebert. LC 68-29016. (American Negro: His History & Literature. Series 1). 1974. reprint ed. 21.95 (0-405-01835-5) Ayer.

Underground Railroad from Slavery to Freedom. Wilbur H. Siebert. (History - United States Ser.). 478p. 1992. reprint ed. lib. bdg. 99.00 (0-7812-6163-5) Rprt Serv.

*Underground Railroad in American History. Sawyer K. Knapp. LC 96-30901. (In American History Ser.). (Illus.). 128p. (YA). (gr. 5 up). 1997. lib. bdg. 18.95 (0-89490-885-5) Enslow Pubs.

Underground Railroad in Montgomery County, Maryland: A History & Driving Guide. rev. ed. Anthony Cohen. 38p. 1995. pap. text ed. 7.00 (0-9601094-0-4) Montgomery Co Hist.

Underground Railroad in Ohio. Wilbur H. Siebert. (Ohio History, Afro-American, Slavery Ser.). (Illus.). 24p. (C). 1993. reprint ed. pap. 2.60 (1-56651-098-8) A W McGraw.

Underground Railroad in Pennsylvania. Charles L. Blockson. LC 80-69847. (Illus.). 225p. 1981. 13.95 (0-933184-21-2); pap. 6.95 (0-933184-22-0) Flame Intl.

*Underground Railroad Tales with Routes Through the Finger Lakes Region. Emerson Klees. LC 97-60426. (Illus.). 184p. (YA). (gr. 7-12). 1997. pap. 17.00 (0-9635990-8-9) Frnds Finger Lks.

Underground Reservation: Osage Oil. Terry P. Wilson. LC 84-26974. 279p. 1985. pap. 79.60 (0-7837-8445-7, 2049250) Bks Demand.

Underground River & Other Stories. Ines Arredondo. Tr. by Cynthia Steele. LC 95-37585. xxiii, 130p. 1996. pap. 12.00 (0-8032-5927-1, Bison Books); text ed. 30.00 (0-8032-1034-5) U of Nebr Pr.

Underground Rock Chambers: Symposium Held During the ASCE National Meeting on Water Resources Engineering, Phoenix, Arizona, Jan. 13-14, 1971. American Society of Chemical Engineers, Underground Rock Chambers Symposium Staff. LC 78-322140. 606p. reprint ed. pap. 172.80 (0-317-08299-X, 2019554) Bks Demand.

Underground Sax Quartet. J. Hartog. 1995. pap. text ed. 20.00 (0-7935-4818-7, 00000640) H Leonard.

*Underground Service Reservoirs: Waterproofing & Repair Manual. Construction Industry Research Staff. 168p. 1996. 99.80 (0-7277-2095-3) Am Soc Civil Eng.

Underground Shadows. Valery Oistenau. 1977. pap. 1.50 (0-9601870-0-6) Pass.

Underground Shopper: Nineteen Ninety-Two Dallas - Ft. Worth Edition. rev. ed. Sue Goldstein. (Illus.). 1992. reprint ed. pap. 6.99 (1-879524-01-5) Great Buys.

Underground Siting of Nuclear Power Plants: Internationales Symposium, 1981. F. Bender. (Illus.). 416p. (ENG & GER.). 1982. 120.00 (3-510-65108-1, Pub. by Schweizerbartsche GW) Lubrecht & Cramer.

Underground Space Design: A Guide to Subsurface Utilization & Design for People in Underground Spaces. John Carmody & Ray Sterling. LC 92-33460. 1993. text ed. 69.95 (0-442-01383-3) Van Nos Reinhold.

*Underground Storage of Natural Gas. Mehmet R. Tek. LC 86-32017. (Contributions in Petroleum Geology & Engineering Ser.: Vol. 3). (Illus.). 399p. reprint ed. pap. 113.80 (0-608-04539-X, 2065281) Bks Demand.

Underground Storage of Natural Gas: Proceedings of the NATO Advanced Study Institute Held in Ankara, Turkey 2-10 May, 1988. M. Rasin Tek. (C). 1989. lib. bdg. 198.00 (0-7923-0338-5) Kluwer Ac.

Underground Storage of Natural Gas & LPG. (ECE Energy Ser.: No. 3). 539p. 1990. 95.00 (92-1-100353-9, GV.90.0.7) UN.

Underground Storage Systems. M. Moreau. (General Engineering Ser.). 1992. text ed. write for info. (0-442-00390-0) Van Nos Reinhold.

Underground Storage Systems - Leak Detection & Monitoring. Todd G. Schwendeman et al. (Illus.). 240p. 1987. 87.95 (0-87371-045-2, L045) Lewis Pubs.

Underground Storage Tank Cleanup: Status & Outlook. 200p. 1995. spiral bd. 225.00 (1-882957-06-7) Environ Info.

Underground Storage Tank Installation Practices. G. Mattney Cole. 192p. 1991. 69.95 (0-87371-596-9, L596) Lewis Pubs.

Underground Storage Tank Liability. Ed. by Diana Kowatch. 55p. 1996. 10.00 (1-56461-167-1) Rough Notes.

Underground Storage Tank Management: A Practical Guide. 4th ed. Joyce A. Rizzo. (Illus.). 420p. 1991. pap. 89.00 (0-86587-271-6) Gov Insts.

Underground Storage Tank Management: Closure & Financial Assurance. Janet E. Robinson. 320p. 1993. 70.00 (0-87371-402-4, L402) Lewis Pubs.

Underground Storage Tanks. Richard K. Miller & Marcia E. Rupnow. (Survey on Technology & Markets Ser.: No. 214). 50p. 1994. pap. text ed. 200.00 (1-55865-245-0) Future Tech Surveys.

Underground Storage Tanks. Richard K. Miller & Terri C. Walker. 226p. 1991. 285.00 (0-89671-120-X) SEAI Tech Pubns.

Underground Storage Tanks Handbook. Paul N. Cheremisinoff. (Illus.). 400p. 1991. text ed. 59.95 (0-925760-56-0) SciTech Pubs.

Underground Storage Tanks Management. Pollution Engineering Staff. 136p. 1994. 29.95 (0-934165-43-2) Gulf Pub.

Underground Stream. Velda Johnston. 1993. mass mkt. 3.99 (0-373-26111-X, 1-26111-4) Harlequin Bks.

Underground Stream: The Life & Art of Caroline Gordon. Nancylee N. Jonza. LC 93-30366. (Illus.). 416p. 1995. 34.95 (0-8203-1628-8) U of Ga Pr.

Underground Structures: Design & Instrumentation. Ed. by R. S. Sinha. (Developments in Geotechnical Engineering Ser.: No. 59A). 460p. 1989. 195.75 (0-444-87462-3) Elsevier.

Underground Structures - Design & Construction. Ed. by R. S. Sinha. (Developments in Geotechnical Engineering Ser.: No. 59B). 530p. 1991. 207.50 (0-444-88991-4) Elsevier.

Underground Systems Reference Book. 592p. 1955. 14.50 (0-317-34113-8, 045516) Edison Electric.

Underground Tank Leak Detection Methods. Shahzad Niaki & John A. Broscious. LC 86-31159. (Pollution Technology Review Ser.: No. 139). (Illus.). 123p. 1987. 36.00 (0-8155-1117-5) Noyes.

Underground Tank Leak Detection Methods: A State-of-the-Art Review. Shahzad Niaki & John A. Broscious. 136p. 1988. 55.95 (0-89116-098-1) Hemisp Pub.

Underground Tea Party. Carol B. Kaplan. Ed. by Janet L. Bolinske. LC 87-62996. (Animal Tales Ser.). (Illus.). 24p. (Orig.). (J). (ps). 1988. pap. 4.95 (0-88335-080-7); spiral bd. 17.95 (0-88335-758-5) Milliken Pub Co.

*Underground Train. Mary Quattlebaum. LC 96-30507. (Illus.). (J). 1997. write for info. (0-385-32204-6) Doubleday.

Underground Transmission of Electric Power. Birron M. Weedy. LC 79-42896. 308p. reprint ed. pap. 87.80 (0-8357-2608-8, 2039928) Bks Demand.

Underground Transportation Infrastructures. 453p. 1993. 140.00 (90-5410-315-9, Pub. by A A Balkema NE) Ashgate Pub Co.

Underground Venus. Tim Kelly & Mark Twain, pseud. 31p. 1996. pap. 3.00 (0-87129-710-8, U23) Dramatic Pub.

Underground Waste Management & Artificial Recharge: Preprints of Papers Presented at the Second International Symposium, 1973, New Orleans, 2 vols., Vol. 1. LC 73-87270. (Illus.). 677p. reprint ed. pap. 160.00 (0-685-24150-5, 2033024) Bks Demand.

Underground Waste Management & Artificial Recharge: Preprints of Papers Presented at the Second International Symposium, 1973, New Orleans, 2 vols., Vol. 2. LC 73-87270. (Illus.). 677p. reprint ed. pap. 71.80 (0-685-24151-3) Bks Demand.

Underground Waters & Subsurface Temperatures of the Woodbine Sand in Northeast Texas. F. B. Plummer & E. C. Sargent. (Bulletin Ser.: BULL 3138). (Illus.). 178p. 1931. pap. 1.00 (0-686-29351-7) Bur Econ Geology.

*Undergrounding Electric Lines. Anthony J. Pansini & Kenneth D. Smalling. 74.00 (0-87814-677-6) PennWell Bks.

Undergrounding Electric Lines. 2nd ed. Anthony J. Pansini & Kenneth D. Smalling. LC 92-41799. 1993. write for info. (0-88173-162-5) PennWell Bks.

Underhill & Hayton: Law Relating to Trusts & Trustees. 14th ed. David J. Hayton. 1987. 290.00 (0-406-40593-X, U.K.) MICHIE.

Underhill & Hayton: Law Relating to Trusts & Trustees. 14th ed. David J. Hayton. 1992. suppl. ed. 45.00 (0-406-00367-X) MICHIE.

*Underhill Genealogy, 4 vols., Vols. I-IV. Ed. by Josephine C. Frost. 2560p. 1996. reprint ed. lib. bdg. 205.00 (0-8328-5455-7) Higginson Bk Co.

Underlay. Barry N. Malzberg. 256p. 1986. pap. 4.95 (0-930330-41-2) Intl Polygonics.

Underlight: Poems. Regina Merzlak. LC 92-44220. 64p. 1993. pap. 12.95 (0-7734-2770-8, Mellen Poetry Pr) E Mellen.

Underlying Molecular, Cellular, & Immunological Factors in Cancer & Aging. Ed. by S. S. Yang. (Advances in Experimental Medicine & Biology Ser.: Vol. 330). (Illus.). 272p. (C). 1993. 95.00 (0-306-44411-9, Plenum Pr) Plenum.

*Undermined Establishment: Church-State Relations in America, 1880-1920. Robert T. Handy. LC 91-10200. (Studies in Church & State). reprint ed. pap. 61.60 (0-608-04584-5, 2065354) Bks Demand.

Undermining Capitalism: State Ownership & the Dialectic of Control in the British Coal Industry. Joel Krieger. LC 83-42563. 334p. 1983. reprint ed. pap. 95.20 (0-7837-9363-4, 2060106) Bks Demand.

*Undermining Gender - Overcoming Sex: Identitat und Autorschaft bei Mary Wilkins Freeman, Edith Wharton und Ellen Glasgow. Marietta Von Lavergne-Peguilhen. (Europaische Hochschulschriften, Reihe 14: Bd. 321). 147p. (GER.). 1997. 35.95 (3-631-30806-X) P Lang Pubng.

Undermining of the Sandinista Revolution. Gary Prevost. 226p. 1997. text ed. 39.95 (0-312-16112-3) St Martin.

Undermining the Centre: The Gulf Migration & Pakistan. Jonathan S. Addleton. 256p. 1992. 45.00 (0-19-577418-3) OUP.

Undermining the Japanese Miracle: Work & Conflict in a Japanese Coalmining Community. Matthew Allen. (Illus.). 360p. (C). 1994. text ed. 57.95 (0-521-45009-8) Cambridge U Pr.

Undermountain Trilogy 2: Maddgot. Steven Schend. 1996. 7.95 (0-7869-0423-2) TSR Inc.

Undermountain Trilogy 3: Stardock. Steven Schend. 1997. 7.95 (0-7869-0451-8) TSR Inc.

Underneath It All. Ed. by Louise Hurren. 80p. (C). 1988. pap. 35.00 (0-7212-0782-0, Pub. by Regency Press UK) St Mut.

Underneath New York. Harry Granick. LC 90-56479. 212p. 1991. pap. 16.95 (0-8232-1312-9) Fordham.

*Underneath Which Rivers Flow: The Symbolism of the Islamic Garden. Emma Clark. 48p. 1996. pap. 16.95 (1-898465-06-1, Pub. by Drake Intl Serv UK) Intl Spec Bk.

*Underpainter. Jane Urquhart. 1997. pap. 22.95 (0-670-87726-3) Viking Penguin.

Underpinning: A Practical Guide. Roger A. Bullivant & H. W. Bradbury. 208p. 1996. text ed. 65.00 (0-632-04004-1) Blackwell Sci.

*Underpinning & Retention. Ed. by Thorburn & Littlejohn. (Illus.). 416p. 1992. text ed. 184.95 (0-7514-0094-7, Pub. by Blackie Acad & Prof UK) Routledge Chapman & Hall.

*Underpinnings of Medical Ethics. Edmond A. Murphy et al. LC 97-1405. 1997. write for info. (0-8018-5568-3) Johns Hopkins.

*Underprivileged Areas & Health Care. 200p. 1997. pap. 18.00 (1-86094-014-5) World Scientific Pub.

Underrepresentation & the Question of Diversity: Women & Minorities in Community Colleges. John Roueche et al. 300p. (C). 1991. text ed. 35.00 (0-87117-225-9, 1316) Am Assn Comm Coll.

Underrunners. Margaret Mahy. 176p. (J). (gr. 5 up). 1994. pap. 3.99 (0-14-036869-8) Puffin Bks.

Underrunners. Margaret Mahy. 192p. (J). (gr. 5-9). 1992. pap. 14.00 (0-670-84179-X) Viking Child Bks.

Underscore. Frank Skinner. 1960. 12.95 (0-910468-09-5) Criterion Mus.

Undersea. Moira Butterfield. (Wildlife World Ser.). (Illus.). 16p. (J). (gr. 1-5). 1992. pap. 6.95 (0-8249-8589-3, Ideals Child) Hambleton-Hill.

U V

Undersea. D. Mackie. (CHP Technology Ser.). (Illus.). 32p. (J). (gr. 4-9). 1987. pap. 5.95 (0-88625-156-7) Durkin Hayes Pub.

*Undersea. Kees Moerbeek. (Open Sesame Bks.). 1997. 10.95 (0-8431-7897-3) Price Stern Sloan.

Undersea. Christopher Pick. (Young Scientist Ser.). (Illus.). 32p. (J). 1976. pap. 6.95 (0-86020-092-2); lib. bdg. 14.95 (0-88110-437-X) EDC.

Undersea Adventure. 35.00 (1-56997-093-9) Knowldge Adv.

Undersea Adventures. Dennis Graham et al. (BrainBooster Ser.). (Illus.). 32p. (J). (gr. 3 up). 1989. 6.95 (0-88679-574-5) Educ Insights.

Undersea Bread: (Three Plays) Vincent Ferrini. 271p. 1989. pap. 12.95 (0-685-33654-9) Univ Conn Lib.

Undersea Britain. Rob Palmer. 160p. (C). 1995. 36.00 (0-907151-52-3, Pub. by IMMEL Pubng UK) St Mut.

*Undersea City: A Story of a Caribbean Coral Reef. Dana M. Rau. LC 96-39099. (Illus.). 36p. (J). (gr. 1-4). 1997. 14.95 (1-56899-433-8); 19.95 incl. digital audio (1-56899-435-4); pap. 5.95 (1-56899-434-6) Soundprints.

*Undersea City: A Story of a Caribbean Coral Reef, Incl. toy. Dana M. Rau. (Illus.). 36p. (J). (gr. 1-4). 1997. 24.95 (1-56899-436-2); write for info. incl. digital audio (1-56899-437-0); pap. 14.95 (1-56899-438-9); pap. write for info. incl. digital audio (1-56899-439-7) Soundprints.

Undersea Discoveries of Jacques-Yves Cousteau, Set. Jacques-Yves Cousteau. 1989. boxed 49.98 (0-88486-017-5) Arrowood Pr.

Undersea Fleet. Frederik Pohl & Jack Williamson. 1982. pap. write for info. (0-345-27552-7) Ballantine.

Undersea Giants. Patrick Geistdoefer. LC 87-34531. (Illus.). 38p. (J). (gr. k-5). 1988. 5.95 (0-944589-02-2, 022) Young Discovery Lib.

Undersea Journey. Jeff Rotman. 1995. 22.98 (0-8317-1038-1) Smithmark.

Undersea Life of America. William Sargent. 1990. 19.99 (0-517-69509-X) Random Hse Value.

Undersea Lightwave Communications. Ed. by Patrick R. Trischitta. LC 86-10670. 644p. 1986. 49.95 (0-87942-201-7, PC01933) Inst Electrical.

*Undersea Magic Window. John Hamburger. (J). Date not set. pap. 4.95 (0-399-21165-9) Putnam Pub Group.

Undersea People. Eve Bunting. (Author's Signature Collection). (Illus.). 64p. (J). (gr. 3-8). 1992. lib. bdg. 12.79 (0-89565-766-X) Childs World.

Undersea Treasures. Emory Kristof. LC 95-17376. (National Geographic Action Bk.). (Illus.). 10p. (J). 1995. 16.00 (0-7922-2977-0) Natl Geog.

Undersea Trilogy. Frederik Pohl & Jack Williamson. 512p. (Orig.). 1992. mass mkt. 5.99 (0-671-72123-2) Baen Bks.

Undersea Vehicles & National Needs. National Research Council Staff. 116p. (Orig.). 1996. pap. text ed. 39.00 (0-309-05384-6) Natl Acad Pr.

Undersea Work Systems. Howard R. Talkington. LC 80-25978. (Ocean Engineering Ser.: No. 1). (Illus.). 179p. reprint ed. pap. 51.10 (0-8357-3580-X, 2034570) Bks Demand.

Undersea World Fact Finders. 1990. 7.99 (0-517-69084-5) Random Hse Value.

Underseas Possessions: Selected Poems. Hans-Juergen Heise. (Modern Poets Ser.: Vol. 1). 1972. pap. 4.95 (0-902675-33-8) Oleander Pr.

Underserved: Our Young Gifted Children. Ed. by Merle B. Karnes. 240p. 1983. pap. text ed. 10.00 (0-86586-147-1, P273) Coun Exc Child.

Undershirts & Other Stories. Cathy Cockrell. 1982. pap. 6.00 (0-914610-30-9) Hanging Loose.

Underside of American History, Vol. I: To 1877. 5th ed. Ed. by Thomas R. Frazier. 482p. (C). 1987. pap. text ed. 19.50 (0-15-592852-X) HB Coll Pubs.

Underside of American History, Vol. II: Since 1865. 5th ed. Ed. by Thomas R. Frazier. 436p. (C). 1987. pap. text ed. 19.50 (0-15-592853-8) HB Coll Pubs.

Underside of High-Tech: Technology & the Deformation of Human Sensibilities. Ed. by John W. Murphy et al. LC 85-27265. (Contributions in Sociology Ser.: No. 59). 226p. 1986. text ed. 59.95 (0-313-24612-2, Greenwood Pr) Greenwood.

Underside of History: A View of Women Through Time, Vol. 1. Elise Boulding. 392p. (C). 1992. 55.00 (0-8039-4768-2); pap. 26.00 (0-8039-4769-0) Sage.

Underside of History: A View of Women Through Time, Vol. 2. Elise Boulding. (Illus.). 372p. 1992. 55.00 (0-8039-4816-6); pap. 26.00 (0-8039-4817-4) Sage.

Underside of Malaysian History: The Pullers, Prostitutes, Plantation Workers. Ed. by Peter J. Rimmer & Lisa M. Allen. 308p. (Orig.). 1990. pap. 39.50 (9971-69-127-2, Pub. by Sgapore Univ SI) Coronet Bks.

Underside of Modernity: Apel, Ricoeur, Rorty, Taylor, & the Philosophy of Liberation. Enrique Dussel. Ed. & Tr. by Eduardo Mendieta. LC 95-32838. 256p. (C). 1996. text ed. 60.00 (0-391-03932-6) Humanities.

Underside of Reconstruction New York: The Struggle Over the Issue of Black Equality. Ena L. Farley. LC 93-20042. (Studies in African American History & Culture). 224p. 1993. Alk. paper. text ed. 56.00 (0-8153-1012-9) Garland.

Undersong: Chosen Poems Old & New. rev. ed. Audre Lorde. 224p. 1992. 19.95 (0-393-03395-3) Norton.

Undersong: Chosen Poems Old & New. rev. ed. Audre Lorde. 224p. 1992. pap. 9.95 (0-393-30975-4) Norton.

Understains: The Sense & Seduction of Advertising. Kathy Myers. (Comedia Bks.). 160p. 1988. pap. text ed. 13.95 (0-906890-98-5, Pub. by Comedia NY) Routledge Chapman & Hall.

Understand & Control Your Asthma. Helene Boutin & Louis-Philippe Boulet. (Illus.). 112p. 1994. 37.95 (0-7735-1210-1, Pub. by McGill CN) U of Toronto Pr.

Understand & Control Your Asthma. Helene Boutin & Louis-Philippe Boulet. (Illus.). 112p. 1995. pap. 14.95 (0-7735-1263-2, Pub. by McGill CN) U of Toronto Pr.

Understand & Develop Your ESP: Based on the Edgar Cayce Readings. Mark Thurston. 80p. (Orig.). 1977. pap. 6.95 (0-87604-097-0, 287) ARE Pr.

*Understand & Treat Alcoholism. Paul Berenson. Date not set. 19.95 (0-465-08875-9) Basic.

*Understand Economics. I. J. Humphreys. Date not set. pap. text ed. write for info. (0-85896-848-7) Addison-Wesley.

Understand Electrical & Electronics Maths. Owen Bishop. 256p. 1993. pap. 36.95 (0-7506-0924-9) Buttrwrth-Heinemann.

Understand Electronic Filters. Owen Bishop. LC 96-8190. 180p. 1996. pap. 24.95 (0-7506-2628-3) Buttrwrth-Heinemann.

*Understand International Relationship. Brown. LC 96-50057. 1997. text ed. 55.00 (0-312-17337-7); text ed. 19.95 (0-312-17338-5) St Martin.

Understand, My Love. large type ed. Peggy Dern. (Linford Romance Library). 320p. 1992. pap. 15.99 (0-7089-7240-3, Linford) Ulverscroft.

*Understand Numbers 1-100 (Math) Jo E. Moore. (Mathematics Ser.). (Illus.). 32p. (J). (gr. 1-2). 1996. teacher ed., pap. 2.95 (1-55799-445-5, 4047) Evan-Moor Corp.

*Understand Numbers 1-1000 (Math) Jo E. Moore. (Mathematics Ser.). (Illus.). 32p. (J). (gr. 2-3). 1996. teacher ed., pap. 2.95 (1-55799-458-7, 4060) Evan-Moor Corp.

Understand Technical Maths. Owen Bishop. 1994. pap. text ed. 32.95 (0-7506-1955-4) Buttrwrth-Heinemann.

Understand This. Jervey Tervalon. LC 94-45600. 272p. 1995. pap. 10.00 (0-385-47824-0, Anchor NY) Doubleday.

*Understand TOEFL. 1987. 13.00 (0-446-73547-7) Warner Bks.

Understand Your Backache: A Guide to Prevention, Treatment, & Relief. Rene Cailliet. LC 83-24071. (Illus.). 194p. 1984. pap. 12.95 (0-8036-1647-3) Davis Co.

Understand Your Dreams: 1500 Basic Dream Images & How to Interpret Them. 2nd ed. Alice A. Parker. Ed. by Nancy Carleton. LC 94-36260. 228p. 1995. pap. 12.00 (0-915811-59-6) H J Kramer Inc.

Understandable Guide to Music Theory: The Most Useful Aspects of Theory for Rock, Jazz & Blues Musicians. 3rd ed. Chaz Bufe. (Illus.). 80p. 1994. reprint ed. pap. 9.95 (1-884365-00-0) See Sharp Pr.

*Understandable History of the Bible. 4th ed. Samuel C. Gipp. 242p. (KOR.). 1987. reprint ed. pap. 10.00 (1-890120-01-4) Frnd To Churches.

Understandable Jung: The Personal Side of Jungian Psychology. Harry A. Wilmer. LC 93-10581. (Illus.). 296p. (Orig.). 1994. pap. 19.95 (0-933029-69-1) Chiron Pubns.

*Understandable Statistics: Concepts & Methods. Charles H. Brase & Corrinne P. Brase. (C). 1995. teacher ed., text ed. 2.66 (0-669-39478-5) HM College Div.

Understandable Statistics: Concepts & Methods. 3rd ed. Charles H. Brase & Corrinne P. Brace. LC 86-81382. 544p. (C). 1987. text ed. 66.36 (0-669-12181-9) HM College Div.

Understandable Statistics: Concepts & Methods. 4th ed. Charles H. Brase & Corrinne P. Brase. LC 90-83093. 616p. (C). 1991. text ed. 66.36 (0-669-24477-5); Instr.'s guide. teacher ed. 2.66 (0-669-24478-3); Study & solutions guide. student ed. 20.36 (0-669-24479-1); Test item file. 2.66 (0-669-27152-7) HM College Div.

*Understandable Statistics: Concepts & Methods. 5th annot. ed. Charles H. Brase & Corrinne P. Brase. (C). 1995. teacher ed., text ed. 64.76 (0-669-35514-3) HM College Div.

Understandable Statistics: Concepts & Methods. 5th ed. Charles H. Brase & Corrinne P. Brase. 832p. (C). 1995. text ed. 66.36 (0-669-35513-5) HM College Div.

*Understandable Statistics: Concepts & Methods: Study & Solutions Guide. 5th ed. Charles H. Brase & Corrinne P. Brase. (C). 1995. text ed. 20.36 (0-669-39479-3) HM College Div.

Understanding. Sandra K. Ziegler. LC 88-23745. (Values to Live By Ser.). (Illus.). 32p. (J). (ps-2). 1989. lib. bdg. 21.36 (0-89565-452-0) Childs World.

*Understanding. 2nd rev. ed. Jane Nelsen. 224p. 1996. pap. 12.00 (0-7615-0559-8) Prima Pub.

Understanding: A Phenomenological-Pragmatic Analysis. LC 81-4233. (Contributions in Philosophy Ser.: No. 19). 344p. 1982. text ed. 49.95 (0-313-22483-8, MUN/, Greenwood Pr) Greenwood.

Understanding: Coming to Grips with Moments of Inadequacy, Neurosis, Isolation, Depression, Masochism, Frustration. Ann Dally. LC 78-66254. 192p. (C). 1983. pap. 6.95 (0-8128-6104-3, Scrbrough Hse) Madison Bks UPA.

Understanding: Eliminating Stress & Finding Serenity in Life & Relationships. rev. ed. Jane E. Nelson. Ed. by Bookman Productions Staff. 192p. 1988. pap. 11.95 (0-914629-72-7) Prima Pub.

Understanding: Statistics in Education. W. James Popham & Kenneth A. Sirotnik. LC 90-63795. (Illus.). 423p. (C). 1992. text ed. 50.00 (0-87581-348-8) IOX Amnt Assocs.

Understanding: The Universal Solvent. L. Ron Hubbard. 484p. 1990. 50.00 (0-88404-640-0) Bridge Pubns Inc.

Understanding a Company. Jeffrey B. Little. (Basic Investor's Library). (Illus.). 48p. 1988. lib. bdg. 12.95 (1-55546-622-2) Chelsea Hse.

Understanding a LAN. Paul Dravilas. Ed. by Jacqueline Jonas & Patricia A. Menges. (Illus.). 150p. (Orig.). (C). 1990. pap. text ed. 245.00 incl. audio (0-917792-77-7) OneOnOne Comp Trng.

Understanding Abilities, Disabilities, & Capabilities: A Guide to Children's Literature. Margaret F. Carlin et al. (Illus.). x, 114p. 1991. lib. bdg. 22.00 (0-87287-717-5) Libs Unl.

*Understanding Abnormal Behavior, 5 Vols. David Sue et al. (C). 1996. student ed., text ed. 18.76 (0-395-78827-7) HM.

*Understanding Abnormal Behavior, 5 Vols. 5th ed. David Sue et al. 570p. (C). 1996. text ed. 65.16 (0-395-78826-9) HM.

*Understanding Abnormal Behavior, 5 Vols. 5th ed. David Sue et al. (C). 1997. teacher ed., text ed. 11.96 (0-395-81860-5) HM.

*Understanding Abnormal Psychology. Neil Frude. (Basic Psychology Ser.). 400p. (C). 1998. text ed. 64.95 (0-631-16194-5) Blackwell Pubs.

*Understanding Abnormal Psychology. Neil Frude. (Basic Psychology Ser.). 400p. (C). 1998. pap. text ed. 34.95 (0-631-16195-3) Blackwell Pubs.

*Understanding Abusive Families: An Ecological Approach to Theory & Practice. James Garbarino. LC 97-20812. 1997. 34.95 (0-7879-1005-8) Jossey-Bass.

Understanding ACARS: Aircraft Communications Addressing & Reporting System. 3rd ed. Ed Flynn. (Illus.). 80p. 1995. pap. 9.95 (1-882123-36-0) Universal Radio Rsch.

Understanding Accounting Principles. Catherine Robinson & Phil Ker. 338p. 1993. pap. 65.00 (0-409-79000-1, NZ) MICHIE.

Understanding Accreditation: Contemporary Perspectives on Issues & Practices in Evaluating Educational Quality. Kenneth E. Young et al. LC 83-11260. (Jossey-Bass Higher Education Ser.). 528p. reprint ed. pap. 150.50 (0-7837-2531-0, 2042690) Bks Demand.

*Understanding Acid-Base. Benjamin Abelow. LC 97-3514. 1997. write for info. (0-683-18272-2) Williams & Wilkins.

*Understanding Acol: The Good Bidding Guide. Eric Crowhurst & Andrew Kambites. 176p. 1997. pap. 13.95 (0-575-06457-9, Pub. by V Gollancz UK) Trafalgar.

Understanding Action: An Essay on Reasons. Frederic Schick. 192p. (C). 1991. text ed. 54.95 (0-521-40330-8); pap. text ed. 16.95 (0-521-40886-5) Cambridge U Pr.

Understanding ADA: A Software Engineering Approach. Gary Bray & David Pokrass. LC 92-9974. 368p. (C). 1992. reprint ed. lib. bdg. 42.50 (0-89464-744-X) Krieger.

Understanding Addictive Disease: A Tool for Preventing Relapse. Terrence Gorski & Merlene Miller. 30p. 1991. pap. 4.00 (0-8309-0608-8) Herald Hse.

Understanding ADHD. Lovorn Bender. LC 96-23914. (C). 1996. pap. text ed. 28.00 (0-13-348731-8) P-H.

*Understanding ADHD: Attention Deficit Hyperactivity Disorder & Feeding the Brain. Sandra K. Woods & Willis H. Ploof. LC 97-4853. 208p. 1997. text ed. 46.00 (0-8039-7422-1); pap. text ed. 21.95 (0-8039-7423-X) Sage.

Understanding Adolescence: Issues & Implications for Effective Schools. Barbara Z. Presseisen. 60p. 1990. reprint ed. pap. 16.95 (1-56602-002-6) Research Better.

Understanding Adolescents & Safety at Home & on the Job. Betty L. Brace & Tonita Croghan. LC 79-21803. (Lifeworks Ser.). (Illus.). 1980. text ed. 13.96 (0-07-060912-8) McGraw.

Understanding Adult Education & Training. Griff Foley. 320p. 1996. pap. 29.95 (1-86373-901-7, Pub. by Allen & Unwin Aust Pty AT) Paul & Co Pubs.

Understanding Adult Memory for Childhood Trauma: An Integrative Analysis. LC 96-10813. 178p. 1996. pap. text ed. 14.95 (1-57230-110-4) Guilford Pr.

Understanding Adventures of Huckleberry Finn: A Student Casebook to Issues, Sources, & Historical Documents. Claudia D. Johnson. LC 95-40031. (Greenwood Press "Literature in Context" Ser.). 272p. 1996. text ed. 35.00 (0-313-29327-9, Greenwood Pr) Greenwood.

Understanding Aerodynamic Characteristics of Windsurfing. Paul Ng. 1992. pap. 12.95 (0-533-10271-5) Vantage.

Understanding Aeronautical Charts. Terry T. Lankford. 1992. pap. 17.95 (0-07-157799-8) McGraw.

Understanding Aeronautical Charts. Terry T. Lankford. (Practical Flying Ser.). 320p. 1992. 27.95 (0-8306-3912-8, 1041); pap. 17.95 (0-8306-3911-X, 1041) McGraw-Hill Prof.

Understanding Aeronautical Charts. 2nd ed. Terry T. Lankford. 1996. pap. text ed. 22.95 (0-07-036467-2) McGraw.

Understanding Aeronautical Charts. 2nd ed. Terry T. Lankford. 1996. text ed. 34.95 (0-07-036468-0) McGraw.

Understanding Africa's Food Problems: Social Policy Perspectives. A. K. Mhina & G. K. Munishi. (African Social Challenges Ser.: No. 1). 259p. 1991. lib. bdg. 60.00 (0-905450-39-6, Pub. by H Zell Pubs UK) Bowker-Saur.

Understanding Ageing. Robin Holliday. LC 94-11727. (Developmental & Cell Biology Ser.: No. 30). (Illus.). 250p. (C). 1995. text ed. 69.95 (0-521-41788-0); pap. text ed. 27.95 (0-521-47802-2) Cambridge U Pr.

*Understanding Aggressive Behavior in Children. Craig F. Ferris & Thomas Grisso. LC 96-34935. (Annals of the New York Academy of Sciences Ser.). 1996. write for info. (1-57331-012-3); pap. write for info. (1-57331-013-1) NY Acad Sci.

Understanding Aging: Images, Attitudes & Professional Practice. Simon J. Biggs. LC 92-46227. 1993. 90.00 (0-335-15725-4, Open Univ Pr); pap. 31.00 (0-335-15724-6, Open Univ Pr) Taylor & Francis.

Understanding Aging Parents. Andrew D. Lester & Judith L. Lester. LC 80-17832. (Christian Care Bks.: No. 8). 120p. reprint ed. pap. 34.20 (0-7837-2636-8, 2042987) Bks Demand.

Understanding Agriculture: New Directions for Education. National Research Council Staff. 80p. 1988. pap. text ed. 16.95 (0-309-03936-3) Natl Acad Pr.

Understanding AIDS. Arun & Anadi K. Dasa. 1987. 11.95 (0-318-36373-9) Asia Bk Corp.

Understanding AIDS: A Guide for Mental Health Professionals. Seth C. Kalichman. (Illus.). 421p. 1995. text ed. 39.95 (1-55798-284-8, 431-7500) Am Psychol.

Understanding Aircraft Composite Construction: Basics of Materials & Techniques for the Non-Engineer. Zeke Smith. LC 94-96418. (Illus.). 200p. (Orig.). 1996. pap. 29.95 (0-9642828-1-X) Aeronaut Pr.

Understanding Aircraft Structures. 2nd ed. John Cutler. (Illus.). 192p. 1992. pap. 34.95 (0-632-03241-3) Blackwell Sci.

Understanding Albert Camus. David R. Ellison. (Understanding Modern European & Latin American Literature Ser.). 247p. (C). 1990. text ed. 29.95 (0-87249-705-4) U of SC Pr.

Understanding Alcoholism: A Starting Point for Families. Ted Lawson. LC 90-64269. 64p. (Orig.). 1991. pap. 1.95 (0-89243-341-8) Liguori Pubns.

Understanding Algebra. John D. Baley & Martin Holstege. 1988. text ed. write for info. (0-07-003566-0) McGraw.

Understanding Algebra for College Students. Lewis R. Hirsch & Arthur Goodman. Ed. by Pullins. LC 93-38909. 780p. (C). 1994. text ed. 57.50 (0-314-02899-4) West Pub.

*Understanding Algebra for College Students. 2nd ed. Goodman. (C). 1998. text ed. 62.95 (0-534-35305-3) Brooks-Cole.

Understanding Algorithms & Data Structures. David Brunskill & John Turner. LC 96-8874. 1996. write for info. (0-07-709141-8) McGraw.

Understanding Allergy, Sensitivity, & Immunity: A Comprehensive Guide. Janice Vickerstaff Joneja & Leonard Bielory. 350p. (Orig.). (C). 1990. pap. 16.95 (0-8135-1521-1); text ed. 45.00 (0-8135-1520-3) Rutgers U Pr.

Understanding Alzheimer's Disease. Neal R. Cutler & John J. Sramek. LC 96-20284. (Understanding Health & Sickness Ser.). 1996. pap. 12.00 (0-87805-911-3); text ed. 28.00 (0-87805-910-5) U Pr of Miss.

Understanding America. Sharp & Alcestis R. Oberg. 1993. pap. text ed. write for info. (0-07-056897-9) McGraw.

*Understanding American Business Jargon: A Dictionary. W. Davis Folsom. LC 96-50211. 264p. 1997. text ed. 65.00 (0-313-29991-9, Greenwood Pr) Greenwood.

Understanding American Democracy. Leon P. Baradat. (C). 1991. text ed. 34.50 (0-06-040478-7); student ed. 16.50 (0-06-500460-4) Addson-Wesley Educ.

Understanding American Economic Decline: A Structural & Institutional Approach. Ed. by Michael A. Bernstein & David E. Adler. 304p. (C). 1994. text ed. 59.95 (0-521-45063-2); pap. text ed. 19.95 (0-521-45679-7) Cambridge U Pr.

Understanding American Education: Its Past, Practices & Promise. Lloyd Duck. (Illus.). 480p. (Orig.). (C). 1996. pap. text ed. 19.95 (0-9639874-8-8) Chatelaine.

Understanding American Government. 2nd ed. Susan Welch et al. Ed. by Baxter. LC 92-43187. 450p. (C). 1993. pap. text ed. 41.00 (0-314-01238-9) West Pub.

Understanding American Government. 3rd ed. John Gruhl et al. LC 94-37653. 666p. (C). 1995. pap. text ed. 43.25 (0-314-04578-3) West Pub.

*Understanding American Government. 4th ed. Susan Welch. LC 96-36719. 550p. 1997. pap. write for info. (0-314-20153-X) West Pub.

Understanding American History Through Children's Literature, Instructional Units, & Activities: Grades K-8. Mary H. Cordier & Maria A. Perez-Stable. LC 94-2636. 328p. 1994. pap. 27.50 (0-89774-795-X) Oryx Pr.

Understanding American Jewish Philanthropy. Marc L. Raphael. 25.00 (0-87068-689-5) Ktav.

Understanding American Jewry. Ed. by Marshall Sklare. LC 81-14795. 300p. 1982. text ed. 39.95 (0-87855-454-8) Transaction Pubs.

Understanding American Judaism: Toward the Description of a Modern Religion: Reform, Orthodoxy, Conservatism, & Reconstructionism, 2 vols., Vol. 2. Jacob Neusner. pap. 16.95 (0-87068-279-2) Ktav.

Understanding American Judaism: Toward the Description of a Modern Religion: The Synagogue & the Rabbi, 2 vols., Vol. 1. Jacob Neusner. pap. 16.95 (0-87068-280-6) Ktav.

Understanding America's Drinking Problem: How to Combat the Hazards of Alcohol. Don Cahalan. LC 87-45418. (Health-Social & Behavioral Science Ser.). 254p. text ed. 34.95 (1-55542-057-5) Jossey-Bass.

Understanding Anaesthesia. 3rd ed. Len E. S. Carrie et al. LC 95-25188. 544p. 1996. pap. text ed. 47.50 (0-7506-2079-X) Buttrwrth-Heinemann.

Understanding Ancient Coins: An Introduction for Archaeologists & Historians. P. J. Casey. LC 86-4028. (Illus.). 168p. 1986. 34.95 (0-8061-2003-7) U of Okla Pr.

Understanding & Accepting Human Needs. Vincent W. Kafka. 12p. 1987. pap. 3.95 (0-913261-17-3) Effect Learn Sys.

Understanding & Accommodating Physical Disabilities: The Manager's Desk Reference. Dorothy Shrout. LC 93-14120. 200p. 1993. text ed. 52.95 (0-89930-814-7, Q814, Quorum Bks) Greenwood.

Understanding & Affecting the Behavior of Young Children. Thomas J. Zirpoli. LC 94-27900. 1994. pap. text ed. 40.00 (0-02-431732-2, Macmillan Coll) P-H.

Understanding & Applying PLCs in Electrical Controls No. 677: Video Booklet/Workbook. L. A. Bryan & E. A. Bryan. Ed. by L. B. Thompson. (Illus.). 52p. (Orig.). 1995. pap. 22.95 (0-944107-19-2) Indust Text.

An Asterisk (*) at the beginning of an entry indicates that the title is appearing in BIP for the first time.

Understanding & Applying the Bible. rev. ed. J. Robertson McQuilkin. (Orig.). 1992. pap. 14.99 (*0-8024-9091-3*) Moody.

Understanding & Applying Value-Added Assessment: Eliminating Business Process Waste. William E. Trischler. LC 96-8811. (Illus.). 127p. (Orig.). 1996. pap. 29.00 (*0-87389-369-7*, H0934) ASQC Qual Pr.

Understanding & Being. Bernard Lonergan. Ed. by Frederick E. Crowe & Robert M. Doran. (Collected Works of Bernard Lonergan: Vol. 5). 476p. 1990. 60.00 (*0-8020-3987-1*); pap. 19.95 (*0-8020-3989-8*) U of Toronto Pr.

Understanding & Being: An Introduction & Companion to Insight. Bernard J. F. Lonergan. Ed. by Elizabeth A. Morelli & Mark D. Morelli. (Toronto Studies in Theology: Vol. 5). xii, 368p. 1980. lib. bdg. 99.95 (*0-88946-909-1*) E Mellen.

Understanding & Being Understood. Sanford Berman. LC 72-75526. 77p. 1972. pap. text ed. 5.00 (*0-918970-13-X*) Intl Gen Semantics.

Understanding & Caring for Human Diseases. 2nd ed. Borgstadt. (Health Occupations Ser.). 56p. 1996. teacher ed., pap. text ed. 12.50 (*0-8273-7431-3*) Delmar.

Understanding & Caring for Human Diseases. 2nd rev. ed. Marcia Borgstadt. LC 95-13518. 464p. (J). 1996. pap. text ed. 25.00 (*0-8273-6605-1*) Delmar.

Understanding & Controlling Crime: Toward a New Research Strategy. David P. Farrington et al. LC 86-11823. (Research in Criminology Ser.). 215p. 1986. 57.95 (*0-387-96298-0*) Spr-Verlag.

Understanding & Controlling the German Cockroach. Ed. by Michael K. Rust et al. (Illus.). 448p. 1995. text ed. 95.00 (*0-19-506495-X*) OUP.

***Understanding & Designing Computer Networks.** write for info. (*0-340-61419-6*, Pub. by E Arnold UK) Routledge Chapman & Hall.

Understanding & Developing Language Tests. C. J. Weir. LC 92-33403. (Language Teaching Methodology Ser.). 1993. 14.50 (*0-13-947532-X*) P-H.

Understanding & Developing the Skills of Oral Communication. 2nd ed. Richard Hunsaker. 208p. 1990. pap. text ed. 15.95 (*0-89582-203-2*) Morton Pub.

Understanding & Diagnosing Pediatric Heart Disease. David W. Sapire. (Illus.). 208p. (C). 1991. pap. text ed. 43.95 (*0-8385-9254-6*, A9254-2) Appleton & Lange.

Understanding & Educating the Deaf-Blind - Severely & Profoundly Handicapped: An International Perspective. Sara R. Walsh & Robert Holzberg. (Illus.). 328p. 1981. pap. 31.95 (*0-398-06478-4*) C C Thomas.

Understanding & Educating the Deaf-Blind - Severely & Profoundly Handicapped: An International Perspective. fac. ed. Sara R. Walsh & Robert Holzberg. (Illus.). 328p. 1981. 47.95 (*0-398-04514-3*) C C Thomas.

Understanding & Encouraging Your Child's Art: How to Enhance Confidence in Drawing. Mia Johnson. (Illus.). 160p. (J). (ps-7). 1994. reprint ed. pap. 13.95 (*1-56565-099-9*) Lowell Hse.

Understanding & Enhancing Self-Esteem. Carol Rogne. 527p. 1991. pap. text ed. 8.95 (*1-881565-00-9*) Discov Counsel.

Understanding & Enjoying Adolescence. William N. Wingerd. (YA). 1988. pap. text ed. 13.05 (*0-8013-0215-3*, 75873) Longman.

***Understanding & Evaluating Education Research.** McMillan & Wergin. 1997. pap. text ed. 19.00 (*0-13-193541-0*) P-H.

Understanding & Evaluating Methodologies: NIMSAD, a Systematic Framework. Nimal Jayaratna. LC 94-10969. (Information Systems, Management). 1994. write for info. (*0-07-707882-9*) McGraw.

Understanding & Experiencing Prayer. E. J. Thomas. (Let's Discuss It Ser.). pap. 3.95 (*0-88172-130-1*) Believers Bkshelf.

Understanding & Explanation. Stephan Strasser. LC 84-21176. (Duquesne Studies: Philosophical: Vol. 39). 196p. 1985. text ed. 18.50 (*0-8207-0173-4*) Duquesne.

Understanding & Explanation: A Transcendental Pragmatic Perspective. Karl-Otto Apel. Tr. by Georgia Warnke from GER. (Studies in Contemporary German Social Thought). 320p. 1984. pap. 14.95 (*0-262-51041-3*) MIT Pr.

Understanding & Facilitating Adult Learning: A Comprehensive Analysis of Principles & Effective Practices. Stephen D. Brookfield. LC 85-23861. (Higher Education Ser.). 391p. text ed. 38.95 (*0-87589-674-X*) Jossey-Bass.

Understanding & Facilitating Adult Learning: A Comprehensive Analysis of Principles & Effective Practices. Stephen D. Brookfield. 375p. 1986. write for info. (*0-335-15226-0*, Open Univ Pr) Taylor & Francis.

Understanding & Facilitating Adult Learning: A Comprehensive Analysis of Principles & Effective Practices. Stephen D. Brookfield. LC 85-23861. (Higher & Adult Education-Management Ser.). 393p. reprint ed. text ed. 25.95 (*1-55542-355-8*) Jossey-Bass.

Understanding & Facilitating Forgiveness. David G. Benner & Robert W. Harvey. LC 96-15340. (Strategic Pastoral Counseling Resources Ser.). 160p. (C). 1996. 16.99 (*0-8010-9019-9*) Baker Bks.

Understanding & Guiding Young Children. 3rd ed. K. Baker & Xenia F. Fane. LC 67-4932. 1975. 26.48 (*0-13-935825-0*) P-H.

Understanding & Healing Codependency with Gospel Principles. John C. Turpin. 1996. pap. 6.95 (*1-55503-401-2*, 01111043) Covenant Comms.

Understanding & Helping Families: A Cognitive-Behavioral Approach. Andrew I. Schwebel & Mark A. Fine. LC 93-32023. 224p. 1994. pap. 24.50 (*0-8058-1449-3*); text ed. 59.95 (*0-8058-1225-3*) L Erlbaum Assocs.

Understanding & Helping the Retarded Reader. Ed. by Ruth M. Strang. LC 64-17275. 130p. reprint ed. pap. 37.10 (*0-317-51993-X*, 2027390) Bks Demand.

Understanding & Helping the Schizophrenic: A Guide for Family & Friends. Silvano Arieti. LC 94-77917. 252p. 1995. pap. text ed. 28.50 (*1-56821-269-0*) Aronson.

Understanding & Helping the Schizophrenic: A Guide for Family & Friends. Silvano Arieti. 222p. 1994. pap. text ed. 32.95 (*1-85575-063-5*, Pub. by Karnac Bks UK) Brunner-Mazel.

***Understanding & Implementing ISO 9000 & Other ISO Standards.** Goetsch & Stanley Davis. (C). 1997. text ed. 40.00 (*0-13-613779-2*) P-H.

Understanding & Implementing Performance Management. Hermann Spangenberg. 318p. 1994. text ed. 70.00 (*0-7021-3182-2*, Pub. by Juta & Co SA) Intl Spec Bk.

Understanding & Implementing Quality Management: A Step-by-Step Approach for Implementing Total Quality Management in Organizations. Johnson A Edosomwan. 32p. 1991. pap. 39.95 (*1-879849-05-4*) Johnsn Johnsn.

***Understanding & Implementing Successful Data Marts.** Douglas Hackney. (C). 1997. pap. text ed. 34.95 (*0-201-18380-3*) Addison-Wesley.

Understanding & Improving Behavior. rev. ed. Herbert Friedman. LC 75-22951. 1980. text ed. 5.00 (*0-9606824-0-6*) Medfd Pr.

Understanding & Installing Home Systems: How to Automate Your Home. 3rd ed. David Gaddis. (Illus.). 29.95 (*0-9632170-1-1*) Home Systs.

Understanding & Learning Statistics by Computer. M. C. Yang et al. (Computer Science Ser.: Vol. IV). 216p. 1986. text ed. 59.00 (*9971-5-0019-1*); pap. text ed. 30.00 (*9971-5-0091-4*) World Scientific Pub.

Understanding & Letting Go of Guilt. Lucy Freeman & Herbert S. Strean. 286p. 1995. pap. 30.00 (*1-56821-628-9*) Aronson.

Understanding & Living with People Who Are Mentally Ill: Techniques to Deal with Mental Illness in the Family. James E. Soukup. LC 94-3543. 192p. (C). 1994. pap. 26.95 (*0-398-05949-7*); text ed. 41.95 (*0-398-05940-3*) C C Thomas.

Understanding & Management of Conflict in Sport Organizations. Earle F. Zeigler. (Monograph Series on Sport & Physical Education Management). 33p. (C). 1995. pap. text ed. 4.40 (*0-87563-566-0*) Stipes.

Understanding & Management of Health Problems in Schools: A Resource Manual for School Personnel. H. Moghadam. 152p. (Orig.). 1995. pap. text ed. 13.95 (*1-55059-121-5*, Pub. by Detselig CN) Temeron Bks.

Understanding & Management of Nausea & Vomiting. Jan Hawthorn. (Illus.). 224p. 1994. pap. 24.95 (*0-632-03819-5*, Pub. by Blckwell Sci Pubns UK) Blackwell Sci.

Understanding & Management of Pain. Bourke. Date not set. write for info. (*0-7506-9550-1*) Buttrwrth-Heinemann.

Understanding & Management of Pain. Jan Hawthorn & Kathy Redmond. 224p. (Orig.). 1996. pap. text ed. 24.95 (*0-632-04033-5*) Blackwell Sci.

Understanding & Managing Child Behavior in the 90's: Positive, Caring Discipline That Works! Ann P. Wildemann. 70p. 1993. pap. text ed. 19.95 (*1-885477-10-4*) Fut Horizons.

***Understanding & Managing Child Sexual Abuse.** Ed. by R. Kim Oates. (Illus.). 422p. 1990. write for info. (*0-7295-0322-4*, Bailliere-Tindall) Saunders.

Understanding & Managing Children's Classroom Behavior. Sam Goldstein. LC 94-9332. (Wiley Series on Personality Processes). 528p. 1994. text ed. 62.50 (*0-471-57946-7*) Wiley.

Understanding & Managing Cholesterol: A Guide for Wellness Professionals. Kevin P. Byrne. LC 90-5195. (Illus.). 344p. (Orig.). 1991. text ed. 42.00 (*0-87322-309-8*, BBYR0309) Human Kinetics.

Understanding & Managing Financial Information: The Non-Financial Manager's Guide. Michael M. Coltman. (Business Ser.). 232p. 1993. pap. 9.95 (*0-88908-297-9*) Self-Counsel Pr.

Understanding & Managing Interest Rate Risks. Ren-Raw Chen. LC 96-9289. (Series in Mathematical Finance). 200p. 1996. write for info. (*981-02-2751-5*) World Scientific Pub.

Understanding & Managing Investment Risk & Return. David L. Scott. (Investor's Self-Teaching Seminar Ser.). 1990. pap. 21.95 (*1-55738-105-4*) Irwin Prof Pubng.

Understanding & Managing Organizational Behavior. George & Jones. Ed. by Michael Payne. 800p. (C). 1996. text ed. 69.95 (*0-201-53210-7*) Addison-Wesley.

Understanding & Managing Organizational Behavior. annot. ed. Jennifer George & Gareth Jones. (C). 1996. teacher ed., text ed. write for info. (*0-201-53211-5*) Addison-Wesley.

Understanding & Managing Organizational Behavior Printed Test Bank. Jennifer George & Gareth Jones. Ed. by Michael Payne. (C). 1996. pap. text ed. write for info. (*0-201-53213-1*) Addison-Wesley.

Understanding & Managing Organizational Behavior Printed Test Bank: Instructor's Manual Restricted. George Jones. Ed. by Michael Payne. 1996. pap. text ed. write for info. (*0-201-53212-3*) Addison-Wesley.

Understanding & Managing Public Organizations. Hal G. Rainey. LC 90-28985. (Public Administration - Management Ser.). 359p. 36.95 (*1-55542-344-2*) Jossey-Bass.

***Understanding & Managing Public Organizations.** 2nd ed. Hal G. Rainey. LC 96-2538. (Public Administration Ser.). 1996. write for info. (*0-7879-0251-9*) Jossey-Bass.

Understanding & Managing Sales & Use Tax. 2nd ed. Fields. 216p. 1992. pap. 32.50 (*0-685-67050-3*, 4702) Commerce.

Understanding & Managing Vision Deficits: A Guide for Occupational Therapists. Mitchell M. Scheiman. LC 96-30414. 426p. 1996. pap. 30.00 (*1-55642-283-0*, 32830) SLACK Inc.

Understanding & Managing Your Anger & Aggression: A Book to Help Prevent the Damage Anger Causes You & Your Relationships. Alfred Nye, Jr. LC 92-75756. (Illus.). 253p. (Orig.). 1993. pap. 14.95 (*0-9635613-5-9*) B C A Pub.

Understanding & Measuring Vibrations. R. H. Wallace. LC 78-135386. (Wykeham Technology Ser.: No. 4). 148p. (C). 1970. pap. 18.00 (*0-8448-1125-4*, Crane Russak) Taylor & Francis.

***Understanding & Meeting the Challenge of Student Cultural Diversity.** Eugene Garcia. 416p. (C). 1994. pap. text ed. 46.76 (*0-395-51735-4*) HM.

Understanding & Modification of Delinquent Behavior. Lanier Morgan. LC 84-90339. 1984. 15.00 (*0-87212-181-X*) Libra.

Understanding & Modification of Delinquent Behavior. rev. ed. Lanier Morgan. LC 91-61814. 1992. 20.00 (*0-87212-251-4*) Libra.

Understanding & Prediction. Stefan Nowak. (Synthese Library: No. 94). 507p. 1981. pap. text ed. 43.00 (*90-277-1199-2*, D Reidel) Kluwer Ac.

Understanding & Prediction Essays in the Methodology of Social & Behavioral Theories. Stefan Nowak. LC 75-44179. (Synthese Library: No. 94). 507p. 1976. lib. bdg. 158.50 (*90-277-0558-5*, D Reidel) Kluwer Ac.

Understanding & Preventing AIDS: A Book for Everyone. rev. ed. Chris Jennings. LC 92-72998. (Illus.). 50p. 1992. 35.00 (*0-936571-04-7*); pap. text ed. 3.50 (*0-936571-03-9*) Health Alert Pr.

Understanding & Preventing AIDS: A Book for Everyone. 2nd ed. Chris Jennings. LC 87-80364. (Illus.). 240p. 1988. pap. text ed. 24.95 (*0-936571-01-2*) Health Alert Pr.

Understanding & Preventing Child Sexual Abuse, 2 vols., Set. Ed. by Christopher Bagley & Wilfreda Thurston. 800p. 1996. text ed. 152.95 (*1-85742-322-4*, Pub. by Arena UK) Ashgate Pub Co.

Understanding & Preventing HIV Risk Behavior. Stuart Oskamp & Suzanne Thompson. LC 96-10121. (Claremont Symposium on Applied Social Science Ser.: Vol. 9). 248p. 1996. 45.00 (*0-8039-7424-8*); pap. 21.95 (*0-8039-7425-6*) Sage.

***Understanding & Preventing Sexual Harassment: The Complete Guide.** Peter Rutter. 272p. 1997. pap. 13.95 (*0-553-37877-5*, Bantam Trade Bks) Bantam.

Understanding & Preventing Suicide: New Perspectives. David Lester. (Illus.). 134p. 1990. pap. 20.95 (*0-398-06235-8*) C C Thomas.

Understanding & Preventing Suicide: New Perspectives. David Lester. (Illus.). 134p. (C). 1990. text ed. 33.95 (*0-398-05709-5*) C C Thomas.

Understanding & Preventing Suicide: Plenary Papers of the First Combined Meeting of the AAS & IASP. Ed. by Ronald W. Maris. LC 88-175957. (Illus.). 142p. reprint ed. pap. 40.50 (*0-7837-1204-9*, 2041736) Bks Demand.

Understanding & Preventing Violence. National Research Council Staff. Ed. by Albert J. Reiss. 480p. 1996. pap. text ed. 24.95 (*0-309-05476-1*) Natl Acad Pr.

Understanding & Preventing Violence, Vol. 2: Biobehavioral Influences. National Research Council, Panel on the Understanding & Control of Violent Behavior Staff. Ed. by Albert J. Reiss, Jr. et al. 560p. (Orig.). (C). 1994. pap. text ed. 45.00 (*0-309-04649-1*) Natl Acad Pr.

Understanding & Preventing Violence, Vol. 3: Social Influences. National Research Council, Panel on the Understanding & Control of Violent Behavior Staff. 592p. (Orig.). (C). 1994. pap. text ed. 45.00 (*0-309-05080-4*) Natl Acad Pr.

Understanding & Preventing Violence, Vol. 4: Consequences & Control. National Research Council, Panel on the Understanding & Control of violent Behavior Staff. Ed. by Albert J. Reiss, Jr. et al. 408p. (Orig.). (C). 1994. pap. text ed. 39.00 (*0-309-05079-0*) Natl Acad Pr.

Understanding & Promotion Transformative Learning: A Guide for Educators of Adult. Patricia Cranton. LC 94-21300. (Higher & Adult Education Ser.). 272p. text ed. 32.95 (*0-7879-0017-6*) Jossey-Bass.

Understanding & Recognizing Creativity: The Emergence of a Discipline. Ed. by Scott G. Isaksen et al. LC 93-29992. (Creativity Research Ser.: Vol. 1). 546p. 1993. pap. 49.50 (*1-56750-006-4*); text ed. 125.00 (*0-89391-982-9*) Ablex Pub.

Understanding & Reducing the Costs of Forscom Installations. John M. Halliday et al. 1996. pap. text ed. 9.00 (*0-8330-2395-0*, MR-730-A) Rand Corp.

Understanding & Reducing Your Electric Bill: For Owners & Managers. Richard L. Hepburn. 126p. 1995. pap. 39.95 (*1-885373-00-7*) Emerald Ink.

Understanding & Reducing Your Home Electric Bill. large type ed. Richard L. Hepburn. Ed. by Christopher Carson & Patrick A. Zale. LC 96-25263. (Illus.). 140p. (Orig.). 1996. pap. 19.95 (*1-885373-01-5*, SAN298-606X) Emerald Ink.

Understanding & Relating to Parents... Professionally. Robert L. DeBruyn. LC 84-62205. 66p. (Orig.). 1985. pap. 4.95 (*0-914607-21-9*) Master Tchr.

Understanding & Repairing CB Radios. Lou Franklin. (Illus.). 384p. (Orig.). 1996. pap. 38.00 (*0-943132-24-X*) CBC Intl.

Understanding & Representing Space: Theory & Evidence from Experiments with Blind & Sighted Children. Susanna Millar. LC 94-10299. (Illus.). 240p. 1994. 75.00 (*0-19-852142-1*, Old Oregon Bk Store) OUP.

Understanding & Selecting Small Business Computers. Glenn A. Gibson & Mary L. Gibson. (Illus.). 400p. (C). 1986. student ed. write for info. (*0-13-937145-1*); text ed. 31.00 (*0-13-937046-3*) P-H.

Understanding & Sense, 2 vols. Ed. by Christopher Peacocke. (International Research Library of Philosophy). 872p. 1993. Set. 229.95 (*1-85521-292-7*, Pub. by Dartmth Pub UK) Ashgate Pub Co.

Understanding & Servicing Alarm Systems. 2nd ed. H. William Trimmer. 250p. 1990. 36.95 (*0-409-90204-7*) Buttrwrth-Heinemann.

Understanding & Servicing CD Players. Ken Clement. (Illus.). 256p. 1994. 49.95 (*0-7506-0934-6*) Buttrwrth-Heinemann.

Understanding & Servicing Fractional Horsepower Motors. Kennard C. Graham. LC 61-11419. 264p. reprint ed. pap. 75.30 (*0-317-10141-2*, 2004575) Bks Demand.

Understanding & Sharing. 5th ed. Judy Pearson & Paul E. Nelson. 544p. (C). 1990. per. write for info. (*0-697-08667-4*) Brown & Benchmark.

Understanding & Sharing. 6th ed. Paul E. Nelson. (C). 1994. audio write for info. (*0-697-26038-0*) Brown & Benchmark.

Understanding & Sharing: An Introduction to Speech. 6th ed. Judy Pearson & Paul E. Nelson. 496p. (C). 1993. per. write for info. (*0-697-21450-8*) Brown & Benchmark.

Understanding & Sharing: An Introduction to Speech Communication. 6th ed. Judy Pearson & Paul E. Nelson. 496p. (C). 1993. per. write for info. (*0-697-13940-9*) Brown & Benchmark.

Understanding & Social Inquiry. Ed. by Fred R. Dallmayr & Thomas A. McCarthy. LC 76-22404. 1977. pap. 16.50 (*0-268-01913-4*) U of Notre Dame Pr.

***Understanding & Standing under the Bhagavad Gita.** Donald Curtis. 111p. (Orig.). 1996. text ed. write for info. (*0-917849-24-8*) Sci of Mind.

Understanding & Teaching Children with Autism. Rita Joran & Stuart Powell. LC 95-3852. 175p. 1995. pap. text ed. 35.00 (*0-471-95714-3*) Wiley.

Understanding & Teaching Children with Autism. Rita Jordan & Stuart Powell. LC 95-3852. 1995. text ed. 50.00 (*0-471-95888-3*) Wiley.

Understanding & Teaching Cohesion Comprehension. Ed. by Judith W. Irwin. LC 85-14340. 144p. reprint ed. pap. 41.10 (*0-8357-4309-8*, 2037106) Bks Demand.

Understanding & Teaching Emotionally Disturbed Children & Adolescents. 2nd rev. ed. Phyllis L. Newcomer. LC 92-33990. (C). 1993. text ed. 41.00 (*0-89079-575-4*, 6575) PRO-ED.

Understanding & Teaching Reading: An Interactive Model. Emerald Dechant. 544p. 1991. pap. 45.00 (*0-8058-0839-6*); text ed. 99.95 (*0-8058-0824-8*) L Erlbaum Assocs.

Understanding & Trading Futures: A Hands-on Study Guide for Investors & Traders. rev. ed. Carl F. Luft. 1994. per. 22.95 (*1-55738-570-X*) Irwin Prof Pubng.

Understanding & Training Your Cat. H. Ellen Whiteley. 1994. pap. 15.00 (*0-517-88182-9*) Crown Pub Group.

Understanding & Training Your Cat or Kitten. E. H. Whiteley. LC 93-2739. 1994. 20.00 (*0-517-59152-9*, Crown) Crown Pub Group.

Understanding & Training Your Dog or Puppy. H. Ellen Whiteley. 288p. 1996. pap. 15.00 (*0-517-88436-4*) Random.

Understanding & Treating ADD. Kirby. (Practitioner Guidebook Ser.). (C). 1992. pap. text ed. 31.50 (*0-205-14391-1*, H4391, Longwood Div) Allyn.

Understanding & Treating Adolescent Substance Abuse. Philip P. Muisener. LC 93-32463. (Sourcebooks for the Human Services Ser.: Vol. 27). (C). 1993. text ed. 52.00 (*0-8039-4275-3*); pap. text ed. 24.95 (*0-8039-4276-1*) Sage.

Understanding & Treating Alcoholism, 2 vols. J. Littrell. (C). 1991. Set. text ed. 99.95 (*0-8058-0872-8*) L Erlbaum Assocs.

Understanding & Treating Alcoholism, Vol. I. J. Littrell. 408p. (C). 1991. Vol. 1. text ed. 75.00 (*0-8058-0870-1*) L Erlbaum Assocs.

Understanding & Treating Alcoholism, Vol. II. J. Littrell. 296p. (C). 1991. Vol. 2. text ed. 49.95 (*0-8058-0871-X*) L Erlbaum Assocs.

***Understanding & Treating Antisocial Personality Disorder: Criminals, Chemical Abusers, & Batterers.** Gregory L. Little & Kenneth D. Robinson. 65p. 1997. pap. 10.00 (*0-940829-17-7*) Eagle Wing Bks.

Understanding & Treating Aspiration. David E. Eibling et al. (Self-Instructional Package Ser.). (Illus.). 69p. (Orig.). (C). 1993. pap. text ed. 25.00 (*1-56772-002-1*) AAO-HNS.

Understanding & Treating Conduct Disorders. Michele Toth. (Child Guidance Mental Health Ser.). 41p. 1990. pap. 9.00 (*0-89079-265-8*, 1507) PRO-ED.

Understanding & Treating Depressed Adolescents & Their Families. Gerald D. Oster & Janice E. Caro. LC 89-37665. (Personality Processes Ser.). 228p. 1990. text ed. 70.00 (*0-471-60897-1*) Wiley.

Understanding & Treating Mental Illness: The Strength & Limits of Modern Psychiatry. J. M. Cleghorn & B. L. Lee. LC 90-4429. 250p. 1991. pap. text ed. 16.95 (*0-920887-73-2*) Hogrefe & Huber Pubs.

Understanding & Treating Tardive Dyskinesia. Dilip V. Jeste & Richard J. Wyatt. LC 81-7059. (Guilford Foundations of Modern Psychiatry Ser.). 363p. 1982. lib. bdg. 52.50 (*0-89862-175-5*) Guilford Pr.

Understanding & Treating the Psychopath. Dennis M. Doren. LC 95-26700. (Master Works). 1996. write for info. (*1-56821-791-9*) Aronson.

Understanding & Troubleshooting the Microprocessors. James W. Coffron. 1980. text ed. 47.00 (*0-13-936625-3*) P-H.

Understanding & Using Appleworks. Frank Short. (Illus.). 352p. (Orig.). (C). 1987. text ed. 23.25 (*0-314-31159-9*); pap. text ed. 20.00 (*0-314-26023-4*); Instr's. manual. teacher ed., pap. text ed. 13.95 (*0-314-33082-8*) West Pub.

Understanding & Using Application Software, Vol. I. Steven C. Ross. 444p. (C). 1988. pap. text ed. 45.25 (*0-314-34739-9*) West Pub.

Understanding & Using Application Software, Vol. II. Steven C. Ross et al. 464p. (C). 1988. pap. text ed. 45.25 (*0-314-34740-2*) West Pub.

Understanding & Using Application Software, Vol. 4. Patsy H. Lund. Ed. by Leyh. 718p. (C). 1990. pap. text ed. 49.25 (*0-314-66777-6*) West Pub.

Understanding & Using Application Software, Vol. 5. Steven C. Ross et al. Ed. by Leyh. 700p. (C). 1991. pap. text ed. 56.00 (*0-314-66779-2*) West Pub.

Understanding & Using Assessment Effectively. Jason K. Feld & John R. Bergan. (Early Childhood Professional Development Ser.: Module 1). 49p. (Orig.). 1994. pap. text ed. 15.00 (*1-888639-02-4*, PDS #1) Assessmnt Tech.

Understanding & Using Autocad. Lea. (West - Engineering Ser.). 1989. text ed. 44.95 (*0-534-93831-0*) PWS Pubs.

Understanding & Using Baptismal Records. John T. Humphrey. 168p. 1996. pap. text ed. 17.95 (*1-887609-10-5*) J T Humphrey.

Understanding & Using Burners. Ralph W. Ritchie. LC 81-90072. (Energy Conservation in the Crafts - Craft Monograph Ser.: No. 4). (Illus.). 60p. (Orig.). 1981. pap. 6.00 (*0-939656-03-5*) Ritchie Unltd.

Understanding & Using ClarisWorks. Gary G. Bitter. Ed. by Leyh. LC 92-31308. (Microcomputing Ser.). 450p. (C). 1993. pap. text ed. 28.75 (*0-314-01249-4*) West Pub.

***Understanding & Using Corel Wp 8.0.** Ouahib. (DF - Computer Applications Ser.). (C). 1998. pap. 79.95 (*0-538-71975-3*) S-W Pub.

Understanding & Using Data Base III: Including D Base II. Steven C. Ross. (Illus.). 196p. (C). 1986. pap. text ed. 28.75 (*0-314-96211-5*) West Pub.

***Understanding & Using Dbase III.** 11th ed. Steven C. Ross. (DF - Computer Applications Ser.). (C). 1987. pap. 18.96 (*0-314-39289-0*) West Pub.

Understanding & Using dBASE III Plus. Steven C. Ross. (Microcomputing Ser.). 283p. (C). 1987. pap. text ed. 20.50 (*0-314-34744-5*) West Pub.

Understanding & Using dBASE III PLUS. 2nd ed. Steven C. Ross. Ed. by Leyh. 368p. (C). 1991. pap. text ed. 28.75 (*0-314-81984-3*) West Pub.

Understanding & Using dBASE IV. Steven C. Ross. Ed. by Leyh. 434p. (C). 1989. pap. text ed. 28.75 (*0-314-47364-5*) West Pub.

Understanding & Using dBASE IV 2.0. Steven C. Ross. Ed. by Leyh. LC 94-8269. (Microcomputing Ser.). 450p. (C). 1994. teacher ed., pap. text ed. 28.75 (*0-314-02871-4*) West Pub.

Understanding & Using Displaywrite 3 & 4. Patsy H Lund & Barbara A. Hayden. 204p. (C). 1988. pap. text ed. 28.75 (*0-314-78996-0*) West Pub.

Understanding & Using Electricity. 2nd ed. Bruce A. McKenzie & Gerald Zachariah. 1982. 13.25 (*0-8134-2204-3*) Interstate.

Understanding & Using English Grammar. 2nd ed. Betty S. Azar. 416p. (C). 1988. pap. text ed. 26.25 (*0-13-943614-6*) P-H.

Understanding & Using English Grammar, Bk. A. 2nd ed. Betty S. Azar. 208p. (C). 1988. pap. text ed. 10.50 (*0-13-943663-4*) P-H.

Understanding & Using English Grammar, Bk. B. 2nd ed. Betty S. Azar. 208p. (C). 1988. pap. text ed. 10.50 (*0-13-943671-5*) P-H.

Understanding & Using English Grammar Chart Book. Betty S. Azar. 144p. pap. write for info. (*0-13-953746-5*) P-H.

Understanding & Using English Grammar Chart Book. 2nd ed. Betty S. Azar. 160p. 1993. pap. text ed. 15.75 (*0-13-948233-4*) P-H.

Understanding & Using Financial Data: An Ernest & Young Guide for Attorneys. Ernst & Young. 120p. 1994. suppl. ed., pap. text ed. 45.00 (*0-471-00814-1*) Wiley.

Understanding & Using Financial Data: An Ernst & Young Guide for Attorneys. Ernst & Young Staff. 384p. 1992. text ed. 115.00 (*0-471-55878-8*) Wiley.

***Understanding & Using Financial Data: An Ernst & Young Guide for Attorneys.** Ernst & Young Staff. 1995. suppl. ed., pap. text ed. 55.00 (*0-471-11535-5*) Wiley.

Understanding & Using Financial Data: An Ernst & Young Guide for Attorneys. 2nd ed. Vincent J. Love & Ernst & Young Staff. LC 96-19756. 1996. text ed. 125.00 (*0-471-16213-2*) Wiley.

Understanding & Using Framework. Karen L. Watterson. (Illus.). 234p. (Orig.). (C). 1986. pap. text ed. 28.75 (*0-314-96219-0*) West Pub.

Understanding & Using Groups. Brenda Vernelle. 212p. 1994. 65.00 (*1-871177-60-X*, Pub. by Whiting & Birch UK); pap. 19.95 (*1-871177-61-8*, Pub. by Whiting & Birch UK) Paul & Co Pubs.

Understanding & Using Information Technology. Judith C. Simon. LC 95-45671. 300p. (C). 1996. pap. text ed. 38.25 (*0-314-06522-9*) West Pub.

Understanding & Using Lotus 1-2-3. Steven C. Ross. (Illus.). 196p. (Orig.). (C). 1986. pap. text ed. 28.75 (*0-314-96209-3*) West Pub.

Understanding & Using Lotus 1-2-3: Advanced Techniques. Judith C. Simon. Ed. by Leyh. 330p. (C). 1992. spiral bd. 28.75 (*0-314-93401-4*) West Pub.

Understanding & Using Lotus 1-2-3: Release 2. Steven C. Ross. (Microcomputing Ser.). 232p. (C). 1987. pap. text ed. 28.75 (*0-314-34741-0*); teacher ed., pap. text ed. write for info. (*0-314-35880-3*) West Pub.

Understanding & Using Lotus 1-2-3 for Windows. Steven C. Ross et al. 544p. (C). 1995. teacher ed., pap. text ed. 28.75 (*0-314-01227-3*) West Pub.

Understanding & Using Lotus 1-2-3 for Windows 5.0. Dolores W. Pusins & Steven C. Ross. 645p. (C). 1996. spiral bd. 28.75 (*0-314-04651-8*) West Pub.

Understanding & Using Lotus 1-2-3 Release 2.3 & 2.4. Steven C. Ross. Ed. by Leyh. LC 92-26257. (Microcomputing Ser.). 416p. (C). 1993. pap. text ed. 28.75 (*0-314-01111-0*) West Pub.

Understanding & Using Lotus 1-2-3 Release 3. Steven C. Ross. Ed. by Leyh. 411p. (C). 1991. pap. text ed. 32.50 (*0-314-47365-3*) West Pub.

Understanding & Using Microcomputers. Steven M. Zimmerman & Leo Conrad. Ed. by Leyh. 436p. (C). 1991. pap. text ed. 54.25 (*0-314-76172-1*) West Pub.

Understanding & Using Microsoft Access. Bruce J. McLaren. Ed. by Leyh. LC 93-38814. 450p. (C). 1993. pap. text ed. 28.75 (*0-314-02586-3*) West Pub.

Understanding & Using Microsoft Access for Windows 95. Bruce J. McLaren. (Microcomputing Ser.). 450p. (C). 1996. spiral bd. write for info. (*0-314-07233-0*) West Pub.

Understanding & Using Microsoft Access 2.0. Bruce J. McLaren. LC 94-31178. (Microcomputing Ser.). 512p. (C). 1995. pap. text ed. 28.75 (*0-314-04653-4*) West Pub.

Understanding & Using MICROSOFT BASIC-IBM PC BASIC. Mary L. Howard. LC 86-26748. (Microcomputing Ser.). 247p. (Orig.). (C). 1987. pap. text ed. 28.75 (*0-314-34632-5*) West Pub.

Understanding & Using Microsoft Excel for Windows 95. Steven C. Ross & Stephen V. Hutson. 450p. (C). 1996. spiral bd. 29.50 (*0-314-07239-X*) West Pub.

Understanding & Using Microsoft Excel 3.0. Steven C. Ross & Stephen V. Hutson. Ed. by Leyh. 410p. (C). 1992. spiral bd. 28.75 (*0-314-93406-5*) West Pub.

Understanding & Using Microsoft Excel 4. Steven C. Ross & Stephen V. Hutson. Ed. by Leyh. LC 93-28874. (Microcomputing Ser.). 400p. (C). 1994. teacher ed., pap. text ed. 28.75 (*0-314-02588-X*) West Pub.

Understanding & Using Microsoft Excel 5.0. Steven C. Ross & Stephen V. Hutson. LC 94-5365. (Microcomputing Ser.). 528p. (C). 1995. pap. text ed. 28.75 (*0-314-04626-7*) West Pub.

Understanding & Using Microsoft Office for Windows 95. Emily M. Ketcham. LC 95-45559. 750p. (C). 1996. pap. text ed. 54.75 (*0-314-07236-5*) West Pub.

Understanding & Using Microsoft Powerpoint for Windows 95. Lisa J. Friedrichsen. LC 95-46505. 150p. (C). 1996. pap. text ed. 21.75 (*0-314-07230-6*) West Pub.

Understanding & Using Microsoft PowerPoint 4.0. Edna Dixon. LC 95-37993. (Microcomputing Ser.). 150p. (C). 1995. pap. text ed. 9.75 (*0-314-04655-0*) West Pub.

Understanding & Using Microsoft QBASIC. Jonathan C. Barron. LC 94-19249. (Microcomputing Ser.). 288p. (C). 1995. pap. text ed. 20.50 (*0-314-03977-5*) West Pub.

Understanding & Using Microsoft Visual BASIC. Jonathan C. Barron. LC 95-38007. 450p. (C). 1996. spiral bd. 26.75 (*0-314-07155-5*) West Pub.

Understanding & Using Microsoft Visual BASIC Version 4.0. Jonathan C. Barron. LC 96-17876. (Microcomputing Ser.). 450p. 1997. pap. write for info. (*0-314-20078-9*) West Pub.

Understanding & Using Microsoft Windows 3. Steven C. Ross & Ronald W. Maestas. Ed. by Leyh. 309p. (C). 1992. spiral bd. 28.75 (*0-314-93375-1*) West Pub.

Understanding & Using Microsoft Windows 3.1. Steven C. Ross & Ronald W. Maestas. Ed. by Leyh. LC 93-8665. 384p. (C). 1994. pap. text ed. 28.75 (*0-314-02589-8*) West Pub.

Understanding & Using Microsoft Windows 4. Steven C. Ross & Ronald W. Maestas. 450p. 1995. write for info. (*0-314-04659-3*) West Pub.

Understanding & Using Microsoft Windows 95. Steven C. Ross & Ronald W. Maestas. LC 95-45674. (Microcomputing Ser.). 400p. (C). 1996. spiral bd. 31.50 (*0-314-07240-3*) West Pub.

Understanding & Using Microsoft Word. Jonathan P. Bacon. 200p. (C). 1988. pap. text ed. 28.75 (*0-314-72625-X*) West Pub.

Understanding & Using Microsoft Word for Windows. Larry Lozuk. Ed. by Leyh. 300p. (C). 1992. spiral bd. 28.75 (*0-314-93443-X*) West Pub.

Understanding & Using Microsoft Word for Windows 2.0. Larry Lozuk & Emily M. Ketcham. Ed. by Leyh. LC 93-1658. (Microcomputing Ser.). 384p. (C). 1993. pap. text ed. 28.75 (*0-314-02473-5*) West Pub.

Understanding & Using Microsoft Word for Windows 6.0. Emily Ketcham. LC 94-8271. (Microcomputing Ser.). 1994. pap. text ed. 28.75 (*0-314-03978-3*) West Pub.

Understanding & Using Microsoft Word for Windows 95. Emily Ketcham. LC 95-46586. 450p. (C). 1996. spiral bd. write for info. (*0-314-07235-7*) West Pub.

Understanding & Using Microsoft Word 5.0. Jonathan P. Bacon. Ed. by Leyh. 350p. (C). 1991. pap. write for info. (*0-318-68307-5*) West Pub.

Understanding & Using Microsoft Works for Windows 3.0. Gary G. Bitter. 450p. (C). 1995. pap. text ed. 31.00 (*0-314-03973-2*) West Pub.

Understanding & Using Microsoft Works 2.0, Macintosh. Gary G. Bitter. Ed. by Leyh. 378p. (C). 1991. pap. text ed. 37.00 (*0-314-76542-5*) West Pub.

Understanding & Using Microsoft Works 2.0, PC. Gary G. Bitter. Ed. by Leyh. 394p. (C). 1991. pap. text ed. 37.00 (*0-314-77286-3*) West Pub.

Understanding & Using Microsoft Works 3.0 on the Macintosh. Gary Bitter. Ed. by Leyh. LC 94-2549. (Microcomputing Ser.). 400p. (C). 1994. pap. text ed. 31.00 (*0-314-02856-0*) West Pub.

Understanding & Using Microsoft Works 3.0 on the PC. Gary G. Bitter. LC 93-43443. (Microcomputing Ser.). 1994. pap. text ed. 31.00 (*0-314-02587-1*) West Pub.

Understanding & Using MS DOS - PC DOS: A Complete Guide. Cody C. Copeland & Jonathan P. Bacon. (Microcomputing Ser.). 262p. (C). 1987. pap. text ed. 28.75 (*0-314-34747-X*) West Pub.

Understanding & Using MS-DOS - PC-DOS: Hard Disk Edition. Cody T. Copeland & Jonathan P. Bacon. Ed. by Leyh. 398p. (C). 1990. pap. text ed. 28.75 (*0-314-66573-0*) West Pub.

Understanding & Using MS-DOS - PC-DOS: The First Steps. 2nd ed. Laura B. Ruff & Mary K. Weitzer. Ed. by Leyh. 118p. (C). 1989. pap. text ed. 19.50 (*0-314-50330-7*) West Pub.

Understanding & Using MS-DOS - PC-DOS 5.0. Jonathan P. Bacon. Ed. by Leyh. LC 92-26261. (Microcomputer Ser.). 450p. (C). 1993. pap. text ed. 28.75 (*0-314-01110-2*) West Pub.

Understanding & Using MS-DOS 6.0. Jonathan P. Bacon. Ed. by Leyh. LC 93-41645. 450p. (C). 1994. pap. text ed. 28.75 (*0-314-02863-3*) West Pub.

***Understanding & Using MS Office 97.** Ketcham. (DF - Computer Applications Ser.). (C). 1998. pap. 50.95 (*0-538-68147-0*) S-W Pub.

***Understanding & Using MS Word 97.** Ketcham. (DF - Computer Applications Ser.). (C). 1998. pap. 50.95 (*0-538-71961-3*) S-W Pub.

***Understanding & Using Ms Word 97.** Ketcham. (DF - Computer Applications Ser.). (C). 1998. pap. 79.95 (*0-538-71970-2*) S-W Pub.

***Understanding & Using Netscape Navigator.** Jonathan P. Bacon & Robert G. Sindt. LC 96-41388. (Microcomputing Ser.). 1996. pap. write for info. (*0-314-20606-X*) West Pub.

Understanding & Using NetWare 3.X. Larry D. Smith. LC 95-33226. (Microcomputing Ser.). 400p. (C). 1996. spiral bd. 26.75 (*0-314-05976-8*) West Pub.

Understanding & Using Networks. E. Joseph Guay. Ed. by Leyh. LC 93-13517. 150p. (C). 1993. pap. text ed. 21.75 (*0-314-01350-4*) West Pub.

Understanding & Using PageMaker 4.0. John R. Nicholson. Ed. by Leyh. LC 92-28569. (Microcomputing Ser.). 416p. (C). 1993. pap. text ed. 28.75 (*0-314-01269-9*) West Pub.

Understanding & Using Pagemaker 5.0. John R. Nicholson. LC 94-11725. (Microcomputing Ser.). 480p. (C). 1995. spiral bd. 28.75 (*0-314-03972-4*) West Pub.

Understanding & Using Paradox 3.5. Larry D. Smith. Ed. by Leyh. LC 92-37389. (Microcomputing Ser.). 450p. (C). 1993. pap. text ed. 28.75 (*0-314-01224-9*) West Pub.

***Understanding & Using Paradox 4.5 for Window.** 11th ed. Smith. (DF - Computer Applications Ser.). 1995. pap. 8.00 (*0-314-02815-3*) West Pub.

Understanding & Using Paradox 4.5 for Windows. Larry D. Smith. Ed. by Leyh. LC 94-8272. (Microcomputing Ser.). 450p. (C). 1994. spiral bd. 28.75 (*0-314-02855-2*) West Pub.

Understanding & Using PFS: File-Report. Laura B. Ruff & Mary K. Weitzer. (Illus.). 253p. (Orig.). (C). 1986. pap. text ed. 28.75 (*0-314-96215-8*) West Pub.

Understanding & Using Quattro Pro for Windows. Larry D. Smith. Ed. by Leyh. LC 93-32088. (Microcomputing Ser.). 450p. (C). 1994. teacher ed., pap. text ed. 28.75 (*0-314-02584-7*) West Pub.

Understanding & Using Quattro Pro 4. Steven C. Ross & Stephen V. Hutson. Ed. by Leyh. LC 92-26259. (Microcomputer Ser.). 416p. (C). 1993. pap. text ed. 28.75 (*0-314-01035-1*) West Pub.

Understanding & Using Quattro Pro 6.0 for Windows. Lisa Friedrichsen. 500p. (C). 1996. spiral bd. 28.75 (*0-314-04658-5*) West Pub.

Understanding & Using RBase 5000. Karen L. Watterson. 242p. (C). 1987. teacher ed. write for info. (*0-318-61427-8*); pap. text ed. 28.75 (*0-314-30118-6*) West Pub.

Understanding & Using Supercalc 3. Steven C. Ross & Judy A. Reinders. (Microcomputing Ser.). 184p. (C). pap. text ed. 28.75 (*0-314-30123-2*) West Pub.

Understanding & Using Supercalc 4. Judy A. Reinders & Steven C. Ross. 212p. (C). 1988. pap. text ed. 28.75 (*0-314-34291-5*) West Pub.

Understanding & Using Symphony. Enzo V. Allegretti. (Microcomputing Ser.). 226p. (C). 1987. pap. text ed. 28.75 (*0-314-34640-6*); Instr's. manual. teacher ed., pap. text ed. write for info. (*0-314-34653-8*) West Pub.

Understanding & Using Technology. Todd. (Tech & Industrial Education Ser.). 1995. teacher ed., pap. 31.95 (*0-8273-6408-3*) Delmar.

Understanding & Using Technology. 2nd ed. Todd. (Tech & Industrial Education Ser.). 1995. text ed. 29.95 (*0-8273-6407-5*) Delmar.

Understanding & Using the Internet. Bruce J. McLaren. (Microcomputing Ser.). 150p. (C). 1996. pap. text ed. 12.25 (*0-314-06411-7*) West Pub.

***Understanding & Using the Internet.** 2nd ed. Bruce J. Mclaren. LC 96-43055. (West's Microcomputing Ser.). 150p. 1997. pap. write for info. (*0-314-20602-7*) West Pub.

Understanding & Using the Macintosh. Barbara Heiman & Nancy McGauley. Ed. by Leyh. LC 93-42969. (Microcomputing Ser.). 400p. (C). 1994. pap. text ed. 28.75 (*0-314-02585-5*) West Pub.

***Understanding & Using Today's Construction Contract Documents.** Hans W. Meier. (Illus.). 123p. (Orig.). 1996. spiral bd., pap. 19.95 (*1-889892-05-X*) Builders Bk Inc.

Understanding & Using Video: A Guide for the Organizational Communicator. 211p. 1985. 34.95 (*0-582-28469-4*) Intl Assn Busn Comm.

Understanding & Using WordPerfect. Patsy H. Lund et al. LC 86-26727. (Microcomputing Ser.). 227p. (C). 1987. pap. text ed. 28.75 (*0-314-30122-4*); teacher ed., pap. text ed. write for info. (*0-314-35883-8*) West Pub.

Understanding & Using WordPerfect for Windows. Jonathan P. Bacon. Ed. by Leyh. LC 92-32700. (Microcomputing Ser.). 400p. (C). 1993. spiral bd. 28.75 (*0-314-93453-7*) West Pub.

Understanding & Using WordPerfect Release 5.1. Cody T. Copeland & Jonathan P. Bacon. Ed. by Leyh. 436p. (C). 1991. pap. text ed. 28.75 (*0-314-81983-5*) West Pub.

Understanding & Using WordPerfect 6.0. Jonathan P. Bacon & Robert G. Sindt. Ed. by Leyh. LC 94-13253. (Microcomputing Ser.). 450p. (C). 1994. spiral bd. 28.75 (*0-314-02868-4*) West Pub.

Understanding & Using WordPerfect 6.0 for Windows. Jonathan P. Bacon. LC 94-13254. (Microcomputing Ser.). 672p. (C). 1995. spiral bd. 28.75 (*0-314-03974-0*) West Pub.

Understanding & Using WordPerfect 6.1. Jonathan P. Bacon. 400p. (C). 1995. pap. text ed. write for info. (*0-314-04660-7*) West Pub.

Understanding & Using WordPerfect 6.1 for Windows. Jonathan P. Bacon. LC 95-8112. (Microcomputing Ser.). 600p. (C). 1995. spiral bd. 28.75 (*0-314-06016-2*) West Pub.

***Understanding & Using Wordperfect 6.1 For Windows: Quick Reference Guide.** Gloria Henderson. (C). 1996. 37.00 (*0-256-23608-9*) Irwin.

Understanding & Using WordStar. Steven C. Ross. (Illus.). 237p. (Orig.). (C). 1986. pap. text ed. 28.75 (*0-314-96207-7*) West Pub.

***Understanding & Using Wordstar.** 11th ed. Lund. (DF - Computer Applications Ser.). (C). 1988. student ed., pap. 31.00 (*0-314-40884-3*) West Pub.

Understanding & Working with Parents & Children from Rural Mexico: What Professionals Need to Know about Child-Rearing Practices, the School Experience, & Health Care Concerns. B. Annye Rothenberg. LC 94-31386. 285p. 1995. per. 27.50 (*0-9642119-0-4*) CHC Ctr.

Understanding & Working with the Japanese Business World. Hiroki Kato. 1992. 19.95 (*0-13-155839-0*, Busn) P-H.

Understanding Anesthesia. 2nd ed. Carrie. 501p. 1988. pap. 70.00 (*0-433-00039-2*) Buttrwrth-Heinemann.

Understanding Anesthesia Equipment. 3rd ed. Jerry A. Dorsch. (Illus.). 736p. 1993. 79.00 (*0-683-02616-X*) Williams & Wilkins.

Understanding Animal Breeding. Bourdon. 608p. (C). 1996. text ed. 73.00 (*0-02-312851-8*, Macmillan Coll) P-H.

***Understanding Anne Frank's The Diary of a Young Girl: A Student Casebook to Issues, Sources & Historical Documents.** Hedda R. Kopf. LC 96-50294. (Greenwood Press Literature in Context Ser.). 1997. text ed. write for info. (*0-313-29607-3*, Greenwood Pr) Greenwood.

Understanding Anne Tyler. Alice H. Petry. (Understanding Contemporary American Literature Ser.). 277p. (C). 1990. pap. 12.95 (*0-87249-742-9*); text ed. 29.95 (*0-87249-716-X*) U of SC Pr.

Understanding Anorexia Nervosa. Felicia F. Romeo. 116p. (C). 1986. 28.95 (*0-398-05191-7*) C C Thomas.

Understanding Antennas for Radar, Communication & Avionics. Gregory A. Robertshaw. (Illus.). 336p. 1987. text ed. 79.95 (*0-442-27772-5*) Van Nos Reinhold.

***Understanding Antique Silver Plate: Reference & Price Guide.** Stephen J. Helliwell. 1996. 49.50 (*1-85149-247-X*) Antique Collect.

Understanding Antique Wine Bottles. R. Dumbrell. (Understanding Ser.). (Illus.). 340p. 1983. 29.50 (*0-907462-14-6*) Antique Collect.

Understanding Aphasia. Harold Goodglass. LC 93-1533. (Foundations of Neuropsychology Ser.). (Illus.). 297p. 1993. text ed. 58.00 (*0-12-290040-5*) Acad Pr.

Understanding Arabic: Essays in Contemporary Arabic Linguistics in Honor of El-Said Badawi. Ed. by Alaa Elgibali. 336p. 1996. 39.00 (*977-424-372-2*, Pub. by Am Univ Cairo Pr UA) Col U Pr.

Understanding Arabs: A Guide for Westerners. Margaret K. Nydell. LC 86-83102. 176p. 1987. pap. text ed. 16.95 (*0-933662-65-3*) Intercult Pr.

Understanding Arabs: A Guide for Westerners. 2nd rev. ed. Margaret K. Nydell. LC 96-9063. (InterAct Ser.). 192p. 1996. 17.95 (*1-877864-46-3*) Intercult Pr.

Understanding Architectural Drawings: A Guide for Non-Architects. John J. Cullinane. (Illus.). 130p. 1995. pap. text ed. 24.95 (*0-471-14429-0*) Wiley.

Understanding Architecture: An Introduction to Architecture & Architectural History. Hazel Conway & Rowan Roenisch. LC 93-47002. (Illus.). 240p. (C). 1994. pap. 19.95 (*0-415-10466-1*, B4445) Routledge.

Understanding Architecture: Its Elements, History, Meaning. Leland M. Roth. LC 88-45540. (Illus.). 576p. 1993. 45.00 (*0-00-001606-3*, PL); pap. 30.00 (*0-06-430158-3*, PL) HarpC.

Understanding Architecture Through Drawing. Brian Edwards. LC 93-35409. 1993. write for info. (*0-419-18640-9*, E & FN Spon) Routledge Chapman & Hall.

Understanding Archives & Manuscripts. James M. O'Toole. (Archival Fundamentals Ser.). 76p. 1990. pap. 25.00 (*0-931828-77-5*) Soc Am Archivists.

Understanding Argument: A Text with Readings. Dorothy U. Seyler. LC 93-10907. (C). 1993. pap. text ed. write for info. (*0-07-056438-8*) McGraw.

***Understanding Arguments.** 5th ed. Fogelin. (C). 1996. teacher ed., pap. text ed. 28.00 (*0-15-505129-6*) HarBrace.

Understanding Arguments. 5th ed. Fogelin. (C). 1997. pap. text ed. write for info. (*0-15-502098-6*) HB Coll Pubs.

Understanding Arguments: An Introduction to Informal Logic. 4th ed. Robert J. Fogelin & Walter Sinnott-Armstrong. 496p. (C). 1990. pap. text ed. 28.75 (*0-15-592672-1*) HB Coll Pubs.

Understanding Arnold Wesker. Robert Wilcher. Ed. by Matthew J. Bruccoli. LC 91-15703. (Understanding Contemporary British Literature Ser.). 194p. 1991. text ed. 29.95 (*0-87249-760-7*) U of SC Pr.

Understanding Art. Ragans. 38.97 (*0-02-662286-6*) Glencoe.

Understanding Art. 4th ed. Lois Fichner-Rathus. LC 94-13304. 533p. 1994. pap. text ed. 58.00 (*0-13-952961-6*) P-H.

Understanding Art. 4th ed. Hewitt. 1994. student ed., pap. text ed. 15.20 (*0-13-400151-6*) P-H.

Understanding Art. 4th ed. Spencer A. Rathus. 1994. student ed., pap. text ed. 18.67 (*0-13-954447-X*) P-H.

Understanding Art. 4th ed. Sandak. 1995. write for info. incl. sl. (*0-13-954405-4*) P-H.

***Understanding Art.** 5th ed. Fichner. LC 97-16039. 1997. pap. text ed. 49.33 (*0-13-645938-2*) P-H.

Understanding Art in Primary Schools. Ed. by Tickle. 292p. (C). 1996. pap. text ed. 22.95 (*0-415-13031-X*) Routledge.

Understanding Art Testing: Past Influences, Norman C. Meier's Contributions, Present Concerns, & Future Possibilities. Enid D. Zimmerman et al. 128p. (C). 1987. pap. 17.00 (*0-937652-40-7*) Natl Art Ed.

Understanding Arthritis. Myron G. Rosenbaum. LC 73-9498. (Illus.). 112p. 1975. 8.50 (*0-87527-121-9*) Green.

***Understanding Arthritis.** large type ed. Ann F. Irving et al. LC 96-48727. (Spec-Hall Ser.). 309p. 1997. lib. bdg. 24.95 (*0-7838-8043-X*, GK Hall) Thorndike Pr.

Understanding Arthritis: What It Is, How To Treat it, How to Cope with It. Arthritis Foundation Editors. (Illus.). 290p. 1986. pap. 12.00 (*0-684-18736-1*) S&S Trade.

Understanding Arthur Miller. Alice Griffin. Ed. by Matthew Broccoli. LC 95-41776. (Understanding Contemporary American Literature Ser.). 220p. 1996. text ed. 34.95 (*1-57003-101-0*) U of SC Pr.

Understanding Asian Americans: A Curriculum Resource Guide. Ed. by Marjorie Li & Peter Li. 185p. (Orig.). 1990. pap. text ed. 35.00 (*1-55570-047-0*) Neal-Schuman.

Understanding Aspects: The Inconjunct. Alan Epstein. 184p. 1995. pap. 12.95 (*0-9649783-0-X*) Trines Pubng.

***Understanding Aspects - the Sextile.** Alan Epstein. 200p. 1997. pap. write for info. (*0-9649783-1-8*) Trines Pubng.

Understanding Assessment & Evaluation in Early Childhood Education. Dominic F. Gullo. LC 93-29495. (Early Childhood Education Ser.). 290p. (C). 1994. text ed. 32.00 (*0-8077-3309-1*); pap. text ed. 16.95 (*0-8077-3308-3*) Tchrs Coll.

Understanding Asset Allocation: What You Need to Know Before Making Investment Decisions. Richard D. Glass & Stan Marshall. (Illus.). 30p. (Orig.). 1995. pap. 6.95 (*0-9638029-3-3*) Invest Horizons.

Understanding Astrology: Practical Guide to the Stars. Sasha Fenton. (Illus.). 1995. pap. 8.00 (*1-85538-065-X*) Thorsons SF.

Understanding ATM. Stanley Schatt. (Illus.). 352p. 1996. pap. text ed. 45.00 (*0-07-057679-3*) McGraw.

Understanding Atmospheric Change: A Survey of the Background Science & Implications of Climate Change & Ozone Depletion. Henry Hengeveld. (Illus.). 68p. (Orig.). (C). 1994. pap. text ed. 30.00 (*0-7881-0635-X*) DIANE Pub.

Understanding Attitudes about War: Modeling Moral Judgments. Gregory G. Brunk et al. LC 95-53043. (Pitt Series in Policy & Institutional). 256p. (C). 1996. text ed. 45.00 (*0-8229-3926-6*); pap. text ed. 19.95 (*0-8229-5585-7*) U of Pittsburgh Pr.

Understanding Attitudes to the European Community: A Social-Psychological Study in Four Member States. Miles Hewstone. (European Monographs in Social Psychology). (Illus.). 300p. 1986. text ed. 69.95 (*0-521-32165-4*) Cambridge U Pr.

***Understanding Audits & the Auditor's Report: A Guide for Financial Statement Users.** 2nd ed. American Institute of Certified Public Accountants Staff. LC 96-31406. 1996. write for info. (*0-87051-180-7*) Am Inst CPA.

Understanding Authority see Lay Counseling Series

Understanding Authority for Effective Leadership. rev. ed. Buddy Harrison. 80p. (Orig.). 1991. pap. 4.99 (*0-89274-869-9*, HH-869) Harrison Hse.

Understanding AutoLISP: Programming for Productivity. William Kramer. LC 92-40585. 225p. 1993. pap. 30.50 (*0-8273-5832-6*) Delmar.

Understanding Automotive Electronics. 4th ed. William B. Ribbens. (Illus.). 392p. (Orig.). 1992. 24.95 (*0-672-27358-6*) Buttrwrth-Heinemann.

Understanding Automotive Emissions Control: Theory, Troubleshooting, Maintenance, Testing, Tuning, Repair. Larry Carley & Bob Freudenberger. LC 94-24720. 176p. (Orig.). 1995. pap. 16.00 (*1-55788-201-0*, HP Books) Berkley Pub.

Understanding Avalanches: A Handbook for Snow Travelers in the Sierra & Cascades. Barbara Diltz-Siler. (Illus.). 32p. 1977. pap. 3.95 (*0-913140-24-4*) Signpost Bk Pub.

Understanding Bacterial Action. Russel. 1990. pap. write for info. (*0-318-68274-5*) P-H.

Understanding Baking. 2nd ed. Joseph Amendola. 300p. 1992. pap. 29.95 (*0-442-00967-4*) Van Nos Reinhold.

Understanding Balance: The Mechanics of Posture & Locomotion. T. D. Roberts. 360p. 1995. pap. 47.99 (*1-56593-416-4*, 1082) Singular Publishing.

Understanding Balance Sheets. George Friedlob. 250p. 1996. text ed. 34.95 (*0-471-13075-3*) Wiley.

Understanding Ballistics: Basic to Advanced Ballistics, Simplified, Illustrated & Explained. 2nd rev. ed. Robert A. Rinker. LC 95-94092. (Illus.). 373p. (Orig.). 1996. pap. 19.95 (*0-9645598-1-1*) Mulberry Hse Pub.

***Understanding Bandwidth.** Cary Lu. LC 97-4204. 1997. pap. text ed. 17.99 (*1-57231-513-X*) Microsoft.

Understanding Bankruptcy in the United States. Albergotti. 1992. 94.95 (*0-631-18125-3*) Blackwell Pubs.

Understanding Bar Code. James R. Plunkett. (Quick Read Ser.). (Illus.). 70p. (Orig.). 1993. pap. 39.95 (*1-884322-17-4*) Duke Commns Intl.

Understanding Basic. Steven L. Mandell. Date not set. text ed. 46.50 (*0-314-89690-2*) West Pub.

Understanding Basic Copyright Law 1995. (Patents, Copyrights, Trademarks, & Literary Property Ser.). 384p. 1995. pap. 99.00 (*0-685-69727-4*, G4-3946) PLI.

Understanding Basic Electronics. 314p. 1996. 20.00 (*0-87259-398-3*) Am Radio.

Understanding Basic Energy Terms. Robert V. Nelson. LC 81-2888. 1981. pap. text ed. 8.00 (*0-86663-807-5*); lib. bdg. 10.00 (*0-86663-806-7*) Ide Hse.

Understanding Basic Estate Planning. (Tax Law & Estate Planning Course Handbook Ser.: Vol. 223). 240p. 1993. 70.00 (*0-685-69748-7*, D4-5239) PLI.

Understanding Basic Mechanics. Frederick Reif. LC 94-44982. 471p. 1995. pap. text ed. write for info. (*0-471-10337-3*); student ed., pap. text ed. 25.95 (*0-471-11624-6*) Wiley.

Understanding Basic Mechanics. Frederick Reif. LC 94-44982. 1911. pap. write for info. (*0-471-11623-8*) Wiley.

Understanding Basic Pharmacology: Practical Approaches for Effective Application. Barbara MacDermott & Judith H. Deglin. 546p. (C). 1994. pap. text ed. 26.95 (*0-8036-5714-5*) Davis Co.

***Understanding Basic Statistics.** Charles Brase & Corrinne Brase. 608p. (C). 1996. text ed. 48.36 (*0-669-39812-8*) HM College Div.

***Understanding Basic Statistics.** Charles Brase & Corrinne Brase. (C). 1996. student ed., text ed. 17.16 (*0-669-39814-4*) HM College Div.

Understanding Basic Statistics. Harvey W. Kushner & Gerald De Maio. LC 78-54195. 1980. text ed. 29.95 (*0-8162-4874-5*); teacher ed. 6.00 (*0-686-76791-8*, 0-8162-8475) Holden-Day.

Understanding Basic Trademark Law 1995. (Patents, Copyrights, Trademarks, & Literary Property Ser.). 510p. 1995. pap. 99.00 (*0-685-69728-2*, G4-3947) PLI.

***Understanding Bats: Discovering the Secret Lives of These Gentle Mammals.** Ron Meis & Kim Williams. Ed. by William H. Thompson, III et al. (Illus.). 32p. (Orig.). 1996. pap. write for info. (*0-614-30206-4*) Bird Watchers.

Understanding Beckett: A Study of Monologue & Gesture in the Works of Samuel Beckett. Peter Gidal. LC 85-8304. 246p. 1986. text ed. 39.95 (*0-312-83080-7*) St Martin.

Understanding Behavior: What Primate Studies Tell Us about Human Behavior. Ed. by James Loy & Calvin B. Peters. (Illus.). 280p. 1991. 60.00 (*0-19-506020-2*) OUP.

Understanding Big Government: The Programme Approach. Richard Rose. LC 83-51198. iii, 261p. 1984. 39.95 (*0-8039-9778-7*); pap. 16.95 (*0-8039-9779-5*) Sage.

Understanding Biology. Peter H. Raven & George B. Johnson. 896p. (C). 1994. text ed. write for info. (*0-697-25448-8*) Wm C Brown Pubs.

Understanding Biology. Peter H. Raven et al. 312p. (C). 1994. student ed., per. write for info. (*0-697-25449-6*) Wm C Brown Pubs.

Understanding Biology. 2nd ed. Johnson & Peter H. Raven. (Illus.). 416p. (C). 1989. student ed. 14.95 (*0-8016-5288-X*) Mosby Yr Bk.

Understanding Biology. 2nd ed. Peter H. Raven & George B. Johnson. 850p. (C). 1994. text ed. write for info. (*0-697-25253-1*) Wm C Brown Pubs.

Understanding Biology. 2nd ed. Peter H. Raven & George B. Johnson. 850p. (C). 1993. text ed. write for info. (*0-697-23503-3*); student ed., spiral bd. write for info. (*0-697-23505-X*) Wm C Brown Pubs.

Understanding Biology. 2nd ed. Peter H. Raven & George B. Johnson. 416p. (C). 1995. student ed., spiral bd. write for info. (*0-697-22217-9*) Wm C Brown Pubs.

Understanding Biology. 3rd ed. Peter H. Raven & George B. Johnson. 968p. (C). 1995. text ed. write for info. (*0-697-22213-6*) Wm C Brown Pubs.

Understanding Biology. 3rd ed. Peter H. Raven & George B. Johnson. 64p. 1995. student ed., spiral bd. write for info. (*0-697-25031-8*) Wm C Brown Pubs.

Understanding Biology. 3rd ed. Peter H. Raven & George B. Johnson. 384p. (C). 1995. student ed., per. write for info. (*0-697-22216-0*) Wm C Brown Pubs.

Understanding Biology, Vol. I. 3rd ed. Peter H. Raven & George B. Johnson. 552p. (C). 1995. per. write for info. (*0-697-26327-4*) Wm C Brown Pubs.

Understanding Biology, Vol. II. 3rd ed. Peter H. Raven & George B. Johnson. 496p. (C). 1995. per. write for info. (*0-697-26328-2*) Wm C Brown Pubs.

Understanding Biology: Study Guide. 2nd ed. Vernon & David C. Whitenack. 448p. 1991. pap. 16.95 (*0-8016-4515-8*) Mosby Yr Bk.

Understanding Biology for Advanced Level. Glenn Toole & Susan Toole. (C). 1987. text ed. 130.00 (*0-7487-0288-1*, Pub. by S Thornes Pubs UK) St Mut.

Understanding Biology for Advanced Level. Glenn Toole & Susan Toole. 712p. (C). 1994. 57.00 (*0-7478-0539-3*, Pub. by Stanley Thornes UK) Trans-Atl Phila.

Understanding Biostatistics. Hassard. (Illus.). 304p. (C). (gr. 13). 1991. pap. text ed. 35.95 (*0-8016-2078-3*) Mosby Yr Bk.

Understanding Biotechnology Law: Protection, Licensing, & Intellectual Property Policies. Ed. by Gale R. Peterson. LC 93-7101. 496p. 1993. 175.00 (*0-8247-8935-0*) Dekker.

Understanding Birth Defects. Karen Gravelle. LC 90-32658. (Illus.). 128p. (YA). (gr. 9-12). 1990. lib. bdg. 22.70 (*0-531-10955-0*) Watts.

Understanding Black Adolescent Male Violence: Its Remediation & Prevention. Amos N. Wilson. 92p. (Orig.). 1992. pap. 5.95 (*1-879164-03-5*) African World.

Understanding Black Africa: Data & Analysis of Social Change & Nation Building. Donald G. Morrison et al. LC 88-33052. (Illus.). 253p. (C). 1989. text ed. 39.50 (*0-8290-2228-7*); pap. text ed. 19.95 (*0-8290-1371-7*) Irvington.

Understanding Black Africa: Data & Analysis of Social Change & Nation Building. Donald G. Morrison et al. LC 88-33052. 255p. 1988. 39.50 (*0-88702-052-6*) Washington Inst Pr.

Understanding Blindness: An Integrative Approach. Mark Hollins. 200p. 1989. 39.95 (*0-89859-952-0*) L Erlbaum Assocs.

Understanding Boat Design. 4th ed. Edward S. Brewer. 1993. pap. text ed. 16.95 (*0-07-007694-4*) McGraw.

Understanding Boat Design. 4th ed. Ted Brewer. 1993. pap. 16.95 (*0-87742-392-X*) Intl Marine.

Understanding Body Movement: An Annotated Bibliography. Martha Davis. LC 73-37652. 1676p. 1979. 23.95 (*0-405-00286-6*) Ayer.

Understanding Bollinger Bands. Edward D. Dobson. (Illus.). 24p. (Orig.). 1994. pap. 8.00 (*0-934380-25-2*, 580) Traders Pr.

Understanding Book. John Pavao. Ed. by Ruth L. Perle. (Illus.). (J). (gr. 1). 1977. pap. text ed. 3.25 (*0-89796-863-8*) New Dimens Educ.

Understanding Book-Collecting. Grant Uden. (Understanding Ser.). (Illus.). 280p. 1986. 29.50 (*0-907462-13-8*) Antique Collect.

***Understanding Boris Pasternak.** Larissa Rudova. LC 96-45786. (Understanding Modern European Literature Ser.). 1997. 29.95 (*1-57003-143-6*) U of SC Pr.

***Understanding Boy Scouts with Handicaps.** (Illus.). 1996. pap. 1.45 (*0-8395-3056-0*, 33056) BSA.

Understanding Brain Damage: A Primer of Neuropsychological Evaluation. 2nd ed. Kevin W. Walsh. (Illus.). 304p. 1991. text ed. 75.00 (*0-443-04320-5*) Churchill.

***Understanding Brands: By Ten Experts Who Do.** Ed. by Con Cowley. (Marketing & Sales Ser.). 1996. pap. 25.00 (*0-7494-2110-X*) Kogan Page Ltd.

Understanding Breast Cancer: Clinical & Laboratory Concepts. Ed. by Marvin A. Rich et al. LC 83-18981. (Illus.). 415p. reprint ed. pap. 118.30 (*0-7837-0673-1*, 2041008) Bks Demand.

Understanding Breast Cancer Risk. Patricia T. Kelly. (Health, Society, & Policy Ser.). 195p. 1991. 49.95 (*0-87722-812-4*); pap. 18.95 (*0-87722-813-2*) Temple U Pr.

Understanding British English. Margaret E. Moore. 1989. pap. 9.95 (*0-8065-1149-4*, Citadel Pr) Carol Pub Group.

***Understanding British English.** rev. ed. Margaret Moore. LC 97-16018. 1997. pap. text ed. 9.95 (*0-8065-1939-8*, Citadel Pr) Carol Pub Group.

Understanding BS5750 & Other Quality Systems. Tony Brown. LC 93-36860. 180p. 1993. 43.95 (*0-566-07454-0*, Pub. by Gower UK); pap. 25.95 (*0-566-07455-9*, Pub. by Gower UK) Ashgate Pub Co.

Understanding Buddhism: Key Themes. Heinrich Dumoulin. Tr. by Joseph S. O'Leary from GER. 192p. (Orig.). 1993. pap. 14.95 (*0-8348-0297-X*) Weatherhill.

Understanding Budgeting. John A. Tracy. LC 96-22265. (Finance Fundamentals for Nonfinancial Managers Ser.). 250p. 1996. pap. text ed. 16.95 (*0-471-10928-2*) Wiley.

Understanding Budgets. Affinity Communications Staff. 1996. pap. 12.00 (*0-614-12589-8*) McGraw.

Understanding Building Automation Systems: Direct Digital Control Energy Management Life Safety. Reinhold A. Carlson & Robert Di Giandomenico. 225p. 1991. 74.95 (*0-87629-211-2*, 67284) ACMDG Co.

Understanding Buildings: A Multidisciplinary Approach. Esmond Reid. (Illus.). 256p. 1988. pap. 18.50 (*0-262-68054-8*) MIT Pr.

Understanding Business. Miller. Date not set. text ed. 46.50 (*0-314-80042-5*) West Pub.

Understanding Business. 3rd ed. Barbara Barrett. 416p. (C). 1992. student ed., per. 16.95 (*0-256-11667-9*) Irwin.

Understanding Business. 3rd ed. William G. Nickels et al. LC 92-17456. 984p. (C). 1992. text ed. 55.95 (*0-256-09548-5*) Irwin.

Understanding Business. 4th ed. William G. Nichels. LC 95-22442. 1995. text ed. write for info. (*0-256-19074-7*) Irwin.

***Understanding Business.** 4th ed. William Nickels & James McHugh. (C). 1996. text ed. 55.95 (*0-256-20282-6*) Irwin.

Understanding Business. 4th ed. William G. Nickels et al. LC 95-22442. 784p. (C). 1995. text ed. 55.95 (*0-256-14054-5*) Irwin.

Understanding Business. 4th ed. William G. Nickels et al. 800p. (C). 1995. 39.95 (*0-256-20215-X*) Irwin.

***Understanding Business.** 4th ed. William G. Nickels. (C). 1996. pap. text ed. 9.95 incl. disk (*0-256-19638-9*) Irwin.

Understanding Business: Electronic Presentation/Power-Point Slide With 3.50 IBM Disks. 4th ed. William G. Nickels. (C). 1995. write for info. incl. 5.25 ld (*0-256-19384-3*) Irwin.

***Understanding Business: Study Guide & Software Package.** 4th ed. William G. Nickels. (C). 1995. 55.95 incl. cd-rom (*0-256-21654-1*) Irwin.

Understanding Business & Consumer Law. 6th ed. R. Robert Rosenberg et al. (Illus.). (YA). (gr. 11-12). 1979. text ed. 25.12 (*0-07-053631-7*) McGraw.

Understanding Business & Finance: An Active-Learning Approach. Jill Hussey. Ed. by P. Cox et al. Tr. by M. Sutcliffe. 400p. (C). 1991. 65.00 (*1-870941-74-8*) St Mut.

Understanding Business & Personal Law. 7th ed. G. W. Brown. 576p. 1983. text ed. 24.28 (*0-07-053635-X*) McGraw.

Understanding Business & Personal Law. 8th ed. G. W. Brown. 608p. 1987. pap. text ed. 23.12 (*0-07-008433-5*) McGraw.

Understanding Business & Personal Law. 8th ed. Paul A. Sukys et al. 1987. pap. text ed. 26.50 (*0-07-008438-6*) Gregg-McGraw.

Understanding Business & Personal Law: Performance Guide. 7th ed. Gordon W. Brown & R. Robert Rosenberg. (Illus.). 144p. 1983. pap. text ed. 9.44 (*0-07-053636-8*) McGraw.

Understanding Business Bankruptcy: How to Handle Everyday Problems. 186p. 1991. pap. text ed. 12.00 (*0-685-49886-7*, A4-4334) PLI.

Understanding Business Bankruptcy 1992: How to Handle Everyday Problems - A Satellite Program. (Commercial Law & Practice Course Handbook Ser.: Vol. 633). 252p. 1992. 70.00 (*0-685-65478-8*, A4-4393) PLI.

Understanding Business Communication. Richard L. Weaver, II. (Illus.). 352p. (C). 1985. text ed. write for info. (*0-13-936998-8*) P-H.

Understanding Business Contracts in China, Nineteen Forty-Nine to Nineteen Sixty-Three. Richard M. Pfeffer. (East Asia Monographs: Vol. No. 53). 147p. 1973. 14.00 (*0-674-92095-3*) HUP.

Understanding Business Forecasting. 2nd ed. Chapman L. Jain. LC 87-82280. 261p. 1988. pap. text ed. 27.95 (*0-932126-15-4*) Graceway.

Understanding Business Forecasting: A Manager's Guide. Ed. by Al Migliaro & Chaman L. Jain. 234p. (Orig.). 1985. pap. 27.95 (*0-932126-12-X*) Graceway.

Understanding Business Getting & Keeping the Job You Want: A Practical Job Search Handbook. 4th ed. William G. Nickels et al. 256p. (C). 1995. 14.95 (*0-256-19362-2*) Irwin.

Understanding Business Objects. Robert E. Shelton. Ed. by Carter Shanklin. 225p. (C). 1997. pap. text ed. 26.95 (*0-201-89547-1*) Addison-Wesley.

***Understanding Business on the Internet.** Bob Norton & Cathy A. Smith. LC 96-32473. (Business Success Ser.). 1997. pap. 6.95 (*0-7641-0069-6*) Barron.

Understanding Business Statistics. John E. Hanke & Arthur G. Reitsch. 896p. (C). 1990. text ed. 61.95 (*0-256-06627-2*, 10-2691-01) Irwin.

***Understanding Business Statistics.** Gareth Lewis. LC 96-6541. (Business Success Ser.). 1997. pap. 6.95 (*0-7641-0257-5*) Barron.

Understanding Business Statistics. Paul Van Ness. 176p. (C). 1991. student ed., text ed. 17.50 (*0-256-09340-7*) Irwin.

Understanding Business Statistics. 2nd ed. John E. Hanke & Arthur G. Reitsch. LC 93-16827. 1024p. (C). 1993. Acid-free paper. text ed. 71.25 (*0-256-11219-3*) Irwin.

Understanding Business Statistics. 2nd ed. Walter Hartman & Paul D. Van Ness. 456p. (C). 1993. student ed. 22.75 (*0-256-12799-9*) Irwin.

Understanding Business Statistics: Selected Chapters. 2nd ed. John Hanke & Arthur G. Reitsch. (C). 1994. pap. text ed. 16.95 (*0-256-18349-X*) Irwin.

Understanding Business Statistics: Student Solutions Manual. 2nd ed. Paul D. Van Ness. 208p. (C). 1993. 18.75 (*0-256-12800-6*) Irwin.

Understanding Business Study Guide. 4th ed. William G. Nickels. 344p. (C). 1995. 16.95 (*0-256-19562-5*) Irwin.

Understanding Business, 1990. 2nd ed. William G. Nickels et al. 884p. (C). 1989. text ed. 55.95 (*0-256-07623-5*) Irwin.

Understanding Business, 1990. 2nd ed. William G. Nickels et al. 542p. (C). 1989. student ed., per. 16.95 (*0-256-08058-5*) Irwin.

***Understanding Caffeine: A Biobehavioral Analysis.** Jack E. James. LC 96-45893. (Behavioral Medicine & Health Psychology Ser.: Vol. 2). 230p. (C). 1997. 46.00 (*0-8039-7182-6*, 71826); pap. 21.95 (*0-8039-7183-4*, 71834) Sage.

Understanding Calcium & Osteoporosis. American Allergy Association Staff. Ed. by Irene T. McPherrin. 16p. 1987. pap. 4.00 (*0-9616708-4-3*) Allergy Pubns.

***Understanding Camilo Jose Cela.** Lucile C. Charlebois. LC 96-51296. 180p. 1997. 29.95 (*1-57003-151-7*) U of SC Pr.

Understanding Canada. Ed. by William Metcalfe et al. 624p. (C). 1982. pap. 22.50 (*0-8147-5383-3*); text ed. 44.00 (*0-8147-5382-5*) NYU Pr.

***Understanding Canada: Building on the New Canadian Political Economy.** Ed. by Wallace Clement. 408p. 1996. pap. 22.95 (*0-7735-1503-8*, Pub. by McGill CN) U of Toronto Pr.

***Understanding Canada: Building on the New Canadian Political Economy.** Ed. by Wallace Clement. 420p. 1996. 55.00 (*0-7735-1502-X*, Pub. by McGill CN) U of Toronto Pr.

***Understanding Canadian Business.** 2nd ed. William G. Nickels et al. 704p. (C). 1997. text ed. 45.95 (*0-256-19444-0*) Irwin.

Understanding Canadian Business: Canadian. William G. Nickels et al. (C). 1994. student ed., text ed. 15.00 (*0-256-10801-3*) Irwin.

Understanding Cancer. Susan N. Terkel & Marlene L. Brazz. LC 92-38715. (Illus.). 56p. (J). (gr. k-4). 1993. lib. bdg. 19.60 (*0-531-11085-0*) Watts.

Understanding Cancer. 4th ed. Mark Renneker. 1994. pap. 39.95 (0-923521-29-1) Bull Pub.

***Understanding Cancer: From Basic Science to Clinical Practice.** Malcolm Alison & Catherine Sarraf. (Postgraduate Medical Science Ser.). (Illus.). 320p. (C). 1997. text ed. 74.95 (0-521-56154-X) Cambridge U Pr.

***Understanding Cancer: From Basic Science to Clinical Practice.** Malcolm Alison & Catherine Sarraf. (Postgraduate Medical Science Ser.). (Illus.). 320p. (C). 1997. pap. text ed. 29.95 (0-521-56751-3) Cambridge U Pr.

Understanding Candida: Treatment & Recipes. Peter De Ruyter. 160p. (Orig.). 1989. pap. write for info. (1-85327-035-0, Pub. by Prism Pr UK) Assoc Pubs Grp.

Understanding Capital. Duncan K. Foley. (Illus.). 208p. 1986. 32.00 (0-674-92087-2); pap. 15.95 (0-674-92088-0) HUP.

Understanding Capitalism. 2nd ed. Samuel Bowles, III & George C. Edwards. (C). 1992. text ed. 55.93 (0-06-500645-3) Addson-Wesley Educ.

Understanding Capitalism: How Economies Work. Brian Kantor. 208p. 1995. pap. 17.95 (0-614-03026-9) M Boyars Pubs.

Understanding Cardiac Pacing: A Guide for Nurses. Kevan Metcalfe. (Illus.). 192p. 1986. pap. text ed. 36.95 (0-8385-9258-9, A9258-3) Appleton & Lange.

Understanding Cash Flow. George T. Friedlob & Franklin J. Plewa. LC 94-45407. 496p. 1995. pap. text ed. 14.95 (0-471-10386-1) Wiley.

Understanding Cash Flow. George T. Friedlob & Franklin J. Plewa. LC 94-45407. 296p. 1995. text ed. 49.95 (0-471-10385-3) Wiley.

Understanding Catastrophe. Ed. by Janine Bourriau. (Darwin College Lectures). (Illus.). 192p. (C). 1992. text ed. 34.95 (0-521-41324-9) Cambridge U Pr.

Understanding Catholic Christianity. Thomas Zanzig. (Illus.). 302p. 1988. pap. text ed. 11.20 (0-88489-182-8); teacher ed., spiral bd. 18.95 (0-88489-183-6) St Marys.

***Understanding Catholic Christianity.** Thomas Zanzig & Barbara Allaire. 352p. 1997. pap. text ed. 13.90 (0-88489-372-3) St Marys.

***Understanding Catholic Christianity.** Thomas Zanzig. 364p. 1997. teacher ed., spiral bd. 24.95 (0-88489-373-1) St Marys.

***Understanding Catholic Morality.** Elizabeth L. Willems. 1997. pap. text ed. 17.95 (0-8245-1725-3) Crossroad NY.

Understanding Catholicism. Monika K. Hellwig. LC 81-80047. 200p. (Orig.). 1981. pap. 10.95 (0-8091-2384-3) Paulist Pr.

Understanding Catholicism. John Honner. 65p. 1989. pap. 22.00 (0-85294-595-7, Pub. by Veritas IE) St Mut.

Understanding Catholicism: A Question & Answer Approach to the Catholic Faith. John Honner. 64p. 1989. pap. 4.95 (0-8146-1776-X) Liturgical Pr.

Understanding Cats: Their History, Nature, & Behavior. Roger K. Tabor. LC 96-25121. 1997. write for info. (0-89577-916-1) RD Assn.

Understanding Causes & Generalizing about Them. Ed. by Lee B. Sechrest & Anne G. Scott. LC 85-644749. (New Directions for Evaluation Ser.: No. 57). 88p. (Orig.). 1993. pap. 19.00 (1-55542-696-4) Jossey-Bass.

Understanding Celine. Philip H. Solomon. Ed. by James N. Hardin. LC 91-36224. (Understanding Modern European & Latin American Literature Ser.). 179p. 1992. text ed. 29.95 (0-87249-814-X) U of SC Pr.

Understanding Cell Structure. M. W. Steer. (Illus.). 120p. 1981. 49.95 (0-521-23745-9) Cambridge U Pr.

Understanding Census Data. Mike Long. 71p. 1990. reprint ed. 25.00 (0-923172-02-5) West Econ Rsch.

Understanding Census Data: A Quick & Simplified Reference. C. Michael Long. 71p. reprint ed. 25.00 (0-685-44383-3) West Econ Rsch.

Understanding Central America. 2nd ed. John A. Booth & Thomas W. Walker. 248p. (C). 1993. pap. text ed. 21.00 (0-8133-8219-X) Westview.

Understanding Challenging Behavior: A Step-by-Step Behavior Analysis Guide. Gerald Groden et al. 125p. 1993. ring bd. 89.00 (1-884937-03-9) Manisses Communs.

Understanding Change: Anthropological & Sociological Perspectives. S. C. Dube. (C). 1992. pap. text ed. 7.95 (0-7069-6396-2) Advent Bks Div.

Understanding Change in Education: Rural & Remote Regions of Canada. Ed. by Earle Newton & Doug Knight. 310p. (Orig.). (C). 1993. pap. text ed. 22.95 (1-55059-059-6) Temeron Bks.

***Understanding Change in Social Attitudes.** Bridget Taylor & Katarina Thomson. (Illus.). 232p. 1996. text ed. 59.95 (1-85521-892-5, Pub. by Dartmth Pub UK) Ashgate Pub Co.

Understanding Changing in Time: The Development of Diachronic Thinking in 7-12 Year Old Children. Jacques Montangero. 240p. 1996. 79.95 (0-7484-0470-8); pap. 24.95 (0-7484-0471-6) Taylor & Francis.

Understanding Characters: Advanced Level. 2nd ed. Ed. by Kraft. (Comprehension Skills Ser.). 64p. 1993. pap. 8.45 (0-89061-615-9) Jamestown Pubs.

Understanding Characters: Introductory Level. Ed. by Kraft. (Comprehension Skills Ser.). 64p. 1993. pap. 7.91 (0-89061-655-8) Jamestown Pubs.

Understanding Characters: Middle Level. 2nd ed. Ed. by Kraft. (Comprehension Skills Ser.). 64p. 1993. pap. 8.31 (0-89061-635-3) Jamestown Pubs.

Understanding Chemical Patents: A Guide for the Inventor. 2nd ed. John T. Maynard & Howard M. Peters. LC 91-24124. 1991. 39.95 (0-8412-1997-4); pap. 29.95 (0-8412-1998-2) Am Chemical.

Understanding Chemical Thermodynamics. George C. Pimentel & Richard D. Spratley. LC 69-13419. (Illus.). (C). 1969. pap. text ed. 22.00 (0-8162-6791-X) Holden-Day.

Understanding Chemistry. Dewey. Date not set. teacher ed., pap. text ed. write for info. (0-314-03268-1) West Pub.

Understanding Chemistry. Dewey. Date not set. student ed., pap. text ed. 17.25 (0-314-03668-7) West Pub.

Understanding Chemistry. George C. Pimentel & Richard D. Spratley. LC 70-142944. (C). 1971. 38.00 (0-8162-6761-8) Holden-Day.

Understanding Chemistry. 2nd ed. J. Dudley Herron. 1986. text ed. write for info. (0-07-554635-3); lab manual ed., pap. text ed. write for info. (0-07-553853-9) McGraw.

Understanding Chemistry. Lawrence P. Lessing. LC 59-14418. 192p. reprint ed. pap. 54.80 (0-317-08764-9, 2007397) Bks Demand.

Understanding Chemistry: A Brief Introduction. Fred M. Dewey. Ed. by Mixter. LC 93-36018. 400p. (C). 1994. pap. text ed. 51.75 (0-314-02893-5) West Pub.

Understanding Chemistry: An Introduction. Fred M. Dewey. Ed. by Mixter. LC 93-33034. 500p. (C). 1994. text ed. 62.75 (0-314-02825-0) West Pub.

Understanding Chemistry: Testbank. Dewey. Date not set. suppl. ed., pap. text ed. write for info. (0-314-03266-5) West Pub.

Understanding Chemistry for A-Level. L. Lister & R. Renshaw. (C). 1990. text ed. 150.00 (0-7487-0216-4, Pub. by Stanley Thornes UK) Trans-Atl Phila.

Understanding Chemistry for Advanced Level. Ted Lister & Janet Renshaw. 608p. (C). 1994. 57.00 (0-7478-0216-5) St Mut.

Understanding Chemsitry. Dewey. Date not set. student ed., pap. text ed. 17.25 (0-314-03669-5) West Pub.

Understanding Cheque Law. Robert Sharrock & Michael Kidd. 227p. 1993. pap. 30.00 (0-7021-2807-4, Pub. by Juta SA) Gaunt.

Understanding Chest Radiographers. Joseph L. Rau. 1985. 23.95 (0-8016-4026-1) Mosby Yr Bk.

Understanding Chicana Elderly: Sociological & Policy Perspectives. Elisa Facio. (Series on Race & Ethnic Relations: Vol. 14). 160p. 1995. 38.00 (0-8039-4580-9); pap. 16.50 (0-8039-4581-7) Sage.

Understanding Chicano Literature. Carl R. Shirley & Paula W. Shirley. Ed. by Matthew J. Bruccoli. (Understanding Contemporary American Literature Ser.). 253p. 1988. text ed. 29.95 (0-87249-575-2) U of SC Pr.

Understanding Child Abuse & Neglect. Waln K. Brown. 20p. 1989. 2.95 (1-56456-017-1, 208) W Gladden Found.

Understanding Child Abuse & Neglect. National Research Council, Panel on Research on Child Abuse & Neglect Staff. LC 93-29640. 408p. (C). 1993. text ed. 44.95 (0-309-04889-3) Natl Acad Pr.

Understanding Child Abuse & Neglect. Cynthia C. Tower. 496p. 1989. pap. text ed. 23.00 (0-205-11767-8, H17676) Allyn.

Understanding Child Abuse & Neglect. 3rd ed. Cynthia C. Tower. LC 95-3501. 1995. pap. text ed. 38.00 (0-205-16814-0) Allyn.

Understanding Child Behavior Disorder. 2nd ed. Gelfand. (C). 1988. teacher ed., pap. text ed. 66.50 (0-03-016619-5) HB Coll Pubs.

Understanding Child Behavior Disorders. 3rd ed. Donna M. Glefand et al. 496p. (C). 1996. text ed. write for info. (0-15-501701-2) HB Coll Pubs.

Understanding Child Behavior Disorders: An Introduction of Child Psychopathology. 2nd ed. Donna M. Gelfand et al. LC 87-19753. (Illus.). 352p. (C). 1988. text ed. 45.25 (0-03-016618-7) HB Coll Pubs.

Understanding Child Custody. Susan N. Terkel. LC 90-48268. (Venture Bks.). 96p. (YA). (gr. 7-12). 1991. lib. bdg. 22.00 (0-531-12521-1) Watts.

Understanding Child Development. Spencer A. Rathus & Peter Favaro. (Illus.). 688p. (C). 1988. text ed. 46.75 (0-03-001837-4) HB Coll Pubs.

Understanding Child Development. Spencer A. Rathus. (C). 1988. student ed., pap. text ed. 24.00 (0-03-001839-0) HB Coll Pubs.

Understanding Child Development. Spencer A. Rathus. (C). 1988. teacher ed. 409.50 (0-03-001843-9) HB Coll Pubs.

Understanding Child Development. 3rd ed. Rosalind Charlesworth. (Orig.). 1992. pap. 40.00 (0-8273-4891-6) Delmar.

Understanding Child Development. 3rd ed. Phyllis M. Click. 1992. student ed., pap. 15.95 (0-8273-4893-2) Delmar.

Understanding Child Development. 4th ed. Charlesworth. (Early Childhood Education Ser.). 96p. (C). 1996. teacher ed. 18.95 (0-8273-7334-1) Delmar.

Understanding Child Development. 4th ed. Delmar Inc. Staff. (Early Childhood Education Ser.). 1996. 15.00 (0-8273-7335-X) Delmar.

Understanding Child Development: For Adults Who Work with Young Children. 4th ed. Rosalind Charlesworth. LC 95-16990. 624p. (C). 1996. pap. 41.95 (0-8273-7332-5) Delmar.

Understanding Child Development: Instructor's Guide & Test Bank. 3rd ed. Rosalind Charlesworth. 1992. pap. 14.95 (0-8273-4892-4) Delmar.

***Understanding Child Molesters: Taking Charge.** Eric Leberg. 232p. 1997. 46.00 (0-7619-0186-8) Sage.

***Understanding Child Molesters: Taking Charge.** Eric Leberg. 232p. 1997. pap. 21.95 (0-7619-0187-6) Sage.

Understanding Child Sexual Abuse: Therapeutic Guidelines for Professionals Working with Children. Thomas McGuire & Faye Grant. 60p. 1990. pap. 13.00 (0-409-89771-X) MICHIE.

Understanding Child Sexual Maltreatment. Kathleen C. Faller. (Sourcebooks for the Human Services Ser.: Vol. 12). (Illus.). 256p. (C). 1990. text ed. 52.00 (0-8039-3841-1); pap. text ed. 24.95 (0-8039-3842-X) Sage.

Understanding Childhood Deafness: A Word in Your Ear. Wilhma R. Quinn. (Illus.). 160p. (Orig.). 1996. pap. 15.00 (0-7225-3302-0) Thorsons SF.

Understanding Childhood Stress. Ron Kerner. (Family Forum Library Ser.). 16p. 1992. 1.95 (1-56688-005-X) Bur For At-Risk.

Understanding Children. Jeannette Harrison. (C). 1990. 60.00 (0-86431-087-0, Pub. by Aust Council Educ Res AT) St Mut.

***Understanding Children.** 2nd ed. Jeannette Harrison. 200p. 1997. text ed. 26.95 (1-85742-387-9, Pub. by Arena UK) Ashgate Pub Co.

Understanding Children. 2nd rev. ed. Judith A. Schickedanz et al. 1993. student ed., pap. text ed. 17.95 (1-55934-178-5, 1178); trans. write for info. (0-615-00313-3); vhs write for info. (0-615-00311-7); disk write for info. (0-615-00312-5) Mayfield Pub.

Understanding Children. 2nd rev. ed. Judith A. Schickedanz et al. LC 92-26573. 768p. (C). 1993. text ed. 55.95 (1-55934-171-8, 1171) Mayfield Pub.

Understanding Children. Richard A. Gardner. LC 84-45133. 258p. 1994. reprint ed. pap. 25.00 (1-56821-225-9) Aronson.

Understanding Children: A Parents Guide to Child Rearing. Richard A. Gardner. LC 79-20004. 258p. 1979. reprint ed. 18.00 (0-933812-01-9) Creative Therapeutics.

Understanding Children: Essays in Honour of Margaret Donaldson. Ed. by Robert Grieve & Martin Hughes. 224p. (Orig.). (C). 1991. pap. text ed. 22.95 (0-631-15388-8) Blackwell Pubs.

Understanding Children: Infancy & Toddlers. 2nd ed. Judith A. Schickedanz et al. 358p. (C). 1993. pap. text ed. 41.95 (1-55934-244-7, 1244) Mayfield Pub.

Understanding Children: Infancy Through Pre-School. 2nd ed. Judith A. Schickedanz et al. 496p. (C). 1993. pap. text ed. 44.95 (1-55934-245-5, 1245) Mayfield Pub.

Understanding Children: Infancy Through School-Age. 2nd ed. Judith A. Schickedanz et al. LC 92-26573. 624p. (C). 1993. pap. text ed. 45.95 (1-55934-246-3, 1246) Mayfield Pub.

Understanding Children: School-Age & Adolescence. 2nd ed. Judith A. Schickedanz et al. 447p. (C). 1993. pap. text ed. 43.95 (1-55934-247-1, 1247) Mayfield Pub.

Understanding Children & Youth with Emotional & Behavioral Problems: A Handbook for Parents & Professionals. Paul Zionts & Richard Simpson. LC 87-29798. 192p. (Orig.). 1988. pap. 26.00 (0-89079-170-8, 1429) PRO-ED.

Understanding Children & Youth with Problems. Neel. (Special Education Ser.). Date not set. text ed. 62.95 (0-534-34404-6) Wadsworth Pub.

Understanding Children, Instructor's Manual. 2nd rev. ed. Judith A. Schickedanz et al. (C). 1993. teacher ed., pap. text ed. write for info. (1-55934-238-2, 1238) Mayfield Pub.

Understanding Children Through Astrology: A Uniquely New Approach. 2nd ed. Samantha A. Davis. Ed. by Alina Nguyen & Judith L. Powell. LC 93-14947. (Illus.). 416p. (Orig.). 1993. pap. 16.95 (1-56087-072-9) Top Mtn Pub.

Understanding Children Through Observation. Sherrill Richarz. 222p. 1980. pap. text ed. 37.00 (0-8299-0337-2) West Pub.

Understanding Children with Special Needs: A Handbook for the Caring Professions. Lorna Selfe & Lynn Stow. 256p. (C). 1990. text ed. 44.95 (0-685-46026-6); pap. text ed. 19.95 (0-04-445367-1) Routledge Chapman & Hall.

Understanding Children with Special Needs: The Caring Professions. Lorna Selfe & Lynn Stow. 256p. 1989. text ed. 55.00 (0-04-445311-6) Routledge Chapman & Hall.

***Understanding Children's Development.** Peter K. Smith et al. (Basic Psychology Ser.). (Illus.). 544p. (C). 1998. pap. text ed. 32.95 (0-631-19412-6) Blackwell Pubs.

Understanding Children's Drawings. Michaela Strauss. Tr. by Pauline Wehrle from GER. (Illus.). 95p. 1988. reprint ed. 24.95 (0-85440-330-2, Steinerbks) Anthroposophic.

Understanding Children's Sandplay Lowenfeld's World Technique. Margaret Lowenfeld. 1993. reprint ed. pap. 19.95 (0-9521788-0-X, Pub. by M Lowenfeld UK) Intl Spec Bk.

Understanding Chimpanzees. Ed. by Paul G. Heltne & Linda A. Marquardt. (Illus.). 432p. 1989. 40.00 (0-674-92091-0) HUP.

Understanding China: A Guide to China's Culture, Economy, & Political Structure. John B. Starr. LC 97-934. (Illus.). 320p. 1996. 25.00 (0-8090-9488-6) Hill & Wang.

Understanding China: Center Stage of the Fourth Power. Yanan Ju. LC 95-52977. (SUNY Series in International Management). 128p. (C). 1996. text ed. 44.50 (0-7914-3121-5); pap. text ed. 14.95 (0-7914-3122-3) State U NY Pr.

Understanding China's Economy. Gregory C. Chow. 250p. 1994. text ed. 61.00 (981-02-1841-9); pap. text ed. 33.00 (981-02-1858-3) World Scientific Pub.

***Understanding China's Socialist Market Economy.** John Wong. 120p. 1993. pap. write for info. (981-210-035-0, Pub. by Times Academic SI) Intl Spec Bk.

Understanding Chinese: A Guide to the Usage of Chinese Characters. Rita M. Choy. 480p. (CHI.). 1989. pap. 15.95 (0-941340-10-4); audio write for info. (0-318-58973-7) China West.

Understanding Chinese Characters by Means of Their Ancestral Forms. rev. ed. Ping-Gam Go. (Illus.). 150p. 1989. pap. 9.95 (0-685-29399-8) Simplex Pubns.

Understanding Chinese Characters by Their Ancestral Forms. 2nd ed. Go. 1992. pap. 13.95 (0-9623113-1-6) Simplex Pubns.

Understanding Chinese Characters by Their Ancestral Forms: What Character is That? 3rd rev. ed. Ping-gam Go. (References Ser.). (Illus.). 128p. (Orig.). (C). 1995. pap. text ed. 13.95 (0-9623113-4-0) Simplex Pubns.

***Understanding Chinese, Japanese, Korean, Vietnamese Processing.** 2nd ed. Ken Lunde. Ed. by Gigi Estabrook. (Illus.). 468p. 1997. pap. 34.95 (1-56592-224-7) OReilly & Assocs.

Understanding Chord Progressions for Guitar. Arnie Berle. (Illus.). 64p. (Orig.). 1996. pap. 4.95 (0-8256-1488-0, AM 931250, Amsco Music) Music Sales.

***Understanding Christa Wolf: Returning Home from a Foreign Land.** Margit Resch. LC 96-51242. (Understanding Modern European Literature Ser.). 190p. 1997. 29.95 (1-57003-148-7) U of SC Pr.

Understanding Christian Ethics. Ed. by William M. Tillman, Jr. LC 87-36752. (Orig.). 1988. pap. 11.99 (0-8054-6129-9, 4261-29) Broadman.

Understanding Christian Spirituality. Michael Downey. 192p. (Orig.). 1997. reprint ed. pap. 12.95 (0-8091-3680-5) Paulist Pr.

Understanding Christianity? Looking Through the Windows of God. Scott Walker. LC 92-12370. 164p. 1992. pap. 9.95 (1-880837-02-1) Smyth & Helwys.

Understanding Christoph Hein. Phillip S. McKnight. LC 94-18721. (Understanding Modern European & Latin American Literature Ser.). 260p. 1994. text ed. 29.95 (1-57003-015-4) U of SC Pr.

Understanding Chronic Illness: The Medical & Psychosocial Dimensions of Nine Diseases. Toba S. Kerson & Lawrence A. Kerson. LC 84-28622. 368p. (C). 1985. 35.00 (0-02-918200-X, Free Press) Free Pr.

Understanding Church Growth. 3rd ed. Donald A. McGavran. (Orig.). 1990. pap. 18.00 (0-8028-0463-2) Eerdmans.

Understanding Civil Liberties. 1991. lib. bdg. 250.00 (0-8490-5182-7) Gordon Pr.

***Understanding Classical Economics: Studies in Long-Period Theory.** Heinz-Diete Kurz & Neri Salvadori. LC 97-18644. 1997. write for info. (0-415-15871-0) Routledge.

Understanding Classical Sociology: Marx, Weber, Durkheim. John Hughes et al. 224p. 1995. text ed. 69.95 (0-8039-8635-1); pap. text ed. 23.95 (0-8039-8636-X) Sage.

Understanding Classroom Behaviour. Maurice Balson. (C). 1990. 75.00 (0-86431-098-6, Pub. by Aust Council Educ Res AT) St Mut.

***Understanding Classroom Behaviour.** 3rd ed. Maurice Balson. 256p. 1997. pap. 26.95 (1-85742-386-0, Pub. by Arena UK) Ashgate Pub Co.

Understanding Claude Simon. Ralph Sarkonak. Ed. by James Hardin. (Understanding Modern European & Latin American Literature Ser.). 237p. 1990. text ed. 29.95 (0-87249-669-4) U of SC Pr.

Understanding Climate: Selected Works of Yale Mintz. Ed. by J. R. Bates et al. (Illus.). 336p. 1993. 62.00 (0-937194-30-1) A Deepak Pub.

Understanding Climate Changes, IUGG 7. Ed. by A. Berger et al. (Geophysical Monograph Ser.: Vol. 52). 188p. 1989. 26.00 (0-87590-457-2) Am Geophysical.

***Understanding Climatic Change.** 1980. 55.00 (0-8103-1019-8, 00008307, Gale Res Intl) Gale.

Understanding Clinical Investigations. Skinner. 1995. pap. text ed. 39.50 (0-7020-1821-X) Saunders.

Understanding Clinical Nutrition. Corinne B. Cataldo et al. Ed. by Marshall. 382p. (C). 1992. pap. text ed. 52.00 (0-314-20865-8) West Pub.

***Understanding Clinical Nutrition.** Sharon R. Rolfes. (Miscellaneous/Catalogs Ser.). 1991. student ed., pap. 9.56 (0-314-89897-2) West Pub.

***Understanding Clinical Nutrition.** 2nd ed. Whitney & Cataldo. (Health Sciences Ser.). (C). 1998. pap. 50.95 (0-534-53341-8) Wadsworth Pub.

Understanding Co-Dependency. Sharon Wegscheider-Cruse & Joseph R. Cruse. 150p. 1990. pap. 7.95 (1-55874-077-5, 0775) Health Comm.

***Understanding Cognitive Performance Modes: Version 2.1.** Claudia Allen et al. Date not set. pap. 35.00 (0-9654111-0-9) Allen Conf.

Understanding Cognitive Psychology. Peter E. Morris & Peter J. Hampson. Ed. by Peter K. Smith. (Basic Psychology Ser.). (Illus.). 399p. (C). 1995. 62.95 (0-631-15749-2); pap. 24.95 (0-631-15751-4) Blackwell Pubs.

Understanding College Mathematics: A Calculator-Based Approach. Marvin Johnson. LC 93-21614. (C). 1993. Student study manual. student ed. 12.50 (0-06-502034-0) Addson-Wesley Educ.

Understanding College Mathematics: A Calculator-Based Approach. Marvin Johnson. LC 93-21614. (C). 1994. text ed. 54.50 (0-06-500885-5) Addson-Wesley Educ.

Understanding College Mathematics: A Calculator-Based Approach. Marvin Johnson. LC 93-21614. (C). 1994. Sale tutorial, Mac. 12.00 (0-06-502192-4); Sale tutorial, IBM. 12.00 (0-06-502191-6) Addson-Wesley Educ.

Understanding Colonial Handwriting. 2nd ed. Harriet Stryker-Rodda. 26p. 1996. reprint ed. pap. 4.50 (0-8063-1153-3, 3647) Genealog Pub.

Understanding Color. rev. ed. William F. Powell. (How to Draw & Paint Ser.). (Illus.). 32p. (Orig.). 1993. pap. 6.95 (1-56010-167-9, HT154) W Foster Pub.

Understanding Color: An Introduction for Designers. Linda Holtzschue. 176p. 1994. pap. 38.95 (0-442-01683-2) Van Nos Reinhold.

Understanding Color Infrared Photography. William H. Klein. (Illus.). 16p. 1982. pap. text ed. 3.00 (0-938361-02-3) Austin Univ Forestry.

UV

An Asterisk (*) at the beginning of an entry indicates that the title is appearing in BIP for the first time.

Understanding Colors, Shapes, & Direction. Helen P. Singletary & Zebrena M. Glover. (Computers & Children Ser.: Bk. II). (Illus.). 31p. (Orig.). (J). (ps-6). 1991. pap. text ed. 20.00 (*1-880850-02-8*) Comp Trng Clinic.

***Understanding COM: A Programmer's Guide to the Component Object Model.** Don Box. 1996. 36.53 (*0-201-63446-5*) Addison-Wesley.

Understanding Comics. 2nd deluxe limited ed. Scott McCloud. Ed. by Mark Martin. (Illus.). 224p. (Orig.). (J). (gr. 4 up). 1993. 34.95 (*0-87816-245-3*) Kitchen Sink.

Understanding Comics. 2nd ed. Scott McCloud. Ed. by Mark Martin. (Illus.). 224p. (Orig.). (J). (gr. 4 up). 1993. reprint ed. 27.95 (*0-87816-244-5*); reprint ed. pap. 19.95 (*0-87816-243-7*) Kitchen Sink.

Understanding Comics: The Invisible Art. Scott McCloud. 1994. pap. 22.50 (*0-06-097625-X*) HarpC.

Understanding Commodity Futures. 53p. 1994. pap. 3.00 (*0-915513-57-9*) Ctr Futures Ed.

Understanding Common Disorders in Reproductive Endocrinology. Ed. by Michael M. Dooley & Mark P. Brincat. LC 93-20863. 250p. 1994. text ed. 67.95 (*0-471-94151-4*) Wiley.

Understanding Communication: A Workbook Approach. Douglas Hoehn. 280p. (C). 1996. per., pap. text ed. 38. 79 (*0-7872-2381-6*) Kendall-Hunt.

Understanding Communication: Hidden Insight into Human Communication. Dana Britton. 35p. (Orig.). 1987. pap. 5.00 (*0-944478-00-X*) Dock Pub Co.

Understanding Communication: The Signifying Web, Vol. 2. D. J. Crowley. (Communication & the Human Condition Ser.). xvi, 212p. 1982. text ed. 87.00 (*0-677-05920-5*) Gordon & Breach.

Understanding Communication in Second Language Classrooms. Karen E. Johnson. (Language Education Ser.). (Illus.). 224p. (C). 1995. text ed. 44.95 (*0-521-45355-0*) Cambridge U Pr.

Understanding Communication in Second Language Classrooms. Karen E. Johnson. Ed. by Makoto Kanazawa & Christopher J. Pinon. (CSLI Lecture Notes Ser.). (Illus.). 224p. (C). 1995. pap. text ed. 17.95 (*0-521-45968-0*) Cambridge U Pr.

Understanding Communications. Osborn. (C). Date not set. pap. write for info. (*0-395-63206-4*) HM.

Understanding Communications. Osborn. (C). Date not set. pap. write for info. (*0-395-67561-8*) HM.

Understanding Communist China: Communist China Studies in the United States & the Republic of China, 1949-1978. Tai-chun Kuo & Ramon H. Myers. 172p. (Orig.). 1986. text ed. 17.95 (*0-8179-8341-4*); pap. text ed. 9.95 (*0-8179-8342-2*) Hoover Inst Pr.

***Understanding Community Librarianship.** Ed. by Alistair Black & David Muddiman. (Studies in Librarianship). (Illus.). 184p. 1997. text ed. 55.95 (*1-85972-243-1*, Pub. by Avebury Pub UK) Ashgate Pub Co.

Understanding Community Policing: A Framework for Action. (Illus.). 69p. (Orig.). (C). 1995. pap. text ed. 25. 00 (*0-7881-1943-5*) DIANE Pub.

Understanding Companies & Markets. Bryan Lowes et al. 350p. 1996. pap. 33.95 (*0-631-19718-4*) Blackwell Pubs.

***Understanding Company Accounts.** 4th ed. B. Rothenberg & J. Newman. (Daily Telegraph Guides Ser.). 1995. pap. 15.95 (*0-7494-1622-X*) Kogan Page Ltd.

Understanding Company Law. 4th ed. Phillip Lipton & Abe Herzberg. 590p. 1991. pap. 49.00 (*0-455-21022-5*, Pub. by Law Bk Co AT) Gaunt.

Understanding Company Law: Supplement, July, 1992. 4th ed. Phillip Lipton & Abe Herzberg. 1992. 15.00 (*0-455-21155-8*, Pub. by Law Bk Co AT) Gaunt.

Understanding Company Law: With Computer Tutorials. 5th ed. Phillip Lipton & Abe Herzberg. 730p. 1993. pap. 69.00 incl. disk (*0-455-21215-5*, Pub. by Law Bk Co AT) Gaunt.

Understanding Company Strategy: An Introduction to Thinking & Acting Strategically. 2nd ed. Brian Houlden. LC 96-6457. 304p. 1996. pap. 36.95 (*0-631-20090-8*) Blackwell Pubs.

***Understanding Comparative History: Britain & America, 1760-1970.** Open University Team Staff & David Englander. LC 96-36470. 1997. write for info. (*0-300-06977-4*); pap. write for info. (*0-300-06978-2*) Yale U Pr.

Understanding Comparative Politics: A Framework for Analysis. Mehran Kamrava. LC 95-12505. 232p. (C). 1995. pap. 16.95 (*0-415-13012-3*) Routledge.

Understanding Comparative Politics: A Framework for Analysis. Mehran Kamrava. LC 95-12505. 232p. (C). (gr. 13). 1995. text ed. 45.00 (*0-415-13011-5*) Routledge.

Understanding Complexity in the Prehistoric Southwest. Ed. by George J. Gumerman & Murray Gell-Mann. LC 94-6317. (Proceedings of the Santa Fe Institute, Studies in the Sciences of Complexity: Vol. 16). 380p. (C). 1994. 55.95 (*0-201-52763-4*); pap. 31.95 (*0-201-52766-9*) Addison-Wesley.

Understanding Compulsive Gambling. Henry Lesieur. 32p. 1994. pap. 2.50 (*0-89486-388-6*, 5497) Hazelden.

Understanding Computer Accounting. M-USA Business Systems, Inc. Staff. (VideoNotes Ser.). (Illus.). (Orig.). 1988. pap. text ed. 9.95 incl. vhs (*0-929978-02-1*) M-USA Busn Systs.

Understanding Computer & Information Processing. 6th ed. Parker. (C). 1995. pap. text ed. 49.25 (*0-03-013827-2*) HB Coll Pubs.

Understanding Computer & Information Processing. 6th ed. Parker. (C). 1996. teacher ed., pap. text ed. 33.75 (*0-03-016433-8*) HB Coll Pubs.

Understanding Computer & Information Processing: Test Bank. 6th ed. Parker. (C). 1996. suppl. ed., pap. text ed. 33.75 (*0-03-016434-6*) HB Coll Pubs.

Understanding Computer Contracts. (Management MR1 Reference Ser.: No. 1). 52p. 1974. pap. 10.50 (*0-318-13885-9*, MRI) Data Process Mgmt.

Understanding Computer Information Systems. Paul W. Ross et al. Ed. by Leyh. 204p. (C). 1992. pap. text ed. 15.75 (*0-314-93437-5*) West Pub.

Understanding Computer Networks. Apple Computer, Inc. Staff. 96p. 1989. pap. 10.95 (*0-201-19773-1*) Addison-Wesley.

Understanding Computer Project Management. M-USA Business Systems, Inc. Staff. (VideoNotes Ser.). (Illus.). (Orig.). 1988. pap. text ed. 9.95 incl. vhs (*0-929978-04-8*) M-USA Busn Systs.

Understanding Computer Science for Advanced Level. R. Bradley. (C). 1987. 140.00 (*0-09-170061-2*, Pub. by S Thornes Pubs UK) St Mut.

Understanding Computer Systems Architecture. Ed. by M. Lacy. 400p. (C). 1991. 75.00 (*1-870941-81-0*) St Mut.

Understanding Computer Telephony. Carlton Cardin. 34.95 (*0-936648-83-X*) Flatiron Pubng.

Understanding Computers. Wade Byrd. (Illus.). 128p. (Orig.). 1995. pap. 9.95 (*0-87573-064-7*) Jain Pub Co.

Understanding Computers. Don Cassel. 576p. (C). 1990. pap. text ed. write for info. (*0-13-946120-5*) P-H.

Understanding Computers. Grace M. Hopper & Steven L. Mandell. (Illus.). 490p. 1984. Instr's. manual. teacher ed., pap. text ed. write for info. (*0-314-79139-6*) West Pub.

Understanding Computers. Steven L. Mandell. Date not set. pap. text ed. 12.25 (*0-314-87930-7*) West Pub.

Understanding Computers. 2nd ed. Hopper. Date not set. student ed., pap. text ed. 26.00 (*0-314-32608-1*) West Pub.

Understanding Computers. 2nd ed. Grace M. Hopper & Steven L. Mandell. LC 86-15914. (Illus.). 527p. (C). 1987. text ed. 54.75 (*0-314-30383-9*) West Pub.

Understanding Computers. 2nd ed. Nathan Shedroff et al. LC 92-82013. 144p. 1993. 12.95 (*0-7821-1284-6*) Sybex.

Understanding Computers. 3rd ed. Hopper. Date not set. teacher ed., pap. text ed. write for info. (*0-314-72092-8*); student ed., pap. text ed. 20.50 (*0-314-72093-6*) West Pub.

Understanding Computers. 3rd ed. Grace M. Hopper & Steven L. Mandell. Ed. by Clyde Perlee. 578p. (C). 1990. pap. text ed. 54.75 (*0-314-66590-0*) West Pub.

Understanding Computers: In a Weekend. 3rd ed. David Traynor. LC 95-92094. (Illus.). 208p. 1995. pap. 12.95 (*0-9629304-3-1*) DOT Pub.

***Understanding Computers: 1998.** 7th ed. Parker. (C). 1997. pap. text ed. 53.25 (*0-03-024481-1*) HB Coll Pubs.

Understanding Computers & Cognition: A New Foundation for Design. Terry Winograd & Fernando Flores. LC 85-3856. 224p. 1986. text ed. 78.50 (*0-89391-050-3*) Ablex Pub.

Understanding Computers & Cognition: A New Foundation for Design. Terry Winograd & Fernando Flores. LC 85-3856. 224p. (C). 1987. pap. text ed. 18.95 (*0-201-11297-3*) Addison-Wesley.

Understanding Computers & Cogniton: A New Foundation for Design. Paul Winograd & Fernando Flores. 207p. (C). 1987. pap. 12.95 (*0-317-62466-0*) Addison-Wesley.

Understanding Computers & Information Processing. 4th ed. Charles S. Parker. 770p. (C). 1992. pap. text ed. 41. 75 (*0-03-055753-4*) Dryden Pr.

Understanding Computers & Information Processing: Today & Tomorrow with Basic. 5th ed. Charles S. Parker. 650p. (C). 1994. text ed. 44.00 (*0-03-097905-6*) Dryden Pr.

Understanding Computers & Information Processing with Basic. 3rd ed. Charles S. Parker. 768p. (C). 1990. text ed. 45.00 (*0-03-030909-3*) Dryden Pr.

Understanding Computers & Information Processing with BASIC. 4th ed. Charles S. Parker. 770p. (C). 1992. text ed. 44.25 (*0-03-055754-2*) Dryden Pr.

Understanding Computers & Information Processing with BASIC. 6th ed. Charles S. Parker. (C). 1995. student ed., pap. text ed. 21.00 (*0-03-016742-6*) HB Coll Pubs.

Understanding Computers with Basic Programming. 3rd ed. Donald D. Spencer. 1996. pap. 22.95 (*0-89218-253-9*) Camelot Pub.

Understanding Conservative Judaism. Robert Gordis. 20.00 (*0-87068-680-1*) Ktav.

Understanding Constitutional Law: 1995 Supplement. Norman Redlich et al. 32p. (C). 1996. pap. text ed. 12. 95 (*0-256-21910-9*) Irwin.

Understanding Construction Drawings. Mark R. Huth. LC 78-60838. (Illus.). 304p. 1983. pap. 37.95 (*0-8273-1584-8*) Delmar.

Understanding Construction Drawings. 2nd ed. Huth. (Construction & Building Trades Ser.). 144p. 1996. teacher ed., text ed. 14.95 (*0-8273-7291-4*) Delmar.

Understanding Construction Drawings. 2nd ed. Mark W. Huth. LC 95-33335. (Construction & Building Trades Ser.). 384p. 1996. pap. 36.50 (*0-8273-7290-6*) Delmar.

Understanding Construction Drawings: Residential. Mark W. Huth. LC 95-42328. 264p. 1996. pap. 26.95 (*0-8273-7643-X*) Delmar.

Understanding Consumer Behavior. J. Paul Peter & Jerry C. Olson. LC 93-13484. 512p. (C). 1993. text ed. 68.95 (*0-256-12278-4*) Irwin.

Understanding Consumption. Angus Deaton. LC 92-30783. (Clarendon Lectures in Economics). 256p. 1993. pap. 22. 00 (*0-19-828824-7*, Old Oregon Bk Store) OUP.

Understanding Contemporary Africa. Ed. by April A. Gordon & Donald L. Gordon. LC 91-42922. 434p. (C). 1992. pap. text ed. 19.95 (*1-55587-299-9*); lib. bdg. 45. 00 (*1-55587-256-5*) Lynne Rienner.

Understanding Contemporary Africa. 2nd ed. Ed. by April A. Gordon & Donald L. Gordon. (Understanding the Contemporary World Ser.). 434p. 1996. 19.95 (*1-55587-547-5*) Lynne Rienner.

Understanding Contemporary American Drama. William Herman. (Understanding Contemporary American Literature Ser.). 307p. 1987. text ed. 29.95 (*0-87249-492-6*) U of SC Pr.

Understanding Contemporary American Literary Theory. Michael P. Spikes. Ed. by Matthew J. Bruccoli. (Understanding Contemporary American Literature Ser.). 150p. 1997. text ed. 24.95 (*1-57003-134-7*) U of SC Pr.

Understanding Contemporary American Science Fiction: The Formative Period, 1926-1970. Thomas D. Clareson. Ed. by Matthew J. Bruccoli. (Understanding Contemporary American Literature Ser.). 307p. (Orig.). 1992. pap. 12.95 (*0-87249-870-0*) U of SC Pr.

Understanding Contemporary Germany. Stuart Parkes. LC 96-7154. 296p. (C). 1996. pap. 19.95 (*0-415-14124-9*) Routledge.

Understanding Contemporary Germany. Stuart Parkes. LC 96-7154. 296p. (C). 1997. text ed. 69.95 (*0-415-14123-0*) Routledge.

Understanding Contemporary Latin America. Ed. by Richard S. Hillman. LC 96-2712. (Understanding Ser.). (Illus.). 375p. 1996. 49.95 (*1-55587-546-7*, 875467); pap. 19.95 (*1-55587-575-0*, 875750) Lynne Rienner.

Understanding Contract Law. 3rd ed. Daniel Khoury. 336p. 1991. pap. 48.00 (*0-409-30353-4*, Austral) MICHIE.

Understanding Contracts & Legal Documents & Understanding Criminal Law. Northwest Regional Educational Laboratory Staff. (Lifeworks Ser.). (Illus.). 1980. text ed. 13.96 (*0-07-060913-6*) McGraw.

Understanding Conversion. Karl F. Morrison. 272p. 1992. text ed. 40.00 (*0-8139-1360-8*) U Pr of Va.

Understanding Copyright: A Practical Guide. Ed. by Eric A. Thorn. (C). 1989. 65.00 (*1-870404-03-3*, Pub. by Jay Bks UK) St Mut.

Understanding CORBA: The Common Object Request Broker Architecture. Randy Otte et al. LC 95-37455. 1995. pap. text ed. 50.00 (*0-13-459884-9*) P-H.

Understanding Corporate Annual Reports: A Practice Set for Financial Accounting. William R. Pasewark. 64p. (C). 1992. 19.95 (*0-256-12339-X*) Irwin.

Understanding Corporate Annual Reports: A Practice Set for Financial Accounting. 2nd ed. William R. Pasewark. 64p. (C). 1995. 20.75 (*0-256-19075-5*) Irwin.

Understanding Corporate Bonds. Harold Kerzner. 1990. 24. 95 (*0-8306-8058-6*) McGraw-Hill Prof.

Understanding Corporate Bonds. Harold Kerzner. 1991. 24. 95 (*0-8306-6736-9*) McGraw-Hill Prof.

Understanding Corporate Criminality. Ed. by Michael B. Blankenship. LC 93-18139. (Current Issues in Criminal Justice Ser.: Vol. 3). (Illus.). 296p. 1993. text ed. 48.00 (*0-8153-0883-3*, SS845) Garland.

Understanding Corporate Criminality. Ed. by Michael B. Blankenship. LC 93-18139. (Current Issues in Criminal Justice Ser.: Vol. 3). (Illus.). 296p. 1995. pap. text ed. 21. 95 (*0-8153-1922-3*, SS845) Garland.

Understanding Corporate Finance. Robert N. Holt. 91p. 1986. ring bd. 295.00 incl. disk (*0-934427-07-0*) Ivy Soft.

Understanding Corporate-Shareholder Taxation. William J. Brown. LC 88-62368. 155p. 1989. pap. 20.00 (*0-916081-16-8*) J Marshall Pub Co.

Understanding Corporation Law. Larry D. Soderquist & A. A. Sommer, Jr. 454p. 1990. 95.00 (*0-614-17137-7*, B1-1330) PLI.

Understanding Countertransference: From Projective Identification to Empathy. Michael J. Tansey & Walter F. Burke. 240p. 1989. pap. text ed. 24.95 (*0-88163-064-0*) Analytic Pr.

***Understanding Countertransference: From Projective Identification to Empathy.** Michael J. Tansey & Walter F. Burke. 240p. 1995. pap. 24.95 (*0-88163-227-9*) Analytic Pr.

Understanding Crime: Theory & Practice. L. Thomas Winfree, Jr. & Howard Abadinsky. 421p. (C). 1996. pap. text ed. 30.95 (*0-8304-1380-4*) Nelson-Hall.

Understanding Crime & Criminal Justice. Ed. by Mark Findlay & Russell Hogg. xiii, 349p. 1988. pap. 49.99 (*0-455-20775-5*, Pub. by Law Bk Co AT) Gaunt.

Understanding Crime Data: Haunted by the Dark Figure. Clive Coleman & Jenny Moynihan. (Crime & Justice Ser.). 160p. 1996. 79.00 (*0-335-19519-9*, Open Univ Pr); pap. 25.95 (*0-335-19518-0*, Open Univ Pr) Taylor & Francis.

Understanding Crime Incidence Statistics. A. D. Biderman et al. (Research in Criminology Ser.). (Illus.). 112p. 1991. 71.95 (*0-387-97045-2*) Spr-Verlag.

Understanding Crime Prevention. National Crime Prevention Institute Staff. (Illus.). 207p. (C). 1986. 32.95 (*0-409-90075-3*) Buttrwrth-Heinemann.

***Understanding Criminal Procedure.** 2nd ed. Joshua Dressler. LC 96-50953. 1997. write for info. (*0-8205-2824-2*) Bender.

***Understanding Criminal Procedures.** 2nd ed. Dressler. (Legal Text Ser.). 1996. text ed. 20.76 (*0-256-22169-3*) McGraw.

***Understanding Criminology: Current Theoretical Debates.** Sandra Walklate. LC 97-15404. 1997. write for info. (*0-335-19362-5*, Open Univ Pr); pap. write for info. (*0-335-19361-7*, Open Univ Pr) Taylor & Francis.

Understanding Crop Production. Neal C. Stoskopf. 420p. 1981. text ed. 50.80 (*0-8359-8027-8*, Reston) P-H.

Understanding Cub Scouts with Handicaps. (Illus.). 12p. (J). (gr. 3-5). 1975. pap. 3.25 (*0-8395-3839-1*, 33839) BSA.

Understanding Cults & New Religions. Irving Hexham & Karla Poewe. LC 86-16231. 180p. (Orig.). reprint ed. pap. 51.30 (*0-7837-6562-2*, 2046127) Bks Demand.

Understanding Cults & Spiritual Movements. Ed. by David C. Lane. (Understanding Cults & Spiritual Movements Ser.). (Illus.). 200p. (Orig.). 1989. pap. 21.95 (*0-9611124-2-5*) Del Mar Pr.

Understanding Cultural Differences: Germans, French & Americans. Edward T. Hall & Mildred R. Hall. LC 89-84388. 208p. (Orig.). (C). 1989. pap. 16.95 (*1-877864-07-2*) Intercult Pr.

Understanding Cultural Diversity. 96p. (Orig.). (C). 1993. pap. text ed. 16.00 (*0-929310-93-4*, 525) Am Correctional.

Understanding Cultures: Perspectives in Anthropology & Social Theory. Robert C. Ulin. LC 83-19783. 220p. (C). 1984. reprint ed. text ed. 19.95 (*0-292-71088-7*) U of Tex Pr.

***Understanding Cultures & Customs.** 2nd ed. L. Gerlach. 1996. pap. text ed. write for info. (*0-07-024557-6*) McGraw.

***Understanding Cultures Through Their Key Words: English, Russian, Polish, German, & Japanese, Vol. 8.** Anna Wierzbicka. LC 96-8915. (Oxford Studies in Anthropological Linguistics). 464p. 1997. 80.00 (*0-19-508835-2*); pap. 35.00 (*0-19-508836-0*) OUP.

Understanding Curriculum: An Introduction to the Study of Historical & Contemporary Curriculum Discourses. William F. Pinar et al. LC 94-44009. (Counterpoints Studies in the Postmodern Theory of Education Ser.: Vol. 17). 1143p. (C). 1995. pap. 49.95 (*0-8204-2601-6*) P Lang Pubng.

Understanding Curriculum as Phenomenological & Deconstructed Text. Ed. by William Reynolds & William F. Pinar. (Critical Issues in Curriculum Ser.: No. 2). 272p. (C). 1991. text ed. 46.00 (*0-8077-3114-5*); pap. text ed. 21.95 (*0-8077-3113-7*) Tchrs Coll.

Understanding Curriculum As Racial Text: Representations of Identity & Difference in Education. Ed. by Louis A. Castenell, Jr. & William F. Pinar. LC 92-38899. (SUNY Series, Feminist Theory in Education). 312p. (C). 1993. text ed. 59.50 (*0-7914-1661-5*); pap. text ed. 19.95 (*0-7914-1662-3*) State U NY Pr.

Understanding Customers. 2nd ed. Rice. 414p. 1996. pap. 34.95 (*0-7506-2322-5*) Buttrwrth-Heinemann.

Understanding Customers Workbook: Revision Tips, Exam Hints, Model Answers. Rosemary Phipps. 240p. 1995. pap. text ed. 26.95 (*0-7506-1996-1*) Buttrwrth-Heinemann.

Understanding Cynthia Ozick. Lawrence S. Friedman. Ed. by Matthew J. Bruccoli. (Understanding Contemporary American Literature Ser.). 189p. 1991. text ed. 29.95 (*0-87249-772-0*) U of SC Pr.

Understanding Dance. Graham McFee. LC 91-44620. 352p. (C). 1992. pap. 24.95 (*0-415-07810-5*) Routledge.

***Understanding Data.** 2nd ed. Bonnie Erickson & Terry Nosanchuk. 400p. 1992. pap. 12.99 (*0-335-09662-X*, Open Univ Pr) Taylor & Francis.

Understanding Data. 2nd ed. Bonnie Erickson & Terry Nosanchuk. 400p. 1992. 60.00 (*0-8020-2877-2*); pap. 24. 95 (*0-8020-7382-4*) U of Toronto Pr.

***Understanding Data Communication & Networks.** 2nd ed. Shay. (Computer Science Ser.). (C). Date not set. text ed. 62.95 (*0-534-95054-X*) PWS Pubs.

Understanding Data Communications. 5th ed. Gilbert Held. (Illus.). 500p. 1997. 35.00 (*0-672-30934-3*) Sams.

***Understanding Data Communications.** 6th ed. Gil Held. 1998. 35.00 (*0-672-31139-9*) Macmillan.

Understanding Data Communications: From Fundamentals to Networking. 2nd ed. Gilbert Held. LC 96-21461. 1996. pap. text ed. write for info. (*0-471-96820-X*) Wiley.

Understanding Data Communications & Networks. William A. Shay. LC 94-31432. 624p. 1995. text ed. 69.95 (*0-534-20244-6*) PWS Pubs.

Understanding Data Pattern Processing: The Key to Competitive Advantage. William H. Inmon & Susan Osterfelt. 155p. 1993. text ed. 39.95 (*0-471-56795-7*) Wiley.

***Understanding Data Storage.** Glatzer. 1997. text ed. 50.00 (*0-13-861691-4*) P-H.

Understanding Database Management: An Insider's Guide to Architectures, Products, & Design. Robert Mattison. LC 92-25971. 1992. text ed. 50.00 (*0-07-040973-0*) McGraw.

Understanding dBASE IV 2.0 for DOS. 4th ed. Alan Simpson. LC 92-82012. 1008p. 1993. 29.95 (*0-7821-1256-0*) Sybex.

Understanding DC & AC Circuits Through Analogies. Joseph P. Kittel. LC 79-65896. (Illus.). viii, 416p. (Orig.). (C). 1983. pap. text ed. 14.95 (*0-9603198-0-8*) B Royal Pr.

Understanding DCE. Ward Rosenberry et al. (Nutshell Handbook Ser.). (Illus.). 266p. (Orig.). 1992. pap. text ed. 24.95 (*1-56592-005-8*) OReilly & Assocs.

Understanding Deafness & the Rehabilitation Process. Ed. by Richard C. Nowell & Laura E. Marshak. LC 93-50768. 1994. text ed. 54.50 (*0-205-15628-2*) Allyn.

Understanding Deafness Socially: Continuities in Research & Theory. 2nd ed. Paul C. Higgins & Jeffery E. Nash. LC 95-42414. (Illus.). 168p. 1996. text ed. 42.95 (*0-398-06569-1*); pap. text ed. 27.95 (*0-398-06570-5*) C C Thomas.

Understanding Death & Grief. David M. Lindsey. 1991. pap. 9.95 (*1-878040-03-0*) Personal Growth.

Understanding Death, Dying & Berevement. 3rd ed. Leming. (C). 1994. teacher ed., pap. text ed. 8.50 (*0-15-501311-4*) HB Coll Pubs.

Understanding Decision Support Systems & Expert Systems. Efrem G. Wallach. LC 93-6186. 704p. (C). 1993. text ed. 67.60 (*0-256-11896-5*) Irwin.

***Understanding Decline: Perceptions & Realities of British Economic Performance.** Ed. by Peter Clarke & Clive Trebilcock. (Illus.). 285p. (C). 1997. write for info. (*0-521-56317-8*) Cambridge U Pr.

Understanding Defeat: How to Recover from Loss in Battle to Gain Victory in War. Trevor N. Dupuy. 1995. reprint ed. pap. 24.95 (*0-9638692-4-8*) NOVA Pubns.

Understanding Delinquency. Barlow & Theodore N. Ferdinand. (C). 1992. text ed. 26.95 (*0-06-042028-6*) Addson-Wesley Educ.

Understanding Deliverance: Workbook & Bible Study. Joan Barr & Jack Barr. Ed. by Maranatha Church Staff. (Illus.). 61p. (Orig.). 1987. student ed. 5.00 (*0-9619102-0-8*) New Life Christ.

Understanding Dementia. 2nd ed. Alan & Jacques. (Illus.). 358p. (Orig.). 1992. pap. text ed. 36.00 (*0-443-04392-2*) Churchill.

***Understanding Democracy: Economic & Political Perspectives.** Albert Breton et al. (Illus.). 320p. (C). 1997. text ed. 54.95 (*0-521-58236-9*) Cambridge U Pr.

Understanding Demography in Organizations. Anne Tsui. (C). 1997. pap. text ed. write for info. (*0-201-82709-3*) Addison-Wesley.

Understanding Demons. Neil C. Ellis. (Orig.). (YA). 1994. 7.95 (*0-925783-11-0*) Natl BIE Pub.

Understanding Denise Levertov. Harry Marten. Ed. by Matthew J. Bruccoli. (Understanding Contemporary American Literature Ser.). 231p. 1989. pap. 12.95 (*0-87249-579-5*); text ed. 29.95 (*0-87249-578-7*) U of SC Pr.

Understanding Dental Caries, Vol. 1: Etiology & Mechanisms. Ed. by G. Nikiforuk. (Illus.). xiv, 306p. 1985. 46.50 (*3-8055-3864-2*) S Karger.

Understanding Dental Caries, Vols. 1 & 2, 2 vols. Ed. by G. Nikiforuk. (Illus.). xxviii, 596p. 1985. Set. 93.00 (*3-8055-3906-1*) S Karger.

***Understanding Dental Health.** Francis G. Serio. LC 97-15276. (Understanding Health & Sickness Ser.). (Illus.). 128p. 1998. pap. 12.00 (*1-57806-010-9*); text ed. 28.00 (*1-57806-009-5*) U Pr of Miss.

Understanding Depression. John Docherty. 160p. (Orig.). 1991. pap. 8.95 (*0-929162-26-9*) PIA Pr.

Understanding Depression. Paul R. Robbins. LC 92-56685. 200p. 1993. lib. bdg. 23.50 (*0-89950-878-2*) McFarland & Co.

Understanding Depression. Siang-Yang Tan & John Ortberg, Jr. LC 95-89. (Strategic Pastoral Counseling Resources Ser.). 128p. (C). 1995. 16.99 (*0-8010-8921-2*) Baker Bks.

Understanding Depression: A Complete Guide to Its Diagnosis & Treatment. Donald F. Klein & Paul H. Wender. 192p. (C). 1994. reprint ed. pap. 7.95 (*0-19-508669-4*, 6287) OUP.

Understanding Depression: A Complete Guide to Its Diagnosis, Course, & Treatment. Donald F. Klein & Paul H. Wender. 192p. 1993. 25.00 (*0-19-507279-0*) OUP.

Understanding Derivatives: What You Really Need to Know about the Wild-Card of Finance. Bob Reynolds & Price Waterhouse Staff. (Illus.). 256p. 1995. 30.00 (*0-273-61378-2*) Pitman Publng.

Understanding Design: The Praxiological-Systemic Perspective. Wojciech Gasparski. (Systems Inquiry Ser.). 209p. 1984. pap. text ed. 13.95 (*0-914105-32-9*) Intersystems Pubns.

Understanding Design & Technology in Primary Schools: Cases from Teachers' Research. Ed. by Les Tickle. 232p. (C). 1996. pap. text ed. 22.95 (*0-415-13032-8*) Routledge.

Understanding Design Fundamentals see Design Fundamentals for the Digital Age

Understanding Desktop Color. Michael Kieran. 608p. 1994. pap. 32.95 (*1-56609-164-0*) Peachpit Pr.

Understanding Development: Theory & Practice in the Third World. John Rapley. LC 96-17326. 205p. 1996. 42.00 (*1-55587-604-8*, 876048); pap. 17.95 (*1-55587-625-0*, 876250) Lynne Rienner.

Understanding Development Regulations. Robert E. Merritt et al. 248p. (Orig.). 1994. pap. 26.00 (*0-923956-19-0*) Solano Pr.

Understanding Deviance: A Guide to the Sociology of Crime & Rule-Breaking. David Downes & Paul E. Rock. 400p. 1997. pap. 24.00 (*0-19-876373-5*) OUP.

Understanding Diabetes. 3rd rev. ed. John W. Stephens. 240p. 1987. pap. 9.95 (*0-911518-71-1*) Touchstone Oregon.

Understanding Differences Between Divorced & Intact Families: Stress, Interaction, & Child Outcomes. Simons, Ronald L., & Assocs. Staff. LC 96-4471. (Understanding Families Ser.: Vol. 5). 216p. 1996. 54.00 (*0-8039-5161-2*); pap. 24.95 (*0-8039-5162-0*) Sage.

***Understanding Differentiation.** Sylvia McNamara & Gill Moreton. 112p. 1996. pap. 24.95 (*1-85346-457-0*, Pub. by D Fulton UK) Taylor & Francis.

Understanding Digital Color. Phil Green. Ed. by Pamela Groff. (Illus.). 343p. 1995. text ed. 59.00 (*0-88362-174-6*) Graphic Arts Tech Found.

***Understanding Digital Electronics.** Sandy Sommer. (Illus.). 24p. (YA). (gr. 10 up). 1987. wbk. ed., pap. 7.00 (*0-8064-0729-8*, E13) Bergwall.

Understanding Digital Electronics. R. H. Warring. (Illus.). 154p. (Orig.). 1984. 13.95 (*0-8306-0193-7*) McGraw-Hill Prof.

Understanding Digital Electronics: How Microcomputers & Microprocessors Work. Patrick J. O'Connor. LC 83-21206. (Illus.). 266p. (C). 1984. 18.50 (*0-13-936964-3*) P-H.

Understanding Digital Signal Processing. James O. Broesch. 288p. 1995. pap. 39.95 (*1-878707-16-7*) HighText.

***Understanding Digital Signal Processing.** Richard G. Lyons. 608p. 1996. text ed. write for info. (*0-201-63467-8*) Addison-Wesley.

Understanding Digital TV: The Route to HDTV. Brian Evans. LC 94-20667. (Understanding Science & Technology Ser.). 256p. 1995. pap. 34.95 (*0-7803-1082-9*, PP04366) Inst Electrical.

Understanding Digitally Programmable Hearing Aids. Ed. by Robert E. Sandlin. LC 93-14194. 325p. 1993. text ed. 75.50 (*0-205-14845-X*) Allyn.

***Understanding Disability.** write for info. (*0-7131-3563-8*, Pub. by E Arnold UK) Routledge Chapman & Hall.

***Understanding Disability: A Lifespan Approach.** Peggy Quinn. LC 97-4852. (Sourcebooks for the Human Services Ser.). 1997. write for info. (*0-7619-0526-X*); pap. write for info. (*0-7619-0527-8*) Sage.

Understanding Disability: From Theory to Practice. Michael Oliver. 1995. text ed. 39.95 (*0-312-15794-0*); text ed. 18.95 (*0-312-15803-3*) St Martin.

Understanding Discourse: The Speech Act & Rhetorical Action. Karl R. Wallace. LC 76-103130. (Illus.). 162p. 1970. reprint ed. pap. 46.20 (*0-7837-9869-5*, 2060595) Bks Demand.

Understanding Disease. John Ball. 111p. 1990. pap. 19.95 (*0-85207-229-5*, Pub. by C W Daniel UK) Natl Bk Netwk.

Understanding Disease: A Health Practitioner's Handbook. John Ball. (Illus.). 264p. (Orig.). pap. 29.95 (*0-8464-4307-4*) Beekman Pubs.

Understanding Disease: Pathology & Prevention. S. Mera. (Illus.). 600p. (C). 1997. pap. text ed. 49.95 (*1-56593-428-8*, 1095) Singular Publishing.

Understanding Dispensationalists. 2nd ed. Vern S. Poythress. LC 93-39295. 1993. 7.99 (*0-87552-374-9*, Pub. by Evangelical Pr) Presby & Reformed.

Understanding Disputes: The Politics of Argument. Ed. by Pat Caplan et al. LC 94-34791. (Explorations in Anthropology Ser.). (Illus.). 248p. 1995. pap. 15.95 (*0-85496-925-X*) Berg Pubs.

Understanding Disputes: The Politics of Argument. Ed. by Patricia Caplan et al. LC 94-34791. (Explorations in Anthropology Ser.). (Illus.). 252p. 1995. 36.95 (*0-85496-924-1*) Berg Pubs.

Understanding Disruption. J. Fitzgerald. (C). 1989. 39.00 (*0-903534-92-4*, Pub. by Brit Ag for Adopt & Fost UK) St Mut.

Understanding Distance Education: A Framework for the Future. D. R. Garrison. 144p. 1989. 45.00 (*0-415-02090-5*, A3259) Routledge.

Understanding Distributed Objects. Daniel Yoder. (C). 1998. pap. text ed. write for info. (*0-201-57166-8*) Addison-Wesley.

Understanding Distributed Process Control. rev. ed. S. M. Herb & J. A. Moore. (Instructional Resource Package Ser.). 212p. 1984. student ed., pap. text ed. 40.00 (*0-87664-785-9*, 1785-9) ISA.

Understanding Diverse Families: An Introduction for Practitioners. Barbara F. Okun. LC 96-35441. 376p. 1996. lib. bdg. 35.00 (*1-57230-056-6*, 0056) Guilford Pr.

Understanding Diversity: Readings, Cases & Exercises. Carol P. Harvey & M. June Allard. LC 94-26136. (C). 1995. text ed. 35.50 (*0-673-46996-4*) Addson-Wesley Educ.

Understanding Divine Healing. Richard M. Sipley. LC 90-80504. 162p. 1990. reprint ed. pap. 7.99 (*0-87509-430-9*) Chr Pubns.

Understanding Division. Christine Losq. (Whole Math Project Ser.). (Illus.). 188p. 1993. teacher ed., spiral bd. 29.95 (*1-56892-000-8*) CSL Assocs.

***Understanding DNA: The Molecule & How It Works.** 2nd ed. Chris R. Calladine & Horace R. Drew. LC 96-37106. (Illus.). 320p. 1997. text ed. 59.95 (*0-12-155087-7*, AP Prof); pap. text ed. 34.95 (*0-12-155088-5*, AP Prof) Acad Pr.

Understanding DNA & Gene Cloning. 2nd ed. Karl Drlica. LC 91-26076. 272p. (C). 1991. Net. pap. text ed. 31.95 (*0-471-62225-7*) Wiley.

Understanding DNA & Gene Cloning: A Guide for the Curious. 3rd ed. Karl Drlica. LC 96-23077. 329p. 1996. pap. text ed. 28.95 (*0-471-13774-X*) Wiley.

Understanding Doctrine: What It Is & Why It Matters. Alister E. McGrath. 192p. 1992. pap. 12.99 (*0-310-47951-7*) Zondervan.

***Understanding Dogmas & Dreams: A Text.** Nancy S. Love. LC 97-4916. (Studies in Political Thinking). 1997. pap. write for info. (*1-56643-044-5*) Chatham Hse Pubs.

Understanding Dolls. Caroline Goodfellow. (Understanding Ser.). (Illus.). 240p. 1995. pap. 19.95 (*1-85149-236-4*) Antique Collect.

Understanding Donald Barthelme. Stanley Trachtenberg. (Understanding Contemporary American Literature Ser.). 275p. (C). 1990. text ed. 29.95 (*0-87249-711-9*) U of SC Pr.

Understanding Doris Lessing. Jean Pickering. (Understanding Contemporary British Literature Ser.). 234p. (C). 1990. pap. 12.95 (*0-87249-743-7*); text ed. 29.95 (*0-87249-710-0*) U of SC Pr.

Understanding DOS 6. Mary Campbell. LC 93-10838. 336p. (C). 1993. pap. text ed. 33.60 (*0-13-098393-4*) P-H Gen Ref & Trav.

Understanding Down Syndrome: An Introduction for Parents. Cliff Cunningham. LC 95-25997. 256p. 1996. pap. 14.95 (*1-57129-009-5*) Brookline Bks.

Understanding Dreams. Mary A. Mattoon. LC 84-5523. Orig. Title: Applied Dream Analysis: A Jungian Approach. vii, 248p. 1978. pap. 19.00 (*0-88214-326-3*) Spring Pubns.

Understanding Dreams: A Concise Guide to Dream Symbols. (Gem Ser.). (Illus.). 256p. (YA). 1994. pap. 5.95 (*1-56138-467-4*) Running Pr.

Understanding Dreams: How to Benefit from the Power of Your Dreams. Nerys Dee. 1995. pap. 10.00 (*1-85538-086-2*) Harper SF.

Understanding Drug Treatment in Mental Health Care. Alyson J. Bond & Malcolm H. Lader. LC 96-1090. (Series in Clinical Psychology). 1996. pap. write for info. (*0-471-96171-X*) Wiley.

Understanding Drug Treatment in Mental Health Care. Alyson J. Bond & Malcolm H. Lader. LC 96-1090. (Series in Clinical Psychology). 237p. 1996. text ed. 54.95 (*0-471-94227-8*) Wiley.

***Understanding Drugs: A Handbook for Parents, Teachers & Other Professionals.** David Emmett & Graeme Nice. 160p. 1996. pap. 24.95 (*1-85302-400-7*, Pub. by J Kingsley Pubs UK) Taylor & Francis.

Understanding Drugs of Abuse: The Processes of Addiction, Treatment & Recovery. Mim J. Landry. LC 93-26208. 363p. 1993. 21.95 (*0-88048-533-7*, 8533) Am Psychiatric.

Understanding Dying & Death. 4th ed. Leming. (C). 1997. text ed. write for info. (*0-15-505174-1*) HarBrace.

Understanding Dying, Death, & Bereavement. Michael Leming & George Dickinson. 552p. (C). pap. text ed. 36.25 (*0-15-500632-0*) HB Coll Pubs.

Understanding Dying, Death & Bereavement. 2nd ed. Michael R. Leming & George E. Dickinson. LC 89-29924. (Illus.). 500p. (C). 1990. text ed. 33.25 (*0-03-028377-9*) HB Coll Pubs.

Understanding Dynamic Systems: Approaches to Modeling, Analysis & Design. Nelson C. Dorny. 640p. 1993. text ed. 85.00 (*0-13-221839-9*) P-H.

Understanding Dyslexia. Ed. by T. R. Miles. (C). 1988. 60.00 (*1-871458-07-2*, Pub. by Bath Educ Pubs UK) St Mut.

Understanding Dyslexia: A Practical Handbook for Parents & Teachers. Anne M. Huston. (Illus.). 368p. 1991. 24.95 (*0-8191-7804-7*) Madison Bks UPA.

Understanding E. L. Doctorow. Douglas Fowler. Ed. by Matthew J. Bruccoli. LC 92-8042. (Understanding Contemporary American Literature Ser.). 182p. 1992. text ed. 29.95 (*0-87249-819-0*) U of SC Pr.

***Understanding Each Other.** Laura Latulippe. 1997. pap. text ed. write for info. (*0-201-84675-6*) Addison-Wesley.

Understanding Each Other: Improving Communication Through Effective Dialogue. Cathrina Bauby. LC 76-43576. (Illus.). 59p. 1976. pap. text ed. 6.00 (*0-317-65121-8*) Intl Gen Semantics.

Understanding Ear Infections. Peter Allen. (Illus.). 28p. (C). 1993. reprint ed. pap. 24.95 (*0-9622326-1-0*) Hear You Are.

Understanding Early Adolescence: A Framework. John P. Hill. 52p. (Orig.). 1980. reprint ed. pap. 8.00 (*1-57482-703-0*) Search Inst.

***Understanding Earth.** Best. Date not set. student ed. write for info. (*0-7167-2804-4*) St Martin.

Understanding Earth. Peacock. 1995. write for info. (*0-7167-2523-1*) W H Freeman.

Understanding Earth. Peacock. write for info. (*0-7167-2525-8*) W H Freeman.

Understanding Earth. Raymond Siever. (C). 1995. Instr.'s Manual. teacher ed., text ed. write for info. (*0-7167-2521-5*); Student Guide. student ed., text ed. write for info. (*0-7167-2522-3*) W H Freeman.

Understanding Earth. 2nd ed. Best. LC 96-43804. 1997. text ed. write for info. (*0-7167-2836-2*) W H Freeman.

***Understanding Eastern Europe.** John Howell & Ernst & Young Staff. (International Business Ser.). 1994. 35.00 (*0-7494-1510-X*) Kogan Page Ltd.

***Understanding Eastern Philosophy.** Ray Billington. 192p. (C). 1997. pap. 18.95 (*0-415-12965-6*, Routledge NY); text ed. 65.00 (*0-415-12964-8*, Routledge NY) Routledge.

Understanding Eating Disorders: Anorexia Nervosa, Bulimia Nervosa, & Obesity. LeeAnn Alexander-Mott & Barry D. Lumsden. LC 94-8719. 49.50 (*1-56032-294-2*); pap. 29.50 (*1-56032-295-0*) Taylor & Francis.

Understanding Eating Disorders: Anorexia Nervosa, Bulimia Nervosa, & Obesity. Ed. by LeeAnn Alexander-Mott & D. Barry. 275p. 1994. 59.50 (*1-56032-249-7*) Taylor & Francis.

Understanding ECGs in Infants & Children. 2nd ed. L. C. Harris & Ellen Feinstein. 1979. text ed. 19.50 (*0-316-34826-0*, Little Med Div) Little.

Understanding Ecology. 1986. teacher ed. 6.96 (*0-88334-070-4*, 76065); student ed. 12.00 (*0-8013-0103-3*, 75767) Longman.

Understanding Economic Behaviour. Ed. by Klaus G. Grunert & Folke Olander. (C). 1989. lib. bdg. 151.00 (*0-7923-0482-9*) Kluwer Ac.

Understanding Economic Policy. Maurice Mullard. (Illus.). 288p. (C). (gr. 13). 1991. text ed. 79.95 (*0-415-06881-9*, A6575) Routledge.

Understanding Economic Policy: A Citizen's Handbook. Alice Rivlin & Carol Cox. 1990. 5.95 (*0-89959-417-4*, 896) LWVUS.

Understanding Economic Process. Ed. by Sutti Ortiz & Susan Lees. LC 92-24047. (Monographs in Economic Anthropology: No. 10). 220p. (Orig.). (C). 1992. pap. text ed. 24.50 (*0-8191-8828-X*, Soc Economic Anthropology); lib. bdg. 51.00 (*0-8191-8827-1*, Soc Economic Anthropology) U Pr of Amer.

Understanding Economics. Vicky Allsopp. LC 95-11819. 480p. (C). 1995. pap. 29.95 (*0-415-09133-0*) Routledge.

Understanding Economics. Vicky Allsopp. LC 95-11819. 480p. (C). (gr. 13). 1995. text ed. 74.95 (*0-415-09132-2*) Routledge.

Understanding Economics. Ken Cole. LC 95-3092. 198p. (C). pap. 16.95 (*0-7453-0893-7*, Pub. by Pluto Pr UK) LPC InBook.

Understanding Economics. Roger L. Miller & Robert W. Pulsinelli. (Illus.). 457p. (C). 1983. text ed. 52.00 (*0-314-69669-5*); teacher ed., pap. text ed. write for info. (*0-314-71114-7*); student ed., pap. text ed. 20.50 (*0-314-71143-0*) West Pub.

***Understanding Economics.** 2nd ed. Ken Heather. LC 96-40928. 1997. 30.00 (*0-13-650169-9*) P-H.

Understanding Economics: Overview for Teachers Experiences for Students. Marilyn L. Kourilsky. 1983. text ed. 10.00 (*0-201-20032-5*) Addison-Wesley.

Understanding Economics Today. 3rd ed. Gary Walton & Frank C. Wykoff. (C). 1990. text ed. 43.95 (*0-256-08976-0*) Irwin.

Understanding Economics Today. 4th ed. Thomas Adams. 224p. (C). 1993. student ed., per. 20.95 (*0-256-13758-7*) Irwin.

Understanding Economics Today. 4th ed. Gary M. Walton & Frank C. Wykoff. LC 93-28102. 496p. (C). 1993. text ed. 48.95 (*0-256-13757-9*) Irwin.

Understanding Economics Today. 5th ed. Gary M. Walton & Frank C. Wykoff. LC 95-21709. 496p. (C). 1995. per. 48.95 (*0-256-17236-6*) Irwin Prof Pubng.

Understanding Economics Today. 5th ed. Gary M. Walton. 236p. (C). 1995. student ed., pap. text ed. 20.95 (*0-256-17237-4*) Irwin.

Understanding Economics Today: Wall Street Journal Edition. 5th ed. Gary M. Walton & Frank C. Wykoff. 496p. (C). 1995. text ed. 53.95 (*0-256-21682-7*) Irwin.

***Understanding Economy.** Dunnett. 1982. pap. text ed. write for info. (*0-582-44646-5*, Pub. by Longman UK) Longman.

Understanding Editorial Text: A Computer Model of Argument Comprehension. Sergio J. Alvarado. (C). 1990. lib. bdg. 93.50 (*0-7923-9123-3*) Kluwer Ac.

Understanding Educational Measurement. Ernest McDaniel. 384p. (C). 1993. text ed. write for info. (*0-697-13208-0*) Brown & Benchmark.

Understanding Educational Reform in Global Context: Economy, Ideology & the State. Mark Ginsburg. LC 91-3812. (Reference Books in International Education: Vol. 22). 424p. 1991. text ed. 58.00 (*0-8240-6896-3*, SS663) Garland.

***Understanding Educational Research.** Ed. by David Scott & Robin Usher. 208p. (C). 1996. pap. 18.95 (*0-415-13131-6*); text ed. 59.95 (*0-415-13130-8*) Routledge.

Understanding Educational Research. 4th ed. D. B. Van Dalen. 1979. text ed. write for info. (*0-07-066883-3*) McGraw.

Understanding Edward Albee. Matthew C. Roudane. Ed. by Matthew J. Bruccoli. (Understanding Contemporary American Literature Ser.). 233p. 1987. pap. 12.95 (*0-87249-503-5*) U of SC Pr.

Understanding Einstein's Theories of Relativity: Man's New Perspective on the Cosmos. Stan Gabilisco. 1991. pap. 6.95 (*0-486-26659-1*) Dover.

Understanding Electrical Diagrams & Control Circuits No. 611: Video Booklet/Workbook. L. A. Bryan & E. A. Bryan. Ed. by L. B. Thompson. (Illus.). 48p. (Orig.). 1995. pap. 22.95 (*0-944107-13-3*) Indust Text.

Understanding Electricity. Gary Gibson. (Science for Fun Ser.). 32p. (J). (gr. 2-4). 1995. lib. bdg. 15.40 (*1-56294-629-3*, Copper Beech Bks) Millbrook Pr.

Understanding Electricity. Gary Gibson. LC 95-41529. (Science for Fun Ser.). (Illus.). 32p. (J). (gr. 2-4). 1996. pap. 4.95 (*0-7613-0462-2*, Copper Beech Bks) Millbrook Pr.

Understanding Electricity & Electrical Terms. 8th ed. G. E. Henderson. Ed. by George W. Smith. 40p. 1993. 7.50 (*0-89606-293-7*, 303); 3.00 (*0-89606-329-1*, 303TK); disk 40.00 (*0-89606-331-3*, 303CSI); Apple II 40.00 (*0-89606-330-5*, 303CS) Am Assn Voc Materials.

Understanding Electricity & Electronics. Dale R. Patrick & Stephen W. Fardo. 550p. 1989. pap. text ed. 73.00 (*0-13-943242-6*) P-H.

Understanding Electricity & Electronics. 3rd ed. Peter Buban, Sr. & Marshall L. Schmitt. (J). 1974. text ed. 28.32 (*0-07-008675-3*) McGraw.

Understanding Electricity & Electronics Technology. 5th ed. Peter Buban, Sr. et al. 544p. (J). 1987. text ed. 19.96 (*0-07-008646-X*) McGraw.

Understanding Electrocardiography. Mary B. Conover. 528p. (C). (gr. 13). 1995. pap. text ed. 36.95 (*0-8151-1927-5*) Mosby Yr Bk.

Understanding Electromagnetic Scattering Using the Moment Method: A Practical Approach. Randy Bancroft. 1996. 77.00 (*0-89006-859-3*) Artech Hse.

Understanding Electromechanical Engineering: An Introduction to Mechatronics. Lawrence J. Kamm. LC 95-16524. 416p. 1995. pap. 44.95 (*0-7803-1031-4*, PP3806) Inst Electrical.

Understanding Electronic & Computer Technology. 3rd ed. Ronald A. Reis. (Illus.). 384p. (Orig.). 1996. pap. text ed. 25.00 (*0-911908-23-4*) Tech Ed Pr.

***Understanding Electronic Commerce.** David R. Kosiur. LC 97-4201. 1997. pap. text ed. 17.99 (*1-57231-560-1*) Microsoft.

Understanding Electronic Communications: Printing in the Information Age. Aisha Ajayi & Pamela Groff. LC 96-75269. (Illus.). 152p. (C). 1997. text ed. 60.00 (*0-88362-182-7*) Graphic Arts Tech Found.

Understanding Electronic Schematics. Lenk. LC 97-15943. Date not set. write for info. (*0-7506-9654-0*) Buttrwrth-Heinemann.

Understanding Electronics. Owen Bishop. (Illus.). 256p. 1995. pap. 27.95 (*0-7506-2100-1*) Buttrwrth-Heinemann.

Understanding Electronics. 2nd ed. R. H. Warring. (Illus.). 210p. 1984. 15.95 (*0-8306-0253-4*) McGraw-Hill Prof.

Understanding Electronics. 3rd ed. R. H. Warring. (Illus.). 230p. pap. 13.95 (*0-8306-9344-0*, 3044) McGraw.

UV

An Asterisk (*) at the beginning of an entry indicates that the title is appearing in BIP for the first time.

Understanding Electronics. 3rd ed. R. H. Warring & G. Randy Slone. 1989. pap. text ed. 14.95 (*0-07-157376-3*) McGraw.

Understanding Electronics. 3rd ed. R. H. Warring. Ed. by G. Randy Slone. (Illus.). 230p. 1989. 18.95 (*0-8306-9044-1*, 3044) McGraw-Hill Prof.

Understanding Elementary Algebra. 2nd ed. Robert G. Moon. 1990. student ed., pap. text ed. write for info. (*0-675-20781-9*, Merrill Coll) P-H.

***Understanding Elementary Algebra.** 3rd ed. Goodman. 1994. 4.95 (*0-314-03792-6*); student ed. 20.95 (*0-314-03995-3*) Wadsworth Pub.

***Understanding Elementary Algebra.** 3rd ed. Goodman. 1996. 17.95 (*0-314-03824-8*) Wadsworth Pub.

***Understanding Elementary Algebra.** 4th ed. Goodman. (Mathematics Ser.). (C). 1998. student ed., pap. 17.95 (*0-534-35502-1*) Brooks-Cole.

Understanding Elementary Algebra: A Course for College Students. 3rd ed. Arthur Goodman & Lewis R. Hirsch. Ed. by Pullins. LC 93-11701. 500p. (C). 1993. text ed. 56.00 (*0-314-02519-7*) West Pub.

Understanding Elementary Algebra: A Text-Workbook. 2nd ed. Arthur Goodman & Lewis R. Hirsch. Ed. by Ricci. 792p. (Orig.). (C). 1991. pap. text ed. 54.25 (*0-314-81299-7*) West Pub.

Understanding Elementary Algebra: Testbank. 3rd ed. Goodman. Date not set. suppl. ed., teacher ed., pap. text ed. write for info. (*0-314-03283-5*) West Pub.

Understanding Elementary Algebra with Geometry. Arthur Goodman & Lewis R. Hirsch. Ed. by Pullins. LC 93-42146. 530p. (C). 1994. text ed. 57.50 (*0-314-02898-6*) West Pub.

***Understanding Elementry Algebra.** 4th ed. Goodman. (C). Date not set. text ed. 62.95 (*0-534-35327-4*) Brooks-Cole.

***Understanding Elementry Algebra: A Course for College Students.** 4th ed. Goodman. (C). 1998. text ed. 54.95 (*0-534-35316-9*) Brooks-Cole.

Understanding Elias Canetti. Richard H. Lawson. Ed. by James N. Hardin. LC 91-13888. (Understanding Modern European & Latin American Literature Ser.). 123p. 1991. text ed. 29.95 (*0-87249-768-2*) U of SC Pr.

Understanding Emerging Network Services, Pricing, & Regulation. Leo A. Wrobel & Eddie M. Pope. LC 95-6096. 168p. 1995. 59.00 (*0-89006-790-2*) Artech Hse.

Understanding Emotions. Keith Oatley & Jennifer M. Jenkins. (Illus.). 512p. (C). 1996. 73.95 (*1-55786-494-2*); pap. 34.95 (*1-55786-495-0*) Blackwell Pubs.

Understanding Employee Ownership. Ed. by Corey Rosen & Karen M. Young. 248p. (Orig.). 1991. 35.00 (*0-87546-171-9*, ILR Press); pap. 16.95 (*0-87546-172-7*, ILR Press) Cornell U Pr.

Understanding Employee Relations: A Behavioural Approach. Derek Rollinson. LC 93-10997. (C). 1993. pap. text ed. 35.50 (*0-201-56892-6*) Addison-Wesley.

Understanding Emptiness: The Think - Feel Conflict. Robert A. Moss. 128p. 1993. pap. 9.95 (*0-9638848-0-8*) R A Moss.

Understanding End Times Prophecy: A Comprehensive Approach. Paul N. Benware. 1995. pap. 15.99 (*0-8024-9077-8*) Moody.

Understanding Energy: Energy, Entropy & Thermodynamics for Every Man. R. Stephen Berry. 150p. (C). 1991. text ed. 43.00 (*981-02-0342-X*); pap. text ed. 23.00 (*981-02-0679-8*) World Scientific Pub.

***Understanding Engine Oil Rheology & Tribology.** 1997. 38.00 (*1-56091-999-X*) Soc Auto Engineers.

Understanding Engineering Design: Context, Theory & Practice. Richard Birmingham. LC 96-19064. 200p. (C). 1996. pap. 53.00 (*0-13-525650-X*) P-H.

Understanding Engineering Systems Via Conservation. 3rd ed. Louis J. Everett. 1994. pap. 42.75 (*0-07-019939-6*) McGraw.

Understanding Engineering Thermo. Octave Levenspiel. LC 96-1546. 1996. text ed. 66.00 (*0-13-531203-5*) P-H.

Understanding English. 4th ed. Kolln. 1994. text ed. 68.20 (*0-02-366074-0*, Macmillan Coll) P-H.

Understanding English: How Sentences Work. Smith. (PS - Communication/English Ser.). 1992. pap. 40.95 (*0-538-70175-7*) S-W Pub.

Understanding English Grammar. 3rd ed. Martha Kolln. (Illus.). 444p. (C). 1989. text ed. write for info. (*0-02-366061-9*, Macmillan Coll) P-H.

Understanding English Grammar. 4th ed. Martha Kolln. LC 93-3099. 496p. (C). 1993. text ed. 51.00 (*0-02-366072-4*, Macmillan Coll) P-H.

***Understanding English Grammar.** 5th ed. Kolln & Funk. LC 97-14410. 1997. text ed. 50.00 (*0-205-26855-2*) P-H.

Understanding English Grammar: A Linguistic Approach. Ronald Wardhaugh. (Illus.). 304p. 1995. pap. 27.95 (*0-631-19642-0*) Blackwell Pubs.

Understanding Enterprise Liability: Rethinking Tort Reform for the 21st Century. Ed. by Virginia E. Nolan & Edmund Ursin. LC 94-2881. 272p. (C). 1994. text ed. 49.95 (*1-56639-230-6*) Temple U Pr.

Understanding Enterprise Networks. Philippe Gomez & Pierre Bichon. (Illus.). 224p. 1996. pap. 29.99 (*1-85032-163-9*) ITCP.

Understanding Environmental Administration & Law. Susan J. Buck. LC 91-15608. 199p. (Orig.). 1991. 34.95 (*1-55963-021-3*); pap. 21.95 (*1-55963-020-5*) Island Pr.

Understanding Environmental Administration & Law. 2nd ed. Susan J. Buck. 224p. (Orig.). (C). 1996. pap. text ed. 24.95 (*1-55963-474-X*) Island Pr.

***Understanding Environmental Pollution: A Primer.** Marquita K. Hill. LC 96-52929. (Illus.). 340p. (C). 1997. text ed. 69.95 (*0-521-56210-4*) Cambridge U Pr.

***Understanding Environmental Pollution: A Primer.** Marquita K. Hill. LC 96-52929. (Illus.). 340p. (C). 1997. pap. text ed. 27.95 (*0-521-56680-0*) Cambridge U Pr.

Understanding Enzymes. 4th ed. Trevor Palmer. 398p. 1995. pap. text ed. 65.33 (*0-13-134470-6*) P-H.

Understanding Epidemiology. Torrence. LC 96-39467. (Biomedical Science Ser.). 160p. (gr. 13). 1997. pap. text ed. 23.00 (*0-8151-8887-0*) Mosby Yr Bk.

***Understanding Equal Education Opportunity: Social Justice, Democracy, & Schooling.** Kenneth R. Howe. LC 96-37710. (Advances in Contemporary Educational Thought Ser.). 207p. (Orig.). 1997. pap. text ed. 21.95 (*0-8077-3599-X*) Tchrs Coll.

***Understanding Equal Education Opportunity: Social Justice, Democracy, & Schooling.** Kenneth R. Howe. LC 96-37710. (Advances In Contemporary Educational Thought Ser.). 207p. 1997. text ed. 50.00 (*0-8077-3600-7*) Tchrs Coll.

Understanding Equal Opportunity Policies. Ken Blakemore & Robert F. Drake. LC 95-47285. (Contemporary Social Policy Ser.). 1996. write for info. (*0-13-433319-5*) P-H.

Understanding Erich Maria Remarque. Hans Wagener. Ed. by James N. Hardin. (Understanding Modern European & Latin American Literature Ser.). 153p. (C). 1991. text ed. 29.95 (*0-87249-740-2*) U of SC Pr.

Understanding ERISA, 1992. (Tax Law & Estate Planning Course Handbook Ser.). 855p. 1992. pap. 70.00 (*0-685-70150-6*) PLI.

Understanding ERISA 1995: An Introduction to Basic Employee Benefits. (Tax Law & Estate Planning Course Handbook Ser.). 1995. pap. 99.00 (*0-685-69747-9*, J4-3677) PLI.

Understanding ESL Writers: A Guide for Teachers. Ilona Leki. LC 91-35814. 151p. 1992. pap. text ed. 23.50 (*0-86709-303-X*, 0303) Boynton Cook Pubs.

Understanding Estate Administration in New York 1992. (Tax Law & Estate Planning Course Handbook Ser.: Vol. 217). 436p. 1992. 70.00 (*0-685-65541-5*, D4-5235) PLI.

Understanding Estate, Gift, & Generation-Skipping Transfer Taxes. (Tax Law & Estate Planning Course Handbook Ser.: Vol. 225). 337p. 1993. 70.00 (*0-685-69750-9*, D4-5244) PLI.

Understanding Estimates of National Health Expenditures under Health Reform. (Illus.). 216p. (Orig.). (C). 1994. pap. text ed. 50.00 (*0-7881-1041-1*) DIANE Pub.

***Understanding Ethics.** Noel Preston. 219p. 1996. pap. 29.00 (*1-86287-227-9*, Pub. by Federation Pr AU) Gaunt.

***Understanding Ethnic Identities: A Psychocontextual.** Carlos M. Alvarez. Ed. by Joe Kincheloe & Shirley R. Steinberg. (Critical Education Practice Ser.). 200p. Date not set. text ed. 30.00 (*0-8153-1646-1*); pap. text ed. 18.95 (*0-8153-2328-X*) Garland.

Understanding Ethnographic Texts. Paul Atkinson. (Qualitative Research Methods Ser.: Vol. 25). 88p. (C). 1992. text ed. 22.95 (*0-8039-3936-1*); pap. text ed. 9.95 (*0-8039-3937-X*) Sage.

Understanding Eugene Ionesco. Nancy Lane. Ed. by James N. Hardin. LC 93-42291. (Understanding Modern European & Latin American Literature Ser.). 200p. (C). 1994. text ed. 29.95 (*0-87249-981-2*) U of SC Pr.

Understanding Europeans. 2nd ed. Stuart Miller. LC 96-6407. 272p. 1996. pap. 14.95 (*1-56261-294-8*) John Muir.

Understanding Events. David R. Heise. LC 78-2417. (American Sociological Assn. Rose Monograph Ser.). (Illus.). 1979. pap. 10.95 (*0-521-29544-0*) Cambridge U Pr.

Understanding Everyday Racism: An Interdisciplinary Theory. Philomena Essed. (Series on Race & Ethnic Relations: Vol. 2). 320p. (C). 1991. 52.00 (*0-8039-4255-9*); pap. 24.00 (*0-8039-4256-7*) Sage.

Understanding Everyday Sesotho: A Vocabulary & Reference Book. 94p. 1994. pap. 16.95 (*0-7818-0305-5*) Hippocrene Bks.

Understanding Evolution. Earl D. Hanson. (Illus.). 556p. (C). 1981. text ed. 31.95 (*0-19-502784-1*) OUP.

Understanding Evolution. 5th ed. E. Peter Volpe. 288p. (C). 1985. per. write for info. (*0-697-04944-2*) Wm C Brown Pubs.

***Understanding Evolution.** 6th ed. Volpe & Rosenbaum. 1998. pap. text ed. 30.00 (*0-697-05137-4*) McGraw.

Understanding Exceptional People. Colleen J. Mandell & Edward D. Fiscus. (Illus.). 517p. (C). 1981. text ed. 56.00 (*0-8299-0394-1*) West Pub.

Understanding Executive Performance: A Life-Story Perspective. Charles J. Palus et al. (Reports: No. 148G). 48p. 1991. pap. 20.00 (*0-912879-45-9*, 148) Ctr Creat Leader.

Understanding Executive Stress. Cary L. Cooper & Judi Marshall. LC 77-16077. 1978. text ed. 17.50 (*0-89433-059-4*) Petrocelli.

***Understanding Exercise for Health & Fitness.** Andrew Jackson & Robert Ross. 178p. (C). 1997. per., pap. text ed. 24.95 (*0-7872-3478-8*) Kendall-Hunt.

***Understanding Exercise for Health & Fitness.** 3rd ed. Jackson & Ross. 182p. (C). 1997. per. 28.95 (*0-7872-3905-4*) Kendall-Hunt.

Understanding Expert Systems: Using Crystal. Mary Jackson. 207p. 1992. pap. text ed. 47.95 (*0-471-93580-8*) Wiley.

Understanding Expository Text: A Theoretical & Practical Handbook for Analyzing Explanatory Text. Ed. by Bruce K. Britton & John B. Black. LC 84-13807. (Psychology of Reading & Reading Instruction Ser.). (Illus.). 421p. reprint ed. pap. 120.00 (*0-8357-4207-5*, 2036984) Bks Demand.

Understanding Exposure: How to Shoot Great Photographs. Peterson & DiAMAR Staff. (Illus.). 144p. 1995. pap. 79.95 incl. cd-rom (*1-886393-00-1*, Amphoto) Watsn-Guptill.

Understanding Exposure: How to Shoot Great Photographs. Bryan F. Peterson. (Illus.). 144p. 1990. pap. 22.50 (*0-8174-3712-6*, Amphoto) Watsn-Guptill.

Understanding Fabrics: From Fiber to Finished Cloth. Debbie A. Gioello. (Language of Fashion Ser.). (Illus.). 325p. (C). 1982. pap. 42.00 (*0-87005-377-9*) Fairchild.

Understanding Face-to-Face Interaction: Issues Linking Goals & Discourse. K. Tracy. 232p. (C). 1991. pap. 24.50 (*0-8058-0907-4*); text ed. 49.95 (*0-8058-0538-9*) L Erlbaum Assocs.

Understanding Families: Diversity, Continuity, & Change. 2nd ed. George E. Dickinson & Michael R. Leming. LC 94-75869. 576p. 1995. 57.75 (*0-15-500577-4*) HarBrace.

Understanding Family. 2nd ed. Dickinson. (C). 1994. teacher ed., pap. text ed. 33.75 (*0-15-502144-3*) HB Coll Pubs.

Understanding Family Care: A Multi-Dimensional Model of Caring & Coping. Mike Nolan et al. LC 96-20513. 192p. 1996. 79.00 (*0-335-19574-1*, Open Univ Pr); pap. 24.95 (*0-335-19573-3*, Open Univ Pr) Taylor & Francis.

***Understanding Family Communication.** 2nd ed. Yerby & Beurkel. 1994. pap. text ed. 40.00 (*0-13-776667-X*) P-H.

Understanding Family Communication. 2nd ed. Janet Yerby et al. LC 94-23164. 325p. 1994. per. 32.95 (*0-89787-355-6*) Gorsuch Scarisbrick.

Understanding Family Policy: Theoretical Approaches. Shirley L. Zimmerman. 200p. (C). 1988. text ed. 42.00 (*0-8039-2798-3*); pap. text ed. 18.95 (*0-8039-3226-X*) Sage.

Understanding Family Policy: Theoretical Approaches. 2nd ed. Shirley L. Zimmerman. LC 95-13488. 256p. (C). 1995. 42.00 (*0-8039-5460-3*); pap. 19.95 (*0-8039-5461-1*) Sage.

Understanding Family Problems: A Psychological Approach. Neil Frude. LC 90-12309. 418p. 1990. text ed. 95.00 (*0-471-91741-9*) Wiley.

Understanding Family Process: The Basics of Family Systems Theory. Carlfred B. Broderick. (Illus.). 296p. 1993. 55.00 (*0-8039-3777-6*); pap. 26.00 (*0-8039-3778-4*) Sage.

Understanding Family Violence within U. S. Refugee Communities: A Training Manual. Refugee Women in Development Staff. Ed. by Beth Richie. 1988. 8.00 (*0-9620653-0-7*) Ref Women Dev.

Understanding Fashion. Elizabeth Rouse. (Illus.). 256p. (C). 1989. pap. text ed. 29.95 (*0-632-01891-7*) Blackwell Sci.

***Understanding Federal Government Contracts.** Whelan. 624p. 1994. pap. 75.00 (*0-8080-0005-5*, BLS-3306) Commerce.

***Understanding Federal Training & Employment Programs, 2 vols.** 1997. lib. bdg. 605.95 (*0-8490-7664-1*) Gordon Pr.

Understanding Federal Training & Employment Programs, 2 vols., Set. 1996. lib. bdg. 600.95 (*0-8490-6880-0*) Gordon Pr.

Understanding Federico Garcia Lorca. Candelas Newton. (Understanding Modern European & Latin American Literature Ser.). 190p. 1995. text ed. 29.95 (*1-57003-020-0*) U of SC Pr.

Understanding Female Sexual Health. Dorothy Baldwin. (Illus.). 300p. 1992. 19.95 (*0-7818-0072-2*) Hippocrene Bks.

***Understanding Fetal Alcohol Syndrome: A Guide for Families & Communities.** Ann P. Streissguth. LC 96-47826. 1997. write for info. (*1-55766-283-5*) P H Brookes.

Understanding FFT Applications: A Tutorial for Laymen, Students, Technicians & Working Engineers. Anders E. Zonst. LC 97-66217. (Illus.). 406p. (Orig.). (C). 1997. pap. text ed. 34.95 (*0-9645681-9-5*) Citrus Pr.

***Understanding Fiber Optics.** Jeff Hecht. 24.95 (*0-614-18440-1*, B11020) Info Gatekeepers.

***Understanding Fiber Optics.** 2nd ed. Hecht. 1997. pap. text ed. 35.93 (*0-13-649070-0*) P-H.

Understanding Fiber Optics on a PC. A. K. Ghatak et al. LC 95-48423. 100p. 1997. write for info. (*981-02-2594-6*) World Scientific Pub.

Understanding Fibonacci Numbers. Edward D. Dobson. 16p. 1984. pap. 5.00 (*0-934380-08-2*, 43-A) Traders Pr.

***Understanding Fibromyalgia: A Guide for Family & Friends.** Betty Dotterer & Paul Davidson. LC 96-77600. 60p. 1996. pap. 9.95 (*0-9653493-0-6*) HlthRd Prods.

Understanding Fiction. 3rd ed. Robert Penn Warren & Cleanth Brooks. 1979. pap. text ed. 41.00 (*0-13-936690-3*) P-H.

Understanding Fiction: Poems, 1986-1996. Henry Taylor. 64p. 1996. pap. 9.95 (*0-8071-2111-8*); text ed. 16.95 (*0-8071-2110-X*) La State U Pr.

Understanding Filipino Values: A Management Approach. Tomas D. Andres. 180p. (C). 1981. 15.00 (*971-10-0117-9*, Pub. by New Day Pub PH) Cellar.

Understanding Financial Derivatives: How to Protect Your Investments. Donald Strassheim. 176p. 1996. text ed. 40.00 (*0-7863-0385-9*) Irwin Prof Pubng.

Understanding Financial Statements. Gus Gordon. (C). 1992. text ed. 39.95 (*0-538-81516-7*, AM67AA) S-W Pub.

Understanding Financial Statements. 4th ed. Lyn M. Fraser. 1994. write for info. (*0-318-72786-2*) P-H.

Understanding Financial Statements. 4th ed. Lyn M. Fraser. 1994. pap. text ed. 34.80 (*0-13-103078-7*) P-H.

***Understanding Financial Statements.** 5th ed. Fraser & Ormiston. 1997. pap. text ed. 34.67 (*0-13-619115-0*) P-H.

Understanding Financial Statements: A Primer of Useful Information. James O. Gill. Ed. by Michael Crisp. LC 89-81248. (Fifty-Minute Ser.). (Illus.). 104p. (Orig.). 1990. pap. 10.95 (*1-56052-022-1*) Crisp Pubns.

Understanding Financial Statements: Through the Maze of a Corporate Annual Report. Adlyn M. Fraser. 1984. 24.95 (*0-8359-8042-1*, Reston); pap. 19.33 (*0-8359-8041-3*, Reston) P-H.

Understanding Financial Statements, 1991: Accounting for Lawyers - A Satellite Program. (Corporate Law & Practice Course Handbook, 1985-86 Ser.). 429p. 1992. pap. 17.50 (*0-685-70151-4*); audio 75.00 (*0-685-70152-2*) PLI.

***Understanding Financial Stewardship: Learn What God Has to Say about Managing Your Money.** Charles Stanley. (In Touch Ser.). 1997. pap. text ed. 6.99 (*0-7852-7274-7*) Nelson.

Understanding Flannery O'Connor. Margaret E. Whitt. LC 94-18748. (Understanding Contemporary American Literature Ser.). 259p. 1995. text ed. 29.95 (*1-57003-036-7*) U of SC Pr.

***Understanding Flannery O'Connor.** Margaret E. Whitt. LC 94-18748. 259p. (C). 1997. pap. 12.95 (*1-57003-225-4*) U of SC Pr.

Understanding Flying. Taylor. 1983. pap. 14.95 (*0-02-616640-2*) Macmillan.

Understanding Flying. Taylor. 1986. 22.50 (*0-02-616650-X*) Macmillan.

Understanding Flying. Richard L. Taylor. LC 91-46837. (Illus.). 342p. 1992. 29.95 (*1-56566-002-1*) Thomasson-Grant.

Understanding Foodservice Financial Management. Jeannie Sneed & Kathryn Kresse. LC 88-22321. 310p. (C). 1988. 60.00 (*0-87189-795-4*) Aspen Pub.

***Understanding Football: A Basic Guide to the Game.** David R. Walker. (Illus.). 204p. (Orig.). 1996. pap. 14.95 (*0-9646388-1-9*) WCB Enter.

Understanding Foreign Policy: The Foreign Policy Systems Approach. Ed. by Michael Clarke & Brian White. 232p. 1989. text ed. 70.00 (*1-85278-123-8*); pap. text ed. 25.00 (*1-85278-125-4*) E Elgar.

Understanding Forfeiture & Related Civil Actions in Criminal Law. (Litigation & Administrative Practice Course Handbook, 1983-84 Ser.). 144p. 1992. pap. 35.00 (*0-685-70153-0*) PLI.

Understanding FORTRAN. 3rd ed. Michel Boillot. (Illus.). 592p. (C). 1985. pap. text ed. 50.75 (*0-314-85219-0*) West Pub.

Understanding FORTRAN 77 & 90. Gene Zirkel & Eli Berlinger. LC 93-20755. 1994. pap. 64.95 (*0-534-93447-1*) PWS Pubs.

Understanding FORTRAN 77 with Structured Problem Solving. Michel Boillot. LC 86-26662. (Illus.). 527p. (C). 1987. Instr's. manual. teacher ed., pap. text ed. write for info. (*0-314-34720-8*) West Pub.

Understanding FORTRAN 77 with Structured Problem Solving. 2nd ed. Michel Boillot. LC 86-26662. (Illus.). 527p. (C). 1987. pap. text ed. 53.25 (*0-314-27031-0*) West Pub.

Understanding Fossils: An Introduction to Invertebrate Palaeontology. Peter Doyle. LC 95-49411. 1996. pap. text ed. 42.95 (*0-471-96351-8*) Wiley.

***Understanding Fractions.** Jo E. Moore. (Mathematics Ser.). (Illus.). 32p. (J). (gr. 3-5). 1997. teacher ed., pap. 2.95 (*1-55799-467-6*, 4069) Evan-Moor Corp.

Understanding Franchise Contracts. David C. Hjelmfelt. LC 84-1848. 45p. 1984. pap. 3.95 (*0-87576-110-0*) Pilot Bks.

Understanding Frank Lloyd Wright's Architecture. Donald Hoffmann. (Illus.). 96p. (Orig.). 1995. pap. text ed. 10.95 (*0-486-28364-X*) Dover.

Understanding Franz Werfel. Hans Wagener. LC 92-41141. (Understanding Modern European & Latin American Literature Ser.). 204p. (C). 1993. text ed. 29.95 (*0-87249-883-2*) U of SC Pr.

Understanding Freelance Graphics for Windows. Katherine Murray. LC 92-83944. 507p. 1993. 26.95 (*0-7821-1231-5*) Sybex.

Understanding French Accounts: Language & Terminology. Silvano Levy. 128p. (Orig.). 1995. pap. 37.50 (*0-273-60307-8*, Pub. by Pitman Pub Ltd UK) Trans-Atl Phila.

Understanding French Poetry: Essays for a New Millennium. Ed. by Stamos Metzidakis. LC 93-50527. (Illus.). 304p. 1994. text ed. 49.00 (*0-8153-0841-8*, H1596) Garland.

***Understanding Freud: The Man.** Garcia. 1997. pap. 20.00 (*0-8147-3109-0*) NYU Pr.

Understanding Freud: The Man & His Ideas. Ed. by Emanuel E. Garcia. 200p. (C). 1992. 40.00 (*0-8147-3045-0*) NYU Pr.

Understanding Fundamental Techniques: Volleyball. Bob Howard. 1995. pap. text ed. 20.00 (*0-205-16558-3*) Allyn.

Understanding Fundamentalism & Evangelicalism. George M. Marsden. 216p. (Orig.). 1990. pap. 11.00 (*0-8028-0539-6*) Eerdmans.

Understanding Futures Markets. 3rd ed. Robert W. Kolb. 1991. 39.95 (*0-13-928631-4*, Busn) P-H.

Understanding Futures Markets. 4th ed. Robert W. Kolb. 640p. pap. text ed. 40.00 (*1-878975-41-2*) Blackwell Pubs.

***Understanding Futures Markets.** 5th rev. ed. Robert W. Kolb. LC 96-29372. (Illus.). 576p. 1997. text ed. 66.95 (*1-57718-065-8*) Blackwell Pubs.

Understanding Gabriel Garcia Marquez. Kathleen McNerney. Ed. by James N. Hardin. (Understanding Contemporary European & Latin American Literature Ser.). 192p. (C). 1989. text ed. 29.95 (*0-87249-563-9*) U of SC Pr.

Understanding Gandhi. Ramashray Roy. (C). 1996. 27.00 (*81-202-0423-9*, Pub. by Ajanta II) S Asia.

Understanding Gangs. Carol Duerksen. (Fast Lane Bible Studies Ser.). 48p. (J). (gr. 7-9). 1995. pap. 9.95 (*0-87303-245-4*) Faith & Life.

Understanding Gary Snyder. Patrick D. Murphy. Ed. by Matthew J. Bruccoli. LC 91-46461. (Understanding Contemporary American Literature Ser.). 199p. 1992. text ed. 29.95 (*0-87249-821-2*) U of SC Pr.

***Understanding Gene Testing.** (Illus.). 31p. (Orig.). 1996. pap. 20.00 (0-7881-3000-5) DIANE Pub.

***Understanding Gene Therapy.** R. G. Vile. (Medical Perspective Ser.). 176p. 1997. pap. 18.95 (1-85996-180-0, Pub. by Bios Scientific UK) Coronet Bks.

***Understanding Gene Therapy.** R. G. Vile. (Medical Perspectives Ser.). 176p. 1997. pap. 38.95 (0-387-91512-5) Spr-Verlag.

Understanding Generalist Practice. Karen K. Kirst-Ashman & Grafton H. Hull, Jr. LC 92-34831. 1993. 46.95 (0-8304-1268-9) Nelson-Hall.

Understanding Genesis: The Heritage of Biblical Israel. Nahum M. Sarna. LC 66-23626. 1970. reprint ed. pap. 14.00 (0-8052-0253-6) Schocken.

Understanding Genetics: A Molecular Approach. Norman V. Rothwell. 672p. 1993. text ed. 64.95 (0-471-58822-9, Wiley-L) Wiley.

Understanding Genital Warts: A Guide for Women. Patricia A. Kuper. (Women's Health Care Ser.). 61p. (Orig.). 1996. pap. 4.95 (1-880906-29-5) IDI Pubns.

***Understanding Geology.** Webster. 1987. pap. text ed. write for info. (0-05-003664-5) Addison-Wesley.

Understanding George Garrett. R. H. Dillard. Ed. by Matthew J. Bruccoli. (Understanding Contemporary American Literature Ser.). 237p. (C). 1988. pap. 12.95 (0-87249-551-5); text ed. 29.95 (0-87249-550-7) U of SC Pr.

Understanding Gerhart Hauptmann. Warren R. Maurer. Ed. by James N. Hardin. LC 92-14308. (Understanding Modern European & Latin American Literature Ser.). 196p. (C). 1992. text ed. 29.95 (0-87249-823-9) U of SC Pr.

Understanding German Accounts: Language & Terminology. Adelheid Hofften & Johanna Edelsbacher. Ed. by Silvano Levy. 128p. (Orig.). 1994. pap. 37.50 (0-273-60309-4, Pub. by Pitman Pub Ltd UK) Trans-Atl Phila.

Understanding Gestational Diabetes. (Illus.). 52p. (Orig.). 1994. pap. text ed. 20.00 (0-7881-1057-8) DIANE Pub.

Understanding Giftedness. Kokot. 258p. 1993. 41.95 (0-409-11163-5) Buttrwrth-Heinemann.

Understanding GIS: The Arc - Info Method for Workstations. 6th rev. ed. 1993. pap. text ed. write for info. (1-879102-07-2) ERS Inst.

Understanding GIS: The Arc-Information Method: PC Version. Environmental Systems Research Institute Staff. 525p. 1993. pap. text ed. 54.95 (0-470-21959-9) Wiley.

Understanding GIS: The ARC/INFO3 Method: Version 7 for UNIX3 & Open VMSTM. Environmental Systems Research Institute Staff. 500p. 1995. pap. text ed. 49.95 (0-470-24987-0) Wiley.

Understanding GIS - The ARC - INFO Method: Host Version. Environmental Systems Research Institute, Inc. Staff. (Illus.). (C). 1990. pap. text ed. 50.00 (1-879102-01-3) ERS Inst.

Understanding GIS - The ARC - INFO Method: PC Version. Environmental Systems Research Institute Staff. (Illus.). (C). 1990. pap. text ed. 50.00 (1-879102-00-5) ERS Inst.

Understanding Global Cultures: Metaphorical Journeys Through 17 Countries. Martin J. Gannon. (C). 1994. text ed. 55.00 (0-8039-5374-7); pap. text ed. 25.50 (0-8039-5375-5) Sage.

***Understanding Globalization: The Social Consequences of Political, Economic & Environmental Change.** Ed. by Robert Schaeffer. LC 96-54822. 368p. (Orig.). 1997. 62.50 (0-8476-8351-6); pap. 21.95 (0-8476-8352-4) Rowman.

Understanding GMDSS. Tetley. (Electrical Engineering Ser.). (C). 1995. 62.95 (0-340-61042-5, Pub. by E Arnold UK) Routledge Chapman & Hall.

***Understanding God & His Covenants.** Patricia B. Gruits. 420p. (YA). (gr. 8 up). 1985. 14.95 (0-935945-00-8) PeterPat Pubs.

***Understanding God & His Covenants: Russian Edition.** Patricia B. Gruits. 450p. (RUS & SPA.). (YA). (gr. 8 up). 1994. 14.95 (0-9639461-1-0) PeterPat Pubs.

***Understanding God's Love: A Study of the Misunderstanding & Misrepresentation of God.** Ronald Greib. vi, 276p. (Orig.). 1997. pap. 14.95 (0-9656403-0-2) Christian Trad Pub.

Understanding God's Word - Chinese Edition. Alan N. Stibbs. Tr. by Daniel Law. 73p. (CHI.). 1975. pap. 3.50 (1-56582-097-5) Christ Renew Min.

***Understanding Governance: Policy Networks, Governance, Reflexivity & Accountability.** R. A. Rhodes. LC 96-49949. (Public Policy & Management Ser.). 1997. write for info. (0-335-19728-0, Open Univ Pr); pap. write for info. (0-335-19727-2, Open Univ Pr) Taylor & Francis.

Understanding GPS: Principles & Applications. Elliott D. Kaplan. 554p. 1996. 99.00 (0-89006-793-7) Artech Hse.

Understanding Graciliano Ramos. Celso L. De Oliveira. (Understanding Contemporary European & Latin Literature Ser.). 188p. (C). 1988. pap. 12.95 (0-87249-561-2); text ed. 29.95 (0-87249-560-4) U of SC Pr.

Understanding Grammar. William L. Rivers & Alison W. Rodriguez. LC 94-27634. 1994. pap. text ed. 30.00 (0-205-14633-3) Allyn.

Understanding Greek Sculpture: Ancient Meanings, Modern Readings. Nigel J. Spivey. LC 95-60560. (Illus.). 240p. 1996. 34.95 (0-500-23710-7) Thames Hudson.

Understanding Greek Sculpture: Ancient Meanings, Modern Readings. Nigel J. Spivey. LC 95-60560. (Illus.). 240p. 1997. pap. 24.95 (0-500-27876-8) Thames Hudson.

***Understanding Green Consumer Behavior: A Qualitative Cognitive Approach.** Sigmund A. Wagner. LC 97-18704. 1997. write for info. (0-415-15732-3) Routledge.

Understanding Grief: Helping Yourself Heal. Alan D. Wolfelt. LC 92-53492. 175p. 1992. pap. text ed. 18.95 (1-55959-038-6) Accel Devel.

Understanding Ground-Water Contamination: An Orientation Manual. Ed. by Paul E. Bailey & William D. Ward. 191p. 1990. 59.95 (1-55840-415-5, P7419) Exec Ent Pubns.

***Understanding Groundwater.** W. Jesse Schwalbaum. (Illus.). 207p. 1996. 35.00 (1-56072-404-8) Nova Sci Pubs.

Understanding Group Behavior, 2 vols., Set. Ed. by Erich H. Witte & James H. Davis, Jr. 1996. pap. 47.50 (0-8058-2176-7) L Erlbaum Assocs.

Understanding Group Behavior, 2 vols., Set. 1. Ed. by Erich H. Witte & James H. Davis, Jr. 1996. write for info. (0-8058-2175-9) L Erlbaum Assocs.

Understanding Group Behavior: A Discussion Guide. rev. ed. Harry L. Miller. 99p. reprint ed. pap. 28.30 (0-317-10607-4, 2000637) Bks Demand.

Understanding Group Behavior Vol. 1: Consensual Action by Small Groups. Ed. by Erich H. Witte & James H. Davis. 320p. 1996. pap. 34.50 (0-8058-1640-2) L Erlbaum Assocs.

Understanding Group Behavior Vol. 1: Consensual Action by Small Groups. Ed. by Erich H. Witte & James H. Davis. 375p. 1996. text ed. 69.95 (0-8058-1639-9) L Erlbaum Assocs.

Understanding Group Behavior Vol. 2: Small Group Processes & Interpersonal Relations. Ed. by Erich H. Witte & James H. Davis. 1996. pap. 34.50 (0-8058-1642-9); text ed. 69.95 (0-8058-1641-0) L Erlbaum Assocs.

Understanding Group Therapy. Yalom. (Counseling Ser.). 1990. student ed., pap. 9.95 (0-534-13521-8) Brooks-Cole.

***Understanding Groupware in the Enterprise.** Joanne Woodcock. LC 97-12282. 1997. pap. text ed. 17.99 (1-57231-561-X) Microsoft.

Understanding Growth Hormone. Neil B. Shulman. 300p. 1992. 19.95 (0-7818-0071-4) Hippocrene Bks.

Understanding Growth Management: Critical Issues & a Research Agenda. Ed. by David J. Brower et al. LC 89-51662. 198p. (Orig.). 1989. pap. text ed. 43.95 (0-87420-691-X, U99) Urban Land.

Understanding Gunter Grass. Alan F. Keele. Ed. by James N. Hardin. (Understanding Contemporary European & Latin Literature Ser.). 255p. (C). 1988. pap. 12.95 (0-87249-547-7); text ed. 29.95 (0-87249-546-9) U of SC Pr.

***Understanding Halal Foods-Falacies & Facts.** Ahmad H. Sakr. 144p. (Orig.). 1996. pap. text ed. 8.95 (0-911119-76-0) Cedar Graphics.

Understanding Harmony. Robert L. Jacobs. LC 85-31691. Orig. Title: Harmony for the Listener. 192p. 1986. reprint ed. text ed. 49.75 (0-313-25092-8, JAHA, Greenwood Pr) Greenwood.

Understanding Harold Pinter. Ronald Knowles. LC 95-4338. (Understanding Contemporary British Literature Ser.). 232p. 1995. text ed. 29.95 (1-57003-044-8) U of SC Pr.

Understanding Health Care Budgeting: An Introduction. Allen G. Herkimer, Jr. 238p. (C). 1988. 55.00 (0-87189-772-5) Aspen Pub.

Understanding Health Care Financial Management: Text, Cases, & Models. 2nd ed. Louis C. Gapenski. 872p. 1996. text ed. 72.00 (1-56793-041-7) Health Admin Pr.

***Understanding Health Care Outcomes Research.** Robert L. Kane. LC 97-6839. 1997. write for info. (0-8342-0959-4) Aspen Pub.

Understanding Health Care Reform. Theodore R. Marmor. 288p. 1994. 40.00 (0-300-05878-0); pap. 15.00 (0-300-05879-9) Yale U Pr.

Understanding Health Policy: A Clinical Approach. Thoams S. Bodenheimer & Grumach. (C). 1995. pap. text ed. 28.95 (0-8385-3678-6) Appleton & Lange.

Understanding Hearing Loss. rev. ed. Kenneth Lysons. 150p. 1995. pap. 18.95 (1-85302-214-4, Pub. by J Kingsley Pubs UK) Taylor & Francis.

Understanding Heart Disease. Arthur Selzer. (Illus.). 325p. 1991. 35.00 (0-520-06560-3) U CA Pr.

Understanding Heart Sounds & Murmurs: With an Introduction to Lung Sounds. 3rd ed. Ara G. Tilkian & Mary B. Conover. (Illus.). 304p. 1993. pap. text ed. 37.50 (0-7216-6784-8) Saunders.

Understanding Heat Pumps, Ground Water, & Wells. Ed. by K. McGray. 39p. 1983. 10.00 (1-56034-048-7, T040) Natl Grnd Water.

Understanding Heinrich Boll. Robert C. Conard. Ed. by James N. Hardin. (Understanding Modern European & Latin American Literature Ser.). 202p. 1992. text ed. 29.95 (0-87249-779-8) U of SC Pr.

Understanding Herbert Hoover: Ten Perspectives. Ed. by Lee Nash. 196p. 1988. 21.95 (0-8179-8541-7) Hoover Inst Pr.

Understanding Herpes: To Conquer a Dragon. 2nd ed. Gilles R. Monif. (Women's Health Care Ser.). (Illus.). 74p. 1996. pap. 4.95 (1-880906-38-4) IDI Pubns.

Understanding Hieroglyphs: A Complete Introductory Guide. Hilary Wilson. 192p. (Orig.). 1995. pap. 14.95 (0-8442-4604-2) NTC Pub Grp.

Understanding HIRF. Gerald L. Fuller. (Illus.). 125p. 1995. pap. 89.00 (1-885544-05-7) Avionics Commun.

Understanding Hispanic Surnaming Methods. Peter E. Carr. (Illus.). 60p. (Orig.). 1995. pap. 17.95 (0-9631209-6-4) TCI Gene Res.

Understanding Historical Research: A Search for Truth. Jack Block. (Illus.). 156p. 1971. pap. text ed. 7.00 (0-9600478-0-8) Research Pubns.

Understanding History: An Introduction to Analytical Philosophy of History. Jonathan Gorman. (Philosophica Ser.: No. 42). 121p. 1992. pap. 15.00 (0-7766-0355-8, Pub. by Univ Ottawa Pr CN) Paul & Co Pubs.

Understanding History: Marxist Essays. 3rd ed. George Novack. LC 75-186684. 210p. 1980. reprint ed. pap. 15.95 (0-87348-605-6); reprint ed. lib. bdg. 50.00 (0-87348-606-4) Pathfinder NY.

Understanding History of Education. 2nd ed. Ed. by Robert R. Sherman. 345p. 1984. text ed. 24.95 (0-87073-338-9); pap. text ed. 18.95 (0-87073-339-7) Schenkman Bks Inc.

Understanding History Through the American Experience. Bernard Norling & Charles Poinsatte. LC 76-637. 208p. 1976. pap. 9.50 (0-268-01911-8) U of Notre Dame Pr.

Understanding HIV-AIDS: A Workbook Suitable for Mainstreamed Students. Lynda L. Arehart & Margaret Torrie. (Contemporary Parenting Choices Ser.). (Illus.). 48p. (YA). (gr. 9-12). 1990. teacher ed., pap. text ed. 8.95 (0-8138-1619-X); student ed., wbk. ed., pap. text ed. 4.95 (0-8138-1618-1) Iowa St U Pr.

Understanding Homeowners Insurance. 211p. 1995. pap. 21.95 (0-7931-1277-X, 5732-0101) Dearborn Finan.

***Understanding Homosexual Problems: How to Help LDS Men Resolve Their Homosexual Problems.** Jason Park. 150p. (Orig.). 1997. pap. 10.95 (0-941846-07-5) Centry Pub.

Understanding Homosexuality. Isabel H. Pinkston. Ed. by Helen Roberts. LC 92-64453. (Researching the Soul with Dr. John Ser.: No. 3). 122p. (Orig.). 1993. pap. 5.95 (0-915151-17-0) Religious Res Pr.

Understanding Homosexuality. Scott Richards. 140p. 1995. pap. 10.95 (1-55517-173-7) CFI Dist.

Understanding Homosexuality: The Pride & the Prejudice. Roger E. Biery. LC 90-39122. 344p. 1990. 23.95 (0-934411-37-9) Edward-William Austin.

Understanding Hospital Financial Management. 2nd ed. Allen G. Herkimer, Jr. 456p. (C). 1986. 62.00 (0-87189-392-4) Aspen Pub.

***Understanding Hospitality Accounting I.** Raymond Cote. LC 97-23155. 1997. write for info. (0-86612-154-4) Educ Inst Am Hotel.

Understanding Hospitality Accounting I. 3rd ed. Raymond Cote. LC 94-37288. 1995. pap. write for info. (0-86612-093-9) Educ Inst Am Hotel.

Understanding Hospitality Accounting II. 2nd ed. Raymond Cote. (Illus.). 403p. 1991. text ed. write for info. (0-86612-063-7) Educ Inst Am Hotel.

***Understanding Hospitality Accounting II.** 3rd ed. Raymond Cote. LC 96-35894. 1996. pap. write for info. (0-86612-135-8) Educ Inst Am Hotel.

Understanding Hospitality Law. 3rd ed. Jack P. Jefferies. LC 94-46501. 1995. pap. write for info. (0-86612-090-4) Educ Inst Am Hotel.

Understanding House Construction. 2nd rev. ed. John A. Kilpatrick. Ed. by Rosanne O'Connor. LC 92-35117. (Illus.). 120p. 1993. pap. 7.95 (0-86718-382-9) Home Builder.

Understanding How Components Fail. 262p. 1985. 84.00 (0-87170-189-8, 6345) ASM.

Understanding How Others Misunderstand You: A Unique & Proven Plan for Strengthening Personal Relationships. rev. ed. Ken Voges & Ron Braund. 305p. 1995. pap. 14.99 (0-8024-1106-1) Moody.

Understanding How Others Misunderstand You Workbook. rev. ed. Ken Voges & Ron Braund. 1995. wbk. ed., pap. 21.99 (0-8024-1105-3) Moody.

Understanding How School Change Really Happens: Reform at Brookville High. Rosetta M. Cohen. LC 95-22652. 168p. 1995. 44.00 (0-8039-6254-1); pap. 20.00 (0-8039-6255-X) Corwin Pr.

Understanding How to Build Guitar Chords & Arpeggios. Michael A. Policastro. LC 93-85006. (C). 1993. pap. text ed. 29.95 (0-9637292-0-9) Silvanus Pub.

Understanding How to Fight the Good Fight of Faith. Kenneth E. Hagin. 1987. pap. 4.95 (0-89276-510-0) Hagin Ministries.

***Understanding Hubert Selby, Jr.** James R. Giles. LC 97-4721. (Understanding Contemporary American Literature Ser.). 166p. 1997. 24.95 (1-57003-176-2) U of SC Pr.

Understanding Human Anatomy & Physiology. Sylvia Mader. 368p. (C). 1991. pap. write for info. (0-697-07856-6) Wm C Brown Pubs.

Understanding Human Anatomy & Physiology. Sylvia Mader. 368p. (C). 1991. student ed., per. write for info. (0-697-12042-2) Wm C Brown Pubs.

Understanding Human Anatomy & Physiology. Eldra P. Solomon & Gloria A. Phillips. (Illus.). 400p. 1987. pap. text ed. 31.50 (0-7216-1994-0) Saunders.

***Understanding Human Anatomy & Physiology.** Eldra P. Solomon & Gloria A. Phillips. (Illus.). 1987. teacher ed., pap. write for info. (0-7216-1995-9) Saunders.

Understanding Human Anatomy & Physiology. Ann Stalheim-Smith & Gregory K. Fitch. Ed. by Westby. LC 92-48865. 1000p. (C). 1993. text ed. 72.50 (0-314-00602-8) West Pub.

Understanding Human Anatomy & Physiology. 2nd ed. Sylvia Mader. 464p. (C). 1994. text ed. write for info. (0-697-22191-1); Study wkbk. student ed., spiral bd. write for info. (0-697-13673-6) Wm C Brown Pubs.

Understanding Human Anatomy & Physiology. 3rd ed. Sylvia Mader & Jay M. Templin. 160p. (C). 1996. student ed., per. write for info. (0-697-25173-X) Wm C Brown Pubs.

Understanding Human Anatomy & Physiology. 3rd ed. Sylvia S. Mader. 480p. (C). 1996. per. write for info. (0-697-25170-5) Wm C Brown Pubs.

Understanding Human Behavior. 7th ed. James V. McConnell & Ronald P. Philipchalk. 750p. (C). 1991. text ed. write for info. (0-318-69127-2) HB Coll Pubs.

Understanding Human Behavior. 8th ed. Philipchal. (C). 1994. teacher ed., pap. text ed. 35.00 (0-15-501419-6) HB Coll Pubs.

Understanding Human Behavior. 8th ed. Philipchal. (C). 1994. student ed., pap. text ed. 24.00 (0-15-501420-X) HB Coll Pubs.

Understanding Human Behavior. 8th ed. Ronald P. Philipchalk & James V. McConnell. (Illus.). 704p. (C). text ed. write for info. (0-15-500991-5) HB Coll Pubs.

Understanding Human Behavior: A Guide for Health Care Providers. 4th ed. Mary E. Milliken. LC 86-16758. 304p. (C). 1987. pap. 28.95 (0-8273-2797-8); text ed. 28.50 (0-8273-2798-6) Delmar.

Understanding Human Behavior: A Guide for Health Care Providers. 4th ed. Mary E. Milliken. LC 86-16758. 304p. (C). 1987. teacher ed. 12.00 (0-8273-2799-4) Delmar.

Understanding Human Behavior: A Guide for Health Care Providers. 5th ed. Mary E. Milliken. LC 92-14880. 78p. 1993. pap. 29.95 (0-8273-5473-8); text ed. 32.95 (0-8273-5474-6) Delmar.

Understanding Human Behavior: A Guide for Health Care Providers. 5th ed. Mary E. Milliken. LC 92-14880. 78p. 1993. student ed., teacher ed., pap. 14.00 (0-8273-5475-4) Delmar.

***Understanding Human Behavior: A Guide for Health Care Providers.** 6th ed. Mary E. Milliken. LC 97-13707. 1997. write for info. (0-8273-8221-9) Delmar.

Understanding Human Behavior: An Introduction to Psychology. 6th ed. James V. McConnell. 768p. (C). 1989. wbk. ed. 12.95 (0-318-43181-5); text ed. 29.95 (0-318-43180-7) HB Coll Pubs.

Understanding Human Behavior: Test Bank. 8th ed. Philipchal. (C). 1994. pap. text ed. 35.00 (0-15-501421-8) HB Coll Pubs.

***Understanding Human Behavior & the Social Environment.** 4th ed. Charles H. Zastrow. LC 96-47768. (Social Welfare Ser.). 1997. 47.95 (0-8304-1483-5) Nelson-Hall.

Understanding Human Behavior & the Social Environment. 4th ed. Charles H. Zastrow. LC 93-4904. (Social Welfare Ser.). 1994. write for info. (0-8304-1397-9); disk write for info. (0-8304-1395-2) Nelson-Hall.

***Understanding Human Behavior & the Social Environment Instructor's Resource Manual & Test Bank.** Charles Zastrow & Karen K. Kirst-Ashman. 1997. write for info. (0-8304-1493-2) Nelson-Hall.

***Understanding Human Behavior & the Social Environment Student Study Guide.** Charles Zastrow & Karen K. Kirst-Ashman. 1997. disk write for info. (0-8304-1510-6) Nelson-Hall.

Understanding Human Behavior & the Social Environment Student Study Guide. 4th ed. Charles H. Zastrow. LC 93-4904. (Social Welfare Ser.). 1997. student ed. 16.95 (0-8304-1396-0) Nelson-Hall.

Understanding Human Behavior for Effective Police Work. 3rd ed. Harold E. Russell & Allan Beigel. LC 90-80676. 464p. 1990. 42.00 (0-465-08859-7) Basic.

Understanding Human Behavior in Health & Illness. 3rd ed. Richard C. Simons. (Illus.). 822p. (C). 1985. text ed. 35.00 (0-683-07741-4) Williams & Wilkins.

Understanding Human Communication. 4th ed. Ronald B. Adler & George Rodman. 464p. (C). 1991. pap. text ed. 28.00 (0-03-049727-2) HB Coll Pubs.

Understanding Human Communication. 5th ed. Ron Adler & George Rodman. (Illus.). 496p. (C). 1993. pap. text ed. 29.00 (0-15-500781-5) HB Coll Pubs.

Understanding Human Communication. 6th ed. Ronald B. Adler & George Rodman. 552p. (C). 1996. pap. text ed. write for info. (0-15-503286-0) HB Coll Pubs.

***Understanding Human Communication: Student Resource Manual.** 6th ed. Walter Nicholson. 390p. (C). 1996. pap. text ed. 17.50 (0-15-504170-3) HR&W Schl Div.

Understanding Human Evolution. 3rd ed. Frank E. Poirier. LC 92-26288. 400p. 1993. pap. text ed. 24.00 (0-13-012477-X) P-H.

***Understanding Human Evolution.** 11th ed. Wetherington. 1992. 15.95 (0-314-01087-4) Wadsworth Pub.

Understanding Human Nature. Alfred Adler. Tr. by Colin Brett from GER. 240p. (C). 1994. pap. 13.95 (1-85168-021-7) Onewrld Pubns.

Understanding Human Nature. George S. Howard. LC 96-586. 1996. write for info. (0-937647-03-9) Academic Pubns.

Understanding Human Relations. Graham. 1989. text ed. 66.00 (0-02-345471-7, Macmillan Coll) P-H.

***Understanding Human Relations & Multicultural Education.** 2nd ed. Douglas F. Warring. 217p. 1996. pap. 25.00 (1-887049-04-5) Leader Scottsdale.

Understanding Human Rights. Ed. by Conor A. Gearty & Adam Tomkins. LC 95-34235. 672p. 1996. 160.00 (0-7201-2295-3, Mansell Pub) Cassell.

Understanding Human Sexuality. 4th ed. Janet S. Hyde. 1990. teacher ed. 15.95 (0-07-031607-4) McGraw.

Understanding Human Sexuality. 5th ed. Janet S. Hyde. LC 93-24355. 1993. text ed. write for info. (0-07-031615-5) McGraw.

Understanding Human Sexuality. 6th ed. Janet S. Hyde. 1996. text ed. write for info. (0-07-031802-6) McGraw.

***Understanding Human Structure & Function.** Valerie C. Scanlon & Tina Sanders. LC 96-37146. (Illus.). 454p. 1997. pap. 28.95 (0-8036-0236-7) Davis Co.

Understanding Human Values: Individual & Societal. Milton Rokeach. LC 78-24753. (Illus.). 1979. 35.00 (0-02-926760-9, Free Press) Free Pr.

U V

An Asterisk (*) at the beginning of an entry indicates that the title is appearing in BIP for the first time.

Understanding Humankind: A Global Introduction to Social Science. Thomas O'Toole. Ed. & Illus. by Davies Group Staff. 278p. (C). 1996. pap. 20.70 (*1-888570-01-6*) Davies Grp.

Understanding Hydropower. Walter C. Eshenaur. 60p. 1984. 9.95 (*0-86619-205-0*, TP5) Vols Tech Asst.

Understanding Hypermedia: From Multimedia to Virtual Reality. Bob Cotton & Richard Oliver. (Illus.). 160p. (C). 1993. pap. 29.95 (*0-7148-2908-0*, Pub. by Phaidon Press UK) Chronicle Bks.

***Understanding Hypermedia 2.0.** 2nd ed. Bob Cotton & Richard Oliver. (Illus.). 192p. 1997. 39.95 (*0-7148-3657-5*, Pub. by Phaidon Press UK) Chronicle Bks.

Understanding Hypertext: Concepts & Applications. Philip Seyer. (Illus.). 288p. 1989. 28.95 (*0-8306-9108-1*, Windcrest); pap. 19.95 (*0-8306-3308-1*, Windcrest) TAB Bks.

Understanding Illness Series, 6 vols., Set. Elaine Landau. (Illus.). 64p. (J). (gr. 5-8). 1994. lib. bdg. 95.88 (*0-8050-3713-6*) TFC Bks NY.

Understanding Illuminated Manuscripts: A Guide to Technical Terms. Michelle P. Brown. LC 93-42239. (Looking at...Ser.). (Illus.). 112p. (Orig.). 1994. pap. 13.95 (*0-89236-217-0*, J P Getty Museum) J P Getty Trust.

Understanding Images: Finding Meaning in Digital Imagery. Ed. by Francis T. Marchese. LC 93-42645. (TELOS - The Electronic Library of Science). 1995. 54.95 (*0-387-94148-7*) Spr-Verlag.

Understanding Immigration Law. 2nd ed. Nancy-Jo Merritt. (Layman's Law Guides Ser.). 128p. 1994. pap. 8.95 (*1-56414-089-X*) Career Pr Inc.

Understanding Immigration Law: How to Enter, Work & Live in the United States. Nancy-Jo Merritt. 96p. 1992. pap. 9.95 (*0-9630356-2-2*) Makai.

Understanding Imperial Russia: State & Society in the Old Regime. Marc Raeff. Tr. by Arthur Goldhammer. LC 83-26241. 240p. 1986. pap. text ed. 17.00 (*0-231-05843-8*) Col U Pr.

Understanding Impoverishment: The Consequences of Development-Induced Displacement. Ed. by Christopher McDowell. LC 96-42. (Refugee & Forced Migration Studies: Vol. 2). 208p. 1996. 45.00 (*1-57181-916-9*); pap. 18.95 (*1-57181-927-4*) Berghahn Bks.

Understanding in Human Context: Themes & Variations in Indian Philosophy. Debabrata Sinha. (New Perspectives in Philosophical Scholarship Series: Texts & Issues: Vol. 5). 208p. (C). 1996. text ed. 44.95 (*0-8204-2723-3*) P Lang Pubng.

Understanding in Mathematics. Anna Sierpinska. LC 94-27248. (Studies in Mathematics Education Ser.: No. 2). 182p. (Orig.). 1994. 55.00 (*0-7507-0334-2*, Falmer Pr) Taylor & Francis.

***Understanding in Mathematics.** Anna Sierpinska. (Studies in Mathematics Education Ser.). 206p. (Orig.). 1996. pap. 24.95 (*0-7507-0568-X*, Falmer Pr) Taylor & Francis.

***Understanding (in 30 Minutes) & Eliminating (in 30 Days) Pain.** Daniel A. Twogood. 42p. (Orig.). 1996. pap. 7.95 (*0-9631125-3-8*) Wilhelmina.

Understanding Indian Classical Music. G. N. Joshi. (Illus.). xii, 46p. (C). 1981. text ed. 25.00 (*0-86590-046-9*, Pub. by Taraporevala II) Apt Bks.

Understanding Indian Classical Music. G. N. Joshi. (Illus.). 110p. 1979. 16.95 (*0-318-36334-8*) Asia Bk Corp.

Understanding Indian History. Ranjit San. (C). 1988. 27.00 (*0-8364-2380-1*, Pub. by Firma KLM II) S Asia.

Understanding Indian Music. Baburao Joshi. LC 73-15055. 102p. (C). 1974. reprint ed. text ed. 45.00 (*0-8371-7156-3*, JOIM, Greenwood Pr) Greenwood.

Understanding Individuals with Low Incidence Handicaps: Categorical & Noncategorical Perspectives. Ed. by Anthony F. Rotatori & Robert A. Fox. (Illus.). 378p. (C). 1989. text ed. 77.95 (*0-398-05538-6*) C C Thomas.

Understanding Indonesia. Ed. by Leslie Palmier. LC 84-21133. 128p. 1985. text ed. 46.95 (*0-566-00784-3*, Pub. by Dartmth Pub UK) Ashgate Pub Co.

Understanding Indoor Air Quality. Bradford O. Brooks. 189p. 1991. 73.00 (*0-8493-8846-5*, TD883) CRC Pr.

Understanding Industrial Designed Experiments. 2nd ed. Stephen Schmidt & Robert G. Launsby. (Illus.). 420p. (C). 1989. text ed. 80.00 (*0-9622176-1-1*) Air Acad Pr.

Understanding Industrial Designed Experiments. 3rd ed. Stephen R. Schmidt & Robert G. Launsby. 575p. (C). 1991. text ed. 80.00 (*0-9622176-2-X*) Air Acad Pr.

Understanding Industrial Designed Experiments. 4th ed. Stephen R. Schmidt & Robert G. Launsby. 768p. (C). 1994. text ed. 69.95 (*1-880156-03-2*) Air Acad Pr.

Understanding Industrial Experimentation. Donald J. Wheeler. 264p. (C). 1988. pap. text ed. 50.00 (*0-945320-03-5*) SPC Pr.

Understanding Industrial Organizations: Theoretical Perspectives in Industrial Sociology. Richard Brown. LC 91-42994. 288p. (C). 1992. pap. 19.95 (*0-415-01782-3*, Routledge NY) Routledge.

Understanding Industrial Relations. 4th ed. D. Farnham & J. Pimlott. 244p. 1990. pap. text ed. 22.50 (*0-304-31794-2*) Cassell.

Understanding Industrial Society: Sociological Guide. Robin Theobald. LC 93-39175. 1994. text ed. 49.95 (*0-312-12067-2*) St Martin.

Understanding Industry & Organizations. Dipboye. (C). 1993. teacher ed., pap. text ed. 35.00 (*0-03-094857-6*) HB Coll Pubs.

Understanding Industry & Organizations. Dipboye. (C). 1994. student ed., pap. text ed. 24.00 (*0-03-094858-4*) HB Coll Pubs.

***Understanding Infertility: Insights for Family & Friends.** Patricia I. Johnston. 32p. 1996. 5.00 (*0-944934-18-8*) Perspect Indiana.

Understanding Inflation & Unemployment. 2nd ed. Allen W. Smith. LC 75-29492. 176p. (C). 1981. text ed. 28.95 (*0-88229-276-5*) Nelson-Hall.

Understanding Information: Business, Technology & Geography. Ed. by Kevin Robins. LC 91-40511. 207p. 1994. text ed. 75.00 (*0-471-94763-6*) Wiley.

***Understanding Information Policy.** Ian H. Rowlands. (British Library Research Ser.). 1997. 60.00 (*1-85739-179-9*) Bowker-Saur.

***Understanding Information Retrieval Interactions: Theoretical & Practical Implications.** Date not set. text ed. 73.25 (*1-56750-305-5*) Ablex Pub.

***Understanding Information Retrieval Interactions: Theoretical & Practical Implications.** Date not set. pap. 39.50 (*1-56750-306-3*) Ablex Pub.

Understanding Information Systems. Steven C. Ross. Ed. by Leyh. LC 93-33048. (Microcomputing Ser.). 224p. (C). 1994. pap. text ed. 17.00 (*0-314-02880-3*) West Pub.

Understanding Infrastructure: A Guide for Architects & Planners. George Rainer. LC 89-36569. 278p. 1990. text ed. 69.95 (*0-471-50546-3*) Wiley.

Understanding Ingeborg Bachmann: Understanding Modern European & Latin American Literature. Karen R. Achberger. LC 94-18679. 230p. 1994. text ed. 29.95 (*0-87249-994-4*) U of SC Pr.

Understanding Injection Molding Technology. Herbert Rees. 128p. 1994. pap. write for info. (*1-56990-130-9*) Hanser-Gardner.

Understanding Instructions. Janis Minton. (Language Arts Ser.). 24p. (gr. 3-6). 1979. student ed. 5.00 (*0-8209-0322-1*, LA-8) ESP.

Understanding Insulin Action. J. Espinal. 1990. boxed write for info. (*0-318-68275-3*) P-H.

***Understanding Insulin Action: Principles & Molecular Mechanisms.** Splittstoesser. (Ellis Horwood Series in Biomedical Sciences). 300p. (C). (gr. 13 up). 1989. text ed. 51.50 (*0-412-02261-3*) Chapman & Hall.

Understanding Insurance Law. 2nd ed. Robert H. Jerry. LC 96-20541. (Legal Text Ser.). 1996. pap. write for info. (*0-8205-2467-0*) Bender.

Understanding Intelligence. Ken Richardson. 192p. 1990. 90.00 (*0-335-09398-1*, Open Univ Pr); pap. 32.00 (*0-335-09397-3*, Open Univ Pr) Taylor & Francis.

Understanding Interaction in Central Australia. Kenneth Liberman. (Studies in Ethnomethodology). 352p. 1985. 67.50 (*0-7102-0473-6*, RKP) Routledge.

Understanding Interdependence: The Macroeconomics of the Open Economy. Ed. by Peter B. Kenen. LC 94-36531. 472p. 1995. text ed. 55.00 (*0-691-03408-7*) Princeton U Pr.

Understanding Interest Rate Swaps. Mary S. Ludwig. LC 92-39058. 1993. text ed. 49.95 (*0-07-039020-7*) McGraw.

Understanding Interfaces: A Handbook of Human-Computer Dialogue. Mark W. Lansdale & Thomas C. Ormerod. (Computers & People Ser.). (Illus.). 304p. 1994. text ed. 48.00 (*0-12-528390-3*) Acad Pr.

Understanding Intergovernmental Relations. 3rd ed. Deil S. Wright. LC 87-36747. 511p. (C). 1988. pap. text ed. 31.00 (*0-534-09012-5*) HarBrace.

Understanding Intermediate Algebra: A Course for College Students. 3rd ed. Lewis R. Hirsch & Arthur Goodman. Ed. by Pullins. LC 93-11707. 750p. (C). 1993. text ed. 56.00 (*0-314-02518-9*) West Pub.

***Understanding Intermediate Algebra: A Course for College Students.** 4th ed. Hirsch. (C). 1998. text ed. 62.95 (*0-534-35338-X*) Brooks-Cole.

Understanding Intermediate Algebra: A Text-Workbook. 2nd ed. Lewis R. Hirsch & Arthur Goodman. Ed. by Ricci. 967p. (C). 1991. pap. text ed. 56.00 (*0-314-81298-9*) West Pub.

Understanding International Conflict: An Introduction to Theory & History. Joseph S. Nye, Jr. LC 92-32174. (C). 1993. text ed. 28.50 (*0-06-500720-4*) Addson-Wesley Educ.

***Understanding International Conflicts: An Introduction to Theory & History.** 2nd ed. Joseph S. Nye. LC 97-33683. (C). 1998. text ed. 26.50 (*0-321-01101-5*) Addson-Wesley Educ.

Understanding International Political Economy, with Readings for the Fatigued. Ralph Pettman. 257p. (Orig.). 1996. pap. text ed. 19.95 (*1-55587-677-3*, 87-677-3) Lynne Rienner.

Understanding International Political Economy, with Readings for the Fatigued. Ralph Pettman. (Orig.). 1996. lib. bdg. 48.00 (*1-55587-666-8*, 87-666-8) Lynne Rienner.

Understanding International Relations. Clark et al. 1993. pap. text ed. write for info. (*0-07-011153-7*) McGraw.

Understanding International Relations: The Value of Alternative Lenses. 2nd rev. ed. Kaufman et al. 1994. pap. text ed. write for info. (*0-07-034049-8*) McGraw.

Understanding Internet. Bruce J. McLaren. Date not set. teacher ed., pap. text ed. write for info. (*0-314-07364-7*) West Pub.

Understanding Interpersonal Communication. 6th ed. Richard L. Weaver, II. (C). 1993. text ed. 37.50 (*0-673-46776-7*) Addson-Wesley Educ.

Understanding Interpersonal Communication. 7th ed. Richard L. Weaver. (C). 1995. teacher ed., pap. write for info. (*0-673-97017-5*) Addson-Wesley Educ.

Understanding Interpersonal Communication. 7th ed. Richard L. Weaver, II. LC 95-35466. (Illus.). 560p. (C). 1996. text ed. 38.50 (*0-673-99581-X*) Addson-Wesley Educ.

Understanding Interracial Unity: A Study of U. S. Race Relations. Richard W. Thomas. (Sage Series on Race & Ethnic Relations: Vol. 16). 320p. 1995. 42.00 (*0-8039-4602-3*); pap. 18.95 (*0-8039-4603-1*) Sage.

Understanding I/O Subsystems. W. David Schwaderer & Andrew W. Wilson, Jr. (Illus.). 375p. (Orig.). 1996. pap. 29.95 (*0-9651911-0-9*) Adaptec Pr.

Understanding IRAs: An Amiable Approach. D. Kirk Buchanan. 110p. 1990. pap. 7.95 (*0-9630879-0-8*) Buchanan Res.

Understanding IRAs & SEPs. Dearborn Staff & R&R Newkirk Staff. 100p. 1996. pap. 24.95 (*0-7931-1484-5*, 5459-0101, R & R Newkirk) Dearborn Finan.

Understanding Iris Murdoch. Cheryl K. Bove. LC 92-35180. (Understanding Contemporary British Literature Ser.). 225p. (C). 1993. text ed. 29.95 (*0-87249-876-X*) U of SC Pr.

Understanding Isaac Bashevis Singer. Lawrence S. Friedman. Ed. by Matthew J. Bruccoli. (Understanding Contemporary American Literature Ser.). 256p. (C). 1988. pap. 12.95 (*0-87249-544-2*); text ed. 29.95 (*0-87249-543-4*) U of SC Pr.

Understanding Islam. Frithjof Schuon. LC 93-26267. 133p. 1994. pap. 12.00 (*0-941532-17-8*) Wrld Wisdom Bks.

***Understanding Islam.** Frithjof Schuon. 204p. 1996. pap. 14.50 (*0-614-21452-1*, 1270) Kazi Pubns.

Understanding Islam: An Approach to Witness. Dwight L. Baker. 125p. (Orig.). 1989. pap. 4.63 (*0-685-29349-1*) Baptist Literacy.

Understanding Islam: An Introduction to the Moslem World. Thomas W. Lippman. LC 81-85142. 208p. 1982. pap. 3.95 (*0-451-62666-4*, ME2079, Ment) NAL-Dutton.

Understanding Islam: An Introduction to the Muslim World. 2nd rev. ed. Thomas W. Lippman. 208p. 1995. pap. 10.95 (*0-452-01160-4*, Plume) NAL-Dutton.

Understanding Islam & Muslims in the Philippines. Ed. by Peter G. Gowing. (Illus.). 186p. (Orig.). (C). 1989. pap. 13.75 (*971-10-0386-4*, Pub. by New Day Pub PH) Cellar.

Understanding ISO 9000 & Implementing the Basics to Quality. Dean H. Stamatis. LC 95-32191. (Quality & Reliability Ser.: Vol. 45). 280p. 1995. 49.75 (*0-8247-9656-X*) Dekker.

Understanding Israel. Sol Scharfstein. LC 94-5791. (J). 1994. 19.95 (*0-88125-448-7*); pap. 14.95 (*0-88125-428-2*) Ktav.

Understanding Italo Calvino. Beno Weiss. LC 92-40941. (Understanding Modern European & Latin American Literature Ser.). 244p. (C). 1993. text ed. 29.95 (*0-87249-858-1*) U of SC Pr.

Understanding Japanese Business. Hirofumi Matsuo. (Illus.). 74p. (Orig.). (C). 1995. pap. text ed. 25.00 (*0-7881-2332-7*) DIANE Pub.

Understanding Japanese Society. Joy Hendry. 240p. 1988. text ed. 49.95 (*0-7099-3788-1*, Pub. by Croom Helm UK); pap. text ed. 13.95 (*0-7099-5703-3*, Pub. by Croom Helm UK) Routledge Chapman & Hall.

Understanding Japanese Society. 2nd rev. ed. Joy Hendry. LC 94-39921. (Nissan Institute-Routledge Japanese Studies). (Illus.). 256p. (gr. 13). 1995. pap. 16.95 (*0-415-10259-6*, C0183) Routledge.

Understanding JCT Standard Building Contracts. 2nd ed. David M. Chappell. 112p. 1991. pap. 27.95 (*0-419-17320-X*, E & FN Spon) Routledge Chapman & Hall.

Understanding JCT Standard Building Contracts. 3rd ed. David M. Chappell. LC 93-12123. (Builder's Bookshelf Ser.). 1993. write for info. (*0-419-18430-9*, E & FN Spon) Routledge Chapman & Hall.

Understanding Jean-Paul Sartre. Philip R. Wood. (Understanding Modern European & Latin American Literature Ser.). 289p. (C). 1991. text ed. 29.95 (*0-87249-703-8*) U of SC Pr.

Understanding Jehovah's Witnesses: Why Jehovah's Witnesses Read the Bible the Way They Do. Robert M. Bowman, Jr. LC 91-3034. 168p. (gr. 10). 1991. pap. 7.99 (*0-8010-0995-2*) Baker Bks.

Understanding Jesus. Alister E. McGrath. 192p. 1990. pap. 14.99 (*0-310-29811-3*) Zondervan.

Understanding Jewelery. rev. ed. David Bennett & Daniela Mascetti. 1994. 79.50 (*1-85149-205-4*) Antique Collect.

Understanding Jewish Ethics. Richard A. Freund. LC 90-46835. 344p. 1990. pap. 34.95 (*0-7734-9894-X*) E Mellen.

Understanding Jewish Ethics, Vol. II: Major Themes & Thinkers. Richard A. Freund. LC 90-46835. 360p. 1993. pap. 34.95 (*0-7734-1972-1*) E Mellen.

***Understanding Jewish History: From the Patriarchs to the Expulsion from Spain.** Sol Scharfstein. 168p. (YA). (gr. 7 up). pap. 15.95 (*0-88125-545-9*) Ktav.

***Understanding Jewish History: Text & Commentaries.** Steven Bayme. 1997. 39.50 (*0-614-27519-9*) Ktav.

***Understanding Jewish History: Text & Commentaries.** Steven Bayme. 1997. pap. 24.95 (*0-614-27520-2*) Ktav.

***Understanding Jewish History: Texts & Commentaries.** Steven Bayme. LC 97-6196. 1997. write for info. (*0-88125-581-5*) Ktav.

Understanding Jewish Mysticism: A Source Reader, No. I. D. R. Blumenthal. (Library of Judaic Learning). 25.00 (*0-87068-334-9*); pap. 14.95 (*0-685-02922-0*) Ktav.

Understanding Jewish Mysticism: The Philosophic-Mystical Tradition & the Hasidic Tradition, Vol.II. David Blumenthal. 25.00 (*0-87068-205-9*); pap. 12.95 (*0-87068-225-3*) Ktav.

Understanding Jewish Theology. Jacob Neusner. 1973. pap. 16.95 (*0-87068-215-6*) Ktav.

Understanding Johannes Bobrowski. David Scrase. LC 95-10398. (Understanding Modern European & Latin American Literature Ser.). 165p. 1995. text ed. 29.95 (*1-57003-028-6*) U of SC Pr.

Understanding John Barth. Stan Fogel & Gordon Slethaug. (Understanding Contemporary American Literature Ser.). 253p. (C). 1990. text ed. 29.95 (*0-87249-660-0*) U of SC Pr.

Understanding John Dewey: Nature & Cooperative Intelligence. James Campbell. 322p. 1995. pap. text ed. 19.95 (*0-8126-9285-3*) Open Court.

Understanding John Fowles. Thomas G. Foster. LC 94-3215. 200p. 1994. text ed. 29.95 (*1-57003-003-0*) U of SC Pr.

Understanding John Gardner. John M. Howell. (Understanding Contemporary American Literature Ser.). 181p. (C). 1993. text ed. 29.95 (*0-87249-872-7*) U of SC Pr.

Understanding John Irving. Edward C. Reilly. Ed. by Matthew J. Bruccoli. LC 91-14616. (Understanding Contemporary American Literature Ser.). 165p. 1991. text ed. 29.95 (*0-87249-770-4*) U of SC Pr.

Understanding John Irving. Edward C. Reilly. LC 91-14616. (Understanding Contemporary American Literature Ser.). 165p. (C). 1993. pap. 12.95 (*0-87249-880-8*) U of SC Pr.

***Understanding John le Carre.** John L. Cobbs. LC 96-4863. (Understanding Contemporary British Literature Ser.). 300p. 1997. 29.95 (*1-57003-168-1*) U of SC Pr.

Understanding Jose Donoso. Sharon Magnarelli. LC 92-19103. (Understanding Modern European & Latin American Literature Ser.). (Illus.). 204p. 1992. text ed. 29.95 (*0-87249-844-1*) U of SC Pr.

Understanding Joseph Heller. Sanford Pinsker. Ed. by Matthew J. Bruccoli. (Understanding Contemporary American Literature Ser.). 200p. 1991. text ed. 29.95 (*0-87249-751-8*) U of SC Pr.

Understanding Journalism: A Guide to Terms. John Wilson. 320p. (C). 1996. pap. 17.95 (*0-415-11599-X*); text ed. 59.95 (*0-415-11598-1*) Routledge.

Understanding Joyce Carol Oates. Greg Johnson. (Understanding Contemporary American Literature Ser.). 224p. (C). 1987. pap. 12.95 (*0-87249-525-6*) U of SC Pr.

Understanding Juan Goytisolo. Randolph D. Pope. Ed. by James Hardin. LC 95-11606. (Understanding Modern European & Latin American Literature Ser.). 190p. 1995. text ed. 29.95 (*1-57003-069-3*) U of SC Pr.

Understanding Judaism: The Basics of Deed & Creed. Benjamin Blech. LC 90-24947. 368p. 1997. pap. 25.00 (*0-87668-291-3*) Aronson.

Understanding Julian Barnes. Merritt Moseley. LC 96-25197. (Understanding Contemporary British Literature Ser.). 200p. 1997. 29.95 (*1-57003-140-1*) U of SC Pr.

***Understanding Just in Time.** Malcolm Wheatley. LC 96-49056. (Business Success Ser.). 1997. pap. text ed. 6.95 (*0-7641-0126-9*) Barron.

Understanding Justice: An Introduction to Ideas, Perspectives & Controversies in Modern Penal Theory. Barbara A. Hudson. LC 95-26511. 160p. (C). 1996. 89.00 (*0-335-19684-5*, Open Univ Pr); pap. 27.00 (*0-335-19329-3*, Open Univ Pr) Taylor & Francis.

Understanding Juvenile Justice. Henri Giller & Alison Morris. 240p. 1987. 47.50 (*0-7099-3832-2*, Pub. by Croom Helm UK) Routledge Chapman & Hall.

Understanding Katherine Anne Porter. Darlene H. Unrue. Ed. by Matthew J. Bruccoli. (Understanding Contemporary American Literature Ser.). 205p. 1988. pap. 12.95 (*0-87249-584-1*); text ed. 29.95 (*0-87249-583-3*) U of SC Pr.

Understanding Kidney Transplantation. Edith T. Oberley & Neal R. Glass. (Illus.). 160p. (C). 1987. 33.95 (*0-398-05277-8*) C C Thomas.

Understanding Kingsley Amis. Merritt Moseley. LC 92-37274. (Understanding Contemporary British Literature Ser.). 201p. (C). 1993. text ed. 29.95 (*0-87249-861-1*) U of SC Pr.

Understanding Korean Literature. Kim Hung-Gyu. Tr. by J. Fouser Robert. LC 97-11941. (New Studies in Asian Culture). 248p. (C). (gr. 13). 1997. pap. text ed. 21.95 (*1-56324-774-7*, East Gate Bk) M E Sharpe.

Understanding Korean Literature. Hung-Gyu Kim. Tr. by Robert J. Fouser. LC 97-11941. (New Studies in Asian Culture). 248p. (C). (gr. 13). 1997. text ed. 62.95 (*1-56324-773-9*, East Gate Bk) M E Sharpe.

Understanding Kurt Vonnegut. William R. Allen. Ed. by Matthew J. Bruccoli. LC 90-12831. (Understanding Contemporary American Literature Ser.). (Illus.). 203p. 1990. text ed. 29.95 (*0-87249-722-4*) U of SC Pr.

***Understanding Laboratory & Diagnostic Tests.** Marie A. Moisio & Elmer W. Moisio. LC 97-13352. (Health Information Management Ser.). 1997. write for info. (*0-8273-7854-8*) Delmar.

Understanding Laboratory Values. Barry Creighton. 60p. 1988. pap. 39.50 (*0-911110-58-5*) MICHIE.

***Understanding Landscape Design.** Manning. (Illus.). 224p. (Orig.). 1997. pap. text ed. 34.50 (*0-419-20260-9*, E & FN Spon) Routledge Chapman & Hall.

Understanding Language. (Odyssey Ser.). (J). 1995. student ed. 5.00 (*0-88106-140-9*, UL10) Charlesbridge Pub.

Understanding Language. (Odyssey Ser.). (J). 1995. teacher ed. 20.00 (*0-88106-139-5*, UL15) Charlesbridge Pub.

Understanding Language. (Odyssey Ser.). (J). 1995. teacher ed. 75.00 (*0-88106-401-7*, UL20) Charlesbridge Pub.

Understanding Language: A Practical Approach. Thompson. (Electronics Technology Ser.). 1998. 41.95 (*0-8273-7808-4*) Delmar.

Understanding Language: A Study of Theories of Language in Linguistics & in Philosophy. Julius M. Moravcsik. (Janua Linguarum, Ser. Minor: No. 169). 95p. 1977. pap. text ed. 29.25 (*90-279-3111-9*) Mouton.

Understanding Language: Man or Machine. John A. Moyne. (Foundations of Computer Science Ser.). 374p. 1985. 79.50 (*0-306-41970-X*, Plenum Pr) Plenum.

U V

Understanding Language Acquisition: The Framework of Learning. Christina E. Erneling. LC 92-22085. (SUNY Series, Literacy, Culture, & Learning: Theory & Practice). 256p. (C). 1993. text ed. 64.50 (*0-7914-1461-2*); pap. text ed. 21.95 (*0-7914-1462-0*) State U NY Pr.

Understanding Language Change. April M. McMahon. 336p. (C). 1994. text ed. 54.95 (*0-521-44119-6*); pap. text ed. 18.95 (*0-521-44665-1*) Cambridge U Pr.

Understanding Language Disorders: The Impact on Learning. Vivienne L. Ratner & Laura R. Harris. LC 93-23636. 1994. text ed. 47.00 (*0-930599-90-X*) Thinking Pubns.

***Understanding Laser Technology, Vol. 206.** 270p. 1991. 59.95 (*0-87814-332-7*) Laser Inst.

Understanding Lasers. Stan Gibilisco. (Illus.). 192p. (Orig.). 1989. pap. 14.95 (*0-8306-3175-5*) McGraw-Hill Prof.

Understanding Lasers: An Entry-Level Guide. 2nd ed. Jeff Hecht. LC 93-24203. (Illus.). 448p. 1994. pap. 39.95 (*0-7803-1005-5*, PP03541) Inst Electrical.

Understanding Latino Families: Scholarship, Policy, & Practice. Ruth E. Zambrana. (Illus.). 244p. 1995. pap. 21.95 (*0-8039-5610-X*) Sage.

Understanding Latino Families: Scholarship, Policy, & Practice. Ed. by Ruth E. Zambrana. LC 95-8202. (Understanding Families Ser.: No. 2). (Illus.). 242p. 1995. 44.00 (*0-8039-5609-6*) Sage.

Understanding Laughter: The Workings of Wit & Humor. Charles R. Gruner. LC 78-16759. 272p. 1978. 36.95 (*0-88229-186-6*) Nelson-Hall.

Understanding Law: An Introduction to Australia's Legal System. 4th ed. Garth Nettheim & R. Chisholm. 160p. 1992. pap. 22.00 (*0-409-30486-7*) MICHIE.

Understanding Law in Micronesia: An Interpretive Approach to Transplanted Law. Brian Z. Tamanaha. LC 93-724. (Studies in Human Society: Vol. 7). ix, 214p. 1993. pap. 57.00 (*90-04-09768-6*) E J Brill.

Understanding Law in Our Changing Society. 2nd ed. Altschuler & Sgroi. 1995. pap. text ed. 55.00 (*0-13-449019-3*) P-H.

Understanding LD (Learning Differences) A Curriculum to Promote LD Awareness, Self Esteem & Coping Skills in Students Ages 8-13. Susan McMurchie. 160p. 1994. pap. 21.95 (*0-915793-75-X*) Free Spirit Pub.

Understanding Leadership: Fresh Perspective on the Essentials of New Testament Leadership. Tom Marshall. 1992. pap. 8.99 (*0-927545-51-9*) YWAM Pub.

Understanding Learning Disabilities. Jane C. Sacknowitz. (Family Forum Library Ser.). 16p. 1992. 1.95 (*1-56688-045-9*) Bur For At-Risk.

***Understanding Learning Disabilities: A Parent Guide & Workbook.** 180p. 1989. pap. 20.00 (*0-614-29486-X*) Orton Dyslexia.

Understanding Learning Disabilities: A Parent Guide & Workbook. Learning Disabilities Council, Inc. Staff. 181p. 1991. pap. 21.70 (*0-9636305-0-4*) Lrning Disabil Coun.

***Understanding Learning Styles in the Second Language Classroom.** Joy M. Reid. LC 97-25281. 1997. write for info. (*0-13-281636-9*) P-H.

Understanding Leisure. Ed. by H. Haywood. (C). 1989. 160.00 (*0-09-182260-2*, Pub. by S Thornes Pubs UK) St Mut.

Understanding Leisure. J. Spink et al. 335p. (C). 1989. pap. 80.00 (*0-7478-0307-2*, Pub. by S Thornes Pubs UK) St Mut.

Understanding Leisure. J. Spink et al. 335p. 1989. 69.00 (*0-7487-0307-1*, Pub. by S Thornes Pubs UK) St Mut.

***Understanding Leisure.** 2nd ed. Les Haywood et al. 272p. (Orig.). 1995. pap. 56.50 (*0-7487-2059-6*, Pub. by Stanley Thornes UK) Trans-Atl Phila.

Understanding Leisure & Recreation: Mapping the Past, Charting the Future. Ed. by Edgar L. Jackson & Thomas L. Burton. LC 89-51320. 653p. (C). 1989. 31.95 (*0-910251-34-7*) Venture Pub PA.

Understanding Lens Surfacing. Clifford W. Brooks. (Illus.). 399p. 1991. 85.00 (*0-7506-9177-8*) Buttrwrth-Heinemann.

Understanding Lens Surfacing Laboratory Exercises: A Laboratory Manual in Lens Surfacing. Clifford W. Brooks. (Illus.). 118p. 1995. lab manual ed., pap. text ed. 27.50 (*0-7506-9617-6*) Buttrwrth-Heinemann.

***Understanding "Les Fleurs du Mal" Critical Readings.** Ed. by William J. Thompson. LC 97-4698. 272p. 1997. 35.95 (*0-8265-1290-9*) Vanderbilt U Pr.

***Understanding "Les Fleurs du Mal" Critical Readings.** Ed. by William J. Thompson. LC 97-4698. 272p. 1997. pap. 18.95 (*0-8265-1297-6*) Vanderbilt U Pr.

***Understanding Liberalism - a History & Analysis of the Last Half Century.** Virgil R. Cowart. LC 96-69084. 240p. Date not set. 21.95 (*1-57197-033-9*) Pentland Pr.

Understanding Life-Style: The Psycho-Clarity Process. Robert L. Powers & Jane Griffith. LC 87-13146. 336p. 1987. text ed. 32.50 (*0-918287-02-2*); pap. text ed. 22.50 (*0-918287-03-0*) AIAS.

Understanding Life Through Universal Metaphysics. Jean Wright. Tr. by Dianna Wright. (Illus.). 120p. (Orig.). (C). 1982. 25.00 (*0-941978-00-1*); pap. 14.00 (*0-941978-01-X*); lib. bdg. 20.00 (*0-941978-02-8*) Airman Universal.

Understanding Lightwave Transmission: Applications of Fiber Optics. William O. Grant. 366p. (C). 1988. text ed. 40.00 (*0-15-592874-0*); pap. text ed. 3.00 (*0-15-592875-9*) SCP.

***Understanding Limited Appraisals & Appraisal Reporting Options.** Stephanie C. Coleman & Joseph L. Minnich. LC 96-31829. 1996. write for info. (*0-922154-31-7*) Appraisal Inst.

***Understanding Literacy: Personality Preference in Rhetorical & Psycholinguistic Contexts.** Alice S. Horning & Ronald A. Sudol. LC 96-40404. 320p. 1997. 65.00 (*1-57273-078-1*); pap. 24.95 (*1-57273-079-X*) Hampton Pr NJ.

Understanding Literacy & Cognition: Theory, Research & Application. Ed. by Che K. Leong & Bikkar S. Randhawa. LC 89-77899. (Illus.). 330p. 1989. 85.00 (*0-306-43489-X*, Plenum Pr) Plenum.

Understanding Literacy Difficulties: Assessment & Instruction. Sally Lipa & Ernest Balajhty. (Illus.). 525p. (C). Date not set. text ed. 45.95 (*0-534-24096-8*) Wadsworth Pub.

Understanding Literary Forms: Advanced Level. 2nd ed. Ed. by Kraft. (Comprehension Skills Ser.). 64p. 1993. pap. 8.45 (*0-89061-623-X*) Jamestown Pubs.

Understanding Literary Forms: Introductory Level. Ed. by Kraft. (Comprehension Skills Ser.). 64p. 1993. pap. 7.91 (*0-89061-663-9*) Jamestown Pubs.

Understanding Literary Forms: Middle Level. 2nd ed. Ed. by Kraft. (Comprehension Skills Ser.). 64p. 1993. pap. 8.31 (*0-89061-643-4*) Jamestown Pubs.

Understanding Living Trusts. 2nd rev. ed. Vickie Schumacher & Jim Schumacher. LC 89-92798. Orig. Title: A Will Is Not the Way, the Living Trust Alternative. (Illus.). 224p. 1990. pap. 19.95 (*0-945811-07-1*) Schumacher Pub.

Understanding Living Trusts: How You Can Avoid Probate, Save Taxes & Enjoy Peace of Mind. 3rd rev. ed. Vickie Schumacher & Jim Schumacher. (Illus.). 224p. 1994. pap. 19.95 (*0-945811-12-8*) Schumacher Pub.

Understanding Living Trusts: How You Can Avoid Probate, Save Taxes & Enjoy Peace of Mind. 4th rev. ed. Vickie Schumacher & Jim Schumacher. (Illus.). 288p. 1996. pap. text ed. 24.95 (*0-945811-19-5*) Schumacher Pub.

Understanding Lloyd's: A Guide to Corporate Membership. Sedgewick Group Plc. Staff. 104p. 1995. pap. 14.95 (*1-899163-14-X*) Cimino Pub Grp.

Understanding Local Area Networks. 5th ed. Stanley Schatt. (Illus.). 336p. 1995. 29.99 (*0-672-30840-1*) Sams.

Understanding Locke. J. J. Jenkins. 192p. 1983. pap. 18.00 (*0-85224-449-5*, Pub. by Edinburgh U Pr UK) Col U Pr.

Understanding Log-Linear Analysis with ILOG: An Interactive Approach. Roger Bakeman & Byron F. Robinson. 160p. 1994. pap. 19.95 (*0-8058-1240-7*); text ed. 36.00 (*0-8058-1239-3*) L Erlbaum Assocs.

Understanding Long-Term Care Insurance. Jeff Sadler. 137p. 1993. pap. 21.95 (*0-87425-194-X*) HRD Press.

Understanding Lotus 1-2-3. M-USA Business Systems, Inc. Staff. (VideoNotes Ser.). (Illus.). (Orig.). 1988. pap. text ed. 9.95 incl. vhs (*0-929978-01-3*) M-USA Busn Systs.

Understanding Low Vision. Randall T. Jose. LC 83-21446. 560p. 1983. text ed. 49.00 (*0-89128-119-3*) Am Foun Blind.

Understanding Luigi Pirandello. Fiora A. Bassanese. Ed. by James N. Hardin. (Understanding Modern European & Latin American Literature Ser.). 200p. 1997. text ed. 29.95 (*1-57003-081-2*) U of SC Pr.

Understanding Luminescence Spectra & Efficiency Using Wp & Related Functions. C. W. Struck & W. H. Fonger. Ed. by C. K. Jorgensen et al. (Inorganic Chemistry Concepts Ser.: Vol. 13). (Illus.). 264p. 1991. 142.95 (*0-387-52766-4*) Spr-Verlag.

Understanding Lung Sounds. 2nd ed. Steven Lehrer. 144p. 1993. pap. text ed. 44.00 (*0-7216-4902-5*) Saunders.

Understanding Lupus: What It Is, How to Treat It, How to Cope with It. Henrietta Aladjem. 247p. 1985. pap. 11.95 (*0-684-18349-8*) S&S Trade.

***Understanding Macbeth: A Student Casebook to Issues, Sources & Historical Documents.** Faith Nostbakken & William Shakespeare. LC 96-35013. (Literature in Context Ser.). 256p. 1997. text ed. 39.95 (*0-313-29630-8*) Greenwood.

Understanding Macroeconomics. 9th ed. Robert Heilbroner & James K. Galbraith. 1989. pap. text ed. 69.00 (*0-13-933359-2*) P-H.

Understanding Macroeconomics: An Introduction to Economic Policy in the 1990's. Ed. by David Gowland. (Illus.). 288p. 1990. text ed. 80.00 (*1-85278-326-5*); pap. text ed. 25.00 (*1-85278-327-3*) E Elgar.

Understanding Major Mental Disorder: The Contribution of Family Interaction Research. Ed. by Kurt Hahlweg & Michael J. Goldstein. 1987. text ed. 30.00 (*0-9615519-4-1*) Family Process.

Understanding Malcolm X: His Controversial Philosophical Changes. Edward R. Leader. 1992. 18.95 (*0-533-09520-4*) Vantage.

***Understanding Male Homosexual Problems: An Introduction for Latter-Day Saints.** Jason Park. 48p. (Orig.). 1997. pap. 2.95 (*0-941846-08-3*) Centry Pub.

Understanding Male Sexual Health. Dorothy Baldwin. 1993. pap. 11.95 (*0-7818-0128-1*) Hippocrene Bks.

***Understanding Managed Health Care: A Guide for Seniors.** William J. Pokluda. LC 96-35275. (Patient Information Series Ser.). 1996. write for info. (*1-57626-021-6*) Quality Med Pub.

Understanding Management. Richard L. Daft. 704p. 1995. text ed. 36.00 (*0-03-098582-X*) Dryden Pr.

Understanding Management. Richard L. Daft. (C). 1994. teacher ed. 122.75 (*0-03-098902-7*) HB Coll Pubs.

Understanding Management. Richard L. Daft. (C). 1995. student ed., pap. text ed. 24.00 (*0-03-098898-5*) HB Coll Pubs.

Understanding Management. Stephen Linstead et al. 256p. 1996. 69.95 (*0-8039-8912-1*) Sage.

Understanding Management. Stephen Linstead et al. 256p. 1996. pap. 24.00 (*0-8039-8913-X*) Sage.

Understanding Management. Thomas W. Shaughnessy et al. 344p. (C). 1995. teacher ed., pap. text ed. 61.00 (*0-03-098897-7*) Dryden Pr.

***Understanding Management.** 2nd ed. Daft. (C). 1997. teacher ed., pap. text ed. 26.75 (*0-03-024734-9*); pap. text ed. 26.75 (*0-03-024736-5*); student ed., pap. text ed. write for info. (*0-03-024737-3*) HB Coll Pubs.

***Understanding Management.** 2nd ed. Richard L. Daft. (C). 1997. text ed. write for info. (*0-03-024593-1*) HB Coll Pubs.

Understanding Management: Test Bank. Richard L. Daft. (C). 1995. suppl. ed., teacher ed., pap. text ed. 33.75 (*0-03-098899-3*) HB Coll Pubs.

Understanding Management Software. Andrew Leigh. 288p. (C). 1985. 69.00 (*0-333-40946-9*) St Mut.

Understanding Man's Best Friend: Why Dogs Look & Act the Way They Do. Ann Squire. LC 90-30631. (Illus.). 128p. (J). (gr. 3-7). 1991. lib. bdg. 14.95 (*0-02-786590-8*, Mac Bks Young Read) S&S Childrens.

Understanding Mantras. Ed. by Harvey P. Alper. LC 87-6481. (SUNY Series in Religious Studies). 530p. 1989. text ed. 34.50 (*0-88706-598-8*) State U NY Pr.

Understanding MAP: Manufacturing Automation Protocol. V. Rizzardi. 264p. 1988. 42.00 (*0-87263-302-0*) SME.

Understanding Maps. Janis Minton. (Social Studies Ser.). 24p. (gr. 4-7). 1979. student ed. 5.00 (*0-8209-0257-8*, SS-24) ESP.

Understanding Maps. 2nd ed. J. S. Keates. 288p. (C). 1996. pap. text ed. 22.50 (*0-582-23927-3*) Longman.

Understanding MARC (Machine Readable Cataloging) 4th ed. Follett Software, Database Development Department et al. LC 94-30508. 1994. write for info. (*0-8444-0820-4*) Lib Congress.

Understanding Marine Biodiversity. National Research Council Staff. LC 94-44420. 180p. (Orig.). (C). 1995. text ed. 29.95 (*0-309-05225-4*) Natl Acad Pr.

Understanding Mario Vargas Llosa. Sara Castro-Klaren. Ed. by James Hardin. (Understanding Modern European & Latin American Literature Ser.). 258p. 1992. pap. 12.95 (*0-87249-848-4*); text ed. 29.95 (*0-87249-668-6*) U of SC Pr.

***Understanding Marketing.** Mark Davies. 1997. pap. text ed. 40.00 (*0-13-490467-2*) P-H.

Understanding Marketing. Alan West. 256p. (C). 1987. pap. 65.00 (*0-06-318384-6*, Pub. by P Chapman Pub UK) St Mut.

Understanding Marriage: A Hong Kong Case Study. Katherine Young. 224p. 1995. pap. 37.50 (*962-209-366-3*, Pub. by Hong Kong Univ Pr HK) Coronet Bks.

Understanding Martin Amis. James Diedrick. Ed. by Matthew J. Bruccoli. LC 95-4367. (Understannding Contemporary British Literature Ser.). 190p. 1995. text ed. 29.95 (*1-57003-058-8*) U of SC Pr.

Understanding Marx. Friedrich W. Sixel. 124p. (Orig.). (C). 1995. pap. text ed. 22.00 (*0-7618-0025-5*); lib. bdg. 42.00 (*0-7618-0024-7*) U Pr of Amer.

Understanding Masculinities: Social Relations & Cultural Arenas. Mairtin Mac An Ghaill. 224p. 1996. 79.00 (*0-335-19461-3*, Open Univ Pr); pap. 21.00 (*0-335-19460-5*, Open Univ Pr) Taylor & Francis.

***Understanding Mass Communication: A Liberal Arts Perspective, Updated 1996 Edition, 5 Vols.** Melvin L. DeFleur & Everette E. Dennis. (C). 1995. teacher ed., text ed. 11.96 (*0-395-76556-0*) HM.

***Understanding Mathematics: From Counting to Calculus.** Keith Kressin. (Illus.). x, 342p. (Orig.). 1997. pap. 19.95 (*0-9657300-1-8*) K Squared Pub.

Understanding Max Frisch. Wulf Koepke. (Understanding Modern European & Latin American Literature Ser.). 198p. (C). 1990. text ed. 29.95 (*0-87249-714-3*) U of SC Pr.

***Understanding Maya Inscriptions: A Hieroglyph Handbook.** John F. Harris & Stephen K. Stearns. (Illus.). x, 162p. 1992. pap. 30.00 (*0-924171-14-6*) U PA Mus Pubns.

Understanding Me: Reproducible Activity Sheets Develop Self-Esteem in Your Secondary Students. Dianne Schilling. 96p. (YA). (gr. 7-12). teacher ed. 13.95 (*1-56499-005-2*) Innerchoice Pub.

Understanding Measuring. Donna Burk et al. (Box It or Bag It Mathematics Ser.). (Illus.). 33p. (Orig.). (C). 1988. teacher ed., ring bd. 3.75 (*1-886131-04-X*, BB3) Math Lrning.

***Understanding Measurment, Evaluation & Essessment.** Ed. by Thompson. (C). 1998. text ed. write for info. (*0-321-01155-4*) Addson-Wesley Educ.

Understanding Media: The Extensions of Man. Marshall McLuhan. 392p. 1994. pap. 14.95 (*0-262-63159-8*) MIT Pr.

Understanding Media: The Extensions of Man. Marshall McLuhan. 320p. 1966. pap. 4.95 (*0-451-62496-3*, ME2170, Ment) NAL-Dutton.

Understanding Media Cultures: Social Theory & Mass Communication. Nick Stevenson. 256p. 1995. 69.95 (*0-8039-8930-X*); pap. 21.95 (*0-8039-8931-8*) Sage.

Understanding Medical Immunology. 2nd ed. Evelyne M. Kirkwood & Catriona J. Lewis. LC 87-31747. 179p. 1991. pap. text ed. 42.95 (*0-471-91577-7*) Wiley.

Understanding Medical Information. Jordan. 1997. pap. text ed. 19.95 (*0-8385-9272-4*, A9272-4) Appleton & Lange.

Understanding Medical Insurance. Rowell. (Medical Assisting Ser.). 1989. pap. 29.95 (*0-8273-3352-8*) Delmar.

Understanding Medical Insurance. Rowell. (Medical Assisting Ser.). 1989. teacher ed., pap. 14.00 (*0-8273-3353-6*) Delmar.

Understanding Medical Insurance. 3rd ed. Rowell. (Medical Assisting Ser.). 1996. teacher ed. 16.00 (*0-8273-7269-8*) Delmar.

Understanding Medical Insurance. 3rd ed. JoAnn C. Rowell. (Medical Assisting Ser.). 384p. 1996. text ed. 35.95 (*0-8273-7268-X*) Delmar.

Understanding Medical Insurance: A Step-by-Step Guide. JoAnn C. Rowell. (Practice Management Ser.). (Illus.). 256p. 1990. text ed. 49.95 (*0-87489-634-7*) Med Econ.

Understanding Medical Insurance: A Step-by-Step Guide. 2nd ed. Joann C. Rowell. LC 93-2680. 336p. 1994. pap. 29.95 (*0-8273-4966-1*) Delmar.

Understanding Medical Research: A Practitioner's Guide. Jane L. Garb. LC 96-17216. 173p. 1996. pap. text ed. 24.95 (*0-316-29169-2*) Lppncott-Raven.

Understanding Medical Terminology. 8th ed. Rose M. Mahoney. 640p. (C). 1990. per. write for info. (*0-697-14056-3*) Wm C Brown Pubs.

Understanding Medical Terminology. 9th ed. Agnes C. Frenay & Rose M. Mahoney. 640p. (C). 1992. per. write for info. (*0-697-14058-X*) Brown & Benchmark.

***Understanding Medical Terminology.** 10th ed. Clare A. Frenay & Maureen R. Mahoney. 640p. (C). 1997. per. write for info. (*0-697-21943-7*) Wm C Brown Pubs.

Understanding Medical Terms: A Guide for Pharmacy Practice. Walter F. Stanaszek et al. LC 91-66131. 315p. (Orig.). 1992. pap. text ed. 29.95 (*0-87762-885-8*) Technomic.

Understanding Medicare. T. J. Steskal. 93p. (Orig.). 1980. pap. 9.95 (*0-937978-00-0*, MC-1) Info Prods.

Understanding Medications: What the Label Doesn't Tell You. Alfred Burger. LC 95-17498. 1995. 39.95 (*0-8412-3210-5*); pap. 21.95 (*0-8412-3246-6*) Am Chemical.

***Understanding Melanoma: What You Need to Know.** Perry Robins & Maritza Perez. (Illus.). 80p. (Orig.). 1996. mass mkt. 10.00 (*0-9627688-2-0*) Skin Cancer Fndtn.

Understanding Menopause: Answers & Advice for Women in the Prime of Life. Janine O. Cobb. LC 93-12308. (Illus.). 336p. 1993. reprint ed. pap. 12.95 (*0-452-27028-6*, Plume) NAL-Dutton.

***Understanding Men's & Women's Behavior.** Parveen Khosla. LC 96-90117. 72p. (Orig.). 1997. pap. 8.00 (*1-56002-659-6*, Univ Edtns) Aegina Pr.

Understanding Mental Disorders Due to Medical Conditions or Substance Abuse: What Every Therapist Should Know. Ghazi Asaad. LC 94-11620. (Basic Principles into Practice Ser.: Vol. 3). (Illus.). 172p. 1995. pap. text ed. 22.95 (*0-87630-751-9*) Brunner-Mazel.

Understanding Mental Illness: For Teens Who Care about Someone with Mental Illness. Julie T. Johnson. (Coping with Modern Problems Ser.). 72p. (J). (gr. 4 up). 1989. lib. bdg. 17.50 (*0-8225-0042-6*, Lerner Publctns) Lerner Group.

Understanding Mental Illness & Its Nursing. 2nd ed. Trick. 1976. pap. 30.00 (*0-8464-0947-X*) Beekman Pubs.

Understanding Mental Objects. Meir Perlow. LC 94-45147. (New Library of Psychoanalysis). 208p. (C). 1995. pap. 19.95 (*0-415-12179-5*, C0225) Routledge.

Understanding Mental Objects. Meir Perlow. LC 94-45147. (New Library of Psychoanalysis). 224p. (C). (gr. 13). 1995. text ed. 59.95 (*0-415-12178-7*, C0224) Routledge.

Understanding Mental Retardation. Edward F. Zigler & Robert M. Hodapp. (Illus.). 288p. 1986. pap. text ed. 22.95 (*0-521-31878-5*) Cambridge U Pr.

Understanding Mentally Retarded Children. Harriet E. Blodgett & Grace J. Warfield. LC 59-12295. (Illus.). (Orig.). 1959. pap. text ed. 5.95 (*0-89197-457-1*) Irvington.

Understanding Mentoring: Reflective Strategies for School-Based Teacher Preparation. Peter Tomlinson. LC 94-27609. 238p. 1994. 29.95 (*0-335-19306-4*, Open Univ Pr) Taylor & Francis.

Understanding Mentoring Relationships. Dale A. Blyth & Rebecca N. Saito. 62p. 1992. pap. text ed. 8.00 (*1-57482-316-7*) Search Inst.

Understanding Metaphor in Literature: An Empirical Approach. Gerard Steen. LC 93-32427. (Studies in Language & Linguistics). 1994. pap. text ed. 25.70 (*0-582-10118-2*, Pub. by Longman UK) Longman.

Understanding Metaphor in Literature: An Empirical Approach. Gerard Steen. LC 93-32427. (Studies in Language & Linguistics). 1994. text ed. write for info. (*0-582-21715-6*, Pub. by Longman UK) Longman.

Understanding Mexico: Historical Perspective & Future Potential. Jose L. Reyna et al. Ed. by Morris M. Blachman et al. LC 85-62047. (Papers on International Issues: No. 7). 63p. (Orig.). 1985. pap. 5.00 (*0-935082-09-3*) Southern Ctr Intl Stud.

Understanding Microbes: Laboratory Textbook for Microbiology. William G. Claus. LC 87-33152. 528p. (C). 1995. pap. text ed. write for info. (*0-7167-1809-X*) W H Freeman.

Understanding Microcomputer Concepts: A Guide for Beginners & Hobbyists. Jefferson C. Boyce. LC 83-62030. (Illus.). 336p. 1984. 18.95 (*0-13-936956-2*) P-H.

Understanding Microcomputers. Dennis Ashworth. Ed. by Richard M. Hylton. 32p. (Orig.). (YA). (gr. 9-12). 1987. pap. text ed. 6.50 (*0-89606-215-5*, 801) Am Assn Voc Materials.

Understanding Microcomputers & Application Software. Marly K. Bergerud et al. 1989. pap. text ed. 34.50 (*0-471-61822-5*) P-H.

Understanding Microcomputers & Applications Software. Bergerud & Busche. (DF - Computer Applications Ser.). 1989. 15.95 (*0-538-70653-8*); 15.95 (*0-538-70654-6*) S-W Pub.

Understanding Microcomputers & Small Computer Systems. Nat Wadsworth. (Quality Paperbacks Ser.). (Illus.). 312p. 1981. reprint ed. pap. 8.95 (*0-306-80143-4*) Da Capo.

Understanding Microprocessor-Based Equipment. Lenk. Date not set. write for info. (*0-7506-9652-4*) Buttrwrth-Heinemann.

U V

An Asterisk (*) at the beginning of an entry indicates that the title is appearing in BIP for the first time.

Understanding Microprocessors. Thompson. (Electronics Technology Ser.). 1995. lab manual ed. 24.50 (*0-8273-7033-4*) Delmar.

Understanding Microprocessors: A Practical Approach. Arthur W. Thompson. LC 94-43495. 1995. text ed. 44.95 (*0-8273-5347-2*) Delmar.

Understanding Microsoft Access 2, Special Edition. Alan Simpson. LC 93-87699. 945p. 1994. pap. 29.99 (*0-7821-1466-0*) Sybex.

Understanding Microwaves. Allan W. Scott. LC 92-16863. 560p. 1993. text ed. 95.00 (*0-471-57567-4*) Wiley.

Understanding Milan Kundera: Public Events, Private Affairs. Fred Misurella. LC 92-27444. (Understanding Modern European & Latin American Literature Ser.). 231p. (C). 1993. text ed. 29.95 (*0-87249-853-0*) U of SC Pr.

Understanding Miniature British Pottery & Porcelain, 1730-Present Day. Maurice Milbourn. 1995. pap. text ed. 29.95 (*1-85149-237-2*) Antique Collect.

Understanding Miniature British Pottery & Porcelain, 1730-the Present Day. Maurice Milbourn & Evelyn Milbourn. (Understanding Ser.). (Illus.). 184p. 1983. 29.50 (*0-907462-30-8*) Antique Collect.

Understanding Ministerial Leadership: Essays Contributing to a Developing Theology of Ministry. Ed. by John A. Esau. (Text Reader Ser.: No. 6). 123p. 1995. pap. 15.00 (*0-936273-22-4*) Inst Mennonite.

***Understanding Misbehavior: Using Misbehavior As a Guide to Children's & Adolescent's Needs.** John F. Taylor. (Illus.). 36p. 1993. 10.95 (*1-884063-80-2*) Mar Co Prods.

Understanding Misbehavior: Using Misbehavior As a Guide to Children's & Adolescent's Needs. John F. Taylor. LC 93-79229. (Counselor Survival Skills Ser.: Vol. 6). 48p. 1993. 10.95 (*1-884063-01-2*) Mar Co Prods.

Understanding Mobility: Guide to Wireless & Personal Communications. A'isha M. Ajayi. write for info. (*0-471-54926-6*) Wiley.

Understanding Modern Architecture. Patrick J. Nuttgens. 220p. 1990. text ed. 45.00 (*0-04-500040-9*) Routledge Chapman & Hall.

Understanding Modern Art. J. Cook. (Understanding the Arts Ser.). (Illus.). 64p. (J). (gr. 5 up). 1992. pap. 9.95 (*0-7460-0475-3*, Usborne); lib. bdg. 17.95 (*0-88110-512-0*, Usborne) EDC.

Understanding Modern Business Data Processing see Introduction to Data Processing

Understanding Modern Juvenile Justice: The Organisational Context of Service. Kevin Haines. (Swansea Social Studies). 239p. 1996. 59.95 (*1-85972-430-2*, Pub. by Avebury Pub UK) Ashgate Pub Co.

Understanding Modernity: Towards a New Perspective Going Beyond Durkheim & Webber. Richard Munch. (International Library of Sociology). 356p. 1988. text ed. 75.00 (*0-415-01283-X*) Routledge.

Understanding Molecular Properties. Ed. by John Avery et al. 1987. lib. bdg. 208.50 (*90-277-2419-9*) Kluwer Ac.

Understanding Molecular Simulation: From Algorithms to Applications. Ed. by Daan Frenkel & Berend Smit. LC 96-19662. (Illus.). 443p. 1996. boxed 65.00 (*0-12-267370-0*) Acad Pr.

Understanding More Quantum Physics, Vol. 1. Michael A. Morrison et al. 1991. pap. text ed. 29.33 (*0-13-928300-5*, 530502) P-H.

Understanding Mormonism: Mormonism & Christianity Compared. 4th rev. ed. Sandra Sundholm & Conrad Sundholm. 190p. 1993. pap. text ed. write for info. (*0-9637182-0-7*) Truth Pub OR.

***Understanding Motivaiton & Emotion.** 2nd ed. Johnmarshall Reeve. 546p. (C). 1996. text ed. write for info. (*0-15-502654-2*) HB Coll Pubs.

Understanding Motivation & Emotion. John M. Reeve. 544p. (C). 1992. text ed. 42.75 (*0-03-030512-8*) HB Coll Pubs.

***Understanding Motor Development: Infants & Children.** 3rd ed. David L. Gallahue & John Ozmun. 592p. (C). 1997. per. write for info. (*0-697-41799-9*) Wm C Brown Pubs.

***Understanding Motor Development: Infants & Children.** 4th ed. David L. Gallahue & John Ozmun. LC 97-10621. 592p. (C). 1997. text ed. write for info. (*0-697-29487-0*) Wm C Brown Pubs.

Understanding Motor Development: Infants, Children. 2nd ed. David L. Gallahue. 562p. (C). 1994. per. write for info. (*0-697-24891-7*) Brown & Benchmark.

Understanding Mourning: A Guide for Those Who Grieve. Glen W. Davidson. LC 84-14527. 112p. (Orig.). 1984. pap. 8.99 (*0-8066-2080-3*, 10-6805, Augsburg) Augsburg Fortress.

Understanding Movies. 7th ed. Louis D. Giannetti. LC 95-13526. (C). 1995. pap. text ed. 42.00 (*0-13-190836-7*) P-H.

Understanding MRI. Newhouse. 1991. 54.95 (*0-316-60474-7*) Little.

Understanding MS Access 2.0 Bundle. Allen Simpson. 1994. pap. 29.99 (*0-7821-1537-3*) Sybex.

Understanding MS-DOS. Ed. by M-USA Business Systems, Inc. Staff. (VideoNotes Ser.). (Illus.). (Orig.). 1988. pap. 9.95 incl. vhs (*0-929978-00-5*) M-USA Busn Systs.

Understanding MSDS: Material Safety Data Sheets. Shirley Ayers. 48p. 1995. pap. write for info. (*0-945790-09-0*) Detrick Lawrence.

Understanding Muscles. B. Kingston. 288p. (Orig.). (C). 1996. pap. text ed. 42.99 (*1-56593-123-8*, 1094) Singular Publishing.

Understanding Music. Carruthers. 1996. student ed., pap. text ed. 17.33 (*0-13-606260-1*) P-H.

Understanding Music. Anthony Hopkins. (Illus.). 256p. (C). pap. write for info. (*0-19-816518-8*) OUP.

Understanding Music. Anthony Hopkins. (Illus.). 256p. (C). 1993. pap. 9.95 (*0-19-521028-X*, 8047) OUP.

Understanding Music. Judy Tatchell. (Understanding the Arts Ser.). (Illus.). 64p. (J). (gr. 4 up). 1990. pap. 9.95 (*0-7460-0302-1*, Usborne); lib. bdg. 17.95 (*0-88110-382-9*, Usborne) EDC.

Understanding Music & Worship in the Local Church. Vernon Whaley. 96p. (Orig.). 1995. pap. text ed. 8.95 (*0-910566-65-8*); teacher ed., ring bd. 19.95 (*0-910566-66-6*) Evang Trg Assn.

Understanding Music Fundamentals. 2nd ed. R. Phyllis Gelineau. 352p. (C). 1992. pap. text ed. 46.67 (*0-13-928722-1*) P-H.

Understanding Music with AI: Perspectives on Music Cognition. Ed. by Mira Balaban et al. (AAAI Press Ser.). (Illus.). 400p. 1992. pap. 42.50 (*0-262-52170-9*) MIT Pr.

Understanding Myself. Dolores Ready. (Discovering Program Ser.). (Illus.). 24p. (Orig.). 1989. 2.80 (*0-88489-196-8*); teacher ed. 6.00 (*0-88489-197-6*) St Marys.

Understanding NAFTA: Mexico, Free Trade, & the New North America. 2nd ed. William A. Orme, Jr. (Illus.). 368p. 1996. pap. 19.95 (*0-292-76046-9*) U of Tex Pr.

Understanding Narrative. Ed. by James Phelan & Peter J. Rabinowitz. (Theory & Interpretation of Narrative Ser.). 256p. 1994. 59.50 (*0-8142-0633-6*); pap. 17.95 (*0-8142-0634-4*) Ohio St U Pr.

Understanding Natural Flavors. J. R. Piggott. 352p. 1994. 145.50 (*0-7514-0180-3*, Pub. by Blackie Acad & Prof UK) Routledge Chapman & Hall.

Understanding Navstar: GPS, GIS, IVHS. 2nd ed. Tom Logsdon. 1995. text ed. 49.95 (*0-442-02054-6*) Van Nos Reinhold.

***Understanding NE Code Rules on Emergency & Standby Power System.** Ed. by Frederic P. Hartwell. (Understanding NE Code Rules on Ser.). 152p. (Orig.). 1996. pap. 18.95 (*0-87288-635-2*) Intertec Pub.

Understanding NE Code Rules on Grounding & Bonding. Ed. by Alfred Berutti. (Understanding NE Code Rules on Ser.). (Illus.). 174p. (Orig.). 1994. pap. 18.95 (*0-87288-543-7*) Intertec Pub.

Understanding NE Code Rules on Hazardous Locations. Ed. by Alfred Berutti & Frederic P. Hartwell. (Illus.). 160p. (Orig.). 1993. pap. 18.95 (*0-87288-513-5*) Intertec Pub.

Understanding NE Code Rules on Lighting. 2nd ed. Ed. by Frederic P. Hartwell. (Understanding NE Code Rules on Ser.). (Illus.). 150p. 1996. pap. 18.95 (*0-87288-612-3*) Intertec Pub.

Understanding NE Code Rules on Medium Voltage Power Systems. Ed. by Frederic P. Hartwell. (Understanding NE Code Rules on Ser.). (Illus.). 201p. (Orig.). 1994. pap. 18.95 (*0-87288-546-1*) Intertec Pub.

Understanding NE Code Rules on Motors & Motor Controls. 2nd ed. Ed. by Frederic P. Hartwell. (Understanding NE Code Rules on Ser.). (Illus.). 152p. 1996. pap. 18.95 (*0-87288-611-5*) Intertec Pub.

Understanding NE Code Rules on Pools, Spas & Hot Tubs. Ed. by Frederic P. Hartwell. (Understanding NE Code Rules on Ser.). (Illus.). (Orig.). 1991. pap. 18.95 (*0-614-14939-8*) Intertec Pub.

Understanding NE Code Rules on Services. Ed. by Alfred Berutti. (Understanding NE Code Rules on Ser.). (Illus.). 123p. (Orig.). 1995. pap. 18.95 (*0-87288-622-0*) Intertec Pub.

Understanding N.E. Code Rules on Transformers. Ed. by Frederic P. Hartwell. (Illus.). 98p. (Orig.). 1993. pap. 18.95 (*0-87288-541-0*) Intertec Pub.

Understanding NEC Calculations. 2nd ed. Michael Holt. 64p. (C). 1996. teacher ed., pap. text ed. 16.00 (*0-8273-7908-0*) Delmar.

Understanding NEC Calculations. 2nd ed. Michael Holt. (Electrical Trades (w-o Electro) Ser.). 304p. 1996. 33.95 (*0-8273-7838-6*) Delmar.

Understanding NECode Calculations. Michael Holt. LC 94-3072. 479p. 1994. pap. 32.50 (*0-8273-6312-5*) Delmar.

Understanding Negotiation: The Academic Contribution. Richard Cottam. (Pew Case Studies in International Affairs). 50p. (C). 1993. pap. text ed. 3.50 (*1-56927-413-4*) Geo U Inst Dplmcy.

Understanding Nervousness in Horses & Riders. Moyra Williams. (Illus.). 129p. 1990. 44.00 (*0-85131-530-5*, Pub. by J A Allen & Co UK); pap. 24.00 (*0-85131-501-1*, Pub. by J A Allen & Co UK) St Mut.

Understanding Network Management: Strategies & Solutions. Stanley Schatt. (Illus.). 288p. 1992. 29.95 (*0-8306-3757-5*, 4085, Windcrest); pap. 19.95 (*0-8306-3727-3*, 4085, Windcrest) TAB Bks.

Understanding Networked Multimedia: Applications & Technology. Francois Fluckiger. LC 95-10212. 550p. (C). 1995. text ed. 52.00 (*0-13-190992-4*) P-H.

***Understanding Networking & the Internet.** Charles S. Parker. 158p. (C). 1997. pap. text ed. write for info. (*0-03-024578-8*) Dryden Pr.

Understanding Networking Technology. Mark Norris. LC 96-26606. 243p. 1996. 49.00 (*0-89006-879-8*) Artech Hse.

***Understanding Neural Networks.** C. Cruz. 156p. 1991. 150.00 (*0-943779-69-3*, Pub. by Elsvr Adv Tech UK) Elsevier.

Understanding Neural Networks: Computer Explorations, 2 vols., Vol. 1. Maureen Caudill. 1992. pap. 45.00 (*0-262-53102-X*, Bradford Bks) MIT Pr.

Understanding Neural Networks: Computer Explorations, 2 vols., Vol. 1: Basic Networks, IBM. Maureen Caudill. 1992. pap. 47.50 (*0-262-53099-6*, Bradford Bks) MIT Pr.

Understanding Neural Networks: Computer Explorations, 2 vols., Vol. 2. Maureen Caudill. 1992. pap. 45.00 (*0-262-53103-8*, Bradford Bks) MIT Pr.

Understanding Neural Networks: Computer Explorations, 2 vols., Vol. 2: Advanced Networks, IBM. Maureen Caudill. 1992. pap. 47.50 (*0-262-53100-3*, Bradford Bks) MIT Pr.

Understanding Neural Networks & Fuzzy Logic: Basic Concepts & Applications. Stamatios V. Kartakapoulos. (IEEE Press Understanding Science & Technology Ser.). 232p. 1995. pap. 39.95 (*0-7803-1128-0*, PP5591) Inst Electrical.

Understanding Neuromuscular Plasticity: A Basis for Clinical Rehabilitation. Kidd. 136p. 1992. pap. 48.00 (*1-56593-570-5*, 0515) Singular Publishing.

Understanding Neuropsychology. Graham J. Beaumont. (Illus.). 160p. (Orig.). 1988. pap. text ed. 28.95 (*0-631-15721-2*) Blackwell Pubs.

Understanding Neuroscience. William R. Klemm. LC 95-36633. (Mosby's Biomedical Science Ser.). 292p. (gr. 13). 1995. pap. text ed. 23.00 (*0-8151-5223-X*) Mosby Yr Bk.

Understanding New Religious Movements. John A. Saliba. LC 96-16344. 250p. (Orig.). 1996. pap. 18.00 (*0-8028-4226-7*) Eerdmans.

***Understanding New Testament Judgments.** unabridged ed. K. D. Anderholm. 100p. (Orig.). Date not set. pap. text ed. 6.99 (*0-9655407-1-5*) True Light Pubns.

Understanding New York State Law, Custom Pub. Pogue & Christoff. 1993. pap. text ed. write for info. (*0-07-050458-X*) McGraw.

Understanding New York's Nonresident Income Allocation Rules: A Guidebook Specially Designed to Assist Taxpayers & Tax Advisors in Understanding & Interpreting New York's Complex Income Sourcing Rules. Paul R. Comeau & Mark S. Klein. Ed. by Sharon M. Kelly. 87p. (Orig.). 1996. pap. 10.95 (*0-9639171-3-7*) Guaranty NY.

Understanding New Zealand. Frederick L. Wood. LC 75-134163. (Essay Index Reprint Ser.). 1977. 23.95 (*0-8369-2097-X*) Ayer.

Understanding News. John Hartley. (Communication Ser.). 160p. (C). 1982. pap. 12.95 (*0-415-03933-9*, NO. 3622) Routledge Chapman & Hall.

***Understanding Nigeria: A Reference Guide to Political Transitions in Nigeria.** Adonis Hoffman. 1997. pap. text ed. 21.00 (*0-87003-112-0*) Brookings.

Understanding NihONSENSE: A Cross-Cultural Encounter. Paul M. Stuart. (Illus.). 104p. (Orig.). (C). 1990. pap. text ed. 8.57 (*1-880596-05-9*) Allegan Educ.

Understanding Non-Western Philosophy: Introductory Readings. Daniel Bonevac & Stephen Phillips. LC 92-39700. 350p. (C). 1993. pap. text ed. 19.95 (*1-55934-077-0*) Mayfield Pub.

Understanding Nonprofit Financial Statements: A Primer for Board Members. John P. Dalsimer. (Nonprofit Governance Ser.: No. 8). 24p. (Orig.). (C). 1995. pap. 10.00 (*0-925299-43-X*) Natl Ctr Nonprofit.

Understanding Nonprofit Financial Statements: A Primer for Board Members. John P. Dalsimer. (Nonprofit Governance Ser.: No. 08). 24p. (Orig.). (C). 1992. reprint ed. pap. text ed. 12.00 (*0-925299-10-3*) Natl Ctr Nonprofit.

Understanding Nonprofit Funding: Managing Revenues in Social Services & Community Development Organizations. Kirsten A. Gronbjerg. LC 92-41368. (Nonprofit Sector-Public Administration Ser.). 397p. text ed. 42.95 (*1-55542-538-0*) Jossey-Bass.

Understanding Normal & Clinical Nutrition. 3rd ed. Eleanor N. Whitney et al. Ed. by Marshall. 954p. (C). 1991. text ed. 65.25 (*0-314-87426-7*) West Pub.

Understanding Normal & Clinical Nutrition. 4th ed. Eleanor N. Whitney et al. LC 94-14940. 1298p. (C). 1995. text ed. 66.50 (*0-314-04178-8*) West Pub.

***Understanding Normal & Clinical Nutrition.** 5th ed. Whitney & Cataldo. 1998. pap. 21.95 (*0-534-53335-3*) Brooks-Cole.

***Understanding Normal & Clinical Nutrition.** 5th ed. Eleanor N. Whitney et al. (Health Sciences Ser.). (C). 1997. text ed. 63.95 (*0-534-53334-5*) Wadsworth Pub.

Understanding Novell NetWare: A Practical Guide for Users & Network Managers. Trevor Chapman. (Illus.). 256p. 1996. pap. 31.95 (*1-85032-236-8*) ITCP.

Understanding Nuclear Power. H. A. Cole. 300p. 1987. text ed. 79.95 (*0-291-39704-2*, Pub. by Gower UK) Ashgate Pub Co.

Understanding Numbers. Patricia Jones & Kathleen Lopez. 1992. 19.00 (*0-536-58326-9*) Ginn Press.

Understanding Numbers. Helen P. Singletary et al. (Computers & Children Ser.: Bk. IV). (Illus.). 47p. (Orig.). (J). (ps-6). 1991. pap. text ed. 20.00 (*1-880850-04-4*) Comp Trng Clinic.

***Understanding Numbers 1-20.** Jo E. Moore. (Mathematics Ser.). (Illus.). 32p. (J). (gr. k-1). 1997. teacher ed., pap. 2.95 (*1-55799-440-4*, 4042) Evan-Moor Corp.

Understanding Numerology: A Power Guide to the Power of Numbers. D. Jason Cooper. (Illus.). 1995. pap. 9.00 (*1-85538-462-0*) Harper SF.

Understanding Nurses: The Social Psychology of Nursing. fac. ed. Ed. by Suzanne Skevington. LC 83-14509. 214p. pap. 61.00 (*0-7837-7368-4*, 2047177) Bks Demand.

Understanding Nursing Care. 3rd ed. Ed. by Anne M. Chilman & Margaret Thomas. LC 85-24653. (Illus.). 681p. (Orig.). 1987. pap. text ed. 43.00 (*0-443-03040-5*) Churchill.

Understanding Nursing Care. 4th ed. Ed. by Stanley Walker & Patricia I. Peattie. 1995. write for info. (*0-443-04636-0*) Churchill.

Understanding Nursing Research. Burns. 1995. student ed., pap. text ed. 17.95 (*0-7216-4437-6*) HarBrace.

Understanding Nursing Research. Nancy Burns & Susan K. Grove. 208p. 1994. teacher ed. write for info. (*0-7216-4439-2*) Saunders.

Understanding Nursing Research. Nancy Burns & Susan K. Grove. (Illus.). 560p. 1995. pap. text ed. 29.95 (*0-7216-4436-8*) Saunders.

Understanding Nutrition. 6th ed. Whitney. Date not set. teacher ed., pap. text ed. write for info. (*0-314-01664-3*) West Pub.

Understanding Nutrition. 6th ed. Whitney. Date not set. student ed., pap. text ed. 20.50 (*0-314-01665-1*) West Pub.

Understanding Nutrition. 6th ed. Eleanor N. Whitney & Sharon R. Rolfes. Ed. by Marshall. 603p. (C). 1993. text ed. 55.25 (*0-314-01239-7*) West Pub.

Understanding Nutrition. 7th ed. Whitney. Date not set. teacher ed., pap. text ed. write for info. (*0-314-08754-0*); student ed., pap. text ed. 20.50 (*0-314-08755-9*) West Pub.

Understanding Nutrition. 7th ed. Eleanor N. Whitney & Sharon R. Rolfes. 925p. (C). 1996. text ed. 57.00 (*0-314-06385-4*) West Pub.

Understanding Object-Oriented Software Engineering: A Practical Approach. Stefan Siegfried. LC 95-1226. (Understanding Science & Technology Ser.). 478p. 1996. pap. 44.95 (*0-7803-1095-0*, PP4507) Inst Electrical.

Understanding Obsessive-Compulsive Behavior. Ed. by Michael A. Jenike & M. Asberg. (Illus.). 60p. 1991. text ed. 16.00 (*0-88937-046-X*) Hogrefe & Huber Pubs.

Understanding Occam & the Transputer: Complete Working Programs. David Ellison. 212p. (Orig.). 1991. pap. 42.50 (*1-85058-206-8*, Pub. by Sigma Press UK) Coronet Bks.

Understanding Occupational Pension Schemes. 5th ed. Maurice Oldfield. 170p. 1994. pap. 100.00 (*0-85459-878-2*, Pub. by Tolley Pubng UK) St Mut.

Understanding of Afrocentric World View: Introduction to an Optimal Psychology. Linda J. Myers. 128p. 1995. per. 20.94 (*0-8403-8342-8*) Kendall-Hunt.

Understanding of Difference in Heidegger & Derrida. Douglas L. Donkel. LC 92-22090. (American University Studies: Philosophy: Ser. V, Vol. 143). 221p. (C). 1993. text ed. 44.95 (*0-8204-1961-3*) P Lang Pubng.

Understanding of Melody & Rhythm. Ed. by Thomas Tighe & W. Jay Dowling. 248p. 1993. pap. 27.50 (*0-8058-0128-6*); text ed. 49.95 (*0-8058-0145-6*) L Erlbaum Assocs.

***Understanding Of Mice & Men, The Red Pony & The Pearl: A Student Casebook to Issues, Sources & Historical Documents.** Claudia D. Johnson. LC 96-41332. (Greenwood Press "Literature in Context" Ser.). 232p. 1997. text ed. 39.95 (*0-313-29966-8*, Greenwood Pr) Greenwood.

Understanding OLE with Active X: A Guide for Managers & Developers. David Chappell. (Strategic Technologies Ser.). 250p. 1996. pap. 17.95 (*1-57231-216-5*) Microsoft.

Understanding One Another: Communicating Interpersonally. Thomas F. Mader & Diane C. Mader. 416p. (C). 1989. per. write for info. (*0-697-06779-3*) Brown & Benchmark.

Understanding Operating Systems. Ida M. Flynn & Ann McHoes. 320p. (C). 1991. text ed. 46.50 (*0-534-15180-9*) PWS Pubs.

Understanding Opportunities & Risks in Futures Trading. 53p. (Orig.). (C). 1994. pap. text ed. 20.00 (*0-7881-0328-8*) DIANE Pub.

***Understanding Opposites.** Playskool Staff. (J). 1997. pap. 5.99 (*0-525-45785-2*) NAL-Dutton.

Understanding Options. (Self-Study Options Ser.). Date not set. 83.00 (*0-614-17084-2*, Pub. by IFR Pub UK) Am Educ Systs.

Understanding Options. Robert Kolb. (Wiley Marketplace Book Ser.). 228p. 1995. text ed. 55.00 (*0-471-08554-5*) Wiley.

***Understanding Ordinary Landscapes.** Paul E. Groth & Todd W. Bressi. LC 97-5776. 1997. write for info. (*0-300-06371-7*); pap. write for info. (*0-300-07203-1*) Yale U Pr.

Understanding Organic Chemistry. Margot K. Schumm. 544p. (C). 1987. text ed. write for info. (*0-02-408200-7*, Macmillan Coll) P-H.

Understanding Organic Chemistry at the Molecular Level. Philip L. Fuchs. (Illus.). 361p. 1994. pap. text ed. 49.95 (*0-87563-532-6*) Stipes.

***Understanding Organic Reaction Mechanisms.** Adam Jacobs. (Illus.). 350p. (C). 1997. text ed. 85.00 (*0-521-46217-7*); pap. text ed. 39.95 (*0-521-46776-4*) Cambridge U Pr.

Understanding Organisations. C. B. Handy. 487p. (C). 1985. 140.00 (*0-685-39851-X*, Pub. by Inst Pur & Supply UK) St Mut.

Understanding Organization: Advanced Level. 2nd ed. Ed. by Kraft. (Comprehension Skills Ser.). 64p. 1993. pap. 8.45 (*0-89061-625-6*) Jamestown Pubs.

Understanding Organization: Introductory Level. Ed. by Kraft. (Comprehension Skills Ser.). 64p. 1993. pap. 7.91 (*0-89061-665-5*) Jamestown Pubs.

Understanding Organization: Middle Level. 2nd ed. Ed. by Kraft. (Comprehension Skills Ser.). 64p. 1993. pap. 8.31 (*0-89061-645-0*) Jamestown Pubs.

Understanding Organizational Behavior: A Casebook. Bud Knudson et al. 320p. (C). 1986. pap. write for info. (*0-675-20481-X*, Merrill Coll) P-H.

Understanding Organizational Change: Converting Theory into Practice. Lynn Fossum. Ed. by Michael G. Crisp. LC 88-72251. (Fifty-Minute Ser.). (Illus.). 85p. (Orig.). 1989. pap. 10.95 (*0-931961-71-8*) Crisp Pubns.

Understanding Organizational Communication: Cases, Commentaries, & Conversations. Pamela Shockley-Zalabak. LC 93-9687. 368p. (C). 1994. pap. text ed. 33.50 (*0-8013-0786-4*, 78804) Longman.

Understanding Organizations. 3rd ed. Charles B. Handy. LC 86-2139. 487p. reprint ed. pap. 138.80 (*0-8357-3444-7*, 2039701) Bks Demand.

U V

Understanding Organizations. 4th ed. Charles Handy. LC 93-5123. (Illus.). 448p. (C). 1993. 30.00 (*0-19-508732-1*, 14617) OUP.

Understanding Organizations: Interpreting Organizational Cultures. Charles R. Bantz. LC 92-44328. (Studies in Communication Processes). (Illus.). 262p. (C). 1993. text ed. 34.95 (*0-87249-879-4*) U of SC Pr.

***Understanding Organized Crime: A Reader.** Patrick J. Ryan & George E. Rush. LC 97-21083. 1997. write for info. (*0-7619-0981-8*); pap. write for info. (*0-7619-0982-6*) Sage.

Understanding Oriental Philosophy. James K. Feibleman. 1984. pap. 9.95 (*0-452-00710-0*, Mer) NAL-Dutton.

Understanding Origins: Contemporary Views on the Origin of Life, Mind & Society. Ed. by Francisco J. Varela. (Boston Studies in the Philosophy of Science). 328p. (C). 1992. lib. bdg. 141.50 (*0-7923-1251-1*, Pub. by Klwr Acad Pubs NE) Kluwer Ac.

***Understanding Orthodontics.** Harold T. Perry & David P. Forbes. LC 96-27508. (Illus.). 52p. (J). 1996. pap. 28.00 (*0-86715-315-6*) Quint Pub Co.

***Understanding Oscillators.** Irving Gottlieb. 1997. pap. text ed. 37.95 (*0-7506-3102-3*) Buttrwrth-Heinemann.

Understanding Oscillators. 2nd ed. Irving M. Gottlieb. (Illus.). 224p. 1987. 16.95 (*0-8306-0715-3*) McGraw-Hill Prof.

***Understanding OSF DCE 1.1 for AIX & OS-2.** Rolf Lendenmann. 1996. pap. text ed. 38.00 (*0-13-493750-3*) P-H.

Understanding OSI. John Larmouth. (Illus.). 320p. 1996. pap. 36.95 (*1-85032-176-0*) ITCP.

Understanding OSI. John Larmouth. 300p. 1994. pap. text ed. 33.00 (*0-13-927765-X*) P-H.

Understanding Osteoporosis. G. Birdwood. (Illus.). 182p. 1995. 55.00 (*1-85070-409-0*) Prthnon Pub.

Understanding Other Minds: Perspectives from Autism. Ed. by Simon Baron-Cohen et al. (Illus.). 544p. 1994. pap. text ed. 45.00 (*0-19-262056-8*) OUP.

Understanding Other People. Stuart Palmer. 208p. 1977. pap. 1.75 (*0-449-30815-4*, Prem) Fawcett.

Understanding Others. Elaine Goley. (Learn the Value Ser.). (Illus.). 32p. (J). (gr. 1-4). 1987. lib. bdg. 15.94 (*0-86592-382-5*); lib. bdg. 11.95 (*0-685-67588-2*) Rourke Corp.

Understanding Others: Cultural & Cross-Cultural Studies & the Teaching of Literature. Ed. by Tilly Warnock. 257p. (Orig.). 1992. pap. 21.95 (*0-8141-5562-6*) NCTE.

Understanding Our Biblical & Early Christian Tradition: An Introductory Textbook in Theology. Jean Laporte & Finian Taylor. LC 91-35645. 368p. 1991. pap. 34.95 (*0-7734-9668-8*) E Mellen.

Understanding Our Environment: An Introduction. William P. Cunningham & Barbara W. Saigo. (Illus.). 408p. (C). 1993. per. write for info. (*0-697-20456-1*) Wm C Brown Pubs.

Understanding Our Environment: An Introduction. William P. Cunningham & Barbara W. Saigo. (Illus.). 408p. (C). 1994. Study guide. student ed., per. write for info. (*0-697-20480-4*) Wm C Brown Pubs.

Understanding Our Fertility. M. Freeman & C. Pyper. 1996. 9.99 (*0-7493-2461-9*, Reed Trade) Buttrwrth-Heinemann.

Understanding Our Sexuality. 2nd ed. Bryan Strong & Christine DeVault. 566p. (C). 1988. text ed. 53.25 (*0-314-62316-7*) West Pub.

Understanding Our Sexuality. 2nd ed. Bryan Strong. Date not set. student ed., pap. text ed. 19.00 (*0-314-79026-8*); teacher ed., pap. text ed. write for info. (*0-314-79027-6*) West Pub.

Understanding Our World: An Integral Ontology. Hendrik Hart. LC 84-17238. 498p. (Orig.). 1985. 62.00 (*0-8191-4257-3*, Inst Christ Stud); pap. 36.00 (*0-8191-4258-1*, Inst Christ Stud) U Pr of Amer.

***Understanding Our World Bk. 1.** Sale et al. Date not set. pap. text ed. write for info. (*0-582-87246-4*, Pub. by Longman UK) Longman.

***Understanding Our World Bk. 2.** Sale et al. Date not set. pap. text ed. write for info. (*0-582-87376-2*, Drumbeat) Longman.

Understanding Our World Through Geography. Jerry Aten. 208p. (J). (gr. 4-8). 1991. 15.99 (*0-86653-592-6*, GA1309) Good Apple.

Understanding Ourselves. Ellen A. Knodt. Date not set. teacher ed., pap. write for info. (*0-673-99236-5*) Addson-Wesley Educ.

Understanding Ourselves: Readings for Writers on Identity in American Society. Ellen A. Knodt. LC 94-49197. (Illus.). 368p. (C). 1996. text ed. 28.50 (*0-673-99235-7*) Addson-Wesley Educ.

Understanding Ourselves as Adults: The Meaning of Emotional Maturity. Helmer R. Myklebust. LC 93-37825. 1994. pap. write for info. (*0-89876-198-0*) Gardner Pr.

Understanding Pacemakers. David Sonnenburg et al. LC 80-22912. (Illus.). 175p. 24.95 (*0-935576-04-5*); pap. 14. 95 (*0-935576-05-3*) Kesend Pub Ltd.

Understanding Pain: Interpretation & Philosophy. Mitchell T. Smolkin. LC 88-23590. 102p. (Orig.). 1989. 14.00 (*0-89464-308-8*) Krieger.

Understanding Paint & Painting Processes. 3rd ed. Gerald L. Schneberger. (Illus.). 176p. (Orig.). pap. 25.00 (*0-933931-05-0*) Hitchcock Pub.

Understanding Palestine: Israel & the U. S. Role. 26p. 1988. pap. 0.50 (*0-89567-087-9*) World View Forum.

Understanding Parenting. 2nd ed. Jaffe. LC 96-41885. 416p. 1996. pap. 44.33 (*0-205-18997-0*) Allyn.

Understanding Partner Violence: Prevalence, Causes, Consequences, & Solutions. Ed. by Sandra M. Stith et al. (Families in Focus Ser.: Vol. 2). 306p. (C). 1995. pap. text ed. 36.95 (*0-916174-50-6*) Natl Coun Family.

Understanding Party System Change in Western Europe. Ed. by Peter Mair & Gordon Smith. 191p. 1990. text ed. 37.50 (*0-7146-3381-X*, Pub. by F Cass Pubs UK) Intl Spec Bk.

Understanding Pascal. Steven L. Mandell. Date not set. text ed. 46.50 (*0-314-89691-0*); teacher ed., pap. text ed. 21.95 (*0-314-87254-X*) West Pub.

***Understanding Pascal: Turbo Version.** 11th ed. Susan K. Baumann. (DF - Computer Applications Ser.). 1990. pap. 35.50 (*0-314-49897-4*) West Pub.

Understanding Patents & Other Protection for Intellectual Property. Thomas A. Penn & Ramon D. Foltz. (Illus.). 100p. (Orig.). (C). 1990. pap. 15.00 (*0-944606-07-5*) Penn Inst.

Understanding Patents & Other Protection for Intellectual Property see Handbook for Protecting Ideas & Inventions

Understanding Pathophysiology. Huether & Kathryn L. McCance. 1248p. (C). (gr. 13). 1995. text ed. 61.00 (*0-8151-4081-9*) Mosby Yr Bk.

Understanding Pathophysiology. Parkinson. 300p. (C). (gr. 13). 1995. student ed., pap. text ed. 19.95 (*0-8151-7299-0*) Mosby Yr Bk.

***Understanding Patient Financial Services.** Christine B. Robinson. LC 97-25029. 350p. 1997. spiral bd. 65.00 (*0-8342-0916-0*, 20916) Aspen Pub.

Understanding Patients. Morrison. 1995. pap. text ed. 16. 95 (*0-7020-1718-3*) HarBrace.

Understanding Patriarchal Blessings. R. Clayton Brough & Thomas W. Grassley. LC 84-81233. 81p. 1984. 12.98 (*0-88290-253-9*) Horizon Utah.

Understanding Paul. Richard L. Anderson. LC 83-72103. xv, 448p. 1990. reprint ed. pap. 8.95 (*0-87579-477-7*) Deseret Bk.

Understanding Paul West. David W. Madden. LC 93-12537. (Understanding Contemporary British Literature Ser.). 183p. (C). 1993. text ed. 29.95 (*0-87249-886-7*) U of SC Pr.

Understanding Paul's Ethics: Twentieth Century Approaches. Ed. by Brian S. Rosner. LC 95-4623. 1995. pap. 22.00 (*0-8028-0749-6*) Eerdmans.

Understanding PCM. 2nd ed. Tom Rogers. (ABC Pocket Guide for the Field Ser.). (Illus.). 56p. (C). 1986. pap. text ed. 6.95 (*1-56016-028-4*) ABC TeleTraining.

Understanding Peasant Agriculture: An Integrated Land-Use Model for the Punjab. Joseph H. Astroth, Jr. (Research Papers). (Illus.). xiii, 173p. 1990. pap. write for info. (*0-89065-127-2*) U Ch Pr.

Understanding Peasant China: Case Studies in the Philosophy of Social Science. Daniel Little. (Illus.). 333p. (C). 1992. reprint ed. pap. text ed. 22.00 (*0-300-05477-7*) Yale U Pr.

Understanding Pedal Power. David G. Wilson. Ed. by Margaret Crouch. (Technical Papers: No. 51). 13p. (Orig.). 1987. 9.95 (*0-86619-268-9*) Vols Tech Asst.

***Understanding Pediatric Heart Sounds.** Steven Lehrer. (Illus.). 248p. 1992. pap. write for info. incl. digital audio (*0-7216-2387-5*) Saunders.

Understanding Pennsylvania Civics. William A. Cornell. (YA). (gr. 7-12). 1987. 10.45 (*0-931992-57-5*); pap. 6.95 (*0-931992-45-1*) Penns Valley.

Understanding Pension Schemes. 4th ed. Maurice Oldfield. 182p. 1992. 45.00 (*1-85190-168-X*, Pub. by Tolley Pubng UK) St Mut.

Understanding People: Children, Youth, Adults. LC 75-172116. 90p. 1990. teacher ed., ring bd. 19.95 (*0-910566-25-9*) Evang Trg Assn.

Understanding People: Children, Youth, Adults. Robert Barron et al. LC 75-172116. 96p. 1989. pap. text ed. 8.95 (*0-910566-15-1*) Evang Trg Assn.

Understanding People: Deep Longings for Relationship. Lawrence J. Crabb, Jr. 224p. 1987. 16.99 (*0-310-22600-7*, 10171) Zondervan.

***Understanding People & Organizations.** Linda Maund. 352p. (Orig.). 1997. pap. 49.50 (*0-7487-2404-4*, Pub. by Stanley Thornes UK) Trans-Atl Phila.

Understanding People & Social Life: An Introduction to Sociology. 2nd ed. H. Paul Chalfant & Emily E. LaBeff. Ed. by LaMarre. 367p. (C). 1991. pap. text ed. 39.75 (*0-314-77342-8*) West Pub.

Understanding Perception: The Concept & Its Conditions. David W. Hamlyn. (Avebury Series in Philosophy). 112p. 1996. 55.95 (*1-85972-375-6*, Pub. by Avebury Pub UK) Ashgate Pub Co.

Understanding Performance Appraisal: Social, Organizational, & Goal-Based Perspectives. Kevin R. Murphy & Jeanette Cleveland. 500p. 1995. text ed. 55. 00 (*0-8039-5474-3*); pap. text ed. 27.95 (*0-8039-5475-1*) Sage.

***Understanding Performance Measures: An Approach to Linking Rewards to the Achievement of Organizational Objectives.** James S. Hillgren & David W. Cheatham. (Building Blocks Ser.: Vol. 33). (Illus.). 24p. (Orig.). 1996. pap. 24.95 (*1-57963-034-0*, A0233) Am Compensation.

Understanding Periodontal Diseases. rev. ed. Joel M. Berns. LC 92-37495. (Illus.). 74p. 1993. pap. 26.00 (*0-86715-239-7*) Quint Pub Co.

Understanding Persecution. Annette Capps. 32p. 1982. pap. 0.99 (*0-89274-214-3*, HH-214) Harrison Hse.

Understanding Personal Auto Insurance. 141p. 1995. pap. 21.95 (*0-7931-1280-X*, 5734-0101) Dearborn Finan.

Understanding Personal Computers: A Home Study Course. Harry M. Brobst. (Home Study Ser.). 36p. 1987. student ed. 30.00 (*0-939926-38-5*); audio (*0-939926-37-7*) Fruition Pubns.

Understanding Personal Umbrella Insurance. LC 95-16211. 100p. 1995. 22.95 (*0-7931-1400-4*, 5731-0101, R & R Newkirk) Dearborn Finan.

Understanding Persons: Personal & Impersonal Relationships. F. M. Berenson. LC 91-35953. 226p. 1991. reprint ed. lib. bdg. 89.95 (*0-7734-9848-6*) E Mellen.

Understanding Persuasion. 4th ed. Raymond S. Ross. LC 93-9103. 1993. pap. text ed. 45.00 (*0-13-501131-0*) P-H.

***Understanding Pesticides in Food.** Christine F. Chaisson. LC 92-230714. 12p. 1991. reprint ed. pap. 25.00 (*0-608-03031-7*, 2063482) Bks Demand.

Understanding Peter Weiss. Robert Cohen. LC 93-17439. (Understanding Modern European & Latin American Literature Ser.). 225p. 1993. text ed. 29.95 (*0-87249-898-0*) U of SC Pr.

Understanding Pharmacology. Susan Turley. 240p. 1993. pap. 28.05 (*0-13-126830-9*) P-H.

Understanding Phrasal Verbs. M. M. Murphy. (C). 1983. 55.00 (*0-7175-1011-5*, Pub. by S Thornes Pubs UK) St Mut.

Understanding Physical Anthropology & Archaeology. 6th ed. William A. Turnbaugh et al. LC 95-25842. 525p. (C). 1996. pap. text ed. 51.50 (*0-314-06941-0*) West Pub.

Understanding Physical Anthropology & Archeology. 5th rev. ed. William A. Turnbaugh et al. Ed. by Clyde Perlee & Simon. LC 92-41998. (Illus.). 525p. (C). 1993. pap. text ed. 52.00 (*0-314-01232-X*) West Pub.

Understanding Physical, Sensory, & Health Impairments: Characteristics & Educational Implications. Kathryn W. Heller et al. LC 95-9010. 410p. 1996. text ed. 64.95 (*0-534-33913-1*) Brooks-Cole.

Understanding Physician: Writings of Charles D. Aring, M.D. enl. rev. ed. Charles D. Aring. LC 73-143496. 220p. reprint ed. pap. 62.70 (*0-685-15663-X*, 2027650) Bks Demand.

Understanding Physics for Advanced Level. J. Breithaupt. (C). 1990. text ed. 130.00 (*0-7487-0510-4*, Pub. by Stanley Thornes UK) Trans-Atl Phila.

Understanding Physics for Advanced Level. Jim Breithaupt. 585p. (C). 1994. 57.00 (*0-7478-0510-5*, Pub. by Stanley Thornes UK) Trans-Atl Phila.

Understanding Piaget. R. Droz & M. Rahmy. Tr. by Joyce Diamanti from FRE. LC 75-18509. Orig. Title: Lire Piaget. 212p. 1976. 35.00 (*0-8236-6690-5*) Intl Univs Pr.

Understanding Pictures. Dominic Lopes. (Oxford Philosophical Monographs). (Illus.). 224p. 1996. text ed. 55.00 (*0-19-824097-X*) OUP.

Understanding Pictures: Theories, Exercises, & Procedures. enl. rev. ed. Stuart A. Oring. LC 91-75593. (Illus.). 233p. 1992. reprint ed. spiral bd. 34.00 (*0-9630896-0-9*) ISIS Visual.

Understanding Pietism. rev. ed. Dale W. Brown. 192p. 1996. pap. 10.00 (*0-916035-64-6*) Evangel Indiana.

Understanding Planetary Placements. rev. ed. Sophia Mason. 86p. 1993. pap. 10.00 (*0-86690-365-8*) Am Fed Astrologers.

Understanding Plato. D. J. Melling. (Illus.). 190p. 1987. pap. text ed. 15.95 (*0-19-289116-2*) OUP.

Understanding Plays. 2nd ed. Milly S. Barranger. LC 93-36946. 1993. pap. text ed. 46.00 (*0-205-15096-9*) Allyn.

Understanding Poetry. 4th ed. Cleanth Brooks & Warren. 602p. (C). 1976. pap. text ed. 28.00 (*0-03-076980-9*) HB Coll Pubs.

Understanding Poets & Prophets. A. G. Auld. 75.00 (*1-85075-427-6*, Pub. by Sheffield Acad UK) CUP Services.

Understanding Police & Police Work: Psychosocial Issues. A. Daniel Yarmey. (C). 1990. 45.00 (*0-8147-9670-2*) NYU Pr.

Understanding Policy Fiascoes. Mark Bovens & Paul't Hart. LC 95-9318. 184p. 1995. 34.95 (*1-56000-214-X*) Transaction Pubs.

Understanding Political Change: The British Voter 1964-1987. Anthony Heath. (Illus.). 348p. 1991. pap. text ed. 27.95 (*0-08-037256-2*, Prgamon Press) Buttrwrth-Heinemann.

Understanding Political Development. Myron Weiner & Samuel P. Huntington. (Illus.). 514p. (C). 1994. reprint ed. pap. text ed. 23.95 (*0-88133-794-3*) Waveland Pr.

Understanding Political Theory: An Introduction. Thomas S. Spragens, Jr. LC 75-33578. 150p. 1976. pap. text ed. 16.00 (*0-312-83195-1*) St Martin.

Understanding Political Variables. 4th ed. William Buchanan. 395p. (C). 1988. pap. text ed. 63.00 (*0-02-316360-7*, Macmillan Coll) P-H.

Understanding Politics. 4th ed. Thomas M. Magstadt. 1995. pap. text ed. 39.50 (*0-312-11593-8*) St Martin.

Understanding Politics. 4th ed. Thomas M. Magstadt. 1995. teacher ed., pap. text ed. 3.37 (*0-312-11613-6*) St Martin.

Understanding Politics: The Cultures of Societies & the Structures of Government. William S. Stewart. Ed. by Victor Jones. LC 88-20431. (Publications in Political Science). (Illus.). 240p. (Orig.). 1988. pap. text ed. 14.95 (*0-88316-558-9*) Chandler & Sharp.

Understanding Polymer Morphology. Arthur E. Woodward. 128p. 1994. pap. text ed. write for info. (*1-56990-141-4*) Hanser-Gardner.

Understanding Popular Culture. John Fiske. 208p. 1989. 39.95 (*0-04-445438-4*); pap. 14.95 (*0-04-445439-2*) Routledge Chapman & Hall.

Understanding Popular Culture. John Fiske. (Illus.). 220p. 1989. pap. 15.95 (*0-415-07876-8*, Routledge NY) Routledge.

Understanding Popular Culture: Europe from the Middle Ages to the Nineteenth Century. Ed. by Steven L. Kaplan. LC 84-1001. (New Babylon Studies in the Social Sciences: No. 40). viii, 311p. 1984. 106.15 (*3-11-009600-5*) Mouton.

Understanding Popular Music. Roy Shuker. LC 94-944. 368p. (C). 1994. pap. 17.95 (*0-415-10723-7*, B4689, Routledge NY) Routledge.

Understanding Popular Music. Roy Shuker. LC 94-944. 368p. (C). (gr. 13). 1994. text ed. 62.95 (*0-415-10722-9*, B4685, Routledge NY) Routledge.

Understanding Population Change. Charles B. Nam. LC 93-71269. 471p. (C). 1994. boxed 50.00 (*0-87581-377-1*) Peacock Pubs.

***Understanding Post-Traumatic Fibromyalgia: A Medical Perspective.** Mark J. Pellegrino. (Illus.). 130p. 1996. pap. 16.25 (*0-9646891-8-9*) Anadem Pubng.

***Understanding Post-Traumatic Stress: A Psychosocial Perspective on PTSD & Treatment.** Stephen Joseph et al. LC 96-41655. 1997. pap. write for info. (*0-471-96801-3*) Wiley.

***Understanding Post-Traumatic Stress: A Psychosocial Perspective on PTSD & Treatment.** Stephen Joseph et al. LC 96-41655. 1997. text ed. 65.00 (*0-471-96800-5*) Wiley.

Understanding Post-War British Society. Ed. by James Obelkevich & Peter Catterall. LC 94-7263. 224p. (C). 1994. pap. 17.95 (*0-415-10940-X*, B4690) Routledge.

Understanding Post-War British Society. Ed. by James Obelkevich & Peter Catterall. LC 94-7263. 224p. (C). (gr. 13). 1994. text ed. 59.95 (*0-415-10939-6*, B4686) Routledge.

Understanding PostScript. 3rd ed. David A. Holzgang. LC 92-80098. 515p. 1992. 29.95 (*0-7821-1059-2*) Sybex.

***Understanding Poverty.** Alcock. 1997. pap. 19.95 (*0-333-56759-5*, Pub. by Macm UK) St Martin.

Understanding Poverty & Dependence. Besharov. 1994. 26. 87 (*0-02-903071-4*) S&S Trade.

Understanding Poverty in Poland. LC 95-629. (Country Study Ser.). 236p. 1995. 13.95 (*0-8213-3368-2*) World Bank.

Understanding Practice: Perspectives on Activity & Context. Ed. by Seth Chaiklin & Jean Lave. LC 92-10606. (Learning in Doing: Social, Cognitive & Computational Perspectives Ser.). (Illus.). 432p. (C). 1993. text ed. 64.95 (*0-521-39263-2*) Cambridge U Pr.

Understanding Practice: Perspectives on Activity & Context. Ed. by Seth Chaiklin & Jean Lave. (Learning in Doing: Social, Cognitive & Computational Perspectives Ser.). (Illus.). 432p. (C). 1996. pap. text ed. 19.95 (*0-521-55851-4*) Cambridge U Pr.

Understanding Pregnancy & Childbirth. Sheldon H. Cherry. LC 72-89700. 1973. 8.95 (*0-672-51614-4*, Bobbs) Macmillan.

Understanding Pregnancy & Childbirth. rev. ed. Sheldon H. Cherry. LC 82-17800. 272p. 1983. write for info. (*0-672-52758-8*) Macmillan.

Understanding Pregnancy & Childbirth. 3rd rev. ed. Sheldon H. Cherry. (Illus.). 288p. 1992. pap. 10.00 (*0-02-030981-3*) Macmillan.

Understanding, Preparing for, & Practicing Christian Worship. 2nd ed. Franklin M. Segler & C. Randall Bradley. LC 95-15291. 320p. 1996. 24.99 (*0-8054-1168-2*, 4211-68) Broadman.

Understanding Presses & Press Operations. Ed. by Donald F. Wilhelm. LC 81-51805. (Manufacturing Update Ser.). (Illus.). 238p. reprint ed. pap. 67.90 (*0-8357-6484-2*, 2035855) Bks Demand.

***Understanding Pride & Prejudice: A Student Casebook to Issues, Sources & Historical Documents.** Debra Teachman. LC 97-5858. (Greenwood Press Literature in Context Ser.). 1997. text ed. write for info. (*0-313-30126-3*, Greenwood Pr) Greenwood.

Understanding Primary Science: A Book for Teachers. Pat Cheek. (Illus.). 112p. (Orig.). 1993. pap. 33.50 (*0-572-01877-0*, Pub. by W Foulsham UK) Trans-Atl Phila.

Understanding Primary Science: Ideas, Concepts & Explanations. Martin Wenham. 224p. 1995. pap. text ed. 24.95 (*1-85396-246-5*, Pub. by Paul Chapman UK) Taylor & Francis.

Understanding Primo Levi. Nicholas Patruno. LC 94-18747. (Understanding Modern European & Latin American Literature Ser.). 170p. 1995. text ed. 34.95 (*1-57003-026-X*) U of SC Pr.

Understanding Principia & Tractatus: Russell & Wittgenstein Revisited. A. P. Rao. LC 97-7115. 268p. 1997. 69.95 (*1-57309-099-9*); pap. 49.95 (*1-57309-098-0*) Intl Scholars.

Understanding Probability & Statistics: A Book of Problems. Ruma Falk. LC 93-21627. (Illus.). 256p. (C). 1993. text ed. 44.00 (*1-56881-018-0*) AK Peters.

Understanding Problem Prophetic Passages: The Olivet Discourse. Noah W. Hutchings. 100p. (Orig.). 1991. pap. 5.95 (*1-879366-10-X*) Hearthstone OK.

Understanding Process Integration II. Ed. by Robin Smith. (European Federation of Chemical Engineering Ser.). 356p. 1988. 126.00 (*0-89116-881-8*) Hemisp Pub.

***Understanding Product Design for Injection Molding.** Herbert Rees. LC 96-32922. (Hanser Understanding Bks.). 1996. write for info. (*1-56990-210-0*) Hanser-Gardner.

Understanding Productivity: An Introduction to the Dynamics of Productivity Change. John W. Kendrick. LC 77-4786. (Policy Studies in Employment & Welfare Ser.: No. 31). (Illus.). 1978. text ed. 32.50 (*0-8018-1996-2*); pap. text ed. 12.95 (*0-8018-1997-0*) Johns Hopkins.

Understanding Program Evaluation, Vol. 31. Leonard Rutman & George Mowbray. 112p. 1983. pap. 17.95 (*0-8039-2093-8*) Sage.

Understanding Programming: An Introduction Using C++ Scott R. Cannon. LC 96-27896. 1996. pap. write for info. (*0-314-20410-5*) West Pub.

Understanding Programming & Problem Solving with C++ Kenneth A. Lambert & Douglas W. Nance. LC 95-34794. 650p. (C). 1996. pap. text ed. 48.00 (*0-314-06743-4*) West Pub.

UV

An Asterisk (*) at the beginning of an entry indicates that the title is appearing in BIP for the first time.

Understanding Programming Languages. Monti Ben-Ari. 350p. 1996. pap. text ed. 54.95 (*0-471-95846-8*) Wiley.

Understanding Psychiatric Medications in the Treatment of Chemical Dependency & Dual Diagnoses. Julia D. Lucas et al. (Illus.). 134p. (C). 1995. pap. text ed. 26.95 (*0-398-05964-0*) C C Thomas.

Understanding Psychiatric Medications in the Treatment of Chemical Dependency & Dual Diagnoses. John D. Preston et al. (Illus.). 134p. (C). 1995. text ed. 37.95 (*0-398-05963-2*) C C Thomas.

Understanding Psychological Preparation for Sport: Theory & Practice of Elite Performers. Lew Hardy et al. LC 96-21493. 1996. text ed. 55.00 (*0-471-95023-8*); pap. text ed. 36.95 (*0-471-95787-9*) Wiley.

Understanding Psychological Research. Miriam Lewin. LC 87-3507. 464p. (C). 1987. reprint ed. lib. bdg. 49.50 (*0-89464-230-8*) Krieger.

Understanding Psychological Science. Janet L. Jones. LC 94-8456. (C). 1995. text ed. 59.95 (*0-06-501459-6*) Addson-Wesley Educ.

Understanding Psychological Testing in Children: A Guide for Health Professionals. Stewart Gabel et al. LC 86-15104. 194p. 1986. 39.50 (*0-306-42244-1*, Plenum Med Bk) Plenum.

Understanding Psychology. Ken Richardson. 160p. 1989. 80.00 (*0-335-09843-6*, Open Univ Pr); pap. 27.00 (*0-335-09842-8*, Open Univ Pr) Taylor & Francis.

Understanding Psychology. 3rd ed. Bishop. 1996. student ed., pap. text ed. 21.00 (*0-13-443508-7*) P-H.

Understanding Psychology. 3rd ed. Robert S. Feldman. LC 92-13181. (C). 1993. pap. text ed. write for info. (*0-07-020659-7*) McGraw.

Understanding Psychology. 3rd ed. Robert S. Feldman. LC 92-13181. (C). 1993. pap. text ed. 10.36 (*0-07-020786-0*) McGraw.

Understanding Psychology. 3rd ed. Charles G. Morris. LC 95-23618. 1995. pap. text ed. 36.80 (*0-13-432998-8*) P-H.

Understanding Psychology. 4th ed. Robert S. Feldman. LC 95-7190. 1996. text ed. write for info. (*0-07-021249-X*) McGraw.

Understanding Psychology. 4th ed. Robert S. Feldman. 1996. student ed., pap. text ed. write for info. (*0-07-021281-3*) McGraw.

Understanding Psychology. 5th ed. Sandra W. Scarr et al. 608p. 1987. text ed. 32.52 (*0-07-555247-7*) McGraw.

Understanding Psychology. 5th ed. Sandra W. Scarr. 1988. student ed., pap. text ed. write for info. (*0-07-553985-3*) McGraw.

Understanding Psychotherapy: The Science Behind the Art. Michael F. Basch. LC 88-47763. (Illus.). 352p. 1990. pap. 16.00 (*0-465-08860-0*) Basic.

Understanding Psychotic Speech: Beyond Freud & Chomsky. Elaine O. Chaika. 342p. 1990. pap. 41.95 (*0-398-06048-7*) C C Thomas.

Understanding Psychotic Speech: Beyond Freud & Chomsky. Elaine O. Chaika. 342p. (C). 1990. text ed. 61.95 (*0-398-05648-X*) C C Thomas.

Understanding Public Opinion. Barbara Norrander. LC 96-23904. 325p. 1996. 37.95 (*1-56802-153-4*); pap. 26.95 (*1-56802-156-9*) Congr Quarterly.

Understanding Public Policy. 8th ed. Thomas R. Dye. LC 94-15650. 1995. write for info. (*0-13-043613-5*) P-H.

Understanding Public Policy. 8th ed. Thomas R. Dye. (Illus.). 342p. (C). 1994. text ed. 58.00 (*0-13-097411-0*) P-H.

*__Understanding Public Policy.__ 9th ed. Dye. LC 97-25918. 1997. text ed. 45.33 (*0-13-639105-2*) P-H.

Understanding Punctuation: Grades 4-7. Bearl Brooks. (English Ser.). 24p. (gr. 4-7). 1979. student ed. 5.00 (*0-8209-0186-5*, E-15) ESP.

Understanding Quantitative & Qualitative Research in Early Childhood Education. William Goodwin & Laura Goodwin. LC 96-23110. (Early Childhood Education Ser.: Vol. 59). 208p. (C). 1996. text ed. 40.00 (*0-8077-3548-5*); pap. text ed. 18.95 (*0-8077-3547-7*) Tchrs Coll.

Understanding Quantitative History. Loren Haskins & Kirk Jeffrey. (New Liberal Arts Ser.). 400p. 1990. pap. text ed. write for info. (*0-07-026972-6*) McGraw.

Understanding Quantitive History. Loren Haskins & Kirk Jeffrey. 400p. 1990. 37.50 (*0-262-08190-3*) MIT Pr.

Understanding Quantum Physics: A User's Manual, Vol. I. Michael A. Morrison. 500p. (C). 1990. text ed. 84.00 (*0-13-747908-5*) P-H.

Understanding QuickBooks. Darleen H. Yourzek. LC 92-63056. 365p. 1992. 19.95 (*0-7821-1164-5*) Sybex.

Understanding R-41C: An Annotated Edition of the Federal Home Loan Bank Boards Standard on Appraisals. Ed. by Stuart M. Bloch. 31p. 1987. 4.95 (*0-318-22826-2*) Land Dev Inst.

Understanding Rabbinic Judaism: From Talmudic to Modern Times. Jacob Neusner. 1974. pap. 19.95 (*0-87068-238-5*) Ktav.

Understanding Race, Ethnicity, & Power: The Key to Efficacy in Clinical Practice. Elaine Pinderhughes. 256p. 1989. 35.00 (*0-02-925341-1*, Free Press) Free Pr.

Understanding Race Relations. Keith Trobe. 80p. (C). 1991. pap. 35.00 (*0-7478-0507-5*, Pub. by Stanley Thornes UK) Trans-Atl Phila.

*__Understanding Racial-Ethnic Differences in Secondary School Science & Mathematics Achievement.__ 1997. lib. bdg. 250.95 (*0-8490-6088-5*) Gordon Pr.

*__Understanding Racial-Ethnic Differences in Secondary School Science & Mathematics Achievement.__ Samuel S. Peng & Susan T. Hill. (Illus.). 80p. 1996. reprint ed. pap. 25.00 (*0-7881-3292-X*) DIANE Pub.

Understanding Radar. 2nd ed. Harry Cole. (Illus.). 300p. 1992. text ed. 59.95 (*0-632-03124-7*) Blackwell Sci.

Understanding Radiation. Bjorn Wahlstrom. LC 95-49913. (Illus.). 110p. (Orig.). (YA). (gr. 7 up). 1996. pap. 17.95 (*0-944838-62-6*, Cogito Bks) Med Physics Pub.

Understanding Radio. Andrew Crisell. (Communication Ser.). 256p. 1987. 32.50 (*0-416-38330-0*, 1067); pap. 11.95 (*0-416-38340-8*, 1085) Routledge Chapman & Hall.

Understanding Radio. 2nd ed. Andrew Crisell. LC 93-43580. (Studies in Culture & Communication). 256p. (C). 1994. pap. 19.95 (*0-415-10315-0*, B3810) Routledge.

Understanding Radioactive Waste. 4th ed. Raymond L. Murray. Ed. by Judith A. Powell. LC 94-9995. (Illus.). 220p. 1994. pap. text ed. 12.50 (*0-935470-79-4*) Battelle.

Understanding Radiography. 3rd ed. Stephen S. Hiss. (Illus.). 574p. (C). 1993. text ed. 61.95 (*0-398-05827-X*) C C Thomas.

Understanding Rainer Werner Fassbinder: Film As Private & Public Art. Wallace S. Watson. LC 95-41780. 338p. 1996. text ed. 34.95 (*1-57003-079-0*) U of SC Pr.

Understanding Randomness: Exercise for Statisticians. Salsburg. (Lecture Notes in Statistics Ser.: Vol. 6). 120p. 1983. 75.00 (*0-8247-7057-9*) Dekker.

Understanding Rational Numbers & Proportions. Frances R. Curcio & Nadine S. Bezuk. LC 94-15966. (Curriculum & Evaluation Standards for School Mathematics Addenda Series, Gr. 5-8). (Illus.). 95p. (Orig.). 1994. pap. 13.00 (*0-87353-325-9*) NCTM.

Understanding Rawls: A Reconstruction & Critique of a Theory of Justice. Robert P. Wolff. 1991. 22.75 (*0-8446-6480-4*) Peter Smith.

Understanding Raymond Carver. Arthur M. Saltzman. Ed. by Matthew J. Bruccoli. (Understanding Contemporary American Literature Ser.). 202p. 1988. text ed. 29.95 (*0-87249-581-7*) U of SC Pr.

Understanding Readers' Understanding: Theory to Practice. Ed. by Robert J. Tierney et al. 344p. (C). 1987. text ed. 69.95 (*0-89859-911-3*) L Erlbaum Assocs.

Understanding Reading. Peter B. Mosenthal. (C). 1994. write for info. (*0-582-28482-1*) Addison-Wesley.

Understanding Reading. 5th ed. Frank Smith. 376p. 1994. pap. 24.95 (*0-8058-1420-5*); text ed. 69.95 (*0-8058-1419-1*) L Erlbaum Assocs.

Understanding Reading: A Psycholinguistic Analysis of Reading & Learning to Read. Frank Smith. 376p. 1988. pap. 24.95 (*0-89859-879-6*) L Erlbaum Assocs.

Understanding Reading Comprehension: Cognition, Language, & the Structure of Prose. Ed. by James Flood. LC 83-10847. 274p. reprint ed. pap. 78.10 (*0-8357-2641-X*, 2040129) Bks Demand.

Understanding Reading Problems. Jean W. Gillet & Charles Temple. (C). 1994. text ed. 60.95 (*0-673-52327-6*) Addson-Wesley Educ.

Understanding Real Time Systems: Management, Computers, Applications. Joseph C. Hassab. LC 96-47400. 352p. 1995. 59.95 (*0-8493-7971-7*, 7971) CRC Pr.

Understanding Reality: A Taoist Alchemical Classic. Chang Po-tuan. Tr. by Thomas Cleary. LC 87-25539. 176p. 1987. pap. text ed. 15.00 (*0-8248-1139-9*) UH Pr.

Understanding Reality Therapy: A Metaphorical Approach. Robert E. Wubbolding. LC 90-55519. 160p. (Orig.). 1991. pap. 11.00 (*0-06-096572-X*, PL) HarpC.

Understanding Reception. Frederick M. Bliss. (Studies in Theology). 180p. (Orig.). 1993. pap. 20.00 (*0-87462-625-0*) Marquette.

*__Understanding Regression Analysis.__ Michael P. Allen. LC 97-20373. 214p. (C). 1997. 42.50 (*0-306-45648-6*, Plenum Pr) Plenum.

Understanding Regression Analysis. Larry D. Schroeder. (Quantitative Applications in the Social Sciences Ser.: Vol. 57). 96p. (Orig.). (C). 1986. pap. text ed. 9.95 (*0-8039-2758-4*) Sage.

Understanding Regression Assumptions. William D. Berry. (Quantitative Applications in the Social Sciences Ser.: Vol. 92). (Illus.). 96p. (C). 1993. pap. text ed. 9.95 (*0-8039-4263-X*) Sage.

Understanding Regulations on OSHA Design Safety Standards. Ed. by Brendan B. Read. (Understanding NE Code Rules on Ser.). (Illus.). 164p. (Orig.). 1991. pap. 15.95 (*0-87288-458-9*) Intertec Pub.

Understanding Regulations on OSHA Electrical Safety for Construction Sites. Ed. by Brendan B. Read. (Illus.). 154p. (Orig.). 1992. pap. 15.95 (*0-87288-460-0*) Intertec Pub.

Understanding Regulations on OSHA Electrical Work Rules. Ed. by Brendan B. Read. (Understanding NE Code Rules on Ser.). (Illus.). 139p. (Orig.). 1991. pap. 15.95 (*0-87288-459-7*) Intertec Pub.

Understanding Relational Databases: With Examples in SQL-92. Fabian Pascal. LC 93-7595. 304p. 1993. pap. text ed. 34.95 (*0-471-58538-6*) Wiley.

Understanding Relationships. Steve Duck. LC 91-6658. 224p. 1991. pap. text ed. 19.95 (*0-89862-470-3*); lib. bdg. 42.00 (*0-89862-758-3*) Guilford Pr.

Understanding Relationships: Selected Readings in Interpersonal Communication. 2nd ed. Benjamin J. Broome. 192p. (C). 1994. per., pap. text ed. 25.14 (*0-8403-9139-0*) Kendall-Hunt.

Understanding Relativity: A Simplified Approach to Einstein's Theories. Leo Sartori. LC 94-49358. 378p. 1995. 50.00 (*0-520-07986-8*); pap. 19.95 (*0-520-20029-2*) U CA Pr.

Understanding Relativity: Origin & Impact of a Scientific Revolution. Stanley Goldberg. LC 83-22368. 494p. 1989. 54.00 (*0-8176-3150-X*) Birkhauser.

Understanding Religious Conversion. Lewis R. Rambo. LC 92-39404. 224p. (C). 1993. text ed. 32.50 (*0-300-05283-9*) Yale U Pr.

Understanding Religious Life. 3rd ed. Frederick J. Streng. 276p. (C). 1985. pap. 27.95 (*0-534-03699-6*) Wadsworth Pub.

Understanding Rent Control: Rental Housing Committee of the Real Estate, Housing & Land Use Section, 1989. 1989. 7.00 (*0-685-57464-4*) DC Bar.

Understanding Reptile Parasites. Roger J. Klingenberg. 81p. 1993. pap. text ed. 11.50 (*1-882770-21-8*) Adv Vivarium.

Understanding Research in Early Education. M. M. Clark. 132, xp. 1989. pap. text ed. 23.00 (*2-88124-730-X*) Gordon & Breach.

*__Understanding Research in Education: A Consumer Guide.__ 4th ed. Wopert & Spiers. 304p. (C). 1997. per. 39.95 (*0-7872-3786-8*) Kendall-Hunt.

Understanding Research in Education: An Introductory Guide to Critical Reading. 3rd ed. Edward M. Wolpert. 304p. 1991. per. 31.44 (*0-8403-6722-8*) Kendall-Hunt.

Understanding Research in Nursing. Shirley Chater. (Offset Publication Ser.: No. 14). 1975. pap. text ed. 3.60 (*92-4-170014-9*, 1120014) World Health.

Understanding Research in Second Language Learning. James D. Brown. LC 85-30569. (New Directions in Language Teaching Ser.). (Illus.). 152p. 1988. pap. text ed. 18.95 (*0-521-31551-4*) Cambridge U Pr.

*__Understanding Research in Second Language Learning: A Teacher's Guide to Statistics & Research Design.__ 240p. 1988. text ed. 47.95 (*0-521-30524-1*) Cambridge U Pr.

*__Understanding Research Methods: An Overview of the Essentials.__ Mildred L. Patten. (Illus.). 136p. (C). 1996. pap. text ed. 20.95 (*1-884585-02-7*) Pyrczak Pub.

Understanding Resource Management: How to Deploy Your People, Products, & Processes for Maximum Productivity. James A. Constantin & Robert F. Lusch. 1994. write for info. (*0-318-72930-X*) Irwin Prof Pubng.

Understanding Resource Management: How to Deploy Your People, Products, & Processing. James A. Constantin. 264p. 1994. text ed. 35.00 (*0-7863-0360-3*) Irwin Prof Pubng.

Understanding-Responding. 2nd ed. Long & Penny Prophit. (Nursing-Health Science Ser.). 1992. pap. text ed. 37.50 (*0-86720-433-8*) Jones & Bartlett.

Understanding-Responding: A Communication Manual for Nurses. Lynette Long & Penny Prophit. LC 80-17977. (C). 1981. pap. text ed. 30.00 (*0-87872-284-X*) Jones & Bartlett.

Understanding Retrogrades. Helen J. Adams. LC 80-51517. 80p. 1980. 9.00 (*0-86690-056-X*, A1006-014) Am Fed Astrologers.

Understanding Rett Syndrome: A Practical Guide for Parents, Teachers & Therapists. Barbro Lindberg. LC 90-34409. (Illus.). 184p. 1992. text ed. 26.00 (*0-88937-033-8*) Hogrefe & Huber Pubs.

Understanding Return on Investment. Franklin J. Plewa & George T. Friedlob, Jr. LC 96-8694. (Finance Fundamentals for Nonfinancial Managers Ser.). 237p. 1996. text ed. 34.95 (*0-471-10381-0*); pap. text ed. 17.95 (*0-471-10372-1*) Wiley.

Understanding Revelation. Charles B. Christian. (Illus.). 168p. 1996. pap. 12.95 (*0-614-97244-2*) Anchor Pub Co.

Understanding Revelation. Gary C. Cohen. 218p. 1992. pap. 6.99 (*0-89957-101-8*) AMG Pubs.

Understanding Reynolds Price. James A. Schiff. LC 96-9971. (Understanding Contemporary American Literature Ser.). 150p. 1996. text ed. 29.95 (*1-57003-126-6*) U of SC Pr.

*__Understanding RF Microelectronics for Wireless Communication: An Entry-Level Guide.__ Donald R. Green. (C). 1997. pap. text ed. 30.00 (*0-13-488131-1*) P-H.

Understanding Rheumatoid Arthritis. Stanton Newman et al. LC 95-16023. 224p. (C). 1995. pap. 18.95 (*0-415-10541-2*); text ed. 69.95 (*0-415-10540-4*) Routledge.

Understanding Rigs & Rigging. rev. ed. Richard Henderson. (Illus.). 272p. 1990. pap. text ed. 24.95 (*0-87742-283-4*) Intl Marine.

Understanding Rigs & Rigging. rev. ed. Richard Henderson. 1991. pap. text ed. 24.95 (*0-07-156304-0*) McGraw.

Understanding RISC Microprocessors. Microprocessor Report Newsletter Staff. 564p. 1993. pap. 79.95 (*1-56276-159-5*, Ziff-Davis Pr) Que.

Understanding Risk. Bernstein. 1995. 24.95 (*0-02-903032-3*) S&S Trade.

Understanding Risk: Informing Decisions in a Democratic Society. National Research Council Staff. 250p. 1996. text ed. 39.95 (*0-309-05396-X*) Natl Acad Pr.

Understanding Rituals. Ed. by Daniel De Coppet. LC 92-5657. (European Association of Social Anthropologists Ser.). (Illus.). 144p. (C). 1992. pap. 15.95 (*0-415-06121-0*, A9650, Routledge NY) Routledge.

Understanding Rituals. Ed. by Daniel De Coppet. LC 92-5657. (European Association of Social Anthropologists Ser.). (Illus.). 144p. (C). (gr. 13). 1992. text ed. 65.00 (*0-415-06120-2*, A9646, Routledge NY) Routledge.

Understanding Robert Bly. William V. Davis. Ed. by Matthew J. Bruccoli. (Understanding Contemporary American Literature Ser.). 196p. 1989. text ed. 29.95 (*0-87249-590-6*) U of SC Pr.

Understanding Robotics. Taylor. 1990. 32.00 (*0-8493-7145-7*, TJ211) CRC Pr.

Understanding Robust & Exploratory Data Analysis. Ed. by David C. Hoaglin et al. (Probability & Mathematical Statistics Ser.). 447p. 1982. text ed. 89.95 (*0-471-09777-2*) Wiley.

*__Understanding Rock Music: Essays in Musical Analysis.__ Ed. by John Covach & Graeme Boone. LC 96-53475. (Illus.). 256p. 1997. 35.00 (*0-19-510004-2*) OUP.

*__Understanding Rock Music: Essays in Musical Analysis.__ Ed. by John Covach & Graeme Boone. LC 96-53475. (Illus.). 256p. 1997. pap. 19.95 (*0-19-510005-0*) OUP.

Understanding Rock 'N' Roll: Popular Music in Britain, 1955-1964. Dick Bradley. (Popular Music in Britain Ser.). 192p. 1992. 90.00 (*0-335-09755-3*, Open Univ Pr); pap. 32.00 (*0-335-09754-5*, Open Univ Pr) Taylor & Francis.

Understanding Roman Catholicism: 37 Roman Catholic Doctrines Explained. Rick Jones. LC 95-92609. 224p. (Orig.). 1995. pap. 9.95 (*0-937958-48-4*) Chick Pubns.

Understanding Roman Inscriptions. Lawrence J. Keppie. (Illus.). 160p. 1992. text ed. 55.00 (*0-8018-4322-7*); pap. text ed. 22.95 (*0-8018-4352-9*) Johns Hopkins.

Understanding Russia's 1993 Parlimentary Elections: Implications for U. S. Foreign Policy. Michael McFaul. LC 94-10757. (Essays in Public Policy Ser.: No. 49). 1994. pap. text ed. 5.00 (*0-8179-5542-9*) Hoover Inst Pr.

Understanding Samuel Beckett. Alan Astro. (Understanding Modern European & Latin American Literature Ser.). 240p. (C). 1990. text ed. 29.95 (*0-87249-686-4*) U of SC Pr.

Understanding Satellite Television Reception. Susan E. Sutphin. (Illus.). 144p. (C). 1986. text ed. 33.00 (*0-317-39622-6*) P-H.

*__Understanding Saving: Evidence from the United States & Japan.__ Fumio Hayashi. LC 96-37681. (Illus.). 492p. 1997. 45.00 (*0-262-08255-1*) MIT Pr.

Understanding Schizophrenia: A Guide to the New Research on Causes & Treatment. Richard S. Keefe & Philip D. Harvey. LC 94-8270. 286p. 1994. 22.95 (*0-02-917247-0*, Free Press) Free Pr.

Understanding School Management. Margaret Preedy et al. 320p. 1987. 85.00 (*0-335-15559-6*, E325, Open Univ Pr); pap. 27.00 (*0-335-15552-9*, Open Univ Pr) Taylor & Francis.

Understanding School System Administration: Studies of the Contemporary Chief Education Officer. Ed. by Kenneth A. Leithwood & Donald F. Musella. 250p. 1991. 55.00 (*1-85000-869-8*, Falmer Pr) Taylor & Francis.

Understanding School System Administration: Studies of the Contemporary Chief Education Officer. Ed. by Kenneth L. Leithwood & Donald F. Musella. 250p. 1991. pap. 27.00 (*1-85000-870-1*, Falmer Pr) Taylor & Francis.

Understanding Schools: The Foundations of Education. Gary K. Clabaug & Edward G. Rozycki. 550p. (C). 1990. text ed. 75.50 (*0-06-041318-2*) Addson-Wesley Educ.

Understanding Science: An Introduction to Concepts & Issues. Arthur Strahler. 409p. (C). 1992. 28.95 (*0-87975-724-8*) Prometheus Bks.

Understanding Scientific Prose. Ed. by Jack Selzer. LC 93-21870. (Rhetoric of the Human Sciences Ser.). (Illus.). 406p. (Orig.). (C). 1993. pap. 27.95 (*0-299-13904-2*) U of Wis Pr.

Understanding Scientific Reasoning. 3rd ed. Ronald N. Giere. (Illus.). 375p. (C). 1991. pap. text ed. 33.25 (*0-03-026419-7*) HB Coll Pubs.

Understanding Scientific Reasoning. 4th ed. Ronald N. Giere. 336p. (C). 1996. pap. text ed. write for info. (*0-15-501625-3*) HB Coll Pubs.

Understanding Scripture. Center for Learning Network Staff. (Adult Workshops Ser.). 97p. 1992. teacher ed., spiral bd. 15.95 (*1-56077-199-2*) Ctr Learning.

Understanding Scripture: Explorations of Jewish & Christian Traditions of Interpretation. Ed. by Clemens Thoma & Michael Wyschgrod. (Stimulus Bks.). 1987. pap. 7.95 (*0-8091-2873-X*) Paulist Pr.

Understanding Scripture: How to Read & Study the Bible. Berkley Mickelson. LC 92-7905. 160p. 1992. pap. 9.95 (*0-943575-84-2*) Hendrickson MA.

Understanding Second Language Acquisition. Rod Ellis. 327p. 1986. pap. 21.95 (*0-19-437081-X*) OUP.

Understanding Second Language Learning Difficulties: Looking Beneath the Surface. Madeline E. Ehrman. 312p. 1996. pap. 25.95 (*0-7619-0191-4*) Sage.

Understanding Second Language Learning Difficulties: Looking Beneath the Surface. Madeline E. Ehrman. 312p. 1996. 55.00 (*0-7619-0190-6*) Sage.

Understanding Sectarian Groups in America. rev. ed. George W. Braswell, Jr. LC 93-24941. 400p. 1994. pap. 21.99 (*0-8054-1047-3*, 4210-47) Broadman.

Understanding Secular Humanistic Judaism. Ed. by Judith Seid. 84p. (Orig.). 1990. pap. 10.00 (*0-9623668-1-1*) Kopinvant Secular.

*__Understanding Secured Transactions.__ William H. Henning et al. LC 97-20820. (Legal Text Series). 1997. write for info. (*0-8205-2659-2*) Bender.

Understanding Securitized Investments & Their Use in Portfolio Management. Ed. by Ken M. Eades et al. (Orig.). 1991. pap. text ed. 30.00 (*1-879087-07-3*) Assn I M&R.

Understanding Seeking Faith Vol. 2: Essays on the Case of Judaism: Literature, Religion & the Social Study of Judaism. Jacob Neusner. LC 86-20316. (Brown Judaic Studies). 250p. 1987. 31.95 (*1-55540-114-7*, 14-00-73) Scholars Pr GA.

Understanding Seeking Faith Essay on the Case of Judaism Vol. 3: Society, History, & the Political & Philosophical Uses of Judaism. Jacob Neusner. LC 86-20316. (Brown Judaic Studies). 334p. 1989. 46.95 (*1-55540-270-4*, 14-01-53) Scholars Pr GA.

*__Understanding Seeking Faith, Essays on the Case of Judaism: Judaism Then & Now, Vol. Four.__ Jacob Neusner. 324p. 1995. 74.95 (*0-7885-0097-X*, 240114) Scholars Pr GA.

Understanding Seeking Faith Essays on the Case of Judaism Vol. 1: Debates on Method Reports of Results. Jacob Neusner. LC 86-20316. (Brown Judaic Studies). 158p. (C). 1986. 27.95 (*1-55540-053-1*, 14-01-16) Scholars Pr GA.

Understanding Self-Esteem. Braham. (YA - Adult Education Ser.). 1993. pap. 5.95 (*0-538-70847-6*) S-W Pub.

***Understanding Self-Similar Fractals.** Roger T. Stevens. 400p. pap. 39.95 incl. disk (*0-87930-451-0*) Miller Freeman.

Understanding "Senility" A Layperson's Guide. Virginia Fraser & Susan M. Thornton. LC 86-30662. (Golden Age Books - Perspectives on Aging Ser.). 101p. 1988. 23.95 (*0-87975-391-9*); pap. 16.95 (*0-87975-392-7*) Prometheus Bks.

Understanding Sensation & Perception. Coren. (C). 1996. write for info. (*0-15-501643-1*) HB Coll Pubs.

Understanding Sergers. Diana Davies. LC 92-70237. (Illus.). 207p. 1993. spiral bd. 24.95 (*0-9634868-0-2*); 24.95 (*0-9634868-1-0*) Acorn Pr MN.

Understanding Serial Communications. 2nd ed. Peter W. Gofton. LC 93-87417. 352p. 1994. 26.99 (*0-7821-1202-1*) Sybex.

Understanding Services Management: Integrating Marketing Organisational Behaviour, Operations & Human Resource Management. Ed. by William J. Glynn & James G. Barnes. 1995. pap. text ed. 50.00 (*0-471-96066-7*) Wiley.

Understanding Sexual Identity. Janice E. Rench. (YA). 1992. pap. 4.95 (*0-8225-9602-4*, Lerner Publctns) Lerner Group.

Understanding Sexual Identity: A Book for Gay Teens & Their Friends. Janice E. Rench. (Coping with Modern Problems Ser.). 72p. (YA). (gr. 4 up). 1990. lib. bdg. 17.50 (*0-8225-0044-2*, Lerner Publctns) Lerner Group.

Understanding Sexual Medicine. I. L. Felstein. 1986. pap. text ed. 61.00 (*0-85200-982-8*) Kluwer Ac.

Understanding Sexual Misconduct by Clergy: A Handbook for Ministers. John A. Loftus. (Orig.). 1994. pap. text ed. 4.95 (*1-56929-024-5*) Pastoral Pr.

Understanding Sexual Violence: A Study of Conviced Rapists. Diana Scully. LC 94-16604. (Perspectives on Gender Ser.: Vol. 3). 208p. (C). 1990. pap. 17.95 (*0-415-91108-7*) Routledge.

Understanding Sexual Violence: A Study of Convicted Rapists. Diana Scully. (Perspectives on Gender Ser.: No. 3). 208p. (C). 1990. pap. text ed. 14.95 (*0-04-445846-0*) Routledge Chapman & Hall.

Understanding Sexuality: The Mystery of Our Lost Identities. rev. ed. Roy Masters. LC 87-83552. 361p. 1988. reprint ed. pap. 15.95 (*0-933900-13-9*) Foun Human Under.

Understanding Shakespeare. Evelyn F. Ludowyk. LC 62-6756. 284p. reprint ed. pap. 81.00 (*0-317-20599-4*, 2024489) Bks Demand.

Understanding Shakespeare's England: A Companion for the American Reader. Jo McMurtry. LC 89-32451. (Illus.). xiii, 254p. (C). 1989. lib. bdg. 37.50 (*0-208-02248-1*, Archon Bks) Shoe String.

Understanding Shakespeare's Julius Caesar: A Student Casebook to Issues, Sources, & Historical Documents. Thomas J. Derrick. LC 96-25005. (Literature in Context Ser.). 256p. 1997. text ed. 39.95 (*0-313-29638-3*) Greenwood.

Understanding Shame. Carl Goldberg. LC 91-13935. 328p. 1991. 40.00 (*0-87668-541-6*) Aronson.

Understanding Shinran: A Dialogical Approach. Hee-Sung Keel. LC 95-13351. (Nanzan Studies in Asian Religions: Vol. 6). 224p. (C). 1996. text ed. 50.00 (*0-89581-937-6*) Asian Humanities.

Understanding Shmittah. David Marchant. 1987. 12.95 (*0-87306-425-9*) Feldheim.

Understanding Sickle Cell Disease. Miriam Bloom. (Understanding Health & Sickness Ser.). 128p. 1995. pap. 11.95 (*0-87805-745-5*); text ed. 25.00 (*0-87805-744-7*) U Pr of Miss.

***Understanding Signals & Systems.** Jack Golten. LC 97-545. 1997. write for info. (*0-07-709320-8*) McGraw.

Understanding Significance Testing. Lawrence B. Mohr. (Quantitative Applications in the Social Sciences Ser.: Vol. 73). (Illus.). 96p. (C). 1990. pap. text ed. 9.95 (*0-8039-3568-4*) Sage.

Understanding Significant Details: Advanced Level. 2nd ed. Ed. by Kraft. (Comprehension Skills Ser.). 64p. 1993. pap. 8.45 (*0-89061-627-2*) Jamestown Pubs.

Understanding Significant Details: Introductory Level. Ed. by Kraft. (Comprehension Skills Ser.). 64p. 1993. pap. 7.91 (*0-89061-667-1*) Jamestown Pubs.

Understanding Significant Details: Middle Level. 2nd ed. Ed. by Kraft. (Comprehension Skills Ser.). 64p. 1993. pap. 8.31 (*0-89061-647-7*) Jamestown Pubs.

Understanding Sikhism. K. S. Grewal. (C). 1991. 17.50 (*81-210-0268-0*, Pub. by Inter-India Pubns) S Asia.

Understanding Sjogren's Syndrome. enl. ed. Sue Dauphin. LC 93-85164. (Illus.). 245p. (Orig.). 1993. pap. 16.95 (*0-9620354-2-4*) Pixel Pr.

***Understanding Sleep: The Evaluation & Treatment of Sleep Disorders.** Ed. by Mark R. Pressman & William C. Orr. LC 97-1393. (Application & Practice in Health Psychology Ser.: Vol. 4). 592p. 1997. 49.95 (*1-55798-419-0*, 4317870) Am Psychol.

Understanding Smart Sensors. Randy Frank. LC 95-48912. 1995. 75.00 (*0-89006-824-0*) Artech Hse.

***Understanding SNMP MIBS.** Evan McGinnis & David Perkins. 400p. (C). 1996. text ed. 58.00 (*0-13-437708-7*) P-H.

Understanding Soccer: Rules & Procedures for Players, Parents & Coaches. Gene S. Kira. LC 93-20748. (Illus.). 84p. (Orig.). (YA). (gr. 5 up). 1994. pap. 9.95 (*0-929637-02-X*) Apples & Oranges Inc.

Understanding Soccer Hooliganism. John H. Kerr. LC 94-27678. 160p. (Orig.). 1994. 79.00 (*0-335-19250-5*, Open Univ Pr); pap. write for info. (*0-335-19249-1*) Taylor & Francis.

Understanding Social Change in the Nineties: Theoretical Approaches & Historiographical Perspectives. Ed. by Valentin De Prada et al. LC 95-3346. 520p. 1995. 97.95 (*0-86078-496-7*, Pub. by Variorum UK) Ashgate Pub Co.

Understanding Social Deviance. Curra. (C). 1993. 46.00 (*0-06-500778-6*) Addson-Wesley Educ.

Understanding Social Deviance: A Lecture Study Guide. 2nd ed. George S. Bridges. 128p. 1995. per. 19.89 (*0-8403-8916-7*) Kendall-Hunt.

Understanding Social Inequality: Modeling Allocation Processes. Hubert M. Blalock. (Library of Social Research: Vol. 188). 256p. (C). 1991. text ed. 54.00 (*0-8039-4339-3*); pap. text ed. 24.95 (*0-8039-4340-7*) Sage.

Understanding Social Issues: Critical Thinking & Analysis. 4th ed. Gai Berlage & William Egelman. LC 95-3495. 1995. pap. text ed. 23.00 (*0-205-16815-9*) Allyn.

Understanding Social Issues: Sociological Fact Finding. 2nd ed. Gai I. Berlage & William Egelman. 150p. 1990. pap. text ed. write for info. (*0-205-12255-8*, H22551) Allyn.

Understanding Social Life. Boudreau. Date not set. teacher ed., pap. text ed. write for info. (*0-314-01714-3*) West Pub.

Understanding Social Life. Boudreau. Date not set. student ed., pap. text ed. 15.75 (*0-314-01716-X*) West Pub.

Understanding Social Life: An Introduction to Sociology. Frances A. Boudreau & William M. Newman. Ed. by Baxter. LC 92-30979. (Illus.). 400p. (C). 1993. pap. text ed. 34.25 (*0-314-01187-0*) West Pub.

Understanding Social Networks. Lambert Maquire. LC 83-4489. (Sage Human Services Guides Ser.: No. 32). 119p. 1983. reprint ed. pap. 34.00 (*0-608-01512-1*, 2059556) Bks Demand.

Understanding Social Policy. 4th ed. Michael Hill. LC 92-26626. 256p. 1993. pap. 25.95 (*0-631-18849-5*) Blackwell Pubs.

Understanding Social Policy. 5th rev. ed. Michael Hill. LC 96-23265. (Illus.). 256p. 1997. pap. text ed. 29.95 (*0-631-20039-8*) Blackwell Pubs.

Understanding Social Problems. Caroline Schacht et al. LC 96-2132. 500p. (C). 1997. pap. text ed. 54.75 (*0-314-06717-5*) West Pub.

Understanding Social Problems, Policies, & Programs. Leon H. Ginsberg. LC 94-12556. 214p. 1994. pap. text ed. 17.95 (*0-87249-998-7*) U of SC Pr.

Understanding Social Problems, Policies, & Programs. 2nd ed. Leon Ginsberg. 250p. 1996. pap. text ed. 18.95 (*1-57003-119-3*) U of SC Pr.

Understanding Social Psychology. 5th ed. Stephen Worchel & Cooper. (Psychology Ser.). 1991. student ed., pap. 19.95 (*0-534-13627-3*) Brooks-Cole.

Understanding Social Science. Keith McKean. 384p. (C). 1995. per., pap. text ed. 48.56 (*0-7872-0250-9*) Kendall-Hunt.

Understanding Social Science: A Philosophical Introduction to the Social Sciences. Roger Trigg. 272p. 1985. pap. 23.95 (*0-631-14161-8*) Blackwell Pubs.

Understanding Social Science Statistics: A Spreadsheet Approach. Roger Bakeman. 464p. 1992. pap. 45.00 (*0-8058-1117-6*); text ed. 89.95 (*0-8058-0623-7*) L Erlbaum Assocs.

Understanding Social Security. (Illus.). 39p. (Orig.). 1995. pap. text ed. 15.00 (*0-7881-2169-3*) DIANE Pub.

Understanding Social Theory. Derek Layder. 240p. (C). 1994. text ed. 65.00 (*0-8039-8448-0*); pap. text ed. 19.95 (*0-8039-8449-9*) Sage.

Understanding Social Welfare. 3rd rev. ed. Ralph Dolgoff et al. 461p. (C). 1993. text ed. 55.50 (*0-8013-0867-4*, 78969) Longman.

Understanding Social Welfare. 4th ed. Ralph Dolgoff. (C). 1997. text ed. 46.95 (*0-8013-1701-0*) Addison-Wesley.

***Understanding Sociology: A Student Workbook for Active Learning.** Armand. (C). 1997. pap. text ed. 19.38 (*0-201-32237-4*) Addison-Wesley.

***Understanding Sociology: Active Learning.** Ed. by Armand. (C). 1996. student ed., wbk. ed., text ed. 20.95 (*0-673-67603-X*) Addison-Wesley.

Understanding Soil Mechanics. Roberts. (Agriculture Ser.). 336p. (C). 1996. text ed. 39.95 (*0-8273-6869-0*) Delmar.

Understanding Soil Mechanics. Roberts. (Agriculture Ser.). 32p. 1996. teacher ed., text ed. 12.95 (*0-8273-6870-4*) Delmar.

Understanding Solar Cookers & Ovens. Thomas Bowman. Ed. by Margaret Crouch. (Technical Papers: No. 36). 26p. (Orig.). 1987. 9.95 (*0-86619-247-6*) Vols Tech Asst.

Understanding Solid & Hazardous Waste Identification & Classification: A Practical Guide to the Waste Generator. Mark S. Dennison. 374p. 1994. ring bd. 135.00 (*0-471-11264-X*) Wiley.

***Understanding Solid State Electronics.** 5th ed. Cannon. 1997. pap. text ed. 33.27 (*0-13-649088-3*) P-H.

Understanding SONET/SDH Vol. 1: Standards & Applications. Ming-Chwan Chow. (Illus.). 504p. 1995. text ed. 65.00 (*0-9650448-2-3*) Andan Pub.

Understanding South Africa's Transitional Bill of Rights. Lourens Du Plessis & Hugh Corder. 224p. 1994. pap. 32.00 (*0-614-04222-4*, Pub. by Juta SA) Gaunt.

Understanding South Asia: Essays in the Memory of Late Professor (Mrs.) Urmila Phadnis. Ed. by S. D. Muni. (C). 1994. 28.00 (*81-7003-173-7*, Pub. by S Asia Pubs II) S Asia.

Understanding Southeast Asian Cultures: Their Cultural Traits & Implications in Casework Practice. Chareundi Van-Si. 108p. 1992. pap. text ed. 12.95 (*0-9633904-0-6*) Asian Am United Pr.

Understanding Soviet Foreign Policy: Readings & Documents. V. Wozniuk. 1990. pap. text ed. write for info. (*0-07-071912-8*) McGraw.

***Understanding Soviet Naval Developments.** 6th ed. (Illus.). 189p. (Orig.). (C). 1996. reprint ed. pap. 45.00 (*0-7881-3009-9*) DIANE Pub.

Understanding Soviet Politics Through Literature. Martin Crouch & Robert Porter. 300p. 1984. pap. text ed. 16.95 (*0-04-320158-X*) Routledge Chapman & Hall.

Understanding Soviet Society. Ed. by Michael P. Sacks & Jerry G. Pankhurst. 320p. (C). 1988. text ed. 44.95 (*0-04-445036-2*); pap. text ed. 17.95 (*0-04-445048-6*) Routledge Chapman & Hall.

Understanding Space: An Introduction to Astronautics. Jerry Sellers & Wiley J. Larson. (Space Technology Ser.). 656p. 1995. pap. text ed. write for info. (*0-07-057027-2*) McGraw.

Understanding Spain. Julian Marias. Tr. by Frances M. Lopez-Morillas from SPA. 464p. (C). 1992. pap. text ed. 24.95 (*0-472-08188-8*) U of Mich Pr.

Understanding Spain. Julian Marias & Michigan University Press Staff. LC 89-77991. 462p. 1990. 32.50 (*0-8477-0888-8*) U of PR Pr.

Understanding Spanish Accounts: Language & Terminology. Peter Donaghy & John Laidler. Ed. by Silvano Levy. 128p. (Orig.). 1994. pap. 37.50 (*0-273-60308-6*, Pub. by Pitman Pub Ltd UK) Trans-Atl Phila.

***Understanding Specific Learning Difficulties.** Margot Prior. 192p. 1996. 45.00 (*0-86377-712-0*) L Erlbaum Assocs.

***Understanding Specific Learning Difficulties.** Margot Prior. 192p. 1996. pap. 21.50 (*0-86377-713-9*) L Erlbaum Assocs.

Understanding Spiritual Power: A Forgotten Dimension of Cross-Cultural Mission & Ministry. Marguerite G. Kraft. (American Society of Missiology Ser.: No. 22). 160p. (Orig.). 1995. pap. 16.95 (*1-57075-036-X*) Orbis Bks.

***Understanding Sport.** Garry Whannel et al. 224p. (Orig.). 1997. pap. text ed. 38.50 (*0-419-13640-1*, E & FN Spon) Routledge Chapman & Hall.

***Understanding Sport Behavior.** Pargman. (C). 1997. pap. text ed. 46.00 (*0-13-149196-2*) P-H.

Understanding Sport Organizations: The Application of Organizational Theory. Trevor Slack. LC 96-26111. (Illus.). 360p. (C). 1996. text ed. 38.00 (*0-87322-948-7*, BSLA0948) Human Kinetics.

Understanding Sports Massage. Patricia Benjamin. LC 95-49158. (Illus.). 168p. (Orig.). 1996. pap. text ed. 22.00 (*0-87322-976-2*, BBEN0976) Human Kinetics.

Understanding SQL. Martin Gruber. LC 89-51772. 434p. (Orig.). 1990. pap. 26.95 (*0-89588-644-8*) Sybex.

Understanding Staff Development. Graham Webb. 144p. 1996. 89.00 (*0-335-19289-0*, Open Univ Pr); pap. 32.00 (*0-335-19288-2*, Open Univ Pr) Taylor & Francis.

Understanding State Economies Through Industry Studies. John Redman. LC 94-5574. 1994. 15.95 (*0-934842-70-1*) CSPA.

Understanding Static Electricity. 2nd ed. (ABC Pocket Guide for the Field Ser.). (Illus.). 60p. (C). 1987. pap. text ed. 6.95 (*1-56016-035-7*) ABC TeleTraining.

Understanding Station Carrier. Kenneth C. Nelson. LC 73-85629. (Basic Ser.). (Illus.). 68p. (Orig.). (C). 1983. pap. 13.95 (*1-56016-005-5*) ABC TeleTraining.

Understanding Statistical Process Control. 2nd rev. ed. Donald J. Wheeler. (Illus.). 406p. (C). 1992. text ed. 45.00 (*0-945320-13-2*) SPC Pr.

Understanding Statistics. Chalmer. (Statistics: Textbooks & Monographs). 448p. 1986. 75.00 (*0-8247-7322-5*) Dekker.

Understanding Statistics. George G. Maltenfort. LC 92-28704. 128p. 1993. 62.00 (*0-9616302-8-0*) Jelmar Pub.

Understanding Statistics. 3rd ed. Gene Zirkel et al. (Illus.). 368p. (C). 1983. text ed. write for info. (*0-07-045863-4*) McGraw.

Understanding Statistics. 4th ed. Arnold Naiman & Robert Rosenfeld. 1996. student ed., pap. text ed. write for info. (*0-07-045996-7*) McGraw.

Understanding Statistics. 4th ed. Arnold Naiman et al. 1996. pap. text ed. write for info. (*0-07-045915-0*) McGraw.

Understanding Statistics. 4th ed. Robert R. Pagano. Date not set. teacher ed., pap. text ed. write for info. (*0-314-03371-8*) West Pub.

Understanding Statistics. 4th ed. Robert R. Pagano. Date not set. student ed., pap. text ed. 21.75 (*0-314-03707-1*) West Pub.

Understanding Statistics. 5th ed. R. Lyman Ott & William Mendenhall. 608p. (C). 1990. text ed. 52.95 (*0-534-92154-X*) Wadsworth Pub.

Understanding Statistics. 6th ed. William Mendenhall & R. Lyman Ott. 598p. 1994. text ed. 70.95 (*0-534-20922-X*) Wadsworth Pub.

Understanding Statistics. 6th ed. Ott & William Mendenhall. (Statistics Ser.). 1994. student ed., pap. 20.95 (*0-534-20924-6*) Wadsworth Pub.

Understanding Statistics: A Guide To Learning. 4th ed. Robert Herrmann. 1996. pap. text ed. write for info. (*0-07-028466-0*) McGraw.

Understanding Statistics: A Research Perspective. Robert E. McGrath. LC 96-557. (C). 1997. text ed. 57.95 (*0-673-99058-3*) Addson-Wesley Educ.

Understanding Statistics: An Informal Introduction for the Behavioral Sciences. R. L. Wright. (Illus.). 500p. (C). 1976. text ed. 40.00 (*0-15-592877-5*) HB Coll Pubs.

Understanding Statistics: An Introduction for the Social Sciences. Daniel B. Wright. 224p. 1996. 69.95 (*0-8039-7917-7*); pap. 22.95 (*0-8039-7918-5*) Sage.

Understanding Statistics in the Behavioral Sciences. 4th ed. Robert R. Pagano. Ed. by Clyde Perlee. LC 93-41157. 550p. (C). 1994. text ed. 61.50 (*0-314-02691-6*) West Pub.

***Understanding Statistics in the Behavioral Sciences.** 5th ed. Pagano. 1998. pap. 20.95 (*0-534-35392-4*); text ed. 59.95 (*0-534-35390-8*) Brooks-Cole.

Understanding Statutes. Justice Crabbe. 260p. 1995. pap. 50.00 (*1-85941-138-X*, Pub. by Cavendish UK) Gaunt.

Understanding Stepfamilies: Implications for Assessment and Treatment. Debra K. Huntley. LC 94-34581. (Family Ser.). 155p. 1995. pap. text ed. 17.95 (*1-55620-142-7*, 72590) Am Coun Assn.

***Understanding Strategic Interaction: Essays in Honor of Reinhard Selten.** Wulf Albers et al. LC 96-38555. (Illus.). 517p. 1996. 149.50 (*3-540-61490-7*) Spr-Verlag.

Understanding Street Gangs. Robert K. Jackson & Wesley D. McBride. LC 84-71475. (Illus.). 136p. (Orig.). (C). 1991. pap. 19.95 (*0-942728-17-3*) Copperhouse.

Understanding Stress. Robert S. Feldman. (Venture Bks.). (Illus.). 112p. (YA). (gr. 7-12). 1992. lib. bdg. 22.00 (*0-531-12531-9*) Watts.

Understanding Stress: A Psychological Perspective for Health Professionals. Cary L. Cooper & Valerie Sutherland. 250p. 1990. pap. 19.95 (*0-412-33930-7*, A4406) Chapman & Hall.

Understanding Stress Using Pointed Illustrations. Ivor L. Livingston & Shaffiran Livingston. (Illus.). 143p. 1994. pap. write for info. (*0-9631535-0-1*) I L Livingston.

Understanding Structural Cobol. 2nd ed. Boillot. Date not set. teacher ed., pap. text ed. 21.95 (*0-314-96598-X*) West Pub.

Understanding Structured COBOL. 2nd ed. Michel Boillot. LC 85-22719. (Illus.). 622p. (C). 1986. pap. text ed. 52.00 (*0-314-93155-4*) West Pub.

***Understanding Structured Programming Basic.** Susan K. Baumann. (DG - Computer Programming Ser.). 1991. text ed. 36.75 (*0-314-67029-7*) West Pub.

Understanding Structured Programming in BASIC, Apple Version. large type ed. Susan K. Baumann & Steven L. Mandell. 1991. 128.00 (*0-614-09878-5*, L-95703-00) Am Printing Hse.

Understanding Student Affairs Organizations. Ed. by George D. Kuh. LC 82-84205. (New Directions for Student Services Ser.: No. SS 23). 1983. 19.00 (*0-87589-971-4*) Jossey-Bass.

Understanding Student & Faculty Life. Leonard Baird & Rodney T. Hartnett. LC 79-24863. (Jossey-Bass Series in Higher Education). 217p. reprint ed. pap. 61.90 (*0-8357-4931-2*, 2037861) Bks Demand.

Understanding Stupidity: An Analysis of the Premaladaptive Beliefs & Behavior of Institutions & Organizations. 5th rev. ed. James F. Welles. 208p. 1995. pap. 8.95 (*0-9617729-0-5*) Mt Pleasant Pr.

Understanding Substance Abuse & Treatment. Ed. by George Pratsinak & Robert Alexander. 212p. (Orig.). 1992. pap. text ed. 26.25 (*0-929310-73-X*, 449) Am Correctional.

***Understanding Success & Failure.** Lois S. Roets. 36p. (YA). (gr. 5 up). 1997. 10.00 (*0-911943-51-X*) Leadership Pub.

Understanding Suicide: A Case Study Approach. David Lester. 221p. (C). 1994. lib. bdg. 79.00 (*1-56072-149-9*) Nova Sci Pubs.

Understanding Supernatural Dreams According to the Bible. David A. Castro. Ed. by Eddie Joe Irish. 286p. 1994. reprint ed. pap. 11.95 (*0-9637001-0-3*) D A Castro.

Understanding Supernatural Visions According to the Bible. David A. Castro. Ed. by Eddie Joe Irish. 122p. (Orig.). 1994. pap. 14.95 (*0-9637001-3-8*) D A Castro.

Understanding Support Networks & Community Care: Network Assessment for Elderly People. G. Clare Wenger. (Care in the Community Studies). 130p. 1994. 51.95 (*1-85628-667-3*, Pub. by Avebury Pub UK) Ashgate Pub Co.

Understanding Supreme Court Opinions. Tyll Van Geel. 143p. (Orig.). (C). 1991. pap. text ed. 29.50 (*0-8013-0308-7*, 78013) Longman.

Understanding Supreme Court Opinions. 2nd ed. T. R. Van Geel. (C). 1997. pap. text ed. 27.50 (*0-8013-1741-X*) Longman.

Understanding Swaps. John F. Marshall & Kenneth R. Kapner. (Finance Editions Ser.). 270p. 1993. text ed. 59.50 (*0-471-30827-7*) Wiley.

Understanding Sybase Sql Server 11 + Cdrom. Sridharan Kotta. (ITCP-US Computer Science Ser.). 1997. pap. 39.95 (*1-85032-852-8*) ITCP.

Understanding Symbolic Logic. 3rd ed. Virginia Klenk. LC 93-36598. 480p. 1994. text ed. 55.00 (*0-13-060767-3*) P-H.

Understanding Systems Failures. Victor Bignell & Joyce Fortune. LC 83-12016. 272p. 1988. text ed. 14.95 (*0-7190-0973-1*, Pub. by Manchester Univ Pr UK) St Martin.

Understanding Taligent Program. David Wilson. 1995. write for info. (*0-679-76189-6*) Random.

Understanding Tarot: A Practical Guide to Tarot Card Reading. Jocelyn Almond & Keith Seddon. (Illus.). 160p. 1992. pap. 9.00 (*1-85538-087-0*, Pub. by Aquarian Pr UK) Harper SF.

Understanding Teacher Development. Andy Hargreaves & Michael G. Fullan. (Teacher Development Ser.). 288p. (C). 1992. text ed. 44.00 (*0-8077-3189-7*); pap. text ed. 21.95 (*0-8077-3188-9*) Tchrs Coll.

Understanding Teacher Education: Case Studies in the Professional Development of Beginning Teachers. James Calderhead & Susan Shorrock. 240p. 1995. 69.95 (*0-7507-0398-9*, Falmer Pr); pap. 26.95 (*0-7507-0399-7*, Falmer Pr) Taylor & Francis.

Understanding Teacher Knowledge - In-Use. Catherine Cornbleth et al. (Special Studies in Teaching & Teacher Education: No. 6). 63p. (Orig.). (C). 1991. pap. text ed. 10.00 (*0-937033-24-3*) SUNY GSE Pubns.

An Asterisk (*) at the beginning of an entry indicates that the title is appearing in BIP for the first time.

Understanding Teaching. Kenneth O. Gangel. LC 68-24579. 96p. 1981. pap. text ed. 8.95 (*0-910566-14-3*) Evang Trg Assn.

Understanding Teaching. Kenneth O. Gangel. LC 68-24579. 90p. 1983. teacher ed., ring bd. 19.95 (*0-910566-26-7*) Evang Trg Assn.

Understanding Teaching: Beyond Expertise. John Olson. (Developing Teachers & Teaching Ser.). 160p. 1991. 90.00 (*0-335-09289-6*, Open Univ Pr); pap. 32.00 (*0-335-09288-8*, Open Univ Pr) Taylor & Francis.

Understanding Teaching: Continuity & Change in Teachers' Knowledge. William Louden. 224p. (C). 1991. text ed. 40.00 (*0-8077-3102-1*); pap. text ed. 18.95 (*0-8077-3101-3*) Tchrs Coll.

Understanding Technical Change: An Evolutionary Process. R. R. Nelson. (Lectures in Economics: Vol. 8). 126p. 1987. pap. 79.25 (*0-444-70207-5*, North Holland) Elsevier.

Understanding Technical Data Rights. 2nd ed. National Contract Management Association Staff. Ed. by Anne M. Rankin. (National Contract Management Association Workshop Ser.). 40p. 1993. pap. 10.95 (*0-940343-38-X*, TDRPG) Natl Contract Mgmt.

Understanding Technical English. R. Sundarsanam. 180p. (C). 1989. text ed. 25.00 (*81-207-0768-0*, Pub. by Sterling Pubs II) Apt Bks.

Understanding Technical English, 3 bks., Bk. 1. Keith Methold et al. (English As a Second Language Bk.). (Illus.). 60p. 1975. pap. text ed. 4.95 (*0-582-69032-3*) Longman.

Understanding Technical English, 3 bks., Bk. 2. Keith Methold et al. (English As a Second Language Bk.). (Illus.). 60p. 1975. pap. text ed. 4.95 (*0-582-69035-8*) Longman.

Understanding Technical English, 3 bks., Bk. 3. Keith Methold et al. (English As a Second Language Bk.). (Illus.). 60p. 1980. pap. text ed. 4.95 (*0-582-69036-6*) Longman.

Understanding Technological Change. Chris De Bresson. 400p. 1987. 39.95 (*0-920057-26-8*, Pub. by Black Rose Bks CN); pap. 19.95 (*0-920057-27-6*, Pub. by Black Rose Bks CN) Consort Bk Sales.

Understanding Technological Politics: A Decision-Making Approach. Patrick W. Hamlett. 264p. (C). 1991. pap. text ed. 23.80 (*0-13-947094-8*) P-H.

Understanding Technology. Wright & Smith. LC 88-31961. (Illus.). 312p. 1993. text ed. 33.28 (*0-87006-905-5*) Goodheart.

***Understanding Technology.** Thomas R. Wright & Bud H. Smith. LC 97-171. 312p. 1998. 34.60 (*1-56637-374-3*) Goodheart.

Understanding Technology. Charles Susskind. LC 72-12344. 175p. reprint ed. pap. 49.90 (*0-317-20640-0*, 2024131) Bks Demand.

Understanding Technology in Education. Ed. by Hughie Mackay & John Beynon. 272p. 1991. 65.00 (*1-85000-887-6*, Falmer Pr); pap. 27.00 (*1-85000-888-4*, Falmer Pr) Taylor & Francis.

Understanding Telecommunications. Ronald R. Thomas. 290p. (Orig.). 1989. 24.95 (*0-8306-9229-0*); pap. 17.95 (*0-8306-3229-8*) McGraw-Hill Prof.

Understanding Telecommunications & Lightwave Systems: An Entry-Level Guide. 2nd ed. John G. Nellist. LC 95-11535. 272p. 1995. pap. 34.95 (*0-7803-1113-2*, PP 4665) Inst Electrical.

***Understanding Telephone Electronics.** 3rd ed. Stephen J. Bigelow. 367p. 1997. pap. text ed. 24.95 (*0-7506-9944-2*) Buttrwrth-Heinemann.

Understanding Telephone Electronics. 3rd ed. John L. Fike et al. (Understanding Ser.). 367p. 1991. 24.95 (*0-672-27350-0*) Buttrwrth-Heinemann.

Understanding Television. Ed. by Andrew Goodwin & Garry Whannel. LC 89-10954. (Studies in Communication). (Illus.). 208p. (C). 1990. pap. text ed. 18.95 (*0-415-01672-X*, A4644) Routledge.

Understanding Television: Essays on Television As a Social & Cultural Force. Ed. by Richard Adler. LC 81-47781. 456p. 1981. text ed. 65.00 (*0-275-90575-6*, C0575, Praeger Pubs) Greenwood.

Understanding Television: Guidelines for Visual Literacy. 2nd ed. Gertruida M. Du Plooy. (Communicamus Ser.: Vol. 4). 111p. (C). 1994. reprint ed. text ed. 29.00 (*0-7021-2255-6*, Pub. by Juta & Co SA) Intl Spec Bk.

***Understanding Temperament: Strategies for Creating Family Harmony.** Lyndall Shick. 1997. 19.95 (*1-884734-33-2*); pap. text ed. 13.95 (*1-884734-32-4*) Parenting Pr.

Understanding Tendering & Estimating. A. A. Kwakye. 328p. 1994. 59.95 (*0-566-07490-7*, Pub. by Gower UK); pap. 24.95 (*0-566-07509-1*, Pub. by Gower UK) Ashgate Pub Co.

Understanding Tennessee Williams. Alice Griffin. LC 94-18690. (Understanding Contemporary America Literature Ser.). 288p. 1994. text ed. 29.95 (*1-57003-017-0*) U of SC Pr.

Understanding Terence. Sander M. Goldberg. LC 85-43285. 246p. reprint ed. pap. 70.20 (*0-8357-4286-5*, 2037085) Bks Demand.

Understanding Terrorism: Groups, Strategies, & Responses. James M. Poland. (Illus.). 288p. (C). 1988. pap. text ed. 43.00 (*0-13-936113-8*) P-H.

Understanding Testing in Occupational Licensing. Jim C. Fortune et al. LC 84-43026. (Jossey-Bass Social & Behavioral Science Ser.). 230p. reprint ed. pap. 65.60 (*0-7837-0167-5*, 2040464) Bks Demand.

Understanding Texas Insurance. Douglas Caddy. LC 83-40499. 180p. 1984. 16.95 (*0-89096-179-4*) Tex A&M Univ Pr.

Understanding Textiles. 5th ed. Phyllis G. Tortora & Billie J. Collier. LC 95-47801. 1996. text ed. 62.00 (*0-13-439225-6*, Merrill Pub Co) Macmillan.

Understanding the ABCs of Alzheimer's Disease: A Guide for Caregivers. Frances Oakley. (Illus.). 20p. (Orig.). 1993. pap. text ed. 6.00 (*0-910317-94-1*) Am Occup Therapy.

Understanding the Admissions Process in U. S. Higher Education: A Case Study Approach. Caroline Aldrich-Langen. LC 93-35556. (PIER World Education Series Special Report). 24p. 1993. pap. text ed. 25.00 (*0-929851-18-8*) Am Assn Coll Registrars.

Understanding the Adolescent. George H. Orvin. LC 95-24033. 224p. 1995. 21.95 (*0-88048-651-1*, 8651) Am Psychiatric.

Understanding the Air Force's Capability to Effectively Apply Advanced Distributed Simulation for Analysis: An Interim Report. Robert Kerchner et al. LC 96-22854. 1996. pap. 9.00 (*0-8330-2410-8*, MR-744-AF) Rand Corp.

Understanding the Alcoholic's Mind: The Nature of Craving & How to Control It. Arnold M. Ludwig. (Illus.). 240p. 1987. reprint ed. 25.00 (*0-19-504878-4*) OUP.

Understanding the Alcoholic's Mind: The Nature of Craving & How to Control It. Arnold M. Ludwig. (Illus.). 240p. 1989. reprint ed. pap. 12.95 (*0-19-505918-2*) OUP.

Understanding the Alphabets. Helen P. Singletary & Zebrena M. Glover. (Computers & Children Ser.: Bk. III). (Illus.). 59p. (Orig.). (J). (ps-6). 1991. pap. text ed. 20.00 (*1-880850-03-6*) Comp Trng Clinic.

***Understanding the AMA Guides in Workers' Compensation.** 2nd ed. Steven J. Babitsky. LC 96-39989. (Personal Injury Library). 1996. text ed. 125.00 (*0-471-15296-X*) Wiley.

Understanding the American Revolution: Issues & Actors. Jack P. Greene. LC 95-8292. 512p. (C). 1995. text ed. 68.50 (*0-8139-1608-9*); pap. text ed. 24.50 (*0-8139-1609-7*) U Pr of Va.

***Understanding the Amish.** Merle Good. (Illus.). 96p. 1997. pap. 9.95 (*1-56148-226-9*) Good Bks PA.

***Understanding the Amish.** Merle Good. (Illus.). 96p. 1997. 16.95 (*1-56148-230-7*) Good Bks PA.

Understanding the Anasazi of Mesa Verde & Hovenweep. Ed. by David G. Noble. LC 92-9279. Orig. Title: Tse Ya Kin. (Illus.). 40p. (Orig.). 1992. reprint ed. pap. 7.95 (*0-941270-71-8*) Ancient City Pr.

Understanding the Anointing. Kenneth E. Hagin. 1983. pap. 4.95 (*0-89276-507-0*) Hagin Ministries.

Understanding the Artificial: On the Future Shape of Artificial Intelligence. Ed. by M. Negrotti. (Artificial Intelligence & Society Ser.). (Illus.). xi, 164p. 1991. pap. 69.00 (*0-387-19612-9*) Spr-Verlag.

Understanding the Asian Manager. Hari Bedi. 192p. (Orig.). pap. 19.95 (*1-86373-029-X*, Pub. by Allen Unwin AT) Paul & Co Pubs.

Understanding the Atonement for the Mission of the Church. John Driver. LC 86-3133. 288p. (Orig.). 1986. pap. 19.99 (*0-8361-3403-6*) Herald Pr.

Understanding the Australian Legal System: A Book for First Time Law Students. 2nd ed. John Carvan. 138p. 1994. pap. 20.00 (*0-455-21282-1*, Pub. by Law Bk Co AT) Gaunt.

Understanding the Autopsy. Samuel B. Burgess. LC 92-74142. (Illus.). 224p. (Orig.). 1993. pap. 22.50 (*0-923687-26-2*) Celo Valley Bks.

Understanding the Beats. Edward H. Foster. Ed. by Matthew J. Bruccoli. LC 91-36122. (Understanding Contemporary American Literature Ser.). 248p. (C). 1992. text ed. 29.95 (*0-87249-798-4*) U of SC Pr.

Understanding the Beats. Edward H. Foster. 248p. (C). 1993. pap. 14.95 (*0-87249-878-6*) U of SC Pr.

Understanding the Bible. 3rd rev. ed. Stephen L. Harris. LC 91-33856. 489p. (C). 1992. pap. text ed. 31.95 (*1-55934-083-5*) Mayfield Pub.

Understanding the Bible. 4th rev. ed. Stephen L. Harris. LC 96-20085. 558p. (C). 1996. pap. text ed. 31.95 (*1-55934-655-8*, 1655) Mayfield Pub.

***Understanding the Bible: A Short Introduction to Biblical Interpretation.** George T. Montague. LC 97-22381. 1997. write for info. (*0-8091-3744-5*) Paulist Pr.

Understanding the Bible: Workbook. Paul A. Mirecki. 144p. (C). 1993. spiral bd. 27.24 (*0-8403-9247-8*) Kendall-Hunt.

Understanding the Bible According to Granny: Themes from Genesis. Susie M. Simpson. (Illus.). 133p. (J). (gr. 1 up). 1992. pap. 10.00 (*1-880892-46-4*) Com Sense FL.

Understanding the Biochemistry of Respiration. David James & Guy Matthews. (Illus.). 96p. (C). 1991. pap. text ed. 15.95 (*0-521-39993-9*) Cambridge U Pr.

Understanding the Bird of Prey: Their Biology, Behavior, Breeding, Captive Management, Rehabilitation, & Falconry Training. Nick Fox. 1995. 49.95 (*0-88839-317-2*) Hancock House.

Understanding the Black Family: A Guide for Scholarship & Research. Wade W. Nobles & Lawford L. Goddard. 137p. 1984. 10.00 (*0-939205-00-9*) Blk Fam Inst Pub.

Understanding the Black Mountain Poets. Edward H. Foster. LC 94-18677. (Understanding Contemporary American Literature Ser.). 224p. 1994. text ed. 29.95 (*1-57003-014-6*) U of SC Pr.

Understanding the Body of Christ: A Pauline Trilogy. Charles F. Baker. 161p. (C). 1985. text ed. 8.95 (*0-912340-04-5*) Grace Bible Coll.

Understanding the Body Organs: And the Eight Laws of Health. Celeste Lee. LC 94-60068. 128p. (YA). 1994. reprint ed. per. 7.95 (*0-945383-44-4*) Teach Servs.

Understanding the Book of Acts. Charles F. Baker. 182p. (C). 1981. text ed. 6.95 (*0-912340-03-7*) Grace Bible Coll.

Understanding the Book of Revelation. Bonell McBroom, Sr. 128p. 1995. pap. text ed. write for info. (*0-9648274-0-9*) D E McBroom.

Understanding the Bottom Line. Randolph Pohlman. (Productivity Ser.). (Illus.). 100p. (Orig.). 1991. pap. 9.95 (*1-55852-034-1*) Natl Pr Pubns.

Understanding the Bottom Line. 2nd ed. Ed. by Career Press Staff. (Business Desk Reference Ser.). 128p. 1993. pap. 8.95 (*1-56414-108-X*) Career Pr Inc.

Understanding the Bottom Line: Finance for Non-Financial Managers & Supervisors. Randolph Pohlman. 1991. pap. 7.95 (*1-55852-057-0*) Natl Pr Pubns.

Understanding the Brain & Its Development: A Chemical Approach. Harun K. Yusuf. 400p. (C). 1992. pap. 37.00 (*981-02-0492-2*); text ed. 114.00 (*9971-5-0756-0*) World Scientific Pub.

Understanding the Brain Through the Hippocampus: The Hippocampal Region As a Model for Studying Brain Structure & Function. Jon Storm-Mathisen et al. Ed. by J. Zimmer & Ole P. Ottersen. (Progress in Brain Research Ser.: No. 83). 488p. 1990. 290.75 (*0-444-81149-4*) Elsevier.

***Understanding the Building Regulations.** Polley. (Illus.). 208p. (Orig.). 1995. pap. text ed. 24.00 (*0-419-19950-0*, E & FN Spon) Routledge Chapman & Hall.

Understanding the Business, Bankruptcy & Securities Aspects of Derivatives. (Commercial Law & Practice Course Handbook Ser.). Date not set. pap. 99.00 (*0-614-17159-8*, A4-4492) PLI.

Understanding the Business of Advertising. Hiroshi Ishii & Robert N. St. Clair. 130p. (Orig.). 1996. pap. 21.75 (*0-935563-00-8*) Social Sys Pr.

Understanding the Business of Library Acquisitions. Ed. by Karen A. Schmidt. LC 90-33772. (Illus.). 336p. 1990. reprint ed. pap. 95.80 (*0-608-01736-1*, 2062393) Bks Demand.

Understanding the Canadian Economy: A Problems Approach to Economic Principles. Roy George. 252p. 1988. pap. text ed. 22.95 (*0-921149-17-4*) Broadview Pr.

Understanding the Cat You Love: A Guide to Preventing & Solving Behavior Problems in Your Cat. Mordecai Siegal. 224p. (Orig.). 1994. mass mkt. 4.99 (*0-425-14498-4*) Berkley Pub.

Understanding the Cell. Denson K. McLain. LC 94-72550. (Illus.). 126p. (Orig.). (C). 1994. pap. 12.99 (*1-884612-01-6*) AudioText.

Understanding the Census: A Guide for Marketers, Planners, Grant Writers & Other Data Users. Michael R. Lavin. LC 92-74697. (Illus.). 535p. (Orig.). 1996. pap. 49.95 (*0-9629586-1-1*) Epoch Bks.

Understanding the Census: A Guide for Marketers, Planners, Grant-Writers & Other Data Users. Michael R. Lavin. 560p. 1996. boxed 59.95 (*0-89774-995-2*) Oryx Pr.

Understanding the Central American Crisis: Sources of Conflict, U. S. Policy, & Options for Peace. Ed. by Kenneth M. Coleman & George C. Herring. LC 91-2974. (Latin American Silhouettes Ser.). 240p. 1991. 40.00 (*0-8420-2382-8*) Scholarly Res Inc.

Understanding the Chambon. Ed. by Hilary Legard & Elizabeth Launder. 88p. (C). 1990. 21.00 (*0-85131-439-2*, Pub. by J A Allen & Co UK) St Mut.

Understanding the Chemistry & Physics of Anesthesia. Stanley Hall et al. 400p. 1996. write for info. (*0-683-03828-1*) Williams & Wilkins.

Understanding the Chicano Experience Through Literature. 2nd ed. write for info. (*0-614-06972-6*) Univ Houston Mex Amer.

Understanding the Chinese Mind: The Philosophical Roots. Ed. by Robert E. Allinson. 328p. 1989. 29.95 (*0-685-47313-9*) OUP.

Understanding the Chinese Mind: The Philosophical Roots. Ed. by Robert E. Allinson. 322p. 1990. reprint ed. pap. 18.95 (*0-19-585022-X*) OUP.

Understanding the Christian Faith. Charles D. Barrett. (Illus.). 1980. text ed. write for info. (*0-13-935882-X*) P-H.

Understanding the Christian Faith. Georgia Harkness. (Abingdon Classics Ser.). 192p. 1992. reprint ed. pap. 2.38 (*0-687-42805-X*) Abingdon.

***Understanding the CISG in Europe: A Compact Guide to the 1980 United Nations Convention on Contracts for the International Sale of Goods.** Herbert Bernstein & Joseph M. Lookofsky. LC 96-6526. 1997. write for info. (*90-411-0951-X*) Kluwer Law Tax Pubs.

Understanding the CISG in the U. S. A. A Compact Guide to the 1980 United Nations Convention on Contracts for the International Sale of Goods. Joseph Lookofsky. LC 95-36819. 1995. write for info. (*90-411-0956-0*) Kluwer Law Tax Pubs.

Understanding the Cold War. Howard Roffman. LC 75-5251. 198p. (C). 1976. 29.50 (*0-8386-1740-9*) Fairleigh Dickinson.

Understanding the Competition: A Practical Guide to Competitive Analysis. Kaiser Associates, Inc. Staff. 180p. 1991. 155.00 (*1-56365-019-3*) Wash Res.

Understanding the Concept of Empathy & Its Foundations in Psychoanalysis. Renuka M. Sharma. LC 93-34149. 132p. 1993. text ed. 69.95 (*0-7734-9375-1*) E Mellen.

Understanding the Constitution. 2nd ed. J. W. Peltason. 512p. (C). 1997. pap. text ed. 17.00 (*0-15-599717-3*) HB Coll Pubs.

Understanding the Constitution. 12th ed. Jack W. Peltason. 398p. (C). 1991. pap. text ed. 18.75 (*0-15-592869-4*) HB Coll Pubs.

Understanding the Constitution. 13th ed. Jack W. Peltason. 432p. (C). 1994. pap. text ed. 20.00 (*0-15-500721-1*) HarBrace.

***Understanding the Consumer Interest in the New Biotechnology Industry.** (Illus.). 53p. (Orig.). 1996. pap. 25.00 (*0-7881-3327-6*) DIANE Pub.

Understanding the Control of Metabolism. Keith Snell. (Frontiers in Metabolism Ser.: No. 2). (Illus.). 300p. (Orig.). (C). 1996. pap. 32.20 (*1-85578-047-X*, Pub. by Portland Pr Ltd UK) Ashgate Pub Co.

Understanding the Creative Activity of Students. Robert J. Kirschenbaum. 58p. 1989. pap. 14.95 (*0-936386-50-9*) Creative Learning.

Understanding the Crisis in the Persian Gulf. Peter Cipkowski. LC 91-39259. 192p. (J). 1992. pap. text ed. 12.95 (*0-471-54816-2*) Wiley.

Understanding the Dead Sea Scrolls: A Reader. Ed. by Hershel Shanks. LC 92-50614. 1993. pap. 13.00 (*0-679-74445-2*, Vin) Random.

Understanding the Developing Metropolis: Lessons from the City Study of Bogota & Cali, Colombia. Rakesh Mohan. (World Bank Publication). 344p. 1994. text ed. 32.95 (*0-19-520882-X*) OUP.

Understanding the Difficult Words of Jesus. David Bivin & Roy Blizzard. 160p. (Orig.). 1994. pap. 9.99 (*1-56043-550-X*) Destiny Image.

Understanding the Dispensation. Dwight McDaniel. 125p. 1993. pap. text ed. 9.95 (*1-883866-00-6*) Clarion Pub.

Understanding the Dog You Love: A Guide to Preventing & Solving Behavior Problems in Your Dog. Mordecai Siegal. 240p. (Orig.). 1994. mass mkt. 5.50 (*0-425-14234-5*) Berkley Pub.

Understanding the Dollar Crisis. enl. ed. Percy L. Greaves, Jr. LC 84-148895. 332p. (gr. 11-12). 1984. reprint ed. 14.00 (*0-930902-02-5*); reprint ed. pap. 7.00 (*0-930902-03-3*) Free Market.

Understanding the Dreams You Dream. Ira Milligan. 280p. (Orig.). 1993. pap. 9.99 (*1-56043-761-8*) Destiny Image.

***Understanding the Dreams You Dream.** rev. ed. Iraa Milligan & Judy Milligan. 1997. pap. 9.99 (*1-56043-284-5*) Destiny Image.

Understanding the E-Meter. L. Ron Hubbard. 222p. 1988. 50.00 (*0-88404-265-0*) Bridge Pubns Inc.

Understanding the Earth. Ed. by Geoffrey C. Brown et al. (Illus.). 450p. (C). 1992. text ed. 140.00 (*0-521-37020-5*); pap. text ed. 49.95 (*0-521-42740-1*) Cambridge U Pr.

Understanding the Earth. Frank Press & Raymond Siever. LC 93-4967. (C). 1995. pap. text ed. write for info. (*0-7167-2239-9*) W H Freeman.

Understanding the Eastern Caribbean & the Antilles, with Checklists Appended. Nelson Marshall. (Illus.). 252p. (Orig.). 1992. pap. write for info. (*0-9628730-0-4*) Th Anchorage.

Understanding the Economy. Mark Brownrigg. (C). 1990. pap. text ed. 37.50 (*0-201-41690-5*) Addison-Wesley.

***Understanding the Effects of Neuropharmacological Agents on Communication Disorders in Adults & Children.** Deanie Vogul & Louise Zingeser. (Illus.). 45p. (C). 1996. ring bd. 45.00 incl. audio (*0-910329-94-X*, 0112020) Am Speech Lang Hearing.

Understanding the Elements of Literature. Richard H. Taylor. LC 81-9295. 256p. 1982. text ed. 24.95 (*0-312-83216-8*) St Martin.

Understanding the Emotionally Depleted Woman. Anne Bowie & P. S. Bowie. LC 95-77815. 221p. 1996. pap. 12.95 (*0-9646913-0-2*) Gldn Quill NV.

Understanding the Enneagram: The Practical Guide to Personality Types. Don R. Riso. (Illus.). 224p. 1990. pap. 12.95 (*0-395-52148-3*) HM.

Understanding the Enterprise Culture: Themes in the Work of Mary Douglas. Ed. by Shaun H. Heap & Angus Ross. (Illus.). 240p. 1992. 49.50 (*0-7486-0323-9*, Pub. by Edinburgh U Pr UK) Col U Pr.

Understanding the Essay. 2nd ed. Ed. by Edward O. Shakespeare et al. 1978. teacher ed. 6.96 (*0-88334-109-3*, 76086); student ed. 9.60 (*0-8013-0104-1*, 75768) Longman.

Understanding the Essay. 3rd ed. Ed. by Edward O. Shakespeare et al. 262p. 1992. pap. 16.57 (*0-8013-0758-9*, 78787) Longman.

Understanding the European Communities. William Nicoll & Trevor C. Salmon. (Illus.). 260p. (C). 1990. pap. 25.50 (*0-86003-709-6*); lib. bdg. 64.50 (*0-389-20912-0*) B&N Imports.

***Understanding the Evolution of Yes!, Pt. 2.** Allan C. Somersall. (Evolution of Yes! Ser.). 250p. 1997. 18.95 (*1-890412-84-8*, 049) Glden Eight Intl.

Understanding the Fabian Essays in Socialism (1889) Clive E. Hill. LC 95-18520. (Studies in British History: Vol. 37). 488p. 1996. text ed. 109.95 (*0-7734-8880-4*) E Mellen.

Understanding the Family. Ed. by John Muncie et al. 320p. 1995. 65.00 (*0-8039-7954-1*) Sage.

Understanding the Family. Ed. by John Muncie et al. 320p. 1995. pap. 21.95 (*0-8039-7955-X*) Sage.

Understanding the Farmers Comprehensive Personal Liability Policy: A Guide for Farmers, Attorneys & Insurance Agents. John D. Copeland. 150p. 1992. pap. 25.00 (*1-882461-00-2*) Natl Ctr Agricult LR&I.

Understanding the Feasts of the Lord, God's Time Clock for the Ages. Roger V. Houtsma. 195p. (Orig.). 1986. pap. 6.95 (*0-9617623-0-6*) World Outreach.

***Understanding the Federal Debt & Deficit.** 1996. lib. bdg. 253.95 (*0-8490-6595-X*) Gordon Pr.

Understanding the Federal Income Tax: A Lawyer's Guide to the Code & Its Provisions. LC 87-73312. 280p. 1988. pap. 39.95 (*0-89707-338-X*, 515-0079-01) Amer Bar Assn.

***Understanding the Federal Retirement Systems.** (Illus.). 58p. (Orig.). (C). 1996. pap. text ed. 9.95 (*0-936295-70-8*) FPMI Comns.

Understanding the FFT: A Tutorial on the Algorithm & Software for Laymen, Students, Technicians & Working Engineers. Anders E. Zonst. LC 95-67942. (Illus.). 180p. (Orig.). (C). 1995. pap. text ed. 29.95 (*0-9645681-8-7*) Citrus Pr.

UV

Understanding the Filipino. Tomas D. Andres & Pilar B. Ilada-Andres. xii, 184p. (Orig.). 1987. pap. 15.00 (*971-10-0337-6*, Pub. by New Day Pub PH) Cellar.

Understanding the Film. 4th ed. Ron Johnson & Jan Bone. 304p. 1995. pap. 24.95 (*0-8442-5694-3*, Natl Textbk) NTC Pub Grp.

Understanding the Film: An Introduction to Film Appreciation. 5th rev. ed. Jan Bone & Ron Johnson. LC 96-13299. 352p. 1996. pap. 29.95 (*0-8442-5797-4*) NTC Pub Grp.

Understanding the Former Prisoner of War: Life after Liberation. Guy Kelnhofer, Jr. Ed. by Amy Lindgren. (Illus.). 196p. (C). 1992. pap. 19.95 (*0-9633008-1-4*, Banfil Street Pr); text ed. 29.95 (*0-9633008-0-6*, Banfil Street Pr) Prototype Career Pr.

Understanding the Fourth Gospel. John Ashton. 624p. (C). 1993. reprint ed. pap. 35.00 (*0-19-826353-8*, 14080) OUP.

Understanding the Free Trade Agreement. Ed. by Donald M. McRae & Debra P. Steger. 254p. 1989. pap. text ed. 23.95 (*0-88645-079-9*, Pub. by Inst Res Pub CN) Ashgate Pub Co.

Understanding the French Revolution. Albert Soboul. Ed. by Betty Smith. Tr. by April A. Knutson from FRE. LC 88-1215. 346p. (Orig.). 1988. reprint ed. pap. 10.95 (*0-7178-0658-8*) Intl Pubs Co.

Understanding the Gender Gap: An Economic History of American Women. Claudia D. Goldin. (National Bureau of Economic Research Ser.). (Illus.). 336p. (C). 1992. reprint ed. pap. text ed. 25.50 (*0-19-507270-7*) OUP.

Understanding the Gift of Life. Michael H. Moler. (Orig.). 1996. pap. write for info. (*1-57553-252-2*) Watermrk Pr.

Understanding the Gifted Adolescent. Ed. by Marlene Bireley & Judy Genshaft. (Education & Psychology of the Gifted Ser.: No. 5). 296p. (C). 1991. pap. text ed. 22.95 (*0-8077-3072-6*) Tchrs Coll.

Understanding the Gospel of John. Arthur H. Maynard. LC 91-37589. 100p. 1991. lib. bdg. 59.95 (*0-7734-9640-8*) E Mellen.

Understanding the Gospels. Charles F. Baker. 324p. 1994. 10.99 (*0-89814-044-7*) Grace Publns.

*__Understanding the GPS: An Introduction to the Global Positioning System.__ Gregory T. French. (Illus.). 300p. (Orig.). 1996. pap. 44.95 (*0-9655723-0-7*); pap. 44.95 (*0-614-25091-9*) GeoResearch.

Understanding the Greek Orthodox Church: Its Faith, History & Practice. Demetrios J. Constantelos. LC 90-22863. 220p. (Orig.). (C). 1990. pap. 14.95 (*0-917653-39-4*) Hellenic Coll Pr.

Understanding the Gyroplane. Paul B. Abbott. 120p. 1994. pap. text ed. 14.95 (*1-888723-01-7*) Abbott Co.

Understanding the Gyroplane. 2nd ed. Paul C. Abbott. (Illus.). 85p. 1994. pap. 14.95 (*0-916413-21-7*) Aviation.

*__Understanding the Healing Power of God! How to Get It & What to Do with It Once You've Got It.__ Douglas E. Jones. vii, 132p. (Orig.). 1997. pap. write for info. (*0-9657595-0-4*) Doug Jones.

Understanding the History & Records of Non-Conformity. (C). 1987. 30.00 (*0-317-89833-7*, Pub. by Birmingham Midland Soc UK) St Mut.

*__Understanding the Holy Spirit.__ Charles H. Spurgeon & G. Campbell Morgan. (Bible Sermon Ser.: Pulpit Legends Colletions). 351p. 14.99 (*0-89957-210-3*) AMG Pubs.

Understanding the Holy Spirit. G. Campbell Morgan & Charles H. Spurgeon. (Classic Library). 500p. 1995. reprint ed. 19.99 (*0-529-10482-2*, UHS) World Publng.

Understanding the Human Being: The Importance of the First Three Years of Life. Silvana Q. Montanaro. (Illus.). 166p. (Orig.). (C). 1991. pap. text ed. 14.95 (*1-879341-00-X*) N Montessori.

*__Understanding the Human Body.__ E. R. Tudor & E. M. Tudor. Date not set. pap. text ed. write for info. (*0-85896-260-8*) Addison-Wesley.

*__Understanding the I Ching.__ Cyrille Javary. LC 96-52862. 128p. 1997. pap. 10.00 (*1-57062-227-2*) Shambhala Pubns.

Understanding the I Ching: The History & Use of the World's Most Ancient System of Divination. Tom Riseman. 1990. pap. 8.00 (*0-85030-985-9*, Pub. by Aquarian Pr UK) Thorsons SF.

Understanding the I Ching: The Wilhelm Lectures on the Book of Changes. H. Wilhelm & R. Wilhelm. Tr. by C. F. Baynes & I. Eber. LC 94-37282. 308p. 1995. pap. text ed. 13.95 (*0-691-00171-5*) Princeton U Pr.

Understanding the Immune System. Lydia W. Schindler. (Illus.). 51p. 1994. pap. text ed. 20.00 (*0-7881-1519-7*) DIANE Pub.

Understanding the Immune System: The Immune System in the Human Body & How It Works. 1984. lib. bdg. 250.00 (*0-87700-620-2*) Revisionist Pr.

Understanding the Infinite. Shaughan Lavine. LC 93-49697. (Illus.). 376p. 1994. text ed. 39.95 (*0-674-92096-1*) HUP.

Understanding the Internet: An SLA Information Kit. Special Libraries Association Staff. 94p. 1996. pap. 20.00 (*0-87111-460-7*) SLA.

Understanding the IRS Separate Lines of Business Regulations. 56p. 1992. pap. 10.00 (*0-685-67051-1*, 4817) Commerce.

Understanding the Japanese Food & Agrimarket: A Multifaceted Opportunity. Ed. by A. Desmond O'Rourke. LC 92-20076. (Illus.). 212p. 1994. lib. bdg. 49.95 (*1-56022-029-5*) Haworth Jrnl Co-Edits.

Understanding the Japanese Mind. James C. Moloney. LC 68-23316. 252p. 1968. reprint ed. text ed. 35.00 (*0-8371-0172-7*, MOJM, Greenwood Pr) Greenwood.

Understanding the Jewish Calendar. Nathan Bushwick. 114p. (YA). (gr. 9-12). 1989. 11.00 (*0-940118-17-3*) Moznaim.

Understanding the L. A. R. E. 3rd ed. Ed. by Elizabeth A. Isbell. (Illus.). 224p. (Orig.). 1994. pap. 94.95 (*1-882998-03-0*); pap. 119.90 incl. vhs (*1-882998-05-7*) Coun Lndscape.

Understanding the Land of the Bible: A Biblical-Theological Guide. O. Palmer Robertson. LC 96-33675. (Illus.). 160p. (Orig.). 1996. pap. 9.99 (*0-87552-399-4*, Pub. by Evangelical Pr) Presby & Reformed.

Understanding the Language of Medicine: A Programmed Learning Text. Patricia J. Bernthal & James D. Spiller. (Illus.). 318p. (C). 1981. pap. text ed. 27.50 (*0-19-502879-1*) OUP.

Understanding the Language of the Metric System: A Guide to the Use of Metric Units. Herbert R. Streb. LC 95-90857. (Illus.). 75p. (Orig.). 1996. pap. 8.95 (*0-533-11701-1*) Vantage.

Understanding the Law. Donald L. Carper et al. Ed. by Clyde Perlee. 536p. (C). 1991. text ed. 43.75 (*0-314-80723-3*) West Pub.

*__Understanding the Law.__ 2nd ed. Carper. (LA - Business Law Ser.). (C). Date not set. text ed. 48.95 (*0-538-88549-1*) S-W Pub.

Understanding the Law. 2nd ed. Donald L. Carper et al. 762p. (C). 1995. text ed. 48.75 (*0-314-04520-1*) West Pub.

Understanding the Law: A Handbook on Educating the Public. Charles J. White et al. LC 84-164846. (Illus.). 232p. 1983. pap. 9.95 (*0-89707-111-5*, 468-0003) Amer Bar Assn.

Understanding the Law: Principles, Problems & Potentials of the American Legal System. Art Wolfe et al. LC 94-32592. 656p. (C). 1995. text ed. 53.25 (*0-314-04580-5*) West Pub.

Understanding the Liver: A History. Thomas S. Chen & Peter S. Chen. LC 83-22631. (Contributions in Medical History Ser.: No. 14). (Illus.). xiii, 293p. 1984. text ed. 69.50 (*0-313-23472-8*, CLV/, Greenwood Pr) Greenwood.

*__Understanding the Mafia.__ Joseph Farrell. LC 97-12985. (Manchester Italian Texts Ser.). 1997. text ed. write for info. (*0-7190-4900-8*, Pub. by Manchester Univ Pr UK); text ed. 19.95 (*0-7190-5171-1*, Pub. by Manchester Univ Pr UK) St Martin.

Understanding the Main Idea: Advanced Level. 2nd ed. Ed. by Kraft. (Comprehension Skills Ser.). 64p. 1993. pap. 8.45 (*0-89061-611-6*) Jamestown Pubs.

Understanding the Main Idea: Introductory Level. Ed. by Kraft. (Comprehension Skills Ser.). 64p. 1993. pap. 7.91 (*0-89061-651-5*) Jamestown Pubs.

Understanding the Main Idea: Middle Level. 2nd ed. Ed. by Kraft. (Comprehension Skills Ser.). 64p. 1993. pap. 8.31 (*0-89061-631-0*) Jamestown Pubs.

Understanding the Male Hustler. Samuel M. Steward. 150p. 1991. pap. 9.95 (*0-918393-96-5*) Harrington Pk.

Understanding the Male Hustler. Samuel M. Steward. 150p. 1991. pap. 29.95 (*1-56024-111-X*) Haworth Pr.

Understanding the Male Temperament: What Every Man Would Like to Tell His Wife about Himself...But Won't. 2nd rev. ed. Tim LaHaye. LC 95-40963. (Illus.). 288p. (gr. 10). 1996. 15.99 (*0-8007-1719-8*) Revell.

Understanding the Man in Your Life. H. Norman Wright. 212p. 1989. pap. 10.99 (*0-8499-3188-6*) Word Pub.

Understanding the Manufacturing Process: Key to Successful CAD-CAM Implementation. Harrington. (Manufacturing Engineering & Materials Processing Ser.: Vol. 12). 240p. 1984. 75.00 (*0-8247-7170-2*) Dekker.

Understanding the Many Faces of the Culture of Higher Education. Ed. by James J. Van Patten. LC 93-26177. 1993. write for info. (*0-7734-9317-4*) E Mellen.

Understanding the Market Economy. Arne J. Isachsen et al. LC 92-24790. (Illus.). 256p. (C). 1993. pap. 19.95 (*0-19-877357-9*) OUP.

Understanding the Mass. Charles Belmonte. 1997. pap. 9.95 (*0-933932-89-8*) Scepter Pubs.

*__Understanding the Mass.__ Maynard Kolodziej. 80p. (Orig.). 1997. pap. 2.95 (*0-89942-106-7*, 106/04) Catholic Bk Pub.

Understanding the Mass. rev. ed. Maynard Kolodziej. 80p. 1987. pap. 1.50 (*1-55805-000-0*) Franc Pubs WI.

*__Understanding the Master's Voice.__ Patricia B. Gruits. 277p. 1994. 14.95 (*0-9639461-2-9*) PeterPat Pubs.

Understanding the Mathematics Teacher: A Study of Practice in First Schools. Charles Desforges & Anne D. Cockburn. 180p. 1987. 55.00 (*1-85000-212-6*, Falmer Pr); pap. 28.00 (*1-85000-213-4*, Falmer Pr) Taylor & Francis.

Understanding the Media: A Sociology of Mass Communication. Joel Smith. Ed. by Lee Becker. LC 95-3103. (Communication Series). 384p. 1995. text ed. 72.50 (*1-57273-004-8*) Hampton Pr NJ.

Understanding the Media: A Sociology of Mass Communication. Joel Smith. Ed. by Lee Becker. LC 95-3103. (Communication Series). 384p. 1995. pap. text ed. 28.50 (*1-57273-005-6*) Hampton Pr NJ.

Understanding the Media: Practical Guide. Andrew W. Hart. (Illus.). 272p. (C). 1991. pap. 22.95 (*0-415-05713-2*, Routledge NY) Routledge.

*__Understanding the Medical Diagnosis of Child Maltreatment: A Guide for the NonMedical Professional.__ 2nd rev. ed. Jean C. Smith et al. (Illus.). iv, 144p. 1997. pap. text ed. write for info. (*0-930915-02-X*, CMD02) Am Humane Assn.

*__Understanding the Mentally Disordered Offenders: A Multi-Agency Perspective.__ Anthony Colombo. (Welfare & Society Ser.). (Illus.). 236p. 1997. text ed. 55.95 (*1-85972-689-5*, Pub. by Avebury Pub UK) Ashgate Pub Co.

*__Understanding the Mind: An Explanation of the Nature & Functions of the Mind.__ 2nd ed. Geshe Kelsang Gyatso. (Illus.). 320p. pap. 19.95 (*0-948006-54-4*, Pub. by Tharpa Pubns UK) ACCESS Pubs Network.

*__Understanding the Mind: An Explanation of the Nature & Functions of the Mind.__ 2nd ed. Geshe Kelsang Gyatso. (Illus.). 320p. 1997. 24.95 (*0-948006-53-6*, Pub. by Tharpa Pubns UK) ACCESS Pubs Network.

Understanding the Mother of Jesus. Eamon R. Carroll. 106p. 1989. pap. 22.00 (*0-89453-101-8*, Pub. by Veritas IE) St Mut.

Understanding the Multicultural Experience in Early Childhood Education. Ed. by Olivia N. Saracho & Bernard Spodek. LC 83-60866. 158p. 1983. pap. text ed. 5.50 (*0-912674-84-9*, NAEYC #125) Natl Assn Child Ed.

Understanding the Musical Experience. Ed. by E. Joseph Smith. (Monographs on Musicology: Vol. 8). 230p. 1989. text ed. 57.00 (*2-88124-204-9*) Gordon & Breach.

Understanding the National Curriculum. Anthony Harnett et al. 162p. 1994. text ed. 55.00 (*0-304-32324-1*); pap. text ed. 18.95 (*0-304-32327-6*) Cassell.

Understanding the National Electric Code. 2nd ed. Michael Holt. (Electrical Trades Ser.). 208p. (C). 1996. wbk. ed., pap. 19.95 (*0-8273-6732-5*) Delmar.

Understanding the National Electric Code. 2nd ed. Michael Holt. (Electrical Trades Ser.). 1996. teacher ed. 19.95 (*0-8273-6806-2*) Delmar.

Understanding the National Electric Code. 2nd ed. Michael Holt. LC 95-21402. (Electrical Trades (w-o Electro) Ser.). 432p. (C). 1996. text ed. 35.00 (*0-8273-6805-4*) Delmar.

Understanding the National Electric Code - CTB. Michael Holt. (Electrical Trades Ser.). 1993. 72.95 (*0-8273-5931-4*) Delmar.

Understanding the National Electrical Code: Instructor's Guide. Michael Holt. 112p. 1993. 17.50 (*0-8273-5329-4*) Delmar.

Understanding the National Electrical Code, 1993 Edition. Charles M. Holt. LC 92-11315. 1993. pap. 31.50 (*0-8273-5328-6*) Delmar.

Understanding the National Electrical Code, 1993 Edition. Charles M. Holt. LC 92-11315. 1993. trans. 147.00 (*0-8273-5614-5*) Delmar.

*__Understanding the National Health Service Reforms: The Creation of Incentives?__ Peter A. West. (State of Health Ser.). 1997. write for info. (*0-335-19244-0*, Open Univ Pr); pap. write for info. (*0-335-19243-2*, Open Univ Pr) Taylor & Francis.

Understanding the Nature of Poverty in Urban America. James Jennings. LC 94-16111. 224p. 1994. text ed. 55.00 (*0-275-94953-2*, Praeger Pubs); pap. text ed. 18.95 (*0-275-94984-2*, Praeger Pubs) Greenwood.

Understanding the Nature of Small Business Module, PACE: A Program for Acquiring Competence in Entrepreneurship, 3 levels. rev. ed. National Center for Research in Vocational Education Staff. 1983. Level 1. write for info. (*0-318-67190-5*, RD240AB1) Ctr Educ Trng Employ.

Understanding the Nature of Small Business Module, PACE: A Program for Acquiring Competence in Entrepreneurship, 3 levels, Level 1. rev. ed. National Center for Research in Vocational Education Staff. 1983. 6.50 (*0-317-06086-4*, RD240AB1) Ctr Educ Trng Employ.

Understanding the Nature of Small Business Module, PACE: A Program for Acquiring Competence in Entrepreneurship, 3 levels, Level 2. rev. ed. National Center for Research in Vocational Education Staff. 1983. 6.50 (*0-317-06087-2*, RD240BB1) Ctr Educ Trng Employ.

Understanding the Nature of Small Business Module, PACE: A Program for Acquiring Competence in Entrepreneurship, 3 levels, Level 3. rev. ed. National Center for Research in Vocational Education Staff. 1983. 6.50 (*0-318-67191-3*, RD240CB1) Ctr Educ Trng Employ.

Understanding the NEC - Testmaker. 2nd ed. Michael Holt. (Electrical Trades Ser.). 1996. text ed. 69.95 (*0-8273-6755-4*) Delmar.

Understanding the NEC Workbook. 1,993th ed. Michael Holt. 197p. 1993. pap. 18.95 (*0-8273-5515-7*) Delmar.

*__Understanding the NEC 2E Transparency Masters.__ Holt. 128p. 1996. 12.95 (*0-8273-8374-6*) Delmar.

Understanding the Nervous System: An Engineering Perspective. Sid Deutsch & Alice Deutsch. LC 92-49854. (Illus.). 408p. (C). 1993. pap. 34.95 (*0-87942-296-3*, PP0291-5) Inst Electrical.

Understanding the Neurotransmitters: Key to the Workings of the Brain. W. Birkmayer & P. Riederer. (Illus.). 160p. 1989. 35.95 (*0-387-82100-7*) Spr-Verlag.

Understanding the New Age. Russell Chandler. 368p. 1993. pap. 10.99 (*0-310-38561-X*) Zondervan.

Understanding the New Economy. Alfred L. Malabre, Jr. 200p. 1988. text ed. 30.00 (*1-55623-117-2*) Irwin Prof Pubng.

Understanding the New Politics of Abortion. Ed. by Malcolm L. Goggin. LC 93-17610. (Illus.). 320p. (C). 1993. 52.00 (*0-8039-5240-6*); pap. 25.50 (*0-8039-5241-4*) Sage.

Understanding the New SQL: A Complete Guide. Jim Melton & Alan Simon. 586p. 1992. pap. 44.95 (*1-55860-245-3*) Morgan Kaufmann.

*__Understanding the New SQL/PSM: A Complete Guide.__ 2nd ed. Jim Melton. 400p. (Orig.). 1997. pap. 29.95 (*1-55860-461-8*) Morgan Kaufmann.

Understanding the New Testament. Stephen Doyle. LC 88-82197. (Catholic Home Library). (Illus.). 128p. 1989. 4.95 (*1-55944-000-7*) Franciscan Comns.

Understanding the New Testament. Vahan H. Tootikian. 304p. 1991. 25.00 (*0-8187-0137-4*) Harlo Press.

Understanding the New Testament. 5th ed. Howard C. Kee. LC 92-16133. 432p. 1993. text ed. 58.00 (*0-13-948266-0*) P-H.

Understanding the New U. S. Transfer Pricing Rules. Deloris R. Wright. Ed. by Jay Stein & Khiem Ting. 136p. (Orig.). pap. 48.00 (*0-8080-0001-2*) Commerce.

*__Understanding the Nigerian Nation Tribes - Why They Boil: Current & Recent Past Events in Context.__ Peter Enyinna Kayang Opara. 150p. (Orig.). 1996. text ed. 15.00 (*0-9653465-4-4*); pap. text ed. 11.99 (*0-9653465-5-2*) Paine Pr.

Understanding the North American Free Trade Agreement: Legal & Business Consequences of NAFTA. Leslie A. Glick. LC 92-45137. 1993. 45.00 (*90-6544-689-3*) Kluwer Law Tax Pubs.

Understanding the North American Free Trade Agreement: Legal & Business Consequences of NAFTA. 2nd ed. Leslie A. Glick. LC 94-27721. 1994. write for info. (*90-6544-846-2*) Kluwer Law Tax Pubs.

*__Understanding the North Sea System.__ Charnock et al. (Illus.). 240p. 1994. text ed. 72.95 (*0-412-55480-1*, Chap & Hall NY) Chapman & Hall.

Understanding the Nursery School: A Sociological Analysis. David Hartley. Ed. by Cedric Cullingford. (Children, Teachers & Learning Ser.). 192p. 1993. text ed. 65.00 (*0-304-32597-X*); pap. text ed. 22.50 (*0-304-32584-8*) Cassell.

Understanding the Nursing Process: Fundamentals of Care Planning. 4th ed. Leslie D. Atkinson & Mary E. Murray. (Illus.). 319p. 1990. pap. text ed. 21.95 (*0-08-040299-2*, Pub. by PPI UK) McGraw.

Understanding the Nursing Process: The Next Generation. 5th ed. Mary E. Murray & Leslie D. Atkinson. LC 93-1938. (Illus.). 192p. 1993. pap. text ed. 24.00 (*0-07-105458-8*) McGraw-Hill HPD.

Understanding the Occults see Deceivers: What Cults Believe; How They Lure Followers

Understanding the Old Testament. 4th abr. ed. Anderson. LC 96-31386. 608p. (C). 1997. pap. text ed. 33.33 (*0-13-948399-3*) P-H.

Understanding the Old Testament. 4th ed. Bernhard W. Anderson. (Illus.). 672p. 1986. text ed. 57.00 (*0-13-935925-7*) P-H.

Understanding the Oracle Server: Covers Version 7.X. Marina Krakovsky. 1995. pap. 25.95 (*0-13-190265-2*) P-H.

*__Understanding the Order of Christian Funerals Vol. 1: Introduction to the CCF, the Vigil & Related Rites.__ Richard Rutherford. Date not set. 39.95 (*0-8146-7910-2*) Liturgical Pr.

*__Understanding the Order of Christian Funerals Vol. II: Funeral Liturgy.__ Richard Rutherford. Date not set. 39.95 (*0-8146-7912-9*) Liturgical Pr.

Understanding the Orthodox Liturgy: A Guide for Participating in the Liturgy of St. John Chrysostom. Michel Najim & T. L. Frazier. (Illus.). 178p. 1995. per. 12.50 (*1-879038-25-0*) Oakwood Pubns.

Understanding the Outboard Motor. Eugene W. Stagner. 1985. text ed. 84.00 (*0-8359-8059-6*, Reston) P-H.

*__Understanding the Parent-Teacher Conference.__ Greg Anderson. (Illus.). 8p. (Orig.). 1996. pap. 2.50 (*1-884241-79-4*, AN1026) Energeia Pub.

Understanding the Past, Managing the Future: The Integration of the Five New Lander into the Federal Republic of Germany. Ed. by Margy Gerber & Roger Woods. LC 94-465. (Selected Papers from the Eighteenth New Hampshire Symposium - Studies in GDR Culture & Society: No. 13). 176p. 1994. lib. bdg. 42.00 (*0-8191-9390-9*) U Pr of Amer.

Understanding the Personal Auto Policy. Richard Marzilli. 164p. 1991. 49.95 (*1-56461-039-X*, 46120) Rough Notes.

Understanding the Petit Basset Griffon Vendeen: Rustic French Hound. Kitty Steidel. Ed. by Jo Ann T. Redditt. (Illus.). 176p. 1987. 25.00 (*0-9618117-0-6*) Orient Pubns VA.

Understanding the Pill: A Consumer's Guide to Oral Contraceptives. Greg Juhn. LC 93-38903. (Illus.). 105p. 1994. pap. 9.95 (*1-56024-908-0*); lib. bdg. 19.95 (*1-56024-851-3*) Haworth Pr.

*__Understanding the Political World.__ 4th ed. James N. Danziger. (C). 1998. pap. text ed. write for info. (*0-8013-1852-1*); pap. text ed. write for info. (*0-8013-1853-X*) Addison-Wesley.

Understanding the Political World: A Comparative Introduction to Political Science. 3rd ed. James N. Danziger. 576p. (C). 1996. pap. text ed. 40.95 (*0-8013-1547-6*) Longman.

Understanding the Political World: An Introduction to Political Science. 2nd ed. James N. Danziger. LC 93-2171. 450p. (Orig.). (C). 1994. teacher ed. write for info. (*0-8013-1180-2*, 79704) Longman.

Understanding the Post-Colonial World: Theory & Method. Ed. by Neera Chandhoke. (C). 1995. 32.00 (*81-207-1718-X*, Pub. by Sterling Plns Pvt II) S Asia.

Understanding the Presidency. Ed. by James P. Pfiffner & Roger H. Davidson. LC 96-15634. (C). 1997. text ed. 29.95 (*0-673-99899-1*) Addson-Wesley Educ.

Understanding the Primary School: A Sociological Analysis. David Hartley. LC 85-11369. 285p. 1985. 34.50 (*0-7099-3742-3*, Pub. by Croom Helm UK) Routledge Chapman & Hall.

Understanding the Principalship: Metaphorical Themes, 1920s-1990s. Lynn G. Beck & Joseph Murphy. 272p. (C). 1992. text ed. 47.00 (*0-8077-3208-7*); pap. text ed. 22.95 (*0-8077-3207-9*) Tchrs Coll.

Understanding the Process of Doing Business in China, Taiwan, & Hong Kong: A Guide for International Executives. Min Chen & Winston Pan. LC 93-29328. 260p. 1993. 89.95 (*0-7734-9404-9*) E Mellen.

Understanding the Process of Operational Research: Collected Readings. Ed. by Paul Keys. LC 94-36547. 340p. 1995. text ed. 65.00 (*0-471-95269-9*) Wiley.

Understanding the Professional Programmer. rev. ed. Gerald M. Weinberg. LC 88-5098. (Illus.). 240p. 1988. reprint ed. pap. 24.00 (*0-932633-09-9*) Dorset Hse Pub Co.

***Understanding the Properties of Matter.** Michael De Podesta. 320p. 1996. 69.95 (*1-56032-614-X*) Hemisp Pub.

***Understanding the Properties of Matter.** Michael De Podesta. 320p. (C). 1996. pap. 29.95 (*1-56032-616-6*) Hemisp Pub.

Understanding the Prophets. Sheldon H. Blank. 144p. (C). 1983. pap. text ed. 4.00 (*0-8074-0250-8*, 382755) UAHC.

***Understanding the Qur'an: Themes & Style.** Muhammad A. Haleem. 256p. 1996. 39.95 (*1-86064-009-5*, Pub. by I B Tauris UK) St Martin.

***Understanding the Rabbinic Mind: Essays on the Hermeneutic of Max Kadushin.** Peter Ochs. LC 90-48284. (University of South Florida Studies in the History of Judaism). 266p. 1990. 59.95 (*1-55540-544-4*, 24 00 14) Scholars Pr GA.

***Understanding the Red Badge of Courage: A Student Casebook to Issues, Sources & Historical Documents.** Claudia D. Johnson. (Greenwood Press Literature in Context Ser.). 1998. text ed. write for info. (*0-313-30122-0*, Greenwood Pr) Greenwood.

Understanding the Representational Mind. Josef Perner. (Bradford LDCC Ser.). (Illus.). 340p. 1991. 44.00 (*0-262-16124-9*, Bradford Bks) MIT Pr.

Understanding the Representational Mind. Josef Perner. (Learning, Development, & Conceptual Change). (Illus.). 340p. 1993. reprint ed. pap. 18.00 (*0-262-66082-2*, Bradford Bks) MIT Pr.

Understanding the Revelation. Dawn R. Ariyavatkul. LC 94-72421. 1995. 8.95 (*0-8158-0506-3*) Chris Mass.

Understanding the Riots: Los Angeles & the Aftermath of the Rodney King Verdict. Los Angeles Times Staff. 160p. 1992. pap. 14.95 (*0-9619095-9-5*) LA Times.

Understanding the Runes: Their Origins & Magical Power. Michael Howard. 144p. 1991. pap. 9.00 (*1-85538-013-7*) Harper SF.

Understanding the Russians: A Study of Soviet Life & Culture. Ed. by Bernhard J. Stern & Samuel Smith. LC 72-167424. (Essay Index Reprint Ser.). 1977. reprint ed. 22.95 (*0-8369-2476-2*) Ayer.

Understanding the Sacraments Today. Lawrence E. Mick. 148p. (Orig.). 1987. pap. 5.95 (*0-8146-1567-8*) Liturgical Pr.

Understanding the Scarlet Letter: A Student Casebook to Issues, Sources & Historical Documents. Claudia D. Johnson. LC 94-39083. (Literature in Context Ser.). 248p. 1995. text ed. 35.00 (*0-313-29328-7*, Greenwood Pr) Greenwood.

Understanding the Second Epidemic: The Status of Research on Women & AIDS in the United States. Hoangmai Pham et al. LC 91-81222. 63p. 1992. 15.00 (*1-877966-11-8*) Ctr Women Policy.

Understanding the Securities Laws. 3rd ed. Larry D. Soderquist. 400p. 1993. ring bd. 135.00 (*0-614-17131-8*, B1-1345) PLI.

Understanding the Securities Laws 1994. (Corporate Law & Practice Course Handbook, 1985-86 Ser.). 656p. 1994. pap. 99.00 (*0-614-17171-7*, B4-7067) PLI.

Understanding the Securities Laws 1995. (Corporate Law & Practice Course Handbook, 1985-86 Ser.). Date not set. pap. 99.00 (*0-614-17193-8*, B4-7094) PLI.

Understanding the Self. Ed. by Richard Stevens. 384p. (C). 1996. 79.95 (*0-7619-5039-7*); pap. 27.95 (*0-7619-5040-0*) Sage.

Understanding the Self-Help Organization: Frameworks & Findings. Ed. by Thomas J. Powell. 345p. 1994. 55.00 (*0-8039-5487-5*); pap. 26.00 (*0-8039-5488-3*) Sage.

Understanding the Sermon on the Mount. Harvey K. McArthur. LC 78-16404. 192p. 1978. reprint ed. text ed. 42.50 (*0-313-20569-8*, MCUS, Greenwood Pr) Greenwood.

***Understanding the Service Economy: Employment, Productivity, Location.** Thomas M. Stanback. LC 79-2372. (Policy Studies in Employment & Welfare: No. 35). 144p. 1979. reprint ed. pap. 41.10 (*0-608-04044-4*, 2064780) Bks Demand.

Understanding the Sky. Dennis Pagen. (Illus.). 290p. 1992. pap. 19.95 (*0-936310-10-3*, Sport Aviation Pubns) Black Mntn.

Understanding the Social Effects of Policy Reform. Ed. by Lionel Demery et al. LC 93-3805. 228p. 1993. 13.95 (*0-8213-2425-X*, 12425) World Bank.

***Understanding the Spanish.** Shaun Taulbut. LC 96-78263. (New American Batsford Chess Library). 128p. 1997. pap. 17.95 (*1-879479-41-9*) ICE WA.

Understanding the Spiritual Nature of Addiction. Thomas S. Baker. 25p. 1994. 24.95 (*1-884937-17-9*) Manisses Communs.

Understanding the Structure of Elementary School Mathematics. Fendel. 512p. 1987. text ed. write for info. (*0-205-08821-X*, H88214) Allyn.

Understanding the Sunday Eucharist. Brian Grenier. 1991. pap. 4.50 (*0-8189-0639-1*) Alba.

***Understanding the Sunday Scriptures: The Synthesis Commentary.** H. King Oehmig et al. 124p. 1996. wbk. ed. 19.00 (*0-935453-79-2*) Pasha Pubns.

Understanding the Swedish Model. Ed. by Jan-Erik Lane. 1991. text ed. 35.00 (*0-7146-3445-X*, Pub. by F Cass Pubs UK) Intl Spec Bk.

Understanding the Talmud. Ernest R. Trattner. LC 77-27887. 211p. 1978. reprint ed. text ed. 35.00 (*0-313-20253-2*, TRUT, Greenwood Pr) Greenwood.

Understanding the Talmud: A Modern Reader's Guide for Study. Edward S. Boraz. LC 96-5142. 232p. 1996. 30.00 (*1-56821-616-5*) Aronson.

***Understanding the Tarot.** Sharman Burke. Date not set. pap. write for info. (*0-312-17913-8*) St Martin.

Understanding the Tax Aspects of Bankruptcy & Workouts. (Commercial Law & Practice Ser.). 387p. 1992. pap. text ed. 70.00 (*0-685-56869-5*, A4-4370) PLI.

Understanding the TI PC: A Programming Digest. J. B. Dawson. 108p. (Orig.). 1985. pap. 19.95 (*0-9615084-0-X*) J B Dawson CA.

Understanding the Time Value of Money. Jack V. Michaels. (Illus.). 382p. (Orig.). 1996. pap. 29.95 (*0-9649133-0-5*) Mgmt Sci FL.

Understanding the Time Zones of God. John Tetsola. Ed. by Perry M. Mallory. 176p. (Orig.). 1993. pap. 9.99 (*0-9634306-1-0*) End-Time Wave.

Understanding the Times. David A. Noebel. LC 94-29314. 1994. 36.99 (*1-56507-268-5*) Harvest Hse.

Understanding the Times: The Religious Worldviews of Our Day & the Search for Truth. abr. ed. David A. Noebel. 1995. pap. write for info. (*0-936163-22-4*) Summit Pr CO.

Understanding the Times of Christ. William W. Menzies. LC 91-70704. 117p. 1991. reprint ed. pap. 2.95 (*0-88243-622-8*, 02-0622) Gospel Pub.

Understanding the Traditional Art of Ghana. Emmanuel V. Asihene. (Illus.). 100p. 1978. 29.50 (*0-8386-2130-9*) Fairleigh Dickinson.

Understanding the Trauma of Childhood Psycho-Sexual Abuse. Elizabeth Adams. 200p. (Orig.). 1994. pap. 12.95 (*0-938179-38-1*) Mills Sanderson.

Understanding the Trinity. Alister E. McGrath. 160p. 1990. pap. 10.99 (*0-310-29681-1*) Zondervan.

Understanding the Twelve Steps. Terence T. Gorski. 208p. 1991. pap. 10.00 (*0-671-76558-2*, Fireside) S&S Trade.

Understanding the Twelve Steps: A Guide for Counselors, Therapists, & Recovering People. Terence T. Gorski. 1989. pap. 8.95 (*0-8309-0559-6*, 17-0187-8) Herald Hse.

***Understanding the U. K.** Rose. Date not set. pap. text ed. write for info. (*0-582-29591-2*, Pub. by Longman UK) Longman.

Understanding the U. K. Economy. Ed. by Peter J. Curwen. LC 90-30893. 376p. 1990. text ed. 55.00 (*0-312-04749-5*) St Martin.

Understanding the U. S. Constitution. James R. Shaver. (J). 1986. pap. 3.25 (*0-87738-023-6*) Youth Ed.

Understanding the United States. C. Cherryholmes. (McGraw-Hill Social Studies). (Illus.). (gr. 5). 1979. text ed. 26.76 (*0-07-011985-6*) McGraw.

Understanding the Universe. David R. Flower. Date not set. student ed., pap. text ed. 18.50 (*0-314-73471-6*) West Pub.

Understanding the Universe. Phillip Flower. Ed. by Marshall. 698p. (C). 1990. text ed. 57.50 (*0-314-57880-3*) West Pub.

***Understanding the Universe.** 2nd ed. Flower. Date not set. text ed. 45.00 (*0-697-24195-5*) McGraw.

Understanding the Universe: The Impact of Space Astronomy. Ed. by Richard M. West. 1983. lib. bdg. 104.50 (*90-277-1647-1*) Kluwer Ac.

Understanding the Universe in Seventh Century Ireland. Marina B. Smyth. (Studies in Celtic History: No. XV). (Illus.). 352p. (C). 1996. 70.00 (*0-85115-313-5*) Boydell & Brewer.

Understanding the Value of ISO 9000: A Management Guide to Higher Quality, Productivity, & Sales. Bryn Owen & Peter M. Malkovich. Ed. by Catherine Malkovich. (Illus.). 195p. (Orig.). 1995. pap. 25.00 (*0-945320-44-2*) SPC Pr.

Understanding the Variety of Nuclear Excitations: Third International Spring Seminar on Nuclear Physics. Aldo Covello. 788p. 1991. text ed. 147.00 (*981-02-0401-9*) World Scientific Pub.

***Understanding the Virtual Organization.** Bob Norton & Cathy Smith. LC 97-24746. 1998. write for info. (*0-7641-0305-9*) Barron.

***Understanding the Voice-Enabled Web.** Edwin Margulies. 500p. 1996. 34.95 (*0-936648-91-0*, P50003) Flatiron Pubng.

***Understanding the Water.** Joan P. Kincaid. (Illus.). 60p. Date not set. pap. write for info. (*1-888832-03-7*) Kings Estate.

Understanding the Weather. rev. ed. Robert C. McNeill. (Illus.). 250p. (C). 1991. pap. text ed. write for info. (*0-9623781-8-6*) Arbor Pubs.

Understanding the Weather. 2nd rev. ed. Robert C. McNeill. (Illus.). 250p. (C). 1991. pap. write for info. (*0-9623781-7-8*) Arbor Pubs.

Understanding the Wholesale Insurance Market: An Educational Program. Academy of Producer Insurance Studies, Inc. Staff. 82p. (Orig.). 1994. pap. text ed. 17.50 (*1-878204-52-1*) APIS Inc.

Understanding the "Why" Chromosome: A Cathy Collection. Cathy Guisewite. (Illus.). 128p. 1995. pap. 8.95 (*0-8362-0423-9*) Andrews & McMeel.

Understanding the Wind Peril. Insurance Institute for Property Loss Reduction Staff. (Illus.). 109p. 1994. write for info. (*1-885312-00-8*) Ins Inst for PLR.

Understanding the Wind Peril. Insurance Institute for Property Loss Reduction Staff. (Illus.). 109p. 1995. reprint ed. write for info. (*1-885312-06-7*) Ins Inst for PLR.

***Understanding the World Economy: Global Issues Shaping the Future.** Tony Cleaver. LC 96-9862. 256p. (C). 1997. pap. write for info. (*0-415-12816-1*) Routledge.

***Understanding the World Economy: Global Issues Shaping the Future.** Tony Cleaver. LC 96-9862. 256p. (C). 1997. text ed. write for info. (*0-415-12815-3*) Routledge.

Understanding the Yacht Racing Rules - 1993-96. Dave Perry. 306p. 1993. reprint ed. pap. 19.95 (*1-882502-02-7*) US Sail Assn.

Understanding the 1994 Amendments to the Bankruptcy Code. (Commercial Law & Practice Course Handbook Ser.). 544p. 1994. pap. 99.00 (*0-614-17150-4*, A4-4481) PLI.

Understanding Theology. R. T. Kendall. 480p. (Orig.). 1996. pap. 18.99 (*0-614-15842-7*, Pub. by Christian Focus UK) Spring Arbor Dist.

Understanding Therapeutic Action: Psychodynamic Concepts of Cure. Ed. by Lawrence Lifson. (PI Ser.: No. 1). 272p. 1996. text ed. 39.95 (*0-88163-205-8*) Analytic Pr.

Understanding Thermodynamics. H. C. Van Ness. 103p. 1983. reprint ed. pap. 3.95 (*0-486-63277-6*) Dover.

Understanding "Things Fall Apart" Selected Essays & Criticisms. Ed. by Solomon O. Iyasere. LC 92-64473. 150p. 1997. write for info. (*0-87875-433-4*) Whitston Pub.

Understanding Third World Politics: Theories of Political Change & Development. B. C. Smith. LC 95-41370. 1996. pap. text ed. 18.95 (*0-253-21013-5*) Ind U Pr.

Understanding Third World Politics: Theories of Political Change & Development. B. C. Smith. LC 95-41370. (C). 1996. 39.95 (*0-253-32954-X*) Ind U Pr.

Understanding Thomas Bernhard. Stephen D. Dowden. Ed. by James N. Hardin. (Understanding Modern European & Latin American Literature Ser.). 117p. 1991. text ed. 29.95 (*0-87249-759-3*) U of SC Pr.

Understanding Thomas Jefferson: Studies in Economics, Law, & Philosophy. Meyer L. Burstein. LC 93-9790. 256p. 1993. text ed. 45.00 (*0-312-08693-8*) St Martin.

Understanding Thomas Pynchon. Robert D. Newman. (Understanding Contemporary American Literature Ser.). 164p. 1986. text ed. 29.95 (*0-87249-485-3*) U of SC Pr.

Understanding Those Who Create. Jane Piirto. LC 91-41971. 380p. 1992. pap. 22.00 (*0-910707-19-7*) Gifted Psych Pr.

Understanding Three-Dimensional Images: Recognition of Abdominal Anatomy from CAT Scans. Uri Shani. LC 83-15818. (Computer Science: Artificial Intelligence Ser.: No. 13). (Illus.). 221p. reprint ed. pap. 63.00 (*0-8357-1521-3*, 2070352) Bks Demand.

Understanding Three Dimensions. Jonathan Block & Jerry Leisure. (Illus.). 150p. (C). 1986. pap. text ed. 33.33 (*0-13-937202-4*) P-H.

Understanding Tim O'Brien. Steven Kaplan. LC 94-3203. (Understanding Contemporary American Literature Ser.). 230p. 1995. text ed. 34.95 (*1-57003-007-3*) U of SC Pr.

Understanding To Kill A Mockingbird: A Student Casebook to Issues, Sources, & Documents. Claudia D. Johnson. LC 94-4793. (Literature in Context Ser.). 248p. 1994. text ed. 35.00 (*0-313-29193-4*, Greenwood Pr) Greenwood.

Understanding Today's Police. Mark L. Dantzker. LC 93-47403. 496p. 1994. pap. text ed. 50.67 (*0-13-951591-7*) P-H.

Understanding Today's Youth Culture. Walt Mueller. LC 94-26142. 448p. 1994. pap. 14.99 (*0-8423-7736-0*) Tyndale.

Understanding Today's Youth Culture Discussion Guide. Walt Mueller. 80p. 1995. 4.99 (*0-8423-7738-7*) Tyndale.

Understanding TOEFL. 1994. 14.00 (*0-446-77730-7*) Warner Bks.

Understanding TOEFL: Test Kit 1. TOEFL Program Staff. (TOEFL Test Kits Ser.). 76p. (Orig.). 1980. pap. text ed. 13.00 (*0-88685-024-X*, IN678528) Educ Testing Serv.

***Understanding Tolowa Histories: Western Hegemonies & Native American Responses.** LC 96-46667. 256p. (C). 1997. text ed. write for info. (*0-415-91207-5*) Routledge.

***Understanding Tolowa Histories: Western Hegemonies & Native American Responses.** James Collins. 256p. (C). 1997. pap. 18.95 (*0-415-91208-3*, Routledge NY) Routledge.

Understanding Torts. John L. Diamond et al. LC 96-21224. (Legal Text Ser.). 1996. pap. write for info. (*0-8205-2486-7*) Bender.

Understanding Toscanini: A Social History of American Concert Life. Joseph Horowitz. LC 93-38873. 1994. pap. 16.00 (*0-520-08542-6*) U CA Pr.

Understanding Tourette Syndrome, Obsessive-Compulsive Disorder & Related Problems: A Developmental & Catastrophe Theory Perspective. John M. Berecz. LC 91-4824. (Illus.). 366p. 1991. 44.95 (*0-8261-7390-X*) Springer Pub.

***Understanding Toxicology: Chemicals, Their Benefits & Risks.** Brono H. Schiefer et al. LC 96-41143. 144p. 1997. 24.95 (*0-8493-2686-9*) CRC Pr.

Understanding Traffic Systems: Data, Analysis & Presentation. Michael Taylor. 464p. 1996. 84.95 (*0-291-39815-4*, Pub. by Avebury Technical UK) Ashgate Pub Co.

Understanding Transmission: Engineering Seminar I. 2nd ed. Eugene W. Riley & Victor E. Acuna. LC 73-85629. (ABC of the Telephone Ser.: Vol. 7). (Illus.). 60p. (C). 1988. pap. text ed. 13.95 (*1-56016-006-3*) ABC TeleTraining.

Understanding Transparent Watercolor. Gerald F. Brommer. LC 92-72328. (Illus.). 192p. 1993. 32.50 (*0-87192-245-2*) Davis Mass.

Understanding Travel Behaviour in an Era of Change. Ed. by Peter Stopher & Martin Lee-Gosselin. LC 96-11486. 628p. 1996. text ed. 96.00 (*0-08-042390-6*, Pergamon Pr) Elsevier.

Understanding Troubled & Troubling Youth: Multiple Perspectives. Ed. by Peter E. Leone. (Focus Editions Ser.: Vol. 116). (Illus.). 320p. (C). 1990. 54.00 (*0-8039-3442-4*); pap. 24.95 (*0-8039-3443-2*) Sage.

Understanding Troubled Minds: A Guide to Mental Illness & Its Treatment. Sidney Bloch & Bruce Singh. 320p. 1997. pap. 17.95 (*0-522-84642-4*, Pub. by Melbourne Univ Pr AT) Paul & Co Pubs.

Understanding Turbo Pascal: Programming & Problem Solving. Douglas W. Nance. Ed. by Westby. LC 93-28875. 650p. (C). 1994. pap. text ed. 50.75 (*0-314-02812-9*) West Pub.

Understanding Twins. Miram P. Braunstein. 1991. 29.95 (*0-904575-56-X*, Coventure Ltd); pap. 15.95 (*0-904575-55-1*, Coventure Ltd) Sigo Pr.

Understanding Type for Desktop Publishing. Paul Luna. 136p. 1992. 29.95 (*0-948905-76-X*) Chapman & Hall.

Understanding Types, Shadows & Names: A Biblical Guide. Kelley Varner. 276p. 1996. 16.99 (*1-56043-165-2*) Destiny Image.

Understanding U. S. & European Environmental Law. Ed. by Turner T. Smith & Pascale Kromarek. (C). 1989. lib. bdg. 102.50 (*1-85333-305-0*) Kluwer Ac.

Understanding U. S. & Global Economic Trends: A Guide for the Non-Economist. Daniel Gaske. 142p. (C). 1996. per., pap. text ed. 20.94 (*0-7872-1986-X*) Kendall-Hunt.

Understanding U. S. Identity Documents. Brent Wade. LC 91-61946. (Illus.). 224p. (Orig.). 1993. pap. 27.95 (*1-55950-071-9*, 61129) Loompanics.

Understanding U. S. Information Policy, 1 vol. 49.95 (*0-317-44249-X*) Info Indus.

Understanding U. S. Information Policy, 1 vol., Vol. I: The Information Policy Primer. 30.00 (*0-685-43516-4*) Info Indus.

Understanding Ultrasound Physics: Fundamentals & Exam Review. 2nd ed. Sidney K. Edelman. (Illus.). 385p. (C). 1994. text ed. 46.00 (*0-9626444-3-9*) ESP TX.

Understanding Unemployment. Ed. by Lawrence H. Summers. 344p. 1990. 37.50 (*0-262-19265-9*) MIT Pr.

Understanding Unemployment. Ed. by Lawrence H. Summers. (Illus.). 384p. 1992. reprint ed. pap. 17.50 (*0-262-69157-4*) MIT Pr.

Understanding Unemployment: New Perspectives on Active Labour Market Policies. Ed. by Eithne McLaughlin. 224p. (C). (gr. 13). 1992. text ed. 74.95 (*0-415-07805-9*, A9693) Routledge.

Understanding United States Government Growth: An Empirical Analysis of the Postwar Era. William Berry & David Lowery. LC 87-11818. 232p. 1987. text ed. 59.95 (*0-275-92509-9*, C2509, Praeger Pubs) Greenwood.

Understanding Universal Health Programs: Issues & Options. Ed. by David A. Kindig & Robert B. Sullivan. LC 92-49882. 287p. (Orig.). 1992. pap. text ed. 37.00 (*0-910701-86-5*, 0919) Health Admin Pr.

Understanding Unix. 2nd rev. ed. Stan Kelly-Bootle. LC 94-683434. 587p. 1994. pap. 29.99 (*0-7821-1499-7*) Sybex.

Understanding Unreliable Narrators: Reading Between the Lines in the Literature Classroom. Michael W. Smith. (Theory & Research into Practice Ser.). 50p. 1991. pap. 8.95 (*0-8141-5566-9*) NCTE.

Understanding Urban Unrest: From Reverend King to Rodney King. Dennis E. Gale. LC 95-50225. 296p. (C). 1996. 48.00 (*0-7619-0094-2*); pap. 22.95 (*0-7619-0095-0*) Sage.

Understanding Urology. S. N. Rous. (Perspectives in Medicine Ser.: No. 5). (Illus.). 1973. 15.25 (*3-8055-0000-9*) S Karger.

Understanding Ursula K. Le Guin. Elizabeth Cummins. 223p. 1990. text ed. 29.95 (*0-87249-687-2*) U of SC Pr.

Understanding Ursula K. Le Guin. rev. ed. Elizabeth Cummins. Ed. by Matthew J. Bruccoli. (Understanding Contemporary American Literature Ser.). 269p. 1992. pap. 12.95 (*0-87249-869-7*) U of SC Pr.

Understanding Us: Family Development 1. 1981. pap. 14.00 (*0-917340-10-8*) Interpersonal Comm.

Understanding Utterances: An Introduction to Pragmatics. Diane Blakemore. (Blackwell Textbooks in Linguistics Ser.). (C). 1992. pap. text ed. 24.95 (*0-631-15867-7*) Blackwell Pubs.

Understanding Value Added Tax (VAT) William Lovell. (NatWest Business Handbook Ser.). 176p. (Orig.). (C). 1991. pap. 36.50 (*0-273-03622-X*, Pub. by Pitman Pub Ltd UK) Trans-Atl Phila.

Understanding Variable Insurance Products. (Commercial Law & Practice Course Handbook Ser.). 216p. 1994. pap. 99.00 (*0-614-17152-0*, A4-4495) PLI.

Understanding Variation: The Key to Managing Chaos. Donald J. Wheeler. (Illus.). 136p. (Orig.). 1993. 29.00 (*0-945320-35-3*) SPC Pr.

Understanding Ventilation: How to Design, Select, & Install Residential Ventilation Systems. John Bower. LC 94-96635. (Illus.). 432p. 1995. 31.95 (*0-9637156-5-8*) Hlthy Hse.

Understanding Verbal Relations. Ed. by Steven C. Hayes & Linda J. Hayes. (International Institute on Verbal Relations Ser.). (Illus.). 224p. (Orig.). (C). 1992. text ed. 49.95 (*1-878978-07-1*); pap. text ed. 29.95 (*1-878978-01-2*) Context Pr.

Understanding Veritatis Splendor. John Wilkins et al. 127p. 1994. 39.00 (*1-85390-217-9*, Pub. by Veritas IE) St Mut.

Understanding Video: Applications, Impact & Theory. Jarice Hanson. LC 87-14136. (Sage Commtext Ser.: No. 19). 135p. 1987. reprint ed. pap. 38.50 (*0-608-01513-X*, 2059557) Bks Demand.

Understanding Video Equipment. Neil Heller. 206p. 1989. student ed. 24.95 (*0-86729-185-0*, Focal) Buttrwrth-Heinemann.

Understanding Vietnam. Neil L. Jamieson. LC 92-20978. 440p. (C). 1993. 35.00 (*0-520-08048-3*) U CA Pr.

Understanding Vietnam. Neil L. Jamieson. 428p. 1995. pap. 15.00 (*0-520-20157-4*) U CA Pr.

UV

*Understanding Violence: An Introduction to Research on Aggressive Individuals, Families, & Groups. Elizabeth Kandel-Englander. 200p. 1997. 45.00 (0-8058-1939-8); pap. 19.98 (0-8058-1940-1) L Erlbaum Assocs.

Understanding Violence Against Women. National Research Council, Panel on Violence Against Women Staff. Ed. by Nancy A. Crowell & Ann W. Burgess. LC 96-17335. 240p. 1996. 29.95 (0-309-05425-7) Natl Acad Pr.

Understanding Vision. Roger Watt. (Illus.). 301p. (C). 1991. text ed. 93.00 (0-12-738500-2); pap. text ed. 50.00 (0-12-738501-0) Acad Pr.

Understanding Vision: An Interdisciplinary Approach. Ed. by Glyn W. Humphreys. (Readings in Mind & Language Ser.). (Illus.). 256p. (C). 1992. pap. 27.95 (0-631-17909-7) Blackwell Pubs.

Understanding Visual Basic. Barron. Date not set. teacher ed., pap. text ed. write for info. (0-314-09375-3) West Pub.

Understanding Visual Basic 3 for Windows. Jim Boyce. LC 94-10169. 428p. 1994. pap. 24.99 (1-56205-310-8) New Riders Pub.

Understanding Vladimir Nabokov. Stephen J. Parker. (Understanding Contemporary American Literature Ser.). 170p. 1987. text ed. 29.95 (0-87249-494-2) U of SC Pr.

Understanding Vladimir Nabokov. Steven J. Parker. (Understanding Contemporary American Literature Ser.). 170p. 1987. pap. 12.95 (0-87249-495-0) U of SC Pr.

Understanding Vocabulary: Advanced Level. 2nd ed. Ed. by Kraft. (Comprehension Skills Ser.). 64p. 1993. pap. 8.45 (0-89061-629-9) Jamestown Pubs.

Understanding Vocabulary: Introductory Level. Ed. by Kraft. (Comprehension Skills Ser.). 64p. 1993. pap. 7.91 (0-89061-669-8) Jamestown Pubs.

Understanding Vocabulary: Middle Level. 2nd ed. Ed. by Kraft. (Comprehension Skills Ser.). 64p. 1993. pap. 8.31 (0-89061-649-3) Jamestown Pubs.

Understanding Voice Problems. Raymond Colton et al. (Illus.). 376p. 1989. pap. 43.00 (0-683-02058-7) Williams & Wilkins.

Understanding Voice Problems: A Physiological Perspective for Diagnosis & Treatment. 2nd ed. Raymond H. Colton & Janina K. Casper. LC 95-33492. 418p. 1996. 45.00 (0-683-02059-5) Williams & Wilkins.

Understanding Vygotsky: A Quest for Synthesis. Rene Van der Veer & Jaan Valsiner. (Illus.). 400p. 1993. pap. text ed. 27.95 (0-631-18955-6) Blackwell Pubs.

*Understanding W. S. Merwin. H. L. Hix. LC 96-51241. (Understanding Contemporary American Literature Ser.). 190p. 1997. 29.95 (1-57003-154-1) U of SC Pr.

Understanding Walker Percy. Linda W. Hobson. Ed. by Matthew J. Bruccoli. (Understanding Contemporary American Literature Ser.). 212p. (C). 1988. text ed. 29.95 (0-87249-548-5); pap. text ed. 12.95 (0-87249-549-3) U of SC Pr.

Understanding Wall Street. rev. ed. Jeffrey B. Little & Lucien Rhodes. 240p. 1991. pap. 9.95 (0-8306-0479-0) McGraw-Hill Prof.

Understanding Wall Street. 2nd ed. Jeffrey B. Little & Lucien Rhodes. 240p. 1987. 19.95 (0-8306-3120-8, Liberty Hse); pap. 9.95 (0-8306-3020-1, 30020, Liberty Hse) TAB Bks.

Understanding Wall Street. 3rd ed. J. B. Little. 1991. pap. text ed. 11.95 (0-07-038102-X) McGraw.

Understanding Wall Street. 3rd rev. ed. Jeffrey B. Little & Lucien Rhodes. 240p. 1991. 21.95 (0-8306-0482-0, 3686) McGraw-Hill Prof.

*Understanding Wall Street. 4th ed. Jeffrey B. Little & Lucien Rhodes. (Illus.). 304p. 1997. pap. text ed. 12.95 (0-07-038111-9) McGraw.

Understanding War. W. B. Gallie. 160p. (C). 1990. pap. text ed. 15.95 (0-415-05640-3, A5196) Routledge.

Understanding War. Koral. (J). 1995. 13.95 (0-689-31698-4, Atheneum Bks Young) S&S Childrens.

Understanding War: Essays on Clausewitz & the History of Military Power. Peter Paret. 239p. 1992. pap. text ed. 15.95 (0-691-00090-5) Princeton U Pr.

Understanding Watercolours. H. L. Mallalieu. (Understanding Ser.). (Illus.). 1985. 49.50 (0-907462-39-1) Antique Collect.

Understanding Weapons & Arms Control: A Guide to the Issues. 4th rev. ed. T. K. Mayers. (Illus.). 157p. 1991. text ed. 9.95 (0-08-037438-7) Brasseys Inc.

*Understanding Weatherfax. Mike Harris. LC 96-51920. (Illus.). 112p. 1997. pap. 16.50 (1-57409-031-3) Sheridan.

*Understanding Whitehead. Victor Lowe. LC 62-15312. 416p. 1966. reprint ed. pap. 118.60 (0-608-03723-0, 2064548) Bks Demand.

Understanding Whitetails. David Samuel. (Complete Bowhunter Ser.). (Illus.). 1996. 19.95 (0-86573-063-6) Cowles Creative.

*Understanding Whitetails. David Samuel. LC 96-25979. (Complete Bowhunter Ser.). 1996. write for info. (0-86573-069-5) Cowles Creative.

*Understanding Who You Are: What Your Relationships Tell You about Yourself. rev. ed. Larry Crabb. LC 96-6536. Orig. Title: Who We Are & How We Relate. 78p. (Orig.). 1997. pap. 9.00 (1-57683-014-4) NavPress.

Understanding Whole Language: From Principles to Practice. Constance Weaver. LC 90-37835. (Illus.). 309p. (Orig.). (C). 1990. pap. text ed. 25.00 (0-435-08535-2, 08535) Heinemann.

Understanding William Kennedy. J. Kenneth Van Dover. Ed. by Matthew J. Bruccoli. (Understanding Contemporary American Literature Ser.). 149p. 1991. text ed. 29.95 (0-87249-663-5) U of SC Pr.

Understanding William Stafford. Judith Kitchen. Ed. by Matthew J. Bruccoli. (Understanding Contemporary American Literature Ser.). 168p. (Orig.). 1989. text ed. 34.95 (0-87249-618-X) U of SC Pr.

Understanding Windows 95. Jim Boyce. 350p. 1994. pap. 24.99 (1-56205-359-0) New Riders Pub.

Understanding Winning Archery. Al Henderson. Ed. by Glenn Helgeland. LC 82-74190. (On Target Ser.). (Illus.). 114p. (Orig.). (C). 1983. pap. 9.95 (0-913305-00-6) Target Comm.

Understanding Witchcraft & Sorcery in Southeast Asia. Ed. by C. W. Watson & Roy Ellen. LC 93-5293. 248p. (C). 1993. text ed. 32.00 (0-8248-1515-7) UH Pr.

Understanding Wittgenstein: Studies of Philosophical Investigations. J. M. Hunter. 246p. 1985. 40.00 (0-85224-497-5, Pub. by Edinburgh U Pr UK) Col U Pr.

Understanding Woman's Behaviour. Parveen Kumar. LC 89-50185. 134p. (Orig.). 1990. pap. 7.00 (0-916383-90-3) Aegina Pr.

Understanding Women in Distress. Ed. by Pamela Ashurst & Zaida Hall. 272p. (C). 1989. pap. text ed. 14.95 (0-415-01833-1) Routledge.

Understanding Women in Distress. Ed. by Pamela Ashurst & Zaida Hall. 272p. 1989. 49.95 (0-415-01832-3) Routledge.

Understanding Wood. R. Bruce Hoadley. (Illus.). 256p. 1981. 31.95 (0-918804-05-1) Taunton.

Understanding Wood Finishing: How to Select & Apply the Right Finish. Bob Flexner. Date not set. pap. 14.95 (0-87596-734-5) Rodale Pr Inc.

Understanding Wood Finishing: How to Select & Apply the Right Finish. Bob Flexner. LC 93-3433. (Illus.). 320p. 1993. 27.95 (0-87596-566-0) Rodale Pr Inc.

*Understanding Woodcarving. Woodcarving Magazine Staff. 1997. pap. text ed. 14.95 (1-86108-045-X, Pub. by Guild Mstr Craftsman UK) Sterling.

*Understanding Woodturning. Ann Phillips. 1997. pap. text ed. 17.95 (1-86108-034-4, Pub. by Guild Mstr Craftsman UK) Sterling.

Understanding Word & Sentence. Ed. by G. B. Simpson. (Advances in Psychology Ser.: No. 77). 400p. 1991. 173.50 (0-444-88487-4, North Holland) Elsevier.

Understanding Workers' Compensation: A Guide for Safety & Health Professionals. Kenneth Wolff. LC 95-8770. 1995. 49.00 (0-86587-464-6) Gov Insts.

Understanding World Politics. Kenneth W. Thompson. LC 74-12569. (International Studies of the Committee on International Relations, University of Notre Dame). 254p. 1975. reprint ed. pap. 72.40 (0-608-00892-3, 2061686) Bks Demand.

Understanding World Religions. rev. ed. George W. Braswell, Jr. LC 93-24944. 244p. (Orig.). 1994. pap. 16.99 (0-8054-1068-6, 4210-68) Broadman.

Understanding Writer's Block: A Therapist's Guide to Diagnosis & Treatment. Martin D. Kantor. LC 95-22005. 208p. 1995. text ed. 57.95 (0-275-94905-2, Praeger Pubs) Greenwood.

Understanding Writing: Ways of Observing, Learning, & Teaching. 2nd ed. Ed. by Thomas Newkirk & Nancie Atwell. LC 87-11872. 312p. (Orig.). 1987. reprint ed. pap. text ed. 23.50 (0-435-08441-0, 08441) Heinemann.

Understanding Written Language: Explorations of Comprehension Beyond the Sentence. Anthony J. Sanford & S. C. Garrod. LC 80-40849. (Illus.). 238p. reprint ed. pap. 67.90 (0-8357-8645-5, 2035069) Bks Demand.

Understanding X.500. Chadwick. (Computer Science Ser.). 1994. text ed. 49.95 (1-85032-281-3) ITCP.

Understanding X.500: The Directory. D. Chadwick. 412p. 1994. text ed. 49.95 (0-412-43020-7) Chapman & Hall.

Understanding X86 Microprocessors. Microprocessor Report Newsletter Staff. 318p. 1993. pap. 49.95 (1-56276-158-7, Ziff-Davis Pr) Que.

Understanding Yacht Racing Rules Thru 1988. Dave Perry. 1985. pap. 18.95 (0-396-08614-4) Putnam Pub Group.

*Understanding Young Children's Behavior: A Guide for Early Childhood Professionals. Jillian Rodd. LC 96-34336. (Early Childhood Education Ser.). 208p. (Orig.). 1996. pap. text ed. 19.95 (0-8077-3595-7) Tchrs Coll.

*Understanding Your Accounts. 3rd ed. John Price. (Small Business Ser.). 1991. pap. 14.95 (0-7494-0368-3) Kogan Page Ltd.

Understanding Your Authority in Christ. Bob Yandian. Ed. by Elizabeth Sherman. (Illus.). 32p. (Orig.). 1994. mass mkt. 2.50 (1-885600-00-3) B Yandian Minist.

*Understanding Your Baby. Lisa Miller. (Understanding Your Child Ser.: Vol. 1). 1997. pap. text ed. 8.95 (1-894020-00-6, Pub. by Warwick Pub CN) Firefly Bks Ltd.

Understanding Your Bible: An Introduction to Dispensationalism. S. C. MacDonald. (Illus.). 177p. (Orig.). 1995. pap. 10.95 (0-912340-05-3) Grace Bible Coll.

Understanding Your Body: Every Woman's Guide to Gynecology & Health. Felicia Stewart et al. 650p. (Orig.). 1987. pap. 17.95 (0-553-34451-X) Bantam.

Understanding Your Body's Architecture see Your Body Intuitive Series

Understanding Your Body's Inner Workings see Your Body Intuitive Series

Understanding Your Body's Vascular Container see Your Body Intuitive Series

Understanding Your Body's Wiring see Your Body Intuitive Series

Understanding Your Brain. Rebecca Treays. (Science for Beginners Ser.). (Illus.). 32p. (J). (gr. 2 up). 1996. lib. bdg. 14.95 (0-88110-799-9, Usborne) EDC.

Understanding Your Brain. Rebecca Treays. (Science for Beginners Ser.). (Illus.). (J). (gr. 2 up). 1996. pap. 6.95 (0-7460-2014-7, Usborne) EDC.

Understanding Your Cat. Michael W. Fox. (Illus.). 224p. 1992. pap. 9.95 (0-312-07107-8) St Martin.

Understanding Your Child From Birth to Sixteen. David Elkind. LC 93-39529. 1994. pap. text ed. 26.00 (0-205-15971-0) Allyn.

Understanding Your Child's Pain. Kenneth Gorfinkle. 1996. write for info. (0-8092-3255-3) Contemp Bks.

*Understanding Your Child's Temperament. William B. Carey & Martha M. Jablow. 1997. 23.95 (0-614-28004-4) Mac Pub USA.

*Understanding Your Child's Temperament. William B. Carey & Martha M. Jablow. LC 97-14347. 256p. 1997. 23.95 (0-02-861664-2) Macmillan.

*Understanding Your Child's Temperament. William B. Curez & Martha M. Jablow. 1997. write for info. (0-614-30158-0) Childrens Hospital of Philadelphia.

*Understanding Your Child's Temperament. expanded rev. ed. Beverly LaHaye. 250p. (Orig.). 1997. pap. 9.99 (1-56507-518-8) Harvest Hse.

Understanding Your Company. Jeffrey B. Little & Lucien Rhodes. 1977. pap. 2.95 (0-8306-3003-1, 30003, Liberty Hse) TAB Bks.

Understanding Your Congregation As a System: The Manual. George D. Parsons & Speed B. Leas. LC 93-73158. 154p. (Orig.). 1994. pap. 18.95 (1-56699-118-8, AL147) Alban Inst.

Understanding Your Digestive System. Michael F. Elmore. (Illus.). 20p. (Orig.). 1991. pap. write for info. (0-9631030-0-8) Creat Ideas.

Understanding Your Divine Nature. Grant Von Harrison. (Personal Enrichment Ser.). 193p. (Orig.). 1985. pap. text ed. 8.95 (0-929985-26-5) Jackman Pubng.

Understanding Your Dog. Michael W. Fox. (Illus.). 256p. 1992. pap. 10.95 (0-312-07108-6) St Martin.

Understanding Your Dreams. Stacey J. Farley. 66p. (YA). (gr. 7-12). 1992. pap. 6.95 (1-57515-023-9) PPI Pubng.

Understanding Your Economy: Using Analysis to Guide Local Strategic Planning. rev. ed. Mary L. McLean & Kenneth P. Voytek. LC 92-73812. (Illus.). 245p. 1992. 52.00 (0-918286-82-4); pap. 38.95 (0-918286-81-6) Planners Pr.

*Understanding Your Health. 4th ed. James F. Mckenzie. 288p. (C). 1994. student ed., per. write for info. (0-8151-5777-0) Wm C Brown Pubs.

Understanding Your Health Study Guide. McKenzie et al. 288p. 1991. pap. 14.95 (0-8016-6654-6) Mosby Yr Bk.

*Understanding Your Horse: How to Overcome Common Behaviour Problems. Lesley Bayley & Richared Maxwell. (Illus.). 160p. 1997. 27.50 (1-57076-073-X, Trafalgar Sq Pub) Trafalgar.

Understanding Your Horses Health: A Practical Guide. Janet L. Eley. (Illus.). 144p. (Orig.). 1996. pap. 19.95 (0-7063-7484-3, Pub. by Ward Lock UK) Sterling.

Understanding Your Horse's Lameness. Diane Morgan. LC 92-13128. (Illus.). 152p. 1992. 19.95 (0-939481-26-X) Half Halt Pr.

Understanding Your Immune System. Eve Potts & Marion Morra. 224p. 1986. pap. 3.95 (0-380-89728-8) Avon.

Understanding Your Income Taxes: Money Management. Ransbottom. (YA - Adult Education Ser.). 1993. wbk. ed., pap. 5.95 (0-538-70840-9) S-W Pub.

Understanding Your Lover: Avoiding Rejection. Deborah Cooper. 21p. 1989. spiral bd., pap. 9.95 (0-9636566-0-0) Schaefer Pubns.

Understanding Your Man. 31p. (Orig.). student ed., pap. 6.95 (0-9645343-1-2) Fairbanks Pub.

Understanding Your Management Style: Beyond the Meyers-Briggs Type Indicator. Robert Benfari. 202p. 24.95 (0-669-24814-2, Lexington) Jossey-Bass.

Understanding Your Mentally Retarded Child: A New Approach. Richard Koch & Kathryn J. Koch. (Illus.). 1974. 10.95 (0-394-48547-5) Random.

*Understanding Your Muscles & Bones. Rebecca Treays. (Science for Beginners Ser.). (Illus.). 32p. (Orig.). (YA). (gr. 3 up). 1997. pap. 6.95 (0-7460-2739-7, Usborne) EDC.

*Understanding Your Muscles & Bones. Rebecca Treays. (Science for Beginners Ser.). (Illus.). 32p. (J). (gr. 3 up). 1997. lib. bdg. 14.95 (0-88110-937-1, Usborne) EDC.

Understanding Your New Life with Dialysis: A Patient Guide for Physical & Psychological Adjustment. 4th ed. Edith T. Oberley & Terry D. Oberley. (Illus.). 194p. (C). 1992. pap. text ed. 31.95 (0-398-05774-5) C C Thomas.

Understanding Your Potential. Myles E. Munroe. 168p. (Orig.). 1992. pap. 8.99 (1-56043-046-X) Destiny Image.

Understanding Your Potential. Myles E. Munroe. 48p. (Orig.). 1992. student ed., wbk. ed., pap. 6.99 (1-56043-092-3) Destiny Image.

Understanding Your Sex Drive. George B. Eager. (Illus.). 29p. (YA). (gr. 6-12). 1993. pap. 3.00 (1-879224-05-4) Mailbox.

Understanding Your Social Agency. 2nd ed. Armand Lauffer. 168p. 1984. pap. 17.95 (0-8039-2349-X) Sage.

Understanding Your Solar Return. Connie Cummings. pap. 7.00 (0-86690-329-1, 2936-014) Am Fed Astrologers.

Understanding Your Spiritual Destiny. Jeffrey B. Krall. (Illus.). 48p. (Orig.). 1996. pap. 4.75 (1-57688-005-2, 005-2) Branch & Vine.

Understanding Your Teen. Wayne Rice. 1992. wbk. ed., pap. 49.99 incl. vhs (0-310-54528-5) Zondervan.

Understanding Your Teenager's Depression: Issues & Insights for Every Parent. Kathleen McCoy. 352p. (Orig.). 1994. pap. 13.00 (0-399-51856-8, Perigee Bks) Berkley Pub.

Understanding Your Temperament: A Self-Analysis with a Christian Viewpoint. Peter Blitchington & Robert J. Cruise. 42p. (Orig.). 1979. pap. 3.99 (0-943872-67-7) Andrews Univ Pr.

Understanding Your Woman. Keith Fairbanks. 31p. (Orig.). 1994. student ed., pap. 6.95 (0-9645343-0-4) Fairbanks Pub.

Understanding Your Worst Enemy. Mel Bond. Ed. by Gale Cox. 130p. (Orig.). 1992. pap. text ed. write for info. (1-882318-00-5) Agape Wrd Minist.

*Understanding Your 1 Year Old. Deborah Steiner. (Understanding Your Child Ser.: Vol. 2). 1997. pap. text ed. 8.95 (1-894020-01-4, Pub. by Warwick Pub CN) Firefly Bks Ltd.

*Understanding Your 10 Year Old. Jonathan Bradley. (Understanding Your Child Ser.: Vol. 11). 1997. pap. 8.95 (1-894020-10-3, Pub. by Warwick Pub CN) Firefly Bks Ltd.

*Understanding Your 11 Year Old. Ellen Orford. (Understanding Your Child Ser.: Vol. 12). 1997. pap. 8.95 (1-894020-11-1, Pub. by Warwick Pub CN) Firefly Bks Ltd.

*Understanding Your 12-14 Year Olds. Margot Waddell. (Understanding Your Child: Vol. 13). 1997. pap. 8.95 (1-894020-12-X, Pub. by Warwick Pub CN) Firefly Bks Ltd.

*Understanding Your 15-17 Year Olds. Jonathan Bradley. (Understanding Your Child Ser.: Vol. 14). 1997. pap. 8.95 (1-894020-13-8, Pub. by Warwick Pub CN) Firefly Bks Ltd.

*Understanding Your 18-20 Year Olds. Gianna Williams. (Understanding Your Child Ser.: Vol. 15). 1997. pap. 8.95 (1-894020-14-6, Pub. by Warwick Pub CN) Firefly Bks Ltd.

*Understanding Your 2 Year Old. Susan Reid. (Understanding Your Child Ser.: Vol. 3). 1997. pap. 8.95 (1-894020-02-2, Pub. by Warwick Pub CN) Firefly Bks Ltd.

*Understanding Your 3 Year Old. Judith Trowell. (Undertanding Your Child Ser.: Vol. 4). 1997. pap. 8.95 (1-894020-03-0, Pub. by Warwick Pub CN) Firefly Bks Ltd.

*Understanding Your 4 Year Old. Lisa Miller. (Understanding Your Child Ser.: Vol. 5). 1997. pap. 8.95 (1-894020-04-9, Pub. by Warwick Pub CN) Firefly Bks Ltd.

*Understanding Your 5 Year Old. Lesley Holditch. (Understanding Your Child Ser.: Vol. 6). 1997. pap. 8.95 (1-894020-05-7, Pub. by Warwick Pub CN) Firefly Bks Ltd.

*Understanding Your 6 Year Old, Vol. 7. Deborah Steiner. (Understanding Your Child Ser.: Vol. 7). 1997. pap. 8.95 (1-894020-06-5, Pub. by Warwick Pub CN) Firefly Bks Ltd.

*Understanding Your 7 Year Old. Elsie Osbourne. (Understanding Your Child Ser.: Vol. 8). 1997. pap. 8.95 (1-894020-07-3) Firefly Bks Ltd.

*Understanding Your 8 Year Old. Lisa Miller. (Understanding Your Child Ser.: Vol. 9). 1997. pap. 8.95 (1-894020-08-1, Pub. by Warwick Pub CN) Firefly Bks Ltd.

*Understanding Your 9 Year Old. Dora Lush. (Understanding Your Child Ser.: Vol. 10). 1997. pap. text ed. 8.95 (1-894020-09-X, Pub. by Warwick Pub CN) Firefly Bks Ltd.

Understanding Yourself: Identifying Your Interests, Skills, Values, & Life-Style Preferences. rev. ed. JIST Works, Inc. Staff & Northern Virginia Community College Staff. (Career Emphasis Ser.). (Illus.). 60p. 1991. pap. text ed. 5.95 (0-942784-12-X, CE11) JIST Works.

Understanding Yourself Through Birth Order. Clifford E. Isaacson. (Illus.). 120p. (Orig.). 1988. pap. 7.95 (0-945156-00-6) Upper Des Moines Counsel.

Understanding Z: A Specification Language & Its Formal Semantics. J. M. Spivey. (Cambridge Tracts in Theoretical Computer Science Ser.: No. 3). 160p. 1988. text ed. 44.95 (*0-521-33429-2*) Cambridge U Pr.

Understanding Zen. Benjamin Radcliff & Amy Radcliff. LC 92-42624. 192p. (Orig.). 1993. pap. 14.95 (*0-8048-1808-8*) C E Tuttle.

Understanding 1-2-3 Release 2.3 & 2.4 for DOS. 2nd ed. Rebecca B. Altman. LC 92-81684. 715p. 1992. pap. 29.95 (*0-7821-1133-5*) Sybex.

Understanding 1-2-3, Release 5 for Windows. Douglas Hergert & Guy Hart-Davis. LC 94-67534. 1320p. 1994. pap. 29.99 (*0-7821-1579-9*) Sybex.

Understanding 1st & 2nd Chronicles: The House of God & Its Service. John Heading. 405p. 1995. reprint ed. pap. 12.50 (*0-937396-10-9*) Walterick Pubs.

Understanding 30 Power & Plant Distribution No. 602: Video Booklet/Workbook. unabridged ed. L. A. Bryan & E. A. Bryan. Ed. by L. B. Thompson. (Illus.). 48p. (Orig.). 1995. pap. 22.95 (*0-944107-10-9*) Indust Text.

***Understanding Stepfamilies: Their Structure & Dynamics.** Ed. by Craig A. Everett. LC 95-52580. (Journal of Divorce & Remarriage: Vol. 24, Nos. 1/2). 196p. (C). 1996. pap. 14.95 (*0-7890-0225-6*) Haworth Pr.

Understaning Stepfamilies: Their Structure & Dynamics. Ed. by Craig A. Everett. LC 95-52580. (Journal of Divorce & Remarriage: Vol. 24, Nos. 1/2). 196p. (C). 1996. 49.95 (*1-56024-769-X*) Haworth Pr.

Understatements & Hedges in English. Alex Huebler. LC 84-10981. (Pragmatics & Beyond Ser.: Vol. IV, No. 6). ix, 192p. (Orig.). 1983. pap. 59.00 (*0-915027-29-1*) Benjamins North Am.

Understood Betsy. Dorothy Canfield. 1976. 17.95 (*0-8488-1261-1*) Amereon Ltd.

Understood Betsy. Dorothy C. Fisher. (J). pap. 4.95 (*0-8167-2903-4*) Troll Communs.

Understood Betsy. Dorothy Canfield. 219p. (J). 1981. reprint ed. lib. bdg. 21.95 (*0-89966-342-7*) Buccaneer Bks.

Understood Betsy. Dorothy Canfield. 213p. (J). 1980. reprint ed. lib. bdg. 21.95 (*0-89967-016-4*) Harmony Raine.

Understory: Poems by Michelle Boisseau. Frwd. by Molly Peacock. 64p. 1996. pap. text ed. 10.95 (*1-55553-286-1*) NE U Pr.

Understructure of Writing for Film & Television. Ben Brady & Lance Lee. 282p. (Orig.). (C). 1988. pap. 14.95 (*0-292-78515-1*); text ed. 28.95 (*0-292-78514-3*) U of Tex Pr.

Understudies. Mary E. Wilkins Freeman. LC 70-86141. (Short Story Index Reprint Ser.). 1977. 21.95 (*0-8369-3045-2*) Ayer.

Undertaker. Edward R. Ricciuti. Ed. by Bruce Glassman. (Face to Face Ser.). 25p. (Orig.). (J). (gr. 5 up). 1994. pap. text ed. 6.95 (*1-56711-074-6*, Topdog) Blackbirch.

Undertaker's Daughter. Susie Mee. 80p. (Orig.). 1992. pap. 9.00 (*1-881523-01-2*) Junction CA.

Undertaker's Garland. John P. Bishop & Edmund Wilson. LC 74-4263. (American Literature Ser.: No. 49). 1974. lib. bdg. 42.95 (*0-8383-2041-4*) M S G Haskell Hse.

Undertaker's Gone Bananas. Paul Zindel. 160p. (YA). (gr. 6-12). 1984. mass mkt. 4.50 (*0-553-27189-X*) Bantam.

***Undertaking: Life Studies from the Dismal Trade.** Thomas Lynch. (Illus.). 160p. 1997. 23.00 (*0-393-04112-3*) Norton.

Undertaking Midwifery Research: A Basic Guide to Design & Analysis. Carolyn M. Hicks. 1996. write for info. (*0-443-05230-1*) Churchill.

Undertaking, Thief, The Pig: Three Plays. David Trainer. LC 68-28570. 176p. 1968. 14.95 (*0-910278-51-2*) Boulevard.

Undertones. Philip E. Duffy. LC 95-69549. xii, 148p. (Orig.). 1996. pap. 10.95 (*0-9629651-1-1*) Chase Pub.

Undertones of Insurrection: Music, Politics, & the Social Sphere in Modern German Narrative. Marc A. Weiner. LC 92-29072. (Texts & Contexts Ser.). (Illus.). xvi, 314p. 1993. text ed. 40.00 (*0-8032-4758-3*) U of Nebr Pr.

Undertow. Susanna Kearsley. 1993. 17.95 (*0-8034-8987-0*) Bouregy.

***Undertow.** Kiki Kjaer. (Illus.). 48p. 1997. pap. 8.95 (*1-56163-185-X*, Amerotica) NBM.

Undertow. Sandra Marshburn. 21p. (Orig.). 1992. pap. 6.00 (*0-9624453-9-8*) March Street Pr.

Undertow. Sally H. Reid. 320p. 1992. mass mkt. 4.50 (*0-8217-3962-X*, Zebra Kensgtn) Kensgtn Pub Corp.

Undertow. C. Simmons. 19.95 (*0-06-019018-3*, HarpT) HarpC.

Undertow. Lynn Stegner. LC 92-74927. 367p. 1993. 21.00 (*1-880909-02-2*) Baskerville.

Undertow. Lynn Stegner. 367p. 1996. pap. 12.00 (*1-880909-42-1*, Basset Bks) Baskerville.

Undertow. Joy Walsh. 100p. pap. 10.00 (*0-938838-54-7*) Textile Bridge.

***Undertow.** limited unabridged ed. Harrison Clark. 210p. 1996. 95.00 (*1-881119-08-4*) Pyncheon Hse.

***Undertow: New & Selected Poems.** John Kinsella. 110p. 1996. pap. 15.95 (*1-900072-07-6*) Dufour.

Underutilized Resources As Animal Feedstuffs. National Research Council Staff. LC 83-13311. 273p. reprint ed. pap. 77.90 (*0-7837-2779-8*, 2043170) Bks Demand.

Underwater. Paul Starry & Andrew Cleave. LC 92-60795. (Nature Search Ser.). (Illus.). 32p. (J). (gr. 4-7). 1992. 14.00 (*0-89577-449-6*) RD Assn.

Underwater Acoustic Data Processing. Ed. by Y. T. Chan. (C). 1989. lib. bdg. 265.00 (*0-7923-0127-7*) Kluwer Ac.

***Underwater Acoustic Modeling: Principles, Techniques & Applications.** 2nd ed. Etter. (Illus.). 360p. 1995. text ed. 129.00 (*0-419-20190-4*, E & FN Spon) Routledge Chapman & Hall.

***Underwater Acoustic Positioning Systems.** P. H. Milne. LC 83-80348. (Illus.). 294p. pap. 83.80 (*0-608-04876-3*, 2065557) Bks Demand.

Underwater Acoustics & Signal Processing. Ed. by L. Bjorno. 1981. lib. bdg. 194.00 (*90-277-1255-7*) Kluwer Ac.

Underwater Acoustics Instrumentation. Vernon M. Albers. LC 76-84217. 99p. reprint ed. pap. 28.30 (*0-317-08626-X*, 2051122) Bks Demand.

Underwater Adventures: Fifty of the World's Greatest! Paul McCallum. (Illus.). 160p. (Orig.). 1992. pap. 19.95 (*1-55870-255-5*, Betrwy Bks) F & W Pubns Inc.

Underwater Alphabet Book. Jerry Pallotta. LC 91-70015. (Jerry Pallotta's Alphabet Bks.). (Illus.). 32p. (J). (ps-8). 1991. 14.95 (*0-88106-461-0*); pap. 6.95 (*0-88106-455-6*); lib. bdg. 15.88 (*0-88106-684-2*) Charlesbridge Pub.

Underwater Animals. Helen Cooney. LC 96-16966. (Young Discoveries Ser.). (Illus.). 32p. (J). (ps-2). 1996. write for info. (*0-7835-4841-9*) Time-Life.

Underwater Archaeology: Exploring the World Beneath the Sea. Jean-Yves Blot. Tr. by Alexandra Campbell. (Discoveries Ser.). (Illus.). 176p. 1996. pap. 12.95 (*0-8109-2859-0*) Abrams.

Underwater California. Wheeler North. LC 75-13153. (California Natural History Guides Ser.: No.39). (Illus.). 1976. pap. 12.00 (*0-520-03039-7*) U CA Pr.

Underwater Communication: A Guide for Scuba & Commercial Divers. Jess F. King. (Illus.). 96p. (Orig.). 1994. pap. 14.95 (*1-884362-00-1*) Butte Pubns.

***Underwater Concreting & Repair.** write for info. (*0-340-54466-X*, Pub. by E Arnold UK) Routledge Chapman & Hall.

Underwater Concreting & Repair. Andrew McLeish. 160p. 1994. text ed. 59.95 (*0-470-23403-2*) Halsted Pr.

Underwater Construction: Development & Potential. Ed. by Society for Underwater Technology Staff. (C). 1987. lib. bdg. 127.00 (*0-86010-861-9*, Pub. by Graham & Trotman UK) Kluwer Ac.

Underwater Crime Scene: Underwater Crime Investigative Techniques. Ronald F. Becker. LC 94-48036. (Illus.). 148p. (C). 1995. text ed. 41.95 (*0-398-05979-9*); pap. text ed. 29.95 (*0-398-05980-2*) C C Thomas.

Underwater Crime Scene Investigation: Organizing, Training & Equipping - The Dive Team on a Budget. Eric Tackett. Ed. by PADI Staff & Ruth Hunsinger. (Emergency Service - Public Safety Dive Teams Ser.). (Illus.). 150p. (Orig.). 1987. teacher ed. 15.95 (*0-943155-05-3*, 1011); pap. 15.95 (*0-943155-00-2*) Laser Tech.

Underwater Dig: Introduction to Marine Archaeology. 2nd ed. Robert F. Marx. 252p. 1990. 19.95 (*1-55992-031-9*, Pisces Bks) Gulf Pub.

Underwater Dive, Version One. Jena Osman. (Illus.). 24p. (Orig.). 1990. pap. 4.00 (*0-945926-22-7*) Paradigm RI.

Underwater Ear & Nose Care. rev. ed. Noel Roydhouse. (Illus.). 78p. (C). 1994. 24.85 (*0-941332-23-3*, D055) Best Pub Co.

Underwater Electroacoustic Measurements. Robert J. Bobber. LC 87-63303. 341p. 1989. reprint ed. 43.95 (*0-932146-19-8*) Peninsula CA.

Underwater Expeditions. Ed. by Robert Palmer. (C). 1990. 30.00 (*0-907649-31-9*, Pub. by Expedit Advisory Centre UK) St Mut.

Underwater Fantasies. Robert L. Nelson. 1995. pap. 10.99 (*1-57081-770-7*) Day Dream SBCA.

Underwater Flies for Trout. Tom Fuller. (Illus.). 192p. 1996. text ed. 24.95 (*0-07-022634-2*, Ragged Mntn) Intl Marine.

Underwater Gourmet: The Great Seafood Book. Young et al. LC 83-81849. (Famous Florida Ser.). (Illus.). 320p. (Orig.). 1986. reprint ed. pap. 14.95 (*0-932855-27-X*) Winner Enter.

Underwater Guide to Hawai'i. Ann Fielding. LC 86-30841. (Illus.). 144p. 1987. 19.95 (*0-8248-1104-6*) UH Pr.

Underwater Guide to Hawaiian Reef Fishes. John E. Randall. LC 79-27625. (Illus.). 72p. 1980. spiral bd. 18.95 (*0-915180-02-2*) Harrowood Bks.

***Underwater Guide to Pacific Coast Fishes.** Daniel W. Gotshall. (Illus.). 26p. 1997. 16.95 (*0-930118-25-1*, 139G) Sea Chall.

Underwater Guide to the Florida Keys. Stephen Frink. Ed. by Robert Haff, Jr. (Illus.). 64p. (Orig.). (C). 1990. pap. 7.95 (*0-9625409-0-0*) Blue Water FL.

Underwater Handbook: A Guide to Physiology & Performance for the Engineer. Ed. by Charles W. Shilling et al. LC 76-7433. (Illus.). 912p. 1977. 155.00 (*0-306-30843-6*, Plenum Pr) Plenum.

Underwater Indonesia: A Guide to the World's Best Diving. David Pickell. 1993. pap. 15.95 (*0-8442-9908-1*, Passport Bks) NTC Pub Grp.

Underwater Indonesia: A Guide to the World's Greatest Diving. 2nd ed. Kal Muller. Ed. by David Pickell. 326p. 1995. pap. 19.95 (*962-593-029-9*) Periplus.

***Underwater Inspection.** 3rd ed. Short & Bax. (Illus.). 229p. 1991. text ed. 78.95 (*0-419-13540-5*, E & FN Spon) Routledge Chapman & Hall.

Underwater Inspection & Repair of Bridge Substructures. (National Cooperative Highway Research Program Report Ser.: No. 088). 77p. 1981. 7.60 (*0-309-03407-8*) Transport Res Bd.

Underwater Intervention Systems. USNA (Hawley) Staff. 246p. (C). 1996. per., pap. text ed. 26.19 (*0-7872-1510-4*) Kendall-Hunt.

***Underwater Investigations: Correspondence Course.** Robert G. Teather. 40p. 1996. text ed. 16.50 (*0-941332-49-7*, D487A) Best Pub Co.

Underwater Investigator. Robert G. Teather. 111p. 1983. pap. text ed. 12.95 (*0-943717-18-3*) Concept Sys.

Underwater Life. Dean Morris. (Read About Ser.). (J). (ps-3). 1990. pap. 4.95 (*0-8114-8219-7*) Raintree Steck-V.

Underwater Logging. John E. Cayford & Ronald E. Scott. LC 64-18585. (Illus.). 93p. reprint ed. pap. 26.60 (*0-7837-6297-6*, 2046012) Bks Demand.

Underwater Minerals. David S. Cronan. (Ocean Science, Resources & Technology Ser.). 1980. text ed. 154.00 (*0-12-197480-4*) Acad Pr.

Underwater Navigator Manual. (Illus.). 76p. 1994. pap. 12.95 (*1-878663-15-1*) PADI.

Underwater Paradise: The World's Best Diving Sites. Robert Boye. (Illus.). 192p. 1989. 39.95 (*0-8109-1159-0*) Abrams.

Underwater Photographer. Martin Edge. (Illus.). 256p. 1996. pap. 39.95 (*0-240-51433-5*, Focal) Buttrwrth-Heinemann.

***Underwater Photography.** Harry Averill. (Specialty Diver Ser.). 128p. 1995. pap. text ed. write for info. (*1-880229-26-9*) Concept Sys.

Underwater Photography. Charles R. Seaborn. (Illus.). 144p. 1988. pap. 18.95 (*0-8174-6336-4*, Amphoto) Watsn-Guptill.

Underwater Photography. Smith. 1984. 62.50 (*0-442-27962-0*) Jones & Bartlett.

Underwater Photography Camera Basics Equipment Care. Geri Murphy. Ed. by Karl Shreeves et al. (Underwater Photography Ser.). (Illus.). 87p. (Orig.). 1989. pap. text ed. 9.95 (*1-878663-03-8*) PADI.

***Underwater Photography Instructor Manual.** Harry Averill. (Specialty Diver Ser.). 52p. 1995. pap. text ed. write for info. (*1-880229-27-7*) Concept Sys.

Underwater Photography Macro. Geri Murphy. Ed. by Mary E. Hurrell et al. (Underwater Photography Ser.). (Illus.). 59p. (Orig.). 1990. pap. text ed. 12.95 (*1-878663-04-6*) PADI.

Underwater Photography Now. Peter J. Diamondis. LC 83-136151. (Illus.). 154p. 1983. 11.95 (*0-9612110-0-8*) P J Diamondis.

Underwater Prospecting Techniques: The Gold Divers Handbook. 10th rev. ed. LC 60-4754. (Illus.). 1983. pap. 3.00 (*0-686-38066-5*) Merlin Engine Wks.

Underwater Range. large type ed. Mark Donovan. 182p. 1994. pap. 17.99 (*1-85389-439-7*, Medcom-Trainex) Ulverscroft.

Underwater Repair Technology: Ninth Annual North American Welding Research Conference. J. H. Nixon. 200p. 1995. boxed 144.00 (*1-85573-239-4*, Pub. by Woodhead Pubng UK) Am Educ Systs.

Underwater Robotics Vehicles: Design & Control. Ed. by Junku Yuh. 361p. (C). 1995. write for info. (*0-614-16441-9*) TSI Pr.

Underwater Robots. George A. Bekey & Tamaki Ura. Ed. by Junku Yuh. LC 96-23420. 256p. (C). 1996. lib. bdg. 130.00 (*0-7923-9754-1*) Kluwer Ac.

Underwater Signal & Data Processing. Joseph C. Hassab. 320p. 1989. 228.95 (*0-8493-6800-6*, QC242) CRC Pr.

Underwater Soil Sampling, Testing, & Construction Control: A Symposium Presented at the Seventy-Fourth Annual Meeting, American Society for Testing & Materials, Atlantic City, 1971. American Society for Testing & Materials Staff. LC 77-185536. (ASTM Special Technical Publication Ser.: 501). 247p. reprint ed. pap. 70.40 (*0-317-26537-7*, 2023988) Bks Demand.

Underwater Technology. Atteraas. 1980. pap. write for info. (*0-08-026142-6*, Pergamon Pr) Elsevier.

Underwater Tools. Donald J. Hackman & Don W. Caudy. LC 81-4399. (Illus.). 152p. 1981. 32.95 (*0-935470-08-5*) Battelle.

Underwater Videographers Handbook. Lynn Laymon. 128p. 1992. pap. 19.95 (*0-936262-18-4*) Amherst Media.

Underwater Warfare in the Age of Soil. Alex Roland. LC 77-74436. (Illus.). 254p. reprint ed. pap. 72.40 (*0-8357-6698-5*, 2056878) Bks Demand.

Underwater Warriors: Midget Submarine Operations in War. Paul J. Kemp. (Illus.). 192p. 1996. 34.95 (*1-55750-857-7*) Naval Inst Pr.

Underwater Weapons. Lynn M. Stone. LC 96-8995. (Animal Weapons Ser.). 1996. write for info. (*1-57103-162-6*) Rourke Pr.

Underwater Welding. Iiw. 1983. pap. 22.50 (*0-08-030539-3*, Pergamon Pr); 45.00 (*0-08-030538-5*, Pergamon Pr) Elsevier.

Underwater Wilderness: Life in America's National Marine Sanctuaries & Reserves. Charles R. Seaborn. LC 96-68565. (Illus.). 192p. (Orig.). 1996. pap. 29.95 (*1-57098-104-3*) Monterey Bay Aquarium.

Underwater Work: A Manual of Scuba Commercial, Salvage, & Construction Operations. 2nd ed. John E. Cayford. LC 66-28081. (Illus.). 244p. reprint ed. pap. 69.60 (*0-7837-6298-4*, 2046013) Bks Demand.

Underwater World. LC 92-25074. (Understanding Science & Nature Ser.). 176p. (J). 1993. 17.95 (*0-8094-9679-8*); lib. bdg. 24.60 (*0-8094-9680-1*) Time-Life.

Underwater World of Sport Diving. Larry S. Roberts. 240p. (gr. 13). 1991. pap. text ed. 14.00 (*0-8016-4130-6*) Mosby Yr Bk.

Underwater Worlds: Marine Life of the Pacific. (Postcard Book Ser.). (Illus.). 50p. 1994. 8.00 (*1-56836-019-3*) Kodansha.

Underwear. Hannant. (Stickers 'N' Shapes Ser.). (J). 1998. 3.99 (*0-689-81106-3*) S&S Childrens.

Underwear! Mary E. Monsell. Ed. by Abby Levine. LC 87-25419. (Illus.). 24p. (J). (ps-2). 1988. lib. bdg. 12.95 (*0-8075-8308-1*) A Whitman.

Underwear! Mary E. Monsell. (J). (ps-3). 1993. pap. 4.95 (*0-8075-8309-X*) A Whitman.

***Underwear.** Jonathan Potter. Ed. by William-Alan Landes. 55p. (Orig.). 1997. pap. 5.00 (*0-88734-369-4*) Players Pr.

Underwear. Jennifer Ruby. (Illus.). (J). (gr. 5-9). 1996. 24.95 (*0-7134-7663-X*, Pub. by Batsford UK) Trafalgar.

***Underwear.** Andrew Santella. 1997. spiral bd. write for info. (*0-201-15170-7*) Addison-Wesley.

Underwhere. Kevin Eastman. 1996. 24.95 (*1-882931-18-1*) Heavy Metal Magazine.

Underwood & Holt's Professional Negligence. Hilton Harrop-Griffiths & Jane Bennington. 136p. 1985. 95.00 (*0-906840-90-2*, Pub. by Fourmat Pub UK) St Mut.

Underwood Biographical Dictionary. Laverne Galeener-Moore. 584p. (Orig.). 1993. pap. text ed. 37.00 (*1-55613-853-9*) Heritage Bk.

Underwood. The Underwood Families of America. L. M. Underwood. Ed. by H. J. Banker. (Illus.). 809p. 1991. reprint ed. pap. 107.50 (*0-8328-2016-4*); reprint ed. lib. bdg. 117.50 (*0-8328-2015-6*) Higginson Bk Co.

Underwood's Children: The Wood Engravings of Gertrude Hermes & Blair Hughes-Stanton. Ed. by Katherine Eustance. (Illus.). 71p. 1996. pap. 12.95 (*1-85444-064-0*, 640-0, Pub. by Ashmolean Mus UK) A Schwartz & Co.

Underworld. William J. Austin. LC 94-65417. 64p. (C). 1994. pap. 7.00 (*1-884970-00-1*) S Press.

***Underworld.** Don DeLillo. 1997. 27.50 (*0-684-84269-6*) S&S Trade.

***Underworld.** Kaz. 80p. 1995. pap. 9.95 (*1-56097-169-X*) Fantagraph Bks.

Underworld. Kelly Klein. LC 95-34169. (Illus.). 180p. 1995. 65.00 (*0-679-43579-4*) Knopf.

***Underworld No. 2: Bare Bulbs.** Kaz. 96p. 1996. pap. 9.95 (*1-56097-258-0*) Fantagraph Bks.

Underworld Dwellers. Ernest Tucker. LC 94-16875. 160p. 1994. 15.95 (*0-944957-22-6*) Rivercross Pub.

***Underworld Enemies.** 1994. 13.00 (*1-55806-197-5*) Iron Crown Ent Inc.

***Underworld Sewer: A Prostitute Reflects on Life in the Trade, 1871-1909.** Josie Washburn. (Illus.). 368p. 1997. pap. 15.00 (*0-8032-9797-1*, Bison Books) U of Nebr Pr.

***Underworld Sourcebook.** FASA Corporation Staff. 1997. pap. text ed. 15.00 (*1-55560-315-7*) FASA Corp.

Underworlds: Organized Crime in the Netherlands, 1650-1800. Florike Egmond. Ed. by Sue Leigh. (Illus.). 268p. 1994. text ed. 55.95 (*0-7456-0644-X*) Blackwell Pubs.

Underwriter. Jack Rudman. (Career Examination Ser.: C-2011). 1994. pap. 29.95 (*0-8373-2011-9*) Nat Learn.

Underwriters Bedside Book. Jonathan Ignarski. 1987. 35.00 (*1-85044-132-4*) LLP.

Underwriting Commercial Liability. Joseph F. Mangan & Connor M. Harrison. LC 95-81905. (Illus.). 347p. (Orig.). (C). 1995. pap. text ed. 26.00 (*0-89462-095-9*, AU66) IIA.

Underwriting Commercial Property. Joseph F. Mangan & Connor M. Harrison. LC 95-814488. (Illus.). 347p. (Orig.). (C). 1995. pap. text ed. 26.00 (*0-89462-093-2*, AU65) IIA.

Underwriting Decisions under Uncertainty: The Catastrophe Market. David E. Ayling. (C). 1984. 275.00 (*0-685-32684-5*, Pub. by Witherby & Co UK) St Mut.

Underwriting in Life & Health Insurance: Course Manual. Ed. by Joyce A. Fleming. 1995. ring bd. 30.00 (*0-939921-67-7*) Life Office.

Underwriting in Life & Health Insurance Companies. Ed. by Richard Bailey. LC 85-50140. (FLMI Insurance Education Program Ser.). 1985. text ed. 55.00 (*0-915322-74-9*) Life Office.

Underwriting Injustice: Aid & El Salvador's Judicial Reform Program. Martha Doggett. Ed. by Michael Posner & William O'Neill. (Illus.). 190p. (Orig.). 1989. pap. text ed. 12.00 (*0-934143-24-2*) Lawyers Comm Human.

Underwriting Principles. Joseph F. Mangan & Connor M. Harrison. LC 95-81452. (Illus.). 201p. (Orig.). (C). 1995. pap. text ed. 26.00 (*0-89462-094-0*, AU65) IIA.

Undescended Testis. Ed. by Eric W. Fonkalsrud & Wolfgang Mengel. LC 80-19479. (Illus.). 295p. reprint ed. pap. 84.10 (*0-8357-7614-X*, 2056937) Bks Demand.

Undeserving Poor: From the War on Poverty to the War on Welfare. Michael B. Katz. 320p. 1990. pap. 17.00 (*0-679-72561-X*) Pantheon.

Undesigning the Bath. Leonard Koren. (Illus.). 112p. (Orig.). 1996. pap. 16.95 (*1-880656-24-8*) Stone Bridge Pr.

Undesirable Journalist. Gunter Wallraff. LC 78-70935. 192p. 1983. pap. 10.95 (*0-87951-169-9*) Overlook Pr.

Undesirables. Y. Fries & T. Bibib. 1985. 24.95 (*0-318-37282-7*) Asia Bk Corp.

***Undesirables.** Mary C. Smith. 470p. 1997. 24.95 (*0-930773-47-0*) Black Heron Pr.

Undesirables: The Expatriation of the Tamil People of Recent Indian Origin from the Plantations in Sri Lanka. Yvonne Fries & T. Bibin. 1985. 18.50 (*0-8364-1344-X*, Pub. by KP Bagchi IA) S Asia.

Undesirables, Early Immigrants & the Anti-Japanese Movement in San Francisco: 1892-1893. Donald T. Hata, Jr. Ed. by Roger Daniels. LC 78-54817. (Asian Experience in North America Ser.). 1979. lib. bdg. 18.95 (*0-405-11273-4*) Ayer.

Undesired Princess & the Enchanted Bunny. L. Sprague De Camp. (J). 1990. mass mkt. 4.99 (*0-671-69875-3*) Baen Bks.

Undetected Enemy: French & American Miscalculations at Dien Bien Phu, 1953. John R. Nordell, Jr. LC 94-37073. (Military History Ser.: No. 39). (Illus.). 224p. 1995. 39.50 (*0-89096-645-1*) Tex A&M Univ Pr.

Undeveloped West; or Five Years in Territories. John H. Beadle. LC 72-9427. (Far Western Frontier Ser.). (Illus.). 828p. 1973. reprint ed. 56.95 (*0-405-04958-7*) Ayer.

Undiet. Kim Jordan. 278p. (Orig.). 1994. pap. text ed. 14.95 (*0-89716-465-2*) P B Pubng.

Undiet Book. Elizabeth Baker. 210p. 1992. pap. 9.95 (*0-937766-17-8*) Drelwood Comns.

Undimensional Scaling. John P. McIver & Edward G. Carmines. (Quantitative Applications in the Social Sciences Ser.: Vol. 24). (Illus.). (C). 1981. pap. 9.95 (*0-8039-1736-8*) Sage.

Undiminished Man: A Political Biography of Robert Walker Kenny. Janet Stevenson. LC 80-10889. (Illus.). 218p. 1980. 10.95 (0-88316-538-4) Chandler & Sharp.

Undimmed by Tears. Ed. by Amnon Katz. 118p. 1992. pap. 15.00 (0-938245-12-0) Inverted-A.

Undine. Michael O'Rourke. 368p. 1996. mass mkt. 5.50 (0-06-100718-8, Harp PBks) HarpC.

Undine. Fouque De La Motte. Ed. by Ben Barkow. (Dedalus European Classics Ser.). (Illus.). 224p. 1997. reprint ed. pap. 11.95 (0-946626-57-X, Pub. by Dedalus UK) Subterranean Co.

Undiplomatic Dialogue: Letters Between Carl Berendsen & Alister McIntosh, 1943-1952. Ed. by Ian McGibbon. (Auckland University Press Book). 336p. 1994. 29.95 (1-86940-095-X) OUP.

Undiplomatic Diary. Harry H. Bandholtz. LC 77-160009. reprint ed. 49.50 (0-404-00494-6) AMS Pr.

Undiplomatic Incidents. Apa B. Pant. 1987. text ed. 12.50 (0-86131-690-8, Pub. by Orient Longman Ltd II) Apt Bks.

Undiscovered Europe. Ed. by Marian V. Cooper. 610p. 1988. 14.95 (0-945332-07-6) Agora Inc MD.

Undiscovered Self: With "Symbols & the Interpretation of Dreams" C. G. Jung. Tr. by R. F. Hull. 166p. (Orig.). 1990. pap. 9.95 (0-691-01894-4) Princeton U Pr.

Undiscovered Self: With "Symbols & the Interpretation of Dreams" Carl G. Jung. Tr. by R. F. Hull. 166p. (Orig.). 1990. text ed. 39.50 (0-691-09968-5) Princeton U Pr.

Undiscovered: The Fascinating World of Undiscovered Places, Graves, Wrecks & Treasure. large type ed. Ian Wilson. 284p. 1990. 19.95 (1-85089-320-9, Pub. by ISIS UK) Transaction Pubs.

Undiscovered Asir. Thierry Mauger. (Illus.). 160p. 1990. boxed 69.95 (0-905743-70-9, Pub. by Stacey Intl UK) Intl Bk Ctr.

Undiscovered Christ. Mark Chironna. 112p. (Orig.). 1992. pap. 7.99 (1-56043-085-0) Destiny Image.

Undiscovered Continent: Emily Dickinson & the Space of the Mind. Suzanne Juhasz. LC 82-49014. 198p. 1983. reprint ed. pap. 56.50 (0-7837-9655-2, 2059288) Bks Demand.

***Undiscovered Country.** Kenneth Haxton. 376p. (Orig.). 1997. pap. 15.00 (1-57502-503-5, P01495) Morris Pubng.

Undiscovered Country. rev. ed. Georges Duquette. LC 93-24146. 64p. 1995. pap. 12.95 (0-7734-2767-8, Mellen Poetry Pr) E Mellen.

Undiscovered Country. William Dean Howells. LC 71-129976. 1971. reprint ed. 24.00 (0-403-00133-1) Scholarly.

Undiscovered Country. William Dean Howells. (Notable American Authors Ser.). 1992. reprint ed. lib. bdg. 75.00 (0-7812-3232-5) Rprt Serv.

Undiscovered Country: Exploring the Promise of Death. Eknath Easwaran. 144p. 1996. 22.00 (0-915132-84-2); pap. 9.95 (0-915132-83-4) Nilgiri Pr.

***Undiscovered Hero.** Stephanie Doyle. (Intimate Moments Ser.: No. 792). 1997. mass mkt. 3.99 (0-373-07792-0, 1-07792-4) Silhouette.

Undiscovered Museums of Florence. 2nd ed. Eloise M. Danto. LC 90-24480. 132p. (Orig.). 1991. pap. 8.95 (0-940625-34-2) Surrey Bks.

Undiscovered Museums of London. 2nd ed. Eloise M. Danto. LC 90-24481. 138p. (Orig.). 1991. pap. 8.95 (0-940625-35-0) Surrey Bks.

Undiscovered Museums of New York. 2nd ed. Eloise M. Danto. LC 90-24479. 144p. (Orig.). 1991. pap. 8.95 (0-940625-36-9) Surrey Bks.

Undiscovered Museums of Paris. 2nd ed. Eloise M. Danto. LC 91-14027. 132p. (Orig.). 1991. pap. 8.95 (0-940625-33-4) Surrey Bks.

Undiscovered Niagara. Linda Bramble. (Illus.). 96p. (Orig.). pap. 16.95 (1-919783-61-X, Pub. by Boston Mills Pr CN) Genl Dist Srvs.

Undiscovered Oil & Gas Resources: An Evaluation of the Department of the Interior's 1989 Assessment Procedures. National Research Council Staff. 192p. 1991. pap. text ed. 23.00 (0-309-04533-9) Natl Acad Pr.

***Undiscovered One.** Raymond D. Kruk. 1997. mass mkt. 4.99 (1-55197-324-3, Pub. by Comnwlth Pub CN) Partners Pubs Grp.

***Undiscovered Petroleum & Mineral Resources: Assessment & Controversy.** Lawrence J. Drew. (Illus.). 205p. (C). 59.50 (0-306-45524-2, Plenum Pr) Plenum.

Undiscovered Self. C. G. Jung. 1976. 17.95 (0-8488-0547-X) Amereon Ltd.

Undiscovered Self. Carl G. Jung. 1959. pap. 5.99 (0-451-62650-8) NAL-Dutton.

Undiscovered Self. Carl G. Jung. 1974. pap. 3.95 (0-451-62539-0, ME1946, Ment) NAL-Dutton.

Undivided Heart: Making Sense of Celibate Chastity. Sean D. Sammon. LC 93-3852. 172p. 1993. pap. 9.95 (0-8189-0674-X) Alba.

Undivided Heart: The Western Monastic Approach to Contemplation. Michael Casey. LC 94-6259. 217p. 1994. pap. 12.95 (1-879007-04-5) St Bedes Pubns.

Undivided Universe. David Bohm & Basil Hiley. 416p. 1995. pap. 18.95 (0-415-12185-X) Routledge.

Undivine "Comedy" Detheologizing Dante. Teodolinda Barolini. LC 92-11859. 360p. 1993. text ed. 60.00 (0-691-06953-0); pap. text ed. 19.95 (0-691-01528-7) Princeton U Pr.

Undocumented Aliens & Crime: The Case of San Diego County. Daniel H. Wolf. (Monographs: No. 29). 54p. (Orig.). 1988. pap. 7.95 (0-935391-77-0, MN-29) UCSD Ctr US-Mex.

Undocumented Aliens in the New York Metropolitan Area. Demetrios G. Papademetriou & Nicholas DiMarzio. LC 85-23385. 292p. (C). 1986. pap. 14.95 (0-913256-99-4) CMS.

Undocumented DOS: A Programmer's Guide to Reserved MS-DOS Functions & Data Structures. 2nd ed. Andrew Schulman et al. 880p. 1993. pap. 44.95 incl. disk (0-201-63287-X) Addison-Wesley.

Undocumented DOS with Disk. Andrew Schulman. 1990. pap. 44.95 (0-201-57064-5) Addison-Wesley.

***Undocumented, Illegal & Scared: The Experiences of an Illegal Alien.** L. Trevor Grant. LC 96-90629. (Illus.). 96p. (Orig.). 1997. pap. 10.00 (0-9653734-1-X) Yacos Publns.

***Undocumented Immigration to California: 1980-1993.** Hans Johnson. 133p. 1996. pap. write for info. (0-9653184-1-9) Pub Policy Inst.

***Undocumented in L. A. An Immigrant's Story.** Dianne W. Hart. LC 96-50993. (Latin American Silhouettes Ser.). 160p. 1997. pap. 16.95 (0-8420-2649-5); text ed. 45.00 (0-8420-2648-7) Scholarly Res Inc.

***Undocumented Java.** Ed Tittel. 1997. pap. 59.99 (0-7645-8007-8) IDG Bks.

Undocumented Love: Amor Indocumentado. Jose A. Burciaga. (Illus.). 173p. 1992. pap. 12.00 (0-9624536-3-3) Chusma Hse.

Undocumented Mexicans in the United States. David M. Heer. (American Sociological Assn. Rose Monograph Ser.). (Illus.). 200p. (C). 1990. text ed. 57.95 (0-521-38247-5) Cambridge U Pr.

Undocumented Migration to the United States: IRCA & the Experience of the 1980s. Ed. by Frank D. Bean et al. LC 90-12967. (Illus.). 240p. (Orig.). (C). 1990. pap. text ed. 23.00 (0-87766-490-0); lib. bdg. 52.00 (0-87766-489-7) Urban Inst.

***Undocumented NetWare.** 512p. 1997. 49.99 (0-7821-1846-1) Sybex.

Undocumented Netwars: A Programmer's Guide to Reserved Networking Apis & Protocals. Tim Farley. 1994. pap. 44.95 (0-201-62645-4) Addison-Wesley.

Undocumented PC. Frank Van Gilluwe. LC 93-33259. 928p. 1993. pap. 49.95 incl. disk (0-201-62277-7) Addison-Wesley.

***Undocumented Peripherals.** Jim Kyle. (C). 1997. pap. text ed. write for info. (0-201-87378-8) Addison-Wesley.

Undocumented Windows: A Programmer's Guide to Reserved Microsoft Windows API Functions. Andrew Schulman et al. 736p. 1992. pap. 44.95 incl. disk (0-201-60834-0) Addison-Wesley.

***Undocumented Windows NT.** Prasad Dabak et al. 1997. pap. write for info. (1-56592-288-3) OReilly & Assocs.

Undoing: Returning to Simplicity. Rudite J. Emir. LC 94-71902. (Illus.). 170p. 1994. pap. 12.00 (0-9641762-1-1) Amber Publish.

Undoing Culture: Globalization, Postmodernism & Identity. Mike Featherstone. (Theory, Culture & Society Ser.). 288p. 1995. 69.95 (0-8039-7605-4); pap. 21.95 (0-8039-7606-2) Sage.

***Undoing Depression: What Therapy Doesn't Teach You & Drugs Can't Give You.** Richard O'Connor. LC 96-50214. 1997. 23.95 (0-316-62643-0) Little.

***Un/Doing Educational Research: Engagements with the Postmodern.** Ian Stronach & Margaret Maclure. LC 96-48465. 1997. write for info. (0-335-19434-6, Open Univ Pr); pap. write for info. (0-335-19433-8, Open Univ Pr) Taylor & Francis.

***Undoing Racism: An International Philosophy of Social Change by the People's Institute for Survival & Beyond.** Michael Washington & Ronald Chisom. 110p. (Orig.). 1996. pap. 10.00 (0-9653305-0-8) Michael Washington.

Undoing the Clinch of Oppression. Philip Lichtenberg. LC 89-48239. (American University Studies: Psychology: Ser. VIII, Vol. 21). 235p. (C). 1990. text ed. 52.95 (0-8204-1301-1) P Lang Pubng.

***(Un)Doing the Missionary Position: Gender Asymmetry in Contemporary Asian American Women's Writing.** Phillipa Kafka. LC 96-27391. (Contributions in Women's Studies). 208p. 1997. text ed. 55.00 (0-313-30161-1) Greenwood.

***Undoing the Social: Towards a Deconstructive Sociology.** Ann Game. 224p. 1991. pap. 13.99 (0-335-09383-3, Open Univ Pr) Taylor & Francis.

Undoing the Social: Towards a Deconstructive Sociology. Ann Game. (Illus.). 224p. 1991. 45.00 (0-8020-5970-8); pap. 18.95 (0-8020-6897-9) U of Toronto Pr.

Undoing Yourself: With Energized Meditation & Other Devices. 6th rev. ed. Christopher S. Hyatt. LC 82-83293. (Illus.). 288p. 1993. pap. 14.95 (1-56184-057-2) New Falcon Pubns.

Undone. Michael Kimball. LC 96-12744. 352p. 1996. 23.00 (0-380-97305-7) Avon.

Undone! More Mad Endings. Paul Jennings. 112p. (YA). (gr. 5 up). 1995. pap. 14.99 (0-670-86005-0) Viking Child Bks.

Undone! More Mad Endings. Paul Jennings. 1997. pap. 3.99 (0-14-038398-0) Viking Penguin.

***UNDP/UNFPA/WHO/World Bank Special Programme of Research, Development & Research Training in Human Reproduction: Biennial Report 1994-1995, UNDP/UNFPA/WHO.** 111p. (Orig.). 1996. pap. 26.00 (92-4-156183-1, 1150443) World Health.

***Undressing Cinema: Clothing & Identity in the Movies.** Stella Bruzzi. LC 97-7260. 216p. 1998. pap. write for info. (0-415-13957-0) Routledge.

***Undressing Cinema: Clothing & Identity in the Movies.** Stella Bruzzi. LC 97-7260. 216p. (C). 1998. text ed. write for info. (0-415-13956-2) Routledge.

Undressing Lesbian Sex. Elaine Creith. 1996. pap. 16.95 (0-304-32849-9, Pub. by Cassell Pubng UK) LPC InBook.

Undressing the American Male: Men with Sexual Problems & What You Can Do to Help Them. Eva L. Margolies. 288p. 1995. pap. 12.95 (0-452-27444-3, Plume) NAL-Dutton.

***Undressing the Dark.** Barbara Carey. 80p. 1986. pap. 12.95 (0-919627-01-3, Pub. by Quarry Pr CN) LPC InBook.

***Undstanding Child Behavior.** 3rd ed. Gelfand. (C). 1997. pap. text ed. 42.00 (0-15-504013-8) HarBrace.

Undue Influence. Miriam Borgenicht. 1990. mass mkt. 3.50 (0-373-26062-8) Harlequin Bks.

Undue Influence. Steve Martini. 480p. 1995. mass mkt. 6.99 (0-515-11605-X) Jove Pubns.

Undue Influence. large type ed. Steve Martini. 567p. 1996. pap. 20.95 (0-7838-1129-2) G K Hall.

Undue Influence. large type ed. Shelby Yastrow. 574p. 1991. reprint ed. lib. bdg. 21.95 (1-56054-132-6) Thorndike Pr.

***Undue Influence: TV Movie Tie-In.** Steve Martini. 1996. mass mkt. 6.99 (0-515-12072-3) Jove Pubns.

Undue Process: A Story of How Political Differences Are Turned into Crimes. Elliott Abrams. 250p. 1992. text ed. 27.95 (0-02-900167-6, Free Press) Free Pr.

***Undue Process: The Untold Story of America's German Alien Internees.** Arnold Krammer. (Illus.). 272p. 1997. 27.95 (0-8476-8518-7) Rowman.

Undulating Weft Effects. Harriet Tidball. LC 76-24001. (Guild Monographs: No. 9). (Illus.). 25p. 1963. pap. 7.95 (0-916658-09-0) Shuttle Craft.

***Undulating Women/Erect Men: The Visual Imagery of Gender, Race & Progress in Reconstructive Illustrations of Human Evolution.** Melanie G. Wiber. (Illus.). 208p. 1997. 24.95 (0-88920-274-5) Wilfrid Laurier.

Undulator Magnets for Synchrotron Radiation & Free Electron Lasers: Symp in the Adriatico Conf. L. Fonda. 280p. 1988. text ed. 93.00 (9971-5-0709-9) World Scientific Pub.

Undulator Radiation & Free-Electron Lasers. Ed. by P. A. Cherenkov. 190p. 1995. pap. 93.00 (1-898326-13-4, Pub. by Cambdge Intl UK) Am Educ Systs.

UnDutchables: An Observation of the Netherlands; Its Culture & Its Inhabitants. 3rd ed. Colin White & Laurie Boucke. LC 96-233338. (Illus.). 250p. 1993. pap. 12.50 (0-9625006-3-1) White-Boucke.

Undying Flame. Ed. by Ellen Garwood. 226p. 1985. 14.95 (0-931727-01-4) Am Studies Ctr.

Undying Glory: The Story of the Massachusetts 54th Regiment. Clinton Cox. 176p. (J). (gr. 4-7). 1993. pap. 3.50 (0-590-44171-X) Scholastic Inc.

Undying Land. William Gilmour. (Illus.). 1985. 20.00 (0-937986-62-3) D M Grant.

Undying Laughter. Kelsey Roberts. (Intrigue Ser.). 1995. mass mkt. 3.50 (0-373-22334-X, 1-22334-6) Harlequin Bks.

Undying Love: The True Story of a Passion That Defied Death. Ben Harrison. 266p. 1996. 23.95 (0-88282-149-0) New Horizon NJ.

Undying Love: True Stories of Love That Survived the Grave. Brad Steiger & Sherry Hansen-Steiger. 240p. (Orig.). 1992. mass mkt. 4.99 (0-425-13536-5) Berkley Pub.

Undying Past of Shenandoah National Park. Darwin Lambert. 352p. 1989. 29.95 (0-911797-58-0); pap. 16.95 (0-911797-57-2) R Rinehart.

Undying Swan: Selected Poems in Russian. Moses S. Altman. Ed. by Ilya A. Mamantov. 254p. (RUS.). reprint ed. pap. 72.40 (0-8357-7065-6, 2008981) Bks Demand.

Une l'Arme see Voix et Silences: Les Meilleures Pieces Radiophoniques Francaises

Une Novice de Sainte Therese see Therese of Lisieux & Marie of the Trinity: A Transformative Relationship

***Unearned Pleasures & Other Stories.** Ursula Hegi. 1997. pap. 11.00 (0-684-84485-0) S&S Trade.

Unearthing Atlantis: An Archaeological Odyssey. Charles R. Pellegrino. LC 92-56364. 1993. pap. 13.00 (0-679-73407-4, Vin) Random.

Unearthing New England's Past: The Ceramic Evidence. Mary C. Beaudry et al. LC 83-51504. 112p. (Orig.). (C). 1984. pap. 16.50 (0-9621107-3-6) Mus Our Natl Hertge.

Unearthing Seeds of Fire: The Idea of Highlander. Frank Adams & Myles Horton. LC 74-16653. 225p. 1975. pap. 7.95 (0-89587-019-3) Blair.

***Unearthing the Invisible Colony: Historical Archaeology in New Jersey.** Ed. by Rebecca Yamin. (Illus.). 112p. (Orig.). 1997. pap. 8.95 (0-614-30725-2) NJ Hist Soc.

Unearthing the Truth: Exhuming a Decade of Terror in Guatemala. Grahame Russell. Ed. by Sarah Kee & Ann Butwell. (Illus.). 48p. (Orig.). 1996. pap. 5.00 (0-918346-16-9) EPICA.

Unearthly Delights: Paintings by Laurie Hogin, David Klamen, David Kroll, Rosalyn Schwartz, Maria Tomasula. Robert Sill et al. Ed. by Kimberly Britton. (Illus.). 22p. 1996. pap. write for info. (0-89792-152-6) Ill St Museum.

Unease. Tadeusz Rozewicz. Tr. by Victor Contoski. 160p. 1980. pap. 5.00 (0-89823-013-6) New Rivers Pr.

Uneaseful Death. large type ed. Mollie Hardwick. 1990. 25.99 (0-7089-2252-X) Ulverscroft.

Uneasful Death. Mollie Hardwick. 1993. mass mkt. 4.50 (0-449-22030-3, Crest) Fawcett.

Uneasily in Love with God: Herman F. Reissig, Pastor & Prophet. 1992. text ed. 20.00 (1-881907-05-8); pap. text ed. 12.00 (1-881907-06-6) Two Bytes Pub.

Uneasy Access: Privacy for Women in a Free Society. Anita L. Allen. (New Feminist Perspectives Ser.). 240p. (C). 1975. lib. bdg. 61.00 (0-8476-7327-8) Rowman.

Uneasy Access: Privacy for Women in a Free Society. Anita L. Allen. (New Feminist Perspectives Ser.). 240p. (C). 1988. pap. text ed. 27.00 (0-8476-7328-6) Rowman.

Uneasy Alliance. Jayne Ann Krentz. (Men Made in America Ser.). 1995. mass mkt. 3.99 (0-373-45187-3, 1-45187-1) Harlequin Bks.

Uneasy Alliance: Religion, Refugee Work, & U. S. Foreign Policy. J. Bruce Nichols. 332p. 1988. 30.00 (0-19-504274-3) OUP.

***Uneasy Alliances.** TSR Inc. Staff. 1997. pap. 1.99 (0-7869-0870-X) TSR Inc.

Uneasy at Home: Antisemitism & the American Jewish Experience. Leonard Dinnerstein. LC 87-521. 272p. 1987. text ed. 42.50 (0-231-06252-4) Col U Pr.

Uneasy Careers & Intimate Lives: Women in Science, 1787-1979. Ed. by Pnina G Abir-Am & Dorinda Outram. (Douglass Series on Women's Lives & the Meaning of Gender). (Illus.). 400p. 1987. text ed. 45.00 (0-8135-1255-7); pap. text ed. 18.95 (0-8135-1256-5) Rutgers U Pr.

Uneasy Case for Progressive Taxation. Walter J. Blum & Harry Kalven. (Phoenix Bks.: P130). 135p. reprint ed. pap. 38.50 (0-685-15667-2, 2026765) Bks Demand.

Uneasy Center: Reformed Christianity in AnteBellum America. Paul K. Conkin. LC 94-12292. 352p. 1995. text ed. 39.95 (0-8078-2180-2); pap. text ed. 16.95 (0-8078-4492-6) U of NC Pr.

Uneasy Century: International Relations, 1900-1990. Margaret MacMillian & Arne Kislenko. 224p. (C). 1996. per., pap. text ed. 34.59 (0-7872-2217-8) Kendall-Hunt.

Uneasy Coalition: The Entente Experience in World War I. Jehuda L. Wallach. LC 93-18144. (Contributions in Military Studies: No. 146). 208p. 1993. text ed. 59.95 (0-313-28879-8, GM8879, Greenwood Pr) Greenwood.

Uneasy Compromise: Problems of a Hybrid Income-Consumption Tax. Ed. by Henry J. Aaron et al. LC 88-464. 441p. 1988. pap. 19.95 (0-8157-0045-8); text ed. 44.95 (0-8157-0046-6) Brookings.

Uneasy Conquest. large type ed. Leila Mackinlay. 368p. 1987. 25.99 (0-7089-1643-0) Ulverscroft.

Uneasy Endings: Daily Life in an American Nursing Home. Renee R. Shield. LC 88-47743. (Anthropology of Contemporary Issues Ser.). 304p. 1988. 42.50 (0-8014-2159-4); pap. 15.95 (0-8014-9490-7) Cornell U Pr.

Uneasy Equilibrium: Private & Public Financing of Health Services in the United States, 1875-1965. Odin W. Anderson. 1968. pap. 9.95 (0-8084-0305-2) NCUP.

Uneasy Lies. Zaremba. 1994. pap. 11.95 (0-929005-17-1, Pub. by Second Story Pr CN) LPC InBook.

***Uneasy Manhood.** Robert M. Hicks. LC 96-24273. 256p. (YA). (gr. 10). 1997. pap. 10.99 (0-8007-5616-9) Revell.

Uneasy Money. P. G. Wodehouse. 252p. 1992. pap. 8.95 (0-14-001273-7, Penguin Bks) Viking Penguin.

Uneasy Narrator: Chinese Fiction from the Traditional to the Modern. Henry Y. Zhao. (London Oriental Ser.). 288p. 1995. 55.00 (0-19-713611-7) OUP.

***Uneasy Neighbors: Cuba & the United States.** Margaret Regler & Rhoda Hoff. (International Affairs Ser.). 1997. lib. bdg. 22.00 (0-531-11326-4) Watts.

Uneasy Partners: Big Business in American Politics, 1945-1990. Kim McQuaid. LC 93-17520. (American Moment Ser.). 272p. (C). 1993. text ed. 38.95 (0-8018-4651-X); pap. text ed. 13.95 (0-8018-4652-8) Johns Hopkins.

Uneasy Partners: The College & the Church. Merrimon Cuninggim. 200p. (Orig.). 1994. pap. 14.95 (0-687-01151-5) Abingdon.

Uneasy Partnership: Social Science & the Federal Government in the Twentieth Century. Gene M. Lyons. LC 72-93761. 394p. 1969. 39.95 (0-87154-561-6) Russell Sage.

Uneasy Public Policy Triangle in Higher Education: Quality, Diversity, & Budgetary Efficiency. David H. Finifter et al. Ed. by Roger G. Baldwin & John R. Thelin. (ACE-Oryx Series on Higher Education). (Illus.). 224p. 1991. 27.95 (0-02-897145-0, ACE-Oryx) Oryx Pr.

Uneasy Relations. John Haylock. 223p. 9300. 30.00 (0-7206-0880-5, Pub. by P Owen Ltd UK) Dufour.

***Uneasy Rider: The Interstate Way of Knowledge.** Mike Bryan. LC 96-38901. 1997. 25.00 (0-679-41671-4) Random.

Uneasy Sensations: Smollett & the Body. Aileen Douglas. LC 95-1786. 232p. pap. text ed. 14.95 (0-226-16052-1) U Ch Pr.

Uneasy Sensations: Smollett & the Body. Aileen Douglas. LC 95-1786. 232p. 1995. 29.95 (0-226-16051-3) U Ch Pr.

Uneasy Solitude: Individual & Society in the Work of Ralph Waldo Emerson. Maurice Connaud. Tr. by Lawrence Rosenwald. 455p. 1987. text ed. 69.50 (0-691-06718-X) Princeton U Pr.

***Uneasy Spirits: Ghost Stories & Haunted Places of Clermont County, Ohio.** Richard Crawford. Date not set. pap. write for info. (1-890538-19-1) Rhiannon Pubns.

Uneasy State: The United States from 1915 to 1945. Barry D. Karl. LC 83-9134. 268p. 1985. pap. text ed. 12.95 (0-226-42520-7) U Ch Pr.

Uneasy Transitions: Disaffection in Post-Compulsory Education & Training. Jenny Corbett. (Education & Alienation Ser.). 208p. 1990. 65.00 (1-85000-795-0, Falmer Pr); pap. 30.00 (1-85000-796-9, Falmer Pr) Taylor & Francis.

Uneasy Verdicts. Tim Wells. Date not set. pap. 19.95 (0-670-81382-6) Viking Penguin.

Uneasy Virtue: The Politics of Prostitution & the American Reform Tradition. Barbara M. Hobson. (Illus.). xviii, 296p. 1990. pap. text ed. 17.95 (0-226-34557-2) U Ch Pr.

Uneasy Warriors: Coming Back Home: The Perilous Journey of the Green Berets. Vincent Coppola. 1995. 19.95 (1-56352-197-0) Longstreet Pr Inc.

UN/ECE Standards for Dry & Dried Fruit. 130p. 1994. 19.00 (92-1-116533-4) UN.

UN/ECE Standards for Fresh Fruit & Vegetables. 419p. 1991. 50.00 (92-1-116532-6) UN.

An Asterisk (*) at the beginning of an entry indicates that the title is appearing in BIP for the first time.

Unechte Korrespondenzen. Theodor Fontane. Ed. by Heide Streiter-Buscher. (Schriften der Theodor Fontane Gesellschaft Ser.: Vol. 1). (Illus.). xii, 1279p. (GER.). (C). 1995. lib. bdg. 129.25 (*3-11-014076-4*) De Gruyter.

Unediting the Renaissance: Shakespeare, Marlowe, Milton. Leah S. Marcus. LC 96-7263. 288p. (C). 1996. pap. 18.95 (*0-415-10053-4*); text ed. 69.95 (*0-415-09934-X*) Routledge.

Unemployed. Ed. by Alex Baskin. LC 74-20094. 1975. 34.95 (*0-914924-01-X*) Archives Soc Hist.

Unemployed Actress & Other Minor Parts. Susann Jacobson. 388p. (Orig.). 1994. pap. 9.95 (*0-9640786-0-0*) S Jacobson.

Unemployed Fortune-Teller: Essays & Memoirs. Charles Simic. LC 94-16088. (Poets on Poetry Ser.). 144p. 1994. pap. 13.95 (*0-472-06569-6*) U of Mich Pr.

Unemployed Fortune-Teller: Essays & Memoirs. Charles Simic. LC 94-16088. (Poets on Poetry Ser.). 144p. 1994. 39.50 (*0-472-09569-2*) U of Mich Pr.

Unemployed? Laid Off? Survival Possibilities for the Unemployed & Similar Situations. rev. ed. Center for Self-Sufficiency Staff. 70p. 1993. ring bd. 25.95 (*0-910811-11-3*) Ctr Self Suff.

Unemployed Man & His Family: The Effect of Unemployment upon the Status of the Man in Fifty-Nine Families. Mirra Komarovsky. LC 79-137174. (Poverty U. S. A. Historical Record Ser.). 1975. reprint ed. 17.95 (*0-405-03113-0*) Ayer.

Unemployed People: Social & Psychological Perspectives. David Fryer & Phillip Ullah. 320p. 1987. 90.00 (*0-335-15507-3*, Open Univ Pr); pap. 34.00 (*0-335-15506-5*, Open Univ Pr) Taylor & Francis.

Unemployment: A Disequilibrium Approach. Mark Casson. (Modern Revivals in Economics Ser.). 280p. 1993. 61.95 (*0-7512-0216-9*, Pub. by Gregg Revivals UK) Ashgate Pub Co.

Unemployment: A Global Challenge. Ed. by Bertram Gross & Alfred Pfaller. (Annals Ser.: Vol. 492). 1987. 26.00 (*0-8039-2933-1*); pap. 17.00 (*0-8039-2934-X*) Sage.

Unemployment: A Problem of Industry. William H. Beveridge. LC 79-95398. (BCL Ser. II). reprint ed. 25.00 (*0-404-00794-5*) AMS Pr.

Unemployment: A Problem of Policy: Analysis of British Experience & Prospects. G. D. Worswick. (National Institute of Economic & Social Research Occasional Papers: No. 35). (Illus.). 375p. (C). 1991. text ed. 59.95 (*0-521-40034-1*) Cambridge U Pr.

Unemployment: A State of Mind. Larry Marks. (Illus.). 80p. 1994. 29.00 (*1-56216-223-3*); pap. 14.00 (*1-56216-224-1*) Systems Co.

Unemployment: An Economic Analysis. K. G. Knight. LC 86-17455. 432p. 1986. 66.00 (*0-389-20661-X*, N8218) B&N Imports.

Unemployment: International Perspectives. Ed. by Morley Gunderson et al. 234p. 1987. 30.00 (*0-8020-5710-1*); pap. 14.95 (*0-8020-6636-4*) U of Toronto Pr.

Unemployment: Macroeconomic Performance & the Labour Market. Richard Layard et al. Ed. by Richard Jackman. (Illus.). 640p. 1991. pap. text ed. 35.00 (*0-19-828434-9*) OUP.

Unemployment: The European Perspective. Angus Maddison. LC 81-21264. 220p. 1982. text ed. 29.95 (*0-312-83261-3*) St Martin.

Unemployment: Theory, Policy & Structure. Ed. by Peder J. Pedersen & Reinhard Lund. (Studies in Organization: No. 10). 353p. (C). 1987. lib. bdg. 113.85 (*3-11-011071-7*) De Gruyter.

Unemployment - Vacancy Curve: Theoretical Foundation & Empirical Relevance. J. Christl. (Studies in Empirical Economics). (Illus.). xvi, 152p. 1992. 69.00 (*0-387-91424-2*) Spr-Verlag.

Unemployment & Adjustment in the Labor Market: A Comparison Between the Regional & National Responses. Houston H. Stokes et al. LC 75-26552. (University of Chicago, Department of Geography, Research Paper Ser.: No. 177). 138p. 1975. reprint ed. pap. 39.40 (*0-608-02265-9*, 2062906) Bks Demand.

Unemployment & American Trade Unions. David P. Smelser. LC 78-63968. (Johns Hopkins University. Studies in the Social Sciences. Thirtieth Ser. 1912: No. 37, 1919: 1). reprint ed. 37.50 (*0-404-61214-8*) AMS Pr.

Unemployment & Female Labor: A Study of Labor Supply in Kingston, Jamaica. Guy Standing. 1981. text ed. 39.95 (*0-312-83266-4*) St Martin.

Unemployment & Growth in Western Economies. Ed. by Andrew J. Pierre. (Europe-America Ser.). 160p. (C). 1984. text ed. 28.00 (*0-8147-6589-0*) NYU Pr.

Unemployment & Inflation: Institutional & Structuralist Views, A Reader in Labor Economics. Ed. by Michael J. Piore. LC 79-55274. 300p. (gr. 13). 1980. pap. text ed. 23.95 (*0-87332-165-0*) M E Sharpe.

Unemployment & Labour Force Behaviour in Young People: Evidence from Canada & Ontario. F. T. Denton et al. (Ontario Economic Council Research Studies). 232p. 1980. pap. 7.95 (*0-8020-3379-2*) U of Toronto Pr.

Unemployment & Labour Market Flexibility: Austria. Ewald Walterskirchen. vi, 133p. 1991. pap. 27.00 (*92-2-107290-8*) Intl Labour Office.

Unemployment & Labour Market Flexibility: Italy. L. De Luca & Mary-Ann S. Bruni. (Illus.). xiv, 214p. (Orig.). 1993. pap. 27.00 (*92-2-108266-0*) Intl Labour Office.

Unemployment & Labour Market Flexibility: Sweden. Guy Standing. x, 149p. (Orig.). 1988. pap. 27.00 (*92-2-106265-1*) Intl Labour Office.

Unemployment & Labour Market Flexibility: The United Kingdom. Guy Standing. viii, 147p. (Orig.). 1986. pap. 27.00 (*92-2-105291-5*) Intl Labour Office.

Unemployment & Labour Market Flexibility in Finland. R. Lilja et al. vi, 222p. 1990. pap. 27.00 (*92-2-107273-8*) Intl Labour Office.

Unemployment & Local Labour Markets. Peter Robinson. (Campaign for Work Ser.). 125p. 1991. text ed. 68.95 (*1-85628-125-6*, Pub. by Avebury Pub UK) Ashgate Pub Co.

Unemployment & Macroeconomics. Assar Lindbeck. LC 92-29465. (Ohlin Lectures: Vol. 3). (Illus.). 120p. 1993. 25.00 (*0-262-12175-1*) MIT Pr.

Unemployment & Public Policy in a Changing Labour Market. Michael White. 216p. (C). 1995. pap. 19.95 (*0-85374-639-7*, Pub. by Pol Studies Inst UK) Brookings.

Unemployment & Social Services. Clive Miller & Lynette Domoney. (C). 1988. 60.00 (*0-685-28600-2*, Pub. by Natl Inst Soc Work) St Mut.

Unemployment & Technical Innovation. Daniel B. Freeman. (C). 1983. text ed. write for info. (*0-86187-212-6*) St Martin.

Unemployment & Technical Innovation: A Study of Long Waves & Economic Development. Ed. by Christopher Freeman et al. LC 82-1113. (Contributions in Economics & Economic History Ser.: No. 50). (Illus.). xiii, 214p. 1982. text ed. 38.50 (*0-313-23601-1*, FUN/) Greenwood.

Unemployment & the Economists. Ed. by Alan Budd et al. LC 96-4213. (Illus.). 176p. (C). 1996. text ed. 70.00 (*1-85898-351-7*) E Elgar.

Unemployment & the Great Depression in Weimar Germany. Ed. by Peter D. Stachura. LC 86-1906. 350p. 1986. text ed. 37.50 (*0-312-83267-2*) St Martin.

Unemployment & Underemployment in Historical Perspective: Proceedings of the Tenth International Economic History Congress, Leuven, Belgium, August 1990. Ed. by E. Aerts & B. Eichengreen. (Studies in Social & Economic History: No. 12). 136p. (Orig.). 1990. pap. 32.50 (*90-6186-384-8*, Pub. by Leuven Univ BE) Coronet Bks.

Unemployment As a World Problem. Ed. by Philip Wright. LC 70-107744. (Essay Index Reprint Ser.). 1977. 20.95 (*0-8369-1689-1*) Ayer.

Unemployment Benefits. Theresa Hernandez & National Employment Law Project Staff. 30p. pap. 3.25 (*0-685-23170-4*, 41,575U) NCLS Inc.

Unemployment Challenge Log Workbook. Frieda Carrol. 60p. 1983. ring bd. 21.95 (*0-939476-86-X*) Prosperity & Profits.

Unemployment Compensation: A Cost You Can Cut. Frick Company Staff. 166p. 1995. pap. 75.00 (*0-685-67825-3*) Amer CC Pubs.

Unemployment Compensation Handbook: A Comprehensive Guide to Unemployment Insurance in Indiana. W. Michael Schiff. 114p. 1996. per. 40.00 (*1-883698-10-3*) IN Chamber Comm.

Unemployment, Crime & Offenders. Iain Crow et al. 216p. 1989. 57.50 (*0-415-01834-X*) Routledge.

Unemployment Crisis. Richard Layard et al. 160p. 1994. 35.00 (*0-19-877395-1*); pap. 14.95 (*0-19-877394-3*) OUP.

***Unemployment Crisis.** Ed. by Brian K. MacLean & Lars Osberg. (Critical Perspectives on Public Affairs Ser.). 280p. 1996. 55.00 (*0-7735-1417-1*, Pub. by McGill CN) U of Toronto Pr.

***Unemployment Crisis: All for Nought?** Ed. by Brian K. MacLean & Lars Osberg. (Critical Perspectives on Public Affairs Ser.). 254p. 1996. pap. 22.95 (*0-7735-1418-X*, HD5707, Pub. by McGill CN) U of Toronto Pr.

Unemployment, Education & Training: Case Studies from North America & Europe. Ed. by Keith Forrester & Kevin Ward. LC 90-85884. 360p. (Orig.). (C). 1991. pap. text ed. 19.95 (*0-9625945-6-3*) Caddo Gap Pr.

Unemployment, Idle Capacity, & the Evaluation of Public Expenditures: National & Regional Analyses. Robert H. Haveman & John V. Krutilla. LC 68-54039. (Resources for the Future Ser.). 169p. 1968. 15.00 (*0-8018-0258-X*) Johns Hopkins.

Unemployment, Imperfect Competition & Macroeconomics: Essays in the Post Tradition. Malcolm C. Sawyer. 224p. 1995. 75.00 (*1-85278-957-3*) E Elgar.

Unemployment in Britain: Between the Wars. Stephen Constantine. (C). 1900. pap. text ed. 12.50 (*0-582-35232-0*) Addison-Wesley.

Unemployment in Capitalist, Communist, & Post-Communist Economies. J. L. Porket. LC 94-34872. 1995. text ed. 75.00 (*0-312-12484-8*) St Martin.

Unemployment in Europe. Ed. by Jonathon Michie & John G. Smith. (Illus.). 384p. 1994. pap. text ed. 32.00 (*0-12-494065-X*) Acad Pr.

Unemployment in Europe: Problems & Policies. Valerie Symes. LC 94-33819. 232p. (C). 1995. pap. 25.00 (*0-415-11825-5*, C0095) Routledge.

Unemployment in Europe: Problems & Policies. Valerie Symes. LC 94-33819. 224p. (C). (gr. 13). 1995. text ed. 69.95 (*0-415-11824-7*, C0094) Routledge.

Unemployment in France, the Federal Republic of Germany & the Netherlands: A Survey of Trends, Causes & Policy Options (WEP Study) Wouter Van Ginneken & Michel Garzuel. 1983. pap. 15.75 (*92-2-103032-6*) Intl Labour Office.

Unemployment in History: Economic Thought & Public Policy. John A. Garraty. 1986. pap. text ed. 10.00 (*0-06-132057-9*) HarpC.

Unemployment in the Learned Professions: An International Study of Occupational & Educational Planning. Walter M. Kotsching. Ed. by Walter P. Metzger. LC 76-55177. (Academic Profession Ser.). (Illus.). 1977. reprint ed. lib. bdg. 29.95 (*0-405-10005-1*) Ayer.

Unemployment in the U. K. Politics & Policies. J. Richardson & Jeremy Moon. 240p. 1985. text ed. 72.95 (*0-566-00892-0*, Pub. by Avebury Pub UK) Ashgate Pub Co.

Unemployment in Transition Countries: Transiet or Persistent? 200p. (Orig.). 1994. pap. 29.00 (*92-64-14076-X*) OECD.

Unemployment Insurance: A Cost You Can Cut. Frick Co. Staff. 121p. (Orig.). (C). 1992. pap. text ed. 35.00 (*1-878630-24-5*) CA Chamber Commerce.

Unemployment Insurance: The American Experience, 1915-1935. Daniel Nelson. LC 69-16114. (Illus.). 323p. reprint ed. pap. 92.10 (*0-7837-1660-5*, 2041957) Bks Demand.

Unemployment Insurance: The Second Half-Century. Ed. by W. Lee Hansen & James F. Byers. LC 89-40257. (Follette Public Policy Ser.). 464p. (Orig.). (C). 1990. pap. text ed. 22.50 (*0-299-12354-5*) U of Wis Pr.

Unemployment Insurance: The Second Half-Century. Ed. by W. Lee Hansen & James F. Byers. LC 89-40257. (Follette Public Policy Ser.). 464p. (Orig.). (C). 1990. text ed. 40.00 (*0-299-12350-2*) U of Wis Pr.

Unemployment Insurance Accounts Examiner. Jack Rudman. (Career Examination Ser.: C-3164). 1994. pap. 27.95 (*0-8373-3164-1*) Nat Learn.

Unemployment Insurance Act & Regulations. annot. ed. Pierre-Yves Bourdeau & Claudine Roy. 700p. 1993. pap. 55.00 (*0-409-91938-1*, CN) MICHIE.

Unemployment Insurance & Active Labor Market Policy: An International Comparison of Financing Systems. Gunther Schmid et al. LC 91-19311. (Labor Economics & Policy Ser.). (Illus.). 314p. 1992. 39.95 (*0-8143-2314-6*) Wayne St U Pr.

Unemployment Insurance & Disability Insurance in California: A Guide for Union Representatives. Paul Chown & Pam Tellew. 65p. 1986. pap. text ed. 7.00 (*0-937817-04-X*) CLRE UCAL Berk.

Unemployment Insurance & the Dutch Labor Market. J. A. Vijlbrief. (Tinbergen Institute Research Ser.). 294p. 1992. pap. 25.00 (*90-5170-165-9*, Pub. by Thesis Pubs NE) IBD Ltd.

Unemployment Insurance Claims Clerk. Jack Rudman. (Career Examination Ser.: C-850). 1994. pap. 23.95 (*0-8373-0850-X*) Nat Learn.

Unemployment Insurance Claims Examiner. Jack Rudman. (Career Examination Ser.: C-851). 1994. pap. 27.95 (*0-8373-0851-8*) Nat Learn.

Unemployment Insurance Hearing Representative. Jack Rudman. (Career Examination Ser.: C-2728). 1994. pap. 29.95 (*0-8373-2728-8*) Nat Learn.

***Unemployment Insurance in the United States: Analysis of Policy Issues.** Ed. by Christopher J. O'Leary & Stephen A. Wandner. 780p. 1997. pap. 30.00 (*0-88099-173-9*) W E Upjohn.

***Unemployment Insurance in the United States: Analysis of Policy Issues.** Ed. by Christopher J. O'Leary & Stephen A. Wandner. 780p. 1997. 40.00 (*0-88099-174-7*) W E Upjohn.

Unemployment Insurance in the United States: The First Half Century. Saul J. Blaustein. LC 93-13480. 367p. 1993. text ed. 30.00 (*0-88099-136-4*); pap. text ed. 20.00 (*0-88099-135-6*) W E Upjohn.

Unemployment Insurance Investigator. Jack Rudman. (Career Examination Ser.: C-2364). 1994. pap. 29.95 (*0-8373-2364-9*) Nat Learn.

Unemployment Insurance Referee. Jack Rudman. (Career Examination Ser.: C-917). 1994. pap. 34.95 (*0-8373-0917-4*) Nat Learn.

Unemployment Insurance Reviewing Examiner. Jack Rudman. (Career Examination Ser.: C-3041). 1994. pap. 29.95 (*0-8373-3041-6*) Nat Learn.

Unemployment Insurance Tax Auditor. (Career Examination Ser.). 1997. pap. 34.95 (*0-8373-3788-7*, C3788) Nat Learn.

Unemployment Insurance Trust Fund Adequacy in the 1990s. Wayne Vroman. LC 90-47790. 160p. 1990. text ed. 23.00 (*0-88099-101-1*); pap. text ed. 13.00 (*0-88099-102-X*) W E Upjohn.

Unemployment, Labour Slack & Labour Market Accounting. Chris De Neubourg. (Contributions to Economic Analysis Ser.: No. 177). 270p. 1988. 133.25 (*0-444-70527-9*, North Holland) Elsevier.

***Unemployment Law & Procedure in South Carolina.** 2nd ed. Everett H. Garner. 1996. pap. 25.00 (*0-943856-95-7*, 603) SC Bar CLE.

***Unemployment Policy: Government Options for the Labour Market.** Ed. by Dennis J. Snower. (Illus.). 500p. (C). 1997. 80.00 (*0-521-57139-1*); pap. 34.95 (*0-521-59921-0*) Cambridge U Pr.

Unemployment Relief in Periods of Depression: A Study of Measures Adopted in Certain Cities, 1857 Through 1922. Leah H. Feder. LC 75-137165. (Poverty U. S. A. Historical Record Ser.). 1978. reprint ed. 31.95 (*0-405-03104-1*) Ayer.

Unemployment, Restructuring, & the Labor Market in Eastern Europe & Russia. Ed. by Simon Commander & Fabrizio Coricelli. LC 94-29583. (EDI Development Studies). 1995. 24.95 (*0-8213-2988-X*, 12988) World Bank.

Unemployment, Search & Labour Supply. Ed. by Richard W. Blundell & Ian Walker. (Illus.). 320p. 1986. 69.95 (*0-521-32027-5*) Cambridge U Pr.

Unemployment, Social Vulnerability & Health in Europe. Ed. by D. Schwefel et al. (Health Systems Research Ser.). (Illus.). 350p. 1987. 152.00 (*0-387-17867-8*) Spr-Verlag.

Unemployment Survival Handbook. Nina Schuyler. LC 92-75525. 144p. 1993. pap. 9.95 (*1-880559-08-0*) Allworth Pr.

Unemployment under Capitalism: The Sociology of British & American Labour Markets. David N. Ashton. LC 85-21874. (Contributions in Economics & Economic History Ser.: No. 65). (Illus.). 225p. 1986. text ed. 27.50 (*0-313-25201-7*, AUT/, Greenwood Pr) Greenwood.

Unemployment upon the Status of the Man in Fifty-Nine Families. LC 79-137174. (Poverty U. S. A. Historical Record Ser.). 1971. reprint ed. 8.00 (*0-685-47396-1*) Ayer.

Unemployment, Vacancies & Local Labor Markets. Harry J. Holzer. LC 89-30636. 87p. 1989. pap. text ed. 9.00 (*0-88099-072-4*) W E Upjohn.

Unended Quest: An Intellectual Autobiography. rev. ed. Karl R. Popper. LC 76-2155. 258p. 1982. 17.95 (*0-87548-366-6*) Open Court.

Unending Blues: Poems. Charles Simic. 64p. 1986. pap. 8.00 (*0-15-692831-0*, Harvest Bks) HarBrace.

Unending Carols. 1995. 8.99 (*0-614-01680-0*, MC-276) Lillenas.

Unending Design: The Forms of Postmodern Poetry. Joseph M. Conte. LC 90-55732. (Illus.). 336p. 1991. pap. 17.95 (*0-8014-9914-3*) Cornell U Pr.

Unending Dialogue: Voices from an AIDS Poetry Workshop. Rachel Hadas. 156p. 1993. pap. 9.95 (*0-571-19804-X*) Faber & Faber.

***Unending Journey of the Black Race.** Dudley Earlington. 175p. (Orig.). 1997. mass mkt. 4.99 (*1-55197-899-7*, Pub. by Comnwlth Pub CN) Partners Pubs Grp.

Unending Lightning: Selected Poems of Miguel Hernandez. Miguel Hernandez. Tr. by Edwin Honig. LC 89-10699. 63p. 1990. pap. 10.95 (*0-935296-86-7*) Sheep Meadow.

Unending Rhythms: Oral Poetry of Indian Tribes. Sitakant Mahapatra. (Tribal Studies of India Ser.: No. T 145). (C). 1992. 32.00 (*81-210-0277-X*, Pub. by Inter-India Pubns) S Asia.

Unending Work & Care: Managing Chronic Illness at Home. Juliet M. Corbin & Anselm Strauss. LC 87-46343. (Health-Management Ser.). 384p. text ed. 45.00 (*1-55542-082-6*) Jossey-Bass.

Unenlightened & Other Korean Short Stories. Yi Kwang-su et al. Tr. by Chang Wang-rok et al. from KOR. (Modern Korean Short Stories Ser.: No. 3). viii, 234p. 1983. 20.00 (*0-89209-204-1*) Pace Intl Res.

***UNEP Biodiversity Programme & Implementation Strategy.** 74p. 1995. pap. text ed. 15.00 (*92-807-1566-6*) UN.

UNEP's New Way Forward: Environmental Law & Sustainable Development. Ed. by Sun Lin et al. (Illus.). 397p. 1995. 80.00 (*92-807-1524-0*) UN.

Unequal Access: Women Lawyers in a Changing America. Frwd. by Ronald Chester & Cynthia F. Epstein. LC 84-9355. 160p. (C). 1984. text ed. 49.95 (*0-89789-052-3*, Bergin & Garvey) Greenwood.

Unequal Access to Information: Problems & Needs of the World's Information Poor. Ed. by Jovian P. Lang. LC 87-34577. 258p. 1988. pap. 35.00 (*0-87650-239-7*) Pierian.

Unequal Alliance: The World Bank, the International Monetary Fund & the Philippines. Robin Broad. (Studies in International Political Economy: Vol. 19). 1988. 45.00 (*0-520-05905-0*); pap. 14.00 (*0-520-06953-6*) U CA Pr.

Unequal Americans: Practices & Politics of Intergroup Relations. John Slawson. LC 78-67909. (Contributions in Political Science Ser.: No. 24). 249p. 1979. text ed. 59.95 (*0-313-21118-3*, SUA/, Greenwood Pr) Greenwood.

Unequal Bargaining: A Study of Vitiating Factors in the Formation of Contracts. John Cartwright. 288p. 1991. 75.00 (*0-19-825243-9*) OUP.

Unequal Beginnings: Agriculture & Economic Development in Quebec & Ontario until 1870. John McCallum. (State & Economic Life Ser.). 1980. pap. 15.95 (*0-8020-6362-4*) U of Toronto Pr.

Unequal Beginnings: Agriculture & Economic Development in Quebec & Ontario until 1870. John McCallum. LC 80-501832. (State & Economic Life Ser.: No. 2). 159p. reprint ed. pap. 45.40 (*0-8357-4026-9*, 2036718) Bks Demand.

Unequal Breadwinner. Ruth Lister & Leo Wilson. 1976. 20.00 (*0-901108-57-X*, Pub. by NCCL UK) St Mut.

Unequal Burden: Economic Crises, Persistent Poverty, & Women's Work. Ed. by Lourdes Beneria & Shelley Feldman. 278p. (C). 1992. pap. text ed. 21.50 (*0-8133-8230-0*) Westview.

Unequal Care: A Case Study of Interorganizational Relations. Murray Milner, Jr. LC 80-15612. (Illus.). 224p. 1980. text ed. 55.00 (*0-231-05006-2*) Col U Pr.

***Unequal Colleagues: The Entrance of Women into the Professions, 1890-1940.** Penina M. Glazer & Miriam Slater. (Illus.). 295p. pap. 15.00 (*0-8135-1187-9*) Rutgers U Pr.

Unequal Education Provision in England & Wales: The Nineteenth-Century Roots. William E. Marsden. (Illus.). 269p. 1987. text ed. 30.00 (*0-7130-0178-X*, Pub. by Woburn Pr UK) Intl Spec Bk.

Unequal Exchange: A Study of the Imperialism of Trade. Emmanuel Arhiri. LC 78-158920. 493p. reprint ed. pap. 140.60 (*0-7837-3924-9*, 2043772) Bks Demand.

Unequal Exchange & the Evolution of the World System: Reconsidering the Impact of Trade on North-South Relations. Kunibert Raffer. LC 86-31306. 336p. 1987. text ed. 45.00 (*0-312-00440-0*) St Martin.

Unequal Giants: Diplomatic Relations Between the United States & Brazil, 1889-1930. Joseph Smith. LC 90-25379. (Latin American Ser.). 352p. (C). 1991. text ed. 49.95 (*0-8229-3676-3*) U of Pittsburgh Pr.

Unequal Homeless: Men on the Streets, Women in Their Place. Joanne Passaro. LC 95-47036. 256p. (C). 1996. pap. 15.95 (*0-415-90903-1*); text ed. 59.95 (*0-415-90902-3*) Routledge.

Unequal Influence: The Revolutionary Ideas Prophecies & Solutions of John Adams. Steven J. Adamski. 304p. 1995. 17.95 (*0-9637891-7-1*) Printed Voice.

Unequal Justice. Robert Perske. 1991. pap. 3.59 (*0-687-42983-8*) Abingdon.

Unequal Justice: A Question of Color. Coramae R. Mann. LC 92-25110. (Blacks in the Diaspora Ser.). 320p. (C). 1993. 35.00 (*0-253-33676-7*); pap. 15.95 (*0-253-20783-5*) Ind U Pr.

Unequal Justice: Lawyers & Social Change in Modern America. Jerold S. Auerbach. LC 75-7364. 412p. 1977. reprint ed. pap. 13.95 (*0-19-502170-3*) OUP.

Unequal Justice: The Prosecution of Child Sexual Abuse. Ellen B. Gray. LC 92-38229. 256p. 1993. 27.95 (*0-02-912663-0*, Free Press) Free Pr.

Unequal Justice: Wayne Dumond, Bill Clinton & the Politics of Rape in Arkansas. Guy Reel. 263p. 1993. 25.95 (*0-87975-841-4*) Prometheus Bks.

Unequal Knowledge Distribution: The Schooling Experience in a Togolese Secondary School. Karen Biraimah. (Special Studies in Comparative Education: No. 9). 56p. (Orig.). pap. text ed. 10.00 (*0-937033-00-6*) SUNY GSE Pubns.

Unequal Laws unto a Savage Race: European Legal Traditions in Arkansas, 1686-1836. Morris S. Arnold. LC 84-168. (Illus.). 262p. 1985. 26.00 (*0-938626-33-7*); pap. 14.00 (*0-938626-76-0*) U of Ark Pr.

Unequal Marriage. large type ed. Emma Tennant. LC 95-722. 1995. lib. bdg. 20.95 (*0-7862-0418-4*) Thorndike Pr.

***Unequal Match.** large type ed. Rachelle Edwards. (Linford Romance Large Print Ser.). 320p. 1997. pap. 16.99 (*0-7089-5082-5*, Linford) Ulverscroft.

Unequal Opportunity: Learning to Read in the U. S. A. Jill Bartoli. (Language & Literacy Ser.). 256p. (C). 1994. text ed. 40.00 (*0-8077-3385-7*); pap. text ed. 19.95 (*0-8077-3384-9*) Tchrs Coll.

Unequal Partnership: U. S. Economic Relations with the Developing Countries. Rudolf Zimenkov. 110p. 1986. text ed. 15.00 (*81-207-0120-8*, Pub. by Sterling Pubs II) Apt Bks.

Unequal Partnerships: The Political Economy of Urban Redevelopment. Ed. by Gregory D. Squires. LC 88-32534. 280p. (C). 1989. text ed. 45.00 (*0-8135-1451-7*); pap. text ed. 16.95 (*0-8135-1452-5*) Rutgers U Pr.

Unequal Protection. Thomas H. Clark. Ed. by Linda Stone. LC 95-96013. (Illus.). 295p. 1996. 23.00 (*0-9649521-4-9*) Delta Pub MD.

Unequal Protection: Environmental Justice & Communities of Color. Robert D. Bullard. (Illus.). 416p. 1996. pap. 16.00 (*0-87156-380-0*) Sierra.

Unequal Protection: Women, Children, & the Elderly in Court. Lois G. Forer. 1991. 22.95 (*0-393-02949-2*) Norton.

Unequal Protection: Women, Children, & the Elderly in Court. Lois G. Forer. 256p. 1993. pap. 10.95 (*0-393-30954-1*) Norton.

Unequal Sisters: A Multicultural Reader in U. S. Women's History. 2nd ed. Ellen C. DuBois. 576p. (gr. 13). 1994. pap. 24.95 (*0-415-90892-2*, Pub. by Tavistock UK) Routledge Chapman & Hall.

Unequal Sisters: A Multicultural Reader in U. S. Women's History. 2nd ed. Ed. by Vicki L. Ruiz & Ellen C. DuBois. LC 94-2430. 1994. write for info. (*0-415-90905-8*); pap. write for info. (*0-415-90906-6*) Routledge.

Unequal Sisters: Multicultural Reader in U. S. Women's History. 2nd ed. Ed. by Ellen C. Dubois & Vicki L. Ruiz. 576p. (C). (gr. 13 up). 1994. text ed. 69.95 (*0-415-90891-4*, Routledge NY) Routledge.

Unequal Taxation: Its Unconstitutionality. 100p. 1981. 65.00 (*0-318-16627-5*) T Jefferson Equal Tax.

Unequal Treaties: China & the Foreigner. Rodney V. Gilbert. LC 75-32314. (Studies in Chinese History & Civilization). 248p. 1976. reprint ed. text ed. 59.95 (*0-313-26960-2*, U6960, Greenwood Pr) Greenwood.

Unequal Treatment. Eileen Nechas. 1994. 22.00 (*0-671-79186-9*) S&S Trade.

Unequal Treatment: A Study in the Neoclassical Theory of Discrimination. Mats Lundahl & Eskil Wadensjo. 336p. (C). 1984. text ed. 44.00 (*0-8147-5012-5*) NYU Pr.

Unequal Victims: Poles & Jews During World War II. Israel Gutman & Shmuel Krakowski. LC 86-81417. 1987. 20.95 (*0-89604-055-0*, Holocaust Library); pap. 13.95 (*0-89604-056-9*, Holocaust Library) US Holocaust.

Unequal Wealth & Incentives to Save. James P. Smith. (Illus.). iii, 37p. (Orig.). 1995. pap. text ed. 6.00 (*0-8330-2289-X*, DB-145-RC) Rand Corp.

Unequal Work. Veronica Beechey. (Questions for Feminism Ser.). 240p. 1987. text ed. 44.95 (*0-86091-149-7*, Pub. by Verso UK); pap. text ed. 14.95 (*0-86091-862-9*, Pub. by Verso UK) Routledge Chapman & Hall.

Unequal Yoke. Edmund W. Gosse. LC 75-31652. 52p. 1975. lib. bdg. 50.00 (*0-8201-1163-5*) Schol Facsimiles.

Unequal Yoke see IVP Booklets

Unequally Yoked Wives. C. S. Lovett. 1968. pap. 7.45 (*0-938148-22-2*) Prsnl Christianity.

Unerring Fire: The Massacre at Fort Pillow. Richard L. Fuchs. LC 93-47915. 1994. 34.50 (*0-8386-3561-X*) Fairleigh Dickinson.

Unersattliche Mensch. Jurgen Lowe. 272p. 1995. text ed. 68.00 (*3-7186-5774-0*, Harwood Acad Pubs); pap. text ed. 30.00 (*3-7186-5700-7*, Harwood Acad Pubs) Gordon & Breach.

UNESCO: In Retrospect & Prospect. Ed. by U. S. Pajpai & S. Viswam. 197p. 1986. 25.00 (*81-7062-000-7*, Pub. by Lancer II) S Asia.

UNESCO: Status of Improvements in Management, Personnel, Financial & Budgeting Practices. (Illus.). 76p. (Orig.). (C). 1992. pap. text ed. 20.00 (*1-56806-057-2*) DIANE Pub.

UNESCO Dictionary of the Social Sciences. Julius Gould & W. J. Kolb. LC 64-20307. 1964. text ed. 49.95 (*0-02-917490-2*, Free Press) Free Pr.

UNESCO General History of Africa Vol. I: Methodology & African Prehistory. Ed. by J. Ki-Zerbo. 1980. 45.00 (*0-520-03912-2*); pap. 13.95 (*0-520-06696-0*) U CA Pr.

UNESCO General History of Africa Vol. II: Ancient Africa. Ed. by G. Mokhtar. 1980. 45.00 (*0-520-03913-0*); pap. 12.00 (*0-520-06697-9*) U CA Pr.

UNESCO General History of Africa Vol. III: Africa from the Seventh to the Eleventh Century. UNESCO Staff & M. El Fasi. (C). 1988. pap. 13.00 (*0-520-06698-7*) U CA Pr.

UNESCO General History of Africa Vol. III: Africa from the Seventh to the Eleventh Century. UNESCO Staff. Ed. by M. El Fasi. 1988. 35.00 (*0-520-03914-9*) U CA Pr.

UNESCO General History of Africa Vol. IV: Africa from the XII to the XVI Century. Ed. by D. T. Niane. 1984. 45.00 (*0-520-03915-7*) U CA Pr.

UNESCO General History of Africa Vol. V: Africa from the Sixteenth to the Eighteenth Century. Ed. by Bethwell A. Ogot. LC 78-57321. (Illus.). 1076p. (C). 1992. 45.00 (*0-520-03916-5*) U CA Pr.

UNESCO General History of Africa Vol. VII: Africa under Colonial Domination, 1880-1935. Ed. by A. Adu Boahen. 1985. 45.00 (*0-520-03918-1*); pap. 13.95 (*0-520-06702-9*) U CA Pr.

UNESCO General History of Africa Vol. VIII: Africa since 1935. Ed. by A. A. Mazrui. 1994. 47.50 (*0-520-03920-3*) U CA Pr.

UNESCO List of Documents & Publications, 1987-1989. UNESCO Staff. 620p. 1993. pap. 85.00 (*92-3-002840-1*, U2840, Pub. by UNESCO-Bangkok TH) Bernan Associates.

***UNESCO Statistical Yearbook: 1996 Edition.** 976p. (ENG, FRE & SPA.). (C). 1996. lib. bdg. 90.00 (*0-89059-064-8*, U3344) Bernan Pr.

UNESCO Statistical Yearbook 1992. 1993. pap. 95.00 (*92-3-002801-0*, U6120, Pub. by UNESCO FR) Bernan Associates.

UNESCO Statistical Yearbook, 1995. United Nations Educational, Scientific & Cultural Organization Staff. 900p. 1995. lib. bdg. 90.00 (*0-89059-049-4*) Bernan Pr.

Unesco World Heritage Desk Diary. 68p. 1995. pap. text ed. 25.00 (*92-3-003026-0*, U3202, Pub. by UNESCO-Bangkok TH) Bernan Associates.

UNESCO Yearbook on Peace & Conflict Studies, 1988. Unesco. 254p. 1990. text ed. 65.00 (*0-313-27461-4*, UN88, Greenwood Pr) Greenwood.

UNESCO Yearbook on Peace & Conflict Studies, 1987. UNESCO Staff. LC 82-642769. 347p. 1989. text ed. 65.00 (*0-313-26485-6*, UN87, Greenwood Pr) Greenwood.

Unesco Yearbook on Peace & Conflict Studies 1985. UNESCO Staff. (Unesco Yearbook of Peace and Conflict Studies). 326p. 1987. text ed. 65.00 (*0-313-26143-1*, Greenwood Pr) Greenwood.

UNESCO Yearbook on Peace & Conflict Studies, 1980. United Nations Educational, Scientific & Cultural Organization Staff. LC 82-642769. 384p. 1981. text ed. 65.00 (*0-313-22922-8*, UN80, Greenwood Pr) Greenwood.

UNESCO Yearbook on Peace & Conflict Studies 1981. United Nations Educational, Scientific & Cultural Organization Staff. LC 82-642769. (United Nations Educational, Scientific & Cultural Organization Annuals Ser.). (Illus.). 576p. 1982. text ed. 65.00 (*0-313-22923-6*, UN81) Greenwood.

UNESCO Yearbook on Peace & Conflict Studies, 1982. United Nations Educational, Scientific & Cultural Organization Staff. LC 82-642769. (United Nations Educational, Scientific & Cultural Organization Annuals Ser.). (Illus.). xiv, 269p. 1983. text ed. 65.00 (*0-313-22924-4*, UN82) Greenwood.

UNESCO Yearbook on Peace & Conflict Studies, 1983. United Nations Educational, Scientific & Cultural Organization Staff. LC 82-642769. (United Nations Educational, Scientific & Cultural Organization Annuals Ser.). (Illus.). xiv, 406p. 1985. text ed. 65.00 (*0-313-24833-8*, UN83) Greenwood.

UNESCO Yearbook on Peace & Conflict Studies 1984. United Nations Educational, Scientific & Cultural Organization Staff. (United Nations Educational, Scientific & Cultural Organization Annuals Ser.). 240p. 1986. text ed. 65.00 (*0-313-25442-7*, UN84/) Greenwood.

UNESCO Yearbook on Peace & Conflict Studies, 1986. United Nations Educational, Scientific & Cultural Organization Staff. 324p. 1988. text ed. 65.00 (*0-313-26217-9*, UN86, Greenwood Pr) Greenwood.

UNESCO Yearbook on Peace & Conflict Studies 1985. United Nations Educational, Scientific & Cultural Organization Staff. 250p. 1987. 49.95 (*0-313-26122-9*, UN85, Greenwood Pr) Greenwood.

Unescorted Women. Ed. by Bibliotheca Press Staff. Date not set. pap. 12.95 (*0-939476-26-6*, Biblio Pr) Prosperity & Profits.

UNESCO's Standard Setting Instruments, Vol. 3. 650p. 1995. 16.00 (*92-3-102942-8*, U2942, Pub. by UNESCO FR) Bernan Associates.

Une'Tete Coupee. Iris Murdoch. 316p. (FRE.). 1988. pap. 15.95 (*0-7859-4303-X*, 2070380777) Fr & Eur.

Uneven & Unequal: Insurance Coverage & Reproductive Health Services. 38p. 1994. pap. 8.00 (*0-939253-35-6*) Guttmacher Inst.

Uneven Development & Regionalism: State, Territory & Class in Southern Europe. Cotis Hadjimichalis. Ed. by Alan Wilson et al. (Geography & Environment Ser.). 352p. (C). 1986. text ed. 59.95 (*0-7099-3700-8*, Pub. by Croom Helm UK) Routledge Chapman & Hall.

***Uneven Development in South East Asia.** Ed. by Chris Dixon & David Drakakis-Smith. 274p. 1997. 63.95 (*1-85972-555-4*, Pub. by Ashgate UK) Ashgate Pub Co.

Uneven Development in Thailand. Ed. by Michael J. Parnwell. 368p. 1996. 72.95 (*1-85972-085-4*, Pub. by Avebury Pub UK) Ashgate Pub Co.

Uneven Development in the Third World: A Study of China & India. 2nd ed. A. S. Bhalla. LC 94-44766. 1995. text ed. 79.95 (*0-312-12469-4*) St Martin.

Uneven Developments: The Ideological Work of Gender in Mid-Victorian England. Mary Poovey. (Women in Culture & Society Ser.). 296p. 1988. pap. text ed. 15.95 (*0-226-67530-0*) U Ch Pr.

Uneven Ground. Paul F. Jamieson. (Illus.). 232p. (Orig.). 1992. pap. text ed. 17.95 (*0-9634028-0-3*) Frnds O D Young Lib.

Uneven Ground: An Appalachian Anthology. Illus. by Jon Howson. LC 85-50640. 250p. (Orig.). 1985. pap. 9.95 (*0-935680-16-0*) Kentucke Imprints.

Uneven Growth Between Interdependent Economies: An Evolutionary View on Technology Gaps, Trade & Growth. Burt Verspagen. 171p. 1993. 67.95 (*1-85628-491-3*, Pub. by Avebury Pub UK) Ashgate Pub Co.

Uneven Reproduction: Industry, Space & Society. Andrew Pratt. (Policy, Planning, & Critical Theory Ser.). 270p. 1994. pap. 57.95 (*0-08-040487-1*, Prgamon Press); pap. text ed. 37.95 (*0-08-040486-3*, Prgamon Press) Buttrwrth-Heinemann.

Uneven Tides: Rising Inequality in America. Sheldon Danziger & Peter Gottschalk. LC 92-14233. (Illus.). 320p. 1992. 45.00 (*0-87154-222-6*) Russell Sage.

Uneven Tides: Rising Inequality in America. Ed. by Sheldon Danziger & Peter Gottschalk. (Illus.). 288p. 1994. reprint ed. pap. 16.95 (*0-87154-227-7*) Russell Sage.

***Uneven Zimbabwe: A Study of Finance, Development, & Underdevelopment.** Patrick Bond. LC 96-35891. 550p. 1996. 79.95 (*0-86543-538-3*); pap. 24.95 (*0-86543-539-1*) Africa World.

Unexamined Wife. Sherril Jaffe. LC 83-11915. 188p. (Orig.). 1983. 14.00 (*0-87685-570-2*); pap. 9.00 (*0-87685-569-9*) Black Sparrow.

Unexamined Wife, signed ed. deluxe ed. Sherril Jaffe. LC 83-11915. 188p. (Orig.). 1983. 25.00 (*0-87685-571-0*) Black Sparrow.

Unexcavated Objects & Ancient Near Eastern Art: Addenda. Oscar W. Muscarella. (Occasional Papers: No. 1-1). 19p. (C). 1979. pap. text ed. 5.25 (*0-685-65599-7*) Undena Pubns.

***Unexpected Addition.** Terese Ramin. (Intimate Moments Ser.: No. 793). 1997. mass mkt. 3.99 (*0-373-07793-9*, 1-07793-2) Silhouette.

***Unexpected Adventures of Cora Louise.** Susan R. Jones. (Illus.). 48p. (Orig.). (J). (gr. 4-12). 1997. mass mkt. 10.00 (*0-9657615-0-9*) Vintage Studio.

Unexpected Answers. Barbara Bartocci. LC 93-87104. 168p. (Orig.). 1994. pap. 7.95 (*0-87973-742-5*, 742) Our Sunday Visitor.

***Unexpected Child.** Kate Walker. 1997. mass mkt. 3.50 (*0-373-11921-6*, 1-11921-3) Harlequin Bks.

Unexpected Community: Portrait of an Old Age Subculture. Arlie R. Hochschild. LC 77-91733. 1978. pap. 12.00 (*0-520-03624-7*) U CA Pr.

Unexpected Company. Susan M. Blair. (Little Girl Ser.). (Illus.). 56p. (J). (ps-7). 1992. 19.95 (*0-9631956-0-3*) Pendant Pr.

Unexpected Delivery. Laurie Paige. (Romance Ser.). 1996. mass mkt. 3.25 (*0-373-19151-0*, 1-19151-9) Silhouette.

Unexpected Destinations: The Poignant Story of Japan's First Vassar Graduate. Akiko Kuno. Ed. by Meagan Calogeras. (Illus.). 256p. 1993. 23.00 (*4-7700-1638-7*) Kodansha.

***Unexpected Eagle: Essays on the Edge of the Wild.** Stephen Bodio. 208p. 1998. 25.00 (*1-55821-648-0*) Lyons & Burford.

Unexpected Eloquence: The Art in American Folk Art. Howard Rose. (Illus.). 160p. 1990. 25.00 (*1-878352-00-8*); pap. 15.00 (*1-878352-01-6*) R Saroff Pub.

Unexpected Engagement. Jessica Steele. 1996. pap. 3.25 (*0-373-03436-9*, 1-03436-2) Harlequin Bks.

***Unexpected Engagement.** large type ed. Jessica Steele. (Mills & Boon Large Print Ser.). 288p. 1997. 22.50 (*0-263-15009-7*) Ulverscroft.

***Unexpected Engagement.** large type ed. Jessica Steele. (Holding Out for a Hero Ser.). 1996. mass mkt. 3.25 (*0-373-15682-0*) Harlequin Bks.

Unexpected Family. Cathy G. Thacker. (American Romance Ser.: No. 407). 1991. mass mkt. 3.29 (*0-373-16407-6*) Harlequin Bks.

***Unexpected Father.** Kelly Jamison. 1997. pap. 3.50 (*0-373-76092-5*, 1-76092-5) Silhouette.

***Unexpected Father.** large type ed. Kathryn Ross. (Mills & Boon Large Print Ser.). 288p. 1997. 22.50 (*0-263-15047-X*) Ulverscroft.

Unexpected Grace: How God Brings Meaning Out of Our Failures. David B. Wyrtzen. LC 92-28415. 160p. 1992. pap. 9.99 (*0-929239-61-X*) Discovery Hse Pubs.

Unexpected Groom. Muriel Jensen. (American Romance Ser.). 1993. mass mkt. 3.50 (*0-373-16507-2*, 1-16507-5) Harlequin Bks.

Unexpected Guests at God's Banquet: Welcoming People with Disabilities in the Church. Brett Webb-Mitchell. 224p. (Orig.). 1994. pap. 17.95 (*0-8245-1440-8*) Crossroad NY.

Unexpected Hanging & Other Mathematical Diversions. Martin Gardner. (Illus.). 264p. 1991. pap. 15.95 (*0-226-28256-2*) U Ch Pr.

Unexpected Japan: Why American Business Should Return to Its Own Traditional Values--& Not Imitate the Japanese. Donald R. Riccomini & Philip M. Rosenzweig. 144p. 1985. 12.95 (*0-8027-0858-7*) Walker & Co.

Unexpected Journeys: The Art & Life of Remedios Varo. Janet Kaplan. (Illus.). 288p. 1988. 24.95 (*0-89659-797-0*) Abbeville Pr.

Unexpected Landlord. Leigh Michaels. (Romance Ser.). 1992. pap. 2.89 (*0-373-03233-1*, 1-03233-3) Harlequin Bks.

Unexpected Legacy. Susan Waggoner. 1997. write for info. (*0-517-70277-0*, Crown) Crown Pub Group.

Unexpected Meditations Late in the Twentieth Century. James V. Schall. 142p. 1986. 4.95 (*0-8199-0885-1*, Frncscn Herld) Franciscan Pr.

Unexpected Mrs. Pollifax. Dorothy Gilman. 1985. mass mkt. 5.99 (*0-449-20828-1*, Crest) Fawcett.

Unexpected Mrs. Pollifax. large type ed. Dorothy Gilman. LC 92-19245. (General Ser.). 400p. 1992. 18.95 (*0-8161-5352-3*) G K Hall.

Unexpected Mrs. Pollifax. Dorothy Gilman. 300p. 1991. reprint ed. lib. bdg. 22.95 (*0-89966-873-9*) Buccaneer Bks.

Unexpected News: Reading the Bible with Third World Eyes. Robert M. Brown. LC 84-2380. 166p. 1984. pap. 13.00 (*0-664-24552-8*, Westminster) Westminster John Knox.

Unexpected Night. Daly. 1995. pap. 6.95 (*1-883402-14-X*) S&S Trade.

Unexpected Night: A Henry Gamadge Mystery. Elizabeth Daly. 240p. 1994. reprint ed. pap. 7.00 (*1-883402-51-4*) S&S Trade.

Unexpected Real Consequences of Floating Exchange Rates. Rachel McCulloch. LC 83-10857. (Essays in International Finance Ser.: No. 153). 28p. 1983. pap. text ed. 8.00 (*0-88165-060-9*) Princeton U Int Finan Econ.

***Unexpected Rendezvous.** Greg Breza. 107p. (Orig.). 1997. mass mkt. 4.99 (*1-55197-728-1*, Pub. by Comnwlth Pub CN) Partners Pubs Grp.

Unexpected Roads: A Personal Success Journal. Arthur Pine. 160p. (Orig.). 1995. pap. 7.95 (*1-57071-070-8*) Sourcebks.

Unexpected Son. Marisa Carroll. (Hometown Reunion Ser.). 1996. mass mkt. 4.50 (*0-373-82549-8*) Harlequin Bks.

Unexpected Tenderness & Fighting over Beverley: Two New Plays by Israel Horovitz. Israel Horovitz. 164p. 1995. 9.99 (*1-56865-131-7*, GuildAmerica) Dblday Direct.

Unexpected Twist Series. Paul J. Payack. (Illus.). 1976. pap. 1.00 (*0-686-16728-7*) Chthon Pr.

Unexpected Universe. Loren Eiseley. LC 67-20308. 239p. 1972. reprint ed. pap. 11.00 (*0-15-692850-7*, Harvest Bks) HarBrace.

Unexpected Universe of Doris Lessing: A Study of in Narrative Technique. Katherine Fishburn. LC 85-9913. (Contributions to the Study of Science Fiction & Fantasy Ser.: No. 17). 184p. 1985. text ed. 45.00 (*0-313-23424-8*, FTW/, Greenwood Pr) Greenwood.

Unexpected Visions: Science Fiction by Classic Writers Not Known for Science Fiction. Ed. by Richard G. Jones. LC 93-45378. 1994. pap. 15.95 (*0-8065-1516-3*, Citadel Pr) Carol Pub Group.

Unexpected Visit: A Tale of Arwen Undomiel. Kerry E. Thompson. 16p. (Orig.). 1996. pap. 3.50 (*1-881799-11-5*) Am Tolkien Soc.

Unexpected Weapon. Connie Griffith. (Tootie McCarthy Ser.: Bk. 1). 128p. (Orig.). (J). (gr. 5-8). 1993. pap. 6.99 (*0-8010-3858-8*) Baker Bks.

Unexplained! Jerome Clark. (Illus.). 443p. 1993. 14.95 (*0-8103-9436-7*, 089174) Visible Ink Pr.

Unexplained see Strange & Unexplained Mysteries of the 20th Century

Unexplained Fever. Isaac & Serge Kernbaum. 560p. 1990. 254.95 (*0-8493-4556-1*, RB129) CRC Pr.

Unexplained Infertility. Patrick J. Taylor & John A. Collins. LC 92-23032. 296p. 1993. 39.95 (*0-19-262290-0*) OUP.

Unexplained Michigan Mysteries. Gary W. Barfknecht. 192p. (Orig.). 1993. pap. 11.95 (*0-923756-05-1*) Friede Pubns.

Unexplained Mysteries of the 20th Century. Janet Bord & Colin Bord. (Illus.). 432p. 1990. pap. 15.95 (*0-8092-4113-7*) Contemp Bks.

Unexplained Mysteries of World War II. Robert Jackson. 96p. 1996. write for info. (*1-57215-147-1*) World Pubns.

Unexplored New Guinea. Wilfred N. Beaver. LC 75-32799. (Illus.). reprint ed. 74.50 (*0-404-14102-1*) AMS Pr.

Unexplored Ocean. Catherine Fisher. 1995. 14.95 (*0-614-07441-X*, Pub. by Seren Bks UK); pap. 14.95 (*1-85411-106-X*) Dufour.

Unfaded Pagent: Edwin Austin Abbey's Shakespearean Subjects. Lucy Oakley. LC 94-75803. (Illus.). 104p. (Orig.). 1994. pap. 25.00 (*1-884919-00-6*) Wallach Art Gallery.

Unfailing Light: Memoirs of an American Rabbi. Bernard Drachman. (American Autobiography Ser.). 456p. 1995. reprint ed. lib. bdg. 99.00 (*0-7812-8501-1*) Rprt Serv.

Unfair Advantage. Tom Miller. 170p. (Orig.). 1986. pap. 17.95 (*0-9613034-1-7*) Unfair Advan Corp.

Unfair Advantage. Tom Miller. 170p. (Orig.). 1986. pap. 17.95 (*0-9613034-2-5*) Unfair Advan Corp.

Unfair Advantage: The Mental Part of Sports & Business. James A. Davis. LC 84-50120. (Illus.). 215p. (Orig.). 1984. 19.95 (*0-915377-00-4*); pap. 13.95 (*0-915377-01-2*) Trad Pub.

Unfair & Deceptive Acts & Practices. 3rd ed. Jonathan Sheldon. LC 91-66366. (Consumer Credit & Sales Legal Practice Ser.). 605p. (Orig.). 1991. pap. 70.00 (*0-943116-95-3*) Nat Consumer Law.

Unfair at Any Gridiron. C. W. Staley. LC 80-66404. 250p. 1981. 14.95 (*0-9604324-0-X*, 8012 800326) CWS Group Pr.

Unfair Competition & Section 43(a) of the Lanham Act. Doris E. Long. LC 93-3995. 540p. 1993. 95.00 (*0-87179-785-2*) BNA Books.

***Unfair Competition Law.** Anselm K. Sanders. 200p. 1997. 95.00 (*0-19-876487-1*) OUP.

An Asterisk (*) at the beginning of an entry indicates that the title is appearing in BIP for the first time.

***Unfair Competition, Student Edition, Restatement of the Law.** American Law Institute Staff. 683p. 1996. reprint ed. student ed., pap. text ed. write for info. (*0-314-20581-0*) West Pub.

Unfair Tactics. 3rd ed. John F. Romano. 1996. text ed. 125. 00 (*0-471-13969-6*) Wiley.

Unfair Tactics in Matrimonial Cases. Lawrence A. Moskowitz. LC 89-24757. (Trial Practice Library). 298p. 1990. text ed. 140.00 (*0-471-50117-4*) Wiley.

Unfair Tactics in Matrimonial Cases. Lawrence A. Moskowitz. 119p. 1994. suppl. ed., pap. 57.00 (*0-471-03224-7*) Wiley.

Unfair Tactics in Matrimonial Cases: 1996 Cumulative Supplement. Lawrence A. Moskowitz. LC 89-24757. 1996. pap. text ed. 82.00 (*0-471-15989-1*, Wiley-Liss) Wiley.

Unfair Trade: The Complete Report on Unfair Trade Policies by Japan's Major Trading Partners. Industrial Structure Council of Japan Staff. 212p. 1993. 85.00 (*1-56072-095-6*) Nova Sci Pubs.

Unfair Trade Practices & Consumer Protection, Cases & Comments. 5th ed. Glen E. Weston et al. (American Casebook Ser.). 957p. (C). 1992. text ed. 50.50 (*0-314-92199-0*) West Pub.

Unfair Trade Practices & Consumer Protection, Cases & Comments. 5th ed. Glen E. Weston et al. (American Casebook Ser.). 135p. 1992. pap. text ed. write for info. (*0-314-00827-6*) West Pub.

Unfair Trade Practices & Intellectual Property. 2nd ed. Roger E. Schechter. LC 93-20284. (Black Letter Ser.). 313p. 1993. pap. 24.50 incl. disk (*0-314-01949-9*) West Pub.

Unfair Trade Practices in a Nutshell. 3rd ed. Charles R. McManis. (Nutshell Ser.). 471p. 1993. pap. 17.00 (*0-314-01122-6*) West Pub.

***Unfair Trade Practices Litigation.** J. Clarke Kelso. 511p. 1995. 105.00 (*1-55834-224-9*, 63815) MICHIE.

***Unfair Trade Practices Litigation.** J. Clarke Kelso. 1996. suppl. ed. write for info. (*0-614-25244-X*, 63816-10) MICHIE.

Unfair Trial Tactics: Recognizing & Avoiding Them in Litigation. Mark A. Dombroff. 1985. 25.00 (*1-55917-781-0*, 5315); audio 125.00 (*1-55917-779-9*); vhs 395.00 (*1-55917-780-2*) Natl Prac Inst.

Unfaithful Angels: How Social Work Has Abandoned Its Mission. Harry Specht & Mark E. Courtney. 1995. pap. 15.00 (*0-02-874086-6*) Free Pr.

Unfaithful Devotion. Lajoya Lynx & Temptra Savage. 176p. 1994. 16.95 (*1-56167-134-7*) Noble Hse MD.

Unfaithful Wife. Lynne Graham. 1995. mass mkt. 3.25 (*0-373-11779-5*, 1-11779-5) Harlequin Bks.

***Unfaithful Wife.** large type ed. Lynne Graham. (Mills & Boon Large Print Ser.). 288p. 1996. 21.50 (*0-263-14575-1*, Pub. by M & B UK) Ulverscroft.

Unfamiliar Masterpieces of Painting. Walter Scheidig. (Illus.). 1965. 43.50 (*0-8079-0163-6*) October.

***Unfamiliar Partners: Asian Parents & U.S. Public Schools.** Bouy Te et al. (Illus.). 118p. (Orig.). 1997. pap. 18.95 (*1-880002-13-2*) Natl Coal Advocates.

Unfashionable Observations. Friedrich Wilhelm Nietzsche. Tr. by Richard T. Gray from GER. LC 94-6177. (Complete Works of Friedrich Nietzsche: Vol. 2). x, 420p. 1995. 29.95 (*0-8047-2382-6*) Stanford U Pr.

Unfastened Heart. Lane Von Herzen. 256p. 1995. pap. 10. 95 (*0-452-27290-4*, Plume) NAL-Dutton.

Unfastened Heart. large type ed. Lane Von Herzen. LC 95-7161. 341p. 1995. lib. bdg. 19.95 (*0-7838-1288-4*, GK Hall) Thorndike Pr.

Unfavorable Result in Plastic Surgery, 2 vols. 2nd ed. Robert M. Goldwyn. 1134p. 1984. boxed 285.00 (*0-316-31975-9*) Little.

Unfeigned Word: Fifteen Years of "New England Review" Ed. by T. R. Hummer & Devon Jersild. LC 92-56906. 315p. (C). 1993. pap. 14.95 (*0-87451-619-6*) U Pr of New Eng.

Unfettered. Sutton E. Griggs. LC 79-144623. reprint ed. 29. 50 (*0-404-00168-8*) AMS Pr.

Unfettered Mind: Writings of the Zen Master to the Sword Master. Takuan Soho. 92p. 1988. pap. 8.00 (*0-87011-851-X*, 300) Kodansha.

Unfettered Word: Confronting the Authority - Inerrancy Question. Robison B. James. 192p. 1994. reprint ed. pap. 11.95 (*1-880837-96-X*) Smyth & Helwys.

***Unfilled Graves.** Ah Cheng. 170p. 1995. pap. 6.95 (*0-8351-3145-9*) China Bks.

Unfilled Orders, Price Changes, & Business Fluctuations. Victor Zarnowitz. (Occasional Papers: No. 84). 32p. 1962. reprint ed. 20.00 (*0-685-66193-8*) Natl Bur Econ Res.

Unfilled Promise: Public Subsidy of the Arts in America. Edward Arian. 120p. 1993. pap. 12.95 (*1-56639-083-4*) Temple U Pr.

Unfinished. Jay B. Laws. 283p. (Orig.). 1993. pap. 9.95 (*1-55583-217-2*) Alyson Pubns.

***Unfinished.** large type ed. Cynthia Harrod-Eagles. (Dales Large Print Ser.). (Illus.). 310p. 1996. pap. 17.99 (*1-85389-449-4*) Ulverscroft.

Unfinished ... Essays in Honor of Ray L. Hart. Ed. by Mark C. Taylor. (JAAR Thematic Studies). 184p. 1981. pap. 20.95 (*0-89130-680-3*, 01-24-81) Scholars Pr GA.

Unfinished Agenda. National Commission on Secondary Vocational Education Staff. 35p. 1985. 4.75 (*0-318-22226-4*, IN289) Ctr Educ Trng Employ.

Unfinished Agenda. Lesslie Newbigin. 352p. 1993. pap. 60. 00 (*0-7152-0687-7*, Pub. by St Andrew UK) St Mut.

Unfinished Agenda: A New Vision for Child Development & Education. 96p. 1991. pap. 12.50 (*0-87186-093-7*); lib. bdg. 15.00 (*0-87186-793-1*) Comm Econ Dev.

Unfinished Agenda: Higher Education & the 1980s. Judith S. Eaton. (ACE-Oryx Series on Higher Education). (Illus.). 192p. 1991. 27.95 (*0-02-897111-6*, ACE-Oryx) Oryx Pr.

Unfinished Agenda: India & the World Economy. A. M. Khusro. 1994. reprint ed. write for info. (*81-224-0605-X*, Pub. by Wiley Estrn II) Franklin.

Unfinished Agenda for Civil Servivce Reform: Implications of the Grace Commission Report. Ed. by Charles H. Levine. LC 85-71183. (Dialogues on Public Policy Ser.). 142p. 1985. pap. 10.95 (*0-8157-5251-2*) Brookings.

Unfinished Assignment: Equal Education for Women. Patricia L. McGrath. 1976. pap. write for info. (*0-916468-06-2*) Worldwatch Inst.

Unfinished Autobiography. Alice A. Bailey. LC 51-32284. 1951. 26.00 (*0-85330-024-0*) Lucis.

Unfinished Autobiography. Alice A. Bailey. LC 51-32284. 1973. pap. 13.00 (*0-85330-124-7*) Lucis.

Unfinished Autobiography. Indira Goswami. 216p. 1990. text ed. 27.95 (*81-207-1173-4*, Pub. by Sterling Pubs II) Apt Bks.

Unfinished Battle: American Women 1848-1865 see Young Oxford History of Women in the United States

Unfinished Building. Henry J. Ambers. LC 74-19535. 400p. 1974. 19.95 (*0-9600874-2-7*) Edelweiss Pr.

Unfinished Building. Toby Olson. LC 93-15299. 96p. (Orig.). 1993. pap. 11.95 (*1-56689-009-8*) Coffee Hse.

Unfinished Business. Susan C. Ramirez. 277p. (Orig.). 1996. mass mkt. 4.99 (*1-55197-212-3*, Pub. by Comnwlth Pub CN) Partners Pubs Grp.

Unfinished Business. Nora Roberts. (Intimate Moments Ser.: No. 433). 1992. mass mkt. 3.39 (*0-373-07433-6*, 5-07433-1) Harlequin Bks.

Unfinished Business. Stephen Robinett. 1990. mass mkt. 3.50 (*0-380-75849-0*) Avon.

Unfinished Business. Maggie Scarf. 1986. mass mkt. 7.99 (*0-345-34248-8*) Ballantine.

Unfinished Business. Larry Strauss. 320p. (Orig.). 1997. mass mkt. 5.99 (*0-87067-849-3*, BH-849-3, Melrose Sq) Holloway.

***Unfinished Business.** Julie H. White. Ed. by Roy Zarauln. (Chapbook Ser.). 32p. 1996. boxed 7.95 (*1-879205-65-3*) Nightshade Pr.

Unfinished Business. large type ed. Nora Roberts. (Popular Ser.). 294p. 1993. reprint ed. lib. bdg. 16.95 (*1-56054-634-4*) Thorndike Pr.

Unfinished Business: A Civil Rights Strategy for America's Third Century. Clint Bolick. LC 90-7332. 220p. (Orig.). (C). 1990. 24.95 (*0-936488-35-2*); pap. 12.95 (*0-936488-36-0*) PRIPP.

Unfinished Business: A Memoir: 1902-1988. John Houseman. (Illus.). 508p. (Orig.). 1989. pap. 19.95 (*1-55783-024-X*) Applause Theatre Bk Pubs.

Unfinished Business: An Intellectual Nonhistory, 1963-1989. Richard Kostelanetz. 130p. (Orig.). 1990. pap. 30. 00 (*0-932360-92-0*) Archae Edns.

***Unfinished Business: From Sarajevo to Dayton.** Richard Holbrooke. 1998. 25.00 (*0-375-50057-X*) Random.

Unfinished Business: Iran, the UAE, Abu Musa & the Tunbs. Richard Schofield. 176p. (C). 1995. pap. 19.95 (*0-905031-90-3*, Pub. by Royal Inst Intl Affairs UK) Brookings.

Unfinished Business: Politics of Class War. Class War Federations Staff. (Illus.). 192p. 1992. pap. 9.00 (*1-873176-45-7*, AK Pr San Fran) AK Pr Dist.

***Unfinished Business: Restoring Your Accusers Dignity - Honor Thyself.** Ricardo A. Scott. (Ras Cardo Speaks Ser.). (Illus.). 100p. (Orig.). Date not set. pap. write for info. (*1-883427-95-9*) Crnerstone GA.

Unfinished Business: The Railroad in American Life. Maury Klein. LC 93-8112. (Illus.). 236p. 1994. text ed. 30.00 (*0-87451-657-9*) U Pr of New Eng.

***Unfinished Business: The Railroad in American Life.** Maury Klein. LC 93-8112. (Illus.). 236p. 1994. pap. 15. 95 (*0-87451-691-9*) U Pr of New Eng.

Unfinished Business: Twenty Years of Socialist Review. Ed. by Socialist Review Collective Staff. LC 91-32878. 300p. (C). 1991. pap. 20.00 (*0-86091-524-7*, A6419, Pub. by Vrso UK) Norton.

Unfinished Business in China. Mary E. Saunders. (Illus.). 304p. 1991. text ed. 9.95 (*0-932727-49-2*) Hope Pub Hse.

Unfinished Business of Civil Service Reform. William S. Carpenter. LC 79-16863. 128p. 1980. reprint ed. text ed. 35.00 (*0-313-22051-4*, CACS, Greenwood Pr) Greenwood.

Unfinished Business of Doctor Hermes. Richard Grossinger. 1976. pap. 4.00 (*0-913028-43-6*) North Atlantic.

Unfinished Business of Living: Helping Aging Parents Help Themselves. Elwood N. Chapman. Ed. by Michael G. Crisp. LC 86-71572. (Illus.). 232p. (Orig.). 1987. pap. 14.95 (*0-931961-19-X*) Crisp Pubns.

Unfinished Cathedral. T. S. Stribling. LC 85-20857. (Library of Alabama Classics). 400p. 1986. pap. 19.95 (*0-8173-0253-0*) U of Ala Pr.

Unfinished Clue. Georgette Heyer. reprint ed. lib. bdg. 24. 95 (*0-89190-648-7*, Rivercity Pr) Amereon Ltd.

Unfinished Conquest: The Guatemalan Tragedy. Victor Perera. LC 93-12054. (Illus.). 297p. 1993. 27.00 (*0-520-07965-5*) U CA Pr.

Unfinished Conquest: The Guatemalan Tragedy. Victor Perera. LC 93-12054. (Illus.). 297p. 1995. pap. 14.95 (*0-520-20349-6*) U CA Pr.

Unfinished Conversations: Mayas & Foreigners Between Two Wars. Paul Sullivan. (Illus.). 294p. 1991. pap. 15. 00 (*0-520-07244-8*) U CA Pr.

Unfinished Democracy. Haavio-Mannila & Skard. Date not set. pap. text ed. write for info. (*0-08-031814-2*, Pergamon Pr) Elsevier.

Unfinished Democracy: Women in Nordic Politics. Ed. by E. Haavio-Mannila. (Illus.). 228p. 1985. text ed. 106.00 (*0-08-031811-8*) Franklin.

Unfinished Design: The Humanities & Social Sciences in Undergraduate Engineering Education. Joseph S. Johnston, Jr. et al. (Illus.). 80p. (Orig.). (C). 1988. pap. text ed. 12.00 (*0-911696-42-3*) Assn Am Coll.

Unfinished Dialogue: Martin Buber & the Christian Way. John M. Oesterreicher. 136p. 1987. reprint ed. pap. 5.95 (*0-8065-1050-1*, Citadel Pr) Carol Pub Group.

Unfinished Dreams: A Poignant Coming-of-Age Novel about Dreams Cut Short by AIDS. Jane B. Zalben. LC 95-44424. 192p. (J). (gr. 3-5). 1996. 16.00 (*0-689-80033-9*, S&S Bks Young Read) S&S Childrens.

Unfinished Evangelism: More Than Getting Them in the Door. Tim Wright. LC 94-43567. 1995. pap. 10.99 (*0-8066-2794-8*) Augsburg Fortress.

Unfinished Funeral. Niccolo Tucci. 192p. 1992. reprint ed. pap. 8.95 (*1-55921-063-X*) Moyer Bell.

Unfinished Gospel: Notes on the Quest for the Historical Jesus. Evan Powell. 347p. (C). 1994. 23.95 (*0-9639650-6-9*) Symposium Bks.

Unfinished Health Agenda: Lessons from Hawai'i. Ed. by Bob Grossman & Jim Shon. 256p. (Orig.). (C). 1994. pap. text ed. 19.00 (*0-8248-1690-0*) UH Pr.

Unfinished Heaven: Durham, North Carolina: a Story of Two Schools. Betsy Holloway. LC 93-87215. (Illus.). 1994. 23.95 (*0-9616500-1-X*) Persimmon Pr.

Unfinished Journey: America since World War II. William H. Chafe. (Illus.). 576p. (C). 1995. pap. text ed. 26.95 (*0-19-508279-6*) OUP.

Unfinished Journey: Restructuring Schools in a Diverse Society. Laurie Olsen et al. 362p. 1994. pap. 27.00 (*1-887039-09-0*) Calif Tomorrow.

Unfinished Journey: Two People, Two Worlds - from Tyranny to Freedom. Nancy Rosenfeld. LC 93-17961. 294p. (Orig.). (C). 1993. pap. text ed. 18.95 (*0-8191-9196-5*); lib. bdg. 47.50 (*0-8191-9195-7*) U Pr of Amer.

***Unfinished Legacy.** 2nd ed. Ed. by Kishlansky. (C). 1997. student ed., pap. text ed. 15.95 (*0-673-98345-5*) Addison-Wesley.

Unfinished Legacy: A Brief History of Western Civilization. 2nd ed. Mark A. Kishlansky et al. LC 96-2526. (C). 1997. text ed. 42.50 (*0-673-98072-3*) Addson-Wesley Educ.

Unfinished Legacy: A Brief History of Western Civilization. Mark Kushlansky et al. 946p. reprint ed. pap. 42.00 (*1-886746-50-8*, 93498) Talman.

Unfinished Liberation of Chinese Women, 1949-1980. Phyllis Andors. LC 81-48323. 221p. reprint ed. pap. 63. 90 (*0-8357-3963-5*, 2057059) Bks Demand.

Unfinished Life: An Autobiography. Ruth St. Denis. (American Biography Ser.). 391p. 1991. reprint ed. lib. bdg. 79.00 (*0-7812-8335-3*) Rprt Serv.

***Unfinished Lives.** 1996. pap. 4.99 (*0-7871-1082-5*, Dove Bks) Dove Audio.

***Unfinished Lives.** Barbara Condos. Date not set. write for info. (*0-688-03761-5*) Morrow.

***Unfinished Lives, 3.** 1997. pap. 4.99 (*0-7871-1084-1*, Dove Bks) Dove Audio.

***Unfinished Lives 2.** 1996. pap. 4.99 (*0-7871-1083-3*, Dove Bks) Dove Audio.

Unfinished Man & the Imagination: Toward an Ontology & a Rhetoric of Revelation. Ray L. Hart. (Reprints & Translations Ser.). 418p. (C). 1985. pap. text ed. 14.95 (*0-89130-937-3*, 00-07-15) Scholars Pr GA.

Unfinished Manner: Essays on the Fragment in the Later Eighteenth Century. Elizabeth W. Harries. (Illus.). 224p. (C). 1994. text ed. 35.00 (*0-8139-1502-3*) U Pr of Va.

Unfinished Murder: The Capture of a Serial Rapist. James Neff. Ed. by William Grose. LC 94-34008. 352p. (Orig.). 1995. 22.00 (*0-671-73185-8*) PB.

Unfinished Murder: The Capture of a Serial Rapist. James Neff. 1996. mass mkt. 5.99 (*0-671-73186-6*) PB.

Unfinished Music, No. 1: An Unauthorized Companion to the Lost Lennon Tapes. L. R. King. 107p. (Orig.). 1990. pap. 10.00 (*0-944692-05-2*) Storyteller Prodns.

Unfinished Music, No. 2: An Unauthorized Companion to Year Two of the Lost Lennon Tapes. L. R. King. 110p. (Orig.). 1992. pap. 11.00 (*0-944692-10-9*) Storyteller Prodns.

***Unfinished Nation.** 2nd ed. Alan Brinkley. 1997. 45.00 (*0-679-45459-4*) Knopf.

Unfinished Nation: A Concise History of the American People. Alan Brinkley. LC 92-26666. 1993. 40.00 (*0-679-42548-9*) Knopf.

Unfinished Nation: A Concise History of the American People, 2 vols., Set. Alan Brinkley. LC 92-26666. 1993. 12.76 (*0-685-61105-1*) McGraw.

***Unfinished Nation: A Concise History of the American People, Vol. 1.** 2nd ed. Alan Brinkley. 1996. text ed. write for info. (*0-07-913182-4*) McGraw.

Unfinished Nation: A Concise History of the American People, Vol. 1: To 1877. Alan Brinkley. LC 92-26666. 1993. Vol. 1, to 1877. pap. text ed. write for info. (*0-07-007871-8*) McGraw.

Unfinished Nation: A Concise History of the American People, Vol. 2. Alan Brinkley. LC 92-26666. 1993. pap. text ed. write for info. (*0-07-007872-6*) McGraw.

Unfinished Nation: A Concise History of the American People, Vol. 3. 2nd ed. Alan Brinkley. 1996. pap. text ed. write for info. (*0-07-008216-2*) McGraw.

Unfinished Nation: A Concise History of the American People, Vol. 3. 2nd ed. Alan Brinkley. 1996. text ed. write for info. (*0-07-008219-7*) McGraw.

Unfinished Nation: A Concise History of the American People, Vol. 4. Alan Brinkley. 1993. text ed. write for info. (*0-07-007873-4*) McGraw.

Unfinished Nation: A Concise History of the American People from 1865, Vol. 3. 2nd ed. Alan Brinkley. 1996. pap. text ed. write for info. (*0-07-008218-9*) McGraw.

***Unfinished Nation: A Concise History of the American People: From 1865, Vol. 3.** 2nd ed. Alan Brinkley. 1996. student ed., pap. text ed. write for info. (*0-07-008221-9*) McGraw.

***Unfinished Nation: A Concise History of the American People: From 1865 with Documents, Vol. 3.** 2nd ed. Alan Brinkley. 1996. pap. text ed. write for info. (*0-07-913180-8*) McGraw.

Unfinished Nation: A Concise History of the American People from 1877, Vol. 2. 2nd ed. Alan Brinkley. 1996. pap. text ed. write for info. (*0-07-008217-0*) McGraw.

***Unfinished Nation: A Concise History of the American People to 1877, Vol. 2.** 2nd ed. Alan Brinkley. 1996. student ed., pap. text ed. write for info. (*0-07-008220-0*) McGraw.

***Unfinished Nation: A Concise History of the American People to 1877, Vol. 2.** 2nd ed. Alan Brinkley. 1996. pap. text ed. write for info. (*0-07-913179-4*) McGraw.

***Unfinished Nation Combined Edition: A Concise History of the American People, Vol. 1.** 2nd ed. Alan Brinkley. 1996. student ed., pap. text ed. write for info. (*0-07-015105-9*) McGraw.

***Unfinished Nation Commbined Edition: A Concise History of the American People, Vol. 1.** 2nd ed. Alan Brinkley. 1996. pap. text ed. write for info. (*0-07-913181-6*) McGraw.

Unfinished Nation Vol. 1: A Concise History of the American People. Alan Brinkley. 1993. pap. text ed. write for info. (*0-07-015065-6*) McGraw.

Unfinished Nation Vol. 3: A Concise History of the American People, Vol. 3. Alan Brinkley. 1993. pap. text ed. write for info. (*0-07-015033-8*) McGraw.

Unfinished Nation Vol. II: A Concise History of the American People, Vol. 2. Alan Brinkley. 1993. pap. text ed. write for info. (*0-07-015066-4*) McGraw.

Unfinished Novels. Charlotte Bronte. LC 93-26286. (Pocket Classics Ser.). 1993. 6.00 (*0-7509-0481-X*, Pub. by Sutton Pubng UK) Bks Intl VA.

Unfinished Painting. Mary J. Salter. 1989. 18.95 (*0-394-57417-6*) Knopf.

Unfinished People: Eastern European Jews Encounter America. Ruth Gay. 308p. 1996. 27.50 (*0-393-03991-9*) Norton.

Unfinished Portrait. Richard Peck. 176p. (J). 1993. mass mkt. 3.99 (*0-440-21886-1*) Dell.

Unfinished Quest of Richard Wright. 2nd ed. Michel Fabre. Tr. by Isabel Barzun from FRE. LC 92-14493. (Illus.). 696p. 1992. 54.95 (*0-252-01985-7*); 19.95 (*0-252-06264-7*) U of Ill Pr.

Unfinished Reformation. Charles C. Morrison. LC 68-20322. (Essay Index Reprint Ser.). 1977. 20.95 (*0-8369-0723-X*) Ayer.

***Unfinished Republic.** Gregory. 1997. student ed., pap. text ed. 16.00 (*0-13-613951-5*) P-H.

***Unfinished Republic: American Government in the Twenty-First Century.** Kenneth R. Mladenka. LC 96-32393. 1996. pap. 33.33 (*0-13-124496-5*) P-H.

Unfinished Revolution: Education & Politics in the Thought of Thomas Jefferson. Harold Hellenbrand. LC 88-40466. 208p. 1990. 36.50 (*0-87413-370-X*) U Delaware Pr.

Unfinished Revolution: Russia, 1917-1967. Isaac Deutscher. LC 67-23012. 124p. 1969. reprint ed. pap. 7.95 (*0-19-500786-7*) OUP.

Unfinished Revolution: Women & Health Care in America. Emily Friedman. LC 94-5940. 304p. 1994. pap. 20.00 (*1-881277-17-8*) United Hosp Fund.

Unfinished Road: Jewish Survivors of Latvia Look Back. Ed. by Gertrude Schneider. LC 91-3343. 232p. 1991. text ed. 49.95 (*0-275-94093-4*, C4093, Praeger Pubs) Greenwood.

Unfinished Sequence. Edward Butscher. Ed. by Stanley H. Barkan. (Cross-Cultural Review Chapbook Ser.: No. 6). 20p. 1980. 15.00 (*0-89304-849-6*, CCC131) Cross-Cultrl NY.

Unfinished Sequence. Edward Butscher. Ed. by Stanley H. Barkan. (Cross-Cultural Review Chapbook Ser.: No. 6: American Poetry 3). 20p. 1980. pap. 5.00 (*0-89304-805-4*); audio 10.00 (*0-89304-830-5*) Cross-Cultrl NY.

***Unfinished Society, Vol. 1.** Schultz. Date not set. pap. text ed. write for info. (*0-312-07602-9*) St Martin.

Unfinished Stories. Sybille Pearson. 1993. pap. 5.25 (*0-8222-1351-6*) Dramatists Play.

Unfinished Stories for Facilitating Decision Making in the Elementary Classroom. Ed. by Elizabeth H. Weiner. 78p. 1980. pap. 9.95 (*0-8106-1678-5*) NEA.

***Unfinished Symphony.** Andrews. 1997. 23.00 (*0-671-53469-6*, PB Hardcover); mass mkt. 7.50 (*0-671-53473-4*) PB.

Unfinished Tales. J. R. R. Tolkien. 512p. 1988. mass mkt. 5.99 (*0-345-35711-6*) Ballantine.

Unfinished Tales. J. R. R. Tolkien. Ed. by Christopher Tolkien. (Illus.). 368p. 1982. pap. 14.95 (*0-395-32441-6*) HM.

Unfinished Tasks: The New International Trade Theory & the Post-Uruguay Round Challenges. F. M. Scherer & Richard S. Belous. 64p. (Orig.). 1994. pap. text ed. 9.00 (*0-89068-126-0*, NPA 271) Natl Planning.

Unfinished Universe. Louise B. Young. (Illus.). 240p. 1993. 10.95 (*0-19-508039-4*) OUP.

Unfinished Voyages. John P. Fish. LC 88-84151. 310p. 1989. 35.00 (*0-936972-10-6*) Lower Cape.

Unfinished Voyages: Western Australian Shipwrecks, 1851-1880. 2nd ed. Graeme Henderson & Kandy-Jane Henderson. 1988. 35.00 (*0-85564-282-3*, Pub. by Univ of West Aust Pr AT) Intl Spec Bk.

Unfinished Voyages Vol. 3: Western Australian Shipwrecks 1881-1900. Lynne Cairns & Graeme Henderson. 383p. (C). 1995. 45.00 (*1-875560-24-6*, Pub. by Univ of West Aust Pr AT) Intl Spec Bk.

Unfinished War: Vietnam & the American Conscience. 2nd ed. Walter H. Capps. LC 81-66193. 224p. 1983. pap. 14.00 (*0-8070-0411-1*, BP 657) Beacon Pr.

Unfinshed Lives: What if They Hadn't Died When They Did? 336p. 1995. pap. 19.95 (*0-7871-0299-7*, Dove Bks) Dove Audio.

Unfired Food & Tropho Therapy, Food Cure. George J. Drews. 324p. 1963. reprint ed. spiral bd. 15.00 (*0-7873-0296-1*) Hlth Research.

Unfired Food Diet. James Faulkner. 1991. lib. bdg. 79.95 (*0-8490-4535-5*) Gordon Pr.

Unfired Food Diet Simplified. James Faulkner. 47p. 1968. reprint ed. spiral bd. 6.50 (*0-7873-0322-4*) Hlth Research.

Unfit for Heroes: Reconstruction & Soldier Settlement in the Empire Between the Wars. Kent Fedorowich. LC 94-27753. 1995. text ed. 69.95 (*0-7190-4108-2*, Pub. by Manchester Univ Pr UK) St Martin.

Unfit Mothers. Sue Mahan. Ed. by Robert D. Reed. LC 81-83616. (Illus.). 125p. (C). 1982. pap. 12.95 (*0-88247-622-X*) R & E Pubs.

***Unflinching Gaze: Morrison & Faulkner Re-Envisioned.** Carol A. Kolmerten et al. LC 96-35243. 1997. 45.00 (*0-87805-955-5*); pap. 18.00 (*0-87805-956-3*) U Pr of Miss.

Unfold the Sky. Tobi J. Kumar. (Orig.). 1996. pap. write for info. (*1-57553-251-4*) Watermrk Pr.

Unfolded Tales: Essays on Renaissance Romance. Ed. by George M. Logan & Gordon Teskey. LC 88-47920. (Illus.). 368p. 1989. 45.00 (*0-8014-2268-X*) Cornell U Pr.

Unfolding. Nick Ierullo. 1993. 10.00 (*0-533-10659-1*) Vantage.

Unfolding a Mandala: The Buddhist Cave Temples at Ellora. Geri H. Malandra. LC 92-8142. (SUNY Series in Buddhist Studies). (Illus.). 348p. (C). 1993. text ed. 89.50 (*0-7914-1355-1*); pap. text ed. 29.95 (*0-7914-1356-X*) State U NY Pr.

Unfolding & Determinacy Theorems for Subgroups of A & K. James Damon. LC 84-9333. (Memoirs of the American Mathematical Society Ser.: No. 50/306). 88p. 1984. pap. 17.00 (*0-8218-2306-X*, MEMO/50/306) Am Math.

Unfolding Beauty: The Art of The Fan. Janet G. Silver. LC 86-63853. (Illus.). 264p. 1987. 29.95 (*0-87846-279-1*); pap. 45.00 (*0-685-17968-0*) Mus Fine Arts Boston.

Unfolding Destiny: The Messages from the Guardian of the Baha'i Faith to the Baha'i Community of the British Isles. Shoghi Effendi. 531p. 1983. 21.95 (*0-900125-43-8*) Bahai.

Unfolding Drama: Studies in U. S. History by Herbert Aptheker. Herbert Aptheker. Ed. by Bettina Aptheker. LC 78-21025. 188p. 1979. pap. 3.50 (*0-7178-0501-8*) Intl Pubs Co.

Unfolding Drama of Redemption. W. Graham Scroggie. 1456p. 1995. 41.99 (*0-8254-3774-1*, Kregel Class) Kregel.

Unfolding Drama of the Bible: Eight Studies Introducing the Bible as a Whole. 3rd ed. Bernhard W. Anderson. LC 87-45884. 96p. 1988. pap. 10.00 (*0-8006-2098-4*, 1-2098, Fortress Pr) Augsburg Fortress.

Unfolding God of Jung & Milton. James P. Driscoll. LC 92-21769. (Studies in the English Renaissance). 248p. (C). 1993. text ed. 33.00 (*0-8131-1809-3*) U Pr of Ky.

***Unfolding Mallarme: The Development of a Poetic Art.** Roger Pearson. 326p. 1997. 80.00 (*0-19-815917-X*) OUP.

Unfolding Meaning. David Bohm. 192p. 1996. pap. 14.95 (*0-415-13638-5*) Routledge.

Unfolding Mystery: Discovering Christ in the Old Testament. Edmund P. Clowney. (Orig.). 1991. pap. 9.99 (*0-87552-174-6*, Pub. by Evangelical Pr) Presby & Reformed.

Unfolding of Anarchism: Its Origins & Historical Development to the Year 1864. Max Nettlau. (Men & Movements in the History & Philosophy of Anarchism Ser.). 1978. lib. bdg. 49.95 (*0-685-06650-9*) Revisionist Pr.

Unfolding of the Seasons. Ralph Cohen. LC 70-82867. 350p. reprint ed. pap. 99.80 (*0-317-19884-X*, 2023088) Bks Demand.

Unfolding Self: Psychosynthesis & Counseling. Molly Y. Brown. LC 83-61449. (Illus.). 181p. (C). reprint ed. pap. 20.00 (*0-9611444-0-8*) Psychosynth Pr.

Unfolding Self: Separation & Individuation. Mara Sidoli. 203p. (C). 1991. 29.95 (*0-938434-66-7*) Sigo Pr.

Unfolding Self: Separation & Individuation. Mara Sidoli. 203p. (Orig.). 1990. pap. 16.95 (*0-938434-65-9*) Sigo Pr.

***Unfolding Self: Varieties of Transformative Experience.** Ralph Metzner. LC 97-19672. 1997. pap. 12.95 (*1-57983-000-5*) Origin Pr CA.

Unfolding Splendor: A Biography of Laura Ophelia Reynolds Hughes. Annrey Nolds & Helen A. Reynolds. Ed. by G. M. Carlock & B. Holbrook Browne. (Illus.). 319p. (C). 1992. 29.95 (*1-880926-01-6*) Four Star SC.

Unfolding the Revelation. Roy A. Anderson. LC 61-10884. (Dimension Ser.). 223p. 1961. reprint ed. pap. 7.99 (*0-8163-0027-5*, 21400-7) Pacific Pr Pub Assn.

Unfolding the Third Eye. Robert G. Chaney. (Adventures in Esoteric Learning Ser.). 48p. 1970. pap. 4.95 (*0-918936-18-7*) Astara.

Unfolding Universe: A Stellar Journey. Lloyd Motz & Jefferson H. Weaver. (Illus.). 379p. 1989. 24.50 (*0-306-43264-1*, Plenum Pr) Plenum.

Unfoldings & Bifurcations of Quasi-Periodic Tori. H. Broer et al. LC 89-18093. (Memoirs Ser.). 175p. 1990. pap. 24.00 (*0-8218-2483-X*, MEMO/83/421) Am Math.

***Unfoldment & Manifestation.** L. Van der Hammen. (Illus.). xi, 181p. 1988. pap. 44.00 (*90-5103-008-8*, Pub. by SPB Acad Pub NE) Balogh.

Unfoldment of Man. Ida Mingle. 45p. 1987. reprint ed. spiral bd. 10.00 (*0-7873-0617-7*) Hlth Research.

***Unfoldment of the Great Within: Experienced Thinking for Your Self Development.** Bernard Jensen. (Dr. Jensen's Health Handbooks Ser.: Vol. 1). (Illus.). 120p. (Orig.). 1992. pap. 8.00 (*0-932615-24-4*, P-0284) B Jensen.

Unforeseen. Dorothy Macardle. reprint ed. lib. bdg. 23.95 (*0-89190-113-2*, Rivercity Pr) Amereon Ltd.

Unforeseen Joy: Serving a Friends Meeting As Recording Clerk. Damon D. Hickey. (Illus.). 40p. 1987. pap. text ed. 2.00 (*0-942727-16-9*) NC Yrly Pubns Bd.

Unforeseen Tendencies of Democracy. E. L. Godkin. 1976. lib. bdg. 59.95 (*0-8490-2784-5*) Gordon Pr.

Unforeseen Tendencies of Democracy. Edwin L. Godkin. LC 76-37153. (Essay Index Reprint Ser.). 1977. reprint ed. 23.95 (*0-8369-2500-9*) Ayer.

Unforeseen Tendencies of Democracy. Edwin L. Godkin. (Notable American Authors Ser.). 1992. reprint ed. lib. bdg. 75.00 (*0-7812-2926-X*) Rprt Serv.

Unforeseen Wilderness: Kentucky's Red River Gorge. Wendell Berry. (Illus.). 160p. (Orig.). 1991. reprint ed. pap. 19.95 (*0-86547-462-1*, North Pt Pr) FS&G.

Unforgettable. F. Rosanne Bittner. 480p. 1994. mass mkt. 5.50 (*0-8217-4423-2*, Zebra Kensgtn) Kensgtn Pub Corp.

Unforgettable. Caroline B. Cooney. 272p. (J). (gr. 7-9). 1994. pap. 3.95 (*0-590-47877-X*) Scholastic Inc.

Unforgettable. Molly Rice. 1995. mass mkt. 3.50 (*0-373-22348-X*) Harlequin Bks.

***Unforgettable.** Meryl Sawyer. 1998. mass mkt. 5.99 (*0-8217-5830-6*, Zebra Kensgtn) Kensgtn Pub Corp.

Unforgettable: The Life & Mystique of Nat King Cole. Leslie Gourse. (Illus.). 336p. 1992. pap. 12.95 (*0-312-07877-3*) St Martin.

Unforgettable! The 100 Greatest Moments in Los Angeles Sports History. Richard B. Perelman & Mark Meyers. LC 95-36666. (Moments in Sports Ser.). (Illus.). 224p. 1995. 39.95 (*1-881096-21-1*) Towery Pub.

Unforgettable Army: Slim's XIV Army. Spellmount Ltd. Publishers Staff. (C). 1986. 125.00 (*0-685-60236-2*, Pub. by Spellmount UK) St Mut.

Unforgettable Army: Slim's XIVth Army in Burma. Michael Hickey. (Illus.). 320p. 1994. 24.95 (*1-885119-10-0*) Sarpedon.

Unforgettable Army: Slim's 14th Army-Burma. Michael Hickey. 256p. (C). 1991. 130.00 (*1-873376-10-3*, Pub. by Spellmount UK) St Mut.

Unforgettable Characters. Nancy Polette. (Illus.). 48p. (Orig.). 1991. pap. 5.95 (*0-913839-97-3*) Pieces of Lrning.

Unforgettable Grady. Victoria Lee. Date not set. pap. write for info. (*1-888225-05-X*) A Touch of Heart.

Unforgettable Man. large type ed. Penny Jordan. (Harlequin Romance Ser.). 1996. lib. bdg. 19.95 (*0-263-14550-6*, Pub. by Mills & Boon UK) Thorndike Pr.

Unforgettable Man (Dangerous Liaisons) Penny Jordan. 1996. mass mkt. 3.50 (*0-373-11805-8*, 1-11805-8) Harlequin Bks.

Unforgettable Months & Years. Vo-Nguyen-Giap. (Cornell University, Southeast Asia Program, Data Paper Ser.: No. 99). 124p. reprint ed. pap. 35.40 (*0-317-29631-0*, 2021847) Bks Demand.

Unforgettable Musical Memories. Reader's Digest Editors. (Illus.). 252p. 1984. spiral bd. 29.95 (*0-89577-178-0*, Random) RD Assn.

Unforgettable Pacific Northwest Camping Vacations. Kiki Canniff. LC 94-18169. 144p. 1994. pap. 10.95 (*0-941316-11-4*) F Amato Pubns.

Unforgettable Pacific Northwest Camping Vacations. Kiki Canniff. 1995. pap. 10.95 (*0-941361-14-4*, KUCV) KITwo Enter.

Unforgettable Pen Pal Activity Guide: A Story about Prejudice & Discrimination. Joy Berry. Ed. by Cathy Vertuca. (Human Race Club Ser.). (Illus.). 20p. (Orig.). (J). (gr. k-6). 1991. pap. 12.99 (*0-923790-30-6*) Kids Media Group.

Unforgettable Radio, Vol. I: A Program Chronicle of WKBB, 1933-1941. Len Kruse. (Illus.). 224p. (Orig.). 1993. pap. write for info. (*0-9639249-0-7*) L Kruse.

***Unforgettable Seafaring Adventures from a Storyteller.** Tristan Jones. 1996. text ed. 23.50 (*0-07-063339-8*) McGraw.

Unforgettable Strategies for Success. George R. Allen. 96p. (Orig.). 1987. pap. 6.95 (*0-933554-50-8*) Tech-Ed Pub.

Unforgetting Heart: An Anthology of Short Stories by African American Women, 1859-1992. Ed. by Asha Kanwar. LC 93-3240. 276p. (Orig.). 1993. pap. 10.95 (*1-879960-30-3*); lib. bdg. 20.95 (*1-879960-31-1*) Aunt Lute Bks.

***Unforgivable.** Joyce McGill. 1997. pap. 3.99 (*0-373-48349-X*, 1-48349-4) Harlequin Bks.

Unforgiveness. Kenneth Hagin, Jr. 1983. pap. 0.75 (*0-89276-716-2*) Hagin Ministries.

Unforgiving Bride. Joan Johnston. (Desire Ser.). 1994. mass mkt. 2.99 (*0-373-05878-0*, 1-05878-3) Silhouette.

Unforgiving Land. Paul Sullivan. Ed. by Myrna Kemnitz. 220p. (Orig.). (YA). 1996. pap. 7.00 (*0-88092-256-7*) Royal Fireworks.

***Unforgiving Minute.** Jerome Reyer. 139p. (Orig.). 1997. mass mkt. 4.99 (*1-55197-888-1*, Pub. by Comnwlth Pub CN) Partners Pubs Grp.

***Unforgotten.** Tamara Leigh. 1997. mass mkt. 5.50 (*0-06-108448-4*, Harp PBks) HarpC.

Unforgotten Dreams: Poems by the Zen Monk Shotetsu. Steven D. Carter. (Translations from the Asian Classics Ser.). 240p. 1996. 49.00 (*0-231-10576-2*); pap. 16.50 (*0-231-10577-0*) Col U Pr.

Unformed & Unfilled: A Critique of the Gap Theory. John C. Whitcomb. 245p. 1994. reprint ed. pap. 8.00 (*0-9641659-0-2*) Burgener.

Unformulated Experience. Donnel B. Stern. LC 97-25923. (RPBS Ser.). 1997. write for info. (*0-88163-141-8*) Analytic Pr.

Unfortunate Emigrants: Narratives of the Donner Party. Ed. by Kristin Johnson. (Illus.). 320p. 1996. 35.95 (*0-87421-204-9*) Utah St U Pr.

Unfortunate Emigrants: Narratives of the Donner Party. Ed. by Kristin Johnson. (Illus.). 320p. 1996. pap. 19.95 (*0-87421-208-1*) Utah St U Pr.

Unfortunate Fall: Theodicy & the Moral Imagination of Andrew Marvell. John Klause. LC 83-13521. xi, 208p. (C). 1984. lib. bdg. 32.50 (*0-208-02026-8*, Archon Bks) Shoe String.

***Unfortunate Prairie Occurrence.** Jamie Harrison. 304p. 1998. 22.95 (*0-7868-6260-2*) Hyperion.

Unfortunate Traveller & Other Works. Thomas Nashe. Ed. & Intro. by J. B. Steane. (English Library). 512p. 1972. pap. 12.95 (*0-14-043067-9*, Penguin Classics) Viking Penguin.

Unfortunate Woman. Barry Gifford. LC 83-82560. 192p. (Orig.). 1984. 14.95 (*0-916870-73-1*); pap. 7.95 (*0-916870-74-X*) Creat Arts Bk.

***Unfortunates.** William Baer. LC 97-11544. 76p. 1997. 25.00 (*0-943549-46-9*) TJU Pr.

***Unfortunates.** William Baer. LC 97-11544. 76p. (Orig.). 1997. pap. 15.00 (*0-943549-47-7*) TJU Pr.

Unfought War: Japan 1941-1942. Alvin D. Coox. 65p. 1992. 27.50 (*1-879691-06-X*) SDSU Press.

Unfought War: Japan 1941-1942. Alvin D. Coox. (University Research Lecture Ser.). 76p. (C). 1992. lib. bdg. 27.50 (*0-685-52078-1*) Wright State Univ Pr.

Unfought War of Nineteen Sixty-Two. J. R. Saigal. 180p. 1979. 11.95 (*0-318-36616-9*) Asia Bk Corp.

Unfound Treasures of Mexico. Charles A. Kenworthy. (Illus.). 96p. (Orig.). (SPA.). 1995. pap. 13.95 (*0-9632156-4-7*) Quest Pubns.

Unfounded Fears: Myths & Realities of a Constitutional Convention. A. Perry Barbara. LC 89-7502. (Contributions in Legal Studies: No. 55). 192p. 1989. text ed. 49.95 (*0-313-26717-0*, WKC, Greenwood Pr) Greenwood.

Unfounded Fears: Myths & Realities of a Constitutional Convention. Paul J. Weber & Barbara A. Perry. LC 89-8479. 192p. 1989. pap. text ed. 12.95 (*0-275-93347-4*, WKC/, Praeger Pubs) Greenwood.

Unframed Originals: Recollections. W. S. Merwin. LC 81-70063. 256p. 1983. 14.95 (*0-689-11284-X*, Atheneum S&S) S&S Trade.

Unfree Associations. Michael Covino. 64p. (Orig.). 1982. pap. 5.95 (*0-917658-17-5*) BPW & P.

Unfree Labor: American Slavery & Russian Serfdom. Peter Kolchin. 536p. 1990. pap. 17.95 (*0-674-92098-8*) HUP.

Unfree Labour in the Development of the Atlantic World. Ed. by Paul E. Lovejoy & Nicholas Rogers. LC 94-31528. (Studies in Slave & Post-Slave Societies & Cultures). (Illus.). 272p. (Orig.). 1995. 35.00 (*0-7146-4579-6*, Pub. by F Cass Pubs UK) Intl Spec Bk.

Unfree Labour in the Development of the Atlantic World. Ed. by Paul E. Lovejoy & Nicholas Rogers. (Illus.). 272p. (Orig.). 1995. pap. 20.00 (*0-7146-4152-9*, Pub. by F Cass Pubs UK) Intl Spec Bk.

Unfree Professions: German Lawyers, Teachers, & Engineers, 1900-1950. Konrad H. Jarausch. 368p. 1990. 65.00 (*0-19-504482-7*) OUP.

Unfriendly Fire: A Mother's Memoir. Albert E. Stone. LC 94-48108. (Singular Lives: The Iowa Series in North American Autobiography). (Illus.). 175p. 1995. 22.95 (*0-87745-506-6*); pap. 12.95 (*0-87745-507-4*) U of Iowa Pr.

Unfriendly Governor. Anthony A. Lee. (Stories about 'Abdu'l-Baha Ser.). (Illus.). 24p. (J). (gr. k-5). 1980. pap. 3.00 (*0-933770-02-2*) Kalimat.

Unfriendly Proposition. Jessica Steele. (Romance Ser.: No. 3095). 1990. pap. 2.50 (*0-373-03095-9*) Harlequin Bks.

Unfriendly Proposition. large type ed. Jessica Steele. 1990. reprint ed. lib. bdg. 18.95 (*0-263-12232-8*, Pub. by Mills & Boon UK) Thorndike Pr.

Unfriendly Skies: Saga of Corruption. 3rd ed. Rodney Stich. LC 90-80467. (Illus.). 656p. 1991. pap. 25.00 (*0-932438-02-4*) Diablo West Pr.

Unfulfilled Expectations: Home & School Influences on Literacy. Catherine E. Snow et al. LC 90-4814. (Illus.). 251p. 1991. 37.50 (*0-674-92110-0*, SNOUNF) HUP.

***Unfulfilled Indian Summer of 1996.** Russell Schneider. (Illus.). 280p. (Orig.). 1996. 16.95 (*0-9649813-1-9*) R Schneider.

Unfulfilled Promise: Public Subsidy of the Arts in America. Edward Arian. 120p. (C). 1989. 22.95 (*0-87722-612-1*) Temple U Pr.

Unfulfilled Promise: Rescue & Resettlement of Jewish Refugee Children in the United States, 1934-1945. Judith T. Baumel. LC 90-32118. (Illus.). 227p. (Orig.). (C). 1990. pap. 27.50 (*0-938737-21-X*) Denali Press.

Unfulfilled Promise of Synthetic Fuels: Technological Failure, Policy Immobilism, or Commercial Illusion. Ed. by Ernest J. Yanarella & William C. Green. LC 87-247. (Contributions in Political Science Ser.: No. 179). 243p. 1987. text ed. 59.95 (*0-313-25666-7*, YUN/) Greenwood.

Unfurl the Flags: Remembrances of the American Civil War. Ed. by William E. Edmonston, Jr. LC 89-84086. v, 90p. (Orig.). 1989. pap. 4.95 (*0-9622393-0-5*) Edmonston Pub.

Unga Island Girl (Ruth's Book) Jacquelin R. Pels. LC 94-96375. (Illus.). 312p. (Orig.). 1995. pap. 24.50 (*0-9625429-7-0*) Hardscratch Pr.

Ungarische Grammatik. Jozsef Tompa. (Janua Linguarum, Series Practica: No. 96). 1968. 95.40 (*90-279-0674-2*) Mouton.

Ungeduld des Herzens. Stefan Zweig. 456p. (GER.). 1995. pap. 18.00 (*3-596-21679-6*, Pub. by Fischer Taschbch Verlag GW) Intl Bk Import.

Unger's Bible Handbook: A Best-Selling Guide to Understanding the Bible. Merrill F. Unger. LC 66-16224. 1988. mass mkt., pap. 11.99 (*0-8024-9013-1*) Moody.

Unger's Bible Handbook see Manual Biblico de Unger

Unger's Concise Bible Dictionary: With Complete Pronunciation Guide to Bible Names by W. Murray Severance. Merrill F. Unger. 296p. (gr. 10). 1985. pap. 14.99 (*0-8010-9208-6*) Baker Bks.

Unglued Empire: The Soviet Experience with Communications Technologies. Gladys D. Ganley. (Communication, Culture & Information Studies Ser.). 220p. 1996. pap. 39.50 (*1-56750-198-2*); text ed. 73.25 (*1-56750-197-4*) Ablex Pub.

Ungodliness. Leslie A. Miller. LC 93-73475. (Poetry Ser.). 80p. (Orig.). 1994. 20.95 (*0-88748-172-8*); pap. 11.95 (*0-88748-173-6*) Carnegie-Mellon.

Ungodly Rage: The Hidden Face of Catholic Feminism. Donna M. Steichen. LC 90-84593. 420p. (Orig.). 1991. pap. 14.95 (*0-89870-348-4*) Ignatius Pr.

Ungodly Women: Genger & the First Wave of American Fundamentalism. Betty A. Deberg. LC 90-35589. 176p. 1990. pap. 12.00 (*0-8006-2439-4*, 1-2439) Augsburg Fortress.

Ungovernable People: The English & Their Law in the Seventeenth & Eighteenth Centuries. Ed. by John Brewer & John Styles. 1980. 50.00 (*0-8135-0891-6*) Rutgers U Pr.

Ungovernable Rock: A History of the Anglo-Corsian Kingdom & Its Role in Britain's Mediterranean Strategy During the Revolutionary War. Desmond Gregory. LC 83-49345. (Illus.). 216p. 1986. 32.50 (*0-8386-3225-4*) Fairleigh Dickinson.

Ungoverned Imaginings: James Mill's the History of British India & Orientalism. Javed Majeed. (Oxford English Monographs). 270p. 1992. 65.00 (*0-19-811786-8*) OUP.

Ungrateful Governess. Mary Balogh. 1988. pap. 4.99 (*0-451-15727-3*, Sig) NAL-Dutton.

Ungrounded Empires: The Cultural Politics of Modern Chinese Transnationalism. Ed. by Ong. 250p. (C). 1996. pap. 21.95 (*0-415-91543-0*, Routledge NY); text ed. 74.95 (*0-415-91542-2*, Routledge NY) Routledge.

Unguarded Moments: Behind-the-Scenes Photographs of President Ronald Reagan. Pete Souza. (Illus.). 160p. 1992. 39.95 (*1-56530-023-8*) Summit TX.

Unguarded Moments: Behind the Scenes Photographs of President Ronald Reagan. Pete Souza. 1992. 195.95 (*1-56530-024-6*) Summit TX.

Unguided Tour. Sylvia Plachy. 1990. 39.95 (*0-89381-393-1*) Aperture.

Unguided Tour. Photos by Sylvia Plachy. (Illus.). 144p. 1991. pap. 29.95 (*0-89381-431-8*) Aperture.

Ungulate Behavior & Management: Proceedings of the Conference College Station, TX, 23-27 May, 1988. Ed. by E. C. Mungall. 540p. 1991. reprint ed. 223.75 (*0-444-88995-7*) Elsevier.

Unhallowed Intrusions, a History of Cherokee Families in Forsyth County, Georgia. Don Shadburn. 800p. (C). 1996. text ed. write for info. (*1-883793-00-9*) Wolfe Pubng.

Unhappily Unwed. Toni Collins. 1995. mass mkt. 3.50 (*0-373-52006-9*, 1-52006-3) Silhouette.

Unhappy Children: Reasons & Remedies. Heather Smith. 250p. (C). 1995. 45.00 (*1-85343-308-X*); pap. 24.95 (*1-85343-301-2*) NYU Pr.

Unhappy Consciousness: Bankimchandra Chattopadhyay & the Formation of Discourse in India. Sudipta Kaviraj. (SOAS Studies on South Asia). 250p. 1995. 22.00 (*0-19-563294-X*) OUP.

Unhappy Consciousness: The Poetic Plight of Samuel Beckett. Eugene F. Kaelin. 350p. 1981. lib. bdg. 129.50 (*90-277-1313-8*, D Reidel) Kluwer Ac.

Unhappy India. 2nd enl. rev. ed. Lala Lajpat Rai. LC 72-171642. reprint ed. 49.50 (*0-404-03803-4*) AMS Pr.

Unhappy Kashmir: The Hidden Story. Dina N. Raina. 1990. text ed. 30.00 (*81-85047-69-3*, Pub. by Reliance Pub Hse II) Apt Bks.

Unhappy Kashmir: The Hidden Story. Dina N. Raina. (C). 1990. text ed. 29.00 (*0-685-39106-X*, Pub. by BR Pub II) S Asia.

Unhappy Landings: Why Airplanes Crash. Thomas W. Watson. LC 92-16913. 372p. 1992. pap. 16.95 (*0-9630891-0-2*) Harbor City.

Unhappy Medium: Spiritualism & the Life of Margaret Fox. Earl W. Fornell. LC 64-10317. 220p. reprint ed. pap. 62.70 (*0-317-10609-0*, 2000824) Bks Demand.

Unhappy Valley: Clan, Class, & State in Colonial Kenya. Bruce Berman & John Lonsdale. LC 91-28362. (Eastern African Studies). 521p. (Orig.). (C). 1991. text ed. 50.00 (*0-8214-1016-4*) Ohio U Pr.

Unhappy Valley: Clan, Class, & State in Colonial Kenya, 1. Bruce Berman & John Lonsdale. LC 91-28362. (Eastern African Studies). 521p. (Orig.). (C). 1992. pap. text ed. 19.95 (*0-8214-1017-2*) Ohio U Pr.

Unhappy Valley: Clan, Class, & State in Colonial Kenya, 2. Bruce Berman & John Lonsdale. LC 91-28362. (Eastern African Studies). 521p. (Orig.). (C). 1992. pap. text ed. 19.95 (*0-8214-1025-3*) Ohio U Pr.

***UNHCR & Voluntary Repatriation of Regugees.** Zieck. 1997. write for info. (*90-411-0409-7*) Kluwer Law Tax Pubs.

Unhealthy Alliances: Bureaucrats, Interest Groups, & Politicians in Health Reform. Henry N. Butler. (Special Studies in Health Reform). 100p. (Orig.). 1994. pap. 9.95 (*0-8447-7022-1*, AEI Pr) Am Enterprise.

An Asterisk (*) at the beginning of an entry indicates that the title is appearing in BIP for the first time.

Unhealthy Housing: Research, Remedies, & Reform. Ed. by Roger Burridge & David Ormandy. LC 92-21146. 1993. write for info. (*0-419-15410-8*, E & FN Spon) Routledge Chapman & Hall.

Unhealthy Societies: From Inequality to Well-Being. Richard G. Wilkinson. LC 96-21560. 272p. (C). 1996. pap. 17.95 (*0-415-09235-3*); text ed. 69.95 (*0-415-09234-5*) Routledge.

Unheard Cry. Cleta B. Lee. Ed. by Caroline Tresidder. (Cleta's Story Ser.: Vol. 3). (Illus.). 240p. (Orig.). 1995. pap. 12.95 (*0-9649047-3-X*) Cletas Desk Top.

Unheard Melodies: Narrative Film Music. Claudia Gorbman. LC 86-45941. (Illus.). 200p. 1987. 27.50 (*0-253-33987-1*); pap. 10.95 (*0-253-20436-4*, MB-436) Ind U Pr.

***Unheard Music: Photographs 1991-1997.** Christina Piper. Ed. by Glenn Maryansky & Sara Brownell. (Illus.). 160p. (Orig.). 1997. pap. 9.00 (*0-9657534-0-9*) P A Kane.

Unheard Of: Voices from the College. Katherine Kehoe & Michele Angers. Ed. by Priscilla F. Sears & Charlotte Houde-Quimbey. 102p. (Orig.). 1996. pap. 20.00 (*0-9650844-0-X*) Whipple Hse.

Unheard Voice. Lemlem Tsegaw. 60p. 1994. pap. 7.00 (*1-56411-092-3*) Untd Bros & Sis.

***Unheard Voice Vol. 1: Portraits of Childhood.** Colin Finlay. Ed. by Alison Morley. (Illus.). 72p. 1996. 25.00 (*0-9654124-0-7*) Browning-Cohen.

Unheard Voices. Judy Baer. (Cedar River Daydreams Ser.: Vol. 16). 144p. (Orig.). (J). (gr. 7-10). 1992. mass mkt. 4.99 (*1-55661-257-5*) Bethany Hse.

Unheard Voices: American Indian Responses to the Columbian Quincentenary. Ed. by Carole M. Gentry & Donald A. Grinde, Jr. LC 94-72032. (National Conference Proceedings Ser.: 3). 221p. 1994. pap. 15.00 (*0-935626-39-5*) U Cal AISC.

Unheard Voices: The First Historians of Southern Women. Ed. by Anne F. Scott. LC 92-26552. (Feminist Issues Ser.). 216p. 1993. text ed. 29.95 (*0-8139-1432-9*); pap. text ed. 14.50 (*0-8139-1433-7*) U Pr of Va.

Unheavenly City Revisited: A Revision of The Unheavenly City. Edward C. Banfield. 358p. (C). 1990. reprint ed. pap. text ed. 16.95 (*0-88133-529-0*) Waveland Pr.

Unheeded Cry. Abraham Fuchs. (ArtScroll History Ser.). (Illus.). 288p. 1984. 19.99 (*0-89906-468-X*); pap. 16.99 (*0-89906-469-8*) Mesorah Pubns.

Unheeded Teachings of Christ or Christ Rejected. Emanuel M. Josephson. 1979. 250.00 (*0-685-96472-8*) Revisionist Pr.

Unheeded Teachings of Jesus: Christ Rejected. Emanuel M. Josephson. (Illus.). 50.00 (*0-685-07976-7*) Chedney.

Unheeded Teachings of Jesus Christ or Christ Rejected: The Strangest Story Never Told. Emanuel Josephson. LC 59-15870. (Blacked-Out History Ser.). (Illus.). 96p. 1959. 10.00 (*0-686-32441-2*); pap. 10.00 (*0-686-32442-0*) A-albionic Res.

Unheeded Warning. Manes Sperber. LC 90-5399. (All Our Yesterdays Ser.: Vol. 2). 224p. (C). 1991. 27.95 (*0-8419-1032-4*) Holmes & Meier.

Unheeded Warning: The Inside Story of American Eagle Flight 4184. S. A. Frederick. LC 96-20857. (Illus.). 324p. 1996. text ed. 22.95 (*0-07-021951-6*) McGraw.

Unheralded Triumph: City Government in America, 1870-1900. Jon C. Teaford. LC 83-12082. 416p. 1984. pap. text ed. 16.95 (*0-8018-3063-X*) Johns Hopkins.

***Unheroic Conduct: The Rise of Heterosexuality & the Invention of the Jewish Man.** Daniel Boyarin. LC 96-46047. (Contraversions Ser.: Vol. 8). (Illus.). 1997. 50.00 (*0-520-20033-0*); pap. 18.95 (*0-520-21050-6*) U CA Pr.

Unheroic Muse. Barriss Mills. 1978. 20.00 (*0-686-59681-1*); pap. 8.00 (*0-686-59682-X*) Elizabeth Pr.

Unholy Alliance. (Illus.). 28p. 1995. pap. 16.95 (*90-6918-136-3*) Dist Art Pubs.

***Unholy Alliance.** LC 96-86319. 316p. (Orig.). 1996. pap. 15.95 (*0-9652651-0-2*) Aunt Hagars Chaps.

Unholy Alliance. Susanna Gregory. LC 96-27965. 288p. 1996. 23.95 (*0-312-14752-X*) St Martin.

Unholy Alliance. Peter Levenda. 400p. (Orig.). 1995. mass mkt. 6.99 (*0-380-77722-3*) Avon.

***Unholy Alliance: Religion & Atrocity in Our Time.** Marc H. Ellis. 1997. pap. 18.00 (*0-8006-3080-7*, Fortress Pr) Augsburg Fortress.

Unholy Alliance: Stalin's Pact with Hitler. Geoffrey Roberts. LC 89-15456. 314p. 1989. 39.95 (*0-253-35117-0*) Ind U Pr.

Unholy Alliances: New Women's Fiction. Ed. by Louise Rafkin. 168p. (Orig.). (C). 1988. pap. 9.95 (*0-939416-15-8*) Cleis Pr.

Unholy Allies Bk. 2: Vampire: Masquerade of the Red Death Trilogy. Robert Weinberg. 1995. pap. 5.99 (*1-56504-841-5*, 12401) White Wolf.

Unholy Angels. Kate Gallison. 266p. 1996. mass mkt. 5.50 (*0-440-22220-6*) Dell.

"Unholy" Apostles: Tales of Chequamegon Shipwrecks. James Keller. (Illus.). 160p. (Orig.). 1984. pap. text ed. 5.95 (*0-933577-00-1*) Apostle Isl Pr.

Unholy Bible: Blake, Jung & the Collective Unconscious. June Singer. LC 85-22139. (Illus.). 272p. (Orig.). 1986. 32.00 (*0-938434-24-1*); pap. 15.95 (*0-938434-25-X*) Sigo Pr.

Unholy Bible: Hebrew Literature of the Early Kingdom Period. Jacob Rabinowitz. 156p. Date not set. 7.00 (*1-57027-015-5*) Autonomedia.

Unholy Bible: The Truth about the Old Testament with an Afterword on the New Testament. David S. Sommers. LC 95-90320. 1995. 19.95 (*0-533-11537-X*) Vantage.

***Unholy Drawers: Let the Parody Begin.** Starla K. Immak. 36p. (YA). 1996. write for info. (*1-889494-02-X*) Sword Publng.

Unholy Dying. R. T. Campbell. 128p. 1985. reprint ed. pap. 5.95 (*0-486-24977-8*) Dover.

Unholy Fire. 5.98 (*0-8317-3545-7*) Smithmark.

Unholy Fire. Whitley Strieber. 416p. 1993. pap. 5.99 (*0-451-17496-8*, Sig) NAL-Dutton.

***Unholy Ghosts.** Richard Zimler. 256p. 1996. pap. 14.95 (*0-85449-233-X*, Pub. by Gay Mens Pr UK) LPC InBook.

Unholy Grail: A Social Reading of Chretien de Troyes's 'Conte du Graal' Brigitte Cazelles. LC 95-1781. (Figurae Ser.). 414p. 1995. 42.50 (*0-8047-2481-4*) Stanford U Pr.

Unholy Hands on the Bible: An Examination of Major Modern Versions, Vol. II. Ed. by Green & Johnston. 768p. 1990. 24.95 (*0-685-35683-3*) Sovereign Grace Trust Fund.

Unholy Hands on the Bible: An Examination of the Six Major New Versions, Vol. II. Peter J. Johnston & Jay P. Sr. Green. 768p. 1992. 29.95 (*1-878442-65-1*) Sovereign Grace Trust Fund.

Unholy Hands on the Bible: The Works of John W. Burgon, Vol. 1. abr. ed. John W. Burgon. (New Testament Text Ser.). 608p. (C). 1989. text ed. 24.95 (*0-685-30023-4*) Sovereign Grace Trust Fund.

***Unholy in Holy Scripture: The Dark Side of the Bible.** Gerd Ludemann. LC 96-52254. (Orig.). 1997. pap. 14.00 (*0-664-25739-9*) Westminster John Knox.

Unholy Spirits: Occultism & New Age Humanism. Gary North. 426p. (Orig.). 1991. reprint ed. pap. 12.95 (*0-930462-53-X*) Inst Christian.

Unholy Tricks: More Miraculous Card Play. Terence Reese & David Bird. 128p. 1995. pap. 13.95 (*0-575-05944-3*, Pub. by V Gollancz UK) Trafalgar.

***Unholy Trinity.** Aarons. Date not set. pap. write for info. (*0-312-18199-X*) St Martin.

Unholy Trinity: The Vatican, the Nazis, & Soviet Intelligence. Mark Aarons & John Loftus. 368p. 1991. 22.95 (*0-312-07111-6*) St Martin.

Unholy Trinity: The Vatican, the Nazis, & Soviet Intelligence. Mark Aarons & John Loftus. (Illus.). 372p. 1993. pap. 15.95 (*0-312-09407-8*) St Martin.

***Unholy War: BYU vs. Utah.** Phil Miller & Dick Rosetta. LC 97-13814. (Illus.). 224p. (Orig.). 1997. pap. 14.95 (*0-87905-560-X*, Peregrine Smith) Gibbs Smith Pub.

Unhooked: Staying Sober & Drug-Free. James Christopher. 184p. 1989. pap. 16.95 (*0-87975-564-4*) Prometheus Bks.

Unhurried View of Copyright. Benjamin Kaplan. LC 67-13539. (James S. Carpentier Lectures, 1966). 158p. reprint ed. pap. 45.10 (*0-685-10851-1*, 2055780) Bks Demand.

Unhurried Years. Pierce Butler. (American Autobiography Ser.). 198p. 1995. reprint ed. lib. bdg. 69.00 (*0-7812-8470-8*) Rprt Serv.

Uni- the New International Language. Elisabeth Wainscott. (Illus.). 346p. 1974. 10.95 (*0-912904-00-3*); pap. 5.95 (*0-912904-01-1*) Uniline Div.

Unica Reconciliacion Nacional: La Reconciliacion Con La Ley. Jose Sanchez-Boudy. (Coleccion Cuba y Sus Jueces). 22p. (SPA.). 1992. pap. 2.00 (*0-89729-644-3*) Ediciones.

UNICEF for Beginners. Illus. & Text by Christian Clark. 160p. 1995. pap. 11.00 (*0-86316-197-9*) Writers & Readers.

***Unicity: A Collection of Photographs of Ostad Elahi.** Bahram Elahi. 147p. 1995. 65.00 (*0-614-31090-3*, Pub. by R Laffont FR) Baker & Taylor.

Unicity Precept & the Socio-Scientific Order. Masudul A. Choudhury. LC 93-6688. 194p. (C). 1993. lib. bdg. 42.50 (*0-8191-9079-9*) U Pr of Amer.

Unicode Standard: Worldwide Character Encoding, Version 1.1. 2nd ed. Unicode Staff. LC 96-18831. (C). 1996. pap. text ed., pap. 57.95 incl. cd-rom (*0-201-48345-9*) Addison-Wesley.

Unicon II. David J. Schlink. 1983. reprint ed. 4.95 (*0-912327-00-6*) Unicon Ent.

***Unicor 1996 ICD-9-CM Easy Coder.** 49.95 (*0-614-19634-5*, OP080196WE) AMA.

Unicorn. Sri Donato. Ed. by Morningland Publications, Inc. Staff. (Illus.). 207p. (Orig.). 1981. pap. 10.00 (*0-935146-16-4*) Morningland.

Unicorn. Nancy Hathaway. 192p. 1984. 12.98 (*0-517-44902-1*) Random Hse Value.

Unicorn. Iris Murdoch. 312p. 1987. pap. 10.95 (*0-14-002476-X*, Penguin Bks) Viking Penguin.

Unicorn. Martin Walser. Tr. by B. Ellis-Jones from GER. 283p. 1983. pap. 7.95 (*0-7145-0886-1*) M Boyars Pubs.

Unicorn Alphabet. Marianna Mayer. (Illus.). 32p. (J). (gr. 1 up). 1989. lib. bdg. 14.89 (*0-8037-0373-2*) Dial Bks Young.

Unicorn Alphabet. Marianna Mayer. (Illus.). 32p. (J). 1993. pap. 5.99 (*0-14-054922-6*, Puff Pied Piper) Puffin Bks.

Unicorn & Dragon, Vol. 1. Lynn Abbey. 240p. 1987. mass mkt. 3.50 (*0-380-75567-X*) Avon.

Unicorn & Dragon Vol. II: Conquest. Lynn Abbey. 272p. 1988. pap. 6.95 (*0-380-75354-5*) Avon.

Unicorn & Other Poems. Anne M. Lindbergh. LC 56-9810. 112p. 1993. 14.00 (*0-679-42540-3*) Pantheon.

Unicorn & Other Poems. Anne M. Lindbergh. LC 72-4548. 1972. pap. 8.00 (*0-394-71822-4*, Vin) Random.

Unicorn & the Dancing Girl: Poems of Faiz Almed Faiz, with Original Text. Ed. by Khalid Hasan. Tr. by Daud Kamal. (C). 1988. 17.50 (*0-8364-2360-7*, Pub. by Allied II) S Asia.

Unicorn & the Garden. Ed. by Betty Parry. LC 78-64531. (Illus.). 1978. per. 15.00 (*0-915380-04-8*) Word Works.

Unicorn & the Lake. Marianna Mayer. LC 81-5469. (Pied Piper Bks.). (Illus.). 32p. (J). (gr. k up). 1987. pap. 4.95 (*0-8037-0436-4*) Dial Bks Young.

Unicorn & the Lake. Marianna Mayer. (J). (ps-3). 1990. pap. 17.99 (*0-8037-0844-0*) Dial Bks Young.

Unicorn & the Lake. Marianna Mayer. 1992. pap. 5.99 (*0-14-054718-5*) NAL-Dutton.

Unicorn & the Moon. Tomie De Paola. LC 94-20297. (Illus.). (J). 1995. 12.95 (*0-382-24659-4*, Silver Pr NJ); lib. bdg. 14.95 (*0-382-24658-6*) Silver Burdett Pr.

Unicorn & the Moon. David M. McPhail. LC 94-20298. (Illus.). 32p. (J). 1994. pap. 13.95 (*0-382-24660-8*) Silver Burdett Pr.

Unicorn at the Manger: Yearlong Stories of the Holy Night. Roger Robbennolt. LC 96-9658. (Illus.). 104p. (Orig.). 1996. pap. 16.95 (*0-8298-1146-X*) Pilgrim OH.

Unicorn Bride. Claire Delacroix. 1994. mass mkt. 3.99 (*0-373-28823-9*, 1-28823-2) Harlequin Bks.

Unicorn Captured. Michael L. Johnson. 80p. (Orig.). 1980. per. 4.00 (*0-685-30033-1*) Cottonwood KS.

Unicorn Coloring Book. Christine Gansberger. (Color & Story Bks.). (Illus.). 32p. (Orig.). (J). (gr. 1-6). 1985. pap. 5.95 (*0-8431-1755-9*, Troubador) Price Stern Sloan.

Unicorn Crossing. Nancy Luenn. 64p. (J). (gr. 2-9). 1996. reprint ed. pap. 2.50 (*0-8167-1321-9*) Troll Communs.

Unicorn Dilemma. John Lee. (Unicorn Ser.: No. 2). 384p. 1992. mass mkt. 4.99 (*0-8125-2092-0*) Tor Bks.

***Unicorn Dreams.** Dyan Sheldon. LC 96-54226. (Illus.). (J). 1997. pap. 14.99 (*0-8037-2284-2*) Dial Bks Young.

***Unicorn Girl: An Illustrated Novel.** Anne McCaffrey. 1997. 22.00 (*0-06-105540-9*, HarperPrism) HarpC.

Unicorn Highway. David L. Jones. 352p. (Orig.). 1992. mass mkt. 4.99 (*0-380-76506-3*, AvoNova) Avon.

Unicorn in the Sanctuary: The Impact of the New Age Movement on the Catholic Church. rev. ed. Randy England. LC 91-66615. 161p. (Orig.). 1992. reprint ed. pap. 9.00 (*0-89555-451-8*) TAN Bks Pubs.

Unicorn Island. Francis G. Hutchins. 208p. 1993. 15.00 (*0-935100-06-7*) Amarta Pr.

Unicorn Murders. Carter Dickson. 192p. 1989. reprint ed. pap. 5.95 (*1-55882-015-9*, Lib Crime Classics) Intl Polygonics.

Unicorn Named Beulah Mae. Jane H. Stroschin. 32p. (J). (gr. k-6). 1993. lib. bdg. 15.00 (*1-883960-04-5*) Henry Quill.

Unicorn Named Beulah Mae. rev. ed. Jane H. Stroschin. (Illus.). 32p. (J). (gr. k-6). 1996. lib. bdg. 15.00 (*1-883960-14-2*) Henry Quill.

Unicorn Named Beulah Mae Returns. Jane H. Stroschin. (Illus.). 32p. (J). (gr. k-6). 1995. lib. bdg. 15.00 (*1-883960-05-3*) Henry Quill.

Unicorn of Kilimanjaro. Robert Vavra. (Illus.). 216p. 1991. 17.99 (*0-517-05755-7*) Random Hse Value.

Unicorn of the West: El Unicornio del Oeste. Alma F. Ada. Tr. by Rosa Zubizarreta. LC 92-7425. (Illus.). 40p. (J). (gr. 1-3). 1994. English ed. text ed. 14.95 (*0-689-31778-6*, Atheneum Bks Young); Spanish ed. text ed. 14.95 (*0-689-31916-9*, Atheneum Bks Young) S&S Childrens.

Unicorn Peace. John Lee. 352p. 1993. mass mkt. 4.99 (*0-8125-1981-7*) Tor Bks.

Unicorn Peak. Adams. 1993. 20.00 (*0-8212-2029-2*) Bulfinch Pr.

Unicorn Poem & Flowers & Songs of Sorrow. E. A. Mares. 78p. (Orig.). 1992. pap. 8.95 (*0-931122-65-1*) West End.

Unicorn Point. Piers Anthony. (Apprentice Adept Fantasy Ser.: No. 6). 1990. mass mkt. 5.99 (*0-441-84563-0*) Ace Bks.

Unicorn Quest. John Lee. (Unicorn Ser.: No. 1). 1992. mass mkt. 3.99 (*0-8125-2055-6*) Tor Bks.

Unicorn Rampant. Nigel Tranter. 1984. 14.95 (*0-340-33720-6*) Beaufort Bks NY.

Unicorn Riders of the Orb. Michael G. Moore. (Illus.). 227p. 1986. pap. 2.95 (*0-9613282-1-5*) MGM Bks.

***Unicorn Ship.** Barbara Berger. Date not set. 15.95 (*0-399-22035-6*) Putnam Pub Group.

Unicorn Solution. John Lee. 1991. pap. 3.95 (*0-8125-0346-5*) Tor Bks.

Unicorn Sonata. Peter S. Beagle. LC 96-16007. (Illus.). 160p. 1996. 19.95 (*1-57036-288-2*) Turner Pub GA.

***Unicorn Summer.** large type ed. Rhona Martin. (Ulverscroft Large Print Ser.). 544p. 1997. 27.50 (*0-7089-3724-1*) Ulverscroft.

Unicorn Variations. Roger Zelazny. 256p. 1987. mass mkt. 3.50 (*0-380-70287-8*) Avon.

Unicorn Vengeance. Claire Delacroix. 1995. mass mkt. 4.50 (*0-373-28893-X*) Harlequin Bks.

Unicorn War. John Lee. 1996. mass mkt. 5.99 (*0-8125-3639-8*) Tor Bks.

Unicorn Was There. Elizabeth Pool. LC 81-4747. (Illus.). 64p. 1981. reprint ed. pap. 5.95 (*0-87233-061-3*) Bauhan.

Unicorn Whispers. Rohini Godneratne-Cooray. 50p. (Orig.). 1995. pap. 15.00 (*0-9645560-0-6*) R Gooneratne-Cooray.

Unicorn Without a Name. Sharon L. Karim. LC 93-73171. (Unicorn Ser.: Bk. 1). (Illus.). 32p. (J). (ps-3). 1995. 12.95 (*1-883703-00-X*) Big Heart Pub.

Unicornis: On the History & Truth of the Unicorn. rev. ed. Michael Green. Tr. by James ODonnell. (Illus.). 128p. 1994. pap. 14.95 (*1-56138-514-X*) Running Pr.

Unicorns. Ariel Books Staff. (Illus.). 80p. 1992. 4.95 (*0-8362-3020-5*) Andrews & McMeel.

Unicorns. James G. Huneker. LC 72-6581. reprint ed. 32.50 (*0-404-10529-7*) AMS Pr.

Unicorns. James G. Huneker. (BCL1-PS American Literature Ser.). 361p. 1992. reprint ed. lib. bdg. 89.00 (*0-7812-6749-8*) Rprt Serv.

Unicorns: Opposing Viewpoints. Norma Gaffron. LC 89-11660. (Great Mysteries Ser.). (Illus.). 112p. (J). (gr. 5-8). 1989. lib. bdg. 17.96 (*0-89908-063-4*) Greenhaven.

Unicorns & Dreams. Wanda W. Waller. Ed. by Ron Lopez. (Illus.). 39p. (Orig.). (J). (gr. k-6). 1985. pap. 4.95 (*0-930825-00-4*) Lola Library.

Unicorns & Other Fabulous Creatures. Heather Lowenberg. (Tattoo Tales Ser.). (Illus.). 24p. (Orig.). (J). (ps-3). 1994. pap. 4.99 (*0-679-86437-7*) Random Bks Yng Read.

Unicorns & Rainbows. Sondra J. Short. LC 92-60808. 223p. (J). (gr. 3 up). 1993. 9.95 (*1-55523-537-9*) Winston-Derek.

Unicorns Are Real: A Right-Brained Approach to Learning. Barbara M. Vitale. LC 82-83064. (Right Brain-Whole Brain Learning Ser.). (Illus.). 144p. (Orig.). 1982. pap. 12.95 (*0-915190-35-4*, JP9035-4) Jalmar Pr.

Unicorns at War: Special Edition. Francine Pascal. (Unicorn Club Ser.). 176p. (J). (gr. 4-7). 1995. pap. 3.99 (*0-553-48222-X*) Bantam.

***Unicorns Blood.** Finney. Date not set. write for info. (*0-312-18201-5*) St Martin.

Unicorns-Coloring Book. J. K. Anderson. (J). 1985. pap. 4.95 (*0-88388-086-5*) Bellerophon Bks.

Unicorns for Everyone. large type ed. Marilyn R. Riddle. (Illus.). 24p. (Orig.). 1980. pap. 7.00 (*0-9603748-1-7*) Sandpiper OR.

Unicorns Go Hawaiian. Francine Pascal. (Sweet Valley Twins & Friends Ser.). 192p. (J). (gr. 4-7). 1991. pap. 3.99 (*0-553-15948-8*) Bantam.

Unicorns I Have Known. Robert Vavra. LC 83-61566. (Illus.). 200p. 1983. 45.00 (*0-688-02203-0*) Morrow.

Unicorns in Love. Francine Pascal. (Unicorn Club Ser.: No. 5). 144p. (J). (gr. 4-7). 1995. pap. 3.50 (*0-553-48218-1*) Bantam.

Unicorns in Soft Sculpture, Bk. 1. Bonnie Arthur. (Illus.). (Orig.). 1982. pap. 3.50 (*0-941284-14-X*) J Shaw Studio.

***Unicorns! Unicorns!** Geraldine McCaughrean. LC 97-5296. (Illus.). 32p. (J). (ps-3). 1997. lib. bdg. 15.95 (*0-8234-1319-5*) Holiday.

Unicycles & Artistic Bicycles Illustrated. Jack Wiley. LC 86-61015. (Illus.). 168p. (YA). (gr. 7 up). 1986. pap. 26.95 (*0-913999-15-6*) Solipaz Pub Co.

Unidad Cristiana. D. Martyn Lloyd-Jones. 68p. (SPA.). 1973. pap. 2.25 (*0-8254-1449-0*, Edit Portavoz) Kregel.

Unidad de Dios. David K. Bernard. Tr. by Kelley Nix from ENG. 343p. (Orig.). (SPA.). 1996. pap. 8.99 (*1-56722-186-6*) Word Aflame.

Unidad Y La Unanimidad Segun La Aspiracion Del Senor Y La Vida Y El Servicio Del Cuerpo Segun Su Deleite. Witness Lee. 54p. (SPA.). per. 2.00 (*0-87083-516-5*, 08029002) Living Stream Ministry.

Unidades Habitacionales en Tula, Hidalgo. Blanca L. Paredes. 248p. 1990. pap. 10.00 (*968-6487-39-5*, IN015) UPLAAP.

Unidades Habitacionales Mesoamericanas y Sus Areas de Actividad. Ed. by Linda Manzanilla. 470p. 1986. pap. 4.50 (*968-837-585-3*, UN011) UPLAAP.

Unidentified Drawings. Ed. by Franz Schulze & George E. Danforth. LC 86-9980. (Mies Van Der Rohe Archive Series An Illustrated Catalog of the Mies Van Der Rohe Drawing in the Museum of Modern Art, Pt. II, 1938-1967: Vol. 20). (Illus.). 400p. 1993. text ed. 300.00 (*0-8153-0121-9*) Garland.

Unidentified Flying Objects. 1991. lib. bdg. 250.00 (*0-8490-4918-0*) Gordon Pr.

UFOs: A Manual for the Millenium. Phil Cousineau. LC 95-7239. 272p. 1995. pap. 5.99 (*0-06-258638-6*) HarpC.

Unidentified Flying Objects: A Selected Bibliography. 1992. lib. bdg. 250.00 (*0-8490-8767-8*) Gordon Pr.

Unidentified Flying Objects: Fact or Fiction? Lillian C. Desguin. (Illus.). (Orig.). 1992. pap. 19.80 (*0-89412-188-X*) Aegean Park Pr.

Unidentified Human Remains & the True Nature of Love. Fraser. Date not set. per. 10.95 (*0-921368-11-9*, Pub. by Blizzard Pub CN) Genl Dist Srvs.

Unidentified Particles of Time. Phyllis R. Weprin. 40p. (Orig.). 1990. pap. 6.00 (*0-9623552-2-4*, Border Pr) Ed Arcas.

Unidentified Sign. Henry F. Lutz. LC 72-995. (University of California Publications in Social Welfare: Vol. 10, No. 2). 4p. reprint ed. pap. 25.00 (*0-317-10202-8*, 2021473) Bks Demand.

Unidentified Woman. Mignon G. Eberhart. 176p. 1988. mass mkt. 4.99 (*0-446-31461-7*) Warner Bks.

***Unidentified Woman.** large type ed. Mignon G. Eberhart. LC 96-37565. 325p. 1997. pap. 21.95 (*0-7838-8055-3*, GK Hall) Thorndike Pr.

Unidimensional Scaling of Social Variables: Concepts & Procedures. Raymond L. Gorden. LC 76-26443. 1977. 22.95 (*0-02-912580-4*, Free Press) Free Pr.

UNIDIR Repertory of Disarmament Research: 1990. 402p. 1990. 45.00 (*92-9045-043-6*, GV.90.0.10) UN.

***UNIDO: Central Asian Republics, 2 vols.** Date not set. 285.00 (*0-614-24745-4*, M305) Economist Intell.

***UNIDO: China.** 1996. 445.00 (*0-85058-929-0*, M307) Economist Intell.

UNIDO Guides to Information Sources: Beer & Wine Industry, No. 25. pap. 4.00 (*92-1-106163-6*, ID/190) UN.

UNIDO Guides to Information Sources: Cement & Concrete Industry, No. 2. pap. 4.00 (*92-1-106125-3*, ID/185) UN.

UNIDO Guides to Information Sources: Ceramics Industry, No. 17. pap. 4.00 (*92-1-106152-0*, ID/143) UN.

UNIDO Guides to Information Sources: Coffee, Cocoa, Tea & Spices Industry, No. 28. pap. 4.00 (*92-1-106162-8*, ID/198) UN.

UNIDO Guides to Information Sources: Dairy Products Manufacturing Industry, No. 23. mass mkt. 4.00 (*92-1-106166-0*, ID/177) UN.

UNIDO Guides to Information Sources: Foundry Industry, No. 5. rev. ed. 87p. pap. 4.00 (*92-1-106137-7*, ID/192) UN.

UNIDO Guides to Information Sources: Industrial Maintenance & Repair, No. 36. 86p. mass mkt. 4.00 (*92-1-106178-4*, ID/236) UN.

UNIDO Guides to Information Sources: Leather & Leather Products, No. 3. 85p. 1980. pap. 4.00 (*92-1-106136-9*, ID/226) UN.

UNIDO Guides to Information Sources: Pharmaceutical Industry, No. 20. pap. 4.00 (*92-1-106150-4*, ID/162) UN.

U V

An Asterisk (*) at the beginning of an entry indicates that the title is appearing in BIP for the first time.

UNIDO Guides to Information Sources: Soap & Detergent Industry, No. 24. pap. 4.00 (92-1-106156-3, ID/181) UN.

UNIDO Guides to Information Sources, No. 1: Meat Processing Industry. pap. 4.00 (92-1-106138-5, ID/163) UN.

UNIDO Guides to Information Sources, No. 10: Pesticides Industry. rev. ed. 4.00 (92-1-106142-3) UN.

UNIDO Guides to Information Sources, No. 14: Printing & Graphics Industry. pap. 4.00 (92-1-106148-2, ID/135) UN.

UNIDO Guides to Information Sources, No. 15. (Non-Alcoholic Beverages Industry Ser.). pap. 4.00 (92-1-106147-4, ID136) UN.

UNIDO Guides to Information Sources, No. 16: Glass Industry. pap. 4.00 (92-1-106146-6, ID/138) UN.

UNIDO Guides to Information Sources, No. 18: Paint & Varnish Industry. pap. 4.00 (92-1-106145-8, ID/150) UN.

UNIDO Guides to Information Sources, No. 19: Canning Industry. 4.00 (92-1-106143-1) UN.

UNIDO Guides to Information Sources, No. 21: Fertilizer Industry. 4.00 (92-1-106141-5) UN.

UNIDO Guides to Information Sources, No. 26: Iron & Steel Industry. 4.00 (92-1-106160-1) UN.

UNIDO Guides to Information Sources, No. 27: Packaging Industry. pap. 4.00 (92-1-106165-2, ID/194) UN.

UNIDO Guides to Information Sources, No. 29: Petrochemical Industry. mass mkt. 4.00 (92-1-106164-4, ID/199) UN.

UNIDO Guides to Information Sources, No. 31: Woodworking Industry Machinery. mass mkt. 4.00 (92-1-106159-8, ID/214) UN.

UNIDO Guides to Information Sources, No. 32: Electronics Industry. 4.00 (92-1-106139-3) UN.

UNIDO Guides to Information Sources, No. 33: Bioconversion of Agricultural Wastes. mass mkt. 4.00 (92-1-106154-7) UN.

UNIDO Guides to Information Sources, No. 34: Natural & Synthetic Rubber Industry. pap. 4.00 (92-1-106155-5, ID/230) UN.

UNIDO Guides to Information Sources, No. 35: Utilization of Agricultural Residues for the Production of Panels, Pulp & Paper. 4.00 (92-1-106173-3) UN.

UNIDO Guides to Information Sources, No. 37: Industrial Training. pap. 4.00 (92-1-106168-7, ID/237) UN.

UNIDO Guides to Information Sources, No. 38: Essential Oils. 4.00 (92-1-106177-6) UN.

UNIDO Guides to Information Sources, No. 4: Furniture & Joinery Industry. pap. 4.00 (92-1-106135-0, ID/188) UN.

UNIDO Guides to Information Sources, No. 40: Grain Processing & Storage. 4.00 (92-1-106179-2) UN.

UNIDO Guides to Information Sources, No. 8: Agricultural Implements & Machinery Industry. 4.00 (92-1-106134-2) UN.

Unification & Comparative Law in Theory & Practice. Ed. by C. S. Hondius. 1984. lib. bdg. 104.00 (90-6544-173-5) Kluwer Law Tax Pubs.

Unification & Conquest: A Political & Social History of England in the Tenth & Eleventh Centuries. Pauline Stafford. 240p. 1995. text ed. 19.95 (0-7131-6532-4, A4088, Pub. by E Arnld UK) St Martin.

Unification & Differentiation in Socialist Criminal Justice. T. Szabo. 260p. (C). 1979. 70.00 (963-05-1685-3, Pub. by Akad Kiado HU) St Mut.

Unification & Division of India. B. B. Misra. 456p. 1991. 32.00 (0-19-562615-X) OUP.

Unification & Supersymmetry. R. N. Mohapatra. (Contemporary Physics Ser.). (Illus.). xiv, 328p. 1986. 44.00 (0-387-96285-9) Spr-Verlag.

Unification & Supersymmetry: The Frontiers of Quark-Lepton Physics. 2nd ed. R. N. Mohapatra. (Graduate Texts in Contemporary Physics Ser.). (Illus.). 424p. 1996. 49.95 (0-387-97646-9) Spr-Verlag.

Unification & the Fundamentals of Quantum Physics: The First of the 1988 Dirac Memorial Lectures. Abdus Salam. (Illus.). 100p. (C). 1990. text ed. 19.95 (0-521-37140-6) Cambridge U Pr.

Unification Church. J. Isamu Yamamoto. (Guide to Cults & Religious Movements Ser.). 64p. 1995. pap. 5.99 (0-310-70381-6) Zondervan.

Unification Church, Vol. II. Ed. by J. Gordon Melton. (Cults & New Religions Ser.: Vol. 16). 600p. 1990. reprint ed. text ed. 40.00 (0-8240-4490-8) Garland.

Unification Church Policy on South Africa. Dibinga wa Said. (Christian Churches Policies on South Africa Ser.). 14p. (Orig.). 1986. pap. write for info. (0-943324-26-2) Omenana.

Unification Church, Vol. III: Outreach. James R. Lewis. (Cults & New Religions Ser.). 616p. 1990. reprint ed. text ed. 50.00 (0-8240-4491-6) Garland.

Unification of a Slave State: The Rise of the Planter Class in the South Carolina Backcountry, 1760-1808. Rachel N. Klein. LC 89-16684. (Institute of Early American History & Culture Ser.). (Illus.). xii, 332p. (C). 1990. 45.00 (0-8078-1899-2) U of NC Pr.

Unification of a Slave State: The Rise of the Planter Class in the South Carolina Backcountry, 1760-1808. Rachel N. Klein. LC 89-1668. 1992. pap. 14.95 (0-8078-4369-5) U of NC Pr.

Unification of China & the Problem of Public Opinion in the Republic of China in Taiwan. Thomas A. Metzger. LC 92-10214. (Essays in Public Policy Ser.: No. 32). 1992. pap. text ed. 5.00 (0-8179-5372-8) Hoover Inst Pr.

Unification of Divorce Laws in India. Shiv S. Singh. (C). 1993. 40.00 (81-7100-592-6, Pub. by Deep II) S Asia.

Unification of Elementary Forces & Gauge Theories: Proceedings of the Ben Lee Memorial International, Weak Neutral Currents & Gauge Theories, Held at the Fermi National Accelerator Laboratory, Oct 20-22, 1977. Ed. by D. B. Cline & F. E. Mills. xx, 770p. 1980. text ed. 253.00 (0-906346-00-2) Gordon & Breach.

Unification of German Education. Val D. Rust & Diane Rust. LC 94-26651. (Reference Books in International Education: Vol. 32). 384p. 1995. text ed. 57.00 (0-8153-1705-0, SS960) Garland.

Unification of Germany: The Anatomy of a Peaceful Revolution. Peter Neckermann. 160p. 1992. text ed. 32.50 (0-88033-230-1) Col U Pr.

Unification of Germany, 1815-1871. Michael J. Gorman. (Cambridge Topics in History Ser.). (Illus.). 112p. (C). 1989. pap. text ed. 15.95 (0-521-31730-4) Cambridge U Pr.

Unification of Germany, 1848-1871. Ed. by Otto Pflanze. LC 78-23470. (European Problem Studies). 128p. 1979. reprint ed. pap. 10.50 (0-88275-803-9) Krieger.

Unification of Italy, Eighteen Fifty-Nine to Eighteen Sixty-One. Ed. by Charles F. Delzell. LC 76-15352. (European Problem Studies). 126p. 1976. reprint ed. pap. text ed. 8.50 (0-88275-658-3) Krieger.

***Unification of Law in International Protection of Industrial Property.** Endre Lontai. LC 89-26461. 1990. write for info. (0-7923-0545-0) Kluwer Ac.

Unification of Law in the Field of International Industrial Property. E. Lontai. 230p. 1994. 35.00 (963-05-6741-5, Pub. by A K HU) Intl Spec Bk.

Unification of Spacetime, the Forces, Matter & Energy. Randell L. Mills & William R. Good. (Illus.). 224p. 1992. 25.00 (0-9635171-0-4) BlckLight Power.

Unification Process in Germany: From Dictatorship to Democracy. Gert-Joachim Glaessner. Tr. by Colin B. Grant from GER. LC 92-16646. 1992. text ed. 45.00 (0-312-08570-2) St Martin.

Unification Theology & Christian Thought. Young O. Kim. pap. 4.00 (0-686-13407-9) Unification Church.

Unification Thought. 1975. pap. 5.00 (0-686-13405-2); Study Guide. student ed., pap. text ed. 1.50 (0-686-13406-0) Unification Church.

***Unification Through Division: Histories of the Division of American Psychological Association, Vol. 2.** Donald A. Dewsbury. 1997. pap. text ed. 24.95 (1-55798-430-1) Am Psychol.

***Unification Through Division Vol. 1: Histories of the Divisions of the American Psychological Association.** Donald A. Dewsbury. LC 96-41480. 317p. 1996. 24.95 (1-55798-379-8) Am Psychol.

Unificationism: A New Philosophy & Worldview. Sebastian A. Matczak. LC 81-86036. (Philosophical Questions Ser.: No. 11). 500p. 1982. 55.00 (0-912116-14-5) Learned Pubns.

UNIFIED--A Course on Truth & Practical Guidance from Babaji. Roger G. Lanphear. LC 86-72570. 160p. (Orig.). 1987. pap. 8.95 (0-87516-585-0) DeVorss.

***Unified Algebraic Approach to Control Design.** Robert E. Skelton. 256p. 1997. 59.95 (0-7484-0592-5, Pub. by Tay Francis Ltd UK) Taylor & Francis.

Unified Analysis & Solutions of Heat & Mass Diffusion. M. D. Mikhailov & M. Necati Ozisik. LC 93-34237. (Illus.). 524p. 1994. reprint ed. pap. text ed. 15.95 (0-486-67876-8) Dover.

Unified Approach to Interior Point Algorithms for Linear Complementarity Problems. Nimrod Megiddo et al. (Lecture Notes in Computer Science Ser.: Vol. 538). ,p. 1991. 22.00 (0-387-54509-3) Spr-Verlag.

Unified Approach to the Engineering of Measurement Systems for Test & Evaluation: Basic Principles. Peter K. Stein. (LF-MSE Publications). 134p. 1992. pap. 20.00 (1-881472-00-0) Stein Eng Servs.

Unified Approach to Uniqueness, Expansion & Approximation Problems. Chin-Cheng Chang. 120p. 1994. text ed. 36.00 (981-02-1805-2) World Scientific Pub.

Unified Computation Laboratory: Modelling, Specifications, & Tools. Ed. by Charles Rattray & Robert G. Clark. (Institute of Mathematics & Its Applications Conference Series, New Ser.: New Series 34). (Illus.). 480p. 1992. 110.00 (0-19-853684-4) OUP.

***Unified Computational Approach to Optimal Control Problems.** K. L. Teo et al. LC 91-13182. (Pitman Monographs & Surveys in Pure Applied Mathematics: No. 55). (Illus.). 345p. pap. 98.40 (0-608-05243-4, 2065780) Bks Demand.

Unified Constitutive Laws of Plastic Deformation. Ed. by A. S. Krausz & K. Krausz. (Illus.). 463p. 1996. boxed 129.00 (0-12-425970-7) Acad Pr.

Unified Development Ordinance. Michael Brough. LC 85-70182. (Illus.). 240p. (Orig.). 1985. pap. 39.95 (0-918286-39-5) Planners Pr.

Unified English Composition. 4th ed. Gerald D. Sanders et al. LC 66-13967. 1966. text ed. 9.95 (0-89197-458-X); student ed. 5.95 (0-89197-459-8) Irvington.

Unified Equilibrium Calculations. William B. Guenther. LC 91-9414. 336p. 1991. text ed. 105.00 (0-471-53854-X) Wiley.

Unified Field. Mark Leon. 288p. (Orig.). 1996. mass mkt. 5.99 (0-380-78651-6, AvoNova) Avon.

Unified Field. Joseph A. Uphoff, Jr. LC 88-2440. 32p. 1988. pap. text ed. 2.00 (0-943123-06-2) Arjuna Lib Pr.

Unified Field Theories: In the First Third of the Twentieth Century. Vladimir P. Vizgin. Tr. by Julian B. Barbour from RUS. LC 93-48725. (Science Networks Series: Historical Studies: Vol. 13). 360p. 1994. 159.00 (0-8176-2679-4) Birkhauser.

Unified Field Theories of More Than Four Dimensions Including Exact Solutions: Proceedings of the 8th Course of the International School Cosmology & Gravitation Erice, Trapani, Siciliy, May 20-June 1, 1982. Ed. by Venzo De Sabbata & E. Schmutzer. 458p. 1983. 86.00 (9971-950-50-2) World Scientific Pub.

Unified Field Theory. (Wilhelm Reich - Nikola Tesla Alternate Energy Ser.). 1991. lib. bdg. 250.00 (0-8490-4265-8) Gordon Pr.

Unified Field Theory. J. G. Gallimore. 123p. 1974. reprint ed. spiral bd. 21.00 (0-7873-0340-2) Hlth Research.

Unified Gas Supply System of the U. S. S. R., Vol. 2. Ed. by L. A. Melentiev. (Soviet Technology Reviews Ser.: Vol. 2). 316p. 1985. text ed. 415.00 (3-7186-0152-4) Gordon & Breach.

Unified Grand Tour of Theoretical Physics. I. D. Lawrie. LC 89-24740. (Illus.). 392p. 1990. 180.00 (0-85274-014-X) IOP Pub.

Unified Grand Tour of Theoretical Physics. I. D. Lawrie. LC 89-24740. (Illus.). 392p. 1990. pap. 55.00 (0-85274-015-8) IOP Pub.

Unified in Hope: Arabs & Jews Talk about Peace. Carol J. Birkland. 160p. 1987. reprint ed. pap. 8.95 (0-377-00177-5) Friendship Pr.

Unified Introduction to Linear Algebra: Models, Methods & Theory. Alan Tucker. (C). 1987. pap. write for info. (0-02-421580-5, Macmillan Coll) P-H.

Unified List of United States Companies Doing Business in South Africa. 3rd ed. Ed. by Richard Knight. 90p. 1990. 30.00 (0-685-39025-X) Africa Fund.

Unified Mathematics, Book 1. Rising. 1984. text ed. 47.88 (0-395-36085-4) HM.

Unified Mathematics. Rising. 1990. student ed., pap. 7.48 (0-395-55066-1) HM.

Unified Mathematics, Vol. 3. Rising. 1990. teacher ed., pap. 16.76 (0-395-55070-X) HM.

Unified Mathematics, Vol. 2. Rising. 1990. teacher ed., pap. 16.76 (0-395-55068-8) HM.

Unified Mathematics. Rising. 1990. teacher ed., pap. 16.76 (0-395-55064-5) HM.

Unified Mathematics, Book 2. Rising. 1985. text ed. 48.20 (0-395-36086-2) HM.

***Unified Medical Dictionary: English, Arabic, French.** 1983. text ed. write for info. (88-7674-000-7) World Health.

Unified Methods for VLSI Simulation & Test Generation. Kwang-Ting Cheng & Vishwani D. Agrawal. (C). 1989. lib. bdg. 60.00 (0-7923-9025-3) Kluwer Ac.

Unified Model of the Universe: The Geometrically Unified Field Solution. Sean Sheeter. LC 80-27648. (Unified Theory of Process Ser.: Vol. 1, No. 1). (Illus.). 170p. 1981. pap. 9.50 (0-9605378-1-3) Process Pr.

***Unified Modeling Language Users Guide.** Grady Booch. (C). 1998. pap. text ed. write for info. (0-201-57168-4) Addison-Wesley.

Unified Numbering System for Metals & Alloys: And Cross Index of Chemically-Similar Specification - A Joint Activity of the Society of Automotive Engineers, American Society for Testing & Materials. American Society for Testing & Materials Staff. LC 77-89064. (American Society for Testing & Materials Special Technical Publication Ser.: No. DS-56A). 288p. reprint ed. pap. 82.10 (0-317-29433-4, 2024296) Bks Demand.

Unified Numbering System for Metals & Alloys: Metals & Alloys Currently Covered by UNS Numbers, July, 1974. American Society for Testing & Materials Staff. LC 75-309848. 186p. reprint ed. pap. 53.10 (0-317-11264-3, 2021525) Bks Demand.

***Unified Objects: Object-Oriented Programming Using C++** Babak Sadr. LC 96-45236. 464p. 1997. 40.00 (0-8186-7733-3) IEEE Comp Soc.

Unified Planning & Budgeting in a Free Society. Herman I. Shaller. LC 76-49389. 1977. 15.00 (0-9601104-1-0) Oakview.

***Unified Process: A Software Engineering Process Using the Unified Modelling Language.** Ivar Jacobson. (C). 1998. text ed. write for info. (0-201-57169-2) Addison-Wesley.

Unified Reading. Fred Justus. (Early Education Ser.). 24p. (gr. 2). 1981. student ed. 5.00 (0-8209-0212-8, K-14) ESP.

Unified Ring: Narrative Art & the Science-Fiction Novel. Frank Sadler. LC 84-16232. (Studies in Speculative Fiction: No. 11). 133p. reprint ed. pap. 38.00 (0-8357-1598-1, 2070522) Bks Demand.

Unified River Basin Management: Proceedings of a Symposium Held in Gatlinburg, Tennessee, May 4-7, 1980. Ed. by Ronald M. North et al. LC 81-69176. (American Water Resources Association Technical Publication Ser.: No. TPS-81-3). (Illus.). 666p. reprint ed. pap. 180.00 (0-8357-3163-4, 2039426) Bks Demand.

Unified River Basin Management, Stage 2: Proceedings of a Symposium Held in Atlanta, Georgia, October 4-8, 1981. Ed. by David J. Allee et al. LC 82-72088. (Illus.). 510p. reprint ed. pap. 145.40 (0-8357-3162-6, 2039425) Bks Demand.

Unified Rules: Inland, Western & Great Lakes, Complies with the Requirements That All Vessels Over. Greg Szczurek. 1994. pap. 19.95 (0-932889-33-6) Examco Inc.

Unified Science. Ed. by Brian F. McGuinness. 328p. (C). 1987. lib. bdg. 194.00 (90-277-2484-9, D Reidel) Kluwer Ac.

Unified Separation Science. J. Calvin Giddings. LC 90-38149. 320p. 1991. text ed. 69.95 (0-471-52089-6) Wiley.

Unified String Theories: Proceedings of the Workshop on Unified String Theories, Santa Barbara, July 29-August 16,1985. Ed. by M. B. Green. 760p. 1986. pap. 60.00 (9971-5-0032-9); text ed. 159.00 (9971-5-0031-0) World Scientific Pub.

Unified Symmetry: In the Small & in the Large. Ed. by Behram N. Kursunoglu & A. Perlmutter. (Illus.). 414p. (C). 1994. lib. bdg. 115.00 (1-56072-156-1) Nova Sci Pubs.

Unified Symmetry: In the Small & in the Large. Ed. by Behram N. Kursunoglu et al. LC 95-6218. (Illus.). 264p. (C). 1995. 85.00 (0-306-44914-5, Plenum Pr) Plenum.

Unified Symmetry, in the Small & in the Large Vol. 2: Proceedings of the 23rd Coral Gables Conference Held in Coral Gables, Florida, February 2-5, 1995, Vol. 2. Ed. by Behram N. Kursunoglu et al. (Illus.). 260p. (C). 1995. 85.00 (0-306-45189-1, Plenum Pr) Plenum.

Unified Technical Concepts in Physics. 3rd ed. Center for Occupational Research & Development Staff. (Illus.). 520p. 1990. Incl. suppl. suppl. ed., text ed. 30.00 (1-55502-353-3) CORD Commns.

Unified Technical Concepts in Physics - Instructor's Guide with Solutions. Center for Occupational Research & Development Staff. (Unified Technical Concepts Ser.). 171p. 1991. pap. text ed. 20.00 (1-55502-415-7) CORD Commns.

Unified Technical Concepts in Physics--Laboratory Exercises Manual. 3rd ed. Center for Occupational Research & Development Staff. (Unified Technical Concepts Ser.). (Illus.). 1990. pap. text ed. 35.00 (1-55502-393-2) CORD Commns.

Unified Theories of Cognition. Allen Newell. (Illus.). 549p. 1990. 47.00 (0-674-92099-6) HUP.

Unified Theories of Cognition. Allen Newell. 549p. 1994. pap. 21.00 (0-674-92101-1) HUP.

Unified Theory & Strategies of Survey Sampling. A. B. Chaudhuri & J. W. Vos. (North-Holland Series in Statistics & Probability: No. 4). 414p. 1988. 152.50 (0-444-70357-8, North Holland) Elsevier.

Unified Theory for Reinforced Concrete. Thomas T. Hsu. (New Directions in Civil Engineering Ser.). 336p. 1992. 77.00 (0-8493-8613-6, TA863) CRC Pr.

Unified Theory of Ether, Field & Matter. 3rd ed. R. B. Driscoll. 310p. 1966. pap. 20.00 (0-9601374-1-6) R B Driscoll.

Unified Theory of Global Development. Van B. Weigel. LC 88-25211. (Illus.). 292p. 1989. text ed. 59.95 (0-275-93134-X, C3134, Praeger Pubs) Greenwood.

Unified Theory of Nonlinear Operator & Evolution Equations with Applications: A New Approach to Nonlinear Partial Differential Equations. Altman. (Pure & Applied Mathematics Ser.: Vol. 103). 312p. 1986. 145.00 (0-8247-7613-5) Dekker.

Unified Theory of Refining. Alan J. Pearson. (Pulp & Paper Technology Ser.: No. 6). 128p. 1990. 15.00 (0-919893-79-1, 0101JT06) TAPPI.

Unified Theory of Refining. Alan J. Pearson. (Pulp & Paper Technology Ser.: No. 6). (Illus.). reprint ed. pap. 35.40 (0-8357-4081-1, 2036771) Bks Demand.

Unified Theory of Syntactic Categories. Joseph E. Emonds. (Studies in Generative Grammar: No. 19). 360p. 1985. pap. 83.10 (90-6765-092-7) Mouton.

Unified Theory of the Mechanical Behavior of Matter. M. J. Marcinkowski. LC 78-27799. 275p. reprint ed. pap. 78.40 (0-317-28028-7, 2055722) Bks Demand.

Unified Valence Bond Theory of Electronic Structure. N. B. Epictis et al. (Lecture Notes in Chemistry Ser.: Vol. 29). 303p. 1982. 42.95 (0-387-11491-2) Spr-Verlag.

Unified View of the Macro- & Micro-Cosmos. Ed. by A. de Rujula. 680p. (C). 1987. pap. 64.00 (9971-5-0394-8); text ed. 153.00 (9971-5-0393-X) World Scientific Pub.

Uniform Algebras. 2nd ed. Theodore W. Gamelin. LC 83-72339. 270p. text ed. 19.95 (0-8284-0311-2) Chelsea Pub.

Uniform Algebras & Jensen Measures. Theodore W. Gamelin. LC 78-16213. (London Mathematical Society Lecture Note Ser.: 32). 170p. reprint ed. pap. 48.50 (0-317-20600-1, 2024488) Bks Demand.

Uniform Anatomical Gift Act: A State-by-State Guide. Roger A. Kessinger. 170p. (Orig.). 1990. pap. 19.95 (0-922802-07-6) Kessinger Pub.

Uniform & Reciprocal Motor Carrier Programs under ISTEA. (State Legislative Reports: Vol. 19, No. 16). 7p. 1994. 5.00 (1-55516-384-X, 7302-1916) Natl Conf State Legis.

Uniform Approach to Rate & Ratio Problems. James R. Rogers. (Hi Map Ser.: No. 15). (Illus.). 60p. pap. text ed. 11.99 (0-614-05311-0, HM 5615) COMAP Inc.

Uniform Building Code, Vol. 2. 1339p. 1994. pap. text ed. 77.65 (1-884590-35-7, 10/594) Intl Conf Bldg Off.

Uniform Building Code Application Interpretation Manual: 1991 Edition. 1991. 30.10 (1-884590-18-7, 123L91) Intl Conf Bldg Off.

Uniform Building Code Application/Interpretation Manual, 1994. 149p. 1994. ring bd. 30.10 (1-884590-62-4) Intl Conf Bldg Off.

Uniform Building Code Standards. 1994. 68.75 (1-884590-19-5, 102S94) Intl Conf Bldg Off.

Uniform Building Code, 1994, Vol 1. 574p. 1994. pap. text ed. 58.75 (1-884590-36-5); ring bd. 67.55 (1-884590-42-X) Intl Conf Bldg Off.

Uniform Building Code, 1994, Vol. 2. 1339p. 1994. ring bd. 89.25 (1-884590-43-8) Intl Conf Bldg Off.

Uniform Building Code, 1994, Vol. 3. 836p. 1994. pap. text ed. 68.75 (1-884590-38-1); ring bd. 79.00 (1-884590-44-6) Intl Conf Bldg Off.

Uniform Building Security Code. LC 81-86613. (Illus.). 1994. 12.65 (1-884590-20-9, 117S94) Intl Conf Bldg Off.

Uniform Building Security Code, 1994. 22p. 1994. pap. text ed. 12.65 (1-884590-52-7) Intl Conf Bldg Off.

Uniform Business Rate: A Practical Guide. William McClusky & Peter Moss. 180p. 1992. 66.00 (1-85190-149-3, Pub. by Tolley Pubng UK) St Mut.

Uniform Child Custody Jurisdiction Act: A State-by-State Guide. Roger A. Kessinger. 266p. (Orig.). 1990. pap. 45.00 (0-922802-05-X) Kessinger Pub.

An Asterisk (*) at the beginning of an entry indicates that the title is appearing in BIP for the first time.

Uniform Civil Jury Instruction: 1991 Supplement. rev. ed. 1990. ring bd. 105.00 (0-685-59614-1) Oregon St Bar.

Uniform Code for Building Conservation 1994. 34.65 (1-884590-21-7, 231S94) Intl Conf Bldg Off.

Uniform Code for Building Conservation, 1994. 304p. 1994. pap. text ed. 34.65 (1-884590-53-5) Intl Conf Bldg Off.

Uniform Code for the Abatement of Dangerous Buildings. 1994. 12.65 (1-884590-22-5, 105S94) Intl Conf Bldg Off.

Uniform Code for the Abatement of Dangerous Buildings, 1994. 18p. 1994. pap. text ed. 12.65 (1-884590-54-3) Intl Conf Bldg Off.

***Uniform Color Scales.** 1996. ring bd. 450.00 (1-55752-268-5) Optical Soc.

Uniform Commercial Code, 11 vols. Ronald A. Anderson. 1992. boxed 1,000.00 (0-685-63104-4) Clark Boardman Callaghan.

Uniform Commercial Code. Dolan. 1991. 25.95 (0-316-18905-7) Little.

Uniform Commercial Code. Robert S. Summers & James J. White. (Hornbook Ser.). 930p. 1993. Student Edition. student ed., text ed. 41.00 (0-314-38503-7) West Pub.

Uniform Commercial Code. 4th ed. James White & Robert S. Summers. (Hornbook Ser.). 1043p. 1995. text ed. 41.00 (0-314-06903-8) West Pub.

Uniform Commercial Code, 4 vols., Vol. 1. 4th ed. James J. White & Robert S. Summers. (Practitioner Treatise Ser.). 2251p. 1995. text ed. write for info. (0-314-06355-2) West Pub.

Uniform Commercial Code, 4 vols., Vol. 2. 4th ed. James J. White & Robert S. Summers. (Practitioner Treatise Ser.). 2251p. 1995. text ed. write for info. (0-314-06356-0) West Pub.

Uniform Commercial Code, 4 vols., Vol. 3. 4th ed. James J. White & Robert S. Summers. (Practitioner Treatise Ser.). 2251p. 1995. text ed. write for info. (0-314-06357-9) West Pub.

Uniform Commercial Code, 4 vols., Vol. 4. 4th ed. James J. White & Robert S. Summers. 2251p. 1995. text ed. write for info. (0-314-06932-1) West Pub.

Uniform Commercial Code: An Operational Translation. Robert LeVine. LC 80-68569. 1980. pap. 16.50 (0-933718-00-4) Browning Pubns.

Uniform Commercial Code: Annual Edition. Gould Editorial Staff. 950p. ring bd., pap. 18.95 (0-87526-251-1) Gould.

Uniform Commercial Code: Official Text with Comments. 994p. 1978. write for info. (0-318-57521-3) West Pub.

Uniform Commercial Code: State Variations Service, 3 vols. Ed. by Pike & Fischer, Inc. Staff. LC 82-9735. 1992. 425.00 (0-317-12222-3) Clark Boardman Callaghan.

Uniform Commercial Code, Article 9: Appendices to Article 9 Study Group Report. 1992. pap. 30.00 (0-614-00945-6, 5424) Am Law Inst.

Uniform Commercial Code, Article 9: Study Group Report. xii, 249p. 1992. pap. 20.00 (0-614-00944-8, 5423) Am Law Inst.

Uniform Commercial Code, Article 9 Reprint, 1962 Official Text with Comments: Secured Transactions; Sale of Accounts Contract Rights & Chattel Paper. 1976. pap. 1.95 (0-685-71471-3) West Pub.

Uniform Commercial Code Case Citations, 4 vols. Shepard's Citation, Inc. Staff. 1988. Set. 520.00 (0-685-23120-8) Shepards.

Uniform Commercial Code Case Digest & Code Service, 33 vols. Ed. by Pike & Fischer, Inc. Staff. LC 70-126080. 1992. 1,850.00 (0-317-11804-8) Clark Boardman Callaghan.

Uniform Commercial Code Citations, 2 vols. Shepard's Citation, Inc. Staff. 1991. 74.00 (0-685-67701-X) Shepards.

Uniform Commercial Code Confidential Drafts: Issued by the American Law Institute & the National Conference of Commissioners on Uniform State Laws Through the 1977 Revisions of Article 8, 10 vols., Set. Compiled by Elizabeth S. Kelly & Ann Puckett. LC 93-41511. 1995. 795.00 (0-8377-1241-6) Rothman.

Uniform Commercial Code Drafts: Issued by the American Law Institute & the National Conference of Commissioners on Uniform State Laws Through the 1962 Official Text with Comments, 23 vols. Elizabeth S. Kelly. 1984. Set. text ed. 1,150.00 (0-8377-1235-1) Rothman.

Uniform Commercial Code Filing Guide, 5 vols., Set. LC 91-52948. 1992. write for info. (1-881627-00-4) UCC Guide.

Uniform Commercial Code Filing Guide, Vol. 1. LC 91-52948. 1992. write for info. (1-881627-01-2) UCC Guide.

Uniform Commercial Code Filing Guide, Vol. 2. LC 91-52948. 1992. write for info. (1-881627-02-0) UCC Guide.

Uniform Commercial Code Filing Guide, Vol. 3. LC 91-52948. 1992. write for info. (1-881627-03-9) UCC Guide.

Uniform Commercial Code Filing Guide, Vol. 4. LC 91-52948. 1992. write for info. (1-881627-04-7) UCC Guide.

Uniform Commercial Code Filing Guide, Vol. 5. LC 91-52948. 1992. write for info. (1-881627-05-5) UCC Guide.

Uniform Commercial Code in a Nutshell. 3rd ed. Bradford Stone. (Nutshell Ser.). 580p. 1993. reprint ed. pap. text ed. 18.00 (0-314-56271-0) West Pub.

Uniform Commercial Code in a Nutshell. 4th ed. Bradford Stone. LC 95-3049. (Nutshell Ser.). 579p. (C). 1995. pap. text ed. 19.00 (0-314-05351-4) West Pub.

Uniform Commercial Code Law Journal. Ed. by Louis F. Del Duca. 145.00 (0-685-69641-3, UCLJ) Warren Gorham & Lamont.

Uniform Commercial Code Law Journal: 1968-1996/97, 29 vols. Bound set. 2,320.00 (0-8377-9167-7) Rothman.

Uniform Commercial Code Law Letter. Thomas M. Quinn. 180.00 (0-685-69642-1, UCLL) Warren Gorham & Lamont.

Uniform Commercial Code Legal Forms, 2 vols. 3rd ed. Deborah L. Nelson & Jennifer L. Howicz. LC 94-37285. 1994. 200.00 (0-615-00337-0) Clark Boardman Callaghan.

Uniform Commercial Code of Kentucky. 2nd ed. David J. Liebson & Richard H. Nowka. 1151p. 1992. 95.00 (0-87473-852-0) MICHIE.

Uniform Commercial Code of the State of California: Annotated. Bancroft-Whitney Staff. 7p. write for info. (0-318-62081-2) Bancroft Whitney Co.

Uniform Commercial Code Reporting Service: 1965-1992, 63 vols. Ed. by Pike & Fischer, Inc. Staff. Set. 2,650.00 (0-318-42414-2) Clark Boardman Callaghan.

Uniform Commercial Code Series, 12 vols. William D. Hawkland et al. LC 82-9735. 1992. 1,000.00 (0-317-12224-X) Clark Boardman Callaghan.

Uniform Commercial Code Simplified. Jesse S. Raphael. LC 67-15469. 416p. reprint ed. pap. 118.60 (0-317-09564-1, 2012370) Bks Demand.

Uniform Commercial Code Transaction Guide: Analysis & Forms, 4 vols. Peter Alces et al. 1992. 420.00 (0-685-28166-3) Clark Boardman Callaghan.

Uniform Commercial Code, Vol. 1 & 2: 1994 Pocket Parts, 2 vols. James J. White & Robert S. Summers. 1994. write for info. (0-318-72774-9) West Pub.

Uniform Commercial Law in the 21st Century: Proceedings of Conference. 1994. write for info. (92-1-133472-1, E. 94.V.12) UN.

Uniform CPA Examination: May 1985-May 1989: Selected Questions & Unofficial Answers. Indexed to Content Specification Outlines: Accounting Practice, Accounting Theory, Auditing, Business Law. American Institute of Certified Public Accountants Staff. Ed. by Examinations Division Staff. 645p. pap. 180.00 (0-7837-0275-2, 2040586) Bks Demand.

Uniform CPA Examination, May 1982 to November 1983: Questions. American Institute of Certified Public Accountants Staff. 256p. reprint ed. pap. 73.00 (0-8357-6422-2, 2035790) Bks Demand.

Uniform CPA Examination, May 1984-May 1988: Selected Questions & Unofficial Answers: Indexed to Content Specification Outlines. Ed. by American Institute of Certified Public Accountants Staff. 642p. reprint ed. pap. 180.00 (0-8357-3041-7, 2039296) Bks Demand.

***Uniform Crime Reports, 2 vols.** 1997. lib. bdg. 600.95 (0-8490-8220-X) Gordon Pr.

Uniform Crime Reports: Crime in the United States. 1996. lib. bdg. 259.95 (0-8490-6906-8) Gordon Pr.

***Uniform Crime Reports for the United States, 1993.** Justice Dept., F. B. I. Staff. (Illus.). 405p. 1994. per., pap. 24.00 (0-16-045321-6, 027-001-00066-1) USGPO.

***Uniform Crime Reports for the United States, 1994.** Justice Dept., F. B. I. Staff. (Illus.). 407p. 1995. per., pap. 25.00 (0-16-048362-X, 027-001-00069-6) USGPO.

***Uniform Crime Reports for the United States, 1995.** Justice Dept., F. B. I. Staff. (Illus.). 399p. 1996. per., pap. 32.00 (0-16-048756-0) USGPO.

Uniform Crime Reports of U. S. 1996. pap. 32.00 (0-87511-853-4) Claitors.

Uniform Criminal Jury Instruction: 1991 Supplement. rev. ed. 1990. ring bd. 105.00 (0-685-59615-X) Oregon St Bar.

Uniform Deterrence of Nuclear First Use. Robert A. Levine. LC 93-25248. 1993. pap. 15.00 (0-8330-1401-3, MR-231) Rand Corp.

Uniform Distribution of Sequences. Lauwerens Kuipers & H. Niederreiter. LC 73-20497. (Pure & Applied Mathematics (Wiley) Ser.). 404p. reprint ed. pap. 115.20 (0-317-08710-X, 2055524) Bks Demand.

Uniform Distribution of Sequences of Integers in Residue Classes. Wladyslaw Narkiewicz. (Lecture Notes in Mathematics Ser.: Vol. 1087). vii, 125p. 1984. 29.95 (0-387-13872-2) Spr-Verlag.

Uniform Drug Code. 2nd rev. ed. Peter D. Hays. 10p. (Orig.). 1994. pap. 3.00 (1-885554-02-8) P D Hays.

Uniform Evidence Law. Stephen Odgers. 353p. 1995. 74.00 (1-86287-187-6, Pub. by Federation Pr AU) Gaunt.

***Uniform Evidence Law.** 2nd ed. Stephen Odgers. 372p. 1996. 79.00 (1-86287-237-6, Pub. by Federation Pr AU) Gaunt.

Uniform Federal Accessibility Standards. (Illus.). 89p. (Orig.). (C). 1994. pap. text ed. 25.00 (0-7881-0483-7) DIANE Pub.

Uniform Fire Code. 1991. pap. 55.65 (1-884590-33-0, 108S94); ring bd. 63.70 (1-884590-32-2, 108L94) Intl Conf Bldg Off.

Uniform Fire Code Standards: 1991 Edition. 1991. 89.45 (1-884590-24-1, 119S94) Intl Conf Bldg Off.

Uniform Fire Code, 1994. (Uniform Fire Code Ser.). 1016p. 1994. ring bd. 97.50 (1-884590-49-7) Intl Conf Bldg Off.

Uniform Fire Code, 1994, Vol. 1. 550p. 1994. ring bd. 63.70 (1-884590-47-0) Intl Conf Bldg Off.

Uniform Fire Code, 1994, Vol. 1. 550p. 1995. pap. text ed. 55.65 (1-884590-46-2) Intl Conf Bldg Off.

Uniform Fire Code, 1994, Vol. 2. 1016p. 1994. pap. text ed. 89.45 (1-884590-48-9) Intl Conf Bldg Off.

Uniform Frechet Algebras. H. Goldmann. (North-Holland Mathematics Studies: No. 162). 356p. 1990. 149.50 (0-444-88488-2, North Holland) Elsevier.

Uniform Housing Code 1994. 1994. 12.65 (1-884590-25-X, 104S94) Intl Conf Bldg Off.

Uniform Housing Code, 1994. 28p. 1994. pap. text ed. 12.65 (1-884590-55-1) Intl Conf Bldg Off.

Uniform Investment Adviser Home Study Course. 260p. 1993. pap. 75.00 (0-915513-50-1) Ctr Futures Ed.

Uniform Land Transactions Act, Uniform Simplification of Land Transfers Act, Uniform Condominium Act: 1877 Official Text with Comments. 462p. 1978. pap. write for info. (0-318-57527-2) West Pub.

Uniform Law for International Sales. rev. ed. John Honnold. 450p. 1991. pap. 97.00 (90-6544-555-2) Kluwer Law Tax Pubs.

Uniform Law for International Sales. 2nd rev. ed. John Honnold. 450p. 1991. 121.00 (90-6544-473-4) Kluwer Law Tax Pubs.

Uniform Laws Annotated: Uniform Commercial Code. write for info. (0-318-57513-2) West Pub.

Uniform Limit Theorems for Sums of Independent Random Variables. T. Arak & A. Zaitsev. LC 88-10443. (Proceedings of the Steklov Institute of Mathematics Ser.: Vol. 174). 222p. 1988. reprint ed. pap. text ed. 124.00 (0-8218-3118-6, STEKLO/174) Am Math.

Uniform Marking of Fire Hydrants. (Twenty Ser.). 1988. pap. 16.75 (0-685-58114-4, 291-88) Natl Fire Prot.

Uniform Mechanical Code: 1991 Edition. 1994. pap. 44.65 (1-884590-27-6, 103S94); ring bd. 51.45 (1-884590-26-8, 103L94) Intl Conf Bldg Off.

Uniform Mechanical Code Applications Manual, 1994. 71p. 1994. ring bd. 29.65 (1-884590-64-0) Intl Conf Bldg Off.

Uniform Mechanical Code, 1994. 336p. 1994. ring bd. 51.45 (0-614-09341-4) Intl Conf Bldg Off.

Uniform Mechanical Code, 1994. 336p. 1994. pap. text ed. 44.65 (1-884590-40-3) Intl Conf Bldg Off.

Uniform Pharmaceutical Pricing: An Economic Analysis. Ernst R. Berndt. 40p. 1994. pap. 9.95 (0-8447-7028-0) Am Enterprise.

Uniform Plumbing Code: 1991 Edition. 1991. pap. 49.90 (1-884590-29-2, 113S94); ring bd. 59.25 (1-884590-28-4, 113L94) Intl Conf Bldg Off.

Uniform Probate Code in a Nutshell. 3rd ed. Lawrence H. Averill, Jr. LC 93-31236. (Nutshell Ser.). 576p. 1993. pap. text ed. 19.00 (0-314-02476-X) West Pub.

Uniform Probate Code in a Nutshell. 4th ed. Lawrence H. Averill. LC 93-31236. (Nutshell Ser.). 566p. 1996. pap. 19.50 (0-314-07083-4) West Pub.

Uniform Probate Code, Official 1993 Text with Comments. 979p. 1993. pap. 22.00 (0-314-04481-7) West Pub.

Uniform Random Numbers: Theory & Practice. Shu Tezuka. LC 95-10562. (International Series in Engineering & Computer Science). 224p. (C). 1995. lib. bdg. 105.00 (0-7923-9572-7) Kluwer Ac.

Uniform Reciprocal Enforcement of Support Act: A State-by-State Guide. Roger A. Kessinger. 290p. (Orig.). 1990. pap. 45.00 (0-922802-06-8) Kessinger Pub.

Uniform Rules for Collections. Bernard Wheble & Hon Fib. 1985. 70.00 (0-85297-088-9, Pub. by Inst Bankers UK) St Mut.

Uniform Rules for Collections: Whebles Guide Notes. W. Wheble. (C). 1989. 60.00 (0-85297-257-1, Pub. by Inst Bankers UK) St Mut.

Uniform Rules of Criminal Procedure for All Courts. Russell Chapin & Graham Hueber. LC 83-72139. (AEI Studies: No. 388). 79p. reprint ed. pap. 25.00 (0-8357-4538-4, 2037427) Bks Demand.

Uniform Securities Agent Examination Home Study Course. 120p. 1996. pap. 25.00 (0-915513-62-5) Ctr Futures Ed.

Uniform Sign Code 1994. 1994. 12.65 (1-884590-30-6, 106S94) Intl Conf Bldg Off.

Uniform Sign Code, 1994. 20p. 1994. pap. text ed. 12.65 (1-884590-56-X) Intl Conf Bldg Off.

Uniform Simplification in a Full Neighborhood of a Transition Point. Yasataka Sibuya. LC 74-11246. (Memoirs Ser.: No. 1/149). 106p. 1974. pap. 17.00 (0-8218-1849-X, MEMO/1/149) Am Math.

Uniform Spaces. John R. Isbell. LC 64-16541. (Mathematical Surveys & Monographs: No. 12). 175p. 1964. 35.00 (0-8218-1512-1, SURV/12) Am Math.

Uniform Spaces & Transformation Groups. Hidegoro Nakano. LC 68-13935. 269p. reprint ed. pap. 76.70 (0-7837-3776-9, 2043595) Bks Demand.

***Uniform Standards of Professional Appraisal Practice.** 4th rev. ed. Tosh & Rayburn. 182p. 1997. pap. text ed. 21.95 (0-7931-2656-8, 1556-184A, Real Estate Ed) Dearborn Finan.

Uniform Standards of Professional Appraisal Practice: Applying the Standards. 4th ed. Dennis S. Tosh & William B. Rayburn. LC 96-977. (Illus.). (Orig.). 1996. pap. 21.95 (0-7931-2192-2, 1556-1804, Real Estate Ed) Dearborn Finan.

Uniform Stationary Phase Method. V. A. Borovikov. (IEE Electromagnetic Waves Ser.: No. 40). 240p. 1994. boxed 95.00 (0-85296-812-4) Inst Elect Eng.

Uniform System of Accounts for Restaurants. rev. ed. Laventhol & Horwath Staff. 160p. 1996. pap. 39.95 (0-317-57883-9, MG936) Natl Restaurant Assn.

***Uniform System of Accounts for the Lodging Industry.** 9th rev. ed. Ed. by Timothy J. Eaton. (Illus.). 238p. 1996. write for info. (0-86612-128-5) Educ Inst Am Hotel.

***Uniform System of Citation, 14 vols.** Harvard Law Review Editors. Date not set. reprint ed. write for info. (1-57588-376-7, 310670) W S Hein.

Uniform System of Financial Reporting for Clubs. CMAA (Club Managers Association of America) Staff. 112p. 1996. pap. text ed. 39.95 (0-7872-2147-3) Kendall-Hunt.

Uniform Vehicle Code & Model Traffic Ordinance 1992. National Committee on Uniform Traffic Laws & Ordinances Staff. (Orig.). 1992. pap. 22.00 (0-317-05952-1) Natl Comm Traffic.

Uniform Zoning Code, 1994. 42p. 1994. pap. text ed. 17.85 (1-884590-57-8) Intl Conf Bldg Off.

Uniformed Court Officer. Jack Rudman. (Career Examination Ser.: C-852). 1994. pap. 23.95 (0-8373-0852-6) Nat Learn.

Uniformed Forces Administrative Aide. (Career Examination Ser.: C-3654). pap. 23.95 (0-8373-3654-6) Nat Learn.

***Uniformed Services Almanac.** Sol Gordon. 252p. 1997. 6.25 (1-888096-54-3) Uniformed Srvs.

Uniformity & Diversity: Development of Classification Concepts in Double Entry Accounting. Hans P. Hain. Ed. by Richard P. Brief. LC 80-1498. (Dimensions of Accounting Theory & Practice Ser.). 1980. lib. bdg. 62.95 (0-405-13492-4) Ayer.

Uniformity Efforts in Oversize-Overweight Permits. (National Cooperative Highway Research Program Report Ser.: No. 143). 79p. 1988. 10.00 (0-309-04553-3) Transport Res Bd.

Uniformity of Cement Strength. Ed. by Emery Farkas & Paul Klieger. LC 87-17469. (Special Technical Publication Ser.: No. 961). (Illus.). 105p. 1987. text ed. 18.00 (0-8031-0961-X, 04-961000-07) ASTM.

Uniformity with God's Will. St. Alphonsus de Liguori. 1977. reprint ed. pap. 1.50 (0-89555-019-9) TAN Bks Pubs.

Uniforms & Equipment of the Last Campaign 1916: The Pursuit of Pancho Villa. William C. Machado. (Illus.). 112p. (Orig.). (C). 1993. pap. 20.00 (0-9636005-0-8) W C Machado.

Uniforms & Insignia of the Luftwaffe Vol. 2: 1940-1945. Brian L. Davis. (Illus.). 320p. 1995. 65.00 (1-85409-107-7, Pub. by Arms & Armour UK) Sterling.

Uniforms & Nonuniforms: Communication Through Clothing. Nathan Joseph. LC 86-7677. (Contributions in Sociology Ser.: No. 61). 257p. 1986. text ed. 59.95 (0-313-25195-9, JUN/, Greenwood Pr) Greenwood.

Uniforms & Traditions of the Luftwaffe, Vol. 1. John R. Angolia. (Illus.). 592p. 1996. 54.95 (0-912138-64-5) Bender Pub CA.

Uniforms of Napoleon's Russian Campaign. Philip J. Haythornthwaite & Michael Chappell. (Illus.). 208p. 1996. pap. 19.95 (1-85409-309-6, Pub. by Arms & Armour UK) Sterling.

***Uniforms of the Armed Forces of Eastern European Countries.** (Illus.). 148p. 1997. reprint ed. pap. text ed. 60.00 (0-7881-3807-3) DIANE Pub.

Uniforms of the Civil War in Color. Philip J. Haythornthwaite. LC 89-22035. (Illus.). 128p. (Orig.). 1990. pap. 14.95 (0-8069-5846-4) Sterling.

Uniforms of the Civil War in Color. Philip J. Haythornthwaite. LC 89-22035. (Illus.). 128p. (Orig.). (C). 1990. reprint ed. lib. bdg. 33.00 (0-8095-7580-9) Borgo Pr.

Uniforms of the Continental Army. Philip R. Katcher. LC 80-54450. (Illus.). 230p. 1981. 40.00 (0-87387-036-0) Shumway.

Uniforms of the Peninsular Wars 1807-1814. rev. ed. Philip J. Haythornthwaite & Michael Chappel. (Illus.). 192p. 1995. pap. 19.95 (1-85409-271-5) Sterling.

***Uniforms of the SS.** Taylor Mollo et al. 528p. 1997. 75.00 (1-85915-048-9, Pub. by W & G UK) Motorbooks Intl.

Uniforms of the SS Vol. 5: Sicherheitscdienst und Sicherheitspolizei 1931-1945. Andrew Mollo. (Illus.). 64p. 1992. 29.95 (1-872004-62-8, Pub. by Windrow & Green UK) Motorbooks Intl.

***Uniforms of the Third Reich: A Study in Photographs.** Arthur Hayes & Jon Maguire. 200p. 1997. 69.95 (0-7643-0358-9) Schiffer.

***Uniforms of Waterloo.** Philip J. Haythornthwaite et al. (Illus.). 192p. 1997. pap. 19.95 (1-85409-394-0, Pub. by Arms & Armour UK) Sterling.

Uniforms, Organization & History of the LAH (Leibstandarte SS Adolf Hitler) Stan Cook & Roger J. Bender. (Illus.). 432p. 1994. 44.95 (0-912138-55-6) Bender Pub CA.

Uniforms, Organization & History of the Legion Condor. Roger J. Bender. (Illus.). 324p. 1992. 34.95 (0-912138-50-5) Bender Pub CA.

Uniforms, Organization & History of the NSKK-NSFK. John R. Angolia & David Littlejohn. (Illus.). 464p. 1994. 44.95 (0-912138-56-4) Bender Pub CA.

UniForum Guide to Graphical User Interfaces. Eric Nee. Ed. by Jordan Gold. (Illus.). 25p. (Orig.). pap. text ed. 9.95 (0-936593-16-4) UniForum.

UniForum Technology Guide: Electronic Mail Demystified. Smoot Carl-Mitchell & John S. Quarterman. 34p. pap. text ed. 10.00 (0-936593-15-6) UniForum.

UniForum Technology Guide: Internationalization Explored. Sandra Martin. 40p. 1992. pap. text ed. 10.00 (0-936593-18-0) UniForum.

UniForum Technology Guide: Network Applications. John S. Quarterman. 34p. pap. text ed. 10.00 (0-936593-13-X) UniForum.

UniForum Technology Guide: Network Substrata. John S. Quarterman. 30p. pap. text ed. 10.00 (0-936593-14-8) UniForum.

Unifying Behavior Therapy: Contributions of Paradigmatic Behavior. Ed. by Georg H. Eifert & Ian M. Evans. LC 90-9408. (Behavior Therapy & Behavioral Medicine Ser.). 392p. 1990. 48.95 (0-8261-4740-2) Springer Pub.

Unifying Biology: The Evolutionary Synthesis & Evolutionary Biology. Vassiliki B. Smocovitis. 248p. 1996. text ed. 29.95 (0-691-03343-9) Princeton U Pr.

Unifying Concept: Approaches to the Structure of Cervantes' Comedias. Edward H. Friedman. LC 81-50484. 186p. 1981. 18.00 (0-938972-00-6) Spanish Lit Pubns.

Unifying Concepts of Leukemia: Proceedings of the International Symposium on Comparative Leukemia Research, 5th, Padova, Venice, 1971. International Symposium on Comparative Leukemia Research Staff. Ed. by R. M. Dutcher. (Bibliotheca Haematologica Ser.: No. 39). 1973. 181.00 (3-8055-1383-6) S Karger.

U V

Unifying Factor: A Review of Kabbalah. Nekhama Schoenburg. LC 95-9630. 288p. 1996. 30.00 (1-56821-562-2) Aronson.

Unifying Framework for Structured Systems Development Models. T. H. Tse. (Tracts in Theoretical Computer Science Ser.: No. 11). (Illus.). 250p. (C). 1991. text ed. 42.95 (0-521-39196-2) Cambridge U Pr.

Unifying Individual & Family Therapies. David M. Allen. LC 87-46328. (Jossey-Bass Social & Behavioral Science Ser.). 389p. reprint ed. pap. 110.90 (0-7837-6531-2, 2045643) Bks Demand.

Unifying Moment: The Psychological Philosophy of William James & Alfred North Whitehead. Craig R. Eisendrath. LC 70-135550. 308p. 1971. 33.95 (0-674-92100-3) HUP.

Unifying Nursing Practice & Theory. Ed. by Judith Lathlean & Barbara Vaughan. LC 93-48048. (Illus.). 192p. 1994. pap. text ed. 30.00 (0-7506-1593-1) Buttrwrth-Heinemann.

Unifying Political Methodology: The Likelihood Theory of Statistical Inference. Gary King. (Illus.). 288p. (C). 1989. pap. text ed. 19.95 (0-521-36697-6) Cambridge U Pr.

Unifying Political Methodology: The Likelihood Theory of Statistical Inference. Gary King. (Illus.). 288p. (C). 1989. text ed. 69.95 (0-521-36622-4) Cambridge U Pr.

***Unifying Theory of ADHD: Inhibition, Self-Control & Time.** Russell A. Barkley. LC 97-25931. 1997. lib. bdg. 40.00 (1-57230-250-X, o250) Guilford Pr.

Unifying Your Family: Parents & Teenagers - Chinese Edition. Ed. by Jay Kesler. Tr. by May-Chun Kay. 90p. (CHI.). 1994. pap. 5.00 (1-56582-020-7) Christ Renew Min.

UNIK: United Nations Operations in Iraq & Kuwait, 1991-1992. (Illus.). 81p. (Orig.). (C). 1995. pap. text ed. 30.00 (0-7881-1756-4) DIANE Pub.

Unilateral Application of Antitrust & Trade Laws: Toward a New Economic Relationship Between the United States & Japan. Ed. by Henry B. Cortesi. LC 93-47931. 1994. 95.00 (1-883223-04-0) Pacific NY.

Unilateral Nuclear Disarmament Measures. (Disarmament Studies: No. 13). 5.00 (92-1-142078-4, E.85.IX.2) UN.

Unilateral Problems in Structural Analysis IV: Proceedings of the Fourth Meeting on Unilateral Problems in Structural Analysis, Capri, June 14-16, 1989. Ed. by G. Del Piero & Franco Maceri. (International Series of Numerical Mathematics: Vol. 101). 240p. 1991. 91.00 (0-8176-2487-2) Birkhauser.

Unilateral Problems in Structural Analysis 2. Ed. by G. Del Piero & Franco Maceri. (CISM Ser.: Vol. 304). (Illus.). vi, 314p. 1988. 68.95 (0-387-82036-1) Spr-Verlag.

Unilateral Renal Function Studies: Proceedings of the International Symposium, 1st, Monecatini Terme, May, 1977. International Symposium on Unilateral Renal Function Studies Staff et al. Ed. by S. Giovannetti et al. (Contributions to Nephrology Ser.: Vol. 11). (Illus.). 1978. 62.50 (3-8055-2858-2) S Karger.

Unilever U. S., Inc. A Report on the Company's Environmental Policies & Practices. (Illus.). 23p. (C). 1994. reprint ed. pap. text ed. 250.00 (0-7881-0930-8, Coun on Econ) DIANE Pub.

UNILEX, International Case Law & Bibliography on the U. N. Convention on Contracts for the International Sale of Goods. Michael J. Bonell. LC 95-39727. 1995. ring bd. 275.00 (1-57105-022-1) Transnatl Pubs.

Unillustrious Alliance: The African American & Jewish American Communities. William M. Phillips, Jr. LC 91-17126. (Contributions in Afro-American & African Studies: No. 146). 176p. 1991. text ed. 49.95 (0-313-27776-1, PUL, Greenwood Pr) Greenwood.

***Unimaginable Life: Lessons Learned on the Path of Love.** Kenny Loggins & Julia Loggins. 1997. 24.00 (0-614-28269-1) Avon.

***Unimaginable Life: Lessons Learned on the Way to Love.** Kenny Loggins & Julia Loggins. LC 97-3220. 1997. write for info. (0-380-97531-9) Avon.

Unimaginable Storms: A Search for Meaning in Psychosis. Murray Jackson & Paul Williams. 254p. 1994. pap. text ed. 38.50 (1-85575-075-9, Pub. by Karnac Bks UK) Brunner-Mazel.

UNIMARC - Authorities: Universal Format for Authorities Recommended by the IFLA Steering Group on a UNIMARC Format for Authorities. Ed. by Standing Committee of the IFLA Sections on Cataloguing & Information Technology Staff. 93p. 1991. lib. bdg. 45.00 (3-598-10986-5) K G Saur.

UNIMARC & CDS/ISIS. Ed. by Marie-France Plassard. (UBCIM Publications). 92p. 1994. 35.00 (3-598-11210-6) K G Saur.

UNIMARC Manual. rev. ed. Ed. by International Federation of Library Associations & Institutions. v, 498p. 1987. pap. 46.00 (3-598-10960-1) K G Saur.

UNIMARC Manual: Bibliographic Format. Ed. by Marie-France Plassard. (UBCIM Publications). 100p. 1994. 35.00 (3-598-11211-4) K G Saur.

UNIMARC/CCF: Proceedings of the Workshop Held in Florence, 5-7 June 1991. Ed. by Marie-France Plassard & Diana M. Brooking. (UBCIM Publications). 150p. 1993. 60.00 (3-598-11140-1) K G Saur.

Unimodal Log-Concave & Polya Frequency Sequences in Combinatorics. F. Brenti. LC 89-15137. (Memoirs Ser.: Vol. 81/413). 106p. 1989. pap. 19.00 (0-8218-2476-7, MEMO/81/413) Am Math.

Unimodality, Convexity & Applications. Ed. by Sudhakar Dharmadhikari & Kumar Joag-dev. (Probability & Mathematical Statistics Ser.: Vol. 27). 278p. 1988. text ed. 116.00 (0-12-214690-5) Acad Pr.

***Unimodality of Probability Measures.** Emile M. Bertin. LC 96-21369. (Mathematics & Its Applications Ser.). 268p. (C). 1996. lib. bdg. 136.00 (0-7923-4318-2) Kluwer Ac.

Unimolecular & Biomolecular Ion-Molecule Reaction Dynamics. Ed. by Cheuk-Yiu Ng et al. LC 93-46718. (Ion Chemistry & Physics Ser.). 503p. 1994. text ed. 145.00 (0-471-93831-9) Wiley.

Unimolecular Reaction Dynamics: Theory & Experiments. Tomas Baer & William Hase. (International Series of Monographs on Chemistry: Vol. 31). (Illus.). 448p. (C). 1996. 75.00 (0-19-507494-7) OUP.

Unimolecular Reactions. 2nd rev. ed. K. A. Holbrook et al. LC 95-40902. Orig. Title: Unimolecular Reactions. 417p. 1996. text ed. 165.00 (0-471-92268-4) Wiley.

Unimolecular Reactions see Unimolecular Reactions

***Unincorporated Business Entities.** Larry E. Ribstein. LC 96-21369. 518p. 1996. teacher ed., pap. 34.00 (0-87084-766-X) Anderson Pub Co.

Uninformed Choice: The Failure of the New Presidential Nominating System. Scott Keeter & Cliff Zukin. (American Political Parties & Elections Ser.). 272p. 1983. text ed. 45.00 (0-275-91022-9, C1022, Praeger Pubs) Greenwood.

Uninhabited House see Five Victorian Ghost Novels

Uninhabited Ocean Islands. Jon Fisher. LC 91-61945. (Illus.). 168p. (Orig.). 1991. pap. 16.95 (1-55950-074-3, 17059) Loompanics.

Uninhabited, Robust, & Wide Open: Mr. Justice Brennan's Legacy to the First Amendment. Robert D. Richards. LC 94-4973. 163p. 1994. pap. 35.00 (0-9635752-4-4) Pkway Pubs.

UnInstaller 3: Uncluttering Your PC. Valda Hilley. 1995. pap. text ed. 19.95 (0-7615-0094-4) Prima Pub.

Uninstalling Windows Applications. James McCord. (Illus.). 223p. (Orig.). 1995. 19.99 (0-7897-0358-0) Que.

Uninsured & Underinsured Motorist Insurance, Vol. 1. rev. ed. Alan I. Widiss. 1995. text ed. 375.00 (0-87084-938-7) Anderson Pub Co.

Uninsured Families: Problems & Solutions. Ed. by Carol Huber. 69p. (Orig.). 1988. pap. 10.00 (0-932622-13-5) Ctr Public Rep.

Unintellectual Freedoms: Opinions of a Public Librarian. Will Manley. LC 90-53505. (Illus.). 174p. 1991. lib. bdg. 23.95 (0-89950-575-9) McFarland & Co.

***Unintended Consequences.** Edward Harper. LC 96-71054. 432p. 1997. 20.95 (1-887750-42-8) Rutledge Bks.

Unintended Consequences. Susan Lee. 1999. pap. 12.95 (0-14-016774-9) Viking Penguin.

***Unintended Consequences.** Susan Lee. 1999. pap. 23.95 (0-670-84358-X) Viking Penguin.

Unintended Consequences. T. Naftali & A. Fursenko. Date not set. 25.00 (0-517-59741-1) Random Hse Value.

Unintended Consequences. John Ross. 861p. (C). 1996. 28.95 (1-888118-04-0) Accurate Pr.

Unintended Consequences: Illegal Drugs & Drug Policies in Nine Countries. F. Lamond Tullis. LC 95-3464. (Studies on the Impact of the Illegal Drug Trade: Vol. 4). 229p. 1995. lib. bdg. 45.00 (1-55587-549-1) Lynne Rienner.

***Unintended Impacts of Restructuring.** Ed. by Dianna Gordon. (Restructure? What Then? Ser.). 22p. 1996. 15.00 (1-55516-811-6, 4120) Natl Conf State Legis.

Unintended Reader: Feminism & "Manon Lescaut" Naomi Segal. (Cambridge Studies in French: No. 13). 275p. 1986. 69.95 (0-521-30723-6) Cambridge U Pr.

Unintended Thought. Ed. by James S. Uleman & John A. Bargh. LC 89-7582. 469p. 1989. lib. bdg. 55.00 (0-89862-379-0) Guilford Pr.

Uninterrupted Prose: Selected Writings of Paul Eluard. Paul Eluard. Tr. by Lloyd Alexander from FRE. LC 77-22122. 218p. 1977. reprint ed. text ed. 55.00 (0-8371-9779-1, ELSW, Greenwood Pr) Greenwood.

Uninterruptible Power Supplies. (Electrical Engineering Ser.). 1991. text ed. write for info. (0-442-00220-3) Van Nos Reinhold.

Uninterruptible Power Supplies. J. Platts & J. D. St. Aubyn. (IEE Power Engineering Ser.: No. 14). 168p. 1992. text ed. 70.00 (0-86341-263-7) Inst Elect Eng.

Uninterruptible Power Supplies: Power Conditioners for Critical Equipment. Griffith. (Electrical Engineering & Electronics Ser.: Vol. 58). 544p. 1989. 150.00 (0-8247-8076-0) Dekker.

Uninterruptible Power Supply Systems Directory. FMJ Intl. Publ. Ltd. Staff. (C). 1990. 295.00 (0-685-46633-7, Pub. by Fuel Metallurgical Jrnl UK) St Mut.

Uninterruptible Power Systems. 1983. 15.00 (0-318-18030-8, PE 1-1983) Natl Elec Mfrs.

Uninvited. James G. Berman. 240p. 1996. mass mkt. 5.99 (0-446-60329-5) Warner Bks.

Uninvited. adapted ed. Dorothy Macardle. 1979. pap. 5.25 (0-8222-1196-3) Dramatists Play.

Uninvited. Dorothy Macardle. 342p. 1976. reprint ed. lib. bdg. 25.95 (0-89244-068-6, Queens House) Amereon Ltd.

Uninvited Dilemma: A Question of Gender. rev. ed. Kim E. Stuart. 192p. 1997. pap. 14.95 (1-55552-013-8) Metamorphous Pr.

Uninvited Guest. Barbara Kennedy. 256p. 1981. mass mkt. 2.50 (0-449-14421-6, GM) Fawcett.

Uninvited Guest & Other Jewish Holiday Tales. Nina Jaffe. LC 92-36308. 80p. (J). 1993. 16.95 (0-590-44653-3) Scholastic Inc.

Uninvited Guests: A Documented History of U. F. O. Sightings, Alien Encounters & Coverups. Richard Hall. 384p. 1988. pap. 14.95 (0-943358-32-9) Aurora Press.

Uninvited Guests: The Parasitic Connection to Unexplained Illness. Ann L. Giltleman. (Good Health Guide Ser.). 48p. (Orig.). 1996. pap. 3.95 (0-87983-736-5) Keats.

Uninvited Memories. Ina Smith. LC 92-21767. 120p. 1992. 9.95 (0-944957-12-9) Rivercross Pub.

Uninvited Tenant. Mary S. Colquett. 286p. 1997. 18.00 (0-9648890-1-3) Southern Ink.

***Unio Mystica.** Boris Vukov. 150p. 1996. pap. write for info. (0-9657106-5-3) Zona Incerta.

Union: A Guide to Federal Archives Relating to the Civil War. Kenneth W. Munden & Henry P. Beers. LC 86-8363. 721p. 1986. reprint ed. text ed. 25.00 (0-911333-46-0, 100050) National Archives & Recs.

***Union a Dieu Chez Denys l'Areopagite.** Ysabel De Andia. (Philosophia Antiqua Ser.: Vol. 71). 528p. (FRE.). 1996. 170.50 (90-04-10656-1) E J Brill.

Union & Anti-Slavery Speeches. Charles D. Drake. LC 77-83961. (Black Heritage Library Collection). 1977. 20.95 (0-8369-8552-4) Ayer.

Union & Communion. Hudson Taylor. 96p. 1971. reprint ed. mass mkt. 4.99 (0-87123-571-4) Bethany Hse.

***Union & Emancipation: Essays on Politics & Race in the Civil War Era.** Ed. by David W. Blight & Brooks D. Simpson. LC 96-34978. 1997. 35.00 (0-87338-565-9) Kent St U Pr.

Union & Liberty: The Political Philosophy of John C. Calhoun. John C. Calhoun. Ed. by Ross M. Lence. LC 92-10391. 656p. 1992. 25.00 (0-86597-102-1); pap. 9.50 (0-86597-103-X) Liberty Fund.

Union & the Coal Industry. Morton S. Baratz. LC 82-25141. (Yale Studies in Economics: No. 4). xvii, 170p. (C). 1983. reprint ed. text ed. 52.50 (0-313-23698-4, BAUC, Greenwood Pr) Greenwood.

Union Army Black. Lucille Travis. LC 95-10349. (Ben & Zack Ser.: Bk. 4). 168p. (Orig.). (J). (gr. 4-8). 1995. pap. 5.99 (0-8010-4037-X) Baker Bks.

Union Army Camp Cooking. rev. ed. Patricia B. Mitchell. 1991. pap. 4.00 (0-925117-41-2) Mitchells.

Union Army Operations in the Southwest. LC 61-18715. 140p. 1982. reprint ed. lib. bdg. 33.00 (0-89370-739-2) Borgo Pr.

Union Army, 1861-1865: Organization & Operations, Vol. II: The Western Theater. Frank J. Welcher. 1088p. 1993. 75.00 (0-253-36454-X) Ind U Pr.

Union Army, 1861-1865: Organizations & Operation: The Eastern Theater, Vol. 1. Frank J. Welcher. LC 88-45749. 1084p. 1989. 75.00 (0-253-36453-1) Ind U Pr.

Union As It Is: Constitutional Unionism & Sectional Compromise, 1787-1861. Peter B. Knupfer. LC 91-50254. xvi, 286p. (C). 1991. 34.95 (0-8078-1996-4) U of NC Pr.

Union at Risk: Jacksonian Democracy, States' Right & the Nullification Crisis. Richard E. Ellis. 280p. 1989. pap. 18.95 (0-19-506187-X) OUP.

Union Authorization Cards & the NLRB: A Study of Congressional Intent, Administrative Policy, & Judicial Review. Alan R. McFarland & Wayne S. Bishop. LC 70-78136. (Labor Relations & Public Policy Ser.: No. 2). 112p. reprint ed. pap. 32.00 (0-8357-3160-X, 2039423) Bks Demand.

Union Bay: The Life of a City Marsh. Harry W. Higman & Earl J. Larrison. LC 51-13089. (Illus.). 325p. 1951. 15.00 (0-295-73976-2) U of Wash Pr.

Union Belle. Gilbert Morris. (House of Winslow Ser.: No. 11). 336p. (Orig.). 1992. pap. 9.99 (1-55661-186-2) Bethany Hse.

Union Bible Companion. Samuel A. Allibone. (Principle Works of Samuel Austin Allibone). 1989. reprint ed. lib. bdg. 79.00 (0-7812-1786-5) Rprt Serv.

Union Bibliography of Ohio Printed State Documents, 1803-1970. Ohio Historical Society Staff. 750p. 1973. 20.00 (0-318-03190-6) Ohio Hist Soc.

Union Bookshelf: A Selected Civil War Bibliography. Michael A. Mullins & Rowena Reed. LC 82-71852. (Illus.). 100p. 1982. pap. text ed. 25.00 (0-916107-12-4) Broadfoot.

Union Bride: A Story about Workers, Unions, Employers, & the Changing Labor Scene. Susan S. Bright. LC 95-61075. 368p. (Orig.). 1996. pap. 10.95 (1-896560-06-7) Tll Pubng.

Union Business: Trade Union Organisation & Financial Reform in the Thatcher Years. Paul Willman et al. (Cambridge Studies in Management: No. 19). 272p. (C). 1993. text ed. 59.95 (0-521-41725-2) Cambridge U Pr.

Union Busting in the Tri State: The Oklahoma, Kansas, & Missouri Metal Workers Strike of 1935. George G. Suggs, Jr. LC 86-6910. (Illus.). 296p. 1986. 27.95 (0-8061-2012-6) U of Okla Pr.

Union Calvaryman 1861-1865. Philip R. Katcher. (Warrior Ser.). (Illus.). 64p. 1995. pap. 12.95 (1-85532-462-8, 9610) Stackpole.

Union Camp Corp. A Report on the Company's Environmental Policies & Practices. (Illus.). 50p. (C). 1994. reprint ed. pap. text ed. 250.00 (0-7881-0970-7, Coun on Econ) DIANE Pub.

Union Camp Papers. D. R. Wagner. 1968. pap. 4.00 (0-912136-02-2) Twowindows Pr.

Union Carbide: A Report on the Company's Environmental Policies & Practices. (Illus.). 51p. (C). 1994. reprint ed. pap. text ed. 250.00 (0-7881-0926-X, Coun on Econ) DIANE Pub.

Union Cases: A Collector's Guide to the Art of America's First Plastics. Clifford Krainik & Carl Walvoord. LC 88-71215. (Illus.). 240p. 1988. 85.00 (0-931838-12-6, CP3812, Amphoto) Watsn-Guptill.

Union-Castle Line. A. S. Mallett. 1990. 59.00 (0-9516038-1-7, Pub. by Ship Pictorial Pubng UK) St Mut.

Union Catalog of Clemens Letters. Ed. by Paul Machlis. (UC Publications in Catalogs & Bibliographies: Vol. 1). 1986. 60.00 (0-520-09688-6) U CA Pr.

Union Catalog of Letters to Clemens. Paul Machlis. LC 92-1225. (UC Publications in Catalogs & Bibliographies: Vol. 8). 407p. 1992. 60.00 (0-520-09743-2) U CA Pr.

Union Catalogue of Philosophical Periodicals. Ed. by S. C. Biswas. (C). 1989. 11.00 (0-685-30704-2, Pub. by Munshiram Manoharial II) S Asia.

Union Catalogues of Serials: Guidelines for Creation & Maintenance, with Recommended Standards for Bibliographic & Holdings Control. Jean Whiffin. LC 83-8586. (Serials Librarian Ser.: Vol. 8, No. 1). 138p. 1983. text ed. 39.95 (0-86656-238-9) Haworth Pr.

Union Cavalry in the Civil War Vol. 1: From Fort Sumter to Gettysburg. Stephen Z. Starr. LC 78-26751. (Illus.). xiv, 522p. 1979. 39.95 (0-8071-0484-1) La State U Pr.

Union Cavalry in the Civil War Vol. 2: The War in the East, from Gettysburg to Appomattox, 1863-1865. Stephen Z. Starr. LC 78-26751. (Illus.). xvi, 568p. 1981. 39.95 (0-8071-0859-6) La State U Pr.

Union Cavalry in the Civil War Vol. 3: The War in the West, 1861-1865. Stephen Z. Starr. LC 78-26751. xv, 616p. 1985. 45.00 (0-8071-1209-7) La State U Pr.

Union Cemetery, Leesburg, Loudoun County, Virginia: Plats A & B, 1784-1995. Elizabeth R. Frain. 350p. 1995. pap. 30.00 (1-888265-04-3) Willow Bend.

Union College: Celebrating Two Centuries, 1795-1995. Peter Blankman et al. LC 94-19426. (Illus.). 1994. write for info. (0-89865-906-X) Donning Co.

Union Contract Application & Interpretation. Charles E. Hooper. 53p. 1978. 4.50 (0-318-13503-5) Assn U Busn & Econ Res.

Union Cook Book. 1987. 3.00 (0-317-55310-0) United Elec R&M.

Union Corporate Campaigns. Charles R. Perry. LC 86-82727. (Employee Relations & Collective Bargaining Ser.). (Orig.). 1987. pap. 30.00 (0-89546-065-3) U PA Ctr Hum Res.

Union County, South Carolina, Will Abstracts 1787-1849. Brent H. Holocomb. 175p. 1987. 25.00 (0-913363-09-X) SCMAR.

Union County (TN) Faces of War: A Pictorial History of Union Countians Involvement in the Military Service of Our Country. Bonnie H. Peters & Winnie P. McDonald. LC 95-92282. (Illus.). 256p. 1995. lib. bdg. 35.00 (0-9636662-1-5) Peters McDonald.

Union Dale Cemeteries, Vol. 2. Ed. by Kenneth T. McFarland. 112p. per. 11.95 (0-933227-25-6) Closson Pr.

Union Dale Cemetery, Vol. I. Ed. by Kenneth T. McFarland. 109p. pap. text ed. 11.95 (0-933227-24-8) Closson Pr.

Union Democracy & Landrum Griffin. Clyde W. Summer et al. 52p. 1986. pap. 3.00 (0-9602244-3-2) Assn Union Demo.

Union Democracy & Liberal Corporatism: Exit Voice & Wage Regulation in Postwar Europe. Peter Lange. (Western Societies Papers). 117p. 1984. 11.95 (0-8014-9636-5) Cornell U Pr.

Union Democracy in the Construction Trades. Ed. by Herman Benson et al. 33p. 1985. pap. 2.00 (0-9602244-2-4) Assn Union Demo.

Union Democracy Review. 200p. 7.00 (0-318-13505-1); 10.00 (0-318-13506-X); 10.00 (0-318-13508-6); ring bd. 35.00 (0-318-13507-8) Assn Union Demo.

Union Democracy Review: 27-49; 1982-1985. 1987. 35.00 (0-9602244-5-9); 10.00 (0-9602244-6-7) Assn Union Demo.

Union Education in Britain. John Holford. 315p. 1994. 45.00 (1-85041-074-7, Pub. by U Nottingham UK); pap. 19.95 (1-85041-073-9, Pub. by U Nottingham UK) Paul & Co Pubs.

Union, Essex & Hudson County see Hagstrom Atlases

Union Fires. John Barnes. 1992. mass mkt. 3.50 (0-373-63606-7, 1-63606-7) Harlequin Bks.

Union for Empire: Political Thought & the British Union of 1707. Ed. by John Robertson. 336p. (C). 1995. text ed. 59.95 (0-521-43113-1) Cambridge U Pr.

Union Forever. William R. Forstchen. (Lost Regiment Ser.: No. 2). 464p. (Orig.). 1991. pap. 5.99 (0-451-45060-4, ROC) NAL-Dutton.

Union Ghosts. Susan Crites. 48p. 1993. pap. 5.00 (1-881562-06-9) Butternut Pubns.

Union Government & Organization. Jim Wallihan. LC 85-10980. 270p. 1985. text ed. 30.00 (0-87179-460-8, 0460); pap. text ed. 28.00 (0-87179-461-6, 0461) BNA Books.

Union Government & Organization in the United States. James Wallihan. LC 85-10980. 272p. 1985. reprint ed. pap. 77.60 (0-608-00710-2, 2061483) Bks Demand.

Union Government & the Law: British & American Experiences. Joseph R. Grodin. (Monograph & Research Ser.: No. 8). 209p. 1961. 5.00 (0-89215-010-6) U Cal LA Indus Rel.

Union Guide to Photographic Collections in the Pacific Northwest. (Illus.). 434p. 1978. pap. 15.00 (0-87595-065-5) Oregon Hist.

Union Home Prayerbook. 204p. 1951. 1.00 (0-916694-19-4) Central Conf.

Union Home Prayerbook. deluxe ed. 204p. 1951. 2.00 (0-916694-60-7) Central Conf.

***Union in Peril: The Crisis over British Intervention in the Civil War.** Howard Jones. LC 96-49131. (Illus.). xiii, 302p. 1997. pap. 15.95 (0-8032-7597-8, Bison Books) U of Nebr Pr.

Union in Peril: The Crisis over British Intervention in the Civil War. Howard Jones. LC 92-53619. (H. Eugene & Lillian Youngs Lehman Ser.). (Illus.). xvi, 300p. (C). 1992. 37.50 (0-8078-2048-2) U of NC Pr.

Union in Truth: A History of the Restoration Movement. James B. North. Ed. by Jonathan Underwood. 416p. (Orig.). 1994. pap. 17.99 (0-7847-0197-0, 88577) Standard Pub.

Union Indian Brigade in the Civil War. Wiley Britton. (Illus.). 474p. (C). 1995. text ed. 40.00 (1-878882-06-6) KS Heritage Pr.

Union Inspiration in American Politics: The Autoworkers & the Making of a Liberal Industrial Order. Stephen Amberg. (Labor & Social Change Ser.). 336p. (C). 1994. text ed. 59.95 (1-56639-189-X) Temple U Pr.

Union Jack - the New York City Ballet. Ed. by Lincoln Kirstein. LC 77-94845. 1977. pap. 15.00 (0-87130-047-8) Eakins.

Union, Justice & Bonnie & Clyde: A Louisiana Legacy. William P. Watson. LC 89-84604. 145p. 1989. lib. bdg. 9.95 (0-944419-19-4) Everett Cos Pub.

Union Kommando in Auschwitz: The Auschwitz Munition Factory Through the Eyes of Its Former Slave Laborers. Ed. & Tr. by Lore Shelley. LC 95-45494. (Studies in the Shoah). (C). 1995. pap. text ed. 39.50 (0-7618-0195-2) U Pr of Amer.

Union Kommando in Auschwitz: The Auschwitz Munition Factory Through the Eyes of Its Former Slave Laborers, Vol. XIII. Ed. by Lore Shelley. LC 95-45494. (Studies in the Shoah). 442p. (C). 1995. lib. bdg. 58.00 (0-7618-0194-4) U Pr of Amer.

Union League Movement in the Deep South: Politics & Agricultural Change During Reconstruction. Michael W. Fitzgerald. LC 88-38406. xii, 304p. 1989. text ed. 37.50 (0-8071-1526-6) La State U Pr.

Union League of Philadelphia: 125 Years. Union League of Philadelphia Staff. (Illus.). 264p. 1987. write for info. (0-318-66927-7) Union League PA.

Union List of Arabic Serials in the United States: The Arabic Serials Holdings of Seventeen Libraries. Mohamed M. El-Hadi. LC 67-157. (University of Illinois, Graduate School of Library Science Occasional Papers: No. 75). 62p. reprint ed. pap. 25.00 (0-317-29753-8, 2017405) Bks Demand.

Union List of Artist Names. Getty. 1994. 495.00 incl. 3.5 hd (0-8161-0879-X, Hall Reference) Macmillan.

Union List of Artist Names, Vol. 2. large type ed. 1994. 123.75 (0-7838-2136-0, GK Hall) Thorndike Pr.

Union List of Artist Names, Vol. 3. large type ed. 1994. 123.75 (0-7838-2137-9, GK Hall) Thorndike Pr.

Union List of Artist Names, Vol. 4. large type ed. 1994. 123.75 (0-7838-2138-7, GK Hall) Thorndike Pr.

Union List of Artist Names: Vol. 1: Aa-Dzw, Set. Ed. by James M. Bower & Murtha B. Getty. LC 93-46729. 2912p. 1994. 495.00 (0-8161-0725-4, GK Hall) Thorndike Pr.

Union List of Artist Names Printed Version, Vol 1. Getty. 1994. 123.75 (0-7838-2135-2, Biblio Guides) G K Hall.

***Union List of Artist Names Single User Version.** Getty. 1994. 195.00 (0-8161-0726-2) Mac Lib Ref.

Union List of Film Periodicals: Holdings of Selected American Collections. Ed. by Anna Brady et al. LC 83-22585. xxvi, 316p. 1984. text ed. 47.95 (0-313-23702-6, BRL/, Greenwood Pr) Greenwood.

Union List of Korean Serials in East Asian Libraries in the United States. Compiled by Yong Kyu Choo. 263p. 1994. pap. 20.00 (0-924304-21-9) Assn Asian Studies.

Union List of Legislative Histories: 47th Congress, 1881-101st Congress, 1990. 6th ed. Compiled by Law Librarians' Society of the District of Columbia Staff. LC 91-31271. xxix, 605p. ring bd. 95.00 (0-8377-2705-7) Rothman.

Union List of Population-Family Planning Periodicals. Ed. by Susan K. Pasquariella. 135p. 1978. 25.00 (0-318-03477-8, LC-78-60528); 10.00 (0-318-03478-6) Assn Pop Lib.

Union List of Sanborn Fire Insurance Maps Held by Institutions in the United States & Canada: Alabama to Missouri, Vol.1. R. Philip Hoehn. LC 76-6129. (Occasional Papers: No. 2). (Illus.). 195p. 1976. fiche 4.00 (0-939112-16-7) Western Assn Map.

Union List of Sanborn Fire Insurance Maps Held by Institutions in the United States & Canada: Volume 2 (Montana to Wyoming, Canada & Mexico, with a Supplement & Corrigenda to Volume 1. rev. ed. William S. Peterson-Hunt & Evelyn L. Woodruff. LC 76-6129. (Occasional Papers: No. 3). (Illus.). 216p. (Orig.). 1977. pap. 6.00 (0-939112-03-5) Western Assn Map.

Union List of South Asian Periodicals in Western Languages in British Libraries. Hedley Sutton & Dipali Ghosh. 304p. 1994. text ed. 120.00 (0-7201-2107-8, Mansell Pub) Cassell.

Union Lists: Issues & Answers. Ed. by Dianne Ellsworth. LC 82-81471. (Current Issues in Serials Management Ser.: No. 2). 1982. 24.50 (0-87650-141-2) Pierian.

Union Maids Not Wanted: Organizing Domestic Workers Eighteen Seventy to Nineteen Forty. Donna Van Raaphorst. LC 87-25899. 328p. 1988. text ed. 49.95 (0-275-92288-X, C2288, Praeger Pubs) Greenwood.

Union Makes & Us Strong: Radical Unionism on the San Francisco Waterfront. David Wellman. LC 94-10286. (Illus.). 384p. (C). 1995. text ed. 59.95 (0-521-45005-5) Cambridge U Pr.

***Union Makes Us Strong: Radical Unionism on the San Francisco Waterfront.** 384p. 1997. pap. text ed. 19.95 (0-521-62968-3) Cambridge U Pr.

Union-Management Cooperation: Structure, Process, Impact. Michael H. Schuster. LC 84-17373. 235p. 1984. text ed. 23.00 (0-88099-023-6); pap. text ed. 13.00 (0-88099-024-4) W E Upjohn.

Union-Management Cooperation on the Railroads. Louis A. Wood. LC 74-22765. (Labor Movement in Fiction & Non-Fiction Ser.). reprint ed. 52.50 (0-404-58518-3) AMS Pr.

Union-Management in a Changing Economy. Alan Balfour. (Illus.). 464p. 1987. text ed. write for info. (0-13-938804-4) P-H.

Union Mas Perfecta: La Historia de Nuestra Constitucion. Betsy Maestro & Giulio Maestro. Tr. by Aida E. Marcuse. (Illus.). 48p. (J). (gr. 5). 1992. 13.95 (0-9625162-8-7) Lectorum Pubns.

Union Membership & Earnings Data Book: Compilations from the Current Population Survey. Barry T. Hirsch & David A. MacPherson. 132p. 1996. 60.00 (1-55871-325-5, XCMP 40) BNA Plus.

***Union Membership & Earnings Data Book: Compilations from the Current Population Survey.** 1,997th ed. Barry T. Hirsch & David A. Macpherson. 141p. 1997. 65.00 (1-55871-352-2, XCMP 42) BNA Plus.

Union Membership & Earnings Data Book 1993: Compilations from the Current Population Survey. Barry T. Hirsch & David A. Macpherson. LC 94-38227. 128p. 1994. 55.00 (1-55871-310-7, XCMP 26) BNA Plus.

Union Membership & Earnings Data Book 1994: Compilations from the Current Population Survey. Barry T. Hirsch & David A. Macpherson. 130p. 1995. 55.00 (1-55871-317-4, XCMP 19) BNA Plus.

Union Membership in Great Britain & the United States. Leo Wolman. (NBER Bulletin Ser.: No. 68). 1937. reprint ed. 20.00 (0-685-61186-8) Natl Bur Econ Res.

Union Mergers in Hard Times: The View from Five Countries. Gary N. Chaison. LC 96-28101. (IRL Press Book/Cornell International Reports: No. 31). (Illus.). 256p. 1996. 39.95 (0-8014-3330-4); pap. 16.95 (0-8014-8380-8) Cornell U Pr.

Union Nationale: Quebec Nationalism from Duplessis to Levesque. 2nd enl. ed. Herbert F. Quinn. LC 80-472454. 356p. reprint ed. pap. 101.50 (0-8357-8359-6, 2033981) Bks Demand.

Union, NJ. D. Johnson. (Images of America Ser.). 1994. pap. 14.99 (0-7524-0095-9, Arcdia) Chalford.

Union Obrera Democratica: First Filipino Labor Union. William H. Scott. 85p. (Orig.). 1993. pap. 8.75 (971-10-0488-7, Pub. by New Day Pub PH) Cellar.

Union of Bliss & Emptiness. Dalai Lama. Ed. by Christine Cox. Tr. & Intro. by Thupten Jinpa. LC 88-31948. 91p. (Orig.). 1988. pap. 14.95 (0-937938-69-6) Snow Lion Pubns.

Union of Diversities: Style in the Music of Charles Ives. Larry Starr. 192p. 1992. 38.00 (0-02-872465-8) Schirmer Bks.

Union of Honour. James Yorke. LC 72-240. (English Experience Ser.: No. 148). 76p. 1969. reprint ed. 58.00 (90-221-0148-7) Walter J Johnson.

Union of Interests: Political & Economic Thought in Revolutionary America. Cathy D. Matson & Peter S. Onuf. LC 89-16749. (American Political Thought Ser.). x, 238p. 1990. 25.00 (0-7006-0417-0) U Pr of KS.

Union of Lublin: Polish Federalism in the Golden Age. Harry E. Dembkowski. (East European Monographs: No. 116). 380p. 1982. text ed. 73.50 (0-88033-009-0) East Eur Monographs.

***Union of Mahamudra & Dzogchen.** Chokyi N. Rinpoche. 240p. 1996. pap. 18.00 (962-7341-21-5, Pub. by Rang Jung Yshe HK) Bookpeople.

***Union of Multiple Identities.** Brockliss. LC 97-10563. 1997. text ed. 69.95 (0-7190-5046-4, Pub. by Manchester Univ Pr UK) St Martin.

Union of Parts: Labor Politics in Postwar Germany. Kathleen Thelen. LC 91-55050. (Cornell Studies in Political Economy). 264p. 1991. 37.50 (0-8014-2586-7) Cornell U Pr.

Union of Professionals: Labor Relations & Educational Reform. Charles T. Kerchner et al. LC 92-43304. (Series on School Reform). 240p. (C). 1993. text ed. 42.00 (0-8077-3266-4); pap. text ed. 19.95 (0-8077-3265-6) Tchrs Coll.

Union of Tanganyika & Zanzibar: A Study in Political Integration. Martin Bailey. (Foreign & Comparative Studies Program, Eastern Africa Ser.: No. 9). 114p. 1973. pap. 3.00 (0-915984-06-7) Syracuse U Foreign Comp.

Union of Words: A History of Presidential Eloquence. Wayne Fields. 350p. 1995. text ed. 24.95 (0-02-910162-X, Free Press) Free Pr.

Union of Words: A History of Presidential Eloquence. Wayne Fields. 352p. 1996. 25.00 (0-684-82285-7) Free Pr.

Union of Words & Music in Medieval Poetry. Ed. by Rebecca A. Baltzer et al. (Illus.). 167p. (C). 1991. text ed. 45.00 (0-292-78519-4) U of Tex Pr.

Union of Youth: A Society of Artists of the Early Twentieth Century Russian Avant Garde. Jeremy Howard. (Illus.). 224p. 1992. text ed. 59.95 (0-7190-3731-X, Pub. by Manchester Univ Pr UK) St Martin.

***Union Officer in the Reconstruction.** John W. De Forest. Ed. by James H. Croushore & David M. Potter. LC 96-29715. 248p. 1997. pap. 12.95 (0-8071-2183-5) La State U Pr.

Union on the King's Highway. Dean Mills. LC 87-72772. (Campbell-Stone Heritage of Unity Ser.). 188p. 1987. 12.99 (0-89900-286-2) College Pr Pub.

Union Organizing: Management & Labor Conflict. William E. Fulmer. LC 82-16172. 240p. 1982. text ed. 55.00 (0-275-90797-X, C0797, Praeger Pubs) Greenwood.

Union Organizing & Public Policy: Failure to Secure First Contracts. William N. Cooke. LC 85-3239. 159p. (C). 1985. text ed. 22.00 (0-88099-026-0); pap. text ed. 12.00 (0-88099-027-9) W E Upjohn.

Union Organizing & Staying Organized. Kenneth Gagala. (C). 1983. text ed. 24.33 (0-8359-8064-2, Reston) P-H.

Union Organizing in the Public Sector: An Analysis of State & Local Elections. Kate Bronfenbrenner & Tom Juravich. (ILR Press Book: No. 70). 112p. 1995. pap. 15.95 (0-87546-347-9) Cornell U Pr.

Union Organizing in the Public Sector: An Analysis of State & Local Elections. Kate Bronfenbrenner & Tom Juravich. LC 95-17967. (ILR Bulletin Ser.: Vol. 70). 1995. pap. 15.95 (0-614-07799-0, ILR Press) Cornell U Pr.

Union Pacific. Marie Cahill & Lynne Piade. (Great Rails Ser.). 128p. 1994. 14.98 (0-8317-3799-9) Smithmark.

Union Pacific - 1990. George R. Cockle & Paul K. Withers. (Illus.). 208p. 1991. 42.50 (0-9618503-8-8) Withers Pub.

Union Pacific Business Cars 1870-1991. Ralph L. Barger. (Illus.). 208p. 1992. 49.95 (0-89778-281-X, 10-7570, Greenberg Books) Kalmbach.

Union Pacific Cheyenne West, Pt. 1. Wesley Fox. (Illus.). 96p. 1996. 37.95 (1-884831-02-8) Fox Pubns.

***Union Pacific Country.** Robert G. Athearn. LC 75-11707. (Illus.). 480p. 1976. reprint ed. pap. 136.80 (0-608-03987-X, 2064719) Bks Demand.

Union Pacific Forties...on the Move. George R. Cockle. LC 81-65096. (Overland Railbook Ser.). (Illus.). 208p. 1985. pap. 23.50 (0-916160-10-6) G R Cockle.

Union Pacific Freight Cars, 1936-1951. Terry Metcalfe. (Illus.). 200p. 1989. per. 24.95 (0-9623347-0-7) Metcalfe Pubns.

Union Pacific Motive Power in Transition: 1936-1960. Lloyd E. Stagner. Ed. by James J. Reisdorff. (Illus.). 64p. 1993. pap. 17.95 (0-942035-24-0) South Platte.

Union Pacific Official Color Photography. Robert A. Le Massena & Robert J. Yanosey. (Illus.). 128p. 1993. 49.95 (1-878887-25-4) Morning NJ.

Union Pacific Railroad: A Case in Premature Enterprise. Robert W. Fogel. LC 78-64234. (Johns Hopkins University. Studies in the Social Sciences. Thirtieth Ser. 1912: 2). reprint ed. 37.50 (0-404-61339-X) AMS Pr.

Union Pacific Railway. John P. Davis. LC 73-2501. (Big Business; Economic Power in a Free Society Ser.). 1979. reprint ed. 20.95 (0-405-05082-8) Ayer.

Union Pacific Steam in Color. Lloyd E. Stagner. (Illus.). 1995. 49.95 (1-878887-44-0) Morning NJ.

Union Pacific...Nineteen Seventy-Seven to Nineteen Eighty. George R. Cockle. LC 77-81546. (Illus.). 208p. 1980. pap. 18.95 (0-916160-03-3) G R Cockle.

Union Pacific's Snow Fighters. G. R. Cockle. LC 81-65095. (Overland Railbook Ser.). (Illus.). 208p. 1984. pap. 23.50 (0-916160-09-2) G R Cockle.

Union Pacific's West. Donald Sims. LC 91-2894. (Illus.). (YA). (gr. 11). 1991. 42.95 (0-87046-098-6) Pentrex Pub.

***Union Parish, Louisiana Marriage Records 1839-1900.** John C. Head. 102p. 1990. pap. text ed. 16.00 (1-57088-012-3) J&W Ent.

***Union, Past & Present: An Illustrated History of the Town of Union, from Earliest Times.** 96p. 1997. reprint ed. pap. 16.00 (0-8328-5918-4) Higginson Bk Co.

Union Peligrosa. Helen Bianchin. (Bianca Ser.). 1996. mass mkt. 3.50 (0-373-33371-4, 1-33371-5) Harlequin Bks.

Union Perspectives on New Work-Based Youth Apprenticeship Initiatives. Carol Shenon. 46p. 1992. pap. 10.00 (1-887410-70-8) Jobs for Future.

Union Policies & Industrial Management. Sumner H. Slichter. LC 73-89763. (American Labor, from Conspiracy to Collective Bargaining Ser., No. 1). 611p. 1970. reprint ed. 35.95 (0-405-02148-8) Ayer.

Union Policy & Incentive Wage Methods. Van Dusen Kennedy. LC 68-58598. (Columbia University. Studies in the Social Sciences: No. 513). reprint ed. 29.50 (0-404-51513-4) AMS Pr.

Union Policy & the Older Worker. Melvin K. Bers. LC 76-14986. 87p. 1976. reprint ed. text ed. 45.00 (0-8371-8655-2, BEUP, Greenwood Pr) Greenwood.

Union Politic: The CIO Political Action Committee. James C. Foster. LC 74-22240. 258p. 1975. 34.95 (0-8262-0171-7) U of Mo Pr.

Union Portraits. Gamaliel Bradford. LC 68-29194. (Essay Index Reprint Ser.). 1977. 20.95 (0-8369-0243-2) Ayer.

Union Portraits. Gamaliel Bradford. (History - United States Ser.). 330p. 1992. reprint ed. lib. bdg. 89.00 (0-7812-6174-0) Rprt Serv.

Union Power & American Democracy: The UAW & the Democratic Party, 1972-83. Dudley W. Buffa. 296p. 1984. 39.50 (0-472-10053-X) U of Mich Pr.

Union Power & New York: Victor Gotbaum & District Council 37. Jewel Bellush & Bernard Bellush. LC 84-15926. 496p. 1984. text ed. 59.95 (0-275-91126-8, C1126, Praeger Pubs) Greenwood.

Union Prayerbook, 1. 365p. 1977. 16.00 (0-916694-09-7) Central Conf.

Union Professional: The Staff Rep in Action. Duane Beeler. 109p. 1977. pap. 3.95 (0-317-12247-9) Union Rep.

***Union Reader.** Ed. by Richard Harwell. 384p. 1997. reprint ed. 10.98 (0-614-30889-5) W S Konecky Assocs.

Union Reader: As the North Saw the War. unabridged ed. Ed. by Richard B. Harwell. (Illus.). 384p. 1996. reprint ed. pap. text ed. 9.95 (0-486-29145-6) Dover.

***Union Recreation Area.** 3rd ed. Anne Temte & Camille S. Feltner. 55p. 1985. pap. 24.00 (0-923276-23-8) Assn Coll Unions Intl.

Union Regulations see NEA Series

Union Relative Wage Effects: A Survey. H. Gregg Lewis. LC 85-8663. 240p. 1986. lib. bdg. 45.00 (0-226-47721-5) U Ch Pr.

***Union, Religion & Revolution in 17th Century Scotland.** David Stevenson. (Collected Studies Ser.: No. 570). 336p. 1997. text ed. 98.95 (0-86078-642-0, Pub. by Variorum UK) Ashgate Pub Co.

Union Representation Elections: Law & Reality. Julius G. Getman et al. LC 78-13271. 218p. 1976. 29.95 (0-87154-302-8) Russell Sage.

Union Representative's Guide to Federal Labor Relations. Dennis K. Reischl. (Illus.). 100p. (Orig.). 1988. pap. text ed. 9.95 (0-936295-05-8) FPMI Comns.

Union Representative's Guide to NLRB RC & CA Cases. Gloria Busman. (Policy & Practice Publication). 112p. 1984. 10.00 (0-89215-089-0) U Cal LA Indus Rel.

Union Republics in Soviet Diplomacy: A Study of Soviet Federalism in the Service of Soviet Foreign Policy. Vernon V. Aspaturian. LC 83-22696. 228p. 1984. reprint ed. text ed. 35.00 (0-313-24368-9, ASUP, Greenwood Pr) Greenwood.

Union Resilience in Troubled Times: The Story of the Operating Engineers, AFL-CIO, 1960-1993. Garth L. Mangum & John Walsh. LC 94-10047. (Labor & Human Resources Ser.). (Illus.). 294p. (gr. 13). 1994. text ed. 62.95 (1-56324-452-7); pap. text ed. 25.95 (1-56324-453-5) M E Sharpe.

Union Retirees: Enriching Their Lives, Enhancing Their Contribution, 2 vols. Ivan Charner et al. 500p. 1990. Set. 37.50 (0-86510-061-6); write for info. (0-318-68441-1) Natl Inst Work.

Union Retirees: Enriching Their Lives, Enhancing Their Contribution, 2 vols., Vol. II. Ivan Charner et al. 250p. 1990. 20.00 (0-89492-096-0) Natl Inst Work.

Union Retirees - Enriching Their Lives, Enhancing Their Contribution: Executive Summary. Ivan Charner et al. 66p. 1990. 3.50 (0-89492-094-4) Natl Inst Work.

Union Retreat & the Regions: The Shrinking Landscape of Organised Labour. Ron Martin et al. (Regional Policy & Development Ser.: No. 8). 144p. 1996. pap. 34.95 (1-85302-255-1) Taylor & Francis.

***Union Sisters: Women in the Labour Movement.** Ed. by Linda Briskin. 424p. reprint ed. pap. 10.95 (0-88961-079-7, Pub. by Wmns Pr CN) LPC InBook.

***Union Soldier in Battle: Enduring the Ordeal of Combat.** Earl J. Hess. (Modern War Studies). (Illus.). 264p. 1997. 29.95 (0-7006-0837-0) U Pr of KS.

Union Soldier Returns South: The Civil War Letters & Diary of Alfred C. Willett, 113th Ohio Volunteer Infantry. Charles E. Willett. (Illus.). 136p. 1994. 14.95 (1-57072-005-3) Overmountain Pr.

Union Square. Meredith Tax. 432p. 1990. mass mkt. 4.95 (0-380-70906-6) Avon.

Union Square. Albert Halper. (Proletarian Literature Ser.). xxiv, 393p. 1990. reprint ed. lib. bdg. 38.00 (1-55888-273-1) Omnigraphics Inc.

Union Square Cafe Cookbook. D. Meyer. LC 94-1110. 320p. 1994. 30.00 (0-06-017013-1, HarpT) HarpC.

Union Station: A Decorative History of Washington's Grand Terminal. Carol M. Highsmith & Ted Landphair. (Illus.). 100p. 1989. pap. 19.95 (0-685-21898-8) Chls Pub Inc.

***Union Station Massacre: The Making of J. Edgar Hoover's FBI.** Robert Unger. LC 97-18630. (Illus.). 256p. 1997. 22.95 (0-8362-2773-5) Andrews & McMeel.

Union Station Remembered. 2nd ed. Joseph Pallotta. (Illus.). 173p. 1985. pap. 19.95 (0-9616091-0-9) J & C Bks.

Union Strategies for a High Tech Era. Ed. by Gloria Busman. (Current Issues Ser.: No. 10). 106p. 1993. reprint ed. 15.00 (0-89215-150-1) U Cal LA Indus Rel.

Union Strategy & Industrial Change. Ed. by Stephen Frenkel. 192p. 1987. pap. 27.95 (0-86840-250-8, Pub. by New South Wales Univ Pr AT) Intl Spec Bk.

Union Tactics & Economic Change: A Case Study of Three Philadelphia Textile Unions. Gladys L. Palmer. LC 71-156438. (American Labor Ser., No. 2). 1978. reprint ed. 19.95 (0-405-02936-5) Ayer.

Union, the Confederacy, & the Atlantic Rim. James M. McPherson et al. Ed. by Robert E. May. LC 94-32424. (Illus.). 181p. 1995. pap. 12.95 (1-55753-061-0) Purdue U Pr.

Union, the Confederacy, & the Atlantic Rim. James M. McPherson et al. Ed. by Robert E. Mayed. LC 94-32424. (Illus.). 181p. 1995. 24.95 (1-55753-060-2) Purdue U Pr.

Union Violence: The Record & the Response by Courts, Legislatures & the NLRB. Armand J. Thieblot & Thomas R. Haggard. LC 83-81085. (Labor Relations & Public Policy Ser.: No. 25). 560p. (Orig.). 1983. reprint ed. pap. 159.60 (0-608-00878-8, 2061672) Bks Demand.

Union Voices: Labor's Responses to Crisis. Ed. by Glenn Adler & Doris Suarez. LC 91-38444. (SUNY Series in the Anthropology of Work). 321p. (C). 1992. text ed. 64.50 (0-7914-1247-4); pap. text ed. 21.95 (0-7914-1248-2) State U NY Pr.

Union with Christ: John Calvin & the Mysticism of St. Bernard. Dennis E. Tamburello. LC 94-9324. (Columbia Series in Reformed Theology). 192p. 1994. 18.00 (0-664-22054-1) Westminster John Knox.

Union with God. Jeanne Guyon. Ed. by Gene Edwards. 117p. 1981. pap. 8.95 (0-940232-05-7) Seedsowers.

Union with the Church. Henry Harbaugh. (Notable American Authors Ser.). 1992. reprint ed. lib. bdg. 75.00 (0-7812-3008-X) Rprt Serv.

Unionisation & Policisation of Peasants & Agricultural Labourers in India. Jose George. (C). 1992. 24.00 (81-7169-187-0, Commonwealth) S Asia.

Unionism & Relative Wages in the United States: An Empirical Inquiry. Harold G. Lewis. LC 63-20915. (Studies in Economics of the Economics Research Center of the University of Chicago). 325p. reprint ed. pap. 92.70 (0-685-23873-3, 2056657) Bks Demand.

Unionism, Economic Stabilization & Incomes Policies: European Experience. Robert J. Flanagan et al. LC 83-71459. 705p. 1983. 44.95 (0-8157-2856-5); pap. 19.95 (0-8157-2855-7) Brookings.

Unionism in Modern Ireland: New Perspectives on Politics & Culture. Ed. by Richard English & Graham Walker. LC 96-10387. 224p. 1996. text ed. 65.00 (0-312-15979-X) St Martin.

Unionism, International Trade, & Trade Policy. rev. ed. Robert J. Riley. LC 94-35675. (Foreign Economic Policy of the United States Ser.). (Illus.). 208p. 1995. text ed. 59.00 (0-8153-1993-2) Garland.

UV

An Asterisk (*) at the beginning of an entry indicates that the title is appearing in BIP for the first time.

*__Unionist Politics & the Politics of Unionism.__ Feargal Cochrane. 320p. 1997. 69.95 (1-85918-138-4, Pub. by Cork Univ IE) Intl Spec Bk.

*__Unionist Politics & the Politics of Unionism.__ Feargal Cochrane. 320p. 1997. pap. 24.95 (1-85918-139-2, Pub. by Cork Univ IE) Intl Spec Bk.

Unionists Divided: Arthur Balfour, Joseph Chamberlain & the Unionist Free Traders. Richard A. Rempel. (Library of Politics & Society Ser.). 236p. (C). 1972. 35.00 (0-208-01308-3, Archon Bks) Shoe String.

Unionization & Deunionization: Strategy, Tactics, & Outcomes. John J. Lawler. (Studies in Industrial Relations). 300p. (C). 1990. text ed. 34.95 (0-87249-662-7) U of SC Pr.

Unionization of Teachers: A Case Study of the UFT. Stephen Cole. Ed. by Harriet Zuckerman & Robert K. Merton. LC 79-8986. (Dissertations on Sociology Ser.). 1980. reprint ed. lib. bdg. 25.95 (0-405-12959-9) Ayer.

Unionization of the Maquiladora Industry: The Tamaulipan Case in National Context. Edward J. Williams & John T. Passe-Smith. (Border Studies Ser.: No. 4). 134p. (Orig.). 1992. pap. 9.50 (0-925613-08-8) SDSU Inst Reg Studies.

*__Unionizing the Jungles: Labor & Community in the Twentieth-Century Meatpacking Industry.__ Ed. by Shelton Stromquist & Marvin Bergman. LC 96-53293. 288p. 1997. 32.95 (0-87745-589-9) U of Iowa Pr.

Unions Against Revolution. John Zerzan. 1975. pap. 1.25 (0-934868-12-3) Black & Red.

Unions & Communities under Siege: American Communities & the Crisis of Organized Labor. Gordon L. Clark. (Cambridge Human Geography Ser.). (Illus.). 328p. (C). 1989. text ed. 69.95 (0-521-36516-3) Cambridge U Pr.

Unions & Economic Competitiveness. Ed. by Lawrence R. Mishel & Paula Voos. LC 91-21335. (Economic Policy Institute Ser.). 368p. (gr. 13). 1991. text ed. 59.95 (0-87332-827-2); pap. text ed. 24.95 (0-87332-828-0) M E Sharpe.

Unions & Economic Competitiveness: 1990-91 Edition. Lawrence R. Mishel & David M. Frankel. Ed. by Paula Voos. (Economic Policy Institute Ser.). 550p. (gr. 13). 1991. 65.95 (0-87332-812-4); pap. 25.95 (0-87332-813-2) M E Sharpe.

Unions & Economic Crisis: Britain, West Germany & Sweden. George Ross et al. 250p. 1984. text ed. 44.95 (0-04-331094-X) Routledge Chapman & Hall.

Unions & Free Trade: Solidarity vs. Competition. Kim Moody & Mary McGinn. LC 92-70092. (Illus.). 84p. (Orig.). 1992. pap. 7.00 (0-914093-05-3) Labor Notes.

Unions & Immigrants: Organizations & Struggle. George E. Pozzetta. LC 90-49263. (Immigration & Ethnicity Ser.: Vol. 7). 368p. 1991. reprint ed. text ed. 62.00 (0-8240-7407-6) Garland.

Unions & Industrial Relations: Recent Trends & Prospects. Ed. by Roger Blanpain. (Bulletin of Comparative Labour Relations Ser.: Vol. 16). 220p. 1987. pap. 62.00 (90-6544-294-4) Kluwer Law Tax Pubs.

Unions & Politics in Mexico: The Case of the Automobile Industry. Ian Roxborough. (Cambridge Latin American Studies: No. 49). (Illus.). 224p. 1984. text ed. 80.00 (0-521-25987-8) Cambridge U Pr.

Unions & Public Policy. Ed. by Lawrence G. Flood. (Orig.). 1989. pap. 15.00 (0-944285-13-9) Pol Studies.

Unions & Public Policy: The New Economy, Law, & Democratic Politics. Ed. by Lawrence G. Flood. LC 95-22976. (Contributions in Political Science Ser.: Vol. 364). 224p. 1995. text ed. 59.95 (0-313-29800-9, Greenwood Pr) Greenwood.

Unions & the Cities. Harry H. Wellington & Ralph K. Winter, Jr. LC 79-179327. (Brookings Institution Studies of Unionism in Government). 240p. reprint ed. pap. 68.40 (0-685-10707-8, 2025417) Bks Demand.

Unions & Workers: Limitations & Possibilities. Martin Glaberman. 18p. 1994. pap. 3.00 (0-935590-22-6) Bewick Edns.

*__Unions & Workplace Reorganization.__ Ed. by Bruce Nissen. LC 97-15001. 224p. (Orig.). 1998. pap. 22.95 (0-8143-2703-6) Wayne St U Pr.

Unions for Academic Library Support Staff: Impact on Workers & the Workplace. James M. Kusack. LC 86-7709. (New Directions in Information Management Ser.: No. 10). 121p. 1986. text ed. 42.95 (0-313-24991-1, KUA/, Greenwood Pr) Greenwood.

*__Unions in a Changing World: Problems & Prospects in Selected Industrialized Countries.__ Shauna L. Olney. xii, 99p. 1996. pap. 18.00 (92-2-109504-5) Intl Labour Office.

Unions in Conflict: A Comparative Study Four South Indian Textile Centres, 1918-1939. Eamon Murphy. 1982. 18.00 (0-8364-0874-8) S Asia.

Unions in Crisis & Beyond. Richard C. Edwards et al. LC 85-26646. 400p. (C). 1986. text ed. 42.95 (0-86569-127-4, Auburn Hse) Greenwood.

Unions in Emerging Societies: Frustration & Politics. Sidney C. Sufrin. LC 64-14084. 130p. reprint ed. pap. 37.10 (0-317-52020-2, 2027414) Bks Demand.

*__Unions in Politics: Britain, Germany & the United States in the Nineteenth & Early Twentieth Centuries.__ Gary W. Marks. LC 88-25054. (Illus.). 294p. 1989. reprint ed. pap. 83.80 (0-608-02526-7, 2063170) Bks Demand.

Unions in Teachers' Professional Lives: Social, Intellectual, & Practical Concerns. Nina Bascia. LC 93-45998. (Series on School Reform). 128p. (C). 1994. text ed. 34.00 (0-8077-3339-3); pap. text ed. 15.95 (0-8077-3338-5) Tchrs Coll.

Unions, Management, & Quality: Opportunities for Innovation & Excellence. Edward Cohen-Rosenthal, Jr. & Frank J. Wayno. LC 94-27614. 324p. 1994. text ed. 35.00 (0-7863-0157-0) Irwin Prof Pubng.

Unions, Management & Quality: Opportunities for Innovation & Excellence. Edward Cohen-Rosenthal. 275p. 35.00 (0-614-04832-X, DJ21H) Assn Qual & Part.

Unions of States: Theory & Practice of Confederation. Murray G. Forsyth. LC 80-29044. 360p. (C). 1981. 42.50 (0-8419-0691-2); pap. 19.50 (0-8419-0729-3) Holmes & Meier.

Unions on Campus. Frank R. Kemerer & J. Victor Baldridge. LC 75-24009. (Jossey-Bass Higher Education Ser.). 263p. reprint ed. pap. 75.00 (0-685-16214-1, 2027758) Bks Demand.

Unions, Parties, & Political Development: A Study of Mineworkers in Zambia. Robert H. Bates. LC 78-158135. 303p. reprint ed. pap. 86.40 (0-317-29593-4, 2021980) Bks Demand.

Unions' Rights to Company Information. rev. ed. James T. O'Reilly & Jodi C. Aronson. LC 85-82257. (Labor Relations & Public Policy Ser.). 300p. 1987. pap. 30.00 (0-89546-060-2) U PA Ctr Hum Res.

Unions' Rights to Company Information. James T. O'Reilly & Gale P. Simon. LC 80-53300. (Labor Relations & Public Policy Ser.: No. 21). 292p. reprint ed. pap. 83.30 (0-317-41895-5, 2025913) Bks Demand.

Unions, Wages & Inflation. Daniel J. Mitchell. LC 79-3776. 304p. 1980. pap. 16.95 (0-8157-5751-4) Brookings.

Unions, Workers, & the Law. Betty W. Justice. LC 82-22826. 307p. 1983. reprint ed. pap. 87.50 (0-608-00711-0, 2061484) Bks Demand.

Uniontown, Maryland: A Walking Tour. Joseph M. Getty. LC 83-61818. 54p. (Orig.). 1983. pap. 10.00 (0-913281-00-X) Hist Soc Carroll.

*__UNIPAC 1: The Hospice/Palliative Approach to Caring for the Terminally Ill.__ Porter Storey & Carol F. Knight. 80p. (Orig.). 1997. pap. 20.00 (1-889296-01-5) Acad Hospice.

*__UNIPAC 2: Psychological, Spiritual, & Physiological Aspects of Dying & Bereavement.__ Porter Storey & Carol F. Knight. (Hospice/Palliative Care Training for Physicians Ser.: Vol. 2). 80p. (Orig.). 1997. pap. 20.00 (1-889296-02-3) Acad Hospice.

*__Unipac 3: Assessment & Treatment of Pain in the Terminally Ill.__ Porter Storey & Carol F. Knight. (Hospical/Palliative Care Training for Physicians Ser.: Vol. 3). 86p. (Orig.). 1996. pap. text ed. 20.00 (1-889296-03-1) Acad Hospice.

*__Unipac 4: Management of Selected Nonpain Symptoms in the Terminally Ill.__ Porter Storey & Carol F. Knight. (Hospice/Palliative Care Training for Physicians Ser.: Vol. 4). 80p. (Orig.). 1996. pap. text ed. 20.00 (1-889296-04-X) Acad Hospice.

*__UNIPAC 5: Caring for the Terminally Ill: Communication & the Interdisciplinary Team Approach.__ Porter Storey & Carol F. Knight. (Hospice/Palliative Care Training for Physicians Ser.: Vol. 5). 80p. (Orig.). 1997. pap. 20.00 (1-889296-05-8) Acad Hospice.

*__Unipac 6: Ethical & Legal Decision Making When Caring for the Terminally Ill.__ Porter Storey & Carol F. Knight. (Hospice/Palliative Care Training for Physicians Ser.: Vol. 6). 112p. (Orig.). 1996. pap. text ed. 20.00 (1-889296-06-6) Acad Hospice.

Uniplex: A Guide to Integrated Office Automation. Nigel Girling. 300p. 1991. pap. text ed. 32.00 (0-13-929910-6) P-H.

Uniplex II Plus Word Processing Guide. 2nd ed. Martin J. Penning & John Humphries. LC 92-21946. 1992. pap. text ed. 36.00 (0-13-953902-6) P-H.

Uniplex II Plus Wordprocessing Guide. John Humphries & Martin J. Penning. 250p. 1990. pap. 32.00 (0-13-946294-5) P-H.

Unique & Unusual Places in the Mid-Atlantic Region. William N. Hoffman. 160p. (Orig.). 1995. pap. 9.95 (0-9612050-6-7) Spring Garden Pubns.

Unique Animal. Don D. Davis. (Illus.). 336p. 1981. 25.00 (0-907152-02-3); pap. 12.95 (0-907152-01-5) Prytaneum Pr.

Unique Arizona: A Guide to the State's Quirks, Charisma, & Character. Tom Barr. LC 94-20034. (Illus.). 112p. (Orig.). 1994. pap. 10.95 (1-56261-178-X) John Muir.

Unique California: A Guide to the State's Quirks, Charisma, & Character. Richard Harris. LC 94-20048. (Illus.). 112p. (Orig.). 1994. pap. 10.95 (1-56261-179-8) John Muir.

Unique Chemical Labs. Louis Casimir. 107p. 1994. pap. text ed. 8.95 (0-87563-511-3) Stipes.

Unique Christ in Our Pluralistic World. Ed. by Bruce J. Nicholls. LC 94-36248. (World Evangelical Fellowship Ser.). 288p. (C). 1995. pap. 14.99 (0-8010-2013-1) Baker Bks.

Unique Colorado: A Guide to the State's Quirks, Charisma, & Character. Sarah Lovett. LC 93-13452. (Unique Travel Ser.). (Illus.). 112p. (Orig.). 1993. pap. 10.95 (1-56261-103-8) John Muir.

Unique Continent. Ed. by Jeremy Smith. (Orig.). 1992. pap. 16.95 (0-7022-2475-8, Pub. by Univ Queensland Pr AT) Intl Spec Bk.

Unique Experience. Carolyn T. Anderson. 173p. (Orig.). 1987. pap. 6.00 (0-935132-08-2) C H Fairfax.

Unique Florida: A Guide to the State's Quirks, Charisma & Character. Sarah Lovett. LC 93-3232. (Unique Travel Ser.). (Illus.). 112p. (Orig.). 1993. pap. 10.95 (1-56261-104-6) John Muir.

*__Unique Galilean.__ 1986. pap. 0.99 (0-8341-1175-6) Nazarene.

Unique Georgia: A Guide to the State's Quirks, Charisma, & Character. Tom Barr. LC 95-7321. (Illus.). 112p. 1995. pap. 11.95 (1-56261-240-9) John Muir.

Unique Ghost Towns & Mountain Spots. Caroline Bancroft. (Illus.). 96p. 1961. pap. 5.95 (0-933472-24-2) Johnson Bks.

Unique Golf Resorts of the World. Gwen Williams. 204p. 1983. 34.95 (0-9612294-0-3) Unique Golf Res.

Unique Golf Resorts of the World. 2nd ed. Gwen Williams. 1987. 34.95 (0-9612294-2-X) Unique Golf Res.

Unique Golf Resorts of World. Gwen Williams. 1990. pap. 34.95 (0-9612294-3-8) Unique Golf Res.

Unique Gospel Outlines & Addresses. J. W. Jordan. 1991. reprint ed. pap. 5.99 (0-88019-283-6) Schmul Pub Co.

Unique Health Guide for Young People. Betty Y. Ho. (System of Government in the Living Body Ser.). (Illus.). 60p. (Orig.). (J). (gr. 3 up). 1994. pap. 8.00 (1-884996-00-0) Juvenescent.

Unique Hopewellian Mask-Headdress. Raymond Baby. (Illus.). 2p. 1956. reprint ed. pap. 0.50 (0-318-00853-X) Ohio Hist Soc.

Unique Meeting Places in Baltimore: Distinctive Conference & Party Facilities from Downtown to the Eastern Shore. Elise Ford. LC 92-6070. (Illus.). 256p. 1992. pap. 11.95 (0-939009-61-7) EPM Pubns.

*__Unique Meeting, Wedding & Party Places in Greater Washington: Distinctive Conference & Party Facilities Found Only in the Capital Area.__ Elise Ford. LC 96-42291. (Illus.). 400p. 1996. 18.95 (1-889324-02-7) EPM Pubns.

Unique Meeting, Wedding & Party Places in Greater Washington: Distinctive Conference & Party Facilities Found Only in the Capital Area. 3rd ed. Elise Ford. LC 93-12781. (Illus.). 272p. 1993. pap. 12.95 (0-939009-76-5) EPM Pubns.

Unique New England: A Guide to the Region's Quirks, Charisma, & Character. Sarah Lovett. LC 93-32352. (Unique Travel Ser.). 112p. (Orig.). 1994. pap. 10.95 (1-56261-146-1) John Muir.

Unique New Mexico: A Guide to the State's Quirks, Charisma & Character. Sarah Lovett. LC 93-3003. (Unique Travel Ser.). (Illus.). 112p. (Orig.). 1993. pap. 10.95 (1-56261-102-X) John Muir.

*__Unique One-Recipe, Three-Meal Family Cookbook.__ Sara Lewis. 1996. 12.98 (0-7651-9789-8); 12.98 (0-8317-7290-5) Smithmark.

Unique Oregon: A Guide to the State's Quirks, Charisma, & Character. Richard Harris. LC 95-52136. (Unique Travel Guides Ser.). (Illus.). 112p. 1996. pap. 9.95 (1-56261-247-6) John Muir.

Unique Parish: St. Anne's, Walnut Creek, California. Joseph A. King. LC 93-94215. (Illus.). 125p. 1994. 25.00 (0-9608500-7-4) K & K Pubns.

Unique Perspective of Television & Its Effect: A Pilot Study. Kurt Lang & Gladys E. Lang. (Reprint Series in Social Sciences). (C). 1993. reprint ed. pap. text ed. 1.00 (0-8290-3797-7, S-160) Irvington.

Unique Physician Identification Number for All States, 2 vols., Set. 1994. lib. bdg. 495.00 (0-8490-8402-4) Gordon Pr.

Unique Position: A Biography of Edith Dircksey Cowan, 1861-1932. Peter Cowan. 1979. 29.75 (0-85564-135-5, Pub. by Univ of West Aust Pr AT) Intl Spec Bk.

Unique Program for Staying Healthy, Young, & Trim. Riette Ormond & George Ormond. 44p. (Orig.). 1982. pap. 6.95 (0-9620518-0-2) Ormond Assocs.

Unique Properties of Melanocytes: Proceedings of the International Pigment Cell Conference, Houston, Texas, Jan., 1975. International Pigment Cell Conference Staff. Ed. by V. Riley. (Pigment Cell Ser.: Vol. 3). (Illus.). 1977. 122.50 (3-8055-2371-8) S Karger.

Unique Relationship: The United & the Republic of China under the Taiwan Relations Act. Ed. by Ramon H. Myers. 370p. 1989. 25.95 (0-8179-8871-8); pap. 15.95 (0-8179-8872-6) Hoover Inst Pr.

Unique Science: Demonstrations & Laboratories for the Physics Instructor. E. M. Kinsman & C. Waters. (Illus.). 220p. 1991. pap. 14.00 (0-9630142-0-X) Kinsman Physics.

Unique Services & Your Success. rev. ed. Paul Harris. Ed. by Sally M. Corngold. (Introduction to Behavioral Optometry Ser.). (Illus.). 64p. 1989. reprint ed. pap. text ed. 180.00 (0-943599-06-7) OEPF.

Unique Solutions for Strategic Games. W. Guth & B. Kalkofen. (Lecture Notes in Economics & Mathematical Systems Ser.: Vol. 328). vii, 200p. 1989. 34.70 (0-387-50974-7) Spr-Verlag.

Unique Texas: A Guide to the State's Quirks, Charisma, & Character. Sarah Lovett. LC 93-30384. (Unique Travel Ser.). 112p. (Orig.). 1994. pap. 10.95 (1-56261-145-3) John Muir.

Unique Three-in-One Research & Development Directory: Annual. 640p. 1987. pap. 15.00 (0-318-00176-4) Gov Data Pubns.

*__Unique Voice of Hillary Rodham Clinton: A Portrait in Her Own Words.__ Ed. by Claire G. Osborne. LC 96-46399. 224p. 1997. 18.00 (0-380-97416-9) Avon.

Unique Washington: A Guide to the States Quirks, Charisma, & Character Unique. Tom Barr. LC 94-23407. (Illus.). 112p. 1995. pap. 10.95 (1-56261-192-5) John Muir.

*__Unique Way to Make Money at the Racetrack.__ Ed P. Gambera. (Illus.). 204p. (Orig.). 1996. pap. 20.00 (0-9656580-0-7) Hillsdale Pr.

Unique Woman. Ed Cole & Nancy Cole. 180p. Date not set. pap. 8.99 (1-56292-010-3, HB-010) Honor Bks OK.

Unique Wood Duck: Tableau of a Field Trip with Frank Bellrose & Scott Nielsen. Richard E. McCabe. LC 92-46903. (Illus.). 136p. 1993. pap. 24.95 (0-8117-3099-9) Stackpole.

Unique World of Women. large type ed. Eugenia Price. 1995. 21.95 (0-7838-1194-2, GK Hall) Thorndike Pr.

Uniquely Gifted: Discovering Your Spiritual Gifts. Stuart Calvert. Ed. by Judith Edwards. 140p. (Orig.). 1993. pap. 7.95 (1-56309-061-9, New Hope) Womans Mission Union.

Uniquely Human: The Evolution of Speech, Thought, & Selfless Behavior. Philip Lieberman. LC 90-38130. (Illus.). 210p. 1991. 34.95 (0-674-92182-8, LIEUNI) HUP.

Uniquely Human: The Evolution of Speech, Thought, & Selfless Behavior. Philip Lieberman. (Illus.). 210p. (C). 1993. pap. 14.95 (0-674-92183-6) HUP.

Uniquely Oregon. Larry King. 192p. (C). 1994. spiral bd. 25.14 (0-8403-7326-0) Kendall-Hunt.

Uniquely You Comprehensive Profile: Combining Personalities, Spiritual Gifts, Talents, & Interests. Mels Carbonell. 72p. (Orig.). 1995. pap. text ed. 9.95 (0-9627245-5-6) Uniquely You.

Uniquely Yours: A Collection of over 700 Suggestions to Individualize Your Wedding. Michelle M. Pattarozzi. 104p. 1983. 9.95 (0-317-00911-7) M M Pattarozzi.

Uniqueness: Problem or Paradox in Jewish & Christian Traditions. Gabriel Moran. LC 92-13009. (Faith Meets Faith Ser.). 215p. 1992. 40.00 (0-88344-830-0); pap. 20.00 (0-88344-829-7) Orbis Bks.

Uniqueness: The Human Pursuit of Difference. C. R. Snyder & Howard L. Fromkin. LC 79-18764. (Perspectives in Social Psychology Ser.). (Illus.). 250p. 1980. 39.50 (0-306-40376-5, Plenum Pr) Plenum.

Uniqueness & Diversity in Human Evolution: Morphometric Studies of Australopithecines. Charles E. Oxnard. LC 74-16689. viii, 144p. 1975. lib. bdg. 21.00 (0-226-64253-4) U Ch Pr.

Uniqueness & Nonuniqueness Criteria for Ordinary Differential Equations. Ravi P. Agarwal & V. Lakshmikantham. (Series in Real Analysis). 324p. 1993. text ed. 86.00 (981-02-1357-3) World Scientific Pub.

Uniqueness of Biological Materials. A. Needham & G. A. Kerkut. LC 64-21694. (International Series of Monographs on Pure & Applied Mathematics: Vol. 25). 1965. 268.00 (0-08-010748-6, Pub. by Pergamon Repr UK) Franklin.

Uniqueness of Jesus. Navpress Staff. (Radical Relationships Ser.). 1996. pap. 7.00 (0-89109-863-1) NavPress.

*__Uniqueness of Jesus: A Dialogue with Paul Knitter.__ Ed. by Leonard Swidler & Paul Mojzes. LC 97-11275. (Faith Meets Faith Ser.). (Orig.). 1997. pap. 20.00 (1-57075-123-4) Orbis Bks.

Uniqueness of Jesus: The Life & Teachings of Jesus Introduction. Bill Bright. Ed. by Don Tanner et al. (Ten Basic Steps Toward Christian Maturity Ser.). (Illus.). 80p. (Orig.). 1994. pap. text ed. 5.99 (1-56399-029-6) NewLife Pubns.

Uniqueness of Jesus Christ in the Theocentric Model of the Christian Theology of World Religions: An Elaboration & Evaluation of the Position of John Hick. Gregory H. Carruthers. 378p. (C). 1990. lib. bdg. 53.00 (0-8191-7889-6) U Pr of Amer.

Uniqueness of Man. John Lewis. 1974. 24.95 (0-8464-0948-8) Beekman Pubs.

Uniqueness of the Individual. Peter B. Medawar. 192p. 1981. reprint ed. pap. 6.95 (0-486-24042-8) Dover.

Uniqueness of the Injective III1 Factor. S. Wright. (Lecture Notes in Mathematics Ser.: Vol. 1413). iii, 108p. 1989. 26.50 (0-387-52130-5) Spr-Verlag.

Unit & Bulk Materials Handling: Presented at the Materials Handling Conference, ASME Century 2 - Emerging Technology Conferences, San Francisco, CA, August 19-21, 1980. Materials Handling Conference Staff. Ed. by F. J. Loeffler & C. R. Proctor. LC 80-66042. 297p. reprint ed. pap. 84.70 (0-8357-8772-9, 2033642) Bks Demand.

*__Unit-Based Nursing Staff Development.__ Joan S. Lockhart. 300p. 1997. pap. 42.00 (0-8342-0887-3, 20887) Aspen Pub.

Unit Based Planning: A Guide for the Secondary English Teacher. Susan E. Lake. 135p. (Orig.). (C). 1994. pap. 15.00 (1-881459-10-1) Eagle Pr SC.

Unit Based Quality Assurance: A Patient-Centered Approach. Connington & Hector Dupuis. 180p. 1990. 74.00 (0-8342-0153-4, 20153) Aspen Pub.

Unit Conversions for Scientists, Engineers & Students. Daniel R. Singer & Asha Narayana. 152p. 1992. 9.99 (0-9635043-1-2) U S Enterprises.

*__Unit Cost 96 Environmental Restoration, Vol. 3.__ Ed. by Richard R. Rast. 1997. ring bd. 150.00 (0-87629-456-5, 64017) ACMDG Co.

Unit Costs of Salaries in Teachers College & Normal Schools. Herman J. MaGee. LC 73-177046. (Columbia University. Teachers College. Contributions to Education Ser.: No. 489). reprint ed. 37.50 (0-404-55489-X) AMS Pr.

Unit Fines. Ed. by Chris Bazell & Ian S. Lomax. 60p. 1992. 45.00 (1-85190-177-9, Pub. by Tolley Pubng UK) St Mut.

Unit Groups of Classical Rings. Gregory Karpilovsky. 384p. 1988. 120.00 (0-19-853557-0) OUP.

Unit Histories of the United States Air Forces: Including Privately Printed Personal Narratives & United States Air Force History: a Guide to Documentary Sources. Charles E. Dornbusch & Lawrence J. Paszek. Ed. by James B. Gilbert. LC 79-7247. (Flight: Its First Seventy-Five Years Ser.). (Illus.). 1979. reprint ed. lib. bdg. 28.50 (0-405-12159-8) Ayer.

Unit History 283rd Field Artillery Battalion. 2nd rev. ed. Ed. by Frank H. Armstrong. (Illus.). 91p. 1995. pap. text ed. 17.95 (0-9632448-3-3) Bull Run VT.

*__Unit Issues in Archaeology: Measuring Time, Space & Material.__ Ann F. Ramenofsky. 1997. 55.00 (0-87480-547-3); pap. text ed. 25.00 (0-87480-548-1) U of Utah Pr.

Unit-Load & Package Conveyors: Application & Design. Henry C. Keller. LC 66-21856. (Illus.). 249p. reprint ed. pap. 71.00 (0-317-11121-3, 2012434) Bks Demand.

Unit Management: The Decentralisation of Decision Making. Hans Wissema. 224p. 1992. 105.00 (*0-273-60033-8*, Pub. by Pitman Pubng UK) St Mut.

Unit Manufacturing Processes: Issues & Opportunities in Research. National Research Council, Unit Manufacturing Committee. 228p. (Orig.). (C). 1995. pap. text ed. 39.00 (*0-309-05192-4*) Natl Acad Pr.

Unit Method of Clothing Construction. 7th rev. ed. Phyllis Brackelsberg & Ruth Marshall. LC 89-24710. (Illus.). 288p. (C). 1990. pap. text ed. 29.95 (*0-8138-1711-0*) Iowa St U Pr.

Unit of Measure. Marilyn R. Rosenberg. 18p. 1977. pap. 8.00 (*0-913615-04-8*) Marilyn R Rosenberg.

Unit Operations & Processes in Environmental Engineering. Reynolds. 1982. text ed. 63.50 (*0-8185-0493-5*) PWS Pubs.

Unit Operations & Processes in Environmental Engineering. 2nd ed. Reynolds. 1996. text ed. 80.95 (*0-534-94884-7*) Wadsworth Pub.

Unit Operations for the Food Industries. Wilber A. Gould. 192p. 1995. 74.00 (*0-930027-29-9*, 027299) CTI Pubns.

Unit Operations Handbook, Vol. 1. Ed. by John J. McKetta. LC 92-25562. 1017p. 1992. 175.00 (*0-8247-8669-6*) Dekker.

Unit Operations Handbook, Vol. 2. Ed. by John J. McKetta. LC 92-25562. 742p. 1992. 175.00 (*0-8247-8670-X*) Dekker.

Unit Operations in Cane Sugar Production. J. H. Payne. (Sugar Technology Ser.: Vol. 4). 204p. 1982. 157.50 (*0-444-42104-1*) Elsevier.

Unit Operations in Chemical Engineering. 5th ed. Warren L. McCabe et al. LC 92-36218. (McGraw-Hill Chemical Engineering Ser.). 1993. text ed. write for info. (*0-07-044844-2*) McGraw.

Unit Operations in Environmental Engineering. Ed. by Robert Noyes. LC 94-1324. (Illus.). 498p. 1994. 76.00 (*0-8155-1343-7*) Noyes.

Unit Operations Models for Solid Waste Processing. George M. Savage. LC 86-5154. (Pollution Technology Review Ser.: No. 133). (Illus.). 214p. 1986. 36.00 (*0-8155-1086-1*) Noyes.

Unit Operations of Sanitary Engineering. Linvil G. Rich. LC 61-15410. (C). 1961. pap. 20.00 (*0-686-11818-9*) Rich SC.

Unit Origami: Multidimensional Transformations. Tomoko Fuse. (Illus.). 240p. (Orig.). 1990. pap. 19.00 (*0-87040-852-6*) Japan Pubns USA.

Unit Pricing for Dressmaking. Karen Howland. 39p. 1994. pap. 10.00 (*0-9648964-0-0*) Kensinger.

Unit Processes in Drinking Water Treatment. Willy J. Masschelein. LC 92-20757. (Environmental Science & Pollution Ser.: Vol. 3). 656p. 1992. 210.00 (*0-8247-8678-5*) Dekker.

Unit Processes in Hydrometallurgy: Papers, Dallas, Texas, February 24-28, 1963. Ed. by Milton E. Wadsworth & Franklin T. Davis. LC 65-7413. (Metallurgical Society Conference Ser.: Vol. 24). 1008p. reprint ed. pap. 180.00 (*0-317-10396-2*, 2001512) Bks Demand.

Unit Processes of Sanitary Engineering. Linvil G. Rich. LC 63-14067. (C). 1963. pap. 20.00 (*0-686-15000-7*) Rich SC.

Unit Six-George-Ninety, Signal Forty-Four: Oh God, Please Tell Me Where You Are. Laurie Balbach-Taylor. LC 94-70554. 96p. (Orig.). 1994. pap. 4.50 (*1-880033-13-5*) Faith Pub OH.

Unit Study Book. Valerie Bendt. 105p. 1993. reprint ed. spiral bd. 14.00 (*1-880892-43-X*) Com Sense FL.

Unit Study Journal: Record Keeping for All Unit Studies. Amanda Bennett. (Unit Study Adventures Ser.). 88p. 1996. pap. text ed. 7.99 (*1-888306-02-5*, Home School Pr) GCB.

***Unit Study Planning Workbook Vol. 1.** Beverly L. Adams-Gordon. 164p. 1996. wbk. ed. 17.95 (*1-888827-17-3*) Castlemoyle Bks.

Unit, Symbols & Terminology for Plant Physiology: A Reference for the Presentation of Research Results in the Plant Science. Frank B. Salisbury. (Illus.). 256p. 1996. pap. 29.95 (*0-19-509445-X*) OUP.

Unit Treatment Processes in Water & Wastewater Engineering. T. J. Casey. LC 96-15921. (Series in Water Resources Engineering). 1996. pap. text ed. 72.95 (*0-471-96693-2*) Wiley.

Unit Two Thousand: A Nursing Unit Design Symposium Addressing Patient Beds for the Future. Ed. by Kirkham R. Hamilton. 391p. 1993. 35.00 (*0-9636950-0-2*) W C H Architects.

Unit 731: Testimony: Japan's Wartime Human Experimentation & the Post-War Cover-Up. Hal Gold. 1995. pap. text ed. 9.95 (*4-900737-39-9*, Pub. by Yen Bks JA) C E Tuttle.

Unitarian Conscience. Daniel W. Howe. LC 75-116737. 1970. 15.00 (*0-674-92121-6*) HUP.

Unitarian Conscience: Harvard Moral Philosophy, 1805-1861. Daniel W. Howe. LC 87-34089. 415p. 1988. pap. 19.95 (*0-8195-6201-7*, Wesleyan Univ Pr) U Pr of New Eng.

Unitarian Controversy: Essays on American Unitarian History. Conrad Wright. 256p. 1994. pap. 19.00 (*1-55896-290-5*, Skinner Hse Bks) Unitarian Univ.

Unitarian Universalism. Alan W. Gomes. (Zondervan Guide to Cults & Religious Movements Ser.). 96p. 1996. pap. 5.99 (*0-310-48891-5*) Zondervan.

Unitarian Universalism & the Quest for Racial Justice. 280p. 1993. pap. 10.00 (*1-55896-318-9*) Unitarian Univ.

Unitarian Universalist Pocket Guide. 2nd ed. Ed. by William F. Schulz. LC 93-22694. 1994. pap. 4.00 (*1-55896-319-7*, Skinner Hse Bks) Unitarian Univ.

Unitarian Universalist Poets: A Contemporary American Survey. Ed. by Jennifer Bosveld et al. 208p. (Orig.). 1996. per. 18.95 (*0-614-10187-5*) Pudding Hse Pubns.

Unitarianism in America. George W. Cooke. LC 72-155153. reprint ed. 34.50 (*0-404-01699-5*) AMS Pr.

Unitarians & India: A Study in Encounter & Response. 3rd ed. Spencer Lavan. LC 90-86029. (Illus.). 217p. 1991. reprint ed. pap. 18.95 (*0-913552-46-1*) Exploration Pr.

Unitarians & the Universalists. David Robinson. LC 84-9031. (Denominations in America Ser.: No. 1). xiii, 368p. 1985. text ed. 45.00 (*0-313-20946-4*, RUN/) Greenwood.

Unitarians & the Universalists. David Robinson. LC 84-9031. (Denominations in America Ser.: No. 1). xiii, 368p. 1985. pap. text ed. 39.95 (*0-313-24893-1*, RUNPB) Greenwood.

Unitary Dilations of Hilbert Space Operators & Related Topics. B. Sz-Nagy. LC 73-17332. (CBMS Regional Conference Series in Mathematics: No. 19). 54p. 1974. reprint ed. pap. 22.00 (*0-8218-1669-1*, CBMS/19) Am Math.

Unitary Representation Theory for Solvable Lie Groups. Jonathan Brezin. LC 52-42839. (Memoirs Ser.: No. 79). 122p. 1968. pap. 16.00 (*0-8218-1279-3*, MEMO/1/79) Am Math.

Unitary Representation Theory of Exponential Lie Groups. Horst Leptin & Jean Ludwig. LC 94-27983. (Expositions in Mathematics Ser.: Vol. 18). 210p. (C). 1994. lib. bdg. 98.95 (*3-11-013938-3*) De Gruyter.

Unitary Representations & Harmonic Analysis. 2nd ed. M. Sugiura. (North-Holland Mathematical Library: No. 44). 452p. 1990. 178.50 (*0-444-88593-5*, North Holland) Elsevier.

Unitary Representations of Maximal Parabolic Subgroups of the Classical Groups. J. A. Wolf. LC 76-44397. (Memoirs Ser.: No. 8/180). 193p. 1976. pap. 23.00 (*0-8218-2180-6*, MEMO/8/180) Am Math.

Unitary Representations of Reductive Lie Groups. David A. Vogan, Jr. Ed. by William Browder et al. (Annals of Mathematics Studies: No. 118). 319p. 1988. text ed. 75.00 (*0-691-08481-5*); pap. text ed. 35.00 (*0-691-08482-3*) Princeton U Pr.

Unitary Representations of Solvable Lie Groups. Louis Auslander & C. C. Moore. (Memoirs Ser.: No. 1/62). 199p. 1990. reprint ed. pap. 19.00 (*0-8218-1262-9*, MEMO/1/62) Am Math.

Unitary Representations of the Poincare Group & Relativistic Wave Equations. Y. Ohnuki. 228p. (C). 1988. text ed. 54.00 (*9971-5-0250-X*) World Scientific Pub.

Unitary Representations on Partially Holomorphic Cohomology Spaces. Joseph A. Wolf. LC 73-21505. (Memoirs Ser.: No. 1/138). 152p. 1974. pap. 18.00 (*0-8218-1838-4*, MEMO/1/138) Am Math.

Unitas: Building Healing Communities for Children. Edward P. Eismann. xiii, 210p. (Orig.). 1996. pap. 22.50 (*0-8232-1686-1*) Fordham.

Unitas: Hispanic & Black Children in a Healing Community. Anne Farber & Lloyd H. Rogler. 128p. 1982. 18.95 (*0-87073-505-5*); pap. 11.95 (*0-87073-506-3*) Schenkman Bks Inc.

Unite & Conquer. Murphy & Sapir. (Destroyer Ser.: Vol. 102). 1996. mass mkt. 4.99 (*0-373-63217-7*, 1-63217-3, Wrldwide Lib) Harlequin Bks.

Unite d'Habitation: Marseilles 1945-52 Le Corbusier. David Jenkins. (Architecture in Detail Ser.). (Illus.). 60p. (C). 1993. pap. 29.95 (*0-7148-2770-3*, Pub. by Phaidon Press UK) Chronicle Bks.

Unite d'Habitation, Reze-les-Nantes. Ed. by H. Allen Brooks. LC 83-9074. (Le Corbusier Archieve Ser.). 1983. lib. bdg. 95.00 (*0-8240-5070-3*) Garland.

Unite Monetaire Europeenne: Au Profit De Qui? see European Monetary Unity: For Whose Benefit?

Unite (1942-1944) see Memoires de Guerre

UNITECR 'Eighty-Nine Proceedings, Vol. 1. UNITECR '89 Staff. Ed. by L. J. Trostel, Jr. (Illus.). 945p. reprint ed. pap. 180.00 (*0-7837-4338-6*, 2044049) Bks Demand.

UNITECR 'Eighty-Nine Proceedings, Vol. 2. UNITECR '89 Staff. Ed. by L. J. Trostel, Jr. (Illus.). 950p. reprint ed. pap. 180.00 (*0-7837-4339-4*, 2044049) Bks Demand.

United American Healthcare Corporation Collection. Luisa W. Chapman. LC 93-61338. (Illus.). 84p. (Orig.). 1994. pap. text ed. 24.95 (*0-8143-2532-7*) Wayne St U Pr.

United & Separate Parliaments. Andrew Fletcher. 34p. 1985. 20.00 (*0-85411-025-9*, Pub. by Saltire Soc) St Mut.

United & Uniting: The Meaning of An Ecclesial Journey (United Church of Christ 1957-1987) Louis H. Gunneman. LC 87-14718. 224p. 1987. pap. 12.95 (*0-8298-0757-8*) Pilgrim OH.

United Arab Emirates. Frank A. Clements. (World Bibliographical Ser.: No. 43). 161p. 1983. lib. bdg. 45.00 (*0-903450-74-7*) ABC-CLIO.

United Arab Emirates. Julia Johnson. (Let's Visit Places & Peoples of the World Ser.). (Illus.). 96p. (J). (gr. 5 up). 1988. lib. bdg. 19.95 (*1-55546-178-6*) Chelsea Hse.

United Arab Emirates: An Economic & Social Survey. 2nd ed. Kevin G. Fenelon. LC 75-42139. 170p. reprint ed. pap. 48.50 (*0-685-16374-1*, 2027712) Bks Demand.

United Arab Emirates: Heritage & Modern Development. Peter Vine et al. 160p. (C). 1995. 105.00 (*0-907151-85-X*, Pub. by IMMEL Pubng UK) St Mut.

United Arab Republic-Egypt. Ed. by Donald N. Wilber et al. LC 68-22208. (Area & Country Surveys Ser.). 479p. 1969. 20.00 (*0-87536-927-8*) HRAFP.

United Artists. S. X. Rosenstock. Ed. by Richard Howard. (James Dickey Contemporary Poetry Ser.). 70p. 1996. pap. 9.95 (*1-57003-131-2*); text ed. 15.95 (*1-57003-130-4*) U of SC Pr.

United Artists: The Company Built by the Stars. Tino Balio. LC 75-12208. (Illus.). 344p. 1976. 16.95 (*0-299-06940-0*) U of Wis Pr.

United Artists: The Company Built by the Stars. Tino Balio. LC 75-12208. (Illus.). 344p. 1979. pap. 14.95 (*0-299-06944-3*) U of Wis Pr.

United Artists: The Company That Changed the Film Industry. Tino Balio. LC 87-40138. (Illus.). 496p. 1987. text ed. 19.95 (*0-299-11440-6*) U of Wis Pr.

United Arts Fundraising: 1989 Campaign Analysis. Ed. by Amy Segal. 55p. (Orig.). 1989. pap. 28.00 (*0-685-38222-2*, ACA Bks) Am Council Arts.

United Arts Fundraising in the 1990s: Serving the Community Arts System in an Era of Change. James L. Shanahan. LC 93-9496. 1993. 15.95 (*1-879903-13-X*) Am Council Arts.

United Arts Fundraising, 1990. Ed. by Amy Segal. (Illus.). 55p. (Orig.). 1991. pap. 28.00 (*1-879903-00-8*, ACA Bks) Am Council Arts.

United Arts Fundraising 1991. Anita McGlynn. (Illus.). 58p. (Orig.). 1992. spiral bd. 100.00 (*1-879903-08-3*) Am Council Arts.

United Brotherhood of Carpenters: The First Hundred Years. Walter Galenson. (Wertheim Publications in Industrial Relations). (Illus.). 454p. 1983. 27.50 (*0-674-92196-8*) HUP.

United Church of Christ: Studies in Identity & Polity. Ed. by Dorothy C. Bass & Kenneth B. Smith. LC 86-83022. (Studies in Ministry & Parish Life). 107p. (C). 1987. text ed. 22.95 (*0-913552-37-2*) Exploration Pr.

United Church of Christ Hymnal. Ed. by John Ferguson & William Nelson. LC 74-12571. 1974. Pew Edition. 10.95 (*0-8298-4141-5*); spiral bd. 16.00 (*0-8298-0300-9*) Pilgrim OH.

United Empire Loyalists. Arthur G. Bradley. LC 75-136413. (BCL Ser. I). reprint ed. 20.00 (*0-404-00927-1*) AMS Pr.

United Empire Loyalists: Enquiry into the Losses & Services in Consequence of Their Loyalty, Evidence in Canadian Cliams, Second Report of the Bureau of Archives for the Province of Ontario, 2 vols., Set. Alexander Fraser. 1994. 87.50 (*0-614-03812-X*, 2065) Genealog Pub.

United for a Better World. Carol A. Wehrheim. LC 94-41696. (Illus.). (J). (gr. 3-5). 1995. pap. 3.95 (*0-377-00294-1*) Friendship Pr.

United for Kids. Life Touch Nation School Studio Staff. (Illus.). 56p. 1991. teacher ed., pap. 8.95 (*0-943535-13-1*) Primarius Ltd.

United Front: The TUC & the Russians, 1923-1928. Daniel F. Calhoun. LC 75-23486. (Soviet & East European Studies). 462p. reprint ed. pap. 131.70 (*0-317-20618-4*, 2024572) Bks Demand.

United Fruit Company in Latin America. National Planning Association Staff. Ed. by Stuart Bruchey & Eleanor Bruchey. LC 76-5023. (American Business Abroad Ser.). (Illus.). 1976. reprint ed. 31.95 (*0-405-09290-3*) Ayer.

United Germany: The Past, Politics, Prospects. H. G. Wallach & Ronald A. Francisco. LC 91-39645. (Contributions in Politicel Science Ser.: No. 297). 192p. 1992. text ed. 55.00 (*0-313-27619-6*, WPA/, Greenwood Pr); pap. text ed. 15.95 (*0-275-94288-0*, B4288, Greenwood Pr) Greenwood.

United Germany & the United States. Michael A. Freney & Rebecca S. Hartley. LC 91-60520. (Committee on Changing International Realities Ser.: No. 21). 178p. (Orig.). 1991. pap. text ed. 17.50 (*0-89068-107-4*, CIR 21 (NPA250)) Natl Planning.

United Germany the First Five Years: Performance & Policy Issues. Robert Corker et al. LC 95-18140. (Occasional Paper Ser.: No. 125). 1995. 15.00 (*1-55775-472-1*) Intl Monetary.

United Government & Foreign Policy in Russia, 1900-1914. David M. McDonald. 276p. (C). 1992. 45.00 (*0-674-92239-5*) HUP.

United in Christ. Josephine Clemson. (C). 1988. 45.00 (*0-85439-196-7*, Pub. by St Paul Pubns UK) St Mut.

United in His Name: Jesus in Our Midst in the Writings of Chiara Lubich. Judith Povilus. Tr. by Jerry Hearne from ITA. 160p. (Orig.). 1992. pap. 8.95 (*1-56548-003-1*) New City.

United in Marriage: A Guide to Premarital Counseling. Richard T. Ulyat. 47p. 1984. pap. 4.75 (*0-86544-023-9*) Salv Army Suppl South.

United in Service: Reflections on the Presbyteral Council. National Conference of Catholic Bishops Staff. 20p. (Orig.). (C). 1992. pap. 1.95 (*1-55586-482-1*) US Catholic.

***United Irishmen: Republicanism, Radicalism & Rebellion.** David Dickson & Daire Keogh. 378p. 9300. pap. 31.95 (*1-874675-19-8*) Dufour.

United Jerusalem: The Story of Ateret Cohanim. Ann Johnson. LC 92-21906. 1992. 25.00 (*0-88125-424-X*) Ktav.

United Keetoowah Band of Cherokee Indians in Oklahoma. Georgia R. Leeds. LC 95-36888. (American University Studies XI: Vol. 67). 320p. (C). 1997. 49.95 (*0-8204-2720-9*) P Lang Pubng.

United Kingdom? E. Ellis Cashmore. 208p. 1989. text ed. 44.95 (*0-04-305014-X*) Routledge Chapman & Hall.

United Kingdom. David Flint. LC 93-13610. (Country Fact Files Ser.). (J). 1994. lib. bdg. 24.26 (*0-8114-1849-9*) Raintree Steck-V.

United Kingdom: Medical Laboratory Science, Occupational Therapy, Physiotherapy. Alan M. Margolis & Thomas J. Monahan. LC 79-49614. (World Education Ser.). 192p. reprint ed. pap. 54.80 (*0-8357-7534-8*, 2036247) Bks Demand.

***United Kingdom: Racist Violence in the United Kingdom.** 102p. (Orig.). 1997. pap. 10.00 (*1-56432-202-5*) Hum Rts Watch.

United Kingdom Air Arms 1993. Mach III Plus Staff. (C). 1993. 30.00 (*0-9515462-7-9*, Pub. by Mach III Plus UK) St Mut.

United Kingdom & EC Membership Evaluated. Ed. by Simon Bulmer et al. LC 91-41425. (EC Membership Evaluated Ser.). 300p. 1992. text ed. 55.00 (*0-312-07917-6*) St Martin.

***United Kingdom Balance of Payments: The Pink Book, 1996.** Central Statistical Office Staff. 80p. 1996. pap. 60.00 (*0-11-620776-0*, HM07760, Pub. by Stationery Ofc UK) Bernan Associates.

United Kingdom Balance of Payments "The Pink Book" 1994. Central Statistical Office Staff. 80p. 1994. pap. 30.00 (*0-11-620651-9*, HM06519, Pub. by Stationery Ofc UK) Bernan Associates.

***United Kingdom Bistros, Bars & Cafes 1997.** Egon Ronay Staff. (Travel Guides 1997 Ser.). (Illus.). 416p. (Orig.). 1997. pap. 14.95 (*1-898718-54-7*, Pub. by Ringpr Bks UK) Seven Hills Bk.

United Kingdom Business Finance Directory 1990. 544p. 1990. 265.00 (*0-685-49075-0*, 100769-99584, Pub. by Graham & Trotman UK) Gale.

United Kingdom Card Decks: Rates & Data. (Illus.). 76p. (Orig.). (C). 1993. pap. text ed. 50.00 (*1-56806-381-4*) DIANE Pub.

United Kingdom Confronts the European Convention on Human Rights: A Liberal State Confronts the European Convention on Human Rights. Donald W. Jackson. LC 96-21379. 224p. 1997. lib. bdg. 49.95 (*0-8130-1487-5*) U Press Fla.

U. K. Economics Decline: Key Texts. David Coates. Ed. by John Hillard. LC 95-12507. 1995. pap. text ed. 43.00 (*0-13-342775-7*) P-H.

U. K. Economy Today. Ken Holden et al. LC 94-41832. 1995. text ed. 39.95 (*0-7190-4306-9*, Pub. by Manchester Univ Pr UK); text ed. 15.00 (*0-7190-4307-7*) St Martin.

U. K. Environmental Policy in the 1990s. Tim S. Gray. LC 95-5580. 1995. text ed. 75.00 (*0-312-12672-7*) St Martin.

United Kingdom Financial System: Theory & Practice. 2nd ed. M. J. Buckle & J. L. Thompson. 336p. 1996. text ed. 24.95 (*0-7190-4816-8*, Pub. by Manchester Univ Pr UK) St Martin.

United Kingdom Financial System in Transition: Theory & Practice. M. Buckle & John L. Thompson. 304p. 1992. text ed. 75.00 (*0-7190-3028-5*, Pub. by Manchester Univ Pr UK) St Martin.

***United Kingdom-Hong Kong: Recent Economic Developments.** Bankim Chadha. (IMF Staff Country Report Ser.: Vol. 96/29). 102p. pap. 29.10 (*0-608-04853-4*, 2065512) Bks Demand.

***United Kingdom Hotels & Restaurants 1997.** Egon Ronay Staff. (Travel Guides 1997 Ser.). (Illus.). 1008p. (Orig.). 1997. pap. 24.95 (*1-898718-44-X*, Pub. by Ringpr Bks UK) Seven Hills Bk.

United Kingdom, Human Rights Concerns. 66p. 1991. 6.00 (*0-939994-66-6*) Amnesty Intl USA.

***United Kingdom National Accounts: The Blue Book, 1996.** HMSO Staff. 144p. 1996. pap. 60.00 (*0-11-620777-9*, HM07779, Pub. by Stationery Ofc UK) Bernan Associates.

United Kingdom National Accounts "The Blue Book," 1993. HMSO Staff. 144p. 1993. pap. 30.00 (*0-11-620598-9*, HM05989, Pub. by Stationery Ofc UK) Bernan Associates.

United Kingdom National Accounts "The Blue Book" 1994. HMSO Staff. 144p. 1994. pap. 35.00 (*0-11-620652-7*, HM06527, Pub. by Stationery Ofc UK) Bernan Associates.

United Kingdom Oil & Gas Fields: Twenty-Five Years Commemorative Volume. Ed. by I. L. Abbotts. (Geological Society Memoirs Ser.: No. 14). (Illus.). 582p. 1991. 134.00 (*0-903317-62-1*, 265, Pub. by Geol Soc Pub Hse UK) AAPG.

United Kingdom Publications & Theses on Africa, 1963. Standing Conference On Library Materials Staff. 94p. 1966. pap. 35.00 (*0-7146-2992-8*, Pub. by F Cass Pubs UK) Intl Spec Bk.

United Kingdom Publications & Theses on Africa, 1964. Standing Conference On Library Materials Staff. 89p. 1966. pap. 35.00 (*0-7146-2993-6*, Pub. by F Cass Pubs UK) Intl Spec Bk.

United Kingdom Publications & Theses on Africa, 1965. Standing Conference On Library Materials Staff. 92p. 1967. pap. 35.00 (*0-7146-2994-4*, Pub. by F Cass Pubs UK) Intl Spec Bk.

United Kingdom Publications & Theses on Africa, 1966. Standing Conference On Library Materials Staff. 96p. 1969. pap. 35.00 (*0-7146-2995-2*, Pub. by F Cass Pubs UK) Intl Spec Bk.

United Kingdom Publications & Theses on Africa, 1967-1968. Standing Conference On Library Materials Staff. 1968. pap. 15.00 (*0-7146-2998-7*, Pub. by F Cass Pubs UK) Intl Spec Bk.

***United Kingdom Pubs & Inns 1997: Pubs & Inns.** Egon Ronay Staff. (Travel Guides 1997 Ser.). (Illus.). 504p. (Orig.). 1997. pap. 19.95 (*1-898718-49-0*, Pub. by Ringpr Bks UK) Seven Hills Bk.

United Kingdom Sea Fishery Statistics: Sea Fisherues Stat Yables 1994. 90p. 1995. pap. text ed. 30.00 (*0-11-243001-5*, HM30015, Pub. by Stationery Ofc UK) Bernan Associates.

***United Kingdom Sea Fishery Statistics 1995.** 90p. 1996. pap. 45.00 (*0-11-243018-X*, HM3018X, Pub. by Stationery Ofc UK) Bernan Associates.

United Kingdom Securities & Investments Regulation Handbook. Ed. by Peter Farmery & Keith Walmsley. LC 92-13555. (International Securities & Investments Regulation Ser.). 1992. Set. write for info. (*1-85333-738-2*, Pub. by Graham & Trotman UK); write for info. (*1-85333-632-7*, Pub. by Graham & Trotman UK) Kluwer Ac.

UV

United Kingdom Taxation on the Profits from North Sea Oil. Ed. by Waterhouse Staff. (C). 1990. lib. bdg. 134.50 (*1-85333-397-2*, Pub. by Graham & Trotman UK) Kluwer Ac.

***United Kingdom 1995-1996.** 160p. 1996. 26.00 (*92-64-14874-4*, 10-96-28-1, Pub. by Org for Econ FR) OECD.

***United Lutheran Church in America, 1918-1962.** E. Theodore Bachmann et al. LC 97-20819. 1997. write for info. (*0-8006-2925-6*, Fortress Pr) Augsburg Fortress.

United Methodism in America: A Compact History. Ed. by John G. McEllhenney et al. 160p. (Orig.). 1992. pap. 10.95 (*0-687-43170-0*) Abingdon.

United Methodist Altars: A Guide for the Local Church. Hoyt L. Hickman. LC 83-21554. 96p. 11.85 (*0-687-42985-4*) Abingdon.

United Methodist Alters. 2nd ed. Hoyt L. Hickman. 112p. (Orig.). 1996. pap. 10.95 (*0-687-00562-0*) Abingdon.

United Methodist Book of Worship. Ed. by Andy Langford. LC 92-28537. 1992. 24.95 (*0-687-03572-4*) Abingdon.

United Methodist Book of Worship. deluxe ed. Ed. by Andy Langford. LC 92-28537. 1992. lthr. 49.95 (*0-687-03573-2*) Abingdon.

***United Methodist Book of Worship: Accompanist Edition.** 1996. 9.95 (*0-687-03574-0*) Abingdon.

***United Methodist Book of Worship: Pastor's Pocket Edition.** 1996. 14.95 (*0-687-03575-9*) Abingdon.

United Methodist Doctrine. Thomas F. Chilcote. LC 89-51191. 80p. 1990. pap. 5.95 (*0-88177-080-9*, DR080) Discipleship Res.

United Methodist Heritage Book. General Commission Archives & History, the United Methodist Church Staff. 1994. pap. 4.10 (*1-55673-829-3*) CSS OH.

***United Methodist Hymnal: Pew Edition.** 1996. lthr. 64.95 (*0-687-43156-5*) Abingdon.

***United Methodist Hymnal: Pew Edition, Black.** 1996. bond lthr. 36.95 (*0-687-43140-9*) Abingdon.

***United Methodist Hymnal: Pew Edition, Bright Red.** 1996. 14.00 (*0-687-43134-4*) Abingdon.

***United Methodist Hymnal: Pew Edition, Bright Red.** large type ed. 1996. 15.95 (*0-687-43154-9*) Abingdon.

***United Methodist Hymnal: Pew Edition, Dark Red.** 1996. 14.00 (*0-687-43133-6*) Abingdon.

***United Methodist Hymnal: Pew Edition, Dark Red.** 1996. bond lthr. 36.95 (*0-687-43145-X*) Abingdon.

***United Methodist Hymnal: Pew Edition, Dark Red.** large type ed. 1996. 15.95 (*0-687-43143-3*) Abingdon.

***United Methodist Hymnal: Pew Edition, Gray.** 1996. 17.50 (*0-687-43136-0*) Abingdon.

***United Methodist Hymnal: Pew Edition, Green.** 1996. 17.50 (*0-687-43135-2*) Abingdon.

***United Methodist Hymnal: Pew Edition, Ivory.** 1996. 17.50 (*0-687-43137-9*) Abingdon.

***United Methodist Hymnal: Pew Edition, Maroon.** 1996. 17.50 (*0-687-43138-7*) Abingdon.

***United Methodist Hymnal: Pew Edition, Navy Blue.** 1996. 14.00 (*0-687-43132-8*) Abingdon.

***United Methodist Hymnal: Pew Edition, Navy Blue.** 1996. bond lthr. 36.95 (*0-687-43144-1*) Abingdon.

***United Methodist Hymnal: Pew Edition, Navy Blue.** large type ed. 1996. 15.95 (*0-687-43153-0*) Abingdon.

***United Methodist Hymnal: Pew Edition, Purple.** 1996. 14.00 (*0-687-43139-5*) Abingdon.

***United Methodist Hymnal: Pew Edition, Purple.** large type ed. 1996. 15.95 (*0-687-43155-7*) Abingdon.

***United Methodist Music & Worship Planner, 1996-97.** 1996. spiral bd. 15.95 (*0-687-10951-5*) Abingdon.

United Methodist Primer. 3rd ed. Chester E. Custer. LC 85-73470. 112p. (Orig.). 1986. pap. 5.95 (*0-88177-024-8*, DR024) Discipleship Res.

***United Methodist Studies: Basic Bibliographies.** 4th ed. Ed. & Compiled by Kenneth E. Rowe. (Wesleyan/Methodist Studies). 1996. pap. 9.95 (*0-687-24994-5*) Abingdon.

United Methodist Studies, Basic Bibliographies. 3rd ed. Kenneth E. Rowe. 96p. 1992. pap. 7.95 (*0-687-43165-4*) Abingdon.

***United Methodist Worship.** Hoyt L. Hickman. 112p. 5.95 (*0-687-43196-4*) Abingdon.

***United Mind Workers: Unions & Teaching in the Knowledge Society.** Charles T. Kerchner et al. LC 97-4636. (Education Ser.). 1997. write for info. (*0-7879-0829-0*) Jossey-Bass.

United Mine Workers of America: A Model of Industrial Solidarity? Ed. by John M. Laslett. LC 95-39732. 1996. 65.00 (*0-271-01537-3*) Pa St U Pr.

United Nations. LC 96-45364. (At Issue Ser.). (J). (gr. 5-12). 1996. pap. 8.96 (*1-56510-547-8*) Greenhaven.

United Nations. LC 96-45364. (At Issue Ser.). (J). (gr. 5-12). 1996. lib. bdg. 14.96 (*1-56510-548-6*) Greenhaven.

United Nations. Ann Armbruster. (First Bks.). (Illus.). 64p. (J). (gr. 4-6). 1995. lib. bdg. 21.00 (*0-531-20201-1*) Watts.

United Nations. R. Conrad Stein. LC 93-37030. (Cornerstones of Freedom Ser.). (Illus.). 32p. (J). (gr. 3-6). 1994. lib. bdg. 18.00 (*0-516-06677-3*) Childrens.

United Nations. Adam Woog. LC 93-3767. (Overview Ser.). (J). (gr. 5-8). 1994. lib. bdg. 17.96 (*1-56006-145-6*) Lucent Bks.

***United Nations: A Family of Nations?: A Seminar on the Address of His Holiness Pope John Paul II to the United Nations Organization: Trusteeship Council Chamber, United Nations Headquarters, New York City, Wednesday, 8 May 1996.** Catholic Church Staff & Path to Peace Foundation Staff. LC 96-28118. 1996. pap. 20.00 (*0-9651613-1-5*) Path to Peace.

United Nations: A Pictorial Book. (Illus.). 32p. 1987. 4.95 (*92-1-002050-2*) UN.

United Nations: A Place of Promise & of Mischief. Richard S. Williamson. 248p. (C). 1990. pap. text ed. 23.50 (*0-8191-7951-5*, Hudson Instit IN); lib. bdg. 41.50 (*0-8191-7950-7*, Pub. by Hudson Inst) U Pr of Amer.

United Nations: A Working Paper for Restructuring. Harold Stassen. LC 93-47910. (Illus.). 128p. 1994. pap. 14.95 (*0-8225-3149-6*, Lerner Publctns) Lerner Group.

United Nations: Background, Organization, Functions, Activities. Amry Vandenbosch. LC 70-100183. 456p. 1970. reprint ed. text ed. 75.00 (*0-8371-4050-1*, VAUN, Greenwood Pr) Greenwood.

United Nations: Constitutional Developments, Growth & Possibilities. Benjamin V. Cohen. LC 61-16691. (Oliver Wendell Holmes Lectures: 1961). 116p. 1961. 20.00 (*0-674-92265-4*) HUP.

United Nations: Disarmament & Security, Evolution & Prospects. 155p. Date not set. 26.00 (*92-9045-054-1*, E. GV.91.0.13) UN.

United Nations: How It Works & What It Does. 2nd ed. Evan Luard. Ed. by Derek Heater & Pauline Williamson. LC 93-15601. 1994. text ed. 15.95 (*0-312-10060-4*) St Martin.

United Nations: International Organization & World Politics. Robert E. Riggs & Jack C. Plano. 399p. (C). 1988. pap. text ed. write for info. (*0-534-10804-0*) HarBrace.

United Nations: International Organization & World Politics. 2nd ed. Robert E. Riggs & Jack C. Plano. 364p. (C). 1993. pap. text ed. 38.25 (*0-534-19704-3*) HarBrace.

United Nations: Issues of Peace & Conflict, 1989: The Study & Background Guide, Set. Ed. by Daniel S. Papp & John Diehl. LC 89-64408. 1990. 60.00 (*0-935082-15-8*) Southern Ctr Intl Stud.

United Nations: Law, Policies & Practice. rev. ed. Ed. by Rudiger Wolfrum & Christiane Philipp. LC 95-11889. 1995. lib. bdg. 304.00 (*0-7923-2717-9*, Pub. by M Nijhoff NE) Kluwer Ac.

United Nations: Organizations That Help the World. Michael Pollard. (YA). 1995. pap. 7.95 (*0-382-24764-7*, New Dscvry Bks) Silver Burdett Pr.

United Nations: Structure & Functions of an International Organization. Rumki Basu. (C). 1993. text ed. 40.00 (*81-207-1472-5*, Pub. by Sterling Pubs II) Apt Bks.

***United Nations: The First Fifty Years.** Stanley Meisler. 416p. 1997. reprint ed. pap. 15.00 (*0-87113-656-2*, Atlntc Mnthly) Grove-Atltic.

***United Nations: The First 25 Years.** Date not set. 15.95 (*0-8464-4428-3*) Beekman Pubs.

United Nations: Towards the Fiftieth Anniversary. Geoff Simons. LC 93-48287. 1994. text ed. 49.95 (*0-312-12134-2*) St Martin.

***United Nations: U. S. Participation in the Fourth World Conference on Women.** (Illus.). 65p. (Orig.). (C). 1996. pap. 25.00 (*0-7881-3228-8*) DIANE Pub.

United Nations see Strategy of World Order

United Nations Action in the Field of Human Rights. 389p. 37.00 (*92-1-154043-7*, E.83.XIV.2) UN.

United Nations Action in the Field of Human Rights. 359p. 1988. 80.00 (*92-1-154067-4*, E.88.XIV.2) UN.

United Nations Action in the Field of Human Rights. 417p. 1994. 80.00 (*92-1-154107-7*) UN.

United Nations & Afghanistan Crisis. Mohammed Khaliq Ma'aroof. 1990. 40.00 (*81-7169-044-0*, Commonwealth) S Asia.

***United Nations & Apartheid.** Boutros Boutros-Ghali. 220p. 1996. pap. 29.95 (*92-1-100614-7*, 71474) UN.

United Nations & Apartheid 1948-1994. United Nations Staff. (United Nations Blue Bks.: Vol. I). 565p. (Orig.). 1995. 29.95 (*92-1-100546-9*, E.95.1.7) UN.

United Nations & Cambodia, 1991-1995, Vol.II. United Nations Staff. (United Nations Blue Bks.: Vol. II). 360p. 1995. 29.95 (*92-1-100548-5*, E.95.I.9) UN.

United Nations & Changing World Politics. Thomas G. Weiss et al. LC 94-16161. (C). 1994. pap. text ed. 22.00 (*0-8133-1761-4*) Westview.

***United Nations & Changing World Politics.** 2nd ed. Thomas G. Weiss & Roger A. Coate. LC 97-15192. 6p. (C). 1997. pap. text ed. 22.95 (*0-8133-9962-9*) Westview.

United Nations & Civil Wars. Ed. by Thomas G. Weiss. (Emerging Global Issues Ser.). 360p. 1995. lib. bdg. 43.00 (*1-55587-527-0*) Lynne Rienner.

United Nations & Collective Management of International Conflict. 73p. 1992. 20.00 (*0-685-52978-9*) UN.

United Nations & Decision-Making: The Role of Women, 2 vols., I. 10.00 (*92-1-157012-3*, E.78.XV.CR/10) UN.

United Nations & Decision-Making: The Role of Women, 2 vols., II. 12.00 (*92-1-157010-7*, E.78.XV.CR/11) UN.

United Nations & Dependent Peoples: A Greenwood Archival Edition. Emil J. Sady. LC 74-4730. 205p. 1974. reprint ed. text ed. 69.50 (*0-8371-7483-X*, SAUN, Greenwood Pr) Greenwood.

United Nations & Disarmament: Nineteen Forty-Five to Nineteen Eighty-Five. 1986. 22.50 (*0-685-13460-1*, E. 85.IX.6); pap. 16.95 (*92-1-142112-8*) UN.

United Nations & Drug Abuse Control. 102p. 12.00 (*92-1-100428-4*, E.90.I.3) UN.

United Nations & Drug Abuse Control. 100p. 1992. 12.00 (*92-1-100502-7*, E.92I.31) UN.

United Nations & El Salvador, 1990-1995. The United Nations Staff. (United Nations Blue Bks.: Vol. IV). 611p. 1995. 29.95 (*92-1-100552-3*, E.95.1.12) UN.

United Nations & Electoral Assistance. (United Nations Blue Bks.). 1996. pap. write for info. (*92-1-100601-5*, E. 96.I.7) UN.

United Nations & Foreign Military Interventions: A Comparative Study of the Application of the Charter. 2nd ed. Ramses Amer. 314p. (Orig.). 1994. pap. 68.00 (*91-90610-27-X*, Pub. by Uppsala Universitet SW) Coronet Bks.

United Nations & Haiti. (United Nations Blue Bks.). 1996. pap. write for info. (*92-1-100606-6*, E.96.I.11) UN.

United Nations & Human Rights. James F. Green. (Brookings Institution Reprint Ser.). 1958. reprint ed. lib. bdg. 39.50 (*0-697-00155-5*) Irvington.

United Nations & Human Rights: A Critical Appraisal. Ed. by Philip Alston. 784p. 1995. pap. 45.00 (*0-19-826001-6*) OUP.

United Nations & Human Rights, 1945-1995, Vol. 7. United Nations Staff. (United Nations Blue Bks.: Vol. VII). 536p. 1995. 29.95 (*92-1-100560-4*, JX1977) UN.

United Nations & International Business. Sidney Dell. LC 89-27999. 204p. (C). 1990. text ed. 29.95 (*0-8223-0957-2*) UN.

***United Nations & International Law.** 2nd ed. Ed. by Christopher C. Joyner. 450p. (C). 1997. text ed. 64.95 (*0-521-58379-9*) Cambridge U Pr.

***United Nations & International Law.** 2nd ed. Ed. by Christopher C. Joyner. 450p. (C). 1997. pap. text ed. 24.95 (*0-521-58659-3*) Cambridge U Pr.

United Nations & International Law. Brian Urquhart. LC 87-4503. (Rede Lecture Ser.: No. 1985). 22p. reprint ed. pap. 25.00 (*0-318-34672-9*, 2031738) Bks Demand.

United Nations & International Peacekeeping. Agostinho Zacarias. 204p. 1996. text ed. 59.50 (*1-86064-065-6*, Pub. by I B Tauris UK) St Martin.

United Nations & Mozambique, 1992-1995. Intro. by Boutros Boutros-Ghali. (United Nations Blue Bks.: Vol. V). 321p. 1995. 29.95 (*92-1-100559-0*, E.95.1.20) UN.

United Nations & NATO Force Structure & Military Operations in the Mediterranean. 52p. (Orig.). (C). 1994. pap. text ed. 25.00 (*0-7881-1243-0*) DIANE Pub.

United Nations & Nuclear Non-Proliferation Treaty. The United Nations Staff. (United Nations Blue Bks.: Vol. III). 200p. 1995. 29.95 (*92-1-100557-4*, E.95.I.17) UN.

***United Nations & Rwanda, 1993-1996.** Ed. by Boutros Boutros-Ghali. (United Nations Blue Bks.: Vol. X). 739p. 1996. pap. text ed. 29.95 (*92-1-100561-2*, E.96.I.20) UN.

United Nations & Somalia, 1992-1996. United Nations Staff. (United Nations Blue Bks.: VIII). 518p. 1996. pap. 29.95 (*92-1-100566-3*, E.96.I.8) UN.

United Nations & the Advancement of Women, 1945 - 1996. Intro. by Boutros Boutros-Ghali. (United Nations Blue Bks.: Vol. VI). 852p. 1996. pap. 49.95 (*92-1-100603-1*, E.96.I.9) UN.

United Nations & the Advancement of Women, 1945-1995. (United Nations Blue Bks.: Vol. VI). 689p. 1995. 29.95 (*92-1-100567-1*) UN.

United Nations & the Bretton Woods Institutions: New Challenges for the Twenty-First Century. Ed. by Mahbub ul Haq et al. LC 94-36892. 1995. text ed. 55.00 (*0-312-12449-X*); text ed. 19.95 (*0-312-12450-3*) St Martin.

United Nations & the Control of International Violence: A Legal & Political Analysis. John F. Murphy. LC 81-69989. 224p. 1983. text ed. 53.00 (*0-86598-079-9*) Rowman.

United Nations & the Independence of Eritrea. (Blue Bks.: Vol. 12). 1996. pap. 29.95 (*92-1-100605-8*, E.96.I.10) UN.

United Nations & the International Tribunals for the Former Yugoslavia & Rwanda. (United Nations Blue Bks.). 1996. pap. write for info. (*92-1-100598-1*, E.96. I.5) UN.

***United Nations & the Iran-Iraq War.** R. P. King. 39p. 1996. reprint ed. pap. 20.00 (*0-7881-3002-1*) DIANE Pub.

United Nations & the Iraq-Kuwait Conflict, 1990-1996. (United Nations Blue Bks.: Vol. 9). 844p. 1996. 49.95 (*92-1-100596-5*, E.96.I.3) UN.

United Nations & the Maintenance of International Peace & Security. 73p. 1986. 20.00 (*92-1-157092-1*) UN.

United Nations & the Maintenance of International Peace & Security. N. D. White. (Melland Schill Monographs in International Law). 1990. text ed. 59.95 (*0-7190-3227-X*, Pub. by Manchester Univ Pr UK) St Martin.

United Nations & the Maintenance of International Security: A Challenge to Be Met. James S. Sutterlin. LC 94-40038. 160p. 1995. text ed. 57.95 (*0-275-95052-2*, Praeger Pubs); pap. text ed. 16.95 (*0-275-95053-0*, Praeger Pubs) Greenwood.

United Nations & the Quest for Nuclear Disarmament. Dimitris Bourantonis. 218p. 1993. 59.95 (*1-85521-344-3*, Pub. by Dartmth Pub UK) Ashgate Pub Co.

United Nations & the Super-Powers: China, Russia, & America. 4th ed. John G. Stoessinger. 1977. pap. text ed. write for info. (*0-07-553679-X*) McGraw.

***United Nations & the United States.** Ostrower. 1998. 26.95 (*0-8057-7937-X*) Mac Lib Ref.

United Nations & the World's Religions: Proceedings of a Conference Held October 7, 1994, at Columbia University. Ed. by Nancy Hodes & Michael Hays. 141p. (Orig.). 1995. pap. text ed. 7.00 (*1-887917-00-4*) Boston RCFT-FC.

United Nations & Transnational Organized Crime. Ed. by Philip Williams & Ernesto U. Savona. 208p. (C). 1996. 37.50 (*0-7146-4733-0*, Pub. by F Cass Pubs UK); pap. 19.50 (*0-7146-4283-5*, Pub. by F Cass Pubs UK) Intl Spec Bk.

United Nations Archives, New York: United Nations War Crimes Commission. Ed. by George J. Lankevich. LC 89-16915. (Archives of the Holocaust Ser.: Vol. 16). 400p. 1990. reprint ed. text ed. 100.00 (*0-8240-5498-9*) Garland.

United Nations As a Dispute Settlement System: Improving Mechanisms for the Prevention & Resolution of Conflict. Connie Peck. LC 96-18022. (Legal Aspects of International Organization Ser.: Vol. 29). 1996. write for info. (*90-411-0248-5*) Kluwer Law Tax Pubs.

United Nations As a Political Institution. 5th ed. H. G. Nicholas. 272p. 1975. pap. 16.95 (*0-19-519826-3*) OUP.

United Nations at Age Fifty: A Legal Perspective. Ed. by Christian Tomuschat. (Legal Aspects of International Organization Ser.: Vol. 23). 327p. 1996. 130.00 (*90-411-0145-4*) Kluwer Law Tax Pubs.

***United Nations at Fifty: Retrospect & Prospect.** Ed. by Ramesh Thakur. 334p. 1996. pap. 39.95 (*1-877133-03-5*, Pub. by U Otago Pr NZ) Intl Spec Bk.

United Nations at Fifty: Sovereignty, Peacekeeping, & Human Rights. Ed. by Don M. Snider & Stuart J. Schwartzstein. LC 95-15805. (Report Ser.). 74p. (Orig.). (C). 1995. pap. 10.95 (*0-89206-268-1*) CSI Studies.

United Nations at Forty: A Foundation to Build On. 160p. 1985. 15.00 (*0-685-50215-5*) UN.

United Nations at the Crossroads of Reform. Wendell Gordon. LC 94-19451. (Studies in Institutional Economics). 296p. (gr. 13). 1994. pap. 24.95 (*1-56324-401-2*) M E Sharpe.

United Nations at the Crossroads of Reform. Wendell Gordon. LC 94-19451. (Studies in Institutional Economics). 296p. (C). (gr. 13). 1994. 58.95 (*1-56324-400-4*) M E Sharpe.

United Nations at Work: The Challenge of Building Global Peace. Amy Edwards et al. LC 95-1895. 32p. (YA). (gr. 7-12). 1995. pap. 6.95 (*0-932765-63-7*, 1665-95) Close Up Fnd.

United Nations Bibliographic Information Systems Thesaurus, English Edition: Trilingual List (English, French, Spanish) of Terms Used in Subject Analysis of Documents & Other Materials Relevant to United. . . 3rd ed. 758p. 1995. 65.00 (*92-1-100573-6*) UN.

United Nations Code of Conduct on Transnational Corporations. (UNCTC Current Studies A: No. 4). 80p. 1986. pap. 9.50 (*92-1-104191-0*, E.86.II.A.15) UN.

United Nations Code of Conduct on Transnational Corporations. UN Centre on Transnational Corporations Staff. (C). 1988. pap. text ed. 48.50 (*1-85333-085-X*, Pub. by Graham & Trotman UK) Kluwer Ac.

United Nations Commission on International Trade Law: Case Law on Uncitral Text. 47p. 1994. 15.00 (*92-1-133475-6*, E.94.V.8) UN.

United Nations Commission on International Trade Law: Case Law on UNcitral Text: Abstracts of Case 4 & 5. 19p. 1995. 15.00 (*92-1-133479-9*, E.95.V.1) UN.

United Nations Commission on International Trade Law: UNCITRAL. 199p. 1987. 15.00 (*92-1-133284-2*, E.86. V.8) UN.

United Nations Commission on International Trade Law Vol. 25: Yearbook 1994. 446p. 1994. 60.00 (*92-1-133500-0*) UN.

United Nations Commission on International Trade Law Yearbook, 14 bks., Set. LC 94-78586. 1994. 1,250.00 (*0-89941-905-4*, 308430) W S Hein.

United Nations Commission on International Trade Law Yearbook: 1986, Vol. XVII. 1988. 54.00 (*92-1-133307-5*, E.88.V.4) UN.

***United Nations Commission on International Trade Law, Yearbook Vol. 26: 1995.** 399p. 1997. pap. 60.00 (*92-1-133510-8*, K1005) UN.

United Nations Commission on International Trade Law Yearbook, 1987, Vol. XVIII. 50.00 (*92-1-133317-2*) UN.

United Nations Commission on International Trade Law, Yearbook, 1988, Vol. XIX. 228p. 50.00 (*92-1-133321-0*, E.89.V.8) UN.

United Nations Commission on International Trade Law Yearbook, 1989, Vol. XX. 280p. 1989. 50.00 (*92-1-133402-0*, 90.V.9) UN.

United Nations Compensation Commission: 13th Sokol Colloquium. Ed. by Richard B. Lillich. LC 94-44756. 486p. 1995. 95.00 (*0-941320-73-1*) Transnatl Pubs.

United Nations Conference for the Adoption of a Convention Against Illicit Traffic in Narcotic Drug & Psychotropic Substances. Vienna, 25 November-20 December 1988, Vol.I. 221p. Date not set. 45.00 (*92-1-148092-2*, E.94.XI.5) UN.

United Nations Conference for the Adoption of a Convention Against Illicit Traffic in Narcotic Drugs & Psychtropic Substance, Vol.II. 333p. Date not set. 50.00 (*92-1-148084-1*, E.94,XI.5) UN.

United Nations Conference on Environment & Development: Process & Documentation. Shanna L. Halpern. (Reports & Papers 1993: No. 2). 60p. (C). 1993. pap. text ed. 10.00 (*1-880660-05-9*) Acad Coun UN Syst.

United Nations Conference on Human Settlements, Vancouver, B. C., 1976: Human Settlements, National Reports: Summaries & Reference Guides. International Institute for Environment & Development (I.I.E.D.) Staff. Ed. by Signe R. Ottersen. LC 76-14569. 1976. pap. 69.00 (*0-08-021243-3*, Pergamon Pr) Elsevier.

***United Nations Conference on Straddling Fish Stocks & Highly Migratory Fish Stocks: Selected Documents.** Jean-Pierre Levy & Gunnar G. Schram. LC 96-28964. 1996. lib. bdg. 322.00 (*90-411-0270-1*, Pub. by M Nijhoff NE) Kluwer Ac.

United Nations Conference on Succession of States in Respect of State Property, Archives & Debts. 461p. Date not set. 45.00 (*92-1-133467-5*, E.94.V.6) UN.

United Nations Conference on the Carriage of Goods by Sea, Official Records. 434p. 26.00 (*92-1-139014-1*) UN.

United Nations Conference on the Liability of Operations of Transport Terminals in International Trade. 219p. 1993. 25.00 (*92-1-148089-2*, E.93.V.14) UN.

United Nations Conference on the Standardization of Geographical Names, Vol. II, No. 5. 477p. 1990. 50.00 (*92-1-002053-7*, 90.I.21) UN.

UV

An Asterisk (*) at the beginning of an entry indicates that the title is appearing in BIP for the first time.

United Nations Conference on the Standardization of Geographical Names: 6th Conference, Vol. I. 61p. Date not set. 12.00 (*92-1-100516-7*, E.93.I.23) UN.

United Nations Conference on the Standardization of Geographical Names, Vol. I: Report of the 5th Conference. 101p. 1988. 12.00 (*92-1-100326-1*, E.88.I.7) UN.

United Nations Conference on the Standardization of Geographical Names, 4th: Report of the Conference, Vol. 1. 79p. 1983. pap. text ed. 10.00 (*92-1-100124-2*, E.83.1.7) UN.

United Nations Conference on the Standardization of Geographical Names, 4th: Technical Papers. Geneva, 24 August-14 September 1982, Vol. II. 409p. 1987. 45.50 (*92-1-002049-9*, E/F/S.86.I.21) UN.

United Nations Conference on Trade & Development: Rules of Procedure. 2nd rev. ed. 37p. 1987. 10.00 (*92-1-112230-9*, E.87.II.D.4) UN.

United Nations Conflict Management: An Institutionalist Perspective. Signe Burgstaller. (Illus.). 91p. (Orig.). (C). 1995. pap. text ed. 25.00 (*0-7881-2177-4*) DIANE Pub.

United Nations Congress on the Prevention of Crime & the Treatment of Offenders: 8th Report. 282p. 1991. 20.00 (*92-1-130143-2*) UN.

United Nations Congress on the Prevention of Crime & the Treatment of Offenders - The 7th Report. 182p. 16.50 (*92-1-130108-4*) UN.

United Nations Conspiracy: Wars, Police Actions, Growing Instability, an Epidemic of Terrorism, Hostility to American Ideals, & Decline in America's Influence. 1991. lib. bdg. 75.00 (*0-8490-5099-5*) Gordon Pr.

United Nations Convention Against Illicit Traffic in Narcotic Drugs & Psychotropic Substances. 29p. 1991. pap. 15.00 (*92-1-148083-3*) UN.

United Nations Convention on Contracts for the International Sale of Goods. 192p. 1993. 25.00 (*92-1-033070-6*, M.93.V.4) UN.

United Nations Convention on Contracts for the International Sale of Goods. 29p. 1995. 29.00 (*92-1-133492-6*, E.95.V.12) UN.

United Nations Convention on International Bills of Exchange & International Promissory Notes. 44p. 1995. 7.50 (*92-1-133496-9*, E.95.V.16) UN.

United Nations Convention on the Carriage of Goods by Sea, 1978 (Hamburg Rules) 20p. 1995. 7.50 (*92-1-133494-2*, E.95.V.14) UN.

United Nations Convention on the Elimination of All Forms of Racial Dicrimination. Natan Lerner. LC 80-51738. 278p. 1980. lib. bdg. 87.50 (*90-286-0160-0*) Kluwer Ac.

United Nations Convention on the Law of the Sea. 2nd ed. Ed. by Shabtai Rosenne & Louis B. Sohn. (C). 1989. lib. bdg. 225.50 (*90-247-3719-2*) Kluwer Ac.

United Nations Convention on the Law of the Sea 1982. Ed. by Myron H. Nordquist. 1985. lib. bdg. 233.00 (*90-247-3145-3*) Kluwer Ac.

United Nations Convention on the Law of the Sea, 1982: A Commentary Volume II Article 1 to 85 Annexes I & II Final Act, Annex II. Ed. by Myron H. Nordquist. 1088p. (C). 1993. lib. bdg. 253.00 (*0-7923-2471-4*) Kluwer Ac.

United Nations Convention on the Law of the Sea, 1982 & the Agreement Relating to the Implementation of Part XI of the Convention, 1994, Set. Ed. by Kenneth R. Simmonds & Brian H. Hill. 30p. 1995. boxed, ring bd. 80.00 incl. disk (*1-898029-12-1*, Pub. by Simmonds & Hill Pubng UK) Gaunt.

United Nations Convention on the Law of the Sea, 1982, Vol. IV: A Commentary, Articles 192 to 278 Final Act, Annex VI. Ed. by Myron H. Nordquist. (C). 1990. lib. bdg. 271.00 (*0-7923-0764-X*) Kluwer Ac.

United Nations Convention on the Liability of Operators of Transport Terminals in International Trade. 20p. 1995. 7.50 (*92-1-133495-0*, E.95.V.15) UN.

United Nations Convention on the Limitation Period in the International Sale of Goods. 17p. 1995. 7.50 (*92-1-133493-4*, E.95.V.13) UN.

United Nations Correspondece Manual: A Compendium of Rules Relating to the Drafting, Typing & Dispatch of Official United Nations Communications. LC 84-46787. 108p. 9.00 (*92-1-100253-2*, E.84.I.11) UN.

United Nations Crime Prevention & Criminal Justice Program: Formulation of Standards & Efforts at Their Implementation. Roger S. Clark. (Procedural Aspects of International Law Ser.). 352p. (C). 1994. text ed. 47.50 (*0-8122-3269-0*) U of Pa Pr.

***United Nations Curriculum Guide.** UNA of USA Staff. 240p. 1996. per., pap. text ed. 35.00 (*0-7872-2586-X*) Kendall-Hunt.

United Nations Decade for Women World Conference. Ed. by Naomi B. Lynn. LC 84-4559. (Women & Politics Ser.: Vol. 4, No. 1). 93p. 1984. text ed. 32.95 (*0-86656-150-1*) Haworth Pr.

United Nations Decade of International Law: Reflections on International Dispute Settlement. Ed. by Marcel Brus. 168p. (C). 1991. lib. bdg. 102.50 (*0-7923-1220-1*) Kluwer Ac.

United Nations Decision Making. John Kaufmann. 300p. 1980. lib. bdg. 53.00 (*90-286-0410-3*) Kluwer Ac.

United Nations Disability Statistics Data Base, 1975-1986: Technical Manual. 86p. 1988. pap. 10.00 (*92-1-161298-5*, E.88.XVII.12) UN.

***United Nations Disarmament Yearbook.** 329p. 1996. pap. text ed. 50.00 (*92-1-142218-3*, JX1901) UN.

United Nations Disarmament Yearbook, 18. 419p. 1994. 50.00 (*92-1-142204-3*) UN.

United Nations Disarmament Yearbook, Vol. 10. 577p. 1985. pap. 35.00 (*92-1-142121-7*, E.86.IX.7) UN.

United Nations Disarmament Yearbook, Vol. 11, 1986. 492p. 1987. 37.50 (*92-1-142129-2*, E.87.IX.1) UN.

United Nations Disarmament Yearbook, Vol. 15. 549p. 1991. 45.00 (*92-1-142170-5*, 91.IX.8) UN.

United Nations Disarmament Yearbook, Vol. 16. 513p. 1991. 45.00 (*92-1-142182-9*, E.92.IX.1) UN.

United Nations Disarmament Yearbook, Vol. 17. 392p. 1992. 50.00 (*92-1-142193-4*, E.93.IX.1) UN.

United Nations Disarmament Yearbook, 1987, Vol. 12. (ENG, FRE & SPA.). 1988. pap. 37.50 (*92-1-142136-5*, E.88.IX.2) UN.

United Nations Disarmament Yearbook, 1988, Vol. 13. 461p. 45.00 (*92-1-142148-9*, E.89.IX.5) UN.

United Nations Disarmament Yearbook, 1989, Vol. 14. 463p. 1989. 45.00 (*92-1-142154-3*, 90.IX.4) UN.

United Nations Disarmament Yearbook, 1994, Vol. 19. 376p. 1995. pap. 50.00 (*92-1-142214-0*, UN95 9 1) UN.

United Nations, Divided World: The U. N.'s Roles in International Relations. 2nd ed. Ed. by Adam Roberts & Benedict Kingsbury. 396p. 1994. pap. 22.00 (*0-19-827926-4*) OUP.

United Nations Document Series Symbols, 1978-1984. 168p. 1985. 18.50 (*92-1-100281-8*, E.85.I.21) UN.

United Nations Documentation: A Basic Guide. Marian Shaaban & Robert Goehlert. (MacArthur Scholar Series, Occasional Paper: No. 16). 96p. (Orig.). 1993. pap. 3.00 (*1-881157-17-2*) In Ctr Global.

United Nations Editorial Manual. 532p. 1983. 50.00 (*92-1-100185-4*, E.83.1.16) UN.

United Nations Efforts to Control Arms in Outer Space: A Brief History with Key Documents. P. K. Menon. LC 87-24727. (Studies in World Peace: Vol. 1). 212p. 1989. lib. bdg. 89.95 (*0-88946-587-8*) E Mellen.

***United Nations Electoral Assistance & the Evolving Right to Democratic Governance.** Timothy C. Evered. 79p. (Orig.). 1996. pap. 10.00 (*1-881520-05-6*) Ctr U N Reform Educ.

United Nations Emergency Force: Basic Documents. Compiled by E. Lauterpacht. (International & Comparative Law Quarterly Supplement Publication Ser.: No. 3). 1974. reprint ed. pap. 25.00 (*0-8115-3194-5*) Periodicals Srv.

United Nations Fiftieth Anniversary Book. Barbara Brenner. LC 94-12784. (J). (gr. 3-7). 1995. text ed. 19.95 (*0-689-31912-6*) Macmillan.

***United Nations for the Twenty-First Century: Peace, Security & Development.** Dimitris Bourantonis & Marios L. Evriviades. LC 96-48835. 1997. 235.00 (*90-411-0312-0*) Kluwer Law Tax Pubs.

United Nations General Assembly & Disarmament 1985. 309p. 1987. 30.00 (*92-1-142126-8*, E.86.IX.11) UN.

United Nations General Assembly & Disarmament, 1986. 229p. 1987. 23.50 (*92-1-142132-2*, E.87.IX.6) UN.

United Nations General Assembly & Disarmament, 1988. 207p. 21.00 (*92-1-142149-7*, E.89.IX.6) UN.

United Nations General Assembly & Disarmament, 1989. 250p. 1990. 21.00 (*92-1-142155-1*, 90.IX.5) UN.

United Nations General Assembly Resolutions in Our Changing World. Blaine Sloan. 592p. (C). 1991. lib. bdg. 95.00 (*0-941320-55-3*) Transnatl Pubs.

United Nations High Commissioner for Refugees. Leslie Burger & Debra L. Rahm. LC 95-45058. (J). 1996. lib. bdg. 16.13 (*0-8225-2699-9*) Lerner Group.

United Nations High Commissioner for Refugees. Jean Trier. LC 94-5772. (Organizations That Help the World Ser.). 64p. (J). 1995. lib. bdg. 13.95 (*0-02-726335-5*, New Dscvry Bks) Silver Burdett Pr.

United Nations High Commissioner for Refugees. Jean Trier. LC 94-5772. (Organizations That Help the World Ser.). (Illus.). 64p. (J). (gr. 6 up). 1995. pap. 7.95 (*0-382-24982-8*, New Dscvry Bks) Silver Burdett Pr.

United Nations in a New World Order. Edwin M. Smith et al. LC 93-50867. (Keck Center for International & Strategic Studies: No. 6). viii, 91p. 1994. pap. 10.95 (*0-930607-17-1*) Keck Ctr.

United Nations in a Turbulent World. James N. Rosenau. LC 91-45522. (International Peace Academy Occasional Paper Ser.). 88p. 1992. pap. text ed. 8.95 (*1-55587-330-8*) Lynne Rienner.

United Nations in Action. Sohn. 1968. pap. text ed. 18.50 (*0-88277-401-8*) Foundation Pr.

United Nations in Action. David J. Whittaker. LC 95-20701. (Illus.). 288p. (gr. 13). 1995. 69.95 (*1-56324-742-9*) M E Sharpe.

United Nations in Action. David J. Whittaker. LC 95-20701. (Illus.). 288p. (gr. 13). 1995. pap. text ed. 24.95 (*1-56324-743-7*) M E Sharpe.

United Nations in Bangladesh. Thomas W. Oliver. LC 77-85554. 253p. 1978. reprint ed. pap. 72.20 (*0-7837-9408-8*, 2060153) Bks Demand.

United Nations in New World Order: The World Organization at Fifty. Ed. by Dimitris Bourantonis & Jarrod Wiener. 230p. 1996. text ed. 19.95 (*0-312-16118-2*) St Martin.

***United Nations in the Contemporary World.** David J. Whittaker. LC 97-2973. (Making of the Contemporary World Ser.). 120p. (C). 1997. pap. write for info. (*0-415-15317-4*) Routledge.

United Nations in the New World Order: The World Organization at Fifty. Dimitrs Bourantonis & Jarrod Wiener. LC 94-48398. 1995. text ed. 45.00 (*0-312-12617-4*) St Martin.

United Nations in the Post-Cold War Era. Karen A. Mingst & Margaret P. Karns. Ed. by George A. Lopez. LC 95-5657. (Dilemmas in World Politics Ser.). (Illus.). 200p. (C). 1995. pap. text ed. 15.95 (*0-8133-2261-8*) Westview.

United Nations in the World Political Economy: Essays in Honour of Leon Gordenker. Ed. by David P. Forsythe. LC 89-30610. (International Political Economy Ser.). 300p. 1989. text ed. 45.00 (*0-312-03106-8*) St Martin.

United Nations in the 1990s. Peter R. Baehr & Leon Gordenker. LC 93-39269. 1994. text ed. 49.95 (*0-312-12070-2*) St Martin.

United Nations Industrial Development Organization: UNIDO & Problems of International Industrial Development. Youry Petchenkine. LC 93-2859. 224p. 1993. text ed. 59.95 (*0-275-94496-4*, C4496, Praeger Pubs) Greenwood.

United Nations International Court of Justice Yearbook: 1946-1994, 14 bks., Set, Vols. 1-48. 1996. reprint ed. 1, 795.00 (*1-57588-098-9*, 310440) W S Hein.

United Nations, Iran, & Iraq: How Peacemaking Changed. Cameron R. Hume. LC 93-26951. 292p. 1994. 31.50 (*0-253-32874-8*) Ind U Pr.

United Nations Juridical Yearbook, 13 bks., Set. LC 94-77940. 1994. 1,365.00 (*0-89941-901-1*, 308440) W S Hein.

United Nations Juridical Yearbook: 1985 Edition. 239p. 1992. 49.00 (*92-1-133415-2*) UN.

United Nations Juridical Yearbook: 1986 Edition. 412p. 1994. 55.00 (*92-1-133457-8*) UN.

United Nations Juridical Yearbook: 1990 Edition. 389p. 1993. 55.00 (*92-1-133438-1*) UN.

United Nations Juridical Yearbook, 1982. 282p. 1989. 40. 00 (*92-1-133314-8*, 89.V.1) UN.

***United Nations Juridical Yearbook, 1991.** 449p. 1996. pap. text ed. 55.00 (*92-1-133499-3*) UN.

United Nations Law. 2nd ed. Sohn. 1967. text ed. 36.00 (*0-88277-399-2*) Foundation Pr.

United Nations Law: Basic Documents Supplement. 2nd ed. Sohn. 1967. pap. text ed. 13.00 (*0-88277-400-X*) Foundation Pr.

United Nations Law Making: Cultural & Ideological Relativism & International Law for an Era of Transition. Edward McWhinney. 310p. (C). 1984. 34.50 (*0-8419-0948-2*); pap. 24.50 (*0-8419-1008-1*) Holmes & Meier.

United Nations Legal Order Vols. 1 & 2, 2 vols., Set. Ed. by Oscar Schachter & Christopher Joyner. 900p. (C). 1995. 190.00 (*0-521-46522-2*) Cambridge U Pr.

United Nations Library on Transnational Corporations: International Business & the Development of the World Economy, 20 vols., Set. Ed. by John Dunning. 8275p. (C). 1994. text ed. 2,995.00 (*0-415-08559-4*, B4705) Routledge.

United Nations List of National Parks & Protected Areas, 1993 - Liste des Nations Unies des Parcs Nationaux & des Aires Protegees, 1993. World Conservation Monitoring Centre Staff & IUCN Commission on National Parks & Protected Areas. 313p. (Orig.). (FRE.). 1994. pap. 30.00 (*2-8317-0190-2*, Pub. by IUCN SZ) Island Pr.

United Nations Mission in El Salvador: A Humanitarian Law Perspective. Tathiana F. Acuna. LC 95-37528. (Nijhoff Law Specials Ser.: Vol. 14). 1995. pap. text ed. 92.00 (*90-411-0123-3*) Kluwer Ac.

United Nations of Time Square. Bruce Benderson. LC 87-42542. 24p. 1987. pap. 3.00 (*0-87376-056-5*) Red Dust.

***United Nations Past, Present & Future.** LC 96-38074. 1996. pap. text ed. 88.00 (*90-411-0337-6*) Kluwer Ac.

United Nations Peacekeeper of American Policies & Uncivilizations. Durch. LC 96-34880. 1996. text ed. 49. 95 (*0-312-12930-0*) St Martin.

United Nations Peacekeeping: Information Notes. 244p. Date not set. 19.95 (*92-1-137028-0*, E.95.VII.1) UN.

United Nations Peacekeeping after Suez: UNEF 1 - The Swedish Involvement. Nils Skold. 256p. 1996. text ed. 55.00 (*0-312-12819-3*) St Martin.

United Nations Peacekeeping & the Non-Use of Force. F. T. Liu. LC 92-6760. (International Peace Academy Occasional Paper Ser.). 47p. 1992. pap. text ed. 6.95 (*1-55587-337-5*) Lynne Rienner.

United Nations Peacemaking: The Conciliation Commission for Palestine. David P. Forsythe. LC 71-181557. 222p. reprint ed. pap. 63.30 (*0-317-42329-0*, 2025814) Bks Demand.

United Nations Philately, 2 vols. Ed. by Arleigh Gaines. (Illus.). 1200p. 1990. Set. 99.00 (*0-685-45866-0*) R & D Pubns.

United Nations Philately. 16th rev. ed. Arleigh Gaines. (Illus.). 1500p. 1996. ring bd. 129.00 (*0-938152-05-X*) R & D Pubns.

United Nations Reference Guide in the Field of Human Rights. 124p. 1993. 25.00 (*92-1-154097-6*) UN.

United Nations Regional Cartographic Conference for Asia & the Pacific: Bangkok, 17-28 January 1983, Vol. II. 813p. 1987. 75.00 (*92-1-000067-6*, E/F.86.I.11) UN.

United Nations Regional Cartographic Conference for Asia & the Pacific: 12th Conference. 54p. Date not set. pap. 12.00 (*92-1-100539-6*, E.94.I.19) UN.

United Nations Regional Cartographic Conference for Asia & the Pacific, 10th, Vol. I. 42p. 1992. 6.00 (*92-1-100107-2*) UN.

United Nations Regional Cartographic Conference for the Americas: 4th Conference, Vol. II. 133p. Date not set. 25.00 (*92-1-100469-1*, T.92.I.2) UN.

United Nations Regional Cartographic Conference for the Americas: 5th Conference, Vol. I. 31p. Date not set. pap. 7.50 (*92-1-100521-3*, E.94.I.4) UN.

United Nations Regional Cartographic Conference for the Americas, 4th Conference, Vol. I. 7.50 (*92-1-100413-6*) UN.

United Nations Regional Cartographic Conference for the Fourth Americas: 3rd Conference, Vol. I. 64p. 8.50 (*92-1-100271-0*) UN.

United Nations Regional Cartographic Conference(s) for Asia & the Pacific, Vol. II: Eleventh Conference: Technical Papers. 1987. 39.50 (*92-1-000068-4*, EF.88.I.18) UN.

United Nations Representatives, Foreign Ambassadors to the United States: Names, Addresses, Phone & FAX Numbers. rev. ed. Ed. by Rick Lawler. 36p. (Orig.). 1996. pap. 6.75 (*0-9624394-3-6*) MinRef Pr.

United Nations Resolutions on Palestine & the Arab-Israeli Conflict: 1987-1991. Ed. by Jody Boudreault. (U. N. Resolutions on Palestine & the Arab-Israeli Conflict Ser.: Vol. 4). (Orig.). (C). 1993. text ed. 29.95 (*0-88728-240-7*); pap. text ed. 19.95 (*0-88728-241-5*) Inst Palestine.

United Nations Resolutions on Palestine & the Arab-Israeli Conflict, 1947-74, Vol. 1. George J. Tomeh. LC 88-2791. 294p. 1988. 29.95 (*0-88728-161-3*); pap. 19.95 (*0-88728-171-0*) Inst Palestine.

United Nations Resolutions on Palestine & the Arab-Israeli Conflict, 1975-81, Vol. 2. Ed. by Regina Sharif. LC 88-2791. 333p. 1988. 29.95 (*0-88728-162-1*); pap. 19.95 (*0-88728-172-9*) Inst Palestine.

United Nations Resolutions on Palestine & the Arab-Israeli Conflict, 1982-1986, Vol. 3. Ed. by Michael Simpson. LC 88-2791. 340p. 1988. pap. 19.95 (*0-88728-173-7*); text ed. 29.95 (*0-88728-163-X*) Inst Palestine.

United Nations' Role in World Affairs: A Renewed Role in World Affairs. Ed. by Donald Altschiller. LC 93-21142. (Reference Shelf Ser.: Vol. 65, No. 2). 1993. 15.00 (*0-8242-0841-2*) Wilson.

United Nations' Search for a Definition of Aggression. Nicolas Nyiri. (American University Studies: Political Science: Ser. X, Vol. 22). 412p. (C). 1989. text ed. 53.95 (*0-8204-0869-7*) P Lang Pubng.

United Nations Secretariat, Vol. 4. Wallace S. Sayre. LC 78-2884. (Carnegie Endowment for International Peace, United Nations Studies: No. 4). 96p. 1978. reprint ed. text ed. 45.00 (*0-313-20331-8*, UNNS) Greenwood.

United Nations Security Council. 19p. 1989. pap. 5.00 (*92-1-100421-7*) UN.

United Nations Security Council Official Records, 31st Year. Incl. Meeting Number 1941 - July 12, 1976. 21p. 1985. 4.00 (*0-685-43467-2*); Meeting Number 1942 - July 13, 1976. 24p. 1985. 4.00 (*0-685-43468-0*); Meeting Number 1954 - August 31, 1976. 10p. 1985. 3.00 (*0-317-41002-4*); Meeting Number 1957 - September 30, 1976. 13p. 1985. 3.00 (*0-317-41005-9*); 1985. write for info. (*0-318-60318-7*) UN.

United Nations Security Council Reform & Restructuring. Walter Hoffmann. (CURE Monographs: No. 14). 77p. 1994. pap. text ed. 5.00 (*1-881520-04-8*) Ctr U N Reform Educ.

United Nations Statement of Treaties & Agreements Annual Cumulation, 10 bks., Set. Igor I. Kavass. 1996. reprint ed. 1,050.00 (*1-57588-097-0*, 310450) W S Hein.

United Nations Studies, 11 vols. Carnegie Endowment for International Peace Staff. 1980. text ed. 495.00 (*0-313-20320-2*, UNSS, Greenwood Pr) Greenwood.

United Nations System: An Annotated Bibliography. Compiled by Joseph P. Baratta. LC 94-41759. (International Organizations Ser.: Vol. 10). 1995. 89.95 (*1-56000-216-6*) Transaction Pubs.

United Nations System: Monographs and Articles in Collective Volumes 1976-1980, 5. 420p. 1993. 195.00 (*3-598-11111-8*) K G Saur.

***United Nations System & Its Predecessors: Basic Documents, Vol. I.** Ed. by Volker Rittberger et al. 1000p. 1997. 185.00 (*0-19-876448-0*) OUP.

***United Nations System & Its Predecessors: Basic Documents, Vol. II.** Ed. by Volker Rittberger et al. 1000p. 1997. 185.00 (*0-19-876449-9*) OUP.

United Nations System & Nutrition: The Need for Change in a More Democratic World. E. J. Heyward. (Martin J. Forman Memorial Lectures). 40p. (Orig.). 1992. pap. 7.50 (*0-915173-20-4*) Helen Keller Intl.

United Nations System at Geneva: Scope & Practices of Multilateral Diplomacy & Co-Operation. 1991. write for info. (*0-318-68987-1*, 91.III.K.LS6) UN.

United Nations System-International Bibliography - das System der Vereinigten Nationen: Learned Journal, 1981-1985. Klaus Hufner & Jens Neumann. (United Nations System Ser.: Vol. 4, Pt. B). 600p. (ENG & GER.). 1990. lib. bdg. 205.00 (*3-598-10994-6*) K G Saur.

United Nations System International Bibliography - das System der Vereinigten Nationen: Learned Journals. Compiled by Klaus Hufner. (IFLA Publication Ser.). 566p. (ENG & GER.). 1991. Vol. 4, Pt. A: 1976-1980, 566p.; Vol. 4, Pt. B: 1981-1985, 498p. lib. bdg. 205.00 (*3-598-10993-8*) K G Saur.

***United Nations, the Great Powers & Middle East Peacemaking, 1948-1954.** LC 96-39814. (Futile Diplomacy Ser.). 1997. pap. write for info. (*0-7146-4317-3*) Intl Spec Bk.

United Nations Transitional Authority in Cambodia: Debriefing & Lessons. Ed. by Nassrine Azimi. LC 96-29. 304p. 1996. 123.00 (*90-411-0886-6*) Kluwer Law Tax Pubs.

United Nations Treaty Series. Incl. Vol. 1024. . 435p. 1985. (0-318-60337-3); Vol. 1027. . 419p. 1985. (0-318-60338-1); Vol. 1032. . 379p. 1985. (0-318-60339-X); Vol. 1040. . 394p. 1985. (0-318-60340-3); Vol. 1052. . 435p. 1985. (0-318-60341-1); Vol. 1059. . 477p. 1985. (0-318-60342-X); Vol. 1067. . 382p. 1985. (0-318-60343-8); Vol. 1072. . 413p. 1985. (0-318-60344-6); Vol. 1083. . 375p. 1985. (0-318-60345-4); Vol. 1090. . 381p. 1985. (0-318-60346-2); Vol. 1106. . 413p. 1985. (0-318-60347-0); Vol. 1110. . 388p. 1985. (0-318-60348-9); Vol. 1111. . 475p. 1985. (0-318-60349-7); Vol. 1115. . 371p. 1985. (0-318-60350-0); Vol. 1130. . 361p. 1985. (0-318-60351-9); Vol. 1132. . 446p. 1985. (0-318-60352-7); Vol. 1089. . 408p. 1986. 22.00 (0-685-73833-7); Vol. 1098. . 399p. 1986. 22.00 (0-685-73834-5); Vol. 1105. . 438p. 1986. (0-318-61532-0); Vol. 1108. . 457p. 1986. (0-318-61533-9); Vol. 1139. . 427p. 1986. (0-318-61534-7); Volume 1113. 370p. (0-318-62514-8); Volume 1119. 389p. (0-318-62515-6); Volume 1125. 699p. (0-318-62516-4); Volume 1126. 458p. (0-318-62517-2); Volume 1129. 412p. (0-318-62518-0); Volume 1137. 949p. (0-318-62519-9); Volume 1143. 373p. (0-318-62520-2); Volume 1144. 410p. (0-318-62521-0); Volume 1163. 386p. (0-318-62522-9); Volume 1187. 412p. (0-318-62523-7); Volume 1191. 441p. (0-318-62524-5); write for info. (0-318-61531-2) UN.

United Nations Treaty Series. Incl. Vol. 1024. . 435p. 1985. (0-318-60337-3); Vol. 1027. . 419p. 1985. (0-318-60338-1); Vol. 1032. . 379p. 1985. (0-318-60339-X); Vol. 1040. . 394p. 1985. (0-318-60340-3); Vol. 1052. . 435p. 1985. (0-318-60341-1); Vol. 1059. . 477p. 1985. (0-318-60342-X); Vol. 1067. . 382p. 1985. (0-318-60343-8); Vol. 1072. . 413p. 1985. (0-318-60344-6); Vol. 1083. . 375p. 1985. (0-318-60345-4); Vol. 1090. . 381p. 1985. (0-318-60346-2); Vol. 1106. . 413p. 1985. (0-318-60347-0); Vol. 1110. . 388p. 1985. (0-318-60348-9); Vol. 1111. . 475p. 1985. (0-318-60349-7); Vol. 1115. . 371p. 1985. (0-318-60350-0); Vol. 1130. . 361p. 1985. (0-318-60351-9); Vol. 1132. . 446p. 1985. (0-318-60352-7); Vol. 1089. . 408p. 1986. 22.00 (0-685-73833-7); Vol. 1098. . 399p. 1986. 22.00 (0-685-73834-5); Vol. 1105. . 438p. 1986. (0-318-61532-0); Vol. 1108. . 457p. 1986. (0-318-61533-9); Vol. 1139. . 427p. 1986. (0-318-61534-7); Volume 1113. 370p. (0-318-62514-8); Volume 1119. 389p. (0-318-62515-6); Volume 1125. 699p. (0-318-62516-4); Volume 1126. 458p. (0-318-62517-2); Volume 1129. 412p. (0-318-62518-0); Volume 1137. 949p. (0-318-62519-9); Volume 1143. 373p. (0-318-62520-2); Volume 1144. 410p. (0-318-62521-0); Volume 1163. 386p. (0-318-62522-9); Volume 1187. 412p. (0-318-62523-7); Volume 1191. 441p. (0-318-62524-5); 1985. 22.00 (0-685-73766-7) UN.

United Nations Treaty Series. Incl. Vol. 1024. . 435p. 1985. (0-318-60337-3); Vol. 1027. . 419p. 1985. (0-318-60338-1); Vol. 1032. . 379p. 1985. (0-318-60339-X); Vol. 1040. . 394p. 1985. (0-318-60340-3); Vol. 1052. . 435p. 1985. (0-318-60341-1); Vol. 1059. . 477p. 1985. (0-318-60342-X); Vol. 1067. . 382p. 1985. (0-318-60343-8); Vol. 1072. . 413p. 1985. (0-318-60344-6); Vol. 1083. . 375p. 1985. (0-318-60345-4); Vol. 1090. . 381p. 1985. (0-318-60346-2); Vol. 1106. . 413p. 1985. (0-318-60347-0); Vol. 1110. . 388p. 1985. (0-318-60348-9); Vol. 1111. . 475p. 1985. (0-318-60349-7); Vol. 1115. . 371p. 1985. (0-318-60350-0); Vol. 1130. . 361p. 1985. (0-318-60351-9); Vol. 1132. . 446p. 1985. (0-318-60352-7); Vol. 1089. . 408p. 1986. 22.00 (0-685-73833-7); Vol. 1098. . 399p. 1986. 22.00 (0-685-73834-5); Vol. 1105. . 438p. 1986. (0-318-61532-0); Vol. 1108. . 457p. 1986. (0-318-61533-9); Vol. 1139. . 427p. 1986. (0-318-61534-7); Volume 1113. 370p. (0-318-62514-8); Volume 1119. 389p. (0-318-62515-6); Volume 1125. 699p. (0-318-62516-4); Volume 1126. 458p. (0-318-62517-2); Volume 1129. 412p. (0-318-62518-0); Volume 1137. 949p. (0-318-62519-9); Volume 1143. 373p. (0-318-62520-2); Volume 1144. 410p. (0-318-62521-0); Volume 1163. 386p. (0-318-62522-9); Volume 1187. 412p. (0-318-62523-7); Volume 1191. 441p. (0-318-62524-5); 1987. 22.00 (0-317-64632-X) UN.

United Nations Urban Agglomeration Chart, 1990. 1990. 7.95 (0-685-39233-3, 90.XIII.6) UN.

United Nations Women's Guild Cookbook: Collection of International Recipes. 240p. 1992. 14.95 (0-9632500-0-0) UN Wom Guild.

United Nations World Conference on Human Rights. Ed. by William J. Butler. LC 93-10785. 1993. write for info. (0-916265-05-6) Am Assn Intl Comm Jurists.

***United Nations World Drug Report.** United Nations Drug Control Programme Staff. (Illus.). 300p. 1997. pap. 29.95 (0-19-829299-6) OUP.

***United Nations World Drug Report.** United Nations Drug Control Programme Staff. (Illus.). 300p. 1997. 75.00 (0-19-829320-8) OUP.

United Nations World Hearings on Development: Expressing a Need for Change & Reform. H. E. Samuel et al. Ed. by Miriam Friedmann. 68p. (Orig.). 1995. pap. write for info. (0-9645188-0-5) F Ebert Found.

United Nations World Population Chart, 1990. 1990. 5.95 (0-685-39234-1, 90.XIII.4) UN.

United Nations 1990s. 2nd ed. Baehr. 1994. text ed. 18.95 (0-312-12071-0) St Martin.

United Negro College Fund Archives: A Guide & Index to the Microfiche. (Illus.). 422p. 1985. 95.00 (0-8357-0678-8) Univ Microfilms.

United Order among the Mormons (Missouri Phase) An Unfinished Experiment in Economic Organization. Joseph A. Geddes. LC 72-8247. reprint ed. 39.50 (0-404-11001-0) AMS Pr.

United Press International Book of the Congressional Medal of Honor. Bill Harris. 1990. 9.99 (0-517-69323-2) Random Hse Value.

United Press International Stylebook: The Authoritative Handbook for Writers, Editors, & News Directors. 3rd ed. United Press International Staff. 432p. 1994. pap. 12. 95 (0-8442-5337-5, Natl Textbk) NTC Pub Grp.

United Republic of Tanzania: Tanzania. (Case Studies in Population Policy). 42p. pap. 7.50 (92-1-151216-6, 90. XIII.29) UN.

United Roumania. Charles U. Clark. LC 79-135799. (Eastern Europe Collection). 1971. reprint ed. 28.95 (0-405-02741-9) Ayer.

United Santas of America. Bernie Fass & Mack Wolfson. 48p. (J). (gr. 3-12). 1987. pap. 16.95 (0-86704-038-6); student ed. 2.95 (0-86704-039-4) Clarus Music.

***United State Experience in South Africa 1784-1870.** Alan R. Booth. (South African Biographical & Historical Studies: No. 22). 256p. 1976. 60.00 (0-86961-062-7, Pub. by A A Balkema NE) Ashgate Pub Co.

United States. Denise Allard. LC 96-2615. (Postcards from Ser.). (J). 1997. lib. bdg. 21.40 (0-8172-4019-5) Raintree Steck-V.

United States. Amoco Pathfinder Staff. 1992. pap. 1.00 (0-671-84027-4) S&S Trade.

United States. John D. Baines. LC 93-26533. (Country Fact Files Ser.). (J). 1993. lib. bdg. 24.26 (0-8114-1857-X) Raintree Steck-V.

United States. Philip Brooks. LC 95-49450. (Games People Play Ser.). (Illus.). 64p. (J). (gr. 4 up). 1996. lib. bdg. 22. 00 (0-516-04442-7) Childrens.

United States. Chantal Deltenre & Martine Noblet. (Tintin's Travel Diaries Ser.). (Illus.). 76p. (J). (gr. 5 up). 1994. 11.95 (0-8120-6428-3); pap. 6.95 (0-8120-1867-2) Barron.

United States. Thomas L. Dumm. (Contestations Ser.). (Illus.). 256p. 1994. 39.95 (0-8014-3002-X); pap. 16.95 (0-8014-8190-2) Cornell U Pr.

United States, 3 vols. Ed. by Godfrey Hodgson. (Handbooks to the Modern World Ser.). 1840p. 1992. Set. lib. bdg. 150.00 (0-8160-1621-6) Facts on File.

United States. Cass R. Sandak. LC 96-8358. (Modern Industrial World Ser.). (J). 1997. lib. bdg. 24.26 (0-8172-4556-1) Raintree Steck-V.

United States. Cass R. Sandak. LC 93-40251. (Discovering Science Ser.). (Illus.). 32p. (J). (gr. 4 up). 1994. text ed. 13.95 (0-89686-776-5, Crstwood Hse) Silver Burdett Pr.

United States. 2nd ed. Passport Books Editors. 48p. 1994. pap. 8.95 (0-8442-0724-1) NTC Pub Grp.

United States. 4th ed. Winthrop D. Jordan & Leon F. Litwack. LC 93-11597. 544p. 1993. pap. text ed. 33.60 (0-13-035981-5) P-H.

United States, 2 vols. 7th enl. ed. Winthrop D. Jordan & Leon F. Litwack. 1990. text ed. 69.33 (0-13-933524-2, 686104) P-H.

United States, 2 vols., Vol. I: Conquering a Continent. 7th enl. ed. Winthrop D. Jordan & Leon F. Litwack. 1990. pap. text ed. 54.00 (0-13-933516-1, 680102) P-H.

United States, 2 vols., Vol. II: Becoming a World Power. 7th enl. ed. Winthrop D. Jordan & Leon F. Litwack. 1990. pap. text ed. 52.00 (0-13-933490-4, 680103) P-H.

***United States: A Contemporary Human Geography.** Paul L. Knox et al. LC 87-3166. (Illus.). 299p. pap. 85.30 (0-608-05251-5, 2065789) Bks Demand.

United States: A Guide to Library Holdings in the United Kingdom. Compiled by Peter G. Snow. 744p. 1982. text ed. 85.00 (0-313-28130-0, SZR/, Greenwood Pr) Greenwood.

United States: A Hopeful Future. Peter Duignan. LC 93-12868. (Hoover Essays Ser.: No. 4). 1993. pap. 5.00 (0-8179-3672-6) Hoover Inst Pr.

***United States: Abuses in the State of Georgia: Modern Capital of Human Rights?** 214p. (Orig.). 1996. pap. 15. 00 (1-56432-169-X) Hum Rts Watch.

United States: Brief Edition, Vol. 1. Winthrop D. Jordan et al. (Illus.). 272p. (C). 1987. pap. text ed. write for info. (0-13-939109-6) P-H.

United States: Essays, 1951-1991. Gore Vidal. 1993. 37.50 (0-679-41489-4) Random.

United States: Essays: 1952-1992. Gore Vidal. 1995. pap. 23.00 (0-679-75572-1) Random.

United States: Government & Citizenship. Darryl Stacy. (Illus.). 176p. (J). (gr. 7-9). 1992. text ed. 21.95 (0-911981-67-5); student ed., pap. text ed. 5.95 (0-911981-71-3); teacher ed., pap. text ed. 8.95 (0-911981-70-5) Cloud Pub.

United States: Grade 5. Harcourt Brace Staff. 1985. student ed. 45.50 (0-15-373205-9) HB Schl Dept.

United States: Its History & Constitution. Alexander Johnston. (Notable American Authors Ser.). 1992. reprint ed. lib. bdg. 75.00 (0-7812-3505-7) Rprt Serv.

United States: Its Land & People. Sidney E. Zimmerman. 1991. student ed., pap. text ed. 9.95 (0-87594-344-6) Book-Lab.

United States: Policeman of the World. Gerald Kurland. (Topics of Our Times Ser.: No. 10). 32p. lib. bdg. 7.25 (0-87157-811-5) SamHar Pr.

***United States: Sexual Abuse of Women in U. S. State Prisons All Too Familiar.** Womens Rights Project Staff. 366p. (Orig.). 1996. pap. 20.00 (1-56432-153-3) Hum Rts Watch.

United States: Social Studies 1985. Harcourt Brace Dept. 1985. wbk. ed., pap. 11.00 (0-15-373237-7) HB Schl Dept.

United States Study Guide. Jordan. 1991. pap. text ed. 54. 00 (0-13-062283-4) P-H.

United States see Women in Society - Group 3

United States - Ambition. Alan Ehrenhalt. 1992. pap. 13.00 (0-8129-2027-9, Times Bks) Random.

United States - Breach of Trust: Physician Participation in Executions in the United States. Physicians for Human Rights Staff et al. 80p. (Orig.). 1994. pap. 7.00 (1-56432-125-8) Hum Rts Watch.

United States - Canadian Agricultural Trade Challenges: Developing Common Approaches - Proceedings of a Symposium Held at Spring Hill Conference Center, Wayzata, Minnesota, July 22-24, 1987, Cosponsored by National Center for Food & Agricultural Policy at Resources for the Future & C. D. Howe Institute. Ed. by Kristen Allen & Katie Macmillan. LC 88-10299. 230p. reprint ed. pap. 65.60 (0-8357-3283-5, 2039506) Bks Demand.

United States - Comanche Relations: The Reservation Years. William T. Hagan. LC 89-29029. (Illus.). 352p. 1990. pap. 14.95 (0-8061-2275-7) U of Okla Pr.

United States - European Monetary Relations. Ed. by Samuel I. Katz. LC 79-11718. (AEI Symposia Ser.: No. 79B). (Illus.). 294p. reprint ed. pap. 83.80 (0-8357-4540-6, 2037432) Bks Demand.

United States - Japanese Political Relations: The Critical Issues Affecting Asia's Future. Center for Strategic & International Studies Staff. LC 80-12143. (Center for Strategic Studies, Georgetown University Special Report: No. 7). ix, 104p. 1980. reprint ed. text ed. 49.75 (0-313-22376-9, CSUS) Greenwood.

United States - Mexico Border Statistics since 1900. Ed. by David E. Lorey. 512p. 1993. pap. 35.00 (0-87903-251-0) UCLA Lat Am Ctr.

United States - Taiwan Security Ties: From Cold War to Beyond Containment. Dennis V. Hickey. LC 93-1649. 208p. 1993. text ed. 52.95 (0-275-94672-X, Praeger Pubs) Greenwood.

United States - Third World Relations in the New World Order. Abbas P. Grammy & C. Kaye Bragg. LC 96-20518. (Illus.). 325p. (C). 1996. lib. bdg. 59.00 (1-56072-350-5) Nova Sci Pubs.

United States--Japan Relations & International Institutions after the Cold War. Ed. by Peter Gourevitch et al. 406p. (Orig.). (C). 1995. pap. write for info. (0-9637158-1-X) U CA Grad Schl.

United States--Vulnerable. 2nd ed. Eli Raitport. Ed. by F. R. Duplantier. (United States in Crises Ser.). 221p. (Orig.). (C). 1989. reprint ed. pap. 19.50 (0-944182-02-X) Raitport Co.

United States Abridged Life Tables: 1919-1920. U. S. Department of Commerce, Bureau of the Census Staff & Elbertie Foudray. LC 75-37268. (Demography Ser.). (Illus.). 1976. reprint ed. 17.95 (0-405-08000-X) Ayer.

United States Activity & Coloring Book. Anne M. Eccles. (Illus.). 36p. (J). (ps-8). 1992. pap. 2.95 (0-9618555-2-5) Anne M Eccles.

United States Administrative Citations, 5 vols. Shepard's Citation, Inc. Staff. (Specialized Citations Ser.). 1989. 550.00 (0-685-47142-X) Shepards.

***United States Admiralty Law.** 1997. lib. bdg. 121.00 (90-411-0417-8) Kluwer Ac.

United States after the World War. James C. Malin. LC 77-37897. (Select Bibliographies Reprint Ser.). 1977. reprint ed. 31.95 (0-8369-6735-6) Ayer.

United States after War. A. H. Hansen et al. LC 69-18571. (Essay Index Reprint Ser.). 1977. 18.95 (0-8369-1069-9) Ayer.

United States Agricultural Export Policy. Ed. by Sheila M. Geoghegan. (Wisconsin International Law Journal, 1982 Ser.: Vol. 1). 150p. (Orig.). 1983. pap. text ed. 8.00 (0-933431-00-7) U Wisc Law Madison.

United States Air Force: A Dictionary. Bruce W. Watson & Susan M. Watson. LC 91-42269. (Series on Military Affairs: Vol. 4). 896p. 1992. text ed. 35.00 (0-8240-5539-X, SS696) Garland.

United States Air Force Fighter Support in Operation Desert Storm. Hyman L. Shulman. LC 95-33017. 126p. (Orig.). 1995. pap. text ed. 13.00 (0-8330-2291-1, MR-468-AF) Rand Corp.

United States Air Force in Korea, 1950-1953. rev. ed. Robert F. Futrell. 823p. 1996. reprint ed. pap. text ed. 48.00 (0-912799-71-4) Off Air Force.

United States Air Force in Southeast Asia, 1961-73: An Illustrated Account. Ed. by Carl Berger. 381p. 1984. write for info. (0-912799-16-1) Off Air Force.

United States Air Force Operations in Laos: 1 January 1970-30 June 71. Headquarters PACAF Staff. 285p. 1994. reprint ed. pap. 29.50 (0-923135-26-X) Dalley Bk Service.

United States Air Force 1993. Ed. by Mach III Plus Staff. (C). 1993. pap. 40.00 (0-9515462-9-5, Pub. by Mach III Plus UK) St Mut.

United States Air Forces: Basic Documents on Roles & Missions. 455p. 1987. write for info. (0-912799-54-4) Off Air Force.

United States Air National Guard: World Air Power. Rene J. Francillon. (Illus.). 224p. 1993. 29.95 (1-880588-03-X) AIRtime Pub.

United States among the Nations. California University Committee on International Relations. LC 68-54336. (Essay Index Reprint Ser.). 1977. 18.95 (0-8369-0271-8) Ayer.

United States & Africa. American Assembly Staff. LC 75-117751. (Essay Index Reprint Ser.). 1977. 21.95 (0-8369-1781-2) Ayer.

United States & Africa. rev. ed. American Assembly Staff. Ed. by Walter Goldschmidt. LC 63-20154. 316p. reprint ed. pap. 90.10 (0-685-20469-3, 2029868) Bks Demand.

United States & Africa: A History. Peter Duignan & Lewis H. Gann. (Illus.). 464p. 1987. pap. 21.95 (0-521-33571-X) Cambridge U Pr.

United States & Africa: Into the Twenty-First Century. Carol J. Lancaster. LC 93-19138. (Policy Essay Ser.: No. 7). (Illus.). 72p. (C). 1993. pap. text ed. 9.95 (1-56517-010-5) Overseas Dev Council.

United States & Anastasio Somoza: Dealing with Friendly Dictators Who Are Losing Authority. Doug A. Chalmers. (Pew Case Studies in International Affairs). 50p. (C). 1992. pap. text ed. 3.50 (1-56927-105-4) Geo U Inst Dplmcy.

United States & Arab Nationalism: The Syrian Case. Bonnie F. Saunders. LC 95-34201. 128p. 1996. text ed. 49.95 (0-275-95426-9, Praeger Pubs) Greenwood.

United States & Argentina, 1945-47: A Case Study in Diplomatic Practice. Constantine L. Richardson. 1993. 15.95 (0-533-10495-5) Vantage.

***United States & Arms Control: The Challenge of Leadership.** Allan S. Krass. LC 97-8863. 1997. text ed. write for info. (0-275-95947-3, Praeger Pubs) Greenwood.

United States & Brazil: Limits of Influence. Robert Wesson. LC 80-27514. 186p. 1981. text ed. 31.95 (0-275-90739-2, C0739, Praeger Pubs) Greenwood.

United States & Britain. Clarence C. Brinton. LC 75-97340. 312p. 1970. reprint ed. text ed. 59.75 (0-8371-2964-8, BRUS, Greenwood Pr) Greenwood.

United States & Bulgaria in World War I. Petko Petkov. 224p. 1991. text ed. 40.00 (0-88033-203-4) Col U Pr.

United States & Burma. John F. Cady. LC 75-22256. (American Foreign Policy Library). 315p. 1976. reprint ed. pap. 89.80 (0-7837-6081-7, 2059127) Bks Demand.

United States & Canada. (Airport & Handling Agents 94-95 Ser.). 1996. pap. text ed. 350.00 (0-7106-1143-9) Janes Info Group.

United States & Canada. Ed. by John S. Dickey. LC 64-21215. 1964. 3.95 (0-317-02965-7, C-93839); pap. 1.95 (0-317-02966-5, P-93838) Am Assembly.

United States & Canada. Gerald M. Craig. LC 67-30826. (American Foreign Policy Library). 376p. reprint ed. pap. 107.20 (0-7837-4459-5, 2057989) Bks Demand.

***United States & Canada: A Systematic Approach.** D. Gordon Bennett & Jeffrey Patton. 200p. 1996. per., pap. text ed. 36.69 (0-7872-2633-5) Kendall-Hunt.

United States & Canada: The Land & the People. Arthur Getis. 64p. 1994. student ed., spiral bd. write for info. (0-697-26314-2) Wm C Brown Pubs.

United States & Canada: The Land & the People. Arthur Getis et al. 464p. (C). 1994. per. write for info. (0-697-20039-6) Wm C Brown Pubs.

United States & Canada: The Land & the People. Arthur Getis et al. 480p. 1995. write for info. (0-697-28226-0) Wm C Brown Pubs.

United States & Canada: The Quest for Free Trade. Paul Wonnacott. LC 87-2660. (Policy Analysis in International Economics Ser.: No. 16). 173p. (Orig.). (C). 1987. pap. 10.00 (0-88132-056-0) Inst Intl Eco.

United States & Central America, 1944-1949: Perceptions of Political Dynamics. Thomas M. Leonard. LC 83-5032. (Illus.). 232p. 1984. text ed. 28.50 (0-8173-0190-9) U of Ala Pr.

***United States & Central America, 1944-1949: Perceptions of Political Dynamics.** Thomas M. Leonard. LC 83-5032. 230p. pap. 65.60 (0-608-05134-9, 2065695) Bks Demand.

United States & China. Arnold X. Jiang. (United States in the World: Foreign Perspectives). xvi, 216p. 1988. 26.50 (0-226-39947-8) U Ch Pr.

United States & China. 4th enl. ed. John K. Fairbank. (Illus.). 664p. (C). 1983. pap. text ed. 14.95 (0-674-92438-X) HUP.

United States & China in the Twentieth Century. 2nd ed. Michael Schaller. (Illus.). 264p. (C). 1990. pap. text ed. 16.95 (0-19-505866-6) OUP.

United States & China Relations at a Crossroads. Ed. by David M. Lampton & Alfred D. Wilhelm, Jr. 306p. (Orig.). (C). 1995. pap. 34.00 (0-8191-9889-7) U Pr of Amer.

United States & China since 1949: A Troubled Affair. Robert Garson. 256p. 1995. 38.50 (0-8386-3610-1) Fairleigh Dickinson.

United States & China, 1944-1946. James R. Howard & David S. Painter. (Pew Case Studies in International Affairs). 50p. (C). 1995. pap. text ed. 3.50 (1-56927-345-6) Geo U Inst Dplmcy.

United States & Civilization. 2nd rev. ed. John U. Nef. LC 67-28465. 451p. reprint ed. pap. 128.60 (0-317-09261-8, 2020136) Bks Demand.

United States & Cuba. Harry F. Guggenheim. LC 79-111715. (American Imperialism: Viewpoints of United States Foreign Policy, 1898-1941 Ser.). 1970. reprint ed. 20.95 (0-405-02024-4) Ayer.

United States & Cuba: A Study in International Relations. Harry F. Guggenheim. LC 78-102242. (Select Bibliographies Reprint Ser.). 1977. 26.95 (0-8369-5127-1) Ayer.

United States & Cuba: A Study in International Relations. Harry F. Guggenheim. LC 79-131730. 1970. reprint ed. 22.00 (0-403-00617-1) Scholarly.

United States & Cuba: Business & Diplomacy, 1917-1960. Robert F. Smith. (Orig.). 1960. pap. 9.95 (0-8084-0306-0) NCUP.

An Asterisk (*) at the beginning of an entry indicates that the title is appearing in BIP for the first time.

United States & Cuba: Hegemony & Dependent Development, 1880-1934. Jules R. Benjamin. LC 77-74550. (Pitt Latin American Ser.). 280p. reprint ed. pap. 79.80 (*0-7837-2142-0*, 2042428) Bks Demand.

United States & Cuba after the Cold War: The 1994 Refugee Crisis. William M. LeoGrande. (Pew Case Studies in International Affairs). 50p. (C). 1995. pap. text ed. 3.50 (*1-56927-367-7*, GU Schl Foreign) Geo U Inst Dplmcy.

United States & Cuba under Reagan & Shultz: A Foreign Service Officer Reports. Kenneth N. Skoug, Jr. LC 95-42964. 256p. 1996. text ed. 57.95 (*0-275-95467-6*, Praeger Pubs) Greenwood.

United States & Democracy in Chile. Paul E. Sigmund. LC 92-39230. (Twentieth Century Fund Book Ser.). 256p. 1993. text ed. 42.50 (*0-8018-4580-7*); pap. text ed. 14.95 (*0-8018-4581-5*) Johns Hopkins.

United States & East Asia. Richard W. Van Alstyne. (Library of World Civilization). (Illus.). (C). 1973. pap. text ed. 9.95 (*0-393-09368-9*) Norton.

***United States & East Asia: Conflict & Co-Operation.** Tommy T. Koh. 300p. 1996. reprint ed. pap. 12.50 (*981-210-084-9*, Pub. by Times Academic SI) Intl Spec Bk.

United States & East Asia since 1945. Charles M. Dobbs. LC 90-20213. (Studies in American History: Vol. 5). 248p. 1991. lib. bdg. 89.95 (*0-88946-505-3*) E Mellen.

United States & Eastern Europe. Ed. by Robert F. Byrnes. LC 67-23502. 1967. pap. 1.95 (*0-936904-04-6*) Am Assembly.

United States & Eastern Europe. American Assembly Staff. Ed. by Robert F. Byrnes. LC 67-23502. (Illus.). 191p. reprint ed. pap. 54.50 (*0-685-20470-7*, 2029869) Bks Demand.

United States & Egypt: An Essay on Policy for the 1990s. William B. Quandt. 82p. (C). 1990. pap. 8.95 (*0-8157-7295-5*) Brookings.

United States & Ethiopia: Military Assistance & the Quest for Security, 1953-1993. Baffour Agyeman-Duah. LC 94-8023. 274p. (C). 1994. lib. bdg. 48.50 (*0-8191-9523-5*) U Pr of Amer.

United States & Europe after the Cold War: A New Alliance? John W. Holmes. LC 95-50216. 210p. 1997. text ed. 34.95 (*1-57003-107-X*) U of SC Pr.

United States & Europe, 1815-1823. Edward H. Tatum. (History - United States Ser.). 315p. 1993. reprint ed. lib. bdg. 89.00 (*0-7812-4836-1*) Rprt Serv.

***United States & European Reconstruction: The Case of Norway, 1945-1953.** Kai R. Pedersen. 286p. 1997. pap. 54.95 (*1-57292-078-5*) Austin & Winfield.

***United States & European Reconstruction: The Case of Norway, 1945-1953.** Kai R. Pedersen. 286p. 1997. 74.95 (*1-57292-079-3*) Austin & Winfield.

United States & Fascist Italy, 1922-1940. David F. Schmitz. LC 87-19032. xii, 273p. (C). 1988. text ed. 39.95 (*0-8078-1766-X*) U of NC Pr.

United States & France. Donald C. McKay. LC 83-1558. xvii, 334p. (C). 1983. reprint ed. text ed. 65.00 (*0-313-23885-5*, MCUW, Greenwood Pr) Greenwood.

United States & French Security: 1917-1921, a Study in American Diplomatic History. Louis A. Yates. 252p. 1957. text ed. 29.50 (*0-8290-0214-6*) Irvington.

United States & German-American Relations Through German Eyes. Ed. by Cord Jakobeit & Ute Sacksofsky. 179p. 1995. 67.00 (*1-56072-261-4*) Nova Sci Pubs.

United States & Germany: A Diplomatic History. Manfred Jonas. LC 83-15278. 336p. (C). 1985. pap. 18.95 (*0-8014-9890-2*) Cornell U Pr.

***United States & Global Economy since 1945.** Henry C. Dethloff et al. 208p. (C). 1997. pap. text ed. write for info. (*0-15-502854-5*) HB Coll Pubs.

United States & Huerta. Kenneth J. Grieb. LC 69-10906. (Illus.). 251p. reprint ed. pap. 71.60 (*0-8357-6836-8*, 2035523) Bks Demand.

United States & India: The Dimensions of Influence. Norman D. Palmer. LC 84-8272. (Studies of Influence in International Relations). 316p. 1984. text ed. 49.95 (*0-275-91240-X*, C1240, Praeger Pubs); pap. text ed. 18.95 (*0-275-91624-3*, B1624, Praeger Pubs) Greenwood.

United States & India & Pakistan see United States & India, Pakistan, Bangladesh

United States & India, Pakistan, Bangladesh. 3rd ed. W. Norman Brown. LC 72-81270. (American Foreign Policy Library). Orig. Title: The United States & India & Pakistan. (Illus.). 462p. 1972. 39.95 (*0-674-92446-0*) HUP.

United States & India, Seventeen Seventy-Six to Nineteen Seventy-Six. M. V. Kamath. 182p. 1976. 24.95 (*0-318-37275-4*) Asia Bk Corp.

***United States & Iran.** Goode. Date not set. text ed. 39.95 (*0-312-17272-9*) St Martin.

United States & Iran: A Documentary History. Yonah Alexander & Allan Nanes. LC 80-53318. 524p. 1980. text ed. 95.00 (*0-313-27095-3*, U7095); pap. text ed. 24.95 (*0-313-27054-6*, P7054) Greenwood.

United States & Ireland. Donald H. Akenson. LC 73-82348. (American Foreign Policy Library). 322p. reprint ed. pap. 91.80 (*0-7837-4444-7*, 2057974) Bks Demand.

United States & Israel: Influence in the Special Relationship. Bernard Reich. LC 83-24795. (Studies of Influence in International Relations). 254p. 1984. text ed. 31.95 (*0-275-91247-7*, C1247, Praeger Pubs) Greenwood.

United States & Israel: The Limits of the Special Relationship. Abraham Ben-Zvi. LC 92-46441. 312p. 1993. 37.50 (*0-231-08184-7*) Col U Pr.

United States & Italy. 3rd enl. ed. H. Stuart Hughes. LC 79-63706. (American Foreign Policy Library). 336p. (C). 1979. 34.50 (*0-674-92545-9*) HUP.

United States & Italy, 1940-1950: The Politics & Diplomacy of Stabilization. James E. Miller. LC 85-10035. xv, 356p. 1986. 45.00 (*0-8078-1673-6*) U of NC Pr.

United States & Japan: Changing Relations. Ed. by Chae-Jin Lee. (Keck Center for International & Strategic Studies: No. 2). viii, 75p. 1992. pap. 9.95 (*0-930607-13-9*) Regina Bks.

United States & Japan: Cooperative Leadership for Peace & Global Prosperity. Atlantic Council of the United States Staff. 125p. (C). 1990. pap. text ed. 11.75 (*0-8191-7693-1*); pap. text ed. 11.75 (*0-8191-7713-X*) Atl Coun US.

United States & Japan: Cooperative Leadership for Peace & Global Prosperity. Atlantic Council of the United States Staff. 138p. 1990. text ed. 32.50 (*0-8191-7712-1*) U Pr of Amer.

United States & Japan: Shared Progress in Technology Management. Fred Y. Phillips et al. 429p. 1993. pap. 25.00 (*1-887406-03-4*) ICTwo Inst.

***United States & Japan in Asia.** Alan Romberg et al. Ed. by Christopher Twomey & Michael Stankeiwicz. (IGCC Policy Papers: No. 10). 50p. (Orig.). 1994. pap. 3.50 (*0-934637-25-3*) U of CA Inst Global.

United States & Japan in the International Monetary System: 1946-1985. Robert V. Roosa. (Occasional Papers: No. 21). 75p. 1986. pap. write for info. (*1-56708-020-0*) Grp of Thirty.

United States & Japan in the Pacific. Jiuji G. Kasai. LC 72-111759. (American Imperialism: Viewpoints of United States Foreign Policy, 1898-1941 Ser.). 1977. reprint ed. 21.95 (*0-405-02030-9*) Ayer.

United States & Japan in the Postwar World. Akira Iriye. 256p. 1989. pap. 18.95 (*0-8131-0826-8*) U Pr of Ky.

United States & Lafayette. Louis Gottschalk. LC 58-49303. (Augustana College Library Occasional Papers, Wallin Lecture: No. 3). 19p. 1958. pap. 1.00 (*0-910182-24-8*) Augustana Coll.

United States & Latin America. rev. ed. Ed. by Herbert L. Matthews. LC 59-15330. 1963. reprint ed. pap. 1.95 (*0-317-02968-1*, 93840-C) Am Assembly.

***United States & Latin America: A Select Bibliography.** John A. Britton. LC 96-42962. (Magill Bibliographies Ser.). 1997. write for info. (*0-8108-3248-8*) Scarecrow.

United States & Latin America: Myths & Stereotypes of Civilization & Nature. Fredrick B. Pike. LC 91-42454. (Illus.). 464p. 1992. pap. 19.95 (*0-292-78524-0*); text ed. 40.00 (*0-292-78523-2*) U of Tex Pr.

United States & Latin America: Redefining U. S. Purposes in the Post-Cold War Era. Ed. by G. Pope Atkins. (Tom Slick World Peace Ser.). 176p. 1992. pap. 12.50 (*0-89940-426-X*) LBJ Sch Pub Aff.

United States & Latin America in the Nineteen Nineties: Beyond the Cold War. Ed. by Augusto Varas et al. LC 92-29400. xiv, 328p. (C). 1993. 45.00 (*0-8078-2070-9*); pap. 17.95 (*0-8078-4402-0*) U of NC Pr.

United States & Lithuania: The Stimson Doctrine of Nonrecognition. Robert A. Vitas. LC 89-16063. 184p. 1990. text ed. 49.95 (*0-275-93412-8*, C3412, Praeger Pubs) Greenwood.

United States & Malaysia. James W. Gould. LC 76-78518. (American Foreign Policy Library). (Illus.). 281p. 1969. 25.00 (*0-674-92615-3*) HUP.

United States & Mexico. rev. ed. James F. Rippy. LC 73-137281. reprint ed. 37.50 (*0-404-05337-8*) AMS Pr.

United States & Mexico. Josefina Z. Vazquez & Lorenzo Meyer. LC 85-1061. (United States in the World: Foreign Perspectives). xiv, 234p. 1987. reprint ed. pap. text ed. 13.95 (*0-226-85205-9*) U Ch Pr.

United States & Multilateral Institutions: Patterns of Changing Instrumentality & Influence. Ed. by Margaret Karnes & Karen A. Mingst. 384p. (C). 1992. pap. 24.95 (*0-415-08110-6*, Routledge NY) Routledge.

United States & Multilateral Resource Management: Marine Minerals, Food, & Energy. Robert S. Jordan et al. 192p. 1985. text ed. 45.00 (*0-275-90125-4*, C0125, Praeger Pubs) Greenwood.

United States & NATO: The Formative Years. Lawrence S. Kaplan. LC 84-5087. 288p. 1984. pap. 12.00 (*0-8131-0159-X*) U Pr of Ky.

United States & NATO in an Undivided Europe. 1991. 9.95 (*0-685-52085-4*) JH FPI SAIS.

United States & Neutral Reunited Korea: Search for a New Basis of American Strategy. In K. Hwang. 224p. (C). 1990. pap. text ed. 25.00 (*0-8191-7915-9*); lib. bdg. 50.00 (*0-8191-7914-0*) U Pr of Amer.

United States & Nicaragua: Anatomy of a Failed Negotiation for Regime Change, 1977-1979. Alex R. Hybel. (Pew Case Studies in International Affairs). 50p. (C). 1988. pap. text ed. 3.50 (*1-56927-327-8*) Geo U Inst Dplmcy.

United States & North Africa: A Cognitive Approach to Foreign Policy. Azzedine Layachi. LC 89-22962. 217p. 1990. text ed. 55.00 (*0-275-93365-2*, C3365, Greenwood Pr) Greenwood.

United States & North Africa: Morocco, Algeria, & Tunisia. Charles F. Gallagher. LC 63-20766. (American Foreign Policy Library). 292p. (C). reprint ed. 83.30 (*0-8357-9182-3*, 2016539) Bks Demand.

United States & Northeast Asia. Ed. by Robert Puckett. 280p. 1993. pap. text ed. 21.95 (*0-8304-1279-4*) Nelson-Hall.

United States & Pakistan: The Evolution of an Influence Relationship. Shirin Tahir-Kheli. Ed. by Alvin Z. Rubinstein. LC 81-21160. (Studies of Influence in International Relations). 192p. 1982. text ed. 49.95 (*0-275-90914-X*, C0914, Praeger Pubs); pap. text ed. 16.95 (*0-275-91555-7*, B1555, Praeger Pubs) Greenwood.

United States & Poland. Piotr S. Wandycz. LC 79-11998. (American Foreign Policy Library). (Illus.). 474p. 1980. 42.50 (*0-674-92685-4*) HUP.

United States & Puerto Rico. L. S. Rowe. 1976. lib. bdg. 59.95 (*0-8490-1242-2*) Gordon Pr.

United States & Puerto Rico. Leo S. Rowe. LC 74-14249. (Puerto Rican Experience Ser.). 290p. 1975. reprint ed. 23.95 (*0-405-06235-4*) Ayer.

United States & Puerto Rico: Decolonization Options & Prospects. Roland I. Perusse. 192p. (Orig.). (C). 1987. pap. text ed. 22.00 (*0-8191-6658-8*) U Pr of Amer.

United States & Puerto Rico: The Struggle for Equality. Roland I. Perusse. LC 89-48583. (Anvil Ser.). 188p. (C). 1990. pap. 12.50 (*0-89464-396-7*) Krieger.

***United States & Puerto Rico Commission on the Status of Puerto Rico.** Date not set. write for info. (*0-405-06239-7*) Ayer.

United States & Russia: The Beginning of Relations, U. S. Department of State. Ed. by Nina H. Bashkina & David F. Trask. LC 80-607939. 1982. reprint ed. lib. bdg. 80.00 (*0-89941-229-7*, 201510) W S Hein.

United States & Somoza, 1933-1956: A Revisionist Look. Paul C. Clark. LC 92-8399. 264p. 1992. text ed. 49.95 (*0-275-94334-8*, C4334, Praeger Pubs) Greenwood.

United States & South Africa: The 1985 Sanctions Debate. Gregory F. Treverton & Pamela Varley. (Pew Case Studies in International Affairs). 50p. (C). 1992. pap. text ed. 3.50 (*1-56927-443-6*) Geo U Inst Dplmcy.

United States & Soviet Relations. 2nd ed. Karl W. Ryavec. (C). 1996. pap. text ed. write for info. (*0-8013-0688-4*) Addison-Wesley.

United States & Thailand: Alliance Dynamics, 1950-1985. R. Sean Randolph. LC 86-82389. (Research Papers & Policy Studies: No. 12). (Illus.). x, 246p. (Orig.). 1987. pap. 7.50 (*0-912966-92-0*) IEAS.

United States & the African Slave Trade, 1619-1862. Peter Duignan & Clarence Clendenen. LC 77-20159. (Hoover Institution Studies). 72p. 1978. reprint ed. text ed. 35.00 (*0-313-20009-2*, DUUS, Greenwood Pr) Greenwood.

United States & the Andean Republics: Peru, Bolivia & Ecuador. Frederick B. Pike. (American Foreign Policy Library). 493p. 1977. 64.00 (*0-674-92300-6*) HUP.

United States & the Balkan Crisis of 1940-41. Peter B. Lane. LC 88-11062. (Modern American History Ser.). 336p. 1988. 20.00 (*0-8240-4332-4*) Garland.

United States & the Berlin Blockade, 1948-1949: A Study in Crisis Decision-Making. Avi Shlaim. LC 81-19636. (International Crisis Behavior Ser.: Vol. 2). 440p. (C). 1983. pap. 15.00 (*0-520-06619-7*) U CA Pr.

United States & the Caribbean. rev. ed. Dexter Perkins. LC 67-12532. (American Foreign Policy Library). 213p. 1966. reprint ed. pap. 60.80 (*0-7837-4176-6*, 2059025) Bks Demand.

United States & the Caribbean. Ed. by Tad Szulc. LC 79-140265. 224p. 1971. reprint ed. 63.90 (*0-8357-9034-7*, 2007849) Bks Demand.

United States & the Caribbean: Challenges of an Asymmetrical Relationship. Anthony P. Maingot. LC 94-28673. (C). 1994. pap. text ed. 21.00 (*0-8133-2241-3*) Westview.

United States & the Caribbean in the Twentieth Century. 4th ed. Lester D. Langley. LC 89-4660. 360p. 1989. pap. 20.00 (*0-8203-1154-5*) U of Ga Pr.

United States & the Caribbean Republics, 1921-1933. Dana G. Munro. LC 73-16767. 405p. 1974. reprint ed. pap. 115.50 (*0-7837-9397-9*, 2060142) Bks Demand.

United States & the Cold War in the High North. Rolf Tamnes. 388p. 1991. text ed. 64.95 (*1-85521-223-4*, Pub. by Dartmth Pub UK) Ashgate Pub Co.

United States & the Cuban Revolution, 1958-1960. Abraham F. Lowenthal & Pamela K. Starr. (Pew Case Studies in International Affairs). 50p. (C). 1994. pap. text ed. 3.50 (*1-56927-328-6*) Geo U Inst Dplmcy.

United States & the Developing Countries. Edwin M. Martin. 150p. 1977. pap. 5.95 (*0-317-33700-9*) Atl Coun US.

United States & the Developing Economies. rev. ed. Gustav Ranis. (Problems of Modern Economy Ser.). (C). 1973. text ed. 8.95 (*0-393-05461-6*); pap. text ed. 5.95 (*0-393-09999-7*) Norton.

United States & the Direct Broadcast Satellite: The Politics of International Broadcasting in Space. Sara F. Luther. (Illus.). 238p. 1988. 55.00 (*0-19-505138-6*) OUP.

United States & the End of the Cold War: Implications, Reconsiderations, Provocations. John L. Gaddis. 320p. 1992. 30.00 (*0-19-505201-3*) OUP.

United States & the End of the Cold War: Implications, Reconsiderations, Provocations. John L. Gaddis. 320p. 1994. reprint ed. pap. 13.95 (*0-19-508551-5*) OUP.

United States & the European Community: Policies for a Changing World Economy. 75p. 1971. pap. 1.50 (*0-87186-044-9*, 044P) Comm Econ Dev.

United States & the European Community in the 1990s. Kevin Featherstone & Roy H. Ginsberg. LC 92-32753. 1993. write for info. (*0-333-52346-6*, Pub. by Macmillan UK) Macmillan.

United States & the European Community in the 1990's: Partners in Transition, Vol. 1. Kevin Featherstone & Roy H. Ginsberg. 320p. 1996. text ed. 17.95 (*0-312-12366-3*) St Martin.

United States & the European Pillar: The Strained Alliance. William C. Cromwell. 304p. 1992. text ed. 55.00 (*0-312-06831-X*) St Martin.

United States & the European Trade Union Movement, 1944-1951. Federico Romero. Tr. by Harvey Fergusson, II. LC 92-27645. xvi, 292p. (C). 1993. 45.00 (*0-8078-2065-2*) U of NC Pr.

United States & the Far East. rev. ed. Ed. by Willard L. Thorp. LC 62-12831. 1962. reprint ed. pap. 1.95 (*0-317-02967-3*, 93827-C) Am Assembly.

United States & the Far East. 2nd ed. American Assembly Staff. Ed. by Willard L. Thorp. LC 62-12831. 192p. reprint ed. pap. 54.80 (*0-317-08145-4*, 2050840) Bks Demand.

United States & the Far Eastern Crisis of 1933-1938: From the Manchurian Incident Through the Initial Stage of the Undeclared Sino-Japanese War. Dorothy Borg. LC 64-13421. (Harvard East Asian Ser.: No. 14). 684p. 1964. pap. 180.00 (*0-7837-4100-6*, 2057923) Bks Demand.

United States & the Genocide Convention. Lawrence J. LeBlanc. LC 90-45572. 303p. 1991. text ed. 44.95 (*0-8223-1109-7*) Duke.

United States & the Global Environment: A Guide to American Organizations Concerned with International Environment Issues. Pref. by Thaddeus C. Trzyna. LC 79-53313. (Who's Doing What Ser.: No. 9). 72p. (Orig.). 1983. pap. 25.00 (*0-912102-45-4*) Cal Inst Public.

United States & the Global Struggle for Minerals. Alfred E. Ackes. LC 78-11082. 365p. 1979. pap. 104.10 (*0-7837-8955-6*, 2049668) Bks Demand.

United States & the Global Struggle for Minerals. Alfred E. Eckes, Jr. LC 78-11082. 365p. 1979. pap. 9.95 (*0-292-78511-9*) U of Tex Pr.

United States & the Greek War for Independence 1821-1828. Paul Pappas. 1985. text ed. 46.00 (*0-88033-065-1*, 173) Col U Pr.

United States & the Hawaiian Kingdom: A Political History. Merze Tate. LC 80-14045. (Illus.). ix, 374p. 1980. reprint ed. text ed. 65.00 (*0-313-22441-2*, TAUS, Greenwood Pr) Greenwood.

***United States & the Horn of Africa: An Analytical Study of Pattern & Process.** Yohannes Okbazghi. LC 97-15186. (C). 1997. text ed. 65.00 (*0-8133-3361-X*) Westview.

United States & the Integration of Europe: Legacies of the Postwar Era. Ed. by Francis H. Heller & John R. Gillingham. (Franklin & Eleanor Roosevelt Institute Series on Diplomatic & Economic History). 416p. 1996. text ed. 49.95 (*0-312-12414-7*) St Martin.

United States & the Integration of Europe: Legacies of the Postwar Era. Ed. by Francis H. Heller & John R. Gillingham. LC 95-51441. 1996. write for info. (*0-614-10493-9*) St Martin.

United States & the Inter-American System: Are There Functions for the Forms?, No. 17. Tom J. Farer. (Studies in Transnational Legal Policy). 71p. 1978. 3.50 (*0-318-13190-0*) Am Soc Intl Law.

United States & the Italo-Ethiopian Crisis. Brice Harris, Jr. vi, 187p. 1964. 32.50 (*0-8047-0243-8*) Stanford U Pr.

United States & the Korean Problem, Documents, 1943-1953. U. S. Congress, Senate Committee on Foreign Relations. LC 72-38089. reprint ed. 42.50 (*0-404-56962-5*) AMS Pr.

United States & the Latin American Sphere of Influence: The Era of Caribbean Intervention, 1890-1930, 1. Ed. by Robert F. Smith. 104p. 1981. pap. 8.50 (*0-89874-153-X*) Krieger.

United States & the Latin American Sphere of Influence: The Era of Good Neighbors, Warriors & Hairshirts, 1930-1982, 2. Ed. by Robert F. Smith. 160p. 1983. pap. 9.50 (*0-89874-154-8*) Krieger.

United States & the Law of the Sea Treaty. Steven R. David & Peter Digeser. (Pew Case Studies in International Affairs). 50p. (Orig.). (C). 1990. pap. text ed. 3.50 (*1-56927-418-5*) Geo U Inst Dplmcy.

United States & the Law of the Sea Treaty. Steven R. David & Peter Digeser. LC 89-23366. (FPI Case Studies: No. 14). 52p. (Orig.). (C). 1990. pap. text ed. 15.75 (*0-941700-54-2*) JH FPI SAIS.

United States & the Making of Postwar France, 1945-1954. Irwin M. Wall. 400p. (C). 1991. text ed. 69.95 (*0-521-40217-4*) Cambridge U Pr.

United States & the Materials Advance in Russia, 1881-1906. George S. Queen. Ed. by Stuart Bruchey & Eleanor Bruchey. LC 76-5030. (American Business Abroad Ser.). (Illus.). 1976. lib. bdg. 24.95 (*0-405-09297-0*) Ayer.

United States & the Middle East. Ed. by Georgiana G. Stevens. LC 64-14027. 1964. 4.95 (*0-936904-05-4*) Am Assembly.

United States & the Middle East. American Assembly Staff & G. G. Stevens. (New Reprints in Essay & General Literature Index Ser.). 1977. reprint ed. 22.95 (*0-518-10195-9*, 10195) Ayer.

United States & the Middle East. American Assembly Staff. LC 64-14027. 192p. reprint ed. pap. 54.80 (*0-685-20471-5*, 2029870) Bks Demand.

United States & the Middle East: A Search for New Perspectives. Ed. by Hooshang Amirahmadi. LC 91-38541. 512p. (C). 1992. text ed. 74.50 (*0-7914-1225-3*); pap. text ed. 24.95 (*0-7914-1226-1*) State U NY Pr.

United States & the Near East. rev. ed. Ephraim A. Speiser. LC 73-100244. (Illus.). 283p. 1971. reprint ed. text ed. 59.75 (*0-8371-4031-5*, SPUS, Greenwood Pr) Greenwood.

United States & the New Europe, 1945-1993. Peter Duignan & L. H. Gann. LC 93-17859. (Illus.). 288p. 1994. 61.95 (*1-55786-518-3*); pap. 25.95 (*1-55786-519-1*) Blackwell Pubs.

United States & the Origins of the Cold War, 1941-1947. John L. Gaddis. LC 75-186388. (Contemporary American History Ser.). 396p. (C). 1972. text ed. 59.50 (*0-231-03289-7*); pap. text ed. 17.50 (*0-231-08302-5*) Col U Pr.

United States & the Origins of the Cuban Revolution: An Empire of Liberty in an Age of National Liberation. Jules R. Benjamin. (Illus.). 241p. 1990. text ed. 42.50 (*0-691-07836-X*); pap. text ed. 16.95 (*0-691-02536-3*) Princeton U Pr.

United States & the Pacific Basin: Changing Economic & Security Relationships. Ed. by Mary B. Bullock & Robert S. Litwak. (Woodrow Wilson Center Special Studies: No. 2). 80p. 1991. pap. text ed. 7.00 (*0-943875-31-5*, Johns Hopkins) W Wilson Ctr Pr.

UV

United States & the Pacific Economy in the 1980's. Ed. by Kermit Hanson & Thomas W. Roehl. 160p. (C). 1980. pap. text ed. write for info. (0-318-51127-4) Macmillan.

United States & the Pacific Islands. John C. Dorrance. LC 92-19951. (Washington Papers: No. 158). 192p. 1992. text ed. 45.00 (0-275-94471-9, C4471); pap. text ed. 16.95 (0-275-94472-7, B4472) CSI Studies.

United States & the Persian Gulf: An ANVIL Original. Joseph S. Roucek & Michael V. Belok. LC 84-19366. (Anvil Ser.). 208p. (C). 1985. reprint ed. pap. text ed. 11.50 (0-89874-574-8) Krieger.

United States & the Persian Gulf Crisis. Alvin J. Cottrell. 45p. 1982. pap. 24.95 (0-87855-909-4) Transaction Pubs.

United States & the Philippine Bases. Evelyn Colbert. (Orig.). (C). 1987. pap. text ed. 12.75 (0-941700-26-7) JH FPI SAIS.

United States & the Philippines. Ed. by Frank H. Golay. LC 66-22802. 1966. 3.95 (0-936904-06-2) Am Assembly.

United States & the Philippines. American Assembly Staff. Ed. by Frank H. Golay. LC 66-22802. 192p. reprint ed. pap. 54.80 (0-685-20472-3, 2029871) Bks Demand.

United States & the Politicization of the World Bank: Issues of International Law & Policy. Bartram S. Brown. 350p. 1992. 89.95 (0-7103-0424-2, A6709) Routledge Chapman & Hall.

United States & the Republic of China: Democratic Friends, Strategic Allies & Economic Partners. Ed. by Steven W. Mosher. 176p. (C). 1991. text ed. 39.95 (0-88738-410-2) Transaction Pubs.

United States & the Republic of Panama. William D. McCain. LC 72-111724. (American Imperialism: Viewpoints of United States Foreign Policy, 1898-1941 Ser.). 1970. reprint ed. 21.95 (0-405-02036-8) Ayer.

United States & the Second Hague Peace Conference: American Diplomacy & International Organization, 1899-1914. Calvin D. Davis. LC 75-17353. ix, 398p. 1976. text ed. 46.95 (0-8223-0346-9) Duke.

United States & the State of Israel. David Schoenbaum. 424p. 1993. pap. 19.95 (0-19-504576-9) OUP.

***United States & the States under the Constitution.** Christopher S. Patterson. LC 97-1955. xxxi, 290p. 1997. reprint ed. lib. bdg. 45.00 (0-8377-2559-3) Rothman.

United States & the Struggle for Southeast Asia: 1945-1975. Alan J. Levine. LC 95-6928. 200p. 1995. text ed. 52.95 (0-275-95124-3, Praeger Pubs) Greenwood.

United States & the United Nations. William A. Scott & Stephen B. Withey. LC 74-7383. (National Studies on International Organization-Carnegie Endowment for International Peace). (Illus.). 314p. 1974. reprint ed. text ed. 59.75 (0-8371-7537-2, SCUS) Greenwood.

***United States & the United Nations.** Ed. by Francis O. Wilcox & H. Field Haviland, Jr. LC 61-16652. 198p. 1961. reprint ed. pap. 56.50 (0-608-04047-9, 2064783) Bks Demand.

United States & the United Nations Treaty on Racial Discrimination, No. 9. (Studies in Transnational Legal Policy). 94p. 1975. 3.00 (0-318-13191-9) Am Soc Intl Law.

United States & the Unity of Europe. Max Beloff. LC 75-31355. 124p. 1976. reprint ed. text ed. 45.00 (0-8371-8507-6, BEUS, Greenwood Pr) Greenwood.

United States & the Vatican Policies, 1914-1918. Dragan R. Zivojinovic. LC 78-52438. (Illus.). 250p. reprint ed. pap. 71.30 (0-8357-5522-3, 2035138) Bks Demand.

United States & the Washington Conference, 1921-1922. Thomas H. Buckley. LC 79-100409. 236p. reprint ed. pap. 67.30 (0-317-20137-9, 2023166) Bks Demand.

United States & the World. Marilyn Thypin & Lynne Glasner. (History of the U. S. Ser.: Bk. 4). (Illus.). 1982. pap. text ed. 6.00 (0-941342-04-2, 1024) Entry Pub.

United States & the World Court As a Supreme Court of the Nations' Dreams, Illusions & Disillusion: Dreams, Illusions, & Disillusion. Michia Pomerance. LC 96-4896. (Legal Aspects of International Organization Ser.: No. 26). 524p. 1996. 207.00 (90-411-0204-3) Kluwer Law Tax Pubs.

United States & the World Economy: The Postwar Years. Leonard S. Silk. 1976. 27.95 (0-405-06671-6) Ayer.

United States & the 1958 Lebanon Crisis: American Intervention in the Middle East. Erika G. Alin. LC 93-36101. 170p. (C). 1994. lib. bdg. 39.00 (0-8191-9332-1) U Pr of Amer.

United States & the 1982 Law of the Sea Convention: The Cases Pro & Con. George Galdorisi et al. (Occasional Papers: 38). 79p. 1994. 10.00 (0-911189-28-9) Law Sea Inst.

United States & Turkey. Bruce R. Kuniholm. 1998. 26.95 (0-8057-7908-6, Twayne) Scribnrs Ref.

United States & United Nations: A Brief History of a Tumultuous Relationship. Jean M. Coicaud. (Concepts Ser.). 128p. (Orig.). 1996. pap. 12.00 (1-887933-06-9) Diderot Pubs.

United States & Vietnam: The Question of Diplomatic Relations, 1975-1979. Joseph J. Zasloff. (Pew Case Studies in International Affairs). 65p. (C). 1988. pap. text ed. 3.50 (1-56927-417-7) Geo U Inst Dplmcy.

United States & Vietnam from War to Peace: Papers from an Interdisciplinary Conference on Reconciliation. Ed. by Robert M. Slabey. LC 96-28830. 288p. 1996. lib. bdg. 38.50 (0-7864-0227-X) McFarland & Co.

***United States & Vietnam 1787-1941, 2 vols.** Ed. by Robert H. Miller. (Illus.). 334p. 1990. pap. text ed. 50.00 (1-57979-151-4) BPI Info Servs.

United States & World Development: Agenda 1979. Overseas Development Council Staff & Martin M. McLaughlin. LC 78-71589. 348p. 1979. text ed. 59.95 (0-275-90392-3, C0392, Praeger Pubs) Greenwood.

United States & World Development: Agenda 1980. John W. Sewell. LC 80-82415. 256p. 1980. pap. 15.95 (0-03-058992-4, Praeger Pubs) Greenwood.

United States & World Organization, 1920-1933. Denna F. Fleming. LC 70-168040. reprint ed. 41.50 (0-404-02435-1) AMS Pr.

United States & World Poverty: A Survey of the History, Current Operations & Issues of the U. S. Foreign Assistance Program. E. Boyd Wennergren et al. Ed. by Jane Gold. LC 89-10757. 201p. 1989. pap. 13.95 (0-932020-76-3) Seven Locks Pr.

United States Antarctic Research Report to the Scientific Committee on Antarctic Research (SCAR) Number 32-1990, No. 32, 1990. National Research Council Staff. 104p. 1991. pap. text ed. 19.00 (0-309-04626-2) Natl Acad Pr.

United States Anti-Apartheid Movement: Local Activism in Global Politics. Janice Love. LC 85-3564. 316p. 1985. text ed. 59.95 (0-275-90139-4, C0139, Praeger Pubs) Greenwood.

United States Arctic Interests: The 1980's & 1990's. Ed. by W. E. Westermeyer & K. M. Shusterich. (Illus.). 304p. 1984. 118.95 (0-387-96009-0) Spr-Verlag.

***United States Armory at Harper's Ferry, 1799-1860.** James B. Whisker. LC 97-10542. 220p. 1997. text ed. 89.95 (0-7734-8603-8) E Mellen.

***United States Armory at Springfield, 1795-1865.** James B. Whisker. LC 97-10540. 268p. 1997. text ed. 89.95 (0-614-30267-6) E Mellen.

United States Arms Sales: The China-Taiwan Tangle. A. Doak Barnett. LC 82-72117. (Studies in Defense Policy). 78p. reprint ed. pap. 25.00 (0-685-23672-2, 2027972) Bks Demand.

United States Arms Sales Policy: Background & Issues. Roger P. Labrie et al. LC 87-72491. (AEI Studies: No. 359). 96p. reprint ed. pap. 27.40 (0-8357-4539-2, 2037430) Bks Demand.

United States Army Air Arm: April 1861 to April 1917. Juliette A. Hennessy. (USAF Historical Studies: No. 98). 271p. 1958. reprint ed. pap. text ed. 40.95 (0-89126-014-5) MA-AH Pub.

United States Army Air Service: Wing Badges - Uniforms & Insignia 1913-1918. Terry R. Morris. 128p. 1996. 39.95 (1-888722-06-1) S A Duff.

United States Army & Counterinsurgency in the Philippine War, 1899-1902. Brian M. Linn. LC 88-20741. (Illus.). 276p. 1989. reprint ed. pap. 77.60 (0-7837-9038-4, 2049789) Bks Demand.

United States Army & Navy Directory of Airfields, Continental United States, 1944. U. S. Civil Aeronautics Administration Staff. 166p. 1992. pap. 27.00 (0-938242-23-7) Portrayal.

United States Army & Reconstruction, 1865-1877. James E. Sefton. LC 80-15136. (Illus.). xx, 284p. 1980. reprint ed. text ed. 55.00 (0-313-22602-4, SEUS, Greenwood Pr) Greenwood.

United States Army & the Motor Truck: A Case Study in Standardization. Marc K. Blackburn. LC 95-24770. (Contributions in Military Studies: No. 163). 128p. 1996. text ed. 55.00 (0-313-29808-4, Greenwood Pr) Greenwood.

United States Army in Peacetime. Ed. by Robin Higham & Carol Brandt. 1975. 9.95 (0-686-00372-1) AG Pr.

United States Army in Peacetime: Essays in Honor of the Bicentennial 1775-1975. Ed. by Robin Higham & Carol Brandt. (Illus.). 234p. (Orig.). 1975. 14.95 (0-89126-018-8); pap. 9.00 (0-89126-019-6) MA-AH Pub.

United States Army in the Korean War: Ebb & Flow, Nov. 1950-July 1951. Billy C. Mossman. LC 89-600137. (Illus.). 569p. 1990. per. 36.00 (0-16-023487-5, 008029002116) USGPO.

United States Army in the Korean War: Medic's War. Albert E. Cowdrey. (Center for Military History Publication German Report Series, DA Pam: No. 20-5). (Illus.). 409p. 1987. text ed. 27.00 (0-16-001949-4, 008-029-00147-1) USGPO.

United States Army in the World War, 1917-1919. 1996. lib. bdg. 750.99 (0-8490-6918-1) Gordon Pr.

United States Army in the World War, 1917-1919, Vol. 1: Organization of the American Expeditionary Forces. LC 88-600367. (Center for Military History Publication German Report Series, DA Pam: No. 23-6). (Illus.). 462p. 1989. reprint ed. 42.00 (0-16-001978-8, S/N008029001764) USGPO.

United States Army in World War II Special Studies Employment of Negro Troops, 2 vol. set. 1995. lib. bdg. 599.99 (0-8490-6552-6) Gordon Pr.

United States Army in World War 2: A Pictorial Record, 3 vols. Compiled by United States Army, Center of Military History Staff. (Illus.). 1426p. 1990. 39.98 (0-89660-010-6, Artabras) Abbeville Pr.

United States Army in World War 2: European Theater of Operations, Cross-Channel Attack. Gordon A. Harrison. LC 51-61669. (Illus.). 519p. 1985. reprint ed. 38.00 (0-16-001881-1, S/N 008-029-00020-2) USGPO.

United States Army in World War 2, Pictorial Record, War Against Germany: Europe & Adjacent Areas. Ed. by Kenneth E. Hunter et al. 460p. 1985. reprint ed. 20.00 (0-16-001895-1, S/N 008-029-00042-3) USGPO.

United States Army in World War 2. Special Studies, Manhattan: The Army & the Atomic Bomb. Vincent C. Jones. LC 84-12407. (Illus.). 682p. 1985. 27.00 (0-16-001939-7, S/N 008-029-00132-2) USGPO.

United States Army in World War 2, War in the Pacific: Campaign in the Marianas. Philip A. Crowl. LC 60-60000. (Center for Military History Publication German Report Series, DA Pam: No. 5-7). (Illus.). 505p. 1985. reprint ed. 46.00 (0-16-001893-5, S/N 008-029-00040-7) USGPO.

United States Army Invades the New River Valley, May 1864. LC 86-51170. 137p. 1986. reprint ed. pap. 12.00 (0-9614765-7-5) Walpa Pub.

United States Army Logistics: The Normandy Campaign, 1944. Steve R. Waddell. LC 93-49615. (Contributions in Military Studies: Vol. 155). 216p. 1994. text ed. 55.00 (0-313-29054-7, Greenwood Pr) Greenwood.

United States Army Mobilization & Logistics in the Korean War: A Research Approach. Terrence J. Gough. LC 87-1781. (Center for Military History Publication German Report Series, DA Pam: No. 70-19). (Illus.). 134p. (Orig.). 1988. pap. 5.50 (0-16-001956-7, S/N 008-029-00154-3) USGPO.

United States Army Signals Intelligence in World War II: A Documentary History. 1996. lib. bdg. 251.95 (0-8490-6923-8) Gordon Pr.

United States Army Special Operations in World War II. 1996. lib. bdg. 253.95 (0-8490-6919-X) Gordon Pr.

United States Army Special Warfare Counter-Insurgency Planning Guide. 1982. lib. bdg. 250.00 (0-87700-374-2) Revisionist Pr.

United States Army Unit Histories: A Reference & Bibliography. Compiled by James T. Controvich. 600p. 1983. pap. 82.00 (0-89126-121-4) MA-AH Pub.

United States Army Unit Histories: A Reference & Bibliography, Suppl. C. Compiled by James T. Controvich. 115p. 1996. pap. 29.95 (0-89126-195-8) MA-AH Pub.

United States Army Unit Histories: A Reference & Bibliography, Suppl. A. Compiled by James T. Controvich. 136p. 1987. Supplement A, 1987, 136p. pap. 32.00 (0-89126-166-4) MA-AH Pub.

United States Army Unit Histories: A Reference & Bibliography, Suppl. B. Compiled by James T. Controvich. 600p. 1992. Supplement B, 1992, 136p. pap. 32.00 (0-89126-174-5) MA-AH Pub.

United States As a Developing Country: Studies in U. S. History in the Progressive Era & the 1920's. Martin J. Sklar. 256p. (C). 1992. pap. text ed. 17.95 (0-521-40922-5) Cambridge U Pr.

United States As a Developing Country: Studies in U. S. History in the Progressive Era & the 1920's. Martin J. Sklar. 256p. (C). 1992. text ed. 69.95 (0-521-40060-0) Cambridge U Pr.

United States As a World Power. Archibald C. Coolidge. (History - United States Ser.). 385p. 1992. reprint ed. lib. bdg. 89.00 (0-7812-6211-9) Rprt Serv.

United States As Seen by Spanish American Writers: 1776-1890. Jone De Onis. 226p. 1952. 4.00 (0-318-14313-5) Hispanic Inst.

United States As Seen by Spanish American Writers (1776-1890) Jose De Onis. LC 74-26684. (Cultural Relations Between the U. S. & the Hispanic World Ser.: Vol. 1). 236p. (C). 1975. reprint ed. 40.00 (0-87752-184-0) Gordian.

United States-Asian Relations in the 20th Century. Young H. Kim. LC 95-19576. 432p. 1996. 109.95 (0-7734-8832-4) E Mellen.

United States at War. United States Bureau of the Budget, Committee on Records of War Administration. LC 79-169909. (FDR & the Era of the New Deal Ser.). 553p. 1972. reprint ed. lib. bdg. 65.00 (0-306-70330-0) Da Capo.

United States at War, 1941-1945. Gary R. Hess. Ed. by John H. Franklin & A. S. Eisenstadt. LC 85-20728. (American History Ser.). 184p. (C). 1986. pap. text ed. write for info. (0-88295-834-8) Harlan Davidson.

United States Atlas for Young People. Kathie B. Smith. LC 90-675059. (Illus.). 128p. (J). (gr. 3-7). 1991. lib. bdg. 15.50 (0-8167-2195-5) Troll Communs.

United States Atlas for Young People. Kathie B. Smith. LC 90-675059. (Illus.). 128p. (J). (gr. 3-7). 1996. pap. 9.95 (0-8167-2196-3) Troll Communs.

United States Atlases. Ed. by Clara E. Le Gear. LC 71-154058. (Library of Congress Publications in Reprint). 1971. reprint ed. 23.95 (0-405-03424-5) Ayer.

United States Attitudes Toward China: The Impact of American Missionaries. Ed. by Patricia Neils. LC 89-78510. (Studies on Modern China). 304p. (gr. 13). 1990. text ed. 57.95 (0-87332-632-6, East Gate Bk) M E Sharpe.

United States, Australia, & Regional Nation Defense Interactions in Asia Pacific. William Pendley et al. 1993. write for info. (1-884296-01-7) Austlia-NZ Studies.

United States Bar Review Multistate Questions. Michael Cantarutti. 500p. (Orig.). (C). 1993. reprint ed. pap. text ed. write for info. (1-879563-37-1) Lexicon CA.

United States Beet Sugar Industry & the Tariff. Roy G. Blakey. LC 77-76717. (Columbia University. Studies in the Social Sciences: No. 119). reprint ed. 37.50 (0-404-51119-8) AMS Pr.

United States, Britain & Appeasement 1936-1939. C. A. MacDonald. LC 79-27121. 224p. 1981. text ed. 32.50 (0-312-83313-X) St Martin.

United States Business History, 1602-1988: A Chronology. Richard B. Robinson, Jr. LC 90-34102. 656p. 1990. text ed. 69.50 (0-313-26095-8, RUB/, Greenwood Pr) Greenwood.

United States, Canada & the New International Economic Order. Ed. by Ervin Laszlo & Joel Kurtzman. (Policy Studies). 1979. 52.00 (0-08-025113-7, Pergamon Pr) Elsevier.

United States, Canada, & the World Economy. Charles Doran & Alvin Drischler. 100p. 1991. pap. 14.95 (0-941700-73-9) JH FPI SAIS.

United States-Canada Free Trade: An Evaluation of the Agreement. Jeffrey J. Schott. LC 88-9106. (Policy Analyses in International Economics Ser.: No. 24). 51p. (Orig.). reprint ed. pap. 25.00 (0-7837-4213-4, 2043902) Bks Demand.

United States-Canada Free Trade Act: A Legislative History of the US-Canada Free Trade Agreement Implementation Act of 1988, Pub. L. 100-449, 13 vols., Set. Ed. by Bernard D. Reams, Jr. & Mary A. Nelson. LC 89-81792. (Federal Legislative Histories of Laws & Legislation on Trade Law & Economic Policy Ser.: Pt. 2). 12084p. 1990. lib. bdg. 1,050.00 (0-89941-728-0, 306450) W S Hein.

United States Cancellarions 1845-1869. Hubert C. Skinner & Amos Eno. (APS Handbook Ser.). (Illus.). 1980. 22.00 (0-933580-04-5) Am Philatelic Society.

United States Capitol. Fred J. Maroon. LC 92-35906. (Illus.). 192p. 1993. 45.00 (1-55670-316-3); pap. 24.95 (1-55670-319-8) Stewart Tabori & Chang.

United States Cartridge Co.-Lowell, Mass: Catalog 1891. (Illus.). pap. 3.50 (0-686-20762-9) Sand Pond.

United States Catholic & Secondary Schools Finances 1994. Frederick H. Brigham, Jr. (Illus.). 35p. (Orig.). 1995. pap. 13.30 (1-55833-159-X) Natl Cath Educ.

United States Catholic Elementary & Secondary Schools, 1990-91. Intro. by Alice Gallin. (Data Bank Ser.). 54p. (Orig.). 1991. pap. 6.50 (1-55833-110-7) Natl Cath Educ.

United States Catholic Elementary & Secondary Schools, 1990-91: Annual Statistical Report on Schools, Enrollment & Staffing. Frederick H. Brigham, Jr. 1991. 9.30 (1-55833-100-X) Natl Cath Educ.

United States Catholic Elementary & Secondary Schools, 1992-1993. Frederick H. Brigham, Jr. 62p. (Orig.). 1993. pap. text ed. 10.00 (1-55833-098-4) Natl Cath Educ.

United States Catholic Elementary & Secondary Schools 1993-1994. Frederick H. Brigham, Jr. (Illus.). 32p. (Orig.). 1994. pap. 12.00 (1-55833-134-4) Natl Cath Educ.

United States Catholic Elementary Schools & Their Finances 1984. 6.00 (0-318-03695-9) Natl Cath Educ.

United States Catholic Elementary Schools & their Finances, 1986. Frank H. Bredweg. 1986. 6.00 (0-318-20577-7) Natl Cath Educ.

United States Catholic Elementary Schools & Their Finances 1988. Frank H. Bredeweg. (Data Bank Ser.). 14p. 1988. pap. 6.60 (1-55833-006-2) Natl Cath Educ.

United States Catholic Elementary Schools & Their Finances 1989. Robert J. Kealey. (Data Bank Ser.). 57p. (Orig.). 1990. pap. 9.00 (1-55833-052-6) Natl Cath Educ.

United States Catholic Elementary Schools & Their Finances, 1991. Robert J. Kealey. (Data Bank Ser.). (Illus.). 53p. (Orig.). 1992. pap. 7.25 (1-55833-119-0) Natl Cath Educ.

United States Census Key, 1850, 1860 & 1870. American Genealogical Lending Library Staff. 193p. 1987. pap. 14.95 (0-932022-32-4) Precision Indexing.

United States Census of Putnam County Tennessee, 1870. Norman T. McGee & G. Kay McGee. LC 89-80386. (Illus.). 170p. (Orig.). 1989. pap. 25.00 (0-9622403-1-1) Lilac Hill Pubns.

United States Census of Putnam County Tennessee, 1880. Illus. by Ernest L. Jackson. LC 89-80385. 290p. 1989. pap. 30.00 (0-9622403-0-3) Lilac Hill Pubns.

United States Census 1818 Pensioners Lists. (Illus.). 1988. lib. bdg. 58.00 (0-89593-501-5) Accelerated Index.

United States Census 1850 Slave Schedules. (Illus.). lib. bdg. 410.00 (0-89593-502-3) Accelerated Index.

United States Chess Championship, 1845-1996. 2nd ed. Andrew Soltis. LC 96-35534. (Illus.). 247p. 1996. lib. bdg. 45.00 (0-7864-0248-2) McFarland & Co.

United States Chess Federation's Official Rules of Chess. 4th ed. Compiled by United States Chess Federation Staff. LC 92-40961. 1994. pap. 16.00 (0-8129-2217-4, Times Bks) Random.

***United States Children's Bureau, 1912-1972.** Julia C. Lathrop. Date not set. 26.95 (0-405-05988-4) Ayer.

United States Children's Bureau, 1912-1972: An Original Anthology. LC 74-1712. (Children & Youth Ser.: Vol. 16). (Illus.). 1974. 16.00 (0-685-50597-9) Ayer.

United States, China & Arms Control. Ralph N. Clough et al. LC 75-15650. 165p. reprint ed. pap. 47.10 (0-317-20793-8, 2025370) Bks Demand.

United States-China Nuclear Bilateral Accord. Michael J. Brenner. (Pew Case Studies in International Affairs). 50p. (C). 1986. pap. text ed. 3.50 (1-56927-106-2) Geo U Inst Dplmcy.

United States China Policy: Building a New Consensus. Center for Strategic & International Studies Staff. (Asian Studies Report). 117p. 1994. reprint ed. pap. 33.40 (0-608-00206-2, 2060989) Bks Demand.

United States Citations, 32 vols. Shepard's Citation, Inc. Staff. 1986. 2,976.00 (0-685-58455-0) Shepards.

***United States Citizenship Education & Naturalization Information: An English As a Second Language Text.** 1997. lib. bdg. 251.95 (0-8490-6209-8) Gordon Pr.

United States Citizenship Examination. Jack Rudman. (Career Examination Ser.: C-3487). 1994. pap. 23.95 (0-8373-3487-X) Nat Learn.

United States Civil Service Commission: Its History, Activities & Organization. Darrell H. Smith. LC 72-3065. (Brookings Institution. Institute for Government Research. Service Monographs of the U. S. Government: No. 49). reprint ed. 45.00 (0-404-57149-2) AMS Pr.

United States Civil War Revenue Stamp Taxes. Michael D. Mahler. LC 88-72215. (C. & S. Revenue Ser.). (Illus.). 384p. 1988. 49.95 (0-9603498-3-9) Castenholz Sons.

United States Clad Coinage. Ginger Rapsus. (Illus.). 184p. (Orig.). 1992. pap. text ed. 12.95 (0-943161-42-8) Bowers & Merena.

United States Clock Co. Catalogue. (Illus.). 15p. pap. 3.00 (0-930163-67-2) Arlington Bk.

An Asterisk (*) at the beginning of an entry indicates that the title is appearing in BIP for the first time.

United States Coal & the Electric Power Industry. Richard L. Gordon. LC 74-24403. 232p. reprint ed. pap. 66.20 (*0-8357-4677-1*, 2037624) Bks Demand.

United States Coal Industry 1970-1990: Two Decades of Change. 1995. lib. bdg. 250.00 (*0-8490-6504-6*) Gordon Pr.

United States Coal Reserves: An Update by Heat & Sulfur Content. 1995. lib. bdg. 250.00 (*0-8490-6505-4*) Gordon Pr.

United States Coastal Charts, 1783-1860. Peter Guthorn. LC 84-51187. (Illus.). 272p. 1984. 59.00 (*0-88740-019-1*) Schiffer.

United States Code Annotated: Crimes and Criminal Procedure, 15 vols. write for info. (*0-318-57482-9*) West Pub.

United States Code Service: Lawyers Edition, 184 vols., Set. LC 72-76254. 1991. suppl. ed. 2,000.00 (*0-318-57187-0*) Lawyers Cooperative.

United States Code Unannotated, 14 vols., Set. Gould Editorial Staff. 449.00 (*0-87526-359-3*) Gould.

United States Code, 1994 Vol. 49: General Index A-B. 1001p. 1996. boxed 60.00 (*0-16-024146-4*, 0S2-001-00418-3) USGPO.

***United States Code, 1994 Edition Vol. 1: General Provisions; The Congress; The President; Flag & Sea, Seat of Government, & the States; Government Organization & Employees; Surety Bonds (Repealed)** 1688p. 1995. 65.00 (*0-614-24628-8*, 052-001-00390-0) USGPO.

***United States Code, 1994 Edition Vol. 3: Aliens & Nationality; Arbitration; Armed Forces, Sections 101 to 3000.** 1414p. 1995. 62.00 (*0-614-24630-X*, 052-001-00392-6) USGPO.

***United States Code, 1994 Edition Vol. 4: Armed Forces, Sections 3001 to End; Bankruptcy.** 1078p. 1995. 53.00 (*0-614-24631-8*, 052-001-00393-4) USGPO.

***United States Code, 1994 Edition Vol. 5: Banks & Banking; Census.** 1628p. 1995. 66.00 (*0-614-24632-6*, 052-001-00394-2) USGPO.

***United States Code, 1994 Edition Vol. 6: Coast Guard; Commerce & Trade.** 1618p. 1995. 66.00 (*0-614-24633-4*, 052-001-00395-1) USGPO.

***United States Code, 1994 Edition Vol. 7: Conservation, Sections 1 to 790.** 1121p. 1995. 59.00 (*0-614-24634-2*, 052-001-00396-9) USGPO.

***United States Code, 1994 Edition Vol. 8: Conservation, Sections 791 to End; Copyrights.** 1068p. 1995. 53.00 (*0-614-24635-0*, 052-001-00397-7) USGPO.

***United States Code, 1994 Edition Vol. 9: Crimes & Criminal Procedure; Customs Duties.** 1600p. 1995. 66.00 (*0-614-24636-9*, 052-001-00398-5) USGPO.

***United States Code, 1994 Edition Vol. 10: Education.** 1492p. 1995. 65.00 (*0-614-24637-7*, 052-001-00399-3) USGPO.

***United States Code, 1994 Edition Vol. 11: Food & Drugs; Foreign Relations & Intercourse.** 1718p. 1995. 69.00 (*0-614-24638-5*, 052-001-00400-1) USGPO.

***United States Code, 1994 Edition Vol. 12: Highways; Hospitals & Asylums; Indians.** 992p. 1995. 52.00 (*0-614-24639-3*, 052-001-00401-9) USGPO.

***United States Code, 1994 Edition Vol. 13: Internal Revenue Code, Sections 1 to 1000.** 1563p. 1995. 65.00 (*0-614-24640-7*, 052-001-00402-7) USGPO.

***United States Code, 1994 Edition Vol. 14: Internal Revenue Code, Sections 1001 to End.** 1565p. 1995. 66.00 (*0-614-24641-5*, 052-001-00403-5) USGPO.

***United States Code, 1994 Edition Vol. 15: Intoxicating Liquors; Judiciary & Judicial Procedure.** 1145p. 1995. 60.00 (*0-614-24642-3*, 052-001-00404-3) USGPO.

***United States Code, 1994 Edition Vol. 16: Labor; Mineral Lands & Mining; Money & Finance; National Guard.** 1589p. 1995. 66.00 (*0-614-24643-1*, 052-001-00405-1) USGPO.

***United States Code, 1994 Edition Vol. 17: Navigation & Navigable Waters; Navy; Patents; Patriotic Societies & Observances; Pay & Allowances of the Uniformed Services.** 1178p. 1995. 59.00 (*0-614-24644-X*, 052-001-00406-0) USGPO.

***United States Code, 1994 Edition Vol. 18: Veterans' Benefits, & Appendix; Postal Service; Public Buildings, Property, & Works, & Appendix; & Public Contracts.** 1354p. 1995. 63.00 (*0-614-24645-8*, 052-001-00407-8) USGPO.

***United States Code, 1994 Edition Vol. 19: The Public Health & Welfare, Sections 1 to 300.** 907p. 1995. 51.00 (*0-614-24646-6*, 052-001-00408-6) USGPO.

***United States Code, 1994 Edition Vol. 20: The Public Health & Welfare, Sections 301 to 1399.** 404p. 1995. 63.00 (*0-614-24647-4*, 052-001-00409-4) USGPO.

***United States Code, 1994 Edition Vol. 21: The Public Health & Welfare, Sections 1400 to 4000.** 278p. 1995. 61.00 (*0-614-24648-2*, 052-001-00410-8) USGPO.

***United States Code, 1994 Edition Vol. 22: The Public Health & Welfare, Sections 4001 to 7700.** 295p. 1995. 61.00 (*0-614-24649-0*, 052-001-00411-6) USGPO.

***United States Code, 1994 Edition Vol. 23: The Public Health & Welfare, Sections 7701 to End.** 1079p. 1995. 58.00 (*0-614-24650-4*, 052-001-00412-4) USGPO.

***United States Code, 1994 Edition Vol. 24: Public Lands; Public Printing & Documents; Railroads; Shipping & Appendix.** 1412p. 1995. 67.00 (*0-614-24651-2*, 052-001-00413-2) USGPO.

***United States Code, 1994 Edition Vol. 25: Telegraphs, Telephones, & Radiotelegraphs; Territories & Insular Possessions; Transportation.** 1471p. 1995. 67.00 (*0-614-24652-0*, 052-001-00414-1) USGPO.

***United States Code, 1994 Edition Vol. 26: War & National Defense, & Appendix; & Popular Names.** 1157p. 1995. 62.00 (*0-614-24653-9*, 052-001-00415-9) USGPO.

***United States Code, 1994 Edition Vol. 27: Tables.** 1996. 65.00 (*0-614-24654-7*, 052-001-00416-7) USGPO.

***United States Code, 1994 Edition Vol. 28: Tables.** 1996. 66.00 (*0-614-24655-5*, 052-001-00417-5) USGPO.

United States Coins by Design Types: An Action Guide for the Collector & Investor. rev. ed. Q. David Bowers. (Illus.). 248p. 1988. reprint ed. pap. 9.95 (*0-943161-13-4*) Bowers & Merena.

***United States Coins 1998.** Marc Hudgeons. 1997. pap. 6.99 (*0-676-60067-0*) Random.

United States Colored Troops, 1863-1867. William A. Gladstone. (Illus.). 132p. (C). 1990. pap. text ed. 16.95 (*0-939631-16-4*) Thomas Publications.

United States-Comanche Relations: The Reservation Years. William T. Hagan. LC 76-43318. (Yale Western Americana Ser.: No. 28). 352p. reprint ed. pap. 100.40 (*0-8357-8360-X*, 2033738) Bks Demand.

United States Combat Aircrew Survival Equipment, WW II to the Present: A Reference Guide for Collectors. Michael S. Breuninger. LC 93-90752. (Illus.). 208p. (Orig.). 1995. pap. 29.95 (*0-88740-791-9*) Schiffer.

***United States Commission on Minority Business Development: Final Report.** (Illus.). 300p. (C). 1996. reprint ed. pap. 40.00 (*0-7881-3144-3*) DIANE Pub.

United States Commission on Minority Business Development, Final Report. 1995. lib. bdg. 250.00 (*0-8490-6553-4*) Gordon Pr.

United States, Common Market & International Antitrust: A Comparative Guide. Barry E. Hawk. write for info. (*0-318-66009-1*) P-H.

United States, Common Market, & International Antitrust: A Comparative Guide, 3 vols. 2nd ed. Barry E. Hawk. LC 84-27790. 1985. Supplements avail. suppl. ed. 225.00 (*0-15-004385-6*, #H43856) HarBrace.

United States, Communism & the Emergent World. Bernard P. Kiernan. LC 72-75636. 256p. reprint ed. 73.00 (*0-8357-9251-X*, 2015826) Bks Demand.

United States Congress. Dennis Hale. LC 83-7992. 360p. 1984. pap. 24.95 (*0-87855-939-6*) Transaction Pubs.

United States Congress: Proceedings of the Thomas P. O'Neill, Jr., Symposium on the U. S. Congress, Boston College, 1981. Ed. by Dennis Hale. LC 82-71847. 360p. (Orig.). (C). 1982. pap. text ed. 10.00 (*0-943360-00-5*) BU Poli Sci.

United States Congress & the Making of U. S. Policy Toward Mexico. Donald L. Wyman. (Research Reports: No. 13). 74p. (Orig.). (C). 1981. ring bd. 5.00 (*0-935391-12-6*, RR-13) UCSD Ctr US-Mex.

United States Congress, Immigration Hearings. Ed. by Carlos E. Cortez. LC 80-7793. (Hispanics in the United States Ser.). 1981. reprint ed. lib. bdg. 25.95 (*0-405-13186-0*) Ayer.

United States Congress, Immigration 1976. Ed. by Carlos E. Cortez. LC 80-7794. (Hispanics in the United States Ser.). 1981. lib. bdg. 28.95 (*0-405-13187-9*) Ayer.

United States Congress in a Transitional Era, 1800-1841: The Interplay of Party, Faction & Section, 2 vols. Joel H. Silbey. LC 90-28961. (Congress of the United States, 1789-1989 Ser.: Vol. 5). 603p. 1991. Set. 150.00 (*0-926019-32-5*) Carlson Pub.

United States Congressional Directories, 1789-1840. Ed. by James S. Young et al. 417p. 1973. text ed. 95.00 (*0-231-03365-6*) Col U Pr.

United States Congressional Districts, 1788-1841. Stanley B. Parsons et al. LC 77-83897. (Illus.). 416p. 1978. text ed. 105.00 (*0-8371-9828-3*, PUS/, Greenwood Pr) Greenwood.

United States Congressional Districts, 1883-1913. Stanley B. Parsons et al. LC 89-675315. 464p. 1990. text ed. 115.00 (*0-313-26482-1*, PUC/, Greenwood Pr) Greenwood.

United States Congressional Elections, 1788-1996: The Official Results of the Elections of the 1st Through 105th Congresses. Michael J. Dubin. LC 96-9841. 1152p. 1997. lib. bdg. 175.00 (*0-7864-0283-0*) McFarland & Co.

United States Conquest of California: An Original Anthology. Lewis & Emory. Ed. by Carlos E. Cortes. LC 76-7303. (Chicano Heritage Ser.). (Illus.). 1977. 57.95 (*0-405-09542-2*) Ayer.

United States Constitution: Its Birth, Growth & Influence in Asia. Ed. by J. Barton Starr. 322p. (Orig.). 1988. pap. 37.50 (*962-209-201-2*, Pub. by Hong Kong Univ Pr HK) Coronet Bks.

United States Constitution: Personalities, Principles, & Issues. Walter B. Mead. LC 87-16162. 236p. (C). 1987. pap. text ed. 14.95 (*0-87249-523-X*) U of SC Pr.

United States Constitution: Supreme Court Cases. Denis Killeen. 374p. (Orig.). 1987. pap. 19.95 (*0-944830-00-5*) Hartfordshire.

United States Constitution Study Guide. 2nd ed. 106p. (Orig.). (C). 1996. pap. 13.95 (*0-9635364-3-5*) Academic Solutions.

United States Constitutional Convention. David W. Felder. 52p. 1996. pap. text ed. 8.95 (*0-910959-61-7*, B&G 25B) Wellington Pr.

United States Contract Law. E. Allan Farnsworth. 200p. 1991. 70.00 (*0-929179-29-3*) Juris Pubng.

United States Control of Petroleum Imports: A Study of the Federal Government's Role in the Management of Domestic Oil Supplies. Torleif Meloe. Ed. by Stuart Bruchey. LC 78-22701. (Energy in the American Economy Ser.). (Illus.). 1979. lib. bdg. 28.95 (*0-405-12003-6*) Ayer.

United States Copper Cents Eighteen Sixteen to Eighteen Fifty-Seven. Howard R. Newcomb. LC 81-50923. (Illus.). 288p. 1981. reprint ed. lib. bdg. 50.00 (*0-88000-127-5*) Quarterman.

United States Copper Cents (1816-1857) Howard R. Newcomb. (Illus.). 1988. reprint ed. lib. bdg. 45.00 (*0-942666-51-8*) S J Durst.

United States County Encyclopedia, Ser. 1, Vol. 1. Ronald V. Jackson. LC 77-77313. (Illus.). lib. bdg. 45.00 (*0-89593-159-1*) Accelerated Index.

United States County Encyclopedia & State Maps. 1977. 50.00 (*0-89593-644-5*) Accelerated Index.

United States County Guide to All Fifty States. 1987. 15.00 (*0-89593-645-3*) Accelerated Index.

United States Court Case Names Citator, 2 vols. Shepard's Citation, Inc. Staff. 1987. 114.00 (*0-685-23126-7*) Shepards.

United States Crude Oil, Natural Gas & Natural Gas Liquids Reserves. 1995. lib. bdg. 250.00 (*0-8490-6506-2*) Gordon Pr.

United States: Cruel & Inhuman Treatment: The Use of Four-Point Restraint in the Onondaga County Public Safety Building. Physicians for Human Rights Staff. LC 93-84902. (Illus.). 67p. 1993. pap. 7.00 (*1-879707-16-0*) Phy Human Rights.

United States Crusade in China, 1938-1945. Michael Schaller. LC 78-15032. 380p. reprint ed. pap. 108.30 (*0-8357-3581-8*, 2034612) Bks Demand.

***United States Cryptographic Patents, 1861-1989.** Jack Levine. (Illus.). 125p. 1991. reprint ed. pap. 35.70 (*0-608-03153-4*, 2063606) Bks Demand.

United States Cultural History: A Guide to Information Sources. Ed. by Philip I. Mitterling. LC 79-24061. (American Government & History Information Guide Ser.: Vol. 5). 592p. 1980. 68.00 (*0-8103-1369-3*) Gale.

United States Custom Service: A Bicentennial History. 1990. lib. bdg. 79.95 (*0-8490-4005-1*) Gordon Pr.

United States Customs & International Trade Guide, 4 vols. Peter B. Feller. 1979. Set. Updates. ring bd. write for info. (*0-8205-1757-7*) Bender.

***United States Customs Service Guide for Private Flyers.** 1997. lib. bdg. 251.75 (*0-8490-8106-8*) Gordon Pr.

United States, Cyprus & the Rule of Law, 1974-1994: Twenty Years of Turkish Aggression & Occupation. Ed. by Eugene T. Rossides. LC 96-20080. 320p. 1996. text ed. 40.00 (*0-89241-569-X*) Caratzas.

United States Decision to Resist Aggression in Korea: The Application of an Analytical Scheme. Richard C. Snyder & Glenn D. Paige. (Reprint Series in Social Sciences). (C). 1993. reprint ed. pap. text ed. 1.00 (*0-8290-2763-7*, PS-268) Irvington.

United States Decorated Stoneware. Carmen A. Guappone. (Orig.). 1988. pap. 24.95 (*0-9615230-9-3*) Guappones Pubs.

United States Defense Spending: How Much Is Enough? Ed. by Carol C. Collins. LC 83-20603. (Illus.). 256p. reprint ed. pap. 73.00 (*0-7837-5330-6*, 2045070) Bks Demand.

United States Democratic Review, 42 vols., lacks vol. 39. reprint ed. Set. lib. bdg. 3,200.00 (*0-404-19561-X*) AMS Pr.

United States Department of Agriculture: A Study in Administration. William L. Wanlass. LC 78-63970. (Johns Hopkins University. Studies in the Social Sciences. Thirtieth Ser. 1912: 1). 136p. (C). 1982. reprint ed. 37.50 (*0-404-61216-4*) AMS Pr.

United States Department of Agriculture Pomological Watercolor Collection Index. Compiled by Patricia L. Morelli. 211p. 1987. 105.00 (*0-85964-206-2*) Chadwyck-Healey.

United States Dependency on Canadian Natural Resources: Extent & Significance: Seminar Proceedings, April 7, 1979. Ed. by Frank J. Convery & Boyd R. Strain. 72p. reprint ed. pap. 25.00 (*0-7837-6047-7*, 2045860) Bks Demand.

United States Destroyer Operations in World War II. Theodore Roscoe. LC 53-4273. (Illus.). 581p. 1953. 44.95 (*0-87021-726-7*) Naval Inst Pr.

United States Development Assistance Policy: The Domestic Politics of Foreign Economic Aid. Vernon W. Ruttan. LC 95-6422. (Studies in Development). 568p. 1995. text ed. 65.00 (*0-8018-5051-7*) Johns Hopkins.

United States Dictionary of Places. LC 87-32065. 644p. 1988. lib. bdg. 145.00 (*0-403-09899-8*) Somerset Pub.

United States Dimes. Abe Kosoff. pap. 8.00 (*0-317-27389-2*) S J Durst.

United States Diplomatic Codes & Ciphers, 1775-1938. Ralph E. Weber. (Illus.). 656p. 1979. 44.95 (*0-913750-20-4*) Transaction Pubs.

United States Diplomatic History, Vol. 1: From Revolution to Empire to 1914. Gerard H. Clarfield. 368p. (C). 1991. pap. text ed. 26.80 (*0-13-029190-0*) P-H.

United States Diplomatic History, Vol. 2: The Age of Ascendancy since 1900. Gerard H. Clarfield. 512p. (C). 1991. pap. text ed. 33.00 (*0-13-029232-X*) P-H.

***United States Direct Investment Abroad: Operations of United States Parent Companies & Their Foreign Affiliates.** 1997. lib. bdg. 250.95 (*0-8490-6100-8*) Gordon Pr.

United States Direct Tax of 1798: Tax Lists for Cumberland Co., PA. Wilbur J. McElwain. (Illus.). 231p. (Orig.). 1995. pap. text ed. 33.00 (*0-7884-0118-1*) Heritage Bk.

United States District Court for the Northern District of Ohio Rules. Lawyers Cooperative Publishing Staff. 1993. ring bd. 39.50 (*0-317-05383-3*) Lawyers Cooperative.

United States Documents in the Propaganda Fide Archives: A Calendar, Vol. 1. Ed. by Finbar Kenneally et al. 1987. 50.00 (*0-614-05564-4*) AAFH.

United States Documents in the Propaganda Fide Archives: A Calendar, Vol. 2. Ed. by Finbar Kenneally et al. 1987. 50.00 (*0-614-05565-2*) AAFH.

United States Documents in the Propaganda Fide Archives: A Calendar, Vol. 3. Ed. by Finbar Kenneally et al. 1987. 50.00 (*0-614-05566-0*) AAFH.

United States Documents in the Propaganda Fide Archives: A Calendar, Vol. 4. Ed. by Finbar Kenneally et al. 1987. 50.00 (*0-614-05567-9*) AAFH.

United States Documents in the Propaganda Fide Archives: A Calendar, Vol. 5. Ed. by Finbar Kenneally et al. 1987. 50.00 (*0-614-05568-7*) AAFH.

United States Documents in the Propaganda Fide Archives: A Calendar, Vol. 6. Ed. by Finbar Kenneally et al. 1987. 50.00 (*0-614-05569-5*) AAFH.

United States Documents in the Propaganda Fide Archives: A Calendar, Vol. 7. Ed. by Finbar Kenneally et al. 1987. 50.00 (*0-614-05570-9*) AAFH.

United States Documents in the Propaganda Fide Archives: A Calendar, Vol. 8. Ed. by Debevec et al. 1980. 50.00 (*0-88382-208-3*) AAFH.

United States Documents in the Propaganda Fide Archives: A Calendar, Vol. 9. Ed. by Debevec et al. 1982. 50.00 (*0-88382-210-5*) AAFH.

United States Documents in the Propaganda Fide Archives: A Calendar, Vol. 10. Ed. by Mathias Kiemen et al. 1984. 50.00 (*0-88382-211-3*) AAFH.

United States Documents in the Propaganda Fide Archives: Index to Vols. 1-7. Finbar Kenneally. (Propaganda Fide Ser.). 1981. 50.00 (*0-88382-209-1*) AAFH.

United States Dressage Federation Calender of Competitions. 180p. write for info. (*0-318-60030-7*) US Dressage Fed.

United States Earthquakes. (Disaster Ser.). 1990. lib. bdg. 79.95 (*0-8490-4051-5*) Gordon Pr.

United States Earthquakes, 1986. Carl W. Stover & Lindie R. Brewer. Vol. 2089. write for info. (*0-318-72734-X*) US Geol Survey.

United States Economic Measures Against Cuba: Proceedings in the United Nations & International Law Issues. Michael Krinsky & David Golove. LC 92-43229. 1993. 35.00 (*1-880831-02-3*); pap. 15.00 (*1-880831-01-5*) Aletheia Pr.

United States Economy: Performance & Issues. International Monetary Fund Staff & Yusuke Horiguchi. 599p. 1992. pap. 35.00 (*1-55775-231-1*) Intl Monetary.

United States Educational System: Marxist Approaches. Ed. by Marvin J. Berlowitz & Frank E. Chapman, Jr. LC 80-12394. (Studies in Marxism: Vol. 6). 221p. 1980. pap. 7.50 (*0-930656-11-3*) MEP Pubns.

United States Electoral Systems: Their Impact on Women & Minorities. Ed. by Wilma Rule & Joseph F. Zimmerman. LC 91-34481. (Contributions in Political Science Ser.: No. 294). 264p. 1992. text ed. 59.95 (*0-313-27730-3*, ZIU/, Greenwood Pr); pap. text ed. 18.95 (*0-275-94240-6*, B4240, Greenwood Pr) Greenwood.

United States Electricity Trade with Canada & Mexico. 1994. lib. bdg. 259.95 (*0-8490-5626-8*) Gordon Pr.

United States' Emergence As a Southeast Asian Power, 1940-1950. Gary R. Hess. LC 86-18861. 448p. 1987. text ed. 66.00 (*0-231-06190-0*) Col U Pr.

United States Employment & Training Programs: A Selected Annotated Bibliography. Compiled by Frederick A. Raffa et al. LC 82-25108. xvi, 152p. 1983. text ed. 42.95 (*0-313-23872-3*, RUE/, Greenwood Pr) Greenwood.

United States Energy Policies: An Agenda for Research. Resources for the Future, Inc. Staff. LC 68-28767. 166p. reprint ed. pap. 47.40 (*0-317-26477-X*, 2023812) Bks Demand.

United States Energy R & D Policy: The Role of Economics. John E. Tilton. LC 74-21753. (Resources for the Future, RFF Working Papers: EN-4). 142p. reprint ed. pap. 40.50 (*0-317-26483-4*, 2023817) Bks Demand.

***United States Entry & Work Permits.** Liam Schwartz & Tsvi Kantor. LC 97-19439. 1997. write for info. (*90-411-0431-3*) Kluwer Law Tax Pubs.

United States Ethnic Heritage Studies Center. U. S. House of Representatives General Subcommittee on Education & Labor. Ed. by Francesco Cordasco. LC 77-90564. (Bilingual-Bicultural Education in the U. S. Ser.). 1978. reprint ed. lib. bdg. 36.95 (*0-405-11102-9*) Ayer.

United States-European Community Relations: Past, Present, Future. Leon Hurwitz. Ed. by S. Victor Papacosma. (Occasional Papers). 1993. pap. 5.00 (*1-882160-02-9*) Kent St U L L Lemnitzer.

United States-European Community Trade Directory. William S. Loiry. 416p. 1993. text ed. 55.00 (*0-471-55667-X*) Wiley.

United States Expansionism: The Imperialist Urge in the 1890s. David Healy. LC 71-121769. (Illus.). 325p. reprint ed. pap. 92.70 (*0-8357-6801-5*, 2035480) Bks Demand.

United States Expansionism & British North America, 1775-1871. Reginald C. Stuart. LC 87-25506. xvi, 374p. (C). 1988. 55.00 (*0-8078-1767-8*) U of NC Pr.

United States Exploring Expedition During the Years 1838, 1839, 1840, 1841, 1842 under the Command Charles Wilkes, U.S.N., 2 Vols., Vol. 8. John Cassin. Ed. by Keir B. Sterling. LC 77-81079. (Biologists & Their World Ser.). (Illus.). 1979. reprint ed. lib. bdg. 52.95 (*0-405-10656-4*) Ayer.

United States Exploring Expedition During the Years 1838, 1839, 1840, 1841, 1842 under the Command of Charles Wilkes, U.S.N, Vol. 8. Titian R. Peale. Ed. by Keir B. Sterling. LC 77-81078. (Biologists & Their World Ser.). (Illus.). 1978. reprint ed. lib. bdg. 35.95 (*0-405-10646-7*) Ayer.

United States Exploring Expedition During the Years 1838, 1839, 1840, 1841, 1842 under the Command of Charles Wilkes, U.S.N. Herpetology, 2 Vols., Vol. 20. Charles Girard. Ed. by Keir B. Srling. LC 77-81095. (Biologists & Their World Ser.). (Illus.). 1979. reprint ed. lib. bdg. 55.95 (*0-405-10678-5*) Ayer.

U
V

United States Exploring Expedition During the Years 1838-1842 under the Command of Charles Wilkes: Botanical Section, Set. Incl. Vol. 15. Phanoregamia. A. Gray. 1968. 288.00 (3-7682-0714-5); Vol. 16. Cryptogamia, Filices, Lycopodiaceae & Hydropterides. W. D. Brackenridge. (Illus.). 1968. 108.00 (3-7682-0715-3); Vol. 17. Cryptogamia Musci, Lichenes, Algae, Fungi Phanerogamia of Pacific North America. W. B. Sullivent et al. (Illus.). 1968. 120.00 (3-7682-0716-1); 1968. reprint ed. 650.00 (3-7682-0709-9) Lubrecht & Cramer.

United States Export Control Policy: The National Organization of Power. William J. Long. 200p. 1989. text ed. 45.00 (0-231-06798-4) Col U Pr.

United States Export Policy on Technology Transfer. Ed. by Laura S. Lengjak. (Wisconsin International Law Journal, 1982 Ser.: Vol. 1983). 228p. (Orig.). 1984. pap. 8.00 (0-933431-01-5) U Wisc Law Madison.

United States External Adjustment & the World Economy. William R. Cline. LC 89-2038. 392p. (Orig.). (C). 1989. pap. 25.00 (0-88132-048-X) Inst Intl Eco.

United States Federal Census Microfilms, 1790-1910. 1983. 10.00 (0-89593-646-1) Accelerated Index.

United States Federal Census Place Enrollment Schedules, 1790-1830 Inclusive, Vol. 1. Ronald V. Jackson. 1991. 90.00 (0-89593-830-8) Accelerated Index.

United States Federal Census Place Enrollment Schedules, 1840-1850 Inclusive, Vol. 2. Ronald V. Jackson. 1991. 90.00 (0-89593-831-6) Accelerated Index.

United States Federal Census Place Enrollment Schedules, 1860, Vol. 3. Ronald V. Jackson. 1991. 90.00 (0-89593-832-4) Accelerated Index.

United States Federal Census Place Enrollment Schedules, 1870, Vol. 4. Ronald V. Jackson. 1991. 190.00 (0-89593-833-2) Accelerated Index.

United States Federal System: Legal Integration in the American Experience. Peter Hay & Ronald D. Rotunda. LC 82-8271. (Studies in Comparative Law: No. 22). 366p. 1983. lib. bdg. 40.00 (0-379-20800-8) Oceana.

United States Firms in South Africa. Donald McHenry. (African Humanities Ser.). 74p. (Orig.). 1975. pap. text ed. 4.00 (0-941934-15-2) Indiana Africa.

United States First-Class Mail Permit Stamp Catalog, Including Business Reply Mail. Richard Stambaugh. (Illus.). 150p. (Orig.). 1989. pap. 29.50 (0-9622935-0-4) R Stambaugh.

United States First Three Hundred Years of the 2000 Most Common Surnames in the United States. 1990. 30.00 (0-89593-634-8) Accelerated Index.

United States Flagbook: Everything about Old Glory. Robert L. Loeffelbein. LC 96-20026. (Illus.). 247p. 1996. pap. 35.00 (0-7864-0156-7) McFarland & Co.

United States Flea Market Directory. Albert LaFarge. 432p. (Orig.). 1993. pap. 7.00 (0-380-77079-2, Confident Collect) Avon.

*__United States Flea Markets.__ 6th ed. Kitty Werner. 1998. pap. write for info. (0-676-60139-1) Random.

United States Food Laws, Regulations & Standards, 2 vol. set. 2nd ed. Yiu H. Hui. 1586p. 1986. Set. text ed. 195.00 (0-471-84846-8) Wiley.

United States Force Structure in NATO: An Alternative: A Staff Paper. Richard D. Lawrence & Jeffrey Record. LC 74-1436. (Studies in Defense Policy). (Illus.). 148p. reprint ed. pap. 42.20 (0-685-23673-0, 2027968) Bks Demand.

United States Forces Travel Guide to Overseas U. S. Military Installations. William R. Crawford & Lela A. Crawford. Ed. by Donna L. Russell. LC 96-21223. 1996. write for info. (0-914862-43-X) Military Living Pubns.

United States Foreign Oil Policy, 1919-1948: For Profits & Security. Stephen J. Randall. 336p. 1985. 55.00 (0-7735-0449-4, Pub. by McGill CN) U of Toronto Pr.

United States Foreign Policy & Peru. Ed. by Daniel A. Sharp. LC 73-39097. (Special Publication of the Institute of Latin American Studies, University of Texas at Austin). 511p. reprint ed. pap. 145.70 (0-685-15660-5, 2027333) Bks Demand.

United States Foreign Policy & the Law of the Sea. Ann L. Hollick. LC 80-8554. 510p. reprint ed. pap. 145.40 (0-7837-0042-3, 2040277) Bks Demand.

United States Foreign Policy & the United Nations System. Ed. by C. William Maynes & Richard S. Williamson. 352p. 1996. 27.50 (0-393-03907-2) Norton.

United States Foreign Policy & World Order. 4th ed. James A. Nathan & James K. Oliver. (C). 1989. text ed. 44.50 (0-673-39689-4) Addson-Wesley Educ.

United States Foreign Policy at the Crossroads. Ed. by George Schwab. LC 82-15588. (Contributions in Political Science Ser.: No. 96). xxvii, 268p. 1982. text ed. 55.00 (0-313-23270-9, SFP/, Greenwood Pr) Greenwood.

United States Foreign Policy in the Caribbean, Cuba, & Central America. James N. Cortada & James W. Cortada. LC 84-26629. 270p. 1985. text ed. 59.95 (0-275-90078-9, C0078, Praeger Pubs) Greenwood.

United States Foreign Policy Regarding Greece, Turkey & Cyprus: The Rule of Law & American Interests. DeVallon Bolles et al. 127p. (Orig.). 1989. 15.00 (0-941882-00-4) Amer Hellenic Inst.

*__United States Foreign Policy Toward Africa: Incrementalism, Crisis & Change.__ 373p. 1994. pap. text ed. 29.95 (0-521-46677-6) Cambridge U Pr.

United States Foreign Policy Toward Africa: Incrementalism, Crisis & Change. Peter J. Schraeder. LC 93-21590. (Studies in International Relations: No. 13). (Illus.). 336p. (C). 1994. 59.95 (0-521-44439-X); pap. write for info. (0-521-46673-3) Cambridge U Pr.

United States Foreign Policy Toward India: A Diagnosis of the American Approach. M. J. Vinod. (C). 1991. 28.00 (81-7095-021-X, Pub. by Lancer II) S Asia.

United States Foreign Policy Towards India, 1947-1954. Srinivas Mudumbai. 1985. 12.00 (0-8364-1335-0, Pub. by Manohar II) S Asia.

United States Forest Policy. John Ise. LC 72-2845. (Use & Abuse of America's Natural Resources Ser.). 400p. 1972. reprint ed. 25.95 (0-405-04511-5) Ayer.

United States Free Market Money: The Check Clearing Mechanism. 1992. lib. bdg. 250.00 (0-8490-8722-8) Gordon Pr.

United States Geography. John Carratello & Patty Carratello. (Illus.). 48p. (J). (gr. 3-6). 1989. student ed. 7.95 (1-55734-160-5) Tchr Create Mat.

United States Geological Survey's National Water Quality Assessment Program (NAWQA) fac. ed. Ed. by P. Patrick Leahy et al. (AWRA Monograph Ser.: No. 19). 186p. 1993. reprint ed. pap. 53.10 (0-608-01000-6, 2061858) Bks Demand.

United States-German Economic Yearbook 1996: Deutsch-Amerikanisches Wirtschaftsjahrbuch, Vol. 21. 22th ed. Ed. by Richard C. Jacob. (Illus.). 216p. (Orig.). 1996. pap. 45.00 (0-86640-060-5) German Am Chamber.

*__United States Global Trade Outlook, 1995-2000: Toward the 21st Century.__ 1997. lib. bdg. 250.95 (0-8490-6091-5) Gordon Pr.

United States Government - New Customer! A Step-by-Step Guide for Selling Your Product or Service to Uncle Sam. Robert Sullivan. LC 96-94438. 540p. (Orig.). 1997. pap. 27.95 (1-882480-20-1) Info Intl.

*__United States Government & the Vietnam War: Executive & Legislative Roles & Relationships, Pt. 1.__ William C. Gibbons. LC 86-3270. 378p. 1986. reprint ed. pap. 107.80 (0-608-03752-4, 2064576) Bks Demand.

*__United States Government & the Vietnam War: Executive & Legislative Roles & Relationships, Pt. 2.__ William C. Gibbons. LC 86-3270. 438p. 1986. reprint ed. pap. 124.90 (0-608-03753-2, 2064576) Bks Demand.

United States Government Documents on Women, 1800-1990: A Comprehensive Bibliography, Vol. II: Labor, Vol. 2. Mary E. Huls. LC 92-38990. (Bibliographies & Indexes in Women's Studies: No. 18). 500p. 1993. text ed. 79.50 (0-313-28157-2, HGK, Greenwood Pr) Greenwood.

United States Government Documents on Women, 1800-1990: Social Issues & Labor, Set, Vols. I-II. Mary E. Huls. LC 92-38990. (Bibliographies & Indexes in Women's Studies: Vol. 18). 1993. text ed. 159.00 (0-313-29016-4, Greenwood Pr) Greenwood.

United States Government Documents on Women, 1800-1990 Vol. 1: A Comprehensive Bibliography - Social Issues. Mary E. Huls. LC 92-38990. (Bibliographies & Indexes in Women's Studies: No. 17). 520p. 1993. text ed. 79.50 (0-313-26712-X, HGB/) Greenwood.

United States Government Information Policies: Views & Perspectives. Ed. by Charles R. McClure et al. LC 88-35081. (Information Management, Policies & Services Ser.: Vol. 5). 352p. (C). 1989. text ed. 73.25 (0-89391-563-7) Ablex Pub.

United States Government Manual. annuals 860p. 1934. pap. 36.00 (0-16-045055-1) Office Fed Register.

United States Government Manual, 1993-94. Office of the Federal Register, National Archives & Records Administration Staff. (Illus.). 1000p. 1993. reprint ed. pap. 30.00 (0-89059-016-8); reprint ed. lib. bdg. 30.00 (0-89059-019-2) Bernan Pr.

United States Government Manual 1994-95. Office of the Federal Register, National Archives & Records Administration Staff. (Illus.). 1000p. 1994. reprint ed. pap. 29.95 (0-89059-031-1) Bernan Pr.

United States Government Manual, 1995-1996: Laminated Edition. Office Of the Federal Register Staff. 1995. 29.95 (0-89059-045-1) Bernan Pr.

United States Government Manual 1995-96. Ed. by National Archives & Records Administration Staff. (Illus.). 904p. 1995. reprint ed. pap. 33.00 (0-89059-057-5) Bernan Pr.

*__United States Government Manual, 1996-1997.__ Bernan Press Staff. 1996. pap. 36.00 (0-89059-067-2) Bernan Pr.

United States Government Market for Wind Energy Systems. U. S. Department of Energy Staff. 110p. 1981. pap. 55.00 (0-88016-015-2) WindBks.

United States Government Periodicals Index 1993. Ed. by Congressional Information Service, Inc. Staff. 1026p. 1995. write for info. (0-88692-327-1) Cong Info.

United States Government Periodicals Index 1994, 2 vols. Ed. by Congressional Information Service, Inc., Staff. 1026p. 1995. write for info. (0-88692-317-4) Cong Info.

United States Government Policy & Supporting Positions. 1993. 262.95 (0-8490-8914-X) Gordon Pr.

*__United States Government Policy & Supporting Positions: The Plum Book.__ 1997. lib. bdg. 250.99 (0-8490-7662-5) Gordon Pr.

United States Government Printing Office: Style Manual. LC 84-600037. 488p. 1984. pap. 24.00 (0-16-002858-2, 021-000-00120-1) USGPO.

United States Government Publications Catalogs. Steven D. Zink. LC 81-18352. (SLA Bibliographies Ser.: No. 8). 119p. reprint ed. pap. 34.00 (0-317-27926-2, 2025125) Bks Demand.

*__United States Government Structure.__ 1997. lib. bdg. 251.95 (0-8490-7756-7) Gordon Pr.

United States Government Structure: An English As a Second Language Text. (Illus.). 186p. 1989. per. 12.00 (0-16-003710-7, 027-002-00380-2) USGPO.

*__United States Government Structure: An English As a Second Language Text.__ 1997. lib. bdg. 251.95 (0-8490-6208-X) Gordon Pr.

United States, Great Britain, & Egypt, 1945-1956: Strategy & Diplomacy in the Early Cold War. Peter L. Hahn. LC 90-47616. xiv, 360p. (C). 1991. pap. text ed. 15.95 (0-8078-1942-5) U of NC Pr.

United States, Great Britain & Mossadegh. David S. Painter. (Pew Case Studies in International Affairs). 50p. (C). 1993. pap. text ed. 3.50 (1-56927-332-4) Geo U Inst Dplmcy.

United States, Great Britain, & the Cold War, 1944-1947. Terry H. Anderson. LC 80-25838. 270p. reprint ed. pap. 77.00 (0-7837-4206-1, AU00436) Bks Demand.

United States Great Britain & the Sovietization of Hungary 1945-1948. Stanley M. Max. 1985. text ed. 52.50 (0-88033-069-4, 177) Col U Pr.

United States, Greece & Turkey: The Troubled Triangle. Theodore A. Couloumbis. Ed. by Alvin Z. Rubinstein. (Studies of Influence in International Relations). 256p. 1983. pap. 16.95 (0-275-91566-2, B1566, Praeger Pubs) Greenwood.

United States-Grenada Relations, 1979-1983: American Foreign Policy Towards a "Backyard" Revolution. William R. Nylen. (Pew Case Studies in International Affairs). 50p. (C). 1988. pap. text ed. 3.50 (1-56927-306-5) Geo U Inst Dplmcy.

United States Half Cents. Illus. by D. Bowers & J. Ruddy. LC 83-51003. 1984. pap. 10.00 (0-317-27384-1) S J Durst.

United States Half Dimes. Daniel W. Valentine. LC 74-80917. (Illus.). 384p. 1975. reprint ed. 40.00 (0-88000-049-X) Quarterman.

United States Half Dimes. Daniel W. Valentine et al. LC 84-70699. 1984. reprint ed. lib. bdg. 35.00 (0-942666-39-9) S J Durst.

United States Health Care Laws & Rules. Ed. by Peter A. Pavarini. 1700p. 1995. 75.00 (0-314-06827-9) Natl Health Lawyers.

United States Higher Civil Service Study: Careers of High-Level Employees, 1963. David T. Stanley. 1973. write for info. (0-89138-064-7) ICPSR.

United States History. (Advanced Placement (AP) Test Ser.). 1997. pap. 23.95 (0-8373-6212-1, AP-12) Nat Learn.

United States History. Burns & Dunfey. 1996. write for info. (0-679-82752-8) Knopf.

United States History. Dibacco. (C). 1990. student ed., pap. 54.52 (0-395-48751-X) HM.

United States History. Reich. 1988. text ed. 76.25 (0-03-014627-5); text ed. 62.00 (0-03-014808-1); teacher ed., wbk. ed., pap. text ed. 17.75 (0-03-014807-3) HR&W Schl Div.

United States History: A Resource Book for Secondary Schools. James R. Giese & Laurel R. Singleton. (Social Studies Resources for Secondary School Librarians, Teachers, & Students). 1987. Set. lib. bdg. 66.50 (0-87436-525-2) ABC-CLIO.

United States History: A Selective Guide to Information Sources. Ronald Blazek & Anna H. Perrault. xxviii, 411p. 1994. lib. bdg. 55.00 (0-87287-984-4) Libs Unl.

United States History: In the Course of Human Events. Matthew T. Downey et al. 1995. text ed. write for info. (0-314-04021-8) West Pub.

United States History: To 1877, Vol. 1. 4th ed. Klose. 1983. pap. 12.95 (0-8120-2250-5) Barron.

United States History & Government. (Regents Competency Test Ser.). 1997. pap. 23.95 (0-8373-6406-X, RCT-6) Nat Learn.

United States History & Government: A Competency Review Text. 2nd ed. Paul Stich et al. Ed. by Wayne Garnsey. (Illus.). 384p. (YA). (gr. 7-12). 1992. pap. text ed. 12.95 (0-935487-20-4) N & N Pub Co.

United States History & Government: A Review Text. 6th ed. Paul Stich et al. Ed. by Wayne Garnsey. (Illus.). 416p. (YA). (gr. 7-12). 1992. pap. text ed. 9.95 (0-935487-21-2) N & N Pub Co.

United States History & Government: Ten Day Competency Review. rev. ed. Paul Stich et al. Ed. by Wayne Garnsey. (Illus.). 128p. (YA). (gr. 7-12). 1992. pap. text ed. 7.95 (0-935487-54-9) N & N Pub Co.

United States History & Government: Ten Day Review. rev. ed. Paul Stich et al. Ed. by Wayne Garnsey. (Illus.). 128p. (YA). (gr. 7-12). 1992. pap. text ed. 7.95 (0-935487-49-2) N & N Pub Co.

*__United States History Beginning - 1877.__ Downey & Giese. Date not set. 53.95 (0-314-22321-5) Wadsworth Pub.

United States History Simulation: Based on President John F. Kennedy's Pulitzer Prize Book. Richard W. Hostrop. LC 94-46804. 1995. pap. 22.95 (0-88280-127-9) ETC Pubns.

United States History Simulation: The Waterloo of a President. LC 75-33806. (ETC Simulations Ser.: No. 1). 32p. 1975. pap. 14.95 (0-88280-041-8) ETC Pubns.

United States History Simulations, 1787-1868. Ed. by Richard W. Hostrop. LC 87-24370. (ETC Simulations Ser.: No. 2). 1989. pap. 19.95 (0-88280-091-4) ETC Pubns.

United States History Simulations, 1925-1964. Richard W. Hostrop. 64p. (Orig.). 1990. pap. 19.95 (0-88280-095-7) ETC Pubns.

United States History to 1877. Nelson Klose & Robert F. Jones. (College Review Ser.). 362p. 1994. pap. 11.95 (0-8120-1834-6) Barron.

United States History to 1877. 5th ed. Nelson Klose & Curt Lader. (College Review Ser.: Vol. 2). 528p. (C). 1994. pap. 11.95 (0-8120-1835-4) Barron.

United States History to 1877. 8th ed. Arnold M. Rice et al. LC 90-56006. (College Outline Ser.). (Illus.). 320p. (Orig.). 1991. pap. 14.00 (0-06-467111-9, Harper Ref) HarpC.

*__United States History 1877 - Present.__ Downey & Giese. Date not set. 53.95 (0-314-22320-7) Wadsworth Pub.

*__United States Holocaust Memorial Museum.__ Philip Brooks. (Cornerstones of Freedom Ser.). 32p. (J). 1997. pap. 4.95 (0-516-26071-5) Childrens.

United States Holocaust Memorial Museum: Washington DC, 1993. Adrian Dannatt. (Architecture in Detail Ser.). (Illus.). 60p. 1995. pap. 29.95 (0-7148-2939-0, Pub. by Phaidon Press UK) Chronicle Bks.

United States Holocaust Memorial Museum & Washington, D. C. Guide. Oscar Israelowitz. 126p. 7.95 (1-878741-16-0) Israelowitz Pub.

United States House of Representatives. James T. Currie. LC 87-16898. (Anvil Ser.). 248p. 1988. pap. 16.00 (0-89874-882-8) Krieger.

United States House of Representatives Telephone Directory. 1990. lib. bdg. 75.00 (0-8490-3995-9) Gordon Pr.

United States Household Consumption, Income, & Demographic Changes, 1975-2025. Philip Musgrove. LC 81-86060. (Illus.). 263p. reprint ed. pap. 75.00 (0-8357-4684-4, 2037631) Bks Demand.

United States Immigration History Timeline. Eric Lefcowitz. (Illus.). 1990. 5.95 (0-943249-03-1) Terra Firma Bks.

United States Immigration Policy: Restoring Credibility. 1996. lib. bdg. 255.95 (0-8490-5972-0) Gordon Pr.

*__United States Immigration Policy: Restoring Credibility.__ 1997. lib. bdg. 250.95 (0-8490-7754-0) Gordon Pr.

United States Import Trade Regulation. Eugene T. Rossides. LC 84-23748. 768p. reprint ed. pap. 180.00 (0-7837-4597-4, 2044316) Bks Demand.

United States Imports & Exports, 7 vols. 1991. Set. lib. bdg. 995.75 (0-8490-5086-3) Gordon Pr.

United States in a Disarmed World: A Study of the U. S. Outline for General & Complete Disarmament. Washington Center of Foreign Policy Research Staff et al. LC 66-16036. 250p. reprint ed. pap. 71.30 (0-317-19862-9, 2023114) Bks Demand.

United States in Africa: A Historical Dictionary. David Shavit. LC 88-7707. 320p. 1989. text ed. 69.50 (0-313-25887-2, SVU, Greenwood Pr) Greenwood.

United States in Asia: A Historical Dictionary. David Shavit. LC 90-36740. 648p. 1990. text ed. 79.50 (0-313-26788-X, SQA, Greenwood Pr) Greenwood.

United States in Central America: An Analysis of the Kissinger Commission Report. Larry G. Hufford. LC 87-25704. (Edwin Mellen Text Ser.). 280p. 1987. lib. bdg. 89.95 (0-88946-006-X) E Mellen.

United States in Central America, 1860-1911: Episodes of Social Imperialism & Imperial Rivalry in the World System. Thomas D. Schoonover. LC 91-12687. (Illus.). 269p. 1991. text ed. 37.95 (0-8223-1160-7) Duke.

United States in Crisis: Marxist Analysis. Ed. by Lajos Biro & Marc J. Cohen. LC 78-61686. (Studies in Marxism: Vol. 4). 245p. 1979. 8.95 (0-930656-08-3); pap. 3.00 (0-930656-07-5) MEP Pubns.

United States in Crisis - the Communist Solution. 1969. pap. 0.75 (0-87898-042-3) New Outlook.

United States in Cuba, 1898-1902: Generals, Politicians, & the Search for Policy. David Healy. LC 63-13742. 272p. reprint ed. pap. 77.60 (0-7837-2643-0, 2042997) Bks Demand.

United States in International Banking. Siegfried Stern. Ed. by Stuart Bruchey & Eleanor Bruchey. LC 76-5036. (American Business Abroad Ser.). 1976. reprint ed. 41.95 (0-405-09302-0) Ayer.

United States in Latin America: A Historical Dictionary. David Shavit. LC 91-32403. 496p. 1992. text ed. 79.50 (0-313-27595-5, SVG/, Greenwood Pr) Greenwood.

United States in Old Maps & Prints. Edward Van Erman. 1993. 50.00 (0-528-83619-6) Rand McNally.

United States in Pictures. Lerner Geography Department Staff. LC 94-44841. (Visual Geography Ser.). (J). 1995. lib. bdg. 14.96 (0-8225-1896-1) Lerner Group.

United States in Prague, 1945-1948. Walter Ullmann. (East European Monographs: No. 36). 205p. 1978. text ed. 58.00 (0-914710-29-X) East Eur Monographs.

United States in Prophecy: The Role & Destiny of the United States of America. Edward Aguirre. (Illus.). 166p. (Orig.). 1996. mass mkt. 9.95 (0-9650765-4-7) Shiloh Pubng.

*__United States in the Changing Global Economy: Policy Implications & Issues.__ George Macesich. LC 96-44686. 136p. 1997. text ed. 49.95 (0-275-95705-5, Praeger Pubs) Greenwood.

United States in the First World War: An Encyclopedia. Ed. by Anne C. Venzon. LC 95-1782. (Military History of the U. S. Ser.: Vol. 3). (Illus.). 856p. 1995. text ed. 95.00 (0-8240-7055-0) Garland.

United States in the Global Economy: Challenges & Policy Choices. John J. Accordino. LC 92-11399. (Last Quarter Century: a Guide to the Issues & the Litereature Ser.: No. 2). 450p. (C). 1992. pap. text ed. 18.00 (0-8389-0591-9) ALA.

United States in the International Telecommunication Union & in Pre-ITU Conferences. Mildred L. B. Feldman. LC 76-2971. 1976. 10.00 (0-9606700-0-9) Feldman.

United States in the Middle East: A Historical Dictionary. David Shavit. LC 87-24965. 465p. 1988. text ed. 79.50 (0-313-25341-2, SHV/, Greenwood Pr) Greenwood.

United States in the Middle East: Interests & Obstacles. Seth P. Tillman. LC 81-47777. 352p. 1982. 35.00 (0-253-36172-9) Ind U Pr.

United States in the Middle East: Interests & Obstacles. Seth P. Tillman. LC 81-47777. 352p. 1984. pap. 13.95 (0-253-20335-X, MB-335) Ind U Pr.

United States in the New Global Economy: A Rallier of Nations. Research & Policy Committee of the Committee for Economic Development. LC 92-34022. 90p. 1992. pap. 17.50 (0-87186-094-5) Comm Econ Dev.

An Asterisk (*) at the beginning of an entry indicates that the title is appearing in BIP for the first time.

United States in the Pacific: Private Interests & Public Policies, 1784-1899. Donald D. Johnson. LC 94-41799. 248p. 1995. text ed. 59.95 (*0-275-95055-7*, Praeger Pubs) Greenwood.

United States in the Supreme War Council: American War Aims & Inter-Allied Strategy 1917-1918. David F. Trask. LC 77-16237. 244p. 1978. reprint ed. text ed. 35.00 (*0-313-20006-8*, TRUS, Greenwood Pr) Greenwood.

United States in the Twentieth Century. Melvyn Dubofsky et al. LC 77-13246. (Illus.). 1978. pap. text ed. write for info. (*0-13-938712-9*) P-H.

United States in the World. Brands. (C). 1993. teacher ed., pap. 5.96 (*0-395-62182-8*) HM.

United States in the World. Brands. (C). 1993. pap. 25.56 (*0-395-62180-1*) HM.

United States in the World Vol. 2. Brands. (C). 1993. pap. 30.36 (*0-395-62181-X*) HM.

United States in the World Economy. Martin Feldstein. (National Bureau of Economic Research Conference Report Ser.). 704p. 1988. pap. text ed. 30.00 (*0-226-24078-9*) U Ch Pr.

United States in the World Economy. Hal B. Lary et al. LC 75-26859. (Economic Handbook Ser.: No. 23). 216p. 1975. reprint ed. text ed. 55.00 (*0-8371-8257-3*, LAUS, Greenwood Pr) Greenwood.

United States in the World Political Economy. Ed. by Theodore Rueter. LC 93-1129. 1993. pap. text ed. write for info. (*0-07-054259-7*) McGraw.

United States in the 19th Century. David Rubel. (Scholastic Timelines Ser.). 192p. (J). (gr. 4-7). 1996. 18.95 (*0-590-72564-5*, Scholastic Ref) Scholastic Inc.

United States in the 1980s. Ed. by Peter Duignan & Alvin Rabushka. LC 79-5475. (Publication Ser.: No. 228). 1980. 8.00 (*0-8179-7281-1*) Hoover Inst Pr.

United States in the 20th Century. David Rubel. LC 94-45702. (Scholastic Timeliness Ser.). (Illus.). 192p. (YA). (gr. 4 up). 1995. 16.95 (*0-590-27134-2*, Scholastic Ref) Scholastic Inc.

United States in World Affairs: Leadership, Partnership, or Disengagement. Ed. by Robert A. Bauer. LC 74-14990. (Essays on Alternatives of U. S. Foreign Policy Ser.). 144p. reprint ed. pap. 41.10 (*0-685-16261-3*, 2027724) Bks Demand.

United States in 1800. Henry Adams. 142p. 1955. pap. 9.95 (*0-8014-9014-6*) Cornell U Pr.

United States in 1800: Henry Adams Revisited. Noble E. Cunningham. LC 88-5514. (Douglas Southall Freeman Lectures: No. 1986). 83p. reprint ed. pap. 25.00 (*0-7837-4348-3*, 2044058) Bks Demand.

United States Income Tax Treaties. Klaus Vogel et al. 500p. 1990. ring bd. 226.00 (*90-6544-969-8*) Kluwer Law Tax Pubs.

United States Index 1840 Pensioners Lists. (Illus.). lib. bdg. 50.00 (*0-89593-503-1*) Accelerated Index.

United States Index 1890 Miscellaneous Veterans. (Illus.). lib. bdg. 45.00 (*0-89593-504-X*) Accelerated Index.

United States Index 1890 Vessels & Navy. (Illus.). lib. bdg. 45.00 (*0-89593-505-8*) Accelerated Index.

United States, India & the Bomb. Shelton L. Williams. LC 74-79299. (Washington Center of Foreign Policy Research. Studies in International Affairs: No. 12). 93p. reprint ed. pap. 26.60 (*0-317-08622-7*, 2016058) Bks Demand.

United States Industrial Outlook. 1991. lib. bdg. 88.00 (*0-8490-5058-8*) Gordon Pr.

United States Industrial Outlook: Prospects for over 350 Industries. 1992. lib. bdg. 148.95 (*0-8490-8742-2*) Gordon Pr.

United States Infantry Regiments. C. Gallagher & R. Pigeon. 1986. 14.98 (*0-685-16802-6*, 614944) Random Hse Value.

United States Intelligence: An Encyclopedia. Bruce W. Watson et al. LC 89-28206. (Series on U. S. Military Affairs: Vol. 1). 896p. 1990. text ed. 35.00 (*0-8240-3713-8*, 589) Garland.

***United States Intelligence & the Soviet Strategic Threat.** 2nd ed. Lawrence Freedman. LC 85-43345. reprint ed. pap. 76.70 (*0-608-04651-5*, 2065337) Bks Demand.

United States Intelligence Community: Woodrow Wilson School, Undergraduate Policy Conference Report - Including Comments by Robert M. Gates, the Deputy Director of Central Intelligence Agency. United States Intelligence Community Staff. (Policy Memorandum Ser.: No. 43). 96p. reprint ed. pap. 27.40 (*0-7837-2611-2*, 2042775) Bks Demand.

United States Internal Revenue Tax-Paid Stamps Printed on Tin-Foil & Paper Tobacco Wrappers. John A. Hicks. LC 87-82283. (Illus.). 217p. 1989. 95.00 (*0-9619611-0-4*) Hicks Philatelic.

United States International Economic Policy in an Interdependent World, 4 vols. Commission of International Trade & Investment Policy Staff. (Final Reports & Compendium of Papers: Nos. 1 & 2). 1985. reprint ed. Set. lib. bdg. 205.00 (*0-89941-420-6*, 201700) W S Hein.

United States International Revenue Tax System. Charles W. Eldridge. LC 94-76048. x, 722p. 1994. reprint ed. 75.00 (*0-89941-879-1*, 308210) W S Hein.

United States International Trade Laws. Ed. by Alan M. Stowell. LC 85-11371. 510p. reprint ed. pap. 145.40 (*0-7837-4611-3*, 2044330) Bks Demand.

United States International Visitor Program: Strengthening the Community Organization. John S. Gibson. 108p. 1979. 1.00 (*0-318-15385-8*) Natl Coun Intl Visitors.

United States Investment in the Forest-Based Sector in Latin America: Problems & Potentials. Hans M. Gregersen & Arnoldo Contreras. LC 74-21754. reprint ed. pap. 34.60 (*0-7837-3131-0*, 2042856) Bks Demand.

***United States Involvement in Vietnam: Role Play Peacegame.** David W. Felder. 56p. 1997. pap. text ed. 8.95 (*1-57501-105-0*, 25E) Wellington Pr.

United States, Italy & NATO, 1947-52. E. Timothy Smith. LC 90-44809. 260p. 1991. text ed. 59.95 (*0-312-05559-5*) St Martin.

United States, It's History & Neighbors: HBJ Social Studies Landmark Edition. 88th ed. Stephanie Hirsh. (J). (gr. 5). 1988. text ed. 48.00 (*0-15-372905-8*) HarBrace.

United States, Japan, & Asia: Challenges in the Policy. Gerald L. Curtis. 1994. 28.00 (*0-393-03633-2*) Norton.

United States, Japan, & Asia: Challenges in the Policy. Gerald L. Curtis. (C). 1994. pap. text ed. 9.95 (*0-393-96583-X*) Norton.

United States, Japan, & the Future of Nuclear Weapons: Report of the U. S.-Japan Study Group on Arms Control & Non-Proliferation after the Cold War. Selig S. Harrison. LC 95-6459. 192p. (C). 1995. pap. 12.95 (*0-87003-060-4*) Carnegie Endow.

United States-Japan Economic Problem. 2nd ed. C. Fred Bergsten & William R. Cline. LC 86-83417. (Policy Analyses in International Economics Ser.: No. 13). 182p. reprint ed. pap. 51.90 (*0-7837-6142-2*, 2043499) Bks Demand.

United States-Japan Relations: A Surprising Partnership-- Annual Review, 1986. Ed. by Richard B. Finn. (U. S. Japan Relations Ser.). 288p. 1987. pap. 21.95 (*0-88738-685-7*) Transaction Pubs.

United States-Japan Seminar on Host-Guest Chemistry. Ed. by George W. Gokel & Kenji Koga. (C). 1989. lib. bdg. 141.50 (*0-7923-0262-1*) Kluwer Ac.

United States-Japan Trade in Telecommunications: Conflict & Compromise. Ed. by Meheroo Jussawalla. LC 92-35597. (Contributions in Economics & Economic History Ser.: No. 145). 208p. 1993. text ed. 52.95 (*0-313-28718-X*, GM8718, Greenwood Pr) Greenwood.

United States-Japanese Relations: The 1970's. Ed. by Priscilla Clapp & Morton H. Halperin. LC 74-80441. 256p. (C). 1974. 32.00 (*0-674-92571-8*) HUP.

***United States Jewish Travel Guide.** 4th ed. (Illus.). 400p. (Orig.). 1997. per., pap. 19.95 (*1-878741-31-4*) Israelowitz Pub.

United States Jewry, 1776-1985, Vol. I: The Sephardic Period. Jacob R. Marcus. LC 89-5723. (Illus.). 856p. 1989. 49.95 (*0-8143-2186-0*) Wayne St U Pr.

United States Jewry, 1776-1985, Vol. II: The Germanic Period, Pt. 1. Jacob R. Marcus. LC 89-5723. (Illus.). 452p. 1990. text ed. 39.95 (*0-8143-2187-9*) Wayne St U Pr.

United States Jewry 1776-1985, Vol. III: The Germanic Period, Pt. 2. Jacob R. Marcus. LC 89-5723. (Illus.). 958p. 1993. text ed. 59.95 (*0-8143-2188-7*) Wayne St U Pr.

United States Jewry, 1776-1985, Vol. IV: The East European Period, the Emergence of the American Jew, Epilogue. Jacob R. Marcus. (Illus.). 982p. 1993. 64.95 (*0-8143-2189-5*) Wayne St U Pr.

United States Labor & Employment Laws. fac. ed. Ed. by Ruth C. West. LC 89-17406. 654p. 1991. pap. 180.00 (*0-7837-7705-1*, 2047464) Bks Demand.

United States Labor Movement. Robert N. Stern. 356p. 1996. 45.00 (*0-8161-7277-3*, Hall Reference) Macmillan.

United States Large Cents 1793-1857. Ed. by Warren A. Lapp & Herbert A. Silberman. LC 74-27611. (Gleanings from the Numismatist Ser.). (Illus.). 640p. 1975. 50.00 (*0-88000-058-9*) Quarterman.

United States Large Size National Bank Notes. Peter W. Huntoon. 283p. 1995. lib. bdg. 49.95 (*0-9648774-1-4*) Soc Paper Money.

United States-Latin American Relations, 1800-1850: The Formative Generations. Ed. by T. Ray Shurbutt. LC 89-38363. 344p. 1991. text ed. 39.95 (*0-8173-0482-7*) U of Ala Pr.

United States Legislation on Foreign Relations & International Commerce: 1789-to Date, 6 vols. Ed. by Igor I. Kavass & Michael J. Blake. LC 76-51898. 1977. Set. lib. bdg. 750.00 (*0-930342-00-3*, 300760) W S Hein.

United States Letter Rates to Foreign Destinations, 1847 to GPU-UPU. Charles J. Starnes. Ed. by Leonard H. Hartmann. LC 82-80070. (Illus.). 160p. 1982. 27.50 (*0-917528-04-2*) L H Hartmann.

***United States Life-Saving Service.** Ralph C. Shanks. 1996. pap. text ed. 21.95 (*0-07-057829-X*) McGraw.

United States Life-Saving Service: Eighteen Eighty. J. H. Merryman. Ed. by William R. Jones. (Illus.). 1981. pap. 6.95 (*0-89646-071-1*) Vistabooks.

United States Life Tables: 1890, 1901, 1910, & 1901-1910. U. S. Department of Commerce, Bureau of the Census Staff & James W. Glover. LC 75-37267. (Demography Ser.). (Illus.). 1976. reprint ed. 51.95 (*0-405-07997-4*) Ayer.

United States Lifesaving Association Manual of Open Water Lifesaving. Ed. by B. Chris Brewster. LC 95-11842. 1995. pap. 13.50 (*0-8359-4919-2*) P-H.

United States Local Histories in the Library of Congress: A Bibliography, 5 vols., Set. Ed. by Jack Kaminkow. 5000p. 1976. 300.00 (*0-614-10566-8*, 8510) Genealog Pub.

United States Local History Catalog. New. 1980. 200.00 (*0-8161-1285-1*, Hall Library) G K Hall.

United States Magistrates in the Federal Courts: Subordinate Judges. Christopher E. Smith. LC 89-16214. 208p. 1990. text ed. 49.95 (*0-275-93396-2*, C3396, Praeger Pubs) Greenwood.

United States Mail Order Industry. Sroge, Maxwell H., Staff. 240p. 1991. per. 55.00 (*1-55623-486-4*) Irwin Prof Pubng.

United States Mail Order Industry. 2nd ed. Sroge, Maxwell H., Staff. 240p. 1995. 54.95 (*0-8442-3451-6*, NTC Busn Bks) NTC Pub Grp.

United States Map. Little Golden Books Staff. (J). 1906. pap. 2.59 (*0-307-04560-9*, Golden Pr) Western Pub.

***United States Marine Corps.** Charles H. Cureton. LC 97-19007. (G. I. Series). 1997. pap. write for info. (*1-85367-289-0*, Pub. by Greenhill Bks UK) Stackpole.

***United States Marine Corps Book of Lists.** Albert A. Nofi. 1997. pap. 12.95 (*0-614-27675-6*) Combined Pub.

United States Marine Corps in the Civil War: The First Year: 1861. David M. Sullivan. LC 97-19798. 390p. 1996. 40.00 (*1-57249-040-3*) White Mane Pub.

***United States Marine Corps in the Civil War - The Second Year.** David M. Sullivan. (Illus.). 332p. Date not set. write for info. (*1-57249-055-1*, WM Kids) White Mane Pub.

United States Marine Corps VHPA. Turner Publishing Company Staff. LC 95-60546. 112p. 1995. 48.00 (*0-614-05328-5*) Turner Pub KY.

United States Marines Force Recons: A Black Hero's Story. Amankwa Adeduro. 300p. (Orig.). 1994. pap. 16.95 (*0-86626-009-9*) McKinzie Pub.

United States Marines in North China. John A. White. Date not set. reprint ed. 23.95 (*0-614-07618-8*) Zenger Pub.

United States Marines Seventeen Seventy-Five to Nineteen Seventy-Five. E. H. Simmons. 342p. 1976. lib. bdg. 2.95 (*0-670-74101-9*) Marine Corps.

United States Marshal. Jack Rudman. (Career Examination Ser.: C-853). 1994. pap. 27.95 (*0-8373-0853-4*) Nat Learn.

United States Martial Flintlocks. Robert M. Reilly. LC 86-60684. (Illus.). 263p. 1997. reprint ed. 40.00 (*0-917218-21-3*) A Mowbray.

United States Match & Medicine Stamps. Christopher West. LC 80-80786. (C. & S. Revenue Ser.). (Illus.). 144p. 1980. 24.95 (*0-9603498-1-2*) Castenholz Sons.

***United States Merchant Marine: Guide to Seaman Opportunities.** 2nd ed. Jerald P. Dyrek. LC 94-92148. (Illus.). 432p. 1997. pap. 69.95 (*0-9645447-4-1*) Dyrek-Seaways.

United States Merchant Marine: Guide to Seaman Opportunities. 2nd rev. ed. Jerald P. Dyrek. LC 94-92148. 432p. 1996. pap. text ed. 69.95 (*0-9645447-0-9*) Dyrek-Seaways.

United States Metallurgical Coal Industry. James E. Spearman. 209p. 1980. 10.00 (*0-937058-00-9*) West Va U Pr.

***United States Meter Stamps: First Days & Earliest-Known Uses.** Douglas A. Kelsey. (Illus.). 32p. (Orig.). 1996. pap. 6.00 (*1-879390-21-3*) Am First Day.

United States-Mexico Border Environmental Geographic Information System. Ed. by Richard D. Wright et al. 44p. (Orig.). (C). 1993. pap. text ed. 5.00 (*0-925613-11-8*) SDSU Inst Reg Studies.

United States-Mexico Border Statistics since 1900: 1990 Update. Ed. by David E. Lorey. LC 93-24225. (Statistical Abstract of Latin America Supplement Ser.: Vol. 13). 1993. pap. 32.50 (*0-87903-256-1*) UCLA Lat Am Ctr.

United States-Middle East Diplomatic Relations 1784-1978: An Annotated Bibliography. Thomas A. Bryson. LC 78-26754. 219p. 1979. lib. bdg. 29.50 (*0-8108-1197-9*) Scarecrow.

United States Military Aircraft: Directory. M. G. Jennings. 84p. (C). 1990. text ed. 110.00 (*0-9515462-0-1*, Pub. by Mach III Plus UK) St Mut.

United States Military Aircraft Directory 1993. Mach III Plus Staff. (C). 1993. pap. 55.00 (*0-9515462-5-2*, Pub. by Mach III Plus UK) St Mut.

United States Military Almanac. Walt Lang. 1989. 24.99 (*0-517-68846-8*) Random Hse Value.

United States Military Medals 1939-1994: U. S. Decorations & Service Medals. Lawrence H. Borts & Frank C. Foster. LC 93-80445. (Illus.). 80p. (Orig.). 1993. 24.95 (*1-884452-09-4*). pap. 19.95 (*1-884452-08-6*) MOA Press.

***United States Military Medical Facilities Map.** William R. Crawford & Lela A. Crawford. 1994. write for info. (*0-914862-54-5*) Military Living Pubns.

United States Military Records Catalog. 1983. 10.00 (*0-89593-647-X*) Accelerated Index.

United States Military Road Atlas. William Crawford & Ann C. Crawford. Ed. by R. J. Crawford. LC 94-44407. 1995. write for info. (*0-914862-51-0*) Military Living Pubns.

United States Military Saddles, 1812-1943. Randy Steffan. LC 72-9268. (Illus.). 176p. 1988. pap. 19.95 (*0-8061-2102-5*) U of Okla Pr.

United States Military Small Arms, 1816-1865. Robert M. Reilly. 1983. 39.95 (*0-88227-019-2*) Gun Room.

United States Military under the Constitution of the United States, 1789-1989. Ed. by Richard H. Kohn. 424p. (C). 1991. text ed. 36.00 (*0-8147-4615-2*) NYU Pr.

United States Military under the Constitution of the United States, 1789-1989. Ed. by Richard H. Kohn. 424p. (C). 1992. pap. text ed. 16.00 (*0-8147-4638-1*) NYU Pr.

United States Mineral Lands. Henry N. Copp. Ed. by Stuart Bruchey. LC 78-53539. (Development of Public Land Law in the U. S. Ser.). 1979. reprint ed. lib. bdg. 49.95 (*0-405-11373-0*) Ayer.

United States Minerals Issues--the Seventies, a Review; the Eighties, a Preview: 6th Annual Mineral Economics Symposium, November 12, 1980, Washington DC. Ed. by W. Hibbard. 1981. pap. 33.00 (*0-08-027593-1*, Pergamon Pr) Elsevier.

United States Monetary Policy. rev. ed. American Assembly Staff. Ed. by Neil H. Jacoby. LC 64-7956. (Illus.). 255p. reprint ed. pap. 72.70 (*0-685-20473-1*, 2029872) Bks Demand.

United States Monetary Policy. rev. ed. Ed. by Neil H. Jacoby. LC 59-6614. 1964. reprint ed. pap. 2.25 (*0-317-02969-X*) Am Assembly.

United States Multinational Companies. 1986. lib. bdg. 79.95 (*0-8490-3783-2*) Gordon Pr.

United States Music: Sources of Bibliography. Richard Jackson. LC 73-80637. (I.S.A.M. Monographs: No. 1). 80p. (Orig.). 1973. pap. 10.00 (*0-914678-00-0*) Inst Am Music.

United States National Bank Notes & Their Seals. Dewitt G. Prather. Ed. by J. S. Prather & Angela Prather. (Illus.). 200p. 1986. 40.00 (*0-9616836-0-0*); 60.00 (*0-317-58449-9*) D G Prather.

United States National Interests in a Changing World. Donald E. Nuechterlein. LC 73-77255. 215p. reprint ed. pap. 61.30 (*0-8357-8595-5*, 2034969) Bks Demand.

United States National Report to International Union of Geodesy & Geophysics: 1971-1974, 2 Vols., Vol. 1. (Special Publications Reprints: Antarctic Research Series). 504p. reprint ed. pap. 10.00 (*0-317-32678-3*, SP0005) Am Geophysical.

United States National Report to International Union of Geodesy & Geophysics: 1971-1974, 2 Vols., Vol. 2. (Special Publications Reprints: Antarctic Research Series). 1108p. 1974. reprint ed. 20.00 (*0-87590-751-2*, SP006) Am Geophysical.

United States National Security Policy & Aid to the Thailand Police. Thomas Lobe. (Monograph Series in World Affairs: Vol. 14, 1976-77 Ser., Bk. 2). 161p. (Orig.). 1977. pap. 5.95 (*0-87940-051-X*) Monograph Series.

United States Naval Academy: A Pictorial Celebration of One Hundred Fifty Years. Gale G. Kohlhagen & Ellen Boraz. LC 94-25955. 1995. 49.50 (*0-8109-3932-0*) Abrams.

***United States Naval Air Stations: Of World War II-Western States, Vol. 2.** M. L. Shettle. 1997. 34.95 (*0-9643388-1-5*) M L Shettle.

***United States Naval Aviation, 1910-1995.** 4th ed. Roy A. Grossnick & William J. Armstrong. LC 96-37481. 1997. write for info. (*0-945274-34-3*) Naval Hist Ctr.

United States Naval History: A Bibliography. 7th ed. Ed. by John E. Vajda. LC 92-40017. (Naval History Bibliogrpahies Ser.: No. 1). 182p. 1993. pap. text ed. 6.50 (*0-945274-12-2*) Naval Hist Ctr.

United States Naval Institute, Intellectual Forum of the New Navy: 1873-1889. Lawrence C. Allin. 381p. (Orig.). 1978. pap. 47.95 (*0-89126-066-8*) MA-AH Pub.

United States Naval Power in a Changing World. Edwin B. Hooper. LC 87-29942. 320p. 1988. text ed. 65.00 (*0-275-92738-5*, C2738, Praeger Pubs) Greenwood.

United States Naval Vessels: The Official United States Navy Reference Manual Prepared by the Division of Naval Intelligence 1 September 1945. Intro. by Samuel L. Morison. (Illus.). 672p. 1996. 75.00 (*0-7643-0090-3*) Schiffer.

United States Navy: A Dictionary. Bruce W. Watson & Susan M. Watson. LC 90-20079. (Series on U. S. Military Affairs: Vol. 3). 978p. 1991. text ed. 35.00 (*0-8240-5538-1*, SS695) Garland.

United States Navy, a History. Carroll S. Alden. (History - United States Ser.). 508p. 1993. reprint ed. lib. bdg. 99.00 (*0-7812-4838-8*) Rprt Serv.

United States Navy Aircraft Since 1911. 3rd ed. Gordon Swanborough & Peter M. Bowers. (Illus.). 520p. 1990. 41.95 (*0-87021-792-5*) Naval Inst Pr.

United States Navy & Defense Unification, 1947-1953. Paolo E. Coletta. LC 77-74410. (Illus.). 550p. 1981. 55.00 (*0-87413-126-X*) U Delaware Pr.

United States Navy & Marine Corps Bases, Domestic. Ed. by Paolo E. Coletta & K. Jack Bauer. LC 84-4468. xv, 740p. 1985. text ed. 125.00 (*0-313-23133-8*, CUN/, Greenwood Pr) Greenwood.

United States Navy & Marine Corps Bases, Overseas. Ed. by Paolo E. Coletta & K. Jack Bauer. LC 84-4470. 480p. 1985. text ed. 105.00 (*0-313-24504-5*, COU/, Greenwood Pr) Greenwood.

***United States Navy Diving Manual, 3 vols.** 1997. lib. bdg. 900.95 (*0-8490-8125-4*) Gordon Pr.

United States Navy in the Pacific, 1897-1909. William R. Braisted. LC 70-90473. (Illus.). 1958. reprint ed. 16.50 (*0-8290-0373-8*); reprint ed. pap. text ed. 12.95 (*0-89197-971-9*) Irvington.

United States Navy in the Pacific, 1897-1909. William R. Braisted. LC 57-12530. 294p. 1977. reprint ed. pap. text ed. 17.50 (*0-292-78505-4*) U of Tex Pr.

United States Navy in the Pacific, 1909-1922. William R. Braisted. 753p. 1971. 35.00 (*0-292-70037-7*) U of Tex Pr.

United States Navy in World War I with over 600 Photos. J. C. Russel & William E. Morse. 1977. lib. bdg. 175.00 (*0-8490-2785-3*) Gordon Pr.

United States Navy Patches: Command & Support/ Amphibious Forces/SEAL Teams/Fleets/Flotillas. Michael L. Roberts. (Illus.). 160p. 1996. 29.95 (*0-7643-0068-7*) Schiffer.

***United States Navy Patches Vol. V: Ships: Battleships/ Cruisers/Destroyers/LSTs/Etc.** Michael L. Roberts. (Illus.). 208p. 1997. 39.95 (*0-7643-0144-6*) Schiffer.

***United States Navy Patches Vol. VI: Submarines.** Michael L. Roberts. (Illus.). 176p. 1997. 35.00 (*0-7643-0186-1*) Schiffer.

United States Navy Wings of Gold: From 1917 to the Present. Ron L. Willis & Thomas Carmichael. LC 95-67629. (Illus.). 224p. 1995. 49.95 (*0-88740-795-1*) Schiffer.

United States Newspaper Program: Cataloging Aspects. Ed. by Ruth C. Carter. LC 86-4828. (Cataloging & Classification Quarterly Ser.: Vol. 6, No. 4). 119p. 1986. text ed. 29.95 (*0-86656-576-0*) Haworth Pr.

United States Nickel Five-Cent Piece: A Date-By-Date Analysis & History. Michael Wescott. (Illus.). 192p. (Orig.). 1991. pap. text ed. 14.95 (*0-943161-33-9*) Bowers & Merena.

U V

United States Notes. John J. Knox. LC 78-54681. 1978. reprint ed. lib. bdg. 25.00 (*0-915262-17-7*) S J Durst.
United States Numismatic Auction Catalogs: A Bibliography. Lorraine S. Durst. lib. bdg. 25.00 (*0-915262-44-4*) S J Durst.
United States Occupation of Haiti, 1915-1934. Stephen J. Solarz. 303p. 1995. pap. 15.95 (*0-8135-2203-X*) Rutgers U Pr.
United States of Ambition: Politicians, Power, & the Pursuit of Office. Alan Ehrenhalt. 1991. 23.00 (*0-8129-1894-0*) Random.
United States of America. Sheila R. Herstein & Naomi C. Robbins. (World Bibliographical Ser.: No. 16). 307p. 1982. lib. bdg. 60.00 (*0-903450-29-1*) ABC-CLIO.
United States of America. Chester Krone. LC 89-26177. (World in View Ser.). (Illus.). 96p. (YA). (gr. 6-12). 1990. lib. bdg. 25.68 (*0-8114-2434-0*) Raintree Steck-V.
United States of America. Satyaprakash. 1984. 38.50 (*0-8364-1107-2*, Pub. by Indian Doc Serv II) S Asia.
United States of America. R. Conrad Stein. LC 93-35492. (Enchantment of the World Ser.). (Illus.). 128p. (J). (gr. 5-9). 1994. lib. bdg. 30.00 (*0-516-02623-2*) Childrens.
United States of America: Are We a Nation of Fools Before God? George G. Gregg. 164p. 1994. pap. write for info. (*0-9631249-9-4*) Morris Pubng.
United States of America: Death Penalty Briefing. Amnesty International Staff. (Illus.). 245p. (Orig.). 1987. pap. 4.00 (*0-939994-26-7*, Pub. by Amnesty Intl Pubns UK) Amnesty Intl USA.
***United States of America: I: The People & the Federal Constitution; II: Elections, Parties & Pressure; III: Congress, Presidency & Administration, 3 vols.** Alan Ware. (International Library of Politics & Comparative Government). 1500p. 1997. text ed. 337.50 (*1-85521-774-0*, Pub. by Dartmth Pub UK) Ashgate Pub Co.
United States of America: Income Taxation of Private Investments in Developing Countries. 5.00 (*92-1-159028-0*, E.76.XVI.1) UN.
United States of America Vol. 1: Agriculture 1878-90. (British Parliamentary Papers). Date not set. write for info. (*0-614-16231-9*, Pub. by Irish Acad Pr IE) Intl Spec Bk.
United States of America Vol. 2-6: Seal Fisheries in the Bering Sea 1890-98. (British Parliamentary Papers). Date not set. write for info. (*0-614-16232-7*, Pub. by Irish Acad Pr IE) Intl Spec Bk.
United States of America Vol. 15: Central & South America, 1850-96. (British Parliamentary Papers). Date not set. write for info. (*0-614-16235-1*, Pub. by Irish Acad Pr IE) Intl Spec Bk.
United States of America Vol. 41: Education, 1867-99. (British Parliamentary Papers). Date not set. write for info. (*0-614-16238-6*, Pub. by Irish Acad Pr IE) Intl Spec Bk.
United States of America Vol. 46: Fugitive Criminals & the Slave Trade, 1842-90. (British Parliamentary Papers). Date not set. write for info. (*0-614-16240-8*, Pub. by Irish Acad Pr IE) Intl Spec Bk.
United States of America Vol. 47: Immigration, 1870-98. (British Parliamentary Papers). Date not set. write for info. (*0-614-16241-6*, Pub. by Irish Acad Pr IE) Intl Spec Bk.
United States of America Vol. 48: Industry, 1854-99. (British Parliamentary Papers). Date not set. write for info. (*0-614-16242-4*, Pub. by Irish Acad Pr IE) Intl Spec Bk.
United States of America Vol. 49: Postal Services 1846-92. (British Parliamentary Papers). Date not set. write for info. (*0-614-16243-2*, Pub. by Irish Acad Pr IE) Intl Spec Bk.
United States of America Vol. 50: The Samoan Question 1881-99. (British Parliamentary Papers). Date not set. write for info. (*0-614-16244-0*, Pub. by Irish Acad Pr IE) Intl Spec Bk.
United States of America Vol. 51: Social Conditions 1834-99. (British Parliamentary Papers). Date not set. write for info. (*0-614-16245-9*, Pub. by Irish Acad Pr IE) Intl Spec Bk.
United States of America Vol. 60: Miscellaneous Documents 1842-98. (British Parliamentary Papers). Date not set. write for info. (*0-614-16248-3*, Pub. by Irish Acad Pr IE) Intl Spec Bk.
United States of America Vols. 7-10: Anglo-American Relations, 1802-31. (British Parliamentary Papers). Date not set. write for info. (*0-614-16233-5*, Pub. by Irish Acad Pr IE) Intl Spec Bk.
United States of America Vols. 11-14: American-Canadian Relations, 1819-94. (British Parliamentary Papers). Date not set. write for info. (*0-614-16234-3*, Pub. by Irish Acad Pr IE) Intl Spec Bk.
United States of America Vols. 16-18: The Civil War & Its Aftermath, 1861-70. (British Parliamentary Papers). Date not set. write for info. (*0-614-16236-X*, Pub. by Irish Acad Pr IE) Intl Spec Bk.
United States of America Vols. 19-40: Commercial Reports, 1854-99. (British Parliamentary Papers). Date not set. write for info. (*0-614-16237-8*, Pub. by Irish Acad Pr IE) Intl Spec Bk.
United States of America Vols. 42-45: International Exhibitions, 1874-77. (British Parliamentary Papers). Date not set. write for info. (*0-614-16239-4*, Pub. by Irish Acad Pr IE) Intl Spec Bk.
United States of America Vols. 52-55: Trade & Tariffs 1846-92. (British Parliamentary Papers). Date not set. write for info. (*0-614-16246-7*, Pub. by Irish Acad Pr IE) Intl Spec Bk.
United States of America Vols. 56-59: The Treaty of Washington 1871-97. (British Parliamentary Papers). Date not set. write for info. (*0-614-16247-5*, Pub. by Irish Acad Pr IE) Intl Spec Bk.

U
V

United States of America Stories, Maps, Activities in Spanish & English: For Ages 10 to Adult, Bk. 1. large type ed. Kathleen Fisher. 136p. (Orig.). 1996. pap. text ed. 14.95 (*1-878253-10-7*) Fisher Hill.
United States of America Stories, Maps, Activities in Spanish & English: For Ages 10 to Adult, Bk. 2. large type ed. Kathleen Fisher. 140p. (Orig.). 1997. pap. text ed. 14.95 (*1-878253-11-5*) Fisher Hill.
***United States of America Stories, Maps, Activities in Spanish & English: For Ages 10 to Adult, Bk. 3.** large type ed. Kathleen Fisher. 140p. (Orig.). (ENG & SPA.). 1997. pap. text ed. 14.95 (*1-878253-12-3*) Fisher Hill.
***United States of America Stories, Maps, Activities in Spanish & English: For Ages 10 to Adult, Bk. 4.** large type ed. Kathleen Fisher. 140p. (Orig.). (ENG & SPA.). 1997. pap. text ed. 14.95 (*1-878253-13-1*) Fisher Hill.
United States of America vs. Motion Picture Patents Company & Others (1914) (Special Issue of Film History Ser.: Vol. 1, No. 3). 304p. 1987. pap. 29.00 (*0-8448-1546-2*, Crane Russak) Taylor & Francis.
United States of America vs. One Book Entitled Ulysses by James Joyce: Documents & Commentary : 50-Year Retrospective. Michael Moscato & Leslie LeBlanc. LC 83-25929. 482p. 1984. text ed. 79.50 (*0-313-27065-1*, U7065) Greenwood.
United States of America, 1802-1899, 60 vols., Set. (British Parliamentary Papers). Date not set. 6,250.00 (*0-614-16230-0*, Pub. by Irish Acad Pr IE) Intl Spec Bk.
United States of Americas Congressional Medal of Honor Recipients: And Their Official Citations. rev. ed. Ed. by R. J. Proft & Mitch Demars. (Illus.). 1119p. 1994. 39.00 (*0-9644590-0-0*) Highland House.
United States of Brazil. Charles W. Domville-Fife. 1976. lib. bdg. 59.95 (*0-8490-1243-0*) Gordon Pr.
United States of Europe. Victor Hugo. 1972. 59.95 (*0-8490-1244-9*) Gordon Pr.
United States of Europe. rev. ed. Ernest Wistrich. LC 93-23856. 176p. (C). 1993. pap. 16.95 (*0-415-09324-4*, B0778) Routledge.
United States of Europe & Other Papers. James A. Salter. LC 74-117837. (Essay Index Reprint Ser.). 1977. 21.95 (*0-8369-1718-9*) Ayer.
***United States of Jasper Johns.** John Yau. LC 96-47265. 1997. write for info. (*0-944072-75-5*) Zoland Bks.
***United States of Jasper Jones.** John Yau. 1997. pap. 16.95 (*0-614-28147-4*) Zoland Bks.
United States of North America. Achille Murat. 1977. text ed. 23.95 (*0-8369-9231-8*, 9085) Ayer.
United States of Poetry. Joshua Blum et al. LC 95-6263. (Illus.). 176p. 1996. 29.95 (*0-8109-3927-4*) Abrams.
United States Official Documents on the Armenian Genocide, 5 vols., Set. Compiled & Intro. by Ara Sarafian. LC 93-1863. (Archival Collections on the Armenian Genocide). pap. 75.00 (*0-935353-05-4*) Armenian Revw.
United States Official Documents on the Armenian Genocide Vol. 1: The Lower Euphrates. Compiled & Intro. by Ara Sarafian. LC 93-1863. (Archival Collections on the Armenian Genocide). (Illus.). 218p. (Orig.). 1994. pap. 15.00 (*0-935353-00-3*) Armenian Revw.
United States Official Documents on the Armenian Genocide Vol. 2: The Peripheries. Compiled & Intro. by Ara Sarafian. LC 93-1863. (Archival Collections of the Armenian Genocide). 1995. pap. 15.00 (*0-935353-01-1*) Armenian Revw.
United States Official Documents on the Armenian Genocide Vol. 3: The Central Lands. Compiled & Intro. by Ara Sarafian. LC 93-1863. (Archival Collections on the Armenian Genocide). 1995. pap. 15.00 (*0-935353-02-X*) Armenian Revw.
United States Official Documents on the Armenian Genocide Vol. 4: Non-Consulor Reports. Compiled & Intro. by Ara Sarafian. LC 93-1863. (Archival Collections on the Armenian Genocide). 1997. pap. 15.00 (*0-935353-03-8*) Armenian Revw.
United States Official Documents on the Armenian Genocide Vol. 5: Ambassador Morgenthau's Reports. Compiled & Intro. by Ara Sarafian. LC 93-1863. (Archival Collections on the Armenian Genocide). pap. 15.00 (*0-935353-04-6*) Armenian Revw.
United States Oil Pipe Lines. George S. Wolbert, Jr. 556p. 1979. 19.00 (*0-317-33104-3*, 877-76000) Am Petroleum.
United States Oil Policy. John Ise. LC 72-2846. (Use & Abuse of America's Natural Resources Ser.). (Illus.). 584p. 1972. reprint ed. 37.95 (*0-405-04512-3*) Ayer.
United States Oil Policy & Diplomacy: A Twentieth Century Overview. Edward W. Chester. LC 82-9379. (Contributions in Economics & Economic History Ser.: No. 52). (Illus.). 384p. 1983. text ed. 55.00 (*0-313-23174-5*, CUO/, Greenwood Pr) Greenwood.
United States Overseas Basing: An Anatomy of the Dilemma. James R. Blaker. LC 90-35145. 206p. 1990. text ed. 45.00 (*0-275-93665-1*, C3665, Praeger Pubs) Greenwood.
***United States Paper Money 1998.** Marc Hudgeons. 1997. pap. 6.99 (*0-676-60070-0*) Random.
United States Park Police Officer. Jack Rudman. (Career Examination Ser.: C-1989). 1994. pap. 23.95 (*0-8373-1989-7*) Nat Learn.
United States: Part 1 see Encyclopedia of World Geography
United States: Part 2 see Encyclopedia of World Geography
United States Passenger Rail Technologies. 1986. lib. bdg. 79.95 (*0-8490-3799-9*) Gordon Pr.
United States Patchwork Pattern Book: Fifty Quilt Blocks for Fifty States from "Hearth & Home" 1907-1912. Ed. by Barbara Bannister & Edna P. Ford. LC 75-2821. 128p. (Orig.). 1976. pap. 4.95 (*0-486-23243-3*) Dover.
United States Patent Classification to International Patent Classification, 1995: Concordance. 198p. 1995. pap. 13.00 (*0-16-045497-2*, 003004006765) USGPO.

United States Patents & Trademarks Citations, 10 vols. Shepard's Citation, Inc. Staff. 1988. Set. 990.00 (*0-685-23136-4*) Shepards.
United States Policies & the Latin American Economies. Ed. by Werner Baer & Donald V. Coes. LC 90-31182. 208p. 1990. text ed. 55.00 (*0-275-93502-7*, C3502, Praeger Pubs) Greenwood.
United States Policies Toward Mexico: Perceptions & Perspectives. Ed. by Richard D. Erb & Stanley R. Ross. LC 79-23112. (AEI Symposia Ser.: No. 79H). 71p. reprint ed. pap. 25.00 (*0-8357-4541-4*, 2037433) Bks Demand.
United States Policy & the Future of the United Nations. Roger Coate. 284p. 1993. pap. 14.95 (*0-87078-175-8*) TCFP-PPP.
United States Policy & the Partition of Turkey, 1914-1924. Laurence Evans. LC 65-11660. (Johns Hopkins University Studies in Historical & Political Science: Ser. 82, No. 2). 448p. reprint ed. pap. 127.70 (*0-317-55758-0*, 2029284) Bks Demand.
***United States Policy for the Changing Realities of East Asia: Toward a New Consensus.** unabridged ed. Daniel I. Okimoto et al. xii, 64p. (Orig.). 1996. pap. 10.00 (*0-9653935-0-X*, 96-04) Asia-Pacific Res.
United States Policy in Latin America: A Decade of Crisis & Challenge. Ed. by John D. Martz. LC 94-40410. xvii, 407p. (C). 1995. text ed. 55.00 (*0-8032-3162-8*); pap. text ed. 25.00 (*0-8032-8189-7*, Bison Books) U of Nebr Pr.
United States Policy in the Middle East, September 1956-June 1957: Documents. U. S. Department of State Staff. LC 68-55122. (Illus.). 425p. 1969. reprint ed. text ed. 75.00 (*0-8371-0707-5*, USPM, Greenwood Pr) Greenwood.
United States Policy on Immigration: An Overview of the Issues Affecting the Immigration Policy of the United States. Robert C. Rowland. 148p. 1995. pap. 23.95 (*0-8442-5837-7*) NTC Pub Grp.
United States Policy Toward Latin America: A Study in Domestic & International Politics. R. Harrison Wagner. LC 79-107651. x, 246p. 1970. 39.50 (*0-8047-0730-8*) Stanford U Pr.
United States Policy Toward South Africa: Is an Effective One Possible? William J. Foltz. (CISA Working Papers: No. 43). 42p. (Orig.). 1983. pap. 15.00 (*0-86682-056-6*) Ctr Intl Relations.
United States Policy Toward the People's Republic of China. Robert C. Rowland. 160p. 1995. pap. text ed. 25.25 (*0-8442-5840-7*) NTC Pub Grp.
United States Policy Toward Vietnam 1940-1945. Edward R. Drachman. LC 71-86293. 470p. 1975. 29.50 (*0-8386-7535-2*) Fairleigh Dickinson.
***United States Policy Towards Southeast Asia, 1943-1968: A Chronological Compedium.** Robert F. Futrell. 652p. 1968. reprint ed. pap. 75.00 (*0-923135-32-4*) Dalley Bk Service.
United States Politics & Elections: A Guide to Information Sources. Ed. by David J. Maurer. LC 78-13669. (American Government & History Information Guide Ser.: Vol. 3). 232p. 1978. 68.00 (*0-8103-1367-7*) Gale.
United States Pony Club Manual of Horsemanship: Basics for Beginners-D Level. Susan E. Harris. (Illus.). 288p. 1994. pap. 17.00 (*0-87605-952-3*) Howell Bk.
United States Pony Club Manual of Horsemanship: Intermediate Horsemanship/C Level. Susan E. Harris et al. (Illus.). 384p. 1995. 17.95 (*0-87605-977-9*) Howell Bk.
United States Post-Office Guide. Eli Bowen. LC 75-22802. (America in Two Centuries Ser.). 1976. reprint ed. 30.95 (*0-405-07674-6*) Ayer.
United States Post Offices, 1828-1832. T.L.C. Genealogy Staff. LC 92-64442. 224p. (Orig.). 1992. spiral bd., pap. 16.00 (*1-886633-00-2*) TLC Genealogy.
United States Postage Stamps of the Nineteenth Century, 3 vols., I. Lester G. Brookman. LC 89-62408. (Illus.). 882p. 1989. reprint ed. write for info. (*1-877998-01-X*) D G Phillips.
United States Postage Stamps of the Nineteenth Century, 3 vols., II. Lester G. Brookman. LC 89-62408. (Illus.). 882p. 1989. reprint ed. write for info. (*1-877998-02-8*) D G Phillips.
United States Postage Stamps of the Nineteenth Century, 3 vols., III. Lester G. Brookman. LC 89-62408. (Illus.). 882p. 1989. reprint ed. write for info. (*1-877998-03-6*) D G Phillips.
United States Postage Stamps of the Nineteenth Century, 3 vols., Set. Lester G. Brookman. LC 89-62408. (Illus.). 882p. 1989. reprint ed. text ed. 120.00 (*0-685-28852-8*) D G Phillips.
United States Postage Stamps of 1869. Jon Rose. (Linn's Handbook Ser.: No. 5). (Illus.). 200p. (Orig.). 1996. 30.00 (*0-940403-67-6*); pap. 14.95 (*0-940403-66-8*) Linns Stamp News.
United States Postage Stamps, 1902-1935: Regular Issues, Parcel Post, Airmails. Max G. Johl. LC 75-18276. (Illus.). 512p. 1976. reprint ed. 50.00 (*0-88000-069-4*) Quarterman.
United States Postal History. Richard B. Graham. (Illus.). 200p. (Orig.). 1990. pap. 14.95 (*0-940403-30-7*) Linns Stamp News.
United States Postal History. Richard B. Graham. (Illus.). 200p. (Orig.). 1990. 30.00 (*0-940403-39-0*) Linns Stamp News.
United States Postal Policy. Clyde Kelly. 1977. lib. bdg. 59.95 (*0-8490-2786-1*) Gordon Pr.
United States Postal Slogan Cancel Catalog. rev. ed. Moe Luff. LC 68-2266. 128p. 1977. pap. text ed. 5.75 (*0-9600162-0-1*) M Luff.
United States Power Squadrons' Boating Course for Power & Sail. 1989. 39.95 (*0-688-09126-1*) Morrow.
***United States Presidents, 7 vols.** (Illus.). (YA). (gr. 5 up). 1997. lib. bdg. 132.65 (*0-89490-912-6*) Enslow Pubs.

United States Prison Law: Sentencing to Prison, Prison Conditions, & Release - The Court Decisions, 15 vols. Ed. by Erwin C. Surrency & Sol Rubin. LC 74-23142. 1975. lib. bdg. 855.00 (*0-379-10050-9*) Oceana.
United States Productivity Growth: Who Benefited? Lawrence P. Brunner. LC 83-9108. (Research in Business Economics & Public Policy Ser.: No. 3). 160p. reprint ed. pap. 45.60 (*0-8357-1442-X*, 2070364) Bks Demand.
United States-Puerto Rico Relations. Ed. by Raoul Gordon. 1976. lib. bdg. 59.95 (*0-8490-1245-7*) Gordon Pr.
United States Pulp & Paper Industry: Global Challenges & Strategies. Jeffrey S. Arpan et al. LC 86-19296. 324p. 1987. text ed. 75.00 (*0-87249-501-9*) U of SC Pr.
United States Relations with Mexico: Context & Content. Ed. by Richard D. Erb & Stanley R. Ross. LC 81-210953. 295p. reprint ed. pap. 84.10 (*0-8357-4705-0*, 2037434) Bks Demand.
United States Relations with Russia & the Soviet Union: A Historical Dictionary. David Shavit. LC 93-9313. 256p. 1993. text ed. 59.95 (*0-313-28469-5*, SXN/, Greenwood Pr) Greenwood.
United States Response to Turkish Nationalism & Reform, 1914-1939. Roger R. Trask. LC 74-153505. 290p. reprint ed. pap. 82.70 (*0-317-29475-X*, 2055923) Bks Demand.
United States Responses to Excessive Maritime Claims. 2nd ed. J. Ashley Roach & Robert W. Smith. 1996. lib. bdg. 204.00 (*90-411-0225-6*, Pub. by M Nijhoff NE) Kluwer Ac.
United States, Revolutionary Russia, & the Rise of Czechoslovakia. Betty M. Unterberger. LC 88-38687. (Supplementary Volumes to the Papers of Woodrow Wilson). (Illus.). xvi, 464p. (C). 1989. text ed. 65.00 (*0-8078-1853-4*) U of NC Pr.
United States Road Atlas. rev. ed. 80p. 1984. 2.95 (*0-88098-074-5*, H M Gousha) P-H Gen Ref & Trav.
United States Sailing Association 1995 Directory. U. S. Sailing Staff. pap. text ed. 5.00 (*1-882502-23-X*) US Sail Assn.
United States Sailing Association 1996 Directory. U. S. Sailing Staff. (Illus.). 304p. 1996. write for info. (*1-882502-33-7*) US Sail Assn.
United States Sales Tax Tokens & Stamps: A History & Catalog. Merlin K. Malehorn & Tim Davenport. LC 93-79632. (Illus.). 403p. 1993. text ed. 49.95 (*0-942596-05-6*) Jade Hse Pubns.
United States Sanctions & South Africa: A Selected Legal Bibliography. Compiled by Terrel D. Hale. LC 92-8787. (Bibliographies & Indexes in Law & Political Science Ser.: No. 18). 192p. 1993. text ed. 69.50 (*0-313-28521-7*, HUD, Greenwood Pr) Greenwood.
United States Savings Bond Program in the Postwar Period. George Hanc. (Occasional Papers: No. 81). 124p. 1962. reprint ed. 32.30 (*0-87014-395-6*) Natl Bur Econ Res.
United States Scientific & Technical Information Policies: Views & Perspectives. Ed. by Charles R. McClure & Peter Hernon. LC 89-278. (Information Management, Policies & Services Ser.: Vol. 8). 336p. (C). 1989. text ed. 73.25 (*0-89391-571-8*) Ablex Pub.
United States Security Agreements & Commitments Abroad: Kingdom of Laos: Hearings April 3rd, 1970. Ed. by U. S. Senate Committee on Foreign Relations Staff. 241p. 1991. reprint ed. pap. 28.50 (*0-923135-25-1*) Dalley Bk Service.
United States Sentencing Commission Unpublished Public Hearings, 1986. U. S. Sentencing Commission Staff. LC 88-80878. iii, 601p. 1988. lib. bdg. 60.00 (*0-89941-639-X*, 305580) W S Hein.
United States Service Industries Handbook. Ed. by Wray O. Candilis. LC 87-7292. 254p. 1988. text ed. 59.95 (*0-275-92367-3*, C2367, Praeger Pubs) Greenwood.
United States Shipping Board: Its History, Activities & Organization. Darrell H. Smith & Paul V. Betters. LC 72-3080. (Brookings Institution. Institute for Government Research. Service Monographs of the U. S. Government: No. 63). reprint ed. 62.50 (*0-404-57163-8*) AMS Pr.
United States Shipping Policies & the World Market. Ed. by William A. Lovett. LC 95-37483. 336p. 1996. text ed. 75.00 (*0-89930-945-3*, Quorum Bks) Greenwood.
United States Shipping Policy. Wytze Gorter. LC 77-6767. 230p. 1977. reprint ed. text ed. 59.75 (*0-8371-9657-4*, GOUS, Greenwood Pr) Greenwood.
United States Since 1945. D. B. O'Callahan. 1983. pap. text ed. 9.75 (*0-582-22181-1*, 70893) Longman.
United States, Soviet Union, Cuba & South Africa on Angola: Negotiator's Nightmare; Diplomat's Dilemma, 1974-1980. Pamela S. Falk. (Pew Case Studies in International Affairs). 50p. (C). 1988. pap. text ed. 3.50 (*1-56927-405-3*) Geo U Inst Dplmcy.
United States, Soviet Union, Cuba & South Africa in Angola: The Quagmire of Four Party Negotiations, 1981-88. Kurt N. Campbell & Pamela Falk. (Pew Case Studies in International Affairs). 50p. (C). 1988. pap. text ed. 3.50 (*1-56927-429-0*) Geo U Inst Dplmcy.
United States Space Directory - 1996/97. Scott Sacknoff. 276p. 1996. pap. 97.00 (*1-887022-03-1*) Space Pubns.
United States Space Law: National & International Regulation, 5 binders. Ed. by Stephen Gorove. LC 81-22465. 1982. Set. ring bd. 625.00 (*0-379-20695-1*) Oceana.
United States Spanish-American War Fortifications at the Sabine Pass, Texas. Mildred S. Wright & William D. Quick. LC 82-99801. (Illus.). x, 50p. (Orig.). (C). 1982. pap. 15.00 (*0-917016-23-8*) M S Wright.
United States-Spanish Relations: Wolfram & World War II. John W. Cortrada. 134p. 1971. 10.00 (*0-939738-11-2*) Zubal Inc.

An Asterisk (*) at the beginning of an entry indicates that the title is appearing in BIP for the first time.

United States Special Operations Command Resource Management Process: An Application of the Strategy-to-Tasks Framework. Leslie Lewis et al. LC 94-17803. 1994. pap. 15.00 (0-8330-1557-5, MR-445-A/SOCOM) Rand Corp.

***United States Stamps 1922-26.** Gary Griffith. LC 97-17184. (Illus.). 400p. 1997. 30.00 (0-940403-74-9) Linns Stamp News.

***United States Stamps 1922-26.** Gary Griffith. LC 97-17184. (Illus.). 400p. 1997. pap. 14.95 (0-940403-75-7) Linns Stamp News.

United States Steel Corporation: A Study of the Growth & Influence of Combination in the Iron & Steel Industry. Abraham Berglund. LC 72-76677. (Columbia University. Studies in the Social Sciences: No. 73). 1968. reprint ed. 39.50 (0-404-51073-6) AMS Pr.

United States Store Cards. Edgar Adams. LC 80-70824. 1981. reprint ed. pap. 12.00 (0-915262-60-6) S J Durst.

United States Strategic Reconnaissance: Photographic - Imaging Satellites. Jeffrey T. Richelson. (CISA Working Papers: No. 38). 51p. (Orig.). 1983. pap. 15.00 (0-86682-050-7) Ctr Intl Relations.

United States Submarine Operations in World War II. Theodore Roscoe. LC 50-5198. (Illus.). 577p. 1949. 44.95 (0-87021-731-3) Naval Inst Pr.

United States Supreme Court, 10 vols., Set. (Illus.). 3000p. 1994. lib. bdg. 229.00 (0-7172-7439-X) Grolier Educ.

United States Supreme Court: An Historical & Political Analysis. 2nd ed. Robert Langran. 1992. 30.00 (0-536-57699-8) Ginn Pr.

United States Supreme Court: From the Inside Out. Phillip Cooper & Howard Ball. LC 95-7018. 400p. (C). 1995. pap. text ed. 32.00 (0-13-063850-1) P-H.

United States Supreme Court Case Names Citator, 2 vols. Shepard's Citation, Inc. Staff. 1987. 114.00 (0-685-67702-8) Shepards.

United States Supreme Court Cases & Comments: Criminal Law & Procedure, 3 vols. William H. Erickson. 1985. Looseleaf. ring bd. write for info. (0-8205-1765-8) Bender.

United States Supreme Court Decisions: An Index to Excerpts, Reprints & Discussions. 2nd ed. Nancy A. Guenther. LC 82-10518. (Illus.). 864p. 1983. 79.50 (0-8108-1578-8) Scarecrow.

United States Supreme Court Justices Biographical Data, 1789-1958. John R. Schmidhauser. 1972. write for info. (0-89138-052-3) ICPSR.

United States Synchronized Swimming Directory, 1991. U. S. Synchronized Swimming Staff. 92p. 1991. 4.00 (0-911543-12-0) US Synch Swim.

United States Synchronized Swimming Official Rules, 1991-1992. U. S. Synchronized Swimming Staff. 200p. 1991. 10.00 (0-911543-11-2) US Synch Swim.

United States Synchronized Swimming 1987 Directory. U. S. Synchronized Swimming Staff. 50p. (Orig.). 1987. pap. 5.00 (0-911543-06-6) US Synch Swim.

United States Synchronized Swimming 1987-1988 Official Rules. U. S. Synchronized Swimming Staff. 139p. (Orig.). 1987. pap. 10.00 (0-911543-02-3) US Synch Swim.

United States, Syria, & the Lebanese Crisis. R. D. Tschurgi. (Research Note Ser.: No. 8). 32p. (Orig.). 1982. pap. 5.00 (0-86682-039-6) Ctr Intl Relations.

United States Taekwon-Do Federation Handbook of Tournament Rules & Regulations. rev. ed. 94p. pap. text ed. 10.00 (0-9639671-5-0) Access Pubng.

United States Taekwon-Do Federation Handbook of Tournament Rules & Regulations. 4th ed. Freddie C. Akard et al. Ed. by Charles E. Sereff. (Illus.). 94p. (Orig.). 1993. per. 6.00 (0-9622129-6-2) Lilley Gulch.

United States Taekwon-Do Federation Patterns Workout Book. Richard L. Mitchell. Ed. by Freddie C. Akard & Charles E. Sereff. 139p. (Orig.). 1992. per. 6.00 (0-9622129-4-6) Lilley Gulch.

United States Taekwon-Do Federation Patterns Workout Book. rev. ed. 140p. pap. text ed. 10.00 (0-9639671-4-2) Access Pubng.

United States Taekwon-Do Federation Step-Sparring Handbook: 9th GUP, White Belt Through 2nd Dan, Black Belt. rev. ed. 69p. pap. text ed. 10.00 (0-9639671-6-9) Access Pubng.

United States Taekwon-Do Federation Testing Requirements: 1st Dan, Black Belt Through 4th Dan, Black Belt. rev. ed. 52p. pap. text ed. 10.00 (0-9639671-8-5) Access Pubng.

United States Taekwon-Do Federation Testing Requirements: 9th GUP, White Belt Through 1st Dan, Black Belt. rev. ed. 59p. pap. text ed. 10.00 (0-9639671-7-7) Access Pubng.

United States Tax Treaties. Kees Van Raad & Richard L. Doernberg. 714p. 1991. pap. 38.00 (90-6544-528-5) Kluwer Law Tax Pubs.

United States Taxation of Foreign Investment Income: Issues & Arguments. Peggy B. Musgrave. LC 68-58098. (Illus.). 186p. (Orig.). 1969. pap. 6.00 (0-915506-10-6) Harvard Law Intl Tax.

United States Technology Export Control: An Assessment. Douglas E. McDaniel. LC 91-45608. 304p. 1993. text ed. 59.95 (0-275-94164-7, C4164, Praeger Pubs) Greenwood.

United States Telegraph Stamps & Franks: (Incl. Pricing Guide & Control Number Guide) George J. Kramer. (Illus.). 190p. 1992. 55.00 (0-912574-44-5) Collectors.

United States Telegraph Stamps & Franks: (Incl. Pricing Guide & Control Number Guide) George J. Kramer. 190p. 1992. lthr. 85.00 (0-912574-45-3) Collectors.

United States-Thailand Relations. Ed. by Karl D. Jackson & Wiwat Mungkandi. LC 86-82801. (Research Papers & Policy Studies: No. 20). xii, 332p. (Orig.). 1986. pap. 10.00 (0-912966-95-5) IEAS.

***United States the Eastern States: Freewheeling Made Easy.** FT Publications Staff. (Smooth Ride Guides Ser.). 1996. pap. 22.50 (0-9521982-2-3, Pub. by FT Publishing UK) Seven Hills Bk.

United States, the United Nations, & Human Rights: The Eleanor Roosevelt & Jimmy Carter Eras. A. Glenn Mower, Jr. LC 78-22134. (Studies in Human Rights: No. 4). xii, 215p. 1979. text ed. 49.95 (0-313-21090-X, MUH/, Greenwood Pr) Greenwood.

United States Theatre Cloth. Silvester. 400p. 1993. 160.00 (0-7838-2059-3) G K Hall.

***United States-Third World Relations in the Post - Cold War Era.** Ed. by Harold Isaacs. (Journal of Third World Studies: Vol. IX, No. 2). (Orig.). pap. 18.25 (0-614-30668-X) Assn Third Wld.

***United States-Third World Relations in the Post-Cold War Era.** Ed. by Harold Isaacs. (Journal of Third World Studies: Vol. IX, No. 2). 570p. 1992. pap. 18.25 (0-931971-16-0) Assn Third Wld.

United States Three-Cent & Five-Cent Pieces: An Action Guide for the Collector & Investor. Intro. by Q. David Bowers. (Illus.). 168p. 1988. reprint ed. pap. text ed. 9.95 (0-943161-06-1, BBM-303) Bowers & Merena.

United States Today: An Atlas of Reproducible Pages. World Eagle Staff. LC 89-675449. (World Eagle's Today Ser.: No. 6). (Illus.). 182p. (Orig.). 1990. ring bd. 29.50 (0-930141-28-8) World Eagle.

United States Trade & Investment in Latin America: Opportunities for Business in the 1990s. Chris C. Carvounis & Brinda Z. Carvounis. LC 92-12719. 256p. 1992. text ed. 55.00 (0-89930-786-8, CUT/, Quorum Bks) Greenwood.

United States Trade Deficit of the 1980's: Origins, Meanings, & Policy Responses. Chris C. Carvounis. LC 87-2561. 197p. 1987. text ed. 55.00 (0-89930-219-X, CTD/, Quorum Bks) Greenwood.

United States Trade in Transition, 2 vols. 1992. lib. bdg. 300.00 (0-8490-5512-1) Gordon Pr.

***United States Trade Relations with the Newly Industrializing Countries in the Pacific Basin.** rev. ed. Won Kwang Paik. LC 96-48393. (Financial Sector of the American Economy Ser.). (Illus.). 177p. 1997. text ed. 50.00 (0-8153-2597-5) Garland.

United States Trade Tokens 1866-1889. 2nd ed. Russell Rulau. LC 83-81009. (Illus.). 332p. 1988. pap. 17.95 (0-87341-115-3, TT02) Krause Pubns.

United States Trade with Puerto Rico & United States Possessions. 1996. lib. bdg. 255.95 (0-8490-5971-2) Gordon Pr.

United States Treasure Atlas, Set. rev. ed. Thomas P. Terry. Incl. Vol. 1. United States Treasure Atlas. 103p. (Orig.). 1985. pap. 9.95 (0-939850-16-8); Vol. 2. United States Treasure Atlas. rev. ed. 111p. (Orig.). pap. 9.95 (0-939850-17-6); Vol. 3. United States Treasure Atlas. rev. ed. 119p. (Orig.). 1985. pap. 9.95 (0-939850-18-4); Vol. 4. United States Treasure Atlas. rev. ed. 119p. (Orig.). 1985. pap. 9.95 (0-939850-19-2); Vol. 5. United States Treasure Atlas. rev. ed. 103p. (Orig.). 1985. pap. 9.95 (0-939850-20-6); Vol. 6. United States Treasure Atlas. rev. ed. 111p. (Orig.). 1985. pap. 9.95 (0-939850-21-4); Vol. 7. United States Treasure Atlas. rev. ed. 119p. (Orig.). 1985. pap. 9.95 (0-939850-22-2); Vol. 8. United States Treasure Atlas. rev. ed. 111p. (Orig.). 1985. pap. 9.95 (0-939850-23-0); Vol. 9. United States Treasure Atlas. rev. ed. 119p. (Orig.). 1985. pap. 9.95 (0-939850-24-9); Vol. 10. United States Treasure Atlas. rev. ed. 103p. (Orig.). 1985. pap. 9.95 (0-939850-25-7); 1127p. (Orig.). 1985. Set pap. 99.50 (0-939850-26-5) Spec Pub.

United States Treasure Atlas see United States Treasure Atlas

United States Treasury System: Debt Bondage or a Debtless Economy. Silas W. Adams. 1979. lib. bdg. 59.95 (0-8490-3012-9) Gordon Pr.

United States Treaty Index: 1995 Revision, 13 vols., Vols. 6 & 7. Igor I. Kavass. LC 91-21983. 1996. 1,495.00 (0-89941-770-1, 307200) W S Hein.

***United States Tsunamis (Including United States Possessions) 1690-1988.** James F. Lander & Patricia A. Lockridge. (Illus.). 265p. (C). 1997. reprint ed. pap. text ed. 50.00 (0-7881-3932-0) DIANE Pub.

United States v. Crime in the Streets. Thomas E. Cronin et al. LC 80-8842. 224p. reprint ed. pap. 63.90 (0-685-16403-9, 2056221) Bks Demand.

United States v. Nixon: Watergate & the President. D. J. Herda. LC 95-31629. (Landmark Supreme Court Cases Ser.). (Illus.). 112p. (YA). (gr. 6 up). 1996. lib. bdg. 18.95 (0-89490-753-0) Enslow Pubs.

United States v. Nixon 1974: Presidential Powers. Mark E. Dudley. LC 94-21863. 96p. (YA). (gr. 6 up). 1994. lib. bdg. 15.98 (0-8050-3658-X) TFC Bks NY.

United States v. Peters. 4th rev. ed. Kenneth S. Broun & James H. Seckinger. 126p. 1992. pap. 18.95 (1-55681-307-4) Natl Inst Trial Ad.

United States v. Peters Teaching Notes. 4th rev. ed. Kenneth S. Broun & James H. Seckinger. 52p. 1993. teacher ed., pap. 8.95 (1-55681-443-7) Natl Inst Trial Ad.

United States vs. Charles J. Guiteau: Supreme Court Holding a Criminal Term No. 14056. District of Columbia Supreme Court Staff et al. 141.00 (0-685-11341-8) Ayer.

United States vs. Hip Hop Music. Julian Dillard. (Orig.). 1992. pap. 4.95 (1-56411-027-3) Untd Bros & Sis.

United States vs. United Shoe Machinery Corporation: An Economic Analysis of an Anti-Trust Case. Carl Kaysen. LC 56-7215. (Economic Studies: No. 99). 415p. 1956. 27.50 (0-674-92895-4) HUP.

United States Vulnerability to an Oil Import Curtailment: The Oil Replacement Capability. 1990. lib. bdg. 75.00 (0-87700-910-4) Revisionist Pr.

***United States Walks Out of the IAEA.** Roger Kirk. (Pew Case Studies in International Affairs). 50p. (C). 1996. text ed. 3.50 (1-56927-470-3) Geo U Inst Dplmcy.

United States, Western Europe & Military Intervention Overseas. Ed. by Christopher Coker. LC 87-26111. 200p. 1988. text ed. 45.00 (0-312-01620-4) St Martin.

United States Wheel of Destiny. Diana Stone. LC 76-23512. 132p. 1976. 7.00 (0-86690-162-0, S1469-014) Am Fed Astrologers.

United States Will Planning Guide. Jens C. Appel & F. Bruce Gentry. 40p. (Orig.). 1987. student ed. 9.25 (0-936499-01-X) Spectrum Bus Syst.

United States with an Excursion into Mexico see Baedeker's U. S. A.

United States Women in Aviation 1919-1929. Kathleen Brooks-Pazmany. LC 82-10812. Orig. Title: Smithsonian Studies in Air & Space Number 5. (Illus.). 62p. 1991. pap. 11.95 (0-87474-378-8) Smithsonian.

United States Women in Aviation 1930-1939. Claudia M. Oakes. LC 85-600019. Orig. Title: Smithsonian Studies in Air & Space Number 6. (Illus.). 84p. 1991. pap. 11.95 (0-87474-380-X) Smithsonian.

United States Women in Aviation, 1930-1939. Claudia M. Oakes. LC 85-600019. (Smithsonian Studies in Air & Science: No. 6). 74p. (Orig.). reprint ed. pap. 25.00 (0-317-41864-5, 2026175) Bks Demand.

United States Women in Aviation, 1940-1985. Deborah G. Douglas. Orig. Title: Smithsonian Studies in Air & Space, No. 7. (Illus.). 152p. 1991. pap. 12.95 (0-87474-382-6) Smithsonian.

***United States 1 Cent Franklin 1861-1867: And an Introduction to the Postal History of the Period.** Don L. Evans. (Illus.). 340p. 1997. pap. 30.00 (0-940403-70-6) Linns Stamp News.

***United States 1 Cent Franklin 1861-1867: And an Introduction to the Postal History of the Period.** Don L. Evans. (Illus.). 340p. 1997. 60.00 (0-940403-71-4) Linns Stamp News.

United States, 1830-1850: The Nation & Its Sections. Frederick J. Turner. (History - United States Ser.). 602p. 1993. reprint ed. lib. bdg. 109.00 (0-7812-4886-8) Rprt Serv.

United States, 1985. Steve Birnbaum. (Birnbaum's Travel Guides Ser.). pap. 11.95 (0-685-09374-3) HM.

United States, 1989. Stephen Birnbaum. (Birnbaum's Travel Guides Ser.). 1008p. 1988. pap. 12.95 (0-318-35549-3) HM.

United States/Canada/Mexico Sticker Atlas. Rand McNally Staff. 1995. pap. text ed. 4.95 (0-528-83721-4) Rand McNally.

United Synod: The Southern New School Presbyterian Church. Harold M. Parker, Jr. LC 87-37564. (Contributions to the Study of Religion Ser.: No. 20). 363p. 1988. text ed. 55.00 (0-313-26289-6, PSY/, Greenwood Pr) Greenwood.

United Technologies: A Report on the Company's Environmental Policies & Practices. (Illus.). 50p. (C). 1994. reprint ed. pap. text ed. 250.00 (0-7881-0911-1, Coun on Econ) DIANE Pub.

United Theological Seminary of the Twin Cities: An Ecumenical Venture. Arthur L. Merrill. LC 92-41819. (Illus.). 340p. 1993. text ed. 99.95 (0-7734-9201-1) E Mellen.

United They Hate: White Supremacists in America. Michael Kronenwetter. 133p. (J). 1992. 14.95 (0-8027-8162-4); lib. bdg. 15.85 (0-8027-8163-2) Walker & Co.

United Way: Dilemmas of Organized Charity. Eleanor L. Brilliant. 382p. (C). 1993. pap. text ed. 19.00 (0-231-05623-0) Col U Pr.

United We Fall. Ed. by Pat Works & Jan Works. LC 77-84030. (C). 17.95 (0-930438-03-5); pap. 11.95 (0-930438-02-7) RWU Parachuting Pubns.

United We Solve: 116 Math Problems for Groups, Grades 5-10. Tim Erickson. 192p. (Orig.). 1996. teacher ed., pap. text ed. 19.95 (0-9648496-0-7, eeps media) Epistemol Eng.

United We Stand. Alvin R. Cunningham. LC 90-70673. (Illus.). 126p. (Orig.). 1991. pap. 7.00 (1-56002-014-8) Aegina Pr.

United We Stand. rev. ed. Arthur L. Clanton & Charles Clanton. LC 95-24156. 336p. 1995. text ed. 14.99 (1-56722-134-3) Word Aflame.

United We Stand: Collaboration for Child Care & Early Education Services, Vol. 33. Lynn Kagan. (Early Childhood Education Ser.). 168p. (C). 1991. text ed. 24.00 (0-8077-3135-8) Tchrs Coll.

United We Stand: The Role of Polish Workers in the New York Mills Textile Strikes, 1912 & 1916. James S. Pula & Eugene E. Dziedzic. (East European Monographs: No. 286). 320p. 1990. 53.50 (0-88033-183-6) Col U Pr.

United We Stand: The Unprecedented Story of GM & UAW Finally Working Together. Thomas L. Weekley. 1996. text ed. 24.95 (0-07-068958-X) McGraw.

***United World.** Scott Nearing. 265p. pap. 10.00 (0-614-30476-8) Good Life Ctr.

Unites States-China Nuclear Cooperative Agreement of 1985. James Reardon-Anderson. (Pew Case Studies in International Affairs). 50p. (C). 1993. pap. text ed. 3.50 (1-56927-110-0) Geo U Inst Dplmcy.

Unites States Congress, Western Hemisphere Immigration. Ed. by Carlos E. Cortez. LC 80-7795. (Hispanics in the United States Ser.). 1981. reprint ed. lib. bdg. 40.95 (0-405-13188-7) Ayer.

***Uniting Agriculture: Proceedings, 38th Annual Meeting of the Agricultural Research Institute, October 10-12, 1989.** 256p. pap. 25.00 (0-614-24234-7) Agri Research Inst.

Uniting Communities for Youth: Mobilizing All Sectors to Create a Positive Future. Peter L. Benson. (Everyone's an Asset-Builder Ser.). 1995. pap. 4.50 (1-57482-327-2) Search Inst.

***Uniting Communities Through Crime Prevention.** 2nd ed. Jean O'Neil. Ed. by Judy Kirby. (Special Focus Ser.). 80p. (Orig.). 1994. reprint ed. pap. 14.95 (0-934513-07-4, M35) Natl Crime DC.

Uniting Germany: Actions & Reactions. Pekka K. Hamalainen. LC 94-33704. (C). 1994. pap. text ed. 23.00 (0-8133-2536-6) Westview.

Uniting Germany: Documents & Debates, 1944-1993. Konrad H. Jarausch & Volker Gransow. LC 94-20694. 304p. (C). 1994. text ed. 64.00 (1-57181-010-2); pap. text ed. 18.95 (1-57181-011-0) Berghahn Bks.

***Uniting of Europe: From Discord to Concord.** Stanley Henig. LC 97-14344. (Making of the Contemporary World Ser.). 144p. (C). 1997. pap. write for info. (0-415-13693-8) Routledge.

Uniting of Europe: Political, Social, & Economic Forces, 1950-1957. rev. ed. Ernst B. Haas. xl, 552p. 1968. 62.50 (0-8047-0515-1) Stanford U Pr.

Uniting of Europe: Political, Social, & Economic Forces, 1950-1957. Ernst B. Haas. LC 58-9450. 592p. 1958. reprint ed. pap. 30.00 (0-7837-8938-6, 2049648) Bks Demand.

***Uniting Psychology & Biology: Integrative Perspectives on Human Development.** Nancy L. Segal et al. LC 97-10903. 1997. write for info. (1-55798-428-X) Am Psychol.

Uniting Sex, Self, & Spirit. Genia P. Haddon. LC 92-61120. (Illus.). 263p. 1993. pap. 15.95 (1-881311-13-9) Plus Pubns CT.

Uniting the Dual Torah: Sifra & the Problem of the Mishnah. Jacob Neusner. 272p. (C). 1990. text ed. 80.00 (0-521-38125-8) Cambridge U Pr.

Uniting the Kingdom? The Making of British History. Keith J. Stringer. LC 95-34971. 336p. (C). (gr. 13). 1995. 39.95 (0-415-13041-7) Routledge.

Uniting the Peoples & Nations, Vol. 2: Readings in World Federalism. Ed. by Barbara Walker. 364p. (Orig.). (C). pap. 15.00 (0-685-71547-7) Wrld Federal.

Uniting the Tailors. Anne J. Kershen. 1995. pap. 22.50 (0-7146-4145-6, Pub. by F Cass Pubs UK) Intl Spec Bk.

Uniting the Tailors: Trade Unionism among the Tailoring Workers of London & Leeds, 1870-1939. Anne J. Kershen. LC 94-3697. 272p. 1995. 39.50 (0-7146-4596-6, Pub. by F Cass Pubs UK) Intl Spec Bk.

***Uniting Two Worlds, Vol. 6.** Satsvarupa Dasa Goswami. 1997. 50.00 (0-89213-287-6) Bhaktivedanta.

***Unititled II, Veterinarian Romance.** Leslie Brannen. 288p. 1997. mass mkt. 5.99 (0-515-12188-6) Jove Pubns.

Unitization of Oil & Gas Fields in Texas: A Study of Legislative, Administrative, & Judicial Policies. Jacqueline L. Weaver. LC 85-24475. 555p. 1986. lib. bdg. 37.50 (0-915707-20-9) Resources Future.

Unitized Experiments in Organic Chemistry. 4th ed. Ray Q. Brewster et al. 577p. (C). 1977. pap. 50.95 (0-534-21051-1) Wadsworth Pub.

Unitizing Investment Pools. Paul V. Silva. Ed. by Anne Kendrick. 48p. 1993. 45.00 (0-614-17596-8) NACUBO.

Unitl the Mashiach: The Life of Rabbi Nachman. Chaim Kramer. 379p. 1986. text ed. 15.00 (0-930213-08-4) Breslov Res Inst.

***Unitool Method.** M. L. Baxter. (Technical Papers: Vol. 129.11). 1954. pap. text ed. 30.00 (1-55589-158-6) AGMA.

Units. Dianne DeTommaso. (Illus.). 192p. (Orig.). 1994. spiral bd. 24.00 (1-884135-03-X) Mayer-Johnson.

Units & Standards of Electromagnetism. P. Vigoreaux. (Wykeham Science Ser.: No. 15). 82p. 1971. pap. 18.00 (0-85109-190-3) Taylor & Francis.

Units & Standards of Electromagnetism. P. Vigoureux & R. A. Tricker. LC 77-153869. (Wykeham Science Ser.: No. 15). 82p. (C). 1971. 18.00 (0-8448-1117-3, Crane Russak) Taylor & Francis.

Units Based on a Theme. 1984. Eleven Topics. 3.50 (0-939418-54-1) Ferguson-Florissant.

Units Calculator. Scott Ferson & Rudiger Kuhn. 35p. 1993. 99.00 (1-884977-08-1) Applied Biomath.

Units in Mandarin Conversation: Prosody, Discourse & Grammar. Hongyin Tao. LC 96-3779. (Studies in Discourse & Grammar: Vol. 5). xvi, 226p. 1996. lib. bdg. 77.00 (1-55619-371-8) Benjamins North Am.

***Units of Biodiversity: Species in Practice.** Ed. by Claridge et al. (Systematics Association Ser.). (Illus.). 386p. (C). 1997. text ed. 69.00 (0-412-63120-2, Chap & Hall NY) Chapman & Hall.

Units of Evolution: Essays on the Nature of the Species. Marc Ereshefsky. (Illus.). 424p. 1991. 52.50 (0-262-05044-7, Bradford Bks); pap. 30.00 (0-262-55020-2, Bradford Bks) MIT Pr.

Units of Expression for Wastewater Management. rev. ed. (Manual of Practice Ser.: No. 6). 47p. (C). 1982. pap. text ed. 11.00 (0-943244-06-4, M0006) Water Environ.

Units of Lovers. Doug Dahl. 1994. 8.95 (0-533-10754-7) Vantage.

Units of Measure. Fred Justus. (Math Ser.). 24p. (gr. 3-5). 1979. student ed. 5.00 (0-8209-0120-2, A-30) ESP.

Units of Measure & the Metric System see Basic Mathematics

Units of Measurement: An Encyclopaedic Dictionary of Units, Both Scientific & Popular, & the Quantities They Measure. Stephen Dresner. LC 72-187346. 303p. reprint ed. pap. 86.40 (0-317-26195-9, 2052071) Bks Demand.

Units of the Confederate States Army. Joseph Crute, Jr. 504p. 1988. 45.00 (0-942211-53-7) Olde Soldier Bks.

Units of the Royal Australian Air Force Vol. 1: A Concise History: Introduction, Bases, Supporting Organisations. Royal Australian Air Force Historical Section Staff. LC 94-31303. (Illus.). 243p. (Orig.). 1995. pap. 24.95 (*0-644-42792-2*, 9431303, Pub. by AGPS Pr AT) Intl Spec Bk.

Units of the Royal Australian Air Force Vol. 2: A Concise History: Fighter Units. Royal Australian Air Force Historical Section Staff. LC 94-31315. 187p. (Orig.). 1995. pap. 24.95 (*0-644-42794-9*, 9431315, Pub. by AGPS Pr AT) Intl Spec Bk.

Units of the Royal Australian Air Force Vol. 3: A Concise History: Bomber Units. Royal Australian Air Force Historical Section Staff. LC 94-31327. (Illus.). 191p. (Orig.). 1995. pap. 24.95 (*0-644-42795-7*, 9431327, Pub. by AGPS Pr AT) Intl Spec Bk.

Units of the Royal Australian Air Force Vol. 4: Maritime & Transport Units. Royal Australian Air Force Historical Section Staff. LC 94-31339. (Illus.). 221p. (Orig.). 1995. pap. 24.95 (*0-644-42796-5*, 9431339, Pub. by AGPS Pr AT) Intl Spec Bk.

Units of the Royal Australian Air Force Vol. 5: A Concise History: Radar Units. Royal Australian Air Force Historical Section Staff. LC 94-31340. (Illus.). 190p. (Orig.). 1995. pap. 24.95 (*0-644-42797-3*, 9431340, Pub. by AGPS Pr AT) Intl Spec Bk.

Units of the Royal Australian Air Force Vol. 6: A Concise History: Logistics Units. Royal Australian Air Force Historical Section Staff. LC 94-31352. (Illus.). 176p. (Orig.). 1995. pap. 24.95 (*0-644-42798-1*, 9431352, Pub. by AGPS Pr AT) Intl Spec Bk.

Units of the Royal Australian Air Force Vol. 7: A Concise History: Maintenance Units. Royal Australian Air Force Historical Section Staff. LC 94-31364. (Illus.). 157p. (Orig.). 1995. pap. 24.95 (*0-644-42799-X*, 9431364, Pub. by AGPS Pr AT) Intl Spec Bk.

Units of the Royal Australian Air Force Vol. 8: A Concise History: Training Units. Royal Australian Air Force Historical Section Staff. LC 94-31376. (Illus.). 237p. (Orig.). 1995. pap. 24.95 (*0-644-42800-7*, 9431376, Pub. by AGPS Pr AT) Intl Spec Bk.

Units of the Royal Australian Air Force Vol. 9: A Concise History: Ancillary Units. Royal Australian Air Force Historical Section Staff. LC 94-3139. (Illus.). 255p. (Orig.). 1995. pap. 24.95 (*0-644-42802-3*, 943139X, Pub. by AGPS Pr AT) Intl Spec Bk.

Units of the Royal Australian Air Force Vol. 10: A Concise History: Chiefs of the Air Staff, Aircraft, Bibliography. Royal Australian Air Force Historical Section Staff. LC 94-31388. (Illus.). 150p. (Orig.). 1995. pap. 24.95 (*0-644-42801-5*, 9431388, Pub. by AGPS Pr AT) Intl Spec Bk.

Unity. David Miller. 32p. (Orig.). 1981. pap. 3.00 (*0-935162-03-8*) Singing Horse.

Unity: A Celebration of Gay Games IV & Stonewall. Ed. by Lisa Labrecque. 168p. (Orig.). 1994. pap. 29.95 (*0-9643182-0-2*) Labrecque Pub.

Unity: A Quest for Truth. Eric Butterworth. (Orig.). 1965. pap. 4.00 (*0-8315-0020-4*) Speller.

Unity: A Quest for Truth. rev. ed. Eric Butterworth. LC 85-50997. 94p. (Orig.). 1994. pap. 8.95 (*0-87159-177-4*) Unity Bks.

***Unity Amid Diversity: Ministry in an Age of Pluralism, Vol. VII, No. 4.** Bernard F. Stratman. (Illus.). 50p. 1996. pap. 6.00 (*0-9653675-1-7*) NFPC.

Unity & Design in Horace's Odes. Matthew S. Santirocco. LC 85-20964. x, 251p. (C). 1986. 34.95 (*0-8078-1691-4*) U of NC Pr.

Unity & Disintegration in International Alliances. Ole R. Holsti et al. (Illus.). 306p. 1985. reprint ed. pap. text ed. 25.00 (*0-8191-4387-1*) U Pr of Amer.

Unity & Diversity: Essays in the History, Literature, & Religion of the Ancient Near East. Ed. by Hans Goedicke & J. J. Roberts. LC 74-24376. (Johns Hopkins University Near Eastern Studies). 240p. reprint ed. pap. 68.40 (*0-317-11301-1*, 2016572) Bks Demand.

Unity & Diversity: Local Cultures & Identities in China. A. Liu. 328p. (Orig.). 1996. pap. 39.50 (*962-209-402-3*, Pub. by Hong Kong Univ Pr HK) Coronet Bks.

Unity & Diversity in the Church: Papers Read at the 1994 Summer Meeting & the 1995 Winter Meeting of the Ecclesiastical History Society. Ed. by Robert N. Swanson. LC 95-33575. (Ecclesiastical History Ser.: Vol. 32). (Illus.). 576p. (C). 71.95 (*0-631-19892-X*) Boydell & Brewer.

Unity & Diversity in the New Testament: An Inquiry into the Character of Earliest Christianity. 2nd ed. James Dunn. LC 89-20659. 528p. (C). 1990. pap. text ed. 24.95 (*0-334-02436-6*) TPI PA.

Unity & Diversity of Membrane Function. Ed. by Gerhard H. Giebisch & J. F. Hoffman. (Journal: Renal Physiology & Biochemistry: Vol. 17, No. 3-4, 1994). (Illus.). 110p. 1994. pap. 38.50 (*3-8055-5980-1*) S Karger.

Unity & Identity in Aristotle's Metaphysics. Theodore Scaltsas. 368p. 1994. 58.00 (*0-19-824067-8*) OUP.

Unity & Plurality: Mission in the Bible. Lucien Legrand. LC 90-38940. 1990. pap. 20.00 (*0-88344-692-8*) Orbis Bks.

Unity & Struggle: Speeches & Writings. Amilcar Cabral. Tr. by Michael Wolfers. LC 79-2337. 334p. 1979. reprint ed. pap. 95.20 (*0-7837-9602-1*, 2060359) Bks Demand.

Unity & Variety: A History of the Church in Devon & Cornwall. Ed. by Orme. 256p. 1991. pap. text ed. 21.95 (*0-85989-355-3*, Pub. by Univ Exeter Pr UK) Northwestern U Pr.

Unity & Variety in Muslim Civilization. Armand Abel et al. Ed. by Gustave E. Von Grunebaum. LC 55-11191. (Comparative Studies of Cultures & Civilizations: No. 7). 397p. reprint ed. pap. 113.20 (*0-317-11328-3*, 2013614) Bks Demand.

Unity Guide to Healing. Connie Fillmore. LC 89-50699. 128p. 1989. pap. 4.95 (*0-87159-167-7*) Unity Bks.

Unity Guide to Prosperous Living. Connie Fillmore. LC 89-51221. 124p. 1990. pap. 4.95 (*0-87159-168-5*) Unity Bks.

Unity, Heresy, & Reform, 1378-1460. Christopher Crowder. 1987. pap. 12.50 (*0-919642-10-1*) Limestone Pr.

Unity in Christ. Leonard Mullens. 1958. 3.00 (*0-88027-053-5*) Firm Foun Pub.

Unity in Creation. Russell Maatman. 143p. (Orig.). 1978. pap. 4.95 (*0-932914-00-4*) Dordt Coll Pr.

Unity in Diversity. Ben M. Carter. 102p. (C). 1991. lib. bdg. 36.00 (*0-8191-8314-8*) U Pr of Amer.

Unity in Diversity: A Story of Apuleius' "Metamorphoses" Paula James. (Altertumswissenschaftliche Texte und Studien: Vol. 16). viii, 272p. (GER.). 1987. 25.87 (*3-487-07820-1*) G Olms Pubs.

Unity in Diversity: Papers Presented to Simon C. Dik on His 50th Birthday. Ed. by Harm Pinkster & Inge Genee. viii, 313p. (Orig.). (C). 1990. pap. text ed. 69.25 (*3-11-013353-9*) Mouton.

Unity in Hardy's Novels: Repetitive Symmetries. Peter J. Casagrande. xii, 252p. 1982. 29.95 (*0-7006-0209-7*) U Pr of KS.

***Unity in Science & Nature.** George Smoot. (A Science Master Ser.). 176p. Date not set. pap. write for info. (*0-465-08874-0*) Basic.

***Unity in Science & Nature.** George Smoot. (Science Master Ser.). 176p. 1998. 25.00 (*0-465-08873-2*) Basic.

Unity in Shakespearian Tragedy. Brents Stirling. LC 66-19086. 212p. 1966. reprint ed. 45.00 (*0-87752-105-0*) Gordian.

Unity in the Church or the Principles of Catholicism: Presented in the Spirit of the Church Fathers of the First Three Centuries. Johann A. Mohler. Tr. by Peter Erb from GER. LC 95-7264. 487p. (YA). 1996. 49.95 (*0-8132-0621-9*) Cath U Pr.

Unity in the Ghazals of Hafez. Michael C. Hillmann. LC 74-27614. (Studies in Middle Eastern Literatures: No. 6). 1976. pap. 20.00 (*0-88297-010-0*) Bibliotheca.

Unity in the Trinity. Ian McCrimmon. (C). 1992. text ed. 30.00 (*0-9514698-4-3*, Pub. by Cosmatom UK) St Mut.

Unity in Truth. D. Martyn Lloyd-Jones. 1991. pap. 11.99 (*0-85234-288-8*, Pub. by Evangelical Pr) Presby & Reformed.

Unity, Liberty, & Charity: Building Bridges under Icy Waters. William J. Abraham. Ed. by Donald E. Messer. LC 96-11266. 1996. pap. 12.95 (*0-687-03306-3*) Abingdon.

Unity of All Religions & Atheism. Aratis. 8p. (Orig.). 1995. pap. 2.00 (*0-938075-66-7*) Ocean View Bks.

Unity of Anglicanism: Catholic & Reformed. Henry R. McAdoo. LC 82-62392. 48p. (Orig.). 1983. pap. 4.95 (*0-8192-1324-1*) Morehouse Pub.

Unity of Being. Esme Wynne-Tyson. 230p. reprint ed. pap. 65.60 (*0-8357-6656-X*, 2035325) Bks Demand.

Unity of Environmentalism. Bryan Norton. (Illus.). 272p. 1991. 34.00 (*0-19-506112-8*) OUP.

Unity of Evolutionary Biology: Proceedings of the Fourth International Congress of Systematic & Evolutionary Biology, 2 vols. Ed. by Elizabeth Dudley. LC 90-27811. (Illus.). 1160p. 1992. Set. 125.00 (*0-931146-19-4*, Dioscorides) Timber.

Unity of Forces in the Universe, 2 vols., 1. A. Zee. 1104p. 1982. text ed. write for info. (*9971-950-14-6*); pap. text ed. write for info. (*9971-950-15-4*) World Scientific Pub.

Unity of Forces in the Universe, 2 vols., 2. A. Zee. 1104p. 1982. text ed. 140.00 (*9971-950-38-3*); pap. text ed. 62.00 (*9971-950-39-1*) World Scientific Pub.

Unity of Good. Mary Baker Eddy. reprint ed. pap. 5.00 (*0-87952-053-1*) Eddy Wrtngs M B Eddy.

Unity of Good. Mary M. Eddy. (Notable American Authors Ser.). 1992. reprint ed. lib. bdg. 75.00 (*0-7812-2750-X*) Rprt Serv.

Unity of Homer. John A. Scott. LC 65-15246. 1921. 30.00 (*0-8196-0152-7*) Biblo.

Unity of Isaiah. Oswald T. Allis. 1952. pap. 7.99 (*0-87552-105-3*, Pub. by Evangelical Pr) Presby & Reformed.

Unity of Kant's Critique of Pure Reason: Experience, Language, & Knowledge. Terence C. Williams. (Studies in the History of Philosophy: No. 4). 1986. lib. bdg. 99.95 (*0-88946-301-8*) E Mellen.

Unity of Law: As Exhibited in the Relation of Physical, Social, Mental & Moral Science. Henry C. Carey. LC 67-18575. (Reprints of Economic Classics Ser.). (Illus.). xxiii, 433p. 1967. reprint ed. 49.50 (*0-678-00247-9*) Kelley.

Unity of Man's Trinity. Glenn F. Casey. 68p. (Orig.). 1992. pap. text ed. 5.95 (*0-9633714-0-1*) G F Casey.

Unity of Mistakes: A Phenomenological Interpretation of Medical Work. Marianne A. Paget. LC 87-26716. 224p. (C). 1988. 32.95 (*0-87722-533-8*) Temple U Pr.

Unity of Nature & History in Pannenberg's Theology. Cornelius A. Buller. 224p. (C). 1996. pap. text ed. 22.95 (*0-8226-3055-9*); lib. bdg. 57.50 (*0-8226-3054-0*) Rowman.

Unity of Reality: God, God-Experience & Meditation in the Hindu-Christian Dialogue. Michael Von Bruck. Tr. by James V. Zeitz. 1991. pap. 19.95 (*0-8091-3214-1*) Paulist Pr.

Unity of Reason: Essays on Kant's Philosophy. Dieter Henrich. Ed. by Richard L. Velkley. Tr. by Jeffrey Edwards et al. LC 93-34705. 255p. 1994. 45.00 (*0-674-92905-5*) HUP.

Unity of Reason: Rereading Kant. Susan Neiman. 288p. 1994. 45.00 (*0-19-506768-1*) OUP.

***Unity of Reason: Rereading Kant.** Susan Neiman. 224p. 1997. reprint ed. pap. 14.95 (*0-19-511388-8*) OUP.

Unity of Science. Robert L. Causey. (Synthese Library: No. 109). 192p. 1977. lib. bdg. 88.00 (*90-277-0779-0*, D Reidel) Kluwer Ac.

***Unity of Science: 1934 Edition.** Rudolf Carnap. Tr. & Intro. by M. Black. (Key Texts Ser.). 101p. 1996. reprint ed. pap. write for info. (*1-85506-391-3*) Bks Intl VA.

Unity of Self. Stephen L. White. (Illus.). 464p. 1991. 42.50 (*0-262-23162-X*) MIT Pr.

Unity of the Bible. Harold H. Rowley. LC 78-2684. 201p. 1978. reprint ed. text ed. 38.50 (*0-313-20346-6*, ROUB, Greenwood Pr) Greenwood.

Unity of the Bible: Unfolding God's Plan for Humanity. Daniel P. Fuller. 336p. 1992. 24.99 (*0-310-53300-7*) Zondervan.

Unity of the Common Law: Studies in Hegelian Jurisprudence. Alan Brudner. LC 94-37053. (Philosophy, Social Theory & the Rule of Law Ser.: Vol. 2). 368p. 1995. 45.00 (*0-520-08596-5*) U CA Pr.

Unity of the Hebrew Bible. David N. Freedman. (Distinguished Senior Faculty Lectures). 128p. (C). 1993. pap. text ed. 19.95 (*0-472-08241-8*) U of Mich Pr.

Unity of the Mind. D. H. Brooks. LC 93-37499. 1994. text ed. 69.95 (*0-312-12017-6*) St Martin.

Unity of the Moral & Spiritual Life. William E. May. (Synthesis Ser.). 1978. pap. 1.00 (*0-8199-0745-6*, Frncscn Herld) Franciscan Pr.

Unity of the Muslim World. 3.00 (*0-933511-81-7*) Kazi Pubns.

Unity of the "Odyssey" George E. Dimock. LC 88-14824. 360p. (Orig.). (C). 1989. pap. 18.95 (*0-87023-721-7*, X1989) U of Mass Pr.

Unity of the Platonic Dialogue: The Cratylus, the Protagoras, the Parmenides. Rudolph H. Weingartner. LC 73-186244. 1973. text ed. 29.50 (*0-672-51658-6*) Irvington.

Unity of the Platonic Dialogue: The Cratylus, the Protagras, the Parmenides. Ed. by Rudolph H. Weingartner. 1973. pap. 4.50 (*0-672-61310-7*, LLA224, Bobbs) Macmillan.

Unity of the Stream. Vernon Watkins. 108p. (C). 1978. pap. 20.00 (*0-85088-820-4*, Pub. by Gomer Pr UK) St Mut.

Unity of Torah, Vol. 1. Yehoshua Hoenigwachs. 1991. 18.95 (*0-87306-802-5*) Feldheim.

Unity of Western Civilization. Ed. by Francis S. Marvin. LC 77-128277. (Essay Index Reprint Ser.). 1977. 21.95 (*0-8369-1889-4*) Ayer.

Unity of Western Europe. Ed. by Jack D. Dowell. LC 76-13400. 65p. reprint ed. pap. 25.00 (*0-685-24157-2*, 2033031) Bks Demand.

Unity, Our Adventure: The Focolare Movement. (Illus.). 80p. 1987. 14.90 (*0-911782-56-7*) New City.

***Unity Out of Diversity: The Origins & Development of the University of Humberside.** David Foster. LC 97-461. (Illus.). 180p. 1997. 57.50 (*0-485-11513-1*, Pub. by Athlone Pr UK) Humanities.

Unity, Plurality & Politics. Ed. by J. M. Porter & Richard Vernon. LC 85-26262. 256p. 1986. text ed. 32.50 (*0-312-83331-8*) St Martin.

Unity Temple: Frank Lloyd Wright & Architecture for Liberal Religion. Joseph M. Siry. (Illus.). 400p. (C). 1996. text ed. 75.00 (*0-521-49542-3*) Cambridge U Pr.

***Unity Temple: Oak Park, Illinois, 1905: Frank Lloyd Wright.** Robert McCarter. (Architecture in Detail Ser.). (Illus.). 60p. 1997. pap. 29.95 (*0-7148-3629-X*, Pub. by Phaidon Press UK) Chronicle Bks.

Unity We Seek. Robert Runcie. LC 90-31506. 169p. (Orig.). 1990. pap. 7.95 (*0-8192-1521-X*) Morehouse Pub.

Unity with Diversity in the European Economy: The Community's Southern Frontier. Ed. by Christopher Bliss & Jorge B. De Macedo. (Illus.). 391p. (C). 1990. text ed. 69.95 (*0-521-39520-8*) Cambridge U Pr.

Unity Without Uniformity: History of the Rhinebeck, N. Y. Church Community, 1718-1918. Althea Lawrence. LC 91-33508. 184p. 1992. 30.00 (*0-912526-54-8*) Lib Res.

Unity Without Uniformity: The Story of Rhinebeck Churches. Thea Lawrence. (Illus.). (Orig.). (C). 1990. pap. write for info. (*0-318-65920-4*) Dawn Treader.

Univalent Functions. P. L. Duren. (Grundlehren der Mathematischen Wissenschaften Ser.: Vol. 259). (Illus.). 382p. 1983. 99.95 (*0-387-90795-5*) Spr-Verlag.

Univalent Functions, 2 vols. A. W. Goodman. 1983. Set. 35.00 (*0-936166-12-6*) Polygonal Pub.

Univalent Functions, 2 vols., Vol. I. A. W. Goodman. 264p. 1983. 20.00 (*0-936166-10-X*) Polygonal Pub.

Univalent Functions, 2 vols., Vol. II. A. W. Goodman. 323p. 1983. 20.00 (*0-936166-11-8*) Polygonal Pub.

Univalent Functions & Orthonormal Systems. Isaak M. Milin. LC 77-1198. (Translations of Mathematical Monographs: Vol. 49). 202p. 1977. 62.00 (*0-8218-1599-7*, MMONO/49) Am Math.

Univalent Functions & Teichmuller Spaces. O. Lehto. (Graduate Texts in Mathematics Ser.: Vol. 109). (Illus.). 270p. 1986. 54.95 (*0-387-96310-3*) Spr-Verlag.

Univariate Discrete Distributions. 2nd ed. Norman L. Johnson et al. LC 92-11685. (Probability & Mathematical Statistics: Applied Probability & Statistics Section Ser.). 565p. 1993. text ed. 94.95 (*0-471-54897-9*) Wiley.

Univariate Tests for Time Series Models. Jeff B. Cromwell & Walter C. Labys. (Quantitative Applications in the Social Sciences Ser.: Vol. 99). (C). 1994. pap. text ed. 9.95 (*0-8039-4991-X*) Sage.

Univariate Time-Series Analysis of Quarterly Earnings: Some Unresolved Issues. Wm S. Hopwood & James C. McKeown. (Studies in Accounting Research: No. 25). 52p. 1986. 12.00 (*0-86539-059-2*) Am Accounting.

Univers de la Psychologie, 1: Champ, Histoire et Methodes de la Psychologie. Ed. by Yves Pelicier. 512p. (FRE.). 1977. 150.00 (*0-8288-5525-0*, M6537) Fr & Eur.

Univers de la Psychologie, 2: La Vie Psychologique Normale. Ed. by Yves Pelicier. 509p. (FRE.). 1977. 150.00 (*0-8288-5526-9*, M6538) Fr & Eur.

Univers de la Psychologie, 3: Le Development Psychologique Normale, Lavie Psychologie Pathologique. Ed. by Yves Pelicier. 523p. (FRE.). 1977. 150.00 (*0-8288-5527-7*, M6539) Fr & Eur.

Univers Leibnizien. Joseph Moreau. 256p. 1988. reprint ed. write for info. (*3-487-07903-8*) G Olms Pubs.

Univers Theatral De Corneille: Paradoxe et Subtilite Heroiques. A. S. Goulet. LC 78-1756. (Studies in Romance Languages: No. 33). 232p. 1978. 14.00 (*0-674-92928-4*) HUP.

Universal Abandon? The Politics of Postmodernism. Ed. by Andrew Ross. LC 88-10134. (Cultural Politics Ser.). xviii, 300p. (Orig.). 1989. pap. 16.95 (*0-8166-1680-9*) U of Minn Pr.

Universal Access to E-Mail: Feasibility & Societal Implications. Robert H. Anderson et al. LC 95-53853. 295p. (Orig.). 1995. pap. 20.00 (*0-8330-2331-4*, MR-650-RC) Rand Corp.

Universal Access to Outdoor Recreation: A Design Guide. PLAE, Inc. Staff. (Illus.). 300p. 1993. pap. 44.95 (*0-944661-25-4*) MIG Comns.

Universal Access to Outdoor Recreation: A Pocket Guide. PLAE, Inc. Staff. (Illus.). 64p. (Orig.). 1994. pap. text ed. 9.95 (*0-944661-28-9*) MIG Comns.

Universal Accountant, & Complete Merchant, Vol. 2. William Gordon. LC 86-18419. (Accounting Thought & Practice Ser.). 488p. 1986. text ed. 20.00 (*0-8240-7879-9*) Garland.

Universal Algebra, Algebraic Logic, & Databases. B. I. Plotkin. LC 93-44246. 438p. 1994. lib. bdg. 225.50 (*0-7923-2665-2*) Kluwer Ac.

Universal Algebra & Lattice Theory. Ed. by S. D. Comer. (Lecture Notes in Mathematics Ser.: Vol. 1149). vi, 282p. 1985. pap. 38.40 (*0-387-15691-7*) Spr-Verlag.

Universal Algebra & Lattice Theory. Ed. by R. S. Freese & O. C. Garcia. (Lecture Notes in Mathematics Ser.: Vol. 1004). 308p. 1983. 42.95 (*0-387-12329-6*) Spr-Verlag.

Universal Algebra for Computer Scientists. W. Wechler. Ed. by W. Brauer et al. (EATCS Monographs on Theoretical Computer Science: Vol. 25). 352p. 1992. 61.00 (*0-387-54280-9*) Spr-Verlag.

Universal Almanac: 1997 Edition. Ed. by John Wright. (Illus.). 768p. (Orig.). 1996. 22.95 (*0-8362-2236-9*); pap. 12.95 (*0-8362-2187-7*) Andrews & McMeel.

Universal & Applied Algebra: Proceedings of the 5th International Algebra Symposium. Ed. by K. Halkowska & B. Stawski. 416p. (C). 1989. text ed. 117.00 (*9971-5-0837-0*) World Scientific Pub.

Universal Appeal: Aspects of the Revival of Monasticism in the West in 19th & Early 20th Centuries. Rene Kollar. (Catholic Scholars Press Ser.). (Illus.). 312p. (Orig.). 1996. text ed. 64.95 (*1-57309-003-4*, Cath Scholar Pr); pap. text ed. 44.95 (*1-57309-002-6*, Cath Scholar Pr) Intl Scholars.

Universal Appeal: The Bottom Line Benefit of Diversity. GEBS by Dorsey. 208p. 1994. boxed, per. 21.95 (*0-8403-9688-0*) Kendall-Hunt.

Universal Assembly Language. Robert M. Fitz & Larry Crockett. (Illus.). 260p. 1986. 27.95 (*0-8306-1730-2*) McGraw-Hill Prof.

Universal Atlas of Cape Cod & Southeastern Massachusetts with Part of Rhode Island. 2nd ed. Alfred Glassman. Ed. by Michail Glassman. (Illus.). 136p. 1991. pap. 12.95 (*0-932427-16-2*) Univ Pub MA.

Universal Atlas of Metropolitan Boston & Eastern Massachusetts. 28th ed. Alfred Glassman. Ed. by Michail Glassman. (Illus.). 212p. (Orig.). 1995. spiral bd. 18.95 (*0-932427-22-7*) Univ Pub MA.

Universal Atlas of Southern New Hampshire. 5th ed. Alfred Glassman. Ed. by Michail Glassman. (Illus.). 120p. 1994. pap. 12.95 (*0-932427-20-0*) Univ Pub MA.

Universal Atlas of Western Massachusetts. Alfred Glassman. Ed. by Michail Glassman. (Illus.). 120p. 1992. pap. 10.95 (*0-932427-18-9*) Univ Pub MA.

Universal Bach. Michael Korn et al. LC 86-71071. (Special Publications: No. 43). 1986. pap. 8.00 (*0-87169-436-0*, A043-BAC) Am Philos.

***Universal Banking: International Comparisons & Theoretical Perspectives.** Jordi Canals. (Illus.). 384p. 1997. 85.00 (*0-19-877506-7*); pap. 24.95 (*0-19-877505-9*) OUP.

Universal Banking in the Twentieth Century. Ed. by Alice Teichova et al. 328p. 1994. 95.00 (*1-85278-977-8*) E Elgar.

Universal Banking in the United States: What Could We Gain? What Could We Lose? Anthony Saunders & Ingo Walter. LC 92-41473. 288p. 1994. 45.00 (*0-19-508069-6*) OUP.

Universal Baseball Association Inc., J. Henry Waugh, Prop. Robert Coover. 1971. pap. 11.95 (*0-452-26030-2*, Plume) NAL-Dutton.

Universal Baseball Association, Incorporated. Robert Coover. 1983. mass mkt. 6.95 (*0-452-25553-8*, Plume) NAL-Dutton.

***Universal Bath Planning.** Mary J. Peterson. (Illus.). 285p. (Orig.). 1996. pap. text ed. 50.00 (*1-887127-01-1*, 5253) Natl Kit Bath.

Universal Bead. Joan M. Erikson. (Illus.). 192p. 1993. pap. 17.95 (*0-393-31005-1*) Norton.

Universal Bible Dictionary: Dictionnaire Biblique Universel. Louis Monloubou. 772p. (FRE.). 1985. 150.00 (*0-8288-1203-9*, F10644) Fr & Eur.

Universal Cards - Angelically Inspired. 3rd expanded rev. ed. Nora Monaco & Juliet Hubbs. (Illus.). 128p. 1997. 28.50 (*0-9631714-1-0*) AngelStar.

***Universal Catechism: A Homily Sourcebook.** N. Abeyasingha. 65p. 1993. pap. write for info. (*1-56929-010-5*) Pastoral Pr.

Universal Childbirth Picture Book. Fran P. Hosken. (Illus.). 76p. (Orig.). (C). 1981. pap. text ed. 7.00 (*0-942096-01-0*) WINNEWS.

Universal Childbirth Picture Book. Fran P. Hosken. Tr. by Hawa Mohamed from ENG. (Illus.). 84p. (Orig.). (SOM.). 1993. 7.00 (*0-942096-07-X*) WINNEWS.

Universal City & North Hollywood. Tom Link. 1991. 27.95 (*0-89781-393-6*) Am Historical Pr.

***Universal Compassion: Transforming Your Life Through Love & Compassion.** 3rd ed. Geshe K. Gyatso. 176p. 1997. 19.95 (*0-948006-57-9*, Pub. by Tharpa Pubns UK) ACCESS Pubs Network.

***Universal Compassion: Transforming Your Life Through Love & Compassion.** 3rd ed. Geshe K. Gyatso. 176p. 1997. pap. 14.95 (*0-948006-58-7*, Pub. by Tharpa Pubns UK) ACCESS Pubs Network.

Universal Compression & Retrieval. Rafael Krichevsky. LC 93-45682. (Mathematics & Its Applications Ser.). 228p. (C). 1994. lib. bdg. 109.50 (*0-7923-2672-5*) Kluwer Ac.

Universal Computer Interfaces. R. F. Dheere. (European Patent Office Ser.: No. 11). (Illus.). 394p. 1988. 215.00 (*0-08-036610-4*, Pergamon Pr) Elsevier.

Universal Databank. 1992. pap. 5.95 (*0-426-20370-4*, Dr Who) Carol Pub Group.

Universal Decimal Classification: Theory & Practice. 2nd enl. rev. ed. H. Bose. 200p. 1990. text ed. 30.00 (*81-207-1255-2*, Pub. by Sterling Pubs II) Apt Bks.

Universal Declaration of Human Rights: A Commentary. Asbjorn Eide et al. (Scandinavian University Press Publication). 474p. (C). 1992. 49.50 (*82-00-21339-0*, 14456) Scandnvan Univ Pr.

Universal Declaration of Human Rights: An Adaptation for Children. 46p. (J). 1990. 9.95 (*92-1-100424-1*, 89.I.19); pap. 9.95 (*0-685-47757-6*, 90.I.20) UN.

Universal Declaration of Human Rights: An Adaptation for Children. 46p. 1989. pap. text ed. 9.95 (*92-1-100423-3*) UN.

Universal Design: Creative Solutions for ADA Compliance. Ed. by Roberta L. Null & Kenneth F. Cherry. LC 95-23842. (Illus.). 352p. 1996. 54.95 (*0-912045-86-8*) Prof Pubns CA.

Universal Dictionary of History: Dictionnaire d'Histoire Universelle. Michel Mourre. (FRE.). 1981. 125.00 (*0-8288-1489-9*, F700) Fr & Eur.

Universal Dictionary of Literature: Diccionario de Literatura Universal. Jesus Bustos Tovar. 657p. (SPA.). 1985. 49.50 (*0-8288-1576-3*, S60726) Fr & Eur.

***Universal Dictionary of Science & Technology: English/Dutch.** G. Schuurmans-Stekhoven. 968p. (DUT & ENG.). 1993. 250.00 (*0-7859-9304-5*) Fr & Eur.

Universal Didactic Encyclopedia: Enciclopedia Didactica Universa, 4 vols. Vox Staff. (SPA.). 1980. 175.00 (*0-8288-4695-2*, S35422) Fr & Eur.

***Universal Difference.** Nash. Date not set. text ed. 65.00 (*0-312-21004-3*) St Martin.

***Universal Dominion of Christ: A Study in Psalm 2.** H. Rondel Rumburg. 159p. (YA). 1996. 16.95 (*0-9639730-2-9*) Soc Bibl & So Stud.

***Universal Donor.** Craig Nova. 1997. 23.00 (*0-395-70938-5*) HM.

Universal Dream Book. Foulsham Editors. 144p. 1995. pap. 4.95 (*0-572-00179-7*, Pub. by Foulsham UK) Assoc Pubs Grp.

Universal Drug Infusion Ruler. Sota Omoigui. (Illus.). 4p. 1995. spiral bd. 29.00 (*0-9650767-0-9*) St-of-the-Art Tech.

Universal Education in the South, 2 Vols. Charles W. Dabney. LC 70-89170. (American Education: Its Men, Institutions, & Ideas. Series 1). 1970. reprint ed. Set. 60.95 (*0-405-01408-2*) Ayer.

Universal Elixir & Other Computing Projects Which Failed. Robert L. Glass. 1977. 10.00 (*0-942337-00-X*) Computing Trends.

Universal English-Gujarati Dictionary. Tr. by P. G. Deshpande. 968p. (ENG & GUJ.). 1989. 35.00 (*0-19-561828-9*) OUP.

Universal Etymological English Dictionary. Nathan Bailey. (Anglistica & Americana Ser.: No. 52). 982p. 1969. reprint ed. 240.00 (*0-317-05068-0*, 05102625) G Olms Pubs.

Universal Experience of Adolescence. Norman Kiell. LC 63-22359. 942p. 1964. 72.50 (*0-8236-6720-0*) Intl Univs Pr.

Universal Exposition of Nineteen Hundred: Two Catalogues. Ed. by Peter C. Bunnell & Robert A. Sobieszek. LC 76-23041. (Sources of Modern Photography Ser.). (Illus.). 1979. lib. bdg. 20.95 (*0-405-09603-8*) Ayer.

Universal Faith? Peoples, Cultures, Religions, & the Christ. Ed. by Catherine Cornille & Valeer Neckebrouck. (Louvain Theological & Pastoral Monographs). 198p. (Orig.). 1993. pap. 25.00 (*0-8028-0569-8*) Eerdmans.

Universal Fascism: The Theory & Practice of the Fascist International, 1928-1936. Michael A. Ledeen. LC 70-185794. xxi, 200p. 1996. reprint ed. lib. bdg. 35.00 (*0-86527-202-6*) Fertig.

Universal Film Lexicon. Frank Arnau. 1972. 69.95 (*0-8490-1246-5*) Gordon Pr.

Universal Flame. Ed. by L. H. Leslie-Smith. 263p. 1975. 9.95 (*0-8356-7506-8*) Theos Pub Hse.

Universal Fly Tying Guide. 2nd rev. ed. Dick Stewart. 156p. pap. 12.95 (*0-936644-20-6*) Mtn Pond Pub.

Universal Frame: Historical Essays in Astronomy. J. D. North. 400p. 1989. text ed. 60.00 (*0-907628-95-8*) Hambledon Press.

Universal Genius Letter, Vol. I. Musical Lynn. (Illus.). 22p. (Orig.). (C). 1992. pap. 12.95 (*1-880718-04-9*) Genius New.

Universal Gita. Eric J. Sharpe. LC 85-5062. 188p. 1985. 38.95 (*0-8126-9001-X*); pap. 17.95 (*0-8126-9129-6*) Open Court.

Universal Gnosis. Catharose De Petri & Jan Van Rijckenborgh. (Orig.). 1986. pap. 14.00 (*90-70196-57-3*) Rosycross Pr.

Universal God: Justice, Love, & Peace in the Global Village. James E. Will. LC 94-523. 304p. (Orig.). 1994. pap. 25.00 (*0-664-25560-4*) Westminster John Knox.

Universal Grammar. Martin. 1991. pap. text ed. 46.50 (*0-7923-1420-4*) Kluwer Ac.

Universal Grammar: Fifteen Essays. Edward L. Keenan. 448p. 1987. 85.00 (*0-7099-3109-3*, Pub. by Croom Helm UK) Routledge Chapman & Hall.

Universal Grammar & American Sign Language: Setting the Null Argument Parameters. Diane C. Lillo-Martin. (Studies in Theoretical Psycholinguistics). 264p. (C). 1991. lib. bdg. 113.50 (*0-7923-1419-0*) Kluwer Ac.

Universal Grammar & Language Learnability. Anjum P. Saleemi. (Studies in Linguistics: No. 61). 180p. (C). 1992. 49.95 (*0-521-40075-9*) Cambridge U Pr.

Universal Grammar & Narrative Form. David Herman. LC 95-6223. (Roman Jakobson Series in Linguistics & Poetics). 320p. 1995. text ed. 49.95 (*0-8223-1656-0*); pap. text ed. 19.95 (*0-8223-1668-4*) Duke.

Universal Grammar & Second Language Acquisition. Lydia White. LC 89-48055. (Language Acquisition & Language Disorders (LALD) Ser.: Vol. 1). xii, 194p. 1989. 56.00 (*1-55619-092-1*); pap. 19.95 (*1-55619-093-X*) Benjamins North Am.

Universal Grammar in Child Second Language Acquisition: Null Subjects & Morphological Uniformity. Usha Lakshmanan. LC 94-26067. (Language Acquisition & Language Disorders (LALD) Ser.: 10). x, 162p. 1994. 35.00 (*1-55619-247-9*) Benjamins North Am.

***Universal Grammar of English.** Quirk. Date not set. pap. text ed. write for info. (*0-582-55207-9*, Pub. by Longman UK) Longman.

Universal Guide to High Pressure & Steam Cleaner Repair. 332p. 1994. pap. text ed. write for info. (*0-9646327-0-5*) Journey Ga.

Universal Guide to Success in Any Endeavor. Don Page. (Illus.). 106p. (Orig.). 1986. pap. text ed. 12.00 (*0-937514-49-7*) Prime Pubs.

Universal Health Insurance Coverage Using Medicare's Payment Rates. (Illus.). 61p. (Orig.). (C). 1992. pap. text ed. 20.00 (*1-56806-125-0*) DIANE Pub.

Universal Healthcare Almanac: Quarterly Updates. Linda L. Cherner. 480p. 1989. ring bd. 180.00 (*0-9645024-0-2*) Silver Cherner.

Universal History - 1949, Vol. 2. Eugen Rosenstock-Huessy. (Eugen Rosenstock-Huessy Lectures). 141p. pap. 60.00 incl. audio (*0-614-05349-8*); pap. 35.00 (*0-912148-21-7*); audio 35.00 (*0-614-05348-X*) Argo Bks.

Universal History - 1951, Vol. 3. Eugen Rosenstock-Huessy. (Eugen Rosenstock-Huessy Lectures). 22p. pap. 10.00 incl. audio (*0-614-05351-X*); pap. 7.50 (*0-912148-22-5*); audio 5.00 (*0-614-05350-1*) Argo Bks.

Universal History - 1954, Vol. 12. Eugen Rosenstock-Huessy. (Eugen Rosenstock-Huessy Lectures). 540p. pap. 200.00 incl. audio (*0-614-05370-6*); pap. 125.00 (*0-912148-31-4*); audio 130.00 (*0-614-05369-2*) Argo Bks.

Universal History - 1955, Vol. 14. Eugen Rosenstock-Huessy. (Eugen Rosenstock-Huessy Lectures). 91p. pap. 35.00 incl. audio (*0-614-05374-9*); pap. 20.00 (*0-912148-33-0*); audio 20.00 (*0-614-05373-0*) Argo Bks.

Universal History - 1956, Vol. 17. Eugen Rosenstock-Huessy. (Eugen Rosenstock-Huessy Lectures). 218p. pap. 80.00 incl. audio (*0-614-05380-3*); pap. 45.00 (*0-912148-36-5*); audio 55.00 (*0-614-05379-X*) Argo Bks.

Universal History - 1957, Vol. 18. Eugen Rosenstock-Huessy. (Eugen Rosenstock-Huessy Lectures). 595p. pap. 220.00 incl. audio (*0-614-05382-X*); pap. 130.00 (*0-912148-37-3*); audio 145.00 (*0-614-05381-1*) Argo Bks.

Universal History - 1967, Vol. 32. Eugen Rosenstock-Huessy. (Eugen Rosenstock-Huessy Lectures). 396p. pap. 155.00 incl. audio (*0-614-05410-9*); pap. 90.00 (*0-912148-51-9*); audio 100.00 (*0-614-05409-5*) Argo Bks.

Universal History of Linguistics: India, China, Arabia, Europe. Esa Itkonen. LC 91-30574. (Studies in the History of the Language Sciences: No. 65). ix, 368p. 1991. 74.00 (*1-55619-360-2*) Benjamins North Am.

Universal History of Music: Compiled from Diverse Sources Together with Various Original Notes on Hindu Music. Sourindro M. Tagore. (C). 1990. reprint ed. 12.50 (*81-85418-54-3*, Pub. by Low Price II) S Asia.

Universal Horrors: The Studio's Classic Films, 1931-1946. Michael Brunas et al. LC 89-42706. (Illus.). 624p. 1990. lib. bdg. 55.00 (*0-89950-369-1*) McFarland & Co.

Universal Human: The Evolution of Individuality. Rudolf Steiner. Tr. by Gilbert Church et al. from GER. 96p. 1990. 16.95 (*0-88010-350-7*) Anthroposophic.

Universal Human Rights in Theory & Practice. Jack Donnelly. LC 89-7057. 304p. 1989. pap. 14.95 (*0-8014-9570-9*) Cornell U Pr.

Universal Humanism: Selected Social Writings of P. R. Sarkar. Prabhat Rainjan Sarkar. Ed. by Tim Anderson & Gary Coyle. 108p. (Orig.). (C). 1983. pap. 4.95 (*0-9591792-0-8*) Proutist Universal.

Universal Ice: Science & Ideology in the Nazi State. Robert Bowen. LC 92-43689. 195p. 1993. text ed. 59.00 (*1-85293-190-6*) St Martin.

Universal Indian Sign Language of the Plains Indians of North America see Indian Sign Language

***Universal Interviewing & Communications: A Preemployment Application.** 2nd ed. Donald W. Slowik. LC 97-60044. (Unicom Series in Human Resource Development). 484p. 1997. boxed 45.00 (*1-883342-04-X*) Evergrn Pr CO.

Universal Jesus. Meg Chignell. (C). 1989. pap. 24.00 (*1-85072-067-3*, Pub. by W Sessions UK) St Mut.

Universal Joint & Driveshaft Design Manual. LC 79-63005. 440p. 1991. Forty-one papers. pap. 89.00 (*0-89883-007-9*, AE7) Soc Auto Engineers.

Universal Joints & Driveshafts: Analysis, Design, Applications. F. Schmelz et al. (Illus.). 272p. 1992. 126.95 (*0-387-53314-1*) Spr-Verlag.

Universal Journalist. David Randall. LC 96-8113. 216p. 1996. write for info. (*0-7453-1108-3*, Pub. by Pluto Pr UK) LPC InBook.

Universal Journalist. David Randall. 216p. 1996. pap. text ed. 17.95 (*0-7453-1109-1*, Pub. by Pluto Pr UK) LPC InBook.

Universal Key (to Self-Mastership) Darwin Gross. 190p. (Orig.). (C). 1988. pap. 19.95 (*0-931689-07-4*) D Gross.

Universal Kinship: The Bond Between All Living Things. Latham Foundation Staff. LC 91-50981. (Illus.). 200p. 1992. text ed. 22.95 (*0-88247-918-0*, 918); pap. text ed. 11.95 (*0-88247-917-2*, 917) R & E Pubs.

***Universal Kitchen.** Elizabeth Rozin. 1997. pap. 13.95 (*0-14-025782-9*) Viking Penguin.

Universal Kitchen: A 250-Recipe Tour of World Cooking. Elizabeth Rozin. 384p. 1996. pap. 27.95 (*0-670-85404-2*) Viking Penguin.

Universal Kitchen Planning: Design That Adapts to People. Mary J. Peterson. (Illus.). 220p. (Orig.). (C). 1995. pap. text ed. 50.00 (*1-887127-00-3*) Natl Kit Bath.

Universal Language. David B. Axelrod. 30p. (Orig.). (C). 1993. pap. text ed. 5.00 (*1-878173-30-8*) Birnham Wood.

Universal Language. David B. Axelrod. (Orig.). 1993. pap. 6.00 (*0-614-14277-6*) Writers Ink Pr.

Universal Language of Cabalah: The Master Key to the God Consciousness. William Eisen. LC 87-51656. (Illus.). 368p. (Orig.). 1989. pap. 24.95 (*0-87516-613-X*) DeVorss.

Universal Language of Mind: The Book of Matthew Interpreted. Daniel R. Condron. 310p. 1994. pap. 13.00 (*0-944386-15-6*) SOM Pub.

Universal Law. (Illus.). 147p. 1990. reprint ed. pap. 9.95 (*1-55705-074-0*) Adamis Intl.

Universal Law of Cosmic Cycles. Robert A. Ferguson. 1980. 4.95 (*0-13-938738-2*, Parker Publishing Co) P-H.

Universal Laws Never Before Revealed: Keely's Secrets: Understanding & Using the Science of Sympathetic Vibration. rev. ed. Dale Pond et al. LC 94-77879. (Illus.). 288p. 1995. pap. 19.95 (*1-57282-003-9*) Message NM.

Universal Laws of Success. Brian S. Tracy. 140p. (Orig.). pap. text ed. 5.95 (*1-880461-37-4*) Celebrat Excell.

Universal Layman. Pat Keith & Shelly Arney. (Illus.). 62p. (Orig.). 1991. pap. 6.95 (*0-9629553-0-2*) P Keith-M Arney.

Universal Layout Sheet. Raymond Dorn. (Illus.). 14p. 1983. pap. text ed. 20.00 (*0-931368-13-8*) Ragan Comm.

Universal Life Insurance Ripoff: Money Down the Drain. Ray Combs. LC 95-68227. 72p. (Orig.). 1995. pap. 9.95 (*1-884570-26-7*) Research Triangle.

Universal Limited Art Editions: A History & Catalogue. The First Twenty-Five Years. Esther Sparks. (Illus.). 552p. 1989. 95.00 (*0-8109-1732-7*) Abrams.

Universal Love. Sheng Liang. 200p. (Orig.). (CHI.). 1995. pap. 20.00 (*0-9642790-3-7*) Sayinga.

Universal Love: Neo-Mohism. 2nd ed. Sheng Liang. 300p. (CHI.). 1996. pap. 20.00 (*0-9642790-4-5*) Sayinga.

***Universal Love: Neo-Mohism.** 3rd ed. Sheng Liang. Ed. by Sam Heye. 300p. (CHI.). 1996. pap. 20.00 (*0-9642790-5-3*) Sayinga.

***Universal Love: Neo-Mohism.** 4th ed. Sheng Liang. Ed. by Sam Heye. LC 97-72839. 300p. (CHI.). 1997. reprint ed. pap. 20.00 (*0-9642790-6-1*) Sayinga.

***Universal Machine: A Multimedia Approach to Computing.** Glenn Blank & Robert Barnes. LC 97-22132. 1997. write for info. (*0-256-21140-X*) Irwin Prof Pubng.

***Universal Man.** Abd A. Al-Jili. Tr. by Titus Burckhardt & Angela Culme-Seymour from ARA. (Illus.). 104p. 1983. reprint ed. pap. 12.50 (*0-904975-15-0*, Pub. by Beshara UK) Beshara Fndtn.

Universal Man. Florence DeGroat. LC 80-69413. 117p. 1981. reprint ed. pap. 6.50 (*0-87516-428-5*) DeVorss.

Universal Man: Tagore's Vision of the Religion of Humanity. Santi N. Chattopadhyay. (C). 1987. 27.50 (*81-85169-16-0*, Pub. by Naya Prokash IA) S Asia.

Universal Man: Theodore von Karman's Life in Aeronautics. Michael H. Gorn. LC 91-5099. (History of Aviation Ser.). (Illus.). 215p. 1992. 27.50 (*1-56098-165-2*) Smithsonian.

Universal Meaning of the Kabbalah. Leo Schaya. 1972. 6.95 (*0-8216-0167-9*, Univ Bks) Carol Pub Group.

Universal Medical Device Nomenclature System. ECRI Staff. Tr. & Intro. by Guy Knickerbocker. (Illus.). 187p. (ENG & RUS.). 1991. pap. text ed. 25.00 (*0-941417-24-7*) ECRI.

Universal Medical Device Nomenclature System. ECRI Staff. 300p. (ENG & SPA.). 1994. pap. 95.00 (*0-941417-30-1*) ECRI.

Universal Meditation. Aliyoshi Kawahata. Tr. by Diane T. Ooka. 116p. (Orig.). pap. 7.95 (*0-89346-243-8*) Heian Intl.

Universal Method for Saxophone. Paul DeVille. 320p. 1907. pap. 22.95 (*0-8258-0146-X*, 0532) Fischer Inc NY.

Universal Multiplication of Intelligence. Glenn Doman & J. Michael Armentrout. LC 80-66236. (Gentle Revolution Ser.). 223p. 1980. 12.50 (*0-936676-02-7*) Better Baby.

Universal Myths: Heroes, Gods, Tricksters & Others. Alexander Eliot. 252p. 1990. pap. 12.95 (*0-452-01027-6*, Mer) NAL-Dutton.

Universal Natural History & Theory of the Heaven. Immanuel Kant. Tr. by W. Hastie & Milton K. Munitz. LC 70-629269. (Ann Arbor Paperbacks Ser.: No. 158). 206p. reprint ed. pap. 58.80 (*0-317-09540-4*, 2055666) Bks Demand.

***Universal Newborn Hearing Screening: A Practical Guide.** Lynn Spivak. LC 97-22870. (Illus.). 256p. 1997. 49.00 (*0-86577-699-7*) Thieme Med Pubs.

Universal One. Walter Russell. (Illus.). 266p. 1974. reprint ed. text ed. 200.00 (*1-879605-08-2*) U Sci & Philos.

Universal Path. rev. ed. Jan Van Rijckenborgh & Catharose De Petri. (Cornerstone Ser.: No. 2). 99p. 1986. reprint ed. pap. 11.00 (*90-6732-007-2*) Rosycross Pr.

Universal Path of Natural Life. Hua C. Ni. LC 95-36374. (Course for Total Health Ser.). 1996. pap. 9.50 (*0-937064-76-9*) SevenStar Comm.

Universal Path to Enlightenment: The Eastern Answers to the Mysteries of Life. Stephen Knapp. (Illus.). 373p. 1992. pap. 14.95 (*0-9617410-2-3*) World Relief.

Universal Pattern of Consciousness. Louis F. Wilson. LC 92-81895. (Illus.). 1994. 24.95 (*0-8158-0486-5*) Chris Mass.

Universal Patterns. rev. ed. Rochelle Newman & Martha Boles. LC 85-60105. (Illus.). 266p. 1990. pap. text ed. 32.95 (*0-9614504-3-6*) Pythagorean Pr.

Universal Penman. George Bickham. (Illus.). 1941. pap. 15.95 (*0-486-20616-5*) Dover.

Universal Pictures in the Twenties & Thirties, 2 vols. Ed. by R. Gordon. 1976. lib. bdg. 200.00 (*0-8490-2787-X*) Gordon Pr.

Universal Pictures of Nineteen Thirty-Two to Nineteen Thirty-Three. Ed. by R. F. Gordon. 1976. lib. bdg. 78.00 (*0-8490-2788-8*) Gordon Pr.

Universal Playground: A Planning Guide. 45p. (Orig.). (C). 1996. pap. text ed. 30.00 (*0-7881-2692-X*) DIANE Pub.

Universal Prayers. Tr. by Swami Yatiswarananda from SAN. 261p. 1950. Bilingual ed. pap. 3.00 (*0-87481-443-X*, Pub. by Ramakrishna Math II) Vedanta Pr.

Universal Pressure Supercritical Boiler Fundamentals: Babcock & Wilcox Design, 4 vols. (Illus.). 1979. Set. ring bd. 250.00 (*0-87683-214-1*) GP Courseware.

Universal Pressure Supercritical Boiler Fundamentals: Combustion Engineering Design, 4 vols. (Illus.). 1979. ring bd. 250.00 (*0-87683-219-2*) GP Courseware.

Universal Primacy of Christ. Francesco S. Pancheri. Tr. by Juniper B. Carol from ITA. Orig. Title: Il Primato universale de Christo. 144p. (Orig.). (C). 1984. pap. 6.95 (*0-931888-16-6*) Christendom Pr.

Universal Product Code. Lawrence E. Hicks. LC 75-34999. (AMA Management Briefing Ser.). (Illus.). 48p. reprint ed. pap. 25.00 (*0-317-09590-0*, 2051518) Bks Demand.

Universal Pronouncing Dictionary of Biography & Mythology, 2 vols. Joseph Thomas. 1976. reprint ed. Set. 210.00 (*1-55888-239-1*) Omnigraphics Inc.

Universal Prototype: An Islamic Perspective. Murtaza Mutahhari. Tr. by Laleh Bakhtiar from PER. 112p. (Orig.). (C). 1989. pap. 10.00 (*1-871031-04-4*) Abjad Bk.

Universal Reality: Physics-Religion-Psychology. Harold S. Cober. (Illus.). 96p. (Orig.). (C). 1994. pap. 5.99 (*1-877633-23-2*) Luthers.

Universal Realization: A Unified Theory. Paul H. Weber. LC 94-90473. (Illus.). 210p. (C). 1994. pap. text ed. 15.00 (*0-9643517-0-6*) P H W Ent.

Universal Reflections. Ray Reardon. 90p. 1993. pap. 120.00 (*0-949823-33-3*, Pub. by Deakin Univ AT) St Mut.

Universal Register of the Baptist Denomination in North America for the Years 1790, 1791, 1792, 1793, & Part of 1794. John Asplund. Ed. by Edwin S. Gaustad. LC 79-52581. (Baptist Tradition Ser.). 1980. reprint ed. lib. bdg. 17.95 (*0-405-12448-1*) Ayer.

Universal Religion: The Final Destiny of Mankind. Christopher A. Anderson. LC 93-74928. (Illus.). 135p. (Orig.). 1994. pap. 12.00 (*0-931353-38-6*) Andersons Pubns.

Universal Remedy. Jan Van Rijckenborgh. 47p. (Orig.). 1986. pap. 8.00 (*90-70196-58-1*) Rosycross Pr.

Universal Reproductive & Human Rights: Ordering Corrective Action Against North American Circumcisers. Anastasios Zavales. 52p. (Orig.). (C). 1995. pap. text ed. 28.95 (*1-884090-09-5*) Ecumenics Intl.

Universal Salvation Agency. Tim Adams. Ed. by Alice Hardy. LC 78-74426. 9.00 (*0-686-24153-3*); pap. 1.50 (*0-686-24154-1*) Central FL Voters.

Universal Scenarios of Transitions to Chaos Via Homoclinic Bifurations, Vol. 8. D. V. Lyubimov et al. (SSR: SEC Mathematical Physics Review Ser.: Vol. 8, Pt. 4). ii, 78p. 1989. pap. text ed. 70.00 (*3-7186-4867-9*) Gordon & Breach.

Universal School of Street Fighting. Frank DeGourville. (Illus.). 1984. pap. 7.95 (*0-931981-03-4*) Am Martial Arts Pub.

Universal Schoolhouse: Spiritual Awakening Through Education. James Moffett. LC 93-40694. (Education-Higher Education Ser.). 391p. 1994. pap. 29.00 (*1-55542-607-7*) Jossey-Bass.

Universal Secrets. 2nd ed. Michael J. Kurban. (Illus.). 115p. 1991. pap. 12.00 (*0-938863-02-9*) Libra Press Chi.

Universal Self: A Study of Paul Valery. Agnes E. Mackay. 263p. 1982. 45.00 (*0-85335-235-6*, Pub. by Stuart Titles Ltd UK) St Mut.

Universal Self: A Study of Paul Valery. Agnes E. Mackey. LC 61-65142. 279p. reprint ed. pap. 79.60 (*0-685-15380-0*, 2026530) Bks Demand.

Universal Serial Business System Architecture. Mindshare Inc. Staff. LC 96-52321. (C). 1997. pap. text ed. 29.95 (*0-201-46137-4*) Addison-Wesley.

Universal Service: Competition, Interconnection & Monopoly in the Making of the American Telephone System. Milton Mueller. LC 96-35151. (AEI Studies in Telecommunications Deregulation). (Illus.). 170p. 1996. 40.00 (*0-262-13327-X*) MIT Pr.

Universal Service & Rate Restructuring in Telecommunications. OECD Staff. (Information Computer Communications Policy Ser.: No. 23). 193p. (Orig.). 1991. pap. 52.00 (*92-64-13497-2*) OECD.

Universal Service Obligations in a Competitive Telecommunications Environment. (Information Computer Communications Policy Ser.: No. 38). 152p. (Orig.). (ENG & FRE.). 1995. pap. 42.00 (*92-64-14664-4*, Pub. by Org for Econ FR) OECD.

***Universal Sherlock Holmes, 5 vols.** Ronald B. De Waal. (Illus.). 1440p. 1994. spiral bd., pap. 150.00 (*1-896032-00-1*) Battered Silicon.

***Universal Sherlock Holmes, the Index, Vol. 5.** George A. Vanderburgh. (Illus.). 382p. 1995. pap. 30.00 (*1-896032-22-2*) Battered Silicon.

Universal Showstoppers. Ed. by Carol Cuellar. (Showstoppers Ser.). 276p. (Orig.). (YA). 1994. pap. text ed. 18.95 (*0-89898-832-2*, F3409SMX) Warner Brothers.

Universal Sikhism. A. S. Sethi. 1972. 5.95 (*0-88253-767-9*) Ind-US Inc.

Universal Soil Loss Equation: Past, Present & Future. Ed. by A. E. Peterson & J. B. Swan. 53p. 1979. pap. 3.75 (*0-89118-766-9*) Soil Sci Soc Am.

Universal Spanish--Cambios: Descubriendo lo Mejor Que Hay en Ti. Bill Cosby et al. Ed. by Juan Callejas et al. Tr. by Pierre Trevant from ENG. (Destrezas para la Adolescencia Ser.). (Illus.). 181p. (Orig.). (SPA.). (YA). (gr. 6-8). 1988. pap. text ed. 6.85 (*0-933419-44-9*) Quest Intl.

Universal Spanish--Los anos Sorprendentes: Como Comprender los Cambios en Su Adolescente. Cliff Schimmels & Hank Resnik. Ed. by Juan Callejas et al. Tr. by Judith Ferdinandi from ENG. (Destrezas para la Adolescencia Ser.). (Illus.). 128p. (Orig.). (SPA.). 1988. pap. text ed. 6.85 (*0-933419-45-7*) Quest Intl.

Universal Speaking Pictures. Art Freifeld. (Illus.). 60p. (Orig.). 1982. pap. text ed. 8.95 (*0-916177-00-9*) Am Eng Pubns.

Universal Speaking Pictures, No. 2. Natalie Gast. (Illus.). 36p. (Orig.). 1984. student ed. 7.95 (*0-916177-01-7*); pap. 1.45 (*0-685-50631-2*) Am Eng Pubns.

Universal Stamping Machine Co. Bart Billings. (Illus.). 250p. 1994. pap. 20.00 (*1-880065-10-X*) Machine Cancel Soc.

Universal Stamping Machine Co. Machines & Postal Markings, Catalog Revision No. 1. Bart Billings. (Illus.). 120p. (Orig.). 1990. pap. text ed. 7.00 (*0-9621481-2-1*) Machine Cancel Soc.

Universal Stamping Machine Company: Machines & Postal Markings, 1909-1920. Bart Billings. Ed. by Reg Morris & Robert J. Payne. (Illus.). 121p. (Orig.). (C). 1988. pap. text ed. 7.00 (*0-9621481-0-5*) Machine Cancel Soc.

Universal Standard Benefits Set, Enrollee Cost Sharing & Affordability Report. (Illus.). 99p. (Orig.). (C). 1995. pap. text ed. 30.00 (*0-7881-2365-3*) DIANE Pub.

Universal Style: Dress for Who You Are & What You Want. Alyce Parsons & Diane Parente. (Illus.). (Orig.). 1991. pap. 19.95 (*0-9627405-0-0*) A Parsons.

Universal Style for Men: Dress for Who You Are & What You Want. Alyce Parsons et al. (Illus.). (Orig.). 1992. pap. 12.95 (*0-9627405-1-9*) A Parsons.

Universal Subgoaling & Chunking: The Automatic Generation & Learning of Goal Hierarchies. John Laird et al. 1986. lib. bdg. 84.00 (*0-89838-213-0*) Kluwer Ac.

***Universal Sufism.** Witteveen. LC 97-2609. 1997. pap. 15.95 (*1-86204-093-1*) Element MA.

Universal Tarot Package. Maxwell Miller. (Illus.). 144p. (Orig.). 1996. pap. 25.00 (*0-87728-840-2*) Weiser.

Universal Teaching Strategies. 2nd ed. H. Jerome Freiberg & Amy Driscoll. LC 95-11982. 1995. pap. text ed. 52.00 (*0-205-16722-5*) Allyn.

***Universal Teachings of Life: From Christina a Highly Evolved Spiritual Being.** LC 96-61346. (Orig.). 1996. pap. 19.95 (*0-9654080-1-9*) Tall Tree Pubng.

Universal Theory of Automata. H. Ehrig. (Illus.). 1976. pap. 27.75 (*3-519-02054-8*) Adlers Foreign Bks.

Universal Theosophy. Robert Crosbie. 171p. 1963. pap. 5.00 (*0-938998-31-5*) Theosophy.

Universal Trail Assessment Coordinator Training Workshop: Training Manual. rev. ed. Mindy Pasternak et al. (Illus.). 62p. (Orig.). 1996. pap. text ed. 30.00 (*1-882632-06-0*) PAX Pr.

Universal Traveler: A Soft-Systems Guide to Creativity, Problem-Solving & the Process of Reaching Goals. 7th ed. Don Koberg & Jim Bagnall. LC 91-18321. 150p. 1991. pap. 13.95 (*1-56052-045-0*) Crisp Pubns.

Universal Traveller. Charles A. Goodrich. (Notable American Authors Ser.). 1992. reprint ed. lib. bdg. 75.00 (*0-7812-2934-0*) Rprt Serv.

Universal Treatise of Nicholas of Autrecourt. Leonard Kennedy. LC 70-155364. (Medieval Philosophical Texts in Translation Ser.). 172p. 1971. pap. 15.00 (*0-87462-220-4*) Marquette.

Universal Turing Machine: A Half-Century Survey. 2nd ed. Ed. by R. Herken. 661p. 1995. 98.00 (*3-211-82628-9*) Spr-Verlag.

Universal Turing Machine: A Half-Century Survey. 2nd ed. Ed. by R. Herken. 661p. 1995. 49.00 (*3-211-82637-8*) Spr-Verlag.

Universal Typing. 3rd ed. Edith Mackay. 192p. 1988. 32.50 (*0-273-02706-9*, Pub. by Pitman Pub Ltd UK) Trans-Atl Phila.

Universal Typing: Advanced. 2nd ed. Edith Mackay. 192p. 1990. pap. text ed. 27.50 (*0-273-02707-7*, Pub. by Pitman Pub Ltd UK) Trans-Atl Phila.

Universal Typing: Study Key & Notes. Edith Mackay. 128p. (Orig.). 1988. pap. 17.95 (*0-273-02956-8*, Pub. by Pitman Pub Ltd UK) Trans-Atl Phila.

Universal Variable Life Insurance Pocket Guide. Rich White. write for info. (*0-318-59654-7*) S&S Trade.

Universal Vocabulario de Alfonso de Palencia: Registro de Voces Internas. John M. Hill. 212p. (SPA.). 1968. 125.00 (*0-614-00122-6*) Elliots Bks.

Universal Waite Tarot. Arthur E. Waite. 24p. 1991. pap. 12.95 (*0-88079-496-8*) US Games Syst.

Universal Waite Tarot Deck-Book Set. Arthur E. Waite. (Illus.). 340p. 1991. pap. 19.95 (*0-88079-416-X*) US Games Syst.

***Universal Web Design.** Crystal Waters. LC 97-8937. 450p. 1997. 39.99 (*1-56205-738-3*) Mac Comp Pub.

Universalism & Spirituality. Ralph Hetherington. LC 93-84361. (Orig.). 1993. pap. 3.00 (*0-87574-309-9*) Pendle Hill.

Universalism Versus Relativism in Language & Thought: Proceedings of a Colloquium on the Sapir-Whorf Hypothesis. Ed. by Rik Pinxten. (Contributions to the Sociology of Language Ser.: No. 11). 1977. text ed. 63.10 (*90-279-7791-7*) Mouton.

Universalism vs. Communitarianism: Contemporary Debates in Ethics. Ed. by David Rasmussen. 250p. 1990. 32.50 (*0-262-18140-1*); pap. 17.00 (*0-262-68063-7*) MIT Pr.

***Universalismo del Pensamiento Cristiano de Don Luigi Sturzo.** Filippo M. Toscano. LC 97-2373. (Roman Catholic Studies: Vol. 9). 220p. (SPA.). 1997. text ed. 89.95 (*0-7734-8685-2*) E Mellen.

***Universalismus und Neuaristotelismus in der Zeitgenossischen Ethik.** Osvaldo Guariglia. (Philosophische Texte und Studien: Vol. 40). 177p. (GER.). 1995. write for info. (*3-487-10067-3*) G Olms Pubs.

Universalist & Unitarian Women Ministers. Catherine F. Hitchings. (Illus.). 165p. (Orig.). (C). 1985. pap. 7.95 (*0-317-91176-7*) UUHS.

Universalist Church of America: A Short History. Clinton L. Scott. 124p. (Orig.). 1960. pap. 4.00 (*0-317-91175-9*) UUHS.

Universality & the Liar: An Essay on Truth & the Diagonal Argument. Keith Simmons. LC 92-28986. 240p. (C). 1993. text ed. 64.95 (*0-521-43069-0*) Cambridge U Pr.

Universality in Chaos. 2nd ed. Predrag Cvitanovic. (Illus.). 648p. 1989. pap. 56.00 (*0-85274-260-6*) IOP Pub.

Universality in Statistical Physics & Synergetics: A Comprehensive Approach to Modern Theoretical Physics. Volker Weberrub. 263p. 1993. 56.00 (*3-528-06513-3*, Pub. by Vieweg & Sohn GW) Informatica.

Universality of Man: Message of Romain Rolland. Addresses & Papers of International Seminar Organised Jointly by the Sahitya Akademi & Festival of France in India 15-17 Jan. 1990. (C). 1992. pap. text ed. 8.00 (*81-7201-095-8*, Pub. by National Sahitya Akademi II) S Asia.

Universality of Tagore: Souvenir of a Symposium. Luciana Colussi. (C). 1991. 19.50 (*0-8364-2754-8*, Pub. by Firma KLM II) S Asia.

Universalizability. Wlodzimierz Rabinowicz. (Synthese Library: No. 141). 190p. 1979. lib. bdg. 64.50 (*90-277-1020-1*, D Reidel) Kluwer Ac.

Universals: An Opinionated Introduction. D. M. Armstrong. 148p. (C). 1989. pap. text ed. 19.95 (*0-8133-0772-4*) Westview.

Universals: Studies in Indian Logic & Linguistics. Frits Staal. (Illus.). x, 280p. 1988. lib. bdg. 57.00 (*0-226-76999-2*) U Ch Pr.

Universals & Property Instances. John Bacon. LC 94-28779. (Aristotelian Society Ser.: 15). Orig. Title: Relations Particularized. 200p. 1995. 57.95 (*0-631-19629-3*) Blackwell Pubs.

Universals & Scientific Realism, Vol. 1: Nominalism & Realism. D. M. Armstrong. LC 77-80824. 164p. 1980. pap. text ed. 21.95 (*0-521-28033-8*) Cambridge U Pr.

Universals & Scientific Realism, Vol. 2: A Theory of Universals. D. M. Armstrong. LC 77-80824. 200p. 1978. text ed. 54.95 (*0-521-21950-7*) Cambridge U Pr.

Universals & Scientific Realism, Vol. 2: A Theory of Universals. D. M. Armstrong. LC 77-80824. 197p. 1980. pap. text ed. 18.95 (*0-521-28032-X*) Cambridge U Pr.

Universals of Human Language, 4 vols., Set. Incl. Vol. I. Method & Theory. Charles A. Ferguson. Ed. by Joseph H. Greenberg & Edith Moravcsik. LC 77-89179. xviii, 286p. 1978. 42.50 (*0-8047-0965-3*); Vol. II. Phonology. Ed. by Joseph H. Greenberg et al. LC 77-89179. xviii, 590p. 1978. 62.50 (*0-8047-0966-1*); Vol. III. Word Structure. Charles A. Ferguson. Ed. by Joseph H. Greenberg & Edith Moravcsik. LC 77-89179. xvi, 463p. 1978. 59.50 (*0-8047-0968-8*); Vol. IV. Syntax. LC 77-89179. xviii, 667p. 79.50 (*0-8047-0969-6*); LC 77-89179. 1978. 229.50 (*0-8047-1012-0*) Stanford U Pr.

Universals of Psychoanalysis: In the Treatment of Psychotic & Borderline States. Henri Rey. Ed. by Jeanne Magagna. 319p. (C). 1994. pap. 37.00 (*1-85343-370-5*) NYU Pr.

Universe. Eric J. Chaisson. (Illus.). 544p. (C). 1988. text ed. 72.00 (*0-13-938391-3*) P-H.

Universe. Kaufmann & Carlson. 1995. teacher ed. write for info. (*0-7167-2532-0*) W H Freeman.

Universe. John Maguire. 106p. 1989. 19.95 (*0-9621826-0-5*) Ash Pr.

Universe. Christopher Maynard & Jean-Pierre Verdet. LC 94-9085. (First Facts Ser.). (Illus.). 128p. (J). (gr. k-4). 1994. pap. 5.95 (*1-85697-527-4*, Kingfisher LKC) LKC.

Universe. Enrico Miotto. LC 94-3839. (Beginnings Origins & Evolution Ser.). (J). 1994. lib. bdg. 24.26 (*0-8114-3334-X*) Raintree Steck-V.

Universe. Ed. by Patrick Moore & Laian Nicolson. (Illus.). 256p. 1985. 60.00 (*0-02-922110-2*, Free Press) Free Pr.

***Universe.** Scholastic Inc., Staff. (J). 1997. 11.95 (*0-590-96212-4*) Scholastic Inc.

***Universe.** Seymour Simon. LC 97-20489. 1998. write for info. (*0-688-15301-1*, Morrow Junior) Morrow.

***Universe.** Seymour Simon. LC 97-20489. 1998. lab manual ed. write for info. (*0-688-15302-X*, Morrow Junior) Morrow.

Universe. Constantin Stoicescu. (Orig.). 1995. pap. write for info. (*1-57553-081-3*) Watermrk Pr.

Universe. rev. ed. Larry Ciupik. LC 87-20805. (Read about Science Ser.). (Illus.). 48p. (J). (gr. 2-6). 1987. pap. 4.95 (*0-8114-8221-9*) Raintree Steck-V.

Universe. 4th ed. Kaufman. LC 93-27842. (C). text ed. write for info. (*0-7167-2519-3*) W H Freeman.

Universe. 4th ed. William J. Kaufmann, III. LC 93-27842. (C). 1995. text ed. write for info. (*0-7167-2379-4*) W H Freeman.

***Universe.** 5th ed. Kaufmann. 1998. write for info. (*0-7167-2826-5*) W H Freeman.

Universe. Scudder Klyce. LC 75-3217. reprint ed. 54.00 (*0-404-59213-9*) AMS Pr.

Universe... And Beyond. rev. ed. Terence Dickinson. 1992. 29.95 (*0-921820-51-8*, Pub. by Camden Hse CN); pap. 24.95 (*0-921820-53-4*, Pub. by Camden Hse CN) Firefly Bks Ltd.

Universe: From Chaos to Consciousness. Thomas M. Corwin & Dale G. Wachowiak. 421p. (C). 1989. pap. text ed. 39.00 (*0-15-592942-9*) SCP.

Universe: God, Science & the Human Person. Adam Ford. LC 87-50830. 228p. (C). 1986. reprint ed. pap. 9.95 (*0-89622-336-1*) Twenty-Third.

***Universe: Origins & Evolution.** Snow. (Astronomy Ser.). (C). 1997. pap. 57.95 incl. cd-rom (*0-534-53286-1*) Wadsworth Pub.

Universe: Origins & Evolution. Theodore P. Snow & Kenneth R. Brownsberger. LC 96-14610. 600p. 1997. pap. write for info. (*0-314-09838-0*) West Pub.

Universe: The Infinite Front. Coast Community College Staff. (Astronomy Ser.). 250p. 1995. student ed., pap. 20.95 (*0-534-20610-7*) Wadsworth Pub.

Universe: The Latest Secrets Revealed in the Light of Recent Scientific Discoveries. Nigel Hawkes. LC 95-13396. (Mysteries of...Ser.). (Illus.). 40p. (J). (gr. 4-6). 1995. lib. bdg. 17.40 (*1-56294-939-X*, Copper Beech Bks) Millbrook Pr.

Universe: Theoretical Physics for the Young Adult. William Bockus, Jr. LC 95-92361. (Illus.). 190p. (Orig.). (YA). (gr. 6-12). Date not set. pap. write for info. (*0-9647151-1-2*) Print Place.

Universe: Think Big! Jeanne Bendick. (Early Bird Astronomy Ser.). (Illus.). 32p. (J). (gr. k-2). 1991. pap. 4.95 (*1-878841-49-1*) Millbrook Pr.

Universe: Think Big! Jeanne Bendick. (Early Bird Astronomy Ser.). (Illus.). 32p. (J). (gr. k-2). 1991. lib. bdg. 14.90 (*1-878841-01-7*) Millbrook Pr.

Universe-a Unified Theory of Mass Energy Space-Time Frame Mechanics Relativity or the Universe is God. Allen C. Goodrich. (Illus.). 440p. (C). 1995. 35.00 (*0-9644267-0-6*); 100.00 (*0-9644267-9-X*); pap. 30.00 (*0-9644267-3-0*); lib. bdg. 35.00 (*0-9644267-1-4*) New Allen Goodrich.

***Universe Alternatives: Emerging Concepts of Size, Age, Structure & Behavior.** 2nd ed. Billy L. Farmer. LC 96-95447. 129p. (Orig.). 1997. pap. 8.00 (*0-9649983-4-3*) B L Farmer.

Universe & Creed. Stanley Jaki. LC 92-60286. (Pere Marquette Lectures). 1992. 15.00 (*0-87462-547-5*) Marquette.

Universe & Dr. Einstein. Lincoln Barnett. 18.95 (*0-8488-0146-6*); pap. 12.95 (*0-685-73713-6*) Amereon Ltd.

Universe & I Teacher Guide. Mike Howard et al. (Universe & I TV Ser.). 96p. 1987. pap. 3.50 (*0-910475-38-5*) KET.

Universe & Life. Herbert S. Jennings. (Select Bibliographies Reprint Ser.). 1977. reprint ed. 17.95 (*0-8369-6695-3*) Ayer.

Universe & Life: Origins & Evolution. G. Siegfried Kutter. 1986. pap. 52.50 (*0-86720-033-2*) Jones & Bartlett.

Universe & Other Fictions. Paul West. LC 87-42889. 224p. 1988. 17.95 (*0-87951-303-9*) Overlook Pr.

Universe & Other Fictions. Paul West. LC 87-42889. 224p. 1989. Tusk. pap. 10.95 (*0-87951-316-0*) Overlook Pr.

Universe & the Light. Nicholas Hagger. 1993. pap. 24.95 (*1-85230-404-9*); pap. 15.95 (*1-85230-413-8*) Element MA.

Universe As Journey: Conversations with W. Norris Clarke, S.J. Ed. by Gerald A. McCool. LC 88-80357. viii, 183p. (C). 1988. text ed. 60.00 (*0-8232-1208-4*) Fordham.

Universe As Pictured in Milton's Paradise Lost: An Illustrated Study for Personal & Class Use. William F. Warren. LC 68-59037. (Illus.). 80p. (C). 1968. reprint ed. 40.00 (*0-87752-117-4*) Gordian.

Universe at High-Z, Large-Scale Structure & the Cosmic Microwave Background: Proceedings of an Advanced Summer School, Held at Laredo, Cantabria, Spain, 4-8 September 1995, Vol. 470. E. Martinez-Gonzalez & J. L. Sanz. LC 96-20317. (Lecture Notes in Physics Ser.). 254p. 1996. 73.00 (*3-540-61225-4*) Spr-Verlag.

***Universe at Large: Key Issues in Astronomy & Cosmology.** Ed. by Guido Munch et al. (Illus.). 400p. (C). 1997. pap. text ed. 24.95 (*0-521-58944-4*) Cambridge U Pr.

***Universe at Large: Key Issues in Astronomy & Cosmology.** Ed. by Guido Munch et al. (Illus.). 400p. (C). 1997. text ed. 69.95 (*0-521-55367-9*) Cambridge U Pr.

Universe at Your Fingertips: An Astronomy Activity & Resource Notebook. Ed. by Andrew Fraknoi. 813p. 1995. pap. 29.95 (*1-886733-00-7*) Astron Soc Pacific.

***Universe Below: Discovering the Secrets of the Deep Sea.** William J. Broad. LC 96-50337. (Illus.). 432p. 1997. 30.00 (*0-684-81108-1*) S&S Trade.

Universe City. Randy Russell. 48p. (Orig.). 1987. pap. 3.00 (*0-944388-00-0*) TBS Pubns.

Universe Cycle - Earth (Fifth) 1992. 45.00 (*1-56638-070-7*) Math Sci Nucleus.

Universe Cycle - Earth (Fourth) 1992. 25.00 (*1-56638-066-9*) Math Sci Nucleus.

Universe Cycle - Earth (Third) 1992. 35.00 (*1-56638-063-4*) Math Sci Nucleus.

Universe Cycle - Geography (Fifth) 1992. 60.00 (*1-56638-071-5*) Math Sci Nucleus.

Universe Cycle - Geography (First) 1992. 35.00 (*1-56638-060-X*) Math Sci Nucleus.

Universe Cycle - Geography (Fourth) Plus Maps. 1992. 50.00 (*1-56638-067-7*) Math Sci Nucleus.

Universe Cycle - Geography (Second) 1992. 25.00 (*1-56638-061-8*) Math Sci Nucleus.

Universe Cycle - Geography (Sixth) 1992. 35.00 (*1-56638-073-1*) Math Sci Nucleus.

Universe Cycle - Geography (Third) 1992. 25.00 (*1-56638-064-2*) Math Sci Nucleus.

Universe Cycle - Literature Books (K-Sixth) 1992. 250.99 (*1-56638-201-7*) Math Sci Nucleus.

Universe Cycle - Search for Our Beginning. J. R. Blueford et al. (J). (gr. k-6). 1992. 20.95 (*1-56638-055-3*) Math Sci Nucleus.

Universe Cycle - Solar System (Fifth) 1992. 40.00 (*1-56638-069-3*) Math Sci Nucleus.

Universe Cycle - Solar System (First) 1992. 30.00 (*1-56638-059-6*) Math Sci Nucleus.

Universe Cycle - Solar System (Fourth) 1992. 25.00 (*1-56638-065-0*) Math Sci Nucleus.

Universe Cycle - Solar System (Second) 1992. 35.00 (*1-56638-062-6*) Math Sci Nucleus.

Universe Cycle - Solar System (Sixth) 1992. 45.00 (*1-56638-072-3*) Math Sci Nucleus.

Universe Cycle - Universe (Fifth) 1992. 45.00 (*1-56638-068-5*) Math Sci Nucleus.

Universe Cycle - Universe (First) 1992. 25.00 (*1-56638-058-8*) Math Sci Nucleus.

Universe Cycle - Universe (K) 1992. 25.00 (*1-56638-056-1*) Math Sci Nucleus.

Universe down to Earth. Neil D. Tyson. LC 93-32259. 277p. 1994. 29.95 (*0-231-07560-X*) Col U Pr.

Universe Down to Earth. Neil D. Tyson. 236p. 1995. pap. 15.95 (*0-231-07561-8*) Col U Pr.

Universe Earth & Man. Rudolf Steiner. (Russian Language Ser.). 136p. 1985. pap. 15.95 (*0-89345-903-8*, Steiner) Garber Comm.

Universe Earth & Man: In Their Relationship to Egyptian Myths & Modern Civilization. Rudolf Steiner. (Russian Language Ser.). 174p. 1987. pap. 15.95 (*0-85440-606-9*) Anthroposophic.

Universe Explained: The Earth-Dweller's Guide to the Mysteries of Space. Ed. by Colin A. Ronan. LC 94-16294. 192p. 1994. 35.00 (*0-8050-3488-9*) H Holt & Co.

***Universe Explained: The Earth-Dweller's Guide to the Mysteries of Space.** Colin A. Ronan. 1996. pap. 22.50 (*0-614-20832-7*, Owl) H Holt & Co.

Universe for the Beginner. Patrick Moore. (Illus.). 48p. (C). 1992. text ed. 13.95 (*0-521-41834-8*) Cambridge U Pr.

Universe from Your Backyard: A Guide to Deep Sky Objects from Astronomy Magazine. David J. Eicher. LC 88-8920. (Illus.). 188p. 1988. 29.95 (*0-913135-13-5*, 18037) Kalmbach.

Universe, God, & God-Realization: From the Viewpoint of Vedanta. Swami Satprakashananda. LC 77-79829. 310p. 1977. 12.50 (*0-916356-57-4*) Vedanta Soc St Louis.

Universe in a Handkerchief: Lewis Carroll's Mathematical Recreations, Games, Puzzles, & Word Play. Martin Gardner. LC 95-51303. (Copernicus Bks.). (Illus.). 200p. 1996. text ed. 19.00 (*0-387-94673-X*) Spr-Verlag.

Universe in a Handkerchief: Lewis Carroll's Mathematical Recreations, Games, Puzzles & Word Plays. Martin Gardner. 1996. 19.00 (*0-614-97165-9*) Copernicus Systs.

Universe Is a Green Dragon: A Cosmic Creation Story. Brian Swimme. LC 84-72255. (Illus.). 176p. (Orig.). 1984. pap. 10.95 (*0-939680-14-9*) Bear & Co.

Universe is Broken: Who on Earth Can Fix It? Moishe Rosen. LC 91-67710. (Illus.). 52p. (Orig.). 1991. pap. write for info. (*0-9616148-8-9*) Purple Pomegranate.

Universe Is Calling: Opening to the Divine Through Prayer. Eric Butterworth. LC 91-59028. 192p. 1994. pap. 10.00 (*0-06-250094-5*) Harper SF.

Universe is My Home: A Children's Adventure Story. Bill Fletcher & Sally Fletcher. (Illus.). 34p. (J). (gr. k-5). 1993. 14.95 (*0-9634622-0-2*) Sci & Art Prods.

Universe Lost: Reclaiming a World View. Stuart D. Cook. 192p. (Orig.). (C). 1992. pap. 8.99 (*0-89900-404-0*) College Pr Pub.

***Universe Maker.** A. E. Van Vogt. 3.95 (*0-7867-0841-7*) Carroll & Graf.

Universe Maker. A. E. Van Vogt. 192p. 1992. pap. 3.95 (*0-88184-841-7*) Carroll & Graf.

Universe Next Door. rev. ed. James W. Sire. LC 88-8852. 246p. 1988. pap. 12.99 (*0-8308-1220-2*, 1220) InterVarsity.

***Universe Next Door: A Basic Worldview Catalog.** 3rd ed. James W. Sire. LC 97-10670. 264p. 1997. pap. 13.99 (*0-8308-1899-5*, 1899) InterVarsity.

Universe Observers Handbook. David R. Flower. Date not set. pap. text ed. 7.50 (*0-314-73281-0*) West Pub.

Universe of Babies: In the Beginning There Were No Words. Caleb Gattegno. 133p. 1973. pap. 10.95 (*0-87825-023-9*) Ed Solutions.

Universe of Cartoons. Jack Nemec. LC 87-91984. (Illus.). 120p. (Orig.). 1987. pap. 3.95 (*0-9618998-3-2*) Nemec Pub.

U V

An Asterisk (*) at the beginning of an entry indicates that the title is appearing in BIP for the first time.

Universe of Discourses: Issues & Features. Evan Blythin. LC 94-22106. 1994. 29.50 (*0-8191-9638-X*) U Pr of Amer.

Universe of Galaxies. Ed. by Paul W. Hodge. (Readings from Scientific American Ser.). (Illus.). 113p. (C). 1996. text ed. write for info. (*0-7167-1676-3*) W H Freeman.

Universe of Motion. Dewey B. Larson. LC 79-88078. (Illus.). 460p. 1984. 28.00 (*0-913138-11-8*) North Pacific.

Universe of Numbers. Ed. by Ralph M. Lewis. LC 83-51126. 209p. (Orig.). 1984. pap. 12.95 (*0-912057-11-4*, 501920) RO AMORC.

Universe of Science. H. Levy. LC 74-26272. (History, Philosophy & Sociology of Science Ser.). 1975. reprint ed. 23.95 (*0-405-06600-7*) Ayer.

Universe of Shabbetai Donnolo. A. Sharf. 20.00 (*0-87068-485-X*) Ktav.

Universe of the Mind. George E. Owen. LC 76-125674. (Seminars in the History of Ideas Ser.: No. 4). (Illus.). 368p. 1971. pap. 15.95 (*0-8018-1179-1*) Johns Hopkins.

Universe of the Mind: A Semiotic Theory of Culture. Yuri Lotman. Tr. by Ann Shukman. LC 90-39870. (Second World Ser.). 300p. 1991. 45.00 (*0-253-33608-2*) Ind U Pr.

Universe of the Warramirri. John Cawte. 1992. 22.95 (*0-86840-013-0*, Pub. by New South Wales Univ Pr AT) Intl Spec Bk.

Universe Story: From the Promordial Flaring Forth to the Ecozoic Era- A Celebration of the Unfolding of the Cosmos. Brian Swimme & Thomas Berry. LC 91-58907. 320p. 1994. reprint ed. pap. 14.00 (*0-06-250835-0*) Harper SF.

Universe That Isn't. J. H. Hacsi. 236p. (Orig.). 1985. pap. 9.95 (*0-9612146-1-9*) Champagne Pr.

***Universe Unfolding.** Ed. by Hermann Bondi & Elizabeth M. Weston-Smith. (Illus.). 416p. 1997. 35.00 (*0-19-851188-4*) OUP.

Universe Upstairs: A Cartoon Guide to World Views. Merve Jones. 128p. (Orig.). 1992. pap. 5.99 (*0-8308-5467-3*, 5467, Pub. by IVP UK) InterVarsity.

Universe Within: An Exploration of the Human Spirit. Anjam Khursheed. 220p. 1995. pap. 11.95 (*1-85168-075-6*) Onewrld Pubns.

Universes. John Leslie. 256p. (C). 1990. text ed. 25.00 (*0-415-04144-9*, A4027) Routledge.

Universes. John Leslie. 256p. 1996. pap. 16.95 (*0-415-13955-4*) Routledge.

Universes of E. E. Smith. Ron Ellik & Bill Evans. LC 66-9092. (Illus.). 1968. reprint ed. pap. 9.00 (*0-911682-03-1*) Advent.

Universitaets-Klinik und Poliklinik fuer Hals -, Nasen- und Ohren-Krankheiten Basel 1876-1976. 1976. 15.25 (*3-8055-2405-6*) S Karger.

***Universitas: The Social Restructuring of American Higher Education.** Thomas E. Boudreau. LC 97-23660. 1998. text ed. write for info. (*0-275-95584-2*, Praeger Pubs) Greenwood.

Universitas, Enciclopedia Cultural, Vol. 1. Salvat Staff. 112p. 1987. 19.95 (*0-7859-5951-3*, 8434547422) Fr & Eur.

Universitas, Enciclopedia Cultural, Vol. 2. Salvat Staff. 112p. 1987. 19.95 (*0-7859-5952-1*, 8434547430) Fr & Eur.

Universitas, Enciclopedia Cultural, Vol. 4. Salvat Staff. 112p. 1987. 19.95 (*0-7859-5954-8*, 8434547457) Fr & Eur.

Universitas, Enciclopedia Cultural, Vol. 5. Salvat Staff. 112p. 1987. 19.95 (*0-7859-5955-6*, 8434547465) Fr & Eur.

Universitas, Enciclopedia Cultural, Vol. 6. Salvat Staff. 112p. 1987. 19.95 (*0-7859-5956-4*, 8434547473) Fr & Eur.

Universitas, Enciclopedia Cultural, Vol. 7. Salvat Staff. 112p. 1987. 19.95 (*0-7859-5950-5*, 8434547325) Fr & Eur.

Universitas, Enciclopedia Cultural, Vol. 8. Salvat Staff. 112p. 1987. 19.95 (*0-7859-6468-1*) Fr & Eur.

Universitas, Enciclopedia Cultural, Vol. 9. Salvat Staff. 112p. 1987. 19.95 (*0-7859-5957-2*, 8434547503) Fr & Eur.

Universitas, Enciclopedia Cultural, Vol. 10. Salvat Staff. 112p. 1987. 19.95 (*0-7859-5958-0*, 8434547511) Fr & Eur.

Universitas, Enciclopedia Cultural, Vol. 12. Salvat Staff. 112p. 1987. 19.95 (*0-7859-5959-9*, 8434547538) Fr & Eur.

Universitas, Enciclopedia Cultural, Vol. 13. Salvat Staff. 112p. 1987. 19.95 (*0-7859-5960-2*, 8434547546) Fr & Eur.

Universitas, Enciclopedia Cultural, Vol. 14. Salvat Staff. 112p. 1987. 19.95 (*0-7859-5961-0*, 8434547554) Fr & Eur.

Universitas, Enciclopedia Cultural, Vol. 15. Salvat Staff. 112p. 1987. 19.95 (*0-7859-5962-9*, 8434547562) Fr & Eur.

Universitas, Enciclopedia Cultural, Vol. 16. Salvat Staff. 112p. 1987. 19.95 (*0-7859-5963-7*, 8434547570) Fr & Eur.

Universitas, Enciclopedia Cultural, Vol. 17. Salvat Staff. 112p. 1987. 19.95 (*0-7859-5964-5*, 8434547589) Fr & Eur.

Universitas, Enciclopedia Cultural, Vol. 18. Salvat Staff. 112p. 1987. 19.95 (*0-7859-5965-3*, 8434547597) Fr & Eur.

Universitas, Enciclopedia Cultural, Vol. 19. Salvat Staff. 112p. 1987. 19.95 (*0-7859-5966-1*, 8434547600) Fr & Eur.

Universitas, Enciclopedia Cultural, Vol. 21. Salvat Staff. 112p. 1987. 19.95 (*0-7859-5968-8*, 8434547627) Fr & Eur.

Universitas, Enciclopedia Cultural, Vol. 22. Salvat Staff. 112p. 1987. 19.95 (*0-7859-5969-6*, 8434547635) Fr & Eur.

Universitas, Enciclopedia Cultural, Vol. 24. Salvat Staff. 112p. 1987. 19.95 (*0-7859-5971-8*, 8434547651) Fr & Eur.

Universitas 15: Enciclopedia Cultural, 15 vols. 4500p. (SPA.). 1971. Set. 695.00 (*0-8288-6484-5*, S-50485) Fr & Eur.

Universitats-Selbstwerwaltung: Ihre Geschichte und Gegenwartige Rechtsform. Alexander Kluge. Ed. by Walter P. Metzger. LC 76-55205. (Academic Profession Ser.). 1977. reprint ed. lib. bdg. 23.95 (*0-405-10033-7*) Ayer.

Universitatsbibliotheken Heidelberg, Jena und Koln unter dem Nationalsozialismus. Lothar Bohmuller et al. (Illus.). 448p. (GER.). 1989. lib. bdg. 54.00 (*3-598-10858-3*) K G Saur.

Universite de la Parole. Dick Eastman. Ed. by Annie Cosson. Tr. by Vera Sayous from ENG. Orig. Title: The Universoty of the WORD. 240p. (FRE.). 1986. pap. 2.95 (*0-8297-0441-8*) Life Pubs Intl.

Universite, la Societe & le Gouvernment: Rapport de la Commission d'Etude sur les Relations Entre les Universites & les Gouvernements, Commissaires, Rene Hurtubise, Donald C. Rowat. Commission on the Relations Between Universities & Governments. LC 70-875960. 282p. (FRE.). 1970. reprint ed. pap. 80.40 (*0-608-02203-9*, 2062873) Bks Demand.

Universites Americaines: Dynamismes et Traditions. J. Bodelle et al. 416p. (Orig.). (FRE.). 1985. pap. 30.00 (*0-318-18948-8*, Pub. by Technique et Documentation) S M P F Inc.

Universites Francaises au Moyen Age. Jacques Verger. (Education & Society in the Middle Ages & Renaissance Ser.: No. 7). 320p. 1995. 95.00 (*90-04-10312-0*) E J Brill.

Universities: American, English, German. rev. ed. Abraham Flexner. 400p. (C). 1994. pap. 29.95 (*1-56000-737-0*) Transaction Pubs.

Universities: Commonwealth & American; a Comparative Study. Oliver C. Carmichael. LC 70-167323. (Essay Index Reprint Ser.). 1977. reprint ed. 22.95 (*0-8369-2760-5*) Ayer.

Universities, Adult Education & Social Criticism. S. Raybould. (Tolley Medal Ser.). 1970. 1.50 (*0-686-52207-9*, WPT 3) Syracuse U Cont Ed.

Universities & Educational Systems of the British Empire see British Empire

Universities & Elites in Britain Since 1800. R. D. Anderson. (New Studies in Economic & Social History: No. 16). 88p. (C). 1995. text ed. 34.95 (*0-521-55275-3*) Cambridge U Pr.

Universities & Elites in Britain Since 1800. R. D. Anderson. (New Studies in Economic & Social History: No. 16). 88p. (C). 1996. pap. text ed. 10.95 (*0-521-55778-X*) Cambridge U Pr.

***Universities & Empire.** Christopher Simpson. Date not set. 27.50 (*1-56584-387-8*) New Press NY.

Universities & Industrial Research. Ewald Konecny et al. 181p. 1995. 75.00 (*0-85404-407-8*) CRC Pr.

Universities & Scientific Life in the United States. Maurice Caullery. LC 74-26257. (History, Philosophy & Sociology of Science Ser.). 1975. reprint ed. 26.95 (*0-405-06585-X*) Ayer.

Universities & Scientific Life in the United States. Maurice J. Caullery. LC 72-94312. (American Scientific Community, 1790-1920 Ser.). 1973. reprint ed. lib. bdg. 30.00 (*0-8420-1677-5*) Scholarly Res Inc.

Universities & State Governments: Study in Policy Analysis. Irwin Feller. LC 86-520. 188p. 1986. text ed. 49.95 (*0-275-92094-1*, C2094, Praeger Pubs) Greenwood.

Universities & the Capitalist State: Corporate Liberalism & the Reconstruction of American Higher Education, 1894-1928. Clyde W. Barrow. (History of American Thought & Culture Ser.). 350p. (Orig.). (C). 1990. text ed. 39.50 (*0-299-12400-2*); pap. text ed. 17.25 (*0-299-12404-5*) U of Wis Pr.

Universities & the Future of America. Derek Bok. LC 89-49196. 128p. (C). 1990. text ed. 16.95 (*0-8223-1036-8*) Duke.

***Universities & the Global Knowledge Economy: A Triple Helix of University-Industry-Government.** Henry Etzkowitz & Loet A. Leydesdorff. LC 96-39272. (Science, Technology & the International Political Economy Ser.). 224p. 1997. 83.60 (*1-85567-421-1*, Pub. by Pntr Pubs UK) Bks Intl VA.

Universities & the International Distribution of Knowledge. Ed. by Irving J. Spitzberg, Jr. LC 80-16569. 222p. 1980. text ed. 55.00 (*0-275-90556-X*, C0556, Praeger Pubs) Greenwood.

Universities & the Military. Ed. by David A. Wilson. (Annals Ser.: Vol. 502). 1989. 26.00 (*0-8039-3175-1*); pap. 17.00 (*0-8039-3176-X*) Sage.

Universities & the Myth of Cultural Decline. Jerry S. Herron. LC 88-10081. 144p. 1988. 24.95 (*0-8143-2068-6*); pap. 14.95 (*0-8143-2069-4*) Wayne St U Pr.

Universities & Their Communities: The Challenge for Lifelong Learning. Ed. by Jane Elliott et al. 224p. 1996. pap. 25.00 (*0-85315-850-9*, Pub. by Lawrence & Wishart UK) NYU Pr.

Universities & Women Faculty: Why Some Organizations Discriminate More Than Others. Robert F. Szafran. LC 83-23104. 1984. text ed. 49.95 (*0-275-91282-5*, C1282, Praeger Pubs) Greenwood.

Universities Education & the National Economy. Ed. by Michael D. Stephens. 224p. 1989. 47.50 (*0-415-01951-6*) Routledge.

Universities for All. George Z. Bereday. LC 72-11624. (Jossey-Bass Higher Education Ser.). 175p. reprint ed. pap. 49.90 (*0-685-16353-9*, 2027746) Bks Demand.

Universities in Africa: Strategies for Stabilization & Revitalization. William S. Saint. LC 92-41398. (Technical Paper Ser.: No. 194). 165p. 1992. 10.95 (*0-8213-2310-5*, 12310) World Bank.

Universities in Germany. Ed. by Werner Becker et al. (Illus.). 304p. (ENG & GER.). 1995. 55.00 (*3-7913-1496-3*, Pub. by Prestel GW) te Neues.

Universities in Politics: Case Studies from the Late Middle Ages & Early Modern Period. Ed. by John W. Baldwin & Richard A. Goldthwaite. LC 73-183041. (Johns Hopkins Symposia in Comparative History Ser.). 144p. reprint ed. pap. 41.10 (*0-317-41614-6*, 2025829) Bks Demand.

Universities in Saudi Arabia: Their Role in Science, Technology, & Development. Ali N. Alghafis. 114p. (C). 1992. lib. bdg. 39.50 (*0-8191-8831-X*) U Pr of Amer.

Universities in the Business of Repression: The Academic-Military-Industrial Complex & Central America. Jonathan Feldman. LC 89-4156. 250p. 1989. 30.00 (*0-89608-355-1*); pap. 14.00 (*0-89608-354-3*) South End Pr.

Universities in the Late Middle Ages. Ed. by J. Ijsewijn & J. Paquet. No. 6. 672p. (Orig.). 1978. pap. 92.50 (*90-6186-055-5*, Pub. by Leuven Univ BE) Coronet Bks.

Universities in the Twenty-First Century. Ed. by Steven Muller. LC 95-31519. (International Political Currents Ser.: Vol. II). 182p. 1996. 39.95 (*1-57181-026-9*) Berghahn Bks.

Universities in Transition: The U. S. Presence in Latin American Higher Education. Latin American Conference Staff. Ed. by Richard R. Renner. LC 73-8234. 156p. reprint ed. pap. 44.50 (*0-7837-5085-4*, 2044783) Bks Demand.

Universities in Tudor England. Craig R. Thompson. LC 79-65982. (Folger Guides to the Age of Shakespeare Ser.). 1979. pap. 4.95 (*0-918016-09-6*) Folger Bks.

Universities, Information Technology, & Academic Libraries: The Next 20 Years. Robert M. Hayes. LC 85-22879. (Libraries & Information Science). 180p. 1986. text ed. 73.25 (*0-89391-266-2*) Ablex Pub.

Universities of Ancient Greece. John W. Walden. LC 70-109635. (Select Bibliographies Reprint Ser.). 1977. 35.95 (*0-8369-5244-8*) Ayer.

Universities of Europe. S. Willis Rudy. LC 82-49281. 176p. 1984. 22.50 (*0-685-07997-X*) Fairleigh Dickinson.

Universities of Europe, Eleven Hundred to Nineteen Fourteen: A History. S. Willis Rudy. 176p. 1984. 29.50 (*0-8386-3177-0*) Fairleigh Dickinson.

Universities of Puerto Rico: A Historical, Sociological & Cultural Study Including a Directory of Puerto Rico Scholars. Winifred Melendez. 1979. lib. bdg. 250.00 (*0-8490-1247-3*) Gordon Pr.

University. John Jory. 1983. 5.25 (*0-87129-518-0*, U16) Dramatic Pub.

University. Bentley Little. 416p. (Orig.). 1995. mass mkt., pap. 4.99 (*0-451-18390-8*) NAL-Dutton.

University: An Owner's Manual. Henry Rosovsky. 1991. pap. 11.95 (*0-393-30783-2*) Norton.

University - a Regional Booster? Economic Impacts of Academic Knowledge Infrastructure. Raymond Florax. 346p. 1992. 68.95 (*1-85628-342-9*, Pub. by Avebury Pub UK) Ashgate Pub Co.

University - Government - Industry Microelectronics Symposium, 1993. IEEE, (Electron Devices Society) Staff. Ed. by IEEE, (Institute of Electrical & Electronics Engineers, Inc.) Staff. 250p. 1993. pap. text ed. write for info. (*0-7803-0990-1*); lib. bdg. write for info. (*0-7803-0991-X*, 93CH3273-0); fiche write for info. (*0-7803-0992-8*) Inst Electrical.

University - 1968, Vol. 34. Eugen Rosenstock-Huessy. (Eugen Rosenstock-Huessy Lectures). 8p. pap. 10.00 incl. audio (*0-614-05414-1*); pap. 7.50 (*0-912148-53-5*); audio 5.00 (*0-614-05413-3*) Argo Bks.

University Administration in India & U. S. A. Pradeep Mehendiratta. 1985. 28.50 (*0-8364-1308-3*, Pub. by Oxford IBH II) S Asia.

University Adult Education: The Career for Experiment in Education. A. A. Liveright. 1961. 2.50 (*0-87060-080-X*, PUC 21) Syracuse U Cont Ed.

University Adult Education in China. M. D. Stephens & S. Stephens. (C). 1992. 45.00 (*1-85041-061-5*, Pub. by Univ Nottingham UK) St Mut.

University Adult Education in England & the U. S. A. A Reappraisal of the Liberal Tradition. Richard Taylor et al. LC 85-8743. (Radical Forum on Adult Education Ser.). 272p. 1985. 37.50 (*0-7099-2431-3*, Pub. by Croom Helm UK) Routledge Chapman & Hall.

***University & College Governing Boards: From the Middle Ages to the Twentieh Century.** E. D. Duryea. Ed. by Philip Altbach. (Garland Studies in Higher Education). 200p. 1997. text ed. 30.00 (*0-8153-2119-8*) Garland.

University & College Museums, Galleries, & Related Facilities: A Descriptive Directory. Victor J. Danilov. LC 95-20544. 696p. 1996. text ed. 99.50 (*0-313-28613-2*, Greenwood Pr) Greenwood.

***University & College Stress.** David C. Rainham. (Illus.). 16p. (Orig.). 1996. pap. 3.00 (*1-884241-32-8*, SPSO314) Energeia Pub.

University & Colleges of Cambridge. Rodney Tibbs. 104p. (C). 1988. 70.00 (*0-900963-38-7*, Pub. by T Dalton UK) St Mut.

University & Colleges of Oxford. John R. Thackrah. 160p. (C). 1988. 100.00 (*0-86138-002-9*, Pub. by T Dalton UK) St Mut.

University & Community Education. Kenneth Haygood. 1962. 2.50 (*0-8156-7017-6*, NES 36) Syracuse U Cont Ed.

University & Community Service: Perspectives for the Seventies. J. Whipple & Doris S. Chertow. LC 74-118676. (Notes & Essays Ser.: No. 64). (C). pap. text ed. 2.50 (*0-87060-028-1*, NES 64) Syracuse U Cont Ed.

University & Government in Mexico: Autonomy in a Authoritarian System. Daniel C. Levy. LC 79-21134. 190p. 1980. text ed. 49.95 (*0-275-90512-8*, C0512, Praeger Pubs) Greenwood.

University & Historical Addresses. James B. Bryce. LC 68-55842. (Essay Index Reprint Ser.). 1977. 23.95 (*0-8369-0262-9*) Ayer.

University & Research Library Studies: Contributions University Sheffield Post-Graduate School Librarianship. W. L. Saunders & George Chandler. LC 68-21388. (International Series of Monographs in Library & Information Science: Vol. 8). 1968. 108.00 (*0-08-012726-6*, Pub. by Pergamon Repr UK) Franklin.

University & Society: Essays on the Social Role of Research & Higher Education. Ed. by Martin A. Trow & Thorsten Nybom. (Higher Education Policy Ser.: No. 12). 256p. 1991. 62.00 (*1-85302-525-9*) Taylor & Francis.

University & the City: From Medieval Origins to the Present. Ed. by Thomas Bender. 328p. (C). 1991. reprint ed. pap. text ed. 18.95 (*0-19-506775-4*) OUP.

University & the Man of Tomorrow. 1967. 11.95 (*0-8156-6008-1*, Am U Beirut) Syracuse U Pr.

University Associates Training Technologies, 7 vols., Set. J. William Pfeiffer & Arlette C. Ballew. 1988. Boxed set. boxed 139.00 (*0-88390-286-9*, Pfffr & Co) Jossey-Bass.

University at Prayer. Alfred C. Payne. LC 86-14613. (Illus.). 1987. 13.95 (*0-9617635-0-7*) VA Tech Found.

University at the Crossroads: Addresses & Essays. Henry E. Sigerist. LC 73-167419. (Essay Index Reprint Ser.). 1977. reprint ed. 18.95 (*0-8369-2861-X*) Ayer.

University Budgeting for Critical Mass & Competition. L. R. Jones. LC 84-26416. 304p. 1985. text ed. 59.95 (*0-275-90124-6*, C0124, Praeger Pubs) Greenwood.

University-Business Partnership: An Assessment. Norman E. Bowie. 300p. (C). 1994. pap. text ed. 24.95 (*0-8476-7897-0*); lib. bdg. 64.50 (*0-8476-7896-2*) Rowman.

University Chemical Dependency Project. Steven Ungerleider & Steven A. Bloch. 113p. (Orig.). 1987. write for info. (*0-943277-00-0*) Integrated Res Servs.

University Chemistry. 3rd ed. Bruce M. Mahan. LC 74-19696. (C). 1975. text ed. write for info. (*0-201-04405-6*) Addison-Wesley.

University Chemistry. 4th ed. Bruce M. Mahan & Rollie J. Myers. LC 86-14063. (Chemistry Ser.). (Illus.). 1076p. (C). 1987. text ed. 55.95 (*0-201-05833-2*); student ed. 17.25 (*0-201-05835-9*); 15.00 (*0-201-05838-3*) Benjamin-Cummings.

University Chemistry. 4th ed. Bruce M. Mahan. (C). 1987. pap. text ed. 51.95 (*0-201-05846-4*) Addison-Wesley.

University Club of San Francisco Centennial History 1890-1990: With an Appendix on the Clubhouse. Mitchell P. Postel. (Illus.). 112p. 1990. 30.00 (*0-9627540-0-5*) Univ Club.

University College of Swansea. David Dykes. (Illus.). 224p. 1992. 36.00 (*0-86299-904-9*, Pub. by Sutton Pubng UK) Bks Intl VA.

***University Community Collaborations for the Twenty-First Century: Outreach Scholarship for Youth & Families.** Richard M. Lerner & Lou Anna Simon. Ed. by Michigan State University Staff. (MSU Series on Children, Youth & Families: Vol. 4). 475p. 1998. text ed. 60.00 (*0-8153-2445-6*) Garland.

University-Community Relations: Living Together Effectively. David Nichols. 142p. 1990. pap. 21.95 (*0-398-06307-9*) C C Thomas.

University-Community Relations: Living Together Effectively. David Nichols. 142p. (C). 1990. text ed. 32.95 (*0-398-05680-3*) C C Thomas.

University Control. J. McKeen Cattell. Ed. by Walter P. Metzger. LC 76-55179. (Academic Profession Ser.). 1977. reprint ed. lib. bdg. 40.95 (*0-405-10007-8*) Ayer.

University Council on Education for Public Responsibility, 1961-1975. Granville D. Davis. LC 75-2281. 130p. 1975. pap. 2.75 (*0-87060-068-0*, OCP 43) Syracuse U Cont Ed.

University Course in English Grammar. Angela Downing & Philip Locke. LC 92-13623. 1994. pap. text ed. 33.75 (*0-13-952490-8*) P-H.

University Curriculum on Transnational Corporations, 3 vols. 1991. Set. 50.00 (*92-1-104367-0*, 91.II.A.8) UN.

University Curriculum on Transnational Corporations. 188p. Date not set. 20.00 (*92-1-104364-6*, E.91.II.A.5) UN.

University Curriculum on Transnational Corporations, 3 vols., Vol. 1. 206p. 1991. 20.00 (*0-685-74333-0*, 91.II. A.5) UN.

University Curriculum on Transnational Corporations, 3 vols., Vol. 2. 168p. 1991. Vol. III: 168p. 20.00 (*92-1-104365-4*, 91.II.A.6) UN.

University Curriculum on Transnational Corporations, 3 vols., Vol. 3. 192p. 1991. Vol. II: 192p. 20.00 (*92-1-104366-2*, 91.II.A.7) UN.

University Development in the Third World: The Rockefeller Foundation Experience. James S. Coleman & David Court. LC 93-14907. 350p. 1993. 89.95 (*0-08-041936-4*, Prgamon Press) Buttrwrth-Heinemann.

University Drama in the Tudor Age. Frederick S. Boas. LC 65-20049. (Illus.). 1979. 30.95 (*0-405-08277-0*, Pub. by Blom Pubns UK) Ayer.

University Drama in the Tudor Age. Frederick S. Boas. (BCL1-PR English Literature Ser.). 414p. 1992. reprint ed. lib. bdg. 99.00 (*0-7812-7101-0*) Rprt Serv.

University Education. Henry P. Tappan. LC 78-89243. (American Education: Its Men, Institutions, & Ideas. Series 1). 1975. reprint ed. 17.95 (*0-405-01480-5*) Ayer.

University Education for Business. James H. Bossard & J. Frederic Dewhurst. LC 73-1993. (Big Business; Economic Power in a Free Society Ser.). 1973. reprint ed. 40.95 (0-405-05076-3) Ayer.

University Education for Management Consulting: Position Paper & Conference Report. fac. ed. American Institute of Certified Public Accountants Staff. Ed. by Monroe S. Kuttner. 154p. pap. 43.90 (0-7837-8239-X, 2049003) Bks Demand.

University Education for Management Consulting: Position Paper & Conference Report. Ed. by Monroe S. Kuttner. (Illus.). 154p. reprint ed. pap. 43.90 (0-8357-6421-4, 2035788) Bks Demand.

University Education Uses of Visualization: Proceedings of the IFIP WG 3.2 Working Conference on Visualization in Scientific Computing, Uses in University Education. Ed. by Stephen D. Franklin et al. LC 94-20016. (IFIP Transactions A: Computer Science & Technology Ser.: Vol. A-48). 222p. 1994. 100.75 (0-444-81543-0) Elsevier.

***University Experience.** Ohio University Staff. 302p. (C). 1997. per. 25.95 (0-7872-3794-9) Kendall-Hunt.

University Experience. 3rd ed. Ohio University Staff. 304p. (C). 1996. pap. text ed. 26.25 (0-7872-2373-5) Kendall-Hunt.

***University Gallery Presents a One-Man Retrospective Exhibition of Works by Hiram Williams.** Hiram Williams. LC 83-154413. (Illus.). 40p. reprint ed. pap. 25.00 (0-608-04507-1, 2065252) Bks Demand.

University Gradebook-Class Recordkeeping Software. Herrick. (C). 1987. text ed. 53.75 (0-8053-2268-X) Benjamin-Cummings.

***University Health Services.** (Technical Report Ser.: No. 320). 21p. 1966. pap. text ed. 3.00 (92-4-120320-X) World Health.

University Hospitals & School Managers Guide to Environment: A Guide for University, Hospital, & School Managers. James T. O'Reilly. LC 95-38757. (Industrial Health & Safety Ser.). 448p. 1996. text ed. 74.95 (0-442-02123-2) Van Nos Reinhold.

University in a Changing World. Ed. by Walter M. Kotsching & Elined Prys. LC 71-86766. (Essay Index Reprint Ser.). 1977. 19.95 (0-8369-1183-0) Ayer.

University in a Liberal State. Ed. by Bob Brecher et al. (Avebury Series in Philosophy). 160p. 1996. 55.95 (1-85628-987-7, Pub. by Avebury Pub UK) Ashgate Pub Co.

University in Its Region: The Extra-Mural Contribution. A. H. Thornton & M. D. Stephens. (C). 1977. 39.00 (0-902031-39-2, Pub. by Univ Nottingham UK); text ed. 50.00 (0-685-22164-4, Pub. by Univ Nottingham UK) St Mut.

University in Process. John O. Riedl. LC 65-19126. (Aquinas Lectures). 1965. 15.00 (0-87462-130-5) Marquette.

University in Ruins. Bill Readings. 256p. 1996. 29.95 (0-674-92952-7) HUP.

***University in Ruins.** Bill Readings. 1997. pap. text ed. 15.95 (0-674-92953-5) HUP.

University in the Forest. John T. Cunningham. Ed. by Ruth La Clair. (Illus.). 384p. 1990. write for info. (0-89359-017-7) Afton Pub.

University in the Urban Community: Responsibilities for Public Health. Ed. by John R. Hogness et al. LC 95-5244. 250p. 1995. pap. write for info. (1-879694-09-3) AAH Ctrs.

University in the 1870s: (1) William Hammond Hall & the Original Campus Plan, (2) The University & the Constitutional Convention of 1878. Kent Watson & Peter S. Van Houten. LC 96-8769. (Chapters in the History of the University of California Ser.: No. 6). (Illus.). 90p. (Orig.). (C). 1996. pap. 10.00 (0-87772-370-2) UCB IGS.

University in Transition. James A. Perkins. LC 66-15804. (Stafford Little Lectures: No. 1965). 100p. reprint ed. pap. 28.50 (0-8357-4651-8, 2037582) Bks Demand.

University-Industry Research Partnerships: The Major Legal Issues in Research & Development Agreements. Bernard D. Reams, Jr. LC 85-9589. (Illus.). 365p. 1986. text ed. 69.50 (0-89930-121-5, RUI/, Quorum Bks) Greenwood.

University Librarianship. Ed. by John F. Stirling. LC 81-138917. (Handbooks on Library Practice). 245p. reprint ed. pap. 69.90 (0-7837-7013-8, 2046827) Bks Demand.

University Libraries & Scholarly Communication: Study Prepared for the Andrew W. Mellon Foundation. Anthony M. Cummings et al. LC 92-44941. 205p. 1992. pap. 8.00 (0-918006-22-8) Assn Res Lib.

University Libraries & the Antiquarian Book Trade: Fragments of Library History. Lawrence S. Thompson. (University of Kentucky Libraries Occasional Papers: No. 4). 26p. 1983. pap. 5.00 (0-317-27435-X) U of KY Libs.

University Libraries in Developing Countries: Structure & Function in Regard to Information Transfer for Science & Technology. Ed. by Anthony J. Loveday & Gunter Gattermann. (IFLA Publication Ser.: Vol. 33). 183p. 1985. lib. bdg. 25.00 (3-598-20397-7) K G Saur.

University Library Building Planning. Heather M. Edwards. LC 89-24261. (Illus.). 145p. 1990. 29.50 (0-8108-2225-3) Scarecrow.

University Library Practices in Developing Countries. Nazir Ahmad. (Illus.). 220p. 1985. 55.00 (0-7103-0058-1) Routledge Chapman & Hall.

University Library System in India. K. S. Deshpande. 1985. text ed. 25.00 (0-86590-697-1, Pub. by Sterling Pubs II) Apt Bks.

University-Linked Retirement Communities: Student Visions of Eldercare. Ed. by Benyamin Schwarz. LC 93-40379. (Journal: Housing for the Elderly). (Illus.). 166p. 1994. 49.95 (1-56024-570-0) Haworth Pr.

University Malpractice: Essays. Jack N. Formacarr. LC 90-56277. 160p. 1991. 44.50 (1-55914-336-3); pap. 39.50 (1-55914-337-1) ABBE Pubs Assn.

University of Alabama: A Guide to the Campus. Robert Mellown. LC 87-26205. (Illus.). 128p. 1988. pap. 9.50 (0-8173-0395-2) U of Ala Pr.

University of Alabama: A Pictorial History. Suzanne R. Wolfe. LC 82-2626. (Illus.). 264p. 1983. pap. 75.30 (0-7837-8417-1, 2059228) Bks Demand.

University of Alabama: College of Commerce & Business Administration. Morris F. Mayer & Richard Melancon. (First 75 Years Ser.). 250p. 1995. 49.95 (0-9644291-0-1) U Ala Coll of C & B A.

University of Alaska Anthropological Papers: An Index. David A. Hales et al. LC 79-624596. (Elmer E. Rasmuson Library Occasional Papers: No. 6). 198p. 1979. pap. text ed. 7.50 (0-937592-02-1) U Alaska Rasmuson Lib.

University of Alberta. Photos by Phil Schofield. (Illus.). 112p. 1990. 49.00 (0-916509-52-4) Harmony Hse Pub.

University of British Columbia Hispanic Studies. Ed. by Harold U. Livermore. (Monografias A Ser.: Vol. XL). 250p. (Orig.). (ENG & SPA.). (C). 1974. pap. 27.00 (0-900411-82-1, Pub. by Tamesis Bks Ltd UK) Boydell & Brewer.

University of Calgary. Creasia. (C). (gr. 13). 1994. 4.50 (0-8151-1922-4) Mosby Yr Bk.

University of California: A Pictorial History. Albert G. Pickerell & May Dornin. (Illus.). 1968. 40.00 (0-520-01010-8) U CA Pr.

University of California Davis Book of Dogs: A Complete Medical Reference Guide for Dogs & Puppies. University of California Davis, School of Veterinary Medicine Faculty & Staff. Ed. by Mordecai Siegal. 560p. 1995. 27.50 (0-06-270136-3, Harper Ref) HarpC.

University of California Press: The Early Years, 1893-1953. Albert Muto. LC 92-20506. (C). 1993. 30.00 (0-520-07732-6) U CA Pr.

University of California San Diego Nutrition Book. Paul Saltman et al. 1993. pap. 14.95 (0-316-76981-9) Little.

University of California Sotheby Book of California Wine. Ed. by Doris Muscatine et al. LC 83-47666. (Illus.). 640p. 1984. 25.00 (0-520-05085-1) U CA Pr.

University of Cambridge & the English Revolution, 1625-1688. John Twigg. (History of the University of Cambridge: Texts & Studies). 364p. 1991. 99.00 (0-85115-497-2) Boydell & Brewer.

University of Chicago. Photos by Dan Dry. (Illus.). 112p. 1992. 39.95 (0-916509-67-2) Harmony Hse Pub.

University of Chicago Faculty: A Centennial View. Frank Yoder. LC 91-31994. 1991. pap. 7.00 (0-943056-15-2) Univ Chi Lib.

University of Chicago Graduate Problems in Physics with Solutions. Jeremiah A. Cronin et al. 272p. 1979. pap. text ed. 15.95 (0-226-12109-7, P809) U Ch Pr.

University of Chicago Law Review: 1933-1996, 63 vols. Bound set. 2,992.50 (0-8377-9174-X) Rothman.

University of Chicago Reading in Western Civilization, Vol. 9: Twentieth Century Europe. Ed. by John W. Boyer et al. LC 85-16328. (Readings in Western Civilization Ser.). 640p. (C). 1987. pap. text ed. 17.95 (0-226-06954-0) U Ch Pr.

University of Chicago Readings in Western Civilization: Medieval Europe, Vol. 4. Ed. by John W. Boyer et al. LC 85-16328. x, 462p. 1986. pap. text ed. 16.95 (0-226-06943-5); lib. bdg. 36.00 (0-226-06942-7) U Ch Pr.

University of Chicago Readings in Western Civilization: The Church in the Roman Empire, Vol. 3. Ed. by John W. Boyer et al. LC 85-16328. 256p. 1986. pap. text ed. 12.95 (0-226-06939-7); lib. bdg. 24.00 (0-226-06938-9) U Ch Pr.

University of Chicago Readings in Western Civilization: The Greek Polis, Vol. 1. Ed. by John W. Boyer et al. LC 85-16328. (Readings in Western Civilization Ser.). viii, 360p. (C). 1986. pap. text ed. 11.95 (0-226-06935-4); lib. bdg. 30.00 (0-226-06934-6) U Ch Pr.

University of Chicago Readings in Western Civilization: The Renaissance, Vol. 5. Ed. by John W. Boyer et al. LC 85-16328. (Readings in Western Civilization Ser.). x, 448p. (C). 1986. pap. text ed. 16.95 (0-226-06945-1); lib. bdg. 36.00 (0-226-06944-3) U Ch Pr.

University of Chicago Readings in Western Civilization, Vol. 2: Rome: Late Republic & Principate. Ed. by John W. Boyer et al. LC 85-16328. (Readings in Western Civilization Ser.). vii, 316p. (C). 1986. pap. text ed. 12.95 (0-226-06937-0); lib. bdg. 30.00 (0-226-06936-2) U Ch Pr.

University of Chicago Readings in Western Civilization, Vol. 6, Early Modern Europe: Crisis of Authority. Ed. by John W. Boyer et al. LC 85-16328. (Readings in Western Civilization Ser.). x, 618p. (C). 1987. pap. text ed. 17.95 (0-226-06948-6) U Ch Pr.

University of Chicago Readings in Western Civilization, Vol. 7: The Old Regime & the French Revolution. Ed. by John W. Boyer et al. LC 85-16328. (Readings in Western Civilization Ser.). x, 480p. (C). 1987. pap. text ed. 13.95 (0-226-06950-8); lib. bdg. 40.00 (0-226-06949-4) U Ch Pr.

University of Chicago Readings in Western Civilization, Vol. 8, Nineteenth-Century Europe: Liberalism & Its Critics. Ed. by John W. Boyer et al. LC 86-16328. (Readings in Western Civilization Ser.). x, 584p. (C). 1987. pap. text ed. 18.95 (0-226-06952-4); lib. bdg. 45.00 (0-226-06951-6) U Ch Pr.

University of Chicago Spanish Dictionary. 4th ed. Ed. by Chicago Editorial Staff. (Illus.). viii, 484p. (C). 1987. pap. 8.95 (0-226-10402-8) U Ch Pr.

University of Chicago Spanish Dictionary. 4th ed. Ed. by Chicago Editorial Staff. (Illus.). viii, 484p. (ENG & SPA.). (C). 1987. 23.95 (0-226-10400-1) U Ch Pr.

University of Chicago Spanish Dictionary: A New Concise Spanish-English & English-Spanish Dictionary of Words & Phrases Basic to the Written & Spoken Language of Today, 7 vols. large type ed. Castillo & Bond. 1740p. (YA). (gr. 9 up). 1967. reprint ed. Set. 434.00 (0-317-01954-6, J-23870-00) Am Printing Hse.

University of Chicago Spanish-English, English-Spanish Dictionary. 3rd ed. Carlos Castillo & Otto F. Bond. pap. 3.95 (0-317-56745-4) PB.

University of Cincinnati Law Review: 1927-1995/96, Vols. 1-64. Bound set. 3,040.00 (0-8377-9175-8) Rothman.

University of Colorado-Boulder. Photos by Jim Richardson. (Illus.). 112p. 1990. 39.00 (0-916509-54-0) Harmony Hse Pub.

University of Colorado Investigations of Paleolithic & Epipaleolithic Sites in the Sudan, Africa. Lee F. Irwin. (Nubian Ser.: No. 3). reprint ed. 20.00 (0-404-60699-7) AMS Pr.

University of Colorado Library & Its Makers, 1876-1972. Ellsworth Mason. LC 93-33714. (Illus.). 401p. 1994. 45.00 (0-8108-2685-2) Scarecrow.

University of Delaware. Photos by Kevin Fleming. (First Edition Ser.). (Illus.). 112p. 1988. 39.00 (0-916509-43-5) Harmony Hse Pub.

University of Florida. Photos by Tommy Thompson. (Illus.). 112p. 1991. 39.00 (0-916509-69-9) Harmony Hse Pub.

University of Georgia. Photos by Sam Abell. (Illus.). 112p. 1987. 37.50 (0-916509-22-2) Harmony Hse Pub.

University of Georgia: A Bicentennial History, 1785-1985. Thomas G. Dyer. LC 84-232. 448p. 1985. 34.95 (0-8203-0725-4) U of Ga Pr.

University of Guelph. Photos by John DeVisser & John De Visser. (Illus.). 112p. 1990. 49.00 (0-916509-58-3) Harmony Hse Pub.

University of Hard Knocks: Learning to Do What Winners Do. Ralph Parlette. (Illus.). 1966. 9.99 (0-915720-05-1) Brownlow Pub Co.

University of Hard Knocks: Learning to Do What Winners Do. deluxe ed. Ralph Parlette. (Illus.). 1966. 9.99 (0-915720-03-5) Brownlow Pub Co.

University of Hong Kong: An Informal History, 2 vols. Bernard Mellor. (Illus.). 428p. 1980. Set. 87.50 (962-209-023-0, Pub. by Hong Kong Univ Pr HK) Coronet Bks.

***University of Illinois.** Nardulli. Date not set. lab manual ed., pap. text ed. write for info. (0-312-17070-X) St Martin.

University of Illinois: Past & Present. (Illus.). 156p. 1995. 49.00 (1-886154-09-0) Phoenix IL.

***University of Iowa Family Practice.** Graber et al. (Illus.). 672p. (C). (gr. 13). 1997. pap. text ed. 36.95 (0-8151-2395-7, 30999) Mosby Yr Bk.

University of Iowa Football: The Hawkeyes. Chuck Bright. LC 82-50031. (College Sports Bks.). 1982. 10.95 (0-87397-233-3, Strode Pubs) Circle Bk Service.

University of Iowa in the Twentieth Century: An Institutional History. Stow Persons. LC 90-10771. (Illus.). 354p. 1990. 38.95 (0-87745-282-2) U of Iowa Pr.

University of Kansas Medical Center: A Pictorial History. Lawrence H. Larsen & Nancy J. Hulston. LC 91-44669. (Illus.). x, 222p. 1992. 35.00 (0-7006-0539-8) U Pr of KS.

University of Kentucky: A Pictorial History. Carl B. Cone. LC 89-36823. 248p. 1990. text ed. 35.00 (0-8131-1696-1) U Pr of Ky.

University of Kentucky - Then & Now. Photos by Bill Luster. (Illus.). 112p. 1993. 39.95 (1-56469-004-0) Harmony Hse Pub.

University of Kentucky Elder Care Handbook: Resources & Guidance for University Employees Helping Older Family Members. Ronald L. Burdon. 88p. 1995. pap. write for info. (0-9647559-0-4) Am Wellness.

University of Life. Mehdi Bahadori. LC 93-41303. (Illus.). 96p. (Orig.). 1993. pap. 7.95 (0-931892-70-8) B Dolphin Pub.

University of Life. Mehdi N. Bahadori. (Illus.). 83p. (Orig.). 1988. pap. 6.75 (0-9620384-0-7) M N Bahadori.

University of London & the World of Learning, 1836-1986. Ed. by F. M. Thompson. 304p. 1990. boxed 45.00 (1-85285-032-9) Hambledon Press.

***University of London Legal Series, 12 vols.** Incl. Vol. 1 Public Policy: A Comparative Study in English & French Law. Dennis Lloyd. xxii, 166p. 1996. reprint ed. 48.00 (1-56169-242-5); Vol. 2 Status in the Common Law. R. H. Graveson. xxiv, 151p. 1996. reprint ed. 48.00 (1-56169-239-5); Vol. 3 The History of Negotiable Instruments in English Law. J. Milnes Holden. xxxix, 350p. 1996. reprint ed. 95.00 (1-56169-270-0); Vol. 4 The Transfer of Chattels in Private International Law. G. A. Zaphiriou. xix, 227p. 1996. reprint ed. 75.00 (1-56169-240-9); Vol. 5 The Right to Membership of a Trade Union. R. W. Rideout. xlii, 243p. 1996. reprint ed. 85.00 (1-56169-236-0); Vol. 6 The Concept of Matrimonial Cruelty. John M. Biggs. xix, 228p. 1996. reprint ed. 75.00 (1-56169-237-9); Vol. 7 Lectures in Jurisprudence. H. F. Jolowicz. xxi, 391p. 1996. reprint ed. 125.00 (1-56169-241-7); Vol. 8 The Constructive Trust: The Case for a New Approach to English Law. D. W. Waters. xxiii, 353p. 1996. reprint ed. 110.00 (1-56169-233-6); Vol. 9 The Charter Controversy in the City of London, 1660-1688, & Its Consequences. Jennifer Levin. 119p. 1996. reprint ed. 40.00 (1-56169-235-2); Vol. 10 Law Reporting in England, 1485-1585. L. W. Abbott. xxi, 372p. 1996. reprint ed. 120.00 (1-56169-243-3); Vol. 11 Law Reform in the Muslim World. Norman Anderson. xi, 235p. 1996. reprint ed. 75.00 (1-56169-232-8); Vol. 12 The Court of King's Bench, 1450-1550. Marjorie Blatcher. xiv, 181p. 1996. reprint ed. 60.00 (1-56169-238-7); 1996. 950.00 (1-56169-234-4) Gaunt.

University of Louisville Journal of Family Law: 1961-1994/95, 33 vols., Set. Bound set. 1,562.50 (0-8377-9091-3) Rothman.

University of Melborune - Nucleus Multi-Electrode Cochlear Implant. G. M. Clark et al. (Advances in Oto-Rhino-Laryngology Ser.: Vol. 38). (Illus.). x, 190p. 1987. 107.25 (3-8055-4575-4) S Karger.

University of Miami. Photos by Brian Smith. (First Edition Ser.). (Illus.). 112p. 1988. 39.00 (0-916509-34-6) Harmony Hse Pub.

University of Miami Dictionary: English Spanish - Spanish English. 4th ed. Editorial America, S. A. Staff. Ed. by Maria E. Alvarez del Real. 592p. 1991. pap. 3.95 (1-56259-009-X) Editorial Amer.

University of Miami Hispanic-American Studies. Miami University, Hispanic American Institute Staff. Ed. by R. E. McNicoll & J. R. Owre. LC 70-117825. (Essay Index Reprint Ser.). 1977. 23.95 (0-8369-1997-1) Ayer.

University of Miami Law Center's Philip E. Heckerling Institute on Estate Planning. annuals John T. Gaubatz. 1975. Annual. ring bd. write for info. (0-8205-1755-0) Bender.

University of Michigan: Its Legal Profile. William B. Cudlip. (University of Michigan Legal Publications). xv, 367p. 1994. 38.50 (1-57588-377-5, 300190) W S Hein.

University of Missouri: An Illustrated History. James C. Olson & Vera B. Olson. LC 88-1158. (Illus.). 312p. 1988. 29.95 (0-8262-0678-6) U of Mo Pr.

University of Missouri, One Hundred Fifty Years. Audrey Walsworth. Ed. by Bill Kuykendall. 112p. 1989. text ed. 42.75 (0-940213-32-X) Walsworth Pub.

University of Montana: A Pictorial History. Stan B. Cohen & Don C. Miller. LC 80-53616. (Illus.). 96p. 1980. pap. 5.95 (0-933126-12-3) Pictorial Hist.

University of Nebraska National Championship 1994. Tom Vint. Ed. by Amy Vail & Jeff Huneycutt. 184p. 1995. text ed. 39.95 (0-943860-10-5) UMI Pubns.

University of Nevada, Reno, Oral History, 1970-71. Ed. by Mary E. Glass. (History Ser.). 157p. 1971. lib. bdg. 34.50 (1-56475-111-2); fiche write for info. (1-56475-112-0) U NV Oral Hist.

University of Nevada, Reno, Oral History, 1971-72. Ed. by Mary E. Glass. 432p. 1972. lib. bdg. 62.50 (1-56475-125-2); fiche write for info. (1-56475-126-0) U NV Oral Hist.

University of Nevada, Reno, Oral History, 1972-73. Ed. by Mary E. Glass. (University History Ser.). 321p. 1973. lib. bdg. 50.50 (1-56475-134-1); fiche write for info. (1-56475-135-X) U NV Oral Hist.

University of Nevada, Reno, Oral History, 1973-74. Ed. by Mary E. Glass. (University History Ser.). 523p. 1974. lib. bdg. 70.50 (1-56475-138-4); fiche write for info. (1-56475-139-2) U NV Oral Hist.

University of New South Wales: The Baxter Years. A. H. Willis. (Illus.). 27.95 (0-614-13108-1, Pub. by New South Wales Univ Pr AT) Intl Spec Bk.

University of Newark Law Review: 1936-1942, Vols. 1-7. Bound set. 85.00 (0-8377-9213-4) Rothman.

University of Northern Iowa Department of Art Annual Faculty Exhibition. Daniel E. Stetson. Ed. by Kevin Boatright. LC 82-50565. 16p. (Orig.). 1982. pap. text ed. 2.00 (0-685-05598-1) U of NI Dept Art.

University of Notre Dame: A Contemporary Portrait. Robert Schmuhl. LC 86-40246. 160p. 1986. text ed. 19.50 (0-268-01916-9) U of Notre Dame Pr.

University of Notre Dame: A Contemporary Portrait. 2nd ed. Robert P. Schmuhl. LC 86-40246. (Illus.). (C). 1988. pap. text ed. 11.50 (0-268-01918-5) U of Notre Dame Pr.

University of Pennsylvania & the U. S. Navy: The V-12 at Penn in World War II. Robert B. Hamilton, Jr. LC 95-94809. 250p. 1995. 20.00 (0-9648802-0-2) Hamilton Bks.

University of Pennsylvania Law Review: 1852-1995/96, 144 vols. Bound set. 7,730.00 (0-8377-9178-2) Rothman.

University of Pennsylvania Library: Philadelphia, 1888-1891. Edward Bosley. (Architecture in Detail Ser.). 60p. (Orig.). 1996. pap. 29.95 (0-7148-3389-4, Pub. by Phaidon Press UK) Chronicle Bks.

UV

An Asterisk (*) at the beginning of an entry indicates that the title is appearing in BIP for the first time.

University of Pittsburgh - Then & Now. Photos by Scott Goldsmith. (First Edition Ser.). (Illus.). 112p. 1992. 39. 00 (*0-916509-88-5*) Harmony Hse Pub.

University of Puget Sound Law Review: 1977-1993, 19 vols. Set. 762.50 (*0-8377-9221-5*) Rothman.

University of Redlands - Then & Now. Photos by Bob Holmes. (First Edition Ser.). (Illus.). 112p. 1992. 39.95 (*0-916509-99-0*) Harmony Hse Pub.

University of Rochester. Photos by Ira Block. (First Edition Ser.). (Illus.). 112p. 1988. 39.00 (*0-916509-36-2*) Harmony Hse Pub.

University of San Francisco. Photos by Phil Schermeister. (Illus.). 112p. 1987. 37.50 (*0-916509-24-9*) Harmony Hse Pub.

University of San Francisco Law Review: 1966-1995/96, 30 vols. Bound set. 1,325.00 (*0-8377-9179-0*) Rothman.

University of Santa Clara: A History, 1851-1977. Gerald McKevitt. LC 78-65396. (Illus.). xii, 385p. 1979. 47.50 (*0-8047-1024-4*) Stanford U Pr.

University of Spiritualism. Harry Boddington. 1972. 59.95 (*0-8490-1248-1*) Gordon Pr.

University of Success. Og Mandino. 544p. 1983. pap. 15.95 (*0-553-34535-4*) Bantam.

University of Tennessee, Memphis 75th Anniversary: Medical Accomplishments. James E. Hammer, III. LC 86-16170. (Illus.). 320p. 1986. 25.00 (*0-9616311-3-9*) Univ TN Alumni.

University of Texas at Austin: A History of Campus Buildings, 1883-1992. Margaret C. Berry. Ed. by Richard Pennington. 195p. 1992. text ed. 50.00 (*0-9623171-9-5*) LBCo Pub.

University of Texas Buildings: A History. Margaret C. Berry. (Illus.). 200p. 1994. 25.00 (*0-614-04440-5*) LBCo Pub.

University of the Future: Problems & Prospects. Ed. by Marilyn R. Waldman. 142p. (Orig.). 1989. pap. 10.00 (*0-9625041-0-6*) OSU Ctr CSITH.

University of the Future: The Yugoslav Experience. Miroslav Pecujlit. Tr. by Tanja Lorkovic. LC 86-31899. (Contributions to the Study of Education Ser.: No. 22). 211p. 1987. text ed. 49.95 (*0-313-25430-3*, PUF/, Greenwood Pr) Greenwood.

University of the State of New York: History of Higher Education in the State of New York. Sidney Sherwood. 538p. 1993. reprint ed. lib. bdg. 99.00 (*0-7812-5321-7*) Rprt Serv.

University of Toronto. Ed. by William Strode & William Butler. (Illus.). 112p. 1990. 49.00 (*0-916509-61-3*) Harmony Hse Pub.

University of Toronto Doctoral Theses, 1897-1967: A Bibliography. Judy Mills & Irene Dombre. LC 75-354611. 197p. reprint ed. pap. 56.20 (*0-317-41719-3*, 2055822) Bks Demand.

University of Toulouse in the Middle Ages. Cyril E. Smith. 1959. 20.00 (*0-87462-402-9*) Marquette.

University of Utah Anthropological Papers, 81 vols., Set. Utah University, Department Of Anthropology Staff. Incl. Set. Glen Canyon Series. , 32 vols. LC 78-123. reprint ed. 1,089.00 (*0-404-60630-X*); Upper Colorado Series. , 9 vols. LC 78-123. reprint ed. Set. 252.00 (*0-404-60670-9*); Nubian Series. , 4 vols. LC 78-123. reprint ed. Set. 116.50 (*0-404-60690-3*); LC 78-123. reprint ed. 2,425.00 (*0-404-60600-8*) AMS Pr.

University of Vermont Graduate Theses on Vermont Topics, 1975-1992. Ed. by Kristin Peterson-Ishaq. (Ocassional Papers: No. 15). 246p. 1993. pap. 17.00 (*0-944277-24-1*) U VT Ctr Rsch VT.

University of Vermont Libraries Folklore & Oral History Catalogue. rev. ed. Intro. by Connell B. Gallagher. 133p. 1991. pap. text ed. 10.00 (*0-944277-22-5*) U VT Ctr Rsch VT.

University of Vermont Student Research on Vermont Topics. Ed. by Carolyn Perry. (Occasional Papers: No. 1). 66p. (Orig.). 1979. pap. text ed. 4.00 (*0-944277-02-0*, U52) U VT Ctr Rsch VT.

University of Virginia: Charlottesville 1817-26 Thomas Jefferson. Michael Brawne. (Architecture in Detail Ser.). (Illus.). 60p. (C). 1994. pap. 29.95 (*0-7148-2752-5*, Pub. by Phaidon Press UK) Chronicle Bks.

University of Virginia - Then & Now. Charles Shoftner et al. (Illus.). 112p. 1988. 39.00 (*0-916509-49-4*) Harmony Hse Pub.

University of Virginia Edition of the Works of Stephen Crane, Vol. 5: Tales of Adventure. Stephen Crane. Ed. by Fredson Bowers. LC 68-8536. 440p. reprint ed. pap. 125.40 (*0-7837-2432-2*, 2042580) Bks Demand.

University of Virginia's Impact on the Charlottesville & Metropolitan Areas. 1990. 12.00 (*0-317-69878-8*) U VA Ctr Pub Serv.

University of Western Ontario. John De Visser. (First Edition Ser.). (Illus.). 112p. 1988. 49.00 (*0-916509-38-9*) Harmony Hse Pub.

University of Wisconsin: A History, 1848-1925, Vol. 1. Merle E. Curti & Vernon Carstensen. LC 48-47638. 759p. 1974. reprint ed. pap. 180.00 (*0-608-01862-7*, 2062513) Bks Demand.

University of Wisconsin: A Pictorial History. Arthur Hove. LC 90-26466. (Illus.). 366p. 1991. 50.00 (*0-299-13000-2*) U of Wis Pr.

University of Wisconsin: Madison Department of Art Quadrennial Exhibition. (Illus.). (Orig.). 1994. pap. text ed. 12.95 (*0-932900-37-2*) Elvehjem Mus.

University of Wisconsin: One Hundred & Twenty-Five Years. Ed. by Allan G. Bogue & Robert Taylor. LC 74-27306. (Illus.). 302p. 1975. 17.50 (*0-299-06840-4*) U of Wis Pr.

University of Wisconsin Vol. III: A History: Politics, Depression, & War, 1925-1945. E. David Cronon & John W. Jenkins. LC 48-47638. (Illus.). 920p. 1994. 35. 00 (*0-299-14430-5*) U of Wis Pr.

University of Wisconsin-Madison & the Local & State Economies: A Second Look. William A. Strang et al. 1985. pap. 10.00 (*0-86603-019-0*) Bur Busn Wis.

University of Wisconsin Medical School: A Chronicle, 1848-1948. Paul F. Clark. LC 67-12004. (Illus.). 311p. reprint ed. pap. 88.70 (*0-8357-4742-5*, 2037663) Bks Demand.

University of Wisconsin, Vol. 2: A History, 1848-1925. Merle E. Curti. 678p. 1949. 22.50 (*0-299-80572-7*) U of Wis Pr.

University on Trial: The Case of the University of North Carolina. Robert A. Dentler et al. 212p. 1984. reprint ed. lib. bdg. 58.50 (*0-8191-4083-X*) U Pr of Amer.

University Outside Europe. Ed. by Edward Bradby. LC 71-107684. (Essay Index Reprint Ser.). 1977. 23.95 (*0-8369-1548-8*) Ayer.

University Physics. Harris Benson. 114p. 1991. Net. 13.00 (*0-471-53954-6*) Wiley.

University Physics. Harris Benson. 149p. 1991. trans. 55.00 (*0-471-51872-7*) Wiley.

University Physics. Edwin Jones. (C). 1997. text ed. write for info. (*0-201-56981-7*) Addison-Wesley.

University Physics. William Moebs & Jeff Sanny. 350p. 1995. student ed., pap. text ed. write for info. (*0-697-05886-7*) Wm C Brown Pubs.

University Physics. William Moebs & Jeff Sanny. 224p. (C). 1995. student ed., per. write for info. (*0-697-23258-1*) Wm C Brown Pubs.

University Physics. William Moebs & Jeff Sanny. 1072p. (C). 1995. text ed. write for info. (*0-697-05884-0*) Wm C Brown Pubs.

***University Physics.** Sanny & Moebs. 1995. teacher ed., pap. text ed. 28.75 (*0-697-05887-5*) McGraw.

University Physics. Francis W. Sears et al. LC 81-17551. (Physics Ser.). (Illus.). 900p. 1982. student ed., teacher ed. 1.00 (*0-201-07226-2*); student ed. write for info. (*0-201-07224-6*); student ed. 9.95 (*0-201-07225-4*) Addison-Wesley.

University Physics. expanded ed. Edwin R. Jones. (C). 1997. text ed. write for info. (*0-201-82325-X*) Addison-Wesley.

University Physics. expanded ed. Jeff Sanny & William Moebs. 1000p. (C). 1996. text ed. write for info. (*0-697-27337-7*) Wm C Brown Pubs.

University Physics, 2 vols. 2nd ed. George B. Arfken et al. 1000p. (C). 1989. Set. text ed. 61.25 (*0-15-592977-1*) SCP.

University Physics. 2nd ed. Hudson. (C). 1990. student ed., pap. text ed. 20.75 (*0-03-046984-8*) HB Coll Pubs.

University Physics. 2nd ed. Hudson. (C). 1990. teacher ed., pap. text ed. 34.00 (*0-03-047172-9*) HB Coll Pubs.

University Physics. 2nd ed. Hudson. (C). 1990. pap. text ed. 20.75 (*0-03-046987-2*) HB Coll Pubs.

University Physics, 2 vols. 2nd ed. Alvin Hudson & Rex Nelson. 992p. (C). 1990. Set. text ed. 57.25 (*0-03-046979-1*) SCP.

University Physics. 6th ed. Francis W. Sears et al. LC 81-17551. (Physics Ser.). (Illus.). 900p. (C). 1982. text ed. 48.50 (*0-201-07195-9*) Addison-Wesley.

University Physics. 7th ed. Francis W. Sears et al. LC 85-28801. (Illus.). 976p. (C). 1987. Answer guide. 2.25 (*0-201-06685-8*) Addison-Wesley.

University Physics. 8th ed. Hugh D. Young. (C). 1992. text ed. 69.95 (*0-201-19651-4*) Addison-Wesley.

University Physics. 8th ed. Hugh D. Young. (C). 1992. student ed., pap. text ed. 16.95 (*0-201-19652-2*) Addison-Wesley.

***University Physics.** 9th ed. Hugh D. Young. (C). 1996. pap. text ed. write for info. (*0-201-31132-1*) Addison-Wesley.

University Physics. 9th ed. Hugh D. Young. (C). 1996. text ed. 77.50 (*0-201-57157-9*); text ed. 84.95 (*0-201-57158-7*) Addison-Wesley.

***University Physics.** 9th ed. Hugh D. Young. (C). 1996. text ed. 98.95 (*0-201-18563-6*) Addison-Wesley.

University Physics. 9th ed. Hugh D. Young. (C). 1996. student ed., pap. text ed. 15.95 (*0-201-64059-7*) Addison-Wesley.

University Physics, Extend. Version. 9th expanded ed. Hugh D. Young & Roger A. Freedman. LC 95-15917. (C). 1996. text ed. 80.50 (*0-201-64044-9*) Addison-Wesley.

University Physics, No. 1. Ulrich Eschholz. 95p. (C). 1993. student ed. 13.84 (*1-56870-074-1*) RonJon Pub.

University Physics, Std. Version. 9th ed. Hugh D. Young & Roger A. Freedman. (C). 1996. text ed. 69.95 (*0-201-50583-5*) Addison-Wesley.

University Physics, Vol. 1. 2nd ed. George B. Arfken et al. 467p. (C). 1989. text ed. 37.25 (*0-15-592974-7*) HB Coll Pubs.

University Physics, Vol. 1. 8th ed. Hugh D. Young. (C). 1992. text ed. 45.95 (*0-201-52195-4*) Addison-Wesley.

University Physics, Vol. 1. 9th ed. Hugh D. Young. (C). 1996. text ed. 55.50 (*0-201-57155-2*); pap. text ed. 42.50 (*0-201-87446-6*) Addison-Wesley.

University Physics, 2 vols., Vol. 1: Chapters 1-23. 2nd ed. Alvin Hudson & Rex Nelson. 452p. (C). 1990. text ed. 39.00 (*0-03-046982-1*) SCP.

University Physics, Vol. 2. Hugh D. Young. (C). 1992. student ed., pap. text ed. 19.50 (*0-201-55709-6*) Addison-Wesley.

University Physics, 2 vols., Vol. 2. rev. ed. Harris Benson. 1996. text ed. write for info. (*0-471-15264-1*) Wiley.

University Physics, 2 vols., Vol. 2. rev. ed. Harris Benson. LC 95-41514. 1024p. 1995. pap. text ed. 54.50 (*0-471-00689-0*) Wiley.

University Physics, Vol. 2. 8th ed. Hugh D. Young. (C). 1992. text ed. 43.95 (*0-201-52196-2*) Addison-Wesley.

University Physics, Vol. 2. 9th ed. Young. (C). 1996. text ed. 48.95 (*0-201-64046-5*) Addison-Wesley.

University Physics, Vol. 2. 9th ed. Hugh D. Young. (C). 1996. text ed. 55.50 (*0-201-57156-0*); pap. text ed. 42.50 (*0-201-87447-4*) Addison-Wesley.

University Physics, Vol. 2. 9th ed. Hugh D. Young & Freedman. Ed. by Julie Berrisford. (C). 1996. pap. text ed. 15.95 (*0-201-44168-3*) Addison-Wesley.

University Physics, Vol. 2. 9th ed. Hugh D. Young & Freedman. Ed. by Julie Berrisford. (C). 1996. student ed., pap. text ed. 20.50 (*0-201-64058-9*) Addison-Wesley.

University Physics, 2 vols., Vol. 2: Chapters 23-42. 2nd ed. George B. Arfken et al. 1000p. (C). 1989. text ed. 37.25 (*0-15-592975-5*) SCP.

University Physics, 2 vols., Vol. 2: Chapters 24-45. 2nd ed. Alvin Hudson & Rex Nelson. 540p. (C). 1990. text ed. 39.00 (*0-03-046983-X*) SCP.

***University Physics, Vol. III.** Jeff Sanny & William Moebs. 24p. (C). 1996. student ed. write for info. (*0-697-34338-3*) Wm C Brown Pubs.

University Physics: An Extended Version. 8th ed. Hugh D. Young. (C). 1992. text ed. 46.95 (*0-201-52981-5*) Addison-Wesley.

University Physics: Models & Applications. William P. Crummett & Arthur B. Western. (Illus.). 1248p. (C). 1994. text ed. write for info. (*0-697-11199-7*) Wm C Brown Pubs.

University Physics: Models & Applications. William P. Crummett & Arthur B. Western. (Illus.). 1248p. (C). 1994. Study guide. student ed., spiral bd. write for info. (*0-697-11204-7*) Wm C Brown Pubs.

University Physics: Models & Applications. William P. Crummett & Arthur B. Western. 100p. 1994. student ed. write for info. (*0-697-27240-0*) Wm C Brown Pubs.

University Physics: Models & Applications. William P. Crummett & Arthur B. Western. (Illus.). 1248p. (C). 1995. Solutions manual. student ed., spiral bd. write for info. (*0-697-16426-8*) Wm C Brown Pubs.

University Physics: Updated Problems Version, 2 vols. Hugh D. Young & Roger A. Freedman. Incl. University Physics Vol. 1: Updated Problems Version. 8th ed. 672p. (C). 1994. text ed. (*0-201-59327-0*); University Physics Vol. 2: Updated Problems Version. 8th ed. 784p. (C). 1994. text ed. (*0-201-59328-9*); write for info. (*0-201-59325-4*) Addison-Wesley.

University Physics Part. 1, Vol. 1. 9th ed. Hugh D. Young et al. (C). 1996. student ed., pap. text ed. 19.50 (*0-201-64057-0*) Addison-Wesley.

University Physics Vol. 1, Vol. 1. 9th ed. Hugh D. Young et al. 688p. (C). 1996. text ed. 47.95 (*0-201-64045-7*) Addison-Wesley.

University Physics Vol. I: Mechanics & Thermo Dynamics. Jeff Sanny & William Moebs. 456p. (C). 1995. per. write for info. (*0-697-29949-X*) Wm C Brown Pubs.

University Physics Vol. II: Electricity, Magnetism & Optics. Jeff Sanny & William Moebs. 424p. (C). 1995. per. write for info. (*0-697-29950-3*) Wm C Brown Pubs.

University Physics Vol. III: Modern Physics. Jeff Sanny & William Moeb. 240p. (C). 1995. write for info. (*0-697-29951-1*) Wm C Brown Pubs.

University Physics Extended: Updated Problems Version. 8th ed. Hugh D. Young & Roger A. Freedman. 2456p. (C). 1994. text ed. write for info. (*0-201-59326-2*) Addison-Wesley.

University Physics I. Kenneth E. Jesse. (College Outline Ser.). 306p. (C). 1987. pap. text ed. 12.25 (*0-15-601668-0*) HarBrace.

University Physics II. Kenneth E. Jesse. (HBJ College Outlines Ser.). 376p. (C). 1992. pap. text ed. 14.50 (*0-15-601685-0*) Dryden Pr.

University Physics Student Solutions Manual. 8th ed. Hugh D. Young. (C). 1992. pap. text ed. 19.50 (*0-201-19653-0*) Addison-Wesley.

University Physics, Vol. 1, Updated Problems Version see University Physics: Updated Problems Version

University Physics, Vol. 2, Updated Problems Version see University Physics: Updated Problems Version

University Politics: F. M. Cornford's Cambridge & His Advice to the Young Academic Politician. Gordon Johnson. (Illus.). 128p. (C). 1994. pap. text ed. 14.95 (*0-521-46919-8*) Cambridge U Pr.

University Politics: F. M. Cornford's Cambridge & His Advice to the Young Academic Politician. Gordon Johnson. 120p. (C). 1994. text ed. 39.95 (*0-521-47547-3*) Cambridge U Pr.

University President in Arizona, 1945-1980: An Oral History. Michael V. Belok & Thomas H. Metos. LC 89-49146. (Studies in Education: Vol. 7). 296p. 1990. lib. bdg. 89.95 (*0-88946-942-3*) E Mellen.

University Press of America Publication Masnavi Ravayeh. Ali N. Salaheddin. 60p. (Orig.). 1990. 34.00 (*0-910735-31-X*); pap. 19.25 (*0-910735-32-8*) MTO Printing & Pubn Ctr.

University Problems in the United States. Daniel C. Gilman. LC 75-89182. (American Educatio: Its Men, Institutions, & Ideas. Series 1). 1978. reprint ed. 18.95 (*0-405-01419-8*) Ayer.

University Problems in the United States. Daniel C. Gilman. 1972. reprint ed. lib. bdg. 29.00 (*0-8422-8058-8*) Irvington.

University Programs in Computer-Aided Engineering, Design, & Manufacturing. Ed. by Ken P. Chong et al. 346p. 1989. pap. text ed. 44.00 (*0-87262-709-8*) Am Soc Civil Eng.

***University Records Retention & Disposition Schedule.** 236p. 1991. ring bd. 8.00 (*0-86526-246-2*) NC Archives.

University Reform of Tsar Alexander I, 1802-1835. James T. Flynn. LC 88-3184. 299p. 1988. reprint ed. pap. 85. 30 (*0-7837-9121-6*, 2049922) Bks Demand.

University Research: Social & Political Implications: A Bibliography. Ed. by Joan Nordquist. (Contemporary Social Issues: A Bibliographic Ser.: No. 3). 1986. pap. 15.00 (*0-937855-05-7*) Ref Rsch Serv.

University Research Park: The First Twenty Years. Dean W. Colvard et al. 128p. 1988. 19.95 (*0-945344-00-7*) UNC Charlotte Urban Inst.

University Science & Engineering Libraries. 2nd ed. Ellis Mount. LC 84-6530. (Contributions in Librarianship & Information Science Ser.: No. 49). (Illus.). x, 303p. 1985. text ed. 59.95 (*0-313-23949-5*, MOU/, Greenwood Pr) Greenwood.

University Science Facilities: 100 Project Profiles. Ed. by Holly Lloyd & Lee Ingalls. (Illus.). 250p. (Orig.). 1992. pap. 95.00 (*0-9627204-1-0*) Tradeline.

University Secrets: Your Guide to Surviving a College Education. Robert D. Honigman. 352p. (Orig.). 1997. pap. 19.95 (*0-9648846-5-8*) Honey Pubng.

University Services & Auxiliary Enterprises: A Case Study. Archie W. Earl, Sr. (Higher Education Ser.). 100p. (C). 1993. text ed. 34.95 (*1-884169-12-0*); pap. text ed. 19.95 (*1-884169-13-9*) Intl Educ Improve.

University Spin-off Companies: Economic Development, Faculty Entrepreneurs, & Technology Transfer. Ed. by Alistair Brett et al. 240p. (C). 1990. lib. bdg. 59.00 (*0-8476-7646-3*) Rowman.

University Student: A Study of Behavior & Values. Charles D. Bolton & Kenneth C. Kammeyer. 1967. pap. 19.95 (*0-8084-0308-7*) NCUP.

University Student: Background Profile & Stance. Krishna Chakrabortty. 1985. 10.00 (*0-8364-1480-2*, Pub. by KP Bagchi IA) S Asia.

University Students & African Politics. Ed. by William J. Hanna. LC 73-89778. 400p. 1975. 37.95 (*0-8419-0145-7*, Africana) Holmes & Meier.

University Students & Revolution in Cuba, 1920-1968. Jaime Suchlicki. LC 69-19866. 1969. 10.95 (*0-87024-108-7*) U of Miami Pr.

University Success: The Christian Perspective. Josephine Shangkuan-Ong. 192p. (C). 1996. per. 26.19 (*0-8403-7652-9*) Kendall-Hunt.

***University Success: The Christian Perspective.** Josephine Shangkuan-Ong. 256p. (C). 1996. per., pap. text ed. 26. 95 (*0-7872-2788-9*) Kendall-Hunt.

University System & Economic Development in Mexico since 1929. David E. Lorey. LC 93-20289. 288p. (C). 1993. 39.50 (*0-8047-2124-6*) Stanford U Pr.

University Teacher As Artist. Joseph Axelrod. LC 73-3773. (Jossey-Bass Higher Education Ser.). 262p. reprint ed. pap. 74.70 (*0-317-42098-4*, 2052159) Bks Demand.

University Teaching: A Guide for Graduate Students. Ed. by Leo Lambert et al. 200p. 1995. pap. 15.00 (*0-8156-2637-1*) Syracuse U Pr.

University Wine Course. Marian Baldy. (Illus.). 380p. 1992. pap. 24.95 (*0-932664-67-9*) Wine Appreciation.

University Wine Course. Marian Baldy. LC 92-50668. 426p. 1993. 24.95 (*0-932664-69-5*) Wine Appreciation.

University Work of the United Lutheran Church in America: A Study of the Work among Lutheran Students at Non-Lutheran Institutions. Howard M. Le Sourd. LC 70-176990. (Columbia University. Teachers College. Contributions to Education Ser.: No. 377). reprint ed. 37.50 (*0-404-55377-X*) AMS Pr.

***University/Industry Materials Research Exchange.** 72p. 1996. pap. 40.00 (*1-86125-017-7*, Pub. by Inst Materials UK) Ashgate Pub Co.

Universo: Look Up, Level 2. Richard Vaughan. (Let Me Read Ser.). (J). 1996. 2.95 (*0-673-36329-5*, GoodYrBooks) Addison-Wesley Educ.

Universoty of the WORD see Universite de la Parole

Universtat Unterm Hakenkreuz, Teil 1: Der Professor im Dritten Reich. 650p. (GER.). 1991. lib. bdg. 198.00 (*3-598-22629-2*) K G Saur.

Univex Story. Cynthia A. Repinski. LC 91-71477. (Illus.). 272p. 1991. 34.95 (*0-931838-17-7*) Centennial Photo Serv.

UNIX. Richard K. Miller & Terri C. Walker. LC 88-82060. (Survey on Technology & Markets Ser.: No. 84). 50p. 1989. pap. text ed. 200.00 (*1-55865-083-0*) Future Tech Surveys.

UNIX: A Minimal Manual. Jim Moore. LC 88-29943. 238p. (C). 1995. pap. text ed. write for info. (*0-7167-8195-6*) W H Freeman.

UNIX: Essentials. North. 1996. pap. text ed. 34.00 (*0-13-123738-1*) P-H.

***UNIX: Its Use, Control & Audit.** Coopers & Lybrand LLP Staff. Ed. by Lee A. Campbell. 136p. 1995. pap. 65.00 (*0-89413-344-6*, A899) Inst Inter Aud.

UNIX: Self Teaching Guide. George W. Leach. 272p. 1992. pap. text ed. 22.95 (*0-471-57924-6*) Wiley.

UNIX: Self-Teaching Guide & Portable UNIX, 2 vols., Set. George W. Leach & Douglas W. Topham. 560p. 1993. pap. text ed. 34.90 (*0-471-59678-7*) Wiley.

UNIX: The Basics. Kevin Reichard. LC 94-30873. 1995. pap. 19.95 (*1-55828-362-5*) MIS Press.

UNIX: The Book. Banahan. 265p. 1987. teacher ed. 25.00 (*0-318-33343-0*, Pub. by Sigma Pr UK) Bk Clearing Hse.

UNIX: The Book. Banahan. 265p. 1987. reprint ed. text ed. 20.08 (*0-905104-21-8*, Pub. by Sigma Pr UK) Bk Clearing Hse.

UNIX: Working with UNIX & XENIX. (Prisma Computer Courses Ser.). (Illus.). 200p. (Orig.). 1995. pap. 12.95 (*1-85365-380-2*, Pub. by Spectrum UK) Seven Hills Bk.

Unix - An Open Systems Dictionary: The Authoritative Source of Jargon-Free Definitions for More Than Six Thousand Common & Uncommon Open Systems Terms. William H. Holt & Rockie J. Morgan. LC 95-100611. 512p. 1994. pap. 24.95 (*0-945264-14-3*) Resolution Busn Pr.

UV

UNIX - the Complete Book: A Guide for the Professional User. Jason J. Manger. 468p. (Orig.). 1991. pap. 67.50 (*1-85058-219-X*, Pub. by Sigma Press UK) Coronet Bks.
UNIX Administration Guide for System V. Rebecca Thomas & Rick Farrow. (Illus.). 500p. 1992. pap. 34.95 (*0-13-942889-5*) P-H.
UNIX Administration Guide for System V, Version IV. 2nd ed. Rebecca Thomas & Rick Farrow. 750p. pap. 37.00 (*0-13-932385-6*) P-H.
UNIX & TCP/IP for the Mainframer. David B. Horvath. (Illus.). 300p. 1996. pap. 35.00 (*1-878956-64-7*) CBM Bks.
***Unix & Windows NT.** Williams G. Robert. (C). 1997. pap. text ed. write for info. (*0-201-18536-9*) Addison-Wesley.
UNIX & X Command Compendium: A Dictionary for High Level Computing. Alan Southerton & Edwin C. Perkins, Jr. 623p. 1994. text ed. 49.95 (*0-471-01281-5*); pap. text ed. 19.95 (*0-471-30982-6*) Wiley.
UNIX Audit: Using UNIX to Audit UNIX. Michael G. Grottola. 1993. pap. text ed. 32.95 (*0-07-025127-4*) McGraw.
Unix Benchmark & Test Suite. Rodney C. Wilson. 1995. pap. text ed. 52.00 (*0-13-125634-3*) P-H.
Unix Book of Games. Janice Winsor. LC 96-3207. 1996. pap. text ed. 29.95 incl. cd-rom (*0-13-490079-0*) P-H.
UNIX Book of Games. Janice Winsor. 1996. 29.95 incl. cd-rom (*0-614-14487-6*) P-H Pro Soft.
UNIX by Example: A Handbook for New Users. P. K. McBride. 250p. 1993. pap. 31.95 (*0-7506-0637-1*) Buttrwrth-Heinemann.
UNIX C Shell Desk Reference. Martin R. Arick. 224p. 1993. pap. text ed. 34.95 (*0-471-55680-7*, GD3234) Wiley.
UNIX C Shell Field Guide. Gail Anderson & Paul Anderson. (Illus.). 374p. (C). 1992. 44.95 (*0-13-937468-X*) P-H.
UNIX Companion. John Colasante. 1995. ring bd. 89.00 (*0-929321-16-2*) WEKA Pub.
UNIX Companion: A Handbook for Everyone. Harley Hahn. 832p. 1995. pap. text ed. 29.95 (*0-07-882149-5*) Osborne-McGraw.
UNIX Desk Reference: The Human Pages. Peter Dyson. 523p. 1996. pap. text ed. 29.99 (*0-7821-1658-2*) Sybex.
UNIX Desktop Handbook (SVR4.2 MP) Unix System Laboratories Staff. (Illus.). 608p. (C). 1994. pap. text ed. 62.00 (*0-13-157892-8*) P-H.
Unix Desktop Quickstart. Unix System Laboratories Staff. 1993. pap. text ed. 18.00 (*0-13-176538-8*) P-H.
UNIX Developer's Tool Kit. Kevin E. Leininger. LC 93-44068. (J. Ranade Workstation Ser.). 1994. text ed. 65.00 (*0-07-911836-4*); pap. text ed. 49.95 (*0-685-70129-8*) McGraw.
UNIX Dictionary of Commands, Terms & Acronyms. John Levine & Margaret L. Young. 1996. text ed. 39.50 (*0-07-037643-3*); pap. text ed. 24.95 (*0-07-037644-1*) McGraw.
UNIX Distributed Programming. Chris Brown. LC 93-49622. 250p. 1994. pap. text ed. 44.00 (*0-13-075896-5*) P-H Gen Ref & Trav.
UNIX Document Processing & Typesetting. Ed. by B. Srinivasan & K. Ranai. 200p. (C). 1993. text ed. 48.00 (*981-02-0605-4*) World Scientific Pub.
UNIX Environment. A. N. Walker. LC 84-13046. (Illus.). 163p. reprint ed. pap. 46.50 (*0-7837-4397-1*, 2044137) Bks Demand.
Unix for Application Developers. William A. Parrette. 352p. 1991. pap. text ed. 32.95 (*0-07-031697-X*) McGraw.
UNIX for Dummies. John Levine & Margaret L. Young. (Illus.). 375p. 1993. pap. 19.95 (*1-878058-58-4*) IDG Bks.
UNIX for Dummies. 2nd ed. John Levine. 384p. 1995. pap. 19.99 (*1-56884-905-2*) IDG Bks.
***UNIX for Dummies.** 3rd ed. John Levine & Margaret L. Young. 384p. 1997. pap. 19.99 (*0-7645-0130-5*, Dummies Tech) IDG Bks.
Unix for Dummies Quick Reference. 2nd ed. Margaret Levine-Young. 1995. pap. 12.99 (*1-56884-979-6*) IDG Bks.
Unix for Engineers. D. C. Williams. (C). 1997. pap. text ed. write for info. (*0-8053-6487-0*) Addison-Wesley.
UNIX for MVS Users. Harry S. Singh. LC 96-19154. 536p. (C). 1996. pap. text ed. 40.00 (*0-13-442989-3*) P-H.
UNIX for Programmers & Users: A Complete Guide. Graham Glass. 592p. 1993. pap. text ed. 44.33 (*0-13-480880-0*) P-H.
UNIX for Software Developers. Gary Perlman. 250p. 1993. pap. 24.00 (*0-13-932997-8*) P-H.
UNIX for the IBM-PC. Paul M. Chirlian. 192p. (C). 1990. pap. text ed. 46.00 (*0-675-20785-1*, Merrill Coll) P-H.
Unix for the Impatient. Paul W. Abrahams & Bruce R. Larson. LC 95-14174. (Illus.). 400p. (C). 1992. pap. text ed. 29.25 (*0-201-55703-7*) Addison-Wesley.
***UNIX for the Impatient.** Paul W. Abrahams & Bruce R. Larson. Ed. by Karen Wernholm. 896p. 1996. pap. text ed. 49.44 (*0-201-41979-3*) Addison-Wesley.
UNIX for the Impatient. 2nd ed. Abrahams. 1995. pap. text ed. 29.25 (*0-201-60965-7*) Addison-Wesley.
Unix for the Impatient. 2nd ed. Paul W. Abrahams & Bruce R. Larson. LC 95-14174. (C). 1996. pap. text ed. 26.95 (*0-201-82376-4*) Addison-Wesley.
***Unix for the Mainframer: The Essential Reference for Commands, Conversions & TP, IP.** David B. Horvath. LC 97-14545. (C). 1997. 49.00 (*0-13-632837-7*) P-H.
UNIX for the MS-DOS User. Kenneth Pugh. LC 93-46801. 240p. 1994. pap. 22.95 (*0-13-146077-3*) P-H.
UNIX for VMS Users. Philip E. Bourne. (VAX Users Ser.). (Illus.). 368p. (Orig.). (C). 1989. 36.95 (*1-55558-034-3*, EY-C177E-DP, Digital DEC) Buttrwrth-Heinemann.
UNIX Guide for DOS Users. Allen G. Taylor. 1990. pap. 21.95 (*1-55828-024-3*) MIS Press.
UNIX-Hater Handbook. Simson Garfinkle. 288p. 1994. pap. 16.95 (*1-56884-203-1*) IDG Bks.
UNIX in a Nutshell: System V Edition. 2nd ed. Daniel Gilly. Ed. by O'Reilly & Associates Staff & Mike Loukides. (Nutshell Handbook Ser.). (Illus.). 444p. 1992. pap. text ed. 9.95 (*1-56592-001-5*) OReilly & Assocs.
UNIX in Easy Steps. M. Azam. 1993. write for info. (*81-224-0552-5*, Pub. by Wiley Estrn II) Franklin.
Unix in Plain English. Kevin Reichard & Eric F. Johnson. 304p. 1994. pap. 14.95 (*1-55828-345-5*) MIS Press.
***UNIX in Plain English.** 2nd ed. Kevin Reichard & Eric Foster-Johnson. 1997. pap. write for info. (*0-614-28502-X*) MIS Press.
***UNIX in Plain English.** 2nd ed. Kevin Reichard. LC 97-19174. 1997. pap. text ed. 14.95 (*1-55828-549-0*) MIS Press.
Unix Industry & Open Systems in Transition: A Guidebook to Managing Change. 2nd ed. Edward Dunphy. 616p. 1994. text ed. 39.95 (*0-471-60608-1*) Wiley.
UNIX Installation Security & Integrity. David Ferbrache & Gavin Shearer. 1993. pap. text ed. 37.60 (*0-13-015389-3*) P-H.
UNIX Internals: A Practical Approach. Steve Pate. (C). 1996. text ed. 39.95 (*0-201-87721-X*) Addison-Wesley.
Unix Internals: A Systems Operations Handbook. Myril C. Shaw & Susan S. Shaw. (Illus.). 320p. 1987. pap. 19.95 (*0-8306-2951-3*) McGraw-Hill Prof.
UNIX Internals: The New Frontiers. Uresh Vahalia. LC 95-25213. 1995. text ed. 49.00 (*0-13-101908-2*) P-H.
UNIX Internetworking. Uday O. Pabrai. LC 93-7164. 1993. text ed. 65.00 (*0-89006-685-X*) Artech Hse.
UNIX Internetworking. 2nd ed. Uday O. Pabrai. 1995. 67.00 (*0-89006-778-3*) Artech Hse.
UNIX Made Easy: The Basics & Beyond! 2nd ed. John Muster. (Made Easy Ser.). 720p. 1996. pap. text ed. 34.95 (*0-07-882173-8*) McGraw.
Unix Network Programming. W. Richard Stevens. 1990. text ed. 68.00 (*0-13-949876-1*) P-H.
***Unix Network Programming.** 2nd ed. Richard Stevens. (C). 1997. text ed. 54.00 (*0-13-490012-X*) P-H.
UNIX NROFF-TROFF: A User's Guide. Kevin P. Roddy. LC 85-27223. 362p. (C). 1986. pap. text ed. 29.00 (*0-03-000167-6*) HB Coll Pubs.
Unix Online Library. Unix System Laboratories Staff. 1994. Incl. disk. 105.00 incl. disk (*0-13-108952-8*) P-H.
UNIX Operating System. 3rd ed. Christian Kaare & Susan Richter. 544p. 1993. text ed. 49.95 (*0-471-58683-8*); pap. text ed. 29.95 (*0-471-58684-6*) Wiley.
UNIX Operating System Notes. Raul A. Salazar. Ed. by Jeanette H. Lawrence. 200p. (C). student ed. 33.95 (*1-887459-00-6*) Aurora Pub.
***UNIX Performance Tuning.** Ed. by System Admin Magazine Editors. (Sys Admin Essential Reference Ser.: Vol. 3). (Illus.). 230p. (Orig.). 1997. pap. 29.95 incl. disk (*0-87930-470-7*) R & D Books.
UNIX Philosophy. Mike Gancarz. LC 94-25893. 176p. 1995. pap. 21.95 (*1-55558-123-4*, Digital DEC) Buttrwrth-Heinemann.
UNIX, POSIX, & Open Systems: The Open Standards Puzzle. John S. Quarterman. (Illus.). 384p. (C). 1993. text ed. 44.25 (*0-201-52772-3*) Addison-Wesley.
UNIX Power Tools. Jerry Peek. 1184p. 1993. pap. 60.00 (*0-679-79073-X*) Random.
UNIX Productivity Tools. Gerald Tan. (C). 1992. pap. text ed. 30.25 (*0-201-55612-X*) Addison-Wesley.
UNIX Program Design & Development for IBM PC's. Thomas Yager. 1991. pap. 24.95 (*0-201-57727-5*) Addison-Wesley.
UNIX Programmer's Manual, Vol. 4. AT&T Staff. (C). 1986. pap. text ed. 38.75 (*0-03-011207-9*) HB Coll Pubs.
UNIX Programmer's Manual, Vol. 5. AT&T Staff. (C). 1986. pap. text ed. 42.75 (*0-03-011204-4*) HB Coll Pubs.
***UNIX Programmer's Reference.** John Muster. (Illus.). 288p. (Orig.). 1997. pap. 14.99 (*0-07-882366-8*, Oracle Press) Osborne-McGraw.
UNIX Programming: Methods & Tools. James F. Peters, III. 464p. (C). 1995. pap. text ed. 35.00 (*0-15-593021-4*) OUP.
UNIX Programming Environment. Brian W. Kernighan & Robert Pike. LC 83-62851. (Software Ser.). 368p. (C). 1983. 38.95 (*0-13-937681-X*); text ed. 58.00 (*0-13-937699-2*) P-H.
***UNIX Programming for Dummies.** (For Dummies Ser.). 1996. pap. 24.99 (*0-7645-0061-9*) IDG Bks.
UNIX, Quick! Andrew Feibus. LC 91-2183. (Illus.). 249p. 1991. pap. 30.00 (*1-878956-01-9*) CBM Bks.
UNIX Quick Reference Guide. 5th ed. Anatole Olczak. 237p. 1996. pap. text ed. 9.95 (*0-935739-25-4*) ASP.
UNIX Quick Reference Guide for BSD. 128p. 9.95 (*0-935739-24-6*) ASP.
Unix-R System V Programmer's Guide. American Telephone & Telegraph Staff. (Illus.). 848p. 1987. pap. text ed. 34.95 (*0-317-58031-0*) P-H.
UNIX Reference Guide. McNulty Development Incorporated Staff. (Illus.). 100p. 1986. 33.95 (*0-13-938952-0*) P-H.
UNIX Relational Database Management: Application Development in the UNIX Environment. Rod Manis. 1988. pap. text ed. 75.00 (*0-13-938622-X*) P-H.
Unix Research System Vol. 1: Programmer's Manual. 2nd ed. M. D. McIroy. (Unix Programmer's Ser.: Vol. I). 702p. (C). 1990. pap. text ed. 43.00 (*0-03-047532-5*) SCP.
Unix Secrets. James Armstrong. 1996. pap. 49.99 (*1-56884-499-9*) IDG Bks.
***UNIX Security.** Ed. by System Admin Magazine Editors. (Sys Admin Essential Reference Ser.: Vol. 4). (Illus.). 245p. (Orig.). 1997. pap. 29.95 incl. disk (*0-87930-471-5*) R & D Books.
UNIX Security - Course Notes. H. Podell et al. (Illus.). 416p. (Orig.). (C). 1995. pap. 45.76 (*0-942891-63-5*) Comp Educ.
Unix Security Audit. Sunsoft Inc. Staff. (C). 1997. pap. text ed. 24.00 (*0-13-494998-6*) P-H.
UNIX Shell Programming. rev. ed. Stephen G. Kochan & Patrick H. Wood. (Illus.). 460p. (C). 1989. 29.95 (*0-672-48448-X*) Sams.
UNIX Shell Programming. 3rd ed. Lowell J. Arthur & Edward N. Burns. 462p. 1994. pap. text ed. 39.99 (*0-471-59941-7*) Wiley.
***UNIX Shell Programming.** 4th ed. Lowell J. Arthur et al. LC 97-11528. 448p. 1997. pap. 39.99 (*0-471-16894-7*) Wiley.
UNIX Shells by Example. Ellie Quigley. 1996. pap. 49.95 (*0-13-460866-6*) P-H.
Unix Software Development Tools. Unix System Laboratories Staff. 1993. pap. text ed. 32.00 (*0-13-177049-7*) P-H.
UNIX Software Development Tools (UNIX SVR 4.2 MP) Unix System Laboratories Staff. (Illus.). 672p. (C). 1994. pap. text ed. 65.00 (*0-13-157926-6*) P-H.
UNIX Survival Guide. Joseph Nichols et al. 352p. (C). 1987. pap. text ed. 28.00 (*0-03-000773-9*) HB Coll Pubs.
UNIX Survival Guide. Timothy Parker. 1990. pap. 24.95 (*0-201-57078-5*) Addison-Wesley.
UNIX SVR4 Migration Guide. Specialized Systems Consultants, Inc. Staff. 8p. (Orig.). (C). 1992. pap. 2.00 (*0-916151-60-3*) Specialized Sys.
UNIX SVR4 Migration Pack. Specialized Systems Consultants, Inc. Staff. 80p. (Orig.). (C). 1992. pap. 23.50 (*0-916151-57-3*) Specialized Sys.
UNIX System. S. R. Bourne. (C). 1983. pap. text ed. 25.75 (*0-201-13791-7*) Addison-Wesley.
UNIX System Administration. Frank Burke. 175p. (C). 1987. text ed. write for info. (*0-318-61789-7*); pap. text ed. 17.50 (*0-15-593025-7*) SCP.
***UNIX System Administration for the Enterprise: Intelligent UNIX Procedures & Automated Tools.** John R. Wetsch. 1997. pap. text ed. 49.95 incl. disk (*0-87930-458-8*) R & D Books.
Unix System Administration Handbook. 2nd ed. Evi Nemeth. 816p. 1995. pap. 63.33 (*0-13-151051-7*) P-H.
UNIX System Administrator's Companion. Michael R. Ault. LC 95-37073. 384p. 1995. pap. text ed. 39.95 (*0-471-11144-9*) Wiley.
UNIX System Administrator's Guide. AT&T Staff. 1988. pap. 34.95 (*0-13-936139-1*) P-H.
UNIX System Administrator's Reference Manual. AT&T Staff. 1988. pap. 24.95 (*0-13-936147-2*) P-H.
UNIX System Architecture. Prabhat K. Andleigh. 1989. 32.95 (*0-13-949843-5*) P-H.
UNIX System Architecture, System V, Version IV. 2nd ed. Prabhat K. Andleigh. 270p. 1993. pap. 35.00 (*0-13-948423-X*) P-H.
UNIX System Book. Peter P. Silvester. (Books on Professional Computing). (Illus.). 230p. 1984. pap. 18.50 (*0-387-90906-0*) Spr-Verlag.
UNIX System Command Summary for Berkeley 4.2 & 4.3 BSD. Specialized Systems Consultants, Inc. Staff. 52p. (Orig.). (C). 1986. pap. 6.00 (*0-916151-17-4*) Specialized Sys.
***UNIX System Command Summary for Solaris 2.5.** 176p. (Orig.). 1996. pap. 10.00 (*0-916151-91-3*) Specialized Sys.
UNIX System Command Summary for SUR4.2-Solaris 2.1. Specialized Systems Consultants, Inc. Staff. 160p. (Orig.). (C). 1993. pap. 10.00 (*0-916151-61-1*) Specialized Sys.
UNIX System Five: A Practical Guide. 3rd ed. Mark G. Sobell. 864p. (C). 1995. pap. text ed. 35.50 (*0-8053-7566-X*) Benjamin-Cummings.
UNIX System Five Network Programming. Spephen A. Rago. LC 92-45276. (Professional Computing Ser.). 784p. (C). 1993. text ed. 49.95 (*0-201-56318-5*) Addison-Wesley.
Unix System Five Release Four Integrated Software Development Guide for Motorola Processors. Unix System Laboratories Staff. pap. text ed. 30.00 (*0-13-587684-2*) P-H.
UNIX System Five Release Four Programmer's Guide: ANSI C & Programming Support Tools for Motorola Processors. Unix System Laboratories Staff. 1992. pap. text ed. 40.00 (*0-13-587635-4*) P-H.
Unix System Five Release Four Programmer's Guide: Streams for Motorola Processors. Unix System Laboratories Staff. pap. text ed. 36.00 (*0-13-587676-1*) P-H.
UNIX System Five Release Four System Administrator's Guide for Motorola Processors. Unix System Laboratories Staff. 1992. pap. text ed. 42.00 (*0-13-587726-1*) P-H.
UNIX System Guidebook. 2nd ed. Peter P. Silvester. (Books on Professional Computing). (Illus.). xiv, 338p. 1988. 53.95 (*0-387-96489-4*) Spr-Verlag.
UNIX System Price Performance Guide. Jim Geers. (Illus.). (Orig.). Date not set. 12.45 (*1-881351-19-X*) AIM Tech.
UNIX System Price Performance Guide. Jim Geers. (Summer 1996 Ser.). (Illus.). 145p. (Orig.). Date not set. pap. 12.45 (*1-881351-20-3*) AIM Tech.
UNIX System Price Performance Guide: Winter 1996. Ed. by Tammy L. Bauer. (Illus.). 175p. (Orig.). 1995. pap. 39.95 (*1-881351-18-1*) AIM Tech.
Unix System Programming. 2nd ed. Keith Haviland. (C). 1996. pap. text ed. write for info. (*0-201-87758-9*) Addison-Wesley.
UNIX System Programming: A Programmer's Guide to Software Development. Ben Salama & Keith Haviland. (C). 1987. pap. text ed. 33.50 (*0-201-12919-1*) Addison-Wesley.
UNIX System Programming Using C++ Terrence Chan. LC 96-30559. 598p. (C). 1996. pap. text ed. 48.00 (*0-13-331562-2*) P-H.
UNIX System Security. Rick Farrow. 1990. pap. 24.95 (*0-201-57030-0*) Addison-Wesley.
Unix System Security: A Guide for Users & System Administrators. David A. Curry. (Illus.). 256p. (C). 1992. text ed. 32.95 (*0-201-56327-4*) Addison-Wesley.
UNIX System Security Essentials. Christoph Braun. LC 94-31241. (C). 1995. pap. text ed. 21.95 (*0-201-42775-3*) Addison-Wesley.
UNIX System User's Handbook. AT&T Bell Laboratories Staff & Morris I. Bolsky. 98p. 1986. 21.50 (*0-13-937764-6*) P-H.
UNIX System V Command Summary. rev. ed. Specialized Systems Consultants, Inc. Staff. 60p. (C). 1987. pap. 6.00 (*0-916151-23-9*) Specialized Sys.
Unix System V Commands. Baird Peterson. 1992. pap. 36.95 (*0-442-00998-4*) Van Nos Reinhold.
Unix System V for MS DOS Programmers. Jon Tulk. 1994. pap. text ed. 26.25 (*0-13-123431-5*) P-H.
UNIX System V Release 3.2 Series: Administrator's Guide, Version 386. AT&T Staff. 1988. pap. text ed. 61.00 (*0-13-944893-4*) P-H.
UNIX System V Release 3.2 Streams Programmer's Guide. AT&T Staff. 256p. 1989. pap. 24.95 (*0-685-27161-7*) P-H.
UNIX System V Release 4: An Introduction. 2nd ed. Kenneth H. Rosen et al. 1250p. 1996. pap. text ed. 39.95 (*0-07-882130-4*) McGraw.
UNIX System V Release 4: XII-News Graphical Windowing System News. 1990. pap. 32.00 (*0-13-931825-9*) P-H.
UNIX System V Release 4: XII-News Graphical Windowing System Service. 1990. pap. 21.00 (*0-13-931833-X*) P-H.
UNIX System V Release 4 Commands Reference Manual: Commands A-L for Motorola Processors, Vol. 1. Motorola UNIX Staff. 800p. (C). 1992. pap. text ed. 55.00 (*0-13-088832-X*) P-H.
UNIX System V Release 4 Commands Reference Manual: Commands M-Z for Motorola Processors, Vol. 2. Motorola UNIX Staff. 784p. (C). 1992. pap. text ed. 55.00 (*0-13-088840-0*) P-H.
Unix System V Release 4 Network User's & Administrator's Guide. 1990. pap. text ed. 68.00 (*0-13-933813-6*) P-H.
Unix System V Release 4 Programmer's Guide: XII-News Graphical Windowing System X View. 1990. pap. 32.00 (*0-13-931841-0*) P-H.
Unix System V Release 4 System Administrator's Guide. 1990. pap. text ed. 68.00 (*0-13-947086-7*) P-H.
Unix System V Release 4 System Administrator's Reference Manual. 1990. pap. text ed. 44.20 (*0-13-947011-5*) P-H.
UNIX System V Release 4 System Calls & Library Functions Reference Manual for Motorola Processors. Motorola UNIX Staff. 1104p. (C). 1992. pap. text ed. 61.00 (*0-13-035841-X*) P-H.
UNIX System V Release 4 System Files & Devices Reference Manual for Motorola Processors. Motorola UNIX Staff. 464p. (C). 1992. pap. text ed. 55.00 (*0-13-035874-6*) P-H.
UNIX System V Release 4 User's Guide. 1990. pap. text ed. 63.00 (*0-13-947052-2*) P-H.
UNIX System V Release 4.0 Pattern Matching. Sally Browning. 1993. pap. 27.95 (*0-13-091117-8*) P-H.
UNIX System V Software Catalog. AT&T Information Systems, Inc. Staff. 1986. 19.95 (*0-8359-8068-5*) S&S Trade.
Unix System V 386 Release 4 Multibus Installation & Configuration Guide. AT&T UNIX Software Operation Staff. 1990. pap. 21.00 (*0-13-957499-9*) P-H.
UNIX System V-386 Release 4.0 Version 4.0 System Files & Devices Reference Manual (TMAC) Unix System Laboratories Staff. 1992. pap. 12.00 (*0-13-031337-8*) P-H.
UNIX System V-386 System Administrator's Guide. AT&T Staff. 1988. pap. 34.95 (*0-13-940891-6*) P-H.
UNIX System V.4 Command Summary. rev. ed. Specialized Systems Consultants, Inc. Staff. 80p. (C). 1990. pap. 8.00 (*0-916151-44-1*) Specialized Sys.
UNIX System V.4 Command Summary. rev. ed. Specialized Systems Consultants, Inc. Staff. 80p. 1993. pap. 8.00 (*0-916151-63-8*) Specialized Sys.
UNIX System 5 (Bourne) Shell Tutorial. rev. ed. Specialized Systems Consultants, Inc. Staff. 49p. (C). 1990. pap. 6.00 (*0-916151-39-5*) Specialized Sys.
UNIX System 5 Release 4 Streams. Unix System Laboratories Staff. 1993. pap. text ed. 60.00 (*0-13-020660-1*) P-H.
UNIX Systems. Bruce H. Hunter. 448p. (C). 1991. pap. text ed. 43.51 (*0-02-358950-7*, Macmillan Coll) P-H.
UNIX Systems Administrators Guide to X Windows with CD ROM. Kevin Reichard & Eric F. Johnson. 1994. pap. 44.95 (*1-55828-347-1*) MIS Press.
UNIX Systems for Modern Architectures: Symmetric Multiprocessing & Caching for Kernel Prog... Curt Schimmel. 1994. 47.95 (*0-201-63338-8*) Addison-Wesley.
UNIX Systems Programming for SVR4. Dave Curry. (Illus.). 620p. (Orig.). 1996. pap. 34.95 (*1-56592-163-1*) OReilly & Assocs.
UNIX Tools. Rosenburg. 1996. write for info. (*0-201-41854-1*) Addison-Wesley.
***UNIX Tools.** 2nd ed. Jerry Peek. 1997. pap. text ed. 59.95 incl. cd-rom (*1-56592-260-3*) OReilly & Assocs.
UNIX Tools for Musical Research: The Humdrum Toolkit Reference Manual. David Huron. 551p. (Orig.). 1994. pap. text ed. 25.00 (*0-936943-10-6*) CCARH.

An Asterisk (*) at the beginning of an entry indicates that the title is appearing in BIP for the first time.

*UNIX Unbounded. 2nd ed. Afzal. LC 97-3551. 1997. pap. text ed. 62.00 (0-13-621632-3) P-H.
UNIX Unbounded. 2nd ed. Amir Afzal. LC 97-3551. 400p. 1995. pap. text ed. 65.00 (0-13-328246-5) P-H.
UNIX Unleashed. Emmett Dulaney. 1620p. 1994. 49.99 (0-672-30402-3) Sams.
*UNIX Unleashed. 2nd ed. Dave Taylor et al. 1600p. 1997. 59.99 (0-672-30952-1) Mac Comp Pub.
UNIX User's Handbook. Ed. by Lance A. Leventhal. LC 91-53067. (Lance A. Leventhal Microtrend Ser.). 600p. (Orig.). 1992. pap. 29.95 (0-915391-47-3, Microtrend) Slawson Comm.
UNIX V Environment. S. R. Bourne. 368p. (C). 1986. pap. text ed. 26.95 (0-201-18484-2) Addison-Wesley.
*UNIX Web Server Administration. Leavitt. Ed. by Linda Mui. (Illus.). 325p. (Orig.). 1997. pap. 32.95 (1-56592-217-4) OReilly & Assocs.
*UNIX Web Server Book. 2nd ed. LC 96-34305. 750p. 1996. 49.99 (1-56604-480-4) Ventana Communs.
Unix Webmaster Bible. Naba Barkakati. 1996. pap. 44.99 (0-7645-3016-X) IDG Bks.
UNIX Workshop. Pilavakis. 1989. 32.00 (0-8493-7104-X, QA76) CRC Pr.
UNIX Workstations. Richard K. Miller & Marcia E. Rupnow. LC 90-83862. (Survey on Technology & Markets Ser.: No. 155). 50p. 1991. pap. text ed. 200.00 (1-55865-182-9) Future Tech Surveys.
UNIX, XENIX & VENIX: Introduction, Applications Tips & Tricks. Sam D. Roberts. (Illus.). 206p. 1985. pap. 12. 95 (3-88963-064-2) Elcomp.
Unix-Xenix Text Processing Reference. rev. ed. Specialized Systems Consultants, Inc. Staff. 32p. 1987. pap. 6.00 (0-916151-22-0) Specialized Sys.
UNIX(R) Security Handbook. David S. Bauer. (Illus.). 117p. (C). 1991. 49.00 (1-878108-12-3) Bellcore.
UNIX(r) System Five Release Four Device Driver Interface-Driver Kernel Interface Reference Manual for Intel Processors. Unix System Laboratories Staff. 400p. 1991. pap. text ed. 43.00 (0-13-879529-0) P-H.
UNIX(r) System Five Release Four Migration & Compatibility Guide for Motorola Processors. Unix System Laboratories Staff. 1992. pap. text ed. 37.00 (0-13-587700-8) P-H.
Unix(r) System Five Release Four User's Reference Manual-System Administrator's Reference Manual (Commands A-L) for Intel Processors. Unix System Laboratories Staff. 848p. 1991. pap. text ed. 63.00 (0-13-951310-8) P-H.
Unix(r) System Five Release Four User's Reference Manual-System Administrator's Reference Manual (Commands M-Z) for Intel Processors. Unix System Laboratories Staff. 832p. 1991. pap. text ed. 63.00 (0-13-951328-0) P-H.
UNIXV Pocket Reference. Sam D. Roberts. (Info Compact Ser.). 88p. 1992. pap. 5.00 (0-911827-14-5) Elcomp.
UNIX3 for DOS Users. Martin R. Arick. LC 95-14629. 230p. 1995. pap. text ed. 24.95 (0-471-04988-3) Wiley.
Unjust Death. Richard Berman. 352p. (Orig.). 1995. mass mkt. 5.50 (0-380-77812-2) Avon.
Unjust Dismissal, 2 vols. Lex K. Larson & Philip Borowsky. 1985. Updates available. ring bd. write for info. (0-8205-1779-8) Bender.
*Unjust Enrichment: A Study of Private Law & Public Values. Hanoch Dagan. (Studies in International & Comparative Law). (Illus.). 185p. (C). 1997. text ed. 59. 95 (0-521-58468-X) Cambridge U Pr.
Unjust Punishments: Mandatory HIV Testing of Women Sex Workers & Pregnant Women. Lisa Bowleg. (Women & AIDS Ser.). (Orig.). (C). 1992. pap. 15.00 (1-877966-13-4) Ctr Women Policy.
Unjust Relations: Aboriginal Rights in Canadian Courts. Ed. by Peter Kulchyski. 380p. 1994. pap. 32.00 (0-19-540985-X) OUP.
Unjustified Enrichment. 1992. pap. write for info. (0-7021-2933-X, Pub. by Juta SA) Gaunt.
Unjustified Enrichment: A Casebook. Sieg Eiselen. 658p. 1993. pap. 116.00 (0-409-02692-1, SA) MICHIE.
*Unjustified Enrichment: A Comparative Study of the Law of Restitution. Ed. by P. W. Russell. 96p. 1997. pap. 17.50 (90-5383-478-8, Pub. by VUB Univ Pr BE) Paul & Co Pubs.
Unkept Promises, Unclear Consequences: U. S. Economic Policy & the Japanese Response. Ed. by Ryuzo Sato & John A. Rizzo. (Illus.). 210p. 1989. text ed. 47.95 (0-521-35201-0) Cambridge U Pr.
Unkind Word & Other Stories. Dinah M. Craik. LC 70-101278. (Short Story Index Reprint Ser.). 1977. 23.95 (0-8369-3215-3) Ayer.
Unkind Words: Ethnic Labeling from Redskin to WASP. Irving L. Allen. LC 90-32392. 52p. 1990. text ed. 45.00 (0-89789-217-8, H217, Bergin & Garvey); pap. text ed. 14.95 (0-89789-220-8, G220, Bergin & Garvey) Greenwood.
Unkindest Cut: How a Hatchet-Man Critic Made His Own $7,000 Movie & Put It All on His Credit Card. Joseph Queenan. (Illus.). 304p. 1996. 22.95 (0-7868-6090-1) Hyperion.
*Unkindest Cut: How a Hatchet-Man Critic Made His Own $7,000 Movie & Put It All on His Credit Card. Joseph Queenan. 320p. 1997. pap. 11.95 (0-7868-8198-4) Hyperion.
Unkindest Cut: Life in the Backrooms of Medicine. Marcia Millman. LC 76-18726. 1978. pap. 8.20 (0-688-08120-7, Quill) Morrow.
Unkindness of Ravens. Ruth Rendell. 352p. 1986. mass mkt. 5.99 (0-345-32746-2) Ballantine.
Unknowable Light of the Alien. Stanley Nelson. LC 80-53431. 180p. (Orig.). 1981. pap. 7.50 (0-912292-65-2) Smith.
Unknowing Sage: The Life & Work of Baba Fagir Chand. Ed. by David C. Lane. (Enchanted Land Book Ser.). (Illus.). 63p. (Orig.). 1989. pap. 11.95 (0-9611124-1-7) Del Mar Pr.
Unknowledge & Choice in Economics. Ed. by Stephen F. Frowen. LC 88-26543. 250p. 1990. text ed. 45.00 (0-312-02768-0) St Martin.
Unknown. Benito Perez Galdos. Tr. by Karen Austin from SPA. LC 91-38448. (Hispanic Literature Ser.: Vol. 14). 252p. 1991. lib. bdg. 89.95 (0-7734-9444-8) E Mellen.
Unknown: A Monument by R. V. Greeves. John Running. LC 86-61592. (Illus.). (Orig.). (C). 1986. pap. 9.75 (0-9616999-0-6) R V Greeves.
Unknown Ambassadors: A Saga of Citizenship. Phyllis Michaux. LC 95-83659. 175p. (Orig.). 1996. pap. 15.95 (0-9639260-2-0) Aletheia.
Unknown Army: Mutinies in the British Army in World War I. Gloden Dallas & Douglas Gill. 178p. 1985. text ed. 44.95 (0-86091-106-3, A0681, Pub. by Verso UK); pap. text ed. 14.95 (0-86091-814-9, A1010, Pub. by Verso UK) Routledge Chapman & Hall.
Unknown Arthur: Forgotten Tales of the Round Table. John Matthews. (Illus.). 172p. 1996. 27.95 (0-7137-2476-5, Pub. by Blandford Pr UK) Sterling.
*Unknown Biography of Jesus Christ: A Treasure of Stories about Jesus Christ You Have Never Read! P. Bellavitis. Ed. by R. E. Payne. (Illus.). 100p. (Orig.). Date not set. pap. write for info. (1-885308-08-6) Sr Polit Action.
Unknown Brahms. Robert H. Schauffler. LC 70-152602. (Illus.). 560p. 1972. reprint ed. text ed. 85.00 (0-8371-6037-5, SOCB, Greenwood Pr) Greenwood.
Unknown California. Jonathan Eisen et al. Ed. by Dorszynski. 416p. 1985. 17.26 (0-02-535150-8, Collier S&S) S&S Trade.
Unknown Capablanca. David Hooper & Dale Brandreth. (Illus.). 201p. 1993. reprint ed. pap. 6.95 (0-486-27614-7) Dover.
Unknown Christ of Hinduism. Raimundo Panikkar. LC 81-2886. 208p. (Orig.). 1981. reprint ed. pap. 18.00 (0-88344-523-9) Orbis Bks.
*Unknown Coleridge: The Life & Times of Derwent Coleridge, 1800-1883. Raymonde Hainton & Godfrey Hainton. (Illus.). 316p. 1997. pap. 18.95 (1-85756-288-7, Pub. by Janus Pubng UK) Paul & Co Pubs.
Unknown Colour: Paintings, Letters & Writings. Winifred Nicholson. Ed. by Andrew Nicholson. (Illus.). 256p. 1987. 47.50 (0-571-14950-2) Faber & Faber.
Unknown Constellations. Harvey Swados. LC 95-6021. 224p. 1995. 16.95 (0-252-06486-0); text ed. 34.95 (0-252-02130-4) U of Ill Pr.
Unknown Country. large type ed. Audrey Slaughter. 1996. 25.99 (0-7505-0863-9, Pub. by Magna Print Bks UK) Ulverscroft.
Unknown Country: Canada & Her People. Bruce Hutchison. LC 76-58025. 420p. 1977. reprint ed. text ed. 65.00 (0-8371-9451-2, HUUC, Greenwood Pr) Greenwood.
Unknown Craftsman: A Japanese Insight into Beauty. Soetsu Yanagi. LC 72-77798. (Illus.). 232p. 1990. pap. 32.00 (0-87011-948-6) Kodansha.
Unknown Distance: From Consciousness to Conscience, Goethe to Camus. Edward Engelberg. LC 74-188974. 308p. 1972. 33.95 (0-674-92965-9) HUP.
Unknown Dreams. Kristin Hungenberg. 1993. 17.95 (0-8034-8984-6) Bouregy.
Unknown East: Forgotten Foes of the Bright Empire. Lawrence Whitaker. Ed. by Lynn Willis. (Elric Roleplaying Game Ser.). (Illus.). 96p. (Orig.). 1995. pap. 16.95 (1-56882-032-1, 2907) Chaosium.
Unknown Fleet: The Army's Civilian Seamen in War & Peace. Reg Cooley. LC 93-20778. 1993. 30.00 (0-7509-0384-8, Pub. by Sutton Pubng UK) Bks Intl VA.
Unknown Forest. Anne-Marie Edwards. 96p. 1987. 45.00 (0-905392-08-6) St Mut.
Unknown God: Negative Theology in the Platonic Tradition: Plato to Eriugena. Deirdre Carabine. (Louvain Theological & Pastoral Monographs: Vol. 19). 358p. 1996. pap. 23.00 (0-8028-0558-2) Eerdmans.
Unknown God: W. T. Smith & the Thelemites. Martin P. Starr. (Illus.). 1998. write for info. (0-933429-07-X) Teitan Pr.
Unknown Guest. Leslie A. Shepard. 1975. 7.95 (0-8216-0220-9, Univ Bks) Carol Pub Group.
Unknown Hitler: His Private Life & Fortune. Wulf Schwarzwaller. 240p. (Orig.). 1989. 17.95 (0-915765-63-2) Natl Pr Bks.
Unknown Homeland. Tr. by Marite Sapiets. 254p. (Orig.). 1980. pap. 7.95 (0-87243-082-0) Templegate.
Unknown in the Underground. Alfred c. Maevis. 5.00 (0-614-05243-2, UNK10791M) ASFE.
Unknown Indian. G. B. Brown. 1977. lib. bdg. 59.95 (0-8490-2789-6) Gordon Pr.
Unknown Journey: A History of Croatians in Canada. Gabriele P. Scardellato. 1995. 32.00 (0-919045-64-2) U of Toronto Pr.
Unknown Lenin: From the Secret Archive. Ed. by Richard Pipes et al. LC 96-8415. (Annals of Communism Ser.). 256p. 1996. 27.50 (0-300-06919-7) Yale U Pr.
*Unknown Lenin: From the Secret Archive. Ed. by Richard Pipes. (Illus.). 204p. Date not set. 27.50 (0-614-22118-8) Yale U Pr.
Unknown Life of Jesus Christ. Nicolas T. Notovitch. 1973. 250.00 (0-87968-073-3) Gordon Pr.
Unknown Life of Jesus Christ. 2nd rev. ed. Nicolas Notovitch. Ed. by Bianca Leonardo. LC 96-23833. (Illus.). 56p. 1980. pap. 10.00 (0-9602850-1-6) Tree Life Pubns.
Unknown Life of Jesus Christ. Tr. by Nicolas Notovitch & Alexina Loranger. 66p. 1959. reprint ed. spiral bd. 7.00 (0-7873-0637-1) Hlth Research.
Unknown Light. Fray L. De Leon. Tr. by Willis Barnstone. LC 79-15030. 175p. 1979. pap. text ed. 19.95 (0-87395-419-X) State U NY Pr.
Unknown Man, No. 89. Elmore Leonard. 272p. 1984. mass mkt. 6.50 (0-380-67041-0) Avon.
Unknown Man Number 89. large type ed. Elmore Leonard. LC 92-35897. (General Ser.). 379p. 1993. pap. 17.95 (0-8161-5696-4, GK Hall) Thorndike Pr.
Unknown Mexico, 2 vols. Carl Lumholtz. 1973. 500.00 (0-8490-1249-X) Gordon Pr.
Unknown Mexico: A Record of Five Years' Exploration among the Tribes of the Western Sierra Madre, in the Tierra Caliente of Tepic & Jalisco, & Among the Tarascos of Michoacan, 2 vols. Karl S. Lumholtz. LC 72-5010. (Antiquities of the New World Ser.: Vol. 15). (Illus.). reprint ed. Set. 125.00 (0-404-57315-0) AMS Pr.
Unknown Mexico: Explorations in the Sierra Madre & Other Regions, 1890-1898, 2 vols., Vol. 1. Carl Lumholtz. 576p. 1987. reprint ed. pap. 15.95 (0-486-25364-3) Dover.
Unknown Mexico: Explorations in the Sierra Madre & Other Regions, 1890-1898, 2 vols., Vol. 2. Carl Lumholtz. 544p. 1987. reprint ed. pap. 15.95 (0-486-25413-5) Dover.
Unknown Modigliani: Drawings from the Collection of Paul Alexandre. Noel Alexandre. LC 93-1141. 1993. 95.00 (0-8109-3642-9) Abrams.
*Unknown Mongolia: A Record of Travel & Exploration in the North West Mongolia & Dzungaria. Douglas Carruthers. (C). 1994. reprint ed. write for info. (81-206-0857-7, Pub. by Asian Educ Servs II); reprint ed. write for info. (81-206-0859-3, Pub. by Asian Educ Servs II) S Asia.
Unknown Murderer. Theodor Reik. 1978. pap. 24.95 (0-8236-8320-6, 26700) Intl Univs Pr.
Unknown Oman. Wendel Phillips. (Arab Background Ser.). 319p. 1972. 16.00 (0-86685-025-2, LDL0252, Pub. by Librairie du Liban FR) Intl Bk Ctr.
Unknown O'Neill: Unpublished & Unfamiliar Writings of Eugene O'Neill. Eugene O'Neill. Ed. by Travis Bogard. LC 87-24637. 352p. (C). 1988. 50.00 (0-300-03985-9) Yale U Pr.
Unknown Orwell & Orwell: The Transformation. Peter Stansky. xxii, 302p. 1994. pap. 17.95 (0-8047-2342-7) Stanford U Pr.
Unknown Pahari Wall Paintings in North India. K. C. Aryan. (Illus.). 122p. 1992. 37.00 (81-900003-6-5, Pub. by Rekha Prakashn II) Nataraj Bks.
Unknown Patton. Charles M. Province. (Illus.). 272p. 1988. 5.99 (0-517-45595-1) Random Hse Value.
Unknown Pauline Smith: Unpublished & Out of Print Stories, Diaries & Other Prose Writings (Including Her Arnold Bennett Memoir) Pauline Smith. Ed. by Ernest Pereira. 254p. 1993. pap. 23.00 (0-86980-885-0, Pub. by Univ Natal Pr SA) Intl Spec Bk.
Unknown Philosopher: Louis Claude de Saint Martin. Arthur E. Waite. LC 70-130815. 464p. 1987. pap. 17.95 (0-89345-244-0, Steinerbks) Garber Comm.
Unknown Philosopher: The Life of Louis Claude de Saint-Martin & the Substance of His Transcendental Doctrine. Arthur E. Waite. 464p. 1995. pap. 27.00 (1-56459-485-8) Kessinger Pub.
Unknown Poe. Edgar Allan Poe. Ed. by Raymond Foye. LC 80-2431. 1980. pap. 7.95 (0-87286-110-4) City Lights.
Unknown Powers. Brown Landone. 17p. 1994. reprint ed. spiral bd. 6.00 (0-7873-1252-5) Hlth Research.
Unknown Prophet Jakob Lorber. Kurt Eggenstein. LC 79-89530. 78p. (Orig.). 1979. pap. 10.00 (0-912760-99-0) Valkyrie Pub Hse.
Unknown Puccini: A Historical Perspective on the Songs Including Little-Known Music from "Edgar" & "La Rondine" Michael Kaye. (Illus.). 256p. 1987. 49.95 (0-19-385745-6) OUP.
Unknown Quantity. Eberhart. 1999. mass mkt. 2.95 (0-446-35258-6) Warner Bks.
Unknown Quantity. Hermann Broch. Tr. by Willa Muir & Edwin Muir from GER. LC 87-63049. 240p. 1988. reprint ed. pap. 10.95 (0-910395-36-5) Marlboro Pr.
Unknown Reality Vol. I: A Seth Book. Jane Roberts. 304p. (Orig.). 1996. reprint ed. pap. 17.95 (1-878424-25-4) Amber-Allen Pub.
Unknown Reality Vol. II: A Seth Book. Jane Roberts. 560p. (Orig.). 1996. reprint ed. pap. 19.95 (1-878424-26-2) Amber-Allen Pub.
*Unknown Regions. Robert Holdstock. 1996. mass mkt. 5.99 (0-614-20520-4, ROC) NAL-Dutton.
Unknown Revolution: 1917-1922. Voline. Tr. by Fredy Perlman from FRE. 717p. 1975. 38.99 (0-919618-26-X, Pub. by Black Rose Bks CN); pap. 19.99 (0-919618-25-1, Pub. by Black Rose Bks CN) Consort Bk Sales.
Unknown Rider. rev. ed. Scott Anderson. 205p. 1995. pap. 12.50 (0-9644521-0-3) DENNOCH.
Unknown Rilke. enl. ed. Franz Wright & Rainer M. Wilke. (Field Translation Ser.: No. 17). 175p. (Orig.). 1990. pap. 12.95 (0-932440-56-8) Oberlin Coll Pr.
Unknown Samuel Johnson. Ed. by John J. Burke & Donald Kay. LC 81-70159. 195p. reprint ed. pap. 55.60 (0-685-16438-1, 2027363) Bks Demand.
Unknown Sanctuary. Aime Palliere. Tr. by Louise W. Wise. LC 79-150294. 243p. 1985. pap. 8.95 (0-8197-0498-9) Bloch.
Unknown Self. George Frankl. (Psychoanalysis & Society Ser.). 240p. 1990. 39.95 (1-871871-05-0, Pub. by Open Gate Pr UK); pap. 18.95 (1-871871-18-2, Pub. by Open Gate Pr UK) Paul & Co Pubs.
*Unknown Shore. Patrick O'Brian. 1996. text ed. 23.00 (0-07-048221-7) McGraw.
Unknown Shore. Patrick O'Brian. 288p. 1995. 23.00 (0-393-03859-9) Norton.
Unknown Shore. Patrick O'Brian. 316p. 1996. pap. 12.95 (0-393-31538-X) Norton.
*Unknown Shore. large type ed. Patrick O'Brian. LC 96-32354. 1996. 24.95 (1-56895-360-7, Compass) Wheeler Pub.
Unknown Soldier. Mickey Z. Reichert. 320p. (Orig.). 1994. mass mkt. 4.99 (0-88677-600-7) DAW Bks.
*Unknown Soldier: Book One of the Cogal. Sean Williams & Shane Dix. 361p. (Orig.). pap. 10.00 (1-875346-11-2, Pub. by Aphelion AT) Firebird Dist.
*Unknown Soldiers. Chris Neterer. 1996. mass mkt. 4.99 (1-55197-041-4, Pub. by Comnwlth Pub CN) Partners Pubs Grp.
Unknown Soldiers: African-American Troops in World War I. Arthur E. Barbeau & Florette Henri. LC 95-45862. (Illus.). 320p. 1996. reprint ed. pap. 14.95 (0-306-80694-0) Da Capo.
Unknown South of France: A History Buff's Guide. Henry S. Reuss & Margaret M. Reuss. LC 90-47384. (Illus.). (Orig.). 1991. pap. 12.95 (1-55832-030-X) Harvard Common Pr.
Unknown Spirit: The Unity of Matter & Spirit in Space & Time. Jean Charon. 1991. pap. 9.95 (0-904575-18-7, Coventure Ltd) Sigo Pr.
Unknown Swedes: A Book about Swedes & America, Past & Present. Vilhelm Moberg. Ed. & Tr. by Roger McKnight. LC 88-1731. 210p. (C). 1988. text ed. 24.95 (0-8093-1486-X) S Ill U Pr.
Unknown Thomas Hardy: Lesser Known Aspects of Hardy's Life & Career. Harold Orel. LC 86-4653. 256p. 1987. text ed. 39.95 (0-312-00538-5) St Martin.
Unknown Virginia Woolf. 4th ed. Rogers Poole. 320p. (C). 1996. pap. text ed. 18.95 (0-521-48402-2) Cambridge U Pr.
Unknown War: The Miskito Nation, Nicaragua, & the United States. Bernard Nietschmann. LC 89-7831. (Focus on Issues Ser.: No. 8). (Illus.). 120p. (Orig.). (C). 1989. pap. text ed. 16.50 (0-932088-42-2); lib. bdg. 37. 00 (0-932088-41-4) Freedom Hse.
Unknown Washington. John R. Corbin. LC 72-1273. (Select Bibliographies Reprint Ser.). 1977. reprint ed. 23.95 (0-8369-6823-9) Ayer.
Unknown Woman. Alice Koller. 320p. 1991. pap. 10.95 (0-553-35482-5) Bantam.
Unknown Works: Previously Unpublished Articles from the Turn of the Century. deluxe limited ed. Frederick C. Selous. (Illus.). 275p. 1996. boxed 75.00 (1-57157-004-7) Safari Pr.
Unknown Worlds: Second Series. Stanley Schmidt. 1989. 9.98 (0-88365-728-7) Galahad Bks.
Unkonventionelle Rheumatherapie. Ed. by W. Muller et al. (Fortbildungskurse fuer Rheumatologie Ser.: Vol. 7). (Illus.). viii, 192p. (GER.). 1985. pap. 60.00 (3-8055-4005-1) S Karger.
Unk's Fiddle...And Other Stories. Steven E. Burt. 96p. 1995. 9.95 (0-9649283-0-2) S E Burt.
Unladylike & Unprofessional: Academic Women & Academic Unions. fac. ed. Ed. by Elaine Reuben & Leonore Hoffmann. 63p. 1975. reprint ed. pap. 25.00 (0-7837-8033-8, 2047789) Bks Demand.
Unlawful Gain & Legitimate Profit in Islamic Law: Riba, Gharar, & Islamic Banking. 2nd ed. Nabil A. Saleh. LC 92-18224. (Arab & Islamic Laws Ser.). 176p. (C). 1992. lib. bdg. 109.00 (1-85333-721-8, Pub. by Graham & Trotman UK) Kluwer Ac.
Unlawful Occasions see Henry Cecil Reprint Series
Unlawfullness of Adultery & Fornication & Their Dangers. Bader F. El-Suwailem. 42p. (Orig.). (ARA.). 1996. mass mkt. write for info. (1-56923-033-1) Inst Islamic.
Unlawfully Wedded. Kelsey Roberts. (Intrigue Ser.). 1995. mass mkt. 3.50 (0-373-22330-7, 1-22330-4) Harlequin Bks.
Unlearned Language: New Studies in Xenoglossy. Ian Stevenson. LC 83-12525. 223p. 1984. text ed. 30.00 (0-8139-0994-5) U Pr of Va.
Unlearned Lessons: Current & Past Reforms for School Improvement. Barbara Z. Presseisen. LC 85-29659. 258p. 1985. 55.00 (1-85000-079-4, Falmer Pr); pap. 28. 00 (1-85000-080-8, Falmer Pr) Taylor & Francis.
Unlearning Violence: A Breakthrough Book for Violent Men & All Those Who Love Them. Paul Kivel. 1995. 7.98 (1-56731-082-6, MJF Bks) Fine Comms.
Unleash the Enterpreneur Within: How to Make Everyone an Entrepreneur & Stay Efficient. Mitch McCrimmon. 240p. 1995. 29.95 (0-273-61456-8) Natl Bk Netwk.
*Unleash the Potential: Unlocking the Mystery of Motivation. David Zimmerman. 139p. 1997. 39.95 (1-882987-05-5) Zimmerman & Assocs.
Unleash the Power: How to Learn a Power Golf Swing. Don A. Wiseman. Incl. Common Sense Golf: A New Concept in Golf: Basic Laws of Physics & Geometry Combined with Common Sense. 44p. (Orig.). 1994. student ed. 19.95 (0-9642645-0-1); 1994. Set student ed. 59.95Set incl. vhs (0-9642645-2-8) Golf Sci Multimed.
Unleash the Power of UIM: The Complete Guide to Creating Customized Help Support. Richard Shaler. (Illus.). 221p. (Orig.). 1994. pap. 99.00 (1-883884-19-5) Midrange Comput.
Unleash the Scoring. Don A. Wiseman. 1995. 59.95 incl. vhs (0-9642645-5-2) Golf Sci Multimed.
Unleash the Tremendous Potential Within You & Achieve the Success You've Always Dreamed Of! Bill W. Wayman. 190p. 1987. pap. 10.95 (0-941155-01-3) Positive Liv Pubns.
Unleashed. Sam Robins. LC 95-44473. 384p. (Orig.). 1997. pap. 18.95 (0-86534-035-8) Sunstone Pr.
Unleashed: Poems by Writers' Dogs. Amy Hempel & Jim Shepard. 176p. 1995. 19.00 (0-517-70140-5, Crown) Crown Pub Group.

U
V

Unleashing America's Potential: A Pro-Growth, Pro-Family Tax System for the 21st Century. National Commission of Economics. 1996. pap. 9.99 (0-312-14618-3) St Martin.

Unleashing Feminism: A Critique of Lesbian Sadomasochism in the Gay Nineties. Ed. by Irene Reti. 160p. 1993. pap. 8.95 (0-939821-04-4) HerBooks.

Unleashing Multiplication. Daniel Sueltz. 1985. 22.95 (0-13-937228-8) P-H.

Unleashing Our Unknown Selves: An Inquiry into the Future of Feminity & Masculinity. France Morrow. LC 90-39262. 288p. 1990. text ed. 59.95 (0-275-93587-6, C3587, Praeger Pubs); pap. text ed. 19.95 (0-275-93837-9, B3837, Praeger Pubs) Greenwood.

Unleashing Productivity: Prescription for Manufacturing Survival. Timothy E. Fleskes. LC 95-60771. 192p. 1995. 29.95 (0-9645305-1-1); pap. 21.95 (0-9645305-0-3) TFME Pr.

Unleashing Productivity! Your Guide to Unlocking the Secrets of Super Performance. Richard Ott & Martin Snead. LC 93-11585. 264p. 1993. text ed. 24.95 (1-55623-931-9) Irwin Prof Pubng.

Unleashing Rights: Law, Meaning, & the Animal Rights Movement. Helena Silverstein. LC 96-10321. (Law, Meaning, & Violence Ser.). (C). 1995. 39.50 (0-472-10685-6) U of Mich Pr.

Unleashing SuperCalc. Daniel Sueltz & Bruce Kinder. 1985. 22.95 (0-13-937269-5); pap. 14.95 (0-685-08088-9) P-H.

Unleashing the Genius. Roberta DePorter. (Learning Forum Products Ser.). 1989. 9.95 (0-945525-15-X) Supercamp.

***Unleashing the Lay Potential in Sunday School.** 88p. 1986. pap. 5.99 (0-8341-1129-2) Nazarene.

Unleashing the Power of Praying in the Spirit. Oral Roberts. 160p. 1993. pap. 8.99 (0-89274-678-5, HH-678) Harrison Hse.

Unleashing the Power of the Gospel. 160p. 1994. pap. text ed. 5.99 (0-8407-2087-4) Nelson.

Unleashing the Right Side of the Brain: The LARC Creativity Program. Robert Williams & John Stockmyer. 1987. pap. 9.95 (0-317-61853-9) Viking Penguin.

Unleashing the Scripture: Freeing the Bible from Captivity to America. Stanley Hauerwas. LC 93-11107. 144p. (Orig.). 1993. pap. 13.95 (0-687-31678-2) Abingdon.

Unleashing the Sex Goddess. Olivia St. Claire. 1996. 18.00 (0-517-70438-2) Random.

Unleashing the Truth: How to Be Intimate with God. Clive E. Neil. 128p. (Orig.). 1996. pap. 8.99 (0-9634306-8-8) End-Time Wave.

Unleavened Bread. Robert Grant. LC 68-20014. (Americans in Fiction Ser.). 431p. reprint ed. lib. bdg. 29.00 (0-8398-0665-5) Irvington.

Unleavened Bread. Robert Grant. 431p. (C). 1986. reprint ed. pap. text ed. 6.95 (0-8290-2046-2) Irvington.

Unleaving. Jill Paton Walsh. 1990. pap. 3.50 (0-374-48068-0) FS&G.

Unless & Until: A Baha'i Focus on the Environment. Arthur L. Dahl. 96p. 1990. pap. 10.95 (1-870989-09-0) Bahai.

Unless One Is Born Anew. Dorothy Hutchinson. LC 65-26994. (Orig.). 1965. pap. 3.00 (0-87574-143-6) Pendle Hill.

Unless the Wind Turns. Mildred Walker. LC 96-780. xiii, 235p. 1996. pap. 12.00 (0-8032-9781-5, Bison Books) U of Nebr Pr.

Unless We Become Wise. El Seti Anu Ali El. 158p. 1992. pap. 10.95 (0-9632256-0-X) Amurru Pub.

Unless You Become Like This Child. Hans U. Von Balthasar. Tr. by Erasmo Leiva from GER. LC 91-73329. 75p. (Orig.). 1991. pap. 8.95 (0-89870-379-4) Ignatius Pr.

***Unless You Believe, You Shall Not Understand: Logic, University, & Society in Late Medieval Vienna.** Michael H. Shank. LC 87-36889. 275p. 1988. reprint ed. pap. 78.40 (0-608-02997-1, 2063254) Bks Demand.

***Unless You Repent.** 2nd ed. Henry A. Ironside. Ed. by J. B. Nicholson. Orig. Title: Except Ye Repent. 151p. 1994. reprint ed. 8.95 (1-882701-07-0) Uplook Min.

Unless You Take Up Your Cross: Lenten Reflection & Devotion. Robert D. Eimer & Sarah A. P'Malley. 104p. (Orig.). 1992. pap. 4.95 (0-8146-2063-9) Liturgical Pr.

***Unlevel Playing Fields: Understanding Wage Inequality & Discrimination.** Randy Albelda et al. LC 96-36356. (Illus.). 256p. 1996. pap. text ed. 27.25 (0-07-000968-6) McGraw.

***Unlike Normal Women.** Vernella Fuller. 330p. 1997. pap. 13.95 (0-7043-4431-9, Pub. by Womens Press UK) Trafalgar.

Unlike Subjects: Women, Theory, Fiction. Gerardine Meaney. LC 92-36699. (Gender, Culture, Difference Ser.). 264p. (C). 1993. pap. 18.95 (0-415-07099-6, B0709, Routledge NY) Routledge.

Unlike Subjects: Women, Theory, Fiction. Gerardine Meaney. LC 92-36699. (Gender, Culture, Difference Ser.). 264p. (C). (gr. 13). 1993. text ed. 62.95 (0-415-07098-8, B0705, Routledge NY) Routledge.

Unlike the Lilies: Doukhobor Textile Traditions in Canada. Dorothy K. Burnham. 112p. 1994. pap. 24.95 (0-88854-322-0, Pub. by Royal Ont Mus CN) U of Toronto Pr.

Unlikely Affair: The Irving Layton - Dorothy Rath Correspondence. Intro. by Adrienne Clarkson. 230p. 8.95 (0-88962-101-2) Mosaic.

Unlikely Angel. Betina M. Krahn. 528p. 1996. mass mkt. 5.99 (0-553-56524-9, Fanfare) Bantam.

Unlikely Beginnings. Gerald H. Bidlack. LC 82-90984. 1984. 10.95 (0-87212-164-X) Libra.

***Unlikely Conversations about Jesus: Six Dramas for Lent.** Jon L. Joyce. LC 96-37175. 74p. (Orig.). 1997. reprint ed. pap. 8.75 (0-89536-244-9) CSS OH.

Unlikely Cupid. Catherine George. (Romance Ser.: No. 177). 1992. pap. 2.79 (0-373-03177-7, 1-03177-2) Harlequin Bks.

Unlikely Duchess. Mary Balogh. 224p. 1990. pap. 4.50 (0-451-16739-2, Sig) NAL-Dutton.

Unlikely Eden. Anne M. Winston. (Desire Ser.). 1993. mass mkt. 2.99 (0-373-05827-6, 5-05827-6) Silhouette.

Unlikely Hero. Eastwood-Stokes. 1996. mass mkt. 4.99 (0-451-19001-7, Sig) NAL-Dutton.

Unlikely Heroines: Nineteenth-Century Women Writers & the Woman Question. Ann R. Shapiro. LC 86-22750. (Contributions in Women's Studies: No. 81). 163p. 1987. text ed. 45.00 (0-313-25422-2, SUH/, Greenwood Pr) Greenwood.

Unlikely Liberators: The Men of the 100th & the 442nd. Masayo U. Duus. Tr. by Peter Duus from JPN. LC 87-6013. (Illus.). 288p. 1987. 23.95 (0-8248-1081-3) UH Pr.

Unlikely Ones. Mary Brown. 432p. 1987. mass mkt. 4.99 (0-671-65361-X) Baen Bks.

Unlikely Pioneer: Building Opera from the Pacific Through the Prairies. David Watmough. (Illus.). 185p. 1995. lib. bdg. 35.00 (0-8095-4919-0) Borgo Pr.

Unlikely Pioneer: Building Opera from the Pacific Through the Prairies. David Watmough. (Illus.). 185p. pap. 12.95 (0-88962-285-X) Mosaic.

Unlikely Romance. large type ed. Betty A. Neels. 1992. reprint ed. lib. bdg. 18.95 (0-263-13091-6, Pub. by Mills & Boon UK) Thorndike Pr.

Unlikely Romance of Kate Bjorkman. Louise Plummer. LC 94-49614. 176p. (YA). (gr. 7 up). 1995. 15.95 (0-385-32049-3, Delacorte Pr Bks) BDD Bks Young Read.

***Unlikely Romance of Kate Bjorkman.** Louise Plummer. 192p. (YA). (gr. 7 up). 1997. mass mkt. 4.50 (0-440-22704-6) BDD Bks Young Read.

Unlikely Sailor. J. Edward Day. 1990. pap. 10.95 (0-9626033-0-9) McClain.

Unlikely Santa. Leigh Michaels. 1995. mass mkt. 2.99 (0-373-03388-5, 1-03388-5) Harlequin Bks.

***Unlikely Spy.** Daniel Silva. 1996. 24.00 (0-553-47734-X) Bantam.

Unlikely Spy. Daniel Silva. LC 96-27961. 1997. 25.00 (0-679-45562-0, Villard Bks) Random.

***Unlikely Spy.** large type ed. Daniel Silva. LC 97-8194. 1997. 27.95 (0-7862-1101-6, Thorndike Lrg Prnt) Thorndike Pr.

***Unlikely Stories: Causality & the Nature of Modern Narrative.** Brian Richardson. LC 96-30906. 224p. 1997. 36.00 (0-87413-609-1) U Delaware Pr.

Unlikely Unions: The Angela Nugent Story. Charles Niedrich. 150p. (Orig.). 1996. pap. 15.95 (1-57502-202-8, D0834) Morris Pubng.

Unlimit Your Life: Setting & Getting Goals. James Fadiman. LC 89-31702. 224p. 1995. pap. 12.95 (0-89087-562-6) Celestial Arts.

***Unlimited Access: An FBI Agent Inside the Clinton White House.** Gary Aldrich. 1997. pap. 12.95 (0-89526-406-4) Regnery Pub.

Unlimited Access: An FBI Agent Inside the Clinton White House. Gary W. Aldrich. LC 95-26817. 1996. 24.95 (0-89526-454-4) Regnery Pub.

Unlimited Community: A Study of the Possibility of Social Science. Julius W. Friend & James K. Feibleman. LC 75-3144. reprint ed. 49.50 (0-404-59152-3) AMS Pr.

Unlimited Dream Co. J. G. Ballard. 1993. reprint ed. lib. bdg. 18.95 (0-89968-391-6, Lghtyr Pr) Buccaneer Bks.

Unlimited Empowerment: Discovering & Enhancing Your Personal Professional Life Via the Enneagram. Patrick J. Aspell & Denise D. Aspell. (Illus.). 1992. student ed., ring bd. 29.95 (1-881773-00-0) Lifewings.

Unlimited Human Potential: A New Definition. John S. Morgan. LC 94-7645. 224p. (Orig.). 1994. pap. 14.95 (1-56825-019-3) Rainbow Books.

Unlimited Options: Career Strategies to Last a Lifetime. Lily Maestas & Lorelei Snyder. 256p. (Orig.). 1996. per., pap. 14.97 (0-9651077-5-2) Prsprity Pr.

Unlimited Options for Aging: Commonsense Answers from Scandinavia. Joseph Carella. 120p. (Orig.). 1995. pap. write for info. (1-884186-01-7, Hollis Pubng) Puritan Pr.

Unlimited Partners: Our American Story. Bob Dole & Elizabeth Dole. 384p. 1996. 24.00 (0-684-83401-4) S&S Trade.

Unlimited Partnership: God & the Businessman. Bob Yandian. 72p. (Orig.). 1996. mass mkt. write for info. (1-885600-01-1) B Yandian Minist.

***Unlimited Power.** Robbins. 1997. pap. 13.00 (0-684-84577-6) S&S Trade.

Unlimited Power. Anthony Robbins. 1987. pap. 12.50 (0-449-90280-3) Fawcett.

***Unlimited Power: A Black Choice.** Robbins & McClendon. 1997. pap. 13.00 (0-684-83872-9) S&S Trade.

***Unlimited Power: A Black Choice.** Anthony Robbins & Joseph McClendon, III. LC 96-39232. 1997. 24.00 (0-684-82436-1) S&S Trade.

***Unlimited Power 1998.** Robbins. 1997. pap. 9.95 (0-684-83326-3, S&S Editions) S&S Trade.

Unlimited Purpose. Joshua K. Ogawa. 1986. pap. 4.95 (9971-972-46-8) OMF Bks.

Unlimited Referrals: Secrets That Turn Your Business Relationships to Gold! Bill Cates. 200p. 1996. 24.95 (1-888970-07-3) Thndr Hill Pr.

Unlimited Selling Power: How to Master Hypnotic Skills. Donald J. Moine & Kenneth Lloyd. 288p. 1990. pap. 12.95 (0-13-689126-8) P-H.

Unlimited Sex: Beck's Three-Step Method for Achieving Unlimited Male Potency Forever. Francine Beck. 1996. pap. text ed. 14.95 (0-935016-37-6, Barclay House) Arrowood Pr.

Unlimited Visibility: 26 Lessons & Processes for Being in the Science of Mind. Stephanie Sorensen. LC 96-83746. 262p. (Orig.). 1996. pap. 12.95 (0-87516-687-3) DeVorss.

Unlimited Wealth: The Theory & Practice of Economic Alchemy. Paul Z. Pilzer. 1991. 22.00 (0-517-58211-2, Crown) Crown Pub Group.

Unlisted Legion. Jock Purves. 1978. pap. 6.99 (0-85151-245-3) Banner of Truth.

***Unlisted Lives.** David H. Flaherty. 1987. mass mkt. 3.95 (0-671-63984-6) PB.

Unlisted Numbers. Eleanor R. May. 59p. (Orig.). 1995. pap. 10.00 (1-880994-15-1) Mt Olive Coll Pr.

Unlit Lamp. Radclyffe Hall. 1988. reprint ed. lib. bdg. 80.00 (0-7812-0150-0) Rprt Serv.

Unlit Lamp: A Novel. Radclyffe Hall. LC 74-145067. 343p. 1972. reprint ed. 49.00 (0-403-01010-1) Scholarly.

Unlived Affections. George Shannon. LC 95-33606. 93p. (YA). (gr. 8-12). 1995. reprint ed. pap. 8.95 (1-55583-299-7) Alyson Pubns.

Unlived Lives. Michael Nava. 1997. write for info. (0-517-70572-9) Random.

Unlock My Heart. large type ed. Honor Vincent. (Linford Romance Library). 288p. 1984. pap. 15.99 (0-7089-6010-3) Ulverscroft.

Unlock the Power of Family: Discover God's Design for Lasting Relationships. Daniel Brown. LC 94-17643. 1994. 10.95 (0-917143-30-2) Sparrow TN.

Unlock the Power of Your Paycheck Now! 10 Easy Steps You Can Take for On-Time Bill Paying & Debt-Free Living. David M. Katz. Ed. by Jack Johnson. Orig. Title: Pay Your Bills on Time!. (Illus.). 160p. 1996. ring bd. 29.95 (0-9642399-7-3) Right Track.

Unlock Your Happiness. Baker E. Morten. 104p. 1994. pap. 10.95 (0-9633004-8-2) Integ Pub DC.

Unlock Your Mind & Be Free! A Practical Approach to Hypnotherapy. Edgar Barnett. 153p. 1984. reprint ed. pap. 8.95 (0-930298-49-7) Westwood Pub Co.

Unlock Your Personal Best: From the Inside Out. John Ross. (Illus.). 264p. (Orig.). 1995. pap. 12.95 (1-879868-02-4) Mentor Group.

Unlock Your Potential: Know Your Brain & How to Use It. Margaret A. Golton. LC 82-2490. 80p. (Orig.). 1982. pap. 5.95 (0-942952-00-6) Frank Pubns.

Unlock Your Psychic Powers. Richard Lawrence. 1995. mass mkt. 4.99 (0-312-95412-3) St Martin.

Unlocked Book: A Memoir of John Wilkes Booth by His Sister. Asia Clarke. LC 74-88533. (Illus.). 206p. 1972. 24.95 (0-405-08363-7, Pub. by Blom Pubns UK) Ayer.

Unlocked Door & Other Short Stories. Donald Deffner. 1995. pap. 4.99 (0-570-09529-8, 20-2620) Concordia.

Unlocked Dreams: A Collection of Poems. Catherine Marshall. 64p. 1995. 9.99 (0-7852-7940-7) Nelson.

***Unlocking Christ's Parables: A Guide for Aligning Our Lives with the Wisdom of Jesus' Parables, Vol. 2.** Rogie Spon. Ed. by Kelly Mullins. LC 96-90621. (Illus.). 135p. (Orig.). 1996. wbk. ed., pap. text ed. write for info. (0-9653376-0-X) Truthought Grp.

***Unlocking Church Doors: Ten Keys to Positive Change.** Paul Mundey. Ed. by Herb Miller. LC 96-42569. (Leadership Insight Ser.). 168p. 1997. pap. 14.95 (0-687-03087-0) Abingdon.

***Unlocking DCOM.** Joseph Van Dertol. 1997. 45.00 (1-56205-758-8) Macmillan.

Unlocking Doors to Self-Esteem: Supportive Counseling for Professionals & Families. C. Lynn Fox & Francine L. Weaver. (YA). (gr. 7-12). 1990. pap. 16.95 (0-915190-60-5, JP 9060-5) Jalmar Pr.

Unlocking Japan's Markets: Seizing Marketing & Distribution Opportunities in Today's Japan. Michael R. Czinkota & Jon Woronoff. 225p. 1991. text ed. 29.95 (1-55738-213-1) Irwin Prof Pubng.

Unlocking Japan's Markets: Seizing Marketing & Distribution Opportunities in Today's Japan. Michael R. Czinkota & Jon Woronoff. 228p. 1993. pap. 12.95 (0-8048-1899-1) C E Tuttle.

Unlocking Mallarme. Graham Robb. LC 95-46661. (C). 1996. text ed. write for info. (0-03-000648-1) Yale U Pr.

Unlocking Mallarme. Graham Robb. 1996. 35.00 (0-300-06486-1) Yale U Pr.

Unlocking Microsoft Internet Information Server. Riders Development Group Staff. 350p. 1996. pap. text ed. 40.00 (1-56205-605-0) New Riders Pub.

Unlocking Patients' Records in General Practice for Research, Medical Education & Quality Assurance: The Registration Network Family Practices. Job FM Metsemakers Staff. 200p. 1994. pap. 23.50 (90-5170-279-5, Pub. by Thesis Pubs NE) IBD Ltd.

Unlocking Personal Creativity: A Course in Idea Mapping. David D. Thornburg. (Illus.). 124p. (Orig.). (C). 1986. pap. 8.95 (0-942207-00-9) Starsong CA.

Unlocking Powerhouse. Ramon A. Alino. 408p. (C). 1992. pap. 39.95 (1-882498-12-7) Sftware Visions.

***Unlocking Profits: The Strategic Advantage of Key Account Management.** Lisa Napolitano & Mike Pusateri. Ed. by Ginger Conlon. (Illus.). (Orig.). 1997. pap. 14.95 (0-9657422-0-2) Natl Acct Mgmt.

Unlocking the Adoption Files. Paul Sachidev. 247p. pap. 13.95 (0-669-24780-4, Lexington) Jossey-Bass.

***Unlocking the Air.** Ursula K. Le Guin. Date not set. mass mkt. 6.99 (0-06-105801-7, HarperPrism) HarpC.

Unlocking the Air & Other Stories. Ursula K. Le Guin. LC 95-36012. 224p. 1996. 22.00 (0-06-017260-6, HarpT) HarpC.

***Unlocking the Air & Other Stories.** Ursula K. Le Guin. 224p. 1997. pap. 12.00 (0-06-092803-4, PL) HarpC.

Unlocking the Door to Higher Compensation: Your Key to the Salary Maze. Ernst & Young. 64p. 1996. pap. 28.00 (0-87111-454-2) SLA.

Unlocking the English Language. Robert Burchfield. 1992. pap. 12.00 (0-374-52339-8, Noonday) FS&G.

Unlocking the Files of the FBI: A Guide to Its Records & Classification System. Gerald K. Haines & David A. Langbart. LC 92-16728. 352p. 1993. 60.00 (0-8420-2338-0) Scholarly Res Inc.

Unlocking the Golden Cage: An Intimate Biography of Hilde Bruch, M. D. Joanne H. Bruch. LC 96-75699. (Illus.). 336p. 1996. 29.95 (0-936077-16-6, HIL) Gurze Bks.

***Unlocking the Infrastructure: The Reform of Public Utilities in Australia.** Rodney Maddock & Stephen King. 200p. 1997. pap. 29.95 (1-86448-114-5, Pub. by Allen Unwin AT) Paul & Co Pubs.

Unlocking the Iron Gage: The Men's Movement, Gender Politics, & American Culture. Michael Schwalbe. 304p. 1996. 30.00 (0-19-509229-5) OUP.

Unlocking the Japanese Business Mind. Gregory R. Tenhover. Ed. by Lane Jennings & Richard Matthews. 273p. (Orig.). 1994. pap. 17.95 (0-930124-10-3) Transemantics.

Unlocking the Mysteries of God's Word. Bill R. Swetmon. 136p. 1995. pap. 8.95 (1-55622-036-7, Seaside Pr) Wordware Pub.

***Unlocking the Mysteries of Sensory Dysfunction.** Elizabeth Anderson & Pauline Emmons. 91p. (Orig.). 1996. pap. 19.95 (1-885477-25-2) Fut Horizons.

Unlocking the Mystery of Revelation. James H. Knotek. (Illus.). 145p. (Orig.). 1987. teacher ed. 7.95 (0-939925-03-6); pap. 5.95 (0-939925-02-8) R C Law & Co.

Unlocking the Mystery of Revelation. deluxe ed. James H. Knotek. (Illus.). 145p. (Orig.). 1987. Set. teacher ed. 49.00 (0-939925-07-9) R C Law & Co.

Unlocking the Old Testament. Victor L. Ludlow. LC 81-68266. (Illus.). 239p. 1981. 11.95 (0-87747-873-2) Deseret Bk.

Unlocking the Power Within. Shifra Stein. 1996. pap. text ed. 12.95 (1-878686-22-4) Two Lane Pr.

Unlocking the Powers of Faith. Garth Allred. 1993. pap. 10.95 (1-55503-584-1, 01111248) Covenant Comms.

Unlocking the Puzzle Box. Harold Klemp. (Mahanta Transcripts Ser.: Bk. 6). 309p. 1992. pap. 14.00 (1-57043-007-1) ECKANKAR.

Unlocking the Secret to Tax Free Wealth Transfer: Family Limited Partnerships. Irving L. Blackman & Brian T. Whitlock. (BK Special Reports). 1995. pap. 29.00 (0-916181-37-5) Blackman Kallick Bartelstein.

Unlocking the Secret World: A Unique Christian Ministry to Abused, Abandoned, & Neglected Children. Wayne Tesch & Diane Tesch. LC 94-45046. 1995. pap. 9.99 (0-8423-7735-2) Tyndale.

Unlocking the Secrets in Old Photographs. Karen Frisch-Ripley. (Illus.). 202p. (Orig.). 1991. pap. 14.95 (0-916489-50-7) Ancestry.

***Unlocking the Secrets of Aiki-Jujutsu.** H. E. Davey. LC 97-2289. (Illus.). 256p. (Orig.). 1997. pap. 17.95 (1-57028-121-1) Masters Pr IN.

***Unlocking the Secrets of Time: Maryland's Hidden Heritage.** Ed. by Jean B. Russo. (Illus.). 106p. (Orig.). 1991. pap. 10.95 (0-938420-43-7) MD Hist.

Unlocking the Secrets of Your Childhood Memories. Kevin Leman & Randy Carlson. 288p. 1990. mass mkt. 5.99 (0-671-70317-X) PB.

Unlocking the Secrets of Your Childhood Memories Workbook. Kevin Leman. 1994. pap. 14.99 (0-8407-3446-8) Nelson.

Unlocking the Stories Within You. Jewell R. Coburn. LC 86-70472. (Illus.). 142p. (Orig.). 1986. pap. text ed. 7.95 (0-918060-05-2) Burn Hart.

Unlocking the Text: Fundamental Issues in Literary. Jeremy Hawthorn. 144p. 1995. text ed. 12.95 (0-7131-6427-1, Pub. by E Arnld UK) St Martin.

Unlocking the Unconscious: Selected Papers of Habib Davanloo, MD. Habib Davanloo. 344p. 1995. pap. text ed. 38.95 (0-471-95611-2) Wiley.

Unlocking the Will to Learn. Christine A. Johnston. (1-Off Ser.). (Illus.). 160p. 1996. 54.95 (0-8039-6437-4); pap. 24.95 (0-8039-6392-0) Corwin Pr.

***Unlocking the Zen Koan: A New Translation of the Zen Classic Wumenguan.** 2nd ed. Wumen Huikai. Tr. by Thomas Cleary. 213p. (Orig.). 1997. pap. 12.95 (1-55643-247-X) North Atlantic.

Unlocking Your Bowels for Better Health. Salem Kirban. 1981. pap. 5.00 (0-912582-41-3) Kirban.

***Unlocking Your Career Potential.** Jane Ballback & Jan Slater. (Personal Growth & Development Collection). (Illus.). 118p. (Orig.). 1996. pap. 14.95 (1-883553-77-6) R Chang Assocs.

Unlocking Your Child's Learning Potential: How to Equip Kids to Succeed in School & Life. Cheri Fuller. LC 94-17148. 205p. (Orig.). 1994. pap. 14.00 (0-89109-834-8) Pinon Press.

Unlocking Your Creative Power. Peter Jacoby. 127p. 1993. pap. 14.95 (1-883368-00-6) Ramsey Pr.

Unlocking Your Potential. Charles S. Gifford & Glenn A. Schiro. viii, 88p. 1995. pap. text ed. 2.50 (0-8134-3032-1) Interstate.

Unlocking Your Potential. Harold Sala. 1996. pap. 11.99 (1-885305-46-X) Multnomah Pubs.

Unlocking Your Potential: A Handbook for Personal Growth. Joan P. Lonergan. (Illus.). 72p. 1993. student ed. 9.95 (1-884168-00-0) Chameleon Pub.

Unloosing Monsters: Plunging to the Depths of Human Wisdom. Fred Leavitt. LC 84-90338. 1984. 10.00 (0-87212-179-8) Libra.

Unloved. John Saul. 368p. 1988. mass mkt. 6.99 (0-553-27261-6) Bantam.

Unloved: From the Diary of Perla S. Arnost Lustig. LC 96-25849. (Jewish Lives Ser.). 196p. 1996. pap. 14.95 (0-8101-1347-3) Northwestern U Pr.

An Asterisk (*) at the beginning of an entry indicates that the title is appearing in BIP for the first time.

Unlovelinesse of Love-Lockes. William Prynne. LC 76-57410. (English Experience Ser.: No. 825). 1977. reprint ed. lib. bdg. 25.00 (*90-221-0825-2*) Walter J Johnson.

***Unlucky Seven: A Gil Yates Private Investigator Novel.** Alistair Boyle. LC 96-51686. 176p. 1997. 20.00 (*1-888310-77-4*) A A Knoll Pubs.

Unmade Bed: Sensual Writing on Married Love. Laura Chester. LC 91-50461. 304p. 1993. pap. 11.00 (*0-06-092366-0*, PL) HarpC.

Unmaking Mimesis: Essays on Feminism & Theater. Elin Diamond. LC 96-8881. 224p. (C). 1997. pap. write for info. (*0-415-01229-5*); text ed. write for info. (*0-415-01228-7*) Routledge.

***Unmaking of a Colony.** Motyl. (C). 1992. pap. text ed. 14.36 (*0-8147-5486-4*) NYU Pr.

Unmaking of a Whig & Other Essays in Self-Definition. fac. ed. Edwin M. Yoder. LC 89-71493. 232p. 1990. reprint ed. pap. 94.70 (*0-7837-7789-2*, 2047544) Bks Demand.

Unmaking of Adolf Hitler. Eugene Davidson. (Illus.). 536p. (C). 1997. 29.95 (*0-8262-1045-7*) U of Mo Pr.

Unmaking of God. William F. Nietmann. LC 93-49437. 240p. (Orig.). (C). 1994. pap. text ed. 28.50 (*0-8191-9436-0*); lib. bdg. 49.50 (*0-8191-9435-2*) U Pr of Amer.

Unmaking of Palestine. W. F. Abboushi. 1992. pap. 12.50 (*0-915597-74-8*) Amana Bks.

Unmaking of the President, 1996. William L. Rivera. 240p. 1995. mass mkt. 4.99 (*1-896329-69-1*, Pub. by Comnwlth Pub CN) Partners Pubs Grp.

Unmanageable Consumer: Contemporary Consumption & Its Fragmentations. Yiannis Gabriel & Tim Lang. 224p. 1995. 69.95 (*0-8039-7744-1*); pap. 21.95 (*0-8039-7745-X*) Sage.

Unmanageable Revolutionaries. Margaret Ward. 1996. pap. text ed. 17.95 (*0-7453-1084-2*, Pub. by Pluto Pr UK) LPC InBook.

Unmanly Man: Concept of Sexual Defamation in Early Northern Society. Preben M. Sorensen. 115p. (Orig.). 1983. pap. 37.50 (*87-7492-436-2*, Pub. by Odense Universitets Forlag DK) Coronet Bks.

Unmanned Aircraft. Michael Armitage. Ed. by R. A. Mason. (Air Power Ser.: Vol. 3). (Illus.). 137p. 1988. 40.00 (*0-08-034743-6*, Pub. by Brasseys UK); 25.00 (*0-08-034744-4*, Pub. by Brasseys UK) Brasseys Inc.

Unmanned Aircraft. A. Reed. 110p. 1979. 35.95 (*0-08-027026-3*, Pergamon Pr) Elsevier.

Unmanned Exploration of the Solar System. Ed. by George W. Morgenthaler & R. G. Morra. (Advances in the Astronautical Sciences Ser.: Vol. 19). 1965. 45.00 (*0-87703-021-9*) Univelt Inc.

Unmanned Vehicle Systems: Military & Civil Robots for the 21st Century & Beyond. Robert Finkelstein & Steven Shaker. (Illus.). 1994. pap. 248.00 (*0-935453-70-9*) Pasha Pubns.

***Unmanning Modernism: Gendered Re-Readings.** Elizabeth J. Harrison & Shirley Peterson. LC 97-4761. 1997. write for info. (*0-87049-985-8*) U of Tenn Pr.

Unmapped Territories: New Women's Fiction from Japan. Tr. & Intro. by Yukiko Tanaka. 162p. (Orig.). 1991. pap. 10.95 (*1-879679-00-0*) Women Translation.

Unmarked: The Politics of Performance. Peggy Phelan. LC 92-7895. (Illus.). 224p. (C). 1993. pap. 16.95 (*0-415-06822-3*, A9654) Routledge.

Unmarked: The Politics of Performance. Peggy Phelan. LC 92-7895. (Illus.). 224p. (C). (gr. 13). 1993. text ed. 59.95 (*0-415-06821-5*, A6278) Routledge.

Unmarried America: How Singles Are Changing & What It Means for the Church. Telford Work. Ed. by George Barna. (Illus.). 110p. (Orig.). 1993. spiral bd. 22.00 (*1-882297-03-2*) Barna Res Grp.

Unmarried Bride. large type ed. Emma Goldrick. (Harlequin Ser.). 1994. lib. bdg. 19.95 (*0-263-13649-3*) Thorndike Pr.

Unmarried Couples: A Guide to Your Legal Rights & Obligations. Elliot D. Samuelson. (Illus.). 312p. (C). 1992. 24.95 (*0-306-44322-8*, Plenum Insight) Plenum.

***Unmarried Couple's Legal Survival Guide: Your Rights & Obligations.** Elliot D. Samuelson. LC 96-45421. 1996. pap. text ed. 16.95 (*0-8065-1845-6*, Citadel Pr) Carol Pub Group.

Unmarried in Later Life. Pat M. Keith. LC 88-28854. 232p. 1989. text ed. 55.00 (*0-275-92620-6*, C2620, Praeger Pubs) Greenwood.

Unmarried Man. Patrick Smith. 224p. 1995. pap. 17.95 (*0-224-03680-7*, Pub. by Jonathan Cape UK) Trafalgar.

Unmarried Mother: A Study of 500 Cases. Percy G. Kammerer. LC 69-14935. (Criminology, Law Enforcement, & Social Problems Ser.: No. 58). 1969. reprint ed. 24.00 (*0-87585-058-8*) Patterson Smith.

Unmarried Mother in German Literature. O. H. Werner. 1973. 75.00 (*0-8490-1250-3*) Gordon Pr.

Unmarried Mothers. Clark E. Vincent. LC 80-16580. x, 308p. 1980. reprint ed. text ed. 59.75 (*0-313-22474-9*, VIMO, Greenwood Pr) Greenwood.

Unmarried with Children. Victoria Pade. (Special Edition Ser.). 1993. mass mkt. 3.50 (*0-373-09852-9*, 5-09852-0) Silhouette.

Unmarried Working Women. Majula Rathaur. 165p. 1988. text ed. 18.95 (*81-7027-134-7*, Pub. by Radiant Pubs II) S Asia.

***Unmasked.** 1997. mass mkt. 6.99 (*1-55166-272-8*, 1-66272-5, Mira Bks) Harlequin Bks.

Unmasking. Kevin Flynn. 352p. 1994. mass mkt. 5.99 (*0-7860-0053-8*, Pinncle Kensgtn) Kensgtn Pub Corp.

Unmasking. Jan Van Rijckenborgh. 70p. 1987. pap. 7.50 (*0-317-56231-2*) Rosycross Pr.

Unmasking: Married to a Rapist. Kevin Flynn. 1993. text ed. 24.95 (*0-02-910315-0*, Free Press) Free Pr.

Unmasking a Virginia Myth: Who Visited First the Virgin Valley? What the Schools Did Not Teach. Gene P. Hammond. Ed. by Evelyn E. Hammond & Rachael W. Hammond. LC 93-94170. (Illus.). 70p. (YA). (gr. 8-12). 1993. pap. 14.00 (*1-878014-07-2*) G P Hammond Pub.

Unmasking & Triumphing over the Spirit of Antichrist. Jack Van Impe. 224p. 1991. pap. 7.00 (*0-934803-82-X*) J Van Impe.

Unmasking Japan: Myths & Realities about the Emotions of the Japanese. David R. Matsumoto. 1996. 29.50 (*0-8047-2719-8*); pap. write for info. (*0-8047-2755-4*) Stanford U Pr.

Unmasking Japan Today: The Impact of Traditional Values on Modern Japanese Society. Fumie Kumagai & Donna J. Keyser. LC 95-23224. 208p. 1996. text ed. 39.95 (*0-275-95144-8*, Praeger Pubs) Greenwood.

Unmasking Masculinity: A Critical Autobiography. David Jackson. (Critical Studies on Men & Masculinities: No. 2). 240p. (C). 1990. pap. text ed. 17.95 (*0-04-445552-6*) Routledge Chapman & Hall.

Unmasking of Drama: Contested Representation in Shakespeare's Tragedies. Jonathan Baldo. 240p. 1996. 39.95 (*0-8143-2598-X*) Wayne St U Pr.

Unmasking of Medicine: A Searching Look at Health Care Today. Ian Kennedy. 256p. 1983. pap. 9.00 (*0-586-08433-9*, Pub. by Granada UK) Academy Chi Pubs.

Unmasking PMS. Joseph Martorano et al. LC 93-72. 240p. 1993. 21.95 (*0-87131-692-7*) M Evans.

Unmasking PMS: The Complete PMS Medical Treatment Plan. Morgan & Joseph Martorano. 272p. 1994. mass mkt. 5.99 (*0-425-14401-1*, Berkley Trade) Berkley Pub.

***Unmasking Sexual Con Games: Helping Teens Identify Good & Bad Relationships.** 2nd rev. ed. Ron W. Herron & Kathleen M. Sorensen. 1997. pap. text ed. 29.95 (*1-889322-04-0*, 25-008) Boys Town Pr.

Unmasking Sexual Con Games: Student Guide. Ed. by Ronald W. Herron. 28p. 1993. pap. text ed. 4.50 (*0-938510-44-4*, 25-002) Boys Town Pr.

***Unmasking Sexual Con Games: Student Guide.** 2nd ed. (YA). (gr. 7-12). 1997. pap. 4.50 (*1-889322-07-5*, 25-009) Boys Town Pr.

***Unmasking the Book of Revelation.** Charles W. Weller. 162p. (Orig.). 1995. 15.00 (*0-9653851-0-8*) Not I But Christ.

Unmasking the Cults. Alan W. Gomes. (Zondervan Guide to Cults & Religious Movements Ser.). 96p. 1995. pap. 5.99 (*0-310-70441-3*) Zondervan.

Unmasking the Enemy. Nelson S. Pacheco & Tommy R. Blann. (Illus.). 406p. (Orig.). 1994. pap. 14.95 (*1-885152-01-9*) Bendan Pr.

Unmasking the Idols. Douglas Gwyn. LC 88-35548. 190p. (Orig.). 1989. pap. 10.95 (*0-944350-04-6*) Friends United.

***Unmasking the Internet for Research Using Hands-On Active Learning Exercises.** Ed. by Marilyn Whitmore. LC 97-72733. (Active Learning Ser.: No. 2). 288p. 1997. spiral bd. 50.00 (*0-9652711-1-0*) Lib Instruct.

Unmasking the Magistrates: The "Custody-or-Not" Decision in Sentencing Young Offenders. Howard Parker & Graham Jarvis. 176p. 1989. 90.00 (*0-335-09936-X*, Open Univ Pr); pap. 32.00 (*0-335-09935-1*, Open Univ Pr) Taylor & Francis.

Unmasking the New Age. Douglas Groothuis. LC 85-23832. 194p. (Orig.). 1986. pap. 10.99 (*0-87784-568-9*, 568) InterVarsity.

Unmasking the Powers: The Invisible Forces That Determine Human Existence. Walter Wink. LC 85-45480. 224p. 1993. pap. 16.00 (*0-8006-1902-1*, 1-1902, Fortress Pr) Augsburg Fortress.

Unmasking the Psychopath: Antisocial Personality & Related Syndromes. Ed. by William H. Reid et al. (Professional Bks.). 1986. 34.95 (*0-393-70025-9*) Norton.

Unmasterable Past: History, Holocaust, & German National Identity. Charles S. Maier. LC 88-11690. 240p. 1988. 33.95 (*0-674-92975-6*) HUP.

Unmasterable Past: History, Holocaust, & German National Identity. Charles S. Maier. 240p. 1990. pap. text ed. 12.00 (*0-674-92976-4*) HUP.

Unmastered Past: The Autobiographical Reflections of Leo Lowenthal. Leo Lowenthal. LC 86-24942. (Illus.). 240p. 1987. 35.00 (*0-520-05638-8*) U CA Pr.

Unmatchable Miss Mirabella. Gillian Grey. 176p. (Orig.). 1993. mass mkt. 3.99 (*0-380-77399-6*) Avon.

Unmedical Book. Elizabeth Baker & Elton Baker. 263p. (Orig.). 1987. pap. 11.95 (*0-918880-14-9*) Drelwood Comns.

Unmedical Miracle - Oxygen. rev. ed. Elizabeth Baker. 150p. 1994. pap. 11.95 (*0-937766-12-7*) Drelwood Comns.

***UnMedical Miracle Oxygen.** Elizabeth Baker. 119p. (Orig.). 1996. pap. 12.95 (*1-57901-010-5*) Intl Promotions.

Unmeltable Ethnics: Politics & Culture in American Life. 2nd ed. Michael Novak. 512p. (C). 1996. pap. text ed. 21.95 (*1-56000-773-7*) Transaction Pubs.

Unmentionable! More Amazing Stories. Paul Jennings. 128p. (J). 1995. pap. 3.99 (*0-14-037399-3*) Puffin Bks.

Unmentionable Cuisine. Calvin W. Schwabe. LC 79-15957. (Illus.). 476p. (Orig.). 1979. pap. 16.95 (*0-8139-1162-1*) U Pr of Va.

Unmentionable Man: Five Short Stories. Edward Upward. 102p. 9500. pap. 13.95 (*1-870612-64-7*, Pub. by Enitha Pr UK) Dufour.

Unmentionables: A Brief History of Underwear. Elaine Benson. 160p. 1996. 30.00 (*0-684-82266-0*) S&S Trade.

***Unmerited Favor: Teaching Sermons on the Love & Grace of God.** David A. Farmer. Ed. by Ronald J. Allen. LC 96-47763. (Teaching Sermon Ser.: Vol. 1). 96p. 1997. pap. 9.95 (*0-687-01788-2*) Abingdon.

Unmet Needs: The Growing Crisis in America. League of Women Voters Education Fund Staff. 71p. 1988. pap. 5.00 (*0-89959-409-3*, 853) LWVUS.

Unmet Promise of Alternatives to Incarceration. Barry Krisberg & Jim Austin. 1982. 4.50 (*0-318-02054-8*) Natl Coun Crime.

Unmodern Observations. Friedrich Wilhelm Nietzsche. Ed. by William Arrowsmith. 424p. (C). 1990. text ed. 47.50 (*0-300-04311-2*) Yale U Pr.

Unmotivated Child. Natalie Rathvon. 1996. pap. 12.00 (*0-684-80306-2*) S&S Trade.

Unmusical New York: A Brief Criticism of Triumphs, Failures, & Abuses. Herman Klein. LC 79-1278. (Music Reprint Ser.). 1979. reprint ed. lib. bdg. 25.00 (*0-306-79517-5*) Da Capo.

Unmuzzled Ox Anthology, No. 7. Ed. by Michael Andre. (Illus.). 78p. 1974. pap. 10.95 (*0-934450-13-7*) Unmuzzled Ox.

Unmuzzled Ox Anthology, No. 13. Ed. by Michael Andre et al. 1980. pap. 19.95 (*0-934450-06-4*) Unmuzzled Ox.

Unmuzzled Ox Anthology, No. 14. William Stafford et al. Ed. by Michael Andre et al. (Illus.). 1980. pap. 19.95 (*0-934450-07-2*) Unmuzzled Ox.

Unmuzzled Ox Anthology, No. 15. Djuna Barnes et al. Ed. by Michael Andre. (Illus.). pap. 19.95 (*0-934450-08-0*) Unmuzzled Ox.

Unmysterious Universe: An Introduction to D. B. Larson's New, Unified, General Theory. Ronald W. Satz. (Illus.). 80p. (Orig.). (C). 1971. pap. text ed. 6.50 (*1-880845-00-8*) Transpower.

Unnam'd Form: Blake & Textuality. Nelson Hilton. 1985. 45.00 (*0-520-05298-6*) U CA Pr.

Unnatural. David Prill. 1995. 21.00 (*0-312-11910-0*) St Martin.

Unnatural: Techno-Theory for a Contaminated Culture. Matthew Fuller. (Illus.). 80p. (Orig.). 1994. pap. 15.00 (*1-899037-00-4*, Pub. by Underground UK) AK Pr Dist.

Unnatural Act of Management. Everett T. Suters. LC 89-50277. 382p. 1989. boxed 18.95 (*0-9621571-0-4*) Curry Pub.

Unnatural Acts. Dylan Jones. LC 96-27966. 320p. 1996. 22.95 (*0-312-14753-8*) St Martin.

Unnatural Acts. Susan Shellogg. LC 93-43563. 304p. 1994. 21.00 (*1-56980-000-6*) Barricade Bks.

Unnatural Acts & Other Stories. Lucy Taylor. (Orig.). 1994. 12.95 (*1-56333-181-0*, R Kasak Bks) Masquerade.

***Unnatural Acts & Other Stories.** 2nd ed. Lucy Taylor. (Orig.). 1997. reprint ed. mass mkt. 7.95 (*1-56333-552-2*, Rhinoceros) Masquerade.

Unnatural Causes. P. D. James. 256p. 1988. mass mkt. 5.99 (*0-446-31219-3*) Warner Bks.

Unnatural Causes: The Three Leading Killer Diseases in America. Ed. by Russell C. Maulitz. 210p. 1989. text ed. 37.00 (*0-8135-1405-3*); pap. text ed. 16.00 (*0-8135-1406-1*) Rutgers U Pr.

Unnatural Death: A Lord Peter Wimsey Mystery. Dorothy L. Sayers. 288p. 1995. mass mkt. 4.99 (*0-06-104358-3*, Harp PBks) HarpC.

Unnatural Death: Confessions of a Medical Examiner. Michael M. Baden & Judith A. Hennesee. 240p. 1990. mass mkt. 5.99 (*0-8041-0599-5*) Ivy Books.

Unnatural Deaths in the U. S. S. R., 1928-1954. Iosif G. Dyadkin. Tr. by Tania Deruguine from RUS. LC 82-8455. (Illus.). 80p. (Orig.). 1983. pap. text ed. 21.95 (*0-87855-919-1*) Transaction Pubs.

Unnatural Disasters: Recent Writings from the Golden State. Ed. by Nicole Panter. 250p. (Orig.). 1996. pap. 15.00 (*1-884615-16-3*) Incommcdo San Diego.

Unnatural Disease. Noel Hume. Date not set. pap. write for info. (*0-679-44636-2*) Random.

Unnatural Doubts: Epistemological Realism & the Basis of Skepticism. Michael Williams. 416p. (C). 1996. pap. text ed. 19.00 (*0-691-01115-X*) Princeton U Pr.

Unnatural Dykes to Watch Out For: Cartoons. Alison Bechdel. LC 95-36092. 144p. 1995. pap. 10.95 (*1-56341-067-2*) Firebrand Bks.

Unnatural Emotions: Every Day Sentiments on a Micronesian Atoll & Their Challenge to Western Theory. Catherine A. Lutz. (Illus.). 286p. 1988. pap. text ed. 16.95 (*0-226-49722-4*) U Ch Pr.

Unnatural Enemy: Essays on Hunting. Vance N. Bourjaily. LC 84-8640. (Illus.). 195p. 1984. reprint ed. pap. 55.60 (*0-608-00728-5*, 2061504) Bks Demand.

***Unnatural Exposure.** limited ed. Patricia Cornwell. 352p. 1997. 150.00 (*0-399-14295-9*) Putnam Pub Group.

***Unnatural Exposure: A Kay Scarpetta Mystery.** Patricia D. Cornwell. LC 96-54064. 1997. 28.95 (*0-7838-8087-1*); write for info. (*0-7838-8088-X*) G K Hall.

***Unnatural Exposure: A Kay Scarpetta Mystery.** Patricia D. Cornwell. LC 96-38460. 352p. 1997. 25.95 (*0-399-14285-1*, Putnam) Putnam Pub Group.

Unnatural History of Death Valley: With Reflections on the Valley's Varmints, Virgins, Vandals & Visionaries. Paul Bailey. LC 78-21578. (Illus.). 84p. 1978. pap. 5.95 (*0-912494-31-X*) Death Valley Fortyniners.

Unnatural Lives: Studies in Australian Convict Fiction. Laurie Hergenhan. (Orig.). 1993. pap. 29.95 (*0-7022-2258-5*, Pub. by Univ Queensland Pr AT) Intl Spec Bk.

Unnatural Lottery: Character & Moral Luck. Claudia Card. LC 96-1316. 1996. 59.95 (*1-56639-452-X*); pap. 22.95 (*1-56639-453-8*) Temple U Pr.

Unnatural Mothers: A Novel. Renate Dorrstein. Tr. by Wanda Boeke. LC 94-16877. 232p. 1994. pap. 11.95 (*1-879679-06-X*) Women Translation.

Unnatural Nature of Science. Lewis Wolpert. LC 92-40510. 205p. (C). 1993. text ed. 19.95 (*0-674-92980-2*) HUP.

Unnatural Nature of Science. Lewis Wolpert. (Illus.). 205p. 1994. pap. text ed. 12.95 (*0-674-92981-0*, WOLUNX) HUP.

***Unnatural Order: Why We Are Destroying the Planet & Each Other.** Jim Mason. 352p. 1997. pap. text ed. 17.95 (*0-8264-1028-6*) Continuum.

Unnatural Relations. Seabrook. 1996. pex. 14.95 (*0-85449-116-3*, Pub. by Gay Mens Pr UK) LPC InBook.

Unnatural Selection: Technology, Politics, & Plant Evolution. Cary Fowler. LC 94-17304. (International Studies in Global Change). 352p. 1994. text ed. 50.00 (*2-88124-640-0*); pap. text ed. 20.00 (*2-88124-639-7*) Gordon & Breach.

Unnatural Selections: A Far Side Collection. Gary Larson. (Illus.). 112p. (Orig.). 1991. pap. 8.95 (*0-8362-1881-7*) Andrews & McMeel.

Unnatural Wolf Transplant in Yellowstone National Park. Troy R. Mader. (C). 1990. pap. text ed. 3.50 (*0-944402-04-6*) Cmmn Man Inst.

***Unnaturals (33012)** (Bloodshadows Ser.). 15.00 (*0-87431-382-1*, 31011) West End Games.

Unneccessary Losses: Costs to Americans of the Lack of Family & Medical Leave: Executive Summary. Roberta M. Spalter-Roth & Heidi Hartmann. 18p. 1988. pap. 5.00 (*0-685-29930-9*) Inst Womens Policy Rsch.

Unneccessary Losses: The Costs to Workers in the States of the Lack of Family & Medical Leave. Roberta M. Spalter-Roth et al. 150p. 1989. pap. 25.00 (*0-685-29939-2*) Inst Womens Policy Rsch.

Unnecessary Cesarean Sections: Curing a National Epidemic. enl. ed. Mary Gabay & Sidney M. Wolfe. 589p. (C). 1994. pap. text ed. 60.00 (*0-937188-55-7*) Pub Citizen Inc.

Unnecessary Cesareans: Ways to Avoid Them. Diony Young & Charles Mahan. 27p. 1980. 1.50 (*0-934024-00-6*) Intl Childbirth.

***Unnecessary Debts.** Ed. by Lars Osberg & Pierre Fortin. 200p. pap. 19.95 (*1-55028-496-7*, Pub. by J Lorimer CN) Formac Dist Ltd.

***Unnecessary Debts.** Ed. by Lars Osberg & Pierre Fortin. 200p. bds. 24.95 (*1-55028-497-5*, Pub. by J Lorimer CN) Formac Dist Ltd.

Unnecessary Losses: Costs to Americans of the Lack of Family & Medical Leave. Roberta M. Spalter-Roth & Heidi Hartmann. LC 89-82427. 73p. 1990. pap. 15.00 (*1-878428-00-4*) Inst Womens Policy Rsch.

Unnecessary Problem of Edith Stein. Harry J. Cargas. (Studies in the Shoah). 135p. (C). 1994. lib. bdg. 37.50 (*0-8191-8781-X*) U Pr of Amer.

Unnecessary Suffering: Management, Markets & the Liquidation of Solidarity. Maurice Glasman. LC 96-48704. 192p. (C). 1996. text ed. 60.00 (*1-85984-976-8*, C0521, Pub. by Vrso UK); pap. text ed. 18.00 (*1-85984-071-X*, C0522, Pub. by Vrso UK) Norton.

Unnecessary War: Proceedings of the Belgrano Enquiry, November 1986. Ed. by Belgrano Action Group Staff. 184p. 1988. 42.50 (*0-85124-455-6*, Pub. by Spokesman Bks UK) Coronet Bks.

Unnecessary Wars? Causes & Effects of United States Wars from the Revolution to Vietnam. Peter M. Rinaldo. LC 93-70883. (Illus.). 168p. (C). 1993. 14.95 (*0-9622123-7-7*) DorPete Pr.

Unnormalized Relational Data Model: For Office Form Processor Design. H. Kitagawa. Ed. by Toshiyasu L. Kunii. (Computer Science Workbench Ser.). xiii, 164p. 1990. 71.95 (*0-387-70049-8*) Spr-Verlag.

Unnoticed Challenge: Soviet Maritime Strategy & the Global Choke Points. Robert J. Hanks. LC 80-83751. (Special Report Ser.). 66p. 1980. 11.95 (*0-89549-025-0*) Inst Foreign Policy Anal.

Unnoticed Majority in Psychiatric Inpatient Care. Charles A. Kiesler & C. G. Simpkins. (Stress & Coping Ser.). (Illus.). 260p. (C). 1993. 39.50 (*0-306-44363-5*, Plenum Pr) Plenum.

Uno: Guida Per l'Insegnante. Gruppo Meta. (Illus.). 154p. (C). 1994. pap. text ed. 36.95 (*0-521-46812-4*) Cambridge U Pr.

Uno: Guida Per l'Insegnante, No. 3. Gruppo Meta. (Illus.). 154p. (C). 1994. digital audio 14.95 (*0-521-46816-7*) Cambridge U Pr.

Uno: Guida Per l'Insegnante, Nos. 1 & 2. Gruppo Meta. (Illus.). 154p. (C). 1994. pap. 23.95 (*0-521-46815-9*) Cambridge U Pr.

Uno: Libro Degli Esercizi e Sintesi di Grammatica. Gruppo Meta. (Illus.). 168p. (C). 1994. pap. text ed. 16.95 (*0-521-46813-2*) Cambridge U Pr.

Uno: Libro Dello Studente. Gruppo Meta. (Illus.). 216p. (C). 1994. pap. text ed. 19.95 (*0-521-46814-0*) Cambridge U Pr.

Uno Arriba, Uno Abajo. Carol Snyder. Tr. by Alma F. Ada. (Illus.). (SPA.). (J). (ps-3). 1995. 16.00 (*0-689-31994-0*, Atheneum Bks Young) S&S Childrens.

Uno, Dos, Cuatro: A Guide to the Number Stations. Havana Moon. 76p. (Orig.). 1987. pap. 13.95 (*0-936653-06-X*) Tiare Pubns.

Uno, Dos, Tres: One, Two, Three. Pat Mora. LC 94-15337. (Illus.). 43p. (J). (ps-3). 1996. 14.95 (*0-395-67294-5*, Clarion Bks) HM.

Unobserved Heritage of Texas Tech. Nolan E. Barrick. LC 84-51938. (Illus.). 64p. 1985. pap. 5.00 (*0-89672-125-6*) Tex Tech Univ Pr.

Unobstructed Shortest Paths in Polyhedral Environments. V. Akman. (Lecture Notes in Computer Science Ser.: Vol. 251). vii, 103p. 1987. 26.00 (*0-387-17629-2*) Spr-Verlag.

Unobstructed Universe. Stewart E. White. 350p. 1988. reprint ed. pap. 9.95 (*0-89804-152-X*) Ariel GA.

Unobtrusive Researcher: A Guide to Methods. Allan Kellehear. 192p. pap. 19.95 (*1-86373-513-5*, Pub. by Allen Unwin AT) Paul & Co Pubs.

Unobtrusive Testing & Library Reference Services. Peter Hernon & Charles R. McClure. LC 86-28736. 256p. (C). 1987. text ed. 73.25 (*0-89391-383-9*) Ablex Pub.

Unocal Corp. A Report on the Company's Environmental Policies & Practices. (Illus.). 26p. (C). 1994. reprint ed. pap. text ed. 250.00 (*0-7881-0986-3*, Coun on Econ) DIANE Pub.

Unocal Environmental Loss Control Management Audit Working Copy. Date not set. spiral bd. write for info. (*0-88061-172-3*) Intl Loss Cntrl.

Unocal Loss Control Management Audit Working Copy. Date not set. spiral bd. write for info. (*0-88061-171-5*) Intl Loss Cntrl.

Unoccupied Electronic States: Fundamentals for XANES, EELS, IPS & BIS. Jeanne Somers. Ed. by J. E. Inglesfield. (Topics in Applied Physics Ser.: Vol. 69). (Illus.). 336p. 1992. 90.95 (*0-387-54162-4*) Spr-Verlag.

Unoccupied Mission Fields of Africa & Asia. Samuel M. Zwemer. 1977. 22.95 (*0-8369-9197-4*, 9066) Ayer.

Unofficial Guide to Life at Harvard. Let's Go, Inc. Editorial Staff. 327p. 1995. pap. 7.95 (*0-9634820-0-9*) Harvard Student Agencies Inc.

Unofficial Atlanta. 3rd ed. Bob Sehlinger. 1996. 15.95 (*0-02-861243-4*) Mac Pub USA.

Unofficial Atlanta Souvenir Guide. Kudzu Undercover Staff. 160p. 1993. pap. 17.95 (*0-89804-825-7*, Enthea Pr) Ariel GA.

Unofficial Branson, Missouri. (Unofficial Guides Ser.). 1995. 10.00 (*0-02-860078-9*) Macmillan.

Unofficial Chicago. Bob Sehlinger. 1995. pap. 14.00 (*0-671-89862-0*) S&S Trade.

Unofficial Christmas Survival Guide. 78p. (Orig.). 1991. pap. 7.95 (*1-56245-024-7*) Great Quotations.

Unofficial Diplomats. Ed. by Maureen R. Berman & Joseph E. Johnson. LC 77-9376. 1977. text ed. 49.50 (*0-231-04396-1*); pap. text ed. 17.00 (*0-231-04397-X*) Col U Pr.

***Unofficial Disney Reader.** Eve Zibart. (Unofficial Guides Ser.). 1997. pap. 11.95 (*0-02-861557-3*) Macmillan.

Unofficial Documents of the Democracy Movement in Communist China 1978-1981: A Checklist of Chinese Materials in the Hoover Institution on War, Revolution & Peace. I-mu. 100p. 1986. pap. text ed. 10.95 (*0-8179-2672-0*) Hoover Inst Pr.

Unofficial Ethnic Dining in America. (Unofficial Guides Ser.). 1995. 13.00 (*0-02-860067-3*) Macmillan.

Unofficial Gay Manual: Living the Lifestyle (or At Least Appearing To) Kevin DiLallo & Jack Krumholtz. LC 94-10769. (Illus.). 240p. 1994. pap. 12.95 (*0-385-47445-8*) Doubleday.

Unofficial Gilligan's Island Handbook: A Castaway's Companion to the Longest Running Shipwreck in Television History. Joey Green. (Illus.). 384p. (Orig.). 1988. pap. 8.95 (*0-446-38668-5*) Warner Bks.

Unofficial Guide to America's Ethnic Dining. Bob Sehlinger. 1994. pap. 13.00 (*0-671-89213-4*, P-H Travel) P-H Gen Ref & Trav.

Unofficial Guide to Atlanta 1996. Fred Brown. 1995. 14.95 (*0-02-860665-5*) Macmillan.

Unofficial Guide to Branson, Missouri. Bob Sehlinger. 1995. pap. 10.00 (*0-671-89214-2*, P-H Travel) P-H Gen Ref & Trav.

Unofficial Guide to Chicago. Bob Sehlinger. 1995. pap. 11.00 (*0-671-89216-9*, P-H Travel) P-H Gen Ref & Trav.

***Unofficial Guide to Chicago: Save Money, Best Hotel Values Restaurants Ranked & Rated.** 2nd ed. Bob Sehlinger. 1997. pap. text ed. 14.95 (*0-02-862032-1*) Macmillan.

Unofficial Guide to Chicago, 1996. Bob Sehlinger. 1995. 14.00 (*0-02-860494-6*) Macmillan.

Unofficial Guide to Cruises. Bob Sehlinger. 1995. pap. 18.00 (*0-671-89703-9*, P-H Travel) P-H Gen Ref & Trav.

Unofficial Guide to Cruises. Kay Showker. 1995. 18.00 (*0-02-860495-4*) Macmillan.

***Unofficial Guide to Cruises: Lowest Fares, Best Cruise Deals, Lines & Ships Ranked & Rated.** 2nd ed. Bob Sehlinger. 1997. pap. text ed. 18.95 (*0-02-862033-X*) Macmillan.

Unofficial Guide to Dining in L. A. Bob Sehlinger. 200p. 1997. 11.00 (*0-02-860899-2*) Macmillan.

Unofficial Guide to Dining in Miami. Bob Sehlinger. 1994. pap. 11.00 (*0-671-89211-8*, P-H Travel) P-H Gen Ref & Trav.

Unofficial Guide to Dining in San Francisco. Richard Sterling. 200p. 1997. 11.00 (*0-02-860898-4*) Macmillan.

***Unofficial Guide to Disneyland.** Bob Sehlinger. 1997. pap. text ed. 13.95 (*0-02-862030-5*) Macmillan.

Unofficial Guide to Disneyland 1996. Bob Sehlinger. 1995. 13.95 (*0-02-860664-7*) Macmillan.

Unofficial Guide to Disneyland 1997. Bob Sehlinger. (Illus.). 1996. 13.95 (*0-02-861271-X*, P-H Travel) P-H Gen Ref & Trav.

Unofficial Guide to Las Vegas. Bob Sehlinger. (Illus.). 1994. pap. 13.00 (*0-671-86846-2*, P-H Travel) P-H Gen Ref & Trav.

***Unofficial Guide to Las Vegas: Gambling Tips, the Best Hotel Values, Casinos Ranked & Rated.** Bob Sehlinger. 1997. pap. text ed. 16.95 (*0-02-862037-2*) Macmillan.

Unofficial Guide to Las Vegas: 1996. Bob Sehlinger. 576p. 1995. 15.95 (*0-02-860706-6*) Macmillan.

Unofficial Guide to Las Vegas 1995. 4th ed. Bob Sehlinger. 1995. pap. 14.00 (*0-671-50308-1*) S&S Trade.

Unofficial Guide to Las Vegas '97. Bob Sehlinger. (Illus.). 1997. 16.95 (*0-02-861272-8*, P-H Travel) P-H Gen Ref & Trav.

Unofficial Guide to Miami & the Keys. Bob Sehlinger. 1994. pap. 15.00 (*0-671-89212-6*, P-H Travel) P-H Gen Ref & Trav.

Unofficial Guide to Miami & the Keys. 2nd ed. Bob Sehlinger. (Illus.). 1996. 15.95 (*0-02-861270-1*, P-H Travel) P-H Gen Ref & Trav.

Unofficial Guide to Skiing in the West. Lito Tejada-Flores. 1995. 14.00 (*0-02-860493-8*) Macmillan.

***Unofficial Guide to Skiing in the West: Save Money Hotel & Condo Deals When & How to Ski the Slopes.** 2nd ed. Lito Tejada-Flores. 1997. pap. text ed. 16.95 (*0-02-861914-5*) Macmillan.

***Unofficial Guide to the Great Smokey & Blue Ridge Mountains.** 2nd ed. Bob Sehlinger. 1997. 15.95 (*0-02-861897-1*) Macmillan.

Unofficial Guide to the Great Smokey Mountains & Blue Ridge Parkway. Bob Sehlinger. 1995. pap. 16.00 (*0-671-89215-0*, P-H Travel) P-H Gen Ref & Trav.

Unofficial Guide to the Great Smoky & Blue Ridge Mountains. Bob Surkiewicz. (Unofficial Guides Ser.). 400p. 1995. 16.00 (*0-02-860079-7*) Macmillan.

***Unofficial Guide to Walt Disney World & Epcot: Tips & Warnings Save Money & Time on All Attractions.** Bob Sehlinger. 1997. pap. text ed. 15.95 (*0-02-862031-3*) Macmillan.

Unofficial Guide to Walt Disney World 1996. Bob Sehlinger. 1995. 14.95 (*0-02-860663-9*) Macmillan.

Unofficial Guide to Walt Disney World 1997. Bob Sehlinger. (Illus.). 1996. 15.95 (*0-02-861240-X*, P-H Travel) P-H Gen Ref & Trav.

Unofficial Guide to Washington, D. C. Bob Sehlinger. (Illus.). 1996. 15.95 (*0-02-861242-6*, P-H Travel) P-H Gen Ref & Trav.

***Unofficial Guide to Washington, D. C. Save Money, Best Hotel Values, Restaurants Ranked & Rated.** 3rd ed. Bob Sehlinger. 1997. pap. text ed. 14.95 (*0-02-862036-4*) Macmillan.

Unofficial Guide to Washington, D.C. 1996. Bob Sehlinger. 1995. 14.95 (*0-02-860666-3*) Macmillan.

Unofficial IEEE Brainbuster Gamebook: Mental Workouts for the Technically Inclined. Donald R. Mack. LC 92-4724. (Illus.). 144p. 1992. pap. 12.95 (*0-7803-0423-3*, PP0318-6) Inst Electrical.

***Unofficial Kern County Activity Guide.** Jim Duriga. (Illus.). 193p. (Orig.). 1996. lab manual ed., ring bd., pap. 4.95 (*1-889991-01-5*) Seneca-Secor.

Unofficial Liberal Joke Book: For the Politically Incorrect. Bob Phillips. 1994. pap. 7.99 (*1-56507-278-2*) Harvest Hse.

Unofficial Macintosh Guide to America Online. Charles E. Flynn. LC 94-46229. 364p. 1995. pap. text ed. 19.95 (*0-471-06482-3*) Wiley.

***Unofficial Mini-Mickey: The Pocket-Sized Guide to Walt Disney World.** 2nd ed. Bob Sehlinger. 1997. pap. text ed. 10.95 (*0-02-862035-6*) Macmillan.

Unofficial Mother's Handbook. Art Peterson & Norma Peterson. (Illus.). 128p. 1991. mass mkt. 6.95 (*0-452-25213-X*, Plume) NAL-Dutton.

***Unofficial Murder She Wrote Casebook.** James R. Parish. 384p. 1997. pap. 15.00 (*1-57566-210-8*, Knsington) Kensgtn Pub Corp.

***Unofficial Rilke.** Ranier M. Rilke & Michael Hamburger. 116p. 1992. pap. 13.95 (*0-85646-077-X*, Pub. by Anvil Press UK) Dufour.

Unofficial Rose. Iris Murdoch. 334p. 1987. pap. 10.95 (*0-14-002154-X*, Penguin Bks) Viking Penguin.

Unofficial Secretary's Handbook. Richard Mintzer. (Illus.). 112p. 1991. mass mkt. 6.95 (*0-452-25180-X*, Plume) NAL-Dutton.

Unofficial Sensuous Women Sexual Men User's Manual: For Women Only. Garrett Brandon. 62p. 1993. pap. 2.95 (*0-9638612-0-4*) Amer Press.

Unofficial Ski Resorts of the West. Bob Sehlinger. 1994. pap. 13.00 (*0-671-79828-6*) S&S Trade.

Unofficial Suitor. Charlotte L. Dolan. (Regency Romance Ser.). 224p. (Orig.). 1992. pap. 3.99 (*0-451-17300-7*, Sig) NAL-Dutton.

Unofficial Test for Stress. Debbie Hansen. (Illus.). 78p. 1993. pap. 7.95 (*1-56245-063-8*) Great Quotations.

Unofficial Women's Divorce Guide. Mary B. Shank & Suzanne Tumy. Ed. by Cliff Carle. 1991. pap. 5.95 (*0-918259-31-2*) CCC Pubns.

Unofficial X-Files Companion: An X-Phile's Guide to the Mysteries, Conspiracies, & Really Strange Truths Behind the Show. N. E. Genge. LC 95-34598. (Illus.). 256p. (Orig.). 1995. pap. 15.00 (*0-517-88601-4*) Crown Pub Group.

Unofficial X-Files Companion II. N. E. Genge. (Orig.). 1996. pap. 14.00 (*0-380-79024-6*) Avon.

***Unofficial 3rd Rock from the Sun.** Fran W. Golden. 1997. pap. write for info. (*0-609-80064-7*, Crown) Crown Pub Group.

Unopened Letters. Linda Zisquit. LC 96-29253. 88p. (Orig.). 1996. pap. 12.95 (*1-878818-61-9*) Sheep Meadow.

Unordinary Man: A Life of Father John LaFarge, S. J. Robert A. Hecht. LC 95-38738. (ATLA Monographs: No. 39). 304p. 1995. 67.50 (*0-8108-3094-9*) Scarecrow.

Unordnung und Fruehes Leid: Erzaehlungen 1910-1930. Thomas Mann. 240p. (GER.). 1991. pap. 13.50 (*3-596-29441-X*, Pub. by Fischer Taschbch Verlag GW) Intl Bk Import.

Unoriented Bordism & Actions of Finite Groups. R. E. Stong. LC 52-42839. (Memoirs Ser.: No. 1/103). 80p. 1970. pap. 16.00 (*0-8218-1803-1*, MEMO/1/103) Am Math.

***Unorthodox Book of Jewish Records & Lists.** Allan Gould & Danny Siegel. (Illus.). 192p. pap. text ed. 14.95 (*1-888820-04-7*, S Wachtmans) Millennium Calif.

***Unorthodox Chess Openings.** Eric Schiller. LC 96-71755. (Illus.). 480p. 1997. pap. 22.95 (*0-940685-73-6*) Cardoza Pub.

Unorthodox Judaism. Norman B. Mirsky. LC 78-8683. 227p. 1978. reprint ed. pap. 64.70 (*0-608-00917-2*, 2061711) Bks Demand.

***Unorthodox Lawmaking: New Legislative Processes in the U. S. Congress.** Barbara Sinclair. LC 96-54276. 1997. write for info. (*1-56802-277-8*); pap. write for info. (*1-56802-276-X*) Congr Quarterly.

Unorthodox Marxism: An Essay on Capitalism, Socialism, & Revolution. Michael Albert & Robin Hahnel. LC 78-53575. 380p. 1978. 35.00 (*0-89608-005-6*); pap. 8.50 (*0-89608-004-8*) South End Pr.

Unorthodox Methods. Deborah Valentine. 192p. (Orig.). 1991. mass mkt. 3.99 (*0-380-76286-2*) Avon.

Unorthodox Practices. Marissa Piesman. 224p. 1989. mass mkt. 4.99 (*0-671-67315-7*) PB.

Unorthodox Strategies for the Everyday Warrior: Ancient Wisdom for the Modern Competitor. Ralph D. Sawyer. 224p. 1996. text ed. 25.00 (*0-8133-2860-8*) Westview.

Unpackaged Tours: World Travels off the Beaten Track. Edwin Morrisby. (Illus.). 400p. 1988. 17.95 (*0-8008-7939-2*) Taplinger.

Unpacking Duchamp: Art in Transit. Dalia Judovitz. LC 94-26724. (Illus.). 310p. 1995. 34.95 (*0-520-08809-3*) U CA Pr.

Unpaid Costs of Electrical Energy: Health & Environmental Impacts from Coal & Nuclear Power. William Ramsay. LC 78-15668. 180p. 1978. pap. 14.95 (*0-8018-2230-0*) Resources Future.

Unpaid Ransom. Marcus Lehman. Tr. by Nissan Mindel from GER. (Illus.). 74p. (YA). reprint ed. 10.00 (*0-8266-0338-6*, Merkos LInyonei Chinuch) Kehot Pubn Soc.

Unpaid Work in the Household: A Review of Economic Evaluation Methods. 4th ed. Luisella Goldschmidt-Clermont. (Women, Work & Development Ser.: No. 1). xi, 137p. 1989. 15.75 (*92-2-103085-7*) Intl Labour Office.

Unpainted Aristocracy: The Beach Cottages of Old Nags Head. Catherine Bishir. (Illus.). 28p. 1992. pap. 3.00 (*0-86526-105-9*) NC Archives.

Unpainted Portrait: Contemporary Portraiture in Nontraditional Media. (Illus.). 48p. 1979. pap. 7.50 (*0-932718-04-3*) Kohler Arts.

Unpainted to the Last: Moby-Dick & Twentieth-Century American Art. Elizabeth A. Schultz. LC 94-43810. (Illus.). 398p. (C). 1995. 65.00 (*0-7006-0741-2*); pap. 35.00 (*0-7006-0742-0*) U Pr of KS.

***Unparalleled Danger Unsurpassed Courage: Recipients of the Indian Order of Merit in the Second World War.** Compiled by Christopher M. Peterson. 200p. (Orig.). 1997. pap. 19.95 (*0-9656205-0-6*) C Peterson.

Unpardonable Sins: A Father's Fight for Justice. Robert M. McQueeney & Bob Vacon. LC 91-68140. 1992. 21.95 (*0-88282-068-0*) New Horizon NJ.

Unpath'd Waters. Frank Harris. LC 78-122714. (Short Story Index Reprint Ser.). 1977. 18.95 (*0-8369-3547-0*) Ayer.

Unperfect Poet: Another Way of Speaking. Robin Deschamps. 1995. pap. 7.95 (*0-533-11335-0*) Vantage.

Unperfected Treaties of the United States of America 1776-1976, 9 vols. Christian L. Wiktor. LC 76-2647. 1991. Set. lib. bdg. 400.00 (*0-379-00560-3*) Oceana.

Unplanned Audition. Claudine W. Larson. (Illus.). 24p. (J). (gr. 3-5). 1995. pap. 7.00 (*0-8059-3699-8*) Dorrance.

Unplanned Parenthood: The Confessions of a Septuagenarian Surrogate Mother. Liz Carpenter. 1994. 20.00 (*0-679-42798-8*) Random.

Unplanned Parenthood: The Confessions of a Seventysomething Surrogate Mother. Liz Carpenter. 256p. 1995. pap. 11.00 (*0-449-90995-6*) Fawcett.

Unplanned Pregnancy: Your Choices. Ann Furedi. (Illus.). 176p. 1996. pap. 19.95 (*0-19-262445-8*) OUP.

Unplanned Society. Janine Wedel. 1992. text ed. 37.00 (*0-231-07372-0*) Col U Pr.

Unplanned Suburbs: Toronto's American Tragedy, 1900-1950. Richard Harris. LC 95-31010. (Creating the North American Landscape Ser.). (Illus.). 352p. (C). 1996. text ed. 39.95 (*0-8018-5142-4*) Johns Hopkins.

Unplayable Lie: The Untold Story of Women & Discrimination in American Golf. Marcia Chambers. Ed. by Donna Ruvituso. 208p. 1995. 21.00 (*0-671-50151-8*) PB.

Unplayable Lie: The Untold Story of Women & Discrimination in American Golf. Marcia Chambers. 240p. 1996. pap. 12.00 (*0-671-50155-0*) S&S Trade.

Unpleasant Profession of Jonathan Hoag. Robert A. Heinlein. 1987. mass mkt. 5.99 (*0-441-85457-5*) Ace Bks.

Unpleasant Ways to Die. Elan Fleisher. (Illus.). 112p. (Orig.). 1989. pap. 7.95 (*0-312-03269-2*) St Martin.

Unpleasantness at the Bellona Club. Dorothy L. Sayers. 256p. 1995. mass mkt. 4.99 (*0-06-104354-0*, Harp PBks) HarpC.

Unplug the Christmas Machine: A Complete Guide to Putting Love & Joy Back into the Season. rev. ed. Jo Robinson & Jean C. Staeheli. 256p. 1991. pap. 9.00 (*0-688-10961-6*, Quill) Morrow.

Unplug the Christmas Machine: How to Really Participate in the Joys of Christmas. Jean C. Staeheli. LC 82-13154. 1982. pap. 8.95 (*0-688-01461-5*, Quill) Morrow.

Unplugged. rev. ed. Ed. by Aaron Stang. 128p. (Orig.). 1995. pap. text ed. 14.95 (*0-89724-618-7*, GF0621A) Warner Brothers.

***Unplugged! The Bare Facts on Toilets Through the Ages.** Anna Ciddor. (True Stories Ser.). (Illus.). 100p. (Orig.). (J). (gr. 3-8). 1997. pap. 6.95 (*1-86448-454-3*, Pub. by Allen & Unwin Aust Pty AT) IPG Chicago.

Unplugged Acoustic Rock Guitar Hits: With Notes & Tablature. 96p. 1992. pap. 12.95 (*0-7935-1604-8*, 00694839) H Leonard.

Unplugged Kitchen: A Return to the Simple, Authentic Joys of Cooking. Viana La Place. 1996. 25.00 (*0-614-95779-6*) Morrow.

Unplugged Kitchen: A Return to the Simple, Authentic Joys of Cooking. Viana La Place, pseud. 320p. 1996. 25.00 (*0-688-11313-3*) Morrow.

Unplugged Tough-Love Therapy for New Technology. Jerome. 1996. pap. write for info. (*0-201-41044-3*) Addison-Wesley.

***UNPO Yearbook 1996.** 1997. lib. bdg. write for info. (*90-411-0439-9*) Kluwer Law Tax Pubs.

***Unpopular Culture: Lesbian Writing after the Sex Wars.** Kathleen Martindale. 1997. 18.95 (*0-614-22147-1*) St U NY Geneseo.

Unpopular Culture: The Birth of Law & Popular Culture. Steve Redhead. 1995. text ed. 49.95 (*0-7190-3651-8*); text ed. 19.95 (*0-7190-3652-6*) St Martin.

Unpopular Essays. Russell. 208p. (C). 1996. pap. 15.95 (*0-415-11963-4*) Routledge.

Unpopular Essays on Technological Progress. Nicholas Rescher. LC 79-21648. (Illus.). 132p. 1980. 49.95 (*0-8229-3411-6*) U of Pittsburgh Pr.

Unpopular Government in the United States. Albert M. Kales. LC 73-19155. (Politics & People Ser.). (Illus.). 272p. 1974. reprint ed. 21.95 (*0-405-05877-2*) Ayer.

Unpossessed. Tess Slesinger. LC 84-20840. (Novels of the Thirties Ser.). 412p. (C). 1984. reprint ed. pap. 9.95 (*0-935312-21-8*) Feminist Pr.

Unposted Letters. Donald W. Baker. LC 83-173208. 64p. (Orig.). (C). 1984. pap. 6.95 (*0-935306-23-4*) Barnwood Pr.

Unprecedented Realism: The Work of Machado & Silvetti. Ed. by K. Michael Hays. LC 94-26739. (Illus.). 280p. (Orig.). 1994. 60.00 (*1-56898-003-5*); pap. 40.00 (*0-910413-60-6*) Princeton Arch.

Unpredictable. Patt Bucheister. 1994. mass mkt. 3.50 (*0-373-09899-5*, 1-09899-5) Harlequin Bks.

Unpredictable Adventure: A Comedy of Women's Independence. Claire M. Owens. (Utopianism & Communitarianism Ser.). (Illus.). 1992. reprint ed. pap. 16.95 (*0-8156-2583-9*) Syracuse U Pr.

Unpredictable Certainty: Information Infrastructure Through 2000. National Research Council, NII 2000 Steering Committee. 304p. (Orig.). 1996. pap. 24.95 (*0-309-05432-X*) Natl Acad Pr.

Unpredictable Past: Explorations in American Cultural History. Lawrence W. Levine. 384p. 1993. pap. 17.95 (*0-19-508297-4*) OUP.

Unprejudiced Palate: Classic Thoughts on Food & the Good Life. Angelo M. Pellegrini. LC 83-60691. (Cook's Classic Library). 256p. 1997. 14.95 (*1-55821-199-3*) Lyons & Burford.

Unprejudiced Eye: The Drawings of Jasper F. Cropsey. Kenneth W. Maddox. LC 79-90970. (Illus.). 72p. (Orig.). 1979. pap. 5.00 (*0-943651-07-7*) Hudson Riv.

Unpremeditated Art: The Cadenza in the Classical Keyboard Concerto. Philip J. Whitmore. (Oxford Monographs on Music). (Illus.). 248p. 1991. 75.00 (*0-19-315263-0*) OUP.

Unprepared: A Husband's Story of Coping with His Wife's Stroke. Ellwyn Collins. 208p. 1992. pap. 9.95 (*0-925190-50-0*) Fairview Press.

Unpriced Values: Decisions Without Market Prices. J. A. Sinden & Albert C. Worrell. LC 78-24183. (Illus.). 527p. reprint ed. pap. 149.70 (*0-8357-3582-6*, 2056807) Bks Demand.

Unprofessional Behavior: Confessions of a Public Librarian. Will Manley. LC 91-40350. (Illus.). 208p. 1992. lib. bdg. 23.95 (*0-89950-690-9*) McFarland & Co.

Unprofitable Servants: Conferences on Humility. Nivard Kinsella. 105p. 1981. 2.95 (*0-8199-0807-X*, Frncscn Herld) Franciscan Pr.

Unpromised Land: Agrarian Reform & Conflict Worldwide. Demetrios Christodoulou. LC 88-31885. 256p. (C). 1990. pap. 19.95 (*0-86232-779-2*, Pub. by Zed Bks Ltd UK); text ed. 55.00 (*0-86232-778-4*, Pub. by Zed Bks Ltd UK) Humanities.

Unpromised Land: The Struggle of Messianic Jews Gary & Shirley Beresford. Linda Alexander. 207p. 1994. pap. 10.95 (*1-880226-56-1*) M J Pubs.

Unprotected: Or, Mistakes of the Republican Party. Bryan W. Herring. LC 74-83892. (Black Heritage Library Collection). 1977. 20.95 (*0-8369-8599-0*) Ayer.

Unprotected Witness. Guy Slaughter. 264p. 1995. 19.95 (*1-885173-04-0*) Write Way.

***Unprotected Witness.** James Stevenson. LC 96-39130. 176p. (J). (gr. 5 up). 1997. 15.00 (*0-688-15133-7*) Greenwillow.

***Unpublishable! Rejected Writers from Jane Austen to Zane Grey.** Elaine Borish. 1997. pap. text ed. 12.95 (*0-9524881-1-6*, Pub. by Fidelio Pr UK) IPG Chicago.

Unpublished Activities of World War II. Earl J. Roberts. LC 87-61783. (Illus.). 341p. 1988. 13.55 (*0-940553-00-7*) Scanly Pr.

Unpublished & Forgotten Writings: Editor's Text in English. Volodymyr Mijakovs'kyj. Ed. by Marc Antonovych. (Sources of Modern History of the Ukraine Ser.). (Illus.). 516p. (UKR.). 1984. 30.00 (*0-916381-02-1*) Ukrainian Arts Sci.

Unpublished & Uncollected Letters. William Cowper. (BCL1-PR English Literature Ser.). 85p. 1992. reprint ed. lib. bdg. 59.00 (*0-7812-7338-2*) Rprt Serv.

Unpublished Coins of the Medieval Kingdom of Cyprus. Paul Lambros. Tr. by Michael Toumazou from GRE. (Illus.). 170p. (ENG, FRE & GRE.). 1980. 30.00 (*0-916710-76-9*) Obol Intl.

Unpublished Coins Struck at Glarentza in Imitation of Venetian by Robert of Taranto, Sovereign of the Peloponnese: 1346-1364. Paul Lambros. Tr. by B. Gardiakos. (Illus.). 30p. 1969. pap. 5.00 (*0-916710-01-7*) Obol Intl.

Unpublished Dispositions: Problems of Access & Use in the Courts of Appeals. Donna Stienstra. 1985. write for info. (*0-318-60800-6*) Bates Info Serv.

Unpublished J. B. S. Haldane. Haldane. 1994. pap. text ed. 14.95 (*0-226-31313-1*); lib. bdg. 31.00 (*0-226-31312-3*) U Ch Pr.

An Asterisk (*) at the beginning of an entry indicates that the title is appearing in BIP for the first time.

Unpublished Lectures of William Morris. William Morris. LC 69-19307. 332p. reprint ed. pap. 94.70 (*0-7837-3609-6*, 2043475) Bks Demand.

Unpublished Letters of Charles Dickens: To Mark Lemon. Charles Dickens. LC 76-155146. (Studies in Dickens: No. 52). 1971. reprint ed. lib. bdg. 59.95 (*0-8383-1281-0*) M S G Haskell Hse.

Unpublished Memoirs. Abraham S. Rosenbach. (American Biography Ser.). 151p. 1991. reprint ed. lib. bdg. 59.00 (*0-7812-8330-2*) Rprt Serv.

Unpublished Opinions of the Burger Court. Bernard Schwartz. (Illus.). 496p. 1988. 55.00 (*0-19-505317-6*) OUP.

Unpublished Opinions of the Rehnquist Court. Bernard Schwartz. 512p. 1996. 45.00 (*0-19-509332-1*) OUP.

Unpublished Opinions of the Warren Court. Bernard Schwartz. 479p. 1985. 55.00 (*0-19-503563-1*) OUP.

Unpublished Orations: The Discovery of the Columbia River & the Whitman Controversy, the Crispus Attucks Memorial & Columbus Memorial. John Fiske. LC 77-168031. reprint ed. 31.50 (*0-404-02403-3*) AMS Pr.

***Unpublished Papers of T.R. Malthus in the Collection of Kanto Gakuen University.** J. M. Pullen. 160p. (C). 1997. text ed. 49.95 (*0-521-58138-9*) Cambridge U Pr.

Unpublished Personal Name Indexes in Record Offices & Libraries in Great Britain. 2nd ed. Jeremy S. Gibson. 40p. 1989. 6.00 (*0-8063-1244-0*, 2182) Genealog Pub.

Unpublished Personal Names Indexes in Record Offices & Libraries. (C). 1987. 45.00 (*0-317-89813-2*, Pub. by Birmingham Midland Soc UK) St Mut.

Unpublished Philosophical Essays. Kurt Godel. Ed. & Intro. by Francisco A. Rodriguez-Consuegra. 235p. 1996. pap. 69.50 (*0-8176-5310-4*) Birkhauser.

Unpublished Plays of Richard Cumberland, 2 vols., Set. Ed. by Richard J. Dircks. (Studies in the Eighteenth Century: No. 17). 1992. 115.00 (*0-404-63517-2*) AMS Pr.

Unpublished Plays of Thomas Holley Chivers. Thomas H. Chivers. LC 79-29747. 1980. 75.00 (*0-8201-1350-6*) Schol Facsimiles.

Unpublished Poetry of Charles Wesley, 3 vols., Set. Ed. by S. T. Kimbrough, Jr. & Oliver A. Beckerlegge. (Kingswood Ser.). (Orig.). 1993. pap. 49.95 (*0-687-43315-0*) Abingdon.

Unpublished Poetry of Charles Wesley, Vol. 1. Ed. by S. T. Kimbrough, Jr. & Oliver A. Beckerlegge. (Kingwood Ser.). 325p. (Orig.). 1988. pap. 17.95 (*0-687-43310-X*) Abingdon.

Unpublished Poetry of Charles Wesley: Hymns & Poems for Church & World. Ed. by S. T. Kimbrough, Jr. & Oliver A. Beckerlegge. (Kingwood Ser.: Vol. 3). 511p. (Orig.). 1992. pap. 24.95 (*0-687-43312-6*) Abingdon.

Unpublished Poetry of Charles Wesley: Hymns & Poems on Holy Scripture. Ed. by S. T. Kimbrough, Jr. & Oliver A. Beckerlegge. (Kingwood Ser.: Vol. 2). 475p. (Orig.). 1990. pap. 22.95 (*0-687-43311-8*) Abingdon.

Unpublished Roll of Honor. Compiled by Mark Hughes. 341p. 1996. 35.00 (*0-8063-1487-7*) Genealog Pub.

Unpublished Velins of Lamarck, 1802 to 1809: Illustrations of Fossils of the Paris Basin Eocene. Katherine V. Palmer. (Illus.). 67p. 1977. 21.00 (*0-87710-373-9*) Paleo Res.

***Unpunished: A Mystery.** Charlotte Perkins Gilman et al. LC 96-53526. 1997. 18.95 (*1-55861-170-3*) Feminist Pr.

Unpuzzling Your Past: A Basic Guide to Genealogy. 3rd ed. Emily A. Croom. LC 95-18210. (Illus.). 180p. 1995. pap. 14.99 (*1-55870-396-9*, Betrwy Bks) F & W Pubns Inc.

Unpuzzling Your Past Workbook: Essential Forms & Letters for All Genealogists. Emily A. Croom. 320p. 1996. wbk. ed., pap. 15.99 (*1-55870-423-X*, Betrwy Bks) F & W Pubns Inc.

Unquenchable. David Dvorkin. 352p. 1995. mass mkt. 4.50 (*0-8217-4974-9*, Pinncle Kensgtn) Kensgtn Pub Corp.

Unquenchable Black Fires. Leedell W. Neyland. 204p. 1994. write for info. (*0-9641539-0-4*); pap. write for info. (*0-9641539-1-2*) Leney Educ.

Unquenchable Fire. Rachel Pollack. LC 91-37756. 390p. 1992. 23.95 (*0-87951-447-7*) Overlook Pr.

Unquenchable Fire. Rachel Pollack. LC 91-37756. 390p. 1994. pap. 13.95 (*0-87951-530-9*, Penguin Bks) Overlook Pr.

Unquestionable Lady. Rosina Pyatt. 1994. pap. 3.99 (*0-8217-4444-5*) NAL-Dutton.

Unquestionable Right to Be Free: Black Theology from South Africa. Ed. by Itumeleng J. Mosala & Buti Tlhagale. LC 87-102501. 224p. 1986. reprint ed. pap. 63.90 (*0-7837-9813-X*, 2060542) Bks Demand.

Unquestioned Loyalty: A Teal Stewart Mystery. J. Dayne Lamb. 352p. 1996. mass mkt. 4.99 (*1-57566-054-7*, Knsington) Kensgtn Pub Corp.

Unquestioning Obedience to the President: The ACLU Case Against the Legality of the War in Vietnam. Leon Friedman & Burt Neuborne. LC 76-169004. (C). 1972. pap. text ed. 3.95 (*0-393-05470-5*) Norton.

Unquiet Border. S. K. Ghosh. (Illus.). xvi, 108p. (C). 1993. 17.00 (*81-7024-526-5*, Pub. by Ashish Pub Hse II) Nataraj Bks.

***Unquiet Dead.** Edith Fiore. 1997. pap. 12.00 (*0-345-42021-7*) Ballantine.

Unquiet Dead: A Psychologist Treats Spiritual Possession. Edith Fiore. 1988. mass mkt. 5.99 (*0-345-35083-9*) Ballantine.

Unquiet Earth. Denise Giardina. 480p. 1992. 22.95 (*0-393-03096-2*) Norton.

Unquiet Earth. Denise Giardina. 352p. 1994. mass mkt. 5.99 (*0-8041-1144-8*) Ivy Books.

Unquiet Eye: Vera Berdich, a Retrospective. Intro. by Lanny Silverman. (Illus.). 24p. 1995. pap. 10.00 (*0-938903-18-7*) Cty of Chicago.

Unquiet Ghost: Russians Remember Stalin. Adam Hochschild. (Illus.). 336p. (Orig.). 1995. pap. 13.95 (*0-14-015795-6*, Penguin Bks) Viking Penguin.

Unquiet Grave. Cyril Connolly. 156p. 1982. reprint ed. pap. 9.95 (*0-89255-058-9*) Persea Bks.

Unquiet Graves: The Search for the Disappeared in Iraqi Kurdistan. Ed. by Human Rights Watch Staff. 50p. (Orig.). 1992. pap. 5.00 (*1-56432-057-X*) Hum Rts Watch.

Unquiet Heart: Reflections on Love & Sexuality. Jordan Aumann. Ed. by Conrad Baars. LC 91-27910. 1991. pap. 9.95 (*0-8189-0619-7*) Alba.

Unquiet Mind: A Memoir of Moods & Madness. Kay R. Jamison. 220p. 1995. 22.00 (*0-679-44374-6*) Random.

Unquiet Mind: A Memoir of Moods & Madness. Kay R. Jamison. 240p. 1997. pap. 12.00 (*0-679-76330-9*, Vin) Random.

Unquiet Minds: The World of Forensic Psychiatry. Hugh Miller. 304p. 1996. pap. 11.95 (*0-7472-4646-7*, Pub. by Headline UK) Trafalgar.

Unquiet Pedagogy: Transforming Practice in the English Classroom. Eleanor Kutz & Hephzibah Roskelly. LC 90-24244. 357p. (Orig.). (C). 1991. pap. text ed. 32.50 (*0-86709-277-7*, 0277) Boynton Cook Pubs.

Unquiet Suitcase. large type ed. Gerald Priestland. 224p. 1991. 19.95 (*1-85089-306-3*, Pub. by ISIS UK) Transaction Pubs.

***Unquiet Time: Alabama & the Civil Rights Movement, 1950-1968.** Donald E. Collins. LC 96-49402. 1997. write for info. (*1-881320-97-9*, Black Belt) Black Belt Comm.

Unquiet Waters. Cecil Cahoon, 2nd. (Illus.). 83p. (Orig.). 1994. pap. text ed. 10.00 (*1-880994-21-6*) Mt Olive Coll Pr.

Unquiet Waves. Romen Basu. 120p. 1996. mass mkt. write for info. (*0-932377-53-X*) Facet Bks.

Unquiet Woods: Ecological Change & Peasant Resistance in the Himalaya. Ramachandra Guha. 1990. 38.00 (*0-520-06501-8*) U CA Pr.

UNR Index of Chemical & Physical Data. Arthur M. James & M. P. Lord. LC 92-25365. 1992. text ed. 79.95 (*0-442-30895-7*) Van Nos Reinhold.

Unratified Treaty Between the Kiowas, Comanches & Apaches & the United States of 1863. R. J. DeMallie. (Treaty Manuscripts Ser.: No. 24). 8p. 5.00 (*0-944253-46-6*) Inst Dev Indian Law.

Unraveling DNA. Maxim D. Frank-Kamenetskii. Tr. by Lev Liapin. LC 93-17544. 1993. 27.95 (*1-56081-617-1*, VCH) Wiley.

***Unraveling DNA.** 2nd ed. Maxim D. Frank-Kamenetskii. (C). 1997. pap. write for info. (*0-201-15584-2*) Addison-Wesley.

***Unraveling DNA: Molecular Biology for the Laboratory.** Michael R. Winfrey et al. LC 96-36610. 1997. pap. 45.00 (*0-13-270034-4*) P-H.

Unraveling Fatherhood. Ed. by T. Knyn & A. C. Mulder. (Women's Studies). viii, 180p. 1986. pap. 42.35 (*90-6765-278-4*) Mouton.

Unraveling Fibers. Patricia A. Keeler & Francis X. McCall, Jr. LC 93-13906. (Illus.). 35p. (J). (gr. 3-5). 1995. text ed. 16.00 (*0-689-31777-8*) Macmillan.

Unraveling Mathematical Concepts. Edith Silver & Betty Cornelius. 1978. spiral bd. 42.65 (*0-88252-084-9*) Paladin Hse.

Unraveling of America: A History of Liberalism in the 1960s. Allen J. Matusow. LC 83-48019. (New American Nation Ser.). 560p. 1986. pap. text ed. 16.00 (*0-06-132058-7*, TB2058, Torch) HarpC.

Unraveling Piltdown: The Fraud of the Century & Its Solution. John E. Walsh. 304p. 1996. 25.95 (*0-679-44444-0*) Random.

Unraveling the Asian Miracle: Explorations in Development Strategies, Geopolitics & Regionalism. Abeysinghe M. Navaratna-Bandara. Ed. by Jayant Lele & Kwasi Ofori-Yeboah. 248p. 1996. text ed. 62.95 (*1-85521-740-6*, Pub. by Dartmth Pub UK) Ashgate Pub Co.

Unraveling the Integral Knot Concordance Group. N. Stoltzfus. LC 77-10133. (Memoirs Ser.: No. 12/192). 91p. 1977. pap. 21.00 (*0-8218-2192-X*, MEMO/12/192) Am Math.

Unraveling the "Model Minority" Stereotype: Listening to Asian American Youth. Stacey J. Lee. 160p. (C). 1996. text ed. 39.00 (*0-8077-3510-8*); pap. text ed. 17.95 (*0-8077-3509-4*) Tchrs Coll.

Unraveling the Mystery of Health: How People Manage Stress & Stay Well. Aaron Antonovsky. LC 86-27386. (Social & Behavioral Science Ser.). 238p. text ed. 34.95 (*1-55542-028-1*) Jossey-Bass.

***Unraveling the Mystery of the Blood Covenant.** John Osteen. Date not set. mass mkt. 2.99 (*0-912631-34-1*) J O Pubns.

Unravelled. David Goldschlag et al. 30p. 1992. 2.00 (*1-881168-03-4*) Red Danceflr.

***Unravelling.** Elizabeth Graver. 304p. 1997. 22.95 (*0-7868-6281-5*) Hyperion.

***Unravelling Animal Behviour.** 2nd ed. Marian S. Dawkins. (C). 1995. pap. text ed. 27.50 (*0-582-21875-6*, Pub. by Longman UK) Longman.

Unravelling Global Apartheid: An Overview of World Politics. Titus Alexander. 288p. (C). 1996. 57.95 (*0-7456-1352-7*) Blackwell Pubs.

Unravelling Global Apartheid: An Overview of World Politics. Titus Alexander. 288p. (C). 1996. pap. 23.95 (*0-7456-1353-5*) Blackwell Pubs.

Unravelling Japan's Mystique. John R. Terry. (Illus.). 200p. 1988. pap. 9.95 (*0-933704-33-X*) Dawn Pr.

Unravelling Social Policy. enl. rev. ed. David G. Gil. 350p. (C). 1992. pap. text ed. 19.95 (*0-87047-057-4*) Schenkman Bks Inc.

Unravelling Social Policy. 5th enl. rev. ed. David G. Gil. 350p. (C). 1992. text ed. 29.95 (*0-87047-056-6*) Schenkman Bks Inc.

Unravelling the Franklin Mystery: Inuit Testimony. David C. Woodman. 408p. 1991. 42.95 (*0-7735-0833-3*, Pub. by McGill CN) U of Toronto Pr.

Unravelling the Franklin Mystery: Inuit Testimony. David C. Woodman. 408p. 1992. pap. 19.95 (*0-7735-0936-4*, Pub. by McGill CN) U of Toronto Pr.

Unravelling the Mind of God. Robert Matthews. 1995. mass mkt. 6.95 (*0-86369-671-6*, Pub. by Virgin Pub UK) London Brdge.

***Unravelling the South China Miracle: Two Worlds of Factory Women.** Ching K. Lee. LC 97-25832. 1998. write for info. (*0-520-21125-1*); pap. write for info. (*0-520-21127-8*) U CA Pr.

Unravelling Words & Weaving Water. Cecilia Vicuna. 176p. 1992. pap. 12.00 (*1-55597-166-0*) Graywolf.

Unreachable Star. large type ed. Anne Durham. 1990. 25.99 (*0-7089-2170-1*) Ulverscroft.

***Unreached Peoples.** Ed. by Patrick Johnstone et al. 120p. (Orig.). 1996. pap. 8.99 (*0-927545-98-5*) YWAM Pub.

Unread Herrings: Thomas Nashe & the Prosaics of the Real. James Nielson. LC 93-31708. (Renaissance & Baroque Studies & Texts: Vol. 11). 224p. 1994. 43.95 (*0-8204-2254-1*) P Lang Pubng.

Unreadable Shores of Love: Turkish Modernity & Mystic Romance. Victoria R. Holbrook. LC 93-37046. 256p. (Orig.). (C). 1994. pap. 19.95 (*0-292-73082-9*); text ed. 37.50 (*0-292-73080-2*) U of Tex Pr.

Unreadable Writin's of Spur-Track Jack. Jack Blankenship. 72p. 1994. text ed. 24.95 (*0-9644081-8-X*) Sarpy Creek.

Unreal! Eight Surprising Stories. Paul Jennings. 112p. (J). 1995. pap. 3.99 (*0-14-037577-5*) Puffin Bks.

Unreal! Hennepin County Library Subject Headings for Fictional Characters & Places. 2nd ed. LC 92-53596. 155p. 1992. lib. bdg. 35.00 (*0-89950-733-6*) McFarland & Co.

***Unreal: The Official Strategy Guide.** 240p. 1997. per. 19.99 (*0-7615-1029-X*) Prima Pub.

***Unreal America, Architecture & Illusion.** Ada L. Huxtable. (Illus.). 188p. 1997. 30.00 (*0-614-28058-3*) New Press NY.

Unreal Cities: Urban Figuration in Wordsworth, Baudelaire, Whitman, Eliot, & Williams. William C. Sharpe. LC 89-24616. 256p. 1990. text ed. 39.95 (*0-8018-3972-6*) Johns Hopkins.

***Unreal City.** Thomas E. Kennedy. 196p. 1996. 11.95 (*1-877655-17-1*) Wordcraft Oregon.

Unreal City. Powell. Date not set. per. 12.95 (*1-873741-04-9*, Pub. by Millvres Bks UK) LPC InBook.

Unreal City. Robert Liddell. 238p. 9300. reprint ed. 30.00 (*0-7206-0884-8*, Pub. by P Owen Ltd UK) Dufour.

Unreal Estate. Brian Swann. LC 82-2799. (Illus.). 45p. (Orig.). 1982. pap. 8.50 (*0-915124-40-8*, Toothpaste) Coffee Hse.

Unreal Estate: The Eastern Shore. Robert De Gast. (Illus.). 96p. 1993. pap. 29.95 (*0-8018-4591-2*); text ed. 59.95 (*0-8018-4412-6*) Johns Hopkins.

Unreal God of Modern Theology: Bultmann, Barth, & the Theology of Atheism: a Call to Recovering the Truth of God's Reality. Klaus Bockmuehl. Tr. by Geoffrey W. Bromiley from GER. LC 88-24679. 192p. (Orig.). 1988. pap. 18.95 (*0-939443-11-2*) Helmers Howard Pub.

Unreal Past & Other Poems. K. R. Narayanaswamy. 6.75 (*0-89253-710-8*); 3.00 (*0-89253-711-6*) Ind-US Inc.

Unreal World of Real Estate. Earle S. Smith. (Illus.). 64p. 1989. pap. 4.95 (*0-931474-38-8*) TBW Bks.

***Unreal 1.** Oltion. 1997. mass mkt. 6.99 (*0-671-01881-7*) PB.

***Unreal 2.** Smith. 1997. mass mkt. 6.99 (*0-671-01882-5*) PB.

Unrealists. Harvey Wickham. LC 78-105051. (Essay Index Reprint Ser.). 1977. 21.95 (*0-8369-1736-7*) Ayer.

Unreality: The Metaphysics of Fictional Objects. Charles Crittenden. LC 90-55739. 192p. 1991. 35.00 (*0-8014-2520-4*); pap. 13.95 (*0-8014-9754-X*) Cornell U Pr.

Unreality & Time. Robert S. Brumbaugh. LC 83-5084. (SUNY Series in Philosophy). 164p. 1984. text ed. 69.50 (*0-87395-799-7*); pap. text ed. 24.95 (*0-87395-798-9*) State U NY Pr.

Unreality Industry. Ian I. Mitroff & Warren Bennis. Ed. by Stewart Richardson. 292p. 1989. 17.95 (*1-55972-014-X*, Birch Ln Pr) Carol Pub Group.

Unreality Industry: The Deliberate Manufacturing of Falsehood & What It Is Doing to Our Lives. Ian I. Mitroff & Warren G. Bennis. LC 92-44601. 256p. (C). 1993. pap. 11.95 (*0-19-508398-9*) OUP.

Unreason Within Reason: Essays on the Outskirts of Rationality. A. C. Graham. LC 92-24269. 309p. 1992. 59.95 (*0-8126-9166-0*); pap. 21.95 (*0-8126-9167-9*) Open Court.

Unreasonable Effectiveness of Number Theory. Ed. by Stefan A. Burr et al. LC 92-24328. (Proceedings of Symposia in Applied Mathematics Ser.: Vol. 46). 125p. 1992. 28.00 (*0-8218-5501-8*, PSAPM/46) Am Math.

Unreasonable Men. Victor J. Seidler. LC 93-3492. 288p. (C). 1993. pap. 17.95 (*0-415-08294-3*) Routledge.

Unreasonable Men. Victor J. Seidler. LC 93-3492. 288p. (C). (gr. 13). 1993. text ed. 69.95 (*0-415-08293-5*) Routledge.

Unreasonable Sufficiency? Assessing the New Soviet Strategy. William E. Odom. (C). 1990. 35.00 (*0-907967-13-2*, Pub. by Inst Euro Def & Strat UK) St Mut.

Unreasonable Summer. Dixie Browning. 1980. pap. 1.50 (*0-373-58013-4*) Harlequin Bks.

Unreasoning Earth. large type ed. Jean Chapman. 384p. 1986. 25.99 (*0-7089-1553-1*) Ulverscroft.

Unrecognized Precursors of Montemayor's Diana. Elizabeth Rhodes. 280p. (C). 1992. text ed. 32.50 (*0-8262-0818-5*) U of Mo Pr.

Unreconstructed Rebel. Diana L. Johnson. LC 91-67913. (Illus.). 124p. (Orig.). 1993. pap. 10.00 (*1-56002-173-X*, Univ Edtns) Aegina Pr.

Unreconstructed Rebel: The Life of General John McCausland. Michael J. Pauley. LC 92-61980. (Illus.). 112p. (Orig.). 1993. pap. 9.95 (*0-929521-65-X*) Pictorial Hist.

Unrecorded Media: Industry & Trade Summary. Douglas J. Puffert. (Illus.). 22p. (Orig.). (C). 1995. pap. text ed. 20.00 (*0-7881-2102-2*) DIANE Pub.

Unredeemed Captive: A Family Story from Early America. John Demos. 1995. pap. 13.00 (*0-679-75961-1*, Vin) Random.

Unredeemed Captive: A Family Story from Early America. John P. Demos. LC 93-23907. 1994. 27.50 (*0-394-55782-4*) Knopf.

Unredeemed Rhetoric: Thomas Nashe & the Scandal of Authorship. Jonathan V. Crewe. LC 82-6554. 135p. reprint ed. pap. 38.50 (*0-8357-6608-X*, 2035253) Bks Demand.

Unreformed Cambridge: A Study of Certain Aspects of the University in the Eighteenth Century. D. A. Winstanley. Ed. by Walter P. Metzger. LC 76-55194. (Academic Profession Ser.). 1977. reprint ed. lib. bdg. 35.95 (*0-405-10023-X*) Ayer.

Unreformed House of Commons: Parliamentary Representation Before 1832, 2 vols., Set. Edward Porritt. LC 63-21104. 1963. reprint ed. 150.00 (*0-678-00012-3*) Kelley.

***Unregenerate South: The Agrarian Thought of John Crowe Ransom, Allen Tate, & Donald Davidson.** Mark G. Malvasi. LC 97-10950. (Southern Literary Studies). 296p. 1997. text ed. 35.00 (*0-8071-2143-6*) La State U Pr.

Unrelated Adults in Adolescents' Lives: Perspectives from Four Countries. Ed. by Stephen Hamilton. (Cornell University's Western Societies Papers: Vol. 26). 110p. (Orig.). 1990. pap. 11.95 (*0-8014-9649-7*) Cornell U Pr.

***Unrelated Business Income Tax Issues in Health Care.** Brian D. Lepard & Frederick J. Gerhart. (BNA's Health Law & Business Ser.: No. 2000). 1996. 125.00 (*1-55871-342-5*) BNA.

Unrelated Kin: Race & Gender in Women's Personal Narratives. Ed. by Gwendolyn Etter-Lewis & Michele Foster. 224p. (C). (gr. 13). 1995. text ed. 59.95 (*0-415-91138-9*, B4908, Routledge NY) Routledge.

Unrelated Kin: Race & Gender in Women's Personal Narratives. Ed. by Gwendolyn Etter-Lewis & Michele Foster. 224p. (C). (gr. 13). 1995. pap. 16.95 (*0-415-91139-7*, B4912, Routledge NY) Routledge.

Unrelenting Power of Words. Lillian Caesar-Sutherland. 75p. 1995. 10.95 (*0-932831-14-1*) Eastern Caribbean Inst.

Unreliable Sources: A Guide to Detecting Bias in News Media. Martin A. Lee. 320p. 1990. 19.95 (*0-8184-0521-X*) Carol Pub Group.

Unreliable Sources: A Guide to Detecting Bias in News Media. Martin A. Lee & Norman Solomon. 448p. 1991. reprint ed. pap. text ed. 12.95 (*0-8184-0561-9*, Citadel Pr) Carol Pub Group.

Unrelieved Paradox: Studies in the Theology of Franz Bibfeldt. Ed. by Martin E. Marty & Jerald Brauer. (Illus.). 1994. pap. text ed. 15.00 (*0-8028-0745-3*) Eerdmans.

Unreluctant Years: A Critical Approach to Children's Literature. Lillian H. Smith. LC 90-23850. (C). 1991. text ed. 25.00 (*0-8389-0557-9*, 0557-9) ALA.

Unremarkable Wordsworth. Geoffrey H. Hartman. LC 86-24887. (Theory & History of Literature Ser.: Vol. 34). 276p. (Orig.). 1987. pap. text ed. 14.95 (*0-8166-1176-9*) U of Minn Pr.

Unremembered Country. Susan Griffin. LC 86-73197. 144p. (Orig.). 1987. 15.00 (*1-55659-000-8*) Copper Canyon.

***Unrepeatered Submarine Fiber Optic Systems.** 1993. 1,995.00 (*0-614-18345-6*, IGIC-63) Info Gatekeepers.

***Unrepeatered Submarine Fiber Optic Systems (1996)** 2,995.00 (*0-614-26453-7*) Info Gatekeepers.

Unrepentant Leftist: A Lawyer's Memoir. Victor Rabinowitz. (Illus.). 352p. 1996. 29.95 (*0-252-02253-X*) U of Ill Pr.

Unrepentant, Self-Affirming, Practicing: Lesbian/Bisexual/Gay People Within Organized Religion. Gary D. Comstock. 336p. 1996. 29.95 (*0-8264-0881-8*) Continuum.

***Unrepresented Nations & Peoples Organization Yearbook 1995.** Date not set. text ed. 275.00 (*90-411-0223-X*) Kluwer Law Tax Pubs.

Unrequited Toil: Denial of Labor Rights in Mexico & Implications for NAFTA. Jerome I. Levinson. Ed. by Andrew A. Reding. (North America Project Special Report Ser.). 28p. 1993. pap. 5.00 (*0-911646-53-1*) World Policy.

Unresolvable Plot: Reading Contemporary Fiction. Elizabeth Dipple. 288p. 1988. text ed. 49.50 (*0-415-00661-9*); pap. text ed. 14.95 (*0-415-00662-7*) Routledge.

Unresolved Conflict: India & China. Bhim Sandhu. 300p. 1988. text ed. 30.00 (*81-7027-116-9*, Pub. by Radiant Pubs II) S Asia.

***Unresolved Dilemmas: Women, Work & the Family in the United States, Europe & the Former Soviet Union.** Ed. by Kaisa Kauppinen & Tuula Gordon. (Illus.). 252p. 1997. text ed. 55.95 (*0-614-28622-0*, Pub. by Ashgate UK) Ashgate Pub Co.

Unresolved Grief: A Practical, Multicultural Approach for Health Professionals. Gunzburg. 416p. 1993. pap. 54.25 (*1-56593-198-X*, 0513) Singular Publishing.

UV

Unresolved Issues in Arms Control. Ed. by Kenneth W. Thompson. LC 88-20569. (W. Alton Jones Foundation Series on Arms Control: Vol. VIII). 174p. (Orig.). (C). 1988. pap. text ed. 19.50 (*0-8191-7132-8*, Pub. by White Miller Center); lib. bdg. 41.00 (*0-8191-7131-X*, Pub. by White Miller Center) U Pr of Amer.

Unresolved Past: A Debate in German History. Ed. by Gina Thomas. LC 90-19422. (Conference Sponsored by the Wheatland Foundation Ser.). 146p. 1991. text ed. 45.00 (*0-312-05796-2*) St Martin.

Unresolved Question: The Anglo-Irish Settlement & Its Undoing 1912-72. Nicholas Mansergh. 384p. (C). 1991. text ed. 42.00 (*0-300-05069-0*) Yale U Pr.

Unresolved Questions in the Freud-Jung Debate: On Psychosis, Sexual Identity & Religion. P. Vandermeersch. (Louvain Philosophical Studies: No. 4). 304p. (Orig.). 1991. pap. 47.50 (*90-6186-436-4*, Pub. by Leuven Univ BE) Coronet Bks.

Unresponsive - Resistant or Neglected: Homogeneous Unit Principal Illustrated by the Hakka Chinese in Taiwan. David Liao. LC 73-175494. 160p. 1979. reprint ed. pap. 6.95 (*0-87808-735-4*) William Carey Lib.

Unrest in the Middle East. Francis Neilson. 1979. lib. bdg. 250.00 (*0-685-96646-1*) Revisionist Pr.

Unresting Transformation: The Theology & Spirituality of Maude Petre. Ellen Leonard. 256p. (Orig.). (C). 1991. pap. text ed. 29.00 (*0-8191-8221-4*); lib. bdg. 51.00 (*0-8191-8220-6*) U Pr of Amer.

UnRetirement: A Career Guide for the Retired...the Soon-to-Be Retired...the Never Want-to-Be-Retired. Catherine D. Fyock & Anne M. Dorton. LC 93-49657. 1994. pap. 17.95 (*0-8144-7865-4*) AMACOM.

Unrevised History of the War for Southern Independence. Betty Lawrence. 1996. 29.50 (*0-89896-431-8*) Larksdale.

Unrevolutionary England, 1603-42. Conrad Russell. 343p. 1990. boxed 60.00 (*1-85285-025-6*) Hambledon Press.

***Unriddling: All Sorts of Riddles to Puzzle Your Guessery.** Susan G. Truesdale. (Illus.). (J). (gr. 4-7). Date not set. 14.89 (*0-397-32029-9*) Lppncott-Raven.

Unriddling of Christian Origins: A Secular Account. Joel Carmichael. LC 95-2879. 425p. 1995. 34.95 (*0-87975-952-6*) Prometheus Bks.

Unripe Gold. large type ed. Geoffrey Jenkins. 480p. 1984. 25.99 (*0-7089-1103-X*) Ulverscroft.

Unrolithiasis Research. Nath & Thind, S. K. Staff. (C). 1989. 34.00 (*81-7024-244-4*, Pub. by Ashish II) S Asia.

Unrolling Time: Christiaan Huygens & the Mathematization of Nature. Joella G. Yoder. (Illus.). 264p. 1989. text ed. 52.95 (*0-521-34140-X*) Cambridge U Pr.

Unromantic Agony: An Exhibition. Intro. by Dominique De Menil. (Illus.). 1965. pap. 6.95 (*0-914412-26-4*) Inst for the Arts.

Unruly Child: A History of Law in Australia. Bruce Kercher. 272p. 1996. pap. 29.95 (*1-86373-891-6*, Pub. by Allen & Unwin Aust Pty AT) Paul & Co Pubs.

Unruly Corporatism: Associational Life in Twentieth-Century Egypt. Robert Bianchi. (Illus.). 280p. 1989. 48.00 (*0-19-506031-8*) OUP.

Unruly Eloquence: Lucian & the Comedy of Traditions. R. Bracht Branham. Ed. by Glen W. Bowersock. LC 88-24297. (Revealing Antiquity Ser.: No. 2). (Illus.). 296p. 1989. 36.00 (*0-674-93035-5*) HUP.

Unruly Emotions. (Cross Training Ser.: Vol. 1). 64p. (YA). (gr. 10-12). 1994. pap. 29.95 (*1-57405-010-9*) CharismaLife Pub.

Unruly Examples: On the Rhetoric of Exemplarity. Ed. by Alexander Gelley. LC 94-26822. xii, 376p. 1995. 49.50 (*0-8047-2400-8*); pap. 18.95 (*0-8047-2490-3*) Stanford U Pr.

Unruly Gods: Divinity & Society in China. Ed. by Meir Shahar & Robert P. Weller. LC 96-5144. (Illus.). 304p. 1996. text ed. 32.00 (*0-8248-1724-9*) UH Pr.

Unruly Practices: Power, Discourse & Gender in Contemporary Social Theory. Nancy Fraser. 208p. 1989. pap. 15.95 (*0-8166-1778-3*); text ed. 39.95 (*0-8166-1777-5*) U of Minn Pr.

Unruly Queen: The Life of Queen Caroline. Flora Fraser. (Illus.). 537p. 1996. 35.00 (*0-394-56146-5*) Knopf.

***Unruly Queen: The Life of Queen Caroline.** Flora Fraser. LC 97-11950. 1997. pap. write for info. (*0-520-21275-4*) U CA Pr.

Unruly Voice: Rediscovering Pauline Elizabeth Hopkins. John C. Gruesser. 248p. 1996. pap. text ed. 16.95 (*0-252-06554-9*) U of Ill Pr.

Unruly Woman: Gender & the Genres of Laughter. Kathleen Rowe. LC 94-13656. (Texas Film Studies). (Illus.). 272p. 1995. pap. 17.95 (*0-292-77069-3*); text ed. 37.50 (*0-292-79072-4*) U of Tex Pr.

Unruly Women: The Politics of Confinement & Resistance. Karlene Faith. 1993. pap. 21.95 (*0-88974-050-X*, Pub. by Press Gang CN) LPC InBook.

Unruly Women: The Politics of Social & Sexual Control in the Old South. Victoria E. Bynum. LC 91-33851. (Gender & American Culture Ser.). (Illus.). xvi, 234p. (C). 1992. 37.50 (*0-8078-2016-4*); pap. 13.95 (*0-8078-4361-X*) U of NC Pr.

Unruly Women of Paris: Images of the Commune. Gay L. Gullickson. LC 96-19780. (Illus.). 304p. 1996. 39.95 (*0-8014-3228-6*); pap. 16.95 (*0-8014-8318-2*) Cornell U Pr.

***Unruly World? Globalization, Governance & Geography.** Andrew Herod et al. LC 97-8550. 1997. write for info. (*0-415-16931-3*); pap. write for info. (*0-415-16932-1*) Routledge.

UNS 1994 Update. 25p. 1994. 40.00 (*0-87180-518-9*) Economist Intell.

Unsafe & Unsatisfactory? The Independent Inquiry into the Working Practices of the West Midlands Police Serious Crime Squad. Tim Kaye. 80p. (C). 1991. text ed. 50.00 (*0-900137-35-5*, Pub. by NCCL UK) St Mut.

Unsafe Keeping. Carol Cail. 304p. 1996. mass mkt. 5.50 (*0-440-22298-2*) Dell.

Unsafe Keeping. Carol Cail. LC 95-1739. 1995. 20.95 (*0-312-13198-4*) St Martin.

Unsafe on Any Sea-L.H.A. Ships of the U. S. Navy. Earl Kent. 1976. pap. text ed. 25.00 (*0-918782-00-7*) E Kent.

Unsatisfied Judgement Funds. Hallman. (C). 1968. 11.95 (*0-256-00645-8*) Irwin.

***Unsaturated Fatty Acids: Nutritional & Physiological Significance.** Ed. by M. Ashwell. (British Nutrition Foundation Task Force Reports). (Illus.). 224p. (C). (gr. 13 up). text ed. 103.95 (*0-412-45750-4*, Chap & Hall NY) Chapman & Hall.

Unsaturated Fatty Acids in Foods: The Report of the British Nutrition Foundation's Task Force. British Nutrition Foundation Staff. 300p. 1992. 89.95 (*0-442-31621-6*) Chapman & Hall.

Unsaturated Flow in Hydrologic Modeling: Theory & Practice. Ed. by Hubert J. Morel-Seytoux. (C). 1989. lib. bdg. 216.00 (*0-7923-0211-7*) Kluwer Ac.

Unsaturated Polyester Technology. Paul F. Bruins. LC 74-12774. 438p. 1976. text ed. 244.00 (*0-677-21160-0*) Gordon & Breach.

***Unsaturated Soil Engineering Practice: Committee Report by the Subcommittee on Unsaturated Soils (Committee on Soil Properties) & the Committee on Shallow Foundations.** Sandra L. Houston et al. LC 97-20892. (Geotechnical Special Publication Ser.). 1997. write for info. (*0-7844-0259-0*) Am Soc Civil Eng.

Unsaturated Soils: Proceedings: International Conference (1st: 1995: Paris, France), 3 vols., Set. Ed. by E. E. Alonso & P. Delage. (Illus.). 1500p. (C). Date not set. 190.00 (*90-5410-583-6*, Pub. by A A Balkema NE) Ashgate Pub Co.

Unsaturated Soils: Proceedings of a Session Sponsored by the Subcommittee on Unsaturated Soils (Committee on Soil Properties) & the Committee on Shallow Foundations of the Geotechnical Engineering Division of the American Society of Civil Engineers, in Conjunction with the ASCE Convention in Dallas, Texas, October 24-28, 1993. Ed. by Sandra L. Houston & Warren K. Wray. LC 93-31662. (Geotechnical Special Publications: No. 39). 1993. 23.00 (*0-87262-988-0*) Am Soc Civil Eng.

Unsaturated Zone Hydrology. Gary L. Guyman. 224p. 1994. text ed. 81.00 (*0-13-369083-0*) P-H.

Unscheduled Departures: The Asylum Anthology of Short Fiction. Ed. by Greg Boyd. LC 90-86266. 112p. (Orig.). 1991. pap. 7.95 (*1-878580-11-6*) Asylum Arts.

Unschooled Mind: How Children Think & How Schools Should Teach. Howard Gardner. LC 91-70058. 320p. 1993. pap. 16.00 (*0-465-08896-1*) Basic.

Unscientific Essays. Frederic W. Jones. LC 67-23236. (Essay Index Reprint Ser.). 1977. reprint ed. 18.95 (*0-8369-0578-4*) Ayer.

Unscientific Psychology: A Cultural-Performatory Approach to Understanding Human Life. Fred Newman & Lois Holzman. LC 96-2801. 224p. 1996. text ed. 55.00 (*0-275-95412-9*, Praeger Pubs) Greenwood.

***Unscrupulous Uncle.** Allison Lane, pseud. 1997. mass mkt. 4.99 (*0-451-19159-5*, Sig) NAL-Dutton.

Unsealed Fountain: Essays on the Christian Spiritual Tradition. Ed. by M. Couve De Murville. 155p. (Orig.). 1987. pap. 11.95 (*0-86217-243-8*, Pub. by Veritas Publns IE) Ignatius Pr.

Unsealed Sources see Manual on Radiation Protection in Hospitals & General Practice

Unsearchable Riches: The Symbolic Nature of Liturgy. David N. Power. 240p. 1992. pap. 14.95 (*0-8146-6062-2*, Pueblo Bks) Liturgical Pr.

Unsearchable Riches of Christ: An Exposition of Ephesians 3. D. Martyn Lloyd-Jones. 320p. 1980. 24.99 (*0-8010-5597-0*) Baker Bks.

Unsearchable Wisdom of God: A Study of Providence in Richardson's Pamela. James L. Fortuna. LC 80-14919. (University of Florida Humanities Monographs: No. 49). 142p. reprint ed. pap. 40.50 (*0-7837-5071-4*, 2044769) Bks Demand.

Unseasonable Truths: The Life of Robert Maynard Hutchins. Harry S. Ashmore. 1989. 27.50 (*0-316-05396-1*) Little.

Unsecular Media: Making News of Religion in America. Mark Silk. LC 94-45939. (Public Expressions of Religion in America Ser.). 184p. 1995. 19.95 (*0-252-01904-0*) U of Ill Pr.

***Unseemly Man.** Larry Flynt. 1996. pap. 17.95 (*0-7871-1178-3*) Kensgtn Pub Corp.

***Unseemly Man: My Life As a Pornographer, Pundit & Social Outcast.** Larry Flynt. 1996. pap. 22.95 (*0-7871-1143-0*, Dove Bks) Dove Audio.

Unseemly Woman. Esther W. Bennett. 176p. 1994. text ed. 13.95 (*0-8059-3499-5*) Dorrance.

Unseen. Nanni Balestrini. Tr. by Liz Heron from ITA. 272p. 1989. 18.95 (*0-86091-242-6*, A3312, Pub. by Verso UK) Routledge Chapman & Hall.

Unseen. Janet Lunn. LC 97-13620. (J). 1997. pap. 3.99 (*0-14-038067-1*) Viking Penguin.

Unseen America: The Greatest Cult Exploitation Magazines, 1950-1966. Alan Betrock. LC 90-91696. (Illus.). 112p. (Orig.). 1990. pap. 11.95 (*0-9626833-0-2*) Shake Bks.

Unseen Beauty & the Beast. Ed. by Edward Gross. (Illus.). 112p. (Orig.). 1991. pap. 12.95 (*0-9627508-4-0*) Image NY.

Unseen Beings Unseen Worlds Vol. 1: A Look at the Realms of the Great Unknown. Tom Dongo. (Illus.). 122p. (Orig.). 1994. pap. 9.95 (*0-9622748-3-6*) T Dongo.

Unseen Bird. S. C. Saha. 6.75 (*0-89253-727-2*); 4.00 (*0-89253-728-0*) Ind-US Inc.

Unseen Elderly: A Study of Marginally Subsistent Hotel Dwellers. J. Kevin Eckert. (Illus.). 244p. (Orig.). 1980. 37.50 (*0-916304-47-7*); pap. 18.75 (*0-916304-45-0*) SDSU Press.

Unseen Hand. Assembly of Elementary Schools Staff. 87p. 6.50 (*0-318-14824-2*, AES 4); 3.50 (*0-318-14825-0*) Mid St Coll & Schl.

Unseen Hand: An Introduction to the Conspiratorial View of History. A. Ralph Epperson. (Illus.). 474p. (Orig.). 1985. pap. 15.95 (*0-9614135-0-6*) Publius Pr.

Unseen Hand & the Other Plays. Sam Shepard. LC 95-47723. 383p. 1996. pap. 14.00 (*0-679-76789-4*, Vin) Random.

Unseen Hands: The Story of Revival in Ethiopia. Nona Freeman. Ed. by Nell Perry. LC 87-23263. (Illus.). 224p. (Orig.). 1987. pap. 8.99 (*0-932581-22-6*) Nonas Bk Sales.

Unseen Hands & Unknown Hearts: A Miracle of Healing Created Through Prayer. Kathy L. Callahan. 258p. 1995. pap. text ed. 14.95 (*0-87604-330-9*, 419) ARE Pr.

Unseen Israelis: The Jews from Turkey in Israel. Walter F. Weiker. LC 88-20749. 144p. (Orig.). (C). 1989. pap. text ed. 17.00 (*0-8191-7173-5*); lib. bdg. 34.50 (*0-8191-7172-7*) U Pr of Amer.

Unseen King. Tyson Blue. LC 88-1074. (Starmont Studies in Literary Criticism: No. 26). viii, 200p. 1989. pap. 23.00 (*1-55742-072-6*); lib. bdg. 31.00 (*1-55742-073-4*) Borgo Pr.

Unseen Peninsula. Robert Buelteman. Ed. by Robert McDonald. LC 94-26284. 1994. 65.00 (*1-881529-02-9*) Custom & Limited.

Unseen Peninsula. limited ed. Robert Buelteman. Ed. by Robert McDonald. LC 94-26284. 1994. 350.00 (*1-881529-03-7*) Custom & Limited.

Unseen Power: Public Relations. A History. Scott M. Cutlip. (Communication Ser.). 808p. 1994. pap. 45.00 (*0-8058-1465-5*); text ed. 135.00 (*0-8058-1464-7*) L Erlbaum Assocs.

***Unseen Powers, Vol. 3.** M. C. Sumner. (Extreme Zone Ser.). (YA). (gr. 6 up). 1997. mass mkt. 3.99 (*0-671-00243-0*, Archway) PB.

***Unseen Presence: The Buddha & Sanchi.** Ed. by Vidya Dehejia. (C). 1996. 98.00 (*81-85026-32-7*, Pub. by Marg) S Asia.

***Unseen Rain.** Tr. by Coleman Books & John Moyne. 96p. 1996. pap. 9.00 (*0-614-21375-4*, 1273) Kazi Pubns.

Unseen Rain: Quatrains of Rumi. Mevlana J. Rumi. Tr. by John Moyne & Coleman Barks from PER. LC 86-50782. 96p. (Orig.). 1986. 15.00 (*0-939660-17-2*); pap. 9.00 (*0-939660-16-4*) Threshold VT.

Unseen Rainbows, Silent Songs: The World Beyond Your Senses. Susan Goodman. LC 94-10209. (J). (gr. 3-7). 1995. text ed. 16.00 (*0-689-31892-8*, Atheneum S&S) S&S Trade.

***Unseen Self.** Brian Snellgrove. 144p. 1996. 15.95 (*0-85207-277-5*, Pub. by C W Daniel UK) Natl Bk Netwk.

***Unseen Universe: Of Mind & Matter.** 2nd rev. ed. Daniel W. Miller. 330p. (Orig.). 1996. reprint ed. pap. 16.45 (*0-9638055-1-7*) Beyond Realm.

Unseen War in Europe: Espionage & Conspiracy in the Second World War. John H. Waller. LC 95-32723. (Illus.). 512p. 1996. 35.00 (*0-679-44826-8*) Random.

Unseen Warfare. Lorenzo Scupoli. 280p. 1978. pap. 11.95 (*0-913836-52-4*) St Vladimirs.

Unseen Warhol. John O'Connor & Benjamin Liu. LC 96-19379. (Illus.). 208p. 1996. 50.00 (*0-8478-1967-1*) Rizzoli Intl.

Unseen World. John Fiske. (Notable American Authors Ser.). 1992. reprint ed. lib. bdg. 75.00 (*0-7812-2842-5*) Rprt Serv.

Unseen World: Catholic Theology & Spiritualism. A. M. Lepicier. 1972. 69.95 (*0-8490-1251-1*) Gordon Pr.

***Unselected Poems.** Philip Levine. (Orig.). 1997. pap. 13.95 (*0-9655239-0-X*) Greenhouse Review Pr.

Unselfish Patriot. Michael J. Thorn. 136p. (Orig.). (C). 1991. pap. 16.95 (*1-56485-391-8*) Stone Pubns.

Unselfishness: The Role of the Vicarious Affects in Moral Philosophy & Social Theory. Nicholas Rescher. LC 75-9123. 138p. 1975. 49.95 (*0-8229-3308-X*) U of Pittsburgh Pr.

Unselfishness of God. Hannah W. Smith. (Christian Library). 204p. 1989. 8.97 (*1-55748-419-8*) Barbour & Co.

Unsent Letters: Irreverent Notes from a Literary Life. Malcolm Bradbury. 224p. 1989. pap. 7.95 (*0-14-010705-3*, Penguin Bks) Viking Penguin.

Unsentimental Education: Writers & Chicago. Molly McQuade. LC 94-43441. 270p. 1995. 18.95 (*0-226-56210-7*) U Ch Pr.

Unsentimental Journey. Albert Drach. Tr. by Harvey I. Dunkle. (Studies in Austrian Literature, Culture, & Thought. Translation Ser.). 352p. 1991. pap. 22.00 (*0-929497-47-3*) Ariadne CA.

***Unsentimental Journey.** large type ed. Vera Cowie. (Black Satin Romance Ser.). 501p. 1996. 25.99 (*1-86110-020-5*) Ulverscroft.

***Unsentimental Reformer: The Life of Josephine Shaw Lowell.** Joan Waugh. LC 97-15647. 1997. write for info. (*0-674-93036-3*) HUP.

***Unser Buch, 2 vols.** 10th ed. Y. Y. Lifshitz. Incl. Vol. 2. . 10th ed. (YID.). 48p. 1969. reprint ed. pap. text ed. 2.00 (*0-8266-0210-X*, Merkos LInyonei Chinuch); Vol. 1. . 10th ed. (YID.). 64p. 1969. reprint ed. pap. text ed. 2.00 (*0-8266-0209-6*, Merkos LInyonei Chinuch); write for info. (*0-8266-0208-8*) Kehot Pubn Soc.

Unser Planet Erde: Ursprung & Dynamik. Klaus Strobach. (Illus.). 253p. (GER.). 1991. pap. 40.00 (*3-443-01028-8*) Lubrecht & Cramer.

Unsers. Karen Bentley. LC 95-18676. (Race Car Legends Ser.). 64p. (J). 1996. lib. bdg. 15.95 (*0-7910-3186-1*) Chelsea Hse.

Unsettled Accounts. Peter Stambler. (QRL Poetry Bks.: Vol. XXVII). 1987. 35.00 (*0-614-06423-6*) Quarterly Rev.

Unsettled Affinities. Reinhard Bendix. Ed. by Rudolph Von Thadden. LC 92-43184. 302p. (C). 1993. text ed. 44.95 (*1-56000-101-1*) Transaction Pubs.

Unsettled Country: Changing Landscapes of the American West. Donald Worster. LC 93-30331. (Calvin P. Horn Lectures in Western History & Culture). 163p. 1994. 32.50 (*0-8263-1481-3*); pap. 15.95 (*0-8263-1482-1*) U of NM Pr.

***Unsettled Frontiers & Transnational Linkages: New Tasks for the Historian of Modern Asia.** Ed. by Leo Douw. (Comparative Asian Studies: No. 19). 120p. 1997. pap. 19.50 (*90-5383-536-9*, Pub. by VU Univ Pr NE) Paul & Co Pubs.

***Unsettled Matters: The Life & Death of Bruce Lee.** Tom Bleecker. LC 96-94563. 228p. (Orig.). 1996. pap. text ed. 7.99 (*0-9653132-0-4*) Gilderoy Publns.

Unsettled Relationship: Labor Migration & Economic Development. Ed. by Demetrious G. Papademetriou & Philip L. Martin. LC 90-45603. (Contributions in Labor Studies: No. 33). 336p. 1991. text ed. 65.00 (*0-313-25463-X*, PDA, Greenwood Pr) Greenwood.

Unsettled States, Disputed Lands: Britain & Ireland, France & Algeria, Israel & the West Bank/Gaza. Ian S. Lustick. (Wilder House Series in Politics, History, & Culture). (Illus.). 592p. 1993. 45.00 (*0-8014-2840-8*) Cornell U Pr.

Unsettled States, Disputed Lands: Britain & Ireland, France & Algeria, Israel & the West Bank/Gaza. Ian S. Lustick. (Wilder House Ser.). (Illus.). 592p. 1995. pap. 19.95 (*0-8014-8088-4*) Cornell U Pr.

***Unsettled Subjects: Race, Class, Nation, & the Politics of Female Subjectivity.** Susan Lurie. LC 97-3845. 216p. 1997. text ed. 49.95 (*0-8223-2003-7*); pap. text ed. 16.95 (*0-8223-1999-3*) Duke.

Unsettling America: Race & Ethnicity in Contemporary American Poetry. Ed. by Maria M. Gillan & Jennifer Gillan. LC 94-722. 432p. 1994. pap. 14.95 (*0-14-023778-X*, Viking) Viking Penguin.

Unsettling of America: Culture & Agriculture. Wendell Berry. 236p. 1996. pap. 12.00 (*0-87156-877-2*) Sierra.

***Unsettling Relations: The University As a Site of Feminist Struggles.** Himani Bannerji et al. 144p. (Orig.). pap. write for info. (*0-88961-160-2*, Pub. by Wmns Pr CN) LPC InBook.

Unsettling Relations: The University As a Site of Feminist Struggles. Himani Bannerji et al. 160p. (Orig.). 1992. 30.00 (*0-89608-453-1*); pap. 12.00 (*0-89608-452-3*) South End Pr.

Unsettling Season. Donald J. Shelby. LC 88-51469. 128p. (Orig.). 8.95 (*0-8358-0596-4*) Upper Room Bks.

***Unsettling Season.** Donald J. Shelby. 10.35 (*0-687-61230-6*) Abingdon.

Unsettling Settler Societies: Articulations of Gender, Race, Ethnicity & Class. Daiva Stasiulis & Nira Yuval-Davis. (Series on Race & Ethnic Relations). 336p. 1995. text ed. 69.95 (*0-8039-8693-9*); pap. text ed. 26.50 (*0-8039-8694-7*) Sage.

Unsettling Statecraft: Democracy & Neoliberalism in the Central Andes. Catherine M. Conaghan & James M. Malloy. (Latin American Ser.). 320p. (Orig.). (C). 1994. 49.95 (*0-8229-3786-7*); pap. 22.95 (*0-8229-5532-6*) U of Pittsburgh Pr.

Unsex'd Revolutionaries: Five Women Novelists of the 1790s. Eleanor Ty. 192p. 1993. 40.00 (*0-8020-2949-3*); pap. 18.95 (*0-8020-7774-9*) U of Toronto Pr.

Unshackled Organization: Facing the Challenge of Unpredictability Through Spontaneous Reorganization. Jeffrey Goldstein. LC 94-983. (Illus.). 189p. 1994. 25.00 (*1-56327-048-X*) Prod Press.

Unshackling the Private Sector: A Latin American Story. Paul Holden & Sarath Rajapatirana. LC 95-22319. (Directions in Development Ser.). 120p. 1995. 10.95 (*0-8213-3336-4*, 13336) World Bank.

***Unshakable Faith.** Mark Finley & Steven R. Mosley. LC 96-48049. 1996. pap. write for info. (*0-8163-1381-4*) Pacific Pr Pub Assn.

Unshakable Man: A Stable Spiritual Force in the Home, Vol. 1. Ron Auch. 176p. 1996. pap. text ed. 9.95 (*0-89221-323-X*) New Leaf.

Unshakable Peace. Kelley Varner. 322p. (Orig.). 1994. pap. 10.99 (*1-56043-137-7*) Destiny Image.

Unshakeable Kingdom. Ed. by Clarence M. Wagner. 90p. pap. 4.00 (*0-317-39376-6*) Tru-Faith.

Unshaken Friend: A Profile of Maxwell Perkins. Malcolm Cowley. (Illus.). 48p. 1985. 14.50 (*0-911797-15-7*) R Rinehart.

***Unshed Tears: Deora Nar Caoineadh.** Aine Ni Ghlinn. 80p. 9700. 24.95 (*1-873790-68-6*); pap. 12.95 (*1-873790-67-8*) Dufour.

Unsigned Rappers' Guide to Gettin' a Record Deal. Mike Eliot et al. Ed. by Tracey Mitchell. (Illus.). 96p. (Orig.). 1992. pap. 14.95 (*0-9631220-0-2*) M Three Comms.

Unsigned Rappers Guide to Getting a Record Deal. Elliot. Date not set. pap. 10.00 (*0-684-81558-3*) S&S Trade.

Unsigned, Unsung . . . Whereabouts Unknown: Make-Do Art of the American Outlands. Jim Roche. (Illus.). 80p. 1994. pap. 19.95 (*0-295-97343-9*) U of Wash Pr.

***Unsilenced: The Spirit of Women.** Mollie C. Bryan. LC 97-3126. (Illus.). 256p. (Orig.). 1997. pap. 14.95 (*1-881394-11-5*) Commune-A-Key.

Unsilent Revolution: Television News & American Public Life, 1948-1991. Robert Donovan & Ray Scherer. (Woodrow Wilson Center Ser.). 500p. (C). 1992. text ed. 69.95 (*0-521-41829-1*); pap. text ed. 20.95 (*0-521-42862-9*) Cambridge U Pr.

An Asterisk (*) at the beginning of an entry indicates that the title is appearing in BIP for the first time.

Unsinkable Bambi Lake: A Fairy Tale Containing the Dish on Cockettes, Punks & Angels. Bambi Lake & Alvin Orloff. LC 96-10093. (Illus.). 160p. (Orig.). 1996. pap. 11.95 (*0-916397-42-4*) Manic D Pr.

Unsinkable Charlie Brown. Charles M. Schulz. (Illus.). (J). 1994. pap. 7.95 (*0-8050-3311-4*) H Holt & Co.

Unsinkable Fleet: The Politics of U. S. Navy Expansion in World War II. Joel R. Davidson. LC 96-13714. (Illus.). 264p. 1996. 28.95 (*1-55750-156-4*) Naval Inst Pr.

Unsinkable Molly Brown. (Vocal Score Ser.). 164p. 1982. pap. 40.00 (*0-88188-212-7*, 00448710) H Leonard.

Unsinkable Molly Brown. Al Hine. 18.95 (*0-8488-0166-0*) Amereon Ltd.

Unsinkable Molly Brown. Al Hine. 1993. reprint ed. lib. bdg. 14.95 (*1-56849-204-9*) Buccaneer Bks.

Unsinkable Molly Brown: Vocal Selections. (Illus.). 048p. 1982. pap. 8.95 (*0-88188-207-0*, 00447210) H Leonard.

Unsinkable Molly Brown Cookbook. May B. Wills & Caroline Bancroft. (Illus.). 118p. (Orig.). 1966. pap. 8.95 (*0-914248-18-9*) Hist Denver.

Unsinkable Mrs. Brown. Caroline Bancroft. (Illus.). 44p. 1963. pap. 3.95 (*0-933472-25-0*) Johnson Bks.

Unsinkable Titanic Thompson. Carlton Stowers. 256p. 1992. reprint ed. pap. 14.95 (*0-9634015-8-0*) Palmer Magic.

Unskilled Labor for Development: Its Economic Cost. Orville J. McDiarmid. LC 76-47398. 219p. reprint ed. pap. 62.50 (*0-7837-4276-2*, 2043968) Bks Demand.

Unsmiling Faces: Creating Preschools That Heal. Lesley Koplow. 288p. (C). 1995. text ed. 54.00 (*0-8077-3471-3*); pap. text ed. 22.95 (*0-8077-3470-5*) Tchrs Coll.

***Unsnarling the World-Knot: Consciousness, Freedom & the Mind-Body Problem.** David R. Griffin. LC 97-8390. 1998. write for info. (*0-520-20944-3*) U CA Pr.

Unsocial Socialist. George Bernard Shaw. (BCL1-PR English Literature Ser.). 250p. 1992. reprint ed. lib. bdg. 79.00 (*0-7812-7646-2*) Rprt Serv.

Unsold Television Pilots, 1955-1989. Lee Goldberg. LC 89-42717. 655p. 1990. lib. bdg. 55.00 (*0-89950-373-X*) McFarland & Co.

Unsold TV Pilots: The Almost Complete Guide to Everything You Never Saw on TV. Lee Goldberg. 1991. pap. 12.95 (*0-8065-1242-3*, Citadel) Carol Pub Group.

Unsolicited Advice: Observations of a Public Librarian. Will Manley. LC 92-50311. (Illus.). 208p. 1992. lib. bdg. 23.95 (*0-89950-745-X*) McFarland & Co.

Unsolicited Chronicler: An Account of the Gunnison Massacre, Its Causes & Consequences, Utah Territory, 1847-1859: a Narrative History. Robert K. Fielding. LC 92-29398. (Illus.). 450p. (C). 1993. text ed. 49.95 (*0-912111-38-0*) Paradigm Publns.

Unsolved! George Sullivan. 112p. (YA). (gr. 7-9). 1992. pap. 3.50 (*0-590-42990-6*, Point) Scholastic Inc.

***Unsolved.** Kirk Wilson. 10.95 (*0-7867-0703-8*) Carroll & Graf.

Unsolved: Great Mysteries of the Twentieth Century. Kirk Wilson. 264p. 1991. pap. 10.95 (*0-88184-703-8*) Carroll & Graf.

Unsolved Case of Sherlock Holmes. Alan Sharp. 1984. pap. 8.95 (*0-521-27708-6*) Cambridge U Pr.

Unsolved Chocolate Pudding Files. Alex Gabbard. 128p. (Orig.). 1994. pap. 9.95 (*0-9622608-5-1*) Gabbard Pubns.

Unsolved Crimes. Time-Life Books Editors. Ed. by Laura Foreman. LC 93-9604. (True Crime Ser.). (Illus.). 192p. 1993. 12.99 (*0-7835-0012-2*); lib. bdg. 17.45 (*0-7835-0013-0*) Time-Life.

Unsolved II. George Sullivan. 112p. (J). (gr. 7-9). 1995. pap. 2.99 (*0-590-20357-6*) Scholastic Inc.

***Unsolved Miracles.** Compiled by John Van Diest. LC 97-19581. 224p. 1997. 18.99 (*1-57673-150-2*, Multnomah Bks) Multnomah Pubs.

***Unsolved Mysteries.** LC 96-41216. (It's a Fact! Ser.). (J). 1997. lib. bdg. 14.95 (*0-88682-862-7*) Creative Ed.

***Unsolved Mysteries.** McCallum. 1992. student ed., pap. text ed. write for info. (*0-17-555897-3*) Addison-Wesley.

Unsolved Mysteries. Colin Wilson. 1992. 9.98 (*0-88365-790-2*) Galahad Bks.

***Unsolved Mysteries of American History: An Eye-Opening Journey Through 500 Years of Disappearances & Baffling Discoveries.** Paul Aron. LC 97-7319. 256p. 1997. 22.95 (*0-471-15369-9*) Wiley.

Unsolved Mysteries of the Arctic. Vilhjalmur Stefansson. LC 72-278. (Essay Index Reprint Ser.). 1977. reprint ed. 34.95 (*0-8369-2828-8*) Ayer.

Unsolved Mysteries of the Arctic. Vilhjalmur Stefansson. (Illus.). 320p. (J). 1985. reprint ed. pap. 12.95 (*0-938271-02-4*) Press N Amer.

Unsolved Mysteries Past & Present. Colin Wilson. 400p. 1992. pap. 13.95 (*0-8092-4091-2*) Contemp Bks.

***Unsolved Mystery Diseases.** large type ed. Katherine E. Anderson. (Illus.). 240p. (Orig.). 1996. spiral bd., pap. 24.95 (*1-57876-900-0*) Triple U Prods.

***Unsolved Problems in Astrophysics.** John N. Bahcall & Jeremiah P. Ostriker. LC 96-45581. (Princeton Series in Astrophysics). 1996. write for info. (*0-691-01607-0*); pap. write for info. (*0-691-01606-2*) Princeton U Pr.

Unsolved Problems in Geometry. H. T. Croft et al. (Problem Books in Mathematics, Subseries: Unsolved Problems in Intuitive Mathematics: No. II). (Illus.). 240p. 1994. 48.95 (*0-387-97506-3*) Spr-Verlag.

Unsolved Problems in Intuitive Mathematics: Unsolved Problems in Number Theory, Vol. 1. H. T. Croft & R. K. Guy. (Problem Books in Mathematics). (Illus.). 160p. 1981. 29.00 (*0-387-90593-6*) Spr-Verlag.

Unsolved Problems in Number Theory. Richard K. Guy. LC 94-3818. (Problem Books in Mathematics). (Illus.). xii, 291p. 1994. 43.95 (*0-387-94289-0*) Spr-Verlag.

Unsolved Problems in the Bibliography of J. J. Rousseau. R. A. Leigh. Ed. by John Leigh. (Sandars Lectures in Bibliography). (Illus.). 164p. (C). 1990. text ed. 80.00 (*0-521-38481-8*) Cambridge U Pr.

***Unsolved Problems of Noise in Physics Biology.** 348p. 1997. text ed. 54.00 (*981-02-3199-7*) World Scientific Pub.

Unsolved Problems of the Milky Way. Ed. by Leo Blitz & Peter Teuben. 725p. 1996. lib. bdg. 208.00 (*0-7923-4039-6*) Kluwer Ac.

Unsolved Problems Related to Smarandache Function. R. Muller. (Illus.). 66p. (Orig.). 1993. pap. text ed. 9.85 (*1-879585-37-5*) Erhus Univ Pr.

***Unsolved Shadow.** James W. Fraley. 180p. (Orig.). 1998. mass mkt. 6.99 (*1-58006-000-5*, Sherlock Pr) Sovereign.

Unsolved Texas Mysteries. Wallace O. Chariton et al. (Illus.). 272p. 1990. pap. 12.95 (*1-55622-256-4*); boxed 16.95 (*1-55622-136-3*) Wordware Pub.

Unsophisticated Investor. Gary Arthur Tupper. LC 94-90099. 187p. 1994. pap. 19.95 (*0-9642503-0-6*) Shear Pr.

***Unsorted Drawer.** Rita Summers. Ed. by Victoria Rivas. (Illus.). 36p. 1996. pap. 4.50 (*1-889289-06-X*) Ye Olde Font Shoppe.

Unsounded Centre: Jungian Studies in American Romanticism. Martin Bickman. LC 79-26042. 192p. reprint ed. pap. 54.80 (*0-8357-3895-7*, 2036627) Bks Demand.

***Unsparing Scourge: Australian Satirical Texts.** Vincent O'Sullivan. pap. 12.95 (*0-86422-056-1*, Pub. by Univ of West Aust Pr AT) Intl Spec Bk.

***Unspeakable.** Charles L. Calia. Date not set. write for info. (*0-688-15119-1*) Morrow.

Unspeakable: Discourse, Dialogue, & Rhetoric in the Postmodern World. Stephen A. Tyler. LC 87-40149. (Rhetoric of the Human Sciences Ser.). (Illus.). 224p. (C). 1988. pap. text ed. 17.75 (*0-299-11274-8*) U of Wis Pr.

Unspeakable: The Rise of Gay & Lesbian Press in America. Rodger Streitmatter. (Illus.). 394p. 1995. 27.95 (*0-571-19873-2*) Faber & Faber.

Unspeakable Acts: Why Men Sexually Abuse Children. Douglas W. Pryor. 300p. (C). 1996. 26.95 (*0-8147-6637-4*) NYU Pr.

Unspeakable Gift: A Miraculous Testimony of Conversion. Mary Ellis. LC 93-31506. 227p. (Orig.). 1994. pap. 8.99 (*1-56722-015-0*) Word Aflame.

Unspeakable Images: Ethnicity & the American Cinema. Ed. by Lester D. Friedman. (Illus.). 456p. 1991. text ed. 44.95 (*0-252-01575-4*); pap. text ed. 18.95 (*0-252-06152-7*) U of Ill Pr.

***Unspeakable Losses.** Kim Kluger-Bell. Date not set. write for info. (*0-393-04572-2*) Norton.

Unspeakable Mating. T. H. Cornell. 1989. pap. 8.00 (*0-941179-27-3*) Latitudes Pr.

Unspeakable Mother: Forbidden Discourse in Jean Rhys & H.D. Deborah K. Kloepfer. LC 89-7182. (Reading Women Writing Ser.). 224p. 1989. 35.00 (*0-8014-2306-6*) Cornell U Pr.

Unspeakable Sadness: The Dispossession of the Nebraska Indians. David J. Wishart. LC 94-4611. (Illus.). xv, 311p. 1995. text ed. 50.00 (*0-8032-4774-5*) U of Nebr Pr.

***Unspeakable Sadness: The Dispossession of the Nebraska Indians.** David J. Wishart. LC 94-4611. (Illus.). xv, 311p. 1997. pap. 18.00 (*0-8032-9795-5*, Bison Books) U of Nebr Pr.

Unspeakable Strangers: Poems about the Holocaust. Van K. Brock. Ed. by Rick Campbell. LC 95-83122. 108p. (Orig.). 1996. pap. 12.00 (*0-938078-42-9*) Anhinga Pr.

***Unspeakable Subjects: The Genealogy of the Event in Early Modern Europe.** Jacques Lezra. LC 96-38471. 1997. write for info. (*0-8047-2778-3*) Stanford U Pr.

***Unspeakable Truths & Happy Endings: Human Cruelty & the New Trauma Therapy.** Rebecca Coffey. 320p. (Orig.). 1998. write for info. (*1-886968-04-7*) Sidran Pr.

***Unspeakable Truths & Happy Endings: Human Cruelty & the New Trauma Therapy.** Rebecca Coffey. 320p. (Orig.). 1998. pap. write for info. (*1-886968-05-5*) Sidran Pr.

Unspeakable Women: Selected Short Stories Written by Italian Women During Fascism. Robin Pickering-Iazzi. 176p. 1993. 35.00 (*1-55861-062-6*); pap. 14.95 (*1-55861-063-4*) Feminist Pr.

Unspeakably Gross Jokes. Julius Alvin. (Gross Jokes Ser.: No. 20). 160p. 1995. mass mkt. 3.99 (*0-8217-5009-7*, Zebra Kensgtn) Kensgtn Pub Corp.

Unspeakably Rotten Cartoons. J. Kohl. 96p. 1994. pap. 5.95 (*0-88032-455-4*) Ivory Tower Pub.

Unspiked Rail: Memoir of a Nevada Rebel. Sally S. Zanjani. LC 80-39920. (Lancehead Ser.). (Illus.). 424p. 1981. 21.95 (*0-87417-064-8*) U of Nev Pr.

Unspoiled Heart: The Journal of Charles Mattocks of the 17th Maine. Ed. by Philip N. Racine. LC 93-21274. (Voices of the Civil War Ser.). (Illus.). 480p. (C). 1994. 36.00 (*0-87049-834-7*) U of Tenn Pr.

Unspoiled Umbria. Paul Hofmann. 1996. pap. 14.95 (*0-8050-4679-8*) H Holt & Co.

Unspoiled Umbria. Paul Hofmann. 1997. 25.00 (*0-8050-4678-X*) H Holt & Co.

Unspoiled West: The Western Landscape As Seen by Its Greatest Photographers. Jerome Prescott. (Illus.). 128p. 1995. 15.98 (*0-8317-9058-X*) Smithmark.

***Unspoken Art: Profiles of Veterinary Life.** Lee Gutkind. (Illus.). 1997. 25.00 (*0-614-28262-4*) H Holt & Co.

Unspoken Bequest: The Contribution of German Jews to German Culture. Hugo Munsterberg. (Illus.). 224p. (YA). (gr. 10 up). 1995. 20.00 (*1-878352-10-5*) McPherson & Co.

Unspoken Bond. 2nd ed. Gloria J. Black. (Illus.). 80p. (Orig.). 1986. pap. 6.00 (*0-9616466-1-6*) G Black.

Unspoken Confessions. Kelsey Roberts. (Intrigue Ser.). 1995. mass mkt. 3.50 (*0-373-22326-9*, 1-22326-2) Harlequin Bks.

Unspoken Desire. Penny Jordan. (Presents Ser.: No. 1404). 1991. pap. 2.79 (*0-373-11404-4*) Harlequin Bks.

Unspoken for Time. Jeff Barker. 86p. 1996. pap. 5.25 (*0-87129-646-2*, U21) Dramatic Pub.

Unspoken Hunger. Terry T. Williams. 1995. pap. 10.00 (*0-679-75256-0*) Random.

Unspoken Language of Children. Suzanne Szasz. (Illus.). 160p. 1980. reprint ed. pap. 10.95 (*0-393-00989-0*) Norton.

***Unspoken Promise.** Georgia Bockoven. 368p. 1997. mass mkt. 5.99 (*0-06-108439-5*, Harp PBks) HarpC.

Unspoken Sermons, Vol. 1. George MacDonald. 1989. 24.50 (*0-940652-80-3*) Sunrise Bks.

Unspoken Sermons, Vol. 2. George MacDonald. 1989. 24.50 (*0-940652-81-1*) Sunrise Bks.

Unspoken Sermons, Vol. 3. George MacDonald. 1996. 24.50 (*0-940652-82-X*) Sunrise Bks.

Unspoken Sermons - Series I, II, III, Vols. 1-3. George MacDonald. (George MacDonald Original Works: Series VIII). 560p. 1997. 24.00 (*1-881084-48-5*) Johannesen.

Unspoken Sermons (Series Three) The Sermons of George MacDonald. George MacDonald. 250p. (C). 1987. reprint ed. pap. 14.95 (*0-944724-06-X*) J J Flynn.

Unspoken Sermons (Series Two) The Sermons of George MacDonald. George MacDonald. 250p. (C). 1987. reprint ed. pap. 14.95 (*0-944724-05-1*) J J Flynn.

Unspoken Visions: An Inner Journey. Kikanza N. Robins. LC 95-29996. (Illus.). 128p. (Orig.). 1996. pap. 12.95 (*0-918949-88-2*) Papier-Mache Press.

Unspoken Way: Haragei, or the Role of Silent Communication in Japanese Business & Society. Michihiro Matsumoto. LC 88-80138. 200p. 1988. pap. 10.00 (*0-87011-889-7*) Kodansha.

Unspoken Wisdom: Truths My Father Taught Me. Ray S. Anderson. LC 94-44754. 128p. 1995. pap. 9.99 (*0-8066-2811-1*, Augsburg) Augsburg Fortress.

Unspoken Word. Ricardo A. Davis. Ed. by Sharon L. Goodman. (Orig.). 1986. pap. text ed. 3.50 (*0-935369-04-X*) In Tradition Pub.

Unspoken Words. Cida Goncalves. 67p. 1994. pap. 10.36 (*0-9646884-0-9*) In-Site Pr.

Unsportsmanlike Conduct: Exploiting College Athletes. Walter Byers & Charles Hammer. LC 95-16973. (C). 1995. 29.95 (*0-472-10666-X*) U of Mich Pr.

***Unsportsmanlike Conduct: Exploiting College Athletes.** Walter Byers. (C). 1997. pap. 18.95 (*0-472-08442-9*) U of Mich Pr.

Unsportsmanlike Conduct: The National Collegiate Athletic Association & the Business of College Football. Paul R. Lawrence. LC 87-12496. 200p. 1987. text ed. 49.95 (*0-275-92725-3*, C2725, Praeger Pubs) Greenwood.

UNS/SABIR United Nations System Selected Agencies Bibliographic Information Records. 110p. Date not set. 195.00 incl. cd-rom (*92-1-100669-4*) UN.

Unstable Adams Spectral Sequence for Free Iterated Loop Spaces. Robert J. Wellington. LC 81-20515. (Memoirs Ser.: Vol. 36/258). 225p. 1982. pap. 23.00 (*0-8218-2258-6*, MEMO/36/258) Am Math.

Unstable Agriculture & Droughts. Hanumantha Rao. 155p. 1988. text ed. 25.00 (*0-7069-4041-5*, Pub. by Vikas II) S Asia.

Unstable & Turbulent Motion of Fluid - Proceedings of the Conference: RIMS, Kyoto University, 19-30 October 1992. Ed. by Shigeo Kida. LC 93-30498. 328p. 1993. text ed. 95.00 (*981-02-1546-0*) World Scientific Pub.

Unstable Angina. 1995. lib. bdg. 251.95 (*0-8490-6848-7*) Gordon Pr.

Unstable Angina. Rutherford. (Fundamental & Clinical Cardiology Ser.: Vol. 4). 328p. 1991. 125.00 (*0-8247-8618-1*) Dekker.

***Unstable Angina: Diagnosis & Management: Commentary on the Agency for Health Care Policy & Research Clinical Practice Guidelines, No. 10.** Michael H. Crawford. LC 96-26865. (Clinical Practice Guidelines Ser.). 1996. 34.95 (*0-412-09771-0*) Chapman.

Unstable Angina Order. Adelman. 1981. lib. bdg. 135.00 (*90-247-2486-4*, Pub. by M Nijhoff NE) Kluwer Ac.

Unstable Bodies: Victorian Representations of Sexuality & Maternity. Jill L. Matus. LC 94-22957. 1995. text ed. 69.95 (*0-7190-4347-6*, Pub. by Manchester Univ Pr UK); text ed. 24.95 (*0-7190-4348-4*) St Martin.

Unstable Current Systems & Plasma Instabilities in Astrophysics. Ed. by Mukul R. Kundu & Gordon D. Holman. 1984. pap. text ed. 84.50 (*90-277-1887-3*); lib. bdg. 175.00 (*90-277-1886-5*) Kluwer Ac.

Unstable Dollar: Domestic & International Issues. Randall W. Hinshaw. 320p. 1988. pap. 24.95 (*0-88738-228-2*) Transaction Pubs.

Unstable Frontiers: Technomedicine & the Cultural Politics of "Curing" AIDS. John N. Erni. LC 94-773. 1994. text ed. 39.95 (*0-8166-2380-5*) U of Minn Pr.

Unstable Frontiers: Technomedicine & the Cultural Politics of "Curing" AIDS. John N. Erni. 1994. pap. 15.95 (*0-8166-2381-3*) U of Minn Pr.

Unstable Ideas: Temperament, Cognition, & Self. Jerome Kagan. LC 88-28376. (Illus.). 328p. 1989. 36.50 (*0-674-93038-X*) HUP.

Unstable Ideas: Temperament, Cognition, & Self. Jerome Kagan. (Illus.). 328p. 1992. pap. 15.95 (*0-674-93039-8*) HUP.

Unstable Modules over the Steenrod Algebra & Sullivan's Fixed Point Set Conjecture. Lionel Schwartz. LC 93-48596. (Chicago Lectures in Mathematics). 240p. 1994. pap. text ed. 16.95 (*0-226-74203-2*) U Ch Pr.

Unstable Modules Over the Steenrod Algebra & Sullivan's Fixed Point Set Conjecture. abr. ed. Lionel Schwartz. LC 93-48596. (Chicago Lectures in Mathematics). 240p. 1994. lib. bdg. 40.00 (*0-226-74202-4*) U Ch Pr.

Unstable Nuclei in Astrophysics. Ed. by T. Kajino et al. 400p. (C). 1992. text ed. 114.00 (*981-02-0782-4*) World Scientific Pub.

Unstable Shoulder. Ed. by Louis U. Bigliani. LC 96-2510. (American Academy of Orthopaedic Surgeons Monograph). 90p. 1996. pap. 35.00 (*0-89203-120-4*) Amer Acad Ortho Surg.

***Unstable Tendencies: Feminism, Deconstruction & the History of Philosophy.** Penelope Deutscher. LC 97-7477. 208p. (C). 1997. pap. write for info. (*0-415-13945-7*); text ed. write for info. (*0-415-13944-9*) Routledge.

***Unstately Power: Local Causes of China's Economic Reforms.** Lynn T. White, III. 768p. (C). (gr. 13). 1997. pap. text ed. 34.95 (*0-7656-0045-5*, East Gate Bk) M E Sharpe.

***Unstately Power: Local Causes of China's Economic Reforms.** Lynn T. White, III. 550p. (C). (gr. 13). 1997. text ed. 62.95 (*0-7656-0044-7*, East Gate Bk) M E Sharpe.

***Unstately Power: Local Causes of China's Intellectual, Legal, & Regime Reforms.** Lynn T. White, III. 750p. (C). (gr. 13). 1997. text ed. 62.95 (*0-7656-0148-6*, East Gate Bk) M E Sharpe.

Unsteady Aerodynamics & Aeroelasticity of Turbomachines: Proceedings of the 7th International Symposium, Fukuoka Sun Palace, September 25-29, 1994. Seventh International Symposium Staff. Ed. by Yoshimichi Tanida & M. Namba. LC 95-12218. 820p. 1995. 353.25 (*0-444-81900-2*) Elsevier.

Unsteady Aerodynamics & Aeroelasticity of Turbomachines & Propellers: Proceedings of the Fifth International Symposium, Beijing, China, 18-21 September, 1989. Ed. by Tianmin Pan et al. (International Academic Publishers Ser.). 528p. 1990. 135.00 (*0-08-040187-2*, Pub. by IAP UK) Elsevier.

Unsteady Combustion: Proceedings of the NATO Advanced Study Institute, Praia da Granja, Portugal, September 6-17, 1993. Ed. by F. Culick et al. (NATO ASI Series E: Applied Sciences: Vol. 306). 568p. (C). 1996. lib. bdg. 275.00 (*0-7923-3888-X*) Kluwer Ac.

Unsteady Flow & Fluid Transients: Proceedings of the International Conference Durham, U. K. 29 September - 1 October 1992. Ed. by Roger Bettes & Jacqueline Watts. (Illus.). 380p. (C). 1992. text ed. 95.00 (*90-5410-046-X*, Pub. by A A Balkema NE) Ashgate Pub Co.

Unsteady Flows - 1995. Ed. by W. L. Keith et al. LC 84-72442. (1995 ASME/JSME Fluids Engineering Conference Ser.: FED-Vol. 216). 204p. 1995. 100.00 (*0-7918-1471-8*, G00966) ASME.

Unsteady Flows in Aeropropulsion: 1994 International Mechanical Engineering Congress & Exposition, Chicago, Illinois - November 6-11, 1994. (AD Ser.: Vol. 40). 204p. 1994. 74.00 (*0-7918-1417-3*, G00912) ASME.

Unsteady Flows, 1993. Ed. by W. L. Keith & T. Wei. LC 86-72518. (FED Ser.: Vol. 157). 239p. 1993. pap. 45.00 (*0-7918-0965-X*, H00797) ASME.

Unsteady Flows, 1993. Ed. by D. C. Wiggert & Frederick J. Moody. 501p. 1993. pap. 30.00 (*0-7918-1014-3*) ASME.

Unsteady Flows 1994. Ed. by T. Wei et al. LC 84-72442. (Fluid Engineering Division Conference Ser.: Vol. 192). 69p. 1994. pap. 25.00 (*0-7918-1375-4*) ASME.

Unsteady Heat Mass Transfer. Dzyubenko et al. 1990. 142.00 (*0-89116-884-2*) Hemisp Pub.

Unsteady Interaction of Shock & Detonation Waves in Gases. V. P. Korobeinikov. Tr. by Jamil I. Ghojel from RUS. (Illus.). 330p. 1989. 137.00 (*0-89116-751-X*) Hemisp Pub.

Unsteady March. Klinkner. 1997. 25.00 (*0-02-874028-9*) Free Pr.

Unsteady March. Klinkner. 1998. 25.00 (*0-684-82727-1*) Free Pr.

Unsteady Motions of Compressible Media with Blast Waves: Proceedings. Ed. by Leond I. Sedov. (Proceedings of the Steklov Institute of Mathematics Ser.: No. 87). 144p. 1967. 50.00 (*0-8218-1887-2*, STEKLO/87) Am Math.

Unsteady State Processes in Catalysis. Yu S. Matros. (Illus.). 724p. 1990. 245.00 (*90-6764-127-8*, Pub. by VSP NE) Coronet Bks.

Unsteady Turbulent Shear Flows: Proceedings. Ed. by R. Michel et al. (International Union of Theoretical & Applied Mechanics Symposia Ser.). 450p. 1982. 76.95 (*0-387-11099-2*) Spr-Verlag.

Unsteady Viscous Flows. D. Telionis. (Computational Physics Ser.). (Illus.). 320p. 1981. 118.95 (*0-387-10481-X*) Spr-Verlag.

***Unstoppable: The Story of George Mikan, the First NBA Superstar.** George Mikan. 1997. pap. text ed. 16.95 (*1-57028-132-7*) Masters Pr IN.

***Unstoppable: To Be Determined.** Cynthia Kersey. 256p. 1997. 12.95 (*1-890043-00-1*) Spectrum Pub.

Unstretched Surfaces/Surface Lisses, Los Angeles-Paris, Vol. 1. Text by Jean-Luc Bordeaux & Alfred Pacquement. (Illus.). 47p. (Orig.). (ENG & FRE.). 1977. pap. 20.00 (*0-911291-02-4*) Fellows Cont Art.

Unstructured Scientific Computation on Scalable Multiprocessors. Ed. by Piyush Mehrotra et al. LC 91-48051. (Scientific & Engineering Computation Ser.). 405p. 1992. 39.95 (*0-262-13272-9*, Q183) MIT Pr.

Unstrung Heroes. Franz Lidz. 176p. 1991. 17.95 (*0-394-56988-1*) Random.

Unstrung Heros. Franz Lidz. 1995. mass mkt. 4.99 (*0-451-18442-4*) NAL-Dutton.

Unstuck: Risking Change in Adult Life Passages: Hope for Anyone Who Feels Stuck Between the Pain of the Past & the Promise of the Future. Carolyn A. Koons. 220p. 1995. pap. 12.99 (*0-89283-866-3*, Vine Bks) Servant.

UV

Unsubmissive Women: Chinese Prostitutes in Nineteenth-Century San Francisco. Benson Tong. LC 94-16168. (Illus.). 320p. 1994. 24.95 (*0-8061-2653-1*) U of Okla Pr.

Unsuccess: How to Be a Complete Screwup. Benjamin P. Yarbrough. 67p. (Orig.). (C). 1986. pap. 4.95 (*0-9618422-0-2*) Sunshine CA.

Unsuccessful Ladies. Jane-Eliza Hasted. LC 73-148216. (Biography Index Reprint Ser.). 1977. 25.95 (*0-8369-8063-8*) Ayer.

Unsui: A Diary of Zen Monastic Life. Giei Sato & Eshin Nishimura. Ed. by Bardwell L. Smith. LC 73-78112. (Illus.). 142p. 1973. pap. 16.95 (*0-8248-0272-1*) EW Ctr HI.

Unsuitable Arrangements. Keverne Barrett. 352p. (Orig.). 1993. pap. 14.99 (*1-85242-248-3*) Serpents Tail.

Unsuitable for Ladies: An Anthology of Women Travelers. Selected by Jane Robinson. (Illus.). 496p. 1995. pap. 14.95 (*0-19-282489-9*) OUP.

Unsuitable for Ladies: An Anthology of Women Travellers. Selected by Jane Robinson. LC 93-34644. (Illus.). 496p. 1994. 35.00 (*0-19-211681-9*) OUP.

Unsuitable Job for a Woman. P. D. James. 288p. 1988. mass mkt. 5.99 (*0-446-31517-6*) Warner Bks.

Unsuitable Match. Date not set. pap. 5.50 (*0-451-18801-2*, Sig) NAL-Dutton.

***Unsuitable Match.** Patricia Oliver. 1997. pap. 5.50 (*0-451-18800-4*, Sig) NAL-Dutton.

Unsuitable Match. large type ed. Alice Thornton. 350p. 1996. 21.50 (*0-263-14522-0*, Pub. by M & B UK) Ulverscroft.

***Unsuitable Suitor.** Marilyn Clay. 256p. 1997. mass mkt. 4.99 (*0-8217-5755-5*, Zebra Kensgtn) Kensgtn Pub Corp.

Unsuitable Wife. Lindsay Armstrong. (Presents Ser.). 1995. pap. 2.99 (*0-373-11713-2*, 1-11713-4) Harlequin Bks.

Unsuitable Wife. large type unabridged ed. (Harlequin Ser.). 1994. lib. bdg. 19.95 (*0-263-13893-3*, Pub. by Mills & Boon UK) Thorndike Pr.

Unsung: A History of Women in American Music. Christine Ammer. LC 79-52324. (Contributions in Women's Studies: No. 14). 317p. 1980. text ed. 42.95 (*0-313-22007-7*, AMU/) Greenwood.

Unsung: A History of Women in American Music. Christine Ammer. LC 79-52324. (Contributions in Women's Studies: No. 14). 317p. 1980. pap. text ed. 7.95 (*0-313-22909-0*, AMUPB) Greenwood.

Unsung Americans: A Teacher's Guide. 57p. (Orig.). 1995. teacher ed., pap. 14.95 (*1-886747-02-4*) Ward Hill Pr.

***Unsung Creatures from A to Z.** Katherine H. Brooks. (Illus.). 44p. (Orig.). 1996. pap. 4.00 (*1-886467-09-9*) WJM Press.

Unsung Heart of Black America: A Middle-Class Church at Midcentury. Dona L. Irvin. (Illus.). 256p. 1992. 32.50 (*0-8262-0841-X*) U of Mo Pr.

Unsung Heart of Black America: A Middle-Class Church at Midcentury. Dona L. Irvin. (Illus.). 256p. (Orig.). (C). 1992. pap. 18.95 (*0-8262-0902-5*) U of Mo Pr.

Unsung Heroes. Kenneth E. Sibley. (Illus.). 34p. 1989. pap. 6.50 (*0-9619934-2-1*) K E Sibley.

Unsung Heroes: A Decade of Writings. Michael K. Blanchard. LC 95-43135. (Illus.). 208p. 1995. pap. 10.00 (*1-883551-10-2*) Attic Studio Pub.

Unsung Heroes: Combat Nurses & Army Wives. LaVada B. Aquilina. LC 95-62217. (Illus.). 208p. (Orig.). 1996. pap. 12.95 (*0-9636577-3-9*) Trego-Hill.

Unsung Heroes: Federal Execucrats Making a Difference. Norma M. Riccucci. LC 95-7073. 266p. 1995. 45.00 (*0-87840-592-5*); pap. 17.95 (*0-87840-595-X*) Georgetown U Pr.

Unsung Heroes: The Women Behind the Men of God. 169p. (Orig.). 1996. pap. 5.95 (*0-9627838-3-8*) B B Kelly.

Unsung Heroes: Unheralded People Who Invented Famous Products. Nathan Aaseng. (Inside Business Ser.). (Illus.). 80p. (J). (gr. 5 up). 1989. lib. bdg. 18.95 (*0-8225-0676-9*, Lerner Publctns) Lerner Group.

Unsung Heroes, Negroes Domestic Service in U. S. African-American Women Writers by Haynes. Gates. LC 96-43477. 1996. 25.00 (*0-7838-1432-1*, Hall Reference) Macmillan.

Unsung Heroes of Rock 'n' Roll. Nick Tosches. 1991. pap. 10.00 (*0-517-58052-7*, Harmony) Crown Pub Group.

Unsung Heroes of Texas. Ann Ruff. LC 85-17606. (Illus.). 112p. (Orig.). 1985. pap. 9.95 (*0-88415-864-0*) Gulf Pub.

Unsung Heroines: The Women Who Won the War. large type ed. Vera Lynn et al. 222p. 1993. 22.95 (*1-85089-596-1*, Pub. by ISIS UK) Transaction Pubs.

***Unsung Heroines of the South Carolina Carolina Frontier: A Curriculum Resource Document Packet No. 9.** Alexia J. Helsley. 1997. wbk. ed., pap. 16.95 (*1-880067-41-2*) SC Dept of Arch & Hist.

Unsung Role of the Career Assistant Principal. Catherine Marshall. 68p. (Orig.). (C). 1993. pap. text ed. 11.00 (*0-88210-272-9*) Natl Assn Principals.

Unsung Sailors: The Naval Armed Guard in World War II. Justin F. Gleichauf. LC 89-13767. (Illus.). 480p. 1990. 32.95 (*0-87021-770-4*) Naval Inst Pr.

Unsung Season: Gardens & Gardeners in Winter. Sydney Eddison. (Illus.). 186p. 1995. 29.95 (*0-395-71551-2*) HM.

Unsung Voices: Opera & Musical Narrative in the Nineteenth Century. Carolyn Abbate. 304p. 1991. text ed. 49.50 (*0-691-09140-4*) Princeton U Pr.

Unsung Voices: Opera & Musical Narrative in the Nineteenth Century. Carolyn Abbate. 304p. 1991. pap. text ed. 16.95 (*0-691-02608-4*) Princeton U Pr.

Unsung Women: The Anonymous Female Voice in Troubadour Poetry. Tr. by Carol Nappholz from PRO. LC 93-37317. (Studies in the Humanities: Literature-Politics-Society: Vol. 13). 140p. (C). 1994. text ed. 39.95 (*0-8204-2376-9*) P Lang Pubng.

Unsupervised Estimation & Processing of Unknown Signals. E. A. Patrick & J. P. Costello. LC 71-136727. 207p. 1970. 19.00 (*0-403-04528-2*) Scholarly.

Unsupported Assertions: Essays. Hugh Hood. 121p. 1991. pap. 12.95 (*0-317-05588-7*, Pub. by Hse of Anansi Pr CN) Genl Dist Srvs.

Unsupported Assertions: Essays. Hugh Hood. 121p. 1991. 19.95 (*0-88784-505-3*, Pub. by Hse of Anansi Pr CN) Genl Dist Srvs.

***Unsupported Middle: Future Developments in a Primary Care-LED NHS.** Geoff Meads. LC 97-5138. 1997. write for info. (*1-85775-109-4*, Radcliffe Med Pr) Scovill Paterson.

Unsuspected. Charlotte Armstong. 1990. reprint ed. lib. bdg. 15.95 (*0-89968-474-2*) Buccaneer Bks.

Unsuspected Eloquence: A History of the Relations Between Poetry & Music. James A. Winn. LC 80-27055. 395p. 1981. pap. 112.60 (*0-7837-8419-8*, 2082307) Bks Demand.

***Unsuspecting Viewers.** Anthony Knopps. 387p. (Orig.). 1997. pap. 19.95 (*0-9646898-8-X*) Leathers Pub.

Unsuspended Animation. Craig Watson. 20p. (Orig.). 1990. pap. 4.00 (*0-945926-24-3*) Paradigm RI.

UNTAG in Namibia - A New Nation Is Born. 113p. 1990. 20.00 (*92-1-100434-9*, 90.I.10); pap. 14.00 (*0-685-39237-6*, 90.I.10) UN.

***Untam'd Desire: Sex in Elizabethan England.** Alan Haynes. 1997. 29.95 (*0-8117-1524-8*) Stackpole.

Untameables. Filippo T. Marinetti. Tr. by Jeremy Parzen from ITA. (Sun & Moon Classics Ser.: No. 28). 236p. 1994. pap. 10.95 (*1-55713-064-7*) Sun & Moon CA.

Untamed. Max Brand. LC 94-13997. xiv, 374p. 1994. pap. 10.95 (*0-8032-6117-9*, Bison Books) U of Nebr Pr.

Untamed. Elizabeth Lowell. 416p. (Orig.). 1993. mass mkt. 6.50 (*0-380-76953-0*) Avon.

Untamed. Kasey Michaels. 307p. 1996. mass mkt. 5.99 (*0-671-50115-1*) PB.

Untamed. Nora Roberts. (NR Flowers Ser.: No. 28). 1993. mass mkt. 3.59 (*0-373-51028-4*, 1-51028-8) Silhouette.

Untamed. Joann Ross. (Temptation Ser.). 1996. mass mkt. 3.50 (*0-373-25705-8*, 1-25705-4) Harlequin Bks.

Untamed. large type ed. Max Brand. (Sagebrush Large Print Westerns Ser.). 320p. 1995. lib. bdg. 18.95 (*1-57490-000-5*) T T Beeler.

Untamed. large type ed. Elizabeth Lowell. LC 93-13230. (Orig.). 1993. lib. bdg. 22.95 (*1-56054-757-X*) Thorndike Pr.

Untamed. large type ed. Helga Moray. 512p. 1983. 25.99 (*0-7089-1046-7*) Ulverscroft.

***Untamed Alaska.** Steve Kaufman & Yogi Kaufman. LC 97-16755. 1997. write for info. (*1-890674-00-1*, T-G & Lickle) Lickle Pubng.

Untamed Alaska. Yogi Kaufman & Steve Kaufman. LC 87-50137. 126p. 1987. 34.00 (*0-934738-28-9*) Lickle Pubng.

Untamed & Unabashed: Essays on Women & Humor in British Literature. Regina Barreca. LC 93-30645. (Humor in Life & Letters Ser.). 192p. 1994. text ed. 29.95 (*0-8143-2136-4*) Wayne St U Pr.

***Untamed Angel.** Elaine Fox. 320p. (Orig.) 1997. mass mkt. 4.99 (*0-8439-4274-6*, Leisure Bks) Dorchester Pub Co.

Untamed Breed. Gordon D. Shirreffs. 352p. 1994. mass mkt., pap. text ed. 4.50 (*0-8439-3696-7*) Dorchester Pub Co.

Untamed Coast: Pictures of Rare People & Places along the Edge of America. Peter Jenkins. LC 95-38102. (Illus.). 176p. 1995. 29.95 (*1-55853-347-8*) Rutledge Hill Pr.

Untamed Garden & Other Personal Essays. David R. Wallace. LC 86-21667. 203p. 1986. 35.00 (*0-8142-0423-6*) Ohio St U Pr.

Untamed Glory. Suzannah Davis. 368p. 1988. pap. 3.95 (*0-380-75397-9*) Avon.

***Untamed God: Unleashing the Supernatural in the Body of Christ.** Neil B. Wiseman. LC 96-46719. 176p. (Orig.). 1996. 15.99 (*0-8341-1629-4*) Beacon Hill.

Untamed Heart. Georgina Devon. 1994. mass mkt. 4.99 (*0-373-31215-6*, 1-31215-6) Harlequin Bks.

***Untamed Heart.** Kit Gardner. 1997. mass mkt. 4.99 (*0-373-28990-1*, 1-28990-9) Harlequin Bks.

Untamed Heart: A Book of Heartfelt Illustrations. Peter Georgeson. (Illus.). 40p. 1997. 6.95 (*0-8362-2143-5*) Andrews & McMeel.

Untamed Hearts. Wendy Garrett. 384p. 1996. mass mkt. 4.99 (*0-8217-5421-1*, Zebra Kensgtn) Kensgtn Pub Corp.

Untamed Land. Lauraine Snelling. (Red River of the North Ser.: Vol. 1). 352p. (Orig.). 1996. pap. 9.99 (*1-55661-576-0*) Bethany Hse.

***Untamed Land, a New Day Rising & Land To Call Home, 3 Vols.** Lauraine Snelling. (Red River of the North Ser.). 1997. pap. text ed. 29.99 (*0-7642-8150-X*) Bethany Hse.

***Untamed Lover.** Sharon Kendrick. (Harlequin Romance Ser.). 1996. 19.95 (*0-263-14716-9*) Thorndike Pr.

Untamed Tongue: A Dissenting Dictionary. Thomas Szasz. 272p. 1990. pap. 17.95 (*0-8126-9104-0*) Open Court.

***Untamed World, 12 vols.** (Untamed World Ser.). (Illus.). (J). 221.76 (*0-8172-4574-X*) Raintree Steck-V.

Untamed Years: Wild Silver. Iris Johansen et al. (Delaneys Ser.). 256p. 1988. pap. 3.50 (*0-685-20087-6*) Bantam.

Untangling Japanese I: Beginning Japanese. rev. ed. Seiko Huntington. Orig. Title: Untangling Nihongo One. (Illus.). 128p. 1991. pap. 17.95 (*0-936845-11-2*) Sakura Press.

Untangling Japanese II: Beginning Japanese. Seiko Huntington. (Illus.). 128p. (Orig.). 1992. pap. 17.95 (*0-936845-12-0*) Sakura Press.

Untangling Japanese III: Beginning Japanese. Seiko Huntington. (Illus.). 128p. (Orig.). 1992. pap. 17.95 (*0-936845-13-9*) Sakura Press.

Untangling Nihongo: Beginning Japanese. Seiko Huntington. LC 85-63445. (Illus.). 412p. (Orig.). (ENG & JPN.). 1987. pap. 29.95 (*0-936845-04-X*) Sakura Press.

Untangling Nihongo One see Untangling Japanese I: Beginning Japanese

Untangling Organizational Gridlock: Strategies for Building a Customer Focus. Michele L. Bechtell. LC 92-46118. 337p. 1993. 27.95 (*0-87389-147-3*, H0685) ASQC Qual Pr.

Untangling Organizational Gridlock: Strategies for Building a Customer Focus. Michelle L. Bechtell. 224p. 1993. 27.95 (*0-8144-0203-8*) AMACOM.

Untangling Our Faith. Elbert Dempsey, Jr. LC 93-28843. 1993. pap. 21.00 (*0-8309-0640-1*) Herald Hse.

Untangling the Family Finances: Divorce Simulation. David W. Felder. 44p. 1996. pap. text ed. 8.95 (*0-910959-92-7*, B&G 18C) Wellington Pr.

Untangling the Income Tax. David F. Bradford. 386p. 1986. lib. bdg. 29.95 (*0-87186-246-8*) Comm Econ Dev.

Untangling the Income Tax. David F. Bradford. LC 85-27078. 400p. 1988. reprint ed. pap. 17.95 (*0-674-93041-X*) HUP.

Untangling the Sexual Revolution. Henry W. Spaulding, II. 112p. 1989. pap. 6.99 (*0-8341-1305-8*) Beacon Hill.

***Untangling the Web.** Werner. 1996. pap. text ed. 1.00 (*0-312-15257-4*) St Martin.

Untapped Maps. Maureen Owen. 96p. (Orig.). 1993. pap. 9.50 (*0-937013-44-7*) Potes Poets.

Untapped Power in Praise. Kenneth Hagin, Jr. 1990. pap. 4.95 (*0-89276-725-1*) Hagin Ministries.

Untapped Power of the Press: Explaining Government to the People. Lewis W. Wolfson. LC 85-9471. 208p. 1985. text ed. 55.00 (*0-275-90237-4*, C0237, Praeger Pubs); pap. text ed. 18.95 (*0-275-91678-2*, B1678, Praeger Pubs) Greenwood.

Untapped Profits by Profession. abr. rev. ed. Intro. by Luanna C. Blagrove. (Illus.). 250p. 1988. 29.95 (*0-939776-15-4*) Blagrove Pubns.

Untapped Resource: The Final Report of the Americans over 55 at Work Program. (Illus.). 72p. (Orig.). (C). 1994. pap. text ed. 25.00 (*0-7881-0562-0*) DIANE Pub.

Untapped Resource: Working with Volunteers Who Are Mentally Ill. John D. Weaver. (C). 1993. pap. 10.95 (*0-945795-10-6*) MBA Pub.

Untaught History of Money. A. N. Field. 1991. lib. bdg. 77.95 (*0-8490-4418-9*) Gordon Pr.

Untaught History of Money. A. N. Field. 1992. lib. bdg. 79.96 (*0-8490-5424-9*) Gordon Pr.

Untaught Lessons. Philip W. Jackson. 128p. (C). 1992. text ed. 24.00 (*0-8077-3194-3*); pap. text ed. 13.95 (*0-8077-3193-5*) Tchrs Coll.

Untempered Wind: Forty Years in Palestine. Christine H. Jones. 238p. reprint ed. pap. 67.90 (*0-685-16286-9*, 2027719) Bks Demand.

Untended Gate: The Mismanagement of the Press. Norman E. Isaacs. LC 85-13296. 192p. 1986. text ed. 49.50 (*0-231-05876-4*) Col U Pr.

Untended Gates: The Mismanaged Press. Norman E. Isaacs. 258p. 1988. pap. text ed. 16.50 (*0-231-05877-2*) Col U Pr.

Unter der Erde. (Meyers Kleine Kinderbibliothek Ser.). 24p. 1991. 13.25 (*3-411-08481-2*, Pub. by Bibliogr Inst Brockhaus GW) Langenscheidt.

Untergang Des Abendlandes. Oswald Spengler. pap. 29.95 (*3-423-00838-5*) Adlers Foreign Bks.

Untergang Des Abendlandes. Oswald Spengler. 1989. 63.50 (*3-406-02531-5*) Adlers Foreign Bks.

Unteritalischen Dialekte. Theodor Mommsen. (Illus.). viii, 368p. reprint ed. write for info. (*0-318-71603-8*) G Olms Pubs.

***Unternehmenskultur: Entwicklung und Gestaltung aus Interaktionistischer Sicht.** Niels Jacobsen. (Europaische Hochschulschriften: Reihe 5: Bd. 1873). (Illus.). 211p. (GER.). 1996. pap. 42.95 (*3-631-50046-7*) P Lang Pubng.

Unternehmer & Marktdynamik. Israel M. Kirzner. Tr. by Gerd Reese & Rudi Schadt. (International Carl Menger Library). 300p. (GER.). 1988. 85.00 (*3-88405-036-2*) Philosophia Pr.

Unternehmung in der Demokratischen Gesellschaft see Business Corporation in the Democratic Society

Unterrichten - Grundzuge und Gestaltungsformen Des Lehrens und Lernens. Karl G. Poppel. (Hildesheimer Beitrage Ser.: Bd. 27). 192p. (GER.). 1992. write for info. (*3-487-09033-3*) G Olms Pubs.

Untersuchengen zu den Totenbuch-Papyri der 18 Dyn. Irmtraut Munro. 300p. (GER.). 1988. lib. bdg. 125.00 (*0-7103-0288-6*) Routledge Chapman & Hall.

Untersuchungen. M. Kreeb. pap. 25.00 (*0-89005-481-9*) Ares.

Untersuchungen an Gesteinsbewohnenden Xanthonhaltigen Sippen der Flechtengattung Lecidella (Lecanoraceae, Lecanorales) Johannes G. Knoph. (Bibliotheca Lichenologica Ser.: No. 36). (Illus.). 183p. 1990. pap. text ed. 52.00 (*3-443-58015-7*, Pub. by Cramer-Borntraeger GW) Lubrecht & Cramer.

Untersuchungen Uber Das "Argumentum e Consensu Omnium" Ruth Schian. (Spudasmata Ser.: Bd. 28). x, 201p. (GER.). 1973. write for info. (*3-487-04499-4*) G Olms Pubs.

Untersuchungen ueber die Grundfragen des Sprachlebens, Vol. 5. Phillip Wegener. LC 90-357. (Classics in Psycholinguistics Ser.). xlviivii, 214p. (GER.). 1991. reprint ed. 59.00 (*90-272-1894-3*) Benjamins North Am.

Untersuchungen Uber Plutarchs Biographische Technik. Adolf Weizsaecker. 122p. 1980. write for info. (*3-296-15880-4*) G Olms Pubs.

Untersuchungen ueber die Lebermoose. H. Leitgeb. 1970. 160.00 (*3-7682-7187-0*) Lubrecht & Cramer.

Untersuchungen ueber Hoehere Arithmetik: including Disquisitionea Arithmeticae. 2nd ed. Karl Gauss. Tr. by H. Maser. LC 65-17614. 695p. (GER.). 1981. text ed. 39.50 (*0-8284-0191-8*) Chelsea Pub.

Untersuchungen ueber Veraenderungen in den Buchenschuerzen der Kalk-Buchenwaelder des Teutoburger Waldes. Heinz Neite. (Dissertationes Botanicae Ser.: Vol. 108). (Illus.). 104p. 1987. pap. text ed. 50.00 (*3-443-64020-6*) Lubrecht & Cramer.

Untersuchungen Zu Cassiusi Dios Sicht der Romischen Republik. Detlef Fechner. (Altertumswissenschaftliche Texte und Studien: Bd. 14). xii, 265p. (GER.). 1986. write for info. (*3-487-07761-2*) G Olms Pubs.

Untersuchungen Zu Ciceros Philosophiscshen Schriften, 3 vols. Rudolf Hirzel. 1753p. 1964. reprint ed. Set. write for info. (*0-318-71144-3*) G Olms Pubs.

Untersuchungen Zu Den "Argonautica" Des Valerius Flaccus. Ratis O. Vincet. Ed. by Matthias Korn & Hans J. Tschiedel. (Spudasmata Ser.: Bd. XLVIII). 200p. (GER.). 1991. write for info. (*3-487-09410-X*) G Olms Pubs.

Untersuchungen Zu Den Athetesen Aristarchs in der Ilias und Zu Ihrer Behandlung Im Corpus der Exegetischen Scholien. Dietrich Luhrs. (Beitrage Zur Altertumswissenschaft Ser.: Bd. 11). xviii, 286p. (GER.). 1992. write for info. (*3-487-09629-3*) G Olms Pubs.

Untersuchungen Zu Fortpflanxung und Ploidie Verschiedener Ascomyceten. Evi Weber. (Bibliotheca Mycologica Ser.: Vol. 140). (Illus.). 186p. (GER.). 1992. pap. 59.40 (*3-443-59041-1*, Pub. by Cramer-Borntraeger GW) Lubrecht & Cramer.

Untersuchungen zu Gorgias' Schrift Ueber das Nichtseiende. Hans-Joachim Newiger. (C). 1973. 89.25 (*3-11-003432-8*) De Gruyter.

Untersuchungen Zu Lucilius. Conrad Cichorius. ix, 364p. 1964. 80.00 (*3-296-11610-9*) G Olms Pubs.

Untersuchungen Zu Senecas "Epistulae Morales" Hildegard Cancik. x, 163p. (GER.). 1967. 40.00 (*0-318-70622-9*) G Olms Pubs.

Untersuchungen zum Abbau der Buchenblattstreu Durch Pilze - Unter Besonderer Beruecksichtigung der Ascomyceten. Martina Kloidt. (Dissertationes Botanicae Ser.: Vol. 130). (Illus.). 184p. (GER.). 1989. spiral bd. 66.00 (*3-443-64042-7*, Pub. by Cramer GW) Lubrecht & Cramer.

Untersuchungen Zum Begriff Des Gottgeziemenden in der Antike. Oskar Dreyer. viii, 164p. (GER.). 1970. write for info. (*0-318-70626-1*) G Olms Pubs.

***Untersuchungen zum DDR-Berufskabarett der Ara Honecker.** Dietmar Jacobs. Ed. by Volker Neuhaus. (Kolner Studien zur Literaturwissenschaft: Bd. 8). 309p. (GER.). 1996. 57.95 (*3-631-30546-X*) P Lang Pubng.

Untersuchungen zum Einfluss der Kombinierten Nutzung als Kuehl-und Abwasserteich auf den Stoffhaushalt Eines Braunkohlerestgewaessers. R. Dietrich. (Dissertationes Botanicae Ser.: Vol. 129). (Illus.). 176p. (GER.). 1989. spiral bd. 46.00 (*3-443-64041-9*, Pub. by Cramer GW) Lubrecht & Cramer.

Untersuchungen zum Einfluss von Rhizosphaeren-organismen der Fichte (Picea abies (L.) H. Karst.) auf den Rotfaeuleerreger Fomes Annosus (Fr.) B. Karst., sowie die Identifikation von Gliotoxin als Stoffwechselprodukt von Penicillium spinolosum Thom. Erich Falk. (Bibliotheca Mycologica Ser.: Vol. 111). (Illus.). 170p. (GER.). 1987. pap. text ed. 42.00 (*3-443-59012-8*) Lubrecht & Cramer.

Untersuchungen Zum Nerobild der Spatantike. Waltraud Jakob-Sonnabend. (Altertumswissenschaftliche Texte und Studien: Bd. 18). viii, 216p. (GER.). 1990. write for info. (*3-487-09297-2*) G Olms Pubs.

Untersuchungen Zum Serapiontischen Prinzip E.T.A. Hoffmans. Ilse Winter. (De Proprietatibus Litterarum Ser.: No. 111). 90p. (Orig.). 1976. pap. text ed. 29.25 (*90-279-3434-7*) Mouton.

Untersuchungen Zum Sozialverhalten Des Rindes. V. Reinhardt. (Tierhaltung Ser.: No. 10). (Illus.). 96p. (GER.). 1980. 32.50 (*0-8176-1138-X*) Birkhauser.

Untersuchungen zum Wasserhaushalt der Vegetation im Nordwestargentinischen Andenhochland. Erika Geyger. (Dissertationes Botanicae Ser.: 88). 228p. (GER.). 1985. pap. text ed. 60.00 (*3-443-64002-8*) Lubrecht & Cramer.

Untersuchungen zum Wasserhaushalt von Myrceugenia exsucca und Temu divaricatum in Relation zur Morphologie und Anatomie der Wurzel an Ueberflutungsstandorten. R. Debus. (Dissertationes Botanicae Ser.: Vol. 100). (Illus.). 154p. (GER.). (C). 1987. pap. text ed. 56.00 (*3-443-64012-5*) Lubrecht & Cramer.

***Untersuchungen Zur Antiken Veroffentlichung der Catullgedichte.** Johannes Scherf. (Spudasmata Ser.: Band 61). 108p. (GER.). 1996. write for info. (*3-487-10157-2*) G Olms Pubs.

Untersuchungen zur Biologie der: Begleitflora Mediterraner Wein und Getreidekulturen im Westlichen Sizilien. Karl-Georg Bernhardt. (Dissertationes Botanicae Ser.: Vol. 103). (Illus.). 138p. 1987. pap. 48.00 (*3-443-64015-X*) Lubrecht & Cramer.

Untersuchungen Zur Biologie der Erdkrote Bufo Bufo L. Unter Besonderer Berucksichtigung des Einflusses Von Migrationshindernissen Auf das Wanderverhalten und Die Entwicklung Von Vier Erdkrotenpopulationen Im Stadtgebiet Von Osnabruck. Karl-Robert Wolf. 440p. (GER.). 1994. pap. 109.95 (*0-7734-4050-X*) E Mellen.

Untersuchungen zur Blueten-und Infloresz Enzmorphologie, Embryologie und Systematic der Restionaceen im Vergleich mit Gramineen und verwandten Familiem. Peter Kircher. (Dissertationes Botanicae Ser.: Vol. 94). (Illus.). 22p. 1986. 40.00 (*0-685-14381-3*) Lubrecht & Cramer.

Untersuchungen zur Byzantinischen Provinzverwaltung VI-XIII Jahrhundert: Gesammelte Aufsatze. Jadran. Ferluga. vii, 672p. (GER.). 1992. pap. 154.00 (*90-256-0992-9*, Pub. by A M Hakkert NE) Benjamins North Am.

Untersuchungen zur Eigenart des Buches Qohelet. Diethelm Michel. (Beiheft zur Zeitschrift fuer die Alttestamentliche Wissenschaft Ser.: No. 183). vii, 329p. (C). 1989. lib. bdg. 95.40 (*3-11-012161-1*) De Gruyter.

Untersuchungen zur Embryologie, Bluetenmorphologie und Systematik der Rapateaceen und der Xyridaceen-Gattung Abolboda: Monocotyledoneae. A. Tiemann. (Dissertatones Botanicae Ser.: No. 82). (Illus.). 202p. 1985. pap. text ed. 64.00 (*3-7682-1436-2*) Lubrecht & Cramer.

Untersuchungen zur Entstehung und Stabilitaet der Panaschierungen bei Hedera. Garry Grueber. (Illus.). 112p. (GER.). 1983. Color. pap. 85.00 (*0-937323-24-2*); B&W. pap. 50.00 (*0-937323-23-4*) Am Ivy Soc.

Untersuchungen zur Expression & Funktion des Linearen, Mitochondrialen Plasmidespcki von Claviceps Purpurea. Katrin Gessner-Ulrich. (Bibliotheca Mycologica Ser.: Vol. 148). (Illus.). 83p. (GER.). 1992. pap. 49.00 (*3-443-59049-7*, Pub. by Cramer-Borntraeger GW) Lubrecht & Cramer.

Untersuchungen zur Fruehzeit des franzoesischen Fuerstentums (9-10 Jahrhundert) Karl F. Werner. LC 79-8375. reprint ed. 18.50 (*0-404-18357-3*) AMS Pr.

***Untersuchungen zur Funktion des Emphatischen Do Im Englischen.** Jurgen Gerner. Ed. by Peter Godgluck. (Sprachwelten Ser.: Bd. 10). 276p. (GER.). 1996. 54.95 (*3-631-30603-2*) P Lang Pubng.

Untersuchungen Zur Genetik Des Fortpflanzungsverhaltens und der Fruchtkoerper- und Antibiotikabbildung Des Basidiomyceten Agrocybe Aegerita. F. Meinhardt. (Bibliotheca Mycologica Ser.: No. 75). (Illus.). 128p. (GER.). 1981. pap. text ed. 32.00 (*3-7682-1275-0*) Lubrecht & Cramer.

Untersuchungen Zur Geschichte der Griechischen Sprache. Karl Dieterich. xxiv, 326p. 1970. reprint ed. write for info. (*0-318-70911-2*) G Olms Pubs.

Untersuchungen Zur Geschichte der Internationalen Rezeption Uwe Johnsons. Nicolai Riedel. (Germanistische Texte und Studien: Vol. 21). xiii, 672p. 1985. write for info. (*3-487-07624-1*) G Olms Pubs.

Untersuchungen Zur Geschichte Des Kaisers Hadrian. Wilhelm Weber. vii, 288p. 1973. reprint ed. write for info. (*3-487-04699-7*) G Olms Pubs.

Untersuchungen Zur Geschichte Des Kaisers Septimius Severus. Johannes Hasebroek. LC 75-7321. (Roman History Ser.). (GER.). 1975. reprint ed. 19.95 (*0-405-07085-3*) Ayer.

Untersuchungen zur Geschichte Einer Fragestellung. Adolf Kleingunther. LC 75-13276. (History of Ideas in Ancient Greece Ser.). (GER.). 1976. reprint ed. 13.95 (*0-405-07316-X*) Ayer.

Untersuchungen Zur Geschichte und Verwaltung Agyptens Unter Romischer Herrschaft. Arthur Stein. xi, 260p. 1974. reprint ed. write for info. (*3-487-05306-3*) G Olms Pubs.

***Untersuchungen Zur Gotterwelt Des Altsumerischen Stadtstaates von Lagas.** Gebhard Selz. (Occasional Publications of the Samuel Noah Kramer Fund: No. 13). 1996. 65.00 (*0-924171-00-6*) U PA Mus Pubns.

***Untersuchungen zur Grammatik von Adjunkten im Deutschen.** Frank Beckmann. 298p. (GER.). (C). 1997. lib. bdg. 146.70 (*3-11-014594-4*) De Gruyter.

Untersuchungen Zur Hypotaxe Im Vedischen. Heinrich Hettrich. (Studies in Indo-European Language & Culture NF: Vol. 4). xix, 862p. (C). 1988. lib. bdg. 311.55 (*3-11-010844-5*) De Gruyter.

Untersuchungen zur Immissionsbelastung der Berliner Forsten: Deposition & Bioindikation. Kristina Markan & Uwe Fischer. (Dissertationes Botanicae Ser.: Vol. 170). (Illus.). 258p. (GER.). 1991. pap. 63.00 (*3-443-64082-6*, Pub. by Cramer-Borntraeger GW) Lubrecht & Cramer.

***Untersuchungen Zur Komposition der Jakoberzahlungen: Auf der Suche Nach der Endgestalt des Genesisbuches.** Thomas Nauerth. (Beitrage zur Erforschung des Alten Testaments & Antiken Judentums Ser.: Bd. 27). 318p. (GER.). 1997. 57.95 (*3-631-30220-7*) P Lang Pubng.

Untersuchungen Zur Lyrischen Kunst Des P. P. Statius. Hubert Cancik. 155p. (GER.). 1965. 32.00 (*0-318-70486-2*) G Olms Pubs.

Untersuchungen zur Oekologischen & Geographischen Gliederung der Strassenbegleit-Vegetation Innerhalb Eines Nord-Sued-Transekts Zwischen dem Nordwestdeutschen Tiefland & der Mediterranean Kuestenebene. Baerbl Heindl. (Dissertationes Botanicae Ser.: Vol. 186). (Illus.). 250p. (GER.). 1992. pap. text ed. 84.50 (*3-443-64098-2*, Pub. by Cramer-Borntraeger GW) Lubrecht & Cramer.

Untersuchungen zur Phylogenese Linearer Element: Extrachromosomale DNA des Ascomyceten Morchella Conica. M. Rohe. (Bibliotheca Mycologica Ser.: Vol. 146). (Illus.). 118p. (GER.). 1992. pap. text ed. 42.00 (*3-443-59047-0*, Pub. by Cramer-Borntraeger GW) Lubrecht & Cramer.

Untersuchungen zur Populationsdynamyk am Beginn von Sekundaersukzessionen. Beseutung von Samenbank und Samenniederschlag. Anton Fischer. (Dissertations Botanicae Ser.: Vol. 110). (Illus.). 234p. (GER.). 1987. pap. text ed. 60.00 (*0-318-32760-0*) Lubrecht & Cramer.

Untersuchungen zur Production und Reingung eines gelben Farbstoffes des Basidiomyceten: Pleurotus ostreatus (Jacq. ex Fr.) Kummer. Wolfgang Margraf. (Bibliotheca Mycologica Ser.: No. 93). (Illus.). 95p. (GER.). 1984. 26.00 (*3-7682-1412-5*) Lubrecht & Cramer.

Untersuchungen zur Redaktionsgeschichte des Pentateuch. Peter Weimar. (C). 1977. 91.55 (*3-11-006731-5*) De Gruyter.

Untersuchungen zur Reliefbedingten Variation von Vegetation & Standort. Karl H. Biederbick. (Dissertationes Botanicae Ser.: Vol. 176). (Illus.). 189p. (GER.). 1991. pap. 50.00 (*3-443-64088-5*) Lubrecht & Cramer.

Untersuchungen Zur Romischen Zenturienverfassung. Arthur Rosenberg. LC 75-7337. (Roman History Ser.). (GER.). 1975. reprint ed. 13.95 (*0-405-07058-6*) Ayer.

Untersuchungen Zur Selbstdarstellung Alterer Romischer Dichter. Werner Suerbaum. xxvii, 393p. (GER.). 1968. write for info. (*0-318-70623-7*) G Olms Pubs.

Untersuchungen zur Spaet- und Postglazialen Vegetationsgeschichte des Bayerischen Wald. H. Stalling. (Dissertationes Botanicae Ser.: Vol. 105). (Illus.). 201p. (GER.). 1987. pap. 56.00 (*3-443-64017-6*) Lubrecht & Cramer.

Untersuchungen Zur Spanischen Syntax Auf Grund der Werke Des Cervantes. L. Weigert. vii, 241p. 1973. reprint ed. write for info. (*3-487-04795-0*) G Olms Pubs.

Untersuchungen zur Spaten Eisenzeit in Syrien und Libanon: Stratigraphie und Keramikformen Zwischen ca. 720 bis 300 v. Chr. Gunnar Lehmann. (Altertumskunde Des Vorderen Orients Ser.: No. 5). (Illus.). x, 548p. 1996. 141.00 (*3-927120-33-2*, Pub. by UGARIT GW) Eisenbrauns.

Untersuchungen Zur Sprache der Euripideisschen Lyrik. Wilhelm Breitenbach. xviii, 293p. 1967. reprint ed. 65.00 (*0-318-70883-3*) G Olms Pubs.

Untersuchungen zur Textkritischen Methode des Zenodotos von Ephesos. Klaus Nickau. (Untersuchungen zur Antiken Literatur und Geschichte Ser.: Vol. 16). (C). 1977. 103.10 (*3-11-001827-6*) De Gruyter.

Untersuchungen zur Vegetation Ostliguriens (Italien) Bernd Nowak. (Dissertationes Botanicae Ser.: Vol. 111). (Illus.). 264p. (GER.). 1987. pap. text ed. 86.00 (*3-443-64023-0*) Lubrecht & Cramer.

Untersuchungen Zur Vergleichenden Entwicklungsgeschichte Von Scrophulaiceen-Blueten: Die Entwicklung der Blueten Von Digitalis Lanata, Digitalis Lutea Etc. U. Wunderlin. (Dissertationes Botaincae Ser.: Vol. 188). (Illus.). 313p. (GER.). 1992. pap. text ed. 94.50 (*3-443-64100-8*, Pub. by Cramer-Borntraeger GW) Lubrecht & Cramer.

Untertaneneid & Treuvorbehalt in Frankreich & England. Walther Kienast. LC 80-2022. reprint ed. 34.50 (*0-404-18572-X*) AMS Pr.

Untheory of Evolution: And Other Scientific Studies Including Hunting, Fishing & Sex. William C. Berdine. LC 91-90760. 248p. 1992. 19.95 (*0-9631802-0-7*) Berdine.

Untherapeutic Community: Organizational Behaviour in a Failed Addiction Treatment Program. Robert S. Weppner. LC 83-1270. 285p. reprint ed. pap. 81.30 (*0-7837-6167-8*, 2045889) Bks Demand.

Unthinkable Swift: Jonathan Swift & the Ideological Crisis of Church & State, 1688-1730. 152p. (C). 1994. pap. 17.95 (*1-85984-000-0*, B4691, Pub. by Verso UK) Routledge Chapman & Hall.

Unthinkable Swift: Jonathan Swift & the Ideological Crisis of Church & State, 1688-1730. Warren Montag. 152p. (C). (gr. 13). 1994. text ed. 60.00 (*1-85984-900-8*, B4687, Pub. by Vrso UK) Norton.

***Unthinkable Tenderness: Selected Poems.** Juan Gelman. Ed. & Tr. by Joan Lindgren from SPA. LC 96-46859. 1997. 45.00 (*0-520-20586-3*); pap. 16.95 (*0-520-20587-1*) U CA Pr.

Unthinking Eurocentrism: Multiculturalism & the Media. Ella Shohat & Robert Stam. LC 93-41501. (Sightlines Ser.). (Illus.). 336p. (gr. 13). 1994. pap. 18.95 (*0-415-06325-6*, A6574, Routledge NY) Routledge.

Unthinking Eurocentrism: Multiculturalism & the Media. Ella Shohat & Robert Stam. LC 93-41501. (Sightlines Ser.). (Illus.). 336p. (C). (gr. 13). 1994. text ed. 74.95 (*0-415-06324-8*, A6570, Routledge NY) Routledge.

Unthinking Faith & Enlightenment: Nature & Politics in a Post-Hegelian Era. Jane Bennett. 192p. (C). 1987. text ed. 32.00 (*0-8147-1095-6*) NYU Pr.

Unthinking Modernity: Innis, McLuhan, & the Frankfurt School. Judith Stamps. 224p. 1995. 49.95 (*0-7735-1232-2*, Pub. by McGill CN) U of Toronto Pr.

Unthinking Social Science: The Limits of Nineteenth-Century Paradigms. Immanuel Wallerstein. 220p. (C). 1991. pap. text ed. 24.95 (*0-7456-0911-2*) Blackwell Pubs.

Unthinking the Unthinkable: Nuclear Weapons & Western Culture. Jeff Smith. LC 88-45458. 208p. 1989. 27.50 (*0-253-35353-X*) Ind U Pr.

Unthinking Thinking: Jorge Luis Borges, Mathematics, & the New Physics. Floyd Merrell. LC 90-20128. (Illus.). 320p. 1991. 29.50 (*1-55753-011-4*) Purdue U Pr.

***Untidy Bride.** Sandra Nicholls. 72p. 1991. pap. 12.95 (*1-55082-021-4*, Pub. by Quarry Pr CN) LPC InBook.

Untidy Candles: Anthology of Contemporary Maine Poets. Ed. by Julie Zimmerman. LC 94-74204. (Illus.). 112p. 1995. pap. 10.00 (*1-879418-17-7*) Biddle Pub.

Untidy Murder. large type ed. Frances Lockridge & Richard Lockridge. LC 92-23912. 333p. 1992. reprint ed. lib. bdg. 17.95 (*1-56054-298-5*) Thorndike Pr.

Untidy Pilgrim. Eugene Walter. 250p. (C). 1988. pap. 9.95 (*0-413-55340-X*, A0304, Pub. by Methuen UK) Heinemann.

Untidy Pilgrim. Eugene Walter. LC 87-5881. (Library of Alabama Classics). 264p. 1987. reprint ed. pap. 14.95 (*0-8173-0370-7*) U of Ala Pr.

***Untie the Ribbons.** Sharon Hoffman. LC 97-9386. 1997. write for info. (*0-88368-480-2*) Whitaker Hse.

***Untie the Ribbons: Charished Gifts.** Sharon Hoffman. 167p. (Orig.). 1996. pap. 9.99 (*0-88368-471-3*) Whitaker Hse.

Until: The Coming of Messiah & His Kingdom. Robert Shank. LC 81-72098. 520p. 1982. pap. 11.95 (*0-911620-04-4*) Westcott.

Until Darkness Holds No Fear: The Healing of a Multiple Personality. Elizabeth J. Mikal. Ed. by Judith Rydlun. LC 95-80336. (Illus.). 304p. (Orig.). 1995. pap. 16.95 (*1-883862-08-6*) Bks Beyond Brdrs.

Until Death. Polly Whitney. 320p. 1994. 21.95 (*0-312-11089-8*, Thomas Dunne Bks) St Martin.

Until Death. Polly Whitney. 1996. mass mkt. 4.99 (*0-373-26219-1*, 1-26219-5, Wrldwide Lib) Harlequin Bks.

Until Death & After: How to Live with a Dying Intimate. Jayne M. Murdock. Ed. by Dick Murdock & Jayne Murdock. LC 79-90348. (Illus.). 64p. 1979. pap. 4.00 (*0-932916-05-8*) May-Murdock.

Until Death Do Us Part. McGuire. 1997. mass mkt. 6.50 (*0-671-53618-4*) PB.

Until Death Do Us Part. Joyce J. Tyra. 85p. (Orig.). 1989. pap. 5.95 (*0-89265-135-0*) Randall Hse.

Until Forever. Johanna Lindsey. 416p. (Orig.). 1995. mass mkt. 6.50 (*0-380-76259-5*) Avon.

***Until I Have No Country: A Novel of King Philip's War in New England.** Michael J. Tougias. 256p. (Orig.). 1996. pap. 12.95 (*0-924771-80-1*, Covered Brdge Pr) D C Press.

***Until I Met Dudley: How Every Day Things Really Work.** Roger McGough. LC 96-47900. (Illus.). 32p. (J). (gr. 1-5). 1997. 15.95 (*0-8027-8623-5*); lib. bdg. 16.85 (*0-8027-8624-3*) Walker & Co.

Until I Return. Laura Simon. 480p. 1987. mass mkt. 3.95 (*0-373-97051-X*) Harlequin Bks.

Until I Saw the Sea: A Collective of Seashore Poems. Alison Shaw. (Illus.). 32p. (J). 1995. 15.95 (*0-8050-2755-6*) H Holt & Co.

Until It Changes. Stephen-Paul Martin. 48p. 1988. pap. 3.00 (*0-926935-07-0*) Runaway Spoon.

***Until It Hurts: An Ike & Abby Mystery.** Polly Whitney. 1997. 22.95 (*0-312-15237-X*) Thomas Dunne Bks.

Until It's Time to Die. Ricardo F. Henry. 1996. 16.95 (*0-533-11657-0*) Vantage.

Until Justice Is Done. Christine McGuire. 1995. pap. 6.50 (*0-671-53052-6*) PB.

Until Justice Rolls Down: The Birmingham Church Bombing Case. Frank Sikora. LC 90-37498. 192p. 1991. 24.95 (*0-8173-0520-3*) U of Ala Pr.

Until My Eyes Are Closed with Shards. Manes Sperber. Tr. by Harry Zohn from GER. (All Our Yesterdays Ser.: Vol. 3). 240p. (C). 1994. 34.95 (*0-8419-1033-2*) Holmes & Meier.

***Until Next Year: Letter Writing & the Mails in the Canadas, 1640-1830.** Jane E. Harrison. (Illus.). xx, 155p. 1997. 49.95 (*0-88920-284-2*) Wilfrid Laurier.

Until Proven Guilty. J. A. Jance. (J. P. Beaumont Ser.). 208p. 1985. mass mkt. 6.50 (*0-380-89638-9*) Avon.

Until Proven Guilty. Christine McGuire. Ed. by Julie Rubenstein. 384p. 1995. mass mkt. 5.99 (*0-671-75012-7*) PB.

Until Proven Innocent. Art Harris. 408p. (Orig.). 1995. mass mkt. 5.99 (*0-380-77733-9*) Avon.

Until the Cure: Caring for Women with HIV. Ed. by Ann Kurth. 336p. 1993. 42.50 (*0-300-05806-3*); pap. 17.00 (*0-300-05835-7*) Yale U Pr.

Until the Day. large type ed. Muriel Howe. 416p. 1988. 25.99 (*0-7089-1799-2*) Ulverscroft.

Until the Day Break. Louis Bromfield. 25.95 (*0-8488-0250-0*) Amereon Ltd.

***Until the End.** Harold Coyle. 1997. mass mkt. 6.99 (*0-671-89017-4*) PB.

Until the End. Harold Coyle. 464p. 1996. 25.00 (*0-684-81140-5*) S&S Trade.

Until the End of Summer. Elizabeth Ogilvie. 19.95 (*0-8488-1119-4*) Amereon Ltd.

***Until the End of the World.** Garth Ennis. (Preacher Ser.). 1997. pap. text ed. 14.95 (*1-56389-312-6*) DC Comics.

***Until the End of Time.** Polly Whitney. 1997. mass mkt. 4.99 (*0-373-26233-7*, 1-26233-6, Wrldwide Lib) Harlequin Bks.

Until the End of Time. Polly Whitney. LC 95-14709. 272p. 1995. 21.95 (*0-312-13199-2*) St Martin.

Until the End of Time: Revealing the Future of Humankind (Dan. & Rev.) 160p. 1994. pap. text ed. 6.99 (*0-8407-2081-5*) Nelson.

Until the Hour Decides. Robert V. Danso. (Orig.). 1996. pap. write for info. (*1-57553-213-1*) Watermrk Pr.

Until the Karma Ends. Paul Adirex. 246p. 1995. 24.95 (*974-89245-2-1*, Pub. by Aries Bks TH) Weatherhill.

Until the King Comes. Theodore F. Schneider. 1991. pap. 9.75 (*1-55673-316-X*, 9137) CSS OH.

***Until the Last Arrow.** Percy T. Booth. 1997. pap. text ed. 19.95 (*1-885813-06-6*) B & B Pubng.

Until the Last Leaf Falls. Clue Tyler Dennis. 1995. 10.95 (*0-943873-28-2*) Elder Bks.

Until the Morning After: Selected Poems 1963-1985. Kofi Awoonor. LC 87-80177. 212p. (Orig.). 1987. pap. 10.95 (*0-912678-69-0*, Greenfld Rev Pr) Greenfld Rev Lit.

Until the Stars Appear: From the Hills of Middle America, the Enduring Power of Prayer Moves Mountains in Southern Africa. Randy Sprinkle. Ed. by Susan Hansen. 128p. (Orig.). 1994. pap. 8.95 (*1-56309-092-9*, New Hope) Womans Mission Union.

Until the Sun Dies. Robert Jastrow. (Illus.). 1977. 12.95 (*0-393-06415-8*) Norton.

Until the Twelfth of Never. Bella Stumbo. Ed. by Judith Regan. 800p. 1994. reprint ed. pap. 6.50 (*0-671-72668-4*) PB.

Until Then... Lair. 1993. pap. 8.95 (*1-883748-00-3*) Chrstian Stewardshp.

Until They Are Five: A Parents' Guide. Angela Phillips. 208p. (Orig.). 1989. pap. 10.95 (*0-04-440361-5*) Routledge Chapman & Hall.

***Until They Bring the Streetcars Back.** Stanley G. West. LC 96-95370. 296p. (Orig.). 1997. pap. 12.00 (*0-9656247-6-5*) Lexington Marshall.

Until Tomorrow. F. Rosanne Bittner. 400p. 1995. mass mkt. 5.99 (*0-8217-5064-X*, Zebra Kensgtn) Kensgtn Pub Corp.

Until Tomorrow. Jill M. Landis. 368p. (Orig.). 1994. mass mkt. 6.50 (*0-515-11403-0*) Jove Pubns.

Until Tomorrow. Charlotte J. Long. 48p. (Orig.). 1983. pap. 3.95 (*0-88100-036-1*) Marsh Creek.

Until Victory: Horace Mann & Mary Peabody. Louise H. Tharp. LC 77-6360. (Illus.). 367p. 1977. reprint ed. text ed. 65.00 (*0-8371-9653-1*, THUV, Greenwood Pr) Greenwood.

Until We Are Free: Study Guide to South Africa's Moment of Truth. Patricia De Beer & John De Beer. 40p. 1988. pap. 3.95 (*0-377-00183-X*) Friendship Pr.

***Until We Are Parted by Death.** Kenya McCullum. 150p. (Orig.). 1998. pap. 11.95 (*1-58006-027-7*, Sherlock Pr) Sovereign.

***Until We Are Strong Together: Women Writers in the Tenderloin.** Caroline Heller. LC 97-3210. (Language & Literacy Ser.). 262p. (Orig.). 1997. pap. 19.95 (*0-8077-3646-5*) Tchrs Coll.

***Until We Are Strong Together: Women Writers in the Tenderloin.** Caroline Heller. (Language & Literacy Ser.). 262p. 1997. 42.00 (*0-8077-3647-3*) Tchrs Coll.

Until We Meet Again. large type ed. Ann Farrington. (Romance Ser.). 320p. 1993. 25.99 (*0-7089-2951-6*) Ulverscroft.

Until We Meet Again: A True Story of Love & Survival in the Holocaust. Michael Korenblit & Kathleen Janger. (Illus.). 336p. (Orig.). 1995. pap. 13.95 (*0-9647124-0-7*) C River Pr.

Until We Met. large type ed. Anne Weale. 318p. 1980. 25.99 (*0-7089-0511-0*) Ulverscroft.

Until You. Illus. by Flavia. 32p. 1994. 6.95 (*0-8362-4726-4*) Andrews & McMeel.

***Until You.** Sandra Marton. 416p. 1997. mass mkt. 5.50 (*0-7860-0372-3*, Pinncle Kensgtn) Kensgtn Pub Corp.

Until You. Judith McNaught. Ed. by Linda Marrow. 464p. 1995. mass mkt. 6.50 (*0-671-88060-8*, Pocket Star Bks) PB.

Until You. large type ed. Judith McNaught. LC 94-40738. 1994. 26.95 (*1-56895-160-4*) Wheeler Pub.

Until You Are Dead: The Book of Executions in America. Frederick Drimmer. 1990. 19.95 (*0-8065-1184-2*, Citadel Pr) Carol Pub Group.

Until Your Heart Stops. T. M. McNally. 804p. 1994. mass mkt. 5.99 (*0-8041-1243-6*) Ivy Books.

Untilled Field. George Moore. LC 70-125233. (Short Story Index Reprint Ser.). 1977. 30.95 (*0-8369-3600-0*) Ayer.

***Untimely Death: A Novel.** Fred Yager & Jan Yager. 305p. 1997. 24.95 (*1-889262-01-3*) Hannacroix.

Untimely Loss: A Passage to the Gentle Side of Grief. Linda G. Zelenka. 64p. (Orig.). 1996. pap. 4.95 (*0-8091-3671-6*) Paulist Pr.

***Untimely Meditations.** Friedrich Nietzsche. Ed. by Daniel Breazeale. Tr. by R. J. Hollingdale. (Texts in the History of Philosophy Ser.). 336p. (C). 1997. text ed. 44.95 (*0-521-58458-2*) Cambridge U Pr.

***Untimely Meditations.** Friedrich Nietzsche. Ed. by Daniel Breazeale. Tr. by R. J. Hollingdale. (Texts in the History of Philosophy Ser.). 336p. (C). 1997. pap. text ed. 15.95 (*0-521-58584-8*) Cambridge U Pr.

Untimely Meditations. Friedrich Wilhelm Nietzsche. Tr. by R. J. Hollingdale. LC 83-6604. (Texts in German Philosophy Ser.). 250p. 1984. pap. text ed. 18.95 (*0-521-28927-0*) Cambridge U Pr.

Untimely Thoughts: Essays on Revolution, Culture & the Bolsheviks, 1917-1918. Maxim Gorky. 1995. pap. text ed. 14.00 (*0-300-06069-6*) Yale U Pr.

Untimely Tracts. Scruton. 1987. 19.95 (*0-333-43862-0*, Pub. by Macm UK) St Martin.

***Untitle Valentine Anthology.** Katherine Sutcliffe. 1998. mass mkt. write for info. (*0-515-12226-2*) Jove Pubns.

***Untitled.** Kevin J. Anderson & Rebecca Moesta. (Star Wars Ser.: No. 11). 1998. mass mkt. write for info. (*1-57297-331-5*) Blvd Books.

***Untitled.** Lizi Boyd. 1999. pap. write for info. (*0-670-85384-4*) Viking Penguin.

Untitled. Timothy Bush. Date not set. write for info. (*0-517-79984-7*, Crown); lib. bdg. write for info. (*0-517-79985-5*, Crown) Crown Pub Group.

***Untitled.** Mary Cantwell. 1999. pap. 22.95 (*0-670-85231-7*) Viking Penguin.

***Untitled.** Casanova. 1998. 14.95 (*0-7868-0324-X*) Hyperion.

***Untitled.** Deborah Chester. (Lucasfilm Alien Chronicles Bk.: No. I). 1997. mass mkt. 5.99 (*1-57297-278-5*) Blvd Books.

***Untitled.** Mark Edmundson. 1997. pap. write for info. (*0-670-84540-X*) Viking Penguin.

***Untitled.** Thomas Eidson. 1998. pap. 22.95 (*0-525-94249-1*) NAL-Dutton.

***Untitled.** Tess Galati. 1998. pap. 22.95 (*0-670-87219-9*) Viking Penguin.

***Untitled.** James Gleick. 1999. pap. 10.00 (*0-14-011871-3*); pap. 25.00 (*0-670-82650-2*) Viking Penguin.

***Untitled.** Goodman. 1996. 35.00 (*0-8050-4081-1*) St Martin.

***Untitled.** Ed. by Martin H. Greenberg. (Murder She Wrote Anthology Ser.: No. 2). 1998. mass mkt. write for info. (*1-57297-339-0*) Blvd Books.

***Untitled.** Higgins. 1996. pap. 14.00 (*0-8050-4818-9*) St Martin.

***Untitled.** Jones. 1996. 22.00 (*0-8050-4273-3*) St Martin.

U V

An Asterisk (*) at the beginning of an entry indicates that the title is appearing in BIP for the first time.

***Untitled.** David Leavitt. 1999. pap. 22.95 (0-670-85447-6) Viking Penguin.
***Untitled.** McCarty. 1996. pap. 15.95 (0-8050-4620-8) St Martin.
***Untitled.** McKnight. 1996. 22.95 (0-8050-4828-6) St Martin.
***Untitled.** McKnight. LC 97-19096. 1997. 22.95 (0-8050-4829-4) St Martin.
***Untitled.** Mori. 1997. 22.50 (0-8050-4080-3) St Martin.
***Untitled.** Darian North. 1998. pap. 23.95 (0-525-94201-7) Viking Penguin.
***Untitled.** Petersen. 1996. 30.00 (0-8050-4774-3) St Martin.
***Untitled.** Pitt. 1997. 25.00 (0-684-83837-0) S&S Trade.
***Untitled.** Thomas Pynchon. 1999. pap. write for info. (0-670-81374-5) Viking Penguin.
Untitled. Anna Quindlen. Date not set. write for info. (0-517-59663-6) Crown Pub Group.
***Untitled.** Nancy T. Rosenberg. 1998. pap. 24.95 (0-525-94315-3) NAL-Dutton.
***Untitled.** Slotkin. 1996. 35.00 (0-8050-4124-9) St Martin.
***Untitled.** Spurr. 1996. pap. 12.00 (0-8050-4633-X) St Martin.
***Untitled.** Spurr. 1997. 22.50 (0-8050-4632-1) St Martin.
Untitled. Trice D. Turner. Date not set. write for info. (0-517-70589-3) Crown Pub Group.
Untitled. Nina Vida. Date not set. write for info. (0-517-70072-7) Crown Pub Group.
***Untitled.** Fay Weldon. 1999. pap. 19.95 (0-670-84948-0) Viking Penguin.
***Untitled.** Wiggins. 1996. 22.00 (0-8050-4418-3) St Martin.
***Untitled.** Winner. 1996. write for info. (0-8050-4834-0) St Martin.
Untitled, Bk. 2. D. Cragg & D. Sherman. Date not set. pap. write for info. (0-345-40623-0) Ballantine.
Untitled, No. 1. Justine Korman. (J). Date not set. pap. write for info. (0-679-87755-X, Bullseye Bks) Random Bks Yng Read.
Untitled, No. 2. Tara K. Harper. Date not set. pap. write for info. (0-345-40635-4) Ballantine.
Untitled, No. 2. Justine Korman. (J). Date not set. pap. write for info. (0-679-87756-8, Bullseye Bks) Random Bks Yng Read.
Untitled, No. 3. Tara K. Harper. Date not set. pap. write for info. (0-345-40636-2) Ballantine.
Untitled, No. 3. Justine Korman. (J). Date not set. pap. write for info. (0-679-87757-6, Bullseye Bks) Random Bks Yng Read.
Untitled, No. 4. Tara K. Harper. Date not set. pap. write for info. (0-345-40637-0) Ballantine.
Untitled, No. 5. Tara K. Harper. Date not set. pap. write for info. (0-345-40638-9) Ballantine.
Untitled: Elmo Beginner Book. Jane E. Gerver. 1997. 7.99 (0-679-88157-3) McKay.
Untitled: Elmo Beginner Book. Jane E. Gerver. (J). 1997. lib. bdg. 11.99 (0-679-98157-8) McKay.
Untitled: John Henry. Diaz. write for info. (0-15-200403-3) HarBrace.
***Untitled No. 5.** Suzanne Forster. 1998. mass mkt. write for info. (0-425-16185-4) Berkley Pub.
Untitled - C. F. Mills. Ed. by C. F. Mills et al. 1004p. 1985. 130.00 (0-85198-553-X, Pub. by CAB Intntl UK) OUP.
Untitled - Christopher Pike. Christopher Pike. 1997. 14.00 (0-671-55056-X, PB Hardcover) PB.
Untitled - Irene Dische. Irene Dische. Date not set. pap. 8.95 (0-14-014983-X) Viking Penguin.
Untitled - Kate Saunders Novel. Kate Saunders. Date not set. pap. write for info. (0-525-94171-1) NAL-Dutton.
Untitled - Linda Collins Novel. Linda Collins. Date not set. pap. write for info. (0-670-81355-9) Viking Penguin.
Untitled - McGaughey. McGaughey. 1998. 21.00 (0-684-19762-6) S&S Trade.
Untitled - Nye Anthology. Nye. LC 97-18622. (J). 1998. 19.95 (0-689-81233-7) S&S Childrens.
Untitled - Nye Poetry Collection. Nye. (J). 1998. 17.00 (0-689-81232-9) S&S Childrens.
Untitled - Paul, Bk. 2. Paul. LC 96-37258. 1997. 21.00 (0-684-19716-2) S&S Trade.
Untitled - Simon Picture Book. Simon. (J). Date not set. 16.00 (0-689-81238-8) S&S Childrens.
Untitled # 2. Sid Hite. 1996. 15.95 (0-8050-5055-8, Bks Young Read) H Holt & Co.
Untitled Alan Furst Novel. Alan Furst. Date not set. write for info. (0-679-45193-5) Random.
***Untitled Alther.** Lisa Alther. 1996. pap. write for info. (0-452-15527-4, Plume) NAL-Dutton.
Untitled Anne Lamott Non-Fiction. Anne Lamott. 1998. write for info. (0-679-44240-5) Random.
Untitled Anthology of Original Mysteries. Duncan. 1997. 3.99 (0-689-80724-4) S&S Childrens.
Untitled Autobiography. Christopher Reeve. Date not set. write for info. (0-679-45235-4) McKay.
***Untitled Beavis & Butt Head.** MTV Staff. 1997. pap. 12.00 (0-671-01533-8, PB Trade Paper) PB.
Untitled Bernard Lewis on the Middle East. Bernard Lewis. Date not set. write for info. (0-679-45191-9) Random.
Untitled, Black - White. Janelle Reiring. (Illus.). 1978. pap. text ed. 4.95 (0-931706-03-3) L Lawler.
Untitled Book. Adam Gussow. Date not set. pap. write for info. (0-679-77177-8) McKay.
***Untitled Book about the Golden Age of America's Railroads & Their Decline.** Buckley. 1994. 22.50 (0-684-19502-X) S&S Trade.
Untitled Book Non-Fiction. Edmund O. Wilson. Date not set. pap. write for info. (0-679-76811-4) McKay.
***Untitled Book of Novellas.** Richard Ford. 1997. pap. write for info. (0-679-77668-0, Vin) Random.
Untitled Book on Coming-of-Age Ceremonies. Strom. (J). 1997. 18.00 (0-689-80073-8) S&S Childrens.
Untitled Book on Economic Philosophy. Steven E. Landsburg. 1997. 24.00 (0-684-82755-7) S&S Trade.
Untitled Book on Preserving Wildlife. James Arnosky. (J). 1998. 13.00 (0-689-80474-1) S&S Childrens.
Untitled Book on Religion #1. Moser. (J). Date not set. 25.00 (0-689-80576-4) S&S Childrens.
Untitled Book on Religion #2. Moser. (J). Date not set. 16.00 (0-689-80562-4) S&S Childrens.
***Untitled Book #1.** Drescher. (J). 1900. 14.95 (0-7868-0343-6); lib. bdg. 14.89 (0-7868-2282-1) Hyprn Child.
***Untitled Book #2.** Drescher. (J). 1998. 14.95 (0-7868-0344-4); lib. bdg. 14.89 (0-7868-2283-X) Hyprn Child.
Untitled Boy Talk, No. 10. Betsy Haynes. (J). 1996. pap. write for info. (0-679-88052-6, Bullseye Bks) Random Bks Yng Read.
Untitled Budgie Book #1. H. R. H. the Duchess of York. (J). 1997. 15.00 (0-689-81313-9); pap. 5.99 (0-689-81314-7) S&S Childrens.
Untitled Budgie Book #2. H. R. H. the Duchess of York. (J). 1997. 15.00 (0-689-81315-5) S&S Childrens.
Untitled Budgie Book #2. H. R. H. the Duchess of York. (J). 1998. pap. 5.99 (0-689-81316-3) S&S Childrens.
Untitled Carter Bugs Book #3. Carter. (J). 1997. 12.95 (0-689-80435-0) S&S Childrens.
Untitled Cats Book, Steps 4. Cindy Wheeler. (J). 1996. pap. write for info. (0-679-87786-X, Bullseye Bks) Random Bks Yng Read.
***Untitled Cecil Dawkins Novel.** Cecil Dawkins. 1997. mass mkt. 5.99 (0-8041-1433-1) Ivy Books.
Untitled Chandler. Chandler. Date not set. 30.00 (0-02-905305-6) S&S Trade.
***Untitled Chap Book.** Pinkney. (J). 1998. pap. 3.95 (0-7868-1217-6); lib. bdg. 13.89 (0-7868-2266-X) Hyprn Child.
Untitled Charlotte Dolan. Charlotte L. Dolan. Date not set. pap. 4.99 (0-451-17727-4) NAL-Dutton.
Untitled Chris Bohjalian. Chris Bohjalian. 1997. write for info. (0-517-70586-9) Random Hse Value.
Untitled Christmas Ornament. (J). 1996. write for info. (0-679-87816-5, Bullseye Bks) Random Bks Yng Read.
Untitled Christmas Ornament, No. 3. (J). 1996. write for info. (0-679-87817-3, Bullseye Bks) Random Bks Yng Read.
Untitled Christmas Ornament, No. 4. (J). 1996. write for info. (0-679-87818-1, Bullseye Bks) Random Bks Yng Read.
Untitled Claire Harman Biography on Fanny Burney. Claire Harman. Date not set. pap. write for info. (0-679-44658-3) Random.
Untitled Clay Reynolds Novel. Clay Reynolds. Date not set. pap. 21.95 (0-525-93916-4) NAL-Dutton.
Untitled Collection. Michael Kimmelman. Date not set. write for info. (0-679-45219-2) McKay.
Untitled Collection of Poems. Federico G. Lore. LC 96-53684. 1997. pap. 9.00 (0-679-77634-6) Random.
Untitled Collection of Short Stories. Joy Williams. Date not set. pap. write for info. (0-679-44647-8) McKay.
Untitled Collection of the Family. Sharon S. Fiffer & Steve Fiffer. 1997. pap. 13.00 (0-679-77274-X) McKay.
Untitled Commonwealth Novel. Alan Dean Foster. 1998. mass mkt. write for info. (0-345-40645-1) Ballantine.
Untitled Cookbook. Piero Seluaggio. 1996. write for info. (0-679-45242-7) McKay.
Untitled Daranna G. Bradley. Daranna G. Bradley. Date not set. pap. 19.95 (0-525-93736-6) NAL-Dutton.
Untitled David Adler. David Adler. LC 96-48205. 1997. lib. bdg. 17.99 (0-679-94699-3) Random.
Untitled David Adler #4. David Adler. LC 96-48205. 1997. pap. 3.99 (0-679-84699-9) Random.
Untitled David Blum Non-Fiction on Longevity. David Blum. Date not set. write for info. (0-679-45170-6) Random.
Untitled Deepak Chopra Nonfiction. Deepak Chopra. 1998. write for info. (0-517-70623-7) Random Hse Value.
Untitled Deepak Chopra Nonfiction. Deepak Chopra. 1999. write for info. (0-517-70624-5) Random Hse Value.
Untitled Diane Ackerman. Diane Ackerman. 1996. write for info. (0-679-44879-9) Random.
Untitled Dinotopia, No. 6. Scott Ciencin. (J). 1996. pap. write for info. (0-679-88264-2) Random Bks Yng Read.
Untitled Dinotopia #5. Scott Cienein. 1996. pap. write for info. (0-679-87428-3) Random.
Untitled Elephant. Roger Caras. 1999. pap. 20.00 (0-670-83386-X) Viking Penguin.
***Untitled Elizabeth Elliott, Historical Romance #4.** Elizabeth Elliott. 1997. mass mkt. 5.99 (0-553-57567-8, Fanfare) Bantam.
Untitled Elizabeth Hewitt. Elizabeth Hewitt. 1999. pap. 5.99 (0-451-40655-9, Onyx) NAL-Dutton.
***Untitled Essays - Michael Ryan.** Michael Ryan. 1999. pap. 9.95 (0-14-013229-5); pap. 19.95 (0-670-83258-8) Viking Penguin.
Untitled Essex Hemphill Fiction. 1999. pap. 23.95 (0-525-94189-4) NAL-Dutton.
***Untitled Fairy Tale.** Berenzy. 1996. pap. 15.95 (0-8050-4024-2) St Martin.
***Untitled, Fayrene Preston #3.** Fayrene Preston. 1997. mass mkt. 3.50 (0-553-44533-2, Loveswept) Bantam.
***Untitled Follett Fiction #2.** Ken Follett. 1997. write for info. (0-517-70297-5, Crown) Crown Pub Group.
Untitled Frank Wilson. Frank Wilson. Date not set. pap. 17.95 (0-670-83163-8) Viking Penguin.
Untitled Frederick Manfred. Frederick Manfred. Date not set. pap. write for info. (0-451-18135-2, Sig) NAL-Dutton.
***Untitled Freedman Novel 2.** J. F. Freedman. Date not set. pap. 21.95 (0-670-85348-8) Viking Penguin.
***Untitled Frontier Novel No. 2.** Jim R. Woolard. 1998. mass mkt. write for info. (0-425-16082-3) Berkley Pub.
Untitled Garrett Files. Glen Cook. Date not set. pap. 5.99 (0-451-45479-0, ROC) NAL-Dutton.
Untitled Gerald Early: On Fisk College. Gerald Early. 1995. write for info. (0-201-62685-3) Addison-Wesley.
Untitled-GLB. Anna Quindlen. 1996. lib. bdg. write for info. (0-517-59664-4) Crown Pub Group.
Untitled Helene M. Viramontes Novel. 1998. pap. 21.95 (0-525-93953-9) NAL-Dutton.
***Untitled (Inch)** Peter Ganick. 28p. 1996. pap. 4.50 (1-889289-12-4) Ye Olde Font Shoppe.
Untitled Irene Dische. Irene Dische. 1999. pap. 18.95 (0-670-83866-7) Viking Penguin.
Untitled James Herriot. large type ed. James Herriot. 1992. 22.00 (0-8161-5216-0) G K Hall.
Untitled Janet Ciccone. Janet Ciccone. 1999. pap. 5.99 (0-451-40630-3) NAL-Dutton.
Untitled Janet Flanner Biography. Murray. 1993. 24.95 (0-13-511973-1) P-H.
Untitled Jeffery Greene. Jeffrey Greene. (J). 1998. 15.00 (0-671-51097-5) S&S Childrens.
***Untitled Jerry Jones.** Jerry Jones. 1997. 23.00 (0-671-01710-1) PB.
***Untitled Joseph Brodsky Poetry Collection.** Joseph Brodsky. 1998. pap. 9.95 (0-14-086530-6) Viking Penguin.
***Untitled Joyce Maynard.** Joyce Maynard. Date not set. pap. write for info. (0-449-90942-5) Fawcett.
***Untitled Krentz.** Krentz. Date not set. 24.00 (0-671-52306-6, Pocket Books) PB.
Untitled Lane Novel. Allison Lane. 1998. pap. 4.99 (0-451-19158-7, Sig) NAL-Dutton.
Untitled Larry Collins Novel. Larry Collins. 1998. pap. 24.95 (0-525-94172-X) NAL-Dutton.
Untitled Lee Gruenfeld. Lee Gruenfeld. 1998. pap. 24.95 (0-525-94132-0) NAL-Dutton.
***Untitled Lewis.** Lewis. (J). 1997. 15.00 (0-671-88317-8) S&S Childrens.
Untitled-Lillian Faderman. Lillian Faderman. Date not set. pap. 11.95 (0-14-017249-1) Viking Penguin.
Untitled Lillian Faderman Reader. Lillian Faderman. Date not set. pap. 24.95 (0-670-84639-2) Viking Penguin.
***Untitled Linn.** Linn. 1980. mass mkt. 1.95 (0-671-82556-9, Pocket Books) PB.
Untitled Mark Leyner #2. Mark Leyner. 1997. write for info. (0-517-70102-2) Random.
Untitled Mary Willis Novel. Mary P. Willis. Date not set. pap. write for info. (0-679-44696-6) Random.
Untitled Mathematics. 97th ed. HRW Staff. 1997. 26.75 (0-03-095790-7) HarBrace.
Untitled McGraw. McGraw. (J). 1998. 16.00 (0-689-80512-8, S&S Bks Young Read) S&S Childrens.
Untitled McGraw #2. McGraw. (J). 1997. 16.00 (0-689-80572-1) S&S Childrens.
***Untitled Memoirs.** Joni Mitchell. 1997. write for info. (0-609-60006-0) Random Hse Value.
***Untitled Middle Grade.** Kathryn Lasky. (J). 1900. 14.95 (0-7868-0337-1); pap. 4.50 (0-7868-1223-0); lib. bdg. 14.89 (0-7868-2278-3) Hyprn Child.
Untitled Middle Grade Novel. Marino. (J). 1998. 16.00 (0-689-80067-3) S&S Trade.
***Untitled Morgantina Studies, Vol. 6.** Princeton University Staff. (Morgantina Studies: No. 6). 1996. 85.00 (0-691-04017-6) Princeton U Pr.
***Untitled Morgantina Studies, Vol. 7.** Princeton University Staff. (Morgantina Studies: No. 7). 1999. 85.00 (0-691-04018-4) Princeton U Pr.
Untitled Moser Counting Book. Moser. (J). 1998. 15.00 (0-689-80511-X, S&S Bks Young Read) S&S Childrens.
Untitled Naipaul Non-Fiction on the Middle East. V. S. Naipaul. Date not set. write for info. (0-679-45207-9) Random.
Untitled Nancy Collins. Nancy Collins. Date not set. pap. 17.95 (0-670-82082-2) Viking Penguin.
Untitled Nicholasa Mohr. 1998. pap. 14.99 (0-670-86220-7) Viking Penguin.
Untitled Nina Blanchard. 1998. pap. 21.95 (0-525-93797-8) NAL-Dutton.
Untitled Non-Fiction. Roger Cohen. 1997. write for info. (0-679-45243-5) McKay.
***Untitled Nonfiction.** Mary Matalin. 1997. write for info. (0-679-45705-4) Random.
Untitled Nonfiction Book on Eating Disorders. Bode. LC 96-29186. (J). 1997. 16.00 (0-689-80272-2) S&S Childrens.
***Untitled Novel.** John Bennett. 1997. write for info. (0-679-45700-3) Random.
Untitled Novel. Rupert Holmes. Date not set. write for info. (0-679-45220-6) McKay.
Untitled Novel. Mazer. (J). Date not set. mass mkt. 3.95 (0-689-80752-X) S&S Childrens.
Untitled Novel. Mazer. (J). 1998. 16.00 (0-689-80751-1) S&S Childrens.
Untitled Novel. Georgia E. Taylor. Date not set. pap. 19.95 (0-525-93746-3) Viking Penguin.
Untitled Novel. Hunter S. Thompson. 1998. write for info. (0-679-40694-8) McKay.
Untitled Novel. Sabin Willett. 1997. write for info. (0-679-44853-5) Random.
Untitled Novel. Joy Williams. Date not set. pap. write for info. (0-679-44646-X) McKay.
Untitled Novel #2. Nicholas Kilmer. 1996. 23.00 (0-8050-5034-5) H Holt & Co.
Untitled Nude. Carol Doumani. LC 94-61117. (Illus.). 352p. 1995. 25.00 (0-9642359-6-X) Wave Pubng.
Untitled Oates Biography. Greg Johnson. 1998. pap. 27.95 (0-525-94161-4) NAL-Dutton.
Untitled on Balanchine. Suki Schorer. Date not set. pap. write for info. (0-679-45060-2) McKay.
***Untitled On Children.** Billy Shore. 1997. write for info. (0-679-45706-2) Random.
***Untitled on Gay Marriage.** Andrew Sullivan. LC 96-51881. 1997. pap. 14.00 (0-679-77637-0, Vin) Random.
***Untitled on Interview Skills.** L. I. Lishing. 1997. pap. 4.95 (0-679-77875-6) Random.
Untitled on Joe McCarthy. Ted Morgan. 1997. write for info. (0-679-44399-1) Random.
***Untitled on Networking.** L. I. Lishing. 1997. pap. 4.95 (0-679-77877-2) Random.
Untitled on Nutrition. American Academy of Pediatrics. Date not set. pap. write for info. (0-679-44869-1) McKay.
***Untitled on Resumes.** L. I. Lishing. 1997. pap. 4.95 (0-679-77872-1) Random.
Untitled on Russia. Robert Haupt. 1997. 25.00 (0-8050-5111-2) H Holt & Co.
Untitled on Symptoms. American Academy of Ped. Date not set. pap. write for info. (0-679-44868-3) McKay.
***Untitled on Teenagers & Parent.** Lis Harris. 1997. write for info. (0-517-70727-6) Crown Pub Group.
Untitled on the Creation of the Interstate System see Divided Highways: Building the Interstate Highways, Transfroming American Life
Untitled on the Media. Todd Gitlin. Date not set. 5.95 (0-8050-4898-7) H Holt & Co.
***Untitled on the South.** Tony Horwitz. 1998. pap. write for info. (0-679-75833-X) Knopf.
***Untitled on U. S. - Africa Policy.** Oudes. 1996. 27.50 (0-8050-4066-8) St Martin.
***Untitled On Women And Personal Finance.** Judy Resnick. LC 97-25527. 1998. write for info. (0-307-44005-2, Golden Books) Western Pub.
Untitled on Women, Cancer, & the Environment. Steingraber. 1996. write for info. (0-201-48333-5) Addison-Wesley.
Untitled on Wyoming. C. Vetter. Date not set. pap. write for info. (0-670-80460-6) Viking Penguin.
Untitled One: Poems for the Search & Finding. Laura Cruger. per., pap. write for info. (0-9643566-1-9) Awake VA.
***Untitled Pears, No. 3.** Iain Pears. Date not set. 20.00 (0-684-81461-7) S&S Trade.
***Untitled Photo Essay on Archaeological Dig in Jerusalem.** Bernard Wolf. 1998. pap. 15.99 (0-525-45738-0) NAL-Dutton.
Untitled Picture Book. (J). 1998. lib. bdg. 14.89 (0-7868-2250-3) Hyprn Child.
***Untitled Picture Book.** Gorton. (J). 1998. 14.95 (0-7868-0327-4); lib. bdg. 14.89 (0-7868-2272-4) Hyprn Child.
Untitled Picture Book, No. 1. Tryon. 1998. 16.00 (0-689-81136-5) S&S Childrens.
Untitled Picture Book #1. McDermott. (J). 1997. 17.00 (0-689-80706-6) S&S Childrens.
Untitled Picture Book #2. McDermott. (J). 1998. 16.00 (0-689-80707-4) S&S Childrens.
Untitled Picture Book #3. McDermott. (J). Date not set. 16.00 (0-689-80708-2) S&S Childrens.
Untitled Picture Book #4. McDermott. (J). Date not set. 16.00 (0-689-80709-0) S&S Childrens.
Untitled Picture Book #5. (J). Date not set. 16.00 (0-689-80710-4) S&S Childrens.
Untitled Picture Book #6. McDermott. (J). Date not set. 16.00 (0-689-80711-2) S&S Childrens.
***Untitled Pincus.** Pincus. 1987. pap. 5.95 (0-671-65942-1); mass mkt. 4.95 (0-671-65939-1) PB.
Untitled Poetry. Diane Ackerman. 1997. write for info. (0-679-44878-0) Random.
Untitled-Poetry Atlas of the U. S. Hopkins. (J). Date not set. 19.95 (0-689-81247-7) S&S Childrens.
Untitled Price. Price. 1994. 19.18 (0-02-925453-1) S&S Trade.
***Untitled Prison Diaries.** 1990. 17.95 (0-671-61802-4) S&S Trade.
Untitled Quebec. Ron Graham. Date not set. pap. 22.00 (0-670-84005-X) Viking Penguin.
Untitled Raeburn. Raeburn. 1992. 19.95 (0-13-019613-4) S&S Trade.
Untitled, Red - Blue, 2 vols. Louise Lawler. LC 78-59796. (Illus.). 1978. Set. pap. text ed. 7.95 (0-931706-00-9) L Lawler.
Untitled, Red - Blue, 2 vols, 1. Louise Lawler. LC 78-59796. (Illus.). 1978. write for info. (0-931706-01-7) L Lawler.
Untitled, Red - Blue, 2 vols, 2. Louise Lawler. LC 78-59796. (Illus.). 1978. write for info. (0-931706-02-5) L Lawler.
Untitled Rikki Lake. (J). 1996. pap. write for info. (0-679-87960-9, Bullseye Bks) Random Bks Yng Read.
Untitled Robert Cowley on the Western Front. Robert Cowley. 1995. write for info. (0-201-62639-X) Addison-Wesley.
Untitled Robert MacNeil Novel. Robert MacNeil. Date not set. pap. write for info. (0-670-83178-6) Viking Penguin.
Untitled Robert McCloskey. Robert McCloskey. 1998. pap. 15.95 (0-670-84827-1) NAL-Dutton.
Untitled Robert O. Kaplan. Robert O. Kaplan. Date not set. write for info. (0-679-45190-0) Random.
***Untitled Ruth Rendell.** Ruth Rendell. LC 97-1200. 1997. 25.00 (0-609-60056-7) Random Hse Value.
Untitled Scarry #6. Richard Scarry. (J). 1997. mass mkt. 3.25 (0-689-80992-1) S&S Childrens.
Untitled-Science Anthology. Hopkins. Date not set. 17.00 (0-689-81283-3) S&S Childrens.
Untitled Science Fiction Novel. Alan Dean Foster. Date not set. pap. write for info. (0-345-40646-X) Ballantine.
Untitled Selina Hastings. Selina Hastings. Date not set. pap. 22.95 (0-670-81643-4) Viking Penguin.
Untitled Sequel to Purple Coat. Hest. LC 96-53145. (J). 1998. 16.00 (0-689-80573-X) S&S Childrens.
Untitled Sex Book. Olivia St. Claire. 1996. write for info. (0-517-70192-8, Harmony) Crown Pub Group.

An Asterisk (*) at the beginning of an entry indicates that the title is appearing in BIP for the first time.

Untitled Stechen. Joanna Stechen. Date not set. pap. write for info. (*0-679-45076-9*) McKay.

Untitled Steingraber: Women, Cancer & the Environment. Steingraber. 1997. 24.00 (*0-201-48303-3*) Addison-Wesley.

Untitled Steven Saylor Texas Novel. Steven Saylor. 1997. write for info. (*0-517-70629-6*) Random Hse Value.

Untitled Stories. Rebecca West. Date not set. pap. 17.95 (*0-670-81387-7*) Viking Penguin.

Untitled Thriller. Ed Bungert. Date not set. pap. 4.99 (*0-451-17719-3*, Sig) NAL-Dutton.

Untitled Thriller. Greg Iles. 1998. pap. 21.95 (*0-525-93793-5*) Viking Penguin.

***Untitled Time Passages.** Angie Ray. 1998. mass mkt. write for info. (*0-515-12227-0*) Jove Pubns.

***Untitled Walcott Poetry.** Derek Walcott. 1998. pap. 9.95 (*0-14-086529-2*) Viking Penguin.

Untitled Western Front. Robert Cowley. Date not set. pap. 27.95 (*0-670-86724-1*) Viking Penguin.

Untitled William Norris. William Norris. Date not set. pap. write for info. (*0-670-81931-X*) Viking Penguin.

Untitled Work. Adam Gussow. Date not set. pap. write for info. (*0-679-45022-X*) McKay.

Untitled Work. Julee Rosso. 1997. write for info. (*0-517-70288-6*) Crown Pub Group.

Untitled Work. 4th ed. Julee Rosso. 1997. pap. write for info. (*0-517-88526-3*, Crown) Crown Pub Group.

Untitled Work, No. 3. American Academy of Pediatrics. Date not set. pap. write for info. (*0-679-76981-1*) McKay.

Untitled Work, No. 4. American Academy of Pediatrics Staff. Date not set. pap. write for info. (*0-679-76982-X*) McKay.

Untitled Work, No.5. Julee Rosso. 1997. pap. write for info. (*0-517-88527-1*, Crown) Crown Pub Group.

Untitled X-Files No. 4 see Tiger, Tiger

Untitled Yoshi Picture Book. Yoshi. (J). Date not set. 15. 00 (*0-689-80567-5*) S&S Childrens.

Untitled Yoshi Picture Book #1. Yoshi. (J). 1997. 15.00 (*0-689-80574-8*) S&S Childrens.

Untitled Young Indiana Jones. Bill Mccay. (J). 1996. pap. write for info. (*0-679-87907-2*, Bullseye Bks) Random Bks Yng Read.

***Untitled Zindel #1.** Paul Zindel. (J). 1998. 14.95 (*0-7868-0338-X*) Hyprn Child.

***Untitled Zindel #1.** Paul Zindel. (J). 1999. pap. 4.95 (*0-7868-1224-9*) Hyprn Child.

***Untitled Zindel #2.** Paul Zindel. (J). 1999. 14.95 (*0-7868-0339-8*); pap. 4.95 (*0-7868-1225-7*) Hyprn Child.

***Untitled Zindel #3.** Paul Zindel. (J). 1900. 15.95 (*0-7868-0340-1*) Hyprn Child.

***Untitled Zindel #3.** Paul Zindel. (J). 1901. pap. 5.95 (*0-7868-1226-5*) Hyprn Child.

***Untitled 1.** Adams Round Table Staff. LC 97-23375. 1998. write for info. (*0-425-16146-3*, Prime Crime) Berkley Pub.

Untitled 1. Krentz. 1997. pap. 6.99 (*0-671-52420-8*) PB.

Untitled 2. Krentz. Date not set. 23.00 (*0-671-52310-4*) PB.

Untitled 2. Krentz. Date not set. pap. 6.99 (*0-671-52409-7*) PB.

Untitled 3. Krentz. Date not set. 23.00 (*0-671-52308-2*) PB.

Untitled 3. Krentz. Date not set. pap. 7.99 (*0-671-52309-0*) PB.

***Untitled #4.** Krentz. Date not set. pap. 7.99 (*0-671-52307-4*) PB.

***Unto a Good Land.** Vilhelm Moberg. 1984. 3.62 (*0-446-38116-0*) Warner Bks.

Unto a Good Land. Vilhelm Moberg. 1994. reprint ed. lib. bdg. 29.95 (*1-56849-313-4*) Buccaneer Bks.

Unto a Good Land. Vilhelm Moberg. LC 95-15847. (Emigrant Novels Ser.: Bk. 2). xxvii, 372p. 1995. reprint ed. pap. 15.95 (*0-87351-320-7*, Borealis Book) Minn Hist.

Unto a Perfect Man. 4th ed. Carl Coffman. 212p. 1982. pap. 13.99 (*0-943872-83-9*) Andrews Univ Pr.

Unto Caesar: The Political Relevance of Christianity. David McLellan. LC 92-53753. (Frank M. Covey, Jr., Loyola Lectures in Political Analysis). (C). 1993. text ed. 23.00 (*0-268-01900-2*) U of Notre Dame Pr.

Unto Christ. H. L. Heijkoop. 47p. pap. 0.60 (*0-88172-087-9*) Believers Bkshelf.

Unto Dust You Shall Return. Norman Geller. (Illus.). 16p. (J). (gr. 6-10). 1986. pap. 4.95 (*0-915753-11-1*) N Geller Pub.

Unto Him: Homage to Swami Chinmayananda & His Teaching. Ed. by Anjli Singh. (Illus.). 160p. (Orig.). 1994. pap. 25.00 (*1-880687-03-8*) Chinmaya Pubns.

***Unto Him Vol. 1: Biblical Ballads of People & Events in God's Word.** Orlando. (Illus.). vii, 51p. (Orig.). 1997. pap. 6.95 (*0-9658387-0-6*) desktop.

Unto the Churches: Jesus Christ, Christianity, & the Edgar Cayce Readings. Richard H. Drummond. 206p. 1978. pap. 7.95 (*0-87604-102-0*, 289) ARE Pr.

Unto the Hills. Juliet B. Ballard. 251p. 1982. pap. 9.95 (*0-87604-144-6*, 317) ARE Pr.

Unto the Hills. Billy Graham. 375p. 1993. 4.99 (*0-8499-5031-7*) Word Pub.

Unto the Hills. Sara Yoder. 1985. pap. 3.25 (*0-87813-523-5*) Christian Light.

Unto the Hills. rev. ed. Billy Graham. 375p. 1996. 21.99 (*0-8499-1334-9*) Word Pub.

Unto the Least of These: Special Education in the Church. Andrew H. Wood. LC 84-16077. 143p. 1984. pap. 4.95 (*0-87227-099-8*, RBP5127) Reg Baptist.

Unto the Least Seattle Ryther Center. Cora G. Chase. 152p. reprint ed. pap. 5.95 (*0-8466-0283-0*, S283) Shorey.

Unto the Sons. Gay Talese. 1992. 25.00 (*0-679-41034-1*) Knopf.

Unto the Sons. Gay Talese. 640p. 1993. mass mkt. 5.99 (*0-8041-1033-6*) Ivy Books.

***Unto the Soul.** Aharon Appelfeld. 1998. pap. write for info. (*0-8052-1097-0*) Schocken.

Unto the Thousandth Generation: Conceptualizing Intergenerational Justice, Vol. 43. Bruce E. Auerbach. LC 93-2300. (American University Studies, Political Science Ser.: Ser. X, Vol. 42). 288p. (C). 1995. 46.95 (*0-8204-2228-2*) P Lang Pubng.

Unto the Uttermost. Claude Sumerline. 1996. 17.95 (*0-533-11624-4*) Vantage.

Unto Thee I Grant. 32th ed. Rev. by Sri Ramatherio. LC 49-15007. 96p. 1925. 16.95 (*0-912057-02-5*, 501620) RO AMORC.

Unto Themselves: Recapturing Control of Our Legal System from the Self-Serving Legal Profession. Perry Turner. 364p. 1994. 29.95 (*0-9642689-0-6*) Telic Pub Co.

***Unto This Hour: A Novel by Tom Wicker.** Tom Wicker. LC 97-13718. 656p. 1997. reprint ed. pap. 24.95 (*0-8203-1964-3*, Brown Thrasher) U of Ga Pr.

***Unto This Last: Four Essays on the First Principles of Political Economy.** John Ruskin. Ed. & Intro. by Lloyd J. Hubenka. LC 67-12118. 143p. pap. 40.80 (*0-608-04826-7*, 2065483) Bks Demand.

Unto This Last & Other Stories. John Ruskin. Ed. & Intro. by Clive Wilmer. (Classics Ser.). 368p. 1986. pap. 11.95 (*0-14-043211-6*, Penguin Classics) Viking Penguin.

Unto Us a Child: Meditations for Advent. Jeffrey Devries. LC 96-24444. 111p. (Orig.). 1996. pap. 7.95 (*1-56212-191-X*, 1701-0670) CRC Pubns.

***Unto Us a Child Is Born.** 4.15 (*0-687-43123-9*) Abingdon.

Unto Us a Child Is Born. W. Jeffrey Marsh. 1994. 10.95 (*0-88494-937-0*) Bookcraft Inc.

Unto Us a Child is Born. J. W. Roberts et al. 126p. (Orig.). 1982. pap. 2.95 (*0-88027-109-4*) Firm Foun Pub.

***Unto Whom Much Is Given.** Shelia P. Spencer. 76p. 1995. 10.00 (*0-9653688-0-7*) P & P Ent.

Untold Decades: Seven Comedies of Gay Romance. Robert Patrick. (Stonewall Inn Editions Ser.). (Illus.). 240p. 1989. pap. 7.95 (*0-312-03447-4*) St Martin.

Untold Facts about the Small Business Game: How to Be Competent in Business. abr. rev. ed. Intro. by Luanna C. Blagrove. (Illus.). 250p. 1988. 24.95 (*0-939776-14-6*) Blagrove Pubns.

Untold Legend of the Batman. Len Wein. 128p. 1992. pap. 3.50 (*0-8125-2042-4*) Tor Bks.

Untold Millions. Franklin F. Ellis. (J). (gr. k-6). 1972. 4.50 (*3-901170-07-3*) CEF Press.

Untold Millions: Positioning Your Business for the Gay & Lesbian Consumer Revolution. Grant Lukenbill. LC 95-24276. (Illus.). 288p. 1995. 25.00 (*0-88730-699-3*) Harper Busn.

Untold Mystery Novels, Vol. 1. 1991. 17.95 (*0-671-69231-3*) Summit Bks.

***Untold Sisters: Hispanic Nuns in Their Own Works.** Ed. by Electra Arenal & Stacey Schlau. Tr. by Amanda Powell. LC 88-34947. (Illus.). 464p. 1989. reprint ed. pap. 132.30 (*0-608-04147-5*, 2064880) Bks Demand.

Untold Stories. William Slaughter. LC 90-80869. 100p. (Orig.). 1990. 20.00 (*0-912887-23-0*); pap. 10.00 (*0-912887-24-9*) Empty Bowl.

Untold Stories of Advent. Mark Vincent. LC 93-72479. 77p. (Orig.). (YA). 1993. pap. 8.95 (*0-87303-207-1*) Faith & Life.

Untold Story: Jesus Son of God. Clarice Albritton. LC 83-73188. 1983. pap. 5.95 (*0-318-00817-3*) W P Brownell.

Untold Story: The Life of Isadora Duncan 1921-1927. Mary Desti. LC 80-26739. (Series in Dance). (Illus.). 281p. 1981. reprint ed. lib. bdg. 35.00 (*0-306-76044-4*) Da Capo.

Untold Story: Women & Theory in Golden Age Texts. Mary S. Gossy. (Women & Culture Ser.). 160p. 1990. text ed. 32.50 (*0-472-10132-3*) U of Mich Pr.

Untold Story of Blacks in Islam. Salim Abdul-Khaliq. 110p. (Orig.). 1994. pap. 7.00 (*1-56411-073-7*) Untd Bros & Sis.

Untold Story of Cinderella. Russell Shorto. (Upside Down Tales Ser.). (Illus.). (J). 1992. pap. 8.95 (*0-8065-1298-9*, Citadel Pr) Carol Pub Group.

***Untold Story of the Iroquois Influence on Early Feminists: Essays by Sally Roesch Wagner.** 48p. 1996. pap. 7.00 (*1-880589-30-3*) Sky Carrier Pr.

Untold Studio Secret, a Fantasy: Portrait for Barley. Donald S. Vogel. Ed. by Peggy Goad. LC 90-71584. (Illus.). 65p. (Orig.). 1991. write for info. (*1-879154-00-5*) Vlly Hse Gllry.

Untold Studio Secret, a Fantasy: Portrait for Barley. Donald S. Vogel. Ed. by Peggy Goad. LC 90-71584. (Illus.). 65p. (Orig.). 1993. text ed. 14.00 (*1-879154-01-3*) Vlly Hse Gllry.

Untold Tale. Jonathan Strong. LC 93-14209. 240p. 1993. 19.95 (*0-944072-32-1*) Zoland Bks.

Untold Tales. William J. Brooke. LC 91-4179. 160p. (J). (gr. 5 up). 1992. lib. bdg. 14.89 (*0-06-020272-6*) HarpC Child Bks.

***Untold Tales of Spider-Man.** Kurt Busiek. 1997. pap. text ed. 16.95 (*0-7851-0263-9*) Marvel Entmnt.

***Untold Tales of Spider-Man.** Ed. by Stan Lee & Kurt Busiek. 320p. 1997. pap. 13.00 (*1-57297-294-7*) Blvd Books.

Untold Tales, Unsung Heroes: An Oral History of Detroit's African American Community, 1918-1967. Elaine L. Moon. LC 93-26073. (African American Life Ser.). (Illus.). 410p. (C). 1994. pap. text ed. 19.95 (*0-8143-2465-7*) Wayne St U Pr.

Untold Terror: Violence Against Women in Peru's Armed Conflict. Ed. by Human Rights Watch Staff. 70p. (Orig.). 1992. pap. 7.00 (*1-56432-093-6*) Hum Rts Watch.

Untold Truth about Fatness. Dean Kimmel. 42p. (Orig.). 1988. pap. 2.95 (*0-9621446-0-6*) Corbin Hse.

Untouchable. Mulk R. Anand. (Mayfair Paperbacks Ser.). 226p. 1983. pap. 5.00 (*0-86578-068-4*) Ind-US Inc.

Untouchable. John Banville. LC 96-49637. 368p. 1997. 25. 00 (*0-679-45108-0*) Knopf.

***Untouchable.** John Banville. 1998. pap. write for info. (*0-679-76747-9*, Vin) Random.

Untouchable. Mulk Raj Anand. (Classics Ser.). 160p. 1990. pap. 10.95 (*0-14-018395-7*, Penguin Classics) Viking Penguin.

Untouchable. Mulk R. Anand. (C). 1970. reprint ed. pap. text ed. 6.00 (*0-8364-2848-X*, Pub. by Arnold Pubs II) S Asia.

Untouchable: A Biography of Robert De Niro. Andy Dougan. LC 96-26805. 1997. 24.95 (*1-56025-136-0*) Thunders Mouth.

Untouchable: An Indian Life History. James M. Freeman. LC 78-55319. (Illus.). x, 427p. 1979. 55.00 (*0-8047-1001-5*); pap. 18.95 (*0-8047-1103-8*) Stanford U Pr.

Untouchable Community in South India: Structure & Consensus. Michael Moffatt. LC 78-51183. 368p. 1979. reprint ed. pap. 104.90 (*0-7837-9392-8*, 2060137) Bks Demand.

***Untouchable Pasts: Religion, Identity, & Power among a Central Indian Community, 1780-1950.** Saurabh Dube. (SUNY Series in Hindu Studies). (Illus.). 320p. (C). 1998. text ed. 71.50 (*0-7914-3687-X*) State U NY Pr.

***Untouchable Pasts: Religion, Identity, & Power among a Central Indian Community, 1780-1950.** Saurabh Dube. (SUNY Series in Hindu Studies). (Illus.). 320p. (C). 1998. pap. text ed. 23.95 (*0-7914-3688-8*) State U NY Pr.

Untouchable Story. D. P. Das. 1985. 16.00 (*0-8364-1494-2*, Pub. by Allied II) S Asia.

Untouchables. Boileau-Narcejac. 256p. (FRE.). 1984. pap. 10.95 (*0-7859-2000-5*, 2070375951) Fr & Eur.

Untouchables. Eliot Ness & Oscar Fraley. 224p. 1987. mass mkt. 4.99 (*0-671-64449-1*) PB.

Untouchables. Oscar Fraley & Eliot Ness. reprint ed. lib. bdg. 21.95 (*0-89190-483-2*, Rivercity Pr) Amereon Ltd.

Untouchables. Elliott Ness & Oscar Fraley. 1993. reprint ed. lib. bdg. 25.95 (*1-56849-198-0*) Buccaneer Bks.

Untouchables: Mission Accomplished. Brian Shul & Walter L. Watson, Jr. (Illus.). 216p. 1993. 43.00 (*0-929823-12-5*) Mach One.

Untouchables in Contemporary India. Ed. by J. Michael Mahar. LC 79-152039. (Illus.). 528p. reprint ed. pap. 150.50 (*0-317-58770-6*, 2029654) Bks Demand.

***Untouched.** Sandra Field. 1997. mass mkt. 3.50 (*0-373-11919-4*, 1-11919-7) Harlequin Bks.

Untouched. large type ed. Sandra Field. (Harlequin Romance Ser.). 1995. 20.95 (*0-263-14260-4*, Pub. by Mills & Boon UK) Thorndike Pr.

Untouched Key: Tracing Childhood Trauma in Creativity & Destructiveness. Alice Miller. 208p. 1991. pap. 12.00 (*0-385-26764-9*, Anchor NY) Doubleday.

Untouched Thoughts. Perman Eubanks, Jr. (Orig.). 1996. pap. write for info. (*1-57553-129-1*) Watermrk Pr.

***Untrammeled Approaches.** Jacques Maritain. Ed. by Bernard Doering. LC 96-26434. (Collected Works of Jacques Maritain: Vol. 20). Orig. Title: Approaches San Entraves. 528p. (C). 1996. text ed. 35.00 (*0-268-04300-0*) U of Notre Dame Pr.

Untrampled Ground. Albert Krassner. (Illus.). 96p. 1985. pap. 10.95 (*0-912061-07-3*) Veridon Edns.

Untrapping Your Inventiveness. J. DiSilvestro & J. Riley. 1992. pap. 19.95 (*0-936386-61-4*) Creative Learning.

Untriangulated Stars. Edwin A. Robinson. (American Autobiography Ser.). 348p. 1995. reprint ed. lib. bdg. 89. 00 (*0-7812-8626-3*) Rprt Serv.

Untrodden Fields of Anthropology. Doctor Jacobus. 1977. lib. bdg. 75.00 (*0-8490-2790-X*) Gordon Pr.

***Untrodden Ways.** Kate Fielding. 384p. 1997. pap. 17.95 (*0-7528-0135-X*, Pub. by Orion Bks UK) Trafalgar.

Untuning of the Sky: Ideas of Music in English Poetry, 1500-1700. John Hollander. LC 92-7084. (Illus.). 498p. (C). 1992. reprint ed. lib. bdg. 47.50 (*0-208-02351-8*, Archon Bks) Shoe String.

Untutored Eye: Childhood in the Films of Cocteau, Cornell, & Brakhage. Marjorie Keller. LC 85-47628. (Illus.). 272p. 1986. 42.50 (*0-8386-3242-4*) Fairleigh Dickinson.

Untwisting Twisted Relationships. William Backus & Candace Backus. LC 88-4579. 176p. (Orig.). 1988. pap. 8.99 (*0-87123-998-1*) Bethany Hse.

Untwisting Twisted Relationships: Study Guide. William Backus. 64p. 1989. student ed. 4.99 (*1-55661-089-0*) Bethany Hse.

Untying the Afghan Knot: Negotiating Soviet Withdrawal. Riaz M. Khan. LC 91-11624. (Institute for the Study of Diplomacy Book Ser.). 416p. 1991. text ed. 54.95 (*0-8223-1155-0*) Duke.

Untying the Apron Strings: Anti-Sexist Provision for the Under-Five. Ed. by Naima Brown & Pauline France. LC 86-5102. 160p. 1986. pap. 27.00 (*0-335-15232-5*, Open Univ Pr) Taylor & Francis.

Untying the Knot. George E. Vandeman. (Outreach Ser.). 48p. 1988. pap. 1.49 (*0-8163-0736-9*) Pacific Pr Pub Assn.

Untying the Knot: A Short History of Divorce. Roderick Phillips. (Canto Book Ser.). 255p. (C). 1991. pap. text ed. 11.95 (*0-521-42370-8*) Cambridge U Pr.

Untying the Knot: On Riddles & Other Enigmatic Modes. Galit Hasan-Rokem & David Shulman. 384p. 1996. 65. 00 (*0-19-510186-3*) OUP.

Untying the Knot: On Riddles & Other Enigmatic Modes. Galit Hasan-Rokem & David Shulman. 384p. 1996. pap. 29.95 (*0-19-510856-6*) OUP.

Untying the Knot of War: A Bargaining Theory of International Crises. T. Clifton Morgan. 240p. (C). 1994. text ed. 49.50 (*0-472-10277-X*) U of Mich Pr.

Untying the Text: A Post-Structuralist Anthology. Ed. by Robert Young. 320p. 1981. pap. 13.95 (*0-7100-0805-8*, RKP) Routledge.

Unuminutaj Noveloj. Istvan Orkeny. Ed. & Intro. by Istvan Ertl. 120p. (ESP.). 1995. pap. 7.95 (*1-882251-06-7*) Eldonejo Bero.

Unusable Past: America's Puritan Tradition, 1830-1930. Jan C. Dawson. LC 83-27091. (Studies in Humanities). 150p. (C). 1984. pap. 16.95 (*0-89130-722-2*, 00 01 04) Scholars Pr GA.

Unusable Past: Theory & the Study of American Literature. Russell J. Reising. 224p. 1986. text ed. 35.00 (*0-416-01311-2*, 9811) Routledge Chapman & Hall.

Unused. Date not set. pap. 4.99 (*0-451-18936-1*, Sig) NAL-Dutton.

Unused. 1999. pap. 5.50 (*0-451-45582-7*, ROC) NAL-Dutton.

Unused. Dan Gutman. Date not set. pap. 12.95 (*0-14-025175-8*) Viking Penguin.

Unused. Laura Jones. 1999. pap. 10.95 (*0-14-043618-9*) Viking Penguin.

Unused. Andrew Morehead. 1376p. 1996. pap. 24.95 (*0-670-86962-7*) Viking Penguin.

Unused. Barrymore L. Scherer. Date not set. pap. 18.95 (*0-525-94074-X*) Viking Penguin.

Unused. William N. Yeomans. Date not set. pap. 24.95 (*0-525-94038-3*) Viking Penguin.

Unused Alibis, Creative Personalities, Vol. 7. Ed. by Philip H. Lotz. LC 79-126322. (Biography Index Reprint Ser.). 1977. 17.95 (*0-8369-8028-X*) Ayer.

Unused Dinosaurs. Elizabeth Macleod. Date not set. pap. 4.99 (*0-14-037659-3*) Viking Penguin.

Unused Intelligence: Physical Thinking for 21st Century Leadership. Andy Bryner & Dawna Markova. 262p. (Orig.). 1996. 45.00 (*0-8095-6054-2*) Borgo Pr.

Unused Intelligence: Physical Thinking for 21st Century Leadership. Peter M. Senge. (Illus.). 300p. (Orig.). 1996. pap. 18.95 (*0-943233-97-6*) Conari Press.

Unusual, No. II. Ven Shen Kai. LC 91-61740. (Illus.). 250p. (CHI.). 1991. write for info. (*1-56369-001-2*) Jen Chen Buddhism.

Unusual Affair. Lindsay Armstrong. (Presents Ser.). 1993. mass mkt. 2.99 (*0-373-11593-8*, 1-11593-0) Harlequin Bks.

Unusual & Most Popular Baby Names. rev. ed. Consumer Guide Editors. 192p. 1995. 5.99 (*0-451-18363-0*, Sig) NAL-Dutton.

Unusual Associates: A Festschrift for Frank Barron. Ed. by Alfonso Montuori. LC 96-6381. 480p. 1996. 89.50 (*1-881303-57-8*); pap. 34.50 (*1-881303-58-6*) Hampton Pr NJ.

Unusual Company. Margaret Erhart. 250p. 1988. pap. 7.95 (*0-452-26144-9*, Plume) NAL-Dutton.

Unusual Court. Torkom Saraydarian. LC 77-86720. 1979. pap. 5.00 (*0-911794-44-1*) Aqua Educ.

Unusual DNA Structures. Ed. by R. D. Wells & S. C. Harvey. (Illus.). 320p. 1987. 87.95 (*0-387-96631-5*) Spr-Verlag.

Unusual Events, 5 novels. Earl Thomas. (Illus.). 48p. (J). (gr. 2-9). 1986. Set. pap. 17.00 (*0-87879-530-8*) High Noon Bks.

Unusual Friendships: Symbiosis in the Animal World. Larry D. Brimner. LC 92-24953. (First Bks.). (Illus.). 64p. (J). (gr. 4-6). 1993. lib. bdg. 21.00 (*0-531-20106-6*) Watts.

Unusual Friendships: Symbiosis in the Animal World. Larry D. Brimner. (First Bks.). (Illus.). 64p. (J). (gr. 5-8). 1993. pap. 6.95 (*0-531-15675-3*) Watts.

Unusual Inheritance. Rebecca Robbins. 224p. (Orig.). 1994. mass mkt. 3.99 (*0-380-77670-7*) Avon.

Unusual Life of Tristan Smith. Peter Carey. 432p. 1996. pap. 13.00 (*0-679-76036-9*) Random.

Unusual Life of Tristan Smith: A Novel. Peter Carey. 1995. 24.00 (*0-679-43888-2*) Knopf.

Unusual Mathematical Puzzles, Tricks, & Oddities. Matthew Mandl. (Illus.). 128p. 1984. 19.95 (*0-13-938150-3*); pap. 15.95 (*0-13-938101-5*) P-H.

Unusual Microorganisms: Gram-Negative Fastidious Species. Ed. by Edward J. Bottone. LC 83-1933. (Microbiology Ser.: No. 10). 136p. reprint ed. pap. 38.80 (*0-7837-3361-5*, 2043319) Bks Demand.

Unusual Occurrences of Cancer As a Clue of Cancer Etiology: Proceedings of the 18th International Symposium of the Princess Takamatsu Cancer Research Fund, November 1987, Tokyo. Joseph F. Fraumeni, Jr. et al. 350p. 1989. 130.00 (*0-85066-459-4*) Taylor & Francis.

Unusual Persons of the Civil War: Fascinating Tales, Infamous Characters, & Strange Coincidences. Webb Garrison. (Illus.). 320p. (Orig.). 1996. pap. 9.95 (*1-887901-08-6*) Sergeant Kirk.

Unusual Rattle from the Etowah Site. L. H. Larson et al. (Missouri Archaeologist Ser.: Vol. 19, No. 4). 1957. pap. 1.00 (*0-943414-79-2*, 111904) MO Arch Soc.

***Unusual Secretory Pathways: From Bacteria to Man.** Karl Kuchler & Anna Rubartelli. LC 97-13250. (Molecular Biology Intelligence Unit Ser.). 221p. 1997. 89.95 (*1-57059-445-7*) R G Landes.

***Unusual Secretory Pathways: From Bacteria to Men.** Karl Kuchler & Anna Rubartelli. (Molecular Biology Intelligence Unit Ser.). 221p. 1997. 89.95 (*0-412-10941-7*) Chapman & Hall.

Unusual Stories from Many Lands. Arlo T. Janssen. (Illus.). 192p. (C). 1984. pap. text ed. 18.00 (*0-13-937707-7*) P-H.

Unusual Stories from Texas' History. Patrick M. Reynolds. (Texas Lore Ser.: Vol. 6). (Illus.). 56p. (Orig.). 1988. pap. 3.75 (*0-932514-18-9*) Red Rose Studio.

Unusual Suspects. Joyce Carol Oates & Andrew Vachss. Ed. by James Grady. 1996. pap. 13.00 (*0-614-97800-9*) Vintage NY.

Unusual Suspects: An Anthology of Crime Stories from Black Lizard. Ed. by James Grady. 352p. 1996. pap. 13.00 (*0-679-76788-6*, Vin) Random.

Unusual Techniques & New Applications of Metallography: Papers Taken from the Metallography Symposia Held at the ASM Metals Congress, St. Louis, Missouri, 27 October 1982 & Philadelphia, Pennsylvania, 4-5 October 1983, 2 Vols., 1. American Society for Metals Staff. LC 85-71946. (Illus.). 149p. reprint ed. pap. 38.80 (*0-318-39727-7*, 2033086) Bks Demand.

Unusual Techniques & New Applications of Metallography: Papers Taken from the Metallography Symposia Held at the ASM Metals Congress, St. Louis, Missouri, 27 October 1982 & Philadelphia, Pennsylvania, 4-5 October 1983, 2 Vols., 2. American Society for Metals Staff. LC 85-71946. (Illus.). 149p. reprint ed. pap. 44.50 (*0-318-39728-5*) Bks Demand.

Unusual Telescopes. Peter L. Manly. (Illus.). 200p. (C). 1992. text ed. 49.95 (*0-521-38200-9*) Cambridge U Pr.

Unusual Telescopes. Peter L. Manly. (Illus.). 238p. (C). 1995. pap. text ed. 20.95 (*0-521-48393-X*) Cambridge U Pr.

Unusual Vintage Tractors. Charles H. Wendel. 1996. pap. text ed. 19.95 (*0-87341-410-1*) Krause Pubns.

Unvanquished. Howard Fast. LC 97-12876. 224p. (gr. 13). 1997. 59.95 (*1-56324-594-9*) M E Sharpe.

Unvanquished. Howard Fast. LC 97-12876. 224p. (C). (gr. 13). 1997. pap. 17.95 (*1-56324-595-7*) M E Sharpe.

Unvanquished. William Faulkner. LC 91-50010. (Vintage International Ser.). 304p. 1991. pap. 11.00 (*0-679-73652-2*, Vin) Random.

Unvanquished Notes. James L. Roberts. 87p. (Orig.). (C). 1980. pap. text ed. 4.50 (*0-8220-1316-9*) Cliffs.

Unvanquished Puritan: A Portrait of Lyman Beecher. Stuart C. Henry. LC 85-30520. 299p. 1986. reprint ed. text ed. 59.75 (*0-313-25097-9*, HEUN, Greenwood Pr) Greenwood.

Unvarnished Doctrine: Locke, Liberalism, & the American Revolution. Steven M. Dworetz. LC 89-35756. 248p. 1990. 39.50 (*0-8223-0961-0*) Duke.

Unvarnished Doctrine: Locke, Liberalism, & the American Revolution. Steven M. Dworetz. LC 89-35756. 264p. 1994. pap. text ed. 16.95 (*0-8223-1470-3*) Duke.

Unvarnished Gospels. Tr. by Andy Gaus from GRE. LC 87-51539. 272p. 1988. pap. 15.00 (*0-939660-25-3*) Threshold VT.

Unvarnished New Testament. Tr. by Andy Gaus from GRE. LC 91-26924. 400p. (Orig.). 1991. pap. 19.95 (*0-933999-99-2*) Phanes Pr.

***Unveiled, Vol. 1.** Mosteshar. 1997. mass mkt. 6.99 (*0-312-96288-6*) St Martin.

Unveiled: Nuns Talking. Mary Loudon. 290p. 1993. pap. 14.95 (*0-87243-201-7*) Templegate.

Unveiled: One Woman's Nightmare in Iran. Cherry Mosteshar. 368p. 1996. 23.95 (*0-312-14061-4*) St Martin.

Unveiled at Last: Discover God's Hidden Message from Genesis to Revelation. Bob Sjogren. 184p. 1992. pap. 7.99 (*0-927545-37-3*) YWAM Pub.

***Unveiled Hope: Eternal Encouragement from the Book of Revelation.** Scotty Smith & Michael Card. LC 96-52485. 256p. 1997. 16.99 (*0-7852-7209-7*) Nelson.

Unveiled Ladies of Stamboul. Demetra Vaka. LC 71-165810. (Select Bibliographies Reprint Ser.). 1977. reprint ed. 24.95 (*0-8369-5967-1*) Ayer.

Unveiled Mysteries (Original) Godfre R. King. LC 84-50381. (Saint Germain Ser.: Vol. 1). (Illus.). 292p. 1982. 21.00 (*1-878891-00-6*); pap. 10.00 (*1-878891-01-4*) St Germain Pr.

Unveiling. Rita Kiefer. LC 93-6285. (Crimson Edge Chapbook Ser.). 1993. 7.95 (*0-9619111-7-4*) Chicory Blue.

***Unveiling.** Jay Zinn. LC 97-60469. 400p. (Orig.). 1997. pap. 12.99 (*1-57921-015-5*) WinePress Pub.

Unveiling: Exploring the Nature of God. Curt Simmons. 203p. 1995. pap. 10.99 (*1-884553-59-1*) Discipleshp.

Unveiling a Parallel. Alice I. Jones & Ella Merchant. Ed. by Carol A. Kolmerten. (Utopianism & Communitarianism Ser.). 296p. (C). 1991. reprint ed. pap. 14.95 (*0-8156-0259-6*); reprint ed. text ed. 39.95 (*0-8156-2538-3*) Syracuse U Pr.

Unveiling Chicago. Roger Jennings. 505p. 1994. 24.99 (*0-7897-0061-1*) Que.

Unveiling Islam. Roger Du Pasquier. 138p. (Orig.). 1992. pap. 9.95 (*0-946621-32-2*, Pub. by Islamic Texts UK) Intl Spec Bk.

Unveiling Large-Scale Structures Behind the Milky Way. Ed. by C. Balkowski & R. C. Kraan-Korteweg. (ASP Conference Series Proceedings: Vol. 67). 318p. 1994. 28.00 (*0-937707-86-4*) Astron Soc Pacific.

***Unveiling Man's Origins: Ten Decades of Thought about Human Evolution.** Louis S. Leakey & Vanne M. Goodall. LC 68-24269. (Illus.). 239p. reprint ed. pap. 68.20 (*0-608-05332-5*, 2065037) Bks Demand.

Unveiling of Arabia. Reginald H. Kiernan. LC 70-180353. reprint ed. 49.50 (*0-404-56285-X*) AMS Pr.

Unveiling of End-Time Events. Walter L. Mahan. LC 92-61369. 392p. 1992. pap. 12.95 (*1-55523-562-X*) Winston-Derek.

Unveiling of Lhasa. 3rd ed. Edmund Candler. (Illus.). 304p. 1987. reprint ed. 19.95 (*0-9617066-2-7*); reprint ed. pap. 12.95 (*0-9617066-1-9*) Snow Lion-SLG Bks.

Unveiling of Love. Muzaffer O. Al-Jerrahi. (Roots of Wisdom Bks.). 210p. 1988. pap. 9.95 (*0-916349-59-4*) Amity Hse Inc.

***Unveiling of Secrets: Diary of a Sufi Master.** Ruzbihan Baqli. Tr. & Pref. by Carl W. Ernst. xi, 150p. (Orig.). 1997. pap. 15.95 (*0-9644362-1-3*) Parvardigar Pr.

***Unveiling of Timbuctoo.** Galbraith Welch. 11.95 (*0-7867-0790-9*) Carroll & Graf.

Unveiling of Timbuctoo. Galbraith Welch. (Illus.). 352p. 1991. pap. 11.95 (*0-88184-790-9*) Carroll & Graf.

Unveiling the Apocalyptic Paul: Paul's Interpreters & the Rhetoric of Criticism. R. Barry Matlock. (Journal for the Study of the New Testament, Supplement Ser.: No. 127). 350p. 1996. 64.00 (*1-85075-590-6*, Pub. by Sheffield Acad UK) CUP Services.

Unveiling the Arctic. Ed. by Louis Rey et al. (Illus.). 292p. 1985. 55.00 (*0-919034-09-8*) U of Alaska Pr.

Unveiling the Cosmic Infrared Background: Proceedings of the Conference on Unveiling the Cosmic Infrared Background, College Park, MD, 1995. Ed. by Eli Dwek. (AIP Conference Proceedings Ser.: No. 348). 354p. 1995. 135.00 (*1-56396-508-9*) Am Inst Physics.

Unveiling the Edge of Time: Black Holes, White Holes, Worm Holes. John Gribbin. LC 92-10485. 1992. 20.00 (*0-517-58591-X*, Harmony) Crown Pub Group.

Unveiling the Edge of Time: Black Holes, White Holes, Worm Holes. John Gribbin. 1994. pap. 13.00 (*0-517-88170-5*, Crown) Crown Pub Group.

***Unveiling the Heart: How to Overcome Evil.** Pat Collins. 130p. 1996. pap. text ed. 12.95 (*1-85390-239-X*) Ignatius Pr.

***Unveiling the Hidden Words: The Norms Used by Shoghi Effendi in His Translation of the Hidden Words.** Diana L. Malouf. (Baha'i Studies: No. 2). 240p. (Orig.). 1997. pap. 18.95 (*0-85398-414-X*) G Ronald Pub.

***Unveiling the Informal Sector.** Ed. by Bohuslav Herman & Wim Stoffers. 264p. 1996. text ed. 68.95 (*1-85972-444-2*, Pub. by Avebury Pub UK) Ashgate Pub Co.

Unveiling the Microcosmos: Essays on Science & Technology from the Royal Institution. Ed. by Peter Day. (Illus.). 200p. 1996. pap. 19.95 (*0-19-855937-2*) OUP.

Unveiling the Mystical Light, No. 1. Terri Glass. 48p. 1991. pap. 8.00 (*0-9630532-0-5*) F & D Graphics.

Unveiling the Universe: An Introduction to Astronomy. J. E. Van Zyl. LC 96-13944. 1996. 39.95 (*3-540-76023-7*) Spr-Verlag.

***Unveiling Windows NT X.** Chronister. 600p. 1997. 29.99 (*0-7897-1329-2*) Que.

Unvented Hot Water Systems. 1987. pap. 50.00 (*0-86022-119-9*, Pub. by Build Servs Info Assn UK) St Mut.

Unvented Hot Water Systems. D. Gregory. (C). 1984. 40.00 (*0-685-33905-X*, Pub. by Build Servs Info Assn UK) St Mut.

Unvented Hot Water Systems in the UK: A Review of the Market Potential, 6 vols. A. Giles. (C). 1987. Set. 10,000.00 (*0-318-66894-7*, Pub. by Build Servs Info Assn UK) St Mut.

Unverganglich Geometrie. 2nd rev. ed. H. S. Coxeter. (Wissenschaft und Kultur Ser.: 17). 552p. (C). 1980. 118.00 (*0-8176-1195-9*) Birkhauser.

***Unverified Sightings: From Dakota East.** Geraldine A. Sanford. 40p. (Orig.). 1996. pap. write for info. (*1-57579-015-7*) Pine Hill Pr.

Unvividness Paradox: Dynamics of Imagery Formation. Akhter Ahsen. LC 89-62540. 250p. 1990. pap. text ed. 24.95 (*0-913412-46-5*) Brandon Hse.

Unvollendete Geschichte. Volker Braun. Ed. by Andy Hollis. LC 88-12740. (New German Texts Ser.). 160p. 1989. text ed. 16.95 (*0-7190-2402-1*, Pub. by Manchester Univ Pr UK) St Martin.

Unvollendete Trauerarbeit in der DDR-Literatur: Ein Studium der Vergangenheitsbewaltigung. Ingrid Dinter. LC 93-12391. (DDR Studien-East German Studies: Vol. 7). 149p. (GER.). (C). 1994. text ed. 45.95 (*0-8204-2182-0*) P Lang Pubng.

Unwanted. John Saul. 339p. 1987. mass mkt. 6.50 (*0-553-26657-8*) Bantam.

Unwanted: Dead or Alive. Gene Shelton. 240p. (Orig.). 1996. mass mkt. 4.99 (*0-515-11826-5*) Jove Pubns.

Unwanted: European Refugees in the Twentieth Century. Michael R. Marrus. (Illus.). 371p. 1985. 30.00 (*0-19-503615-8*) OUP.

Unwanted Attentions. K. K. Beck. 192p. 1988. 17.95 (*0-8027-5729-4*) Walker & Co.

Unwanted Attentions. large type ed. K. K. Beck. LC 89-4340. 329p. 1989. reprint ed. lib. bdg. 17.95 (*0-89621-868-6*) Thorndike Pr.

Unwanted Boy: The Autobiography of Governor Ben W. Hooper. Ben W. Hooper. Ed. by Everett R. Boyce. LC 63-14135. 280p. reprint ed. 79.80 (*0-685-15982-5*, 2027555) Bks Demand.

Unwanted Effects of Cosmetics & Drugs Used in Dermatology. 3rd rev. ed. Ed. by A. C. De Groot et al. 782p. 1993. 307.00 (*0-444-89775-5*) Elsevier.

***Unwanted Gift, 29.** Lois G. Leppard. (J). 1997. pap. 4.99 (*1-55661-556-6*) Bethany Hse.

Unwanted Harvest? Brad Sargent & Mona Riley. LC 95-12240. 216p. 1995. pap. 12.99 (*0-8054-6156-6*, 4261-56) Broadman.

Unwanted Mexican Americans in the Great Depression: Repatriation Pressures, 1929-1939. Abraham Hoffman. LC 73-86448. 207p. 1974. pap. 15.95 (*0-8165-0366-4*) U of Ariz Pr.

Unwanted Pregnancies & Public Policy: An International Perspective. Ed. by Hector Correa. 222p. 1994. lib. bdg. 69.00 (*1-56072-136-7*) Nova Sci Pubs.

Unwanted Symbol: American Foreign Policy, the Cold War & Korea, 1945-1950. Charles M. Dobbs. LC 81-6261. 253p. reprint ed. pap. 72.20 (*0-685-23370-7*, 2032482) Bks Demand.

Unwanted War: The Diplomacy of the United States & Spain over Cuba, 1895-1898. John L. Offner. LC 91-48198. (Illus.). xiv, 306p. (C). 1992. 45.00 (*0-8078-2038-5*); pap. 16.95 (*0-8078-4380-6*) U of NC Pr.

Unwanted Wedding. Penny Jordan. (Harlequin Presents Ser.: No. 1821). 1996. mass mkt. 3.50 (*0-373-11821-X*, 1-11821-5) Harlequin Bks.

Unwanted Wedding. large type ed. Penny Jordan. 1995. 21.50 (*0-263-14237-X*, Pub. by M & B UK) Ulverscroft.

***Unwashed Children of Eve: The Production, Dissemination & Reception of Popular Literature in Post-Reformation Iceland.** Matthew J. Driscoll. 356p. 1996. 60.00 (*1-874312-30-3*, Pub. by Drake Intl Serv UK) Intl Spec Bk.

Unwed Mother. Ed. by Robert W. Roberts. LC 80-20554. (Readers in Social Problems). viii, 270p. 1980. reprint ed. text ed. 59.75 (*0-313-22677-6*, ROUM, Greenwood Pr) Greenwood.

Unwelcome Companion: An Insider's View of Tourette Syndrome. rev. ed. Rick Fowler. LC 96-68438. 155p. (Orig.). 1996. pap. 12.95 (*0-9646376-9-3*) Silver Run Pubns.

Unwelcome Immigrant: The American Image of the Chinese, 1785-1882. Stuart C. Miller. LC 76-81763. 271p. reprint ed. pap. 77.30 (*0-685-23355-3*, 2032284) Bks Demand.

Unwelcome Intruder: Freud's Struggle with Cancer. Sharon Romm. LC 83-13649. (Illus.). 188p. 1983. text ed. 55.00 (*0-275-91409-7*, C1409, Praeger Pubs) Greenwood.

Unwelcome Invader. large type ed. Angela Devine. 288p. 1995. 21.50 (*0-263-14259-0*, Pub. by M & B UK) Ulverscroft.

Unwelcome Presence. large type ed. Malcolm Gray. (Linford Mystery Library). 432p. 1993. pap. 15.99 (*0-7089-7354-X*, Linford) Ulverscroft.

Unwelcome Words. Paul Bowles. 100p. (Orig.). 1987. pap. 8.00 (*0-939180-44-8*) Tombouctou.

Unwept: Black American Soldiers & the Spanish American War. Edward Van Zile Scott. 240p. 1996. 24.95 (*1-881320-62-6*, Black Belt) Black Belt Comm.

Unwicked Witch. Madge Miller. (J). (gr. 1-7). 1964. 5.00 (*0-87602-216-6*) Anchorage.

Unwilling Bride. Jo Beverley. 1994. pap. 3.99 (*0-8217-4475-5*) NAL-Dutton.

Unwilling Bride. Jennifer Greene. (Desire Ser.). 1996. mass mkt. 3.50 (*0-373-75998-3*, 1-075998-4) Silhouette.

Unwilling Captive. Norma Woodburn. LC 94-90556. (Illus.). 72p. (Orig.). (J). (gr. 3-6). 1996. pap. 9.00 (*1-56002-517-4*, Univ Edtns) Aegina Pr.

***Unwilling Conquest.** large type ed. Stephanie Laurens. (Mills & Boon Large Print Ser.). 350p. 1996. 21.50 (*0-263-14896-3*, Pub. by M & B UK) Ulverscroft.

***Unwilling Dictator.** Jules Verne. lib. bdg. 22.95 (*0-8488-2053-3*) Amereon Ltd.

Unwilling Guest. Grace L. HIll. (Grace Livingston Hill Ser.: Vol. 65). 1993. pap. 4.99 (*0-8423-7772-7*) Tyndale.

Unwilling Guest. Grace L. Hill. 1976. reprint ed. lib. bdg. 24.95 (*0-89190-024-1*, Rivercity Pr) Amereon Ltd.

Unwilling Journey: A Diary from Russia. Helmut Gollwitzer. LC 74-7610. 316p. 1975. reprint ed. text ed. 38.50 (*0-8371-7585-2*, GOUJ, Greenwood Pr) Greenwood.

Unwilling Mistress. Lindsay Armstrong. 1994. mass mkt. 2.99 (*0-373-11656-X*, 1-11656-5) Harlequin Bks.

Unwilling Mistress. large type ed. Lindsay Armstrong. (Harlequin Ser.). 1994. lib. bdg. 19.95 (*0-263-13773-2*) Thorndike Pr.

Unwilling Wife. Carolyn Zane. (Romance Ser.). 1995. pap. 2.99 (*0-373-19063-8*, 1-19063-6) Silhouette.

***Unwilling Witch, Vol. 2.** David Lubar. (The Accidental Monsters Ser.). (J). 1997. pap. text ed. 3.99 (*0-590-90719-0*) Scholastic Inc.

Unwillingly to Earth. Pauline Ashwell. 288p. 1992. mass mkt. 3.99 (*0-8125-1929-9*) Tor Bks.

Unwillingly to School. 4th ed. Ed. by Ian Berg & Jean Nursten. 336p. 1996. pap. 37.50 (*0-88048-648-1*, 8648, Pub. by Royal Coll Psych UK) Am Psychiatric.

Unwind: Turkeys Do Fly. Merrie Farrell. LC 94-29892. 1994. 15.95 (*1-885275-59-5*) C J Howie.

***Unwinding Corner.** large type ed. Alice Dwyer-Joyce. LC 96-53908. 1997. pap. 20.95 (*0-7862-1043-5*, Thorndike Lrg Prnt) Thorndike Pr.

Unwinding the Vietnam War: From War into Peace. Ed. by Reese Williams. LC 87-12142. 456p. (Orig.). 1987. pap. 5.00 (*0-941104-21-4*) Real Comet.

Unwinding Threads. Charlotte Bruner. (African Writers Ser.). 224p. 1994. pap. 10.95 (*0-435-90989-4*, 90989) Heinemann.

Unwinding Threads: Writing by Women in Africa. Ed. by Charlotte H. Bruner. LC 83-17175. (African Writers Ser.). 208p. (C). 1984. pap. 8.95 (*0-435-90256-3*, 90256) Heinemann.

Unwise Wanderer. large type ed. Leila Mackinlay. 432p. 1986. 25.99 (*0-7089-1492-6*) Ulverscroft.

Unwitting Influences in Theatre: Exchanges within Europe & Between Europe & the United States. Ed. by Dina Hellemans & Ronald Geerts. 144p. 1995. pap. 14.95 (*90-5487-062-1*) Paul & Co Pubs.

Unwomanly Conduct: The Challenges of Intentional Childlessness. Carolyn M. Morell. LC 93-45984. 240p. (C). 1994. pap. 16.95 (*0-415-90678-4*, Routledge NY) Routledge.

Unwordly Wise: As the Owl Remarked to the Rabbit O. O. O. Wei Wu-wei. 90p. (C). 1974. pap. text ed. 30.00 (*0-85656-103-7*, Pub. by Hong Kong U Pr HK) St Mut.

Unworld People. Joyce L. Heatherley. 258p. 1987. 11.95 (*0-06-252001-6*) Balcony Pub Inc.

Unwound Way. Bill Adams & Cecil Brooks. 352p. 1991. mass mkt. 4.99 (*0-345-37238-7*, Del Rey) Ballantine.

Unwrap the Mummy! A Four-Foot-Long, Fact-Filled, Pop-Up Mummy to Explore! Ian Dicks & Davod Hawcock. LC 94-69547. (Illus.). (J). 1995. 20.00 (*0-679-87028-8*) Random Bks Yng Read.

Unwrap Your Spiritual Gifts. Kenneth O. Gangel. 120p. 1983. pap. 9.99 (*0-88207-102-5*, 6-2102, Victor Bks) Chariot Victor.

Unwrapping a Mummy: The Life, Death, & Embalming of Horemkenesi. John H. Taylor. (Egyptian Bookshelf Ser.). (Illus.). 116p. (Orig.). (C). 1996. pap. 18.95 (*0-292-78141-5*) U of Tex Pr.

Unwrapping Balzac: A Reading of La Peau de Chagrin. Samuel Weber. LC 79-21801. (University of Toronto Romance Ser.: No. 39). 187p. reprint ed. pap. 53.30 (*0-8357-6405-2*, 2035765) Bks Demand.

Unwrapping Christmas. Ed. by Daniel Miller. (Studies in the Anthropology of Cultural Forms). (Illus.). 284p. 1993. 45.00 (*0-19-827903-5*) OUP.

Unwrapping Christmas. Ed. by Daniel Miller. (Oxford Studies in Social & Cultural Anthropology). (Illus.). 256p. 1995. pap. 21.00 (*0-19-828066-1*) OUP.

Unwrapping Japan: Society & Culture in Anthropological Perspective. Ed. by Eyal Ben-Ari et al. LC 89-35666. 266p. 1991. pap. text ed. 18.00 (*0-8248-1412-6*) UH Pr.

Unwrapping Little Gifts: Making the Gospel Come Alive for Children. Mary Budden & Nancy Baize. LC 94-32839. (Healing Presence Ser.). 216p. 1994. teacher ed., pap. 19.95 (*0-89390-290-X*) Resource Pubns.

Unwrapping Spheres of Clouds & Skulls. deluxe limited ed. Guy R. Beining. 1994. spiral bd. 22.00 (*1-884185-07-X*) O Zone.

Unwritten Alliance: Riobanco & Brazilian-American Relations. E. Bradford Burns. LC 65-25661. (Institute of Latin American Studies). (Illus.). 305p. 1966. text ed. 49.50 (*0-231-02855-5*) Col U Pr.

Unwritten Chronicles of Robert E. Lee. Lamar Herrin. 1991. pap. 9.95 (*0-312-05983-3*) St Martin.

Unwritten Constitution of the United States. Christopher G. Tiedeman. Ed. by Roy M. Mersky & J. Myron Jacobstein. LC 74-16910. (Classics in Legal History Reprint Ser.: Vol. 27). 165p. 1974. reprint ed. lib. bdg. 43.50 (*0-89941-026-X*, 301660) W S Hein.

Unwritten Law: Criminal Justice in Victorian Kent. Carolyn A. Conley. (Illus.). 256p. 1991. 42.00 (*0-19-506338-4*) OUP.

Unwritten Laws: The Unofficial Rules of Life as Handed Down by Murphy & Other Sages. Hugh Rawson. LC 97-6402. 1997. 25.00 (*0-517-59279-7*, Crown) Crown Pub Group.

Unwritten Laws of Engineering. 49p. 1944. 5.00 (*0-317-33632-0*, 100006) ASME.

Unwritten Literature of Hawaii: The Sacred Songs of the Hula. Nathaniel Emerson. (Bureau of American Ethnology Bulletins Ser.). 288p. 1995. lib. bdg. 89.00 (*0-7812-4038-7*) Rprt Serv.

Unwritten Literature of Hawaii: The Sacred Songs of the Hula. Nathaniel B. Emerson. LC 65-12971. (Illus.). 340p. 1965. reprint ed. pap. 9.95 (*0-8048-1067-2*) C E Tuttle.

Unwritten Literature of Hawaii: The Sacred Songs of the Hula. Nathaniel B. Emerson. reprint ed. 59.00 (*0-403-03720-4*) Scholarly.

Unwritten Literature on the Hopi. Hattie G. Lockett. LC 76-43767. (Arizona Univ. Social Science Bulletin Ser.: No. 2). reprint ed. 36.00 (*0-404-15621-5*) AMS Pr.

Unwritten Philosophy & Other Esssays. Francis M. Cornford. LC 68-78120. 159p. reprint ed. pap. 45.40 (*0-685-15568-4*, 2026337) Bks Demand.

Unwritten Rules of the Game. Peter B. Scott-Morgan. 1994. text ed. 21.95 (*0-07-057075-2*) McGraw.

Unwritten Stories of the Surui Indians of Rondonia. Betty Mindlin. (Illus.). 160p. (Orig.). 1994. pap. 16.95 (*0-292-75191-5*) U of Tex Pr.

Unwritten War: American Writers & the Civil War. Daniel Aaron. LC 86-40486. 402p. 1987. reprint ed. text ed. 37.50 (*0-299-11390-6*); reprint ed. pap. text ed. 15.95 (*0-299-11394-9*) U of Wis Pr.

***Unzipped: Scorching Tales of Lust & Desire from Men Magazine.** Ed. by Gerry Kroll & Fred Goss. LC 97-18781. 256p. (Orig.). 1997. pap. 11.95 (*1-55583-402-7*) Alyson Pubns.

Unzipped: The Popes Bare All - A Frank Study of Sex & Corruption in the Vatican. Arthur F. Ide. LC 87-19575. (Illus.). 189p. (Orig.). 1987. pap. 12.00 (*0-910309-43-4*, 5510) Am Atheist.

***Unzipped Genes: Taking Charge of Baby-Making.** Martine A. Rothblatt. LC 96-35970. (America in Transition Ser.). 1997. 49.95 (*1-56639-522-4*); pap. 18.95 (*1-56639-554-2*) Temple U Pr.

Unzipped Souls: A Jazz Journey Through the Soviet Union. William Minor. LC 94-37345. (Illus.). 256p. (C). 1995. 27.95 (*1-56639-324-8*) Temple U Pr.

Uomini E No see Men & Not Men

Up a Country Lane Cookbook. Evelyn Birkby. LC 93-20659. (Bur Oak Original Ser.). (Illus.). 276p. 1993. 22.95 (*0-87745-420-5*) U of Iowa Pr.

***Up a Cranberry Tree II: Piney Poems.** Harry S. Monesson. (Illus.). 96p. (Orig.). 1997. pap. write for info. (*0-614-29773-7*) H S Monesson.

Up a Creek. Marshall Saper. 208p. (Orig.). 1989. pap. 12.00 (*0-685-29798-5*) M Saper.

***Up a Rainforest Tree.** Rod Theodorou & Carole Telford. LC 97-13743. (Amazing Journeys Ser.). (J). 1997. lib. bdg. write for info. (*1-57572-156-2*) Rigby Interact Libr.

Up a Road Slowly. Irene Hunt. (J). pap. 1.95 (*0-590-03171-6*) Scholastic Inc.

Up a Road Slowly. Irene Hunt. LC 92-47118. 192p. (J). 1993. 10.95 (*0-382-24366-8*) Silver Burdett Pr.

Up a Road Slowly. Estelle Kleinman. Ed. by J. Friedland & R. Kessler. (Novel-Ties Ser.). 1994. student ed., pap. text ed. 15.95 (*1-56982-075-9*) Lrn Links.

Up a Tree. Kay Cheever. (Illus.). 55p. (Orig.). 1995. pap. write for info. (1-57579-005-X) Pine Hill Pr.

Up a Tree. Patricia Lakin. LC 93-49847. (My School Ser.). (Illus.). (J). 1994. lib. bdg. 21.40 (0-8114-3868-6) Raintree Steck-V.

Up above the World. Paul Bowles. 223p. 1995. pap. 15.00 (0-88001-302-8) Ecco Pr.

Up above the World. Paul Bowles. 223p. 1996. pap. 15.00 (0-88001-500-4) Ecco Pr.

Up Against Apartheid: The Role & the Plight of the Press in South Africa. Richard Pollak. LC 80-22363. (Science & International Affairs Ser.). 167p. 1981. 19.95 (0-8093-1013-9) S Ill U Pr.

Up Against Foucault: Explorations of Some Tensions Between Foucault & Feminism. Ed. by Caroline Ramazanoglu. LC 93-9861. 304p. (C). (gr. 13). 1993. pap. 17.95 (0-415-05011-1); text ed. 69.95 (0-415-05010-3) Routledge.

Up Against It. J. Phillip. 1995. 8.50 (1-871676-54-1, Pub. by Christian Focus UK) Spring Arbor Dist.

Up Against It: Children & the Law in Canada. Jeffery Wilson. 166p. (Orig.). 1980. pap. 8.95 (0-88784-076-0, Pub. by Hse of Anansi Pr CN) Genl Dist Srvs.

Up Against It! Photographs of the Berlin Wall. Photos by Leland D. Rice. LC 91-295. (Illus.). 156p. 1991. 16.95 (0-8263-1291-8) U of NM Pr.

Up Against Odds: Autobiography of an Indian Scientist. Piara S. Gill. (C). 1992. 21.00 (81-7023-364-X, Pub. by Allied II) S Asia.

Up Against the Corporate Wall: Cases in Business & Society. 6th ed. S. Prakash Sethi & Paul Steidlmeier. LC 96-895. 496p. (C). 1996. pap. text ed. 45.33 (0-13-488371-3) P-H.

Up Against the Fences: Poverty, Passes & Privilege in South Africa. Ed. by Hermann Giliomee & Lawrence Schlemmer. LC 85-2349. 368p. 1985. text ed. 39.95 (0-312-83380-6) St Martin.

***Up Against the Law: Affirmative Action & the Supreme Court.** Lincoln Caplan. LC 97-13214. 1997. write for info. (0-87078-409-9) TCFP-PPP.

Up Against the Wal-Marts: How Your Business Can Prosper in the Shadow of the Retail Giants. Dan Taylor & Jeanne S. Archer. 256p. 1996. pap. 14.95 (0-8144-7916-2) AMACOM.

Up Against the Wal-Marts: How Your Business Can Prosper in the Shadow of the Retail Giants. Don Taylor & Jeanne S. Archer. LC 94-31697. 256p. 1994. 21.95 (0-8144-0238-0) AMACOM.

Up Against the Wall. Arthur Crossmen & Anthony Hill. 116p. (Orig.). 1995. pap. text ed. 10.00 (1-887333-00-2) Touch Down Prodns.

Up Against the Wall. June Hubbard & Jawanza Kunjufu. 1991. pap. 4.95 (0-913543-22-5) African Am Imag.

***Up All Night.** Karen Michaels. (Love Stories Ser.: No. 17). 192p. 1997. mass mkt. 3.99 (0-553-57047-1) BDD Bks Young Read.

Up & at 'Em. Harold E. Hartney. Ed. by James B. Gilbert. LC 79-7269. (Flight: Its First Seventy-Five Years Ser.). (Illus.). 1980. reprint ed. lib. bdg. 33.95 (0-405-12179-2) Ayer.

***Up & Away! Taking a Flight.** Meredith Davis. LC 96-44026. (Illus.). 1997. pap. write for info. (1-57255-214-X) Mondo Pubng.

***Up & Away with Arabic Numbers Coloring Book.** 3rd rev. ed. Saba Ghazi & Amal M. El-Naggar. (Illus.). 26p. (J). (ps-k). 1988. pap. 4.00 (1-56316-002-1) Iqra Intl Ed Fdtn.

***Up & Doing: Canadian Women & Peace.** Ed. by Janice Williamson & Deborah Gorham. 262p. pap. 14.95 (0-88961-130-0, Pub. by Wmns Pr CN) LPC InBook.

Up & Doing: The Vermont Historical Society, 1838-1970. Weston A. Cate, Jr. 128p. 1988. pap. 11.95 (0-934720-32-0) VT Hist Soc.

***Up & Down.** Mouseworks Staff. (J). 1997. 7.98 (1-57082-613-7) Mouse Works.

Up & Down. Elizabeth J. Blake. LC 78-144726. (Yale Series of Younger Poets: No. 19). reprint ed. 18.00 (0-404-53819-3) AMS Pr.

Up & down California in Eighteen Sixty to Eighteen Sixty-Four: The Journal of William H. Brewer. 3rd ed. William H. Brewer. Ed. by Francis P. Farquhar. LC 66-26246. 625p. reprint ed. pap. 178.20 (0-685-23674-9, 2029040) Bks Demand.

Up & down California in Eighteen Sixty to Eighteen Sixty-Four: The Journal of William H. Brewer. William H. Brewer. Ed. by Francis P. Farquhar. LC 66-26246. (Illus.). 1974. reprint ed. pap. 17.00 (0-520-02762-0) U CA Pr.

Up & Down, Dainty Dinosaur. (Illus.). (J). (ps-2). 1991. pap. 5.10 (0-8136-5711-3) Modern Curr.

Up & down in California, 1860-1864: The Journal of William H. Brewer. William H. Brewer. (American Biography Ser.). 583p. 1991. reprint ed. lib. bdg. 99.00 (0-7812-8039-7) Rprt Serv.

Up & down on the Merry-Go-Round. Bill Martin, Jr. & John Archambault. LC 87-28836. (Illus.). 32p. (J). (ps-2). 1988. 14.95 (0-8050-0681-8, Bks Young Read) H Holt & Co.

Up & Down on the Merry-Go-Round. Bill Martin, Jr. & John Archambault. LC 87-28836. (Illus.). 32p. (J). (ps-2). 1991. pap. 4.95 (0-8050-1638-4, Bks Young Read) H Holt & Co.

***Up & Down Spring.** Johanna Hurwitz. (J). Date not set. lib. bdg. write for info. (0-688-11923-9, Morrow Junior) Morrow.

Up & Down Spring. Johanna Hurwitz. LC 92-21337. (Illus.). 112p. (J). (gr. 3 up). 1993. 14.00 (0-688-11922-0, Morrow Junior) Morrow.

Up & down Spring. Johanna Hurwitz. 112p. (J). (gr. 4-7). 1994. pap. 3.25 (0-590-47736-6) Scholastic Inc.

Up & down the Beach. June Methot. LC 88-51108. (Illus.). 208p. 1988. write for info. (0-318-64042-2) Whip Pubs.

Up & Down the Mountain. Donald W. Dotterer. 1991. pap. 5.95 (1-55673-391-7, 9209) CSS OH.

Up & Down the Mountain: Helping Children Cope with Parental Alcoholism. Pamela L. Higgins. LC 94-66763. (Illus.). 36p. (J). (ps-4). 1994. pap. 8.95 (0-88282-133-4) New Horizon NJ.

Up & down the Number Line: Changes. Cornelia Tierney et al. Ed. by Priscilla C. Samii et al. (Investigations in Number, Data, & Space Ser.). (Illus.). 98p. (Orig.). 1994. teacher ed., pap. 22.95 (0-86651-804-5, DS21242) Seymour Pubns.

Up & down with the Rolling Stones: The Inside Story. Tony Sanchez. (Illus.). 320p. 1996. reprint ed. pap. 14.95 (0-306-80711-4) Da Capo.

Up & Over: The Story of the Lost Sheep, 3 bks. in 1. Mack Thomas. (J). 1995. 9.99 (0-88070-759-3, Gold & Honey) Multnomah Pubs.

Up & Run with Paradox Version 4.0. Elf. (C). 1994. pap. text ed. 35.00 (0-03-001742-4) HB Coll Pubs.

Up & Running: Integrating Information Technology & the Organization. Richard E. Walton. 1989. text ed. 27.95 (0-07-103275-4) McGraw.

Up & Running: Maintaining, Servicing & Enhancing the PC. John Woram. 320p. 1986. 19.95 (0-933186-08-8) IBM Corp Pub.

Up & Running: Microcomputer Applications. Marilyn K. Popyk. LC 86-26620. (C). 1987. pap. text ed. 35.50 (0-201-06274-7) Addison-Wesley.

Up & Running: PC Applications for DOS, Lotus 1-2-3, WordPedrfect, & dBase IV. D. Michael Werner & Thomas W. Warrner. (C). 1991. text ed. 29.50 (0-673-46359-1) Addson-Wesley Educ.

Up & Running in Fifteen Minutes. David T. Anderson & Charles Seiter. (Illus.). 200p. (Orig.). 1988. pap. text ed. 12.95 (0-915835-11-8) PC Software.

***Up & Running in 30 Days: Como Triunfar en La Venta De Propiedades.** Carla Cross. 161p. (SPA.). 1996. pap. 19.95 (0-7931-2351-8, 1913-4601) Dearborn Finan.

Up & Running in 30 Days: Making Money Your First Month in Real Estate. Carla Cross. 161p. 1995. pap. 24.95 (0-7931-1348-2, 1907-1301, Real Estate Ed) Dearborn Finan.

Up & Running with DOS 6.0. Elf. (C). 1994. teacher ed., pap. text ed. 29.50 (0-03-098513-7) HB Coll Pubs.

Up & Running with DOS 6.0 & 3.5. Elf. (C). 1994. pap. text ed. 17.50 (0-03-098512-9) HB Coll Pubs.

Up & Running with DOS 6.2. 3rd ed. Alan Simpson. LC 93-86593. 179p. 1993. 9.99 (0-7821-1443-1) Sybex.

Up & Running with Excel 4.0 & Mac 3.5. Elf. (C). 1994. pap. text ed. 17.50 (0-03-098528-5) HB Coll Pubs.

Up & Running with Excel 4.0 for Macintosh. Elf. 68p. (C). 1994. teacher ed., pap. text ed. 35.00 (0-03-098529-3) HB Coll Pubs.

Up & Running with Excel 5 for Windows. Sheila Dienes. LC 93-87247. 113p. 1994. pap. 9.99 (0-7821-1422-9) Sybex.

Up & Running with Excel 5.0 for Windows. Elf. (C). 1995. pap. text ed. write for info. (0-03-015017-5) HarBrace.

Up & Running with Harvard Graphics V1.03 for Windows. Electronic Learning Facilitators, Inc. Staff. LC 92-72956. 176p. (C). 1993. 5.25 hd 19.00 (0-03-097653-7) Dryden Pr.

Up & Running with Harvard Graphics V1.03 for Windows. Electronic Learning Facilitators, Inc. Staff. LC 92-72956. 176p. (C). 1994. pap. text ed. 17.50 (0-03-096899-2) Dryden Pr.

Up & Running with Harvard Graphics V1.03 for Windows. Electronic Learning Facilitators, Inc. Staff. LC 92-72956. 176p. (C). 1994. teacher ed., pap. text ed. 35.00 (0-03-097018-0) Dryden Pr.

Up & Running with Internet. Elf. (C). 1995. pap. text ed. 15.75 incl. 3.5 hd (0-03-017187-3) HB Coll Pubs.

Up & Running with Lotus 1-2-3 Release 4/Windows. 68p. (C). 1994. teacher ed., pap. text ed. 32.25 (0-03-098542-0) Dryden Pr.

***Up & Running with Lotus 123 Windows 3.5.** Elf. (C). 1994. 26.95 (0-03-098541-2) HB Coll Pubs.

Up & Running with Mathlab. Pratap. (C). 1995. pap. text ed. 18.00 (0-03-017884-3) HB Coll Pubs.

Up & Running with Microsoft Access 2.0 for Windows. Elf. 158p. (C). 1995. pap. text ed. 18.50 (0-03-015013-2) Dryden Pr.

Up & Running with Microsoft Access 2.0 for Windows. Elf. (C). 1995. teacher ed., pap. text ed. 31.00 (0-03-015014-0) HB Coll Pubs.

Up & Running with Microsoft Works 2.0 for Windows. Elf. (C). 1994. teacher ed., pap. text ed. 35.00 (0-03-098554-4) HB Coll Pubs.

Up & Running with MicroSoft Works 3.0 (DOS) & 3.5. Elf. (C). 1994. pap. text ed. 17.50 incl. 3.5 hd (0-03-001826-9) HB Coll Pubs.

Up & Running with MS Works 2.0 & WIN 3.5. Elf. (C). 1994. pap. text ed. 17.50 (0-03-098553-6) HB Coll Pubs.

Up & Running with PageMaker 5.0 for Macintosh. 152p. (C). 1994. pap. text ed. 17.50 (0-03-098531-5) Dryden Pr.

Up & Running with Pagemaker 5.0 for Macintosh. Elf. 64p. (C). 1994. teacher ed., pap. text ed. 35.00 (0-03-098532-3) HB Coll Pubs.

Up & Running with Pagemaker 5.0 for Windows. Electronic Learning Facilitators, Inc. Staff. 320p. (C). 1994. pap. text ed. 17.50 (0-03-096900-X) Dryden Pr.

Up & Running with Paradox 4.0 (DOS) & 3.5. Elf. (C). 1994. pap. text ed. 17.50 incl. 3.5 hd (0-03-001668-1) HB Coll Pubs.

Up & Running with Paradox 4.5 for Windows. 56p. (C). 1994. teacher ed., pap. text ed. 30.25 (0-03-098546-3) Dryden Pr.

***Up & Running with Paradox 4.5 Windows 3.5.** Elf. (C). 1994. 26.95 (0-03-098545-5) HB Coll Pubs.

Up & Running with Quattro 1.0 & Win 3.5. Elf. (C). 1994. pap. text ed. 17.50 (0-03-098549-8) HB Coll Pubs.

Up & Running with Windows 3.1. Joerg Schieb. LC 92-81039. 149p. (Orig.). 1992. pap. 10.95 (0-89588-843-2) Sybex.

Up & Running with Windows 4.0. Elf. (C). 1995. pap. write for info. (0-03-015092-2) HarBrace.

Up & Running with Windows 4.0. Elf. (C). 1995. teacher ed., pap. text ed. write for info. (0-03-015093-0) HarBrace.

Up & Running with Windows 5.2 & 3.5. Elf. (C). 1994. pap. text ed. 17.50 (0-03-098508-0) HB Coll Pubs.

Up & Running with Word 5.1 & MAC 3.5. Elf. (C). 1994. pap. text ed. 17.50 (0-03-098534-X) HB Coll Pubs.

Up & Running with Word 6 for Windows. Rita Belserene. LC 93-86590. 129p. 1993. 9.99 (0-7821-1421-0) Sybex.

Up & Running with WordPerfect 5.0. Elf. (C). 1994. teacher ed., pap. text ed. 35.00 (0-03-098509-9) HB Coll Pubs.

Up & Running with WordPerfect 5.1 for DOS. Rita Belserene. LC 91-65241. 164p. (Orig.). 1991. pap. 10.95 (0-89588-828-9) Sybex.

Up & Running with WordPerfect 6.0 for Windows. 320p. (C). 1995. pap. text ed. 11.00 (0-03-098520-X) Dryden Pr.

Up & Running with Works 3.0 for DOS. 74p. (C). 1994. teacher ed., pap. text ed. 36.75 (0-03-001831-5) Dryden Pr.

Up & Running with XTreeGold 2. Robin Merrin. LC 91-65166. 144p. (Orig.). 1991. pap. 9.95 (0-89588-820-3) Sybex.

Up & Running with Your Personal Computer: A Beginner's Guide to Buying, Using & Enjoying an IBM or Compatible Personal Computer. Mark Mathosian. (Illus.). 168p. 1992. pap. 16.95 (0-9631924-0-X) Inkwell Pubs.

Up at Altitude: A Celebration of Life in the High Country. M. John Fayhee. LC 94-42568. 224p. (Orig.). 1994. pap. 14.95 (1-55566-134-3) Johnson Bks.

***Up at Lighthouse Hill.** John Sampson. (Illus.). 200p. 1998. 8.95 (0-9613075-7-9) Thornfield Pr.

Up at the Villa. W. Somerset Maugham. LC 75-25366. (Works of W. Somerset Maugham). 1977. reprint ed. 23.95 (0-405-07824-2) Ayer.

Up at Two. Frances Phillips. 1991. 15.00 (0-914610-90-2); pap. 9.00 (0-914610-89-9) Hanging Loose.

Up Before Daylight: Life Histories from the Alabama Writers' Project, 1938-1939. Ed. by James S. Brown, Jr. LC 81-21988. (Illus.). 273p. 1982. pap. 77.90 (0-7837-8365-5, 2059174) Bks Demand.

Up Came Hill. Martin Schenk. 31.00 (0-8488-1157-7) Amereon Ltd.

Up Came Hill. Martin Schenck. 344p. 1958. reprint ed. 25.00 (0-942211-24-3) Olde Soldier Bks.

Up Close. Elizabeth Bevarly. (Special Edition Ser.: No. 737). 1992. mass mkt. 3.39 (0-373-09737-9, 5-09737-3) Harlequin Bks.

Up Close. Charles Sinks. Ed. by Ruth N. Raulston. (Illus.). 150p. (Orig.). 1993. pap. 24.95 (0-9638786-1-1) Artist Res Grp.

Up Close & Personal. Wayne Rice. 160p. 1989. pap. 12.99 (0-310-52491-1) Zondervan.

***Up Close & Personal: Experiential Exercises for Building a Spiritual Community.** Donna J. Moore. (Illus.). 80p. (Orig.). 1997. pap. text ed. 15.00 (0-614-26981-4) D J Moore.

Up Close from Afar: Using Remote Sensing to Teach the American Landscape. T. Cary et al. Ed. by Paul Baumann. (Pathways in Geography Ser.: No. 8). (Illus.). 83p. (Orig.). 1994. pap. text ed. 17.50 (0-9627379-9-2) NCFGE.

Up Close with God. Elliot Johnson & Al Schierbaum. (Gameday Devotions Ser.). 178p. (Orig.). (YA). (gr. 6 up). 1994. pap. 8.95 (1-887002-13-8) Cross Trng.

Up Close with the Savior. Elliot Johnson & Al Schierbaum. (Gameday Devotions Ser.). 212p. (Orig.). (YA). (gr. 6 up). 1994. pap. 8.95 (1-887002-14-6) Cross Trng.

Up Close with the Spirit. Elliot Johnson & Al Schierbaum. (Gameday Devotions Ser.). 158p. (Orig.). (YA). (gr. 6 up). 1994. pap. 8.95 (1-887002-15-4) Cross Trng.

UP Color Guide to Freight & Passenger Equipment. Lloyd E. Stagner & Robert J. Yanosey. (Illus.). 128p. 1993. 49.95 (1-878887-26-2) Morning NJ.

***Up Color Guide to Freight & Passenger Equipment, Vol. 2.** Lou Schmitz. (Illus.). 1996. 49.95 (1-878887-68-8) Morning NJ.

Up Country. (Illus.). 242p. 1987. 9.95 (1-55971-016-0) NorthWord.

Up Cutshin & down Greasy. Leonard W. Roberts. LC 87-29600. 176p. 1988. 22.00 (0-8131-1638-4) U Pr of Ky.

Up Cutshin & down Greasy: Folkways of a Kentucky Mountain Family. Leonard W. Roberts. LC 87-29600. (Illus.). 176p. 1997. pap. 15.95 (0-8131-0176-X) U Pr of Ky.

Up-Date. Dee W. Hadley. LC 81-65308. 112p. (YA). (gr. 9 up). 1988. reprint ed. pap. 5.95 (0-87747-847-3) Deseret Bk.

Up, down, & Around the Raintree. Charlotte Graeber. (Illus.). 60p. (J). (gr. 2). 1984. pap. 6.00 (1-880892-94-4) Com Sense FL.

***Up, Down & Sideways.** Robert H. Patton. LC 96-27409. 1997. 22.00 (1-877946-91-5) Permanent Pr.

Up, Down, Left & Right of Giving, Writing, & Following Directions. Sharon L. Wadle & Michael Turok. (Illus.). 129p. 1992. pap. 19.95 (0-9626939-4-4) Janelle Pubns.

Up Eel River. Margaret P. Montague. LC 77-150552. (Short Story Index Reprint Ser.). (Illus.). 1977. reprint ed. 19.95 (0-8369-3849-6) Ayer.

***Up for Grabs.** Kristen Robinette. (Loveswept Ser.: No. 821). 240p. 1997. mass mkt. 3.50 (0-553-44571-5, Loveswept) Bantam.

Up for Grabs - Hot on His Trail, 2 bks. in 1. Lori Copeland. 368p. 1995. mass mkt., pap. text ed. 4.99 (0-505-52007-9, Love Spell) Dorchester Pub Co.

Up from Agony: A Novel of Americanization. John Harms. 1971. 250.00 (0-685-26305-3) Revisionist Pr.

Up from Communism. John P. Diggins. 544p. 1994. 49.50 (0-231-08488-9); pap. 19.50 (0-231-08489-7) Col U Pr.

***Up from Conservatism.** Lind. 1997. pap. 13.00 (0-684-83186-4) S&S Trade.

Up from Conservatism: Why the Right Is Wrong for America. Michael Lind. 1996. 25.00 (0-02-874109-9); 23.00 (0-684-82761-1) Free Pr.

Up from Depression. Leonard Cammer. 1990. mass mkt. 5.99 (0-671-73482-2) PB.

Up from Eden: A Transpersonal View of Human Evolution. Ken Wilber. LC 95-49090. (Illus.). 372p. 1996. pap. 16.00 (0-8356-0731-3, Quest) Theos Pub Hse.

Up from Grief. large type ed. Bernardine Kreis & Alice Pattie. 208p. 1985. reprint ed. pap. 9.95 (0-8027-2486-8) Walker & Co.

Up from Grief: Patterns of Recovery. Bernadine Kreis & Alice Pattie. 160p. 1985. reprint ed. pap. 11.00 (0-86683-893-7, AY7442) Harper SF.

Up from Harlem. Granville Burnett. 80p. 1991. pap. 5.95 (0-936369-21-3) Son Rise Pubns.

***Up from Insanity: One Man's Triumph over Obsessive-Compulsive Disorder.** Reagan Smith. 203p. 1997. 19.95 (0-9658288-0-8) Emerald Pub TX.

Up from Jericho Tel. E. L. Konigsburg. LC 85-20061. 192p. (YA). (gr. 5 up). 1986. text ed. 17.00 (0-689-31194-X, Atheneum Bks Young) S&S Childrens.

Up from Mount Misery: The Blossoming of North Carolina's Sandhills. Chris Florance. Ed. by Jerry Bledsoe. LC 90-60350. (Illus.). 228p. 1990. 19.95 (0-9624255-3-2) Down Home NC.

***Up from Poverty.** Ed. by Hans F. Sennholz. LC 96-61933. (Freeman Classics Ser.). 208p. 1997. pap. 14.95 (1-57246-060-1) Foun Econ Ed.

Up from Scapegoating: Awakening Consciousness in Groups. Arthur D. Colman. LC 95-14098. 160p. (Orig.). 1995. pap. 19.95 (0-933029-95-0) Chiron Pubns.

Up from Slavery. Booker T. Washington. (Classics Ser.). (YA). (gr. 5 up). 1967. mass mkt. 3.95 (0-8049-0157-0, CL-157) Airmont.

Up from Slavery. Booker T. Washington. 1989. pap. 7.95 (0-8216-0184-9, Univ Books) Carol Pub Group.

Up from Slavery. Booker T. Washington. LC 92-38741. (Library of America). 1993. 6.99 (0-517-09122-4) Random Hse Value.

Up from Slavery. Booker T. Washington & Louis R. Harlan. LC 85-16712. (Classics Ser.). 336p. 1986. pap. 9.95 (0-14-039051-0, Penguin Classics) Viking Penguin.

Up from Slavery. Booker T. Washington. Ed. by William L. Andrews. 232p. 1995. pap. 7.95 (0-19-282348-5) OUP.

Up from Slavery. unabridged ed. Booker T. Washington. (Thrift Editions Ser.). 160p. 1995. reprint ed. pap. text ed. 2.00 (0-486-28738-6) Dover.

Up from Slavery. Booker T. Washington. Date not set. reprint ed. lib. bdg. 20.95 (0-89190-799-8, Am Repr) Amereon Ltd.

Up from Slavery. Booker T. Washington. 1995. reprint ed. lib. bdg. 18.95 (0-89968-556-0) Buccaneer Bks.

Up from Slavery. Booker T. Washington. 330p. 1971. reprint ed. 24.00 (0-87928-021-2) Corner Hse.

Up from Slavery: An Authoritative Text, Contexts & Composition History, Criticism. 2nd ed. Ed. by William L. Andrews. LC 95-1724. (Critical Editions Ser.). (C). 1995. pap. text ed. 8.95 (0-393-96725-5) Norton.

Up from Slavery: An Autobiography. large type ed. Booker T. Washington. LC 96-20240. 261p. 1996. text ed. 26.95 (1-56000-544-0) Transaction Pubs.

Up from Slavery: An Autobiography. Booker T. Washington. (American Biography Ser.). 243p. 1991. reprint ed. lib. bdg. 69.00 (0-7812-8043-1) Rprt Serv.

Up from Slavery see Three Negro Classics

Up from the Ashes: The Rise of the Steel Minimill in the United States. Donald F. Barnett & Robert W. Crandall. LC 85-48201. 135p. 1986. 28.95 (0-8157-0834-3); pap. 10.95 (0-8157-0833-5) Brookings.

Up from the Ashes: There Is Life after a Stroke. James A. Young. Ed. by BookWorld Staff. (Illus.). 147p. (Orig.). 1996. pap. 14.95 (0-9651506-0-7) Inner Path.

Up from the Cradle of Jazz: New Orleans Music since World War II. Jason Berry et al. (Illus.). 299p. 1992. reprint ed. pap. 16.95 (0-306-80493-X) Da Capo.

***Up from the Dust.** Lonnie L. Clayton. 196p. (Orig.). 1997. mass mkt. 4.99 (1-55197-932-2, Pub. by Comnwlth Pub CN) Partners Pubs Grp.

Up from the Eagles' Nest. Larry G. Coleman. (Illus.). 44p. (J). 1996. 12.95 (0-9629978-8-9) Sights Prods.

***Up from the Eagle's Nest: A Collection of Stories.** Larry Coleman. LC 96-33350. (Storytellers Ser.). (Illus.). (J). 1996. write for info. (0-929978-88-9) Sights Prods.

Up from the Mines: Images of the Appalachian Mining Experience. James B. Goode. Ed. by James M. Gifford. LC 93-18597. (Illus.). 144p. 1993. 19.95 (0-945084-37-4) J Stuart Found.

Up from the Roots: Growing a Vocabulary. Bob Moore & Maxine Moore. 1993. 13.95 (0-942257-20-0) New Chapter Pr.

Up from the Rubble. Peter Dyck & Elfrieda Dyck. LC 91-12848. (Illus.). 384p. (Orig.). 1991. pap. 14.99 (0-8361-3559-8) Herald Pr.

***Up from TQM: Up from Total Quality Management.** John T. Atkins, Jr. (Orig.). 1997. pap. 8.95 (0-533-12307-0) Vantage.

***Up from Under.** Michael Daly. Date not set. write for info. (*0-688-08818-X*, Beech Tree Bks) Morrow.

Up from Underachievement: How Teachers, Students, & Parents Can Work Together to Promote Student Success. Diane Heacox. Ed. by Pamela Espeland. LC 91-19069. 144p. (Orig.). (J). 1991. pap. 16.95 (*0-915793-35-0*) Free Spirit Pub.

Up from Uzam. Alta M. Rymer. (Tharma Lo Fairyland Ser.: Story 1). (Illus.). 28p. (Orig.). (J). (gr. 2-4). pap. 20.00 (*0-9600792-8-9*) Rymer Bks.

Up from Washington: William Pickens & the Negro Struggle for Equality, 1900-1954. Sheldon Avery. 1989. 39.50 (*0-87413-361-0*) U Delaware Pr.

Up Front. Bill Mauldin. (Illus.). 240p. 21.95 (*0-89190-896-X*) Amereon Ltd.

Up Front. Bill Mauldin. 1994. lib. bdg. 24.95 (*1-56849-444-0*) Buccaneer Bks.

Up Front. 50th fac. ed. Bill Mauldin. 240p. 1995. 19.95 (*0-393-03816-5*) Norton.

Up Front! Becoming the Complete Choral Conductor. Ray Robinson et al. (Illus.). 304p. (Orig.). (C). 1994. pap. 27.95 (*0-911318-19-4*) E C Schirmer.

Up-Front Sleeper: The Federal Witness "Protection" Program: True Involvement with Rapico Picnocrap - A "Letter" to Janet Reno. Martin J. Porozynski. LC 94-74031. (Judicial Network Under Scrutiny Ser.). 200p. (Orig.). 1995. pap. 14.95 (*0-9644416-3-2*) Doublenight Pr.

Up Goes Mr. Downs. Jerry Smath. LC 93-13041. (Parents Magazine Read Aloud Original Ser.). (J). 1993. lib. bdg. 17.27 (*0-8368-0979-3*) Gareth Stevens Inc.

Up Goes Mr. Downs. Jerry Smath. LC 84-1199. (Illus.). 48p. (J). (ps-3). 1985. 5.95 (*0-8193-1137-5*) Parents.

Up Goes the Skyscraper! Gail Gibbons. LC 85-16245. (Illus.). 32p. (J). (gr. k-3). 1986. 14.95 (*0-02-736780-0*, Four Winds Pr) S&S Childrens.

Up Goes the Skyscraper! Gail Gibbons. LC 90-31777. (Illus.). 32p. (J). (gr. k-3). 1990. reprint ed. pap. 5.95 (*0-689-71411-4*, Aladdin Paperbacks) S&S Childrens.

Up Here. Donald Schenker. Ed. by Orvis Burmaster. LC 88-71125. (Ahsahta Press Modern & Contemporary Poets of the West Ser.). 50p. (Orig.). 1988. pap. 6.95 (*0-916272-36-2*) Ahsahta Pr.

Up Hill, down Dale: A Volume of Short Stories. 2nd ed. Eden Phillpotts. LC 79-150558. (Short Story Index Reprint Ser.). 1977. reprint ed. 20.95 (*0-8369-3855-0*) Ayer.

Up in a Balloon. Leonard Cottrell. LC 69-17423. (Illus.). (J). (gr. 8 up). 1970. 27.95 (*0-87599-142-4*) S G Phillips.

Up in Arms: A Common Cause Guide to Understanding Nuclear Arms Policy. Sandra Secacca. (Illus.). 130p. 1984. pap. text ed. 3.50 (*0-914389-01-7*) Common Cause.

Up in Bed. Stuart Friebert. LC 74-620108. (CSU Poetry Ser.: No. I). 83p. 1974. pap. 4.95 (*0-914946-01-3*) Cleveland St Univ Poetry Ctr.

***Up in Harm's Way: Flying with the Fleet Air Arm.** R. M. Crosley. 256p. 1995. write for info. (*1-85310-555-4*, Pub. by Airlife UK) Motorbooks Intl.

Up in Smoke. H. William Stine. (Brains & Parker McGoohan Ser.). 77p. (J). (gr. 4-6). 1993. pap. 3.95 (*1-56801-067-2*) Sundance Pub.

Up in the Air. (Big Picture Paperbacks Ser.). (Illus.). 32p. (J). (ps-3). 1994. pap. 4.95 (*1-56458-732-0*) DK Pub Inc.

Up in the Air. Myra C. Livingston. LC 88-23293. (Illus.). 32p. (J). (ps-3). 1989. lib. bdg. 14.95 (*0-8234-0736-5*) Holiday.

Up in the Air: The Story of Bessie Coleman. Philip S. Hart. (J). 1996. lib. bdg. 16.13 (*0-87614-949-2*, Carolrhoda) Lerner Group.

Up in the Air: The Story of Bessie Coleman. Philip S. Hart. (J). (gr. 3-6). 1996. pap. text ed. 6.95 (*0-87614-978-6*) Lerner Group.

Up in the Attic. Sesame Street Staff. (Popular Characters/Author Collection). (Illus.). 24p. (J). (ps-2). 1995. bds. 1.59 (*0-307-01008-2*, Golden Books) Western Pub.

Up in the Morning Early: Vermont Farm Families in the Thirties. Scott E. Hastings, Jr. & Elsie R. Hastings. LC 92-53861. (Illus.). 160p. 1992. pap. 24.95 (*0-87451-598-X*) U Pr of New Eng.

Up in the Old Hotel. Joseph Mitchell. LC 92-50835. 1993. pap. 15.00 (*0-679-74631-5*, Publishers Media) Random.

Up in the Sky. Iqbal J. Unus. (Illus.). 24p. (Orig.). (J). (gr. 3-6). 1983. pap. 2.00 (*0-89259-054-8*) Am Trust Pubns.

***Up Is Not the Only Way: A Guide to Developing Workforce Talent.** 2nd rev. ed. Beverly V. Kaye. LC 96-40276. 272p. 1997. 25.95 (*0-89106-099-5*, 7751) Davies-Black.

Up Is the Mountain & Other Views. Erwin Rieger. LC 73-89240. (Illus.). 200p. 1973. 12.95 (*0-8323-0235-X*) Binford Mort.

***Up Island.** Anne R. Siddons. LC 97-5849. 320p. 1997. 23.00 (*0-06-017615-6*) HarpC.

***Up Jumped the Devil.** Blair S. Walker. LC 97-3155. 1997. write for info. (*0-380-97420-7*) Avon.

Up Jumps the Devil. Margaret Maron. 256p. 1996. 20.00 (*0-89296-568-1*) Warner Bks.

Up Jumps the Devil. Margaret Maron. 304p. 1997. mass mkt. 5.99 (*0-446-60406-2*) Warner Bks.

Up Late with Joe Franklin: Stories of the Greats, the Near Greats, the Ingrates. Joe Franklin & R. J. Marx. 1995. 20.00 (*0-02-540775-9*) S&S Trade.

Up-Lot Reveries: A Sense of Place. Maria Parson. 24.95 (*0-8488-0186-5*) Amereon Ltd.

Up-Lot Reveries: An Oral History of the North Fork. Maria Parson. 22.95 (*0-8488-0122-9*) Amereon Ltd.

Up Mount Everest Without a Paddle. large type ed. Derek Nimmo. 168p. 1989. reprint ed. 19.95 (*1-85089-325-X*, Pub. by ISIS UK) Transaction Pubs.

Up My Coast. Joanne Kyger. (Illus.). 24p. (Orig.). 1981. pap. 5.00 (*0-912449-05-5*) Floating Island.

Up North. Sam Cook. LC 86-62906. (Illus.). 192p. 1987. 16.95 (*0-938586-09-2*) Pfeifer-Hamilton.

Up North. Del Hamilton. LC 95-90849. 1996. 18.95 (*0-533-11732-1*) Vantage.

Up North. John S. Wade. (W.N.J. Ser.: No. 12). 1980. pap. 6.00 (*1-55780-061-8*) Juniper Pr WI.

***Up North: Memorable Experiences of Great Deer Hunting.** (Illus.). 224p. (Orig.). 1996. per., pap. 9.95 (*0-939330-07-5*) W H Hull.

***Up North Again: More of Ontarios Wilderness from Pickerel to the Pleiades.** Doug Bennet. 1997. pap. text ed. 18.95 (*0-7710-1115-6*) McCland & Stewart.

Up North at the Cabin. Marsha W. Chall. LC 91-3035. (Illus.). (J). (ps-3). 1992. lib. bdg. 15.93 (*0-688-09733-2*) Lothrop.

Up North at the Cabin. Marsha W. Chall. LC 91-3035. (J). (ps-8). 1992. 16.00 (*0-688-09732-4*) Lothrop.

Up North Big City Streets. Zack Gilbert. 64p. 1987. 9.95 (*0-910671-09-5*) Path Pr Chicago.

Up North in Winter. Deborah Hartley. (Illus.). 32p. (J). (ps-3). 1993. pap. 4.99 (*0-14-054943-9*, Puff Unicorn) Puffin Bks.

Up North on the Mary. Tod Schacht. LC 87-92100. 1989. 17.50 (*0-87212-213-1*) Libra.

Up on Dog Creek: A Time Remembered Foyil, Oklahoma. Bonnie S. Speer. (Illus.). 120p. (Orig.). 1995. pap. 8.95 (*0-9646489-0-3*) Martain Pub.

***Up on Melody Mountain.** Betty J. Robinson. 1997. 14.99 (*0-88419-453-1*) Creation House.

Up on the Housetop. Benjamin R. Hanby. (Illus.). 24p. (Orig.). (J). (ps-2). 1991. pap. 3.95 (*0-8249-8521-4*, Ideals Child) Hambleton-Hill.

Up on the Mountain. Kenneth Roberts. LC 92-64000. 184p. (Orig.). 1992. pap. 8.95 (*1-55725-053-7*) Paraclete MA.

Up or Out: How to Get Promoted As the Army Draws Down. Wilson L. Walker. LC 93-18015. 128p. 1993. 13.95 (*0-942710-91-6*) Impact VA.

Up Periscope! & Other Stories. Alec Hudson. LC 92-3744. 256p. 1992. 24.95 (*1-55750-377-X*) Naval Inst Pr.

Up Pop the Monsters 1 2 3! A Pop-Up Counting Book. Carla Dijs. 22p. (J). 1996. 8.95 (*0-590-84762-7*, Cartwheel) Scholastic Inc.

Up-Pops: Paper Engineering with Elastic Bands. Mark Hiner. 1993. pap. 11.95 (*0-906212-79-0*, Pub. by Tarquin UK) Parkwest Pubns.

Up-Rising in Dying. Ed. by Christy Barnes & Janet Hutchinson. 86p. 1990. pap. 10.95 (*0-932776-16-7*) Adonis Pr.

Up River. Frank Asch. LC 93-38687. (Illus.). (J). 1995. 16.00 (*0-671-88703-3*, S&S Bks Young Read) S&S Childrens.

Up River: The Story of a Maine Fishing Community. Olive Pierce. LC 95-47137. (Library of New England). (Illus.). 131p. (C). 1996. pap. 19.95 (*0-87451-756-7*) U Pr of New Eng.

Up Rode the Troopers: The Black Police in Queensland. Bill Rosser. 1990. pap. 16.95 (*0-7022-2224-0*, Pub. by Univ Queensland Pr AT) Intl Spec Bk.

Up Rose a Burning Man. Ev Miller. 55p. (Orig.). 1996. pap. 6.00 (*0-88734-209-4*) Players Pr.

U.P. Sales Tax Act, 1948, Together with Rules & Notifications. 8th ed. P. L. Malik. (C). 1989. 50.00 (*0-685-38630-9*) St Mut.

Up Saskatchewan Way: An Anthology of Short Stories. J. Paul Loomis. (Illus.). 152p. 1985. 15.00 (*0-317-59459-1*) G K Westgard.

Up She Flew: Poems. Michael Gorman. 90p. 1991. pap. 10.95 (*0-948339-68-3*, Pub. by Salmon Pubng IE) Dufour.

***Up Shit Creek: A Collection of Horrifyingly True Toilet Misadventures.** Joe Lindsay. LC 97-9464. (Illus.). 96p. (Orig.). 1997. pap. 6.95 (*0-89815-939-3*) Ten Speed Pr.

Up Sometimes, Sometimes Down. Irene Senior-Pomeroy. LC 95-91052. (Orig.). 1996. pap. 8.95 (*0-533-11839-5*) Vantage.

Up South: Blacks in Chicago's Suburbs (1719-1983) James Dorsey. LC 86-50583. (Illus.). 113p. (Orig.). 1986. pap. text ed. 19.95 (*0-932269-93-1*) Wyndham Hall.

Up South: Stories, Studies, & Letters of This Century's African American Migrations. Ed. by Malaika Adero. LC 92-53733. (Illus.). 238p. 1992. 25.00 (*1-56584-020-8*) New Press NY.

Up South: Stories, Studies, & Letters of This Century's African American Migrations. Ed. by Malaika Adero. LC 92-53733. (Illus.). 238p. 1993. pap. 12.95 (*1-56584-168-9*) New Press NY.

Up Spake the Cabin Boy. Robert Harbinson. 251p. 1988. pap. 10.95 (*0-85640-400-4*, Pub. by Blackstaff Pr IE) Dufour.

Up Stream: An American Chronicle. Ludwig Lewisohn. LC 24-11220. reprint ed. 29.00 (*0-403-00655-4*) Scholarly.

Up Sun. Max Chennault et al. Ed. by Charles Goodman & Wallace H. Little. (American Heroes Ser.). 142p. 1990. pap. 9.95 (*0-916693-14-7*) Castle Bks.

Up the Agency: The Funny Business of Advertising. Peter Mayle. 1994. pap. 8.95 (*0-312-11911-9*) St Martin.

Up the Coast & into the Past: Hamakua to Waipio. Faith M. Roelofs. (Exploring the Islands: Island of Hawai'i Ser.). 1994. pap. write for info. (*1-882163-31-1*) Moanalua Grdns Fnd.

Up the Country: A Saga of Pioneering Days. Miles Franklin. (Illus.). 256p. 1987. 15.95 (*0-8253-0417-2*) Beaufort Bks NY.

Up the Country: Selected Poems 1992-94. Shane P. Plank. 32p. 1995. pap. 5.00 (*1-885710-10-0*) Geekspeak Unique.

Up the Creek: A Paddler's Guide to Ontario. Kevin Callan. (Illus.). 120p. (Orig.). 1996. pap. 13.50 (*1-55046-167-2*, Pub. by Boston Mills Pr CN) Genl Dist Srvs.

Up the Cut: An Anthology of Inland Waterways. Ivan E. Broadhead. (Illus.). 224p. 1994. 30.00 (*0-7509-0585-9*, Pub. by Sutton Pubng UK) Bks Intl VA.

Up the down Escalator: Development & the Economy, a Jamaican Case Study. Michael Manley. (Illus.). 320p. 1987. 27.50 (*0-88258-112-0*) Howard U Pr.

Up the Down Staircase. Bel Kaufman. 1969. pap. 5.25 (*0-87129-281-5*, U12) Dramatic Pub.

Up the down Staircase. Bel Kaufman. 1993. reprint ed. lib. bdg. 21.95 (*1-56849-148-4*) Buccaneer Bks.

Up the Down Staircase: With a New Introduction by the Author. Bel Kauffman. LC 90-56104. (Illus.). 352p. 1991. reprint ed. pap. 13.00 (*0-06-097361-7*, PL) HarpC.

***Up the Flagpole: A Guide for Women School Administrators.** Beverly M. Enwall & Carolyn O. Fabal. LC 96-37172. 1997. 24.95 (*0-88280-132-5*) ETC Pubns.

Up the Hollow from Lynchburg. Photos by Joe Clark. (Illus.). 128p. 1975. 15.00 (*0-07-062210-8*) McGraw.

Up the HRD Ladder: A Guide to Professional Growth. N. Chalofsky & C. I. Lincoln. 1983. 16.76 (*0-201-04998-8*) Addison-Wesley.

***Up the I. R. S.** Max. (Illus.). 50p. (Orig.). 1997. pap. 30.00 (*0-922070-43-1*) M Tecton Pub.

Up the Infinite Corridor: MIT & the Technical Imagination. Fred Hapgood. 1993. pap. 12.00 (*0-201-62610-1*) Addison-Wesley.

Up the Inward Path. Richard F. Kingsley. 42p. 1989. pap. 7.95 (*0-912132-21-3*) Dominion Pr.

Up the Koyukuk. Alaska Geographic Staff. LC 83-15343. (Alaska Geographic Ser.: Vol. 10, no. 4). (Illus.). 152p. 1983. pap. 19.95 (*0-88240-200-5*) Alaska Geog Soc.

Up the Ladder, down the Slide. Everitt. LC 96-54861. 1998. write for info. (*0-15-292886-3*) HarBrace.

Up the Ladder in Foreign Missions. Lewis G. Jordan. Ed. by Edwin S. Gausted. LC 79-52596. (Baptist Tradition Ser.). (Illus.). 1980. reprint ed. lib. bdg. 26.95 (*0-405-12463-5*) Ayer.

Up the Lake Road: The First Hundred Years of the Adirondack Mountain Reserve 1887-1987. Edith Pilcher. (Illus.). 208p. 1987. 35.00 (*0-9618456-0-0*); pap. 17.50 (*0-9618456-1-9*) Adk Mtn Reserve.

Up the Learning Ladder: How to Boost Your Child's Study Power. Lois D. Glass. LC 88-62652. (Illus.). 146p. (Orig.). 1988. pap. 7.95 (*0-9618766-0-3*) Carriage Pr.

***Up the Loyalty Ladder.** Neil Raphel & Murray. Date not set. write for info. (*0-688-13695-8*) Morrow.

Up the Loyalty Ladder: Turning Some-Time Customers into Full-Time Advocates for Your Business. Neil Raphel & Murray Raphel. LC 94-43548. 288p. 1995. 23.00 (*0-88730-725-6*) Harper Busn.

Up the Loyalty Ladder: Turning Sometime Customers into Full-Time Advocates of Your Business. Murray Raphel. 304p. 1996. pap. 13.00 (*0-88730-786-8*) Harper Busn.

Up the Mainstream: The Rise of Toronto's Alternative Theatres. Denis W. Johnston. 344p. 1990. 35.00 (*0-8020-5834-5*); pap. 18.95 (*0-8020-6741-7*) U of Toronto Pr.

Up the Math Ladder: Activity Based Ideas for Teaching Math to Primary Grades. Lynn Molyneux. (Illus.). 160p. (J). (gr. k-4). 1984. per. 9.95 (*0-685-29137-5*) Trellis Bks Inc.

Up the Neck. Janet Davis. 1993. 9.95 (*1-56222-572-3*, 94820); audio 9.98 (*1-56222-571-5*, 94820C) Mel Bay.

***Up the Neck.** Janet Davis. 1993. 18.95 incl. audio (*0-7866-1123-5*, 94820P) Mel Bay.

Up the Reading Ladder: Activity Based Ideas for Teaching Reading to Primary Grades. Lynn Molyneux & Fran Lipson. (Illus.). 160p. 1984. per. 9.95 (*0-685-29142-1*) Trellis Bks Inc.

Up the Rent. Tim Kelly. 1970. pap. 3.00 (*0-87129-353-6*, U13) Dramatic Pub.

Up the Rough Side. Charles Perry. LC 85-61878. (Illus.). 96p. 1985. pap. 5.95 (*0-9615139-0-X*) C Perry Pub.

Up the Science Ladder: Activity Based Ideas for Teaching Science to Primary Grades. Lynn Molyneux. (Illus.). 128p. 1988. per. 9.95 (*0-685-29136-7*) Trellis Bks Inc.

***Up the Shankill.** Paul Hamilton. (Illus.). 114p. Date not set. pap. 13.95 (*0-85640-178-1*) Dufour.

***Up the Slot: Marines in the Central Solomons.** Charles D. Melson. (Illus.). 37p. 1996. pap. 25.00 (*0-7881-3522-8*) DIANE Pub.

Up the Social Studies Ladder: Activity Based Ideas for Teaching Social Studies to Primary Grades. Lynn Molyneux. (Illus.). 128p. 1988. per. 9.95 (*0-685-29135-9*) Trellis Bks Inc.

Up the Stairs. Sally F. Odgers. LC 92-21395. (Voyages Ser.). (Illus.). (J). 1993. 4.25 (*0-383-03601-1*) SRA McGraw.

Up the Swiftwater: A Pictorial History of the Colorful Upper St. Joe River Country. Sandra A. Crowell & David O. Asleson. (Illus.). 150p. 1995. reprint ed. pap. 19.95 (*0-9643647-3-5*) Mus North Idaho.

Up the Tall Tree. Rosie Hankin. LC 94-28179. (Read All about It Ser.). (Illus.). (J). 1995. lib. bdg. 21.40 (*0-8114-5738-9*) Raintree Steck-V.

Up the Tall Tree. Rosie Hankin. (J). 1995. pap. text ed. 4.95 (*0-8114-3748-5*) Raintree Steck-V.

Up the University: Re-Creating Higher Education in America. Robert Solomon & Jon Solomon. (Illus.). 336p. 1994. pap. 14.95 (*0-201-62691-8*) Addison-Wesley.

Up the University: Recreating Higher Education in America. Robert C. Solomon & Jon Solomon. (Illus.). 256p. 1992. 24.95 (*0-201-57719-4*) Addison-Wesley.

Up the Wall. Nicholas Heller. LC 91-14783. 24p. (J). 1992. lib. bdg. 13.93 (*0-688-10634-X*) Greenwillow.

Up There & Other Strange Directions. Donald A. Wollheim. 148p. 1988. 15.00 (*0-915368-39-0*) New Eng SF Assoc.

Up Through the Water. Darcey Steinke. Ed. by Jane Rosenman. 176p. 1991. reprint ed. pap. 7.95 (*0-671-70647-0*, WSP) PB.

***Up-Tight: The Velvet Underground Story.** (Illus.). 136p. 1996. 11.95 (*0-7119-0168-6*, OP 42142) Omnibus NY.

***Up to Alaska.** Billie J. Jensen & Reece C. Jensen. (Illus.). 312p. (Orig.). 1996. pap. 24.95 (*1-886278-05-9*) Ghastly Gallimaufry.

Up-to-Date Set of the Rules of the Superior Court, DC Court of Appeals, U. S. District Court, DC Circuit Court for the District of Columbia. LC 82-134872. 1987. 67.00 (*0-317-03281-X*) Rules Serv Co.

***Up to Low.** Brian Doyle. 120p. (J). (gr. 4-6). 1996. pap. 5.95 (*0-88899-264-5*, Pub. by Groundwood-Douglas & McIntyre CN) Firefly Bks Ltd.

Up to Mametz. Wyn Griffith. 288p. 1988. 95.00 (*0-947893-08-3*, Pub. by Gliddon Bks UK) St Mut.

Up to Now: An Autobiography. Alfred E. Smith. (History - United States Ser.). 434p. 1992. reprint ed. lib. bdg. 99.00 (*0-7812-6216-X*) Rprt Serv.

Up to Ten & down Again. Lisa C. Ernst. LC 84-21852. (Illus.). 40p. (J). (ps up). 1995. pap. 4.95 (*0-688-14391-1*, Mulberry) Morrow.

Up to the Lake. Tom Hegg. (Illus.). 48p. 1986. 10.95 (*0-931674-09-3*) Waldman Hse Pr.

Up to the Mountains & down to the Villages: The Transfer of Youth from Urban to Rural China. Thomas P. Bernstein. LC 77-76291. (Illus.). 1977. 47.50 (*0-300-02135-6*) Yale U Pr.

Up to the Plate: The All American Girls Professional Baseball League. Margot F. Galt. LC 94-10636. (Sports Legacy Ser.). (Illus.). 96p. (YA). (gr. 5 up). 1995. lib. bdg. 22.95 (*0-8225-3326-X*, Lerner Publctns) Lerner Group.

Up to the Sky in Ships: In & Out of Quandry. A. Bertram Chandler & Lee Hoffman. Ed. by Charles J. Hitchcock. LC 82-60702. 172p. 1982. 13.00 (*0-915368-16-1*) New Eng SF Assoc.

Up to There in Alligators. Patrick Oliphant. (Illus.). 160p. (Orig.). 1987. pap. 8.95 (*0-8362-2095-1*) Andrews & McMeel.

Up to Your Armpits in Alligators? How to Sort Out What Risks Are Worth Worrying About! John Paling & Sean Paling. (Illus.). 155p. 1994. pap. 15.00 (*0-9642236-0-0*) J Paling & Co.

***Up to Your Armpits in Alligators? How to Sort Out What Risks Are Worth Worrying About!** 2nd rev. ed. John Paling. (Illus.). 176p. 1997. per., pap. 22.50 (*0-9642236-6-X*) J Paling & Co.

***Up Turtle Creek.** Tom Von Kamecke. (Illus.). 128p. (Orig.). 1996. pap. 7.95 (*0-9653285-0-3*) Park Lake Pub.

Up, Up & Away. Catherine Ennis. 224p. 1994. pap. 9.95 (*1-56280-065-5*) Naiad Pr.

Up, up & Away. Margaret Hillert. (Illus.). (J). (ps-2). 1982. pap. 5.10 (*0-8136-5596-X*); lib. bdg. 7.95 (*0-8136-5096-8*) Modern Curr.

Up, Up & Away: A Book about Adverbs. Ruth Heller. (Ruth Heller Language Ser.). (Illus.). 48p. (J). (gr. 1 up). 1991. 15.95 (*0-448-40249-1*, G&D) Putnam Pub Group.

Up, up & Away: A Book about Adverbs. Ruth Heller. (Illus.). 48p. (J). (gr. 1 up). 1993. pap. 7.95 (*0-448-40159-2*, Sandcastle Bks) Putnam Pub Group.

Up, up, & Away: The Science of Flight. David Darling. LC 91-4000. (Experiment! Ser.). (Illus.). 60p. (J). (gr. 4-6). 1991. lib. bdg. 13.95 (*0-87518-479-0*, Dillon Silver Burdett) Silver Burdett Pr.

Up up & Away: Universalist Journeys for Ages 8 to 10. Margaret K. Gooding. 1994. pap. 30.00 (*1-55896-287-5*) Unitarian Univ.

Up, up in a Plane! Illus. by Dorothy Stott. (Pudgy Board Bks.). 18p. (J). (ps). 1995. bds. 3.50 (*0-448-40880-5*, G&D) Putnam Pub Group.

Up Went the Goat. Barbara Gregorich. Ed. by Joan Hoffman. (Start to Read! Ser.). (Illus.). 16p. (Orig.). (J). (gr. k-2). 1984. pap. 2.25 (*0-88743-002-3*, 06002) Sch Zone Pub Co.

Up Went the Goat. Barbara Gregorich. Ed. by Joan Hoffman. (Start to Read! Ser.). (Illus.). 32p. (Orig.). (J). (gr. k-2). 1992. pap. 3.95 (*0-88743-400-2*, 06052) Sch Zone Pub Co.

Up Where I Used to Live: Stories. Max Schott. LC 78-11619. (Illinois Short Fiction Ser.). 144p. 1978. 9.95 (*0-252-00720-4*) U of Ill Pr.

Up with Math: Basic Skills Step by Step. 2nd rev. ed. Roland C. McCully. Ed. by Russell F. Jacobs. (Illus.). 292p. (Orig.). (YA). (gr. 5-12). 1994. pap. 12.95 (*0-918272-22-X*, 115) Jacobs.

***Up with Parents.** Larry Koenig & Rodney Kennedy. 88p. 1997. pap. text ed. 10.95 (*1-886901-07-4*) Up With Youth.

***Up with Youth: Participant Workbook.** Larry Koenig. 25p. (J). (gr. 4-8). 1985. pap. write for info. (*1-886901-05-8*) Up With Youth.

***Up with Youth Math Facts Method: Addition & Subtraction Math Facts.** Larry Koenig. (Illus.). 50p. 1990. pap. text ed. 7.95 (*1-886901-02-3*) Up With Youth.

***Up with Youth Math Facts Method: Multiplication & Division Math Facts.** Larry Koenig. (Illus.). 50p. 1990. pap. text ed. 7.95 (*1-886901-03-1*) Up With Youth.

Up Your Asteroid! A Science Fiction Farce. C. Everett Cooper. LC 77-866. 47p. 1977. pap. 13.00 (*0-89370-206-4*); lib. bdg. 23.00 (*0-89370-106-8*) Borgo Pr.

Up Your Attitude! Changing the Way You Look at Life. Elwood N. Chapman. LC 93-13315. 1993. pap. 12.95 (*1-56052-234-8*) Crisp Pubns.

***Up Your Career.** 4th rev. ed. Dean C. Dauw. (Illus.). 200p. (C). 1997. pap. 24.95 (*1-884094-12-0*) Ft Dearborn.

Up Your Cash Flow: Text & Accompanying Workbook. Harvey A. Goldstein. LC 84-82281. 176p. (Orig.). 1986. pap. 12.95 (*0-931349-04-4*); 19.95 (*0-931349-02-8*) Granville Pubns.

Up Your Ear! William Flygare. 150p. 1985. pap. 7.50 (*0-933704-86-0*) Dawn Pr.

Up Your Equity: Build up Your Personal Net Worth. rev. ed. Victor I. Eber. LC 72-95079. (Illus.). 1972. 12.95 (*0-686-05084-3*) Finan Pr FL.

Up Your Gas: Sixty-One Ways to Cut Gas Consumption, Increase Your Mileage, Chop Costs & Minimize Waiting in Gas Lines! Plus Eleven Ways to Find a Good Mechanic & Save Money! John V. Kamin. Incl. Sixty-One Ways to Cut Gas Consumption. 1979. lib. bdg. (*0-318-51906-2*); Increase Your Mileage, Chop Costs & Minimize Waiting in Gas Lines. 1979. lib. bdg. (*0-318-51907-0*); Eleven Ways to Find a Good Mechanic & Save Money. 1979. lib. bdg. (*0-318-51908-9*); 52p. 1979. lib. bdg. 6.00 (*0-911353-07-0*) Forecaster Pub.

Up Your Grades! Proven Strategies for Academic Success. Ann M. Tufariello. LC 96-8126. 192p. 1996. 12.95 (*0-8442-4189-X*, VGM Career Bks) NTC Pub Grp.

Up Your Own Organization: A Handbook for Today's Entrepreneur. Donald M. Dible. 23.95 (*0-8359-8086-3*) S&S Trade.

Up Your Productivity. Kurt Hanks. LC 91-17268. (Quick-Read Ser.). 126p. 1990. pap. 13.95 (*0-931961-49-1*, CR66) Crisp Pubns.

Up Your Punctuation! An Almost Non-Grammatical Approach to Punctuation. Edgar C. Alward & E. Dale. 112p. (Orig.). (YA). (gr. 9-12). 1988. pap. 12.95 (*0-9620092-0-2*) Pine Isl Pr.

Up Yours! Guide to Advanced Revenge Techniques. George Hayduke. 220p. 1982. text ed. 19.95 (*0-87364-249-X*) Paladin Pr.

Upa Gurus. David G. Eberhart. 10.00 (*0-89253-679-9*) Ind-US Inc.

Upadesa Sahasri of Sri Sankaracharya: A Thousand Teachings. Shankara. Tr. by Swami Jagadananda. 1941. Bilingual ed. pap. 5.95 (*0-87481-423-5*, Pub. by Ramakrishna Math II) Vedanta Pr.

Upamana in Indian Philosophy. Shiv Kumar. xiv, 181p. (C). 1994. 18.00 (*81-85133-79-4*, Pub. by Estrn Bk Linkers II) Nataraj Bks.

Upanayanam (Thread Marriage) Panduranga R. Malyala. (Illus.). 20p. 1983. pap. text ed. 2.00 (*0-938924-15-X*) Sri Shirdi Sai.

Upanisads. Tr. by Patrick Olivelle from HIN. (World's Classics Ser.). (Illus.). 320p. 1996. pap. 6.95 (*0-19-282292-6*) OUP.

Upanisads. 2nd ed. Tr. by Srisa Chandra Vasu. LC 73-4980. (Sacred Books of the Hindus: No. 1). reprint ed. 34.50 (*0-404-57801-2*) AMS Pr.

Upanisads: The Selections from 108 Upanisads. T. M. Mahadevan. 240p. (Orig.). 1975. pap. 3.20 (*0-88253-985-X*) Ind-US Inc.

***Upanishad Vahini (Writings on the Upanishads)** Sai B. Sathya. Date not set. pap. 2.00 (*0-614-19046-0*, BA-315) Sathya Sai Bk Ctr.

Upanishads. Tr. & Intro. by Eknath Easwaran. LC 87-14216. 1987. 18.00 (*0-915132-40-0*); pap. 9.95 (*0-915132-39-7*) Nilgiri Pr.

Upanishads. Juan Mascaro. (Orig.). 1976. 18.95 (*0-8488-0339-6*) Amereon Ltd.

Upanishads, 2 vols. F. Max Muller. 1974. lib. bdg. 500.00 (*0-8490-1252-X*) Gordon Pr.

Upanishads, 2 vols. Tr. by Max Muller. 1975. Set. lib. bdg. 600.00 (*0-87968-548-4*) Krishna Pr.

Upanishads. Thomas Wyatt. Tr. by Juan Mascaro. (Classics Ser.). 144p. (Orig.). 1965. pap. 7.95 (*0-14-044163-8*, Penguin Classics) Viking Penguin.

Upanishads. 4th ed. Swami Paramananda. 1981. 6.95 (*0-911564-02-0*); 5.95 (*0-685-05242-7*) Vedanta Ctr.

Upanishads. Sri Aurobindo. 466p. (ENG & SAN.). 1981. reprint ed. 17.00 (*0-89744-026-9*, Pub. by Sri Aurob Ashram Trust II); reprint ed. pap. 14.95 (*0-89744-025-0*, Pub. by Sri Aurob Ashram Trust II) Auromere.

Upanishads, 2 vols. G. R. Mead. 237p. 1992. reprint ed. Set. pap. 14.95 (*0-922802-77-7*) Kessinger Pub.

Upanishads, 2 Vols, 1. F. Max Muller. 1963. reprint ed. text ed. 8.95 (*0-486-20993-8*) Dover.

Upanishads, 2 Vols, 2. F. Max Muller. 1963. reprint ed. text ed. 8.95 (*0-486-20992-X*) Dover.

Upanishads, Set, 4 vols., Set. Tr. by Swami Nikhilananda. LC 49-9558. 1994. 60.00 (*0-911206-14-0*) Ramakrishna.

Upanishads, Vol. I. Ed. by Joseph Campbell. Tr. by Swami Nikhilananda. LC 49-9558. 333p. 1990. 15.00 (*0-911206-15-9*) Ramakrishna.

Upanishads, Vol. II. Ed. by Joseph Campbell. Tr. by Swami Nikhilananda. LC 49-9558. 400p. 1990. 15.00 (*0-911206-16-7*) Ramakrishna.

Upanishads, Vol. III. Ed. by Joseph Campbell. Tr. by Swami Nikhilananda. LC 49-9558. 408p. 1990. 15.00 (*0-911206-17-5*) Ramakrishna.

Upanishads, Vol. IV. Ed. by Joseph Campbell. Tr. by Swami Nikhilananda. LC 49-9558. 424p. 1994. 15.00 (*0-911206-18-3*) Ramakrishna.

Upanishads: A New Translation. Tr. by Alistair Shearer & Peter Russell from HIN. (Illus.). 112p. (Orig.). 1989. pap. 17.95 (*0-04-440521-9*) Routledge Chapman & Hall.

Upanishads: Breath of the Eternal. Tr. by Swami Prabhavananda & Frederick Manchester. 128p. 1957. pap. 4.99 (*0-451-62607-9*, MJ2298, Ment) NAL-Dutton.

Upanishads: Breath of the Eternal. Tr. by Swami Prabhavananda et al. LC 48-5935. 232p. (C). 1947. pap. 7.95 (*0-87481-040-X*) Vedanta Pr.

Upanishads: Gateways of Knowledge. M. P. Pandit. LC 88-83077. 270p. (Orig.). 1988. pap. 9.95 (*0-941524-44-2*) Lotus Light.

Upanishads: Texts, Translations & Commentaries, Pt. 1. Sri Aurobindo. 466p. 1986. 17.95 (*0-89071-295-6*, Pub. by SAA II); pap. 14.95 (*0-89071-294-8*, Pub. by SAA II) Aurobindo Assn.

Upanishads: The Vedic Bibles. Swami Babaji Giri. LC 92-82900. (Complete Works of Lahiri Mahasay: Vol. 3). (Illus.). 136p. (Orig.). 1992. pap. text ed. 15.00 (*1-877854-19-0*) Sanskrit Classics.

***Upanishads: With Sanskrit Text, Translation & Sri Aurobindo's Commentary.** unabridged ed. Sri Aurobindo. LC 96-75803. 466p. 1997. pap. 17.95 (*0-914955-23-3*) Lotus Light.

Upanishads & Early Buddhism. Sanjay G. Deodikar. xi, 223p. 1992. 22.00 (*0-685-62637-7*, Pub. by Estrn Bk Linkers II) Nataraj Bks.

Upas Tree. large type ed. Eva Hanagan. 1990. 25.99 (*0-7089-2120-5*) Ulverscroft.

Upbeat, Downbeat: Basic Conducting Patterns & Techniques. Sandra Willetts. LC 93-8284. 96p. (Orig.). 1993. pap. 9.95 (*0-687-43191-3*) Abingdon.

Upbringing. James Stenson. 176p. 1992. pap. 8.95 (*0-933932-52-9*) Scepter Pubs.

Upbuilding Discourses in Various Spirits. Soren Kierkegaard. Ed. by Edna H. Hong. Tr. by Howard V. Hong & Edna H. Hong. LC 92-33248. (Kierkegaard's Writings: Vol. XV). 490p. (C). 1993. text ed. 47.50 (*0-691-03274-2*) Princeton U Pr.

UPC Coupon Code Guidelines Manual. 1994. 30.00 (*0-318-39847-8*) Uniform Code.

UPC Data Communications Guidelines for General Merchandise & Apparel. 1995. 30.00 (*0-318-50026-4*) Uniform Code.

UPC Film Master Verification Manual. 1991. 50.00 (*0-318-39845-1*) Uniform Code.

UPC Guidelines Manual. 1994. 30.00 (*0-318-39843-5*) Uniform Code.

UPC Implementation Guide. 1991. 30.00 (*0-614-15094-9*) Uniform Code.

UPC Industrial & Commercial Guidelines. 1995. reprint ed. 30.00 (*0-318-39848-6*) Uniform Code.

UPC Marking Guidelines for General Merchandise & Apparel. 1989. 30.00 (*0-318-50027-2*) Uniform Code.

UPC Symbol Location Guidelines Manual. 1992. 30.00 (*0-318-39844-3*) Uniform Code.

UPC Symbol Specification Manual. 1995. reprint ed. 30.00 (*0-318-39842-7*) Uniform Code.

Upcoming Changes: Prophecy & Pragmatism for the Late Nineties. expanded rev. ed. Joya Pope. (Michael Book Ser.). 280p. 1995. pap. 13.95 (*0-942531-38-8*) Emerald Wave.

UPCO's Review of Biology. 2nd ed. Sylvan Alcabes. (Upco's Science Ser.). (Illus.). 288p. (YA). (gr. 9-12). 1988. pap. text ed. 3.00 (*0-937323-05-5*) United Pub Co.

UPCO's Review of Biology: UPCO's Review of Chemistry. UPCO's Review of Biology Staff & Sylvan Alcabes. Ed. by UPCO's Review of Chemistry Staff & Robert M. Capie. Tr. by Freelance Editors Staff. (UPCO's Review Ser.). (Orig.). 1986. pap. text ed. 3.00 (*0-937323-00-4*); pap. text ed. 3.00 (*0-937323-01-2*) United Pub Co.

UPCO's Review of Chemistry. 2nd rev. ed. (Upco's Science Ser.). 256p. 1988. pap. text ed. 3.00 (*0-937323-04-7*) United Pub Co.

UPCO's Review of Comprehensive English. G. A. Kratzenberg & J. D. Vine. (Illus.). 360p. (Orig.). 1991. pap. text ed. 4.95 (*0-937323-09-8*) United Pub Co.

UPCO's Review of Earth Science. Robert B. Sigda. Ed. by Freelance Staff. (UPCO's Review Ser.). 1987. pap. text ed. 3.00 (*0-937323-03-9*) United Pub Co.

UPCO's Review of Physics. Herbert H. Gottlieb. Ed. by Freelance Staff. (UPCO's Review Ser.). 1986. pap. text ed. 3.00 (*0-937323-02-0*) United Pub Co.

Upcountry. Robert Kimber. 180p. 1991. 18.95 (*1-55821-121-7*) Lyons & Burford.

Updata Index to U. S. Department of Agriculture Handbooks, No. 1-540. Ed. by Sara K. Ferguson & Herbert Sclar. 80p. 1981. lib. bdg. 50.00 (*0-9607840-0-4*) Updata Pubns.

Update: Launching the Clinton Administration. Greenberg & Page. (C). 1993. pap. text ed. 7.00 (*0-06-502259-9*) Addison-Wesley Educ.

Update: Pulmonary Diseases & Disorders. 2nd ed. Ed. by Alfred P. Fishman. 512p. 1991. text ed. 95.00 (*0-07-021147-7*) McGraw-Hill HPD.

Update - Belgium. rev. ed. Marvina A. Shilling. LC 88-45505. (Country Orientation Ser.). 118p. 1989. pap. text ed. 9.95 (*0-933662-74-2*) Intercult Pr.

Update - Hong Kong. rev. ed. Martin F. Bennett. LC 92-9174. (Country Orientation Ser.). 178p. (Orig.). 1992. pap. text ed. 9.95 (*1-877864-02-1*) Intercult Pr.

Update - Japan. rev. ed. Aaron R. Hoopes. LC 92-7343. (Country Orientation Ser.). 174p. 1992. pap. text ed. 9.95 (*0-933662-99-8*) Intercult Pr.

Update - Saudi Arabia. rev. ed. Joy McGregor & Margaret K. Nydell. LC 90-83788. (Country Orientation Ser.). 192p. 1990. pap. text ed. 9.95 (*0-933662-90-4*) Intercult Pr.

***Update for the MRCP.** Thomasin C. Andrews. LC 96-30950. 1996. write for info. (*0-443-05589-0*) Churchill.

Update Guide for Autocad R13. 2nd abr. ed. Sham L. Tickoo. 128p. 1995. pap. 24.95 (*0-8273-7433-X*) Delmar.

Update in Critical Care Medicine: Management of the Critical Care Patient. Pierre Casthely et al. LC 89-91693. (Illus.). 200p. (Orig.). 1989. 59.00 (*0-9623083-0-7*) P A Castheley.

Update in Duplex, Power, & Color Flow Imaging Course Syllabus. Date not set. 54.00 (*0-614-14620-8*) Am Inst Ultrasound.

Update in Intensive Care & Emergency Medicine. Ed. by J. L. Vincent. (Anaesthesiology & Intensive Care Medicine Ser.: Vol. 178). (Illus.). xiv, 304p. 1985. 70.95 (*0-387-15261-X*) Spr-Verlag.

Update in Intensive Care & Emergency Medicine, 1986. J. L. Vincent. 588p. 1986. 79.95 (*0-387-16508-8*) Spr-Verlag.

Update in Intensive Care, Vol. 8, 1989. Ed. by J. L. Vincent. (Illus.). xx, 636p. 1989. 112.00 (*0-387-50879-1*) Spr-Verlag.

***Update in Stroke Prevention: Problems of the Stroke Recurrence: Sanofi Winthrop Symposium to the 3rd World Stroke Congress & the 5th European Stroke Conference, Munich, September 1996.** Ed. by J. Bogousslavsky & J. D. Easton. (Journal Ser.: Vol. 7, Supplement 1, 1997). (Illus.). iv, 28p. 1997. pap. 21.75 (*3-8055-6462-7*) S Karger.

Update Map Co. Dale Prevost. 102p. reprint ed. spiral bd. 18.00 (*0-685-29952-X*) Update Map.

***Update on Adolescent Gynecology & Endocrinology: Basic & Clinical Aspects.** Ed. by George Creatsas et al. LC 97-13702. 1997. 140.00 (*1-57331-038-7*) NY Acad Sci.

Update on Adult Learning Theory. Ed. by Sharan B. Merriam. LC 85-644750. (New Directions for Adult & Continuing Education Ser.: No. 57). 116p. (Orig.). 1993. pap. 19.00 (*1-55542-684-0*) Jossey-Bass.

Update on Childhood Asthma. Ed. by M. H. Schoni & R. Kraemer. LC 93-12413. vii, 221p. 1993. 81.50 (*0-8176-2867-3*, Pub. by Birkhauser Vlg SZ) Birkhauser.

Update on El Salvador: The Human Rights Crisis Continues in the Wake of the FMLN Offensive. Ed. by Human Rights Watch Staff. 94p. (Orig.). 1989. pap. 7.00 (*1-56432-005-7*) Hum Rts Watch.

Update on General Medicine: Section Ten. (Basic & Clinical Science Course (1989-90) Ser.). 210p. (C). 1989. pap. text ed. 45.00 (*0-685-26054-2*) Am Acad Ophthal.

Update on Hemostasis. David H. Boldt. (Contemporary Management in Internal Medicine Ser.: Vol. 1, No. 2). (Illus.). 240p. 1990. text ed. 35.00 (*0-443-08823-3*) Churchill.

***Update on Hepatobiliary Diseases 1996.** Ed. by S. K. Lam. (Falk Symposium Ser.). 336p. (C). 1997. lib. bdg. 150.00 (*0-7923-8715-5*) Kluwer Ac.

Update on Hormonal Treatment in the Menopause. Ed. by M. L'Hermite. (Progress in Reproductive Biology & Medicine Ser.: Vol. 13). (Illus.). viii, 108p. 1989. 78.50 (*3-8055-4904-0*) S Karger.

Update on Low-Level Waste Compact Activities. (State Legislative Reports: Vol. 15, No. 17). 26p. 1990. 5.00 (*1-55516-273-8*, 7302-1517) Natl Conf State Legis.

Update on Modern Inhalation Anesthetics. Giorgio Torri. Ed. by Giorgio Damia. 208p. pap. text ed. 25.00 (*0-685-30429-9*) Worldwide Medical Comns.

Update on Non-Narcotic Analgesic Research: Fiuggi, Italy, October 2-3, 1992. Ed. by Giuseppe Nappi & W. D. Gerber. LC 93-11312. 1993. write for info. (*0-8176-2917-3*) Birkhauser.

Update on Strabismus & Pediatric Ophthalmology: Proceedings of the June, 1994 Joint ISA & AAPO&S Meeting, Vancouver, Canada. Ed. by Gunnar Lennerstrand & American Association for Pediatric Ophthalmology & Strabismus Staff. LC 94-46587. 752p. 1995. 199.95 (*0-8493-8961-5*, 8961) CRC Pr.

Update One - Federal Fisheries Management: A Guidebook to the Magnuson Fishery Conservation & Management Act. rev. ed. Ed. by Keith Bartholomew & Samantha McCarthy. 1987. reprint ed. pap. 2.00 (*0-945216-01-7*) U OR Ocean & Law Ctr.

Update, Set One, 1981. New York Times Staff. (Great Contemporary Issues Ser.). 55.95 (*0-405-13941-1*) Ayer.

Update, Set Two, 1980. New York Times Staff. (Great Contemporary Issues Ser.). 1980. 38.95 (*0-405-13781-8*) Ayer.

***Update to Accompany Abnormal Psychology & Modern Life: 1998 Update.** 10th ed. Carson. (C). 1998. student ed., pap. text ed. write for info. (*0-321-01731-5*) Addison-Wesley Educ.

Update to Glaucoma, Ocular Blood Flow & Drug Treatment. Ed. by S. M. Drance. LC 95-17698. (Illus.). 144p. 1995. text ed. 47.00 (*90-6299-124-6*, Pub. by Kugler NE) Kugler Pubns.

Update to Joint Commission Hospital Accreditation Standards: Supplement to the Elements of Quality in Pharmaceutical Care. Charles P. Coe. (Orig.). 1994. pap. text ed. 35.00 (*1-879907-45-3*) Am Soc Hlth-Syst.

Update to Law of Public Communication. 4th ed. Kent R. Middleton. (C). 1997. pap. text ed. write for info. (*0-8013-1737-1*) Addison-Wesley.

Update to Maine & Missouri Reports on Alternative Regulation Plans in Telecommunications. 95p. 1993. 20.00 (*0-317-05550-X*) NARUC.

Update to Redbook on Transport, No. 1. 2nd ed. L. Bierlein. (Industrial Health & Safety Ser.). 1990. text ed. write for info. (*0-442-20576-7*) Van Nos Reinhold.

Update to Redbook on Transport, No. 2. 2nd ed. L. Bierlein. (Industrial Health & Safety Ser.). 1990. text ed. write for info. (*0-442-20577-5*) Van Nos Reinhold.

Update 1980. Ed. by Arleen Kaylin & Douglas J. Bowen. LC 79-27511. (Great Contemporary Issues Ser.). (Illus.). 1980. write for info. (*0-405-13086-4*) Ayer.

Update 1991. Ed. by J. L. Vincent. (Update in Intensive Care & Emergency Medicine Ser.: Vol. 14). (Illus.). 608p. 1991. 130.00 (*0-387-53672-8*) Spr-Verlag.

Update 1995: White Columns Annual Catalogue. Ed. by Jenny Laden & Elaine Tin Nyo. 56p. (Orig.). 1995. pap. 15.00 (*0-9648468-0-2*) White Columns.

***Update '95.** 641p. 1995. 30.00 (*0-614-26751-X*, 1076) NYS Bar.

***Update '95.** 641p. 1995. 175.00 incl. vhs (*0-614-26752-8*, 30766) NYS Bar.

Updated & Annotated Check List of the Vascular Plants of the Galapagos Islands. annot. ed. J. E. Lawesson et al. Ed. by Benjamin Ollgaard. (Reports from the Botanical Institute, University of Aarhus: No. 16). 74p. (C). 1987. pap. 12.95 (*87-87600-23-4*, Pub. by Aarhus Univ Pr DK) David Brown.

Updated ENT. 3rd ed. G. G. Browning. (Illus.). 184p. 1994. pap. text ed. 30.00 (*0-7506-1921-X*) Buttrwrth-Heinemann.

Updated General Chemistry. Joseph Topping. 1995. write for info. (*0-7167-2516-9*) W H Freeman.

Updated Illustrations of Management's Discussion & Analysis of Financial Condition & Results of Operations: A Survey of the Application of Recently Amended Rules 14a-3 & 14c-3 of the Securities & Exchange Act of 1934 in Annual Reports to Shareholders. American Institute of Certified Public Accountants Staff. Ed. by Hortense Goodman & Leonard Lorensen. (Financial Report Survey Ser.: No. 26). 93p. reprint ed. pap. 26.60 (*0-7837-3734-3*, 2043400) Bks Demand.

Updated Illustrations of Reporting Accounting Changes: A Survey of the Application of APB Opinion No. 20, As Amended. fac. ed. Hal G. Clark & Leonard Lorensen. LC 88-137081. (Financial Report Survey Ser.: No. 36). 92p. 1987. reprint ed. pap. 26.30 (*0-7837-8223-3*, 2047983) Bks Demand.

Updated Poverty Tables for New York City with March 1994 Current Population Survey Estimates. Terry J. Rosenberg. 28p. 1995. 5.00 (*0-88156-170-3*) Comm Serv Soc NY.

Updated Price Guide to Elvis Collectibles. Rosalind Cranor & Steve Templeton. 48p. 1992. pap. 4.95 (*0-932807-81-X*) Overmountain Pr.

Updated Realistic Rock Drum Method. Carmine Appice. (Illus.). 76p. (Orig.). 1979. pap. 7.95 (*0-89705-012-6*) Almo Pubns.

Updated X-Rated Mother Goose, Humorous. Richard M. Greene, Jr. (Illus.). 1990. pap. 4.95 (*0-934487-57-X*) R M Greene.

Updates in Colo-Proctology. Ed. by J. C. Givel et al. LC 92-49863. 210p. 1993. 158.00 (*0-387-55327-4*) Spr-Verlag.

***Updates on Clostridium Difficile.** Ed. by J. P. Rambaud & J. T. LaMont. (Illus.). 145p. 1996. 80.00 (*2-287-59639-9*, Pub. by Spr France FR) Spr-Verlag.

Updates on Human Immuno-Deficiency Virus Which Causes the A.I.D.S. Disease & the Third World. Michael Akpan & Juliana Akpan. 88p. (Orig.). 1993. pap. 8.95 (*1-56411-048-6*) Untd Bros & Sis.

***Updating Ergonomics.** Ulrich Burandt. 1996. pap. text ed. 29.00 (*3-931126-05-6*, Pub. by Die Gestalten GW) Consort Bk Sales.

Updating of Data Concerning Impact of Certain Dangerous Substances Aquatic Environment. European Communities Staff. 460p. 1994. pap. 95.00 (*92-826-7138-0*, CR-81-93-648ENC, Pub. by Europ Com UK) Bernan Associates.

Updating of Subsurface Samplings of Soils & Rocks & Their Insitu Testing. Ed. by Surendra K. Saxena. LC 85-70351. 516p. 1985. pap. 25.00 (*0-939204-25-8*, 82-04) Eng Found.

Updating Standard Cost Systems. Carole B. Cheatham & Leon R. Cheatham. LC 92-34376. 256p. 1993. text ed. 59.95 (*0-89930-716-7*, CUC, Quorum Bks) Greenwood.

Updating Teachers for Tomorrow's Technology: A Strategy for Action. James B. Hamilton & Michael E. Wonacott. 71p. 1984. 4.95 (*0-318-22228-0*, RD242) Ctr Educ Trng Employ.

Updating Teachers for Tomorrow's Technology: Programs & Practices. James B. Hamilton & Michael E. Wonacott. 66p. 1983. 5.75 (*0-318-22227-2*, RD241) Ctr Educ Trng Employ.

Updating the Core Psychology Course: Integrating Gender into the Curriculum. Toby R. Silverman-Dresner. (American University Studies: Psychology: Ser. VIII, Vol. 16). 115p. (C). 1989. text ed. 24.95 (*0-8204-1098-5*) P Lang Pubng.

***Updating the Literary West: Western Literature Association.** Thomas J. Lyon et al. LC 97-9120. 1024p. 1997. 79.50 (*0-87565-175-5*) Tex Christian.

Updating Wilkinson: An Annotated Bibliography of Reference Works on Imperial China Published Since 1973. James H. Cole. LC 91-91848. viii, 111p. (Orig.). (C). 1991. pap. text ed. 12.00 (*0-9629122-0-4*) J H Cole.

Updike & the Patriachal Dilemma: Masculinity in the Rabbit Novels. Mary O'Connell. LC 94-39038. 288p. (C). 1995. 34.95 (*0-8093-1949-7*) S Ill U Pr.

Updike's Novels: Thorns Spell a Word. Jeff H. Campbell. 250p. 1987. 17.50 (*0-915323-02-8*) Midwestern St U Pr.

Updike's Version: Rewriting "The Scarlet Letter" James A. Schiff. 176p. 1992. text ed. 24.95 (*0-8262-0871-1*) U of Mo Pr.

Upgrade: The High-Tech Road to School Success. Claudine G. Wirths & Mary Bowman-Kruhm. LC 94-33802. 132p. (Orig.). (J). (gr. 6-9). 1995. pap. 11.95 (*0-89106-069-3*, 7191) Davies-Black.

Upgrade & Maintain Your PC. James Karney. 815p. 1993. pap. 34.95 (*1-55828-294-7*) MIS Press.

Upgrade & Maintain Your PC. 2nd ed. James Karney. 832p. 1996. pap. 39.95 incl. cd-rom (*1-55828-460-5*) MIS Press.

***Upgrade & Repair Your PC on a Shoestring.** Wayne N. Kawamoto. LC 96-35964. 400p. 1996. 29.99 (*1-56604-529-0*) Ventana Communs.

Upgrade or Repair Your PC. 4th ed. Aubrey Pilgrim. LC 94-23468. 1995. pap. text ed. 26.95 (*0-07-050114-9*) McGraw-Hill Prof.

***Upgrade or Repair Your PC & Save a Bundle.** Aubrey Pilgrim. (McGraw Hill Save a Bundle Ser.). 1997. pap. text ed. 34.95 incl. cd-rom (*0-07-913668-0*) McGraw.

Upgrade or Repair Your PC & Save a Bundle. 3rd ed. Aubrey Pilgrim. LC 92-46786. 245p. 1993. 29.95 (*0-8306-4215-3*, Windcrest); pap. 19.95 (*0-8306-4214-5*, Windcrest) TAB Bks.

Upgrade Your Computer Printer & Save a Bundle. Horace W. LaBadie, Jr. (Illus.). 288p. 1992. 29.95 (*0-8306-3954-3*, 4144, Windcrest); pap. 19.95 (*0-8306-3955-1*, 4144, Windcrest) TAB Bks.

Upgrade Your IBM Compatible & Save a Bundle. Aubrey Pilgrim. (Illus.). 240p. 1990. 26.95 (*0-8306-8468-9*, 3468, Windcrest); pap. 16.95 (*0-8306-3468-1*, Windcrest) TAB Bks.

Upgrade Your IBM Compatible & Save a Bundle. 2nd ed. Aubrey Pilgrim. (Illus.). 272p. 1991. 28.95 (*0-8306-8828-5*, 3828, Windcrest); pap. 19.95 (*0-8306-3828-8*, Windcrest) TAB Bks.

Upgrade Your Italian: A Review Grammar. Gifford P. Orwen. 1983. pap. 12.95 (*0-913298-12-3*) S F Vanni.

***Upgrade Your Job: How to Market Your Services Profitably.** James J. Rago. 116p. 1996. wbk. ed. 34.95 (*0-9653992-0-6*) Wrk Smart Pr.

Upgrade Your Macintosh & Save a Bundle. Bob Brant. (Illus.). 352p. 1991. 28.95 (*0-8306-7770-4*, 3770, Windcrest); pap. 21.95 (*0-8306-3770-2*, Windcrest) TAB Bks.

Upgrade Your Own PC. Linda Rohrbough. 1996. pap. 29.99 (*1-56884-831-5*) IDG Bks.

***Upgrade Your PC in a Weekend.** Elaine Marmel. 400p. 1997. per. 19.99 (*0-7615-1138-5*) Prima Pub.

Upgraded Commodities Compete with Engineering Resins. BCC Staff. 126p. 1989. 1,950.00 (*0-89336-691-9*, P-208) BCC.

Upgrading & Fixing Macs for Dummies. Kearney Rietmann. 384p. 1994. pap. 19.95 (*1-56884-189-2*) IDG Bks.

Upgrading & Fixing Macs for Dummies. 2nd ed. Kearney Rietmann. 1996. pap. 19.99 (*1-56884-615-0*) IDG Bks.

Upgrading & Fixing PCs for Dummies. Andy Rathbone. (Illus.). 356p. 1993. pap. 19.95 (*1-56884-002-0*) IDG Bks.

Upgrading & Fixing PCs for Dummies. 2nd ed. Andy Rathbone. 384p. 1995. pap. 19.99 (*1-56884-903-6*) IDG Bks.

***Upgrading & Fixing PCs for Dummies.** 3rd ed. Andy Rathbone. 384p. 1997. pap. 19.99 (*0-7645-0129-1*, Dummies Tech) IDG Bks.

Upgrading & Fixing PCs for Dummies. 4th ed. Andy Rathbone. 1996. pap. 19.99 (*1-56884-643-6*) IDG Bks.

***Upgrading & Maintaining Your PC.** 6th ed. H. Veddeler & U. Schueller. LC 97-10465. (Illus.). 850p. 1997. 44.95 incl. cd-rom (*1-55755-329-7*) Abacus MI.

Upgrading & Maintaining Your PC w/CD ROM. H. Veddeler & U. Schueller. 1995. 34.95 incl. cd-rom (*1-55755-300-9*) Abacus MI.

Upgrading & Migrating to Sybase Sol Server 11. Michael Gurspan. (ITCP-US Computer Science Ser.). (Illus.). 350p. 1996. pap. 39.95 (*1-85032-861-7*) ITCP.

Upgrading & Refurbishing the Older Fiberglass Sailboat. William D. Booth. LC 84-46109. (Illus.). 287p. 1985. 24.50 (*0-87033-335-6*) Cornell Maritime.

Upgrading & Repairing Macs 2D. 750p. 1995. 35.00 (*1-56830-249-5*) Hayden.

Upgrading & Repairing Networks. Adam Engst et al. (Illus.). 1128p. (Orig.). 1996. 59.99 (*0-7897-0181-2*) Que.

Upgrading & Repairing P. C.'s. 5th ed. Scott Mueller. (Illus.). 1394p. (Orig.). 1995. pap. 49.99 (*0-7897-0321-1*) Que.

***Upgrading & Repairing PCs.** 6th ed. 1996. 90.00 (*1-57576-695-7*) Sams.

Upgrading & Repairing PCs. 6th ed. Scott Mueller. 1464p. 1996. 49.99 (*0-7897-0825-6*) Mac Comp Pub.

***Upgrading & Repairing PCs.** 6th ed. Scott Mueller. 1996. 65.00 incl. cd-rom (*0-7897-1053-6*) Que.

***Upgrading & Repairing PCs.** 6th ed. Que Education & Training Staff. 1997. pap. text ed. 39.99 incl. disk (*1-57576-697-3*) Que Educ & Trng.

***Upgrading & Repairing PCS.** 6th ed. Que Education & Training Staff. 1997. pap. text ed. 30.00 (*1-57576-687-6*) Que Educ & Trng.

***Upgrading & Repairing PCs.** 8th ed. Scott Mueller. 1997. 49.99 (*0-7897-1295-4*) Macmillan.

Upgrading & Repairing PCs: Acad Edition. 5th ed. Que Education & Training Staff. 1996. pap. text ed. 72.00 (*1-57576-063-0*) Que Educ & Trng.

Upgrading & Trouble Shooting Your PC. Steve Beyer. Ed. by Kevin C. Hanson. (Illus.). (Orig.). 1990. pap. text ed. write for info. (*0-929978-27-7*) M-USA Busn Systs.

Upgrading Blue Collar & Service Workers. Charles Brecher. LC 79-186512. (Policy Studies in Employment & Welfare: No. 12). 127p. reprint ed. pap. 36.20 (*0-317-09670-2*, 2020494) Bks Demand.

Upgrading Coal Liquids. Ed. by Richard F. Sullivan. LC 81-1277. (ACS Symposium Ser.: No. 156). 1981. 31.95 (*0-8412-0629-5*) Am Chemical.

***Upgrading Coal Liquids: Based on a Symposium.** Ed. by Richard F. Sullivan. LC 81-1277. (ACS Symposium Ser.: Vol. 156). 287p. 1981. reprint ed. pap. 81.80 (*0-608-03041-4*, 2063494) Bks Demand.

Upgrading Existing or Designing New Drinking Water Treatment Facilities. James E. Smith et al. LC 90-23205. (Pollution Technology Review Ser.: No. 198). (Illus.). 384p. 1991. 62.00 (*0-8155-1262-7*) Noyes.

Upgrading, Maintaining, & Servicing IBM PC's & Compatibles. Julian V. Moss. Ed. by Lance A. Leventhal. LC 92-24227. (Lance A. Leventhal Microtrend Ser.). 400p. (Orig.). 1992. pap. 29.95 (*0-915391-70-8*, Microtrend) Slawson Comm.

Upgrading Netware Problems & Solutions. Michael F. Hordeski. 1995. pap. 36.00 (*0-13-625112-9*) P-H.

Upgrading of Wastewater Treatment Plants 1993. Hegemann. (Water Science & Technology Ser.: 29). 292p. 1995. pap. 135.00 (*0-08-042546-1*, Pergamon Pr) Elsevier.

***Upgrading PCs Illustrated.** Jim Boyce. 744p. 1997. 34.99 (*0-7897-0986-4*) Mac Comp Pub.

Upgrading Petroleum Residues & Heavy Oils. Murray R. Gray. LC 94-803. (Chemical Industries Ser.: Vol. 56). 368p. 1994. 150.00 (*0-8247-9211-4*) Dekker.

Upgrading Residues & By-Products for Animals. J. T. Huber. 144p. 1981. 86.00 (*0-8493-5445-5*, SF99, CRC Reprint) Franklin.

Upgrading Textile Printing Equipment see Pocket Printer Series

Upgrading the IBM PC Family 8088 to 486. Michael F. Hordeski. 384p. 1993. text ed. 34.00 (*0-13-948217-2*) P-H.

Upgrading the Microsoft Windows 95 Step by Step. Catapult, Inc., Staff. (Step by Step Ser.). 224p. 1995. pap. 19.95 (*1-55615-816-5*) Microsoft.

Upgrading to AutoCAD 13. Randy Maxey. (Illus.). 400p. (Orig.). 1995. pap. 30.00 (*1-56205-249-7*) New Riders Pub.

Upgrading to DOS 6.2. Weber Knox. (C). 1994. pap. 21.95 (*0-929704-23-1*) Weber Systems.

Upgrading to Excel 5.0 for Windows. Randall Farrar & Bethany Sunny. (Quicksteps to Learning Ser.). 162p. 1994. spiral bd. 22.95 (*1-56951-026-1*) Sftware Trng.

Upgrading to FORTRAN 90. Cooper Redwine. LC 95-12917. (Illus.). 416p. 1995. 44.95 (*0-387-97995-6*) Spr-Verlag.

Upgrading to MS-DOS 6. 1998. 14.95 (*1-56529-264-2*) Que.

Upgrading to Windows 95: Special Edition. deluxe ed. Sharon Crawford & Charlie Russel. LC 95-69364. 496p. 1995. 22.99 (*0-7821-1703-1*) Sybex.

Upgrading to Word 6.0 for Windows. Bethany Sunny. (Quicksteps to Learning Ser.). 162p. 1994. spiral bd. 22.95 (*1-56951-025-3*) Sftware Trng.

Upgrading Wastewater Treatment Plants. Ed. by Glen T. Daigger & John A. Buttz. LC 92-53518. (Water Quality Management Library: Vol. 2). 225p. 1992. text ed. 89.95 (*0-87762-880-7*) Technomic.

Upgrading Wastewater Treatment Plants: Proceedings of the First International Specialized Conference on Upgrading Wastewater Treatment Plants Held in Munich, FRG, September 1989. Ed. by W. Hegemann et al. (Water Science & Technology Ser.: No. 22). (Illus.). 334p. 1990. pap. 155.00 (*0-08-040777-3*, Pergamon Pr) Elsevier.

Upgrading Your College Reading: Study Skills. Harold Newman. 108p. (Orig.). (C). 1984. pap. 15.00 (*0-9613577-0-3*) Prestige Educ.

Upgrading Your PC to Multimedia. Que Development Group Staff & Thompson. (Illus.). 368p. (Orig.). 1994. 24.99 (*1-56529-937-X*) Que.

Upgrading Your 486: Buying & Replacing with Confidence. Arnie Lee. 1997. pap. text ed. 24.95 (*1-55755-323-8*) Abacus MI.

Upham Genealogy: The Descendants of John Upham of Massachusetts, Who Came from England in 1635 & Lived in Weymouth & Malden. F. K. Upham. 573p. 1989. reprint ed. pap. 85.00 (*0-8328-1193-9*); reprint ed. lib. bdg. 93.00 (*0-8328-1192-0*) Higginson Bk Co.

Upham Hotel: Celebrating 125 Years of Santa Barbara Hospitality. Laura K. Fraser. 48p. 1996. pap. 7.95 (*0-9652847-0-0*) Vintage Publng.

Upheaval Against the Plan: Eastern Europe on the Eve of the Storm. Ed. by Peter R. Weilemann & Georg Brunner. 208p. 1991. 19.95 (*0-85496-743-5*) Berg Pubs.

Upheaval in the Quiet Zone: A History of Hospital Workers' Union, Local 1199. Leon Fink & Brian Greenberg. LC 88-20743. (Working Class in American History Ser.). (Illus.). 320p. 1989. pap. text ed. 11.95 (*0-252-06047-4*) U of Ill Pr.

Upheavals. Ed. by Dan Garrett. (Drama Workshop Plays Ser.). (Illus.). 96p. (Orig.). 1990. pap. 15.00 (*0-333-36057-5*, Pub. by Macmillan Ed UK) Players Pr.

Uphill All The Way. O. A. Battista. 1993. 24.95 (*0-915074-14-1*) Knowledge Bk Pubs.

***Uphill & into the Wind.** Willard Helmuth. 189p. (YA). (gr. 6 up). 1996. pap. 7.99 (*0-88092-322-9*); lib. bdg. 19.99 (*0-88092-323-7*) Royal Fireworks.

Uphill Both Ways. Marion Merritt. LC 85-13349. (Illus.). 100p. 1985. pap. 6.95 (*0-916897-05-2*) Andrew Mtn Pr.

Uphill Both Ways: Hiking Colorado's High Country. Robert L. Brown. LC 73-83111. (Illus.). 1976. pap. 7.95 (*0-87004-249-1*) Caxton.

Uphill Climb. Dave Sargent. 344p. (YA). 1992. pap. write for info. (*1-56763-001-4*); lib. bdg. write for info. (*1-56763-000-6*) Ozark Pub.

Uphill Home. James Hayford. LC 92-81709. 80p. (Orig.). 1992. pap. 9.95 (*0-933050-97-6*) New Eng Pr VT.

Uphill View. Jere Knight. 39p. (Orig.). pap. 5.00 (*0-9625348-5-4*) P Goodrich.

Uphill with the Ski Troups. Oley Kohlman. 144p. 1995. per. 10.95 (*0-9648705-0-9*) O Kohlman.

***Upholding Mystery: An Anthology of Contemporary Christian Poetry.** Ed. by David Impastato. 288p. 1996. 25.00 (*0-19-510400-5*) OUP.

Upholding the Common Life: The Community of Mirabai. Parita Mukta. (Illus.). 272p. 1995. 28.00 (*0-19-563115-3*) OUP.

***Upholsterers & Their Work in England: 1530-1840.** Geoffrey W. Beard. LC 96-39874. (Bard Studies in the Decorative Arts Ser.). 1997. write for info. (*0-300-07135-3*) Yale U Pr.

Upholsterer's Pocket Reference Book: Materials, Measurements, Calculations. David James. (Illus.). 192p. 1995. pap. 9.95 (*0-946819-71-8*, Pub. by Guild Mstr Craftsman UK) Sterling.

Upholstering. 3rd ed. James E. Brumbaugh. (Illus.). 416p. 1992. 30.00 (*0-02-517862-8*) Macmillan.

Upholstering Methods. Fred W. Zimmerman. 192p. 1992. 26.60 (*0-87006-959-4*) Goodheart.

***Upholstery.** LC 96-41052. (For Your Home Ser.). 1997. write for info. (*1-56799-331-1*) M Friedman Pub Grp Inc.

Upholstery: A Complete Course. David James. (Illus.). 296p. 1993. pap. 19.95 (*0-946819-19-X*, Pub. by Guild Mstr Craftsman UK) Sterling.

Upholstery: A Practical Guide. David Broan & Freda Broan. (Illus.). 119p. 1987. 13.95 (*0-900873-48-5*, Pub. by Bishopsgte Pr UK); pap. 11.95 (*0-900873-49-3*, Pub. by Bishopsgte Pr UK) Intl Spec Bk.

Upholstery: A Practical Guide. Desmond Gaston. (Illus.). 192p. 1994. 22.00 (*0-00-412912-1*, Pub. by HarpC UK) HarpC.

***Upholstery Basics.** Cowles Creative Publishing Staff. LC 97-14879. (Singer Sewing Reference Library). (Illus.). 128p. 1997. write for info. (*0-86573-318-X*) Cowles Creative.

***Upholstery Basics.** Cowles Creative Publishing Staff. LC 97-14879. (Singer Sewing Reference Library). (Illus.). 128p. 1997. pap. write for info. (*0-86573-319-8*) Cowles Creative.

Upholstery in America & Europe. Ed. by Edward S. Cooke, Jr. (Illus.). 1987. 35.00 (*0-393-02469-5*) Norton.

***Upholstery Made Easy.** Herbert Bast. 200p. 1997. reprint ed. pap. 19.95 (*1-57002-059-0*) Univ Publng Hse.

***Upholstery Restoration.** David James. 1997. pap. text ed. 17.95 (*1-86108-052-2*, Pub. by Guild Mstr Craftsman UK) Sterling.

Upholstery Styles: A Design Sourcebook. Gillian Walking. (Illus.). 144p. (gr. 13). 1989. text ed. 17.95 (*0-442-23844-4*) Chapman & Hall.

Upholstery Techniques & Projects. David James. (Illus.). 256p. 1994. pap. 19.95 (*0-946819-41-6*, Pub. by Guild Mstr Craftsman UK) Sterling.

Upholstery Techniques Illustrated. W. Lloyd Gheen. (Illus.). 352p. 1986. pap. 19.95 (*0-8306-0402-2*) McGraw-Hill Prof.

Upholstery Techniques Illustrated. 2nd ed. W. Lloyd Gheen. 1994. text ed. 34.95 (*0-07-023622-4*); pap. text ed. 21.95 (*0-07-023623-2*) McGraw.

Upholstery Techniques Illustrated. 2nd ed. W. Lloyd Gheen. LC 93-44951. (Illus.). 1995. 35.00 (*0-07-236224-3*); pap. 21.95 (*0-07-236232-4*) McGraw-Hill Prof.

UPI Stylebook. UPI Editorial Staff. 1999. pap. 9.95 (*0-14-046861-7*) Viking Penguin.

***Upland Archeology in the East - A Symposium, Vol. 38, No. 1.** Contrib. by Michael B. Barber et al. (Illus.). 458p. (Orig.). 1996. pap. 22.00 (*1-884626-29-7*) Archeolog Soc.

***Upland Archeology in the East - A Symposium, Vol. 38, No. 2.** Contrib. by Michael B. Barber et al. (Illus.). 290p. (Orig.). 1996. pap. 16.00 (*1-884626-30-0*) Archeolog Soc.

***Upland Archeology in the East - A Symposium, Vol. 38, No. 3.** Contrib. by Michael B. Barber et al. (Illus.). 356p. (Orig.). 1996. pap. 20.00 (*1-884626-31-9*) Archeolog Soc.

***Upland Archeology in the East - A Symposium, Vol. 38, No. 4.** Contrib. by Michael B. Barber et al. (Illus.). 336p. (Orig.). 1996. pap. 18.00 (*1-884626-32-7*) Archeolog Soc.

***Upland Archeology in the East - A Symposium, Vol. 38, No. 5.** Contrib. by Michael B. Barber et al. (Illus.). 256p. (Orig.). 1996. pap. 14.00 (*1-884626-33-5*) Archeolog Soc.

***Upland Archeology in the East - A Symposium, Vol. 38, No. 6.** Contrib. by Michael B. Barber et al. (Illus.). 244p. (Orig.). 1996. pap. 12.00 (*1-884626-34-3*) Archeolog Soc.

***Upland Bird Art of Maynard Reece.** Illus. by Maynard Reece. LC 96-27150. 160p. 1997. 49.50 (*0-8109-3936-3*) Abrams.

Upland Britain: A Natural History. Margaret Atherden. (Illus.). 240p. (C). 1993. text ed. 27.95 (*0-7190-3494-9*, Pub. by Manchester Univ Pr UK) St Martin.

Upland Communities: Environment, Population & Social Structure in the Alps since the Sixteenth Century. Pier P. Viazzo. (Cambridge Studies in Population, Economy & Society in Past Time: No. 8). (Illus.). 340p. (C). 1989. text ed. 65.00 (*0-521-30663-9*) Cambridge U Pr.

Upland Equation: A Modern Bird Hunter's Code. Charles Fergus. LC 95-12399. 88p. 1995. 20.00 (*1-55821-363-5*) Lyons & Burford.

Upland Field & Forest Wildflowers. J. E. Underhill. 64p. pap. 4.95 (*0-88839-174-9*) Hancock House.

Upland Forests of West Virginia. Ed. by Steven L. Stephenson. 308p. (C). 1993. 28.50 (*0-87012-509-5*) McClain.

Upland Game Bird Carving. Rosalyn L. Daisey. LC 91-67015. (Illus.). 240p. 1992. text ed. 49.95 (*0-88740-349-2*) Schiffer.

Upland Game Birds. Dick Sternberg. LC 95-4066. (Hunting & Fishing Library). 128p. 1995. 19.95 (*0-86573-042-3*) Cowles Creative.

Upland Game Birds, Vol.1. (Illus.). 174p. 1982. pap. 9.95 (*0-686-47255-1*) Rolfs Gall.

Upland Game Birds: Their Breeding & Care. Leland B. Hayes. (Illus.). 360p. 1996. pap. 29.95 (*0-9633196-2-0*) L B Hayes.

Upland Game Hunter's Journal. Leisure. 1995. pap. 5.95 (*1-886558-07-8*) Paladin Wrldwide.

Upland Idyll: Images of Cazenovia, New York. Russell A. Grills. Ed. by William Strode. (Illus.). 208p. 1993. write for info. (*1-56469-019-9*) Harmony Hse Pub.

Upland Outlaws. Dave Duncan. (Handful of Men Ser.: Pt. 2). 288p. 1993. mass mkt. 5.99 (*0-345-38477-6*, Del Rey) Ballantine.

Upland Passage: A Field Dog's Education. Robert F. Jones. 1992. 17.00 (*0-374-19444-0*) FS&G.

***Upland Passage: A Field Dog's Education.** Robert F. Jones. 1997. pap. text ed. 10.00 (*0-374-52502-1*, Noonday) FS&G.

Upland Stream: Notes on the Fishing Passion. W. D. Wetherell. 1993. pap. 11.95 (*0-316-93175-6*) Little.

Uplands Haunted by the Sea. Walt Franklin. (Illus.). 90p. 1992. pap. 8.00 (*0-945251-10-6*) Great Elm.

Uplands of Dream. Edgar E. Saltus. Ed. by Charles Honce. LC 78-93776. reprint ed. 37.50 (*0-404-05550-8*) AMS Pr.

Uplift Behavior of Anchor Foundations in Soil: Proceedings of a Session Sponsored by the Geotechnical Engineering Division. Ed. by Samuel P. Clemence. 126p. 1985. 17.00 (*0-87262-496-X*) Am Soc Civil Eng.

Uplift War. David Brin. (Uplift Trilogy Ser.). 672p. 1987. mass mkt. 6.50 (*0-553-27971-8*, Bantam Classics) Bantam.

Uplift War. David Brin. 1987. 22.00 (*0-932096-44-1*) Phantasia Pr.

Uplifted Atmospheres, Borrowed Taste. Howard Halle. (Illus.). 33p. (Orig.). 1986. pap. write for info. (*0-936739-04-5*) Hallwalls Inc.

Uplifting the Race: Black Leadership, Politics, & Culture in the Twentieth Century. Kevin K. Gaines. LC 95-7956. (Illus.). 342p. (C). 1996. lib. bdg. 45.00 (*0-8078-2239-6*) U of NC Pr.

Uplifting the Race: Black Leadership, Politics, & Culture in the Twentieth Century. Kevin K. Gaines. LC 95-7956. (Illus.). 342p. (C). 1996. pap. 17.95 (*0-8078-4543-4*) U of NC Pr.

***Upon a Midnight Clear.** Deveraux. 1997. 16.00 (*0-671-01374-2*) PB.

***Upon a Mystic Tide.** Victoria Barrett. (Seascape Ser.). 1996. mass mkt. 5.99 (*0-312-96038-7*) St Martin.

Upon a Quiet Landscape: The Photographs of Frank Sadorus. Ed. by Raymond Bial & Frederick A. Schlipf. LC 83-72993. (Champaign County Historical Archives Historical Publications Ser.: No. 6). (Illus.). 155p. 1983. 18.00 (*0-9609646-1-4*) Urbana Free Lib.

Upon a Stone Altar: A History of the Island of Pohnpei to 1890. David Hanlon. LC 87-34288. (Pacific Islands Monographs: No.5). 352p. 1988. text ed. 34.00 (*0-8248-1124-0*) UH Pr.

Upon Further Reflection. B. F. Skinner. 224p. 1986. 24.80 (*0-13-938986-5*) P-H.

Upon My Husband's Death: Widows in the Literature & Histories of Medieval Europe. Louise Mirrer. (Illus.). 350p. (C). 1992. text ed. 49.50 (*0-472-10257-5*) U of Mich Pr.

Upon My Words. Alexander S. Kohanski. 1988. 29.95 (*0-8197-0553-5*); pap. 19.95 (*0-8197-0550-0*) Bloch.

***Upon Our Parting.** Christian Hawkes. 50p. (Orig.). 1997. pap. 6.50 (*1-57688-012-5*, 80125) Branch & Vine.

Upon Stormy Downs. large type ed. Cynthia S. Roberts. (Romance Suspense Ser.). 1990. 25.99 (*0-7089-2256-2*) Ulverscroft.

Upon the Buffalo: Life in the Big Buffalo Valley 1839-1922. (Illus.). 117p. Date not set. lib. bdg. write for info. (*0-9646489-2-X*) Martain Pub.

Upon the Doorposts of Thy House: Jewish People, Places, Perception, & Memory in Central Europe. Ruth E. Gruber. 320p. 1994. text ed. 24.95 (*0-471-59568-3*) Wiley.

Upon the Fields of Time: Four Minds of Man. J. R. Challacombe. LC 95-92532. 257p. (Orig.). (C). 1995. pap. 19.95 (*1-886287-23-6*) Clair Studies.

Upon the Head of the Goat: A Childhood in Hungary 1939-1944. Aranka Siegal. LC 81-12642. 214p. (YA). (gr. 7 up). 1981. 16.00 (*0-374-38059-7*) FS&G.

Upon the Head of the Goat: A Childhood in Hungary 1939-1944. Aranka Siegal. (Illus.). 192p. (YA). (gr. 9-12). 1968. pap. 3.95 (*0-451-15535-1*, Sig) NAL-Dutton.

Upon the Head of the Goat: A Childhood in Hungary 1939-1944. Aranka Siegal. 192p. 1983. pap. 2.25 (*0-451-12084-1*, Sig Vista) NAL-Dutton.

Upon the Head of the Goat: A Childhood in Hungary 1939-1944. Aranka Siegal. 224p. (YA). (gr. 7 up). 1994. pap. 4.99 (*0-14-036966-X*) Puffin Bks.

Upon the Objects to Be Attained by the Establishment of a Public Library: Report of the Trustees of the Public Library of the City of Boston, 1852. reprint ed. 3.50 (*0-686-70431-2*) Boston Public Lib.

Upon the Shoulders of Giants: The Shaping of the Modern Mind. 2nd ed. Richard Hardison. 468p. (C). 1988. pap. text ed. 32.00 (*0-8191-6738-X*); lib. bdg. 58.50 (*0-8191-6737-1*) U Pr of Amer.

Upon the Storm. Justine Davis. (Desire Ser.: No. 712). 1992. pap. 2.89 (*0-373-05712-1*, 5-05712-0) Harlequin Bks.

Upon the Tented Field. Bernard A. Olsen. LC 93-80311. (Illus.). 336p. 1993. 59.95 (*0-9638729-0-7*) Historic Proj.

Upon This Mountain. Timothy Wangusa. (African Writers Ser.). 122p. (Orig.). (C). 1989. pap. 10.95 (*0-435-90542-2*, 90542) Heinemann.

Upon This Rock. Eric Gosden. 160p. 1987. pap. 5.95 (*0-87508-186-X*, 186) Chr Lit.

Upon This Rock. Charles E. Hill. 1965. pap. 3.95 (*0-89137-207-5*) Quality Pubns.

Upon This Rock. Valentine Long. 255p. 1983. 12.00 (*0-8199-0834-7*, Frncscn Herld) Franciscan Pr.

Upon This Rock, 3 vols., 1. C. T. Davidson. 692p. 1973. 19.95 (*0-934942-16-1*) White Wing Pub.

Upon This Rock, 3 vols., 2. C. T. Davidson. 692p. 1973. 14.95 (*0-934942-17-X*) White Wing Pub.

Upon This Rock, 3 vols., 3. C. T. Davidson. 692p. 1973. 17.95 (*0-934942-18-8*) White Wing Pub.

Upon This Rock: A New History of the Trenton Diocese. James O'Neill, Jr. et al. (Illus.). 593p. 1993. 39.00 (*0-9638128-0-7*) Diocese of Trenton.

Upon This Rock: The Church, Work, Money & You. Tim Unsworth & Jean M. Unsworth. 120p. (Orig.). 1991. pap. 8.95 (*0-87946-059-8*, 125) ACTA Pubns.

Upon This Rock: The Miracles of a Black Church. Samuel G. Freedman. LC 92-53323. 384p. 1994. pap. 13.00 (*0-06-092459-4*, PL) HarpC.

Upon This Rock Cocaine Satan Builds His Church. Cynthia Jackson. 99p. 1993. text ed. 8.00 (*0-9639563-0-2*, TXU552-019) Cindy Pubns.

***Upon Waking.** Michael Davis. (Premier Ser.: Vol. 8). (Illus.). 21p. 1997. 5.00 (*0-9654421-6-0*) Mica Press.

Upon What Pretext? The Book & Literary History. Larzer Ziff. 29p. 1986. pap. 6.00 (*0-912296-81-X*) Am Antiquarian.

Upon Your Sword. Patrick S. Cauchi. (Illus.). 92p. (Orig.). 1993. pap. 8.95 (*1-878116-18-5*) JVC Bks.

Uposatha Ceremony: The Earliest Traditions & Later Developments. Jayeeta Gangopadhyay. (C). 1991. 22.50 (*81-217-0087-6*, Pub. by Bharat Vidya II) S Asia.

Uppark. (Illus.). 96p. 1995. pap. 9.95 (*0-7078-0198-2*, Pub. by Natl Trust UK) Trafalgar.

***Uppark Restored.** Christopher Rowell & John M. Robinson. (Illus.). 224p. 1997. 40.00 (*0-7078-0252-0*, Pub. by Natl Trust UK) Trafalgar.

***Upper Airways & Artificial Airways.** Gloria Kellum et al. 120p. 1997. pap. 68.00 incl. audio (*0-910329-95-8*, 0112025) Am Speech Lang Hearing.

Upper Alabama: Poems Out of Light. Ralph Hammond. 142p. (Orig.). 1993. pap. 10.00 (*0-9627960-1-8*) Clemmons Crk Pr.

Upper Arkansas River: Rapids, History & Nature Mile by Mile. Frank Staub. LC 87-27439. (Fulcrum's Guide Ser.). (Illus.). 288p. 1988. pap. 14.95 (*1-55591-021-1*) Fulcrum Pub.

Upper Atlantic: New Jersey, New York. Thomas G. Aylesworth & Virginia L. Aylesworth. LC 94-45826. (Discovering America Ser.). (J). 1995. pap. 8.95 (*0-7910-3417-8*); lib. bdg. 19.95 (*0-7910-3399-6*) Chelsea Hse.

Upper Atmosphere: Data Analysis & Interpretation. Ed. by W. Dieminger et al. LC 94-6896. 1994. write for info. (*3-540-57562-6*) Spr-Verlag.

Upper Atmosphere: Data Analysis & Interpretation. Ed. by W. Dieminger et al. LC 94-6896. (Illus.). 650p. 1996. 394.00 (*0-387-57562-6*) Spr-Verlag.

Upper Atmosphere in Motion. Ed. by C. O. Hines et al. LC 74-28234. (Geophysical Monograph Ser.: Vol. 18). (Illus.). 1027p. 1974. 29.00 (*0-87590-018-6*) Am Geophysical.

Upper Atmosphere Models & Research: Proceedings of Workshops X, XI, & of Topical Meeting of the COSPAR Interdisciplinary Scientific Commission C (Meeting C1) of the COSPAR Twenty-Seventh Plenary Meeting Held in Espoo, Finland, 18-29 July, 1988. Ed. by G. M. Keating et al. (Advances in Space Research Ser.: No. 10). (Illus.). 618p. 1989. pap. 95.00 (*0-08-040167-8*, Pergamon Pr) Elsevier.

Upper Atmosphere Research in Antarctica. Ed. by L. J. Lanzerotti & C. Park. (Antarctic Research Ser.: Vol. 29). (Illus.). 264p. 1977. 50.00 (*0-87590-141-7*) Am Geophysical.

Upper Berth. Francis M. Crawford. (Works of Francis Marion Crawford Ser.). 1990. reprint ed. lib. bdg. 79.00 (*0-7812-2546-9*) Rprt Serv.

Upper Body Workout. (Great Shapes Ser.). Date not set. pap. write for info. (*0-614-14298-9*) Personal Fitness Pub.

Upper Brandon. Robert P. Hilldrup. Ed. by Nelson D. Lankford. (Illus.). 98p. 1987. 19.95 (*0-9619387-0-6*) J River VA.

Upper Cambrian Conodonts from Sweden. Klaus J. Muller & Ingelore Hinz. (Fossils & Strata: No. 28). 153p. 1991. pap. 46.00 (*82-00-37475-0*) Scandnvan Univ Pr.

Upper Cambrian Rehbachiella & the Phylogeny of Branchiopoda & Crustacea. Dieter Walossek. (Fossils & Strata: No. 32). 202p. 1993. pap. 52.00 (*82-00-37487-4*) Scandnvan Univ Pr.

Upper Canada Trade, Eighteen Thirty-Four to Seventy-Two: A Study of the Buchanans' Business. Douglas McCalla. LC 79-323032. 239p. reprint ed. pap. 68.20 (*0-8357-8361-8*, 2034006) Bks Demand.

***Upper Cape Cod.** Cheryl J. Huban. (Twelve Short Hikes Ser.). (Illus.). 32p. 1997. pap. 4.95 (*1-57540-094-4*) Chockstone Pr.

Upper Cervical Syndrome: Chiropractic Diagnosis & Treatment. Howard Vernon. (Illus.). 272p. 1988. 62.00 (*0-683-08591-3*) Williams & Wilkins.

Upper Chehalis Dictionary. M. Dale Kinkade. LC 91-65372. (Occasional Papers in Linguistics). xv, 378p. 1991. pap. 20.00 (*1-879763-07-9*) U MT UMOPL.

Upper Chesapeake Bay Decoys & Their Makers. David Hagan & Joan Hagan. LC 90-60738. (Illus.). 216p. 1990. 59.95 (*0-88740-258-5*) Schiffer.

Upper Circle: A Theatrical Chronicle. large type ed. Kitty Black. 416p. 1993. 23.95 (*1-85695-020-4*, Pub. by ISIS UK) Transaction Pubs.

Upper Colorado Series see University of Utah Anthropological Papers

Upper Continental Margin Sedimentation off Brazil. Ed. by John D. Milliman & C. P. Summerhays. (Contributions to Sedimentology Monograph: No. 4). (Illus.). 175p. 1975. pap. text ed. 55.25 (*3-510-57004-9*) Lubrecht & Cramer.

Upper Cretaceous & Cenozoic Geology of the Southeastern Atlantic Coastal Plain, N. T172. Ed. by Harris. (IGC Field Trip Guidebooks Ser.). 104p. 1989. 28.00 (*0-87590-617-6*) Am Geophysical.

Upper Cretaceous & Paleogene Biostratigraphy & Lithostratigraphy of the Eastern Gulf Coastal Plain, No. T372. Ed. by Mancini. (IGC Field Trip Guidebooks Ser.). 128p. 1989. 28.00 (*0-87590-561-7*) Am Geophysical.

Upper Cretaceous Depositional Systems, Southern California - Northern Baja California. Ed. by Patrick L. Abbott. (Illus.). 140p. (Orig.). 1984. pap. 5.00 (*1-878861-36-0*) Pac Section SEPM.

Upper Cretaceous Foraminifera of the Gulf Coastal Region. J. A. Cushman. 1965. reprint ed. 21.80 (*0-934454-79-5*) Lubrecht & Cramer.

Upper Cretaceous Spumellariina from the Great Valley Sequence, California Coast Ranges, No. 276 see Bulletins of American Paleontology: Vol. 63

Upper Crud Cookbook: The Fine Art of Dining Rather Than Merely Eating. Carlo DiNapoli. Ed. by R. Constantine. (Illus.). 275p. 1992. pap. 15.95 (*0-9627946-4-3*) Hawk FL.

Upper Crust: A Slice of the South. Johnson City Junior League High South Publications Staff. 323p. 1986. write for info. (*0-9616492-1-6*) Starr-Toof.

Upper Cumberland. William L. Montell. LC 93-6972. (Folklife in the South Ser.). (Illus.). 256p. 1993. pap. 16.95 (*0-87805-631-9*); text ed. 37.50 (*0-87805-630-0*) U Pr of Miss.

Upper Digestive Surgery. Taylor. 1997. text ed. write for info. (*0-7020-1434-6*) HarBrace.

Upper Egypt: Its People & Its Products. Karl B. Klunzinger. LC 76-44747. 1984. reprint ed. 62.50 (*0-404-15866-8*) AMS Pr.

Upper Egypt Chief Temples. Porter. (Topographical Bibliography of Ancient Egyptian Hieroglyphic Texts Ser.: Reliefs & Paintings, Vol. 6). 1970. 75.00 (*0-900416-30-0*, Pub. by Aris & Phillips UK) David Brown.

Upper Elementary Children Moving & Learning. Rae Pica. LC 92-43855. (Illus.). 136p. 1993. ring bd. 49.00 (*0-87322-468-X*, BPIC0468) Human Kinetics.

Upper-Elementary Meetings. (Illus.). 126p. (Orig.). 1989. pap. 13.99 (*0-931529-86-7*) Group Pub.

Upper Eocene Foraminifera of the Southeastern U. S. J. A. Cushman. 1971. reprint ed. 15.20 (*0-934454-80-9*) Lubrecht & Cramer.

Upper Extremities Orthotics. fac. ed. Miles H. Anderson. (Illus.). 476p. 1979. 66.95 (*0-398-00044-1*) C C Thomas.

***Upper Extremity Disorders: Frequency, Impact & Cost.** LC 96-53383. 1997. write for info. (*0-443-07912-9*) Churchill.

Upper Extremity in Sports Injuries. Frank W. Jobe. Ed. by Marilyn M. Pink. 650p. (C). (gr. 13). 1995. text ed. 195.00 (*0-8016-7207-4*) Mosby Yr Bk.

Upper Extremity in Sports Medicine. 2nd ed. Ed. by James A. Nicholas et al. LC 95-6355. 960p. (C). (gr. 13). 1995. text ed. 190.00 (*0-8151-6392-4*) Mosby Yr Bk.

Upper Extremity Injuries in the Athlete. Ed. by Arthur M. Pappas et al. LC 94-33757. (Illus.). 514p. 1995. 159.00 (*0-443-08836-5*) Churchill.

***Upper Extremity Neuroanatomy & Clinical Examination: A Programmed Text.** David P. Nichols. 50p. 1997. spiral bd. 24.95 (*90-5702-530-2*, Harwood Acad Pubs) Gordon & Breach.

Upper Extremity Reconstruction. Herndon. 1996. text ed. 175.00 (*0-8385-9304-6*) P-H.

***Upper Gastrointestinal Surgery.** Ed. by Michael Griffin & Stephen Raimes. (Companion Guide to Specialist Surgical Practice Ser.: Vol. 2). (Illus.). 380p. 1997. write for info. (*0-7020-2141-5*, Pub. by W B Saunders UK) Saunders.

Upper Great Lakes Best Bed & Breakfasts: Delightful Places to Stay & Great Things to do When You Get There. 3rd ed. Fodor's Travel Staff. (Bed & Breakfasts & Country Inn Ser.). 1997. pap. 17.00 (*0-679-03293-2*) Fodors Travel.

Upper Great Ouse. Wilson Ltd. Staff & Imray L. Norie. (C). 1984. 45.00 (*0-85288-114-2*, Pub. by Imray Laurie Norie & Wilson UK) St Mut.

Upper House in Revolutionary America, 1763-1788. Jackson T. Main. LC 67-20753. 323p. reprint ed. pap. 92.10 (*0-317-09462-9*, 2004974) Bks Demand.

***Upper Intermediate Matters.** Bell & Gower. 1994. student ed., pap. text ed. write for info. (*0-582-04664-5*) Addison-Wesley.

***Upper Intermediate Matters: No Key.** Bell & Gower. 1994. wbk. ed., pap. text ed. write for info. (*0-582-04666-1*, Pub. by Longman UK) Longman.

Upper Iowa University: Doc Dorman's Peacocks. Fred Breckner. LC 81-52627. (College Sports Bks.). 1981. 10.95 (*0-87397-195-7*, Strode Pubs) Circle Bk Service.

***Upper Kennebec Valley, ME.** J. Hall. (Images of America Ser.). 1997. pap. 16.99 (*0-7524-0470-9*, Arcdia) Chalford.

Upper Layer Protocols: Proceedings of the IFIP International Conference on Upper Layer Protocols, Architectures & Applications, Vancouver, B.C., Canada, 27-29 May, 1992. Ed. by Gerald G. Neufeld & Bernhard Plattner. LC 92-37889. (IFIP Transactions C: Communication Systems Ser.). 1992. pap. 152.50 (*0-444-89766-6*, North Holland) Elsevier.

Upper Layer Protocols, Architectures, & Applications: Proceedings of the IFIP TC6-WG6.5 International Working Conference on Upper Layer Protocols, Architectures, & Applications, Barcelona, Spain, 1-3 June, 1994. IFIP TC6-WG6.5 International Working Conference Staff. Ed. by Manuel Medina & Nathaniel Borenstein. (IFIP Transactions C: Communication Systems Ser.: Vol. C-25). 436p. 1994. pap. 152.50 (*0-444-82047-7*) Elsevier.

Upper Layers of Open Systems Interconnection. Ed. by Rainer W. Herbers. 1987. lib. bdg. 129.50 (*90-277-2447-4*) Kluwer Ac.

Upper Leadership Management: The Transitional Process. Dahk Knox. 95p. 1993. pap. text ed. 11.95 (*1-881116-11-5*, 018) Black Forest Pr.

Upper Limb see Physiology of the Joints

Upper Limb Deficiencies in Children. Douglas W. Lamb & Hamish Law. 152p. 1987. 100.00 (*0-316-51269-9*, Little Med Div) Little.

***Upper Limb Orthotics.** Wilton. 1997. text ed. write for info. (*0-7020-2214-4*, Bailliere-Tindall) Saunders.

Upper Limit Music: The Writing of Louis Zukofsky. Ed. by Mark Scroggins. LC 96-17168. 304p. 1997. pap. text ed. 34.95 (*0-8173-0826-1*) U of Ala Pr.

Upper Main Sequence Stars with Anomalous Abundances. Ed. by C. R. Cowley et al. 1986. lib. bdg. 184.00 (*90-277-2296-X*) Kluwer Ac.

Upper Management Related Reports & Directories. George Allen. Ed. by Nancy Bowman. (Monograph Ser.: No. 4). 30p. (C). 1993. 25.00 (*1-878350-04-8*) PMN Pub.

Upper Mantle Structure Studies by Explosion Seismology in the U. S. S. R. Vladislav Ryaboy. Ed. by Erika D. Nobel. (Illus.). 141p. (Orig.). 1989. pap. text ed. 75.00 (*1-55831-091-6*) Delphic Associates.

Upper Mesosphere & Lower Thermosphere: A Review of Experiment & Theory. Ed. by R. M. Johnson & T. L. Killeen. LC 95-9945. (Geophysical Monographs: Vol. 87). 356p. 1995. 80.00 (*0-87590-044-5*) Am Geophysical.

Upper Midwest Flies that Catch Trout & How to Fish Them. Ross A. Mueller. 112p. 1995. pap. write for info. (*0-9648047-0-0*) R Mueller.

Upper Midwest German Biographical Index. Don H. Tolzmann. 125p. (Orig.). 1993. pap. text ed. 23.00 (*1-55613-884-9*) Heritage Bk.

Upper Mississippi River History: Fact-Fiction-Legend. Ron Larson. LC 94-92055. (Illus.). 140p. 1995. 45.00 (*0-9640937-0-7*) Steamboat Pr.

Upper Mississippi River Rafting Steamboats. Edward A. Mueller. (Illus.). 350p. 1995. text ed. 44.95 (*0-8214-1113-6*) Ohio U Pr.

Upper Motor Neurons Functions & Dysfunctions. Ed. by John Eccles & M. R. Dimitrijevic. (Recent Achievements in Restorative Neurology Ser.: Vol. 1). (Illus.). xvii, 346p. 1985. 223.25 (*3-8055-4020-5*) S Karger.

Upper New England. Peter Andrews et al. LC 79-22906. (Country Inns of America Ser.). (Illus.). 96p. (Orig.). 1980. pap. 9.95 (*0-03-043711-3*) H Holt & Co.

Upper Nile Province Handbook: A Report of Peoples & Government in the Southern Sudan, 1931. Ed. by Douglas H. Johnson. (Oriental & African Archives: British Academy Ser.: No. 3). (Illus.). 504p. 1996. 90.00 (*0-19-726146-9*) OUP.

Upper Palaeolithic Age in Britain. Dorothy A. Garrod. LC 76-44722. reprint ed. 47.50 (*0-404-15926-5*) AMS Pr.

Upper Paleolithic of the Central Russian Plain. Olga Soffer. (Studies in Archaeology). 1985. text ed. 83.00 (*0-12-654270-8*) Acad Pr.

Upper Peninsula of Michigan. rev. ed. John S. Penrod. (YA). (gr. 7 up). 1988. pap. 5.00 (*0-942618-11-4*) Penrod-Hiawatha.

Upper Peninsula's Wolverine. (Copper Country Local History Ser.: Vol. 41). (Illus.). 120p. 1992. 3.00 (*0-942363-40-X*) C J Monette.

Upper Places: Nazareth, Gnadenthal & Christian's Spring. Elizabeth L. Myers. 10p. (Orig.). 1978. reprint ed. pap. text ed. 3.00 (*1-877701-04-1*) NCH&GS.

Upper Pleistocene Prehistory of Western Eurasia. Ed. by Harold L. Dibble & Anta Montet-White. (University Museum Monographs: University Museum Symposium Ser.: No. 54). 500p. 1988. text ed. 50.00 (*0-934718-53-9*) U PA Mus Pubns.

Upper Reaches of the River Medway. Imray L. Norie & Wilson, Ltd., Staff. (C). 1980. 25.00 (*0-85288-113-4*, Pub. by Imray Laurie Norie & Wilson UK) St Mut.

Upper Respiratory & Head & Neck Infections. Ed. by Gerald L. Mandell & Itzhak Brook. LC 95-1977. (Atlas of Infectious Diseases Ser.: Vol. 4). 1995. 125.00 (*0-443-07710-X*) Current Med.

Upper Room. J. C. Ryle. 1983. pap. 16.99 (*0-85151-376-X*) Banner of Truth.

***Upper Room Book of Christmas Carols.** pap. 2.00 (*0-8358-0199-3*) Upper Room Bks.

Upper Room Disciplines 1996. 392p. 1995. pap. text ed. 7.95 (*0-8358-0727-4*) Upper Room Bks.

Upper Room Disciplines 1997. 392p. 1996. pap. 7.95 (*0-8358-0747-9*) Upper Room Bks.

***Upper Room Disciplines 1998.** Ed. by Rita Collett. 384p. (Orig.). 1997. pap. 7.95 (*0-8358-0811-4*, UR811) Upper Room Bks.

***Upper Room Spiritual Classics: Series 1, 5 bks.** Incl. Longing for Holiness: Selected Writings of John Wesley. John Wesley. Ed. by Timothy K. Jones. LC 96-52167. 72p. (Orig.). 1997. pap. 4.95 (*0-8358-0827-0*, UR827); Soul's Passion for God: Selected Writings of Teresa of Avila. Ed. by Timothy K. Jones. LC 96-53279. 72p. (Orig.). 1997. pap. 4.95 (*0-8358-0828-9*, UR828); Sanctuary of the Soul: Selected Writings of Thomas Kelly. Ed. by Timothy K. Jones. LC 97-12531. 72p. (Orig.). 1997. pap. 4.95 (*0-8358-0829-7*, UR829); Hungering for God: Selected Writings of Augustine. Ed. by Timothy K. Jones. LC 97-9244. 96p. (Orig.). 1997. pap. 4.95 (*0-8358-0830-0*, UR830); Making Life a Prayer: Selections from the Writings of John Cassian. Ed. by Timothy K. Jones. LC 97-10158. 72p. (Orig.). 1997. pap. 4.95 (*0-8358-0831-9*, UR831); 23.95 (*0-8358-0832-7*) Upper Room Bks.

***Upper Room Worship Book.** 14.80 (*0-687-61245-4*) Abingdon.

Upper Room Worshipbook. Compiled by Elise S. Eslinger. 208p. (Orig.). 1985. pap. 9.95 (*0-8358-0515-8*) Upper Room Bks.

Upper Tertiary & Quaternary Depositional Systems, Central Coastal Plain, Texas--Regional Geology of the Coastal Aquifer & Potential Liquid-Waste Repositories. R. F. Solis. (Report of Investigations Ser.: RI 108). (Illus.). 89p. 1981. pap. 3.00 (*0-318-03239-2*) Bur Econ Geology.

Upper Tertiary Arcacea of the Mid-Atlantic Coastal Plain see Palaeontographica Americana: Vol. 5

Upper Thames & Vale. Mary Webb et al. LC 94-27145. (Oxfordshire Country Walks Ser.: No. 4). (Illus.). 128p. 1994. pap. 10.00 (*0-7509-0576-X*, Pub. by Sutton Pubng UK) Bks Intl VA.

Upper Thames Valley Today. Harry Knights. 80p. 1987. pap. 40.00 (*0-946163-02-2*) St Mut.

Upper Triassic Flora of Arizona. Lyman H. Daugherty. LC 41-9472. (Carnegie Institution of Washington Publication Ser.: No. 526). 150p. reprint ed. pap. 42.80 (*0-7837-5945-2*, 2045744) Bks Demand.

Upper Valley: An Illustrated Tour along the Connecticut River Before the Twentieth Century. Jerold Wikoff. LC 85-4706. (Illus.). 192p. 1985. reprint ed. pap. 54.80 (*0-608-00544-4*, 2061423) Bks Demand.

***Upper Waters of the Intertropical Pacific Ocean.** Mizuki Tsuchiya. LC 68-9513. (Johns Hopkins Oceanographic Studies: No. 4). (Illus.). 66p. 1968. reprint ed. pap. 25.00 (*0-608-04055-X*, 2064791) Bks Demand.

Upper West Side Story: A History & Guide. Peter Salwen. (Illus.). 376p. 1989. 29.95 (*0-89659-894-2*) Abbeville Pr.

Upper West Side Story: A History & Guide. Peter Salwen. (Illus.). 376p. 1993. pap. 19.95 (*1-55859-429-9*) Abbeville Pr.

Upper Yukon Basin. Ed. by Alaska Geographic Staff. LC 72-92087. (Alaska Geographic Ser.: Vol. 14, No. 4). (Illus.). 120p. 1987. pap. 19.95 (*0-88240-183-1*) Alaska Geog Soc.

***Upper Zohar, an Early Byzantine Fort in Palaestina Tertia: Final Report of Excavations in 1985-1986.** Richard P. Harper. (British Academy Monographs in Archaeology: No. 9). (Illus.). 172p. 1997. 120.00 (*0-19-727008-5*) OUP.

Uppers, Downers, All Arounders. Darryl S. Inaba & William E. Cohen. Ed. by Michael Holstein. (Illus.). 380p. (Orig.). (C). 1993. pap. text ed. 34.00 (*0-926544-11-X*) CNS.

Uppers, Downers, All Arounders. 3rd ed. Darry S. Inaba et al. (Illus.). 496p. (Orig.). 1996. pap. text ed. 38.00 (*0-926544-25-X*) CNS.

Uppers, Downers, All Arounders CD-ROM-Book. 2nd ed. CNS Publications Staff. LC 93-72219. (Illus.). (C). pap. text ed. 195.00 incl. cd-rom (*0-926544-14-4*) CNS.

Uppity Women of Ancient Times. Vicki Leon. 256p. 1995. lib. bdg. 35.00 (*0-8095-5896-3*) Borgo Pr.

Uppity Women of Ancient Times. Vicki Leon. (Illus.). 256p. 1995. pap. 12.95 (*1-57324-010-9*) Conari Press.

***Uppity Women of Medieval Times.** Vicki Leon. (Illus.). 256p. (Orig.). 1997. pap. 14.95 (*1-57324-039-7*) Conari Press.

Uppsala Addresses: And Other Recent Essays & Reviews on Judaism Then & Now. Jacob Neusner. LC 96-15401. (South Florida Studies in the History of Judaism: No. 137). 172p. (C). 1996. 69.95 (*0-7885-0270-0*, 240137) Scholars Pr GA.

Uppsala Report, 1968: Official Report of the Fourth Assembly of the World Council of Churches, Uppsala July 4-20, 1968. World Council of Churches, Fourth Assembly Staff. LC 71-453731. 533p. reprint ed. pap. 152.00 (*0-7837-6003-5*, 2045813) Bks Demand.

Uppsala, Universitetsbiblioteket, MS Vokalmusic i Handskrift 76a. Ed. by Howard M. Brown et al. (Renaissance Music in Facsimile Ser.). 192p. 1987. text ed. 30.00 (*0-8240-1468-5*) Garland.

Uppsala, Universitetsbiblioteket, MS Vokalmusik i Handskrift 76b. Ed. by Brown et al. LC 86-753539. (Renaissance Music in Facsimile Ser.: Vol. 20). 352p. 1987. text ed. 35.00 (*0-8240-1469-3*) Garland.

***Upright Children.** Ed. by Barbara Westberg. (Kid's Power Hour Ser.: No. VI). 128p. 1997. teacher ed., per. 14.95 (*1-56722-194-7*) Word Aflame.

Upright Lives: Documents Concerning the Natural Virtue & Wisdom of the Indians. Intro. by Thomas Hahn. LC 92-2399. (Augustan Reprints Ser.: Nos. 209-210). 1992. reprint ed. 21.50 (*0-404-70209-0*, BJ122) AMS Pr.

Upright Piano. Judith Jerome. 1985. 24.45 (*0-671-60735-9*) S&S Trade.

***Uprising.** Yusuf Jah. 1997. pap. 12.00 (*0-684-82537-6*, Touchstone Bks) S&S Trade.

Uprising. Abigail McDaniels. 320p. 1994. mass mkt. 4.50 (*0-8217-4501-8*, Zebra Kensgtn) Kensgtn Pub Corp.

Uprising. Joseph Nazel. 224p. (Orig.). 1987. mass mkt. 2.50 (*0-87067-295-9*, BH295) Holloway.

Uprising. Liviu Rebreanu. Tr. by P. Crandjean & S. Hartauer from RUM. 384p. 1964. 30.00 (*0-7206-9382-9*, Pub. by P Owen Ltd UK) Dufour.

Uprising: Crips & Bloods Tell the Story of America's Youth in Crossfire. Yusuf Jah & Sister Shah'Keyah. 352p. 1995. 23.00 (*0-684-80460-3*) S&S Trade.

Uprising! One Nation's Nightmare: Hungary 1956. David Irving. (Illus.). 628p. 1986. 16.95 (*0-949667-91-9*, Pub. by Veritas Pub AT) Legion Survival.

Uprising of a Great People: The United States in 1861 to Which Is Added a Word of Peace Between England & the United States. Agenor De Gasparin. Tr. by Mary L. Booth. LC 75-95066. (Select Bibliographies Reprint Ser.). 1977. 29.95 (*0-8369-5068-2*) Ayer.

Uprising of June Twentieth, 1792. Laura B. Pfeiffer. LC 78-115360. reprint ed. 29.50 (*0-404-05019-0*) AMS Pr.

Uprising of the Twenty Thousand. Donna Ippolito. Ed. by Anne Pride. 29p. (Orig.). (C). 1979. pap. 3.00 (*0-934238-00-6*) Motheroot.

Uprisings: The Whole Grain Bakers Book. Ed. by Cooperative Whole Grain Education Association Staff. LC 90-1030. (Illus.). 288p. (Orig.). 1990. pap. 13.95 (*0-913990-70-1*) Book Pub Co.

Uproar at Dancing Rabbit Creek: Enviromental Justice & Race. Colin Crawford. 384p. 1996. 24.00 (*0-201-62723-X*) Addison-Wesley.

Uprooted. Istvan I. Mocsy. 1983. text ed. 52.50 (*0-88033-039-2*, 147) Col U Pr.

Uprooted, Vol. 1. 2nd ed. Oscar Handlin. 1973. pap. 14.95 (*0-316-34313-7*) Little.

Uprooted: A Hitler Legacy - Voices of Those Who Escaped Before the "Final Solution" D. B. Whiteman. (Illus.). 446p. (C). 1993. 28.95 (*0-306-44467-4*, Plenum Insight) Plenum.

Uprooted: Braceros in the Hermanos Mayo's Lense. John Mraz & Jaime V. Storey. LC 96-12337. 1996. 39.95 (*1-55885-167-4*); pap. 18.95 (*1-55885-178-X*) Arte Publico.

***Uprooted! Refugees & Forced Migrants.** Elizabeth G. Ferris. LC 97-18121. 1998. write for info. (*0-377-00319-0*) Friendship Pr.

Uprooted: Refugees & the United States - A Multidisciplinary Teaching Guide. David M. Donahue & Nancy Flowers. LC 95-5134. (Illus.). 224p. (Orig.). (YA). (gr. 7-12). 1995. pap. 15.95 (*0-89793-122-X*) Hunter Hse.

Uprooted: Refugees & the United States - A Multidisciplinary Teaching Guide. David M. Donahue & Nancy Flowers. LC 95-5134. 224p. 1995. spiral bd. 22.95 (*0-89793-179-3*) Hunter Hse.

Uprooted: Refugees & the United States: A Resource Curriculum. David M. Donahue & Nancy Flowers. 224p. 1992. lib. bdg. 41.00 (*0-8095-6339-8*) Borgo Pr.

Uprooted: Translation of the Original Novel Vamshavriksha in Kannada. S. L. Bhyrappa. Tr. by K. Raghavendra Rao. (C). 1992. 17.50 (*81-7018-734-6*, Pub. by BR Pub II) S Asia.

Uprooted Americans: The Japanese Americans & the War Relocation Authority During World War II. Dillon S. Myer. LC 76-125169. (Illus.). 390p. reprint ed. pap. 111.20 (*0-317-58772-2*, 2029656) Bks Demand.

Uprooted in Old Age: Russian Jews & Their Social Networks in Israel. Howard Litwin. LC 94-29825. (Contributions to the Study of Aging Ser.: Vol. 25). 208p. 1995. text ed. 55.00 (*0-313-29280-9*, Greenwood Pr) Greenwood.

Uprooted of the Western Sahel: Migrants' Quest for Cash in the Senegambia. Lucie G. Colvin et al. LC 81-5005. 400p. 1981. text ed. 75.00 (*0-275-90597-7*, C0597, Praeger Pubs) Greenwood.

Uprooted People: Displacement, Resettlement & Development. Ed. by V. Surdarsen & M. A. Kalam. 1990. 18.50 (*81-212-0329-5*, Pub. by Gian Publng Hse II) S Asia.

***Uprooted Women: Migrant Domestics in the Caribbean.** Paula L. Aymer. LC 96-53939. 1997. text ed. write for info. (*0-275-95883-3*, Praeger Pubs) Greenwood.

Uprooting & Surviving: Adaptation & Resettlement of Migrant Families. Richard C. Nann. 1982. lib. bdg. 88.00 (*90-277-1339-1*) Kluwer Ac.

Uprooting Leninsim, Cultivating Liberty. Ed. by W. Vladimir Tismaneanu & Patrick Clawson. LC 92-16098. 104p. (C). 1992. pap. text ed. 13.50 (*0-8191-8730-5*); lib. bdg. 35.00 (*0-8191-8729-1*) U Pr of Amer.

Uprooting of Desire: The Words of Sri Aurobindo. 40p. 1.00 (*81-7060-054-5*) Aurobindo Assn.

Uprooting Racism: How White People Can Work for Racial Justice. Paul Kivel. 208p. 1995. pap. 16.95 (*0-86571-338-3*) New Soc Pubs.

Uprooting Racism: How White People Can Work for Racial Justice. Paul Kivel. 208p. 1995. lib. bdg. 39.95 (*0-86571-337-5*) New Soc Pubs.

Uprooting the Spirit of Fear. Creflo A. Dollar. 96p. 1994. pap. 6.99 (*0-89274-686-6*) Harrison Hse.

Uprooting Violence: Building Nonviolence. Pat Patfoort. (Illus.). 1995. pap. 10.00 (*0-89166-015-1*) Cobblesmith.

Uprooting War. Brian Martin. 298p. (Orig.). 1984. pap. 10.00 (*0-900384-26-3*) Left Bank.

Ups & Downs. Pam Adams. (J). (gr. 4 up). 1985. 4.99 (*0-85953-257-7*) Childs Play.

Ups & Downs. Grace Cluster. LC 93-30581. (Lewiston Poetry Ser.: Vol. 21). 64p. 1993. pap. 12.95 (*0-7734-2791-0*, Mellen Poetry Pr) E Mellen.

Ups & Downs. Sheryl Prenzian. (Kid Sisters Ser.: No. 12). (Illus.). 117p. (Orig.). (J). (gr. 3-5). 1995. pap. 6.95 (*0-614-08413-X*) Targum Pr.

***Ups & Downs: A Book About Floating & Sinking.** Scholastic Inc. Staff. (Magic School Bus Ser.). 1997. pap. 2.99 (*0-590-92158-4*) Scholastic Inc.

***Ups & Downs in a Flying Fortress: "Were Those Trips Necessary"** Bud Lembke. (Illus.). 200p. (Orig.). 1997. pap. 24.95 (*0-9657814-0-2*) Pulse Pr.

Ups & Downs of Indo-U. S. Relations, 1948-1983. P. K. Goswami. 1984. 12.00 (*0-8364-1122-6*, Pub. by Mukhopadhyaya II) S Asia.

Ups & Downs of Life in the Indies. P. A. Daum. Ed. by E. M. Beekman. Tr. by Elsje Sturtevant & Donald Sturtevant from DUT. LC 86-16807. (Library of the Indies). 216p. 1987. lib. bdg. 27.50 (*0-87023-551-6*) U of Mass Pr.

***Ups & Downs of Simpson Snail: Level 2.** John Himmelman. (Puffin Easy-to-Read Program Ser.). (J). 1997. pap. text ed. 3.99 (*0-14-038726-9*) Puffin Bks.

UPS Guide to Owning & Managing a B & B. Lisa A. Rogak. 250p. 1994. pap. 15.95 (*0-936894-65-2*, 610059-01, Upstart) Dearborn Finan.

UPS Guide to Owning & Managing a Bar or Tavern. Roy S. Alonzo. 250p. 1994. pap. 15.95 (*0-936894-67-9*, 610058-01, Upstart) Dearborn Finan.

UPS Guide to Owning & Managing a Desktop Publishing Business. Dan Ramsey. 250p. 1994. pap. 15.95 (*0-936894-68-7*, 610060-01, Upstart) Dearborn Finan.

UPS Guide to Owning & Managing a Resume Service. Dan Ramsey. 250p. 1994. pap. 15.95 (*0-936894-69-5*, 6100-6201, Upstart) Dearborn Finan.

UPS Guide to Owning & Managing an Antiques Business. Lisa A. Rogak. 250p. 1994. pap. 15.95 (*0-936894-66-0*, 610061-01, Upstart) Dearborn Finan.

UPS (Uninterrupted Power Supply) Bible. (Illus.). 38p. (Orig.). 1995. pap. text ed. 20.00 (*0-7881-2349-1*) DIANE Pub.

Upscale One-Pocket. Jack H. Koehler. LC 95-92468. (Illus.). (Orig.). 1995. pap. 14.95 (*0-9622890-3-5*) Sportology Pubns.

Upscale Outdoor Cookbook. Cari Taylor-Carlson. 1992. write for info. (*0-9629452-1-8*) Serendpty Ink.

Upscale Sales Training Workbook. Laddie F. Hutar. 96p. 1990. spiral bd. 85.00 (*0-918896-04-5*) Hutar.

Upscaling Downtown: Stalled Gentrification in Washington, D. C. Brett Williams. LC 87-27350. (Anthropology of Contemporary Issues Ser.). 176p. 1988. 32.50 (*0-8014-2106-3*); pap. 12.95 (*0-8014-9419-2*) Cornell U Pr.

Upset Book: A Guide for Dealing with Upset People. Pennie Myers & Don W. Nance. (Illus.). 222p. (Orig.). 1986. pap. 8.95 (*0-937647-01-2*) Academic Pubns.

Upset Book: How to Deal with Upset People. rev. ed. Pennie Myers & Don W. Nance. 218p. (Orig.). 1991. pap. 12.95 (*0-9620723-4-6*) MAS.

Upset Workbook: Client Service Edition for Insurance Companies & Agencies. Pennie Myers & Don W. Nance. 118p. 1989. student ed. 50.00 (*0-9620723-1-1*) MAS.

Upset Workbook: Health Care Edition. Pennie Myers & Don W. Nance. 118p. 1989. 50.00 (*0-9620723-2-X*) MAS.

Upset Workbook: Insurance Claims Edition. Pennie Myers & Don W. Nance. 132p. (Orig.). 1988. student ed. 50.00 (*0-9620723-0-3*) MAS.

Upset Workbook: Patient Representative Edition. Pennie Myers & Don W. Nance. 130p. 1990. 50.00 (*0-9620723-3-8*) MAS.

Upsetting the Applecart: A Common Sense Approach to Successful Hotel Operations in the 90's. Bill Scatchard. Ed. by Maggie Baker. (Illus.). 272p. (Orig.). 1992. pap. text ed. 24.95 (*0-9640151-1-0*) Applecart Hotel.

Upsetting the Balance: German & British Security Interests in the 19th & 20th Century. (Prince Albert Studies Ser.: Vol. 8). Orig. Title: Das Gestorte Gleichgewicht. 160p. (GER.). 1990. Earlier vols. avail. 55.00 (*3-598-21408-1*) K G Saur.

Upsherin: Ephraim's First Haircut. Beverly Geller. 44p. (J). 8.95 (*0-935063-70-6*) CIS Comm.

Upshur Brothers of the Blue & Grey. Betty Hornbeck. 259p. 1995. pap. 14.95 (*0-87012-022-0*) McClain.

Upshur County Death Records: An Alphabetical Listing of Deaths Recorded in the Upshur County Courthouse, Buckhannon, West Virginia, 1853-1928. Paul C. Hawkins & Judith Hawkins. iv, 163p. (Orig.). 1993. pap. text ed. 25.00 (*1-55613-756-7*) Heritage Bk.

Upshur County, West Virginia Births 1853-1897. Billie F. Drost & Karon King. 224p. (Orig.). 1993. pap. text ed. 30.00 (*1-55613-877-6*) Heritage Bk.

Upshur Document Exercise. Date not set. wbk. ed., pap. text ed. write for info. (*0-314-05888-5*) West Pub.

Upshur World History, Vol. 1. 2nd ed. Date not set. student ed., pap. text ed. 17.75 (*0-314-05501-0*); suppl. ed., pap. text ed. 6.75 (*0-314-05914-8*) West Pub.

Upshur World History, Vol. 2. 2nd ed. Date not set. suppl. ed., pap. text ed. 6.75 (*0-314-05915-6*) West Pub.

***Upside Down.** Carr. 1997. pap. 4.95 (*0-7868-4128-1*) Disney Pr.

Upside Down. Mary J. Miller. 121p. (J). (gr. 3-7). 1994. pap. 3.99 (*0-14-034624-4*) Puffin Bks.

Upside Down & Inside Out: Poems for All Your Pockets. Bobbi Katz. LC 91-68197. (Illus.). 48p. (J). (ps-3). 1992. lib. bdg. 14.95 (*1-56397-122-4*, Wordsong) Boyds Mills Pr.

***Upside-Down Christmas.** Sandi Olsen. (Illus.). 32p. 1996. pap. 6.95 (*0-89036-634-9*) Hawkes Pub Inc.

Upside down Circle: Zen Laughter. Zen Master Gilbert. LC 88-7455. (Illus.). 176p. (Orig.). 1989. pap. 12.95 (*0-931892-18-X*) B Dolphin Pub.

Upside down Day. Mike Thaler. (Snuggle & Read Story Bks.). 32p. (J). (gr. k-3). 1986. pap. 2.95 (*0-380-89999-X*, Camelot) Avon.

Upside down in the Dark. Carol Potter. (Orig.). 1995. pap. 9.95 (*1-882295-05-6*) Alicejamesbooks.

Upside down, Inside Out, & Backwards. Duane Michals. 80p. (J). 1994. pap. 19.95 (*0-9638863-0-4*) Sonny Boy Bks.

Upside-Down Kids: Helping Dyslexic Children Understand Themselves & Overcome Their Disorder. Harold N. Levinson & Addie Sanders. LC 91-4420. 168p. 1991. 17.95 (*0-87131-625-0*) M Evans.

Upside-Down Kingdom. rev. ed. Donald B. Kraybill. LC 90-33783. 320p. 1990. pap. 14.99 (*0-8361-3522-9*) Herald Pr.

Upside down Leadership: The Rules Have Changed! Jerry Patterson. 112p. (Orig.). 1995. pap. write for info. (*0-9646020-0-8*) Transit Pr WI.

Upside down Mad Libs. Leonard Stern & Roger Price. 48p. (J). (gr. 2 up). 1995. pap. 3.50 (*0-8431-3935-8*) Price Stern Sloan.

Upside down Management: The Only Way to Win. John Lorriman et al. LC 95-16851. 1995. pap. write for info. (*0-07-709067-5*) McGraw.

Upside-down Marketing: Turning Your Ex-Customers into Your Best Customers. George R. Walther. LC 93-45916. 1994. text ed. 19.95 (*0-07-068047-7*) McGraw.

Upside-down Marketing: Turning Your Ex-Customers into Your Best Customers. George R. Walther. LC 93-45916. 224p. 1996. pap. text ed. 12.95 (*0-07-068048-5*) McGraw.

Upside-Down Sloth. Fay Robinson. LC 93-18981. (Rookie Read-about Science Ser.). (Illus.). 32p. (J). (ps-2). 1993. pap. 3.95 (*0-516-46018-8*); lib. bdg. 17.30 (*0-516-06018-X*) Childrens.

Upside down Tapestry Mosaic History. Leslie A. Reese. LC 87-71058. 53p. (YA). (gr. 12 up). 1987. pap. 5.00 (*0-940713-00-4*) Broadside Pr.

Upside-Downs of Jealousy, Possessiveness & Insecurity. Stuart J. Faber & Teddi Levison. 100p. 1975. pap. text ed. 4.95 (*0-89074-012-7*) Charing Cross.

Upside of Down: Finding Hope When It Hurts. Joseph M. Stowell. 1991. pap. 10.99 (*0-8024-8533-2*) Moody.

Upside of Downsizing: Using Library Instruction to Cope. Ed. by Cheryl LaGuardia. LC 95-13157. 250p. 1995. pap. 39.95 (*1-55570-217-1*) Neal-Schuman.

Upside Your Head! Rhythm & Blues on Central Avenue. Johnny Otis. LC 93-13611. (Music - Culture Ser.). (Illus.). 212p. 1993. pap. 16.95 (*0-8195-6287-4*, Wesleyan Univ Pr) U Pr of New Eng.

Upsize Selling: Increase Your Sales with the Mix of Six. Stephen M. Gower. 136p. 1994. 20.00 (*1-880150-80-8*) Lectern Pub.

Upsizing the Individual in the Downsized Organization. Robert Johnansen. 1994. 24.00 (*0-201-62712-4*) Addison-Wesley.

Upsizing the Individual in the Downsized Organization: Managing in the Wake of Reengineering, Globalization, & Overwhelming Technological Change. Robert Johansen & Rob Swigart. 1996. pap. 14.00 (*0-201-48940-6*) Addison-Wesley.

Upson Family in America. Compiled by Upson Family Assoc Staff. (Illus.). 624p. 1992. reprint ed. pap. 94.00 (*0-8328-2206-X*); reprint ed. lib. bdg. 104.00 (*0-8328-2205-1*) Higginson Bk Co.

Upstaged. Jacqueline Shannon. 192p. 1987. mass mkt. 2.50 (*0-380-75245-X*, Flare) Avon.

Upstaged, No. 6. Elle Wolfe. (Palm Beach Prep Ser.: No. 6). (J). (gr. 4-7). 1990. pap. 2.95 (*0-8125-1077-1*) Tor Bks.

Upstaging Big Daddy: Directing Theater As If Gender & Race Matter. Ed. by Ellen Donkin & Susan Clement. LC 92-38338. (Illus.). 276p. 1993. text ed. 44.50 (*0-472-09503-X*); pap. text ed. 17.95 (*0-472-06503-3*) U of Mich Pr.

Upstaging God. Pelle Karlsson. 156p. 1996. pap. 8.99 (*0-8499-3955-0*) Word Pub.

Upstairs Cat. Karla Kuskin. LC 95-50523. (Illus.). (J). 1997. 15.00 (*0-395-70146-5*, Clarion Bks) HM.

Upstairs Connection. Barbara Davoll. (Molehole Mystery Ser.: Vol. 5). (J). (gr. 4-7). 1993. pap. 6.99 (*0-8024-2704-9*) Moody.

Upstairs in the Garden. Robin Morgan. 1991. pap. 9.95 (*0-393-30760-3*) Norton.

Upstairs Lover. Emma Darcy. (Presents Ser.). 1993. pap. 2.89 (*0-373-11555-5*, 1-11555-9) Harlequin Bks.

Upstairs Lover. large type ed. Emma Darcy. LC 93-3644. 1993. lib. bdg. 18.95 (*1-56054-733-2*) Thorndike Pr.

Upstairs Room. Johanna Reiss. LC 77-187940. 196p. (YA). (gr. 7 up). 1972. 15.00 (*0-690-85127-8*) HarpC Child Bks.

Upstairs Room. Johanna Reiss. LC 77-187940. (Trophy Bk.). 208p. (YA). (gr. 7 up). 1990. pap. 3.95 (*0-06-440370-X*, Trophy) HarpC Child Bks.

Upstairs Room. Johanna Reiss. LC 77-187940. (Trophy Keypoint Bk.). 192p. (YA). (gr. 7 up). 1987. reprint ed. pap. 3.95 (*0-06-447043-1*, Trophy) HarpC Child Bks.

Upstairs to Downstairs: Advice to Servant Girls & Weary Mothers. Ed. by James Drummond. (SWSS Ser.). 96p. 1991. pap. text ed. 7.90 (*0-08-041204-1*, Pub. by Aberdeen U Pr) Macmillan.

***Upstart.** 1997. 29.95 (*0-593-02848-1*) Bantam.

***Upstart Guide to Buying, Valuing & Selling Your Business.** Scott Gabehart. LC 97-19701. 304p. (Orig.). 1997. pap. 29.95 incl. 3.5 ld (*1-57410-087-4*, 5615-8401, Upstart) Dearborn Finan.

Upstart Guide to Owning & Managing a Consulting Service. Dan Ramsey. 214p. 1995. pap. 15.95 (*0-936894-81-4*) Upstart Pub.

Upstart Guide to Owning & Managing a Florist Service. Dan Ramsey. 210p. 1995. pap. 15.95 (*0-936894-82-2*) Upstart Pub.

Upstart Guide to Owning & Managing a Mail Order Business. Dan Ramsey. (Upstart Guide to Owning & Managing...Ser.). 208p. (Orig.). 1995. pap. 15.95 (*0-936894-97-0*, 5614-41-01) Upstart Pub.

Upstart Guide to Owning & Managing a Newsletter Business. Lisa A. Rogak. 213p. 1995. pap. 15.95 (*0-936894-87-3*) Upstart Pub.

Upstart Guide to Owning & Managing a Restaurant. Roy S. Alonzo. 224p. 1995. pap. 15.95 (*0-936894-89-X*, 6100-85-01) Upstart Pub.

Upstart Guide to Owning & Managing a Travel Service. Dan Ramsey. 210p. 1995. pap. 15.95 (*0-936894-83-0*) Upstart Pub.

***Upstart Small Business Legal Guide.** 2nd ed. Robert Friedman. 360p. 1998. pap. 29.95 (*1-57410-092-0*, 5615-6202, Upstart) Dearborn Finan.

Upstart Spring. James Nora. 352p. 1989. 16.95 (*0-922811-00-8*) Mid-List.

Upstate. 2nd ed. Sallie Bingham. LC 92-34345. 128p. 1993. pap. 16.00 (*1-877946-50-8*) Permanent Pr.

Upstate: Records & Recollections of Northern New York. Edmund Wilson. (New York Classics Ser.). (Illus.). 424p. 1990. reprint ed. pap. text ed. 15.95 (*0-8156-2499-9*) Syracuse U Pr.

Upstate Anecdotes. Robert B. Walker. 1994. pap. 1.25 (*0-9603088-1-4*) Martingale.

Upstate Arcadia: Landscape, Aesthetics, & the Triumph of Social Differentiation in America. Peter J. Hugill. (Geographical Perspectives on the Human Past Ser.). 210p. (Orig.). (C). 1995. pap. text ed. 24.95 (*0-8476-7856-3*); lib. bdg. 61.50 (*0-8476-7855-5*) Rowman.

Upstate Echos. Arch Merrill. (Arch Merrill's New York Ser.: Vol. 9). (Illus.). 168p. 1992. reprint ed. pap. 12.95 (*1-55787-003-9*, 76043, Empire State Bks) Hrt of the Lakes.

Upstate Literature: Essays in Memory of Thomas F. O'Donnell. Ed. by Frank Bergmann. LC 84-26853. (New York State Bks.). 256p. 1985. pap. text ed. 16.95 (*0-8156-2331-3*) Syracuse U Pr.

Upstate New York Business Directory, 1996-97, Vol. 3 Upstate. rev. ed. 2240p. 1996. boxed 430.00 (*1-56105-788-6*) Am Busn Direct.

***Upstate New York Business Directory 1997.** rev. ed. American Business Directories Staff. 2240p. 1996. boxed 430.00 (*1-56105-871-8*) Am Busn Direct.

Upstate New York Business Directory 1998 see New York Business Directory 1998

Upstate New York City Street Maps. DeLorme Staff. 1990. pap. 9.95 (*0-89933-300-1*) DeLorme Map.

Upstate New York in the Seventeen Sixties. Florence Christoph. LC 91-68234. (Illus.). 320p. 1992. 39.50 (*0-929539-90-7*, 1328) Picton Pr.

Upstate New York Jobbank, 1997. Adams Publishing Staff. 1996. pap. text ed. 15.95 (*1-55850-666-7*) Adams Media.

***Upstate Odyssey: The Lehigh Valley Railroad in Western New York.** Mary H. Dann. LC 96-71260. (Illus.). 144p. (Orig.). 1997. pap. 29.95 (*1-884650-05-8*) Railroad Res.

Upstate Travels: British Views of Nineteenth-Century New York. Ed. by Roger M. Haydon. LC 82-3312. (New York State Bks.). (Illus.). 320p. 1982. pap. 16.95 (*0-8156-0175-1*) Syracuse U Pr.

***Upstream.** Sharon Butala. 256p. 1997. pap. 14.00 (*0-00-648113-2*) HarperColl Wrld.

Upstream. Ludwig Lewisohn. 1992. reprint ed. lib. bdg. 250.00 (*0-8490-8904-2*) Gordon Pr.

Upstream: Salmon & Society in the Pacific Northwest. National Research Council Protection & Management of Pacific Northwest Salmonids Committee. 450p. 1996. 44.95 (*0-309-05325-0*) Natl Acad Pr.

Upstream - Downstream: Issues in Environmental Ethics. Ed. by Donald Scherer. 288p. 1990. 44.95 (*0-87722-747-0*) Temple U Pr.

Upstream - Downstream: Issues in Environmental Ethics. Ed. by Donald Scherer. 288p. 1993. pap. 19.95 (*1-56639-079-6*) Temple U Pr.

Upstream People: An Annotated Research Bibliography of the Omaha Tribe. Michael L. Tate. LC 90-24533. (Native American Bibliography Ser.: No. 14). (Illus.). 522p. 1991. 62.50 (*0-8108-2372-1*) Scarecrow.

***Upsurge: A Novel.** J. M. Harcourt. pap. 2.00 (*0-85564-244-0*, Pub. by Univ of West Aust Pr AT) Intl Spec Bk.

Uptake & Storage of Noradrenaline in Sympathetic Nerves. Leslie L. Iverson. LC 67-12318. 267p. reprint ed. pap. 76.10 (*0-685-16034-3*, 2027233) Bks Demand.

Uptaught. Ken Macrorie. (Innovators in Education Ser.). 188p. 1996. pap. 14.95 (*0-86709-396-X*, 0396) Boynton Cook Pubs.

Uptight: The Story of the Velvet Underground. Victor Backriss & Gerard Malanga. (Illus.). 208p. (Orig.). pap. 12.95 (*0-7119-5223-X*, OP 47794) Omnibus NY.

***Uptime.** Horton. 1997. pap. text ed. 42.00 (*0-13-631789-8*) P-H.

Uptime: Strategies for Excellence in Maintenance Management. John D. Campbell. (Illus.). 250p. 1994. 35.00 (*1-56327-053-6*) Prod Press.

Upton & the Army. Stephen E. Ambrose. LC 64-21590. (Illus.). 190p. (C). 1993. pap. 9.95 (*0-8071-1850-8*) La State U Pr.

Upton Family Records: Being Genealogical Collections for an Upton Family History. W. H. Upton. (Illus.). 534p. 1989. reprint ed. pap. 80.00 (*0-8328-1197-1*); reprint ed. lib. bdg. 88.00 (*0-8328-1196-3*) Higginson Bk Co.

Upton Memorial: A Genealogical Record of the Descendants of John Upton of North Reading, Massachusetts, Together with Short Genealogies of the Putnam, Stone & Bruce Families. J. A. Vinton. (Illus.). 556p. 1989. reprint ed. pap. 82.50 (*0-8328-1195-5*); reprint ed. lib. bdg. 90.50 (*0-8328-1194-7*) Higginson Bk Co.

Upton-on-Severn Words & Phrases. Robert Lawson. (English Dialect Society Publications: No. 42). 1974. reprint ed. pap. 25.00 (*0-8115-0468-9*) Periodicals Srv.

Upton Sinclair: A Descriptive Annotated Bibliography. John Ahouse. 180p. (C). 1994. 55.00 (*0-923980-35-0*) Arundel Pr.

Upton Sinclair: A Study in Social Protest. Floyd Dell. LC 73-133826. reprint ed. 24.50 (*0-404-02076-3*) AMS Pr.

Upton Sinclair: An Annotated Checklist. Ronald Gottesman. LC 72-634010. (Serif Ser.: No. 24). 564p. reprint ed. pap. 160.80 (*0-8357-9375-3*, 2014598) Bks Demand.

Upton Sinclair: The Forgotten Socialist. Ivan Scott. LC 95-39548. 1996. lib. bdg. write for info. (*0-7618-0176-6*) U Pr of Amer.

Upton Sinclair Presents William Fox. Upton Sinclair. LC 78-124037. (Literature of Cinema, Ser. 1). 1970. reprint ed. 26.95 (*0-405-01637-9*) Ayer.

An Asterisk (*) at the beginning of an entry indicates that the title is appearing in BIP for the first time.

***Upton Sinclair, the Forgotten Socialist.** Ivan Scott. LC 97-2194. (Studies in American Literature: Vol. 23). 412p. 1997. text ed. 109.95 (*0-7734-8679-8*) E Mellen.

Upton's Heritage: The History of a Massachusetts Town. Donald B. Johnson. LC 84-16659. (Illus.). 280p. 1984. 20.00 (*0-914659-08-1*) Phoenix Pub.

Uptown: Character Monologues for Actors. Glenn Alterman. LC 92-37750. (Monologue Audition Ser.). 86p. 1992. pap. 8.95 (*1-880399-08-3*) Smith & Kraus.

Uptown & Downtown. Stanley Fischler. pap. 12.95 (*0-8015-8196-6*, Dutton) NAL-Dutton.

Uptown Country: Food with Style. Donald Lewis. 1991. 12.95 (*5-550-37028-X*) Precision Foods.

Uptown Country Food with Style. Donald Lewis. (Illus.). 165p. 1995. reprint ed. 12.95 (*0-9646944-0-9*) Uptown Cntry.

Uptown down South. 198p. 1986. 10.95 (*0-9608172-1-2*) Greenville SC Jr League.

***Uptown Heads.** R. K. Byers. 192p. 1996. pap. 9.95 (*1-874509-30-1*) LPC InBook.

Uptown Squares: A Big Coloring Book. Donald E. Jones. (Illus.). 48p. (J). (ps up). 4.00 (*0-9645737-0-9*) Uptown Sq.

***Uptown/Downtown: Growing up in New Orleans.** rev. ed. Elsie Martinez & Margaret LeCorgne. (Illus.). 177p. 1996. pap. 10.00 (*1-887366-06-7*) U of SW LA Ctr LA Studies.

Upturned Stone. Scott Hampton. Ed. by Paul Jenkins. (Illus.). 64p. 1993. reprint ed. 14.95 (*0-87816-225-9*) Kitchen Sink.

UPU Mail: Annual Tables of Exchange Rates & of Postage Rates to the U.S., 1881-1953. Intro. by Robert D. Harris. (Illus.). 200p. 1989. pap. 45.00 (*0-941480-04-6*, Postilion Pubns) Subway Stamp.

***Upward Bound.** Curtis L. Meeks. 1997. 19.95 (*0-533-12338-0*) Vantage.

***Upward Call.** John Coblentz. 240p. (Orig.). (YA). 1997. pap. 9.95 (*0-87813-567-7*) Christian Light.

Upward Call: Spiritual Formation & the Holy Life. Morris Weigelt et al. 256p. 1993. pap. 12.99 (*0-8341-1516-6*) Beacon Hill.

Upward Climb: An Epic Poem. Judith D. Parr. 55p. 1994. pap. 4.50 (*0-941971-10-4*) Peacock CO.

Upward-Communication Programs in American Industry. Allen I. Kraut & Frank H. Freeman. (Reports: No. 152G). (Illus.). 81p. 1992. pap. text ed. 30.00 (*0-912879-46-7*) Ctr Creat Leader.

***Upward, Inward, Outward: A Course in Maturing Disciples in Christ.** Milton Jones. 64p. (Orig.). 1984. pap. 2.00 (*0-940999-11-0*, C-2081) Star Bible.

Upward Journey: The Story of Internal Medicine at Georgetown: 1851-1981. John F. Stapleton. LC 96-76436. (Illus.). 304p. (C). 1996. write for info. (*0-9652807-0-5*) Georgetown U Med.

Upward Mobility in Coaching Basketball. Bill Foster. 84p. 1994. pap. text ed. 9.95 (*0-9644407-0-9*) BF Pub.

Upward Moving & Emergence Way: The Gishin Biye' Version. Berard Haile. LC 81-7441. (American Tribal Religions Ser.: No. 7). 255p. reprint ed. pap. 72.70 (*0-7837-6457-X*, 2046461) Bks Demand.

Upward Panic: The Autobiography of Eva Palmer-Sikelianos, Vol. 4. Ed. by John P. Anton. (Choreography & Dance Studies). 252p. 1993. text ed. 64.00 (*3-7186-5264-1*) Gordon & Breach.

Upward Panic: The Autobiography of Eva Palmer-Sikelianos, Vol. 4. Intro. by John P. Anton. (Choreography & Dance Studies). 252p. 1993. pap. text ed. 34.00 (*3-7186-5310-9*) Gordon & Breach.

Upward Path. Jim Lewis. LC 82-60277. 150p. (Orig.). 1982. pap. 7.95 (*0-942482-04-2*) Unity Church Denver.

Upward Path: Daily Inspirations from the Works of Henry van Dyke. Henry Van Dyke. LC 95-17800. 192p. 1995. 14.99 (*0-87788-249-5*) Shaw Pubs.

Upward Trend. Harvey Jackins. 1993. pap. write for info. (*91-971405-0-3*) Rational Isl.

Upward Trend. Harvey Jackins. 1994. 13.00 (*1-885357-04-4*) Rational Isl.

Upward Trend. 2nd ed. Harvey Jackins. LC 78-109407. 1977. reprint ed. 13.00 (*0-911214-57-7*); reprint ed. pap. 10.00 (*0-911214-81-X*) Rational Isl.

***Upwards & Onwards.** Reynnie. LC 95-90626. 72p. (Orig.). 1996. pap. 7.95 (*1-56002-599-9*) Aegina Pr.

Upwelling in the Ocean: Modern Processes & Ancient Records. C. P. Summerhayes et al. LC 95-23821. (Dahlem Workshop Reports Enviornmental Science Ser.: Vol. 18). 422p. 1996. text ed. 165.00 (*0-471-96041-1*) Wiley.

Upwelling Systems: Evolution Since the Early Miocene. Ed. by C. P. Summerhayes et al. (Geological Society Special Publications: No. 64). (Illus.). vi, 520p. (C). 1992. 110.00 (*0-903317-78-8*, 277, Pub. by Geol Soc Pub Hse UK) AAPG.

Upwellings: First Expressions of Unbelief in the Printed Literature of the French Renaissance. Max Gauna. LC 90-56223. 320p. 1992. 45.00 (*0-8386-3439-7*) Fairleigh Dickinson.

***Upwind & High-Resolution Schemes.** M. Yousuff Hussaini et al. LC 96-39965. 504p. 1997. 199.00 (*3-540-61655-1*) Spr-Verlag.

Uqalukutuat: Elders' Conference, Women's Session, 1980. Dorothy P. Edwardson. (Illus.). 230p. (Orig.). 1993. pap. write for info. (*1-881246-01-9*) Arctic Sivunmun.

Uqiuvanqmiut Quliapyuit King Island Tales. Frank Ellanna et al. Ed. by Lawrence D. Kaplan. Tr. by Margaret Seeganna & Gertrude Analoak. (Illus.). xii, 259p. (Orig.). (ENG & ESK.). 1988. pap. 19.95 (*1-55500-019-3*) Alaska Native.

Ur: Buildings of the Third Dynasty. Leonard Woolley. (Ur Excavations Ser.: Archaeology, No. 6). (Illus.). x, 110p. 1974. 60.00 (*0-686-17772-X*) U PA Mus Pubns.

***Ur-ine Trouble: Think You Would Pass a Drug Test? Don't Be So Sure!** Kent Holtorf & Stephanie Cartozian. (Illus.). 165p. (Orig.). 1997. 24.95 (*0-9657467-3-9*) Vandalay Pubs.

Urach Geothermal Project: Swabian Alb, Germany. Ed. by Ralph Haenel. (Illus.). 419p. 1982. pap. text ed. 96.60 (*3-510-65107-3*) Lubrecht & Cramer.

Uraguay Round & Beyond. Ed. by John Whalley. LC 89-5203. (Studies In International Trade Policy). 224p. (C). 1989. Vol. 3--The Uruguay Round & Beyond; Final Report of a Ford Foundation Project, 224 pgs. text ed. 47.50 (*0-472-10151-X*) U of Mich Pr.

Ural-Altaische Jahrbucher, Vol. 64, 1992. Ed. by Gyula Decsy & A. J. Bodrogligeti. 210p. 1991. 74.00 (*0-931922-44-5*) Eurolingua.

Ural-Altaische Jahrbucher: Altaic Yearbook, Vol. 63, 1991. Ed. by Gyula Decsy & A. J. Bodrogligeti. 248p. 1990. 74.00 (*0-931922-39-9*) Eurolingua.

Ural-Altaische Jahrbucher: Ural Altaic Yearbook, Vol. 58. Ed. by Gyula Decsy & A. J. Bodrogligeti. 172p. 1986. 48.00 (*0-931922-22-4*) Eurolingua.

Ural-Altaische Jahrbucher: Ural-Altaic Yearbook, Vol. 59. Ed. by Gyula Decsy & A. J. Bodrogligeti. 172p. 1987. 48.00 (*0-931922-23-2*) Eurolingua.

Ural-Altaische Jahrbucher: Ural-Altaic Yearbook, Vol. 61. Ed. by Gyula Decsy & A. J. Bodrogligeti. 187p. 1989. 74.00 (*0-931922-34-8*) Eurolingua.

Ural-Altaische Jahrbucher: Ural-Altaic Yearbook 1984, Vol. 56. Ed. by Gyula Decsy & A. J. Brodrogligeti. 187p. 1985. 48.00 (*0-931922-17-8*) Eurolingua.

Ural-Altaische Jahrbucher: Ural Altaic Yearbook, 1985, Vol. 57. Ed. by Gyula Decsy & A. J. Bodrogligeti. 180p. 1980. 48.00 (*0-931922-20-8*) Eurolingua.

Ural-Altaische Jahrbucher: 1977, Vol. 49. Ed. by Gyula Decsy & A. J. Bodrogligeti. 177p. 1977. 48.00 (*3-447-01806-2*) Eurolingua.

Ural-Altaische Jahrbucher: 1978, Vol. 50. Ed. by Gyula Decsy & A. J. Bodrogligeti. 207p. 1978. 48.00 (*3-447-01891-7*) Eurolingua.

Ural-Altaische Jahrbucher: 1979, Vol. 51. Ed. by Gyula Decsy & A. J. Brodrogligeti. 183p. 1979. 48.00 (*0-931922-00-3*) Eurolingua.

Ural-Altaische Jahrbucher: 1980, Vol. 52. Ed. by Gyula Decsy & A. J. Bodrogligeti. 191p. 1980. 48.00 (*0-931922-05-4*) Eurolingua.

Ural-Altaische Jahrbucher: 1981, Vol. 53. Ed. by Gyula Decsy & A. J. Bodrogligeti. 172p. 1981. 48.00 (*0-931922-08-9*) Eurolingua.

Ural-Altaische Jahrbucher: 1982, Vol. 54. Ed. by Gyula Decsy & A. J. Bodrogligeti. 172p. 1982. 48.00 (*0-931922-09-7*) Eurolingua.

Ural-Altaische Jahrbucher: 1983, Vol. 55. Ed. by Gyula Decsy & A. J. Bodrogligeti. 174p. 1983. 48.00 (*0-931922-14-3*) Eurolingua.

Ural-Altaische Jahrbucher - Ural-Altaic Yearbook, Vol. 62, 1990. Ed. by Gyula Decsy & A. J. Bodrogligeti. 188p. 1990. 74.00 (*0-931922-37-2*) Eurolingua.

Ural-Altaische Jahrbucher - Ural-Altaic Yearbook, 1988, Vol. 60. anniversary ed. Ed. by Gyula Decsy & A. J. Bodrogligeti. 224p. 1988. Anniversary vol. 74.00 (*0-931922-30-5*) Eurolingua.

Uralic & Altaic Series: An Analytical Index. Ed. by John R. Krueger. LC 68-66742. (Uralic & Altaic Ser.: Vol. 100). 81p. 1970. 11.00 (*0-87750-000-2*) Res Inst Inner Asian Studies.

***Uralic Languages.** Daniel M. Abondolo. LC 96-29898. (Routledge Language Family Descriptions Ser.). 656p. (C). 1998. text ed. write for info. (*0-415-08198-X*) Routledge.

Uralic Protolanguage: A Comprehensive Reconstruction. (Bibliotheca Nostratica Ser.: Vol. 9). 148p. 1990. 26.00 (*0-931922-38-0*) Eurolingua.

Urania: A Choice Collection of Psalm-Tunes, Anthems & Hymns. James Lyon. LC 69-11667. (Music Reprint Ser.). 198p. 1974. reprint ed. lib. bdg. 37.50 (*0-306-71198-2*) Da Capo.

Uranian Worlds: A Guide to Alternative Sexuality in Science Fiction, Fantasy & Horror. 2nd ed. Ed. by Eric Garber & Lyn Paleo. 325p. 1990. 40.00 (*0-8161-1832-9*, Hall Reference) Macmillan.

Urania's Daughters: A Checklist of Women Science Fiction Writers, 1692-1982. Roger C. Schlobin. LC 83-2467. (Starmont Reference Guides Ser.: No. 1). (Illus.). xiv, 79p. (Orig.). 1983. pap. 15.00 (*0-916732-56-8*); lib. bdg. 25.00 (*0-916732-57-6*) Borgo Pr.

Uranium. J. H. Gittus. LC 64-9713. (Metallurgy of the Rarer Metals Ser.: No. 8). 637p. reprint ed. pap. 180.00 (*0-317-42150-6*, 2025762) Bks Demand.

Uranium, Pt. C, Section 3. Planck, Max, Society for the Advancement of Science, Gmelin Institute for Inorganic Chemistry Staff. (Illus.). 360p. 1975. 540.00 (*0-387-93290-9*) Spr-Verlag.

Uranium: Economic & Political Instability in a Strategic Commodity Market. Marian Radetzki. 1981. text ed. 39.95 (*0-312-83424-1*) St Martin.

Uranium Carbides, Nitrides & Silicides. Compiled by V. Maximov. (Bibliographical Ser.: No. 14). 175p. 1964. pap. 17.00 (*92-0-044064-9*, ISP21 14, Pub. by IAEA AU) Bernan Associates.

Uranium Carbides, Nitrides & Silicides. Compiled by V. Maximov. (Bibliographical Ser.: No. 33). 110p. 1968. pap. 16.00 (*92-0-044368-0*, ISP21 33, Pub. by IAEA AU) Bernan Associates.

Uranium Carbides, Nitrides & Silicides II, 1963-1965. Compiled by V. Maximov. (Bibliographical Ser.: No. 21). 172p. 1966. pap. 17.00 (*92-0-044166-1*, ISP21 21, Pub. by IAEA AU) Bernan Associates.

Uranium-Carbon & Plutonium-Carbon Systems: A Thermochemical Assessment. (Technical Reports: No. 14). (Illus.). 44p. 1963. pap. 11.00 (*92-0-145063-X*, IDC14, Pub. by IAEA AU) Bernan Associates.

Uranium Development in Less Developed Countries: A Handbook of Concerns. David M. Erickson. (Lincoln Institute Monograph Ser.: No. 81-4). 91p. reprint ed. pap. 26.00 (*0-7837-2165-X*, 2042471) Bks Demand.

Uranium Enrichment. Ed. by S. Villani. (Topics in Applied Physics Ser.: Vol. 35). (Illus.). 1979. 73.95 (*0-387-09385-0*) Spr-Verlag.

Uranium Enrichment: Process to Privatize the U. S. Enrichment Corporation Needs to Be Strengthened. (Illus.). 70p. (Orig.). (C). 1996. pap. text ed. 25.00 (*0-7881-2734-9*) DIANE Pub.

***Uranium Enrichment: Process to Privatize the U. S. Enrichment Corporation Needs to Be Strengthened.** (Illus.). 70p. 1995. pap. text ed. 35.00 (*1-57979-095-X*) BPI Info Servs.

Uranium Enrichment & Nuclear Weapon Proliferation. Allan S. Krass et al. LC 83-8486. 270p. 1983. 45.00 (*0-85066-219-2*) Taylor & Francis.

Uranium Enrichment & Nuclear Weapon Proliferation. Allan S. Krass et al. 270p. 1983. 45.00 (*0-8002-3079-5*) Taylor & Francis.

Uranium Enrichment & Other Technical Problems Relating to Nuclear Weapons Proliferation. Robert F. Mozley. 64p. (Orig.). 1994. pap. 9.00 (*0-935371-30-3*) CFISAC.

Uranium Geology & Mines, South Texas. D. H. Eargle et al. (Guidebook Ser.: GB 12). (Illus.). 59p. 1971. pap. 1.75 (*0-686-29320-7*) Bur Econ Geology.

Uranium Industry Annual. 1994. lib. bdg. 250.00 (*0-8490-8603-5*) Gordon Pr.

Uranium Industry Annual 1993. (Illus.). 152p. (Orig.). (C). 1994. pap. text ed. 40.00 (*0-7881-1129-9*) DIANE Pub.

***Uranium Industry Annual (1995)** (Illus.). 66p. (Orig.). (C). 1996. pap. 25.00 (*0-7881-3517-1*) DIANE Pub.

***Uranium Mill Tailings: Cleanup Continues, but Future Costs Are Uncertain.** (Illus.). 48p. (Orig.). (C). 1996. pap. 20.00 (*0-7881-3021-8*) DIANE Pub.

Uranium Mill Tailings Management: Proceedings of the Fifth Symposium, 1982. 557p. 1982. 30.00 (*0-910069-06-9*) Geotech Engineer Prog.

Uranium Mill Tailings Management: Proceedings of the First Symposium, 1978, 2 vols. Set. 17.00 (*0-910069-11-5*) Geotech Engineer Prog.

Uranium Mill Tailings Management: Proceedings of the First Symposium, 1978, 2 vols., Vol. 1. 172p. write for info. (*0-910069-00-X*) Geotech Engineer Prog.

Uranium Mill Tailings Management: Proceedings of the First Symposium, 1978, 2 vols., Vol. 2. 141p. write for info. (*0-910069-01-8*) Geotech Engineer Prog.

Uranium Mill Tailings Management: Proceedings of the Fourth Symposium, 1981. 729p. 1981. 28.00 (*0-910069-04-2*) Geotech Engineer Prog.

Uranium Mill Tailings Management: Proceedings of the Second Symposium, 1979. 331p. 1979. 20.00 (*0-910069-02-6*) Geotech Engineer Prog.

Uranium Mill Tailings Management: Proceedings of the Third Symposium, 1980. 573p. 1980. 25.00 (*0-910069-03-4*) Geotech Engineer Prog.

Uranium Mineralization: New Aspects on Geology, Minerology, Geochemistry & Exploration Methods. G. Friedrich et al. (Monograph Series on Mineral Deposits: No. 27). (Illus.). 197p. 1987. pap. text ed. 87.50 (*3-443-12027-X*) Lubrecht & Cramer.

Uranium, Nuclear Power, & Canada-U. S. Energy Relations. Hugh C. McIntyre. LC 78-54112. (Canadian-American Committee Ser.). 80p. 1978. 4.00 (*0-88806-035-1*) Natl Planning.

***Uranium Ore Deposits.** 1993. 262.95 (*0-387-53264-1*) Spr-Verlag.

Uranium Ore Deposits. F. J. Dahlkamp. (Illus.). 512p. 1993. 262.95 (*3-540-53264-1*) Spr-Verlag.

Uranium Ore Processing. (Panel Proceedings Ser.). (Illus.). 238p. 1977. pap. 60.00 (*92-0-041176-2*, ISP453, Pub. by IAEA AU) Bernan Associates.

Uranium Poems. Judith J. Sherwin. reprint ed. 31.50 (*0-404-53864-9*, PS35) AMS Pr.

Uranium Provinces of North America: Their Definition, Distribution, & Models. Warren I. Finch. LC 95-37553. (U. S. Geological Survey Bulletin Ser.: Vol. 2141). 1996. write for info. (*0-614-08570-5*) US Geol Survey.

Uranium Resources, Production & Demand, 1993. OECD Staff. 314p. (Orig.). 1994. pap. 59.00 (*92-64-14019-0*) OECD.

Uranium Technology. AEC Technical Information Center Staff et al. (National Nuclear Energy Ser.: Div. VII, Vol. 2A). 238p. 1951. pap. 36.50 (*0-87079-227-X*, TID-5231); fiche 9.00 (*0-87079-463-9*, TID-5231) DOE.

Uranium Trade Issues: The U. S. Uranium Industry & Imports from the Soviet Union. 29p. (Orig.). (C). 1992. pap. text ed. 25.00 (*1-56806-033-5*) DIANE Pub.

Uranium (VI) -Oxygen Chemistry: Uranyl Hydroxo Complexes, Uranates, Oxides. Vaclav Baran. 135p. (Orig.). 1993. pap. text ed. 60.00 (*0-911767-62-2*) Hadronic Pr Inc.

Uranium 1995 Resources, Production & Demand. OECD Nuclear Energy Agency Staff & International Atomic Energy Agency Staff. 364p. (Orig.). 1996. pap. 86.00 (*92-64-14875-2*, Pub. by Org for Econ FR) OECD.

Uranometria. Joannes Bayer. (Mapping of the Stars Ser.). (Illus.). 216p. (GRE & LAT.). (C). 1989. reprint ed. 495.00 (*1-85297-021-9*, Pub. by Archival Facs UK) St Mut.

Uranometria Two Thousand Point Zero, Vol. 1: The Northern Hemisphere to Minus 6 Degrees. Wil Tirion et al. LC 87-14769. (Illus.). 300p. 1987. text ed. 39.95 (*0-943396-14-X*) Willmann-Bell.

Uranometria Two Thousand Point Zero, Vol. 2: The Southern Hemisphere to Plus 6 Degrees. Wil Tirion et al. 1988. 39.95 (*0-943396-15-8*) Willmann-Bell.

Urantia: The Great Cult Mystery. Martin Gardner. LC 95-2019. (Illus.). 400p. 1995. 25.95 (*0-87975-955-0*) Prometheus Bks.

Urantia Book. LC 55-10554. 2097p. 1955. 54.00 (*0-911560-02-5*) Urantia Foun.

Urantia Book. LC 55-10554. 2097p. 1995. pap. 19.95 (*0-911560-50-5*) Urantia Foun.
URANTIA Foundation is the original publisher of The URANTIA Book & has been since 1955. The URANTIA Book addresses a broad range of subjects, including philosophy, religion, science, sociology, & cosmology. Among other things, The URANTIA Book discusses: the origin, history, & destiny of humankind; the nature of God; the relationship of God to the world & to people; & the life & teachings of Jesus of Nazareth. 370, 000 copies in print & English edition now in the thirteenth printing. 40% discount available to all bookstores. Also available: The URANTIA Book in hardcover, El Libro de URANTIA, Spanish Translation, ISBN 1-883395-01-1; Le Livre d'URANTIA, Revised French Translation, ISBN 0-911560-05-X; URANTIA-kirja, Finnish Translation, ISBN 0-911560-03-3; URANTIA-kirja Hakemisto, Finnish Index, ISBN 0-911560-04-1; Russian Translation 0-911560-80-7 & the URANTIA Book Concordance, ISBN 0-911560-00-9 an alphabetical, comprehensive, easy-to-read, reference tool to aid in the research & the study of The URANTIA Book. Softcover (0-911560-50-5) $19.95. For more information, please contact: URANTIA Foundation, 533 Diversey Parkway, Chicago, IL 60614. (800) 525-3319; FAX (773) 525-7739. ***Publisher Provided Annotation.***

Urantia Book: Electronic Version. 1995. 75.00 (*0-911560-01-7*) Urantia Foun.

***Urantia Book: Leather Collector's Edition.** Urantia Foundation Staff. 1997. 75.00 (*0-911560-75-0*) Urantia Foun.

***Urantia Book: Russian.** 2097p. (RUS.). 1997. 54.00 (*0-911560-80-7*) Urantia Foun.

Urantia Book - A Revelation for Humanity. Uversa Revelatory Corps Staff et al. 1996p. (Orig.). 1996. 24.95 (*0-9651972-0-4*); pap. 18.95 (*0-9651972-1-2*) Uversa Pr.

Urantia Book Concordance. 1584p. 1993. 65.00 (*0-911560-00-9*) Urantia Foun.

Urantia-Kirja. 2097p. (FIN.). 1993. 90.00 (*0-911560-03-3*) Urantia Foun.

Uranus. Marcel Ayme. 384p. (FRE.). 1990. pap. 11.95 (*0-7859-1712-8*, 2070362248) Fr & Eur.

Uranus. Marcel Ayme. (Folio Ser.: No. 224). 376p. (FRE.). 1948. pap. 9.95 (*2-07-036224-8*) Schoenhof.

Uranus. Ed. by Jay T. Bergstralh et al. LC 90-21185. (Space Science Ser.). 1076p. (YA). 1991. 82.00 (*0-8165-1208-6*) U of Ariz Pr.

Uranus. Ellis D. Miner. 1990. pap. write for info. (*0-318-68273-7*) P-H.

Uranus. Donna W. Shepherd. LC 93-6097. (First Bks.). (Illus.). 64p. (J). (gr. 5-8). 1994. lib. bdg. 21.00 (*0-531-20167-8*) Watts.

Uranus. Seymour Simon. LC 86-31223. (Illus.). 32p. (J). (ps-3). 1987. 16.00 (*0-688-06582-1*, Morrow Junior); lib. bdg. 15.93 (*0-688-06583-X*, Morrow Junior) Morrow.

Uranus. Seymour Simon. LC 86-31223. (Illus.). 32p. (J). (ps-3). 1990. pap. 6.95 (*0-688-09929-7*, Morrow Junior) Morrow.

Uranus. Gregory L. Vogt. LC 92-30184. (Gateway Solar System Ser.). (Illus.). 32p. (J). (gr. 2-4). 1993. pap. 6.95 (*1-56294-802-4*); lib. bdg. 14.90 (*1-56294-330-8*) Millbrook Pr.

Uranus. rev. ed. Dennis B. Fradin. LC 89-9984. (New True Bks.). (Illus.). 48p. (J). (gr. k-4). 1990. pap. 5.50 (*0-516-41177-2*); lib. bdg. 19.00 (*0-516-01177-4*) Childrens.

Uranus. Walsh Shepherd. (First Bks.). (Illus.). 64p. (J). (gr. 4-6). 1996. reprint ed. pap. 6.95 (*0-531-15775-X*) Watts.

***Uranus: The Planet, Rings & Satellites.** LC 96-51980. (Wiley-Praxis Series in Astronomy & Astrophysics). 1997. write for info. (*0-471-97398-X*) Wiley.

Uranus & the Outer Planets: Proceedings of the IAU-RAS Colloquium, No. 60. IAU-RAS Colloquium (60th: 1981: University of Bath) Staff. Ed. by Garry Hunt. LC 81-17047. 317p. reprint ed. pap. 90.40 (*0-318-34809-8*, 2031672) Bks Demand.

Uranus-Neptune Influence. Joy Michaud. LC 94-16827. (Illus.). 208p. (Orig.). 1994. pap. 11.95 (*0-87728-806-2*) Weiser.

Uranus-Neptune-Pluto: The Spiritual Trinity. Ted George. LC 79-53906. 234p. 1980. 17.00 (*0-932782-01-9*, G1144-034) Am Fed Astrologers.

Uranus Run. Daniel F. Mitchell. LC 94-90891. 152p. (Orig.). 1996. pap. 8.00 (*1-56002-549-2*, Univ Edtns) Aegina Pr.

Urashima & the Kingdom Beneath the Sea. Roaph F. McCarthy. Ed. by Ogawa & Pockell. LC 93-18500. (Children's Classics Ser.). (Illus.). 48p. (J). 1994. 13.00 (*4-7700-1757-X*) Kodansha.

Urashima Taro & Other Japanese Children's Stories. Ed. by Florence Sakade. (Illus.). 58p. (J). (gr. 1-6). 1958. pap. 9.95 (*0-8048-0609-8*) C E Tuttle.

***U.R.B.** James M. Cox. (Orig.). 1997. 14.99 (*1-889501-10-7*); mass mkt. 8.99 (*1-889501-08-5*, Midnight Tales) Sovereign.

Urban - Suburban Composter: The Complete Guide to Backyard, Balcony, & Apartment Composting. Mark Cullen & Lorraine Johnson. (Illus.). 192p. 1993. pap. 13.95 (*0-312-10530-4*) St Martin.

Urban Aboriginals: A Celebration of Leathersexuality. Geoffrey Mains. (Illus.). 192p. (Orig.). 1991. reprint ed. pap. 14.95 (*0-917342-38-0*) Gay Sunshine.

Urban Affairs Subject Headings. Ed. by Mary Kalb & Letitia Mutter. LC 75-33026. vi, 34p. (Orig.). 1975. text ed. 42.95 (*0-8371-8537-8*, ICSH, Greenwood Pr) Greenwood.

Urban African American Health Care. Eric J. Bailey. 206p. (Orig.). (C). 1991. pap. 23.50 (*0-8191-8277-X*); lib. bdg. 49.00 (*0-8191-8276-1*) U Pr of Amer.

Urban Agglomeration & Economic Growth. Ed. by Herbert Giersch. LC 95-5875. (Publications of the Egon-Sohmen-Foundation). 1995. 98.00 (*3-540-58690-3*) Spr-Verlag.

Urban Agriculture in Zimbabwe: Implications for Urban Management, Urban Economy, Urban Poverty, the Environment & Gender. Beacon Mbiba. 240p. 1995. 59.95 (*1-85628-857-9*, Pub. by Avebury Pub UK) Ashgate Pub Co.

Urban Air Pollution. (UNEP/GEMS Environment Library: No. 4). 40p. 1995. 10.00 (*92-1-100576-0*) UN.

*__Urban Air Pollution.__ Bloemen. (Illus.). 304p. 1997. text ed. write for info. (*0-7514-0381-4*, Pub. by Blackie Acad & Prof UK) Routledge Chapman & Hall.

Urban Air Pollution: Monitoring & Control Strategies. Ed. by Ivo Allegrini & Franco De Santis. LC 95-48078. (NATO ASI Series, Partnership 2: Vol. 8). 477p. 1996. 219.00 (*3-540-60707-2*) Spr-Verlag.

Urban Air Pollution: Proceedings of the WHO Expert Committee with Particular Reference to Motor Vehicles, Geneva, 1968. WHO Staff. (Technical Report Ser.: No. 410). 53p. 1969. pap. text ed. 5.00 (*92-4-120410-9*, 1100410) World Health.

Urban Air Pollution Vol. 1. Ed. by N. Moussiopoulos et al. LC 94-68174. (Urban Air Pollution Ser.: No. 1). 300p. 1994. 161.00 (*1-56252-255-8*, 3315) Computational Mech MA.

Urban Air Pollution Vol. 2. Ed. by H. Power & N. Moussiopoulos. LC 94-6817. (Urban Air Pollution Ser.: No. 2). 260p. 1995. 137.00 (*1-56252-296-5*, 3722) Computational Mech MA.

Urban Air Pollution in Megacities of the World: Eartheatch: Global Environment Monitoring System. UNEP Staff. LC 92-19968. 1992. pap. 37.95 (*0-631-18404-X*) Blackwell Pubs.

*__Urban Air Pollution, 1973-1980.__ WHO Staff. 96p. 1984. 11.00 (*92-4-156082-7*) World Health.

Urban Air Traffic & City Planning: Case Study of Los Angeles County. Melville C. Branch. LC 73-1090. (Special Studies in U. S. Economic, Social & Political Issues). 1973. 49.50 (*0-275-28701-7*) Irvington.

Urban Alcoholism. Sloan T. Letman. 104p. (C). 1993. pap. text ed. 25.00 (*1-884028-00-4*) SL Pubs.

Urban Alternatives: Public & Private Markets in the Provision of Local Services. Robert Stein. LC 90-33959. (Policy & Institutional Studies). 240p. 1992. pap. 19.95 (*0-8229-5476-1*) U of Pittsburgh Pr.

Urban Amazons. Green. Date not set. text ed. 39.95 (*0-312-16470-X*) St Martin.

Urban Amenities & Economic Development, Vol. 2. Ed. by A. Tappan Wilder. (Livability Digest Ser.: No. 1). 80p. 1982. pap. 6.00 (*0-317-44279-1*) Partners Livable.

Urban America: Documenting the Planners. Elaine D. Engst & H. Thomas Hickerson. LC 85-73105. (Illus.). 44p. (Orig.). pap. 5.00 (*0-935995-00-5*) Cornell Manu.

Urban America: Institutions & Experience. Michael Lewis. LC 72-10944. 526p. reprint ed. pap. 150.00 (*0-317-07770-8*, 2013723) Bks Demand.

Urban America: Policy Choices for Los Angeles & the Nation. Mary E. Vaiana. 378p. 1992. pap. text ed. 20.00 (*0-8330-1281-9*) Rand Corp.

Urban America & the Foreign Traveler, 1815-1855. Eugene P. Moehring. LC 73-13465. (Foreign Travelers in America, 1810-1935 Ser.). 334p. 1974. reprint ed. 25.95 (*0-405-05468-8*) Ayer.

Urban America in the Eighties: Perspectives & Prospects. Ed. by Donald A. Hicks. LC 81-2984. 132p. reprint ed. pap. 37.70 (*0-7837-2123-4*, 2042405) Bks Demand.

Urban America in the Modern Age, 1920 to the Present. Carl Abbott. Ed. by John H. Franklin & A. S. Eisenstadt. LC 86-6363. (American History Ser.). (Illus.). 192p. (Orig.). (C). 1987. pap. text ed. write for info. (*0-88295-840-2*) Harlan Davidson.

Urban America in Transition: Perspectives on Urban Policy & Development. Benjamin S. Kleinberg. 320p. 1994. 52.00 (*0-8039-5295-3*); pap. 25.00 (*0-8039-5296-1*) Sage.

Urban Analysis for Branch Library System Planning. R. E. Coughlin et al. LC 71-133496. (Contributions in Librarianship & Information Science Ser.: No. 1). 167p. (C). 1972. text ed. 45.00 (*0-8371-5161-9*, CLP/, Greenwood Pr) Greenwood.

Urban & Agricultural Water Reuse. 1992. pap. 150.00 (*0-943244-86-2*) Water Environ.

Urban & Community Development in Atlantic Canada, 1867-1991: Enterprise in a Maritime Setting, 1787-1920. Carleton University History Collaborative Staff. (Mercury Ser.: No. 44). (Illus.). 146p. 1993. pap. 19.95 (*0-660-14017-9*, Pub. by Can Mus Civil CN) U of Wash Pr.

Urban & Regional Change in Southern Africa. Ed. by David Drakakis-Smith. LC 91-24981. 240p. (C). (gr. 13). 1992. text ed. 79.95 (*0-415-05441-9*, A6707) Routledge.

Urban & Regional Conflict Resolution in Water Related Issues. Ed. by Charles H. King, Jr. & Donald K. Frevert. LC 91-33565. 90p. 1991. pap. text ed. 17.00 (*0-87262-853-1*) Am Soc Civil Eng.

Urban & Regional Economics. Ed. by Paul Cheshire & Alan Evans. (International Library of Critical Writings in Economics Ser.: No. 14). 416p. 1991. text ed. 150.00 (*1-85278-181-5*) E Elgar.

Urban & Regional Economics: A Guide to Information Sources. Ed. by Jean A. Shackelford. LC 74-11556. (Economics Information Guide Ser.: Vol. 14). 190p. 1980. 68.00 (*0-8103-1303-0*) Gale.

Urban & Regional Economics: Marxist Perspectives, Vol. 47. Matthew Edel. (Fundamentals of Pure & Applied Economics Ser.). 158p. 1991. text ed. 22.00 (*3-7186-5102-5*, Harwood Acad Pubs) Gordon & Breach.

Urban & Regional Models in Geography & Planning. Alan G. Wilson. LC 73-8200. 432p. reprint ed. pap. 123.20 (*0-317-30329-5*, 2024807) Bks Demand.

Urban & Regional Planning. 2nd ed. Peter Hall. (Illus.). 336p. 1985. reprint ed. pap. text ed. 16.95 (*0-04-711014-7*) Routledge Chapman & Hall.

Urban & Regional Planning. 3rd ed. Peter Hall. LC 92-24743. (Illus.). 304p. (C). 1992. pap. 19.95 (*0-415-07624-2*, A8508) Routledge.

Urban & Regional Planning in an Age of Austerity. Ed. by Pierre Clavel & William W. Goldsmith. LC 79-21416. (Policy Studies in Urban Affairs). 402p. 1980. text ed. 100.00 (*0-08-025539-6*, Pergamon Pr); pap. text ed. 19.50 (*0-08-025540-X*, Pergamon Pr) Elsevier.

Urban & Regional Planning in Canada. J. Barry Cullingworth. 460p. 1987. 49.95 (*0-88738-135-9*) Transaction Pubs.

*__Urban & Regional Planning Periodicals with Book Reviews.__ Laura J. Clarke & Deborah Thompson-Wise. 19p. 1993. pap. 10.00 (*0-614-25157-5*) Coun Plan Librarians.

Urban & Regional Planning Periodicals with Book Reviews. Laura J. Clarke & Deborah Thompson-Wise. LC 93-42458. (CPL Bibliographies Ser.: No. 297). 1993. 10.00 (*0-86602-297-X*, Sage Prdcls Pr) Sage.

Urban & Regional Policy. Ed. by Jon Pierre. LC 94-22993. (International Library of Comparative Public Policy: Vol. 2). 688p. 1995. 200.00 (*1-85278-909-3*) E Elgar.

Urban & Regional Studies at United States Universities: A Report Based on a 1963 Survey of Urban & Regional Research. Ed. by Scott Keyes. 141p. reprint ed. pap. 40.20 (*0-317-26467-2*, 2023803) Bks Demand.

Urban & Rural Change in West Germany. Ed. by Trevor Wild. LC 83-6350. 272p. (C). 1983. text ed. 56.00 (*0-389-20392-0*, N7270) B&N Imports.

Urban & Rural Development in Third World Countries: Problems of Population in Developing Nations. Ed. by Valentine U. James. LC 90-53499. (Illus.). 365p. 1991. lib. bdg. 49.95 (*0-89950-584-8*) McFarland & Co.

Urban & Spatial Development in Mexico. Ian Scott. LC 80-8023. 442p. reprint ed. pap. 126.00 (*0-7837-4463-3*, 2043949) Bks Demand.

Urban Anthropology: A Research Bibliography, Nos. 944-945. William W. Pilcher. 1975. 10.50 (*0-686-20380-1*, Sage Prdcls Pr) Sage.

Urban Anthropology in China. Ed. by Greg Guldin & Aidan Southall. LC 92-36147. (Studies in Human Society: Vol. 6). (Illus.). xv, 429p. 1993. pap. 107.00 (*90-04-09620-5*) E J Brill.

Urban Applications of Satellite Remote Sensing & GIS Analysis. Bengt Paulsson. LC 92-33642. (Urban Management Program Ser.: Vol. 9). 71p. 1992. 6.95 (*0-8213-2266-4*, 12266) World Bank.

Urban Astronomer: A Practical Guide to Celestial Objects for Observers in Cities & Suburbs. Gregory L. Matloff. LC 91-9316. (Science Editions Ser.: No. 1800). 224p. 1991. text ed. 39.95 (*0-471-53142-1*); pap. text ed. 16.95 (*0-471-53143-X*) Wiley.

Urban Atlanta: Redefining the Role of the City. Ed. by Andrew M. Hamer. LC 79-27699. (Research Monograph: No. 84). 256p. 1980. spiral bd. 19.95 (*0-88406-125-6*) GA St U Busn Pr.

*__Urban Atmosphere & Its Effects, 1.__ 300p. 1997. text ed. 33.00 (*1-86094-064-1*) World Scientific Pub.

Urban Australia. Brownlow & Reid. (Spotlight Australia Ser.). 1996. pap. write for info. (*0-08-020938-6*, Pergamon Pr) Elsevier.

Urban Australia. Ed. by Steve Hamnett & R. Bunker. 200p. 1987. pap. text ed. 90.00 (*0-7201-1843-3*, Mansell Pub) Cassell.

*__Urban Bikers' Tricks & Tips: Low-Tech & No-Tech Ways to Find, Ride & Keep a Bicycle.__ Dave Glowacz. 1997. pap. 14.95 (*0-9651728-0-5*) Wrdspace Pr.

Urban Biophysical Environments. Howard Bridgman et al. (Meridian Australian Geographical Perspectives Ser.). (Illus.). 166p. (C). 1996. pap. text ed. 29.95 (*0-19-553611-8*) OUP.

Urban Black Politics. Ed. by John R. Howard & Robert C. Smith. LC 78-56922. (Annals Ser.: No. 439). 1978. 28.00 (*0-87761-230-7*); pap. 18.00 (*0-87761-231-5*) Am Acad Pol Soc Sci.

Urban Bliss. Janice Eidus. 208p. 1994. 19.95 (*0-88064-159-2*) Fromm Intl Pub.

Urban Blues. 2nd ed. Charles Keil. (Illus.). 243p. 1968. pap. 15.95 (*0-226-42960-1*, P291) U Ch Pr.

Urban Blues for Guitar. 112p. 1988. per. 12.95 (*0-7935-0799-5*, 00028000) H Leonard.

Urban Business Profiles. LC 79-14909. (Small-Business Library: Vol. 1). 400p. 1979. 99.00 (*0-8103-1027-9*) Gale.

Urban Caldron: The Second Annual Donald G. Hagman Commemorative Conference. Donald G. Hagman Commemorative Conference Staff et al. Ed. by Joseph DiMento. LC 85-21641. (Lincoln Institute of Land Policy Book Ser.). 160p. reprint ed. pap. 45.60 (*0-7837-5774-3*, 2045439) Bks Demand.

Urban Campus: Educating the New Majority for the New Century. Peggy G. Elliott. LC 94-5958. (American Council on Education-Oryx Press Series on Higher Education). (Illus.). 184p. 1994. 29.95 (*0-89774-818-2*) Oryx Pr.

Urban Capitalists: Entrepreneurs & City Growth in Pennsylvania's Lackawanna & Lehigh Regions, 1800-1920. Burton W. Folsom. LC 80-8864. (Studies in Industry & Society: No. 1). 205p. 1981. pap. 58.50 (*0-7837-7452-4*, 2049174) Bks Demand.

*__Urban Caribbean: Transition to the New Global Economy.__ Ed. by Alejandro Portes et al. LC 96-35184. 296p. 1997. text ed. 48.50 (*0-8018-5517-9*) Johns Hopkins.

*__Urban Caribbean: Transition to the New Global Economy.__ Ed. by Alejandro Portes et al. LC 96-35184. 296p. 1997. pap. text ed. 17.95 (*0-8018-5519-5*) Johns Hopkins.

*__Urban Challenge in Africa: Growth & Management of Its Large Cities.__ Carole Rakodi. LC 97-4603. 100p. 1997. pap. 40.00 (*92-808-0952-0*, UNUP-0952, Pub. by UN Univ JA) UN.

Urban Change & Renewal: The Paradox of Place. Ed. by Philip Garragan & Paul Stewart. (Studies in Urban Continuity & Revival). 1994. 55.95 (*1-85628-648-7*, Pub. by Avebury Pub UK) Ashgate Pub Co.

Urban Change & the Planning Syndrome. Ed. by George F. Mott & Richard D. Lambert. LC 72-93250. (Annals of the American Academy of Political & Social Science Ser.: No. 405). 250p. (C). 1973. 28.00 (*0-685-00185-7*, 87761); pap. 18.00 (*0-87761-157-2*) Am Acad Pol Soc Sci.

Urban Change in China: Politics & Development in Tsinan, Shantung, 1890-1949. David D. Buck. LC 76-11309. 313p. 1978. reprint ed. pap. 89.30 (*0-608-01907-0*, 2062559) Bks Demand.

Urban Change in the United States & Western Europe: Comparative Analysis & Policy. Anita A. Summers. LC 93-16113. 770p. (Orig.). 1993. lib. bdg. 72.00 (*0-87766-592-3*) Urban Inst.

Urban Children in Distress: Global Predicaments & Innovative Strategies. Cristina S. Blanc et al. LC 94-401. 481p. 1994. text ed. 50.00 (*2-88124-622-2*); pap. text ed. 25.00 (*2-88124-623-0*) Gordon & Breach.

Urban Christian. Raymond Bakke. LC 87-30861. 202p. 1987. reprint ed. pap. 11.99 (*0-87784-523-9*, 523) InterVarsity.

Urban Church Education. Ed. by Donald B. Rogers. LC 89-4024. 213p. 1989. 16.95 (*0-89135-070-5*) Religious Educ.

Urban Classroom Portraits: Teachers Who Make a Difference. Mary E. Bredemeier. (American University Studies: Language: Ser. XIV, Vol. 11). 279p. (C). 1988. text ed. 38.50 (*0-8204-0651-1*) P Lang Pubng.

Urban Climate. Helmut Landsberg. LC 80-2766. (International Geophysics Ser.). 1981. text ed. 75.00 (*0-12-435960-4*) Acad Pr.

*__Urban Coastal Area Management: The Experience of Singapore.__ Chia L. Sien. (ICLARM Conference Proceedings Ser.: No. 25). 128p. 1991. per. write for info. (*971-10-2287-7*, Pub. by ICLARM PH) Intl Spec Bk.

Urban Cognition. T. Garling. (Readings in Environmental Psychology Ser.). (Illus.). 203p. 1995. text ed. 24.95 (*0-12-276040-9*) Acad Pr.

Urban Community. Ed. by Ernest W. Burgess. LC 71-175038. (BCL Ser. I). reprint ed. 39.50 (*0-404-01235-3*) AMS Pr.

Urban Community: A Guide to Information Sources. Ed. by Anthony Filipovitch & Earl Reeves. LC 78-13171. (Urban Studies Information Guide Ser.: Vol. 4). 296p. 1978. 68.00 (*0-8103-1429-0*) Gale.

Urban Community: Housing & Planning in the Progressive Era. Roy Lubove. LC 81-6328. (American Historical Sources: Research & Interpretation Ser.). ix, 148p. 1981. reprint ed. text ed. 49.75 (*0-313-22731-4*, LUUC, Greenwood Pr) Greenwood.

Urban Community Development. Jacob Z. Thudipara. (C). 1993. 18.50 (*81-7033-217-6*, Pub. by Rawat II) S Asia.

Urban Consumer Theory. Jeffrey Turnbull. 170p. 1995. pap. text ed. 25.50 (*0-87766-645-8*); lib. bdg. 57.50 (*0-87766-644-X*) Urban Inst.

Urban Context: Ethnicity, Social Networks, & Situational Analysis. Ed. by Alisdair Rogers et al. LC 94-25313. (Explorations in Anthropology Ser.). (Illus.). 320p. 1995. 45.95 (*0-85496-317-0*); pap. 19.95 (*1-85973-072-8*) Berg Pubs.

Urban Crime: Global Trends & Policies. 450p. 1989. 45.00 (*92-808-0679-3*, 89.III.A.1) UN.

Urban Crime, Criminals & Victims: The Swedish Experience in an Anglo-American Comparative Perspective. P. O. Wikstrom. Ed. by A. Blumstein & David P. Farrington. (Research in Criminology Ser.). (Illus.). viii, 269p. 1990. 91.95 (*0-387-97405-9*) Spr-Verlag.

*__Urban Crisis: Linking Research to Action.__ Burton A. Weisbrod. LC 96-41992. 236p. 1997. pap. 22.50 (*0-8101-1390-2*) Northwestern U Pr.

*__Urban Crisis: Linking Research to Action.__ Ed. by Burton A. Weisbrod & James C. Worthy. LC 96-41992. 236p. 1997. 69.95 (*0-8101-1389-9*) Northwestern U Pr.

Urban Crucible: The Northern Seaports & the Origins of the American Revolution. Gary B. Nash. (Illus.). 300p. 1986. pap. 15.95 (*0-674-93059-2*) HUP.

Urban Dances for Brass Quintet, Score & Parts. R. Danielpour. 72p. 1992. pap. 35.00 (*0-7935-1244-1*) H Leonard.

Urban Danger: Life in a Neighborhood of Strangers. Sally E. Merry. 278p. 1986. pap. 18.95 (*0-87722-425-0*) Temple U Pr.

Urban Decay in India. R. S. Sharma. 1988. 40.00 (*81-215-0045-1*, Pub. by Munshiram Manoharial II) S Asia.

Urban Decision Making...a Guide to Information Sources. Ed. by Mark Drucker. LC 80-19252. (Urban Studies Information Guide Ser.: Vol. 13). 208p. 1981. 68.00 (*0-8103-1481-9*) Gale.

Urban Decline: The British Experience. David Clark. 160p. 1989. 52.50 (*0-415-03031-5*, A3289) Routledge.

Urban Decline & the Future of American Cities. Katherine J. Bradbury et al. LC 82-70888. 309p. 1982. 36.95 (*0-8157-1054-2*); pap. 16.95 (*0-8157-1053-4*) Brookings.

Urban Decline in Early Modern Germany: Schwabisch Hall & Its Region, 1650-1750. Terence McIntosh. LC 96-13722. (James Sprunt Studies in History & Political Science: Vol. 62). 368p. (C). (gr. 13). 1997. lib. bdg. 34.95 (*0-8078-5063-2*) U of NC Pr.

Urban Design: A Comprehensive Reference. Hamid Shirvani. (CPL Bibliographies Ser.: No. 46). vi, 80p. 1981. 10.00 (*0-86602-046-2*, Sage Prdcls Pr) Sage.

Urban Design: Green Dimensions. James C. Moughtin. (Illus.). 224p. 1996. text ed. 56.95 (*0-7506-2659-3*) Buttrwrth-Heinemann.

Urban Design: Ornament & Decoration. Taner Oc et al. LC 94-47287. (Illus.). 224p. 1995. 56.95 (*0-7506-0792-0*) Buttrwrth-Heinemann.

Urban Design: Street & Square. James C. Moughtin. (Illus.). 224p. 1992. 78.95 (*0-7506-0416-6*) Buttrwrth-Heinemann.

Urban Design: The American Experience. Jon T. Lang. LC 93-15893. 509p. 1994. pap. 62.95 (*0-442-01360-4*) Van Nos Reinhold.

Urban Design: Visions & Reflections. Ed. by Iris Miller & Robert A. Busser. 160p. (Orig.). (C). 1991. pap. text ed. write for info. (*0-9635710-1-X*) Iris Miller.

*__Urban Design Downtown: Poetics & Politics of Form.__ Anastasia Loukaitou-Sideris & Tridib Banerjee. LC 97-10758. 1998. write for info. (*0-520-20930-3*) U CA Pr.

Urban Design in Western Europe: Regime & Architecture, 900-1900. Wolfgang Braunfels. Tr. by Kenneth J. Northcott. (Illus.). xvi, 422p. 1990. pap. text ed. 30.00 (*0-226-07179-0*) U Ch Pr.

Urban Design Manhattan. Rai Y. Okamoto & Frank E. Williams. (Illus.). 130p. (C). 1969. text ed. 10.00 (*0-318-19021-4*) Regional Plan Assn.

Urban Designer. Jack Rudman. (Career Examination Ser.: C-1527). 1994. pap. 27.95 (*0-8373-1527-1*) Nat Learn.

Urban Development: Theory, Fact, & Illusion. J. Vernon Henderson. (Illus.). 256p. (C). 1991. reprint ed. pap. text ed. 21.00 (*0-19-506902-1*) OUP.

Urban Development Action Grant Program. Richard P. Nathan & Jerry A. Webman. 125p. 1980. pap. text ed. 21.95 (*0-938882-01-5*) Transaction Pubs.

Urban Development & the Royal Fine Art Commission. A. J. Youngson. 186p. 1990. 45.00 (*0-7486-0114-7*, Pub. by Edinburgh U Pr UK) Col U Pr.

Urban Development & the Royal Fine Art Commissions. A. J. Youngson. (Illus.). 186p. 1992. pap. 25.00 (*0-7486-0153-8*, Pub. by Edinburgh U Pr UK) Col U Pr.

Urban Development in Nigeria: Planning, Housing & Land Policy. Robert W. Taylor. 240p. 1992. 59.95 (*1-85628-456-5*, Pub. by Avebury Pub UK) Ashgate Pub Co.

Urban Development in the Muslim World. Ed. by Hooshang Amirahmadi & Salah S. El-Shakhs. LC 92-20103. 290p. (C). 1993. text ed. 34.95 (*0-88285-141-1*) Ctr Urban Pol Res.

Urban Development in the Third World. Ed. by Pradip K. Ghosh. LC 83-22859. (International Development Resource Bks.: No. 2). (Illus.). xviv, 546p. 1984. text ed. 69.50 (*0-313-24138-4*, GUD/, Greenwood Pr) Greenwood.

Urban Development in the U. S. A. & Hungary. Gy Enyedi. (Studies in Geography in Hungary: No. 14). 311p. 1978. 81.00 (*963-05-1514-8*, Pub. by Akad Kiado HU) St Mut.

Urban Development Issues: What Is Controversial in Urban Sprawl? Ivonne Audirac & Maria Zifou. (Bureau of Economic & Business Research Monographs). 52p. (Orig.). 1989. pap. text ed. 12.00 (*0-930885-02-3*) Bur Econ & Bus Res.

Urban Development Law & Policy. Patricia Ryan. cxiii, 473p. 1987. 129.50 (*0-455-20750-X*, Pub. by Law Bk Co AT); pap. 84.00 (*0-455-20749-6*, Pub. by Law Bk Co AT) Gaunt.

Urban Development Models. Ed. by Richard Baxter et al. LC 79-301020. (Cambridge University Centre for Land Use & Built Form Studies Conference Proceedings: No. 3). 343p. reprint ed. pap. 97.80 (*0-317-27680-8*, 2025216) Bks Demand.

Urban Development Planning: Lessons for the Economic Reconstruction of South Africa's Cities. Richard Tomlinson. LC 95-13016. (Illus.). 288p. (C). 1995. pap. 25.00 (*1-85649-308-3*, Pub. by Zed Bks Ltd UK) Humanities.

*__Urban Development, Planning & Development of Urban & Rural Settlements: Snip 2.07.01-89.__ Russia's Minstroy Staff. (Snip Building Codes of Russia Ser.). (Illus.). iv, 68p. (Orig.). 1996. ring bd. 269.95 (*1-57937-007-1*) Snip Register.

Urban Disaster Mitigation: The Role of Engineering & Technology. Ed. by F. Y. Cheng & M. S. Sheu. LC 95-12167. 340p. 1995. 132.25 (*0-08-041920-8*, Pergamon Pr) Elsevier.

Urban Discharges & Receiving Water Quality Impacts: Proceedings of a Seminar Organized by the IAWPRC-IAHR Sub-Committee for Urban Runoff Quality, Data, As Part of the IAWPRC 14th Biennial Conference, Brighton, UK, July 18-21, 1988. Ed. by J. B. Ellis. (Advances in Water Pollution Control Ser.). 198p. 1989. 53.25 (*0-08-037376-3*, Pergamon Pr) Elsevier.

Urban Disorder & the Shape of Belief: The Great Chicago Fire, the Haymarket Bomb. Carl Smith. (Illus.). 396p. (C). 1996. pap. text ed. 18.95 (*0-226-76417-6*) U Ch Pr.

An Asterisk (*) at the beginning of an entry indicates that the title is appearing in BIP for the first time.

Urban Disorder & the Shape of Belief: The Great Chicago Fire, the Haymarket Bomb & the Model Town of Pullman. Carl Smith. (Illus.). 408p. 1994. 35.00 (*0-226-76416-8*) U Ch Pr.

Urban District Heating Using Nuclear Heat. (Panel Proceedings Ser.). (Illus.). 207p. 1977. pap. text ed. 40.00 (*92-0-051077-9*, ISP461, Pub. by IAEA AU) Bernan Associates.

*__Urban Districts & Drug Scenes: Prevention of Drug Dependence.__ 288p. 1996. pap. 15.00 (*92-827-7759-6*, CE91-95-576-ENC, Pub. by Europ Com UK) Bernan Associates.

*__Urban Dominance & Labour Market Differentiation of a European Capital City: Lisbon 1890-1990.__ Ed. by Pedro T. Pereira & Maria E. Mata. LC 96-46652. 200p. (C). 1996. lib. bdg. 79.95 (*0-7923-9830-0*) Kluwer Ac.

Urban Drainage Catchments: Selected Worldwide Rainfall-Runoff Data. Ed. by C. Maksimovic & M. Radojkovic. (Illus.). 382p. 1986. 174.00 (*0-08-034086-5*, Pub. by PPL UK) Franklin.

Urban Drainage Modelling--Urban Drainage Catchments. C. Maksimovic. 1986. 150.00 (*0-08-034333-3*, Pergamon Pr) Elsevier.

Urban Drainage Rehabilitation Programs & Techniques: Selected Papers on Urban Drainage Rehabilitation from 1988-1993 Water Resources Planning & Management Division Conference Sessions. American Society of Civil Engineers, Task Committee on Marines 2000 Staff et al. LC 94-5426. 1994. 25.00 (*0-7844-0038-5*) Am Soc Civil Eng.

*__Urban Dweller Who Is Looking for Alternatives.__ John Hanna. Ed. by Liz Lake. 204p. (Orig.). 1997. pap. write for info. (*0-89716-755-4*) P B Pubng.

Urban Dynamics. Jay W. Forrester. (Illus.). 256p. 1994. reprint ed. 45.00 (*1-56327-058-7*) Prod Press.

Urban Dynamics: A Real Estate Perspective. Erwin Van der Krabben. 251p. 1995. pap. 26.50 (*90-5170-390-2*, Pub. by Thesis Pubs NE) IBD Ltd.

Urban Dynamics: Expansions & Reflections. Ed. by Kan Chen. 1971. 7.50 (*0-911302-18-2*); pap. 5.00 (*0-317-58564-9*) San Francisco Pr.

Urban Dynamics & Spatial Choice Behaviour. Joost Hauer et al. 320p. 1989. lib. bdg. 123.50 (*0-7923-0391-1*) Kluwer Ac.

Urban Dynamics & Urban Externalities, Vol. 11. Takahiro Miyao & Yoshitsugu Kanemoto. (Fundamentals of Pure & Applied Economics Ser.: Volume 11). 1987. pap. text ed. 43.00 (*3-7186-0333-0*) Gordon & Breach.

Urban Ecology. Ed. by H. Sukopp & S. Hejny. (Illus.). viii, 281p. 1990. pap. 60.00 (*90-5103-040-1*, Pub. by SPB Acad Pub NE) Balogh.

Urban Ecology: A Teacher's Resource Book. Martin Collins. (Illus.). 160p. 1984. pap. text ed. 19.95 (*0-521-27803-1*) Cambridge U Pr.

Urban Ecology & Health in the Third World. Ed. by Lawrence M. Schell et al. (Society for the Study of Human Biology Symposium Ser.: No. 32). (Illus.). 325p. (C). 1993. text ed. 90.00 (*0-521-41159-9*) Cambridge U Pr.

Urban Ecology As the Basis of Urban Planning. Ed. by A. Huber et al. (Illus.). 218p. 1995. pap. 55.00 (*90-5103-096-7*, Pub. by SPB Acad Pub NE) Balogh.

Urban Economic & Planning Models: Assessing the Potential for Cities in Developing Countries. LC 78-8437. (World Bank Staff Occasional Papers: No. 25). 194p. reprint ed. pap. 55.30 (*0-7837-4267-3*, 2043959) Bks Demand.

Urban Economic Change: Five City Studies. Ed. by Members of ESRC Inner Cities Research Programme Staff & Victor A. Hausner. (ESRC Inner Cities Research Programme Ser.: No. 2). (Illus.). 280p. 1988. 69.00 (*0-19-823280-2*) OUP.

Urban Economic Development. Ed. by Richard D. Bingham & John P. Blair. LC 84-11456. (Urban Affairs Annual Reviews Ser.: No. 27). 287p. 1984. reprint ed. pap. 81.80 (*0-608-01514-8*, 2059558) Bks Demand.

Urban Economic Development, 2 bks., Set. Roger L. Kemp. 158p. (Orig.). (C). 1995. pap. text ed. 21.95 (*0-943025-65-6*) Cummngs & Hath.

Urban Economic Theory: Land Use & City Size. Masahisa Fujita. (Illus.). 320p. (C). 1989. text ed. 89.95 (*0-521-34662-2*) Cambridge U Pr.

Urban Economic Theory: Land Use & City Size. Masahisa Fujita. (Illus.). 320p. (C). 1991. pap. text ed. 29.95 (*0-521-39645-X*) Cambridge U Pr.

Urban Economics. 2nd ed. Arthur M. O'Sullivan. LC 92-17150. 768p. (C). 1992. text ed. 64.95 (*0-256-09617-1*) Irwin.

Urban Economics. 3rd ed. Arthur M. O'Sullivan. LC 95-37278. (Irwin Series in Economics). 768p. (C). 1995. 67.50 (*0-256-16072-4*) Irwin.

Urban Economics. 5th ed. Edwin S. Mills & Hamilton. 480p. (C). 1994. text ed. 71.95 (*0-673-46867-4*) Addson-Wesley Educ.

*__Urban Economics.__ Werner Z. Hirsch. (Illus.). 464p. (C). 1992. reprint ed. text ed. 55.00 (*1-878907-65-4*) TechBooks.

Urban Economics & Real Estate Markets. William Wheaton & Denise DiPasquale. LC 95-32621. 400p. (C). 1995. text ed. 70.00 (*0-13-225244-9*) P-H.

Urban Economy. Ed. by Harold M. Hochman. (Problems of the Modern Economy Ser.). (Illus.). 320p. (C). 1976. pap. text ed. 6.95 (*0-393-09243-7*) Norton.

Urban Economy & Regional Trade Liberalization. Peter K. Kresl. LC 91-45611. 224p. 1992. text ed. 55.00 (*0-275-94289-9*, C4289, Praeger Pubs) Greenwood.

Urban Education. Noguera. 1996. pap. text ed. 27.00 (*0-205-18937-7*) Allyn.

Urban Education: A Guide to Information Sources. Ed. by Donald W. Mocker & George E. Spear. LC 78-13627. (Urban Studies Information Guide Ser.: Vol. 3). 216p. 1978. 68.00 (*0-8103-1431-2*) Gale.

Urban Education: A Workbook of Activities for Classroom Teachers. Stephanie Evans. 140p. (C). 1996. spiral bd. 40.89 (*0-7872-2013-2*) Kendall-Hunt.

Urban Education Bibliography. (Urban Education Reports Ser.: No. 1). 4p. 1980. 1.00 (*0-685-09450-2*) I N Thut World Educ Ctr.

Urban Education in the Nineteenth Century. Ed. by D. A. Reeder. LC 77-26280. 1978. text ed. 29.95 (*0-312-83446-2*) St Martin.

Urban Elders: Family, Work & Welfare among Boston's Aged, 1890 to 1950. Brian Gratton. LC 85-14791. 1986. 34.95 (*0-87722-390-4*) Temple U Pr.

*__Urban Elections in Democratic Latin America.__ Ed. by Henry A. Dietz & Gil Shidlo. LC 97-13454. (Latin American Silhouettes Ser.). 264p. (C). 1997. text ed. 50.00 (*0-8420-2627-4*, SR Bks); pap. text ed. 18.95 (*0-8420-2628-2*, SR Bks) Scholarly Res Inc.

Urban Elements: Furniture & Microarchitecture. Josep M. Serra. (Illus.). 304p. 1996. pap. text ed. 60.00 (*84-252-1679-6*) Watsn-Guptill.

Urban Elites & Mass Transportation: The Dialectics of Power. J. Allen Whitt. LC 81-47958. (Illus.). 245p. 1982. reprint ed. pap. 69.90 (*0-7837-9482-7*, 2060224) Bks Demand.

Urban Enclave: Lithuanian Refugees in Los Angeles. Liucija Baskauskas. LC 83-45348. (Immigrant Communities & Ethnic Minorities in the U. S. & Canada Ser.: No. 7). 1985. 39.50 (*0-404-19402-8*) AMS Pr.

Urban Enclaves. Mark Abrahamson. 1996. pap. 16.95 (*0-312-13837-7*) St Martin.

Urban Enclaves: Identity & Place in America. Mark Abrahamson. 1995. text ed. 39.95 (*0-312-12794-4*) St Martin.

Urban Encounters: Art Architecture Audience. Lawrence Alloway et al. (Illus.). 64p. (Orig.). 1980. pap. 15.00 (*0-88454-055-3*) U of Pa Contemp Art.

Urban Energy Planning. L. Kwit. write for info. (*0-275-90019-3*, C0019, Praeger Pubs) Greenwood.

Urban Entertainment Graphics: Theme Parks & Entertainment Environments. Wayne Hunt. (Illus.). 224p. 1997. 45.00 (*0-942604-49-0*) Madison Square.

Urban Entomology: Interdisciplinary Perspectives. Ed. by Gordon W. Frankie & Carl S. Koehler. LC 83-2407. 512p. 1983. text ed. 50.00 (*0-275-90981-6*, C0981, Praeger Pubs) Greenwood.

Urban Environment & Population Relocation. Michael M. Cernea. (Discussion Paper Ser.: No. 152). 56p. 1993. 6.95 (*0-8213-2057-2*, 12057) World Bank.

Urban Environmental Education. Jeffrey Frank & Michael Zamm. (EEToolbox-Workshop Resource Manual Ser.). 48p. 1994. teacher ed. 8.00 (*1-884782-06-X*) Natl Consort EET.

Urban Environmental Education. NCEET Staff. 52p. (C). 1996. 8.00 (*0-7872-2199-6*) Kendall-Hunt.

Urban Environmental Management: Environmental Change & Urban Design. Rodney R. White. LC 94-9553. 192p. 1994. text ed. 52.95 (*0-471-95001-7*) Wiley.

*__Urban Environmental Planning: Policies, Instruments & Methods in an International Perspective.__ Ed. by Donald Miller & Gert De Roo. 336p. 1997. 72.95 (*1-85972-593-7*, Pub. by Avebury Pub UK) Ashgate Pub Co.

Urban Environments. 5p. 1994. 39.00 (*1-56290-099-4*, 6037) Crystal.

Urban Environments in Emerging Economies. David L. McKee. LC 94-7430. 192p. 1994. text ed. 52.95 (*0-275-94938-9*, Praeger Pubs) Greenwood.

Urban Establishment: Upper Strata in Boston, New York, Charleston, Chicago, & Los Angeles. Frederic C. Jaher. LC 80-18925. 790p. 1981. text ed. 49.95 (*0-252-00827-8*); pap. text ed. 19.95 (*0-252-00932-0*) U of Ill Pr.

Urban Establishment: Upper Strata in Boston, New York, Charleston, Chicago, & Los Angeles. fac. ed. Frederic C. Jaher. LC 80-18925. 789p. reprint ed. pap. 180.00 (*0-7837-8071-0*, 2047824) Bks Demand.

Urban Ethos in the South, Nineteen Twenty to Nineteen Thirty. Blaine A. Brownell. LC 74-82003. 262p. reprint ed. pap. 74.70 (*0-317-28674-9*, 2055299) Bks Demand.

*__Urban Europe 1500-1700.__ pap. write for info. (*0-340-66324-3*, Pub. by E Arnold UK) Routledge Chapman & Hall.

*__Urban Europe 1500-1700.__ write for info. (*0-7131-6529-4*, Pub. by E Arnold UK) Routledge Chapman & Hall.

*__Urban Evidence: Contemporary Artists Reveal Cleveland.__ Gary Sangster et al. LC 96-33452. 1996. write for info. (*0-940717-35-2*) Cleveland Mus Art.

Urban Excess & the Law. Christopher Stanley. 244p. 1996. pap. 40.00 (*1-85941-209-2*, Pub. by Cavendish UK) Gaunt.

Urban Experience. David Harvey. LC 88-46118. 285p. 1989. pap. text ed. 16.95 (*0-8018-3849-5*) Johns Hopkins.

Urban Experience. 2nd ed. Claude S. Fischer & Robert K. Merton. 371p. (Orig.). (C). 1984. pap. text ed. 20.00 (*0-15-593498-8*) HB Coll Pubs.

*__Urban Experience: A People-Environment Perspective.__ Ed. by Neary et al. (Illus.). 544p. 1995. text ed. 86.50 (*0-419-20160-2*, E & FN Spon) Routledge Chapman & Hall.

Urban Experience: Calcutta: Essays in Honour of Professor Nisith Ranjan Ray. Ed. by Sinha Padip. 186p. (C). 1987. 17.50 (*0-685-19667-4*, Pub. by KP Bagchi IA) S Asia.

Urban Experience: Essays in Honour of Professor Nisith R. Ray. Nisith R. Ray. 1987. 17.50 (*0-8364-2276-7*, Pub. by Rddhi IA) S Asia.

Urban Families: Conjugal Roles & Social Networks. Elizabeth Bott. (Reprint Series in Social Sciences). (C). 1993. reprint ed. pap. text ed. 2.90 (*0-8290-2679-7*, S-554) Irvington.

Urban Family: A Study of Hindu Social System. A. K. Lal. 1990. 21.00 (*0-317-99587-1*, Pub. by Concept II) S Asia.

Urban Family & Family Planning in India. A. R. Desai. 224p. 1980. reprint ed. 22.95 (*0-940500-70-1*) Asia Bk Corp.

Urban Family Medicine. Ed. by R. Birrer. (Illus.). 350p. 1986. 139.00 (*0-387-96301-4*) Spr-Verlag.

Urban Family Practice - A Resource Monograph. 168p. 1994. 20.00 (*0-614-01879-X*) Soc Tchrs Fam Med.

Urban Finance Policy & Administration: A Guide to Information Sources. Jerry L. McCaffery & John L. Mikesell. (Urban Studies Information Guide Ser.: Vol. 12). 240p. 1980. 68.00 (*0-8103-1464-9*) Gale.

Urban Finance under Siege. Ed. by Thomas R. Swartz & Frank J. Bonello. LC 92-40741. 208p. (C). (gr. 13). 1993. text ed. 58.95 (*1-56324-224-9*); pap. text ed. 23.95 (*1-56324-225-7*) M E Sharpe.

Urban Financial Management: A Training Manual. James McMaster. (EDI Technical Materials Ser.). 192p. 1991. 10.95 (*0-8213-1615-X*, 11615) World Bank.

Urban Financial Stress: Why Cities Go Broke. Joan Martin. LC 81-20659. 198p. 1982. text ed. 49.95 (*0-86569-084-7*, Auburn Hse) Greenwood.

Urban Flood Loss Prevention & Mitigation. (Water Resources Ser.: No. 68). 92p. 1991. 15.00 (*92-1-119570-5*, 91.II.F.6) UN.

Urban Flood Protection Benefits: A Project Appraisal Guide. Dennis Parker et al. Orig. Title: The Indirect Benefits of Urban Flood Alleviation. 1987. text ed. 159.95 (*0-291-39707-7*, Pub. by Avebury Technical UK) Ashgate Pub Co.

Urban Forest: Comprehensive Management. rev. ed. Gene W. Grey. LC 95-10875. Orig. Title: Urban Forestry. 208p. 1995. text ed. 69.95 (*0-471-12275-0*) Wiley.

Urban Forest Landscapes: Integrating Multidisciplinary Perspectives. Ed. by Gordon A. Bradley. LC 94-23781. 240p. 1995. 40.00 (*0-295-97438-9*); pap. 20.00 (*0-295-97439-7*) U of Wash Pr.

Urban Forester. Jack Rudman. (Career Examination Ser.: C-2905). 1994. pap. 27.95 (*0-8373-2905-1*) Nat Learn.

Urban Forestry. 2nd ed. Gene W. Grey & Frederick J. Deneke. LC 91-46194. 316p. (C). 1992. reprint ed. 45.00 (*0-89464-704-0*) Krieger.

Urban Forestry. 2nd ed. Robert W. Miller. 480p. (C). 1996. text ed. 89.00 (*0-13-458522-4*) P-H.

Urban Forestry: A Bibliography. Jean Albrecht. 73p. (C). 1993. pap. text ed. 15.00 (*1-881956-03-2*) Int Soc Arboricult.

Urban Forestry: Building Sustainable Communities, an Environmental Guide for Local Government. Center for the Study of Law & Politics Staff. 112p. 1991. 40.00 (*1-880386-07-0*) Ctr Study Law.

Urban Forestry see Urban Forest: Comprehensive Management

Urban Forestry Conference: Proceedings. 1973. 1.50 (*0-686-20725-4*) SUNY Environ.

*__Urban Forms & Colonial Confrontations: Algiers under French Rule.__ Zeynep Celik. LC 96-37606. (Illus.). 1997. 40.00 (*0-520-20457-3*) U CA Pr.

Urban Forms, Suburban Dreams. Ed. by Malcolm Quantrill & Bruce Webb. LC 92-43269. (Studies in Architecture & Culture: No. 2). (Illus.). 232p. 1993. 50.00 (*0-89096-535-8*) Tex A&M Univ Pr.

Urban Fortunes: The Political Economy of Place. Ed. by John R. Logan & Harvey L. Molotch. (C). 1987. pap. 14.00 (*0-520-06341-4*) U CA Pr.

Urban Foxes. Stephen Harris. (Illus.). 128p. text ed. 19.95 (*0-905483-47-2*, Pub. by Whittet Bks UK) Diamond Farm Bk.

Urban Freight Transport: Problems & Some Possible Solutions. Alan R. Boyland. (C). 1977. 29.00 (*0-685-30306-3*, Pub. by Oxford Polytechnic UK) St Mut.

Urban Frontier: The Rise of Western Cities, 1790-1830. Richard C. Wade. LC 59-9285. (Historical Monographs: No. 41). 372p. 1959. 25.00 (*0-674-93075-4*) HUP.

Urban Frontier: The Rise of Western Cities, 1790-1830. Richard C. Wade. 384p. 1996. pap. text ed. 18.95 (*0-252-06422-4*) U of Ill Pr.

Urban Future. Ed. by Ely Chinoy. (Controversy Ser.). 200p. 1973. 12.95 (*0-88311-200-0*); pap. 6.95 (*0-88311-201-9*) Lieber-Atherton.

Urban Futures for Central Canada: Perspectives on Forecasting Urban Growth & Form. Ed. by Larry S. Bourne et al. LC 73-92297. 376p. reprint ed. pap. 107.20 (*0-317-26899-6*, 2023595) Bks Demand.

Urban Futures Observed: In the Asian Third World. Richard L. Meier. LC 79-28624. (Policy Studies on International Development). 256p. 1980. 78.00 (*0-08-025954-5*, Pergamon Pr) Elsevier.

Urban General Plan. T. J. Kent, Jr. LC 90-83694. 213p. 1990. reprint ed. pap. 29.95 (*0-918286-73-5*); reprint ed. lib. bdg. 45.00 (*0-918286-74-3*) Planners Pr.

Urban Geographic Information Systems: Methods & Applications. Ed. by Peng Gong. (Illus.). (Orig.). (CHI.). 1996. pap. write for info. (*0-9651441-7-8*) Assoc Chinese Prof.

*__Urban Geography.__ Tim Hall. LC 97-15274. (Routledge Contemporary Human Geography Ser.). 1998. write for info. (*0-415-14084-6*); pap. write for info. (*0-415-14085-4*) Routledge.

Urban Geography. 2nd ed. Ray M. Northam. LC 78-12335. (Illus.). 524p. reprint ed. pap. 149.40 (*0-7837-3496-4*, 2057829) Bks Demand.

Urban Geography: An Analytical Approach. Martin Cadwallader. LC 95-4904. 1995. text ed. 69.00 (*0-13-341637-2*) P-H.

Urban Geography: An Introductory Guide. David Clark. 256p. 1982. text ed. 40.00 (*0-8018-2965-8*) Johns Hopkins.

Urban Geography in the Soviet Union & the United States. Ed. by Craig Zubrunnen. 172p. (C). 1992. 49.50 (*0-8476-7568-8*) Rowman.

Urban Geography of England & Wales in the Nineteenth Century. Harold Carter & C. Roy Lewis. (Illus.). 256p. 1990. pap. 22.50 (*0-7131-6549-9*, A5497, Pub. by E Arnold UK) Routledge Chapman & Hall.

Urban Geomorphology: Proceedings of the Symposium, Miami Beach, Fl, 1974. Urban Geomorphology Symposium Staff. Ed. by Donald R. Coates. LC 76-4242. (Geological Society of America, Special Paper Ser.: No. 174). 170p. reprint ed. pap. 48.50 (*0-317-29094-0*, 2023740) Bks Demand.

*__Urban Geoscience.__ G. J. McCall & E. F. De Mulder. (AGID Special Publication Ser.: No. 20). 280p. 1996. 67.00 (*90-5410-643-3*, Pub. by A A Balkema NE) Ashgate Pub Co.

*__Urban Geoscience.__ G. J. McCall & E. F. De Mulder. (AGID Special Publication Ser.: No. 20). 280p. 1996. pap. 38.00 (*90-5410-647-6*, Pub. by A A Balkema NE) Ashgate Pub Co.

Urban Ghetto Riots, 1965-1968: A Comparison of Soviet & American Press Coverage. Ann K. Johnson. 200p. 1996. 28.00 (*0-88033-334-0*) Col U Pr.

Urban Girls: Resisting Stereotypes, Creating Identities. Ed. by Bonnie J. Leadbeater & Niobe Way. 408p. (C). 1996. 60.00 (*0-8147-5107-5*); pap. 24.95 (*0-8147-5108-3*) NYU Pr.

Urban Goods Movement: A Guide to Policy & Planning. Ken W. Ogden. 256p. 1991. 74.95 (*1-85742-029-2*, Pub. by Avebury Pub UK) Ashgate Pub Co.

Urban Government: Supplementary Report of the Urbanism Committee to the National Resources Committee, Vol. 1. United States National Resources Committee. LC 77-74951. (American Federalism-the Urban Dimension Ser.). (Illus.). 1978. reprint ed. lib. bdg. 26.95 (*0-405-10509-6*) Ayer.

Urban Government Finance: Emerging Trends. Ed. by Roy W. Bahl. LC 80-39559. (Urban Affairs Annual Reviews Ser.: No. 20). 287p. reprint ed. pap. 81.80 (*0-8357-8468-1*, 2034736) Bks Demand.

Urban Growth & Change in Britain: An Introduction. Paul Lawless & Frank Brown. 256p. (C). 1986. pap. 36.00 (*0-06-318336-6*, Pub. by P Chapman Pub UK) St Mut.

Urban Growth & City-Systems in the United States, 1840-1860. Allan R. Pred. LC 80-12098. (Studies in Urban History). (Illus.). 297p. 1980. text ed. 38.50 (*0-674-93091-6*) HUP.

Urban Growth & Housing Policy in Algeria: A Case Study of a Migrant Community in the City of Cons. Rabah Boudebaba. 300p. 1991. 69.95 (*1-85628-247-3*, Pub. by Avebury Pub UK) Ashgate Pub Co.

Urban Growth & Rural Stagnation: Studies in the Economy of an Indian Coalfield & Its Hinterland. Ed. by Dietmar Rothermund et al. 1980. 36.00 (*0-8364-0662-1*, Pub. by Manohar II) S Asia.

Urban Growth & Sustainable Habitats: Case Studies of Policy Conflicts in South Florida's Coastal Environment. Daniel O. Suman. (Illus.). 176p. (Orig.). 1995. pap. 10.00 (*0-9642315-1-4*) U Miami Div Marine.

Urban Growth & the Circulation of Information: The United States System of Cities, 1790-1840. Allan R. Pred. LC 73-76384. (Studies in Urban History). 384p. (C). 1973. text ed. 39.95 (*0-674-93090-8*) HUP.

Urban Growth & Urban Planning: Political Context & People's Priorities. Ed. by Alfred DeSouza. 1984. pap. 6.00 (*0-8364-1242-7*, Pub. by Indian Soc Inst II) S Asia.

Urban Growth in Austin. Nancy G. Bunch. (Special Project Report). 189p. 1986. pap. 8.00 (*0-89940-853-2*) LBJ Sch Pub Aff.

Urban Growth in the Age of Sectionalism: Virginia, 1847-1861. David R. Goldfield. LC 77-3514. 368p. 1977. pap. 105.27 (*0-7837-8465-1*, 2049270) Bks Demand.

Urban Harvest. Roy Joslin. 1982. pap. 13.99 (*0-85234-159-8*, Pub. by Evangelical Pr) Presby & Reformed.

Urban Harvest: Recycling as a Peasant Industry in Northern Vietnam. Michael R. DiGregorio. LC 94-23197. (Occasional Papers: No. 17, September 1994). 1994. pap. 5.00 (*0-86638-164-3*) EW Ctr HI.

*__Urban Hassle.__ Allen Elkin. 1998. pap. 10.95 (*0-452-27741-8*, Plume) NAL-Dutton.

Urban Health Crisis: Strategies for Health for All in the Face of Rapid Urbanization. xvi, 80p. 1993. pap. text ed. 20.00 (*92-4-156159-9*, 1150402) World Health.

Urban Health in Developed Countries. Harpham. 1995. text ed. 49.95 (*0-312-15831-9*) St Martin.

Urban Health Research in Developing Countries: Implications for Policy. Ed. by S. Atkinson et al. 208p. 1996. 65.00 (*0-85199-135-1*, Pub. by CAB Intntl UK) OUP.

*__Urban Health Services.__ (Technical Report Ser.: No. 250). 35p. 1963. pap. text ed. 4.00 (*92-4-120250-5*) World Health.

*__Urban Heroes.__ Peter Regan. Date not set. pap. 8.95 (*0-947962-62-X*) Dufour.

Urban History: A Guide to Information Sources. Ed. by John Buenker et al. LC 80-19643. (American Government & History Information Guide Ser.: Vol. 9). 464p. 1981. 68.00 (*0-8103-1479-7*) Gale.

Urban History: Reviews of Recent Research. Ed. by Patricia J. Rosof et al. LC 80-27903. (Trends in History Ser.: Vol. 2, No. 1). 97p. 1981. text ed. 39.95 (*0-917724-26-7*) Haworth Pr.

Urban History of India (A Case Study) Deepali Barua. (C). 1995. 22.50 (*81-7099-538-8*, Pub. by Motilal Banarsidass II) S Asia.

Urban History Yearbook, 1988. Ed. by Richard Rodger. 280p. 1989. 39.00 (*0-7185-6088-4*) St Martin.

Urban History Yearbook, 1989. Richard Rodger. 280p. 1989. 42.00 (*0-7185-6089-2*) St Martin.

Urban History Yearbook, 1990. Ed. by Richard Rodger. (Illus.). 300p. 1990. 39.00 (*0-7185-6090-6*) St Martin.

Urban History Yearbook, 1991. Ed. by Richard Rodger. (Illus.). 300p. 1992. text ed. 65.00 (*0-7185-6091-4*) St Martin.

Urban Homesteading: Programs & Policies. Mittie O. Chandler. LC 88-15481. 164p. 1988. text ed. 45.00 (*0-313-26338-8*, Greenwood Pr) Greenwood.

Urban Hospital Location. Leslie Mayhew. LC 85-15820. (London Research Series in Geography: No. 4). (Illus.). 176p. 1985. text ed. 60.00 (*0-04-362054-X*) Routledge Chapman & Hall.

Urban Housing--Public & Private: A Guide to Information Sources. Ed. by John E. Rouse, Jr. LC 79-100279. (Urban Studies Information Guide Ser.: Vol. 5). 336p. 1978. 68.00 (*0-8103-1398-7*) Gale.

Urban Housing & Neighborhood Revitilization: Turning a Federal Program into Local Projects. Donald B. Rosenthal. LC 87-32259. (Contributions in Political Science Ser.: No. 208). 238p. 1988. text ed. 59.95 (*0-313-26148-2*, RND/, Greenwood Pr) Greenwood.

Urban Housing Crisis: Economic, Social, & Legal Issues & Proposals. Arlene Zarembka. LC 89-38226. (Contributions in Sociology Ser.: No. 90). 206p. 1990. text ed. 49.95 (*0-313-26691-3*, ZHU/, Greenwood Pr) Greenwood.

Urban Housing in the Nineteen Eighties: Markets & Policies. Margery A. Turner & Raymond J. Struyk. LC 84-21942. 113p. (C). 1984. lib. bdg. 24.50 (*0-87766-371-8*) Urban Inst.

Urban Housing Markets: Recent Directions in Research & Policy: Proceedings of a Conference Held at the University of Toronto, October 27-29, 1977. Ed. by Larry S. Bourne & John R. Hitchcock. LC 79-310508. 342p. reprint ed. pap. 97.50 (*0-8357-8362-6*, 2034053) Bks Demand.

Urban Housing Policy. William G. Grigsby & Louis Rosenburg. 350p. 1975. 29.95 (*0-87855-117-4*) Transaction Pubs.

Urban Housing Segregation of Minorities in Western Europe & the United States. Ed. by Elizabeth Huttman et al. LC 90-3221. 444p. (C). 1991. text ed. 64.95 (*0-8223-1060-0*) Duke.

Urban Hydrology. Ed. by Harry C. Torno. 270p. 1983. pap. 25.00 (*0-87262-388-2*) Am Soc Civil Eng.

Urban Hydrology. rev. ed. Timothy Lazaro. LC 89-51913. 260p. 1990. 89.95 (*0-87762-547-6*) Technomic.

Urban Hydrology: Symposium Proceedings, Hyatt Regency Denver, Denver, CO, November 4-8, 1990. Urban Hydrology Symposium Staff. Ed. by Marshall E. Jennings. LC 90-84160. (American Water Resources Association Technical Publication Ser.: Vol. TPS-91-4). (Illus.). 349p. 1991. reprint ed. pap. 99.50 (*0-7837-9220-4*, 2049971) Bks Demand.

Urban Illusions: New Approaches to Inner City Unemployment. Michael Bernick. LC 87-7208. 256p. 1987. text ed. 55.00 (*0-275-92804-7*, C2804, Praeger Pubs) Greenwood.

Urban Image of Augustan Rome. Diane Favro. (Illus.). 368p. (C). 1996. 70.00 (*0-521-47071-4*) Cambridge U Pr.

Urban Image of Augustan Rome. Diane Favro. (Illus.). 368p. 1996. text ed. 80.00 (*0-521-45083-7*) Cambridge U Pr.

Urban Impact of Federal Policies. Ed. by Norman J. Glickman. LC 79-2368. (Johns Hopkins Studies in Urban Affairs). 648p. reprint ed. pap. 180.00 (*0-317-41638-3*, 2025837) Bks Demand.

Urban Indians: Drums from the Cities. Gregory W. Frazier. (Illus.). 500p. (Orig.). (C). 1993. pap. 19.95 (*0-935151-17-6*) Arrowstar Pub.

Urban Indians see **Indians of North America**

Urban Indicators: A Guide to Information Sources. Ed. by Thomas P. Murphy. LC 80-13333. (Urban Studies Information Guide Ser.: Vol. 10). 256p. 1980. 68.00 (*0-8103-1451-7*) Gale.

Urban-Industrial Frontier: Essays on Social Trends & Institutional Goals in Modern Communities. Ed. by David Popenoe. LC 73-75680. 191p. reprint ed. pap. 54.50 (*0-7837-5636-4*, 2050631) Bks Demand.

Urban Industrial Parks. Joseph Rosenblum. Ed. by Stephanie Bell. 8p. (Orig.). 1978. pap. 8.00 (*0-317-05496-1*) Natl Coun Econ Dev.

***Urban Inequality under Socialism: Case Studies from Eastern Europe & the Soviet Union.** 80p. 1989. pap. text ed. 15.95 (*0-521-36679-8*) Cambridge U Pr.

Urban Influence on Farm Family Size. Nathan Keyfitz. Ed. by Harriet Zuckerman & Robert K. Merton. LC 79-9009. (Dissertations on Sociology Ser.). 1980. lib. bdg. 16.95 (*0-405-12977-7*) Ayer.

Urban Informal Sector. Surjit Singh. (C). 1995. 22.00 (*81-7033-245-1*, Pub. by Rawat II) S Asia.

Urban Informal Sector in Africa in Retrospect & Prospect: An Annotated Bibliography. (International Labour Bibliography Ser.: No. 10). x, 86p. 1991. pap. 15.75 (*92-2-107747-0*) Intl Labour Office.

Urban Informal Sector in Asia: An Annotated Bibliography. (International Labour Bibliography Ser.: No. 13). v, 161p. (Orig.). 1992. pap. 20.25 (*92-2-108259-8*) Intl Labour Office.

Urban Informal Sector Information: Needs & Methods. H. Haan. Ed. by J. B. Celestin. vi, 44p. (Orig.). 1989. pap. 11.25 (*92-2-107004-2*) Intl Labour Office.

Urban Information Thesaurus: A Vocabulary for Social Documentation. Ed. by Baltimore Region Institutional Studies Center Staff et al. LC 76-52604. 375p. 1977. text ed. 59.95 (*0-8371-9483-0*, UTH, Greenwood Pr) Greenwood.

Urban Infrastructure. Sanders. Date not set. 25.00 (*0-02-927665-9*, Free Press) Free Pr.

Urban Infrastructure: Finance & Management. OECD Staff. 92p. (Orig.). 1991. pap. 22.00 (*92-64-13584-7*) OECD.

Urban Innovation: Creative Strategies for Turbulent Times. Ed. by Terry N. Clark. LC 94-13485. (Urban Innovation Ser.: Vol. 3). 348p. 1994. 49.95 (*0-8039-3800-4*); pap. 24.95 (*0-8039-3801-2*) Sage.

Urban Innovation Abroad: Problem Cities In Search of Solutions. Ed. by Thomas L. Blair. 424p. 1984. 95.00 (*0-306-41492-9*, Plenum Pr) Plenum.

Urban Innovation & Autonomy: Political Implications of Policy Change. Ed. by Susan E. Clarke. (Urban Innovation Ser.: Vol. 1). 320p. (C). 1989. text ed. 36.00 (*0-8039-3139-5*); pap. text ed. 17.95 (*0-8039-3140-9*) Sage.

***Urban Innovation & Autonomy: Political Implications of Policy Change.** Ed. by Susan E. Clarke. LC 89-10513. (Urban Innovation Ser.: No. 1). (Illus.). 288p. pap. 82.10 (*0-608-05074-1*, 2065629) Bks Demand.

***Urban Integrated Pest Management: A Guide for Commercial Applicators.** Eugene Wood & Lawrence Pinto. Ed. by Jann Cox. (Illus.). 200p. (C). 1996. reprint ed. pap. 40.00 (*0-7881-3165-6*) DIANE Pub.

Urban Interiors in Italy, Vol. 2. San Pietro. (Illus.). 256p. 1996. 59.95 (*88-7685-075-9*, Pub. by LArchivoto IT) Bks Nippan.

***Urban Interiors in New York.** L'Archivolto Editorial Staff. (Illus.). 260p. 1997. 79.95 (*88-7685-086-4*, Pub. by LArchivoto IT) Bks Nippan.

Urban Intersections: Meetings of Life & Literature in United States Cities. Sidney H. Bremer. 280p. (C). 1992. text ed. 32.50 (*0-252-01886-9*) U of Ill Pr.

Urban Japanese Housewives: At Home & in the Community. Anne E. Imamura. LC 86-27262. 224p. (C). 1992. reprint ed. pap. text ed. 15.00 (*0-8248-1499-1*) UH Pr.

Urban Kill. Joe Barfield. 220p. 1996. pap. 9.95 (*1-884797-04-0*) Moran Pub.

Urban Labor Markets & Job Opportunity. Ed. by George E. Peterson & Wayne Vroman. LC 92-10899. (Urban Opportunity Ser.). 342p. (Orig.). (C). 1992. pap. text ed. 26.50 (*0-87766-567-2*); lib. bdg. 61.00 (*0-87766-566-4*) Urban Inst.

Urban Land & Property Markets in France. Rodrigo Acosta & Vincent Renard. (European Urban Land & Property Markets Ser.: No. 3). 256p. 1993. 75.00 (*1-85728-050-4*, Pub. by UCL Pr UK) Taylor & Francis.

Urban Land & Property Markets in Germany. Harmut Dieterich et al. 256p. 1993. 75.00 (*1-85728-049-0*, Pub. by UCL Pr UK) Taylor & Francis.

***Urban Land & Property Markets in Italy.** Ed. by Gastone Ave. (European Land & Property Markets Ser.: No. 5). 256p. 1996. 90.00 (*1-85728-053-9*, Pub. by UCL Pr UK) Taylor & Francis.

Urban Land & Property Markets in Sweden. Han Mattsson & Thomas Kalbro. 256p. 1995. 75.00 (*1-85728-052-0*, Pub. by UCL Pr UK) Taylor & Francis.

Urban Land & Property Markets in the Netherlands. Barrie Needham & Patrick Koenders. 240p. 1993. 75.00 (*1-85728-051-2*, Pub. by UCL Pr UK) Taylor & Francis.

Urban Land & Property Markets in the U. K. Richard Williams & Barry Wood. (Evaluating the Fluidized Bed Combustion Option Ser.: No. 4). 256p. 1993. 75.00 (*1-85728-048-2*, Pub. by UCL Pr UK) Taylor & Francis.

Urban Land Economics. Herbert B. Dorau & Albert G. Hinman. Date not set. write for info. (*0-8434-0053-6*, Pub. by McGrath NH) Ayer.

Urban Land Economics: Principles & Policy. Graham Hallett. LC 79-65820. (Illus.). xv, 274p. (C). 1979. 35.00 (*0-208-01834-4*, Archon Bks) Shoe String.

Urban Land Markets: Policies for the 1990s. 151p. (Orig.). 1992. pap. 42.00 (*92-64-13640-1*) OECD.

Urban Land Markets: Price Indices, Supply Measures & Public Policy Effects. Michael A. Goldberg et al. Ed. by James Thomas Black & James E. Hoben. LC 80-53134. (ULI Research Reports: No. 30). (Illus.). 238p. reprint ed. pap. 67.90 (*0-8357-6768-X*, 2035443) Bks Demand.

Urban Land Policy for the 1980s: The Message for State & Local Government. Ed. by George Lefcoe. LC 82-48492. (Lincoln Institute of Land Policy Book Ser.). 233p. reprint ed. pap. 66.50 (*0-7837-3269-4*, 2043288) Bks Demand.

Urban Land-Use & Transport Interaction: Policies & Models. F. V. Webster et al. 534p. 1988. text ed. 79.95 (*0-566-05726-3*, Pub. by Avebury Pub UK) Ashgate Pub Co.

Urban Land Use Planning. 3rd ed. F. Stuart Chapin, Jr. & Edward J. Kaiser. LC 64-18666. (Illus.). 672p. 1986. pap. 22.50 (*0-252-01257-7*) U of Ill Pr.

Urban Land Use Planning. 4th ed. Edward J. Kaiser et al. LC 93-44787. 464p. 1994. text ed. 35.00 (*0-252-02101-0*) U of Ill Pr.

Urban Landscape Management. James Hitchmough. 600p. 1994. pap. 160.00 (*0-409-30748-3*) Buttrwrth-Heinemann.

***Urban Landscape Management.** Kendle. (Illus.). 256p. 1997. text ed. 47.50 (*0-419-19300-6*, E & FN Spon) Routledge Chapman & Hall.

Urban Landscapes: A New Jersey Portrait. George A. Tice. LC 75-30549. (Illus.). reprint ed. 28.00 (*0-8357-9529-2*, 2050675) Bks Demand.

Urban Landscapes: International Perspectives. Ed. by Peter J. Larkham & Jeremy W. Whitehand. LC 92-12622. (Geography & Environment Ser.). (Illus.). 288p. (C). (gr. 13). 1992. text ed. 79.95 (*0-415-07074-0*, A9702) Routledge.

Urban Law: A Guide to Information Sources. Ed. by Thomas P. Murphy & Robert D. Kline. (Urban Studies Information Guide Ser.: Vol. 11). 352p. 1980. 68.00 (*0-8103-1409-6*) Gale.

Urban Learners. Robert DeLucia. 224p. 1996. pap. text ed. 26.00 (*0-13-104456-7*) P-H.

Urban Legends & the Japanese Tale. David Shaefer. 31p. 1990. pap. 6.00 (*0-904674-19-3*, Pub. by Octagon Pr UK) ISHK.

Urban Leviathan: Mexico City in the Twentieth Century. Diane E. Davis. LC 93-23069. (Illus.). 464p. 1994. 59.95 (*1-56639-150-4*); pap. 24.95 (*1-56639-151-2*) Temple U Pr.

Urban Life. Linda Leuzzi. LC 94-24617. (Life in America 100 Years Ago Ser.). (Illus.). (YA). (gr. 5 up). 1995. lib. bdg. 19.95 (*0-7910-2841-0*) Chelsea Hse.

Urban Life: Readings in Urban Anthropology. 3rd rev. ed. Ed. by George Gmelch & Walter P. Zenner. (Illus.). 603p. (Orig.). (C). 1995. pap. text ed. 25.95 (*0-88133-860-5*) Waveland Pr.

Urban Life in Contemporary China. Martin K. Whyte & William L. Parish. LC 83-7779. (Illus.). xii, 420p. 1984. 39.00 (*0-226-89546-7*) U Ch Pr.

Urban Life in Contemporary China. Martin K. Whyte & William L. Parish. LC 83-7779. (Illus.). xii, 420p. 1985. pap. text ed. 18.00 (*0-226-89549-1*) U Ch Pr.

Urban Life in Kingston, Jamaica, Vol. 3. Diane J. Austin. (Caribbean Studies: Vol. 3). xxvi, 282p. 1984. text ed. 96.00 (*2-88124-006-2*) Gordon & Breach.

Urban Life in Mediterranean Europe: Anthropoligical Perspectives. Ed. by Michael Kenny & David I. Kertzer. LC 82-1890. 352p. reprint ed. pap. 100.40 (*0-7837-5740-9*, 2045401) Bks Demand.

Urban Life in the Renaissance. Ed. by Susan Zimmerman & Ronald F. Weissman. LC 86-40595. (Illus.). 304p. 1989. 50.00 (*0-87413-323-8*) U Delaware Pr.

Urban Life in Transition. Ed. by M. Gottdiener & C. G. Pickvance. (Urban Affairs Annual Review Ser.: Vol. 39). 300p. (C). 1991. text ed. 58.00 (*0-8039-3974-4*); pap. text ed. 24.95 (*0-8039-3975-2*) Sage.

***Urban Life in Transition.** Ed. by M. Gottdiener & Chris G. Pickvance. LC 91-25273. (Urban Affairs Annual Reviews Ser.: No. 39). (Illus.). 253p. 1991. reprint ed. pap. 72.20 (*0-608-04310-9*, 2065089) Bks Demand.

***Urban Living.** Walmsley. 1988. pap. text ed. write for info. (*0-582-30167-X*, Pub. by Longman UK) Longman.

Urban Low-Income Housing & Development: A Case Study in Peninsular Malaysia. Emiel A. Wegelin. 1978. lib. bdg. 64.00 (*90-207-0729-9*) Kluwer Ac.

Urban Low Income Housing in Zambabwe. Christopher J. Mafico. 176p. 1991. 68.95 (*1-85628-226-0*, Pub. by Avebury Pub UK) Ashgate Pub Co.

Urban Management. Ed. by David R. Morgan. LC 72-8662. 183p. 1973. text ed. 34.50 (*0-8422-5065-4*); pap. text ed. 9.95 (*0-8422-0249-8*) Irvington.

Urban Management: A Guide to Information Sources. Ed. by Bernard H. Ross. LC 78-10310. (Urban Studies Information Guide Ser.: Vol. 8). 304p. 1979. 68.00 (*0-8103-1430-4*) Gale.

Urban Management: Policies & Innovations in Developing Countries. Ed. by G. Shabbir Cheema. LC 92-18365. 352p. 1993. text ed. 65.00 (*0-275-94085-3*, C4085, Praeger Pubs) Greenwood.

Urban Management: The Challenge of Growth. Ed. by Kenneth Davey. 320p. 1996. 68.95 (*1-85972-063-3*, Pub. by Avebury Pub UK) Ashgate Pub Co.

Urban Markets: Developing Informal Retailing. David Dewar & Venessa Watson. 160p. (C). (gr. 13). 1990. text ed. 69.95 (*0-415-03813-8*, A3770) Routledge.

Urban Mass Transit: A Guide to Organizations & Information Resources. Thomas N. Trzyna & Joseph R. Beck. LC 78-12497. (Who's Doing What Ser.: No. 5). 1979. pap. 25.00 (*0-912102-38-1*) Cal Inst Public.

Urban Mass Transportation: A Dozen Years of Federal Policy. George M. Smerk. LC 73-21242. 404p. reprint ed. pap. 115.20 (*0-685-23899-7*, 2056721) Bks Demand.

Urban Mass Transportation Planning. Alan Black. 1995. text ed. write for info. (*0-07-005557-2*) McGraw.

Urban Masses & Moral Order in America, 1820-1920. Paul Boyer. (Illus.). 432p. (C). 1992. pap. 17.95 (*0-674-93110-6*) HUP.

Urban Medical Centers. Eli Ginzberg. 1996. text ed. 58.50 (*0-8133-2883-7*) Westview.

Urban Millennium: The City-Building Process from the Early Middle Ages to the Present. Josef W. Konvitz. LC 84-13908. 289p. 1985. text ed. 24.95 (*0-8093-1201-8*) S Ill U Pr.

Urban Minority Administrations: Politics, Policy, & Style. Ed. by Albert K. Karnig & Paula D. McClain. LC 88-21349. (Contributions in Political Science Ser.: No. 228). 182p. 1988. text ed. 45.00 (*0-313-25852-X*, KUY/, Greenwood Pr) Greenwood.

Urban Models. Janet R. Pack. (Monograph Ser.: No. 7). 1978. 27.50 (*1-55869-129-4*) Regional Sci Res Inst.

Urban Mortgage Lending: Comparative Markets & Experience. J. E. Morton. (Financial Research Program IV: Studies in Urban Mortgage Financing: No. 6). 212p. 1956. reprint ed. 55.20 (*0-87014-144-9*) Natl Bur Econ Res.

Urban Mortgage Lending by Life Insurance Companies. Raymond J. Saulnier. (Financial Research Program IV: Studies in Urban Mortgage Financing: No. 1). 202p. 1950. reprint ed. 52.60 (*0-87014-139-2*) Natl Bur Econ Res.

Urban Mosaic: Towards a Theory of Residential Differentiation. Duncan Timms. LC 70-123665. (Cambridge Geographical Studies: No. 2). 285p. reprint ed. pap. 81.30 (*0-685-15670-2*, 2026354) Bks Demand.

***Urban Muse: Stories on the American City.** Ed. by Ilan Stavans. 352p. 1998. pap. 12.95 (*0-385-31368-3*) Doubleday.

Urban Nationalism: A Study of Political Development in Trinidad. Alvin Magid. LC 86-33978. 314p. 1988. 49.95 (*0-8130-0853-0*) U Press Fla.

Urban Native Men & Women: Differences in Their Work Adaptations. Dorothy M. Jones. LC 76-620028. (Occasional Papers: No. 12). 45p. 1976. pap. 1.00 (*0-88353-021-X*) U Alaska Inst Res.

Urban Neighborhoods: Research & Policy. Ed. by Ralph B. Taylor. LC 85-28311. 397p. 1986. text ed. 59.95 (*0-275-92017-8*, C2017, Praeger Pubs) Greenwood.

Urban Networks in Russia, 1750-1800, & Premodern Periodization. Gilbert Rozman. LC 75-3472. 349p. reprint ed. pap. 99.50 (*0-8357-6932-1*, 2037991) Bks Demand.

Urban Networks: The Structure of Activity Patterns see **Progress in Planning**

***Urban Nightmares.** Ed. by Josepha Sherman & Keith DeCandido. 288p. 1997. mass mkt. 5.99 (*0-671-87851-4*) Baen Bks.

Urban Notions. Stephen Marc. LC 84-180996. (Illus.). 70p. 1983. 15.00 (*0-915109-01-8*); pap. 8.00 (*0-915109-02-6*) Ataraxia.

***Urban Oasis: Guideways & Greenways in the Human Environment.** Roxanne Warren. LC 97-24539. 1997. write for info. (*0-07-068331-X*) McGraw.

Urban Odyssey: A Multicultural History of Washington, D.C. Ed. by Francine C. Cary. LC 94-44018. 320p. 1996. 34.95 (*1-56098-545-3*) Smithsonian.

Urban Open Spaces. Ed. by Lisa Taylor. LC 81-655475. (Immovable Objects Ser.). (Illus.). 64p. 1979. 2.50 (*0-910503-27-3*) Cooper-Hewitt Museum.

Urban Opportunity: The Work of NECs in Cities of the South. Nicolas Hall et al. 160p. (Orig.). 1996. pap. 18.95 (*1-85339-347-9*, Pub. by Intermed Tech UK) Women Ink.

***Urban Oracles: Short Stories.** Mayra S. Febres. LC 97-246. 220p. (Orig.). 1997. pap. 15.95 (*1-57129-034-6*) Brookline Bks.

Urban Order. John R. Short. (Illus.). 352p. (C). 1996. 69.95 (*1-55786-360-1*); pap. 27.95 (*1-55786-361-X*) Blackwell Pubs.

Urban Outcomes: Schools, Streets, & Libraries. Frank S. Levy et al. (Oakland Project Ser.). 1974. pap. 14.00 (*0-520-03045-1*) U CA Pr.

Urban Pagan: Magical Living in a 9-to-5 World. Patricia Telesco. LC 93-15787. (Illus.). 336p. 1993. pap. 13.00 (*0-87542-785-5*) Llewellyn Pubns.

***Urban Parent Education: Dilemmas & Resolutions.** Louis Smith & Wilma L. Wells. LC 97-14141. (Qualitative Studies on Schools & Schooling). (Illus.). 320p. (C). 1997. text ed. 65.00 (*1-57273-165-6*) Hampton Pr NJ.

***Urban Parent Education: Dilemmas & Resolutions.** Louis M. Smith & Wilma L. Wells. LC 97-14141. (Qualitative Studies on Schools & Schooling). (Illus.). 320p. (C). 1997. pap. text ed. 26.50 (*1-57273-166-4*) Hampton Pr NJ.

Urban Park Officer. Jack Rudman. (Career Examination Ser.: C-1995). 1994. pap. 23.95 (*0-8373-1995-1*) Nat Learn.

Urban Park Patrol Sergeant. Jack Rudman. (Career Examination Ser.: C-2541). 1994. pap. 29.95 (*0-8373-2541-2*) Nat Learn.

Urban Park Program Coordinator. (Career Examination Ser.). pap. 29.95 (*0-8373-3783-6*, C3783) Nat Learn.

Urban Park Ranger. Jack Rudman. (Career Examination Ser.: C-3267). 1994. pap. 23.95 (*0-8373-3267-2*) Nat Learn.

***Urban Parks, 2.** Arco Editorial Staff. (Urban Spaces Ser.). 1997. 80.00 (*84-8185-006-3*) Watsn-Guptill.

***Urban Parks & Open Spaces.** Gayle Berens et al. 1997. pap. write for info. (*0-87420-809-2*) Urban Land.

Urban Patronage & Social Authority: The Management of the Duke of Devonshire's Towns in Ireland, 1764-1891. Lindsay J. Proudfoot. LC 94-22416. 398p. 1995. 69.95 (*0-8132-0819-X*) Cath U Pr.

Urban Pattern. 6th ed. Simon Eisner. 1993. pap. 44.95 (*0-442-00752-3*) Van Nos Reinhold.

Urban Patterns: Studies in Human Ecology. rev. ed. Ed. by George A. Theodorson. LC 81-83145. (Illus.). 475p. (C). 1982. 40.00 (*0-271-00297-2*) Pa St U Pr.

Urban Peasant: 220 Fast & East Recipes from the Popular, Fun-Loving TV Chef. James Barber. 1995. pap. 16.95 (*0-8038-9370-1*) Hastings.

Urban Permaculture: A Practical Handbook for Sustainable Living. David Watkins. 1993. pap. text ed. 13.99 (*1-85623-002-3*) Permaculture.

Urban Pest Control in Australia. 3rd rev. ed. John Gerozisis & Philip Hadlington. 294p. 1995. 42.95 (*0-86840-334-2*, Pub. by New South Wales Univ Pr AT) Intl Spec Bk.

Urban Pest Control in Australia. P. Hadlington & J. Gerozisis. 1988. reprint ed. pap. 34.95 (*0-86840-027-0*, Pub. by New South Wales Univ Pr AT) Intl Spec Bk.

Urban Planner. Jack Rudman. (Career Examination Ser.: C-854). 1994. pap. 27.95 (*0-8373-0854-2*) Nat Learn.

Urban Planning. 2nd ed. Anthony J. Catanese & J. C. Synder. 416p. 1988. text ed. write for info. (*0-07-010229-5*) McGraw.

Urban Planning: A Guide to Information Sources. J. Alexander et al. LC 78-13462. (Urban Studies Information Guide Ser.: Vol. 2). 184p. 1979. 68.00 (*0-8103-1399-5*) Gale.

Urban Planning & Civic Order in Germany, 1860-1914. Brian Ladd. (Historical Studies: Vol. 105). (Illus.). 326p. 1990. 37.50 (*0-674-93115-7*) HUP.

Urban Planning & Land Development Control Law: Practitioner's Edition. 2nd ed. Donald G. Hagman & Julian C. Juergensmeyer. (Hornbook Ser.). 984p. 1986. text ed. write for info. (*0-314-26013-7*) West Pub.

***Urban Planning & Politics.** 2nd ed. William C. Johnson. LC 97-71685. Orig. Title: The Politics of Urban Planning. (Illus.). 250p. 1997. pap. write for info. (*1-884829-14-7*) Planners Pr.

***Urban Planning & Politics.** 2nd ed. William C. Johnson. LC 97-71685. Orig. Title: The Politics of Urban Planning. (Illus.). 250p. 1997. lib. bdg. write for info. (*1-884829-15-5*) Planners Pr.

Urban Planning & Public Transport. Ed. by Roy Cresswell. (Illus.). 172p. 1980. text ed. 38.00 (*0-86095-849-3*) Longman.

Urban Planning & Real Estate Development. John Ratcliffe & Michael Stubbs. (Natrual & Built Environment Ser.: Vol. 8). 512p. 1996. text ed. 95.00 (*1-85728-563-8*, Pub. by UCL Pr UK); pap. text ed. 34.95 (*1-85728-564-6*, Pub. by UCL Pr UK) Taylor & Francis.

***Urban Planning & the African American Community: In the Shadows.** Ed. by June M. Thomas & Marsha Ritzdorf. LC 96-25329. 320p. 1996. 49.95 (*0-8039-7233-4*); pap. 23.95 (*0-8039-7234-2*) Sage.

Urban Planning & the Development Process. C. David Adams. LC 94-36313. 224p. 1994. 75.00 (*1-85728-021-0*, Pub. by UCL Pr UK); pap. 27.00 (*1-85728-022-9*, Pub. by UCL Pr UK) Taylor & Francis.

Urban Planning for Arid Zones: American Experiences & Directions. Ed. by Gideon Golany. LC 77-10472. 267p. reprint ed. pap. 76.10 (*0-317-28052-X*, 2055775) Bks Demand.

Urban Planning for Latin America: The Challenge of Metropolitan Growth. Francis Violich. LC 86-2394. 435p. (C). 1987. text ed. 26.25 (*0-89946-213-8*) Lincoln Inst Land.

Urban Planning Guide. rev. ed. LC 86-17335. 592p. 1986. 45.00 (*0-87262-546-X*) Am Soc Civil Eng.

***Urban Planning in China & Sweden in a Comparative Perspective.** A. Khakee. 140p. 1996. pap. 100.75 (*0-08-043083-X*, Pergamon Pr) Elsevier.

Urban Planning in Europe: International Competition, National Systems, & Planning Projects. Andy Thornley & Peter Newman. 304p. (C). 1996. pap. 19.95 (*0-415-11179-X*); text ed. 65.00 (*0-415-11178-1*) Routledge.

Urban Planning in Malaysia: History, Assumptions & Issues. Goh Ban Lee. 230p. 1995. pap. 9.95 (*983-888-009-4*, Pub. by Delta Edits MY) Weatherhill.

Urban Planning in Pre-Columbian America. Jorge Hardoy. LC 68-24700. (Planning & Cities Ser.). (Illus.). 128p. 1968. 7.95 (*0-8076-0466-6*) Braziller.

***Urban Planning in Western Europe Since 1945.** Albers. 400p. 1997. text ed. write for info. (*0-419-20220-X*, E & FN Spon) Routledge Chapman & Hall.

Urban Planning Law in East Africa see Progress in Planning

Urban Plunge: Meeting the Challenge of a Divided City. Ed. by Veritas Publications Staff. 96p. 1989. pap. 22.00 (*1-85390-026-5*, Pub. by Veritas IE) St Mut.

Urban Police: Selected Surveys on Police Problems in Newark & a Reorganization Plan for the Chicago Police Department. Bureau of Municipal Research, Newark, NJ Staff et al. (Police in America Ser.). 1971. reprint ed. 33.95 (*0-405-03375-3*, 16954) Ayer.

Urban Policing in Canada: Anatomy of an Aging Craft. Maurice A. Martin. 232p. 1995. 49.95 (*0-7735-1284-5*, Pub. by McGill CN); pap. 18.95 (*0-7735-1294-2*, Pub. by McGill CN) U of Toronto Pr.

Urban Policy: A Guide to Information Sources. Ed. by Dennis Palumbo & George A. Taylor. LC 78-25957. (Urban Studies Information Guide Ser.: Vol. 6). 216p. 1979. 68.00 (*0-8103-1428-2*) Gale.

Urban Policy & Economic Development: An Agenda for the 1990s. (Policy Paper Ser.). 95p. 1991. 7.95 (*0-8213-1816-0*, 11816) World Bank.

Urban Policy & Politics in a Bureaucratic Age. 2nd ed. Clarence N. Stone et al. (Illus.). 400p. (C). 1985. pap. text ed. 42.80 (*0-13-939562-8*) P-H.

Urban Policy Evaluation: Challenge & Change. Ed. by Robin Hambleton & Huw Thomas. 272p. 1995. pap. text ed. 29.95 (*1-85396-271-6*, Pub. by Paul Chapman UK) Taylor & Francis.

Urban Policy in a Changing Federal System. National Research Council Staff. 278p. 1985. pap. text ed. 24.95 (*0-309-03591-0*) Natl Acad Pr.

Urban Policy in Britain: The City, the State & the Market. Rob Atkinson & Graham Moon. LC 93-27202. 1994. text ed. 59.95 (*0-312-10627-0*) St Martin.

Urban Policy in Practice. Tim Blackman. LC 94-9428. (Illus.). 320p. (C). 1994. pap. text ed. 24.95 (*0-415-09300-7*, C0288, Routledge NY) Routledge.

Urban Policy in Practice. Tim Blackman. LC 94-9428. (Illus.). 320p. (C). (gr. 13). 1994. text ed. 79.95 (*0-415-09299-X*, C0289, Routledge NY) Routledge.

Urban Policy in Twentieth-Century America. Ed. by Arnold R. Hirsch & Raymond A. Mohl. LC 92-9429. (C). 1993. pap. 16.00 (*0-8135-1906-3*); text ed. 42.00 (*0-8135-1905-5*) Rutgers U Pr.

Urban Policy Problems. Ed. by Robert L. Lineberry & Louis H. Masotti. (C). 1975. pap. 15.00 (*0-918592-11-9*) Pol Studies.

Urban Policy Problems. Mark S. Rosentraub. (Orig.). 1984. pap. 15.00 (*0-918592-67-4*) Pol Studies.

Urban Policy Problems: Federal Policy & Institutional Change. Ed. by Mark S. Rosentraub. LC 86-596. 270p. 1986. text ed. 49.95 (*0-275-92120-4*, C2120, Praeger Pubs) Greenwood.

Urban Policy under Capitalism. Ed. by Norman I. Fainstein & Susan S. Fainstein. LC 81-23185. (Urban Affairs Annual Reviews Ser.: No. 22). (Illus.). 303p. reprint ed. pap. 86.40 (*0-8357-8459-2*, 2034724) Bks Demand.

Urban Political Economy: Broward County, Florida. Ronald K. Vogel. (Illus.). 176p. (C). 1992. lib. bdg. 29.95 (*0-8130-1112-4*) U Press Fla.

Urban Politics. Fuchs. (Political Pampheleteer Ser.). (C). 1995. text ed. 3.95 (*0-673-99785-5*) Addson-Wesley Educ.

Urban Politics: A Guide to Information Sources. Ed. by Thomas P. Murphy. LC 78-54117. (Urban Studies Information Guide Ser.: Vol. 1). 272p. 1978. 68.00 (*0-8103-1395-2*) Gale.

Urban Politics: Power in Metropolitan America. 5th rev. ed. Bernard H. Ross & Myron A. Levine. LC 95-69692. 539p. (C). 1995. pap. text ed. 35.00 (*0-87581-397-6*) Peacock Pubs.

Urban Politics Dictionary. John W. Smith & John S. Klemanski. LC 90-37221. 613p. 1990. pap. text ed. 36.00 (*0-87436-534-1*) ABC-CLIO.

Urban Politics Dictionary. John W. Smith & John S. Klemanski. LC 90-37221. 613p. 1990. lib. bdg. 65.00 (*0-87436-533-3*) ABC-CLIO.

Urban Politics, New York Style. Ed. by Jewel Bellush & Dick Netzer. LC 89-77913. 480p. (C). (gr. 13). 1990. pap. 25.95 (*0-87332-603-2*) M E Sharpe.

Urban Poor: Slum & Pavement Dwellers in the Major Cities of India. Andre M. Singh & Alfred De Souza. 1981. 14.00 (*0-8364-0694-X*, Pub. by Manohar II) S Asia.

Urban Poor: Their Housing Needs & Government Response. Promila Suri. (C). 1994. 34.00 (*81-241-0226-0*, Pub. by Har-Anand Pubns II) S Asia.

Urban Poor of Puerto Rico: A Study in Development & Inequality, 1974. Safa. 116p. (C). 1974. pap. text ed. 13.50 (*0-03-085360-5*) HB Coll Pubs.

Urban Ports & Harbor Management: Responding to Change Along U. S. Waterfronts. Ed. by Marc J. Hershman. 366p. (C). 1988. 73.00 (*0-8448-1547-0*, Crane Russak); pap. text ed. 36.00 (*0-8448-1548-9*, Crane Russak) Taylor & Francis.

Urban Poverty & the Labour Market: Access to Jobs & Incomes in Asian & Latin American Cities. Ed. by Gerry Rodgers. vi, 257p. (Orig.). 1989. 42.75 (*92-2-106499-9*); pap. 31.50 (*92-2-106500-6*) Intl Labour Office.

Urban Poverty & the Underclass: A Reader. Enzo Mingione. (Studies in Urban & Social Change Ser.). (Illus.). 240p. Date not set. 54.95 (*0-631-20036-3*); pap. 22.95 (*0-631-20037-1*) Blackwell Pubs.

***Urban Poverty & Violence in Jamaica.** Caroline Moser & Jeremy Holland. 56p. 1997. 20.00 (*0-8213-3870-6*, 13870) World Bank.

Urban Poverty Database Inventory. Ed. by William H. Scarbrough. LC 91-34536. (Illus.). 380p. 1992. ring bd. 35.00 (*0-926582-04-6*) NCCP.

Urban Poverty in Asia: A Survey of Critical Issues. Ernesto M. Pernia. 300p. 1995. 55.00 (*0-19-586770-X*) OUP.

Urban Poverty in the Caribbean: The Martinican Experience. Michel S. Laguerre. LC 89-77908. 180p. 1990. text ed. 49.95 (*0-312-04495-X*) St Martin.

Urban Predicament. Ed. by William Gorham & Nathan Glazer. 368p. (Orig.). 1976. pap. text ed. 28.00 (*0-87766-160-X*); lib. bdg. 71.00 (*0-87766-161-8*) Urban Inst.

Urban Principal's Handbook. Hamilton J. McMaster. (C). 1988. 21.25 (*0-932957-28-5*) Natl School.

Urban Privatisation in Europe. Dominique Loffain & Gerry Stoker. (SCWE Ser.). 192p. (C). 1997. pap. 24.95 (*1-85567-365-7*, Pub. by Pntr Pubs UK); text ed. 60.00 (*1-85567-364-9*, Pub. by Pntr Pubs UK) Bks Intl VA.

Urban Problems & Economic Development. Lata Chatterjee & Peter Nijkamp. (NATO Advanced Study, Behavioral & Social Sciences Ser.: No. 6). 359p. 1981. lib. bdg. 93.00 (*90-286-2661-1*) Kluwer Ac.

Urban Problems & Policy Perspectives. Ed. by Gopal Bhargava. 1981. 38.00 (*0-8364-0720-2*, Pub. by Abhinav II) S Asia.

Urban Problems & Policy Perspectives. Bhargava Gopal. 531p. (Orig.). 1981. 49.95 (*0-940500-15-9*, Pub. by Abhinav Pub II) Asia Bk Corp.

Urban Problems & Public Policy. Ed. by Robert L. Lineberry & Louis H. Masotti. 240p. 1976. boxed 34.95 (*0-669-00017-5*) Transaction Pubs.

Urban Problems & Public Policy. Robert L. Lineberry & Louis H. Masotti. 240p. 1985. reprint ed. lib. bdg. 37.50 (*0-8191-5142-4*, Pol Studies) U Pr of Amer.

Urban Problems in Sociological Perspective. 2nd ed. Thomas A. Shannon et al. (Illus.). 335p. (C). 1991. pap. text ed. 14.95 (*0-88133-584-3*) Waveland Pr.

***Urban Problems in Sociological Perspective.** 3rd rev. ed. Thomas R. Shannon et al. (Illus.). 384p. (C). 1997. pap. text ed. 17.95 (*0-88133-959-8*) Waveland Pr.

Urban Problems in Western Europe: An Economic Analysis. Paul C. Cheshire & Dennis G. Hay. 256p. 1989. text ed. 70.00 (*0-04-445010-9*) Routledge Chapman & Hall.

Urban Process & Power. Peter Ambrose. LC 93-44565. (Illus.). 264p. (C). 1994. pap. 18.95 (*0-415-00851-4*, B3829, Routledge NY) Routledge.

Urban Process & Power. Peter Ambrose. LC 93-44565. (Illus.). 264p. (C). (gr. 13). 1994. text ed. 59.95 (*0-415-00850-6*, B3825, Routledge NY) Routledge.

Urban Property Tax Reform: Guidelines & Recommendations. William Dillinger. 59p. 1992. pap. 6.95 (*0-8213-2065-3*, 12065) World Bank.

Urban Protest in Seventeenth-Century France: The Culture of Retribution. William Beik. LC 96-2951. (Illus.). 288p. (C). 1997. pap. text ed. 19.95 (*0-521-57585-0*) Cambridge U Pr.

Urban Protest in Seventeenth-Century France: The Culture of Retribution. William Beik. LC 96-2951. (Illus.). 288p. (C). 1997. text ed. 59.95 (*0-521-57308-4*) Cambridge U Pr.

Urban Public Finance, Vol. 10. David A. Wildasin. LC 86-14981. (Fundamentals of Pure & Applied Economics Ser.: Vol. 10). 176, viiip. 1986. pap. text ed. 55.00 (*3-7186-0334-9*) Gordon & Breach.

Urban Public Policy: Historical Modes & Methods. Ed. by Martin V. Melosi. LC 93-15358. (Issues in Policy History Se.: No. 3). 206p. 1993. pap. 13.95 (*0-271-01093-2*) Pa St U Pr.

Urban Public Transport Today. Barry J. Simpson. LC 93-32186. 1993. write for info. (*0-419-18780-4*, E & FN Spon) Routledge Chapman & Hall.

Urban Public Transportation. Vukan Vuchic. (Illus.). 672p. 1981. text ed. 115.00 (*0-13-939496-6*) P-H.

Urban Public Transportation: Planning & Service Operation Issues. (Research Record Ser.: No. 1108). 72p. 1987. 10.00 (*0-309-04456-1*) Transport Res Bd.

Urban Public Transportation Glossary. 74p. 1989. 14.00 (*0-309-04718-8*) Transport Res Bd.

Urban Public Transportation Research 1990. (Transportation Research Record Ser.: No. 1266). 311p. 1990. 45.00 (*0-309-05018-9*) Transport Res Bd.

Urban Public Works Administration. International City Management Association Staff. Ed. by William E. Korbitz. LC 76-11639. (Municipal Management Ser.). (Illus.). 563p. (C). 1981. reprint ed. text ed. 30.00 (*0-87326-013-9*) Intl City-Cnty Mgt.

Urban Race Riots. Ed. by Michal R. Belknap. LC 92-3617. (Civil Rights, White House & Justice Dept. Ser.: Vol. 11). 304p. 1991. text ed. 79.00 (*0-8240-3380-9*) Garland.

Urban Railways & the Civil Engineer: Conference Proceedings. 264p. 1987. 79.00 (*0-7277-1337-X*) Am Soc Civil Eng.

Urban Rank-Size Hierarchy: A Mathematical Interpretation. James W. Fonseca. (Monograph Ser.: No. 8). (Illus.). 86p. (Orig.). (C). 1989. pap. 15.95 (*1-877751-16-2*); pap. text ed. 15.95 (*1-877751-17-0*) Inst Math Geo.

Urban Reader. Marback & Bruch. LC 97-16287. 1997. pap. text ed. 25.00 (*0-205-18456-1*) Allyn.

Urban Real Estate Markets: Characteristics & Financing. Ernest M. Fisher. (Financial Research Program IV: Studies in Urban Mortgage Financing: No. 3). 208p. 1951. reprint ed. 54.10 (*0-87014-141-4*) Natl Bur Econ Res.

Urban Redevelopment: Problems & Practices. Ed. by Coleman Woodbury. LC 53-7678. 541p. reprint ed. pap. 154.20 (*0-317-41816-5*, 2024108) Bks Demand.

Urban Reform & Its Consequences: A Study in Representation. Susan Welch & Timothy Bledsoe. (Illus.). xx, 176p. 1988. pap. text ed. 13.50 (*0-226-89300-6*); lib. bdg. 33.00 (*0-226-89299-9*) U Ch Pr.

***Urban Regeneration.** Central Office of Info. (Aspects of Britain Ser.). (Illus.). 85p. 1995. pap. 12.00 (*0-11-701927-5*, HM19275, Pub. by Stationery Ofc UK) Seven Hills Bk.

Urban Regeneration. Ian Colquhoun. (Illus.). 176p. 1996. 100.00 (*0-7134-7087-9*, Pub. by Batsford UK) Trafalgar.

Urban Regeneration: Property Investment & Development. Ed. by Jim Berry et al. LC 92-36203. 1993. write for info. (*0-419-18310-8*, E & FN Spon) Routledge Chapman & Hall.

Urban Regeneration & Central-Local Government Relation: East Manchester. Tye & Williams. (Progress in Planning Ser.: No. 42). 102p. 1994. pap. 69.25 (*0-08-042533-X*, Pergamon Pr) Elsevier.

Urban Regimes & Strategies: Building Europe's Central Executive District in Brussels. Alex G. Papadopoulos. (Illus.). 288p. 1996. pap. text ed. 23.00 (*0-226-64559-2*) U Ch Pr.

Urban-Regional Economics, Social Systems Accounts, & Eco-Behavioral Science. Ed. by James R. Prescott et al. LC 94-8239. (Illus.). 1994. text ed. 52.95 (*0-8138-2338-2*) Iowa St U Pr.

Urban Regional Environmental Issues. Raven. (C). 1997. pap. text ed. write for info. (*0-03-004608-4*) HB Coll Pubs.

Urban Religion & the Second Great Awakening. Terry D. Bilhartz. LC 83-49455. 240p. 1986. 36.50 (*0-8386-3227-0*) Fairleigh Dickinson.

Urban Relocation in Archaic & Classical Greece: Flight & Consolidation. Nancy H. Demand. LC 89-40737. (Oklahoma Series in Classical Culture: Vol. 6). (Illus.). 256p. 1990. 42.95 (*0-8061-2278-1*) U of Okla Pr.

Urban Renegades: The Cultural Strategy of American Indians. Jeanne Guillemin. LC 74-30434. 336p. 1975. text ed. 49.50 (*0-231-03884-4*) Col U Pr.

Urban Renewal. George Griffin. (Illus.). 104p. (Orig.). 1989. pap. 4.95 (*0-941104-46-X*) Real Comet.

Urban Renewal: The Indian Experience. Ed. by D. Ravindra Prasad. 304p. 1989. text ed. 30.00 (*81-207-0950-0*, Pub. by Sterling Pubs II) Apt Bks.

Urban Renewal Administration: Practices, Procedures, Record Keeping. Emanuel Gorland. LC 79-111041. 183p. reprint ed. 52.20 (*0-685-16213-3*, 2027596) Bks Demand.

Urban Renewal & the Small Firm Cardiff Docklands. H. Thomas et al. (C). 1989. 29.00 (*0-685-30239-3*, Pub. by Oxford Polytechnic UK) St Mut.

Urban Republicanism in the South. Donald S. Strong. LC 76-49535. 69p. 1977. reprint ed. text ed. 45.00 (*0-8371-9359-1*, STUR, Greenwood Pr) Greenwood.

Urban Research & Policy Planning. Ed. by Leo F. Schnore & Henry Fagin. LC 67-18420. (Urban Affairs Annual Reviews Ser.: Vol. 1). 638p. reprint ed. pap. 180.00 (*0-317-08744-4*, 2021956) Bks Demand.

Urban Revisions: Current Projects for the Public Realm. Ed. by Russell Ferguson. LC 94-4197. 1994. write for info. (*0-914357-34-4*) Los Angeles Mus Contemp.

Urban Revitalization: Israel's Project Renewal & Other Experiences. Ed. by Daniel J. Elazar. 607p. 1991. 59.50 (*0-8191-8134-X*); pap. 39.50 (*0-8191-8135-8*) U Pr of Amer.

Urban Revitalization: Policies & Practices. Fritz W. Wagner et al. 215p. 1995. text ed. 45.00 (*0-8039-5869-2*); pap. text ed. 21.50 (*0-8039-5870-6*) Sage.

Urban Revolt in South Africa, Nineteen Sixty to Nineteen Sixty-Four: A Case Study. Edward Feit. LC 78-138921. 387p. reprint ed. pap. 110.30 (*0-317-11314-3*, 2016706) Bks Demand.

Urban Riots in the 20th Century: A Social History. James N. Upton, Jr. LC 89-40364. 73p. (C). 1989. text ed. 34.95 (*1-55605-091-7*); pap. text ed. 14.95 (*1-55605-092-5*) Wyndham Hall.

Urban Rivalries in the French Revolution. Ted W. Margadant. LC 92-9563. (Illus.). 504p. (C). 1992. pap. text ed. 26.95 (*0-691-00891-4*) Princeton U Pr.

Urban River. Margaret Tsuda. (Illus.). 96p. 1976. 4.95 (*0-913976-03-2*) Discovery Bks.

***Urban Rock: Stoney Point Top Rope Guide.** 2nd rev. ed. Chris Owen. (Illus.). 84p. 1994. pap. 12.95 (*0-9654448-0-5*) C Owen.

Urban Romance. Nelson George. 1994. reprint ed. pap. 12.98 (*1-879360-36-5*) Noble Pr.

Urban Romance: a Novel of New York in the '80s. Nelson George. LC 93-2469. 288p. 1994. 24.95 (*0-399-13865-X*, Putnam) Putnam Pub Group.

Urban Romances. Yury Miloslavsky. 1995. 22.95 (*0-87501-062-8*) Ardis Pubs.

Urban Roosts: Where Birds Nest in the City. Barbara Bash. (Illus.). 32p. (J). (gr. 4-7). 1992. mass mkt. 6.95 (*0-316-08312-7*) Little.

Urban Roots of Indian Nationalism. Rajat Ray. 246p. 1979. 18.95 (*0-318-36867-6*) Asia Bk Corp.

***Urban Runoff & Stormwater Management Handbook.** 15p. 1990. pap. 4.50 (*0-614-30371-0*, H1) Terrene Inst.

Urban Runoff Quality-Impact & Quality Enhancement Technology. Ed. by Ben Urbonas & Larry A. Roesner. (Conference Proceedings Ser.). 486p. 1986. 41.00 (*0-87262-577-X*) Am Soc Civil Eng.

Urban Runoff Quality Management. Water Environment Federation Staff & American Society of Civil Engineers Staff. LC 96-21244. (Asce Manual & Report on Engineering Practice Ser.). 1996. write for info. (*1-57278-039-8*) Water Environ.

Urban-Rural Connexions: Perspectives from Environmental Archaeology. Ed. by A. R. Hall & H. K. Kenward. (Oxbow Monographs in Archaeology: No. 47). (Illus.). 176p. 1995. pap. 40.00 (*0-946897-81-6*, Pub. by Oxbow Bks UK) David Brown.

Urban-Rural Integration in Regional Development: A Case Study of Saurashtra, India, 1800-1960. Howard Spodek. LC 75-40468. (University of Chicago, Department of Geography, Research Paper Ser.: No. 171). 158p. 1976. reprint ed. pap. 45.10 (*0-608-02272-1*, 2062913) Bks Demand.

Urban Sanctuaries: Neighborhood Organizations in the Lives & Futures of Inner-City Youth. Milbrey W. McLaughlin et al. LC 93-40706. (social & Behavioral Science Ser.). 272p. pap. 27.00 (*1-55542-599-2*) Jossey-Bass.

Urban Schooling. Bash et al. 1985. pap. text ed. 24.95 (*0-03-910609-8*) Cassell.

***Urban Schools: The Challenge of Location & Poverty.** 1997. lib. bdg. 251.95 (*0-8490-6242-X*) Gordon Pr.

***Urban Schools: The Challenge of Location & Poverty.** Laura Lippman et al. (Illus.). 196p. (Orig.). (C). 1996. pap. 35.00 (*0-7881-3632-1*) DIANE Pub.

Urban Self-Management: Planning for a New Society. Simona Ganassi Agger. LC 78-73223. 245p. reprint ed. 69.90 (*0-685-16307-5*, 2027616) Bks Demand.

Urban Service Distributions. Ed. by Richard Rich. (Orig.). (C). 1981. pap. 15.00 (*0-918592-46-1*) Pol Studies.

Urban Shaman. Serge K. King. 256p. 1990. pap. 11.00 (*0-671-68307-1*) S&S Trade.

Urban Shelter & Services: Public Policies & Management Approaches. G. Shabbir Cheema. LC 87-6982. 240p. 1987. text ed. 55.00 (*0-275-92653-2*, C2653, Praeger Pubs) Greenwood.

Urban Signal Systems & Transportation Systems Management. (Research Record Ser.: No. 1142). 62p. 1987. 10.50 (*0-317-93790-1*) Transport Res Bd.

Urban Snow. George Bowering. 112p. (Orig.). 1993. pap. 10.95 (*0-88922-305-X*) Genl Dist Srvs.

Urban, Social & Educational Issues. Leonard Golbchick & Burry Pensly. LC 87-30649. (Under the Doctorate Assoc. of New York Education Ser.). 308p. 1988. 15.00 (*0-89529-377-3*) Avery Pub.

Urban Social Geography: An Introduction. 3rd ed. Paul Knox. LC 94-7618. (C). 1995. pap. text ed. 40.95 (*0-582-22937-5*, Pub. by Longman UK) Longman.

Urban Social Movements in Jerusalem: The Protest of the Second Generation. Shlomo Hasson. LC 92-15120. (SUNY Series in Israeli Studies). 198p. 1993. text ed. 59.50 (*0-7914-1427-2*); pap. text ed. 19.95 (*0-7914-1428-0*) State U NY Pr.

Urban Social Structure. James M. Beshers. LC 80-27972. vii, 207p. 1981. reprint ed. text ed. 55.00 (*0-313-22714-4*, BEUR, Greenwood Pr) Greenwood.

***Urban Society.** annuals 8th ed. Fred Siegel. 256p. (C). 1996. per. write for info. (*0-697-36343-0*) Brown & Benchmark.

Urban Society: An Ecological Approach. 2nd ed. Amos H. Hawley. LC 80-17925. (Illus.). 394p. reprint ed. pap. 112.30 (*0-7837-3487-5*, 2057820) Bks Demand.

Urban Society in Roman Italy. University College, London Staff. Ed. by Tim Cornell & K. Lomas. LC 94-34480. 221p. 1995. text ed. 55.00 (*0-312-12416-3*) St Martin.

Urban Sociology: Images & Structure. 2nd ed. William G. Flanagan. LC 94-8906. 1994. text ed. 58.00 (*0-205-15461-1*) Allyn.

Urban Sociology, Capitalism, & Modernity. Mike Savage & Alan Warde. LC 93-9816. 224p. 1993. 22.95 (*0-8264-0587-8*) Continuum.

Urban Soil in Landscape Design. Phillip J. Craul. LC 91-36557. 416p. 1992. text ed. 79.95 (*0-471-80598-X*) Wiley.

Urban South. Ed. by Rupert B. Vance & Nicholas J. Demerath. LC 75-134147. (Essay Index Reprint Ser.). 1977. 23.95 (*0-8369-2032-5*) Ayer.

Urban South: A Bibliography. Compiled by Catherine L. Brown. LC 89-2151. (Bibliographies & Indexes in American History Ser.: No. 12). 465p. 1989. text ed. 85.00 (*0-313-26154-7*, BRJ/, Greenwood Pr) Greenwood.

Urban South: A History. Lawrence H. Larsen. LC 89-34162. 224p. 1990. text ed. 25.00 (*0-8131-0309-6*) U Pr of Ky.

Urban Space. Rob Krier. LC 79-64347. (Illus.). 174p. 1993. pap. 29.95 (*0-8478-0236-1*) Rizzoli Intl.

Urban Spaces in Contemporary China: The Potential for Autonomy & Community in Post-Mao China. Ed. by Richard Kraus et al. (Woodrow Wilson Center Press Ser.). (Illus.). 350p. (C). 1995. 59.95 (*0-521-47410-8*) Cambridge U Pr.

Urban Spaces in Contemporary China: The Potential for Autonomy & Community in Post-Mao China. Ed. by Richard Kraus et al. (Woodrow Wilson Center Press Ser.). (Illus.). 350p. (C). 1995. pap. 18.95 (*0-521-47943-6*) Cambridge U Pr.

Urban State Universities: An Unfinished National Agenda. Arnold B. Grobman. LC 87-32670. 140p. 1988. text ed. 49.95 (*0-275-92934-5*, C2934, Praeger Pubs) Greenwood.

Urban Statistical Surveys: Proceedings of the U. S. Bureau of the Census on General Statistics of Cities, 1909-1976 & 1916-1976 & Historical Statistics on State Local Government Finances, 1902-1953. U. S. Bureau of the Census Staff. Ed. by United States Bureau of the Census Historical Statistics on State Local Government Finances, 1902-1953. (America in Two Centuries Ser.). 1976. 31.95 (*0-405-07750-5*, 10174) Ayer.

Urban Storm Drainage. Ed. by Carlo Cao et al. 320p. 1993. text ed. 45.00 (*0-918334-75-6*) WRP.

Urban Storm Drainage, No. WST29/1-2. J. Marsalek & Harry C. Torno. (Water Science & Technology Ser.: No. 29/1-2). 466p. 1995. pap. 220.00 (*0-08-042498-8*, Pergamon Pr) Elsevier.

Urban Storm Modeling & Stimulation. Nix. 224p. 1994. 69.95 (*0-87371-527-6*, L527) Lewis Pubs.

Urban Storm Water Quality & Ecological Effects upon Receiving Waters: Proceedings of the Second IAWPRC Conference, Held in Wageningen, The Netherlands, 20-22 September 1989. Ed. by R. H. Aalderink et al. (Water Science & Technology Ser.: No. 22). (Illus.). 318p. 1990. pap. 139.00 (*0-08-040161-9*, Pergamon Pr); pap. 60.00 (*0-08-040162-7*, Pergamon Pr) Elsevier.

Urban Stormwater Hydrology. D. K. Kibler. (Water Resources Monograph Ser.: Vol. 7). 271p. 1982. pap. 18.00 (*0-87590-308-8*) Am Geophysical.

Urban Stormwater Hydrology: A Guide to Engineering Calculations. A. Osman Akan. LC 92-62441. 275p. 1992. text ed. 89.95 (*0-87762-967-6*) Technomic.

Urban Stormwater Management. American Public Works Association Staff. (Special Reports: No. 49). (Illus.). 312p. (Orig.). 1981. pap. text ed. 45.00 (*0-917084-41-1*) Am Public Works.

Urban Stormwater Management in Coastal Areas. Ed. by Chin Y. Kuo. LC 80-66949. 442p. 1980. pap. 32.00 (*0-87262-247-9*) Am Soc Civil Eng.

***Urban Stormwater Management, 2nd International Symposium, 1995: Integrated Management of Urban Environments.** Contrib. by Tony H. Wong. (National Conference Proceedings 95 Ser.: Vol. 3). (Illus.). 564p. 1995. pap. 108.00 (*0-85825-628-2*, Pub. by Inst Engrs Aust-EA Bks AT) Accents Pubns.

Urban Stormwater Quality Enhancement: Source Control, Retrofitting & Combined Sewer Technology. Ed. by Harry C. Torno. LC 90-654. 585p. 1990. pap. text ed. 37.00 (*0-87262-759-4*) Am Soc Civil Eng.

Urban Stormwater Treatment at Coyote Hills Marsh. 181p. 1986. 20.00 (*1-888028-24-6*, P86001WAT) Assn Bay Area.

Urban Strategies: Bringing the Gospel to the Cities. David Mendez. 72p. (Orig.). 1990. pap. 8.00 (*1-56428-000-4*) Logos Intl Pub.

Urban Stress: Experiments on Noise & Social Stressors. David C. Glass & Jerome E. Singer. LC 78-182640. 196p. 1972. reprint ed. pap. 55.90 (*0-608-00686-6*, AU00472) Bks Demand.

Urban Strike Official Power Play Guide with Desert & Jungle. Carlton Books Staff. 1994. pap. 12.95 (*1-55958-687-7*) Prima Pub.

Urban Structure & the Labour Market: Worker Mobility, Commuting, & Underemployment in Cities. Wayne Simpson. 192p. 1992. 55.00 (*0-19-828358-X*) OUP.

***Urban Student: Being Your Best at College & Life.** Jerry S. Thornton et al. LC 96-48945. (Freshman Orientation Ser.). (C). 1997. pap. text ed. 25.95 (*0-534-52893-7*) Wadsworth Pub.

***Urban Studies.** (Information Guide Ser.). 1978. 62.00 (*0-8103-4394-0*, 00005983, Gale Res Intl) Gale.

Urban Studies. W. Andrews et al. 1976. teacher ed. 8.44 (*0-13-939454-0*); pap. text ed. 20.04 (*0-13-939280-7*) P-H.

Urban Studies Pak. Roberta Steinbacher & Virginia Benson. 112p. (C). 1995. student ed. write for info. (*0-7872-0570-2*); 46.20 (*0-7872-0571-0*) Kendall-Hunt.

Urban-Suburban Problems. Bernard J. Frieden. (Task Force on the Eighties Ser.). 34p. 1981. pap. 2.50 (*0-87495-038-4*) Am Jewish Comm.

Urban Surface Water Management. Stuart G. Walesh. LC 88-27704. 518p. 1989. text ed. 99.95 (*0-471-83719-9*) Wiley.

Urban Survival: The World of Working-Class Women. Ruth Sidel. LC 95-17950. xvii, 182p. (C). 1995. pap. 10.00 (*0-8032-9239-2*, Bison Books) U of Nebr Pr.

Urban Survival Arsenal: The Best Guns for Self-Preservation. F. Rexer. 1986. lib. bdg. 79.95 (*0-8490-3817-0*) Gordon Pr.

Urban Survival Handbook. John Wiseman. (Illus.). 320p. (Orig.). 1992. pap. 20.00 (*0-00-272164-3*, Pub. by HarpC UK) HarpC.

Urban Symbolism. Ed. by Peter J. Nas. LC 93-16885. (Studies in Human Society: No. 8). (Illus.). 393p. 1993. pap. 89.00 (*90-04-09855-0*) E J Brill.

Urban System & Networks of Corporate Control, Vol. 11. Christopher Ross. (Contemporary Studies in Sociology). 170p. 1992. 73.25 (*1-55938-474-3*) Jai Pr.

Urban System of a Developing Economy. H. N. Misra. 1988. 32.00 (*0-8364-2312-7*, Heritage) S Asia.

Urban Systems: Contemporary Approaches to Modelling. Ed. by C. S. Bertuglia et al. 688p. (C). 1987. text ed. 125.00 (*0-7099-3971-X*, Pub. by Croom Helm UK) Routledge Chapman & Hall.

***Urban Targeting & BMP Selection.** 54p. 1990. pap. 10.00 (*0-614-30380-X*, S3) Terrene Inst.

Urban Technology: A Second Primer on Problems. Herbert Fox. LC 75-1686. (Urban Problems & Urban Technology Ser.: No. 2). 191p. reprint ed. pap. 54.50 (*0-7837-0919-6*, 2027128) Bks Demand.

Urban Terrorism. Ed. by A. E. Sadler & Paul A. Winters. LC 96-11849. (Current Controversies Ser.). 176p. (J). (gr. 5-12). 1996. pap. text ed. 12.96 (*1-56510-410-2*) Greenhaven.

Urban Terrorism. Ed. by A. E. Sadler & Paul A. Winters. LC 96-11849. (Current Controversies Ser.). 176p. (J). (gr. 5-12). 1996. lib. bdg. 20.96 (*1-56510-411-0*) Greenhaven.

Urban Texas: Politics & Development. Ed. by Char Miller & Heywood T. Sanders. LC 89-33948. (Southwestern Studies: No. 8). (Illus.). 224p. 1989. pap. 15.95 (*0-89096-397-5*) Tex A&M Univ Pr.

Urban Tourism: Performance & Strategies in Eight European Cities. Leo Van den Berg et al. 240p. 1995. 55.95 (*1-85972-152-4*, Pub. by Avebury Pub UK) Ashgate Pub Co.

Urban Traffic Networks: Dynamic Flow Modeling & Control. International Seminar on Urban Traffic Networks Staff. Ed. by Nathan H. Gartner & Gennaro Improta. LC 95-10070. (Transportation Analysis Ser.). 375p. 1995. 122.00 (*3-540-59073-0*) Spr-Verlag.

Urban Transformation of the Developing World. Ed. by Josef Gugler. (Illus.). 352p. (C). 1996. 65.00 (*0-19-874158-8*); pap. text ed. 19.95 (*0-19-874159-6*) OUP.

Urban Transit: The Private Challenge to Public Transportation. Ed. by Charles A. Lave. LC 84-21529. (Illus.). 372p. 1985. 29.95 (*0-936488-62-X*); pap. 14.95 (*0-936488-63-8*) PRIPP.

***Urban Transport: A Century of Progress?** Ed. by Kevin Hey & John Sheldrake. (Illus.). 144p. 1997. text ed. 55.95 (*1-85972-466-3*, Pub. by Ashgate UK) Ashgate Pub Co.

***Urban Transport: An Annotated International Bibliography.** J. McConville & John Sheldrake. LC 96-32816. 1997. write for info. (*0-7201-2335-6*, Mansell Pub) Cassell.

Urban Transport & Planning: A Bibliography with Abstracts. D. Banister & L. Pickup. 360p. 1989. text ed. 90.00 (*0-7201-1627-9*, Mansell Pub) Cassell.

Urban Transport & the Environment for the 21st Century: Proceedings of the International Conference. L. Sucharov & C. A. Brebbia. LC 95-67484. 474p. 1995. 190.00 (*1-56252-247-7*, 3234) Computational Mech MA.

Urban Transport & the Environment for the 21st Century II: Proceedings of the Second International Conference, Southampton, U. K., 1996. Ed. by L. J. Sucharov et al. (Urban Transport Ser.: Vol. 2). 602p. 1996. 239.00 (*1-85312-451-6*, 4516) Computational Mech MA.

Urban Transport & the Environment for the 21st Century III. (Urban Transport Ser.: Vol. 3). 450p. 1997. 202.50 (*1-85312-464-8*, 4648) Computational Mech MA.

Urban Transport Development with Particular Reference to Developing Countries. 53p. 1989. mass mkt. 7.50 (*92-1-104313-1*, E. 89. II.A.7) UN.

Urban Transport Economics. Ed. by David A. Hensher. LC 76-11061. 285p. reprint ed. pap. 81.30 (*0-685-44042-7*, 2030599) Bks Demand.

Urban Transport Future. Ed. by Tony Young & Roy Cresswell. LC 81-19560. (Illus.). 214p. reprint ed. pap. 61.00 (*0-685-20292-5*, 2030326) Bks Demand.

Urban Transport Planning: A Developmental Approach. Harry T. Dimitriou. LC 91-21438. 320p. (C). (gr. 13). 1992. text ed. 110.00 (*0-415-03857-X*, A6786) Routledge.

Urban Transport Planning: Theory & Practice. Ed. by John Black. LC 80-8860. (Illus.). 257p. (C). 1981. pap. text ed. 15.95 (*0-8018-2604-7*) Johns Hopkins.

Urban Transport Planning: Theory & Practice. John Black. LC 80-8860. 248p. reprint ed. pap. 70.70 (*0-317-41621-9*, 2025831) Bks Demand.

***Urban Transportation: Metropolitan Planning Organizations' Efforts to Meet Federal Planning Requirements.** (Illus.). 59p. (Orig.). (C). 1996. pap. 25.00 (*0-7881-3582-1*) DIANE Pub.

Urban Transportation Economics, Vol. 51. Kenneth A. Small. (Fundamentals of Pure & Applied Economics Ser.). 185, xvp. 1992. pap. text ed. 44.00 (*3-7186-5169-6*, Harwood Acad Pubs) Gordon & Breach.

Urban Transportation Efficiency. 442p. 1977. pap. 22.00 (*0-87262-174-X*) Am Soc Civil Eng.

Urban Transportation Financing. LC 80-66290. 312p. 1980. pap. 28.00 (*0-87262-241-X*) Am Soc Civil Eng.

Urban Transportation Financing: Theory & Policy in Ontario. Mark W. Frankena. (Ontario Economic Council Research Studies). 248p. 1982. pap. 6.95 (*0-8020-3380-6*) U of Toronto Pr.

Urban Transportation Innovation. Compiled by Daniel Brand. 445p. 1970. pap. 21.00 (*0-87262-044-1*) Am Soc Civil Eng.

Urban Transportation of Irradiated Fuels. Ed. by John Surrey. LC 83-40490. 300p. 1984. text ed. 29.95 (*0-312-83481-0*) St Martin.

Urban Transportation Planning. Compiled by Harold Deutschman. 106p. 1968. pap. 10.00 (*0-87262-019-0*) Am Soc Civil Eng.

Urban Transportation Planning. M. Meyer & E. Miller. 544p. 1984. text ed. write for info. (*0-07-041752-0*) McGraw.

Urban Transportation Planning: Traffic Management. 1992. lib. bdg. 350.00 (*0-8490-5603-9*) Gordon Pr.

Urban Transportation Planning in the United States: An Historical Overview. Edward Weiner. LC 86-30343. 135p. 1987. text ed. 49.95 (*0-275-92493-9*, C2493, Praeger Pubs); pap. text ed. 11.95 (*0-275-92544-7*, B2544, Praeger Pubs) Greenwood.

Urban Transportation Planning in the 1980s. (Special Reports: No. 196). 52p. 1982. 7.80 (*0-309-03404-3*) Transport Res Bd.

Urban Transportation Problem. John R. Meyer et al. LC 65-13848. (Rand Corporation Research Studies). (Illus.). 427p. 1965. pap. 16.50 (*0-674-93121-1*) HUP.

Urban Travel & Sustainable Development. 238p. (Orig.). 1995. pap. 48.00 (*92-64-14370-X*, Pub. by Org for Econ FR) OECD.

Urban Travel Demand Modeling: From Individual Choices to General Equilibrium. Robert Oppenheim. 456p. 1995. text ed. 69.95 (*0-471-55723-4*) Wiley.

Urban Travel Forecasting. (Research Record Ser.: No. 1139). 47p. 1987. 7.50 (*0-309-04650-5*) Transport Res Bd.

Urban Treasure Hunter. Michael Chaplan. 100p. 1992. 9.95 (*1-882279-00-X*) Whites Elect.

Urban Trees: A Guide for Selection, Maintenance, & Master Planning. Leonard E. Phillips, Jr. LC 92-43723. 1993. text ed. 37.00 (*0-07-049835-0*) McGraw.

Urban Underclass. Ed. by Christopher Jencks & Paul E. Peterson. 490p. 1991. pap. 19.95 (*0-8157-4605-9*) Brookings.

Urban Underclass. fac. ed. Ed. by Christopher Jencks & Paul E. Peterson. LC 90-23619. (Illus.). 504p. 1991. pap. 143.70 (*0-7837-7679-9*, 2047432) Bks Demand.

Urban Underground Space Design in China: Vernacular & Modern Practice. Gideon S. Golany. LC 87-40708. (Illus.). 160p. 1989. 35.00 (*0-87413-345-9*) U Delaware Pr.

***Urban Unemployment.** Hasluck. 1987. pap. text ed. write for info. (*0-582-29668-4*, Pub. by Longman UK) Longman.

Urban University in America. Maurice R. Berube. LC 77-87917. 149p. 1978. text ed. 45.00 (*0-313-20031-9*, BUU/, Greenwood Pr) Greenwood.

Urban Unrest in the Middle East: A Comparative Study of Informal Networks in Egypt, Iran, & Lebanon. Guilain Denoeux. LC 92-25353. (SUNY Series in the Social & Economic History of the Middle East). 310p. (C). 1993. text ed. 64.50 (*0-7914-1523-6*); pap. text ed. 21.95 (*0-7914-1524-4*) State U NY Pr.

Urban Utopias in the Twentieth Century: Ebenezer Howard, Frank Lloyd Wright, Le Corbusier. Robert Fishman. (Illus.). 384p. (C). 1982. pap. 20.00 (*0-262-56023-2*) MIT Pr.

***Urban Vector & Pest Control: Eleventh Report of the WHO Expert Committee on Vector Biology & Control.** WHO Staff. (Technical Report Ser.: No. 767). 77p. 1988. 9.00 (*92-4-120767-1*) World Health.

***Urban Vegetarian.** Nancy M. Forte & James Forte. 210p. (Orig.). 1992. pap. 15.95 (*1-889560-07-3*) Wildflower Pub.

Urban Vegetation: A Review & Chicago Case Study. James A. Schmid. LC 74-84781. (University of Chicago, Department of Geography, Research Paper Ser.: No. 161). (Illus.). 280p. reprint ed. pap. 79.80 (*0-7837-0406-2*, 2040727) Bks Demand.

Urban Verbs: Arts & Discourses of American Cities. Kevin R. McNamara. LC 95-42932. 1996. 39.50 (*0-8047-2645-0*) Stanford U Pr.

Urban Vigilantes in the New South: Tampa, 1882-1936. Robert P. Ingalls. LC 93-7217. (Florida Sand Dollar Bk.). (Illus.). 312p. 1993. pap. 16.95 (*0-8130-1223-6*) U Press Fla.

Urban Vigilantes in the New South: Tampa, 1882-1936. Robert P. Ingalls. LC 87-30077. (Illus.). 310p. 1988. text ed. 36.00 (*0-87049-571-2*) U of Tenn Pr.

Urban Village: Community & Family in Germantown, Pennsylvania, 1683-1800. Stephanie G. Wolf. LC 76-3025. 376p. 1976. pap. text ed. 17.95 (*0-691-00590-7*) Princeton U Pr.

Urban Villagers. 2nd expanded rev. ed. Herbert J. Gans. LC 82-8577. (Illus.). 456p. (C). 1982. pap. 15.95 (*0-02-911240-0*, Free Press) Free Pr.

Urban Voodoo. Edgardo Cozarinsky. 120p. (Orig.). 1991. pap. 9.95 (*0-930829-15-8*) Lumen Inc.

Urban Voodoo: A Beginner's Guide to Afro-Caribbean Magic. S. Jason Black & Christopher S. Hyatt. LC 94-66064. (Illus.). 188p. (Orig.). 1995. pap. 14.95 (*1-56184-059-9*) New Falcon Pubns.

Urban Warrior's Book of Solutions: Staying Healthy, Fit & Sane in the Business Jungle. Michael McGannon. 240p. 1996. 22.00 (*0-273-61307-3*) Pitman Publng.

Urban Wastes in Coastal Marine Environments: Oceanic Processes in Marine Pollution, Vol. 5. Ed. by Douglas A. Wolfe & Thomas P. O'Connor. LC 87-22831. 292p. (C). 1988. lib. bdg. 65.00 (*0-89874-963-8*) Krieger.

Urban Water Conservation: Increasing Efficiency-in-Use Residential Water Demand. J. Ernest Flack. LC 82-70113. 111p. 1982. pap. 14.00 (*0-87262-296-7*) Am Soc Civil Eng.

***Urban Water Demand Management & Planning.** Duane D. Baumann et al. (Illus.). 350p. 1997. text ed. 59.95 (*0-07-050301-X*) McGraw.

Urban Water Infrastructure: Planning, Management, & Operations. Neil S. Grigg. LC 91-46196. 342p. (C). 1992. reprint ed. 52.50 (*0-89464-705-9*) Krieger.

Urban Water Infrastructure: Proceedings of the NATO Advanced Research Workshop Held on the Isle of Man, U. K., 22-27 June 1989. Ed. by Kyle E. Schilling & Eric Porter. (C). 1990. lib. bdg. 141.50 (*0-7923-0686-4*) Kluwer Ac.

Urban Water Resources Management. (Water Resources Ser.: No. 72). 160p. 1993. 30.00 (*92-1-119621-3*) UN.

Urban Water Supply Alternatives: Perception & Choice in the Grand Basin, Ontario. Ian MacIver. LC 70-115926. (University of Chicago, Department of Geography, Research Paper Ser.: No. 126). (Illus.). 193p. reprint ed. pap. 55.10 (*0-7837-0402-X*, 2040723) Bks Demand.

Urban Waterfront. B. Fisher. 1998. text ed. 39.95 (*0-442-22496-6*) Van Nos Reinhold.

Urban Waterfront Development. Douglas M. Wrenn et al. LC 82-84340. (Illus.). 224p. (Orig.). reprint ed. pap. 63.90 (*0-7837-3938-9*, 2043693) Bks Demand.

Urban Waterfront Resource Materials. 50p. 1988. 30.00 (*0-685-24939-5*) Waterfront DC.

Urban Waterfronts: Accent on Access. Ann Breen & Dick Rigby. (Illus.). 100p. 1989. pap. 24.95 (*0-935957-05-7*) Waterfront DC.

Urban Waterfronts '84: Toward New Horizons. Ann Breen & Dick Rigby. (Illus.). 100p. 1985. pap. 24.95 (*0-935957-00-6*) Waterfront DC.

Urban Waterfronts '85: Water Makes a Difference! Ann Breen & Dick Rigby. (Illus.). 134p. (Orig.). 1986. pap. 24.95 (*0-935957-02-2*) Waterfront DC.

Urban Waterfronts '86: Developing Diversity. Ann Breen & Dick Rigby. (Illus.). 100p. (Orig.). 1987. pap. 24.95 (*0-935957-03-0*) Waterfront DC.

Urban Waterfronts '87: Water - The Ultimate Amenity. Ann Breen & Dick Rigby. (Illus.). 100p. 1988. pap. 24.95 (*0-935957-04-9*) Waterfront DC.

Urban Web: Politics, Policy, & Theory. Lawrence J. Herson & John M. Bolland. (Political Science Ser.). (Illus.). 512p. 1990. 39.95 (*0-8304-1078-3*); pap. text ed. 28.95 (*0-8304-1220-4*) Nelson-Hall.

Urban West: Managing Growth & Decline. James B. Wetherby & Stephanie L. Witt. LC 93-43062. 168p. 1994. text ed. 49.95 (*0-275-93998-7*, Praeger Pubs) Greenwood.

Urban Wilderness: A History of the American City. Sam B. Warner, Jr. LC 95-3437. (Classics in Urban History Ser.: Vol. 5). 1995. pap. 14.95 (*0-520-20224-4*) U CA Pr.

Urban Wilderness: Nature in New York City. Jean Gardner. (Illus.). 132p. 1988. 39.95 (*0-317-91298-4*) Earth Environmental.

***Urban Wildland Interface Code.** 64p. (C). 1997. pap. 25.00 (*1-884590-73-X*) Intl Conf Bldg Off.

Urban Wildlife. Peter Shirley. (Illus.). 128p. 1996. pap. 19.95 (*1-873580-23-1*, Pub. by Whittet Bks UK) Diamond Farm Bk.

Urban Wildlife Habitats: A Landscape Perspective. Lowell W. Adams. LC 93-44211. (Wildlife Habitats Ser.: No. 3). 1994. pap. 16.95 (*0-8166-2213-2*) U of Minn Pr.

Urban Workers & Labor Unions in Chile, 1902-1927. Peter DeShazo. LC 82-70557. (Illus.). 384p. 1983. 32.50 (*0-299-09220-8*) U of Wis Pr.

Urban Workers on Relief, 2 Vols. in 1. Gladys L. Palmer & Katherine D. Wood. LC 75-165688. (Research Monographs: Vol. 4). 1971. reprint ed. Set. lib. bdg. 59.50 (*0-306-70336-X*) Da Capo.

Urban World. 5th ed. J. John Palen. LC 96-5369. 1996. text ed. write for info. (*0-07-048168-7*) McGraw.

Urban World, Global City. David Clark. LC 95-26472. 224p. (C). 1996. pap. 17.95 (*0-415-14437-X*); text ed. 55.00 (*0-415-14436-1*) Routledge.

Urban Youth & the Frail Elderly: Reciprocal Giving & Receiving. rev. ed. Doris Schindler. LC 95-48373. (Studies on the Elderly in America). (Illus.). 136p. 1996. text ed. 47.00 (*0-8153-2331-X*) Garland.

Urbana: A Pictorial History. Raymond Bial. (Illinois Pictorial History Ser.). (Illus.). 1994. write for info. (*0-943963-38-9*) G Bradley.

Urbana Municipal Documents Center Manual. Jean E. Koch et al. LC 86-51179. (Illus.). 260p. 1987. 50.00 (*0-9609646-6-5*) Urbana Free Lib.

Urbana Scripta: Studies of Fire Living Poets & Other Essays. Arthur H. Galton. 1977. text ed. 16.95 (*0-8369-8160-X*, 8300) Ayer.

Urbana, University of Illinois, MS X786. 4108 - M319 ("Woodcock MS") Ed. by Alexander Silbiger. LC 87-754779. (Seventeenth-Century Keyboard Music Ser.: Vol. 20). 880624p. 1988. text ed. 20.00 (*0-8240-8019-X*) Garland.

***Urbane Imagination: Ideas of Civilization in the Chinese.** Daniel Kwok. 200p. (C). 1997. per. 29.95 (*0-7872-3742-6*) Kendall-Hunt.

An Asterisk (*) at the beginning of an entry indicates that the title is appearing in BIP for the first time.

Urbane Tales. Raymond Johnson. LC 90-38358. 76p. 1991. 12.95 (*0-933532-77-6*) BkMk.

Urbanisation: Trends, Perspectives & Challenges. Ed. by Jaymala Diddee. (C). 1993. 30.00 (*81-7033-185-4*, Pub. by Rawat II) S Asia.

Urbanisation & Industrial Estates: The U. S. A., the U. K. & Indian Experience. K. K. Khakhar. 1985. 18.50 (*0-8364-1512-4*, Pub. by Ashish II) S Asia.

Urbanisation in Ancient India. Vijay K. Thakur. 1981. 25.00 (*0-8364-0814-4*, Pub. by Abhinav II) S Asia.

Urbanising Britain: Essays on Class & Community in the Nineteenth Century. Ed. by Gerry Kearns & Charles W. Withers. (Studies in Historical Geography: No. 17). (Illus.). 192p. (C). 1991. text ed. 54.95 (*0-521-36499-X*) Cambridge U Pr.

***Urbanism.** Links Editors. (Illus.). 238p. 1997. 85.00 (*1-56970-548-8*, Pub. by Links SP) Bks Nippan.

Urbanism: An Architectural Design Profile. David Gosling & Barry Maitland. (Illus.). 88p. 1984. pap. 19.95 (*0-312-83485-3*) St Martin.

Urbanism & Industrial Culture - Industry & Urban Culture. 120p. 1992. 33.00 (*0-8176-2724-3*) Birkhauser.

Urbanism As a Way of Life. Louis Wirth. (Reprint Series in Sociology). (C). 1993. reprint ed. pap. text ed. 1.90 (*0-8290-2639-8*, S-320) Irvington.

Urbanism as Delinquency: Compromising the Agenda for Social Change. William J. Mackey et al. 184p. (C). 1993. lib. bdg. 49.50 (*0-8191-9102-7*) U Pr of Amer.

Urbanism, Colonialism & the World Economy. Anthony D. King. 208p. 1989. 49.95 (*0-415-00884-0*, A2383) Routledge.

Urbanism, Colonialism & the World Economy: Cultural & Spatial Foundations of the World Urban System. Anthony D. King. (International Library of Sociology). 208p. (C). 1991. pap. 16.95 (*0-415-06240-3*, A5697) Routledge.

Urbanists, Eighteen Sixty-Five to Nineteen Fifteen. Dana F. White. LC 88-24703. (Contributions in American Studies: No. 94). 302p. 1989. text ed. 65.00 (*0-313-25256-4*, WUR/, Greenwood Pr) Greenwood.

***Urbanitat und Stadtentwicklung.** Erwin Ruegg. (Europaische Urbanitat-Politik der Stadte Ser.). (GER.). 1996. text ed. 56.00 (*90-5708-005-2*); pap. text ed. 25.00 (*90-5708-006-0*) Gordon & Breach.

Urbanities. Edward V. Lucas. LC 79-128272. (Essay Index Reprint Ser.). 1977. 19.95 (*0-8369-1888-6*) Ayer.

Urbanities: Visions of the Metropolis. Ed. by Patra McSharry & Roger Rosen. (Icarus World Issues Ser.). (Illus.). (YA). (gr. 7-12). 1993. pap. 8.95 (*0-8239-1388-0*); lib. bdg. 16.95 (*0-8239-1387-2*) Rosen Group.

***Urbanizacion.** G. Carney. (SPA.). 1.50 (*0-8297-1958-X*) Life Pubs Intl.

Urbanization. Clandion Carney. Ed. by Stephen Hayner & Gordon Aeschliman. (Global Issues Bible Study Ser.). 48p. (Orig.). 1990. wbk. ed., pap. 4.99 (*0-8308-4904-1*, 4904) InterVarsity.

Urbanization: An Introduction to Urban Geography. Paul L. Knox. LC 93-27070. 436p. (C). 1993. text ed. 69.00 (*0-13-953357-5*) P-H.

Urbanization: IGU Congress, Moscow, Proceedings, Pt. 3. Ed. by Yuri Medvedkov. 1977. pap. 23.00 (*0-08-021324-3*, Pergamon Pr) Elsevier.

Urbanization, Agricultural Development, & Land Allocation. Dipasis Bhadra & Antonio S. Brandao. LC 93-17320. (Discussion Paper Ser.: Vol. 201). 71p. 1993. 6.95 (*0-8213-2456-X*, 12456) World Bank.

Urbanization & Cancer Mortality: The United States Experience, 1950-1975. Michael R. Greenberg. (Monographs in Epidemiology & Biostatistics: No. 4). (Illus.). 128p. 1983. 45.00 (*0-19-503173-3*) OUP.

Urbanization & Counterurbanization. Ed. by Brian J. Berry. LC 76-15864. (Urban Affairs Annual Reviews Ser.: No. 11). (Illus.). 334p. reprint ed. pap. 95.20 (*0-8357-4736-0*, 2037653) Bks Demand.

Urbanization & Crime: Germany 1871-1914. Eric A. Johnson. (Illus.). 293p. (C). 1995. text ed. 49.95 (*0-521-47017-X*) Cambridge U Pr.

***Urbanization & Economic Growth.** Vibhooti Shukla. Ed. by Tara Shukla & Satchit Srinivasan. (Illus.). 512p. 1997. 35.00 (*0-19-563725-9*) OUP.

Urbanization & Environmental Quality. T. R. Lakshmanan & Lata Chatterjee. Ed. by Salvatore J. Natoli. LC 76-57032. (Resource Papers for College Geography). (C). 1977. pap. text ed. 15.00 (*0-89291-122-0*) Assn Am Geographers.

Urbanization & Family Change. M. S. Gore. 1990. 27.50 (*0-86132-262-2*, Pub. by Popular Prakashan II) S Asia.

Urbanization & Inequality: The Political Economy of Urban & Rural Development in Latin America. Ed. by Wayne A. Cornelius & Felicity M. Trueblood. LC 74-83000. (Latin American Urban Research Ser.: Vol. 5). (Illus.). 318p. reprint ed. pap. 90.70 (*0-317-08989-7*, 2021879) Bks Demand.

***Urbanization & Its Implications for Child Health Potential for Action.** WHO Staff. 86p. 1988. 16.00 (*92-4-156123-8*) World Health.

Urbanization & Planning in the Third World: Spatial Perspectives & Public Participation. Robert B. Potter. LC 85-10924. 284p. 1985. text ed. 39.95 (*0-312-83497-7*) St Martin.

Urbanization & Population Redistribution in Mongolia. Ricardo Neupert & Sidney Goldstein. LC 94-39475. (Occasional Papers: No. 122). 1994. pap. text ed. write for info. (*0-86638-166-X*) EW Ctr HI.

Urbanization & the Growth of Cities. Ed. & Des. by Neil L. Shumsky. LC 95-38493. (American Cities Ser.: Vol. 1). (Illus.). 536p. 1995. reprint ed. text ed. 90.00 (*0-8153-2186-4*) Garland.

Urbanization & Urban Growth in the Caribbean. Malcolm Cross. LC 78-67307. (Urbanization in Developing Countries Ser.). 186p. reprint ed. pap. 53.10 (*0-317-26045-6*, 2024438) Bks Demand.

Urbanization & Urban Planning in Capitalist Societies. Michael J. Dear & Allen J. Scott. 1981. pap. 19.95 (*0-416-74650-0*, NO. 6382) Routledge Chapman & Hall.

Urbanization & Urban Problems. Edwin S. Mills & Byung-Nak Song. (East Asian Monographs: No. 88). 329p. 1979. 17.50 (*0-674-93133-5*) HUP.

Urbanization & Urban Systems in India. R. Ramachandran. (Illus.). 380p. 1990. 26.00 (*0-19-562140-9*) OUP.

Urbanization & Values. Ed. by George F. McLean & John Kromkowski. (Cultural Heritage & Contemporary Change Ser.: No. 5). 380p. (Orig.). 1991. 45.00 (*1-56518-011-9*, HT361.U725) Coun Res Values.

Urbanization & Values. Ed. by George F. McLean & John Kromkowski. (Cultural Heritage & Contemporary Change Series VI: Foundations of Moral Education,: Vol. I, No. 5). 380p. (Orig.). 1991. pap. 17.50 (*1-56518-010-0*) Coun Res Values.

Urbanization & Water Quality: A Guide to Protecting the Urban Environment. Ed. by Roberta F. Schulman. (Illus.). 67p. (Orig.). 1994. pap. 12.95 (*0-614-14312-8*) Terrene Inst.

***Urbanization & Water Quality: A Guide to Protecting the Urban Environment.** TTI (Taggart) Staff. 80p. 1996. per., pap. text ed. 12.95 (*0-7872-2909-1*) Kendall-Hunt.

Urbanization & Water Quality Control. Ed. by William Whipple, Jr. 310p. reprint ed. pap. 88.40 (*0-317-11243-0*, 2017813) Bks Demand.

Urbanization, Capital Formation & Labour Productivity in Agriculture. G. C. Srivastava. 205p. 1986. text ed. 22.50 (*81-7027-096-0*, Pub. by Radiant Pubs II) S Asia.

Urbanization in Africa: A Handbook. Ed. by James D. Tarver. LC 93-11853. 536p. 1994. text ed. 115.00 (*0-313-27760-5*, Greenwood Pr) Greenwood.

Urbanization in China: New Insights from the 1982 Census. Sidney Goldstein. LC 85-13120. (Papers of the East-West Population Institute: No. 93). (Illus.). 73p. (Orig.). 1985. pap. 3.00 (*0-86638-067-1*) EW Ctr HI.

Urbanization in Contemporary Latin America: Critical Approaches to the Analysis of Urban Issues. Alan Gilbert. LC 81-21876. (Illus.). 302p. reprint ed. pap. 86.10 (*0-8357-6708-6*, 2035339) Bks Demand.

Urbanization in Developing Countries: An International Bibliography. Stanley D. Brunn. LC 79-172535. (Latin American Studies Center Research Report: No. 8). 711p. reprint ed. pap. 180.00 (*0-8357-4336-5*, 2037137) Bks Demand.

Urbanization in Europe: Selected Papers of the European Regional Conference of the International Geographical Union. B. Starfalvi. 314p. (ENG, FRE & GER.). (C). 1975. 51.00 (*963-05-0490-1*, Pub. by Akad Kiado HU) St Mut.

Urbanization in Garhwal Himalaya: A Geographical Interpretation. Surendra Singh. 303p. 1995. pap. 225.00 (*81-85880-69-7*, Pub. by Print Hse II) St Mut.

Urbanization in Garhwal Himalaya: A Geographical Interpretation. Surendra Singh. 303p. 1995. pap. 200.00 (*0-614-09720-7*, Pub. by Print Hse II) St Mut.

Urbanization in History: A Process of Dynamic Interactions. Ed. by Ad Van Der Woude et al. (International Studies in Demography). (Illus.). 387p. 1995. pap. 26.00 (*0-19-828958-8*) OUP.

Urbanization in India: A Study of Sibsagar-Assam. Manirul Huda. 1990. 32.50 (*81-7099-209-5*, Pub. by Mittal II) S Asia.

Urbanization in India: Spatial Dimensions. Prakasa Rao. 1983. 24.00 (*0-8364-1033-5*) S Asia.

***Urbanization in Large Developing Countries: China, Indonesia, Brazil & India.** Ed. by Gavin M. Jones & Pravin Visaria. (Illus.). 376p. 1997. 75.00 (*0-19-828974-X*) OUP.

Urbanization in Nepal. Pitamber Sharma. LC 89-11878. (Papers of the East-West Population Institute: No. 110). x, 162p. 1989. 3.00 (*0-86638-115-5*) EW Ctr HI.

Urbanization in Papua New Guinea: A Study of Ambivalent Townsmen. H. B. Levine & Marlene W. Levine. LC 78-58795. 169p. reprint ed. pap. 48.20 (*0-318-34817-9*, 2031682) Bks Demand.

Urbanization in the Americas from Its Beginnings to the Present. Ed. by Richard P. Schaedel et al. (World Anthropology Ser.). (Illus.). xii, 676p. 1978. 69.25 (*90-279-7530-2*) Mouton.

Urbanization in the Third World: A Case Study of Lahore, Pakistan. Mohammad A. Qadeer. LC 82-15117. 300p. 1983. text ed. 65.00 (*0-275-91061-X*, C1061, Praeger Pubs) Greenwood.

Urbanization in the World Economy. Michael Timberlake. (Studies in Social Discontinuity). 1985. text ed. 61.00 (*0-12-691290-4*) Acad Pr.

Urbanization in Twentieth Century Latin America: A Working Bibliography. Denton R. Vaughan. LC 72-206165. 132p. reprint ed. pap. 37.70 (*0-685-15626-5*, 2027328) Bks Demand.

Urbanization in West Africa. Ruth P. Simms. 109p. 1965. 29.00 (*0-89771-007-X*) St Mut.

Urbanization in West Africa: A Review of Current Literature. Ruth P. Simms. LC 65-19464. 132p. reprint ed. pap. 37.70 (*0-317-10334-2*, 2006372) Bks Demand.

Urbanization of an African Community. Claude Meillassoux. LC 84-45538. (American Ethnological Society Monographs: No. 45). 1988. reprint ed. 30.00 (*0-404-62943-1*) AMS Pr.

Urbanization of Capital: Studies in the History & Theory of Capitalist Urbanization. David Harvey. LC 85-9795. (Illus.). 259p. reprint ed. pap. 73.90 (*0-8357-6747-7*, 2035402) Bks Demand.

***Urbanization of Injustice.** Andy Merrifield & E. Swyngedouw. LC 96-47841. 1997. 50.00 (*0-8147-5575-5*); pap. 16.95 (*0-8147-5576-3*) NYU Pr.

Urbanization of Injustice. Ed A. Merrifield. (C). 1996. pap. write for info. (*0-85315-842-8*, Pub. by Lawrence & Wishart UK) NYU Pr.

Urbanization of Japanese Labor, Eighteen Sixty-Eight to Nineteen Fifty-Five. Thomas O. Wilkinson. LC 65-26242. (Illus.). 262p. 1965. 30.00 (*0-87023-018-2*) U of Mass Pr.

Urbanization of Modern America: A Brief History. 2nd ed. Zane L. Miller & Patricia M. Melvin. 264p. (C). 1987. pap. text ed. 16.00 (*0-15-593657-3*) HB Coll Pubs.

***Urbanization of Opera.** Gerhard. 1997. 45.00 (*0-226-28857-9*); pap. text ed. 26.00 (*0-226-28858-7*) U Ch Pr.

Urbanization of Prime Agricultural Land in the United States: A Statistical Analysis. Daniel R. Vining, Jr. et al. (Discussion Paper Ser.: No. 99). 1977. pap. 10.00 (*1-55869-130-8*) Regional Sci Res Inst.

Urbanization of Rural Dialect Speakers: A Sociolinguistic Study in Brazil. Stella Bortoni-Ricardo. (Cambridge Studies in Linguistics: Supplementary Volumes). 350p. 1985. text ed. 65.00 (*0-521-30404-0*) Cambridge U Pr.

Urbanization, Planning & Development in the Caribbean. Ed. by R. B. Potter. 336p. 1989. text ed. 90.00 (*0-7201-2012-8*, Mansell Pub) Cassell.

Urbanization, Planning, & National Development. John Friedman. LC 72-84049. 352p. reprint ed. pap. 100.40 (*0-317-07764-3*, 2021901) Bks Demand.

Urbanization, Population Growth & Economic Deveopment in the Philippines. Ernesto D. Pernia. LC 77-24588. (Studies in Population & Urban Demography: No. 3). 213p. 1977. text ed. 55.00 (*0-8371-9721-X*, PEU/, Greenwood Pr) Greenwood.

Urbanization Primer: Project Assessment, Site Analysis, Design Criteria for Site & Services or Similar Dwelling Environments in Developing Areas, with a Documentary Collection of Photographs on Urbanization. Horacio Caminos & Reinhard Goethert. (Illus.). 1978. 45.00 (*0-262-03066-7*) MIT Pr.

Urbanization Revolution: Planning a New Agenda for Human Settlements. R. May, Jr. (Urban Innovation Abroad Ser.). (Illus.). 288p. 1989. 75.00 (*0-306-43222-6*, Plenum Pr) Plenum.

***Urbanization Without Cities: The Rise & Decline of Citizenship.** Murray Bookchin. 316p. 1996. 48.99 (*1-895431-01-8*, Pub. by Black Rose Bks CN) Consort Bk Sales.

Urbanizing China. Gregory E. Guldin. LC 91-24837. (Contributions in Asian Studies: No. 1). 272p. 1992. text ed. 59.95 (*0-313-26813-4*, GUB, Greenwood Pr) Greenwood.

Urbanizing World: Global Report on Human Settlements 1996. U. N. Centre for Human Settlements (Habitat) Staff. (Illus.). 600p. 1996. 75.00 (*0-19-823347-7*) OUP.

Urbanizing World: Global Report on Human Settlements 1996. U. N. Centre for Human Settlements (Habitat) Staff. (Illus.). 600p. 35.00 (*0-19-823346-9*) UN.

Urbanna, Virginia: A Port Town since 1860. David D. Ryan. (Illus.). 1995. pap. 12.00 (*0-87517-074-9*) Dietz.

Urbild des Gottesbewusstseins: Zur Entwicklung der Religionstheorie & Christologie Schleiermachers Von der Ersten zur Zweiten Auflage der Glaubenslehre. Maureen Junker. (Schleiermacher-Archiv Ser.: Band 8). xi, 236p. (C). 1990. lib. bdg. 64.65 (*3-11-012312-6*) De Gruyter.

Urbs Antiqua. Paul Whalen. 96p. (C). 1990. pap. text ed. 10.95 (*0-521-37739-0*) Cambridge U Pr.

Urbs Prima in India: An Epoch in the History of Bombay, 1840-1865. Teresa Albuquerque. 1985. 28.00 (*81-85002-00-2*, Pub. by Promilla) S Asia.

Urchin in the Storm: Essays about Books & Ideas. Stephen J. Gould. (Illus.). 1988. pap. 9.95 (*0-393-30537-6*) Norton.

***Urda.** Sarah Belle. LC 96-90814. (Illus.). 91p. (Orig.). (J). (gr. 4-8). 1996. pap. 12.95 (*0-9655316-0-0*) Urda Pub.

***Urdu.** (Teach Yourself Ser.). pap. 34.95 (*0-8442-3716-7*) NTC Pub Grp.

Urdu, Vol. I. Muhammad A. Barker et al. 497p. 1975. pap. 185.00 incl. audio (*0-88432-106-1*, AFU200) Audio-Forum.

Urdu, Vol. II. Muhammad A. Barker et al. 568p. (C). 1976. pap. text ed. 115.00 incl. audio (*0-88432-107-X*, AFU250) Audio-Forum.

Urdu: Grammar & Reader. Ernest Bender. LC 66-20832. (Illus.). 491p. reprint ed. pap. 140.00 (*0-317-10103-X*, 2051185) Bks Demand.

Urdu: Readings in Literary Urdu Prose. Gopi C. Narang. LC 70-2757. 396p. reprint ed. pap. 112.90 (*0-317-10097-1*, 2004657) Bks Demand.

Urdu Encyclopedia: Pictorial, 4 Color. Ferozsons. 120.00 (*0-933511-82-5*) Kazi Pubns.

Urdu-English Dictionary. (ENG & URD.). 35.50 (*0-933511-83-3*) Kazi Pubns.

Urdu-English Dictionary. Abul Haq. 688p. 1993. 24.95 (*0-7818-0222-9*) Hippocrene Bks.

Urdu-English Dictionary. S. Sangaji. (ENG & URD.). 1983. 49.95 (*0-8288-1111-3*, F140706) Fr & Eur.

Urdu-English Dictionary, Romanized. (ENG & URD.). 42.50 (*0-87557-090-9*) Saphrograph.

Urdu-English Vocabulary: Student's Dictionary. M. A. Barker et al. LC 79-92847. 382p. (ENG & URD.). 1980. pap. text ed. 15.00 (*0-87950-438-2*) Spoken Lang Serv.

Urdu for Beginners. Krawaja M. Zakariya. (Orig.). 1992. pap. 12.95 (*1-56744-448-2*) Kazi Pubns.

***Urdu for Children: Book One.** Ed. by Sajida Alvi. 174p. 1997. teacher ed., pap. 24.95 (*0-7735-1622-0*, Pub. by McGill CN) U of Toronto Pr.

***Urdu for Children: Book One.** Ed. by Sajida Alvi. 96p. 1997. wbk. ed., pap. 6.95 (*0-7735-1623-9*, Pub. by McGill CN) U of Toronto Pr.

***Urdu for Children: Book One, Vol. 1.** Ed. by Sajida Alvi. 90p. 1997. pap. 14.95 (*0-7735-1620-4*, Pub. by McGill CN) U of Toronto Pr.

***Urdu for Children: Book One, Vol. 2.** Ed. by Sajida Alvi. 78p. 1997. pap. 14.95 (*0-7735-1621-2*, Pub. by McGill CN) U of Toronto Pr.

***Urdu Ghazals: An Anthology from 16th to 20th Century.** K. C. Kanda. (C). 1995. 15.00 (*81-207-1826-7*, Pub. by Sterling Plns Pvt II) S Asia.

Urdu Language & Literature: A Bibliography of Sources in European Languages. Shabana Mahmud. 352p. 1992. text ed. 100.00 (*0-7201-2143-4*, Mansell Pub) Cassell.

Urdu Language & Literature: A Critical Perspective. Gopi C. Narang. 224p. 1991. text ed. 27.95 (*81-207-1124-6*, Pub. by Sterling Pubs II) Apt Bks.

Urdu Letters of Mirza Asadu'llah Khan Ghalib. Annemarie Schimmel. LC 87-6447. 628p. 1987. text ed. 29.50 (*0-88706-412-4*) State U NY Pr.

Urdu Literature: A Bibliography of English Language Sources. Frances W. Pritchett. 1979. 15.00 (*0-8364-0534-X*) S Asia.

Urdu Manual of the Phonetic Inductive or Direct Method: With a Progressive Introduction to the Constructions of the Urdu Language. Thomas F. Cummings. (C). 1993. 20.00 (*81-206-0856-9*, Pub. by Asian Educ Servs II) S Asia.

Urdu Newspaper Articles (For Reading Comprehension) 160p. 1987. P. 160. teacher ed. 17.00 (*0-9617188-5-4*); P. 80. student ed. 11.00 (*0-9617188-4-6*) H J Dhillon.

Urdu Newspaper Reader. 1985. audio 15.00 (*0-931745-12-8*) Dunwoody Pr.

Urdu Newspaper Reader. Mumtaz Ahmad. LC 85-70269. xiii, 322p. 1985. text ed. 43.00 (*0-931745-06-3*) Dunwoody Pr.

Urdu Newspaper Reader. Muhammad A. Barker et al. LC 74-21940. (Spoken Language Ser.). (Illus.). 472p. 1974. reprint ed. pap. 20.00 (*0-87950-337-8*); reprint ed. pap. 85.00 incl. audio (*0-87950-339-4*); reprint ed. audio 65.00 (*0-87950-338-6*) Spoken Lang Serv.

Urdu, Turkish, Beugali, Amharic, Indonesian, Telegu, Estonian see Verb Be & Its Synonyms

Urdu Verse in English. Ed. by David Matthews. 144p. (ENG & URD.). 1995. 17.95 (*0-19-563462-4*) OUP.

Urdu Writing System. William Bright & Saeed A. Kahn. LC 76-40672. 48p. (C). 1976. reprint ed. pap. 5.00 (*0-87950-256-8*) Spoken Lang Serv.

Urea Cycle. Santiago Grisolia et al. LC 76-7382. (Wiley-Interscience Publications). 601p. reprint ed. pap. 171.30 (*0-317-26102-9*, 2025174) Bks Demand.

Urea-Formaldehyde Resins. Beat Meyer. (Illus.). 1979. text ed. write for info. (*0-201-04558-3*) Addison-Wesley.

Uremic Toxins. Ed. by S. Ringoir et al. LC 87-25936. (Illus.). 308p. 1987. 85.00 (*0-306-42771-0*, Plenum Pr) Plenum.

Ureter. Ed. by H. Bergman. (Illus.). 780p. 1981. 250.00 (*0-387-90561-8*) Spr-Verlag.

Ureteroscopy. Jeffry Huffman et al. (Illus.). 200p. 1987. pap. text ed. 65.00 (*0-7216-2148-1*) Saunders.

Urethane Chemistry & Applications. Ed. by Kenneth N. Edwards. LC 81-15070. (ACS Symposium Ser.: No. 172). 1981. 65.95 (*0-8412-0664-3*) Am Chemical.

***Urethane Chemistry & Applications.** Ed. by Kenneth N. Edwards. LC 81-15070. (ACS Symposium Ser.: No. 172). (Illus.). 603p. 1981. reprint ed. pap. 171.90 (*0-608-03251-4*, 2063770) Bks Demand.

Urethane Technology. enl. rev. ed. Ed. by George Epstein & Louis Rubin. 141p. 1989. reprint ed. pap. 34.00 (*0-938648-08-X*) T-C Pr CA.

Urfaust. Johann Wolfgang Von Goethe. Tr. by Scott. 1977. pap. 5.95 (*0-8120-0213-X*) Barron.

Urge to Punish: New Approaches to the Problem of Mental Irresponsibility for Crime. Henry Weihofen. LC 78-11363. 213p. 1979. reprint ed. text ed. 55.00 (*0-313-21069-1*, WEUP, Greenwood Pr) Greenwood.

Urgency Addiction: How to Slow Down Without Sacrificing Success. Nina Tassi. 272p. 1993. pap. 4.99 (*0-451-17563-8*, Sig) NAL-Dutton.

Urgency of Change. William J. Cook, Jr. Ed. by Stephanie Hirsch. 73p. (Orig.). 1988. pap. 6.95 (*0-317-91172-4*) Underdog Pr.

Urgency of Change: America's Schools in Transition. William J. Cook, Jr. Ed. by Stephanie Hirsch. LC 88-50676. 80p. 1988. pap. 4.95 (*0-929570-00-6*) Underdog Pr.

Urgency of Identity: Contemporary English-Language Poetry from Wales. Ed. by David Lloyd. (TriQuarterly Bks.). 200p. (Orig.). 1994. 39.95 (*0-8101-5032-8*); pap. 14.95 (*0-8101-5007-7*) Northwestern U Pr.

Urgent Advice & Probing Question: Collected Writings on Old Testament Wisdom. James L. Crenshaw. LC 95-13926. 620p. (C). 1995. text ed. 45.00 (*0-86554-483-2*, MUP/H379) Mercer Univ Pr.

Urgent & Emergency Admissions to Hospital: The Report of a CSAG Committee. 96p. 1995. pap. 25.00 (*0-11-321835-4*, HM18354, Pub. by Stationery Ofc UK) Bernan Associates.

Urgent Endoscopy of Digestive & Abdominal Diseases: New Fields of Gastrointestinal Endoscopy. (Illus.). 260p. 1972. 99.25 (*3-8055-1349-6*) S Karger.

Urgent Fury: The Battle for Grenada: The Truth Behind the Largest U. S. Military Operation since Vietnam. Mark Adkin. (Illus.). 391p. 1989. 42.50 (*0-85052-023-1*, Pub. by L Cooper Bks UK) Trans-Atl Phila.

***Urgent Images.** 1995. 49.95 (*0-688-14057-2*) Morrow.

Urgent Longings: Reflections on Infatuation, Intimacy, & Sublime Love. rev. ed. Thomas J. Tyrrell. LC 93-61903. 128p. 1994. pap. 7.95 (*0-89622-573-9*) Twenty-Third.

Urgent Task: What Bishops & Priests Say about Religious Education Programs. J. Stephen O'Brien. 90p. (Orig.). 1989. pap. 8.00 (1-55833-020-8) Natl Cath Educ.

Urgings of Conscience: A Theory of Punishment. Jacob Adler. (C). 1992. 54.95 (0-87722-826-4) Temple U Pr.

Urgings of the Heart: A Spirituality of Integration. Wilkie Au & Noreen Cannon. LC 95-35391. 192p. (Orig.). 1996. pap. 14.95 (0-8091-3604-X) Paulist Pr.

***Urheberrechte, Computerprogramme & Internet.** Bernd Grzeszick. (GER.). Date not set. 25.00 (0-86640-058-3) German Am Chamber.

Urho Saari: Olympian. Jim Norris & Lynne Norris. LC 88-19538. (Illus.). 200p. (Orig.). 1988. 25.00 (0-933380-35-6) Olive Pr Pubns.

URICA: A Guide for Librarians & System Managers. Keith E. Jones & Gavin A. Rea. 209p. 1989. text ed. 49.95 (0-566-05492-2, Pub. by Gower UK) Ashgate Pub Co.

Uriel's Eye: Miltonic Stationing & Statuary in Blake, Keats, & Shelley. Nancy M. Goslee. LC 84-8815. 279p. reprint ed. pap. 79.60 (0-608-03968-3, 2062323) Bks Demand.

Urim & Thummim: An Old Testament Means of Revelation. Cornelis Van Dam. LC 96-39803. 300p. 1997. text ed. 34.50 (0-931464-83-8) Eisenbrauns.

Urinalysis. Sheryl Whitlock & John Flynn. (Clinical Laboratory Manual Ser.). (Illus.). 128p. 1996. pap. text ed. 21.95 (0-8273-7196-9) Delmar.

Urinalysis: Methods, Diagnostics, Influence of Sexually Transmitted Diseases & Abuse-Injury Implications. Shelly S. Scarre. LC 95-15409. 1995. 47.50 (0-7883-0720-7); pap. 44.50 (0-7883-0721-5) ABBE Pubs Assn.

Urinalysis & Body Fluids. Mobley. (Medical Lab Technician Ser.). Date not set. lab manual ed., pap. 32.95 (0-8273-5951-9) Delmar.

Urinalysis & Body Fluids. Karen M. Ringsrud. 284p. (gr. 13). 1994. pap. text ed. 42.00 (0-8016-7043-8) Mosby Yr Bk.

Urinalysis & Body Fluids. 3rd ed. Susan K. Strasinger. LC 94-18792. 233p. 1994. pap. 33.95 (0-8036-8103-8) Davis Co.

***Urinalysis & Body Fluids: A Case-Oriented Approach.** Landy J. McBride. (Illus.). 352p. 1997. pap. text ed. 34.95 (0-397-55231-9) Lppncott-Raven.

Urinary & Fecal Incontinence: Nursing Management. Doughty. 304p. (C). (gr. 13). 1991. text ed. 45.00 (0-8016-1444-9) Mosby Yr Bk.

***Urinary & Fecal Incontinence: Nursing Management.** 2nd ed. Doughty. 384p. (C). (gr. 13). 1998. text ed. 41.95 (0-8151-2912-2) Mosby Yr Bk.

Urinary Calculi: ESWL, Endourology, & Medical Therapy. James E. Lingeman et al. Ed. by Mary B. Moster. LC 88-38144. 476p. reprint ed. pap. 135.70 (0-7837-2725-9, 2043105) Bks Demand.

Urinary Calculi: Recent Advances in Aetiology, Stone Structure & Treatment, Proceedings of the Renal Stone Research Symposium, Madrid, Sept. 1972. Renal Stone Research Symposium Staff. Ed. by L. Cifuentes Delatte et al. (Illus.). 1973. 104.00 (3-8055-1618-5) S Karger.

Urinary Calculus: Proceedings of the International Urinary Stone Conference, Australia, 1979. International Urinary Stone Conference Staff et al. 518p. 1989. 59.50 (0-88416-294-X, Yr Bk Med Pubs) Mosby Yr Bk.

Urinary Concentrating Mechanisms. Ed. by R. K. Kinne. (Comparative Physiology Ser.: Vol. 2). (Illus.). 148p. 1990. 115.00 (3-8055-5026-X) S Karger.

Urinary Continence: Assessment & Promotion. Mary Palmer. 256p. 1996. 35.00 (0-8342-0747-8, 20747) Aspen Pub.

Urinary Cytology: Manual & Atlas. 2nd rev. ed. P. Rathert et al. Tr. by Terry C. Telger from GER. LC 92-49568. 1992. 158.00 (0-387-53312-5) Spr-Verlag.

Urinary Cytology: Phase-Contrast Microscopy & Analysis of Stained Smears. H. J. De Voogt et al. (Illus.). 1977. 114.00 (0-387-08042-2) Spr-Verlag.

Urinary Diversion. Ed. by M. H. Ashken. (Clinical Practice in Urology Ser.). (Illus.). 143p. 1982. 114.00 (0-387-11273-1) Spr-Verlag.

Urinary Enzymes in Clinical & Experimental Medicine. Ed. by K. Jung et al. (Illus.). 248p. 1992. 136.00 (0-387-53188-2) Spr-Verlag.

***Urinary Incontinence.** Ed. by James G. Malone-Lee & Adrian Wagg. (Greenwich Medical Media Ser.). (Illus.). 256p. 1997. pap. text ed. 59.50 (1-900151-16-2) OUP.

Urinary Incontinence. O'Donnell. 550p. (C). (gr. 13). 1997. text ed. 84.95 (0-8151-6517-X) Mosby Yr Bk.

Urinary Incontinence. Ed. by Adolphe Steg. (International Society of Urology Reports). (Illus.). 304p. 1993. text ed. 95.00 (0-443-04643-3) Churchill.

Urinary Incontinence & How to Overcome It. 1991. lib. bdg. 250.00 (0-8490-5123-1) Gordon Pr.

Urinary Incontinence in Adults. 1995. lib. bdg. 251.95 (0-8490-6803-7) Gordon Pr.

***Urinary Incontinence in Adults No. 2: Acute & Chronic.** USPHS Staff. Date not set. pap. 7.50 (1-883205-26-3) Intl Med Pub.

***Urinary Incontinence in the Elderly: Pharmacotherapy Treatment.** James Cooper. LC 97-16252. (Journal of Geriatric Drug Therapy Ser.). 1997. write for info. (0-7890-0327-9) Haworth Pr.

***Urinary Incontinence in Women: A Guide for Women.** Joseph Khoury. Ed. by G. D. Webster. (Urology Ser.). (Illus.). 32p. (Orig.). 1997. pap. text ed. 2.95 (1-885274-41-6) HIN.

Urinary Proteins. Ed. by L. Migone. (Contributions to Nephrology Ser.: Vol. 26). (Illus.). viii, 124p. 1981. pap. 66.50 (3-8055-1848-X) S Karger.

Urinary Sediment. G. B. Fogazzi. 160p. (gr. 13). 1994. text ed. 90.95 (0-412-59300-9) Chapman & Hall.

Urinary Sediment. Patrick C. Ward. (C). 1991. 400.00 incl. disk (1-56815-009-1) Mosby Yr Bk.

Urinary Sediment: A Textbook Atlas. Meryl H. Haber. LC 81-4413. (Illus.). 126p. 1981. pap. 60.00 (0-89189-103-X); sl. 180.00 (0-89189-106-4) Am Soc Clinical.

Urinary Sediment & Urinalysis: A Practical Guide for the Health Science Professional. Thomas A. Stamey & Robert W. Kindrachuk. (Blue Bk.). (Illus.). 109p. 1985. text ed. 39.00 (0-7216-1412-4) Saunders.

Urinary Stones: Diagnosis, Treatment, & Prevention of Recurrence. Ed. by A. Hesse et al. (Illus.). 208p. 1996. pap. 34.00 (3-8055-6346-9) S Karger.

***Urinary System.** Ed. by R. D. Hunt et al. (Illus.). xviii, 405p. 1986. 250.00 (3-540-16591-6, 165916) Spr-Verlag.

Urinary System. Ed. by Thomas C. Jones et al. (Monographs on Pathology of Laboratory Animals). (Illus.). 405p. 1986. 316.00 (0-387-16591-6) Spr-Verlag.

***Urinary System.** 2nd ed. Ed. by R. D. Hunt et al. Date not set. write for info. (0-614-22658-9) ILSI.

***Urinary System.** 2nd ed. Thomas C. Jones et al. LC 97-25783. (Monographs on Pathology of Laboratory Animals). 1997. write for info. (0-944398-76-6) ILSI.

***Urinary System.** 2nd ed. Thomas C. Jones et al. LC 97-25783. (Monographs on Pathology of Laboratory Animals). 1997. spiral bd. write for info. (3-540-61847-3) Spr-Verlag.

Urinary System & Others, Pt. 16. Ed. by Daniel Bergsma. (Alan R. Liss Ser.: Vol. 10, No. 4). 1974. 48.00 (0-686-23126-0) March of Dimes.

Urinary System Malformations in Children. Ed. by Daniel Bergsma. (Alan R. Liss Ser.: Vol. 13, No. 5). 1977. 70.00 (0-686-23127-9) March of Dimes.

Urinary Tract & the Catheter: Infection & Other Problems. Norman Slade & William A. Gillespie. LC 84-25650. (Illus.). 138p. reprint ed. pap. 39.40 (0-7837-1881-0, 2042082) Bks Demand.

***Urinary Tract Cancer: State of the Art EORTC GU Group Seminar.** Ed. by Louis Denis. (Journal Ser.: Vol. 31, Supplement 1, 1997). (Illus.). vi, 82p. 1997. pap. 69.75 (3-8055-6466-X) S Karger.

***Urinary Tract Infections.** Ed. by Tom Bergan. LC 97-2774. (Infectiology Ser.: Vol. 1, 1997). (Illus.). viii, 142p. 1997. 97.50 (3-8055-6440-6) S Karger.

Urinary Tract Infections. Ed. by Graeme R. Catto. (New Clinical Applications Nephrology Ser.). (C). 1989. lib. bdg. 92.00 (0-7462-0115-X) Kluwer Ac.

Urinary Tract Infections: Detection, Prevention, & Management. 5th ed. Calvin M. Kunin. LC 96-26585. 419p. 1996. pap. 49.00 (0-683-18102-5) Williams & Wilkins.

Urinary Tract Infections: Molecular Pathogenesis & Clinical Management. Ed. by Harry L. Mobley & John W. Warren. LC 95-24719. 1995. 79.00 (1-55581-093-4) Am Soc Microbio.

Urinary Tract Infections in Children. Stanley Hellerstein. LC 82-2791. (Illus.). 153p. 1982. reprint ed. pap. 43.70 (0-8357-7619-0, 2056942) Bks Demand.

***Urinary Tract Pathology: An Illustrated Practical Guide to Diagnosis.** Ed. by Jay Bernstein et al. LC 91-4872. (Illus.). reprint ed. pap. 75.30 (0-608-04727-9, 2065448) Bks Demand.

Urine - Therapy - It May Save Your Life. Beatrice Bartnett. 52p. (Orig.). 1992. pap. 5.90 (0-9622182-3-5) Lifestyle Inst.

Urine & Polymedicine: Guidebook with Bibiliography. rev. ed. Gwen V. Hassig. LC 87-47634. 160p. 1991. 44.50 (1-55914-216-2); pap. 39.50 (1-55914-217-0) ABBE Pubs Assn.

***Urine Drug Testing in the Clinical Laboratory Proposed Guideline (1993)** Contrib. by M. Jeffery Shoemaker. 1993. 85.00 (0-614-20207-8, T/DM8-P) Natl Comm Clin Lab Stds.

Urine Studies in Labs & Practice: Index of Modern Authors & Subjects with Guide for Rapid Research. Jerry C. Ewald. LC 90-56292. 160p. 1991. 44.50 (1-55914-378-9); pap. 39.50 (1-55914-379-7) ABBE Pubs Assn.

Urine Testing for Drugs of Abuse. 1991. lib. bdg. 250.00 (0-8490-4349-2) Gordon Pr.

Urine-Therapy: It May Save Your Life. 7th rev. ed. Beatrice Barnett. 56p. 1992. pap. 9.95 (0-9622182-5-1) Lifestyle Inst.

Urine Therapy for AIDS & Cancer. 1991. lib. bdg. 250.00 (0-8490-5032-4) Gordon Pr.

Urinzytologie. 1995. 194.00 (3-540-59248-2) Spr-Verlag.

Uristen Az Abece Minden Betuje. Endre Enczi. LC 68-8924. (HUN.). 1968. pap. 6.00 (0-911050-31-0) Occidental.

Urkunden der Ptolemaeerzeit (Aeltere Funde), 2 vols. Ulrich Wilcken. Incl. Vol. 1. Papyri aus Unteraegypten. x, 676p. 1977. reprint ed. 519.00 (3-11-005711-5); Vol. 2. Papyri aus Oberaegypten. viii, 333p. 1977. reprint ed. 267.00 (3-11-005712-3); (Illus.). (C). 1977. write for info. (0-318-51651-9) De Gruyter.

Urkunden des Babylonischen Geschaftsmannes Iddin-Marduk: Zum Handel Mit Naturalien Im 6. Jahrhundert v. Chr. Cornelia Wunsch. xxix, 486p. 1993. pap. text ed. 95.00 (90-72371-64-X, Pub. by Styx NE) Eisenbrauns.

Urkunden Dramatischer Auffuehrungen in Griechenland. Hans J. Mette. (Texte und Kommentare Ser.: Vol. 8). (C). 1977. 134.60 (3-11-006782-X) De Gruyter.

Urn Burial. Patrick Ruell. 224p. 1994. 18.50 (0-7451-8628-9, Black Dagger) Chivers N Amer.

***Urn Burial.** Robert Westall. (J). Date not set. lib. bdg. 99.98 (0-688-07596-7) Greenwillow.

Uroboros - Out of Delinquency: A True Story. Waln K. Brown. 20p. 1983. 2.95 (1-56456-011-2, 205) W Gladden Found.

Urodynamic & Reconstructive Surgery: The Practice of Surgery. A. R. Mundy. (Illus.). 348p. 1993. text ed. 235.00 (0-443-03348-X) Churchill.

Urodynamics. P. H. Abrams. (Clinical Practice in Urology Ser.). (Illus.). 236p. 1986. 106.00 (0-387-11903-5) Spr-Verlag.

***Urodynamics.** 2nd ed. Paul Abrams. LC 96-51999. 1997. write for info. (3-540-19678-1) Spr-Verlag.

Urodynamics: Principles, Practice, & Application. 2nd ed. Ed. by A. R. Mundy et al. (Illus.). 542p. 1994. pap. 149.95 (0-443-04081-8) Churchill.

Urodynamics: The Mechanics & Hydrodynamics of the Lower Urinary Tract. D. J. Griffiths. LC 80-8228. (Medical Physics Handbks.: No. 4). (Illus.). 149p. 1980. reprint ed. pap. 42.50 (0-7837-4502-8, 2044279) Bks Demand.

***Urodynamics & the Evaluation of Female Incontinence.** Peter K. Sand & Donald R. Ostergard. (Illus.). 271p. 1995. 89.00 (3-540-19904-7) Spr-Verlag.

Urodynamics & the Evaluation of Female Incontinence: A Practical Guide. Peter K. Sand & Donald R. Ostergard. LC 94-24640. 1995. 89.00 (0-387-19904-7) Spr-Verlag.

Urodynamics Made Easy. Christopher R. Chapple & Timothy J. Christmas. (Illus.). 92p. 1990. pap. text ed. 19.95 (0-443-04356-6) Churchill.

Urogenital Infections. Ed. by A. Bondi et al. LC 87-14209. (Advances in Experimental Medicine & Biology Ser.: Vol. 224). (Illus.). 146p. 1988. 65.00 (0-306-42799-0, Plenum Pr) Plenum.

Urogenital Manipulation. Jean-Pierre Barral. LC 93-72643. (Illus.). 249p. (C). 1993. text ed. 48.00 (0-939616-18-1) Eastland.

Urogenital Pathology. Murphy. 560p. 1989. pap. text ed. 169.00 (0-7216-2417-0) Saunders.

Urogenital System. Braem. 1994. pap. text ed. 19.95 (1-878576-33-X) Flash Anatomy Inc.

Urogynecologic Surgery. W. Glenn Hurt. LC 92-7378. (Principles & Techniques of Gynecologic Surgery Ser.). 224p. 1992. text ed. 110.50 (0-8342-0339-1, 20339) Lppncott-Raven.

***Urogynecology: Diagnosis & Treatment of Female Incontinence.** Ed. by Gretchen M. Lentz. LC 97-6755. 300p. 1997. 79.95 (0-412-06691-2) Chapman & Hall.

Urogynecology & Urodynamics. 3rd ed. Donald R. Ostergard & Alfred E. Bent. (Illus.). 692p. 1991. 98.00 (0-683-06647-1) Williams & Wilkins.

Urogynecology & Urodynamics: Theory & Practice. 4th ed. Ed. by Donald R. Ostergard & Alfred E. Bent. LC 95-47708. 726p. 1996. 109.00 (0-683-06648-X) Williams & Wilkins.

Urohyal of Fishes. Takaya Kusaka. LC 75-307339. 333p. 1974. reprint ed. pap. 95.00 (0-608-01240-8, 2061928) Bks Demand.

Uroki po Pastirskomu Bogosloviju. Basil Boshtchanovsky. 100p. 1961. pap. text ed. 5.00 (0-317-30267-1) Holy Trinity.

Urokinase: Basic & Clinical Aspects. Ed. by P. M. Mannucci & A. D'Angelo. LC 81-68958. (Serono Symposia Ser.: Vol. 48). 276p. 1982. text ed. 99.00 (0-12-469280-X) Acad Pr.

Urolithiasis. Donald Resnick & Charles Y. Pak. (Illus.). 352p. 1990. text ed. 110.00 (0-7216-2439-1) Saunders.

Urolithiasis. Ed. by R. A. Sutton. (Journal: Mineral & Electrolyte Metabolism: Vol. 13, No. 4, 1987). 96p. 1987. pap. 89.75 (3-8055-4567-3) S Karger.

Urolithiasis. Ed. by V. R. Walker et al. (Illus.). 1102p. 1989. 165.00 (0-306-43249-8, Plenum Pr) Plenum.

Urolithiasis 2: Proceedings of the International Symposium on Urolithiasis, 7th, Cairns, Australia, Held August 1992. Ed. by Rosemary Ryall et al. (Illus.). 696p. (C). 1994. text ed. 159.50 (0-306-44727-4, Plenum Pr) Plenum.

Urologic Cancer. Marc S. Ernstoff. LC 96-34918. 1996. 165.00 (0-86542-497-7) Blackwell Sci.

Urologic Cancer. Ed. by Richard E. Peschel et al. 500p. (C). 1995. write for info. (0-393-71029-7, Norton Medical Bks) Norton.

Urologic Cancer: A Multidisciplinary Approach. Ed. by Marc Garnick & Jerome Richie. LC 83-17720. 288p. 1983. 69.50 (0-306-41473-2, Plenum Med Bk) Plenum.

Urologic Cancer: Chemotherapeutic Principles & Management. Ed. by F. M. Torti. (Recent Results in Cancer Research Ser.: Vol. 85). (Illus.). 151p. 1983. 76.00 (0-387-12163-3) Spr-Verlag.

Urologic Disorders. Jonathan I. Epstein. LC 91-35399. (Differential Diagnosis in Pathology Ser.). (Illus.). 208p. 1992. 89.00 (0-89640-222-3) Igaku-Shoin.

Urologic Endocrinology. Jacob Rajfer. (Illus.). 448p. 1986. text ed. 110.00 (0-7216-7426-7) Saunders.

Urologic Endoscopy: A Manual & Atlas. Demetrius H. Bagley et al. 336p. 1985. 165.00 (0-316-07518-3) Little.

Urologic Laparoscopic Surgery. Ed. by Raul Parra. 250p. 1995. text ed. 135.00 (0-07-048580-1) McGraw-Hill HPD.

Urologic Malignancies: Quality of Life Issues. Ed. by Emil A. Tanagho & P. R. Carroll. (Journal: Urologia Internationalis: Vol. 46, No. 3, 1991). (Illus.). 68p. 1991. pap. 69.75 (3-8055-5399-4) S Karger.

Urologic Oncology. Ed. by William J. Catalona & T. Ratliff. (Cancer Treatment & Research Ser.). 1984. lib. bdg. 154.50 (0-89838-628-4) Kluwer Ac.

Urologic Oncology. Ed. by Herbert Lepor & William L. McGuire. (Cancer Treatment & Research Ser.). (C). 1989. lib. bdg. 143.50 (0-7923-0161-7) Kluwer Ac.

Urologic Oncology. Joseph E. Oesterling & Jerome Richie. Ed. by Richard Zorab. LC 96-41702. 864p. 1997. text ed. 159.00 (0-7216-6347-8) Saunders.

Urologic Oncology. Ed. by Sam D. Graham, Jr. LC 85-28150. 557p. 1986. reprint ed. pap. 158.80 (0-608-00396-4, 2061110) Bks Demand.

Urologic Pathology. 2nd ed. Petersen. (Illus.). 800p. 1992. text ed. 149.00 (0-397-51063-2) Lppncott-Raven.

Urologic Pathology: The Prostate. Ed. by Myron Tannenbaum. LC 76-5466. (Illus.). 431p. reprint ed. pap. 122.90 (0-8357-7662-X, 2056989) Bks Demand.

Urologic Surgery. Jackson E. Fowler, Jr. LC 91-45996. (Mastery of Surgery Ser.). 734p. 1992. text ed. 125.00 (0-316-29011-4) Lppncott-Raven.

Urologic Surgery. 4th ed. Glenn. (Illus.). 1142p. 1991. text ed. 195.00 (0-397-50995-2) Lppncott-Raven.

Urologic Surgery. 5th ed. James Glenn. 1998. text ed. write for info. (0-397-58737-6) Lppncott-Raven.

Urologic Surgery: Diagnosis, Techniques, & Postoperative Treatment. Georges Mayor & Ernst J. Zingg. LC 75-36660. 643p. reprint ed. pap. 180.00 (0-317-07965-4, 2016475) Bks Demand.

***Urologic Surgery in Infants & Children.** Lowell R. King. Ed. by Stephanie Donley. LC 97-4118. 320p. 1997. text ed. write for info. (0-7216-6857-7) Saunders.

Urologic Surgery in Neonates & Young Infants. Lowell King. (Illus.). 432p. 1989. text ed. 120.00 (0-7216-2370-0) Saunders.

Urologic Surgery of the Dog & Cat. Elizabeth Stone & Jeanne Barasanti. (Illus.). 320p. 1992. text ed. 69.00 (0-8121-1431-0) Williams & Wilkins.

Urologic Surgical Pathology. Young. Ed. by David G. Bostwick & John N. Eble. 788p. (C). (gr. 13). 1996. text ed. 230.00 (0-8016-7503-0) Mosby Yr Bk.

Urological Complications in Gynecological Surgery & Radiotherapy. J. Kunz. (Contributions to Gynecology & Obstetrics Ser.: Vol. 11). (Illus.). viii, 220p. 1984. 108.00 (3-8055-3759-X) S Karger.

***Urological Disease in the Fetus & Infant: Diagnosis & Management.** D. F. Thomas. LC 97-26049. 1997. write for info. (0-7506-0768-8) Buttrwrth-Heinemann.

Urological Pathology. 2nd ed. William M. Murphy. Ed. by Leslie Day. LC 96-46546. 656p. 1997. text ed. 195.00 (0-7216-6029-0) Saunders.

Urological Pathology: Based on the Proceedings of the Sixtieth Annual Anatomic Pathology Slide Seminar of the American Society of Clinical Pathologists: October 27 & 28, 1994, Washington, DC. Contrib. by William M. Murphy et al. 112p. 1995. 40.00 (0-89189-393-8) Am Soc Clinical.

Urological Prostheses, Appliances & Catheters. Ed. by J. P. Pryor & G. D. Chisholm. (Clinical Practice in Urology Ser.). (Illus.). xii, 288p. 1992. 196.00 (0-387-17490-7) Spr-Verlag.

Urological Radiology: Radiological Diagnosis of Urological Diseases: Plain Film, Sonography, Angiography, CT, & MRI. Ed. by Eberhard Lohr & Klaus Sievers. LC 94-34633. (Illus.). 256p. 1995. text ed. 89.00 (0-88937-131-8) Hogrefe & Huber Pubs.

Urological Research: Papers Presented in Honor of William W. Scott. William W. Scott. LC 73-179757. 236p. reprint ed. pap. 67.30 (0-317-30344-9, 2024716) Bks Demand.

Urology. Ed. by Elroy D. Kursh & Martin I. Resnick. (Problems in Primary Care Ser.). 352p. (Orig.). 1987. pap. 43.95 (0-87489-419-0) Med Econ.

Urology. 2nd ed. Michael Macfarlane. (House Officer Ser.). 304p. 1994. 21.95 (0-683-05325-6) Williams & Wilkins.

Urology. 2nd rev. ed. Jurgen Sokeland. Tr. by Claus Rohrborn. (Flexibook Ser.). 427p. 1989. text ed. 30.00 (0-86577-321-1) Thieme Med Pubs.

Urology: A Core Textbook. 2nd ed. Stephen N. Rous. LC 95-39429. (Illus.). 365p. 1996. pap. text ed. 44.95 (0-86542-493-4) Blackwell Sci.

Urology: Core Textbook. Stephen N. Rous. Date not set. pap. write for info. (0-393-71033-5) Norton.

Urology: From Antiquity to the 20th Century. Leonard P. Wershub. LC 71-78017. (Illus.). 320p. 1970. 18.50 (0-87527-086-7) Green.

Urology: Illustrated Case Histories. Helen Parkhouse & Krishna Sethia. 92p. (gr. 13). 1995. 30.00 (0-7234-2234-6, Pub. by Wolfe Pub UK) Mosby Yr Bk.

Urology & Reproduction. 3rd ed. LC 92-48863. (Regents - Prentice-Hall Medical Assistant Kit Ser.). 1993. pap. 16.60 (0-13-035676-X) P-H.

Urology Annual, 1987, Vol. 1. Stephen N. Rous. (Illus.). 336p. (C). 1987. text ed. 90.00 (0-8385-9318-6, A9318-5) Appleton & Lange.

Urology Annual, 1988, Vol. 2. Stephen N. Rous. (Illus.). 304p. (C). 1988. text ed. 90.00 (0-8385-9319-4, A9319-3) Appleton & Lange.

Urology Annual, 1989, Vol. 3. Stephen N. Rous. (Illus.). 356p. 1989. text ed. 90.00 (0-8385-9320-8, A9320-1) Appleton & Lange.

Urology Annual, 1990, Vol. 4. Stephen N. Rous. (Illus.). 300p. 1989. text ed. 90.00 (0-8385-9322-4, A9322-7) Appleton & Lange.

Urology Annual, 1991, Vol. 5. Stephen N. Rous. (Illus.). 288p. (C). 1990. text ed. 90.00 (0-8385-9323-2, A9323-5) Appleton & Lange.

Urology Annual 1995, Vol. 9. Ed. by Stephen N. Rous. 300p. (C). 1995. 85.00 (0-393-71022-X, Norton Medical Bks) Norton.

Urology Annual 1996, Vol. 10. Stephen N. Rous. 368p. 1996. 95.00 (0-86542-488-8) Blackwell Sci.

Urology Annual 1996, Vol. 10. Stephen N. Rous. Date not set. write for info. (0-393-71034-3) Norton.

***Urology Annual 1997, Vol. 11.** Ed. by Stephen N. Rous. (Illus.). 321p. 1997. 125.00 (0-86542-567-1) Blackwell Sci.

***Urology for Nurses.** J. P. Blandy & J. Moors. (Illus.). 276p. 1989. pap. write for info. (0-632-01686-8) Blackwell Sci.

Urology for Nurses. 3rd ed. Mitchell. 380p. 1980. 15.00 (0-7236-0528-9) Buttrwrth-Heinemann.

Urology for the House Officer. Michael Macfarlane. (House Officer Ser.). (Illus.). 300p. (Orig.). (C). 1988. pap. 20.00 (0-683-05324-8) Williams & Wilkins.

Urology in Childhood see Encyclopedia of Urology

U V

An Asterisk (*) at the beginning of an entry indicates that the title is appearing in BIP for the first time.

***Urology Office Manual.** Neil Baum. (Office Manual Ser.). 200p. 1994. ring bd. 145.00 (*1-890018-04-X*) Anadem Pubng.

Urology Secrets: Questions You Will Be Asked on Rounds, in the OR, in the Clinic. Ed. by Martin I. Resnick & Andrew C. Novick. (Secrets Ser.). (Illus.). 420p. (Orig.). 1994. pap. text ed. 33.95 (*1-56053-108-8*) Hanley & Belfus.

Uromastyx & Butterfly Agamas. Jerry G. Walls. (Illus.). 64p. 1996. pap. 9.95 (*0-7938-2074-X*, RE162) TFH Pubns.

Uropathology, 2 vols. Ed. by Gary S. Hill. (Illus.). 1427p. 1989. Set. text ed. 302.00 (*0-443-08194-8*) Churchill.

Uropathology, Vol. 1. Ed. by Gary S. Hill. LC 88-22940. (Illus.). 685p. reprint ed. pap. 180.00 (*0-7837-6828-1*, 2046658) Bks Demand.

Uropathology, Vol. 2. Ed. by Gary S. Hill. LC 88-22940. (Illus.). 819p. reprint ed. pap. 180.00 (*0-7837-6829-X*, 2046658) Bks Demand.

Urquhart of Arnhem: The Life & Times of Major General R. E. Urquhart, CB DSO. John Baynes. (Illus.). 285p. 1993. 41.00 (*0-08-041318-8*, Pub. by Brasseys UK) Brasseys Inc.

Urs Jaeggi: Eine Wekbiographie. Irmgard E. Hunt. LC 92-39172. (American University Studies: Germanic Languages & Literature: Ser. I, Vol. 101). 236p. (GER.). (C). 1993. text ed. 45.95 (*0-8204-2010-7*) P Lang Pubng.

Ursa Major Stream. David A. Wilson. 48p. (Orig.). 1995. pap. 6.00 (*0-934852-40-5*) Lorien Hse.

Ursa Minor & Other Poems. Takis Papatsonis. Tr. by Kimon Friar & Kostas Myrsiades. (Modern Greek History & Culture Ser.). 103p. 1988. 25.00 (*0-932963-05-6*) Nostos Bks.

Ursachen des Terrorismus in der Bundesrepublik Deutschland. (Sammlung Goeschen Ser.: Vol. 2806). (C). 1978. 12.95 (*3-11-007702-7*) De Gruyter.

Ursinus College: A History of Its First Hundred Years. Calvin D. Yost. (Illus.). 224p. 1985. lib. bdg. 28.00 (*0-685-28057-8*) Ursinus College.

Ursi's Amazing Fur Coat. David R. Collins. (Illus.). (J). (ps-2). 1987. pap. 5.10 (*0-8136-5686-9*); lib. bdg. 7.95 (*0-8136-5186-7*) Modern Curr.

Ursprung der Woerter: Etymologisches Woerterbuch der Deutschen Sprache. Lutz Mackensen. 446p. (GER.). 1985. 49.95 (*0-7859-8406-2*, 3517008583) Fr & Eur.

Ursule Mirouet. Honore De Balzac. write for info. (*0-318-63612-3*, 2449) Fr & Eur.

Ursule Mirouet. Honore De Balzac. (FRE.). 1981. pap. 12.95 (*0-7859-1937-6*, 2070373002) Fr & Eur.

Ursule Mirouet. Honore De Balzac. (Folio Ser.: No. 1300). (FRE.). pap. 9.95 (*2-07-037300-2*) Schoenhof.

Ursule Mirouet. Honore De Balzac. Tr. by Donald Adamson. (Classics Ser.). 272p. 1976. pap. 9.95 (*0-14-044316-9*, Penguin Classics) Viking Penguin.

Urszula Koziol: Polish Poetry in Bilingual. Urszula Koziol. Ed. by Joe Bratcher & Elzbieta Szoka. Tr. by Regina Grol-Prokopczyk from POL. (Illus.). 120p. (C). 1989. pap. 10.00 (*0-924047-02-X*) Host Pubns.

Urteil ohne Richter: Psychishe Integration oder Charakterentfaltung im Werke Franz Kafkas. Evelyn W. Asher. LC 83-48884. (Stanford German Studies: Vol. 20). 139p. (GER.). (C). 1984. pap. text ed. 14.75 (*0-8204-0062-9*) P Lang Pubng.

Urteil und Andere Erzaehlungen. Franz Kafka. 189p. (GER.). 1994. pap. 11.75 (*3-596-20019-9*, Pub. by Fischer Taschbch Verlag GW) Intl Bk Import.

Urth of the New Sun. Gene Wolfe. 384p. 1988. pap. 3.95 (*0-8125-5817-0*) Tor Bks.

***Urth of the Sun.** Wolfe. LC 97-22177. 1997. pap. 14.95 (*0-312-86394-2*) St Martin.

***Urticaria.** B. M. Henz et al. LC 97-20558. 1997. write for info. (*3-540-62973-4*) Spr-Verlag.

Uruguay. Marion Morrison. LC 91-35144. (Enchantment of the World Ser.). 128p. (J). (gr. 5-9). 1992. lib. bdg. 30.00 (*0-516-02607-0*) Childrens.

Uruguay. annot. ed. Ed. by Henry Finch & Alicia C. De Barran. (World Bibliographical Ser.: No. 102). 234p. 1989. lib. bdg. 60.00 (*1-85109-098-3*) ABC-CLIO.

Uruguay. Rosa Q. Mesa. LC 73-180800. (Latin American Serial Documents Ser.: Vol. 11). 193p. reprint ed. pap. 55.10 (*0-317-10313-X*, 2013553) Bks Demand.

Uruguay. George Pendle. LC 85-24780. 136p. 1986. reprint ed. text ed. 49.75 (*0-313-24981-4*, PEUR, Greenwood Pr) Greenwood.

Uruguay: The Politics of Failure. Martin E. Weinstein. LC 74-19809. (Illus.). 190p. 1975. text ed. 29.95 (*0-8371-7845-2*, WPF/, Greenwood Pr) Greenwood.

Uruguay: The Private Sector. (Country Study Ser.). 142p. 1994. 9.95 (*0-8213-2730-5*, 12730) World Bank.

Uruguay see Statements of the Laws of the OAS Member States in Matters Affecting Business

Uruguay in Pictures. Lerner Geography Department Staff. (Visual Geography Ser.). (Illus.). 64p. (YA). (gr. 5 up). 1994. lib. bdg. 19.95 (*0-8225-1823-6*, Lerner Publctns) Lerner Group.

Uruguay in Transition: From Civilian to Military Rule. Edy Kaufman. LC 78-55939. 200p. 1979. 34.95 (*0-87855-242-1*) Transaction Pubs.

Uruguay Nunca Mas: Human Rights Violations, 1972-1985. Servicio Paz Y. Justicia-Uruguay Staff. (Illus.). 360p. (C). 1992. 59.95 (*0-87722-953-8*) Temple U Pr.

Uruguay Nunca Mas: Human Rights Violations, 1972-1985. Servicio Paz Y. Justicia-Uruguay Staff. (Illus.). 360p. (C). 1993. pap. 22.95 (*1-56639-146-6*) Temple U Pr.

Uruguay Round: A Preliminary Evaluation of the Impacts of the Agreement on Agriculture in the OECD Countries. OECD Staff. 99p. (Orig.). 1995. pap. 25.00 (*92-64-14582-6*, Pub. by Org for Econ FR) OECD.

Uruguay Round: An Assessment. Jeffrey J. Schott. LC 94-5627. 219p. 1994. pap. 19.95 (*0-88132-206-7*) Inst Intl Eco.

Uruguay Round: Statistics on Tariff Concessions Given & Received. J. Michael Finger et al. LC 95-11817. 210p. 1996. 11.95 (*0-8213-3211-2*, 13211) World Bank.

***Uruguay Round: Widening & Deepening the World Trading System.** Will Martin & L. Alan Winters. (Directions in Development Ser.). 40p. 1995. 7.95 (*0-8213-3488-3*, 13488) World Bank.

Uruguay Round Agreements Act: A Legislative History of Public Law No. 103-465, 14 vols., 17 bks., Set. Ed. by Jon S. Schultz & Bernard D. Reams, Jr. 16000p. 1995. 1,650.00 (*0-89941-968-2*, 308720) W S Hein.

Uruguay Round & the Arab Countries, Seminar. Ed. by S. El-Naggar. 1996. pap. 20.00 (*1-55775-497-7*) Intl Monetary.

***Uruguay Round & the Developing Countries.** Ed. by Will Martin & L. Alan Winters. 472p. 1997. pap. text ed. 27.95 (*0-521-58601-1*) Cambridge U Pr.

Uruguay Round & the Developing Countries. Ed. by Will Martin & L. Alan Winters. 472p. (C). 1997. text ed. 69.95 (*0-521-57235-5*) Cambridge U Pr.

Uruguay Round & the Developing Economies. Ed. by Will Martin & L. Alan Winters. (World Bank Discussion Papers: Vol. 307). 476p. 1995. 25.95 (*0-8213-3469-7*, 13469) World Bank.

Uruguay Round Midterm Review, 1988-1989: A Case Study of Multilateral Trade Negotiations. Karin L. Kizer & Gilbert R. Winham. LC 93-20116. (FPI Case Studies: No. 20). 1993. write for info. (*0-941700-82-8*) JH FPI SAIS.

Uruguayan Literature: A Selective Bibliography. Walter Rela. LC 86-15989. (Special Studies: No. 26). 86p. 1987. pap. 10.00 (*0-87918-060-9*) ASU Lat Am St.

Uruguayan Paper Money. Dale A. Seppa. (Illus.). 60p. 1974. pap. 5.00 (*0-916710-15-7*) Obol Intl.

Uruk Document of the Time of Cambyses. Henry F. Lutz. (University of California Publications in Social Welfare: Vol. 10, No. 8). 10p. reprint ed. pap. 25.00 (*0-317-10219-2*, 2021479) Bks Demand.

Uruk World System: The Dynamics of Early Mesopotamian Civilization. Guillermo Algaze. LC 92-27445. (Illus.). 174p. (C). 1993. 39.95 (*0-226-01381-2*) U Ch Pr.

Urushi: Proceedings of the 1985 Urushi Study Group. Ed. by Norman S. Brommelle & Perry Smith. LC 85-21394. (Illus.). 260p. 1988. pap. 50.00 (*0-89236-096-8*, Getty Conservation Inst) J P Getty Trust.

Urushi: The Technology of Japanese Lacquer. John J. Quin. Ed. & Intro. by Jack C. Thompson. LC 95-71506. (Illus.). v, 53p. (C). 1995. reprint ed. pap. 8.95 (*1-887719-01-6*) Caber Pr.

***Urwind.** Bo Carpelan. Tr. by David McDuff from FIN. 220p. 1997. pap. 24.95 (*1-85754-250-9*, Pub. by Carcanet Pr UK) Paul & Co Pubs.

Us. Ralph Burns. (CSU Poetry Ser.: No. XII). 43p. (Orig.). 1983. pap. 4.50 (*0-914946-38-2*) Cleveland St Univ Poetry Ctr.

US. Michael Castro. 28p. (Orig.). 1991. pap. text ed. 5.00 (*1-56439-003-9*) Ridgeway.

US & the EU: Economic Relations in a World of Transition. Ed. by Norman Levine. LC 96-21502. 358p. 1996. pap. text ed. 39.50 (*0-7618-0398-X*); lib. bdg. 64.50 (*0-7618-0397-1*) U Pr of Amer.

Us & Them. David Campton. 1982. 3.00 (*0-87129-426-5*, U15) Dramatic Pub.

Us & Them: A History of Intolerance in America. Jim Carnes. (Illus.). 136p. (J). 1996. lib. bdg. 22.00 (*0-19-510378-5*) OUP.

Us & Them: A Study of Group Consciousness. W. A. Elliott. 224p. 1986. text ed. 27.90 (*0-08-032438-X*, Pub. by Aberdeen U Pr) Macmillan.

Us & Them: The Psychology of Ethnonationalism. Group for the Advancement of Psychiatry Staff. LC 87-17872. (Group for the Advancement of Psychiatry, Symposium Ser.: No. 123). 159p. reprint ed. pap. 45.40 (*0-7837-2096-3*, 2042372) Bks Demand.

Us & Them in Modern Societies: Ethnicity & Nationalism in Mauritius, Trinidad, & Beyond. Thomas H. Eriksen. (Scandinavian University Press Publication). 208p. (C). 1992. 29.50 (*82-00-21550-4*, 14455) Scandnvan Univ Pr.

Us & Uncle Fraud. Lois Lowry. LC 84-12783. 192p. (gr. 5-9). 1984. 14.95 (*0-395-36633-X*) HM.

Us &...Our Good Stuff. Janeway Riley. (Illus.). 176p. (J). 1993. 19.95 (*0-9637378-1-3*) Janeway Riley.

Us Four: A Senator, His Family, Their Brain-injured Child. Marion Menning. (Illus.). 160p. 1986. pap. write for info. (*0-9615632-0-6*) Alpha Pub MN.

Us Henry Kids. Belle T. Hinther. (Illus.). 202p. (Orig.). 1986. pap. 10.95 (*0-9619970-1-X*) Blue Sky Bks.

US in the Twentieth Century. Olson. Date not set. pap. text ed. 34.20 (*0-312-13796-6*) St Martin.

US-MARC Code List for Countries, 1993. Prod. by MARC Standards Office Staff. LC 93-38625. 1993. write for info. (*0-8444-0825-5*) Lib Congress.

U.S. Progressive Periodicals Directory see Progressive Periodicals Directory

***US Supreme Court.** McKeever. Date not set. text ed. 59.95 (*0-7190-4081-7*, Pub. by Manchester Univ Pr UK); text ed. 22.50 (*0-7190-4082-5*) St Martin.

U.S taxation of International Transactions. Samuel C. Thompson, Jr. LC 94-48752. (American Casebook Ser.). 610p. (C). 1995. text ed. 44.00 (*0-314-04745-X*) West Pub.

Us Women. Marjorie Fletcher. LC 73-86245. (Illus.). 64p. 1973. pap. 3.95 (*0-914086-00-6*) Alicejamesbooks.

***Usa a Personas Que No Son Perfectas - God Uses People Who Are Not Perfect.** Fernandez. (SPA.). 1996. write for info. (*0-7899-0140-4*) Editorial Unilit.

USA Crosswords, No. 18. Charles Preston. 80p. (Orig.). 1995. pap. 7.95 (*0-399-51963-7*, Perigee Bks) Berkley Pub.

***USA Today: The Complete Four Sport Stadium Guide.** Fodors Travel Guide Staff. (Illus.). pap. 16.95 (*0-614-25657-7*) Fodors Travel.

USA Today: The Complete Four Sport Stadium Guide: Everything You Ever Wanted to Know about All of the Major League Baseball & Football Stadiums & Hockey & Basketball Arenas. USA Today Sports Staff. (Illus.). 1994. pap. 14.95 (*0-679-02849-8*) Fodors Travel.

USA Today Atlas of the Great Outdoors. Gousha. 1995. 12.95 (*0-671-50061-9*) S&S Trade.

USA Today Crossword Companion, Vol. 1. 1995. pap. 25.00 (*1-57495-014-2*) Herbko Intl.

USA Today Crossword Companion, Vol. 2. 1995. pap. 12.00 (*1-57495-015-0*) Herbko Intl.

USA Today Crossword Companion, Vol. 3. 1995. pap. 12.00 (*1-57495-016-9*) Herbko Intl.

USA Today Crossword Companion, Vol. 4. 1995. pap. 12.00 (*1-57495-017-7*) Herbko Intl.

USA Today Crossword Companion, Vol. 5. 1995. pap. 12.00 (*1-57495-018-5*) Herbko Intl.

USA Today Crossword Companion, Vol. 6. 1995. pap. 12.00 (*1-57495-019-3*) Herbko Intl.

USA Today Crossword Companion, Vol. 7. 1995. pap. 12.00 (*1-57495-020-7*) Herbko Intl.

USA Today Crossword Companion, Vol. 8. 1995. pap. 12.00 (*1-57495-021-5*) Herbko Intl.

USA Today Crossword Companion, Vol. 9. 1995. pap. 12.00 (*1-57495-022-3*) Herbko Intl.

***USA Today Crosswords No. 22.** Charles Preston. 80p. 1997. pap. 7.95 (*0-399-52315-4*, Perigee Bks) Berkley Pub.

***U.S.A Today Crosswords No. 23.** Charles Preston. 1998. pap. write for info. (*0-399-52381-2*, Perigee Bks) Berkley Pub.

USA Today Design & Layout Manual. Richard A. Curtis. Ed. by Jacqueline Blais & Lynne Perri. (Illus.). 52p. 1995. pap. text ed. 10.00 (*0-944347-03-7*) USA Today Bks.

USA Today Read All about It: Mastering Reading Comprehension & Critical Thinking Skills. Ethel Tiersky. 192p. 1995. pap. text ed. (*0-8442-5870-9*) NTC Pub Grp.

***USA Today: Read All about It: Mastering Reading Comprehension & Critical Thinking Skills, 3 cass.** Ethel Tiersky & Esther Dickstein. 192p. pap. 39.95 incl. audio (*0-8442-5875-X*) NTC Pub Grp.

USA Today Sports Atlas: Where to Find Every Sport in America. F-Stop Fitzgerald. Ed. by Will Balliett. 224p. 1992. pap. 12.95 (*0-13-948258-X*, H M Gousha) P-H Gen Ref & Trav.

USA Today Weather Almanac, 1995. Jack Williams. 1994. pap. 14.00 (*0-679-75547-0*, Vin) Random.

USA Today Weather Book. Jack Williams. (Illus.). 212p. 1992. pap. 20.00 (*0-679-73669-7*, Publishers Media) Random.

***USA Today Weather Book.** Jack Williams. 1997. pap. 20.00 (*0-679-77665-6*, Vin) Random.

USA Today Weather Book. 2nd ed. Jack Williams. 1996. pap. write for info. (*0-679-76794-0*) Random.

***USA Today's Baseball Weekly 1997 Almanac.** Paul White & Baseball Weekly Staff. 1997. pap. text ed. 12.95 (*0-8050-5147-3*) H Holt & Co.

***USAAF Aircraft Markings & Camouflage 1941-1947: The History of USAAF Aircraft Markings, Insignia, Camouflage & Colors.** Robert D. Archer & Victor G. Archer. 352p. 1997. 79.95 (*0-7643-0246-9*) Schiffer.

***USAAF Handbook 1939-45.** Martin W. Bowman. LC 96-48473. (Illus.). 288p. 1997. 29.95 (*0-8117-1822-0*) Stackpole.

Usability: Turning Technologies into Tools. Ed. by Paul S. Adler & Terry Winograd. (Illus.). 208p. 1992. 55.00 (*0-19-507510-2*) OUP.

Usability Engineering. Jakob Nielsen. (Illus.). 362p. 1994. pap. text ed. 29.95 (*0-12-518406-9*, AP Prof) Acad Pr.

Usability Evaluation in Industry. Ed. by Patrick W. Jordan et al. 224p. 1996. 59.95 (*0-7484-0314-0*, Pub. by Tay Francis Ltd UK); pap. 29.95 (*0-7484-0460-0*, Pub. by Tay Francis Ltd UK) Taylor & Francis.

Usability in Practice: How Companies Develop User-Friendly Products. Michael E. Wiklund. (Illus.). 609p. 1994. pap. text ed. 39.95 (*0-12-751250-0*, AP Prof) Acad Pr.

Usability Inspection Methods. Jakob Nielsen & Robert L. Mack. 413p. 1994. text ed. 49.95 (*0-471-01877-5*) Wiley.

Usability Testing & System Evaluation: A Guide for Designing Useful Computer Systems. Gitte Lindgaard. LC 94-142590. (Computing Ser.). 416p. 1993. pap. 59.95 (*0-412-46100-5*) Chapman & Hall.

***Usable Knowledges As the Goal of University Education: Innovations in the Academic Enterprise Culture.** Ed. by K. Moti Gokulsing & Cornel DaCosta. LC 97-21657. (Studies in Education: Vol. 33). 280p. 1997. text ed. 89.95 (*0-7734-8619-4*) E Mellen.

Usable Past: Essays in European Cultural History. William J. Bouwsma. 1990. 52.00 (*0-520-06438-0*); pap. 17.00 (*0-520-06990-0*) U CA Pr.

Usable Past: Essays on Modern & Contemporary Poetry. Paul J. Mariani. LC 84-2613. 280p. 1984. lib. bdg. 32.50 (*0-87023-445-5*) U of Mass Pr.

***Usable Past: The Imagination of History in Recent Fiction of the Americas.** Lois P. Zamora. 256p. (C). 1997. text ed. 49.95 (*0-521-58253-9*) Cambridge U Pr.

***Usable Pasts: Traditions & Group Expressions in North America.** Ed. by Tad Tuleja. LC 96-51304. 352p. (Orig.). 1997. pap. 19.95 (*0-87421-226-X*) Utah St U Pr.

***Usable Pasts: Traditions & Group Expressions in North America.** Ed. by Tad Tuleja. 352p. (Orig.). 1997. 39.95 (*0-87421-225-1*) Utah St U Pr.

USAF Colors & Markings in the 1990s. Dana Bell. 176p. 1992. 34.95 (*1-85367-112-6*, 5447) Stackpole.

USAF Colors & Markings in the 1990s. Dana Bell. LC 93-45331. (Illus.). 178p. 1994. pap. 24.95 (*1-85367-171-1*, 5600) Stackpole.

USAF for the 21st Century: Super Wing: Total Force Integration. Jim Benson. (Illus.). 128p. 1996. pap. 18.95 (*1-85532-617-5*, Pub. by Osprey Pubng Ltd UK) Motorbooks Intl.

USAF Plus Fifteen: A Photo History 1947-1962. David W. Menard. LC 92-63123. (Illus.). 144p. (Orig.). 1993. pap. 24.95 (*0-88740-483-9*) Schiffer.

USAF Scientific Advisory Board: Its First Twenty Years, 1944-1964. Thomas A. Sturm. (Illus.). 194p. 1985. reprint ed. pap. write for info. (*0-912799-18-8*) Off Air Force.

USAF Today. Walter Wright. (Osprey Colour Library). (Illus.). 128p. 1992. pap. 15.95 (*1-85532-223-4*, Pub. by Osprey Pubng Ltd UK) Motorbooks Intl.

USAF 1947 - A Retrospect. (Illus.). 86p. 1987. reprint ed. pap. 9.95 (*0-89745-103-1*) Sunflower U Pr.

USAFE in Color, Vol. 2. Robbie Robinson. (Fighting Colors Ser.). (Illus.). 32p. 1990. pap. 9.95 (*0-89747-250-0*, 6563) Squad Sig Pubns.

Usage & Abusage: How to Pick the Right Words & Avoid the Wrong Ones in Speech & Writing. Eric Partridge. 400p. 1995. 27.50 (*0-393-03761-4*) Norton.

Usage de la Parole. Nathalie Sarraute. (Folio Ser.: No. 1435). (FRE.). pap. 8.95 (*2-07-037435-1*) Schoenhof.

***Usage de la Parole.** Nathalie Sarraute. 1983. pap. 10.95 (*0-8288-3742-2*) Fr & Eur.

Usage in Dictionaries & Dictionaries of Usage. Thomas J. Creswell. (Publications of the American Dialect Society: Nos. 63 & 64). (Illus.). 213p. 1975. pap. text ed. 18.80 (*0-8173-0662-5*) U of Ala Pr.

Usage Indicators: A New Foundation for Information Technology Policies. OECD Staff. 132p. (Orig.). 1993. pap. 24.00 (*92-64-13814-5*) OECD.

Usage of Traditions of the Prophet in Contemporary Indonesia. Howard M. Federspiel. iii, 159p. (Orig.). 1993. pap. 12.95 (*1-881044-11-4*) ASU Prog SE Asian.

Usage Prudent de la Vitamine A. J. Christopher Bauernfeind. Ed. by G. Arroyave et al. Tr. by Marc Vincent. (Illus.). 77p. (Orig.). (FRE.). 1984. pap. text ed. 3.50 (*0-935368-39-6*) ILSI.

Usagi Yojimbo, Bk. 1. Stan Sakai. (Illus.). 152p. (Orig.). 1987. pap. 10.95 (*0-930193-35-0*) Fantagraph Bks.

Usagi Yojimbo, Bk. 2. Stan Sakai. (Illus.). 144p. (Orig.). 1989. pap. 10.95 (*0-930193-88-1*) Fantagraph Bks.

Usagi Yojimbo, Bk. 3. Stan Sakai. (Illus.). 152p. (Orig.). 1989. pap. 10.95 (*1-56097-009-X*) Fantagraph Bks.

Usagi Yojimbo, Bk. 4. Stan Sakai. (Illus.). 188p. (Orig.). 1990. 35.95 (*1-56097-055-3*) Fantagraph Bks.

***Usagi Yojimbo, Bk. 6.** Stan Sakai. 144p. (Orig.). 1994. pap. 12.95 (*1-56097-146-0*) Fantagraph Bks.

***Usagi Yojimbo, Bk. 6.** Stan Sakai. 160p. (Orig.). 1994. 39.95 (*1-56097-147-9*) Fantagraph Bks.

***Usagi Yojimbo, Bk. 7.** Stan Sakai. 184p. (Orig.). 1996. pap. 16.95 (*1-56097-304-8*) Fantagraph Bks.

***Usagi Yojimbo, Bk. 7.** Stan Sakai. 192p. (Orig.). 1996. 39.95 (*1-56097-305-6*) Fantagraph Bks.

Usagi Yojimbo: Lone Goat & Kid, Bk. 5. Stan Sakai. 152p. 1992. 35.00 (*1-56097-084-7*) Fantagraph Bks.

Usagi Yojimbo: Lone Goat & Kid, Bk. 5. Stan Sakai. 160p. 1992. pap. 13.95 (*1-56097-088-X*) Fantagraph Bks.

***Usagi Yojimbo Roleplaying Game.** Greg Stolze. (Illus.). 96p. (Orig.). 1997. pap. 16.00 (*1-890305-02-2*) Gold Rush.

USAID in South Africa: Learning Lessons, Continuing Debates. Douglas J. Tilton. Ed. by Jim Cason. 110p. (Orig.). (C). 1995. pap. 8.95 (*0-9634238-3-5*) Africa Policy Info.

Usando Bien la Palabra De Verdad. Ralph V. Reynolds. Ed. by Darry Geissler & Kimberly Geissler. Tr. by Darry Crossley. 220p. (Orig.). (SPA.). (YA). pap. 14.95 (*1-877917-12-5*) Alpha Bible Pubns.

Usando Bien la Palabra De Verdad. Ralph V. Reynolds. Ed. by Darry Geissler & Kimberly Geissler. Tr. by Darry Crossley from ENG. (Dividing the World of Truth Ser.). 220p. (Orig.). (SPA.). (C). 1988. pap. 14.95 (*0-685-27251-6*) Alpha Bible Pubns.

***Usando Su Dinero Sabiamente - Using Your Money Wisely.** Burkett. (SPA.). 1995. write for info. (*1-56063-503-7*) Editorial Unilit.

USAREUR Force Structure. Robert D. Howe & William D. O'Malley. LC 93-2733. 1993. pap. 7.50 (*0-8330-1321-1*, MR-104-A) Rand Corp.

Usarufas & Their Music. Vida Chenoweth. (Museum of Anthropology Publications: No. 5). 258p. 1979. fiche 12.00 (*0-88312-242-1*) Summer Instit Ling.

Usatges of Barcelona: The Fundamental Law of Catalonia. Tr. by Donald J. Kagay. (Middle Ages Ser.). 160p. (Orig.). (C). 1995. text ed. 29.95 (*0-8122-3256-9*); pap. text ed. 14.95 (*0-8122-1535-4*) U of Pa Pr.

***USB Drivers.** David Lawrence. 1997. pap. text ed. 49.95 incl. disk (*0-929392-40-X*) Annabooks.

***USB Peripheral Developer's Guide.** John Koon. 1997. pap. text ed. 49.95 (*0-929392-46-9*) Annabooks.

***Usbekistan, 1925-1940.** Max Penson. 1997. 60.00 (*3-7165-0997-3*, Pub. by Benteli Verlag SZ) Dist Art Pubs.

Usborne Children's Encyclopedia. J. Elliot. (Encyclopedias Ser.). (Illus.). 128p. (J). (gr. 3-6). 1987. pap. 14.95 (*0-7460-0000-6*) EDC.

Usborne Children's Encyclopedia. Jane Elliot. (Encyclopedias Ser.). (Illus.). 128p. (J). (gr. 3-6). 1987. lib. bdg. 22.95 (*0-88110-265-2*) EDC.

USCG Captain's License. Wing. 1997. pap. text ed. 34.95 (*0-07-071093-7*) McGraw.

USCG Examination Questions & Answers: Navigation for Master-Mate Less Than 1600 Gross Tons. 308p. 1988. 29.95 (*0-932889-02-6*) Examco Inc.

U
V

USCG Examination Questions & Answers: Navigation for 100 Ton Master & Uninspected Passenger Vessel Operator. 172p. 1988. 19.95 (*0-932889-03-4*) Examco Inc.

USCG Examination Questions & Answers: Rules of the Road. (Illus.). 188p. 1988. 24.95 (*0-932889-06-9*) Examco Inc.

USCTA Book of Eventing: The Official Handbook of the United States Combined Training Association, Inc. 2nd ed. Ed. by Sally O'Connor. LC 86-51445. (Illus.). 288p. 1987. reprint ed. 18.95 (*0-9617826-0-9*) USCTA.

USDA Choice Flesh. Don Krow. 32p. (Orig.). pap. 2.00 (*1-881541-04-5*, 401) A Wommack.

Use & Abuse of America's Natural Resources, 41 bks. Ed. by Stuart Bruchey & Eleanor Bruchey. 1972. Set. 1,506. 50 (*0-405-04500-X*) Ayer.

Use & Abuse of Art. Jacques Barzun. LC 73-16780. (A. W. Mellon Lectures in the Fine Arts, 1989: Bollingen Ser.: Vol. 35, No. 22). 150p. 1974. pap. text ed. 10.95 (*0-691-01804-9*) Princeton U Pr.

Use & Abuse of Biology: An Anthropological Critique of Sociobiology. Marshall D. Sahlins. 1976. pap. 13.95 (*0-472-76600-7*) U of Mich Pr.

Use & Abuse of Eschatology in the Middle Ages. Ed. by W. Verbeke. No. 15. 522p. (Orig.). 1988. pap. 97.50 (*90-6186-259-0*, Pub. by Leuven Univ BE) Coronet Bks.

Use & Abuse of History: Nietzsche. Adrian Collins. 88p. (C). 1957. pap. text ed. 8.60 (*0-02-323730-9*, Macmillan Coll) P-H.

Use & Abuse of Medicine. Marten DeVries et al. LC 82-7563. 316p. 1982. text ed. 75.00 (*0-275-91362-7*, C1362, Praeger Pubs) Greenwood.

Use & Abuse of Oral Evidence. Roy Hay. (C). 1986. 30.00 (*0-7300-0226-8*, Pub. by Deakin Univ AT) St Mut.

Use & Abuse of Social Science. 2nd ed. Ed. by Irving L. Horowitz. 520p. 1975. pap. 24.95 (*0-87855-599-4*) Transaction Pubs.

Use & Abuse of Sovietology. Leopold Labedz. 372p. 1988. 49.95 (*0-88738-252-5*) Transaction Pubs.

Use & Abuse of Statistical Methods in the Earth Sciences. Ed. by William B. Size. (International Association for Mathematical Geology: Studies in Mathematical Geology: No. 1). (Illus.). 192p. 1987. 55.00 (*0-19-504963-2*) OUP.

Use & Abuse of Television: A Social Psychological Analysis of the Changing Screen. Joseph M. Wober. 256p. 1988. 49.95 (*0-89859-662-9*) L Erlbaum Assocs.

Use & Abuse of the English Language. Robert Graves & Alan Hodge. 290p. 1995. pap. 12.95 (*1-56924-849-4*) Marlowe & Co.

Use & Approval of Antihypertensive Agents & Surrogate Endpoints for the Approval of Drugs Affecting Antiarrhythmic Heart Failure & Hypolipidemia: Proceedings of the Tenth Annual Symposium on New Drugs & Devices, Oct. 31-Nov. 1, 1989. Ed. by Joel Morganroth & E. Neil Moore. (C). 1990. lib. bdg. 110. 50 (*0-7923-0756-9*) Kluwer Ac.

Use & Care of Handtools & Measuring Tools. 1991. lib. bdg. 79.95 (*0-8490-4280-1*) Gordon Pr.

Use & Care of Handtools & Measuring Tools. 1995. lib. bdg. 268.99 (*0-8490-6569-0*) Gordon Pr.

Use & Comply with Administrative Mechanisms Module, Competency-Based Career Guidance (CBCG) - Category B: Supporting. National Center for Research in Vocational Education Staff. 1985. 7.95 (*0-317-03922-9*, CB100B05) Ctr Educ Trng Employ.

Use & Conservation of Natural Gas in the Glass Industry. D. M. Haines & Dynatech R-D Company. 115p. 1977. pap. 8.50 (*0-318-12726-1*, M60277) Am Gas Assn.

Use & Conservation of Natural Gas in the Steel Industry. Dynatech R-D Company Staff & D. H. Walker. 115p. 1977. pap. 5.50 (*0-318-12727-X*, M60377) Am Gas Assn.

***Use & Control of Performance Indicators in the Public Sector.** William A. Hillison et al. Ed. by Lee A. Campbell. 63p. 1996. pap. 50.00 (*0-89413-343-8*, A300) Inst Inter Aud.

Use & Costs of Chiropractic Care in the Health Insurance Experiment. Paul G. Shekelle. LC 94-43279. (MR-401-CCR/AHCPR Ser.). 104p. (Orig.). 1994. pap. text ed. 9.00 (*0-8330-1608-3*, MR-401-CCR/AHCR) Rand Corp.

Use & Disposal of Wastes from Phosphoric Acid & Titanium Dioxide Production. 1988. 32.00 (*92-1-116433-8*, E.88.II.E.27) UN.

Use & Disposal of Wastewater Sludge in Illinois. (Illus.). 214p. (Orig.). (C). 1993. pap. text ed. 50.00 (*1-56806-655-4*) DIANE Pub.

Use & Effectiveness of Videodisc Training: A Status Report. rev. ed. Michael DeBloois. Ed. by Rockley L. Miller et al. (Illus.). 120p. 1991. spiral bd. 49.95 (*0-938907-10-7*) Future Syst.

Use & Function of Tattooing on Moroccan Women, 3 Vols. Susan Searight. (Ethnography Ser.). 1984p. 66.00 (*0-317-07534-9*) HRAFP.

Use & Impact of Computers in Clinical Medicine. Ed. by J. G. Anderson & S. J. Jay. (Computers & Medicine Ser.). (Illus.). 375p. 1986. 58.00 (*0-387-96362-6*) Spr-Verlag.

Use & Management of Criminal History Record Information: A Comprehensive Report. (Illus.). 148p. (Orig.). (C). 1995. pap. text ed. 30.00 (*0-7881-2293-2*) DIANE Pub.

Use & Misuse of People: The Indian Case. A. K. Dasgupta. (C). 1989. 30.00 (*81-7018-550-5*, Pub. by BR Pub II) S Asia.

Use & Misuse of the Seafloor: Report of the Dahlem Workshop on Use & Misuse of Seafloor, Berlin, March 17-22, 1991. Ed. by Kenneth J. Hsu et al. LC 92-14115. (Environmental Sciences Research Report Ser.: No. ES11). 440p. 1992. text ed. 265.00 (*0-471-93191-8*) Wiley.

Use & Standardization of Chemically Defined Antigens. Ed. by W. Hennessen & Girish N. Vyas. (Developments in Biological Standardization Ser.: Vol. 63). (Illus.). viii, 176p. 1986. pap. 65.75 (*3-8055-4280-1*) S Karger.

Use & Standardization of Combined Vaccines. Ed. by A. L. Van Wezel & W. Hennessen. (Developments in Biological Standardization Ser.: Vol. 65). (Illus.). viii, 288p. 1987. 112.00 (*3-8055-4461-8*) S Karger.

Use & Training of the Human Voice. Arthur Lessac. LC 67-28352. 297p. (C). 1967. pap. text ed. 32.95 (*0-87484-845-8*, 845) Mayfield Pub.

Use & Training of the Human Voice: A Bio-Dynamic Approach to Vocal Life. 3rd rev. ed. Arthur Lessac. LC 96-18629. (Illus.). 291p. (Orig.). 1996. pap. text ed. 32. 95 (*1-55934-696-5*, 1696) Mayfield Pub.

Use & Value of Special Libraries. Donald W. King & Jose-Marie Griffiths. 150p. 1986. 36.50 (*0-313-25781-7*, Greenwood Pr) Greenwood.

Use Both Brains. Joseph P. Reel. LC 80-82602. (Illus.). 104p. (Orig.). 1980. pap. 14.95 (*0-938024-00-0*) Human Dev Pr.

Use Both Sides of Your Brain. rev. ed. Tony Buzan. (Illus.). 1983. pap. 7.95 (*0-525-48229-6*, Dutton) NAL-Dutton.

Use Both Sides of Your Brain. 3rd ed. Tony Buzan. (Illus.). 1991. pap. 12.95 (*0-452-26603-3*, Plume) NAL-Dutton.

Use Case Maps for Object-Oriented Systems. R. J. Buhr & R. S. Casselman. LC 95-31100. 1995. text ed. 46.00 (*0-13-456542-8*) P-H.

***Use Enough Gun: On Hunting Big Game.** R. Ruark. 35.00 (*1-57157-059-4*) Safari Pr.

Use for Journal Keeping: An Ethnography of Writing in a University Science Class. Anne C. Johnstone. LC 94-9942. (Writing Research Ser.). 192p. 1994. pap. 39.50 (*1-56750-052-8*); text ed. 73.25 (*0-89391-888-1*) Ablex Pub.

Use It or Lose It: The Word of Faith. Roy H. Hicks. 68p. (Orig.). 1976. pap. 4.99 (*0-89274-002-7*) Harrison Hse.

Use-It Report: Education & Instruction Through Telecommunications: Distance Learning for All Learners. Frank Withrow. 92p. (Orig.). 1995. pap. 20. 00 (*0-614-14608-9*) Coun Chief St Schl Offs.

Use-It Report - Education & Instruction Through Telecommunications: Distance Learning for All Learners. Frank Withrow. 92p. 1995. pap. 10.00 (*1-884037-07-0*) Coun Chief St Schl Offs.

Use-It-Up Cookbook: A Guide for Minimizing Food Waste. 2nd ed. Lois C. Willand. LC 85-60649. 190p. 1985. reprint ed. spiral bd. 12.95 (*0-9614556-0-8*) Practical Cookbks.

Use, Maintenance, & Service Testing of Fire Department Ground Ladders. National Fire Protection Association Staff. 1989. 16.75 (*0-317-63564-6*, 1932-89) Natl Fire Prot.

***Use of a PC Printer Port for Control & Data Acquisition.** Peter H. Anderson. LC 96-96562. (Illus.). 150p. (Orig.). (C). 1996. pap. 15.00 (*0-9653357-0-4*) P H Anderson.

Use of a Wall Mirror. Adrian Morrien. Tr. by Ria Leigh-Loohuizen. 1970. pap. 6.00 (*0-912136-17-0*) Twowindows Pr.

Use of Abuse: The Polemics of the Dreyfus Affair & Its Aftermath. Richard Griffiths. LC 89-17566. (French Studies). 221p. 1991. 19.95 (*0-85496-626-9*) Berg Pubs.

Use of ACE Inhibitors in General Practice. George Strube & Gillian Strube. 128p. 1992. pap. text ed. 37.50 (*0-7923-8963-8*) Kluwer Ac.

Use of Adsorbents for the Removal of Pollutants from Wastewater. Ed. by Gordon McKay. 208p. 1995. 69.95 (*0-8493-6920-7*, 6920) CRC Pr.

Use of Aircraft for Mosquito Control, Oct. 1982. N. B. Akesson & W. E. Yates. 96p. 10.00 (*0-686-84357-6*) Am Mosquito.

Use of Anchors in Offshore Petroleum Operations. Alain Puech. (Illus.). 160p. (C). 1984. 280.00 (*2-7108-0453-0*, Pub. by Edits Technip FR) St Mut.

***Use of Anchors in Offshore Petroleum Operations.** Alain Puech. Tr. by Nissim Marshall from FRE. LC 84-71684. (Illus.). 155p. 1984. reprint ed. pap. 44.20 (*0-608-04201-3*, 2064936) Bks Demand.

Use of Animal Models for Research in Human Nutrition. Ed. by A. C. Beynen & C. E. West. (Comparative Animal Nutrition Ser.: Vol. 6). (Illus.). v, 190p. 1989. 134.50 (*3-8055-4802-8*) S Karger.

Use of Animals & Plants in School Science: A Joint Statement from ASE, JOB, UFAW. Ed. by Universities Federation for Animal Welfare Staff. 1984. 16.00 (*0-317-43893-X*) St Mut.

***Use of Animals in Scientific Procedures.** F. Kim. 1994. pap. 23.00 (*0-900767-84-7*, Pub. by Univs Fed Animal Welfare UK) St Mut.

***Use of Antibiotics: A Clinical Review of Antibacterial, Antifungal & Antiviral Drugs.** 5th ed. A. Kucers. LC 97-21384. 1997. write for info. (*0-7506-0155-8*) Buttrwrth-Heinemann.

Use of Anticonvulsants in Psychiatry: Recent Advances. Post et al. Ed. by Pope. LC 88-60179. 192p. 1988. 22.50 (*0-945986-00-9*) Health Care NJ.

Use of Antistripping Additives in Asphaltic Concrete Mixtures - Laboratory Phase. (National Cooperative Highway Research Program Report Ser.: No. 274). 50p. 1984. 7.60 (*0-309-03858-8*) Transport Res Bd.

Use of Applicable Biotechnological Methods for Diagnosing Haemoparasites. Ed. by G. Uilenberg & A. Permin. 188p. 1994. pap. 20.00 (*92-5-103503-2*, F35032, Pub. by FAO IT) Bernan Associates.

Use of Aquatic Invertebrates As Tools for Monitoring of Environmental Hazards. Ed. by Werner E. Muller. (Illus.). 288p. 1995. 65.00 (*3-437-30791-6*, Pub. by G Fischer Verlag GW) Lubrecht & Cramer.

Use of Arabic in Biblical Hebrew Lexicography. John Kaltner. LC 95-45182. (Catholic Biblical Quarterly Monographs: No. 28). (ARA & HEB.). 1996. 7.50 (*0-915170-27-2*) Catholic Bibl Assn.

Use of Arthurian Legend in Hollywood Film: From Connecticut Yankees to Fisher Kings. Rebecca A. Umland & Samuel J. Umland. LC 96-5835. (Contributions to the Study of Popular Culture Ser.: No. 57). 224p. 1996. text ed. 55.00 (*0-313-29798-3*, Greenwood Pr) Greenwood.

Use of Artificial Satellites for Geodesy. Ed. by Soren Henriksen et al. LC 72-88669. (Geophysical Monograph Ser.: Vol. 15). (Illus.). 298p. 1972. 35.00 (*0-87590-015-1*) Am Geophysical.

Use of Assessment Techniques by Applied Psychologists. Paula S. Wise. 148p. (C). 1989. pap. 28.95 (*0-534-09750-2*) Brooks-Cole.

Use of Beneficial Organisms in the Control of Crop Pests: Proceedings of the Joint American-Soviet Conference. rev. ed. Ed. by Jack R. Coulson et al. 105p. 1985. 9.00 (*0-685-14295-7*, SOU) Entomol Soc.

Use of Bioassay Procedures for Assessment of Internal Radionuclide Deposition. LC 86-33136. (Report Ser.: No. 87). 86p. 1987. pap. text ed. 40.00 (*0-913392-83-9*) NCRP Pubns.

Use of Biological Specimens for the Assessment of Human Exposure to Environmental Pollutants. A. Berlin et al. 1979. lib. bdg. 123.50 (*90-247-2168-7*) Kluwer Ac.

Use of Biomarkers in Assessing Health & Environmental Impacts of Chemicals & Pollutants. Ed. by Curtis C. Travis. (NATO ASI Series A, Life Sciences: Vol. 250). 1993. 95.00 (*0-306-44539-5*, Plenum Pr) Plenum.

Use of Books & Libraries. 10th ed. Raymond H. Shove et al. LC 63-16070. 128p. reprint ed. pap. 36.50 (*0-317-29481-4*, 2055916) Bks Demand.

Use of Both the Globes. Thomas Hood. LC 70-38111. (English Experience Ser.: No. 389). 54p. 1971. reprint ed. 20.00 (*90-221-0389-7*) Walter J Johnson.

Use of Boundary Elements for the Determination of the Geometry Factor. Sandeep M. Vijayakar & Donald R. Houser. (Fall Technical Meeting Papers). (Illus.). 9p. 1986. pap. 30.00 (*1-55589-474-7*, 86FTM10) AGMA.

Use of Calcium Antagonists in Cardiology: Proceedings of the 1st International Symposium on Tiapamil, Lausanne, April 1981. B. N. Singh. (Journal: Cardiology: Vol. 69, Suppl. 1, 1982). (Illus.). xii, 242p. 1982. pap. 60.00 (*3-8055-3588-0*) S Karger.

Use of Cannabis: Proceedings of the WHO Scientific Group, Geneva, 1970. WHO Staff. (Technical Report Ser.: No. 478). 1971. pap. text ed. 5.00 (*92-4-120478-8*, 1100478) World Health.

Use of Cantilever Jack-up Drilling Rigs for Cost Effective Satellite & Marginal Field Developments. Ed. by Rustem Akcora. (C). 1989. 95.00 (*0-89771-727-9*, Pub. by Lorne & MacLean Marine) St Mut.

Use of Ceramics in Surgical Implants. S. F. Hulbert & F. A. Young, Jr. LC 73-99078. 270, viiip. 1978. text ed. 216.00 (*0-677-13870-9*) Gordon & Breach.

Use of Chemicals in Oil Spill Response. Ed. by Peter Lane. LC 95-22156. (STP Ser.: No. 1252). 340p. 1995. 89.00 (*0-8031-1999-2*, 04-012520-48) ASTM.

Use of Ciprofloxacin in the Treatment of Chronic Otitis & Sinusitis & Malignant External Otitis. Ed. by F. Legent. (Journal: Chemotherapy: Vol. 40, Suppl. 1, 1994). (Illus.). iv, 42p. 1994. pap. 74.00 (*3-8055-6071-0*) S Karger.

Use of Coconut Oil/Diesel Blends As a Fuel for Compression Ignition Engines. J. M. Jones et al. 1990. pap. 49.00 (*0-85954-266-1*, Pub. by Nat Res Inst UK) St Mut.

Use of Color. (Shorewood Art Programs for Education Ser.). 8p. 1974. teacher ed. 107.00 (*0-88185-021-7*); 143. 00 (*0-685-07219-3*) Shorewood Fine Art.

Use of Color in the Verse of English Romantic Poets from Langland to Keats. Alice E. Pratt. (English Literature Ser.: No. 33). 1970. reprint ed. pap. 39.95 (*0-8383-0061-8*) M S G Haskell Hse.

Use of Color Terms in the Greek Poets. Alice E. Kober. viii, 124p. 1989. reprint ed. text ed. 25.00 (*0-89241-474-X*) Caratzas.

Use of Compensatory Strategies by Dutch Learners of English. Nanda Ponlisse. (Studies on Language Acquisition). 1990. pap. 53.85 (*3-11-013110-2*) Mouton.

Use of Complexing Agents to Modify the Aging Behavior of Insulating Enamel on Copper Wire. 85p. 1983. write for info. (*0-318-60085-4*, 319) Intl Copper.

Use of Computers & Statistics in Toxicology, Vol. 10. Ed. by M. J. Ord et al. 102p. 1985. 32.00 (*0-85066-977-4*) Taylor & Francis.

Use of Computers for Laboratory Automation. S. P. Maj. 380p. 1993. 63.00 (*0-85186-744-8*, R6744) CRC Pr.

Use of Computers in Analysis of Experimental Data & the Control of Nuclear Facilities: Proceedings. Bernard I. Spinrad. LC 67-60057. (AEC Symposium Ser.). 290p. 1967. pap. 15.75 (*0-87079-214-8*, CONF-660527); fiche 9.00 (*0-87079-215-6*, CONF-660527) DOE.

Use of Computers in Civil Litigation (1990) 63p. 1988. pap. text ed. 15.00 (*1-56986-042-4*) Federal Bar.

Use of Computers in External Beam Radiotherapy Procedures with High Energy Photons & Electrons. ICRU Staff. LC 87-16975. (ICRU Report Ser.: No. 42). 1987. 55.00 (*0-685-18557-5*) Intl Comm Rad Meas.

Use of Computers in General Practice. 2nd ed. John F. Preece. (Illus.). 256p. 1989. pap. text ed. 48.00 (*0-443-04258-6*) Churchill.

Use of Computers in High Schools. Joe E. Crick & Lawrence M. Stolurow. LC 74-121200. 172p. 1965. 25. 00 (*0-403-04492-8*) Scholarly.

Use of Computers in Managing Material Property Data: Presented at the Winter Annual Meeting of the American Society of Mechanical Engineers, Chicago, Illinois, November 16-21, 1980. American Society of Mechanical Engineers Staff. Ed. by James A. Graham. LC 80-69196. (MPC Ser.: No. 14). (Illus.). 72p. reprint ed. pap. 25.00 (*0-8357-2902-8*, 2039138) Bks Demand.

Use of Computers in the Coal Industry: Proceedings of the 3rd Conference on the Use of Computers in the Coal Industry, W. Virginia University, Morgantown, 28-30 July 1986. Ed. by Y. Wang et al. 342p. (C). 1986. text ed. 160.00 (*90-6191-655-0*, Pub. by A A Balkema NE) Ashgate Pub Co.

Use of Computers in the Coal Industry 1990: Proceedings of the 4th Conference, Morgantown, WV, 20-22 June 1990. Ed. by Y. J. Wang et al. (Illus.). 280p. (C). 1990. text ed. 105.00 (*90-6191-117-6*, Pub. by A A Balkema NE) Ashgate Pub Co.

Use of Computers in the Fatigue Laboratory - STP 613. Ed. by H. Mindlin & R. W. Longdgraf. 172p. 1976. 20.00 (*0-8031-0593-2*, 04-613000-30) ASTM.

Use of Consultants for Construction Engineering Inspection. (National Cooperative Highway Research Program Report Ser.: No. 146). 64p. 1989. 9.00 (*0-309-04556-8*) Transport Res Bd.

Use of Contilever Jack-up Drilling Rigs for Cost Effective Satellite & Marginal Field Development. Rustem Akcora. 1989. 125.00 (*90-6314-552-7*, Pub. by Lorne & MacLean Marine) St Mut.

Use of Contrast Coefficients: Supplement to McNeil, Kelly, & McNeil, "Testing Research Hypotheses Using Multiple Linear Regression" Ernest L. Lewis & John T. Mouw. LC 77-16406. 80p. 1978. pap. text ed. 6.95 (*0-8093-0868-1*) S Ill U Pr.

Use of Counseling Skills: A Guide for Therapists. John Swain. (Skills for Practice Ser.). 224p. 1995. pap. 30.00 (*0-7506-1618-0*) Buttrwrth-Heinemann.

Use of CPM in Construction. 192p. 1976. 12.00 (*0-317-01171-5*) Assn Gen Con.

Use of Credit Instruments in Payments in the United States. David Kinley. LC 68-27848. (Library of Money & Banking History). vi, 229p. 1970. reprint ed. 35.00 (*0-678-00546-X*) Kelley.

Use of DEAE: Cellulose to Extract Anionic Organic Material from Groundwaters. B. Smith & P. Moody. 53p. 1994. pap. 10.00 (*92-826-6475-9*, CD-NA-14968-ENC, Pub. by Europ Com UK) Bernan Associates.

Use of Debonded Strands in Pretensioned Bridge Members. (PCI Journal Reprints Ser.). 18p. 1981. pap. 12.00 (*0-318-19800-2*, JR289) P-PCI.

Use of Definite & Indefinite Reference in Young Children: An Experimental Study of Semantic Acquisition. Michael P. Maratsos. 158p. reprint ed. pap. 45.10 (*0-317-27554-2*, 2024500) Bks Demand.

Use of Digital Computers in Process Control. Theodore J. Williams. LC 84-6649. 393p. reprint ed. pap. 112.10 (*0-7837-5157-5*, 2044886) Bks Demand.

Use of Dipmeters in Stratigraphic & Depositional Interpretation of Natural Gas Reservoirs of the Oligocene Vicksburg Formation: An Example from McAllen Ranch Field, Hidalgo County, Texas. R. P. Langford et al. (Geological Circular Ser.: No. GC 94-1). (Illus.). 39p. 1994. pap. 5.50 (*0-614-01871-4*) Bur Econ Geology.

Use of Drugs in Food Animals: Benefits & Risks. National Research Council Staff. 290p. 1997. 34.95 (*0-309-05434-6*) Natl Acad Pr.

Use of Drugs in Psychiatry. 2nd ed. John L. Crammer et al. 268p. reprint ed. pap. 76.40 (*0-8357-7775-8*, 2036135) Bks Demand.

Use of Early Release & Sentencing Guidelines to Ease Prison Crowding: The Shifting Sands of Reform. 8.00 (*0-318-21764-3*) Natl Coun Crime.

Use of Economists in Antitrust Litigation. American Bar Association Staff. LC 84-71278. 81p. 1984. pap. 35.00 (*0-89707-145-X*, 503-0054) Amer Bar Assn.

***Use of Electronic Data Processing in Aircraft Gear Manufacturing.** T. M. Englehart. (Technical Papers). 1957. pap. text ed. 30.00 (*1-55589-461-5*) AGMA.

Use of Energeology for Low Energy Synthetics: Uses of Energy Masses for Synthetic Atomic Production. Troy C. Guillory. (Illus.). (C). 1989. text ed. 99.95 (*0-9622829-8-7*) Guillory Operations.

Use of Energeology for Synthetic Atomic Physics: Uses of Energy Masses for Synthetic Atomic Production. Troy C. Guillory. (Illus.). 54p. (Orig.). (C). 1989. 79.50 (*0-317-93973-4*); text ed. 89.99 (*0-317-93974-2*); pap. text ed. 80.95 (*0-317-93975-0*) Guillory Operations.

***Use of English.** Afolaian & Newsum. 1983. pap. text ed. write for info. (*0-582-64236-1*, Pub. by Longman UK) Longman.

Use of English. Daniel Jones. 1985. teacher ed., pap. 14.95 (*0-521-26977-6*); student ed., pap. 11.95 (*0-521-26976-8*) Cambridge U Pr.

Use of English Grammar. Ed. by R. O'Neill et al. (C). 1988. 60.00 (*0-685-37720-2*, Pub. by S Thornes Pubs UK) St Mut.

Use of English Grammar. Guy Wellman & Michael Duckworth. 320p. (C). 1988. 49.00 (*1-870511-20-4*, Pub. by S Thornes Pubs UK) St Mut.

Use of EOS for Studies of Atmospheric Physics: Varenna on Lake Como, Villa Monastero, 26 June-6 July 1990. Ed. by J. C. Gille & G. Visconti. LC 92-41017. (Proceedings of the International School of Physics "Enrico Fermi" Ser.: Course 115). 580p. 1993. 272.25 (*0-444-89896-4*, North Holland) Elsevier.

***Use of Epidemiology in Local Health Planning: A Training Manual.** Axel Kroeger et al. LC 96-36126. 192p. 1997. 55.00 (*1-85649-481-0*, Pub. by Zed Bks Ltd UK) Humanities.

*__Use of Epidemiology in Local Health Planning: A Training Manual.__ Axel Kroeger et al. LC 96-36126. 192p. 1997. pap. 22.50 (*1-85649-482-9*, Pub. by Zed Bks Ltd UK) Humanities.

Use of Essential Drugs: Model List of Essential Drugs (Eighth List) Sixth Report of the WHO Expert Committee. (Technical Report Ser.: No. 850). iv, 138p. (FRE & SPA.). (C). 1995. pap. text ed. 21.00 (*92-4-120850-3*, 1100850) World Health.

Use of Essential Drugs: Model List of Essential Drugs Fourth Report of the WHO Expert Committee. (Technical Report Ser.: No. 796). 57p. 1990. pap. text ed. 8.00 (*92-4-120796-5*, 1100796) World Health.

*__Use of Essential Drugs Model List of Essential Drugs (9th List) Seventh Report of the WHO Expert Committee.__ WHO Staff. (Technical Report Ser.: No. 867). 0080p. 1997. 15.00 (*92-4-120867-8*) World Health.

*__Use of Essential Drugs (The) Model List of Essential Drugs (Fifth List) Third Report of the WHO Expert Committee.__ WHO Staff. (Technical Report Ser.: No. 770). 0063p. 1988. 8.00 (*92-4-120770-1*) World Health.

*__Use of Essential Drugs (The) Model List of Essential Drugs (Seventh List) Fifth Report of the WHO Expert Committee, 1991.__ WHO Staff. (Technical Report Ser.: No. 825). 79p. 1992. 10.00 (*92-4-120825-2*) World Health.

Use of Expert Systems in a Water Utility. Richard M. Males et al. (Illus.). 120p. (Orig.). (C). 1994. pap. text ed. 40.00 (*0-7881-0277-X*) DIANE Pub.

Use of Expert Systems in Management Accounting. Germain Boer. Ed. by Claire Barth. 55p. (Orig.). 1989. pap. 20.00 (*0-86641-173-9*, 89230) Inst Mgmt Account.

Use of Experts by International Tribunals. Gillian M. White. LC 65-15853. xv, 259p. Date not set. 50.00 (*1-57588-378-3*, 306640) W S Hein.

Use of Factory Statistics in the Investigation of Industrial Fatigue. Philip S. Florence. LC 76-76627. (Columbia University. Studies in the Social Sciences: No. 190). reprint ed. 39.50 (*0-404-51190-2*) AMS Pr.

Use of Family Planning Services in the United States 1982 & 1988: PHS 90-1250. No. 184. write for info. (*0-318-69625-8*) Natl Ctr Health Stats.

Use of Film Badges for Personnel Monitoring. (Safety Ser.: No. 8). 1962. pap. 16.00 (*92-0-123162-8*, ISP43, Pub. by IAEA AU) Bernan Associates.

Use of Fire. Reynolds Price. 160p. 1990. 19.95 (*0-689-12109-1*, Pub. by Ctrl Bur voor Schimmel NE) Macmillan.

Use of Flocculants to Control Turbidity in Placer Mining Effluents. Yun-Hwei Shen. (MIRL Reports: No. 78). (Illus.). 50p. (Orig.). (C). 1988. pap. 5.00 (*0-911043-07-1*) UAKF Min Ind Res Lab.

Use of Fly Ash in Concrete. (National Cooperative Highway Research Program Report Ser.: No. 127). 66p. 1986. 8.40 (*0-309-04401-4*) Transport Res Bd.

Use of Force: Military Power & International Politics. 4th ed. Ed. by Robert J. Art & Kenneth N. Waltz. 620p. (C). 1993. pap. text ed. 23.95 (*0-8191-8864-6*) U Pr of Amer.

*__Use of Force: The Practice of States, 1945-1991.__ A. Mark Weisburd. LC 96-44645. 1997. 65.00 (*0-271-01679-5*); pap. 25.00 (*0-271-01680-9*) Pa St U Pr.

Use of Formal Specification of Software. Ed. by H. K. Berg & Wolfgang K. Giloi. (Informatik-Fachberichte Ser.: Vol. 36). 388p. 1981. 38.00 (*0-387-10442-9*) Spr-Verlag.

Use of Fragrance in Consumer Products. Joseph S. Jellinek. LC 75-2106. (Wiley-Interscience Publications). 231p. reprint ed. pap. 65.90 (*0-317-27938-6*, 2055981) Bks Demand.

Use of Fungi As Food & in Food Processing, Pt. 2. William D. Gray. (Monotopic Reprint Ser.). 1973. 22.00 (*0-8493-0118-1*, CRC Reprint) Franklin.

Use of Gold & Other Metal among the Ancient Inhabitants of Chiriqui, Isthmus of Darien. William H. Holmes. (Bureau of American Ethnology Bulletins Ser.). 99p. 1995. lib. bdg. 69.00 (*0-7812-4003-4*) Rprt Serv.

Use of Government Publications of Social Scientist. Peter Hernon. LC 79-16144. (Libraries & Librarianship Ser.). 1979. text ed. 73.25 (*0-89391-024-4*) Ablex Pub.

Use of Group Services in Permanency Planning for Children. Ed. by Sylvia Morris. LC 82-23389. (Social Work with Groups Ser.: Vol. 5, No. 4). 109p. 1983. text ed. 32.95 (*0-86656-199-4*) Haworth Pr.

Use of Growth Factors in Cancer Therapy. 1994. lib. bdg. 258.95 (*0-8490-8525-X*) Gordon Pr.

Use of Growth Factors in Cancer Therapy. 1995. lib. bdg. 250.99 (*0-8490-7582-3*) Gordon Pr.

Use of Hand Woodworking Tools. 2nd ed. L. P. McDonnell & A. I. Kaumeheiwa. LC 76-48504. 301p. (C). 1978. teacher ed. 13.50 (*0-8273-1099-4*); pap. 25.50 (*0-8273-1098-6*) Delmar.

*__Use of Health Service Facilities in Medical Education: Sixteenth Report of the WHO Expert Committee on Professional & Technical Education of Medical & Auxiliary Personnel.__ (Technical Report Ser.: No. 355). 0065p. 1967. pap. text ed. 5.00 (*92-4-120355-2*, 1100355) World Health.

Use of Herbicides in the Forest: Forestry Commission Field Book 8. 2nd ed. I. Willoughby & J. Dewar. (Forestry C Ser.). 328p. 1995. pap. 25.00 (*0-11-710330-6*, HM03306, Pub. by Stationery Ofc UK) Bernan Associates.

Use of Heteroploid & Other Cell Substrates for the Production of Biologicals. Ed. by W. Hennessen. (Developments in Biological Standardization Ser.: Vol. 50). (Illus.). x, 402p. 1982. pap. 68.00 (*3-8055-3472-8*) S Karger.

Use of High Purity Oxygen in the Activated Sludge Process, 2 vols., Vol. 1. Ed. by J. R. McWhirter. (Uniscience Ser.). 296p. 1978. 89.00 (*0-8493-5101-4*, TD756, CRC Reprint) Franklin.

Use of High Purity Oxygen in the Activated Sludge Process, 2 vols., Vol. 2. Ed. by J. R. McWhirter. (Uniscience Ser.). 292p. 1978. 89.00 (*0-8493-5102-2*, CRC Reprint) Franklin.

Use of Human Beings in Research. Ed. by Stuart F. Spicker et al. 312p. 1988. lib. bdg. 127.00 (*1-55608-043-3*, D Reidel) Kluwer Ac.

*__Use of Human Immunoglobulin.__ (Technical Report Ser.: No. 327). 29p. 1966. pap. text ed. 3.00 (*92-4-120327-7*) World Health.

Use of Human Tissues & Organs for Therapeutic Purposes: A Survey of Existing Legislation. (International Digest of Health Legislation Ser: Vol. 20, No. 1). 1969. pap. text ed. 5.00 (*92-4-169201-4*, 1956901) World Health.

Use of Humor in Psychotherapy. Herbert S. Strean. LC 93-25547. 248p. 1994. pap. 25.00 (*1-56821-084-1*) Aronson.

Use of In Situ Tests in Geotechnical Engineering. Ed. by Samuel P. Clemence. (Conference Proceedings Ser.). 1284p. 1986. 106.00 (*0-87262-541-9*) Am Soc Civil Eng.

Use of Incentives to Attain Specified Performance Standards in Collective Bargaining for Mass Transit. (National Cooperative Transit Research Program Synthesis Ser.: No. 13). 68p. 1987. 9.20 (*0-309-04420-0*) Transport Res Bd.

Use of Individual Quotas in Fisheries Management. OECD Staff. 224p. (Orig.). 1993. pap. 26.00 (*92-64-13940-0*) OECD.

Use of Instructional Television in Adult Education. Robert J. Blakely. LC 73-13295. (Occasional Papers: No. 40). 1974. pap. text ed. 2.00 (*0-87060-064-8*, OCP 40) Syracuse U Cont Ed.

Use of Instrumentation to Optimize the Continuous Casting Process, Vol. 9: Process Technology Conference: 9th Proceedings, Detroit Meeting, March 25-28, 1990. AIME Iron & Steel Society Staff. LC 82-197229. 203p. pap. 57.90 (*0-7837-2203-6*, 2042541) Bks Demand.

Use of International Law. Philip C. Jessup. LC 88-61810. (Michigan Legal Publications). xiii, 164p. 1988. reprint ed. lib. bdg. 38.50 (*0-89941-659-4*, 305670) W S Hein.

Use of International Law. Philip C. Jessup. LC 79-173670. 164p. 1971. reprint ed. lib. bdg. 27.50 (*0-306-70407-2*) Da Capo.

Use of Interpretation in Treatment: Technique & Art. Ed. by Emanuel F. Hammer. LC 93-30193. 392p. 1993. pap. 35.00 (*1-56821-111-2*) Aronson.

Use of Ion Implantation to Modify the Para-Surface Properties of Copper. 74p. 1982. write for info. (*0-318-60073-0*) Intl Copper.

Use of Irradiation As a Quarantine Treatment of Food & Agricultural Commodities. 220p. 1992. pap. 70.00 (*92-0-102992-6*, STI/PUB/873, Pub. by IAEA AU) Bernan Associates.

Use of Irradiation to Control Infectivity of Food - Borne Parasites. IAEA Staff. 139p. 1994. pap. 40.00 (*92-0-103193-9*, STI/PUB/933, Pub. by IAEA AU) Bernan Associates.

Use of Knowledge in Analogy & Induction. Ed. by Stuart J. Russel. 200p. (C). 1989. pap. text ed. 190.00 (*0-273-08814-9*, Pub. by Pitman Pubng UK) St Mut.

Use of Knowledge in Analogy & Induction. Stuart Russell. (Research Notes in Artificial Intelligence Ser.). 1989. 29. 95 (*1-55860-089-2*) Morgan Kaufmann.

Use of Landfarming to Remediate Soil Contaminated by Pesticide Waste. Allan S. Felsot et al. (Illus.). 53p. (Orig.). (C). 1994. pap. text ed. 30.00 (*0-7881-1348-8*) DIANE Pub.

Use of Landfarming to Remediate Soil Contaminated by Pesticides. Dwight J. Roberts. (Illus.). 42p. (Orig.). (C). 1995. pap. text ed. 25.00 (*0-7881-2615-6*) DIANE Pub.

Use of LANDSAT Data in Forestry, Vol. 2. Ed. by Josef Cihlar. (Remote Sensing Reviews Ser.: Vol. 1, Pt. 3). 258p. 1986. pap. text ed. 220.00 (*3-7186-0307-1*) Gordon & Breach.

Use of Language in Clinical Practice Guidelines. (Medical Ser.). 1995. lib. bdg. 253.99 (*0-8490-6840-1*) Gordon Pr.

Use of Lateral Thinking. Edward De Bono. 1990. 25.00 (*0-317-90555-4*) Intl Ctr Creat Think.

Use of Legislative History in Statutory Interpretation Cases in the 1992 U. S. Supreme Court Term. 44p. 1993. 15.00 (*0-317-05924-6*, PB-20) Natl Attys General.

Use of Less-Than-Fee Acquisition for the Preservation of Open Space. Robert E. Coughlin & Thomas Plaut. (Discussion Paper Ser.: No. 101). 1977. pap. 10.00 (*1-55869-131-6*) Regional Sci Res Inst.

*__Use of Library Materials: The University of Pittsburgh Study.__ Allen Kent et al. LC 79-11513. (Books in Library & Information Science: No. 26). 288p. 1979. reprint ed. pap. 82.10 (*0-608-04200-5*, 2064935) Bks Demand.

Use of Line. (Shorewood Art Programs for Education Ser.). 8p. 1974. teacher ed. 107.00 (*0-88185-022-5*); 143.00 (*0-685-07220-7*) Shorewood Fine Art.

Use of Literacy: Media. Ed. by Peter Davison et al. LC 77-90618. (Literary Taste, Culture & Mass Communication Ser.: Vol. 9). 299p. 1978. lib. bdg. 100.00 (*0-85964-044-2*) Chadwyck-Healey.

Use of Local Minerals in the Treatment of Radioactive Waste. (Technical Reports: No. 136). (Illus.). 128p. (Orig.). 1972. pap. 25.00 (*92-0-125172-6*, IDC136, Pub. by IAEA AU) Bernan Associates.

Use of Longer-Acting Agents in Cardiac Therapy: Recent Advances. Abrams et al. Ed. by Stanley B. Garbus. 1989. 25.00 (*0-945986-11-4*) Health Care NJ.

*__Use of Macrophytes in Water Pollution Control.__ D. Athie & C. C. Cerri. (Water Science & Technology Ser.: Vol. 19). 186p. 1988. 61.00 (*0-08-035594-3*, Pergamon Pr) Elsevier.

Use of Manuscripts in Literary Research: Problems of Access & Literary Property Rights. 2nd ed. James E. Thorpe. LC 79-87584. 40p. reprint ed. pap. 25.00 (*0-8357-8572-6*, 2034938) Bks Demand.

Use of Mechanistic Information in Risk Assessment: Proceedings of the 1993 EUROTOX Congress Meeting Held in Uppsala, Sweden, June 30-July 3, 1993. Ed. by H. M. Bolt et al. LC 93-44609. (Archives of Toxicology Ser.: Suppl. 16). 1994. write for info. (*3-540-57442-5*); 122.00 (*0-387-57442-5*) Spr-Verlag.

Use of Medical Evidence: Low-Back Permanent Partial Disability Claims in Maryland. Leslie I. Boden. 60p. (Orig.). 1986. pap. 25.00 (*0-935149-02-3*, SP-86-1) Workers Comp Res Inst.

Use of Medical Evidence: Low-Back Permanent Partial Disability Claims in New Jersey. Leslie I. Boden. LC 87-31628. (Orig.). 1987. 25.00 (*0-935149-07-4*, WC-87-2) Workers Comp Res Inst.

Use of Mercury & Alternative Compounds As Seed Dressings: Report of the FAO-WHO Meeting, Geneva, 1974. FAO-WHO Meeting Staff. (Technical Report Ser.: No. 555). 1974. pap. text ed. 5.00 (*92-4-120555-5*, 1100555) World Health.

Use of Microcomputers in Geology. Ed. by Daniel F. Merriam & Hans Kurzl. LC 92-29735. (Computer Applications in the Earth Sciences Ser.). 1992. 95.00 (*0-306-44310-4*, Plenum Pr) Plenum.

Use of Microphysiological Recordings During Stereotactic Neurosurgery Journal: Stereotactic & Functional Neurosurgery, 1989, Vol. 52, No. 2-4. Ed. by P. L. Gildenberg et al. (Illus.). 200p. 1989. pap. 84.00 (*3-8055-5039-1*) S Karger.

Use of Microprocessors. Michel Aumiaux. LC 79-42904. (Wiley Series in Computing). 208p. reprint ed. pap. 59. 30 (*0-318-34898-5*, 2031295) Bks Demand.

*__Use of Multispectral Digital Imagery in Archeological Investigations.__ Ed. by W. Fredrick Limp. (Illus.). 121p. 1989. pap. 16.00 (*1-56349-062-5*, RS34) AR Archaeol.

Use of Music & Recordings for Teaching about the Middle Ages. John W. Barker. 1988. pap. 8.00 (*0-614-01298-8*) Medieval Inst.

Use of Myth to Create Suspense. William W. Flint. (Studies in Comparative Literature: No. 35). 1970. reprint ed. pap. 24.95 (*0-8383-0030-8*) M S G Haskell Hse.

Use of Natural Pozzolans in Concrete: ACI Committee 232. 18p. 1994. 19.50 (*0-614-11128-5*, 232194.BOW6) ACI.

Use of Neuroleptics in Children. Ed. by Mary A. Richardson & Gary Haugland. (Clinical Practice Ser.: No. 37). 256p. 1995. text ed. 34.00 (*0-88048-475-6*, 8475) Am Psychiatric.

Use of Non-Conventional Water Resources in Developing Countries. (Natural Resources-Water Ser.: No. 14). 278p. 1984. 27.00 (*92-1-104234-8*, 84.II.A.14) UN.

Use of Non-Lethal Force: A Manual. 1991. lib. bdg. 79.95 (*0-8490-5167-3*) Gordon Pr.

Use of Nuclear Meters in Soils Investigations. P. C. Smith et al. LC 67-13261. (American Society for Testing & Materials Special Technical Publication Ser.: Special Technical Publication, No. 412). 142p. reprint ed. pap. 40.50 (*0-317-11246-5*, 2000938) Bks Demand.

Use of Numbers & Quantifications in the Assyrian Royal Inscriptions. Marco De Odorico. (State Archives of Assyria Ser.: Vol. 3). xxxii, 206p. 1995. pap. 37.50 (*951-45-7125-8*, Pub. by Neo-Assyrian Text FI) Eisenbrauns.

Use of Optical Disks for Public Records. C18.2 Committee on Digital Imaging for Public Records Staff. (Technical Reports). (Illus.). (Orig.). (C). 1995. 45.00 (*0-89258-214-6*, TR25) Assn Inform & Image Mgmt.

*__Use of Oversize Hobs to Cut Worm Gears.__ John R. Colbourne. (1989 Fall Technical Meeting). 1989. pap. text ed. 30.00 (*1-55589-534-4*) AGMA.

Use of Ozone in Medicine: A Practical Handbook. 2nd ed. Renate Viebahn. (Illus.). 187p. (Orig.). (GER.). 1994. pap. text ed. 29.95 (*3-7760-1481-4*, Pub. by K F Haug Pubs) Medicina Bio.

Use of Ozone in the Treatment of Swimming Pool Waters: Proceedings of 6th Ozone World Congress Ozone-Chlorine Dioxide Oxidation Products of Organic Materials - Ozone Systems Design Guidance Manual. 1990. 50.00 (*0-317-07462-8*) Pan Am Intl Ozone.

Use of Performance Indicators in Higher Education: A Critical Analysis of Developing Practice. Martin Cave et al. (Higher Education Policy Ser.: No. 34). 160p. 1996. pap. 34.95 (*1-85302-345-0*, Pub. by J Kingsley Pubs UK) Taylor & Francis.

Use of Performance Indicators in Higher Education: A Critical Analysis of Developing Practice. 2nd ed. Martin Cave et al. (Higher Education Policy Ser.: No. 3). 144p. 1991. 51.00 (*1-85302-518-6*) Taylor & Francis.

Use of Performance Measures. James B. Edwards. 114p. 1985. pap. 20.00 (*0-86641-129-1*, 85168) Inst Mgmt Account.

Use of Personal Monitors to Estimate Effective Dose Equivalent & Effective Dose to Workers for External Exposure to Low-LET Radiation. LC 95-26433. (NCRP Reports: Vol. 122). 64p. (Orig.). 1995. pap. 25.00 (*0-929600-50-9*) NCRP Pubns.

Use of Personality Measures in the Leadership Development Program. David Campbell & Ellen Van Velsor. (Special Reports: No. 308G). 72p. 1985. pap. 10. 00 (*0-912879-57-2*) Ctr Creat Leader.

Use of Personnel in Child Welfare Agencies: Proceedings of the Arden House Conference, October 1966. Arden House Conference Staff. Ed. by Helen Fradkin. 1966. 2.00 (*0-686-16767-8*) Univ Bk Serv.

Use of Phosphate Rock for Sustainable Agriculture in West Africa. Ed. by Henry Gerner & A. Uzo Mokwunye. LC 95-13400. (Miscellaneous Fertilizer Sector Studies: No. 11). (ENG & FRE.). 1995. write for info. (*0-88090-111-X*) Intl Fertilizer.

Use of Physicians' Services by Low-Income Children. Margo L. Rosenbach. LC 92-48901. (Children of Poverty Ser.). 200p. 1993. text ed. 56.00 (*0-8153-1113-3*) Garland.

*__Use of Plane Parallel Ionization Chambers in High Energy Electron & Photon Beams.__ International Atomic Energy Agency Staff. (Technical Report Ser.: No. 381). 125p. 1996. pap. 50.00 (*92-0-104896-3*, STI/DOC/381, Pub. by IAEA AU) Bernan Associates.

Use of Plant Genetic Resources. Ed. by A. H. Brown et al. 376p. (C). 1989. pap. text ed. 25.95 (*0-521-36886-3*) Cambridge U Pr.

Use of Plant Genetic Resources. Ed. by A. H. Brown et al. 376p. (C). 1989. text ed. 69.95 (*0-521-34584-7*) Cambridge U Pr.

Use of Plant Introductions in Cultivar Development. 182p. 1991. 30.00 (*0-89118-528-3*) Soil Sci Soc Am.

Use of Plastics & Plastic Composites: Materials & Mechanical Issues. Ed. by V. K. Stokes. LC 93-73609. 677p. pap. 100.00 (*0-7918-1252-9*) ASME.

Use of Plastics in Agriculture: Proceedings of the XI International Congress, 26 February - 2 March 1990, 2 vols. (Illus.). 1300p. (C). 1990. Set. text ed. 95.00 (*90-6191-998-3*, Pub. by A A Balkema NE) Ashgate Pub Co.

Use of Plastics Materials in Building. EEMUA Staff. 1973. 135.00 (*0-85931-082-5*, Pub. by EEMUA UK) St Mut.

Use of Poetry & the Use of Criticism. T. S. Eliot. 160p. 1986. pap. text ed. 11.95 (*0-674-93150-5*) HUP.

Use of Polymers in Highway Concrete. (National Cooperative Highway Research Program Report Ser.: No. 190). 77p. 1978. 5.60 (*0-309-02778-0*) Transport Res Bd.

Use of Prestressed Concrete & Epoxies to Expedite Construction of I-87. (PCI Journal Reprints Ser.). 16p. 1967. pap. 12.00 (*0-686-39993-5*, JR45) P-PCI.

Use of Probabilistic Safety Assessment for Operational Safety. IAEA Staff. 859p. 1992. pap. 300.00 (*92-0-000292-7*, STI/PUB/878, Pub. by IAEA AU) Bernan Associates.

Use of Projective Geometry in Computer Graphics. I. Herman. Ed. by G. Goos & J. Hartmanis. (Lecture Notes in Computer Science Ser.: Vol. 564). viii, 146p. 1992. 35.00 (*0-387-55075-5*) Spr-Verlag.

*__Use of Projective Techniques with Persons with Mental Retardation: A Guide for Assessment Instrument Selection.__ Paul E. Panek. LC 96-53508. (Illus.). 188p. 1997. text ed. 45.95 (*0-398-06756-2*); pap. text ed. 33.95 (*0-398-06757-0*) C C Thomas.

Use of Pspice in Circuit Analysis. Franz Monssen. 1992. pap. text ed. 47.00 (*0-675-21376-2*, Merrill Coll) P-H.

Use of Psychological Testing for Treatment Planning & Outcome Assessment. Ed. by Mark E. Maruish. 624p. 1994. text ed. 135.00 (*0-8058-1162-1*) L Erlbaum Assocs.

Use of Psychotropic Drugs in the Medically Ill. Ed. by G. A. Fava & H. Freyberger. (Journal: Psychotherapy & Psychosomatics: Vol. 49, No. 2, 1988). (Illus.). 80p. 1988. pap. 45.00 (*3-8055-4927-X*) S Karger.

Use of Public Attitude Assessment in the Development of Emergency Service Policy for the City of Austin, Texas. William E. Coll. 218p. 1989. pap. 10.00 (*0-89940-865-6*) LBJ Sch Pub Aff.

Use of Pulsating Stars in Fundamental Problems of Astronomy: International Astronomical Union Colloquium, No. 111. Ed. by Edward G. Schmidt. (Illus.). 30p. (C). 1990. 64.95 (*0-521-37023-X*) Cambridge U Pr.

Use of Pyrotechnics Before a Proximate Audience. 17p. 1992. 16.75 (*0-685-64962-8*, 1126-92) Natl Fire Prot.

Use of Quinolones in Travel Medicine: Second Conference on International Travel Medicine. Ed. by H. L. DuPont. (Illus.). 56p. 1992. 21.95 (*0-387-54778-9*) Spr-Verlag.

Use of Radioactive Isotopes in the Life Sciences. J. M. Chapman & G. Ayrey. (Illus.). (C). 1981. pap. text ed. 24.95 (*0-04-570012-5*) Routledge Chapman & Hall.

Use of Reclaimed Water & Sludge in Food Crop Production. National Research Council Staff. 192p. (Orig.). 1996. pap. text ed. 29.00 (*0-309-05479-6*) Natl Acad Pr.

*__Use of Recycled-Concrete Aggregate from Concrete Exhibiting Alkali-Silica Reactivity.__ 14p. 1996. pap. 19. 00 (*0-89312-145-2*, RD114T) Portland Cement.

*__Use of Remote Sensing in the Modeling of Forest Productivity.__ Henry L. Gholz et al. LC 96-38601. (Forest Resources Ser.). 1996. write for info. (*0-07-923478-X*) McGraw.

*__Use of Remote Sensing in the Modeling of Forest Productivity.__ Ed. by Henry L. Gholz. LC 96-38601. (Forestry Sciences Ser.). 336p. (C). 1996. lib. bdg. 162. 50 (*0-7923-4278-X*) Kluwer Ac.

Use of Resealed Erythrocytes As Carriers & Bioreactors. Ed. by M. Magnani & J. R. DeLoach. (Advances in Experimental Medicine & Biology Ser.: Vol. 326). (Illus.). 357p. (C). 1993. 95.00 (*0-306-44345-7*, Plenum Pr) Plenum.

Use of Research in Social Work Practice: A Case Example from School Social Work. Nancy F. Chavkin. LC 93-19111. 168p. 1993. text ed. 59.95 (*0-275-94648-7*, C4648, Praeger Pubs) Greenwood.

Use of Reservoir Water for Hydroelectric Power Generation. John E. Gessford. Ed. by Stuart Bruchey. LC 78-22684. (Energy in the American Economy Ser.). (Illus.). 1979. lib. bdg. 15.95 (*0-405-11987-9*) Ayer.

Use of Restricted Significance Tests in Clinical Trials. D. Salsburg & Stephen E. Fienberg. Ed. by J. O. Berger et al. (Series in Statistics in the Health Sciences). (Illus.). 184p. 1992. 53.95 (*0-387-97798-8*) Spr-Verlag.

Use of Riches. J. I. Stewart. (Phoenix Fiction Ser.). 246p. 1983. pap. 8.50 (*0-226-77403-1*) U Ch Pr.

U V

An Asterisk (*) at the beginning of an entry indicates that the title is appearing in BIP for the first time.

Use of Saline Water for Crop Production. F.A.O. Staff et al. 1994. pap. 125.00 (*81-7233-093-6*, Pub. by Scientific Pubs II) St Mut.

Use of Saline Waters for Crop Production. J. D. Rhoades et al. (Irrigation & Drainage Papers: No. 48). 149p. 1992. pap. 17.00 (*92-5-103237-8*, F32378, Pub. by FAO IT) Bernan Associates.

Use of Sampling in Archaeological Survey. James W. Mueller. (Memoir Ser.: No. 28). 104p. 1974. 6.00 (*0-932839-07-X*) Soc Am Arch.

Use of Scripture in the Damascus Document 1-8, 19-20. Jonathan G. Campbell. LC 95-5898. (Beihefte zur Zeitschrift fuer die Alttestamentliche Wissenschaft Ser.: No. 228). 230p. 1995. lib. bdg. 85.50 (*3-11-014240-6*) De Gruyter.

Use of Selected Medical Device Implants in the United States, 1988: PHS 91-1250. No. 191. 1991. write for info. (*0-318-69598-7*) Natl Ctr Health Stats.

Use of Self in Therapy. Virginia M. Satir. LC 87-90. (Journal of Psychotherapy & the Family: Vol. 3, No. 1). 155p. (Orig.). 1987. text ed. 39.95 (*0-86656-544-2*); pap. text ed. 19.95 (*0-86656-545-0*) Haworth Pr.

Use of Shotcrete for Underground Structural Support Staff: Proceedings of the Engineering Foundation Conference, Berwick Academy, South Berwick, Maine, July 16-20, 1973 - with the Cooperation of ASCE & ACI. Engineering Foundation Conference on Use of Shotcrete for Underground Structural Support Staff. (American Concrete Institute Publication Ser.: SP-45). (Illus.). 475p. reprint ed. pap. 135.40 (*0-317-10278-8*, 2019550) Bks Demand.

Use of Silence. Geoffrey Hoyland. (C). 1955. pap. 3.00 (*0-87574-083-9*) Pendle Hill.

Use of Small-Scale Specimens for Testing Irradiated Material- STP 888. Ed. by W. R. Corwin & G. E. Lucas. LC 85-27487. (Illus.). 375p. 1986. text ed. 52.00 (*0-8031-0440-5*, 04-888000-35) ASTM.

Use of Social Research in Community Education Programme (UNESCO) (Education Studies & Documents: No. 10). 1974. reprint ed. pap. 25.00 (*0-8115-1334-3*) Periodicals Srv.

***Use of Social Science Data in Supreme Court Decisions.** Rosemary J. Erickson & Rita J. Simon. LC 97-4657. 1998. write for info. (*0-252-02355-2*); pap. write for info. (*0-252-06661-8*) U of Ill Pr.

Use of Soil for Treatment & Final Disposal Effluents & Sludge: Proceedings of an IAWPRC Seminar Held in Salvador, Brazil, 13-15 August 1986. Ed. by P. R. Oliveira & S. A. Almeida. LC 82-645900. (Water Science & Technology Ser.: Vol. 19). (Illus.). 224p. 1988. pap. 61.00 (*0-08-035590-0*, Pergamon Pr) Elsevier.

Use of Space Dependent on Development of Space Law. 137p. (Orig.). (C). 1994. pap. text ed. 50.00 (*0-941375-88-9*) DIANE Pub.

Use of Space Systems for Planetary Geology & Geophysics. Ed. by Robert D. Enzmann. (Science & Technology Ser.: Vol. 17). 1967. 45.00 (*0-87703-045-6*); suppl. ed. 15.00 incl. fiche (*0-87703-135-5*) Univelt Inc.

Use of "Spoudaiogeloion" in Greek & Roman Literature. Lawrence Giangrande. LC 78-182466. (Studies in Classical Literature: Vol. 6). 1972. pap. text ed. 21.55 (*3-10-800271-6*) Mouton.

Use of State High School Examinations As an Instrument for Judging the Work of Teachers. Henry M. Davis. LC 77-176713. (Columbia University. Teachers College. Contributions to Education Ser.: No. 611). reprint ed. 37.50 (*0-404-55611-6*) AMS Pr.

Use of Statistics in Equal Employment Opportunity Litigation. Walter B. Connolly, Jr. & David W. Peterson. 750p. 1980. ring bd. 90.00 (*0-318-20279-4*, 00553) NY Law Pub.

Use of Statistics to Develop & Evaluate Analytical Methods. Grant Wernimont & William Spendley. (Illus.). xvi, 183p. 1985. pap. 65.00 (*0-935584-31-5*) AOAC Intl.

Use of Steel. J. Barba. (Works of J. Barba). ix, 110p. 1985. reprint ed. lib. bdg. 39.00 (*0-932051-61-8*) Rprt Serv.

Use of Subcontractors in Management Consulting. James H. Kennedy. 1987. ring bd. 89.00 (*0-916654-49-4*) Kennedy Info.

***Use of Sugars & Other Carbohydrates in the Food Industry: A Collection of Papers.** American Chemical Society, Division of Agricultural & Food Chemistry Staff. LC 55-4135. (Advances in Chemistry Ser.: No. 12). (Illus.). 146p. 1955. reprint ed. pap. 41.70 (*0-608-03266-2*, 2063785) Bks Demand.

Use of Superconductivity in Energy Storage. P. Komarek & W. Maurer. 425p. 1995. text ed. 124.00 (*981-02-2182-7*) World Scientific Pub.

Use of Surface Enhanced Raman Spectroscopy in the Study of Corrosion, Inhibition & Passivation Process on Copper & Copper-Based Alloys. SRI International Staff. 41p. 1983. write for info. (*0-318-60415-9*) Intl Copper.

***Use of Synthetic Antigens for Diagnosis of Infectious Diseases: Report of a WHO Scientific Group, 1987.** (Technical Report Ser.: No. 784). 74p. 1989. pap. text ed. 9.00 (*92-4-120784-1*, 1100784) World Health.

Use of Synthetic Environments for Corrosion Testing. Ed. by P. E. Francis & T. S. Lee. (Special Technical Publication Ser.: No. 970). (Illus.). 300p. 1988. text ed. 42.00 (*0-8031-0977-6*, 04-970000-27) ASTM.

***Use of Tapered Roller Bearings in Gear Reduction Units.** S. M. Weckstein. (Technical Papers). 1936. pap. text ed. 30.00 (*1-55589-362-7*) AGMA.

Use of Technology in the Care of the Elderly & the Disabled. Ed. by Jean Bray & Sheila Wright. LC 80-17847. xii, 267p. 1980. text ed. 55.00 (*0-313-22616-4*, BTC/, Greenwood Pr) Greenwood.

Use of the Army in Certain of the Southern States: 44th Congress, Second Session, Executive Document No. 30. U. S. House of Representatives Staff. LC 75-90201. (Mass Violence in America Ser.). 1969. reprint ed. 21.95 (*0-405-01314-0*) Ayer.

Use of the Bible in Milton's Prose. Harris F. Fletcher. 1973. lib. bdg. 250.00 (*0-87968-014-8*) Gordon Pr.

Use of the Bible in Milton's Prose. H. Fletcher. LC 75-95425. (Studies in Milton: No. 22). (C). 1970. reprint ed. lib. bdg. 75.00 (*0-8383-0974-7*) M S G Haskell Hse.

Use of the Bible in Milton's Prose, with an Index of the Biblical Quotations & Citations Arranged in the Chronological Order of the Prose Works. Harris F. Fletcher. (BCL1-PR English Literature Ser.). 176p. 1992. reprint ed. lib. bdg. 69.00 (*0-7812-7383-8*) Rprt Serv.

Use of the Body in Relation to the Mind. George Moore. LC 78-72812. reprint ed. 32.50 (*0-404-60882-5*) AMS Pr.

Use of the Eyes in Movement. Jack Heggie. 54p. (Orig.). 1985. pap. 9.95 (*0-939866-03-X*) Woodstone Bks.

Use of the Film. Basil Wright. LC 75-169356. (Arno Press Cinema Program Ser.). 76p. 1972. reprint ed. 7.00 (*0-405-03927-1*) Ayer.

Use of the Infinitive Instead of a Finite Verb in French. Benjamin F. Luker. LC 16-16932. (Columbia University. Studies in Romance Philology & Literature: No. 18). reprint ed. 27.50 (*0-404-50618-6*) AMS Pr.

Use of the Labscope & Auto Diagnosis. (C). 1997. pap. text ed. 19.95 (*0-8273-7903-X*) Delmar.

Use of the Labscope & Auto Diagnosis. (C). 1997. teacher ed., pap. text ed. 69.95 (*0-8273-7904-8*) Delmar.

Use of the Microcomputer in Teaching & Learning. J. J. Beishuizen et al. xiv, 258p. 1988. 42.50 (*90-265-0894-8*) Swets.

Use of the Mind in the Martial Arts. 1991. lib. bdg. 79.95 (*0-8490-4754-4*) Gordon Pr.

Use of the Oxygen Electrode & Fluorescence Probes in Simple Measurements of Photosynthesis. David Walker. 204p. (C). 1991. text ed. 120.00 (*1-870232-00-3*, Pub. by Surrey Beatty & Sons AT) St Mut.

Use of the Physical & Social Environment of the General Hospital for Therapeutic Purposes see Newer Dimensions of Patient Care

Use of the Self: Countertransference & Communication in the Analytic Situation. Theodore Jacobs. LC 90-4926. 224p. 1991. 35.00 (*0-8236-6710-3*) Intl Univs Pr.

Use of Time: Daily Activities of Urban & Suburban Populations in Twelve Countries. Ed. by Alexander Szalai et al. 1972. text ed. 126.95 (*90-279-7146-3*) Mouton.

Use of Time & Resources by Provisioned Troops of Monkeys: Social Behaviour, Time & Energy in the Barbary Macaque (Macaca Sylanus L.) at Gibraltar. John E. Fa. (Contributions to Primatology Ser.: Vol. 23). (Illus.). xii, 380p. 1986. 138.50 (*3-8055-4263-1*) S Karger.

Use of Tissue Culture & Photoplasts in Plant Pathology. Ed. by John P. Helgeson & B. J. Deverall. 208p. 1983. text ed. 69.00 (*0-12-338650-0*) Acad Pr.

Use of Tools by Human & Non-Human Primates. Ed. by Arlette Berthelet & Jean Chavaillon. LC 92-26903. (Fyssen Foundation Symposium Ser.). (Illus.). 432p. 1993. 105.00 (*0-19-852263-0*) OUP.

Use of Tora by Isaiah: His Debate with the Wisdom Tradition. Joseph Jensen. LC 73-83134. (Catholic Biblical Quarterly Monographs: No. 3). ix, 156p. 1973. 3.00 (*0-915170-02-7*) Catholic Bibl Assn.

Use of Underground Space to Achieve National Goals. 353p. 1972. pap. 24.00 (*0-87262-045-X*) Am Soc Civil Eng.

Use of Vegetation in Civil Engineering. N. J. Coppin et al. (Illus.). 292p. 1990. 84.95 (*0-408-03849-7*) Buttrwrth-Heinemann.

Use of Vernacular Languages in Education. United Nations Educational, Scientific & Cultural Organization Staff. Ed. by Francesco Cordasco. LC 77-90566. (Bilingual-Bicultural Education in the U. S. Ser.). 1978. reprint ed. lib. bdg. 21.95 (*0-405-11105-3*) Ayer.

Use of Vibration Measurements in Structural Evaluation. Ed. by John R. Hall, Jr. 64p. 1987. 12.00 (*0-87262-586-9*) Am Soc Civil Eng.

***Use of Victim-Offender Communication in the Treatment of Sexual Abuse: Three Intervention Models.** W. Bera et al. 112p. (Orig.). 1990. pap. 17.50 (*1-884444-29-6*) Safer Soc.

Use of Viruses for the Control of Insect Pests & Disease Vectors: Report of the FAO-WHO Meeting on Insect Viruses, Geneva, 1972. FAO-WHO Meeting on Insect Viruses Staff. (Technical Report Ser.: No. 531). 1973. pap. text ed. 4.00 (*92-4-120531-8*, 1100531) World Health.

Use of Waste & Recycled Materials As Aggregaes: Standards & Specifications. 70p. 1995. pap. 65.00 (*0-11-752953-2*, HM29532, Pub. by Stationery Ofc UK) Bernan Associates.

Use of Waste Materials in Highway Construction. Imtiaz Ahmed. LC 92-541. (Illus.). 114p. 1993. 45.00 (*0-8155-1315-1*) Noyes.

Use of Waste Materials in Hot-Mix Asphalt. Ed. by Fred H. Waller. LC 93-23992. (STP Ser.: Vol. 1193). (Illus.). 306p. 1993. text ed. 56.00 (*0-8031-1881-3*, 04-011930-08) ASTM.

Use of Welsh. Ed. by Martin J. Ball. 1988. 99.00 (*0-905028-99-6*, Pub. by Multilingual Matters UK); pap. 39.95 (*0-905028-98-8*, Pub. by Multilingual Matters UK) Taylor & Francis.

Use of Wetlands for Controlling Stormwater Pollution. Eric W. Strecker et al. 66p. (Orig.). 1992. pap. 10.00 (*0-614-14302-0*) Terrene Inst.

Use of Wetlands for Water Pollution Control. 261p. 1981. 25.00 (*0-317-05652-2*, P90004HAZ) Assn Bay Area.

Use of Words in Context: The Vocabulary of College Students. John W. Black et al. (Cognition & Language: A Series in Psycholinguistics). 276p. 1985. 70.00 (*0-306-42206-9*, Plenum Pr) Plenum.

Use of X-Ray Diffraction in the Study of Protein & Nucleic Acid Structure. rev. ed. K. C. Holmes & D. M. Blow. Ed. by D. Glick. LC 79-20293. 132p. 1979. lib. bdg. 15.00 (*0-89874-046-0*) Krieger.

Use of Yeast Biomass in Food Production. Halasz. 1990. 230.00 (*0-8493-5866-3*, TP248) CRC Pr.

USE Quick Reference Guide. Mark Hanna. 135p. (C). 1993. pap. 19.95 (*0-940479-03-6*) M Hanna & Assocs.

Use the News: Teaching Basic Skills with Creative Newspaper Activities. Joan Groeber. Ed. by Catherine Aldy. (Illus.). 96p. (Orig.). 1995. pap. text ed. 9.95 (*0-86530-336-3*, IP 336-3) Incentive Pubns.

Use Their Heads. Tristan Howard. (Leftovers Ser.: No. 3). 1996. pap. text ed. 2.99 (*0-590-89896-5*) Scholastic Inc.

Use Value Assessment: Its Causes, Its Characteristics, Its Effects. Gregory Beattie & Richard Ransom. (Land Policy Roundtable Case Studies Ser.: No. 302). 47p. reprint ed. pap. 25.00 (*0-7837-2157-9*, 2042459) Bks Demand.

Use-Wear Analysis of Flaked Stone Tools. Patrick Vaughan. LC 85-989. 204p. 1985. 54.50 (*0-8165-0861-5*) U of Ariz Pr.

Use with Care: Managing Australia's Natural Resources in the Twenty-First Century. Doug Cocks. (Illus.). pap. 32.95 (*0-86840-308-3*, Pub. by New South Wales Univ Pr AT) Intl Spec Bk.

Use Your Anger: A Woman's Guide to Empowerment. Thomas Jefferson & Cheryl Jefferson. 320p. 1996. pap. 12.00 (*0-671-51973-5*) PB.

Use Your Computer. Ronald W. Fry. (How to Study Ser.). 128p. (Orig.). 1996. pap. 6.99 (*1-56414-235-3*) Career Pr Inc.

Use Your Foreign Language! Raymond G. Scheuerman. 95p. (Orig.). 1991. pap. write for info. (*0-9626091-0-2*) Bilingual Comns Serv.

Use Your Head, Dear. Aliki. LC 82-11911. (Illus.). 48p. (J). (gr. k-3). 1983. lib. bdg. 15.93 (*0-688-01812-2*) Greenwillow.

***Use Your Head, Molly Malone!** Linda L. Maifair. LC 96-37828. (Winners! Ser.). 64p. (Orig.). (J). (gr. 2-5). 1997. pap. 3.99 (*0-310-20704-5*) Zondervan.

Use Your Illusion I & II (Piano - Vocal) Guns N' Roses. Ed. by Mark Phillips & Milton Okun. (Illus.). 68p. (Orig.). 1994. pap. text ed. 17.95 (*0-89524-734-8*) Cherry Lane.

Use Your Perfect Memory. 2nd ed. Tony Buzan. (Illus.). 256p. 1987. pap. 10.95 (*0-525-48284-9*, 01063-320, Dutton) NAL-Dutton.

Use Your Perfect Memory. 3rd ed. Tony Buzan. (Illus.). 1991. pap. 12.95 (*0-452-26606-8*, Plume) NAL-Dutton.

Use Your Perfect Memory: A Complete Program of New Techniques for Remembering. Tony Buzan. (Illus.). 288p. 1984. pap. 9.95 (*0-525-48112-5*, 0966-290, Dutton) NAL-Dutton.

Useable Portable Guide: Microsoft Windows, WordPerfect for Windows & Excel. Jon Haber & Herbert R. Haber. 448p. 1992. 19.00 (*1-55623-619-0*) Irwin Prof Pubng.

Useable Portable Guide: Microsoft Windows 3, Word for Windows & Excel. Jon Haber & Herbert R. Haber. Ed. by Susan Glinert. 300p. 1992. per. 19.00 (*1-55623-618-2*) Irwin Prof Pubng.

Useable Portable Guide: Microsoft Windows 3, Word for Windows & Excel. Jon Haber & Herbert R. Haber. Ed. by Susan Glinert. 300p. 1992. text ed. 95.00 (*1-55623-631-X*) Irwin Prof Pubng.

Useable Portable Guide: Microsoft Windows 3, WordPerfect for Windows, & Excel. Jon Haber & Herbert R. Haber. 1992. text ed. 95.00 (*1-55623-632-8*) Irwin Prof Pubng.

Useable Portable Guide: MS-DOS - WordPerfect - Lotus 1-2-3, Bryant & Stratton Business Institute Edition. Jon Haber & Herbert Haber. (C). 1994. 20.15 (*0-7863-0468-5*) Irwin Prof Pubng.

Useable Portable Guide: MS-DOS, WordPerfect, & Lotus 1-2-3. Jon Haber & Herbert R. Haber. Ed. by Susan Glinert. 300p. 1991. per. 19.00 (*1-55623-617-4*); 95.00 (*1-55623-630-1*) Irwin Prof Pubng.

Useable Portable Guide: Multimate Advantage. Jon Haber & Herbert Haber. 1989. pap. 5.95 (*0-685-35391-5*) Useable Portable Pubns.

Useable Portable Guide: WordPerfect 5.0 & 5.1. Jon Haber & Herbert Haber. 1989. pap. 5.95 (*0-685-35392-3*) Useable Portable Pubns.

***Used & Abused.** Pam Mitchell. Ed. by Publishers Design Works Staff. (Illus.). 169p. (Orig.). 1996. pap. 12.95 (*0-9653527-0-6*) Bordertown Pr.

***Used & Rare.** Goldstone. LC 96-30081. 1997. 22.95 (*0-312-15682-0*) St Martin.

Used Book Lover's Guide to New England. 2nd rev. ed. David S. Siegel & Susan Siegel. 383p. (Orig.). 1995. pap. 16.95 (*0-9634112-4-1*) Book Hunter Pr.

Used Book Lover's Guide to the Central States. David S. Siegel & Susan Siegel. 464p. (Orig.). 1996. pap. 18.95 (*0-9634112-6-8*) Book Hunter Pr.

***Used Book Lover's Guide to the Mid Atlantic States: New York, New Jersey, Pennsylvania & Delaware.** rev. ed. David S. Siegel & Susan Siegel. 410p. 1997. pap. 18.95 (*0-9634112-7-6*) Book Hunter Pr.

Used Book Lover's Guide to the Midwest. David S. Siegel & Susan Siegel. 449p. (Orig.). 1994. pap. 17.95 (*0-9634112-3-3*) Book Hunter Pr.

Used Book Lover's Guide to the Pacific Coast States. David S. Siegel & Susan Siegel. 474p. (Orig.). 1995. pap. 18.95 (*0-9634112-5-X*) Book Hunter Pr.

Used Book Lover's Guide to the South Atlantic States: Maryland, Washington, DC, Virginia, North Carolina, South Carolina, Georgia & Florida. David S. Siegel & Susan Siegel. 316p. (Orig.). 1994. pap. 15.95 (*0-9634112-2-5*) Book Hunter Pr.

***Used Book Lover's Guide to the South Atlantic States: Maryland, Washington, DC, Virginia, North Carolina, South Carolina, Georgia & Florida.** rev. ed. David S. Siegel & Susan Siegel. 316p. 1998. pap. 17.95 (*0-9634112-8-4*) Book Hunter Pr.

Used Book Price Guide: Five Year Edition, 2 vols., Set. Ed. by Mildred S. Mandeville. Incl. A-K May 1967 to May 1972. 376p. 1977. (*0-318-55347-3*); L-Z May 1968 to May 1973. 368p. 1977. reprint ed. (*0-911182-72-1*); 1977. 59.00 (*0-911182-73-X*) Price Guide.

Used Book Price Guide: Five Year Edition, 1977 Supplement. Ed. by Mildred S. Mandeville. 479p. 1977. 49.00 (*0-911182-76-4*) Price Guide.

Used Book Price Guide: Five Year, 1983 Edition. Ed. by Mildred S. Mandeville. 536p. 1983. 79.00 (*0-685-05650-3*) Price Guide.

Used Book Sales: Less Work & Better Profits. D. Keith Crotz. 80p. 1995. pap. 11.00 (*0-917846-32-X*, 95584) Highsmith Pr.

Used Car Book: 1996 Edition. Consumer Guide Edition Staff. 1996. pap. 8.99 (*0-451-18738-5*, Sig) NAL-Dutton.

Used Car Book, 1993. Consumer Guide Editors. (Illus.). 192p. (Orig.). 1993. pap. 7.99 (*0-451-82259-5*, 4014100, Sig) NAL-Dutton.

Used Car Book, 1995. Consumer Guide Editors. 160p. (Orig.). 1995. pap. 7.99 (*0-451-82298-6*, Sig) NAL-Dutton.

***Used Car Book, 1997-1998.** Jack Gillis. 1997. pap. text ed. 12.95 (*0-06-273452-0*, Harper Ref) HarpC.

***Used Car Book, 1998.** Jack Gillis. 224p. 1998. pap. 12.95 (*0-06-273444-X*, PL) HarpC.

***Used Car Book, 1999.** Jack Gillis. 224p. Date not set. pap. 12.95 (*0-06-273445-8*, PL) HarpC.

Used Car Buyer's Manual: How to Find the Best Buy on a Used Car. David J. Buechel. LC 95-70448. (Illus.). 176p. (Orig.). 1995. pap. 9.95 (*0-9647780-0-9*) Pyramid West Pubng.

Used Car Buyer's Manual II: How to Get the Best Buy on a Private-Party Sale. David J. Buechel. LC 96-92359. (Illus.). 123p. (Orig.). 1996. pap. 7.95 (*0-9647780-1-7*) Pyramid West Pubng.

***Used Car Buying Guide.** Consumer Reports Staff. 1997. pap. 8.99 (*0-89043-861-7*) Consumer Reports.

Used Car Buying Guide 1996. 1996. pap. 8.99 (*0-89043-816-1*) Consumer Reports.

***Used Car Buying Guide 1997.** Consumer Guide Editorial Staff. 1997. pap. 8.99 (*0-451-82338-9*) NAL-Dutton.

Used Car for Sale. Lewis J. Carlino. 1959. pap. 3.25 (*0-8222-1197-1*) Dramatists Play.

***Used Car Prices: U. S. & Import Cars, Vans & Trucks, 1983-1996.** Vechicle Market Research Staff. (VMR Standard Auto Guides Ser.). 1997. pap. text ed. 4.99 (*1-883899-15-X*) VMR Intl.

***Used Car Reliability & Safety Guide.** 2nd ed. Adam Berliant. 384p. 1997. pap. 14.99 (*1-55870-438-8*, Betrwy Bks) F & W Pubns Inc.

Used Car Seller's Guide. Kirk Martensen. 144p. (Orig.). 1990. pap. text ed. 6.95 (*0-9624853-0-6*) Green Light Pr.

Used Cars: How to Buy One. rev. ed. Darrell B. Parrish. (Illus.). 235p. 1995. mass mkt. 5.95 (*0-9612322-9-3*) Bk Express.

***Used Cars: How to Buy One.** 3rd rev. ed. Illus. by Richard Chan. 250p. 1997. pap. 9.95 (*0-9612322-6-9*) Bk Express.

***Used Cars 1997.** Consumer Guide Staff. 1997. pap. 6.99 (*0-451-19199-4*, Sig) NAL-Dutton.

Used Dry Cell Batteries: Is a Collection Program Right for Your Community? (Illus.). 56p. (Orig.). (YA). (gr. 12 up). 1994. pap. text ed. 25.00 (*0-7881-0835-2*) DIANE Pub.

Used Guns: How to Buy & Sell Them. 1991. lib. bdg. 75.00 (*0-8490-4983-0*) Gordon Pr.

Used Intercity Bus Pricing 1978-1986. Larry Plachno. Ed. by Jackie Plachno. LC 87-19189. (Illus.). 40p. 1987. pap. 20.00 (*0-933449-03-8*) Transportation.

***Used Math.** Clifford E. Swartz. (Illus.). 264p. (Orig.). 1993. pap. 25.00 (*0-917853-50-4*, OP59) Am Assn Physics.

Used Math for the First Two Years of College Science. Clifford E. Swartz. (Illus.). 320p. 1973. pap. write for info. (*0-13-939736-1*) P-H.

Used Numbers - Measuring: From Paces to Feet. Corwin et al. 100p. 1990. 12.95 (*0-86651-503-8*, DS01025) Seymour Pubns.

Used Oil: Disposal Options, Management Practices & Potential Liability. 3rd ed. John J. Nolan. Ed. by Law Firm of Schmeltzer, Aptaker & Sheppard Staff. 321p. 1990. 69.00 (*0-86587-234-1*) Gov Insts.

Used Oil Management: A Best Management Practices Handbook. 100p. 1993. pap. text ed. 17.95 (*0-88711-208-0*) Am Trucking Assns.

Used Sorbent Disposal: Is It a Hazardous Waste? T. D. Herod. 75p. 1992. pap. 49.95 (*1-878985-03-5*) Compliance Tech.

Used Tire Recycling & Resource Recovery. Richard K. Miller & Marcia E. Rupnow. LC 90-83879. (Survey on Technology & Markets Ser.: No. 175). 50p. 1991. pap. text ed. 200.00 (*1-55865-199-3*) Future Tech Surveys.

Used-to-Be Lovers. Linda L. Miller. 1995. mass mkt. 4.99 (*1-55166-037-7*, 1-66037-2, Mira Bks) Harlequin Bks.

Used to Kill. Lillian O'Donnell. 1995. mass mkt. 4.99 (*0-449-22249-7*, Crest) Fawcett.

Used to Kill. large type ed. Lillian O'Donnell. LC 93-17005. 1993. lib. bdg. 21.95 (*1-56054-736-7*) Thorndike Pr.

An Asterisk (*) at the beginning of an entry indicates that the title is appearing in BIP for the first time.

Used to the Dark. 2nd rev. ed. Vicky J. Edmonds. 112p. 1994. reprint ed. pap. 11.00 (*0-9639918-1-7*) E All Above.

Useful Adversaries: Grand Strategy, Domestic Mobilization, & Sino-American Conflict, 1947-1958. Thomas J. Christensen. LC 96-8082. (Studies in International History & Politics). 352p. 1996. text ed. 49.50 (*0-691-02638-6*); pap. text ed. 19.95 (*0-691-02637-8*) Princeton U Pr.

Useful & Harmful Interactions of Antibiotics. M. Neuman. LC 84-1607. 288p. 1985. 164.00 (*0-8493-6061-7*, CRC Reprint) Franklin.

Useful Animals 1860-1970. John Jesse. (Illus.). 120p. 1987. pap. 15.00 (*0-614-16853-8*, Pub. by R Dennis UK) Antique Collect.

Useful Arts. Jacob Bigelow. LC 72-5034. (Technology & Society Ser.). (Illus.). 762p. 1972. reprint ed. 46.95 (*0-405-04687-1*) Ayer.

Useful Beauty: Turning Practical Items on a Wood Lathe. Photos & Text by Alison Levie. LC 95-22738. (Illus.). 64p. (Orig.). 1995. pap. write for info. (*0-88740-851-6*) Schiffer.

Useful Cobbler: Edmund Burke & the Politics of Progress. James Conniff. LC 93-16994. 363p. (C). 1994. text ed. 59.50 (*0-7914-1843-X*); pap. text ed. 19.95 (*0-7914-1844-8*) State U NY Pr.

Useful Economics. E. C. Harwood. 53p. 1970. 6.00 (*0-318-12796-2*) Am Inst Econ Res.

Useful Gifts. Carole L. Glickfeld. LC 88-17099. (Flannery O'Connor Award for Short Fiction Ser.). 224p. 1989. 19.95 (*0-8203-1041-7*) U of Ga Pr.

Useful Guide to Irish Crochet Lacemaking. Margaret Cussen. 87p. (C). 1989. pap. 40.00 (*0-7223-2096-5*, Pub. by A H S Ltd UK) St Mut.

Useful Information on Alzheimer's Disease: Diagnosis, Causes, Treatment & Research. 1991. lib. bdg. 65.00 (*0-8490-4336-0*) Gordon Pr.

Useful Inheritance: Evolutionary Aspects of the Theory of Knowledge. Nicholas Rescher. LC 89-27509. 148p. (C). 1990. lib. bdg. 46.50 (*0-8476-7615-3*) Rowman.

***Useful Knowledge.** Gertrude Stein. 1998. pap. text ed. 15.95 (*1-886449-63-5*) Barrytown Ltd.

Useful Knowledge. Gertrude Stein. 240p. 1988. reprint ed. 19.95 (*0-88268-075-7*) Station Hill Pr.

Useful Measurements for Violin Makers: A Reference for Shop Use. 3rd rev. ed. LC 89-90382. (Illus.). 46p. 1989. pap. 12.50 (*0-9620673-2-6*) H A Strobel.

Useful Optics. Walter T. Welford. LC 91-8355. (Chicago Lectures in Physics Ser.). (Illus.). 150p. 1991. pap. text ed. 15.00 (*0-226-89306-5*); lib. bdg. 34.50 (*0-226-89305-7*) U Ch Pr.

Useful Palms of the World: A Synoptic Bibliography. Ed. by Hans T. Beck. 752p. 1990. text ed. 58.50 (*0-231-06676-7*) Col U Pr.

Useful Patchwork Gifts. Chuck Nohara. (Illus.). 96p. (Orig.). 1993. pap. 18.95 (*0-87040-907-7*) Japan Pubns USA.

Useful Plant of India. C. H. Drury. 513p. 1991. 225.00 (*81-7089-155-8*, Pub. by Intl Bk Distr II) St Mut.

Useful Plants of Brazil. Walter B. Mors & Carlos T. Rizzini. LC 66-17891. 181p. reprint ed. pap. 51.60 (*0-317-28317-0*, 2016293) Bks Demand.

Useful Plants of India. Ed. by C. H. Drury. (C). 1988. 75.00 (*0-317-92327-7*, Pub. by Scientific UK) St Mut.

Useful Plants of India. Ed. by C. H. Drury. 513p. (C). 1978. text ed. 260.00 (*0-89771-600-0*, Pub. by Intl Bk Distr II) St Mut.

Useful Plants of India. C. H. Drury. 513p. 1978. reprint ed. 260.00 (*0-685-54028-6*, Pub. by Intl Bk Distr II) St Mut.

Useful Plants of India & Pakistan. J. F. Dastur. (C). 1988. 40.00 (*0-317-92328-5*, Pub. by Scientific UK) St Mut.

Useful Plants of Neotropical Origin. H. Brucher. (Illus.). 335p. 1989. 196.95 (*0-387-18743-X*) Spr-Verlag.

Useful Plants of West Tropical Africa Vol. 1: Families A-D. H. M. Burkill. (Illus.). 960p. 1985. 140.00 (*0-947643-01-X*, Pub. by Royal Botnic Grdns UK) Balogh.

***Useful Plants of West Tropical Africa Vol. 2: Families E - I.** H. M. Burkill. xii, 636p. 1994. 100.00 (*0-947643-56-7*, Pub. by Royal Botnic Grdns UK) Balogh.

***Useful Plants of West Tropical Africa Vol. 3: Families J-L.** H. M. Burkill. (Illus.). xi, 855p. 1995. 120.00 (*0-947643-64-8*, Pub. by Royal Botnic Grdns UK) Balogh.

Useful Procedures in Medical Practice. Ed. by Paul W. Roberts. LC 85-4534. (Illus.). 632p. reprint ed. pap. 180.00 (*0-7837-1495-5*, 2057191) Bks Demand.

***Useful Programs for the Psion Series 3a & 3c.** Mike Shaw. (Illus.). 1996. pap. 34.95 (*0-614-30728-7*, Pub. by Capall Bann Pubng UK) Holmes Pub.

Useful Science. Linda A. Wesner. (Illus.). 92p. 1983. 1.25 (*0-88323-132-8*, 222); pap. 4.25 (*0-88323-181-6*, 216) Pendergrass Pub.

Useful Servants: Psychodynamic Theories from a Clinical Perspective. Susan Levine. 320p. 1996. 40.00 (*1-56821-844-3*) Aronson.

***Useful Sinner.** J. David Hawkins. 112p. (Orig.). 1996. pap. 6.95 (*0-88028-176-6*, 1395) Forward Movement.

Useful Spanish for Medical & Hospital Personnel. Francesco Cordasco. 146p. 1977. pap. 14.95 (*1-879170-62-0*) St Aedans Pr & Bk.

Useful Spelling: Levels 2-8. Bradley M. Loomer & Maxine G. Strege. (J). (gr. 2-8). 1990. write for info. (*1-878712-03-9*) Useful Lrn.

Useful Tables. Nathaniel Bowditch. (Works of Nathaniel Bowditch). 1989. reprint ed. lib. bdg. 79.00 (*0-7812-2023-8*) Rprt Serv.

Useful Toil: Autobiographies of Working People from the 1820s to the 1920s. John Burnett. LC 93-39961. 352p. (C). 1994. pap. 22.95 (*0-415-10399-1*, B4447) Routledge.

Useful Toil: Autobiographies of Working People from the 1820s to the 1920s. John Burnett. LC 93-39961. 400p. (C). (gr. 13). 1994. text ed. 85.00 (*0-415-10398-3*, B4443) Routledge.

Useful Wild Plants of Texas, the Southeastern & Southwestern United States, the Southern Plains, & Northern Mexico. Scooter Cheatham et al. LC 95-16542. 1995. 125.00 (*1-887292-01-2*) Useful Wild Plants.

Useful Woodturning Projects: The Best from Woodturning Magazine. Woodturning Magazine Staff. (Illus.). 128p. 1995. pap. 12.95 (*0-946819-80-7*, Pub. by Guild Mstr Craftsman UK) Sterling.

Usefulness & Necessity of a Liberal Education for Clergymen see Argument to Prove That the Tragedy of Douglas Ought to Be Publickly Burned by the Hands of the Hangman

***Usefulness of Corporate Annual Reports to Shareholders in Australia, New Zealand & the United States: In Preparation, Winter 1996, Vol. 4.** Ray H. Anderson. LC 96-48394. 1996. 73.25 (*0-7623-0162-7*) Jai Pr.

Usefulness to Investors & Creditors of Information Provided by Financial Reporting. Paul A. Griffin. LC 87-81637. (Financial Accounting Standards Board Research Report Ser.). 294p. 1987. pap. 20.00 (*0-910065-24-1*) Finan Acct Found.

Usefulness to Investors & Creditors of Information Provided by Financial Reporting: A Review of Empirical Accounting Research. Paul A. Griffin & Michael O. Alexander. LC 82-71093. (Financial Accounting Standards Board Research Report Ser.). (Illus.). 232p. (Orig.). 1982. pap. 20.00 (*0-910065-15-2*) Finan Acct Found.

***Useh Ov Eh Unkehrut: Haykahkan Johghohvurtakahn Badmoutiun.** Alidz Agbabian. (Illus.). 32p. (Orig.). (ARM.). (J). (ps-2). 1996. pap. 12.00 (*0-9655507-1-0*) Dziludzar.

Useless Dog. 2nd ed. Billy C. Clark. LC 96-14489. (Illus.). (YA). (gr. 4 up). 1996. reprint ed. pap. 8.50 (*0-945084-57-9*) J Stuart Found.

Useless Guide to Windblows 95. Jeff Yoder & Jim Motavalli. Ed. by Deborah Werksman. (Illus.). 104p. (Orig.). 1996. pap. 7.95 (*1-887166-04-1*, Hysteria Pubns) Rose Commns.

Useless Hands. Charles Bargone. LC 74-15969. (Science Fiction Ser.). 300p. 1975. reprint ed. 28.95 (*0-405-06289-3*) Ayer.

Useless Servants. Rolando Hinojosa. LC 93-12812. 200p. (Orig.). (C). 1993. 17.95 (*1-55885-068-6*) Arte Publico.

UseNet: NetNews for Everyone. Jenny A. Fristrup. LC 94-15379. 416p. 1994. 24.95 (*0-13-123167-7*) P-H Gen Ref & Trav.

USENET Book: Finding, Using, & Surviving Newsgroups on the Internet. Bryan Pfaffenberger. LC 94-38690. 496p. 1995. pap. 26.95 (*0-201-40978-X*) Addison-Wesley.

Usenet Navigator Kit. Steve Davis. 1995. pap. 29.95 (*1-55958-745-8*) Prima Pub.

Usenet News & Inn. Randall L. Else & Trent R. Hein. 1996. pap. 24.95 (*0-13-456758-7*) P-H.

USENET Starter Kit for Macintosh. Don Rittner. (Illus.). 350p. (Orig.). 1995. pap. text ed. 25.00 (*1-56830-130-8*) Hayden.

Usenix C Plus Plus Conference Proceedings: Cambridge, MA. (Illus.). 281p. (Orig.). 1994. pap. text ed. 28.00 (*1-880446-60-X*) USENIX Assn.

USENIX C Plus Plus Conference Proceedings: Portland, OR. 352p. (Orig.). 1992. pap. text ed. 39.00 (*1-880446-45-6*) USENIX Assn.

Usenix Conference on Object-Oriented Technologies (COOTS) 204p. (Orig.). 1995. pap. text ed. 24.00 (*1-880446-71-5*) USENIX Assn.

Usenix Distributed & Multiprocessor Systems (SEDMS III) Symposium Proceedings, Newport Beach, CA. 332p. (Orig.). 1992. pap. text ed. 30.00 (*1-880446-41-3*) USENIX Assn.

USENIX Distributer & Multiprocessor Systems Symposium Proceedings, San Diego. 304p. (Orig.). 1993. pap. text ed. 32.00 (*1-880446-54-5*) USENIX Assn.

USENIX Filesystems Workshop Proceedings: Ann Arbor, MI. 152p. (Orig.). 1992. pap. text ed. 20.00 (*1-880446-43-X*) USENIX Assn.

USENIX First Symposium on Operating Systems Designs & Implementation (OSDI) Proceedings: Monterey, CA. 280p. 1994. pap. text ed. 27.00 (*1-880446-66-9*) USENIX Assn.

USENIX High-Speed Networking Symposium Proceedings: Berkeley, CA. 128p. 1994. pap. text ed. 20.00 (*1-880446-63-4*) USENIX Assn.

USENIX MACH III Symposium Proceedings: Santa Fe, NM. 324p. (Orig.). 1993. pap. text ed. 39.00 (*1-880446-49-9*) USENIX Assn.

USENIX Mobile & Location-Independent Computing Symposia Proceedings: Cambridge, MA. 144p. (Orig.). 1993. pap. text ed. 20.00 (*1-880446-51-0*) USENIX Assn.

USENIX Summer Conference Proceedings, 1992: San Antonio, TX. 253p. (Orig.). 1992. pap. text ed. 30.00 (*1-880446-44-8*) USENIX Assn.

USENIX Summer Conference Proceedings, 1993: Cincinnati, OH. 322p. (Orig.). 1993. pap. text ed. 33.00 (*1-880446-50-2*) USENIX Assn.

USENIX Summer 1994 Conference Proceedings: Boston, Massachusetts. 324p. (Orig.). 1994. pap. text ed. 33.00 (*1-880446-62-6*) USENIX Assn.

USENIX Symposium on Microkernels & Other Kernel Architectures (II) Proceedings: San Diego, CA. 144p. (Orig.). 1993. pap. text ed. 20.00 (*1-880446-52-9*) USENIX Assn.

USENIX System Administration Conference Proceedings (USA VIII) San Diego, CA. 204p. (Orig.). 1994. pap. text ed. 22.00 (*1-880446-64-2*) USENIX Assn.

USENIX Systems Administration Conference Proceedings: LISA VI, Long Beach, CA. 268p. (Orig.). 1992. pap. text ed. 30.00 (*1-880446-47-2*) USENIX Assn.

USENIX Unix Applications Development Symposium Proceedings: Toronto, Ontario, Canada. (Illus.). 189p. (Orig.). 1994. pap. text ed. 20.00 (*1-880446-61-8*) USENIX Assn.

USENIX UNIX Security Symposium: Baltimore, MD. 352p. (Orig.). 1992. pap. text ed. 39.00 (*1-880446-46-4*) USENIX Assn.

USENIX Unix Security Symposium IV: Santa Clara, CA. 160p. (Orig.). 1993. pap. text ed. 20.00 (*1-880446-55-3*) USENIX Assn.

USENIX Very High Level Languages Symposium Proceedings (VHLL) Santa Fe, NM. 232p. (Orig.). 1994. pap. text ed. 30.00 (*1-880446-65-0*) USENIX Assn.

USENIX Winter Conference Proceedings, 1993: San Diego, CA. 530p. (Orig.). 1993. pap. text ed. 40.00 (*1-880446-48-0*) USENIX Assn.

USENIX Winter 1994 Conference Proceedings San Francisco, CA. 372p. (Orig.). 1994. pap. text ed. 39.00 (*1-880446-58-8*) USENIX Assn.

USENIX Workshop Proceedings on Micro-Kernels & Other Kernel Architectures: Seattle, WA. 308p. (Orig.). 1992. pap. text ed. 30.00 (*1-880446-42-1*) USENIX Assn.

USENIX 1996 Annual Technical Conference Proceedings, San Diego, CA. 360p. 1996. pap. text ed. 40.00 (*1-880446-76-6*) USENIX Assn.

***USENIX 1997 Annual Technical Conference.** Ed. by John Kohl. 330p. 1997. pap. 40.00 (*1-880446-84-7*) USENIX Assn.

User. Bruce Benderson. 240p. 1995. pap. 10.95 (*0-452-27461-3*, Plume) NAL-Dutton.

User & Geoscience Information. Geoscience Information Society Staff. Ed. by Robert A. Bier, Jr. (Geoscience Information Society Proceedings Ser.: No. 17). 123p. reprint ed. pap. 35.10 (*0-8357-2797-1*, 2039924) Bks Demand.

User Applications of Alloy Phase Diagrams: Proceedings of an International Conference on User Applications of Alloy Phase Diagrams. International Conference on User Applications of Alloy Phase Diagrams (1986: Lake Buena Vista, FL) Staff. Ed. by Larry Kaufman. LC 87-70845. (Illus.). 271p. reprint ed. pap. 77.30 (*0-318-39729-3*, 2033087) Bks Demand.

User Aspects of Phase Diagrams. F. H. Hayes. 1991. 80.00 (*0-901462-91-8*, Pub. by Inst Materials UK) Ashgate Pub Co.

User-Centered Application Design with Visual Basic. Peter D. Varhol. LC 95-14640. 325p. 1995. pap. text ed. 29.95 (*0-471-11522-3*) Wiley.

User-Centered Requirements: The Scenario-Based Engineering Process Approach. Karen McGraw. Ed. by Karan Harbison. LC 96-31004. 384p. 1997. 79.95 (*0-8058-2064-7*); pap. 45.00 (*0-8058-2065-5*) L Erlbaum Assocs.

User-Centered Requirements for Software Engineering Environments. Ed. by David J. Gilmore et al. LC 94-2918. (NATO ASI Ser.: Vol. 123). 1994. 107.95 (*0-387-57653-3*) Spr-Verlag.

User Centered System Design. Donald A. Norman & Stephen Draper. (New Perspectives on Human-Computer Interaction Ser.). 544p. (C). 1986. pap. 49.95 (*0-89859-872-9*) L Erlbaum Assocs.

User Conference Proceedings 1994, Vol. 1. Ed. by Mike Livingston. (Illus.). 872p. (Orig.). (C). 1994. pap. text ed. 25.00 (*1-879102-22-6*) ERS Inst.

User Conference Proceedings 1994, Vol. 2. Ed. by Mike Livingston. (Illus.). 808p. (Orig.). (C). 1994. pap. text ed. 25.00 (*1-879102-23-4*) ERS Inst.

User Conference Proceedings 1994 & 1994 User Conference Technical Handouts, 3 vols. Ed. by Mike Livingston. (Illus.). 590p. (Orig.). (C). 1994. pap. text ed. 25.00 (*1-879102-19-6*); cd-rom 30.00 (*1-879102-20-X*) ERS Inst.

User Conference Proceedings 1994 & 1994 User Conference Technical Handouts, 3 vols., Set. Ed. by Mike Livingston. (Illus.). (Orig.). (C). 1994. pap. text ed. 75.00 (*1-879102-21-8*) ERS Inst.

User-Directed Competitive Intelligence: Closing the Gap Between Supply & Demand. Walter D. Barndt. LC 93-49030. 208p. 1994. text ed. 49.95 (*0-89930-781-7*, Quorum Bks) Greenwood.

User-Driven Innovation: The World's First Business Computer. David Caminer et al. 1995. write for info. (*0-07-709236-8*) McGraw.

User Education for Online Systems in Libraries: A Selective Bibliography, 1970-1988. Judith M. Pask. LC 90-9102. 220p. 1990. 25.00 (*0-8108-2378-0*) Scarecrow.

User Education in Health Sciences Libraries: A Reader. Ed. by M. Sandra Wood. (Illus.). 298p. (C). 1995. pap. text ed. 14.95 (*1-56024-995-1*); lib. bdg. 39.95 (*1-56024-964-1*) Haworth Pr.

User-Fee-Funded Stormwater Utilities. 84p. 1994. pap. 35.00 (*0-685-72645-2*) Water Environ.

User Friendly. Jim Ciano. 75p. (Orig.). 1994. pap. 9.95 (*1-888672-01-3*) J Ciano Pubng.

User-Friendly: Hands-On Exhibits that Work. Jeff Kennedy. (Illus.). 88p. 1990. 35.00 (*0-944040-22-5*) AST Ctrs.

User-Friendly: Workbook & ASP Tutorial. Harry Frank & Steven C. Althoen. 232p. (C). 1994. pap. text ed. 21.95 (*0-521-44571-X*) Cambridge U Pr.

User Friendly Cookbook: Easy to Use Recipes for Busy People. Eleanor Copley. 200p. 1985. 14.95 (*0-943066-05-0*) CareerTrack Pubns.

User Friendly Evaluation: Improving the Work of Pastors, Programs & Laity. C. Jeff Woods. Date not set. pap. 14.95 (*1-56699-154-4*) Alban Inst.

User Friendly Fund-Raising: A Step-by-Step Guide to Profitable Special Events. Warrene Williams. LC 94-60483. 144p. (Orig.). 1994. pap. 12.95 (*1-56664-065-2*) WorldComm.

User-Friendly Greek: A Commonsense Approach to the Greek New Testament. Kendell H. Easley. LC 93-33580. 1994. 14.99 (*0-8054-1043-0*, 4210-43) Broadman.

User Friendly Guide to Good English. Rose Grossfeld. 249p. 1993. pap. text ed. 26.00 (*0-7021-3030-3*, Pub. by Juta & Co SA) Intl Spec Bk.

User Friendly Guide to Managing Employees. William H. Truesdell. 200p. 1991. pap. text ed. 44.95 (*1-879876-25-6*) Mgmt Advantage.

***User Friendly Home Care Handbook.** Wendy Anemaet & Michelle Moffa-Trotter. 430p. 1997. text ed. 149.00 (*0-9643582-2-0*) Learn Pubns.

User-Friendly Hydraulics Specifications. James E. Anders, Sr. 292p. 1993. 30.00 (*0-9636737-0-X*) Hydraulics.

User-Friendly Irrigation Designs. Nirmal Sengupta. LC 92-32460. (Illus.). 152p. (C). 1993. text ed. 27.50 (*0-8039-7459-0*) Sage.

***User-Friendly Justice: Making Courts More Accessible, Easier to Understand, & Simpler to Use.** Ed. by Jona Goldschmidt & Ira Pilchen. LC 96-85175. (Illus.). 62p. (Orig.). 1996. pap. text ed. 9.50 (*0-938870-75-0*) Am Judicature.

***User Friendly Prophecy.** Larry Randolph. 210p. 1996. pap. 10.00 (*0-614-23037-3*, LRI-001) Morning NC.

***User-Friendly Psychology for Managing Your Medical Practice.** Roger Reid & Alys Novak. (Illus.). 256p. 1995. 49.00 (*1-56829-045-4*, 4813) Med Group Mgmt.

User Guide. IPM Staff. (C). 1994. pap. 65.85 (*0-08-042170-9*, Pub. by IPM Hse UK) St Mut.

User Guide: NRF Color & Size Codes. National Retail Federation Staff. 111p. 1997. pap. 235.00 (*0-9645599-0-0*) Nat Retail Fed.

User Guide - Saunders College. Saundersco. (C). 1994. pap. text ed. 32.00 (*0-03-006613-1*) HB Coll Pubs.

User Guide & Index: For the A. F. Whiting Collection of Ethnographic Notes & Papers. P. David Seaman. (Anthropological Papers: No. 3). xiv, 142p. (Orig.). 1993. pap. 16.00 (*0-910953-02-3*) N Arizona U Bkstore.

User Guide on Process Integration for the Efficient Use of Energy. rev. ed. 290p. 1994. pap. 32.00 (*0-85295-343-7*, 9CH106) Gulf Pub.

User Guide to Clip Art Folio: Library Of Desktop Publishing. Inhouse Staff. (DF-Computer Applications Ser.). 1991. pap. 12.25 (*0-538-60797-1*) S-W Pub.

User Guide to Focus. R. P. Lipton. 272p. 1987. pap. text ed. 29.95 (*0-07-038006-6*) McGraw.

User Instruction in Academic Libraries: A Century of Selected Readings. Ed. by Larry L. Hardesty et al. LC 86-960. 326p. 1986. 32.50 (*0-8108-1881-7*) Scarecrow.

User Interface: Concepts & Design. Lon Barfield. (C). 1993. pap. text ed. 37.75 (*0-201-54441-5*) Addison-Wesley.

User Interface Design. Ray E. Eberts. LC 93-29743. (International Industrial & Systems Engineering Ser.). 672p. 1994. text ed. 59.00 (*0-13-140328-1*) P-H.

User Interface Design: A Structured Approach. S. Treu. (Languages & Information Systems Ser.). (Illus.). 351p. (C). 1994. 79.50 (*0-306-44681-2*, Plenum Pr) Plenum.

User Interface Design Book. Harold Thimbleby. (Illus.). 500p. (C). 1990. text ed. 37.75 (*0-201-41618-2*) Addison-Wesley.

***User Interface Design in Delphi 3.** Warren Kovach & Ludovic Dubois. LC 97-22361. 1997. pap. write for info. (*0-13-617960-6*) P-H.

User Interface Evaluation: A Structured Approach. S. Treu. (Languages & Information Systems Ser.). (Illus.). 290p. (C). 1994. text ed. 69.50 (*0-306-44746-0*, Plenum Pr) Plenum.

User Interface in C. Mark Goodwin. 1988. 49.95 (*1-55828-036-7*) MIS Press.

User Interface Management & Design: Proceedings of the Workshop on User Interface Management Systems & Environments Lisbon, Portugal, June 4-6, 1990. Ed. by D. A. Duce et al. (Eurographic Seminars Ser.). (Illus.). 344p. 1991. 82.95 (*0-387-53454-7*) Spr-Verlag.

User Interface Management Systems; Models & Algorithms. Dan R. Olsen. LC 91-41076. (Morgan Kaufmann Series in Computer Graphics & Geometric Modeling). 231p. 1991. 49.95 (*1-55860-220-8*, QA76.9) Morgan Kaufmann.

User-Interface Screen Design. 4th ed. Wilbert O. Galitz. 1992. 44.95 (*0-89435-406-X*) Wiley.

User-Interface Screen Design. 4th ed. Wilbert O. Galitz. 532p. 1993. pap. text ed. 44.95 (*0-471-56156-8*) Wiley.

User Interface Software. Leonard J. Bass & Prasun Dewan. LC 93-9748. 201p. (Orig.). 1993. pap. text ed. 65.00 (*0-471-93784-3*) Wiley.

***User Interfaces for Virtual Reality Applications.** Chris Esposito & Lisbeth Duncan-Lacoste. 400p. (C). 1998. pap. 44.95 (*1-55860-493-6*) Morgan Kaufmann.

User Interfaces in C Plus Plus: Objects-Oriented Programming. Mark Goodwin. 375p. 1988. 53.95 (*1-55828-037-5*) MIS Press.

User Involvement in Social Services: An Annotated Bibliography. Tessa Harding & Angela Upton. 1991. pap. 30.00 (*0-902789-76-7*, Pub. by Natl Inst Soc Work) St Mut.

User Involvement in Social Services: An Annotated Bibliography. Tessa Harding & Angela Upton. (C). 1991. 60.00 (*0-7855-0098-7*, Pub. by Natl Inst Soc Work) St Mut.

User Involvement in Social Services Pt. 2: An Annotated Bibliography: 1992-1993, Pt. 2: 1992-1993. Angela Upton. 1994. pap. 24.00 (*0-902789-86-4*, Pub. by Natl Inst Soc Work) St Mut.

***User-Led Services, the Standards We Expect: What Service Users & Careers Want from Social Services Workers.** Tessa Harding & Peter Beresford. 1990. pap. 26.00 (*1-899942-05-X*, Pub. by Natl Inst Soc Work) St Mut.

User Manual for FEMA CYL: A FE-BI Numerical Laboratory for Cavity-Backed Antennas in a Circular Cylinder Version 1.5. fac. ed. Leo C. Kempel et al. (University of Michigan Report: No. 031307-1-T). 64p. 1994. pap. 25.00 (*0-7837-7695-0*, 2047452) Bks Demand.

User Manual with Ibm 3" - Lindo 6.0. Schrage. (Quantitative Techniques Ser.). 1998. pap. 42.95 (*0-7895-0159-7*) Wadsworth Pub.

User Modeling in Text Generation. Cecile L. Paris. (Communication in Artificial Intelligence Ser.). 240p. 1993. text ed. 79.00 (*0-86187-809-4*) St Martin.

User Models in Dialog Systems. Ed. by A. Kobsa & Wolfgang Wahlster. (Symbolic Computation - Artificial Intelligence Ser.). (Illus.). 465p. 1989. 122.95 (*0-387-18380-9*) Spr-Verlag.

User Needs in IT Standards. Ed. by Brian Meek et al. (Illus.). 320p. 1993. pap. 99.95 (*0-7506-1559-1*) Buttrwrth-Heinemann.

User-Network Interface (UNI) Specification Version 3.1. ATM Forum Technical Committee Staff. LC 95-18452. 1995. pap. text ed. 49.00 (*0-13-393828-X*) P-H Gen Ref & Trav.

User-Oriented Command Language: Requirements & Designs for a Standard Job Control Language. Ed. by K. Hopper. LC 81-21160. (Monographs in Informatics). (Illus.). 122p. reprint ed. pap. 34.80 (*0-685-23437-1*, 2032684) Bks Demand.

User-Oriented Evaluation of Information Resources. David Bawden. 200p. 1990. text ed. 54.95 (*0-566-05209-1*, Pub. by Gower UK) Ashgate Pub Co.

User-Oriented Methodology & Techniques of Decision Analysis & Support: Proceedings of the International IIASA Workshop, Held in Serock, Poland, September 9-13, 1991. Ed. by Jaap Wessels & P. Wierzbicki. LC 92-42974. (Lecture Notes in Economics & Mathematical Systems Ser.: Vol. 397). 1993. write for info. (*3-540-56382-2*); 69.95 (*0-387-56382-2*) Spr-Verlag.

User Participation & the Success of Information System Development: An Integrated Model of User-Specialist Relationships. Lei Lei. (Tinbergen Research Institute Research Ser.: No. 73, Series B). 257p. 1994. pap. 28.00 (*90-5170-285-X*, Pub. by Thesis Pubs NE) IBD Ltd.

User Participation in Building Design & Management: A Generic Approach to Building Evaluation. 2nd ed. David Kernoham et al. (Illus.). 166p. 1996. pap. 24.95 (*0-7506-2888-X*, Butterwrth Archit) Buttrwrth-Heinemann.

User Precision Performance of Clinical Chemistry Devices: Tentative Guideline, Vol. 4. 2nd ed. National Committee for Clinical Laboratory Standards. 1992. 85.00 (*1-56238-145-8*, EP5-T2) Natl Comm Clin Lab Stds.

***User Study: Informational Needs of Remote National Archives & Records Administration Customers.** Judi Moline & Steve Otto. (Illus.). 106p. (C). 1996. reprint ed. pap. 25.00 (*0-7881-3065-X*) DIANE Pub.

User Support & Information Sources in Europe: A Status Report. 2nd ed. Ed. by Jill Foster. 75p. (C). 1993. pap. text ed. 40.00 (*0-7881-0037-8*) DIANE Pub.

User Surveys in College Libraries. Compiled by Mignon Adams & Jeffrey Beck. (CLIP Note Ser.: No. 23). 90p. (Orig.). (C). 1995. pap. 24.95 (*0-8389-7825-8*) Assn Coll & Res Libs.

***User Training for Windows NT: Version 3.5X.** Pinnacle Communications Staff. Ed. by Natalie B. Young. (Illus.). 100p. (Orig.). 1996. pap. 195.00 (*1-56562-083-6*) OneOnOne Comp Trng.

User Tutorial see **Hewlett Packard HP-UX CMW**

***Users.** Brian Case. 190p. 9700. pap. 12.95 (*1-899344-05-5*) Dufour.

Users & Abusers of Psychiatry: A Critical Look at Traditional Psychiatric Practice. Lucy Johnstone. 288p. 1989. 45.00 (*0-415-02839-6*) Routledge.

Users & Abusers of Psychiatry: A Critical Look at Traditional Psychiatric Practice. Lucy Johnstone. 288p. (C). 1989. pap. text ed. 16.95 (*0-415-02840-X*) Routledge.

Users' Directory of Computer Networks. Tracy L. LaQuey. (Illus.). 630p. (Orig.). 1990. 41.95 (*1-55558-047-5*, EY-C200E-DP, Digital DEC) Buttrwrth-Heinemann.

User's Fuel Handbook. Ralph W. Ritchie. LC 81-90075. (Energy Conservation in the Crafts - Craft Monograph Ser.: No. 7). (Illus.). (Orig.). 1981. pap. 6.00 (*0-939656-06-X*) Ritchie Unltd.

User's Guide. Common Desktop Environment Documentation Group Staff. LC 95-11127. (Common Desktop Environment 1.0 Ser.). 368p. (C). 1995. pap. text ed. 25.95 (*0-201-48951-1*) Addison-Wesley.

User's Guide. Unix System Laboratories Staff. 1993. pap. text ed. 32.00 (*0-13-177205-8*) P-H.

User's Guide: Shareware, Freeware, & Public Domain Software. Bruce Jackson. 222p. (Orig.). 1987. pap. 25.00 (*0-939731-01-0*) South Moulton Pr.

User's Guide: UNIX SVR 4.2. Unix System Laboratories Staff. 1993. pap. text ed. 34.00 (*0-13-017708-3*) P-H.

***User's Guide Algebraic.** Dodson. 1997. pap. text ed. 69.00 (*0-7923-4293-3*) Kluwer Ac.

***User's Guide Exp 5.0.** 8th ed. Smith. (Mathematics Ser.). 1997. pap. 35.95 (*0-534-34887-4*) Brooks-Cole.

User's Guide for All 1997 Windows. 97th ed. 1997. pap. text ed. 7.00 (*0-03-018314-6*) HR&W Schl Div.

User's Guide (SVR4.2 MP) Unix System Laboratories Staff. (Illus.). 560p. (C). 1994. pap. text ed. 65.00 (*0-13-157918-5*) P-H.

User's Guide to a Better Bod: "Wisdom for Facing the Trials of Creating a Healthier, Happier You" Jo Elder & M. I. Wiser. LC 92-21172. (Illus.). 160p. 1993. pap. 6.50 (*0-941361-96-9*) One More Pr.

***User's Guide to Algebraic Topology.** C. T. Dodson & Phillip E. Parker. LC 96-43438. (Mathematics & Its Applications Ser.). 1996. lib. bdg. 209.00 (*0-7923-4292-5*) Kluwer Ac.

Users Guide to Another Millenium. Patty Sausage & Link Sausage. 128p. (Orig.). Date not set. pap. 12.50 (*0-9639544-5-8*) A F A B.

***User's Guide to Astrology.** Bruce Scofield. (Illus.). 144p. (Orig.). 1997. pap. 10.00 (*0-9628031-3-8*) One Reed Pubns.

User's Guide to Bypass Surgery. Ted Klein. LC 95-48908. 175p. (Orig.). 1996. pap. 14.95 (*0-8214-1143-8*) Ohio U Pr.

User's Guide to Capitalism & Schizophrenia: Deviations from Deleuza & Guattari. Brian Massumi. 1992. 26.95 (*0-262-13282-6*); pap. 13.95 (*0-262-63143-1*) MIT Pr.

User's Guide to College - Making Notes & Taking Tests: Conversations with Dr. Walter Pauk. Walter Pauk. (Illus.). 128p. (C). 1988. pap. text ed. 6.75 (*0-89061-481-4*) Jamestown Pubs.

User's Guide to Community Entry for the Severely Handicapped. Ed. by Ernest Pancsofar & Robert Blackwell. LC 84-24139. (SUNY Series in Special Education). 182p. 1985. text ed. 64.50 (*0-88706-034-X*); pap. text ed. 21.95 (*0-88706-035-8*) State U NY Pr.

User's Guide to Computer Peripherals. Donald Eadie. (Illus.). 224p. 1982. text ed. 47.00 (*0-13-939660-8*) P-H.

User's Guide to Contemporary Russian Vocabulary: Lexical Semantics. Yuri D. Apresjan. Tr. by Alexander Lehrman from RUS. (Linguistica Extranea: Studia Ser.: No. 13). 636p. (C). 1992. 185.00 (*0-89720-039-X*); disk 175.00 (*0-685-57744-9*) Karoma.

User's Guide to Cost-Care. Terrill A. Mast. (Cost Containment Learning Modules Ser.). 59p. (Orig.). 1985. pap. text ed. 12.50 (*0-931369-17-7*) Southern IL Univ Sch.

User's Guide to Dust & Fume Control. ICHEM Engineers Staff. (Institution of Chemical Engineers Symposium Ser.). 1983. pap. 20.00 (*0-08-031408-2*, Pergamon Pr) Elsevier.

User's Guide to Ellipsometry. Harland G. Tompkins. (Illus.). 260p. 1992. text ed. 56.00 (*0-12-693950-0*) Acad Pr.

User's Guide to Federal Architect-Engineer Contracts. 2nd ed. James B. Goodowens. 494p. 1996. 112.00 (*0-7844-0145-4*) Am Soc Civil Eng.

***User's Guide to Federal Architect-Engineer Contracts.** James B. Goodowens. LC 89-17818. (Illus.). 624p. 1989. reprint ed. pap. 177.90 (*0-608-04431-8*, 2059668) Bks Demand.

Users Guide to FOCUS. 2nd ed. Russell C. Lipton. (Illus.). 320p. 1988. pap. text ed. 24.95 (*0-07-038013-9*) McGraw.

***User's Guide to German Cultural Studies.** Ed. by Scott D. Denham et al. LC 97-4768. (Social History, Popular Culture, & Politics in Germany Ser.). (C). 1997. pap. 23.95 (*0-472-06656-0*); text ed. 59.50 (*0-472-09656-7*) U of Mich Pr.

User's Guide to Ghostwriter DOS 3" Hajduk. (EC - HS Communication/Engl Ser.). Date not set. text ed. 49.95 (*0-538-85969-5*) S-W Pub.

***Users' Guide to GPS: The Global Positioning System.** Bonnie Dahl. Ed. by Steve Ault et al. (Illus.). 253p. 1993. pap. 24.95 (*0-932647-12-X*) Richardsons Marine.

User's Guide to Hot Dip Galvanizing for Corrosion Protection in Atmospheric Service, TPC 9. (Illus.). 35p. 1983. 32.00 (*0-915567-60-1*) NACE Intl.

User's Guide to Love: "Wisdom for Facing the Trials of Intimate Relationships" Jo Elder & M. I. Wiser. LC 92-21184. (Illus.). 160p. 1993. pap. 6.50 (*0-941361-97-7*) One More Pr.

***Users Guide to Millenium.** Ballard. 1997. pap. 14.00 (*0-312-15683-9*) St Martin.

User's Guide to Money: Wisdom for Facing the Trials of Making, Keeping & Spending It. Jo Elder & M. I. Wiser. (Illus.). 160p. 1993. 6.50 (*0-941361-94-2*) One More Pr.

User's Guide to New York City Public Elementary & Intermediate Schools: Selected Statistics, 1992-1993. Laurie R. Beck et al. 106p. 1995. 17.50 (*0-88156-165-7*) Comm Serv Soc NY.

User's Guide to Old Age: "Wisdom for Facing the Trials of Growing Older" rev. ed. Jo Elder & M. I. Wiser. LC 92-27867. (Illus.). 160p. 1993. pap. 6.50 (*0-941361-98-5*) One More Pr.

User's Guide to Operator Algebras. Peter A. Fillmore. LC 95-38340. (Canadian Mathematical Society Ser. & Advanced Texts). 172p. 1996. text ed. 59.95 (*0-471-31135-9*) Wiley.

User's Guide to Parenthood: "Wisdom for Facing the Trials of Raising Kids" rev. ed. Jo Elder & M. I. Wiser. LC 92-27868. (Illus.). 160p. 1993. pap. 6.50 (*0-941361-99-3*) One More Pr.

User's Guide to Patents. M'Caw & Co. Staff. 1995. pap. text ed. write for info. (*0-406-01307-1*, UK) MICHIE.

User's Guide to Pets: Wisdom for Facing the Trials of Living with Dogs & Cats. Jo Elder & M. I. Wiser. LC 93-20558. (Illus.). 160p. 1993. 6.50 (*0-941361-95-0*) One More Pr.

User's Guide to Powder Coating. 2nd fac. ed. Ed. by Emery P. Miller. LC 87-61422. (Illus.). 176p. 1987. reprint ed. pap. 50.20 (*0-7837-8189-X*, 2047894) Bks Demand.

User's Guide to Powder Coating. 3rd ed. Ed. by D. L. Ulrich. LC 93-85795. 113p. 1993. pap. text ed. 34.00 (*0-87263-444-2*) SME.

User's Guide to Powder Coating. Ed. by Emery P. Miller. LC 85-71675. (Illus.). 176p. 1975. reprint ed. pap. 50.20 (*0-8357-6481-8*, 2035852) Bks Demand.

User's Guide to Principal Components. J. Edward Jackson. LC 90-28108. (Series in Probability & Mathematics). 569p. 1991. text ed. 132.00 (*0-471-62267-2*) Wiley.

User's Guide to Resume Writer DOS 3" Hajduk. (EC - HS Communication/English Ser.). Date not set. text ed. 55.95 (*0-538-85968-7*) S-W Pub.

User's Guide to Salary Survey Applications. 32p. 1991. 15.00 (*1-878240-01-3*) Coll & U Personnel.

User's Guide to Spectral Sequences. John McCleary. LC 85-63230. (Mathematics Lectures: No. 12). xvi, 423p. 1985. 40.00 (*0-914098-21-7*) Publish or Perish.

***User's Guide to Spectral Sequences.** John McCleary. (Studies in Advanced Mathematics: Vol. 58). (Illus.). 450p. (C). 1997. write for info. (*0-521-56141-8*) Cambridge U Pr.

***User's Guide to Spectral Sequences.** John McCleary. (Studies in Advanced Mathematics: Vol. 58). (Illus.). 450p. (C). 1997. pap. write for info. (*0-521-56759-9*) Cambridge U Pr.

User's Guide to Statistics Programs: The Rapidata Timesharing System. Bruce Bosworth. 1982. pap. text ed. 9.95 (*0-89529-167-3*) Avery Pub.

User's Guide to the "Bluebook" 15th rev. ed. Alan L. Dworsky. LC 91-31634. vi, 54p. 1991. pap. 5.50 (*0-8377-0558-4*) Rothman.

***User's Guide to the Bluebook.** 16th rev. ed. Alan L. Dworsky. LC 96-48351. vi, 58p. 1996. pap. 6.50 (*0-8377-0563-0*) Rothman.

***User's Guide to the Book of Common Prayer: Holy Eucharist, Rites I & II.** Christopher L. Webber. 96p. (Orig.). pap. 6.95 (*0-8192-1695-X*) Morehouse Pub.

***User's Guide to the Book of Common Prayer: Morning Prayer Rites I & II & Baptism.** Christopher L. Webber. 96p. (Orig.). pap. 6.95 (*0-8192-1696-8*) Morehouse Pub.

***User's Guide to the Brain.** John J. Ratey. 1997. write for info. (*0-679-45309-1*) Pantheon.

User's Guide to the Ecu. Ralph J. Mehnert. 250p. (C). 1992. lib. bdg. 78.00 (*1-85333-742-0*, Pub. by Graham & Trotman UK) Kluwer Ac.

Users Guide to the Family. Kathleen Gilbert. 140p. (C). 1995. pap. text ed., spiral bd. 19.89 (*0-8403-9921-9*) Kendall-Hunt.

User's Guide to the "Gottman-Williams Time Series Analysis Computer Programs for Social Scientists" Esther A. Williams & John M. Gottman. 86p. 1982. pap. text ed. 15.95 (*0-521-28059-1*) Cambridge U Pr.

Users Guide to the Highway Concrete (HWYCON) Expert System. Lawrence J. Kaetzel et al. (SHRP Ser.: C-406). (Illus.). 82p. (Orig.). (C). 1994. pap. text ed. 35.00 (*0-309-05822-8*) Natl Res Coun.

User's Guide to the IBM Portable PC. Herb Friedman. write for info. (*0-318-58194-9*) P-H.

User's Guide to the Loran-C. 2nd rev. ed. Bonnie Dahl. Ed. by Wally Haskins & Hal Sherman. (Illus.). 263p. (Orig.). 1991. reprint ed. pap. 19.95 (*0-932647-09-X*) Richardsons Marine.

Users Guide to the Maintenance & Inspection of Above-Ground Vertical Cylindrical Steel Storage Tanks. EEMUA Staff. 1994. 190.00 (*0-85931-219-4*, Pub. by EEMUA UK) St Mut.

Users Guide to the Maintenance & Inspection of above Ground Vertical Cylindrical Steel Storage Tanks. EEMUA Staff. 1994. 125.00 (*0-85931-079-5*, Pub. by EEMUA UK) St Mut.

***User's Guide to the Millennium.** J. G. Ballard. 1997. pap. 14.00 (*0-614-27420-6*, Picador USA) St Martin.

User's Guide to the Millennium: Essays & Reviews. J. G. Ballard. 288p. 1996. 23.00 (*0-312-14440-7*) St Martin.

User's Guide to the Millennium: Essays & Reviews. J. G. Ballard. 1996. 23.00 (*0-614-96854-2*, Picador USA) St Martin.

User's Guide to the Occupational Performance History Interview. Gary Keilhofner et al. 49p. (Orig.). (C). 1989. pap. text ed. 7.00 (*0-910317-47-X*) Am Occup Therapy.

User's Guide to the Official Records of the American Civil War. Alan C. Aimone & Barbara A. Aimone. LC 93-9261. (Illus.). 125p. (C). 1993. pap. 12.00 (*0-942597-38-9*) White Mane Pub.

User's Guide to the Scientific & Clinical Literature on Dog & Cat Behavior. 2nd ed. Richard H. Polsky. 97p. (C). 1995. pap. text ed. 69.95 (*0-614-04772-2*) Animal Behav.

User's Guide to the Scientific & Clinical Literature on Dog & Cat Behavior. 2nd ed. Richard H. Polsky. 92p. 1995. write for info. (*0-614-13694-6*) Animal Behav.

User's Guide to the View Camera. Jim Stone. (C). 1987. pap. text ed. 36.50 (*0-673-39617-7*) Addson-Wesley Educ.

User's Guide to the View Camera. rev. ed. Jim Stone. 1996. pap. text ed. 36.50 (*0-8230-4988-4*, RAC Bks) Watsn-Guptill.

User's Guide to the View Camera. 2nd ed. Jim Stone. LC 96-19182. (C). 1997. 39.95 (*0-673-52006-4*) Addson-Wesley Educ.

User's Guide to Trade Marks: The New Law. Julian Gyngell. 340p. 1994. pap. text ed. 55.00 (*0-406-00577-X*, UK) MICHIE.

User's Guide to Vacuum Technology. 2nd ed. John F. O'Hanlon. LC 88-27327. 481p. 1989. text ed. 77.95 (*0-471-81242-0*) Wiley.

User's Guide to Wheels & Rims. (Illus.). 93p. 1994. pap. text ed., spiral bd. 65.00 (*0-88711-239-0*) Am Trucking Assns.

User's Guide, Windows Office Pro V4.3 Academic Edition 3.5. Microsoft Press Staff. (NO - Novell/Wordperfect Ser.). 1995. text ed. 121.95 (*0-538-66027-9*) S-W Pub.

User's Handbook of D-A & A-D Converters. Eugene R. Hnatek. LC 86-7205. 488p. 1988. reprint ed. text ed. 62.50 (*0-89874-953-0*) Krieger.

User's Introduction to UNIX V. Richard H. Balay. 128p. 1988. spiral bd. 17.32 (*0-8403-4671-9*) Kendall-Hunt.

User's Manual: Authority Reference Tool, Version 2.0, for the Art & Architecture Thesaurus. Getty Art History Information Program. (Illus.). 128p. 1994. 12.95 (*0-19-508883-2*) OUP.

User's Manual: 80C186-C188, 80C186XL-188XL. Intel Corporation Staff. 1992. pap. 27.95 (*1-55512-163-2*) Intel Corp.

User's Manual, Advanced FORTRAN IV Utilities for Data General Computers. Ed. by Emma Duchane. (Illus.). viii, 223p. 1980. pap. 20.00 (*0-938876-03-1*) Entropy Ltd.

User's Manual for Conducting Child Nutrition Surveys in Developing Countries. CFNPP Staff & Victoria Quinn. (Working Papers). (C). 1992. pap. text ed. 7.00 (*1-56401-121-6*) Cornell Food.

User's Manual for Optical Waveguide Communications. Institute for Telecommunication Sciences Staff. (Fiber Optics User's Manual & Design Ser.: Vol. I). 287p. 1975. 75.00 (*0-918435-81-1*, 152U01) Info Gatekeepers.

Users' Manual for the Job Descriptive Index (JDI; 1997 Revision) & the Job in General (JIG) Scales. 2nd rev. ed. William K. Balzer et al. (Illus.). 273p. (Orig.). 1997. pap. 35.00 (*0-9627727-0-4*) BGSU Dept Psy.

User's Manual for the MicroCAT Testing System. rev. ed. Assessment Systems Corporation. (Illus.). 1996. ring bd. 30.00 (*0-924724-00-5*) Assmnt Systs.

User's Manual Linear, Integer, & Quadratic Programming with LINDO: Student Edition. 5th ed. Linus E. Schrage. 132p. (C). 1991. pap. 34.00 (*0-89426-196-7*) Course Tech.

Users Manual 80960CA. Intel Corporation Staff. 672p. (Orig.). (C). 1989. pap. 29.95 (*1-55512-099-7*, 270710) Intel Corp.

Uses. James L. Weil. (Vagrom Chap Bk.: No. 16). (Illus.). 49p. (Orig.). 1981. pap. 6.00 (*0-935552-06-5*) Sparrow Pr.

Uses, Abuses, & Future of Great Lakes Modeling: Report. fac. ed. Great Lakes Science Advisory Board, Modeling Task Force Staff. (Illus.). 107p. 1986. pap. 30.50 (*0-7837-8625-5*, 2075236) Bks Demand.

Uses & Abuse of Criminal Statistics. Ed. by Kenneth Pease. (International Library of Criminology, Criminal Justice & Penology). (Illus.). 500p. 1996. text ed. 127.95 (*1-85521-408-3*, Pub. by Dartmth Pub UK) Ashgate Pub Co.

Uses & Abuses of Air: Showing Its Influence in Sustaining Life & Producing Disease. John H. Griscom. LC 79-125743. (American Environmental Studies). 1972. reprint ed. 19.95 (*0-405-02668-4*) Ayer.

Uses & Abuses of Economics: Contentious Essays on History & Method. Terence Hutchison. LC 94-2482. 336p. (C). (gr. 13). 1994. text ed. 74.95 (*0-415-09404-6*, B4449) Routledge.

***Uses & Abuses of Knowledge: Proceedings of the 23rd Annual Scholars' Conference on the Holocaust & the German Church Struggle.** Ed. by Henry F. Knight & Marcia S. Littell. LC 96-45423. (Studies in the Shoah: Vol. XVII). 478p. 1997. text ed. 64.50 (*0-7618-0629-6*) U Pr of Amer.

Uses & Abuses of Profiling: A Handbook on Reviewing & Recording Student Experience & Achievement. Ed. by Bill Law. 192p. (C). 1984. 50.00 (*0-06-318300-5*, Pub. by P Chapman Pub UK) St Mut.

Uses & Abuses of Social Research in Social Work. Tony Tripodi & Phillip Fellin. LC 73-17280. 208p. 1974. pap. text ed. 17.50 (*0-231-03663-9*) Col U Pr.

Uses & Actions of 1,25 Dihyroxyvitamin D3 in Uremia. Ed. by Shaul G. Massry & J. W. Coburn. (Contributions to Nephrology Ser.: Vol. 18). (Illus.). x, 218p. 1980. 65.00 (*3-8055-3064-1*) S Karger.

Uses & Effects of Cultured Fishes in Aquatic Ecosystems. Ed. by R. G. Piper & H. L. Schramm, Jr. LC 95-60393. (Symposium Ser.: No. 15). 606p. 1995. 53.50 (*0-913235-91-1*) Am Fisheries Soc.

***Uses & Limitations of Transmission Error.** J. D. Smith. (1987 Fall Technical Meeting). 1987. pap. text ed. 30.00 (*1-55589-481-X*) AGMA.

Uses & Limits of Intelligence. rev. ed. Walter Laqueur. LC 92-32932. 445p. (C). 1993. pap. 24.95 (*1-56000-594-7*) Transaction Pubs.

Uses & Misuses of Tests. Ed. by Charles W. Daves. LC 84-47982. (Jossey-Bass Social & Behavioral Science Ser.). 155p. reprint ed. pap. 44.20 (*0-7837-0166-7*, 2040463) Bks Demand.

Uses & Standardization of Vertebrate Cell Cultures. 1984. 65.00 (*0-931767-00-8*) Soc In Vitro Biol.

Uses for Mooses & Other Popular Pets. Mike Thaler. LC 93-25542. (Laffalong Bk.). (Illus.). 32p. (J). (ps-3). 1993. lib. bdg. 12.50 (*0-8167-3301-5*) Troll Communs.

Uses for Mooses & Other Popular Pets. Mike Thaler. LC 93-25542. (Laffalong Bk.). (Illus.). 32p. (J). (ps-3). 1996. pap. 2.95 (*0-8167-3302-3*) Troll Communs.

Uses of Abundance: A History of New Jersey's Economy. Paul G. Clemens. LC 92-38149. (New Jersey History Ser.: No. 2). 1992. 9.00 (*0-89743-078-6*) NJ Hist Com.

Uses of Adversity: Essays on the Fate of Central Europe. Timothy G. Ash. 1989. 19.95 (*0-394-57573-3*) Random.

Uses of Adversity: Failure & Accommodation in Reader Response. Ed. by Ellen Spolsky. LC 88-43297. 216p. 1990. 38.50 (*0-8387-5112-1*) Bucknell U Pr.

UV

An Asterisk (*) at the beginning of an entry indicates that the title is appearing in BIP for the first time.

Uses of Anachrohism on Cultural Methodological Diversity in Islamic Art. J. M. Rogers. (C). 1994. 8.50 (*0-7286-0225-3*, Pub. by Sch Orient & African Stud UK) S Asia.

Uses of Antiquity: The Scientific Revolution & the Classical Tradition. Ed. by Stephen Gaukroger. (Australasian Studies in History & Philosophy of Science: No. 10). 284p. (C). 1991. lib. bdg. 133.00 (*0-7923-1130-2*, Pub. by Klwr Acad Pubs NE) Kluwer Ac.

Uses of Argument. Stephen E. Toulmin. 272p. (C). 1958. pap. text ed. 24.95 (*0-521-09230-2*) Cambridge U Pr.

Uses of Art: Medieval Metaphor in the Michigan Law Quadrangle. Ilene H. Forsythe. (Distinguished Senior Faculty Lectures). (Illus.). 120p. 1993. text ed. 29.95 (*0-472-09506-4*) U of Mich Pr.

Uses of Autobiography. Ed. by Julia Swindells. 192p. 1996. 75.00 (*0-7484-0365-5*); pap. 21.95 (*0-7484-0366-3*) Taylor & Francis.

Uses of Bank Funds. Waldo F. Mitchell. Ed. by Stuart Bruchey. LC 80-1162. (Rise of Commercial Banking Ser.). (Illus.). 1981. reprint ed. lib. bdg. 18.95 (*0-405-13669-2*) Ayer.

Uses of Beauty & Order. Harvey Jackins. 1967. pap. 2.00 (*0-911214-15-1*) Rational Isl.

Uses of Bryophytes. Janice M. Glime & Dinesh Saxena. (Illus.). 100p. 1992. 25.00 (*1-55528-261-X*, Pub. by Today & Tomorrows P & P II) Scholarly Pubns.

Uses of Bryophytes. Dinesh Saxena. (Illus.). 99p. 1991. text ed. 25.00 (*0-685-55200-4*, Pub. by Today Tomorrow II) Lubrecht & Cramer.

Uses of Census Data for Demographic Research & Development Planning in Africa: Aspects of Technical Co-operation. 24p. 1986. pap. 4.00 (*92-1-123104-3*, E. 86.II.H.1) UN.

Uses of Charity: The Poor on Relief in the Nineteenth-Century Metropolis. Ed. by Peter Mandler. LC 90-30496. (Shelby Cullom Davis Center Ser.). (Illus.). 264p. (C). 1990. text ed. 36.50 (*0-8122-8214-0*) U of Pa Pr.

Uses of Comparative Mythology: Essays on the Work of Joseph Campbell. Ed. by Kenneth L. Golden. LC 92-10581. 296p. 1992. text ed. 49.00 (*0-8240-7092-5*, H1338) Garland.

Uses of Countertransference. Michael Gorkin. 1996. pap. text ed. 30.00 (*1-56821-835-4*) Aronson.

Uses of Countertransference: Working with the Therapist's Response. Michael Gorkin. LC 87-1068. 312p. 1987. 40.00 (*0-87668-970-5*) Aronson.

*__Uses of Culture: Education & the Limits of Ethnic Affiliation.__ Cameron McCarthy. LC 97-19763. (Critical Social Thought Ser.). 192p. (C). 1997. pap. write for info. (*0-415-91300-4*); text ed. write for info. (*0-415-91299-7*) Routledge.

Uses of Decadence: Wilde, Yeats, Joyce. Richard Ellmann. (Chapbooks in Literature Ser.). (Illus.). 25p. 1990. pap. text ed. 5.00 (*0-9614940-7-7*) Bennington Coll.

Uses of Discretion. Ed. by Keith Hawkins. LC 92-28309. (Oxford Socio-Legal Studies). 448p. 1993. 55.00 (*0-19-825762-7*, Clarendon Pr) OUP.

Uses of Discretion. Ed. by Keith Hawkins. (Socio-Legal Studies). 448p. 1995. reprint ed. pap. 26.00 (*0-19-825950-6*) OUP.

Uses of Disorder: Personal Identity & City Life. Richard Sennett. LC 92-13142. 216p. 1992. pap. 8.95 (*0-393-30909-6*) Norton.

Uses of Ecology: Lake Washington & Beyond. W. T. Edmondson. LC 90-47158. (Jessie & John Danz Lectures). (Illus.). 352p. 1991. 25.00 (*0-295-97024-3*) U of Wash Pr.

Uses of Ecology: Lake Washington & Beyond. W. T. Edmondson. LC 90-47158. (Jessie & John Danz Lectures). (Illus.). 352p. 1996. pap. 12.95 (*0-295-97569-5*) U of Wash Pr.

Uses of Elemental Diets in Clinical Situations. Ed. by Gustavo Bounous. LC 87-24283. 352p. 1992. 235.00 (*0-8493-6680-1*, RM229, CRC Reprint) Franklin.

Uses of Enchantment: The Meaning & Importance of Fairy Tales. Bruno Bettelheim. 1989. pap. 13.00 (*0-679-72393-5*, Vin) Random.

Uses of Energy. Ed Catherall. LC 90-46703. (Exploring Science Ser.). (Illus.). 48p. (J). (gr. 4-8). 1990. lib. bdg. 24.26 (*0-8114-2598-3*) Raintree Steck-V.

Uses of Epidemiology in Housing Programmes & in Planning Human Settlements: Proceedings of the WHO Expert Committee on Housing & Health, Geneva, 1972. WHO Staff. (Technical Report Ser.: No. 544). 1974. pap. text ed. 6.00 (*92-4-120544-X*, 1100544) World Health.

*__Uses of Epidemiology in the Study of the Elderly.__ (Technical Report Ser.: No. 706). 84p. 1984. pap. text ed. 10.00 (*92-4-120706-X*) World Health.

Uses of Error. Frank Kermode. LC 90-47100. 432p. 1991. 32.00 (*0-674-93152-1*, KERUSE) HUP.

Uses of Experiment: Studies in the Natural Sciences. Ed. by David Gooding et al. (Illus.). 400p. 1989. 99.95 (*0-521-33185-4*); pap. text ed. 38.95 (*0-521-33768-2*) Cambridge U Pr.

Uses of Fiction. Douglas Jefferson & Graham Martin. 364p. 1982. 95.00 (*0-335-10181-X*, Open Univ Pr) Taylor & Francis.

Uses of Force & Wilsonian Foreign Policy. Frederick S. Calhoun. LC 92-31632. (American Diplomatic History Ser.: No. 6). 184p. (Orig.). 1993. pap. 15.00 (*0-87338-464-4*) Kent St U Pr.

Uses of Geographical Information Systems in Socio-Economic Studies. P. Daplyn et al. 1994. pap. 49.00 (*0-85954-372-2*, Pub. by Nat Res Inst UK) St Mut.

Uses of Gothic: Planning & Building the Campus of the University of Chicago, 1892-1932. Jean F. Block. LC 83-6545. (Illus.). 284p. 1985. pap. 23.95 (*0-226-06004-7*) U Ch Pr.

Uses of Greek Mythology. Ken Dowden. LC 91-38305. (Approaching the Ancient World Ser.). 144p. (C). 1992. pap. 13.95 (*0-415-06135-0*, A7500) Routledge.

Uses of Haiti. Paul Farmer. 300p. 1994. pap. 14.95 (*1-56751-034-5*); lib. bdg. 29.95 (*1-56751-035-3*) Common Courage.

*__Uses of Health Systems Research.__ C. Taylor. (Public Health Papers: No. 78). 49p. 1984. pap. text ed. 9.00 (*92-4-130078-7*, 1110078) World Health.

Uses of History: Essays in Intellectual & Social History, Presented to William J. Bossenbrook. Compiled by Hayden V. White. LC 68-12852. 286p. reprint ed. pap. 81.60 (*0-7837-3596-0*, 2043461) Bks Demand.

Uses of History: Marxism, Postmodernism & the Renaissance. Ed. by Francis Barker et al. LC 91-17278. (Literature, Politics, Theory: the Essex Symposia Ser.). 192p. 1991. text ed. 49.95 (*0-7190-3512-0*, Pub. by Manchester Univ Pr UK) St Martin.

Uses of History in the Novels of Vardis Fisher. George F. Day. (Vardis Fisher Ser.). 1974. lib. bdg. 250.00 (*0-87700-225-8*) Revisionist Pr.

Uses of Immobilized Biological Compounds: Proceedings of the NATO Advanced Research Workshop on Uses of Immobilized Biological Compounds for Detection, Medical, Food & Environmental Analysis, Brixen, Italy, May 9-14, 1993. Ed. by George G. Guilbault. LC 93-33128. (NATO Advanced Science Institutes Series C: Mathematical & Physical Sciences). 600p. (C). 1993. lib. bdg. 289.00 (*0-7923-2529-X*) Kluwer Ac.

Uses of Ineptitude, or How Not to Want to Do Better. Nicholas Samstag. 1962. 10.95 (*0-8392-1123-6*) Astor-Honor.

Uses of Johnson's Criticism. Leopold Damrosch. LC 75-19431. 250p. reprint ed. pap. 71.30 (*0-318-34977-9*, 2030788) Bks Demand.

Uses of Juices. 8th ed. C. E. Clinkard. 32p. 1993. reprint ed. spiral bd. 6.00 (*0-7873-0178-7*) Hlth Research.

Uses of Knowledge: Selections from the Idea of a University. John H. Newman. Ed. by Leo L. Ward. (Crofts Classics Ser.). 128p. 1948. pap. text ed. write for info. (*0-88295-063-0*) Harlan Davidson.

Uses of Life. John Lubbock. LC 72-4585. (Essay Index Reprint Ser.). 1977. reprint ed. 23.95 (*0-8369-2961-6*) Ayer.

Uses of Life: A Conversation with Ruth H. Cooke & Jacob Needleman. LC 90-80872. 1995. pap. 5.00 (*0-914480-11-1*) Far West Edns.

Uses of Life: A History of Biotechnology. Robert Bud. LC 92-19513. (Illus.). 304p. (C). 1993. text ed. 59.95 (*0-521-38240-8*) Cambridge U Pr.

Uses of Life: A History of Biotechnology. Robert Bud. (Illus.). 320p. (C). 1994. pap. text ed. 20.95 (*0-521-47699-2*) Cambridge U Pr.

Uses of Life Assurance & Pensions in Tax Planning. Tony Wickendon & M. Chapman. (C). 1987. 230.00 (*0-685-32683-7*, Pub. by Witherby & Co UK) St Mut.

Uses of Literacy. Richard Hoggart. 319p. (C). 1991. pap. 24.95 (*0-88738-892-2*) Transaction Pubs.

*__Uses of Literacy.__ Richard Hoggart. LC 97-13291. (Classics in Communication & Mass Culture Ser.). 1997. pap. write for info. (*0-7658-0421-2*) Transaction Pubs.

Uses of Literacy in Early Medieval Europe. Ed. by Rosamond McKitterick. (Illus.). 361p. (C). 1992. pap. text ed. 22.95 (*0-521-42896-3*) Cambridge U Pr.

Uses of Literary History. Ed. by Marshall Brown. LC 95-42027. (Illus.). 290p. 1995. text ed. 49.95 (*0-8223-1704-4*); pap. text ed. 16.95 (*0-8223-1714-1*) Duke.

Uses of Literature. Italo Calvino. Tr. by Patrick Creagh. 1987. pap. 12.00 (*0-15-693250-4*, Harvest Bks) HarBrace.

Uses of Literature. Ed. by Monroe Engel. LC 73-82627. (English Studies: No. 4). 256p. 1960. pap. 5.95 (*0-674-93155-6*) HUP.

Uses of Manuscripts in Literary Studies: Essays in Memory of Judson Boyce Allen. Ed. by Charlotte C. Morse et al. (Studies in Medieval Culture: No. 31). 1992. pap. 15.00 (*1-879288-14-1*); boxed 35.00 (*1-879288-13-3*) Medieval Inst.

Uses of National Income in Peace & War. Simon Kuznets. (Occasional Papers: No. 6). 47p. 1942. reprint ed. 20.00 (*0-87014-321-2*); reprint ed. mic. film 20.00 (*0-685-61233-3*) Natl Bur Econ Res.

Uses of Passion. Angie Estes. LC 95-13158. (Peregrine Smith Poetry Contest Ser.). 64p. 1995. pap. 9.95 (*0-87905-684-3*) Gibbs Smith Pub.

Uses of Plants by the Indians of the Missouri River Region. enl. ed. Melvin R. Gilmore. LC 90-25514. (Illus.). xviii, 165p. 1991. reprint ed. pap. 10.00 (*0-8032-7034-8*, Bison Books); reprint ed. text ed. 30.00 (*0-8032-2146-0*) U of Nebr Pr.

Uses of Psychiatry in Smaller General Hospitals. Raymond M. Glasscote et al. LC 82-22719. 141p. reprint ed. pap. 40.20 (*0-8357-7797-9*, 2036160) Bks Demand.

Uses of Psychiatry in the Law: A Clinical View of Forensic Psychiatry. Walter Bromberg. LC 78-22724. (Illus.). x, 442p. 1979. text ed. 69.50 (*0-89930-000-6*, BRP/, Quorum Bks) Greenwood.

Uses of Randomness in Algorithms & Protocols. Joe Kilian. (ACM Distinguished Dissertation, 1989 Ser.). 250p. 1990. 35.95 (*0-262-11153-5*) MIT Pr.

Uses of Reform: "Godly Discipline" & Popular Behavior in Scotland & France, 1560-1610. Michael F. Graham. LC 96-5481. (Studies in Medieval & Reformation Thought: Vol. 58). 376p. 1996. 87.50 (*90-04-10261-2*) E J Brill.

Uses of Reminiscence: New Ways of Working with Older Adults. Ed. by Marc Kaminsky. LC 84-4520. (Journal of Gerontological Social Work: Vol. 7, Nos. 1-2). 245p. 1984. text ed. 39.95 (*0-86656-272-9*) Haworth Pr.

*__Uses of Reminiscence: New Ways of Working with Older Adults.__ Ed. by Marc Kaminsky. 245p. 1984. pap. 19.95 (*0-86656-285-0*) Haworth Pr.

Uses of Risk Analysis to Achieve Balanced Safety in Building Design an Operations. National Research Council Staff. Ed. by Bruce D. McDowell & Andrew C. Lemers. (Studies in Management of Building Technicians). 84p. (C). 1992. pap. text ed. 19.00 (*0-309-04680-7*) Natl Acad Pr.

Uses of Schooling. Harry S. Broudy. 160p. 1988. text ed. 19.95 (*0-415-00176-5*) Routledge.

Uses of "Structure" in Communication Studies. Ed. by Richard L. Conville. LC 93-19112. 240p. 1993. text ed. 59.95 (*0-275-94407-7*, C4407, Praeger Pubs) Greenwood.

Uses of Style in Archaeology. Ed. by Margaret W. Conkey & Christine A. Hastorf. (New Directions in Archaeology Ser.). 280p. (C). 1990. 65.00 (*0-521-35061-1*) Cambridge U Pr.

Uses of Style in Archaeology. Ed. by Margaret W. Conkey & Christine A. Hastorf. (New Directions in Archaeology Ser.). 146p. (C). 1993. pap. text ed. 20.95 (*0-521-44576-0*) Cambridge U Pr.

Uses of Supernatural Power: The Transformation of Popular Religion in Medieval & Early Modern Europe. Gabor Klaniczay. Ed. by Karen Margolis. Tr. by Susan Singerman from HUN. 300p. (C). 1990. text ed. 49.50 (*0-691-07377-5*) Princeton U Pr.

Uses of Talent. Dael L. Wolfle. LC 71-143817. 214p. 1971. 35.00 (*0-691-08603-6*) Princeton U Pr.

Uses of Talent. Dael L. Wolfle. LC 71-143817. (Illus.). 214p. 1971. reprint ed. pap. 61.00 (*0-7837-9488-6*, 2060231) Bks Demand.

Uses of Television in American Higher Education. James Zigerell. LC 90-36600. 192p. 1990. text ed. 49.95 (*0-275-93318-0*, C3318, Praeger Pubs) Greenwood.

Uses of the Canon. Howard Felperin. 208p. 1992. pap. 21.00 (*0-19-812265-9*) OUP.

Uses of the Canon: Elizabethan Literature & Contemporary Theory. Howard Felperin. 208p. 1990. 45.00 (*0-19-812244-6*) OUP.

Uses of the Past: Essays on Irish Culture. Ed. by Audrey S. Eyler & Robert F. Garratt. LC 86-40601. 200p. 1988. 32.50 (*0-87413-326-2*) U Delaware Pr.

Uses of the Past in the Novels of William Faulkner. Carl E. Rollyson. LC 84-2745. (Studies in Modern Literature: No. 37). 234p. reprint ed. pap. 66.70 (*0-8357-1554-X*, 2070598) Bks Demand.

Uses of the Seas. Ed. by Edmund A. Gullion. LC 69-11361. 1968. 4.95 (*0-317-02970-3*, C-93937); pap. 2.45 (*0-317-02971-1*, P-93936) Am Assembly.

Uses of the Spirit: Religious Impulse in Selected Autobiographies of American Women, 1630-1893. Phebe Davidson. LC 93-5973. (Studies in Women & Religion: Vol. 33). 228p. 1993. text ed. 89.95 (*0-7734-9354-9*) E Mellen.

Uses of the Unfashionable: The Pre-Raphaelites in Nineteenth-Century Culture. Morse Peckham. LC 92-33625. 1993. 10.95 (*0-935061-50-9*) Contemp Res.

Uses of the University. 3rd ed. Clark Kerr. 224p. 1982. pap. 15.95 (*0-674-93171-8*) HUP.

Uses of the University. 4th ed. Clark Kerr. (Godkin Lectures). (Illus.). 244p. 1995. pap. text ed. 15.95 (*0-674-93172-6*, KERUSY) HUP.

Uses of Tradition: Arts of Italian Americans in Philadelphia. Dorothy Noyes. (Illus.). 80p. (Orig.). (C). 1991. pap. 16.95 (*0-8122-1387-4*) U of Pa Pr.

*__Uses of Tradition: Arts of Italian Americans in Philadelphia.__ Dorothy Noyes. (Illus.). 79p. 1997. reprint ed. pap. text ed. 30.00 (*0-7881-3771-9*) DIANE Pub.

Uses of Tradition: Jewish Continuity in the Modern Era. Ed. by Jack Wertheimer. LC 92-33133. (Jewish Theological Seminary of America Ser.). 510p. (C). 1993. text ed. 45.00 (*0-674-93157-2*) HUP.

Uses of Writing in Psychotherapy. Ed. by Patricia Kelley. LC 89-26938. (Journal of Independent Social Work: Vol. 4, No. 2). 160p. (C). 1990. text ed. 39.95 (*0-86656-967-7*) Haworth Pr.

USFHA Coaches Manual. Boudewijn Castelijn. 100p. 1988. 19.00 (*0-318-49983-5*) US Field Hockey.

USFHA Umpiring Manual. 97p. 1988. 10.00 (*0-318-17592-4*); suppl. ed. write for info. (*0-318-60093-5*) US Field Hockey.

USFK Strategy-to-Tasks Resource Management. John Y. Schrader et al. LC 96-22431. 109p. (Orig.). 1996. pap. text ed. 13.00 (*0-8330-2353-5*, MR-654-USFK) Rand Corp.

USGF Junior Olympic Rhythmic Gymnastics Compulsory Program 1992-1996. United States Gymnastics Federation Staff. 118p. 1992. pap. 29.95 (*1-885250-32-0*) USA Gymnastics.

USGF Professional Development Program: USGF Coaches Education. U. S. A. Gymnastics Staff. (Coaches Accreditation Course Workbook Ser.: Level I). 24p. 1993. 20.00 (*1-885250-18-5*) USA Gymnastics.

USGF Women's Technical Committee Element Supplement 1993-96. USGF WTC Staff. 52p. 1993. pap. 10.00 (*1-885250-09-6*) USA Gymnastics.

Usher. Matthew Condon. (Orig.). 1993. pap. 14.95 (*0-7022-2421-9*, Pub. by Univ Queensland Pr AT) Intl Spec Bk.

Ushering in His Excellence: An Usher's Manual. Ron Kite. 128p. (Orig.). 1982. pap. 4.50 (*0-942847-00-8*) Nugget Truth Minist.

Usher's Book of the Mass. Modern Liturgy Editors. LC 96-4891. 31p. (Orig.). 1996. pap. 5.95 (*0-89390-364-7*) Resource Pubns.

Usher's Manual. Leslie Parrott, III. 48p. 1970. pap. 5.99 (*0-310-30651-5*, 10513P) Zondervan.

Usher's Passing. Robert R. McCammon. Ed. by Sally Peters. 416p. 1992. reprint ed. mass mkt. 6.99 (*0-671-76992-8*) PB.

Usher's Syndrome: What It Is, How to Cope, & How to Help. Earlene Duncan et al. (Illus.). 106p. 1988. pap. 20.95 (*0-398-06099-1*) C C Thomas.

Usher's Syndrome: What It Is, How to Cope, & How to Help. Earlene Duncan et al. (Illus.). 106p. (C). 1988. text ed. 32.95 (*0-398-05481-9*) C C Thomas.

Ushkuiniki. Aleksandr V. Tufanov. Ed. by Tatiana Nikolskaia. (Modern Russian Literature & Culture, Studies & Texts: Vol. 27). (Illus.). 197p. (Orig.). (RUS.). 1991. pap. 16.00 (*0-933884-77-X*) Berkeley Slavic.

USIA: New Directions for a New Era. Ed. by Henry B. Ryan. (ISD Reports). 56p. (Orig.). 1993. pap. text ed. 3.00 (*0-934742-76-6*) Geo U Inst Dplmcy.

USIA: Public Diplomacy in the Computer Age. 2nd ed. Allen C. Hansen. LC 89-3586. 262p. 1989. text ed. 59.95 (*0-275-93112-9*, C3112, Praeger Pubs) Greenwood.

USIA Economic Analysis of North American Ski Areas: 1989-90 Season. C. R. Goeldner et al. 150p. 1991. pap. 75.00 (*0-89478-021-2*) U CO Busn Res Div.

USIA Economic Analysis of North American Ski Areas: 1990-91 Season. C. R. Goeldner et al. 159p. 1992. pap. text ed. 100.00 (*0-89478-050-6*) U CO Busn Res Div.

*__Using a Client's 1040 to Generate Tax Planning Ideas.__ Practitioners Publishing Company Staff. 1996. write for info. (*0-7646-0090-7*) Prctnrs Pub Co.

Using a Computer in Church Ministry. James P. Emswiler. 1986. pap. 6.95 (*0-87193-248-2*) Dimension Bks.

Using a Computer Simulation to Teach General Equilibrium Concepts. Scott Magruder. 63p. 1989. pap. text ed. 26.50 (*0-931179-03-3*) Bus Account Pubns.

Using a Family Perspective in Catholic Social Justice & Family Ministries. Ed. by Patricia Voydanoff & Thomas M. Martin. LC 93-36835. (Roman Catholic Studies: Vol. 6). 228p. 1993. text ed. 89.95 (*0-7734-9428-6*) E Mellen.

Using a Gebra Named Al in the Classroom. Wendy Isdell. 32p. (Orig.). 1993. teacher ed., pap. 6.95 (*0-915793-59-8*) Free Spirit Pub.

Using a Law Library. 3rd ed. Paul Hasse. (Citizens Legal Manual Ser.). 174p. 1988. pap. write for info. (*0-910073-10-4*) HALT DC.

Using a Lawyer. Kay A. Ostberg. (Random House Practical Law Manual Ser.). 146p. 1990. pap. write for info. (*0-679-72970-4*) HALT DC.

Using a Map & Compass. Don Geary. LC 95-3069. (Illus.). 160p. 1995. pap. 14.95 (*0-8117-2591-X*) Stackpole.

Using a Medical Library. 1991. write for info. (*0-944093-18-3*) Am Brain Tumor.

Using a Microcomputer in the Classroom. Gary G. Bitter & Ruth A. Camuse. (J). (gr. k-12). 1983. pap. text ed. 25.00 (*0-8359-8144-4*, Reston) P-H.

Using a Microcomputer in the Classroom. 2nd ed. Gary G. Bitter & Ruth A. Camuse. (Illus.). 384p. 1988. pap. text ed. 38.67 (*0-13-938978-4*) P-H.

Using a Microcomputer in the Classroom. 3rd ed. Gary G. Bitter et al. LC 92-39102. 1993. pap. text ed. 49.00 (*0-205-14758-5*) Allyn.

Using a Multicultural Calendar. (Ethnic Studies Bulletins: No. 2). 14p. 1982. 2.00 (*0-685-05161-7*) I N Thut World Educ Ctr.

*__Using a pH Meter.__ Norman E. Griswold & M. L. Gillette. Ed. by C. L. Stanitski. (Modular Laboratory Program in Chemistry Ser.). 12p. (C). 1997. pap. text ed. 1.35 (*0-87540-489-8*) Chem Educ Res.

Using a Table Saw. Nick Engler. (Workshop Companion Ser.). 1995. pap. 12.95 (*0-87596-609-8*) Rodale Pr Inc.

Using a TI Graphing Calculator. James Maratta. 92p. (C). 1995. spiral bd. 12.07 (*0-7872-1654-2*) Kendall-Hunt.

Using Access for Windows 95. 5th ed. Roger Jennings et al. (Illus.). 1290p. (Orig.). 1995. 44.99 (*0-7897-0184-7*) Que.

*__Using Microsoft Access 97.__ Scott F. Barker. 432p. 1997. 24.99 (*0-7897-1050-1*) Mac Comp Pub.

Using Access 2 for Windows. 2nd ed. Roger Jennings. 1254p. 1994. 34.99 (*1-56529-628-1*) Que.

Using Access 2 with Office Companion. R. Jennings et al. 1995. student ed. 39.99 incl. cd-rom (*0-7897-0350-5*) Que.

Using Access 95. Robert Schneider & Que Staff. (Illus.). 385p. (Orig.). 1995. 24.99 (*0-7897-0185-5*) Que.

*__Using Access 97.__ Roger Jennings. 1997. 65.00 (*0-7897-1411-6*) Que.

*__Using Access 97: Special Edition.__ 2nd ed. Roger Jennings. 1997. 49.99 (*0-7897-1452-3*) Que.

Using Accounting Information: An Interactive Learning Approach. Linda M. Plunkett et al. Ed. by Horan. 200p. (C). 1993. pap. text ed. 20.50 (*0-314-02184-1*) West Pub.

Using Acid-Base Indicators to Visually Estimate the pH of Solutions. Marcia L. Gillette. (Modular Laboratory Program in Chemistry Ser.). 12p. (C). 1995. pap. text ed. 1.35 (*0-87540-465-0*, EQUL 465-0) Chem Educ Res.

Using Act! Que Development Group Staff. (Illus.). 374p. (Orig.). 1995. 19.99 (*0-7897-0254-1*) Que.

*__Using Active Server Pages.__ Scott Johnson. 1997. 49.99 (*0-7897-1389-6*) Que.

Using ActiveX Special Edition. Que Development Group Staff. 408p. 1996. pap. text ed. 39.99 incl. cd-rom (*0-7897-0886-8*) Que.

Using Activity Based Management for Continuous Improvement. Tom Pryor & Julie Sahm. (Illus.). 190p. 1995. pap. 29.95 (*1-886933-00-6*) ICMS TX.

Using Adult Learning Principles Workshop. Sharon G. Fisher. 174p. 1989. ring bd. 99.95 (*0-87425-081-1*) HRD Press.

Using Advanced Revelation Applications I Training Manual. Revelation Technologies Staff. 100p. 1989. 30.00 (*0-923387-26-9*) Rev Tech Inc.

UV

An Asterisk (*) at the beginning of an entry indicates that the title is appearing in BIP for the first time.

Using Advanced Revelation Applications I Training Manual (Instructor Manual) Revelation Technologies Staff. 75p. 1989. 60.00 (0-923387-27-7) Rev Tech Inc.

Using Algebra. Ethan D. Bolker. LC 90-50000. 305p. (Orig.). (C). 1990. pap. text ed. 19.95 (1-55605-134-4) Wyndham Hall.

***Using Alternative Assessments in Vocational Education.** Brian M. Stecher et al. LC 97-16695. (Illus.). xvii, 176p. 1997. pap. 15.00 (0-8330-2489-2, MR-836-NCRVE) Rand Corp.

Using Alternative Dispute Resolution in the Federal Government. Daniel R. Levinson et al. 40p. 1993. pap. text ed. 9.95 (0-936295-41-4) FPMI Comns.

Using America Online. 2nd ed. Gene Steinberg & Que Staff. (Illus.). 450p. 1994. 19.99 (0-7897-0078-6) Que.

***Using America Online.** 3rd ed. Gene Steinberg. 1000p. 1997. 39.99 (0-7897-1254-7) Que.

Using America Online. 3rd ed. Gene Steinberg. 400p. 1996. pap. text ed. 24.99 (0-7897-0826-4) Que.

***Using America Online.** 4th ed. Gene Steinberg. 1997. pap. text ed. 19.99 incl. cd-rom (0-7897-1424-8) Que.

Using America Online with Windows 95. Gene Steinberg. (Illus.). 400p. (Orig.). 1995. 24.99 (0-7897-0594-X) Que.

***Using American Law Books: Including Online & CD-ROM Services.** 4th ed. Alfred J. Lewis. 198p. 1995. pap. 26.88 (0-7872-0735-7) Kendall-Hunt.

Using an Art Technique to Facilitate Leadership Development. Cheryl De Ciantis. LC 95-31264. 1995. 30.00 (1-882197-09-7) Ctr Creat Leader.

Using an Impact Measurement System to Evaluate Land Development. Philip S. Schaenman. (Land Development Impact Ser.). 106p. (Orig.). 1976. pap. text ed. 14.50 (0-87766-172-3) Urban Inst.

Using an Offshore Bank for Profit, Privacy & Tax Protection. Jerome Schneider. Ed. by Max Benavidez & Kate Vozof2. (Illus.). 259p. 1982. 15.00 (0-933560-03-6) Wilshire CA.

Using & Assessing CBI Data at the Bank of England. B. Pesaran & C. B. Wright. (Bank of England Technical Ser.: Vol. 37). 28p. 1991. reprint ed. pap. 25.00 (0-608-00690-4, 2061461) Bks Demand.

Using & Extending C++ Standard. Skaller. 1996. pap. text ed. 38.00 (0-13-461682-0) P-H.

Using & Managing UUCP. unabridged ed. Ed Ravin et al. (Illus.). 424p. (Orig.). 1996. pap. 29.95 (1-56592-153-4) OReilly & Assocs.

Using & Misusing Environmental Marketing Terms: An Evaluation by EPA. Environmental Protection Agency Staff. 196p. 1993. pap. text ed. 69.00 (0-86587-348-8) Gov Insts.

***Using & Porting GNU CC, Version 2.7.2.** Richard M. Stallman. 512p. 1996. pap. 50.00 (1-882114-36-1) Free Software.

***Using & Programming the Psion Siena.** (Illus.). (Orig.). 1997. pap. 39.95 (0-614-30729-5, Pub. by Capall Bann Pubng UK) Holmes Pub.

Using & Troubleshooting the MC68000. James W. Coffron. 1983. pap. 20.50 (0-8359-8159-2, Reston) P-H.

Using & Troubleshooting the Z-8000. James W. Coffron. 1982. text ed. 34.00 (0-8359-8157-6, Reston); pap. text ed. 19.95 (0-8359-8156-8, Reston) P-H.

Using & Understanding Maps, 12 vols., Set. Ed. by Scott Morris. (Illus.). 48p. (YA). (gr. 5 up). 1994. lib. bdg. 203.40 (0-7910-1800-8) Chelsea Hse.

Using & Understanding Medical Statistics. 2nd rev. ed. D. E. Matthews & V. T. Farewell. (Illus.). xii, 228p. 1988. 32.00 (3-8055-4719-6) S Karger.

Using & Understanding Medical Statistics. 3rd rev. ed. D. E. Matthews & V. T. Farewell. (Illus.). xiv, 246p. 1996. pap. 35.00 (3-8055-6276-4) S Karger.

Using Animator Studio: Special Edition. Denise Tyler. 1996. pap. text ed. 49.99 incl. cd-rom (0-7897-0582-6) Que.

Using Appleworks: The Complete Guide to Applications. Richard Loggins. 1985. 17.95 (0-89303-911-X) S&S Trade.

Using Application Software. Edward G. Martin. 192p. 1991. pap. 18.95 (0-87835-564-2) Course Tech.

Using Application Software: Featuring DOS 5.0 & 6.0, WordPerfect 6.0, Lotus 1-2-3 2.4, & dBASE IV 2.0. Edward G. Martin. LC 93-34932. 1994. pap. 18.95 (0-87709-550-7) Course Tech.

Using Application Software: Featuring Windows 3.1, Wordperfect 6.0 for Windows, Excel for Windows 5.0, Paradox for Windows 4.5. Edward G. Martin. LC 94-25499. 1995. pap. 18.95 (0-87709-553-1) Course Tech.

Using Application Software: Lotus SmartSuite Edition. Edward G. Martin. (DF - Computer Applications Ser.). (Illus.). 463p. 1996. teacher ed., text ed. 23.95 incl. 3.5 ld (0-7895-0575-4) Course Tech.

Using Application Software: PC Type, PC-Calc, PC-File, PC-DIAL. James Shuman. 256p. (Orig.). 1986. pap. text ed. 17.95 (0-938188-43-7); disk write for info. (0-318-61056-6) Mitchell Pub.

Using Application Software, Alternate Edition: Alternate Edition Featuring DOS 5.0, WordPerfect 5.1, Lotus 1-2-3, Release 2.2-2.3, & dBASE IV, Version 1.1. Edward G. Martin. LC 92-21995. 1993. pap. 18.95 (0-87835-964-8) Course Tech.

Using Applications Software. Donald H. Beil. 355p. 1986. pap. text ed. 27.95 (0-07-004427-9) McGraw.

Using Applications Software: Microsoft Office Professional Edition. Edward G. Martin. (DF - Computer Applications Ser.). 256p. 1996. pap. 22.95 (0-7895-0096-5) Course Tech.

Using Applications Software: Microsoft Office 95. Edward G. Martin. (DF - Computer Applications Ser.). 320p. 1996. teacher ed., pap. 18.95 (0-7895-0675-0) S-W Pub.

Using Applied Psychology in Personnel Management. Daena Farrow. (C). 1982. write for info. (0-8359-8131-2, Reston) P-H.

Using Art in Sunday Worship. Eileen Gurak. LC 90-8949. 88p. (Orig.). (C). 1990. pap. 7.95 (0-89390-186-5) Resource Pubns.

Using Assembly Language. 3rd ed. Allen L. Wyatt, Sr. (Using Ser.). (Illus.). 900p. (Orig.). 1992. 29.95 (0-88022-884-9) Que.

Using Assessment Results for Career Development. 4th ed. Vernon G. Zunker. LC 93-20947. 201p. 1994. pap. 26.95 (0-534-21204-2) Brooks-Cole.

Using Assessment Results in Career Counseling. 3rd ed. Vernon G. Zunker. LC 89-23873. 185p. (C). 1990. pap. 18.95 (0-534-12109-8) Brooks-Cole.

Using Assessment to Improve Instruction. K. Patricia Cross. (DeGarmo Lectures: No. 12). 1987. 3.00 (0-685-31370-0) Soc Profs Ed.

Using Astrology. Mae R. Wilson-Ludlam. LC 82-72553. 192p. 1985. 16.00 (0-86690-287-2, W2649-014) Am Fed Astrologers.

Using Audits - Inspections to Ensure Your OSHA Compliance. Steve Weisz. 22p. 1994. pap. text ed. 17.50 (0-86587-432-8) Gov Insts.

Using AutoCAD: Engineering Drawing & Design Problem Workbook (Release 11) Michael A. Jordan. 1992. 16.95 (0-8273-5406-1) Delmar.

Using Autocad: Engineering Drawing Problems Workbook; Instructor's Guide. Michael A. Jordan. 1992. teacher ed. 16.00 (0-8273-5565-3) Delmar.

Using AutoCAD: Release 11.0. 4th ed. James E. Fuller. 570p. 1991. pap. 37.95 (0-8273-4568-2) Delmar.

Using AutoCAD: Release 11.0. 4th ed. James E. Fuller. 570p. 1992. pap. 20.95 (0-8273-4755-3) Delmar.

Using AutoCAD: Release 13. Ed. by James E. Fuller. LC 94-46214. 1995. pap. 40.95 (0-8273-6972-7) Delmar.

Using AutoCAD: Release 13 for DOS. Ralph Grabowski & James E. Fuller. LC 94-46214. (Blueprint Reading & Drafting Ser.). 1995. pap. 40.95 (0-8273-6824-0) Delmar.

Using AutoCAD for Windows. Que Development Group Staff. 1281p. 1995. 39.99 (1-56529-887-X) Que.

Using AutoCAD Release 11. 5th ed. James Fuller. 1992. pap. 36.95 (0-8273-5344-8) Delmar.

Using AutoCAD Release 11 Trade Version. 4th ed. James E. Fuller. 1991. pap. 39.95 (0-8273-4753-7) Delmar.

Using AUTOCAD Release 12: Instructor's Guide. James E. Fuller. 57p. 1993. 14.00 (0-8273-6014-2) Delmar.

Using Autocad Release 12: With AME, AutoLISP & Customizing. 6th ed. James Fuller. 1993. text ed. 42.95 (0-8273-5838-5) Delmar.

Using AutoCAD Release 13. Fuller. (ID - CAD/CAM Ser.). 64p. 1995. teacher ed., text ed. 19.00 (0-8273-6825-9) Delmar.

***Using AutoCAD Release 14.** Ralph Grabowski. LC 97-25349. 1997. write for info. (0-7668-0127-6) Autodesk.

Using AutoCad R12 Engineering Drawing Problems Workbook. Michael A. Jordan. 132p. 1993. pap. 20.95 (0-8273-5922-5) Delmar.

Using Autocad R12 Engineering Drawing Problems Workbook Inst. Guide. Michael A. Jordan. 49p. 1993. teacher ed. 16.00 (0-8273-6361-3) Delmar.

***Using AutoCAD R13 DOS.** Fuller. 96p. 1995. teacher ed., pap. text ed. 19.95 (0-8273-7696-0) Delmar.

Using AutoCAD R13 for Windows/3. Fuller. (CAD/CAM Ser.). 1996. 40.95 (0-8273-7500-X) Van Nos Reinhold.

Using AutoCAD R13 Windows. Fuller & Grabowski. LC 96-20291. (CAD/CAM Ser.). (Illus.). 1024p. 1996. text ed. 40.95 incl. disk (0-8273-7499-2) Delmar.

Using Autosketch. Fuller. LC 88-33610. (C). 1990. teacher ed., pap. text ed. 8.00 (0-8273-3243-2) Delmar.

Using Autosketch. Monson. LC 88-33610. (C). 1990. pap. text ed. 21.95 (0-8273-3242-4) Delmar.

***Using BackOffice Vol. 2: Back Office, Vol. 2.** 2nd ed. G. A. Sullivan. (Special Edition Ser.). 960p. 1997. 75.00 (0-7897-1130-3) Mac Comp Pub.

***Using Backstage.** Rick Darnell. 600p. 1996. 49.99 (0-7897-0931-7) Mac Comp Pub.

Using Bandages. Crystal Stevens et al. (Taking Care of Simple Injuries Ser.). (Illus.). 88p. (Orig.). 1978. Set. pap. text ed. 149.00 (0-685-05765-8) PRO-ED.

Using Banks & Credit Services. Cheryl S. Johnson & Richard L. Johnson. (Living Skills Ser.). 99p. 1993. teacher ed. 8.95 (1-884245-28-5); pap. text ed. 7.95 (1-884245-27-7) Life Choices.

Using Bar Code: Why It's Taking Over. 2nd ed. David J. Collins & Nancy N. Whipple. (Illus.). 328p. (C). 1994. reprint ed. pap. 34.95 (0-9627406-1-6) Data Capture Pr.

Using Base-Ten Blocks: To Develop Number-Sense, Place Value, Addition & Subtraction of Whole Numbers. William L. Swart. 31p. 1992. pap. text ed. 5.75 (1-883547-05-9) Tricon Pub.

Using BASIC: An Introduction to Computer Programming. 3rd ed. Julien Hennefeld. 348p. 1985. pap. 54.95 (0-87150-846-X) PWS Pubs.

Using Basic English Grammar: Form & Function. Edward G. Woods & Nicole J. McLeod. LC 92-29721. 1992. 11.95 (0-13-952664-1) P-H.

Using BBC BASIC. Pete J. Cockerell. LC 83-10607. 392p. reprint ed. pap. 111.80 (0-8357-6936-4, 2037995) Bks Demand.

Using Beneficial Insects: Garden Soil Builders, Pollinators, & Predators. Rhonda M. Hart. Ed. by Heather Clemon. (Country Wisdom Bulletin Ser.). (Illus.). 32p. 1991. 2.95 (0-88266-676-2, Storey Pub) Storey Comm Inc.

Using Biblical Hebrew in Ministry: A Practical Guide for Pastors, Seminarians, & Bible Students. Don Parker. 278p. (Orig.). (C). 1995. pap. text ed. 26.50 (0-7618-0124-3) U Pr of Amer.

Using Bibliotherapy in Clinical Practice: A Guide to Self-Help Books. John T. Pardeck. LC 93-20499. (Contributions in Psychology Ser.: No. 22). 160p. 1993. text ed. 55.00 (0-313-27991-8, PUB/, Greenwood Pr) Greenwood.

***Using Big Books & Predictable Books.** Priscilla Lynch. (FRE.). pap. 7.99 (0-590-71984-X) Scholastic Inc.

Using Biographical Methods to Understand Managerial Behavior & Personality. Joan R. Kofodimos. (Technical Reports: No. 139G). 45p. 1990. pap. 7.50 (0-912879-37-8) Ctr Creat Leader.

Using Biography. William Empson. 280p. 1985. 33.95 (0-674-93160-2) HUP.

Using Blackbird: Special Edition. Mike Morrison. 900p. 1997. pap. text ed. 49.99 incl. cd-rom (0-7897-0762-4) Que.

Using Borland's Quattro. R. Taylor. Ed. by Jose Hurtado. (Logic Ware Ser.). (Illus.). 1989. 24.95 (0-929978-11-0) M-USA Busn Systs.

Using Building Systems: Modular, Panelized, Log, Dome. James Carper. 118p. 1990. pap. 10.00 (0-86718-314-4) Home Builder.

Using Business Statistics: A Guide for Beginners. Terry Dickey. Ed. by Chris Carrigan. LC 93-72980. (Fifty-Minute Ser.). (Illus.). 115p. (Orig.). 1994. pap. 10.95 (1-56052-250-X) Crisp Pubns.

Using C-Kermit. 2nd ed. Frank Da Cruz & Christine M. Gianone. (Illus.). 514p. (Orig.). 1993. 41.95 (1-55558-108-0, EY-J896E-DP, Digital DEC) Buttrwrth-Heinemann.

Using C-Kermit Communication Software. 2nd ed. Frank Da Cruz & Christine M. Gianone. LC 96-38354. (Illus.). 620p. 1996. pap. 39.95 (1-55558-164-1, Digital DEC) Buttrwrth-Heinemann.

Using C with Curses, Lex & Yacc: Building a Window Shell for UNIX System V. Axel T. Schreiner. 300p. 1990. pap. text ed. 58.00 (0-13-932864-5) P-H.

Using CA-Unicenter, Special Edition. Que Development Group Staff. 1996. pap. 59.99 incl. cd-rom (0-7897-0691-1) Que.

Using CADkey. Paul J. Resetarits. (CAD/CAM Ser.). 1987. teacher ed. 16.00 (0-8273-2967-9) Delmar.

Using CADKEY. 2nd ed. Paul J. Resetarits & Gary R. Bertoline. 400p. 1991. pap. 42.95 (0-8273-3632-2) Delmar.

Using CADKEY: Version 7. Paul J. Resetarits & Gary Bertoline. (Illus.). 832p. 1996. pap. 44.95 incl. disk (0-8273-7009-1) Delmar.

Using CADKey & Its Applications, Vols. 5-6. Paul J. Resetarits & Gary Bertoline. 36p. 1993. teacher ed. 16.00 (0-8273-5718-4) Delmar.

Using CADKEY & Its Applications Versions 5 & 6. 4th ed. Paul J. Resetarits & Gary R. Bertoline. LC 92-21484. 652p. 1994. pap. 43.95 (0-8273-5607-2) Delmar.

Using Cadkey Light. Paul J. Resetarits & Gary R. Bertoline. 301p. 1991. pap. 41.95 (0-8273-4735-9) Delmar.

Using CADkey Light. Paul J. Resetarits. (CAD/CAM Ser.). 1991. teacher ed., pap. 16.00 (0-8273-4736-7) Delmar.

Using Cadkey 4.0: Instructor's Guide. 3rd ed. Paul J. Resetarits. 1991. pap. 15.00 (0-8273-4946-7) Delmar.

Using Calculators. (J). 1993. pap. 9.95 (0-590-49233-0) Scholastic Inc.

Using Calculators for Business Problems. 3rd ed. Gary Berg & Leo Gafney. 276p. 1993. teacher ed. 8.00 (1-56118-578-7); pap. text ed. 18.95 (1-56118-577-9) Paradigm MN.

Using California Law Books. Alfred J. Lewis. 100p. (C). 1994. per., pap. text ed. 17.32 (0-8403-2982-2) Kendall-Hunt.

Using Calligraphy: A Workbook of Alphabets, Projects, & Techniques. Margaret Shepherd. 160p. 1979. pap. 14.00 (0-02-081970-6) Macmillan.

Using Case Studies, Simulations & Games in Human Resource Developments. J. William Pfeiffer & Arlette C. Ballew. LC 88-50384. (Training Technologies Set Ser.). 124p. (Orig.). 1988. Set, 7 bks. & index. pap. 139.00 (0-88390-222-2, Pfffr & Co) Jossey-Bass.

Using CASE Tools in Systems Development: Their Scope & Value. Ed. by Richard Williams. (Illus.). 125p. 1990. text ed. 55.95 (0-566-09053-8, Pub. by Avebury Pub UK) Ashgate Pub Co.

Using CGI, Special Ed. Michael Erwin & Jeffrey Dwight. 1996. 49.99 incl. cd-rom (0-614-14451-5) Macmillan.

Using Charts & Graphs: One Thousand Ideas for Getting Attention. Jan V. White. 201p. 1984. pap. 39.95 (0-8352-1894-5) Bowker.

***Using Chemoffice with Biochemistry.** Garrett. (C). 1995. pap. text ed. 13.50 (0-03-017958-0) HB Coll Pubs.

Using Chemoffice with Organic Chemistry. Brown. (C). 1995. pap. text ed. 7.00 (0-03-017959-9) HB Coll Pubs.

Using Chicago Multimedia Special Edition. Que Development Group Staff. 1996. pap. 39.99 incl. cd-rom (0-7897-0058-1) Que.

Using Children's Books in Preschool Settings: A How-to-Do-It Manual. Steven Herb & Sara Willoughby-Herb. 181p. 1994. pap. 32.50 (1-55570-156-6) Neal-Schuman.

Using Children's Books in Reading - Language Arts Programs: A How-to-Do-It Manual for School & Public Librarians. Diane D. Canavan & LaVonne H. Sanborn. (How-to-Do-It Ser.). 216p. 1992. 35.00 (1-55570-101-9) Neal-Schuman.

Using Children's Literature. 1991. 7.50 (0-910857-80-6) Educ Impress.

Using Children's Literature to Learn about Disabilities & Illness. Joan K. Blaska. 168p. (C). 1996. pap. text ed. 19.95 (1-886979-07-3) Practicl Pr.

***Using Civil Remedies for Criminal Behavior.** 92p. 1994. pap. text ed. 30.00 (1-57979-192-1) BPI Info Servs.

Using Clarion Database Developer: Includes Version 3. 2nd ed. Mark S. Burgess. 1995. pap. write for info. (0-201-63297-7) Addison-Wesley.

Using Clarion Professional Developer. Mark S. Burgess. 1991. pap. 28.95 (0-201-57054-8) Addison-Wesley.

Using ClarisWorks. Laurie M. Love. 1992. pap. 24.95 (0-201-57017-3) Addison-Wesley.

Using ClarisWorks 2.0 for the Macintosh. 2nd ed. Laurie M. Love. 1993. pap. 24.95 (0-201-62629-2) Addison-Wesley.

Using Clinical Practice Guidelines to Evaluate Quality of Care: Issues & Methods, 2 vols., Set. (Illus.). 166p. (Orig.). (C). 1995. pap. text ed. 40.00 (0-7881-2474-9) DIANE Pub.

Using Cognitive Approaches with the Seriously Mentally Ill: Dialogue Across the Barrier. Barbara A. Olevitch. LC 95-6348. 192p. 1995. text ed. 57.95 (0-275-95244-4, Praeger Pubs) Greenwood.

Using Cointegration Analysis in Econometric Modelling. Richard I. Harris. LC 94-45273. (C). 1995. pap. text ed. 32.00 (0-13-355892-4) P-H.

Using Communication Theory: An Introduction to Planned Communication. Sven R. Windhal et al. (Illus.). 256p. 1992. 55.00 (0-8039-8430-8); pap. 22.00 (0-8039-8431-6) Sage.

Using Community Resources. Nancy A. Osborn & Martha C. Monroe. (EEToolbox-Workshop Resource Manual Ser.). 44p. 1994. 8.00 (1-884782-08-6) Natl Consort EET.

Using CompuServe. 3rd ed. Mike Miller. (Illus.). 400p. (Orig.). 1996. 24.99 (0-7897-0595-8) Mac Comp Pub.

Using Compuserve Special Edition. Que Staff. 875p. 1995. pap. 29.99 incl. cd-rom (0-7897-0280-0) Que.

Using Computer Bulletin Boards. 2nd rev. ed. John V. Hedtke. 422p. 1992. pap. 29.95 (1-55828-196-7) MIS Press.

Using Computer Bulletin Boards. 3rd ed. John V. Hedtke. 1995. pap. 29.95 (1-55828-391-9) MIS Press.

Using Computer Color Effectively: An Illustrated Reference to Computer Color Interface. Lisa G. Thorell & Wanda J. Smith. (Illus.). 224p. 1989. 49.95 (0-13-939878-3); pap. 29.95 (0-13-939852-X) P-H.

Using Computer in Environmental Education: Interactive Multimedia & On-Line Learning. NCEET Staff. 76p. (C). 1996. 8.00 (0-7872-2193-7) Kendall-Hunt.

Using Computer Screens. Larry Mikulecky. 1990. 12.50 (0-13-852252-9) P-H.

Using Computers: A Gateway to Information. 2nd ed. Gary B. Shelly. 1996. text ed. 47.35 (0-7895-0009-4) S-W Pub.

***Using Computers: A Gateway to Information (Brief) & Microsoft Works for Windows 95, Incl. instr. resource pkg, inst. manuals.** Gary B. Shelly et al. (Illus.). 1232p. 1996. student ed., text ed. write for info. incl. 3.5 ld (0-7895-1237-8); student ed., spiral bd. write for info. incl. 3.5 ld (0-7895-1238-6) Course Tech.

***Using Computers: A Gateway to Information (Brief) & Microsoft Works (Short Course) for Windows 95, Incl. instr. resource pkg, inst. manuals.** Gary B. Shelly et al. (Illus.). 880p. 1996. student ed., text ed. write for info. incl. 3.5 ld (0-7895-1234-3); student ed., spiral bd. write for info. incl. 3.5 ld (0-7895-1235-1) Course Tech.

***Using Computers: A Gateway to Information Brief Edition & Microsoft Office: Introductory Concepts & Techniques, Incl. instr. manual & supporting materials.** Gary B. Shelly et al. (Illus.). 1996. text ed. write for info. incl. 3.5 hd (0-7895-0313-1) Course Tech.

***Using Computers: A Gateway to Information Brief Edition & Microsoft Works 3, Incl. instr. manuals, labs.** Gary B. Shelly et al. (Illus.). 1224p. 1996. student ed., text ed. write for info. incl. 3.5 ld (0-7895-0311-5) Course Tech.

***Using Computers: A Gateway to Information Brief Edition & Microsoft Works 3, Incl. instrs. manuals, labs.** Gary B. Shelly et al. (Illus.). 1224p. 1996. student ed., spiral bd. write for info. incl. 3.5 ld (0-7895-0312-3) Course Tech.

Using Computers: Gateway to Information. Gary B. Shelly et al. LC 96-33778. 1996. pap. 43.35 (0-7895-1185-1); suppl. ed., pap. 33.95 (0-7895-1191-6) S-W Pub.

Using Computers: Gateway to Information. 2nd ed. Gary B. Shelly. (Shelly-Cashman Ser.). 1996. pap. 44.65 (0-87709-411-X) S-W Pub.

Using Computers: Gateway to Information - Brief. 2nd ed. Gary B. Shelly. 1996. pap. 33.95 (0-7895-0315-8) S-W Pub.

Using Computers: Gateway to Information & Programming in Qbasic. 2nd ed. Gary B. Shelly. 1996. pap. 49.35 (0-7895-0309-3) S-W Pub.

Using Computers: Human Factors in Information Systems. Raymond S. Nickerson. 22.50 (0-317-42856-X) McGraw.

Using Computers: Human Factors in Information Systems. Raymond S. Nickerson. 456p. 1987. reprint ed. pap. 14.50 (0-262-64022-8, Bradford Bks) MIT Pr.

Using Computers: Lab Manual. 2nd ed. Martin. 288p. 1991. pap. 18.95 (0-87835-689-4) Course Tech.

Using Computers: World Wide Web Ed. Gary B. Shelly. 1996. student ed., pap. 18.95 (0-7895-1270-X) S-W Pub.

Using Computers - All 95 Titles. 2nd ed. Gary B. Shelly. 1996. student ed., pap. 18.95 (0-7895-0411-1) S-W Pub.

Using Computers & Applications Software Featuring VP Planner, dBASE III-III Plus & WordPerfect. Lon Ingalsbe et al. 800p. (C). 1989. pap. write for info. (0-675-21097-6, Merrill Coll) P-H.

Using Computers & Information. Jack B. Rochester. 1996. student ed. 32.00 (1-57576-329-X) Mac Pub USA.

Using Computers & Information. annot. ed. Jack B. Rochester. 1996. teacher ed., pap. text ed. 80.00 (1-57576-060-6) Que Educ & Trng.

Using Computers & Information: Tools for Knowledge Workers. Jack B. Rochester. 1996. pap. text ed. 72.00 (1-57576-059-2) Que Educ & Trng.

Using Computers & Speech Synthesis to Facilitate Communicative Interaction with Young & or Severely Handicapped Children. Linda J. Burkhart. LC 87-71763. (Illus.). (C). 1987. student ed. 24.95 (0-9619338-0-1) L J Burkhart.

An Asterisk (*) at the beginning of an entry indicates that the title is appearing in BIP for the first time.

Using Computers, Brief + MS Office Introduction. 2nd ed. Gary B. Shelly. 1995. pap. 45.00 (*0-7895-0314-X*) S-W Pub.

Using Computers in an Information Age. Brightman. (DC - Introduction to Computing Ser.). 1988. text ed. 51.95 (*0-538-10260-8*) S-W Pub.

***Using Computers in Architectural Practice.** Woodward. (Illus.). 224p. 1997. text ed. write for info. (*0-419-21310-4*, E & FN Spon) Routledge Chapman & Hall.

***Using Computers in Chemistry & Chemical Education.** Theresa J. Zielinski & Mary L. Swift. LC 97-14325. (ACS Professional Reference Books). 1997. write for info. (*0-8412-3465-5*) Am Chemical.

Using Computers in Clinical Practice: Psychotherapy & Mental Health Applications. Ed. by Marc D. Schwartz. LC 83-18648. 510p. 1984. text ed. 89.95 (*0-86656-208-7*) Haworth Pr.

Using Computers in English: A Practical Guide. Phil Moore. (Teaching Secondary English Ser.). 200p. 1986. pap. 14.95 (*0-416-36190-0*, 9929) Routledge Chapman & Hall.

Using Computers in Environmental Education: Interactive Multimedia & On-Line Learning. W. J. Rohwedder. (EEToolbox-Workshop Resource Manual Ser.). 72p. 1994. teacher ed. 8.00 (*1-884782-11-6*) Natl Consort EET.

Using Computers in History: A Practical Guide. M. J. Lewis & Roger Lloyd-Jones. LC 95-20050. 256p. (C). 1996. pap. 18.95 (*0-415-10312-6*); text ed. 59.95 (*0-415-10311-8*) Routledge.

Using Computers in Hospitality & Tourism. Peter O'Connor. LC 95-10738. (Illus.). 256p. 1995. 60.00 (*0-304-33296-8*); pap. 24.95 (*0-304-33299-2*) Cassell.

Using Computers in Human Resources: How to Select & Make the Best Use of Automated HR Systems. Stephen E. Forrer & Zandy B. Leibowitz. LC 90-19954. (Management Ser.). 232p. text ed. 32.95 (*1-55542-318-3*) Jossey-Bass.

Using Computers in Legal Research: A Guide to LEXIS & WESTLAW. Christopher G. Wren & Jill R. Wren. LC 93-40352. (Illus.). 815p. (Orig.). (C). 1994. pap. text ed. 19.95 (*0-916951-21-9*) Adams & Ambrose.

***Using Computers in Linguistics: A Practical Guide.** John Lawler & Helen A. Dry. LC 97-23787. 1998. write for info. (*0-415-16792-2*); pap. write for info. (*0-415-16793-0*) Routledge.

Using Computers in Mathematics. 2nd ed. G. Elgarten. 1986. text ed. 38.24 (*0-201-20793-1*) Addison-Wesley.

Using Computers in Our Society. Kelly. (Introduction to Computing Ser.). 1988. text ed. 43.95 (*0-538-10740-5*) S-W Pub.

Using Computers in Physics. John R. Merrill. LC 80-5681. 271p. 1980. pap. text ed. 23.00 (*0-8191-1134-1*) U Pr of Amer.

Using Computers in Qualitative Research. Ed. by Nigel G. Fielding & Raymond M. Lee. 224p. (C). 1991. text ed. 69.95 (*0-8039-8424-3*); pap. text ed. 19.95 (*0-8039-8425-1*) Sage.

Using Computers in Society. Kelly. (DC - Introduction to Computing Ser.). 1988. student ed., pap. 15.95 (*0-538-10741-3*) S-W Pub.

Using Computers in Society. Kelly. (DC - Introduction to Computing Ser.). 1988. 73.95 (*0-538-10742-1*) S-W Pub.

Using Computers in the Classroom. William L. Callison. (Illus.). 192p. 1985. 18.50 (*0-13-940214-4*) P-H.

Using Computers in the Language Classroom. C. Jones & S. Fortescue. (Handbooks for Language Teachers Ser.). 1987. pap. text ed. 21.95 (*0-582-74617-5*, 74760) Longman.

Using Computers in the Law: Law Office Without Walls. 3rd ed. Mary A. Mason & Robert Harris. LC 93-41189. 284p. 1993. pap. text ed. 23.00 (*0-314-02396-8*) West Pub.

Using Computers in the Law Office. 2nd ed. Brent D. Roper. LC 95-39259. 500p. (C). 1996. pap. text ed. 52.50 (*0-314-06519-9*) West Pub.

Using Computers in the Social Studies. Howard Budin et al. (Computers & the Curriculum Ser.). 118p. (Orig.). 1986. pap. text ed. 14.95 (*0-8077-2781-4*) Tchrs Coll.

***Using Computers in the Social Studies.** Howard Budin et al. LC 85-27779. (Computers in the Curriculum Ser.). (Illus.). 128p. pap. 36.50 (*0-608-05094-6*, 2065650) Bks Demand.

Using Computers in the Teaching of Reading. Dorothy S. Strickland et al. LC 86-14567. (Computers in the Curriculum Ser.). 254p. reprint ed. pap. 72.40 (*0-7837-3887-0*, 2043735) Bks Demand.

Using Computers to Combat Welfare Fraud: The Operation & Effectiveness of Wage Matching. David Greenberg & Douglas J. Wolf. LC 85-30221. (Studies in Social Welfare Policies & Programs: No. 2). (Illus.). 279p. 1986. text ed. 55.00 (*0-313-24870-2*, GRU/) Greenwood.

Using Computers with Pascal Programming. 2nd ed. Donald D. Spencer. 1996. pap. 24.95 (*0-89218-254-7*) Camelot Pub.

Using Concurrent PC DOS. Mark Dahmke. 160p. 1986. pap. text ed. 26.95 (*0-07-015073-7*, BYTE Bks) McGraw.

***Using Conflict in Organizations.** Ed. by Carsten K. De Dreu & Evert Van De Vliert. 240p. 1997. 75.00 (*0-7619-5090-7*) Sage.

***Using Conflict in Organizations.** Ed. by Carsten K. De Dreu & Evert Van De Vliert. 240p. 1997. pap. 26.95 (*0-7619-5091-5*) Sage.

Using Consensus Building to Improve Utility Regulation. Jonathan Raab. LC 94-15737. 317p. (Orig.). (C). 1994. pap. 31.00 (*0-918249-19-8*) Am Coun Energy.

Using Consultants & Experts Effectively in Legal Services: A Desk Reference of Information Sources. Barbara Skolnick. 68p. 1983. 12.00 (*0-941077-09-8*, 35,970) NCLS Inc.

Using Consultants & Experts Effectively in Legal Services: A Desk Reference of Information Sources, 4 vols., Set. Barbara Skolnick. 68p. 1983. 40.00 (*0-685-15208-1*) NCLS Inc.

Using Consultants for Materials Development. R. Soedharno & Nancy Bergau. (Technical Notes Ser.: No. 19). (Illus.). 18p. (Orig.). (C). 1982. pap. 2.00 (*0-932288-65-0*) Ctr Intl Ed U of MA.

Using Consultants in Libraries & Information Centers: A Management Handbook. Ed. by Edward D. Garten. LC 92-12279. (Library Management Collection). 304p. 1992. text ed. 55.00 (*0-313-27878-4*, GLN/, Greenwood Pr) Greenwood.

Using Consultants Successfully. Ed. by Jon F. Wergin. LC 85-644752. (New Directions for Higher Education Ser.: No. HE 73). 1991. 19.00 (*1-55542-789-8*) Jossey-Bass.

Using Copyrighted Videocassettes in Classrooms, Libraries, & Training Centers. 2nd ed. Jerome K. Miller. LC 87-24572. (Copyright Information Bulletin Ser.: No. 3). 131p. 1988. 19.95 (*0-914143-14-X*, Copy Info Svc) Assn Ed Comm Tech.

***Using Corel Wordperfect Suite X.** Bill Bruck. 1997. 39.99 (*0-7897-1328-4*) Que.

***Using Corel Wordperfect Suite 7: Special Edition.** Bill Bruck. 1996. pap. text ed. 39.99 (*0-7897-0999-6*) Que.

***Using Corel Wordperfect X.** Gordon McComb. 1997. 39.99 (*0-7897-1300-4*) Que.

***Using Corel WordPerfect 7 for Windows 95.** 416p. Date not set. 24.99 (*0-614-19923-9*) Que.

Using CorelDRAW! 5.0. Ed Paulson. 1994. 39.99 (*1-56529-764-4*) Que.

Using Corpora for Language Research: Studies in Honour of Geoffrey Leech. Ed. by Jenny Thomas & Mick Short. LC 95-42488. 1996. write for info. (*0-582-24878-7*, Pub. by Longman UK) Longman.

Using Correct Sentence Structure. Contemporary Book Editors. 1993. pap. 2.50 (*0-8092-3747-4*) Contemp Bks.

Using CPT for Cardiothoracic Reimbursement: A Manual for Surgeons & Insurance Billing Specialists. Ed. by Sidney Levitsky & Jeanne T. Fitzgerald. 105p. (Orig.). 1990. 25.00 (*0-9626174-0-7*) Soc Thor Surgeons.

Using Cramm with SSADM. 69p. 1994. pap. 60.00 (*0-11-330629-6*, HM06296, Pub. by Stationery Ofc UK) Bernan Associates.

Using CRC Cards: An Informal Approach to Object-Oriented Development. Nancy M. Wilkinson. LC 95-3987. (Advances in Object Technology Ser.: Vol. 6). (Illus.). 230p. (Orig.). (C). 1995. pap. 29.00 (*1-884842-07-0*) SIGS Bks & Multimedia.

Using Cream Antiseptic. James Lent et al. (Taking Care of Simple Injuries Ser.). (Illus.). 32p. (Orig.). 1978. Set. pap. text ed. 149.00 (*0-685-05766-6*) PRO-ED.

Using Credit & Banking Services & Understanding Income Tax. Northwest Regional Educational Laboratory Staff. (Lifeworks Ser.). (Illus.). 1980. text ed. 13.96 (*0-07-047306-4*) McGraw.

Using CSH & TCSH. Paul DuBois & Joseph Radin. 242p. (Orig.). 1995. pap. 24.95 (*1-56592-132-1*) OReilly & Assocs.

Using Data to Identify & Target Local Line Problems: Four Case Studies. 150p. 1982. 25.00 (*0-318-17359-X*, DG/82-600) Pub Tech Inc.

***Using Datablades.** George W. Anderson. (McGraw Hill Series on Data Warehousing). 1997. pap. text ed. 39.95 (*0-07-001737-9*) McGraw.

Using dBase for Database Applications. William O. Drum. 1993. pap. 27.95 (*0-538-61589-3*) S-W Pub.

Using dBASE for DOS. Que Development Group Staff. 1994. 39.99 (*1-56529-728-8*) Que.

Using dBase Four Version 1.1. 576p. (C). 1992. disk 35.00 (*0-685-61608-8*); disk 22.92 (*0-685-61609-6*); disk 18.00 (*0-685-61610-X*) Course Tech.

Using dBase Four Version 1.1. 576p. (C). 1992. student ed., pap. 49.95 (*0-87835-822-6*) Course Tech.

Using dBase Four Version 1.1. 576p. (C). 1992. pap. 30.95 (*0-87835-793-9*) Course Tech.

Using dBASE III on the IBM PC. Darrell Davisson. write for info. (*0-318-59638-5*) S&S Trade.

Using DBase III Plus. 1988. 36.95 (*0-13-943382-1*) P-H.

Using dBase III Plus. Ernest S. Colantonio. (Software Guide Ser.). 118p. (C). 1989. pap. text ed. 19.16 (*0-669-19956-7*); Software. disk write for info. (*0-318-70085-9*) HM College Div.

Using dBASE III PLUS. James Pratt. 324p. 1991. 15.50 (*0-685-47883-1*) Course Tech.

Using Dbase III Plus. Software Solutions Staff. (C). 1987. pap. 14.36 (*0-395-47796-4*) HM.

Using dBASE III Plus: Limited Use Version & Manual. Lawrence C. Metzelaar & Marianne B. Fox. 210p. (C). 1987. pap. text ed. 23.75 (*0-8053-6742-X*) Benjamin-Cummings.

Using dBASE IV. Steve Beyer. Ed. by Kevin C. Hanson. (Logic Ware Ser.). (Illus.). 1990. 24.95 (*0-929978-22-6*) M-USA Busn Systs.

Using Dbase IV. Presby. (C). 1989. pap. 14.36 (*0-395-51580-7*) HM.

Using dBASE IV for Windows. Pawick. 1994. 34.99 (*1-56529-630-3*) Que.

Using dBASE IV, Version 2.0. Philip J. Pratt. LC 94-1006. 1994. write for info. (*0-87709-514-0*) Course Tech.

Using dBase IV, Version 2.0. Philip J. Pratt. 1995. pap. 24.95 (*0-87709-540-X*) Course Tech.

Using DBase Version 5 for Windows: A How-to-Do-It Manual for Librarians. E. Sonny Butler & Barbara Scanio. (Illus.). 105p. (Orig.). 1995. pap. 35.00 (*1-55570-079-9*) Neal-Schuman.

Using dBase 4 for Windows. Neil J. Salkind. 1996. pap. 21.00 (*0-02-405355-4*, Macmillan Coll) P-H.

Using Dbase 5 for DOS. James Pratt. (Df-Computer Applications Ser.). 1996. pap. 30.95 (*0-7895-0083-3*) S-W Pub.

Using dBase 5.0 for Windows. James Pratt. (Computer Applications Ser.). 1996. pap. 24.95 (*0-7895-0079-5*) Course Tech.

***Using dBase 5.0 for Windows.** Neil J. Salkind. 192p. (C). 1996. pap. text ed. 17.16 (*0-395-74401-6*) HM.

Using DB2 to Build Decision Support Systems. William H. Inmon. 364p. 1993. 49.95 (*0-471-56778-7*) Wiley.

Using DEC Windows Motif for OpenVMS. Margie Sherlock. LC 93-816. (X Window & Motif Ser.). (Illus.). 350p. 1993. pap. 41.95 (*1-55558-114-5*, EY-M743E-DP, Digital DEC) Buttrwrth-Heinemann.

Using Decimals see Key to Decimals Series

Using Delphi-Special Edition. Jon Matcho. 1995. 29.99 (*1-56529-823-3*) Que.

Using Deming to Improve Quality in Colleges & Universities. William C. Merrick et al. 113p. 1990. pap. 39.95 (*0-912150-13-0*) Magna Pubns.

Using Desalination Technologies for Water Treatment. 1992. lib. bdg. 79.99 (*0-8490-8789-9*) Gordon Pr.

Using Design Basics to Get Creative Results, Vol. 28, No. 12. Bryan F. Peterson. (Illus.). 144p. 1996. 29.99 (*0-89134-651-1*, North Lght Bks) F & W Pubns Inc.

***Using Design Protection in the Fashion Industry.** Ulla V. Lane-Rowley. LC 97-21574. pap. text ed. 60.00 (*0-471-96925-7*) Wiley.

Using Designed Experiments to Shrink Healthcare Costs. M. Daniel Sloan. LC 96-17217. (Illus.). 215p. 1996. pap. 40.00 (*0-87389-367-0*, H0931) ASQC Qual Pr.

***Using Desktop Publishing to Create Newsletters, Handouts, & Web Pages: A How-To-Do-It Manual for Librarians.** John Maxymuk. LC 97-3980. (How-to-Do-It Manuals Ser.). 200p. 1997. pap. 49.95 (*1-55570-265-1*) Neal-Schuman.

Using Digital & Analog Integrated Circuits. L. Shacklette & H. Ashworth. (Illus.). 1978. pap. text ed. 35.20 (*0-13-939488-5*) P-H.

Using Digital Video. Arch C. Luther. (Illus.). 320p. 1994. pap. text ed. 34.95 (*0-12-460432-3*, AP Prof) Acad Pr.

Using Digital Video. Arch C. Luther. 1995. pap. text ed. 20.00 (*0-12-784818-5*) Acad Pr.

Using Discussion in Classrooms. James T. Dillon. LC 94-11822. 160p. 1994. 60.00 (*0-335-19325-0*, Open Univ Pr); pap. 19.95 (*0-335-19324-2*, Open Univ Pr) Taylor & Francis.

Using Discussion to Promote Reading Comprehension. Donna E. Alvermann et al. LC 87-3107. 74p. reprint ed. pap. 25.00 (*0-7837-6200-3*, 2045922) Bks Demand.

Using Disk & RAM Utilities. Sinclair. 287p. 1990. pap. 38.95 (*0-434-91892-X*) Buttrwrth-Heinemann.

Using DOS. Gerry Routledge. (Illus.). 419p. (Orig.). 1995. 19.99 (*0-7897-0095-6*) Que.

Using DOS in Court Reporting. Steven B. Larson. 122p. 1994. pap. text ed. 21.95 (*1-881859-07-X*) Natl Ct Report.

Using DOS with OS-2. Ernest S. Colantonio. (Software Guide Ser.). 124p. (C). 1989. pap. text ed. 19.16 (*0-669-20510-9*) HM College Div.

Using Drawings in Assessment & Therapy: A Guide for Mental Health Professionals. Gerald D. Oster & Patricia Gould. LC 86-30958. (Illus.). 208p. 1987. pap. text ed. 24.95 (*0-87630-478-1*) Brunner-Mazel.

Using DSM-IV: A Clinician's Guide to Psychiatric Diagnosis. Anthony L. Labruzza & Jose M. Mendez-Villarrubia. LC 94-28534. (Illus.). 459p. 1995. 47.50 (*1-56821-333-6*) Aronson.

***Using DSM-IV: A Clinician's Guide to Psychiatric Diagnosis.** Anthony L. LaBruzza. 472p. 1996. pap. 40.00 (*0-7657-0053-0*) Aronson.

Using E-MAIL & UUCP. Debra Herman. 1992. pap. write for info. (*0-13-015579-9*) P-H.

Using Early Release - A Dilemma in Public Policy. 8.00 (*0-318-20316-2*) Natl Coun Crime.

Using Econometrics. 2nd ed. A. H. Studenmund. (C). 1991. text ed. 70.00 (*0-673-52125-7*) Addson-Wesley Educ.

Using Econometrics: A Beginner's Guide. Henry J. Cassidy. (C). 1981. teacher ed. write for info. (*0-8359-8136-3*, Reston) P-H.

Using Econometrics: A Practical Guide. 3rd ed. A. H. Studenmund. LC 96-7815. (C). 1997. text ed. 74.50 (*0-673-52486-8*) Addson-Wesley Educ.

Using Economic Incentives to Regulate Toxic Substances. Molly K. Macauley et al. 140p. 1992. lib. bdg. 24.95 (*0-915707-65-9*) Resources Future.

***Using Educational Technology with At-Risk Students: A Guide for Library Media Specialists & Teachers.** Roxanne B. Mendrinos. LC 96-51139. (Greenwood Professional Guides in School Librarianship). 232p. 1997. text ed. 39.95 (*0-313-29369-4*, Greenwood Pr) Greenwood.

Using Electronic Mail & News. Evan Leibovitch. 1993. pap. write for info. (*0-13-016791-6*) P-H.

Using Electronic Mail in an Educational Setting. Dan H. Wishnietsky. LC 91-60203. (Fastback Ser.: No. 316). (Orig.). 1991. pap. 3.00 (*0-87367-316-6*) Phi Delta Kappa.

Using Email Effectively. Linda Lamb & Jerry Peek. 160p. 1995. pap. text ed. 14.95 (*1-56592-103-8*) OReilly & Assocs.

Using ENABLE: An Introduction to Integrated Software. Paul W. Ross. 448p. 1988. pap. 28.50 (*0-87835-295-3*) Course Tech.

Using ENABLE: An Introduction to Integrated Software. 2nd ed. Paul W. Ross. 352p. (C). 1991. pap. 49.95 (*0-87835-441-7*, BF4417) Course Tech.

Using Enable - OA. 2nd ed. Paul W. Ross. 416p. 1991. text ed. 74.95 (*0-87835-557-X*, BF557X) Course Tech.

Using Energy. Sally Morgan & Adrian Morgan. LC 93-20407. (Designs in Science Ser.). (Illus.). 48p. (J). (gr. 4 up). 1993. 14.95 (*0-8160-2984-9*) Facts on File.

Using Energy. Julian Rowe & Molly Perham. LC 94-13911. (First Science Ser.). (Illus.). 32p. (J). (gr. 1-4). 1994. pap. 4.95 (*0-516-48140-1*); lib. bdg. 19.90 (*0-516-08140-3*) Childrens.

Using English. Ed. by Maybin. 352p. (C). 1996. pap. 24.95 (*0-415-13120-0*); text ed. 65.00 (*0-415-13119-7*). Routledge.

Using English. 2nd ed. Danielson & Porter. 1990. pap. text ed. 21.60 (*0-13-947367-X*) P-H.

Using English: Grammar & Writing Skills. Adrian B. Sanford. 420p. (C). 1979. pap. text ed. 2.75 (*0-15-594482-7*) HB Coll Pubs.

Using English: Your Second Language. Dorothy Danielson & Rebecca W. Hayden. (Illus.). 228p. (C). 1973. pap. text ed. write for info. (*0-13-939678-0*) P-H.

Using English Words. Corson. 1996. pap. text ed. 49.95 (*0-7923-3711-5*) Kluwer Ac.

Using English Words. David Corson. LC 95-36587. 236p. (C). 1995. lib. bdg. 120.00 (*0-7923-3710-7*) Kluwer Ac.

Using Environmental Archaeology. Myra L. Shackley. LC 85-27927. (Illus.). 162p. 1986. text ed. 22.50 (*0-312-83538-8*) St Martin.

Using Environmental Management Systems to Improve Profits. Brian Pearson et al. (C). 1992. spiral bd. 265.00 (*1-85333-754-4*) Kluwer Ac.

***Using Epi Info: A Step by Step Guide.** Melissa Alperin & Kathleen Miner. Ed. by Netha Thacker. (Illus.). 424p. (Orig.). 1997. pap. text ed. 54.95 (*1-57931-010-9*) ToucanEd Pubns.

***Using Eudora.** 2nd ed. Que Development Group Staff. 350p. 1997. 24.99 (*0-7897-1166-4*) Mac Comp Pub.

Using Europe, Abusing the Europeans: Britain & European Integration, 1945-63. Wolram Kaiser. LC 96-23297. (Contemporary History in Context Ser.). 1997. text ed. 59.95 (*0-312-16350-9*) St Martin.

Using Excel for Windows. Steve Gregory. Ed. by Taylor R. Taylor. (LogicNotes Ser.). (Illus.). (Orig.). 1991. pap. text ed. write for info. (*0-929978-50-1*) M-USA Busn Systs.

Using Excel for Windows. Neil J. Salkind. 1996. pap. 21.00 (*0-02-405431-3*, Macmillan Coll) P-H.

Using Excel for Windows 95. Josh C. Nossiter. (Illus.). 427p. (Orig.). 1995. 19.99 (*0-7897-0111-1*) Que.

Using Microsoft Excel 97. Joshua C. Nossiter. 432p. 1996. 24.99 (*0-7897-0955-4*) Mac Comp Pub.

***Special Edition Using Microsoft 97.** Ron Person. 1312p. 1996. 34.99 (*0-7897-0960-0*) Mac Comp Pub.

Using Excel Visual Basic for Applications. Elizabeth Boonin. (Illus.). 432p. 1995. 24.99 (*0-7897-0325-4*) Que.

Using Excel 5 for the Macintosh. Christopher Van Buren. (Illus.). 994p. (Orig.). 1994. 29.99 (*1-56529-539-0*) Que.

Using Excel 5 for Windows. Josh C. Nossiter. (Illus.). 360p. (Orig.). 1995. 19.99 (*0-7897-0288-6*) Que.

Using Excel 5 for Windows. Ron Pearson. (Illus.). 1276p. 1993. pap. 34.99 (*1-56529-459-9*) Que.

Using Excelator for Systems Analysis & Design. Jeffrey L. Whitten et al. (C). 1987. 18.95 (*0-685-38302-4*) Irwin.

Using Excelerator for Windows. Anthony C. Connor & Margaret A. Batchelor. LC 94-23579. 141p. (C). 1995. 23.95 (*0-256-18187-X*) Irwin.

Using Experience for Learning. Ed. by David Bout et al. LC 92-47423. 1993. 85.00 (*0-335-19096-0*, Open Univ Pr); pap. 29.50 (*0-335-19095-2*, Open Univ Pr) Taylor & Francis.

***Using Exponential Notation & Significant Figures.** Norman E. Griswold. Ed. by C. L. Stanitski. (Modular Laboratory Program in Chemistry Ser.). 12p. (C). 1997. pap. text ed. 1.35 (*0-87540-490-1*) Chem Educ Res.

Using Farmer Participatory Research to Improve Seed & Food Grain Production in Senegal. Tom Osborn & Alphonse Gaye. (Development Studies Paper). 25p. (Orig.). 1991. pap. 6.00 (*0-933595-57-3*) Winrock Intl.

Using Fast Plants & Bottle Biology in the Classroom. 1994. 24.00 (*0-941212-17-3*) Natl Assn Bio Tchrs.

Using Fastback Plus. Kate L. Johnson. 1990. pap. 14.95 (*0-201-57045-9*) Addison-Wesley.

Using Favorite Picture Books to Stimulate Discussion & Encourage Critical Thinking. Imogene Forte & Sandra Schurr. Ed. by Leslie Britt & Karla Westerman. (Illus.). 128p. (Orig.). 1995. pap. text ed. 10.95 (*0-86530-314-2*, 1P314-2) Incentive Pubns.

Using Federalism to Improve Environmental Policy. Henry N. Butler & Jonathan R. Macey. 150p. 1996. pap. text ed. 12.95 (*0-8447-3963-4*) Am Enterprise.

Using Film in the High School Curriculum: A Practical Guide for Teachers & Librarians. Kenneth E. Resch & Vicki D. Schicker. LC 92-50316. (Illus.). 176p. 1992. pap. 32.50 (*0-89950-750-6*) McFarland & Co.

Using Filters. Eastman Kodak Company Staff. LC 95-68106. (Kodak Workshop Ser.). (Illus.). 96p. (Orig.). (C). 1995. pap. 14.95 (*0-87985-751-X*, KW-13, Kodak) Saunders Photo.

Using Financial Accounting, Ch. 1-12. Murray. Date not set. pap. text ed. 48.00 (*0-314-06934-8*) West Pub.

***Using Financial Accounting: An Introduction.** Dennis F. Murray et al. LC 96-38399. 650p. 1997. write for info. (*0-314-06125-8*) West Pub.

Using Financial Information to Your Clients' Advantage. (Corporate Law & Practice Course Handbook, 1985-86 Ser.). Date not set. pap. 99.00 (*0-614-17202-0*, B4-7121) PLI.

Using Financial Information to Your Clients' Advantage 1996. (Corporate Law & Practice Course Handbook, 1985-86 Ser.). Date not set. pap. 99.00 (*0-614-17219-5*, B4-7149) PLI.

Using Finite Elements in Mechanical Design. J. Toby Mottram & Christopher T. Shaw. 1996. write for info. (*0-07-709093-4*) McGraw.

U V

An Asterisk (*) at the beginning of an entry indicates that the title is appearing in BIP for the first time.

Using Flexible Working Arrangements to Combat Stress: A Manager's Guide. Raymond H. Gottlieb. Date not set. text ed. 55.00 (*0-471-96228-7*) Wiley.

Using Fodder from Trees & Shrubs to Feed Livestock in the Tropics. 50p. 1994. pap. 50.00 (*0-11-330598-2*, HM05982, Pub. by Stationery Ofc UK) Bernan Associates.

Using Fodder from Trees & Shrubs to Feed Livestock in the Tropics. O. B. Smith. (Better Farming Ser.: No. 42). 52p. 1994. pap. 5.00 (*92-5-103476-1*, F34761, Pub. by FAO IT) Bernan Associates.

Using Folk Literature in the Classroom. Carolyn V. Spillman & Frances S. Goforth. LC 94-18808. (Illus.). 240p. 1994. pap. 26.50 (*0-89774-747-X*) Oryx Pr.

Using Formal Description Techniques: An Introduction to Estelle Lotos & SDL. Kenneth J. Turner. (Communication & Distributed Systems Ser.). 431p. 1993. text ed. 98.00 (*0-471-93455-0*) Wiley.

Using FoxPro for Windows Special Edition. Bob Grommes. 1995. pap. 39.99 incl. cd-rom (*0-7897-0076-X*) Que.

Using Framemaker 2.0 for the Macintosh. Katherine Minden. 1990. pap. 22.95 (*0-201-57026-2*) Addison-Wesley.

Using Framework II. 1988. 36.95 (*0-13-943390-2*) P-H.

Using Freelance Graphics Release 2.0 for Windows. Steve Sagman. (Using Ser.). (Illus.). 556p. (Orig.). 1993. 27.95 (*1-56529-259-6*) Que.

Using French. Anthony Bulger. (With Ease Ser.). (Illus.). 357p. 1985. 24.95 (*2-7005-0109-8*, Pub. by ASSIMIL FR) Distribks Inc.

Using French: A Guide to Contemporary Usage. R. E. Batchelor & Malcolm H. Offord. 288p. (C). 1993. text ed. 59.95 (*0-521-44361-X*); pap. text ed. 20.95 (*0-521-44821-2*) Cambridge U Pr.

Using French: Intermediate French for English Speakers. Assimil Staff. (ENG & FRE.). 28.95 (*0-8288-4351-1*, F9010); audio 125.00 (*0-685-53021-3*) Fr & Eur.

Using French: Level 2, 4 cass. (Illus.). (ENG & FRE.). 1997. pap. 59.95 incl. audio (*2-7005-1312-6*, Pub. by ASSIMIL FR) Distribks Inc.

*__Using French (Level II)__ (FRE.). 69.95 incl. audio compact disk (*2-7005-1084-4*, Pub. by ASSIMIL FR) Distribks Inc.

Using French Synonyms. R. E. Batchelor & Malcolm H. Offord. 600p. (C). 1993. text ed. 75.00 (*0-521-37277-1*); pap. text ed. 25.95 (*0-521-37878-8*) Cambridge U Pr.

*__Using FrontPage 97.__ Eric Maloney & Josh C. Nossiter. 456p. 1997. 24.99 (*0-7897-1134-6*) Mac Comp Pub.

Using G. N. N. Gene Steinberg. (Illus.). (Orig.). 1996. 24.99 (*0-7897-0676-8*) Que.

*__Using Geochemical Data: Evaluation, Presentation, Interpretation.__ Hugh R. Rollinson. (Longman Geochemistry Ser.). 1990. pap. 63.95 (*0-582-06701-4*) Longman.

Using German, 4 cass. (ENG & GER.). pap. 59.95 incl. audio (*2-7005-1363-0*, Pub. by ASSIMIL FR) Distribks Inc.

Using German: A Guide to Contemporary Usage. Martin Durrell. 288p. (C). 1992. text ed. 69.95 (*0-521-42077-6*); pap. text ed. 24.95 (*0-521-31556-5*) Cambridge U Pr.

Using God's Resources Wisely: Isaiah & Urban Possibility. Walter Brueggemann. LC 93-3260. 96p. (Orig.). 1993. pap. 10.00 (*0-664-25460-8*) Westminster John Knox.

Using God's World in Christian Education. Elaine M. Ward. 12p. (Orig.). (J). (gr. 1-8). 1987. pap. 5.75 (*0-940754-40-1*) Ed Ministries.

Using Government Documents: A How-to-Do-It Manual for School & Public Librarians. Melody S. Kelly. (How-to-Do-It Ser.). 176p. 1992. 32.50 (*1-55570-106-X*) Neal-Schuman.

Using Government Information Sources: Print & Electronic. 2nd ed. Jean L. Sears & Marilyn K. Moody. LC 93-30859. (Illus.). 552p. 1994. 115.00 (*0-89774-670-8*) Oryx Pr.

Using Government Money to Borrow Your Way to Real Estate Riches. 8th ed. Tyler G. Hicks. 150p. 1996. pap. 15.00 (*1-56150-163-8*) Intl Wealth.

*__Using Government Money to Borrow Your Way to Real Estate Riches.__ 9th ed. Tyler G. Hicks. 150p. 1998. pap. 15.00 (*1-56150-213-8*) Intl Wealth.

Using GPS. Conrad Dixon. LC 94-5802. (Illus.). 96p. 1994. pap. 14.95 (*0-924486-70-8*) Sheridan.

Using Graphs. (Open Learning for Supervisory Management). 1986. pap. text ed. 19.50 (*0-08-070031-4*, Pergamon Pr) Elsevier.

Using Graphs. Nebsm. (Open Learning for Supervisory Management). 1986. pap. text ed. 19.50 (*0-08-033966-2*, Pergamon Pr) Elsevier.

Using Grief to Grow: How You Can Help - How to Get Help, Vol. 1. Johnette Hartnett. LC 93-90774. (Good Mourning Ser.). 100p. 1993. pap. 6.95 (*1-883171-96-2*) Good Mourning.

*__Using Groups to Help People.__ D. S. Whitaker. (International Library of Group Psychotherapy & Group Process Ser.). 448p. (C). 1987. pap. 19.95 (*0-415-04283-6*) Routledge.

Using Groups to Help People. Dorothy S. Whitaker. 448p. 1987. pap. 17.95 (*0-7102-1095-7*, RKP) Routledge.

Using Guidance Skills in the Classroom. Lawrence L. Litwack et al. (Illus.). 314p. 1982. pap. 32.95 (*0-398-06283-8*) C C Thomas.

Using Guidance Skills in the Classroom. Lawrence L. Litwack et al. (Illus.). 314p. (C). 1982. 46.95 (*0-398-04597-6*) C C Thomas.

Using Gypsum Board for Wall & Ceilings. (Illus.). 41p. 1991. reprint ed. pap. 5.75 (*1-56532-001-8*, GA-201) Gypsum Assn.

Using Hard Disks with PCs: IBM-PC Edition. Allen G. Taylor. (Illus.). 160p. 1986. 29.95 (*0-13-939869-4*) P-H.

Using Hard Problems to Create Pseudorandom Generators. Noam Nisan. (ACM Distinguished Dissertation, 1990 Ser.). 76p. 1992. 20.00 (*0-262-14051-9*) MIT Pr.

Using Harvard Graphics. Kevin C. Hauson. Ed. by Taylor R. Taylor. (LogicNotes Ser.). (Illus.). (Orig.). 1991. pap. text ed. write for info. (*0-929978-58-7*) M-USA Busn Systs.

Using Harvard Graphics for Business Presentations. Barker & Ott. 272p. 1990. 16.00 (*0-87835-548-0*) Course Tech.

*__Using Herbs in the Home.__ Anthony Gardiner. 1997. 7.98 (*0-7858-0711-X*) Bk Sales Inc.

Using Herbs in the Landscape: How to Design & Grow Gardens of Herbal Annuals, Perennials, Shrubs, & Trees. Debra Kirkpatrick. LC 91-90155. (Illus.). 224p. 1992. pap. 19.95 (*0-8117-3043-3*) Stackpole.

Using Historical Sources in Anthropology & Sociology. David C. Pitt. (George & Louise Spindler Case Studies in Cultural Anthropology). 92p. (C). reprint ed. pap. write for info. (*0-8290-0587-0*) Irvington.

Using Hops: The Complete Guide to Hops for the Craft Brewer. Mark Garetz. (Illus.). 240p. (Orig.). 1994. pap. 16.95 (*0-9640785-0-3*) HopTech.

*__Using HTML.__ Que Development Staff. 1997. 49.99 (*0-7897-1449-3*) Que.

Using HTML. Tom Savola. (Illus.). (Orig.). 1995. 24.99 (*0-7897-0622-9*) Que.

*__Using HTML.__ 2nd ed. Neil Randall. 400p. 1996. 24.99 (*0-7897-0985-6*) Que.

Using HTML Special Edition. Tom Savola. 673p. 1995. pap. 39.99 incl. cd-rom (*0-7897-0236-3*) Que.

*__Using HTML, Java & CGI, Platinum Edition.__ Eric Ladd et al. 1996. 69.99 incl. cd-rom (*0-614-20289-2*, Que New Media) MCP SW Interactive.

*__Using HTML 3.2.__ Que Development Staff. 1997. 19.99 (*0-7897-1450-7*) Que.

Using Humor for a Change: 101 Clever Ideas to "Lighten up" the Workload. Scott Friedman. (Illus.). (Orig.). 1994. reprint ed. pap. 10.95 (*0-9645212-0-2*) Scott Friedman.

Using Hypnosis in Family Therapy. Michele Ritterman. LC 83-48162. (Social & Behavioral Science Ser.). 374p. 1983. 36.95 (*0-87589-581-6*) Jossey-Bass.

Using Hypnosis in Family Therapy. Michele Ritterman. LC 83-48162. (Jossey-Bass Social & Behavioral Science Ser.). 375p. reprint ed. pap. 106.90 (*0-7837-6525-8*, 2045637) Bks Demand.

Using IBM Displaywrite 5. M-USA Video Staff. (LogicNotes Ser.). (Illus.). (Orig.). 1991. pap. text ed. write for info. (*0-929978-32-3*) M-USA Busn Systs.

Using IBM Microcomputers in Business: Decision Making with Lotus 1-2-3 & dBASE III Plus. John O. Mason, Jr. 922p. (C). 1991. pap. text ed. 44.00 (*0-15-594489-4*) Dryden Pr.

Using IBM Netware. Stanley Schatt. (Using LANS Ser.). 272p. 1991. pap. text ed. 19.00 (*0-13-950288-2*, 250501) P-H.

Using IBM PC Storyboard: The Guide to Applications. Marketing Graphics Corporation Staff & Jan Lewis. 320p. (C). 1988. pap. 24.95 (*0-685-19365-9*) P-H.

Using Illustrations to Preach with Power. Bryan Chapell. 224p. 1993. pap. 12.99 (*0-310-58461-2*) Zondervan.

Using Imagery in Creative Problem Solving. Michael T. Bagley. 1986. pap. 9.99 (*0-89824-104-9*) Trillium Pr.

Using Imagery to Develop Memory. Michael T. Bagley. 118p. 1987. pap. 9.99 (*0-89824-040-9*) Trillium Pr.

Using Industrial Hydraulics. T. C. Frankenfield. LC 84-81279. (Illus.). 406p. (C). 1985. 54.00 (*0-932905-01-3*) Penton Pub.

*__Using Inferno.__ Que Development Group Staff. 500p. 1997. pap. text ed. 34.99 (*0-7897-0966-X*) Que.

Using Informal Education. Ed. by Tony Jeffs & Mark K. Smith. (Innovations in Education Ser.). 176p. 1990. 90.00 (*0-335-09266-7*, Open Univ Pr); pap. 32.00 (*0-335-09265-9*, Open Univ Pr) Taylor & Francis.

Using Information in Career Development: From Cognitions to Computers. Ed. by Lenore W. Harmon et al. 57p. 1983. 4.25 (*0-318-22229-9*, IN262) Ctr Educ Trng Employ.

Using Information Technology. 2nd ed. Stacey C. Sawyer. 544p. (C). 1996. 43.95 (*0-256-20981-2*) Irwin.

Using Information Technology: A Practical Introduction to Computers & Communications. Stacey C. Sawyer et al. LC 94-48219. (Telecommunication Systems Ser.). 1995. write for info. (*0-256-18956-0*) Irwin.

Using Information Technology: A Practical Introduction to Computers & Communications. Stacey C. Sawyer et al. 384p. (C). 1995. 30.95 (*0-256-19205-7*) Irwin.

Using Information Technology: A Practical Introduction to Computers & Communications. Brian K. Williams et al. LC 94-40842. 704p. (C). 1995. 43.95 (*0-256-15350-7*) Irwin.

Using Information Technology: A Practical Introduction to Computers & Communications. 2nd ed. Brian K. Williams et al. LC 96-2239. 336p. (C). 1996. 30.95 (*0-256-20980-4*) Irwin.

Using Information Technology: Brief Edition With DOS 6.0, Wordperfect 6.0, Lotus 2.3, DBase IV, & CD ROM. Brian Williams et al. (C). 1995. 50.33 (*0-256-20808-5*) Irwin.

*__Using Information Technology: With Information Technology CD-ROM for Mac.__ 2nd ed. Stacey C. Sawyer et al. (C). 1996. pap. text ed. 41.95 (*0-256-24881-8*) Irwin.

Using Information to Manage. Arthur B. Toan, Jr. LC 68-28846. 165p. reprint ed. pap. 47.10 (*0-8357-9527-6*, 2012374) Bks Demand.

*__Using Informix Data Blades.__ Database Consulting Group Staff. 1997. 39.99 (*0-7897-1418-3*) Que.

*__Using Informix Online DSA.__ Carlton Doe. LC 97-12291. 1997. pap. 49.95 (*0-13-605296-7*) P-H.

Using Informix, Special Edition. James Fischer. 1996. pap. text ed. 59.99 incl. audio compact disk (*0-7897-0660-1*) Que.

Using Informix Sql. 2nd ed. Jonathan Leffler. (C). 1991. pap. text ed. 32.25 (*0-201-56509-9*) Addison-Wesley.

*__Using Informix Universal Server.__ 1997. 59.99 (*0-7897-1342-X*) Que.

Using Instruments in Human Resource Development. J. William Pfeiffer & Arlette C. Ballew. LC 87-40359. (Training Technologies Set Ser.). 116p. (Orig.). 1988. pap. text ed. 139.00 (*0-88390-210-9*, Pfffr & Co) Jossey-Bass.

Using Integraph Microstation PC. Foger. (CAD/CAM Ser.). 1990. pap. 39.95 (*0-8273-3685-3*); teacher ed., pap. 16.00 (*0-8273-3686-1*) Delmar.

*__Using Intelligence Data for Environmental Needs: Balancing National Interests.__ Scott Pace et al. LC 96-51134. xviii, 75p. 1996. pap. 15.00 (*0-8330-2476-0*, MR-799-CMS) Rand Corp.

Using Interactive Video in Education. Penelope Semrau & Barbara A. Boyer. LC 93-23444. 1993. pap. text ed. 35.00 (*0-205-15257-0*) Allyn.

*__Using Internet Explorer.__ Peter Kent. 400p. 1997. 24.99 (*0-7897-1102-8*) Mac Comp Pub.

Using Internet Explorer. Que Development Group Staff. (Illus.). 350p. (Orig.). 1995. 24.99 (*0-7897-0551-6*) Que.

*__Using Internet Explorer to Browse the Internet.__ Dustin Sullivan. LC 96-41793. (Illus.). 321p. 1996. pap. 24.95 (*0-12-676140-X*, AP Prof) Acad Pr.

Using Internet Works. Que Development Group Staff. (Illus.). 416p. (Orig.). 1995. 19.99 (*0-7897-0283-5*) Que.

Using Intranet HTML, Special Ed. Mark Brown. 1128p. 1996. pap. text ed. 59.99 incl. cd-rom (*0-7897-0852-3*) Que.

*__Using ISETL 3.0: A Language for Learning.__ Dautermann. 1992. pap. 27.95 (*0-314-01327-X*) Wadsworth Pub.

Using ISO 9000 to Improve Business Processes. Sandford Liebesman. Ed. by Robert K. Wright. (AT&T Quality Library). (Illus.). 256p. (Orig.). 1994. pap. 24.95 (*0-932764-46-0*) AT&T Customer Info.

Using It Effectively in Teaching & Learning: Studies in Pre-Service & In-Service Teacher Education. Bridget Somekh & Niki Davis. LC 96-19655. 288p. (C). 1997. text ed. write for info. (*0-415-12131-0*); pap. text ed. write for info. (*0-415-12132-9*) Routledge.

Using IT in Primary School History. Lez Smart. (Children, Teachers & Learning Ser.). (Illus.). 144p. 1996. 80.00 (*0-304-32827-8*); pap. 19.95 (*0-304-32829-4*) Cassell.

Using Jakarta. Greg M. Perry. 408p. 1996. pap. text ed. 34.99 (*0-7897-0899-X*) Que.

Using Japanese Slang: A Comprehensive Guide. Anne Kasschau & Susumu Eguchi. 264p. (Orig.). (ENG & JPN.). 1995. pap. 12.95 (*0-8048-2009-0*) C E Tuttle.

Using Japanese Slang: A Comprehensive Guide. Anne Kasschau. 1995. pap. text ed. 12.95 (*4-900737-36-4*, Pub. by Yen Bks JA) C E Tuttle.

*__Using Java Class Libraries.__ Krishan Sankar. 1997. 59.99 (*0-7897-1292-X*) Que.

*__Using Java Development Tools.__ Clayton Walnum. 1997. 49.99 (*0-7897-1317-9*) Macmillan.

*__Using Java NC Server.__ Que Development Group Staff. 1997. pap. text ed. 49.99 (*0-7897-1279-2*) Que.

*__Using Java Network: Special Edition.__ Jake Reichert. 1997. pap. text ed. 44.99 incl. cd-rom (*1-56276-569-8*, Ziff-Davis Pr) Que.

*__Special Edition Using Java 1.1.__ 3rd ed. Joseph Weber et al. 1296p. 1997. 49.99 (*0-7897-1094-3*) Mac Comp Pub.

*__Using Java Server.__ Allan Williamson. 1997. 49.99 (*0-7897-1319-5*) Macmillan.

Using Java, Special Ed. Alex Newman. 1996. 49.99 incl. cd-rom (*0-614-14450-7*) Macmillan.

Using Java Workshop. Clayton Walnum. 456p. 1996. pap. text ed. 34.99 (*0-7897-0900-7*) Que.

*__Using Javabeans: Special Edition.__ Barbara White. 1997. 49.99 (*0-7897-1460-4*) Que.

Using Javascript Special Edition. Gordon McComb. 864p. 1996. pap. text ed. 49.99 incl. cd-rom (*0-7897-0789-6*) Que.

*__Using JDBC Special Edition Using Enterprise Java.__ Jeff Schneider & Rajeev Aurora. 500p. 1997. 49.99 (*0-7897-0887-6*) Mac Comp Pub.

*__Using Jigsaw.__ Que Development Group Staff. 1996. pap. text ed. 34.99 (*0-7897-0968-6*) Que.

*__Using Jolly Phonics: A Guide for Teaching Reading & Writing.__ Sue Lloyd & Sara Wernham. (Jolly Phonics Ser.). 1997. 14.99 (*1-870946-72-3*, JL723, Pub. by Jolly Lrning UK) Am Intl Dist.

Using JustWrite for Windows. 1991. 24.95 (*0-88022-878-4*) Que.

Using Knowledge about Creativity see Reaching for the Stars Series: A Minicourse for Education of Gifted Students

Using Knowledge about Intelligence see Reaching for the Stars Series: A Minicourse for Education of Gifted Students

Using Knowledge from Social Science in Development Projects. Michael Cernea. (Discussion Paper Ser.: No. 114). 62p. 1991. 6.95 (*0-8213-1754-7*, 11754) World Bank.

Using Lacan, Reading Fiction. James M. Mellard. 264p. 1991. text ed. 36.50 (*0-252-01786-2*); pap. text ed. 14.95 (*0-252-06173-X*) U of Ill Pr.

Using Language. Herbert H. Clark. 300p. (C). 1996. text ed. 54.95 (*0-521-56158-2*); pap. text ed. 19.95 (*0-521-56745-9*) Cambridge U Pr.

Using Language: The Structures of Speech Acts. John T. Kearns. LC 83-14491. (SUNY Series in Philosophy). 457p. 1985. text ed. 64.50 (*0-87395-808-X*); pap. text ed. 21.95 (*0-87395-809-8*) State U NY Pr.

Using Language Experience with Adults. 1993. 3.75 (*0-88336-556-1*) New Readers.

Using Language in the Classroom. Jay L. Lemke. (Language Education Ser.). 60p. 1989. pap. text ed. 7.95 (*0-19-437157-3*) OUP.

Using Language in the Classroom. Jay L. Lemke. (C). 1985. pap. 38.00 (*0-7300-0308-6*, ECS805, Pub. by Deakin Univ AT) St Mut.

Using Large Corpora. Ed. by Susan Armstrong. (Illus.). 300p. 1994. pap. 40.00 (*0-262-51082-0*, Bradford Bks) MIT Pr.

Using Latte. Que Development Group Staff. 1996. pap. text ed. 29.99 (*0-7897-0880-9*) Que.

Using Latte, Special Edition. Que Development Group Staff. 800p. 1997. pap. text ed. 49.99 incl. cd-rom (*0-7897-0892-2*) Que.

Using Law-Related Education in Georgia Studies Curriculum Supplement. Ann Blum et al. LC 93-31320. 290p. 1993. ring bd. 22.50 (*0-89854-169-7*) U of GA Inst Govt.

*__Using Learning Contracts.__ George Boak. LC 97-20723. 1997. write for info. (*0-566-07927-5*, Pub. by Gower UK) Ashgate Pub Co.

Using Learning Contracts: Practical Approaches to Individualizing & Structuring Learning. Malcolm S. Knowles. LC 86-45621. (Higher Education Ser.). 278p. text ed. 50.00 (*1-55542-016-8*) Jossey-Bass.

Using Lecturettes, Theory, & Models in Human Resource Development. J. William Pfeiffer & Arlette C. Ballew. LC 87-40533. (Training Technologies Set Ser.). 92p. (Orig.). 1988. pap. text ed. 139.00 (*0-88390-213-3*, Pfffr & Co) Jossey-Bass.

Using Light. Sally Morgan & Adrian Morgan. LC 93-21535. (Designs in Science Ser.). (Illus.). 48p. (J). 1993. 14.95 (*0-8160-2980-6*) Facts on File.

Using Linux: Special Edition. 2nd ed. Jack Tackett. 792p. 1996. 59.99 (*0-7897-0742-X*) Que.

Using Literature & Poetry Affectively. Ed. by Jon E. Shapiro. LC 79-9902. 126p. (Orig.). reprint ed. pap. 36.00 (*0-8357-8657-9*, 2035104) Bks Demand.

Using Literature in Language Teaching: A Guide for Teachers & Trainers. Gillian Lazar. LC 92-8942. (Teacher Training & Development Ser.). 228p. (C). 1993. text ed. 49.95 (*0-521-40480-0*); pap. text ed. 19.95 (*0-521-40651-X*) Cambridge U Pr.

Using Literature in the Middle Grades: A Thematic Approach. Joy Moss. 252p. (J). (gr. 3-8). 1994. text ed. 27.95 (*0-926842-38-2*) CG Pubs Inc.

Using Literature to Learn about Children Around the World: A Thematic Approach to Cultural Awareness. Judith Cochran. Ed. by Jan Keeling. (Illus.). 80p. (Orig.). 1993. pap. text ed. 9.95 (*0-86530-261-8*) Incentive Pubns.

Using Literature to Learn about the First Americans: A Thematic Approach to Cultural Awareness. Judith Cochran. Ed. by Jan Keeling. (Illus.). 80p. (Orig.). 1993. pap. text ed. 9.95 (*0-86530-262-6*) Incentive Pubns.

Using Literature to Learn America's Story. Judith Cochran. Ed. by Anna Quinn. (Illus.). 96p. (Orig.). 1995. pap. text ed. 9.95 (*0-86530-335-5*, IP 335-5) Incentive Pubns.

Using Literature to Teach Middle Grades about War. Phyllis K. Kennemer. LC 92-31932. 236p. 1992. pap. 29.95 (*0-89774-778-X*) Oryx Pr.

Using Literature to Unite the Curriculum Vol. 1: A Teacher's Resource Book for Grades K-2. Catherine R. Ney. vii, 118p. (Orig.). 1996. teacher ed., pap. 15.95 (*0-9651236-0-X*) BEM Pub Inc.

Using Literature to Unite the Curriculum Vol. 2: A Teacher's Resource Book for Grades 3-5. Catherine R. Ney. vii, 128p. (Orig.). 1996. teacher ed., pap. 15.95 (*0-9651236-1-8*) BEM Pub Inc.

Using Literature to Unite the Curriculum Vols. 1 & 2: A Teacher's Resource Book for Grades K-2 & Grades 3-5, 2 vols., Set. Catherine R. Ney. xiv, 246p. (Orig.). 1996. teacher ed., pap. 31.00 (*0-9651236-2-6*) BEM Pub Inc.

Using Literature with Young Children. Ed. by Leland B. Jacobs. LC 65-24617. (Illus.). (Orig.). 1965. pap. 12.95 (*0-8077-1557-3*) Tchrs Coll.

Using Literature with Young Children. 4th ed. Betty Coody. 320p. (C). 1991. per. write for info. (*0-697-10086-3*) Brown & Benchmark.

Using Literature with Young Children. 5th ed. Betty Coody. 320p. (C). 1996. per. write for info. (*0-697-24142-4*) Brown & Benchmark.

Using LLA's Guidelines for Effective Tutor Workshops. Jane Hugo. 19p. 1993. pap. text ed. write for info. (*0-9623561-5-8*) Laubach Literacy.

Using Local History Sources: A Teacher's Guide for the National Curriculum. James Griffin & D. Eddershaw. (Illus.). 109p. 1994. pap. 27.00 (*0-614-03386-1*, Pub. by Hodder & Stoughton Ltd UK) Lubrecht & Cramer.

Using Lotus Adgenda. R. Taylor & June Kanai. Ed. by Jose Hurtado. (Logic Ware Ser.). (Illus.). 1990. 24.95 (*0-929978-24-2*) M-USA Busn Systs.

*__Using Lotus Notes as an Intranet.__ Mike Falkner. LC 96-47741. 480p. 1997. pap. text ed. 44.95 incl. cd-rom (*0-471-17548-X*) Wiley.

Using Lotus Notes & Domino 4.5: *Special Edition. Cate Richards. 1232p. 1996. 59.99 (*0-7897-0943-0*) Mac Comp Pub.

*__Using Lotus Notes 4.5.__ 2nd ed. Cate Richards. 500p. 1996. 29.99 (*0-7897-0942-2*) Mac Comp Pub.

Using Lotus 1-2-3 for Windows: A How-to-Do-It Manual for Librarians. Robert Machalow. LC 94-25790. 268p. 1994. pap. 35.00 (*1-55570-187-6*) Neal-Schuman.

Using Lotus Organizer for Windows. Que Development Group Staff & Cathy Kenney. (Illus.). (Orig.). 1995. 24.99 (*1-56529-891-8*) Que.

Using Lotus Smartsuite for Windows 95. Nancy Stevenson. 1008p. 1997. pap. text ed. 39.99 (*0-7897-0851-5*) Que.

Using Lotus SmartSuite, Special Edition. Andy Shafran. (Illus.). (Orig.). 1994. 34.99 (*1-56529-747-4*) Que.

Using Lotus 1-2-3: A How-to-Do-It Manual for Library Applications. Robert Machalow. Ed. by Bill Katz. (How-to-Do-It Ser.: No. 1). (Illus.). 166p. (Orig.). 1989. pap. text ed. 39.95 (*1-55570-033-0*) Neal-Schuman.

Using Lotus 1-2-3 Applications for Reinforcement. Anderson. (DF - Computer Applications Ser.). 1995. 60.95 (*0-538-63353-0*); pap. 27.95 (*0-538-62909-6*) S-W Pub.

Using Lotus 1-2-3 for DOS. Que Corporation Staff. 1999. pap. write for info. (*0-395-63911-5*) HM.

Using Lotus 1-2-3 for DOS Release 3.1 Plus. Keiko Pitter & Richard Pitter. 264p. 1993. text ed. write for info. (*0-07-050296-X*) McGraw.

***Using Lotus 1-2-3 for Windows, Release 5.** Neil J. Salkind. 224p. (C). 1995. pap. text ed. 17.16 (*0-395-73674-9*) HM.

Using Lotus 1-2-3 Macros: Step-by-Step. Ian R. Sinclair. 256p. 1991. pap. 41.95 (*0-7506-0198-1*) Buttrwrth-Heinemann.

Using Lotus 1-2-3, SuperCalc 4, WordPerfect, WordStar, & dBase III Plus. 2nd ed. D. Michael Werner & Thomas W. Warrner. (C). 1989. pap. text ed. 35.50 (*0-673-38891-3*) Addson-Wesley Educ.

Using Lotus 1-2-3 to Solve Your Business Problems: Planning, Budgeting, Forecasting, Capital Investment Analysis A Practical Guide to Spreadsheet Planning. George W. Gershefski. LC 84-10671. 156p. (C). 1984. pap. text ed. 38.50 (*0-8476-7346-4*) Rowman.

Using Lotus 1-2-3, Version 2.2. June Kanai. Ed. by R. Taylor. (LogicNotes Ser.). (Illus.). (Orig.). 1990. pap. text ed. write for info. (*0-929978-33-1*) M-USA Busn Systs.

Using Lotus 1-2-3 (Version 2.2) Thomas W. Warrner & D. Michael Werner. (C). 1990. pap. text ed. 24.50 (*0-673-38980-4*) Addson-Wesley Educ.

Using Lotus 1-2-3, Version 3.0. June Kanai. Ed. by R. Taylor. (LogicNotes Ser.). (Illus.). (Orig.). 1990. pap. text ed. write for info. (*0-929978-26-9*) M-USA Busn Systs.

Using Lotus 1-2-3 2.2. Nelda Shelton & Sharon Burton. (C). 1990. pap. 15.16 (*0-395-55321-0*) HM Soft Schl Col Div.

Using Lotus 1-2-3, 2.2 for the IBM Pc. 2nd ed. Keiko Pitter. 1990. pap. text ed. write for info. (*0-07-050258-7*) McGraw.

Using Lotus 1-2-3, 3.0. Nelda Shelton. (C). 1989. pap. 13.16 (*0-395-53255-8*) HM Soft Schl Col Div.

Using Macromedia Authorware, Special Edition. Robert Zielinski. 800p. 1996. pap. text ed. 59.99 incl. cd-rom (*0-7897-0791-8*) Que.

Using Macromedia Director. Que Development Group Staff. 700p. 1998. Incl. CD-ROM. 49.99 incl. cd-rom (*1-56529-781-4*) Que.

Using Main Street: Historic Preservation in Your Downtown. Donald W. Watts. (Local History Technical Leaflets Ser.). 15p. (Orig.). 1985. pap. 1.50 (*0-931406-09-9*) Idaho State Soc.

Using Make for Unix. Technical Ease Corporation Staff. 200p. 1996. pap. 17.95 (*0-13-176488-8*) P-H.

Using Management Games. 2nd ed. Chris Elgood. 136p. 1996. pap. 22.95 (*0-566-07736-1*, Pub. by Gower UK) Ashgate Pub Co.

Using Management Science: A Workbook, Vol. I. John J. Dinkel & Gary A. Kochenberger. LC 79-67422. (Illus.). 234p. (Orig.). 1980. pap. text ed. 13.95 (*0-931920-15-9*) Dame Pubns.

***Using Maple for College Algebra.** Brooks Staff. (Mathematics Ser.). 1997. student ed., pap. 18.95 (*0-534-34757-6*) Brooks-Cole.

Using Maps & Aerial Photography in Your Genealogical Research-With Supplement on Foreign Aerial Photography. rev. ed. Marilyn Lind. LC 85-80941. (Illus.). 217p. (Orig.). 1985. pap. text ed. 15.50 (*0-937463-06-X*) Linden Tree.

***Using Maps & Photographs.** McMaster. Date not set. pap. text ed. write for info. (*0-582-00341-5*, Pub. by Longman UK) Longman.

***Using Maps Workbook.** Hans J. Stolle. 196p. (C). 1996. per., pap. text ed. 29.34 (*0-7872-3427-3*) Kendall-Hunt.

Using Market Research to Grow Your Business. Robin Birn. (Institute of Management Ser.). 192p. (Orig.). 1994. pap. 39.50 (*0-273-60507-0*, Pub. by Pitman Pub Ltd UK) Trans-Atl Phila.

Using Market Research to Improve Management of Transportation Systems. (National Cooperative Highway Research Program Report Ser.: No. 329). 75p. 1990. 10.00 (*0-309-04852-4*) Transport Res Bd.

***Using Math in Economics.** Thomas. 1989. pap. text ed. write for info. (*0-582-02520-6*, Pub. by Longman UK) Longman.

Using Math in Food Service Skillbook. Educational Foundation of the National Restaurant Association Staff. (Management Skills Program Ser.). 54p. (Orig.). 1992. pap. text ed. 10.95 (*0-915452-48-0*) Educ Found.

Using Mathematics in Business. Arthur H. Boiselle et al. LC 80-16710. (Illus.). 384p. (C). 1981. teacher ed. write for info. (*0-201-00099-7*); pap. write for info. (*0-201-00098-9*); 3.00 (*0-201-00041-5*) Addison-Wesley.

Using Matlab for Differential Equations. John Polking. (C). 1995. text ed. 25.00 (*0-13-133944-3*) P-H.

Using MATLAB, Simulink, & Control Toolbox: A Practical Approach. Alberto Cavallo et al. LC 96-7204. 405p. 1996. pap. 48.00 (*0-13-261058-2*) P-H.

Using MATLAB to Analyze & Design Control Systems. William Levine. (C). 1992. pap. text ed. 13.95 (*0-8053-5423-9*) Addison-Wesley.

Using Media for Creative Teaching. Tom Concannon. 76p. 1979. pap. text ed. 7.95 (*0-932720-85-4*) New Plays Inc.

Using Media in Religious Education. Ronald A. Sarno. LC 86-33844. 290p. (Orig.). 1987. pap. 17.95 (*0-89135-058-6*) Religious Educ.

Using Metaphors in Psychotherapy. Philip Barker. LC 85-15171. 236p. 1992. pap. text ed. 28.95 (*0-87630-716-0*) Brunner-Mazel.

Using Metlab to Analyze & Design Control Systems. 2nd ed. Naomi E. Leonard. (C). 1995. pap. text ed. 22.95 (*0-8053-2193-4*) Benjamin-Cummings.

Using Micro Computers in Social Science Research. Mark Shermis et al. 1991. pap. text ed. 42.00 (*0-13-933573-0*, 710303) P-H.

Using Microcomputer Applications: A Computer Lab Manual with DOS, WordPerfect, VPPlannerPlus & dBASE III Plus. Douglas F. Robertson & Donald R. Robertson. (C). 1990. pap. text ed. 24.00 (*0-15-594510-6*) Dryden Pr.

Using Microcomputer Applications: A Computer Lab Manual with DOS, WordPerfect, VPPlannerPlus & dBASE III Plus. Douglas F. Robertson & Donald R. Robertson. 250p. (C). 1990. disk 26.75 (*0-15-594515-7*) HB Coll Pubs.

Using Microcomputer Applications: A Computer Lab Manual with DOS, WordPerfect 5.1, Lotus 1-2-3, & dBASE IV. Douglas F. Robertson & Donald R. Robertson. 475p. (C). 1992. teacher ed. 10.75 (*0-685-70051-8*); pap. text ed. 27.00 (*0-15-594509-2*) Dryden Pr.

Using Microcomputer Applications: A Computer Lab Manual with DOS, WordPerfect 5.1, Lotus 1-2-3, & dBASE IV. 2nd ed. Douglas F. Robertson & Donald R. Robertson. LC 92-72685. 592p. (C). 1992. pap. text ed. 25.50 (*0-15-500765-3*) Dryden Pr.

Using Microcomputer Applications: A Computer Lab Manual with PC-TypePlus, PC-CalcPlus, & PC-FilePlus. Douglas F. Robertson. 250p. (C). 1990. Incl. software. student ed. 17.50 incl. disk (*0-15-594511-4*) Dryden Pr.

Using Microcomputers: A Guidebook for Writers, Teachers, & Researchers in the Social Sciences. Blaine A. Brownell. LC 84-27668. 320p. reprint ed. pap. 91.20 (*0-7837-1120-4*, 2041650) Bks Demand.

Using Microcomputers: An Apple Lab Manual. Keiko Pitter. 237p. 1984. pap. text ed. 17.95 (*0-938188-21-6*) Mitchell Pub.

Using Microcomputers: An IBM PC Lab Manual. Keiko Pitter & Richard Pitter. 280p. 1984. pap. text ed. 17.95 (*0-938188-22-4*) Mitchell Pub.

Using Microcomputers: An IBM-PC Lab Manual. 2nd ed. Keiko Pitter & Richard Pitter. 256p. (Orig.). (C). 1986. pap. text ed. 19.95 (*0-938188-38-0*) Mitchell Pub.

Using Microcomputers for Teaching Reading in the Middle School. Rosemary L. Potter. LC 89-61967. (Fastback Ser.: No. 296). 40p. (Orig.). (C). 1989. pap. 3.00 (*0-87367-296-8*) Phi Delta Kappa.

Using Microcomputers in Managerial Accounting. George Hildebrand. (Microcomputers in Business Ser.). (Illus.). 288p. 1985. write for info. (*0-938188-28-3*); student ed. 13.95 (*0-938188-27-5*) Mitchell Pub.

Using Microcomputers in Managerial Accounting. Mark W. Lehman et al. 406p. (C). 1987. spiral bd. 36.50 (*0-314-98515-8*) West Pub.

Using Microcomputers in Physical Education & the Sport Sciences. Joseph E. Donnelly. LC 86-20096. (Illus.). 288p. 1987. text ed. 35.00 (*0-87322-083-8*, BDON0083) Human Kinetics.

Using Microcomputers in Research. Thomas W. Madron et al. (Quantitative Applications in the Social Sciences Ser.: Vol. 52). 1985. 9.95 (*0-8039-2457-7*) Sage.

Using Microcomputers in Social Agencies. James B. Taylor. LC 81-1759. (Sage Human Services Guides Ser.: No. 19). (Illus.). 119p. reprint ed. pap. 34.00 (*0-7837-1133-6*, 2041663) Bks Demand.

Using Microcomputers in the Lab. Robert F. Tinker. (C). 1990. pap. 18.00 (*0-685-71882-4*) Addson-Wesley Educ.

Using Microcosms to Teach about the Environment. Two Herons Staff. 58p. 1996. pap. text ed. 17.95 (*0-7872-2245-3*) Kendall-Hunt.

Using Microfocus COBOL Workbench. Mark Smith & Doug Coker. 148p. (C). 1993. spiral bd. 22.11 (*0-697-21294-7*) Bus & Educ Tech.

Using Microfocus Personal COBOL. Mark Smith & Doug Coker. 112p. (C). 1994. spiral bd. 14.86 (*0-697-22645-X*) Bus & Educ Tech.

Using Microfocus Personal COBOL. Mark Smith & Doug Coker. 144p. (C). 1994. pap. text ed. 58.72 incl. disk (*0-697-23812-1*) Irwin.

Using MicroFocus Workbench for COBOL. Leona Roen. LC 94-25416. 1994. write for info. (*0-87709-813-1*) Course Tech.

Using Microprocessors & Microcomputers: The Motorola Family. 2nd ed. Joseph D. Greenfield & William C. Wray. LC 87-28020. 718p. 1988. text ed. 49.50 (*0-471-87954-1*) P-H.

Using Microprocessors & Microcomputers: The Motorola Family. 3rd ed. William C. Wray. 736p. 1994. text ed. 87.00 (*0-13-594391-4*) P-H.

***Using Microscale Techniques.** Joe Jeffers. (Modular Laboratory Program in Chemistry Ser.). 16p. (C). 1997. pap. text ed. 1.75 (*0-87540-702-1*) Chem Educ Res.

Using Microsoft Access. Philip J. Pratt. 1994. 24.95 (*0-87709-391-1*) Course Tech.

Using Microsoft Access: A How-to-Do-It Manual for Librarians. E. Sonny Butler. (How-to-Do-It Manuals Ser.). 125p. 1996. pap. 35.00 (*1-55570-268-6*) Neal-Schuman.

Using Microsoft Access, 2.0. Phillip J. Pratt. 1995. pap. 24.95 (*0-87709-565-5*) Course Tech.

***Using Microsoft Excel.** Wilson. 1998. pap. text ed. 28.41 (*0-697-27374-1*) McGraw.

Using Microsoft Excel: A How-to-Do-It Manual for Librarians. Robert Machalow. LC 90-21524. 175p. 1991. 35.00 (*1-55570-075-6*) Neal-Schuman.

Using Microsoft Excel 4.0 for Windows. James E. Shuman. 1993. pap. text ed. write for info. (*0-07-057586-X*) McGraw.

Using Microsoft Excel 4.0 for Windows: The Basics. Keiko Pitter & Richard Pitter. 1993. pap. text ed. write for info. (*0-07-050295-1*) McGraw.

***Using Microsoft Excel 5.0 for Windows.** Jerry Murphy. (C). 1995. pap. text ed. 17.56 (*0-395-35738-1*) HM.

Using Microsoft Exchange Server Special Edition. Mark J. Kapczynski. 896p. 1996. 49.99 (*0-7897-0687-3*) Que.

Using Microsoft Frontpage, Special Ed. Neil Randall. 1996. pap. text ed. 49.99 incl. cd-rom (*0-7897-0821-3*) Que.

***Using Microsoft Frontpage 97: Special Edition.** Neil Randall. 1997. 49.99 (*0-7897-1343-8*) Que.

***Using Microsoft Internet Security Framework.** Leland Hoover. 1996. pap. text ed. 49.99 incl. cd-rom (*0-7897-0969-4*) Que.

Using Microsoft Money. Linda Flanders. (Illus.). 316p. (Orig.). 1995. 19.99 (*0-7897-0606-7*) Que.

Using Microsoft Network. Peter Kent. (Illus.). 374p. (Orig.). 1995. 19.99 (*0-7897-0398-X*) Que.

Using Microsoft Office. Ed Bott. (Illus.). 412p. (Orig.). 1994. 19.99 (*0-7897-0091-3*) Que.

Using Microsoft Office: Special Edition. Sue Plumley. 994p. 1994. pap. 34.99 (*1-56529-721-0*) Que.

Using Microsoft Office: Special Edition. Rick Winter & Patty Winter. (Illus.). 1048p. (Orig.). 1995. 34.99 (*0-7897-0146-4*) Que.

Using Microsoft Office for Windows 95. Ed Bott. (Illus.). 508p. (Orig.). 1995. 19.99 (*0-7897-0176-6*) Que.

Using Microsoft Office 97. Ed Bott. 500p. 1996. 24.99 (*0-7897-0954-6*) Mac Comp Pub.

Using Microsoft Office Professional for Windows 95. Rick Winter. 1255p. 1996. pap. text ed. 39.99 (*0-7897-0854-X*) Que.

***Using Microsoft Office Small Business Edition: Special Edition.** Rick Winter & Patty Winter. 1008p. 1997. 34.99 (*0-7897-1356-X*) Que.

***Using Microsoft Office 97.** Nelson Howell. 1997. 19.99 (*0-7897-1442-6*) Que.

***Using Microsoft Office 97 Platinum Edition.** Que Development Group Staff. 1200p. 1997. 60.00 (*0-7897-1301-2*) Que.

***Using Microsoft Office 97 Professional: Special Edition, Best Seller Edition.** 2nd ed. Jim Boyce. 1997. 39.99 (*0-7897-1396-9*) Que.

***Special Edition Using Microsoft Outlook 97.** Gordon Padwick. 888p. 1997. 34.99 (*0-7897-1096-X*) Mac Comp Pub.

***Using Microsoft Outlooks 97.** Que Development Group Staff. 400p. 1997. 24.99 (*0-7897-1257-1*) Que.

***Using Microsoft Powerpoint.** Nancy Stevenson. 720p. 1996. pap. text ed. 34.99 (*0-7897-0961-9*) Que.

Using Microsoft Project for Windows 95. Ed Willett & Peter Rogers. (Illus.). (Orig.). 1996. 24.99 (*0-7897-0395-5*) Que.

***Using Microsoft Project X.** Tim Pyron. 400p. 1997. 24.99 (*0-7897-1258-X*) Que.

Using Microsoft Project 4 for Windows. Tim Pyron. 780p. 1994. 29.99 (*1-56529-594-3*) Que.

Using Microsoft Publisher for Windows 95. Ed Willet. (Illus.). 326p. (Orig.). 1995. 19.99 (*0-7897-0635-0*) Que.

***Using Microsoft Publisher 97.** Ed Willett. 358p. 1997. 24.99 (*0-7897-1220-2*) Que.

***Using Microsoft Site Server: Special Edition.** Barry Wadman. 1997. pap. text ed. 59.99 incl. cd-rom (*0-7897-1157-5*) Que.

Using Microsoft System Management Server. Que Development Group Staff. 744p. 1996. pap. text ed. 59.99 incl. cd-rom (*0-7897-0820-5*) Que.

Using Microsoft Windows. Taylor R. Taylor. (LogicNotes Ser.). (Illus.). (Orig.). 1990. pap. text ed. write for info. (*0-929978-28-5*) M-USA Busn Systs.

Using MicroSoft Word. Nelda Shelton & Sharon Burton. (C). 1989. pap. 15.16 (*0-395-50549-6*) HM.

Using Microsoft Word. R. Taylor. Ed. by Jose Hurtado. (Logic Ware Ser.). (Illus.). 1989. 24.95 (*0-929978-09-9*) M-USA Busn Systs.

Using Microsoft Word for Windows. 2nd ed. Janet R. Wilson. 512p. (C). 1998. pap. write for info. (*0-697-27372-5*) Bus & Educ Tech.

Using Microsoft Word Version 4.0 Advanced Functions - Macintosh. Janet R. Wilson & Patricia A. Shepard. 256p. (C). 1991. spiral bd. write for info. (*0-697-11710-3*) Bus & Educ Tech.

Using Microsoft Word Version 4.0 Basic Functions: Macintosh Version. Janet R. Wilson & Patricia A. Shepard. 176p. (C). 1991. spiral bd. write for info. (*0-697-11706-5*) Bus & Educ Tech.

Using Microsoft Word Version 5.0: IBM Version. Janet R. Wilson & Patricia A. Shepard. 224p. (C). 1991. spiral bd. write for info. (*0-697-11704-9*) Bus & Educ Tech.

Using Microsoft Word Version 5.0 Advanced Functions - IBM. Janet R. Wilson & Patricia A. Shepard. 320p. (C). 1991. spiral bd. write for info. (*0-697-11708-1*) Bus & Educ Tech.

Using Microsoft Word Version 5.5 IBM. Janet R. Wilson & Patricia A. Shepard. 448p. (C). 1992. spiral bd. 26.82 (*0-697-14775-4*) Bus & Educ Tech.

Using Microsoft Word 2.0 for Windows. Janet R. Wilson & Patricia A. Shepard. 432p. (C). 1992. spiral bd. 29.72 (*0-697-14773-8*) Bus & Educ Tech.

***Using Microsoft Word 6.0 for Windows.** Jerry Horazdovsky. 224p. (C). 1995. pap. text ed. 17.56 (*0-395-72135-0*) HM.

***Using Microsoft Word 97.** Laurie A. Ulrich. 1997. 19.99 (*0-7897-1441-8*) Que.

Using Microsoft Words for Windows 3.0. Glenn T. Smith & Richard T. Christoph. LC 94-21974. 1994. pap. text ed. 35.20 (*0-13-123886-8*) P-H.

Using Microsoft Work 3.0 for Dos. Vivian Frederick & Phyllis S. Yasuda. 1994. pap. text ed. write for info. (*0-07-015666-2*) McGraw.

Using Microsoft Works. R. Taylor. Ed. by Jose Hurtado. (Logic Ware Ser.). (Illus.). 1989. 24.95 (*0-929978-08-0*) M-USA Busn Systs.

Using Microsoft Works: A How-to-Do-It Manual for Librarians. Robert Machalow. 276p. 1992. 35.00 (*1-55570-110-8*) Neal-Schuman.

Using Microsoft Works: An Introduction to Computing. Gwynne Larsen et al. LC 92-25313. 1993. pap. 38.95 (*0-87835-884-6*) Course Tech.

Using Microsoft Works Effectively: Windows Version. Paul W. Ross & P. Whitcomb Ross. 288p. (C). 1993. spiral bd. 22.47 (*0-697-17143-4*) Brown & Benchmark.

Using Microsoft Works Effectively - IBM Version. Paul W. Ross. 272p. (C). 1992. spiral bd. 22.47 (*0-697-15384-3*) Irwin.

Using Microsoft Works for the IBM PC & Compatibles. James Shuman. (Illus.). 288p. (C). 1991. text ed. 22.50 (*0-256-10724-6*, 14-3646-01) Irwin.

Using Microsoft Works for Windows Version 4.0. Larsen & Kathryn A. Marold. (DF - Computer Applications Ser.). 1997. text ed. 32.95 (*0-7895-0168-6*) Course Tech.

Using Microsoft Works for Windows 95. Kathy M. Sabotin & Murray. (Illus.). 354p. (Orig.). 1995. 19.99 (*0-7897-0457-9*) Que.

Using Microsoft Works on the IBM PC. Vivian Frederick & Phyllis S. Yasuda. 1989. pap. text ed. write for info. (*0-07-909409-0*) McGraw.

Using Microsoft Works on the Macintosh. Vivian Frederick & Phyllis S. Yasuda. 1989. pap. text ed. write for info. (*0-07-909408-2*) McGraw.

***Using Microsoft Works X.** Debbie Walkowski. 1997. 29.99 (*0-7897-1308-X*) Que.

Using Microsoft Works 2. 0. Nelda Shelton & Sharon Burton. 1992. pap. 11.56 (*0-395-59240-2*) HM.

Using Microsoft Works 2.0 on the Mac. 2nd ed. Phyllis S. Yasuda. 1991. pap. 19.95 (*0-07-911014-2*) McGraw.

Using Microsoft Works 3.0. James Shuman & Heidi Sewall. LC 93-47665. 304p. (C). 1994. per. 32.50 (*0-256-15889-4*) Irwin.

Using Microsoft Works 3.0. Glenn T. Smith & Richard T. Christoph. 475p. 1993. pap. text ed. write for info. (*0-13-953688-4*) P-H.

Using Microsoft Works 3.0: An Introduction to Computing. Kenneth D. Shaw et al. LC 93-4735. 1993. write for info. (*0-87709-284-2*) Course Tech.

Using MicroSoft Works 3.0 for Windows. Vivian Frederick & Phyllis S. Yasuda. 1994. pap. text ed. write for info. (*0-07-015693-X*) McGraw.

Using Microsoft Works 3.0 for Windows. Larsen & Shaw. (Computer Applications Ser.). 1995. pap. 37.95 incl. 3.5 ld (*0-87709-287-7*) Course Tech.

Using Microsoft Works 3.0 for Windows. Jim Shuman & Heidi Sewall. LC 94-26233. 296p. (C). 1994. 32.50 (*0-256-17446-6*) Irwin.

Using Microsoft Works 3.0 for Windows: An Introduction to Computing. Gwynne Larsen et al. LC 94-21639. 583p. 1994. 36.00 (*0-87709-845-X*) Course Tech.

Using Microsoft Works 30 on the Macintosh. Vivian Frederick. 336p. 1993. pap. text ed. write for info. (*0-07-911509-8*) McGraw.

Using Microsoft Works 4 for MacIntosh. Montes. 1994. 27.99 (*1-56529-920-5*) Que.

***Using Microsoft Works 4.0 for Windows 95.** Gwynne Larsen & Kathryn A. Marold. 516p. (C). 1996. text ed. write for info. (*0-03-020614-6*) HB Coll Pubs.

Using Microsoft Works 4.0 for Windows 95. Glenn T. Smith & Richard T. Christoph. LC 96-15545. 450p. 1996. pap. text ed. 35.20 (*0-13-456344-1*) P-H.

Using Microsoft's Word for DOS 5.0. M-USA Video Staff. (LogicNotes Ser.). (Illus.). (Orig.). 1991. pap. text ed. write for info. (*0-929978-63-3*) M-USA Busn Systs.

Using MIL-STD-810 D in Aquisition Management. Ed. by Howard C. Schafer. (Illus.). 277p. (C). 1987. student ed. 100.00 (*0-918247-06-3*) Tustin Tech.

***Using Military Capabilities to Help Young Adults in U. S. Inner City Areas.** William J. Taylor, Jr. 54p. 1997. pap. text ed. 17.95 (*0-89206-327-0*) CSI Studies.

Using Modula-2. Riley. 1987. pap. 57.95 (*0-87835-236-8*) PWS Pubs.

Using Modula 2. Riley. 1987. pap. 12.25 (*0-87835-237-6*) PWS Pubs.

Using Motif with C Plus Plus. Daniel J. Bernstein. LC 94-44611. (Advances in Object Technology Ser.: Vol. 5). (Illus.). 400p. (Orig.). 1995. pap. 39.00 (*1-884842-06-2*) SIGS Bks & Multimedia.

Using Motif with C Plus Plus. Daniel J. Bernstein. (C). 1995. pap. text ed. 39.00 (*0-13-207390-0*) P-H.

Using Movement Creatively in Religious Education. Pat Sonen. 1963. pap. 3.00 (*0-941500-53-5*) Sharing Co.

Using MPI: Portable Parallel Programming with the Message - Passing Interface. William Gropp et al. 300p. 1994. pap. 28.50 (*0-262-57104-8*) MIT Pr.

***Using MS Access 97.** 1997. 19.99 (*0-7897-1439-6*) Que.

Using MS-DOS. Nelda Shelton & Sharon Burton. (C). 1989. pap. 15.16 (*0-395-50550-X*) HM.

Using MS-DOS Kermit: Connecting Your PC to the Electronic World. 2nd ed. Christine M. Gianone. (Networking Ser.). (Illus.). 345p. (Orig.). 1992. pap. 41.95 (*1-55558-082-3*, EY-H893E-DP, Digital DEC) Buttrwrth-Heinemann.

Using MS-DOS on a Hard Disk. Patricia A. Menges. 80p. (Orig.). 1988. pap. text ed. 175.00 incl. digital audio (*0-917792-61-0*) OneOnOne Comp Trng.

Using MS-DOS 4.01. R. R. Taylor. (LogicNotes Ser.). (Illus.). (Orig.). 1990. pap. text ed. write for info. (*0-929978-25-0*) M-USA Busn Systs.

U
V

Using MS-DOS 6: Special Edition. Que Development Group Staff. 1993. pap. 29.95 (*1-56539-020-2*) Color Cnty.

Using MS-DOS 6.2. Que Development Group Staff. 1115p. 1993. 29.95 (*1-56529-646-X*) Que.

***Using MS Excel 97.** Conrad Carlberg. 1997. 19.99 (*0-7897-1440-X*) Que.

***Using MS Excel 97.** 2nd ed. 1997. 39.99 (*0-7897-1399-3*) Mac Comp Pub.

***Using MS Front Pad.** Dave Karlins. 1997. 19.99 (*0-7897-1322-5*) Macmillan.

***Using MS Internet Info Server 4.** Ben Forta. 1997. 49.99 (*0-7897-1263-6*) Macmillan.

***Using MS Netshow 2.0.** 1997. 39.99 (*0-7897-1410-8*) Que.

***Using MS Powerpoint 97.** Steve Rindsberg. 1997. 19.99 (*0-7897-1438-8*) Que.

***Using MS Word 97.** 2nd ed. 1997. 39.99 (*0-7897-1398-5*) Mac Comp Pub.

Using MSC-NASTRAN: Statics & Dynamics. A. O. Cifuentes. (Illus.). xiv, 458p. 1989. 65.95 (*0-387-97032-0*) Spr-Verlag.

***Using Multiethnic Literature in the K-8 Classroom.** Ed. by Violet J. Harris. 296p. (Orig.). 1997. teacher ed., pap. text ed. 29.95 (*0-926842-60-9*) CG Pubs Inc.

Using Multimate Advantage II. R. Taylor. Ed. by Jose Hurtado. (Logic Ware Ser.). (Illus.). 1989. 24.95 (*0-929978-10-2*) M-USA Busn Systs.

***Using Multimedia for Distance Learning in Adult, Career, & Vocational Education.** Ronald M. Stammen. 75p. (C). 1996. reprint ed. pap. 25.00 (*0-7881-3694-1*) DIANE Pub.

***Using Multimedia Tools & Applications on the Internet.** Dennis O. Gehris. (Illus.). 302p. (C). 1997. pap. text ed. 25.95 (*0-534-51939-3*) Wadsworth Pub.

***Using Multivariate Statistic: SAS Workbook.** 3rd ed. Tabachnick. (C). 1997. pap. text ed. 18.75 (*0-321-01323-9*) Addson-Wesley Educ.

Using Multivariate Statistics. 2nd ed. Barbara G. Tabachnick & Linda S. Fidell. 746p. (C). 1989. text ed. 74.00 (*0-06-046571-9*) Addson-Wesley Educ.

Using Multivariate Statistics. 3rd ed. Barbara G. Tabachnick & Linda S. Fidell. LC 95-16499. 848p. (C). 1996. text ed. 72.95 incl. disk (*0-673-99414-7*) Addson-Wesley Educ.

Using Multivariate Statistics: Computer Manual. Linda S. Fidell & Barbara G. Tabachnick. 1996. text ed. write for info. incl. disk (*0-673-98133-9*) Addson-Wesley Educ.

Using Murder: The Social Construction of Serial Homicide. Philip Jenkins. LC 93-50051. (Social Problems & Social Issues Ser.). 271p. 1994. pap. text ed. 22.95 (*0-202-30525-2*); lib. bdg. 45.95 (*0-202-30499-X*) Aldine de Gruyter.

Using Museums As an Educational Resource. Graeme K. Talboys. 200p. 1996. 51.95 (*1-85742-344-5*, Pub. by Arena UK) Ashgate Pub Co.

Using National Data Bases. Ed. by Charles S. Lenth. LC 85-645339. (New Directions for Institutional Research Ser.: No. IR 69). 1991. 19.00 (*1-55542-791-X*) Jossey-Bass.

Using National Data Bases in Educational Research. Thomas Hilton. 312p. 1992. text ed. 59.95 (*0-8058-0840-X*) L Erlbaum Assocs.

***Using Netscape Communicator 4.** Peter Kent. 400p. 1997. 19.99 (*0-7897-0982-1*) Mac Comp Pub.

***Using Netscape Composer.** Que Development Group Staff. 250p. 1997. 19.99 (*0-7897-1266-0*) Que.

Using Netscape Livewire Pro: Special Edition. Que Development Group Staff. 608p. 1996. pap. text ed. 49.99 incl. cd-rom (*0-7897-0743-8*) Que.

***Using Netscape Messenger Email.** Todd Stauffer. 250p. 1997. 19.99 (*0-7897-1250-4*) Que.

***Using Netscape Navigator Gold 3: Special Edition.** Que Publishing Staff. 1996. pap. text ed. 59.99 (*0-7897-1180-X*) Que.

***Using Netscape Netcaster.** Wes Thomas. 1997. 39.99 (*0-7897-1409-4*) Que.

***Using Netscape Suitespot 3, Vol. 1.** Mike Morgan. 750p. 1997. 75.00 (*0-7897-1229-6*) Que.

***Using Netscape Suitespot 3, Vol. 2.** Mike Morgan. 650p. 1997. 75.00 (*0-7897-1230-X*) Que.

Using Netscape 3. Peter Kent. 432p. 1996. 24.99 (*0-7897-0905-8*) Mac Comp Pub.

Using Netscape with Windows 95. 1998. 19.99 (*0-7897-0652-0*) Que.

Using Netscape 2: Special Edition. Que Development Group Staff. (Illus.). 992p. (Orig.). 1996. 49.99 (*0-7897-0612-1*) Que.

Using Netscape 2 for Macs. Que Development Group Staff. 350p. 1996. 24.99 (*0-7897-0729-2*) Que.

Using Netscape 2 for Windows. Warren Ernst. 342p. 1996. 24.99 (*0-7897-0728-4*) Que.

***Using Netscape 3.** Mark Brown. 1997. pap. text ed. 59.99 (*0-7897-1186-9*) Que.

Using Netscape 3, Special Edition. Mark Brown. 880p. 1996. pap. text ed. 49.99 incl. cd-rom (*0-7897-0904-X*) Que.

Using Netware 3.X: Special Edition. Bill Lawrence. 1118p. 1994. 39.99 (*1-56529-627-3*) Que.

Using Netware 4.1, Special Edition. Bill Lawrence. 1455p. 1996. pap. text ed. 59.99 incl. cd-rom (*0-7897-0810-8*) Que.

Using New Communications Technologies: A Guide for Organizations. Media Institute Staff. LC 85-63320. 70p. (Orig.). 1986. pap. 12.95 (*0-937790-30-3*, 4250) Media Institute.

Using New Testament Greek in Ministry: The Practical Guide for Students & Pastors. David Alan Black. LC 92-42175. 128p. (Orig.). (C). 1993. pap. 9.99 (*0-8010-1043-8*) Baker Bks.

Using Newspapers & Magazines to Enrich Curriculum for Elementary Students: An Enrichment Guide for Elementary Teachers (K-6) Lynn E. Johnson. (Illus.). 100p. (Orig.). 1991. teacher ed., pap. 20.00 (*1-878276-41-7*) Educ Systs Assocs Inc.

Using NMAKE. Steven Lally. (C). 1996. pap. text ed. write for info. (*0-201-63350-7*) Addison-Wesley.

Using Nonfiction in the Classroom. Eileen Burke. 96p. 1994. pap. 9.95 (*0-590-49352-3*) Scholastic Inc.

Using Nonfiction Trade Books in the Elementary Classroom: From Ants to Zeppelins. Ed. by Evelyn B. Freeman & Diane G. Person. (Illus.). 183p. 1992. pap. 11.95 (*0-8141-1811-9*) NCTE.

Using Norton Utilities, Special Edition. Rowlan Prollop. 1995. pap. 29.99 incl. cd-rom (*0-7897-0686-5*) Que.

Using Novell GroupWise. Bill Bruck. (Illus.). 450p. (Orig.). 1994. 24.99 (*0-7897-0086-7*) Que.

Using Novell Groupwise XTD, Special Edition. Bill Bruck. 1998. 39.99 (*0-7897-0690-3*) Que.

Using Novell Netware. Stanley Schatt. 224p. 1991. pap. text ed. 40.00 (*0-13-950296-3*) P-H.

Using Novell PerfectOffice for Windows 95. Que Development Group Staff. 1996. 34.99 (*0-7897-0463-3*) Que.

Using Nursing Case Management to Improve Health Outcomes: Recasting Theory, Tools & Care Delivery. Michael Newell. 304p. 52.00 (*0-8342-0623-4*, 20623) Aspen Pub.

Using Nursing Research. Ed. by Christine Tanner & Carol A. Lindeman. 507p. 1989. 35.95 (*0-88737-414-X*) Natl League Nurse.

Using OCLC: A How-to-Do-It Manual for Librarians. Robert T. Warwick & Patricia E. Jensen. (How-to-Do-It Ser.). 145p. (Orig.). 1990. pap. text ed. 39.95 (*1-55570-037-3*) Neal-Schuman.

Using OCLC under Prism: A How-To-Do-It Manual for Librarians. rev. ed. Robert T. Warwick & Kenneth Carlborg. LC 96-44332. (How-to-Do-It Manuals Ser.). 225p. 1997. pap. 45.00 (*1-55570-179-5*) Neal-Schuman.

***Using ODF: The OpenDoc Development Framework.** Jesse Feiler. LC 97-14005. (Illus.). 500p. 1997. pap. text ed. 39.95 (*0-12-251333-9*, AP Prof) Acad Pr.

Using ODF: Using the Open Doc Parts Framework on Macintosh. Jesse Feiler & Julie McKeehan. (Illus.). 400p. 1997. pap. text ed. 39.95 (*0-12-484806-0*, AP Prof) Acad Pr.

Using of Financial Information in Continuing Education: Accepted Methods & New Approaches. Gary W. Matkin. LC 96-36577. 334p. 1997. boxed 39.95 (*0-89774-941-3*) Oryx Pr.

***Using Oil Spill Dispersants on the Sea.** National Research Council Staff. LC 88-38879. 351p. 1989. reprint ed. pap. 100.10 (*0-608-02776-6*, 2063843) Bks Demand.

Using OLE in Visual BASIC 4. Bill Shadish et al. LC 96-9188. (Special Reports). 1996. write for info. (*1-880935-48-1*) Pinnacle WA.

Using Online Scientific & Engineering Databases. Harley Bjelland. 232p. 1992. pap. 26.95 (*0-8306-3056-2*, 3967, Windcrest) TAB Bks.

Using Online Scientific & Engineering Databases. Harley Bjelland. 1992. pap. text ed. 26.95 (*0-07-005854-7*) McGraw-Hill Prof.

***Using Open View.** Stephens. Ed. by Mike Loukides. (Illus.). (Orig.). 1998. pap. write for info. (*1-56592-317-0*) OReilly & Assocs.

Using Optima++ Special Edition. Raghuram Bala. 656p. 1996. pap. text ed. 49.99 incl. cd-rom (*0-7897-0894-9*) Que.

Using Options. (Self-Study Options Ser.). Date not set. 83.00 (*0-614-17087-7*, Pub. by IFR Pub UK) Am Educ Systs.

***Using Oracle Cartridges.** Steve Shiflett. 1997. 39.99 (*0-7897-1417-5*) Que.

Using Oral History in Community History Projects. Laurie Mercier & Madeline Buckendorf. (Pamphlet Ser.: Vol. 4). (Orig.). 1992. pap. text ed. 8.00 (*0-615-00633-7*) Oral Hist.

Using Oral History in Educational Studies. rev. ed. Frank A. Stone. 29p. 1989. 2.50 (*0-918158-87-7*) I N Thut World Educ Ctr.

***Using Orchestral Excerpts As Study Material for Violin.** James E. Smith. 2.50 (*0-614-25504-X*, 1926S) Am String Tchrs.

Using Outplacement Services Effectively. Marilyn M. Kennedy. Ed. by Wesley Curry. LC 91-75795. 20p. (Orig.). (C). 1991. pap. text ed. 5.95 (*0-924674-11-3*) Am Coll Phys Execs.

Using Oxygen Equipment. Saint Elizabeth Hospital Medical Center Staff. (Respiratory Patient Education Ser.). (Illus.). 22p. 1992. pap. text ed. 5.95 (*1-56077-238-7*) Ctr Learning.

Using Pacioli 2000: Computerized Accounting Today. Jose M. Hurtado. 400p. pap. 21.33 (*0-13-650631-3*) P-H.

Using PageMaker 3.0. R. Taylor & June Kanai. Ed. by Jose Hurtado. (Logic Ware Ser.). (Illus.). 1989. 24.95 (*0-929978-18-8*) M-USA Busn Systs.

***Using Pagemaker 4.0 on the Macintosh.** Jan Eakins. 1992. text ed. write for info. (*0-07-911209-9*) McGraw.

Using Pagemaker 5 for the Mac, Special Edition. Sharyn Venit. 800p. (Orig.). 1993. pap. 29.95 (*0-685-70410-6*) Que.

***Using Pagemill 2.** Todd Stauffer. 1996. pap. text ed. 24.99 (*0-7897-0964-3*) Que.

Using Paradox for Windows. James Pratt & Last. (C). 1994. text ed. write for info. (*0-318-70355-6*, BF3962) S-W Pub.

Using Paradox for Windows. Philip J. Pratt. 1994. 24.95 (*0-87709-396-2*) Course Tech.

Using Paradox for Windows. Levi Reiss. 1993. pap. text ed. write for info. (*0-07-052018-6*) McGraw.

Using Paradox 3.5. Janet R. Wilson & Patricia A. Shepard. 384p. (C). 1991. spiral bd. 28.27 (*0-697-13349-4*) Bus & Educ Tech.

Using Paradox 4.x. Karen E. Hannum. Ed. by Sally Hargrave. 100p. (Orig.). 1993. pap. text ed. 95.00 (*1-56562-022-4*) OneOnOne Comp Trng.

Using Paradox 4.0. Philip J. Pratt. LC 92-27539. (C). 1994. pap. 30.95 (*0-87835-960-5*, BF9605) S-W Pub.

Using Paradox 4.0. Levi Reiss. 448p. 1993. text ed. write for info. (*0-07-051848-3*) McGraw.

Using Paradox 4.0 DOS. James Pratt. (Computer Applications Ser.). 1994. pap. 24.95 incl. 3.5 ld (*0-87709-093-9*) Course Tech.

Using Paradox 5.0 for Windows. James Pratt. (Computer Applications Ser.). 1996. pap. 30.95 (*0-7895-0119-8*) Course Tech.

***Using Paradox 5.0 for Windows.** Neil J. Salkind. 224p. (C). 1996. pap. text ed. 17.16 (*0-395-74404-0*) HM.

Using Pascal: An Introduction to Computer Science I. David D. Riley. 608p. 1987. teacher ed., pap. 12.75 (*0-87835-235-X*) PWS Pubs.

***Using Patents in Business.** Jim Kinnier-Wilson et al. pap. text ed. 42.00 (*0-471-97050-6*) Wiley.

Using PC-Calc Plus. Ernest S. Colantonio. 128p. (C). 1989. Software. disk write for info. (*0-318-70082-4*) HM College Div.

Using PC-File Plus. Ernest S. Colantonio. 110p. (C). 1989. Software. disk write for info. (*0-318-70084-0*) HM College Div.

Using PC Tools 6. Pat Reeder. Ed. by Kevin C. Hanson. (LogicNotes Ser.). (Illus.). (Orig.). 1990. pap. text ed. write for info. (*0-929978-30-7*) M-USA Busn Systs.

Using PC-Type Plus. Ernest S. Colantonio. 106p. (C). 1989. Software. disk write for info. (*0-318-70081-6*) HM College Div.

***Using PC's.** Jim Boyce. 1997. pap. text ed. 19.99 (*0-7897-1451-5*) Que.

***Using PCs.** Jim Boyce. 1997. 19.99 (*0-7897-1454-X*) Que.

Using PCX Graphics Files. Roger Stevens. 1996. pap. text ed. 45.00 incl. cd-rom (*0-13-476359-9*) P-H.

Using PCX Graphics Files. Roger Stevens. 1996. pap. text ed. 49.95 incl. cd-rom (*0-87930-432-4*) R & D Books.

Using Percent. JoAnne S. Grouney. (Hi Map Ser.: No. 5). (Illus.). 60p. pap. text ed. 9.99 (*0-614-05318-8*, HM 5605) COMAP Inc.

Using Perfect Office, Special Edition. Bill Bruck et al. (Illus.). 804p. (Orig.). 1995. 34.99 (*0-7897-0089-1*) Que.

Using Performance Indicators to Guide Strategic Decision Making. Ed. by Victor M. Borden & Trudy W. Banta. LC 85-645339. (New Directions for Institutional Research Ser.: No. 82). 124p. (Orig.). 1994. pap. 19.00 (*0-7879-9964-4*) Jossey-Bass.

Using Performance Measurement in Local Government. 2nd ed. Paul D. Epstein. 1988. 19.95 (*0-916450-47-3*) Nat Civic League.

Using Performance Measurement in Urban Government. 250p. 1983. 40.00 (*0-318-17358-1*, DG/83-202) Pub Tech Inc.

Using Performance Measures in the Federal Budget Process. Philip Joyce. 52p. (Orig.). (C). 1994. pap. text ed. 30.00 (*0-7881-0531-0*) DIANE Pub.

Using Personality to Individualize Instruction. James A. Wakefield, Jr. LC 78-74138. 1979. 12.00 (*0-912736-21-6*) EDITS Pubs.

Using PFS: First Choice. R. Taylor. Ed. by Jose Hurtado. (Logic Ware Ser.). (Illus.). 1989. 24.95 (*0-929978-06-4*) M-USA Busn Systs.

Using PFS: First Choice Tutorial. Drum. (DF - Computer Applications Ser.). 1991. pap. 27.95 (*0-538-60700-9*) S-W Pub.

Using PFS: First Publisher. R. Taylor & June Kanai. Ed. by Jose Hurtado. (Logic Ware Ser.). (Illus.). 1989. 24.95 (*0-929978-14-5*) M-USA Busn Systs.

Using Phonics. Bearl Brooks. (Phonics Ser.). 24p. (gr. 1-4). 1978. student ed. 5.00 (*0-8209-0334-5*, P-6) ESP.

***Using Photoshop for Web Graphics.** (Orig.). pap. write for info. (*1-56592-350-2*) OReilly & Assocs.

Using Picture Story Books to Teach Literary Devices, Vol. 2. Sue Hall. LC 94-32803. (Illus.). 256p. 1994. pap. 29.95 (*0-89774-849-2*) Oryx Pr.

Using Picture Storybooks to Teach Literary Devices: Recommended Books for Children & Young Adults, Vol. 1. Susan Hall. LC 89-8574. (Illus.). 176p. 1990. pap. 29.95 (*0-89774-582-5*) Oryx Pr.

***Using PLAPACK.** Robert A. Van De Geijn. LC 96-38064. (Scientific & Engineering Computation Ser.). 224p. 1997. pap. 27.50 (*0-262-72026-4*) MIT Pr.

***Using Play to Say Goodbye: Planned, Unplanned, & Premature Endings in Child Psychotherapy.** Donna Cangelosi. LC 96-49473. 1997. 35.00 (*1-56821-677-7*) Aronson.

Using Poetry Across the Curriculum: A Whole Language Approach. Barbara Chatton. LC 93-1428. 240p. 1993. pap. 28.50 (*0-89774-715-1*) Oryx Pr.

Using Poetry to Teach Reading & Language Arts: A Handbook for Elementary School Teachers. Richard J. Smith. (C). 1984. pap. text ed. 15.95 (*0-8077-2708-3*) Tchrs Coll.

Using Policy Simulation Analysis to Guide Correctional Reform - Utah. 7.00 (*0-318-20317-0*) Natl Coun Crime.

Using Polyethylene As a Coagulent for Reducing Turbidity from Placer Mining Discharge. Ray-Her Fan. (MIRL Reports: No. 79). (Illus.). 47p. (Orig.). (C). 1987. pap. 5.00 (*0-911043-06-3*) UAKF Min Ind Res Lab.

***Using Portfolios in the English Classroom.** Ed. by Alan C. Purves et al. 288p. (Orig.). 1996. teacher ed., pap. text ed. 27.95 (*0-926842-62-5*) CG Pubs Inc.

Using Powerbuilder: Special Edition. 2nd ed. Chuck Wood. 898p. 1996. pap. text ed. 59.99 incl. cd-rom (*0-7897-0754-3*) Que.

***Using Powerbuilder 6.** Charles Wood. 1997. 59.99 (*0-7897-1437-X*) Que.

Using Powerpoint for Windows. 2nd ed. Que Development Group Staff. 698p. 1994. 29.99 (*1-56529-651-6*) Que.

Using PowerPoint for Windows 95. Liz Reding. (Illus.). 343p. (Orig.). 1995. 19.99 (*0-7897-0365-3*) Que.

***Using Microsoft PowerPoint 97.** Barbara Kasser. 24.99p. 1996. 24.99 (*0-7897-0934-1*) Mac Comp Pub.

Using Prepositions & Particles. J. B. Heaton. (English As a Second Language Bk.). 1965. 3.25 (*0-582-52120-3*) Longman.

Using Prepositions & Particles, No. 1. J. B. Heaton. (English As a Second Language Bk.). 1965. student ed. 3.25 (*0-582-52122-X*) Longman.

Using Prepositions & Particles, No. 2. J. B. Heaton. (English As a Second Language Bk.). 1965. student ed. 3.25 (*0-582-52123-8*) Longman.

Using Prepositions & Particles, No. 3. J. B. Heaton. (English As a Second Language Bk.). 1965. student ed. 3.25 (*0-582-52124-6*) Longman.

Using Prime Information: Applications & Programs. Robert N. Watkins. (Illus.). 352p. (Orig.). 1989. 29.95 (*0-8306-3209-3*, 3209) McGraw-Hill Prof.

Using Procedure Information. Multimedia Development Services Staff. (Plant Fundamentals Ser.: Vol. IX, Module III). (Illus.). 1995. teacher ed. 65.00 (*1-57431-070-4*); student ed. 30.00 (*1-57431-030-5*) Tech Trng Systs.

Using Process Safety Information. Multimedia Development Services Staff. (Plant Fundamentals Ser.: Vol. IX, Module II). (Illus.). 1995. teacher ed. 65.00 (*1-57431-069-0*); student ed. 30.00 (*1-57431-029-1*) Tech Trng Systs.

Using Professional Standards in Student Affairs. Ed. by William A. Bryan et al. LC 85-644751. (New Directions for Student Services Ser.: No. 53). 1991. 19.00 (*1-55542-797-9*) Jossey-Bass.

Using Program Theory in Evaluation. Ed. by Leonard Bickman. LC 85-644749. (New Directions for Evaluation Ser.: No. 33). 1987. 19.00 (*1-55542-968-8*) Jossey-Bass.

Using Programmed Instruction see Educational Technology Reviews Ser.

Using Projective Techniques with Children: A Guide to Clinical Assessment. Louis A. Chandler & Virginia J. Johnson. (Illus.). 140p. 1991. pap. 20.95 (*0-398-06051-7*) C C Thomas.

Using Projective Techniques with Children: A Guide to Clinical Assessment. Louis A. Chandler & Virginia J. Johnson. (Illus.). 140p. (C). 1991. text ed. 32.95 (*0-398-05726-5*) C C Thomas.

***Using Psychometrics.** Robert Edenborough. (Human Resource Management Ser.). 1994. 40.00 (*0-7494-1302-6*) Kogan Page Ltd.

Using Psychosocial Counselling Techniques in Primary Health Care. Ellen Jespersen & P. F. Pegg. 230p. 1988. text ed. 63.95 (*0-566-05463-9*) Ashgate Pub Co.

***Using Public Records to Find or Investigate Anyone.** Robert Berko. 210p. 1997. pap. 25.00 (*0-614-23615-0*) Consumer Ed Res.

Using Publish It! Steve Gregory. Ed. by Taylor R. Taylor. (LogicNotes Ser.). (Illus.). (Orig.). 1991. pap. text ed. write for info. (*0-929978-62-5*) M-USA Busn Systs.

Using Published Data: Errors & Remedies. Herbert Jacob. LC 84-50250. (Quantitative Applications in the Social Sciences Ser.: Vol. 42). 63p. 1984. pap. 9.95 (*0-8039-2299-X*) Sage.

Using Puppetry in the Church. Ed. by Everett Robertson. LC 78-72842. 1979. pap. 7.99 (*0-8054-7517-6*, 4275-17) Broadman.

Using Puppets in Missions - El Uso de Titeres en la Obra Misionera. Dennis Hale. (Illus.). 96p. (SPA.). 1991. pap. 4.50 (*0-311-11072-X*) Casa Bautista.

Using Qualitative Methods in Institutional Research. Ed. by David M. Fetterman. LC 85-645339. (New Directions for Institutional Research Ser.: No. IR 72). 1991. 19.00 (*1-55542-774-X*) Jossey-Bass.

Using Quality to Redesign School Systems: The Cutting Edge of Common Sense. Peggy M. Siegel & Sandra Byrne. LC 93-40965. (Higher & Adult Education Ser.). 190p. text ed. 28.95 (*1-55542-649-2*) Jossey-Bass.

Using Quark Xpress 3.2 for the Mac. 1992. 39.95 (*1-56529-176-X*) Que.

***Using QuarkXpress for the Macintosh.** Cheryl L. Willis & Jerry Waite. (Illus.). 304p. 1996. teacher ed., text ed. write for info. incl. 3.5 ld (*0-7600-4160-1*) Course Tech.

Using Quarkxpress for Windows. Willis. (DF - Computer Applications Ser.). 1996. pap. 27.95 (*0-7895-0572-X*) S-W Pub.

Using Quattro Pro. Murphy. (C). 1995. pap. 13.16 (*0-395-71402-8*) HM.

Using Quattro Pro for IBM. Murphy. (C). 1995. pap. 17.16 (*0-395-38112-6*) HM.

Using Quattro Pro for Windows. Neil J. Salkind. 1996. pap. 21.00 (*0-02-405391-0*, Macmillan Coll) P-H.

Using Quattro Pro for Windows. Brian Underdahl et al. (Illus.). 898p. (Orig.). 1994. 29.99 (*1-56529-761-X*) Que.

Using Query/400. Patrice Gapen & Catherine Stoughton. LC 94-44462. 92p. (C). 1995. pap. text ed. 35.00 (*1-882419-12-X*, Duke Pr) Duke Commns Intl.

***Using Quickbooks 4.0 in the First Accounting Course.** Glen Owen & Paul Solomon. LC 97-12692. 1997. write for info. (*0-538-86559-8*) S-W Pub.

Using Quicken. R. Taylor & June Kanai. Ed. by Jose Hurtado. (Logic Ware Ser.). (Illus.). 1989. 24.95 (*0-929978-12-9*) M-USA Busn Systs.

Using Quicken for DOS, New Edition. rev. ed. Linda Flanders. (Illus.). 1994. 19.99 (*1-56529-934-5*) Que.

Using Quicken for Windows, New Edition. Que Development Group Staff & Linda Flanders. (Illus.). (Orig.). 1994. 19.99 (*1-56529-933-7*) Que.

U V

An Asterisk (*) at the beginning of an entry indicates that the title is appearing in BIP for the first time.

Using Quicken for Windows 95. Linda Flanders. (Illus.). 416p. (Orig.). 1995. 19.99 (0-7897-0631-8) Que.

Using Quicken On the Mac: Tips & Techniques to Enhance Your Business Productivity. Steve Adams. 1990. pap. 19.95 (0-685-32930-5) P-H.

*Using Quicken X for Windows.** Linda Flanders. 432p. 1996. pap. text ed. 19.99 (0-7897-0996-1) Que.

Using R: BASE 3.0. Janet R. Wilson & Patricia A. Shepard. 368p. (C). 1991. spiral bd. write for info. (0-697-12173-9) Bus & Educ Tech.

Using Rational-Emotive Therapy Effectively: A Practitioner's Guide. Ed. by Michael E. Bernard. (Illus.). 370p. 1991. 75.00 (0-306-43754-6, Plenum Pr); pap. 37.50 (0-306-43755-4, Plenum Pr) Plenum.

Using Real-Time Information in 2-Way Amateur Radio Communications--A 20+ Year Experiment. Leonard C. Silvern. 1997. pap. 15.00 (0-87657-127-5, 00018545) Ed & Training.

Using Reality Therapy. Robert E. Wubbolding. LC 87-46183. 192p. 1988. pap. 11.50 (0-06-096266-6, PL-6266, PL) HarpC.

*Using REBT with Common Psychological Problems.** Ed. by Joseph Yankura & Windy Dryden. LC 97-14148. (Illus.). 256p. 1997. write for info. (0-8261-9800-7) Springer Pub.

Using Recycled Materials. 1991. lib. bdg. 77.95 (0-8490-4674-2) Gordon Pr.

*Using Red Hat Linux.** Que Development Staff. 1998. 39.99 (0-7897-1458-2) Que.

Using REDUCE in High Energy Physics. A. G. Grozin. (Illus.). 350p. (C). 1997. text ed. 80.00 (0-521-56002-0) Cambridge U Pr.

Using References see Skillbooster Series Level C

Using References see Skillbooster Series, Level E

Using References see Skillbooster Series, Level F

Using Research: A Primer for Law Enforcement Managers. 2nd rev. ed. John E. Eck & Nancy La Vigne. 180p. (Orig.). 1994. pap. 22.00 (1-878734-33-4) Police Exec Res.

Using Research for Strategic Planning. Ed. by Norman P. Uhl. LC 82-84191. (New Directions for Institutional Research Ser.: No. IR 37). 1983. 19.00 (0-87589-955-2) Jossey-Bass.

Using Research in Public Relations: Applications to Program Management. Glen M. Broom & David Dozier. 450p. 1989. text ed. 40.51 (0-13-939166-5) P-H.

Using Robots. Carroll Morgan. 250p. 1985. 94.95 (0-387-12584-1) Spr-Verlag.

Using Role Plays in Human Resource Development. J. William Pfeiffer & Arlette C. Ballew. LC 87-40534. (Training Technologies Set Ser.). 129p. (Orig.). 1988. pap. 139.00 (0-88390-214-1, Pfffr & Co) Jossey-Bass.

Using Russian: A Guide to Contemporary Usage. Derek C. Offord. 440p. (C). 1996. pap. text ed. 24.95 (0-521-45760-2) Cambridge U Pr.

Using Russian: A Guide to Contemporary Usage. Derek C. Offord. 440p. (C). 1997. text ed. 64.95 (0-521-45130-2) Cambridge U Pr.

*Using Sap R-3: Special Edition.** 2nd ed. Que Development Group Staff. 1997. 85.00 (0-7897-1351-9) Que.

*Using SAP R/3 FI: Beyond Business Process Reengineering.** Benjamin W. Rockefeller. LC 97-4236. 1997. write for info. (0-471-17996-5) Wiley.

Using SAP R/3, Special Edition. Ron Taylor. 1184p. 1996. 75.00 (0-7897-0689-X) Que.

Using SAP's R-3 Client Server Tool. Thomas Curran. LC 97-13166. (C). 1997. pap. text ed. 48.00 (0-13-521147-6) P-H.

Using Sartre: An Analytical Introduction to Early Sartrean Themes. Gregory McCulloch. LC 93-33903. 160p. (C). 1994. pap. 16.95 (0-415-10954-X, B3955) Routledge.

Using Sartre: An Analytical Introduction to Early Sartrean Themes. Gregory McCulloch. LC 93-33903. 160p. (C). (gr. 13). 1994. text ed. 49.95 (0-415-10953-1, B3951) Routledge.

Using Science & Technology Information Sources. Ellis Mount & Beatrice Kovacs. LC 90-21836. 200p. 1991. pap. 26.95 (0-89774-593-0) Oryx Pr.

Using Scripture in Pastoral Counseling. Edward P. Wimberly. LC 93-28847. 128p. (Orig.). 1994. pap. 13.95 (0-687-00251-6) Abingdon.

Using Secondary Data in Marketing Research: United States & Worldwide. Gordon L. Patzer. LC 94-40460. 184p. 1995. text ed. 55.00 (0-89930-961-5, Quorum Bks) Greenwood.

Using Self Psychology in Child Psychotherapy. Jule P. Miller, 3rd. LC 95-22943. 1996. pap. 45.00 (1-56821-492-8) Aronson.

Using Self Psychology in Psychotherapy. Ed. by Helene Jackson. LC 90-1236. 280p. 1991. 35.00 (0-87668-621-8) Aronson.

Using Self Psychology in Psychotherapy. Ed. by Helene Jackson. LC 90-1236. 296p. 1994. pap. 35.00 (1-56821-044-2) Aronson.

Using Self-Reports to Predict Student Performance. Leonard L. Baird. (Research Monographs: No. 7). 92p. 1976. pap. 5.00 (0-87447-098-6, 251701) College Bd.

Using Set-Off As Security: A Comparative Survey for Practitioners. Ed. by Francis W. Neate. (C). 1990. lib. bdg. 183.00 (1-85333-363-8, Pub. by Graham & Trotman UK) Kluwer Ac.

*Using Slackwave Linux.** Que Development Staff. 1998. 39.99 (0-7897-1459-0) Que.

Using Social Science Research in Policy Making. Ed. by Carol H. Weiss. (Organization Ser.). 256p. 1977. 15.00 (0-317-35635-6) Pol Studies.

Using Social Thought: The Nuclear Issue & Other Concerns. R. P. Cuzzort. LC 88-34581. 342p. (C). 1989. pap. text ed. 31.95 (0-87484-800-8, 800) Mayfield Pub.

*Using Sociology: A Bicultural & Binational Approach.** Ed. by Richardson. (C). 1995. text ed. 39.50 (0-673-99848-7) Addison-Wesley.

Using Sociology: An Introduction from the Applied & Clinical Perspectives. 2nd ed. Ed. by Roger A. Straus. LC 93-79474. 320p. (Orig.). 1994. text ed. 39.95 (1-882289-11-0); pap. text ed. 24.95 (1-882289-10-2) Gen Hall.

Using Sociology to Understand Your Life: Theories, Methods, & Strategies for Career Planning. Susan R. Takata & Jeanne Curran. LC 93-13865. 580p. 1993. pap. 49.95 (0-7734-1966-7) E Mellen.

*Using Solstice Workshop: Special Edition.** Que Development Group Staff. 1996. pap. text ed. 49.99 incl. cd-rom (0-7897-0967-8) Que.

Using Sophisticated Models in Resolution Theorem Proving. D. M. Sandford. (Lecture Notes in Computer Science Ser.: Vol. 90). (Illus.). 239p. 1980. 25.00 (0-387-10231-0) Spr-Verlag.

Using Sound. Sally Morgan & Adrian Morgan. LC 93-31720. (Designs in Science Ser.). (Illus.). 48p. (YA). (gr. 5-9). 1994. 14.95 (0-8160-2981-4) Facts on File.

Using Spanish, 4 cass. (ENG & SPA.). pap. 59.95 incl. audio (2-7005-1364-9, Pub. by ASSIMIL FR) Distribks Inc.

Using Spanish: A Guide to Contemporary Usage. R. E. Batchelor & Christopher J. Pountain. 336p. (C). 1992. 65.00 (0-521-42123-3); pap. 20.95 (0-521-26987-3) Cambridge U Pr.

Using Spanish Synonyms. R. E. Batchelor. 600p. (C). 1994. pap. text ed. 25.95 (0-521-44694-5) Cambridge U Pr.

Using Spanish Synonyms. R. E. Batchelor. 600p. (C). 1995. text ed. 80.00 (0-521-44160-9) Cambridge U Pr.

Using Specific Capacity to Estimate Transmissivity: Field & Computer Methods (Plus Computer Program) Michael Kasenow & Paul Pare. 96p. 1995. spiral bd. 40.00 (0-918334-95-0, USCET) WRP.

Using Speech Recognition. Judith Markowitz. 1995. pap. text ed. 38.60 (0-13-186321-5) P-H.

Using Sports & Physical Education to Strengthen Reading Skills. Lance M. Gentile. LC 80-36805. (IRA Reading Aids Ser.). (Illus.). 90p. (Orig.). reprint ed. pap. 25.70 (0-8357-8654-4, 2035099) Bks Demand.

*Using Spreadsheets Correctly.** 2nd ed. Erickson. (C). 1996. pap. text ed. write for info. (0-03-020148-9) HB Coll Pubs.

*Using SPSS for the Macintosh: Analyzing & Understanding Data.** Samuel B. Green. LC 96-29368. 1997. 33.33 (0-13-462367-3) P-H.

Using SPSS for Windows: Analyzing & Understanding Data. Samuel B. Green et al. LC 96-9439. 416p. (C). 1997. pap. text ed. 35.00 (0-02-346434-8) P-H.

Using SQL Windows & Centura: Techniques for Building Client/Server Solutions. Sanjiv Purba. LC 96-21161. 416p. 1996. pap. 44.95 incl. disk (0-471-13089-3) Wiley.

Using SQL with R: BASE. Janet R. Wilson & Patricia A. Shepard. 144p. (C). 1991. spiral bd. write for info. (0-697-12821-0) Bus & Educ Tech.

Using Statistics. Kenneth J. Travers. 1985. 42.50 (0-201-20070-8) Addison-Wesley.

Using Statistics. 2nd ed. (Open Learning Super Ser.). 1991. pap. text ed. 26.00 (0-08-041614-4, Pergamon Pr) Elsevier.

Using Statistics to Solve Problems in Psychology. 4th ed. Eric F. Ward. 1985. pap. text ed. 7.50 (0-89917-457-4) Tichenor Pub.

Using Structured Experiences in Human Resource Development. J. William Pfeiffer & Arlette C. Ballew. LC 87-40530. (Training Technologies Set Ser.). 109p. (Orig.). 1988. pap. text ed. 139.00 (0-88390-212-5, Pfffr & Co) Jossey-Bass.

Using Structured Interviewing Techniques. 99p. (Orig.). (C). 1993. pap. text ed. 20.00 (1-56806-615-5) DIANE Pub.

Using Student-Centered Methods with Teacher-Centered ESL Students. Marilyn Lewis. 112p. 1996. pap. 16.00 (0-88751-068-X, Pub. by Dominie Pr CN) Alemany Pr.

Using Study Skills & Learning Strategies in the Classroom: A Teacher's Handbook. John J. Hoover. LC 90-80215. 113p. (C). 1990. pap. text ed. 16.50 (0-940059-09-6) Hamilton Pubns.

Using Subject Headings for Online Retrieval: Theory, Practice & Potential. Karen M. Drabenstott & Diane Vizine-Goetz. (Library & Information Science Ser.). (Illus.). 365p. 1994. text ed. 58.00 (0-12-221570-2) Acad Pr.

Using Surveys to Value Public Goods: The Contingent Valuation Method. Robert C. Mitchell & Richard T. Carson. LC 87-28633. 463p. 1988. 45.00 (0-915707-32-2) Resources Future.

Using Systems Analysis to Implement Cost-Effectiveness & Program Budgeting in Education. John P. Van Gigch & Richard E. Hill. LC 71-153558. 64p. 1971. pap. 19.95 (0-87778-007-2) Educ Tech Pubns.

Using TACT with Electronic Texts: A Guide to "Text-Analysis Computing Tools" Ian Lancashire et al. LC 95-48850. xiii, 361p. (Orig.). 1996. pap. 50.00 incl. cd-rom (0-87352-569-8, NTACT) Modern Lang.

Using Tandy's Deskmate. R. Taylor. Ed. by Jose Hurtado. (Logic Ware Ser.). (Illus.). 1989. 24.95 (0-929978-07-2) M-USA Busn Systs.

*Using TCP/IP.** Joern Wettern. 1997. 49.99 (0-7897-1362-4) Que.

Using Technical Analysis: A Step-by-Step Guide to Understanding & Applying Stock Market. Clifford Pistolese. (C). 1994. per. 24.95 (1-55738-527-0) Irwin Prof Pubng.

*Using Technical Writing for Learning Across the Curriculum.** Howard Wills & ERIC Clearinghouse on Reading, English & Communication Staff. LC 96-35660. 1997. pap. write for info. (1-883790-22-0, EDINFO Pr) Grayson Bernard Pubs.

Using Technology for Education & Training. LC 83-81648. 248p. 1983. 25.00 (0-317-36884-2); 22.00 (0-317-36885-0) Assn Ed Comm Tech.

Using Technology in Physical Education. Bonnie S. Mohnsen. LC 94-4550. (Illus.). 168p. 1994. pap. text ed. 15.00 (0-87322-661-5, BMOH0661) Human Kinetics.

*Using Technology in the Classroom.** Ed. by D. LaMont Johnson et al. LC 97-2326. (Computers in the Schools Monograph Ser.: Vol. 13, Nos. 1-2). 242p. (C). 1997. 49.95 (0-7890-0311-2) Haworth Pr.

*Using Technology in the Classroom.** D. Lamont Johnson et al. LC 97-2326. 1997. write for info. (0-7890-0352-X) Haworth Pr.

*Using Technology in the Classroom.** 4th ed. Bitter. 1997. pap. text ed. 47.00 (0-205-27565-6) P-H.

Using Technology to Support Education Reform. 1994. lib. bdg. 250.00 (0-8490-5776-0) Gordon Pr.

Using Technology to Support Educational Reform. 1995. lib. bdg. 250.95 (0-8490-6855-X) Gordon Pr.

Using Ten-Key Electronic Desktop Calculators. John Kimmel. 207p. 1983. pap. text ed. 11.95 (0-89420-235-9, 126520); audio 95.95 (0-89420-242-1, 126500) Natl Book.

Using Tests & Other Information in Counseling: A Decision Model for Practitioners. James M. Schuerger & David G. Watterson. LC 77-71888. 1977. pap. text ed. 4.40 (0-918296-08-0) Inst Personality & Ability.

Using Tests to Improve Training: The Complete Guide to Selecting, Developing, & Using Training Instruments. William J. Reddin. LC 94-5600. 1994. write for info. (0-13-108556-5) P-H.

Using the Absolute Weapon: Early Ideas of Bernard Brodie on Atomic Strategy. Barry H. Steiner. (CISA Working Papers: No. 44). 49p. (Orig.). 1984. pap. 15.00 (0-86682-057-4) Ctr Intl Relations.

Using the Appropriateness Method in Clinical Practice Guideline Development. Paul G. Shekelle & David L. Schriger. 85p. (Orig.). 1995. pap. text ed. 13.00 (0-8330-1458-7, MR-233-AHCPR) Rand Corp.

Using the Aquatic Environment for Teaching Handicapped Children: A Manual for Teachers & Parents. Michael A. Horvat & William R. Forbus. (Illus.). 101p. (Orig.). 1989. teacher ed. 25.00 (1-878276-02-6) Educ Systs Assocs Inc.

Using the Arts & Humanities to Teach Nursing: A Creative Approach. Theresa M. Valiga & Elizabeth R. Bruderle. LC 96-26797. (Teaching of Nursing Ser.). (Illus.). 312p. 1996. 33.95 (0-8261-9420-6) Springer Pub.

Using the AS-400: An Introduction. Patrice Gapen & Catherine Stoughton. LC 92-22205. 176p. 1993. pap. 22.95 (0-87835-952-4) Course Tech.

Using the Band Saw. Nick Engler. (Workshop Companion Ser.). Date not set. pap. 12.95 (0-87596-608-X) Rodale Pr Inc.

Using the Band Saw: Techniques for Better Woodworking. Nick Engler. (Workshop Companion Ser.). (Illus.). 128p. 1992. 19.95 (0-87596-140-1, 14-778-0) Rodale Pr Inc.

Using the BBI Combinatory Dictionary of English: A Workbook with Exercises. Morton Benson et al. x, 58p. (Orig.). 1991. pap. text ed. 6.95 (1-55619-094-8) Benjamins North Am.

Using the Bible in Groups. Roberta Hestenes. LC 84-15291. 118p. (Orig.). 1985. pap. 10.00 (0-664-24561-7, Westminster) Westminster John Knox.

Using the Bio-Dynamic Compost Preparations & Sprays in Garden, Orchard & Farm. 2nd ed. E. E. Pfeiffer. 64p. (C). reprint ed. pap. 4.75 (0-938250-26-4) Bio-Dynamic Farm.

Using the Biological Literature: A Practical Guide. 2nd expanded rev. ed. Elisabeth B. Davis. LC 95-11639. (Books in Library & Information Sciences: Vol. 57). 440p. 1995. 85.00 (0-8247-9477-X) Dekker.

Using the Calculator: To Develop Multiplication & Division of Whole Numbers. William L. Swart. 28p. 1989. pap. text ed. 6.75 (1-883547-01-6) Tricon Pub.

Using the Cantonese Tape Set with the Interpreter's Edge Generic Edition, 3 cass. Holly M. Mikkelson. 122p. (C). 1994. spiral bd. 35.00 incl. audio (1-880594-12-9) ACEBO.

Using the Chemical Literature: A Practical Guide. Henry M. Woodburn. (Books in Library & Information Science: Vol. 11). 314p. 1974. pap. 65.00 (0-8247-7455-8) Dekker.

Using the Chemy Called Al in the Classroom. Wendy Isdell. Ed. by Pamela Espeland. 32p. (Orig.). 1996. teacher ed., pap. 6.95 (0-915793-97-0) Free Spirit Pub.

Using the Commodore 64 in the Home. Hank Librach & William Behrendt. (Illus.). 100p. 1984. pap. 10.95 (0-685-06718-1) P-H.

Using the Commodore 64 Without Learning BASIC. Tim Kelly. 1984. 15.95 (0-685-09770-6) P-H.

Using the Compass. Jude LaClaire. (Life Weaving Ser.: Vol. 2). (Illus.). 64p. 1995. spiral bd. 9.95 (0-9629385-2-1) Heartlnd Personal.

Using the Computer for Offensive Football Scouting. Charles Frazier & Alan Hatfield. (Illus.). 256p. 1984. 24.95 (0-13-940198-9) P-H.

Using the Computer in Education: A Briefing for School Decision Makers. Paul G. Watson. LC 72-86779. 144p. 1972. pap. 21.95 (0-87778-042-0) Educ Tech Pubns.

Using the Cranmer Abacus for the Blind. large type ed. F. Gissoni. 40p. reprint ed. 10.50 (0-317-01958-9, 4-27110-00) Am Printing Hse.

Using the Creative Arts in Therapy: A Practical Introduction. 2nd ed. Ed. by Bernie Warren. LC 92-48527. 208p. (C). 1993. pap. 17.95 (0-415-08814-3, B0886) Routledge.

Using the Cuisenaire Rods: A Photo-Text Guide for Teachers. Jessica Davidson. (Illus.). 150p. (J). (gr. 1-8). 1983. pap. text ed. 16.95 (0-914040-04-9) Cuisenaire.

Using the Data Warehouse. William H. Inmon & Richard D. Hackathorn. 285p. 1994. text ed. 49.95 (0-471-05966-8) Wiley.

Using the Dataease Query Language. Jeff Roberts & Frank Davis. 1988. pap. 21.95 (0-916515-50-8) Mercury Hse Inc.

Using the Dictionary. Wood. (YA - Adult Education Ser.). 1993. pap. 5.95 (0-538-70779-8) S-W Pub.

Using the Drill Press: Techniques for Better Woodworking. Nick Engler. LC 95-8114. (Workshop Companion Ser.). (Illus.). 1995. write for info. (0-87596-721-3) Rodale Pr Inc.

Using the Earth to Heat & Cool Homes. 22p. 1983. 4.00 (0-317-53924-8, EC-5) NCAT.

Using the Family History Library Computer System: Including the Library Catalog, Ancestral File, International Genealogical Index. Nancy E. Carlberg. 90p. (Orig.). 1991. pap. 15.00 (0-944878-08-3) Carlberg Pr.

Using the Freedom of Information Act: A Step by Step Guide. 16p. 1992. pap. 4.00 (0-86566-042-5) ACLU DC.

Using the Freedom of Information Act: A Step by Step Guide. ACLU Staff. 16p. 1992. pap. 4.00 (0-86566-062-X) ACLU DC.

*Using the Freedom of Information Act As a Strategic Business Tool.** Burt A. Braverman et al. 1997. write for info. (1-56726-043-8) Holbrook & Kellogg.

Using the Hazardous Waste Manifest: A Manual of Federal & State Requirements. Inter-Face Associates Staff. 270p. 1985. ring bd. 55.00 (0-317-56114-6) Interface Assocs.

Using the HR Consultant Achieving Results-Adding Value. Michael Armstrong. 160p. 1993. pap. 120.00 (0-85292-546-8, Pub. by IPM Hse UK) St Mut.

Using the IBM PC-AT. Thor Petersen. (Illus.). 144p. 1987. 17.95 (0-13-939471-0) P-H.

Using the ICL Data Dictionary: Proceedings of the ICL DDS User Group. Ed. by A. T. Windsor. 160p. 1980. 29.95 (0-906812-06-2) Birkhauser.

*Using the Internet.** Dk Publishing, Inc. Staff. LC 96-6497. (101 Essential Tips Ser.: Vol. 28). 72p. 1997. pap. 6.95 (0-7894-1462-7) DK Pub Inc.

Using the Internet. Bill Eager & Que Staff. (Illus.). 400p. (Orig.). 1994. 19.99 (0-7897-0096-4) Que.

*Using the Internet.** Mary Micco & Therese O'Neil. 184p. (C). 1996. pap. text ed. 18.36 (0-395-77057-2) HM.

*Using the Internet.** 2nd ed. Jerry Honeycutt. 408p. 1996. pap. text ed. 24.99 (0-7897-0963-5) Que.

Using the Internet. 2nd ed. Que Development Group Staff. (Illus.). 1188p. 1995. 39.99 (0-7897-0077-8) Que.

*Using the Internet.** 3rd ed. Jerry Honeycutt. 1997. 19.99 (0-7897-1406-X) Que.

*Using the Internet.** 4th ed. Jerry Honeycutt. 1997. 39.99 (0-7897-1403-5) Que.

Using the Internet & the World-Wide Web in Your Job Search. 2nd ed. Fred E. Jandt & Mary B. Nemnich. LC 96-46178. Orig. Title: Using the Internet in Your Job Search. (Illus.). 300p. 1996. pap. 16.95 (1-56370-292-4, J2924) JIST Works.

Using the Internet for Social Science Research. 2nd ed. Kardas. (Sociology Ser.). Date not set. pap. 25.95 (0-534-52353-6) Wadsworth Pub.

Using the Internet for Social Science Research & Practice. Edward P. Kardas & Tommy M. Milford. (Sociology Ser.). 221p. (C). 1996. pap. text ed. 26.95 incl. disk (0-534-51388-3) Wadsworth Pub.

Using the Internet in Your Job Search see Using the Internet & the World-Wide Web in Your Job Search

Using the Internet, Online Services, & CD-ROMs to Write Research & Term Papers. Ed. by Charles Harmon. (Illus.). 170p. 1996. pap. 29.95 (1-55570-238-4) Neal-Schuman.

Using the Internet with Windows 95. Bill Eager. (Illus.). 376p. (Orig.). 1995. 24.99 (0-7897-0402-1) Que.

Using the Internet with Your Mac. Todd Stauffer. (Illus.). 308p. (Orig.). 1995. 24.99 (0-7897-0665-2) Que.

Using the Korean Tape Set with the Interpreter's Edge Generic Edition, 3 cass. Holly M. Mikkelson. 92p. (KOR.). (C). 1994. spiral bd. 35.00 incl. audio (1-880594-10-2) ACEBO.

Using the Latest Discoveries in Neuroscience: Nutrients & Safe Drugs. 1991. lib. bdg. 79.95 (0-8490-4727-7) Gordon Pr.

Using the Learning Cycle to Teach Physical Science: A Hands on Approach for the Middle Grades. Paul C. Beisenherz & Marylou Dantonio. LC 95-24856. 256p. 1996. pap. text ed. 26.50 (0-435-08376-7, 08376) Heinemann.

Using the Lecture in Teaching & Training see Pedagogia Ilustrada: La Conferencia en la Ensenanza, Tomo 2

Using the Library to Find Out about Parapsychology. Rhea A. White. 40p. (Orig.). 1989. pap. 5.00 (0-944446-16-7) EHE Network.

Using the Los Angeles Family History Center. rev. ed. Nancy E. Carlberg. 160p. 1991. reprint ed. pap. 15.00 (0-944878-03-2) Carlberg Pr.

Using the Magic of Word Power to Multiply Real Estate Sales. Les Davidson. 1973. 49.50 (0-685-01591-2) Exec Reports.

Using the Magnetic Forces of Your Mind. Pritchard. 1957. pap. 4.95 (0-87505-094-8) Borden.

UV

***Using the Mandarin Tape Set with the Interpreter's Edge Generic Edition, 3 cass.** Holly Mikkelson. 103p. (C). 1997. spiral bd. 35.00 incl. audio (*1-880594-17-X*) ACEBO.

Using the Math Explorer Calculator: A Sourcebook for Teachers. Gary G. Bitter. 1990. pap. text ed. 26.00 (*0-201-23389-4*) Addison-Wesley.

Using the Mathematical Literature: A Practical Guide. Barbara K. Schaefer. LC 78-24537. (Bks. in Library & Information Science: No. 25). 155p. reprint ed. pap. 44.20 (*0-685-23675-7*, 2029014) Bks Demand.

Using the Microcomputer in Financial Accounting: Lotus 1-2-3 Edition. Mark W. Lehman & Carol M. Lehman. (Illus.). 308p. (Orig.). (C). 1986. pap. text ed. 36.50 (*0-314-98514-X*) West Pub.

Using the Microscope: A Guide for Naturalists. Eric V. Grave. (Illus.). 224p. reprint ed. pap. 9.95 (*0-486-26916-7*) Dover.

Using the M68HC11 Microcontroller: A Guide to Interfacing & Programming the M68HC11 Microcontroller. John C. Skroder. LC 96-10489. 1996. text ed. 80.00 (*0-13-120676-1*) P-H.

Using the Natural Light: Selected Poems. Nancy Cardozo. LC 91-61718. (Orig.). 1991. pap. 7.95 (*0-9621570-3-1*) North Lights.

Using the New AACR2: An Expert Systems Approach to the Use of Access Points. David Smith et al. 192p. 1993. pap. 65.00 (*1-85604-086-0*, LAP0860, Pub. by Library Association UK) Bernan Associates.

Using the New DB2: IBM's Object-Relational Database System. Donald Chamberlin. 600p. 1996. pap. 44.95 (*1-55860-373-5*) Morgan Kaufmann.

Using the Newspaper in the Writing Process. Carney. (Illus.). (J). (gr. 3-5). 1996. wbk. ed., pap. 9.95 (*1-55734-479-5*) Tchr Create Mat.

Using the Newspaper to Teach ESL Learners. Rafael A. Olivares. LC 93-988. 104p. 1993. pap. 11.95 (*0-87207-237-1*) Intl Reading.

Using the Newspaper to Teach Reading Skills. Carney. (Illus.). (J). (gr. 3-5). 1996. wbk. ed., pap. 9.95 (*1-55734-466-3*) Tchr Create Mat.

Using the Nineteen Ninety-Two IGI on Microfiche. Nancy E. Carlberg. 55p. 1993. pap. 3.00 (*0-944878-29-6*) Carlberg Pr.

Using the Office Telephone Effectively. Patricia A. Garner. LC 92-15979. 128p. (C). 1992. pap. text ed. 17.40 (*0-13-953704-X*) P-H.

Using the Oracle Toolset. Mike Krohn. (Illus.). 320p. (C). 1993. text ed. 33.50 (*0-201-56538-2*) Addison-Wesley.

Using the Orange Family History Center. Nancy E. Carlberg. 160p. 1992. pap. 10.00 (*0-944878-23-7*) Carlberg Pr.

Using the Oscilloscope. Ray Iddings. LC 94-22269. 128p. 1994. pap. text ed. 49.00 (*0-13-148362-5*) P-H.

Using the Past to Serve the Present: Historiography & Politics in Contemporary China. Ed. by Jonathan Unger. LC 93-15256. (Contemporary China Papers - Australian National University Ser.). 304p. (C). (gr. 13). 1993. text ed. 67.95 (*0-87332-747-0*, East Gate Bk); pap. text ed. 25.95 (*0-87332-748-9*, East Gate Bk) M E Sharpe.

Using the Personal Ancestral File. Nancy E. Carlberg. 120p. (Orig.). 1991. pap. 15.00 (*0-944878-09-1*) Carlberg Pr.

Using the Power of Prayer. Leona S. Murphy. 143p. (Orig.). 1987. pap. 5.95 (*0-937580-06-6*) LeSEA Pub Co.

Using the Power of the Psalms As Your Daily Guide. Terry Latterman & Maya Perez. LC 94-61162. 127p. 1995. pap. 6.95 (*1-55523-727-4*) Winston-Derek.

Using the Private Sector to Deter Crime. Morgan O. Reynolds. 42p. (Orig.). 1994. pap. text ed. 10.00 (*1-56808-015-8*, 181) Natl Ctr Pol.

***Using the Psion Series 3a.** Bill Aitkan. (Orig.). 1996. pap. 34.95 (*1-898307-26-1*, Pub. by Capall Bann Pubng UK) Holmes Pub.

Using the Public Library in the Computer Age: Present Patterns, Future Possibilities. Alan F. Westin & Anne L. Finger. LC 91-12332. (Illus.). 80p. 1991. reprint ed. pap. 25.00 (*0-608-01733-7*, 2062390) Bks Demand.

***Using the Russian Tape Set with the Interpreter's Edge Generic Edition, 3 cass.** Holly Mikkelson. 96p. (C). 1996. spiral bd. 35.00 incl. audio (*1-880594-15-3*) ACEBO.

Using the Scroll Saw. Nick Engler. LC 94-14418. (Workshop Companion Ser.). 1994. 19.95 (*0-87596-654-3*) Rodale Pr Inc.

Using the Soil Survey for Equalizing Agricultural Property Taxes in South Dakota. Norman R. Kempf. 1985. 5.00 (*1-55614-013-4*) U of SD Gov Res Bur.

***Using the STL: The C++ Standard Template Library.** Robert Robson. LC 97-8921. 1997. pap. write for info. (*0-387-98204-3*) Spr-Verlag.

Using the Story. Robert G. Davidson. (Leadership Ser.). 1987. pap. 5.50 (*0-940754-44-4*, 4013) Ed Ministries.

Using the Supportive Play Model: Individualized Intervention in Early Childhood Practice. Margaret Sheridan et al. (Early Childhood Education Ser.). 168p. (C). 1994. pap. text ed. 25.95 (*0-8077-3422-5*) Tchrs Coll.

Using the Table Saw. Nick Engler. LC 91-33469. (Illus.). 128p. 1992. 19.95 (*0-87596-127-4*, 14-776-0) Rodale Pr Inc.

Using the Talent Profiles in Counseling: A Supplement to the Career Data Book. Robert J. Rossi et al. 1975. pap. 5.25 (*0-89785-516-7*) Am Inst Res.

Using the Target Language. Carol Macdonald. 1994. pap. 35.00 (*1-85234-507-1*, Pub. by Stanley Thornes UK) Trans-Atl Phila.

Using the Telephone for Business Results. Judith E. Fisher. LC 93-7. 112p. 1993. per. 10.00 (*1-55623-858-4*) Irwin Prof Pubng.

***Using the Telephone More Effectively.** 2nd ed. Madeline Bodin. LC 97-13910. (Business Success Ser.). 1997. pap. text ed. 6.95 (*0-8120-9897-8*) Barron.

Using the TI-82 to Explore Precalculus & Calculus. George W. Best & David A. Penner. 204p. 1994. write for info. (*1-886018-06-5*) Venture Pubng.

Using the TI-85 to Explore Precalculus & Calculus. George W. Best & Sally Fischback. 198p. (C). 1994. 25.00 (*1-886018-05-7*) Venture Pubng.

Using the Turbo Debugger. Philip Seyer. (Illus.). 272p. 1989. pap. 19.95 (*0-8306-7394-6*) TAB Bks.

Using the Twelve Steps to Grow Spiritually: A Guide for Women. Patricia F. Wallace & Mary Winifred. 1992. pap. 14.95 (*0-87193-279-2*) Dimension Bks.

Using the Unix System. Richard Gauthier. 1981. pap. 21.50 (*0-8359-8162-2*, Reston) P-H.

***Using the Vietnamese Tape Set with the Interpreter's Edge Generic Edition, 3 cass.** Holly Mikkelson. 98p. (C). 1996. spiral bd. 35.00 incl. audio (*1-880594-16-1*) ACEBO.

Using the View Camera. rev. ed. Steve Simmons. (Illus.). 144p. 1992. pap. 22.50 (*0-8174-6353-4*, Amphoto) Watsn-Guptill.

Using the Whole Brain: Integrating the Right & Left Brain with Hemi-Sync Sound Patterns. Ed. by Ronald Russell. 264p. (Orig.). 1993. pap. 14.95 (*1-878901-86-9*) Hampton Roads Pub Co.

Using the Windows NT 4.0 Registry Special Edition. Jerry Honeycutt. 800p. 1996. pap. text ed. 39.99 incl. cd-rom (*0-7897-0842-6*) Que.

Using the Windows 95 Registry. Windows Magazine Staff. 816p. 1996. pap. text ed. 59.99 incl. cd-rom (*0-7897-0785-3*) Que.

Using the Win32 API with Visual Basic 4, Special Ed. Ward Hitt. 1996. pap. text ed. 49.99 incl. cd-rom (*0-7897-0816-7*) Que.

Using the World Wide Web & Creating Home Pages: A How-To-Do-It Manual for Librarians. Ray E. Metz & Gail Junion-Metz. (Illus.). 290p. (Orig.). 1996. pap. 49.95 (*1-55570-241-4*) Neal-Schuman.

Using the World Wide Web, Special Edition. 2nd ed. Bill Eager. 1100p. 1996. pap. text ed. 49.99 incl. cd-rom (*0-7897-0788-8*) Que.

Using the 1-2-3 Solver. Jack McGrath. (Illus.). (Orig.). 1991. pap. 44.95 (*0-13-635335-5*) Brady Pub.

Using the 1990 U.S. Census for Research. Richard E. Barrett. LC 94-17655. (Guides to Major Social Science Data Bases Ser.: Vol. 3). 104p. 1994. 26.00 (*0-8039-5389-5*); pap. 10.95 (*0-8039-5390-9*) Sage.

Using Theory to Improve Program & Policy Evaluations. Ed. by Huey-tsyh Chen & Peter H. Rossi. LC 91-27813. (Contributions in Political Science Ser.: No. 290). 288p. 1992. text ed. 69.50 (*0-313-28346-X*, CTV/, Greenwood Pr) Greenwood.

Using Title XX to Serve Children & Youth. Mott-McDonald Associates Staff. LC 76-357536. 80p. reprint ed. pap. 25.00 (*0-317-29896-8*, 2019375) Bks Demand.

Using Tobacco During Youth. J. Frederick Garman & Waln K. Brown. 20p. 1991. 2.95 (*1-56456-003-1*, 241) W Gladden Found.

Using Tofu, Tempeh & Other Soyfoods in Restaurants, Delis & Cafeterias. William Shurtleff & Akiko Aoyagi. (Soyfoods Production Ser.: No. 5). (Illus.). 135p. (Orig.). 1982. spiral bd. 32.95 (*0-933332-07-6*) Soyfoods Center.

Using Toolpack Software Tools. Ed. by A. A. Pollicini. (C). 1988. lib. bdg. 162.50 (*0-7923-0033-5*) Kluwer Ac.

Using Transportation. McVey & Associates Staff. (Follet Coping Skills Ser.). 64p. 1988. pap. text ed. 5.50 (*0-8428-2330-1*) Cambridge Bk.

Using Transportation Control Measures to Reduce Motor Vehicle Emissions. (Illus.). 54p. (Orig.). (C). 1994. pap. text ed. 30.00 (*0-7881-0209-5*) DIANE Pub.

Using TraX: A Tutorial to Accompany TraX, a Program for the Simulation & Analysis of Dynamical Systems, Version 1.2. Alexander I. Khibnik. Ed. by Jeffrey A. Millstein. 72p. 1990. write for info. (*1-884977-12-X*); teacher ed. write for info. (*1-884977-13-8*) Applied Biomath.

Using Turbo Assembler. Philip Seyer. (Illus.). 272p. 1990. pap. 19.60 (*0-8306-3396-0*, 3396) McGraw-Hill Prof.

Using Turbo C Plus Plus. Hennefeld. (Computer Science Ser.). 1998. pap. 44.95 (*0-534-95591-6*) PWS Pubs.

Using TURBO, IBM, & MICROSOFT PASCAL: An Applications Approach. Bruce P. Douglass. write for info. (*0-318-59639-3*) S&S Trade.

Using Turbo Pascal. 2nd ed. Julien Hennefeld. 464p. 1992. pap. 41.25 (*0-534-92710-6*) PWS Pubs.

***Using Turbo Pascal.** 4th ed. Hennefeld. (Computer Science Ser.). (C). Date not set. pap. 29.95 (*0-534-95055-8*) PWS Pubs.

Using Turbo Pascal 6.0-7.0. 3rd ed. Julien O. Hennefeld. LC 94-21767. 544p. 1995. pap. 53.95 incl. disk (*0-534-94398-5*) PWS Pubs.

Using Type Right: One Hundred Twenty-One No-Nonsense Rules for Working with Type. Philip Brady. 128p. 1994. 24.95 (*0-8442-3375-7*, NTC Busn Bks) NTC Pub Grp.

Using Type Well. A. Haley. 1992. pap. write for info. (*0-442-23740-5*) Van Nos Reinhold.

Using UNIX. Phillip Laplante & Robert Martin. Ed. by Robert J. Gordon. LC 93-9501. 225p. (C). 1993. pap. text ed. 24.50 (*0-314-01262-1*) West Pub.

Using UNIX. Christopher Negus & Larry Schulmer. (Illus.). 384p. (Orig.). 1995. 19.99 (*0-7897-0290-8*) Que.

Using Unix by Example. P. C. Poole & Nicola Poole. 416p. (C). 1986. pap. text ed. 26.95 (*0-201-18535-0*) Addison-Wesley.

Using USGS Topographic Maps, Vol. 20. W. Jack Hranicky. 80p. 1990. pap. 17.00 (*1-884626-18-1*) Archeolog Soc.

Using Ventura Publisher. A. Colin Day. (Illus.). 160p. 1989. 49.95 (*0-19-853816-2*) OUP.

Using VersaCAD. Fuller. (CAD/CAM Ser.). 1987. teacher ed., pap. 15.00 (*0-8273-2973-3*) Delmar.

Using VersaCAD. James E. Fuller. 275p. (C). 1987. pap. 39.95 (*0-8273-2972-5*) Delmar.

Using VersaCAD. 2nd ed. James E. Fuller. 275p. 1988. disk 30.00 (*0-8273-2974-1*) Delmar.

Using VersaCAD. 2nd ed. James E. Fuller. 275p. 1990. pap. 41.95 (*0-8273-4165-2*) Delmar.

Using VersaCAD. 2nd ed. James E. Fuller. 275p. 1990. teacher ed., pap. 16.00 (*0-8273-4166-0*) Delmar.

Using VHF Radio. Brian Faulkner. (Illus.). 96p. 1992. pap. 16.50 (*0-7136-3610-6*) Sheridan.

Using Video: Interactive & Linear Designs. Joseph W. Arwady & Diane M. Gayeski. LC 88-31105. (Techniques in Training & Performance Development Ser.). (Illus.). 190p. 1989. 39.95 (*0-87778-199-0*) Educ Tech Pubns.

Using Video: Psychological & Social Applications. Ed. by Peter W. Dowrick & Simon J. Biggs. LC 82-20058. (Illus.). 251p. reprint ed. pap. 71.60 (*0-7837-6372-7*, 2046084) Bks Demand.

Using Video in Training & Education. Ashly Pinnington. 1991. pap. text ed. 24.95 (*0-07-707384-3*) McGraw.

Using Visual Aids. rev. ed. Claire Raines & Linda Williamson. Ed. by Tony Hicks. LC 94-80034. (Fifty-Minute Ser.). (Illus.). 84p. (Orig.). 1995. pap. 10.95 (*1-56052-326-3*) Crisp Pubns.

Using Visual BASIC Script, Special Edition. Clayton Walnum. 624p. 1996. pap. text ed. 49.99 incl. cd-rom (*0-7897-0809-4*) Que.

Using Visual Basic with Client Access APIs. Ron Jones. 600p. (Orig.). 1995. pap. 89.00 (*1-882419-28-6*, Duke Pr) Duke Commns Intl.

Using Visual Basic Writing Windows Applications. William Murray. 1992. pap. 34.95 (*0-201-58145-0*) Addison-Wesley.

Using Visual Basic 3: Special Edition. Que Staff. 1995. 39.99 (*0-7897-0326-2*) Que.

***Using Visual Basic 5.** Andrew Brust. 1997. 60.00 (*0-7897-1412-4*) Que.

***Using Visual Basic 5.** Que Development Group Staff. 1997. pap. text ed. 19.99 incl. cd-rom (*0-7897-1453-1*) Que.

***Using Visual Basic 5.** 2nd ed. Mike McKelvy. 1997. 39.99 (*0-7897-1288-1*) Macmillan.

Using Visual Basic 95. Mike McKelvy. (Illus.). 669p. (Orig.). 1995. 24.99 (*0-7897-0266-5*) Que.

***Using Visual Basics.** 2nd ed. Jennings. (DF-Computer Applications Ser.). 1998. wbk. ed., pap. 15.95 (*0-538-67887-9*); text ed. 46.95 (*0-538-67886-0*) S-W Pub.

SpecialVisual C++ 4.2. Kate Gregory. 840p. 1996. 49.99 (*0-7897-0893-0*) Mac Comp Pub.

***Special Editon Using Visual C++ 9597.** Kate Gregory. 992p. 1997. 39.99 (*0-7897-1145-1*) Mac Comp Pub.

***Using Visual Studio.** G. A. Sullivan. 1997. 49.99 (*0-7897-1260-1*) Que.

Using Volumetric Glassware to Measure, Dilute, & Titrate an Acid Solution. Richard S. Mitchell. Ed. by H. Anthony Neidig. (Modular Laboratory Program in Chemistry Ser.). 11p. (C). 1992. pap. text ed. 1.35 (*0-87540-417-0*, ANAL 417-0) Chem Educ Res.

Using VP-Expert. Ernest S. Colantonio. 116p. (C). 1989. Software. disk write for info. (*0-318-70086-7*) HM College Div.

Using VP-Expert in Business. Thom Luce. 1992. pap. text ed. write for info. (*0-07-038984-5*) McGraw.

Using VRML. Que Development Group Staff. 1996. 24.99 (*0-7897-0730-6*) Que.

Using Water Efficiently: Technological Options. Guy J. Le Moigne et al. LC 93-15614. (Technical Paper Ser.: Vol. 205). 61p. 1993. 6.95 (*0-8213-2455-1*, 12455) World Bank.

Using Water Resources. 146p. 1977. per. 8.25 (*0-86619-058-9*, 11038-BK) Vols Tech Asst.

***Using Waves & VHDL for Effective Design & Testing.** James P. Hanna. LC 96-44342. 328p. (C). 1996. lib. bdg. 145.00 (*0-7923-9799-1*) Kluwer Ac.

***Using Weather Satellite Images.** David Huggins. 171p. 9200. pap. 120.00 (*0-7487-1471-5*) Dufour.

***Using Web Board 2.0.** Susan Peck & Beverly Scherf. (Illus.). (Orig.). 1997. pap. write for info. (*1-56592-318-9*) OReilly & Assocs.

***Using Web Graphics.** T. Michael Clark. 1997. 24.99 (*0-7897-1401-9*); pap. text ed. 19.99 (*0-7897-1397-7*) Que.

***Using Web Mapper.** Matthew E. Brown. 1997. pap. 19.99 (*0-7897-1335-7*) Macmillan.

Using What We Know about At-Risk Youth: Lessons from the Field. Ed. by Robert C. Morris. 272p. 1994. pap. 29.95 (*1-56676-147-6*) Technomic.

Using What We Know about Teaching. Ed. by Philip L. Hosford. LC 83-73411. (Nineteen Eighty-Four Yearbook). 216p. 1984. pap. text ed. 14.95 (*0-87120-122-4*, 610-84322) Assn Supervision.

Using Wild & Wayside Plants. Nelson Coon. (Illus.). 288p. 1980. reprint ed. pap. 6.95 (*0-486-23936-5*) Dover.

***Using Windows-Based Applications.** Ronald A. Goodman. 256p. (C). 1996. pap. text ed. 18.36 (*0-395-71664-0*) HM.

Using Windows for Library Administration. Kenneth E. Marks & Steven P. Nielson. LC 96-24956. 140p. 34.95 (*1-57387-029-3*) Info Today Inc.

Using Windows NT: The Essentials for Professionals. Marshall Brain & Kelly Campbell. LC 93-4999. 208p. (C). 1993. pap. text ed. 28.20 (*0-13-091977-2*) P-H.

***Using Windows NT Server 4: Platinum Edition.** Jerry Honeycutt. 1997. 65.00 incl. cd-rom (*0-7897-1436-1*) Que.

***Using Windows NT Server 4: Special Edition.** 2nd ed. Roger Jennings. 1100p. 1997. 49.99 (*0-7897-1388-8*) Que.

***Using Windows NT Workstation 4: Special Edition.** 2nd ed. Paul Sanna. 1997. 49.99 (*0-7897-1384-5*) Que.

Using Windows NT 4.0. Ed Bott. 480p. 1996. 24.99 (*0-7897-0674-1*) Que.

Using Windows 3.0-3.1 Effectively. Paul W. Ross & P. Whitcomb Ross. 272p. (C). 1992. spiral bd. 22.47 (*0-697-14535-2*) Bus & Educ Tech.

Using Windows 3.1. 3rd ed. Que Development Group Staff. 1101p. 1994. 34.99 (*1-56529-807-1*) Que.

Using Windows 3.11. Suzanne Weixel et al. (Illus.). 389p. (Orig.). 1995. 19.99 (*0-7897-0324-6*) Que.

Using Windows 95. Ed Bott. (Illus.). 486p. 1995. 19.99 (*0-7897-0092-1*) Que.

***Using Windows 95.** Ron Person. 1997. pap. text ed. 19.99 (*0-7897-1462-0*) Que.

***Using Windows 95.** 2nd ed. Ed Bott. 504p. 1997. 24.99 (*0-7897-1162-1*) Mac Comp Pub.

***Using Windows 95: Platinum Edition.** Ron Person. 1464p. 1996. 65.00 (*0-7897-1052-8*) Que.

***Using Windows 95: Platinum Edition.** 2nd ed. Ron Person. 1550p. 1997. 60.00 (*0-7897-1383-7*) Que.

Using Windows 95: Special Edition. Ron Person et al. (Illus.). 1344p. (Orig.). (SPA.). 1995. pap. 39.99 (*1-56529-921-3*) Que.

***Using Windows 95: Special Edition.** 2nd ed. Ron Person. 1200p. (Orig.). 1997. 39.99 (*0-7897-1381-0*) Que.

Using Windows 95 Multimedia. Date not set. 19.99 (*0-7897-0399-8*) Que.

Using Windows 95, Platinum Edition. Ron Person. 1416p. 1996. pap. text ed. 60.00 incl. cd-rom (*0-7897-0797-7*) Que.

Using Wireless Communications in Business. Andrew M. Seybold. LC 94-7271. 216p. 1994. pap. 34.95 (*0-442-01877-0*) Van Nos Reinhold.

Using Word for Macintosh. Que Development Group Staff. 1054p. 1994. 29.99 (*1-56529-647-8*) Que.

Using Word for Windows. Neil J. Salkind. 1996. pap. 21.00 (*0-02-405313-9*, Macmillan Coll) P-H.

Using Word for Windows. Taylor R. Taylor. (LogicNotes Ser.). (Illus.). (Orig.). 1991. pap. text ed. write for info. (*0-929978-49-8*) M-USA Busn Systs.

Using Word for Windows 95. E. Maloney. (Illus.). 466p. (Orig.). 1995. 19.99 (*0-7897-0085-9*) Que.

Using Word for Windows 95: Special Edition. Ron Person. (Illus.). 1226p. (Orig.). 1995. 34.99 (*0-7897-0084-0*) Que.

Using Word 97. Joshua C. Nossiter & Eric Maloney. 523p. 1996. 24.99 (*0-7897-0956-2*) Mac Comp Pub.

***Using Word 97.** Ron Person & Que Development Group Staff. 1295p. 1996. 34.99 (*0-7897-0962-7*) Mac Comp Pub.

Using Word Pro for Windows 95: User Friendly Reference. Nancy Stevenson. (Illus.). 400p. (Orig.). 1995. 19.99 (*0-7897-0175-8*) Que.

Using Word Version 6 for Windows. 2nd ed. Ron Person et al. 1212p. 1993. 34.99 (*1-56529-469-6*) Que.

Using Word 6 for Windows. Nancy Stevenson. (Illus.). 368p. (Orig.). 1995. 19.99 (*0-7897-0289-4*) Que.

Using Wordless Picture Books: Authors & Activities. Katharyn Tuten-Puckett & Virginia H. Richey. xxi, 233p. (Orig.). 1993. pap. text ed. 23.00 (*0-87287-877-5*) Teacher Ideas Pr.

Using WordPerfect for Windows. Verlene Leeburg & Gwynne Larsen. 532p. 1993. pap. text ed. write for info. (*0-07-037586-0*) McGraw.

Using WordPerfect for Windows for Desktop Publishing, Version 6.0. Dennis Gehris. LC 94-21894. 1995. text ed. 30.95 (*0-538-62870-7*) S-W Pub.

Using WordPerfect in Compositions. Halio & Druliner. (C). 1994. text ed. 4.50 (*0-673-52448-5*) Addson-Wesley Educ.

Using WordPerfect in Your Job Search. David F. Noble. 454p. (Orig.). 1995. pap. 19.95 (*1-56370-177-4*, J1774) JIST Works.

Using WordPerfect 4.2. Sherman. (C). 1989. teacher ed., pap. 1.56 (*0-395-52392-3*) HM.

Using WordPerfect 4.2. Software Solutions Staff. (C). 1988. pap. 15.16 (*0-395-47798-0*) HM.

Using WordPerfect 5.0. Ernest S. Colantonio. (Software Guide Ser.). 148p. (C). 1989. pap. text ed. 19.16 (*0-669-19948-6*); Software. disk write for info. (*0-318-70083-2*) HM College Div.

Using WordPerfect 5.0. Nelda Shelton & Sharon Burton. (C). 1989. pap. 15.16 (*0-395-50947-5*) HM.

Using WordPerfect 5.0. R. Taylor. Ed. by Jose Hurtado. (Logic Ware Ser.). (Illus.). 1989. 24.95 (*0-929978-05-6*) M-USA Busn Systs.

Using Wordperfect 5.0. D. Michael Werner et al. (C). 1990. pap. text ed. 27.00 (*0-673-38981-2*) Addson-Wesley Educ.

Using Wordperfect 5.0/5.1: Applications. Wynema Anderson. (DF - Computer Applications Ser.). 1993. pap. 27.95 (*0-538-61755-1*) S-W Pub.

Using WordPerfect 5.1. 1994. teacher ed. 39.99 (*1-56529-483-1*) Que.

Using WordPerfect 5.1. Sharon Burton & Nelda Shelton. (C). 1991. pap. 15.16 (*0-395-56952-4*) HM Soft Schl Col Div.

Using WordPerfect 5.1. Don Cassel. 160p. pap. text ed. write for info. (*0-13-951666-2*) P-H.

Using Wordperfect 5.1. R. R. Taylor. (LogicNotes Ser.). (Illus.). (Orig.). 1990. pap. text ed. write for info. (*0-929978-42-0*) M-USA Busn Systs.

Using WordPerfect 6 for Windows, Special Edition. Que Development Group Staff. (Using Ser.). (Illus.). 1102p. (Orig.). 1993. 29.95 (*1-56529-138-7*) Que.

U V

An Asterisk (*) at the beginning of an entry indicates that the title is appearing in BIP for the first time.

Using WordPerfect 6.0 for DOS. Verlene Leeburg & Peggy Purvis. 1994. pap. text ed. write for info. (*0-07-037625-5*) McGraw.

***Using WordPerfect 6.0 for DOS.** Alan Rowland. 200p. (C). 1995. pap. text ed. 17.56 (*0-395-72128-8*) HM.

Using WordPerfect 6.0 for Windows. Gwynne Larsen & Kenneth Shaw. 1994. pap. text ed. write for info. (*0-07-036602-0*) McGraw.

Using WordPerfect 6.1 for Windows. Kinney et al. (Illus.). 1179p. (Orig.). 1994. 34.99 (*0-7897-0083-2*) Que.

Using WordPerfect 6.1 for Windows. Josh C. Nossiter. (Illus.). 406p. (Orig.). 1995. 19.99 (*0-7897-0293-2*) Que.

***Using WordPerfect 6.1 for Windows.** Alan Rowland. 224p. (C). 1995. pap. text ed. 17.16 (*0-395-72132-6*) HM.

Using Wordperfect 6.1 for Windows & for Desktop Publishing. Gehris. (DF - Computer Applications Ser.). 1997. pap. 31.95 (*0-538-66561-0*) S-W Pub.

Using Wordstar 5.5. R. Taylor & June Kanai. Ed. by Jose Hurtado. (Logic Ware Ser.). (Illus.). 1990. 24.95 (*0-929978-23-4*) M-USA Busn Systs.

Using WORKBENCH Development Tools: Micro Focus Plus Third-Party COBOL Add-Ons & Accessories. Jonathan S. Sayles & Peter Molchan. LC 93-438. 464p. 1993. pap. text ed. 44.95 (*0-471-59370-2*) Wiley.

Using Workperfect Advanced Vol. 4: IBM 5.1. Susan Nelle. 1991. pap. 24.75 (*0-07-909587-9*) McGraw.

Using Workperfect IBM 5.1 with Disk: Beginner's Edition. Susan Nelle. 1991. pap. 27.75 incl. disk (*0-07-909583-6*) McGraw.

***Using Works 3.0.** rev. ed. Smith & Christoph. 453p. (C). 1996. pap. text ed. 35.20 (*0-13-606807-3*, Prentice Hall) P-H.

Using World Wide Web. 2nd ed. Eager. 502p. 1995. 24.99 (*0-7897-0645-8*) Que.

Using WP 6 for Windows NE. 1994. 29.99 (*1-56529-835-7*) Que.

Using Writing Portfolios to Enhance Instruction & Assessment. Marjorie Frank. Ed. by Jan Keeling. LC 93-80014. (Illus.). 160p. (Orig.). 1994. pap. text ed. 14.95 (*0-86530-281-2*) Incentive Pubns.

Using Writing to Teach Mathematics. Ed. by Andrew Sterrett. LC 90-61126. (MAA Notes Ser.). 160p. (Orig.). 1990. pap. 29.95 (*0-88385-066-4*, NTE-16) Math Assn.

Using X: Troubleshooting X Windows, Mofit, Open Systems. Kevin Reichard & Eric F. Johnson. 1992. pap. 29.95 (*1-55828-212-2*) MIS Press.

Using Xerox Ventura Publisher 2.0. R. Taylor & June Kanai. Ed. by Jose Hurtado. (Logic Ware Ser.). (Illus.). 1989. 24.95 (*0-929978-16-1*) M-USA Busn Systs.

***Using XML.** Patricia Ju. 1997. 29.99 (*0-7897-1408-6*) Que.

Using Your Autofocus 35mm Camera. 4th rev. ed. Eastman Kodak Company Staff. LC 96-71257. (Kodak Workshop Ser.). (Illus.). 96p. (C). 1997. pap. 17.95 (*0-87985-652-1*, KW-11, Kodak) Saunders Photo.

Using Your Brain - for a Change. Richard Bandler. Ed. by Connirae Andreas & Steve Andreas. (Illus.). 159p. (Orig.). 1985. 14.00 (*0-911226-26-5*); pap. 10.50 (*0-911226-27-3*) Real People.

Using Your Camera: A Basic Guide to 35mm Photography. George Schaub. (Illus.). 144p. 1990. pap. 18.95 (*0-8174-6351-8*, Amphoto) Watsn-Guptill.

Using Your Chemistry. P. Scott. (C). 1990. text ed. 70.00 (*0-7487-0437-X*, Pub. by Stanley Thornes UK) Trans-Atl Phila.

Using Your Chemistry - Answer Book. Ed. by P. Scott. (C). 1990. text ed. 40.00 (*0-7487-0438-8*, Pub. by Stanley Thornes UK) Trans-Atl Phila.

Using Your Chemistry Comprehension Questions for Advanced Level. Peter Scott. 96p. (C). 1994. student ed. 21.00 (*0-7478-0437-0*, Pub. by Stanley Thornes UK); teacher ed. 21.00 (*0-7478-0438-9*, Pub. by Stanley Thornes UK) Trans-Atl Phila.

Using Your Computer for Fun & Profit. Debbie St. George. LC 91-92468. (Illus.). 104p. (C). 1992. pap. 19.95 (*0-9627484-7-1*) Amer Word.

Using Your Computer for Fun & Profit. 2nd ed. Debbie St. George. (Illus.). 104p. pap. 29.95 incl. 3.5 hd (*0-9627484-9-8*) Amer Word.

Using Your Guitar. Brook Hendick. 1980. pap. 4.95 (*0-8256-2378-2*, AM35783) Music Sales.

Using Your Head: An Owner's Manual. Jeanne E. Ormrod. LC 89-30780. (Illus.). 224p. 1989. 24.95 (*0-87778-216-4*) Educ Tech Pubns.

Using Your HP-41 Advantage: Statics for Students. Ted Wadman & Chris Coffin. (Using Your HP-41 Advantage Ser.). (Illus.). (Orig.). 1985. pap. 9.95 (*0-931011-04-3*) Grapevine Pubns.

Using Your HP 95LX. Lori Monday & Tracy Robinson. (Hewlett-Packard Ser.). 416p. 1991. pap. 28.95 (*0-201-56338-X*) Addison-Wesley.

Using Your Mac. Que Development Group Staff. (Illus.). 450p. (Orig.). 1995. 19.99 (*0-7897-0094-8*) Que.

Using Your Medicines Wisely: A Passport to Good Health Care. 1990. lib. bdg. 75.00 (*0-8490-3999-1*) Gordon Pr.

Using Your Money Wisely: Biblical Principles under Scrutiny. Larry Burkett. 1990. pap. 10.99 (*0-8024-3429-0*) Moody.

Using Your Overhead Projector & Other Visual Aids. C. Waller. (C). 1983. 170.00 (*0-86221-016-X*, Pub. by S Thornes Pubs UK) St Mut.

Using Your P. C. 2nd ed. Que Development Group Staff. (Illus.). 444p. (Orig.). 1995. 24.99 (*0-7897-0637-7*) Que.

Using Your Portable Studio: Techniques for Musicians. Peter Mclan. (Illus.). 128p. (Orig.). pap. 24.95 (*0-8256-1437-6*, AM92232) Omnibus NY.

***Using Your 401(k) Plan Wisely.** McCarthy. 88p. 1994. pap. 5.00 (*0-614-26855-9*, BLS-3329) Commerce.

Using Youth Apprenticeship to Improve the Transition to Work: An Evaluation of System Development in Eight States. 132p. 1994. pap. write for info. (*1-884037-03-8*) Coun Chief St Schl Offs.

Using Z: Specification, Refinement, & Proof. J. C. Woodcock & Jim Davies. 386p. 1996. pap. text ed. 34.00 (*0-13-948472-8*) P-H.

Using 1-2-3 for Windows. Que Development Group Staff. 1190p. 1994. pap. 34.99 (*1-56529-743-1*) Que.

Using 1-2-3 for Windows 95. E. Maloney. (Illus.). 416p. (Orig.). 1995. 21.99 (*0-7897-0142-1*) Que.

USKids History: Book of the American Revolution. Howard Egger-Bovet. (J). (gr. 4-7). 1994. 12.95 (*0-316-22204-6*) Little.

Uskoks of Senj: Piracy, Banditry, & Holy War in the Sixteenth- Century Adriatic. Catherine W. Bracewell. LC 91-55548. (Illus.). 352p. 1992. 49.95 (*0-8014-2674-X*) Cornell U Pr.

USL Journalism Manual of Style & Format. Russell A. Mann. LC 86-90665. 115p. (Orig.). 1986. pap. 9.95 (*0-940205-00-9*) Journalism Style.

USM Company Performance. Ed. by ICC Information Group Staff. 1987. 375.00 (*0-86261-865-7*, Pub. by ICC Info Group Ltd UK) St Mut.

USMARC Code List for Geographic Areas. Ed. by Network Development & MARC Standards Office Staff. LC 94-9550. 1994. write for info. (*0-8444-0812-3*) Lib Congress.

***USMARC Code List for Relators, Sources, Description Conventions.** Library of Congress Staff. LC 97-14263. 1997. pap. write for info. (*0-8444-0944-8*) Lib Congress.

USMARC Code List for Relators, Sources, Description Conventions. Network Development Staff & MARC Standards Office Staff. LC 93-30404. 1993. write for info. (*0-8444-0806-9*) Lib Congress.

USMARC Format for Authority Data: Including Guidelines for Content Designation. Network Development & MARC Standards Office. LC 93-26502. 1993. write for info. (*0-8444-0802-6*) Lib Congress.

USMARC Format for Community Information: Including Guidelines for Content Designation. Network Development & MARC Standards Office. LC 92-45199. 1993. write for info. (*0-8444-0779-8*) Lib Congress.

USMARC Format for Holdings & Locations: Development, Implementation & Use. Intro. by Barry B. Baker. LC 88-16383. (Technical Services Quarterly Supplement Ser.: No. 2). 231p. 1988. text ed. 49.95 (*0-86656-695-3*) Haworth Pr.

USMARC Specifications for Record Structure, Character Sets & Exchange Media. LC 94-41522. 1994. write for info. (*0-8444-0746-1*) Lib Congress.

USMC Field Manual *see* **U. S. M. C. Sniping: FMFM 1-3B**

USMC in Color Photographs. Yves Debay. (Europa Militaria Ser.: No. 5). (Illus.). 66p. 1990. pap. 15.95 (*1-872004-50-4*) Motorbooks Intl.

USMC Phantoms in Combat. Lou Drendel. (Vietnam Studies Group). (Illus.). 80p. 1990. pap. 9.95 (*0-89747-235-7*, 6353) Squad Sig Pubns.

USMC Rifle & Pistol Marksmanship, 1935: The Old Corps Method of Precision Shooting. U. S. Marine Corps Staff. (Illus.). 104p. 1991. reprint ed. pap. 11.95 (*0-935856-07-2*) Lancer.

USMLE Step 1. Schwenker. 160p. 1995. pap. text ed. 19.95 (*0-316-77600-9*) Lppncott-Raven.

USMLE Step 1: The Study Guide. Joel S. Goldberg. LC 95-41811. (United States Medical Licensing Examination Ser.). 473p. 1996. pap. 32.95 (*0-8039-7284-9*) Sage.

***USMLE Success.** 3rd rev. ed. FMSG, Inc. Staff & Stanley Zaslau. (Illus.). 280p. (C). 1996. wbk. ed., pap. text ed. 38.00 (*1-886468-09-5*) FMSG.

USN Phantoms in Combat. Lou Drendel. (Vietnam Studies Group). (Illus.). 80p. 1988. pap. 9.95 (*0-89747-213-6*, 6352) Squad Sig Pubns.

USNP National Unionfest 1989. 3rd ed. Onlinecomputer Library Center, Inc. Staff. 2000p. 1989. 275.00 incl. fiche (*1-55653-074-9*) OCLC Online Comp.

Uso de la Tierra Agricola en Mexico: The Use of Agricultural Land in Mexico. David Barkin. (Research Reports: No. 17). 37p. (Orig.). (SPA.). (C). 1981. pap. 5.00 (*0-935391-16-9*, RR-17) UCSD Ctr US-Mex.

Uso del Conocimiento Local en el Desarrollo Agropecuario. Michael Warren. Tr. by Consuelo Quiroz. (Studies in Technology & Social Change: No. 24). 48p. (SPA.). (C). 1995. pap. 8.00 (*0-945271-39-5*) ISU-CIKARD.

Uso delle Preposizioni in Italiano: The Use of Prepositions in Italian. Luisa Polesini Karumanchiri & Jana Vizmuller-Zocco. 120p. (Orig.). (C). 1984. pap. text ed. 14.95 (*0-8020-6551-1*) U of Toronto Pr.

***Uso Delle Preposizioni in Italiano/The Use of Prepositions in Italian.** 2nd ed. Luisa Polesini et al. (Toronto Italian Studies). 152p. 1996. pap. 16.95 (*0-8020-7931-8*) U of Toronto Pr.

Uso Magico y Ritual de las Hierbas-The Magic & Ritual Use of Herbs. Richard A. Miller. 1995. pap. 9.95 (*0-89281-467-5*) Inner Tradit.

Usonia: Frank Lloyd Wright's Design for America. Alvin Rosenbaum. LC 93-7612. (Illus.). 216p. 1995. text ed. 29.95 (*0-471-14430-4*) Wiley.

USOP Handbook: A Guide to Designing Universal Share Ownership Plans for the United States & Great Britain. Stuart M. Speiser. (Illus.). 168p. (Orig.). 1986. pap. 3.95 (*0-936876-46-8*) LRIS.

Usos y Costumbres de las Tierras Biblicas. Fred H. Wight. Orig. Title: Manners & Customs of Bible Lands. 336p. (SPA.). 1981. pap. 9.99 (*0-8254-1873-9*, Edit Portavoz) Kregel.

USP DI Vol. I: Drug Information for the Health Care Professional, 1995 Edition. 1995. 109.00 (*0-913595-83-7*) US Pharmacopeia.

USP DI Vol. II: Advice for the Patient. United States Pharmacopeial Convention. 1995. 54.00 (*0-913595-84-5*) US Pharmacopeia.

USP DI Vol. III: Approved Drug Products & Legal Requirements. 1995. 98.00 (*0-913595-85-3*) US Pharmacopeia.

USP Dictionary of USAN & International Drug Names, 1995 Edition. 919p. 1994. pap. 109.00 (*0-913595-82-9*) US Pharmacopeia.

USP Guide to Heart Medicines: U. S. Pharmacopeia. U. S. Pharmacopeia Staff. (Illus.). 624p. (Orig.). 1996. mass mkt. 6.99 (*0-380-78094-1*) Avon.

USP Guide to Medicines. U. S. Pharmacopeia Staff. 1996. mass mkt. 6.99 (*0-380-78092-5*) Avon.

USP Guide to Vitamins & Minerals. Contrib. by U. S. Pharmacopeia Staff. 400p. (Orig.). 1996. pap. 6.99 (*0-380-78093-3*) Avon.

USP People, Policies, & Procedures. 128p. 1994. pap. 25.00 (*0-614-06364-7*, 931934) US Pharmacopeia.

USP Pill Book of Prescription Drugs, Bk. 1. United States Pharmacopeial Convention, Inc. Staff. (Orig.). 1994. pap. write for info. (*0-446-60032-6*) Warner Bks.

USP Reference Standards. 1994. write for info. (*0-614-06361-2*) US Pharmacopeia.

USP XXII-NF XVII: The 1990 U. S. Pharmacopeia & the National Formulary. 2067p. 1989. 525.00 (*0-913595-37-3*); lthr. write for info. (*0-913595-38-1*) US Pharmacopeia.

***USPC Guide to Bandaging Your Horse.** Susan E. Harris. LC 97-19351. 1997. pap. 8.95 (*0-87605-638-9*) Macmillan.

***USPC Guide to Confirmation & Movement.** Susan E. Harris. LC 97-3310. 1997. pap. 8.95 (*0-87605-639-7*) Macmillan.

***USPC Guide to Longeing & Ground Training.** Susan E. Harris. LC 97-9403. (United States Pony Club Guides Ser.). (Illus.). 64p. 1997. pap. 8.95 (*0-87605-640-0*) Howell Bk.

Uspenije Presvjatija Bogorodits. M. Skaballanovitch. 114p. reprint ed. pap. 4.00 (*0-317-29164-5*) Holy Trinity.

USPF Yearbook. 80p. write for info. (*0-318-60029-3*) US Dressage Fed.

USS Arizona. R. Conrad Stein. LC 91-44646. (Cornerstones of Freedom Ser.). (Illus.). 32p. (J). (gr. 3-6). 1992. lib. bdg. 18.00 (*0-516-06656-0*) Childrens.

***USS Arizona's Last Band: The History of U. S. Navy Band Number 22.** (Illus.). 384p. 1996. 25.00 (*0-9654199-0-8*) Silent Song.

USS Constitution - "Old Ironsides" An Artist's Sketchbook. John C. Roach & Tyrone G. Martin. 56p. 1994. pap. 9.50 (*1-884824-04-8*) Tryon Pubng.

USS Coral Sea CV-CVA-CVB-43. Turner Publishing Company Staff. LC 91-67152. (Illus.). 112p. 1992. 48.00 (*1-56311-049-0*) Turner Pub KY.

USS Enterprise: CVA(N)-65 to CV(N)-65. Bert Kinzey. (Detail & Scale Ser.: Vol. 39). (Illus.). 62p. 1991. pap. 10.95 (*0-8306-9953-8*, 25052) McGraw-Hill Prof.

USS Enterprise CV-6. Steve Ewing. (Illus.). 9.95 (*0-614-13195-2*, 21-37107) EAA Aviation.

USS Forrestal. Bert Kinzey. (Detail & Scale Ser.: Vol. 36). (Illus.). 72p. 1990. pap. 10.95 (*0-8306-7049-1*, 25049) TAB Bks.

USS Fulton As-11 Fiftieth Anniversary. Turner Publishing Company Staff. LC 91-75255. 88p. 1991. 34.95 (*1-56311-062-8*) Turner Pub KY.

USS Intrepid (CV 11) Warship's Data, No. 4. Robert F. Sumrall. LC 89-60851. (Illus.). 54p. (Orig.). 1990. pap. 9.95 (*0-929521-20-X*) Pictorial Hist.

USS Kidd & Fletcher Class Destroyers. Turner Publishing Company Staff. LC 91-75215. 136p. 1991. 45.00 (*1-56311-039-3*) Turner Pub KY.

USS North Carolina: Symbol of a Vanished Age. Joe A. Mobley. (Illus.). 16p. 1996. reprint ed. pap. 2.00 (*0-86526-219-5*) NC Archives.

USS Pensacola (CA-24) Turner Publishing Company Staff. LC 91-67157. (Illus.). 200p. 1992. 48.00 (*1-56311-050-4*) Turner Pub KY.

USS San Diego: The Last Armored Cruiser. Gary Gentile. (Illus.). 120p. 1989. pap. 20.00 (*0-9621453-1-9*) GGP.

USS Saratoga: Remembering One of America's Great Aircraft Carriers. Jane Tanner. 144p. 1994. 25.00 (*1-56352-189-X*) Longstreet Pr Inc.

USS Saratoga (CV-3) An Illustrated History of the Legendary Aircraft Carrier 1927-1946. John Fry. (Illus.). 176p. 1996. 39.95 (*0-7643-0089-X*) Schiffer.

USS Yorktown (CV10) Robert F. Sumrall. LC 90-63444. (Warship's Data Ser.: No. 5). (Illus.). 60p. 1993. pap. 9.95 (*0-929521-45-5*) Pictorial Hist.

USSF Sports Medicine Book of Soccer. Ed. by William E. Garrett, Jr. et al. LC 96-1088. 1996. write for info. (*0-683-18249-8*) Williams & Wilkins.

UST Inc. A Report on the Company's Environmental Policies & Practices. (Illus.). 23p. (C). 1994. reprint ed. pap. text ed. 250.00 (*0-7881-0990-1*, Coun on Econ) DIANE Pub.

***Ust-Ordynskiy Autonomous Okrug: Economy, Industry, Government, Business.** 2nd rev. ed. Russian Information & Business Center, Inc. Staff. (Russian Regional Business Directories Ser.). (Illus.). 200p. 1997. pap. 99.00 (*0-614-30771-6*) Russ Info & Busn Ctr.

USTA College Tennis Guide. 1990. pap. 5.50 (*0-938822-81-0*) USTA.

USTA Guide to Forming a Community Association. rev. ed. (Illus.). 54p. 1988. reprint ed. 2.00 (*0-938822-89-6*) USTA.

USTA Guide to Fund Raising for Community Associations. rev. ed. (Illus.). 56p. 1988. reprint ed. 2.00 (*0-938822-90-X*) USTA.

USTA Official Yearbook. 1990. pap. 11.00 (*0-938822-82-9*) USTA.

USTA Recreational Tennis Curriculum. rev. ed. (Illus.). 108p. 1990. reprint ed. 3.50 (*0-938822-93-4*) USTA.

USTA Schools Program Tennis Curriculum. rev. ed. (Illus.). 66p. 1991. reprint ed. 3.50 (*0-938822-92-6*) USTA.

USTA Scorebook for Coaches. 48p. 1984. 4.50 (*0-938822-42-X*) USTA.

Ustages de Barcelona. Ed. by Ramon D'Abadal y Vinyals & Ferran V. Taberner. LC 80-1999. reprint ed. 26.00 (*0-404-18552-5*) AMS Pr.

Usted. Carlos Gonzalez. (SPA.). 1983. write for info. (*1-56491-002-4*) Imagine Pubs.

Usted es Sanado. Kenneth Copeland. Tr. by Copeland, Kenneth, Publications Staff. 18p. (Orig.). (SPA.). 1985. pap. 1.00 (*0-88114-306-5*) K Copeland Pubns.

***Usted Es Testigo de Cristo.** Billy Graham. pap. 4.95 (*0-8297-0970-3*) Life Pubs Intl.

Usted Puede Ganar En la Vida. Victor Ricardo. 26p. 1992. pap. 1.15 (*1-885630-11-5*) HLM Producciones.

***Usted Puede Hacer la Diferencia.** Gary R. Collins. 295p. (SPA.). write for info. (*1-56063-506-1*) Editorial Unilit.

Usted Puede Tener lo Que Diga. Kenneth E. Hagin. (SPA.). 1983. pap. 0.75 (*0-89276-154-7*) Hagin Ministries.

***Usted Se Enoja Porque Quiere.** Tim LaHaye. (Orig.). (SPA.). pap. 5.95 (*0-8297-1402-2*) Life Pubs Intl.

Usted y Su Artritis. Barbara Marquez et al. 97p. (Orig.). (SPA.). 1986. 7.50 (*1-879552-20-5*) Stanford CRDP.

Usted y Su Familia. 4p. write for info. (*0-318-68829-8*) Inter-Am Safety.

Usted y Su Hijo. Charles R. Swindoll. 164p. (SPA.). 1992. pap. 4.99 (*1-56063-215-1*, 498468) Editorial Unilit.

Usted y Yo: Primer Paso. Zenia S. Da Silva. (SPA.). 1975. write for info. (*0-02-270900-2*) Macmillan.

Ustilaginales on PolyPolygonaceae - A Taxonomic Revision. F. Oberwinkler & K. Vanky. (Nova Hedwigia Ser.: 107). (Illus.). 96p. 1994. pap. 59.95 (*3-443-51029-9*) Lubrecht & Cramer.

Ustinov Still at Large. Peter Ustinov. LC 94-40932. 218p. 1995. pap. 15.95 (*0-87975-967-4*) Prometheus Bks.

***Usage & Abusage.** Eric Partridge. Date not set. pap. write for info. (*0-393-31709-9*) Norton.

Usual Lunacy. D. G. Compton. LC 78-14953. (Illus.). 191p. 1978. pap. 21.00 (*0-89370-225-0*); lib. bdg. 31.00 (*0-89370-125-4*) Borgo Pr.

Usul al-Fiqh al-Islami, 2 vols., Set. Wahbah al-Zuhayli. 1986. 33.95 (*1-57547-161-2*) Dar Al-Fikr.

Usul al-Fiqh al-Islami, Vol. 1. Wahbah al-Zuhayli. 1986. write for info. (*1-57547-162-0*) Dar Al-Fikr.

Usul al-Fiqh al-Islami, Vol. 2. Wahbah al-Zuhayli. 1986. write for info. (*1-57547-163-9*) Dar Al-Fikr.

Usul al Fiqh al Islami: Manhaj Bahth Wa Mar'ifah (Source Methodology in Islamic Jurisprudence) 2nd rev. ed. Taha Jabir al 'Alwani. (Abhath Ilmiyah Research Monographs: No. 1). 64p. 1994. pap. text ed. 5.00 (*0-912463-57-0*) IIIT VA.

Usul al-Tarbiyah al-Islamiyah wa-Asalibuha fi al-Bayt wa-al-Madrasah wa-al-Mujtama. Abd-al-Rahman Al-Nihlawi. 1983. pap. 4.95 (*1-57547-008-X*) Dar Al-Fikr.

Usurer's Daughter: Male Friendship & Fictions of Women in Sixteenth Century England. Lorna Hutson. LC 93-28752. 300p. (C). (gr. 13). 1994. text ed. 74.95 (*0-415-05049-9*, Routledge NY) Routledge.

***Usurer's Daughter: Male Friendship & Fictions of Women in Sixteenth-Century England.** Lorna Hutson. LC 96-44587. 308p. (C). 1997. pap. write for info. (*0-415-16261-0*) Routledge.

Usurpers. Francisco Ayala. Tr. & Intro. by Carolyn Richmond. 1996. pap. 10.95 (*0-14-018977-7*) Viking Penguin.

Usurpers. Francisco Ayala. 1999. pap. write for info. (*0-14-025419-6*) Viking Penguin.

Usurpers of Freedom in Conspiracy. Gyeorgos C. Hatonn. (Phoenix Journals). 203p. 1994. pap. 6.00 (*1-56935-051-5*) Phoenix Source.

Usury: Destroyer of Nations. 1992. lib. bdg. 250.00 (*0-8490-5251-3*) Gordon Pr.

Usury & Usury Laws. F. W. Ryan. 1977. lib. bdg. 200.00 (*0-8490-2791-8*) Gordon Pr.

Usury As the Root Cause of the Injustices of Our Time: The Economic Background of Unemployment, Crime, Bankruptcy, Family Breakdown, Debt. 1992. lib. bdg. 250.95 (*0-8490-8903-4*) Gordon Pr.

Usury Debate after Adam Smith: Two Nineteenth Century Essays. LC 72-38472. (Evolution of Capitalism Ser.). 106p. 1972. reprint ed. 18.95 (*0-405-04139-X*) Ayer.

Usury Debate in the Seventeenth Century: Three Arguments. LC 76-38473. (Evolution of Capitalism Ser.). 236p. 1972. reprint ed. 23.95 (*0-405-04140-3*) Ayer.

USX Corp. A Report on the Company's Environmental Policies & Practices. (Illus.). 30p. (C). 1994. reprint ed. pap. text ed. 250.00 (*0-7881-0987-1*, Coun on Econ) DIANE Pub.

USY Parshat HaShavuan Series. 10.00 (*0-686-96100-5*) USCJE.

Ut Austin: Traditions & Nostalgia. rev. ed. Margaret C. Berry. LC 75-8061. (Illus.). 142p. 1992. reprint ed. pap. 9.95 (*0-89015-410-4*) Sunbelt Media.

U.T. El Paso 2001: A Diamond Jubilee Commission Report. Ed. by R. Milton Leech. 1990. 10.00 (*0-87404-217-8*) Tex Western.

***UT History 101: Highlights of the History of the University of Texas.** Margaret C. Berry. LC 97-14498. (Illus.). 96p. 1997. pap. 9.95 (*1-57168-188-4*, 188-4, Eakin Pr) Sunbelt Media.

***Ut Poesis Pictura: J. M. W. Turner's Illustrations to the British Poets.** Sharon Church et al. Ed. by Max F. Schulz. (Illus.). 96p. (Orig.). 1997. pap. 20.00 (*0-945192-19-3*) USC Fisher Gallery.

***Ut Unum Sint: On Commitment to Ecumenism.** Pope John Paul, II. 110p. pap. 2.95 (*0-8198-8029-9*) Pauline Bks.

Ut Unum Sint Que Todas Sean Uno: Sobre el Empeno Ecumenico. Pope John Paul, II. 114p. (Orig.). (SPA.). 1995. pap. 6.95 (*1-57455-051-9*) US Catholic.

Ut Videam: Contributions to an Understanding of Linguistics for Pieter Verburg on the Occasion of His 70th Birthday. Ed. by Werner Abraham. 300p. 1975. pap. 44.00 (*0-685-53313-1*) Benjamins North Am.

Utah. Dennis B. Fradin. LC 92-36370. (From Sea to Shining Sea Ser.). (Illus.). 64p. (J). (gr. 3-5). 1993. lib. bdg. 24.00 (*0-516-03844-3*) Childrens.

***Utah.** Dennis B. Fradin. (From Sea to Shining Sea Ser.). 1997. pap. 5.95 (*0-516-26201-7*) Childrens.

Utah. Karen Sirvaitis. (Hello U. S. A. Ser.). (Illus.). 72p. (J). (gr. 3-6). 1991. lib. bdg. 18.95 (*0-8225-2707-3*, Lerner Publctns) Lerner Group.

Utah. Karen Sirvaitis. (Hello U. S. A. Ser.). (J). (gr. 3-6). pap. 5.95 (*0-614-15670-X*, First Ave Edns) Lerner Group.

Utah. Kathleen Thompson. (Portrait of America Library). 48p. (J). (gr. 3 up). 1996. lib. bdg. 22.83 (*0-8114-7390-2*) Raintree Steck-V.

Utah. Kathleen Thompson. (Portrait of America Library). 48p. (J). (gr. 3 up). 1996. pap. text ed. 5.95 (*0-8114-7471-2*) Raintree Steck-V.

Utah. Tom Wharton & Gayen Wharton. Ed. by Barry Parr & Peter Zimmerman. (Discover America Ser.). (Illus.). 370p. (Orig.). 1992. pap. 14.95 (*1-878867-09-1*) Fodors Travel.

Utah. rev. ed. Betty McCarthy. LC 89-35083. (America the Beautiful Ser.). (Illus.). 144p. (J). (gr. 4 up). 1991. lib. bdg. 28.30 (*0-516-00490-5*) Childrens.

Utah. 3rd ed. Tom Wharton & Gayen Wharton. LC 95-8301. (Compass American Guides Ser.). (Illus.). 1995. pap. 17.95 (*1-878867-73-3*, Compass Amrcn) Fodors Travel.

***Utah: A Celebration of the Landscape.** Brooke Williams. (Illus.). 112p. 1997. pap. 29.95 (*1-56579-240-8*) Westcliffe Pubs.

Utah: A Family Travel Guide. Tom Wharton. 1987. pap. 8.50 (*0-915272-31-8*) Wasatch Pubs.

Utah: A Guide to the State. rev. ed. Ward J. Roylance. 1982. reprint ed. 25.00 (*0-914740-23-7*, 884P.); reprint ed. pap. 11.95 (*0-914740-25-3*, PT. 2, TOUR SECTION, 400P.) Western Epics.

Utah: A Guide to the State. Federal Writers' Project Staff & Writers Program-WPA Staff. (American Guide Ser.). 1989. reprint ed. lib. bdg. 69.00 (*0-7812-1043-7*, 1043) Rprt Serv.

Utah: A People's History. Dean May. LC 87-17898. (Bonneville Bks.). (Illus.). 1987. pap. 15.95 (*0-87480-284-9*) U of Utah Pr.

Utah: A Portrait. William B. Smart. LC 94-48005. (Illus.). 256p. 1995. 39.95 (*0-87480-451-5*) U of Utah Pr.

Utah: A State Guide. Federal Writers' Project Staff. 1941. reprint ed. 79.00 (*0-403-02193-6*) Somerset Pub.

Utah: Great Things to See & Do for the Entire Family. Margaret Godfrey. (Family Adventure Guide Ser.). (Illus.). 160p. (Orig.). 1997. pap. 9.95 (*1-56440-870-1*) Globe Pequot.

Utah: Hello U. S. A. Karen Sirvaitis. (J). 1996. pap. text ed. 5.95 (*0-8225-9724-1*) Lerner Group.

Utah: Off the Beaten Path: A Guide to Unique Places. Ted Brewer. LC 95-43698. (Off the Beaten Path Ser.). (Illus.). 192p. (Orig.). 1996. pap. 10.95 (*1-56440-853-1*) Globe Pequot.

Utah: Photos of David Muench. Photos by David Meunch. LC 89-81615. (Illus.). 160p. 1990. 39.95 (*1-55868-024-1*) Gr Arts Ctr Pub.

Utah: Sex & Travel Guide. Calvin Grondahl. LC 93-40831. (Illus.). 96p. (Orig.). 1993. pap. 9.95 (*1-56085-041-8*) Signature Bks.

Utah: The Struggle for Statehood. Ken Verdoia & Richard Firmage. LC 95-49921. (Illus.). 216p. (C). 1996. 34.95 (*0-87480-506-6*) U of Utah Pr.

***Utah: The Struggle for Statehood.** Ken Verdoia & Richard Firmage. (Illus.). 216p. (C). 1996. pap. 21.95 (*0-87480-532-5*) U of Utah Pr.

Utah: Unusual Beginning to Unique Present. Wayne K. Hinton. (Illus.). 192p. (YA). (gr. 7 up). 1988. 29.95 (*0-89781-247-6*) Am Historical Pr.

Utah - Collected Works of Federal Writers Project. Federal Writers' Project Staff. 1991. reprint ed. lib. bdg. 98.00 (*0-7812-5791-3*) Rprt Serv.

Utah, a Centennial Celebration. Brooke Williams. 144p. 1995. 45.00 (*1-56579-116-9*) Westcliffe Pubs.

Utah Administrative Code, 1994 Edition, 4 vols., Set. 195.00 (*1-55834-141-2*) MICHIE.

Utah & All That Jazz. Calvin Grondahl. LC 89-70028. (Illus.). 96p. 1989. pap. 6.95 (*0-941214-86-9*) Signature Bks.

Utah & Nevada Camping: The Complete Guide to More Than 25,000 Campsites. Deke Castleman et al. (Complete Guide Ser.). (Illus.). 352p. (Orig.). 1997. pap. 18.95 (*1-57354-012-9*) Foghorn Pr.

Utah & Other State Greats (Biographies) Carole Marsh. (Carole Marsh Utah Bks.). (Illus.). (J). 1994. pap. 19.95 (*0-7933-2130-1*); lib. bdg. 29.95 (*0-7933-2129-8*); disk 29.95 (*0-7933-2131-X*) Gallopade Pub Group.

Utah & Queensland Coal: A Study in the Micro Political Economy of Modern Capitalism & the State. Brian Galligan. 250p. (Orig.). 1989. text ed. 29.95 (*0-7022-2190-2*, Pub. by Univ Queensland Pr AT) Intl Spec Bk.

Utah & the Mormons. Donald W. Hemingway. (Illus.). 1979. pap. 2.50 (*0-686-30193-5*) D W Hemingway.

Utah & the Mormons. B. G. Ferris. LC 77-134394. reprint ed. 57.50 (*0-404-08436-2*) AMS Pr.

Utah Art see Utah Painting & Sculpture

Utah Atlas & Gazetteer. DeLorme Staff. (Illus.). 64p. (Orig.). 1995. pap. 16.95 (*0-89933-243-9*, 5203) DeLorme Map.

Utah Bandits, Bushwackers, Outlaws, Crooks, Devils, Ghosts, Desperadoes & Other Assorted & Sundry Characters! Carole Marsh. (Carole Marsh Utah Bks.). (Illus.). (J). 1994. lib. bdg. 29.95 (*0-7933-1106-3*); disk 29.95 (*0-7933-1107-1*) Gallopade Pub Group.

Utah Bandits, Bushwackers, Outlaws, Crooks, Devils, Ghosts, Desperadoes & Other Assorted & Sundry Characters! Carole Marsh. (Carole Marsh Utah Bks.). (Illus.). (J). 1997. pap. 19.95 (*0-7933-1105-5*) Gallopade Pub Group.

Utah Beach to Cherbourg. Ed. by Historical Section European Theater of Operations Staff. (Combat Arms Ser.: No. 9). (Illus.). 214p. 1984. reprint ed. 32.50 (*0-89839-079-6*, 0-89839796) Battery Pr.

Utah Bicentennial & History. 1984. pap. 7.95 (*0-393-30221-0*) Norton.

Utah Birds: A Revised Checklist. William H. Behle et al. pap. 6.25 (*0-940378-07-8*) Utah Mus Natural Hist.

Utah Birds: Geographic Distribution & Systematics. William H. Behle. pap. 12.95 (*0-940378-06-X*) Utah Mus Natural Hist.

Utah Birds: Guide, Checklist & Occurrence Charts. William H. Behle & Michael L. Perry. pap. 5.00 (*0-940378-25-6*) Utah Mus Natural Hist.

Utah Birds: Historical Perspective & Bibliography. William H. Behle. 25.00 (*0-940378-11-6*) Utah Mus Natural Hist.

Utah Blaine. Louis L'Amour. 176p. 1984. pap. 3.99 (*0-553-24761-1*) Bantam.

Utah Bookstore Book: A Surprising Guide to Our State's Bookstores & Their Specialties for Students, Teachers, Writers & Publishers. Carole Marsh. (Utah Bks.). (Illus.). 1994. pap. 19.95 (*0-7933-2988-4*); lib. bdg. 29.95 (*0-7933-2987-6*); disk 29.95 (*0-7933-2989-2*) Gallopade Pub Group.

Utah Business Directory 1996-97. rev. ed. American Business Directories Staff. 752p. 1996. boxed 295.00 (*1-56105-840-8*) Am Busn Direct.

***Utah Business Directory 1997-1998.** rev. ed. American Business Directories Staff. 800p. 1997. boxed 295.00 (*1-56105-927-7*) Am Busn Direct.

Utah Byways Vol. 1: Backcountry Drives for the Whole Family. Tony Huegel. Ed. by Mei-Mei Chan. (Byways Guidebooks Ser.). (Illus.). 168p. (Orig.). 1996. pap. 16.95 (*0-9636560-8-2*) Post ID.

Utah Canyon Country. F. A. Barnes. LC 85-52187. (Utah Geographic Ser.: Vol. 1). (Illus.). 120p. (Orig.). 1986. pap. 9.95 (*0-936331-00-3*) Am Wrld Geog.

Utah Celebrities: A Guide to the Stars. Boyd Payne. LC 95-43320. (Illus.). 176p. (Orig.). 1995. pap. 10.95 (*1-56085-052-3*, Telestial Bks) Signature Bks.

Utah Celebrity & Local Heroes Cookbook. Sheila Liermann & Nancy Reid. (Illus.). 144p. (Orig.). 1995. pap. 20.00 (*0-9649428-0-1*) Lost Trail.

Utah Census Index 1850 Mortality Schedule. (Illus.). 1980. lib. bdg. 28.00 (*0-89593-506-6*) Accelerated Index.

Utah Census Index 1854 Parowan, Iron County. (Illus.). lib. bdg. 49.00 (*0-89593-507-4*) Accelerated Index.

Utah Census Index 1860 Mortality Schedule. (Illus.). lib. bdg. 29.00 (*0-89593-508-2*) Accelerated Index.

Utah Census Index 1870 Mortality Schedule. (Illus.). lib. bdg. 33.00 (*0-89593-510-4*) Accelerated Index.

Utah Census Index, 1880. (Illus.). 1989. lib. bdg. 189.00 (*0-89593-511-2*) Accelerated Index.

Utah Census Index 1880 Mortality Schedule. (Illus.). lib. bdg. 35.00 (*0-89593-512-0*) Accelerated Index.

Utah Census Index 1890 Union Veterans. Ronald V. Jackson. (Illus.). lib. bdg. 49.00 (*0-89593-789-1*) Accelerated Index.

Utah Civil Practice. David A. Thomas. 1049p. 1992. 95.00 (*0-87473-775-3*) MICHIE.

Utah Classic Christmas Trivia: Stories, Recipes, Activities, Legends, Lore & More! Carole Marsh. (Carole Marsh Utah Bks.). (Illus.). (J). 1994. pap. 19.95 (*0-7933-1108-X*); lib. bdg. 29.95 (*0-7933-1109-8*); disk 29.95 (*0-7933-1110-1*) Gallopade Pub Group.

Utah Coastales. Carole Marsh. (Carole Marsh Utah Bks.). (Illus.). (J). 1994. pap. 19.95 (*0-7933-2124-7*); lib. bdg. 29.95 (*0-7933-2123-9*) Gallopade Pub Group.

Utah Coastales. Carole Marsh. (Carole Marsh Utah Bks.). (Illus.). (J). 1997. disk 29.95 (*0-7933-2125-5*) Gallopade Pub Group.

Utah Coastales! Carole Marsh. (Utah Bks.). (J). 1994. lib. bdg. 29.95 (*0-7933-7309-3*) Gallopade Pub Group.

Utah Code Annotated. 1953. write for info. (*0-87473-000-7*) MICHIE.

Utah Code Annotated. write for info. (*0-614-05989-5*) MICHIE.

Utah-Colorado Mountain Biking Trail System, Route 1 - Moab to Loma, Kokopelli's Trail. Peggy Utesch. Ed. by F. A. Barnes. LC 90-81500. (Canyon Country Ser.: No. 22). (Illus.). 80p. (Orig.). 1990. pap. 5.00 (*0-9614586-9-0*) Canyon Country Pubns.

Utah Corporations & Business Laws, 1992 Edition. 8.00 (*0-614-05990-9*) MICHIE.

Utah Court Rules Annotated, 1994 Edition. Michie Butterworth Editorial Staff. pap. 65.00 (*1-55834-092-0*) MICHIE.

Utah Crime Perspective 1996. Ed. by Kathleen O. Morgan et al. 24p. 1996. pap. 19.00 (*1-56692-543-6*) Morgan Quitno Corp.

***Utah Crime Perspective 1997.** Ed. by Kathleen O. Morgan & Scott E. Morgan. 24p. 1997. pap. 19.00 (*1-56692-793-5*) Morgan Quitno Corp.

Utah Criminal & Traffic Code, 1993 Edition. 30.00 (*0-614-05991-7*) MICHIE.

Utah Criminal Code. Loren D. Martin. (Orig.). spiral bd. 12.50 (*0-9608244-3-X*) Valiant Pubns.

Utah "Crinkum-Crankum" A Funny Word Book about Our State. Carole Marsh. (Utah Bks.). (Illus.). (J). (gr. 3-12). 1994. 29.95 (*0-7933-4940-0*); pap. 19.95 (*0-7933-4941-9*); disk 29.95 (*0-7933-4942-7*) Gallopade Pub Group.

Utah Dingbats! Bk. 1: A Fun Book of Games, Stories, Activities & More about Our State That's All in Code! for You to Decipher. Carole Marsh. (Utah Bks.). (Illus.). (J). (gr. 3-12). 1994. pap. 19.95 (*0-7933-3906-5*); lib. bdg. 29.95 (*0-7933-3905-7*); disk 29.95 (*0-7933-3907-3*) Gallopade Pub Group.

Utah Dining Car. Junior League of Ogden, Utah, Inc. Staff. Ed. by Many King. 300p. 1984. 12.95 (*0-9613453-0-6*) Jr League Ogden.

Utah Discovery Guide: A Remarkably Useful Travel Companion for Motorists, RVers & Other Explorers. Don W. Martin & Betty W. Martin. (Discovery Guide Ser.: No. 4). (Illus.). 352p. (Orig.). 1995. pap. 13.95 (*0-942053-18-4*) Pine Cone Pr CA.

Utah Early Census Index. 1983. 58.00 (*0-89593-567-8*) Accelerated Index.

Utah Entrepreneur's Guide. University MT Staff. 1995. pap. text ed. 19.95 (*0-9624819-3-9*) University MT.

Utah Environmental Law Handbook. Parsons et al. (State Environmental Law Ser.). 180p. 1991. pap. 79.00 (*0-86587-341-0*) Gov Insts.

***Utah Expedition, 1857-1858: Letters of Part. Jesse A. Gove, of Concord, to Mrs. Gove, & Special Correspondence of the N. Y. Herald.** Ed. by Otis G. Hammond. (Illus.). 442p. 1997. reprint ed. lib. bdg. 47.50 (*0-8328-5969-9*) Higginson Bk Co.

Utah Facts & Factivities. Carole Marsh. (Carole Marsh State Bks.). (Illus.). 1996. 29.95 (*0-614-11555-8*, C Marsh) Gallopade Pub Group.

Utah Facts & Factivities. Carole Marsh. (Carole Marsh State Bks.). (Illus.). (J). 1996. teacher ed., pap. 19.95 (*0-7933-7935-0*, C Marsh) Gallopade Pub Group.

Utah Federal Census Index, 1850. Ronald V. Jackson. LC 77-86077. (Illus.). 1978. lib. bdg. 59.00 (*0-89593-140-0*) Accelerated Index.

Utah Federal Census Index, 1860. Ronald V. Jackson. (Illus.). 1979. lib. bdg. 129.00 (*0-89593-788-3*) Accelerated Index.

Utah Federal Census Index, 1870. (Illus.). 1979. lib. bdg. 133.00 (*0-89593-509-0*) Accelerated Index.

Utah Festival Fun for Kids! Carole Marsh. (Utah Bks.). (Illus.). (YA). (gr. 3-12). 1994. pap. 19.95 (*0-7933-4059-4*); lib. bdg. 29.95 (*0-7933-4058-6*); disk 29.95 (*0-7933-4060-8*) Gallopade Pub Group.

Utah Ghost Rails. Stephen L. Carr & Robert W. Edwards. LC 89-51670. (Illus.). 208p. (Orig.). 1990. pap. 19.95 (*0-914740-34-2*) Western Epics.

***Utah Government! The Cornerstone of Everyday Life in Our State!** Carole Marsh. (Carole Marsh Utah Bks.). (Illus.). (J). (gr. 3-12). 1996. pap. 19.95 (*0-7933-6314-4*); lib. bdg. 29.95 (*0-7933-6313-6*); disk 29.95 (*0-7933-6315-2*) Gallopade Pub Group.

Utah Guide. Allan K. Powell. (Travel Ser.). (Illus.). 534p. 1995. pap. 18.95 (*1-55591-130-7*) Fulcrum Pub.

***Utah Guide to Alternative Health Care.** Lisa Kingsbury & Cam Williams. Ed. by Connie Adler & Mary Kingsbury. 300p. 1996. pap. 14.95 (*0-9653267-0-5*) S L C Pubns.

***Utah Handbook.** 5th ed. Bill Weir & W. C. McRae. 456p. 1997. pap. text ed. 17.95 (*1-56691-087-0*) Moon Trvl Hdbks.

Utah Health Care Perspective 1996. Ed. by Kathleen O. Morgan et al. 24p. 1996. pap. 19.00 (*1-56692-643-2*) Morgan Quitno Corp.

***Utah Health Care Perspective 1997.** Ed. by Kathleen O. Morgan & Scott E. Morgan. 24p. 1997. pap. 19.00 (*1-56692-743-9*) Morgan Quitno Corp.

Utah Historical & Biographical Index, Vol. 1. Ronald V. Jackson. LC 78-53720. (Illus.). 1984. lib. bdg. 30.00 (*0-89593-202-4*) Accelerated Index.

***Utah History! Surprising Secrets about Our State's Founding Mothers, Fathers & Kids!** Carole Marsh. (Carole Marsh Utah Bks.). (Illus.). (J). (gr. 3-12). 1996. pap. 19.95 (*0-7933-6161-3*); lib. bdg. 29.95 (*0-7933-6160-5*); disk 29.95 (*0-7933-6162-1*) Gallopade Pub Group.

Utah History Encyclopedia. Ed. by Allan K. Powell. LC 94-18977. (Illus.). 605p. 1994. 50.00 (*0-87480-425-6*) U of Utah Pr.

Utah Hot Air Balloon Mystery. Carole Marsh. (Carole Marsh Utah Bks.). (Illus.). (J). (gr. 2-9). 1994. 29.95 (*0-7933-2714-8*); pap. 19.95 (*0-7933-2715-6*); disk 29.95 (*0-7933-2716-4*) Gallopade Pub Group.

Utah in Perspective 1996. Ed. by Kathleen O. Morgan et al. 26p. 1996. pap. 19.00 (*1-56692-593-2*) Morgan Quitno Corp.

***Utah in Perspective 1997.** Ed. by Kathleen O. Morgan & Scott E. Morgan. 26p. 1997. pap. 19.00 (*1-56692-693-9*) Morgan Quitno Corp.

Utah in the 1990's: A Demographic Perspective. Ed. by Tim B. Heaton et al. LC 96-14313. (Illus.). 302p. (Orig.). 1996. pap. 19.95 (*1-56085-021-3*) Signature Bks.

Utah Indian Dictionary for Kids! Carole Marsh. (Carole Marsh State Bks.). (J). (gr. 2-9). 1996. 29.95 (*0-7933-7776-5*, C Marsh); pap. 19.95 (*0-7933-7777-3*, C Marsh) Gallopade Pub Group.

Utah Is for Kids! Bobbi Salts. (Illus.). 32p. (Orig.). (J). (gr. 1-6). 1991. pap. 3.95 (*0-929526-06-6*) Double B Pubns.

***Utah Jazz.** Paul Joseph. LC 97-1337. (Inside the NBA Ser.). (J). 1997. write for info. (*1-56239-776-1*) Abdo & Dghtrs.

Utah Jazz. Richard Rambeck. (NBA Today Ser.). 32p. (J). (gr. 4). 1993. lib. bdg. 14.95 (*0-88682-525-3*) Creative Ed.

***Utah Jazz.** Richard Rambeck. LC 96-52961. (NBA Today Ser.). (J). 1997. write for info. (*0-88682-893-7*) Creative Ed.

Utah Jeopardy! Answers & Questions about Our State! Carole Marsh. (Utah Bks.). (Illus.). (J). (gr. 3-12). 1994. pap. 19.95 (*0-7933-4212-0*); lib. bdg. 29.95 (*0-7933-4211-2*); disk 29.95 (*0-7933-4213-9*) Gallopade Pub Group.

Utah "Jography" A Fun Run Thru Our State! Carole Marsh. (Carole Marsh Utah Bks.). (Illus.). (J). 1994. pap. 19.95 (*0-7933-2107-7*); lib. bdg. 29.95 (*0-7933-2106-9*); disk 29.95 (*0-7933-2108-5*) Gallopade Pub Group.

Utah Kid's Cookbook: Recipes, How-to, History, Lore & More! Carole Marsh. (Carole Marsh Utah Bks.). (Illus.). (J). 1994. pap. 19.95 (*0-7933-1117-9*); lib. bdg. 29.95 (*0-7933-1118-7*); disk 29.95 (*0-7933-1119-5*) Gallopade Pub Group.

Utah Library Book: A Surprising Guide to the Unusual Special Collections in Libraries Across Our State for Students, Teachers, Writers & Publishers - Includes Reproducible Mailing Labels Plus Activities for Young People! Carole Marsh. (Utah Bks.). (Illus.). 1994. pap. 19.95 (*0-7933-3138-2*); lib. bdg. 29.95 (*0-7933-3137-4*); disk 29.95 (*0-7933-3139-0*) Gallopade Pub Group.

***Utah Limited Liability Company Forms & Practice Manual.** Preston C. Regehr. LC 97-571. 606p. 1997. ring bd. 149.95 (*1-57400-025-X*) Data Trace Pubng.

Utah, Magnificent Wilderness. Tom Till. (Illus.). 112p. 1989. pap. 19.95 (*0-929969-08-1*) Westcliffe Pubs.

***Utah Manufacturers Register, 1997.** 2nd ed. Ed. by Kathleen Scott. 336p. 1995. pap. 70.00 (*1-57541-024-9*) Database Pub Co.

Utah Media Book: A Surprising Guide to the Amazing Print, Broadcast & Online Media of Our State for Students, Teachers, Writers & Publishers - Includes Reproducible Mailing Labels Plus Activities for Young People! Carole Marsh. (Utah Bks.). (Illus.). 1994. pap. 19.95 (*0-7933-3294-X*); lib. bdg. 29.95 (*0-7933-3293-1*); disk 29.95 (*0-7933-3295-8*) Gallopade Pub Group.

***Utah Mineral Activity Summary for 1995.** Roger L. Bon et al. (Circular of the Utah Geological Survey Ser.: Vol. 91). (Illus.). 15p. (Orig.). 1996. pap. 4.60 (*1-55791-377-3*, C91) Utah Geological Survey.

***Utah Mountaineering Guide.** 3rd ed. Michael R. Kelsey. Orig. Title: Utah Mountaineering Guide & Best Canyon Hikes. (Illus.). 192p. 1997. pap. 12.95 (*0-944510-14-0*) Kelsey Pub.

Utah Mountaineering Guide & Best Canyon Hikes see Utah Mountaineering Guide

Utah Mystery Van Takes Off! Book 1: Handicapped Utah Kids Sneak Off on a Big Adventure. Carole Marsh. (Utah Bks.). (Illus.). (J). (gr. 3-12). 1994. 29.95 (*0-7933-5093-X*); pap. 19.95 (*0-7933-5094-8*); disk 29.95 (*0-7933-5095-6*) Gallopade Pub Group.

Utah P. R. Finder Binder: 1997. Ed. by Alexander M. Brown. xxxiv, 638p. 1997. lib. bdg. 130.00 (*0-9650510-3-X*); vinyl bd. 110.00 (*0-9650510-2-1*) J Brown & Assocs.

***Utah Painting & Sculpture.** rev. ed. William C. Seifrit et al. LC 97-11331. Orig. Title: Utah Art. (Illus.). 320p. 1997. 60.00 (*0-87905-817-X*, Peregrine Smith) Gibbs Smith Pub.

Utah People in the Nevada Desert: Homestead & Community on a Twentieth Century Farmers' Frontier. Marshall E. Bowen. (Illus.). 150p. (C). 1994. 15.00 (*0-87421-168-9*) Utah St U Pr.

Utah Photographs of George Edward Anderson. Rell G. Francis. LC 79-1123. (Illus.). xii, 155p. 1979. text ed. 30.00 (*0-8032-1952-0*) U of Nebr Pr.

Utah Place Names. John W. Van Cott. LC 90-52741. (Illus.). 466p. (Orig.). 1990. pap. 14.95 (*0-87480-345-4*) U of Utah Pr.

Utah Poems. Marek Lugowski. 40p. 1995. pap. 3.00 (*1-888431-00-8*) Small Garlic.

Utah P.R. Finder Binder: 1996. Ed. by Alexander M. Brown. xvi, 421p. 1996. 110.00 (*0-9650510-0-5*); lib. bdg. 125.00 (*0-9650510-1-3*) J Brown & Assocs.

***Utah PR Finder Binder: 1998.** Ed. by Alexander M. Brown. 685p. 1997. lib. bdg. write for info. (*0-9650510-5-6*) J Brown & Assocs.

***Utah PR Finder Binder: 1998.** 3rd ed. Ed. by Alexander M. Brown. 685p. 1997. write for info. (*0-9650510-4-8*) J Brown & Assocs.

***Utah Publicity Source Book.** Ed. by Scott S. Jackson. Tr. by Larry J. Orton. 456p. 1998. ring bd. 130.00 (*1-884689-06-X*) Orton Grp.

Utah Publicity Source Book, 1995. James W. Brown. 1995. lib. bdg. 115.00 (*1-884689-03-5*); ring bd. 130.00 (*1-884689-02-7*) Orton Grp.

Utah Publicity Source Book, 1996. rev. ed. Norma Lloyd. 1995. lib. bdg. 100.00 (*1-884689-05-1*) Orton Grp.

Utah Publicity Source Book, 1996. 15th rev. ed. Norma Lloyd & James W. Brown. 1995. 130.00 (*1-884689-04-3*) Orton Grp.

Utah Quiz Bowl Crash Course! Carole Marsh. (Carole Marsh Utah Bks.). (Illus.). (J). 1994. pap. 19.95 (*0-7933-2121-2*); lib. bdg. 29.95 (*0-7933-2120-4*); disk 29.95 (*0-7933-2122-0*) Gallopade Pub Group.

Utah Reflections: Littlebook. Photos by Tom Till. (Illus.). 64p. 1996. 14.95 (*1-56579-141-X*) Westcliffe Pubs.

Utah Remembers World War Two. Allan K. Powell. (Illus.). 280p. 1991. 29.95 (*0-87421-152-2*) Utah St U Pr.

***Utah Retirement & Relocation Guide.** Leigh Gieringer. (Illus.). 350p. (Orig.). 1997. pap. 19.95 (*1-56559-105-4*) HGI Mrktng.

Utah Roadside History: Monuments, Markers & Sites. Gary L. Gregerson. Ed. by Luree G. Porter. (Illus.). 250p. (Orig.). 1996. pap. 19.95 (*1-888721-00-6*) Griffin UT.

Utah Rollercoasters! Carole Marsh. (Utah Bks.). (Illus.). (YA). (gr. 3-12). 1994. pap. 19.95 (*0-7933-5357-2*); lib. bdg. 29.95 (*0-7933-5356-4*); disk 29.95 (*0-7933-5358-0*) Gallopade Pub Group.

An Asterisk (*) at the beginning of an entry indicates that the title is appearing in BIP for the first time.

Utah Salt Lake County Tax List, 1851-1856. (Illus.). lib. bdg. 65.00 (*0-89593-513-9*) Accelerated Index.

Utah School Trivia: An Amazing & Fascinating Look at Our State's Teachers, Schools & Students! Carole Marsh. (Carole Marsh Utah Bks.). (Illus.). (J). 1994. pap. 19.95 (*0-7933-1114-4*); lib. bdg. 29.95 (*0-7933-1115-2*); disk 29.95 (*0-7933-1116-0*) Gallopade Pub Group.

Utah Science Core Series, 6 vols., Set. B. K. Hixson. (Illus.). 576p. pap. text ed. 130.00 (*1-57156-018-1*) Wild Goose UT.

Utah Silly Basketball Sportsmysteries, Vol. 1. Carole Marsh. (Carole Marsh Utah Bks.). (Illus.). (J). 1994. pap. 19.95 (*0-7933-1111-X*); lib. bdg. 29.95 (*0-7933-1112-8*); disk 29.95 (*0-7933-1113-6*) Gallopade Pub Group.

Utah Silly Basketball Sportsmysteries, Vol. 2. Carole Marsh. (Carole Marsh Utah Bks.). (Illus.). (J). 1994. pap. 19.95 (*0-7933-2133-6*); lib. bdg. 29.95 (*0-7933-2132-8*); disk 29.95 (*0-7933-2134-4*) Gallopade Pub Group.

Utah Silly Football Sportsmysteries, Vol. 1. Carole Marsh. (Carole Marsh Utah Bks.). (Illus.). (J). 1994. pap. 19.95 (*0-7933-2112-3*); lib. bdg. 29.95 (*0-7933-2111-5*); disk 29.95 (*0-7933-2113-1*) Gallopade Pub Group.

Utah Silly Football Sportsmysteries, Vol. 2. Carole Marsh. (Carole Marsh Utah Bks.). (Illus.). (J). 1994. pap. 19.95 (*0-7933-2115-8*); lib. bdg. 29.95 (*0-7933-2114-X*); disk 29.95 (*0-7933-2116-6*) Gallopade Pub Group.

Utah Silly Trivia! Carole Marsh. (Carole Marsh Utah Bks.). (Illus.). (J). 1994. pap. 19.95 (*0-7933-2104-2*); lib. bdg. 29.95 (*0-7933-2103-4*); disk 29.95 (*0-7933-2105-0*) Gallopade Pub Group.

Utah Slickrock Country: Littlebook. Photos by Tom Till. (Illus.). 64p. 1996. 14.95 (*1-56579-142-8*) Westcliffe Pubs.

Utah State Census, 1856. (Illus.). lib. bdg. 170.00 (*0-89593-514-7*) Accelerated Index.

Utah State Fare: A Centennial Recipe Collection. Paula Julander & Joanne Milner. LC 95-35785. (Illus.). 1995. pap. 16.95 (*1-57345-082-0*) Deseret Bk.

Utah State Parks: A Complete Recreation Guide. Jan Bannan. (Illus.). 224p. 1995. pap. 14.95 (*0-89886-421-6*) Mountaineers.

Utah Statehood Census Index, 1856 (Every Name) Ronald V. Jackson. (Illus.). lib. bdg. 179.00 (*0-89593-787-5*) Accelerated Index.

Utah Statistical Abstract 1983. 9th ed. Ed. by Bureau of Economic & Business Research Staff, University of Utah Staff. (Illus.). 396p. (Orig.). 1983. 25.00 (*0-942486-04-8*) Univ Utah.

Utah Survival. Betty L. Hall. 160p. (Orig.). (gr. 10-12). 1979. pap. text ed. 5.84 (*0-03-046981-3*) Westwood Pr.

Utah, the Right Place: The Official Centennial History. rev. ed. Thomas G. Alexander. (Illus.). 488p. 1996. pap. 29.95 (*0-87905-767-X*) Gibbs Smith Pub.

Utah Timeline: A Chronology of Utah History, Mystery, Trivia, Legend, Lore & More. Carole Marsh. (Utah Bks.). (Illus.). (J). (gr. 3-12). 1994. pap. 19.95 (*0-7933-6008-0*); lib. bdg. 29.95 (*0-7933-6007-2*); disk 29.95 (*0-7933-6009-9*) Gallopade Pub Group.

Utah Trackdown. Jon Sharpe. (Trailsman Ser.: No. 170). 176p. 1996. mass mkt., pap. 4.99 (*0-451-18538-2*, Sig) NAL-Dutton.

***Utah Trivia.** Kent Powell & Mariam B. Murphy. LC 97-2995. 192p. 1997. pap. 6.95 (*1-55853-464-4*) Rutledge Hill Pr.

Utah Wildflowers: A Field Guide to Northern & Central Mountains & Valleys. Richard J. Shaw. LC 94-13838. 1995. pap. 12.95 (*0-87421-170-0*) Utah St U Pr.

Utah Wildflowers: Littlebook. Photos by Tom Till. (Illus.). 64p. 1996. 14.95 (*1-56579-140-1*) Westcliffe Pubs.

Utah Wildlife Viewing Guide. Jim Cole. LC 90-80041. (Watchable Wildlife Ser.). (Illus.). 88p. 1990. pap. 8.95 (*1-56044-023-6*) Falcon Pr MT.

Utah Women & the Law. Utah Governor's Commission on the Status of Women. LC 87-5075. 176p. reprint ed. pap. 50.20 (*0-8357-7066-4*, 2033359) Bks Demand.

Utahraptor: The Deadliest Dinosaur. Don Lessom. (J). (gr. 2-5). 1996. lib. bdg. 14.96 (*0-87614-988-3*, Carolrhoda) Lerner Group.

***Utah's Aerospace Heritage: The Aircraft & Artifacts of Hill Aerospace Museum.** Ed. by Paul F. Anderson et al. LC 96-80367. (Illus.). 144p. (Orig.). 1996. pap. 11.95 (*0-9656079-0-9*, UAH-1) Persistence of Vision.

Utah's Audacious Stockman, Charlie Redd. Leonard J. Arrington. (Illus.). 282p. 1995. pap. 19.95 (*0-87421-177-8*) Utah St U Pr.

Utah's Biggest Bucks. 2nd rev. ed. Robert L. Warren. (Illus.). 400p. (C). 1988. 26.95 (*0-317-91343-3*) R L Warren.

Utah's "Dixie" Birthplace, Vol. III. 2nd rev. ed. Harold P. Cahoon & Priscilla J. Cahoon. LC 96-60234. (Illus.). 282p. 1996. pap. 29.95 (*1-888106-20-4*) Custom Fmly.

Utah's High Technology Directory 1993. Jan Crispin-Little & Gary K. Ricks. Ed. by Diane Gillam. 100p. (Orig.). 1993. pap. 10.00 (*0-942486-09-9*) Univ Utah.

***Utah's High Technology Directory 1996.** Jan Crispin-Little & Gary K. Ricks. Ed. by Diane S. Gillam. 104p. (Orig.). 1996. pap. 15.00 (*0-942486-12-9*) Univ Utah.

Utah's Historic Architecture 1847-1940: A Guide. Thomas Carter & Peter Goss. LC 87-34526. (Illus.). 192p. 1991. reprint ed. pap. 19.95 (*1-880351-00-5*) Schl of Arch.

Utah's History. rev. ed. Ed. by Richard D. Poll et al. (Illus.). 757p. (C). 1989. pap. text ed. 29.95 (*0-87421-142-5*) Utah St U Pr.

Utah's (Most Devastating!) Disasters & (Most Calamitous!) Catastrophies! Carole Marsh. (Carole Marsh Utah Bks.). (Illus.). (J). 1994. pap. 19.95 (*0-7933-1102-0*); lib. bdg. 29.95 (*0-7933-1103-9*); write for info. (*0-7933-1104-7*) Gallopade Pub Group.

Utah's National Parks: Hiking & Vacationing in Utah's Canyon Country - Zion, Bryce, Arches, Canyonlands & Capitol Reef. Ron Adkison. LC 91-28496. (Illus.). 320p. (Orig.). 1991. pap. 14.95 (*0-89997-126-1*) Wilderness Pr.

Utah's Road to Statehood. Kenneth R. Williams. (Illus.). 48p. 1995. pap. 3.50 (*0-87421-194-8*) Utah St U Pr.

Utah's Unsolved Mysteries (& Their "Solutions") Includes Scientific Information & Other Activities for Students. Carole Marsh. (Utah Bks.). (Illus.). (J). (gr. 3-12). 1994. pap. 19.95 (*0-7933-5855-8*); lib. bdg. 29.95 (*0-7933-5854-X*); disk 29.95 (*0-7933-5856-6*) Gallopade Pub Group.

***Utamakura, Allusion, & Intertextuality in Traditional Japanese Poetry.** LC 96-44433. 1997. write for info. (*0-300-06808-5*) Yale U Pr.

Utamaro: Portraits from the Floating World. Tadashi Kobayashi. Ed. by Barry Lancet. Tr. by Mark A. Harbison. (Illus.). 96p. 1993. 40.00 (*4-7700-1667-0*) Kodansha.

Utamaro & Hiroshige: In a Survey of Japanese Prints from the James Michener Collection of the Honolulu Academy of Arts. (Illus.). 54p. 1977. pap. 15.00 (*0-614-02676-8*) Japan Soc.

***Utatti Asfet: The Eye of Wicked Sight.** Owen Guthrie & Toivo Luick. (Call of Cthulhu Roleplaying Game System Ser.). (Illus.). 156p. (Orig.). 1996. pap. 20.95 (*1-56882-056-9*, 2360) Chaosium.

Ute. Katherine M. Doherty & Craig A. Doherty. LC 93-37999. (J). 1994. write for info. (*0-86625-530-3*) Rourke Pubns.

***Ute Indians of Colorado in the Twentieth Century.** Richard K. Young. LC 97-2381. 384p. 1997. 29.95 (*0-8061-2968-9*) U of Okla Pr.

UTE Mountain Tribal Park: The Other Mesa Verde. Jean Akens. (Illus.). 96p. (Orig.). 1995. pap. 8.50 (*0-944123-00-7*) Four Crnrs UT.

Ute Pass. Jan Pettit. (Illus.). 64p. (Orig.). 1979. pap. 4.50 (*0-936564-12-1*) Little London.

Ute Tales. Photos by Edward Sapir & Alden Hayes. LC 92-53607. (American West Ser.: Vol. 29). (Illus.). 175p. 1992. 24.95 (*0-87480-404-3*) U of Utah Pr.

Ute Tales. Compiled by Anne M. Smith. (Illus.). 174p. 1993. reprint ed. pap. 12.95 (*0-87480-442-6*) U of Utah Pr.

UTEP: A Pictorial History of the University of Texas at El Paso. Nancy Hamilton. 1988. 35.00 (*0-87404-208-9*) Tex Western.

Uterine & Embryonic Factors in Early Pregnancy. Ed. by Jerome F. Strauss, III & C. R. Lyttle. (Reproductive Biology Ser.). (Illus.). 276p. 1991. 85.00 (*0-306-44042-3*, Plenum Pr) Plenum.

Uterine Circulation. Ed. by Charles Rosenfeld. LC 89-16219. (Reproductive & Perinatal Medicine Ser.: No. X). 1989. 102.50 (*0-916859-30-4*) Perinatology.

Uterine Contractility: Mechanisms of Control. Ed. by Robert E. Garfield. (Serono Symposia, USA Ser.). (Illus.). 400p. (C). 1990. text ed. 70.00 (*1-878601-05-9*) Serono Symposia USA.

***Uterine Fibroids: What Every Woman Needs to Know.** Nelson H. Stringer. (Illus.). 128p. (Orig.). 1996. pap. 17.95 (*0-924428-10-4*) Phys Sci Pub.

Uterine Function: Molecular & Cellular Aspects. Ed. by M. E. Carsten & J. D. Miller. LC 90-6882. (Illus.). 628p. 1990. 149.50 (*0-306-43446-6*, Plenum Pr) Plenum.

***Uterine Natural Killer Cells.** Ed. by Anne Croy. (Journal Ser.: Vol. 15, No. 1, 1996-97). (Illus.). 70p. 1997. pap. 26.25 (*3-8055-6395-7*) S Karger.

Uterus. Ed. by T. Chard & J. G. Grudzinskas. (Cambridge Reviews in Human Reproduction Ser.). (Illus.). 320p. (C). 1995. text ed. 125.00 (*0-521-41403-2*); pap. text ed. 44.95 (*0-521-42453-4*) Cambridge U Pr.

Uterus: Pathology, Diagnosis & Management. Ed. by A. Altcheck et al. (Clinical Perspectives in Obstetrics & Gynecology Ser.). (Illus.). 504p. 1991. 129.00 (*0-387-97422-9*) Spr-Verlag.

***Utes.** Alice Flanagan. LC 97-15089. (True Book Ser.). 1997. write for info. (*0-516-20455-6*) Childrens.

Utes: The Mountain People. rev. ed. Jan Pettit. LC 90-91905. 224p. 1990. pap. 11.95 (*1-55566-065-7*) Johnson Bks.

Uther, the Half Dead King. Ed. by Bo Hampton & Dan Abnett. 64p. 1994. pap. 11.95 (*1-56163-110-8*) NBM.

Uther, the Half Dead King. deluxe ed. Ed. by Bo Hampton & Dan Abnett. 64p. 1994. 45.00 (*1-56163-111-6*) NBM.

Uthman ibn Affan: The Third Caliph of Islam. Abdur Rehman Shad. 96p. (YA). (gr. 10-12). 1985. pap. 3.50 (*1-56744-409-1*) Kazi Pubns.

Utica: The Upper Mohawk Country. David M. Ellis. 1982. 22.95 (*0-89781-054-6*, 5063) Am Historical Pr.

Utica Dine-a-Mate. 224p. 1994. pap. 20.00 (*1-57393-015-6*) Dine-A-Mate.

***Utica Dine-a-Mate Book.** 200p. 1996. pap. text ed. 25.00 (*1-57393-071-7*) Dine-A-Mate.

***Utilisation de la Statistique Dans la Gestion de l'Information.** Kenneth Huggins et al. Ed. by Joel Basarich. (FLMI Ser.). 90p. (FRE.). 1995. pap. text ed. 15.00 (*0-939921-83-9*) Life Office.

Utilisation of Electric Power: Including Electric Drives & Electric Traction. N. V. Suryanarayana. 1994. write for info. (*81-224-0546-0*, Pub. by Wiley Estrn II) Franklin.

Utilisation of Natural Resources: Chemical Engineering Approach. H. S. Ray & A. K. Mitra. (International Series on Chemical Engineering). 1994. write for info. (*81-7236-099-1*, Pub. by Wiley Estrn II) Franklin.

Utilisation of Remote Sensing in the South Pacific. D. Van Classen. (C). 1992. text ed. 100.00 (*1-86320-059-2*, Pub. by ACIAR) St Mut.

Utilisation of Sewage Sludge on Land: Rates of Application & Long-Term Effects of Metals. Ed. by S. Berglund et al. 1983. lib. bdg. 123.50 (*90-277-1701-X*) Kluwer Ac.

Utiliser la Connaisance Endogene dans le Developpement Agricole. D. Michael Warren. (Studies in Technology & Social Change). 48p. (FRE.). (C). 1995. pap. 8.00 (*0-945271-36-0*) ISU-CIKARD.

Utilitarian Confucianism: Ch'en Liang's Challenge to Chu Hsi. Hoyt C. Tillman. (East Asian Monographs: No. 101). 300p. 1982. 26.00 (*0-674-93176-9*) HUP.

Utilitarian Ethics. Anthony Quinton. 128p. 1988. pap. 14.95 (*0-8126-9052-4*) Open Court.

Utilitarian Response: The Contemporary Viability of Utilitarian Political Philosophy. Ed. by Lincoln Allison. (Modern Politics Ser.: Vol. 24). 218p. (C). 1990. text ed. 45.00 (*0-8039-8273-9*) Sage.

Utilitarianism. John Stuart Mill. Ed. by George Sher. LC 78-74450. (HPC Classics Ser.). 80p. (C). 1979. pap. text ed. 3.95 (*0-915144-41-7*) Hackett Pub.

Utilitarianism. John Stuart Mill. 1974. pap. 11.95 (*0-452-00970-7*, Mer) NAL-Dutton.

Utilitarianism. John Stuart Mill. LC 86-62704. (Great Books in Philosophy). 83p. pap. 4.95 (*0-87975-376-5*) Prometheus Bks.

Utilitarianism. John Stuart Mill. Ed. by Mary Warnock. Bd. with On Liberty.; Essay on Bentham.; Selected Writings of Jeremy Bentham & John Austin. Set mass mkt. 6.95 (*0-452-00598-1*, F598, Mer) NAL-Dutton.

Utilitarianism. Geoffrey F. Scarre. LC 95-38889. 216p. (C). 1996. text ed. 55.00 (*0-415-09527-1*) Routledge.

Utilitarianism. Geoffrey F. Scarre. 216p. (C). 1996. pap. 17.95 (*0-415-12197-3*) Routledge.

Utilitarianism: A Contemporary Statement. Robin Barrow. 208p. 1991. text ed. 70.00 (*1-85278-097-5*) E Elgar.

Utilitarianism: For & Against. J. J. Smart & Bernard Williams. LC 73-80487. 180p. 1973. pap. text ed. 16.95 (*0-521-09822-X*) Cambridge U Pr.

Utilitarianism: Mill. Ed. by Oskar Piest. 88p. (C). 1957. pap. text ed. 5.00 (*0-02-395670-4*, Macmillan Coll) P-H.

Utilitarianism & All That. Raghavan N. Iyer. xi, 132p. (C). 1983. pap. 8.75 (*0-88695-003-1*) Concord Grove.

Utilitarianism & Beyond. Ed. by Amartya K. Sen & Bernard Williams. LC 81-17981. 304p. 1982. pap. text ed. 32.95 (*0-521-28771-5*) Cambridge U Pr.

Utilitarianism & Coordination. Allan Gibbard. (Harvard Dissertations in Philosophy Ser.). 264p. 1990. reprint ed. text ed. 20.00 (*0-8240-3202-0*) Garland.

Utilitarianism & Other Essays. John Stuart Mill et al. Ed. & Intro. by Alan Ryan. 352p. 1987. pap. 11.95 (*0-14-043272-8*, Penguin Classics) Viking Penguin.

Utilitarianism As a Public Philosophy. Robert E. Goodin. (Cambridge Studies in Philosophy & Public Policy). 368p. (C). 1995. pap. 18.95 (*0-521-46806-X*); text ed. 59.95 (*0-521-46263-0*) Cambridge U Pr.

***Utilitarianism, Hedonism, & Desert: Essays in Moral Philosophy.** Fred Feldman. (Studies in Philosophy). (Illus.). 220p. (C). 1997. text ed. 54.95 (*0-521-59155-4*) Cambridge U Pr.

***Utilitarianism, Hedonism, & Desert: Essays in Moral Philosophy.** Fred Feldman. (Studies in Philosophy). (Illus.). 220p. (C). 1997. pap. text ed. 17.95 (*0-521-59842-7*) Cambridge U Pr.

***Utilitarianism, Institutions, & Justice.** James W. Bailey. 240p. 1997. 49.95 (*0-19-510510-9*) OUP.

Utilitarianism, On Liberty, Considerations on Representative Government. John Stuart Mill. Ed. by Geraint Williams. 512p. 1993. pap. 6.95 (*0-460-87346-6*, Everyman's Classic Lib) C E Tuttle.

Utilities As Catalysts in Economic Development. James Breagy & Jenny Murphy. 34p. (Orig.). 1989. pap. 21.50 (*0-317-04805-8*) Natl Coun Econ Dev.

Utilities Service Worker. Jack Rudman. (Career Examination Ser.: C-3161). 1994. pap. 27.95 (*0-8373-3161-7*) Nat Learn.

Utility & Choice in Social Interaction. Lynne Ofshe & Richard Ofshe. LC 70-101539. (Illus.). 1970. 39.50 (*0-13-939645-4*) Irvington.

***Utility & Independent Power: Concept for a New Millenium.** F. William Payne. LC 97-7709. 1997. write for info. (*0-88173-267-2*) Fairmont Pr.

***Utility & Independent Power: Concepts for the New Millenium.** Ed. by Payne & Fairmont Press Staff. (C). 1997. text ed. 79.00 (*0-13-645573-5*) P-H.

***Utility Boats: Owner's Manual.** TAL Marketing Services Staff. (Illus.). 85p. (Orig.). 1996. pap. 6.95 (*1-887960-02-3*, 596-207B) TotalConcepts.

***Utility Business Architecture: Designing & Change.** EMA Services, Inc. Staff & AWWA Research Foundation Staff. LC 97-17110. 1997. write for info. (*0-89867-903-6*) Am Water Wks Assn.

Utility Gas Analysis by Gas Chromatography. D. V. Kniebes. (Technical Reports: No. 4). vi, 32p. 1962. pap. 1.00 (*0-317-56935-X*) Inst Gas Tech.

Utility Holding Companies: A Modern View of the Business, Financial, SEC, Corporate Law, Tax, & Accounting Aspects of Their Establishment, Operation, Reputation, & Role in Diversification. Douglas W. Hawes. LC 84-292. 1984. 140.00 (*0-87632-434-0*) Clark Boardman Callaghan.

Utility Maintenance Technician. William Thomas. (Illus.). 205p. (C). 1988. lib. bdg. 45.00 (*0-943863-14-7*) Marsh-Wentworth.

Utility Manual. Fairmont Press Staff & John M. Studebaker. 1993. text ed. 74.00 (*0-13-927740-4*) P-H.

Utility Mapping & Record Keeping for Infrastructure. David F. Pickering et al. LC 93-10646. (Urban Management Programme Paper Ser.: No. 10). 86p. 1993. 7.95 (*0-8213-2426-8*, 12426) World Bank.

Utility Marketing Strategies: Competition & the Economy. Clark Gellings. LC 93-25333. 282p. 1993. 95.00 (*0-88173-156-0*) PennWell Bks.

Utility Marketing 2000. 306p. (Orig.). 1991. pap. text ed. 60.00 (*0-929569-01-6*) Synergic Resc.

Utility Meter Reading Systems. Richard K. Miller & Marcia E. Rupnow. LC 89-85445. (Survey on Technology & Markets Ser.: No. 137). 50p. 1991. pap. text ed. 200.00 (*1-55865-162-4*) Future Tech Surveys.

Utility of Prayers. Afzalur Rahman. pap. 4.50 (*0-933511-84-1*) Kazi Pubns.

Utility of Regional Gravity & Magnetic Anomaly Maps. Ed. by W. J. Hinze. LC 84-52447. (Illus.). 468p. 1985. text ed. 25.00 (*0-931830-34-6*, 512) Soc Expl Geophys.

Utility of Splendor: Ceremony, Social Life, & Architecture at the Court of Bavaria, 1600-1800. Samuel J. Klingensmith. Ed. by Christian F. Otto & Mark Ashton. LC 93-17138. (Illus.). 356p. 1993. 47.50 (*0-226-44330-2*) U Ch Pr.

Utility Outreach & Education Specialist. (Career Examination Ser.: C-3659). pap. 27.95 (*0-8373-3659-7*) Nat Learn.

Utility Promotion of Investment in Energy Efficiency: Engineering, Legal & Economic Analysis. 416p. 26.00 (*0-318-17529-0*) Alliance Save Ener.

Utility Regulatory Policy in the U. S. & Canada, 1994-1995. 800p. 1995. 75.00 (*0-317-05554-2*) NARUC.

Utility-Scale Energy Storage. Richard K. Miller & Marcia E. Rupnow. LC 90-83919. (Survey on Technology & Markets Ser.: No. 114). 50p. 1991. pap. text ed. 200.00 (*1-55865-137-3*) Future Tech Surveys.

Utility Security Operations Management: For Gas, Water, Electric & Nuclear Utilities. Ed. by Clay E. Higgins. (Illus.). 462p. (C). 1989. text ed. 86.95 (*0-398-05576-9*) C C Thomas.

Utility Security Operations Management: For Gas, Water, Electric & Nuclear Utilities. Ed. by Clay E. Higgins. (Illus.). 462p. 1989. pap. 49.95 (*0-398-06390-7*) C C Thomas.

Utility Vehicle Design Handbook, No. 16. 2nd ed. Ed. by Hohn F. Hoelzle et al. (Advances in Engineering Ser.). 560p. 1991. text ed. 39.00 (*1-56091-134-4*, AE-16) Soc Auto Engineers.

Utility's Development & Use of Prestressed Concrete Poles. Prestressed Concrete Institute Staff. (PCI Journal Reprints Ser.). 8p. 1972. pap. 10.00 (*0-318-19837-1*, JR114) P-PCI.

Utilization & Recycle of Agricultural Wastes & Residues. Michael Schuler. 304p. 1980. 174.00 (*0-8493-5569-9*, TD930, CRC Reprint) Franklin.

***Utilization Case Management.** Olga Cotera. 121p. 1996. spiral bd. 110.00 (*1-879575-77-9*) Acad Med Sys.

Utilization-Focused Evaluation. 2nd ed. Michael Q. Patton. LC 85-27817. 352p. (C). 1986. text ed. 52.00 (*0-8039-2779-7*); pap. text ed. 25.00 (*0-8039-2566-2*) Sage.

Utilization-Focused Evaluation: The New Century Text. 3rd ed. Michael Q. Patton. LC 96-25310. 640p. 1996. 69.95 (*0-8039-5264-3*); pap. 29.95 (*0-8039-5265-1*) Sage.

Utilization Management: A Handbook for Psychiatrists. APA Committee on Managed Care. LC 91-47117. 65p. 1992. pap. text ed. 12.00 (*0-89042-235-4*, 2235) Am Psychiatric.

Utilization, Misuse & Development of Human Resources in the Early West Indian Colonies. M. Kazim Bacchus. 480p. (C). 1990. pap. 19.95 (*0-88920-982-0*) Wilfrid Laurier.

Utilization of Acidic Soils for Crop Production. Ed. by Robert J. Wright et al. (Developments in Plant & Soil Sciences Ser.). 1128p. (C). 1991. lib. bdg. 666.00 (*0-7923-1105-1*) Kluwer Ac.

Utilization of Agency for Health Care Policy & Research Guidelines. American Nurses Association Staff. 1994. 13.95 (*0-614-02744-6*, NP-99) Am Nurses Pub.

Utilization of Amateur Radio in Disaster Communications. Lynn E. Edwards. (Illus.). 88p. (Orig.). (C). 1994. pap. text ed. 25.00 (*0-7881-1097-7*) DIANE Pub.

Utilization of Classroom Peers As Behavior Change Agents. Ed. by Phillip S. Strain. (Applied Clinical Psychology Ser.). 376p. 1981. 65.00 (*0-306-40618-7*, Plenum Pr) Plenum.

***Utilization of Genograms & Eco-Maps to Assess American Indian Families Who Have a Member with a Disability (Making Visible the Invisible)** C. T. Goodluck. 100p. 1991. pap. text ed. write for info. (*1-888557-15-X*, 100107) No Ariz Univ.

***Utilization of Genograms & Eco-Maps to Assess American Indian Families Who Have a Member with a Disability (Making Visible the Invisible) Training Curriculum.** C. T. Goodluck. 75p. 1990. pap. text ed. write for info. (*1-888557-47-8*) No Ariz Univ.

Utilization of Geothermal Energy for Electric Power Production & Space Heating. Ed. by E. Barbier & M. Trindade. (Selected Papers from the UNECE Seminar Held in Florence, Italy 14-17 May 1984). 392p. 1985. pap. 61.00 (*0-08-032638-2*, Pergamon Pr) Elsevier.

Utilization of High-Strength Concrete: Second International Symposium. 794p. 1990. 59.75 (*0-685-60168-4*, SP-121BOW6) ACI.

Utilization of Industrial By-Products for Construction Materials: Proceedings of the Session Sponsored by the Materials Engineering Division in Conjunction with the ASCE National Convention in Dallas, Texas, October 24-28, 1993. Ed. by Nader Ghafoori. LC 93-29984. 1993. 13.00 (*0-87262-977-5*) Am Soc Civil Eng.

Utilization of Low-Grade Southern Hardwoods. 289p. 1981. 25.00 (*0-935018-08-5*) Forest Prod.

***Utilization of Multidimensional Engine Modeling.** 38p. 1997. 38.00 (*1-56091-968-X*) Soc Auto Engineers.

Utilization of Ocean Waves - Wave to Energy Conversion. Ed. by Michael E. McCormick & Young C. Kim. 212p. 1987. 24.00 (*0-87262-624-5*) Am Soc Civil Eng.

U
V

Utilization of One & Two Chronicles in the Reconstruction of Israelite History of the Nineteenth Century. Matt P. Graham. (Society of Biblical Literature Dissertation Ser.). 430p. 1990. 25.95 (1-55540-354-9, 06 21 16); pap. 16.95 (1-55540-355-7) Scholars Pr GA.

Utilization of Protein Resources. D. W. Stanley et al. 403p. 1981. 77.00 (0-917678-12-5) Food & Nut Pr.

Utilization of Residual Forest Biomass. P. Hakkila. (Wood Science Ser.). (Illus.). 575p. 1989. 318.95 (0-387-50299-8) Spr-Verlag.

Utilization of Secondary & Trace Elements in Agriculture: Proceedings of Symposium, 12-16 January 1987, Geneva. United Nations, Economic Commission for Latin America. (Developments in Plant & Soil Sciences Ser.). (C). 1987. lib. bdg. 129.50 (90-247-3546-7) Kluwer Ac.

Utilization of Services by Omaha's Older Mexican-Americans. Genevieve Burch & Carole M. Davis. 72p. (Orig.). 1979. pap. 4.50 (1-55719-096-8) U NE CPAR.

Utilization of Space Shuttle & Spacelab: Proceedings of an International Meeting Held in Bonn, 1976. Deutsche Gesellschaft Fur Luft und Raumfahrt. (Illus.). 1976. pap. 30.00 (3-88135-034-9) Univelt Inc.

Utilization of Squid. M. Sugiyama et al. (Illus.). 266p. (C). 1989. text ed. 85.00 (90-6191-479-5, Pub. by A A Balkema NE) Ashgate Pub Co.

Utilization of Squid. M. Sugiyama et al. (C). 1989. 50.00 (81-7087-042-9, Pub. by Oxford IBH II) S Asia.

Utilization of the Cook-Freeze Catering System for School Meals. Janice Millross & Alan Speht. 212p. 1974. text ed. 30.00 (0-87936-007-0) Scholium Intl.

***Utilization of the Family As a Resource in American Indian Vocational Rehabilitation Projects (Section 130 Projects) Final Report.** C. A. Marshall & M. Johnson. 95p. 1996. pap. text ed. write for info. (1-888557-64-8) No Ariz Univ.

Utilization of Thorium in Power Reactors. (Technical Reports: No. 52). (Illus.). 376p. 1966. pap. 50.00 (92-0-055066-5, IDC52, Pub. by IAEA AU) Bernan Associates.

***Utilization of Tropical Foods: Animal Products.** 57p. 1990. 9.00 (92-5-102878-8, F8788, Pub. by FAO IT) Bernan Associates.

***Utilization of Tropical Foods: Cereals.** 149p. 1989. 12.00 (92-5-102774-9, F7749, Pub. by FAO IT) Bernan Associates.

***Utilization of Tropical Foods: Fruits & Leaves.** 67p. 1990. 9.00 (92-5-102874-5, Pub. by FAO IT) Bernan Associates.

***Utilization of Tropical Foods: Roots & Tubers.** 77p. 1989. 9.00 (92-5-102775-7, Pub. by FAO IT) Bernan Associates.

***Utilization of Tropical Foods: Sugars, Spices & Stimulants.** 75p. 1989. 9.00 (92-5-102837-0, F8370, Pub. by FAO IT) Bernan Associates.

***Utilization of Tropical Foods: Trees.** 63p. 1989. 9.00 (92-5-102776-5, F7765, Pub. by FAO IT) Bernan Associates.

***Utilization of Tropical Foods: Tropical Beans.** 92p. 1989. 9.00 (92-5-102777-3, F7773, Pub. by FAO IT) Bernan Associates.

***Utilization of Tropical Foods: Tropical Oil-Seeds.** 97p. 1989. 9.00 (92-5-102800-1, F8001, Pub. by FAO IT) Bernan Associates.

Utilization of Waste Materials in Civil Engineering Construction: Proceedings of Sessions Sponsored by the Materials Engineering Division of the American Society of Civil Engineers in Conjunction with the ASCE National Convention, New York, September 13-17, 1992. Ed. by Hilary I. Inyang & Kenneth L. Bergeson. LC 92-28866. 360p. 1992. 36.00 (0-87262-907-4) Am Soc Civil Eng.

Utilization Review Coordinator. Jack Rudman. (Career Examination Ser.: C-3262). 1994. pap. 27.95 (0-8373-3262-1) Nat Learn.

Utilizing Community Resources: An Overview of Human Services. Ed. by William Crimando & T. F. Riggar. 370p. 1995. pap. 32.95 (1-57444-020-9) St Lucie Pr.

Utilizing Consultants Successfully: A Guide for Management in Business, Government, the Arts & Professions. Herman R. Holtz. LC 85-9526. (Illus.). xiv, 221p. 1985. text ed. 55.00 (0-89930-098-7, HMG/, Quorum Bks) Greenwood.

Utilizing Education & Human Resource Sector Analyses. F. Kemmerer. (Fundamentals of Educational Planning Ser.: No. 47). 97p. 1994. pap. 11.00 (92-803-1151-4, U5111, Pub. by UNESCO-Bangkok TH) Bernan Associates.

Utilizing Multimedia Tool Book 3.0. Hall. (Computer Applications Ser.). 1996. pap. 39.95 (0-7895-0031-0) Course Tech.

Utilizing New Information Technology in Teaching of International Business: A Guide for Instructors. Ed. by Fahri Karakaya. LC 93-27148. (Journal of Teaching in International Business: Vol. 4, Nos. 3-4). (Illus.). 156p. 1993. lib. bdg. 29.95 (1-56024-416-X) Haworth Pr.

Utilizing Outward Influence. Jin Jiang & Zhao Zheng. Ed. by Craig R. Hutchinson. Tr. by Sidney W. Yuan from CHI. (Illus.). 140p. (Orig.). 1995. pap. text ed. 14.95 (0-9641847-6-1) Yutopian Ent.

Utilizing Scientific Information in Environmental Quality Planning: Proceedings of the Symposium Held in Las Vegas, Nevada, Sept. 26-27, 1979. Ed. by William J. Greeney. LC 81-68086. (American Water Resources Association Technical Publication Ser.: No. TPS81-2). (Illus.). 216p. reprint ed. pap. 61.60 (0-317-09806-3, 2022208) Bks Demand.

Utilizing Switch Interfaces with Children Who Are Severely Physically Challenged. Carl Goosens & Sharon S. Crain. LC 91-35836. 326p. 1992. pap. text ed. 49.00 (0-89079-516-9, 2075) PRO-ED.

Utilizing Task Teams for Profit Improvement. Ronald F. Norris. LC 93-46223. 46p. 1994. 7.95 (0-87576-179-8) Pilot Bks.

Utilizing the Strategic Marketing Organization: The Modernization of the Marketing Mindset. Joseph P. Stanco. LC 95-6819. (Illus.). 294p. (C). 1995. lib. bdg. 29.95 (1-56024-912-9) Haworth Pr.

***Utmost Savagery.** Joseph H. Alexander. 1997. mass mkt. 5.99 (0-8041-1559-1) Ivy Books.

Utmost Savagery: The Three Days of Tarawa. Joseph H. Alexander. (Illus.). 304p. (C). 1995. pap. text ed. 50.00 (0-7881-2537-0) DIANE Pub.

Utmost Savagery: The Three Days of Tarawa. Joseph H. Alexander. LC 95-15534. (Illus.). 328p. 1995. 31.95 (1-55750-031-2) Naval Inst Pr.

Utopia. Isaac Asimov & Roger M. Allen. (Caliban Ser.: No. 3). 320p. (Orig.). 1993. pap. 9.95 (0-441-09079-6) Ace Bks.

***Utopia.** Isaac Asimov & Roger M. Allen. (Caliban Ser.: No. 3). 320p. (Orig.). 1996. pap. 13.00 (0-614-17312-4) Ace Bks.

Utopia. Thomas Moore. Tr. by Paul Turner. (Classics Ser.). 160p. 1965. pap. 6.95 (0-14-044165-4, Penguin Classics) Viking Penguin.

Utopia. Thomas More. Date not set. lib. bdg. 18.95 (0-8488-0836-3) Amereon Ltd.

Utopia. Thomas More. Ed. by George M. Logan & Robert M. Adams. (Cambridge Texts in the History of Political Thought Ser.). 200p. (C). 1989. text ed. 29.95 (0-521-34573-1); pap. text ed. 8.95 (0-521-34797-1) Cambridge U Pr.

Utopia. Thomas More. 1992. 15.00 (0-679-41076-7) McKay.

Utopia. Thomas More. Ed. & Tr. by H. V. Ogden. (Crofts Classics Ser.). 96p. 1949. pap. write for info. (0-88295-062-2) Harlan Davidson.

Utopia. Thomas More. Tr. by Peter K. Marshall. mass mkt. 4.99 (0-671-72653-6, WSP) PB.

Utopia. Thomas More. Ed. by Edward Surtz. (Selected Works of St. Thomas More: No. 2). (Illus.). (C). 1964. 7.95 (0-300-00238-6, Y119) Yale U Pr.

Utopia. Thomas More. Ed. by David H. Sacks. 208p. 1995. pap. text ed. 7.50 (0-312-10145-7) St Martin.

Utopia. large type ed. Thomas More. 206p. 1996. text ed. 21.95 (1-56000-545-9) Transaction Pubs.

Utopia. 2nd ed. Thomas More. Tr. by John Sheehan & John Donnelly. 190p. 1984. reprint ed. pap. 10.00 (0-87462-448-7) Marquette.

Utopia. 2nd ed. Thomas More. Ed. & Tr. by Robert M. Adams. (Critical Editions Ser.). (C). 1991. pap. text ed. 7.95 (0-393-96145-1) Norton.

Utopia. Thomas More. Tr. by P. Marshall. 150p. 1990. reprint ed. lib. bdg. 18.95 (0-89966-706-6) Buccaneer Bks.

***Utopia.** Thomas H. More. LC 97-25114. 224p. 1997. reprint ed. pap. text ed. 2.00 (0-486-29583-4, 706420Q) Dover.

Utopia: And Other Essential Writings. Thomas More. Ed. by James Greene. 304p. 1984. mass mkt. 5.95 (0-452-00920-0, Mer) NAL-Dutton.

Utopia: And Other Writings. Thomas More. Ed. by James Greene & John P. Dolan. 304p. 1984. mass mkt. 4.95 (0-452-00687-2, Mer) NAL-Dutton.

Utopia: Dokumente der Wirklichkeit. Ed. by Bruno Adler. (Bauhaus Ser.). 1990. reprint ed. pap. 110.00 (3-601-00284-1) Periodicals Srv.

Utopia: Latin Text & English Translation. Thomas More. Ed. by George M. Logan et al. LC 93-42534. 272p. (C). 1995. text ed. 80.00 (0-521-40318-9) Cambridge U Pr.

Utopia: Nowhere: Now Here. Solange Hertz. 208p. 1993. pap. 12.50 (1-883511-03-8) Veritas Pr CA.

Utopia: The Psychology of a Cultural Fantasy. David Bleich. LC 84-2537. (Studies in Speculative Fiction: No. 5). 160p. reprint ed. pap. 45.60 (0-8357-1574-4, 2070530) Bks Demand.

Utopia see **Famous Utopias of the Renaissance**

Utopia - Fact or Fiction? Lorainne G. Stobbart. (Illus.). 160p. 1992. 33.00 (0-7509-0077-6, Pub. by Sutton Pubng UK) Bks Intl VA.

Utopia Achieved: A Novel of the Future. Herman H. Brinsmade. LC 74-154431. (Utopian Literature Ser.). 1975. reprint ed. 24.95 (0-405-03514-4) Ayer.

Utopia & a Dialogue of Comford Against Tribulation. Thomas More. 440p. 1994. pap. 5.95 (0-460-87431-4, Everyman's Classic Lib) C E Tuttle.

Utopia & Counterutopia in the "Quixote" Jose A. Maravall. Tr. by Robert W. Felkel from SPA. LC 90-20768. 256p. 1991. text ed. 29.95 (0-8143-2294-8) Wayne St U Pr.

Utopia & Dissent: Art, Poetry, & Politics in California. Richard Candida-Smith. (Illus.). 560p. 1996. pap. 19.95 (0-520-20699-1) U CA Pr.

Utopia & Dissent: Art, Poetry, & Politics in California. Richard C. Smith. (Illus.). 560p. 1995. 35.00 (0-520-08517-5) U CA Pr.

Utopia & History in Mexico: The First Chronicles of Mexican Civilization, 1520-1569. Georges Baudot. Tr. by Bernard R. Ortiz De Montellano & Thelma Ortiz De Montellano. 730p. 1995. 49.95 (0-87081-401-X) Univ Pr Colo.

Utopia & Reform in the Enlightenment. Franco Venturi. LC 71-123676. 166p. reprint ed. pap. 47.40 (0-317-27093-1, 2024554) Bks Demand.

Utopia & Revolution: On the Origins of a Metaphor or Some Illustrations of Political Temperament & Intellectual Climate & How Ideas, Ideals & Ideologies Have Been Historically Related. Melvin J. Lasky. LC 75-27893. xiv, 740p. 1985. pap. text ed. 36.00 (0-226-46911-5) U Ch Pr.

Utopia & Utopian Literature Notes. Harold M. Priest. 64p. (Orig.). 1975. pap. text ed. 4.50 (0-8220-1318-5) Cliffs.

Utopia, Community Care & the Retreat from the Asylums. Dylan Tomlinson. 192p. 1991. 90.00 (0-335-09623-9, Open Univ Pr); pap. 34.00 (0-335-09622-0, Open Univ Pr) Taylor & Francis.

Utopia II: An Investigation into the Kingdom of God. John Schmidt. (Orig.). 1986. pap. 3.50 (0-89540-154-1, SB-154) Sun Pub.

Utopia in Chains: An American's Experience in Red Russia. Morris Gordin. 1976. lib. bdg. 59.95 (0-8490-2792-6) Gordon Pr.

Utopia in Upper Michigan. Olive M. Anderson. LC 81-84595. 1982. pap. 5.95 (0-918616-10-7) Northern Mich.

Utopia in Zion: The Israeli Experience with Worker Cooperatives. Raymond Russell. LC 94-19576. (SUNY Series in Israeli Studies). 330p. (C). 1995. text ed. 59.50 (0-7914-2443-X); pap. text ed. 19.95 (0-7914-2444-8) State U NY Pr.

Utopia, Incorporated: Manuscript Edition. Kurtz Gordon. 1964. pap. 13.00 (0-8222-1198-X) Dramatists Play.

Utopia Lost: The United Nations & World Order. Rosemary Righter. LC 94-33886. 421p. (C). 1995. 29.95 (0-87078-358-0) TCFP-PPP.

Utopia Lost: The United Nations & World Order. Rosemary Righter. LC 94-33886. 421p. (C). 1995. pap. 12.00 (0-87078-359-9) TCFP-PPP.

Utopia Now. James Carroll. 160p. 1977. pap. 1.95 (0-89826-001-9) Natl Paperback.

Utopia of Usurers, & Other Essays. Gilbert K. Chesterton. LC 67-26724. (Essay Index Reprint Ser.). 1977. 18.95 (0-8369-0299-8) Ayer.

Utopia, Paraiso e Historia Inscripciones del Mito en Garcia Marquez, Rulfo y Cortazar. Lida Aronne-Amestoy. LC 85-30723. (Purdue University Monographs in Romance Languages: Vol. 19). xi, 167p. (Orig.). 1986. pap. 41.00 (0-915027-68-2) Benjamins North Am.

Utopia Parkway: The Life & Work of Joseph Cornell. Deborah Solomon. LC 95-18258. (Illus.). 426p. 1997. 30.00 (0-374-18012-1) FS&G.

Utopia Post Utopia. David Ross. (Illus.). 1988. 12.95 (0-685-26094-1) ICA Inc.

Utopia, the Perennial Heresy. rev. ed. Thomas Molnar. 260p. (C). 1990. reprint ed. text ed. 43.00 (0-8191-7667-2); reprint ed. pap. text ed. 24.00 (0-8191-7668-0) U Pr of Amer.

Utopia TV Store. Maxine Chernoff. LC 79-14606. 1979. pap. 3.00 (0-916328-13-9) Yellow Pr.

Utopia Unarmed: The Latin American Left after the Cold War. Jorge G. Castaneda. 1994. pap. 15.00 (0-679-75141-6, Vin) Random.

Utopia Undone: The Fall of Uruguay in the Novels of Carlos Martinez Moreno. Kenton V. Stone. LC 93-36324. (C). 1994. 35.00 (0-8387-5193-8) Bucknell U Pr.

Utopia y el Teatro: La Obra Dramatica de Ramon Gomez de la Serna. Carmen H. Vecino. LC 95-68170. 279p. (SPA.). 1995. 50.00 (0-89295-081-1) Society Sp & Sp-Am.

Utopian Alternative: Fourierism in Nineteenth-Century America. Carl Guarneri. LC 90-56085. (Illus.). 544p. 1994. pap. 17.95 (0-8014-8197-X) Cornell U Pr.

Utopian Alternative: Fourierism in Nineteenth-Century America. Carl J. Guarneri. LC 90-56085. (Illus.). 544p. 1991. 55.00 (0-8014-2467-4) Cornell U Pr.

Utopian & Science Fiction by Women: Worlds of Difference. Ed. by Jane L. Donawerth & Carol A. Kolmerten. LC 93-33840. (Utopianism & Communitarianism Ser.). 296p. 1994. text ed. 39.95 (0-8156-2619-3); pap. text ed. 16.95 (0-8156-2620-7) Syracuse U Pr.

Utopian Communism & Political Thought in Early Modern England. Timothy Kenyon. 272p. 1990. text ed. 42.50 (0-86187-772-1) St Martin.

Utopian Dream: Photography in Soviet Russia, 1918-1939. Max Kozloff. (Illus.). 56p. 1992. pap. 20.00 (1-882277-00-7) Schickler-Lafaille.

Utopian-Dystopian Literature: A Bibliography of Literary Criticism. Paul G. Haschak. LC 93-30232. 379p. 1994. 52.50 (0-8108-2752-2) Scarecrow.

Utopian Episodes: Daily Life in Experimental Colonies Dedicated to Changing the World. Seymour R. Kesten. (Utopianism & Communitarianism Ser.). (Illus.). 296p. (C). 1993. text ed. 45.00 (0-8156-2593-6) Syracuse U Pr.

Utopian Episodes: Daily Life in Experimental Colonies Dedicated to Changing the World. Seymour R. Kesten. (Utopianism & Communitarianism Ser.). (C). 1996. pap. 16.95 (0-8156-0381-9, KEUEP) Syracuse U Pr.

Utopian Experiment in Kentucky: Integration & Social Equality at Berea, 1866-1904. Richard Sears. LC 96-2537. (Contributions in American History Ser.: No. 170). 228p. 1996. text ed. 59.95 (0-313-30040-2, Greenwood Pr) Greenwood.

Utopian Feminism: Women's Movements in Fin-de-Siecle Vienna. Harriet Anderson. LC 92-5739. (Illus.). 368p. (C). 1993. text ed. 40.00 (0-300-05736-9) Yale U Pr.

Utopian Flight from Unhappiness: Freud Against Marx on Social Progress. Martin G. Kalin. (Quality Paperback Ser.: No. 314). 231p. 1975. pap. 8.00 (0-8226-0314-4) Littlefield.

Utopian Function of Art & Literature: Selected Essays. Ernst Bloch. Tr. by Jack D. Zipes & Frank Mecklenburg from GER. (Studies on Contemporary German Social Thought). 360p. 1989. pap. 17.50 (0-262-52139-3) MIT Pr.

Utopian Imagination & Eighteenth-Century Fiction. Christine Rees. LC 95-13096. (Studies in Eighteenth & Nineteenth-Century Literature Ser.). 288p. (C). 1995. text ed. 49.95 (0-582-06735-9); pap. text ed. 23.50 (0-582-06736-7) Longman.

Utopian Literature, 41 Bks. Ed. by Arthur O. Lewis. 1971. Set. 932.50 (0-405-03510-1) Ayer.

Utopian Literature: A Selection. James Weldon Johnson. 1968. pap. text ed. write for info. (0-07-553667-6) McGraw.

Utopian Mind & Other Papers: A Critical Study in Moral & Political Philosophy. Aurel Kolnai. Ed. by Francis Dunlop. LC 94-23954. 256p. (C). 1995. text ed. 85.00 (0-485-11232-9, Pub. by Athlone Pr UK) Humanities.

Utopian Moment in Contemporary American Poetry. rev. ed. Norman Finkelstein. LC 91-47176. 184p. 1993. 32.50 (0-8387-5247-0) Bucknell U Pr.

Utopian Movement. Daniel W. Hollis. Date not set. lib. bdg. 57.00 (0-87436-882-0) ABC-CLIO.

Utopian Novel in America, Eighteen Sixty-Five to Nineteen Hundred. Robert L. Shurter. LC 72-2944. reprint ed. 47.50 (0-404-10710-9) AMS Pr.

Utopian Novel in America, 1886-1896: The Politics of Form. Jean Pfaelzer. LC 84-40094. 223p. (C). 1994. reprint ed. pap. 14.95 (0-8229-5413-3) U of Pittsburgh Pr.

Utopian Studies, 2 bks., Set, Nos. III & IV. Ed. by Michael S. Cummings & Nicholas D. Smith. 242p. (C). 1990. lib. bdg. 49.50 (0-8191-7841-1) U Pr of Amer.

Utopian Tales. Jack D. Zipes. 1990. pap. 13.95 (0-7486-6094-1, Pub. by Edinburgh U Pr UK) Col U Pr.

Utopian Thought in the Western World. Frank E. Manuel & Fritzie P. Manuel. LC 79-12382. 902p. 1979. 50.00 (0-674-93185-8) Belknap Pr.

Utopian Thought in the Western World. Frank E. Manuel & Fritzie P. Manuel. LC 79-12382. 902p. 1982. pap. 23.50 (0-674-93186-6) Belknap Pr.

Utopian Thought of St. Thomas More & Its Development in Literature. Mardelle L. Fortier & Robert F. Fortier. LC 92-27794. 128p. 1992. text ed. 59.95 (0-7734-9611-4) E Mellen.

Utopian Vision: Seven Essays on the Quincentennial of Sir Thomas More. Ed. by Edward D. Sullivan. LC 82-50755. (Chataqua Ser.: No. 1). 392p. (Orig.). 1983. 37.50 (0-916304-51-5); pap. 18.75 (0-916304-52-3) SDSU Press.

Utopian Vision of Charles Fourier: Selected Texts on Work, Love & Passionate Attraction. Ed. by Jonathon F. Beecher & Richard Bienvenu. Tr. by Richard Bienvenu. LC 83-5897. 448p. 1982. text ed. 42.00 (0-8262-0426-0); pap. text ed. 17.50 (0-8262-0413-9) U of Mo Pr.

Utopian Vision of Moholy-Nagy. Joseph H. Caton. Ed. by Diane Kirkpatrick. LC 83-18182. (Studies in Photography: No. 5). 200p. reprint ed. 57.00 (0-8357-1528-0, 2070440) Bks Demand.

Utopian Visions. Time-Life Books Editors. (Mysteries of the Unknown Ser.). (Illus.). 144p. 1990. 14.95 (0-8094-6376-8); lib. bdg. write for info. (0-8094-6377-6) Time-Life.

Utopian Vistas: The Mabel Dodge Luhan House & the American Counterculture. Lois P. Rudnick. (Illus.). 224p. 1996. 35.00 (0-8263-1650-6) U of NM Pr.

***Utopianism.** Krishan Kumar. Ed. by Frank Parkin. (Concepts in the Social Sciences Ser.). 144p. 1991. 32.50 (0-335-15362-3, Open Univ Pr); pap. 9.99 (0-335-15361-5, Open Univ Pr) Taylor & Francis.

Utopianism. Krishan Kumar. (Concepts in Social Thought Ser.). 142p. (C). 1991. pap. text ed. 13.95 (0-8166-1975-1) U of Minn Pr.

Utopianism & Education: Robert Owen & the Owenites. Ed. by John F. Harrison. LC 68-54675. (Classics in Education Ser.: No. 37). 268p. (Orig.). 1968. reprint ed. pap. 76.40 (0-7837-9183-6, 2049882) Bks Demand.

Utopianism & Marxism. Vincent Geoghegan. 176p. 1988. text ed. 39.50 (0-416-08062-6); pap. text ed. 11.95 (0-416-08072-3) Routledge Chapman & Hall.

***Utopianism & Radicalism in a Reforming America, 1888-1918.** Francis R. Shor. LC 97-9380. (Contributions in American History: Vol. 178). 1997. text ed. write for info. (0-313-30379-7, Greenwood Pr) Greenwood.

Utopianism & the Emergence of the Colonial Legal Profession: New York, 1664-1710. John R. Aiken. (Outstanding Studies in Early American History). 305p. 1989. reprint ed. 20.00 (0-8240-6170-5) Garland.

Utopias: Schemes of Social Improvement since Sir Thomas More. Moritz Kaufman. 1972. 59.95 (0-8490-1253-8) Gordon Pr.

Utopias & the Millennium. Krishan Kumar et al. 224p. 1993. 45.00 (0-948462-45-0, Pub. by Reaktion Bks UK); pap. 24.50 (0-948462-44-2, Pub. by Reaktion Bks UK) Consort Bk Sales.

Utopias, Dolphins, & Computers: Some Problems in Philosophical Plumbing. Mary Midgley. 192p. 1996. 22.95 (0-415-13377-7) Routledge.

Utopias for a Dying World: Contemporary German Science Fiction's Pleas for a New Ecological Awareness. Amy Stapleton. LC 92-18696. (German Life & Civilization Ser.: Vol. 13). 158p. (C). 1993. text ed. 37.95 (0-8204-1922-2) P Lang Pubng.

Utopias in Conflict: Religion & Nationalism in Modern India. Ainslie T. Embree. 125p. 1990. 22.50 (0-520-06866-1) U CA Pr.

Utopias of the British Enlightenment. Ed. by Gregory Claeys. (Texts in the History of Political Thought Ser.). 356p. (C). 1994. text ed. 59.95 (0-521-43084-4); pap. text ed. 19.95 (0-521-45590-1) Cambridge U Pr.

Utopias on Puget Sound, 1885-1915. Charles P. Lewarne. (Illus.). 346p. 1995. pap. 18.95 (0-295-97444-3) U of Wash Pr.

Utopie. Michael Stott. (Learning Resources Ser.). (Illus.). 120p. 1995. pap. 15.95 (1-869890-57-4, Pub. by Hawthorn Press UK) Anthroposophic.

Utopie Hoffnumg bei Luise Rinser: Eine Soziopsychologische Studie. Gundrun Gill. LC 90-35885. (American University Studies: Germanic Languages & Literature: Ser. I, Vol. 92). 290p. (C). 1991. text ed. 39.95 (0-8204-1366-6) P Lang Pubng.

U V

***Utopische Inseln: Beitrage Zu Ihrer Geschichte und Theorie.** Horst A. Glaser. (Illus.). 241p. (GER.). 1996. 48.95 (*3-631-48965-X*) P Lang Pubng.

Utos Ng Hari at Iba Pang Kuwento. Jun C. Reyes. (Illus.). 130p. (TAG.). 1981. pap. 10.75 (*971-10-0221-3*, Pub. by New Day Pub PH) Cellar.

***Utrecht Psalter in Medieval Art: Picturing the Psalms of David.** Koert Van der Horst et al. (Illus.). 271p. 1996. 115.00 (*1-872501-69-9*, Pub. by Harvey Miller UK) Gordon & Breach.

Utrillo. Gabriel-Joseph Gros. (Illus.). 131p. (FRE.). 1947. lib. bdg. 17.95 (*0-8288-3986-7*) Fr & Eur.

Utrillo: Paris. R. Charmet. (Rhythem & Color One Ser.). 1970. 9.95 (*0-8288-9510-4*) Fr & Eur.

Utrillo's Mother. Sarah Baylis. (Fiction Ser.). 246p. 1989. 18.95 (*0-8135-1431-2*) Rutgers U Pr.

Utrpenie a Prenasledovanie. 2nd ed. Vladimir Uhri. 72p. (SLO.). 1995. pap. 3.50 (*1-56983-038-X*) New Creat WI.

Uttar Pradesh Agrarian Change & Electoral Politics. Sudha Pai. (Illus.). 183p. 1993. 18.00 (*81-85402-21-3*, Pub. by Shipra Pubns II) Nataraj Bks.

Uttar Pradesh Agricultural Credit Act, 1973. B. C. Shukla. (C). 1988. 60.00 (*0-685-44303-5*) St Mut.

Uttar Pradesh Bhoomi Prabandhak Samiti Niyam Sangraph (U.P. Gaon Samaj Manual in Hindi) B. N. Upadhyaya. 1980. 50.00 (*0-317-57747-6*) St Mut.

Uttar Pradesh Bhoomi Vidhi (U.P. Land Laws in Hindi) R. P. Singh. 350p. 1974. 50.00 (*0-317-57689-5*) St Mut.

Uttar Pradesh Dookan aur Vanijya Adhishthan Adhiniyam, 1962: (U. P. Shops & Commercial Establishments Act in English) 3rd ed. K. D. Srivastava. (C). 1984. 55.00 (*0-685-39557-X*) St Mut.

Uttar Pradesh Dookan aur Vanijya Adhishthan Adhiniyam, 1962: U.P. Shops & Commercial Establishments Act in English. 3rd ed. K. D. Srivastava. (C). 1984. 25.00 (*0-685-38614-7*) St Mut.

Uttar Pradesh Dookan aur Vanijya Adhisthan Adhiniyam, 1962 (U.P Shop & Commercial Extablishments Act in English) K. D. Srivastava. 410p. 1984. 150.00 (*0-317-57726-3*) St Mut.

Uttar Pradesh in Statistics. Kripa Shankar. 1986. 24.00 (*0-317-56193-6*, Pub. by Ashish II) S Asia.

Uttar Pradesh Industrial Disputes. K. D. Srivastava. (C). 1987. 75.00 (*0-685-38613-9*) St Mut.

Uttar Pradesh Industrial Disputes Act, 1947. Eastern Book Company Staff. 1987. 60.00 (*0-317-57727-1*) St Mut.

Uttar Pradesh Industrial Disputes Act, 1947. K. D. Srivastava. (C). 1991. 175.00 (*0-89771-785-6*, Pub. by Eastern Book II) St Mut.

Uttar Pradesh Industrial Disputes Act, 1947. 4th ed. K. D. Srivastava. (C). 1987. 150.00 (*0-685-39645-2*) St Mut.

Uttar Pradesh Land Revenue Act, 1901. 7th rev. ed. H. Hasain. (C). 1991. 130.00 (*0-685-39639-8*) St Mut.

Uttar Pradesh Local Acts. S. M. Husain. (C). 1991. text ed. 120.00 (*0-89771-480-6*) St Mut.

Uttar Pradesh Local Acts, 13 vols. 5th rev. ed. Ed. by S. M. Husain. (C). 1981. Set. 515.00 (*0-685-74317-9*) St Mut.

Uttar Pradesh (Nirmanya-Karya Viniyman) Adhiniyam, 1958 & Uttar Pradesh Nagar Yojna aur Vikas Adhiniyam, 1973. Uma Shanakar. 386p. 1983. 120.00 (*0-317-57739-5*) St Mut.

Uttar Pradesh (Nirmanya-Karya Viniyman) Adhiniyam, 1958 & Uttar Pradesh Habar Yojna aur Vikas Adhiniyam, 1973 with Rules, Regulations, Case-Law & Notifications (U. P. Regulation of Building Operations Act, 1958 & U. P. Urban Planning & Development Act, 1973) 2nd ed. Ed. by Uma Shanker. (HIN.). (C). 1991. text ed. 200.00 (*0-89771-517-9*) St Mut.

Uttar Pradesh Regulation of Building Operations Act, 1958: And U.P. Urban Planning & Development Act, 1973. Ed. by Uma Shankar. (C). 1990. 113.00 (*0-685-38611-2*) St Mut.

Uttar Pradesh Sahkari Samiti Adhiniyam, 1965: (Uttar Pradesh Co-Operative Societies Act, 1965 in Hindi) 4th ed. Ed. by Mahavir Singh. (HIN.). (C). 1991. 95.00 (*0-685-39783-1*) St Mut.

Uttar Pradesh Sahkari Samiti Adhinyam, 1965 (Uttar Pradesh Co-operative Societies Act, 1965 in Hindi) Mahavir Singh. 1980. 240.00 (*0-317-57684-4*) St Mut.

Uttara Kalamrita. Kalidasa. Tr. & Illus. by P. S. Sastri. (C). 1994. 16.00 (*0-8364-2902-8*, Pub. by Ranjan Pubs II) S Asia.

Uttara Tantra: A Treatise on Buddha Nature. Rinpoche Khenchen Thrangu. (C). 1995. 15.00 (*81-7030-401-6*, Pub. by Sri Satguru Pubns II) S Asia.

Uttarakhand: Land & People. S. S. Negi. 149p. 1995. pap. 100.00 (*81-85880-73-5*, Pub. by Print Hse II) St Mut.

Uttaratantra of Maitreya. H. S. Prasad. (Bibliotheca Indo-Buddhica Ser.: No. 79). 436p. (C). 1991. text ed. 30.00 (*81-7030-263-3*) S Asia.

Uttaratantra, or Ratnagotravibhaga: Sublime Science of the Great Vehicle to Salvation. Aryasanga Maitreya. Tr. by E. Obermiller from TIB. 225p. 1984. reprint ed. lib. bdg. 27.50 (*0-88181-001-0*) Canon Pubns.

Utter. limited ed. John Byrum & Arleen Hartman. 60p. 1995. 18.00 (*0-937013-63-3*) Potes Poets.

Utter Antiquity: Perceptions of Prehistory in Renaissance England. Arthur B. Ferguson. LC 92-12470. (Monographs in Medieval & Renaissance Studies). 176p. 1992. text ed. 26.95 (*0-8223-1275-1*) Duke.

Utter Disaster on the Oregon Trail: The Utter & Van Ornum Massacres of 1860. 2nd ed. Donald H. Shannon. LC 93-83498. (Snake Country Ser.: Vol. II). 236p. 1993. pap. text ed. 16.95 (*0-9635828-2-8*) Snake Cntry.

Utterance Particles in Cantonese Conversation. Kang K. Luke. LC 90-31714. (Pragmatics & Beyond Ser.: Vol. 9). xvi, 329p. 1990. 76.00 (*1-55619-275-4*) Benjamins North Am.

Utterance Structure: Developing Grammars Again. Wolfgang Klein & Clive Perdue. LC 92-12958. (Studies in Bilingualism: No. 5). xvi, 354p. 1992. 74.00 (*1-55619-349-1*) Benjamins North Am.

***Utterances: Malfuzat.** Shaykh Jilani. 160p. 1996. pap. 16.00 (*0-614-21376-2*, 1444) Kazi Pubns.

Utterback: History & Genealogy of the Utterback Family in America, 1622-1937. William I. Utterback. (Illus.). 470p. 1995. reprint ed. pap. 72.00 (*0-8328-4857-3*); reprint ed. lib. bdg. 82.00 (*0-8328-4856-5*) Higginson Bk Co.

Utterly Other Discourse: The Texts of Christine Brooke-Rose. Ellen G. Friedman & Richard Martin. LC 94-36950. 235p. 1995. 29.95 (*1-56478-079-1*) Dalkey Arch.

Utterly Yours, Booker Jones. Betsy Duffey. (Illus.). 128p. (YA). (gr. 5 up). 1995. pap. 13.99 (*0-670-86007-7*) Viking Child Bks.

***Utterly Yours Booker Jones.** Betsy Duffey. 1997. pap. 3.99 (*0-14-037496-5*) Viking Penguin.

Uttermost Farthing. R. Austin Freeman. 1974. 8.50 (*0-685-41690-9*) Bookfinger.

Uttermost Mark: The Dramatic Criticism of Gerard Manley Hopkins, His Dramatic Works & the Performance Thereof. Ernest Ferlita. 246p. (Orig.). (C). 1990. lib. bdg. 45.00 (*0-8191-7706-7*) U Pr of Amer.

Uttermost Part. rev. ed. Eunice V. Pike. LC 91-75053. 274p. 1991. fiche 12.00 (*0-88312-714-8*) Summer Instit Ling.

Uttermost Part. 2nd rev. ed. Eunice V. Pike. LC 91-75053. 274p. 1991. pap. 8.00 (*0-88312-810-1*) Summer Instit Ling.

***Uttermost Part of the Earth.** E. Lucas Bridges. pap. 13.95 (*0-486-25751-7*) Dover.

Utuado Ceremonial Park. Ricardo E. Alegria. (Puerto Rico Ser.). 1979. lib. bdg. 59.95 (*0-8490-3013-7*) Gordon Pr.

Utwory Poetyckie: Poems. Alexander M. Schenker. 1976. 25.00 (*0-930042-22-0*) Mich Slavic Pubns.

Utz. large type ed. Bruce Chatwin. 130p. 1990. 17.95 (*1-85089-328-4*, Pub. by ISIS UK) Transaction Pubs.

Utz Site: An Oneota Village in Central Missouri. Robert T. Bray. Ed. by Jeffrey K. Yelton. (Missouri Archaeologist Ser.: Vol. 52). (Illus.). 146p. (Orig.). 1993. pap. 7.50 (*0-943414-75-X*) MO Arch Soc.

UV-A: Biological Effects of Ultraviolet Radiation with Emphasis on Human Responses to Longwave Ultraviolet. John A. Parrish et al. LC 78-14968. 272p. reprint ed. pap. 77.60 (*0-317-26187-8*, 2052076) Bks Demand.

UV & EB Curing Formulation for Printing Inks, Coatings & Paints. FMJ Intl. Publ. Ltd. Staff. 239p. (C). 1989. 300.00 (*0-685-36804-1*, Pub. by Fuel Metallurgical Jrnl UK) St Mut.

UV & X-Ray Spectroscopy of Laboratory & Astrophysical Plasmas. Ed. by Eric H. Silver & Steven M. Kahn. (Illus.). 627p. (C). 1994. text ed. 89.95 (*0-521-43470-X*) Cambridge U Pr.

***UV-B & Biosphere.** Ed. by J. Rozema et al. (Advances in Vegetation Science Ser.: No. 17). 230p. 1997. lib. bdg. 208.00 (*0-7923-4422-7*) Kluwer Ac.

UV-B Radiation: Effects on Humans, Animals, Plants, Microorganisms, & Materials. Ed. by Manfred Tevini. 256p. 1993. 94.95 (*0-87371-911-5*, L911) Lewis Pubs.

***UV-B Radiation & Immunosuppression.** Frances P. Noonan. (Medical Intelligence Unit Ser.). 250p. 89.95 (*0-412-11611-1*) Chapman & Hall.

UV Curing: Science & Technology. Ed. by S. Peter Pappas. LC 78-56293. (Illus.). 1978. per. 95.00 (*0-936840-04-8*) Tech Marketing.

UV Curing in Screen Printing for Printed Circuits & the Graphic Arts. S. Wentink & S. Koch. LC 80-80985. 1981. 92.00 (*0-936840-00-5*) Tech Marketing.

UV Curing, Vol. 2: Science & Technology. Ed. by S. Peter Pappas. 360p. 1985. text ed. 99.00 (*0-936840-08-0*) Tech Marketing.

UV Lasers: Effects & Applications in Materials Science. W. W. Duley. (Illus.). 320p. (C). 1996. text ed. 95.00 (*0-521-46498-6*) Cambridge U Pr.

***UV-VIS Atlas of Organic Compounds.** 2nd ed. Heinz-Helmut Perkampus. (Illus.). 1532p. 1992. 500.00 (*3-527-28510-5*, VCH) Wiley.

UV-VIS Spectroscopy & Its Applications. Heinz-Helmut Perkampus. Tr. by H. Charlotte Grinter & T. L. Threlfall. LC 92-20077. (Illus.). ix, 240p. 1994. 139.95 (*0-387-55421-1*) Spr-Verlag.

UV/EB Curing Primer: Inks, Coatings & Adhesives. 4th ed. Camille J. Kallendorf et al. 87p. 1995. 35.00 (*1-878664-13-1*) RadTech Intl North Amer.

***UV/EB Curing Primer: Inks, Coatings & Adhesives.** 5th ed. Camille Rechel et al. 90p. 1997. 35.00 (*1-878664-17-4*) RadTech Intl North Amer.

Uveitis: A Clinical Approach to Diagnosis & Management. 2nd ed. Ronald E. Smith & Robert A. Nozik. (Illus.). 288p. 1988. 87.00 (*0-683-07769-4*) Williams & Wilkins.

Uveitis: A Clinical Manual for Ocular Inflammation. E. Mitchel Opremack. LC 94-13826. (Illus.). 278p. 1994. 142.00 (*0-387-94247-5*) Spr-Verlag.

Uveitis: Fundamentals & Clinical Practice. 2nd ed. Robert B. Nussenblatt et al. 384p. (C). (gr. 13). 1995. text ed. 115.00 (*0-8151-6446-7*) Mosby Yr Bk.

Uveitis Vol. 2: Therapy. Manfred Zeirhut. 176p. 1996. pap. text ed. 50.00 (*0-7506-9815-2*) Buttrwrth-Heinemann.

Uveitis Scoring System. R. B. Nussenblatt et al. 20p. 1991. 20.00 (*0-387-54957-9*) Spr-Verlag.

Uveitus Vol.1: Differential Diagnosis, Vol. 1. Manfred Zierhut. 190p. 1995. pap. text ed. 42.50 (*0-7506-9589-7*) Buttrwrth-Heinemann.

Uwe Johnson Zwischen Vormoderne und Postmoderne: Internationales Uwe-Johnson-Symposium 22.-24.9.1994. Ed. by Carsten Gansel & Nicolai Riedel. xiv, 347p. (GER.). (C). 1995. lib. bdg. 98.50 (*3-11-014671-1*) De Gruyter.

***Uwe Ommer's Black Ladies, Vol. 2.** Uwe Ommer. 1995. 29.95 (*3-8228-8674-2*) Taschen Amer.

Uwharrie. Eugene E. Pfaff, Jr. & Michael Causey. 256p. 1993. 19.95 (*0-936389-30-3*) Tudor Pubs.

UXB: Poems & Translations. Patricia Dobler. Ed. by Peter Oresick & Anthony Petrosky. 64p. (C). 1991. pap. 10.00 (*0-9626023-3-7*); text ed. 20.00 (*0-9626023-2-9*) Mill Hunk Bks.

***Uxbridge 1950-1970: The Changing Town.** K. R. Pearce. (Illus.). 128p. 1997. 16.95 (*0-7509-1310-X*, Pub. by Sutton Pubng UK) Bks Intl VA.

***U*X*L Science Fact Finder.** Ed. by Phillis Engelbert. 672p. 1997. 79.95 (*0-7876-1727-X*) Gale.

Uxpanapa: Agricultural Development in the Mexican Tropics. Peter T. Ewell & Thomas T. Poleman. LC 80-12208. (Policy Studies). 220p. 1980. 68.00 (*0-08-025967-7*, Pergamon Pr) Elsevier.

UY Ranch: Reminiscences of a Montana Stockman's Wife - 1912-1921. Helen A. Howard. (Illus.). 160p. 1989. pap. 17.95 (*0-89745-123-6*) Sunflower U Pr.

Uyghur-English Dictionary. Henry G. Schwarz. (East Asian Research Aids & Translations Ser.: Vol. 3). (Illus.). xxiv, 1083p. (C). 1993. 120.00 (*0-914584-89-8*) WWUCEAS.

Uzailand. Craig Hiler. LC 90-72002. 145p. (Orig.). 1992. pap. 9.00 (*1-56002-083-0*, Univ Edtns) Aegina Pr.

Uzbek, Colloquial. Kurtulus Oztopcu. 64p. 1994. pap. text ed. 75.00 incl. audio (*0-88432-743-4*, AFUZ10) Audio-Forum.

Uzbek-English Dictionary. Natalie Waterson. 190p. (ENG & UZB.). 1980. 85.00 (*0-8288-1732-4*, M9428) Fr & Eur.

Uzbek-English Dictionary. Natalie Waterson. 210p. (ENG & UZB.). 1980. 60.00 (*0-19-713597-8*) OUP.

***Uzbek-English Dictionary.** rev. ed. Karl A. Krippes. 246p. (UZB.). 1996. text ed. 64.00 (*1-881265-45-5*) Dunwoody Pr.

Uzbek-English, English-Uzbek Concise Dictionary. Kamran Khakimov. (Concise Dictionaries Ser.). 329p. (Orig.). 1993. pap. 11.95 (*0-7818-0165-6*) Hippocrene Bks.

Uzbekistan. Ed. by Lerner Geography Department Staff. (Then & Now Ser.). (Illus.). 64p. (YA). (gr. 5 up). 1993. lib. bdg. 22.95 (*0-8225-2812-6*, Lerner Publctns) Lerner Group.

***Uzbekistan.** Calum MacLeod & Bradley Mayhew. 328p. 1997. pap. 19.95 (*0-8442-4852-5*) NTC Pub Grp.

Uzbekistan: An Agenda for Economic Reform. (Country Study Ser.). 342p. 1993. 19.95 (*0-8213-2673-2*, 12673) World Bank.

Uzbekistan: An Agenda for Economic Reform (Russian Edition) (Country Study Ser.). 360p. 1993. 21.95 (*0-8213-2717-8*, 12717) World Bank.

***Uzbekistan: Heir to the Silk Road.** Johannes Kalter & Margareta Pavaloi. LC 96-62027. (Illus.). 368p. 1997. 60.00 (*0-500-97451-9*) Thames Hudson.

Uzbekistan: IMF Economic Review. International Monetary Fund Staff. 44p. 1992. pap. 10.00 (*1-55775-264-8*) Intl Monetary.

Uzbekistan in the Twentiety Century: Political Development & the Evolution of Power. Roger D. Kangas. 304p. 1994. text ed. 49.95 (*0-312-09679-8*) St Martin.

Uzdravenie, 2 vols., Set. 2nd ed. Vladimir Uhri. 145p. (SLO.). 1996. pap. 6.50 (*1-56983-039-8*) New Creat WI.

Uzertoons "Kid & Parent" Cartoon Computer Guide, 2 vols., Vol. 1. Janice B. Weigle. Ed. by Charles W. Weigle et al. (Illus.). 94p. (Orig.). (J). (gr. 3 up). 1994. pap. text ed. 5.95 (*0-9640569-1-7*) Uzertoons Pubng.

Uzertoons "Kid, Parent & Teacher" Fun Computer Learning Guide. Ed. by Charles W. Weigle. (Illus.). 44p. (Orig.). (J). (gr. 3 up). 1994. teacher ed., pap. 15.95 (*0-685-71541-8*); student ed., pap. 5.95 (*0-685-71542-6*) Uzertoons Pubng.

Uzi & the Stone: Images of Gaza. Rhona Davies & Peter R. Johnson. (Illus.). 256p. (Orig.). 1991. pap. 19.95 (*1-55059-025-1*) Temeron Bks.

***Uzo Egonu: An African Artist in the West.** Olu Oguibe. 176p. 1995. 32.95 (*0-947753-08-7*, Pub. by Kala Pr UK) SPD-Small Pr Dist.

Uzsienio Lietuviu Svietimo Ir Pedagogines Minties Istorijos Metmenys: A Historical Outline of Lithuanian Educational Thought Outside of Lithuania. Kestutis Peckus & Jonas Rackauskas. LC 94-73757. (Illus.). 78p. (LIT.). 1995. pap. 5.00 (*0-929700-12-0*) Lith Res & Studies.

***U2.** (Photo Bks.). (Illus.). 1996. 11.95 (*1-870049-53-5*, OB 11017, Pub. by Oliver Bks UK) Music Sales.

U2. Bill Graham. (Complete Guides to the Music Of...Ser.). (Illus.). 118p. (Orig.). pap. 7.95 (*0-7119-4302-8*, OP 47736, Pub. by Omnibus Press UK) Omnibus NY.

U2. Mark Taylor. (CD Bks.). (Illus.). 120p. 1994. pap. 7.99 (*1-886894-18-3*, MBS Paperbk) Mus Bk Servs.

U2: Faraway. Fallon. 1994. pap. 151.60 (*0-316-27395-3*) Little.

U2: Faraway So Close. B. P. Fallon. 1994. pap. 18.95 (*0-316-27392-9*) Little.

U2: Joshua Tree with Notes & Tablature. 120p. 1987. per. 19.95 (*0-88188-769-2*, 00694411) H Leonard.

U2: Rattle & Hum. 1989. pap. 17.95 (*0-7935-0268-3*, 00490160) H Leonard.

***U2: The Road to Pop.** Alan Carter. 1997. pap. text ed. 14.95 (*0-571-19930-5*) Faber & Faber.

U2 - Achtung Baby: Achtung Baby. Ed. by Michael Lefferts. 96p. (Orig.). (C). 1997. pap. text ed. 26.95 (*0-7935-2071-1*, 00308174) H Leonard.

U2 - Joshua Tree: The Joshua Tree. Ed. by Michael Lefferts. 32p. (Orig.). (C). 1997. pap. text ed. 17.95 (*0-7935-1937-3*, 00308525) H Leonard.

U2 - The Rolling Stone Files: The Ultimate Compendium of Interviews, Articles, Facts & Opinions from the Files of "Rolling Stone" Rolling Stone Editors. 256p. 1994. pap. 12.95 (*0-7868-8001-5*) Hyperion.

U2 at the End of the World. Bill Flanagan. LC 94-42846. 544p. 1995. 22.95 (*0-385-31154-0*) Delacorte.

U2 at the End of the World. Bill Flanigan. 544p. 1996. pap. 13.95 (*0-385-31157-5*, Delta) Dell.

U2: Burning Desire: The Complete U2 Story. Sam Goodman. (Illus.). 224p. 1993. pap. 14.00 (*0-685-72584-7*, Pub. by Castle Communs UK) Viking Penguin.

V

V. Thomas Pynchon. 1994. reprint ed. lib. bdg. 39.95 (*1-56849-321-5*) Buccaneer Bks.

V. Thomas Pynchon. LC 85-45222. 496p. 1990. reprint ed. pap. 13.50 (*0-06-091308-8*, PL 1308, PL) HarpC.

V: A Novel. Thomas Pynchon. 492p. (C). 1991. reprint ed. lib. bdg. 35.00 (*0-8095-9031-X*) Borgo Pr.

V: Below the Threshold. Allen L. Wold. 256p. 1988. pap. 3.50 (*0-8125-5732-8*) Tor Bks.

V: Path to Conquest. Howard Weinstein. 288p. 1987. pap. 2.95 (*0-8125-5725-5*) Tor Bks.

V: The Oregon Invasion. Jayne Tannhill. 1988. pap. 3.50 (*0-8125-5729-8*) Tor Bks.

V: To Conquer the Throne. Timothy R. Sullivan. 1987. pap. 2.95 (*0-8125-5727-1*) Tor Bks.

V - STOL Design Concepts for the Custom Aircraft Builder. 2nd ed. Philip Terpstra. (Illus.). 134p. (C). 1992. pap. 23.00 (*0-9626287-0-0*) Spirit Pub HI.

V. A. Caused Me to Live a Sham These Past Four Decades. Paul Sperandeo. 200p. 1994. pap. write for info. (*0-9631249-5-1*) Morris Pubng.

V. A. Meien's Fish Culture in Rice Fields. Ed. by H. S. Forest & C. H. Fernando. 117p. 1993. 2.00 (*1-883641-00-4*) St U NY Geneseo.

V & A Indian Art Day Book. 1992. 14.99 (*1-85145-625-2*, Pavilion Bks) Viking Penguin.

V. & Other Poems. Tony Harrison. 1989. 14.95 (*0-374-28206-4*) FS&G.

V. & Other Poems. Tony Harrison. 96p. 1991. pap. 12.95 (*0-374-52273-1*, Noonday) FS&G.

V-Bombs & Weathermaps: Reminiscences of World War II. Brock McElheran. 199p. 1995. 26.95 (*0-7735-1330-2*, Pub. by McGill CN) U of Toronto Pr.

V. C. Andrews: A Critical Companion. E. D. Huntley. LC 95-38655. (Critical Companions to Popular Contemporary Writers Ser.). 168p. 1996. text ed. 29.95 (*0-313-29448-8*, Greenwood Pr) Greenwood.

***V. C. Andrews Omnibus Edition.** V. C. Andrews. 1997. 14.00 (*0-671-01688-1*, PB Trade Paper) PB.

V. C. Andrews Trivia & Quiz Book. Stephen J. Spignesi. 368p. (Orig.). 1994. pap. 3.99 (*0-451-17925-0*, Sig) NAL-Dutton.

V D I Steam Tables up to Eight Hundred Degrees Centigrade & 1000 at Kcal. at. 7th rev. ed. E. Schmidt. (Illus.). 1968. 51.95 (*0-387-04372-1*) Spr-Verlag.

V. D. Nabokov & the Russian Provisional Government, 1917. Vladimir Nabokov. Ed. by Virgil D. Medlin & Steven L. Parsons. LC 75-18177. 196p. reprint ed. pap. 55.90 (*0-8357-8363-4*, 2033823) Bks Demand.

V. D. Romans & Aliens. J. P. Balsdon. LC 79-14471. x, 310p. 1980. 39.95 (*0-8078-1383-4*) U of NC Pr.

V-Discs: A History & Discography. Richard S. Sears. LC 80-1022. (Discographies Ser.: No. 5). (Illus.). xciii, 1166p. 1980. text ed. 135.00 (*0-313-22207-X*, SHD/, Greenwood Pr) Greenwood.

V-Discs: First Supplement. Compiled by Richard S. Sears. LC 86-19529. (Discographies Ser.: No. 25). 300p. 1986. text ed. 105.00 (*0-313-25421-4*, SDN/, Greenwood Pr) Greenwood.

V-Eight. Dennis Teichman. (Illus.). 64p. 1989. pap. 6.00 (*0-9622474-0-5*) Past Tents Pr.

V-Eight Affair: An Illustrated History of the Pre-War Ford V-8. Ray Miller & Glenn Embree. LC 70-174898. (Ford Road Ser: Vol. 3). (Illus.). 303p. 1972. pap. 29.95 (*0-913056-02-2*) Evergreen Pr.

V. F. Calverton: Radical in the American Grain. Leonard Wilcox. (Critical Prospectives on the Past Ser.). 400p. (C). 1992. 54.95 (*0-87722-929-5*) Temple U Pr.

V-F Validation: The Feil Method. Naomi Feil. (Orig.). 1982. pap. write for info. (*1-878169-00-9*) E Feil Prodns.

V for Vanishing: An Alphabet of Endangered Animals. Patricia Mullins. LC 93-8181. (Illus.). 32p. (J). (ps-2). 1994. 15.00 (*0-06-023556-X*); lib. bdg. 14.89 (*0-06-023557-8*) HarpC Child Bks.

V for Vanishing: An Alphabet of Endangered Animals. Patricia Mullins. LC 93-8181. (Trophy Picture Bk.). (Illus.). 32p. (J). (ps-2). 1997. pap. 6.95 (*0-06-443471-0*, Trophy) HarpC Child Bks.

V for Vendetta. Alan Moore. Ed. by KC Carlson. (Illus.). 288p. 1990. pap. 14.95 (*0-930289-52-8*, Vertigo) DC Comics.

V for Vendetta. Alan Moore & David Lloyd. 288p. 1990. pap. 14.95 (*0-446-39190-5*) Warner Bks.

V for Victor. Mark Childress. 256p. 1990. mass mkt. 5.99 (*0-345-35427-3*) Ballantine.

V for Victory. Francine Pascal. (Sweet Valley High Ser.: No. 114). 208p. (YA). (gr. 7-12). 1995. 3.99 (*0-553-56632-6*) Bantam.

V for Victory: America's Home Front During World War II. Stan Cohen. LC 91-60428. (Illus.). 416p. 1991. pap. 29.95 (*0-929521-51-X*) Pictorial Hist.

V. G. Ramachandran's Law of Writs. 4th ed. C. K. Thakker. (C). 1990. 315.00 (*0-685-37466-1*) St Mut.

V. I. Lenin: An Annotated Bibliography of English-Language Sources to 1980. David R. Egan et al. LC 82-659. 516p. 1982. 42.50 (*0-8108-1526-5*) Scarecrow.

V Is for Vampire: The A-to-Z Guide to Everything Undead. David J. Skal. LC 95-15522. (Illus.). 304p. (Orig.). 1996. pap. 15.95 (*0-452-27173-8*, Plume) NAL-Dutton.

*__V Is for Victory.__ Mark Childress. 1997. pap. 12.00 (*0-345-42005-5*) Ballantine.

V Is for Victory: America Remembers World War II. Kathleen Krull. 128p. 1995. 24.00 (*0-679-86198-X*) Random.

V Is for Victory: The American Homefront During World War II. Sylvia Whitman. (People's History Ser.). (Illus.). 80p. (YA). (gr. 5 up). 1992. lib. bdg. 19.95 (*0-8225-1727-2*, Lerner Publctns) Lerner Group.

V. K. Dmitriev. D. M. Nuti. (Modern Revivals in Economics Ser.). 231p. 1992. 59.95 (*0-7512-0095-6*, Pub. by Gregg Pub UK) Ashgate Pub Co.

*__V. K. Krishna Menon.__ Janaki Ram. (Illus.). 192p. 1997. 17.95 (*0-19-564228-7*) OUP.

V. K. Krishna Menon: India & Kashmir Problem. S. R. Bakshi. (C). 1994. text ed. 50.00 (*81-7041-705-8*, Pub. by Anmol II) S Asia.

V. K. Wellington Koo's Foreign Policy: Some Selected Documents. V. K. Wellington. Ed. by Wuncz King. LC 75-32324. (Studies in Chinese History & Civilization). 141p. 1976. reprint ed. text ed. 55.00 (*0-313-27016-3*, U7016, Greenwood Pr) Greenwood.

V. L. Parrington: Through the Avenue of Art. H. Lark Hall. LC 93-9201. (Illus.). 416p. 1994. 39.00 (*0-87338-480-6*) Kent St U Pr.

V. M. Bekhterev's Collective Reflexology. Ed. by L. H. Strickland & E. Lockwood. 257p. 1993. lib. bdg. 75.00 (*1-56072-142-1*) Nova Sci Pubs.

*__V. M. I. Civil War Dictionary, Vol. 1.__ Victor L. Dupras. 633p. (Orig.). 1997. mass mkt. 5.99 (*1-55197-680-3*, Pub. by Comnwlth Pub CN) Partners Pubs Grp.

*__V. M. I. Civil War Dictionary, Vol. 2.__ Victor L. Pupras. 633p. (Orig.). 1997. mass mkt. 5.99 (*1-55197-682-X*, Pub. by Comnwlth Pub CN) Partners Pubs Grp.

V-Missiles of the Third Reich, the V-1 & V-2. Dieter Holsken. LC 83-61696. (Illus.). 356p. 1994. 49.95 (*0-914144-21-9*) Monogram Aviation.

V Moskve Vse Spokoino (All Is Calm in Moscow) Roman (A Novel) Dimitri Sesemann. Ed. by A. Jurovskii & V. Rybakov. LC 89-60955. 222p. (Orig.). (RUS.). (YA). (gr. 9-12). 1990. pap. 12.50 (*0-911971-47-5*) Effect Pub.

V. N. Soroka-Rosinsky (1882-1960), Soviet Teacher, in Fact & Fiction: The Double Exposure of Vikniksor. John Dunstan. LC 91-14083. (Slavic Studies: Vol. 2). 140p. 1991. lib. bdg. 69.95 (*0-7734-9779-X*) E Mellen.

V. O. C. A. B. Vocabulary for College & Beyond. Rhonda H. Atkinson & Debbie G. Longman. Ed. by Baxter. 294p. (C). 1990. pap. text ed. 31.00 (*0-314-56885-9*) West Pub.

V. O. Key, Jr. & the Study of American Politics. Walter D. Burnham et al. (Evron M. Kirkpatrick Monograph Ser.). xx, 57p. (Orig.). (C). 1988. pap. text ed. 2.00 (*0-915654-83-0*) Am Political.

V. O. Kliuchevskii, Historian of Russia. Robert F. Byrnes. LC 95-18202. 288p. 1995. 29.95 (*0-253-32940-X*) Ind U Pr.

V-One - V-Two: Hitler's Vengeance on London. David Johnson. LC 81-48451. (Illus.). 206p. 1982. pap. 10.95 (*0-8128-8527-9*, Scrbrough Hse) Madison Bks UPA.

V. S. Naipaul. Peter Hughes. (Contemporary Writers Ser.). 96p. (Orig.). 1988. pap. text ed. 9.95 (*0-415-00654-6*) Routledge.

V. S. Naipaul. Fawzia Mustafa. (Studies in African & Caribbean Literature: Vol. 4). 245p. (C). 1995. text ed. 59.95 (*0-521-40378-2*) Cambridge U Pr.

V. S. Naipaul. Fawzia Mustafa. (Studies in African & Caribbean Literature: Vol. 4). 245p. (C). 1995. pap. text ed. 18.95 (*0-521-48359-X*) Cambridge U Pr.

V. S. Naipaul: A Materialist Reading. Selwyn R. Cudjoe. LC 87-35768. 304p. (Orig.). (C). 1988. 35.00 (*0-87023-619-9*); pap. text ed. 17.95 (*0-87023-620-2*) U of Mass Pr.

V. S. Naipaul: A Selective Bibliography with Annotations, 1957-1987. Kelvin Jarvis. LC 89-10057. (Author Bibliographies Ser.: No. 83). 229p. 1989. 30.00 (*0-8108-2190-7*) Scarecrow.

V. S. Naipaul: A Study in Expatriate Sensibility. Sudha Rai. (Indian Writers Ser.: Vol. 19). 136p. 1982. 12.00 (*0-86578-143-5*) Ind-US Inc.

V. S. Naipaul: Displacement & Autobiography. Judith Levy. LC 94-37551. 176p. 1994. text ed. 30.00 (*0-8153-1468-X*, H1781) Garland.

V. S. Naipaul: The Voice of Exile. Chandra B. Joshi. 200p. (C). 1995. 27.00 (*81-207-1346-X*, Pub. by Sterling Plns Pvt II) S Asia.

V. S. Pritchett, Lasting Impressions: Essays 1961-1987. write for info. (*0-318-68253-2*) Random.

V Series Recommendations: Standards for Data Communications over the Telephone Network. 2nd ed. Ulysses D. Black. LC 94-39989. (Ulysses Black Series on Computer Communications). 1995. text ed. 45.00 (*0-07-005592-0*) McGraw.

V Teni Bol'Shogo Doma. Kirill Kostsinskii. Ed. by Gessen Elena. LC 87-22790. (Illus.). 135p. (RUS.). 1988. pap. 8.50 (*0-938920-91-X*) Hermitage.

V-Time: A New Way to Work. 76p. 1985. 10.00 (*0-940173-02-6*) New Ways Work.

V-Twin Thunder. Mike Arman & Carl McClanahan. (Illus.). 56p. (Orig.). 1984. pap. 11.00 (*0-933078-12-9*) M Arman.

V-Twin Tuner's Handbook. D. William Denish. 51p. 1994. spiral bd. 17.95 (*0-9640115-1-4*) Crystal Publns.

V2 - Dawn of the Rocket Age. Joachim Engelmann. LC 90-60472. (Illus.). 48p. 1990. pap. 9.95 (*0-88740-233-X*) Schiffer.

V. V. Vereshchagin: Artist at War. Vahan D. Barooshian. LC 92-32515. (Illus.). 216p. (C). 1993. lib. bdg. 39.95 (*0-8130-1178-7*) U Press Fla.

V Venke Iz Voska; Dirizhabl' Neizvestnogo Napravleniia. 2nd ed. Boris I. Poplavskii. Ed. by Simon Karlinsky. (Modern Russian Literature & Culture Studies & Texts: Vol. 9). (Illus.). 123p. (RUS.). 1981. pap. 7.50 (*0-933884-19-2*) Berkeley Slavic.

V Was for Victory: Politics & American Culture During World War II. John M. Blum. LC 77-3426. 372p. 1977. pap. 14.00 (*0-15-693628-3*, Harvest Bks) HarBrace.

V Zashchitu Marksizma: (Russian Original of "In Defence of Marxism") Leon Trotsky & J. P. Cannon. Tr. & Intro. by Felix Kreisel. LC 94-78935. (Illus.). 250p. (Orig.). (RUS.). 1994. pap. 15.00 (*1-883468-03-5*) Iskra Res.

V Zashchitu Pravoslavnoj Vjeri ot Sektantov. Michael Polsky. 1950. pap. 1.00 (*0-317-30261-2*) Holy Trinity.

V-12 Program. James G. Schneider. (Education for Victory in World War II Ser.). (Illus.). 544p. 1987. text ed. 29.95 (*0-317-57602-X*) HM.

V-2 Rockets. Paula Younkin. LC 94-18475. (J). 1994. pap. 5.95 (*0-614-09467-4*, Crstwood Hse) Silver Burdett Pr.

V 29 den' mesiatsa avgusta slovo Ioanna Zlatoustogo na useknovenie glavy see Sermon on the Decollation of St. John the Baptist, & on Herodias, & on Good & Evil Women

V-6 Performance. Pat Ganahl. (Illus.). 128p. 1982. 18.95 (*0-931472-13-X*) Motorbooks Intl.

Va de Cuento. R. Charran & B. Maharaj. (Illus.). 1977. pap. text ed. 10.40 (*0-582-76616-8*, 74839) Longman.

Va-Et-Vient see Comedies et Actes Divers

VA Foreclosure Packet. 243p. 1987. 17.50 (*0-685-30199-0*, 40,060) NCLS Inc.

VA Health Care: Albuquerque Medical Center Not Recovering Full Costs of Lithotripsy Services. (Illus.). 50p. (Orig.). (C). 1995. pap. text ed. 20.00 (*0-7881-2240-1*) DIANE Pub.

*__VA Health Care: Effects of Facility Realignment on Construction Needs Are Unknown.__ (Illus.). 43p. (Orig.). (C). 1996. pap. 25.00 (*0-7881-3229-6*) DIANE Pub.

*__VA Health Care: Issues Affecting Eligibility Reform Efforts.__ (Illus.). 148p. (Orig.). (C). 1996. pap. 35.00 (*0-7881-3591-0*) DIANE Pub.

*__VA Health Care: Need for Brevard Hospital Not Justified.__ (Illus.). 60p. 1996. reprint ed. pap. 20.00 (*0-7881-3206-7*) DIANE Pub.

*__VA Health Care: Opportunities for Service Delivery Efficiencies Within Existing Resources.__ (Illus.). 64p. (Orig.). (C). 1996. pap. 25.00 (*0-7881-3459-0*) DIANE Pub.

VA Health Care: Retargeting Needed to Better Meet Veterans' Changing Needs. (Illus.). 72p. (Orig.). (C). 1995. pap. text ed. 25.00 (*0-7881-1816-1*) DIANE Pub.

Va Jouer avec Cette Poussiere: Carnets (1958-1964) Henri De Montherlant. (FRE.). 1966. 7.95 (*0-8288-9640-2*, F115570) Fr & Eur.

Va Lettre Va: The French Verse Epistle (1400-1550) Yvonne LeBlanc. LC 94-74076. 268p. 1995. lib. bdg. 41.95 (*1-883479-04-5*) Summa Pubns.

VA Mycorrhiza. Conway L. Powell & D. Joseph Bagaraj. 240p. 1984. 163.95 (*0-8493-5694-6*, QK604) CRC Pr.

Va Va Voom! Bombshells, Pin-Ups, Sexpots & Glamour Girls. Steve Sullivan. Ed. by Harold Bronson & Colby Allerton. LC 95-77537. (Illus.). 256p. 1995. pap. 17.95 (*1-881649-60-1*) Genl Pub Grp.

VA (Veterans Administration) Health Care: Comparison of VA Benefits with Other Public & Private Programs. (Illus.). 89p. (Orig.). (C). 1994. pap. text ed. 30.00 (*0-7881-0197-8*) DIANE Pub.

VA (Veterans Administration) Health Care: Variabilities in Outpatient Care, Eligibility & Rationing Decisions. (Illus.). 56p. (Orig.). (C). 1994. pap. text ed. 30.00 (*0-7881-0216-8*) DIANE Pub.

Vaaldorp Diamond. large type ed. Eva Dane. 384p. 1985. 25.99 (*0-7089-1279-6*) Ulverscroft.

Vac: The Concept of the Word in Selected Hindu Tantras. Andre Padoux. Tr. by Jacques Gontier. LC 89-11436. (SUNY Series in the Shaiva Traditions of Kashmir). 460p. 1990. text ed. 64.50 (*0-7914-0257-6*); pap. text ed. 21.95 (*0-7914-0258-4*) State U NY Pr.

Vaca Que Decia Oink. Bernard Most. Tr. by Teresa Mlawer from ENG. (Illus.). 32p. (SPA.). (J). 1994. 12.95 (*1-880507-14-5*) Lectorum Pubns.

Vacaciones de Paddington - Paddington Abroad. Michael Bond. 1996. pap. text ed. 8.95 (*84-279-3703-2*) Lectorum Pubns.

Vacances a Tous Prix. Pierre Daninos. (FRE.). 1972. 10.95 (*0-8288-9182-6*, F97980) Fr & Eur.

*__Vacances d'Amelie.__ Christine L'Heureux. (Illus.). 24p. (FRE.). (J). (ps up). pap. 4.95 (*2-89021-033-2*, Pub. by Les Editions CN) Firefly Bks Ltd.

Vacances de Maigret. Georges Simenon. pap. 3.95 (*0-685-11613-1*) Fr & Eur.

*__Vacances de Rosalie.__ Ginette Anfousse. (Novels in the Roman Jeunesse Ser.). 96p. (FRE.). (J). (gr. 4-7). 1996. pap. 7.95 (*2-89021-116-9*, Pub. by Les Editions CN) Firefly Bks Ltd.

Vacances de Zephyr. Jean De Brunhoff. 40p. (J). 1983. 24.95 (*0-7859-8797-5*) Fr & Eur.

Vacances du Petit Nicolas. Jean-Jacques Sempe & R. Goscinny. (Folio - Junior Ser: No. 457). 186p. (FRE.). (J). (gr. 5-10). 1987. pap. 9.95 (*2-07-033457-0*) Schoenhof.

Vacancies. Dennis Koran. (Mother's Hen Bk.). 60p. 1975. pap. 6.00 (*0-915572-45-1*) Panjandrum.

Vacant Chair: The Northern Soldier Leaves Home. Reid Mitchell. (Illus.). 240p. 1995. pap. 12.95 (*0-19-509643-6*) OUP.

*__Vacant Eden.__ Abigail Gumbiner & Carol Hayden. LC 96-78617. (Illus.). 96p. (Orig.). 1997. pap. 23.50 (*0-9643119-5-X*) Balcony Pr.

*__Vacant Lot.__ Harlow Rockwell. (J). Date not set. write for info. (*0-688-80259-1*); lib. bdg. write for info. (*0-688-84259-3*) Greenwillow.

Vacant Lot, School Yard, & Back Alley Games of the Midwest Years Ago. Rebecca J. Wilson. (Illus.). 179p. 1992. pap. text ed. 9.95 (*1-87488-70-8*) Quixote Pr IA.

Vacant Places. Stanley Middleton. 238p. (C). 1990. 16.95 (*0-941533-78-6*) New Amsterdam Bks.

Vacant Places. Stanley Middleton. 1992. 9.95 (*1-56131-036-0*) New Amsterdam Bks.

Vacant Thrones: A Volume of Political Portraits. Ian Z. Malcolm. LC 67-28760. (Essay Index Reprint Ser.). 1977. 20.95 (*0-8369-0672-1*) Ayer.

Vacas (Cows) L. Stone. (Spanish Language Books, Set 1: Animales de Granja (Farm Animals)). (J). 1991. 8.95 (*0-86592-952-1*) Rourke Enter.

Vacas Para Helados y Overjas Para. Jane B. Moncure. LC 87-14603. (Castillo Magico Ser.). (Illus.). 32p. (SPA.). (J). (ps-2). 1987. lib. bdg. 21.36 (*0-89565-915-8*) Childs World.

Vacation. Greg Lee. LC 92-45692. (Little Jokester Ser.). (J). 1993. 12.67 (*0-86593-270-0*); 9.50 (*0-685-66420-1*) Rourke Corp.

*__Vacation America.__ Rand McNally Staff. 1996. pap. text ed. 14.95 (*0-528-81520-2*) Rand McNally.

Vacation & Second Homes: 345 Designs for Recreation Retirement & Leisure Living 480 to 4,135 Square Feet. Home Planners, Inc. Staff. 310p. 1995. pap. 8.95 (*1-881955-19-2*) Home Planners.

Vacation & Travel Photography. Sean Hargrave. LC 95-1419. (Point & Shoot Ser.). (Illus.). 96p. 1995. pap. 11.95 (*0-8174-5487-X*, Amphoto) Watsn-Guptill.

Vacation-Condo Game. Donald K. Rose. LC 84-60563. (Illus.). 126p. 1984. pap. 11.95 (*0-88100-042-6*) Natl Writ Pr.

Vacation Cooking: Good Food! Good Fun! Florence H. Boss & Ruth A. Kendrick. 80p. 1991. pap. 6.98 (*0-88290-349-7*) Horizon Utah.

Vacation Dreams. James W. Colegrove. (Illus.). 66p. (Orig.). 1984. pap. 10.00 (*0-918855-01-2*) Aldin Pub.

Vacation from Worry. Larry G. Stenzel. 32p. 1984. pap. 3.00 (*0-910021-03-1*) Samuel P Co.

Vacation Fun Mad Libs. Roger Price & Leonard Stern. (Mad Libs Ser.). 48p. (Orig.). (J). (gr. 3 up). 1987. bds. 3.50 (*0-8431-1921-7*) Price Stern Sloan.

Vacation Getaway: A Journal of Your Travel Memories. Bruce A. Moulton. 36p. 1992. 6.95 (*0-9633573-0-1*) Lakeland Color.

Vacation Home Exchange & Hospitality Guide. John Kimbrough. LC 91-90005. 172p. (Orig.). 1991. pap. 14.95 (*0-9628199-0-5*) Kimco Comns.

*__Vacation Home Furnishings.__ Cy DeCosse Incorporated Staff. LC 96-30485. (Portable Workshop Ser.). (Illus.). 96p. 1996. 14.95 (*0-86573-673-1*) Cowles Creative.

Vacation Homes. Ed. by National Plan Service, Inc. Staff. (Illus.). 32p. reprint ed. pap. 3.95 (*0-934039-14-3*, A50) Natl Plan Serv.

Vacation Homes America: The Complete Rental Guide to Hundreds of All-Season Resort Homes, Villas, Condos & Chalets. Bill Gleeson. 128p. 1991. pap. write for info. (*0-9630092-3-0*) Second Star.

Vacation Homes & Cabins: Sixteen Complete Plans. U. S. Department of Agriculture Staff. (USDA Material Ser.). (Illus.). 1978. pap. 5.95 (*0-486-23631-5*) Dover.

Vacation Notebook Vol. 15: A Translation of Quadern de Vacances. Miguel Marti i Pol. Ed. by Lourdes Manye i Marti. Tr. by Wayne Cox from SPA. (Catalan Studies: Translation & Criticism). 120p. (C). 1995. pap. text ed. 19.95 (*0-8204-2598-2*) P Lang Pubng.

Vacation of a Lifetime. Abigail Sommers. 105p. 1995. spiral bd. 6.95 (*1-888038-01-2*) Rubenesque.

Vacation of the Kelwyns. William Dean Howells. (Notable American Authors Ser.). 1992. reprint ed. lib. bdg. 75.00 (*0-7812-3264-3*) Rprt Serv.

Vacation Puzzle & Fun Book. Elvira Gamiello. (Illus.). (Orig.). (J). (gr. 4-6). 1989. pap. 1.95 (*0-942025-63-6*) Kidsbks.

Vacation, Retirement & Leisure Home Plans. 4th ed. LC 94-73701. (Illus.). 256p. 1995. pap. 6.95 (*0-938708-61-9*) L F Garlinghouse Co.

*__Vacation Sticker Passport.__ (J). (ps-2). 1997. pap. 3.50 (*0-614-28914-9*) Rand McNally.

Vacation Study Abroad, 1991. 41th rev. ed. Ed. by Sara J. Steen & Ed Battle. 278p. 1991. pap. 26.95 (*0-87206-179-5*) Inst Intl Educ.

Vacation Time: Poems for Children. Nikki Giovanni. LC 79-91643. (Illus.). 32p. (YA). (gr. 7 up). 1981. pap. 6.00 (*0-688-00507-1*, Quill) Morrow.

Vacation Time Sharing: Is It Right for You? Al Nunes-Vais. (Illus.). 1983. pap. 9.95 (*0-910793-02-6*) Marlborough Pr.

Vacation to Marsailles. Roxanne Vallet. (Illus.). 15p. (J). (gr. k-3). 1992. pap. 13.95 (*1-895583-38-1*) MAYA Pubs.

Vacation Towns of California. 3rd ed. Ed. by B. Sangwan. (California Ser.). (Illus.). 200p. (Orig.). 1993. pap. 10.95 (*0-916841-31-6*) Indian Chief.

*__Vacation Towns of California.__ 4th ed. B. Sangwan. 1997. pap. text ed. 11.95 (*0-916841-65-0*) Indian Chief.

Vacation with Love. large type ed. Peggy O'More. (Linford Romance Library). 1990. pap. 15.99 (*0-7089-6917-8*, Trailtree Bookshop) Ulverscroft.

Vacationer's Choice. John Nemec. (Illus.). 163p. (Orig.). 1989. pap. 4.45 (*0-9618998-5-9*) Nemec Pub.

*__Vacationers from Outer Space.__ Edward Valfre. LC 97-1351. (J). 1997. 14.95 (*0-8118-1717-2*) Chronicle Bks.

*__Vacationing with Your Pet! Eileen's Directory of Pet-Friendly Lodging in the United States & Canada.__ 3rd ed. Eileen Barish. LC 96-70502. (Illus.). 720p. (Orig.). 1997. pap. 19.95 (*1-884465-07-2*) Pet-Friendly.

Vacations Can Be Murder: The Second Charlie Parker Mystery. Connie Shelton. Ed. by Leslie Lenz. (Charlie Parker Mysteries Ser.). 216p. 1995. 21.95 (*0-9643161-1-0*) Columb Pub.

*__Vacations Can Be Murder: The Second Charlie Parker Mystery.__ Connie Shelton. 272p. 1997. reprint ed. mass mkt. 5.50 (*1-890768-01-4*, Intrigue Pr) Columb Pub.

Vacations in the Maritimes: A Tourbook of Nova Scotia, Prince Edward Island, New Brunswick Plus Newfoundland & Labrador. Laurie Fullerton. LC 92-41441. (Travel Guide Ser.). 288p. (Orig.). 1993. pap. 14.95 (*0-89909-356-6*) Yankee Bks.

Vacations, Parties, People, & Places. (Alan Snow's World of Words Ser.). 24p. (J). (ps-1). 1989. 5.98 (*0-517-68229-X*) Random Hse Value.

Vacations That Can Change Your Life: Adventures, Retreats & Workshops for the Mind, Body & Spirit. Ellen Lederman. LC 96-32057. (Change Your Life Ser.). 448p. (Orig.). 1996. pap. 16.95 (*1-57071-124-0*) Sourcebks.

Vacations with a Purpose: Encourage & Challenge Singles to Give of Themselves. Chris Eaton & Kim Hurst. teacher ed. 19.99 (*0-7814-5042-X*, 87544) Cook.

Vacations with a Purpose: Encourage & Challenge Singles to Give of Themselves. Chris Eaton & Kim Hurst. 1994. student ed. 7.99 (*0-7814-5041-1*, 87536) Cook.

*__Vacationscape: Developing Tourist Areas.__ 3rd ed. LC 96-44472. 1997. boxed write for info. (*1-56032-519-4*) Hemisp Pub.

*__Vacationscape: Developing Tourist Areas.__ 3rd ed. LC 96-44472. 1997. pap. write for info. (*1-56032-520-8*) Hemisp Pub.

Vaccari's Standard Japanese-English Dictionary. Oreste Vaccari & E. E. Vaccari. 1860p. (ENG & JPN.). 1990. 195.00 (*0-8288-7339-9*, F1260) Fr & Eur.

Vaccinating Against Brain Syndromes: The Campaign Against Measles & Rubella. Ed. by Ernest M. Gruenberg et al. (Monographs in Epidemiology & Biostatistics: No. 9). (Illus.). 181p. 1986. 29.95 (*0-19-503631-X*) OUP.

Vaccination Against Brucellosis in Ruminants Using Inactivated H38 Vaccine. Amargies. (C). 1987. 12.50 (*0-317-66877-3*, Pub. by Oxford IBH II) S Asia.

Vaccination Against Pregnancy: Miracle or Menace? Judith Richter. 192p. (C). 1996. text ed. 55.00 (*1-85649-281-8*, Pub. by Zed Bks Ltd UK) Humanities.

Vaccination Against Pregnancy: Miracle Or Menance? Judith Richter. 192p. (C). 1996. pap. 17.50 (*1-85649-282-6*, Pub. by Zed Bks Ltd UK) Humanities.

Vaccination Against Smallpox. Edward Jenner. 78p. 1996. pap. text ed. 5.95 (*1-57392-064-9*) Prometheus Bks.

*__Vaccination Against Tuberculosis.__ (Technical Report Ser.: No. 651). 21p. 1980. pap. text ed. 2.00 (*92-4-120651-9*) World Health.

Vaccination & Control of Aujeszky's Disease. Ed. by J. T. Van Oirschot. (Current Topics in Veterinary Medicine & Animal Science Ser.). (C). 1989. lib. bdg. 132.00 (*0-7923-0184-6*) Kluwer Ac.

Vaccination & Immunisation: Dangers, Delusions & Alternatives (What Every Parent Should Know) 5th ed. Leon Chaitow. 192p. pap. 20.95 (*0-8464-4308-2*) Beekman Pubs.

Vaccination & Immunization. Leon Chaitow. 64p. 1990. pap. 13.95 (*0-85207-191-4*, Pub. by C W Daniel UK) Natl Bk Netwk.

Vaccination & World Health: The LSHTM Fourth Annual Public Health Forum. Ed. by Felicity T. Cutts & Peter G. Smith. LC 94-37790. 294p. 1995. text ed. 69.95 (*0-471-95242-7*) Wiley.

Vaccination, Social Violence & Criminality: The Medical Assault on the American Brain. Harris L. Coulter. LC 90-7991. 300p. (Orig.). 1990. 25.00 (*1-55643-103-1*); pap. 14.95 (*1-55643-084-1*) Ctr Emp Med.

Vaccination Strategies of Tropical Diseases. Ed. by F. Y. Liew. 304p. 1989. 206.00 (*0-8493-6189-3*, RC119) CRC Pr.

Vaccinations: Rest of the Story. 1993. pap. 10.95 (*0-914257-00-5*) Mothering Magazine.

Vaccinations & Immune Malfunction. 3rd ed. Harold E. Buttram & John C. Hoffman. 75p. (Orig.). 1987. pap. 3.00 (*0-916285-36-7*) Humanitarian.

Vaccine & Serum Evils. Herbert M. Shelton. 46p. 1966. reprint ed. spiral bd. 6.50 (*0-7873-0784-X*) Hlth Research.

Vaccine Design. Fred Brown et al. LC 93-9132. (Molecular Medical Science Ser.). 130p. 1993. text ed. 72.95 (*0-471-93727-4*) Wiley.

Vaccine Design: The Subunit & Adjuvant Approach. Mark J. Newman. LC 95-16401. (Pharmaceutical Biotechnology Ser.: Vol. 6). 949p. 1995. 145.00 (*0-306-44867-X*, Plenum Pr) Plenum.

Vaccine Exemptions: A State-by-State Summary of Legal Exemptions to "Mandatory" Vaccine Laws. New Atlantean Press Staff. 16p. (Orig.). 1995. pap. 10.00 (*1-881217-07-8*) New Atlantean.

Vaccine Guide: Making an Informed Choice. Randall Neustaedter. LC 95-48308. Orig. Title: The Immunization Decision. 250p. (Orig.). 1996. pap. 14.95 (*1-55643-215-1*) North Atlantic.

Vaccine Protocols. Ed. by Andrew Robinson et al. LC 96-6818. (Methods in Molecular Medicine Ser.: Vol. 4). (Illus.). 328p. 1996. spiral bd. 89.00 (*0-89603-334-1*) Humana.

Vaccine Research & Development, Vol. 1. Ed. by Koff & Six. 264p. 1992. 160.00 (*0-8247-8619-X*) Dekker.

Vaccine Roulette: Gambling with Your Child's Life. Neil Z. Miller. 32p. (Orig.). 1995. pap. 5.95 (*1-881217-09-4*) New Atlantean.

Vaccine Seminar: Critical Data for New Parents & Health Practitioners. Neil Z. Miller. 40p. (Orig.). 1995. pap. 6.95 (*1-881217-08-6*) New Atlantean.

Vaccine Supply & Innovation. Institute of Medicine Staff. 210p. 1985. pap. text ed. 21.00 (*0-309-03544-9*) Natl Acad Pr.

U V

An Asterisk (*) at the beginning of an entry indicates that the title is appearing in BIP for the first time.

Vaccines. 2nd ed. Stanley A. Plotkin & Edward A. Mortimer, Jr. LC 93-10761. (Illus.). 1024p. 1994. reprint ed. text ed. 179.00 (*0-7216-6584-5*) Saunders.

***Vaccines.** 3rd ed. Plotkin. 1998. text ed. write for info. (*0-7216-7443-7*) Saunders.

Vaccines: Are They Really Safe & Effective? 7th ed. Neil Z. Miller. LC 92-81105. (Illus.). 80p. 1996. reprint ed. pap. 8.95 (*1-881217-10-8*) New Atlantean.

***Vaccines: New Advances in Technologies & Applications.** Ed. by Rebecca Ostriker. (Biomedical Library). 356p. 1996. pap. 795.00 (*1-57936-013-0*) IBC USA.

Vaccines: New Approaches to Immunological Problems. Ronald W. Ellis. 496p. 1991. 52.95 (*0-7506-9265-0*) Buttrwrth-Heinemann.

Vaccines: New Generation Immunological Adjuvants: Proceedings of a NATO ASI Held in Cape Sounion, Greece, June 24-July 5, 1994. Ed. by Gregory Gregoriadis et al. (NATO ASI Series A: Vol. 282). 175p. 1996. 75.00 (*0-306-45283-9*) Plenum.

Vaccines: Preventing Disease. Michael C. Burge. LC 92-27851. (Encyclopedia of Discovery & Invention Ser.). (Illus.). 96p. (J). (gr. 5-8). 1992. lib. bdg. 18.96 (*1-56006-223-1*) Lucent Bks.

Vaccines: Recent Trends & Progress. Ed. by Gregory Gregoriadis et al. (NATO ASI Series A, Life Sciences: Vol. 215). (Illus.). 148p. 1991. 75.00 (*0-306-44044-X*, Plenum Pr) Plenum.

***Vaccines Vol. II: New Advances in Technologies & Applications.** (Biomedical Library). 1997. pap. write for info. (*1-57936-033-5*) IBC USA.

Vaccines Against Virally Induced Cancers: Symposium No. 187. CIBA Foundation Staff. LC 94-33207. (CIBA Foundation Symposium Ser.: Vol. 187). 326p. 1995. text ed. 84.95 (*0-471-95026-2*) Wiley.

Vaccines & Immunotherapy. Ed. by S. J. Cryz. 496p. 1991. text ed. 94.50 (*0-07-105380-8*) McGraw-Hill HPD.

Vaccines & Immunotherapy. S. J. Cryz. (Illus.). 448p. 1991. 94.50 (*0-08-036083-1*, Pub. by PPI UK) McGraw.

Vaccines & Their Alternatives. Business Communications Co., Inc. Staff. 256p. 1985. pap. 1,750.00 (*0-89336-425-8*, C-057) BCC.

Vaccines & World Health: Science, Policy, & Practice. Paul F. Basch. LC 93-23283. 288p. 1994. 49.95 (*0-19-508532-9*) OUP.

Vaccines Are Dangerous: A Warning to the Black Community. Curtis Cost. 199p. 1992. pap. text ed. 9.95 (*1-881316-08-4*) A&B Bks.

Vaccines Eighty-Nine: Modern Approaches to New Vaccines Including the Prevention of AIDS. Ed. by Richard A. Lerner et al. (Illus.). 1989. pap. 100.00 (*0-87969-323-1*) Cold Spring Harbor.

Vaccines Eighty-Seven: Modern Approaches to New Vaccines: Prevention of AIDS & Other Viral, Bacterial, & Parasitic Diseases. Ed. by Robert M. Chanock et al. (Illus.). 461p. (C). 1987. pap. 95.00 (*0-87969-302-9*) Cold Spring Harbor.

Vaccines for Children Program: A Critique. Robert Goldberg. 36p. 1995. pap. 9.95 (*0-8447-7052-3*) Am Enterprise.

Vaccines for Sexually Transmitted Diseases. Raymond E. Spier. (Illus.). 315p. 1990. 140.00 (*0-408-04755-0*) Buttrwrth-Heinemann.

***Vaccines for the 21st Century: A Tool for Setting Priorities.** Ed. by Kathleen R. Stratton et al. 300p. (C). 1997. 42.95 (*0-309-05646-2*, Joseph Henry Pr) Natl Acad Pr.

Vaccines for Vet Applications. Ed. by A. R. Peters. (Illus.). 304p. 1993. 115.00 (*0-7506-1126-X*) Buttrwrth-Heinemann.

Vaccines in Agriculture: Immunological Applications to Animal Health & Production. Ed. by P. R. Wood et al. 1994. 120.00 (*0-643-05535-5*, Pub. by CSIRO AT) Aubrey Bks.

Vaccines Ninety: Modern Approaches to New Vaccines Including Prevention of AIDS. Ed. by Fred Brown et al. (Illus.). 528p. 1990. pap. 100.00 (*0-87969-341-X*) Cold Spring Harbor.

Vaccines Ninety One: Modern Approaches to New Vaccines Including Prevention of AIDS. Ed. by Robert M. Chanock et al. (Illus.). 425p. 1991. pap. text ed. 85.00 (*0-87969-367-3*) Cold Spring Harbor.

Vaccines Ninety-Three: Modern Approaches to New Vaccines Including Prevention of AIDS. Harold S. Ginsberg et al. LC 93-2729. (Illus.). 480p. 1993. reprint ed. pap. 136.80 (*0-7837-8111-3*, 2047918) Bks Demand.

***Vaccines, Vaccination & the Immune Response.** G. L. Ada & Alistair J. Ramsay. LC 96-31613. 272p. 1996. text ed. 89.00 (*0-397-58761-9*) Lppncott-Raven.

Vaccines, 1992: Modern Approaches to New Vaccines Including Prevention of AIDS. Ed. by Fred Brown et al. (Illus.). 400p. (C). 1992. text ed. 100.00 (*0-87969-405-X*) Cold Spring Harbor.

Vaccines 85: Molecular & Chemical Basis of Resistance to Parasitic, Bacterial & Viral Diseases. Ed. by Richard A. Lerner et al. LC 84-29372. 407p. (Orig.). 1985. pap. 75.00 (*0-87969-181-6*) Cold Spring Harbor.

Vaccines 86: New Approaches to Immunization--Developing Vaccines Against Parasitic, Bacterial & Viral Diseases. Ed. by Fred Brown et al. LC 86-2589. 418p. (Orig.). 1986. pap. 75.00 (*0-87969-190-5*) Cold Spring Harbor.

Vaccines 88, New Chemical & Genetic Approaches to Vaccination: Prevention of Aids & Other Viral, Bacterial & Parasitic Diseases. Ed. by Robert Chanock et al. LC 87-13175. (Vaccines Ser.). (Illus.). 460p. 1987. pap. text ed. 95.00 (*0-87969-310-X*) Cold Spring Harbor.

Vaccines 94: Modern Approaches to New Vaccines Including Prevention of AIDS. Ed. by Erling Norrby et al. (Vaccines Ser.: Vol. 94). 423p. 1994. reprint ed. pap. 120.60 (*0-608-00717-X*, 2061491) Bks Demand.

Vaccines 95: Molecular Approaches to the Control of Infectious Diseases. Ed. by Robert M. Chanock et al. LC 93-2729. (Illus.). 441p. (Orig.). 1995. pap. text ed. 100.00 (*0-87969-467-X*) Cold Spring Harbor.

Vaccines 96: Molecular Approaches to the Control of Infectious Diseases. Ed. by Fred Brown et al. (Illus.). 364p. (C). 1996. pap. text ed. 100.00 (*0-87969-479-3*) Cold Spring Harbor.

***Vaccines 97: Molecular Approaches to the Control of Infectious Diseases.** Ed. by Fred Brown et al. (Illus.). 367p. (C). 1997. pap. text ed. 100.00 (*0-87969-516-1*) Cold Spring Harbor.

***Vaccinia, Vaccination, Vaccinology: Jenner, Pasteur & Their Successors.** Ed. by S. A. Plotkin & B. Fantini. 380p. 1996. pap. text ed. 110.00 (*2-906077-83-6*) Elsevier.

Vachel. Vachel Lindsay. Ed. by R-Lou Barker & Roanna Victor. (Illus.). 54p. (C). 1995. lib. bdg. 9.95 (*0-9648065-0-9*) V Lindsay Assn.

Vachel Lindsay: A Poet in America. Edgar L. Masters. LC 68-56452. (Illus.). 1969. reprint ed. 30.00 (*0-8196-0239-6*) Biblo.

Vachel Lindsay: Poet in Exile. Mildred Weston. 94p. 1987. 14.95 (*0-87770-408-2*) Ye Galleon.

Vachel Lindsay: The Poet As Film Theorist. Glenn J. Wolfe. LC 72-554. (Dissertations on Film Ser.). 250p. 1974. 18.95 (*0-405-04097-0*) Ayer.

Vacherie, St. James Parish, Louisiana: History & Genealogy. Elton J. Oubre. LC 86-62380. (Illus.). 576p. 1986. 30.00 (*0-9617559-0-3*) Oubres Bks.

***Vacher's European Companion, Vol. 96.** 300p. 1997. pap. 19.50 (*0-614-24981-3*, Pub. by Dods Parliament UK) Intl Spec Bk.

Vaches. Marcel Ayme. (Folio - Cadet Bleu Ser.: No. 215). (Illus.). 72p. (FRE.). (J). (gr. 1-5). 1990. pap. 9.95 (*2-07-031215-1*) Schoenhof.

Vacillations of Poppy Carew. Mary Wesley. 1987. pap. 10.95 (*0-552-99258-5*) Bantam.

Vacillations of Poppy Carew. Mary Wesley. LC 87-30838. 224p. 1988. pap. 11.95 (*0-14-010828-9*, Penguin Bks) Viking Penguin.

Vaclav Havel & the Velvet Revolution. Jeffrey B. Symynkywicz. LC 94-2384. (People in Focus Ser.). (Illus.). (J). (gr. 5-5). 1995. pap. 7.95 (*0-382-24966-6*, Dillon Silver Burdett) Silver Burdett Pr.

Vaclav Havel & the Velvet Revolution. Jeffrey B. Symynkywicz. LC 94-2384. (People in Focus Ser.). (Illus.). (YA). (gr. 5 up). 1995. lib. bdg. (*0-87518-607-6*, Dillon Silver Burdett) Silver Burdett Pr.

Vacuum & Surface Analysis, Vol. 1: Proceedings of the Chinese-Japanese Joint Seminar. Ed. by Z. Y. Hua. 376p. (C). 1988. text ed. 89.00 (*9971-5-0459-6*) World Scientific Pub.

Vacuum & Surface Analysis, Vol. 2: Proceedings of the Sino-U. S. Joint Seminar. Ed. by Z-Y Hua. 448p. (C). 1988. text ed. 108.00 (*9971-5-0590-8*) World Scientific Pub.

Vacuum & Surface Analysis, Vol. 3: Proceedings of Sino-German Joint Seminar (VASA-88) Ed. by Z. Y. Hua. 410p. (C). 1989. text ed. 151.00 (*9971-5-0853-2*) World Scientific Pub.

Vacuum & Thin Film Technology. Ed. by J. Yarwood. 1978. 30.00 (*0-08-022112-2*, Pergamon Pr) Elsevier.

Vacuum & Vacua: The Physics of Nothing; Proceedings of the International School of Subnuclear Physics. Antonio L. Zichichi. LC 96-9523. (The Subnuclear Ser.). 1996. write for info. (*981-02-2839-2*) World Scientific Pub.

Vacuum Cantos. Lawrence McGaugh. 1969. pap. 1.50 (*0-685-04679-6*) Oyez.

Vacuum Cleaner Maintenance: How to Fix & Care for Them. 5th ed. Florencio O. Garcia. 105p. 1992. pap. 14.00 (*0-929928-14-8*) Fog Pubns.

Vacuum Cleaner Revelation. Barbara Wallace. Ed. by W. B. Knox & Anita Pearson. (Illus.). 100p. (Orig.). 1996. pap. 8.95 (*1-881116-74-3*) Black Forest Pr.

***Vacuum Cleaners.** Elaine M. Alphin. LC 96-36457. (Household History Ser.). (J). 1997. write for info. (*1-57505-018-8*, Carolrhoda) Lerner Group.

Vacuum Degassing of Steel. R. J. Fruehan. LC 90-83280. 212p. 1990. 55.00 (*0-932897-57-6*) Iron & Steel.

Vacuum Design of Advanced & Compact Synchrotron Light Sources. Ed. by H. J. Halama et al. LC 88-71824. (AIP Conference Proceedings Ser.: No. 171). 390p. 1988. lib. bdg. 65.00 (*0-88318-371-4*) Am Inst Physics.

Vacuum Design of Synchrotron Light Sources: AIP Conference Proceedings, No. 236. Ed. by Yeldez G. Amer et al. LC 91-55527. (American Vacuum Society Ser.: No. 12). (Illus.). 448p. 1991. lib. bdg. 85.00 (*0-88318-873-2*) Am Inst Physics.

Vacuum Devices: Proceedings of the Conference, University of Cambridge, 25-27 March 1980. J. Yarwood. 144p. 1981. pap. 26.00 (*0-08-027330-0*, Pergamon Pr) Elsevier.

Vacuum, Eighty-Four: Technological Aspects of Surface Treatment & Analysis: Proceedings of the Conference Held at the University of York, 1-4 April 1984. Ed. by W. A. Grant. 204p. 1985. pap. 50.00 (*0-08-032555-6*, Pergamon Pr) Elsevier.

Vacuum Eighty-Two: Proceedings of the Biennial Conference of the Vacuum Group of the Institute of Physics, Chester, 29-31 March 1982. Ed. by W. A. Grant et al. 112p. 1983. pap. 31.00 (*0-08-029999-7*, Pergamon Pr) Elsevier.

Vacuum Electron & Ion Technologies. Ed. by D. S. Karpuzov. 472p. (C). 1995. lib. bdg. 98.00 (*1-56072-242-8*) Nova Sci Pubs.

Vacuum Engineering Calculations, Formulas, & Solved Exercises. Armand Berman. (Illus.). 257p. 1992. text ed. 83.00 (*0-12-092455-2*) Acad Pr.

Vacuum-Industry-Energy: Proceedings of Second Joint Meeting of the Roland Eotvos Physical Society (Vacuum Physics & Thin Films Section) & the Austrian Vacuum Society, held Niederosterreich, Austria, 27-29 October, 1981. Ed. by R. Dobrozemsky. 128p. 1983. pap. 31.00 (*0-08-029993-8*, Pergamon Pr) Elsevier.

Vacuum Mechatronics. Majid Shirazi et al. (Materials Library). 388p. 1990. text ed. 19.00 (*0-89006-456-3*) Artech Hse.

Vacuum Mechatronics, First International Workshop. Majid Shirazi. LC 89-45905. (AIP Conference Proceedings Ser.: No. 192). 192p. 1990. lib. bdg. 70.00 (*0-88318-394-3*) Am Inst Physics.

Vacuum Metallurgy. A. Choudhury. 248p. 1990. 87.00 (*0-87170-398-X*, 6101) ASM.

***Vacuum Metallurgy.** Ashok Choudhury. LC 90-83642. (Illus.). 255p. 1990. reprint ed. pap. 72.70 (*0-608-02631-X*, 2063289) Bks Demand.

Vacuum Metallurgy Conference on Specialty Metals Melting & Processing: Pittsburgh, Pennsylvania, June 9-11, 1986. fac. ed. Vacuum Metallurgy Conference on Specialty Metals Melting & Processing Staff. LC 86-81028. (Illus.). 229p. 1987. pap. 65.30 (*0-7837-8236-5*, 2049000) Bks Demand.

Vacuum Metallurgy Conference on Specialty Metals Melting & Processing Proceedings: Pittsburgh, Pennsylvania, June 11-13, 1984. Vacuum Metallurgy Conference on Specialty Metals Melting & Processing Staff. LC 85-152302. (Illus.). 229p. reprint ed. pap. 65.30 (*0-8357-8600-5*, 2034984) Bks Demand.

***Vacuum Methods in Electron Microscopy.** W. C. Bigelow. Ed. by A. M. Glauert. (Practical Methods in Electron Microscopy Ser.: Vol. 15). (Illus.). 512p. (Orig.). (C). 1994. pap. text ed. 76.50 (*1-85578-052-6*, Pub. by Portland Pr Ltd UK) Ashgate Pub Co.

***Vacuum Methods in Electron Microscopy.** W. C. Bigelow. Ed. by A. M. Glauert. (Practical Methods in Electron Microscopy Ser.: Vol. 15). (Illus.). 512p. (Orig.). (C). 1994. text ed. 187.00 (*1-85578-053-4*, Pub. by Portland Pr Ltd UK) Ashgate Pub Co.

Vacuum Physics & Technology. T. A. Delchar. LC 92-21136. (Physics & Its Applications Ser.: Vol. 6). 272p. (gr. 13). 1993. pap. text ed. 25.95 (*0-412-46590-6*) Chapman & Hall.

Vacuum Problems & Techniques. AEC Technical Information Center Staff et al. (National Nuclear Energy Ser.: Division I, Vol. 11). 289p. 1950. 36.50 (*0-87079-356-X*, TID-5210); fiche 9.00 (*0-87079-357-8*, TID-5210) DOE.

Vacuum Pumper's Handbook. 4th rev. ed. Gary Griffin. 96p. 1993. pap. 9.95 (*1-879967-07-3*) Added Dimensns.

Vacuum Science & Technology: Pioneers of the 20th Century. Ed. by Paul A. Readhead. LC 93-28714. (History of Vacuum Science & Technology Ser.: Vol. 2). (Illus.). 300p. 1993. pap. text ed. 35.00 (*1-56396-248-9*, AIP) Am Inst Physics.

Vacuum Sealing Techniques. A. Roth. LC 93-27399. (American Vacuum Society Classics Ser.). (Illus.). 864p. 1994. pap. text ed. 35.00 (*1-56396-259-4*, AIP) Am Inst Physics.

Vacuum Seventy-Eight: Selected Proceedings of the Conference on Medium High & Ultra-High Vacuum Technology, Oxford, England, 1978. G. S. Grossart. Ed. by J. Yarwood. (Illus.). 1979. pap. 32.00 (*0-08-024229-4*, Pergamon Pr) Elsevier.

Vacuum Structure & QCD Sum Rules. Ed. by Mikhail A. Shifman. LC 92-22078. (Current Physics Sources & Comments Ser.: No. 10). 516p. 1992. 218.00 (*0-444-89745-3*, North Holland) Elsevier.

Vacuum Structure & QCD Sum Rules. Ed. by Mikhail A. Shifman. LC 92-22078. (Current Physics Sources & Comments Ser.: No. 10). 516p. 1993. pap. 102.50 (*0-444-89746-1*, North Holland) Elsevier.

Vacuum Structure in Intense Fields. Ed. by H. M. Fried & B. Muller. (NATO ASI Series B, Physics: Vol. 255). (Illus.). 436p. 1991. 125.00 (*0-306-43910-7*, Plenum Pr) Plenum.

Vacuum Switchgear. Allan Greenwood. (Power Engineering Ser.: No. 18). 283p. 1994. boxed 99.00 (*0-85296-855-8*) Inst Elect Eng.

Vacuum Technology. 3rd enl. ed. A. Roth. 572p. 1990. 139.00 (*0-444-88010-0*, North Holland) Elsevier.

Vacuum Technology: An Introduction. 2nd fac. ed. L. G. Carpenter. LC 83-153551. (Illus.). 128p. 1983. reprint ed. pap. 36.50 (*0-7837-7987-9*, 2047743) Bks Demand.

Vacuum Technology: Practical Heat Treating & Brazing. Ed. by Roger Fabian. LC 93-71050. 253p. 1993. 90.00 (*0-87170-477-3*, 6091) ASM.

***Vacuum Technology: Practical Heat Treating & Brazing.** Ed. by Roger Fabian. LC 93-71050. (Illus.). 271p. 1993. reprint ed. pap. 77.30 (*0-608-03985-3*, 2064717) Bks Demand.

Vacuum Technology: Selected Proceedings of the 6th Israeli Vacuum Congress, Haifa, Israel, 4-5 April, 1982. Ed. by E. Grunbaum. 64p. 1983. pap. 15.50 (*0-08-030567-9*, Pergamon Pr) Elsevier.

Vacuum Technology & Space Simulation. D. J. Santeler et al. LC 92-46419. (AVS Classics of Ser.). (Illus.). 350p. 1993. pap. text ed. 35.00 (*1-56396-123-7*, AIP) Am Inst Physics.

Vacuum Technology, Thin Films, & Sputtering: An Introduction. R. V. Stuart. LC 82-13748. 1983. text ed. 60.00 (*0-12-674780-6*) Acad Pr.

Vacuum Tube & Guitar & Bass Amplifier Servicing. Tino Zottola. (Illus.). 100p. (Orig.). 1996. pap. 10.95 (*0-933224-97-4*) Bold Strummer Ltd.

Vacuum Tube Guitar & Bass Amplifier Theory. Tino Zottola. (Guitar History Ser.). (Illus.). 80p. 1996. pap. 10.95 (*0-933224-96-6*) Bold Strummer Ltd.

Vacuum Tube Tesla Coils. James F. Corum & Kenneth L. Corum. Ed. by Corum & Associates, Inc. Staff. LC 88-92704. (Illus.). 130p. (Orig.). (C). 1988. pap. text ed. 55.00 (*0-924758-00-7*) Corum & Assocs.

Vacuum Ultraviolet Photoionization & Photodissociation of Molecules & Clusters. Ed. by Cheuk-Yiu Ng. 580p. (C). 1991. pap. 48.00 (*981-02-0431-0*); text ed. 150.00 (*981-02-0430-2*) World Scientific Pub.

Vacuum Ultraviolet Radiation Physics. T. Miyahara et al. 1748p. 1996. text ed. 460.00 (*0-444-82245-3*) Elsevier.

Vacuum Ultraviolet Radiation Physics Ten: Proceedings of the Conference. F. Wuileumier et al. 700p. 1993. text ed. 178.00 (*981-02-1252-6*) World Scientific Pub.

***Vacuum Vapor Extraction.** Timothy B. Holbrook et al. Ed. by William C. Anderson. (Innovative Site Remediation Technology Ser.). (Illus.). 200p. 1998. 70.00 (*1-883767-23-7*) Am Acad Environ.

***Vacuum Vapor Extraction: Design & Application.** Tim B. Holbrook et al. (Innovative Site Remediation Technology: Vol. 7). (Illus.). 300p. 1998. write for info. (*0-614-30720-1*) Am Acad Environ.

Vacuums. David Wellen. (Illus.). 64p. (Orig.). 1988. pap. 4.50 (*0-9620605-0-X*) Vacuum Bks.

Vadanyaya: A Glimpse of Nyaya-Buddhist Controversy. Mangala R. Chinchore. (Bibliotheca Indo-Buddhica Ser.: No. 36). (C). 1988. text ed. 15.00 (*0-685-66323-X*) S Asia.

Vadanyaya of Dharmakirti: The Logic of Debate. Tr. by Pradeep P. Gokhale. (Bibliotheca Indo-Buddhica Ser.: No. 126). (C). 1993. 27.50 (*81-7030-380-X*) S Asia.

Vade-Mecum pour le Releve Methodique de la Vegetation et du Milieu. 170p. (FRE.). 1970. pap. 12.50 (*0-686-57240-8*, M-6541) Fr & Eur.

Vadecum del Cuidador de Caballos. L. S. McKibbin. (SPA.). pap. 56.95 (*84-200-0435-9*); pap. write for info. (*0-8288-7896-X*) Fr & Eur.

Vadecum del Productor de Cerdos. P. Zert. 424p. (SPA.). pap. 75.00 (*0-686-92188-7*) Fr & Eur.

Vadecum del Productor de Cerdos. 2nd ed. P. Zert. 424p. (SPA.). 1979. pap. 75.00 (*0-7859-5226-8*) Fr & Eur.

Vademecum de la Patologia Infecciosa de las Aves Domesticas. Pastor E. Zarzuelo. 356p. 1982. 55.00 (*0-8288-2392-8*, S39832) Fr & Eur.

Vademecum del Arquitecto de Jardines. N. Claraso. 256p. (SPA.). 1977. pap. 19.95 (*0-8288-5528-5*, S35347) Fr & Eur.

Vademecum del Serviceman de TV. H. O. Algarra. 278p. (SPA.). 1981. 22.50 (*0-8288-1383-3*, M15130) Fr & Eur.

Vademecum Deutscher Lehr und Forschungstaten. 8th ed. 1556p. (GER.). 1985. 450.00 (*0-8288-1390-6*, M 7140) Fr & Eur.

Vademecum du Veterinaire: Therapeutique, Pharmacologie et Hygiene. 14th ed. A. Brion. 816p. 1984. 39.95 (*0-8288-1793-6*) Fr & Eur.

Vademecum Encyclopedique du Medecin Praticien: Encyclopedic Vademecum of Medical Practice. 9th ed. H. Dousset. 1266p. 1980. 110.00 (*0-8288-1801-0*, M15580) Fr & Eur.

Vademecum for Servicemen from TV to Transistors: El Vademecum del Serviceman de TV a Transistores. H. O. Algarra. 254p. (SPA.). 1981. 25.95 (*0-8288-1384-1*, M15131) Fr & Eur.

Vademecum fuer Pilzfreunde: Taschenbuch Zur Bequemen Bestimmung Aller in Mittel-Europa Vorkommenden Ansehnlichen Pilzkoerper. A. Ricken. 1969. reprint ed. 32.00 (*3-7682-0603-3*) Lubrecht & Cramer.

***Vademecum International 1997: Especialidades Farmaceutica.** 1700p. 1997. 295.00 (*0-7859-9486-6*) Fr & Eur.

Vademecum of Antibiotics: Vadecum de los Antibioticos. Newman. (SPA.). 1981. pap. 19.95 (*0-8288-4681-2*, S34979) Fr & Eur.

Vademecum of Pharmacology: Vademecum de Pharmacie. 17th ed. Paul Schiltz & Colette Schiltz. 882p. (FRE.). 1985. 42.50 (*0-8288-1827-4*, M6820) Fr & Eur.

Vademecum of Topography: Vadecum del Topografo. H. Witke. (SPA.). 1981. pap. text ed. 24.95 (*0-7859-0799-8*, S33739) Fr & Eur.

Vademekum der Phonetik. 2nd ed. Eugen Dieth. (GER.). 1968. 49.95 (*0-8288-6666-X*, M-7135) Fr & Eur.

Vademekum fuer Den Pharmazeuten. Rudolf Schmidt-Wetter. 39.95 (*0-8288-7982-6*, M7138) Fr & Eur.

Vademekum fuer den Pharmazeuten. 10th ed. Rudolf Schmidt-Wetter. (GER.). 39.95 (*3-7948-0066-4*, M-7138) Fr & Eur.

Vademekum fuer Pilzfreunde. A. Ricken. (GER.). 1969. 69.95 (*0-8288-6618-X*, M-7137) Fr & Eur.

Vademekum fuer Vermessungstechnik. Heinz Wittke. 334p. (GER.). 1948. 39.95 (*0-7859-0835-8*, M-7134) Fr & Eur.

Vademekum Technische Werte der Getreidemittelverarbeitung und Futtermitteltechnik. Karl Gerecke. 160p. (GER.). 1970. 39.95 (*0-8288-6558-2*, M-7133) Fr & Eur.

Vademekum zum Sammeln Parasitischer Pilze. W. Brandenburger. (GER.). 1963. pap. 29.95 (*0-685-57724-4*, M7136) Fr & Eur.

***Vader's Fortress.** Rebecca Moesta. (Star Wars Ser.: No. 5). 128p. 1997. mass mkt. 4.50 (*1-57297-173-8*) Blvd Books.

***Vader's Fortress.** Rebecca Moesta. (Star Wars: Junior Jedi Knights Ser.). (J). 1997. write for info. (*0-614-29190-9*) Blvd Books.

Vadose Zone Hydrology. Daniel B. Stephens. 368p. 1995. 59.95 (*0-87371-432-6*, L432) Lewis Pubs.

Vaegge/Walls: Projection of Knowledge. Ole M. Jensen. 223p. 1995. 39.90 (*82-00-22593-3*) Scandnvan Univ Pr.

Vaer Sa God: Scandinavian Bake Book. rev. ed. Doris R. Gundersen. (Illus.). 96p. 1991. pap. 9.95 (*0-9631652-0-8*) Weston Pr.

Vagabond. (J). Date not set. pap. 15.00 (*0-590-39625-0*) Scholastic Inc.

Vagabond. Colette. (Twentieth Century Classics Ser.). 192p. 1995. pap. 9.95 (*0-14-018325-6*, Penguin Classics) Viking Penguin.

Vagabond. Colette. 1995. 7.99 (*0-517-12259-6*) Random Hse Value.

Vagabond. Michael T. Miller. 224p. 1990. 15.95 (*0-930545-11-7*) Maple Hill Pr.

Vagabond. Michael T. Miller. Ed. by Jamie Teasley. LC 89-51801. 357p. 1990. pap. 15.95 (*1-55523-289-2*) Winston-Derek.

Vagabond. Alexandra Sellers. (Intimate Moments Ser.). 1994. mass mkt. 3.50 (*0-373-07579-0*, 1-07579-5) Harlequin Bks.

Vagabond. A. P. Wolf. 155p. 1992. pap. 15.95 (*1-872180-18-3*, Pub. by Fourth Estate UK) Trafalgar.

Vagabond Anthology. John Bennett et al. LC 77-90626. 1978. pap. 8.00 (*0-912824-45-X*) Vagabond Pr.

***Vagabond Fitness: A Field Manual for Travelers.** Hank Schacte. (Illus.). 80p. 1996. pap. 9.95 (*1-55143-078-9*) Orca Bk Pubs.

Vagabond Globetrotting: State of the Art. 2nd rev. ed. M. L. Endicott. LC 88-81743. (Illus.). 176p. (Orig.). 1989. pap. 8.95 (*0-916649-01-6*) Enchiridion.

Vagabond Globetrotting: State of the Art. M. L. Endicott. LC 84-80473. 142p. (Orig.). 1984. reprint ed. pap. 8.95 (*0-916649-00-8*) Enchiridion.

Vagabond Hearts. Bobby Hutchinson. (Superromance Ser.: No. 492). 1992. mass mkt. 3.39 (*0-373-70492-5*, 1-70492-3) Harlequin Bks.

Vagabond House. Don Blanding. 1992. reprint ed. lib. bdg. 21.95 (*0-89968-294-4*, Lghtyr Pr) Buccaneer Bks.

Vagabond in Literature. Arthur Rickett. LC 68-8489. (Essay Index Reprint Ser.). 1977. reprint ed. 19.95 (*0-8369-0825-2*) Ayer.

Vagabond Nurse. large type ed. Ann Jones. (Romance Ser.). 1994. pap. 15.99 (*0-7089-7608-5*, Linford) Ulverscroft.

Vagabond of Verse: A Biography of Robert Service. James Mackay. (Illus.). 432p. 1996. pap. 22.95 (*1-85158-849-3*, Pub. by Mnstream UK) Trafalgar.

Vagabond Qui Passe sous une Ombrelle Trouee. Jean D'Ormesson. (FRE.). 1981. pap. 8.95 (*0-7859-4158-4*) Fr & Eur.

Vagabond Solitaire. Jack Kerouac. (FRE.). 1980. pap. 10.95 (*0-7859-2432-9*, 2070371875) Fr & Eur.

Vagabond Stars: A World of Yiddish Theater. Nahma Sandrow. (Illus.). 448p. 1995. pap. 16.95 (*0-8156-0329-0*) Syracuse U Pr.

Vagabond Verse: Secular Latin Poems of the Middle Ages. Edwin H. Zeydel. LC 66-13794. 308p. reprint ed. pap. 87.80 (*0-7837-3623-1*, 2043489) Bks Demand.

Vagabondages Litteraires: Initiation a la litterature d'expression francaise. Scott Carpenter & Francois Denis. 1996. pap. text ed. write for info. (*0-07-011444-7*) McGraw.

Vagabonde. Sidonie-Gabrielle Colette. 256p. (FRE.). 1958. pap. write for info. (*0-7859-4722-1*) Fr & Eur.

Vagabondiana, or Anecdotes of Mendicant Wanderers Through the Streets of London. John T. Smith. LC 70-104959. viii, 52p. 1983. reprint ed. lib. bdg. 45.00 (*0-89370-786-4*) Borgo Pr.

Vagabonds. large type ed. Josephine Cox. 608p. 1994. 25.99 (*0-7089-3073-5*) Ulverscroft.

Vagabonds: America's Oldest Little Theater. Linda L. Koenig. LC 81-72057. 200p. 1983. 26.50 (*0-8386-3124-X*) Fairleigh Dickinson.

Vagabonds All. Edward A. Parry. LC 73-93370. (Essay Index Reprint Ser.). 1977. 23.95 (*0-8369-1425-2*) Ayer.

Vagadu. Pierre J. Jouve. (Adventure de Catherine Crachat Ser.: No. II). 224p. (FRE.). 1989. pap. 11.95 (*0-7859-2580-5*, 2070381994) Fr & Eur.

***Vagadu.** Pierre J. Jouve & Lydia Davis. LC 97-18102. (The Adventure of Catherine Crachat Ser.). 1997. write for info. (*0-8101-6040-4*, Marlboro) Northwestern U Pr.

Vagal Control of the Heart Vol. 7: Experimental Basis & Clinical Implications. Ed. by Peter J. Schwartz & Matthew N. Levy. LC 93-23821. (Bakken Research Center Ser.). (Illus.). 644p. 1993. 115.00 (*0-87993-561-8*) Futura Pub.

Vagaries & Varieties in Constitutional Interpretation. Thomas R. Powell. LC 74-181973. reprint ed. 29.50 (*0-404-05118-9*) AMS Pr.

Vagina: An Owner's Manual. Judson P. Cone. 87p. (Orig.). 1974. pap. 1.95 (*0-89074-007-0*) Charing Cross.

Vaginal Birth after Cesarean: The Smart Women's Guide to VBAC. Elizabeth Kaufmann. LC 96-16960. (Illus.). 224p. (Orig.). 1996. pap. 12.95 (*0-89793-202-1*) Hunter Hse.

Vaginal Birth after Cesarean (VBAC) Experience: Birth Stories by Parents & Professionals. Lynn B. Richards et al. LC 87-15107. (Illus.). 304p. 1987. pap. text ed. 18.95 (*0-89789-120-1*, Bergin & Garvey) Greenwood.

Vaginal Operations: Surgical Anatomy & Technique. 2nd ed. Gunther Reiffenstuhl et al. Ed. by John R. Imig. Tr. by Julika Bond. LC 95-39425. 303p. 1996. 150.00 (*0-683-07285-4*) Williams & Wilkins.

Vaginal Surgery. 3rd ed. David H. Nichols & Clyde L. Randall. (Illus.). 480p. 1989. 89.00 (*0-683-06494-0*) Williams & Wilkins.

Vaginal Surgery. 4th ed. David H. Nicholas & Clyde L. Randall. LC 95-17805. 585p. 1996. 89.00 (*0-683-06491-6*) Williams & Wilkins.

Vaginal Therapeutics Education Course. Competence Assurance Systems Staff. (Illus.). 1984. pap. text ed. 55.00 (*0-89147-110-3*) CAS.

Vaginale Hysterektomie und Inkontinenz-Operationen. Ed. by H. A. Hirsch. (Gynaekologische Rundschau, 1979 Journal: Supplement 1, Vol. 19). (Illus.). 1979. 33.75 (*3-8055-3072-2*) S Karger.

Vaginalmykose und Perinatale Pilzinfektion. J. D. Schnell. (Illus.). x, 142p. 1982. 53.00 (*3-8055-2854-X*) S Karger.

Vaginitis. Elizabeth K. White. (Illus.). 40p. 1994. pap. 3.60 (*0-317-61779-6*) Budlong.

Vaginitis: Medical Subject Analysis with Bibliography. Sandy M. Van Wertz. LC 87-47615. 160p. 1987. 44.50 (*0-88164-528-1*); pap. 39.50 (*0-88164-529-X*) ABBE Pubs Assn.

Vagrancy: Some New Perspectives. Ed. by T. Cook. 1981. pap. text ed. 48.00 (*0-12-187560-1*) Acad Pr.

Vagrant Memories. William Winter. LC 70-121514. (Essay Index Reprint Ser.). 1977. 36.95 (*0-8369-1817-7*) Ayer.

Vagrant Memories, Being Further Recollections of Other Days. William Winter. (American Biography Ser.). 525p. 1991. reprint ed. lib. bdg. 99.00 (*0-7812-8421-X*) Rprt Serv.

Vagrant Mood: Six Essays. W. Somerset Maugham. LC 75-25378. (Works of W. Somerset Maugham). 1977. reprint ed. 23.95 (*0-405-07831-5*) Ayer.

Vagrant Writing: Social & Semiotic Disorders in the English Renaissance. Barry Taylor. (Theory - Culture Ser.). 272p. 1991. 35.00 (*0-8020-5885-X*) U of Toronto Pr.

***Vague: The Fashion Parody.** Thomas Hagey. (Illus.). 80p. 1997. pap. text ed. 12.95 (*1-55209-056-6*) Firefly Bks Ltd.

Vague History of the Kings & Queens of England. Kevin Hassall. (Illus.). 106p. pap. 8.95 (*1-85756-118-X*, Pub. by Janus Pubng UK) Paul & Co Pubs.

Vague Vacation. Joan M. Grant. 1980. 17.95 (*0-405-11793-0*) Ayer.

Vaguely Defined Objects: Representations, Fuzzy Sets & Nonclassical Cardinality Theory. Maciej Wygralak. LC 95-47435. (Theory & Decision Library B: Vol. 33). 288p. (C). 1996. lib. bdg. 147.00 (*0-7923-3850-2*) Kluwer Ac.

Vagueness. Timothy Williamson. LC 93-37968. 288p. (C). (gr. 13). 1994. text ed. 49.95 (*0-415-03331-4*) Routledge.

Vagueness. Timothy Williamson. LC 93-37968. 344p. (C). 1996. pap. 22.95 (*0-415-13980-5*) Routledge.

***Vagueness: A Reader.** Rosanna Keefe & Peter Smith. LC 96-40332. 1997. write for info. (*0-262-11225-6*) MIT Pr.

Vagueness: An Investigation into Natural Languages & the Sorites Paradox. Linda Burns. (Reason & Argument Ser.: No. 4). 216p. 1991. lib. bdg. 104.50 (*0-7923-1489-1*, Pub. by Klwr Acad Pubs NE) Kluwer Ac.

Vai: Sex & Religion with Notes & Tablature. 160p. 1994. otabind 24.95 (*0-7935-2796-1*, 00694904) H Leonard.

Vail. Trevor Hoyle. (Orig.). 1984. pap. 9.95 (*0-7145-4055-2*) Riverrun NY.

Vail. Tracy Salcedo. (Twelve Short Hikes Ser.). (Illus.). 32p. (Orig.). 1995. pap. 4.95 (*0-934641-74-9*) Chockstone Pr.

Vail - Frisco - Dillon, CO. rev. ed. Ed. by Trails Illustrated Staff. 1994. 8.99 (*0-925873-29-2*) Trails Illustrated.

Vail Hiker: Snowshoe/Ski Touring Guide. 2nd rev. ed. Mary E. Gilliland. LC 96-84848. (Illus.). 104p. 1996. spiral bd. 15.95 (*1-889385-00-X*) Alpenrose Pr.

Vail Site: A Palaeo-Indian Encampment in Maine. Richard M. Gramly. LC 83-127191. (Bulletin Ser.: Vol. 30). (Illus.). 169p. (Orig.). (C). 1982. pap. 12.95 (*0-944032-38-9*) Buffalo SNS.

Vail Ski Area Trail Map Jigsaw Puzzle. (Ski Area in a Box Ser.). 1995. write for info. (*1-888270-03-9*) Teewinot Ent.

Vailala Madness & Other Essays. Francis E. Williams. Ed. by Erik Schwimmer. LC 76-41133. 432p. reprint ed. pap. 123.20 (*0-7837-1313-4*, 2041461) Bks Demand.

Vailala Madness & the Destruction of Native Ceremonies in the Gulf Division. Francis E. Williams. LC 75-35166. (Territory of Papua. Anthropological Report Ser.: No. 4). reprint ed. 27.50 (*0-404-14180-3*) AMS Pr.

Vailima Letters, 2 vols. Robert Louis Stevenson. (BCL1-PR English Literature Ser.). 1992. reprint ed. Set. lib. bdg. 150.00 (*0-7812-7669-1*) Rprt Serv.

Vailima Letters, 2 vols. Robert Louis Stevenson. LC 76-115278. 1983. reprint ed. Set. lib. bdg. 17.00 (*0-403-00283-4*) Scholarly.

Vain Delights. large type ed. Leila Mackinlay. 400p. 1988. 25.99 (*0-7089-1902-2*) Ulverscroft.

Vain Endeavor: Robert Lansing's Attempts to End the American-Japanese Rivalry. Burton F. Beers. LC 61-16907. 219p. reprint ed. 62.50 (*0-8357-9119-X*, 2017884) Bks Demand.

Vain Glory. Cynthia R. Wills. 220p. (Orig.). 1995. pap. 12.95 (*0-9648350-0-2*) Vain Glory.

Vainqueur De Coupe. Rachid Boudjedra. 246p. (FRE.). 1989. pap. 11.95 (*0-7859-2116-8*, 2070381374) Fr & Eur.

Vairagya-Satakam: The Hundred Verses on Renunciation. Bhartrihari. Bilingual ed. pap. 2.00 (*0-87481-070-1*, Pub. by Advaita Ashrama II) Vedanta Pr.

Vaisesika Sutras of Kanada: With Commentary of Sankara Misra & Extracts from Gloss, of Jayanarayana & Notes from Commentary of Candrakanta. Incl. Notes from the Commentary of Chandrakanta. LC 73-3791. (*0-318-50737-4*); Miscellaneous Collected Papers., 4 vols. Utah University, Department Of Anthropology Staff. LC 78-123. reprint ed. Set. 93.50 (*0-404-60700-4*); LC 73-3791. (Sacred Books of the Hindus: No. 6). 379p. reprint ed. 42.50 (*0-404-57806-3*) AMS Pr.

***Vaishnavism in Eastern India.** Suresh C. Bhattacharya. (C). 1995. 12.00 (*81-7102-026-7*, Pub. by Firma KLM II) S Asia.

Vaishnavism of the Gowd Saraswat Brahmins & a Few Konkani Folklore Tales. V. P. Chavan. (C). 1991. reprint ed. 11.00 (*0-8364-2647-9*, Pub. by Asian Educ Servs II) S Asia.

***Vaisnava Art & Iconography of Kashmir.** Bansi L. Malla. (C). 1996. 38.00 (*81-7017-305-1*, Pub. by Abhinav II) S Asia.

Vaisnava Iconography in the Tamil Country. A. Champakalakshmi. 135p. 1981. text ed. 50.00 (*0-86131-216-3*, Pub. by Orient Longman Ltd II) Apt Bks.

Vaisnava India. Geary J. Sheridan, Jr. et al. (Illus.). 800p. 1994. text ed. write for info. (*0-945421-00-1*) Vedic Heritage.

Vaisnava Interpretation of the Brahmasutras: Vedanta & Theism. Rampada Chattopadhyay. Tr. by Kanti Chattopadhyay from BEN. LC 91-47654. (Indian Thought Ser.: Vol. 3). xxvi, 299p. 1992. 107.00 (*90-04-09570-5*) E J Brill.

Vaisnavism: Contemporary Scholars Discuss the Gaudiya Tradition. Ed. by Steven J. Rosen. LC 92-71546. 1992. pap. write for info. (*0-9619763-6-5*) Folk Bks.

Vaisnavism: Its Philosophy, Theology, & Religious Discipline. Srinivasa M. Chari. (C). 1994. 32.00 (*81-208-1098-8*, Pub. by Munshiram Manoharial II) S Asia.

Vaisnavism & Society in Northern India. Urmila Bhagowalia. 1980. 22.00 (*0-8364-0664-8*, Pub. by Intellectual II) S Asia.

Vaisnavism in Orissa. Santilata Dei. (C). 1988. 34.00 (*0-685-33355-8*, Pub. by Punthi Pus II) S Asia.

Vaisnavism Saivism & Minor Religious Systems. R. G. Bhandarkar. 238p. 1986. reprint ed. 14.00 (*0-8364-1704-6*, Pub. by Minerva II) S Asia.

***Vaisnavism, Saivism & Minor Religious Systems.** Ramkrishna G. Bhandarkar. (C). 1995. reprint ed. 16.00 (*81-206-0122-X*, Pub. by Asian Educ Servs II) S Asia.

Vaisnavite Poets of Northeastern India: Ananta Kandali. N. C. Sarma. (C). 1991. 25.00 (*81-85094-47-0*, Pub. by Punthi Pus II) S Asia.

Vak: An Anthology of Australian, European & Indian Verse. Ed. by Sibnarayan Ray. 14.00 (*0-89253-623-3*); pap. 8.00 (*0-86578-108-7*) Ind-US Inc.

Vakat. Nan Goldin. 1994. 29.50 (*3-88375-178-2*, Pub. by Walther Konig GW) Dist Art Pubs.

Vakataka - Gupta Age Circa 200-550 A.D. R. C. Majumdar & A. S. Altekar. 515p. 1986. reprint ed. 17.50 (*81-208-0026-5*, Pub. by Motilal Banarsidass II); reprint ed. pap. 12.50 (*81-208-0043-5*, Pub. by Motilal Banarsidass II) S Asia.

Vakyapadiyam of Bhartrhari Brahmakanda. Tr. by Korada Subrahmanyam. (Sri Garib Dass Oriental Ser.: No. 146). (C). 1992. 15.00 (*81-7030-328-1*) S Asia.

Vakyavritti of Sri Sankaracharya. Shankara. 1949. Bilingual ed. pap. 2.00 (*0-87481-424-3*, Pub. by Advaita Ashrama II) Vedanta Pr.

Val. Michael Curnes. LC 95-83611. 410p. 1996. pap. 15.95 (*1-885487-19-3*) Brownell & Carroll.

Val Halen - Diver Down. 1994. pap. 12.95 (*0-685-75230-5*); pap. 19.95 (*0-89524-777-1*) Cherry Lane.

Val McCall, Ace Reporter? Fran Manushkin. LC 95-16162. 1995. pap. 3.99 (*0-14-037201-6*) Puffin Bks.

Val Rosing: Musical Genius. Ruth Rosing. (Illus.). 238p. 1993. pap. 20.95 (*0-89745-167-8*) Sunflower U Pr.

Val Verde Winery. Robert C. Overfelt. (Southwestern Studies: No. 75). 76p. 1985. pap. 5.00 (*0-87404-151-1*) Tex Western.

Valances Etc. Cy DeCosse Incorporated Staff. LC 96-15847. (Creative Touches Ser.). 64p. 1996. pap. 9.95 (*0-86573-998-6*) Cowles Creative.

Valazquez: Painter & Courtier. Jonathan Brown. LC 85-14234. 336p. (C). 1988. reprint ed. 35.00 (*0-300-03894-1*) Yale U Pr.

Valdepenas. Richard Lortz. LC 79-66114. 224p. 1984. 22.00 (*0-933256-06-X*); 5.95 (*0-933256-49-3*) Second Chance.

Valdes Leal, Spanish Baroque Painter. Elizabeth Du Gue Trapier. (Illus.). 1960. 10.00 (*0-87535-112-3*) Hispanic Soc.

***Valdes' Two Catechisms: The Dialogue on Christian Doctrine & the Christian Instruction for Children.** 2nd rev. ed. Jose C. Nieto. Ed. by William B. Jones & Carol D. Jones. (Illus.). 276p. 1993. 25.00 (*0-87291-205-1*) Coronado Pr.

***Valdez: A Brief Oral History.** Karen LaChance. 110p. 1995. pap. 10.00 (*0-9647662-0-5*) Prince William.

Valdez Creek Mining District Alaska. Clyde Ross. 56p. reprint ed. pap. 4.95 (*0-8466-0107-9*, S107) Shorey.

Valdez Gold Rush Trails 1898-99. Jim Lethcoe & Nancy Lethcoe. (Illus.). 144p. (Orig.). 1996. pap. 14.95 (*1-877900-05-2*) Prince W Sound.

Valdez Is Coming. Elmore Leonard. 1993. reprint ed. lib. bdg. 21.95 (*1-56849-176-X*) Buccaneer Bks.

Valdez Is Coming. Elmore Leonard. 1994. reprint ed. lib. bdg. 27.95 (*1-56849-300-2*) Buccaneer Bks.

Valdoro's Mistress. large type ed. Evelyn S. Armstrong. 403p. 1978. 25.99 (*0-7089-0168-9*) Ulverscroft.

Valdosta & Lowndes County: A Ray in the Sunbelt. Louis Schmier. 1988. 26.95 (*0-89781-279-4*, 5302) Am Historical Pr.

Vale la Pena Esperar. Tim Stafford. (SPA.). 1990. pap. 4.99 (*0-945792-26-3*, 490237) Editorial Unilit.

Vale la Pena Esperar. Tim Stafford. 140p. (POR.). 1991. pap. 6.95 (*0-8297-1648-3*) Life Pubs Intl.

Vale of Glamorgan in Old Photographs. Steward Williams. 80p. (C). 1989. 70.00 (*1-870402-10-3*, Pub. by D Brown & Sons Ltd UK) St Mut.

Vale of Lanherne. Ed. by Charles Lee. (C). 1989. 30.00 (*0-907566-45-6*, Pub. by Dyllansow Truran UK) St Mut.

Vale of Tears: A Problem Shared. Ed. by Peter Burton & Richard Smith. 212p. (Orig.). 1992. pap. 13.95 (*1-873741-05-7*, Pub. by Millvres Bks UK) LPC InBook.

Vale of Tears: Revisiting the Canudos Massacre in Northeastern Brazil, 1893-1897. Robert M. Levine. LC 91-36011. (C). 1992. 45.00 (*0-520-07524-2*) U CA Pr.

Vale of Tears: Revisiting the Canudos Massacre in Northeastern Brazil, 1893-1897. Robert M. Levine. LC 91-36011. 365p. 1995. pap. 15.95 (*0-520-20343-7*) U CA Pr.

Vale of Tears & on Quakeresses. Nikolai Leskov. 1991. pap. 16.95 (*0-9517853-0-3*, Pub. by Bramcote Pr UK) Intl Spec Bk.

Vale of the Vole. Piers Anthony. 336p. 1987. mass mkt. 5.99 (*0-380-75287-5*) Avon.

Vale-Royall of England: Or, the County Palatine of Chester Illustrated, 1656. Daniel King. (Printed Sources of Western Art Ser.). (Illus.). 354p. 1981. reprint ed. boxed 60.00 (*0-915346-65-6*) A Wofsy Fine Arts.

Valediction. Robert B. Parker, Jr. 288p. 1992. mass mkt. 6.50 (*0-440-19246-3*) Dell.

Valedictory Verses. Gomer Press Staff. (C). 1978. pap. 20.00 (*0-85088-840-9*, Pub. by Gomer Pr UK) St Mut.

Valence Bond Theory & Chemical Structure. Ed. by Nenad Trinajstic & D. J. Klein. (Studies in Physical & Theoretical Chemistry: No. 64). 630p. 1990. 307.00 (*0-444-88186-7*) Elsevier.

Valence Theory. 2nd ed. John N. Murrell et al. LC 70-129161. 444p. reprint ed. pap. 126.60 (*0-685-15458-0*, 2026688) Bks Demand.

***Valence/Grenoble/Gap Map.** 1997. 6.95 (*2-06-700077-2*, 77) Michelin.

Valencia, Ciudad Rodrigo, Badajos, Salamanca, Madrid, Oct. 1811-Aug. 31, 1812 see History of the Peninsular War

Valencian Painters, 1860-1936: From the Collection of the Diputacin de Valencia. Carmen Gracia Beneyto. (Illus.). 174p. 1993. pap. 29.95 (*0-295-97269-6*) U of Wash Pr.

Valenge Women: The Social & Economic Life of the Valenge Women of Portuguese East Africa; An Ethnographic Study. E. Dora Earthy. (Illus.). 251p. 1968. 45.00 (*0-7146-1660-5*, Pub. by F Cass Pubs UK) Intl Spec Bk.

Valenge Women: The Social & Economic Life of the Valenge Women of Portuguese East Africa; An Ethnographic Study. Emily D. Earthy. LC 34-17943. (Illus.). 263p. reprint ed. pap. 75.00 (*0-8357-3216-9*, 2057088) Bks Demand.

Valentin Bonito, Vol. 7: Pasitos Spanish Language Development Books. Darlyne F. Schott. (Pasitos Hacia la Lectura Ser.). 19p. (J). (gr. k-1). 1990. pap. text ed. 11.00 (*1-56537-056-2*) D F Schott Educ.

Valentin et Orson. (EETS, OS Ser.: No. 204). 1974. reprint ed. 65.00 (*0-527-00204-6*) Periodicals Srv.

***Valentin Haussmann (1565 70-Ca. 1614) A Thematic-Documentary Catalogue of His Works.** Robert B. Lynn & Klaus-Peter Koch. LC 96-39598. (Thematic Catalogues Ser.). (GER.). 1997. 62.00 (*0-945193-91-2*) Pendragon NY.

***Valentin Serov: Artist of Russian Romanticism.** Dmitry Sarabyanov. (Great Painters Ser.). 1996. 40.00 (*1-85995-283-6*) Parkstone Pr.

Valentina. Fern Michaels. 1984. mass mkt. 5.99 (*0-345-31126-4*) Ballantine.

Valentina, Vol 1. Guido Crepax. Tr. by S. Gaudiano from ITA. 96p. 1991. pap. 12.95 (*1-56163-032-2*, Eurotica) NBM.

Valentina, Vol. 2: Magic Lantern. Guido Crepax. 104p. 1994. pap. 11.95 (*1-56163-095-0*, Eurotica) NBM.

Valentina's Italian Family Feast: Festive Cooking for Family Occasions. Valentina Harris. (Illus.). 144p. 1992. 24.95 (*0-671-74530-1*) S&S Trade.

Valentine. 1996. pap. 12.95 (*0-7871-0615-1*, Dove Bks) Dove Audio.

Valentine. 1996. pap. 12.98 (*0-7871-0693-3*, Dove Bks) Dove Audio.

Valentine. Carol Carrick. LC 93-35911. (Illus.). (J). 1995. 14.95 (*0-395-66554-X*, Clarion Bks) HM.

Valentine. Jane Feather. 448p. 1995. mass mkt. 5.99 (*0-553-56470-6*) Bantam.

***Valentine.** Jane Feather. (Five Star Romances Ser.). 1996. lib. bdg. 23.95 (*0-7862-0860-0*, Five Star) Mac Lib Ref.

Valentine. Debra A. Gauvin. (Orig.). 1996. pap. write for info. (*1-57553-184-4*) Watermrk Pr.

Valentine. Emilie Paris. (Orig.). 1994. mass mkt. 5.95 (*1-56201-072-7*) Blue Moon Bks.

Valentine. George Sand, pseud. 255p. (FRE.). 1988. pap. 24.95 (*0-7859-1579-6*, 2903950237) Fr & Eur.

Valentine. Tom Savage. LC 95-35937. 336p. 1996. 20.95 (*0-316-77164-3*) Little.

Valentine. Tom Savage. 1997. pap. 6.99 (*0-451-40719-9*, Onyx) NAL-Dutton.

Valentine. S. P. Somtow. 448p. 1995. mass mkt. 5.99 (*0-8125-1240-5*) Tor Bks.

Valentine. large type ed. Jane Feather. LC 94-40975. (Large Print Bks.). 1995. 23.95 (*1-56895-162-0*) Wheeler Pub.

Valentine. George Sand, pseud. Tr. by George B. Ives from FRE. LC 77-28026. 336p. 1995. reprint ed. pap. 14.00 (*0-915864-59-2*) Academy Chi Pubs.

***Valentine: A Bouquet of Letters & Poetry for Lovers.** Stefan Rudnicki. 1997. pap. 7.95 (*0-7871-1262-3*, Dove Bks) Dove Audio.

***Valentine: Very Easy Coloring Fun.** Standard Publishing Staff. (J). 1997. pap. text ed. 1.49 (*0-7847-0598-4*) Standard Pub.

Valentine & Orson. Nancy E. Burkert. (Floyd Yearout Bk.). 56p. (J). (gr. 5 up). 1989. 16.95 (*0-374-38078-3*) FS&G.

Valentine & Orson, a Study in Late Medieval Romance. Arthur Dickson. LC 75-153315. reprint ed. 32.50 (*0-404-02128-X*) AMS Pr.

Valentine Bachelors: Your Heart's Desire; Mr. Romance; Sleepless in St. Louis, 3 vols. in 1. Elise Title et al. (Promo Ser.). 1995. pap. 4.99 (*0-373-83319-9*, 1-83319-3) Harlequin Bks.

Valentine Bears. Eve Bunting. (Illus.). 32p. (J). (gr. 3). 1984. 14.95 (*0-89919-138-X*, Clarion Bks) HM.

An Asterisk (*) at the beginning of an entry indicates that the title is appearing in BIP for the first time.

Valentine Bears. Eve Bunting. (Illus.). 32p. (J). (gr. 3). 1985. pap. 5.95 (*0-89919-313-7*, Clarion Bks) HM.
***Valentine Bouquet.** Tannerbard et al. 320p. 1997. mass mkt. 4.99 (*0-8217-5577-3*, Zebra Kensgtn) Kensgtn Pub Corp.
Valentine Cat. Clyde R. Bulla. (Illus.). 64p. (J). (gr. k-3). 1996. pap. 12.50 (*0-8167-3702-9*) Troll Communs.
Valentine Cat. Clyde R. Bulla. LC 94-18353. (Illus.). 64p. (J). (gr. k-3). 1995. pap. 4.95 (*0-8167-3599-9*) Troll Communs.
Valentine Cats. Jean Marzollo. LC 94-47816. (Read with Me Paperbacks Ser.). (Illus.). 32p. (J). (ps-2). 1996. pap. 2.99 (*0-590-47596-7*, Cartwheel) Scholastic Inc.
Valentine Child. Jacqueline Baird. (Presents Ser.). 1996. mass mkt. 3.50 (*0-373-11795-7*, 1-11795-1) Harlequin Bks.
Valentine Child. large type ed. Jacqueline Baird. (Harlequin Romance Ser.). 1996. 19.95 (*0-263-14573-5*) Thorndike Pr.
***Valentine Cookies.** Adams Media Staff. (Just Desserts Ser.). 1997. pap. text ed. 4.95 (*1-55850-732-9*) Adams Media.
Valentine Crafts. Judith H. Corwin. LC 93-11970. (Holiday Craft Bks.). 48p. (J). 1994. lib. bdg. 19.80 (*0-531-11146-6*) Watts.
Valentine Crafts. Judith H. Corwin. (Holiday Craft Bks.). (Illus.). 48p. (J). (gr. 3-5). 1994. pap. 5.95 (*0-531-15727-X*) Watts.
Valentine Decorations: Make & Color Your Own. (J). (ps-3). 1996. pap. 1.95 (*0-89375-646-6*) Troll Communs.
***Valentine Delights.** Gina F. Wilkins et al. (Harlequin Promotion Ser.). 1997. pap. 6.99 (*0-373-83324-5*, 1-83324-3) Harlequin Bks.
Valentine Duval: An Autobiography. Anne Manning. (Art, History & the Connoisseur Ser.). (Illus.). 142p. (C). 1990. reprint ed. 19.95 (*1-879080-00-1*) Clios Cabinet.
Valentine Embrace. Ed. by Jennifer Sawyer. 320p. 1995. mass mkt. 3.99 (*0-8217-4813-0*, Zebra Kensgtn) Kensgtn Pub Corp.
Valentine Fantasy. Carolyn Haywood. LC 75-23083. (Illus.). 32p. (J). (gr. k-3). 1976. lib. bdg. 14.93 (*0-688-32055-4*, Morrow Junior) Morrow.
Valentine for Daisy. large type ed. Betty A. Nneels. (Harlequin Ser.). 1994. lib. bdg. 18.95 (*0-263-13723-6*, Pub. by Mills & Boon UK) Thorndike Pr.
Valentine for Daisy: (Kids & Kisses) Betty A. Neels. (Romance Ser.). 1995. pap. 2.99 (*0-373-03347-8*, 1-03347-1) Harlequin Bks.
Valentine for Mr. Wonderful. Helen Frankenthaler. (Illus.). 24p. 1996. 35.00 (*0-8478-1986-8*) Rizzoli Intl.
Valentine for Ms. Vanilla. Harriet Ziefert. (Hello Reading! Ser.). (Illus.). 32p. (J). (ps-3). 1992. pap. 3.50 (*0-14-054460-7*) Puffin Bks.
Valentine for Ms. Vanilla. Harriet Ziefert & Martha Gradisher. (Easy-to-Read Ser.: Level 2, Red). (Illus.). (J). (gr. k-3). 1994. pap. 3.50 (*0-14-036871-X*) Puffin Bks.
Valentine for Noel. Emmett Williams. LC 73-78692. 1973. pap. 25.00 (*0-87110-107-6*) Ultramarine Pub.
***Valentine for Norman Noggs.** Valiska Gregory. LC 96-48589. (Illus.). (J). 1999. write for info. (*0-06-027656-8*); lib. bdg. write for info. (*0-06-027657-6*) HarpC.
Valentine for You. Wendy Watson. (Illus.). 32p. (J). (gr. k-3). 1993. pap. 5.95 (*0-395-66411-X*, Clarion Bks) HM.
Valentine Frankenstein. Maggie Twohill. 144p. (J). (gr. 5-7). 1994. pap. 2.95 (*0-590-46039-0*) Scholastic Inc.
Valentine Friends. Ann Schweninger. (Picture Puffins Ser.). (Illus.). 32p. (J). (ps-1). 1990. pap. 4.99 (*0-14-050662-4*, Puffin) Puffin Bks.
Valentine Fun. Judith H. Corwin. LC 82-6047. (Holiday Fun Ser.). (Illus.). 64p. (J). (gr. 3 up). 1983. pap. 5.95 (*0-671-49755-3*, Julian Messner) Silver Burdett Pr.
Valentine Fun Activity Book. Judith B. Stamper. LC 92-13225. (Illus.). 48p. (J). (gr. 2-5). 1997. pap. 4.95 (*0-8167-2911-5*) Troll Communs.
Valentine Hearts & Flowers. Muriel Jensen. (American Romance Ser.: No. 425). 1992. mass mkt. 3.29 (*0-373-16425-4*, 1-16425-0) Harlequin Bks.
Valentine Holiday Grab Bag. Judith B. Stamper. LC 92-13225. (Illus.). 48p. (J). (gr. 2-5). 1992. lib. bdg. 13.95 (*0-8167-2910-7*) Troll Communs.
***Valentine Hostage.** Dawn Stewardson. (Intrigue Ser.). 1997. 3.75 (*0-373-22406-0*, 1-22406-2) Harlequin Bks.
Valentine Jingo. Gary Grimm & Phoebe Wear. 32p. (J). (gr. k-6). 1993. 12.00 (*1-56490-006-1*) G Grimm Assocs.
Valentine Kiss. Monica Harris. 384p. 1996. mass mkt. 4.99 (*0-7860-0237-9*, Pinncle Kensgtn) Kensgtn Pub Corp.
Valentine Legacy. Catherine Coulter. 432p. 1996. mass mkt. 6.99 (*0-515-11836-2*) Jove Pubns.
Valentine Legacy. Catherine Coulter. LC 95-14698. 400p. 1995. 19.95 (*0-399-14094-8*, Putnam) Putnam Pub Group.
Valentine Legacy. large type ed. Catherine Coulter. 573p. 1995. 25.95 (*0-7838-1497-6*, GK Hall) Thorndike Pr.
Valentine Love. Sara Blayne. 352p. 1996. mass mkt. 4.50 (*0-8217-5199-9*, Zebra Kensgtn) Kensgtn Pub Corp.
Valentine M'Clutchy, the Irish Agent: The Chronicles of Castle Cumber Property, with the Pious Aspirations of Solomon M'Slime, 3 vols. in 2, Set. William Carleton. LC 79-8247. reprint ed. 84.50 (*0-404-61807-3*) AMS Pr.
***Valentine Mice!** Bethany Roberts. LC 96-50889. (Illus.). (J). 1997. 13.00 (*0-395-77518-3*, Clarion Bks) HM.
Valentine Mystery. Joan L. Nixon. Ed. by Kathleen Tucker. LC 79-17055. (Illus.). 32p. (J). (gr. 1-3). 1979. lib. bdg. 8.95 (*0-8075-8450-9*) A Whitman.
***Valentine Picotee.** Dominique Demers. (Novels in the Premier Roman Ser.). 64p. (FRE.). (J). (gr. 2-5). 1996. pap. 7.95 (*2-89021-164-9*, Pub. by Les Editions CN) Firefly Bks Ltd.
Valentine Place: Poems. David Lehman. LC 95-38090. 96p. 1996. 25.00 (*0-684-81570-2*) S&S Trade.
Valentine Place: Poems. David Lehman. 96p. 1996. pap. 14.00 (*0-684-82279-2*) S&S Trade.
Valentine Poems. Myra C. Livingston. LC 85-31723. (Illus.). 32p. (J). (ps-3). 1987. lib. bdg. 15.95 (*0-8234-0587-7*) Holiday.
Valentine Pontifex. Robert Silverberg. 496p. 1996. mass mkt. 5.99 (*0-06-105486-0*) HarpC.
Valentine Prentice, His Origins & the Descsendents of His Grandsons John, Jonathan, Stephan & Thomas, 2 vols. Linus J. Dewald, Jr. (Illus.). 620p. (Orig.). 1993. pap. 60.00 (*1-55613-696-X*) Heritage Bk.
***Valentine Rainbow.** Gaby Goldsack. (Little Valentine Window Bks.). 1998. 3.99 (*1-57584-073-1*) Rdrs Dgst Yng Fam.
Valentine Sampler: Only the Present; The Face of Love, 2 bks. in 1. Noelle B. McCue & Anne N. Reisser. 368p. 1994. mass mkt., pap. text ed. 4.99 (*0-8439-3571-5*) Dorchester Pub Co.
***Valentine School Parties...What Do I Do?** Wilhelminia Ripple. (What Do I Do? Ser.). (Illus.). 175p. (Orig.). 1997. pap. write for info. (*0-9649939-9-6*) Oakbrook Pubng.
Valentine Star. Patricia R. Giff. (Kids of the Polk Street School Ser.: No. 6). (Illus.). 80p. (Orig.). (J). (gr. k-6). 1985. mass mkt. 3.50 (*0-440-49204-1*, YB BDD) BDD Bks Young Read.
Valentine Star see Kids of the Polk Street School
Valentine Sticker Book. Nina Barbaresi. (Illus.). (J). (gr. k-3). 1989. pap. 1.00 (*0-486-26192-1*) Dover.
Valentine Street Hustle. Barbara Boswell. (Desire Ser.: No. 609). 1990. pap. 2.50 (*0-373-05609-5*) Silhouette.
Valentine, Texas. Kate Denton. (Romance Ser.). 1996. mass mkt. 3.25 (*0-373-03398-2*, 1-03398-4) Harlequin Bks.
***Valentine Thoughts.** Illus. by Kathy Mitchell. (Sparkle 'n' Twinkle Bks.). (J). (ps-2). 1997. 4.99 (*0-614-29111-9*, Litl Simon S&S) S&S Childrens.
Valentine Wish. Gina F. Wilkins. (Temptation Ser.). 1996. mass mkt. 3.50 (*0-373-25676-0*, 1-25676-7) Harlequin Bks.
***Valentine Wishes.** Jeanne Savery et al. 256p. 1998. mass mkt. 4.99 (*0-8217-5853-5*, Zebra Kensgtn) Kensgtn Pub Corp.
***Valentines.** Robert Brenner. LC 96-36140. 208p. (YA). (gr. 10). 1997. 49.95 (*0-7643-0195-0*) Schiffer.
Valentines. Anne T. Perkins. (Big Books - Mini Bks.). (Illus.). 8p. (J). (ps). 1994. 12.00 (*1-884204-08-2*) Teach Nxt Door.
Valentines: A Loving Remembrance. Jean Favalora. (Illus.). 112p. 1995. 14.00 (*0-937274-92-5*) Lark Books.
Valentines: With Values. Katherine Kreider. LC 95-45153. (Illus.). 192p. 1996. pap. 19.95 (*0-88740-932-6*) Schiffer.
***Valentine's Child.** Natalie Bishop. 1997. pap. 3.99 (*0-373-24086-4*, 1-24086-0) Silhouette.
Valentine's Day. Judy Beach & Kathleen Spencer. (Teachers' Holiday Helpers Ser.). (J). (gr. 1-3). 1987. pap. 6.99 (*0-8224-6774-7*) Fearon Teach Aids.
Valentine's Day. Horton Foote. 1987. pap. 5.25 (*0-8222-1199-8*) Dramatists Play.
Valentine's Day. Dennis B. Fradin. LC 89-7682. (Best Holiday Bks.). (Illus.). 48p. (J). (gr. 1-4). 1990. lib. bdg. 17.95 (*0-89490-237-7*) Enslow Pubs.
Valentine's Day. Gail Gibbons. LC 85-916. (Illus.). 32p. (J). (ps-3). 1986. lib. bdg. 15.95 (*0-8234-0572-9*) Holiday.
Valentine's Day. Gail Gibbons. LC 85-916. (Illus.). 32p. (J). (ps-3). 1989. pap. 6.95 (*0-8234-0764-0*) Holiday.
Valentine's Day. Gail Gibbons. (Illus.). (J). (gr. k-3). 1990. pap. 15.95 incl. audio (*0-87499-004-1*) Live Oak Media.
Valentine's Day. Gail Gibbons. (Illus.). (J). (gr. k-3). 1990. 22.95 incl. audio (*0-87499-006-8*) Live Oak Media.
Valentine's Day. Joyce K. Kessel. LC 81-3842. (Carolrhoda On My Own Bks.). (Illus.). 48p. (J). (gr. k-3). 1981. lib. bdg. 13.13 (*0-87614-166-1*, Carolrhoda) Lerner Group.
Valentine's Day. Miriam Nerlove. Ed. by Judith Mathews. LC 91-19289. (Illus.). 24p. (J). (ps-1). 1992. lib. bdg. 12.95 (*0-8075-8454-1*) A Whitman.
Valentine's Day. Miriam Nerlove. LC 91-19289. (Albert Whitman Prairie Bks.). (Illus.). 24p. (J). (ps-1). 1994. pap. 4.95 (*0-8075-8455-X*) A Whitman.
Valentine's Day. Shelly Nielsen. (J). 1996. lib. bdg. 13.98 (*1-56239-703-6*) Abdo & Dghtrs.
Valentine's Day. Nancy Reese. Ed. by Alton Jordan. (Holiday Set). (Illus.). (J). (gr. k-3). 1984. 7.95 (*0-89868-029-8*, Read Res); pap. 3.95 (*0-89868-062-X*, Read Res) ARO Pub.
***Valentine's Day.** Anne F. Rockwell. LC 97-17492. (Illus.). (J). 1999. write for info. (*0-06-027794-7*) HarpC.
***Valentines Day.** Wendy Watson. (J). Date not set. write for info. (*0-688-09566-6*); lib. bdg. write for info. (*0-688-09567-4*) Lothrop.
Valentine's Day. Joyce K. Kessel. (Holiday on My Own Bks.). (Illus.). 48p. (J). (gr. k-3). 1988. reprint ed. pap. 5.95 (*0-87614-502-0*, First Ave Edns) Lerner Group.
Valentine's Day, 4 bks., Set. Gail Gibbons. (Illus.). (J). (gr. k-3). 1990. pap. 36.95 incl. audio (*0-87499-005-X*) Live Oak Media.
Valentine's Day: A Thematic Unit. Ireta S. Graube. (Thematic Units Ser.). (Illus.). 80p. (Orig.). (J). (gr. 1-3). 1992. student ed. 9.95 (*1-55734-260-1*) Tchr Create Mat.
Valentine's Day: Stories & Poems. Ed. by Caroline Feller Bauer. LC 91-37641. (Illus.). 96p. (J). (gr. 2-5). 1993. 15.95 (*0-06-020823-6*); lib. bdg. 15.89 (*0-06-020824-4*) HarpC Child Bks.
***Valentine's Day Can Be Murder.** Colleen O. McKenna. 1997. pap. text ed. 3.50 (*0-590-67985-6*) Scholastic Inc.
Valentine's Day Delight. Ed. by Jennifer Sawyer. 320p. 1994. mass mkt. 3.99 (*0-8217-4471-2*, Zebra Kensgtn) Kensgtn Pub Corp.
Valentine's Day Gambit. Mona Gedney. 320p. 1993. mass mkt. 3.99 (*0-8217-4049-0*, Zebra Kensgtn) Kensgtn Pub Corp.
Valentine's Day Grump. Rose Greydanus. LC 81-4712. (Illus.). 32p. (J). (gr. k-2). 1997. pap. 3.95 (*0-89375-516-8*) Troll Communs.
Valentines Day Ideals 1996. Ideals Editorial Staff. (Illus.). 80p. 1995. pap. 5.95 (*0-8249-1133-4*) Ideals.
Valentine's Day Mess. Janet A. Craig. LC 93-2211. (Giant First Start Reader Ser.). (Illus.). 32p. (J). (gr. k-2). 1993. lib. bdg. 12.95 (*0-8167-3254-X*) Troll Communs.
Valentine's Day Mess. Janet A. Craig. LC 93-2211. (Giant First Start Reader Ser.). (Illus.). 32p. (J). (gr. k-2). 1997. pap. 3.95 (*0-8167-3255-8*) Troll Communs.
***Valentines Day Murder.** Lee Harris. 1997. mass mkt. 5.99 (*0-449-14964-1*, GM) Fawcett.
Valentine's Day Mystery. Marion M. Markham. LC 92-8391. (Illus.). 48p. (J). (gr. 2-5). 1992. 13.95 (*0-395-61589-5*) HM.
Valentine's Day Postcard Storybook. Lampl. (J). 1997. 6.99 (*0-689-80720-1*) S&S Childrens.
Valentine's Day Search & Find. 24p. (J). (gr. k-4). 1996. pap. 2.50 (*0-8167-1852-0*) Troll Communs.
***Valentine's Day Surprise.** Marilyn Kaye. (The After School Club Ser.: Vol. 2). (YA). 1997. pap. 3.50 (*0-671-51027-4*, Minstrel Bks) PB.
Valentine's Day Tangle. Ed. by Jennifer Sawyer. 352p. 1993. mass mkt. 3.99 (*0-8217-4050-4*, Zebra Kensgtn) Kensgtn Pub Corp.
***Valentines for Nurse Cleo.** large type ed. Lilian Darcy. (Magna Large Print Ser.). (Illus.). 297p. 1996. 25.99 (*0-7505-1010-2*) Ulverscroft.
Valentines Ideals Magazine, 1995. 1994. pap. 4.95 (*0-8249-1123-7*) Ideals.
Valentines in the Snow. Betty R. Gubler. 144p. 1993. 14.98 (*0-88290-471-X*, 1952) Horizon Utah.
***Valentine's Knight.** Renee Roszel. 1998. mass mkt. 4.50 (*0-373-81061-X*, 1-81061-3) Harlequin Bks.
Valentine's Manuals: A General Index to the Manuals of the Corporation of the City of New York, 1841-1870. Hoe R. Lawrence & Otto Hufeland. LC 81-6437. 157p. 1981. 15.00 (*0-916346-42-0*) NY Bound.
Valentine's Night. Penny Jordan. (Winner's Circle Ser.). 1996. mass mkt. 3.99 (*0-373-60074-7*, 1-60074-1) Harlequin Bks.
Valentine's Summer. Terri Lynn. (Superromance Ser.). 1993. mass mkt. 3.50 (*0-373-70555-7*, 1-70555-7) Harlequin Bks.
Valentino. Bernadine Morris. 80p. 1996. 18.95 (*0-7893-0066-4*) St Martin.
Valentino. Andrea Wolf. Ed. by Elizabeth Bradford. Tr. by Mangold Verlag from GER. LC 91-21301. (Magic Mountain Fables Ser.). (Illus.). 32p. (J). (gr. k-3). 1991. lib. bdg. 14.60 (*1-56074-030-2*) Garrett Ed Corp.
Valentino: Thirty Years of Magic. Marie-Paule Pelle & Patrick Mauries. (Illus.). 336p. 1991. 95.00 (*1-55859-237-7*) Abbeville Pr.
Valentino & the Great Italians. Anthony Valerio. LC 86-7564. 248p. 1986. 17.95 (*0-88191-041-4*) Freundlich.
Valentino & the Great Italians. Anthony Valerio. 248p. 1994. pap. 13.00 (*0-920717-90-X*) Guernica Editions.
Valentino's Hair: A Novel. Yvonne V. Sapia. 157p. 1991. 18.95 (*0-932511-45-7*); pap. 8.95 (*0-932511-46-5*) Fiction Coll.
***Valerian: The Genus Valeriana.** Ed. by Peter Houghton. (Medicinal & Aromatic Plants, Industrial Ser.). 1997. text ed. 75.00 (*90-5702-170-6*, Harwood Acad Pubs) Gordon & Breach.
Valerian: The Relaxing & Sleep Herb. Christopher Hobbs. Ed. by Michael Miour. (Illus.). 53p. 1993. pap. 5.95 (*0-9618470-9-3*) Botanica CA.
Valerie & the Jelly Bean Trail. David E. Page. (Illus.). 24p. (J). (gr. k-3). 1995. pap. 2.99 (*0-87406-732-4*) Willowisp Pr.
Valerie & the Silver Pear. Benjamin Darling. LC 90-24945. (Illus.). 32p. (J). (gr. k-3). 1992. text ed. 14.95 (*0-02-726100-X*, Four Winds Pr) S&S Childrens.
Valerie Jaudon. Rene P. Barilleaux & Anna C. Chave. Ed. by Ginger Tucker. (Illus.). 96p. (Orig.). 1996. pap. 25.00 (*1-887422-00-5*) Miss Mus Art.
Valerie Swane's Rose Room. Valerie Swane. 176p. 1994. 25.00 (*0-207-17916-6*, Pub. by Angus & Robertson AT) HarpC.
Valerio Dorico: Music Printer in Sixteenth-Century Rome. Suzanne G. Cusick. LC 81-4745. (Studies in Musicology: No. 43). (Illus.). 329p. reprint ed. pap. 93.80 (*0-685-20886-9*, 2070262) Bks Demand.
Valerius Flaccus - Concordantiae in Valerii Flacci Argonautica, 2 vols. Ed. by Matthias Korn & Wolfgang Slaby. (Alpha-Omega, Reihe A Ser.: Bd. XCIII). vi, 1555p. 1988. Set. write for info. (*3-487-09053-8*) G Olms Pubs.
Valerius Flaccus, Argonautica Bk. V: A Commentary. H. J. Wijsman. LC 95-45997. (Mnemosyne, Bibliotheca Classica Batava Ser.: Vol. 158). 1996. 105.00 (*90-04-10506-9*) E J Brill.
Valerius Flaccus Argonautica VII: Ein Kommentar. Valerius Flaccus. Ed. by Hubert Stadler. (Spudasmata Ser.: Band 49). xiv, 252p. (GER.). 1993. pap. text ed. 36.95 (*3-487-09709-5*) G Olms Pubs.
Valerius Flaccus, Argonautica 4, 1-343. Ein Kommentar. Matthias Korn. (Spudasmata Ser.: Bd. XLVI). 227p. (GER.). 1989. write for info. (*3-487-09227-1*) G Olms Pubs.
Valerius Maximus & the Rhetoric of the New Nobility. W. Martin Bloomer. LC 92-53628. viii, 288p. (C). 1992. 45.00 (*0-8078-2047-4*) U of NC Pr.
***Valerius Maxiums' Memorable Deeds & Sayings.** Valerius Maximus. Ed. & Tr. by D. Wardle. 250p. 1998. 55.00 (*0-19-815016-4*) OUP.
Valery & Poe: A Literary Legacy. Lois D. Vines. 300p. (C). 1992. 45.00 (*0-8147-8771-1*) NYU Pr.
Valery Carick's Picture Folk-Tales see Picture Folk-Tales
Valery Larbaud et l'Italie. Ruggiero. 26.25 (*0-685-34263-8*) Fr & Eur.
Valet's Tragedy & Other Studies. Andrew Lang. LC 75-112939. (Illus.). reprint ed. 39.00 (*0-404-03865-4*) AMS Pr.
Valett Inventory of Critical Thinking Abilities (VICTA) Robert E. Valett. 1981. 35.00 (*0-87879-288-0*); 15.00 (*0-685-44979-3*); lp 40.00 (*0-87879-289-9*) Acad Therapy.
Valeureaux. Albert Cohen. 344p. (FRE.). 1986. pap. 11.95 (*0-7859-2035-8*, 2070377407) Fr & Eur.
Valhalla. Nathan Archer. Ed. by John Ordover. (Star Trek Ser.). 288p. (Orig.). 1995. mass mkt. 5.50 (*0-671-88115-9*) PB.
Valhalla Exchange. Jack Higgins. 1996. pap. 6.50 (*0-671-00032-2*, PB Trade Paper) PB.
Valhalla's Child. Arthur K. Pirkle. LC 92-62012. 288p. 1994. pap. 12.95 (*1-56002-232-9*, Univ Edtns) Aegina Pr.
Valiant & the Damned. large type ed. Roy Clews. Orig. Title: Young Jethro. 450p. 1982. 25.99 (*0-7089-0740-7*) Ulverscroft.
Valiant Bride. Jane Peart. (Brides of Montclair Ser.: Vol. 1). 192p. 1989. pap. 8.99 (*0-310-66951-0*) Zondervan.
Valiant Bride. large type ed. Jane Peart. LC 93-13240. (Brides of Montclair - EasyRead Type Ser.: Bk. 1). 224p. 1993. reprint ed. pap. 8.95 (*0-8027-2673-9*) Walker & Co.
Valiant Bugles. large type ed. Gordon D. Shirreffs. (Linford Western Library). 320p. 1985. pap. 15.99 (*0-7089-6092-8*) Ulverscroft.
Valiant Captains: Epics of the Gallant Ships That Challenged the English Channel. Sheldon A. Jacobson. Ed. by Kieran O'Mahony. LC 90-80517. 250p. (Orig.). (YA). (gr. 9-12). 1990. 19.95 (*0-944638-03-1*); pap. 12.95 (*0-944638-01-5*) EduCare Pr.
Valiant for the Truth see Treasury of Evangelical Writings: Valiant for the Truth
Valiant for Truth: Clarence True Wilson & Prohibition. Robert D. McNeil. LC 91-68406. (Illus.). 172p. (Orig.). 1992. pap. 9.95 (*0-9632048-0-7*) Rockwood UMC.
Valiant Friend: The Life of Lucretia Mott. Margaret H. Bacon. 265p. 1989. reprint ed. pap. 12.95 (*0-8027-7190-4*) Walker & Co.
Valiant Gunman. Gilbert Morris. LC 93-2416. (House of Winslow Ser.: Bk. 14). 320p. 1993. pap. 9.99 (*1-55661-310-5*) Bethany Hse.
Valiant Heart. Gordon Wallace. 201p. 1982. 12.95 (*0-942078-01-2*) R Tanner Assocs Inc.
Valiant Heart: A Biography of Heinrich Heine. Philip Kossoff. LC 82-46085. 217p. 1983. 14.95 (*0-8453-4762-4*, Cornwall Bks) Assoc Univ Prs.
Valiant Lancer of Prince William Sound. Athena Lethcoe. 12p. 1987. 5.95 (*0-9613146-7-2*) Prince W Sound.
Valiant Muse: An Anthology of Poems by Poets Killed in the (First) World War. Ed. by Frederic W. Ziv. LC 70-167488. (Granger Index Reprint Ser.). 1977. reprint ed. 15.95 (*0-8369-6293-1*) Ayer.
Valiant Ones. large type ed. Norman A. Fox. LC 93-44662. 1994. pap. 17.95 (*0-7862-0038-3*) Thorndike Pr.
Valiant Sailors. large type ed. Vivian Stuart. 1991. 25.99 (*0-7089-2470-0*) Ulverscroft.
Valiant Sixty. 3rd ed. Ernest E. Taylor. (Illus.). (C). 1989. pap. 21.00 (*1-85072-033-9*, Pub. by W Sessions UK) St Mut.
Valiant Vagabonds. Charles J. Finger. LC 68-58789. (Essay Index Reprint Ser.). 1977. 23.95 (*0-8369-0112-6*) Ayer.
Valiant Virginian: Story of Presley Neville O'Bannon, 1776-1850, First Lieutenant U. S. Marine Corps, 1801-1807, to Which Is Added the O'Bannon Family Descendants of Bryan O'Bannon of Ireland & Fanquier Co., Virginia. Trudy J. Sundberg & John K. Gott. (Illus.). 124p. (Orig.). 1994. pap. text ed. 22.50 (*0-7884-0067-3*) Heritage Bk.
Valiant Welshman. LC 76-133753. (Tudor Facsimile Texts. Old English Plays Ser.: No. 132). reprint ed. 49.50 (*0-404-53432-5*) AMS Pr.
Valid Diagnosis in High School Composition. Matthew H. Willing. LC 71-177635. (Columbia University. Teachers College. Contributions to Education Ser.: No. 230). reprint ed. 37.50 (*0-404-55230-7*) AMS Pr.
Validate Me Quick, I'm Double Parked. Toni S. Brown. LC 95-71763. 100p. (Orig.). 1995. pap. text ed. 6.95 (*0-9644552-9-3*) SunRise Pbl.
***Validating Automated Manufacturing & Laboratory Applications: Putting Principles into Practice.** Guy Wingate. LC 97-13236. (Illus.). 1997. 219.00 (*1-57491-037-X*) Interpharm.
Validating Digital Systems in Avionics Flight Control. Ed. by Avionics Communications Staff. 530p. 1994. 95.00 (*1-885544-02-2*) Avionics Commun.
Validating Holistic Scoring for Writing Assessment: Theoretical & Empirical Foundations. Michael M. Williamson & Brian Huot. Ed. by Marcia Farr. LC 92-37934. (Written Language Ser.). 352p. (C). 1993. text ed. 69.50 (*1-881303-94-2*); pap. text ed. 28.50 (*1-881303-95-0*) Hampton Pr NJ.
Validating National Curriculum Indicators. Leigh Burstein et al. 109p. 1995. pap. text ed. 15.00 (*0-8330-2333-0*, MR-658-NSF) Rand Corp.
Validating Social Work Credentials for Human Service Jobs: Report of a Demonstration. Robert J. Teare. LC 87-17031. (Illus.). 24p. reprint ed. pap. 25.00 (*0-7837-6547-9*, 2045684) Bks Demand.
Validating Your Training. Tony Newby. 136p. (C). 1992. pap. 45.00 (*0-7494-0551-1*, Pub. by IPM Hse UK) St Mut.

UV

Validation & Predictability of Laboratory Methods for Assessing the Fate & Effects of Contaminants in Aquatic Ecosystems - STP 865. Ed. by Terence P. Boyle. LC 85-5985. (Illus.). 242p. 1985. text ed. 34.00 (0-8031-0433-2, 04-865000-16) ASTM.

Validation & Verification of Knowledge-Based Systems: Papers from the 1993 Workshop. Ed. by Alun Preece. (Technical Reports). (Illus.). 149p. (Orig.). 1994. spiral bd. 25.00 (0-929280-65-2) AAAI Pr.

Validation Breakthrough: Simple Techniques for Communicating with People with "Alzheimer's-Type Dementia" Naomi Feil. LC 93-4077. 356p. (Orig.). (C). 1993. pap. 22.95 (1-878812-11-4) Hlth Prof Pr.

Validation Compliance Biannual: 1996-1997. 856p. 1996. 195.00 (0-8247-9746-9) Dekker.

Validation for Medical Device & Diagnostic Manufacturers. Carol DeSain & Charmaine V. Sutton. 300p. 1994. 179. 00 (0-935184-64-3) Interpharm.

***Validation in Blood Establishments & Transfusion Services.** Ed. by Sallie M. Holliman. (Illus.). 166p. (Orig.). 1996. pap. text ed. 89.00 (1-56395-056-1, PC97-960080) Am Assn Blood.

Validation in Language Testing. Ed. by Alister Cumming & Richard Berwick. LC 95-6556. (Modern Languages in Practice Ser.: Vol. 2). 1995. write for info. (1-85359-296-X, Pub. by Multilingual Matters UK); pap. write for info. (1-85359-295-1, Pub. by Multilingual Matters UK) Taylor & Francis.

Validation in the Clinical Theory of Psychoanalysis: A Study in the Philosophy of Psychoanalysis. Adolf Grunbaum. (Psychological Issues Monograph: No. 61). 450p. 1993. 52.50 (0-8236-6722-7, BN#06722) Intl Univs Pr.

Validation Numerics: Theory & Applications. R. Albrecht et al. (Computing Ser.: Suppl. 9). (Illus.). 300p. 1993. 126.95 (0-387-82451-0) Spr-Verlag.

Validation of Aseptic Drug Powder Filling Process. PDA Research Task Force on Aseptic Filling. (Technical Reports: No. 6). 30p. 1984. pap. 30.00 (0-939459-05-1) PDA.

Validation of Aseptic Filling for Solution Drug Products. rev. ed. PDA Research Task Group No. 15 on Aseptic Filling Staff. (Technical Monographs: No. 2). 28p. (Orig.). 1980. pap. 30.00 (0-939459-01-9) PDA.

Validation of Aseptic Pharmaceutical Processes. Carleton & Agalloco. 720p. 1986. 225.00 (0-8247-7362-4) Dekker.

***Validation of Bulk Pharmaceutical Chemicals.** Ed. by Ira R. Berry & Daniel Harpaz. LC 97-2463. (Illus.). 350p. 1997. 209.00 (1-57491-042-6) Interpharm.

Validation of Computerized Analytical Systems. Ludwig Huber. 252p. 1995. 189.00 (0-935184-75-9) Interpharm.

Validation of Dry Heat Processes Used for Sterlization & Depyrogenation. PDA Research Task Force No. 16 on Dry Heat Processes. (Technical Reports: No. 3). 55p. (Orig.). 1981. pap. 30.00 (0-939459-02-7) PDA.

Validation of Graphological Judgements: An Experimental Study. Abraham Jansen. LC 76-184573. (Psychological Studies, Major Ser.: No. 8). (Illus.). 189p. (Orig.). 1973. pap. text ed. 26.95 (90-279-7267-2) Mouton.

Validation of Relationships Between Specification Properties & Performance. Rita B. Leahy & Harold Von Quintus. (SHRP Ser.: A-409). (Illus.). 104p. (Orig.). (C). 1994. pap. text ed. 15.00 (0-309-05813-9) Natl Res Coun.

Validation of Smart Sensor Technologies for Instrument Calibration Reduction in Nuclear Power Plants. H. M. Hashemian et al. (Illus.). 162p. (Orig.). 1993. per. write for info. (1-882148-00-2) Analysis & Measurement.

Validation of Steam Sterilization Cycles. rev. ed. PDA Research Task Group on Steam Sterilization. (Technical Monographs: No. 1). 36p. 1978. pap. 30.00 (0-939459-00-0) PDA.

Validation of the Measurement Process. Ed. by James R. De Voe. LC 77-15555. (ACS Symposium Ser.: No. 63). 1977. 32.95 (0-8412-0396-2) Am Chemical.

***Validation of the Measurement Process: A Symposium.** Ed. by James R. DeVoe. LC 77-15555. (ACS Symposium Ser.: No. 63). (Illus.). 215p. 1977. reprint ed. pap. 61.30 (0-608-04341-9, 2065121) Bks Demand.

Validation Practices for Biotechnology Products, Vol. 126. Ed. by James K. Shillenn. LC 96-22130. (Special Technical Publication Ser.: No. 1260). (Illus.). 160p. 1996. text ed. 42.00 (0-8031-2405-8, 04-012600-43) ASTM.

Validation Study of Economic Survey Data. Greg J. Duncan et al. LC 85-14434. 136p. (Orig.). 1985. pap. text ed. 18.00 (0-87944-303-0) Inst Soc Res.

Validation Study of Economic Survey Data. Greg J. Duncan et al. LC 85-14434. (Institute for Social Research, Research Report Ser.). 136p. (Orig.). reprint ed. pap. 38.80 (0-7837-5249-0, 2044985) Bks Demand.

Validation Verification & Tests of Knowledge Based Systems. Marc Ayel & Jean-Pierre Laurent. LC 91-22277. 219p. 1991. pap. text ed. 90.00 (0-471-93018-0) Wiley.

Valide: A Novel of the Harem. Barbara Chase-Riboud. 432p. 1988. mass mkt. 4.95 (0-380-70443-9) Avon.

Validity & the Research Process. David Brinberg & Joseph E. McGrath. 1985. pap. 19.95 (0-8039-3376-2) Sage.

***Validity & the Research Process.** David Brinberg & Joseph E. McGrath. LC 85-1903. (Illus.). 175p. 1985. reprint ed. pap. 49.90 (0-608-04301-X, 2065080) Bks Demand.

Validity in Interpretation. Eric D. Hirsch, Jr. 1973. pap. 15.00 (0-300-01692-1, Y259) Yale U Pr.

Validity Issue: What Should Teacher Certification Tests Measure? Ed. by Michael Chernoff et al. 152p. (C). 1987. text ed. 29.95 (0-89859-947-4) L Erlbaum Assocs.

Validity Issues in Evaluative Research. Ed. by Ilene N. Bernstein. LC 75-32373. (Sage Contemporary Social Science Issues Ser.: No. 23). 134p. reprint ed. pap. 38.20 (0-317-29607-8, 2021870) Bks Demand.

Validity of Miracles. Donna J. Simpson. LC 95-90973. (Orig.). 1996. pap. 10.95 (0-533-11800-X) Vantage.

***Validity of Psychiatric Diagnosis.** Ed. by Lee N. Robins & James E. Barrett. LC 87-43322. (American Psychopathological Association Ser.). 350p. 1989. reprint ed. pap. 99.80 (0-608-03441-X, 2064142) Bks Demand.

Validity of the Case Study: Deviance & Self-Destruction. Daniel L. Haytin. (American University Studies Anthropology & Sociology: Ser. XI, Vol. 23). 217p. (C). 1988. text ed. 32.60 (0-8204-0738-0) P Lang Pubng.

Validtion of Systems Transients Analysis Codes. Ed. by R. R. Schultz et al. LC 95-78825. (1995 ASME/JSME Fluids Engineering Conference Ser.: FED-Vol. 223). 196p. 1995. 96.00 (0-7918-1478-5, G00973) ASME.

Valie Export - Fragments of the Imagination. Rosawitha Mueller. LC 94-6589. (Women Artists in Film Ser.). 256p. 1995. pap. 24.95 (0-253-20925-0) Ind U Pr.

Valie Export - Fragments of the Imagination. Roswitha Mueller. LC 94-6589. (Women Artists in Film Ser.). 256p. 1995. 49.95 (0-253-33906-5) Ind U Pr.

Valie Export und Elfriede Jelinek im Spiegel der Presse: Zur Rezeption der Feministischen Avantgarde Osterreichs. Margarete Lamb-Faffelberger. LC 92-20676. 224p. (C). 1993. text ed. 39.95 (0-8204-1980-X) P Lang Pubng.

Valiente! Heritage of Texas, New Mexico, & Arizona to Statehood. Kita Bargas. (Illus.). 271p. (Orig.). 1985. pap. text ed. 9.75 (0-9618500-0-0) Saxon Pubns.

Valiente: Heritage of Texas, New Mexico, & Arizona to Statehood. Kita Bargas. 271p. (Orig.). 1985. pap. 20.00 (1-887116-10-9) Saxon West Pubns.

Valignano's Mission Principles for Japan: Vol. I (1573-1582), Pt. I - The Problem (1573-1580) Josef F. Schutte. Tr. by John J. Coyne from GER. LC 78-69683. (Modern Scholarly Studies about the Jesuits, in English Translations Series II: No. 3). (Illus.). xxiv, 428p. 1980. 7.00 (0-912422-36-X); pap. 6.00 (0-912422-35-1) Inst Jesuit.

Valignano's Mission Principles for Japan, Vol. 1 (1573-1582) The Solution (1580-1582) Josef F. Schutte. Ed. by G. E. Ganss & P. C. Fischer. Tr. by John J. Coyne from GER. LC 78-69683. (Modern Scholarly Studies about the Jesuits, in English Translations Series II: No. 5). Orig. Title: Valignanos Missionsgrundsatze Fur Japan. xviii, 380p. 1985. pap. 7.00 (0-912422-75-0) Inst Jesuit.

Valignanos Missionsgrundsatze Fur Japan see Valignano's Mission Principles for Japan, Vol. 1 (1573-1582): The Solution (1580-1582)

Valincour: The Limits of Honnetete. Charles G. Williams. LC 89-25205. 338p. 1991. text ed. 49.95 (0-8132-0721-5) Cath U Pr.

Valinda, Our Daughter. Gladys Taylor. (Illus.). 160p. (Orig.). 1993. pap. 15.95 (1-55059-051-0) Temeron Bks.

VALIS. Philip K. Dick. LC 90-55676. 240p. 1991. pap. 11. 00 (0-679-73446-5, Vin) Random.

Valium & Other Tranquilizers. Gail Winger. (Encyclopedia of Psychoactive Drugs Ser.: No. 1). (Illus.). (YA). (gr. 7 up). 1992. lib. bdg. 19.95 (0-87754-759-9) Chelsea Hse.

Valium, Librium, & the Benzodiazepine Blues. rev. ed. Jim Parker. 1997. pap. 0.50 (0-89230-163-5) Do It Now.

Valkyrie. Richard Wagner. Ed. by Nicholas John. Tr. by Andrew Porter from GER. (English National Opera - Royal Opera House Guide Ser.: No. 21). (Illus.). 128p. (Orig.). 1984. pap. 9.95 (0-7145-4019-6) Riverrun NY.

Valkyrie: Prisoner of the Past. Dixon et al. (Illus.). 1990. 19.95 (0-685-47369-4); pap. 6.95 (0-913035-36-X) Eclipse Bks.

Valkyrie North American X-B 70 A. Steve Pace. Ed. by Ernest J. Gentle. (Aero Ser.: Vol. 30). (Illus.). 104p. (Orig.). 1984. pap. 10.95 (0-8168-0610-1, 20610, TAB-Aero) TAB Bks.

Valkyries: An Encounter with Angels. Paulo Coelho. Tr. by Alan R. Clarke. LC 95-5747. 256p. 1996. pap. 12.00 (0-06-251334-6) Harper SF.

Valkyries: The Women Around Jung. Maggy Anthony. 1993. pap. 14.95 (1-85230-187-2) Element MA.

***Valkyries International Edition.** Coelho. 1995. pap. 13.00 (0-06-251333-8) HarpC.

***Vallas Protectoras Del Matrinonio.** J. Jenkins. (SPA.). 5.95 (0-8297-1902-4) Life Pubs Intl.

Vallas Rotas. Fernando Pico et al. LC 82-83477. (Nave y el Puerto Ser.). 238p. (SPA.). 1982. pap. text ed. 7.50 (0-940238-69-1) Ediciones Huracan.

***Valle Crucis.** David W. Yates. LC 97-19071. (Illus.). 1997. 29.95 (0-89587-203-X) Blair.

***Valle de los Huesos Secos - The Valley of Dry Bonds.** Yiye Avila. 48p. (SPA.). 1996. write for info. (0-7899-0072-6) Editorial Unilit.

Valle du Rhone Green Guide French Edition. Michelin Staff. (FRE.). pap. 17.95 (0-7859-7239-0, 2067003739) Fr & Eur.

Valle-Inclan: Plays One. Inclan. 273p. (C). 1993. pap. 15. 95 (0-413-67090-2, A0674, Pub. by Methuen UK) Heinemann.

Valle-Inclan: The Theatre of His Life. Robert Lima. LC 87-19119. (Illus.). 392p. 1988. text ed. 37.50 (0-8262-0661-1) U of Mo Pr.

Valle-Inclan & the Theatre: Innovation in "La Cabeza del Dragon," "El Embrujado," & "La Marquesa Rosalinda" Xavier Vila. LC 93-70385. (Illus.). 168p. 1994. 32.50 (0-8387-5267-5) Bucknell U Pr.

Valle-Inclan's Ruedo Iberico: A Popular View of Revolution. Alison Sinclair. (Monagrafias A Ser.: Vol. XLIII). (Illus.). 133p. (C). 1977. 45.00 (0-7293-0034-X, Pub. by Tamesis Bks Ltd UK) Boydell & Brewer.

***Vallee du Rhone Green Guide.** Michelin Travel Publications, Staff. (Illus.). (FRE.). 1996. per. 20.00 (2-06-037303-4, 373) Michelin.

Vallee du Rhone Green Guide. 2nd ed. Michelin Staff. (FRE.). 1991. pap. 18.95 (0-7859-9170-0) Fr & Eur.

***Vallee du Rhone Map.** 1997. 8.95 (2-06-700246-5, 246) Michelin.

Vallejo: El Tragaluz. Ed. by G. Lyon. (Bristol Spanish Texts Ser.). (SPA.). 1995. pap. 16.95 (1-85399-412-X, Pub. by Brstl Class Pr UK) Focus Pub-R Pullins.

Vallejo & the Four Flags: A True Story of Early California. Esther J. Comstock. LC 79-21636. (Illus.). xvi, 142p. (J). (gr. 4). 1988. pap. 8.75 (0-933994-07-9) Comstock Bon.

Vallejo & the Four Flags see Vallejo y las Cuatro Banderas: Una Historia Verdadera de la California de Antano

Vallejo y las Cuatro Banderas: Una Historia Verdadera de la California de Antano. Esther J. Comstock. Tr. by Marcel Pardo & Ana M. Velasco. LC 95-15440. Orig. Title: Vallejo & the Four Flags. (Illus.). xiv, 152p. (Orig.). (SPA.). (J). (gr. 4 up). 1996. pap. 12.50 (0-933994-13-3) Comstock Bon.

Valley. Rolando Hinojosa. LC 83-70275. 112p. 1983. 18.00 (0-916950-37-9); pap. 10.00 (0-916950-38-7) Biling Rev-Pr.

Valley & Ridge & Blue Ridge Traverse, Central Virginia. Ed. by Spencer. (IGC Field Trip Guidebooks Ser.). 72p. 1989. 21.00 (0-87590-591-9, T157) Am Geophysical.

Valley & Ridge Thrust Belt: Balanced Structural Sections, Pennsylvania to Alabama. Ed. by N. B. Woodward. (Studies in Geology). (Illus.). 64p. (Orig.). 1985. pap. 20. 00 (0-910249-11-3) U of Tenn Geo.

Valley Echoes. Tom Sellers. LC 86-70067. (Illus.). 185p. (Orig.). 1986. pap. 7.95 (0-937089-03-6) Davicone Inc.

Valley Floor. Michael Gregory. (Orig.). 1978. 10.00 (0-934600-07-4) Mother Duck Pr.

Valley for Dreams: Life & Landscape in the Sacramento Valley. Susan W. Hardwick & Donald G. Holtgrieve. 332p. 1996. pap. text ed. 24.95 (0-8476-8286-2); lib. bdg. 67.50 (0-8476-8285-4) Rowman.

Valley Forge. Libby Hughes. LC 92-23391. (Places in American History Ser.). (Illus.). 72p. (J). (gr. 4 up). 1993. lib. bdg. 14.95 (0-87518-547-9, Dillon Silver Burdett) Silver Burdett Pr.

Valley Forge. R. Conrad Stein. LC 94-9490. (Cornerstones of Freedom Ser.). (Illus.). 32p. (J). (gr. 3-6). 1994. lib. bdg. 18.00 (0-516-06683-8) Childrens.

Valley Forge: Making & Remarking a National Symbol. Lorett Treese. LC 94-29460. (Keystone Bk.). (Illus.). 288p. 1995. 15.95 (0-271-01402-4); pap. 45.00 (0-271-01403-2) Pa St U Pr.

Valley Forge: Pinnacle of Courage. John W. Jackson. (Illus.). 330p. (C). 1992. text ed. 24.95 (0-939631-59-8); pap. text ed. 16.95 (0-939631-60-1) Thomas Publications.

Valley Forge Album: Portrait of a Park. Ed. by Lorett Treese. (Illus.). 40p. (C). 1993. pap. text ed. 6.95 (0-939631-62-8) Thomas Publications.

Valley Forge, Crucible of Victory. John F. Reed. LC 70-76769. (Revolutionary War Bicentennial Ser.). (Illus.). 1969. lib. bdg. 11.95 (0-912480-04-1) Freneau.

Valley Forge Orderly Book of General George Weedon of the Continental Army Under Command of Gen. George Washington in the Campaign of 1777-8. George Weedon. LC 72-140885. (Eyewitness Accounts of the American Revolution Ser., No. 1). 1979. reprint ed. 23. 95 (0-405-01229-2) Ayer.

Valley Forge Orderly Book of General George Weedon of the Continental Army under Command of General George Washington, in the Campaign of 1777-78. George Weedon. (American Biography Ser.). 323p. 1991. reprint ed. lib. bdg. 79.00 (0-7812-8407-4) Rprt Serv.

Valley Forgers: History Jokes. Illus. by Gregory Filling. 40p. (J). (gr. 3-7). Date not set. lib. bdg. 13.95 (0-945912-50-1) Pippin Pr.

Valley in Between. Marilyn C. Donahue. (YA). (gr. 5 up). 1987. 14.95 (0-8027-6731-1); lib. bdg. 15.85 (0-8027-6733-8) Walker & Co.

Valley in Bloom. large type ed. Thompson. 1995. 25.99 (0-7089-3285-1) Ulverscroft.

Valley in Italy. Lisa St. Aubin de Teran. 224p. 1995. pap. 12.50 (0-06-092619-8, PL) HarpC.

Valley In the Midst of Violence: Selected Poems 1955-1985. Gosta Agren. Tr. by David McDuff from FIN. 110p. 9300. pap. 16.95 (1-85224-236-1, Pub. by Bloodaxe Bks UK) Dufour.

Valley Justice. Gilbert Morris. LC 94-26129. (Reno Western Saga Ser.: Vol. 5). 256p. 1995. 9.99 (0-8423-7756-5) Tyndale.

***Valley Nearby.** Sok-Kyong Kang. 1997. pap. 14.95 (0-614-27279-3) Heinemann.

***Valley Nearby.** Sok-Kyong Kang. Tr. by Kyong-Do Choi. LC 97-5087. (Asian Writers Ser.). 1997. pap. write for info. (0-435-08146-2, 08146) Heinemann.

Valley Nisenan. fac. ed. A. L. Kroeber. (University of California Publications in American Archaeology & Ethnology: Vol. 24: 4). 40p. (C). 1929. reprint ed. pap. text ed. 3.70 (1-55567-268-X) Coyote Press.

Valley of a Thousand Smokes. large type ed. Dan Cushman. Date not set. 20.00 (0-7838-1674-X, GK Hall) Thorndike Pr.

Valley of a Thousand Smokes: A North-Western Story. Dan Cushman. LC 96-5873. 1996. 16.95 (0-7862-0663-2, Five Star) Mac Lib Ref.

Valley of Bones see Dance to the Music of Time: Third Movement

Valley of Darkness: The Japanese People & World War Two. Thomas R. Havens. (Illus.). 294p. (C). 1986. reprint ed. pap. text ed. 24.50 (0-8191-5495-4) U Pr of Amer.

Valley of Decision. Stanley Middleton. LC 87-20323. 214p. 1987. 15.95 (0-941533-08-5) New Amsterdam Bks.

Valley of Decision. Pauline E. Spray. 210p. Date not set. pap. 11.95 (1-888257-00-8) Cameron Press.

***Valley of Decision.** large type ed. Clare F. Holmes. (Linford Romance Large Print Ser.). 336p. 1997. pap. 16.99 (0-7089-5115-5, Linford) Ulverscroft.

Valley of Decision. Marcia Davenport. LC 78-74648. 1979. reprint ed. lib. bdg. 18.00 (0-8376-0427-3) Bentley.

Valley of Decision. Marcia Davenport. LC 88-33758. 640p. 1989. reprint ed. pap. 19.95 (0-8229-5805-8) U of Pittsburgh Pr.

Valley of Decision, 2 vols. Edith Wharton. 1902. reprint ed. Set. 59.00 (0-403-00190-0) Scholarly.

Valley of Decision: The Siege of Khe Sahn. John Prados. 656p. 1993. mass mkt. 6.50 (0-440-21345-2) Dell.

Valley of Deer. Eileen Dunlop. LC 89-1931. 152p. (J). (gr. 4-7). 1989. 13.95 (0-8234-0766-7) Holiday.

Valley of Discord: Church & Society along the Connecticut River, 1636-1725. Paul R. Lucas. LC 75-22520. 291p. reprint ed. pap. 83.00 (0-7837-6205-4, 2045926) Bks Demand.

Valley of Dry Bones: The Conditions That Face Black People in America. Rudolph R. Windsor. LC 83-90249. (Illus.). 162p. (C). 1988. reprint ed. pap. 10.95 (0-9620881-0-2) Windsors Golden Series.

Valley of Dry Bones: 1920-1965 see Religious Trends in English Poetry

***Valley of Fear.** (Heritage Literary Ser.). Date not set. pap. text ed. write for info. (0-582-34909-5, Pub. by Longman UK) Longman.

Valley of Fear. Arthur Conan Doyle. 1976. 17.95 (0-8488-1288-3) Amereon Ltd.

Valley of Fear. Arthur Conan Doyle. 1988. lib. bdg. 16.95 (0-89966-232-3) Buccaneer Bks.

Valley of Fear. Arthur Conan Doyle. Ed. by Owen D. Edwards. (Oxford Sherlock Holmes Ser.). 208p. (C). 1993. 11.00 (0-19-212314-9, 8951) OUP.

Valley of Fear. large type ed. Arthur Conan Doyle. 1978. 25.99 (0-7089-0086-0) Ulverscroft.

Valley of Fear. Arthur Conan Doyle. Ed. & Intro. by Owen D. Edwards. (World's Classics Ser.). 296p. 1995. reprint ed. pap. 5.95 (0-19-282382-5) OUP.

Valley of Fire. Janelle Taylor. 1992. mass mkt. 3.99 (0-373-83242-7, 1-83242-7) Harlequin Bks.

***Valley of Gold.** Kent Conwell. LC 97-93462. 192p. 1997. lib. bdg. 17.95 (0-8034-9240-5, Avalon Bks) Bouregy.

Valley of Guns - Cast a Long Shadow, 2 vols. in 1. Wayne D. Overholser. 384p. 1994. mass mkt., pap. text ed. 4.99 (0-8439-3655-X) Dorchester Pub Co.

***Valley of Home.** large type ed. Joyce Eaglestone. (Linford Romance Library). 368p. 1996. pap. 15.99 (0-7089-7960-2, Linford) Ulverscroft.

Valley of Horses. Jean M. Auel. 560p. 1984. mass mkt. 7.50 (0-553-25053-1) Bantam.

Valley of Horses. Jean M. Auel. (Earth's Children Ser.). 512p. 1982. 19.95 (0-517-54489-X, Crown) Crown Pub Group.

Valley of Horses. large type ed. Jean M. Auel. 1039p. 1991. lib. bdg. 17.95 (1-56054-982-3) Thorndike Pr.

***Valley of Kings.** Holland. 1997. 21.95 (0-312-86334-9) St Martin.

Valley of Minor Animals. John Woods. LC 82-71647. 88p. 1982. 14.00 (0-937872-08-3); pap. 6.00 (0-937872-09-1) Dragon Gate.

Valley of No Return. abr. ed. Richard A. Booth. (Valley Stories Ser.: Vol. 1). 151p. (Orig.). 1996. pap. 7.95 (1-56901-435-3) B & B Pubng.

Valley of Opportunity: Economic Culture along the Upper Susquhanna, 1700-1800. Peter C. Mancall. LC 90-55719. (Illus.). 253p. 1991. 25.00 (0-8014-2503-4) Cornell U Pr.

Valley of Savage Men. large type ed. Harry Whittington. (Linford Western Library). 1991. pap. 15.99 (0-7089-7020-6) Ulverscroft.

Valley of Shadows. Francis Grierson. Ed. by Harold P. Simonson. (Masterworks of Literature Ser.). 1970. 18.95 (0-8084-0309-5); pap. 14.95 (0-8084-0310-9) NCUP.

Valley of Shadows. Francis Grierson. (American Biography Ser.). 278p. 1991. reprint ed. lib. bdg. 69.00 (0-7812-8157-1) Rprt Serv.

Valley of Shadows: Problems of Leprosy in India. S. D. Gokhale. 132p. 1979. 13.95 (0-318-36374-7) Asia Bk Corp.

Valley of Shadows: Sangamon Sketches. Francis Grierson. (Prairie State Bks.). 184p. 1990. reprint ed. 8.95 (0-252-06103-9) U of Ill Pr.

***Valley of Shining Stone: The Story of Abiquiu.** Lesley Poling-Kempes. LC 97-4621. 1997. pap. write for info. (0-8165-1446-1) U of Ariz Pr.

Valley of Silence: Catholic Thought in Contemporary Poland. Ed. by James J. Zatko. LC 67-12125. 407p. reprint ed. pap. 116.00 (0-317-55790-4, 2029313) Bks Demand.

Valley of the Amazons. Noretta Koertge. 160p. 1984. pap. 8.95 (0-312-83608-2) St Martin.

Valley of the Anointers. Kiarri T-H. Cheatwood. LC 78-70230. 73p. 1979. per. 4.00 (0-916418-19-7) Lotus.

Valley of the Blue Heron. Wilma Taylor. 150p. 1994. 18.95 (1-878208-55-1) Guild Pr IN.

Valley of the Broken Cherry Trees. Lensey Namioka. 176p. (YA). (gr. 6 up). reprint ed. pap. 8.95 (0-936085-32-0) Blue Heron OR.

Valley of the Condor. Jon Albertson. Ed. by Anne Hooper. (Air Adventure Ser.: Vol. III). 300p. (YA). (gr. 12). 1990. write for info. (0-9621448-3-5) Aeolus Bks.

***Valley of the Conemaugh, Pa.** Thomas J. Chapman. (Illus.). 202p. 1997. reprint ed. lib. bdg. 29.00 (0-8328-6376-9) Higginson Bk Co.

An Asterisk (*) at the beginning of an entry indicates that the title is appearing in BIP for the first time.

Valley of the Cranes: Exploring Colorado's San Luis Valley. Virginia M. Simmons. (Illus.). 64p. 1988. pap. 14.95 (*0-911797-49-1*) R Rinehart.

Valley of the Delaware & Its Place in History. John P. Garber. 1993. reprint ed. lib. bdg. 89.00 (*0-7812-5460-4*) Rprt Serv.

Valley of the Devil. Yvonne Whittal. (Presents Ser.: No. 438). 1992. pap. 2.79 (*0-373-11438-9*, 1-11438-8) Harlequin Bks.

Valley of the Devil. large type ed. Yvonne Whittal. 285p. 1991. reprint ed. lib. bdg. 18.95 (*0-263-12722-2*) Thorndike Pr.

***Valley of the Dolls: A Novel.** Jacqueline Susann. LC 97-14268. 448p. 1997. reprint ed. pap. 12.00 (*0-8021-3519-6*, Grove) Grove-Atltic.

Valley of the Dry Bones. 1992. 24.95 (*0-9631631-0-8*); pap. 11.95 (*0-9631631-1-6*) Word Farm.

Valley of the Eagles. Cary Anderson. (Illus.). 24p. (Orig.). 1995. pap. 5.95 (*0-9607358-9-5*) Fathom Pub.

Valley of the Eels: A Science Fiction Mystery. Ty Heintze. LC 93-2906. (Illus.). (J). 1993. 14.95 (*0-89015-904-1*) Sunbelt Media.

Valley of the Far Side. Gary Larson. (Illus.). 104p. (Orig.). 1985. pap. 6.95 (*0-8362-2067-6*) Andrews & McMeel.

***Valley of the Giant.** 216p. (J). 1997. write for info. (*0-7814-3002-X*, Chariot Bks) Chariot Victor.

Valley of the Giant Buddhas: Memoirs & Travel. Morag M. Abdullah. 309p. 1993. 29.00 (*0-86304-065-9*, Pub. by Octagon Pr UK) ISHK.

Valley of the Giants. Peter Kyne. 1976. lib. bdg. 17.25 (*0-89968-056-9*, Lghtyr Pr) Buccaneer Bks.

Valley of the Gray Moon: A Trilogy. Ken Brownlee. 627p. 1994. pap. 22.00 (*0-9644894-0-6*) Valley Enter.

Valley of the Horses. large type ed. Jean M. Auel. LC 83-447. 1039p. 1991. reprint ed. lib. bdg. 23.95 (*0-89621-436-2*) Thorndike Pr.

Valley of the Lawless. Lee Martin. 1993. 17.95 (*0-8034-9018-6*) Bouregy.

***Valley of the Moon.** Jack London. lib. bdg. 32.95 (*0-614-30398-2*) Amereon Ltd.

Valley of the Pyramids. James A. Knight. 145p. 1990. pap. 9.95 (*0-9626603-0-2*) J A Knight.

Valley of the Red Hand. Lowell T. Clay. Ed. by Gertrude Clay. 352p. 1992. pap. 11.95 (*0-9630124-0-1*) Packsaddle.

Valley of the Rogues. Percy T. Booth. 71p. 1993. pap. 6.95 (*1-885813-00-7*) B & B Pubng.

Valley of the Rogues. Percy T. Booth. (Illus.). 71p. 1995. 14.50 (*1-885813-04-X*) B & B Pubng.

***Valley of the Shadow.** Edward Ayers. Date not set. 42.50 (*0-393-04604-4*) Norton.

Valley of the Shadow. Christopher Davis. (Stonewall Inn Editions Ser.). 1988. pap. 7.95 (*0-312-02666-8*) St Martin.

Valley of the Shadow. Edward Y. Hall, Sr. LC 88-171640. (Illus.). 270p. (Orig.). 1988. pap. 4.95 (*0-9622166-0-7*) Honoribus Pr.

Valley of the Shadow. Carol R. Murphy. LC 72-80095. 24p. (Orig.). 1972. pap. 3.00 (*0-87574-184-3*) Pendle Hill.

***Valley of the Shadow, Vol. 2.** Roger Elwood. (Without the Dawn Ser.: Vol. 2). 1997. mass mkt. 2.49 (*1-57748-039-2*) Barbour & Co.

Valley of the Shadow: After the Turmoil My Heart Cries No More. Erich A. Helfert. Ed. by Donald S. Ellis. 364p. (Orig.). text ed. 25.00 (*0-88739-117-6*) Creat Arts Bk.

Valley of the Shadow see Jerusalem Journeys Series

***Valley of the Skunk: The Story of a Haven.** Roland Paulson. Ed. by Jim Ayers. LC 96-69428. (Illus.). 230p. (Orig.). 1996. pap. 13.95 (*0-88100-091-4*) Natl Writ Pr.

Valley of the Spirits: A Journey into the Lost Realm of the Ancient Aymara. Alan L. Kolata. LC 95-20746. (Illus.). 288p. 1996. text ed. 27.95 (*0-471-57507-0*) Wiley.

***Valley of the Squinting Windows.** Brinsley MacNamara. Date not set. pap. 14.95 (*0-900068-83-3*) Dufour.

***Valley of the Squinting Windows.** 2nd ed. Brinsley MacNamara. 224p. 1996. reprint ed. pap. 13.95 (*0-947962-01-8*, Pub. by Anvil Bks Ltd IE) Irish Bks Media.

Valley of the Sun. Louis L'Amour. 224p. 1996. mass mkt. 4.99 (*0-553-57444-2*) Bantam.

Valley of the Sun. large type ed. Hilda A. Durman. 230p. 1993. pap. 17.99 (*1-85389-367-6*, Dales) Ulverscroft.

Valley of the Sun. large type ed. Louis L'Amour. 1996. 21.95 (*0-7862-0587-3*) Thorndike Pr.

Valley of the Sun: Selected Poems. Henry Noyes. 117p. (Orig.). 1993. pap. 9.95 (*0-915117-13-4*) New Earth Pubns.

Valley of the Sun Golf Guide. Mike Armfield & Steve Wardell. 130p. 1994. pap. 12.95 (*0-914846-91-4*) Golden West Pub.

Valley of the Sun Golf Guide. Mike Armfield. 1993. pap. 12.95 (*0-9634127-0-1*) Golf Guys.

Valley of the Sun Kings: New Explorations in the Tombs of the Pharaohs. Ed. by Richard H. Wilkinson. 1995. pap. 40.00 (*0-9649958-0-8*) U AZ Egyptian.

Valley of the Sun Ultimate Golf Guide & Reference. Animated Promotional Maps International Staff. (Illus.). 8p. 1994. 7.95 (*0-9645198-0-1*) Anim Prom Maps.

Valley of the Upper Wabash, Indiana. Henry W. Ellsworth. LC 75-98. (Mid-American Frontier Ser.). 1975. reprint ed. 23.95 (*0-405-06864-6*) Ayer.

Valley of Vanishing Riders. large type ed. Norman A. Fox. LC 94-20148. (Western Societies Papers). 268p. 1994. lib. bdg. 17.95 (*1-56054-713-8*) Thorndike Pr.

***Valley of Vision.** Vardis Fisher. (Testament of Man Ser.). 319p. 1963. pap. 10.95 (*0-614-22029-7*) Idaho Ctr Bk.

Valley of Vision. Arthur Bennett. 240p. 1983. reprint ed. pap. 13.99 (*0-85151-228-3*) Banner of Truth.

***Valley of Vision: A Novel of King Solomon & His Time.** Vardis Fisher. (Testament of Man Ser.). 426p. 1951. 15.95 (*0-614-22028-9*) Idaho Ctr Bk.

Valley Outfitter: Your Complete Recreational Guide to Montana's Flathead Valley. Illus. by Carl Lindeman. 1994. pap. write for info. (*0-9640756-0-1*) Whitefish Mag.

Valley People. Frances Marion. LC 70-144161. (Short Story Index Reprint Ser.). 1977. reprint ed. 20.95 (*0-8369-3776-7*) Ayer.

Valley Renewed: The History of the Muskingum Watershed Conservancy District. Hal Jenkins. LC 76-28950. 234p. reprint ed. pap. 66.70 (*0-7837-1352-5*, 2041500) Bks Demand.

Valley Road: The Story of Virginia Hot Springs. Fay Ingalls. (Illus.). 293p. reprint ed. 18.50 (*0-9627650-1-5*) VA Hot Springs.

Valley So Wild: A Folk History. Alberta Brewer & Carson Brewer. 382p. 1975. 15.00 (*0-941199-01-0*) ETHS.

Valley Song. Athol Fugard. 1996. pap. text ed. 10.95 (*1-55936-119-0*) Theatre Comm.

***Valley Voices: A Radio History.** John R. Ghrist. LC 96-83079. (Illus.). 532p. (Orig.). 1996. pap. 24.95 (*0-9616445-42-9*) Crossroads Comm.

Valley Vultures. large type ed. Max Brand. 374p. 1991. reprint ed. lib. bdg. 17.95 (*1-56054-170-9*) Thorndike Pr.

***Valley Walking: Notes on the Land.** Robert Schnelle. LC 97-269. 1997. 25.00 (*0-87422-151-X*); pap. 12.95 (*0-87422-150-1*) Wash St U Pr.

Valleys. In T. Cheong. (Illus.). 50p. (Orig.). 1989. write for info. (*0-318-65965-4*) Cheong Co.

Valleys. Ed. by John Davies & Mike Jenkins. (Illus.). 141p. 8400. pap. 10.95 (*0-907476-31-7*) Dufour.

Valleys Beyond. large type ed. E. V. Timms. 512p. 1984. 25.99 (*0-7089-1078-5*) Ulverscroft.

***Valley's Legends & Legacies.** Catherine M. Rehart. LC 96-36997. (Illus.). 320p. 1996. pap. 18.95 (*1-884995-12-8*) Word Dancer.

Valleys of the Shadow: The Memoir of Confederate Captain Reuben G. Clark, Company I, 59th Tennessee Mounted Infantry. Comment by Willene B. Clark. LC 93-28758. (Voices of the Civil War Ser.). (Illus.). 200p. (C). 1994. 24.95 (*0-87049-819-3*) U of Tenn Pr.

Valleys of Tirol: Their Traditions & Customs, & How to Visit Them. Rachel H. Busk. LC 77-87725. 488p. reprint ed. 54.50 (*0-404-16513-3*) AMS Pr.

Valliere's Natural Cycles Almanac 1984. James T. Valliere et al. (Illus.). 44p. (Orig.). 1983. pap. 7.95 (*0-913637-02-5*) Astrolabe SW.

Valliere's Natural Cycles Almanac 1985. James T. Valliere et al. (Illus.). 44p. (Orig.). 1984. pap. 7.95 (*0-913637-19-X*) Astrolabe SW.

Valliere's Natural Cycles Almanac 1986. James T. Valliere et al. (Illus.). 44p. (Orig.). 1985. pap. 8.95 (*0-87199-038-5*) Astrolabe SW.

Valliere's Natural Cycles Almanac 1987. James T. Valliere et al. (Illus.). 48p. (Orig.). pap. 8.95 (*0-87199-060-1*) Astrolabe SW.

Valliere's Natural Cycles Almanac 1988. James T. Valliere et al. (Illus.). 48p. pap. 9.95 (*0-87199-062-8*) Astrolabe SW.

Valliere's Natural Cycles Almanac, 1989. Dee Dee Shea et al. (Illus.). 48p. (Orig.). 1988. pap. 9.95 (*0-87199-078-4*) Astrolabe SW.

Valliere's Natural Cycles Almanac 1990. James T. Valliere et al. (Illus.). 10.95 (*0-87199-092-X*) Astrolabe SW.

Vallona Starr Ceramics: With Prices. Bernice Stamper. LC 95-21494. (Illus.). 96p. (Orig.). 1995. pap. 19.95 (*0-88740-871-0*) Schiffer.

Vallum & Intervallum. J. Hajnoczi. 317p. (C). 1988. 90.00 (*963-05-4631-0*, Pub. by Akad Kiado HU) St Mut.

Valmiki Ramayana, 2 Vols., Vol. 1. Retold by Swami Rama. LC 93-26312. 1993. Vol.1. pap. 24.95 (*0-89389-137-1*) Himalayan Inst.

Valmiki Ramayana, 2 Vols., Vol. 2. Retold by Swami Rama. LC 93-26312. 1993. Vol.2. pap. 24.95 (*0-89389-139-8*) Himalayan Inst.

Valmiki Ramayanan. V. Sitaramiah. 1982. reprint ed. 7.00 (*0-317-47015-9*, Pub. by National Sahitya Akademi II) S Asia.

Valmiki's Ramayana. K. D. Bharadwaj. 150p. (C). 1989. 80.00 (*81-209-0731-0*, Pub. by Pitambar Pub II); pap. 25.00 (*81-209-0038-3*, Pub. by Pitambar Pub II) St Mut.

Valmouth & Other Novels. Ronald Firbank. 256p. 1992. pap. 9.95 (*0-14-018055-9*, Penguin Classics) Viking Penguin.

Valois Guyenne: A Study of Politics, Government & Society in Late Medieval France. Robin Harris. LC 94-16556. (Royal Historical Society Studies in History: No. 71). (Illus.). 237p. 1994. 63.00 (*0-86193-226-9*, Royal Historical Soc) Boydell & Brewer.

Valois Tapestries. Frances A. Yates. (Illus.). 232p. 1975. 35.00 (*0-7100-8244-4*, RKP) Routledge.

Valor. rev. ed. Jane B. Moncure. (Valores para la Vida Ser.). (Illus.). 32p. (SPA.). (J). (ps-2). 1981. lib. bdg. 21.36 (*0-89565-935-2*) Childs World.

Valor & Act: A Play in Verse about Edmund Campion. Thomas J. Gardiner. 52p. (Orig.). 1993. pap. 4.50 (*1-57514-126-4*, 1135) Encore Perform Pub.

***Valor & Lace No. 15: The Roles of Confederate Women.** Ed. by Mauriel Joslyn. 1996. 16.95 (*1-889332-01-1*) So Herit Pr.

Valor de lo Femenino (A Woman's Worth) Marianne Williamson. 1994. pap. text ed. 15.95 (*84-7953-070-7*, Pub. by Urano Ediciones SP) Hay House.

Valor de Vida Eterna, Regalo de Dios: Regalo de Dios - Gift of God. (Serie Libros Vida Nueva - New Life Bks.). 12p. (SPA.). 1986. 1.00 (*0-8423-6453-6*, 490280) Editorial Unilit.

***Valor in the Land.** large type ed. Lauran Paine. LC 96-53913. 1997. lib. bdg. 18.95 (*1-57490-059-5*, Sagebrush LP West) T T Beeler.

Valor Literario del Lazaro de 1555: Genero, Evolucion, y Metamorfosis. Pierina E. Beckman. LC 90-35787. (American University Studies: Romance Languages & Literature: Ser. II, Vol. 153). 174p. (C). 1991. text ed. 33.95 (*0-8204-1378-X*) P Lang Pubng.

***Valor Oculto de un Homre.** Gary Smalley & John Trent. 98p. (SPA.). 1995. pap. write for info. (*0-614-27156-8*) Editorial Unilit.

***Valor of Francesco D'Amini.** 2nd ed. 230p. (Orig.). 1979. reprint ed. mass mkt. 3.95 (*0-532-23111-2*) Hillside Pubns.

Valores Cristianos en el Hogar: Christian Values in the Home. Dina Alarcon. (Hogar Cristiano - The Christian Home Ser.). 64p. (Orig.). 1991. pap. 1.65 (*0-311-46210-3*) Casa Bautista.

Valores de Puerto Rico: Spanish Text. Vincente Polanco. LC 74-14242. (Puerto Rican Experience Ser.). 178p. 1975. reprint ed. 17.95 (*0-405-06229-X*) Ayer.

Valoric Fire & a Working Plan for Individual Sovereignty. Valorian Society Staff. LC 83-51820. 128p. (Orig.). 1984. pap. 7.00 (*0-914752-18-9*) Sovereign Pr.

Valor's Reward. Jean R. Ewing. 256p. 1996. mass mkt. 4.50 (*0-8217-5410-6*, Zebra Kensgtn) Kensgtn Pub Corp.

***Valour: A History of the Gurkhas.** E. D. Smith. LC 97-23833. 1998. write for info. (*0-87951-817-0*) Overlook Pr.

Valour & Sacrifice: Famous Regiments of the Indian Army. Gaunam. (C). 1990. 21.50 (*81-7023-140-X*, Pub. by Allied II) S Asia.

Valour & the Horror Revisited. Ed. by David J. Bercuson & S. F. Wise. 192p. 1994. 42.95 (*0-7735-1259-4*, Pub. by McGill CN) U of Toronto Pr.

Valour & the Horror Revisited. Ed. by David J. Bercuson & S. F. Wise. 192p. 1994. pap. 14.95 (*0-7735-1271-3*, Pub. by McGill CN) U of Toronto Pr.

Valour & Wisdom: Genesis & Growth of the Indian Military Academy. B. P. Sinha. (C). 1992. text ed. 27.50 (*81-204-0678-8*, Pub. by Oxford IBH II) S Asia.

Valour Fore & Aft. Hope S. Rider. LC 76-17516. (Illus.). 280p. 1987. 17.00 (*0-934943-12-5*) Thirteen Colonies Pr.

Valparaiso. Duncan McNaughton. (Poetry Ser.: No. 2). 144p. 1995. pap. text ed. 10.00 (*0-9639321-2-8*) Listening Chamber.

Valparaiso. deluxe ed. Duncan McNaughton. 1995. pap. 20.00 (*0-9639321-3-6*) Listening Chamber.

Valperga. Mary Wollstonecraft Shelley. LC 95-24126. (Revolution & Romanticism, 1789-1834 Ser.). 269p. 1995. 85.00 (*1-85477-192-2*, Pub. by Woodstock Bks UK) Cassell.

***Valperga: Or the Life & Adventures of Castruccio, Prince of Lucca.** Mary W. Shelley. Ed. by Stuart Curran. (Women Writers in English 1350-1850 Ser.). 416p. 1997. pap. 16.95 (*0-19-510882-5*) OUP.

***Valperga: Or the Life & Adventures of Castruccio, Prince of Lucca.** Mary W. Shelley. Ed. by Stuart Curran. (Women Writers in English 1350-1850 Ser.). 416p. 1997. 49.95 (*0-19-510881-7*) OUP.

Valperga: Or, the Life & Adventures of Castruccio, Prince of Lucca, 3 vols. in 1. Mary Wollstonecraft Shelley. LC 79-8199. reprint ed. 44.50 (*0-404-62122-8*) AMS Pr.

Val's Book. Valentine Sherman. Ed. by Dorothy Schmidt. (Illus.). 274p. 1987. 14.95 (*0-945199-00-7*) Double SS Pr.

Valse aux Adieux. Milan Kundera. (FRE.). 1978. pap. 11.95 (*0-8288-3702-3*) Fr & Eur.

Valse Aux Adieux. Milan Kundera. 339p. (FRE.). 1978. pap. 11.95 (*0-7859-2404-3*, 2070370437) Fr & Eur.

Valse des Toreadors see Pieces Grincantes

***Valse in Full Score.** M. Ravel. 1997. pap. 11.95 (*0-486-29591-5*, 706121Q) Dover.

***Valse Triste: Songs & Ballads.** Emery E. George. LC 96-42395. 132p. 1997. pap. 24.95 (*0-7734-2691-4*, Mellen Poetry Pr) E Mellen.

Valserine & Other Stories. Marguerite Audoux. LC 73-110178. (Short Story Index Reprint Ser.). 1977. 20.95 (*0-8369-3329-X*) Ayer.

Valtat: The Complete Paintings. Jean Valtat. (Illus.). 367p. (FRE.). 1977. 525.00 (*1-55660-014-3*) A Wofsy Fine Arts.

Valtman: The Editorial Cartoons of Edmund S. Valtman, 1961-1991. Ed. by Jyri Kork et al. (Illus.). 143p. 1991. pap. text ed. 13.95 (*0-9620161-2-8*) Esto Inc.

Valu-Able Ideas for Personal Progress. Gayla Wise & Joanna Lewis. LC 92-73587. 1992. pap. 7.95 (*1-55503-422-5*, 01111116) Covenant Comms.

Valuable Collection of Neat Books Well Chosen: The Pennsylvania Assembly Library. Barbara E. Deibler. 64p. 1994. write for info. (*0-9643048-1-3*) Capitol Preserv.

Valuable Nail: The Selected Poems of Gunter Eich. Gunter Eich. Tr. by David Walker et al. from GER. LC 80-85332. (Field Translation Ser.: No. 5). 150p. (C). 1981. 9.95 (*0-932440-08-8*); pap. 4.95 (*0-932440-09-6*) Oberlin Coll Pr.

Valuable Office Professional: For Administrative Assistants, Office Managers, Secretaries & Other Support Staff. Michelle M. Burke. Ed. by Mary Glenn. 192p. (Orig.). 1996. pap. 17.95 (*0-8144-7888-3*) AMACOM.

Valuable Repetitions for Brass Players. Robert D. Weast. 1986. 10.00 (*0-941084-11-6*) McGinnis & Marx.

Valuable Volunteers. Rita Friedman & Elaine Weimann. (Fables from the Letter People Ser.). (Illus.). 30p. (J). (ps-1). 1989. lib. bdg. 12.95 (*0-89796-021-1*) New Dimens Educ.

Valuation: Its Nature & Laws: Being an Introduction to the General Theory of Value. Wilbur M. Urban. LC 75-3416. reprint ed. 49.50 (*0-404-59413-1*) AMS Pr.

Valuation: Measuring & Managing the Value of Companies. 2nd ed. Tom Copeland et al. (Professional Banking & Finance Ser.). 576p. 1994. text ed. 69.95 (*0-471-00993-8*); text ed. 155.00 incl. disk (*0-471-00994-6*) Wiley.

Valuation: Measuring & Managing the Value of Companies. 2nd ed. Tom Copeland et al. LC 94-8304. 550p. 1995. pap. text ed. 64.95 (*0-471-08627-4*) Wiley.

Valuation Actuary Symposium: Proceedings. 1992. pap. 50.00 (*0-938959-28-X*) Soc Actuaries.

Valuation Actuary Symposium: Proceedings. 1993. pap. text ed. 50.00 (*0-938959-32-8*) Soc Actuaries.

Valuation Actuary Symposium: Proceedings. 1995. pap. text ed. write for info. (*0-938959-35-2*) Soc Actuaries.

***Valuation Actuary Symposium Proceedings.** 1997. pap. text ed. write for info. (*0-938959-47-6*) Soc Actuaries.

Valuation Actuary Symposium Proceedings, 1991. 1991. pap. text ed. 40.00 (*0-938959-23-9*) Soc Actuaries.

Valuation & Distribution of Marital Property, 3 vols. Ed. by Bender's Editorial Staff. 1984. Updates. ring bd. write for info. (*0-8205-1133-1*) Bender.

***Valuation & Insurance of Law Libraries.** Bernard D. Reams, Jr. & Erwin C. Surrency. (Law Library Information Reports: Vol. 3). pap. 100.00 (*0-87802-099-3*) Glanville.

Valuation & Investment Merits of Diamonds. Sarkis J. Khoury. LC 89-10192. 184p. 1990. text ed. 65.00 (*0-89930-456-7*, KIF/, Greenwood Pr) Greenwood.

Valuation & Privatisation. OECD Staff. 120p. (Orig.). 1993. pap. 24.00 (*92-64-13818-8*) OECD.

Valuation & Property Taxation of Extractive Resources: A Bibliography. Robert M. Clatanoff. (Bibliographic Ser.). 47p. 1982. pap. 11.50 (*0-88329-114-2*) IAAO.

Valuation & Property Taxation of Forests, Orchards, & Trees: A Bibliography. Robert M. Clatanoff. (Bibliographic Ser.: No. 4). 77p. 1982. pap. 15.00 (*0-88329-118-5*) IAAO.

Valuation & Property Taxation of Nonrenewable Resources: An Annotated Bibliography. Robert M. Clatanoff. (CPL Bibliographies Ser.: No. 99). 53p. 1983. 10.00 (*0-86602-099-3*, Sage Prdcls Pr) Sage.

Valuation & Rate-Making. Robert L. Hale. LC 71-76710. (Columbia University. Studies in the Social Sciences: No. 185). reprint ed. 29.50 (*0-404-51185-6*) AMS Pr.

Valuation & Selection of Convertible Bonds: Based on Modern Option Theory. Stefan J. Gepts. LC 87-14606. 192p. 1987. text ed. 55.00 (*0-275-92466-1*, C2466, Praeger Pubs) Greenwood.

Valuation in Criticism & Other Essays. Frank R. Leavis. Ed. by G. Singh. (Cambridge Paperback Library). 280p. 1986. 74.95 (*0-521-30966-2*) Cambridge U Pr.

Valuation Mehtods & Policy Making in Environmental Economics: Selected & Integrated Papers from the Congress "Environmental Policy in a Market Economy", Wageningen, the Netherlands, 8-11 Sept., 1987. Ed. by Hendrik Folmer & E. C. Van Ierland. (Studies in Environmental Science: No. 36). 260p. 1989. 140.75 (*0-444-87382-1*) Elsevier.

Valuation of Business, Shares & Property. V. L. Gole. 270p. 1980. pap. 54.00 (*0-409-39098-4*, AT) MICHIE.

***Valuation of Closely-Held Businesses: Legal & Tax Aspects.** Lewis D. Solomon & Lewis J. Saret. (Business Practice Library). text ed. write for info. (*0-471-14876-8*) Wiley.

Valuation of Commercial Sales Property: A Classified Annotated Bibliography. Robert M. Clatanoff. LC 84-29005. (Bibliographic Ser.: No. 10). 57p. 1985. pap. 15.00 (*0-88329-137-1*) IAAO.

Valuation of Commercial Services Property: A Classified Annotated Bibliography. Robert M. Clatanoff. LC 85-89. (Bibliographic Ser.: No. 9). 101p. 1985. 19.00 (*0-88329-136-3*) IAAO.

Valuation of Development Land in Hong Kong. Philip J. Roberts. LC 76-369546. 97p. reprint ed. pap. 27.70 (*0-317-27920-3*, 2025128) Bks Demand.

Valuation of Divorce Assets. Barth H. Goldberg. LC 84-20804. 689p. 1984. text ed. write for info. (*0-314-87659-6*) West Pub.

Valuation of Divorce Assets: 1994 Supplement. Barth H. Goldberg. 590p. 1994. pap. text ed. write for info. (*0-314-03952-X*) West Pub.

Valuation of Firms. Luigi Guatri. 220p. 1994. 60.95 (*0-631-19247-6*) Blackwell Pubs.

Valuation of Fixed Assets: Guidance Notes with Background Papers. International Assets Valuation Standards Committee Staff. (C). 1989. text ed. 125.00 (*0-685-40840-X*, Pub. by Surveyors Pubns) St Mut.

Valuation of Fixed Income Securities & Derivatives. 2nd ed. Frank J. Fabozzi. (Illus.). 260p. (C). 1995. pap. 50.00 (*1-883249-06-6*) F J Fabozzi.

***Valuation of Fixed Income Securities & Derivatives.** 3rd rev. ed. Frank J. Fabozzi. (Illus.). 1997. 60.00 (*1-883249-25-2*) F J Fabozzi.

Valuation of Hospitals & Medical Centers. James J. Unland. (Illus.). 355p. (Orig.). (C). 1989. pap. text ed. 34.95 (*0-9622965-0-3*) HMRI.

Valuation of Hospitals & Medical Centers. James J. Unland. 355p. (Orig.). 1989. 45.00 (*1-882198-11-5*) Hlthcare Fin Mgmt.

Valuation of Hospitals & Medical Centers. James J. Unland. (Orig.). 1993. text ed. 60.00 (*0-7602-0118-8*) Irwin Prof Pubng.

Valuation of Industrial Property: A Classified Annotated Bibliography. Robert M. Clatanoff. LC 87-22660. (Bibliographic Ser.: No. 12). 75p. 1987. pap. 16.50 (*0-88329-144-4*) IAAO.

Valuation of Intellectual Property & Intangible Assets. 2nd ed. Gordon V. Smith & Russell L. Parr. 515p. 1994. text ed. 145.00 (*0-471-30412-3*) Wiley.

*Valuation of Intellectual Property & Intangible Assets - 1997 Cumulative Supplement. 2nd ed. Gordon V. Smith & Russell L. Parr. pap. text ed. 60.00 (0-471-16768-1) Wiley.

Valuation of Interest Rate Derative Securities. Jeroen F. De Munnik. LC 96-6089. (New Advances in Economics Ser.: No. 1). 200p. (C). 1996. text ed. 74.95 (0-415-13727-6) Routledge.

Valuation of Interest Rate Derivative Securities. J. De Munnik. (Tinbergen Institute Ser.). 223p. 1992. pap. 25.00 (90-5170-182-9, Pub. by Thesis Pubs NE) IBD Ltd.

*Valuation of Interest-Sensitive Financial Instruments. David F. Babbel & Craig B. Merrill. (Illus.). 145p. (C). 1997. pap. 55.00 (1-883249-15-5) F J Fabozzi.

*Valuation of Life Insurance Liabilities. 3rd ed. Mark A. Tullis & Philip K. Polkinghorn. (Illus.). 191p. (Orig.). 1996. pap. text ed. 38.50 (1-56698-226-X) Actex Pubns.

Valuation of Nationalized Property in International Law, Vol. 1. Ed. by Richard B. Lillich. LC 70-177376. 188p. reprint ed. pap. 53.60 (0-317-26811-2, 2024314) Bks Demand.

*Valuation of Physician Practices & Clinics. Bruce G. Krider. LC 97-23180. 1997. write for info. (0-8342-0962-4) Aspen Pub.

Valuation of Privately-Owned Businesses. Steven M. Reisinger. 155p. 1981. pap. 24.95 (0-940694-00-X) Acquisition Plan.

Valuation of Real Estate. 4th ed. James H. Boykin & Alfred A. Ring. LC 92-12577. 608p. 1992. text ed. 51.80 (0-13-948431-0) P-H.

Valuation of Resort & Recreational Property: A Classified Annotated Biography. Robert M. Clatanoff. LC 87-30992. (Bibliographic Ser.: No. 14). 54p. 1987. pap. 14.50 (0-88329-065-0) IAAO.

*Valuation of Tropical Coastal Resources: Theory & Application of Linear Programming. Ed. by A. Cruz-Trinidad. (ICLARM Studies Rev.: No. 25). (Illus.). 1995. write for info. (971-8709-72-X, Pub. by ICLARM PH) Intl Spec Bk.

Valuation of Used Capital Assets, Vol. 7. Carl R. Beidleman. (Studies in Accounting Research). 84p. 1973. 12.00 (0-86539-019-3) Am Accounting.

Valuation of Wetlands. David M. Keating. 1995. pap. 19.50 (0-922154-21-X) Appraisal Inst.

Valuation Practice in Estate Planning & Litigation. W. C. Elliott, Jr. et al. 1994. 95.00 (0-318-72822-2) Clark Boardman Callaghan.

Valuation Quarterly. Marshall & Swift. 1996. ring bd. write for info. (1-56842-060-9) Marshall & Swift.

*Valuation Quarterly. Marshall & Swift. 1997. ring bd. write for info. (1-56842-064-1) Marshall & Swift.

Valuation Quarterly. Richard Vishanoff. 275p. 1993. write for info. (1-56842-002-1) Marshall & Swift.

Valuation Quarterly (VQ) 89.95 (1-56842-024-2) Marshall & Swift.

Valuation Strategies in Divorce. R. D. Feder. 112p. 1994. suppl. ed., pap. text ed. 50.00 (0-471-00708-0) Wiley.

*Valuation Strategies in Divorce. 4th ed. LC 96-53166. (Family Law Library). 1997. write for info. (0-471-14737-0) Wiley.

*Valuation Strategies in Divorce, 2 vols., Vol. 2. 4th ed. Robert D. Feder. LC 96-53166. (Family Law Library Ser.). 1997. text ed. 225.00 (0-471-13000-1); text ed. write for info. (0-471-13001-X) Wiley.

Valuation Techniques in Estate Planning. (Tax Law & Estate Planning Course Handbook Ser.). Date not set. pap. 99.00 (0-614-17281-0, D4-5259) PLI.

Valuation Theory. O. Endler. LC 72-92285. (Universitext Ser.). xii, 243p. 1972. 26.95 (0-387-06070-7) Spr-Verlag.

Valuation under Direct Tax Laws. S. Bhattacharyya & H. R. Garg. (C). 1989. 175.00 (0-685-36455-0) St Mut.

Valuations of Skew Fields & Projective Hjelmslev Spaces. K. Mathiak. (Lecture Notes in Mathematics Ser.). vii, 116p. 1986. 29.95 (0-387-16099-X) Spr-Verlag.

Valuator Quarterly. Marshall & Swift Staff. 1995. ring bd. 99.95 (1-56842-041-2) Marshall & Swift.

Value. Michael Allingham. LC 82-6018. 105p. 1983. text ed. 29.95 (0-312-83611-2) St Martin.

Value: Its Measurement, Design & Management. M. Larry Shillito & David J. DeMarle. LC 91-26987. 368p. 1992. text ed. 79.95 (0-471-52738-6) Wiley.

*Value Accounting Practices. Robert F. Reilly & Robert P. Schweihs. LC 96-34963. 288p. 1997. text ed. 85.00 (0-471-17224-3) Wiley.

Value Added Attitude & Action. William I. Gorden. 113p. 1995. pap. 5.95 (0-9643860-1-1) Wego Bks.

Value Added Customer Service: Every Employee's Guide for Creating Satisfied Customers. Tom Reilly. LC 94-79761. 70p. (Orig.). (C). 1995. pap. 5.00 (0-944448-10-0) Motivation Pr.

Value-Added Customer Service: The Employee's Guide for Creating Satisfied Customers. Tom Reilly. 160p. 1996. pap. 11.95 (0-8092-3190-5) Contemp Bks.

Value Added in Manufacturing, Mining, & Agriculture in the American Economy from 1809 to 1839. Barry W. Poulson. LC 75-2592. (Dissertations in American Economic History Ser.). (Illus.). 1975. 20.95 (0-405-07214-7) Ayer.

Value Added in Plastics Compounding. BCC Staff. 275p. 1990. 3,150.00 (0-89336-727-3, P-070R) BCC.

Value-Added Leadership: How to Get Extraordinary Performance in Schools. Thomas J. Sergiovanni. 172p. (C). 1989. text ed. 16.00 (0-15-594702-8) HB Coll Pubs.

*Value-Added Management with Design of Experiments. L. Condra. (Illus.). 240p. 1995. text ed. 49.95 (0-412-57070-X, Chap & Hall NY) Chapman & Hall.

Value-Added Marketing: Marketing Management for Superior Results. Torsten H. Nilson. 1992. text ed. 29.95 (0-07-707655-9) McGraw.

Value Added Processes in Information Systems. Robert S. Taylor. Ed. by Melvin J. Voigt. LC 88-18677. (Communication & Information Science Ser.). 264p. 1986. text ed. 78.50 (0-89391-273-5) Ablex Pub.

*Value-Added Products from Beekeeping. R. Krell. (Agricultural Services Bulletin Ser.: No. 124). 420p. 1996. pap. 42.00 (92-5-103819-8, F38198, Pub. by FAO IT) Bernan Associates.

Value-Added Records Management: Protecting Corporate Assets & Reducing Business Risks. Karen L. Sampson. LC 91-45710. 256p. 1992. text ed. 55.00 (0-89930-676-4, Quorum Bks) Greenwood.

Value-Added Records Management: Protecting Corporate Assets & Reducing Business Risks. Karen L. Sampson. 1992. write for info. (0-318-68965-0, SJZ, Quorum Bks) Greenwood.

Value Added Reporting: Lessons for the U. S. Ahmed R. Belkaoui. LC 91-14827. 192p. 1992. text ed. 49.95 (0-89930-651-9, BVE, Quorum Bks) Greenwood.

Value-Added Sales Management: A Guide for Salespeople & Their Managers. Tom Reilly. LC 92-43380. 192p. 1993. pap. 12.95 (0-8092-3787-3) Contemp Bks.

Value Added Sales Management: A Manager's Guide to Creating the Value Added Sales Culture. Thomas P. Reilly. LC 92-63228. 176p. (C). 1993. 24.95 (0-944448-08-9) Motivation Pr.

Value Added Selling Techniques. Thomas P. Reilly. LC 87-90744. 1987. 19.95 (0-944448-07-0) Motivation Pr.

Value Added Tax: A Model Statute & Commentary. LC 88-71735. 300p. 1989. pap. 50.00 (0-89707-401-7, 547-0294-01) Amer Bar Assn.

Value-Added Tax: Administrative & Policy Issues. Ed. by Alan A. Tait. (Occasional Paper Ser.: No. 88). viii, 92p. 1991. pap. 15.00 (1-55775-184-6) Intl Monetary.

Value-Added Tax: International Practice & Problems. Alan A. Tait. xii, 450p. 1988. pap. 29.50 (1-55775-012-2) Intl Monetary.

Value-Added Tax: International Practice & Problems. Alan A. Tait. LC 88-13135. 462p. reprint ed. pap. 131.70 (0-7837-1262-6, 2041399) Bks Demand.

Value-Added Tax: Orthodoxy & New Thinking. Ed. by Murray L. Weidenbaum et al. (C). 1989. lib. bdg. 64.00 (0-7923-9002-4) Kluwer Ac.

Value Added Tax & Duties Reports Pt. 1, Pt. 1. 143p. 1994. pap. 25.00 (0-11-380081-9, HM00819, Pub. by Stationery Ofc UK) Bernan Associates.

Value Added Tax & Duties Reports 1993, Pt. 4. 143p. 1995. pap. 35.00 (0-11-380086-X, HM0086X, Pub. by Stationery Ofc UK) Bernan Associates.

*Value Added Tax & Duties Reports, 1995, Pt. 3. 143p. 1996. pap. 40.00 (0-11-380098-3, HM00983, Pub. by Stationery Ofc UK) Bernan Associates.

*Value Added Tax & Duties Reports, 1995, Pt. 4. 143p. 1996. pap. 35.00 (0-11-380101-7, HM01017, Pub. by Stationery Ofc UK) Bernan Associates.

*Value Added Tax & Duties Reports 1996, Pt. 2. Stationery Office. Orig. Title: Value Added Tax Tribunals. 143p. 1997. pap. 35.00 (0-11-380103-3, HMO1033, Pub. by Stationery Ofc UK) Bernan Associates.

Value Added Tax Tribunals see Value Added Tax & Duties Reports 1996

Value Added Tax Tribunals Reports, 1992 Part 4. 143p. 1994. pap. 16.00 (0-11-380078-9, HM00789, Pub. by Stationery Ofc UK) Bernan Associates.

Value Added Tax Tribunals Reports 1994, Pt. 1. 143p. 1995. pap. 30.00 (0-11-380091-6, HM00916, Pub. by Stationery Ofc UK) Bernan Associates.

Value Added Tax Tribunals Reports 1994 Part 3. 143p. 1995. pap. text ed. 35.00 (0-11-380093-2, HM00932, Pub. by Stationery Ofc UK) Bernan Associates.

Value Added Taxes: A Comparative Analysis. Tax Executives Institute, Inc. Staff. 152p. (Orig.). 1992. pap. 20.00 (0-915128-03-9) Tax Exec Inst.

Value-Added Wood Products: Manufacturing & Marketing Strategies. Ed. by M. Williston. (Illus.). 216p. 1991. 49.00 (0-87930-229-1, 476) Miller Freeman.

Value Analysis. (Open Learning for Supervisory Management Ser.). 1986. pap. text ed. 19.50 (0-08-034169-1, Pergamon Pr) Elsevier.

Value Analysis. (Open Learning for Supervisory Management Ser.). 1987. pap. text ed. 19.50 (0-08-070046-2, Pergamon Pr) Elsevier.

Value Analysis for Better Management. Warren J. Ridge. LC 75-96142. 207p. reprint ed. pap. 59.00 (0-317-09939-6, 2050439) Bks Demand.

Value Analysis in Design. Theodore C. Fowler. 1990. text ed. 59.95 (0-442-23710-3) Van Nos Reinhold.

Value Analysis in the Furniture Industry. 72p. 1990. 13.00 (92-1-106247-0, 90.III.E.9) UN.

Value Analysis in the Furniture Industry. 69p. 1992. 7.00 (92-1-106267-5) UN.

Value & Capital: Fifty Years Later. Lionel W. McKenzie & Stefano Zamagni. 500p. (C). 1991. text ed. 76.00 (0-8147-5454-6) NYU Pr.

Value & Crisis: Essays on Marxian Economics in Japan. Makoto Itoh. LC 80-8084. 192p. 1980. pap. 10.00 (0-85345-557-0) Monthly Rev.

Value & Distribution: A Critical & Constructive Study. Herbert J. Davenport. LC 64-17406. (Reprints of Economic Classics Ser.). xi, 582p. 1964. reprint ed. 49.50 (0-678-00036-0) Kelley.

Value & Distribution System in Ancient India. B. L. Gupta. (C). 1992. 35.00 (81-212-0405-4, Pub. by Gian Publng Hse II) S Asia.

Value & Goal Program. B. L. Davis. 52p. 1993. student ed., pap. 17.00 (0-9640982-0-2) B L Davis.

Value & Goal Program & Kit. rev. ed. B. L. Davis. 65p. (YA). (gr. 3-12). 1995. reprint ed. teacher ed., pap. text ed. 19.00 (0-9640982-2-9) B L Davis.

Value & Goal Program & Kit: Christian Edition. B. L. Davis. 65p. (J). pap. 19.00 (0-9640982-9-6, Wilson-Davis Cnslts) B L Davis.

Value & Goal Program & Kit: Christian Edition. B. L. Davis. 83p. (YA). 1995. pap. 19.50 (0-9640982-7-X) B L Davis.

Value & Growth Styles in Equity Investing. Ed. by Jan R. Squires. 60p. (Orig.). 1995. pap. text ed. 30.00 (1-879087-54-5) ICFARF.

Value & Impact of Information. Ed. by Mary Feeney & Maureen Grieves. LC 94-43184. (British Library Research). 200p. 1994. 50.00 (1-85739-084-9) Bowker-Saur.

Value & Justification: The Foundations of Liberal Theory. Gerald F. Gaus. (Studies in Philosophy). 592p. (C). 1990. pap. text ed. 32.95 (0-521-39733-2) Cambridge U Pr.

Value & Justification: The Foundations of Liberal Theory. Gerald F. Gaus. (Studies in Philosophy). 592p. (C). 1990. text ed. 85.00 (0-521-37525-8) Cambridge U Pr.

Value & Meaning of Depression. M. Esther Harding. (Orig.). 1985. pap. 3.75 (0-318-04660-1) Analytical Psych.

Value & Opportunity: Comparable Pay for Comparable Worth. Deborah Walker. Ed. by Steve Pejovich & Henry Dethloff. (Series on Public Issues: No. 10). 14p. 1984. pap. 2.00 (0-86599-020-4) PERC.

Value & Plan. Ed. by Gregory Grossman. LC 76-6060. (Russian & East European Studies Ser.). 370p. 1976. reprint ed. text ed. 65.00 (0-8371-8804-0, GRVP, Greenwood Pr) Greenwood.

Value & Price. 2nd rev. ed. LC 73-81132. (Capital & Interest Extract Ser.). 246p. 1973. pap. 9.95 (0-910884-01-3) Libertarian Press.

Value & Requirements: An Inquiry Concerning the Origin of Value. Bernt Osterman. 202p. 1995. text ed. 55.95 (1-85972-028-5, Pub. by Avebury Pub UK) Ashgate Pub Co.

Value & Strategy: Competing Successfully in the Nineties. Michael H. Shenkman. LC 91-39712. 208p. 1992. text ed. 49.95 (0-89930-675-6, SZY/, Quorum Bks) Greenwood.

Value & Understanding: Essays for Peter Winch. Ed. by Raymond Gaita. 272p. (C). (gr. 13). 1990. text ed. 85.00 (0-415-04150-3, A4209) Routledge.

Value & Valuation: Axiological Studies in Honor of Robert S. Hartman. John W. Davis. LC 72-146661. 362p. reprint ed. 103.20 (0-685-16063-7, 2027564) Bks Demand.

*Value & Valuation of Natural Science Collections. Ed. by J. R. Nudds & C. W. Pettitt. 230p. 1996. 92.00 (1-897799-76-4, 239, Pub. by Geol Soc Pub Hse UK) AAPG.

Value & Virtue: Moral Education in the Public School. United States Catholic Conference Administrative Board. (Orig.). 1988. pap. 0.50 (1-55586-189-X) US Catholic.

Value Areas & Their Development. H. J. Hermans. 306p. 1976. 46.75 (90-265-0225-7) Swets.

Value Assumptions in Risk Assessment: A Case Study of the Alachlor Controversy. Conrad G. Brunk et al. 168p. (C). 1991. pap. 19.95 (0-88920-266-4); text ed. 29.95 (0-88920-200-1) Wilfrid Laurier.

*Value at Risk. Marwick. 1997. text ed. 55.00 (0-7863-1254-8) Irwin Prof Pubng.

Value at Risk: The New Benchmark for Controlling Derivatives Risk. Philippe Jorion. LC 96-21381. 336p. 1996. 65.00 (0-7863-0848-6) Irwin Prof Pubng.

Value-Based Cost Management for Healthcare: Linking Costs to Quality & Delivery. Kicab Castaneda-Mendez. 189p. 1996. 32.95 (0-527-76304-7) Qual Resc.

*Value Based Decision Making. 1996. 36.00 (1-56091-836-5, SP-1185) Soc Auto Engineers.

*Value-Based Decisions for Automotive Engineering. 1997. 30.00 (1-56091-978-7) Soc Auto Engineers.

*Value-Based Estate Planning. Fowler. Date not set. pap. text ed. 49.00 (0-15-601990-6) Profess Pubns.

*Value Based Management: Developing A Systematic Approach to Creating Shareholder Value. James A. Knight. LC 97-8662. 1997. 65.00 (0-7863-1133-9) Irwin Prof Pubng.

Value-Based PowerTrading: Using the Overlay Demand Curve (TM) to Pinpoint Trends & Predict Market Turns. Donald L. Jones. 240p. 1993. text ed. 45.00 (1-55738-449-5) Irwin Prof Pubng.

Value Basis for Urban & Regional Planning. John M. Udy. LC 95-3937. 268p. 1995. text ed. 89.95 (0-7734-8958-4) E Mellen.

Value by Design: Landscape, Site Planning, & Amenities. Lloyd W. Bookout et al. LC 94-61233. 154p. 1994. pap. text ed. 32.95 (0-87420-763-0, V05) Urban Land.

Value, Capital & Rent. Knut Wicksell. Tr. by S. H. Frowein. LC 68-58668. (Reprints of Economic Classics Ser.). (Illus.). 180p. 1970. reprint ed. 35.00 (0-678-00652-0) Kelley.

Value Cards: Creating a Culture for Team Effectiveness. Alan Barlow. LC 94-67266. 72p. 1994. ring bd. 99.95 (0-88390-444-6, Pfiffr & Co) Jossey-Bass.

Value Change in Chinese Society. Richard W. Wilson et al. LC 77-83479. (Special Studies). 326p. 1979. text ed. 65.00 (0-275-90437-7, C0437, Praeger Pubs) Greenwood.

Value Change in Global Perspective. Paul R. Abramson & Ronald Inglehart. LC 94-45178. 1995. 47.50 (0-472-09591-9); pap. 17.95 (0-472-06591-2) U of Mich Pr.

Value Conflict in Study of Social Change in India. Girish C. Roy. 272p. 1983. 30.95 (0-318-36870-6) Asia Bk Corp.

Value Controversy in Sociology: A New Orientation for the Profession. Dennis C. Foss. LC 77-82915. (Jossey-Bass Higher Education Ser.). 153p. reprint ed. pap. 43.70 (0-317-41964-1, 2025672) Bks Demand.

Value Dimension. Ed. by Ben Fine. (Economy & Society Paperbacks Ser.). 224p. 1986. pap. 16.95 (0-7102-0766-2, 07622, RKP) Routledge.

Value-Directed Management Organizations, Customers, & Quality. Bernard Arogyaswamy & Ron Simmons. LC 92-1749. 248p. 1993. text ed. 55.00 (0-89930-797-3, AQY, Quorum Bks) Greenwood.

Value-Distribution Theory: Proceedings, Pt. 1. Ed. by Robert O. Kujala & Albert L. Vitter, III. LC 73-89281. (Pure & Applied Mathematics Ser.: No. 25). 285p. 1974. reprint ed. pap. 81.30 (0-608-01037-5, 2041048) Bks Demand.

Value-Distribution Theory: Proceedings Pt. B; Deficit & Bezout Estimates. Tulane University Program on Value-Distribution Theory in Complex Analysis & Related Topics in Differential Geometry Staff. Ed. by Robert O. Kujala & Albert L. Vitter, III. LC 73-89281. (Pure & Applied Mathematics Ser.: No. 25). 287p. reprint ed. pap. 81.80 (0-7837-0724-X, 2041048) Bks Demand.

Value Distribution Theory & Its Applications. Ed. by Chung-Chun Yang. LC 83-21465. (Contemporary Mathematics Ser.: Vol. 25). 253p. 1983. pap. text ed. 40.00 (0-8218-5025-3, CONM/25) Am Math.

Value Distribution Theory & New Research. L. Yang. 281p. 1993. 149.95 (0-387-54379-1) Spr-Verlag.

Value Distribution Theory for Meromorphic Maps. Wilhelm Stoll. (Aspects of Mathematics Ser.: Vol. 7). xii, 347p. 1985. pap. 46.00 (3-528-08906-7, Pub. by Vieweg & Sohn GW) Informatica.

Value Distribution Theory of the Gauss Map of Minimal Surfaces in Rm. Hirotaka Fujimoto. (Aspects of Mathematics Ser.: Vol. E21). xvi, 207p. 1993. 46.00 (3-528-06467-6, Pub. by Vieweg & Sohn GW) Informatica.

Value Driven Bank: Strategies for Total Market Satisfaction. Terry C. Wilson et al. 225p. 1995. text ed. 32.50 (1-55738-773-7) Irwin Prof Pubng.

Value Driven Discipline. Gene Bedley. 150p. 1996. pap. text ed. 24.95 (1-888353-18-X) People-Wise.

Value-Driven Purchasing: Managing the Key Steps in the Acquisition Process. Michiel R. Leenders & Anna E. Flynn. LC 94-21172. (NAPM Professional Development Ser.: 13). 264p. 1994. text ed. 45.00 (0-7863-0236-4) Irwin.

*Value Drivers: The Manager's Framework for Identifying the Drivers of Corporate Value Creation. Mark C. Scott. LC 97-26198. 1998. pap. write for info. (0-471-97878-7) Wiley.

Value Education in Schools & Other Essays. Ed. by M. Mascrranahas & H. R. Justa. 150p. 1989. text ed. 15.95 (81-220-0112-2, Pub. by Konark Pubs Pvt Ltd II) Advent Bks Div.

Value Engineering. James Brown. 352p. 1992. 48.95 (0-8311-3038-5) Indus Pr.

Value Engineering: A Systematic Approach. Arthur E. Mudge. 286p. 1989. reprint ed. text ed. 37.00 (0-939332-17-5) J Pohl Assocs.

Value Engineering for the Practitioner. 2nd ed. J. Jerry Kaufman. LC 89-62777. (Illus.). 202p. (C). 1989. text ed. 40.00 (1-56049-000-4) NCSU CE IES.

*Value Enterprise. Richard Tully. 1997. text ed. 24.95 (0-07-552816-9) McGraw.

Value, Exploitation & Class, Vol. 4. John E. Roemer. (Fundamentals of Pure & Applied Economics Ser.: Vol. 4). 94, viiip. 1986. pap. text ed. 44.00 (3-7186-0278-4) Gordon & Breach.

Value Express 4.0 for DOS: The Instant Business Valuation, Deal Structuring & Appraisal Reporting Software System. Wiley-Valuesource Staff. (ValueSource Accounting Software Products Ser.). 272p. 1995. 245.00 (0-471-12217-3) Wiley.

Value-Focused Supply Management: Getting the Most out of the Supply Function. Alan R. Raedels. LC 94-24842. (NAPM Professional Development Ser.: 3). 192p. 1994. text ed. 45.00 (0-7863-0237-2) Irwin Prof Pubng.

Value-Focused Thinking: A Path to Creative Decisionmaking. Ralph L. Keeney. (Illus.). 416p. (C). 1992. 39.95 (0-674-93197-1) HUP.

Value-Focused Thinking: A Path to Creative Decisionmaking. Ralph L. Keeney. (Illus.). 432p. 1996. pap. 18.95 (0-674-93198-X) HUP.

Value-for-Money Auditing in the Public Sector: Strategies for Accountability in the 1990s. D. R. Sheldon & E. F. McNamara. Ed. by Lee A. Campbell. (IIA Monograph). 53p. 1991. pap. 15.00 (0-89413-247-4, A840) Inst Inter Aud.

Value for Value Psychotherapy: The Economic & Therapeutic Barter. Paul S. Rappoport. LC 82-16573. 208p. 1983. text ed. 49.95 (0-275-91724-X, C1724, Praeger Pubs) Greenwood.

Value Form & the State: The Tendencies of Accumulation & the Determination of Economic Policy in Capitalist Society. Geert Reuten & Mike Williams. 320p. 1989. 75.00 (0-415-00088-2, A3585); pap. 21.95 (0-415-03893-6, A3589) Routledge.

Value-Free Science? Purity & Power in Modern Knowledge. Robert N. Proctor. 331p. (C). 1991. 39.95 (0-674-93170-X) HUP.

Value Guide to Advertising Memorabilia. B. J. Summers. 1993. pap. 18.95 (0-89145-597-3) Collector Bks.

Value Guide to Antique Oak Furniture. Conover Hill. (Illus.). 124p. 1996. pap. 7.95 (0-89145-007-6) Collector Bks.

Value Guide to Gas Station Memorabilia. Wayne Priddy & B. J. Summers. 192p. 1995. 24.95 (0-89145-638-4, 3977) Collector Bks.

U V

An Asterisk (*) at the beginning of an entry indicates that the title is appearing in BIP for the first time.

Value Imperative: Managing for Superior Shareholder Returns. James M. McTaggart et al. 288p. 1994. 40.00 (*0-02-920670-7*, Free Press) Free Pr.

Value in Ethics & Economics. Elizabeth Anderson. 1993. text ed. 37.50 (*0-674-93189-0*) HUP.

Value in Ethics & Economics. Elizabeth Anderson. LC 93-365. 261p. 1993. 35.00 (*0-674-09732-7*) HUP.

Value in Ethics & Economics. Elizabeth Anderson. 264p. 1995. pap. text ed. 17.95 (*0-674-93190-4*) HUP.

Value in the Valley. Iyanla Vanzant. 1996. pap. 12.00 (*0-684-82475-2*) S&S Trade.

Value in the Valley: A Black Woman's Guide Through Life's Dilemmas. Iyanla Vanzant. 1995. 22.00 (*0-684-80287-2*) S&S Trade.

Value Investing Made Easy: Benjamin Graham's Classic Investment Strategy Explained For Everyone. Janet Lowe. (Illus.). 256p. 1996. text ed. 22.95 (*0-07-038859-8*) McGraw.

***Value Investing Made Easy: Benjamin Graham's Classic Investment Strategy Explained for Everyone.** Janet Lowe. 1997. pap. text ed. 14.95 (*0-07-038864-4*) McGraw.

Value Investing Today. Charles H. Brandes. 250p. 1989. text ed. 32.50 (*1-55623-178-4*) Irwin Prof Pubng.

***Value Investing Today.** 2nd ed. Charles H. Brandes. LC 97-26016. 1997. text ed. 29.95 (*0-07-007190-X*) McGraw.

***Value Journey: Using Integrated Leadership & Metrics.** Michael C. Harris. 250p. 1997. text ed. 31.00 (*0-87389-378-6*) ASQC Qual Pr.

Value Judgement: Improving Our Ethical Beliefs. James Griffin. LC 96-10751. 192p. 1996. 29.95 (*0-19-823553-4*, Clarendon Pr) OUP.

Value Judgements. Ellen Goodman. 1993. 22.00 (*0-374-16571-8*) FS&G.

Value Judgment & Income Distribution. Charles W. Anderson. Ed. by Robert A. Solo. LC 81-10553. 410p. 1981. text ed. 65.00 (*0-275-90722-8*, C0722, Praeger Pubs) Greenwood.

Value Judgments. Ellen Goodman. 368p. 1995. pap. 13.00 (*0-06-097659-4*, PL) HarpC.

Value Judgments in Arbitration: A Case Study of Saul Wallen. Brook I. Landis. LC 77-8131. (Cornell Studies in Industrial & Labor Relations: No. 19). 200p. 1977. 14.95 (*0-87546-063-1*, ILR Press) Cornell U Pr.

Value, Language & Life. John T. Goldthwait. 336p. 1985. 36.95 (*0-87975-284-X*) Prometheus Bks.

***Value Management in Design & Construction.** J. Kelly & Steven Male. (Illus.). 196p. (Orig.). pap. text ed. 47.50 (*0-419-15120-6*, E & FN Spon) Routledge Chapman & Hall.

Value Management in Design & Construction: The Economic Management of Projects. John Kelly & Steven Male. LC 92-38111. 1992. write for info. (*0-442-31611-9*) Chapman & Hall.

***Value Management Practice.** Michel Thiry. LC 97-12912. (Illus.). 146p. (Orig.). 1997. pap. 24.95 (*1-880410-14-1*) Proj Mgmt Inst.

Value Migration: How to Think Several Moves Ahead of the Competition. Adrian J. Slywotzky. 336p. 1996. 24.95 (*0-87584-632-7*) Harvard Busn.

Value Migration: Strategies to Preempt the Markets of Tomorrow. Adrian J. Slywotzky. 1995. text ed. 24.95 (*0-07-103649-0*) McGraw.

Value of a Dollar: 1901-1920. Manly Inc. Staff. 400p. 1993. 75.00 (*0-8103-6841-2*, 101638) Gale.

Value of a Pound: Price/Income UK 1900-93. 93th ed. Manchester Business School Staff. 1994. 75.00 (*1-873477-31-7*) Gale.

Value of Advanced Manufacturing Technology: How to Assess the Worth of Computers in Manufacturing. Jerry S. Busby. (Illus.). 208p. 1992. 52.95 (*0-7506-0476-X*) Buttrwrth-Heinemann.

Value of Associations to American Society: A Report by the Hudson Institute. Hudson Institute Staff. 121p. (Orig.). 1990. pap. 66.00 (*0-88034-041-X*) Am Soc Assn Execs.

Value of Commodity Output since 1869. William H. Shaw. (General Ser.: No. 48). 321p. 1947. reprint ed. 83.50 (*0-87014-047-7*) Natl Bur Econ Res.

Value of Compassion. Nancy N. Rue. (Encyclopedia of Ethical Behavior Ser.). (YA). (gr. 7-12). 1991. lib. bdg. 15.95 (*0-8239-1240-X*) Rosen Group.

Value of Convenience: A Genealogy of Technical Culture. Thomas F. Tierney. LC 91-42263. (SUNY Series in Science, Technology, & Society). 281p. (C). 1992. pap. text ed. 21.95 (*0-7914-1244-X*) State U NY Pr.

Value of Convenience: A Genealogy of Technical Culture. Thomas F. Tierney. LC 91-42263. (SUNY Series in Science, Technology, & Society). 281p. (C). 1993. text ed. 64.50 (*0-7914-1243-1*) State U NY Pr.

Value of Corporate Libraries: Findings from a 1995 Survey of Senior Management. James M. Matarazzo & Laurence Prusak. (Illus.). 21p. (Orig.). 1995. pap. 7.50 (*0-87111-449-6*) SLA.

Value of Culture: On the Relationship Between Economics & the Arts. Arjo Klammer & Dierdre McCloskey. (C). 1997. pap. 37.50 (*90-5356-218-4*, Pub. by Amsterdam U Pr NE) U of Mich Pr.

Value of Culture: On the Relationship Between Economics & the Arts. Dierdre McCloskey. Ed. by Arjo Klamer. (C). 1997. text ed. 54.50 (*90-5356-219-2*, Pub. by Amsterdam U Pr NE) U of Mich Pr.

Value of Examinations: A Technical Study Carried Out in the Lebanon (UNESCO) E. Valin. (Education Studies & Documents: No. 40). 1974. reprint ed. pap. 25.00 (*0-8115-1364-5*) Periodicals Srv.

Value of Excellence. Etta Wilson. (Encyclopedia of Ethical Behavior Ser.). (YA). (gr. 7-12). 1991. lib. bdg. 15.95 (*0-8239-1289-2*) Rosen Group.

Value of Family: A Blueprint for the 21st Century. Ruth Westheimer & Ben Yagoda. 224p. 1996. 21.95 (*0-446-51875-1*) Warner Bks.

***Value of Family: A Blueprint for the 21st Century.** Ruth Westheimer & Ben Yagoda. 224p. 1997. pap. 12.99 (*0-446-67336-6*) Warner Bks.

***Value of Family: A Blueprint for the 21st Century.** large type ed. Ruth K. Westheimer. LC 96-30934. (Basic Ser.). 386p. 1996. 25.95 (*0-7862-0837-6*, Thorndike Lrg Prnt) Thorndike Pr.

Value of Family: A Bluprint for the 21st Century. Ruth Westheimer & Ben Yagoda. 1997. mass mkt. write for info. (*0-446-60439-9*) Warner Bks.

Value of Friends. LC 86-24164. (Jataka Tales Ser.). (Illus.). 32p. (Orig.). (J). (gr. k-3). 1986. pap. 7.95 (*0-89800-140-4*) Dharma Pub.

Value of Generosity. Janet Grosshandler. (Encyclopedia of Ethical Behavior Ser.). (YA). (gr. 7-12). 1991. lib. bdg. 15.95 (*0-8239-1287-6*) Rosen Group.

***Value of Good Manners.** Kay Beyer. (Ethics). (Illus.). 160p. (YA). (gr. 7-12). 1991. lib. bdg. 15.95 (*0-614-24284-3*) Rosen Group.

Value of Human Life: A Study of the Story of the Flood (Genesis 6-9) P. J. Harland. LC 95-53246. (Supplements to Vetus Testamentum Ser.: Vol. 64). 1996. 97.00 (*90-04-10534-4*) E J Brill.

Value of Human Life in Soviet Warfare. Amnon Sella. 256p. (C). (gr. 13). 1992. text ed. 52.95 (*0-415-02467-6*, A6676) Routledge.

Value of Justice: Essays on the Theory & Practice of Social Virtue. Ed. by Charles A. Kelbley. LC 78-70563. 256p. reprint ed. pap. 73.00 (*0-7837-5605-4*, 2045511) Bks Demand.

Value of Kindness: Stories. Ellyn Bache. Ed. by Gloria Vando Hickok. 220p. (Orig.). 1993. pap. text ed. 11.95 (*0-9627460-8-8*) Helicon Nine Eds.

Value of Library & Information Services. Ed. by Jeans. 95p. 1992. pap. 30.00 (*0-643-05326-3*, Pub. by CSIRO AT) Aubrey Bks.

Value of Life: An Introduction to Medical Ethics. John Harris. 320p. 1985. pap. 13.95 (*0-7102-0437-X*, RKP) Routledge.

Value of Life: Biological Diversity & Human Existence. Stephen R. Kellert. LC 95-32210. 280p. 1995. 24.95 (*1-55963-317-4*) Island Pr.

***Value of Life: Biological Diversity & Human Society.** Stephen R. Kellert. (Illus.). 263p. 1997. pap. 16.95 (*1-55963-318-2*, Shearwater Bks) Island Pr.

***Value of Life: Introduction to Medical Ethics.** J. Harris. 320p. (C). 1985. pap. text ed. 14.95 (*0-415-04032-9*) Routledge.

Value of Loyalty. Ruth C. Rosen. (Encyclopedia of Ethical Behavior Ser.). (YA). (gr. 7-12). 1991. lib. bdg. 15.95 (*0-8239-1243-4*) Rosen Group.

Value of Names. Jeffrey Sweet. 1986. pap. 5.25 (*0-8222-1200-5*) Dramatists Play.

Value of New Serological Probes for the Study of Putative Periodontal Pathogens: A Survey after Five Years of Application. Rudolf Gmur. 1995. write for info. (*0-86715-316-4*) Quint Pub Co.

Value of Patriotism. Carolyn Simpson. (Encyclopedia of Ethical Behavior Ser.). (YA). (gr. 7-12). 1993. lib. bdg. 15.95 (*0-8239-1288-4*) Rosen Group.

Value of Pensions in Divorce. 2nd ed. Marvin Snyder. LC 92-3889. (Family Law Library: No. 1962). 296p. 1992. text ed. 125.00 (*0-471-57119-9*) Wiley.

Value of Pensions in Divorce: What It Is & How to Use It. Marvin Snyder. (Family Law Library). 142p. 1991. 37.50 (*0-471-55518-5*) Wiley.

***Value of Pensions in Divorce - 1997 Cumulative Supplement.** 2nd ed. Marvin Snyder. 1996. pap. text ed. 64.00 (*0-471-17473-4*) Wiley.

Value of Prayer in Psychological Integration. Manly P. Hall. pap. 4.95 (*0-89314-366-9*) Philos Res.

Value of Preventive Medicine. CIBA Foundation Staff. LC 84-41915. (CIBA Foundation Symposium: New Ser.: No. 110). (Illus.). 266p. reprint ed. pap. 75.90 (*0-8357-7067-2*, 2033613) Bks Demand.

***Value of Psychiatric Treatment: Its Efficacy in Severe Mental Disorders.** Ed. by Samuel J. Keith & Susan M. Matthews. (Illus.). 112p. (C). 1996. reprint ed. pap. 35.00 (*0-7881-3094-3*) DIANE Pub.

Value of Self-Control. Sandra L. Smith. (Encyclopedia of Ethical Behavior Ser.). (YA). (gr. 7-12). 1991. lib. bdg. 15.95 (*0-8239-1270-1*) Rosen Group.

Value of the Bible & the Excellence of the Christian Religion: For the Use of Families & Schools 1834. Noah Webster. LC 93-205671. 112p. 1998. reprint ed. 22.00 (*0-912498-08-0*) F A C E.

Value of the Propodeal Orifice & the Phallic Capsule in Vespid Taxonomy (Hymenoptera, Vespidae) Herbert W. Charnley, Jr. LC 79-301936. (Bulletin of the Buffalo Society of Natural Sciences Ser.: Vol. 26). (Illus.). 79p. (Orig.). (C). 1973. pap. 3.00 (*0-944032-33-8*) Buffalo SNS.

Value of Time in Passenger Transportation: The Demand for Air Travel. Reuben Gronau. (Occasional Papers: No. 109). 88p. 1970. reprint ed. 22.90 (*0-87014-219-4*) Natl Bur Econ Res.

Value of Trust. Ruth C. Rosen. (Encyclopedia of Ethical Behavior Ser.). (YA). (gr. 7-12). 1991. lib. bdg. 15.95 (*0-8239-1285-X*) Rosen Group.

Value of Underground Storage in Today's Natural Gas Industry. (Illus.). 85p. (Orig.). (C). 1995. pap. text ed. 40.00 (*0-7881-2266-5*) DIANE Pub.

Value of Visibility: Economic Theory & Applications for Air Pollution Control. Robert D. Rowe & Lauraline G. Chestnut. (Illus.). 280p. 1984. reprint ed. lib. bdg. 56.50 (*0-8191-4091-0*) U Pr of Amer.

Value of Visibility: Theory & Applications. Robert Rowe. 280p. 1982. text ed. 30.00 (*0-89011-572-9*) Abt Bks.

Value of Voluntary Simplicity. Richard B. Gregg. (C). 1983. pap. 3.00 (*0-87574-003-0*) Pendle Hill.

Value Orientations in Counseling & Psychotherapy: The Meanings of Mental Health. 2nd ed. C. Marshall Lowe. LC 76-25957. 1976. pap. text ed. 19.50 (*0-910328-09-9*) Sulzburger & Graham Pub.

Value Perspectives Today: Toward an Integration with Jean Piaget's New Discipline in Relation to Modern Educational Leaders. John F. Emling. LC 75-39114. 393p. 1978. 40.00 (*0-8386-1905-3*) Fairleigh Dickinson.

Value-Philosophy of Alfred Edward Taylor: A Study in Theistic Implication. Charles W. Mason. LC 79-52512. 1979. pap. text ed. 29.00 (*0-8191-0772-7*) U Pr of Amer.

Value Presuppositions in Theories of Human Development. Leonard Cirillo & Seymour Wapner. 184p. 1986. text ed. 39.95 (*0-89859-753-6*) L Erlbaum Assocs.

Value, Price & Profit. Karl Marx. Ed. by Eleanor M. Aveling. Tr. by Edward Aveling. 128p. 17.95 (*0-88286-030-5*); pap. 5.00 (*0-88286-033-X*) C H Kerr.

***Value Pricing: How to Price Products & Services.** A. C. Fletcher & Neil Jones. (Marketing & Sales Ser.). 1996. pap. 40.00 (*0-7494-1895-8*) Kogan Page Ltd.

Value Pricing for the Design Firm. Frank A. Stasiowski. LC 92-26514. 240p. 1993. text ed. 59.95 (*0-471-57933-5*) Wiley.

Value Retailing in the 90's: Off-Pricers, Factory Outlets, & Closeout Stores. Packaged Facts. 192p. 1994. pap. text ed. 160.00 (*0-471-10915-0*) Wiley.

Value Retention among Young Creoles: Attitudes & Commitment of Contemporary Youth. Frances Woods. LC 89-36156. (Studies in Sociology: Vol. 5). 160p. 1989. lib. bdg. 69.95 (*0-88946-634-3*) E Mellen.

***Value Selection Handbook.** 4th ed. R. W. Zappe. 1998. 70.00 (*0-88415-886-1*) Gulf Pub.

Value, Social Form & the State. Ed. by Michael Williams. LC 87-33094. 224p. 1988. text ed. 45.00 (*0-312-01694-8*) St Martin.

Value, Social Influence, & Power see Revisiting Wertheimer's Seminars

Value Strategies for Classroom Teachers. Ed. by Marion Lemin et al. 200p. 1995. pap. 26.95 (*0-86431-111-7*, Pub. by Aust Coun Educ Res AT) Paul & Co Pubs.

Value Systems & Personality in a Western Civilization: Norwegians in Europe & America. Christen T. Jonassen. LC 83-11391. 400p. 1983. 52.50 (*0-8142-0347-7*) Ohio St U Pr.

Value Systems of Different Classes: A Social Psychological Contribution to the Analysis of Stratification. Herbert H. Hyman. (Reprint Series in Social Sciences). (C). 1993. reprint ed. pap. text ed. 1.90 (*0-8290-3786-1*, S-130) Irvington.

Value, Technical Change, & Crisis: Explorations in Marxist Economic Theory. David Laibman. LC 91-11246. 400p. (gr. 13). 1992. text ed. 75.95 (*0-87332-735-7*); pap. text ed. 29.95 (*0-87332-736-5*) M E Sharpe.

Value Theory & Education. Peter F. Carbone, Jr. LC 86-27822. 288p. 1987. lib. bdg. 28.00 (*0-89874-976-X*) Krieger.

Value Theory in Philosophy & Social Science. Ed. by Ervin Laszlo & James B. Wilbur. LC 73-84239. (Current Topics of Contemporary Thought Ser.). 166p. 1973. text ed. 109.00 (*0-677-14160-2*) Gordon & Breach.

Value Travel Passport Nineteen Eighty-Eight. rev. ed. Rodney E. Rawson. 486p. 1988. pap. 16.95 (*0-941751-01-0*) Aeon Pub.

Value, Welfare, & Morality. Ed. by R. G. Frey & Christopher W. Morris. LC 92-36143. 336p. (C). 1993. text ed. 74.95 (*0-521-41696-5*) Cambridge U Pr.

Value Your Children: Becoming Better Parental Disciple-Makers. Kirby Worthington & Everett L. Worthington, Jr. LC 95-36902. (Strategic Christian Living Ser.). 112p. (Orig.). (gr. 10). 1996. pap. 8.99 (*0-8010-5401-X*) Baker Bks.

Value Your Mate: How to Strengthen Your Marriage. Douglas McMurry & Everett L. Worthington, Jr. LC 93-36060. (Strategic Christian Living Ser.). 128p. (Orig.). (C). 1994. pap. 8.99 (*0-8010-9727-4*) Baker Bks.

Valued Heritage & Veritable Harvest, 2 vols., Set. Harold E. Amstutz. (Illus.). 217p. (Orig.). 1992. pap. text ed. 8.95 (*1-888796-09-X*) ABWE Pubng.

Valued Youth Anthology: Articles on Dropout Prevention. Ed. by Aurelio M. Montemayor & Charles Cavazos. 118p. (Orig.). 1989. pap. text ed. 14.95 (*1-878550-27-6*) Inter Dev Res Assn.

Valueing Useless Knowledge: An Anthropological Inquiry into the Meaning of Liberal Education. Robert B. Graber. (Illus.). 80p. (Orig.). 1995. pap. 10.00 (*0-943549-36-1*) TJU Pr.

Valuer. Ellenberger. 1983. 34.95 (*0-409-02711-1*) Buttrwrth-Heinemann.

Values. Marva Collins. 1996. pap. 17.95 (*0-7871-1007-8*, Dove Bks) Dove Audio.

Values. John B. Keane. 1973. pap. 9.95 (*0-85342-369-5*) Dufour.

***Values: A Book of Family Devotions.** G. A. Barbee. LC 96-96375. 190p. (Orig.). 1996. pap. write for info. (*0-7880-0682-7*) CSS OH.

Values: A Foundation for Success. Mescon Group Staff. (GC - Principles of Management Ser.). 1995. text ed. 16.95 (*0-538-84365-9*) S-W Pub.

Values: A Foundation for Success. Mescon Group Staff. (GC - Principles of Management Ser.). 1995. teacher ed., text ed. 25.95 (*0-538-85040-X*) S-W Pub.

Values: Keys to a Meaningful Life. 220p. 1996. pap. 6.95 (*81-7120-726-X*) Vedanta Pr.

Values: Lighting the Candle of Excellence. Marva Collins. 224p. 1996. pap. 17.95 (*0-7871-1040-X*, Dove Bks) Dove Audio.

Values: What They Are & How We Know Them. John T. Goldthwait. 208p. 1996. pap. 16.95 (*1-57392-007-X*) Prometheus Bks.

***Values Added: Making Ethical Decisions in the Financial Marketplace.** John L. Casey. Ed. by Bruce McCandless, 3rd. LC 96-46347. 264p. 1996. 57.50 (*0-7618-0610-5*); pap. 32.50 (*0-7618-0609-1*) U Pr of Amer.

Values & Assumptions in American Labor Law. James B. Atleson. LC 82-21993. 256p. 1983. pap. 17.95 (*0-87023-390-4*) U of Mass Pr.

Values & Attitudes of Indian Youth. N. Y. Reddy. 244p. 1980. 24.95 (*0-940500-10-8*, Pub. by Light & Life Pubs II) Asia Bk Corp.

Values & Choices Teacher's Manual. John Forliti et al. (Values & Choices Ser.). 212p. 1986. teacher ed., pap. text ed. 35.00 (*1-57482-205-5*) Search Inst.

Values & Community in Multinational Yugoslavia. Gary K. Bertsch. (East European Monographs: No. 17). 160p. 1970. text ed. 59.00 (*0-914710-10-9*) East Eur Monographs.

Values & Economic Theory: The Case of Hedonism. S. A. Drakopoulos. 225p. 1991. 68.95 (*1-85628-200-7*, Pub. by Avebury Pub UK) Ashgate Pub Co.

Values & Ethics for Young Adults. Ed. by Kelly Gorham. (Values & Ethics Ser.). 28p. (YA). (gr. 10 up). 1994. student ed. 7.00 (*0-8064-0011-0*, VE4); audio 329.00 (*0-8064-0010-2*) Bergwall.

Values & Ethics in Organization & Human Systems Development. Ed. by Mark S. Frankel. (AAAS Publication Ser.: No. 87-32). 116p. reprint ed. pap. 33.10 (*0-8357-8564-5*, 2034928) Bks Demand.

Values & Ethics in Organization & Human Systems Development: Responding to Dilemmas in Professional Life. William Gellermann et al. LC 90-4946. (Management-Social & Behavioral Science Ser.). 559p. text ed. 43.95 (*1-55542-296-9*) Jossey-Bass.

Values & Ideals of American Youth. Ed. by Eli Ginzberg. LC 72-6798. (Essay Index Reprint Ser.). 1977. reprint ed. 26.95 (*0-8369-7252-X*) Ayer.

Values & Imperatives: Studies in Ethics. Clarence I. Lewis. Ed. by John Lange. LC 69-13181. xv, 201p. 1969. 32.50 (*0-8047-0687-5*) Stanford U Pr.

Values & Knowledge. Ed. by Edward S. Reed et al. (Jean Piaget Symposia Ser.). 192p. 1996. text ed. 39.95 (*0-8058-1521-X*) L Erlbaum Assocs.

Values & Lifestyles of Singaporeans. Kau A. Keng & Charles Yang. 300p. 1992. 72.50 (*9971-69-170-1*, Pub. by Sgapore Univ SI); pap. 57.50 (*9971-69-154-X*, Pub. by Sgapore Univ SI) Coronet Bks.

Values & Planning. Huw Thomas. 230p. 1994. 59.95 (*1-85628-306-2*, Pub. by Avebury Pub UK) Ashgate Pub Co.

Values & Public Life: An Interdisciplinary Study. Ed. by Gerard Magill & Marie D. Hoff. LC 95-17930. 328p. (C). 1995. 49.50 (*0-8191-9974-5*) U Pr of Amer.

Values & Public Policy. Ed. by Henry J. Aaron et al. 216p. (C). 1994. 34.95 (*0-8157-0056-3*); pap. 14.95 (*0-8157-0055-5*) Brookings.

Values & Public Policy. William J. Bennett et al. (C). 1988. pap. text ed. 9.95 (*1-55872-000-6*) Family Research Council Amer Inc.

Values & Public Policy. Claudia Mills. 700p. (C). 1991. pap. text ed. 29.50 (*0-15-594711-7*) HB Coll Pubs.

Values & Public Policy. Ed. by Claudia Mills. 1992. pap. 29.50 (*0-317-05235-7*) IPPP.

Values & Scientists. John A. White. 88p. (Orig.). 1984. pap. text ed. 14.00 (*0-8191-3585-2*) U Pr of Amer.

Values & the Active Community. Philip E. Jacob. LC 71-136613. 1971. 22.95 (*0-02-915920-2*, Free Press) Free Pr.

Values & the Environment: A Social Science Perspective. Ed. by Yvonne Guerrier et al. LC 95-16830. 256p. 1996. text ed. 95.00 (*0-471-96047-0*) Wiley.

Values & the Search for Self. James A. Bellance. LC 75-12724. 111p. reprint ed. pap. 31.70 (*0-317-42175-1*, 2025922) Bks Demand.

Values & the Social Order: Society & Order, Vol. 2. Gerard Radnitzky & Hardy Bouillon. 216p. 1995. 63.95 (*1-85628-900-1*, Pub. by Avebury Pub UK) Ashgate Pub Co.

Values & the Social Order: Values & Society, Vol. 1. Gerard Radnitzky & Hardy Bouillon. 268p. 1995. 63.95 (*1-85628-899-4*, Pub. by Avebury Pub UK) Ashgate Pub Co.

***Values & the Social Order Vol. 3: Voluntary versus Coercive Orders.** Ed. by Gerard Radnitzky. (Series in Philosophy). 544p. 1997. 93.95 (*1-85972-399-3*, Pub. by Avebury Pub UK) Ashgate Pub Co.

Values & the Social Sciences. E. Carlton. 192p. 1995. pap. 24.95 (*0-7156-2665-5*, Pub. by Duckworth UK) Focus Pub-R Pullins.

***Values & Valuation in the Practice of Educational Administration.** Donald J. Willower & Joseph W. Licata. LC 97-4720. (Illus.). 136p. 1997. pap. 18.95 (*0-8039-6632-6*) Corwin Pr.

***Values & Valuation in the Practice of Educational Administration.** Donald J. Willower & Joseph W. Licata. (Illus.). 136p. 1997. text ed. 42.95 (*0-8039-6631-8*) Corwin Pr.

Values & Value Theory in Twentieth Century America: Essays in Honor of Elizabeth Flower. Ed. by Murray G. Murphey & Ivar Berg. LC 87-33675. 308p. (C). 1988. 39.95 (*0-87722-557-5*) Temple U Pr.

Values & Valuing: Speculations on the Ethical Life of Persons. Graham Nerlich. 232p. 1990. 65.00 (*0-19-824847-4*) OUP.

Values & Violence in Auschwitz: A Sociological Analysis. Anna Pawelczynska. LC 76-3886. 1979. pap. 11.00 (*0-520-04242-5*) U CA Pr.

Values & Visions: Changing Ideas in Services for People with Learning Difficulties. Ed. by Linda Ward & Terry Philpot. 256p. 1995. pap. 37.50 (*0-7506-2248-2*) Buttrwrth-Heinemann.

UV

Values & Voices: A College Reader. 3rd ed. Betty B. Renshaw et al. 372p. (C). 1986. pap. text ed. 20.75 (*0-03-071039-1*) HB Coll Pubs.

Values Are Forever: Becoming More Caring & Responsible. Gary A. Davis. LC 95-90784. 140p. (J). (gr. 4-8). 1996. pap. 15.95 (*1-888115-00-9*) Westwood Pubng.

Values at Risk. Ed. by Douglas MacLean. 1986. 49.00 (*0-317-05233-0*); pap. 22.75 (*0-317-05529-1*) IPPP.

Values at Risk. Ed. by Douglas MacLean. (Maryland Studies in Public Philosophy). 192p. (C). 1986. pap. 25.00 (*0-8476-7415-0*) Rowman.

Values at War: Selected Tanner Lectures on the Nuclear Crisis. Freeman J. Dyson et al. Ed. by Sterling M. McMurrin. LC 83-21705. 142p. (Orig.). reprint ed. pap. 40.50 (*0-8357-3273-8*, 2039494) Bks Demand.

Values Auction see Kadima Kesher Series

Values Based Approach. Terry E. McSweens. (Illus.). 250p. 1995. text ed. 51.95 (*0-442-01945-9*) Van Nos Reinhold.

***Values-Based Financial Planning.** Fowler. Date not set. pap. text ed. 49.00 (*0-15-601980-9*) Profess Pubns.

Values-Based Investing. Fowler. Date not set. pap. text ed. 49.00 (*0-15-601945-0*) Profess Pubns.

Values-Based Leadership: Rebuilding Employee Commitment, Performance & Productivity. Thomas D. Kuczmarski. LC 94-35330. 1994. text ed. 21.95 (*0-13-121856-5*) P-H.

Values Based Planning for Quality Education. Mildred L. Burns. LC 95-60606. 520p. 1995. text ed. 39.95 (*1-56676-284-7*) Technomic.

***Values-Based Retirement Planning.** Fowler. Date not set. pap. text ed. 49.00 (*0-15-601966-3*) Profess Pubns.

Values-Based Teaching Skills: Introduction & Implementation. rev. ed. Larry S. Rosen et al. 180p. 1995. pap. 25.95 (*1-885435-02-9*) Twin Lights.

Values Chauffeur You. Andrew Levy. LC 90-60632. 88p. 1991. 9.00 (*1-882022-06-8*) O Bks.

Values Clarification. Sidney B. Simon et al. 336p. 1995. pap. 12.99 (*0-446-67095-2*) Warner Bks.

Values Clarification: A Handbook of Practical Strategies for Teachers & Students. Sidney B. Simon et al. 400p. 1991. reprint ed. pap. text ed. 12.95 (*1-880424-02-9*) Values.

Values Clarification for Counselors: How Counselors, Social Workers, Psychologists, & Other Human Service Workers Can Use Available Techniques. Gordon M. Hart. (Illus.). 104p. 1978. 22.95 (*0-398-03847-3*) C C Thomas.

Values, Conflict & the Environment. Ed. by Robin Attfield & Katharine Dell. (Avebury Series in Philosophy). 180p. 1996. text ed. 59.95 (*1-85972-491-4*, Pub. by Avebury Pub UK) Ashgate Pub Co.

***Values, Culture, Content: Three Keys to Journalism in a Strategic Newspaper.** Michael P. Smith. 52p. (Orig.). 1997. pap. text ed. write for info. (*0-9656018-0-3*) NMC.

Values, Cultures & Kids: Approaches & Resources for Teaching Child Development & about the Family. Development Educational Centre Staff. 80p. (C). 1989. 60.00 (*0-7487-0024-2*, Pub. by Stanley Thornes UK) Trans-Atl Phila.

Values Development: Diagnostic Sourcebook. Brian Hall et al. 87p. (C). 1990. spiral bd. write for info. (*1-879494-00-0*) MC Intl Values Inst.

Values Driven Leadership: Discovering & Developing Your Core Values for Ministry. Aubrey Malphurs. LC 95-47524. 224p. (C). 1996. pap. 16.99 (*0-8010-9015-6*) Baker Bks.

Values-Driven People. Sharon Johnson. LC 88-32493. 1989. pap. 4.99 (*0-945241-01-1*) Probe Bks.

***Values Driven People: A Christian Approach to Management.** Sharon Johnson. 44p. pap. 4.99 (*0-614-25147-8*) Probe Bks.

Values-Driven Safety: The Key to Optimizing Resources & Controlling Losses. Donald J. Eckenfelder. LC 96-37428. 200p. (Orig.). 1996. pap. text ed. 59.00 (*0-86587-532-4*) Gov Insts.

Values Education & Technology: The Ideology of Dispossession. Peter C. Emberley. (Studies in Education). 330p. 1995. 75.00 (*0-8020-0423-7*) U of Toronto Pr.

Values Education in Australian Schools. Brian Hill. (C). 1992. 75.00 (*0-86431-078-1*, Pub. by Aust Council Educ Res AT) St Mut.

Values, Ethics & Aging, Vol. IV. Ed. by Gari Lesnoff-Caravaglia. (Frontiers in Aging Ser.). (Illus.). 196p. 1985. 35.95 (*0-89885-162-9*) Human Sci Pr.

Values for a New Millennium: Activating the Natural Law to Reduce Violence, Revitalize Our Schools & Promote Cross-Cultural Harmony. Robert L. Humphrey. LC 91-90287. (Illus.). 390p. (Orig.). 1991. pap. 17.95 (*0-915761-04-1*) Life Values Pr.

Values for Life: The Sources of Morality & Ethical Criteria. Jean Desclos. 176p. 1993. 29.00 (*0-85439-440-0*, Pub. by St Paul Pubns UK) St Mut.

Values for Survival: Essays, Addresses, & Letters on Politics & Education. Lewis Mumford. LC 79-167387. (Essay Index Reprint Ser.). 1977. reprint ed. 22.95 (*0-8369-2704-4*) Ayer.

Values for Your Son, Your Daughter, & Yourself. Anne Lyons. 52p. 1993. pap. 12.95 (*0-9638076-0-9*) Fulton Freeman Pubs.

Values from the Heartland: Stories of an American Family. Bettie B. Youngs. 275p. (Orig.). 1995. pap. 11.95 (*1-55874-335-9*, 3359) Health Comm.

Values from the Heartland: Stories of an American Farmgirl. Bettie B. Youngs. 260p. (Orig.). 1995. 22.00 (*1-55874-334-0*, 3340) Health Comm.

Values in a Box - Belief Vol. 14: A Tool Kit for Building Whole People. Harry Heuston. (Illus.). 144p. (Orig.). (J). (gr. 5-9). 1995. pap. 4.75 (*1-57414-084-1*) Value Network.

Values in a Box - Caring Vol. 12: A Tool Kit for Building Whole People. Harry Heuston. (Illus.). 144p. (Orig.). (J). (gr. 5-9). 1995. pap. 4.75 (*1-57414-082-5*) Value Network.

Values in a Box - Confidence Vol. 1: A Tool Kit for Building Whole People. Harry Heuston. (Illus.). 144p. (Orig.). (J). (gr. 5-9). 1995. pap. text ed. 4.75 (*1-57414-071-X*) Value Network.

Values in a Box - Courage Vol. 13: A Tool Kit for Building Whole People. Harry Heuston. (Illus.). 144p. (Orig.). (J). (gr. 5-9). 1995. pap. 4.75 (*1-57414-083-3*) Value Network.

Values in a Box - Determination Vol. 8: A Tool Kit for Building Whole People. Harry Heuston. (Illus.). 144p. (Orig.). (J). (gr. 5-9). 1995. pap. 4.75 (*1-57414-078-7*) Value Network.

Values in a Box - Excellence Vol. 11: A Tool Kit for Building Whole People. Harry Heuston. (Illus.). 144p. (Orig.). (J). (gr. 5-9). 1995. pap. 4.75 (*1-57414-081-7*) Value Network.

Values in a Box - Fairness Vol. 10: A Tool Kit for Building Whole People. Harry Heuston. (Illus.). 144p. (Orig.). (J). (gr. 5-9). 1995. pap. 4.75 (*1-57414-080-9*) Value Network.

Values in a Box - Honesty Vol. 2: A Tool Kit for Building Whole People. Harry Heuston. (Illus.). 144p. (Orig.). (J). (gr. 5-9). 1995. pap. 4.75 (*1-57414-072-8*) Value Network.

Values in a Box - Love Vol. 3: A Tool Kit for Building Whole People. Harry Heuston. (Illus.). 144p. (Orig.). (J). (gr. 5-9). 1995. pap. 4.75 (*1-57414-073-6*) Value Network.

Values in a Box - Loyalty Vol. 5: A Tool Kit for Building Whole People. Harry Heuston. (Illus.). 144p. (Orig.). (J). (gr. 5-9). 1995. pap. 4.75 (*1-57414-075-2*) Value Network.

Values in a Box - Respect Vol. 4: A Tool Kit for Building Whole People. Harry Heuston. (Illus.). 144p. (Orig.). (J). (gr. 5-9). 1995. pap. 4.75 (*1-57414-074-4*) Value Network.

Values in a Box - Responsibility Vol. 6: A Tool Kit for Building Whole People. Harry Heuston. (Illus.). 144p. (Orig.). (J). (gr. 5-9). 1995. pap. 4.75 (*1-57414-076-0*) Value Network.

Values in a Box - Trustworthiness Vol. 7: A Tool Kit for Building Whole People. Harry Heuston. (Illus.). 144p. (Orig.). (J). (gr. 5-9). 1995. pap. 4.75 (*1-57414-077-9*) Value Network.

Values in a Box - Unselfishness Vol. 9: A Tool Kit for Building Whole People. Harry Heuston. (Illus.). 144p. (Orig.). (J). (gr. 5-9). 1995. pap. 4.75 (*1-57414-079-5*) Value Network.

Values in Action, Set. Gene Bedley. LC 93-92737. 411p. 1994. teacher ed. 169.00 (*1-888353-14-7*) People-Wise.

Values in Action: A Middle-School Ethics Course. Carol Eliot et al. 162p. (J). (gr. 7-8). teacher ed. 25.50 (*1-881678-39-3*) CRIS.

Values in Administration. Ed. by Ramesh K. Arora & C. V. Raghavulu. 1990. text ed. 27.50 (*81-7045-017-9*, Pub. by Associated Pub Hse II) Advent Bks Div.

Values in America. Ed. by Donald N. Barrett. LC 61-14877. 192p. 1967. reprint ed. pap. 54.80 (*0-608-00893-1*, 2061687) Bks Demand.

Values in an Age of Confrontation: A Symposium Sponsored by the Religion in Education Foundation. Ed. by Jeremiah W. Canning. LC 72-109054. (Studies of the Person). 216p. reprint ed. pap. 61.60 (*0-317-09226-X*, 2055239) Bks Demand.

Values in Art. Oronzo Abbatecola. (Illus.). 80p. 1995. pap. 20.95 (*0-8059-3533-9*) Dorrance.

***Values in Conflict: An Interdisciplinary Approach.** Phyllis O'Callaghan. LC 97-21706. 1997. write for info. (*0-7618-0819-1*); pap. write for info. (*0-7618-0820-5*) U Pr of Amer.

Values in Conflict: Christian Nursing in a Changing Profession. Judith A. Shelly & Arlene Miller. LC 91-20901. 324p. (Orig.). 1991. pap. 14.99 (*0-8308-1330-6*, 1330) InterVarsity.

Values in Conflict: Christianity, Marxism, Psychoanalysis & Existentialism. Ed. by Victor Comerchero. LC 74-111099. 986p. (Orig.). (C). 1970. pap. text ed. 19.95 (*0-89197-463-6*) Irvington.

Values in Conflict: Resolving Ethical Issues in Health Care. 2nd ed. American Hospital Association Staff. 120p. (Orig.). 1994. pap. 29.00 (*0-87258-668-5*, 025002) Am Hospital.

Values in Education & Education in Values. Ed. by J. Mark Halstead & Monica J. Taylor. 240p. 1996. 78.95 (*0-7507-0509-4*, Falmer Pr); pap. 26.95 (*0-7507-0510-8*, Falmer Pr) Taylor & Francis.

Values in Geography. S. A. Buttimer. (C). 1987. text ed. 30.00 (*81-85046-54-9*, Pub. by Scientific Pubs II) St Mut.

Values in Geography. Annette Buttimer. 1987. reprint ed. 75.00 (*0-317-62325-7*, Pub. by Scientific UK) St Mut.

Values in Health Care: Choices & Conflicts. John G. Bruhn & George Henderson. (Illus.). 420p. 1991. pap. 42.95 (*0-398-06038-X*) C C Thomas.

Values in Health Care: Choices & Conflicts. John G. Bruhn & George Henderson. (Illus.). 420p. (C). 1991. text ed. 67.95 (*0-398-05741-9*) C C Thomas.

Values in Medical Practice: A Statement of Philosophy for Physicians & Model for Teaching a Healing Science. Rudolph J. Napodano. LC 85-19742. 144p. 1986. 32.95 (*0-89885-268-4*) Human Sci Pr.

Values in Modern Medicine. William S. Middleton. LC 72-1379. (Illus.). 321p. reprint ed. pap. 91.50 (*0-8357-4751-4*, 2037673) Bks Demand.

Values in Philippine Culture & Education. Manuel B. Dy. LC 94-4724. (Series III, Asia: Vol. 7). 205p. 1994. 45.00 (*1-56518-040-2*); pap. 17.50 (*1-56518-041-0*) Coun Res Values.

Values in Selected Children's Books of Fiction & Fantasy. Ed. by Carolyn W. Field & Jaqueline S. Weiss. LC 87-3874. 240p. (C). 1987. lib. bdg. 35.00 (*0-208-02100-0*, Lib Prof Pubns) Shoe String.

Values in Sexuality Education: A Philosophical Study. Ronald W. Morris. 132p. (Orig.). 1994. pap. text ed. 19.50 (*0-8191-9557-X*); lib. bdg. 41.00 (*0-8191-9556-1*) U Pr of Amer.

Values in Social Work: A Re-Examination. Ed. by Morton Teicher et al. LC 65-15322. 107p. (C). 1967. pap. text ed. 9.95 (*0-87101-345-2*) Natl Assn Soc Wkrs.

Values in Teaching & Professional Ethics. Ed. by Carlton T. Mitchell. LC 89-29914. (Luce Program on Religion & the Social Crisis Ser.: No. IV). 176p. (C). 1990. 24.95 (*0-86554-362-3*, MUP-H300) Mercer Univ Pr.

Values in the Electric Power Industry. Ed. by Kenneth M. Sayre. LC 76-51829. 310p. reprint ed. pap. 88.40 (*0-317-55791-2*, 2029314) Bks Demand.

Values in the Marketplace: The American Stock Market under Federal Securities Law. James Burk. (Studies on North America: No. 2). x, 207p. (C). 1988. lib. bdg. 79.25 (*3-11-011714-2*) De Gruyter.

Values in the Marketplace: The American Stock Market under Federal Securities Law. James Burk. (Sociology & Economics: Controversy & Integration Ser.). 217p. 1992. reprint ed. pap. text ed. 26.95 (*0-202-30397-7*) Aldine de Gruyter.

Values Leadership: Toward a New Philosophy of Leadership. Gilbert W. Fairholm. LC 91-10664. 264p. 1991. text ed. 55.00 (*0-275-93997-9*, C3997, Praeger Pubs) Greenwood.

Values, Leadership & Quality: The Administration of Higher Education. Lloyd C. Elam et al. (David D. Henry Lectures). 164p. 1991. text ed. 17.95 (*0-252-01893-1*) U of Ill Pr.

Values, Lifestyles & Psychographics. Ed. by Lynn R. Kahle & Larry Chiagouris. LC 96-50053. (Advertising & Consumer Psychology Ser.). 500p. 1996. 79.95 (*0-8058-1496-5*) L Erlbaum Assocs.

Values Matter Most: How Democrats, or Republicans, or a Third Party, Can Win & Renew the American Way of Life. Ben J. Wattenberg. 350p. 1995. 25.00 (*0-02-933795-X*, Free Press) Free Pr.

Values Matter Most: How Republicans, or Democrats, Or a Third Party, Can Win & Renew the American Way of Life. Ben J. Wattenberg. LC 96-23930. 350p. 1996. pap. 14.95 (*0-89526-436-6*) Regnery Pub.

Values, Nature, & Culture in the American Corporation. William C. Frederick. (Ruffin Series in Business Ethics). (Illus.). 320p. 1995. 45.00 (*0-19-509411-5*); pap. 24.95 (*0-19-509674-6*) OUP.

Values of Art. Malcolm Budd. 1997. pap. 12.95 (*0-14-012148-X*) Viking Penguin.

Values of Art: Pictures, Poetry & Music. Malcolm Budd. (Illus.). 224p. 1995. 24.95 (*0-7139-9026-0*) Allen Lane.

Values of Change in Social Work. Steven Shardlow. 256p. 1989. 49.95 (*0-415-01837-4*, A3507) Routledge.

Values of Change in Social Work. Steven Shardlow. 256p. (C). 1989. pap. text ed. 14.95 (*0-415-01838-2*, A3511) Routledge.

Value(s) of Literature. James S. Hans. LC 89-31513. (SUNY Series in Aesthetics & the Philosophy of Art). 166p. 1990. text ed. 64.50 (*0-7914-0205-3*); pap. text ed. 21.95 (*0-7914-0206-1*) State U NY Pr.

***Values of Non-Atomic Games.** R. J. Aumann & L. S. Shapley. LC 72-4038. (Rand Corporation Research Study Ser.). 347p. 1974. reprint ed. pap. 98.90 (*0-608-02884-3*, 2063948) Bks Demand.

Values of Precision. Ed. by M. Norton Wise. LC 94-19562. 368p. 1995. text ed. 55.00 (*0-691-03759-0*) Princeton U Pr.

***Values of Precision.** M. Norton Wise. 380p. 1995. pap. text ed. 22.95 (*0-691-01601-1*) Princeton U Pr.

Values of Psychotherapy. Jeremy Holmes & Richard Lindley. (Studies in Bioethics). 272p. 1989. 33.95 (*0-19-217759-1*) OUP.

Values of Social Science. rev. ed. Ed. by Norman K. Denzin. LC 72-94545. 194p. 1973. reprint ed. pap. 18.95 (*0-87855-547-1*) Transaction Pubs.

Values of Social Science. 2nd rev. ed. Ed. by Norman K. Denzin. LC 72-94545. 194p. 1973. reprint ed. 32.95 (*0-87855-054-2*) Transaction Pubs.

Values of the African American Family: The Kwanzaa Canons. Johnnierenee Nelson. (Illus.). 48p. (Orig.). 1993. pap. 9.00 (*0-9623205-2-8*) House Nia.

Values of the Enterprise Culture: Moral Debate. Ed. by Paul Hellas & Paul Morris. 272p. (C). 1992. pap. text ed. 19.95 (*0-415-07615-3*, Routledge NY) Routledge.

***Values Profile.** 4p. 1994. pap. 8.00 (*1-58034-011-3*, M001V) IML Pubns.

Values, Self, & Society: Toward a Humanist Social Psychology. M. Brewster Smith. 278p. (C). 1990. 39.95 (*0-88738-373-4*) Transaction Pubs.

Values Shift: A Guide to Personal & Organizational Transformation. Brian P. Hall. Ed. by Elaine Brett. 286p. (Orig.). 1994. pap. 28.95 (*1-885435-00-2*) Twin Lights.

Values Symphony: How to Harmonize Faith & Choices in Everyday Living. rev. ed. Lois Qualben. Ed. by R. J. Roberts. (Illus.). 169p. 1993. pap. 8.95 (*1-880292-17-3*) LangMarc.

Values That Last. Ed. by R. M. Davis & P. D. Buford. 160p. reprint ed. pap. 5.99 (*1-56722-063-0*) Word Aflame.

***Values Versus Interests: The U. S. Response to the Tiananmen Square Massacre.** Eric A. Hyer. (Pew Case Studies in International Affairs). 50p. (C). 1996. text ed. 3.50 (*1-56927-170-4*) Geo U Inst Dplmcy.

***Values, Virtues: Classic Quotes, Awesome Thoughts & Humorous Sayings.** Bob Phillips & Howard Hendricks. LC 96-49714. 299p. 1997. 12.99 (*1-57673-086-7*, Multnomah Bks) Multnomah Pubs.

Values Visions & Voices: An Anthology of Socialism. Ed. by Gordon Brown & Tony Wright. 224p. 1996. 35.00 (*1-85158-731-4*, Pub. by Mnstream UK) Trafalgar.

***Values We Live By: What Americans Want from Welfare Reform.** Steve Farkas & Jean Johnson. 50p. (Orig.). 1996. pap. 10.00 (*1-889483-00-1*) Public Agenda.

Valuing a Business: Analysis & Appraisal of Closely Held Companies. 3rd ed. Shannon P. Pratt et al. 785p. 1995. text ed. 95.00 (*1-55623-971-8*) Irwin Prof Pubng.

Valuing a Business: The Analysis & Appraisal of Closely Held Companies. 2nd ed. Shannon P. Pratt. 737p. 1988. text ed. 92.50 (*1-55623-127-X*) Irwin Prof Pubng.

Valuing a Property Management Company. Shannon P. Pratt. 69p. 1988. pap. 32.00 (*0-944298-20-6*) Inst Real Estate.

Valuing Ancient Things: Archaeology & Law. John Carman & Clare Hall. LC 95-24873. 288p. 1996. 120.00 (*0-7185-0012-1*, Pub. by Leicester Univ Pr) Bks Intl VA.

***Valuing Assets & Handling the Valuation Expert in Equitable Distribution Trials.** 373p. 1994. 30.00 (*0-614-26686-6*, 1038) NYS Bar.

***Valuing Assets & Handling the Valuation Expert in Equitable Distribution Trials.** 373p. 1994. 92.00 incl. audio (*0-614-26687-4*, 20381) NYS Bar.

Valuing Banks & Thrifts. William D. Miller. 1990. pap. 69.95 (*1-55840-434-1*) Exec Ent Pubns.

Valuing Children in Litigation: Family & Individual Loss Assessment. John O. Ward & Thomas Ireland. 300p. (Orig.). 1995. pap. text ed. 55.00 (*0-913875-05-8*, 5058) Lawyers & Judges.

Valuing Climate Change. Samuel Fankhauser. 1995. 22.00 (*1-85383-237-5*, Pub. by Erthscan Pubns UK) Island Pr.

***Valuing Closely Held Businesses.** 95th ed. Lockwood. 1995. pap. text ed. 35.00 (*0-15-602407-1*) Profess Pubns.

Valuing Common Stock: The Power of Prudence. George Lasry. LC 78-24023. 270p. reprint ed. pap. 77.00 (*0-317-27196-2*, 2023930) Bks Demand.

Valuing Diversity: New Tools for a New Reality. Ed. by Lewis B. Griggs & Lente-Louise Louw. LC 94-22295. 822. 1994. text ed. 29.95 (*0-07-024778-1*) McGraw.

Valuing Diversity: The Primary Years. Janet B. McCracken. LC 93-84576. (Illus.). 104p. 1993. pap. text ed. 5.00 (*0-935989-55-2*, 238) Natl Assn Child Ed.

Valuing Diversity & Similarity: Bridging the Gap Through Interpersonal Skills. Joe Wittmer. LC 92-71010. 256p. (Orig.). (C). 1992. pap. text ed. 14.95 (*0-932796-37-0*) Ed Media Corp.

***Valuing Diversity in the School System: Facilitator's Guide.** Eleanor R. Rodriguez et al. (Illus.). 129p. 1995. teacher ed., ring bd. 140.00 (*1-57517-017-5*, 1367) IRI-SkyLght.

***Valuing Diversity in the School System: Participant's Manual.** Eleanor R. Rodriguez et al. (Illus.). 97p. 1995. ring bd. 19.95 (*1-57517-018-3*, 1423) IRI-SkyLght.

Valuing Diversity on Campus: A Multicultural Approach. Ed. by Cynthia Woolbright. (College Unions at Work Monographs). 1989. 50.00 (*0-923276-05-X*); pap. 25.00 (*0-923276-04-1*) Assn Coll Unions Intl.

Valuing Emotions. Michael Stocker. (Cambridge Studies in Philosophy). 450p. (C). 1996. text ed. 64.95 (*0-521-56110-8*); pap. text ed. 21.95 (*0-521-56786-6*) Cambridge U Pr.

Valuing English: Reflections on the National Curriculum. Roger Knight. (Quality in Secondary Schools & Colleges Ser.). 160p. 1996. pap. text ed. 24.95 (*1-85346-374-4*, Pub. by D Fulton UK) Taylor & Francis.

Valuing Fixed-Income Investments & Derivative Securities: Cash-Flow Analysis & Calculations. Arnold Kleinstein & Steven Allen. 320p. 1991. 34.95 (*0-13-931775-9*) NY Inst Finance.

Valuing Forests: Context Issues & Guidelines. H. Gregersen et al. (Forestry Papers: Vol. 127). 53p. 1995. pap. 12.00 (*92-5-103699-3*) Food & Agriculture Organization of.

***Valuing Ground Water.** Committee on Valuing Ground Water, National Research Council. LC 97-4837. 230p. (C). 1997. 37.95 (*0-309-05640-3*, Joseph Henry Pr) Natl Acad Pr.

Valuing Health Care: Costs, Benefits, & Effectiveness of Pharmaceuticals & Other Medical Technologies. Ed. by Frank A. Sloan. LC 94-9554. (Illus.). 288p. (C). 1995. text ed. 32.95 (*0-521-47020-X*) Cambridge U Pr.

Valuing Health Care: Costs, Benefits, & Effectiveness of Pharmaceuticals & Other Medical Technologies. Frank A. Sloan. (Illus.). 288p. 1996. pap. text ed. 19.95 (*0-521-57646-6*) Cambridge U Pr.

Valuing Health for Policy: An Economic Approach. Ed. by George Tolley et al. LC 94-9537. 436p. 1994. 55.00 (*0-226-80713-4*) U Ch Pr.

Valuing Health Risks, Costs, & Benefits for Environmental Decision Making: Report of a Conference. Ed. by P. Brett Hammond & Rob Coppock. LC 89-64210. 243p. 1990. reprint ed. pap. 69.30 (*0-608-02332-9*, 2062973) Bks Demand.

Valuing Life. John Kleinig. Ed. by Marshall Cohen. 296p. 1991. text ed. 42.50 (*0-691-07388-0*) Princeton U Pr.

Valuing Local Knowledge: Indigenous Peoples & Intellectual Property Rights. Ed. by Stephen B. Brush & Doreen Stabinsky. 351p. 1996. 50.00 (*1-55963-378-6*); pap. 30.00 (*1-55963-379-4*) Island Pr.

Valuing Natural Assets: The Economics of Natural Resource Damage Assessment. Ed. by Raymond J. Kopp & V. Kerry Smith. LC 92-35479. 358p. 1993. lib. bdg. 75.00 (*0-915707-66-7*) Resources Future.

UV

An Asterisk (*) at the beginning of an entry indicates that the title is appearing in BIP for the first time.

Valuing Natural Assets: The Economics of Natural Resource Damage Assessment. Ed. by Raymond J. Kopp & V. Kerry Smith. LC 92-3547. 358p. 1993. pap. 24.95 (0-915707-67-5) Resources Future.
***Valuing Nature? Ethics, Economics & the Environment.** John Foster. LC 96-41517. 256p. (C). 1997. pap. write for info. (0-415-14875-8); text ed. write for info. (0-415-12978-8) Routledge.
***Valuing Nature: Perspectives & Priorities.** Glenn Adelson & Dan Perlman. LC 97-11468. (Illus.). 208p. (Orig.). 1997. pap. text ed. 36.95 (0-86542-439-X) Blackwell Sci.
Valuing Nature: The Decline & Preservation of Old Growth Forests. Douglas Booth. 245p. (Orig.). (C). 1993. pap. text ed. 24.95 (0-8476-7860-1); lib. bdg. 59.50 (0-8476-7859-8) Rowman.
Valuing Nonperforming Investment Real Estate. Kevin Brown & James R. Cooper. 139p. 1992. spiral bd. 35.00 (0-88406-256-2, RM104) GA St U Busn Pr.
Valuing Professional Practises & Licenses: A Guide for the Matrimonial Practitioner. Ronald L. Brown. LC 87-12620. write for info. (0-13-940669-7) P-H.
Valuing Quality in Early Childhood Services: New Approaches to Defining Quality. Ed. by Peter Moss & Alan R. Pence. (Early Childhood Education Ser.). 192p. (C). 1994. pap. text ed. 19.95 (0-8077-3431-4) Tchrs Coll.
Valuing Small Businesses & Professional Practices. Shannon P. Pratt. 1985. text ed. 90.00 (0-87094-598-X) Irwin Prof Pubng.
Valuing Small Businesses & Professional Practices. 2nd ed. Shannon P. Pratt. 720p. 1993. text ed. 92.50 (1-55623-551-8) Irwin Prof Pubng.
***Valuing Small Businesses & Professional Practices.** 3rd ed. Shannon P. Pratt. (Art of M & A Ser.). 1997. 95.00 (0-7863-1186-X) Irwin Prof Pubng.
Valuing Special Libraries & Information Centers: An SLA Information Kit. 195p. 1993. pap. 20.00 (0-87111-418-6) SLA.
Valuing the Dual-Career Workforce: Business Implications of Spouse Employment Issues in Relocation. Paul R. Wesman & Lillian T. Eby. 75p. (Orig.). 1995. pap. 250.00 (0-9628438-4-9) Right Assocs.
Valuing the Earth: Economics, Ecology, Ethics. Herman E. Daly & Kenneth N. Townsend. (Illus.). 384p. 1992. 42.00 (0-262-04133-2); pap. 21.00 (0-262-54068-1) MIT Pr.
Valuing the Environment. A. Coker. 345p. 1992. 260.00 (81-7089-180-9, Pub. by Intl Bk Distr II) St Mut.
Valuing the Environment. Raino Malnes. (Issues in Environmental Politics Ser.). 160p. 1996. text ed. 59.95 (0-7190-4485-5, Pub. by Manchester Univ Pr UK) St Martin.
Valuing the Environment. Raino Malnes. (Issues in Environmental Politics Ser.). 1996. text ed. 19.95 (0-7190-4486-3, Pub. by Manchester Univ Pr UK) St Martin.
Valuing the Environment: Economic Approaches to Enviromental Evaluation. Ed. by Annabel Coker & Cathy Richards. LC 91-46605. 183p. 1994. text ed. 82.95 (0-471-94803-9) Wiley.
Valuing the Environment: Economic Approaches to Environmental Evaluation. Ed. by Annabel Coker. (Illus.). 192p. 1992. text ed. 49.00 (1-85293-212-0) St Martin.
***Valuing the Environment: Economic Approaches to Environmental Evaluation.** Ed. by Annabel Coker & Cathy Richards. 200p. 1995. pap. text ed. 41.95 (0-471-96112-4, ES21) Wiley.
Valuing the Environment: Methodological & Measurement Issues. Rudiger Pethig. LC 93-38948. 376p. (C). 1994. lib. bdg. 169.00 (0-7923-2602-4) Kluwer Ac.
Valuing the Environment: Proceedings of the First Annual International Conference on Environmentally Sustainable Development. Ed. by Ismail Serageldin & Andrew Steer. LC 94-22189. (Environmentally Sustainable Development Proceedings Ser.: No. 2). 1994. 18.95 (0-8213-2882-4, 12882) World Bank.
Valuing the Privately-Held Business: The Art & Science of Establishing a Company's Worth. rev. ed. Irving L. Blackman. 500p. 1992. text ed. 70.00 (1-55738-287-5) Irwin Prof Pubng.
Valuing the Self: What We Can Learn from Other Cultures. Dorothy Lee. (Illus.). 1986. reprint ed. pap. text ed. 8.50 (0-88133-229-1) Waveland Pr.
Valuing the Timeshare Property. Kathleen Conroy. 97p. 1981. 17.00 (0-911780-50-5) Appraisal Inst.
Valuing Tropical Forests: Methodology & Case Study of Madagascar. Narendra P. Sharma et al. (Environment Paper Ser.: No. 13). 76p. 1995. 7.95 (0-8213-3407-7, 13407) World Bank.
Valuing Useless Knowledge: An Inquiry into the Meaning of Liberal Education. Robert B. Graber. (Illus.). 80p. (Orig.). 1995. 5.00 (0-943549-29-9) TJU Pr.
Valuing Your Customers: Quality Database Marketing. Angus Jenkinson. LC 95-20988. (Quality in Action Ser.). 1995. write for info. (0-07-707950-7) McGraw.
Valuing Your Privately-Held Business: The Art & Science of Establishing Your Company's Worth. Irving L. Blackman. 1995. per. 32.50 (1-55738-879-2) Irwin Prof Pubng.
Valuing Your Privately-Held Business: The Art & Science of Establishing Your Own Company's Worth. Irving L. Blackman. 500p. 1995. 29.95 (1-55738-879-2) Irwin Prof Pubng.
***Valusource III Senior Analyst Manual.** Wiley-Valusource Staff. 1994. pap. write for info. (0-471-10901-0) Wiley.
ValuWriteTM: Financial Report Writer for Windows. Wiley-ValuSource Staff. 160p. 1995. 249.00 (0-471-12212-2) Wiley.
Valva & Treatment of the Patient with Diarrhea. Paul F. Miskovitz & Arnold Rochwarger. (Illus.). 179p. 1992. 55.00 (1-56372-059-0) Buttrwrth-Heinemann.
Valve Amplifiers. Morgan Jones. (Illus.). 272p. 1995. 39.95 (0-7506-2337-3) Buttrwrth-Heinemann.
***Valve Handbook.** Philip L. Skousen. LC 97-14832. 1997. write for info. (0-07-057921-0) McGraw.
Valve Manufacturers. Ed. by ICC Information Group Staff. 1987. 695.00 (1-85319-046-2, Pub. by ICC Info Group Ltd UK) St Mut.
Valve Morphology in the Genus Cymbella: C. A. Agardh. Kurt Krammer. Ed. by J. G. Helmcke. (Micromorphology of Datom Valves Ser.: No. XI). (Illus.). 300p. (Orig.). 1982. 99.00 (3-7682-1333-1) Lubrecht & Cramer.
Valve Primer. Brent T. Stojkov. LC 96-37133. (Illus.). 196p. 1997. 32.95 (0-8311-3077-6) Indus Pr.
Valve Selection & Specification. R. Merrick. 1990. text ed. 69.95 (0-442-31870-7) Chapman & Hall.
Valve Selection Handbook. 3rd ed. R. W. Zappe. 352p. 1991. 75.00 (0-87201-863-6) Gulf Pub.
Valves. Center for Occupational Research & Development Staff. (EUTEC Power Plant Operator Curriculum Ser.). (Illus.). 36p. (C). 1985. pap. text ed. write for info. (1-55502-222-7) CORD Commns.
Valves. Multimedia Development Services Staff. (Plant Fundamentals Ser.). (Illus.). 90p. (Orig.). 1995. student ed. 30.00 (1-57431-010-0) Tech Trng Systs.
Valves, Vol. III, Module III. Multimedia Development Services Staff. (Plant Fundamentals Ser.). (Illus.). (Orig.). 1995. teacher ed. 65.00 (1-57431-050-X) Tech Trng Systs.
Valves for Process Control & Safety. Chemical Engineering Magazine Editors & Jay Matley. 153p. 1990. text ed. 48.00 (0-07-040932-3) McGraw.
Valves Piping & Pipelines Handbook. 3rd ed. Ed. by Dickenson. 1996. text ed. write for info. (1-85617-252-X) Elsevier.
***Valvetrain System Design & Materials: Proceedings from the 1st International Symposium.** 100p. 1997. 78.00 (0-87170-594-X, 6488) ASM.
***Valvetrain System Design & Materials: Proceedings from the 1st International Symposium.** 100p. 1997. 78.00 (0-614-27208-4, 6488) ASM.
Valvular Heart Disease. Ed. by Muayed Al-Zaibag & Carlos Duran. LC 93-46486. (Fundamental & Clinical Cardiology Ser.: Vol. 20). 750p. 1994. 215.00 (0-8247-8861-3) Dekker.
Valvular Heart Disease. James E. Dalen & Joseph S. Alpert. 1986. 125.00 (0-316-17171-9) Little.
Valvular Heart Disease. Otto. Date not set. text ed. write for info. (0-7216-7139-X) HarBrace.
Valvular Heart Disease: Comprehensive Evaluation & Treatment. 2nd ed. Ed. by William S. Frankl & Albert N. Brest. LC 70-6558. (Cardiovascular Clinics Ser.: Vol. 23). (Illus.). 339p. 1992. text ed. 80.00 (0-8036-3792-6) Davis Co.
Valyra & the Dragons: And Other Fanciful Adventure Stories. Highlights Staff. LC 94-72483. (Illus.). 96p. (J). (gr. 2-5). 1995. 2.95 (1-56397-443-6) Boyds Mills Pr.
Vamonos a Recorrer el Ano. Jane B. Moncure. LC 87-13257. (Castillo Magico Ser.). (Illus.). 32p. (SPA.). (J). (ps-2). 1987. lib. bdg. 21.36 (0-89565-914-X) Childs World.
Vamos a Jugar. Bell. 1992. 19.00 (1-56492-047-X) Laredo.
Vamos a Jugar. Clarisa Bell. (This Is Entertainment Ser.). (Illus.). 24p. (Orig.). (SPA.). (J). (gr. 2-6). 1992. lib. bdg. 9.95 (1-56492-048-8) Laredo.
Vamos a Jugar: Big Book. Clarisa Bell. (This Is Entertainment Ser.). (Illus.). 24p. (Orig.). (SPA.). (J). (gr. 2-6). 1992. pap. 19.95 (1-56492-049-6) Laredo.
Vamos a Orar: Oraciones para diferentes ocasiones. John T. Catoir. 90p. (SPA.). 1991. pap. 2.95 (0-8189-0610-3) Alba.
Vamos a Practicar, Custom Pub. 2nd ed. Pesacreta et al. 1994. pap. text ed. write for info. (0-07-049525-4) McGraw.
Vamos a Practicar, Custom Pub. 2nd ed. Pesacreta et al. 1994. wbk. ed., pap. text ed. write for info. (0-07-049527-0) McGraw.
Vamos a Subir la Voz Para Morir Mariposas. Dalia N. Albert. Ed. by Pepe Carvajal. (Illus.). 23p. 1989. pap. write for info. (0-942347-02-1) Ediciones Puerto.
Vamos Amigos: A Beginning Spanish Course. Heloise Lewis. 1986. pap. text ed. 8.70 (0-582-36225-3, 74821) Longman.
Vamp. Margaret Holt. 440p. 1996. mass mkt. 4.99 (1-896329-97-7, Pub. by Comnwlth Pub CN) Partners Pubs Grp.
***Vamp.** Tracy Ryan. 187p. 1997. pap. 16.95 (1-86368-172-8, Pub. by Indra Pub AT) Intl Spec Bk.
Vamp: The Rise & Fall of Theda Bara. Eve Golden. (Illus.). 288p. 1996. 29.95 (1-887322-00-0) Emprise NY.
Vamphyri. Brian Lumley. LC 96-23842. 1996. 24.95 (0-312-86212-1) St Martin.
Vamphyri. Brian Lumley. 1989. mass mkt. 5.99 (0-8125-2126-9) Tor Bks.
Vampire. Richie T. Cusick. Ed. by Patricia MacDonald. 224p. (Orig.). (YA). (gr. 7 up). pap. 3.99 (0-671-70956-9, Archway) PB.
Vampire. Sydney Horler. 1974. 8.50 (0-685-47865-3) Bookfinger.
Vampire. John W. Polidori. LC 88-34078. (Step-up Classic Chillers Ser.). (Illus.). 96p. (J). (gr. 2-6). 1989. pap. 3.50 (0-394-83844-0, Bullseye Bks) Random Bks Yng Read.
Vampire. John W. Polidori. LC 88-34078. (Step-up Classic Chillers Ser.). (Illus.). 96p. (J). (gr. 2-6). 1994. lib. bdg. 5.99 (0-394-93844-5, Bullseye Bks) Random Bks Yng Read.
Vampire: In Legend & Fact. Basil Copper. 1989. pap. 8.95 (0-8065-1126-5, Citadel Pr) Carol Pub Group.
Vampire: The Complete Guide to the World of the Undead. Manuela D. Mascetti. (Illus.). 224p. 1994. pap. 14.95 (0-14-023801-8, Viking Studio) Studio Bks.
Vampire: The Dark Ages. Jennifer Hartshorn et al. (Vampire: the Masquerade Ser.). (Illus.). 272p. 1996. 28.00 (1-56504-275-1, 2800) White Wolf.
Vampire: The Dark Ages - Storyteller's Screen. Jennifer Hartshorn & Ethan Skemp. (Vampire Ser.). (Illus.). (Orig.). 1996. pap. 10.00 (1-56504-276-X, 2801) White Wolf.
***Vampire: The Dark Ages Companion.** Various. 1997. 18.00 (1-56504-279-4) White Wolf.
Vampire: The Dark Ages Storytellers Secrets. Wade Racine & Robert Hatch. (Vampire Ser.). (Illus.). 128p. (Orig.). 1996. pap. 15.00 (1-56504-277-8, 2802) White Wolf.
Vampire: The Masquerade. 2nd ed. Mark Rein-Hagen et al. Ed. by Stephen Wieck. (Vampire: the Masquerade Ser.). (Illus.). 264p. 1993. 28.00 (1-56504-029-5, 2002) White Wolf.
Vampire Angel. Michael Romkey. 1998. mass mkt. 5.99 (0-449-14993-5) Fawcett.
Vampire Babies. Ed. by Jeanne Youngson. 18p. (Orig.). 1986. pap. 2.95 (0-9611944-6-4) Dracula Pr.
***Vampire Barbecue.** Mercer Mayer. LC 96-32606. 1998. lib. bdg. 11.99 (0-679-97376-1) Random Bks Yng Read.
Vampire Bat. Pamela J. Gerholdt. LC 95-8115. (Bats Ser.). (J). (gr. k-3). 1995. lib. bdg. 13.98 (1-56239-505-X) Abdo & Dghtrs.
Vampire Bat: A Field Study in Behavior & Ecology. Dennis C. Turner. LC 74-24396. (Illus.). 159p. reprint ed. pap. 45.40 (0-8357-8364-2, 2034156) Bks Demand.
Vampire Bats & Other Creatures of the Night. Philip Steele. LC 95-6105. (Young Observer Ser.). (Illus.). 40p. (J). (gr. 3-5). 1995. pap. 6.95 (1-85697-575-4, Kingfisher LKC) LKC.
Vampire Book: The Encyclopedia of the Undead. J. Gordon Melton. (Illus.). 792p. 1994. 16.95 (0-8103-2295-1) Visible Ink Pr.
Vampire Book: The Encyclopedia of the Undead. Ed. by J. Gordon Melton. 852p. 1994. 39.95 (0-8103-9553-3, 102149) Gale.
Vampire Breath. R. L. Stine. (Goosebumps Ser.: No. 49). (J). (gr. 2-5). 1996. pap. 3.99 (0-590-56886-8) Scholastic Inc.
Vampire Bugs: Stories Conjured from the Past. Sharon D. Wyeth. 96p. (J). (gr. 2-6). 1996. pap. 3.99 (0-440-41155-6, YB BDD) BDD Bks Young Read.
Vampire Bugs: Stories Conjured from the Past. Sharon D. Wyeth. LC 94-20315. 96p. (J). 1995. 14.95 (0-385-32082-5) Delacorte.
Vampire Cat, No. 1. Louise Folley. 96p. (Orig.). (J). (gr. 3-6). 1995. mass mkt. 3.99 (0-8125-5366-7) Tor Bks.
Vampire Cat, Vol. 1, No. 3. Louise M. Foley. 1996. pap. text ed. 4.50 (0-8125-5368-3) Tor Bks.
Vampire Cat: The Bird-Brained Fiasco. Louise M. Foley. (Vampire Cat Ser.). (J). (gr. 3-7). 1996. pap. 3.99 (0-614-15788-9) Tor Bks.
Vampire Cat #02, Vol. 1. Louise M. Folley. 1996. pap. text ed. 3.99 (0-8125-5367-5) Tor Bks.
***Vampire Cat 4: The Catnap Cat-Astrophe!** Louise M. Foley. 1996. pap. text ed. 4.50 (0-8125-5369-1) Tor Bks.
Vampire Child. Ruby J. Jensen. 1990. mass mkt. 3.95 (0-8217-2867-9, Zebra Kensgtn) Kensgtn Pub Corp.
Vampire Chronicle, 4 vols., Set. Anne O. Rice. 1989. Boxed set. boxed 20.97 (0-345-36422-8) Ballantine.
Vampire Chronicles: Interview with the Vampire, The Vampire Lestat, Queen of the Damned, & Tale of the Body Thief, Set. Anne O. Rice. 1993. pap. 27.96 (0-345-38540-3) Ballantine.
Vampire Coffin. Tri-City Elementary School, Mrs. Spicher's 1994-95 Third-Grade Class Staff. (Wee Write Bks.: No. 21). (Illus.). 35p. (J). (ps-3). 1995. pap. 8.95 (1-884987-73-7) WeWrite.
Vampire Companion. Katherine Ramsland. (Illus.). 640p. 1995. pap. 17.95 (0-345-39739-8) Ballantine.
Vampire Companion: The Official Guide to Anne Rice's The Vampire Chronicles. Katherine Ramsland. LC 93-2378. Date not set. write for info. (0-345-37921-7) Ballantine.
Vampire Detectives. Ed. by Martin H. Greenberg. 320p. (Orig.). 1995. mass mkt., pap. 4.99 (0-88677-626-0) DAW Bks.
Vampire, Dracula & Incest: The Vampire Myth, Stoker's Dracula, & Psychotherapy of Vampiric Sexual Abuse. Daniel Lapin. LC 95-75221. 252p. (Orig.). 1995. pap. 14.95 (0-9644983-0-8) Gargoyle Pub.
Vampire Encyclopedia. Matthew Bunson. LC 92-42005. 1993. pap. 16.00 (0-517-88100-4, Crown) Crown Pub Group.
Vampire Files, No. 01: Bloodlist. P. N. Elrod. 1990. mass mkt. 4.99 (0-441-06795-6) Ace Bks.
Vampire Files, No. 02: Lifeblood. P. N. Elrod. 1990. mass mkt. 4.99 (0-441-84776-5) Ace Bks.
Vampire Files, No. 03: Bloodcircle. P. N. Elrod. 1990. mass mkt. 4.99 (0-441-06717-4) Ace Bks.
Vampire Files, No. 06: Blood on the Water. P. N. Elrod. 1992. mass mkt. 4.99 (0-441-85947-X) Ace Bks.
Vampire Film: From Nosferatu to Bram Stoker's Dracula. rev. ed. Alain Silver & James Ursini. LC 93-14565. (Illus.). 272p. 1993. reprint ed. pap. 20.00 (0-87910-170-9) Limelight Edns.
***Vampire Hunters.** William Hill. 1997. pap. write for info. (0-614-30237-4) Otter Crk Pr.
Vampire in Europe. Montague Summers. 1996. 9.99 (0-517-14989-3) Random.
Vampire in Literature: A Critical Bibliography. Ed. by Margaret L. Carter & Robert Scholes. LC 89-31932. (Studies in Speculative Fiction: No. 21). 144p. reprint ed. 40.80 (0-8357-1998-7, 2070704) Bks Demand.
Vampire in Love. Angela Sommer-Bodenburg. 144p. (J). (gr. 3-6). 1993. pap. 2.99 (0-671-75877-2, Minstrel Bks) PB.
Vampire in Nineteenth-Century England Literature. Carol Senf. LC 87-73508. 204p. (C). 1988. 33.95 (0-87972-424-2) Bowling Green Univ Popular Press.
Vampire in Verse: An Anthology. Ed. by Steven Moore. 196p. (Orig.). 1985. pap. 7.95 (0-9611944-2-1) Dracula Pr.
Vampire Invaders. Edward Packard. (Choose Your Own Adventure Ser.: No. 118). 112p. (J). (gr. 4-7). 1991. pap. 3.50 (0-553-29212-9) Bantam.
Vampire Invaders, Vol. 118. large type ed. Edward Packard. LC 95-22411. (Choose Your Own Adventure Ser.: Vol. 118). (Illus.). 128p. (J). (gr. 4 up). 1995. lib. bdg. 15.93 (0-8368-1409-6) Gareth Stevens Inc.
Vampire Joke Book. Count Trans L. Vania. 100p. 1995. mass mkt. 4.99 (0-7860-0191-7, Pinncle Kensgtn) Kensgtn Pub Corp.
Vampire Junction. S. P. Somtow. Ed. by Kay Reynolds. (Illus.). 280p. 35.00 (0-89865-368-1, Starblaze) Donning Co.
Vampire Junction. S. P. Somtow. 384p. 1995. 5.99 (0-8125-2596-5) Tor Bks.
Vampire Junkies. Norman Spinrad. 80p. 1994. pap. 9.95 (0-936071-37-0) Gryphon Pubns.
Vampire Kingdoms. Kevin Siembieda. Ed. by Alex Marciniszyn & Thomas Bartold. (Rifts World Bks.: No. 1). (Illus.). 176p. (Orig.). (YA). (gr. 8 up). 1991. pap. 15.95 (0-916211-52-5, 802) Palladium Bks.
***Vampire Kittens of Count Dracula.** Stanley. LC 97-10448. (Scaredy Cats Ser.: No. 8). (J). (gr. 2-4). 1997. mass mkt. 3.99 (0-689-81615-4) S&S Childrens.
Vampire Legacy: Blood Secrets. Karen E. Taylor. 304p. 1994. mass mkt. 4.50 (0-8217-4437-2, Zebra Kensgtn) Kensgtn Pub Corp.
***Vampire Lestat.** Anne Rice. 1997. pap. 14.00 (0-345-41964-2) Ballantine.
Vampire Lestat. Anne O. Rice. LC 85-40123. (Chronicles of the Vampires Ser.: Bk. 2). 512p. 1985. 25.00 (0-394-53443-3) Knopf.
Vampire Lestat. Anne O. Rice. 560p. 1986. mass mkt. 6.99 (0-345-31386-0) Ballantine.
Vampire Lestat. Anne O. Rice. (Vampire Chronicles Ser.). 384p. 1991. 39.95 (1-56521-002-6) Innovative.
Vampire Lover: (Presents Plus) Charlotte Lamb. (Presents Ser.). 1995. pap. 3.25 (0-373-11720-5, 1-11720-9) Harlequin Bks.
Vampire Mom. Don Whittington. 160p. (Orig.). (J). (gr. 5-6). 1995. pap. 3.50 (0-380-77936-6, Camelot) Avon.
Vampire Moves In. Angela Sommer-Bodenburg. (Illus.). (J). (gr. 2-6). 1990. pap. 2.99 (0-671-73698-1, Minstrel Bks) PB.
Vampire Nights. Tim Moriarty. 1989. mass mkt. 3.95 (1-55817-180-0, Pinncle Kensgtn) Kensgtn Pub Corp.
Vampire Odyssey. Scott Ciencin. 416p. 1992. mass mkt. 4.50 (0-8217-3853-4, Zebra Kensgtn) Kensgtn Pub Corp.
Vampire of Reason: An Essay in the Philosophy of History. Richard J. Blackburn. 272p. (C). 1990. pap. text ed. 19.00 (0-86091-972-2, A4511, Pub. by Vrso UK) Norton.
Vampire Players Guide. 2nd ed. Illus. by Clyde Caldwell. (Vampire: the Masquerade Ser.). 1994. 22.00 (1-56504-053-8, 2206) White Wolf.
Vampire Princess. Michael Romkey. 1996. mass mkt. 5.99 (0-449-14937-4) Fawcett.
Vampire Squadron: The Saga of the 44th Fighter Squadron. William H. Starke. LC 85-61542. (Illus.). xiv, 208p. 1985. 39.50 (0-918837-02-2) Robinson Typos.
***Vampire State.** Fred Block. Date not set. pap. 16.95 (1-56584-194-8) New Press NY.
Vampire State: And Other Myths & Fallacies about the U. S. Economy. Fred Block. 320p. Date not set. 20.00 (1-56584-193-X) New Press NY.
Vampire State in Africa: The Political Economy of Decline in Ghana. Jonathan H. Frimpong-Ansah. 210p. 1992. 49.95 (0-86543-278-3); pap. 16.95 (0-86543-279-1) Africa World.
Vampire Stories. Ed. by Richard Dalby. 1993. 7.98 (1-55521-900-4) Bk Sales Inc.
Vampire Strike - Pipeline Strike, 2 vols. in 1. David Robbins. (Blade Double Edition Ser.). 384p. 1992. mass mkt., pap. text ed. 4.50 (0-8439-3310-0) Dorchester Pub Co.
Vampire Tapestry. Suzy M. Charnas. 300p. 1993. pap. 13.95 (0-945953-05-4) Living Batch Bks.
Vampire Twins: Bloodliness, No. 1. Janice Harrell. 240p. 1994. mass mkt. 3.99 (0-06-106247-2) HarpC.
Vampire Twins #02: Bloodlust. Janice Harrell. (v). 240p. (YA). 1994. mass mkt. 3.99 (0-06-106246-4, Harp PBks) HarpC.
Vampire Vacation. Thomas McKean. LC 85-48073. 1986. pap. 2.50 (0-380-89808-X, Camelot) Avon.
***Vampire Virus.** Michael Romkey. 1998. mass mkt. 5.99 (0-449-00203-9, Crest) Fawcett.
***Vampire Virus.** Michael Romkey. 1998. mass mkt. write for info. (0-345-42172-8) Ballantine.
Vampire Viscount. Karen Harbaugh. (Regency Romance Ser.). 224p. 1995. pap. 3.99 (0-451-18319-3, Sig) NAL-Dutton.
Vampire Who Came for Christmas. Dian C. Regan. 112p. (J). (gr. 4-6). 1994. pap. 2.95 (0-590-47862-1) Scholastic Inc.
***Vampires.** 1991. 12.00 (0-923763-27-9) Mayfair Games.
***Vampires.** Ariel Books Staff. 1996. 4.95 (0-8362-1525-7) Andrews & McMeel.
***Vampires.** Greenberg. (The Greatest Stories Ser.). 1997. 8.98 (1-56731-167-9) Fine Comms.
Vampires. Martin H. Greenberg. Ed. by Jane Yolen. LC 90-27888. (Trophy Chiller Bk.). 240p. (YA). (gr. 5 up). 1993. pap. 4.50 (0-06-440485-4, Trophy) HarpC Child Bks.
Vampires. Colin Hawkins. (Scary Pop-Up Bks.). (Illus.). 10p. (J). (ps-3). 1994. 3.99 (0-89577-587-5) RD Assn.
Vampires. Vincent Hillyer. LC 88-42434. 128p. (Orig.). 1988. pap. 15.95 (0-944707-03-3) Loose Change.
***Vampires.** Martin Jenkins. (Infomania Ser.). (Illus.). 90p. (J). 1997. 14.99 (0-7636-0315-5) Candlewick Pr.

UV

Vampires. Harry Kondoleon. 1984. pap. 5.25 (0-8222-1201-3) Dramatists Play.

Vampires. John Steakley. 368p. (Orig.). 1992. pap. 5.99 (0-451-45153-8, ROC) NAL-Dutton.

Vampires. Ed. by Jane Yolen & Martin H. Greenberg. LC 90-27888. 240p. (J). (gr. 5 up). 1991. lib. bdg. 14.89 (0-06-026801-8) HarpC Child Bks.

Vampires: An Uneasy Essay on the Undead in Film. Jalal Toufic. LC 93-23052. 1993. 12.95 (0-88268-146-X) Station Hill Pr.

***Vampires: Blood Suckers fom Beyond the Grave.** Rowan Wilson. (Strange but True Ser.). 1997. pap. text ed. 5.95 (0-8069-0575-1) Sterling.

***Vampires: Emotional Predators Who Want to Suck the Life Out of You.** Daniel Rhodes. 1998. 23.95 (1-57392-191-2) Prometheus Bks.

Vampires: Opposing Viewpoints. Daniel C. Scavone. LC 90-40131. (Great Mysteries Ser.). (Illus.). 80p. (J). (gr. 5-8). 1990. lib. bdg. 17.96 (0-89908-080-4) Greenhaven.

Vampires: Restless Creatures of the Night. Jean Marigny. (Discoveries Ser.). (Illus.). 1994. pap. 12.95 (0-8109-2869-8) Abrams.

Vampires: The Occult Truth. Konstantinos. LC 96-12238. 256p. 1996. pap. 12.95 (1-56718-380-8) Llewellyn Pubns.

Vampires among Us. Rosemary E. Guiley. Ed. by Claire Zion. 288p. (Orig.). 1991. mass mkt. 5.50 (0-671-72361-8) PB.

Vampires & Other Creatures of the Night. (J). (gr. 4-7). 1992. pap. 2.95 (0-590-44302-X) Scholastic Inc.

Vampires & Vampirism. Dudley Wright. 1973. 250.00 (0-87968-093-8) Gordon Pr.

Vampires & Violets: Lesbians in Film. Andrea Weiss. LC 93-8634. (Illus.). 160p. 1993. pap. 12.50 (0-14-023100-5, Penguin Bks) Viking Penguin.

Vampires Anonymous. Jeffrey N. McMahan. 252p. (Orig.). 1991. pap. 8.95 (1-55583-183-4) Alyson Pubns.

Vampires Apprentice. Richard L. Byers. 1992. mass mkt. 3.99 (0-8217-3632-9, Zebra Kensgtn) Kensgtn Pub Corp.

Vampires Are. Stephen Kaplan. LC 83-6515. 200p. 1984. 15.95 (0-88280-102-3) ETC Pubns.

Vampires, Burial & Death: Folklore & Reality. Paul Barber. LC 88-143. 1988. 37.50 (0-300-04126-8) Yale U Pr.

Vampires, Burial & Death: Folklore & Reality. Paul Barber. 244p. (C). 1990. reprint ed. pap. 13.00 (0-300-04859-9) Yale U Pr.

Vampires Don't Wear Polka Dots. Debbie Dadey & Marcia Jones. 80p. (Orig.). (J). (gr. 2-5). 1990. pap. 3.50 (0-590-43411-X) Scholastic Inc.

***Vampires Don't Wear Polka Dots.** Marcia Jones & Debbie Dadey. (FRE.). (J). pap. 5.99 (0-590-73545-4) Scholastic Inc.

Vampire's Honeymoon. Cornell Woolrich. 220p. 1985. pap. 3.50 (0-88184-132-3) Carroll & Graf.

Vampire's Kiss. Jesse Harris. LC 92-9019. (Orig.). (YA). 1992. 9.99 (0-679-93669-6) Knopf.

Vampire's Kiss. William Hill. 480p. 1994. mass mkt. 4.50 (1-55817-886-4, Pinncle Kensgtn) Kensgtn Pub Corp.

Vampire's Kiss. Diane Hoh. (Nightmare Hall Ser.: No. 22). 176p. (J). (gr. 7-9). 1995. mass mkt. 3.50 (0-590-25089-2) Scholastic Inc.

Vampires, Mummies, & Liberals: Bram Stoker & the Politics of Popular Fiction. David Glover. LC 95-53796. 240p. (C). 1996. text ed. 49.95 (0-8223-1803-2); pap. text ed. 16.95 (0-8223-1798-2) Duke.

Vampires of the Andes. Douglas A. Menville. LC 77-84206. (Lost Race & Adult Fantasy Ser.). 1978. reprint ed. lib. bdg. 29.95 (0-405-10962-8) Ayer.

Vampires or Gods? William Meyers. 192p. (Orig.). 1993. pap. 15.00 (0-9622937-5-X) III Pub.

Vampires Promise. Caroline B. Cooney. 176p. (J). (gr. 7-9). 1993. pap. 3.50 (0-590-45682-2) Scholastic Inc.

Vampires Unstaked: National Images, Stereotypes & Myths in East Central Europe. Ed. by A. Gerrits & N. Adler. 248p. 1995. 50.00 (0-444-85793-1) Elsevier.

Vampires Went Thataway! Nancy Lamb & Muff Singer. LC 95-14844. (Canal Street Kids Bks.). (Illus.). 80p. (J). (gr. 2-5). 1995. pap. 2.95 (0-8167-3718-5, Little Rainbow) Troll Communs.

Vampires Went Thataway! Nancy Lamb & Muff Singer. LC 95-14844. (Illus.). 80p. (J). (gr. 2-5). 1995. lib. bdg. 10.50 (0-8167-3950-1, Little Rainbow) Troll Communs.

Vampires, Werewolves, & Zombies. Stuart A. Kallen. LC 91-73062. (Ghastly Ghost Stories Ser.). (J). 1991. lib. bdg. 13.98 (1-56239-039-2) Abdo & Dghtrs.

***Vampires, Wine & Roses.** Ed. by John R. Stephens. 384p. (Orig.). 1997. pap. 14.00 (0-425-15741-5, Berkley Trade) Berkley Pub.

Vampiric Jihad. Rickey Shanklin et al. (Illus.). 48p. (Orig.). 1991. pap. 4.95 (0-927203-04-9) Apple Pr PA.

Vampiric Verses. Damien R. Cerberus. LC 94-67174. (Illus.). 120p. (Orig.). 1994. pap. 10.95 (0-9642180-0-3) Sunset Pubng.

Vampirism in Literature: Shadow of a Shade. Margaret L. Carter. 1974. lib. bdg. 250.00 (0-87968-225-6) Gordon Pr.

Vampiro: The Vampire Bat in Fact & Fantasy. David E. Brown. LC 94-75838. (Illus.). 148p. (Orig.). 1994. pap. 10.95 (0-944383-22-X) High-Lonesome.

Vamps. Elaine Lee. Ed. by Bob Kahan. (Illus.). 160p. 1995. pap. 9.95 (1-56389-220-0) DC Comics.

***Vamps: An Illustrated History of the Femme Fatale.** Pam Keesey. 1997. pap. 21.95 (1-57344-026-4) Cleis Pr.

Vamps & Tramps: New Essays. Camille Paglia. 1994. pap. 15.00 (0-679-75120-3, Vin) Random.

Vamps, Virgins & Victims: How Can Women Fight AIDS? Robin Gorna. (Women on Women Ser.). 288p. 1994. pap. 18.95 (0-304-32809-X) LPC InBook.

Vamps, Virgins & Victims: How Can Women Fight AIDS? Robin Gorna. (Women on Women Ser.). 288p. 1994. 55.00 (0-304-32807-3, Pub. by Cassell Pubng UK) LPC InBook.

Vampyre. Tim Kelly. 1988. pap. 5.25 (0-8222-1204-8) Dramatists Play.

Vampyre. John W. Polidori. LC 90-40020. 92p. 1990. reprint ed. 40.00 (1-85477-053-5, Pub. by Woodstock Bks UK) Cassell.

Vampyre see Castle of Otranto (Three Gothic Novels)

Vampyre & Ernestus Berchtold, or the Modern Oedipus. John W. Polidori. Ed. by D. L. Macdonald & Kathleen Scherf. (Illus.). 240p. 1993. 45.00 (0-8020-0506-3); pap. 17.95 (0-8020-7465-0) U of Toronto Pr.

***Vampyre & Other Tales of the Macabre.** Ed. by Chris Baldick & Robert Morrison. (The World's Classics Ser.). 272p. 1997. pap. 9.95 (0-19-283291-3) OUP.

Vampyre by Dr. Polidori. John W. Polidori. Ed. by Donald K. Adams. 1968. 12.50 (0-910330-14-X) Grant Dahlstrom.

Vampyres: Lord Byron to Count Dracula. Ed. by Christopher Frayling. (Illus.). 432p. (Orig.). 1992. pap. 14.95 (0-571-16792-6) Faber & Faber.

Vampyres: 13 Tales of Classic Horror. Ed. by Tom Mason & Mickie Villa. 109p. 1991. pap. 9.95 (0-944735-16-9) Malibu Comics Ent.

Vampyre's Kiss, Vol. 1: The Birth of the Vampyre. Barry Blair. (Illus.). 100p. 1991. pap. 14.95 (0-944735-79-7) Malibu Comics Ent.

Van. Roddy Doyle. 320p. 1993. pap. 11.95 (0-14-017191-6, Penguin Bks) Viking Penguin.

Van. Roddy Doyle. 1997. pap. 11.95 (0-14-026002-1) Viking Penguin.

Van Aaken Method. Ernst Van Aaken. 1983. 4.95 (0-02-499850-8, Macmillan Coll) P-H.

Van Aaken Method. Ernst Van Aaken. 1983. pap. 5.95 (0-02-499860-5, Macmillan Coll) P-H.

Van Arteveldes of Ghent: The Varieties of Vendetta & the Hero in History. David Nicholas. LC 88-3858. (Illus.). 232p. 1988. 35.00 (0-8014-2149-7) Cornell U Pr.

Van Benthuysen Genealogy: Descendants of Paulus Martense Van Benthuysen, Who Settled in Albany, NY, Male & Female Lines; Also Genealogy of Certain Branches of Other Families of Dutch & Huguenot Origin in NY. A. S. Van Benthuysen & E. M. Hall. (Illus.). 592p. 1991. reprint ed. pap. 89.50 (0-8328-1770-8); reprint ed. lib. bdg. 99.50 (0-8328-1769-4) Higginson Bk Co.

Van Bibber & Others, Vol. 1. Richard H. Davis. LC 72-5865. (Short Story Index Reprint Ser.). 1977. reprint ed. 23.95 (0-8369-4208-6) Ayer.

Van Buren: History of Cornelis Maessen Van Buren. H. C. Peckham. (Illus.). 431p. 1990. reprint ed. pap. 64.50 (0-8328-1629-9); reprint ed. lib. bdg. 72.50 (0-8328-1628-0) Higginson Bk Co.

Van Buren County Genealogies, Vol. Two: The Greenman Family of Prospect Lake, Michigan. Compiled by Shirley S. Howe. (Illus.). 100p. (Orig.). 1990. pap. text ed. 15.00 (0-9616538-4-1) Heritage Val Pub.

Van Buren County, Michigan 1880 Federal Census Index. Ann Burton. (Illus.). 190p. 1995. pap. 20.00 (0-937505-14-5) Glyndwr Resc.

Van Buren County Plat Book, Michigan: Completely Indexed - Circa 1933. rev. ed. Intro. by Toni J. Benson. (C). 1988. pap. 10.00 (0-9620998-0-5) F-Ami-Lee.

Van Buren County Poorhouse/Infirmary Records, 2 vols., Set. Toni I. Benson. 500p. 1995. pap. 25.00 (0-9620998-4-8) F-Ami-Lee.

Van Cliburn: A Biography. Howard Reich. LC 92-41082. (Illus.). 448p. 1993. 24.99 (0-8407-7681-0) Nelson.

Van Culemborg: Allied Ancestry of the Van Culemborg of Culemborg, Holland, Being the Ancestry of Sophia Van Culemborg, Wife of Johan de Carpentier, Parents of Maria de Carpentier, Wife of Jean Paul Jaquet. E. J. Sellers. 161p. 1992. reprint ed. pap. 25.00 (0-8328-2749-5); reprint ed. lib. bdg. 35.00 (0-8328-2748-7) Higginson Bk Co.

Van Dale Concise Dutch - English Dictionary. Van Dale. (DUT & ENG.). 1991. 49.95 (0-8288-8522-2) Fr & Eur.

Van Dale Concise Dutch - French Dictionary. Van Dale. (DUT & FRE.). 1991. 49.95 (0-8288-8518-4) Fr & Eur.

Van Dale Concise Dutch - German Dictionary. Van Dale. (DUT & GER.). 1991. 49.95 (0-8288-8520-6) Fr & Eur.

Van Dale Concise Dutch - Spanish Dictionary. Van Dale. (DUT & SPA.). 1991. 49.95 (0-8288-8525-7) Fr & Eur.

Van Dale Concise English - Dutch Dictionary. Van Dale. (DUT & ENG.). 1991. 49.95 (0-8288-8524-9) Fr & Eur.

Van Dale Concise French - Dutch Dictionary. Van Dale. (DUT & FRE.). 1991. 49.95 (0-8288-8519-2) Fr & Eur.

Van Dale Concise German-Dutch Dictionary. Van Dale. (DUT & GER.). 1991. 49.95 (0-8288-8521-4) Fr & Eur.

Van Dale Concise Spanish - Dutch Dictionary. Van Dale. (DUT & SPA.). 1991. 49.95 (0-8288-8526-5) Fr & Eur.

Van Dale Dictionary of the Dutch Language. Van Dale. 1570p. (DUT.). 1984. 150.00 (0-8288-8511-7) Fr & Eur.

Van Dale Dutch - English Dictionary. Van Dale. (DUT & ENG.). 1991. 150.00 (0-8288-8517-6, F93960) Fr & Eur.

Van Dale Dutch - French Dictionary. Van Dale. (DUT & FRE.). 1991. 150.00 (0-8288-8513-3) Fr & Eur.

Van Dale Dutch - German Dictionary. Van Dale. (DUT & GER.). 1991. 150.00 (0-8288-8516-8) Fr & Eur.

Van Dale Etymological Dictionary of the Dutch Language. Van Dale. (DUT.). 1991. 150.00 (0-8288-8523-0) Fr & Eur.

Van Dale French - Dutch Dictionary. Van Dale. (DUT & FRE.). 1991. 150.00 (0-8288-8514-1) Fr & Eur.

Van Dale' Groot Woordenboek der Nederlandse Taal, 3 vols. Van Dale. (C). 1984. text ed. 990.00 (0-685-39402-6, Pub. by S Thornes Pubs UK) St Mut.

Van Dale'Woordenboek Dutch - Englis. Van Dale. (C). 1986. text ed. 600.00 (90-6648-107-2, Pub. by S Thornes Pubs UK) St Mut.

Van Dale'Woordenboek English - Dutch. Van Dale. (C). 1984. text ed. 600.00 (0-685-39401-8, Pub. by S Thornes Pubs UK) St Mut.

***Van Day Truex: A Biography.** Lewin. 1998. 40.00 (0-8050-5468-5) H Holt & Co.

Van De Graaff Book. B. K. Hixson. 8p. 1992. pap. text ed. 2.99 (1-57156-010-6) Wild Goose UT.

Van de Velde Drawings: A Catalogue of Drawings in the National Maritime Museum Made by the Elder & the Younger William Van de Velde, Vol. 2: The Ingram Volume. National Maritime Museum Staff. LC 58-14763. 372p. reprint ed. pap. 106.10 (0-317-27097-4, 2024551) Bks Demand.

Van Dean Lesson Plans. rev. ed. Milady Publishing Company Staff. (Cosmetology Ser.). 1991. pap. 51.95 (0-87350-520-4) Van Nos Reinhold.

Van Dean Manual. Milady Inc. Staff. (Cosmetology Ser.). 1987. text ed. 36.95 (0-87350-368-6) Milady Pub.

Van Dean Manual. rev. ed. Milady Editors. (Illus.). 1990. text ed. 36.95 (0-87350-516-6) Milady Pub.

Van Dean Practical: Answer Key. Milady Inc. Staff. (Cosmetology Ser.). 1975. wbk. ed. 26.95 (0-87350-064-4) Van Nos Reinhold.

Van Dean Practical Workbook. Milady Editors. (Illus.). 1990. teacher ed. 30.95 (0-87350-524-7); pap. 22.95 (0-87350-518-2) Milady Pub.

Van Dean Review Questions & Answers. Milady Inc. Staff. (Cosmetology Ser.). 1990. pap. 2.50 (0-87350-296-5) Van Nos Reinhold.

Van Dean Theory. Milady Inc. Staff. (Cosmetology Ser.). 1975. wbk. ed. 15.50 (0-87350-358-9) Van Nos Reinhold.

Van Dean Theory: Answer Key. Milady Inc. Staff. (Cosmetology Ser.). 1975. wbk. ed. 34.84 (0-87350-065-2) Van Nos Reinhold.

Van Dean Theory Workbook. Milady Editors. (Illus.). 1990. teacher ed. 26.95 (0-87350-523-9); pap. 22.95 (0-87350-519-0) Milady Pub.

Van der Corput's Method for Exponential Sums. S. W. Graham & Grigori Kolesnik. (London Mathematical Society Lecture Note Ser.: No. 126). 200p. 1991. pap. 28.95 (0-521-33927-8) Cambridge U Pr.

Van der Slice & Allied Families. H. Vanderslice & H. N. Monnett. 303p. 1992. reprint ed. pap. 46.00 (0-8328-2601-4); reprint ed. lib. bdg. 56.00 (0-8328-2600-6) Higginson Bk Co.

Van der Waals & Molecular Science. A. Ya Kipnis et al. (Illus.). 330p. 1996. 105.00 (0-19-855210-6) OUP.

Van der Waals & Molecular Sciences. A. Ya. Kipnis et al. LC 95-48336. (C). 1996. write for info. (0-614-95856-3, Clarendon Pr) OUP.

Van der Waals Forces & Schielding Effects. Ed. by P. Diehl et al. LC 75-15821. (NMR-Basic Principles & Progress Ser.: Vol. 10). (Illus.). 140p. 1976. 47.95 (0-387-07340-X) Spr-Verlag.

Van Deusen, Van Deursen Family, 2 vols. in 1. A. H. Van Deusen. (Illus.). 915p. 1989. reprint ed. pap. 140.25 (0-8328-1199-8); reprint ed. lib. bdg. 148.25 (0-8328-1198-X) Higginson Bk Co.

***Van Dongen Nobody Knows: Early & Fauvist Drawings 1895-1912.** Anita Hopmans. (Illus.). 328p. 1997. pap. 50.00 (90-6918-170-3, Pub. by Mus Boymans-van Beuningen NE) U of Wash Pr.

Van Doorn Family, Van Dorn, Van Doren, etc. in Holland & America, 1088-1908. A. Van Doren Honeyman. (Illus.). 765p. 1991. reprint ed. pap. 109.00 (0-8328-1836-4); reprint ed. lib. bdg. 119.00 (0-8328-1835-6) Higginson Bk Co.

Van Dorn: The Life & Times of a Confederate General. Robert G. Hartje. LC 67-16280. 374p. (C). 1994. reprint ed. pap. 16.95 (0-8265-1254-2) Vanderbilt U Pr.

Van Dyck Drawings. Christopher Brown. 1991. 95.00 (0-8109-3914-2) Abrams.

Van Dyck's Prints (L'Iconographie d'Antoine van Dyck), Catalogue Raisonne, 2 vols. 2nd ed. Marie Mauquoy-Hendrickx. (Illus.). 450p. (FRE.). 1991. pap. 120.00 (1-55660-226-X) A Wofsy Fine Arts.

Van Every - Records of the Van Every Family, United Empire Loyalists, N. Y. State, 1653-1784, Canada, 1784-1947. Mary B. Piersol. 131p. 1995. reprint ed. pap. 24.50 (0-8328-4566-3); reprint ed. lib. bdg. 34.50 (0-8328-4565-5) Higginson Bk Co.

Van Evrie's White Supremacy & Negro Subordination: The New Proslavery Argument. Ed. by John D. Smith. LC 92-27188. (Anti-Black Thought, 1863-1925 Ser.: Vol. 3). 456p. 1993. text ed. 73.00 (0-8153-0975-9) Garland.

Van Eyck & the Founders of Early Netherlandish Painting. Otto Pacht. Ed. by Maria Schmidt-Dengler. Tr. by David Britt from GER. (Illus.). 224p. 1995. text ed. 65.00 (1-872501-81-8, Pub. by Harvey Miller UK) Gordon & Breach.

Van Eyck Problem. Maurice W. Brockwell. LC 78-138101. (Illus.). 102p. 1971. reprint ed. text ed. 35.00 (0-8371-5677-7, BRVE, Greenwood Pr) Greenwood.

Van Eyck to Bruegel, 1400-1550: Dutch & Flemish Painting in the Collection of the Museum. Friso Lammertse. (Illus.). 298p. 1995. pap. 40.00 (90-6918-137-1) U of Wash Pr.

Van Eycks & Their Followers. William M. Conway. LC 75-41065. (BCL Ser.: Ii). reprint ed. 47.50 (0-404-14657-0) AMS Pr.

Van Gogh. (Masterworks Ser.). (Illus.). 144p. 1990. 15.99 (0-517-67957-4) Random Hse Value.

Van Gogh. Catherine Barry. (Pocket Painters Ser.). (Illus.). 1994. 6.50 (0-517-59968-6, Clarkson Potter) Crown Bks Yng Read.

***Van Gogh.** Catherine Barry. Date not set. 1.99 (0-517-17607-6) Random Hse Value.

Van Gogh. Bruce Bernard. LC 92-7061. (Eyewitness Art Ser.). (Illus.). 64p. 1992. 16.95 (1-56458-069-5) DK Pub Inc.

Van Gogh. Pascal Bonafoux. (Illus.). 160p. 1990. 29.95 (0-8050-1384-9) H Holt & Co.

Van Gogh. Mila Boutan. (Young Artist's Way Ser.). (Illus.). 14p. (J). (ps-5). 1996. pap. 9.95 (0-8118-1312-6) Chronicle Bks.

Van Gogh. Hans Bronkhorst. 1990. 19.99 (0-517-03560-X) Random Hse Value.

Van Gogh. Enrica Crispino. (Masters of Art Ser.). (Illus.). 64p. (YA). (gr. 6 up). 1996. lib. bdg. 22.50 (0-87226-525-0) P Bedrick Bks.

***Van Gogh.** Michel Ferloni. (Masterworks Ser.). (Illus.). 384p. 1996. 19.98 (1-56852-111-1, Konecky & Konecky) W S Konecky Assocs.

Van Gogh. A. M. Hammacher & Renilde Hammacher. LC 90-70217. (Illus.). 240p. 1990. pap. 24.95 (0-500-27603-X) Thames Hudson.

***Van Gogh.** Nathaniel Harris. (Masterworks Ser.). 1996. 17.98 (0-7651-9694-8) Smithmark.

Van Gogh. Andrew S. Hughes. (Famous Artists Ser.). (Illus.). 32p. (YA). (gr. 5 up). 1994. 10.95 (0-8120-6462-3); pap. 6.95 (0-8120-1999-7) Barron.

***Van Gogh.** Rene Huyghe. Date not set. pap. 4.99 (0-517-17644-0) Random Hse Value.

Van Gogh. Rene Huyghe. (Illus.). 1995. pap. 4.20 (0-517-88412-7) Random.

Van Gogh. Eleanor Marrack. 1992. 5.98 (1-55521-763-X) Bk Sales Inc.

Van Gogh. Melissa McQuillan. (Illus.). 1989. pap. 14.95 (0-500-20232-X) Thames Hudson.

Van Gogh. Rainer Metzger. 1996. pap. text ed. 19.99 (3-8228-8905-9) Taschen Amer.

Van Gogh. Random House Value Publishing Staff. 1996. 9.99 (0-517-18230-0) Random Hse Value.

Van Gogh. Meyer Shapiro. (Masters of Art Ser.). 1983. 22.95 (0-8109-1733-5) Abrams.

Van Gogh. Mike Venezia. LC 88-11842. (Getting to Know the World's Greatest Artists Ser.). (Illus.). 32p. (J). (ps-4). 1988. pap. 6.95 (0-516-42274-X); lib. bdg. 19.50 (0-516-02274-1) Childrens.

***Van Gogh.** I. F. Walthe. 1994. pap. 8.99 (3-8228-9630-6) Taschen Amer.

***Van Gogh.** Ingo F. Walther. 1997. pap. text ed. 7.98 (1-57145-098-X) Advan Mktg Servs.

Van Gogh. Wilhelm Uhde. (Color Library). (Illus.). 128p. (C). 1994. reprint ed. pap. 14.95 (0-7148-2724-X, Pub. by Phaidon Press UK) Chronicle Bks.

Van Gogh: A Postcard Book. (Postcard Book Ser.). (Illus.). 64p. (Orig.). 1988. pap. 7.95 (0-89471-648-4) Running Pr.

Van Gogh: A Retrospective. Susan A. Stein. (Great Masters of Art Ser.). (Illus.). 386p. 1991. 34.99 (0-517-66122-5) Random Hse Value.

Van Gogh: A Self-Portrait. Ed. by W. H. Auden. (Illus.). 302p. 1994. pap. 12.00 (1-56924-862-1) Marlowe & Co.

Van Gogh: An Appreciation of His Art. Gerhard Gruitrooy. 1994. 14.98 (0-8317-5781-7) Smithmark.

***Van Gogh: Art & Emotions.** David Spence. 1997. pap. 5.95 (0-7641-0292-3) Barron.

***Van Gogh: Letters.** Vincent Van Gogh. 1998. pap. 14.95 (0-14-044674-5) Viking Penguin.

Van Gogh: Letters from Provence. Martin Bailey. (Illus.). 1990. 27.50 (0-517-58144-2, C P Pubs) Crown Pub Group.

Van Gogh: Portraits. P. Huisman. (Rhythem & Color One Ser.). 1970. 9.95 (0-8288-9505-8) Fr & Eur.

Van Gogh: The Complete Paintings. Ingo F. Walther. 1994. 24.99 (3-8228-9643-8) Taschen Amer.

Van Gogh: The Passionate Eye. Pascal Bonafoux. (Discoveries Ser.). (Illus.). 176p. 1992. pap. 12.95 (0-8109-2828-0) Abrams.

Van Gogh: Vertigo of Light. Jacqueline Guillaud & Maurice Guillaud. (Illus.). 72p. 1991. 85.00 (0-517-58306-2, C P Pubs) Crown Pub Group.

Van Gogh & God: A Creative Spiritual Quest. Cliff Edwards. LC 89-12744. 220p. (C). 1989. 12.95 (0-8294-0621-2) Loyola Pr.

Van Gogh Cafe. Cynthia Rylant. LC 94-43348. (Illus.). 64p. (J). (gr. 3-7). 1995. 14.00 (0-15-200843-8) HarBrace.

Van Gogh Drawings. Evert Van Uitert. LC 78-4361. (Illus.). 228p. 1979. 22.50 (0-87951-085-4) Overlook Pr.

Van Gogh Drawings. Evert Van Uitert. LC 78-4361. (Illus.). 228p. 1980. pap. 12.95 (0-87951-086-2) Overlook Pr.

Van Gogh Drawings: Forty Three Plates. Vincent Van Gogh. (Art Library). (Illus.). 48p. (Orig.). 1987. pap. 3.95 (0-486-25485-2) Dover.

Van Gogh for Kids. Contrib. by Margaret E. Hyde. LC 95-80609. (Great Art for Kids Ser.). 12p. (J). (ps). 1996. 12.95 (1-888108-04-5) Budding Artists.

Van Gogh in Arles. Alfred Nemeczek et al. (Pegasus Library). (Illus.). 128p. 1995. 25.00 (3-7913-1484-X, Pub. by Prestel GW) te Neues.

Van Gogh in England: Portrait of the Artist As a Young Man. Martin Bailey. (Illus.). 144p. (C). 1992. pap. 39.95 (0-85331-617-1, Pub. by Lund Humphries UK) Antique Collect.

***Van Gogh Notes.** Ed. by Helen Exley. (Artist Notebooks). (Illus.). 80p. 1996. 8.00 (1-85015-780-4) Exley Giftbooks.

***Van Gogh One & Two.** I. F. Walther. 1994. 79.90 (3-8228-0291-3) Taschen Amer.

Van Gogh One Hundred. Ed. by Joseph D. Masheck. LC 94-29206. (Contributions to the Study of Art & Architecture Ser.: No. 4). 416p. 1996. text ed. 75.00 (0-313-29491-7, Greenwood Pr) Greenwood.

Van Gogh: The Touch of Yellow see Art for Children

Van Gogh to Picasso: The Berggruen Collection at the National Gallery. Richard Kendall et al. (Illus.). 210p. 1991. text ed. 55.00 (0-947645-83-7) U of Wash Pr.

Van Gogh, Vincent, Complete Paintings & Drawings, Vol. 1. Sjaar Van Heugten. 272p. 1996. 100.00 (*0-614-16748-5*, Pub. by Lund Humphries UK) Antique Collect.
*__Van Gogh's Bad Cafe: A Love Story.__ Frederic Tuten. LC 96-29649. 1997. 20.00 (*0-688-15134-5*) Morrow.
Van Gogh's Complete Works on Paper, 2 vols. rev. ed. J. B. De La Faille. (Illus.). (ENG & FRE.). 1992. Set: Vol. 1, 544p. Vol. 2, 312p. 295.00 (*1-55660-126-3*) A Wofsy Fine Arts.
*__Van Gogh's Flowers & Landscapes: Celebrated Subjects of the Great Artists.__ Janice Anderson. (Rhemes & Reflections Ser.). 1997. 7.98 (*0-7651-9764-2*) Smithmark.
Van Gogh's Progress: Utopia, Modernity, & Late-Nineteenth-Century Art. Carol M. Zemel. LC 96-4850. (California Studies in the History of Art: Vol. 36). (Illus.). 1997. 45.00 (*0-520-08849-2*) U CA Pr.
Van Gogh's Room at Arles. Stanley Elkin. 320p. 1994. pap. 10.95 (*0-14-023659-7*, Penguin Bks) Viking Penguin.
Van Gogh's Room at Arles: Three Novellas. Stanley Elkin. 256p. 1993. 22.95 (*1-56282-937-8*) Hyperion.
Van Halen. 1985. 7.95 (*0-946391-51-3*) Cherry Lane.
*__Van Halen.__ J. D. Considine. Date not set. write for info. (*0-688-04300-3*) Morrow.
Van Halen. Peter Goddard. (Illus.). 128p. 1984. pap. 9.95 (*0-8253-0242-0*) Beaufort Bks NY.
Van Halen. Ed. by Aaron Stang. (Guitar Anthology Ser.). 240p. (Orig.). 1995. pap. text ed. 24.95 (*0-89724-672-1*, PG9531) Warner Brothers.
Van Halen, Vols. I & II. Ed. by Colgan Bryan. 158p. (Orig.). 1996. pap. 21.95 (*1-57623-430-4*, PG9629) Warner Brothers.
*__Van Halen: 5150 & OU812.__ Ed. by Colgan Bryan. 188p. (Orig.). (YA). 1996. pap. text ed. 24.95 (*1-57623-706-0*, PG9668) Warner Brothers.
*__Van Halen - Diver down & 1984.__ Ed. by Michael Lefferts & Colgan Bryan. (Illus.). 160p. (Orig.). (C). 1997. pap. text ed. 24.95 (*0-7692-0026-5*, 0062B) Warner Brothers.
Van Halen - Fair Warning. 1994. pap. 19.95 (*0-89524-743-7*) Cherry Lane.
Van Halen - Women & Children First. 1994. pap. 12.95 (*0-685-75231-3*); pap. 19.95 (*0-89524-800-X*) Cherry Lane.
Van Halen - 1984. Ed. by Joe Vasko. 1995. pap. text ed. 19.95 (*0-89524-642-2*) Warner Bros.
Van Halen - 25 Great Solos. 63p. (Orig.). (YA). 1994. pap. 14.95 (*0-89524-856-5*, 02506315) Cherry Lane.
Van Halen - 5150. Ed. by Milton Okun. Play-It-Like-It-Is Bass. pap. 14.95 (*0-89524-460-8*) Cherry Lane.
*__Van Halen Live: Right Here, Right Now.__ Ed. by Joe Vasko. 240p. 1995. pap. text ed. 29.95 (*0-7692-1358-8*) Warner Bros.
Van Halen Live - Right Here, Right Now. Ed. by Mark Phillips. 1994. pap. 29.95 (*0-89524-787-9*) Cherry Lane.
*__Van Halen/Van Halen II.__ Ed. by Joe Vasko. 72p. 1995. pap. text ed. 19.95 (*0-7692-1357-X*) Warner Bros.
Van Hecke & Allied Ancestry: Ancestry of Josina Van Heck, Wife of Roeland de Carpentier, Grandparents of Maria de Carpentier, Wife of Jean Paul Jaquet, Vidir Director & Chief Magistrate on the South River of New Netherland, 1655-1657. E. J. Sellers. (Illus.). 154p. 1992. reprint ed. pap. 25.00 (*0-8328-2751-7*); reprint ed. lib. bdg. 35.00 (*0-8328-2750-9*) Higginson Bk Co.
Van Heijenoort: Logic & Its History in the Work & Writings of Jean van Heijenoort. Irving H. Anellis. LC 94-75196. (Illus.). xvi, 341p. (Orig.). 1994. 59.95 (*1-884905-01-3*); pap. 39.95 (*1-884905-00-5*) Modern Logic.
Van Helen - OU812. pap. 14.95 (*0-89524-432-2*) Cherry Lane.
Van Hiele Model of Thinking in Geometry among Adolescents. David Fuys et al. (Journal for Research in Mathematics Education Monograph Ser.: No. 3). 196p. 1988. pap. 8.00 (*0-87353-266-X*) NCTM.
Van Horn Family History. Francis M. Marvin. (Illus.). 464p. 1992. reprint ed. pap. 67.50 (*0-8328-2465-8*); reprint ed. lib. bdg. 77.50 (*0-8328-2464-X*) Higginson Bk Co.
Van Horn Sandstone, West Texas: An Alluvial Fan Model for Mineral Exploration. J. H. McGowen & C. G. Groat. (Report of Investigations Ser.: RI 72). (Illus.). 57p. 1982. reprint ed. pap. 2.50 (*0-318-03173-6*) Bur Econ Geology.
Van Horne's Road: Construction & Early Operation of the Canadian Pacific Railway. Omer Lavallee. (Illus.). 304p. 45.00 (*0-919130-22-4*, Pub. by Boston Mills Pr CN) Genl Dist Srvs.
Van Leeuwen's Newborn Medicine. 2nd ed. Gerard Van Leeuwen. Ed. by Charles L. Paxson. LC 79-15838. (Illus.). 578p. reprint ed. pap. 164.80 (*0-8357-7628-X*, 2056951) Bks Demand.
*__Van Leo: Portraits of Glamour.__ Pierre Gazio. 1997. pap. text ed. 14.95 (*977-424-430-3*, Pub. by Am Univ Cairo Pr UA) Col U Pr.
*__Van Loan's 1879 Catskill Mountain Guide.__ (Illus.). 88p. 1979. reprint ed. pap. 11.95 (*0-614-26409-X*) Purple Mnt Pr.
*__Van Morrison.__ John Robertson. (Illus.). 146p. (Orig.). pap. 7.95 (*0-7119-5600-6*, OP47832) Omnibus NY.
Van Morrison: Enlightenment. (Vocal-Piano-Guitar Ser.). 1991. 14.95 (*0-7935-0876-2*, 00308108) H Leonard.
*__Van Morrison: Inarticulate Speech of the Heart.__ John Collis. (Illus.). 272p. (Orig.). 1997. pap. 14.95 (*0-306-80811-0*) Da Capo.
Van Morrison: The Guitar Collection. Ed. by Aaron Stang. 128p. (Orig.). (YA). 1995. pap. text ed. 21.95 (*0-89724-765-5*, PG9521) Warner Brothers.
Van Morrison: The Mystic's Music. Howard A. DeWitt. (Illus.). 114p. 1994. reprint ed. pap. text ed. 14.95 (*0-938840-02-9*) Horizon Bks CA.
Van Morrison Anthology. 1993. 19.95 (*0-7935-2772-4*, 00308204) H Leonard.
*__Van Morrison Autobiography.__ Van Morrison. 1999. pap. 8.95 (*0-14-013274-0*) Viking Penguin.
Van Nostrand Reinhold Dictionary of Environmental Health & Safety. Ed. by Frank S. Lisella. LC 93-25838. 356p. 1994. text ed. 67.95 (*0-442-00508-3*) Van Nos Reinhold.
Van Nostrand's Scientific Dictionary, 2 vols. 7th ed. Douglas M. Considine. 1990. Set. text ed. write for info. (*0-442-31816-2*) Van Nos Reinhold.
Van Nostrand's Scientific Encyclopedia. 7th ed. Ed. by Douglas M. Considine. LC 88-10601. (Illus.). 3264p. 1989. text ed. 207.95 (*0-442-21750-1*) Van Nos Reinhold.
Van Nostrand's Scientific Encyclopedia, 2 vols., Set. 8th ed. Ed. by Douglas M. Considine & Glenn D. Considine. (Illus.). 3632p. 1995. text ed. 259.95 (*0-442-01864-9*) Van Nos Reinhold.
Van Nostrand's Scientific Encyclopedia, Vol. 1. 7th ed. Douglas M. Considine. (General Science & Technology Ser.). 1989. text ed. write for info. (*0-442-31814-6*) Van Nos Reinhold.
Van Nostrand's Scientific Encyclopedia, 2 Vols., Vol. 1. 8th ed. Ed. by Douglas M. Considine & Glenn D. Considine. 3200p. 1995. text ed. 199.95 (*0-442-01865-7*) Van Nos Reinhold.
Van Nostrand's Scientific Encyclopedia, 2 Vols., Vol. 2. 8th ed. Ed. by Douglas M. Considine & Glenn D. Considine. 3200p. 1995. text ed. 199.95 (*0-442-01868-1*) Van Nos Reinhold.
Van Oil Field, Van Zandt County, Texas. R. A. Liddle. (Bulletin Ser.: BULL 3601). 79p. 1936. pap. 1.50 (*0-318-03307-0*) Bur Econ Geology.
Van Petten's Science. Albert A. Van Petten. LC 89-51501. 328p. (Orig.). 1990. 19.95 (*1-878357-33-6*) Van Petten Co.
Van Reinhold Encyclopedia of Chemistry. 5th ed. Douglas M. Considine. 1990. text ed. 140.00 (*0-442-23978-5*) Van Nos Reinhold.
Van Richten's G Vistani. 1995. 12.95 (*0-7869-0155-1*) TSR Inc.
Van Richten's Guide. TSR Inc. Staff. (Illus.). 1994. 12.95 (*1-56076-819-3*) TSR Inc.
Van Richten's Guide to Friends. TSR Inc. Staff. (Advanced Dungeons & Dragons, 2nd Edition Ser.). 1995. 12.95 (*0-7869-0122-5*) TSR Inc.
Van Sickle's Modern Airmanship. 5th ed. Ed. by John F. Welch. (Illus.). 896p. 1987. 37.50 (*0-8306-2411-2*) McGraw-Hill Prof.
Van Sickle's Modern Airmanship. 6th ed. John F. Welch. 1990. 39.95 (*0-8306-7451-9*) McGraw-Hill Prof.
Van Sickle's Modern Airship. 7th ed. John F. Welch. LC 94-30236. 1996. 44.95 (*0-07-069184-3*) McGraw.
Van Vechten: The Genealogical Records of the Van Vechtens from 1638-1896. P. Van Vechten, Jr. (Illus.). 117p. 1992. reprint ed. pap. 22.00 (*0-8328-2753-3*); reprint ed. lib. bdg. 32.00 (*0-8328-2752-5*) Higginson Bk Co.
Van Vlack Elements of Material Science. 6th ed. Lawrence H. Van Vlack. (C). 1989. pap. text ed. write for info. (*0-201-52822-3*) Addison-Wesley.
Van Voorhees: Genealogy of the Van Voorhees Family in America, or the Descendants of Steven Coerte Van Voorhees. Elias W. Van Voorhis. (Illus.). 380p. 1994. reprint ed. pap. 59.50 (*0-8328-4389-X*); reprint ed. lib. bdg. 69.50 (*0-8328-4388-1*) Higginson Bk Co.
Van Wies of Nine Mile Creek. Nancy L. Breed. LC 94-36960. (J). 1994. pap. 12.50 (*0-925168-12-2*) North Country.
Van Winkle, Genealogy of the Van Winkle Family: Account of Its Origin & Settlement in This Country with Data, 1630-1913. Daniel Van Winkle. (Illus.). 433p. 1994. reprint ed. pap. 66.50 (*0-8328-4040-8*); reprint ed. lib. bdg. 76.50 (*0-8328-4039-4*) Higginson Bk Co.
Van Winkle's Return: Change in American English, 1966-1986. Kenneth G. Wilson. LC 86-40390. 205p. reprint ed. pap. 58.50 (*0-7837-6208-9*, 2045929) Bks Demand.
Van Wolverton's Guide to Windows NT: Easy Directions for Immediate Results. Van Wolverton. 1993. pap. 16.00 (*0-685-66618-2*) Random.
Van Wyck Brooks. James R. Vitelli. (Twayne's United States Authors Ser.). 1969. pap. 13.95 (*0-8084-0001-0*, T134) NCUP.
Van Wyck Brooks. William Wasserstrom. LC 68-64754. (University of Minnesota Pamphlets on American Writers Ser.: No. 71). 48p. (Orig.). reprint ed. pap. 25.00 (*0-7837-2857-3*, 2057598) Bks Demand.
Van Wyck Brooks: In Search of American Culture. James Hoopes. LC 76-8754. (Illus.). 368p. 1977. 37.50 (*0-87023-212-6*) U of Mass Pr.
Van Wyck Brooks: The Early Years, 1908-1925. rev. ed. Ed. by Claire Sprague. 288p. 1993. text ed. 42.50 (*1-55553-174-1*); pap. text ed. 15.95 (*1-55553-175-X*) NE U Pr.
Van Zorn: A Comedy in Three Acts. Edwin Arlington Robinson. LC 72-97890. reprint ed. 29.50 (*0-404-05363-7*) AMS Pr.
Vanadium. (Metals & Minerals Ser.). 1993. lib. bdg. 250.95 (*0-8490-8996-4*) Gordon Pr.
*__Vanadium.__ WHO Staff. (Environmental Health Criteria Ser.: No. 81). 170p. 1988. 30.00 (*92-4-154281-0*) World Health.
Vanadium: International Strategic Minerals Inventory Summary Report. (Illus.). 52p. (Orig.). (C). 1992. pap. text ed. 30.00 (*1-56806-132-3*) DIANE Pub.
Vanadium: Trace Mineral for Health. 1996. lib. bdg. 250.99 (*0-8490-5914-3*) Gordon Pr.
*__Vanadium & Some Vanadium Salts Health & Safety Guide.__ (Health & Safety Guides Ser.: No. 42). 35p. 1990. pap. text ed. 5.00 (*92-4-151042-0*, 1860042) World Health.
Vanadium Compounds: Biochemical & Therapeutic Applications. Ed. by Ashok K. Srivastava & Jean-Louis Chiasson. (Developments in Molecular & Cellular Biochemistry Ser.: Vol. 16). 256p. (C). 1996. lib. bdg. 210.00 (*0-7923-3762-X*) Kluwer Ac.
Vanadium in Biological Systems: Physiology & Biochemistry. Ed. by N. Dennis Chasteen. (C). 1990. lib. bdg. 137.50 (*0-7923-0733-X*) Kluwer Ac.
*__Vanadium in the Environment, Pt. 1.__ Ed. by Jerome O. Nriagu. LC 97-14872. (Advances in Environmental Science & Technology Ser.). 450p. 1998. text ed. 89.95 (*0-471-17778-4*) Wiley.
*__Vanadium in the Environment, Pt. 2.__ Ed. by Jerome O. Nriagu. (Advances in Environmental Science & Technology Ser.). 424p. 1998. text ed. 89.95 (*0-471-17776-8*) Wiley.
Vanaspati Industry: A Historical Review. A. C. Chhatrapate. 1986. 27.50 (*0-8364-1601-5*, Pub. by Popular Prakashan II) S Asia.
Vanbrugh. Kerry Downes. Ed. by John Harris & Alastair Laing. (Studies in Architecture: No. XVI). (Illus.). 280p. 1986. 125.00 (*0-302-02769-6*, Pub. by Zwemmer Bks UK) Sothebys Pubns.
Vance. Vance Inc. Staff. 304p. 1994. per., pap. text ed. 16.95 (*0-8403-9499-3*) Kendall-Hunt.
Vance Cunningham's New Mexico Real Estate Digest. Vance Cunningham & Tom O'Brien. (Illus.). 214p. 1993. pap. text ed. 24.95 (*0-9636213-0-0*) Manzano Mtn.
Vance Packard & American Social Criticism. Daniel Horowitz. LC 93-35608. (Illus.). xx, 376p. (C). 1994. 37.50 (*0-8078-2141-1*) U of NC Pr.
Vance Randolph: An Ozark Life. Robert Cochran. LC 84-8647. (Illus.). 294p. 1985. text ed. 24.95 (*0-252-01164-3*) U of Ill Pr.
Vance Stance. Vance Bonner. LC 92-50281. (Illus.). 256p. 1993. pap. 12.95 (*1-56305-311-X*, 3311) Workman Pub.
Vancouver. (Insight Guides, Windows on the World Ser.). (Illus.). 350p. 1993. pap. 21.95 (*0-395-65990-6*) HM.
Vancouver. (Essential Guides Ser.). (J). (gr. k). 1994. pap. 7.95 (*0-8442-8941-8*, Passport Bks) NTC Pub Grp.
Vancouver: A Visual History. MacDonald. 1994. 42.00 (*0-88922-311-4*) Genl Dist Srvs.
*__Vancouver: The Art of Living Well.__ Peter C. Newman & Eve Lazarus. (Urban Tapestry Ser.). (Illus.). 240p. 1996. 49.95 (*1-881096-34-3*) Towery Pub.
Vancouver: The Ultimate Guide. 3rd rev. ed. Terri Wershler. LC 92-40129. 240p. 1993. pap. 11.95 (*0-8118-0368-6*) Chronicle Bks.
Vancouver: The Ultimate Guide. 5th expanded ed. Terri Wershler & Judi Lees. 240p. 1996. pap. 12.95 (*0-8118-1095-X*) Chronicle Bks.
Vancouver: Ulysses Travel Guide. Paul E. Dumontier et al. (Ulysses Travel Guides Ser.). 1996. pap. 10.95 (*0-614-.2866-8*) Ulysses Travel.
Vancouver & British Columbia. Carol Baker. (Illustrated Travel Guides from Thomas Cook Ser.). (Illus.). 192p. 1994. pap. 12.95 (*0-8442-9035-1*, Passport Bks) NTC Pub Grp.
*__Vancouver & British Columbia: Passport's Illustrated Travel Guide.__ Thomas Cook. 1997. pap. 14.95 (*0-8442-4843-6*) NTC Pub Grp.
Vancouver & Its Region. Ed. by Graeme Wynn & Timothy Oke. (Illus.). 351p. 1992. pap. 29.95 (*0-7748-0421-1*, Pub. by U BC Pr) U of Wash Pr.
*__Vancouver Area Diving Guide.__ Carl Trepanier. (Illus.). 185p. (Orig.). 1997. pap. 19.95 (*0-919574-81-5*) Gordon Soules Bk.
*__Vancouver Best Places: The Most Discriminating Guide to Vancouver's Restaurants, Shops, Hotels, Nightlife, Arts, Sights, & Outings.__ 2nd rev. ed. Ed. by Kasey Wilson. LC 96-53855. 352p. 1997. pap. 16.95 (*1-57061-091-6*) Sasquatch Bks.
Vancouver Best Places: The Most Discriminating Guide to Vancouver's Restaurants, Shops, Hotels, Nightlife, Arts, Sights, & Outings. Ed. by Kasey Wilson & Stephanie Irving. (Best Places Guidebooks Ser.). (Illus.). 320p. (Orig.). 1994. pap. 13.95 (*0-912365-96-X*) Sasquatch Bks.
Vancouver Canucks. Iain MacIntyre. LC 93-48447. (NHL Today Ser.). 32p. (J). 1995. lib. bdg. 15.95 (*0-88682-745-0*) Creative Ed.
*__Vancouver Coastal BC Earthquake: Surviving the Big One.__ Susan Mayse. 1992. pap. 8.95 (*1-55105-003-X*) Lone Pine.
*__Vancouver Grizzlies.__ Michael E. Goodman. LC 97-6652. (NBA Today Ser.). (J). 1997. write for info. (*0-88682-895-3*) Creative Ed.
*__Vancouver Grizzlies.__ Bob Italia. LC 96-39608. (Inside the NBA Ser.). (J). 1997. write for info. (*1-56239-777-X*) Abdo & Dghtrs.
Vancouver Island & British Columbia: Their History, Resources & Prospects. Matthew Macfie. LC 72-9458. (Far Western Frontier Ser.). (Illus.). 600p. 1973. reprint ed. 41.95 (*0-405-04986-2*) Ayer.
*__Vancouver Island Letters of Edmund Hope Verney: 1862-65.__ Ed. by Allan Pritchard. (Pioneers of British Columbia Ser.). (Illus.). 324p. 1996. 65.00 (*0-7748-0554-4*, FC3822, Pub. by U BC Pr) U of Wash Pr.
*__Vancouver Island Letters of Edmund Hope Verney: 1862-65.__ Ed. by Allan Pritchard. (Illus.). 324p. 1996. pap. 24.95 (*0-7748-0573-0*, Pub. by U BC Pr) U of Wash Pr.
Vancouver Island South Explorer: The Outdoor Guide. Mark Zuehlke. 1994. pap. text ed. 12.95 (*1-55110-141-6*, Pub. by Whitecap Bks CN) Gr Arts Ctr Pub.
Vancouver Island Traveler: Guide to the Freshest, Friendliest Place on Earth. 2nd ed. Ellen Searby. (Illus.). 224p. (Orig.). 1997. pap. 12.95 (*0-942297-05-9*) Windham Bay.
Vancouver Meeting: Particles & Fields '91, 2 vols. Ed. by D. Axen et al. 1000p. (C). 1991. text ed. 164.00 (*981-02-0768-9*) World Scientific Pub.
Vancouver Recalled. Derek Pethick. (Illus.). 96p. pap. 3.95 (*0-919654-09-6*) Hancock House.
Vancouver Rendezvous. Liz Johnson Gebhardt. 625p. (Orig.). 1996. mass mkt. 6.99 (*1-55197-201-8*, Pub. by Comnwlth Pub CN) Partners Pubs Grp.
Vancouver Short Stories. Ed. by Carole Gerson. 180p. 1985. pap. 14.95 (*0-7748-0228-6*, Pub. by U BC Pr) U of Wash Pr.
Vancouver Stock Exchange: Listing Rules, Policies & Procedures. Garrod & Watkins. 224p. 1990. 70.00 (*0-409-80949-7*) MICHIE.
Vancouver the Way It Was. Michael Kluckner. 1994. 49.95 (*1-55110-102-5*, Pub. by Whitecap Bks CN) Gr Arts Ctr Pub.
Vancouver's Chinatown: Racial Discourse in Canada, 1875-1980. Kay J. Anderson. (McGill-Queen's Studies in Ethnic History). (Illus.). 1991. text ed. 55.00 (*0-7735-0844-9*, Pub. by McGill CN) U of Toronto Pr.
Vancouver's Chinatown: Racial Discourse in Canada, 1875-1980. Kay J. Anderson. 1995. pap. 19.95 (*0-7735-1329-9*, Pub. by McGill CN) U of Toronto Pr.
Vancouver's Discovery of Puget Sound. George C. Shaw. 28p. (YA). (gr. 9 up). reprint ed. pap. 1.95 (*0-8466-0102-8*, S102) Shorey.
Vancouver's Voyage: Charting the Northwest Coast, 1791-1795. Robin Fisher. LC 92-53590. (Illus.). 144p. 1992. 35.00 (*0-295-97191-6*) U of Wash Pr.
Vandal. Tom Molloy. LC 89-62513. 220p. 1990. 22.00 (*0-932966-98-5*) Permanent Pr.
Vandal. Ann Schlee. LC 81-2859. (Illus.). 192p. (J). (gr. 7 up). 1981. 8.95 (*0-517-54424-5*) Crown Bks Yng Read.
*__Vandal Hearts Unauthorized Secrets & Solutions.__ Anthony Lynch. 128p. 1997. per. 14.99 (*0-7615-1133-4*) Prima Pub.
Vandalia: Wilderness Capital of Lincoln's Land. Mary Burtschi. LC 63-5255. (Illus.). 167p. (C). 1977. 12.00 (*0-9601648-1-2*) Little Brick Hse.
Vandalic War *see* **History of the Wars. Secret History**
Vandalism: Behavior & Motivations. Ed. by Claude Levy-Leboyer. 364p. 1984. 152.50 (*0-444-86775-9*, I-245-84) Elsevier.
Vandalized Lovemaps: Paraphilic Outcome of Seven Cases in Pediatric Sexology. John Money & Margaret Lamacz. 224p. 1989. 31.95 (*0-87975-513-X*) Prometheus Bks.
*__Vandals.__ John A. Vikara. 305p. (Orig.). 1997. mass mkt. 4.99 (*1-55237-047-X*, Pub. by Comnwlth Pub CN) Partners Pubs Grp.

Vandals at the Gates of Medicine: Historic Perspectives on the Battle over Health Care Reform. Miguel Faria, Jr. (Illus.). 403p. 1995. 41.95 (*0-9641077-0-8*) Hacienda Pub.
As we teeter at the brink of major health care reform, what should be the guiding light to lead us away from the precipice of socialized medicine & the total collapse of the American health care delivery system? How can we make sure that in the present battle over health system reform we proceed in the right direction & for the good of the nation? In VANDALS AT THE GATES OF MEDICINE, the author, Miguel A. Faria, Jr., M.D., provides compelling arguments that some of the answers to this great dilemma reside on the pages of history. This fascinating book draws parallels between the past & the present as it takes us on a magical journey through time, traveling the ages & visiting enchanted periods in the annals of history: from the time when the fine line separating myth & history was blurred & indistinguishable to the clearly troubled present... In the process, we learn the ethics & workings of the medical profession & the mind & soul of physicians as they perform their work as healers. This is a momentous book that everyone who believes in the unassailable power of history & who is searching for answers to the moral, social & economic problems of our society, not to mention the perplexing riddle of health system reform, will relish. To order call (912) 757-9873; FAX: (912) 757-9725 or write: Hacienda Publishing, Inc., P.O. Box 13648, Macon, GA 31208-3648 or Publishers Distribution Service, Baker & Taylor, Quality Books, & J.A. Majors & Company. ***Publisher Provided Annotation.***

Vandal's Crown: How Rebel Currency Traders Overthrew the World's Central Banks. Gregory J. Millman. 1995. 23.00 (*0-02-921287-1*, Free Press) Free Pr.
Vandals' Crown: How Rebel Currency Traders Overthrew World's Central Banks. Don Milliman. 1996. pap. 13.00 (*0-02-874122-6*) Free Pr.
Vandals' Crown: How Revel Currency Traders Overthrew World Central Banks. Gregory J. Millman. 1995. 17.00 (*0-671-53744-X*) S&S Trade.
*__Vandas: Their Botany, History & Culture.__ Martin R. Motes. LC 96-32199. 250p. 1997. 44.95 (*0-88192-376-1*) Timber.
Vandas & Ascocendas & Their Combinations with Other Genera. David L. Grove. LC 94-44663. (Illus.). 282p. 1995. 44.95 (*0-88192-316-8*) Timber.
Vandemark Mummy. Cynthia Voigt. 224p. (YA). 1992. mass mkt. 4.50 (*0-449-70417-3*, Juniper) Fawcett.

Vandemark Mummy. Cynthia Voigt. LC 91-7311. 240p. (J). (gr. 5-9). 1991. text ed. 15.95 (*0-689-31476-0*, Atheneum Bks Young) S&S Childrens.

Vandemark's Folly. Herbert Quick. LC 87-10800. (Bur Oak Bk.). 452p. 1987. reprint ed. pap. 14.95 (*0-87745-182-6*) U of Iowa Pr.

Vander Zalm's Northwest Gardner's Almanac. Bill V. Zalm. Ed. by Peggy Cromer. (Illus.). 256p. pap. 12.95 (*0-88839-163-3*) Hancock House.

Vanderbilt Campus: A Pictorial History. Robert A. McGaw. LC 78-9913. (Illus.). 160p. 1979. 24.95 (*0-8265-1210-0*) Vanderbilt U Pr.

***Vanderbilt Cup Race 1936 & 1937 Photo Archive.** Brock Yates. LC 96-78343. (Photo Archive Ser.). (Illus.). 128p. 1997. 45.00 (*1-882256-66-2*) Iconografix.

Vanderbilt Hearing Aid Report II. Ed. by Gerald A. Studebaker et al. LC 91-4894. (Illus.). 334p. 1991. pap. text ed. 51.00 (*0-912752-26-2*) York Pr.

Vanderbilt Studies in the Humanities, Vol. 1. Ed. by Richmond C. Beatty et al. LC 52-1180. 283p. reprint ed. pap. 80.70 (*0-8357-3265-7*, 2039486) Bks Demand.

Vanderbilt Tradition: Essays in Honor of Thomas Daniel Young. Ed. by Mark R. Winchell. LC 90-42822. (Southern Literary Studies). 304p. 1991. text ed. 42.50 (*0-8071-1538-X*) La State U Pr.

Vanderbilts. Jerry E. Patterson. (Illus.). 304p. 1989. 49.50 (*0-8109-1748-3*) Abrams.

Vanderbilts & the Story of Their Fortune. William A. Croffut. LC 75-1837. (Leisure Class in America Ser.). (Illus.). 1975. reprint ed. 32.95 (*0-405-06906-5*) Ayer.

Vanderbilt's Folly: History of Pennsylvania Turnpike. 8th ed. William H. Shank. (C). 1993. 7.00 (*0-933788-41-X*) Am Canal & Transport.

***Vanderbilt's New Shoes.** Richard Scarry. (Read-It-Yourself Ser.: No. 2). (J). 1998. mass mkt. 3.99 (*0-689-81625-1*) S&S Childrens.

Vanderfords: Early Settlers of America. Cheryl L. Jensen. (Illus.). 472p. 1992. pap. text ed. 25.00 (*0-9631323-0-X*) Aurora CA.

VanDerlip: Vanderlip, Van Derlip, Vander Lippe Family in America, Also Including Some Account of the Von der Liipe Family of Lippe, Germany, from Which the Norwegian, Dutch & American Lines Have Their Descent. C. E. Booth. (Illus.). 188p. 1993. reprint ed. pap. 29.00 (*0-8328-3425-4*); reprint ed. lib. bdg. 39.00 (*0-8328-3424-6*) Higginson Bk Co.

VanDerZee: Photographer 1886-1983. Deborah Willis-Thomas. LC 93-18307. (Illus.). 192p. 1993. 45.00 (*0-8109-3923-1*) Abrams.

***Vandevelde U. S. Investment Treaties.** 1992. pap. text ed. 163.50 (*90-6544-576-5*) Kluwer Ac.

Vandover & the Brute. Frank Norris. (BCL1-PS American Literature Ser.). 354p. 1992. reprint ed. lib. bdg. 89.00 (*0-7812-6814-1*) Rprt Serv.

Vane Pursuit. Charlotte MacLeod. 1992. 4.50 (*0-446-77520-7*) Warner Bks.

Vane Shear Strength Testing in the Field & Laboratory. Ed. by Adrian F. Richards. LC 88-7684. (Special Technical Publication Ser.: No. STP 1014). (Illus.). 450p. 1988. text ed. 79.00 (*0-8031-1188-6*, 04-010140-38) ASTM.

Vaneglory. George Turner. 352p. (Orig.). 1996. mass mkt. 5.99 (*0-380-77885-8*, AvoNova) Avon.

Vanek Plays: Four Authors, One Character. Marketa Goetz-Stankiewicz. (Illus.). 328p. 1987. pap. 21.95 (*0-7748-0267-7*) U of Wash Pr.

Vanek Progress in Soil Zoology. 1975. lib. bdg. 194.00 (*90-6193-025-1*) Kluwer Ac.

Vanessa. large type ed. Catherine Fellows. 336p. 1988. 25.99 (*0-7089-1759-3*) Ulverscroft.

Vanessa: Vocal Score. S. Barber. 272p. 1986. pap. 45.00 (*0-7935-5125-0*, 50338080) H Leonard.

Vanessa-Ann's Cozy Crocheted Afghans. Vanessa-Ann Collection Staff. 144p. 1992. 24.99 (*0-8487-1095-9*) Oxmoor Hse.

Vanessa-Ann's Holidays in Cross-Stitch. Vanessa-Ann Collection Staff. LC 86-62285. 144p. 1993. pap. 14.95 (*0-8487-1417-2*) Oxmoor Hse.

Vanessa-Ann's Holidays in Cross Stitch Vol. 1. Vanessa-Ann Collection Staff. 1995. pap. 14.95 (*0-8487-1406-7*) Oxmoor Hse.

Vanessa-Ann's Holidays in Cross-Stitch, 1993. Vanessa-Ann Collection Staff. 144p. 1993. 24.99 (*0-8487-1086-X*) Oxmoor Hse.

Vanessa-Ann's One Hundred One Christmas Ornaments. Vanessa-Ann Collection Staff. 160p. 1992. 24.99 (*0-8487-1080-0*) Oxmoor Hse.

Vanessa-Ann's Victorian Cross-Stitch. Vanessa-Ann Collection Staff. LC 93-86048. 144p. 1993. pap. 14.95 (*0-8487-1425-3*) Oxmoor Hse.

Vanessa Libretto. S. Barber. 48p. 1986. pap. 4.95 (*0-7935-2922-0*, 50340390) H Leonard.

Vanessa's Footsteps. Willie M. Griffin. Ed. & Told to Thyonne Gordon-Sales. (Orig.). 1996. pap. 15.99 (*1-889210-00-5*) A Writ Pl.

Vangie's Kitchen Corner - A Down East Cookbook. Evangeline Knowlton. (Illus.). 325p. (Orig.). 1988. pap. 16.95 (*0-941238-05-9*) Penobscot Bay.

Vanguard. Arnold Bennett. LC 74-17054. (Collected Works of Arnold Bennett: Vol. 85). 1977. reprint ed. 25.95 (*0-518-19166-4*) Ayer.

Vanguard: Battle Station II. David Drake & Bill Fawcett. 272p. (Orig.). 1993. mass mkt. 4.99 (*0-441-86032-X*) Ace Bks.

Vanguard Artist. Bernard Rosenberg & Norris Fliegel. 366p. (C). 1990. reprint ed. pap. 14.95 (*0-941533-97-2*) New Amsterdam Bks.

Vanguard Artist: Portrait & Self-Portrait. Bernard Rosenberg & Norris Fliegel. Ed. by Lewis A. Coser & Walter W. Powell. LC 79-7017. (Perennial Works in Sociology). 1980. reprint ed. lib. bdg. 24.95 (*0-405-12116-4*) Ayer.

Vanguard Daily Performance Management System: How to Improve Productivity & Prevent Formal Disciplinary Actions. Hank Engel & Andrew S. Bargerstock. 74p. 1996. ring bd. 29.00 (*0-9639557-4-8*, Jacob-Cameron) A R K Co.

Vanguard Experiment: John Bogle's Quest to Transform the Mutual Fund Industry. Robert Slater. LC 95-52838. 264p. 1996. text ed. 24.95 (*0-7863-0559-2*) Irwin Prof Pubng.

***Vanguard Guide to Investing During Retirement: Managing Your Assets in Retirement.** 2nd ed. Vanguard Group Staff. 1997. pap. text ed. 17.95 (*0-07-066892-2*) McGraw.

***Vanguard Guide to Planning for Retirement: Building Your Retirement Assets.** 3rd ed. Vanguard Group Staff. 1997. pap. text ed. 17.95 (*0-07-066891-4*) McGraw.

Vanguard Leader. Frank Damazio. 320p. 1994. pap. 10.95 (*0-914936-53-0*) BT Pub.

Vanguard of Empire: Ships of Exploration in the Age of Columbus. Roger C. Smith. (Illus.). 304p. 1993. 39.95 (*0-19-507357-6*) OUP.

Vanguard of Islamic Revolution: The Jamaat-I Islami of Pakistan. Seyyed V. Nasr. LC 93-5403. (Comparative Studies on Muslim Societies: No. 19). 1994. 50.00 (*0-520-08368-7*); pap. 20.00 (*0-520-08369-5*) U CA Pr.

Vanguard of Nazism: The Free Corps Movement in Postwar Germany, 1918-1923. Robert G. Waite. LC 52-5045. (Historical Studies: No. 60). 358p. 1952. 27.50 (*0-674-93142-4*) HUP.

***Vanguard of the Islamic Revolution.** Seyyed V. Nasr. 300p. 1996. pap. 22.50 (*0-614-21501-3*) Kazi Pubns.

Vanguard Parties & Revolutionary Change in the Third World: Soviet Perspectives & Their Implications. David E. Albright. LC 90-82547. (Policy Papers in International Affairs: No. 38). viii, 126p. (C). 1990. pap. text ed. 9.50 (*0-87725-538-5*) U of Cal IAS.

Vanguard Retirement Investing Guide. Vanguard Staff. 232p. 1994. per. 15.00 (*0-7863-0322-0*) Irwin Prof Pubng.

Vanguard Retirement Investing Guide: Charting Your Course to a Secure Retirement. 2nd ed. 256p. 1995. per. 24.95 (*0-7863-0624-6*) Irwin Prof Pubng.

Vanguard Retirement Investing Guide: Charting Your Course to a Secure Retirement. 2nd ed. Vanguard Staff. 240p. 1995. per. 24.95 (*0-7863-0502-9*) Irwin Prof Pubng.

Vanguard Staffing Practices: How Leading Employment Managers Achieve Exceptional Results. Andrew S. Bargerstock. 84p. 1996. ring bd. 29.00 (*0-9639557-6-4*, Jacob-Cameron) A R K Co.

Vanguardism in Latin American Literature, 1920-1945: An Annotated Bibliography. Compiled by Merlin H. Forster & K. David Jackson. LC 90-34103. (Bibliographies & Indexes in World Literature Ser.: No. 27). 256p. 1990. text ed. 55.00 (*0-313-24861-3*, FVG, Greenwood Pr) Greenwood.

Vanguards & Followers: Youth in the American Tradition. Louis Filler. LC 78-5893. 268p. 1978. 29.95 (*0-88229-459-8*) Nelson-Hall.

Vanguards & Followers: Youth in the American Tradition. Louis Filler. LC 94-24051. 270p. 1995. pap. 24.95 (*1-56000-817-2*) Transaction Pubs.

Vanguards of the Frontier: A Social History of the Northern Plains & Rocky Mountains from the Fur Traders to the Sod Busters. Everett N. Dick. LC 41-6157. 594p. reprint ed. pap. 169.30 (*0-7837-4659-8*, 2044383) Bks Demand.

Vanijayik Vidhi ke Sidhant: (Principles of Mercantile Law) 4th ed. Avtar Singh. (HIN.). (C). 1988. 110.00 (*0-685-37443-2*) St Mut.

Vanijayik Vidhi ke Sidhant: (Principles of Mercantile Law in Hindi) 4th ed. Ed. by Avtar Singh. (HIN.). (C). 1988. 110.00 (*0-685-39624-X*) St Mut.

Vanijayik Vidhi ke Sidhant (Principles of Mercantile Law in Hindi) 3rd ed. Avtar Singh. 1128p. 1983. 150.00 (*0-317-54723-2*) St Mut.

Vanila Manilla Folder Games for Young Children. Jane A. Caballero. LC 80-83231. (Illus.). 114p. (J). (ps-2). 1981. pap. 16.95 (*0-89334-059-6*) Humanics Ltd.

Vanilla. Janet Hazen. LC 94-16139. (Illus.). 72p. 1995. 9.95 (*0-8118-0254-X*) Chronicle Bks.

Vanilla Blood. Nancy Martin. 320p. 1996. pap. 10.95 (*0-938711-36-9*) Tecolote Pubns.

Vanilla, Chocolate, & Strawberry: The Story of Your Favorite Flavors. Bonnie Busenberg. LC 93-15101. (YA). (gr. 5 up). 1993. lib. bdg. 23.95 (*0-8225-1573-3*, Lerner Publctns) Lerner Group.

Vanilla Custard. Alexander Morgan. (Orig.). 1987. pap. 10.00 (*0-912449-23-3*) Floating Island.

Vanilla Manila Folder Games for Young Children. Jane A. Caballero. LC 80-83231. (Illus.). 114p. 1981. lib. bdg. 26.95 (*0-89334-182-7*, 182-7) Humanics Ltd.

Vanilla Vocabulary: Visualized-Verbalized Vocabulary Book. Nanci Bell & Phyllis Lindamood. (Illus.). 200p. (J). (gr. 4-7). 1992. pap. 19.00 (*0-945856-03-2*) Nancibell Inc.

Vanio & Zanda Zulan. Asaita Thakur. Tr. by Farley P. Richmond from GUJ. 8.00 (*0-89253-658-6*); 4.80 (*0-89253-659-4*) Ind-US Inc.

Vanish! Disappearance Through ID Acquisition. Johnny Yount. 96p. 1986. pap. 15.00 (*0-87364-398-4*) Paladin Pr.

Vanish in an Instant. Margaret Millar. LC 89-85721. 248p. reprint ed. pap. 7.95 (*1-55882-051-5*, Lib Crime Classics) Intl Polygonics.

Vanish Rain Forests. Aiken. 224p. 1996. pap. 45.00 (*0-19-854959-8*) OUP.

Vanish with the Rose. Barbara Michaels. 432p. 1993. mass mkt. 6.99 (*0-425-13898-4*, Berkley Trade) Berkley Pub.

Vanish with the Rose. Barbara Michaels. 1992. 17.00 (*0-671-75594-3*) S&S Trade.

Vanish with the Rose. large type ed. Barbara Michaels. LC 92-31899. (General Ser.). 548p. 1994. pap. 18.95 (*0-8161-5661-1*) G K Hall.

Vanished! Terry Deary. LC 96-7209. (Classified Ser.). 96p. (J). (gr. 5 up). 1995. pap. 3.95 (*0-7534-5005-4*, Kingfisher LKC) LKC.

Vanished. Dorothy Hoobler & Tom Hoobler. (Fact or Fiction Ser.). 144p. (YA). (gr. 7 up). 1992. 16.95 (*0-8027-8148-9*); lib. bdg. 17.85 (*0-8027-8149-7*) Walker & Co.

Vanished. Danielle Steel. LC 92-37118. 312p. 1993. 23.95 (*0-385-30603-2*) Delacorte.

Vanished. Danielle Steel. 400p. 1994. mass mkt. 6.99 (*0-440-21746-6*) Dell.

***Vanished.** large type ed. Julie Ellis. (Linford Mystery Library). 336p. 1996. pap. 15.99 (*0-7089-7944-0*, Linford) Ulverscroft.

Vanished. limited ed. Danielle Steel. 312p. 1993. 200.00 (*0-385-31046-3*) Doubleday.

Vanished! The Mysterious Disappearance of Amelia Earhart. Monica Kulling. (Step into Reading Ser.). (Illus.). (J). 1996. pap. 3.99 (*0-679-87124-1*) Random.

Vanished! The Mysterious Disappearance of Amelia Earhart. Monica Kulling. (Step into Reading Ser.). (Illus.). (J). 1996. lib. bdg. 11.99 (*0-679-97124-6*) Random.

Vanished Arcadia. R. B. Cunningham Grahame & B. Cunningham. 1973. 59.95 (*0-8490-1254-6*) Gordon Pr.

Vanished Arcadia: Being Some Account of the Jesuits in Paraguay. Robert B. Graham. LC 68-25238. (Studies in Spanish Literature: No. 36). 1969. reprint ed. lib. bdg. 75.00 (*0-8383-0949-6*) M S G Haskell Hse.

Vanished Arizona: Recollections of the Army Life of a New England Woman. Martha Summerhayes. (Illus.). 388p. 1988. reprint ed. Indexed. pap. 12.00 (*0-87380-162-8*) Rio Grande.

Vanished Arizona: Recollections of the Army Life of a New England Woman. Martha Summerhayes. LC 78-26814. (Illus.). xxvi, 341p. 1979. reprint ed. pap. 12.95 (*0-8032-9105-1*, Bison Books) U of Nebr Pr.

Vanished Child. Sarah Smith. (Boston Mysteries Ser.). 1993. mass mkt. 5.99 (*0-345-38164-5*) Ballantine.

Vanished Child. Sarah Smith. 1996. mass mkt. 5.99 (*0-345-90947-X*) Ballantine.

***Vanished Child.** Sarah Smith. 1997. pap. 12.00 (*0-345-41805-0*) Ballantine.

Vanished City: Everyday Life in the Warsaw Ghetto. Michel Mazor. Tr. by David Jacobson from FRE. LC 92-62367. 208p. 1994. 24.00 (*0-941419-93-2*) Marsilio Pubs.

Vanished Halls & Cathedrals of France. G. W. Edwards. 69.95 (*0-8490-1255-4*) Gordon Pr.

Vanished Imam: Musa al Sadr & the Shia of Lebanon. Fouad Ajami. LC 85-48194. (Illus.). 228p. 1992. 35.00 (*0-8014-1910-7*); pap. 15.95 (*0-8014-9416-8*) Cornell U Pr.

Vanished Kingdoms: Irish in Australia & New Zealand. Patrick O'Farrell. 309p. 1990. 39.95 (*0-86840-148-X*, Pub. by New South Wales Univ Pr AT) Intl Spec Bk.

Vanished Library: A Wonder of the Ancient World. Luciano Canfora. Tr. by Martin Ryle. (Hellenistic Culture & Society Ser.). (Orig.). 1990. 28.00 (*0-520-07304-5*); pap. 15.00 (*0-520-07255-3*) U CA Pr.

Vanished Messenger. E. Phillips Oppenheim. reprint ed. lib. bdg. 25.95 (*0-89190-416-6*, Rivercity Pr) Amereon Ltd.

Vanished One. Anne Schraff. Ed. by Carol Newell. (Standing Tall Mystery Ser.). 49p. (Orig.). (J). (gr. 5-9). 1995. pap. 4.95 (*1-56254-159-5*, SP1595) Saddleback Pubns.

Vanished Peoples: The Story of the Beothuck. Peter Such. (Illus.). 96p. (Orig.). pap. 9.95 (*0-919600-83-2*, Pub. by NC Press CN) U of Toronto Pr.

Vanished Present: The Memoirs of Alexander. Alexander Pasternak. Ed. & Tr. by Ann P. Slater. LC 88-43305. (Illus.). 238p. 1989. pap. 15.95 (*0-8014-9576-8*) Cornell U Pr.

Vanished Spendor III: Postcard Memories of Oklahoma City. Jim Edwards et al. LC 82-72945. (Illus.). 64p. 1985. 18.95 (*0-910453-03-9*) Abalache Bkshop.

Vanished Supremacies, Vol. 1. Collected Essays Of Sir Lewis Namier. Lewis B. Namier. LC 73-119603. (Select Bibliographies Reprint Ser.). 1977. 15.95 (*0-8369-5195-6*) Ayer.

Vanished World. Roman Vishniac. LC 83-16420. (Illus.). 192p. 1983. 35.00 (*0-374-28247-1*) FS&G.

Vanished World. Anna G. Sneller. (Utopianism & Communitarianism Ser.). 365p. 1994. reprint ed. pap. 15.50 (*0-8156-2582-0*) Syracuse U Pr.

Vanished Worlds: An Introduction to Historical Geology. Roy R. Lemon. 496p. (C). 1992. per. write for info. (*0-697-11249-7*) Wm C Brown Pubs.

Vanishing. Kirby L. Wilkins. 136p. 1984. pap. 6.95 (*0-935330-01-1*) Blackwells Pr.

Vanishing Aborigines. K. N. Dharmadasa & S. W. Samarasinghe. 1990. text ed. 27.95 (*0-7069-5298-7*, Pub. by Vikas II) S Asia.

Vanishing Act. Richard Greenberg. 1987. pap. 3.25 (*0-8222-1205-6*) Dramatists Play.

***Vanishing Act.** Thomas Perry. 1997. mass mkt. 2.99 (*0-8041-1648-2*) Ivy Books.

Vanishing Act. Thomas Perry. 1996. mass mkt. 5.99 (*0-8041-1387-4*) Ivy Books.

Vanishing Act. large type ed. Thomas Perry. LC 95-17067. (Large Print Bks.). 1995. pap. 21.95 (*1-56895-234-1*) Wheeler Pub.

Vanishing Acts. Michael McFee. LC 89-80713. 64p. (Orig.). 1989. pap. 12.50 (*0-917788-38-9*) Gnomon Pr.

Vanishing Acts: An Odyssey. Helen Ashmore. LC 88-63523. (Illus.). 208p. (Orig.). 1989. 15.00 (*0-938270-04-4*); pap. 10.00 (*0-938270-05-2*) Parkway Pr Ltd.

Vanishing Adolescent. Edgar Z. Friedenberg. LC 85-950. xxvi, 144p. 1985. reprint ed. text ed. 38.50 (*0-313-24920-2*, FRVA, Greenwood Pr) Greenwood.

Vanishing Air. John C. Esposito. 328p. 1970. pap. 0.95 (*0-686-36549-6*) Ctr Responsive Law.

Vanishing American. Zane Grey. 336p. 1991. mass mkt. 3.99 (*0-06-100295-X*, Harp PBks) HarpC.

Vanishing American. Zane Grey. 1976. 24.95 (*0-8488-1030-9*) Amereon Ltd.

Vanishing American: White Attitudes & U. S. Indian Policy. Brian W. Dippie. LC 91-18772. (Illus.). x, 428p. 1991. reprint ed. pap. 14.95 (*0-7006-0507-X*) U Pr of KS.

Vanishing American Barber Shop. Ronald S. Barlow. LC 96-76415. (Illus.). 224p. (Orig.). 1996. pap. 19.95 (*0-9652373-0-3*) W Marvy.

Vanishing American Frontier: Bernarda Bryson Shahn & Her Historical Lithographs Created for the Resettlement Administration of FDR. Jake M. Wien. (Illus.). 64p. (Orig.). 1995. pap. 18.00 (*0-9645581-0-6*) Wien American.

***Vanishing American Jew: In Search of Jewish Idenity for the Next Century.** Alan Dershowitz. LC 96-49292. 432p. 1997. 24.95 (*0-316-18133-1*) Little.

***Vanishing American Jews: Is There a Future for Us?** Alan Dershowitz. 1997. 24.95 (*0-614-27525-3*) Little.

Vanishing American Outhouse: A History of Country Plumbing. large type ed. Ronald S. Barlow. (Illus.). 144p. (Orig.). 1989. pap. 15.95 (*0-933846-02-9*) Windmill Pub Co.

Vanishing Animal Neighbors. Geraldine M. Gutfreund. LC 92-25530. (First Bks.). (Illus.). 64p. (J). (gr. 5-8). 1993. lib. bdg. 21.00 (*0-531-20060-4*) Watts.

Vanishing Animal Neighbors. Geraldine M. Gutfreund. (First Bks.). (Illus.). 64p. (J). (gr. 5-8). 1993. pap. 6.95 (*0-531-15674-5*) Watts.

Vanishing Animal Paper Chains. Stewart Walton. (J). 1996. pap. 7.95 (*0-688-14915-4*, Tupelo Bks) Morrow.

***Vanishing Arctic.** Photos by Bryan Alexander & Cherry Alexander. (Illus.). 1997. 35.00 (*0-8160-3650-0*) Facts on File.

Vanishing Arctic: Alaska's National Wildlife Refuge. T. H. Watkins. (Illus.). 88p. 1988. 39.95 (*0-89381-329-X*) Aperture.

Vanishing Barings & Financial Derivatives. Peter G. Zhang. 150p. 1995. pap. 14.00 (*981-02-2333-1*) World Scientific Pub.

***Vanishing Bile Duct Syndrome - Pathophysiology & Treatment.** Ed. by D. Alvaro. (Falk Symposium Ser.). 272p. (C). 1997. lib. bdg. 123.00 (*0-7923-8721-X*) Kluwer Ac.

Vanishing Boundaries: The Religion of Mainline Protestant Baby Boomers. Dean R. Hoge et al. LC 93-31968. 272p. (Orig.). 1994. pap. 20.00 (*0-664-25492-6*) Westminster John Knox.

Vanishing Breed (The Gold Miner) Jimmy Simpson. 551p. 1996. write for info. (*0-9651227-0-0*) Simpson Publng.

Vanishing Children of Paris: Rumor & Politics Before the French Revolution. Arlette Farge et al. 146p. (C). 1991. 23.50 (*0-674-93193-9*) HUP.

Vanishing Children of Paris: Rumor & Politics Before the French Revolution. Arlette Farge. 146p. 1993. pap. 12.95 (*0-674-93194-7*) HUP.

Vanishing Clues. Gilbert Morris. (Time Navigators Ser.: Vol. 2). 144p. (J). (gr. 6-9). 1996. pap. 5.99 (*1-55661-396-2*) Bethany Hse.

Vanishing Coast. Elizabeth Leland. (Illus.). 142p. (Orig.). 1996. pap. 10.95 (*0-89587-149-1*) Blair.

Vanishing Conscience. John MacArthur. 1995. pap. 10.99 (*0-8499-3678-0*) Word Pub.

Vanishing Culture of Lucknow. Amir Hasan. 1990. 28.50 (*81-7018-573-4*, Pub. by BR Pub II) S Asia.

Vanishing DeKalb. DeKalb Historical Society Staff. (Illus.). 240p. 1985. 30.00 (*0-9615459-0-9*) Dekalb.

Vanishing Diaspora: The Jews in Europe since 1945. Bernard Wasserstein. 352p. 1996. 27.95 (*0-674-93196-3*) HUP.

***Vanishing Diaspora: The Jews in Europe Since 1945.** Bernard Wasserstein. 1997. pap. text ed. 15.95 (*0-674-93199-8*) HUP.

Vanishing Dreams: The Economic Plight of America's Young Families. Children's Defense Fund Staff & Northeastern University Center for Labor Market Studies Staff. 40p. 1992. pap. text ed. 6.50 (*0-938008-93-5*) Childrens Defense.

Vanishing Economy: Television Coverage of Economic Affairs, 1982-1987. Ted J. Smith, III. Ed. by Media Institute Staff. LC 88-63170. 100p. (Orig.). (C). 1988. pap. 10.95 (*0-937790-38-9*, 4310) Media Institute.

Vanishing Emptiness. Willem M. Roggeman. LC 88-8259. 108p. 8900. pap. 16.95 (*0-948259-51-5*) Dufour.

Vanishing Farmland Crisis: Critical Views of the Movement to Preserve Agricultural Land. Ed. by John Baden. LC 84-7472. (Studies in Government & Public Policy). x, 174p. 1984. 25.00 (*0-7006-0253-4*) U Pr of KS.

Vanishing Feast. Dorothy H. Patent. LC 94-2227. (Gulliver Green Book Ser.). 192p. (YA). (gr. 7 up). 1994. 18.00 (*0-15-292867-7*, Gulliver Bks) HarBrace.

Vanishing Flora: Endangered Plants Around the World. Dugald Stermer. LC 94-22873. (Illus.). 1995. 39.95 (*0-8109-3930-4*) Abrams.

Vanishing Footprints. Lois W. Johnson. (Adventures of the Northwoods Ser.: Vol. 4). 160p. (Orig.). (J). (gr. 3-8). 1991. pap. 5.99 (*1-55661-103-X*) Bethany Hse.

An Asterisk (*) at the beginning of an entry indicates that the title is appearing in BIP for the first time.

Vanishing Forest Reserves. Willard G. Van Name. Ed. by Stuart Bruchey. LC 78-56688. (Management of Public Lands in the U. S. Ser.). 1979. reprint ed. lib. bdg. 19.95 (*0-405-11356-0*) Ayer.

Vanishing Forests. Helen J. Challand. LC 91-25863. (Saving Planet Earth Ser.). 128p. (J). (gr. 4-8). 1991. lib. bdg. 29. 30 (*0-516-05505-4*) Childrens.

Vanishing Garden: A Conservation Guide to Garden Plants. Christopher Brickell & Fay Sharman. (Illus.). 261p. 1986. 24.95 (*0-88192-030-4*) Timber.

Vanishing Georgia: Photographs from the Vanishing Georgia Collection, Georgia Department of Archives & History. S. Konter. LC 82-4764. (Brown Thrasher Bks.). (Illus.). 240p. (C). 1994. pap. 19.95 (*0-8203-1631-8*) U of Ga Pr.

Vanishing Greece. Patrick L. Fermor. (Illus.). 192p. pap. 24. 95 (*0-7892-0044-9*) Abbeville Pr.

Vanishing Greece. Patrick L. Fermor. (Illus.). 192p. 1992. 35.00 (*1-55859-410-8*) Abbeville Pr.

Vanishing Gwinnett: Gwinnett County Georgia. 2nd rev. ed. W. Dorsey Stancil. (Illus.). 212p. 1993. text ed. 35.00 (*0-914923-04-8*) Gwinnett Hist.

Vanishing Hero. Sean O'Faolain. LC 71-142686. (Essay Index Reprint Ser.). 1977. 18.95 (*0-8369-2065-1*) Ayer.

Vanishing Hero. Sean O'Faolain. 1991. reprint ed. lib. bdg. 21.95 (*1-56849-074-7*) Buccaneer Bks.

Vanishing Hitchhiker: American Urban Legends & Their Meanings. Jan H. Brunvand. (Orig.). (C). 1989. pap. 10. 95 (*0-393-95169-3*) Norton.

***Vanishing Holes Murders.** large type ed. Peter Chambers. (Linford Mystery Library). 304p. 1996. pap. 15.99 (*0-7089-7942-4*, Linford) Ulverscroft.

***Vanishing Irish: Households, Migration, & the Rural Economy in Ireland, 1850-1914.** Timothy Guinnane. LC 97-5383. (Economic History of the Western World Ser.). 1997. write for info. (*0-691-04307-8*) Princeton U Pr.

Vanishing Japan. Elizabeth Kiritani & Itsuo Kiritani. (Illus.). 196p. (Orig.). 1995. pap. 12.95 (*0-8048-1967-X*) C E Tuttle.

Vanishing Jewels: Central Asian Tribal Weavings. William Wood et al. Ed. by H. J. Swinney. LC 90-62705. (Illus.). 128p. (Orig.). 1990. pap. 39.95 (*0-938551-00-0*) Rochester Mus & Sci Ctr.

***Vanishing Jobs: Canada's Changing Workplaces.** Lars Osberg et al. pap. 19.95 (*1-55028-482-7*, Pub. by J Lorimer CN) Formac Dist Ltd.

***Vanishing Jobs: Canada's Changing Workplaces.** Lars Osberg et al. bds. 29.95 (*1-55028-483-5*, Pub. by J Lorimer CN) Formac Dist Ltd.

Vanishing Ladies. Ed McBain. 160p. 1991. reprint ed. mass mkt. 4.50 (*0-380-71121-4*) Avon.

Vanishing Land. large type ed. Alan White. 528p. 1985. 27. 99 (*0-7089-8239-5*) Ulverscroft.

Vanishing Land: The Corporate Theft of America. Frank Browning. 1990. 12.50 (*0-8446-5166-4*) Peter Smith.

Vanishing Lands: A World Survey of Soil Erosion. Graham V. Jacks & Robert O. Whyte. LC 72-4280. (World Affairs Ser.: National & International Viewpoints). (Illus.). 384p. 1972. reprint ed. 28.95 (*0-405-04573-5*) Ayer.

Vanishing Legion: A History of Mascot Pictures, 1927-1935. Jon Tuska. LC 81-6014. (Illus.). 224p. 1982. lib. bdg. 32.50 (*0-89950-030-7*) McFarland & Co.

Vanishing Life: The Mystery of Mass Extinctions. Jeff Hecht. LC 92-41713. (Illus.). 160p. (YA). (gr. 7 up). 1993. text ed. 15.95 (*0-684-19331-0*, C Scribner Sons Young) S&S Childrens.

Vanishing Lights. Mark Weinrich. LC 93-74959. (Light Chaser Mysteries Ser.: Bk. 1). 88p. (J). 1994. pap. 4.99 (*0-88965-106-X*, Pub. by Horizon Books CN) Chr Pubns.

Vanishing Lives: Style & Self in Tennyson, D. G. Rossetti, Swinburne, & Yeats. James Richardson. LC 87-25269. (Virginia Victorian Studies). 251p. 1988. reprint ed. pap. 71.60 (*0-608-01438-9*, 2062200) Bks Demand.

***Vanishing Lung Syndrome.** Miroslav Holub. Tr. by David Young & Dana Habova from CZE. LC 89-64117. (Field Translation Ser.: No. 16). 110p. 1990. pap. 10.95 (*0-932440-52-5*) Oberlin Coll Pr.

Vanishing Lung Syndrome. Miroslav Holub. Tr. by David Young & Dana Habova from CZE. LC 89-64117. (Field Translation Ser.: No. 16). 110p. 1990. 19.95 (*0-932440-53-3*) Oberlin Coll Pr.

Vanishing Mind: A Practical Guide to Alzheimer's Disease & Other Dementias. Leonard Heston & June A. White. (Illus.). 192p. (C). 1995. text ed. write for info. (*0-7167-2131-7*) W H Freeman.

Vanishing Mind: A Practical Guide to Alzheimer's Disease & Other Dementias. Leonard Heston & June A. White. (Illus.). 192p. (C). 1995. pap. text ed. write for info. (*0-7167-2192-9*) W H Freeman.

Vanishing Ministry. Woodrow M. Kroll. LC 91-11752. 160p. 1992. pap. 9.99 (*0-8254-3057-7*) Kregel.

Vanishing New Jersey Landscape. Clem Fiori. LC 93-43531. (Illus.). 150p. (C). 1994. 32.95 (*0-8135-2091-6*) Rutgers U Pr.

Vanishing New Jersey Landscapes. Clem Fiori. (Illus.). 150p. (Orig.). (C). 1995. pap. 20.00 (*0-8135-2167-X*) Rutgers U Pr.

Vanishing-No-More. Alma Burnette. Ed. by Lafe Miller. (Illus.). 28p. (Orig.). (J). (gr. 1-8). 1994. 2.95 (*1-881652-01-6*) Amer Recycling.

Vanishing Ozone. Laurence Pringle. LC 94-25928. (Save the Earth Ser.). (Illus.). 64p. (J). (gr. 3 up). 1995. lib. bdg. 15.93 (*0-688-04158-2*, Morrow Junior) Morrow.

Vanishing Ozone. Laurence Pringle. LC 94-25928. (Save the Earth Ser.). (Illus.). 64p. (YA). (gr. 3 up). 1995. 16. 00 (*0-688-04157-4*, Morrow Junior) Morrow.

Vanishing Paperclips America's Aerospace Secret. Hans H. Amtmann. Ed. by thomas H. Hitchcock. LC 86-62375. (Illus.). 128p. 1988. 26.95 (*0-914144-35-9*) Monogram Aviation.

Vanishing Picture. Sigmar Polke. 220p. 1996. 85.00 (*1-881616-65-7*, Pub. by Scalo Pubs) Dist Art Pubs.

Vanishing Point. Charmian Astbury. (C). 1989. pap. 50.00 (*0-7223-2357-3*, Pub. by A H S Ltd UK) St Mut.

Vanishing Point. Aristotelis Nikolaidis. Tr. by John Leatham. (Modern Greek Writers Ser.). 304p. pap. 19.95 (*960-04-0915-3*, Pub. by Kedros Pubs GR) Paul & Co Pubs.

Vanishing Point. Michaela Roessner. 1994. pap. 4.99 (*0-8125-1672-9*) Tor Bks.

Vanishing Point. Morris West. 272p. 1996. 23.00 (*0-06-101069-3*, HarperPrism) HarpC.

***Vanishing Point.** Morris West. 336p. 1997. mass mkt. 5.99 (*0-06-101222-X*, Harp PBks) HarpC.

***Vanishing Point.** Morris L. West. LC 97-24382. 1997. write for info. (*1-56895-474-3*) Wheeler Pub.

Vanishing Points. Alice Brown. LC 71-106250. (Short Story Index Reprint Ser.). 1977. 21.95 (*0-8369-3287-0*) Ayer.

Vanishing Points. Martin Jones. 1993. pap. 5.95 (*0-88145-096-0*) Broadway Play.

Vanishing Points: Dickens, Narrative, & the Subject of Omniscience. Audrey Jaffe. LC 90-15492. 200p. 1991. 38.00 (*0-520-06918-8*) U CA Pr.

Vanishing Points: Spirituality & the Avant-Garde. Ed. by Aleka Chase et al. (Review Ser.: No. 10). (Illus.). 300p. (Orig.). 1991. pap. 9.00 (*0-9618409-5-1*) Five Fingers.

Vanishing Pumpkin. Tony Johnston. (J). (ps-3). 1992. pap. text ed. 6.95 (*0-399-22436-X*) Putnam Pub Group.

Vanishing Pumpkin. Tony Johnston. (Illus.). 32p. (J). (ps-3). 1996. pap. 5.95 (*0-698-11414-0*, Paperstar) Putnam Pub Group.

***Vanishing Pumpkin.** A. E. Parker. (Clue Ser.: No. 15). (J). 1997. mass mkt. 3.99 (*0-590-13742-5*) Scholastic Inc.

Vanishing Rain Forests. Paula Hogan. (Environment Alert! Ser.). (Illus.). 32p. (J). (gr. 3-4). 1991. lib. bdg. 18.60 (*0-8368-0477-5*) Gareth Stevens Inc.

Vanishing Rain Forests: The Ecological Transition in Malaysia. S. Robert Aiken & Colin H. Leigh. (Oxford Monographs on Biogeography: No. 5). (Illus.). 224p. 1995. pap. 32.00 (*0-614-05437-0*) OUP.

Vanishing Republic: How Can We Save the American Dream? Mark Anthony. 384p. 1996. 24.97 (*0-9646138-0-8*) M Anthony Commun.

Vanishing Shadow. Margaret Sutton. LC 94-9897. (Judy Bolton Mystery Ser.). 216p. (J). 1994. reprint ed. 12.95 (*1-55709-250-8*) Applewood.

Vanishing Smile. Earl Emerson. LC 95-5594. 272p. 1995. 21.00 (*0-345-38486-5*) Ballantine.

Vanishing Smile. Earl Emerson. 1996. mass mkt. 5.99 (*0-345-40453-X*) Ballantine.

***Vanishing Songbirds: The Six Order, Wood Warblers & Other Passerine Birds.** Eliot Porter. LC 96-24484. (Illus.). 159p. 1996. 37.50 (*0-8212-2225-2*) Bulfinch Pr.

Vanishing Species: The Wildlife Art of Laura Regan. Michelle Minnich. (Illus.). 120p. 1993. pap. 19.95 (*1-55912-377-X*) CEDCO Pub.

Vanishing Star. Judy Baer. (Cedar River Daydreams Ser.: Vol. 12). 160p. (Orig.). (YA). (gr. 7-10). 1991. mass mkt. 4.99 (*1-55661-197-8*) Bethany Hse.

Vanishing Subject: Early Psychology & Literary Modernism. Judith Ryan. LC 90-27330. 278p. 1991. 34. 50 (*0-226-73226-6*) U Ch Pr.

Vanishing Thieves, No. 66. Franklin W. Dixon. (Hardy Boys Ser.). (J). 1987. mass mkt. 3.99 (*0-671-63890-4*) PB.

Vanishing Tower. Michael Moorcock. 176p. 1987. mass mkt. 4.99 (*0-441-86039-7*) Ace Bks.

***Vanishing Tribes of Burma.** Richard K. Diran. 1997. 45.00 (*0-8174-5559-0*) Watsn-Guptill.

Vanishing Tribes of Kenya: A Description of the Manners & Customs of the Primitive & Interesting Tribes Dwelling on the Vast Southern Slopes of Mount Kenya & Their Fast Disappearing Native Methods of Life. J. Orde Browne. (B. E. Ser.: No. 148). 1925. 35.00 (*0-8115-3069-8*) Periodicals Srv.

Vanishing Universe: Adverse Environmental Impacts on Astronomy: Proceedings of the Conference Sponsored by UNESCO Held at UNESCO, Paris, June 30-July 2, 1992. Ed. by Derek McNally. LC 93-41980. (Illus.). 450p. (C). 1994. 85.00 (*0-521-45020-9*) Cambridge U Pr.

Vanishing Values: Louis W. Foster & Twentieth Century American Business. Robert Windeler. (Leaders of Industry Ser.). (Illus.). 180p. 1994. text ed. 19.95 (*1-885637-11-X*) Bluefish Pr.

***Vanishing Vampire, Vol. 1.** David Lubar. (The Accidental Monsters Ser.). (J). 1997. pap. text ed. 3.99 (*0-590-90718-2*) Scholastic Inc.

***Vanishing Vampire Clue.** A. E. Parker. (Clue Ser.). (J). (gr. 4-7). 1997. pap. 3.99 (*0-614-29025-2*, Apple Classics) Scholastic Inc.

Vanishing Vector. John P. Evans & John B. Mannion. 256p. (Orig.). 1981. mass mkt. 2.50 (*0-449-14409-7*, GM) Fawcett.

Vanishing Vests. Elaine Weimann & Rita Friedman. (Read to Me Bks.). (Illus.). 30p. (J). (ps-1). 1978. lib. bdg. 12. 50 (*0-89796-804-2*) New Dimens Educ.

Vanishing Village. S. Dixon. (Puzzle Adventures Ser.). (Illus.). 48p. (J). 1990. pap. 5.50 (*0-7460-0330-7*); lib. bdg. 13.95 (*0-88110-405-1*) EDC.

Vanishing Village. Will Rose. 350p. 1970. 5.50 (*0-9600350-0-1*) Catskill Art.

Vanishing Village: Danish Maritime Community. Robert T. Anderson & Barbara G. Anderson. LC 77-87704. (American Ethnological Society Monographs: No. 39). reprint ed. 39.50 (*0-404-16498-6*) AMS Pr.

Vanishing Villages. Clement Marchand. (Prose Ser.: No. 19). 234p. 1993. pap. 13.00 (*0-920717-73-X*) Guernica Editions.

Vanishing Vision: The Inside Story of Public Television. James Day. LC 94-40304. (Illus.). 453p. 1995. 29.95 (*0-520-08659-7*) U CA Pr.

Vanishing Wetlands. Trent Duffy. LC 93-26332. (Impact Bks.). (Illus.). 112p. (YA). (gr. 7-12). 1994. lib. bdg. 22. 70 (*0-531-13034-7*) Watts.

Vanishing Wetlands. Anita L. McCormick. (Lucent Overview Ser.). (Illus.). (J). (gr. 5-8). 1995. lib. bdg. 17. 96 (*1-56006-162-6*) Lucent Bks.

Vanishing Whores & the Insomniac. Guy R. Beining. (Illus.). 40p. (Orig.). 1991. pap. 3.00 (*0-926935-57-7*) Runaway Spoon.

Vanishing Wilderness: America's Last Wild Places. Janis A. Kraulis. 1989. 19.98 (*0-88486-028-0*) Arrowood Pr.

Vanishing Wildlife. Renee Martig. (Illus.). (Orig.). 1989. pap. 9.95 (*0-9622625-0-1*) Timberline Colorado.

Vanishings. Time Life Staff. (Library of Curious & Unusual Facts). 1990. 17.27 (*0-8094-7687-8*); lib. bdg. 23.27 (*0-8094-7688-6*) Time-Life.

Vanishings from That Neighborhood. Joe Bonomo. LC 95-38198. (Wick Poetry Chapbook Ser.: No. 9). 47p. (Orig.). 1996. pap. 4.75 (*0-87338-544-6*) Kent St U Pr.

Vanishment. Aycliffe. 240p. 1994. mass mkt. 4.50 (*0-06-100658-0*, Harp PBks) HarpC.

Vanitas. Jeffrey Ford. LC 87-20676. (Illus.). 184p. 1988. pap. 7.95 (*0-917053-07-9*) Space And.

***Vanitas.** S. P. Somtow. 1997. mass mkt. 6.99 (*0-8125-2478-0*) Tor Bks.

Vanitas: Designs. Abbeville Press Staff & Gianni Versace. (Illus.). 272p. 1996. 75.00 (*1-55859-804-9*) Abbeville Pr.

Vanitas: Escape from Vampire Junction. S. P. Somtow. 384p. 1995. 23.95 (*0-312-85513-3*) Tor Bks.

Vanitas Still Lifes of Harem Steenwyck: Metamorphic Realism. Kristine Koozin. LC 89-13115. (Illus.). 128p. 1990. lib. bdg. 59.95 (*0-88946-949-0*) E Mellen.

Vanitie & Downe-Fall of Superstitious Popish Ceremonies. Peter Smart. LC 77-7428. (English Experience Ser.: No. 894). 1977. reprint ed. lib. bdg. 20.00 (*90-221-0894-5*) Walter J Johnson.

Vanity. Jane Feather. 416p. 1996. mass mkt. 5.99 (*0-553-57248-2*, Fanfare) Bantam.

Vanity. Vicki Power. (Very Peculiar History Ser.). (Illus.). 48p. (J). (gr. 4-7). 1995. pap. 5.95 (*0-531-15273-1*) Watts.

Vanity. Vicki Power. LC 94-40133. (Very Peculiar History Ser.). (Illus.). 48p. (J). (gr. 5-8). 1995. lib. bdg. 23.00 (*0-531-14356-2*) Watts.

***Vanity.** large type ed. Jane Feather. LC 96-35018. (Star-Romance Ser.). 427p. 1997. 23.95 (*0-7862-0888-0*, Five Star) Mac Lib Ref.

Vanity & Meaning: Discovering Purpose in Life. Ed. by R. C. Sproul, Jr. LC 95-674. 96p. (Orig.). (gr. 10). 1995. pap. 6.99 (*0-8010-5242-4*) Baker Bks.

Vanity & Mischief of the Old Letany see Letany of J. Bastwick

Vanity Dies Hard. Ruth Rendell. 208p. 1987. mass mkt. 5.99 (*0-345-34952-0*) Ballantine.

Vanity Fair. Edgar F. Harden. 1995. pap. 13.95 (*0-8057-4460-6*) Macmillan.

Vanity Fair. Edgar F. Harden. 1995. 23.95 (*0-8057-8390-3*, Twayne) Scribnrs Ref.

***Vanity Fair.** Thacker. pap. 6.95 (*0-460-87725-9*, Everyman's Classic Lib) C E Tuttle.

***Vanity Fair.** Thackeray. 1992. pap. text ed. write for info. (*0-17-556468-X*) Addison-Wesley.

Vanity Fair. William Makepeace Thackeray. (Airmont Classics Ser.). (YA). (gr. 11 up). 1967. mass mkt. 2.50 (*0-8049-0138-4*, CL-138) Airmont.

Vanity Fair. William Makepeace Thackeray. 752p. 1991. 20.00 (*0-679-40566-6*, Everymans Lib) Knopf.

Vanity Fair. William Makepeace Thackeray. Ed. by Geoffrey Tillotson & Kathleen Tillotson. LC 63-3850. (C). 1972. pap. 11.56 (*0-395-05161-4*) HM.

Vanity Fair. William Makepeace Thackeray. 1962. pap. 5.95 (*0-451-52041-6*, CE1726, Sig Classics); mass mkt. 6.95 (*0-451-52489-6*, Sig Classics) NAL-Dutton.

Vanity Fair. William Makepeace Thackeray. Ed. by John Sutherland. (World's Classics Ser.). 944p. 1983. pap. 6.95 (*0-19-281642-X*) OUP.

Vanity Fair. William Makepeace Thackeray. Ed. by J. I. Stewart. (English Library). 816p. 1969. pap. 8.95 (*0-14-043035-0*, Penguin Classics) Viking Penguin.

***Vanity Fair.** William Makepeace Thackeray. 1997. mass mkt. 6.95 (*0-553-21462-4*, Bantam Classics) Bantam.

Vanity Fair. abr. ed. William Makepeace Thackeray. 1997. pap. 23.95 incl. audio (*0-14-086052-5*) Viking Penguin.

Vanity Fair. William Makepeace Thackeray. 1982. reprint ed. lib. bdg. 35.95 (*0-89966-406-7*) Buccaneer Bks.

Vanity Fair: Authoritative Text, Backgrounds, Criticism. William Makepeace Thackeray. Ed. by Peter L. Shillingsburg. LC 93-48019. (C). 1994. pap. text ed. 14. 95 (*0-393-96595-3*) Norton.

Vanity Fair Notes. Mildred R. Bennett. 1982. pap. 3.95 (*0-8220-1320-7*) Cliffs.

Vanity of Dogmatizing: or Confidence in Opinions. Joseph Glanvill. Ed. by Bernhard Fabian. (Collected Works: Vol. I). 256p. 1970. reprint ed. 47.32 (*3-487-02687-2*) G Olms Pubs.

Vanity of Duluoz. Jack Kerouac. 272p. 1994. pap. 11.95 (*0-14-023639-2*, Penguin Bks) Viking Penguin.

Vanity of Power: American Isolationism & the First World War. John M. Cooper, Jr. LC 70-95508. (Contributions in American History Ser.: No. 3). 271p. 1970. text ed. 55.00 (*0-8371-2342-9*, COP/, Greenwood Pr) Greenwood.

Vanity Plate Spotter's Log Book. Robert Haiber & William Haiber. 64p. (Orig.). 1989. per. write for info. (*0-944089-29-1*) Info Devels.

Vanity Will Get You Somewhere. Joseph Cotten. 256p. 1988. mass mkt. 4.50 (*0-380-70534-6*) Avon.

Vanley Burke: A Retrospective. Intro. by Stuart Hall. 112p. (C). 1993. pap. 29.95 (*0-85315-783-9*, Pub. by Lawrence & Wishart UK) NYU Pr.

Vanna's Afghans A to Z: 52 Crochet Favorites. Vanna White. 1995. pap. 14.95 (*0-8487-1476-8*) Oxmoor Hse.

***Vanna's Afghans All Through the House.** 1997. pap. 14.95 (*0-8487-1602-7*) Oxmoor Hse.

***Vannes City Plan.** (Grafocarte Maps Ser.). 1996. 8.95 (*2-7416-0079-1*, 80079) Michelin.

***Vannes/La Baule/Angers Map.** 1996. 6.95 (*2-06-700063-2*, 63) Michelin.

Vannevar Bush Science for the 21st Century No. II: Current & Future Challenges for Federal Support. Ed. by John F. Ahearne & Charles F. Blackburn. 48p. (Orig.). 1996. pap. text ed. write for info. (*0-914446-10-X*) Sigma Xi.

Vanom Ka Manmohak Sansar. D. N. Tewari. 274p. 1992. pap. 100.00 (*81-7089-163-9*, Pub. by Intl Bk Distr II) St Mut.

Vanport, Oregon: Life & Death of an Instant City. Manly Maben. (Illus.). (Orig.). (C). 1987. pap. 15.95 (*0-87595-118-X*) Oregon Hist.

Vanquished. Valerie King. 384p. 1995. mass mkt. 4.99 (*0-8217-5052-6*, Zebra Kensgtn) Kensgtn Pub Corp.

Vanquished Hope: The Movement for Church Renewal in Russia, 1905-1906. James W. Cunningham. LC 81-9077. 384p. 1981. pap. text ed. 12.95 (*0-913836-70-2*) St Vladimirs.

Vanquished Nation, Broken Spirit: The Virtues of the Heart in Formative Judaism. Jacob Neusner. 208p. 1987. text ed. 49.95 (*0-521-32832-2*) Cambridge U Pr.

Van't Hoff - Le Bel Centennial: A Symposium Sponsored by the Division of the History of Chemistry at the 168th Meeting of the American Chemical Society, Atlantic City, NJ, September 11-12, 1974. Ed. by Ogden B. Ramsay. LC 75-9656. (ACS Symposium Ser.: No. 12). (Illus.). 208p. reprint ed. pap. 59.30 (*0-8357-4123-0*, 2052334) Bks Demand.

Vantage Legal Briefs: Do-It-Yourself Personal Injury Settlement Kit. Donald Steward. 1993. write for info. (*0-9636732-0-3*) Vantage Grp.

Vantage Point: Photographs from the Warren J. Coville Collection. 32p. 1992. pap. 7.50 (*1-880337-08-8*) Cranbrook Acad.

Vantage Points. Paul McCusker. 1986. 8.99 (*0-685-68718-X*, MP-636) Lillenas.

Vantage Points: Festschrift for Johan P. Snapper. Ed. by Blake L. Spahr et al. LC 96-20716. (Publications of the American Association for Netherlandic Studies). 286p. 1996. lib. bdg. 48.50 (*0-7618-0421-8*) U Pr of Amer.

Vanuatu: Travel Survival Kit. 2nd ed. David Harcombe & Denis O'Byrne. (Illus.). 304p. 1995. pap. 13.95 (*0-86442-293-8*) Lonely Planet.

Vanwell 2. 5 Litre F1: A Technical Appraisal. Ian Bamsey. (Haynes Constructors Ser.). (Illus.). 96p. 1991. 12.95 (*0-85429-838-X*, Pub. by G T Foulis Ltd) Haynes Pubns.

Vanya. Myrna Grant. LC 73-89729. 223p. (C). pap. text ed. 5.95 (*0-88419-009-9*) Omega Pubns OR.

Vanzetti's Fish Cart. Justin Vitiello. LC 91-45737. 64p. 1992. pap. 12.95 (*0-7734-0004-4*) E Mellen.

Vapor Deposition. Ed. by Carroll F. Powell et al. LC 66-13515. (Electrochemical Society Ser.). (Illus.). 741p. reprint ed. pap. 180.00 (*0-317-11088-8*, 2051258) Bks Demand.

Vapor Dreams in L.A. Terry Schoonhaven's Empty Stage. Museum Studies Class Staff. (Illus.). 40p. 1982. pap. 20. 00 (*0-936270-19-5*) CA St U LB Art.

Vapor-Liquid Equilibrium Data Collection: Organic Hydroxy Compounds. J. Gmehling et al. Ed. by R. Eckermann. (Dechema Chemistry Data Ser.: Vol. I, Pt. 2E, Supplement 3). (Illus.). 700p. 1988. text ed. 295.00 (*3-921567-92-0*, Pub. by Dechema GW) Scholium Intl.

Vapor-Liquid Equilibra for Mixtures of Low Boiling Substances, Vol. 6, Pt. I: Binary Systems. H. Knapp et al. Ed. by D. Berhens & R. Eckermann. (Dechema Chemistry Data Ser.). (Illus.). 910p. 1982. Vol. 6, Pt. I--Binary Systems. 285.00 (*3-921567-38-6*, Pub. by Dechema GW) Scholium Intl.

Vapor-Liquid Equilibria for Mixture of Low Boiling Substances. M. Knapp et al. Ed. by Dieter Behrens & Reiner Eckermann. (Dechema Chemistry Data Ser.: Vol. VI, Pts. 2-4). (Illus.). 1989. Set. 635.00 (*3-926959-10-X*, Pub. by Dechema GW); Vol. VI, Pt. 2, 620p. write for info. (*3-921567-74-2*); Vol. VI, Pt. 3, 573p. write for info. (*3-921567-84-X*); Vol. VI, Pt. 4, 616p. write for info. (*3-921567-90-4*) Scholium Intl.

Vapor-Liquid Equilibria Measurements & Calculations. Andre Muhlbauer & J. D. Raal. (Series in Chemical & Mechanical Engineering). 200p. 1996. text ed. 89.95 (*1-56032-550-X*) Taylor & Francis.

Vapor-Liquid Equilibrium Data. S. Ohe. (Physical Sciences Data Ser.: No. 37). 742p. 1989. 379.50 (*0-444-98876-9*) Elsevier.

Vapor-Liquid Equilibrium Data at High Pressure. S. Ohe. (Physical Sciences Data Ser.: No. 42). 356p. 1990. 288. 75 (*0-444-98797-5*) Elsevier.

Vapor-Liquid Equilibrium Data Collection, 3 pts., Vol. 1, Pt. 6A. 1980. Pt. 6A-Aliphatic Hydrocarbons. lib. bdg. 260.00 (*3-921567-30-0*, Pub. by Dechema GW) Scholium Intl.

Vapor-Liquid Equilibrium Data Collection, 3 pts., Vol. 1, Pt. 6B. 1980. Pt. 6B-Aliphatic Hydrocarbons. lib. bdg. write for info. (*3-921567-31-9*, Pub. by Dechema GW) Scholium Intl.

Vapor-Liquid Equilibrium Data Collection, 3 pts., Vol. 1, Pt. 6C. 1980. Pt. 6C-Supplement1. lib. bdg. 235.00 (*3-921567-51-3*, Pub. by Dechema GW) Scholium Intl.

UV

An Asterisk (*) at the beginning of an entry indicates that the title is appearing in BIP for the first time.

Vapor-Liquid Equilibrium Data Collection: Aldehydes, Ketones, Ethers, Vol. 1, Parts 3 & 4. J. Gmehling et al. Ed. by Dieter Behrens & Reiner Eckermann. LC 79-670289. (Dechema Chemistry Data Ser.). (Illus.). 1979. lib. bdg. 295.00 (*3-921567-14-9*, Pub. by Dechema GW) Scholium Intl.

Vapor-Liquid Equilibrium Data Collection: Aldehydes, Supplement 1. J. Gmehling et al. Ed. by Reiner Eckermann & Gerhard Kreysa. (Dechema Chemistry Data Ser.: Vol. 1, Pt. 3A). (Illus.). 280p. 1993. text ed. 215.00 (*3-921567-93-9*, Pub. by Dechema GW) Scholium Intl.

Vapor-Liquid Equilibrium Data Collection: Aqueous Systems. J. Gmehling et al. Ed. by R. Eckermann. (Dechema Chemistry Data Ser.: Vol. I, Pt 1B, Supplement 2). (Illus.). 650p. 1988. text ed. 260.00 (*3-921567-91-2*, Pub. by Dechema GW) Scholium Intl.

Vapor-Liquid Equilibrium Data Collection: Aqueous Systems, Vol I, Pt. 1. 2nd ed. J. Gmehling. (Dechema Chemistry Data Ser.: Vol. 1, Pt. 1). (Illus.). 700p. 1991. text ed. 310.00 (*3-926959-30-4*, Pub. by Dechema GW) Scholium Intl.

Vapor-Liquid Equilibrium Data Collection: Ketones, Supplement 1. J. Gmehling et al. Ed. by Reiner Eckermann & Gerhard Kreysa. (Dechema Chemistry Data Ser.: Vol. 1, Pt. 3B). (Illus.). 730p. 1993. text ed. 360.00 (*3-926959-44-4*, Pub. by Dechema GW) Scholium Intl.

Vapor-Liquid Equilibrium Data Collection: Volume I, Part 1A - Supplement 1 to Aqueous Organic Systems. J. Gmehling et al. 1981. lib. bdg. write for info. (*3-921567-33-5*, Pub. by Dechema GW) Scholium Intl.

Vapor-Liquid Equilibrium Data Collection: Volume I, Part 2C-Organic Hydroxy Compounds: Alcohols (Supplement 1) J. Gmehling et al. (Dechema Chemistry Data Ser.). (Illus.). 698p. 1982. lib. bdg. 215.00 (*3-921567-29-7*, Pub. by Dechema GW) Scholium Intl.

***Vapor-Liquid Equilibrium Data Collection Supplement 1: Ethers.** J. Gmehling et al. Ed. by Gerhard Kreysa. (Dechema Chemistry Data Ser.: Vol. 1, Pt. 4A). (Illus.). 530p. 1996. text ed. 320.00 (*3-921567-86-6*, Pub. by Dechema GW) Scholium Intl.

Vapor-Liquid Equilibrium Data Collection Organic Hydroxy Compounds: Alcohols & Phenols. J. Gmehling et al. Ed. by Dieter Behrens & Reiner Eckermann. (Dechema Chemistry Data Ser.: Vol. 1, Pt. 2F, Suppl. 4). (Illus.). 712p. 1991. text ed. 305.00 (*3-926959-16-9*, Pub. by Dechema GW) Scholium Intl.

Vapor-Liquid Equilibrium Data Collection Part 2d: Organic Hydroxy Compounds: Alcohols & Phenols (Supplement 2) J. Gmehling et al. (Dechema Chemistry Data Ser.: Vol. I). (Illus.). 800p. 1982. 240.00 (*3-921567-43-2*, Pub. by Dechema GW) Scholium Intl.

Vapor-Liquid Equilibrium Data Collection Part 5: Caroxylic Acids, Anhydrides, Esters, Vol. I. J. Gmehling et al. (Illus.). 715p. 1982. 250.00 (*3-921567-20-3*, Pub. by Dechema GW) Scholium Intl.

Vapor-Liquid Equilibrium Data Collection Tables & Diagrams of Data for Binary & Multicomponent Mixtures up to Moderate Pressures: Constants of Correlation Equations for Computer Use: Part 2a: Organic Hydroxy Compounds: Alcohols, Vol. 1. J. Gmehling & U. Onken. LC 79-670289. (Dechema Chemistry Data Ser.). 1978. text ed. 225.00 (*3-921567-09-2*, Pub. by Dechema GW) Scholium Intl.

Vapor-Liquid Equilibrium Data Collection Tables & Diagrams of Data for Binary & Multicomponent Mixtures up to Moderate Pressures; Constants of Correlation Equations for Computer Use: Part 2b: Organic Hydroxy Compounds: Alcohols & Phenols. Ed. by Gmehling et al. LC 79-670289. (Dechema Chemistry Data Ser.: Vol. 1). 1978. text ed. 270.00 (*3-926959-18-5*, Pub. by Dechema GW) Scholium Intl.

Vapor-Liquid Equilibrium Data Collection, Vol. 1, Pt. 8: Halogen, Nitrogen, Sulfur & Other Compounds. 1984. lib. bdg. 230.00 (*3-921567-24-6*, Pub. by Dechema GW) Scholium Intl.

***Vapor-Liquid Equilibrium Data-Salt Effect.** S. Ohe. (Physical Sciences Data Ser.: Vol. 43). xxx, 360p. 1991. 313.25 (*0-444-98687-1*) Elsevier.

Vapor Permeable Barrier Films & Coatings. 1993. 2,650.00 (*0-89336-934-9*, P-137) BCC.

Vapor Removal from Cooking Equipment. (Eighty-Ninety Ser.). 1991. pap. 20.25 (*0-685-58163-2*, 96-91) Natl Fire Prot.

Vapor Trails. Evelyn Sperber. 122p. 1990. pap. 9.95 (*0-87770-480-5*) Ye Galleon.

Vapor Trails. Louise F. Underhill. 60p. 1989. 15.00 (*0-936204-71-0*) Underhill Ent.

***Vaporetto 13: A Novel.** Robert Girardi. LC 97-8424. 1997. write for info. (*0-385-31938-X*) Delacorte.

Vapour Liquid Equilibrium Data at Normal Pressures. E. Hala & I. Wichterle. LC 67-310760. 1968. 240.00 (*0-08-012652-9*, Pub. by Pergamon Repr UK) Franklin.

Vapour-Liquid Equilibrium Data of Binary Polymer Solutions: Vapour Pressures, Henry-Constants & Segment-Molar Excess Gibbs Free Energies. C. Wohlfarth. LC 94-28929. (Physical Sciences Data Ser.: Vol. 44). 884p. 1994. 556.25 (*0-444-81717-4*) Elsevier.

***Vapourizers.** Smith. 1987. pap. text ed. write for info. (*0-582-49490-7*, Pub. by Longman UK) Longman.

***Vapours.** Larry S. Milner. 1996. mass mkt. 4.99 (*1-55197-109-7*, Pub. by Comnwlth Pub CN) Partners Pubs Grp.

Vaquero of the Brush Country. J. Frank Dobie. 1993. reprint ed. lib. bdg. 75.00 (*0-7812-5926-6*) Rprt Serv.

Vaquero of the Brush Country. James F. Dobie. (BCL1 - United States Local History Ser.). 314p. 1991. reprint ed. lib. bdg. 89.00 (*0-7812-6308-5*) Rprt Serv.

Vaqueros No Lloran. Anne McAllister. (Silhouette Deseo Ser.: No. 147). 1996. mass mkt. 3.50 (*0-373-35147-X*, 1-35147-7) Harlequin Bks.

Vaquita & Other Stories. Edith Pearlman. 208p. 1996. 22.50 (*0-8229-3962-2*) U of Pittsburgh Pr.

Varaha in Indian Art, Culture & Literature. Shanti L. Nagar. (C). 1993. 60.00 (*81-7305-030-9*, Pub. by Aryan Bks Intl II) S Asia.

Varanger Saami: Habitation & Economy AD 1200-1900. Knut Odner. (Scandinavian University Press Publication). (Illus.). 320p. 1992. 39.50 (*82-00-21285-8*) Scandnvan Univ Pr.

Vardis Fisher. Joseph M. Flora. (Twayne's United States Authors Ser.). 1965. pap. 13.95 (*0-8084-0311-7*, T76) NCUP.

Vardis Fisher: Challenge to Evasion. David Rein. 1992. lib. bdg. 79.95 (*0-8490-5475-3*) Gordon Pr.

Vardis Fisher: The Novelist As Poet. Dorys C. Grover. (Vardis Fisher Ser.). 1973. 250.00 (*0-87700-197-9*) Revisionist Pr.

Vardon on Golf. Ed. by Herbert W. Wind & Robert Macdonald. (Illus.). 185p. 1989. 28.00 (*0-940889-24-2*) Classics Golf.

Varela En Su Bicentenari: A Proposito Del Bicentenario Del Padre Felix Varela. Instituto Jacques Maritain Staff. 216p. (Orig.). (SPA.). 1991. pap. 12.00 (*0-917049-53-5*) Saeta.

Varenne Pratique: The Complete Illustrated Guide to the Techniques, Ingredients & Tools of Classics Modern Cooking. Anne Willan. 1989. 60.00 (*0-517-57383-0*, Crown) Crown Pub Group.

Varga. Tom Robotham. 1995. (*0-7858-0217-7*) Bk Sales Inc.

Varga. Tom Robotham. 1995. 14.98 (*0-8317-9088-1*) Smithmark.

Vargas Llosa: Los Cachorros. Ed. by J. Hall. (SPA.). 1997. pap. 14.95 (*1-85399-437-5*, Pub. by Brstl Class Pr UK) Focus Pub-R Pullins.

Vargas Llosa among the Postmodernists. M. Keith Booker. LC 93-34788. 256p. (C). 1994. lib. bdg. 34.95 (*0-8130-1248-1*) U Press Fla.

Vargas Regime. Robert M. Levine. LC 78-115222. (Institute of Latin American Studies). 270p. (C). 1970. text ed. 49.50 (*0-231-03370-2*) Col U Pr.

Varia Africana One. Ed. by Oric Bates & F. H. Sterns. LC 33-6339. (Harvard African Studies: Vol. 1). 1976. reprint ed. 35.00 (*0-527-01024-3*) Periodicals Srv.

Varia Africana Three. Ed. by Earnest A. Hooton & Natica I. Bates. LC 33-6339. (Harvard Sfrican Studies: Vol. 3). 1976. reprint ed. 70.00 (*0-527-01026-X*) Periodicals Srv.

Varia Africana Two. Ed. by Oric Bates. LC 33-6339. (Harvard African Studies: Vol. 2). 1976. reprint ed. 35.00 (*0-527-01025-1*) Periodicals Srv.

Varia Anthropologica. fac. ed. Philip Drucker et al. (University of California Publications in American Archaeology & Ethnology: Vol. 35: 3-5). 27p. (C). 1936. reprint ed. pap. text ed. 2.75 (*1-55567-299-X*) Coyote Press.

Varia Coleccion: Ensayos sobre Literatura Hispano-Americana. Ramona Lagos. (American University Studies: Ser. XXII, Vol. 5). 320p. (C). 1989. text ed. 44.95 (*0-8204-1059-4*) P Lang Pubng.

Varia Folkloria. Ed. by Alan Dundes. (World Anthropology Ser.). (Illus.). xii, 280p. 1978. 50.80 (*90-279-7720-8*) Mouton.

***Varia on the Indo-European Past: Papers in Memory of Marisa Gimbutas.** E. J. Barber et al. Ed. by Miriam R. Dexter & Edgar C. Polome. (Journal of Indo-European Studies Monograph Ser.: No. 19). (Orig.). (C). 1997. pap. 48.00 (*0-941694-58-5*) Inst Study Man.

Variabilitat und Sippenabgrenzung in der Senecio Nemorensis-Gruppe (Compositae) im Europaeischen Teilareal. J. Herborg. (Dissertationes Botanicae Ser.: Vol. 107). (Illus.). 262p. (GER.). 1987. pap. 64.00 (*3-443-64019-2*) Lubrecht & Cramer.

***Variabilitat des Realen Wechselkurses & Ihr Okonomischen Auswirkungen: Eine Untersuchung am Beispiel Korea.** Kyung-Sun Park. (Illus.). 174p. (GER.). 1996. 42.95 (*3-631-49454-8*) P Lang Pubng.

Variability & Motor Control. Karl M. Newell & Daniel M. Corcos. LC 92-33077. (Illus.). 520p. 1993. text ed. 65.00 (*0-87322-424-8*, BNEW0424) Human Kinetics.

Variability in Continuation School Populations: A Study of the Significance of Differences in the Proportions of Child Workers. Anthony M. Goldberger. LC 70-178803. (Columbia University. Teachers College. Contributions to Education Ser.: No. 454). reprint ed. 37.50 (*0-404-55454-7*) AMS Pr.

***Variability in Drug Therapy: Description, Estimation, & Control: A Sandoz Workshop.** Ed. by Malcolm Rowland et al. LC 85-1888. reprint ed. pap. 77.00 (*0-608-04735-X*, 2065456) Bks Demand.

Variability in Early Communicative Development. Larry Fenson et al. (Monographs of the Society for Research in Child Development, Serial No. 242: No. 242, Vol. 59; No. 5, 1994). 189p. 1994. pap. text ed. 15.00 (*0-226-24145-9*) U Ch Pr.

Variability in Grain Yields: Implications for Agricultural Research & Policy in Developing Countries. Ed. by Jock R. Anderson & Peter B. Hazell. LC 88-32079. 384p. 1989. text ed. 45.00 (*0-8018-3793-6*) Johns Hopkins.

Variability in Human Fertility. Ed. by L. Rosetta & C. G. Mascie-Taylor. (Studies in Biological Anthropology: Vol. 19). (Illus.). 240p. (C). 1996. text ed. 54.95 (*0-521-49569-5*) Cambridge U Pr.

Variability in Rangeland Water Erosion Process: Proceedings of a Symposium, "Variability in Rangeland Water Erosion Process," Sponsored by Divisions S-1, S-6, & S-7 of the Soil Science Society of America & the Society for Range Management, held in Minneapolis, Minnesota, 1-6 November 1992. Ed. by W. H. Blackburn. LC 94-26299. 1995. write for info. (*0-89118-812-6*) Soil Sci Soc Am.

Variability in Recognizing Scientific Inquiry: An Analysis of High School Science Textbooks. Richard H. Lampkin. LC 70-176971. (Columbia University. Teachers College. Contributions to Education Ser.: No. 955). reprint ed. 37.50 (*0-404-55955-7*) AMS Pr.

Variability in Response to Anti-Rheumatic Drugs. Ed. by Peter M. Brooks et al. LC 93-2005. (Agents & Actions Supplements Ser.: Vol. 44). xi, 227p. 1993. 81.50 (*0-8176-2869-X*) Birkhauser.

Variability Not Disability: Struggling Readers in a Workshop Classroom. Cathy M. Roller. LC 95-46674. (Orig.). 1996. pap. 21.95 (*0-87207-142-1*) Intl Reading.

Variability of Active Galactic Nuclei. Ed. by H. Richard Miller & Paul J. Wiita. (Illus.). 416p. (C). 1991. text ed. 69.95 (*0-521-41295-1*) Cambridge U Pr.

Variability of Active Galaxies: Proceedings of a Workshop of the Sonderforschungsbereich Held at Heidelberg, Germany, 3-5 September. Ed. by W. J. Duschl et al. (Lecture Notes in Physics Ser.: Vol. 377). xii, 312p. 1991. 50.95 (*0-387-53860-7*) Spr-Verlag.

Variability of Blazars. Ed. by Esko Valtaoja & Mauri Valtonen. (Illus.). 480p. (C). 1992. text ed. 69.95 (*0-521-41351-6*) Cambridge U Pr.

***Variability of Geophysical Log Data & the Signature for Crustal Heterogeneitis: An Example from the German Continental Deep Drilling Program (KTB)** Sabrina Leonardi. (Bonner Geowissen Schaftliche Schriften Ser.: Band 24). 1997. pap. 35.00 (*3-931251-15-2*, Pub. by Martina Galunder GW) Balogh.

Variability of Large Alluvial Rivers. Ed. by Stanley A. Schumm & Brien R. Winkley. LC 94-23128. 1994. 44.00 (*0-7844-0054-7*) Am Soc Civil Eng.

Variability Plants. E. Earle. LC 82-5397. 392p. 1982. text ed. 79.50 (*0-275-90783-X*, C0783, Praeger Pubs) Greenwood.

Variability Within & Among Natural Populations see **Evolution & the Genetics of Populations**

Variable Air Volume Manual. Herbert C. Wendes. (Illus.). 290p. 1991. 69.00 (*0-88173-083-1*, 0256) Fairmont Pr.

Variable Air Volume Manual. 2nd ed. Herbert C. Wendes. LC 94-18941. 1994. write for info. (*0-88173-196-X*) Fairmont Pr.

Variable Air Volume System. 52p. 1981. 10.00 (*0-318-17334-4*, DG/81-319) Pub Tech Inc.

Variable Air Volume Systems for Environmental Quality. Stanley J. Demster & Steve Chen. LC 95-22732. 1995. text ed. 55.00 (*0-07-011085-9*) McGraw.

Variable Annuities & Variable Life Insurance Primer. rev. ed. Ed. by Bernard G. Werbel. 80p. 1989. pap. text ed. 7.95 (*1-884803-13-X*) Werbel Pub.

***Variable Bit Rate Compressed Video.** Patrick Van der Meer. (Illus.). xv, 143p. (Orig.). 1997. pap. 47.50 (*90-407-1424-X*, Pub. by Delft U Pr NE) Coronet Bks.

Variable Capacitance Diodes: The Operation & Characterization of Varactor, Charge Storage & PIN Diodes for RF & Microwave Applications. Kenneth E. Mortenson. LC 74-189395. (Modern Frontiers in Applied Science Ser.). 142p. reprint ed. pap. 40.50 (*0-317-39628-5*, 2025053) Bks Demand.

Variable Cloud. Carmen M. Gaite. Tr. by Margaret J. Costa. 352p. 1996. 26.00 (*1-86046-061-5*) HarpC.

Variable Contracts. 1995. pap. 25.95 (*0-7931-1355-5*, 5444-0101, R & R Newkirk) Dearborn Finan.

Variable Contrast Printing Manual. Steve Anchell. LC 96-46892. (Illus.). 193p. 1996. pap. 24.95 (*0-240-80259-4*, Focal) Buttrwrth-Heinemann.

Variable Draught Semi-Submersible Floating Production System. Steve Walker. 1989. 150.00 (*90-6314-540-3*, Pub. by Lorne & MacLean Marine) St Mut.

Variable Draught Semi-Submersible Floating Production System. Steve Walker. (C). 1989. 95.00 (*0-89771-724-4*, Pub. by Lorne & MacLean Marine) St Mut.

Variable Force Technique. Peter Leighton. LC 87-63607. (Illus.). 199p. 1988. ring bd. 39.95 (*0-945817-01-0*) Origin Bks.

Variable Frequency Motor Drives. Richard K. Miller & Marcia E. Rupnow. (Survey on Technology & Markets Ser.: No. 211). 50p. 1993. pap. text ed. 200.00 (*1-55865-242-6*) Future Tech Surveys.

***Variable Frequency Motor Drives, Report 340.** Richard K. Miller & Christy H. Gunter. (Market Research Survey Ser.: No. 340). 50p. 1997. pap. 200.00 (*1-55865-359-7*) Future Tech Surveys.

Variable Geometry--A Recipe for Europe: A Monitoring European Integration Report. Alan Dashwood et al. 190p. (C). 1996. pap. 14.95 (*1-898128-22-7*) Brookings.

Variable Harvest: Essays & Reviews of Film & Literature. Jon Tuska. LC 89-42760. (Illus.). 383p. 1990. lib. bdg. 43.50 (*0-89950-454-X*) McFarland & Co.

***Variable Pumping Rate Solutions.** Michael Kasenow & Paul Pare. 50p. 1996. reprint ed. pap. 25.00 (*1-887201-04-1*) WRP.

Variable Speed Drive Fundamentals. Clarence A. Phipps. LC 93-50689. 1994. 75.00 (*0-88173-191-9*) Fairmont Pr.

***Variable Speed Drive Fundamentals.** 2nd ed. Clarence A. Phipps. LC 96-52187. 1997. write for info. (*0-88173-258-3*) Fairmont Pr.

***Variable Speed Drive Fundamentals.** 2nd ed. Clarence A. Phipps. 1997. 79.00 (*0-13-636390-3*) P-H.

Variable Speed Drives: Principles & Applications for Energy Cost Savings. 2nd rev. ed. David W. Spitzer. LC 87-3585. 204p. 1991. 56.00 (*1-55617-242-7*, A242-7) ISA.

Variable Star Observing. David H. Levy. 180p. 1989. text ed. 28.95 (*0-521-32113-1*) Cambridge U Pr.

Variable Star Quilts & How to Make Them. Nancy Martin & Marsha R. McCloskey. LC 94-41222. (Illus.). 64p. 1995. pap. text ed. 7.95 (*0-486-28595-2*) Dover.

Variable Star Research: An International Perspective: International Cooperation & Coordination of Variable Star Research. Ed. by John R. Percy et al. (Illus.). 352p. (C). 1991. text ed. 69.95 (*0-521-40469-X*) Cambridge U Pr.

Variable Stars & Galaxies. Ed. by B. Warner. (ASP Conference Series Proceedings: Vol. 29). 375p. 1992. 28.00 (*0-937707-48-1*) Astron Soc Pacific.

Variable Stars & Stellar Evolution: Proceedings of the I. A.U. Symposium, No. 67, Moscow, U. S. S. R., July 29-August 4, 1974. International Astronomical Union Staff. Ed. by L. Plaut. LC 75-8740. 619p. 1975. pap. text ed. 175.00 (*90-277-0579-8*); lib. bdg. 263.50 (*90-277-0578-X*) Kluwer Ac.

Variable Structure Control for Robotics & Aerospace Applications. Ed. by K. David Young. LC 92-37682. (Studies in Automation & Control: Vol. 10). 316p. 1993. 160.00 (*0-444-87446-1*) Elsevier.

Variable Sweep Wings: From Theory to Practice, a Symposium of the Langley Research Center, Hampton, Virginia, March 1981. Langley Research Center Staff. 1981. pap. 23.95 (*0-89126-103-6*) MA-AH Pub.

Variable Syndrome: A Science Fiction Story. Don McGregor. 144p. 1981. pap. 10.00 (*0-934882-05-3*) Fictioneer Bks.

Variable Valve Actuation & Control: Nine Papers. 100p. 1993. 29.00 (*1-56091-341-X*, SP-956) Soc Auto Engineers.

Variable Valve Actuation & Power Boost: 1996 International Congress & Exposition. (Special Publications). 183p. 1996. pap. 49.00 (*1-56091-801-2*, SP-1171) Soc Auto Engineers.

Variables & Patterns: Introducing Algebra. Glenda Lappan et al. Ed. by Catherine Anderson et al. (Connected Mathematics Ser.). (Illus.). 68p. (Orig.). (J). (gr. 7). 1996. teacher ed., pap. 16.50 (*0-614-17412-0*) Seymour Pubns.

Variables & Patterns: Introducing Algebra. Glenda Lappan et al. Ed. by Catherine Anderson et al. (Connected Mathematics Ser.). (Illus.). 68p. (Orig.). (J). (gr. 7). 1996. student ed., wbk. ed. 5.95 (*1-57232-162-8*, 21457) Seymour Pubns.

Variables & Patterns: Introducing Algebra. Glenda Lappan et al. Ed. by Catherine Anderson et al. (Connected Mathematics Ser.). (Illus.). 68p. (Orig.). (J). (gr. 7). 1996. student ed., wbk. ed. 5.95 (*1-57232-162-8*, 21457) Seymour Pubns.

***Variables & Patterns: Introducing Algebra.** Glenda Lappan et al. Ed. by Catherine Anderson et al. (Connected Mathematics Ser.). (Illus.). 130p. (Orig.). 1996. teacher ed. 16.50 (*1-57232-163-6*, 21458) Seymour Pubns.

***Variables & Patterns: Introducing Algebra.** rev. ed. Glenda Lappan et al. Ed. by Catherine Anderson et al. (Connected Mathematics Ser.). (Illus.). 72p. (J). (gr. 7). 1997. student ed., pap. text ed. 5.95 (*1-57232-645-X*, 45840) Seymour Pubns.

***Variables & Patterns: Introducing Algebra.** rev. ed. Glenda Lappan et al. Ed. by Catherine Anderson et al. (Connected Mathematics Ser.). (Illus.). 152p. (J). (gr. 7). 1997. teacher ed., pap. text ed. 16.50 (*1-57232-646-8*, 45841) Seymour Pubns.

Variables of Composition: Process & Product in a Business Setting. Ed. by Glenn J. Broadhead & Richard C. Freed. LC 85-14239. (Studies in Writing & Rhetoric). 184p. (Orig.). (C). 1986. pap. text ed. 12.95 (*0-8093-1262-X*) S Ill U Pr.

Variables, Terms & Expressions Bk. 2. Julie King & Peter Rasmussen. (J). 1990. pap. text ed. 2.10 (*1-55953-002-2*) Key Curr Pr.

Variaciones en Torno a Dios, El Tiempo, la Muerte y Otros Temas. Octavio R. Costa. LC 87-81633. 463p. (Orig.). (SPA.). 1987. pap. 20.00 (*0-89729-450-5*) Ediciones.

Variaciones Sobre una Tempestad: Variations on a Storm. Lucha Corpi. Tr. by Catherine Rodriguez-Nieto. 104p. (Orig.). (ENG & SPA.). 1990. pap. 8.95 (*0-943219-05-1*) Third Woman.

***Variance & Covariance Components.** R. Rao. 350p. 1997. text ed. 64.50 (*0-412-72860-5*, Chap & Hall NY) Chapman & Hall.

Variance Components. Shayle R. Searle et al. LC 91-18067. (Probability & Mathematical Statistics: Applied Probability & Statistics Section Ser.: No. 1346). 528p. 1992. text ed. 95.95 (*0-471-62162-5*) Wiley.

Variant Family Forms. Ed. by Catherine S. Chilman et al. LC 89-111125. (Families in Trouble Ser.: Vol. 5). 336p. 1988. reprint ed. pap. 95.80 (*0-608-01713-2*, 2062368) Bks Demand.

Variant Lifestyles & Relationships. Bram P. Buunk & Barry Van Driel. (Family Studies Text Ser.: Vol. 11). 160p. (C). 1989. text ed. 39.95 (*0-8039-3059-3*); pap. text ed. 17.95 (*0-8039-3060-7*) Sage.

Variant Lifestyles & Relationships. Bram Buunk & Barry Van Driel. LC 89-4309. (Family Studies Text Ser.: No. 11). 160p. 1989. reprint ed. pap. 45.60 (*0-7837-9897-0*, 2060623) Bks Demand.

Variant Readings of the Quran: A Critical Study of Their Historical & Linguistic Origins. Ahmad A. Allah. (Academic Dissertations Ser.: Vol. 4). 1995. write for info. (*1-56564-230-9*); pap. write for info. (*1-56564-231-7*) IIIT VA.

Variant Sexuality: Research & Theory. Ed. by Glenn D. Wilson. LC 86-21102. 272p. 1987. text ed. 45.00 (*0-8018-3464-3*) Johns Hopkins.

UV

An Asterisk (*) at the beginning of an entry indicates that the title is appearing in BIP for the first time.

Variant Versions of Targumic Traditions Within Codex Neofiti 1. Shirley Lund & Julia A. Foster. LC 77-5389. (Society of Biblical Literature. Aramaic Studies: No. 2). 186p. reprint ed. pap. 53.10 (*0-7837-5457-4*, 2045222) Bks Demand.

Variants in the First Quarto of King Lear. Walter Greg. LC 68-1839. (Studies in Shakespeare: No. 24). 1969. reprint ed. lib. bdg. 75.00 (*0-8383-0559-8*) M S G Haskell Hse.

Variation Across Speech & Writing. Douglas Biber. (Illus.). 312p. (C). 1992. pap. text ed. 27.95 (*0-521-42556-5*) Cambridge U Pr.

Variation & Adaptive Expression of Antibodies. George P. Smith. LC 72-95186. 192p. 1973. 25.00 (*0-674-93205-6*) HUP.

Variation & Change in Alabama English: A Sociolinguistic Study of the White Community. Crawford Feagin. LC 79-15701. 419p. reprint ed. pap. 119.50 (*0-7837-6320-4*, 2046035) Bks Demand.

Variation & Change in Geographically Isolated Communities: Appalachian English & Ozark English. Donna Christian et al. (Publications of the American Dialect Society: No. 74). 176p. 1989. pap. text ed. 22.00 (*0-8173-0419-3*) U of Ala Pr.

Variation & Change in Language: Essays by William Bright. William Bright. Ed. by Anwar S. Dil. LC 76-23370. (Language Science & National Development Ser.). 304p. 1976. 45.00 (*0-8047-0926-2*) Stanford U Pr.

Variation & Convergence: Studies in Social Dialectology. Ed. by Peter Auer & Aldo Di Luzio. (Sociolinguistics & Language Contact Ser.: Vol. 4). 320p. (C). 1988. lib. bdg. 142.35 (*3-11-011045-8*) De Gruyter.

Variation & Error: A Sociolinguistic Approach to Language Acquisition in Samoa. Ed. by Ochs & Dan I. Slobin. (Crosslinguistic Study of Language Acquisition Ser.: Vol. 1). 1986. pap. 14.95 (*0-89859-847-8*) L Erlbaum Assocs.

Variation & Evolution in Plants. George L. Stebbins. LC 50-9426. (Columbia Biological Ser.: No. 16). (Illus.). 663p. reprint ed. pap. 180.00 (*0-685-20794-3*, 2030108) Bks Demand.

Variation & Evolution of the Nearctic Harebells: Campanula Subsect. Heterophylla. St. G. Shetler. (Phanerogamarum Monographiae: No. XI). (Illus.). 516p. 1982. lib. bdg. 160.00 (*3-7682-1241-6*) Lubrecht & Cramer.

Variation & Linguistic Theory. Charles J. Bailey. LC 73-84648. 170p. reprint ed. pap. 48.50 (*0-8357-3350-5*, 2039583) Bks Demand.

Variation II Vol. 1: Seven Los Angeles Painters, Vol. II. Contrib. by Roy Dowell et al. LC 83-80463. (Illus.). 51p. (Orig.). 1983. pap. 10.00 (*0-911291-08-3*) Fellows Cont Art.

Variation in an English Dialect: A Sociolinguistic Study. Jenny Cheshire. LC 82-4189. (Cambridge Studies in Linguistics: No. 37). 152p. reprint ed. pap. 43.40 (*0-318-34770-9*, 2031630) Bks Demand.

Variation in Asbestos Litigation, Compensation & Expenses. James S. Kakalik et al. LC 84-9808. 91p. 1984. pap. 7.50 (*0-8330-0571-5*, R-3132-ICJ) Rand Corp.

Variation in Central Javanese Gamelan Music: Dynamics of a Steady State. R. Anderson Sutton. (Special Reports: No. 28). 295p. 1993. pap. 25.00 (*1-877979-78-3*) SE Asia.

Variation in German: A Critical Approach to German Sociolinguistics. Stephen Barbour & Patrick Stevenson. (Illus.). 236p. (C). 1990. text ed. 65.00 (*0-521-35397-1*); pap. text ed. 22.95 (*0-521-35704-7*) Cambridge U Pr.

Variation in Grassland Vegetation on the Central Plateu of Shews, Ethiopis, in Relation to Edaphic Factors & Grazing Conditions. W. Zerihun. (Illus.). 114p. 1985. pap. text ed. 30.00 (*3-7682-1439-7*) Lubrecht & Cramer.

Variation in Interlanguage. Elaine E. Tarone. 160p. (Orig.). 1988. pap. text ed. 15.95 (*0-7131-6598-7*, Pub. by E Arnold UK) Routledge Chapman & Hall.

Variation in Interlanguage Morphology. Richard Young. LC 90-42246. (Theoretical Studies in Second Language Acquisition: Vol. 1). 284p. (C). 1990. text ed. 44.95 (*0-8204-1381-X*) P Lang Pubng.

Variation in Language: Code Switching in Czech As a Challenge for Sociolinguistics. Ed. by Petr Sgall et al. LC 92-3512. (Linguistic & Literary Studies in Eastern Europe: No. 39). xii, 370p. 1992. 100.00 (*1-55619-264-9*) Benjamins North Am.

Variation in Mississippian Settlement Patterns: The Larson Settlement System in the Central Illinois River Valley. Alan D. Harn. LC 94-13889. (Reports of Investigations: No. 50). 1994. write for info. (*0-89792-145-3*) Ill St Museum.

Variation in Second Language Acquisition: Discourse & Pragmatics, Vol. 1. Ed. by Susan M. Gass et al. (Multilingual Matters Ser.: No. 49). 200p. 1989. 99.00 (*1-85359-026-6*, Pub. by Multilingual Matters UK); pap. 39.95 (*1-85359-025-8*, Pub. by Multilingual Matters UK) Taylor & Francis.

Variation in Second Language Aquisition: Psycholinguistic Issues, Vol. 2. Ed. by Susan M. Gass et al. (Multilingual Matters Ser.: No. 50). 200p. 1989. 99.00 (*1-85359-028-2*, Pub. by Multilingual Matters UK); pap. 39.95 (*1-85359-027-4*, Pub. by Multilingual Matters UK) Taylor & Francis.

Variation in the Data: Can Linguistics Ever Become a Science? Charles-James N. Bailey. LC 92-90762. (Linguistics Ser.: No. 1). (Illus.). (Orig.). (C). 1993. pap. write for info. (*1-881309-03-7*) Orchid Land.

Variation in the Form & Use of Language: A Sociolinguistics Reader. fac. ed. Ed. by Ralph W. Fasold. LC 83-20620. (Illus.). 424p. 1983. reprint ed. pap. 120.90 (*0-7837-7778-7*, 2047533) Bks Demand.

Variation in the Human Genome. CIBA Foundation Staff & Kenneth M. Weiss. LC 95-54159. (Ciba Foundation Symposium Ser.: Vol. 197). 300p. 1996. 84.95 (*0-471-96152-3*) Wiley.

Variation in Writing: Functional & Linguistic-Cultural Differences, Vol. 1. Ed. by Marcia F. Whiteman & Joseph F. Dominic. (Writing the Nature, Development, & Teaching of Written Communication Ser.). 224p. 1982. 49.95 (*0-89859-101-5*) L Erlbaum Assocs.

Variation of Basidiospores in the Hymenomycetes & Its Significance to Their Taxonomy. Erast Parmasto & Ilmi Parmesto. (Bibliotheca Mycologica Ser.: Vol. 115). (Illus.). 168p. 1987. pap. 56.00 (*3-443-59016-0*) Lubrecht & Cramer.

Variation of Input-Output Coefficients for Philadelphia Manufacturing. Gerald J. Karaska. (Discussion Paper Ser.: No. 13). 1967. pap. 10.00 (*1-55869-132-4*) Regional Sci Res Inst.

Variation on a Theme. Barbara Delinsky. 304p. 1994. mass mkt. 4.99 (*0-06-104234-X*, Harp PBks) HarpC.

Variation on a Theme. large type ed. Barbara Delinsky. LC 96-11050. 1996. 24.95 (*1-56895-316-X*) Wheeler Pub.

Variation on a Theme: Bilingualism, a Case Study. Aleya Rouchdy. LC 76-47344. (Language Science Monographs: Vol. 17). 1977. pap. text ed. 12.00 (*0-87750-209-9*) Res Inst Inner Asian Studies.

Variation Phonetique dans le Parler Acadien du Nordest du Nouveau Brunswick: Etude Socio-Linguistique. Karin Flikeid. (American University Studies: Linguistics: Ser. XIII, Vol. 1). 496p. (Orig.). (FRE.). 1984. pap. text ed. 39.00 (*0-8204-0066-1*) P Lang Pubng.

Variation, Senescence & Neoplasia in Cultured Somatic Cells. Commonwealth Fund Staff & John W. Littlefield. (Illus.). 147p. 1975. 20.00 (*0-674-93208-0*) HUP.

Variation, Systematics, & Zoogeography of Eleutherodactylus Guentheri & Closely Related Species: Amphibia: Anura: Leptodactylidae. LC 84-600184. (Smithsonian Contributions to Zoology Ser.: No. 402). 46p. reprint ed. pap. 25.00 (*0-317-26747-7*, 2024353) Bks Demand.

Variation Theory & Second Language Acquisition. fac. ed. Hugh D. Adamson. LC 87-34198. (Illus.). 100p. 1988. reprint ed. pap. 28.50 (*0-7837-7799-X*, 2047555) Bks Demand.

Variation, Transformation & Meaning: Studies on Indonesian Literatures in Honour of A. Teeuw. Ed. by J. J. Ras & S. O. Robson. (KILTV Verhandelingen Ser.: No. 144). 236p. (Orig.). 1992. pap. 26.50 (*90-6718-027-0*, Pub. by KITLV Pr NE) Cellar.

Variation Within the Leptodactylus Podicipinus-Wagneri Complex of Frogs (Amphibia, Leptodactylidae) W. Ronald Heyer. LC 93-6156. (Smithsonian Contributions to Zoology Ser.: No. 546). 128p. reprint ed. pap. 36.50 (*0-7837-6455-3*, 2046455) Bks Demand.

Variational Analysis: Critical Extremals & Sturmian Extensions. Marston Morse. LC 72-8368. (Pure & Applied Mathematics Ser.). 272p. reprint ed. pap. 77.60 (*0-8357-9998-0*, 2019523) Bks Demand.

Variational & Finite Element Methods. A. I. Beltzer. (Illus.). 240p. 1990. 87.95 (*0-387-51598-4*) Spr-Verlag.

Variational & Free Boundary Problems. Ed. by Avner Friedman & Joel Spruck. LC 93-5143. (IMA Volumes in Mathematics & Its Applications Ser.: Vol. 53). 1993. 63. 95 (*0-387-94111-8*) Spr-Verlag.

Variational & Hamiltonian Control Systems. P. E. Crouch & A. J. Van Der Schaft. (Lecture Notes in Control & Information Sciences Ser.: Vol. 101). vi, 121p. 1987. 31. 95 (*0-387-18372-8*) Spr-Verlag.

Variational & Local Methods in the Study of Hamiltonian Systems: Proceedings of the Workshop: International Centre for Theoretical Physics, Trieste, Italy, 24-28 October, 1995. Ed. by Antonio Ambrosetti & G. F. Dell'Antonio. LC 95-37192. 224p. 1995. write for info. (*981-02-2490-7*) World Scientific Pub.

Variational & Quasivariational Inequalities: Applications to Free Boundary Problems. Claudio Baiocchi & Antonio Capelo. LC 83-6731. 462p. reprint ed. pap. 131.70 (*0-7837-4020-4*, 2043850) Bks Demand.

Variational Calculations in Quantum Field Theory. Ed. by L. Polley & D. E. Pottinger. 316p. (C). 1988. pap. 51.00 (*9971-5-0501-0*); text ed. 100.00 (*9971-5-0500-2*) World Scientific Pub.

Variational Calculus: Die Streitschriften von Jacob & Johann Bernoulli. Ed. by H. H. Goldstine. 600p. 1992. 222.00 (*0-8176-2348-5*) Birkhauser.

Variational Calculus & Optimal Control: Optimization with Elementary Convexity. 2nd ed. John L. Troutman. Ed. by S. Axler et al. LC 95-12918. (Undergraduate Texts in Mathematics Ser.). (Illus.). 480p. (C). 1995. 54.95 (*0-387-94511-3*) Spr-Verlag.

Variational Calculus with Elementary Convexity. John L. Troutman. (Undergraduate Texts in Mathematics Ser.). (Illus.). 364p. 1983. 42.00 (*0-387-90771-8*) Spr-Verlag.

Variational Inequalities & Complementarity Problems: Theory & Applications. Ed. by Richard W. Cottle et al. LC 79-40108. 426p. reprint ed. pap. 121.50 (*0-685-20460-X*, 2029856) Bks Demand.

Variational Inequalities & Flow in Porous Media. M. Chipot. (Applied Mathematical Sciences Ser.: Vol. 52). (Illus.). 120p. 1984. 49.95 (*0-387-96002-3*) Spr-Verlag.

Variational Inequalities & Network Equilibrium Problems: Proceedings of the International School of Mathematics "G Stampacchia" 19th Course Held in Erice, Italy, June 19-25, 1994. Ed. by F. Giannessi & A. Maugeri. LC 95-6220. 305p. 1995. 89.50 (*0-306-45007-0*, Plenum Pr) Plenum.

Variational Methods. Henri Berestycki. (Progress in Nonlinear Differential Equations & Their Applications Ser.). 1990. 96.50 (*0-8176-3452-5*) Birkhauser.

Variational Methods: Applications to Nonlinear Partial Differential Equations & Hamiltonian Systems. Michael Struwe. (Illus.). xiv, 244p. 1990. 39.50 (*0-387-52022-8*) Spr-Verlag.

Variational Methods: Applications to Nonlinear Partial Differential Equations & Hamiltonian Systems. 2nd expanded rev. ed. Michael Struwe. LC 96-17681. (Series of Modern Surveys in Mathematics: Vol. 34). (Illus.). 288p. 1996. 109.00 (*3-540-58859-0*) Spr-Verlag.

Variational Methods & Complementary Formulations in Dynamics. B. Tabarrok & F. P. Rimrott. LC 94-20075. (Solid Mechanics & Its Applications Ser.: Vol. 6). 380p. (C). 1994. lib. bdg. 183.00 (*0-7923-2923-6*) Kluwer Ac.

Variational Methods for Boundary Value Problems (etc.) M. A. Lavrentev. 1990. pap. 4.95 (*0-486-66170-9*) Dover.

***Variational Methods for Discontinuous Structures: Applications to Image Segmentation, Continuum Mechanics, Homogenization : Villa Olmo, Como, 8-10 September 1994.** Raul Serapioni & Franco Tomarelli. LC 96-35953. (Progress in Nonlinear Differential Equations & Their Applications Ser.). 1996. 89.50 (*0-8176-5273-6*) Birkhauser.

***Variational Methods for Discontinuous Structures: Applications to Image Segmentation, Continuum Mechanics, Homogenization : Villa Olmo, Como, 8-10 September 1994, Vol. 25.** Raul Serapion. LC 96-35953. (Progress in Nonlinear Differential Equations & Their Applications Ser.). 208p. 1996. 89.50 (*3-7643-5273-6*) Birkhauser.

Variational Methods for Eigenvalue Approximation. Hans F. Weinberger. (CBMS-NSF Regional Conference Ser.: No. 15). v, 160p. (Orig.). 1974. pap. text ed. 28.75 (*0-89871-012-X*) Soc Indus-Appl Math.

Variational Methods for Eigenvalue Problems: An Introduction to the Methods of Rayleigh, Ritz, Weinstein & Aronszajn. unabridged ed. S. H. Gould. LC 95-8316. 192p. 1995. reprint ed. pap. text ed. 7.95 (*0-486-68712-0*) Dover.

Variational Methods for Free Surface Interfaces. Ed. by P. Concus & R. Finn. (Illus.). x, 204p. 1986. 65.95 (*0-387-96396-0*) Spr-Verlag.

***Variational Methods for Potential Operator Equations: With Applications to Nonlinear Elliptic Equations.** Jan Chabrowski. LC 97-8060. (De Gruyter Studies in Mathematics). 1997. write for info. (*3-11-015269-X*) De Gruyter.

Variational Methods in Atmospheric Sciences. F. X. Le Dimet & I. M. Navon. 450p. 1994. text ed. 68.00 (*981-02-0890-1*) World Scientific Pub.

Variational Methods in Elasticity & Plasticity. 3rd ed. K. Washizu. (Illus.). 540p. 1982. 284.00 (*0-08-026723-8*, Pub. by Pergamon Repr UK) Franklin.

Variational Methods in Engineering. Ed. by C. A. Brebbia. 500p. 1985. 99.00 (*0-931215-50-1*) Computational Mech MA.

Variational Methods in Engineering. Ed. by Carlos A. Brebbia. 750p. 1985. 190.95 (*0-387-15496-5*) Spr-Verlag.

***Variational Methods in Lorentzian Geometry.** Antonio Maisello. 1994. pap. 50.95 (*0-582-23799-8*, Pub. by Longman UK) Longman.

Variational Methods in Mathematical Physics: A Unified Approach. P. Blanchard & E. Bruning. Ed. by W. Beiglbock et al. (Texts & Monographs in Physics). (Illus.). 300p. 1992. 97.95 (*0-387-16190-2*) Spr-Verlag.

Variational Methods in Mathematics, Science & Engineering. Karel Rektorys. Tr. by Michael Basch from CZE. 572p. 1980. lib. bdg. 101.50 (*90-277-1060-0*) Kluwer Ac.

Variational Methods in Mechanics. Toshio Mura et al. (Illus.). 336p. (C). 1992. text ed. 42.00 (*0-19-506830-0*, 230) OUP.

Variational Methods in Nonconservative Phenomena. Bozidar Vujanovic & Stanley E. Jonas. 371p. 1989. text ed. 108.00 (*0-12-728450-8*) Acad Pr.

Variational Methods in Nonlinear Analysis. Ed. by Antonio Ambrosetti & K. C. Chang. LC 93-45010. 292p. 1995. text ed. 105.00 (*2-88124-937-X*) Gordon & Breach.

Variational Models for Image Segmentation. Jean-Michel Morel & Sergio Solimini. LC 94-36639. (Progress in Nonlinear Differential Equations & Their Applications Ser.: 14). xvi, 245p. 1994. 65.00 (*0-8176-3720-6*) Birkhauser.

Variational Principles & Free-Boundary Problems. Avner Friedman. LC 87-29657. 720p. (C). 1988. reprint ed. lib. bdg. 79.50 (*0-89464-263-4*) Krieger.

Variational Principles. Benjamin L. Moiseiwitsch. LC 66-17233. (Interscience Monographs & Texts in Physics & Astronomy: Vol. 20). 320p. reprint ed. pap. 91.20 (*0-317-11049-7*, 2016148) Bks Demand.

***Variational Principles & the Numerical Solution of Scattering Problems.** Adapted by Sadhan K. Adhikari. 200p. 1998. 84.95 (*0-471-18193-5*, Wiley-Interscience) Wiley.

Variational Principles for Nonpotential Operators. V. Filippov. LC 89-6904. (Translations of Mathematical Monographs: Vol. 77). 239p. 1989. 114.00 (*0-8218-4529-2*, MMONO/77) Am Math.

Variational Principles in Dynamics & Quantum Theory. 3rd ed. Wolfgang Yourgrau & Stanley Mandelstam. LC 78-73521. 1979. reprint ed. pap. text ed. 6.95 (*0-486-63773-5*) Dover.

Variational Principles of Continuum Mechanics with Applications to Structural & Mechanical Engineering: Volume 1: Critical Points Theory. Vadim Komkov. 1986. lib. bdg. 145.00 (*90-277-2157-2*) Kluwer Ac.

Variational Principles of Continuum Mechanics with Engineering Applications: Vol. 2: Introduction to Optimal Design Theory. Vadim Komkov. (C). 1987. lib. bdg. 129.50 (*90-277-2639-6*) Kluwer Ac.

Variational Principles of Dynamics. Boris A. Kuperschmidt. (Advanced Series in Mathematical Physics: Vol. 13). 444p. 1992. text ed. 53.00 (*981-02-0274-1*) World Scientific Pub.

Variational Principles of Mechanics. 2nd ed. Cornelius Lanczos. (Mathematical Expositions Ser.: No. 4). 393p. reprint ed. pap. 112.10 (*0-7837-0497-6*, 2040821) Bks Demand.

Variational Principles of Mechanics. Cornelius Lanczos. 418p. 1986. reprint ed. pap. text ed. 11.95 (*0-486-65067-7*) Dover.

Variational Principles of the Theory of Elasticity with Applications. Haichang Hu. 493p. 1984. text ed. 266.00 (*0-677-31330-6*) Gordon & Breach.

Variational Problems in Topology: The Geometry of Length, Area & Volume. A. T. Fomenko. 226p. 1990. text ed. 229.00 (*2-88124-740-7*) Gordon & Breach.

Variational Theories for Liquid Crystals. Epifanio G. Virga. LC 94-70268. 375p. (gr. 13). 1994. text ed. 88.95 (*0-412-39880-X*) Chapman & Hall.

Variations. Joyce A. Rebaric. (Illus.). 250p. 1998. 20.00 (*0-9635084-4-X*) Nightshadow Prods.

Variations. James G. Huneker. (BCL1-PS American Literature Ser.). 279p. 1992. reprint ed. lib. bdg. 79.00 (*0-7812-6750-1*) Rprt Serv.

Variations: Collected Short Stories. large type ed. Claire Lorrimer. (General Ser.). 368p. 1993. 25.99 (*0-7089-2880-3*) Ulverscroft.

Variations: Five Los Angeles Painters. Susan C. Larsen. LC 80-69334. (Illus.). 51p. (Orig.). 1980. pap. write for info. (*0-911291-05-9*) Fellows Cont Art.

Variations: Knitting Patterns for More Than Fifty Seasonal Designs. Patricia Roberts. 1992. 29.95 (*0-8021-1490-3*, Grove) Grove-Atltic.

Variations: Piano Quartet Violin Viola Cello. K. Huska. 40p. 1992. pap. 40.00 (*0-7935-1739-7*) H Leonard.

Variations: Reading Skills-Oral Communication for Beginning Students of ESL. Patricia Duffy. (Illus.). 224p. (C). 1986. pap. text ed. 16.50 (*0-13-940503-8*) P-H.

Variations: The Systematic Design of Supports. N. John Habraken et al. 1976. pap. 21.00 (*0-262-58032-2*) MIT Pr.

Variations Clarinet in a Violin & Piano: Score & Parts. J. Harbison. 48p. 1987. pap. 24.95 (*0-7935-3511-5*, 50507640) H Leonard.

Variations for Orchestra: Corrected Edition 1967 Study Score. E. Carter. 152p. 1986. per. 60.00 (*0-7935-3121-7*) H Leonard.

Variations for Piano. Andrew Lloyd Webber. 64p. 1988. pap. 9.95 (*0-7935-1939-X*, 00361447) H Leonard.

Variations for Pianoforte. Peter Ballinger. (Contemporary Keyboard Ser.: No. 3). 7p. 1990. pap. text ed. 6.00 (*1-56571-016-9*) PRB Prods.

Variations for the Piano. Ed. by Joel Sachs. LC 89-753585. (J. N. Hummel: The Complete Works for Piano Ser.: Vol. 2). 240p. 1989. text ed. 45.00 (*0-8240-3787-1*) Garland.

Variations III Vol. 1: Emerging Artist in Southern California, Vol. III. Contrib. by Alvaro Asturias et al. LC 87-80526. (Illus.). 79p. (Orig.). 1987. pap. 15.00 (*0-911291-13-X*) Fellows Cont Art.

Variations in Autotrophic Life. Ed. by Jessup M. Shively & Larry L. Barton. 346p. 1991. text ed. 99.00 (*0-12-640360-0*) Acad Pr.

Variations in Black & White Perceptions of the Social Environment. Ed. by Harry C. Triandis. LC 75-29056. 212p. 1976. text ed. 27.50 (*0-252-00515-5*) U of Ill Pr.

Variations in Changing Time. Anthony Hars. LC 96-75311. (Illus.). 220p. (Orig.). 1996. 24.95 (*1-884540-18-X*); pap. 14.95 (*1-884540-19-8*) Haleys.

***Variations in Chenille: Nannette Holmberg's Techniques for Creating Faux Chenille.** Nannette Holmberg. Ed. by Laura Reinstatler. (Illus.). 88p. (Orig.). 1997. pap. 21.95 (*1-56477-206-3*, B318) That Patchwork.

Variations in Earth Rotation. Ed. by D. D. McCarthy & W. E. Carter. (Geophysical Monograph Ser.: Vol. 59/ IUGG 9). 205p. 1990. write for info. (*0-87590-459-9*) Am Geophysical.

Variations in Human Physiology. Ed. by R. M. Case. LC 84-11301. (Integrative Studies in Human Physiology). 241p. 1988. text ed. 29.00 (*0-7190-1086-1*, Pub. by Manchester Univ Pr UK) St Martin.

Variations in Susceptibility to Inhaled Pollutants: Identification, Mechanisms, & Policy Implications. Ed. by Joseph D. Brain et al. LC 87-45484. (Environmental Toxicology Ser.). 528p. 1988. text ed. 85.00 (*0-8018-3503-8*) Johns Hopkins.

Variations in Tectonic Styles in Canada. Ed. by Raymond A. Price & R. J. Douglas. LC 73-331222. (Geological Association of Canada. Special Paper Ser.: No. 11). 698p. reprint ed. pap. 180.00 (*0-685-17104-3*, 2027842) Bks Demand.

Variations in the Global Water Budget. F. A. Street-Perrot et al. 1983. lib. bdg. 182.50 (*90-277-1364-2*) Kluwer Ac.

Variations in the Use of Cesarean Sections: Literature Synthesis. Joanna Z. Heilbrunn & Rolla E. Park. LC 95-35760. 80p. 1995. pap. text ed. 9.00 (*0-8330-2306-3*, MR-330-AHCPR) Rand Corp.

Variations of Falun: A Comparative Anthology for the Advanced German Reader. Ed. by Doris S. Guilloton & Agnes D. Langdon. LC 91-16518. 136p. (Orig.). (C). 1992. text ed. 28.95 (*0-8204-1502-2*) P Lang Pubng.

Variations of the Smooth Bore H & R Handy-Gun: A Pocket Guide to Their Identification. Eric M. Larson. LC 93-91518. (Illus.). 64p. (Orig.). 1993. pap. 10.00 (*0-9636465-0-8*) E M Larson.

Variations on a Theme: Diversity & the Psychology of Women. Ed. by Joan C. Chrisler & Alyce H. Hemstreet. LC 94-26207. (SUNY Series, the Psychology of Women). 238p. (C). 1995. text ed. 59.50 (*0-7914-2435-9*); pap. text ed. 19.95 (*0-7914-2436-7*) State U NY Pr.

U V

An Asterisk (*) at the beginning of an entry indicates that the title is appearing in BIP for the first time.

Variations on a Theme: Figurative Painting. Georgia Coopersmith. (Illus.). 32p. 1985. pap. 8.00 (*0-942746-08-2*) SUNYP R Gibson.
Variations on a Theme: Red House. 1993. pap. 19.95 incl. audio (*0-7935-1718-4*, 00699359) H Leonard.
Variations on a Theme: Red House Jimi Hendrix Reference Library. 1993. pap. 24.95 incl. audio compact disk (*0-7935-1719-2*, 00699358) H Leonard.
Variations on a Theme: World's Fairs of the Eighties--Knoxville, New Orleans, Tsukuba, Vancouver. Photos by Algimantas Kezys. LC 87-82223. (Illus.). 96p. (Orig.). 1987. pap. 15.00 (*0-9617756-0-2*) Galerija.
Variations on a Theme by Haydn for the Piano. J. Brahms. 20p. 1992. pap. 5.95 (*0-7935-2058-4*) H Leonard.
Variations on a Theme by Kepler. V. Guillemin & S. Sternberg. (Colloquium Publications: Vol. 42). 88p. 1990. 19.00 (*0-8218-1042-1*, COLL/42) Am Math.
Variations on a Theme of Euler: Quadratic Forms, Elliptic Curves & Hopf Maps. T. Ono. (University Series in Mathematics). (Illus.). 344p. (C). 1994. 79.50 (*0-306-44789-4*, Plenum Pr) Plenum.
Variations on a Theme Park: Scenes from the New American City. Ed. by Michael Sorkin. (Illus.). 252p. 1992. pap. 15.00 (*0-374-52314-2*, Noonday) FS&G.
Variations on All the Perfect Things. David Gregor. 84p. 1997. 25.00 (*0-9631094-1-3*); pap. 10.00 (*0-9631094-2-1*) Alki Pr.
Variations on Humankind: An Introduction to World Literature. Johnny E. Tolliver. 1136p. (C). 1995. per., pap. text ed. 56.91 (*0-8403-6938-7*) Kendall-Hunt.
Variations on Humankind Valuepack. Ruth Perry & Johnny E. Tolliver. 1168p. (C). 1995. 56.91 (*0-8403-9288-5*) Kendall-Hunt.
Variations on Night & Day. Abdelrahman Munif. 1994. pap. 12.00 (*0-679-75551-9*, Vin) Random.
Variations on Teaching & Supervising Group Therapy. Intro. by Karen G. Lewis. LC 89-19970. (Journal of Independent Social Work: Vol. 3, No. 4). (Illus.). 151p. 1989. text ed. 29.95 (*0-86656-921-9*) Haworth Pr.
Variations on the Hermit. Hilary Ayer. 64p. 1973. pap. 30.00 (*0-87924-025-3*) Membrane Pr.
Variations on the Ordinary: A Woman's Reader. Margo LaGattuta. (Illus.). 220p. (Orig.). 1995. pap. text ed. 17.95 (*0-911051-81-3*) Plain View.
Variations on the Theme of Love. G. M. De Pauligny. 1994. pap. 10.95 (*0-533-10769-5*) Vantage.
Variations on the Theme of Love, Vol. II. G. M. De Pauligny. 1995. pap. 11.95 (*0-533-11288-5*) Vantage.
Variations, Opus 40. D. Kabalevsky. 16p. 1985. pap. 4.95 (*0-7935-3673-1*, 00121142) H Leonard.
Variations 1-4 for Cello & Piano. Andrew Lloyd Webber. 12p. 1992. 4.95 (*0-7935-1784-2*, 00312481) H Leonard.
Variationsrechnung im Grossen. Herbert Seifert & W. Threlfall. LC 77-160837. (GER.). 9.95 (*0-8284-0049-0*) Chelsea Pub.
***Varicelle.** Ginette Anfousse. (Jiji et Pichou Ser.). (Illus.). 24p. (FRE.). (J). (ps up). 1996. pap. 4.95 (*2-89021-016-2*, Pub. by Les Editions CN) Firefly Bks Ltd.
Varicose Veins: A Guide for Patients. Bandyk. Ed. by Ellis & Larry Carey. (Surgery Ser.). (Illus.). 24p. (Orig.). 1995. pap. 2.95 (*1-885274-22-X*) HIN.
Varicose Veins: A Guide to Prevention & Treatment. Howard C. Baron & Barbara A. Ross. LC 95-12535. 160p. 1995. 24.95 (*0-8160-2986-5*) Facts on File.
***Varicose Veins: A Guide to Prevention & Treatment.** M. Howard & C. Baron. 1997. pap. text ed. 17.95 (*0-8160-3652-7*) Facts on File.
Varicose Veins & Related Disorders. David J. Tibbs. 240p. 1992. 350.00 (*0-7506-1032-8*) Buttrwrth-Heinemann.
Varicose Veins & Related Disorders. David J. Tibbs. 592p. 1995. pap. 135.00 (*0-7506-2335-7*) Buttrwrth-Heinemann.
Varicose Veins & Telangiectasias: Diagnosis & Treatment. Ed. by John J. Bergan & Mitchel P. Goldman. LC 92-48328. (Illus.). 448p. 1993. 125.00 (*0-942219-44-9*) Quality Med Pub.
***Varicose Veins, Venous Disorders, & Diseases of the Lower Limb.** David Tibbs et al. (Illus.). 320p. 1997. 198.50 (*0-19-262762-7*) OUP.
Varied Bouquet of Poems. Margaret F. Csovanyos. 96p. 1991. 14.99 (*0-925037-14-1*) Great Lks Poetry.
Varied Harvest. Ed. by Amy Loveman et al. LC 73-134109. (Essay Index Reprint Ser.). 1977. 23.95 (*0-8369-1981-5*) Ayer.
Varied Harvest: The Life & Works of Henry Blake Fuller. Kenneth Scambray. LC 86-30827. (Critical Essays in Modern Literature Ser.). 208p. (C). 1987. 49.95 (*0-8229-3556-2*) U of Pittsburgh Pr.
Varied Kitchens of India: Cuisines of the Anglo-Indians of Calcutta, Bengalis, Jews of Calcutta, Kashmiris, Parsis, & Tibetans of Darjeeling. Copeland Marks. LC 86-2028. 288p. 1986. 19.95 (*0-87131-476-2*) M Evans.
Varied Sociology of Paul Lazarsfeld. Ed. by Patricia K. Lazarsfeld. LC 81-24205. 400p. 1982. text ed. 69.00 (*0-231-05122-0*); pap. text ed. 24.50 (*0-231-05123-9*) Col U Pr.
Varied Types. Gilbert K. Chesterton. LC 68-16919. (Essay Index Reprint Ser.). 1977. 19.95 (*0-8369-0300-5*) Ayer.
***Varied Voices.** Blauton. (College ESL Ser.). (C). 1998. pap. 0.95 (*0-8384-7962-6*) Heinle & Heinle.
Variedad en la Razon. Carla Cordua & Roberto Torretti. 248p. 1992. 18.00 (*0-8477-2835-8*) U of PR Pr.
***Variedades de Citricos del Mundo.** James Sount. (Illus.). 128p. (ENG & SPA.). 1992. 50.00 (*84-88077-01-7*, Pub. by Sinclair Internat UK) FL Sci Source.
Variegated Leaves. Susan Conder & David Joyce. (Illus.). 192p. 1994. text ed. 25.00 (*0-02-273302-7*) Macmillan.
Variegated Verse. Carlota Trejos. 24p. 1987. reprint ed. pap. 3.95 (*0-939551-00-4*) Trejos Lit Cnslt.
***Variegrant - New Dimensions in Traditional Quilts: New Dimensions in Traditional Quilts.** Linda Glantz. 1997. pap. 19.95 (*1-57432-703-8*, 4956, Am Quilters Soc) Collector Bks.
Variete 1 et 2. Paul Valery. (FRE.). 1978. pap. 12.95 (*0-7859-3384-0*) Fr & Eur.
Varietes, 5 tomes. Paul Valery. Set. 34.75 (*0-685-36628-6*) Fr & Eur.
Varietie of Lute Lessons. Robert Dowland. Ed. by Edgar Hunt. 1958. 29.00 (*0-901938-45-9*, ST10441) Eur-Am Music.
Varietie of Lute Lessons. Robert Dowland. LC 79-84102. (English Experience Ser.: No. 921). 76p. 1979. reprint ed. lib. bdg. 20.00 (*90-221-0921-6*) Walter J Johnson.
Varieties of Affect. Claire Armon-Jones. (Studies in Philosophy). 200p. 1992. 50.00 (*0-8020-2823-3*) U of Toronto Pr.
Varieties of American English: Essays by Raven I. McDavid, Jr. Raven I. McDavid, Jr. Ed. by Anwar S. Dil. LC 78-59374. (Language Science & National Development Ser.). 400p. 1980. 49.50 (*0-8047-0982-3*) Stanford U Pr.
Varieties of American Religion. Ed. by Charles S. Braden. LC 76-156616. (Essay Index Reprint Ser.). 1977. reprint ed. 17.95 (*0-8369-2307-3*) Ayer.
Varieties of Attention. Raja Parasuraman & D. R. Davies. (Cognition & Perception Ser.). 1984. text ed. 101.00 (*0-12-544970-4*) Acad Pr.
***Varieties of British Political Thought, 1500-1800.** J. A. Pocock et al. 384p. 1996. pap. text ed. 22.95 (*0-521-57498-6*) Cambridge U Pr.
Varieties of British Political Thought, 1500-1800. J. G. Pocock et al. LC 92-37772. 320p. (C). 1994. text ed. 59.95 (*0-521-44377-6*) Cambridge U Pr.
Varieties of Christian-Marxist Dialogue. Ed. by Paul Mojzes. 210p. (Orig.). 1978. pap. 3.00 (*0-931214-02-5*) Ecumenical Phila.
Varieties of Constructive Mathematics. Douglas Bridges & Fred Richman. LC 85-26904. (London Mathematical Society Lecture Note Ser.: No. 97). 200p. 1987. pap. text ed. 29.95 (*0-521-31802-5*) Cambridge U Pr.
Varieties of Contemporary Marxism. Thomas J. Blakeley & James J. O'Rourke. 379p. 1984. lib. bdg. 149.00 (*90-277-1636-6*, D Reidel) Kluwer Ac.
Varieties of Criminology: Readings from a Dynamic Discipline. Ed. by Gregg Barak. LC 93-14138. (Criminology & Crime Control Policy Ser.). 320p. 1993. text ed. 69.50 (*0-275-94485-9*, C4485, Praeger Pubs); pap. text ed. 24.95 (*0-275-94774-2*, Praeger Pubs) Greenwood.
***Varieties of Cultural History.** Peter Burke. LC 97-15063. 256p. 1997. 42.50 (*0-8014-3491-2*) Cornell U Pr.
***Varieties of Cultural History.** Peter Burke. LC 97-15063. 256p. 1997. pap. 16.95 (*0-8014-8492-8*) Cornell U Pr.
Varieties of Dramatic Structure: A Study of Theory & Practice. Edward Murray. 158p. (Orig.). (C). 1990. pap. text ed. 19.00 (*0-8191-7786-5*); lib. bdg. 38.00 (*0-8191-7785-7*) U Pr of Amer.
Varieties of Enchantment: Early Greek Views of the Nature & Function of Poetry. George B. Walsh. LC 83-6467. ix, 170p. 1988. reprint ed. pap. 13.95 (*0-8078-4206-0*) U of NC Pr.
***Varieties of Environmentalism: A Comparative History.** Ed. by Guha. (C). 1998. text ed. write for info. (*0-321-01169-4*) Addson-Wesley Educ.
Varieties of Ethnic Experience: Kinship, Class, & Gender among California Italian-Americans. Micaela Di Leonardo. LC 83-45929. (Anthropology of Contemporary Issues Ser.). 262p. 1984. pap. 16.95 (*0-8014-9278-5*) Cornell U Pr.
Varieties of Experience: An Introduction to Philosophy. Albert W. Levi. LC 57-6807. 537p. reprint ed. pap. 153.10 (*0-317-08882-3*, 2012555) Bks Demand.
Varieties of Fascism: Doctrines of Revolution in the Twentieth Century. Eugen Weber. LC 81-20922. 192p. 1982. reprint ed. pap. 11.50 (*0-89874-444-X*) Krieger.
Varieties of Fear: Growing up Jewish under Nazism & Communism. Peter Kenez. 228p. (C). 1994. 58.50 (*1-879383-29-2*) Am Univ Pr.
Varieties of Fear: Growing up Jewish under Nazism & Communism. Peter Kenez. 228p. (C). 1995. pap. 26.50 (*1-879383-30-6*) Am Univ Pr.
Varieties of Formal Languages. J. E. Pin. (Foundations of Computer Science Ser.). 180p. 1986. 55.00 (*0-306-42294-8*, Plenum Pr) Plenum.
Varieties of Formal Semantics: Proceedings of the 4th Amsterdam Colloquium. Ed. by T. Landman & F. Veltman. (Groningen-Amsterdam Studies in Semantics). xii, 425p. 1985. pap. 75.40 (*90-6765-007-2*) Mouton.
***Varieties of Goodness: 1963 Edition.** George H. Von Wright. (Key Texts Ser.). 234p. 1996. reprint ed. pap. write for info. (*1-85506-232-1*) Bks Intl VA.
Varieties of Groups. H. Neumann. (Ergebnisse der Mathematik und Ihrer Grenzgebiete Ser.: Vol. 37). 1967. 71.95 (*0-387-03779-9*) Spr-Verlag.
Varieties of History: From Voltaire to the Present. Ed. by Fritz R. Stern. 1973. pap. 17.00 (*0-394-71962-X*, Vin) Random.
Varieties of Hope: An Anthology of Oregon Prose. Ed. & Intro. by Gordon Dodds. (Oregon Literature Ser.: Vol. 3). (Illus.). 352p. 1993. pap. 21.95 (*0-87071-374-4*); text ed. 35.95 (*0-87071-373-6*) Oreg St U Pr.
Varieties of Human Habitation. R. Martin Helick. LC 73-19343. 1970. spiral bd. 17.50 (*0-912710-02-0*) Regent Graphic Serv.
Varieties of Human Value. Charles W. Morris. LC 56-6641. (Midway Reprint Ser.: 1973). 225p. reprint ed. pap. 64.20 (*0-8357-9660-4*, 2016989) Bks Demand.
Varieties of Investigative Evaluation. Ed. by Nick L. Smith. LC 85-644749. (New Directions for Evaluation Ser.: No. PE 56). 100p. 1992. 19.00 (*1-55542-741-3*) Jossey-Bass.
Varieties of Juvenile Delinquency. C. Frankenstein. xii, 252p. 1970. text ed. 144.00 (*0-677-02820-2*) Gordon & Breach.
Varieties of Lattices. Peter Jipsen & Henry Rose. LC 92-39980. 1993. 36.95 (*0-387-56314-8*) Spr-Verlag.
Varieties of Literary Thematics. Theodore J. Ziolkowski. LC 83-42585. 282p. 1983. reprint ed. pap. 80.40 (*0-7837-9491-6*, 2060234) Bks Demand.
Varieties of Man-Boy Love: Modern Western Contexts. 1992. write for info. (*0-9615497-1-8*, W Hamilton Pr) N Am Man-Boy.
Varieties of Marxism. Shlomo Avineri. (Van Leer Jerusalem Foundation Ser.). 414p. 1977. lib. bdg. 93.00 (*90-247-2024-9*, Pub. by M Nijhoff NE) Kluwer Ac.
Varieties of Memory & Consciousness: Essays in Honour of Endel Tulving. Ed. by H. L. Roediger, III & F. I. Craik. 464p. 1989. 89.95 (*0-89859-935-0*) L Erlbaum Assocs.
Varieties of Memory & Consciousness: Essays in Honour of Endel Tulving. Ed. by H. L. Roediger, III & F. I. Craik. 464p. 1989. pap. 45.00 (*0-8058-0546-X*) L Erlbaum Assocs.
Varieties of Metaphysical Poetry. T. S. Eliot. Ed. & Intro. by Ronald Schuchard. 368p. 1996. pap. 15.00 (*0-15-600256-6*, Harvest Bks) HarBrace.
Varieties of Metaphysical Poetry: The Clark Lectures at Trinity College, Cambridge, 1926 & the Turnbull Lectures at the Johns Hopkins University, 1933. T. S. Eliot. LC 94-2959. 1994. 29.95 (*0-15-100096-4*) HarBrace.
Varieties of Monetary Reform: Lessons & Experiences on the Road to Monetary Union. Ed. by Pierre L. Siklos. LC 94-13036. 400p. (C). 1994. lib. bdg. 110.50 (*0-7923-9474-7*) Kluwer Ac.
Varieties of Moral Personality. Owen Flanagan. Date not set. pap. 17.95 (*0-674-93219-6*) HUP.
Varieties of Orthographic Knowledge. Ed. by Virginia W. Berninger. LC 94-30307. 1994. lib. bdg. write for info. (*0-7923-3081-1*) Kluwer Ac.
Varieties of Orthographic Knowledge Vol. 1. Ed. by Virginia W. Berninger. LC 94-30307. 1994. lib. bdg. 148.00 (*0-7923-3080-3*) Kluwer Ac.
Varieties of Orthographic Knowledge II: Relationships to Phonology, Reading, & Writing. Ed. by Virginia W. Berninger. (Neuropsychology & Cognition Ser.). 428p. (C). 1995. lib. bdg. 136.00 (*0-7923-3641-0*) Kluwer Ac.
Varieties of Parable. Louis MacNeice. LC 66-10036. (Clark Lectures, 1963). 165p. reprint ed. pap. 47.10 (*0-317-20590-0*, 2024498) Bks Demand.
Varieties of Poetic Utterance: Quotation in the Brothers Kramazov. Nina Perlina. LC 84-20959. 236p. (Orig.). 1985. pap. text ed. 24.00 (*0-8191-4372-3*) U Pr of Amer.
Varieties of Police Behavior: The Management of Law & Order in Eight Communities. James Q. Wilson. LC 68-54027. (Joint Center for Urban Studies). 320p. 1968. 37.00 (*0-674-93210-2*) HUP.
Varieties of Police Behavior: The Management of Law & Order in Eight Communities. James Q. Wilson. LC 68-54027. (Joint Center for Urban Studies). 320p. 1978. pap. 14.50 (*0-674-93211-0*) HUP.
Varieties of Political Expression in Sociology. Robert K. Merton. LC 72-81104. 239p. reprint ed. pap. 68.20 (*0-685-15775-X*, 2026782) Bks Demand.
Varieties of Postmodern Theology. David R. Griffin et al. LC 88-13923. (SUNY Series in Constructive Postmodern Thought). 164p. (C). 1989. text ed. 59.50 (*0-7914-0050-6*); pap. text ed. 19.95 (*0-7914-0051-4*) State U NY Pr.
Varieties of Prayer: A Survey Report. Margaret M. Poloma & George H. Gallup, Jr. LC 90-28578. 160p. (Orig.). (C). 1991. pap. 14.95 (*1-56338-007-2*) TPI PA.
Varieties of Protestantism see Modern American Protestantism & Its World
Varieties of Protestantism in Nazi Germany: Five Theopolitical Positions. Franz G. Feige. LC 90-34083. (Toronto Studies in Theology: Vol. 50). 500p. 1990. lib. bdg. 119.95 (*0-88946-790-0*) E Mellen.
Varieties of Qualitative Research. John Van Mannen et al. LC 82-10719. (Studying Organizations Ser.: No. 5). 152p. 1982. reprint ed. pap. 43.40 (*0-608-01515-6*, 2059559) Bks Demand.
Varieties of Questions in English Conversation. Elizabeth G. Weber. LC 93-5764. (Studies in Discourse & Grammar (SiDaG): Vol. 3). x, 254p. 1993. 59.00 (*1-55619-369-6*) Benjamins North Am.
Varieties of Reference. Gareth Evans. Ed. by John McDowell. (Illus.). 432p. 1982. pap. 38.00 (*0-19-824686-2*) OUP.
Varieties of Reform Thought. Daniel Levine. LC 79-28658. xiii, 149p. 1980. reprint ed. text ed. 49.75 (*0-313-22345-9*, LEVR, Greenwood Pr) Greenwood.
Varieties of Relativism. Rom Harre & Michael Krausz. 190p. (C). 1996. 47.95 (*0-631-18409-0*); pap. 20.95 (*0-631-18411-2*) Blackwell Pubs.
***Varieties of Religious Conversion in the Middle Ages.** Ed. by James Muldoon. LC 96-39216. 248p. 1997. 49.95 (*0-8130-1509-X*) U Press Fla.
***Varieties of Religious Experience.** James. 1997. pap. 8.00 (*0-684-84297-1*) S&S Trade.
Varieties of Religious Experience. William James. LC 37-27013. 1978. 10.95 (*0-394-60463-6*, Modern Lib) Random.
Varieties of Religious Experience. William James. 1958. pap. 6.99 (*0-451-62743-1*, ME2069, Ment) NAL-Dutton.
Varieties of Religious Experience. William James. LC 90-50183. (Vintage-Library of America Ser.). 544p. 1990. pap. 14.50 (*0-679-72491-5*, Vin) Random.
Varieties of Religious Experience. William James. 616p. 1994. 18.50 (*0-679-60075-2*, Modern Lib) Random.
Varieties of Religious Experience. Ray Ragosta. (Burning Deck Poetry Ser.). 80p. (Orig.). 1993. pap. 8.00 (*0-930901-83-5*) Burning Deck.
Varieties of Religious Experience. limited ed. Ray Ragosta. (Burning Deck Poetry Ser.). 80p. (Orig.). 1993. pap. 15.00 (*0-930901-84-3*) Burning Deck.
Varieties of Religious Experience. William James. (Notable American Authors Ser.). 1992. reprint ed. lib. bdg. 75.00 (*0-7812-3476-X*) Rprt Serv.
Varieties of Religious Experience: A Classic on the Psychology of Religion. William James. 406p. 1991. reprint ed. pap. 10.95 (*0-89243-509-7*, Triumph Books) Liguori Pubns.
Varieties of Religious Experience: A Study in Human Nature. William James. Ed. & Intro. by Martin E. Marty. (American Library). 576p. 1982. pap. 10.95 (*0-14-039034-0*, Penguin Classics) Viking Penguin.
Varieties of Religious Expression see Modern American Protestantism & Its World
Varieties of Representations of Finitely Generated Groups. Alexander Lubotsky & Andy R. Magid. LC 85-21444. (Memoirs Ser.: No. 58/336). 117p. 1985. pap. 18.00 (*0-8218-2337-X*, MEMO/58/336) Am Math.
Varieties of Scientific Contextualism. Ed. by Steven C. Hayes et al. (Illus.). 320p. (C). 1993. text ed. 46.95 (*1-878978-05-5*); pap. text ed. 34.95 (*1-878978-04-7*) Context Pr.
Varieties of Scientific Experience: Emotive Aims in Scientific Hypotheses. Lewis S. Fever. LC 95-1470. 365p. 1995. 39.95 (*1-56000-223-9*) Transaction Pubs.
Varieties of Sensory Experience: A Sourcebook in the Anthropology of the Senses. Ed. by David Howes. (Anthropological Horizons Ser.: No. 1). 250p. 1991. 45.00 (*0-8020-5902-3*); pap. 19.95 (*0-8020-6844-8*) U of Toronto Pr.
Varieties of Sexual Experience: An Anthropological Perspective on Human Sexuality. Suzanne G. Frayser. LC 85-60217. (Comparative Studies). 546p. 1985. pap. 25.00 (*0-87536-342-3*) HRAFP.
Varieties of Sexual Experience: Psychosexuality in Literature. Norman Kiell. LC 74-27787. 753p. 1976. 67.50 (*0-8236-6725-1*) Intl Univs Pr.
Varieties of Social Explanation: An Introduction to the Philosophy of Social Science. Daniel Little. 258p. (C). 1990. pap. text ed. 22.95 (*0-8133-0566-7*) Westview.
Varieties of Southern History: New Essays on a Region & Its People. John A. Salmond. Ed. by Bruce Clayton. LC 95-53106. (Contributions in American History Ser.: Vol. 169). 224p. 1996. text ed. 55.00 (*0-313-29860-2*, Greenwood Pr) Greenwood.
Varieties of Southern Religious Experience. Ed. by Samuel S. Hill. LC 87-32993. 248p. 1988. text ed. 32.50 (*0-8071-1372-7*) La State U Pr.
Varieties of Spoken Standard Chinese, Vol. 2: A Speaker from Taipei. Cornelius C. Kubler & G. Ho. (Publications in Modern Chinese Language & Literature). x, 171p. 1984. pap. 38.50 (*90-6765-040-4*) Mouton.
Varieties of Stabilization Experience: Towards Sensible Macroeconomics in the Third World. Lance Taylor. (WIDER Studies in Development Economics). (Illus.). 192p. 1991. reprint ed. pap. 16.95 (*0-19-828731-3*) OUP.
Varieties of Theatrical Art. 3rd ed. Ed. by August W. Staub. 240p. 1994. 29.95 (*0-89892-121-X*) Contemp Pub Co of Raleigh.
Varieties of Thinking: Essays from Harvard's Philosophy of Education Research Center. Ed. by V. A. Howard. (Philosophy of Education Research Library). 192p. (C). (gr. 13). 1990. text ed. 39.95 (*0-415-90085-9*, A2715, Routledge NY) Routledge.
Varieties of Transition: East European & East German Experience. Claus Offe. LC 96-9046. (Studies in Contemporary German Social Thought). 288p. 1996. 36.00 (*0-262-15048-4*) MIT Pr.
Varieties of Transition: The East European & East German Experience. Claus Offe. LC 96-9046. (Studies in Contemporary German Social Thought). 288p. 1996. pap. 18.00 (*0-262-65048-7*) MIT Pr.
Varieties of Travel. Ed. by Alan Hodge. LC 79-351286. (Selections from History Today Ser.: No. 8). (Illus.). 1969. 10.95 (*0-686-85917-0*) Dufour.
Varieties of Travel. Ed. by Alan Hodge. LC 79-351286. (Selections from History Today Ser.: No. 8). (Illus.). 6900. pap. 9.95 (*0-05-001533-8*) Dufour.
***Varieties of Travel.** Alan Hodge. LC 79-35128. (History Today Ser.). 1969. 14.95 (*0-685-09206-2*) Dufour.
***Varieties of Ultramontanism.** Ed. by Jeffrey P. Von Arx. LC 96-44512. 114p. 1997. 34.95 (*0-8132-0871-8*) Cath U Pr.
***Varieties of Ultramontanism.** Ed. by Jeffrey P. Von Arx. LC 96-44512. 114p. 1997. pap. 19.95 (*0-8132-0872-6*) Cath U Pr.
Varieties of Unbelief: From Epicurus to Sartre. J. C. Gaskin. Ed. by Paul Edwards. (Philosophical Topics Ser.). 326p. (C). 1988. pap. text ed. 15.33 (*0-02-340681-X*, Macmillan Coll) P-H.
***Varieties of Understanding Vols. 1 & 2: English Philosophy since 1898, 2 vols., Vols. 1 & 2.** Nikolay Milkov. xxxii, 893p. 1997. 127.95 (*3-631-48508-5*) P Lang Pubng.
Varieties of Visual Experience. 4th ed. Edmund B. Feldman. (Illus.). 544p. 1992. 60.00 (*0-8109-3922-3*) Abrams.
Varieties of Visual Experience. 4th ed. Edmund B. Feldman. 544p. 1992. pap. text ed. 54.00 (*0-13-953449-0*) P-H.
Varieties of Work. Ed. by Phyllis L. Stewart & Muriel G. Cantor. LC 82-716. 311p. 1982. reprint ed. pap. 88.70 (*0-608-03382-0*, 2059646) Bks Demand.

An Asterisk (*) at the beginning of an entry indicates that the title is appearing in BIP for the first time.

Variety. Ed. by Wolfgang Hageney. (Illus.). 88p. (ENG, FRE, GER, ITA & SPA.). 1985. pap. 18.95 (*88-7070-064-X*) Belvedere USA.

Variety & Daily Variety Obituaries Vol. 15: 1993-1994: With Index, Vol. 15. fac. ed. LC 10-730184. 184p. 1995. text ed. 165.00 (*0-8240-0849-9*) Garland.

Variety & Daily Variety Television Reviews 1993-1994. (Variety Television Reviews Ser.: Vol. 18). 520p. 1996. text ed. 165.00 (*0-8240-3797-9*) Garland.

Variety & Unity in New Testament Thought. John H. Reumann. (Oxford Bible Ser.). (Illus.). 344p. 1991. pap. 24.95 (*0-19-826204-3*) OUP.

Variety Artistes. Tom Wakefield. 192p. (Orig.). 1990. pap. 10.95 (*1-85242-138-X*) Serpents Tail.

Variety Book of Puppet Scripts. Sarah W. Miller. LC 78-57276. 1978. pap. 6.99 (*0-8054-7515-X*, 4275-15) Broadman.

Variety Entertainment & Outdoor Amusements: A Reference Guide. Don B. Wilmeth. LC 81-13417. (American Popular Culture Ser.). xiii, 242p. 1982. text ed. 42.95 (*0-313-21455-7*, WRG/, Greenwood Pr) Greenwood.

Variety, Equity, & Efficiency: Product Variety in an Industrial Society. Kelvin Lancaster. LC 78-24616. 432p. 1979. text ed. 61.50 (*0-231-04616-2*) Col U Pr.

***Variety in Christ's Body: 1 Corinthians 12:2.** Spiros Zodhiates. (1 Corinthians Commentary Ser.). 259p. pap. 6.99 (*0-89957-576-5*) AMG Pubs.

Variety in Contemporary English. W. R. O'Donnell & Loreto Todd. 192p. (Orig.). 1991. pap. 16.95 (*0-04-445737-5*, A8213) Routledge Chapman & Hall.

Variety in Contemporary English. 2nd ed. W. R. O'Donnell & Loreto Todd. LC 92-30151. 192p. (Orig.). (C). 1992. pap. text ed. 18.95 (*0-415-08437-7*, Routledge NY) Routledge.

Variety in Written English. Bex. 240p. (C). 1996. pap. 18.95 (*0-415-10840-3*); text ed. 65.00 (*0-415-10839-X*) Routledge.

Variety International Film Guide 1996. Peter Cowie. (Illus.). 448p. 1995. pap. 18.95 (*0-240-80253-5*, Focal) Buttrwrth-Heinemann.

Variety Movie Guide, 1995. Derek Elley. 1994. pap. 20.00 (*0-517-88265-5*, Crown) Crown Pub Group.

Variety Movie Guide 1997. Ed. by Derek Elley. 1200p. 1996. pap. 19.95 (*0-600-59028-3*, Focal) Buttrwrth-Heinemann.

Variety Movie Guide '96. rev. ed. Derek Elley. 1060p. 1995. pap. 19.95 (*0-600-58705-3*, Reed Trade) Buttrwrth-Heinemann.

Variety Obituaries, 1905-1928. Ed. by Michael Kaplan. LC 87-25931. (Variety Obituaries Ser.: Vol. 1). 648p. 1988. text ed. 80.00 (*0-8240-0835-9*) Garland.

Variety Obituaries, 1905-1990, 13 vols. Ed. by Kaplan. 1989. Set. text ed. 195.00 (*0-8240-0845-6*) Garland.

Variety Obituaries, 1905-1990, 13 vols., Ea. 1989. 165.00 (*0-318-69657-6*) Garland.

Variety Obituaries, 1905-1990, 13 vols., Set. Ed. by Kaplan. 1989. Index Vol. 11. 2,685.00 (*0-8153-0362-9*) Garland.

Variety Obituaries, 1929-38. Ed. by Michael Kaplan. LC 87-25931. (Variety Obituaries Ser.: Vol. 2). 656p. 1988. text ed. 80.00 (*0-8240-0836-7*) Garland.

Variety Obituaries, 1939-47. Ed. by Michael Kaplan. LC 87-25931. (Variety Obituaries Ser.: Vol. 3). 568p. 1988. text ed. 80.00 (*0-8240-0837-5*) Garland.

Variety Obituaries, 1948-56. Ed. by Michael Kaplan. LC 87-25931. (Variety Obituaries Ser.: Vol. 4). 584p. 1988. text ed. 80.00 (*0-8240-0838-3*) Garland.

Variety Obituaries, 1957-63. Ed. by Michael Kaplan. LC 87-25931. (Variety Obituaries Ser.: Vol. 5). 544p. 1988. text ed. 80.00 (*0-8240-0839-1*) Garland.

Variety Obituaries 1964-68. (Variety Obituaries Ser.: Vol. 6). 1988. text ed. 80.00 (*0-8240-0840-5*) Garland.

Variety Obituaries, 1969-74. Ed. by Michael Kaplan. LC 87-25931. (Variety Obituaries Ser.: Vol. 7). 560p. 1988. text ed. 80.00 (*0-8240-0841-3*) Garland.

Variety Obituaries 1975-79. Ed. by Michael Kaplan. LC 87-25931. (Variety Obituaries Ser.: Vol. 8). 560p. 1988. text ed. 80.00 (*0-8240-0842-1*) Garland.

Variety Obituaries, 1980-83. Ed. by Michael Kaplan. LC 87-25931. (Variety Obituaries Ser.: Vol. 9). 536p. 1988. text ed. 80.00 (*0-8240-0843-X*) Garland.

Variety Obituaries, 1984-86. Ed. by Michael Kaplan. LC 87-25931. (Variety Obituaries Ser.: Vol. 10). 456p. 1988. text ed. 80.00 (*0-8240-0844-8*) Garland.

Variety Obituaries 1989-90. (Variety Obituaries Ser.: Vol. 13). 1992. text ed. 165.00 (*0-8240-0847-2*) Garland.

Variety Obituaries, 1991-1992, Vol. 14. Daily Variety Staff. LC 10-730184. 296p. 1994. text ed. 165.00 (*0-8240-0848-0*) Garland.

Variety Obituaries 1993-94, Vol. 15. Date not set. 165.00 (*0-614-14187-7*) Garland.

Variety of American Evangelicalism. Ed. by Donald W. Dayton & Robert K. Johnston. LC 90-36516. 294p. 1991. text ed. 39.95 (*0-87049-659-X*) U of Tenn Pr.

Variety of Attempt: British & American Fiction in the Early Nineteenth Century. Neal F. Doubleday. LC 75-38057. 228p. reprint ed. pap. 65.00 (*0-7837-1819-5*, 2042019) Bks Demand.

Variety of Community Experience: Qualitative Studies of Family & Community Life. Ed. by Steven J. Taylor et al. LC 94-45944. 222p. 1995. pap. 26.00 (*1-55766-191-X*) P H Brookes.

Variety of Life. Robert Stephenson & Roger Browne. LC 92-34357. (Exploring Science Ser.). (Illus.). 48p. (J). (gr. 4-8). 1992. lib. bdg. 24.26 (*0-8114-2606-8*) Raintree Steck-V.

Variety of Nuclear Shapes. Ed. by J. Garrett et al. 572p. (C). 1988. text ed. 138.00 (*9971-5-0416-2*) World Scientific Pub.

Variety of Poems. Robert L. McCormick. (Orig.). 1996. pap. write for info. (*1-57553-291-3*) Watermrk Pr.

***Variety of Poems, No. 2.** Robert L. McCormick. (Orig.). 1997. pap. write for info. (*1-57553-511-4*) Watermrk Pr.

Variety of Ways: Discussion on Six Authors. Bonamy Dobree. LC 67-23204. (Essay Index Reprint Ser.). 1977. 15.95 (*0-8369-0377-3*) Ayer.

Variety Photoplays. Edward Field. 1979. 5.00 (*0-917554-02-7*) Maelstrom.

Variety Television Reviews, 1923-1950. Ed. by Howard H. Prouty. LC 89-17088. (Variety Television Reviews Ser.: Vol. 3). 528p. 1989. text ed. 80.00 (*0-8240-2589-X*) Garland.

Variety Television Reviews, 1923-1990, 16 vols. Ed. by Howard H. Prouty. 1992. Set. 3,015.00 (*0-8153-0363-7*) Garland.

Variety Television Reviews, 1923-1990, 16 vols., Ea. Ed. by Howard H. Prouty. 1992. 165.00 (*0-318-69656-8*) Garland.

Variety Television Reviews, 1946-56. Ed. by Howard H. Prouty. LC 89-17088. (Variety Television Reviews Ser.: Vol. 1). 776p. 1990. text ed. 80.00 (*0-8240-2587-3*) Garland.

Variety Television Reviews, 1951-1953. Ed. by Howard H. Prouty. LC 89-17088. (Variety Television Reviews Ser.: Vol. 4). 528p. 1989. text ed. 80.00 (*0-8240-2590-3*) Garland.

Variety Television Reviews 1954-1956. LC 89-17088. (Variety Television Reviews Ser.: Vol. 5). 496p. 1989. text ed. 80.00 (*0-8240-2591-1*) Garland.

Variety Television Reviews, 1957-1959. Ed. by Howard H. Prouty. LC 89-17088. (Variety Television Reviews Ser.: Vol. 6). 536p. 1989. text ed. 80.00 (*0-8240-2592-X*) Garland.

Variety Television Reviews, 1957-60. Ed. by Howard H. Prouty. LC 88-17088. (Variety Television Reviews Ser.: Vol. 2). 496p. 1990. text ed. 80.00 (*0-8240-2588-1*) Garland.

Variety Television Reviews, 1960-1962. Ed. by Howard H. Prouty. LC 89-17088. (Variety Television Reviews Ser.: Vol. 7). 496p. 1989. text ed. 80.00 (*0-8240-2593-8*) Garland.

Variety Television Reviews, 1963-1965. Ed. by Howard H. Prouty. LC 89-17088. (Variety Television Reviews Ser.: Vol. 8). 520p. 1989. text ed. 80.00 (*0-8240-2594-6*) Garland.

Variety Television Reviews, 1966-1969. Ed. by Howard H. Prouty. LC 89-17088. (Variety Television Reviews Ser.: Vol. 9). 560p. 1989. text ed. 80.00 (*0-8240-2595-4*) Garland.

Variety Television Reviews, 1970-1973. Ed. by Howard H. Prouty. LC 89-17088. (Variety Television Reviews Ser.: Vol. 10). 472p. 1989. text ed. 80.00 (*0-8240-2596-2*) Garland.

Variety Television Reviews, 1974-1977. Ed. by Howard H. Prouty. LC 89-17088. (Variety Television Reviews Ser.: Vol. 11). 464p. 1989. text ed. 80.00 (*0-8240-2597-0*) Garland.

Variety Television Reviews, 1978-1982. Ed. by Howard H. Prouty. LC 89-17088. (Variety Television Reviews Ser.: Vol. 12). 424p. 1989. text ed. 80.00 (*0-8240-2598-9*) Garland.

Variety Television Reviews, 1983-1986. Ed. by Howard H. Prouty. LC 89-17088. (Variety Television Reviews Ser.: Vol. 13). 544p. 1989. text ed. 80.00 (*0-8240-3792-8*) Garland.

Variety Television Reviews, 1987-1988. Ed. by Howard H. Prouty. LC 89-17088. (Variety Television Reviews Ser.: Vol. 14). 328p. 1990. text ed. 80.00 (*0-8240-3793-6*) Garland.

Variety Television Reviews, 1989-1990. Ed. by Howard H. Prouty. LC 89-17088. (Variety Television Reviews Ser.: Vol. 16). 592p. 1992. text ed. 165.00 (*0-8240-3795-2*) Garland.

Variety Television Reviews 1991-1992. (Variety Television Reviews Ser.: Vol. 17). 1994. text ed. 165.00 (*0-8240-3796-0*) Garland.

Variety TV Reviews, Index 1923-1990. Howard H. Prouty. LC 89-17088. (Variety Television Reviews Ser.: Vol. 15). 450p. 1991. reprint ed. text ed. 195.00 (*0-8240-3794-4*) Garland.

Variety with Venison & Other Wild Game. 2nd ed. Delores Green & Connie White. (Illus.). 85p. 1989. pap. 8.95 (*0-9624777-0-2*) Green & White Pub.

Variety's Film Reviews Title Index to Vols. 1-15, Vol. 16. 230.00 (*0-8352-2796-0*) Bowker.

Variety's Film Reviews 1993-1994, Vol. 23. Ed. by Bowker, R. R., Staff. 700p. 1995. 199.00 (*0-8352-3577-7*) Bowker.

Variety's Film Reviews 1995-1996, Vol. 24. Ed. by Bowker, R. R., Staff. 1997. write for info. (*0-8352-3851-2*) Bowker.

Variety's Video Directory PLUS, CD-ROM. 1994. 395.00 (*0-8352-2445-7*) Bowker.

Varificationist. Antrim. 1998. pap. write for info. (*0-517-70311-4*) Random Hse Value.

Variogram Primer: Basics of Using Variograms. Stephen A. Krajewski & Betty L. Gibbs. (Illus.). 94p. (Orig.). (C). 1993. pap. text ed. 25.00 (*0-943909-11-2*) Gibbs Assocs.

Variorum: A Greek Translation Book. J. M. Moore & J. J. Evans. 158p. 1991. pap. 15.95 (*1-85399-190-2*, Pub. by Brstl Class Pr UK) Focus Pub-R Pullins.

Variorum Commentary on the Poems of John Milton, Vol. 1. Ed. by Merritt Y. Hughes. LC 70-129962. 1970. text ed. 145.00 (*0-231-08879-5*) Col U Pr.

Variorum Commentary on the Poems of John Milton, Vol. 2, Pt. 1. Ed. by Merritt Y. Hughes. (C). 1972. 145.00 (*0-318-51418-4*) Col U Pr.

Variorum Commentary on the Poems of John Milton, Vol. 2, Pt. 2. Ed. by Merritt Y. Hughes. LC 70-129962. (C). 1972. Pt. 2. text ed. 145.00 (*0-231-08881-7*) Col U Pr.

Variorum Commentary on the Poems of John Milton, Vol. 2, Pt. 3. Ed. by Merritt Y. Hughes. LC 70-129962. (C). 1972. Pt. 3. text ed. 145.00 (*0-231-08882-5*) Col U Pr.

Variorum Commentary on the Poems of John Milton, Vol. 4. Ed. by Merritt Y. Hughes. LC 70-129962. 400p. 1975. text ed. 145.00 (*0-231-08883-3*) Col U Pr.

Variorum Edition of Tennyson's Idylls of the King. John Pfordresher. LC 73-4852. 1088p. 1973. text ed. 105.00 (*0-231-03691-4*) Col U Pr.

Variorum Edition of the Complete Poems of Thomas Hardy. variorum ed. Ed. by James Gibson. 1,003p. 1979. 167.50 (*0-333-23773-0*, Pub. by Macmlln UK) Trans-Atl Phila.

Variorum Edition of the Poems of W. B. Yeats. Ed. by Peter Allt & Russell K. Alspach. 928p. 1987. 65.00 (*0-02-632700-7*) S&S Trade.

Variorum Edition of the Poetry of John Donne Vol. 6: The Anniversaries & Epicedes & Obsequies, Vol. 6. John Donne. Ed. by Donald R. Dickson et al. LC 93-11800. (Variorum Edition of the Poetry of John Donne Ser.). 754p. 1995. text ed. 49.95 (*0-253-31811-4*) Ind U Pr.

Variorum Edition of the Poetry of John Donne Vol. 8: The Epigrams, Epithalamions, Epitaphs... Stringer. LC 93-11800. 1995. 41.75 (*0-253-31812-2*) Ind U Pr.

Variorum Lilith, 2 vols., Set. George MacDonald. Ed. by Rolland Hein. 800p. 1996. 48.00 (*1-881084-56-6*) Johannesen.

***Variorums: Poems from Hollywood.** Mark Dunster. 29p. (Orig.). (YA). (gr. 9-12). 1997. pap. 5.00 (*0-89642-372-7*) Linden Pubs.

Various & Ingenious Machines of Agostino Ramelli: A Classic Sixteenth-Century Illustrated Treatise on Technology. Agostino Ramelli. (Illus.). 608p. 1994. pap. text ed. 24.95 (*0-486-28180-9*) Dover.

Various Antidotes: Stories. Joanna Scott. 1996. pap. 12.00 (*0-8050-4176-1*) H Holt & Co.

Various Art. Andrew Crozier & Tim Longville. 377p. 1995. pap. 12.95 (*1-85754-103-0*, Pub. by Carcanet Pr UK) Paul & Co Pubs.

Various Bengal: Aspects of Modern History. Tarasankar Banerjee. 328p. 1986. 27.50 (*0-8364-1669-4*, Pub. by Popular Prakashan II) S Asia.

Various Devices. Adriano Spatola. Tr. by Paul Vangelisti. 1978. 15.00 (*0-88031-053-7*); pap. 6.00 (*0-88031-052-9*) Invisible-Red Hill.

Various Envies. Jim Elledge. LC 89-521. 48p. (Orig.). 1989. pap. 6.95 (*0-914278-51-7*) Copper Beech.

Various Fragments. Herbert Spencer. LC 72-14180. (Essay Index Reprint Ser.). 1977. reprint ed. 22.95 (*0-518-10025-1*) Ayer.

Various Interpretations of the Rbhu-Hymns in the Rgveda. G. V. Davane. (C). 1991. 22.00 (*81-7030-292-7*) S Asia.

Various Jangling Keys. Edgar Bogardus. LC 70-144756. (Yale Series of Younger Poets: No. 50). reprint ed. 18.00 (*0-404-53850-9*) AMS Pr.

Various Lives of Marcus Igoe. Brinsley MacNamara. 237p. 9600. pap. 13.95 (*0-8023-1304-3*) Dufour.

Various Miracles. Carol Shields. 192p. 1989. pap. 9.95 (*0-14-011837-3*, Penguin Bks) Viking Penguin.

***Various Miracles.** large type ed. Carol Shields. LC 96-32356. 1996. pap. 22.95 (*1-56895-364-X*, Compass) Wheeler Pub.

Various Positions: A Life of Leonard Cohen. Ira B. Nadel. 1996. 26.00 (*0-679-44235-9*) Random.

Various Positions: A Life of Leonard Cohen. Ira B. Nadel. 1997. pap. write for info. (*0-679-76775-4*) Random.

Various Prospects of Mankind, Nature & Providence. Robert Wallace. LC 69-19550. viii, 406p. 1969. reprint ed. 49.50 (*0-678-00491-9*) Kelley.

Various Provincialisms, from Hearne's Glossaries, 1724-25 see English Dialect Society Publications, No. 2: Glossaries VIII-XIV

Various Styles of the Roman Republican Coinage. Harold B. Mattingly. 18p. 1977. 5.00 (*0-916710-31-9*) Obol Intl.

Various Writings of Cornelius Mathews. Cornelius Mathews. LC 72-144659. 370p. 1972. reprint ed. 47.50 (*0-404-04265-1*) AMS Pr.

Various Writings of Cornelius Mathews. Cornelius Mathews. (BCL1-PS American Literature Ser.). 370p. 1992. reprint ed. lib. bdg. 89.00 (*0-7812-6791-9*) Rprt Serv.

Variowin: Software for Spatial Data Analysis in 2-D. Yvan Paninatier. Ed. by W. Eddy et al. 104p. 1996. 52.95 incl. disk (*0-387-94679-9*) Spr-Verlag.

Varitations sur l'Imposture. Lucie Faure. (FRE.). 1975. pap. 10.95 (*0-7859-2635-6*, 2070367l0X) Fr & Eur.

Varitype Operator. Jack Rudman. (Career Examination Ser.: C-872). 1994. pap. 23.95 (*0-8373-0872-0*) Nat Learn.

Vark' Mastots'i: Life of Mashtots. Koriun. Ed. by Krikor Maksoudian. LC 85-4174. (Classical Armenian Texts Ser.). 1985. 50.00 (*0-88206-030-9*) Caravan Bks.

Varlin Nineteen Hundred to Nineteen Seventy-Seven: Paintings. Peter H. Selz. LC 85-63886. (Illus.). 56p. (Orig.). 1986. pap. 12.00 (*0-936827-01-7*) C Bernard Gallery Ltd.

Varmint & Small Game Rifles & Cartridges. 1993. 26.00 (*1-879356-33-3*) Wolfe Pub Co.

Varna, Castes & Scheduled Castes: A Documentation in Historical Perspective. Shanti S. Gupta. (C). 1991. 20.00 (*81-7022-317-2*, Pub. by Concept II) S Asia.

Varner Families of the South, 2 vols., Set. Gerald H. Varner. 1996. 45.00 (*0-9642353-1-5*) G H Varner.

Varner Families of the South Vol. 1: Varner Families of Oglethorpe County, GA & Their Descendants. Gerald H. Varner. LC 94-60607. 1994. 25.00 (*0-9642353-0-7*) G H Varner.

Varner Families of the South Vol. 2: Varner-Verner Families of Pendleton District, SC & Their Descendants. Gerald H. Varner. 1996. 25.00 (*0-9642353-2-3*) G H Varner.

Varney, the Vampire, or, The Feast of Blood, 3 vols, Set. Thomas P. Prest. Ed. by Devendra P. Varma. LC 70-120557. (Gothic Novels II Ser.). 933p. 1972. reprint ed. boxed 51.95 (*0-405-00801-5*) Ayer.

***Varney's Midwifery.** 3rd ed. Helen Varney. LC 96-38376. (Nursery Ser.). 960p. 1996. 79.95 (*0-86720-748-5*) Jones & Bartlett.

***Varnished Cloth Insulated Wire & Cable for the Transmission & Distribution of Electrical Energy.** 3rd ed. 41.00 (*0-614-18698-6*, S-65-375) Insulated Cable.

Varnished Truth: Truth Telling & Deceiving in Ordinary Life. David Nyberg. LC 92-20637. 254p. (C). 1993. 24.95 (*0-226-61051-9*) U Ch Pr.

Varnished Truth: Truth Telling & Deceiving in Ordinary Life. David Nyberg. 256p. 1994. pap. 12.95 (*0-226-61052-7*) U Ch Pr.

Varnishes of the Italian Violin-Makers of the Sixteenth, Seventeenth & Eighteenth Centuries & Their Influence on Tone. George Fry. (Illus.). 1977. reprint ed. text ed. 26.00 (*0-918624-02-9*) Virtuoso.

Varnums of Oracut (in Massachusetts) A History of George Varnum, His Son Samuel & Grandsons Thomas, John & Joseph, & Their Descendants. J. M. Varnum. (Illus.). 314p. 1989. reprint ed. pap. 47.00 (*0-8328-1201-3*); reprint ed. lib. bdg. 55.00 (*0-8328-1200-5*) Higginson Bk Co.

Varon y Su Temperamento. Tim LaHaye. 217p. 1978. 4.95 (*0-88113-340-X*) Edit Betania.

Varouna. Julien Green. 1984. pap. 16.95 (*0-7859-2698-4*) Fr & Eur.

Varro - Concordantia in Varronis Libros de Re Rustica. Varro. Ed. by Ward W. Briggs. (Alpha-Omega, Reihe A Ser.: Vol. LXV). xii, 366p. 1983. 76.70 (*3-487-07301-3*) G Olms Pubs.

Varro und die Hellenistische Sprachtheorie. Hellfried Dahlmann. 89p. 1964. write for info. (*3-296-12110-2*) G Olms Pubs.

***Varroa Jacobsoni Oud. Affecting Honey Bees: Present Status & Needs: Proceedings of a Meeting of the EC Experts' Group, Wageningen, 7-9 February 1983.** Ed. by R. Cavalloro. 129p. 1983. 70.00 (*90-6191-524-4*, Pub. by A A Balkema NE) Ashgate Pub Co.

Varshaphal or the Hindu Progressed Horoscope. Bangalore V. Raman. (BVR Astrology Ser.). (C). 1992. pap. 5.00 (*81-85674-24-8*, Pub. by UBS Pubs Dist II) S Asia.

Varsity Basketball. Boy Scouts of America Staff. (Illus.). 44p. (Orig.). 1989. pap. 3.15 (*0-8395-3450-7*, 3450) BSA.

***Varsity Debate: Experiences in Advanced Debate Theory & Practice.** William H. Bennett. iv, 244p. (Orig.). (YA). (gr. 7-12). 1996. text ed. 39.00 (*1-889510-22-X*); pap. text ed. 29.00 (*1-889510-23-8*) Chmpionship Debate.

Varsity Letters: Documenting Modern Colleges & Universities. Helen W. Samuels. LC 92-24126. (Society of American Archivists Ser.). (Illus.). 296p. 1992. 35.00 (*0-8108-2596-1*) Scarecrow.

Varsity Rags & Hoaxes. Frank A. Reeve. (Cambridge Town, Gown & County Ser.: Vol. 17). (Illus.). 1977. pap. 4.95 (*0-900891-16-5*) Oleander Pr.

Varsity Scout Leader Fundamentals. Boy Scouts of America Staff. 128p. 1991. pap. 11.98 (*0-8395-3443-4*, 33443) BSA.

***Varsity Scout Leader Guidebook.** 184p. 1996. pap. 6.50 (*0-8395-4827-3*, 34827) BSA.

Varsity Shooting Sports. Boy Scouts of America Staff. (Illus.). 87p. (YA). 1990. pap. 3.15 (*0-8395-3457-4*, 3457) BSA.

Varsity Soccer. Boy Scouts of America Staff. (Illus.). 50p. (Orig.). 1989. pap. 3.15 (*0-8395-3453-1*, 3453) BSA.

Varsity Softball. Boy Scouts of America Staff. (Illus.). 48p. (Orig.). 1989. pap. 3.15 (*0-8395-3452-3*, 3452) BSA.

Varsity Tennis. Boy Scouts of America Staff. (Illus.). 42p. (YA). 1990. pap. 3.15 (*0-8395-3455-8*, 3455) BSA.

Varsity Triathlon. Boy Scouts of America Staff. (Illus.). 41p. (YA). 1990. pap. 3.15 (*0-8395-3456-6*, 3456) BSA.

Varsity Volleyball. Boy Scouts of America Staff. (Illus.). 34p. (Orig.). 1989. pap. 3.15 (*0-8395-3451-5*, 3451) BSA.

Varsouvienne. (Ballroom Dance Ser.). 1986. lib. bdg. 79.95 (*0-8490-3436-1*) Gordon Pr.

Varsouvienne. (Ballroom Dance Ser.). 1985. lib. bdg. 60.00 (*0-87700-760-8*) Revisionist Pr.

***Varuna & Vidusaka: On the Origin of the Sanskrit Drama.** F. B. J. Kuiper. (Verhandelingen der Koninklijke Nederlandse Akademie van Wetenschappen, Afd. Letterkunde, Nieuwe Reeks Ser.: No. 100). 252p. 1979. pap. text ed. 62.50 (*0-7204-8452-9*) Elsevier.

Varya & Her Greenfinch. Leo Tolstoy. (J). (ps-2). 1988. 7.95 (*0-86315-043-8*, 20238, Pub. by Floris Bks UK) Gryphon Hse.

***Varying States of Grace.** Ian Stephen. 1989. 12.00 (*0-7486-6038-0*, Pub. by Polygon UK) Subterranean Co.

Vas Zoltan, the Brain Drain. 1976. lib. bdg. 38.50 (*90-286-0276-3*) Kluwer Ac.

***Vasant Chhalke (Gujerati)** large type ed. Ila A. Mehta. (Charnwood Large Print Ser.). 1990. 27.99 (*0-7089-2269-4*, Charnwood) Ulverscroft.

Vasanta Vilasa. Ed. by W. Norman Brown. (American Oriental Ser.: Vol. 46). (Illus.). 1962. 20.00 (*0-940490-46-3*) Am Orient Soc.

Vasarely. Gaston Diehl. (CAL Art Ser.). (Illus.). 96p. 1985. 18.00 (*0-517-50800-1*, Crown) Crown Pub Group.

Vasarely. Smithmark Staff. 1995. 24.98 (*0-8317-9423-2*) Smithmark.

Vasari on Technique. Giorgio Vasari. Ed. by G. Baldwin Brown. Tr. by Louisa S. Maclehose. pap. 9.95 (*0-486-20717-X*) Dover.

Vasari's Florence: Artists & Literati at the Medicean Court. Maia Gahtan & Phillip J. Jacks. LC 94-60240. (Illus.). 63p. (Orig.). (C). 1994. pap. 7.50 (*0-89467-068-9*) Yale Art Gallery.

U V

***Vasari's Florence: Artists & Literati at the Medicean Court.** Giorgio Vasari & Philip J. Jacks. LC 96-46902. 1997. write for info. (*0-521-58088-9*) Cambridge U Pr.

Vasarnap Farkaspusztan. Fury Lajos. 1978. boxed 12.00 (*0-912404-11-6*) Alpha Pubns.

***Vasa'rnapi Kalauz.** Ed. by Akos Felsovalyi. (Illus.). 900p. (HUN.). 1996. 25.00 (*0-9651859-0-7*) St Stephens Magyar.

Vasavadatta. Subandhu. Tr. by Louis H. Gray. LC 70-181070. (Columbia University. Indo-Iranian Ser.: No. 8). reprint ed. 31.50 (*0-404-50478-7*) AMS Pr.

Vasco Da Gama. David Knight. LC 78-18057. (Illus.). 48p. (J). (gr. 4-7). 1979. lib. bdg. 11.89 (*0-89375-175-8*) Troll Communs.

Vasco da Gama & the Portuguese Explorers. Rebecca Stefoff. Ed. by William H. Goetzmann. (World Explorers Ser.). (Illus.). 112p. (YA). (gr. 5 up). 1993. lib. bdg. 19.95 (*0-7910-1303-0*) Chelsea Hse.

Vasco Da Gama und die Entdeckung Des Seeweges Nach Ostindien. Franz Hummerich. xiv, 203p. 1977. reprint ed. write for info. (*3-487-06293-3*) G Olms Pubs.

Vasco de Quiroga & His Pueblo-Hospitals of Santa Fe. Fintan B. Warren. (Monograph Ser.). (Illus.). 1963. 30.00 (*0-88382-057-9*) AAFH.

Vasconselos: A Romance of the New World. W. Gilmore Simms. LC 70-116016. reprint ed. 29.50 (*0-404-06037-4*) AMS Pr.

Vascos en America. I. Arana Perez. (Gran Enciclopedia de Espana y America Ser.). (Illus.). (SPA.). 1989. 200.00 (*84-87053-14-9*) Elliots Bks.

***Vascular Access.** Ingemar Davidson. (On Call In Ser.). 450p. 1997. spiral bd. 39.95 (*0-412-13551-5*) Chapman & Hall.

Vascular Access: Principles & Practice. 3rd rev. ed. Ed. by Samuel E. Wilson. 000336p. (C). (gr. 13). 1995. text ed. 84.95 (*0-8151-9226-6*) Mosby Yr Bk.

***Vascular Access for Hemodialysis-V.** Mitchell L. Henry & Ronald M. Ferguson. LC 97-19574. 1996. 59.95 (*0-944496-50-4*) Precept Pr.

Vascular Access in Oncologic Therapy. Alexander. (C). 1993. write for info. (*0-318-70301-7*) Lppncott-Raven.

Vascular Access in the Cancer Patient. Richard H. Alexander. (Illus.). 256p. 1994. text ed. 55.00 (*0-397-51316-X*) Lppncott-Raven.

***Vascular Access Surgery.** Rowe. 1997. text ed. 60.00 (*0-8385-9353-4*) P-H.

Vascular Anatomy & Physiology: An Introductory Text. Ann C. Belanger. LC 90-925. 200p. 1990. pap. 39.95 (*0-941022-11-0*) Davies Pubng.

Vascular Anatomy & Physiology: An Introductory Text. 2nd ed. Ann C. Belanger. 1998. pap. 39.95 (*0-941022-40-4*) Davies Pubng.

Vascular Anatomy in Abdominal Surgery. J. P. Van Damme & J. Bonte. (Illus.). 160p. 1990. text ed. 69.00 (*0-86577-353-X*) Thieme Med Pubs.

Vascular Anatomy of the Spinal Cord. A. K. Thron. (Illus.). 150p. 1988. 79.95 (*0-387-82015-9*) Spr-Verlag.

***Vascular & Endovascular Surgery.** Ed. by Jonathon Beard & Peter Gaines. (Companion Guide to Specialist Surgical Practice Ser.: Vol. 6). (Illus.). 380p. 1997. 80.00 (*0-7020-2144-X*, Pub. by W B Saunders UK) Saunders.

***Vascular & Endovascular Surgical Techniques: An Atlas.** 3rd ed. Ed. by Roger M. Greenhalgh. (Illus.). 544p. 1994. write for info. (*0-7020-1901-1*, Pub. by W B Saunders UK) Saunders.

***Vascular & Interventional Radiology: Principles & Practices.** Curtis W. Bakal et al. (Illus.). 568p. 1998. 95.00 (*0-86577-678-4*) Thieme Med Pubs.

Vascular & Neurologic Complications of Diabetes Mellitus. Ed. by F. Belfiore et al. (Frontiers in Diabetes Ser.: Vol. 8). (Illus.). xii, 256p. 1987. 158.50 (*3-8055-4452-9*) S Karger.

Vascular & Peritoneal Access for Dialysis. Ed. by Vittorio E. Andreucci. (Topics in Renal Medicine Ser.). (C). 1989. lib. bdg. 203.50 (*0-7923-0119-6*) Kluwer Ac.

Vascular Andrology: Erectile Dysfunction/Priapism Varicocele. Ed. by A. Ledda. (Illus.). 88p. 1996. pap. 49.50 (*3-540-59472-8*) Spr-Verlag.

Vascular Anesthesia. Ed. by Joel A. Kaplan. (Illus.). 717p. 1991. text ed. 99.50 (*0-443-08713-X*) Churchill.

Vascular Aphasia. Joseph M. Tonkongy. (Illus.). 248p. 1986. 32.50 (*0-262-20054-6*, Bradford Bks) MIT Pr.

Vascular Birthmarks: Pathogenesis & Management. Ed. by Terence J. Ryan & George W. Cherry. (Illus.). 250p. 1987. 75.00 (*0-19-261628-5*) OUP.

Vascular Brain Disease in Old Age. Ed. by W. Meier-Ruge. (Teaching & Training in Geriatric Medicine Ser.: Vol. 2). viii, 188p. 1989. pap. 22.50 (*3-8055-4477-4*) S Karger.

Vascular Brain Stem Diseases. Ed. by B. Hofferberth et al. (Illus.). viii, 282p. 1990. 69.75 (*3-8055-5031-6*) S Karger.

Vascular Cambium. Ed. by M. Iqbal. LC 89-70217. 246p. 1990. text ed. 205.00 (*0-471-92647-7*) Wiley.

Vascular Cambium: Development & Structure. Philip R. Larson. LC 94-7963. (Springer Series in Wood Science). 1994. write for info. (*3-540-57165-5*) Spr-Verlag.

Vascular Cambium: Development & Structure. Philip R. Larson. LC 94-7963. (Springer Series in Wood Science). 1994. 343.95 (*0-387-57165-5*) Spr-Verlag.

Vascular Control of Hemostasis. Ed. by Victor W. Van Hinsbergh. (Advances in Vascular Biology Ser.). 1996. text ed. 110.00 (*3-7186-5796-1*) Gordon & Breach.

Vascular Dementia: A Review of Concepts & Ideas. Ed. by I. Prohovnik et al. LC 95-45454. 1996. text ed. 79.95 (*0-471-95294-X*) Wiley.

Vascular Dementia: Etiological, Pathogenetic, Clinical & Treatment Aspects. Ed. by L. A. Carlson et al. (Journal: Dementia Ser.: Vol. 5, Nos. 3-4, 1994). (Illus.). iv, 86p. 1994. pap. 97.50 (*3-8055-5984-4*) S Karger.

Vascular Diagnosis. 4th ed. Ed. by Eugene F. Bernstein. LC 93-4086. 912p. (C). (gr. 13). 1993. text ed. 250.00 (*0-8016-6557-4*) Mosby Yr Bk.

Vascular Diagnosis with Ultrasound: Clinical Reference with Case Studies. Michael Hennerici & Doris Neuerburg-Heusler. (Illus.). 464p. 1997. text ed. 149.00 (*0-86577-603-2*) Thieme Med Pubs.

Vascular Diagnostics: Noninvasive & Invasive Techniques-Periinterventional Evaluations. Ed. by Peter Lanzer & Josef Roesch. (Illus.). 528p. 1994. 155.00 (*0-387-57939-7*) Spr-Verlag.

***Vascular Diagnostics: Principles & Technology.** Martin J. Lipton & Peter Lanzer. LC 96-41507. 1996. write for info. (*0-387-61541-5*) Spr-Verlag.

***Vascular Diagnostics: Principles & Technology.** Martin J. Lipton & Peter Lanzer. LC 96-41507. 1996. 159.00 (*3-540-61541-5*) Spr-Verlag.

Vascular Differentiation & Plant Growth Regulators. L. W. Roberts et al. (Wood Science Ser.). (Illus.). x, 154p. 1988. 137.95 (*0-387-18989-0*) Spr-Verlag.

Vascular Disease, Vol. VII. Ed. by Mark Creager. LC 95-24438. (Atlas of Heart Diseases Ser.: Vol. 7). (Illus.). 232p. 1996. 99.95 (*1-878132-26-1*) Current Med.

***Vascular Disease: A Multi-Specialty Approach to Diagnosis & Management.** Darwin Eton. (On Call In... Ser.). 718p. 1997. 49.95 (*1-57059-435-X*) R G Landes.

Vascular Disease in the Elderly. Edward A. Stemmer. Ed. by Wilbert S. Aronow et al. LC 96-50375. (Illus.). 576p. 1997. 120.00 (*0-87993-646-0*) Futura Pub.

***Vascular Diseases, Pt. I.** Pierre J. Vinken et al. (Handbook of Clinical Neurology Ser.: Vol. 53(9)). 528p. 1989. 258.25 (*0-444-90481-6*) Elsevier.

Vascular Diseases: Surgical & Interventional Therapy, 2 vols. Ed. by D. Eugene Strandness & Arina Van Breda. (Illus.). 1472p. 1993. Set. text ed. 295.00 (*0-443-08841-1*) Churchill.

***Vascular Diseases in Neonates, Infants & Children: Interventional Neuroradiology Management: P. Lasjaunias.** Pierre L. Lasjaunias. LC 96-29097. 1996. write for info. (*0-387-60845-1*) Spr-Verlag.

***Vascular Diseases in Neonates, Infants & Children: Interventional Neuroradiology Management: P. Lasjaunias.** Pierre L. Lasjaunias. LC 96-29097. 1997. 239.00 (*3-540-60845-1*) Spr-Verlag.

Vascular Diseases in the Limbs: Mechanisms & Principles of Treatment. Ed. by Denis L. Clement & John T. Shepherd. LC 92-19066. 319p. (gr. 13). 1992. text ed. 81.00 (*1-55664-287-3*) Mosby Yr Bk.

***Vascular Diseases of the Nervous System, Pt. I.** Pierre J. Vinken & G. W. Bruyn. (Handbook of Clinical Neurology Ser.: Vol. 11). 719p. 1972. 476.00 (*0-7204-7211-3*) Elsevier.

Vascular Diseases of the Nervous System see Handbook of Clinical Neurology

Vascular Diseases, Part II see Handbook of Clinical Neurology

Vascular Diseases, Part III see Handbook of Clinical Neurology

Vascular Disorders of Childhood. Ed. by Richard H. Dean & James A. O'Neill, Jr. LC 82-191. (Illus.). 217p. reprint ed. pap. 61.90 (*0-7837-1486-6*, 2057181) Bks Demand.

Vascular Disorders of the Ocular Fundus: A Colour Manual of Diagnosis. Rodney H. Grey. (Illus.). 120p. 1991. 95.00 (*0-7506-1033-6*) Buttrwrth-Heinemann.

Vascular Dynamics: Physiological Perspectives. Ed. by N. Westerhof & D. R. Gross. (NATO ASI Series A, Life Sciences: Vol. 166). (Illus.). 334p. 1989. 89.50 (*0-306-43210-2*, Plenum Pr) Plenum.

***Vascular Endothelium: Interactions with Circulating Cells.** J. L. Gordon. (Research Monographs in Cell & Tissue Physiology: Vol. 17). 282p. 1991. 200.00 (*0-444-81156-7*) Elsevier.

Vascular Endothelium: Physiological Basis of Clinical Problems. Ed. by J. D. Catravas et al. (NATO ASI Series A, Life Sciences: Vol. 208). (Illus.). 330p. 1991. 95.00 (*0-306-44012-1*, Plenum Pr) Plenum.

Vascular Endothelium: Physiological Basis of Clinical Problems II. Ed. by A. D. Callow et al. (NATO ASI Series A, Life Sciences: Vol. 257). (Illus.). 230p. (C). 1994. 85.00 (*0-306-44633-2*, Plenum Pr) Plenum.

Vascular Endothelium: Receptors & Transduction Mechanisms. Ed. by J. D. Catravas et al. (NATO ASI Series A, Life Sciences: Vol. 175). (Illus.). 320p. 1989. 89.50 (*0-306-43253-6*, Plenum Pr) Plenum.

Vascular Endothelium: Responses to Injury. Ed. by J. D. Catravas et al. (NATO ASI Series A, Life Sciences: Vol. 281). (Illus.). 345p. (C). 1996. 105.00 (*0-306-45282-0*, Plenum Pr) Plenum.

Vascular Endothelium & Basement Membranes. Ed. by B. M. Altura. (Advances in Microcirculation Ser.: Vol. 9). (Illus.). 1979. 49.00 (*3-8055-3054-4*) S Karger.

Vascular Endothelium in Health & Disease. Ed. by Shu Chien. LC 88-26583. (Advances in Experimental Medicine & Biology Ser.: Vol. 242). (Illus.). 246p. 1988. 75.00 (*0-306-43034-7*, Plenum Pr) Plenum.

Vascular Epiphytes: General Biology & Related Biota. David H. Benzing. (Cambridge Tropical Biology Ser.). (Illus.). 320p. (C). 1990. text ed. 75.00 (*0-521-26630-0*) Cambridge U Pr.

Vascular Flora of Georgia: An Annotated Checklist. Wilbur H. Duncan & John T. Kartesz. LC 80-22014. 158p. (C). 1981. pap. 15.00 (*0-8203-0538-3*) U of Ga Pr.

Vascular Flora of Glen Helen, Clifton Gorge, & John Bryan State Park. Sture F. Anliot. (Biological Notes Ser.: No. 5). 1973. 6.00 (*0-86727-064-0*) Ohio Bio Survey.

Vascular Flora of Pennsylvania: Annotated Checklist & Atlas. Ann F. Rhoads & William M. Klein. LC 92-85316. (Memoirs Ser.: Vol. 207). (Illus.). 600p. (C). 1993. 40.00 (*0-87169-207-4*, M207-RHA) Am Philos.

***Vascular Flora of South Georgia.** W. W. Green. (British Antarctic Survey Report Ser.: No. 45). (Illus.). 86p. 1964. 25.00 (*0-85665-779-4*, Pub. by Brit Antarctic Surv UK) Balogh.

***Vascular Flora of the Falkland Islands.** D. M. Moore. (British Antarctic Survey Report Ser.: No. 60). (Illus.). 214p. 1968. 36.00 (*0-85665-032-3*, Pub. by Brit Antarctic Surv UK) Balogh.

Vascular Flora of the Glaciated Allegheny Plateau Region of Ohio. Barbara K. Andreas. Ed. by Veda M. Cafazzo. LC 87-72905. (Bulletin New Ser.: Vol. 8, No. 1). (Illus.). 191p. (Orig.). 1989. pap. text ed. 15.00 (*0-86727-104-3*) Ohio Bio Survey.

***Vascular Flora of the Southeastern United States Vol. 1: Asteraceae.** Arthur Cronquist. LC 79-769. (Illus.). 277p. 1980. reprint ed. pap. 79.00 (*0-608-03182-8*, 2063635) Bks Demand.

Vascular Flora of the Southeastern United States, Vol. 3, Pt. 2: Leguminosae (Fabaceae) Duane Isely. LC 79-769. (Illus.). xv, 261p. (C). 1990. 45.00 (*0-8078-1900-X*) U of NC Pr.

Vascular Graft Infections. Ed. by T. J. Bunt. (Illus.). 420p. 1994. 69.00 (*0-87993-576-6*) Futura Pub.

Vascular Graft Monitoring. Shushil Gupta. (Medical Intelligence Unit Ser.). 150p. 1993. 89.95 (*1-879702-30-4*) R G Landes.

Vascular Graft Update: Safety & Performance. Helen E. Kambic et al. LC 86-14077. (Special Technical Publication (STP) Ser.: No. 898). (Illus.). 360p. 1986. text ed. 54.00 (*0-8031-0462-6*, 04-898000-54) ASTM.

Vascular Grafting: Clinical Applications & Techniques. Ed. by Creighton B. Wright et al. LC 82-17559. 413p. reprint ed. pap. 117.80 (*0-8357-7872-X*, 2036289) Bks Demand.

Vascular Imaging: Principles & Techniques. Ed. by Bonnie L. Johnson & Thomas J. Fogarty. (Illus.). 400p. 1997. 79.00 (*1-56757-063-1*) Appleton Comms.

Vascular Imaging by Color Doppler & Magnetic Resonance. Ed. by A. P. Yoganathan & Peter Lanzer. (Illus.). xiii, 338p. 1991. 249.00 (*0-387-53320-6*) Spr-Verlag.

Vascular Imaging for Surgeons. Greenhalgh. 1995. text ed. 167.00 (*0-7020-2015-X*) Saunders.

Vascular Injuries & Diseases of the Upper Limb. E. Shaw Wilgis. 183p. 1983. 51.50 (*0-316-94066-6*) Little.

Vascular Injuries in Surgical Practice. Fred Bongard et al. (Illus.). 339p. (C). 1990. text ed. 85.00 (*0-8385-9383-6*, A9383-9) Appleton & Lange.

Vascular Injury & Atherosclerosis. Ed. by Sean Moore. LC 81-15228. (Biochemistry of Disease Ser.: No. 9). (Illus.). 253p. reprint ed. pap. 72.20 (*0-7837-3344-5*, 2043302) Bks Demand.

***Vascular Intervention: A Clinical Approach.** Ed. by Bruce A. Perler & Gary J. Becker. (Illus.). 608p. 1997. 95.00 (*0-86577-694-6*) Thieme Med Pubs.

Vascular Laboratory Operations Manual: A Guide to Survival. Claudia B. Rumwell. 1989. 175.00 (*0-941022-14-5*) Davies Pubng.

Vascular Laboratory Operations Manual: A Guide to Survival. 2nd rev. ed. Ed. by Claudia B. Rumwell. LC 92-48990. (Illus.). 350p. 1997. ring bd. 295.00 (*0-941022-24-2*) Davies Pubng.

Vascular Laboratory Physician's Manual: Indications, Interpretation, & Clinical Decision Making. Marsha M. Neumyer et al. 1998. write for info. (*0-941022-29-3*) Davies Pubng.

Vascular Laboratory Policies & Procedures Manual. Ed. by Claudia B. Rumwell & Michalene McPharlin. 1993. 595.00 (*0-941022-25-0*) Davies Pubng.

Vascular Laboratory Policies & Procedures Manual-MSR 1.1. Ed. by Claudia B. Rumwell & Michalene McPharlin. 1995. ring bd. 795.00 incl. disk (*0-941022-41-2*) Davies Pubng.

Vascular Laboratory Policies & Procedures Manual-Windows 2.1.1. Ed. by Claudia B. Rumwell & Michalene McPharlin. 1995. ring bd. 795.00 incl. disk (*0-941022-42-0*) Davies Pubng.

Vascular Laboratory Quality Assurance Manual. Terence Needham. 1998. write for info. (*0-941022-26-9*) Davies Pubng.

Vascular Malformations & Fistulas of the Brain. Ed. by Robert R. Smith et al. LC 81-40371. (Seminars in Neurological Surgery Ser.). 267p. 1982. reprint ed. pap. 76.10 (*0-608-00449-9*, 2061164) Bks Demand.

Vascular Mechanisms of the Brain. Georgii I. Mchedlishvili. LC 70-141241. 127p. reprint ed. pap. 36.20 (*0-317-07810-0*, 2020684) Bks Demand.

Vascular Medicine. Pearce & Yao. 1996. text ed. 145.00 (*0-8385-9378-X*) P-H.

Vascular Medicine: A Textbook of Vascular Biology & Diseases. 2nd ed. Ed. by Joseph Loscalzo et al. LC 95-39262. 1216p. 1996. text ed. 195.95 (*0-316-53400-5*) Lppncott-Raven.

Vascular Medicine: Proceedings of the Sixteenth World Congress of the International Union of Angiology, Paris, 13-18 September 1992. Ed. by H. Boccalon. LC 92-48404. (International Congress Ser.: No. 1018). 1993. 237.50 (*0-444-89581-7*, Excerpta Medica) Elsevier.

Vascular Neuroeffector Mechanisms. International Symposium on Vascular Neuroeffector Mechanisms Staff. Ed. by John A. Bevan et al. LC 78-69739. (Illus.). 429p. reprint ed. pap. 122.30 (*0-7837-7108-8*, 2046937) Bks Demand.

Vascular Neuroeffector Mechanisms: Proceedings of the Symposium, 2nd International, Odense, July-August, 1955. Vascular Neuroeffector Mechanism Symposium Staff. (Illus.). 300p. 1976. 101.00 (*3-8055-2325-4*) S Karger.

Vascular Neuroeffector Mechanisms: Receptors, Ion-Channels, Second Messengers & Endogenous Mediators. Ed. by J. A. Bevan et al. (ICSU Symposium Ser.). 352p. 1988. pap. 90.00 (*1-85221-095-8*, IRL Pr) OUP.

Vascular Neuroeffector Mechanisms: 4th International Symposium. fac. ed. International Vascular Neuroeffector Mechanisms Symposium Staff. Ed. by John A. Bevan et al. LC 83-4410. (Illus.). 455p. pap. 129.70 (*0-7837-7217-3*, 2047081) Bks Demand.

Vascular Neuroeffector Systems, Physiology & Pharmacology: Proceedings of the Symposium, Interlaken, 1969. Physiology & Pharmacology of Vascular Neuroeffector Systems Symposium Staff. Ed. by J. A. Bevan et al. (Illus.). viii, 350p. 1971. 57.75 (*3-8055-1184-1*) S Karger.

Vascular Neuroeffectors Mechanisms: Journal: Blood Vessels, Vol. 28, No. 103, 1991. Ed. by J. A. Bevan et al. (Illus.). 268p. 1991. pap. 187.00 (*3-8055-5380-3*) S Karger.

Vascular Nursing. 2nd ed. Ed. by Victoria A. Fahey. LC 93-11267. (Illus.). 592p. 1993. text ed. 89.00 (*0-7216-6589-6*) Saunders.

***Vascular Nursing.** 3rd ed. Fahey. Date not set. text ed. write for info. (*0-7216-7657-X*) Saunders.

Vascular Pathology. Ed. by William E. Stehbens & J. T. Lie. LC 94-69665. 797p. (gr. 13). 1994. text ed. 177.95 (*0-412-48640-7*) Chapman & Hall.

Vascular Perfusion in Cancer Therapy. Ed. by K. Schwemmle & K. Aigner. (Recent Results in Cancer Research Ser.: Vol. 86). (Illus.). 280p. 1983. 99.00 (*0-387-12346-6*) Spr-Verlag.

Vascular Physics Review. Ed. by Barton A. Bean et al. (Illus.). 180p. 1995. pap. text ed. 55.00 (*0-941022-36-6*) Davies Pubng.

Vascular Plant Families. James P. Smith, Jr. (Illus.). 320p. (Orig.). (C). 1977. pap. 19.95 (*0-916422-11-9*) Mad River.

Vascular Plant Families & Genera: A Listing of the Genera of Vascular Plants of the World According to Their Families...with an Analysis of Relationships of the Flowering Plant Families According to Eight Systems of Classification. Compiled by R. K. Brummitt. viii, 804p. 1992. 48.00 (*0-947643-43-5*, Pub. by Royal Botnic Grdns UK) Balogh.

***Vascular Plant Taxonomy.** 4th ed. Dirk R. Walters. 636p. (C). 1996. per., pap. text ed. 59.79 (*0-7872-2108-2*) Kendall-Hunt.

Vascular Plant Type Collection at the California Academy of Sciences Index. Compiled by Barbara T. Keller. 288p. 1985. 249.00 (*0-930466-90-X*) Chadwyck-Healey.

Vascular Plant Type Collection of the United States National Arboretum Index. Compiled by James A. Mears. 78p. 1985. 100.00 (*0-930466-94-2*) Chadwyck-Healey.

Vascular Plants As Epiphytes. Ed. by Ulrich Luttge. (Ecological Studies: Vol. 76). (Illus.). 280p. 1989. 139.00 (*0-387-50796-5*) Spr-Verlag.

Vascular Plants of Grand Teton National Park: Annotated Checklist. Richard J. Shaw. (Illus.). 96p. 1992. pap. 9.95 (*0-931895-23-5*) Grand Teton NHA.

Vascular Plants of Iowa: An Annotated Checklist & Natural History. Lawrence J. Eilers & Dean M. Roosa. LC 94-21019. (Bur Oak Original Ser.). 319p. 1994. 29.95 (*0-87745-463-9*); pap. 14.95 (*0-87745-464-7*) U of Iowa Pr.

Vascular Plants of Kentucky: An Annotated Checklist. Edward T. Browne, Jr. & Raymond Athey. LC 91-2499. 200p. 1992. text ed. 20.00 (*0-8131-1675-9*) U Pr of Ky.

Vascular Plants of Minnesota: A Checklist & Atlas. Gerald B. Ownbey & Thomas Morley. 307p. 1993. pap. 29.95 (*0-8166-2354-6*) U of Minn Pr.

Vascular Plants of Northern Utah: An Identification Manual. Richard J. Shaw. (Illus.). 412p. (Orig.). (C). 1989. pap. text ed. 29.95 (*0-87421-141-7*) Utah St U Pr.

Vascular Plants of Russia & Adjacent States (the Former U. S. S. R.) S. K. Czerepanov. (Illus.). 516p. (C). 1995. text ed. 100.00 (*0-521-45006-3*) Cambridge U Pr.

Vascular Plants of Texas: A Comprehensive Checklist Including Synonymy, Bibliography, & Index. Stanley D. Jones et al. LC 96-28571. 1997. write for info. (*0-292-74045-X*) U of Tex Pr.

Vascular Plants of Texas: A Comprehensive Checklist Including Synonymy, Bibliography, & Index. Stanley D. Jones et al. LC 96-28571. (Illus.). 384p. 1997. 55.00 (*0-292-74044-1*) U of Tex Pr.

Vascular Plants of the Leeward Island, Hawaii. E. Christophersen & E. L. Caum. (BMB Ser.). 1974. reprint ed. 25.00 (*0-527-02187-3*) Periodicals Srv.

Vascular Plants of the Medicine Bow Mountains, Wyoming. rev. ed. Burrell E. Nelson. 393p. 1984. pap. text ed. 12.00 (*0-936204-19-2*) Big Horn Booksellers Inc.

Vascular Plants of the Nevada Test Site & Central Southern Nevada: Ecologic & Geographic Distributions. ERDA Technical Information Center Staff & Janice C. Beatley. LC 76-21839. 315p. 1976. pap. 16.00 (*0-87079-033-1*, TID-26881); fiche 9.00 (*0-87079-216-4*, TID-26881) DOE.

Vascular Plants of the Pacific Northwest Vol. 1: Vascular Cryptogams, Gymnosperms, & Monocotyledons. C. Leo Hitchcock et al. LC 56-62679. (Biology Ser.). (Illus.). 925p. 1969. 60.00 (*0-295-73983-5*) U of Wash Pr.

Vascular Plants of the Pacific Northwest Vol. 2: Salicaceae to Saxifragaceae. C. Leo Hitchcock et al. LC 56-62679. (Biology Ser.). (Illus.). 597p. 1964. 60.00 (*0-295-73984-3*) U of Wash Pr.

Vascular Plants of the Pacific Northwest Vol. 3: Saxifragaceae to Ericaceae. C. Leo Hitchcock et al. LC 56-62679. (Biology Ser.). (Illus.). 614p. 1961. 60.00 (*0-295-73985-1*) U of Wash Pr.

Vascular Plants of the Pacific Northwest Vol. 4: Ericaceae Through Companulaceae. C. Leo Hitchcock et al. LC 56-62679. (Biology Ser.). (Illus.). 516p. 1959. 60.00 (*0-295-73986-X*) U of Wash Pr.

UV

An Asterisk (*) at the beginning of an entry indicates that the title is appearing in BIP for the first time.

***Vascular Plants of the Pacific Northwest Vol. 5: Compositae.** C. Leo Hitchcock et al. LC 56-62679. (Biology Ser.). (Illus.). 349p. 1955. 60.00 (*0-295-73987-8*) U of Wash Pr.

Vascular Plants of Unglaciated Ohio. Allison W. Cusick & Gene M. Silberhorn. (Bulletin New Ser.: Vol. 5, No. 4). 1977. 10.00 (*0-86727-081-0*) Ohio Bio Survey.

Vascular Plants of Western Washington. Ed. by Irene Creso. LC 84-72043. (Illus.). 520p. (Orig.). 1984. pap. 14.95 (*0-9613916-0-X*) Creso.

***Vascular Risk Factors & Neuroprotection in Glaucoma: Update 1996.** Stephen M. Drance. LC 97-17662. 1997. write for info. (*90-6299-137-8*) Kugler Pubns.

Vascular Smooth Muscle Cell: Molecular & Biological Responses to the Extracellular Matrix. Ed. by Robert P. Mecham & Stephen M. Schwartz. (Biology of the Extracellular Matrix Ser.). (Illus.). 410p. 1995. boxed 95.00 (*0-12-632310-0*) Acad Pr.

Vascular Smooth Muscle in Culture, 2 vols. Ed. by Julie H. Campbell & Gordon R. Campbell. 1987. Set. 212.00 (*0-8493-4325-9*, QP110, CRC Reprint) Franklin.

Vascular Smooth Muscle in Culture, 2 vols., I. Ed. by Julie H. Campbell & Gordon R. Campbell. 168p. 1987. 98.00 (*0-8493-4327-5*, CRC Reprint) Franklin.

Vascular Smooth Muscle in Culture, 2 vols., Vol. II. Ed. by Julie H. Campbell & Gordon R. Campbell. 384p. 1987. write for info. (*0-318-62354-4*) CRC Pr.

Vascular Smooth Muscle/Culture, Vol. I. Campbell. 200p. 1987. 114.00 (*0-8493-4326-7*) CRC Pr.

Vascular Surgery. Callow & Ernst. (C). 1995. text ed. 225.00 (*0-8385-9384-4*, A9384-7) Appleton & Lange.

Vascular Surgery. Ed. by John B. Chang. LC 85-2319. 271p. 1985. text ed. 48.95 (*0-89335-232-2*) PMA Pub Corp.

Vascular Surgery. Ed. by G. Herberer & R. J. Van Dongen. (Illus.). 860p. 1989. 477.00 (*0-387-18280-2*) Spr-Verlag.

Vascular Surgery. Crawford W. Jamieson & James S. Yao. (Rob & Smith's Operative Surgery Ser.). (Illus.). 700p. 1993. 435.00 (*0-7506-0588-X*) Chapman & Hall.

Vascular Surgery. MacVittie. (Perioperative Nursing Ser.). 375p. (C). (gr. 13). 1997. text ed. 54.95 (*0-8151-7031-9*) Mosby Yr Bk.

Vascular Surgery. Ed. by S. E. Wilson et al. (Illus.). 992p. 1987. text ed. 145.00 (*0-07-070812-6*) McGraw.

Vascular Surgery, 2. 4th ed. Ed. by Robert B. Rutherford. (Illus.). 2033p. 1995. 260.00 (*0-7216-3837-6*) Saunders.

Vascular Surgery, 2 vol., Set. 4th ed. Rutherford. 1994. text ed. 269.00 (*0-7216-3836-8*) HarBrace.

Vascular Surgery: A Comprehensive Review. 4th ed. Ed. by Wesley S. Moore. LC 92-49116. (Illus.). 816p. 1993. text ed. 179.00 (*0-7216-4841-X*) Saunders.

Vascular Surgery: A Comprehensive Review. 5th ed. Wesley S. Moore. Ed. by Lisette Bralow. (Illus.). 832p. 1997. text ed. write for info. (*0-7216-6962-X*) Saunders.

Vascular Surgery: Basic Science & Clinical Correlations. Rodney A. White & Larry H. Hollier. LC 93-41441. (Illus.). 700p. (C). 1994. text ed. 110.00 (*0-397-51280-5*, Lippncott) Lppncott-Raven.

Vascular Surgery: Current Questions. Ed. by Aires A. D'Sa et al. (Illus.). 380p. 1991. 140.00 (*0-7506-1381-5*) Buttrwrth-Heinemann.

Vascular Surgery: Guide & Handbook. Pratt. LC 75-27628. (Illus.). 416p. 1976. 27.60 (*0-87527-138-3*) Green.

Vascular Surgery: Principles & Practice. 2nd ed. Ed. by Frank J. Veith et al. (Illus.). 1270p. 1993. text ed. 179.00 (*0-07-070813-4*) McGraw-Hill HPD.

***Vascular Surgery: Twenty Years of Progress.** James S. Yao & William H. Pearce. LC 96-36611. 1996. boxed 145.00 (*0-8385-9387-9*) Appleton & Lange.

Vascular Surgery Review. Roy L. Tawes, Jr. 144p. 1996. pap. 28.95 (*1-56757-060-7*) Appleton Comms.

Vascular Technology: An Illustrated Review for the Registry Exam. Claudia B. Rumwell & Michalene McPharlin. (Illus.). 267p. 1995. pap. text ed. 57.50 (*0-941022-43-9*) Davies Pubng.

Vascular Technology Review. 3rd ed. Ed. by Barton A. Bean. LC 88-34404. (Orig.). 1989. pap. text ed. 55.00 (*0-941022-15-3*) Davies Pubng.

Vascular Technology Review. 4th ed. Ed. by Barton A. Bean. (Orig.). 1997. pap. text ed. 55.00 (*0-941022-19-6*) Davies Pubng.

***Vascular Trauma.** 2nd ed. Rich. 1998. text ed. write for info. (*0-7216-4071-0*) Saunders.

Vascular Tumors & Malfunctions of the Ocular Fundus. J. D. Delaey & M. Hanssens. (Monographs in Ophthalmology). (C). 1990. lib. bdg. 167.00 (*0-7923-0750-X*) Kluwer Ac.

Vascular Wilt Diseases of Plants. Ed. by E. C. Tjamos & C. H. Beckman. (NATO ASI Series H: Vol. 28). (Illus.). xiv, 590p. 1989. 214.95 (*0-387-18560-7*) Spr-Verlag.

***Vasculitides: Science & Practice.** Ed. by Ansell et al. (Illus.). 480p. 1995. text ed. 102.50 (*0-412-64140-2*, Chap & Hall NY) Chapman & Hall.

Vasculitis, Rheumatic Disease, & the Nervous System. Peter Berlit. Ed. by Patricia Moore. LC 92-48500. 1992. 35.00 (*0-387-54853-X*) Spr-Verlag.

Vase Painting in Italy: Red-Figure & Related Works in the Museum of Arts, Boston. Cornelius C. Vermeule et al. (Illus.). 275p. 1993. pap. 30.00 (*0-87846-406-9*) Mus Fine Arts Boston.

Vasectomy: The Decision-Making Process. S. D. Mumford. (Illus.). 1978. 12.50 (*0-615-00892-5*); pap. 7.50 (*0-911302-33-6*) San Francisco Pr.

Vasectomy & Medicine: Guidebook for Reference & Research. Benard I. Valahos. LC 83-46111. 150p. 1985. 37.50 (*0-88164-156-1*); pap. 29.50 (*0-88164-157-X*) ABBE Pubs Assn.

Vasectomy Blues. Al Blair. 6p. 1990. pap. 3.95 (*0-930366-22-0*) Northcountry Pub.

Vasectomy Counseling. S. D. Mumford. (Illus.). 1977. 10.00 (*0-911302-31-X*); pap. 6.00 (*0-317-58585-1*) San Francisco Pr.

Vases Communicants. Andre Breton. (FRE.). 1970. pap. 10.95 (*0-7859-2837-5*) Fr & Eur.

Vases Communicants: Essai. Andre Breton. (Idees Ser.). (FRE.). pap. 8.95 (*2-07-035223-4*) Schoenhof.

Vasile Alecsandri. Alexandre Cioranescu. LC 79-169637. (Twayne's World Authors Ser.). 1973. lib. bdg. 17.95 (*0-8057-2020-0*) Irvington.

Vasilii Shukshin I Russkoe Dukhovnoe Vozrozhdenie (Vassily Shukshin & the Russian Spiritual Renaissance) Eugene Vertlieb. LC 89-82747. (Illus.). 272p. (RUS.). (C). 1990. pap. text ed. 17.00 (*0-911971-49-1*) Effect Pub.

Vasilii Trediakovsky: The Fool of the "New" Russian Literature. Irina Reyfman. LC 90-9682. (Illus.). 336p. 1991. 42.50 (*0-8047-1824-5*) Stanford U Pr.

***Vasili's Secret.** Timothy W. Gibson. 167p. (Orig.). 1997. mass mkt. 4.99 (*1-55197-992-6*, Pub. by Comnwlth Pub CN) Partners Pubs Grp.

Vasilissa the Beautiful. Post Wheeler. (Creative Short Stories Ser.). (YA). (gr. 4-12). 1989. 13.95 (*0-88682-354-4*, 97226-098) Creative Ed.

Vasiliy Grossman - The Genesis of Evolution of Heresy. Frank Ellis. 1994. 49.95 (*0-85496-830-X*) Berg Pubs.

Vasiliy Pavlovich Aksenov: A Writer in Quest of Himself. Ed. by Edward Mozejko et al. (Illus.). 272p. 1986. 27.95 (*0-89357-141-5*) Slavica.

Vasily Ivanchuk's Best Games. Gufeld. 1996. pap. 19.95 (*1-85744-102-8*, Pub. by Cadogan Books UK) Macmillan.

***Vasily Kandinsky.** LC 96-37573. (Masters of Art Ser.). 1997. write for info. (*0-8109-1228-7*) Abrams.

Vasily Kandinsky: A Colorful Life, the Collection of the Lenbachhaus, Munich. Vivian E. Barnett & Helmut Friedel. (Illus.). 512p. 1996. 95.00 (*0-8109-6319-1*) Abrams.

Vasily Kandinsky-An Introduction to His Work, 1974: An Introduction to His Work. Contrib. by Stephanie Terenzio. (Illus.). 60p. 1974. 3.00 (*0-918386-12-8*) W Benton Mus.

Vasily Kandinsky Compositions. Magdalena Dabrowski. (Illus.). 128p. 1995. 45.00 (*0-8109-6142-3*) Abrams.

***Vasily Smslov - Endgame Virtuoso.** Vasily Smysloz. 1997. pap. 19.95 (*1-85744-198-2*) Macmillan.

Vasily Titov & the Russian Baroque: Selected Choral Works. Ed. & Intro. by Olga Dolskaya. (Monuments of Russian Sacred Music Ser.: Series XIII, Vol. 1). (Illus.). xxix, 204p. (C). 1995. 49.00 (*0-9629460-3-6*) Musica Russica.

Vasistha's Yoga. Swami Venkatesananda. LC 92-3160. 767p. 1993. pap. 19.95 (*0-7914-1364-0*); text ed. 59.50 (*0-7914-1363-2*) State U NY Pr.

Vaskulaere Hirnerkrankung im Alter. Ed. by W. Meier-Ruge. (Geriatrie fuer die Taegliche Praxis Ser.: Vol. 2). viii, 188p. 1989. pap. 19.25 (*3-8055-4508-8*) S Karger.

Vaslav Nijinsky. C. W. Beaumont. LC 74-1080. (Studies in Music: No. 42). (C). 1974. lib. bdg. 75.00 (*0-8383-1752-9*) M S G Haskell Hse.

Vaslav Nijinsky: A Leap into Madness. rev. ed. Peter F. Ostwald. LC 95-9381. (Illus.). 400p. 1996. pap. 14.95 (*0-8065-1681-X*, Citadel Pr) Carol Pub Group.

Vaslav Nijinsky: The Leap into Madness. Peter F. Ostwald. 1990. 19.95 (*0-8184-0535-X*) Carol Pub Group.

Vasn Vardanay Ew Hayots Paterazmin: The History of Vartan & the Armenian War. Eghishe. Ed. by R. W. Thomson. LC 93-24942. (Classical Armenian Texts Ser.). 1993. 50.00 (*0-88206-034-1*) Caravan Bks.

Vasnetsov, Victor. N. Shanina. 132p. (C). 1979. 108.00 (*0-685-34414-2*, Pub. by Collets) St Mut.

Vasnetsov, Yury. V. Petrov. 196p. (C). 1984. 275.00 (*0-685-34413-4*, Pub. by Collets) St Mut.

Vasoactive Factors Produced by the Endothelium. J. Seccombe & H. Schaff. (Medical Intelligence Unit Ser.). 100p. 1994. 89.95 (*1-879702-39-8*) R G Landes.

Vasoactive Intestinal Peptide. Sami I. Said. LC 80-5536. (Advances in Peptide Hormone Research Ser.). 526p. reprint ed. pap. 150.00 (*0-7837-7101-0*, 2046930) Bks Demand.

Vasoactive Moleculaes As Regulators of Cell Growth. Ed. by G. Wolf. (Journal: Experimental Nephrology: Vol. 2, No. 2, 1994). (Illus.). 92p. 1994. pap. 50.50 (*3-8055-5958-5*) S Karger.

Vasoactive Renal Hormones. Ed. by G. M. Eisenbach & J. Brod. (Contributions to Nephrology Ser.: Vol. 12). (Illus.). 1978. pap. 54.50 (*3-8055-2839-6*) S Karger.

Vasodepressor Hormones in Hypertension: Prostaglandins & Kallikrein-Kinins. Ed. by Gerd Bonner. (Agents & Actions Supplements Ser.: No. 22). 380p. 1987. 94.50 (*3-7643-1922-4*) Birkhauser.

Vasodilator Mechanisms. Ed. by P. M. Vanhoutte & St. F. Vatner. (Bibliotheca Cardiologica Ser.: No. 38). (Illus.). viii, 284p. 1985. 110.50 (*3-8055-3903-7*) S Karger.

Vasodilator Substances of Tissues. J. H. Gaddum. (Illus.). 288p. 1987. 69.95 (*0-521-30860-7*) Cambridge U Pr.

Vasomotion & Flow Modulation in the Microcirculation. Ed. by Marcos Intaglietta. (Progress in Applied Microcirculation, Mikrozirkulation in Forschung und Klinik Ser.: Vol. 15). (Illus.). viii, 104p. 1989. 62.50 (*3-8055-5014-6*) S Karger.

Vasomotion & Flow Motion. Ed. by C. Allegra et al. (Progress in Applied Microcirculation Ser.: Vol. 20). (Illus.). viii, 88p. 1993. 85.25 (*3-8055-5750-7*) S Karger.

Vasomotion & Quantitative Kapillaroskopie. Ed. by K. Messmer & F. Hammersen. (Progress in Applied Microcirculation Ser.: Vol. 3). (Illus.). viii, 152p. 1984. pap. 65.75 (*3-8055-3809-X*) S Karger.

Vasopressin. Ed. by Robert W. Schrier. LC 85-10714. (Illus.). 601p. 1985. reprint ed. pap. 171.30 (*0-7837-9576-9*, 2060325) Bks Demand.

***Vasopressin: Cellular & Integrative Functions.** Ed. by Allen W. Cowley, Jr. et al. LC 87-43176. reprint ed. pap. 154.50 (*0-608-04722-8*, 2065443) Bks Demand.

Vasopressin: Disturbed Secretion & Its Effects. L. Kovacs. (Developments in Nephrology Ser.). (C). 1990. lib. bdg. 132.00 (*0-7923-0249-4*) Kluwer Ac.

Vasopressin: Principles & Properties. Ed. by Don M. Gash & G. J. Boer. (Illus.). 626p. 1987. 125.00 (*0-306-42515-7*, Plenum Pr) Plenum.

***Vasquez: California's Forgotten Bandit.** Jack Jones. LC 96-95147. (Illus.). viii, 208p. (Orig.). 1997. pap. 9.95 (*0-9653770-0-8*) Akira Pr.

***Vassalboro Register, 1904 (Town History & Directory)** Compiled by Mitchell & Davis. 132p. 1997. reprint ed. pap. 21.50 (*0-8328-5920-6*) Higginson Bk Co.

Vassals, Heiresses, Crusaders, & Thugs: The Gentry of Angevin Yorkshire, 1154-1216. Hugh M. Thomas. LC 92-42782. (Middle Ages Ser.). 320p. (C). 1993. text ed. 34.95 (*0-8122-3159-7*) U of Pa Pr.

Vassar: A Photographic Celebration. Mark C. Borton. (Illus.). 112p. 1984. 30.00 (*0-930527-01-1*); pap. 20.00 (*0-930527-00-3*) Embassy Marine.

Vassar Stories. Grace M. Gallaher. LC 71-113663. (Short Story Index Reprint Ser.). 1977. 21.95 (*0-8369-3392-3*) Ayer.

Vasse's Bambinelli: The Child Portraits of an Eighteenth-Century French Sculptor Bernard Black. Bernard Black. (Illus.). 100p. (C). 1994. text ed. 49.95 (*0-485-11444-5*, Pub. by Athlone Pr UK) Humanities.

***Vassili Surikov (1848-1916)** Vladimir Kemenov. (Great Painters Ser.). 1997. 40.00 (*1-85995-325-5*) Parkstone Pr.

Vassilisa the Wise. Houghton Mifflin Company Staff. (Literature Experience 1991 Ser.). (J). (gr. 5). 1990. pap. 9.16 (*0-395-55169-2*) HM.

Vassilisa the Wise. Houghton Mifflin Company Staff. (J). (gr. 5). 1992. pap. 9.16 (*0-395-61822-3*) HM.

Vassilisa the Wise: A Tale of Medieval Russia. Illus. by Daniel San Souci. LC 87-8563. 26p. (J). (gr. k-3). 1988. 16.00 (*0-15-293240-2*) HarBrace.

Vassilisa the Wise: A Tale of Medieval Russia. large type ed. Illus. by Daniel San Souci. 1993. 9.50 (*0-614-09858-0*, L-34128-00) Am Printing Hse.

Vassouras, a Brazilian Coffee County, 1850-1900: The Roles of Planter & Slave in a Plantation Society. Stanley J. Stein. LC 85-42659. (Illus.). 356p. 1985. pap. text ed. 19.95 (*0-691-02236-4*) Princeton U Pr.

Vast. Doug Huston & Moore Lande. (Westerns Ser.: No. 1). (Illus.). 157p. (Orig.). 1994. pap. 10.00 (*1-888636-03-3*) Sara Ranchouse.

V.A.S.T. Visual Approach to Systems Thinking. Yvonne M. Hansen. (Illus.). 75p. 1996. pap. text ed. 15.00 (*0-9625347-5-7*) Gemin-Ideas Pr.

Vast Amount of Trouble: A History of the Spring Creek Raid. John W. Davis. (Illus.). 304p. 1994. 24.95 (*0-87081-310-2*) Univ Pr Colo.

***Vast & Ancient Wilderness: Images of the Great Basin.** Claude Fiddler. LC 97-21313. 1997. 45.00 (*0-8118-1502-1*) Chronicle Bks.

Vast Design: Patterns in W. B. Yeats's Aesthetic. 2nd expanded ed. Edward Engelberg. LC 87-35101. 316p. 1988. reprint ed. pap. 90.10 (*0-7837-9122-4*, 2049923) Bks Demand.

Vast Domain of Blood. Don Schellie. LC 68-29143. (Illus.). ixx, 268p. 26.95 (*0-87026-022-7*) Westernlore.

Vast Encyclopedia: The Theatre of Thornton Wilder. Paul Lifton. LC 95-5675. (Contributions in Drama & Theatre Studies: Vol. 61). 240p. 1995. text ed. 59.95 (*0-313-29356-2*, Greenwood Pr) Greenwood.

Vast Illusion: Time According to A Course in Miracles. 2nd ed. Kenneth Wapnick. LC 93-41757. 343p. (Orig.). 1993. pap. 12.00 (*0-933291-09-4*) Foun Miracles.

Vast Sea of Misery: A History & Guide to the Union & Confederate Field Hospitals at Gettysburg, July 1-November 20, 1863. Gregory A. Coco. (Illus.). 224p. (C). 1988. pap. text ed. 21.95 (*0-939631-88-1*) Thomas Publications.

***VAST 30th Anniversary Cookbook 1967-1997.** VAST Membership. (Illus.). x, 125p. 1997. 10.95 (*0-9657216-0-4*, 96: 39: 0844) VT Assn Snow Trvlrs.

Vastu-Sastra, Vol. I: Hindu Science of Architecture. D. N. Shukla. (C). 1993. text ed. 67.50 (*81-215-0611-5*, Pub. by Munshiram Manoharial II) S Asia.

Vastu-Sastra, Vol. II: Hindu Canons of Iconography & Painting. D. N. Shukla. (C). 1993. text ed. 67.50 (*81-215-0612-3*, Pub. by Munshiram Manoharial II) S Asia.

Vastusutra Upanishad: The Essence of Form in Sacred Art. Alice Boner. xii, 192p. 1986. 32.00 (*0-317-56442-0*, Pub. by Motilal Banarsidass II) S Asia.

Vasyl Stus: His Life & Works, Recollections & Essays by His Contemporaries. Ed. by Osyp Zinkewych & Mykola Francuzenko. LC 86-62087. 464p. 1987. 16.25 (*0-914834-57-6*) Smoloskyp.

VAT. Gavin McFarlane. (C). 1991. text ed. 22.00 (*1-85431-134-4*, Pub. by Blackstone Pr UK) Gaunt.

VAT: Veterinary Aptitude Test Practice Examination. David M. Tarlow. (Practice Examination Ser.: No. 3). 40p. 1992. pap. 16.95 (*0-931572-56-8*) Datar Pub.

VAT: Veterinary Aptitude Test Practice Examination, No. 2. David M. Tarlow. (Practice Examination Ser.). 40p. 1992. pap. 16.95 (*0-931572-54-1*) Datar Pub.

VAT & Property. 2nd ed. Howard Scott & Dermot McLennan. 251p. 1992. pap. 93.00 (*0-406-00630-X*, U.K.) MICHIE.

Vat & Vat Planning for Retail Businesses. John Ireland. 1995. pap. text ed. 88.00 (*0-406-03687-X*, UK) MICHIE.

VAT Business Needs Survey. HMSO Staff. 178p. 1995. pap. 55.00 (*0-11-701870-8*, HM18708, Pub. by Stationery Ofc UK) Bernan Associates.

Vat Handbook: A Practical Guide for Business. Coopers & Lybrand Staff. 230p. (Orig.). 1989. pap. text ed. 44.95 (*0-8464-1366-3*) Beekman Pubs.

VAT in the European Community. 2nd ed. Ed. by Alan Buckett. 150p. 1992. pap. 78.00 (*0-406-00852-3*, UK) MICHIE.

VAT in the Single Market: The Price Waterhouse Guide Through the Maze. Ed. by Price Waterhouse Staff. LC 93-39924. 128p. (C). 1993. lib. bdg. 61.00 (*1-85333-923-7*) G & T Inc.

VAT in the Single Market: The Price Waterhouse Guide Through the Maze. Price Waterhouse Staff. 128p. (C). 1993. lib. bdg. 53.00 (*1-85333-944-X*, Pub. by Graham & Trotman UK) Kluwer Ac.

VAT Tribunal Reports 1973-1985, 15 vols. Set. 950.00 (*0-86205-284-X*) MICHIE.

VAT (Veterinary Aptitude Test) David M. Tarlow. (Practice Examination Ser.: No. 4). 40p. 1992. pap. text ed. 16.95 (*0-931572-55-X*) Datar Pub.

VAT (Veterinary Aptitude Test) Practice Examination, No. 1. David M. Tarlow. (Practice Examination Ser.). 40p. (C). 1992. pap. 16.95 (*0-931572-27-4*) Datar Pub.

VAT (Veterinary Aptitude Test) Practice Examination, No. 5. David M. Tarlow. (Practice Examination Ser.). 40p. (C). 1992. pap. text ed. 16.95 (*0-931572-28-2*) Datar Pub.

***Vaterbuch.** Deutschen Akademie der Wissenschaften Staff & Karl Reissenberger. (Deutsche Texte des Mittelalters Ser.: Band XXII). xxv, 634p. (GER.). 1967. write for info. (*3-296-17222-X*, Pub. by Weidmann GW) Lubrecht & Cramer.

Vates. Tomas Blanco. LC 80-67415. (Obras Completas de Tomas Blanco Ser.). 96p. 1981. pap. 7.50 (*0-940238-43-8*) Ediciones Huracan.

Vathek. William Beckford. Ed. by Roger Lonsdale. (World's Classics Paperback Ser.). 216p. 1983. pap. 8.95 (*0-19-281645-4*) OUP.

Vathek: The English Translation by Samuel Henley (1786) & the French Editions of Lausanne & Paris -1787., 3 vols. in 1. William Beckford. LC 72-4324. 768p. (FRE.). 1972. reprint ed. 90.00 (*0-8201-1102-3*) Schol Facsimiles.

Vathek see Three Gothic Novels

Vathek see Castle of Otranto (Three Gothic Novels)

Vathek & Other Stories. William Beckford. Ed. & Intro. by Malcolm R. Jack. 352p. 1995. pap. 9.95 (*0-14-043530-1*, Penguin Classics) Viking Penguin.

Vathek & the Escape from Time: Bicentenary Revaluations. Ed. by Kenneth W. Graham. LC 89-6471. (Studies in the Eighteenth Century: No. 15). 1990. 42.50 (*0-404-63515-6*) AMS Pr.

VATI. Peter Schneider. Ed. by Colin Riordan. (German Texts Ser.). 160p. 1993. text ed. 17.95 (*0-7190-3470-1*, Pub. by Manchester Univ Pr UK) St Martin.

***Vatican.** Francesco Papafava. (Illus.). 191p. 1993. 75.00 (*88-86921-03-9*, Pub. by Musei Vaticani IT); pap. 55.00 (*88-86921-02-0*, Pub. by Musei Vaticani IT) Treasures Inc.

Vatican. large type ed. Jerome Carcopino. (Illus.). 225p. (FRE.). 1958. lib. bdg. 150.00 (*0-8288-3947-6*) Fr & Eur.

Vatican & Communism in World War II: What Really Happened? Robert A. Graham. LC 95-79873. 199p. (Orig.). 1996. pap. 12.95 (*0-89870-549-5*) Ignatius Pr.

Vatican & Hungary 1846-1878: Reports & Correspondence on Hungary of the Apostolic Nuncios in Vienna. Lajos Lukacs. Tr. by Zsofia Kormos. 796p. (C). 1981. 150.00 (*963-05-2446-5*, Pub. by Akad Kiado HU) St Mut.

Vatican & Poland in the Age of the Partitions: Diplomatic & Cultural Encounters at the Warsaw Nunciature. Larry Wolff. (East European Monographs: No. 245). 282p. 1988. text ed. 60.00 (*0-88033-142-9*) East Eur Monographs.

Vatican & Zionism: Conflict in the Holy Land, 1895-1925. Sergio I. Minerbi. Tr. by Arnold Schwartz. (Studies in Jewish History). (Illus.). 272p. 1990. 30.00 (*0-19-505892-5*) OUP.

***Vatican Archives: An Inventory & Guide to Historical Record of the Holly See.** Ed. by Francis X. Blouin, Jr. 840p. 1997. 150.00 (*0-19-509552-9*) OUP.

Vatican, Biblioteca Apostolica, Ms Vat. Mus. 569 (Multi MS) Ed. by Alexander Silbiger. (Seventeenth-Century Keyboard Music Ser.). 871230p. 1987. text ed. 20.00 (*0-8240-8013-0*) Garland.

Vatican, Biblioteca Apostolica Vaticana, MS Chigi Q. IV. 25 (Attributed to Frescobaldi) Ed. by Alexander Silbiger. LC 88-753519. (Seventeenth-Century Keyboard Music Ser.: Vol. 1). 160p. 1989. text ed. 20.00 (*0-8240-8000-9*) Garland.

Vatican Billions. Avro Manhattan. LC 83-72654. 304p. 1983. pap. 11.50 (*0-937958-16-6*) Chick Pubns.

***Vatican City.** Francesco Roncalli. (Illus.). 128p. 1996. pap. 25.00 (*0-614-24670-9*) Sheed & Ward MO.

***Vatican City.** Francesco Roncalli. (Illus.). 126p. 1989. pap. 25.00 (*88-86921-07-1*) Treasures Inc.

Vatican City. V. Volpino. 15.95 (*0-517-62280-7*) Random Hse Value.

Vatican City, Biblioteca Apostolica, MSS Chigi Q. IV. 24, 26-29 & Q. VIII. 205-206, 6 vols. Ed. by Alexander Silbiger. LC 88-753943. (Seventeenth-Century Keyboard Music Ser.: Vol. 15). 980p. 1989. Set. text ed. 75.00 (*0-8240-8014-9*) Garland.

Vatican City State. Michael J. Walsh. (World Bibliographical Ser.: No. 41). 105p. 1983. lib. bdg. 45.00 (*0-903450-72-0*) ABC-CLIO.

Vatican Council II: Basic Education. Ed. by Austin P. Flannery. 1996. pap. 13.95 (*0-8146-2451-0*) Liturgical Pr.

Vatican Council II: The Conciliar & Post Conciliar Documents, No. 1. Ed. by Austin P. Flannery. 1062p. (Orig.). 1987. pap. 15.95 (*0-8146-0885-X*) Liturgical Pr.

UV

An Asterisk (*) at the beginning of an entry indicates that the title is appearing in BIP for the first time.

Vatican Council II Vol. 2: The Conciliar & Post Conciliar Documents, Vol. 2. Ed. by Austin P. Flannery. 994p. (Orig.). 1983. pap. 15.95 (*0-8146-1299-7*) Liturgical Pr.

Vatican Council Two: The Sixteen Council Documents, Basic Edition. Ed. by Austin P. Flannery. 510p. (Orig.). pap. write for info. (*0-8028-0687-2*) Eerdmans.

Vatican Diplomacy: A Study of Church & State on the International Plane. Robert A. Graham. LC 59-13870. 452p. reprint ed. pap. 128.90 (*0-317-08423-2*, 2015012) Bks Demand.

Vatican Empire. 1996. lib. bdg. 251.99 (*0-8490-6934-3*) Gordon Pr.

Vatican Frescoes of Michelangelo, 2 vols. limited ed. Tr. by Raymond Rosenthal from FRE. LC 80-66646. (Illus.). 528p. 1980. bond lthr. 8,500.00 (*0-89659-158-1*) Abbeville Pr.

Vatican I, St. Pius X & the Universal Catechism. Eugene Kevane. (Analecta Ser.: No. III). 40p. (C). 1988. reprint ed. pap. 3.50 (*0-910919-16-X*) Mariel Pubns.

Vatican II: Assessment & Prespectives, Twenty-Five Years After (1962-1987), Vol. II. Ed. by Rene Latourelle. 1988. 25.00 (*0-8091-0413-X*) Paulist Pr.

Vatican II: Assessment & Prespectives, Twenty-Five Years After (1962-1987), Vol. III. Ed. by Rene Latourelle. 1988. 25.00 (*0-8091-0414-8*) Paulist Pr.

Vatican II: It Has Only Just Begun! M. Basil Pennington. 176p. 1994. pap. 13.95 (*0-8245-1410-6*) Crossroad NY.

Vatican II Act II: Work, Convener's Guide. Robert L. Kinast. 80p. (Orig.). 1995. teacher ed., pap. 6.95 (*0-8146-2230-5*) Liturgical Pr.

Vatican II, Act II: Called to Holiness (Covener's Guide) Robert L. Kinast. 80p. (Orig.). 1992. pap. 6.95 (*0-8146-2144-9*) Liturgical Pr.

Vatican II, Act II: Called to Holiness (Participant's Guide) Robert L. Kinast. 64p. (Orig.). 1992. pap. 3.95 (*0-8146-2143-0*) Liturgical Pr.

Vatican II & Phenomenology. John F. Kobler. 254p. 1985. lib. bdg. 101.50 (*90-247-3193-3*, Pub. by M Nijhoff NE) Kluwer Ac.

***Vatican II in Plain English: The Constitutions.** Bill Huebsch. (Vatican II in Plain English - The Collection: Vol. II). (Orig.). 1996. pap. 10.95 (*0-88347-350-X*, 7350) Res Christian Liv.

***Vatican II in Plain English: The Council Itself.** Bill Huebsch. (Vatican II in Plain English - The Collection: Vol. I). (Orig.). 1996. pap. 10.95 (*0-88347-349-6*, 7349) Res Christian Liv.

***Vatican II in Plain English: The Decrees & Declarations.** Bill Huebsch. (Vatican II in Plain English - The Collection: Vol. III). (Orig.). 1996. pap. 10.95 (*0-88347-351-8*, 7351) Res Christian Liv.

***Vatican II in Plain English - The Collection, 3 vols.** Bill Huebsch. (Orig.). 1996. pap. 32.95 (*0-88347-348-8*, 7348) Res Christian Liv.

Vatican II Sunday Missal. 1992. 21.95 (*0-8198-8026-4*) Pauline Bks.

Vatican II Weekday Missal. 1992. 32.95 (*0-8198-8021-3*) Pauline Bks.

Vatican in Politics. 4th ed. Daniel De Leon. 1962. pap. text ed. 0.50 (*0-935534-31-8*) NY Labor News.

Vatican, Islam, & the Middle East. Ed. by Kail C. Ellis & Herman F. Eilts. (Contemporary Issues in the Middle East Ser.). 376p. 1987. text ed. 39.95 (*0-8156-2415-8*) Syracuse U Pr.

Vatican Lifeline '44. William C. Simpson. LC 95-71926. (Illus.). 248p. 1996. 24.95 (*1-885119-22-4*) Sarpedon.

Vatican "One" The Fault Line of Vatican II. Bernard M. Bane. 86p. 1986. pap. 5.00 (*0-930924-25-8*) BMB Pub Co.

Vatican Policy on the Palestinian-Israeli Conflict: The Struggle for the Holy Land. Andrej Kreutz. LC 89-11911. (Contributions in Political Science Ser.: No. 246). 209p. 1990. text ed. 49.95 (*0-313-26829-0*, KRV/, Greenwood Pr) Greenwood.

Vatican Radio: Propagation by the Airwaves. Marilyn J. Matelski. LC 94-22656. (Media & Society Ser.). 224p. 1995. text ed. 57.95 (*0-275-94760-2*, Praeger Pubs) Greenwood.

Vatican Rip. Jonathan Gash. 1983. pap. 5.95 (*0-14-006431-1*, Penguin Bks) Viking Penguin.

Vatican Rip. large type ed. Jonathan Gash. 1984. 15.95 (*0-7089-1101-3*) Ulverscroft.

***Vatican Star, Star of David: The Untold Story of Jewish/ Catholic Relations & the 2nd Vatican Council.** Mark J. Hurley. LC 97-16591. 350p. (Orig.). 1997. pap. 24.95 (*1-55612-967-X*, LL1967) Sheed & Ward MO.

Vatican, the Bishops & Irish Politics: Church & State in Ireland, 1919-1939. Dermot F. Keogh. (Illus.). 318p. 1986. text ed. 69.95 (*0-521-30129-7*) Cambridge U Pr.

Vatican, the Law & the Human Embryo. Michael J. Coughlan. LC 90-70400. 133p. (Orig.). 1990. pap. 10.95 (*0-87745-304-7*) U of Iowa Pr.

Vatican Treasures: 2,000 Years of Art & Culture in the Vatican & Italy. Paul Poupard & Franco Cardini. (Illus.). 304p. 1993. 55.00 (*1-55859-298-9*) Abbeville Pr.

Vatican Two, Act Two: Families, Convener's Guide. Robert L. Kinast. 75p. 1990. pap. 6.95 (*0-8146-1973-8*) Liturgical Pr.

Vatican Two, Act Two: Families, Participant's Guide. Illus. by National Pastoral Life Center Staff. 64p. (Orig.). 1990. pap. 3.95 (*0-8146-1972-X*) Liturgical Pr.

Vatican Two, Act Two: Living in God's World, Convener's Guide. Illus. by National Pastoral Life Center Staff. 74p. (Orig.). 1990. pap. 6.95 (*0-8146-1971-1*) Liturgical Pr.

Vatican Two, Act Two: Living in God's World, Participant's Guide. Illus. by National Pastoral Life Center Staff. 61p. 1990. pap. 3.95 (*0-8146-1970-3*) Liturgical Pr.

Vatican Two Revisited: Reflections by One Who Was There. Aloysius J. Wycislo. LC 87-21325. 186p. 1987. pap. 9.95 (*0-8189-0522-0*) Alba.

Vatican Two, Theophany & the Phenomenon of Man: The Council's Pastoral Servant Leader Theology for the Third Millenium. John F. Kobler. LC 90-25972. (American University Studies: Theology & Religion: Ser. VII, Vol. 100). 350p. (C). 1991. text ed. 48.95 (*0-8204-1492-1*) P Lang Pubng.

Vatican Vergil: A Masterpiece of Late Antique Art. David H. Wright. (Illus.). 148p. 1994. 75.00 (*0-520-07240-5*) U CA Pr.

Vatsana's Lucky New Year. Sara Gogol. LC 92-11243. (YA). (gr. 5 up). 1992. lib. bdg. 19.95 (*0-8225-0734-X*, Lerner Publctns) Lerner Group.

Vatsyayana's Kama Sutra. (Illus.). 102p. 1988. 29.95 (*0-318-36352-6*) Asia Bk Corp.

Vatzlav. Slawomir Mrozek. Tr. by Ralph Manheim from POL. 92p. 1986. pap. 5.95 (*0-936839-50-3*) Applause Theatre Bk Pubs.

Vaudeville & Film. Robert C. Allen. Ed. by Garth S. Jowett. LC 79-6667. (Dissertations on Film, 1980 Ser.). 1980. lib. bdg. 26.95 (*0-405-12901-7*) Ayer.

Vaughan: Environment & Planning Law in the EC. Ed. by David Vaughan. 1991. pap. 175.00 (*0-406-37771-5*) MICHIE.

Vaughan Brothers: Family Style. 136p. 1991. otabind 19.95 (*0-7935-0741-3*, 00694776) H Leonard.

Vaughan Brothers: Family Style. 80p. 1991. otabind 16.95 (*0-7935-0738-3*, 00694779) H Leonard.

Vaughan Brothers: Family Style. 96p. 1992. pap. 14.95 (*0-7935-0796-0*, 00694784) H Leonard.

Vaughan of Virginia Pioneers: William & Fereby Vaughan of Russell County, Virginia, & Their Descendants. Lewis E. Vaughan. 359p. 1994. reprint ed. pap. 42.00 (*0-8328-4087-4*); reprint ed. lib. bdg. 52.00 (*0-8328-4086-6*) Higginson Bk Co.

***Vaughan Pride.** large type ed. Margaret R. Miles. (Linford Romance Large Print Ser.). 288p. 1997. pap. 16.99 (*0-7089-5012-4*, Linford) Ulverscroft.

Vaughan Williams. Alan E. Dickinson. 1988. reprint ed. lib. bdg. 79.00 (*0-7812-0245-0*) Rprt Serv.

Vaughan Williams. Alan E. Dickinson. LC 70-181141. 540p. 1963. reprint ed. 79.00 (*0-403-01542-1*) Scholarly.

Vaughan Williams: A Life in Photographs. Jerrold N. Moore. LC 92-15513. (Illus.). 128p. 1992. 45.00 (*0-19-816296-0*, Old Oregon Bk Store) OUP.

***Vaughan Williams Studies.** Ed. by Alain Frogley. (Illus.). 260p. (C). 1997. text ed. 59.95 (*0-521-48031-0*) Cambridge U Pr.

***Vaughan Williams Symphonies.** Hugh Ottaway. (BBC Music Guides Ser.). 64p. 1996. 7.95 (*0-563-20557-1*, BB 11136, Pub. by BBC UK) Parkwest Pubns.

Vaughan's Freedmen's Pension Bill. Walter R. Vaughan. LC 72-173620. (Black Heritage Library Collection). 1977. reprint ed. 24.95 (*0-8369-8913-9*) Ayer.

Vault Cash & the Role of Commercial Banks in Regional Economic Development: United States, 1870-1913. James A. Xander. LC 77-14808. (Dissertations in American Economic History Ser.). 1978. 19.95 (*0-405-11064-2*) Ayer.

Vault of the Adepti. Michael J. Kell & Jeanne M. Dunworth. (Illus.). 175p. (Orig.). 1995. pap. text ed. 14.95 (*0-9618714-1-5*) Trismegistus Pr.

Vaulting: The Art of Gymnastics on Horseback. Debi Pakizer & Mary A. Sears. Ed. by Julia Anderson & Jackie Barnette. (Illus.). 24p. (Orig.). (J). (gr. k-6). pap. 5.00 (*0-9639785-6-X*) M A Sears.

Vaulting: The Official Instruction Handbook of the German National Equestrian Federation. German National Equestrian Federation Staff. Tr. by Christina Belton from GER. (Illus.). 144p. (Orig.). 1987. pap. 24.95 (*1-872082-37-8*) Half Halt Pr.

Vaulting Ambition: Sociobiology & the Quest for Human Nature. Philip Kitcher. 480p. 1985. 35.00 (*0-262-11109-8*) MIT Pr.

Vaux-le-Vicomte. Anatole France. (FRE.). 1950. pap. 8.95 (*0-7859-5521-6*) Fr & Eur.

Vauxhall. Peter Hall. 1989. pap. 25.00 (*0-7478-0183-5*, Pub. by Shire UK) St Mut.

Vauxhall: The Post War Cars. Trevor Alder. (Illus.). 180p. 1991. 42.95 (*0-85429-746-4*, Pub. by G T Foulis Ltd) Haynes Pubns.

Vauxhall Gardens. T. J. Edelstein & Brian Allen. LC 83-60725. (Illus.). 64p. (Orig.). 1983. pap. 7.50 (*0-930606-43-4*) Yale Ctr Brit Art.

Vauxhall Gardens & the Eighteenth Century Garden Theatre. John D. Hunt. (Theatre in Focus Ser.). (Illus.). 124p. 1985. pap. text ed. 105.00 incl. sl. (*0-85964-161-9*) Chadwyck-Healey.

Vavaldi. Todtri Productions Staff. (Great Composers Ser.). 1996. 10.98 (*0-7651-9368-8*) Smithmark.

Vavara Stepanova: The Complete Works. Aleksander Lavrentiev. (Illus.). 1991. pap. 19.95 (*0-262-62082-0*) MIT Pr.

Vavilov Affair. Mark Popovsky. LC 84-9342. viii, 216p. (C). 1984. lib. bdg. 29.50 (*0-208-02035-7*, Archon Bks) Shoe String.

VAX - VMS: Mastering DCL Commands & Utilities. Daniel A. Sideris. 290p. 1993. pap. text ed. 34.95 (*0-471-59330-3*, GD3173) Wiley.

VAX Architecture Reference Manual. 2nd ed. Ed. by Richard A. Brunner. (VAX-VMS Ser.). (Illus.). 560p. 1991. 62.95 (*1-55558-057-2*, EY-F576E-DP, Digital DEC) Buttrwrth-Heinemann.

VAX Assembly Language. Edwin D. Reilly & Francis D. Federighi. (Illus.). 800p. 1990. Casebound, incl. instr's. manual. teacher ed., boxed write for info. (*0-02-399255-7*, Macmillan Coll) P-H.

VAX Assembly Language. 2nd ed. Sara Baase. 480p. 1992. text ed. 63.00 (*0-13-942152-1*) P-H.

VAX BASIC. Barbara Kursham & David G. Weinman. (C). 1983. text ed. 25.67 (*0-8359-8239-4*, Reston) P-H.

VAX BASIC Programming. Grace L. Greenberg. 432p. (C). 1991. text ed. 47.95 (*0-87835-540-5*) Course Tech.

VAX Book: An Introduction. J. R. Hubbard. (Illus.). 276p. 1991. pap. 22.95 (*0-8306-3652-8*) McGraw-Hill Prof.

VAX Book: An Introduction. J. R. Hubbard. (Illus.). 276p. 1991. 32.95 (*0-8306-7652-X*, 3652) TAB Bks.

Vax Book: An Introduction. J. R. Hubbard. 1991. text ed. 32.95 (*0-07-157653-3*) McGraw.

VAX Datatrieve. Westgate. (DF - Computer Applications Ser.). 1991. text ed. write for info. (*0-87835-514-6*) S-W Pub.

VAX DCL Programmers Reference. K. M. Leisner. 1990. pap. 46.95 (*0-442-31834-0*) Van Nos Reinhold.

VAX FORTRAN. Charlotte Middlebrooks. 1984. text ed. 32.00 (*0-8359-8245-9*, Reston) P-H.

VAX Fortran. 2nd ed. David G. Weinman. 512p. (C). 1991. pap. 59.95 (*0-534-92565-0*) PWS Pubs.

VAX I-O Subsystems: Optimizing Performance. Ken Bates. LC 91-24422. (Illus.). 127p. 1991. pap. 49.00 (*1-878956-02-7*) CBM Bks.

VAX-VMS: An Introduction. 2nd ed. T. W. Sze. 480p. 1991. pap. text ed. 41.95 (*0-8403-7151-9*) Kendall-Hunt.

VAX-VMS: Writing Real Programs in DCL. Paul G. Anagnostopoulos. (VAX Users Ser.). 409p. (Orig.). 1989. 39.95 (*1-55558-023-8*, EY C168E-DP, Digital DEC) Buttrwrth-Heinemann.

VAX-VMS Internals & Data Structures: Version 5.2. Ruth E. Goldenberg et al. (VAX-VMS Ser.). (Illus.). 1464p. 1987. 150.00 (*1-55558-059-9*, EY-C171E-DP, Digital DEC) Buttrwrth-Heinemann.

VAX-VMS Operating Systems Concepts. David D. Miller. (VAX-VMS Ser.). (Illus.). 550p. 1991. 49.95 (*1-55558-065-3*, EY-F590E-DP, Digital DEC) Buttrwrth-Heinemann.

VAX-VMS Primer. 3rd ed. Michael Wright. 218p. 1992. pap. text ed. 17.95 (*0-89892-105-8*) Contemp Pub Co of Raleigh.

VAX-VMS User's Guide. James F. Peters & Patrick Holmay. (VAX Users Ser.). (Illus.). 304p. (Orig.). (C). 1989. 36.95 (*1-55558-014-9*, EY-6739E-DP, Digital DEC) Buttrwrth-Heinemann.

VAX 11 BASIC by Design. Andrew Kitchen. (Illus.). 528p. (C). 1987. pap. text ed. 26.00 (*0-685-14923-4*) P-H.

VAXcluster Principles. Roy G. Davis. LC 93-817. (Alpha-VAX-VMS Ser.). (Illus.). 600p. 1993. 62.95 (*1-55558-112-9*, EY-M740E-DP, Digital DEC) Buttrwrth-Heinemann.

Vay: The Official Strategy Guide. Zach Meston & J. Douglas Arnold. (Gaming Mastery Ser.). (Illus.). 120p. (Orig.). 1994. pap. 12.95 (*1-884364-10-1*) Sandwich Islands.

Vay Kamo, Vay! Clarissa Lewis. Tr. by Aramais Andonian from ENG. (Illus.). 28p. (ARM.). (J). (ps-2). 1995. boxed 14.00 (*1-886434-00-X*) Blue Crane Bks.

Vaya!, Level 1. Anthony et al. 1900. pap. 23.95 (*0-17-439156-0*) Heinle & Heinle.

Vaya!, Level 2. Anthony et al. 1992. pap. 23.95 (*0-17-439157-9*) Heinle & Heinle.

Vaya!, Level 3. Anthony et al. 1900. pap. 23.95 (*0-17-439158-7*) Heinle & Heinle.

Vaya!, Level 4. Anthony et al. 1900. pap. 23.95 (*0-17-439196-X*) Heinle & Heinle.

Vaya! Level Four, Bk. 4. Anthony & Buckby. (Secondary Spanish Ser.). 1900. teacher ed., pap. 59.95 (*0-17-439197-8*) Heinle & Heinle.

Vaya! Level One, Bk. 1. Anthony & Buckby. (Secondary Spanish Ser.). 1900. teacher ed., pap. 59.95 (*0-17-439159-5*) Heinle & Heinle.

Vaya! Level Three, Bk. 3. Anthony & Buckby. (Secondary Spanish Ser.). 1900. teacher ed., pap. 44.95 (*0-17-439193-5*) Heinle & Heinle.

Vaya! Nuevo 3. Anthony. (Secondary Spanish Ser.). 1995. student ed., pap. 15.95 (*0-17-439816-6*) Heinle & Heinle.

Vaya! Nuevo 3. Anthony. (Secondary Spanish Ser.). 1995. teacher ed., pap. 29.95 (*0-17-439817-4*) Heinle & Heinle.

Vaya! Stage 1. 2nd ed. Buckby. (Secondary Spanish Ser.). 1995. student ed., pap. 23.95 (*0-17-439667-8*) Heinle & Heinle.

Vaya! Stage 1. 2nd ed. Buckby. (Secondary Spanish Ser.). 1995. teacher ed., pap. 29.95 (*0-17-439668-6*) Heinle & Heinle.

Vaya! Stage 2. 2nd ed. Anthony & Buckby. (Secondary Spanish Ser.). 1995. student ed., pap. 23.95 (*0-17-439809-3*) Heinle & Heinle.

Vaya! Stage 2. 2nd ed. Anthony & Buckby. (Secondary Spanish Ser.). 1995. teacher ed., pap. 29.95 (*0-17-439810-7*) Heinle & Heinle.

Vaya! Nuevo 3: Copymasters. Anthony. (Secondary Spanish Ser.). 1995. pap. 95.95 (*0-17-439818-2*) Wadsworth Pub.

***Vaya Papaya - Ramon Alejandro.** Intro. by Cabrera Infante. (SPA.). pap. 15.00 (*0-89729-260-X*) Ediciones.

Vaya! Stage 2 Copymasters. 2nd ed. Anthony & Buckby. (Secondary Spanish Ser.). 1995. pap. 99.95 (*0-17-439811-5*) Wadsworth Pub.

Vayikra, Vol. 7. Menachem M. Schneerson. (Likkutei Sichos Ser.). 390p. (HEB & YID.). reprint ed. 15.00 (*0-8266-5725-7*) Kehot Pubn Soc.

Vayikra, Vol. 17. Menachem M. Schneerson. (Likkutei Sichos Ser.). 542p. (HEB & YID.). Date not set. reprint ed. 15.00 (*0-8266-5734-6*) Kehot Pubn Soc.

Vayikra, Vol. 22. Menachem M. Schneerson. (Likkutei Sichos Ser.). 448p. (HEB & YID.). Date not set. reprint ed. 15.00 (*0-8266-5740-0*) Kehot Pubn Soc.

Vayikra, Vol. 27. Menachem M. Schneerson. (Likkutei Sichos Ser.). 401p. (HEB & YID.). Date not set. reprint ed. 15.00 (*0-8266-5750-8*) Kehot Pubn Soc.

Vayikra, Vol. 32. Menachem M. Schneerson. (Likkutei Sichos Ser.). 364p. (HEB & YID.). 1993. 15.00 (*0-8266-5777-X*) Kehot Pubn Soc.

Vayikra-Leviticus: Vayikra-Metzora, 2 vols., I. Nosson Scherman & Hersh Goldwurm. (ArtScroll Tanach Ser.). 340p. 1989. 19.99 (*0-89906-370-5*) Mesorah Pubns.

Vayikra-Leviticus: Vayikra-Metzora, 2 vols., II. Nosson Scherman & Hersh Goldwurm. (ArtScroll Tanach Ser.). 340p. 1989. 19.99 (*0-89906-372-1*) Mesorah Pubns.

Vayu Purana, Pt. 1. Tr. by G. V. Tagare. (Ancient Indian Tradition & Mythology Ser.). (C). 1987. 26.00 (*81-208-0332-9*, Pub. by Motilal Banarsidass II) S Asia.

VB Equals MC2: The Art of Visual BASIC Programming. J. D. Evans, Jr. 474p. 1992. pap. 39.90 (*1-881679-22-5*) ETN.

VB Equals MC4: Visual BASIC Standards & Practices. J. D. Evans, Jr. 1992. pap. 39.90 (*1-881679-44-6*) ETN.

***VB Script for the World Wide Web: Visual Quickstart Guide.** Paul Thurrot. 256p. (C). 1997. pap. text ed. 17.95 (*0-201-68892-1*) Peachpit Pr.

***VB Tips & Tricks, Vol. 1.** David McCarter. Ed. by Zane Thomas & James Shields. (Illus.). 160p. (Orig.). 1997. pap. 24.95 (*1-890422-00-2*) Mabry Sftware.

***Vb 5: Environment Programming & Applications.** Alan Eliason & Ryan Malar. 1997. 80.00 (*1-57576-867-4*) Sams.

***Vb 5 Smartstart.** Que Education & Training Staff. 1997. teacher ed. 39.99 (*1-57576-873-9*) Que Educ & Trng.

***Vb 5 Smartstart.** Salosky. 1997. 34.99 (*1-57576-832-1*) Que Educ & Trng.

***VBA Developer's Handbook.** Ken Getz. 1996. pap. text ed. 49.99 incl. cd-rom (*0-7821-1951-4*) Sybex.

***VBA for Dummies.** Dummies Technology Press Staff. 1997. pap. 29.99 (*0-7645-0258-1*) IDG Bks.

***VBA in a Nutshell.** Lomax. Ed. by Ron Patrusha. (Orig.). pap. write for info. (*1-56592-358-8*) OReilly & Assocs.

***VBAC Companion: The Expectant Mother's Guide to Vaginal Birth after Cesarean.** Diana Korte. (Illus.). 224p. 1997. 21.95 (*1-55832-128-4*) Harvard Common Pr.

***VBAC Companion: The Expectant Mother's Guide to Vaginal Birth after Cesarean.** Diana Korte. (Illus.). 224p. 1997. pap. 10.95 (*1-55832-129-2*) Harvard Common Pr.

Vblizi Vestnikov: Near the Messengers - Vblizi Vestnikov Russian. Ed. by Henry Orlov. LC 88-91215. (Illus.). 325p. (Orig.). (RUS.). 1988. pap. 15.00 (*0-929647-00-9*) H A Frager & Co.

***VBS: A Creative Summer Ministry.** 88p. 1980. 4.99 (*0-8341-0635-3*) Nazarene.

VBS & Other Summer Ministries. 96p. 1994. pap. text ed. 8.95 (*0-910566-57-7*) Evang Trg Assn.

VBS & Other Summer Ministries. 90p. 1994. teacher ed., ring bd. 19.95 (*0-910566-58-5*) Evang Trg Assn.

***VBScript for Dummies.** 2nd ed. John Walkenbach. 1997. pap. 24.99 (*0-7645-0259-X*) IDG Bks.

VBscript Master's Handbook. Christopher Goddard. 720p. 1996. per. 45.00 (*0-7615-0769-8*) Prima Pub.

***VBScript Quick Reference.** David Medineta. 170p. 1997. 19.99 (*0-7897-1131-1*) Mac Comp Pub.

***Vbscript Sourcebook.** Mary J. Mara. LC 97-17967. 1997. pap. text ed. 44.99 incl. cd-rom (*0-471-19106-X*) Wiley.

VBscript Web Page Interactivity. Bill Orvis. 504p. 1996. per. 40.00 incl. cd-rom (*0-7615-0684-5*) Prima Pub.

***VBScript 2 & ActiveX Programming: Master the Art of Creating Interactive Web Pages.** Scott Palmer. 1997. pap. text ed. 39.99 (*1-57610-161-4*) Coriolis Grp.

***Vb5 Unleashed.** 1997. 69.99 (*0-672-31195-X*) Mac Comp Pub.

VC - Cost. KJH Communications Staff. (Illus.). 1994. 295.00 incl. disk (*1-880145-03-0*) KJH Comm.

V.C. Andrews, 4 vols., Set. boxed 15.80 (*0-317-12450-1*) PB.

VCAT Exam No. 1 Annotated Answers (Veterinary College Admission Test) 7th ed. David M. Tarlow. (Orig.). 1996. pap. 5.95 (*1-57732-050-6*) Datar Pub.

VCAT Exam No. 1 (Veterinary College Admission Test) 7th ed. David M. Tarlow. (Illus.). (Orig.). 1996. pap. 19.95 (*1-57732-046-8*) Datar Pub.

VCAT Exam No. 2 Annotated Answers (Veterinary College Admission Test) 7th ed. David M. Tarlow. (Orig.). 1996. pap. 5.95 (*1-57732-051-4*) Datar Pub.

VCAT Exam No. 2 (Veterinary College Admission Test) 7th ed. David M. Tarlow. (Orig.). 1996. pap. 19.95 (*1-57732-047-6*) Datar Pub.

VCAT Exam No. 3 Annotated Answers (Veterinary College Admissions Test) 7th ed. David M. Tarlow. 1996. pap. 5.95 (*1-57732-052-2*) Datar Pub.

VCAT Exam No. 3 (Veterinary College Admission Test) David M. Tarlow. (Orig.). 1996. pap. 19.95 (*1-57732-048-4*) Datar Pub.

VCAT Exam No. 4 Annotated Answers (Veterinary College Admissions Test) 7th ed. David M. Tarlow. 1996. pap. 5.95 (*1-57732-053-0*) Datar Pub.

VCAT Exam No. 4 (Veterinary College Admission Test) David M. Tarlow. 1996. pap. 19.95 (*1-57732-049-2*) Datar Pub.

VCAT Exam No. 5 Annotated Answers (Veterinary College Admissions Test) David M. Tarlow. 1996. pap. 5.95 (*1-57732-054-9*) Datar Pub.

VCAT Exam No. 5 (Veterinary College Admission Test) 7th ed. David M. Tarlow. 1996. pap. 19.95 (*1-57732-045-X*) Datar Pub.

VCAT (Veterinary College Admission Test) For Comprehensive Review. 7th ed. David M. Tarlow. (Illus.). (Orig.). 1996. student ed., pap. 19.95 (*1-57732-044-1*) Datar Pub.

VCCALC: Vertical Coverage Plotting Software & User's Manual. John E. Fielding & Gary D. Reynolds. (Radar Software Library). 50p. 1988. text ed. write for info. (*0-89006-327-3*) Artech Hse.

VCE Mathematics Experiment: An Evaluation. Peter J. Martin. 1993. pap. 45.00 (*0-7300-0814-2*, Pub. by Deakin Univ AT) St Mut.

An Asterisk (*) at the beginning of an entry indicates that the title is appearing in BIP for the first time.

VCR Age. Ed. by Mark R. Levy. (Focus Editions Ser.: Vol. 105). 280p. (C). 1989. text ed. 54.00 (*0-8039-3299-5*); pap. text ed. 24.95 (*0-8039-3300-2*) Sage.

***VCR Age: Home Video & Mass Communication.** Ed. by Mark R. Levy. LC 89-5852. (Sage Focus Editions Ser.: No. 105). (Illus.). 274p. 1989. reprint ed. pap. 78.10 (*0-608-04317-6*, 2065096) Bks Demand.

VCR Troubleshooting & Repair. 2nd ed. Gregory R. Capelo. 286p. 1991. 19.95 (*0-672-22749-5*) Buttrwrth-Heinemann.

***VCR Troubleshooting & Repair.** 3rd ed. Robert C. Brenner & Gregory R. Capello. 350p. Date not set. 35.00 (*0-672-30986-6*) Mac Comp Pub.

VCRs. Gene B. Williams. LC 92-9121. (All Thumbs Guide Ser.). (Illus.). 144p. 1992. pap. 9.95 (*0-8306-4181-5*, 4252) McGraw-Hill Prof.

VCRs & Camcorders for Dummies. Andy Rathbone & Gordon McComb. 300p. 1994. pap. 14.99 (*1-56884-229-5*) IDG Bks.

VCRs & Camcorders for Dummies. 2nd ed. Gordon McComb. 1995. pap. 19.99 (*1-56884-397-6*) IDG Bks.

VCs of the First World War: The Somme. Gerald Gliddon. (Illus.). 224p. 1994. 37.00 (*0-7509-0567-0*, Pub. by Sutton Pubng UK) Bks Intl VA.

VD: The Love Epidemic. rev. ed. Mari Stein. (Illus.). 1977. reprint ed. pap. 3.95 (*0-918546-00-1*) Quarterdeck.

VD Book: For People Who Care about Themselves & Others. Joseph A. Chiappa & Joseph J. Forish. LC 76-17596. (Illus.). 145p. 1977. pap. 3.95 (*0-8290-0287-1*) Irvington.

VDAC: a Mitochondrial Outer Membrane Channel: Physiological Regulation & Biophysical Properties. M. Zizi. No. 101. 131p. (Orig.). 1994. pap. 33.50 (*90-6186-650-2*, Pub. by Leuven Univ BE) Coronet Bks.

VDI Heat Atlas. Ed. by Ernst U. Schlunder. (Illus.). 982p. 1993. 1,320.00 (*3-18-400915-7*, Pub. by Woodhead Pubng UK) Am Educ Systs.

VDI-Lexikon Bauingenieurwesen. Hans-Gustav Olshausen. 649p. (GER.). 1991. 250.00 (*0-7859-8287-6*, 3184008975) Fr & Eur.

VDM Eighty-Seven: VDM-A Formal Method at Work. Ed. by D. Bjorner et al. (Lecture Notes in Computer Science Ser.: Vol. 252). x, 422p. 1987. 45.00 (*0-387-17654-3*) Spr-Verlag.

VDM Reference Guide. John Dawes. 200p. (C). 1990. pap. text ed. 175.00 (*0-273-03151-1*, Pub. by Pitman Pubng UK) St Mut.

VDM '88 - VDM: The Way Ahead. Ed. by R. Bloomfield et al. (Lecture Notes in Computer Science Ser.: Vol. 328). ix, 499p. 1988. 53.00 (*0-387-50214-9*) Spr-Verlag.

VDM '90 VDM & Z - Formal Methods in Software Development: Third International Symposium of VDM Europe Kiel, FRG, April 17-21, 1990 Proceedings. Ed. by D. Bjorner et al. (Lecture Notes in Computer Science Ser.: Vol. 428). xviii, 580p. 1990. 57.90 (*0-387-52513-0*) Spr-Verlag.

VDM '91 Formal Software Development Methods, 4th International Symposium of VDM Europe, Noorwijkerhout, the Netherlands, October 21-25, 1991 Proceedings, Vol. 1: Conference Contributions. Ed. by S. Prehn & W. J. Toetenel. (Lecture Notes in Computer Science Ser.: Vol. 551). xiii, 699p. 1991. 74.95 (*0-387-54834-3*) Spr-Verlag.

VDM '91 Formal Software Development Methods, 4th International Symposium of VDM Europe, Noorwijkerhout, the Netherlands, October 21-25, 1991 Proceedings, Vol. 2: Tutorials. Ed. by S. Prehn & W. J. Toetenel. (Lecture Notes in Computer Science Ser.: Vol. 552). xiv, 430p. 1991. 44.95 (*0-387-54868-8*) Spr-Verlag.

VDT Lighting. Office Lighting Committee Staff. (Recommended Practices Ser.). 25p. 1989. pap. 35.00 (*0-87995-031-5*, RP-24-89) Illum Eng.

VDTs in the Workplace: A Study of the Effects on Employment. (Special Report Ser.). 112p. 1984. 25.00 (*0-87179-927-8*, 45 LDSR 30) BNA Plus.

VDTs in the Workplace: New Issues, New Answers. 2nd ed. 233p. 1987. 55.00 (*0-87179-937-5*, BSP-68) BNA Plus.

VDT's May Be Hazardous to Your Health. (Illus.). 131p. (Orig.). (C). 1994. pap. text ed. 30.00 (*0-7881-1428-X*) DIANE Pub.

VDU Terminal Sickness: Computer Health Risks & How to Protect Yourself. 2nd ed. Peggy Bentham. 1996. pap. text ed. 18.95 (*1-897766-21-1*, Pub. by Jon Pubng UK) LPC InBook.

VE Day in Photographs. Tony Hall. (Illus.). 64p. 1995. 1.50 (*0-517-12156-5*) Random Hse Value.

Ve-Ve Diagrammes Rituels du Voudou. Milo Rigaud. 583p. (ENG, FRE & SPA.). 1992. pap. 59.95 (*0-8288-0000-6*, S10043) Fr & Eur.

***Vea Por Usted Mismo.** Carol Sussman-Skalka. (SPA.). 1995. 50.00 incl. vhs (*1-888504-17-X*, P185) Lighthouse NYC.

Veblen. John A. Hobson. LC 90-44107. (Reprints of Economic Classics Ser.). 227p. 1991. reprint ed. lib. bdg. 35.00 (*0-678-01464-7*) Kelley.

Veblen: A Play in Three Acts. Leonard S. Silk. LC 66-20645. 138p. 1966. 25.00 (*0-678-00153-7*) Kelley.

Veblen Treasury: From Leisure Class to War, Peace, & Capitalism. Ed. by Rick Tilman. LC 93-26762. (Studies in Institutional Economics Ser.). 442p. (gr. 13). 1993. text ed. 72.95 (*1-56324-261-3*); pap. text ed. 29.95 (*1-56324-262-1*) M E Sharpe.

Veblen's Theory of Social Change. Leonard A. Dente. Ed. by Stuart Bruchey. LC 76-39826. (Nineteen Seventy-Seven Disserataions Ser.). (Illus.). 1980. lib. bdg. 31.95 (*0-405-09906-1*) Ayer.

Vebreitungsatlas der Farn- und Blutenpflanzen der Schweiz, 2 Vols., Vol. 2. Ed. by Max Welten. 752p. 1980. 50.00 (*0-8176-1308-0*) Birkhauser.

Vecellio's Renaissance Costume Book. Cesare Vecellio. LC 76-55952. (Pictorial Archive Ser.). (Illus.). 1977. pap. 6.95 (*0-486-23441-X*) Dover.

Veces la Vida Puede Ser Dura Pero Todo Saldra Bien (Life Can Be Hard Sometimes but Its) Ed. by Blue Mountain Arts Staff. LC 93-11131. 1993. pap. 7.95 (*0-88396-367-1*) Blue Mtn Pr CO.

Veces las Cosas Cambian (Sometimes Things Change) Patricia Eastman. LC 83-10090. (Rookie Readers - Spanish Ser.). (Illus.). 32p. (SPA.). (J). (ps-2). 1988. pap. 3.50 (*0-516-52044-X*); lib. bdg. 14.70 (*0-516-32044-0*) Childrens.

Vector. Swigart. 1988. pap. 3.95 (*0-317-65475-6*) St Martin.

Vector Analysis. Lewis Peter. (C). 1989. pap. text ed. 46.95 (*0-201-17577-0*) Addison-Wesley.

Vector Analysis & Cartesian Tensors. 3rd ed. D. Bourne & P. C. Kendall. 288p. (C). (gr. 13). 1992. pap. text ed. 51.95 (*0-412-42750-8*, A7133) Chapman & Hall.

Vector Analysis & Cartesian Tensors: With Selected Applications. Karamcheti Krishnamurty. LC 67-13843. (Holden-Day Series in Mathematical Physics). 268p. reprint ed. pap. 76.40 (*0-317-09182-4*, 2016290) Bks Demand.

Vector Analysis for Mathematicians, Scientists & Engineers. 2nd ed. S. Simons. LC 77-96077. (Pergamon International Science Technical Engineering & Social Studies). 1970. 96.00 (*0-08-006895-2*, Pub. by Pergamon Repr UK) Franklin.

Vector Analysis Problem Solver. rev. ed. Research & Education Association Staff. LC 84-61811. (Illus.). 1296p. 1994. pap. text ed. 29.95 (*0-87891-554-0*) Res & Educ.

Vector Analysis (Vect. Alg. & Vect. Calculus) M. Maity & G. K. Ghosh. (C). 1989. 85.00 (*0-89771-392-3*, Pub. by Current Dist II) St Mut.

***Vector & Parallel Processing-Vecpar 96: Second International Conference on Vector & Parallel Processing-Systems & Applications, Porto, Portugal, September 1996: Selected Papers, Vol. 121.** Palma, Jose M.L.M. Rence on Vector & Parallel Processing-Systems & Applications Staff & J. J. Dongarra. LC 97-8372. (Lecture Notes in Computer Science Ser.). 1997. write for info. (*3-540-62828-2*) Spr-Verlag.

Vector & Tensor Analysis. George E. Hay. 1953. pap. text ed. 5.95 (*0-486-60109-9*) Dover.

Vector & Tensor Analysis. 2nd ed. Eutiguio C. Young. (Pure & Applied Mathematics Ser.: Vol. 172). 520p. 1992. 125.00 (*0-8247-8789-7*) Dekker.

Vector & Tensor Analysis see Introduction to Vectors & Tensors

Vector & Tensor Analysis with Applications. A. I. Borisenko & I. E. Tarapov. LC 79-87809. 257p. (C). 1979. reprint ed. pap. 7.95 (*0-486-63833-2*) Dover.

***Vector-Borne Pathogens: International Trade & Tropical Animal Diseases.** Emmanuel Camus et al. LC 96-31285. (Annals of the New York Academy of Sciences). 1996. write for info. (*0-89766-955-X*); pap. write for info. (*0-89766-956-8*) NY Acad Sci.

Vector Bundles & Differential Equations. Ed. by A. Hirschowitz. (Progress in Mathematics Ser.: No. 7). 255p. 1980. 56.50 (*0-8176-3022-8*) Birkhauser.

Vector Bundles in Algebraic Geometry. Ed. by N. J. Hitchin et al. (London Mathematical Society Lecture Note Ser.: No. 208). 356p. (C). 1995. pap. text ed. 42.95 (*0-521-49878-3*) Cambridge U Pr.

Vector Bundles on Complex Projective Spaces. Christian Okonek et al. (Progress in Mathematics Ser.: No. 3). 396p. 1980. 49.00 (*0-8176-3000-7*) Birkhauser.

***Vector Bundles on Curves - New Directions Vol. VII: Lectures Given at the 3rd Session of the Centro Internazionale Matematico Estivo (C. I. M. E.), Held in Cetraro, Cosenza, Italy, June 19-27, 1995.** S. Kumar et al. LC 96-52371. (Lecture Notes in Mathematics Ser.: Vol. 1649). 193p. 1997. pap. 33.00 (*3-540-62401-5*) Spr-Verlag.

Vector Calculus. Peter Baxandall & Hans Liebeck. (Oxford Applied Mathematics & Computing Science Ser.). (Illus.). 560p. 1987. 95.00 (*0-19-859652-9*) OUP.

***Vector Calculus.** Colley. 1997. text ed. 66.67 (*0-13-149204-7*) P-H.

Vector Calculus. David B. Damiano. (Mathematics Ser.). 1998. text ed. 63.95 (*0-534-95654-8*) PWS Pubs.

Vector Calculus. 3rd ed. Jerrold E. Marsden. (C). 1995. text ed. write for info. (*0-7167-1931-2*) W H Freeman.

Vector Calculus. 3rd ed. Jerrold E. Marsden & Anthony J. Tromba. LC 87-24595. (Illus.). 704p. (C). 1996. text ed. write for info. (*0-7167-1856-1*) W H Freeman.

Vector Calculus. 4th ed. Jerrold E. Marsden. (C). Date not set. teacher ed. write for info. (*0-7167-2445-6*) W H Freeman.

Vector Calculus. 4th ed. Jerrold E. Marsden. (C). Date not set. student ed. write for info. (*0-7167-2433-2*) W H Freeman.

Vector Calculus. 4th ed. Anthony J. Tromba & Jerrold E. Marsden. LC 95-37696. (C). 1996. text ed. write for info. (*0-7167-2432-4*) W H Freeman.

Vector Coherent State Method & Its Application to Problems of Higher Symmetries. K. T. Hecht. (Lecture Notes in Physics Ser.: Vol. 290). v, 154p. 1987. 29.95 (*0-387-18537-2*) Spr-Verlag.

Vector Control. (WHO Bulletin Supplement Ser.: Vol. 29). 1963. pap. text ed. 12.00 (*92-4-068291-0*, 1032901) World Health.

***Vector Control & Dynamics of AC Drives, Vol. 41.** D. W. Novotny & T. A. Lipo. (Monographs in Electrical & Electronic Engineering). (Illus.). 456p. 1996. 90.00 (*0-19-856439-2*) OUP.

Vector Control Assistant. Jack Rudman. (Career Examination Ser.: C-3481). 1994. pap. 23.95 (*0-8373-3481-0*) Nat Learn.

Vector Control for Malaria & Other Mosquito-Borne Diseases: Report of a WHO Study Group. (Technical Report Ser.: Vol. 857). 91p. (FRE & SPA.). (C). 1995. pap. 15.00 (*92-4-120857-0*, 1100857) World Health.

Vector Control in International Health. 144p. 1972. pap. text ed. 32.00 (*92-4-154016-8*, 1150160) World Health.

***Vector Control in Primary Health Care: Report of a WHO Scientific Group, 1987.** WHO Staff. (Technical Report Ser.: No. 755). 61p. 1987. 9.00 (*92-4-120755-8*) World Health.

Vector Control of AC Drives. Syed A. Nasar. 256p. 1992. 110.00 (*0-8493-4408-5*, TK2791) CRC Pr.

Vector Control Supervisor. Jack Rudman. (Career Examination Ser.: C-2763). 1994. pap. 27.95 (*0-8373-2763-6*) Nat Learn.

Vector Ecology: Proceedings of the WHO Scientific Group, Geneva, 1972. WHO Staff. (Technical Report Ser.: No. 501). 1972. pap. text ed. 4.00 (*92-4-120501-6*, 1100501) World Health.

Vector Field Theory with Applications. Leonard Sowerby. LC 73-90574. 258p. reprint ed. pap. 73.60 (*0-317-09319-3*, 2019609) Bks Demand.

Vector Handbook. George Burtt. LC 71-91981. 1969. pap. 3.50 (*0-913596-03-5*) Vector Counsel.

***Vector in the Sky: The Correspondence of James Green & Jean Owens.** 2nd ed. James A. Green & Jean Owens. LC 94-77666. (Literature Ser.: Vol. 2). (Illus.). 265p. 1997. reprint ed. 92.08 (*1-890121-25-8*, 04-02-96) Grnwd Resch.

Vector Lattices & Integral Operators. Ed. by S. S. Kutateladze. (Mathematics & Its Applications Ser.: Vol. 358). 472p. (C). 1996. lib. bdg. 235.00 (*0-7923-3897-9*) Kluwer Ac.

Vector Lyapunov Functions & Stability Analysis of Nonlinear Systems. V. Lakshmikantham et al. (C). 1991. lib. bdg. 97.00 (*0-7923-1152-3*) Kluwer Ac.

Vector Lyapunov Functions in Stability Theory. R. Z. Abdulin et al. (Advanced Series in Mathematical Science & Engineering). 1996. write for info. (*1-885978-20-0*) Wrld Fed Pubs.

Vector Measures. J. Diestel & J. J. Uhl, Jr. LC 77-9625. (Mathematical Surveys Ser.: No. 15). 322p. 1991. reprint ed. pap. 50.00 (*0-8218-1515-6*, SURV/15) Am Math.

Vector Mechanics for Engineers: Combined. 5th ed. Ferdinand Pierre Beer & Johnston E. Russell. 1088p. 1988. text ed. write for info. (*0-07-079923-7*) McGraw.

Vector Mechanics for Engineers: Dynamics. 3rd ed. Ferdinand Pierre Beer & E. Russell Johnston, Jr. (C). 1977. text ed. write for info. (*0-07-004281-0*) McGraw.

Vector Mechanics for Engineers: Dynamics. 5th ed. Ferdinand Pierre Beer & Johnston E. Russell. 592p. 1988. text ed. write for info. (*0-07-079926-1*) McGraw.

Vector Mechanics for Engineers: Dynamics. 5th ed. Ferdinand Pierre Beer & Johnston E. Russell. 592p. 1992. Problems supplement. pap. text ed. write for info. (*0-07-005009-0*) McGraw.

***Vector Mechanics for Engineers: Dynamics.** 6th ed. Ferdinand Pierre Beer et al. LC 96-42905. 1997. text ed. write for info. (*0-07-913034-8*) McGraw.

***Vector Mechanics for Engineers: Dynamics.** 6th ed. Ferdinand Pierre Beer et al. LC 96-42905. 1997. write for info. (*0-07-005366-9*); write for info. (*0-07-005419-3*); text ed. write for info. (*0-07-912637-5*) McGraw.

Vector Mechanics for Engineers: Dynamics, Vol. 2. Ferdinand Pierre Beer & E. Russell Johnston. 1985. Transparency masters. trans. write for info. (*0-07-004447-3*) McGraw.

Vector Mechanics for Engineers: Statics. 5th ed. Ferdinand Pierre Beer & E. Russell Johnston. 1988. text ed. write for info. (*0-07-079946-6*) McGraw.

Vector Mechanics for Engineers: Statics. 5th ed. Ferdinand Pierre Beer & Johnston E. Russell. 496p. 1992. 44.95 (*0-07-004507-0*); pap. text ed. write for info. (*0-07-005011-2*) McGraw.

Vector Mechanics for Engineers: Statics. 6th ed. Ferdinand Pierre Beer et al. 1995. write for info. (*0-07-005367-7*) McGraw.

***Vector Mechanics for Engineers: Statics.** 6th ed. Ferdinand Pierre Beer. 599p. 1996. pap. text ed. 79.75 (*0-07-114057-3*, TA351) McGraw.

***Vector Mechanics for Engineers: Statics.** 6th ed. Ferdinand Pierre Beer & E. Russell Johnston. 1996. text ed. write for info. incl. disk (*0-07-912966-8*) McGraw.

***Vector Mechanics for Engineers: Statics & Dynamics.** 6th ed. Ferdinand Pierre Beer et al. LC 96-42906. 1996. write for info. (*0-07-847126-5*) McGraw.

***Vector Mechanics for Engineers: Statics & Dynamics.** 6th ed. Ferdinand Pierre Beer et al. LC 96-42906. 1997. write for info. (*0-07-005365-0*) McGraw.

Vector Mechanics for Engineers: 800 Solved Problems in Vector Mechanics for Engineers Statistics. 5th ed. Ferdinand Pierre Beer & E. Russell Johnston. 1990. text ed. write for info. (*0-07-909914-9*) McGraw.

***Vector Mechanics for Engineers Statics.** 5th ed. Ferdinand Pierre Beer & E. Russell Johnston. 1992. suppl. ed., pap. text ed. write for info. (*0-07-911462-8*) McGraw.

Vector Models for Data-Parallel Computing. Guy E. Blelloch. (Artificial Intelligence Ser.). (Illus.). 300p. 1990. pap. 42.00 (*0-262-02313-X*) MIT Pr.

Vector Particle Physics: Mathematically Consistent Models for the Structures of Subatomic Particles. Thomas N. Lockyer. LC 91-90733. 112p. (C). 1992. 12.95 (*0-9631546-0-5*); pap. 6.95 (*0-9631546-1-3*) TNL Pr.

Vector Quantization. H. Abut. LC 90-32686. (Illus.). 576p. 1990. text ed. 69.95 (*0-87942-265-3*, PC02550) Inst Electrical.

Vector Quantization & Signal Compression. Allen Gersho & Robert M. Gray. (International Series in Engineering & Computer Science, VLSI, Computer Architecture, & Digital Screen Processing). 760p. (C). 1991. lib. bdg. 93.50 (*0-7923-9181-0*) Kluwer Ac.

Vector Resistance to Pesticides: Fifteenth Report of the WHO Expert Committee on Vector Biology & Control. (Technical Report Ser.: No. 818). v, 62p. (ENG, FRE & SPA.). 1992. pap. text ed. 10.00 (*92-4-120818-X*, 1100818) World Health.

Vector Space & Its Application in Crystal-Structure Investigation. Martin J. Buerger. LC 59-6760. 365p. reprint ed. pap. 104.10 (*0-317-08653-7*, 2011964) Bks Demand.

Vector-Valued Functions & Their Applications. Chuang-Gan Hu. (Mathematics & Its Applications Chinese Ser.). 172p. (C). 1992. lib. bdg. 94.00 (*0-7923-1605-3*) Kluwer Ac.

Vectored Propulsion, Supermaneuverability & Robot Aircraft. B. Gal-Or. (Illus.). 240p. 1991. 98.95 (*0-387-97161-0*) Spr-Verlag.

Vectorial Astrometry. C. A. Murray. (Illus.). 368p. 1983. 40.00 (*0-85274-372-6*) IOP Pub.

Vectors. Anthony Nicolaides. 224p. (C). 1994. pap. 45.00 (*1-872684-03-3*, Pub. by P A S S Pubns UK) St Mut.

Vectors. Toby Olson. 1972. pap. 3.00 (*0-87924-017-2*) Membrane Pr.

Vectors. Raymond A. Barnett. LC 75-12664. 140p. (C). 1976. reprint ed. lib. bdg. 14.00 (*0-88275-290-1*) Krieger.

Vectors: Essential Data. Peter Gacesa & Dipak P. Ramji. (Bios Essential Data Ser.). 166p. 1995. pap. text ed. 22.95 (*0-471-94841-1*) Wiley.

Vectors: The Best of Len Morgan. Len Morgan. 1991. 22.95 (*0-8306-2087-7*); pap. 14.95 (*0-8306-2083-4*) McGraw-Hill Prof.

Vectors & Smoothable Curves: Collected Essays. Bronk. 1995. pap. 12.50 (*1-883689-24-4*) Talisman Hse.

Vectors & Smoothable Curves: Collected Essays. Bronk. 1995. 20.00 (*1-883689-25-2*) Talisman Hse.

Vectors & Smoothable Curves: Collected Essays: New Edition. rev. ed. William Bronk. 228p. 1996. reprint ed. pap. 21.95 (*1-883689-32-5*); reprint ed. lib. bdg. 42.95 (*1-883689-33-3*) Talisman Hse.

Vectors & Tensors in Crystallography. Donald E. Sands. 1982. text ed. write for info. (*0-201-07147-9*, Adv Bk Prog) Addison-Wesley.

Vectors & Tensors in Crystallography. Donald E. Sands. LC 94-40104. (Illus.). 256p. 1995. pap. text ed. 7.95 (*0-486-68505-5*) Dover.

Vectors & Tensors in Engineering & Physics. Donald A. Danielson. 352p. (C). 1992. 49.95 (*0-201-52426-0*, Adv Bk Prog) Addison-Wesley.

Vectors & Tensors in Engineering & Physics. 2nd ed. D. A. Danielson. Ed. by Robbins. 290p. (C). 1997. 45.95 (*0-201-44210-8*) Addison-Wesley.

Vectors & Transformations in Plane Geometry. Philippe Tondeor. (Illus.). x, 135p. (C). 1993. text ed. 20.00 (*0-914098-28-4*) Publish or Perish.

Vectors & Vector Operators. P. G. Dawber. (Student Monographs in Physics). (Illus.). 64p. 1987. pap. 13.00 (*0-85274-585-0*) IOP Pub.

Vectors As Tools for the Study of Normal & Abnormal Growth & Differentiation. Ed. by H. Lother et al. (NATO ASI Series H: Vol. 34). viii, 475p. 1989. 206.95 (*0-387-50419-2*) Spr-Verlag.

Vectors in Virus Biology. Ed. by Michael A. Mayo & K. A. Harrap. (Society for General Microbiology Special Publications: No. 12). 1984. text ed. 95.00 (*0-12-481480-8*) Acad Pr.

Vectors, Matrices & Geometry: Introducing Finite-Dimensional Vector Spaces. K. T. Leung & S. N. Suen. 356p. 1994. pap. 29.50 (*962-209-360-4*, Pub. by Hong Kong Univ Pr HK) Coronet Bks.

***Vectors of Death: The Archaeology of European Contact.** Ann F. Ramenofsky. LC 87-19232. (Illus.). 316p. 1987. reprint ed. pap. 90.10 (*0-608-04148-3*, 2064881) Bks Demand.

Vectors of Disease Agents: Interactions with Plants, Animals, & Men. Ed. by John J. McKelvey, Jr. et al. LC 80-18676. 256p. 1980. text ed. 75.00 (*0-275-90521-7*, C0521, Praeger Pubs) Greenwood.

Vectors Tensors & the Basic Equations. Rutherford Aris. 1989. pap. 7.95 (*0-486-66110-5*) Dover.

Vectors to Spare: The Life of an Air Traffic Controller. Milovan S. Brenlove. LC 92-45892. (Illus.). 240p. (C). 1993. 24.95 (*0-8138-0471-X*) Iowa St U Pr.

Veda & Indian Culture: An Introductory Essay. Kireet Joshi. (C). 1991. pap. 7.50 (*81-208-0889-4*, Pub. by Motilal Banarsidass II) S Asia.

Veda & Torah: Transcending the Textuality of Scripture. Barbara A. Holdrege. LC 92-42599. 765p. 1995. text ed. 59.50 (*0-7914-1639-9*); pap. text ed. 19.95 (*0-7914-1640-2*) State U NY Pr.

***Veda & Vedanta.** Ram M. Sharma. xxi, 160p. 1996. 16.00 (*81-86339-25-6*, Pub. by Estrn Bk Linkers II) Nataraj Bks.

Veda Commentaries of H. P. Blavatsky. H. P. Blavatsky. Ed. by H. J. Spierenburg. 250p. (Orig.). 1996. pap. 13.95 (*0-913004-98-7*) Point Loma Pub.

***Veda-Laksana Vedic Ancillary Literature: A Descriptive Bibliography.** K. Parameswara Aithal. (C). 1993. 54.00 (*81-208-1120-8*, Pub. by Motilal Banarsidass II) S Asia.

Veda Recitation in Varanasi. Wayne Howard. 1986. 42.00 (*0-8364-0872-1*) S Asia.

Vedanta: Heart of Hinduism. Hans Torwesten. Tr. by John Phillips from GER. LC 90-37901. 208p. 1992. pap. 10.95 (*0-8021-3262-6*, Grove) Grove-Atltic.

Vedanta: Voice of Freedom. Swami Vivekananda. Ed. & Intro. by Swami Chetanananda. LC 90-12003. (Illus.). 328p. 1990. reprint ed. 19.95 (*0-916356-62-0*); reprint ed. pap. 11.95 (*0-916356-63-9*) Vedanta Soc St Louis.

UV

Vedanta & Christian Faith. rev. ed. Bede Griffiths. LC 90-27068. (Basket of Tolerance Ser.). (Illus.). 232p. 1991. reprint ed. pap. 12.95 (*0-918801-24-9*) Dawn Horse Pr.

Vedanta & the Future of Mankind. 1.95 (*0-614-17356-6*) Vedanta Pr.

Vedanta Commentaries of H. P. Blavatsky. Compiled by H. J. Spierenburg. 246p. 1996. pap. 12.50 (*0-913004-75-8*) Point Loma Pub.

Vedanta for the West: The Ramakrishna Movement in the United States. Carl T. Jackson. LC 93-24702. (Religion in North America Ser.). 199p. 1994. 31.50 (*0-253-33098-X*) Ind U Pr.

Vedanta for the Western World: A Symposium on Vedanta. Ed. by Christopher Isherwood. LC 46-25052. (C). 1945. pap. 10.95 (*0-87481-000-0*) Vedanta Pr.

Vedanta in Brief. Swami Jyotinmayananda. (Orig.). 1978. pap. 6.99 (*0-934664-37-4*) Yoga Res Foun.

Vedanta in Practice. 3rd ed. Swami Paramananda. 1985. pap. 3.95 (*0-911564-04-7*) Vedanta Ctr.

Vedanta Paribhasa. Dharmaraja Adhvarindra. Tr. by Swami Madhavananda. 263p. 1945. Bilingual ed. pap. 4.95 (*0-87481-072-8*, Pub. by Advaita Ashrama II) Vedanta Pr.

Vedanta Philosophy. F. M. Muller. 182p. 1984. text ed. 27.00 (*0-685-14047-4*) Coronet Bks.

Vedanta Philosophy. Max F. Muller. 173p. 1985. 29.95 (*0-318-37034-4*) Asia Bk Corp.

Vedanta Philosophy: Five Lectures on Reincarnation. 4th ed. Swami Abhedananda. 99p. 1976. reprint ed. spiral bd. 8.00 (*0-7873-0016-0*) Hlth Research.

Vedanta Philosophy: Lectures by the Swami Vivekananda on Raja Yoga Also Patanjali's Yoga Aphorisms, with Commentaries, & Glossary of Sanskrit Terms (1899) Vivekananda. 390p. 1996. pap. 27.00 (*1-56459-797-0*) Kessinger Pub.

Vedanta Philosophy: Lectures on Raja Yoga. 8th ed. Swami Vivekananda. 381p. 1972. reprint ed. spiral bd. 12.50 (*0-7873-0910-9*) Hlth Research.

Vedanta Philosophy Five Lectures on Reincarnation (1908) Swami Abhedananda. 100p. 1996. pap. 14.95 (*1-56459-886-1*) Kessinger Pub.

Vedanta Philosophy for the Unity of Mankind. Adwaita Ganguly. (C). 1995. 18.50 (*0-7069-9705-0*, Pub. by Vikas II) S Asia.

Vedanta Philosophy Lectures on Raja Yoga. Swami Vivekananda. 1991. lib. bdg. 250.00 (*0-8490-4972-5*) Gordon Pr.

Vedanta-Sara-Sangraha. Anantendra-Yati. Tr. by T. M. Mahadevan. 1974. pap. 1.25 (*0-89744-124-9*) Auromere.

Vedanta Sutras. Ed. by G. Thibaut. 1974. lib. bdg. 75.00 (*0-8490-1256-2*) Gordon Pr.

Vedanta Sutras: Sacred Books of the East, 2 pts. Sri Sankaracharya. Tr. by George Thibaut. 1988. reprint ed. Set. 28.00 (*0-8364-2569-3*, Pub. by Motilal Banarsidass II) S Asia.

Vedanta Sutras of Badarayana with the Commentary of Baladeva. Tr. by Srisa Chandra Vasu. LC 73-3790. (Sacred Books of the Hindus: Vol. 5). reprint ed. 74.50 (*0-404-57805-5*) AMS Pr.

***Vedanta Sutras of Maharshi Badarayana.** Ed. & Tr. by Peter Freund from SAN. (Six Darshanas Ser.). 77p. (Orig.). 1996. pap. 12.00 (*0-923569-19-7*, 0-08) Maharishi U Mgmt Pr.

Vedantasara of Sadananda. Sadananda. 1949. pap. 3.00 (*0-87481-073-6*, Pub. by Advaita Ashrama II) Vedanta Pr.

Vedantasutras with the Sribhasya of Ramanujacarya, Vol. 1. Tr. by M. Rangacharya & M. B. Aiyangar. (C). 1988. 36.00 (*81-215-0091-5*, Pub. by Munshiram Manoharial II) S Asia.

Vedantic Priesthood Masterworks Vol. 1. Sriman Praman Tiru-Venkatadasa Adhikari. 280p. (C). 1994. pap. text ed. 17.50 (*1-885525-02-8*) RGVMO Fnd Trust.

Vedantic Tales. Sister Gargi. 145p. 1990. pap. 4.95 (*0-87481-236-4*, Pub. by Advaita Ashrama II) Vedanta Pr.

Vedantic Way of Living. Swami B. Tirtha. (C). 1994. pap. 7.50 (*81-207-1666-3*, Pub. by Sterling Plns Pvt II) S Asia.

Vedas. Jyesht Verman. (C). 1992. 6.50 (*81-204-0661-3*, Pub. by Oxford IBH II) S Asia.

Vedas, Ragas & Storytellers. Judy Mitchell-Miller. (Passages to India Ser.). (C). 1989. spiral bd. 20.00 (*1-56709-012-5*) Indep Broadcast.

Vedauwoo: Earthborn. Harold Gilbert. (Illus.). 228p. (Orig.). 1990. pap. write for info. (*0-9617748-2-7*) Connections Pr WY.

Vedda Villages of Anuradhapura: The Historical Anthropology of a Community in Sri Lanka. James Brow. LC 77-16663. (Publications on Asia of the School of International Studies: No. 33). (Illus.). 288p. 1978. 35.00 (*0-295-95585-6*) U of Wash Pr.

Veddas. Charles G. Seligman & Brenda Z. Seligman. LC 76-44787. reprint ed. 47.50 (*0-404-15970-2*) AMS Pr.

Veddas. C. G. Seligmann & Brenda Z. Seligmann. (C). 1995. reprint ed. 52.00 (*81-7013-111-1*, Pub. by Navrang) S Asia.

Vedebarta Bam: And You Shall Speak of Them. Moshe Bojomisky. (Vayikra Ser.: Vol. III). 205p. 1996. 19.95 (*1-880880-17-2*) Israeli Trad.

Vedi. Ved Mehta. (Illus.). 272p. 1987. reprint ed. pap. 7.95 (*0-393-30417-5*) Norton.

Vedibartha Bam: And You Shall Speak of Them. Moshe Bogomilsky. Ed. by Philip Kaplan. (Moshe Ser.: Bogomilsky). 247p. (C). 1995. 16.95 (*1-880880-14-8*) Israeli Trad.

Vedibartha Bam: And You Shall Speak of Them. Moshe Bogomilsky. Ed. by Philip Kaplan. (Exodus (Shemot) Ser.). 247p. (C). 1996. 16.95 (*1-880880-15-6*) Israeli Trad.

Vedic: Religion & Culture. P. L. Bhargava. (C). 1994. 14.00 (*81-246-0006-6*, Pub. by DK Pubs Dist II) S Asia.

***Vedic Astrology: A Guide to the Fundamentals of Jyotish.** Ronnie G. Dreyer. LC 97-5620. (Illus.). 288p. (Orig.). 1997. pap. 14.95 (*0-87728-889-5*) Weiser.

Vedic Concordance. Maurice Bloomfield. (C). 1990. 58.00 (*81-8518-53-5*, Pub. by Low Price II) S Asia.

Vedic Cosmography & Astronomy. Richard Thompson. 250p. 12.95 (*0-89213-269-8*) Govardhan Hill.

Vedic Declension of the Type Vrkis: A Contribution to the Study of the Feminine Noun Declension in Indo-European. Ruth N. Albright. (LD Ser.: No.1). 1927. pap. 25.00 (*0-527-00747-1*) Periodicals Srv.

Vedic Deities. M. P. Pandit. LC 89-84765. 129p. (Orig.). 1989. pap. 7.95 (*0-941524-45-0*) Lotus Light.

Vedic Experience. Raimundo Panniker. 937p. 1983. 15.00 (*0-89744-011-0*) Auromere.

***Vedic Geometry.** S. K. Kapoor. (Illus.). xii, 523p. 1994. 39.00 (*0-614-21796-2*, Pub. by Arya Bk Depot II) Nataraj Bks.

Vedic Harappans. Bhagwan Singh. (C). 1995. 78.00 (*81-86471-04-9*, Pub. by Aditya Prakashan II) S Asia.

Vedic Heritage Teaching Program, Vol. III. Sunita Ramaswamy & Sundar Ramaswamy. Ed. by Irene Schleicher. 280p. (Orig.). (C). 1994. pap. text ed. write for info. (*1-882325-05-2*) Arsha Vidya.

Vedic Heritage Teaching Program Teaching Manual, Vol. I. Sunita Ramaswamy & Sundar Ramaswamy. Ed. by Irene Schleicher. (Illus.). 294p. (Orig.). 1992. pap. text ed. write for info. (*1-882325-00-1*) Arsha Vidya.

Vedic Heritage Teaching Program Teaching Manual, Vol. II. Sunita Ramaswamy & Sundar Ramaswamy. Ed. by Irene Schleicher. 236p. (Orig.). (C). 1993. pap. text ed. write for info. (*1-882325-03-6*) Arsha Vidya.

Vedic Hermeneutics. K. S. Murty. (C). 1993. 14.00 (*81-208-1105-4*, Pub. by Motilal Banarsidass II) S Asia.

Vedic Hymns, 2 vols. F. Max Muller & Hermann Oldenberg. 1974. lib. bdg. 500.00 (*0-685-01976-4*) Gordon Pr.

Vedic Law of Marriage or the Emancipation of Women. A. Mahadeva Sastri. (C). 1988. reprint ed. 17.50 (*81-206-0406-7*, Pub. by Asian Educ Servs II) S Asia.

Vedic Mathematics, 4 vols., Vol. 1. T. Satyanarayana Raju. iv, 190p. (Orig.). (YA). (gr. 7-12). 1996. pap. 29.95 (*0-9650901-3-2*) Inst of Vedic.

Vedic Mathematics: Sixteen Simple Mathematical Formulae from the Vedas. Jahadhuru Swami Sri Bharati & Krsna Tirthaji Maharaja. Ed. by V. S. Agrawala. 367p. (C). 1994. 16.00 (*81-208-0163-6*, Pub. by Motilal Banarsidass II) S Asia.

Vedic Mathematics: Sixteen Simple Mathematical Formulae from the Vedas. Jagadguru S. Maharaja. Ed. by V. S. Agrawala. 367p. (C). 1992. pap. 12.00 (*81-208-0164-4*, Pub. by Motilal Banarsidass II) S Asia.

Vedic Metaphysics. Bharati K. Tirthaji. (C). 1983. 17.50 (*0-8364-2225-2*, Pub. by Motilal Banarsidass II) S Asia.

Vedic Mythology. Arthur A. MacDonell. 1973. 300.00 (*0-87968-153-5*) Gordon Pr.

Vedic Mythology, 2 vols. Alfred Hillebrandt & S. Rajeswara Sarma. (C). reprint ed. Set. 48.00 (*81-208-0801-0*, Pub. by Motilal Banarsidass II) S Asia.

Vedic Mythology. A. A. Macdonell. (C). 1995. reprint ed. 19.50 (*81-208-1113-5*, Pub. by Motilal Banarsidass II) S Asia.

Vedic Origins of Karma: Cosmos as Man in Ancient Indian Myth & Ritual. Herman W. Tull. LC 88-37610. 181p. 1989. text ed. 24.50 (*0-7914-0094-8*) State U NY Pr.

Vedic Reader for Students. Arthur A. Macdonell. 296p. 1992. pap. 14.95 (*0-19-560038-X*) OUP.

Vedic Reader for Students: Containing Thirty Hymns of the Rigveda in the Original Samhita & Pada Texts, with Transliteration, Translation, Explanatory Notes, Introduction, Vocabulary. Arthur A. Macdonell. (C). 1992. reprint ed. text ed. 14.00 (*81-208-1018-X*, Pub. by Motilal Banarsidass II) S Asia.

Vedic Religion & Philosophy. Swami Prabhavananda. 4.95 (*0-87481-411-1*) Vedanta Pr.

***Vedic Sacrifice: Challenge & Response.** Israel Selvanayagam. 1996. 38.00 (*81-7304-104-0*, Pub. by Manohar II) S Asia.

Vedic Symbolism. Sri Aurobindo. Ed. by M. P. Pandit. LC 88-80999. 122p. (Orig.). (C). 1988. pap. 6.95 (*0-941524-30-2*) Lotus Light.

Vedic Tantrism: A Study of Rgvidhana of Saunaka. M. S. Bhat. 475p. (C). 1987. 31.00 (*81-208-0197-0*, Pub. by Motilal Banarsidass II) S Asia.

Vedic Vision. Ed. by John B. Alphonso-Karkala. 80p. 1980. pap. 4.50 (*0-86578-004-8*) Ind-US Inc.

Veedor the Condor. B. L. Walker. LC 95-42999. 1995. pap. 12.00 (*0-9648959-0-0*) Bliss Bks.

Veerabrahmam: India's Nostradamus Saint. R. N. Pillai. (C). 1991. 19.50 (*81-7017-279-9*, Pub. by Abhinav II) S Asia.

Veg & Two Veg. Cecilia Norman. (Illus.). 160p. (Orig.). 1992. pap. 13.95 (*0-563-36358-4*, BBC-Parkwest) Parkwest Pubns.

Vega: The Story of Marshall Miller of Oldham County, TX. William Miller. (Illus.). 136p. (Orig.). 1995. pap. write for info. (*1-885591-81-0*) Morris Pubng.

Vega Ventura: The Operational Story of Lockheed's Lucky Star. John C. Stanaway. (Illus.). 112p. 1996. pap. 19.95 (*0-7643-0087-3*) Schiffer.

***Vegan: The New Ethics of Eating.** Erik Marcus. LC 97-10398. (Illus.). 224p. 1997. 24.95 (*0-935526-34-X*) McBooks Pr.

***Vegan: The New Ethics of Eating.** Erik Marcus. LC 97-10398. (Illus.). 224p. 1997. pap. 14.95 (*0-935526-35-8*) McBooks Pr.

Vegan Cookbook. Alan Wakeman & Gordon Baskerville. 304p. 1986. pap. 12.95 (*0-571-13820-9*) Faber & Faber.

Vegan Cookbook: With More Than 200 Recipes Using No Animal Produce. 2nd ed. Alan Wakeman & Gordon Baskerville. 364p. 1996. reprint ed. pap. 12.95 (*0-571-17804-9*) Faber & Faber.

Vegan Cooking. Eva Batt. 144p. 1993. pap. 10.00 (*0-7225-1161-2*) Thorsons SF.

Vegan Gourmet: Full Flavor & Variety with over 100 Delicious Recipes. Susann Geiskopf-Hadler & Mindy Toomay. LC 95-3366. 1995. pap. 14.95 (*0-7615-0027-8*) Prima Pub.

Vegan Handbook: Over 200 Delicious Recipes, Meal Plans, & Vegetarian Resources for All Ages. Ed. by Debra Wasserman & Reed Mangels. LC 96-60113. (Vegetarian Journal Reports: Vol. 2). (Illus.). 256p. (Orig.). 1996. 20.00 (*0-931411-17-3*) Vegetarian Resc.

Vegan Kitchen. 12th rev. ed. Freya Dinshah. (Illus.). 96p. (Orig.). 1996. pap. 9.95 (*0-942401-15-8*) Am Vegan Soc.

***Vegan-licious: A Lifestyle Book.** Revel Hesterman & Marie O'Meara. Ed. by Carol Berry. (Illus.). 130p. 1996. pap. 15.95 (*0-9657887-0-9*) Essential Therap.

***Vegan Nutrition: Pure & Simple.** Michael Klaper. Ed. by Cynthia Klaper. (Illus.). 1995. 9.95 (*0-9614248-7-7*) Gentle World.

***Vegan Soul.** Tabatha Crayton. 1998. pap. write for info. (*0-609-80000-0*) Crown Pub Group.

Vegan Vittles: A Collection of Recipes Inspired by the Critters of Farm Sanctuary. Joanne Stepaniak. LC 96-14290. 192p. 1996. pap. text ed. 11.95 (*1-57067-025-0*) Book Pub Co.

***Vegas Heat.** Fern Michaels. 400p. 1997. 25.00 (*1-57566-138-1*, Knsington) Kensgtn Pub Corp.

***Vegas Heat.** Fern Michaels. 480p. 1997. mass mkt. 6.99 (*0-8217-5758-X*, Zebra Kensgtn) Kensgtn Pub Corp.

***Vegas on a Chip: Beat the House with Your Computer.** Thomas A. Turcich. (Illus.). 300p. (Orig.). 1997. pap. 24.95 incl. cd-rom (*1-887132-04-X*) LightSpeed Pub.

Vegas P. I. The Life & Times of America's Greatest Detective. Lake Headley & William Hoffman. 352p. 1993. 22.95 (*1-56025-057-7*) Thunders Mouth.

***Vegas Rich.** 1997. 188.73 (*0-8217-8721-7*) Kensgtn Pub Corp.

Vegas Rich. Fern Michaels. 512p. 1996. 25.00 (*1-57566-057-1*, Knsington) Kensgtn Pub Corp.

***Vegas Rich.** Fern Michaels. 544p. 1997. mass mkt. 6.99 (*0-8217-5594-3*, Zebra Kensgtn) Kensgtn Pub Corp.

***Vegas Rich, Vol. 1.** large type ed. Fern Michaels. LC 96-3208. 1996. 26.95 (*1-56895-370-4*, Compass) Wheeler Pub.

***Vegas Sunrise.** Fern Michaels. 384p. 1997. 25.00 (*1-57566-214-0*, Knsington) Kensgtn Pub Corp.

Vegas Vows. Linda R. Wisdom. (American Romance Ser.). 1994. mass mkt. 3.50 (*0-373-16541-2*, 1-16541-4) Harlequin Bks.

Vegetable Book. Colin Spencer. LC 96-6998. (Illus.). 288p. 1996. 40.00 (*0-8478-1971-X*) Rizzoli Intl.

Vegetable Book: A Texan's Guide to Gardening. Sam Cotner. (Illus.). 422p. 1985. 26.95 (*0-914641-01-8*) TX Gardener Pr.

***Vegetable Book: A Texan's Guide to Gardening.** rev. ed. Sam Cotner. (Illus.). 400p. Date not set. pap. 24.95 (*0-914641-15-8*) TX Gardener Pr.

Vegetable Breeding, 3 vols., Vol. I. G. Kalloo. LC 87-23879. 240p. 1988. Vol. I, 240p. 143.00 (*0-8493-6978-9*, SB324, CRC Reprint) Franklin.

Vegetable Breeding, 3 vols., Vol. II. G. Kalloo. 240p. 1988. 129.00 (*0-8493-6979-7*, SB324, CRC Reprint) Franklin.

Vegetable Breeding, 3 vols., Vol. III. G. Kalloo. 280p. 1988. 109.00 (*0-8493-6980-0*, SB324, CRC Reprint) Franklin.

Vegetable Classification in Australia. Anderson & Gillison. (Australian National University Press Ser.). 1981. text ed. 37.00 (*0-08-032945-4*, Pergamon Pr) Elsevier.

Vegetable Cookbook. 1990. 9.99 (*0-517-02219-2*) Random Hse Value.

Vegetable Crop Pests. McKinley. 1992. 99.00 (*0-8493-7729-3*, SB608) CRC Pr.

Vegetable Crops in India. T. K. Bose & M. G. Som. (Illus.). 770p. (C). 1986. 115.00 (*81-85109-41-9*, Pub. by Naya Prokash IA) S Asia.

***Vegetable Desserts: Beyond Carrot Cake & Pumpkin Pie.** Elisabeth Schager & Jeannette L. Miller. (Illus.). 208p. (Orig.). 1998. pap. 15.95 (*1-56561-135-7*) Chronimed.

***Vegetable Discoveries.** Elizabeth Schneider. Date not set. write for info. (*0-688-15260-0*) Morrow.

Vegetable Diseases & Their Control. 2nd ed. Arden F. Sherf & Alan A. MacNab. LC 86-5586. 728p. 1986. text ed. 95.00 (*0-471-05860-2*) Wiley.

Vegetable Fibres. K. B. R. G. Staff. 280p. (C). 1979. text ed. 175.00 (*0-89771-571-3*, Pub. by Intl Bk Distr II) St Mut.

Vegetable Fibres. KBRG Staff. 280p. 1979. 95.00 (*0-685-21839-2*, Pub. by Intl Bk Distr II) St Mut.

Vegetable Food Products & Luxuries see Chemical Technology: An Encyclopedic Treatment

Vegetable Garden. Melvin Berger. Ed. by Susan Evento. (Early Science Big Bks.). (Illus.). 16p. (J). (ps-2). 1995. pap. 14.95 (*1-56784-024-8*) Newbridge Comms.

Vegetable Garden. Douglas Florian. LC 90-20620. (Illus.). 32p. (J). (ps-3). 1994. pap. 5.00 (*0-15-200051-8*, HB Juv Bks) HarBrace.

Vegetable Garden. Douglas Florian. LC 90-20620. (Illus.). 32p. (J). (ps-3). 1991. 14.00 (*0-15-293383-2*, HB Juv Bks) HarBrace.

Vegetable Garden. Douglas Florian. LC 90-20620. (Illus.). 32p. (J). (ps-3). 1996. pap. 5.00 (*0-15-201018-1*, Voyager Bks) HarBrace.

Vegetable Garden. M. Vilmorin-Andrieux. LC 81-50300. 620p. 1981. reprint ed. pap. 19.95 (*0-89815-041-8*) Ten Speed Pr.

Vegetable Garden: Mini Book. Melvin Berger. Ed. by Susan Evento. (Early Science Big Bks.). 16p. (J). (ps-2). 1995. pap. 2.95 (*1-56784-049-3*) Newbridge Comms.

Vegetable Garden Theme Pack. Melvin Berger. Ed. by Susan Evento. (Macmillan Early Science Big Bks.). (Illus.). (J). (ps-2). 1995. pap. write for info. (*1-56784-181-3*) Newbridge Comms.

Vegetable Gardening: Spring & Fall. John Burrow. Ed. by Pete Billac. LC 95-70123. (Illus.). 128p. (Orig.). 1995. pap. 9.95 (*0-943629-17-9*) Swan Pub.

Vegetable Gardening for Beginners. Hugh Wiberg. 1978. pap. 2.00 (*0-87980-169-7*) Wilshire.

***Vegetable Gardening, Ortho's.** Ortho Books Staff. Date not set. write for info. (*0-89721-324-6*) Ortho Info.

Vegetable Gardening with Derek Fell. Derek Fell. (Illus.). 120p. 1996. 22.50 (*1-56799-253-6*, Friedman-Fairfax) M Friedman Pub Grp Inc.

Vegetable Growing. Arthur Billitt. 96p. 1988. 45.00 (*1-85283-226-6*, Pub. by Boxtree Ltd UK) St Mut.

Vegetable Growing Handbook: Organic & Traditional Methods. 3rd ed. Walter E. Splittstoesser. 362p. (gr. 13). 1996. text ed. 60.95 (*0-442-23971-8*) Chapman & Hall.

Vegetable in the Garden. Pascale De Bourgoing. (First Discovery Bks.). (Illus.). 24p. (J). (ps-2). 1994. 11.95 (*0-590-48326-9*, Cartwheel) Scholastic Inc.

Vegetable Ingredients Cookbook. Christine Ingram. 256p. 1996. 32.50 (*1-85967-264-7*, Lorenz Bks) Anness Pub.

Vegetable Magic. Sheilah Kaufman. Ed. by Martina Boudreau. 64p. (Orig.). 1985. pap. 3.95 (*0-942320-16-6*, SK202) Am Cooking.

Vegetable Markets in the Western Hemisphere. Ed. by Rigoberto A. Lopez & Leo C. Polopolus. LC 90-21777. (Illus.). 266p. 1992. text ed. 36.95 (*0-8138-1052-3*) Iowa St U Pr.

Vegetable Materia Medica of India & Ceylon. E. Roberts. 437p. (C). 1984. 60.00 (*0-685-22358-2*, Pub. by Scientific UK) St Mut.

Vegetable Oils & Agrichemicals, 4. Ed. by John H. Benedict et al. LC 94-29090. (Cotton Foundation Reference Bks.). 1994. write for info. (*0-939809-04-4*) Cotton Found.

Vegetable People: Thirty Original Victorian Postcards from the World-Class Meisler Collection. Alan Meisler. (Original Victorian Postcard Book Series from the World-Class Meisler Collection). (Illus.). 34p. (Orig.). 1994. pap. 8.95 (*1-886584-00-1*) Sentimental Times.

Vegetable Processing. Ed. by David Arthey & Colin Dennis. 279p. 1991. lib. bdg. 130.00 (*1-56081-081-5*, VCH) Wiley.

Vegetable Production. I. L. Nonnecke. (Illus.). 448p. (C). (gr. 13). 1989. text ed. 89.95 (*0-442-26721-5*) Chapman & Hall.

***Vegetable Production in the Tropics.** Williams. 1991. pap. text ed. write for info. (*0-582-60609-8*, Pub. by Longman UK) Longman.

Vegetable Seed Production in the San Francisco Bay Area & Other Warm-Winter Areas in the United States. 4th ed. Craig C. Dremann. 1987. pap. 4.25 (*0-933421-24-9*) Redwood Seed.

Vegetable Show. Laurene K. Brown. (Illus.). (J). (ps-3). 1995. 14.95 (*0-316-11363-8*) Little.

Vegetable Soup/The Fruit Bowl. Dianne Warren & Susan S. Jones. LC 96-69104. (Illus.). 64p. (Orig.). (J). (ps-3). 1996. per., pap. 14.95 (*0-9652736-0-1*) Oasis Publns.

Vegetable Spaghetti Cookbook. Phyllis V. Shaudys. LC 82-90074. (Illus.). 96p. (Orig.). 1982. pap. 4.95 (*0-935238-03-4*) Pine Row.

Vegetable Surrender: or Happiness Is Not Blue. Heart-Master Da. LC 87-72668. (Illus.). 46p. (J). 1987. 10.95 (*0-918801-02-8*) Dawn Horse Pr.

Vegetable Theatre. Smithsonian Staff. 1993. 12.95 (*1-55550-896-0*) Universe.

Vegetables. (Popular Brands Cookbooks Ser.). (Illus.). 24p. 1995. pap. write for info. (*1-56144-676-9*) Modern Pub NYC.

Vegetables. Suzanne F. Bales. (Burpee American Gardening Ser.). (Illus.). 96p. 1991. pap. 9.00 (*0-671-86395-9*, P-H Gardening) P-H Gen Ref & Trav.

Vegetables. Emalee Chapman. Ed. by Laurie Wertz. LC 93-17991. (Williams-Sonoma Kitchen Library). (Illus.). 108p. 17.95 (*0-7835-0254-0*) Time-Life.

Vegetables. Emalee Chapman. Ed. by Laurie Wertz. LC 93-17991. (Williams-Sonoma Kitchen Library). (Illus.). 108p. 1993. lib. bdg. write for info. (*0-7835-0255-9*) Time-Life.

Vegetables. S. J. Fretz. 36p. (Orig.). 1991. pap. 3.25 (*0-940844-46-X*) Wellspring.

Vegetables. Ed. by Kristin Joyce. LC 95-11931. (Cultivated Gardner Ser.). (Illus.). 96p. 1997. 18.95 (*0-00-225045-4*) Collins SF.

Vegetables. Patricia S. Michalak & Cass Peterson. LC 92-31890. (Rodale's Successful Organic Gardening Ser.). (Illus.). 1993. 24.95 (*0-87596-563-6*); pap. 14.95 (*0-87596-564-4*) Rodale Pr Inc.

***Vegetables.** Ortho Books Staff. 1996. pap. text ed. 6.95 (*0-89721-303-3*) Ortho Info.

***Vegetables.** Jillian Powell. (Everybody Eats Ser.). (J). 1997. 21.40 (*0-8172-4768-8*) Raintree Pr.

***Vegetables.** Random House Value Publishing Staff. 1997. pap. 8.99 (*0-517-18398-6*) Random Hse Value.

Vegetables. Ross. Date not set. pap. write for info. (*0-14-046864-1*) Viking Penguin.

***Vegetables.** Ed. by J. S. Siemonsma & Piluek Kasem. (PROSEA Ser.: No. 8). (Illus.). 412p. 1993. pap. 74.00 (*979-8316-22-3*, Pub. by Backhuys Pubs NE) Balogh.

Vegetables. Time Life Staff. Ed. by Catherine Hackett. LC 95-43129. (Great Taste, Low Fat Ser.). (Illus.). 160p. 1997. 14.95 (*0-7835-4554-1*) Time-Life.

An Asterisk (*) at the beginning of an entry indicates that the title is appearing in BIP for the first time.

Vegetables. Susan Wake. (Foods We Eat Ser.). (Illus.). 32p. (J). (gr. 1-4). 1990. lib. bdg. 14.96 (*0-87614-390-7*, Carolrhoda) Lerner Group.

Vegetables: Artichokes to Zucchini. rev. ed. Joe Famularo & Louise Imperiale. LC 93-21986. 256p. 1993. pap. 14.95 (*0-8120-1756-0*) Barron.

Vegetables: Characteristics, Production & Marketing. Lincoln C. Peirce. LC 86-32625. 566p. 1987. Net. text ed. 53.50 (*0-471-85022-5*) Wiley.

Vegetables: Cook Books from Amish Kitchens. Phyllis P. Good & Rachel T. Pellman. (From Amish Kitchens Ser.). 32p. 1996. mass mkt. 2.95 (*1-56148-198-X*) Good Bks PA.

Vegetables & Health Sciences: Index of Modern Information. rev. ed. Victor K. Elwood. LC 92-31218. 144p. 1992. 49.50 (*1-55914-750-4*); pap. 39.50 (*1-55914-751-2*) ABBE Pubs Assn.

Vegetables & Herbs. Cecilia Fitzsimons. (All about Food Ser.). (J). 1996. pap. 7.95 (*0-382-39598-0*); lib. bdg. 14.95 (*0-382-39593-X*) Silver Burdett Pr.

Vegetables & Legumes. Corinne T. Netzer. (Corinne T. Netzer Good Eating Gourmet Ser.: Bk. 6). 1997. mass mkt. 5.99 (*0-440-22343-1*) Dell.

Vegetables & Vegetable Products. Ed. by H. F. Linskens & J. F. Jackson. (Modern Methods of Plant Analysis Ser.: Vol. 16). 208p. 1994. 188.95 (*0-387-55843-8*) Spr-Verlag.

Vegetables Drugs of India, 1984. D. Sanyal. 397p. (C). 1988. 30.00 (*0-685-22357-4*, Pub. by Scientific UK) St Mut.

Vegetables for the Hot, Humid Tropics. Franklin W. Martin et al. (Studies in Tropical Agriculture). 1980. lib. bdg. 59.95 (*0-8490-3071-4*) Gordon Pr.

Vegetables for Today's Gardens. R. Milton Carleton. 1979. pap. 2.00 (*0-87980-226-X*) Wilshire.

Vegetables, Gardener's Collection. Better Homes & Gardens Editors. (Better Homes & Gardens Ser.). (Illus.). 64p. 1995. pap. 4.95 (*0-696-02587-6*) Meredith Bks.

Vegetables, Garnitures, & Food Decorations. Yves Thuries. 1997. text ed. 89.95 (*0-442-01698-0*) Van Nos Reinhold.

***Vegetables, Herbs & Fruit.** (Pleasures of Gardening Ser.). (Illus.). 128p. 12.98 (*0-8317-3629-1*) Smithmark.

Vegetables in Family Meals. 1986. lib. bdg. 79.95 (*0-8490-3787-5*) Gordon Pr.

Vegetables on the Grill: A Menu Cookbook. (Illus.). 1992. pap. 17.00 (*0-06-096889-3*, PL) HarpC.

Vegetables on the Side: The Complete Guide to Buying & Cooking Vegetables. Sallie Y. Williams. LC 94-43366. 1995. pap. 25.00 (*0-02-629115-0*) Macmillan.

Vegetables, Salads, & Greens. 1995. 23.95 (*0-916103-20-X*) Am Express Food.

Vegetables, Stories & Articles, 3 vols., Vols. 16-18. Intro. by Matthew J. Bruccoli. (F. Scott Fitzgerald Manuscripts). 1492p. 1991. Set. text ed. 295.00 (*0-8240-5966-2*) Garland.

Vegetables the Chinese Way. Stephen Yan. (Illus.). 64p. (Orig.). 1989. pap. 5.95 (*0-921053-02-9*) Gordon Soules Bk.

Vegetables, Vegetables. Fay Robinson. LC 94-14075. (Rookie Read-about Science Ser.). (Illus.). 32p. (J). (ps-2). 1994. pap. 3.95 (*0-516-46030-7*); lib. bdg. 17.30 (*0-516-06030-9*) Childrens.

Vegetacion de los Rios, Lagos y Pantanos. Chelsea House Publishers Staff. 1996. lib. bdg. 15.95 (*0-7910-4024-0*) Chelsea Hse.

***Vegetarian.** Time-Life Books Editors. LC 96-32125. (Fanfare Ser.). (Illus.). 60p. 1997. write for info. (*0-7835-4874-5*) Time-Life.

***Vegetarian.** Time-Life Books Editors. (Fanfare Collection). 1997. 12.95 (*0-614-27966-6*) Time-Life.

Vegetarian. Joanne Weir. Ed. by Chuck Williams. LC 95-32818. (Williams-Sonoma Kitchen Library). (Illus.). 108p. 1997. 17.95 (*0-7835-0311-3*) Time-Life.

Vegetarian Associations, Organizations, Periodicals, Cooking Schools & More: A How to Find or Locate Reference. Data Notes Publishing Staff. 60p. 1992. wbk. ed., ring bd. 24.95 (*0-911569-53-7*) Prosperity & Profits.

Vegetarian Baby: A Sensible Guide for Parents. Sharon K. Yntema. LC 79-24623. (Illus.). 224p. 1980. lib. bdg. 14.95 (*0-935526-01-3*) McBooks Pr.

Vegetarian Baby: A Sensible Guide for Parents. Sharon K. Yntema. LC 79-24623. (Illus.). 224p. 1991. pap. 10.95 (*0-935526-02-1*) McBooks Pr.

***Vegetarian Bistro: 250 Authentic French Regional Recipes.** Marlena Spieler. LC 96-51122. 1997. pap. 15.95 (*0-8118-1376-2*) Chronicle Bks.

Vegetarian Burgers: The Healthy, Delicious Way to Eat America's Favorite Food. Bharti Kirchner. 144p. 1996. pap. 12.00 (*0-06-095115-X*) HarpC.

Vegetarian Catering. D. Davies. (C). 1987. 80.00 (*0-948315-10-5*, Pub. by S Thornes Pubs UK) St Mut.

Vegetarian Cats & Dogs. 2nd rev. ed. James A. Pedan. LC 90-82536. (Illus.). 240p. 1995. pap. text ed. 14.95 (*0-941319-02-4*) Harbingers New Age.

Vegetarian Celebrations: Festive Menus for Holidays & Other Special Occasions. Nava Atlas. 288p. 1996. 15.95 (*0-316-05739-8*) Little.

Vegetarian Child. Joy Gross & Karen Freifeld. 224p. 1983. 12.00 (*0-8184-0342-X*) Carol Pub Group.

Vegetarian Child: A Complete Guide for Parents. Lucy Mull. LC 96-1949. 224p. 1997. pap. 12.00 (*0-399-52271-9*, Perigee Bks) Berkley Pub.

Vegetarian Children: A Supportive Guide for Parents. enl. rev. ed. Sharon K. Yntema. (Illus.). 176p. 1995. pap. 9.95 (*0-935526-22-6*) McBooks Pr.

***Vegetarian Chinese Cooking.** Wendy Lee. (Cooking for Today Ser.). 1996. 4.98 (*0-7651-9859-2*) Smithmark.

Vegetarian Classic Cooking. 1996. 7.98 (*0-8317-7382-0*) Smithmark.

Vegetarian Cookbooks Etc: A How to Find or Locate Workbook. Ed. by Bibliotheca Press Research Division Staff. 70p. 1983. ring bd. 24.95 (*0-939476-68-1*) Prosperity & Profits.

Vegetarian Cookery. Janet Walker. 1976. pap. 10.00 (*0-87980-170-0*) Wilshire.

Vegetarian Cooking. Lalita Ahmed. 64p. 1995. write for info. (*1-57215-022-X*) World Pubns.

Vegetarian Cooking. Elizabeth L. Huang. 120p. (CHI & ENG.). 1989. pap. 17.95 (*0-941676-20-X*) Wei-Chuan Pub.

Vegetarian Cooking. Ward. 1995. 6.98 (*0-7858-0494-3*) Bk Sales Inc.

Vegetarian Cooking Around the World. Photos by Robert L. Wolfe & Diane Wolfe. (Easy Menu Ethnic Cookbooks Ser.). (Illus.). 52p. (YA). (gr. 5 up). 1992. lib. bdg. 14.95 (*0-8225-0927-X*, Lerner Publctns) Lerner Group.

Vegetarian Cooking Around the World. Robert L. Wolfe. (YA). (gr. 5 up). 1993. pap. 5.95 (*0-8225-9632-6*, Lerner Publctns) Lerner Group.

Vegetarian Cooking for a Better World. 2nd ed. Muriel C. Golde. Ed. by Jennie O. Collura. 30p. reprint ed. pap. 1.50 (*0-9615401-0-9*) North Amer Veg.

***Vegetarian Cooking for Everyone.** Deborah Madison. LC 97-11138. 1997. write for info. (*0-7679-0014-6*) Broadway BDD.

Vegetarian Cooking for Good Health. Gary Null. 320p. 1991. pap. 14.00 (*0-02-010050-7*) Macmillan.

***Vegetarian Cooking for Healthy Living. Jamie G. Galeana & Mary Ter Meer. Ed. by Linda Hachfeld & Samantha Massaglia. (Illus.). 256p. (Orig.). 1997. pap. 17.95 (*0-9620471-9-8*, 190) Appletree MN.**
The ideal to-the-point guide describing how to remain healthy without eating red meat, fish, or poultry. "Highly recommended!"--Dean Ornish, M.D., President, Preventive Medicine Research Institute. Written by a caring & creative wife committed to her husband's health & a knowledgeable dietitian. All recipes have 4 grams of fat or less & few than 7 mg of cholesterol. The 130+ recipes are creative & easy-to-follow, are ultra low-fat, require common ingredients & follow the heart reversal guidelines advocated by Ornish. Recipe sections include Main Dish: Beans & Legumes; Pasta & Grains; Vegetables-Main Dish & On the Side; Hearty Sandwiches & Substantial Soups; Salads; Breakfasts; Breads & Muffins & Desserts to Live For. "This is 'must' reading for anyone seeking guidance, encouragement or reassurance as they face the lifestyle changes involved in adapting to a reduced-fat cuisine."--Helen A. Guthrie, Ph.D., RD, Professor Emerita Nutrition, Penn State. Watch for more low-fat vegetarian cookbooks to be published in 1998. Order from Appletree Press, 151 Good Counsel Drive #125, Mankato, MN 56001; 507-345-4848; FAX 507-345-3002; 800-322-5679. ***Publisher Provided Annotation.***

Vegetarian Cooking for One Hundred. 2nd ed. Freya Dinshah. 1981. Index card file 151 cds. & box. 24.95 (*0-942401-07-7*) Am Vegan Soc.

Vegetarian Cooking for People with Diabetes. Patricia Leshane. LC 94-16298. 144p. 1994. pap. 10.95 (*0-913990-22-1*) Book Pub Co.

Vegetarian Cooking Made Easy & Delectable. Veronica Vezza. 1978. pap. 3.00 (*0-87980-171-9*) Wilshire.

Vegetarian Cooking Made Simple. Susan Lapp. 94p. (Orig.). 1995. pap. 9.95 (*1-57502-095-5*, Cookbks by Morris) Morris Pubng.

***Vegetarian Cooking of the Mediterranean: From Gibraltar to Istanbul.** Cornelia Schinharl. LC 96-41828. 1997. 14.95 (*0-8120-9807-2*) Barron.

Vegetarian Cooking School Cookbook. rev. ed. Danny Vierra & Charise Vierra. LC 96-60016. (Illus.). 144p. 1996. spiral bd. 11.95 (*1-57258-101-8*) Teach Servs.

Vegetarian Creations. Ed. by Arlene Muska. (Illus.). 272p. (Orig.). 1992. pap. 17.00 (*0-918224-26-8*) S K Pubns.

Vegetarian Dining in New York City: And Not Just the Places the Yuppies Like. 4th ed. Arthur S. Brown & Barbara Holmes. (Illus.). 132p. (Orig.). 1994. pap. 8.95 (*0-9635338-2-7*) Vegetarian Dining.

***Vegetarian Dinner in Minutes: 75 Recipes for Quick & Easy Everyday Meals.** Linda Gassenheimer. LC 96-51121. 1997. pap. 16.95 (*0-8118-1383-5*) Chronicle Bks.

Vegetarian Dishes from Around the World. Rose Elliot. (Illus.). 1982. pap. 16.00 (*0-394-74997-9*) Pantheon.

Vegetarian Entertaining. Vegetarian Times Editors. LC 96-18465. (Illus.). 192p. 1996. write for info. (*0-02-861324-4*) Macmillan.

Vegetarian Entertaining: Menus for All Occasions. Diana Shaw. (Illus.). 144p. 1991. 27.50 (*0-517-57475-6*, Harmony) Crown Pub Group.

***Vegetarian Entertaining: 100 Tempting & Nutritious Ideas for Easy Everyday Dining.** Mathew Drennan & Annie Nichols. 192p. 1997. pap. 16.95 (*1-85967-528-X*, Lorenz Bks) Anness Pub.

Vegetarian Entertaining with Friends. Simon Hope. 1996. pap. 14.95 (*0-614-12639-8*) Newmarket.

Vegetarian Entertaining with Friends: 150 Recipes & Menus for Brunches, Buffets, Picnics & the Holidays. Simon Hope. (Illus.). 1996. pap. 14.95 (*1-55704-278-0*) Newmarket.

Vegetarian Epicure. Anna Thomas. 320p. 1972. pap. 16.00 (*0-394-71784-8*, Vin) Random.

Vegetarian Epicure, Bk. 1. Anna Thomas. (Illus.). 1972. pap. 16.95 (*0-394-47606-9*) Knopf.

Vegetarian Epicure, Bk 2. Anna Thomas. LC 77-16685. (Illus.). 1978. 12.50 (*0-394-41363-6*); pap. 16.00 (*0-394-73415-7*) Knopf.

Vegetarian Epicure, Plain & Fancy: Menus for Family & Friends. Anna Thomas. 1996. 30.00 (*0-614-12636-3*); pap. 19.00 (*0-614-12637-1*) Knopf.

Vegetarian Express: Easy, Tasty & Healthy Menus in 28 Minutes or Less. Nava Atlas & Lillian Kayte. (Illus.). 224p. 1995. pap. 15.95 (*0-316-05740-1*) Little.

Vegetarian Express Lane Cookbook: Really Easy Meals for Really Busy Cooks. Sarah Fritschner. Ed. by Rux Martin. (Illus.). 224p. (Orig.). 1996. pap. 14.95 (*1-57630-002-1*) Chapters Pub.

Vegetarian Fact or Myth - Eating to Live. 2nd rev. ed. Ed. by James C. Williams. LC 78-60663. 1978. pap. 8.95 (*0-931564-03-4*) JBR Pub.

Vegetarian Factfinder. Ellen Klavan. Ed. by Angela Hederman. LC 96-76080. (Factfinder Ser.). (Illus.). 52p. (J). (gr. 1-8). 1996. reprint ed. 19.95 (*0-9641262-1-4*) Little Bkrm.

Vegetarian Fast & Fancy: Great Garden of Eating. Darling. 1996. pap. 16.95 (*0-930440-35-8*) Royal Hse.

Vegetarian Fast Food. Rose Elliott. 1995. pap. 18.00 (*0-679-76207-8*) Random.

Vegetarian Feast. rev. ed. Martha R. Shulman. LC 94-18744. 272p. 1995. pap. 16.00 (*0-06-095001-3*) HarpC.

Vegetarian Food for All: Zesty International Dishes from One of the World's Most Celebrated Natural Foods Restaurants. Annabel Perkins. (Illus.). 192p. (Orig.). 1996. reprint ed. pap. 13.95 (*0-945934-13-0*) New Wrld Lib.

***Vegetarian Food Guide & Nutrition Counter.** Suzanne Havala. 176p. 1997. mass mkt. 5.99 (*0-425-16045-9*) Berkley Pub.

Vegetarian Four Seasons. Rose Elliot. 1994. pap. 18.00 (*0-679-75419-9*) Random.

Vegetarian Gourmet. Florence Bienenfeld & Mickey Bienenfeld. 1987. pap. 14.95 (*0-930440-48-X*) Royal Hse.

Vegetarian Gourmet. Ed. by Cole Group Staff. (Cooking Companion Ser.). 96p. (Orig.). 1995. pap. 7.95 (*1-56426-807-1*) Cole Group.

Vegetarian Gourmet. Roz Denny. (Illus.). 128p. 1995. 14.98 (*0-8317-3857-X*) Smithmark.

Vegetarian Gourmet. Judy Ridgeway. (Illus.). 176p. 1981. 14.95 (*0-13-941492-4*, Spectrum IN) Macmillan Gen Ref.

Vegetarian Guide to Diet & Salad. rev. ed. N. W. Walker. (Illus.). 132p. 1995. pap. 6.95 (*0-89019-034-8*) Norwalk Pr.

Vegetarian Hand Book. rev. ed. Gary Null. 304p. 1996. pap. 13.95 (*0-312-14441-5*) St Martin.

Vegetarian Handbook: Eating Right for Total Health. Gary Null. 288p. 1989. pap. 10.95 (*0-312-03948-4*) St Martin.

Vegetarian Hearth: Recipes & Reflections for the Cold Season. Darra Goldstein. 256p. 1996. 25.00 (*0-06-018760-3*) HarpC.

Vegetarian Indian. Shehzad Husain. 127p. 1995. write for info. (*1-57215-115-3*) World Pubns.

***Vegetarian International Cuisine: An Essential Cookbook.** Cheese Factory Restaurant Chiefs Staff. LC 97-13995. (Illus.). 200p. (Orig.). 1997. pap. 19.95 (*0-9655965-1-6*) Amherst Pr.

Vegetarian Jounal's Guide to Natural Foods Restaurants: In the U. S. & Canada. 2nd ed. Vegetarian Resource Group Staff & Lindsay Wagner. LC 94-33255. 304p. pap. 11.95 (*0-89529-654-3*) Avery Pub.

Vegetarian Journal Reports. Ed. by Charles Stahler et al. (Illus.). 112p. (Orig.). 1990. pap. 10.00 (*0-931411-07-6*) Vegetarian Resc.

Vegetarian Kitchen. Sara H. Brown. 1995. pap. 5.95 (*0-563-37037-8*, BBC-Parkwest) Parkwest Pubns.

Vegetarian Kitchen. Sarah Brown. (Illus.). 240p. 1991. pap. 13.95 (*0-563-21034-6*, BBC-Parkwest) Parkwest Pubns.

***Vegetarian Life: How to Be a Veggie in a Meat-Eating World.** Elizabeth Ferber. 256p. 1997. mass mkt. 5.99 (*0-425-15976-0*) Berkley Pub.

Vegetarian Lunchbasket: 225 Easy, Nutritious Recipes for the Quality-Conscious Family on the Go. Linda Haynes. (Illus.). 198p. 1993. pap. 12.95 (*0-945934-09-2*) New Wrld Lib.

***Vegetarian Magic: At the Regency House Spa.** John B. Nowakowski. (Illus.). 272p. (Orig.). 1996. pap. 19.95 (*0-9654045-0-1*) JBN Prods.

Vegetarian Magic: In Three Easy Steps. Karen Iacobbo & Michael E. Gibson. (Illus.). 130p. (Orig.). 1995. pap. 10.95 (*0-9647941-0-1*) Am Lyceum Pubng.

***Vegetarian Main Meals.** Smithmark Staff. (Cooking for Today Ser.). 1996. 4.98 (*0-7651-9861-4*) Smithmark.

Vegetarian Masterpieces. 2nd ed. Carol V. Tracy & Julie B. Bruton. (Illus.). 403p. (Orig.). 1989. lib. bdg. 13.95 (*0-9622168-2-8*) J Tracy Pub.

Vegetarian Medicines. Clarence Meyer. Ed. by David C. Meyer. (Illus.). 96p. (Orig.). 1981. pap. 5.95 (*0-916638-06-5*) Meyerbooks.

Vegetarian Menu Book: A Comprehensive Guide to Authentic Indian Vegetarian Cuisine. Vasantha Moorthy. (C). 1993. pap. 14.00 (*81-85944-18-0*, Pub. by UBS Pubs Dist II) S Asia.

Vegetarian Menus: One for Each Day in a Month (185 Recipes) Clara L. Bemister. 67p. 1997. pap. 5.00 (*0-89540-280-7*, SB-280) Sun Pub.

Vegetarian Microwave Cookbook. Cecilia Norman. (Illus.). 1993. pap. 12.00 (*0-7225-2761-6*) Thorsons SF.

Vegetarian Mother & Baby. Rose Elliot. 1996. pap. 17.95 (*0-679-77410-6*) Pantheon.

Vegetarian Mother & Baby Book: A Complete Guide to Nutrition, Health, & Diet During Pregnancy & After. Rose Elliot. LC 86-853. 224p. 1987. pap. 15.00 (*0-394-74620-1*) Pantheon.

Vegetarian Nights: Fresh from Hawaii. Bonnie Mandoe. LC 93-49055. (Illus.). 224p. 1995. pap. 17.95 (*0-89087-712-2*) Celestial Arts.

Vegetarian No-Cholesterol Family Style Cookbook. Kate Schumann & Virginia Messina. LC 95-24048. 1995. pap. 9.95 (*0-312-13612-9*, Griffin) St Martin.

***Vegetarian Pasta.** Rose Elliot. LC 97-6636. 1997. pap. 18.00 (*0-679-77826-8*) Random.

Vegetarian Pasta. Sarah Maxwell. 1994. 12.98 (*0-7858-0092-1*) Bk Sales Inc.

***Vegetarian Pasta Recipes.** S. Maxwell. 1996. 6.98 (*0-7858-0674-1*) Bk Sales Inc.

***Vegetarian Pizza Cookbook.** M. Keller. 1996. 12.98 (*0-7858-0552-4*) Bk Sales Inc.

***Vegetarian Planet.** Didi Emmons. LC 97-3654. (Illus.). 576p. 1997. 29.95 (*1-55832-114-4*); pap. 14.95 (*1-55832-115-2*) Harvard Common Pr.

Vegetarian Pleasures: A Menu Cookbook. Jeanne Lemlin. (Illus.). 320p. 1986. pap. 20.00 (*0-394-74302-4*) Knopf.

Vegetarian Pleasures: One Hundred Twenty-Five Delicious Meatless Entrees. Jeanne Lemlin. LC 94-23966. 216p. 1995. pap. 15.00 (*0-06-095022-6*) HarpC.

Vegetarian Pregnancy: The Definitive Nutritional Guide to Having a Healthy Baby. Sharon K. Yntema. LC 94-8073. (Illus.). 336p. (Orig.). 1994. pap. 12.95 (*0-935526-21-8*) McBooks Pr.

Vegetarian Quantity Recipes: From the Vegetarian Resource Group. Debra Wasserman & Reed Mangels. 1991. 15.00 (*0-931411-08-4*) Vegetarian Resc.

***Vegetarian Reasoning.** John McCabe. 300p. (Orig.). 1998. pap. 14.95 (*1-884702-34-1*) Carmania Bks.

***Vegetarian Resource Directory: Guide to Information for a Vegetarian Lifestyle.** 2nd ed. Georgia Wheatley. LC 96-2752. 1996. pap. 9.95 (*1-57067-033-1*) Book Pub Co.

***Vegetarian Revolution.** Giorgio Cerquett. LC 97-19203. 1997. write for info. (*1-887089-00-4*) Torchlght Pub.

Vegetarian Rice Cuisine: From Pancakes to Paella, 125 Delicious recipes. Jay Solomon. LC 95-21231. 1995. pap. text ed. 14.95 (*0-7615-0081-2*) Prima Pub.

Vegetarian Soup Cuisine: 125 Soups & Stews from Around the World. Jay Solomon. 1995. pap. 14.95 (*0-7615-0190-8*) Prima Pub.

Vegetarian Soups for All Seasons. Nava Atlas. LC 95-49915. 176p. 1996. pap. 13.95 (*0-316-05733-9*) Little.

Vegetarian Sourcebook. rev. ed. Keith Akers. (Illus.). 240p. (Orig.). 1986. reprint ed. pap. 10.95 (*0-931411-04-1*) Vegetarian Resc.

Vegetarian Sourcebook: The Nutrition, Ecology, & Ethics of a Natural Foods Diet. 4th rev. ed. Keith Akers. (Illus.). 256p. 1993. pap. 10.95 (*0-945528-00-0*) Vegetarian Pr.

Vegetarian Spa Cuisine from Rancho la Puerta & Deborah Szekely. Deborah Szekely. Ed. by Roberta Ridgely. 144p. 1990. pap. write for info. (*0-9625089-0-X*) Rancho La Puerta.

Vegetarian Student. Jenny Baker. 160p. (Orig.). 1986. pap. 9.95 (*0-571-14525-6*) Faber & Faber.

Vegetarian Table: America. Deborah Madison. LC 95-50303. (Illus.). 144p. 1996. 22.95 (*0-8118-0888-2*) Chronicle Bks.

Vegetarian Table: France. Georgeanne Brennan. LC 95-12941. (Illus.). 144p. 1995. 22.95 (*0-8118-0474-7*) Chronicle Bks.

Vegetarian Table: India. Yamuna Devi. LC 96-18697. 1997. 22.95 (*0-8118-1144-1*) Chronicle Bks.

Vegetarian Table: Italy. Julia Della Croce. Ed. by Bill LeBlond. (Illus.). 168p. 1994. 22.95 (*0-8118-0458-5*) Chronicle Bks.

Vegetarian Table: Mexico. Victoria Wise. LC 94-870. (Vegetarian Table Ser.: Vol. 2). (Illus.). 156p. 1995. 22.95 (*0-8118-0475-5*) Chronicle Bks.

Vegetarian Table: North Africa. Kitty Morse. LC 95-31834. (Illus.). 168p. 1996. 22.95 (*0-8118-0694-4*) Chronicle Bks.

***Vegetarian Table: Thailand.** Jacki Passmore. LC 96-51123. 1997. 24.95 (*0-8118-1214-6*) Chronicle Bks.

Vegetarian Taste of Thailand. Pinyo Srisawat & Yingsak Jonglertjesdawong. Ed. by Roger Williams. LC 96-42142. (Illus.). 224p. (Orig.). 1996. 35.00 (*0-943389-14-3*); pap. 22.00 (*0-943389-13-5*) Snow Lion-SLG Bks.

Vegetarian Teen. Charles A. Salter. (Illus.). 112p. (YA). (gr. 7 up). 1991. lib. bdg. 16.90 (*1-56294-048-1*) Millbrook Pr.

Vegetarian Times Complete Cookbook. Vegetarian Times Editors & Lucy Moll. LC 95-30186. (Illus.). 506p. 1995. pap. 29.95 (*0-02-621745-7*) Macmillan.

Vegetarian Times Cookbook. Vegetarian Times Editors. 352p. 1984. pap. 14.00 (*0-02-010370-0*) Macmillan.

***Vegetarian Times Low-Fat & Fast: 150 Meatless Recipe.** Vegetarian Times Editors. LC 96-43586. 1996. 15.00 (*0-02-861588-3*) Macmillan.

***Vegetarian Times Low-Fat & Fast Asian: 150 Easy Meatless Recipes.** Vegeterian Times Magazine Staff. 1997. 16.00 (*0-02-861983-8*) Macmillan.

***Vegetarian Times Low-Fat & Fast Pasta.** LC 97-391. 1997. 16.00 (*0-02-861728-2*) Macmillan.

Vegetarian Times Vegetarian Beginners Guide. Vegetarian Times Editors. 192p. 1996. 12.95 (*0-02-860386-9*) Macmillan.

***Vegetarian Times Vegetarian Entertaining.** Vegetarian Times Editors. 1996. 27.50 (*0-614-19372-9*) Macmillan.

Vegetarian Traveler: Where to Stay If You're Vegetarian, Vegan, Environmentally Sensitive. Jed Civic & Susan Civic. (Illus.). 300p. (Orig.). 1997. pap. 15.95 (*0-943914-79-5*) Larson Pubns.

Vegetarian Traveler's Guide to North America. C. M. Ohanian. 80p. 1993. pap. 8.95 (1-883138-00-0) Cold Sprng.

Vegetarian Treasure Chest. Winifred Graham. Ed. by Lisa Fraser. LC 82-62710. (Illus.). 224p. 1983. pap. 9.95 (0-930356-33-0) Quicksilver Prod.

Vegetarian Visitor: Where to Stay in Britain if You Don't Eat Meat. Ed. by Weitzel. Date not set. pap. 3.50 (1-897766-13-0, Pub. by Jon Pubng UK) LPC InBook.

Vegetarian Way: Healthy Eating for You & Your Family. Virginia Messina & Mark Messina. LC 95-34599. 448p. 1996. 35.00 (0-517-70427-7) Crown Pub Group.

Vegetarian Way: Total Health for You & Your Family. Virginia Messina & Mark Messina. LC 95-34599. 400p. 1996. pap. 24.00 (0-517-88275-2) Crown Pub Group.

Vegetarian Wonders from Gujarat. Aroona Reejhsinghani. 140p. 1989. 5.95 (0-318-36306-2) Asia Bk Corp.

Vegetariana: A Rich Harvest of Wit, Lore, & Recipes. Nava Atlas. LC 92-13452. (Illus.). 1993. pap. 15.95 (0-316-05743-6) Little.

Vegetarianism. Tej Sheth & Tarang Sheth. 96p. 1995. lib. bdg. 29.00 (0-8095-4838-0) Borgo Pr.

Vegetarianism. Tej Sheth & Tarang Sheth. 160p. pap. 10.95 (0-88962-552-2) Mosaic.

Vegetarianism: A History. Jon Gregerson. LC 94-10691. 160p. (Orig.). 1995. pap. 14.95 (0-87573-030-2) Jain Pub Co.

Vegetarianism: An Annotated Bibliography. Judith C. Dyer. LC 82-3159. 292p. 1982. 22.50 (0-8108-1532-X) Scarecrow.

Vegetarianism: Index of Modern Information. Glenn J. Kuffner. LC 88-47634. 150p. 1988. 44.50 (0-88164-627-X); pap. 39.50 (0-88164-628-8) ABBE Pubs Assn.

Vegetarianism & Occultism. C. W. Leadbeater. 1995. pap. 7.95 (1-56459-490-4) Kessinger Pub.

Vegetarianism & the Jewish Tradition. Louis A. Berman. LC 81-11729. 120p. 1982. 19.95 (0-87068-756-5); pap. 11.95 (0-685-05854-9) Ktav.

Vegetarianism of Jesus Christ: The Pacifism, Communalism & Vegetarianism of Primitive Christianity. Charles Vaclavik. 351p. 1988. 14.95 (0-945146-00-0); pap. 11.95 (0-945146-01-9) Kaweah Pub Co.

Vegetarian's A to Z Guide to Fruits & Vegetables. Kathleen Robinson & Pete Luckett. LC 96-5413. (Illus.). 224p. 1996. pap. text ed. 12.95 (1-55561-091-9) Fisher Bks.

Vegetarian's Ecstasy. James Levin & Natalie Cederquist. (Illus.). 321p. 1992. pap. 16.95 (0-9628698-7-2) GLO Inc.

Vegetarian's Ecstasy: A Healthy Gourmet Celebration of Over 250 No-Cholesterol, No-Dairy, Low-Fat Recipes Devoted to Long Life & Good Taste. James Levin & Natalie Cederquist. (Illus.). 328p. Date not set. pap. 16.95 (0-89529-682-9) Avery Pub.

Vegetarians in the Fast Lane. Carla J. Henry & Travis Henry. LC 96-18882. (Illus.). 240p. (Orig.). 1996. pap. 14.95 (1-56554-135-9) Pelican.

Vegetation. Francis Ponge. Tr. by Lee Fahnestock. 48p. 1987. pap. 4.00 (0-87376-058-1) Red Dust.

Vegetation & Climate Interactions in Semi-Arid Areas: Reprinted from Vegetation, Vol. 91. Ed. by A. Henderson-Sellers & A. J. Pitman. (Advances in Vegetation Science Ser.). (C). 1991. lib. bdg. 222.00 (0-7923-1061-6) Kluwer Ac.

Vegetation & Erosion: Processes & Environments. Ed. by John B. Thornes. LC 89-25010. (British Geomorphological Research Group Symposia Ser.). 518p. 1990. text ed. 285.00 (0-471-92630-2) Wiley.

Vegetation & Flora of Temperate Zones. Ed. by U. Bohn & R. Neuhausl. (Illus.). viii, 83p. 1990. pap. 35.00 (90-5103-034-7, Pub. by SPB Acad Pub NE) Balogh.

Vegetation & Flora of the Sonoran Desert, 2 Vols. Forrest Shreve & Ira L. Wiggins. (Illus.). xv, 1740p. 1964. Set. 169.50 (0-8047-0163-6) Stanford U Pr.

Vegetation & Floristics of Pingos, Central Arctic Coastal Plain, Alaska. Marilyn D. Walker. (Dissertationes Botanicae Ser.: Vol. 149). (Illus.). 284p. 1990. pap. text ed. 112.00 (3-443-64061-3, Pub. by Cramer-Borntraeger GW) Lubrecht & Cramer.

Vegetation & Land Use in the Mathews Range Area, Samburu District, Kenya. G. Bronner. (Dissertationes Botanicae Ser.: Vol. 160). (Illus.). 182p. 1990. pap. text ed. 100.00 (3-443-64072-9, Pub. by Cramer-Borntraeger GW) Lubrecht & Cramer.

Vegetation & Physiography of Sumatra. Yves Laumonier. LC 95-40385. (Geobotany Ser.: Vol. 22). 1997. lib. bdg. 256.00 (0-7923-3761-1) Kluwer Ac.

Vegetation & Production Ecology of an Alaskan Arctic Tundra. Ed. by L. L. Tieszen. LC 78-14039. (Ecological Studies: Vol. 29). (Illus.). 1979. 144.95 (0-387-90325-9) Spr-Verlag.

Vegetation & Soils of Africa. Homer L. Shantz & Curtis F. Marbut. LC 70-170848. reprint ed. 49.50 (0-404-05953-8) AMS Pr.

Vegetation auf Strassenbegleitstreifen in verschiedenen Naturraeumen Suedbadens. Ihre Bewertung fuer den Naruschutz und ihre Bedeutung fuer ein Biotopverbundsystem. Regina Rattay-Prade. (Dissertationes Botanicae Ser.: Vol. 114). (Illus.). 230p. (GER.). 1988. pap. text ed. 105.00 (3-443-64026-5) Lubrecht & Cramer.

Vegetation Between Land & Sea: Structure & Processes. Ed. by A. H. Huiskes. (Geobotany Ser.). (C). 1987. lib. bdg. 253.50 (90-6193-649-7) Kluwer Ac.

Vegetation Cover & Environment in the Mammoth Epoch in Siberia. Valentaina V. Ukraintseva. 309p. 1993. pap. 24.95 (0-9624750-3-3) L Agenbroad.

Vegetation der Erde, 15 vols. Ed. by A. Engler & O. Drude. 1977. reprint ed. Set. 1,300.00 (3-7682-0984-9) Lubrecht & Cramer.

Vegetation des Pelouses Seches a Therophytes. Ed. by J. M. Gehu. (Colloques Phytosociologiques Ser.: No. 6). 1979. lib. bdg. 115.00 (3-7682-1207-6) Lubrecht & Cramer.

Vegetation Description & Analysis. Martin Kent. 370p. 1994. pap. 375.00 (81-7089-149-3, Pub. by Intl Bk Distr II) St Mut.

Vegetation Description & Analysis: A Practical Approach. Martin Kent & Paddy Coker. 1992. 78.95 (0-8493-7756-0, QK901) CRC Pr.

Vegetation Description & Analysis: A Practical Approach. Martin Kent & Paddy Coker. 384p. 1995. pap. text ed. 45.00 incl. disk (0-471-94810-1) Wiley.

Vegetation du Paraguay: Resultats Scientifiques d'une Mission Botanique au Paraguay. R. Chodat & W. Fischer. 1977. reprint ed. 96.00 (3-7682-1106-1) Lubrecht & Cramer.

Vegetation Dynamics. Ed. by Wim G. Beeftink. 135p. 1980. pap. text ed. 82.50 (90-6193-606-3) Kluwer Ac.

Vegetation Dynamics & Global Change. Ed. by Herman H. Shugart & Allen M. Solomon. (Illus.). 364p. (gr. 13). 1992. text ed. 78.95 (0-412-03671-1, A7816, Chapman & Hall); pap. text ed. 36.95 (0-412-03681-9, A9557, Chapman & Hall) Chapman & Hall.

Vegetation Dynamics in Grasslands, Heathlands & Mediterranean Ligneous Formations. Ed. by P. Poissonet. 1982. lib. bdg. 230.00 (90-6193-636-5) Kluwer Ac.

Vegetation Dynamics in Temperate Lowland Primeval Forests. J. B. Falinski. (Geobotany Ser.). 1986. lib. bdg. 387.50 (90-6193-534-2) Kluwer Ac.

Vegetation Ecology of Central Europe. 4th ed. H. H. Ellenberg. Tr. by Gordon K. Strutt. (Illus.). 500p. 1988. 155.00 (0-521-23642-8) Cambridge U Pr.

Vegetation Ecology of the Jebel Marra Massif in the Semiarid Sudan. Sabine Miehe. (Dissertationes Botanicae Ser.: Vol. 113). (Illus.). 208p. 1988. pap. text ed. 105.00 (3-443-64025-7) Lubrecht & Cramer.

Vegetation Flora of Ujjain Distt. V. P. Singh. (C). 1992. 237.50 (81-7136-017-3, Pub. by Periodical Expert II) St Mut.

Vegetation History. Ed. by Brian Huntley & Thompson Webb, III. (Handbook of Vegetation Science Ser.). (C). 1988. lib. bdg. 358.00 (90-6193-188-6) Kluwer Ac.

Vegetation Horizons & Related Phenomena: A Paoecological-Micromorphological Study. J. F. Schoute. (Dissertationes Botanicae Ser.: vol. 81). (Illus.). 243p. 1984. lib. bdg. 96.00 (3-7682-1429-X) Lubrecht & Cramer.

Vegetation in Eastern North America: Vegetation System & Dynamics under Human Activity in the Eastern North American Cultural Region in Comparison with Japan. Akira Miyawaki et al. 515p. 1994. 250.00 (0-86008-494-9, Pub. by U of Tokyo JA) Col U Pr.

Vegetation in Gebiet des Messtischblattes 6434 Hersbruck. J Merkel. (Dissertationes Botanicae Ser.: No. 51). (Illus.). 176p. (GER.). 1980. pap. text ed. 40.00 (3-7682-1235-1) Lubrecht & Cramer.

Vegetation Linienfoermiger Kleinstrukturen in Beziehung zur Landwirtschaftlichen Produktionsintensitaet. Michael Kleyer. (Dissertationes Botanicae Ser.: Vol. 169). (Illus.). 242p. (GER.). 1991. pap. 63.00 (3-443-64081-8, Pub. by Cramer-Borntraeger GW) Lubrecht & Cramer.

***Vegetation Mapping: From Patch to Planet.** Roy Alexander. 1997. text ed. 90.00 (0-471-96592-8) Wiley.

***Vegetation, Modelling & Climatic Change Effects.** F. Veroustraete et al. 250p. 1994. 45.00 (90-5103-090-8, Pub. by SPB Acad Pub NE) Balogh.

Vegetation of Australia. N. C. Beadle. LC 81-2662. (Illus.). 656p. 1981. text ed. 175.00 (0-521-24195-2) Cambridge U Pr.

***Vegetation of China.** Ed. by Vegetation of China Editorial Board Staff. (CHI & LAT.). 1995. 168.00 (0-7855-0519-9, Pub. by Wanhai Books CH) St Mut.

Vegetation of Delta du Saloum National Park, Senegal. Anne M. Lykke. (AAU Reports: No. 33). (Illus.). 90p. (C). 1994. pap. 12.95 (87-87600-42-0, Pub. by Aarhus Univ Pr DK) David Brown.

Vegetation of Egmont National Park, New Zealand. B. D. Clarkson. 1986. 27.50 (0-477-06787-5, Pub. by Manaaki Whenua NZ) Balogh.

Vegetation of Egypt. M. A. Zahran & A. J. Willis. (Illus.). 432p. (gr. 13). 1992. pap. text ed. 58.95 (0-412-31510-6, A9465) Chapman & Hall.

Vegetation of Europe, Its Conditions & Causes. Arthur Henfrey. Ed. by Frank N. Egerton, 3rd. LC 77-74227. (History of Ecology Ser.). 1978. reprint ed. lib. bdg. 33.95 (0-405-10397-2) Ayer.

Vegetation of Hormoz, Queshm & Neighbouring Islands (Southern Persian Gulf Area, No. 6) Gunther Kunkel. (Flora et Vegetatio Mundi Ser.). (Illus.). 186p. 1977. text ed. 48.00 (3-7682-1120-7) Lubrecht & Cramer.

Vegetation of Mongolia. W. Hilbig. (Illus.). iv, 256p. 1995. 85.00 (90-5103-106-8, Pub. by SPB Acad Pub NE) Balogh.

Vegetation of New Jersey. Beryl Robichaud. 1985. pap. 15.00 (0-8135-1020-1) Rutgers U Pr.

Vegetation of New Jersey: A Study of Landscape Diversity. Beryl Robichaud & Murray F. Buell. LC 72-4205. (Illus.). 352p. 1983. reprint ed. pap. 100.40 (0-7837-9210-7, 2049960) Bks Demand.

Vegetation of New Jersey see Plant Communities of New Jersey: A Study in Landscape Diversity

***Vegetation of New Jersey Pine Barrens.** John W. Harshberger. pap. 7.95 (0-486-26199-9) Dover.

Vegetation of New Zealand. Peter Wardle. (Illus.). 608p. (C). 1991. text ed. 245.00 (0-521-25873-1) Cambridge U Pr.

***Vegetation of Ningxia.** Gao Zhen Zhong. (CHI & LAT.). 1988. pap. 118.00 (0-7855-0537-7, Pub. by Wanhai Books CH) St Mut.

Vegetation of Northern Cape Breton Island, Nova Scotia. George E. Nichols. (Connecticut Academy of Arts & Sciences Ser., Trans.: Vol. 22). 1918. pap. 100.00 (0-685-22837-1) Elliots Bks.

Vegetation of Pacific Equatorial Islands. E. Christophersen. (BMB Ser.). 1974. reprint ed. 25.00 (0-527-02147-4) Periodicals Srv.

Vegetation of Peten. Cyrus L. Lundell. LC 77-11507. (Carnegie Institution of Washington. Publications: No. 478). reprint ed. 35.00 (0-404-16270-3) AMS Pr.

Vegetation of Rivers, Lakes, & Swamps. Illus. by Luis Rizo. LC 95-22431. (Incredible World of Plants Ser.). 32p. (J). (gr. 4-6). 1996. lib. bdg. 15.95 (0-7910-3469-0) Chelsea Hse.

Vegetation of Southeastern Spain. M. Peindao et al. (Flora et Vegetatio Mundi Ser.: Vol. 10). (Illus.). 487p. 1992. pap. text ed. 105.00 (3-443-66002-9, Pub. by Cramer-Borntraeger GW) Lubrecht & Cramer.

***Vegetation of Southern Africa.** Ed. by R. M. Cowling et al. (Illus.). 680p. (C). 1997. text ed. 225.00 (0-521-57142-1) Cambridge U Pr.

Vegetation of Stewart Island. H. D. Wilson. 1987. 35.75 (0-477-02516-1, Pub. by Manaaki Whenua NZ) Balogh.

Vegetation of the District Minbu in Upper Burma. A. T. Gage. 141p. (C). 1978. text ed. 150.00 (0-89771-622-1, Pub. by Intl Bk Distr II) St Mut.

Vegetation of the District of Mindu in Upper Burma. A. T. Gate. 141p. 1978. 125.00 (0-685-21755-8, Pub. by Intl Bk Distr II) St Mut.

Vegetation of the Earth & Ecological Systems of the Geobiosphere. 3rd rev. ed. H. Walter. Tr. by O. Muise from GER. (Heidelberg Science Library). (Illus.). 340p. 1994. 57.95 (0-387-13748-3) Spr-Verlag.

Vegetation of the Life Zones in Costa Rica. J. O. Sawyer & A. A. Lindsay. 1971. pap. 8.00 (1-883362-03-2) IN Acad Sci.

Vegetation of the Mineral Springs Region of Adams County, Ohio. E. Lucy Braun. (Bulletin Ser.: No. 15). 1928. 3.00 (0-86727-014-4) Ohio Bio Survey.

***Vegetation of the South Orkney Islands with a Particular Reference to Signy Island.** R. L. Smith. (British Antarctic Survey Report Ser.: No. 68). 136p. 1972. 26.00 (0-85665-012-9, Pub. by Brit Antarctic Surv UK) Balogh.

Vegetation of the Soviet Polar Deserts. Vera Aleksandrova & Doris Love. (Studies in Polar Research). (Illus.). 240p. 1988. text ed. 80.00 (0-521-32998-1) Cambridge U Pr.

Vegetation of the Subantartic Islands & Prince Edward. N. J. Gremmen. 1982. lib. bdg. 129.50 (90-6193-683-7) Kluwer Ac.

Vegetation of the Zemu & Lionakh Valleys of Sikkim. W. W. Smith. (C). 1977. text ed. 100.00 (0-89771-656-6, Pub. by Intl Bk Distr II) St Mut.

Vegetation of the Zemu & Llonakh Valleys of Sikkim. W. W. Smith. (C). 1977. reprint ed. 100.00 (0-685-21812-0, Pub. by Intl Bk Distr II) St Mut.

Vegetation of Wisconsin: An Ordination of Plant Communities. John T. Curtis. (Illus.). 672p. 1959. 35.00 (0-299-01940-3) U of Wis Pr.

Vegetation Productivity. Gareth E. Jones. LC 78-40985. (Topics in Applied Geography Ser.). 112p. reprint ed. pap. 32.00 (0-317-20789-X, 2025270) Bks Demand.

Vegetation Science Applications for Rangeland Analysis Management. Ed. by P. Tueller. (Handbook of Vegetation Science Ser.). (C). 1988. lib. bdg. 293.00 (90-6193-195-9) Kluwer Ac.

Vegetation Science in Forestry: Global Perspective Based on Forest Ecosystems of East & Southeast Asia. Ed. by E. O. Box et al. LC 94-683. (Handbook of Vegetation Science Ser.: Pt. 12). 640p. (C). 1995. lib. bdg. 262.00 (0-7923-2679-2) Kluwer Ac.

Vegetation Structure in Relation to Carbon & Nutrient Economy: Production, Decomposition & Atmospheric Interception. Ed. by G. W. Heil et al. (Illus.). viii, 198p. 1988. pap. 50.00 (90-5103-020-7, Pub. by SPB Acad Pub NE) Balogh.

***Vegetation Surveys of Western Australia Sheet 1: Kimberley.** J. S. Beard. pap. 14.95 (0-85564-091-X, Pub. by Univ of West Aust Pr AT) Intl Spec Bk.

***Vegetation Surveys of Western Australia Sheet 5: Pilbara.** J. S. Beard. pap. 14.95 (0-85564-092-8, Pub. by Univ of West Aust Pr AT) Intl Spec Bk.

Vegetation Surveys of Western Australia Sheet 6: Murchison. J. S. Beard. (Vegetation Surveys of W. Australia Ser.). (Illus.). 1977. pap. 14.95 (0-85564-093-6, Pub. by Univ of West Aust Pr AT) Intl Spec Bk.

Vegetation Surveys of Western Australia Sheet 7: Swan Memoir. J. S. Beard. (Illus.). 1977. pap. 22.50 (0-85564-094-4, Pub. by Univ of West Aust Pr AT) Intl Spec Bk.

Vegetation und Flora im suedwestlichen Saudi-Arabien (Asir, Tihama) Peter Koenig. (Dissertationes Botanicae Ser.: Vol. 101). (Illus.). 258p. (GER.). 1987. pap. text ed. 78.00 (3-443-64013-3) Lubrecht & Cramer.

Vegetation von Afrika. R. Knapp. (Vegetationsmonographien: Vol. 3). (Illus.). 626p. 1973. text ed. 165.00 (3-437-30131-4) Lubrecht & Cramer.

Vegetation von Nord: Und Mittelamarika und der Hawaii Inseln. R. Knapp. (Vegetationsmonographien: vol. 1). (Illus.). 373p. (GER.). 1965. lib. bdg. 83.50 (3-437-30084-9) Lubrecht & Cramer.

Vegetation von Quellgebieten im Raum Trier und Ihre Beeinflussung durch Land-und Fortstwirtschaftliche Bodennutzung der Einzugsgebiete. Hildegard Wey. (Dissertationes Botanicae Band Ser.: No. 125). (Illus.). 170p. (GER.). 1988. spiral bd. 75.00 (3-443-64037-0) Lubrecht & Cramer.

Vegetational & Climatic History of the High Plain of Bogota, Colombia: A Continuous Record of 3,5 Million Years. Henry Hooghiemstra. (Dissertationes Botanicae Ser.: Vol. 79). (Illus.). 368p. 1984. lib. bdg. 136.00 (3-7682-1404-4) Lubrecht & Cramer.

Vegetational Wealth of Himalaya. G. S. Paliwal. (C). 1988. 40.00 (0-317-92315-3, Pub. by Scientific UK) St Mut.

Vegetations Herbacees Basses Amphibies: Sytematique, Structuralisme, Synsytematique. Bruno De Foucault. (Dissertations Botanicae Ser.: Vol. 121). 150p. (FRE.). 1988. pap. text ed. 56.00 (3-443-64033-8) Lubrecht & Cramer.

Vegetationsentwickelung in Abgetorften Hochmooren des Bayerischen Alpenvorlandes unter Besonderer Beruecksichtigung Standorts-Kundlicher und Populationsbiologischer Factoren. P. Poschlod. (Dissertationes Botanicae Ser.: Vol. 152). (Illus.). 332p. 1990. pap. 110.00 (3-443-64064-8, Pub. by Cramer-Borntraeger GW) Lubrecht & Cramer.

Vegetationsgeographische Untersuchungen im Dhaulagiri- und Annapurna-Himalaya, 2 vols. George Miehe. (Dissertationes Botanicae Ser.: No. 66). (Illus.). 500p. 1982. lib. bdg. 128.00 (3-7682-1356-0) Lubrecht & Cramer.

Vegetationsgeschichtliche und Pflanzensoziologische Untersuchungen im Vicente Perez Nationalpark: Chile. M. C. Villagran. (Dissertationes Botanicae Ser.: No. 54). (Illus.). 166p. (GER.). 1981. pap. text ed. 40.00 (3-7682-1265-3) Lubrecht & Cramer.

Vegetationskundlich-Oekologische Untersuchungen in der Alpinen Stufe am SW-Rand der Dolomiten (Prov. Bozen und Trient) C. Wallossek. (Dissertationes Botanicae Ser.: Vol. 154). (Illus.). 140p. 1990. pap. text ed. 62.00 (3-443-64066-4, Pub. by Cramer-Borntraeger GW) Lubrecht & Cramer.

Vegetationskundliche und Oekologische Untersuchungen Zum Vorkommen Gefaehrdeter Pflanzenarten in Feuchtwaeldern Nordwestdeutschlands, 1992. Monika Wulf. (Dissertationes Botanicae Ser.: Vol. 185). (Illus.). 250p. (GER.). 1992. pap. text ed. 65.00 (3-443-64097-4, Pub. by Cramer-Borntraeger GW) Lubrecht & Cramer.

Vegetationskundliche Untersuchungen in Hoehenlohe. Martin Nebel. (Dissertationes Botanicae Ser.: Vol. 97). (Illus.). 262p. (GER.). 1986. pap. text ed. 105.00 (3-443-64009-5) Lubrecht & Cramer.

Vegetationsmosaik im Nordschwarzwaelder Waldgebiet. Luise Murmann-Kristen. (Dissertationes Botanicae Ser.: Vol. 104). (Illus.). 290p. (GER.). 1987. pap. 130.00 (3-443-64016-8) Lubrecht & Cramer.

Vegetative Compatibility Responses in Plants. Ed. by Randy Moore. LC 83-72004. (Illus.). 163p. 1983. pap. 19.50 (0-918954-40-1) Baylor Univ Pr.

***Vegetative Physiologie.** 2nd ed. 1990. text ed. 26.95 (3-540-51955-6) Spr-Verlag.

Vegetative Propagation of Conifers. Carl G. Deuber. (CT Academy of Arts & Science Transactions Ser.: Vol. 34). 1940. pap. 49.50 (0-686-51323-1) Elliots Bks.

Vegetative Propagation of Trees in the 1980s. K. A. Longman. 1980. 75.00 (0-85074-055-X) St Mut.

Vegetative Strukturen der Parmeliaceae und Ihre Entwicklung. H. A. Beltman. (Bibliotheca Lichenologica Ser.: No. 11). (Illus.). 1978. lib. bdg. 48.00 (3-7682-1199-1) Lubrecht & Cramer.

Vegetius: Epitome of Military Science. rev. ed. Tr. by N. P. Milner. 192p. (Orig.). 1996. pap. text ed. 17.95 (0-85323-910-X) U of Pa Pr.

Vegetius - Concordantia in Vegetii Opera. Ed. by D. R. Blackman & G. G. Betts. (Alpha-Omega, Reihe A Ser.: Bd. LXXXV). vi, 830p. (GER.). 1988. 280.00 (3-487-09059-7) G Olms Pubs.

***Veggie Colors.** Phil Vischer. (Illus.). 32p. (J). (ps-2). 1997. 8.99 (0-8499-1487-6) Tommy Nelson.

***Veggie Letters.** Phil Vischer. (Illus.). 32p. (J). (ps-2). 1997. 8.99 (0-8499-1508-2) Tommy Nelson.

Veggie Lovers' Cookbook. Morty Star. 1994. pap. 6.95 (0-914846-77-9) Golden West Pub.

***Veggie Numbers.** Phil Vischer. (Illus.). 32p. (J). (ps-2). 1997. 8.99 (0-8499-1488-4) Tommy Nelson.

***Veggie Shapes.** Phil Vischer. (Illus.). 32p. (J). (ps-2). 1997. 8.99 (0-8499-1507-4) Tommy Nelson.

***Vegitalian: Italian Vegetarian Cooking.** Floria Parmiani. LC 96-96908. (Illus.). 152p. (Orig.). 1996. pap. 18.95 (0-9653783-0-6) Floria Publns.

Vehi Ciosane: Le Mandat. Ousmane Sembene. (FRE.). 1969. pap. 12.95 (0-7859-3458-8) Fr & Eur.

Vehicle Accident Investigation: A Guide for Risk Managers & Claims Personnel. Roland A. Ruhl & Dwayne G. Owen. 137p. 1994. pap. text ed. 29.95 (1-887257-00-4) Ruhl & Assocs.

Vehicle Accident Investigation of Heavy Trucks: A Guide for Risk Managers & Claims Personnel. Asa Ruhl. 250p. 1995. pap. text ed. write for info. (1-887257-02-0) Ruhl & Assocs.

Vehicle Aerodynamics. Ed. by V. Sumantran. 688p. 1995. pap. 79.00 (1-56091-594-3, PT49) Soc Auto Engineers.

Vehicle Aerodynamics: Recent Progress. (Illus.). 184p. 1991. pap. 19.00 (1-56091-119-0, SP-855) Soc Auto Engineers.

Vehicle Aerodynamics: Wake Flows, Computational Fluid Dynamics, & Aerodynamic Testing. 212p. 1992. pap. 19.00 (1-56091-225-1, SP-908) Soc Auto Engineers.

Vehicle Aerodynamics: Wind Tunnels, CFD, Aeroacoustics, & Ground Transportation Systems-1996 International Congress & Exposition. (Special Publications). 291p. 1996. pap. 74.00 (1-56091-775-X, SP-1145) Soc Auto Engineers.

Vehicle & Occupant Kinematics: Simulation & Modeling Engineering, Nine Papers. 76p. 1993. 19.00 (1-56091-360-6, SP-975) Soc Auto Engineers.

An Asterisk (*) at the beginning of an entry indicates that the title is appearing in BIP for the first time.

Vehicle & Traffic Law - Condensed Guide. (New York State Ser.). 50p. 1997. ring bd. 5.95 (*0-930137-17-5*) Looseleaf Law.

Vehicle & Traffic Law, New York State. annuals 310p. 1997. Updated annually. ring bd. 9.95 (*0-930137-05-1*) Looseleaf Law.

Vehicle & Traffic Law Quizzer. 50p. 1997. 6.95 (*0-930137-06-X*) Looseleaf Law.

***Vehicle Axle Drive: Gear Design in the 70s.** W. Coleman. (Technical Papers). 1971. pap. text ed. 30.00 (*1-55589-196-9*) AGMA.

Vehicle Body Building One. 1989. 75.00 (*0-85083-023-0*) St Mut.

Vehicle Body Building Two, 2 vols. 1989. Set. 100.00 (*0-685-05791-7*) St Mut.

Vehicle Body Fitting & Repair: NVQ Levels 2 & 3. Alan Robinson. 320p. 1995. pap. 24.95 (*0-7506-2271-7*) Buttrwrth-Heinemann.

Vehicle Body Refinishing. A. Robinson. 192p. 1995. pap. 18.95 (*0-7506-2270-9*) Buttrwrth-Heinemann.

***Vehicle Builders.** 1997. 16.47 (*0-395-83424-4*) HM.

Vehicle Computer Applications: Vehicle Systems & Driving Simulation-1995 International Congress & Exposition Meeting. 186p. 1995. pap. 56.00 (*1-56091-630-3*, SP1080) Soc Auto Engineers.

Vehicle Crashworthiness Occupant Protection in Frontal Collisions. 180p. 1990. 19.00 (*1-56091-016-X*, SP807) Soc Auto Engineers.

Vehicle Dynamics & Electronic Controlled Suspensions. 168p. 1991. pap. 19.00 (*1-56091-125-5*, SP-861) Soc Auto Engineers.

Vehicle Dynamics & Rollover Propensity Research. 172p. 1992. pap. 19.00 (*1-56091-226-X*, SP-909) Soc Auto Engineers.

Vehicle Dynamics & Simulation: Sixteen Papers. 236p. 1993. 29.00 (*1-56091-335-5*, SP-950) Soc Auto Engineers.

Vehicle Dynamics Related to Braking & Steering. 112p. 1989. 19.00 (*0-89883-792-8*, SP801) Soc Auto Engineers.

Vehicle Electronics Meeting Society's Needs: Energy, Environment, Safety - Proceedings of the International Congress on Transportation Electronics, 1992, Sixty Papers. 492p. 1992. 39.00 (*1-56091-267-7*, P-260) Soc Auto Engineers.

Vehicle Extrication. Steven Kidd & John Czaikowski. LC 89-84561. 260p. 1991. 40.95 (*0-87814-915-5*); student ed. 14.95 (*0-87814-929-5*) Fire Eng.

***Vehicle Extrication & Rescue.** Ronald Moore. (gr. 13). 1997. teacher ed. 65.00 (*0-8151-2274-8*, 31739) Mosby Yr Bk.

Vehicle Fire Fighting. Andy Teeter et al. 1996. teacher ed. 120.00 (*0-87939-120-0*, 35908) IFSTA.

Vehicle Fitting One. 1989. 50.00 (*0-85083-402-3*) St Mut.

Vehicle for God: The Metaphorical Theology of Eberhard Jungel. Roland D. Zimany. LC 93-47161. 1994. 25.00 (*0-86554-444-1*, MUP-H353) Mercer Univ Pr.

Vehicle Fuel Emergency Preparedness: A Project Report. 65p. 1981. 15.00 (*0-318-17725-0*, DG 81-314) Pub Tech Inc.

***Vehicle Gearing.** Darle W. Dudley. (Technical Papers). (Illus.). (Orig.). 1972. pap. text ed. 30.00 incl. audio compact disk (*1-55589-200-0*) AGMA.

Vehicle Heat Exchanger & Transfer Design: 1996 International Congress & Exposition. (Special Publications). 158p. 1996. pap. 49.00 (*1-56091-807-1*, SP-1175) Soc Auto Engineers.

Vehicle Identification: 1938-1968. Lee S. Cole. 75p. 1980. pap. 5.00 (*0-939818-03-5*) Lee Bks.

Vehicle Identification: 1969-1982. Lee S. Cole. 136p. (Orig.). 1982. pap. 6.00 (*0-939818-05-1*) Lee Bks.

Vehicle Identification: 1984-1985. Lee S. Cole. 164p. (Orig.). 1984. pap. 15.00 (*0-939818-09-4*) Lee Bks.

Vehicle Identification Number Decoding. 299p. 1995. per. 24.00 (*1-882437-48-9*) ADP-Hollander.

Vehicle Identification, 1983. Lee S. Cole. (Illus.). 80p. (Orig.). 1983. pap. 6.50 (*0-939818-06-X*) Lee Bks.

Vehicle Identification, 1986-1987. Lee S. Cole. 184p. (Orig.). 1986. pap. 15.00 (*0-939818-12-4*) Lee Bks.

Vehicle Identification, 1988-1989. Lee S. Cole. 183p. (Orig.). 1988. pap. 18.00 (*0-939818-18-3*) Lee Bks.

Vehicle Identification 1990-1991. Lee S. Cole & Gerald D. Boyer. 160p. (Orig.). 1991. pap. 18.00 (*0-939818-22-1*) Lee Bks.

Vehicle Identification 1992-1993. Gerald D. Boyer. 144p. (Orig.). 1993. pap. 18.00 (*0-939818-23-X*) Lee Bks.

Vehicle Identification 1994-1995. Gerald D. Boyer. 1995. pap. 18.00 (*0-939818-26-4*) Lee Bks.

Vehicle Inspection Procedure Booklet & Forms. 1975. 3.50 (*0-686-31444-1*); 2.50 (*0-686-31445-X*) Private Carrier.

Vehicle Jiglets. Christopher Jolly. (Illus.). (J). (ps-1). 1994. 13.50 (*1-870946-34-0*, Pub. by Jolly Lrning UK) Am Intl Dist.

Vehicle Lighting & Driver Visibility for the 1990's. 124p. 1990. 45.00 (*1-56091-022-4*, SP813) Soc Auto Engineers.

Vehicle Lighting Design for Optimal Visibility & Performance. 100p. 1991. pap. 19.00 (*1-56091-121-2*, SP-857) Soc Auto Engineers.

***Vehicle Location & Navigation Systems.** Yilin Zhao. LC 97-4200. (Wireless - Transportation Technology Ser.). 386p. 1997. 79.00 (*0-89006-861-5*) Artech Hse.

Vehicle Log. 1995. spiral bd. 6.95 (*0-87603-148-3*) Am Camping.

Vehicle Maintenance Facilities: A Planning Guide. 195p. 1984. 45.00 (*0-917084-45-4*) Am Public Works.

Vehicle Maintenance Repair Shop Hazardous Materials Program Employee Training Manual. Mike Rager. (Illus.). (Orig.). (C). 1989. pap. write for info. (*0-318-65931-X*) Amer Hazmat.

Vehicle Management Four: Vehicles for Trade & Industry. F. Woodward. 1977. 40.00 (*0-85941-029-3*) St Mut.

Vehicle Manufacturing Technology No. R304: A Worldwide Review of Trends for the Future. 1994. 985.00 (*0-85058-672-0*) Economist Intell.

Vehicle Mileage & Maintenance Record Book. 3rd ed. 85p. (Orig.). 1995. spiral bd. 9.95 (*1-881249-46-8*) Consum Educ Adv.

Vehicle Navigation & Information Systems Conference Proceedings, 1994. IEEE Vehicular Technology Society Staff. Ed. by IEEE Staff. LC 94-78429. 780p. 1994. pap. text ed. write for info. (*0-7803-2105-7*); lib. bdg. write for info. (*0-7803-2106-5*, 94CH35703); fiche write for info. (*0-7803-2107-3*, 94CH35703) Inst Electrical.

Vehicle Navigation & Information Systems Conference, 1993. IEEE, Vehicle Technology Society Staff. Ed. by Institute of Electrical & Electronics Engineers, Inc. Staff. LC 93-77324. 600p. 1993. pap. text ed. write for info. (*0-7803-1235-X*, 93CH3285-4); lib. bdg. write for info. (*0-7803-1236-8*, 93CH3285-4); fiche write for info. (*0-7803-1237-6*, 93CH3285-4) Inst Electrical.

Vehicle Operating Costs Vol. 4: Evidence from Developing Countries. Andrew Chesher & Robert Harrison. LC 87-22178. (Highway Design & Maintenance Standards Ser.). 352p. (Orig.). 1988. pap. text ed. 27.95 (*0-8018-3588-7*, 43588) Johns Hopkins.

Vehicle Painting One. 1989. 75.00 (*0-685-05794-1*) St Mut.

Vehicle Painting Two. 1989. 75.00 (*0-685-05792-5*) St Mut.

Vehicle Refinishing. Pat North. (Illus.). 232p. 1993. 29.95 (*1-85532-238-2*, Pub. by Osprey Pubng Ltd UK) Motorbooks Intl.

Vehicle Rescue. Rescue Training Associates, Ltd. Staff et al. (Illus.). 1975. teacher ed. 7.95 (*0-87618-611-8*); pap. text ed. 35.00 (*0-87618-137-X*); pap. text ed. 24.95 (*0-89303-118-6*) P-H.

Vehicle Rescue. 2nd ed. Gargan. 512p. 1996. pap. 28.35 (*0-8359-8374-9*) P-H.

Vehicle Rescue. 2nd ed. Harvey P. Grant. 1990. pap. 43.33 (*0-89303-932-2*) P-H.

Vehicle Rescue & Extrication. Moore. 319p. (gr. 13). 1990. pap. text ed. 34.95 (*0-8016-3351-6*) Mosby Yr Bk.

Vehicle-Road Interaction. Ed. by Bohdan T. Kulakowski. LC 94-2400. (Special Technical Publications: Vol. 1225). (Illus.). 280p. 1994. pap. text ed. 75.00 (*0-8031-1893-7*, 04-012250-08) ASTM.

Vehicle Routing: Methods & Studies. Ed. by B. L. Golden & A. A. Assad. (Studies in Management Science & Systems: Vol. 16). 480p. 1988. 168.25 (*0-444-70407-8*, North Holland) Elsevier.

Vehicle Routing, Traveler ADIS, Network Modeling, & Advanced Control Systems. LC 92-21411. (Transportation Research Record Ser.: No. 1358). 102p. 1992. 22.00 (*0-309-05224-6*) Transport Res Bd.

Vehicle Routing Two Thousand: Advances in Time-Windows, Optimality, Fast Bounds, & Multi-Depot Routing. Ed. by Bruce L. Golden. LC 94-70173. (Series in Mathematical & Management Sciences: Vol. 33). (Illus.). 200p. 1994. 125.00 (*0-935950-36-2*) Am Sciences Pr.

Vehicle Routing with Time-Window Constraints-- Algorithmic Solutions. Ed. by Bruce L. Golden & Arjang A. Assad. LC 86-71927. (Mathematical & Management Sciences Ser.: Vol. 15). 1987. 125.00 (*0-935950-15-X*) Am Sciences Pr.

Vehicle Safety Technical Representative. (Career Examination Ser.: C-3651). pap. 29.95 (*0-8373-3651-1*) Nat Learn.

Vehicle Search Law Deskbook. Christian A. Fisanick. LC 96-11881. 1996. ring bd. write for info. (*0-8366-1012-1*) Clark Boardman Callaghan.

Vehicle Security Systems: Build Your Own Alarm and Protection Systems. A. L. Brown. (Illus.). 160p. 1996. pap. 28.95 (*0-7506-2630-5*) Buttrwrth-Heinemann.

Vehicle Sizes & Weights Manual: Limitations, Oversize & Overweight Mobile Homes 1M. rev. ed. Keller, J. J., & Assocs., Inc. Staff. LC 74-31863. 586p. 1991. ring bd. 159.00 (*0-934674-21-3*, 1M) J J Keller.

Vehicle Speeds & Operating Costs: Models for Road Planning & Management. Thawat Watanatada et al. LC 87-22176. (Highway Design & Maintenance Standards Ser.). 470p. (Orig.). reprint ed. pap. 134.00 (*0-7837-4246-0*, 2043936) Bks Demand.

Vehicle Stops: Tactical Procedures & Safety Strategies. Gregory Connor. 1993. pap. text ed. 10.80 (*0-87563-443-5*) Stipes.

Vehicle Suspension & Steering Systems: Nine Papers. 100p. 1993. 19.00 (*1-56091-337-1*, SP-952) Soc Auto Engineers.

Vehicle Suspension System Advencements: SAE International Congress & Exposition 1994, 15 papers. (Special Publications). 141p. 1994. pap. 44.00 (*1-56091-483-1*, SP-1031) Soc Auto Engineers.

Vehicle Thermal Management. Ed. by Alex C. Alkidas. LC 93-87769. (Progress in Technology Ser.). 442p. 1994. 29.00 (*1-56091-502-1*, PT-46) Soc Auto Engineers.

Vehicle, Tire, Pavement Interface. Ed. by John J. Henry & James C. Wambold. LC 92-16574. (STP Ser.: Vol. 1164). (Illus.). 180p. 1992. text ed. 43.00 (*0-8031-1483-4*, 04-011640-08) ASTM.

Vehicle Traction Mechanics. Ed. by R. N. Yong et al. (Developments in Agricultural Engineering Ser.: Vol. 3). 308p. 1984. 167.50 (*0-444-42378-8*) Elsevier.

Vehicle Traffic Law. Edward C. Fisher & Robert H. Reeder. LC 74-77463. 360p. 1974. 7.50 (*0-912642-00-9*) Traffic Inst.

Vehicle Tribology. Duncan Dowson et al. (Tribology Ser.: Vol. 18). 526p. 1991. 262.50 (*0-444-88796-2*, TRS 18) Elsevier.

Vehicle Washing Compliance Manual. American Trucking Association Staff & Blymyer Engineers Staff. 1995. ring bd. 69.95 (*0-88711-294-3*) Am Trucking Assns.

Vehicles. (Learners Ser.). 48p. (J). 3.50 (*0-7214-1704-3*, Ladybird) Penguin.

Vehicles: Experiments in Synthetic Psychology. Valentino Braitenberg. 168p. (C). 1986. pap. 13.50 (*0-262-52112-1*, Bradford Bks) MIT Pr.

Vehicles: Land, Sea, Air. (Ladybird Learners Ser.: No. 8911-5). (J). 1991. pap. 3.95 (*0-7214-5322-8*, Ladybrd) Penguin.

Vehicles: Superdoodles. LC 92-74099. (J). (gr. 1-6). 1993. pap. 4.95 (*0-88160-220-5*, LW304) Learning Wks.

Vehicles: The Most Extraordinary Achievements Since the Invention of the Wheel. Nigel Hawkes. (Illus.). 240p. 1991. text ed. 39.95 (*0-02-549106-7*) Macmillan.

Vehicles: Urban Survival. CWL. (Security & Survival Ser.). (Illus.). 48p. (Orig.). 1985. pap. 15.00 (*0-939856-46-8*) Tech Group.

Vehicles & Bridging. I. F. Tytler et al. (Battlefield Weapons Systems & Technology Ser.: Vol. 1). (Illus.). 256p. 1985. text ed. 31.95 (*0-08-028322-5*, Pergamon Pr); pap. text ed. 19.50 (*0-08-028323-3*, Pergamon Pr) Elsevier.

Vehicles At War. Denis Bishop & Christopher Ellis. 25.00 (*0-8453-1699-0*, Cornwall Bks) Assoc Univ Prs.

Vehicles of the Air: A Popular Exposition of Modern Aeronautics with Working Drawings. Victor Lougheed. LC 75-169427. (Literature & History of Aviation Ser.). 1972. reprint ed. 48.95 (*0-405-03770-8*) Ayer.

***Vehicles Starter Set.** (Star Wars Miniatures Ser.). boxed 35.00 (*0-87431-285-X*, 40211) West End Games.

Vehicular Fleet Operation on Natural Gas & Propane: An Overview. Dean B. Taylor et al. (Illus.). 106p. (Orig.). (C). 1995. pap. text ed. 25.00 (*0-7881-1656-8*) DIANE Pub.

Vehicular Fuels-Additives & Substitutes for the Future. Business Communications Co., Inc. Staff. 158p. 1989. 1,950.00 (*0-89336-656-0*, E-047) BCC.

Vehicular Traffic & Air Pollution in El Paso-Cd. Juarez. Robert Gray et al. (Illus.). 160p. (ENG & SPA.). 1989. pap. 12.00 (*0-87404-210-0*) Tex Western.

Veil. Helen Mittermeyer. 384p. (Orig.). 1996. mass mkt. 5.99 (*0-446-60263-9*) Warner Bks.

Veil. Scott. Date not set. pap. text ed. 18.50 (*0-314-03661-X*) West Pub.

***Veil.** Henry Slesar. Ed. by William-Alan Landes. LC 97-1564. 62p. (Orig.). 1997. pap. 6.00 (*0-88734-261-2*) Players Pr.

Veil. Robert Williams. 20p. 1976. pap. 4.25 (*0-89536-247-3*, 2200) CSS OH.

Veil. Bob Woodward. 1994. reprint ed. lib. bdg. 29.95 (*1-56849-570-6*) Buccaneer Bks.

Veil: The Secret Wars of the C. I. A., 1981-1987. Bob Woodward. (Illus.). 1988. reprint ed. mass mkt. 5.99 (*0-671-66159-0*) PB.

Veil & Cowl: Writings from the World of Monks & Nuns. Ed. by James B. Simpson. (Illus.). 272p. 1994. text ed. 22.95 (*1-56663-051-7*) I R Dee.

Veil & the Male Elite: A Feminist Interpretation of Women's Rights in Islam. Fatima Mernissi. (Illus.). 240p. 1992. pap. 14.00 (*0-201-63221-7*) Addison-Wesley.

Veil, Hard Rain. Michael O'Brien. 48p. 1986. pap. 5.00 (*1-886044-01-5*) Cairn Editions.

Veil of Fear. Judi Lind. (Intrigue Ser.). 1995. pap. 3.50 (*0-373-22310-2*, 1-22310-6) Harlequin Bks.

***Veil of Flesh.** 1992. 9.00 (*0-923763-40-6*) Mayfair Games.

Veil of Guilt. large type ed. Rebecca Bennett. (Linford Romance Library). 240p. 1992. pap. 15.99 (*0-7089-7197-0*, Linford) Ulverscroft.

Veil of Isis: A Series of Essays on Idealism. Thomas E. Webb. LC 72-8522. (Essay Index Reprint Ser.). 1977. reprint ed. 25.95 (*0-8369-7337-2*) Ayer.

Veil of Isis: Mysteries of the Druids. W. Winwood Reade. reprint ed. spiral bd. 12.50 (*0-7873-0710-6*) Hlth Research.

Veil of Isis, Mysteries of the Druids. W. Winwood Reade. 1991. lib. bdg. 79.95 (*0-8490-4960-1*) Gordon Pr.

Veil of Isis or Mysteries of the Druids. W. Winwood Reade. 256p. 1992. pap. 9.95 (*0-87877-176-X*) Newcastle Pub.

Veil of Mist. Scott Galloway. LC 87-43086. (Illus.). 136p. (Orig.). 1987. 8.95 (*0-941709-05-1*); pap. 5.95 (*0-941709-04-3*) Solo Pubns.

Veil of Passion. Maura Seger. 1996. pap. 5.99 (*0-451-40621-4*, Onyx) NAL-Dutton.

Veil of Secrets. Maura Seger. (Historical Romance Ser.). 352p. 1996. mass mkt., pap. 5.99 (*0-451-40620-6*, Topaz) NAL-Dutton.

Veil of Signs: Joyce, Lacan, & Perception. Sheldon Brivic. 224p. 1991. text ed. 29.95 (*0-252-01765-X*); pap. text ed. 10.95 (*0-252-06159-4*) U of Ill Pr.

***Veil of Snows.** Mark Helprin & Chris Van Allsburg. LC 96-40040. (Illus.). (J). 1997. pap. 24.00 (*0-670-87491-4*) Viking Child Bks.

Veil of Tears. Connie Rinehold. (American Romance Ser.: No. 380). 1991. pap. 2.95 (*0-373-16380-0*) Harlequin Bks.

Veil of Veronica. Gertrud F. Von Lefort. Tr. by Conrad M. Bonacina. LC 70-126667. 1970. reprint ed. 21.45 (*0-404-03946-4*) AMS Pr.

Veil Too Thin: Reincarnation Out of Control. Betty Riley. LC 84-50090. 96p. 1984. pap. 2.95 (*0-911842-37-3*, B920) Valley Sun.

Veiled: Women in Islam. Juliette Minces. Tr. by A. M. Berrett from FRE. LC 93-28544. 176p. 1994. 35.00 (*0-9628715-5-9*) Blue Crane Bks.

Veiled Desire: Augustine on Women. Kim Power. 240p. 1996. 27.50 (*0-8264-0934-2*) Continuum.

Veiled Dragon. Troy Denning. (Forgotten Realms Harpers Ser.: Bk. 3). 1996. pap. 5.99 (*0-7869-0482-8*) TSR Inc.

Veiled Gazelle: Seeing How to See. Idries Shah. 103p. 1977. 18.00 (*0-900860-58-8*, Pub. by Octagon Pr UK) ISHK.

Veiled Half-Truths. Judy Mabro. 1996. text ed. 19.95 (*1-86064-027-3*) St Martin.

***Veiled Histories: The Body, Place, & Public Art.** Dennis Adams et al. Ed. by Anna Nouokov. (Thinking Publically: Vol. 1). (Illus.). 200p. (Orig.). 1997. pap. 16.95 (*1-883831-07-5*) Critical Pr.

Veiled Images: Titian's Mythological Paintings for Philip II. Jane C. Nash. LC 83-45949. (Illus.). 120p. 1986. 35.00 (*0-87982-511-1*) Art Alliance.

Veiled Mirror & the Woman Poet: H. D., Louise Bogan, Elizabeth Bishop, & Louise Gluck. Elizabeth Dodd. 256p. 1992. text ed. 34.95 (*0-8262-0857-6*) U of Mo Pr.

Veiled One. Ruth Rendell. 320p. 1989. mass mkt. 5.99 (*0-345-35994-1*) Ballantine.

***Veiled Pulse of Time: An Introduction to Biographical Cycles & Destiny.** William Bryant. LC 96-27832. (Spirituality & Social Renewal Ser.). 1996. pap. 16.95 (*0-940262-80-0*) Lindisfarne Bks.

Veiled Reality: An Analysis of Present Day Quantum Mechanical Concepts. Bernard D'Espagnat. (C). 1995. 60.95 (*0-201-56988-4*) Addison-Wesley.

Veiled Sentiments: Honor & Poetry in a Bedouin Society. Lila Abu-Lughod. (Illus.). 317p. 1987. pap. 14.00 (*0-520-06327-9*) U CA Pr.

Veiled Species of Hebeloma in the Western United States. Alexander H. Smith et al. (Illus.). 224p. 1983. text ed. 47.50 (*0-472-10036-X*) U of Mich Pr.

Veiled Sun. Mohammad Al-Rashid. LC 90-44315. 1991. 22.95 (*0-87949-327-5*) Ashley Bks.

Veiled Threats. Frank Simon. LC 96-10577. 356p. 1996. pap. 12.99 (*0-89107-880-0*) Crossway Bks.

Veiled Threats: The Logic of Popular Catholicism in Italy. Michael P. Carroll. (Illus.). 320p. 1996. text ed. 39.95 (*0-8018-5290-0*) Johns Hopkins.

Veiled Vixen. Virginia Bown. 224p. 1992. 19.95 (*0-8027-1189-8*) Walker & Co.

Veiled Woman: Shifting Gender Equations in Rural Haryana, 1880-1990. Prem Chowdhry. (Illus.). 368p. 1994. 29.95 (*0-19-563134-X*) OUP.

***Veilleur de Jours.** Pierre Martory. 155p. (FRE.). 1997. 12.95 (*1-897722-83-4*) Sheep Meadow.

Veilleuses: A Collector's Guide. Harold Newman. (Illus.). 176p. 1988. 45.00 (*0-8453-4755-1*, Cornwall Bks) Assoc Univ Prs.

Veils: Short Stories. Nahid Rachlin. 180p. (Orig.). 1992. pap. 8.95 (*0-87286-267-4*) City Lights.

Veils & Words: The Emerging Voices of Iranian Women Writers. Farzaneh Milani. LC 91-28640. (Contemporary Issues in the Middle East Ser.). 320p. 1992. pap. 16.95 (*0-8156-0266-9*); text ed. 39.95 (*0-8156-2557-X*) Syracuse U Pr.

Veils of Silk. Mary J. Putney. 384p. (Orig.). 1992. mass mkt. 4.99 (*0-451-40348-7*, Onyx) NAL-Dutton.

Vein of Gold: A Journey to Your Creative Heart. Julia Cameron. LC 96-13593. (Inner Work Book Ser.). 304p. 1996. 23.95 (*0-87477-836-0*, Tarcher Putnam) Putnam Pub Group.

***Vein of Gold: A Journey to Your Creative Heart.** Julia Cameron. (Inner Work Bk.). 384p. 1997. 15.95 (*0-87477-879-4*, Tarcher Putnam) Putnam Pub Group.

Vein of Iron. Ellen Glasgow. LC 95-14153. (C). 1995. pap. 14.95 (*0-8139-1636-4*) U Pr of Va.

Vein of Iron. Ellen Glasgow. 1995. reprint ed. lib. bdg. 24.95 (*1-56849-624-9*) Buccaneer Bks.

Veins: Normal & Abnormal Function. James E. Wood. LC 65-25171. 240p. reprint ed. pap. 68.40 (*0-317-29845-3*, 2051910) Bks Demand.

Veins: Their Functional Role in the Circulation. Hirakawa et al. LC 93-36742. 1994. 118.00 (*0-387-70126-5*) Spr-Verlag.

Veins & Thumbtacks. Jonathan M. Sherman. 1992. pap. 5.25 (*0-8222-1207-2*) Dramatists Play.

Veinte Anos de Literatura Cubanoamericana. Ed. by Silvia Burunat & Ofelia Garcia. LC 87-70662. 224p. 1988. 26.00 (*0-916950-77-8*); pap. 16.00 (*0-916950-78-6*) Biling Rev-Pr.

Veinte Anos de Teatro Espanol (1960-1980) Juan E. Aragones. LC 87-60874. 301p. 1987. pap. 35.00 (*0-89295-043-9*) Society Sp & Sp-Am.

Veinte Cuentistas Cubanas. Leonardo Fernandez-Marcane. LC 77-89099. 1978. pap. 6.00 (*0-89729-164-6*) Ediciones.

Veinte Cuentos: Para la Ensenanza del Espanol en una Clase de Adultos. Ana L. Jaramillo. LC 87-82001. (Coleccion Textos). (Illus.). 221p. (Orig.). (SPA.). 1988. pap. 15.00 (*0-89729-455-6*) Ediciones.

Veinte Cuentos Breves de la Revolucion Cubana. Ricardo J. Aguiar. LC 87-80642. (Coleccion Caniqui). (Illus.). 84p. (Orig.). (SPA.). 1987. pap. 9.95 (*0-89729-440-8*) Ediciones.

Veinte Cuentos Hispanoamericanos del Siglo Veinte. Ed. by Enrique Anderson-Imbert & Lawrence B. Kiddle. (Orig.). (SPA.). 1956. pap. text ed. write for info. (*0-13-941575-0*) P-H.

Veinte Enemigos del Matrimonio. Rodolfo Loyola. (Serie Guia - Pocket Guides Ser.). 93p. (SPA.). 1989. pap. 2.49 (*1-56063-106-6*, 498070) Editorial Unilit.

Veinte Mille Leguas de Viaje Submarino see Serie Illustrada, "Now Age"

***20 Poemas De Amor y una Cancion Desesperada.** Mario Broeders. (SPA.). 1996. 40.00 (*0-9654944-0-3*) Music Pub NY.

Veinte Poemas De Amor y una Cancion Desesperada. 3rd ed. Pablo Neruda. 129p. (SPA.). 1991. pap. 10.95 (*0-7859-4995-X*) Fr & Eur.

Veinticinco Estampas de la Espana Antigua. Antonio Garcia y Bellido. (Nueva Austral Ser.: Vol. 181). (SPA.). 1991. pap. text ed. 24.95 (*84-239-1981-1*) Elliots Bks.

Veinticinco Lecciones de Ciudadania, 1994. D. L. Hennessey. 95p. 1993. pap. 4.95 (*1-879773-03-1*) D L Hennessey.

Veinticuatro Horas al Dia. 365p. 1976. pap. 10.00 (*0-89486-099-2*) Hazelden.

***Veiw from the Top: A Panoramic Guide to Finding Britain's Most Beautiful Vistas.** Richard Girling. 1997. 27.50 (*0-8212-2439-5*) Bulfinch Pr.

Vejigante & the Folk Festivals of Puerto Rico. Edwin Fontanez. (Illus.). 28p. (Orig.). (ENG & SPA.). (J). (gr. 4-6). 1994. pap. 6.99 (*0-9640868-0-8*) Exit Studio.

Vejigantes Masquerade. Lulu Delacre. LC 92-15480. (Illus.). 40p. (ENG & SPA.). (J). (gr. k-3). 1993. 15.95 (*0-590-45776-4*) Scholastic Inc.

Vek: Kniga Stikhov. Il'ia Lapirov. LC 85-63414. 208p. (Orig.). (RUS.). 1986. pap. 14.00 (*0-89830-108-4*) Russica Pubs.

Vekhi - Landmarks. Nikolai Berdiaev et al. Ed. & Tr. by Marshall S. Shatz from RUS. Tr. by Judith E. Zimmerman from RUS. LC 94-26039. 224p. (gr. 13). 1994. text ed. 63.95 (*1-56324-390-3*); pap. text ed. 24.95 (*1-56324-391-1*) M E Sharpe.

Vel. Peter Inman. LC 94-80138. 61p. 1995. 8.00 (*1-882022-24-6*) O Bks.

Velazques Dictionary Spanish. rev. ed. Velazque Staff. 1974. 16.95 (*0-695-80472-3*) Follett Pr.

Velazquez. Elizabeth Du Gue Trapier. (Illus.). 1948. 20.00 (*0-87535-062-3*) Hispanic Soc.

Velazquez. Antonio D. Ortiz et al. 1989. 45.00 (*0-87099-554-5*); pap. 19.95 (*0-87099-555-3*) Metro Mus Art.

Velazquez. Maurice Serullaz. (Illus.). 128p. 1987. 22.95 (*0-8109-1729-7*) Abrams.

Velazquez. Aureliano De Beruete y Moret. LC 77-37330. (Select Bibliographies Reprint Ser.). (Illus.). 1977. reprint ed. 41.95 (*0-8369-6677-5*) Ayer.

Velazquez: The Complete Paintings. limited ed. Jose Lopez-Rey. (Illus.). 536p. 1988. 175.00 (*1-55660-013-5*) A Wofsy Fine Arts.

Velazquez in Seville. Ed. by David Davies & Enriqueta Harria. (Illus.). 172p. 1996. 50.00 (*0-300-06949-9*) Yale U Pr.

Velazquez, "Los Borrachos," & Painting at the Court of Philip Fourth. Steven N. Orso. LC 93-493. (Illus.). 264p. (C). 1994. text ed. 75.00 (*0-521-44452-7*) Cambridge U Pr.

Velazquez Spanish & English Dictionary. rev. ed. LC 84-27199. 1488p. (SPA.). (C). 21.95 (*0-8329-0265-9*) New Win Pub.

Velazquez's Bodegones: A Study in Seventeenth-Century Spanish Genre Painting. Barry Wind. LC 85-48037. (Illus.). 236p. (Orig.). 1987. pap. text ed. 26.00 (*0-8026-0007-7*, G Mason Univ Pr); lib. bdg. 51.00 (*0-8026-0006-9*, G Mason Univ Pr) Univ Pub Assocs.

***Velcome.** Kevin O'Malley et al. LC 96-51577. 32p. (J). (ps-3). 1997. 15.95 (*0-8027-8628-6*); lib. bdg. 16.85 (*0-8027-8629-4*) Walker & Co.

Velda Newman: A Painter's Approach to Quilt Design. Velda Newman & Christine Barnes. LC 95-48413. (Illus.). 114p. (Orig.). 1996. pap. 29.95 (*1-56477-119-9*, B236) That Patchwork.

Velika Hrvatska. Ivo Omrcanin. 104p. (CRO.). 1994. pap. 10.00 (*1-878716-15-8*) Ivor Pr.

Veliki Anglesko-Slovenski Slovar. Ed. by A. Grad et al. 1400p. 1994. 70.00 (*86-341-0824-4*) OUP.

Velikovsky & Establishment Science. Lynn E. Rose. LC 77-93288. (Illus.). 1977. pap. 12.00 (*0-917994-04-3*) Kronos Pr.

Velikovsky Reconsidered. Pensee Editors. LC 74-33637. 1994. reprint ed. lib. bdg. 27.95 (*1-56849-530-7*) Buccaneer Bks.

Velimir Khlebnikov: A Critical Study. Raymond Cooke. (Cambridge Studies in Russian Literature). 256p. 1987. text ed. 69.95 (*0-521-32670-2*) Cambridge U Pr.

Velimir Xlebnikov's "Krysa" A Commentary. Ronald Vroon. Ed. by Edward J. Brown et al. LC 89-11346. (Stanford Slavic Studies: Vol. 2). 213p. 1989. pap. text ed. 30.00 (*0-926953-01-X*) Berkeley Slavic.

Velimir Xlebnikov's Shorter Poems: A Key to the Coinages. Ronald Vroon. LC 83-50012. (Michigan Slavic Materials Ser.: No. 22). 1983. pap. 15.00 (*0-930042-50-6*) Mich Slavic Pubns.

Velleii Paterculi Quae Supersunt Ex Historiae Romanae Libris Duobus. Velleius Paterculus. cxliv, 638p. (GER.). reprint ed. write for info. (*0-318-70527-3*) G Olms Pubs.

Velleius Paterculus: The Caesarian & Augustan Narrative. A. J. Woodman. LC 83-1988. (Cambridge Classical Texts & Commentaries Ser.: No. 25). 336p. 1984. text ed. 75.00 (*0-521-25639-9*) Cambridge U Pr.

***Velocidad Del Amor.** Antonio Skarmeta. (SPA.). 1997. pap. text ed. 11.95 (*0-553-06075-9*) Bantam.

***Velociraptor: The Swift Hunter.** (Microfaxc Ser.). (J). 1997. pap. text ed. 0.99 (*0-7894-2123-2*) DK Pub Inc.

***Velociraptor: The Swift Hunter.** LC 96-48743. (Dinosaur Days Ser.: Group 1). (Illus.). 32p. (J). (gr. k-3). 1997. lib. bdg. 14.95 (*0-7614-0603-4*, Benchmark NY) Marshall Cavendish.

Velocities: New & Selected Poems 1966-1992. Stephen Dobyns. 320p. (Orig.). 1994. pap. 15.95 (*0-14-058651-2*, Penguin Bks) Viking Penguin.

Velocities Boxed Set, 5 journals. Ed. by Andrew Joron. (Illus.). 290p. 1987. Set. boxed 25.00 (*0-938075-03-9*) Ocean View Bks.

Velocities of Change: Critical Essays from MLN. Ed. by Richard A. Macksey. LC 72-12343. 397p. 1974. 45.00 (*0-8018-1494-4*); pap. 15.95 (*0-8018-1495-2*) Johns Hopkins.

Velocities of Rage. Charles Fasanaro. 72p. (Orig.). 1993. pap. 8.95 (*0-932274-46-3*) Cadmus Eds.

Velocity. Kristin McCloy. 272p. 1990. pap. 7.95 (*0-671-68920-7*, WSP) PB.

Velocity Analysis on Multichannel Seismic Data. Ed. by B. S. Byun. (Geophysics Reprint Ser.: No. 12). 528p. 1990. pap. text ed. 75.00 (*1-56080-006-2*, 472) Soc Expl Geophys.

***Velocity of Money.** Keith Styrcula. LC 97-20626. 1997. write for info. (*0-688-15538-3*) Morrow.

Velocity Structures in Hydrogen Profiles: A Sky Atlas of Neutral Hydrogen Emission. Merle A. Tuve & Soren Lundsager. (Carnegie Institution of Washington Publication Ser.: No. 630). (Illus.). 188p. reprint ed. pap. 53.60 (*0-317-09033-X*, 2007901) Bks Demand.

VeloNews Training Diary: A Weekly Log For Tracking Your Cycling Fitness. 2nd rev. ed. Velo-News Editors. (Illus.). 240p. 1994. spiral bd., pap. 12.95 (*1-884737-04-8*) VeloPress.

***Veloville.** Raymond Plante. (Novels in the Premier Roman Ser.). 64p. (FRE.). (J). (gr. 2-5). 1996. pap. 7.95 (*2-89021-100-2*, Pub. by Les Editions CN) Firefly Bks Ltd.

Velveeta Creative Cooking. (Favorite All Time Recipes Ser.). (Illus.). 96p. 1993. spiral bd. 3.50 (*0-88176-771-9*, 2107400) Pubns Intl Ltd.

Velvet. Jane Feather. 448p. 1994. mass mkt. 5.99 (*0-553-56469-2*) Bantam.

***Velvet: History, Techniques, Fashions.** Fabrizio De Marinis. (Illus.). 202p. (Orig.). 1996. pap. 35.00 (*0-9627985-1-7*) Idea Bks.

***Velvet & Steel: A Practical Guide for Christian Fathers.** John Ream. (Illus.). 160p. (Orig.). 1997. pap. text ed. 13.95 (*0-89390-408-2*) Resource Pubns.

Velvet Angel. Jude Deveraux. Ed. by Linda Marrow. 1991. pap. 6.99 (*0-671-73973-5*) PB.

Velvet Antlers, Velvet Noses: The Story of a Reindeer Family. Tilly Smith. (Illus.). 184p. 1996. 29.95 (*0-340-63825-7*, Pub. by H & S UK) Trafalgar.

Velvet Bond. Catherine Archer. (Historical Ser.). 1995. mass mkt. 4.50 (*0-373-28882-4*, 1-28882-8) Harlequin Bks.

Velvet Chains. Constance O'Banyon. 1985. mass mkt. 3.95 (*0-8217-1640-9*, Zebra Kensgtn) Kensgtn Pub Corp.

Velvet Dawn. Rowena Summers. 1991. 18.00 (*0-7278-4263-3*) Severn Hse.

Velvet Dawn. large type ed. Rowena Summers. 320p. 1993. 25.99 (*0-7505-0539-7*) Ulverscroft.

Velvet Glove: Paternalism & Conflict in Gender, Class & Race Relations. Mary R. Jackman. LC 93-6064. 432p. 1994. 38.00 (*0-520-08113-7*) U CA Pr.

Velvet Glove: Paternalism & Conflict in Gender, Class, & Race Relations. Mary R. Jackman. (Illus.). 432p. 1996. pap. 17.95 (*0-520-20702-5*) U CA Pr.

Velvet Horn. Andrew Lytle. 370p. 1987. pap. 10.95 (*0-918769-03-5*) Univ South Pr.

***Velvet Increase of Curiosity.** Lise Downe. 76p. 1993. pap. 12.00 (*1-55022-199-X*, Pub. by ECW Press CN) Genl Dist Srvs.

Velvet Mites & Silken Webs: Wonderful Details of Nature in Photographs & Essays. Scott Camazine. LC 91-2395. (Science Editions Ser.). 192p. 1991. text ed. 24.95 (*0-471-61485-8*) Wiley.

Velvet on Iron: The Diplomacy of Theodore Roosevelt. Frederick W. Marks. LC 79-1216. reprint ed. pap. 75.00 (*0-608-01787-6*, AU00457) Bks Demand.

Velvet Paw. Jean Conger. (Illus.). 1963. 14.95 (*0-8392-1125-2*) Astor-Honor.

Velvet Prisoner: Artists under State Socialism. Miklos Haraszti. 165p. 1989. pap. 7.95 (*0-374-52181-6*, Noonday) FS&G.

Velvet Promise. Jude Deveraux. Ed. by Linda Marrow. (Richard Gallen Bks.). 416p. 1991. pap. 6.99 (*0-671-73974-3*); pap. 5.50 (*0-685-47135-7*) PB.

Velvet Room. Zilpha K. Snyder. 224p. (J). (gr. k-6). 1988. pap. 3.50 (*0-440-40042-2*, YB BDD) BDD Bks Young Read.

Velvet Song. Jude Deveraux. Ed. by Linda Marrow. 1991. pap. 6.99 (*0-671-73975-1*) PB.

Velvet Thunder. Teresa Howard. 416p. 1994. mass mkt. 4.50 (*0-8217-4508-5*, Zebra Kensgtn) Kensgtn Pub Corp.

Velvet Tiger. Emma Darcy. (Presents Ser.). 1992. pap. 2.89 (*0-373-11496-6*, 1-11496-6) Harlequin Bks.

Velvet Touch. Catherine Archer. (Historical Ser.). 1996. mass mkt. 4.99 (*0-373-28922-7*, 1-28922-2) Harlequin Bks.

***Velvet Underground.** John Robertson. pap. 7.95 (*0-7119-5596-4*, OP 47828) Omnibus NY.

Velvet Underground Companion. Zak. LC 97-9247. 1997. 15.00 (*0-02-864627-4*) Schirmer Bks.

***Velvet Web.** Christopher Summerisle. 224p. (Orig.). 1997. pap. 9.95 (*0-352-33208-5*, Pub. by Virgin Pub UK) London Brdge.

Velvet Web. large type ed. Rae Foley. LC 94-718. Orig. Title: An Ape in Velvet. 282p. 1994. lib. bdg. 19.95 (*0-7862-0185-1*) Thorndike Pr.

Velvet Years: Warhol's Factory 1965-67. Stephen Shore & Lynne Tillman. (Illus.). 176p. 1995. pap. 24.95 (*1-56025-098-4*) Thunders Mouth.

Velveteen Rabbit. (Little Golden Story Book 'n' Tape Ser.). (Illus.). 24p. (J). (ps-3). 1995. 5.95 incl. audio (*0-307-14455-0*, 14455) Western Pub.

Velveteen Rabbit. (Pocket Play Bks.). (Illus.). 24p. (J). (ps-2). 1996. 9.95 (*0-8362-0955-9*) Andrews & McMeel.

Velveteen Rabbit. (Cherished Fairytale Ser.). 32p. (J). (ps-3). Date not set. text ed., spiral bd. 4.95 (*1-56987-234-1*) Landoll.

***Velveteen Rabbit.** Grahame Baker-Smith. (Illus.). 32p. (J). (gr. 1-4). 1997. 19.95 (*0-370-32420-X*, Pub. by Bodley Head UK) Trafalgar.

Velveteen Rabbit. Margery W. Bianco. LC 97-2313. (Illus.). 32p. (J). (ps-3). 1995. 16.95 (*0-15-200923-X*) HarBrace.

Velveteen Rabbit. Golden Books Staff. (Little Golden Bks.). (Illus.). 24p. (J). (ps-2). 1995. 1.49 (*0-307-00135-0*, Golden Pr) Western Pub.

***Velveteen Rabbit.** Illus. by Melissa B. Mathis. (J). (ps-2). 1998. pap. 5.95 (*0-448-41644-1*) Putnam Pub Group.

***Velveteen Rabbit.** Marty Noble & Margery W. Bianco. LC 97-19551. (J). 1997. pap. write for info. (*0-486-29916-3*) Dover.

Velveteen Rabbit. Adapted by Rose Reed. (Big Golden Bks.). (Illus.). 24p. (J). (ps up). 1990. write for info. (*0-307-12105-4*) Western Pub.

Velveteen Rabbit. Adapted by James Still. 33p. (Orig.). (J). 1990. 5.00 (*0-87602-289-1*) Anchorage.

Velveteen Rabbit. Eric Suben. (Storyshapes Ser.). (Illus.). 24p. (Orig.). (J). (ps-1). 1996. pap. 2.25 (*1-56293-907-6*) McClanahan Bk.

Velveteen Rabbit. Margery Williams. (Knopf Book & Cassette Classics Ser.). (Illus.). 48p. (Orig.). (J). (ps up). 1985. 15.95 (*0-394-87712-8*); 12.00 (*0-394-87711-X*) Knopf Bks Yng Read.

Velveteen Rabbit. Margery Williams. (Children's Classics Ser.). (Illus.). 40p. (Orig.). (J). 1991. 6.95 (*0-8362-4910-0*) Andrews & McMeel.

Velveteen Rabbit. Margery Williams. (Illus.). 80p. (Orig.). (J). 1992. 4.95 (*0-8362-3022-1*) Andrews & McMeel.

Velveteen Rabbit. Margery Williams. (Classic Short Stories Ser.). (Orig.). (J). 1991. lib. bdg. 13.95 (*0-88682-474-5*) Creative Ed.

Velveteen Rabbit. Margery Williams. LC 94-5683. (Illus.). 40p. (Orig.). (J). 1994. 16.95 (*0-88682-732-9*) Creative Ed.

Velveteen Rabbit. Margery Williams. 22p. (Orig.). (J). (gr. 3-9). 1994. pap. 3.50 (*1-57514-239-2*, 1133) Encore Perform Pub.

Velveteen Rabbit. Margery Williams. 24p. (Orig.). (J). (gr. k-3). 1988. pap. 3.95 (*0-8249-8175-8*, Ideals Child) Hambleton-Hill.

Velveteen Rabbit. Margery Williams. (All Aboard Bks.). (Illus.). 32p. (Orig.). (J). (ps-2). 1987. pap. 2.95 (*0-448-19083-4*, G&D) Putnam Pub Group.

Velveteen Rabbit. Margery Williams. (Illus.). (Orig.). (J). 1991. Incl. book, cass. & toy rabbit. 14.99 incl. audio (*0-517-66810-6*) Random Hse Value.

Velveteen Rabbit. Margery Williams. LC 81-1454. (Illus.). (Orig.). (J). (ps up). 7.95 (*0-89471-153-9*) Running Pr.

Velveteen Rabbit. Margery Williams. 48p. (Orig.). (J). 1995. 3.95 (*0-8125-3627-4*) Tor Bks.

Velveteen Rabbit. Margery Williams. (Illus.). 47p. (J). (gr. 3-5). 1958. 10.95 (*0-385-07725-4*) Doubleday.

Velveteen Rabbit. Margery Williams. (J). 1988. 5.99 (*0-517-61813-3*) Random Hse Value.

Velveteen Rabbit. Margery Williams. (Illus.). 32p. (J). (ps-3). 1990. pap. 2.99 (*0-590-42805-5*) Scholastic Inc.

Velveteen Rabbit. Margery Williams. Ed. by Kate Klimo. (Illus.). 48p. (J). 1983. pap. 11.00 (*0-671-44498-0*) S&S Trade.

Velveteen Rabbit. Margery Williams. (J). (ps up). 1988. pap. 3.95 (*0-8125-7890-2*) Tor Bks.

Velveteen Rabbit. Margery Williams. (Illus.). 32p. (J). (ps up). 1994. 16.95 (*1-56846-093-7*) Creative Ed.

Velveteen Rabbit. Margery Williams. (J). 1995. 9.98 (*0-8317-9118-7*) Smithmark.

Velveteen Rabbit. abr. ed. Illus. by Nancy Carpenter. LC 92-6036. (Chunky Shape Bks.). 22p. (J). (ps). 1993. 3.99 (*0-679-83617-9*) Random Bks Yng Read.

Velveteen Rabbit. Margery Williams. LC 85-4257. (Illus.). 48p. (Orig.). (J). (ps-2). 1990. reprint ed. pap. 5.99 (*0-679-80333-5*) Knopf Bks Yng Read.

Velveteen Rabbit. Margery Williams. (Illus.). 40p. (Orig.). (J). (gr. k up). 1979. reprint ed. pap. 2.99 (*0-380-00255-8*, Camelot) Avon.

Velveteen Rabbit. Margery Williams. (Illus.). 40p. (Orig.). (J). (gr. 1-9). 1982. reprint ed. pap. 2.95 (*0-380-58156-6*, Flare) Avon.

Velveteen Rabbit: A Musical. George Gray & Chris Talbert. 50p. (J). 1995. pap. 3.50 (*1-57514-146-9*, 0042) Encore Perform Pub.

Velveteen Rabbit: A Study Guide. Marcia Tretler. (Novel-Ties Ser.). 1987. teacher ed., pap. text ed. 15.95 (*0-88122-064-7*) Lrn Links.

Velveteen Rabbit: Gift Set. Margery Williams. (Illus.). 48p. 1995. 24.98 (*1-56138-656-1*) Courage Bks.

Velveteen Rabbit: Musical. Barnes Boffey & Paul Pilcher. 1974. pap. 5.00 (*0-87129-385-4*, V01) Dramatic Pub.

Velveteen Rabbit: Or How Toys Become Real. Margery W. Bianco. (Illus.). 48p. (J). (ps). 1995. 19.95 (*1-883746-06-X*) Vermilion.

Velveteen Rabbit: Or How Toys Become Real. Margery Williams. LC 81-1454. (Literary Classics Ser.). (Illus.). 48p. (Orig.). (J). (gr. k-12). 1984. 9.98 (*0-89471-266-7*) Courage Bks.

Velveteen Rabbit: Or, How Toys Become Real. Margery Williams. LC 82-15606. (Illus.). 48p. (J). (gr. k up). 1983. 13.95 (*0-8050-0209-X*, Bks Young Read) H Holt & Co.

***Velveteen Rabbit: Or, How Toys Become Real.** Margery Williams. (Children's Illustrated Classics Ser.). (Illus.). 56p. (J). 1997. 9.98 (*0-7624-0174-5*) Courage Bks.

***Velveteen Rabbit: Or, How Toys Become Real.** Margery Wlliams & Loretta Krupinski. LC 96-31209. 32p. (J). 1997. 12.95 (*0-7868-0319-3*) Hyprn Child.

***Velveteen Rabbit: Or How Toys Become Real.** unabridged ed. Margery W. Bianco. (Illus.). 48p. (J). (ps up). 1995. 14.95 (*1-883746-07-8*) Vermilion.

Velveteen Rabbit: Pop-Up. (J). (ps-3). 1993. pap. 4.95 (*0-8167-2928-X*) Troll Communs.

Velveteen Rabbit - Straight. Margery Williams & Phil Grecian. 1995. 5.00 (*0-87129-548-2*, V24) Dramatic Pub.

Velveteen Rabbit Coloring Book. (Illus.). (J). 1984. pap. 2.95 (*0-671-49669-7*, Litl Simon S&S) S&S Childrens.

Velveteen Rabbit Coloring Book. Margery Williams. (Illus.). (J). (gr. k-3). 1989. pap. 2.95 (*0-486-25924-2*) Dover.

Velveteen Rabbit Literature Mini-Unit. Janet Lovelady. (Illus.). 32p. (J). (gr. 3-5). 1990. student ed. 4.95 (*1-56096-011-6*) Mari.

***Velveteen Rabbit Sticker Storybook.** Thea Kliros. (Illus.). 16p. (Orig.). (J). 1997. pap. text ed. 1.00 (*0-486-29543-5*) Dover.

Ven a Mi Casa: Una Busqueda de Tesora Multicultural. Aylette Jenness. LC 93-83997. (J). (gr. 4-7). 1993. 16.95 (*1-56584-118-2*) New Press NY.

Ven Conmigo! 96th ed. HRW Staff. 1996. 175.75 (*0-03-094990-4*); 180.50 (*0-03-095020-1*) HB Coll Pubs.

Ven Conmigo!, Bk. 1. 96th ed. HRW Staff. 1996. pap. text ed. 56.00 (*0-03-095029-5*) HB Coll Pubs.

Ven Conmigo!, Bk. 2. 96th ed. HRW Staff. 1996. pap. text ed. 56.00 (*0-03-095030-9*) HB Coll Pubs.

Ven Conmigo!, Bk. 3. 96th ed. HRW Staff. 1996. pap. text ed. 56.00 (*0-03-095031-7*) HB Coll Pubs.

Ven Conmigo! Holt Spanish. Holt Staff. 1996. teacher ed., text ed. 67.75 (*0-03-096523-3*) HR&W Schl Div.

Ven Conmigo! Holt Spanish. Humbach. 1996. student ed., text ed. 53.25 (*0-03-096522-5*) HR&W Schl Div.

***Ven Conmigo! Holt Spanish.** Humbach. (SPA.). 1996. text ed. 56.00 (*0-03-093990-9*); text ed. 57.25 (*0-03-093992-5*) HR&W Schl Div.

Ven Conmigo: Holt Spanish Assessment Guide 1996. 1996. suppl. ed., pap. text ed. 15.25 (*0-03-094993-9*) HR&W Schl Div.

Ven Conmigo! Holt Spanish 1996. 1996. student ed., wbk. ed., pap. text ed. 13.50 (*0-03-095021-X*) HR&W Schl Div.

***Ven Espiritu Santo, Ayudame.** Ed. by Maria C. Marty. (Fe en Accion Ser.). 100p. (Orig.). (SPA.). 1997. pap. 5.00 (*0-9656265-1-2*) Lion Judah.

Ven. Francisco Marto of Fatima. Joseph A. Cirrincione. 43p. 1995. pap. 1.50 (*0-89555-511-5*) TAN Bks Pubs.

Ven Hacia Arriba. Joy Kim. (J). pap. 3.95 (*0-8167-3259-0*) Troll Communs.

Ven. Jacinta Marto of Fatima. Joseph A. Cirrincione. LC 92-61353. 71p. (Orig.). 1992. pap. 2.00 (*0-89555-480-1*) TAN Bks Pubs.

***Ven Pronto, Senor Jesus: Lo Que Necesita Saber Acerca del Arrebatamiento de la Iglesia.** Charles C. Ryrie. (SPA.). 1997. pap. 6.99 (*0-8254-1638-8*, Edit Portavoz) Kregel.

***Venables: The England Era.** Brian Woolnough. (Illus.). 192p. 1996. 34.95 (*1-85158-756-X*, Pub. by Mnstream UK) Trafalgar.

Venables & Impey: Internal Audit. 4th ed. 502p. 1996. pap. 62.00 (*0-406-06673-6*) MICHIE.

Venables & Imprey: Internal Audit. 3rd ed. J. Venables & Ken Impey. 490p. 1991. pap. 55.00 (*0-406-00205-3*) MICHIE.

Venados (Deer) L. Stone. (Spanish Language Books, Set 2: Animales Norteamericanos (North American Animals)). (J). 1991. 8.95 (*0-86592-831-2*) Rourke Enter.

Venajaa Opiskelevan Sanakirja Venaja-Suomi. A. Mustajoki & E. Nikkila. 534p. (FIN & RUS.). 1982. 49.95 (*0-8288-1076-1*, F 85800) Fr & Eur.

Venality: The Sale of Offices in Eighteenth-Century France. William Doyle. LC 96-7432. (Illus.). 380p. 1997. 85.00 (*0-19-820536-8*, Clarendon Pr) OUP.

Venango County PA Death Book Summary & Index 1893-1905. Joan S. Hanson & Kenneth L. Hanson. 105p. 1995. pap. 9.95 (*1-55856-205-2*) Closson Pr.

Venango County, PA Soldiers. Paul W. Myers. 73p. 1988. pap. text ed. 8.50 (*0-933227-83-3*) Closson Pr.

Venango County, Pennsylvania & Her Pioneers & People, 2 vols., Set. Charles A. Babcock. (Illus.). 1087p. 1994. reprint ed. lib. bdg. 110.00 (*0-8328-4006-8*) Higginson Bk Co.

Venantius Fortunatus: Personal & Political Poems. Tr. by Judith George. 192p. (Orig.). 1996. pap. text ed. 17.95 (*0-85323-179-6*) U of Pa Pr.

Vencedores. Witness Lee. 111p. (SPA.). per. 4.25 (*0-87083-724-9*, 08037002) Living Stream Ministry.

***Venceslas, EFT LXXIX.** Rotrou. Ed. by D. A. Watts. 136p. (FRE.). (C). pap. 19.95 (*0-85989-361-8*, Pub. by Univ Exeter Pr UK) Northwestern U Pr.

Vencido el Fuego de la Especie. Lourdes Gil. Ed. by SLUSA Staff. LC 83-60004. (Poetry Ser.). (Illus.). 90p. (Orig.). (SPA.). 1983. pap. 5.00 (*0-9606758-5-X*) SLUSA.

Venciendo al Adversario. Mark I. Bubeck. Orig. Title: Overcoming the Adversary. 160p. (SPA.). 1992. pap. 6.99 (*0-8254-1094-0*, Edit Portavoz) Kregel.

Venda. Rita Stevens. (Let's Visit Places & Peoples of the World Ser.). (Illus.). 96p. (YA). (gr. 5 up). 1989. lib. bdg. 19.95 (*1-55546-788-1*) Chelsea Hse.

Venda Children's Songs: A Study in Ethnomusicological Analysis. John Blacking. 210p. 1995. pap. text ed. 15.95 (*0-226-05511-6*); lib. bdg. 35.00 (*0-226-05510-8*) U Ch Pr.

Venda Dictionary: Venda-English. Van. 1996. 39.95 (*0-7818-0393-4*) Hippocrene Bks.

Venda en los Ojos. Jose Lopez-Rubio. Ed. by Marion P. Holt. LC 66-21587. (Orig.). (SPA.). 1966. pap. text ed. 5.95 (*0-89197-464-4*) Irvington.

Vendanta & Tagore. B. C. Mukherji. 89p. (C). 1994. 30.00 (*81-85880-42-5*, Pub. by Print Hse II) St Mut.

Vendanta Sutras, 3 vols. Tr. by G. Thibaut. 1974. Set. lib. bdg. 900.00 (*0-87968-562-X*) Krishna Pr.

***Vendedor Mas Grande Del Mundo - The Greatest Salesman in the World: Transform Your Life & Find True Fulfillment with Priceless Wisdom.** Og Mandino. 108p. (SPA.). 1996. pap. 14.95 (*0-8119-0847-X*) LIFETIME.

Vendee. Anthony Trollope. Ed. by W. J. McCormack. LC 93-33210. (World's Classics Ser.). (Illus.). 480p. 1994. pap. 10.95 (*0-19-282838-X*) OUP.

U V

Vendee, 3 Vols. Anthony Trollope. Ed. by N. John Hall. LC 80-1875. (Selected Works of Anthony Trollope). 1981. reprint ed. 115.95 (0-405-14122-X) Ayer.

Vendee: A Sociological Analysis of the Counter-Revolution of 1793. Charles Tilly. LC 64-21247. (Illus.). 384p. 1976. pap. 15.95 (0-674-93302-8) HUP.

Vendetta. (Super Bolan Ser.). 1995. mass mkt. 4.99 (0-373-61441-1, 1-61441-1) Harlequin Bks.

Vendetta. Peter David. Ed. by Dave Stern. (Star Trek Giant Novel Ser.). 416p. (Orig.). 1991. mass mkt. 5.99 (0-671-73305-2) PB.

Vendetta. Michael Dibdin. LC 96-46856. 1998. pap. write for info. (0-679-76853-X, Vin) Random.

Vendetta. Jim Dunn. LC 92-62010. 256p. 1993. pap. 10.95 (1-56002-234-5, Univ Edtns) Aegina Pr.

Vendetta. Derek Lambert. 176p. 1990. 16.95 (0-8027-1120-0) Walker & Co.

***Vendetta! Fidel Castro & the Kennedy Brothers.** William B. Breuer. LC 97-5029. 1997. 29.95 (0-471-18456-X) Wiley.

***Vendetta: Lucky's Revenge.** Jackie Collins. LC 96-43458. 528p. 1997. 25.00 (0-06-039209-6, ReganBooks); pap. write for info. (0-614-18297-2, ReganBooks) HarpC.

***Vendetta: Lucky's Revenge.** Jackie Collins. 1997. mass mkt. 6.99 (0-06-101235-1) HarpC.

***Vendetta: Lucky's Revenge.** large type ed. Jackie Collins. LC 97-2922. (Large Print Book Ser.). 1997. 27.95 (1-56895-435-2) Wheeler Pub.

Vendetta! The Story of One Forgotten. Marie Corelli. 405p. 1972. reprint ed. spiral bd. 12.00 (0-7873-0209-0) Hlth Research.

***Vendetta: The True Story of the Largest Lynching in U. S. History.** Richard Gambino. 1997. pap. text ed. 13.00 (1-55071-039-7) Guernica Editions.

Vendetta see Maison du Chat-qui-pelote

Vendetta Bride. Rebecca King. (Presents Ser.). 1994. mass mkt. 2.99 (0-373-11678-0, 1-11678-9) Harlequin Bks.

Vendetta Castle. large type ed. Ellis. 1995. 23.95 (0-7089-3366-1) Ulverscroft.

Vendetta Con Brio. Beth De Bilio. LC 72-9881. (Black Bat Mystery Ser). 1973. 5.95 (0-672-51791-4, Bobbs) Macmillan.

Vendetta Gold. Mike Blakley. 320p. 1996. mass mkt. 2.50 (0-06-101117-7, Harp PBks) HarpC.

Vendetta Mountain. Carmen A. Fiore. LC 86-24963. 175p. 1987. 12.95 (0-939219-02-6); pap. 5.95 (0-939219-03-4) Townhouse Pub.

Vendetta or the Story of One Forgotten (1896) Marie Corelli. 410p. 1996. pap. 24.95 (1-56459-938-8) Kessinger Pub.

Vendian System, Vol. 2. Ed. by B. S. Sokolov & B. S. Fedonkin. (Illus.). 320p. 1990. 190.95 (0-387-51682-4) Spr-Verlag.

Vendiendo Seguridad. 7.50 (0-318-18011-1) Inter-Am Safety.

***Vending for Investors: How to Spot Phony Deals.** rev. ed. G. R. Schreiber. 96p. (Orig.). 1996. pap. 10.95 (0-9644054-2-3) Sunrise Bk IL.

Vending in the UK. Euromonitor Staff. 120p. (C). 1987. 825.00 (0-685-30323-3, Pub. by Euromonitor Pubns UK) St Mut.

Vending into the Nineteen Nineties: The Complete Vending Report. Euromonitor Staff. (C). 1990. 4,790.00 (0-685-37364-9, Pub. by Euromonitor Pubns UK) Gale.

Vending Operator, Inc. v. Nita Department of Transportation. 3rd ed. Steven Lubet. 238p. 1993. pap. 18.95 (1-55681-368-6) Natl Inst Trial Ad.

Vending Operator, Inc. v. Nita Department of Transportation Teaching Notes. 3rd ed. Steven Lubet. 1993. teacher ed., pap. 8.95 (1-55681-446-1) Natl Inst Trial Ad.

Vending Success Secrets: How Anyone Can Grow Rich in America's Best Cash Business! 3rd rev. ed. Bill Way. (Illus.). 220p. (Orig.). 1996. pap. 25.00 (0-615-10987-X) Freedom Tech Pr.

Vendor & Purchaser. D. E. McMorland. 163p. 1979. pap. 45.00 (0-409-64522-2, NZ) MICHIE.

Vendor Evaluation & Acquisition Budgets. Ed. by Sul H. Lee. LC 92-10146. (Journal of Library Administration: Vol. 16, No. 3). (Illus.). 143p. 1992. 29.95 (1-56024-253-1) Haworth Pr.

Vendor Evaluation & Acquisition Budgets. Ed. by Sul H. Lee. LC 92-10146. (Journal of Library Administration: Vol. 16, No. 3). 143p. 1996. pap. 14.95 (0-7890-0051-2) Haworth Pr.

Vendor of Sweets. R. K. Narayan. 144p. 1983. mass mkt. 5.95 (0-14-006258-0, Penguin Bks) Viking Penguin.

Vendors & Library Acquisitions. Ed. by Bill Katz. LC 90-26656. (Acquisitions Librarian Ser.: Vol. 5). (Illus.). 235p. 1991. text ed. 49.95 (1-56024-121-7) Haworth Pr.

Vendredi ou la Vie Sauvage. Michel Tournier. (Folio - Junior Ser.: No. 445). (Illus.). 191p. (FRE.). (J). (gr. 5-10). 1987. pap. 8.95 (2-07-033445-7) Schoenhof.

Vendredi ou les Limbes du Pacifique. Michel Tournier. (Folio Ser.: No. 959). (FRE.). pap. 8.95 (2-07-036959-5) Schoenhof.

Vendredi, Ou les Limbes du Pacifique. Michel Tournier. (FRE.). 1977. pap. 10.95 (0-8288-3801-1, F129031) Fr & Eur.

Vendredi ou les Limbes du Pacifique, Tournier: Critical Monographs in English. Margaret-Anne Hutton. 95p. 1993. pap. 32.00 (0-85261-345-8, Pub. by Univ of Glasgow UK) St Mut.

Vendredi Thirteen. David Goodis. 218p. (FRE.). 1989. pap. 10.95 (0-7859-2576-7, 2070381854) Fr & Eur.

Veneering & Wood Bending in the Furniture Industry. W. Clark & J. Kape. LC 65-97150. (Pergamon Series of Monographs on Furniture & Timber: Vol. 3). 1965. 60.00 (0-08-011255-2, Pub. by Pergamon Repr UK) Franklin.

Veneering Book. David S. Square. LC 95-9794. (Illus.). 176p. 1995. pap. 22.95 (1-56158-093-7) Taunton.

Veneering, Marquetry & Inlay. Fine Woodworking Magazine Editors. LC 95-41543. (Best of Fine Woodworking Ser.). 96p. 1996. pap. 14.95 (1-56158-119-4, 070250) Taunton.

Venegeance Is Mine. Brian Regrut. LC 94-28133. 296p. (Orig.). 1994. pap. 9.99 (0-8308-1372-1, 1372) InterVarsity.

Venerable Ancestor: The Life & Times of Tz'u Hsi, 1835-1908, Empress of China. Harry Hussey. LC 71-110042. 354p. 1971, reprint ed. text ed. 45.00 (0-8371-4430-2, HUVA, Greenwood Pr) Greenwood.

Venerable Assembly: The History of Venable, Baetjer & Howard. Arthur W. Machen, Jr. 240p. 1991. write for info. (0-9631294-0-6) V B & H.

Venerable Bede: Commentary on the Catholic Epistles. David Hurst. 1985. pap. 12.95 (0-87907-982-7) Cistercian Pubns.

Venerable Master Hua's Talks on Dharma, Vol. 1. 2nd ed. Hsuan Hua. Tr. by Buddhist Text Translation Society Staff from CHI. 240p. (Orig.). 1995. pap. 7.50 (0-88139-025-9) Buddhist Text.

Venerable Master Hua's Talks on Dharma, Vol. 2. 2nd ed. Hsuan Hua. Ed. by Buddhist Text Translation Society Staff. 201p. (Orig.). 1995. pap. 7.50 (0-88139-026-7) Buddhist Text.

Venerable Master Hua's Talks on Dharma, Vol. 3. Hsuan Hua. Ed. & Tr. by Buddhist Text Translation Society Staff. 219p. (Orig.). (CHI & ENG.). 1995. pap. 7.50 (0-88139-027-5) Buddhist Text.

Venerable Master Hua's Talks on Dharma, Vol. 4. Hsuan Hua. Ed. & Tr. by Buddhist Text Translation Society Staff. (Orig.). (CHI & ENG.). 1995. pap. 7.50 (0-88139-028-3) Buddhist Text.

Venerable Master Hua's Talks on Dharma: During the 1993 Trip to Taiwan. Hsuan Hua. Ed. & Tr. by Buddhist Text Translation Society Staff from CHI. Orig. Title: Hsuan Hua Shang Jen Kai Shih. (Illus.). 279p. (Orig.). (CHI & ENG.). 1996. pap. 8.50 (0-88139-023-2) Buddhist Text.

Venerable One. Ann R. Colton. LC 67-66241. 166p. 1963. 5.95 (0-917187-11-3) A R Colton Fnd.

Venerable Relic: The Story of the Liberty Bell. David Kimball. (Illus.). 80p. 1989. pap. 5.50 (0-915992-43-4) Eastern Acorn.

Venerable Tibetan Mastiff. Max Siber. LC 95-37185. (Classic Dog Book Ser.). (Illus.). 192p. (GER.). 1995. reprint ed. 27.95 (0-940269-09-0) OTR Pubns.

Venerate the Plough: A History of the Philadelphia Society for Promoting Agriculture, 1785-1985. Simon Baatz. LC 84-26453. (Illus.). 124p. 1985. 25.00 (0-9614267-0-5) Phila Soc Prom.

Venerated Teachers of the Jains, Sikhs & Parsis. Manly P. Hall. (Adepts Ser.). pap. 8.50 (0-89314-545-9) Philos Res.

Veneration of Divine Justice: The Dead Sea Scrolls & Christianity. Roy A. Rosenberg. LC 95-5266. (Contributions to the Study of Religion Ser.: Vol. 40). 145p. 1995. text ed. 47.95 (0-313-29655-3, Greenwood Pr) Greenwood.

Veneration of Icons. John of Damascus. pap. 0.50 (0-89981-107-8) Eastern Orthodox.

Venereal Disease Bibliography for 1973. Stephen H. Goode. LC 71-189843. xxiii, 276p. 1975. 15.00 (0-87875-058-4) Whitston Pub.

Venereal Disease Bibliography for 1974. Judith Kramer-Greene. LC 71-189843. 1976. 15.00 (0-87875-080-0) Whitston Pub.

Venereal Disease Bibliography for 1975. Judith Kramer-Greene. LC 71-189843. 1977. 25.00 (0-87875-097-5) Whitston Pub.

Venereal Disease Bibliography, 1966-1970. Stephen H. Goode. LC 71-189843. 400p. 1972. 22.50 (0-87875-023-1) Whitston Pub.

Venereal Disease Control: A Survey of Recent Legislation. (International Digest of Health Legislation Ser.: Vol. 26, No. 1). 1975. pap. text ed. 8.00 (92-4-169261-8, 1957501) World Health.

Venereal Diseases: A Social Dilemma. Vijay Narayan. (Illus.). 345p. (C). 1985. 32.95 (0-317-66157-4) Asia Bk Corp.

***Venereal Diseases: A Survey of Existing Legislation.** WHO Staff. (International Digest of Health Legislation Offprints: Vol. 7, No. 2). 44p. 1956. 3.00 (92-4-169072-0) World Health.

Venereology in Practice: The Sexually Committed Diseases. Niels Hjorth & Henning Schmidt. LC 79-10995. (Illus.). 105p. reprint ed. pap. 31.40 (0-8357-7621-2, 2056944) Bks Demand.

Veneris Tribunal. Scriva. (Exeter Hispanic Text Ser.: No. 35). 103p. (SPA.). Date not set. pap. text ed. 19.95 (0-85989-194-1, Pub. by Univ Exeter Pr UK) Northwestern U Pr.

Venetia. large type ed. Georgette Heyer. LC 92-37968. 1993. lib. bdg. 21.95 (1-56054-208-X) Thorndike Pr.

Venetia. Georgette Heyer. 321p. 1983. reprint ed. lib. bdg. 16.95 (0-89966-126-2) Buccaneer Bks.

Venetia, etc. see Works of Benjamin Disraeli

Venetia Redeemed: Franco-Italian Relations, 1864-1866. John W. Bush. LC 67-26918. 176p. reprint ed. pap. 50.20 (0-8357-3978-3, 2036676) Bks Demand.

Venetian & North Italian Schools. Michael Jaffe. (Devonshire Collection of Italian Drawings). (Illus.). 256p. (C). 1994. 95.00 (0-7148-2936-6, Pub. by Phaidon Press UK) Chronicle Bks.

Venetian Art from Bellini to Titian. Johannes Wilde. (Oxford Studies in the History of Art & Architecture). (Illus.). 284p. (C). 1975. pap. text ed. 38.00 (0-19-817331-8) OUP.

Venetian Empire: A Sea Voyage. Jan Morris. (Illus.). 208p. 1990. pap. 12.95 (0-14-011994-9, Penguin Bks) Viking Penguin.

Venetian Empire 1200-1700. David Nicolle. (Men-at-Arms Ser.: No. 210). (Illus.). 48p. pap. 11.95 (0-85045-899-4, 9143, Pub. by Osprey UK) Stackpole.

Venetian Family & Its Fortune, 1500-1900: The Dona & the Conservation of Their Wealth. James C. Davis. LC 74-26309. (American Philosophical Society, Memoirs Ser.: No. 106). (Illus.). 205p. reprint ed. pap. 58.50 (0-8357-7914-9, 2036343) Bks Demand.

Venetian Glass Nephew. Elinor H. Wylie. 182p. 1988. reprint ed. pap. 7.95 (0-89733-112-5) Academy Chi Pubs.

Venetian Glass 1890-1990. Rosa B. Mentasi. (Illus.). 208p. 1992. 95.00 (88-7743-119-9, Pub. by Arsenale Editrice IT) Antique Collect.

Venetian Gros Point Lace. Nenia Lovesey. (Illus.). 75p. 1986. 12.75 (0-85219-631-8, Pub. by Dryad Pr UK) Branford.

Venetian Humanism in an Age of Patrician Dominance. Margaret L. King. LC 85-43294. (Illus.). 575p. 1986. text ed. 90.00 (0-691-05465-7) Princeton U Pr.

***Venetian Humanism in an Age of Patrician Dominance.** Margaret L. King. LC 85-43294. reprint ed. pap. 155.90 (0-608-04649-3, 2065335) Bks Demand.

Venetian Instrumental Music: From Gabrieli to Vivaldi. 3rd enl. rev. ed. Eleanor Selfridge-Field. LC 94-8060. (Illus.). 384p. 1994. reprint ed. pap. 13.95 (0-486-28151-5) Dover.

Venetian Life. William Dean Howells. 1989. pap. 12.50 (0-910395-47-0) Marlboro Pr.

Venetian Life. William Dean Howells. LC 73-153876. reprint ed. 45.00 (0-404-03369-5) AMS Pr.

Venetian Life. William Dean Howells. (Notable American Authors Ser.). 1992. reprint ed. lib. bdg. 75.00 (0-7812-3267-8) Rprt Serv.

Venetian Mask. large type ed. Rosalind Laker. 691p. 1993. reprint ed. lib. bdg. 23.95 (1-56054-585-2) Thorndike Pr.

***Venetian Money Market: Banks, Panics, & the Public Debt, 1200-1500.** Reinhold C. Mueller. LC 96-36921. (Illus.). 568p. 1997. text ed. 65.00 (0-8018-5437-7) Johns Hopkins.

Venetian Narrative Painting in the Age of Carpaccio. Patricia F. Brown. LC 87-10669. 320p. (C). 1988. text ed. 70.00 (0-300-04025-3) Yale U Pr.

Venetian Narrative Painting in the Age of Carpaccio. Patricia F. Brown. 318p. (C). 1990. reprint ed. pap. 32.50 (0-300-04743-6) Yale U Pr.

Venetian Opera in the Seventeenth Century. Simon T. Worsthorne. LC 83-18917. (Music Reprint Ser.). 194p. 1984. reprint ed. lib. bdg. 32.50 (0-306-76227-7) Da Capo.

Venetian Painted Ceilings of the Renaissance. Juergen Schulz. (California Studies in the History of Art: No. IX). (Illus.). 1968. 100.00 (0-520-01154-6) U CA Pr.

Venetian Painting. John Steer. (World of Art Ser.). (Illus.). 216p. 1980. pap. 14.95 (0-500-20101-3) Thames Hudson.

Venetian Palaces. Alvise Zorzi. LC 89-63962. (Illus.). 532p. 1991. 95.00 (0-8478-1200-6) Rizzoli Intl.

Venetian Patriciate: Reality vs. Myth. Donald E. Queller. LC 84-28041. 398p. 1985. text ed. 34.95 (0-252-01144-9) U of Ill Pr.

Venetian Phoenix: Paolo Sarpi & Some of His English Friends, 1606-1700. John L. Lievsay. LC 73-6818. x, 262p. 1973. 29.95 (0-7006-0108-2) U Pr of KS.

***Venetian Prints & Books in the Age of Tiepolo.** Suzanne Boorsch & Metropolitan Museum of Art Staff. LC 96-50879. 1997. write for info. (0-87099-824-2) Metropolitan Music Co.

***Venetian Reckoning.** large type ed. Donna Leon. (Large Print Ser.). 480p. 1997. 27.50 (0-7089-3668-7) Ulverscroft.

Venetian Romance. large type ed. Clover Sinclair. (Linford Romance Library). 272p. 1992. pap. 15.99 (0-7089-7244-6, Trailtree Bookshop) Ulverscroft.

Venetian School of Painting. Evelyn M. Phillipps. LC 70-37907. (Select Bibliographies Reprint Ser.). 1977. reprint ed. 24.95 (0-8369-6745-3) Ayer.

Venetian Ships & Shipbuilders of the Renaissance. Frederic C. Lane. 1979. 28.95 (0-405-10609-2) Ayer.

Venetian Ships & Shipbuilders of the Renaissance. Frederic C. Lane. LC 92-11280. (Softshell Bks.). (Illus.). 296p. 1992. reprint ed. pap. text ed. 15.95 (0-8018-4514-9) Johns Hopkins.

Venetian State Theater & the Games of Siena, 1595-1605: The Grimani Banquet Plays. Jonathan Shiff. LC 93-33672. 200p. 1993. text ed. 89.95 (0-7734-9424-3) E Mellen.

Venetian Taste. Photos by Peter Pioppo. LC 94-6993. 192p. 1994. 35.00 (1-55859-548-1) Abbeville Pr.

***Venetian Taste.** Adam D. Tihany. 1997. 35.00 (0-89660-085-8, Artabras) Abbeville Pr.

Venetian Tornesello: A Medieval Colonial Coinage. Alan M. Stahl. (Numismatic Notes & Monographs: No. 163). 100p. (Orig.). 1986. 20.00 (0-89722-209-1) Am Numismatic.

***Venetian Upper Clergy in the 16th & Early 17th Centuries: A Study in Religious Culture.** Oliver Logan. LC 96-31329. (Texts & Studies in Religion: Vol. 68). 624p. 1997. text ed. 129.95 (0-7734-8927-4) E Mellen.

Venetian Woods. Eamon Baeda. LC 88-81109. ix, 66p. 1988. 10.95 (0-9620529-0-6); pap. 5.95 (0-9620529-1-4) Aldine Pr Ltd.

Venetians. Ron Glowen. 132p. 1989. 50.00 (0-944092-08-X) Twin Palms Pub.

Venetian's Wife: A Strangely Sensual Tale of a Renaissance Explorer, a Computer, & a Metamorphosis. Nick Bantock. LC 95-47243. 132p. 1996. 22.95 (0-8118-1140-9) Chronicle Bks.

Venetic see Mediterranean Studies

Veneto: Splendid Italian Life. Hidenobu Jinnai. (Process Architecture Ser.: No. 109). (Illus.). 155p. 1993. pap. 44.95 (4-89331-109-3, Pub. by Process Archit JA) Bks Nippan.

Venetsianov, Alexei. D. V. Sarab'Ianov. (C). 1988. 50.00 (0-685-34412-6, Pub. by Collets) St Mut.

Venezia One-Hundred-One Disegni. Marie Z. Greene-Mercier. 111p. (Orig.). 1969. pap. 6.00 (0-910790-18-3) Intl Bk Co IL.

Venezuela. L. Dalton. 1976. lib. bdg. 59.95 (0-8490-2793-4) Gordon Pr.

***Venezuela.** Ann Heinrichs. LC 96-31629. (True Bk.). (J). 1997. lib. bdg. 19.00 (0-516-20344-4) Childrens.

Venezuela. Gary Hoover. (Pelham Guides Ser.). 40p. (C). 1996. 22.00 (0-929851-84-6) Am Assn Coll Registrars.

Venezuela. Brian S. McBeth. (Illus.). 210p. 1994. 170.00 (1-85564-251-4, Pub. by Euromoney UK) Am Educ Systs.

Venezuela. Marion Morrison. LC 88-30493. (Enchantment of the World Ser.). (Illus.). 128p. (J). (gr. 5-9). 1989. lib. bdg. 30.00 (0-516-02711-5) Childrens.

Venezuela. annot. ed. Ed. by D. A. Waddell. (World Bibliographical Ser.: No. 110). 208p. 1990. lib. bdg. 59.00 (1-85109-106-8) ABC-CLIO.

Venezuela. 2nd ed. John D. Martz. LC 85-28268. 489p. 1985. text ed. 65.00 (0-275-91815-7, C1815, Praeger Pubs); pap. text ed. 17.95 (0-275-92038-0, B2038, Praeger Pubs) Greenwood.

Venezuela. Edwin Lieuwen. LC 85-24781. xi, 223p. 1986. reprint ed. text ed. 55.00 (0-313-24979-2, LIVE, Greenwood Pr) Greenwood.

Venezuela. Rosa Q. Mesa. LC 73-180800. (Latin American Serial Documents Ser.: Vol. 12). 337p. reprint ed. pap. 96.10 (0-317-10310-5, 2013554) Bks Demand.

Venezuela: A Century of Change. Judith Ewell. LC 83-40093. 272p. 1984. 37.50 (0-8047-1213-1) Stanford U Pr.

Venezuela: Politics in a Petroleum Republic. David E. Blank. LC 83-24469. (Politics in Latin America Ser.). 240p. 1984. text ed. 75.00 (0-275-91129-2, C1129, Praeger Pubs) Greenwood.

Venezuela: The Challenge of Competitiveness. Michael Enright et al. 560p. 1996. text ed. 59.95 (0-312-15851-3) St Martin.

Venezuela: The Democratic Experience. Ed. by John D. Martz & David J. Myers. LC 77-7509. (Praeger Special Studies). 432p. 1977. pap. 18.95 (0-275-91471-2, B1471, Praeger Pubs) Greenwood.

Venezuela: The Political Economy of Oil. Juan Carlos Boue. (Institute for Energy Studies). (Illus.). 250p. 1994. 80.00 (0-19-730012-X) OUP.

Venezuela: Travel Survival Kit. Krzysztof Dydynski. (Illus.). 336p. 1994. pap. 14.95 (0-86442-229-6) Lonely Planet.

Venezuela see Statements of the Laws of the OAS Member States in Matters Affecting Business

Venezuela see Cultures of the World - Group 2

***Venezuela - Punishment Before Trial: Prison Conditions in Venezuela.** 128p. (Orig.). 1997. pap. 10.00 (1-56432-201-7) Hum Rts Watch.

Venezuela, a Country Study. 4th ed. Federal Research Division, Library of Congress Staff. Ed. by Richard A. Haggerty. LC 92-10376. (Area Handbook Ser.). 1992. write for info. (0-8444-0747-X) Lib Congress.

***Venezuela Alive.** 3rd rev. ed. Arnold Greenberg. 420p. 1997. pap. 15.95 (1-55650-800-X) Hunter NJ.

Venezuela Alive. 4th ed. Arnold Greenberg. (Alive Travel Ser.). (Illus.). 1989. pap. 10.95 (0-935572-17-1) Alive Pubns.

Venezuela & Its Ruler. N. Naranjo. 1976. lib. bdg. 59.95 (0-8490-2794-2) Gordon Pr.

Venezuela & the United States: From Monroe's Hemisphere to Petroleum's Empire. Judith Ewell. LC 95-2808. (United States & the Americas Ser.). 1996. 50.00 (0-8203-1782-9); pap. 20.00 (0-8203-1783-7) U of Ga Pr.

Venezuela Company Handbook, 1992-93. 2nd ed. Ed. by IMF Editora Staff. 72p. 1993. pap. 29.95 (1-878753-12-6) Hoovers TX.

Venezuela in Focus: A Guide to the People, Politics, & Culture. (In Focus Ser.). (Illus.). 80p. (Orig.). (C). 1995. pap. text ed. 12.00 (0-85345-908-8) Monthly Rev.

Venezuela in Pictures. Lerner Publications, Department of Geography Staff. (Visual Geography Ser.). (Illus.). 64p. (YA). (gr. 5 up). 1987. lib. bdg. 19.95 (0-8225-1824-4, Lerner Publctns) Lerner Group.

Venezuela in the Wake of Radical Reform. Ed. by Joseph S. Tulchin & Gary Bland. LC 92-33571. (Woodrow Wilson Center Current Studies on Latin America). 192p. 1993. pap. text ed. 11.95 (1-55587-364-2) Lynne Rienner.

Venezuela Through Its History. William D. Marsland & Amy L. Marsland. LC 75-40919. (Illus.). 277p. 1976. reprint ed. text ed. 38.50 (0-8371-8690-0, MAVE, Greenwood Pr) Greenwood.

Venezuela-Trinidad to Curacao. Wilson Ltd. Staff & Imray L. Norie. (C). 1987. 85.00 (0-685-40380-7, Pub. by Imray Laurie Norie & Wilson UK) St Mut.

Venezuela 1994: Challenges for the Caldera Administration. William Perry & Norman A. Bailey. LC 94-44043. (CSIS Report Ser.). 24p. (C). 1994. pap. 10.95 (0-89206-310-6) CSI Studies.

Venezuelan - U. S. Petroleum Relationship: Past, Present, & Future. G. Henry Schuler. (Significant Issues Ser.: Vol. 13, No. 11). 22p. 1991. 6.95 (0-89206-179-0) CSI Studies.

Venezuelan Democracy under Stress. Ed. by Jennifer McCoy et al. LC 94-40527. 300p. (C). 1995. pap. 21.95 (1-56000-770-2) U Miami N-S Ctr.

An Asterisk (*) at the beginning of an entry indicates that the title is appearing in BIP for the first time.

Venezuelan Economic Development: A Politico-Economic Analysis. Ingo I. Walter. LC 76-10395. (Contemporary Studies in Economic & Financial Analysis: Vol. 7). 325p. 1977. 73.25 (0-89232-011-7) Jai Pr.

Venezuelan Law Governing Restrictive Business Practices. Gustavo Brillembourg. LC 85-82448. 398p. 1986. lib. bdg. 20.00 (0-935328-35-1) Intl Law Inst.

Venezuela's Moviemiento al Socialismo: From Guerrilla Defeat to Innovative Politics. Steve Ellner. LC 87-30456. (Illus.). xvi, 263p. (C). 1988. text ed. 53.00 (0-8223-0808-8) Duke.

Venezuela's Pursuit of Caribbean Basin Interests: Implications for United States National Security. David J. Myers. LC 83-19144. 1985. pap. text ed. 4.00 (0-8330-0527-8, R-2994-AF) Rand Corp.

Venezuela's Voice for Democracy: Conversations & Correspondence with Romulo Betancourt. Robert J. Alexander. LC 90-36176. 184p. 1990. text ed. 55.00 (0-275-93728-3, C3728, Praeger Pubs) Greenwood.

Vengador! large type ed. Mark Carrel. (Linford Western Library). 1995. pap. 15.99 (0-7089-7757-X, Linford) Ulverscroft.

***Venganza Apasionada.** Valerie Parv. (SPA.). 1997. mass mkt. 3.50 (0-373-33407-9, 1-33407-7) Harlequin Bks.

Venganza de Angeles. 1994. pap. 16.95 (0-7871-0099-4, Dove Bks) Dove Audio.

Venganza de Don Mendo. Pedro Munoz Seca. (Nueva Austral Ser.: Vol. 30). (SPA.). 1991. pap. text ed. 24.95 (84-239-1830-0) Elliots Bks.

Venganza de Tamar. Tirso De Molina. Ed. by A. K. Paterson. LC 69-10572. 158p. reprint ed. pap. 45.10 (0-317-20843-8, 2024442) Bks Demand.

Vengeance. large type ed. J. Stride. 192p. 1992. pap. 15.99 (0-7089-7152-0, Trailtree Bookshop) Ulverscroft.

Vengeance: Hitler's Nuclear Weapon: Fact or Fiction? Philip Henshall. (Illus.). 224p. 1995. 24.95 (0-7509-0874-2, Pub. by Sutton Pubng UK) Bks Intl VA.

Vengeance: Prelude to Saddam's War. Bob Mendes. Tr. by H. S. Smittenaar from DUT. 303p. 1996. pap. 9.95 (1-881164-71-3) Intercont VA.

Vengeance! The Saga of Poor Tom Cover. Dan L. Thrapp. LC 88-50601. (Montana & the West Ser.: Vol. 6). (Illus.). 347p. 1989. 35.00 (0-912783-12-5) Upton & Sons.

Vengeance & Justice: Crime & Punishment in the 19th Century American South. Edward L. Ayers. 353p. 1985. pap. 18.95 (0-19-503988-2) OUP.

Vengeance & Other Stories. Manoj Das. 106p. 1980. 8.95 (0-86578-191-5) Ind-US Inc.

***Vengeance Canyon.** S. J. Stewart. LC 96-95286. 192p. 1997. 17.95 (0-8034-9196-4, Avalon Bks) Bouregy.

Vengeance Gun. large type ed. Ray Hogan. LC 93-21816. 141p. 1993. reprint ed. lib. bdg. 17.95 (1-56054-576-3) Thorndike Pr.

***Vengeance in Death.** J. D. Robb. 368p. 1997. mass mkt. 6.50 (0-425-16039-4) Berkley Pub.

Vengeance in the Apocalypse. Joel N. Musvosvi. (Andrews University Seminary Doctoral Dissertation Ser.: Vol. 17). 315p. 1993. pap. 19.99 (0-943872-48-0) Andrews Univ Pr.

Vengeance in the Ashes. William W. Johnstone. (Ashes Ser.: No. 16). 352p. 1993. mass mkt. 3.99 (0-8217-4066-0, Zebra Kensgtn) Kensgtn Pub Corp.

Vengeance in the Sun. large type ed. Margaret A. Pemberton. (Dales Large Print Ser.). 306p. 1995. pap. 17.99 (1-85389-490-7, Dales) Ulverscroft.

***Vengeance Is Hers.** Max A. Collins. 1997. pap. 5.99 (0-451-19198-6, Sig) NAL-Dutton.

Vengeance Is Mine. Margaret E. Kelchner. 208p. 1995. per., pap. 9.99 (0-8341-1610-3) Beacon Hill.

***Vengeance Is Mine.** Robert Martin. 220p. (Orig.). 1997. pap. 8.95 (1-57502-468-3, P01399) Morris Pubng.

Vengeance Is Mine. Mickey Spillane. 1989. pap. 2.95 (0-451-14687-5) NAL-Dutton.

Vengeance Is Ours: The Church in Dominion. Albert J. Dager. 288p. 1990. pap. 9.95 (0-9626632-0-4) Sword Pubs.

Vengeance of God: The Meaning of the Root NQM & the Function of the NQM-Texts in the Context of Divine Revelation in the Old Testament. Hendrik G. Peels. LC 94-35317. (Oudtestamentische Studien: Vol. 31). 640p. 1994. 92.00 (90-04-10164-0) E J Brill.

***Vengeance of Hera.** John G. Betancourt. (Hercules Ser.). 1997. mass mkt. 4.99 (0-8125-3911-7) Tor Bks.

Vengeance of Orion. Ben Bova. 352p. 1989. pap. 3.95 (0-8125-3161-2) Tor Bks.

***Vengeance of the Black Donnellys: Canada's Most Feared Family Strikes Back from the Grave.** Thomas P. Kelley. 212p. (Orig.). Date not set. pap. 9.95 (1-895565-55-3) Firefly Bks Ltd.

Vengeance of the Dancing Gods. Jack L. Chalker. (Dancing Gods Ser.). 1985. mass mkt. 5.99 (0-345-31549-9, Del Rey) Ballantine.

Vengeance of the Gods: And Three Other Stories of Real American Color Line Life. William Pickens. LC 72-4612. (Black Heritage Library Collection). 1977. reprint ed. 21.95 (0-8369-9120-6) Ayer.

Vengeance of the Gods & Three Other Stories of Real American Color Line Life. William Pickens. LC 73-18564. reprint ed. 24.50 (0-404-11376-1) AMS Pr.

Vengeance of the Swallows: Memoir of a Polish Family's Ordeal under Soviet Aggression, Ukrainian Ethnic Cleansing & Nazi Enslavement, & Their Emigration to America. Tadeusz Piotrowski. LC 94-24862. (Illus.). 299p. 1995. lib. bdg. 29.95 (0-7864-0001-3) McFarland & Co.

Vengeance of the Tau. Jon Land. (Orig.). 1993. mass mkt. 5.99 (0-449-14776-2, GM) Fawcett.

Vengeance of the Witch-Finder. John Bellairs. LC 93-10081. (Illus.). 176p. (YA). (gr. 5 up). 1993. pap. 14.99 (0-8037-1450-5); lib. bdg. 14.89 (0-8037-1451-3) Dial Bks Young.

Vengeance of the Witch-Finder. John Bellairs. 160p. (J). (gr. 3-7). 1995. pap. 3.99 (0-14-037511-2) Puffin Bks.

Vengeance Trail. large type ed. J. B. Dancer. (Linford Western Library). 1989. pap. 15.99 (0-7089-6761-2) Ulverscroft.

Vengeance Trail. large type ed. Charles N. Heckelmann. (Linford Western Library). 1990. pap. 15.99 (0-7089-6809-0) Ulverscroft.

***Vengeance Trail/Death Hunt.** David Thompson. (Wilderness Ser.: Nos. 7 & 8). 352p. 1997. mass mkt. 4.99 (0-8439-4297-5, Leisure Bks) Dorchester Pub Co.

Vengeful Bride. large type ed. Rosalie Ash. 288p. 1995. 21.50 (0-263-14209-4) Ulverscroft.

Vengeful Flames. large type ed. Alan Sewart. (Linford Mystery Library). 1991. pap. 15.99 (0-7089-7004-4) Ulverscroft.

Vengeful Groom. Sara Wood. 1994. mass mkt. 2.99 (0-373-11692-6, 1-11692-0) Harlequin Bks.

Vengeful Passion. Lynne Graham. 1994. mass mkt. 2.99 (0-373-11696-9, 1-11696-1) Harlequin Bks.

Vengeful Seduction. large type ed. Cathy Williams. 288p. 1995. 21.50 (0-263-14361-9, Pub. by M & B UK) Ulverscroft.

Vengement Alixandre. Gui De Cambrai. Ed. by B. Edwards. (Elliott Monographs: Vol. 20). 1928. 25.00 (0-527-02626-3) Periodicals Srv.

Vengence in His Guns. large type ed. Peter Taylor. (Linford Western Library). 208p. 1992. pap. 15.99 (0-7089-7183-0, Trailtree Bookshop) Ulverscroft.

***Vengence of the Mountain Man, No. 18.** William W. Johnstone. 256p. 1997. mass mkt. 4.99 (0-8217-5681-8, Zebra Kensgtn) Kensgtn Pub Corp.

Vengerova System of Piano Playing. Robert D. Schick. LC 82-80454. (Illus.). 126p. 1982. 25.00 (0-271-00313-8) Pa St U Pr.

Veni Creator Spiritus: An Encyclopedia of the Holy Spirit. Ed. by Michael O'Carroll. 235p. 1990. 29.95 (0-8146-5785-0) Liturgical Pr.

Veni Vidi Vici: Conquer Your Enemies, Impress Your Friends with Everyday Latin. Eugene Ehrlich. LC 94-42354. 224p. 1995. pap. 14.00 (0-06-273365-6, PL) HarpC.

Venice. (Panorama Bks.). (Illus.). (FRE.). 3.95 (0-685-11615-8) Fr & Eur.

Venice. (Insight Guides Ser.). 1993. pap. 21.95 (0-395-66289-3) HM.

Venice. (Baedeker's City Guides Ser.). 1987. pap. 12.95 (0-13-058116-X) P-H.

Venice. 1988. 5.95 (0-671-84407-5) PB.

Venice. Baedeker Staff. (Baedeker's Travel Guides Ser.). 1995. 17.00 (0-02-860085-1) Macmillan.

Venice. Boccazzi-Varotto. 1996. 70.00 (0-679-44284-7) Random Hse Value.

Venice. Susie Bolton. (Illustrated Travel Guides from Thomas Cook Ser.). (Illus.). 192p. 1995. 12.95 (0-8442-9083-1, Passport Bks) NTC Pub Grp.

Venice. Harold Brodkey. 1997. write for info. (0-8050-4833-2) H Holt & Co.

Venice. Jean Cocteau et al. 68p. 1951. 27.50 (0-686-54561-3) Fr & Eur.

Venice. David Hamilton. 1990. pap. 12.99 (0-517-06291-7) Random Hse Value.

Venice. M. Muraro & A. Grabar. 39.95 (0-517-62645-4) Random Hse Value.

***Venice.** Danilo Reato. (Places & History Ser.). (Illus.). 136p. 1997. 24.95 (1-55670-532-8) Stewart Tabori & Chang.

Venice. 2nd ed. Dana Facaros & Michael Pauls. (Cadogan City Guides Ser.). (Illus.). 432p. (Orig.). 1994. pap. 15.95 (1-56440-132-4) Globe Pequot.

Venice. 5th ed. Alta Macadam. (Blue Guides Ser.). 1994. pap. 17.95 (0-393-31189-9) Norton.

Venice, No. 3. Jonathan Buckley & Hilary Robinson. (Rough Guide Ser.). (Illus.). 432p. 1996. pap. 14.95 (1-85828-170-9, Penguin Bks) Viking Penguin.

Venice: A Guide to Paintings in Original Settings. Ed. by Teresio Pignatti. (Illus.). 160p. 1996. pap. 19.95 (88-86502-07-9, Pub. by Canal & Stamperia UK) Antique Collect.

Venice: A Guide to the Principal Buildings, the Canal Guides. Antonio Salvadori. 1996. pap. text ed. 17.95 (88-86502-12-5, Pub. by Canal & Stamperia UK) Antique Collect.

Venice: A Maritime Republic. Frederic C. Lane. LC 72-12342. (Illus.). 518p. 1973. pap. 18.95 (0-8018-1460-X) Johns Hopkins.

***Venice: A New Look.** Reg Butler. (City Breaks Ser.). 1997. pap. 6.95 (1-872876-52-8, Pub. by Settle Pr UK) Assoc Pubs Grp.

Venice: An Architectural Guide. Guido Zucconi. 1996. pap. 17.95 (88-7743-130-X, Pub. by Arsenale Editrice IT) Antique Collect.

Venice: An Artist's Vision. Julian Halsby. 14.99 (0-517-12433-5) Random Hse Value.

Venice: From the Earliest Beginnings to the Fall of the Republic, 2 vols. P. Molmenti. 1977. lib. bdg. 250.00 (0-8490-2795-0) Gordon Pr.

Venice: Hidden Splendors. Cesare M. Cunaccia. (Illus.). 128p. 1996. 35.00 (2-08-013573-2, Pub. by Flammarion FR) Abbeville Pr.

Venice: Journey from Horse & Chaise. Janet S. Matthews. LC 89-60490. (Illus.). 394p. 1989. 20.00 (0-9621986-0-9) Coastal Pr FL.

Venice: Picture Book to Remember Her. 1986. 5.99 (0-517-25023-3) Random Hse Value.

Venice: Tales of the City. Ed. by John Miller & Kristen Miller. LC 93-13594. (Abroad Ser.). 176p. 1994. 13.95 (0-8118-0471-2) Chronicle Bks.

Venice: The American View 1860-1920. Margaretta M. Lovell. LC 84-81857. (Illus.). 174p. 1984. pap. 19.95 (0-88401-044-9) Fine Arts Mus.

Venice: The Art of Living. Frederic Vitoux. (Illus.). 252p. 1995. 45.00 (1-55670-425-9) Stewart Tabori & Chang.

Venice: The Artist's Vision: A Guide to British & American Painters. Julian Halsby. (Illus.). 224p. 1992. 45.00 (0-7134-6606-5, Pub. by Batsford UK) Trafalgar.

Venice: The City & Its Architecture. Richard Goy. (Illus.). 288p. 1997. 69.95 (0-7148-3005-4, Pub. by Phaidon Press UK) Chronicle Bks.

***Venice: The Four Seasons.** Lisa St. Aubin de Teran. (Illus.). 12p. 1997. pap. 22.95 (1-85793-726-0, Pub. by Pavilion UK) Trafalgar.

***Venice: The Travel Notebook.** Pascale Loiseau. 104p. 1997. 14.95 (2-911141-08-3, Pub. by Les Edtns Pascale FR) Assoc Pubs Grp.

Venice see Victorian Venetian Travel Guide

***Venice Adriana.** Morrden. Date not set. write for info. (0-312-18202-3) St Martin.

Venice & Amsterdam: A Study of Seventeenth-Century Elites. Peter Burke. Ed. by Sue Leigh. LC 94-27628. 180p. 1994. pap. 19.95 (0-7456-1324-1) Blackwell Pubs.

Venice & Amsterdam: A Study of Seventeenth-Century Elites. Peter Burke. Ed. by Sue Leigh. LC 94-27628. (Illus.). 180p. 1995. 49.95 (0-7456-1343-8) Blackwell Pubs.

Venice & Antiquity: The Venetian Sense of the Past. Patricia F. Brown. LC 96-3196. (Illus.). 361p. 1996. 60.00 (0-300-06700-3) Yale U Pr.

Venice & History: The Collected Papers of Frederic C. Lane. Frederic C. Lane. LC 66-14160. 582p. reprint ed. pap. 165.90 (0-317-30121-7, 2025304) Bks Demand.

Venice & the Defense of Republican Liberty: Renaissance Values in the Age of the Counter Reformation. William J. Bouwsma. LC 68-14642. (Illus.). 1968. pap. 15.00 (0-520-05221-8) U CA Pr.

***Venice & the Grand Tour.** Bruce Redford. LC 96-26608. (Illus.). 160p. 1996. 30.00 (0-300-06911-1) Yale U Pr.

Venice & the Renaissance. Manfredo Tafuri. Tr. by Jessica Levine. (Illus.). 432p. 1995. pap. 22.50 (0-262-70054-9) MIT Pr.

Venice & The Veneto. LC 94-44310. (Eyewitness Travel Guides Ser.). (Illus.). 312p. 1995. pap. 22.95 (1-56458-861-0) DK Pub Inc.

Venice & the Venice Area. George E. Youngberg, Sr. & W. Earl Aumann. Ed. by B. Larz Newton. LC 95-61748. (Illus.). 75p. (Orig.). 1995. reprint ed. pap. 5.95 (1-885527-06-3) Feather Fables.

Venice, Austria & the Turks in the Seventeenth Century. Kenneth M. Setton. LC 90-55269. (Memoirs Ser.: Vol. 192). 502p. (C). 1991. 35.00 (0-87169-192-2, M192-SEK) Am Philos.

Venice Beach. Photos by Claudio Edinger. LC 85-4015. (Illus.). 168p. 1985. pap. 15.00 (0-89659-520-X) Abbeville Pr.

***Venice Beach.** Mark S. McMahon. 1997. 18.95 (0-533-12292-9) Vantage.

Venice, California - Coney Island of the Pacific. Jeffrey W. Stanton. (Illus.). 232p. (Orig.). 1993. pap. 19.95 (0-9619849-2-9) Donahue Pub.

Venice Desired. Tony Tanner. Ed. by Edward W. Said. (Convergences: Inventories of the Present Ser.). (Illus.). 400p. 1992. 34.50 (0-674-93312-5) HUP.

Venice, Durer & the Oriental Mode. Julian Raby. (Hans Huth Memorial Studies: No. 1). (Illus.). 104p. 1983. text ed. 45.00 (0-85667-162-2) Sothebys Pubns.

Venice for Pleasure. 5th ed. J. G. Links. (Illus.). 272p. 1995. pap. 14.95 (1-55921-143-1) Moyer Bell.

Venice Green Guide. Michelin Travel Publications, Staff. (Illus.). 1996. per. 18.00 (2-06-158701-1, 1587) Michelin.

Venice in Old Photographs Vol. 1: 1841-1920. Dorothea Ritter. (Illus.). 208p. 1994. 35.00 (0-8212-2127-2) Bulfinch Pr.

Venice in the Eighteenth Century. Ed. by Henri Zerner. LC 67-17765. (Illus.). 1967. pap. 4.00 (0-911517-40-5) Mus of Art RI.

Venice in Your Pocket Guide. Michelin Travel Publications, Staff. (In Your Pocket Guides Ser.). (Orig.). 1996. per. 9.95 (2-06-650901-9, 6509) Michelin.

Venice Installation: United States Pavilion, the 44th Venice Biennale. Jenny Holzer. 46p. 1990. 10.00 (0-914782-77-0) Buffalo Fine-Albrght-Knox.

Venice Italy: Cooking with Betty Evans. Betty Evans. LC 86-61768. (Illus.). 112p. 1986. pap. 6.96 (0-931104-18-1) Sunflower Ink.

***Venice Menace.** Nancy Lamb. (J). Date not set. write for info. (0-688-13996-5) Lothrop.

Venice Observed. Mary McCarthy. LC 64-49016. 158p. 1963. pap. 9.00 (0-15-693521-X, Harvest Bks) HarBrace.

***Venice Pocket Guide.** Berlitz Editors. 144p. 1998. pap. 8.95 (2-8315-6353-4) Berlitz.

Venice Pocket Guide. rev. ed. Berlitz Editors. LC 76-21365. (Pocket Guides Ser.). 144p. 1994. pap. 7.95 (2-8315-2544-6) Berlitz.

Venice Preserved. Thomas Otway. Ed. by Malcolm Kelsall. LC 69-12902. (Regents Restoration Drama Ser.). 138p. reprint ed. pap. 39.40 (0-8357-4080-3, 2036770) Bks Demand.

Venice Preserved see Restoration Plays

Venice Preserved see Six Restoration Plays

Venice Rediscovered. Ronald S. Kennedy. 20.00 (0-8453-1484-X, Cornwall Bks) Assoc Univ Prs.

Venice Rediscovered. John Pemble. (Illus.). 220p. 1995. 30.00 (0-19-820501-5) OUP.

Venice Rediscovered. Ronald Shaw-Kennedy. LC 73-22608. (Illus.). 136p. 1978. 20.00 (0-87982-020-9) Art Alliance.

Venice Rediscovered. John Pemble. (Illus.). 256p. 1996. reprint ed. pap. 14.95 (0-19-285328-7) OUP.

Venice Simplon Orient-Express: The Return of the World's Most Celebrated Train. Shirley Shirwood. (Illus.). 1984. 19.95 (0-297-78261-4) Beaufort Bks NY.

Venice Simplon Orient-Express: The World's Most Celebrated Train. Shirley Sherwood. (Illus.). 180p. 1996. 29.95 (0-7603-0266-9) Motorbooks Intl.

Venice Through the Years: A Pictorial History. Prudy T. Board & Esther B. Colcord. LC 95-6483. (Illus.). 1995. write for info. (0-89865-931-0) Donning Co.

Venice Walking Guide. Jeanne B. Oelerich. (Illus.). 16p. 1994. pap. 9.95 (1-882546-06-7) Just Marvelous.

Venice West: The Beat Generation in Southern California. John A. Maynard. LC 90-45114. 264p. (C). 1991. 22.95 (0-8135-1653-6) Rutgers U Pr.

Venice West: The Beat Generation in Southern California. John A. Maynard. LC 90-45114. 264p. 1993. pap. 15.95 (0-8135-1965-9) Rutgers U Pr.

***Venice 360.** Attilo Boccazzi-Varotto. 1996. write for info. (0-679-45665-1) Random.

Venice's Hidden Enemies: Italian Heretics in a Renaissance City. John Martin. LC 92-19220. (Studies on the History of Society & Culture: Vol. 16). 1993. 42.50 (0-520-07743-1) U CA Pr.

Venicewalks. Charles Carner. 1991. pap. 14.95 (0-8050-1139-0, Owl) H Holt & Co.

Venida del Senor. 2nd ed. Jorge Cutting. Ed. by Gordon H. Bennett. Tr. by Sara Bautista from ENG. (Serie Diamante). (Illus.). 48p. (SPA.). 1982. pap. 0.85 (0-942504-10-0) Overcomer Pr.

***Venini Glass.** Franco Deboni. 125.00 (88-422-0613-X) Antique Collect.

***Venir Au Monde.** Marie-Francine Hebert. (Gout De Savoir Ser.). (Illus.). 24p. (FRE.). (J). (ps up). 1996. pap. 4.95 (2-89021-225-4, Pub. by Les Editions CN) Firefly Bks Ltd.

Venise Green Guide. Michelin Travel Publications, Staff. (Illus.). (FRE.). 1996. per. 18.00 (2-06-058701-8, 587) Michelin.

Venison: As You Like It. Ned Dobson. 112p. 1994. pap. 7.95 (0-9641160-0-6) Dobson Ent.

Venison Cookbook. Eileen Clarke. LC 96-23136. (Fish & Game Kitchen Ser.). (Illus.). 128p. 1997. 24.95 (0-89658-331-7) Voyageur Pr.

Venison Cookbook. A. D. Livingston. LC 93-4400. (Illus.). 128p. 1993. pap. 12.95 (0-8117-2594-4) Stackpole.

***Venison Cookery.** Cowles Creative Publishing Staff. LC 97-8256. (Hunting & Fishing Library). (Illus.). 128p. 1997. 19.95 (0-86573-068-7) Cowles Creative.

Venjance Alixandre. Jean Le Nevelon. Ed. by Edward B. Ham. (Elliott Monographs: Vol. 27). 1931. 25.00 (0-527-02630-1) Periodicals Srv.

Venom. Stephen Thomas. 24p. 1991. pap. 5.00 (0-685-54603-9) Current.

Venom: Carnage Unleased. Larry Hama. 1996. pap. text ed. 12.95 (0-7851-0199-3) Marvel Entmnt.

Venom: Deathtrap: The Vault. 64p. 1993. 6.95 (0-87135-975-8) Marvel Entmnt.

Venom: Lethal Protector. David Michelinie. (Illus.). 144p. 1995. pap. 15.95 (0-7851-0107-1) Marvel Entmnt.

Venom House. Arthur Upfield. 22.95 (0-8488-1212-3) Amereon Ltd.

***Venom of the Cobra.** large type ed. Robert Charles. (Linford Mystery Library). 368p. 1996. pap. 15.99 (0-7089-7906-8, Linford) Ulverscroft.

***Venom Phospholipase A 2 Enzymes: Structure, Function & Mechanism.** R. M. Kini. LC 96-27171. 1997. text ed. write for info. (0-471-96189-2) Wiley.

Venom Versus Me. Fred E. Katz. (Spine Chillers Ser.: Bk. 3). 144p. 1996. pap. 5.99 (0-7852-7480-4) Nelson.

***Venom Versus Me.** Fred E. Katz. LC 97-11114. (Spinechillers Ser.). (J). 1997. write for info. (0-8499-4058-3) Word Pub.

Venomous & Poisonous Animals. Anders Edstrom. LC 91-17454. 226p. (C). 1992. lib. bdg. 31.50 (0-89464-627-3) Krieger.

***Venomous & Poisonous Marine Animals: A Medical & Biological Handbook.** 4th ed. John Williamson et al. (Illus.). 800p. 1996. 130.00 (0-86840-279-6, Pub. by New South Wales Univ Pr AT) Intl Spec Bk.

Venomous & Poisonous Marine Invertebrates of the Indian Ocean. Rachakonda Nagabhushanam & F. E. Russell. (Illus.). 300p. 1996. lib. bdg. 115.00 (1-886106-56-8) Science Pubs.

Venomous Animals. Edmund D. Brodie. (Golden Guide Ser.). (Illus.). 160p. (J). (ps-3). 1989. 5.50 (0-307-24074-6, Golden Books) Western Pub.

Venomous Animals & Their Toxins. G. Habermehl. (Illus.). 210p. 1981. 37.95 (0-387-10780-0) Spr-Verlag.

Venomous Creatures of Australia. 3rd ed. Struan K. Sutherland. (Illus.). 128p. 1995. pap. 26.00 (0-19-553700-9) OUP.

Venomous Reptiles of Latin America. Jonathan Campbell & William W. Lamar. LC 88-47934. (Comstock Bk.). (Illus.). 440p. 1989. 65.00 (0-8014-2059-8) Cornell U Pr.

Venomous Reptiles of North America. Carl H. Ernst. LC 91-3535. (Illus.). 248p. 1992. 35.00 (1-56098-114-8) Smithsonian.

Venomous Sea Snakes: A Comprehensive Bibliography. Wendy A. Culotta & George V. Pickwell. 526p. (C). 1993. lib. bdg. 79.50 (0-89464-469-6) Krieger.

***Venomous Snakes: Ecology, Evolution, & Snakebite.** Ed. by Roger S. Thorpe et al. (Symposia of the Zoological Society of London Ser.: No. 70). (Illus.). 320p. 1996. 145.00 (0-19-854986-5) OUP.

Venomous Snakes of the World. W. P. Mara. (TS Ser.). (Illus.). 224p. 1993. text ed. 35.95 (0-86622-522-6, TS-189) TFH Pubns.

An Asterisk (*) at the beginning of an entry indicates that the title is appearing in BIP for the first time.

Venomous Teeth & Other Stories. Ed. by R. C. Sinha. 1989. 16.00 (*81-7001-053-5*, Pub. by Chanakya II) S Asia.

Venomous Woman: Fear of the Female in Literature. Margaret Hallissy. LC 87-10711. (Contributions in Women's Studies: No. 87). 192p. 1987. text ed. 45.00 (*0-313-25919-4*, HYV/, Greenwood Pr) Greenwood.

Venoms of the Hymenoptera. Ed. by Tom Piek. 1986. text ed. 199.00 (*0-12-554770-6*) Acad Pr.

***Venona - Soviet Espionage & American Response.** Michael Warner & Robert L. Benson. (Illus.). 556p. (Orig.). 1996. pap. 46.80 (*0-89412-265-7*, C-75) Aegean Park Pr.

***Venona Project.** Eric Breindel & Herbert Rom. 432p. 1998. 27.50 (*0-465-09842-8*) Basic.

***Venous Clinic.** 100p. 1997. pap. text ed. 11.00 (*1-86094-051-X*) World Scientific Pub.

Venous Disease & Miscellaneous Arte, Vol. 6. Ronald J. Stoney & David J. Effeney. (Illus.). 250p. 1993. text ed. 99.50 (*0-397-51206-6*) Lppncott-Raven.

Venous Disorders. John J. Bergan. (Illus.). 576p. 1990. text ed. 165.00 (*0-7216-3747-7*) Saunders.

Venous Imaging Techniques. Steven R. Talbot. 1992. 99.00 (*0-941022-23-4*) Davies Pubng.

Venous Interventional Radiology with Clinical Perspectives. Ed. by Scott J. Savader & Scott O. Trerotola. LC 95-45009. 1995. 125.00 (*0-86577-599-0*) Thieme Med Pubs.

Venous Leakage: Journal: Urologia Internationalis, Vol. 49, No. 1, 1992. Ed. by W. Weidner & G. Ludwig. (Illus.). 68p. 1992. pap. 74.00 (*3-8055-5643-8*) S Karger.

Venous Problems. Symposium on Venous Problems (1976: Northwestern University Medical School) Staff. Ed. by John J. Bergan & James S. Yao. LC 77-81529. 631p. reprint ed. pap. 179.90 (*0-318-34990-6*, 2030838) Bks Demand.

Venous Surgery in the Lower Extremity. Kenneth G. Swan. LC 74-2564. (Illus.). 442p. 1976. 31.80 (*0-87527-135-9*) Green.

Venous Thromboembolism: An Evidence-Based Atlas. Ed. by Russell D. Hull et al. LC 95-39036. (Illus.). 464p. 1996. 149.00 (*0-87993-633-9*) Futura Pub.

Venous Thromboembolism Natural History Diagnosis: Natural History, Diagnosis, & Management. R. D. Hull. Ed. by Jack Hirsh. LC 87-8043. 192p. 1987. 100.00 (*0-8493-4761-0*, RC697, CRC Reprint) Franklin.

Venous Thrombosis. Kakkar. write for info. (*0-7506-1370-X*) Buttrwrth-Heinemann.

Venous Thrombosis: Causation & Prediction. Derek Ogston. LC 87-8146. (Wiley-Medical Publication Ser.). 258p. reprint ed. pap. 73.60 (*0-8357-3473-0*, 2039735) Bks Demand.

***Venous Thrombosis: From Genes to Clinical Medicine.** Ed. by D. N. Cooper & M. Krawczak. (Human Molecular Genetics Ser.). (Illus.). 352p. 1997. 150.00 (*1-872748-94-5*, Pub. by Bios Sci UK) Bks Intl VA.

Venous Thrombosis & Pulmonary Embolism. Michael Hume et al. LC 70-122215. (Commonwealth Fund Publications). 472p. 1970. 45.00 (*0-674-93320-6*) HUP.

Venous Valves. R. Gottlob & R. May. (Illus.). 250p. 1986. 118.00 (*0-387-81898-7*) Spr-Verlag.

Venquetta. Barbara J. Williams. 120p. 1993. pap. 5.95 (*1-880365-14-6*) Prof Pr NC.

***Vent Book.** 1997. pap. 5.95 (*1-56352-404-X*) Longstreet Pr Inc.

Vent, Chronique, Chant Pour un Equinoxe. Saint-John Perse. (FRE.). 1968. pap. 10.95 (*0-8288-3825-9*, F123930) Fr & Eur.

Vent dans les Voiles. Jacques Perret. (FRE.). 1983. pap. 11.95 (*0-7859-4182-7*) Fr & Eur.

Vent de la Passion. Elizabeth Power. (Azur Ser.). (FRE.). 1994. pap. 3.50 (*0-373-34434-1*, 1-34434-0) Harlequin Bks.

***Vent de Liberte.** Marie-Danielle Croteau. (Novels in the Roman Plus Ser.). 160p. (FRE.). (YA). (gr. 8 up). 1996. pap. 7.95 (*2-89021-204-1*, Pub. by Les Editions CN) Firefly Bks Ltd.

Vent Paraclet. Michel Tournier. (Folio Ser.: No. 1138). (FRE.). pap. 9.95 (*2-07-037138-7*) Schoenhof.

Vent Paraclet. Michel Tournier. (FRE.). 1979. pap. 11.95 (*0-8288-3802-X*, M14979) Fr & Eur.

Vent Sur la Maison. Marilene Clement. 212p. (FRE.). 1979. pap. 10.95 (*0-7859-1882-5*, 2070370615) Fr & Eur.

Venta, Tabasco: A Study of Olmec Ceramics & Art. Philip Drucker. (Bureau of American Ethnology Bulletins Ser.). 257p. 1995. lib. bdg. 89.00 (*0-7812-4153-7*) Rprt Serv.

Ventaglio: Libretto by Domenico Gilardoni, after Carlo Goldoni Music by Pietro First Performance Naples, Teatro, Nuovo, 19 April 1831. Pietro Raimondi. LC 89-753856. (Italian Opera 1810-1840 Ser.: Vol. 40). 368p. 1990. text ed. 35.00 (*0-8240-6589-1*) Garland.

Ventana Secreta, Jardin Secreto. Stephen King. 208p. (SPA.). 1995. pap. 4.99 (*0-451-18657-5*, Sig) NAL-Dutton.

Vente Au Detail: Tous les Secrets Des Vendeurs Au Detail les Mieux Remuneres. John F. Lawhon & Catherine D. Lawhon. (Illus.). 395p. (FRE.). (C). 1990. 29.95 (*0-9616736-2-1*) J Franklin.

Ventilation: A Practical Guide. Nancy Clark et al. LC 84-12680. (Illus.). 128p. (Orig.). 1984. pap. text ed. 18.95 (*0-918875-00-5*) Ctr Occupational Hazards.

Ventilation: A Practical Guide for Artists, Craftspeople & Others in the Arts. Nancy Clark et al. 128p. 1987. reprint ed. pap. 18.95 (*0-941130-44-4*) Lyons & Burford.

Ventilation - Blood Flow & Gas Exchange. 5th ed. J. West. (Illus.). 128p. 1990. pap. 29.95 (*0-632-02855-6*) Blackwell Sci.

Ventilation & Drainage Maintainer. Jack Rudman. (Career Examination Ser.: C-1528). 1994. pap. 23.95 (*0-8373-1528-X*) Nat Learn.

Ventilation & Indoor Air Quality in Hospitals: Proceedings of a NATO Advanced Research Workshop, Held in Milano, Italy, on 13-16 September 1995. LC 96-17215. (NATO ASI Series: Partnership Sub-Series 2: Environment). 341p. 1996. lib. bdg. 178.00 (*0-7923-4076-0*) Kluwer Ac.

Ventilation Effectiveness in Mechanical Ventilation Systems. I. N. Potter. (C). 1988. 115.00 (*0-86022-189-X*, Pub. by Build Servs Info Assn UK) St Mut.

Ventilation for Control of the Work Environment. Richard Burgess et al. LC 88-31463. 496p. 1989. text ed. 84.95 (*0-471-89219-X*) Wiley.

Ventilation Heat Loss in Factories & Warehouses. 1992. 75.00 (*0-86022-206-3*, Pub. by Build Servs Info Assn UK) St Mut.

Ventilation Heat Loss in Factories & Warehouses. N. I. Potter & T. J. Jones. (C). 1992. 110.00 (*0-86022-296-9*, Pub. by Build Servs Info Assn UK) St Mut.

Ventilation of Agricultural Structures. Ed. by Hellickson & Walker. LC 83-72691. 374p. 1983. 40.50 (*0-916150-56-9*, M1083) Am Soc Ag Eng.

Ventilation of Buildings. H. B. Awbi. 384p. 1991. 79.95 (*0-419-15690-9*, E & FN Spon) Routledge Chapman & Hall.

Ventilation of School Buildings: A Study of Present Practices & Costs in the Light of Experimental Research. John R. McLure. LC 72-177035. (Columbia University. Teachers College. Contributions to Education Ser.: No. 157). reprint ed. 37.50 (*0-404-55157-2*) AMS Pr.

Ventilation System Hygiene. 1992. 75.00 (*0-685-68107-6*, Pub. by Build Servs Info Assn UK) St Mut.

Ventilation System Hygiene. 6th ed. S. R. Loyd. (C). 1993. 110.00 (*0-86022-377-9*, Pub. by Build Servs Info Assn UK) St Mut.

Ventilation System Hygiene: A Review. S. R. Loyd. 1993. 100.00 (*0-86022-356-6*, Pub. by Build Servs Info Assn UK) St Mut.

Ventilation, 1988: Proceedings of the 2nd International Symposium on Ventilation Contaminant Control, London 9-88. Ed. by J. Vincent. LC 89-4025. 1989. 255.00 (*0-08-036148-X*, Pub. by Pergamon Repr UK) Franklin.

Ventilations. rev. ed. Wilmot Robertson. LC 74-20120. 115p. 1982. pap. 12.00 (*0-914576-06-2*) Howard Allen.

Ventilator Concepts. 2nd ed. S. Mishoe & Neal Kelsey. 497p. (C). 1987. pap. text ed. 35.95 (*0-933195-15-X*) CA College Health Sci.

Ventilators: Theory & Clinical Applications. 2nd ed. Dupuis. (Illus.). 494p. (gr. 13). 1991. text ed. 58.95 (*0-8016-1462-7*) Mosby Yr Bk.

Ventilators & Muscular Dystrophy. Nancy C. Schock & Agatha P. Colbert. 40p. 1987. 6.00 (*0-931301-03-3*) Gazette Intl.

Ventilatory Failure. Ed. by J. L. Vincent et al. (Update in Intensive Care & Emergency Medicine Ser.: Vol. 15). (Illus.). xii, 456p. 1991. 114.95 (*0-387-54297-3*) Spr-Verlag.

Venting, Pt. 1. 2nd ed. Geoff Lunn. (Dust Explosion Prevention & Protection Guides Ser.). 214p. 1992. 50.00 (*0-85295-293-7*, 9CH1) Gulf Pub.

Venting of Weak Explosions & the Effect of Vent Ducts, Pt. 3. Geoff Lunn. (Dust Explosion Prevention & Protection Guides Ser.). 190p. 1988. pap. 30.00 (*0-85295-230-9*, 9CH33) Gulf Pub.

Ventral Mainstem Mechanisms & Control of Respiration & Blood Pressure. Ed. by C. Ovid Trouth. LC 95-10040. (Lung Biology in Health & Disease Ser.: Vol. 82). 992p. 1995. 195.00 (*0-8247-9514-8*) Dekker.

Ventre de Paris. Emile Zola. (Coll. Diamant). 413p. (FRE.). 1991. pap. 10.95 (*0-7859-1603-2*, 226603670X) Fr & Eur.

Ventre de Paris. Emile Zola. (Folio Ser.: No. 1107). (FRE.). pap. 10.95 (*2-07-037107-7*) Schoenhof.

Ventre de Paris. unabridged ed. Emile Zola. (FRE.). pap. 7.95 (*2-87714-229-9*, Pub. by Bookking Intl FR) Distribks Inc.

***Ventre du Serpent.** Chrystine Brouillet. (Roman Jeunesse Ser.). (Illus.). 96p. (FRE.). (J). (gr. 4 up). 1996. pap. 7.95 (*2-89021-262-9*, Pub. by Les Editions CN) Firefly Bks Ltd.

Ventricle: Basic & Clinical Aspects. Ed. by Herbert J. Levine & William H. Gaasch. LC 85-4976. 1985. lib. bdg. 204.50 (*0-89838-721-3*) Kluwer Ac.

Ventricle of Memory: Personal Recollections of Some Neurologists. Macdonald Critchley. 224p. 1989. text ed. 47.50 (*0-88167-599-7*, 2079) Lppncott-Raven.

Ventricular Arrhythmias of Ischemia & Infarction: Electrophysiological Mechanisms. Andrew L. Wit & Michiel J. Janse. (Illus.). 672p. 1992. 150.00 (*0-87993-376-3*) Futura Pub.

Ventricular Septum of the Heart. Ed. by Arnold C. Wenink et al. 1981. lib. bdg. 135.00 (*90-6021-486-2*) Kluwer Ac.

Ventricular Tachycardias. Ed. by Etienne Aliot & Ralph Lazzara. (Developments in Cardiovascular Medicine Ser.). 1987. lib. bdg. 230.50 (*0-89838-881-3*) Kluwer Ac.

Ventricular Vascular Coupling. Ed. by F. C. Yin. (Illus.). 480p. 1986. 129.00 (*0-387-96279-4*) Spr-Verlag.

Ventriloquism: Magic with Your Voice. George Schindler. (Illus.). 1986. pap. 6.95 (*0-679-14127-8*) McKay.

Ventriloquism for the Total Dummy. Dan Ritchard & Kathleen Moloney. LC 87-40186. 96p. 1987. pap. 7.95 (*0-394-75638-X*, Villard Bks) Random.

Ventriloquism in a Nutshell. Clinton Detweiler. (Illus.). 1974. pap. 5.00 (*0-686-20905-2*, 065) Maher Ventril Studio.

***Ventriloquism Made Easy.** Kolby King. LC 96-52592. 96p. (Orig.). 1997. pap. text ed. 5.95 (*0-486-29683-0*) Dover.

Ventriloquism Made Easy: How to Talk to Your Hand Without Looking Stupid. Paul Stadelman & Bruce Fife. LC 88-13439. (Illus.). 102p. (Orig.). 1989. 14.00 (*0-941599-08-6*, Empire Pub Srvs); pap. 8.00 (*0-941599-06-X*, Empire Pub Srvs) Piccadilly Bks.

Ventriloquist: New & Selected Poems. Robert Huff. LC 77-1338. (Virginia Commonwealth University Series for Contemporary Poetry). 58p. 1977. text ed. 10.95 (*0-8139-0725-X*) U Pr of Va.

Ventriloquist in the Rain: A Collection of Poems by Bruce Meyers. Ed. by Christene Cosbriffe-Meyers. LC 92-72999. (Illus.). 100p. 1992. 14.95 (*0-9623036-3-1*) ConAmore Pub.

Ventriloquists: Anthology. Ed. by David Wilde. (Sun Also Sets Ser.). (Illus.). (Orig.). 1992. pap. 12.95 (*0-9625472-6-3*) Wilde Pub.

Ventriloquized Bodies: Narratives of Hysteria in Nineteenth-Century France. Janet Beizer. (Illus.). 312p. 1994. 47.50 (*0-8014-2914-5*); pap. 17.95 (*0-8014-8142-2*) Cornell U Pr.

Ventriloquized Voices. Harvey. 184p. (C). 1995. pap. 15.95 (*0-415-12793-9*) Routledge.

Ventriloquized Voices: Feminist Theory & English Renaissance Texts. Elizabeth D. Harvey. LC 92-4510. 320p. (C). (gr. 13). 1992. text ed. 59.95 (*0-415-06732-4*, A7976) Routledge.

Ventry. Daniel C. Lynch. 1990. 16.95 (*1-55972-049-2*, Birch Ln Pr) Carol Pub Group.

Vents Chroniques. Saint-John Perse. Bd. with Chronique. (Poesie Ser.). (FRE.). Set pap. 6.95 (*2-07-030247-4*) Schoenhof.

Ventura County Companion. Tom Tuttle. (Illus.). 128p. (Orig.). 1988. pap. 8.95 (*0-945092-02-4*) EZ Nature.

Ventura County Street Guide & Directory: 1997 Edition. (Illus.). 104p. 1996. pap. 16.95 (*0-88130-847-1*) Thomas Bros Maps.

***Ventura County Street Guide & Directory: 1998 Edition.** Thomas Bros. Maps Staff. 104p. 1997. pap. 16.95 (*0-88130-916-8*) Thomas Bros Maps.

Ventura Design Companion. Jesse Berst. 300p. 1990. pap. 24.95 (*1-878567-03-9*) D A Pub.

Ventura Desktop Publishing for the PC. William R. Pasewark. (DF - Computer Applications Ser.). 1993. pap. 21.95 (*0-87835-694-0*) Course Tech.

Ventura Tips & Tricks. 3rd ed. Ted Nace & Daniel Will-Harris. (Illus.). 720p. (Orig.). pap. 27.95 (*0-938151-20-7*) Peachpit Pr.

Ventura 3 by Example: Windows Edition. Webster & Associates Staff. (Illus.). 544p. pap. 24.95 (*0-938151-27-4*) Peachpit Pr.

Venture: A Business Novel about Starting Your Own Company. Jeff Cox. 352p. 1997. 24.00 (*0-446-51641-4*) Warner Bks.

Venture Adventure: Strategies for Thriving in the Jungle of Entrepreneurship. Daryl Bernstein & Joe Hammond. LC 94-44135. (Illus.). 200p. (C). 1996. 18.95 (*1-885223-11-0*); pap. 12.95 (*1-885223-09-9*) Beyond Words Pub.

Venture Books, 3 vols. Orig. Title: Bob. 41.79 (*0-531-06929-X*) Watts.

Venture Capital. Levin. 1995. 125.00 (*0-316-52276-7*) Little.

Venture Capital. Ed. by Mike Wright & Ken Robbie. (International Library of Management). 500p. 1997. text ed. 142.95 (*1-85521-855-0*, Pub. by Dartmth Pub UK) Ashgate Pub Co.

Venture Capital: Law, Business Strategies, & Investments. J. W. Bartlett. 60p. 1992. suppl. ed., pap. text ed. 45.00 (*0-471-03337-5*) Wiley.

***Venture Capital & Junk Bond Financing.** Frederick D. Lipman. 859p. 1996. 90.00 (*0-8318-0712-1*) Am Law Inst.

***Venture Capital & New Technology Based Firms: A U. S.-German Comparison.** O. Pfirrmann et al. Ed. by Fraunhofer Institute for Systems & Innovation Research (ISI) Staff. (Technology, Innovation & Policy Ser.: Vol. 4). (Illus.). xii, 153p. 1997. pap. 59.00 (*3-7908-0968-3*) Spr-Verlag.

Venture Capital & Public Offering Negotiation. annuals Ed. by Michael J. Halloran. 890p. 1983. Annual supplements avail. suppl. ed. 95.00 (*0-15-004282-5*, H42825) HarBrace.

Venture Capital & Public Offering Negotiation. Michael J. Halloran. write for info. (*0-318-66010-5*) P-H.

Venture Capital & Small Business Financings, 5 vols. Robert J. Haft. LC 84-14514. 1984. Set. ring bd. 695.00 (*0-87632-447-2*) Clark Boardman Callaghan.

Venture Capital & the Indian Financial Sector. Srinivasan Ramesh & Arun Gupta. 250p. 1995. 27.00 (*0-19-563633-3*) OUP.

Venture Capital at the Crossroads. William D. Bygrave & Jeffry A. Timmons. LC 92-2603. 368p. 1992. 35.00 (*0-87584-304-2*) Harvard Busn.

Venture Capital at the Crossroads. William D. Bygrave & sJeffry A. Timmon. 1992. text ed. 39.95 (*0-07-103315-7*) McGraw.

***Venture Capital Financing in India.** J. C. Verma. LC 97-9986. 1997. pap. write for info. (*0-8039-9356-0*) Sage.

***Venture Capital Financing in India.** J. C. Verma. LC 97-9986. 244p. 1997. text ed. 28.00 (*0-8039-9355-2*) Sage.

Venture Capital Handbook. rev. ed. David J. Gladstone. (Illus.). 416p. 1987. pap. 32.95 (*0-13-941501-7*) P-H.

Venture Capital in Britain, America & Japan. Rodney Clark. LC 86-28001. 128p. 1987. text ed. 39.95 (*0-312-00505-9*) St Martin.

Venture Capital in High-Tech Companies: The Electronics Business in Perspective. George Young. LC 85-12057. viii, 213p. 1985. text ed. 55.00 (*0-89930-146-0*, YVC/, Quorum Bks) Greenwood.

Venture Capital Inside Out: An Entrepreneur's Guide to How the System Works. Roy G. Helsing. LC 88-50083. 128p. (Orig.). 1988. pap. 10.00 (*0-945901-03-8*) Transwest Ventures.

Venture Capital Investing: The Complete Handbook for Investing in Small Private Businesses for Outstanding Profits. David J. Gladstone. 512p. 1987. 39.95 (*0-13-941428-2*) P-H.

Venture Capital of Higher Education: The Private & Public Sources of Discretionary Funds. Martin Kramer. LC 80-65491. 95p. reprint ed. pap. 27.10 (*0-317-55386-0*, 2029491) Bks Demand.

Venture Capital Process: A Guide for Economic Development Practitioners. Alan Gregerman. Ed. by Jenny Murphy & Andrea Kailo. 30p. (Orig.). 1985. pap. 16.00 (*0-317-04845-7*) Natl Coun Econ Dev.

Venture Capital Sourcebook: The Definitive Guide to Finding Start-Up Funds & Growth Capital. A. David Silver. 450p. 1994. per. 29.95 (*1-55738-558-0*) Irwin Prof Pubng.

Venture Cycling. Boy Scouts of America Staff. (Illus.). 36p. (Orig.). 1989. pap. 3.75 (*0-8395-3437-X*, 3437) BSA.

Venture Discovering Adventure. Boy Scouts of America Staff. (Illus.). 20p. (YA). 1990. pap. 3.75 (*0-8395-3472-8*, 33472) BSA.

Venture Feasibility Plan. Robert C. Ronstadt. 1988. 19.95 (*0-930204-25-5*) Lord Pub.

Venture Feasibility Plan Workbook. 29.95 (*0-685-69353-8*); 39.95 (*0-685-69354-6*) Lord Pub.

Venture Feasibility Planning Guide. Robert C. Ronstadt. 150p. 1988. pap. 19.95 (*0-930204-21-2*) Lord Pub.

Venture Fishing. Boy Scouts of America Staff. (Illus.). 70p. (Orig.). 1989. pap. 3.75 (*0-8395-3438-8*, 3438) BSA.

Venture Freestyle Biking. Boy Scouts of America Staff. (Illus.). 52p. (YA). 1990. pap. 3.75 (*0-8395-3447-7*, 3447) BSA.

Venture into Cultures: A Resource Book of Multicultural Materials & Programs. Ed. by Carla D. Hayden. LC 91-43373. (Illus.). 270p. (C). 1993. pap. text ed. 25.00 (*0-8389-0579-X*) ALA.

Venture Inward. Hugh L. Cayce. LC 95-43166. 238p. 1995. reprint ed. pap. 13.95 (*0-87604-354-6*, 467) ARE Pr.

Venture of Islam, 3 vols. Marshall G. Hodgson. Incl. Vol. 1. Venture of Islam Vol. 1: The Classical Age of Islam. LC 73-87243. (Illus.). xii, 532p. 1977. pap. text ed. 19.95 (*0-226-34683-8*, P716); Vol. 2. Venture of Islam Vol. 2: The Expansion of Islam in the Middle Periods. LC 73-87243. (Illus.). viii, 610p. 1977. pap. text ed. 22.50 (*0-226-34684-6*, P717); Vol. 3. Venture of Islam Vol. 3: Conscience & History in World Civilization. LC 73-87243. (Illus.). vi, 470p. 1977. pap. text ed. 18.95 (*0-226-34685-4*, P718); LC 73-87243. (Illus.). 716p. 1977. Set pap. text ed. write for info. (*0-318-56082-8*) U Ch Pr.

***Venture of Islam: The Gunpowder Empires & Modern Times.** Marshall G. Hodgson. 560p. 1996. pap. 22.50 (*0-614-21174-3*, 1284) Kazi Pubns.

Venture of Islam Vol. 3: Conscience & History in World Civilization, Vol. 3. Marshall G. Hodgson. LC 73-87243. (Venture of Islam). (Illus.). vi, 470p. 1977. pap. text ed. 18.95 (*0-226-34685-4*, P718) U Ch Pr.

***Venture of Islam Vol. I: The Classical Age of Islam.** Marshall G. Hodgson. 532p. 1996. pap. 18.95 (*0-614-21172-7*, 1282) Kazi Pubns.

***Venture of Islam Vol. II: The Expansion of Islam in the Middle Periods.** Marshall G. Hodgson. 550p. 1996. pap. 19.95 (*0-614-21173-5*, 1283) Kazi Pubns.

Venture of Islam, Vol. 1, The Classical Age of Islam see Venture of Islam

Venture of Islam, Vol. 2, The Expansion of Islam in the Middle Periods see Venture of Islam

Venture of Islam, Vol. 3, Conscience & History in World Civilization see Venture of Islam

Venture Orienteering. Boy Scouts of America Staff. (Illus.). 36p. (Orig.). 1989. pap. 3.75 (*0-8395-3439-6*, 3439) BSA.

Venture Snow Camping. Boy Scouts of America Staff. (Illus.). 80p. (Orig.). 1989. pap. 3.75 (*0-8395-3440-X*, 33440) BSA.

***Venture Survival.** Boy Scouts of America Staff. (Illus.). 46p. (Orig.). 1996. pap. 3.75 (*0-8395-3483-3*, 33483) BSA.

***Venture to Oregon.** Gordon Hull. Ed. by Gregory M. Franzwa. 240p. (Orig.). (YA). 1993. pap. 10.95 (*1-880397-04-8*) Patrice Pr.

Venture Whitewater. Boy Scouts of America Staff. (Illus.). 70p. (YA). 1990. pap. 3.75 (*0-8395-3465-5*, 33465) BSA.

Venture with Ideas. Kenneth Walker. 160p. 1996. 30.00 (*1-898942-04-8*); pap. 16.00 (*1-898942-05-6*) Weatherhill.

Ventures in Common Sense. E. W. Howe. (Collected Works of E. W. Howe). 1988. reprint ed. lib. bdg. 59.00 (*0-7812-1297-9*) Rprt Serv.

Ventures in Common Sense see Collected Works of E. W. Howe

Ventures in Discipleship. John R. Martin. LC 84-19140. 304p. (Orig.). 1984. pap. 16.99 (*0-8361-3378-1*) Herald Pr.

Ventures in Social Interpretation. Henry Winthrop. LC 68-24073. (Century Sociology Ser.). (Illus.). (Orig.). (C). 1968. pap. text ed. 9.95 (*0-89197-465-2*) Irvington.

Ventures in Thought. Francis B. Latymer. LC 67-23238. (Essay Index Reprint Ser.). 1977. 20.95 (*0-8369-0610-1*) Ayer.

Ventures into Greek History. Ed. by Ian Worthington. (Illus.). 432p. 1994. 75.00 (*0-19-814928-X*) OUP.

Venture's Story: Life & Times of a Guide Dog. Diana Dawne. 304p. 1997. pap. 19.95 (*0-9644857-3-7*) Wrds & Pict Pr.

VentureTrac (r) Complete Business Development Program. Andrew J. Batchelor, Jr. & Timothy E. Nesmith. (Illus.). 480p. (Orig.). 1994. Incl. software. 129.00 incl. disk (0-9623374-3-9) Tangent Pub.

Venturi - Scott Brown: Two Responses to Some Immediate Issues. (C). 1993. pap. 5.00 (0-88454-070-7) U of Pa Contemp Art.

Venturi Analysis. rev. ed. Ken Venturi & Al Barkow. (Classics of Golf Ser.). (Illus.). 160p. 28.00 (0-940889-08-0) Classics Golf.

***Venturi Scott Brown.** 1992. pap. 38.00 (0-312-07148-5) St Martin.

***Venturi Scott Brown, Vol. 1.** 1992. 55.00 (0-312-07244-9) St Martin.

Venturi, Scott Brown: On Houses & Housing. (Architectural Monographs). (Illus.). 144p. (Orig.). 1992. 55.00 (1-85490-093-5); pap. 38.00 (1-85490-098-6) Academy Ed UK.

Venturing Abroad: Innovation by U. S. Multinationals. Frank C. Schuller. LC 87-37574. 177p. 1988. text ed. 55.00 (0-89930-129-0, SMT/, Quorum Bks) Greenwood.

Venturing Abroad: International Business Expansion Via Joint Ventures. Jack Enen, Jr. 260p. 1990. 27.95 (0-8306-8653-3, 3653) McGraw-Hill Prof.

***Venturing into a Child's World.** 2nd ed. Richard D. Dobbins. 189p. 1992. pap. 8.00 (1-890329-08-8) Totally Alive.

Venturing to Do Justice: Reforming Private Law. Robert E. Keeton. LC 69-18035. 192p. 1969. 25.00 (0-674-93355-9) HUP.

***Venue 1.** 172p. (C). 1997. 10.00 (90-5701-371-1) Dist Art Pubs.

***Venue 2.** 172p. (C). 1997. 10.00 (90-5701-381-9) Dist Art Pubs.

***Venue 3.** 172p. (C). 1997. 10.00 (90-5701-391-6) Dist Art Pubs.

Venues. Mark Dunster. 25p. (Orig.). (YA). (gr. 9-12). 1996. pap. 5.00 (0-89642-311-5) Linden Pubs.

Venus. Duncan Brewer. LC 90-40808. (Planet Guides Ser.). (Illus.). 64p. (J). (gr. 5-9). 1992. lib. bdg. 17.95 (1-85435-370-5) Marshall Cavendish.

Venus. Ed. by Donald M. Hunten et al. LC 83-1064. 1143p. 1983. 76.00 (0-8165-0788-0) U of Ariz Pr.

***Venus.** Steven L. Kipp. LC 97-6923. (Galaxy Ser.). (J). 1998. write for info. (1-56065-609-3) Capstone Pr.

***Venus.** Suzan-Lori Parks. 1997. pap. 5.25 (0-8222-1567-5) Dramatists Play.

***Venus.** Suzan-Lori Parks. LC 97-5739. 96p. (Orig.). 1997. pap. 10.95 (1-55936-135-2) Theatre Comm.

Venus. Muriel Schloss. LC 90-13101. (First Bks.). (Illus.). 64p. (J). (gr. 3-5). 1991. lib. bdg. 21.00 (0-531-20019-1) Watts.

Venus. Seymour Simon. LC 91-12171. (Illus.). 32p. (J). (gr. k up). 1992. 15.00 (0-688-10542-4, Morrow Junior); lib. bdg. 14.93 (0-688-10543-2, Morrow Junior) Morrow.

Venus. Gregory L. Vogt. LC 93-11217. (Gateway Solar System Ser.). (Illus.). 32p. (J). (gr. 2-4). 1994. lib. bdg. 14.90 (1-56294-391-X) Millbrook Pr.

Venus. Gregory L. Vogt. (Gateway Solar System Ser.). (Illus.). 32p. (J). (gr. 2-4). 1996. 6.95 (0-7613-0159-3) Millbrook Pr.

Venus. rev. ed. Dennis B. Fradin. LC 88-39121. (New True Bks.). (Illus.). 48p. (J). (gr. k-4). 1993. pap. 5.50 (0-516-41168-3); lib. bdg. 19.00 (0-516-01168-5) Childrens.

Venus. Muriel Schloss. (First Bks.). (Illus.). 64p. (J). (gr. 4-6). 1996. reprint ed. pap. 5.95 (0-531-15772-5) Watts.

***Venus, Vol. II.** Ed. by Hutton Bougher et al. (Space Science Ser.). (C). Date not set. text ed. 95.00 (0-8165-1841-6) U of Ariz Pr.

Venus: A New Geology. Peter Cattermole. (Illus.). 256p. (C). 1996. reprint ed. pap. text ed. 19.95 (0-8018-5418-0) Johns Hopkins.

Venus: Magellan Explores Our Twin Planet. Franklyn M. Branley. LC 92-32990. (Voyage into Space Bk.). (Illus.). 64p. (J). (gr. 3-6). 1994. lib. bdg. 15.89 (0-06-020384-6) HarpC Child Bks.

Venus: The Gift of Love. Martin Schulman. LC 81-90119. (Illus.). 150p. (Orig.). 1981. pap. 7.95 (0-940086-00-X) Golden Light.

Venus, a New Geology. Peter Cattermole. LC 93-11636. 256p. (C). 1994. 49.95 (0-8018-4787-7) Johns Hopkins.

Venus Aeronomy. C. T. Russell. (C). 1991. lib. bdg. 266.50 (0-7923-1091-8) Kluwer Ac.

Venus after Forty: Sexual Myths, Men's Fantasies, & Truths about Middle-Aged Women. Rita M. Ransohoff. LC 87-12233. 289p. 1987. 20.95 (0-88282-034-6) New Horizon NJ.

Venus after Forty: Sexual Myths, Men's Fantasies & Truths about Middle Aged Women. Rita M. Ransohoff. LC 87-12233. 289p. 1990. pap. 11.95 (0-88282-064-8) New Horizon NJ.

Venus among the Fishes. Elizabeth Hall & Scott O'Dell. LC 94-48133. 160p. (YA). (gr. 5 up). 1995. 15.95 (0-395-70561-4) HM.

Venus Among the Fishes. Elizabeth Hall & Scott O'Dell. 160p. (J). (gr. 4-7). 1996. pap. 3.99 (0-440-41175-0, YB BDD) BDD Bks Young Read.

Venus & Adonis: A Study in Warwickshire Dialect. Ed. by James A. Morgan. LC 76-169261. (Shakespeare Society of New York. Publications: No. 2). reprint ed. 27.50 (0-404-54202-6) AMS Pr.

Venus & Adonis: Critical Essays. Philip C. Kolin. LC 96-37751. (Shakespeare Criticism Ser.: Vol. 16). (Illus.). 448p. 1997. text ed. 75.00 (0-8153-2149-X) Garland.

Venus & Don Juan. Carol Frost. LC 96-23430. 90p. 1996. 29.95 (0-8101-5062-X); pap. 11.95 (0-8101-5063-8) TriQuarterly.

Venus & Mars: Atmospheres, Ionospheres, & Solar Wind Interactions. Ed. by J. G. Luhmann et al. (Geophysical Monograph Ser.: Vol. 66). (Illus.). 448p. 1992. 59.00 (0-87590-032-1) Am Geophysical.

Venus & Mars: Engendering Love & War in Medieval & Early Modern Europe. Ed. by Andrew Lynch & Philippa Maddern. 216p. (C). 1995. pap. 24.95 (1-875560-45-9, Pub. by Univ of West Aust Pr AT) Intl Spec Bk.

Venus & Sothis: How the Ancient Near East Was Rediscovered. Wilbur D. Jones. LC 81-11130. 200p. (C). 1981. text ed. 36.95 (0-88229-691-4) Nelson-Hall.

***Venus & the Rain.** Medbh McGuckian. 56p. 1994. pap. 12.95 (1-85235-143-8) Dufour.

Venus Atmosphere. Ed. by G. M. Keating. (Advances in Space Research Ser.: No. 10). (Illus.). 52p. 1989. pap. 95.75 (0-08-040160-0, Pergamon Pr) Elsevier.

Venus Bound: The Erotic Voyage of the Olympia Press & Its Writers. rev. ed. John De St. Jorre. LC 95-37778. Orig. Title: The Good Ship Venus. (Illus.). 384p. 1996. 27.50 (0-679-44336-3) Random.

Venus Butterfly. 220p. 1989. pap. 3.95 (0-88184-489-6) Carroll & Graf.

Venus Delights. 224p. 1986. pap. 3.95 (0-88184-242-7) Carroll & Graf.

Venus d'Ile et Autres Nouvelles: Dossier de Lectures. Prosper Merimee. (FRE.). 1982. pap. 10.95 (0-7859-2980-0) Fr & Eur.

Venus d'Ille: Les Ames du Purgatoire. Prosper Merimee. (Illus.). 135p. (FRE.). 1991. pap. 8.95 (0-7859-4691-8) Fr & Eur.

Venus Disposes. 240p. 1988. pap. 3.95 (0-88184-426-8) Carroll & Graf.

Venus Envy. Rita Mae Brown. 400p. 1994. mass mkt. 6.50 (0-553-56497-8) Bantam.

***Venus Envy: A History of Plastic Surgery.** Elizabeth Haiken. LC 97-19823. 1997. write for info. (0-8018-5763-5) Johns Hopkins.

Venus Fly Traps & Waterwheels: Spring Traps of the Plant World. Victor Gentle. LC 96-12511. (Bloodthirsty Plants! Ser.). (J). 1996. lib. bdg. 15.93 (0-8368-1659-5) Gareth Stevens Inc.

Venus Geologic Mappers' Handbook. K. L. Tanaka et al. (Illus.). 54p. (Orig.). (YA). (gr. 12 up). 1994. pap. text ed. 35.00 (0-7881-0853-0) DIANE Pub.

Venus Geology, Geochemistry, & Geophysics: Research Results from the Soviet Union. Ed. by V. L. Barsukov et al. LC 91-25232. (Illus.). 421p. 1992. 82.50 (0-8165-1222-1) U of Ariz Pr.

Venus Hottentot. Elizabeth Alexander. Ed. by Charles H. Rowell. (Callaloo Poetry Ser.). 52p. 1990. pap. 8.95 (0-8139-1273-3) U Pr of Va.

Venus in Copper. Lindsey Davis. 1993. mass mkt. 4.50 (0-345-37390-1) Ballantine.

Venus in Furs. Guido Crepax. Ed. by Bernd Metz. Tr. by James Keller from GER. 64p. (Orig.). 1991. pap. 11.95 (0-87416-091-X) Catalan Communs.

Venus in Furs. Guido Crepax & Count Masoch. (Illus.). 64p. (Orig.). 1996. pap. 11.95 (1-56163-147-7, Eurotica) NBM.

***Venus in Furs.** Leopole Von Sacher-Masoch. Tr. by Uwe Moeller & Laura Lundgren. 1997. reprint ed. mass mkt. 7.95 (1-56333-589-1, Rhinoceros) Masquerade.

Venus in Furs & Collected Letters of Sacher-Masoch. Leopold Von Sacher-Masoch. 1989. pap. 9.95 (0-922233-01-2) Blast Bks.

Venus in Furs & Letters of Sacher-Masoch. Leopold Von Sacher-Masoch. 280p. (Orig.). (C). 1989. pap. 9.95 (0-685-22944-0) Blast Bks.

Venus in Hollywood: The Continental Enchantress from Garbo to Loren. Michael Bruno. LC 71-90838. (Illus.). 1970. 6.95 (0-8184-0091-9) Carol Pub Group.

Venus in India. 300p. 1987. pap. 3.95 (0-88184-365-2) Carroll & Graf.

***Venus in Spurs.** Sheila Gillooly. 1997. pap. 12.95 (0-8050-5355-7, Owl) H Holt & Co.

Venus in Spurs: The Secret Female Fear of Commitment, or, Why You Head for the Hills When Love Comes to You. Sheila Gillooly. LC 95-32623. 256p. 1996. 20.00 (0-8050-3552-4) H Holt & Co.

Venus in the Kitchen: Recipes for Seduction. Pilaff Bey, pseud. LC 91-28238. (Illus.). 208p. 1992. pap. 13.95 (1-879904-01-2) Halo Bks.

Venus International Reference Atmosphere. Ed. by A. J. Kliore et al. (Illus.). 314p. 1986. pap. 52.00 (0-08-034631-6, Pub. by PPL UK) Elsevier.

Venus Internationale suivi de Dinah Miami. Pierre M. Orlan. (FRE.). 1981. pap. 11.95 (0-7859-4160-6) Fr & Eur.

Venus Love: Potpourri Poetry. Scentouri Staff. (Orig.). 1985. pap. text ed. 4.50 (0-318-04388-2, Scentouri) Prosperity & Profits.

Venus, Mars & Satellites of the Outer Planets: Proceedings of Symposium 3 of the COSPAR Twenty-Fifth Plenary Meeting Held in Graz, Austria, 25 June-7 July 1984. Ed. by R. W. Shorthill. (Illus.). 132p. 1985. pap. 54.00 (0-08-033197-1, Pub. by PPL UK) Elsevier.

Venus Observed. Christopher Fry. 1953. pap. 5.25 (0-8222-1206-4) Dramatists Play.

Venus of Milo: An Archaeological Study of the Goddess of Womanhood. Paul Carus. 1977. lib. bdg. 59.95 (0-8490-2796-9) Gordon Pr.

Venus on the Half-Shell. Kilgore Trout. 204p. 1992. reprint ed. lib. bdg. 25.95 (0-89968-306-1, Lghtyr Pr) Buccaneer Bks.

***Venus Online.** Alison Tyler. (Orig.). 1997. mass mkt. 6.50 (1-56333-521-2, Rosebud) Masquerade.

Venus Peter Saves the Whale. Christopher Rush. LC 92-7808. (Illus.). 32p. (J). (gr. 4-7). 1992. 14.95 (0-88289-928-7) Pelican.

Venus Plus X. Theodore Sturgeon. 224p. 1988. pap. 3.95 (0-88184-387-3) Carroll & Graf.

Venus Plus X. Richard A. Wright. 21.95 (0-8488-1229-8) Amereon Ltd.

Venus Project: The Redesign of a Culture. Jacque Fresco. (Illus.). 56p. (Orig.). 1995. pap. 14.95 incl. vhs (0-9648806-0-1) Glbl Cyber-Vsns.

Venus Revealed: A New Look below the Clouds of Our Mysterious Twin Planet. David H. Grinspoon. Ed. by Jeffrey Robbins. 304p. (C). 1997. 27.50 (0-201-40655-1) Addison-Wesley.

***Venus Revealed: A New Look Below the Clouds of Our Mysterious Twin Planet.** David H. Grinspoon. 1997. 27.50 (0-614-20425-9) Addison-Wesley.

Venus Rising. 640p. 1996. mass mkt. 7.95 (0-7867-0392-X) Carroll & Graf.

Venus Rising. Flora M. Speer. 368p. 1996. mass mkt. 4.99 (0-505-52116-4, Love Spell) Dorchester Pub Co.

Venus Throw. Steven W. Saylor. LC 94-44488. 1995. 22.95 (0-312-11912-7) St Martin.

Venus Throw. Steven W. Saylor. 416p. 1996. mass mkt. 5.99 (0-312-95778-5) Tor Bks.

Venus Throw. large type ed. Steven W. Saylor. 587p. 1995. 25.95 (0-7838-1443-7, GK Hall) Thorndike Pr.

***Venus to the Hoop: A Gold Medal Year in Women's Basketball.** Sara Corbett. 1997. 23.95 (0-385-48682-0) Doubleday.

Venus Tree. Michael Pritchett. LC 88-21795. (John Simmons Short Fiction Award Ser.). 138p. 1988. 19.95 (0-87745-220-2) U of Iowa Pr.

Venus Wars, Vol. 1. Yoshikazu Yasuhiko. Tr. by Alan Gleason & Toren Smith from JPN. (Illus.). 256p. 1993. pap. 13.95 (1-878574-62-0) Dark Horse Comics.

Venus with Pistol. large type ed. Gavin Lyall. 1975. 25.99 (0-85456-370-9) Ulverscroft.

Venuses Penuses. John Money. 659p. 1986. 41.95 (0-87975-327-7) Prometheus Bks.

Venusian Lullaby. Paul Leonard. (Dr. Who Missing Adventures Ser.). (Illus.). 1995. mass mkt. 5.95 (0-426-20424-7, Pub. by Virgin Pub UK) London Brdge.

Venustiano Carranza's Nationalist Struggle, 1893-1920. Douglas W. Richmond. LC 83-3652. (Illus.). 347p. reprint ed. pap. 98.90 (0-8357-2942-7, 2039198) Bks Demand.

Veo: Un Libro de Adivinanzas Ilustradas. Jean Marzollo. (Illus.). 40p. (J). (ps-3). 1994. 12.95 (0-590-48635-7, Cartwheel) Scholastic Inc.

***Veo Formas.** Marcia Fries. Ed. by Christine Hood. Tr. by Rancho Park Publishing Staff. (Math Spanish Learn to Read Ser.). (Illus.). 8p. (Orig.). (SPA.). (J). (ps-2). 1996. pap. 1.59 (1-57471-153-9, 4079) Creat Teach Pr.

Veo Navidad. Jean Marzolla. 40p. (SPA.). (J). 1995. 12.95 (0-590-50197-6) Scholastic Inc.

Veo, Veo - Semilla: Spanish Take-Home Parent Pack, Set. (Illus.). (Orig.). 1993. pap. 16.95 (1-56334-381-9) Hampton-Brown.

Veo, Veo, Que Veo? (Big Book) Lada J. Kratky. (Rimas y Risas Red Ser.). (Illus.). 16p. (Orig.). (SPA.). (J). (gr. k-3). 1990. pap. text ed. 29.95 (0-917837-57-6) Hampton-Brown.

Veo, Veo, Que Veo? (Small Book) Lada J. Kratky. (Rimas y Risas Red Ser.). (Illus.). 16p. (Orig.). (SPA.). (J). (gr. k-3). 1992. pap. text ed. 6.00 (1-56334-082-8) Hampton-Brown.

Ver Al Abuelito. Bernice Myers. Tr. by Argentina Palachos. (Spanish Whole Language Big Bks.). (Illus.). 16p. (Orig.). (SPA.). (J). (ps-2). 1994. pap. 14.95 (1-56784-095-7) Newbridge Comms.

Ver Hablar. Yves Jacot. 1981. pap. text ed. 123.64 (0-201-03609-6) Addison-Wesley.

Ver Planck: History of Abraham Isaacse Ver Planck & His Male Descendants in America. Wm. E. Ver Planck. 304p. 1994. reprint ed. pap. 47.00 (0-8328-4391-1); reprint ed. lib. bdg. 57.00 (0-8328-4390-3) Higginson Bk Co.

Vera. Elizabeth Von Arnim. Ed. by Donna Ng. 208p. 1995. reprint ed. pap. 12.00 (0-671-88391-7, WSP) PB.

Vera Brittain: A Feminist Life. Deborah Gorham. (Illus.). 368p. 1996. 37.95 (0-631-14715-2) Blackwell Pubs.

Vera Brittain: A Life. Paul Berry & Mark Bostridge. (Illus.). 580p. 1996. 35.00 (0-7011-2679-5, Pub. by Chatto & Windus UK) Trafalgar.

Vera Brittain & Winifred Holtby: A Working Partnershp. Jean E. Kennard. LC 88-40351. (Illus.). 238p. 1989. pap. 17.95 (0-87451-482-7) U Pr of New Eng.

Vera Brittain's Diary: 1939-1945. large type ed. Vera Brittain. 512p. 1993. 27.99 (0-7089-8716-8) Ulverscroft.

Vera Brown's Natural Beauty Book. Vera Brown. 1983. 15.95 (0-02-499870-2, Macmillan Coll) P-H.

Vera Cucina: Traditional Recipes from the Homes & Farms of Italy. Carlo Middione. 416p. 1996. 35.00 (0-684-81206-1, S&S) S&S Trade.

Vera Cucina Italiana. Donaldo Soviero. 352p. 1991. 24.95 (0-02-612570-6) Macmillan.

Vera Greenfeld: A Journey from Godyach to Berkeley. Ida Frank. (Illus.). 130p. 1988. pap. 10.95 (0-943376-40-8) Magnes Mus.

Vera I Obraz: Religioznoe Bessoznatel'noe v Russkoi Kul'ture 20-go Veka. Mikhail Epshtein. LC 94-21383. 270p. (Orig.). (RUS.). 1994. pap. 18.00 (1-55779-070-1) Hermitage.

***Vera in the Washtub.** Marjolein Bastin. (Vera the Mouse Ser.). (J). 1988. 2.95 (0-8120-6088-1) Barron.

Vera: or The Nihilist. Oscar Wilde. Ed. by Frances M. Reed. LC 88-32565. (Studies in British Literature: Vol. 4). (Illus.). 103p. 1989. lib. bdg. 69.95 (0-88946-931-8) E Mellen.

Vera Panova - Stranitsy Zhizni: K Biografii Pisatel'Nitsy. Yurieva Serafima. LC 93-16160. (Illus.). 120p. (Orig.). (RUS.). 1993. pap. 10.00 (1-55779-059-0) Hermitage.

Vera Storia Dei Bonobo Con Gli Occhiali see Real Story of the Bonobos Who Wore Spectacles

Vera Zasulich: A Biography. Jay Bergman. LC 82-80927. 280p. 1983. 42.50 (0-8047-1156-9) Stanford U Pr.

Veracini & His Contemporaries: Continuo Sonatas for Violin. Ed. by Jane Adas. LC 91-752425. (Eighteenth Century Continuo Sonata Ser.: Vol. 2). 296p. 1991. text ed. 90.00 (0-8153-0175-8) Garland.

Veracruz Blues. Mark Winegardner. LC 95-31804. 251p. 1996. pap. 22.95 (0-670-86636-9, Viking) Viking Penguin.

Veracruz Blues. Mark Winegardner. 1997. pap. 11.95 (0-14-026028-5) Viking Penguin.

Veraenderungen der Moosflora von Berlin (West) Annemarie Schaeppe. (Bryophytorum Bibliotheca Ser.: No. 33). (Illus.). 392p. (GER.). 1986. 96.00 (3-443-62005-1) Lubrecht & Cramer.

Veraenderungen im-Gaswechsel bei Laubmoosen nach Experimentellen Belastungen mit Schwermetallverbingungen. H. P. Haseloff. (Bryophytorum Bibliotheca Ser.: No. 19). (Illus.). 1979. pap. text ed. 32.00 (3-7682-1234-3) Lubrecht & Cramer.

Verandah. James P. Hennessy. (Century Classic Ser.). 313p. 1988. pap. 11.95 (0-7126-0401-4, Pub. by Century UK) Trafalgar.

***Veranderte Rubland.** Friedrich C. Weber. 1056p. (GER.). 1992. write for info. (3-487-09445-2) G Olms Pubs.

Veranilda: A Romance. George Gissing. LC 68-54270. reprint ed. 15.00 (0-404-02816-0) AMS Pr.

Veranilda: An Unfinished Romance. George R. Gissing. (BCL1-PR English Literature Ser.). 365p. 1992. reprint ed. lib. bdg. 89.00 (0-7812-7537-7) Rprt Serv.

***Veranito de Maria Isabel y Cuentos para Insomnes Rebeldes.** Carmen A. Paz. 101p. (Orig.). (SPA.). 1996. pap. 9.95 (1-882721-11-X) Edit Ponce de Leon.

Verano. J. M. Parramon et al. (Four Seasons Ser.). 32p. (SPA.). 1987. pap. 6.95 (0-8120-3647-6) Barron.

Verano Incesante. Luis De la Paz. LC 96-83142. (Coleccion Caniqui). 123p. (Orig.). (SPA.). 1996. pap. 12.00 (0-89729-793-8) Ediciones.

Verarbeitung von Nahrungsmitteln ohne Qualitaetseinbusse-Wunschtraum oder Wirklichkeit? Handling of Food without Change of Quality - Dream or Reality? Ed. by J. C. Somogyi. (Bibliotheca Nutritio et Dieta Ser.: No. 34). (Illus.). viii, 112p. 1984. 78.50 (3-8055-3926-6) S Karger.

***Vera's Adventures.** Vera D. Ervine. 224p. (Orig.). 1996. pap. 16.95 (1-881576-93-0, Hillsboro Pr) Providence Hse.

Vera's Return: And Other Incidents in the Life of Frank Johnson. Leon Knight. LC 83-81706. 72p. (Orig.). 1983. pap. 4.50 (0-940248-17-4) Guild Pr.

Vera's Special Hobbies. Marjolein Bastin. (Illus.). 28p. (J). (ps-2). 1985. 2.95 (0-8120-5692-2) Barron.

***Verb & Noun Number in English.** Reid. Date not set. text ed. write for info. (0-582-08616-7, Pub. by Longman UK) Longman.

Verb & Noun Number in English: A Functional Explanation. Wallis Reid. (Linguistics Library). 384p. (C). 1991. pap. text ed. 24.95 (0-582-29158-5) Longman.

Verb Be & Its Synonyms. Ed. by J. W. Verhaar. Incl. Part 5. Urdu, Turkish, Beugali, Amharic, Indonesian, Telegu, Estonian. 233p. 1972. lib. bdg. 82.50 (90-277-0217-9); (Foundations of Language Supplementary Ser.). write for info. (0-318-53992-6) Kluwer Ac.

Verb Be in Ancient Greek. C. H. Kahn. LC 74-183367. (Foundations of Language Supplementary Ser.: No. 16). 486p. 1973. lib. bdg. 63.00 (0-685-02828-3) Kluwer Ac.

Verb Chart Bulletin Board: Visuals. Susan F. Gabriele. (Illus.). (Orig.). 1990. pap. text ed. 24.95 (0-937354-49-X) Delta Systems.

Verb Complementation in Written English. Evert Anderson. 292p. (Orig.). 1985. pap. text ed. 35.00 (0-614-03099-4) Coronet Bks.

Verb in Contemporary English: Theory & Description. Ed. by Bas Aarts & Charles F. Meyer. 408p. (C). 1995. text ed. 64.95 (0-521-46039-5) Cambridge U Pr.

Verb in the Greek Non-literary Papyri. Basil G. Mandilaras. 493p. 1973. 84.00 (0-685-47544-1, Pub. by A M Hakkert NE) Benjamins North Am.

Verb-Intensifier Collocations in English. Sidney Greenbaum. (Janua Linguarum, Series Minor: No. 86). (Orig.). 1970. pap. text ed. 29.25 (90-279-0711-0) Mouton.

Verb Movement. Ed. by David Lightfoot & Norbert Hornstein. LC 93-5481. 384p. (C). 1994. pap. text ed. 24.95 (0-521-45661-4) Cambridge U Pr.

Verb Movement. Ed. by David Lightfoot & Norbert Hornstein. LC 93-5481. 384p. (C). 1994. text ed. 65.00 (0-521-45041-1) Cambridge U Pr.

Verb Movement & Expletive Subjects in the Germanic Languages. Sten Vikner. LC 93-31873. (Studies in Comparative Syntax). 352p. 1995. pap. 35.00 (0-19-508394-6) OUP.

Verb Phrase Patterns in Black English & Creole. Ed. by Walter F. Edwards & Donald Winford. LC 90-45777. 326p. (C). 1991. text ed. 31.95 (0-8143-2276-X) Wayne St U Pr.

Verb Second Phenomena in Germanic Languages. Ed. by H. Haider & M. Prinzhorn. (Publications in Language Sciences). vi, 207p. 1986. pap. 52.35 (90-6765-134-6) Mouton.

Verb Syntax in John Dryden's Prose, Pt. 1. Johannes Soderlind. (Essays & Studies on English Language & Literature: Vol. 10). 1974. reprint ed. pap. 30.00 (0-8115-0208-2) Periodicals Srv.

Verb Syntax in John Dryden's Prose, Pt. 2. Johannes Soderlind. (Essays & Studies on English Language & Literature: Vol. 19). 1974. reprint ed. pap. 25.00 (0-8115-0217-1) Periodicals Srv.

An Asterisk (*) at the beginning of an entry indicates that the title is appearing in BIP for the first time.

Verb System of Present-Day American English. 2nd ed. Robert L. Allen. (Janua Linguarum, Series Practica: No. 24). (Orig.). 1982. pap. text ed. 34.65 (*90-279-0643-2*) Mouton.

Verb "To Be" in Middle English: A Survey of the Forms. G. Forsstrom. (Lund Studies in English: Vol. 15). 1974. reprint ed. pap. 30.00 (*0-8115-0558-8*) Periodicals Srv.

Verb to Love. Barbara Horton. 24p. 1989. 3.00 (*0-943710-03-0*) Silver App Pr.

***Verb und Varietat.** Elisabeth Burr. (Romanistische Texte und Studien: Bd. 5). (GER.). 1993. write for info. (*3-487-09762-1*) G Olms Pubs.

Verbableitung im Fruehneuhochdeutschen. Heinz-Peter Prell & Marietheres Schebben-Schmidt. (Studia Linguistica Germanica: Vol. 41). xxx, 424p. (GER.). 1996. lib. bdg. 196.95 (*3-11-014268-6*) De Gruyter.

Verbal Abuse: Healing the Hidden Wound. Grace H. Ketterman. 238p. 1993. pap. 10.99 (*0-89283-824-8*, Vine Bks) Servant.

Verbal Abuse Survivors Speak Out on Relationship & Recovery. Patricia Evans. 252p. (Orig.). 1993. pap. 9.95 (*1-55850-304-8*) Adams Media.

Verbal Analogies. (General Aptitude & Abilities Ser.: CS-46). 1994. pap. 19.95 (*0-8373-6746-8*) Nat Learn.

Verbal & the Visual: Essays in Honor of William Sebastian Heckscher. Ed. by Karl-Ludwig Selig & Elizabeth Sears. LC 88-82493. (Illus.). 269p. 1996. pap. 25.00 (*0-934977-47-X*) Italica Pr.

Verbal & Visual Art of Alfred Kubin. Phillip H. Rhein. (Studies in Austrian Literature, Culture, & Thought). (Illus.). 188p. 1989. 24.95 (*0-929497-01-5*) Ariadne CA.

Verbal Art As Performance. Richard Bauman. 150p. (C). 1984. reprint ed. pap. text ed. 10.50 (*0-88133-048-5*) Waveland Pr.

Verbal Art in San Blas: Kuna Culture Through Its Discourse. Joel Sherzer. (Studies in Oral & Literate Culture: No. 21). 296p. (C). 1991. 69.95 (*0-521-38513-X*) Cambridge U Pr.

Verbal Art of Jean Francois Regnard, Vol. 1. D. M. Medlin. 156p. 1966. pap. 7.00 (*0-912788-00-3*) Tulane Romance Lang.

Verbal Arts in Madagascar: Performance in Historical Perspective. Lee Haring. LC 91-33129. (Publications of the American Folklore Society, Bibliographical & Special Ser.). 256p. (C). 1992. text ed. 28.95 (*0-8122-3141-4*) U of Pa Pr.

Verbal Aspect in Discourse. Ed. by Nils B. Thelin. LC 90-38712. (Pragmatics & Beyond Ser.: Vol. 5). xviii, 460p. 1990. 144.00 (*1-55619-095-6*) Benjamins North Am.

Verbal Aspect in the Greek of the New Testament, with Reference to Tense & Mood. 2nd ed. Stanley E. Porter. Ed. by D. A. Carson. (Studies in Biblical Greek: Vol. 1). 582p. 1993. 49.95 (*0-8204-2423-4*) P Lang Pubng.

Verbal Behavior. B. F. Skinner. (Illus.). 478p. (C). 1991. reprint ed. pap. 20.00 (*0-87411-591-4*) Copley Pub.

Verbal Behavior & Politics. Doris A. Graber. LC 75-25830. 390p. 1976. text ed. 34.95 (*0-252-00262-8*) U of Ill Pr.

Verbal Builder for Standardized Tests. rev. ed. Research & Education Association Staff. (Illus.). 368p. 1996. pap. 14.95 (*0-87891-875-2*) Res & Educ.

Verbal Correspondences. Carlos F. Navarro. (Start Smart Ser.). (J). (gr. k-2). 1990. student ed. 4.50 (*1-878396-00-5*) Start Smart Bks.

***Verbal Decision Analysis for Unstructured Problems.** Oleg I. Larichev & Helen M. Moshkovich. LC 97-20775. (Theory & Decision Library). 1997. text ed. write for info. (*0-7923-4578-9*) Kluwer Ac.

Verbal Dueling in Heroic Narrative: The Homeric & Old English Traditions. Ward Parks. 232p. 1990. text ed. 37.50 (*0-691-06780-5*) Princeton U Pr.

Verbal Elixirs: Thoughts to Peace of Mind; How to Have Heaven on Earth. Yvonne V. Nielsen. 96p. 1991. pap. 16.95 (*0-9630324-0-2*) YV Prods.

Verbal Expression. James T. Martinoff et al. (Language Rehabilitation Ser.). 352p. 1981. 84.00 (*0-88120-126-X*, 2366) PRO-ED.

Verbal Games of Pre-School Children. Susan Iwamura. LC 79-22384. 1980. text ed. 29.95 (*0-312-83877-8*) St Martin.

Verbal Hygiene. Deborah Cameron. LC 94-39801. (Politics of Language Ser.). 272p. (C). 1995. pap. 17.95 (*0-415-10355-X*, C0119) Routledge.

Verbal Hygiene. Deborah Cameron. LC 94-39801. (Politics of Language Ser.). 272p. (C). (gr. 13). 1995. text ed. 62.95 (*0-415-10354-1*, C0118) Routledge.

Verbal Icon: Studies in the Meaning of Poetry. W. K. Wimsatt. LC 54-7479. 320p. 1982. pap. 15.95 (*0-8131-0111-5*) U Pr of Ky.

Verbal Idioms of the Qur'an. Mustansir Mir. (Michigan Series on the Middle East: No. 1). 378p. (Orig.). 1989. pap. 21.95 (*0-932098-21-5*) UM Ctr MENAS.

Verbal Idioms of the Qur'an. Mustsir Mir. 1989. 21.95 (*0-86685-471-1*) Intl Bk Ctr.

Verbal Imagination: Coleridge & the Language of Modern Criticism. A. C. Goodson. 256p. 1988. 55.00 (*0-19-505450-4*) OUP.

Verbal Information Systems: A Comprehensive Guide to Writing Manuals. (Standards Ser.). 1974. 5.00 (*0-934356-18-1*); 4.00 (*0-686-00292-X*) Assn Syst Mgmt.

Verbal Judo: Redirecting Behavior with Words. George J. Thompson & Michael J. Stroud. Ed. by Helen Moody. (Illus.). 110p. (Orig.). 1984. pap. 6.95 (*0-317-07520-9*) Comm Strat Inc.

Verbal Judo: Redirecting Behavior with Words. George J. Thompson. 140p. (Orig.). (C). 1994. pap. text ed. 6.95 (*1-884566-15-4*) Inst Police Tech.

Verbal Judo: The Gentle Art of Persuasion. George J. Thompson. 1994. pap. 12.00 (*0-688-13786-5*, Quill) Morrow.

Verbal Judo: Words As a Force Option. George J. Thompson. (Illus.). 158p. 1983. pap. 19.95 (*0-398-06456-3*) C C Thomas.

Verbal Judo: Words As a Force Option. George J. Thompson. (Illus.). 158p. (C). 1983. 31.95 (*0-398-04879-7*) C C Thomas.

Verbal Landscape-Dinosaur Sat Down. Nathan Lyons. (Illus.). 30p. 1987. pap. 10.00 (*0-939784-16-5*) CEPA Gall.

Verbal Narcotics. Sean Woodward. (C). 1989. 30.00 (*1-871058-02-3*, Pub. by Dragonheart Pr UK) St Mut.

Verbal Piece in Ebira. John R. Adive. (Publications in Linguistics: No. 85). 150p. 1989. fiche 12.00 (*0-88312-476-9*) Summer Instit Ling.

Verbal Power: Rootword Flashcards. Nanette N. Andrews. LC 91-73379. 332p. 1992. pap. text ed. 16.00 (*0-9630715-0-5*) Guid Acad Achieve.

Verbal Processes in Children: Progress in Cognitive Developmental Research. Ed. by Charles J. Brainerd & M. Pressley. (Cognitive Development Ser.). (Illus.). 289p. 1982. 83.95 (*0-387-90648-7*) Spr-Verlag.

Verbal Protocols of Reading: The Nature of Constructively Responsive Reading. Michael Pressley & Peter Afflerbach. 168p. 1995. pap. 17.50 (*0-8058-1764-6*); text ed. 39.95 (*0-8058-1537-6*) L Erlbaum Assocs.

Verbal Review for Standardized Tests. William A. Covino & Peter Z. Orton. (Cliffs Test Preparation Ser.). (Illus.). 375p. 1986. pap. text ed. 7.95 (*0-8220-2034-3*) Cliffs.

Verbal Skills' PSAT-SAT Preparation Guide. Elissa B. Sommerfield. LC 86-81902. 104p. 1986. pap. text ed. 13.95 (*0-9604058-0-1*) Ed Skills Dallas.

Verbal System of Classical Hebrew in the Joseph Story: An Approach from Discourse Analysis. Y. Endo. (Studia Semitica Neerlandica: Vol. 32). xiii, 351p. 1996. pap. 48.00 (*90-232-3093-0*, Pub. by Van Gorcum NE) Eisenbrauns.

Verbal System of Southern Agaw. Robert Hetzron. LC 70-14968. (University of California Publications, Near Eastern Studies: Vol. 12). 134p. reprint ed. pap. 38.20 (*0-317-10197-8*, 2021379) Bks Demand.

Verbal Text - Non-Verbal Context: Handmade Books by Wisconsin Artists. Janet Treacy. (Illus.). 38p. (Orig.). 1992. pap. 12.00 (*0-944110-40-1*) Milwauk Art Mus.

Verbal Violence in Contemporary Drama: From Handke to Shepard. Jeanette Malkin. 256p. (C). 1992. text ed. 69.95 (*0-521-38335-8*) Cambridge U Pr.

Verbal Workbook for SAT I. 8th ed. Mitchel Weiner & Sharon W. Green. 320p. (YA). (gr. 10-12). 1994. pap. 10.95 (*0-8120-1850-8*) Barron.

***Verbal Workbook for SAT I.** 9th ed. Mitchel Weiner & Sharon Green. LC 96-36295. 1997. pap. 11.95 (*0-8120-9640-1*) Barron.

Verbalism among Blind Children: An Investigation & Analysis. Randall K. Harley. (American Foundation for the Blind Research Ser.: No. 10). 61p. reprint ed. pap. 25.00 (*0-7837-0141-1*, 2040430) Bks Demand.

Verbalkategorien des Deutschen: Ein Beitrang Zur Theorie der Sprachlichen Kategorisierung. Elisabeth Leiss. (Studia Linguistica Germanica: No. 31). vi, 334p. (GER.). (C). 1992. lib. bdg. 107.70 (*3-11-012746-6*) De Gruyter.

Verbally Abusive Relationship: How to Recognize It & How to Respond. 2nd rev. ed. Patricia Evans. 196p. 1996. pap. 9.95 (*1-55850-582-2*) Adams Media.

***Verbandsauberungen & Wettbewerbsrecht.** Peter Kurz. 199p. (GER.). 1996. 42.95 (*3-631-30054-9*) P Lang Pubng.

***Verbatim, Vol. 1 & 2.** 1982. 24.00 (*0-8103-4357-6*, 00006582, Gale Res Intl) Gale.

Verbatim, Vols. I & II. LC 77-20392. 250p. 1979. 20.00 (*0-930454-04-9*) Verbatim Bks.

Verbatim, Vols. III & IV. 356p. 1981. 20.00 (*0-930454-12-X*) Verbatim Bks.

Verbatim, Vols. V & VI. 385p. 1981. 20.00 (*0-930454-13-8*) Verbatim Bks.

Verbatim: A Language Quarterly, 4 vols. Ed. by Laurence Urdang. 1100p. 1982. Vols. 3-4. 24.00 (*0-8103-4358-4*); Vols. 5-6. 24.00 (*0-8103-4359-2*) Gale.

Verbatim: Volumes I-VI Index. 128p. 1981. 20.00 (*0-930454-14-6*) Verbatim Bks.

***Verbatim Index to Volumes 1-6.** 1982. 24.00 (*0-8103-4360-6*, 00006532, Gale Res Intl) Gale.

Verbatim Story: The First Twenty-Five Years. Al Ehrbar. (Illus.). 112p. 1995. write for info. (*0-944641-12-1*) Greenwich Pub Group.

Verbe Francais: Five Tomes in One Volume. Jaime M. Tolentino. LC 78-14928. (Illus.). 536p. 1979. text ed. 8.00 (*0-8477-3322-X*) U of PR Pr.

Verbeck of Japan. William E. Griffis. (Notable American Authors Ser.). 1992. reprint ed. lib. bdg. 75.00 (*0-7812-2965-0*) Rprt Serv.

Verbes de Celine. Alphonse Juilland. (Stanford French & Italian Studies: Vol. 32). 160p. 1985. pap. 46.50 (*0-915838-05-2*) Anma Libri.

Verbes de Celine A-D. Alphonse Juilland. (Verbes de Celine Ser.). 301p. (Orig.). (FRE.). (C). 1988. pap. 24.00 (*1-884868-00-2*) Montparnasse.

Verbes de Celine E-L. Alphonse Juilland. (Verbes de Celine Ser.). 245p. (Orig.). (FRE.). (C). 1989. pap. 24.00 (*1-884868-01-0*) Montparnasse.

Verbes de Celine M-P. Alphonse Juilland. (Verbes de Celine Ser.). 183p. (Orig.). (FRE.). (C). 1990. pap. 24.00 (*1-884868-02-9*) Montparnasse.

Verbes de Mouvement en Francais et en Espagnol: Etude Comparee de Leurs Infinitives. Beatrice Lamiroy. (Lingvisticae Investigationes Supplementa Ser.: No. 11). xiv, 323p. (FRE.). 1983. 62.00 (*90-272-3121-4*) Benjamins North Am.

***Verbeserung von Produktivitat und Wirtschaftlichkeit.** Gunnar Almgren & I. Berge. Ed. by R. Matikainen et al. 760p. 1987. 195.00 (*90-6191-703-4*, Pub. by A A Balkema NE) Ashgate Pub Co.

Verbi Italiani. P. Elia. (Bruno Mondadori Ser.). (ITA.). 15.95 (*88-424-8003-7*) Schoenhof.

Verbi Italiani (et Leurs Equivalents Francais & Their English Equivalents) Leonard G. Sbrocchi. (Pedagogical Ser.: Vol. 1). 200p. (Orig.). (ENG, FRE & ITA.). 1989. pap. 12.00 (*0-921252-08-0*) LEGAS.

Verbiage. Mary Scandrett. (Educational Game Activity Ser.). (YA). (gr. 5-12). 1987. 42.00 (*0-930599-12-8*) Thinking Pubns.

Verbis non Factis: Words Meant to Influence Political Choices in the United States, 1800-1980. Fay M. Blake & H. Morton Newman. LC 84-1325. 143p. 1984. 20.00 (*0-8108-1688-1*) Scarecrow.

Verbivocovisual. Thomasine Rose. (Illus.). 72p. (C). 1982. 9.85 (*0-9606540-3-8*) Classic Nonfic.

Verborgene Heilkuenste: Geschichte der Frauenmedzin im Spaetmittelalter. Britta-Juliane Kruse. (Quellen und Forschungen Zur Literatur- unk Kulturgeschichte, Bd 4(238) Ser.: Band 5 (239)). xii, 498p. (GER.). (C). 1995. lib. bdg. 147.70 (*3-11-014704-1*) De Gruyter.

Verborum Amor: Studien zur Geschichte & Kunst der Deutschen Sprache Festschrift fur Stefan Sonderegger zum 65. Geburstag. Ed. by Harald Berger et al. xiv, 830p. (GER.). (C). 1992. lib. bdg 284.65 (*3-11-011682-0*) De Gruyter.

Verbos Espanoles (et Leurs Equivalents Francais & Their English Equivalents) Rodney Williamson. Ed. by Leonard G. Sbrocchi. (Pedagogical Ser.). 164p. (Orig.). (ENG, FRE & SPA.). 1990. pap. 12.00 (*0-921252-11-0*) LEGAS.

Verbos Ingles. Harraps Staff. 1995. 6.00 (*0-02-860093-2*, Harraps IN) Macmillan Gen Ref.

Verbotene Literatur Von der Klassischen Zeit Bis Zur Gegenwart, 2 vols. Heinrich H. Houben. 1992. reprint ed. Set. write for info. (*3-487-01025-9*) G Olms Pubs.

Verbrachergestal Im Zeitalter des Realismus von Fontane Bis Mann. Annelies Luppa. (Studies in European Thought: Vol. 10). 168p. (GER.). (C). 1995. text ed. 37.95 (*0-8204-2545-1*) P Lang Pubng.

Verbrechensthematik im Modernen Roman. Peter Morris-Keitel. Ed. by Jost Hermand. LC 89-12146. (German Life & Civilization Ser.: Vol. 4). 210p. 1990. text ed. 42.95 (*0-8204-1106-X*) P Lang Pubng.

Verbreitung und Oekologie van Flussufer-Gesellschaften (Chenopodion Rubri) im Mittleren und Westlichen Europa. Rolf Wisskirchen. (Dissertationes Botanica Ser.: Vol. 236). (Illus.). 376p. (GER.). 1995. pap. 165.00 (*3-443-64148-2*, Pub. by Cramer-Borntraeger GW) Lubrecht & Cramer.

Verbreitungsatlas de Grosspilze Deutschlands, West, Vol. 1: Staenderpilze, Teil A: Nichtblaetterpilze, Teil B: Blaetterpilze, 2 vols. German J. Krieglsteiner. (Illus.). 1016p. (GER.). 1991. Set. lib. bdg. 75.00 (*3-8001-3318-0*, Pub. by Ulmer Verlog GW) Lubrecht & Cramer.

Verbreitungsatlas der Farn & Bluetenpflanzen Bayerns. P. Schoenfelder et al. (Illus.). 752p. (GER.). 1990. lib. bdg. 55.00 (*3-8001-3455-1*, Pub. by Ulmer Verlog GW) Lubrecht & Cramer.

Verbs. S. Harold Collins. (Straight Forward English Ser.). 36p. (Orig.). (J). (gr. 4-6). 1990. pap. 3.95 (*0-931993-34-2*, GP-034) Garlic Pr OR.

Verbs. Sheldon L. Tilkin. (Horizons II Ser.). (Illus.). 24p. (J). (gr. 3-4). 1980. student ed., pap. 3.95 (*0-89403-598-3*) EDC.

Verbs & Diachronic Syntax: A Comparative History of English & French. Ian G. Roberts. (Studies in Natural Language & Linguistic Theory). 372p. (C). 1993. lib. bdg. 157.50 (*0-7923-1705-X*) Kluwer Ac.

Verbs & Diachronic Syntax: A Comparative History of English & French. Ian G. Roberts. (Studies in Natural Language & Linguistic Theory). 388p. (C). 1993. pap. text ed. 59.50 (*0-7923-2495-1*) Kluwer Ac.

Verbs & Numbers: A Study of the Frequencies of the Hebrew Verbal Tense Forms in the Books of Samuel, Kings, & Chronicles. Arian J. Verheij. (Studia Semitica Neerlandica Ser.: Vol. 28). iv, 135p. 1990. pap. text ed. 24.00 (*90-232-2572-4*, Pub. by Van Gorcum NE) Eisenbrauns.

Verbs for a Specific Purpose. Sandra L. MccKay. (Illus.). 256p. (C). 1982. pap. text ed. 11.75 (*0-13-941617-X*) P-H.

Verbs in Medieval English: Differences in Verb Choice & Prose. Michiko Ogura. LC 95-4499. (Topics in English Linguistics Ser.: No. 17). xxii, 260p. (C). 1995. lib. bdg. 113.85 (*3-11-014426-3*) Mouton.

Verbs of Eating. Harris Winitz. (Using Verbs Ser.). (Illus.). (Orig.). 1988. pap. text ed. 22.00 (*0-939990-55-5*) Intl Linguistics.

Verbs of Motion in Their Semantic Divergence. K. H. Collitz. (LM Ser.: Vol. 8). 1931. pap. 25.00 (*0-527-00812-5*) Periodicals Srv.

Verbs of Placement. Harris Winitz. (Using Verbs Ser.). (Illus.). (Orig.). 1988. pap. text ed. 22.00 (*0-939990-56-3*) Intl Linguistics.

Verbs of Walking. Harris Winitz. (Using Verbs Ser.). (Illus.). (Orig.). 1988. pap. text ed. 22.00 (*0-939990-54-7*) Intl Linguistics.

Verbs Past & Present. Marilyn M. Toomey. (Illus.). 77p. 1989. 17.95 (*0-923573-09-7*) Circuit Pubns.

Verbs Through Pictures. Harris Winitz. (Language Through Pictures Ser.). (Illus.). 62p. (gr. 2-12). 1982. pap. 4.75 (*0-939990-30-X*) Intl Linguistics.

Verbtabellen Deutsch. Heinz F. Wendt. 71p. 1975. 7.50 (*3-468-34110-5*) Langenscheidt.

***Verbum: Word & Idea in Aquinas, Vol. 2.** Bernard Lonergan. (Collected Works of Bernard Lonergan). 1997. pap. text ed. 24.95 (*0-8020-7988-1*) U of Toronto Pr.

Verbum Caro: An Encyclopedia on Jesus, the Christ. Michael O'Carroll. 216p. (Orig.). 1992. 35.00 (*0-8146-5017-1*, M Glazier) Liturgical Pr.

Vercelli Book. Ed. by George P. Krapp. LC 32-10861. 152p. 1932. text ed. 49.50 (*0-231-08766-7*) Col U Pr.

Vercelli Book Homilies: Translations from the Anglo-Saxon. Lewis E. Nicholson. 184p. (C). 1991. lib. bdg. 39.50 (*0-8191-8116-1*) U Pr of Amer.

Vercoquin et le Plancton. Boris Vian. (FRE.). 1973. pap. 8.95 (*0-7859-2877-4*) Fr & Eur.

Vercoquin et le Plancton. Boris Vian. (Folio Ser.: No. 334). 192p. (FRE.). 1968. 6.95 (*2-07-036374-0*) Schoenhof.

Vercors Caves Vol. 1: Classic French Caving. Des Marshall. 100p. 1996. pap. 13.95 (*1-871890-71-3*) Menasha Ridge.

Vercors, Ecrivain et Dessinateur. Konstantinovic. (Bibliotheque Franc. et Romane. Et. Litter. Ser.). 10.95 (*0-685-36631-6*) Fr & Eur.

Verda: An Artist Sketches Europe, 1951. Illus. by Verda MacNamee. LC 90-70192. 100p. (Orig.). 1990. pap. 14.95 (*0-9625879-0-7*) Wilde Pr.

Verdad os Hara Libres. David T. Demola. 21p. 1987. pap. 2.95 (*0-88144-145-7*) Christian Pub.

Verdad Sobre el Caso Savolta. 17th ed. Eduardo Mendoza. 432p. (SPA.). 1992. pap. 17.95 (*0-7859-0578-2*, S29407) Fr & Eur.

Verdad Sobre la Brujeria Americana: The Truth about Witchcraft. Scott Cunningham. Ed. by Edgar Rojas. (Verdad Sobre Ser.). (SPA.). Date not set. mass mkt. 1.99 (*1-56718-878-8*) Llewellyn Pubns.

Verdad Sobre la Communicacion Con los Espiritus: The Truth about Spirit Communication. Ray Buckland. (Truth About Ser.). (SPA.). 1996. mass mkt. 1.99 (*1-56718-879-6*) Llewellyn Pubns.

Verdad Sobre la Curacion los Cristales: The Truth about Crystal Healing. Phyllis Galde. (Truth About Ser.). (SPA.). 1996. mass mkt. 1.99 (*1-56718-877-X*) Llewellyn Pubns.

Verdad Sobre la Falla San Andres. Teodoro O. Aviles. (Illus.). 64p. (SPA.). 1992. per. 3.95 (*0-9627080-9-7*) In One EAR.

Verdad Sobre las Regresion a las Vidas Pasadas: The Truth about Past Life Regression. Florence W. McClain. (Truth About Ser.). (SPA.). 1996. mass mkt. 1.99 (*1-56718-880-X*) Llewellyn Pubns.

Verdad Sobre los Poderes Psiquicos: The Truth about Psychic Powers. Donald M. Kraid. (Truth About Ser.). (SPA.). 1996. mass mkt. 1.99 (*1-56718-876-1*) Llewellyn Pubns.

Verdad Sospechosa. Juan Ruiz De Alarcon. Ed. by Juan M. Martin Martinez. (Nueva Austral Ser.: Vol. 173). (SPA.). 1991. pap. text ed. 11.95 (*84-239-1973-0*) Elliots Bks.

Verdad Sospechosa, No. 68. Juan Ruiz De Alarcon. 165p. (SPA.). 1969. write for info. (*0-8288-8557-5*) Fr & Eur.

Verdad Tras el Telon. Cristina K. De Sokoluk. 96p. (SPA.). 1991. pap. 5.99 (*0-311-07607-6*) Casa Bautista.

***Verdadera Adoracion.** F. Garcia. (SPA.). 5.95 (*0-8297-2086-3*) Life Pubs Intl.

Verdadera Amistad Siempre Perdura en el Corazon (True Friends Always Remain in Each Others) Ed. by Susan P. Schutz. LC 92-14013. 1992. pap. 7.95 (*0-88396-359-0*) Blue Mtn Pr CO.

Verdadera Devocion a Maria. Mary Frederick. (Queen of Apostles Ser.). (SPA.). 1990. 0.50 (*1-56036-000-3*, 9731) AMI Pr.

Verdadera Historia de los Tres Cerditos: The True Story of the Three Little Pigs. Jon Scieszka. Tr. by Maria Negroni. (Illus.). 32p. (SPA.). (J). 1996. pap. 4.99 (*0-14-055758-X*) Viking Penguin.

Verdadera Liberacion Femenina. Gloria Ricardo. 26p. 1993. pap. 1.15 (*1-885630-04-2*) HLM Producciones.

***Verdadera Prosperidad.** Gene A. Getz. (SPA.). 9.95 (*0-8297-1850-8*) Life Pubs Intl.

Verdadero Ladron: The Real Thief. William Steig. (J). (ps-3). 1993. 15.00 (*0-374-30458-0*, Mirasol) FS&G.

Verdades De la Vida. Buth. (SPA.). 1.50 (*0-685-74985-1*, 497420) Editorial Unilit.

Verdades Que Transforman. Victor Ricardo & Gloria Ricardo. (Estudio Biblico Para Mujeres Ser.). 66p. 1992. pap. 4.00 (*1-885630-28-X*) HLM Producciones.

***Verde.** Karen Bryant-Mole. (Images Ser.). Orig. Title: Green. (SPA.). 1996. pap. text ed. 4.95 (*0-382-39575-1*) Silver Burdett Pr.

***Verde River Kid.** John Kilgore. (Linford Western Large Print Ser.). 256p. 1997. pap. 16.99 (*0-7089-5132-5*, Linford) Ulverscroft.

Verde River Reclamation Survey: Verde River Corridor Study, Tapco to Beasley Flat. Edward Cook et al. 43p. 1991. pap. text ed. 25.00 (*1-884320-07-4*) ASU Herberger Ctr.

Verde River Recreation Guide: Boating, Camping & Outdoor Adventure! Jim Slingluff. LC 90-45887. (Illus.). 176p. (Orig.). 1990. pap. 9.95 (*0-914846-50-7*) Golden West Pub.

Verde River Visual Assessment: Verde River Corridor Study, Tapco to Beasley Flat. Edward Cook et al. 100p. 1991. pap. text ed. 45.00 (*1-884320-06-6*) ASU Herberger Ctr.

Verde Valley: A Geological History. Wayne Ranney. (Plateau Ser.: Vol. 60, No. 3). 32p. 1989. pap. 4.95 (*0-89734-096-5*) Mus Northern Ariz.

Verde, Violeta y Amarillo (Purple, Green & Yellow) Robert Munsch. (Illus.). 32p. (J). (ps-2). 1994. pap. 5.95 (*1-55037-971-2*, Pub. by Annick CN) Firefly Bks Ltd.

Verdes Campos Del Eden. Antonio Gala. 96p. 1983. pap. 12.95 (*0-7859-5181-4*) Fr & Eur.

Verdi. (Portraits of Greatness Ser.). 1987. pap. 12.50 (*0-918367-00-X*) Elite.

Verdi. (Dent Master Musicians Ser.). (Illus.). (C). pap. write for info. (*0-19-816469-6*) OUP.

Verdi. Julian Budden. 416p. 1996. 30.00 (*0-02-864616-9*) Macmillan.

Verdi. Janell Cannon. LC 96-18442. (J). 1997. 16.00 (*0-15-201028-9*) HarBrace.

Verdi. Peter Southwell-Sander. (Illustrated Lives of the Great Composers Ser.). (Illus.). 160p. 1996. 14.95 (*0-7119-0250-X*, OP 42365) Omnibus NY.

***Verdi.** Roland Vernon. (Famous Composers Ser.). (Illus.). 32p. (J). (gr. 4-8). 1997. pap. 8.95 (*0-382-39677-4*); lib. bdg. 14.95 (*0-382-39678-2*) Silver Burdett Pr.

Verdi. Ed. by Franz V. Werfel & Paul Stefan. Tr. by Edward Downes. LC 71-130565. (Select Bibliographies Reprint Ser.). 1977. 29.95 (*0-8369-5538-2*) Ayer.

Verdi. Dyneley Hussey. (Music Book Index Ser.). 355p. 1992. reprint ed. lib. bdg. 89.00 (*0-7812-9502-5*) Rprt Serv.

Verdi: A Biography. Mary J. Phillips-Matz. LC 92-37841. 994p. (C). 1993. 49.95 (*0-19-313204-4*) OUP.

Verdi: A Biography. Mary J. Phillips-Matz. (Illus.). 994p. 1996. reprint ed. pap. 22.50 (*0-19-816600-1*) OUP.

Verdi: His Music, Life & Times. George W. Martin. LC 92-23999. (Illus.). 522p. 1992. reprint ed. pap. 22.95 (*0-87910-160-1*) Limelight Edns.

Verdi: Man & Musician. Frederick J. Crowest. LC 74-24065. reprint ed. 39.50 (*0-404-12890-4*) AMS Pr.

Verdi: Music Book Index. Ferruccio Bonavia. 120p. 1993. reprint ed. lib. bdg. 69.00 (*0-7812-9628-5*) Rprt Serv.

Verdi: Requiem. David Rosen. (Music Handbooks Ser.). 125p. (C). 1995. text ed. 34.95 (*0-521-39448-1*); pap. text ed. 11.95 (*0-521-39767-7*) Cambridge U Pr.

Verdi: Roman der Oper. Franz V. Werfel. LC 75-177861. (GER.). reprint ed. 49.50 (*0-404-06907-X*) AMS Pr.

***Verdi: Scholastic Edition.** Cannon. 1997. write for info. (*0-15-201784-4*) HarBrace.

Verdi: The Man in His Letters. Giuseppe Verdi. 1988. reprint ed. lib. bdg. 49.00 (*0-7812-0099-7*) Rprt Serv.

Verdi: The Man in His Letters. Giuseppe Verdi. LC 76-181289. 469p. 1942. reprint ed. 79.00 (*0-403-01712-2*) Scholarly.

***Verdi: Verdi.** Robert Hardcastle. (Illus.). 144p. (Orig.). pap. 14.95 (*0-7119-5500-X*, OP 47816) Omnibus NY.

Verdi, A Theatre of Music. De Van. 1994. lib. bdg. 65.00 (*0-226-14369-4*) U Ch Pr.

Verdi, a Theatre of Music. De Van. 1994. pap. text ed. 24.95 (*0-226-14370-8*) U Ch Pr.

Verdi & His Major Contemporaries. Tom Kaufman. LC 90-3549. (Annals of Opera Ser.). 624p. 1990. text ed. 30.00 (*0-8240-4106-2*, 1016) Garland.

Verdi & Wagner. Erno Lendvai. Tr. by Monika Palos & Judit Pokoly. 504p. 36.50 (*0-685-30700-X*, Pub. by Intl Hse HU) Pro-Am Music.

Verdi at the Golden Gate: Opera & San Francisco in the Gold Rush Years. George W. Martin. LC 92-18674. 1993. 30.00 (*0-520-08123-4*) U CA Pr.

Verdi Baritone: Studies in the Development of Dramatic Character. Geoffrey Edwards & Ryan Edwards. LC 93-27721. 212p. 1994. 24.95 (*0-253-31949-8*) Ind U Pr.

Verdi-Boito Correspondence. Ed. by Marcello Conati & Mario Medici. Tr. by William Weaver. LC 93-22598. 386p. 1994. 29.95 (*0-226-85304-7*) U Ch Pr.

Verdi Companion. Ed. by William Weaver & Martin Chusid. (Illus.). 1988. pap. 10.95 (*0-393-30443-4*) Norton.

Verdi, His Music, Life & Times. George W. Martin. LC 78-31783. (Music Reprint Ser.). 1979. reprint ed. 59.50 (*0-306-79549-3*) Da Capo.

Verdict. Francine Pascal. (Sweet Valley High Ser.: No. 97). 224p. (YA). 1993. 3.50 (*0-553-29854-2*) Bantam.

Verdict. Barry Reed. 1992. mass mkt. 5.99 (*0-312-92954-4*) St Martin.

Verdict. Lalit Sehgal. Tr. by Suresh Kohli from HIN. 8.00 (*0-89253-656-X*); 3.00 (*0-89253-657-8*) Ind-US Inc.

Verdict: Assessing the Civil Jury System. Ed. by Robert E. Litan. 542p. (C). 1993. 52.95 (*0-8157-5282-2*); pap. 24.95 (*0-8157-5281-4*) Brookings.

Verdict: Matrimony. Joann Ross et al. 1996. mass mkt. 5.99 (*0-373-20127-3*, 1-20127-6) Harlequin Bks.

***Verdict: Parenthood.** Jule McBride. 1997. mass mkt. 3.75 (*0-373-16699-0*, 1-16699-0) Harlequin Bks.

Verdict: The Exclusive Picture Story of the Trial of the Chicago 8. Joseph Okpaku. LC 79-129568. (Illus.). 160p. 1970. 30.00 (*0-89388-008-6*); pap. 20.00 (*0-89388-009-4*) Okpaku Communications.

Verdict at Medicine Springs. R. C. House. 1994. mass mkt. 4.99 (*0-671-87244-3*) PB.

Verdict Is In. Ed. by Kathi Georges & Jennifer Joseph. 96p. (Orig.). 1992. pap. 9.95 (*0-916397-25-4*) Manic D Pr.

Verdict of Bridlegoose. 143p. 1985. 30.00 (*0-317-38815-0*, Pub. by Redcliffe Pr Ltd) St Mut.

Verdict of Fate. Marion Andre. 160p. 1995. lib. bdg. 31.00 (*0-8095-4591-8*) Borgo Pr.

Verdict of Fate. Marion Andre. 160p. pap. 10.95 (*0-88962-375-9*) Mosaic.

***Verdict of History on Sacco & Vanzetti.** Frank M. D'Alessandro. 350p. (Orig.). Date not set. pap. 14.95 (*1-889534-07-2*) Jay St Pubs.

Verdict of Three Decades. Ed. by Julien Steinberg. LC 77-142702. (Essay Index Reprint Ser.). 1977. 31.95 (*0-8369-2077-5*) Ayer.

Verdict of Twelve. Raymond Postgate. 208p. 1986. reprint ed. pap. 5.95 (*0-89733-198-2*) Academy Chi Pubs.

Verdict on Janata. J. P. Chandra. 212p. 1979. 14.95 (*0-318-36630-4*) Asia Bk Corp.

Verdict on Winter. Eileen Dewhurst. 256p. 1996. 22.00 (*0-7278-4888-7*) Severn Hse.

***Verdict Unsafe.** Jill McGown. LC 97-4949. 1997. 22.00 (*0-449-91067-9*) Fawcett.

Verdicts Out of Court. Clarence Darrow. Ed. by Arthur Weinberg & Lila Weinberg. (New Reprints in Essay & General Literature Index Ser.). 1977. reprint ed. 34.95 (*0-518-10198-3*, 10198) Ayer.

Verdicts Out of Court. Clarence Darrow. Ed. by Arthur Weinberg & Lila Weinberg. 444p. 1989. reprint ed. pap. 11.95 (*0-929587-01-4*, Elephant Paperbacks) I R Dee.

Verdienen mit Termindoptionen. Tr. by Jorg Gruhler. 51p. 1994. pap. 7.95 (*0-915513-58-7*) Ctr Futures Ed.

Verdilak. Mark Kneece & Bo Hampton. (Illus.). 72p. 1996. 24.95 (*1-56163-143-4*); pap. 14.95 (*1-56163-146-9*) NBM.

Verdi's Aida. Giuseppe Verdi. 96p. (Orig.). 1983. pap. 2.95 (*0-486-24459-8*) Dover.

Verdi's Aida: The History of an Opera in Letters & Documents. Hans Busch. LC 76-11495. 743p. reprint ed. pap. 180.00 (*0-7837-2974-X*, 2057480) Bks Demand.

***Verdi's Falstaff in Letters & Contemporary Reviews.** Giuseppe Verdi & Hans Busch. LC 96-32273. 1997. write for info. (*0-253-32980-9*); pap. write for info. (*0-253-21034-8*) Ind U Pr.

Verdi's Middle Period 1849-1859. Chusid. LC 96-31949. 1997. pap. text ed. 45.00 (*0-226-10659-4*); lib. bdg. 100.00 (*0-226-10658-6*) U Ch Pr.

Verdi's Rigoletto. Giuseppe Verdi. (Opera Libretto Ser.). 64p. (Orig.). 1983. pap. 2.95 (*0-486-24497-0*) Dover.

Verdon Angster. Marcus Reichert. 247p. (Orig.). 1995. pap. 12.95 (*0-9645655-0-1*) BurnhillWolf.

Verdos Sobre la Magia de las Hierbas: The Truth about Herb Magic. Scott Cunningham. Ed. by Edgar Rojas. (Verdad Sobre Ser.). (SPA.). Date not set. mass mkt. 1.99 (*1-56718-875-3*) Llewellyn Pubns.

Verdun. Jules Romains. 376p. (FRE.). 1964. pap. 17.95 (*0-7859-1598-2*, 208060211X) Fr & Eur.

***Verdun/Metz/Wissembourg Map.** 1996. 6.95 (*2-06-700057-8*, 57) Michelin.

Verdura. Viana La Place. LC 90-49304. (Illus.). 320p. 1991. 22.95 (*0-688-08764-7*) Morrow.

***Verdure! The Art of Italian Vegetables.** Time-Life Books Staff. LC 97-1242. (Pane & Vino Ser.). (Illus.). 128p. 1998. write for info. (*0-7835-5259-9*) Time-Life.

Vereda: A Trail Through Time. Ruth M. Colville. (Illus.). 400p. 1996. 24.95 (*0-9650560-3-1*); pap. 14.95 (*0-9650560-4-X*) S Luis Vly Hist Soc.

Verendrye Overland Quest of Pacific. Grace Flandrau. 64p. reprint ed. pap. 3.95 (*0-8466-0213-X*, S213) Shorey.

***Verfahrensgrammatik: Eine Alternative Grammatikbeschreibung Fur Den Sprachunterricht.** Werner Hackel. 95p. (GER.). 1996. 29.95 (*3-631-49150-6*) P Lang Pubng.

Verfasserlexikon: Die Deutsche Literatur des Mittelalters, 6 vols, Vol. 1. 2nd ed. Ed. by Kurt Ruh et al. (C). 1978. 293.85 (*3-11-007264-5*) De Gruyter.

Verfasserlexikon: Die Deutsche Literatur des Mittelalters, 6 vols, Vol. 2. 2nd ed. Ed. by Kurt Ruh et al. (C). 1980. 293.85 (*3-11-007699-3*) De Gruyter.

Verfasserlexikon: Die Deutsche Literatur des Mittelalters, 6 vols, Vol. 3. 2nd ed. Ed. by Kurt Ruh et al. (C). 1981. 293.85 (*3-11-008778-2*) De Gruyter.

Verfasserlexikon: Die Deutsche Literatur des Mittelalters, 6 vols, Vol. 4. 2nd ed. Ed. by Kurt Ruh et al. (C). 1983. 293.85 (*3-11-008838-X*) De Gruyter.

Verfassungsdebatte bei Herodot & Politisches Denken bei Herodot & Frauenimuncipation in Athen, 3 Vols. Helmut Apffel et al. Ed. by Gregory Vlastos. LC 78-14603. (Morals & Law in Ancient Greece Ser.). 1979. reprint ed. lib. bdg. 21.95 (*0-405-11574-1*) Ayer.

Verfolgung bis zum Massenmord: Holocaust-Diskurse in Deutscher Sprache Aus der Sicht der Verfolgten. Dagmar C. Lorenz. LC 91-37352. (German Life & Civilization Ser.: Vol. 11). 451p. (GER.). (C). 1993. text ed. 66.95 (*0-8204-1751-3*) P Lang Pubng.

Verfuehrte Leser: Johann Karl August Musaeus' Romane und Romankritiken. Barbara M. Carvill. (Canadian Studies in German Language & Literature: Vol. 31). 342p. (GER.). (C). 1985. text ed. 25.50 (*0-8204-0224-9*) P Lang Pubng.

Verga's Milanese Tales. Olga Ragusa. 1964. 15.00 (*0-913298-33-6*) S F Vanni.

Verge of Eden. Mae W. Goodman. 1962. 6.95 (*0-8159-7100-1*) Devin.

Vergeelde Portretten Uit Een Indisch Familie-Album see Faded Portraits

vergessene Prinz. Hans Zeidler. 264p. 1995. pap. text ed. 15.00 (*3-364-00318-1*) Gordon & Breach.

Vergil: Antike Weltliteratur in Ihrer Entstehung und Nachwirkung. Ed. by Johannes Irmscher. 168p. (GER.). 1995. pap. 52.00 (*90-256-1030-7*, Pub. by A M Hakkert NE) Benjamins North Am.

Vergil: Selections. Robert P. Sonkowsky. 44p. (LAT.). 1985. pap. text ed. 39.95 (*0-88432-139-8*, S23685) Audio-Forum.

Vergil: Vergil's Aeneid I & II. Waldo E. Sweet. LC 60-9973. 173p. 1983. 14.00 (*0-86516-023-6*) Bolchazy-Carducci.

Vergil & the English Poets. Elizabeth Nitchie. LC 19-9760. reprint ed. 20.00 (*0-404-04778-5*) AMS Pr.

Vergil at Two Thousand: Commemorative Essays on the Poet & His Influence. Ed. by John D. Bernard & Paul T. Alessi. LC 85-48005. (Ars Poetica Ser.: No. 3). 1986. 39.50 (*0-404-62503-7*) AMS Pr.

***Vergil in the Middle Ages.** Domenico Comparetti. LC 96-3403. 392p. 1997. pap. text ed. 19.95 (*0-691-02678-5*) Princeton U Pr.

Vergil und die Gottlichen Machte. Walter Potscher. (Spudasmata Ser.: Bd. XXXV). vi, 184p. (GER.). 1977. write for info. (*3-487-06410-3*) G Olms Pubs.

***Vergilius: Concordantia Vegiliana.** Manfred Wacht. viii, 1420p. (GER.). 1995. write for info. (*3-487-09848-2*) G Olms Pubs.

Vergilius - Concordantia in Appendicem Vergilianam. Ed. by Hermann Morgenroth & Dietmar Najock. (Alpha-Omega, Reihe A Ser.: Bd. LXVIII). x, 542p. (GER.). 1992. write for info. (*3-487-09592-0*) G Olms Pubs.

Vergil's Aeneid. Vergil. Tr. by L. R. Lind. LC 63-9721. (Greek & Latin Classics Ser.). (Illus.). 328p. 1963. pap. 11.95 (*0-253-20045-8*, MB-45) Ind U Pr.

Vergil's Aeneid: A Poem of Grief & Love. Steven Farron. LC 93-6782. (Mnemosyne, Bibliotheca Classica Batava Ser.: Vol. 122). xii, 174p. 1993. 54.00 (*90-04-09661-2*) E J Brill.

Vergil's Aeneid see Bloom's Notes

Vergil's Aeneid & Fourth ("Messianic") Eclogue in the Dryden Translation. Howard Clarke. LC 88-19769. 428p. 1989. lib. bdg. 45.00 (*0-271-00651-X*) Pa St U Pr.

Vergil's Aeneid Books, Vol. I-VI. Clyde Pharr. 1995. pap. text ed. 20.00 (*0-86516-272-7*) Bolchazy-Carducci.

***Vergil's Eclogues.** Tr. by Barbar H. Fowler. LC 96-36990. 72p. (C). 1997. pap. 9.95 (*0-8078-4653-8*) U of NC Pr.

***Vergil's Eclogues.** Tr. by Barbara H. Fowler. LC 96-36990. 72p. (C). 1997. 22.50 (*0-8078-2347-3*) U of NC Pr.

Vergil's Eclogues: Landscapes of Experience. Eleanor W. Leach. LC 73-17699. 288p. 1974. 45.00 (*0-8014-0820-2*) Cornell U Pr.

Vergils Gedichte, Band 1: Bukolika und Georgika. Ed. by Theodor Ladewig et al. xlii, 292p. (GER.). 1973. write for info. (*3-296-15871-5*) G Olms Pubs.

Vergils Gedichte, Band 2: Buch I-VI der Aneis. Ed. by Theodor Ladewig et al. vi, 341p. (GER.). write for info. (*3-296-15872-3*) G Olms Pubs.

Vergils Gedichte, Band 3: Buch VII-XII der Aneis. Ed. by Theodor Ladewig et al. vi, 308p. (GER.). 1973. write for info. (*3-296-15873-1*) G Olms Pubs.

Vergin' Mary & Madonna. Lyn Lifshin et al. (Elite Chaps: No. 4). 62p. (Orig.). 1986. pap. 3.20 (*0-935839-01-1*) Vergin Pr.

Verging on the Abyss: The Social Fiction of Kate Chopin & Edith Wharton. Mary E. Papke. LC 90-38412. (Contributions in Women's Studies: No. 119). 208p. 1990. text ed. 49.95 (*0-313-26877-0*, PAJ, Greenwood Pr) Greenwood.

Verging on the Pertinent. Carol Emshwiller. 130p. (Orig.). 1989. pap. 9.95 (*0-918273-57-9*) Coffee Hse.

Vergleichende Biologische Formenkunde der Fossilen Niederen Tiere: Biological Comparative Morphology of Lower Fossil Animals. Edgar Dacque. Ed. by Stephen J. Gould. LC 79-8329. (History of Paleontology Ser.). (Illus.). (GER.). 1980. reprint ed. lib. bdg. 81.95 (*0-405-12710-3*) Ayer.

Vergleichende Geschichte der Slavischen Literaturen see Comparative History of Slavic Literatures

Vergleichende Syntax der Uralaltaischen (Turanischen) Sprachen. Wilhelm Prohle. (Bibliotheca Nostratica Ser.: Vol. 4). 229p. 1978. 66.00 (*3-447-02003-2*) Eurolingua.

Vergleichende Untersuchungen der Altanatolischen Sprachen. Bernhard Rosenkranz. (Trends in Linguistics, State-of-the-Art Reports: No. 8). 1978. pap. 66.15 (*90-279-7696-1*) Mouton.

Vergleichende Untersuchungen der Keimung Entfaltung, und Fruchtbildung Hoeherer Kryptogamen (Moose, Farne, Equisetaceen, Rhizocarpeen und Lycopodiaceen) und der Samenbildung der Coniferen. W. Hofmeister. (Historia Naturalis Classica Ser.: No. 105). (Illus.). (GER.). 1979. reprint ed. lib. bdg. 48.00 (*3-7682-1250-5*) Lubrecht & Cramer.

Vergleichende Untersuchungen Extensiver und Intensiver Weidebetriebe Mit Rindern und Schafen Aus Grunlandwirtschaftlicher und Okologischer Sicht An Acht Standorten. Martin Rump. LC 94-5089. 312p. (GER.). 1994. pap. 99.95 (*0-7734-4048-8*) E Mellen.

Vergleichendes und Etymologisches Woerterbuch der Germanischen Starken Verben. Elmar Seebold. (Janua Linguarum, Ser. Practica: No. 85). (GER.). 1970. pap. text ed. 133.85 (*3-10-800135-3*) Mouton.

Vergleichendes Woerterbuch der Indogermanischen Sprachen, 3 vols. Alois Walde. Ed. by Julius Pokorny. (GER.). (C). 1973. reprint ed. Set. 488.50 (*3-11-004556-7*) De Gruyter.

Vergleichsprozesse Bei Evaluativen Urteilen: Der EinfluB der in der Frage Vorgegebenen Vergleichsrichtung. Michaela Wanke. LC 93-32124. 140p. (GER.). 1993. text ed. 69.95 (*0-7734-9365-4*) E Mellen.

Verhaeltnis des Johannesevangeliums zu den Synoptikern: Am Beispiel von Mt. 8, 5-13; Lk. 7, 1-10; Joh. 4, 46-54. Stephan Landis. (Beihefte zur Zeitschrift fuer die Neutestamentliche Wissenschaft Ser.: Bd. 74). 85p. (GER.). (C). 1994. pap. text ed. 36.95 (*3-11-014389-5*) De Gruyter.

Verhaeltnis von Amt und Gemeinde im Neueren Katholizismus. Ursula Schnell. (Theologische Bibliothek Toepelmann Ser.: Vol. 29). (C). 1977. pap. 113.85 (*3-11-004929-5*) De Gruyter.

Verhaltensauffaellige Schueler. B. Meile. (Sozialmedizinische und Paedagogische Jugendkunde Ser.: Band 16). xii, 84p. 1982. pap. 18.50 (*3-8055-3552-X*) S Karger.

Verhaltnis der Verstandeserkenntnis Zur Sinnlichen in der Vorsokratischen Philosophie. Ernst Arndt. (Abhandlungen Zur Philosophie und Ihrer Geschichte Ser.: Bd. 31). 57p. 1975. reprint ed. 20.00 (*3-487-05636-4*) G Olms Pubs.

Verhaltniswörter in den Ostseefinnischen Sprachen. Renate Stoebke. LC 67-66160. (Uralic & Altaic Ser.: Vol. 93). 354p. 1968. 15.00 (*0-87750-038-X*) Res Inst Inner Asian Studies.

Verhandlungen des Sechsten Internationalen Symposiums uber Entonomofaunistik in Mitteleuropa. Ed. by Hans Malicky. 1977. pap. text ed. 129.50 (*90-6193-559-8*) Kluwer Ac.

Verifiable Programming. Ole-Johan Dahl. 350p. 1992. pap. text ed. 39.00 (*0-13-951062-1*) P-H.

Verification: How Much Is Enough? Allan S. Krass. 300p. 1985. 90.00 (*0-85066-305-9*, Crane Russak) Taylor & Francis.

Verification: The Soviet Stance Its Past, Present & Future. 125p. 1990. 19.00 (*92-9045-042-8*, GV.90.0.6) UN.

Verification after the Cold War: Broadening the Process. Ed. by Jurgen Altmann et al. 400p. 1994. pap. 49.50 (*90-5383-291-2*, Pub. by VU Univ Pr NE) Paul & Co Pubs.

Verification & the U. N. The Role of the Organization in Verification of Multilateral Arms Limitation & Disarmament Agreements. 122p. 1991. 17.50 (*92-1-142171-3*, 91.IX.9) UN.

***Verification & Validation.** Schulmeyer. (ITCP-US Computer Science Ser.). 1997. text ed. 59.99 (*1-85032-909-5*) ITCP.

Verification & Validation of Complex Systems: Human Factors Issues. Ed. by John A. Wisee et al. LC 93-4994. (NATO ASI Series F: Computer & Systems Science: Vol. 110). 1993. 187.95 (*0-387-56574-4*) Spr-Verlag.

Verification & Validation of Rule-Based Expert Systems. Suzanne Smith. 224p. 1993. 89.00 (*0-8493-8902-X*, QA76) CRC Pr.

Verification at Vienna: Monitoring Reductions of Conventional Armed Forces. Ed. by Jurgen Altmann. 396p. 1992. text ed. 73.00 (*2-88124-539-0*) Gordon & Breach.

Verification in Economics & History: A Sequel to 'Scientifization' Omar F. Hamouda & B. B. Price. (Illus.). 208p. (C). (gr. 13). 1991. text ed. 69.95 (*0-415-05336-6*, A6324) Routledge.

Verification of a Comprehensive Test Ban Treaty from Space: A Preliminary Study. (UNDIR Research Papers: No. 32). 58p. Date not set. pap. 12.00 (*92-9045-099-1*, E.GV.94.0.30) UN.

Verification of Arms Control Agreements. Ed. by Ian Bellany & Coit D. Blacker. 104p. 1983. 35.00 (*0-7146-3228-7*, Pub. by F Cass Pubs UK) Intl Spec Bk.

Verification of Arms Reduction. Ed. by J. Atlmann & Joseph Rotblat. (Illus.). xiv, 228p. 1989. 52.00 (*0-387-51596-8*) Spr-Verlag.

Verification of Disarmament & Arms Limitations Agreements: Ways, Means & Practices. Serge Sur. (UNIDIR (United Nations Institute for Disarmament Research) Ser.). 450p. 1991. 64.95 (*1-85521-235-8*, Pub. by Dartmth Pub UK) Ashgate Pub Co.

Verification of Disarmament or Limitation of Armaments: Instruments, Negotiations, Proposals. 267p. Date not set. 42.00 (*92-9045-062-2*, E.GV.92.0.10) UN.

Verification of Geotechnical Grouting: A Report from the ASCE Committee on Grouting of the Geotechnical Engineering Division & Papers Presented at the ASCE Convention in San Diego, California, October 23-27, 1995. Ed. by Michael J. Byle & Roy H. Borden. 184p. 1995. 25.00 (*0-7844-0132-2*) Am Soc Civil Eng.

Verification of Mathematical & Physical Models in Hydraulic Engineering. 898p. 1978. pap. 44.00 (*0-87262-131-6*) Am Soc Civil Eng.

Verification of Numerical Procedures for the Analysis of Soil Liquefaction Problems: Proceedings of the International Conference, Davis, California, October 1993, 2 vols. Ed. by Kandish Arulanandan et al. (Illus.). 2000p. (C). 1994. text ed. 180.00 (*90-5410-360-4*, Pub. by A A Balkema NE) Ashgate Pub Co.

Verification of Sequential & Concurrent Programs. Krzystof R. Apt & F. R. Olderog. Ed. by David Gries. (Texts & Monographs in Computer Science). xvi, 441p. 1991. 59.95 (*0-387-97532-2*) Spr-Verlag.

***Verification of Sequential & Concurrent Programs.** 2nd ed. Ernst R. Olderog & K. R. Apt. LC 96-29771. (Graduate Texts in Computer Science Ser.). 356p. 1997. 44.95 (*0-387-94896-1*) Spr-Verlag.

Verification Problems of the Washington Treaty on the Elimination of Intermediate-Range Missiles. (United Nations Institute for Disarmament Research (UNIDIR) Publications). 64p. 1988. 15.00 (*92-9045-030-4*, EGV.88.0.7) UN.

Verification under the Projected Chemical Weapons Convention: On-Site Inspection in Chemical Industry Facilities. Ralf Trapp. (SIPRI Chemical & Biological Warfare Studies). 150p. 1993. pap. 32.00 (*0-19-829160-4*) OUP.

Verification 1996: Arms Control, Peacekeeping, & the Environment. R. Guthrie. Ed. by J. B. Poole. (C). 1996. text ed. 95.00 (*0-8133-9005-2*) Westview.

***Verification 1997: The Vertic Yearbook.** Ed. by Richard Guthrie. (C). 1997. pap. text ed. 45.00 (*0-8133-9987-4*) Westview.

Verificationism: Its History & Prospects. C. J. Misak. LC 95-7728. (Philosophical Issues in Science Ser.). 272p. (C). 1995. pap. 19.95 (*0-415-12598-7*, Routledge NY) Routledge.

Verificationist. David Antrim. Date not set. write for info. (*0-679-76943-9*) McKay.

Verify Those Credentials! Do You Know Who You Are Dealing With. Ed. by Michael Sankey & Carl R. Ernst. 480p. 1997. pap. 19.95 (*1-889150-00-2*) Facts on Demand.

Verifying Concurrent Processes Using Temporal Logic. R. T. Hailpern. (Lecture Notes in Computer Science Ser.: Vol. 129). 208p. 1982. 25.00 (*0-387-11205-7*) Spr-Verlag.

Verifying SALT Agreements. Bruce G. Blair & Garry D. Brewer. (CISA Working Papers: No. 19). 61p. (Orig.). 1980. pap. 15.00 (*0-86682-018-3*) Ctr Intl Relations.

Verifying Temporal Properties of Systems. J. C. Bradfield. (Progress in Theoretical Computer Science Ser.). viii, 113p. 1991. 60.50 (*0-8176-3625-0*) Birkhauser.

Verifying the Vision: A Self-Evaluation for the Catholic Elementary School. 2nd ed. Ed. by Carleen Reck & Judith Coreil. 150p. 1988. reprint ed. pap. 14.00 (*1-55833-003-8*) Natl Cath Educ.

***Verilog Handle Conference, 6th Ieee International.** LC 10-859403. 200p. 1997. pap. 50.00 (*0-8186-7955-7*) IEEE Comp Soc.

Verilog Hardware Description Language. 3rd ed. Donald E. Thomas & Philip R. Moorby. LC 94-25116. 336p. (C). 1996. lib. bdg. 98.00 (*0-7923-9723-1*) Kluwer Ac.

Verilog HDL. Samir Palnitkar. 1996. text ed. 71.00 (*0-13-451675-3*) P-H.

Verilog HDL Conference, 1994. LC 93-74849. 136p. 1994. pap. 40.00 (*0-8186-5655-7*, 5655) IEEE Comp Soc.

Verilog HDL Conference, 1995 International. LC 95-75522. 152p. 1995. pap. 50.00 (*0-8186-7082-7*, PR07082) IEEE Comp Soc.

Verilog HDL Conference, 1996 IEEE International. LC 10-859403. 128p. 1996. pap. 50.00 (*0-8186-7429-6*, PRO7429) IEEE Comp Soc.

***Verilog HDL Primer.** Jayaram Bhasker. 260p. 1997. 49.95 (*0-9656277-4-8*) Star Galaxy Pr.

***Verilog Quickstart.** James M. Lee. LC 97-5202. 1997. text ed. write for info. (*0-7923-9927-7*) Kluwer Ac.

***Verisign Certification Practice Statement.** Michael S. Baum. (Certification Practice Statement Ser.). 80p. (Orig.). 1996. ring bd. write for info. (*0-9653555-0-0*) VeriSign.

Veritable Dynamo: Lloyd Ross & Australian Labour 1901-1987. Stephen Holt. 196p. 1996. pap. 29.95 (*0-7022-2653-X*, Pub. by Univ Queensland Pr AT) Intl Spec Bk.

Veritable Split in the International: Public Circular of the Situationist International. Guy Debord & Gianfranco SanGuinetti. 138p. (Orig.). (C). 1989. pap. 15.95 (*0-9508380-2-0*, Pub. by Chronos Pubns UK) AK Pr Dist.

VeriTales: Beyond the Norm: Short Stories for the Evolving Spirit. Ed. by Helen Wirth. LC 93-37511. 192p. (Orig.). 1994. pap. 14.95 (*0-9632374-3-8*) Fall Creek.

VeriTales: Freed by Choice: Short Stories for the Evolving Spirit. Ed. by Helen Wirth. LC 94-22779. 192p. (Orig.). 1994. pap. 14.95 (*0-9632374-4-6*) Fall Creek.

VeriTales: Note of Hope: Short Stories for the Evolving Spirit. Ed. by Helen Wirth. LC 93-13270. 192p. (Orig.). 1993. pap. 14.95 (*0-9632374-2-X*) Fall Creek.

VeriTales: Ring of Truth: Short Stories for the Evolving Spirit. Ed. by Helen Wirth. (Illus.). 192p. (Orig.). 1993. pap. 14.95 (*0-9632374-1-1*) Fall Creek.

***Veritas.** William Lashner. 352p. 1997. 24.00 (*0-06-039147-2*, ReganBooks) HarpC.

***Veritas.** William Lashner. 1997. mass mkt. 6.50 (*0-06-101023-5*, Harp PBks) HarpC.

Veritas: Revelation of Mysteries Biblical, Historical, & Social, by Means of the Mediann & Persian Laws. Henry Melville. 160p. 1993. reprint ed. pap. 17.95 (*1-56459-396-7*) Kessinger Pub.

Veritas Book of Blessing Prayers. 222p. (Orig.). 1990. pap. 14.95 (*1-85390-040-0*, Pub. by Veritas Publns IE) Ignatius Pr.

Veritas Filia Temporis? Philosophiehistorie Zwischen Wahrheit und Geschichte. Ed. by Rolf W. Puster. 319p. (GER.). (C). 1995. lib. bdg. 133.85 (*3-11-014170-1*) De Gruyter.

Veritas Hymnal. Gerry Threadgold. 1989. Organ ed., 148p. pap. 54.00 (*0-901810-93-2*, Pub. by Veritas IE); People's ed., 128p. pap. 30.00 (*0-901810-62-2*, Pub. by Veritas IE) St Mut.

Veritatis Splendor: A Response. Ed. by Charles Yeats. 1995. pap. 17.95 (*1-85311-093-0*, Pub. by Canterbury Press Norwich UK) Morehouse Pub.

Veritatis Splendor: American Responses. Michael E. Allsopp & John J. O'Keefe. (Illus.). 240p. (Orig.). 1995. pap. 19.95 (*1-55612-760-X*) Sheed & Ward MO.

Veritatis Splendor: Living the Good Life. Alfred A. McBride. (Blackline Master Ser.). 25p. 1996. 9.95 (*0-87973-132-X*) Our Sunday Visitor.

***Veritatis Splendor: The Splendor of Truth: A Study Guide for Pro-Life Americans.** Judie Brown. (Evangelium Vitae Ser.). 20p. (Orig.). 1996. pap. 2.00 (*1-890712-01-9*, EVI) Amer Life League.

Verite, Vol. 1. Emile Zola. (Illus.). 352p. (FRE.). write for info. (*2-86808-075-8*) Intl Scholars.

Verite, Vol. 2. Emile Zola. (Illus.). 360p. (FRE.). write for info. (*2-86808-076-6*) Intl Scholars.

Verite see Quatre Evangiles

Verite en Peinture. Jacques Derrida. (FRE.). 1990. pap. 21.95 (*0-7859-3402-2*) Fr & Eur.

Verite et Verification/Wahrheit und Verifikation. H. L. Van Breda. (Phaenomenologica Ser.: No. 61). 230p. 1974. lib. bdg. 82.50 (*90-247-1702-7*, Pub. by M Nijhoff NE) Kluwer Ac.

Verity Bargate Award Plays, 1983: Shona, Lunch Girls & Shelter. Tony Craze et al. Ed. by Barrie Keeffe. (Methuen New Theatrescripts Ser.). 128p. (C). 1988. pap. 8.95 (*0-413-53850-8*, A0262, Pub. by Methuen UK) Heinemann.

Verity Bargate Award Plays, 1984. Mick Mahoney & Melissa Murray. Ed. by Barrie Keefe. (Methuen New Theatrescripts Ser.). 64p. (C). 1988. pap. 8.95 (*0-413-58930-7*, A0305, Pub. by Methuen UK) Heinemann.

Verity Bargate Award Plays, 1986: Rellevo, Made in Spain, Smith. David Spencer et al. Ed. by Barrie Keeffe. (Methuen New Theatrescripts Ser.). 96p. (C). 1988. pap. 11.95 (*0-413-42120-1*, A0236, Pub. by Methuen UK) Heinemann.

Verity Bargate Award Plays, 1988. Gillian Plowman et al. Ed. by Barrie Keeffe. (Methuen New Theatrescripts Ser.). 110p. (Orig.). (C). 1989. pap. 12.95 (*0-413-62240-1*, A0408, Pub. by Methuen UK) Heinemann.

***Verkehrskonzeptionen fur die Zukunft unter Besonderer Berucksichtigung des Fahrradverkehrs: Eine Okonomisch-Politische Analyse.** Ralk Rockenbauch. (Europaische Hochschulschriften: Reihe 5: Bd. 1976). (Illus.). 362p. (GER.). 1996. pap. 61.95 (*3-631-30475-7*) P Lang Pubng.

Verkehswesen Im Kriege: Die Osterreichischen Eisenbahnen; Militarische Verkehrs Probleme Osterreich-Ungarns. Bruno Enderes et al. (Wirtschafts-Und Sozialgeschichte des Weltkrieges (Osterreichische Und Ungarische Serie)). (GER.). 1931. 100.00 (*0-685-10835-X*) Elliots Bks.

Verklarend Informatica Woordenboek. C. Van Uitert. 1063p. (DUT & ENG.). 1989. pap. 95.00 (*0-8288-8017-4*) Fr & Eur.

Verkundigung Vergils. Richard Faber. (Altertumswissenschaftliche Texte und Studien: Bd. 4). xiv, 445p. 1975. write for info. (*3-487-05755-7*) G Olms Pubs.

***Verleger der Spaetaufklaerung und der Deutschen Klassik Band 3: Repertorium der Verlagskorrespondenz Goeschen (1783 bis 1828)** Georg J. Goeschen. Ed. by Stephan Fuessel. xxiii, 574p. (GER.). (C). 1996. lib. bdg. 233.35 (*3-11-014550-2*) De Gruyter.

Verlobung in St. Domingo: Kleist's Novelle in Translation & as a Basis for Opera & Drama. Almute Wedekind. LC 83-48168. (American University Studies: Germanic Languages & Literature: Ser. I, Vol. 12). 119p. (C). 1983. pap. text ed. 12.65 (*0-8204-0017-3*) P Lang Pubng.

Verlorene Ehre der Katharina Blum, Boll: Critical Monographs in English. Donal McLaughlin. 64p. 1993. pap. 32.00 (*0-85261-257-5*, Pub. by Univ of Glasgow UK) St Mut.

Verlorene Heroische Zeitalter: Held und Volk in Heinrich von Kleists Dramen. Gabriele M. Wickert. LC 82-84612. (American University Studies: Germanic Languages & Literature: Ser. I, Vol. 8). 173p. (Orig.). (C). 1983. pap. text ed. 20.55 (*0-8204-0004-1*) P Lang Pubng.

Verlorene Siege see Lost Victories

Verlorene Sohn see Saemtliche Werke

Vermeer. Martin Bailey. (Color Library). (Illus.). 128p. 1995. pap. 14.95 (*0-7148-3463-7*, Pub. by Phaidon Press UK) Chronicle Bks.

Vermeer. Celeste Brusati. LC 92-36644. (Rizzoli Art Ser.). (Illus.). 24p. 1993. pap. 7.95 (*0-8478-1649-4*) Rizzoli Intl.

***Vermeer.** Lawrence Gowing & Johannes Vermeer. LC 97-20774. 1997. write for info. (*0-520-21276-2*) U CA Pr.

Vermeer. John Nash. (Illus.). 128p. 1991. 25.00 (*1-870248-62-7*) Scala Books.

***Vermeer.** Norbert Schneider. 1994. pap. text ed. 9.99 (*3-8228-9046-4*) Taschen Amer.

Vermeer. Michael Walicki. 138p. (GER.). 1970. 60.00 (*0-317-57369-1*) St Mut.

Vermeer. Arthur K. Wheelock, Jr. (Masters of Art Ser.). (Illus.). 128p. 1988. 22.95 (*0-8109-1737-8*) Abrams.

Vermeer: Consciousness & the Chamber of Being. Martin Pops. Ed. by Donald Kuspit. LC 84-2564. (Studies in the Fine Arts: Criticism: No. 16). 132p. reprint ed. 37.70 (*0-8357-1525-6*, 2070460) Bks Demand.

***Vermeer: Faith in Painting.** Daniel Arasse. 208p. 1994. pap. text ed. 18.95 (*0-691-02930-X*) Princeton U Pr.

Vermeer: Reception & Interpretation. Christine Hertel. (Illus.). 352p. (C). 1996. text ed. 70.00 (*0-521-55020-3*) Cambridge U Pr.

***Vermeer: The Complete Works.** Arthur K. Wheelock & Johannes Vermeer. LC 97-399. 1997. pap. write for info. (*0-8109-2751-9*) Abrams.

Vermeer & His Milieu: A Web of Social History. John M. Montias. (Illus.). 427p. 1989. text ed. 79.50 (*0-691-04051-6*); pap. text ed. 24.95 (*0-691-00289-4*) Princeton U Pr.

Vermeer & the Art of Painting. Arthur K. Wheelock, Jr. LC 94-40119. (Illus.). 240p. 1995. 45.00 (*0-300-06239-7*) Yale U Pr.

***Vermeer in Bosnia.** Lawrence Weschler. 1998. write for info. (*0-679-44270-7*) Knopf.

Vermeer the Magical. Edward V. Lucas. LC 79-37352. (Select Bibliographies Reprint Ser.). (Illus.). 1977. reprint ed. 16.95 (*0-8369-6699-6*) Ayer.

***Vermeers Ambition.** Daniel Arasse. 1996. text ed. 40.00 (*3-364-00327-0*) Gordon & Breach.

Vermicomposting: Selected Articles. Mary Appelhof. 32p. 1982. pap. 10.00 (*0-942256-04-2*, Flower Pr) Flowerfield Ent.

***Vermilion.** Nathan Aldyne. 1997. pap. 9.95 (*1-55583-434-5*) Alyson Pubns.

Vermilion. Phyllis A. Whitney. 320p. 1982. mass mkt. 5.99 (*0-449-24555-1*, Crest) Fawcett.

Vermilion Bird: T'ang Images of the South. Edward H. Schafer. LC 67-10463. 1967. pap. 17.00 (*0-520-05463-6*) U CA Pr.

Vermilion in Season. Barbara K. Swasey. Ed. & Intro. by Diana B. Szambeck. (Illus.). 80p. (Orig.). 1994. pap. write for info. (*0-9641237-0-3*) Knots & Lines.

Vermilion Sands. J. G. Ballard. 208p. 1988. pap. 3.95 (*0-88184-422-5*) Carroll & Graf.

Vermilion Skies: The Tai Chi Classics As Contemplation. Al Stone. 80p. (Orig.). 1993. pap. 6.95 (*1-883380-01-4*) Traffic Lght.

Vermillion County, Indiana, History & Family. Vermillion County Historical Society Staff & Turner Publishing Company Staff. LC 88-51841. 224p. 1989. 48.00 (*0-938021-34-6*) Turner Pub KY.

Vermin & Other Survival Stories: Humanity As an Endangered Species. Harry Willson. LC 96-85282. (Illus.). 194p. (Orig.). 1997. pap. 10.00 (*0-938513-22-2*) Amador Pubs.

Vermin Blond. Richard Davis. 208p. 1993. 23.95 (*0-575-05007-1*, Pub. by V Gollancz UK) Trafalgar.

Vermont. Dan Elish. (Celebrate the States Ser.). (Illus.). 144p. (YA). (gr. 4 up). 1997. lib. bdg. 22.95 (*0-7614-0146-6*, Benchmark NY) Marshall Cavendish.

Vermont. Dennis B. Fradin. LC 92-36371. (From Sea to Shining Sea Ser.). (Illus.). 64p. (J). (gr. 3-5). 1993. lib. bdg. 24.00 (*0-516-03845-1*) Childrens.

***Vermont.** Dennis B. Fradin. (From Sea to Shining Sea Ser.). 1997. pap. 5.95 (*0-516-26202-5*) Childrens.

Vermont. Sylvia McNair. LC 90-21117. (America the Beautiful Ser.). (Illus.). 144p. (J). (gr. 5-8). 1991. lib. bdg. 28.30 (*0-516-00491-3*) Childrens.

Vermont. Kathy Pelta. LC 93-33389. (Hello U. S. A. Ser.). (Illus.). 72p. (J). (gr. 3-6). 1994. lib. bdg. 18.95 (*0-8225-2729-4*, Lerner Publctns) Lerner Group.

Vermont. Kathleen Thompson. LC 95-50027. (Portrait of America Library). 48p. (J). (gr. 3 up). 1996. lib. bdg. 22.83 (*0-8114-7391-0*) Raintree Steck-V.

Vermont. Kathleen Thompson. (Portrait of America Library). 48p. (J). (gr. 3 up). 1996. pap. text ed. 5.95 (*0-8114-7472-0*) Raintree Steck-V.

***Vermont.** 9th ed. (Illus.). 1996. write for info. (*0-89933-016-9*, 5253) DeLorme Map.

Vermont: A Culinary Journey. 2nd rev. ed. Sue B. Schildge. (Illus.). 193p. 1995. 12.95 (*0-614-10456-4*) Schildge Pub.

Vermont: A Guide to the Green Mountain State. Federal Writers' Project Staff & Writers Program-WPA Staff. (American Guide Ser.). 1989. reprint ed. lib. bdg. 69.00 (*0-7812-1044-5*, 1044) Rprt Serv.

Vermont: A Guide to the Green Mountain State. Federal Writers' Project Staff. 1937. reprint ed. 79.00 (*0-403-02194-4*) Somerset Pub.

Vermont: A Harvest of Color. Photos by George B. Robinson. LC 90-60429. (Illus.). 32p. 1990. pap. 8.95 (*0-933050-81-X*) New Eng Pr VT.

Vermont: A Special World. 7th ed. Ralph N. Hill et al. (Illus.). 168p. 21.95 (*0-936896-02-7*) VT Life Mag.

Vermont: A Study of Independence. Rowland E. Robinson. LC 72-3751. (American Commonwealths Ser.: No. 14). reprint ed. 39.50 (*0-404-57214-6*) AMS Pr.

Vermont: A Summer View. Photos by Ramon Scavelli. LC 94-65733. (Illus.). 56p. (Orig.). 1995. pap. 12.95 (*1-881535-10-X*) New Eng Pr VT.

***Vermont: An Explorer's Guide.** 7th ed. Christina Tree & Peter S. Jennison. LC 97-7278. (Explorer's Guide Ser.). (Illus.). 480p. (Orig.). 1997. pap. 18.00 (*0-88150-388-6*) Countryman.

Vermont: An Illustrated History. John Duffy. LC 85-22621. 264p. 1985. 24.95 (*0-89781-159-3*) Am Historical Pr.

Vermont: Off the Beaten Path: A Guide to Unique Places. 2nd ed. Lisa Shaw. LC 95-23872. (Off the Beaten Path Ser.). (Illus.). 160p. 1996. pap. 10.95 (*1-56440-766-7*) Globe Pequot.

Vermont: The State with the Storybook Past. rev. ed. Cora Cheney. LC 86-60341. (Illus.). 288p. (J). (gr. 5-9). 1996. pap. 22.95 (*1-881535-21-5*) New Eng Pr VT.

Vermont: Wilderness to Statehood 1748-1791. Warren W. Dexter & Barbara C. Hanson. LC 89-80734. (Illus.). 180p. (Orig.). 1989. pap. 8.95 (*0-914960-71-7*) Academy Bks.

Vermont - Collected Works of Federal Writers Project. Federal Writers' Project Staff. 1991. reprint ed. lib. bdg. 98.00 (*0-7812-5794-8*) Rprt Serv.

Vermont - Paris Odyssey. Esther. 12p. (Orig.). 1988. pap. text ed. 6.00 (*0-938885-05-7*) Shu Pub.

Vermont Adventure: Turn Left to E. Wallingford. A. F. Joy. (Illus.). 131p. (Orig.). 1985. pap. 4.95 (*0-934703-01-9*) Saturscent Pubns.

Vermont Afternoons with Robert Frost. Vrest Orton. LC 70-134029. 64p. 1981. pap. 4.50 (*0-914960-34-2*) Academy Bks.

Vermont & Other State Greats (Biographies) Carole Marsh. (Carole Marsh Vermont Bks.). (Illus.). (J). 1994. pap. 19.95 (*0-7933-2162-X*); lib. bdg. 29.95 (*0-7933-2161-1*); disk 29.95 (*0-7933-2163-8*) Gallopade Pub Group.

Vermont Atlas & Gazetteer. DeLorme Staff. (Atlas & Gazetteer Ser.). 88p. (Orig.). 1996. pap. 16.95 (*0-89933-005-3*) DeLorme Map.

Vermont Autumn. Jay Woodard. (Illus.). 114p. 1991. text ed. 29.95 (*0-9618888-3-0*) Anglo-Am TX.

Vermont Bandits, Bushwackers, Outlaws, Crooks, Devils, Ghosts, Desperadoes & Other Assorted & Sundry Characters! Carole Marsh. (Carole Marsh Vermont Bks.). (Illus.). (J). 1994. pap. 19.95 (*0-7933-1129-2*); lib. bdg. 29.95 (*0-7933-1130-6*); write for info. (*0-7933-1131-4*) Gallopade Pub Group.

Vermont Bicentennial & History. 1984. pap. 9.95 (*0-393-30223-7*) Norton.

Vermont Blood. Barney Crosier. (Illus.). 128p. 1980. pap. 5.95 (*0-9603900-6-5*) Lanser Pr.

Vermont Bookstore Book: A Surprising Guide to Our State's Bookstores & Their Specialties for Students, Teachers, Writers & Publishers. Carole Marsh. (Vermont Bks.). (Illus.). 1994. pap. 19.95 (*0-7933-2991-4*); lib. bdg. 29.95 (*0-7933-2990-6*); disk 29.95 (*0-7933-2992-2*) Gallopade Pub Group.

***Vermont Business Directory 1997.** rev. ed. American Business Directories Staff. 368p. 1997. boxed 295.00 (*1-56105-919-6*) Am Busn Direct.

Vermont by Choice: The Earliest Years. Bertha S. Dodge. LC 87-62158. 160p. (Orig.). 1987. pap. 9.95 (*0-933050-50-X*) New Eng Pr VT.

Vermont Census Index 1850 Mortality Schedule. (Illus.). lib. bdg. 50.00 (*0-89593-515-5*) Accelerated Index.

Vermont Census Index 1860 Mortality Schedules. (Illus.). lib. bdg. 49.00 (*0-89593-517-1*) Accelerated Index.

Vermont Census Index, 1880, 2 vols., Set. (Illus.). lib. bdg. write for info. (*0-89593-519-8*) Accelerated Index.

Vermont Census Index, 1890: Union Veterans. Ronald V. Jackson. (Illus.). lib. bdg. 50.00 (*0-89593-791-3*) Accelerated Index.

Vermont Chapbook. Compiled by Helen H. Flanders. LC 70-76935. (Granger Index Reprint Ser.). 1977. 16.95 (*0-8369-6016-5*) Ayer.

Vermont Classic Christmas Trivia: Stories, Recipes, Activities, Legends, Lore & More! Carole Marsh. (Carole Marsh Vermont Bks.). (Illus.). (J). 1994. pap. 19.95 (*0-7933-1132-2*); lib. bdg. 29.95 (*0-7933-1133-0*); disk 29.95 (*0-7933-1134-9*) Gallopade Pub Group.

Vermont Coastales. Carole Marsh. (Carole Marsh Vermont Bks.). (Illus.). (J). 1994. pap. 19.95 (*0-7933-2156-5*); lib. bdg. 29.95 (*0-7933-2155-7*); disk 29.95 (*0-7933-2157-3*) Gallopade Pub Group.

Vermont Coastales! Carole Marsh. (Vermont Bks.). (J). 1994. lib. bdg. 29.95 (*0-7933-7310-7*) Gallopade Pub Group.

Vermont Coinage see Colonial Coins of Vermont

Vermont Country Cooking. Aristene Pixley. 1979. reprint ed. pap. 3.50 (*0-486-23803-2*) Dover.

Vermont Court Rules Annotated, 1981-1991. 1994. suppl. ed., ring bd. 50.00 (*0-614-03171-0*) MICHIE.

Vermont Court Rules Annotated, 1981-1991, 2 vols., Set. annot. ed. Ed. by Butterworth Staff. 1000p. 1989. ring bd. 98.00 (*0-88063-547-9*) MICHIE.

Vermont Crime Perspective 1996. Ed. by Kathleen O. Morgan et al. 24p. 1996. pap. 19.00 (*1-56692-544-4*) Morgan Quitno Corp.

***Vermont Crime Perspective 1997.** Ed. by Kathleen O. Morgan & Scott E. Morgan. 24p. 1997. pap. 19.00 (*1-56692-794-3*) Morgan Quitno Corp.

Vermont Criminal Practice & Procedure. William A. Nelson. 830p. 1993. ring bd. 170.00 (*1-56257-360-8*) MICHIE.

Vermont Criminal Practice & Procedure. William A. Nelson. 1993. ring bd. 170.00 (*0-88063-788-9*) MICHIE.

Vermont "Crinkum-Crankum" A Funny Word Book about Our State. Carole Marsh. (Vermont Bks.). (Illus.). (J). (gr. 3-12). 1994. 29.95 (*0-7933-4943-5*); pap. 19.95 (*0-7933-4944-3*); disk 29.95 (*0-7933-4945-1*) Gallopade Pub Group.

Vermont Dingbats! Bk. 1: A Fun Book of Games, Stories, Activities & More about Our State That's All in Code! for You to Decipher. Carole Marsh. (Vermont Bks.). (Illus.). (J). (gr. 3-12). 1994. pap. 19.95 (*0-7933-3909-X*); lib. bdg. 29.95 (*0-7933-3908-1*); disk 29.95 (*0-7933-3910-3*) Gallopade Pub Group.

Vermont Early Census. Ronald V. Jackson. (Illus.). lib. bdg. 50.00 (*0-89593-747-6*) Accelerated Index.

Vermont Environmental Law. Merideth Wright. 1994. write for info. (*1-56257-232-6*) MICHIE.

Vermont Experience. Ed. by Susan B. Weber. (Illus.). 156p. 1987. 24.95 (*0-936896-08-6*) VT Life Mag.

Vermont Facts & Factivities. Carole Marsh. (Carole Marsh State Bks.). (Illus.). 1996. 29.95 (*0-614-11557-4*, C Marsh); teacher ed., pap. 19.95 (*0-7933-7937-7*, C Marsh) Gallopade Pub Group.

Vermont Families in 1791. Ed. by Scott A. Bartley. LC 92-64323. 311p. 1992. 30.00 (*0-89725-086-9*, 1395) Picton Pr.

Vermont Family Law. Ed. by Butterworth Staff. 420p. 1993. pap. 39.00 (*0-88063-617-3*) MICHIE.

Vermont Favorites: A Collection of Favorite Vermont Recipes. Ellen Doon. (Illus.). 48p. (Orig.). 1991. pap. 3.95 (*0-933050-94-1*) New Eng Pr VT.

Vermont Federal Census Index, 1790. Ronald V. Jackson. (Illus.). 1978. lib. bdg. 45.00 (*0-89593-790-5*) Accelerated Index.

Vermont Federal Census Index, 1800. Ronald V. Jackson. (Illus.). 1981. lib. bdg. 49.00 (*0-89593-214-8*) Accelerated Index.

Vermont Federal Census Index, 1810. Ronald V. Jackson. LC 77-86067. (Illus.). lib. bdg. 50.00 (*0-89593-141-9*) Accelerated Index.

Vermont Federal Census Index, 1820. Ronald V. Jackson. LC 77-86068. (Illus.). 1976. lib. bdg. 49.00 (*0-89593-142-7*) Accelerated Index.

Vermont Federal Census Index, 1830. Ronald V. Jackson. LC 77-86069. (Illus.). 1977. lib. bdg. 55.00 (*0-89593-143-5*) Accelerated Index.

Vermont Federal Census Index, 1840. Ronald V. Jackson. LC 77-86070. (Illus.). 1978. lib. bdg. 65.00 (*0-89593-144-3*) Accelerated Index.

Vermont Federal Census Index, 1850. Ronald V. Jackson & Gary R. Teeples. LC 77-86071. (Illus.). 1978. lib. bdg. 83.00 (*0-89593-145-1*) Accelerated Index.

Vermont Federal Census Index, 1860. (Illus.). lib. bdg. 120.00 (*0-89593-516-3*) Accelerated Index.

Vermont Federal Census Index, 1870, 2 vols., Set. (Illus.). lib. bdg. write for info. (*0-89593-518-X*) Accelerated Index.

Vermont Festival Fun for Kids! Carole Marsh. (Vermont Bks.). (Illus.). (YA). (gr. 3-12). 1994. pap. 19.95 (*0-7933-4062-4*); lib. bdg. 29.95 (*0-7933-4061-6*); disk 29.95 (*0-7933-4063-2*) Gallopade Pub Group.

Vermont Folk-Songs & Ballads. Helen H. Flanders & George Brown. LC 68-20768. iv, 264p. 1970. reprint ed. 40.00 (*0-8103-5010-6*) Gale.

Vermont for Every Season. Reeve Brown et al. LC 80-23320. (Illus.). 160p. 1980. 30.00 (*0-936896-00-0*) VT Life Mag.

Vermont from A to Z. Judson J. Conner. (Illus.). 48p. (Orig.). 1990. pap. 4.95 (*0-933050-79-8*) New Eng Pr VT.

Vermont General. Edward H. Ripley. Ed. by Otto Eisenschiml. (Illus.). 1959. 12.50 (*0-8159-7101-X*) Devin.

*__Vermont Government! The Cornerstone of Everyday Life in Our State!__ Carole Marsh. (Carole Marsh Vermont Bks.). (Illus.). (J). (gr. 3-12). 1996. pap. 19.95 (*0-7933-6317-9*); lib. bdg. 29.95 (*0-7933-6316-0*); disk 29.95 (*0-7933-6318-7*) Gallopade Pub Group.

Vermont Governments Performance Standards, 1990. Ed. by Greg Michels. (Governments Performance Standards Ser.). (Illus.). 150p. 1990. text ed. 125.00 (*1-55507-503-7*) Municipal Analysis.

Vermont Harmony, Vol. 2: Selections from the Musical Works of Jeremiah Ingalls & Hezekiah Moors. Intro. by James G. Chapman. (Illus.). 93p. (Orig.). 1991. pap. 7.50 (*0-937243-02-7*) Chapman Assocs.

Vermont Harmony, Vol. 4: The Music of Joel Harmon, Jr. & Uri K. Hill. Intro. by James G. Chapman. 85p. (Orig.). 1990. pap. 7.50 (*0-937243-04-3*) Chapman Assocs.

Vermont Health Care Perspective 1996. Ed. by Kathleen O. Morgan et al. 24p. 1996. pap. 19.00 (*1-56692-644-0*) Morgan Quitno Corp.

*__Vermont Health Care Perspective 1997.__ Ed. by Kathleen O. Morgan & Scott E. Morgan. 24p. 1997. pap. 19.00 (*1-56692-744-7*) Morgan Quitno Corp.

Vermont Heritage Songbook. Margaret Mac Arthur & Gregory Sharrow. 108p. 1994. 9.95 (*0-916718-13-1*) VT Folklife Ctr.

Vermont Historical & Biographical Index, Vol. 1. Ronald V. Jackson. LC 78-53721. (Illus.). 1984. lib. bdg. 30.00 (*0-89593-203-2*) Accelerated Index.

Vermont Historical Gazeteer Vol. III: Orleans & Rutland Counties. Ed. by Abby M. Hemenway. (Illus.). 1245p. 1995. reprint ed. lib. bdg. 125.00 (*0-8382-4654-0*) Higginson Bk Co.

Vermont Historical Gazetteer Vol. I: A Magazine Embracing a History of Each Town, Civil, Ecclesiastical, Biogr. & Military: Addison, Bennington, Caledonia, Chittenden & Essex Cos. Ed. by Abby M. Hemenway. (Illus.). 1092p. 1995. reprint ed. lib. bdg. 105.00 (*0-8328-4658-9*) Higginson Bk Co.

Vermont Historical Gazetteer Vol. II: Franklin, Grand Isle, LaMobile, Orange Counties. Ed. by Abby M. Hemenway. (Illus.). 1200p. 1995. reprint ed. lib. bdg. 117.50 (*0-8328-4653-8*) Higginson Bk Co.

Vermont Historical Gazetteer Vol. IV: Washington Co., Including a County Chapter & the Histories of the Towns... Ed. by Abby M. Hemenway. (Illus.). 932p. 1995. reprint ed. lib. bdg. 92.50 (*0-8328-4660-0*) Higginson Bk Co.

Vermont Historical Gazetteer Vol. V: The Towns of Windham County. Ed. by Abby M. Hemenway. (Illus.). 1204p. 1995. reprint ed. lib. bdg. 115.00 (*0-8328-4655-4*) Higginson Bk Co.

Vermont Historical Markers, Covered Bridges, Historic Sites & Museums. Alexa M. Selph. (Illus.). 128p. (Orig.). 1994. pap. 12.95 (*0-87797-132-3*) Cherokee.

*__Vermont History! Surprising Secrets about Our State's Founding Mothers, Fathers & Kids!__ Carole Marsh. (Carole Marsh Vermont Bks.). (Illus.). (J). (gr. 3-12). 1996. pap. 19.95 (*0-7933-6164-8*); lib. bdg. 29.95 (*0-7933-6163-X*); disk 29.95 (*0-7933-6165-6*) Gallopade Pub Group.

Vermont History Index: The Proceedings of the Vermont Historical Society, 1953-1977, Vols. 21-45. Compiled by Reidun D. Nuquist. 268p. 1979. pap. 3.75 (*0-934720-20-7*) VT Hist Soc.

Vermont History Index, Vols. 46-55: The Proceedings of the Vermont Historical Society, 1978-1987. Compiled by Reidun D. Nuquist. 136p. 1991. pap. 24.95 (*0-934720-34-7*) VT Hist Soc.

Vermont Hot Air Balloon Mystery. Carole Marsh. (Carole Marsh Vermont Bks.). (Illus.). (J). (gr. 2-9). 1994. 29.95 (*0-7933-2723-7*); pap. 19.95 (*0-7933-2724-5*); disk 29.95 (*0-7933-2725-3*) Gallopade Pub Group.

Vermont in Perspective 1996. Ed. by Kathleen O. Morgan et al. 26p. 1996. pap. 19.00 (*1-56692-594-0*) Morgan Quitno Corp.

*__Vermont in Perspective 1997.__ Ed. by Kathleen O. Morgan & Scott E. Morgan. 26p. 1997. pap. 19.00 (*1-56692-694-7*) Morgan Quitno Corp.

Vermont in the Civil War, 2 vols., Set. G. G. Benedict. (Illus.). 1428p. 1995. reprint ed. lib. bdg. 147.00 (*0-8328-5121-3*) Higginson Bk Co.

*__Vermont in the Great Rebellion, Containing Historical & Biographical Sketches.__ Otis F. Waite. 288p. 1997. reprint ed. lib. bdg. 37.50 (*0-8328-6497-8*) Higginson Bk Co.

Vermont in the Victorian Age: Continuity & Change in the Green Mountain State, 1850-1900. LC 85-51147. 182p. 1985. 49.50 (*0-911853-06-5*) Vermont Herit Pr.

Vermont in the Victorian Age: Continuity & Change in the Green Mountain State, 1850-1900. limited ed. LC 85-51147. 182p. 1985. 95.00 (*0-911853-07-3*) Vermont Herit Pr.

Vermont Indian Dictionary for Kids! Carole Marsh. (Carole Marsh State Bks.). (J). (gr. 2-9). 1996. 29.95 (*0-7933-7779-X*, C Marsh); pap. 19.95 (*0-7933-7780-3*, C Marsh) Gallopade Pub Group.

Vermont Inns & Bed & Breakfast Inns. Ed. by New England Press Staff. LC 95-68733. (Illus.). 136p. (Orig.). 1995. pap. text ed. 9.95 (*1-881535-19-3*) New Eng Pr VT.

Vermont Integrated Services Team Approach (VISTA) A Guide to Coordinating Educational Support Services. Michael F. Giangreco. LC 95-9164. 1995. 27.95 (*1-55766-230-4*) P H Brookes.

Vermont Jeopardy! Answers & Questions about Our State! Carole Marsh. (Carole Marsh Vermont Bks.). (Illus.). (J). (gr. 3-12). 1994. pap. 19.95 (*0-7933-4215-5*); lib. bdg. 29.95 (*0-7933-4214-7*); disk 29.95 (*0-7933-4216-3*) Gallopade Pub Group.

Vermont "Jography" A Fun Run Thru Our State! Carole Marsh. (Carole Marsh Vermont Bks.). (Illus.). (J). 1994. pap. 19.95 (*0-7933-2139-5*); lib. bdg. 29.95 (*0-7933-2138-7*); disk 29.95 (*0-7933-2140-9*) Gallopade Pub Group.

Vermont Jury Instructions. Richie E. Berger & Frederick S. Lane, 3rd. 400p. 1993. ring bd. 85.00 (*1-56257-293-8*) MICHIE.

Vermont Jury Instructions, Civil & Criminal. Ed. by John M. Dinse et al. LC 93-28597. 1993. 85.00 (*0-562-57293-7*) MICHIE.

Vermont Kids' Cookbook: Recipes, How-to, History, Lore & More! Carole Marsh. (Carole Marsh Vermont Bks.). (Illus.). (J). 1994. lib. bdg. 29.95 (*0-7933-1142-X*); disk 29.95 (*0-7933-1143-8*) Gallopade Pub Group.

Vermont Kids' Cookbook: Recipes, How-to, History, Lore & More! Carole Marsh. (Carole Marsh Vermont Bks.). (Illus.). (J). 1997. pap. 19.95 (*0-7933-1141-1*) Gallopade Pub Group.

Vermont Kitchens Revisited. Illus. by Margaret Parlour. 288p. (Orig.). 1990. pap. 14.95 (*0-9627253-0-7*) VT Kitchen.

Vermont Law Review: 1976-1995/96, 20 vols. Bound set. 722.50 (*0-8377-9180-4*) Rothman.

Vermont Library Book: A Surprising Guide to the Unusual Special Collections in Libraries Across Our State for Students, Teachers, Writers & Publishers - Includes Reproducible Mailing Labels Plus Activities for Young People! Carole Marsh. (Vermont Bks.). (Illus.). 1994. pap. 19.95 (*0-7933-3141-2*); lib. bdg. 29.95 (*0-7933-3140-4*); disk 29.95 (*0-7933-3142-0*) Gallopade Pub Group.

Vermont Life's Guide to Fall Foliage. Gale Lawrence. LC 84-11890. (Illus.). 64p. 1984. pap. 3.95 (*0-936896-03-5*) VT Life Mag.

Vermont Life's Guide to Fall Foliage. 2nd ed. Gale Lawrence. 1993. pap. 4.95 (*0-936896-25-6*) VT Life Mag.

*__Vermont Manufacturing Directory, 1997-1998.__ Tower Pub. Staff. 370p. Date not set. pap. text ed. 55.00 (*1-881758-30-3*) Tower Pub ME.

Vermont Media Book: A Surprising Guide to the Amazing Print, Broadcast & Online Media of Our State for Students, Teachers, Writers & Publishers - Includes Reproducible Mailing Labels Plus Activities for Young People! Carole Marsh. (Vermont Bks.). (Illus.). 1994. pap. 19.95 (*0-7933-3297-4*); lib. bdg. 29.95 (*0-7933-3296-6*); disk 29.95 (*0-7933-3298-2*) Gallopade Pub Group.

Vermont Mortality Schedule, 1870. Ronald V. Jackson. 1992. 53.00 (*0-89593-860-X*) Accelerated Index.

Vermont Mortality Schedule, 1880. Ronald V. Jackson. 1992. 55.00 (*0-89593-861-8*) Accelerated Index.

Vermont Mountain Biking: The Best Back Road & Trail Rides in Southern Vermont. Dick Mansfield. LC 88-355596. (Illus.). 176p. 1989. pap. 10.95 (*0-937921-48-3*) Acorn Pub.

Vermont Museums, Galleries, & Historic Places. Illus. by Robin Rothman. LC 95-38313. 1995. pap. write for info. (*0-936896-42-6*) VT Life Mag.

Vermont Mystery Van Takes Off! Book 1: Handicapped Vermont Kids Sneak Off on a Big Adventure. Carole Marsh. (Vermont Bks.). (Illus.). (J). (gr. 3-12). 1994. 29.95 (*0-7933-5096-4*); pap. 19.95 (*0-7933-5097-2*); disk 29.95 (*0-7933-5098-0*) Gallopade Pub Group.

Vermont Myth. large type ed. Palma Harcourt. 416p. 1996. 27.99 (*0-7089-8885-7*, Charnwood) Ulverscroft.

Vermont, New Hampshire, Maine Visitor's Guide. (Visitor's Guides Ser.). (Illus.). 224p. (Orig.). 1996. pap. 15.95 (*0-86190-586-5*) Hunter NJ.

Vermont Papers: Recreating Democracy on a Human Scale. Frank Bryan & John McClaughry. LC 89-569. 308p. 1990. reprint ed. pap. text ed. 12.95 (*0-930031-31-8*) Chelsea Green Pub.

Vermont People. 3rd ed. Peter Miller. (Illus.). 128p. 1995. 35.00 (*0-9628064-0-4*) Silver Print.

Vermont Philatelic Index. Karl E. Henson. 200p. 1993. pap. 30.00 (*0-9635562-0-7*) VT Philatelic.

Vermont Place-Names: Footprints of History. Esther M. Swift. LC 76-13815. (Illus.). 705p. reprint ed. 45.00 (*0-8289-0291-7*, 1756) Picton Pr.

Vermont Planning, Development & Land Use Regulation. 1994. pap. 35.00 (*0-614-03172-9*) MICHIE.

Vermont Planning, Development & Land Use Regulation. Ed. by Butterworth Staff. 290p. 1994. pap. 35.00 (*0-88063-551-7*) MICHIE.

Vermont Political Tradition. rev. ed. William T. Doyle. (Illus.). 288p. 1991. 20.00 (*0-9615486-0-6*); pap. 12.50 (*0-9615486-1-4*) W T Doyle.

Vermont Quiz Bowl Crash Course! Carole Marsh. (Carole Marsh Vermont Bks.). (Illus.). (J). 1994. pap. 19.95 (*0-7933-2153-0*); lib. bdg. 29.95 (*0-7933-2152-2*); disk 29.95 (*0-7933-2154-9*) Gallopade Pub Group.

Vermont Recipes: Addison County's Finest. Ed. by Kimberly Werner. (Illus.). 192p. (Orig.). 1995. pap. 12.95 (*0-9645761-0-4*) Palatine Bks.

Vermont Recollections: Sifting Memories Through the Interview Process. Ed. by Jane C. Beck & Edward D. Ives. (Northeast Folklore Ser.: Vol. XXX). (Illus.). 191p. (Orig.). (C). 1995. pap. 15.00 (*0-943197-22-8*) ME Folklife Ctr.

Vermont Renaissance. Coral Crosman. (Illus.). 72p. 1976. pap. 2.50 (*0-913884-01-4*) Porphyrion Pr.

Vermont Reports, Vols. 128-145 & 152-161. Ed. by Butterworth Staff. 900p. 1972. boxed 40.00 (*0-88063-552-5*) MICHIE.

Vermont River. W. D. Wetherell. 160p. 1993. pap. 12.95 (*1-55821-261-2*) Lyons & Burford.

*__Vermont Road Atlas & Guide 1997/98.__ (Illus.). 1997. pap. 15.95 (*0-944187-38-2*) N Cartographic.

Vermont Rollercoasters! Carole Marsh. (Vermont Bks.). (Illus.). (YA). (gr. 3-12). 1994. pap. 19.95 (*0-7933-5360-2*); lib. bdg. 29.95 (*0-7933-5359-9*); disk 29.95 (*0-7933-5361-0*) Gallopade Pub Group.

Vermont Rules of Evidence. Ed. by Butterworth Staff. 200p. 1993. pap. 24.00 (*0-88063-548-7*) MICHIE.

Vermont Saints & Sinners: An Impressive Assortment of Geniuses, Nincompoops, Curmudgeons, Scurvy Knaves, & Characters. Lee D. Goodman. LC 85-72569. (Illus.). 172p. (Orig.). 1985. pap. 12.95 (*0-933050-32-1*) New Eng Pr VT.

Vermont Scenes & Seasons. Photos by George B. Robinson. LC 89-63661. (Illus.). 80p. 1989. pap. 14.95 (*0-933050-65-8*) New Eng Pr VT.

Vermont School Trivia: An Amazing & Fascinating Look at Our State's Teachers, Schools & Students! Carole Marsh. (Carole Marsh Vermont Bks.). (Illus.). (J). 1994. pap. 19.95 (*0-7933-1138-1*); lib. bdg. 29.95 (*0-7933-1139-X*); disk 29.95 (*0-7933-1140-3*) Gallopade Pub Group.

Vermont Schoolmarm & the Contemporary One-Room Schoolhouse: An Ethnographic Study of a Contemporary One-Room Schoolteacher. Jody Kenny. (Occasional Papers: No. 12). (Illus.). 105p. (Orig.). 1990. pap. text ed. 8.50 (*0-944277-20-9*, K46) U VT Ctr Rsch VT.

Vermont Scrapbook: Fifty Vermonters Remember. Ed. by Ellen Sullivan. 292p. 1991. 18.95 (*0-9621455-6-4*) Crane Hill AL.

Vermont Silly Basketball Sportsmysteries, Vol. 1. Carole Marsh. (Carole Marsh Vermont Bks.). (Illus.). (J). 1994. pap. 19.95 (*0-7933-1135-7*); lib. bdg. 29.95 (*0-7933-1136-5*); disk 29.95 (*0-7933-1137-3*) Gallopade Pub Group.

Vermont Silly Basketball Sportsmysteries, Vol. 2. Carole Marsh. (Carole Marsh Vermont Bks.). (Illus.). (J). 1994. pap. 19.95 (*0-7933-2165-4*); lib. bdg. 29.95 (*0-7933-2164-6*); 29.95 (*0-7933-2166-2*) Gallopade Pub Group.

Vermont Silly Football Sportsmysteries, Vol. 1. Carole Marsh. (Carole Marsh Vermont Bks.). (Illus.). (J). 1994. pap. 19.95 (*0-7933-2144-1*); lib. bdg. 29.95 (*0-7933-2143-3*); disk 29.95 (*0-7933-2145-X*) Gallopade Pub Group.

Vermont Silly Football Sportsmysteries, Vol. 2. Carole Marsh. (Carole Marsh Vermont Bks.). (Illus.). (J). 1994. pap. 19.95 (*0-7933-2147-6*); lib. bdg. 29.95 (*0-7933-2146-8*); disk 29.95 (*0-7933-2148-4*) Gallopade Pub Group.

Vermont Silly Trivia! Carole Marsh. (Carole Marsh Vermont Bks.). (Illus.). (J). 1994. pap. 19.95 (*0-7933-2136-0*); lib. bdg. 29.95 (*0-7933-2135-2*); disk 29.95 (*0-7933-2137-9*) Gallopade Pub Group.

Vermont State Constitution: A Reference Guide. William C. Hill. LC 92-10067. (Reference Guides to the State Constitutions of the United States Ser.: No. 6). 208p. 1992. text ed. 65.00 (*0-313-26473-2*, HVT/, Greenwood Pr) Greenwood.

Vermont State Office of Economic Opportunity: A Case Study in Organizational Relationships. Mary Carlson. (Occasional Papers: No. 16). (Illus.). 68p. (Orig.). 1993. pap. 7.00 (*0-944277-25-X*) U VT Ctr Rsch VT.

Vermont Statutes Annotated. 1994. suppl. ed., ring bd. 75.00 (*0-614-03173-7*) MICHIE.

Vermont Statutes Annotated, 25 vols. annot. ed. Ed. by Butterworth Staff. 1994. boxed 800.00 (*0-88063-546-0*) MICHIE.

Vermont Tales: For Fools & Other Lovers. Ruth M. Sprague. Ed. by T. Louise. (Illus.). 87p. 1995. pap. 5.95 (*1-883889-19-7*) TWanda.

Vermont Timeline: A Chronology of Vermont History, Mystery, Trivia, Legend, Lore & More. Carole Marsh. (Vermont Bks.). (Illus.). (J). (gr. 3-12). 1994. pap. 19.95 (*0-7933-6011-0*); lib. bdg. 29.95 (*0-7933-6010-2*); disk 29.95 (*0-7933-6012-9*) Gallopade Pub Group.

Vermont Towns & Counties. Michael J. Denis. (New England Towns & Counties Ser.). 35p. 1983. pap. 4.50 (*0-935207-06-6*) Danbury Hse Bks.

Vermont Trout Streams. Allen Farrow et al. LC 84-62918. (Illus.). 128p. 1985. pap. 24.95 (*0-9606738-7-3*) N Cartographic.

*__Vermont Unveiled: A Photographic Guide to Nudism in the Green Mountain State.__ 2nd ed. Jim C. Cunningham. Ed. by Maggie Cunningham. (Illus.). 96p. (Orig.). 1996. pap. 19.50 (*0-9655540-0-7*) Naturist LIFE.

Vermont Voices: An Anthology. League of Vermont Writers Members. 288p. 1991. pap. 13.95 (*0-9630872-0-7*) League VT Writs.

Vermont Walks: Village & Countryside: Walking Tours of Forty-Three Vermont Villages & Their Surroundings. Marilyn Stout. (Illus.). 1995. write for info. (*0-936896-41-8*) VT Life Mag.

Vermont Warnings Out Vol. 1: Northern Vermont. Alden M. Rollins. 448p. 1995. 39.50 (*0-89725-234-9*, 1619) Picton Pr.

Vermont Weather Book. 2nd rev. ed. David M. Ludlum. LC 85-6223. (Illus.). 302p. 1996. mass mkt., pap. 18.95 (*0-934720-30-4*) VT Hist Soc.

Vermont Wildlife Viewing Guide. Cindy K. Brown. LC 94-19270. (Falcon Guides Ser.). (Illus.). 64p. (Orig.). 1994. pap. 8.95 (*1-56044-291-3*) Falcon Pr MT.

Vermont 1771 Census. Jay M. Holbrook. LC 81-836773. 136p. 1982. lib. bdg. 25.00 (*0-931248-11-6*) Holbrook Res.

Vermonters at Their Craft: Vermont CraftsPeople Talk about Their Life & Work. Catharine Wright & Nancy M. Wright. LC 87-62334. (Illus.). 176p. (Orig.). 1987. pap. 19.95 (*0-933050-51-8*) New Eng Pr VT.

Vermonters' Guide to Computer Lingo. Dave Nilsen. (Illus.). 80p. (Orig.). 1995. pap. 6.95 (*0-9649972-0-7*) Cowsamungus.

Vermont's Burned-Over District: Patterns of Community Development & Religious Activity, 1761-1850. P. Jeffrey Potash. LC 91-28028. (Chicago Studies in the History of American Religion Ser.: Vol. 16). 330p. 1991. 60.00 (*0-926019-52-X*) Carlson Pub.

Vermont's Heritage: A Working Conference for Teachers - Plans, Proposals, & Needs. Ed. by Marshall True et al. (Illus.). 130p. (Orig.). 1983. pap. text ed. 7.00 (*0-944277-10-1*, U47) U VT Ctr Rsch VT.

Vermont's Land & Resources. Harold A. Meeks. LC 86-50973. (Illus.). 336p. (Orig.). 1986. pap. 16.95 (*0-933050-40-2*) New Eng Pr VT.

Vermont's (Most Devastating!) Disasters & (Most Calamitous!) Catastrophies! Carole Marsh. (Carole Marsh Vermont Bks.). (Illus.). (J). 1994. pap. 19.95 (*0-7933-1126-8*); lib. bdg. 29.95 (*0-7933-1127-6*); disk 29.95 (*0-7933-1128-4*) Gallopade Pub Group.

Vermont's Unsolved Mysteries (& Their "Solutions") Includes Scientific Information & Other Activities for Students. Carole Marsh. (Vermont Bks.). (Illus.). (J). (gr. 3-12). 1994. pap. 19.95 (*0-7933-5858-2*); lib. bdg. 29.95 (*0-7933-5857-4*); disk 29.95 (*0-7933-5859-0*) Gallopade Pub Group.

*__Vern Gosdin - Anthology.__ Ed. by Carol Cuellar. 96p. (Orig.). (C). 1992. pap. text ed. 18.95 (*0-7692-0732-4*, VF1836) Warner Brothers.

Vernacular Architecture: Paradigms of Environmental Response. Ed. by Mete Turan. (Ethnoscapes Ser.: No. 4). (Illus.). 378p. 1990. text ed. 69.95 (*0-566-07176-2*, Pub. by Avebury Pub UK) Ashgate Pub Co.

Vernacular Architecture in America: A Selective Bibliography. John A. Cuthbert & Barry J. Ward. 1984. 200.00 (*0-8161-0436-0*, Hall Reference) Macmillan.

*__Vernacular Architecture in Rural & Small Town Missouri: An Introduction.__ Howard W. Marshall. 64p. 1994. pap. 6.00 (*0-614-28313-2*, MP688) Extension Div.

Vernacular Architecture in Southern Illinois: The Ethnic Heritage. John M. Coggeshall & Jo A. Nast. LC 87-26448. (Shawnee Bks.). (Illus.). 218p. 1988. 24.95 (*0-8093-1462-2*); pap. 14.95 (*0-8093-1463-0*) S Ill U Pr.

Vernacular Christianity: Essays in the Social Anthropology of Religion. Ed. by Wendy James & Douglas H. Johnson. 196p. 1989. text ed. 44.00 (*0-936508-23-X*) Barber Pr.

*__Vernacular Christianity among the Mulia Dani: An Ethnography of Religious Belief among the Western Dani of Irian Jaya, Indonesia.__ Douglas J. Hayward. 340p. 1997. 62.50 (*0-7618-0760-8*) U Pr of Amer.

*__Vernacular Christianity among the Mulia Dani: An Ethnography of Religious Belief among the Western Dani of Irian Jaya, Indonesia.__ Douglas J. Hayward. 340p. 1997. pap. 39.50 (*0-7618-0761-6*) U Pr of Amer.

Vernacular Dreams. Angelo Loukakis. LC 85-14088. 228p. 1986. pap. 14.95 (*0-7022-2025-6*, Pub. by Univ Queensland Pr AT) Intl Spec Bk.

Vernacular Garden. Ed. by John D. Hunt & Joachim Wolschke-Bulmahn. LC 92-16306. (Dumbarton Oaks Colloquium on the History of Landscape Architecture Ser.: No. 14). (Illus.). 166p. 1993. 30.00 (*0-88402-201-3*, HUVG) Dumbarton Oaks.

Vernacular Language of Puerto Rico. Ed. by Raoul Gordon. 1976. lib. bdg. 59.95 (*0-8490-1258-9*) Gordon Pr.

*__Vernacular Literacy: A Re-Evaluation.__ Ed. by Andree Tabouret-Keller et al. (Oxford Studies in Anthropological Linguistics: No. 13). (Illus.). 384p. 1997. pap. 35.00 (*0-19-823713-8*) OUP.

*__Vernacular Literacy: A Re-Evaluation.__ Ed. by Andree Tabouret-Keller et al. (Oxford Studies in Anthropological Linguistics: No. 13). (Illus.). 384p. 1997. 95.00 (*0-19-823635-2*) OUP.

*__Vernacular Literary Theory in the Middle Ages: The German Tradition, 800-1300, in Its European Context.__ Walter Haug. (Studies in Medieval Literature: No. 29). 474p. (C). 1997. text ed. 74.95 (*0-521-34197-3*) Cambridge U Pr.

Vernacular Names for Texas Plants see Language Trends in Oil Field Jargon

Vernacular Poetics in the Middle Ages. Ed. by Lois Ebin. LC 83-23606. (Studies in Medieval Culture: No. 16). 1984. pap. 14.95 (*0-918720-19-2*); boxed 24.95 (*0-918720-22-2*) Medieval Inst.

Vernacular Press & the Emergence of Modern Indonesian Consciousness (1855 - 1913) Ahmat Adam. (Studies on Southeast Asia: No. 17). (Orig.). (C). 1995. pap. text ed. 16.00 (*0-87727-716-8*) Cornell SE Asia.

Vernacular Republic. Les Murray. 1982. pap. 8.95 (*0-89255-063-5*) Persea Bks.

Vernacular Veda: Revelation, Recitation, & Ritual. Vasudha Narayanan. LC 93-44400. 260p. (C). 1994. text ed. 42.95 (*0-87249-965-0*) U of SC Pr.

Vernacular Visions: Folk Art of Old Newbury. John H. Wright. (Illus.). 120p. (Orig.). 1994. pap. 18.00 (*1-882266-03-X*) Newburyport.

Vernal Calibrations. Gary W. Kroeker. 100p. 1992. pap. 7.95 (*1-881168-01-8*) Red Danceflr.

Verne Foster & the Nevada Mining Association. Intro. by R. T. King. (Illus.). 112p. 1988. write for info. (*1-56475-329-8*); lib. bdg. 34.50 (*1-56475-328-X*); fiche write for info. (*1-56475-330-1*) U NV Oral Hist.

Verner's Law in Gothic, & Reduplicating Verbs in Germanic. Francis A. Wood. LC 73-173039. (Chicago. University. Germanic Studies: No. 2). reprint ed. 32.50 (*0-404-50272-5*) AMS Pr.

An Asterisk (*) at the beginning of an entry indicates that the title is appearing in BIP for the first time.

Verne's Journey to the Centre of the Self: Space & Time in the Voyages Extraordinaires. William Butcher. LC 90-8899. 290p. 1991. text ed. 65.00 (*0-312-05345-2*) St Martin.

Verney Papers. Ralph Verney. Ed. by John Bruce. (Camden Society, London. Publications, First Ser.: No. 31). reprint ed. 57.50 (*0-404-50131-1*) AMS Pr.

Vernon: An Anecdotal Novel. Osmond Beckwith. LC 81-65121. (Illus.). 204p. 1981. 10.00 (*0-917020-02-2*) Breaking Point.

Vernon: Social Work & the Law. 2nd ed. Stuart Vernon. 384p. 1993. pap. 30.00 (*0-406-01417-5*, U.K.) MICHIE.

VERNON Family Records: Descendants of Robert Vernon (1682) John V. Winterton & Laureen E. Winterton. (Illus.). 125p. 1995. pap. 19.50 (*0-8328-4859-X*) Higginson Bk Co.

Vernon Family Records: Descendants of Robert Vernon (1682) John V. Winterton & Laureen E. Winterton. (Illus.). 125p. 1995. lib. bdg. 29.50 (*0-8328-4858-1*) Higginson Bk Co.

Vernon Fisher. (Contemporary Art Ser.: No. 2). (Illus.). 23p. 1994. pap. write for info. (*1-883015-06-5*) Krannert Art.

Vernon Lee: Violet Paget, 1856-1935. Peter Gunn. LC 75-12323. (Homosexuality Ser.). (Illus.). 1975. reprint ed. 17.95 (*0-405-07357-7*) Ayer.

Vernon W. Prigmore: Just an Auxiliarist: Commander, Vice-Commander, Training Officer. Ed. by Mary E. Glass. 43p. 1977. lib. bdg. 24.50 (*1-56475-165-1*); fiche write for info. (*1-56475-166-X*) U NV Oral Hist.

Vernon's Annotated Missouri Statutes. West Publishing Company Editorial Staff. 1951. write for info. (*0-318-60695-X*) West Pub.

Vernon's Collectors' Guide to Orders, Decorations & Medals (with Valuations) 2nd rev. ed. Sydney B. Vernon. (Illus.). 450p. 1990. write for info. (*0-318-65328-1*) S B Vernon.

Vernon's Collectors' Guide to Orders, Medals & Decorations: (with Valuations) 2nd rev. ed. Sydney B. Vernon. LC 89-51178. (Illus.). 502p. (Orig.). 1990. pap. 28.95 (*0-9623575-0-2*) S B Vernon.

Vernon's Collectors' Guide to Orders, Medals & Decorations: (With Valuations) 3rd rev. ed. Sydney B. Vernon. (Illus.). 512p. 1995. pap. 28.95 (*0-9623575-1-0*) S B Vernon.

Vernon's Jerk Paradise Cookbook: Authentic Jamaican Jerk Cuisine Pioneer of Jerk Style Cooking in the U. S. Allan Vernon. (Illus.). 28p. (Orig.). 1994. pap. 6.95 (*0-9644181-0-X*) Tropical Pub.

Vernon's Texas Code Forms Annotated: Uniform Commercial Code Forms, 2 vols. 2nd ed. 1344p. 1986. 85.00 (*0-317-52121-7*) West Pub.

Vernuenftiges Denken. Ed. by Juergen Mittelstrass & Riedel Manfred. (C). 1978. 119.25 (*3-11-006956-3*) De Gruyter.

Vernuft und Glaube. Franz Von Kutschera. ix, 351p. (Orig.). (GER.). (C). 1991. pap. text ed. 36.95 (*3-11-013206-0*, 161-91) De Gruyter.

Vernunft und Glaube. Franz Von Kutschera. ix, 351p. (C). 1990. lib. bdg. 146.15 (*3-11-012287-1*) De Gruyter.

Vernunft und Welt. Wesley Marx. (Phaenomenologica Ser.: No. 36). 123p. 1970. 90.00 (*90-247-5042-3*, Pub. by M Nijhoff NE) Kluwer Ac.

***Vernunftigen Tadlerienen, 2 vols.** Ed. by J. C. Gottsched. 972p. (GER.). 1993. reprint ed. write for info. (*3-487-09640-4*) G Olms Pubs.

Verona: Travel to Landmarks. Sheila Hale. 1992. 24.95 (*1-85043-225-2*, Pub. by I B Tauris UK) St Martin.

Verona Arena: The Largest Opera House in the World. Roberto Pasini. (Illus.). 220p. Date not set. 45.00 (*88-7743-154-7*, Pub. by Arsenale Editrice IT) Antique Collect.

Verona, Biblioteca Capitolare, Cod. DCCLVII. Ed. by Howard M. Brown. (Renaissance Music in Facsimile Ser.). 152p. 1987. text ed. 20.00 (*0-8240-1473-1*) Garland.

***Veronese & the Venetian Tradition of Allegory, 1985.** C. Hope. (Italian Lectures). 1986. 3.98 (*0-85672-548-X*) David Brown.

Veronese to Franz Kline: Masterworks from the Chrysler Museum at Norfolk. Selected by Denys Sutton. (Illus.). 79p. 1978. pap. 6.00 (*0-940744-18-X*) Chrysler Museum.

***Veronica.** Nicholas Christopher. 400p. 1997. mass mkt. 6.99 (*0-380-72918-0*) Avon.

Veronica. Nicholas Christopher. LC 95-18083. 336p. 1996. 22.95 (*0-385-31471-X*, Dial Pr) Dell.

Veronica Ganz. Marilyn Sachs. (J). (gr. 4-8). 1996. 17.50 (*0-8446-6896-6*) Peter Smith.

Veronica Ganz. Marilyn Sachs. LC 94-30013. 144p. (J). 1995. pap. 3.99 (*0-14-037078-1*) Puffin Bks.

Veronica My Daughter & Other Onitsha Plays & Stories. Ogali Ogali. Ed. by Reinhard W. Sander & Peter K. Ayers. LC 80-80886. 376p. (Orig.). 1980. 18.00 (*0-914478-61-3*, Three Contnts); pap. 10.00 (*0-914478-62-1*, Three Contnts) Lynne Rienner.

***Veronica Webb Sight: Adventures in the Big City.** Veronica Webb. 224p. 1998. 19.95 (*0-7868-6338-2*) Hyperion.

Veronica's First Year. Jean S. Rheingrover. (Illus.). 24p. (J). (gr. k-4). 1996. lib. bdg. 12.95 (*0-8075-8474-6*) A Whitman.

Veronique, Dialoque de L'Histoire et de l'Ame Charnelle. Charles Peguy. 12.75 (*0-685-37046-1*) Fr & Eur.

Verre Contemporain. Jean Lechaczynski & Serge Lechaczynski. 154p. (FRE.). 1993. lib. bdg. 150.00 (*0-7859-3649-1*, 2859171320); lib. bdg. 150.00 (*0-7859-3650-5*, 2859171339) Fr & Eur.

Verrine Orations, 2 Vols, I. Marcus Tullius Cicero. (Loeb Classical Library: No. 221, 293). 530p. 1928. 18.95 (*0-674-99243-1*) HUP.

Verrine Orations, 2 Vols, II. Marcus Tullius Cicero. (Loeb Classical Library: No. 221, 293). 704p. 1935. 18.95 (*0-674-99323-3*) HUP.

Verrines II,i. Marcus Tullius Cicero. Ed. by Mitchell. (Classical Texts Ser.). 1986. 49.95 (*0-85668-252-7*, Pub. by Aris & Phillips UK); pap. 24.95 (*0-85668-253-5*, Pub. by Aris & Phillips UK) David Brown.

Verrocchio's Christ & St. Thomas: A Masterpiece of Sculpture from Renaissance Florence. Ed. by Loretta Dolcini. (Illus.). 125p. 1993. 49.50 (*0-8109-6429-5*) Abrams.

Verrykingsaanspreeklikheid in die Suid-Afrikaanse Reg. W. De Vos. 424p. 1987. write for info. (*0-7021-2002-2*, Pub. by Juta SA); pap. write for info. (*0-7021-1926-1*, Pub. by Juta SA) Gaunt.

Vers de Societe Anthology. Ed. by Carolyn Wells. LC 07-37621. (Granger Poetry Library). 1976. reprint ed. 30.00 (*0-89609-055-8*) Roth Pub Inc.

Vers Ispahan. Loti. Ed. by Aelly & Cameron. (Exeter French Texts Ser.: No. 72). 182p. (FRE.). Date not set. pap. text ed. 19.95 (*0-85989-302-2*, Pub. by Univ Exeter Pr UK) Northwestern U Pr.

Vers Ispahan. 2nd ed. Ed. by Pierre P. Loti-Viaud & Michel Desbrueres. (Around 1900 Collection). (Illus.). 320p. (FRE.). 1995. 69.95 (*2-86808-089-8*) Intl Scholars.

Vers le Renouveau (Mai 58-Juill. 62) see Discours et Messages

Vers le Terme (Jano. 66-Avril 69) see Discours et Messages

Vers le Vrai Racine, 2 tomes. Jasinski. 45.50 (*0-685-34026-0*) Fr & Eur.

Vers l'Invisible 1958-67. Julien Green. 510p. 1967. 29.95 (*0-8288-7433-6*) Fr & Eur.

Vers une Justice Universelle. International Commission of Jurists. 103p. (FRE.). 1993. reprint ed. pap. 29.40 (*0-608-00495-2*, 2061314) Bks Demand.

Vers une Nouvelle Philosophie Transcendantale. T. F. Geraerts. (Phaenomenologica Ser.: No. 39). 227p. 1971. lib. bdg. 73.00 (*90-247-5024-5*, Pub. by M Nijhoff NE) Kluwer Ac.

VersaCAD Corporation's Training Guide: 2D & 3D Tutorials. Maria Morrissey & Jack Mitchell. (Orig.). (C). 1989. teacher ed., pap. 21.00 (*0-8273-3563-6*) Delmar.

VersaCAD on the Mac. Carol Buehrens. (Illus.). 496p. 1990. 34.95 (*0-8306-9514-1*, 3514); pap. 24.60 (*0-8306-3514-9*) McGraw-Hill Prof.

VersaCAD Tutorial: A Practical Approach to Computer-Aided Design. Carol Buehrens. (Illus.). 352p. 1988. 28.95 (*0-8306-0303-4*, 3003); pap. 19.95 (*0-8306-9303-3*) McGraw-Hill Prof.

***Versace.** Martin. 1997. 18.95 (*0-7893-0090-7*) Universe.

Versace Signatures. Gianni Versace & Omar Calabrese. (Illus.). 256p. 1996. 75.00 (*1-55859-596-1*) Abbeville Pr.

Versaille Verdic. Maximilian Montgelas. Ed. by Constance Vesey. LC 74-12765. Orig. Title: Lertfaden Zur Kriegsschuldfrage. 255p. 1975. reprint ed. text ed. 65.00 (*0-8371-7741-3*, MOVV, Greenwood Pr) Greenwood.

Versailles. Jean-Marie P. De Montclos. (Illus.). 424p. 1991. 95.00 (*1-55859-228-8*) Abbeville Pr.

Versailles. Jean-Marie P. De Montclos. (Illus.). 160p. 1994. 29.98 (*0-89660-052-1*, Artabras) Abbeville Pr.

Versailles. Gerald Van Der Kemp. 1988. 29.99 (*0-517-33489-5*) Random Hse Value.

Versailles. Karl F. Nowak. Tr. by Norman M. Thomas & E. W. Dickes. LC 76-175705. (Select Bibliographies Reprint Ser.). 1977. reprint ed. 21.95 (*0-8369-6620-1*) Ayer.

Versailles. Karl F. Nowak. Tr. by Norman F. Thomas & E. W. Dickes from FRE. LC 76-175705. (Select Bibliographies Reprint Ser.). 284p. reprint ed. lib. bdg. 17.50 (*0-8290-0822-5*) Irvington.

Versailles: The History of the Gardens & Their Sculpture. Stephane Pincas. LC 96-60114. (Illus.). 280p. 1996. 75.00 (*0-500-01701-8*) Thames Hudson.

Versailles: The View from Sweden. Elain E. Dee & Guy Walton. Ed. by Nancy Aakre. LC 87-73539. (Exhibition Catalogue Ser.). (Illus.). 112p. 1988. pap. text ed. 17.95 (*0-910503-56-7*) Cooper-Hewitt Museum.

Versailles & After, 1919-1933. 2nd ed. Ruth Henig. LC 94-41756. (Lancaster Pamphlets Ser.). 96p. (C). 1995. pap. 9.95 (*0-415-12710-6*) Routledge.

Versailles, le Petit Trianon: Le Mobilier des Inventaires de 1807-1810. Denise Ledoux-Lebard. 248p. (FRE.). 1993. lib. bdg. 225.00 (*0-7859-3646-7*, 2859170863) Fr & Eur.

Versailles Settlement: Peacemaking in Paris, 1919. Alan Sharp. LC 90-22402. (Making of the Twentieth Century Ser.). (Orig.). (C). 1991. pap. text ed. 18.00 (*0-312-05579-X*) St Martin.

***Versatile Arabian Horse.** Rosemary Archer. 1996. text ed. 90.00 (*0-85131-669-7*, Pub. by J A Allen & Co UK) St Mut.

Versatile Fly Tyer. Richard W. Talleur. (Illus.). 352p. 1990. 34.95 (*1-55821-069-5*) Lyons & Burford.

Versatile Gundog: Training HPR's for Gun, Rifle & Hawk. Guy Wallace. (Illus.). 128p. 1995. 35.00 (*0-948253-75-4*) Trafalgar.

Versatile Labrador Retriever. Nancy A. Martin. Ed. by Marianne Foote. (Pure Breds Ser.). (Illus.). 320p. 1994. pap. 23.50 (*0-944875-43-2*) Doral Pub.

Versatile Labrador Retriever. Nancy A. Martin. Ed. by Luana Luther & Alvin Grossman. (Pure Breds Ser.). (Illus.). 320p. 1994. 28.50 (*0-944875-31-9*) Doral Pub.

Versatile Livelihoods: Strategic Adaptation to Food Insecurity in the Malian Sahel. Susanna Davies. LC 95-8216. 1996. text ed. 79.95 (*0-312-12682-4*) St Martin.

Versatile Millstone Workhorse of Many Industries. Jon A. Sass. LC 84-13839. (Illus.). 83p. (Orig.). 1984. pap. 7.95 (*0-930497-00-7*) Soc Preservation.

Versatile Rice Cooker: Rices - Vegetables - Fruits - Custards - Pilafs - Eggs - Dim Sum - Seafood - Chicken. Bob Simmons & Coleen Simmons. (Illus.). 176p. (Orig.). 1992. pap. 8.95 (*1-55867-068-8*, Nitty Gritty Ckbks) Bristol Pub Ent CA.

Versatile Salesperson: Selling the Way Your Customer Wants To Buy. Roger Wenshlag & Roger Wenschlag. Ed. by Sharyn Skeeter. LC 89-9123. 205p. 1989. pap. text ed. 17.95 (*0-471-50379-7*) Wiley.

***Versatile Solitons.** A. Filippov. (Illus.). 250p. 1997. 34.50 (*0-8176-3635-8*) Spr-Verlag.

Versatile Trophy Hunter. Bill Butler. 208p. 1993. pap. 12.95 (*0-9637553-0-7*) Bill Butler.

***Versatile Vegetables.** (Feast of Good Cooking Ser.). (Illus.). 128p. 1996. 12.99 (*1-57215-069-6*, JG1066) World Pubns.

Versatile Vegetables. Barbara Kyte & Kathy Greenberg. LC 80-83403. (Illus.). 1980. pap. 2.95 (*0-915942-16-X*) SF Design.

Versatile Victorian: Selected Writings of George Henry Lewes. Ed. by R. Ashton. 339p. 1992. 65.95 (*1-85399-090-6*, Pub. by Brstl Class Pr UK) Focus Pub-R Pullins.

Versatile Vizsla. Marion Coffman. LC 91-40141. (Illus.). 272p. 1992. 34.95 (*0-931866-54-5*) Alpine Pubns.

***Versatility: Verse Art-Illery.** Marlon C. Williams. (Illus.). 73p. 1997. pap. 10.00 (*0-9658783-5-X*) Positive Yard.

Versatility of Wetlands in the Agricultural Landscape. Ed. by Kenneth L. Campbell. LC 95-79894. (Illus.). 760p. (Orig.). 1995. pap. 45.00 (*0-929355-69-5*, PO995) Am Soc Ag Eng.

Verschlossene Tur see Mensch und Zeit: An Anthology of German Radio Plays

Verschollene (Amerika) Franz Kafka. 352p. (GER.). 1994. pap. 13.50 (*3-596-12442-5*, Pub. by Fischer Taschbch Verlag GW) Intl Bk Import.

***Verse-a-Tile.** Margaret D. Kadisch. (Orig.). 1996. pap. write for info. (*1-57553-337-5*) Watermrk Pr.

Verse by the Side of the Road. Frank Rowsome, Jr. 1993. reprint ed. lib. bdg. 18.95 (*1-56849-088-7*) Buccaneer Bks.

Verse by the Side of the Road. Frank Rowsome, Jr. 1979. reprint ed. pap. 9.95 (*0-452-26762-5*, Plume) NAL-Dutton.

Verse by the Side of the Road: Burma-Shave Signs & Jingles. Frank Rowsome, Jr. LC 65-24618. 1965. 7.95 (*0-8289-0038-8*) Viking Penguin.

Verse by the Side of the Road: Burma-Shave Signs & Jingles. Frank Rowsome, Jr. LC 65-24618. 1979. pap. 5.95 (*0-8289-0351-4*) Viking Penguin.

Verse Choir Technique. Gertrude D. Enfield. 1973. text ed. 2.25 (*0-686-09412-3*) Expression.

Verse Eines Amerika-Deutschen: The German & English Poetry of Gerhard Rudolf Schade. Richard E. Schade. (New German-American Studies: Vol. 8). 216p. (C). 1996. text ed. 52.95 (*0-8204-2331-9*) P Lang Pubng.

Verse for All My Seasons. Silvia Silk. (Illus.). 39p. (Orig.). (J). (ps-3). 1979. pap. 5.50 (*0-938861-02-6*) Jasmine Texts.

***Verse Funny Side Up.** Ron Jackson. 88p. (Orig.). 1997. mass mkt. 5.99 (*1-55237-211-1*, Pub. by Comnwlth Pub CN) Partners Pubs Grp.

Verse of Greek Comedy. John W. White. 509p. reprint ed. lib. bdg. 83.20 (*0-685-13755-4*, 05102198) G Olms Pubs.

Verse of Greek Comedy. John W. White. xxix, 479p. 1969. reprint ed. write for info. (*0-318-71061-7*) G Olms Pubs.

Verse of Royall Tyler. Royall Tyler. LC 68-14026. (Illus.). 315p. reprint ed. pap. 89.80 (*0-7837-4350-5*, 2044060) Bks Demand.

Verse on Understanding. John Beesley. 68p. 1987. boxed 25.00 (*0-7223-2078-7*, Pub. by A H S Ltd UK) St Mut.

Verse Plays & Epic. Johann W. Von Goethe. Ed. by Cyrus Hamlin & Frank Ryder. Tr. by Michael Hamburger et al. from GER. LC 94-40896. 336p. 1994. pap. text ed. 17.95 (*0-691-04343-4*) Princeton U Pr.

Verse-Satire in England Before the Renaissance. Samuel M. Tucker. reprint ed. 42.50 (*0-404-06526-0*) AMS Pr.

Verse Things I Ever Did. Bruce Williamson. LC 94-78702. 118p. 1994. 14.95 (*0-8233-0494-9*) Golden Quill.

Verse with Prose. V. Balasubrahmanyam. 8.00 (*0-89253-559-8*); 4.00 (*0-89253-560-1*) Ind-US Inc.

Verse with Prose from Petronius to Dante: The Art & Scope of the Mixed Form. Peter Dronke. LC 93-4282. (Carl Newell Jackson Lectures). 160p. 1994. text ed. 32.50 (*0-674-93475-X*) HUP.

Versed Edition: A Potpourri of Poems & Parodies. Carol F. Rosenberg. 264p. 1994. pap. 12.00 (*0-8059-3641-6*) Dorrance.

Versed in Country Things. Robert Frost. (Illus.). 1995. 22.50 (*0-8212-2288-0*) Little.

Versed in Country Things: Poems. Robert Frost. 1996. 22.50 (*0-8212-2288-0*) Bulfinch Pr.

Verseform: A Comparative Bibliography. T. V. Brogan. LC 88-45406. 160p. (C). 1989. text ed. 30.00 (*0-8018-3362-0*) Johns Hopkins.

Verses. V. Balasubrahmanyam. (Writers Workshop Redbird Ser.). 1975. 8.00 (*0-89253-056-1*); 4.00 (*0-89253-562-8*) Ind-US Inc.

Verses. Helen H. Jackson. (Notable American Authors Ser.). 1992. reprint ed. lib. bdg. 75.00 (*0-7812-3345-3*) Rprt Serv.

Verses: Decorations. Ernest Dowson. LC 93-31596. (Decadents, Symbolists, Anti-Decadents Ser.). 1994. 48.00 (*1-85477-142-6*, Pub. by Woodstock Bks UK) Cassell.

Verses & Meditations. Rudolf Steiner. Tr. by George Adams. 253p. 1993. 19.95 (*1-85584-003-0*, Pub. by R Steiner Pr UK) Anthroposophic.

Verses & Reverses. Peg Thornton. LC 92-93763. 72p. (Orig.). 1994. pap. 6.95 (*1-56002-301-5*, Univ Edtns) Aegina Pr.

Verses & Sonnets of Julia Stockton Dinsmore. pap. 9.95 (*0-9624673-6-7*) Picture This Bks.

Verses & Sonnets of Julia Stockton Dinsmore. Julia S. Dinsmore. 200p. 1991. reprint ed. write for info. (*0-9624673-5-9*) Picture This Bks.

Verses for Smiling At. Lee C. Sanders. (Illus.). 96p. (Orig.). 1989. pap. 5.95 (*0-9622568-2-X*) Earthside Pubns.

Verses for the Zodiac. Daisy Aldan. (Illus.). 1975. 12.95 (*0-913152-23-4*); pap. 5.95 (*0-913152-22-6*) Folder Edns.

***Verses for the 21st Century: Adam & Eve on the Internet.** Alfred Israelstam. 128p. (Orig.). 1997. pap. write for info. (*1-886094-61-6*) Chicago Spectrum.

***Verses I Like.** Bowes. Date not set. 18.95 (*0-8369-6324-5*) Ayer.

Verses in a Minor Chord. Sebastian Micklas. 83p. 1985. pap. 1.95 (*0-8199-0888-6*, Frncscn Herld) Franciscan Pr.

Verses in Sermons: "Fasciculus mormum" & Its Middle English Poems. Siegfried Wenzel. LC 78-55887. (Medieval Academy Bks.: No. 87). 1978. 30.00 (*0-910956-66-9*) Medieval Acad.

Verses in the Wind. Maryjane Brewster. LC 84-50316. 48p. 1984. pap. 10.00 (*0-934172-10-2*) WIM Pubns.

Verses of a Marriage. Hans Raimund. Tr. by Robert Dassanowsky. (GER.). 1996. pap. 16.95 (*1-880391-16-3*) Event Horizon.

Verses of Cadence. James G. Southworth. 90p. reprint ed. lib. bdg. 79.00 (*0-7812-0252-3*) Rprt Serv.

Verses of Cadence: An Introduction to the Prosody of Chaucer & His Followers. James G. Southworth. LC 70-161954. 94p. 1954. reprint ed. 29.00 (*0-403-01332-1*) Scholarly.

Verses of Life. unabridged ed. Joseph A. Boyd, Jr. 275p. (Orig.). 1995. pap. write for info. (*1-888781-01-7*) J A Boyd.

***Verses of Serenity, 10 vols.** Ta Lien Shih. Incl. Vol. X. . unabridged ed. (CHI.). 90p. (Orig.). Date not set. pap. (*1-889955-09-4*); Vol. VIII. . unabridged ed. (CHI.). 90p. (Orig.). Date not set. pap. (*1-889955-07-8*); Vol. IV. . unabridged ed. (CHI.). 90p. (Orig.). Date not set. pap. (*1-889955-03-5*); Vol. III. . unabridged ed. (CHI.). 90p. (Orig.). Date not set. pap. (*1-889955-02-7*); Vol. II. . unabridged ed. (CHI.). 90p. (Orig.). 1999. pap. (*1-889955-01-9*); Vol. I. . unabridged ed. LC 96-92818. (CHI.). 86p. (Orig.). 1996. pap. 4.00 (*1-889955-00-0*); write for info. (*1-889955-10-8*) Jen Chen Budd-Houston.

Verses of Vermont II, Vol. II. Robert Gokey. 1997. pap. write for info. (*0-8233-0510-4*) Golden Quill.

Verses on Various Occasions. John H. Newman. 1992. 18.95 (*0-87193-282-2*) Dimension Bks.

***Verses That Hurt.** Trachtenberg. LC 96-45529. 1997. pap. 14.95 (*0-312-15191-8*) St Martin.

Verses to Share (God's Word Translation) Perfect Bible Verses for Special Occasions. LC 96-60871. 128p. (Orig.). 1996. pap. 9.99 (*0-529-10695-7*, VTS) World Publng.

Verses Vice Verses. Richard L. Loughlin. LC 80-81692. 120p. 1981. 12.95 (*0-911906-18-5*); pap. 7.95 (*0-911906-19-3*) Harian Creative Bks.

***Versicherungsaufsichtsrechtliche Fragen der Allfinanzkonzeption.** Cord Imelmann. 311p. (GER.). 1996. 57.95 (*3-631-30711-X*) P Lang Pubng.

Versiculos "Llave" Guillermo Woggon. Tr. by Nola Granberry. (Libros Para Colorear Ser.). (Illus.). 16p. (SPA.). (J). (gr. 1-3). 1987. reprint ed. pap. 2.50 (*0-311-38565-6*) Casa Bautista.

Versiegeltes Buch: Der Naturbegriff in der Theologie J. G. Hamanns (1730-1788) Henri Veldhuis. Tr. by Renate Drewes-Siebel from DUT. (Theologische Bibliothek Toepelmann Ser.: No. 65). xvi, 452p. (GER.). (C). 1994. lib. bdg. 183.10 (*3-11-014443-3*, 116-94) De Gruyter.

***Versificacion de Los Hechos.** L. Bernal. p. (SPA.). 7.95 (*0-8297-1945-8*) Life Pubs Intl.

Versificacion Imitativa en Fernando de Herrera. William Ferguson. (Monagrafias A Ser.: Vol. LXXVII). 136p. (SPA.). (C). 1977. 45.00 (*0-7293-0098-6*, Pub. by Tamesis Bks Ltd UK) Boydell & Brewer.

Versification: A Short Introduction. James McAuley. 88p. 1996. reprint ed. pap. 8.00 (*0-87013-096-X*) Mich St U Pr.

Versification & Syntax in Jeremiah 2-25: Syntactical Constraints in Hebrew Colometry. W. T. Cloete. 257p. 1989. 17.95 (*1-55540-389-1*, 06 21 17); pap. 11.95 (*1-55540-390-5*, 06 21 17) Scholars Pr GA.

Versification of Robert Browning. Harlan H. Hatcher. LC 73-90360. 204p. (C). 1969. reprint ed. 45.00 (*0-87753-021-1*) Phaeton.

Versification of Robert Browning. Harlan H. Hatcher. (BCL1-PR English Literature Ser.). 195p. 1992. reprint ed. lib. bdg. 69.00 (*0-7812-7463-X*) Rprt Serv.

Versified Armenian-Turkish Glossary by Kalayi, ca. 1800. Robert Dankoff et al. (Orig.). (C). 1996. pap. 12.50 (*0-9652548-0-1*) CSU Armenian Pub.

Versings & Conversings. Cora E. Cypser. 1992. pap. 7.95 (*0-9625774-7-2*) Kim Pathways.

Version Three Supplement to Exploring CADKEY. David C. Reichard. 176p. 1988. pap. text ed. 8.40 (*0-13-296120-2*) P-H.

Version Two Supplement to CEO: A Business Simulation for Policy & Strategic Management. Precha Thavikulwat. 30p. (C). 1994. student ed. 2.75 (*1-885303-01-7*) Towson St Univ.

Version 2.0: More BYTE-ing Humor from the 5th Wave. Rich Tennant. (Illus.). 104p. 1995. pap. 6.95 (*0-8362-1783-7*) Andrews & McMeel.

Versiones, Interpretaciones, Creaciones: Instancias de la Traduccion Literaria en Hispanoamerica en el Siglo XX. Frances R. Aparicio. LC 90-85355. 196p. (SPA.). 1991. pap. text ed. 15.00 (*0-935318-18-6*) Edins Hispamerica.

Versions of Deconversion: Autobiography & the Loss of Faith. John D. Barbour. 238p. (C). 1994. text ed. 35.00 (*0-8139-1546-5*) U Pr of Va.

UV

An Asterisk (*) at the beginning of an entry indicates that the title is appearing in BIP for the first time.

Versions of History from Antiquity to the Enlightenment. Ed. by Donald R. Kelley. 528p. (C). 1991. text ed. 47.50 (*0-300-04775-4*); pap. text ed. 20.00 (*0-300-04776-2*) Yale U Pr.

Versions of Our Past: Autobiographical Memory, Fabrication. Engel. Date not set. text ed. write for info. (*0-7167-2997-0*) W H Freeman.

Versions of Primary Education. Robin Alexander. LC 95-8133. 352p. (C). 1995. pap. text ed. 24.95 (*0-415-12838-2*) Routledge.

Versions of Survival: The Holocaust & the Human Spirit. Lawrence L. Langer. LC 81-14560. (SUNY Series in Modern Jewish Literature & Culture). 280p. (C). 1982. text ed. 59.50 (*0-87395-583-8*); pap. text ed. 19.95 (*0-87395-584-6*) State U NY Pr.

***Versions of the Past--Visions of the Future: The Canonical in the Criticism of T. S. Eliot, F. R. Leavis, Northrop Frye, & Harold Bloom.** Lars O. Sauerberg. LC 96-24144. 1996. text ed. 55.00 (*0-312-16420-3*) St Martin.

Versions of the Truth. Richard Parrish. 416p. 1994. pap. 5.99 (*0-451-40523-4*, Onyx) NAL-Dutton.

Versions of the Truth. Jean Young. LC 91-67099. 45p. (YA). (gr. 7 up). 1992. pap. 5.95 (*1-55523-484-4*) Winston-Derek.

Versitos Chistosos de Oaxaca. Daniel Worona. (Illus.). 128p. (Orig.). 1983. pap. 6.95 (*0-915311-00-3*) Oaxacado Pub Co.

Versos. Archer M. Huntington. 1952. pap. 5.00 (*0-87535-071-2*) Hispanic Soc.

Versos De Amor. Nelson Arroyo-Ortiz. 50p. (Orig.). (ENG & SPA.). 1992. pap. 5.95 (*0-9634872-0-5*) Blue Sky TX.

Versos de Cada Dia: Estampas Numeradas. Marigloria Palma, pseud. LC 79-10463. (UPREX, Poesia Ser.: No. 58). 228p. (Orig.). 1980. pap. 1.50 (*0-8477-0058-5*) U of PR Pr.

***Versos de Otono.** Oscar R. Benitez. 128p. (Orig.). (SPA.). 1997. pap. 8.99 (*1-890701-00-9*) La Mancha.

Versos Del Capitan. 2nd ed. Pablo Neruda. 126p. (SPA.). 1977. pap. 19.95 (*0-7859-4998-4*) Fr & Eur.

***Versos Sencillos: Simple Verses.** Jose Marti & Manuel A. Tellechea. LC 97-22189. (Recovering the U. S. - Hispanic Literary Heritage Ser.). (SPA.). 1997. write for info. (*1-55885-218-2*); pap. write for info. (*1-55885-204-2*) Arte Publico.

Versos Sencillos de Jose Marti: Analisis Critico. J. Alberto Hernandez-Chiroldes. LC 80-68758. (Coleccion Polymita). 321p. (Orig.). (SPA.). 1983. pap. 19.95 (*0-89729-266-9*) Ediciones.

Versos y Oraciones De Caminante, Libro II. Poesias De Leon Felipe. 104p. 1.10 (*0-318-14316-X*) Hispanic Inst.

Verspaetete Revolution: Erich von Kahler Wissenschaftseschichte Zwischen Konservativer. Gerhard Lauer. (Revolution und Exil Philosophie und Wissenschaft Ser.: Bd. 6). 566p. (GER.). (C). 1994. pap. text ed. 58.00 (*3-11-014397-6*) De Gruyter.

Versprechen und Verlesen: Eine Psychologisch-Linguistische Studie. Rudolf Meringer & Carl Mayer. (Classics in Psycholinguistics Ser.: No. 2). liv, 207p. 1978. 65.00 (*90-272-0973-1*) Benjamins North Am.

Verstaendigungsprobleme in Shakespeares Dramen. Hans J. Weckermann. (Bochum Studies in English: No. 7). vi, 369p. (Orig.). 1978. pap. 41.00 (*90-6032-105-7*, Pub. by B R Gruener NE) Benjamins North Am.

***Verstandnis Wirtschaftsspezifischer Anglizismen in der Deutschen Sprache bei Unternehmern, Fuhrungskraften & Mitarbeitern der Neuen & Alten Bundeslander.** Andrea Effertz & Ulrike Vieth. (Illus.). 191p. (GER.). 1996. 42.95 (*3-631-49969-8*) P Lang Pubng.

Versteh Mich Bitte: Character und Temperament Typen. Stephen E. Montgomery & Barbara B. Wolf. 207p. (Orig.). (GER.). (C). 1990. pap. 11.95 (*0-9606954-4-3*) Prometheus Nemesis.

***Verstehen & Humane Understanding.** Ed. by Anthony O'Hear. (Royal Institute of Philosophy Supplements Ser.: Vol. 41). (Illus.). 318p. (C). 1997. pap. text ed. 22.95 (*0-521-58742-5*) Cambridge U Pr.

Versuch. Alexander Humboldt. 1100p. (GER.). (C). 1994. text ed. 89.50 (*0-930329-75-9*) Kabel Pubs.

Versuch Einer Academischen Gelehrtengeschichte Von der Georg-Augustus-Universitat Zu Gottingen, 4 vols. Johann S. Putter. reprint ed. Set. write for info. (*0-318-71942-8*) G Olms Pubs.

Versuch Einer Beschreibung Sehenswurdiger Bibliotheken Teutschlands Nach Alphabetischer Ordnung, 4 vols. in 3. Friedrich C. Hirsching. 1971. reprint ed. Set. write for info. (*3-487-04157-X*) G Olms Pubs.

Versuch einer Entwicklungsgeschichte der Pflanzenwelt Insbesondere der Florengebiete Seit der Tertiaerperiode. A. Engler. 1971. 160.00 (*3-7682-0749-8*) Lubrecht & Cramer.

Versuch Einer Historie der Gedruckten Niedersachsischen Bibeln Vom Jahre 1470 - 1621. Johan M. Goeze. xxiv, 412p. 1975. reprint ed. write for info. (*3-487-05908-8*) G Olms Pubs.

Versuch Einer Vollstandigen Litteratur der Deutschen Ubersetzungen der Romer, 3 vols. Johann F. Degen. reprint ed. write for info. (*0-318-71762-X*) G Olms Pubs.

Versuche ueber Pflanzenhybriden. G. Mendel. 1966. reprint ed. pap. 12.00 (*3-7682-0013-2*) Lubrecht & Cramer.

Versuche zu einer Soziologie des Wissens: Preliminary Studies for a Sociology of Knowledge. Max F. Scheler. LC 74-25782. (European Sociology Ser.). 464p. 1975. reprint ed. 39.95 (*0-405-06535-3*) Ayer.

Versuche zur Renaturierung Geduengten Feuchtgruenlandes: Aushagerung und Vegetations Entwicklung. Alois Kapfer. (Dissertations Botanicae Ser.: Vol. 120). 154p. (GER.). 1988. pap. text ed. 71.50 (*3-443-64032-X*) Lubrecht & Cramer.

Vert & Venison: Forest Laws & Resource Management: the English Experience. Frank W. Stanton. 590p. Date not set. pap. text ed. write for info. (*0-9644930-1-2*) Silva Pr.

Vert & Venison: Forest Laws & Resource Management: The English Experience. Frank W. Stanton. 590p. Date not set. lib. bdg. 45.00 (*0-9644930-0-4*) Silva Pr.

***Vert Etait le Paradis.** large type ed. Rose Vincent. 288p. 1996. pap. 25.99 (*2-84011-172-1*) Ulverscroft.

***Vertamae Cooks in the Americas' Family Kitchen.** Vertamae Grosvenor. LC 96-42133. (Illus.). 192p. (Orig.). 1996. pap. 18.95 (*0-912333-88-X*) BB&T Inc.

Vertebrados del Viaje al Pacifico. Espada. 1978. write for info. (*0-916984-04-4*) SSAR.

Vertebrae: Poems 1978-1994. Samuel Green. 61p. 1994. 18.00 (*0-910055-18-1*); pap. 11.00 (*0-910055-17-3*) East Wash Univ.

Vertebral Artery: Surgery & Pathology. B. George & C. Laurian. (Illus.). 300p. 1987. 148.00 (*0-387-81968-1*) Spr-Verlag.

Vertebral Fracture in Osteoporosis. Harry K. Genant et al. (Illus.). 300p. 1995. 135.00 (*0-9646199-5-4*) Radiol Res & Educ Found.

Vertebral Manipulation. 5th ed. G. D. Maitland. (Illus.). 400p. 1986. pap. 47.50 (*0-7506-1333-5*) Buttrwrth-Heinemann.

Vertebral Morphology, Alternation of Neural Spine Height & Structure in Permo-Carboniferous Tetrapods & a Reappraisal of Primitive Modes of Terrestrial Locomotion. Stuart S. Sumida. LC 90-10885. (Publications in Zoology: Vol. 122). 144p. 1990. pap. 18.00 (*0-520-09755-6*) U CA Pr.

Vertebrata of the Tertiary Formations of the West, 1 vol. in two. Edward D. Cope. Ed. by Keir B. Sterling. LC 77-81093. (Biologists & Their World Ser.). (Illus.). 1978. reprint ed. Set. lib. bdg. 95.95 (*0-405-10672-6*) Ayer.

Vertebrata of the Tertiary Formations of the West, 1 vol. in two, 1. Edward D. Cope. Ed. by Keir B. Sterling. LC 77-81093. (Biologists & Their World Ser.). (Illus.). 1978. reprint ed. lib. bdg. 45.95 (*0-405-10673-4*) Ayer.

Vertebrata of the Tertiary Formations of the West, 1 vol. in two, Vol. 2. Edward D. Cope. Ed. by Keir B. Sterling. LC 77-81093. (Biologists & Their World Ser.). (Illus.). 1978. reprint ed. 50.95 (*0-405-10674-2*) Ayer.

***Vertebrate Anatomy: External, Vol. 1.** Abramoff. Date not set. write for info. (*0-7167-9048-3*) St Martin.

Vertebrate Biology. 5th ed. Robert T. Orr. 568p. (C). 1982. text ed. 56.00 (*0-03-057959-7*) SCP.

Vertebrate Blood Cells. Ed. by A. F. Rowley & N. A. Ratcliffe. 450p. 1988. 89.95 (*0-521-26032-9*) Cambridge U Pr.

Vertebrate Body. 6th ed. Alfred S. Romer & Thomas S. Parsons. (Illus.). 656p. (C). 1986. text ed. 57.00 (*0-03-058446-9*) SCP.

Vertebrate Cell Culture I. (Advances in Biochemical Engineering-Biotechnology Ser.: Vol. 34). (Illus.). 180p. 1987. 109.00 (*0-387-17626-8*) Spr-Verlag.

Vertebrate Cell Culture II & Enzyme Technology. (Advances in Biochemical Engineering-Biotechnology Ser.: Vol. 39). (Illus.). 195p. 1989. 109.00 (*0-387-51026-5*) Spr-Verlag.

Vertebrate Dissection. 7th ed. Warren F. Walker, Jr. 408p. (C). 1986. pap. text ed. 38.00 (*0-03-004782-X*) SCP.

Vertebrate Dissection. 8th ed. Warren F. Walker, Jr. & Dominique G. Homberger. 416p. (C). 1992. pap. text ed. 37.25 (*0-03-047434-5*) SCP.

Vertebrate Ecology & Systematics: A Tribute to Henry S. Fitch. Ed. by Richard A. Seigel et al. (Special Publications: No. 10). (Illus.). 278p. (Orig.). 1984. pap. 20.00 (*0-89338-019-9*) U KS Nat Hist Mus.

Vertebrate Ecology in the Northern Neotropics. Ed. by John F. Eisenberg. LC 79-9436. (Research Symposia of the National Zoological Park Ser.: No. 4). (Illus.). 272p. 1979. text ed. 32.50 (*0-87474-410-5*, EIVE) Smithsonian.

Vertebrate Endocrinology. 2nd ed. David O. Norris. LC 84-19425. 517p. reprint ed. pap. 147.40 (*0-7837-2734-8*, 2043114) Bks Demand.

Vertebrate Endocrinology. 3rd ed. Ed. by David O. Norris. (Illus.). 634p. (C). 1996. boxed 69.95 (*0-12-521670-X*) Acad Pr.

Vertebrate Faunal Analysis Coding System: With North American Taxonomy & dBase Support Programs & Procedures. Brian Shaffer & Barry Baker. (Technical Reports: No. 23). xii, 110p. (Orig.). (C). 1992. pap. 12.00 (*0-915703-28-9*) U Mich Mus Anthro.

Vertebrate Faunal Remains from Grasshopper Pueblo, Arizona. John W. Olsen. LC 90-6183. (Anthropological Papers: No. 83). (Illus.). xvi, 200p. (Orig.). 1990. pap. 15.00 (*0-915703-21-1*) U Mich Mus Anthro.

Vertebrate Fetal Membranes Comparative Ontogeny & Morphology: Evolution: Phylogenetic Significance, Basic Functions: Research Opportunities. Harland W. Mossman. 400p. 1987. text ed. 100.00 (*0-8135-1132-1*) Rutgers U Pr.

Vertebrate Flight. U. Norberg. (Zoophysiology Ser.: Vol. 27). (Illus.). 305p. 1990. 227.95 (*0-387-51370-1*) Spr-Verlag.

Vertebrate Fossils & the Evolution of Scientific Concepts. Ed. by William A. Sargeant. 535p. 1996. text ed. 120.00 (*2-88124-996-5*) Gordon & Breach.

Vertebrate Gas Transport Cascade: Adaptations to Environment & Mode of Life, Proceedings of a Meeting Held in Sao Sebastiao, Sao Paulo, Brazil, September 10-15, 1991. Ed. by J. Eduardo & P. W. Bicudo. 400p. 1992. 184.00 (*0-8493-4976-1*, QP121) CRC Pr.

Vertebrate Hard Tissues. L. B. Halstead & R. Hill. (Wykeham Science Ser.: No. 30). 192p. (C). 1974. 18.00 (*0-8448-1157-2*, Crane Russak) Taylor & Francis.

Vertebrate Hard Tissues. L. B. Halstead. (Wykeham Science Ser.: No. 30). 192p. 1974. pap. 18.00 (*0-85109-430-9*) Taylor & Francis.

***Vertebrate Histology.** Barbara Hull. 132p. (C). 1995. spiral bd. 23.62 (*0-7872-1010-2*) Kendall-Hunt.

Vertebrate History: Problems in Evolution. Barbara J. Stahl. (Biology Ser.). 640p. 1985. reprint ed. pap. 16.95 (*0-486-64850-8*) Dover.

Vertebrate Inner Ear. Ed. by Edwin R. Lewis et al. 256p. 1985. 148.00 (*0-8493-6465-5*, QP461, CRC Reprint) Franklin.

Vertebrate Life. 4th ed. F. Harvey Pough et al. LC 95-14458. 960p. (C). 1995. text ed. 73.00 (*0-02-396370-0*, Macmillan Coll) P-H.

Vertebrate Limb & Somite Morphogenesis: The Third Symposium of the British Society for Developmental Biology. British Society for Developmental Biology Staff. Ed. by D. A. Ede et al. LC 76-30451. (British Society for Developmental Biology Symposium Ser.: No. 3). 508p. reprint ed. pap. 144.80 (*0-318-34783-0*, 2031644) Bks Demand.

Vertebrate Limb Regeneration. Hugh Wallace. LC 80-40963. (Illus.). 288p. reprint ed. pap. 82.10 (*0-685-20660-2*, 2030446) Bks Demand.

Vertebrate Locomotion. Ed. by M. H. Day. (Symposia of the Zoological Society of London Ser.: No. 48). 1981. text ed. 235.00 (*0-12-613348-4*) Acad Pr.

Vertebrate Natural History. Mary F. Willson. 621p. (C). 1984. text ed. 53.25 (*0-03-061804-5*) SCP.

***Vertebrate Palaeontology.** Benton. (Illus.). 336p. (C). (gr. 13 up). 1996. pap. text ed. 45.95 (*0-412-54010-X*, Chap & Hall NY) Chapman & Hall.

Vertebrate Palaeontology. Michael J. Benton. 246p. (C). 1990. text ed. 80.00 (*0-04-566001-8*); pap. text ed. 24.95 (*0-04-566002-6*) Routledge Chapman & Hall.

***Vertebrate Palaeontology.** 2nd ed. M. J. Benton. 456p. 1997. pap. 49.95 (*0-412-73810-4*) Chapman & Hall.

Vertebrate Paleontological Techniques Vol. 1: Methods of Obtaining & Preparing Vertebrate Fossils. Ed. by Patrick Leiggi & Peter J. May. (Illus.). 380p. (C). 1995. text ed. 74.95 (*0-521-44357-1*) Cambridge U Pr.

Vertebrate Paleontology & Evolution. Robert L. Carroll. LC 86-31808. (Geology Ser.). (Illus.). 698p. (C). 1995. text ed. write for info. (*0-7167-1822-7*) W H Freeman.

Vertebrate Paleontology in the Neotropics: The Miocene Fauna of a La Venta, Colombia. Ed. by Richard F. Kay et al. LC 94-12118. (Illus.). 496p. 1995. text ed. 80.00 (*1-56098-418-X*) Smithsonian.

Vertebrate Pest Control & Management Materials, Vol. 5. Ed. by Stephen A. Shumake & Roger W. Bullard. LC 87-37424. (Special Technical Publication Ser.: No. 974). (Illus.). 191p. 1988. text ed. 34.00 (*0-8031-0991-1*, 04-974000-48) ASTM.

Vertebrate Pest Control & Management Materials, Vol. 6. Ed. by Kathleen A. Fagerstone & Richard D. Curnow. LC 89-17894. (Special Technical Publication (STP) Ser.: No. STP-1055). (Illus.). 75p. 1989. pap. text ed. 22.00 (*0-8031-1281-5*, 04-010550-48) ASTM.

Vertebrate Pest Control & Management Materials: Third Conference - STP 752. Schafer. 206p. 1981. 23.00 (*0-8031-0760-9*, 04-752000-48) ASTM.

Vertebrate Pest Control & Management Materials Second Conference: STP 680. 330p. 1979. 31.50 (*0-8031-0761-7*, 04-680000-48) ASTM.

Vertebrate Pest Control & Management Materials, 4th Symposium - STP 817. D. E. Kaukeinen. LC 83-70429. 305p. 1984. text ed. 44.00 (*0-8031-0213-5*, 04-817000-48) ASTM.

Vertebrate Pest Management. Ed. by G. A. Norton & R. P. Pech. 1989. pap. 30.00 (*0-643-04946-0*, Pub. by CSIRO AT) Aubrey Bks.

Vertebrate Red Blood Cells. M. Nikinmaa. (Zoophysiology Ser.: Vol. 28). (Illus.). 300p. 1990. 149.00 (*0-387-51590-9*) Spr-Verlag.

Vertebrate Reproduction. V. Blum. Tr. by A. C. Whittle from GER. (Illus.). 400p. 1986. pap. 69.00 (*0-387-16314-X*) Spr-Verlag.

Vertebrate Reproduction. Jameson. LC 88-5891. 526p. 1988. text ed. 159.00 (*0-471-62635-X*) Wiley.

Vertebrate Taphonomy. R. Lee Lyman. LC 93-28675. (Manuals in Archaeology Ser.). (Illus.). 576p. (C). 1994. text ed. 99.95 (*0-521-45215-5*); pap. text ed. 39.95 (*0-521-45840-4*) Cambridge U Pr.

Vertebrate Zoology: An Experimental Field Approach. Nelson G. Hairston, Sr. LC 93-27878. (Illus.). 280p. (C). 1994. pap. write for info. (*0-521-42712-6*); text ed. 39.95 (*0-521-41703-1*) Cambridge U Pr.

Vertebrate Zoology of Sind. J. Murray. 424p. (C). 1988. 275.00 (*81-7089-058-6*, Pub. by Intl Bk Distr II) St Mut.

Vertebrates. Nathan Aaseng. LC 93-13391. (Venture Bks.). (Illus.). 112p. (YA). (gr. 7-12). 1993. lib. bdg. 22.00 (*0-531-12551-3*) Watts.

Vertebrates. Ellen Doris. Date not set. 16.95 (*0-500-19009-7*) Thames Hudson.

Vertebrates. Alvin Silverstein et al. (Taxonomy Ser.). (Illus.). 64p. (J). (gr. 5-8). 1996. lib. bdg. 16.98 (*0-8050-3517-6*) TFC Bks NY.

Vertebrates: A Lab Manual. 2nd ed. Wessels. (C). 1996. pap. text ed. 33.75 (*0-86720-853-8*) Jones & Bartlett.

***Vertebrates: Comparative Anatomy, Function & Evolution.** 2nd ed. Kenneth V. Kardong. LC 97-8400. 800p. (C). 1997. text ed. write for info. (*0-697-28654-1*) Wm C Brown Pubs.

Vertebrates: Comparative Anatomy, Function, Evolution. Kenneth V. Kardong. (Illus.). 720p. 1990. 41.95 (*0-8016-2666-8*) Mosby Yr Bk.

Vertebrates: Comparative Anatomy, Function, Evolution. Kenneth V. Kardong. 800p. (C). 1994. text ed. write for info. (*0-697-21991-7*) Wm C Brown Pubs.

Vertebrates from the Barrier Islands of Tamaulipas, Mexico. Robert K. Selander et al. (Museum Ser.: Vol. 12, No. 7). 37p. 1962. pap. 2.00 (*0-686-79809-0*) U KS Nat Hist Mus.

Vertebrates I: Pisces, Amphibia, Reptile, Aves see Text-Book of Palaeontology

Vertebrates in Complex Tropical Systems. Ed. by M. Harmelin-Viven & F. Bourliere. (Ecological Studies: Vol. 69). (Illus.). 200p. 1988. 144.95 (*0-387-96740-0*) Spr-Verlag.

Vertebrates of Arizona: With Major Section on Arizona Habitats. E. Lendell Cockrun et al. Ed. by Charles H. Lowe. LC 63-11981. 282p. reprint ed. pap. 80.40 (*0-8357-7788-X*, 2036149) Bks Demand.

Vertebrates of Florida: Identification & Distribution. Henry M. Stevenson. LC 75-37723. (Illus.). 631p. reprint ed. pap. 179.90 (*0-8357-3073-5*, 2039330) Bks Demand.

Vertebrates, Phylogeny, & Philosophy. Jason A. Lillegraven et al. Ed. by K. Flanagan. LC 86-50857. (Illus.). 372p. 1986. lib. bdg. 30.00 (*0-941570-02-9*) U of Wyoming.

Vertebrobasilar Arterial Disease. Ramon Berguer & Louis R. Caplan. (Illus.). 299p. 1992. 75.00 (*0-942219-22-8*) Quality Med Pub.

Vertebrobasilar Arterial Occlusive Disease: Medical & Surgical Management. Ed. by Ramon Berguer & Raymond B. Bauer. LC 83-22900. 352p. 1984. reprint ed. pap. 100.40 (*0-608-00432-4*, 2061147) Bks Demand.

Vertellingen Van de Buddha: Borobudur. John Miksic. (Illus.). 160p. 1991. 4.95 (*0-945971-25-7*) Periplus.

Vertesszolos: Site, Man & Culture. Miklos Kretzoi & Viola T. Dobost. (Illus.). 554p. (C). 1990. 189.00 (*963-05-4713-9*, Pub. by Akad Kiado HU) St Mut.

***Vertex Algebra for Beginners.** Victor G. Kac. LC 96-35736. (University Lectures: Vol. 10). 141p. 1996. pap. 25.00 (*0-8218-0643-2*) Am Math.

Vertex Algebras & Integral Bases for the Enveloping Algebras of Affine Lie Algebras. S. Prevost. LC 91-44874. (Memoirs Ser.). 97p. 1977. pap. 25.00 (*0-8218-2527-5*, MEMO/96/466) Am Math.

Vertex Detectors. Ed. by F. Villa. LC 87-34301. (Ettore Majorana International Science Series, Life Sciences: Vol. 34). (Illus.). 376p. 1988. 95.00 (*0-306-42798-2*, Plenum Pr) Plenum.

Vertex Operator Algebras & the Monster. Igor Frenkel et al. (Pure & Applied Mathematics Ser.: Vol. 134). 508p. 1989. text ed. 129.00 (*0-12-267065-5*) Acad Pr.

Vertex Operators in Mathematics & Physics. Ed. by I. M. Singer et al. (Mathematical Sciences Research Institute Publications: Vol. 3). (Illus.). xiv, 482p. 1985. 53.95 (*0-387-96121-6*) Spr-Verlag.

Vertex Traditionis: Die Gattung der Altchristlichen Kirchenordnungen. Bruno Steimer. (Beihefte zur Zeitschrift fuer die Neuetestamentliche Wissenschaft Ser.: Bd. 63). xvi, 402p. (GER.). (C). 1992. lib. bdg. 113.85 (*3-11-013460-8*, 271-91) De Gruyter.

Vertical & Horizontal Deformations of Foundations & Embankments: Proceedings of Settlement '94. Ed. by Albert T. Yeung & Guy Y. Felio. LC 94-20011. 1994. 160.00 (*0-7844-0027-X*) Am Soc Civil Eng.

Vertical & Horizontal Mechanisms. Aron I. Katsenelinboigen. 360p. 1988. pap. text ed. 15.95 (*0-685-25891-2*) Intersystems Pubns.

Vertical Antenna Classics. 1995. pap. 12.00 (*0-87259-521-8*) Am Radio.

Vertical Boring. 1983. 100.00 (*0-685-05800-X*) St Mut.

Vertical Cavity Surface Emitting Lasers. Terence E. Sale. (Electronic & Electrical Engineering Research Ser.: Optoelectronics Ser.: Vol. 2). 1995. text ed. 94.95 (*0-471-95740-2*) Wiley.

Vertical Challenge: The Hiller Aircraft Story. Jay P. Spenser. LC 92-7525. (Illus.). 240p. (C). 1992. 30.00 (*0-295-97203-3*) U of Wash Pr.

Vertical Compressions of Soils. E. J. Den Haan. 96p. 1994. pap. 57.50 (*90-407-1062-7*, Pub. by Delft U Pr NE) Coronet Bks.

Vertical File & Its Alternatives: A Handbook. Clara L. Sitter. xv, 256p. 1992. lib. bdg. 32.50 (*0-87287-910-0*) Libs Unl.

Vertical File Index. pap. 50.00 (*0-686-76913-9*) Wilson.

Vertical Fiscal Imbalance & the Assignment of Taxing Powers in Australia. Charles E. McClure, Jr. LC 93-2405. (Essays in Public Policy Ser.: No. 40). 1993. pap. text ed. 5.00 (*0-8179-5452-X*) Hoover Inst Pr.

***Vertical Food Web Interactions: Evolutionary Patterns & Driving Forces.** K. Dettner et al. LC 97-6984. (Ecological Studies). 1997. write for info. (*3-540-62561-5*) Spr-Verlag.

Vertical Fruit of the Horizontal Tree. Howard V. Hendrix. 52p. (Orig.). 1994. pap. 5.95 (*0-9626708-6-3*) Talisman IN.

Vertical Heartland: A Rock Climber's Guide to Southern Illinois. 2nd rev. ed. Eric Ulner. (Illus.). 178p. 1996. pap. 25.95 (*0-9648053-0-8*) Sec West Pub.

Vertical-Horizontal Illusion see Scientific Study of the College Student

Vertical Integration & Joint Ventures in the Aluminum Industry. John A. Stuckey. (Economic Studies: No. 152). (Illus.). 360p. 1983. 30.00 (*0-674-93490-3*) HUP.

Vertical Integration & Technological Innovation: A Transaction Cost Approach. Yeong H. Lee. LC 93-38432. (Studies on Industrial Productivity). 144p. 1994. text ed. 42.00 (*0-8153-1569-4*) Garland.

Vertical Integration in Cable Television. David Waterman & Andrew A. Weiss. LC 96-51422. (AEI Studies in Telecommunications Deregulation). (Illus.). 150p. 1997. 30.00 (*0-262-23190-5*) MIT Pr.

Vertical Integration in the Oil Industry. Ed. by Edward J. Mitchell. LC 76-20267. (National Energy Study Ser.: No. 11). 220p. reprint ed. pap. 62.70 (*0-8357-4542-2*, 2037438) Bks Demand.

Vertical Labyrinth. Aldo Carotenuto. pap. 16.00 (*0-919123-19-8*, Pub. by Inner City CN) BookWorld Dist.

Vertical Loom: Principles & Construction. Jules Kliot. 12p. 1976. 5.00 (*0-916896-09-9*) Lacis Pubns.

An Asterisk (*) at the beginning of an entry indicates that the title is appearing in BIP for the first time.

Vertical Mammaplasty & Liposuction. Madeleine Lejour. LC 93-11760. (Illus.). 238p. 1994. 245.00 incl. vhs (*0-942219-55-4*); vhs 75.00 (*0-614-08703-1*) Quality Med Pub.

Vertical Man. John C. Whitehouse. LC 90-44343. (Studies in Comparative Literature). 228p. 1990. reprint ed. 20.00 (*0-8240-5467-9*) Garland.

Vertical Milling in the Home Workshop. 3rd ed. Arnold Throp. (Workshop Practice Ser.: No. 2). (Illus.). 96p. 1984. pap. 18.50 (*0-85242-843-X*, Pub. by Nexus Special Interests UK) Trans-Atl Phila.

Vertical Milling Machine Explained. Leo Rizzo. LC 79-731074. (Orig.). 1978. student ed. 6.00 (*0-8064-0241-5*, 512); audio 319.00 (*0-8064-0242-3*) Bergwall.

Vertical Milling Machines. 1996. lib. bdg. 251.99 (*0-8490-8342-7*) Gordon Pr.

Vertical Mosaic: An Analysis of Social Class & Power in Canada. John Porter. LC 65-3947. 1965. pap. 21.95 (*0-8020-6055-2*) U of Toronto Pr.

Vertical Mosaic: An Analysis of Social Class & Power in Canada. John A. Porter. LC 78-418980. (Studies in the Structure of Power: Decision-Making in Canada: No. 2). (Illus.). 646p. reprint ed. pap. 180.00 (*0-8357-6365-X*, 2035719) Bks Demand.

Vertical Price Fixing in Australia. Philip H. Clarke. 244p. 1991. 68.00 (*1-86287-054-3*, Pub. by Federation Pr AU) Gaunt.

Vertical Pump Standards for Nomenclature, Definitions, Application, & Operation, No. 2.1-2.5. (Hydraulic Institute Ser.: No. 2.1-2.5). 83p. 1994. 59.00 (*1-880952-04-1*, S109) Hydraulic Inst.

Vertical Pump Test Standard, No. 2.6. (Hydraulic Institute Ser.: No. 2.6). 31p. 1994. 39.00 (*1-880952-05-X*, S110) Hydraulic Inst.

Vertical Restrictions upon Buyers Limiting Purchases of Goods from Others. American Bar Association. Section of Antitrust Law Staff & Lynn H. Pasahow. LC 82-72695. xii, 99p. 1982. pap. 20.00 (*0-89707-081-X*, 503-0043) Amer Bar Assn.

Vertical River. Walter Bargen. 45p. (Orig.). 1996. pap. 10.00 (*0-944048-08-0*) Timberline Missouri.

Vertical Run. Joseph R. Garber. 352p. 1996. mass mkt. 6.50 (*0-553-57392-6*) Bantam.

Vertical Run. large type ed. Joseph R. Garber. 451p. 1996. 24.95 (*0-7838-1592-1*, GK Hall) Thorndike Pr.

Vertical Seismic Profiling. Balch & Lee. 488p. 1988. text ed. 120.00 (*0-13-945122-6*) P-H.

Vertical Seismic Profiling. E. I. Galperin. Ed. by J. E. White. Tr. by Alfred J. Hermont from RUS. LC 74-83416. 278p. 1974. 19.00 (*0-931830-06-0*, 524) Soc Expl Geophys.

Vertical Seismic Profiling Vol. 14, Pt. A: Principles. B. Hardage & K. Helbig. (Handbook of Geophysical Exploration Ser.). 1985. 232.00 (*0-946631-28-X*, Pub. by Pergamon Repr UK) Franklin.

Vertical Seismic Profiling & Its Exploration Potential. E. I. Galperin. 1985. lib. bdg. 194.00 (*90-277-1450-9*) Kluwer Ac.

Vertical Seismic Profiling, Pt. A: Principles. 2nd ed. B. A. Hardage. LC 91-25739. (Handbook of Geophysical Exploration Ser.). 509p. 1992. 92.00 (*0-08-036950-2*, Pergamon Pr) Elsevier.

Vertical Solitude: Managing in the Public Sector. David Zussman & Jak Jabes. (Illus.). 220p. 1990. pap. text ed. 29.95 (*0-88645-094-2*, Pub. by Inst Res Pub CN) Ashgate Pub Co.

Vertical Structure in Aquatic Environments & Its Impact on Tropical Likages & Nutrient Fluxes. C. S. Reynold. Ed. by Y. Watanage. (Advances in Limnology Ser.: No. 35). (Illus.). 159p. 1992. pap. 60.00 (*3-510-47036-2*, Pub. by E Schweizerbartsche GW) Lubrecht & Cramer.

Vertical Transportation: Elevators & Escalators. 2nd ed. George R. Strakosch. LC 82-10866. 495p. 1983. text ed. 125.00 (*0-471-86733-0*) Wiley.

Vertical Transportation for Buildings. Rodney R. Adler. LC 73-104976. (Elsevier Architectural Science Ser.). 238p. reprint ed. pap. 67.90 (*0-317-11060-8*, 2007760) Bks Demand.

Vertical World of Yosemite. Ed. by Galen A. Rowell. LC 73-85098. (Illus.). 218p. (Orig.). 1974. reprint ed. pap. 24.95 (*0-911824-87-1*) Wilderness Pr.

Vertically Integrated Project Management: An Enterprise Management Systems Approach. Lee E. Heindel & Vincent A. Kasten. LC 95-22608. 240p. 1995. 75.00 (*0-8144-0301-8*) AMACOM.

Vertically Transmitted Diseases. Stavros N. Busenberg & Kenneth Cooke. LC 92-49541. (Biomathematics Ser.: Vol. 23). 1993. write for info. (*3-540-52004-X*); 126.95 (*0-387-52004-X*) Spr-Verlag.

Vertige. P. Liard et al. (Illus.). xii, 96p. 1993. pap. 33.25 (*3-8055-5822-8*) S Karger.

***Vertigo.** Louise Desalvo. 1997. pap. 11.95 (*0-452-27324-2*, Plume) NAL-Dutton.

Vertigo. Ed. by M. R. Dix & J. D. Hood. LC 83-10393. (Wiley-Medical Publication Ser.). 501p. reprint ed. pap. 142.80 (*0-8357-3469-2*, 2039731) Bks Demand.

Vertigo: A Memoir. Louise DeSalvo. 288p. 1996. pap. 23.95 (*0-525-93908-3*) NAL-Dutton.

Vertigo: Its Multisensory Syndromes. T. Brandt. Ed. by John P. Conomy & Michael Swash. (Clinical Medicine & the Nervous System Ser.). (Illus.). 344p. 1992. 125.00 (*0-387-19636-6*) Spr-Verlag.

***Vertigo: Its Multisensory Syndromes.** 2nd ed. Thomas Brandt. (Clinical Medicine & the Nervous System Ser.). 352p. 1996. 100.00 (*3-540-19934-9*) Spr-Verlag.

Vertigo & Dizziness. Lucy Yardley. LC 94-6512. (Experience of Illness Ser.). 176p. (C). (gr. 13). 1994. pap. 16.95 (*0-415-10209-X*, B4375) Routledge.

Vertigo, Nausea, Tinnitus & Hearing Loss in Central & Peripheral Vestibular Diseases: Proceedings of the XXIInd Annual Meeting of the International Neurootologic & Equilibriometric Society, Hakone, Japan, 6-9 April 1995. Ed. by Claus-Frenz Claussen et al. LC 95-23632. (International Congress Ser.: No. 1087). 414p. 1995. text ed. 214.25 (*0-444-82193-7*, Excerpta Medica) Elsevier.

Vertigo, Nausea, Tinnitus & Hypoacusia Due to Head & Neck Trauma. C. F. Claussen. (International Congress Ser.: Vol. 929). 1991. 207.00 (*0-444-81150-8*) Elsevier.

Vertigo Park: And Other Tall Tales. Mark O'Donnell. 160p. 1994. pap. 9.95 (*0-312-11363-3*) St Martin.

Vertigo Verite: Seven Miles a Second. David Wojnarowicz. (Illus.). 64p. 1996. pap. text ed. 7.95 (*1-56389-247-2*, Vertigo) DC Comics.

***Vertisols & Technologies for Their Management.** Ed. by N. Ahmad & A. Mermut. (Developments in Soil Science Ser.: Vol. 24). 566p. 1996. 309.50 (*0-444-88789-X*) Elsevier.

Vertrauensmann (Man of Confidence) The Story of an American Ex-Prisoner of World War II. Henry Kaufman. LC 94-27834. (Illus.). 1995. 17.50 (*0-944957-47-1*) Rivercross Pub.

Vertreibung der Deutschen aus dem Osten: Ursachen, Ereignisse, Folgen. Ed. by Wolfgang Benz. (GER.). 1995. pap. 15.25 (*3-596-12784-X*, Pub. by Fischer Taschbch Verlag GW) Intl Bk Import.

Vertue Betray'd: or Anna Bullen: A Tragedy. John Banks. LC 92-25500. (Augustan Reprints Ser.: Nos. 205-206). 1981. reprint ed. 21.50 (*0-404-70205-8*, PR3316) AMS Pr.

Vertue Rewarded: or The Irish Princess: A New Novel. Ed. by Hubert McDermott. 107p. 1994. lib. bdg. 42.00 (*0-86140-305-3*, Pub. by C Smythe Ltd UK) B&N Imports.

Vertue XXXV. Humphrey Barton. 180p. 1985. 18.95 (*0-916025-05-5*) Armchair Sail Pub.

Vertuose Boke of Distyllasyon. Von Braunschweig Hieronymus. Tr. by L. Andrewe. LC 72-6006. (English Experience Ser.: No. 532). 276p. 1973. reprint ed. 60.00 (*90-221-0532-6*) Walter J Johnson.

Vertus de l'Enfer. Pierre Boulle. 272p. (FRE.). 1976. pap. 29.95 (*0-7859-1165-0*, 2080606921) Fr & Eur.

Veruca Salt American Thighs: American Thighs. 93p. (YA). pap. 19.95 (*0-89524-952-9*, 02501261) Cherry Lane.

Verulamium: A Belgic & Two Roman Cities. Robert E. Wheeler & T. V. Wheeler. (Society of Antiquaries of London, Research Committee Reports: No. 11). 426p. reprint ed. pap. 121.50 (*0-317-28843-1*, 2020784) Bks Demand.

***Verulamium Excavations, Vol. I.** Ed. by Sheppard Frere. (Illus.). 384p. 1972. 30.00 (*0-85431-007-X*, Pub. by Soc Antiquaries UK) David Brown.

***Verulamium Excavations, Vol. II.** Sheppard Frere. (Illus.). 392p. 1983. 29.98 (*0-85431-235-8*, Pub. by Soc Antiquaries UK) David Brown.

Verulamium Excavations, Vol. III. Sheppard Frere. (Illus.). 300p. 1984. 29.98 (*0-947816-01-1*, Pub. by Oxford Univ Comm Arch UK) David Brown.

***Verus Israel: A Study of Relations Between Christians & Jews in the Roman Empire, 135-425.** Marcel Simon. Tr. by H. McKeating from FRE. 550p. (Orig.). 1996. pap. 24.95 (*1-874774-27-7*, Pub. by Littman Lib UK) Intl Spec Bk.

Verve: The Ultimate Review of Art & Literature, 1937-1960. Michel Anthonioz. Tr. by I. Mark Paris et al. 1988. 95.00 (*0-8109-1743-2*) Abrams.

Verwaltung uund Wissenschaftliche Erschliebung von Nachlassen in Literaturarchiven: Osterreichisch Richtlinien als Modell. Christoph Konig & Methlagl. (Illus.). 175p. (GER.). 1988. lib. bdg. 43.00 (*3-598-10741-2*) K G Saur.

***Verwaltungskultur in den Neuen Bundeslandern: Werte und Einstellungen von Fuhrungskraften in den Ministerialverwaltungen von Brandenburg und Sachsen.** Horst Damskis & Barbel Moller. (Berliner Schriften zur Demokratieforschung Ser.: Bd. 4). 191p. (GER.). 1997. pap. 42.95 (*3-631-49997-3*) P Lang Pubng.

Verwandlung. Franz Kafka. Ed. by Vladimir Nabokov. 140p. (GER.). 1995. pap. 9.00 (*3-596-25875-8*, Pub. by Fischer Taschbch Verlag GW) Intl Bk Import.

Verwandlung. Franz Kafka. Ed. by Marjorie L. Hoover. (C). 1960. pap. text ed. 9.95 (*0-393-09533-9*) Norton.

Verwehte Zest Erwacht I see Past Eras Awaken: Krishna - Nahome - Cassandra - Mary of Magdala

***Very.** Brad Leithauser. 1998. write for info. (*0-375-40141-5*) Knopf.

***Very Air.** Bauer. LC 97-22106. 1997. pap. 23.00 (*0-8050-4301-2*) St Martin.

***Very Air.** Douglas Bauer. 380p. 4.98 (*0-8317-8604-3*) Smithmark.

Very Angry Day That Amy Didn't Have. Lawrence E. Shapiro. (Illus.). 30p. (Orig.). (J). (ps-6). 1994. pap. 10.95 (*1-882732-18-9*) Ctr Applied Psy.

Very Bad Bunny. Marilyn Sadler. LC 84-3319. (Beginner Bks.). (Illus.). 48p. (J). (ps-3). 1984. 7.99 (*0-394-86861-7*); lib. bdg. 11.99 (*0-394-96861-1*) Beginner.

Very Bad Poetry. Kathryn Petras. LC 96-51788. 1997. pap. 10.00 (*0-679-77622-2*) Random.

***Very Berry Cookbook.** Judith Bosley. (Illus.). 59p. (Orig.). 1991. pap. 8.95 (*0-930809-10-6*) Kitch Cupbd Cookbks.

Very Best: Mexican Restaurants & Where to Find Them. Herbert Wolff & Carol T. Robbins. LC 83-90979. 230p. (Orig.). 1983. pap. 7.95 (*0-911729-01-1*) Very Best.

Very Best Baby Name Book in the Whole Wide World. Bruce Lansky. 1996. write for info. (*0-88166-247-X*) Meadowbrook.

Very Best Baby Name Book in the Whole Wide World. rev. ed. Bruce Lansky. 280p. 1996. pap. 8.00 (*0-671-56113-8*) Meadowbrook.

Very Best Book. Dina Rosenfeld. LC 94-80242. (Illus.). 32p. (J). 1997. 11.95 (*0-922613-76-1*) Hachai Pubns.

***Very Best Book.** Weir. 4.99 (*0-8307-1633-5*) Regal.

Very Best Book of Baby Names. Barbara K. Turner. 320p. (Orig.). 1994. mass mkt. 5.99 (*0-425-14130-6*) Berkley Pub.

Very Best Christmas Present. Jim Razzi. LC 87-83045. (Golden Look-Look Bks.). (Illus.). 24p. (Orig.). (J). (ps-3). 1988. pap. write for info. (*0-307-11711-1*, Golden Books) Western Pub.

***Very Best Easter Bunny.** Golden Books Staff. (Disney's Pooh Ser.). (J). 1997. 1.99 (*0-307-98795-7*, Golden Books) Western Pub.

***Very Best Mama: Peek-a-Pooh.** Walt Disney. (J). 1997. 6.98 (*1-57082-525-4*) Mouse Works.

Very Best Me. C. Urbach. 1993. 14.99 (*0-89906-141-9*); 11.99 (*0-89906-142-7*) Mesorah Pubns.

Very Best Me: Growing up Drug Free. Ann T. Weikel. (Illus.). 60p. (Orig.). (J). (gr. k-3). 1991. pap. 3.95 (*0-935357-11-4*) CRIC Prod.

Very Best Men: Four Who Dared: The Early Years of the CIA. Evan Thomas. LC 95-21316. (Illus.). 448p. 1995. 27.50 (*0-684-81025-5*, S&S) S&S Trade.

Very Best Men: Four Who Dared: The Early Years of the CIA. Evan Thomas. (Illus.). 1996. pap. 15.00 (*0-684-82538-4*) S&S Trade.

Very Best of Children's Book Illustration. Compiled by Society of Illustrators Staff. (Illus.). 144p. 1993. 29.95 (*0-89134-540-X*, 30513, North Lght Bks) F & W Pubns Inc.

Very Best of Foster & Allen. 14.25 (*0-7866-1593-1*, 95178WW) Mel Bay.

Very Best of Friends. Margaret Wild. LC 89-36464. (Illus.). 32p. (J). (ps-3). 1994. pap. 5.00 (*0-15-200077-1*, Gulliver Bks) HarBrace.

Very Best of Gerry Mulligan. 19.95 (*0-7935-4013-5*, 00672302) H Leonard.

Very Best of Lee Greenwood. Lee Greenwood. (Piano-Vocal-Guitar Personality Folio Ser.). (Illus.). 72p. 1986. pap. 12.95 (*0-88188-436-7*, HL00356845) H Leonard.

Very Best of Lee Greenwood, Vol. 103. 56p. 1986. pap. 7.95 (*0-7935-3119-5*, 00100592) H Leonard.

Very Best of Paul Simon. Contrib. by Paul Simon. 1994. pap. 15.95 (*0-8256-3315-X*, PS11345) Music Sales.

Very Best of Ricky Skaggs. Ricky Skaggs. (Piano-Vocal-Guitar Ser.). (Illus.). 64p. 1986. per. 12.95 (*0-88188-435-9*, HLOO358178) H Leonard.

Very Best of Spider-Man. Stan Lee. (Illus.). 176p. 1994. pap. 15.95 (*0-7851-0045-8*) Marvel Entmnt.

Very Best of X: Lifestyles in Christ Meditations on Orthodox Christian Living. James C. Meena. 118p. (Orig.). 1995. pap. 8.95 (*0-9634940-5-8*) York Pub.

Very Best Place for a Penny. Dina H. Rosenfeld. (Illus.). 32p. (J). 1984. reprint ed. 10.00 (*0-8266-0362-9*, Merkos Llnyonei Chinuch) Kehot Pubn Soc.

Very Brady Guide to Life. Jennifer Briggs. (Illus.). 224p. 1996. pap. 7.95 (*1-55853-447-4*) Rutledge Hill Pr.

Very British Miracle: The Failure of Thatcherism. Edgar Wilson. 240p. (C). 59.00 (*0-7453-0653-5*, Pub. by Pluto Pr UK); pap. 18.95 (*0-7453-0654-3*, Pub. by Pluto Pr UK) LPC InBook.

Very British Subject: Telling Tales. Barnet Litvinoff. LC 96-1903. (Illus.). 216p. (Orig.). 1996. pap. 25.00 (*0-85303-293-9*, Pub. by Vallentine Mitchell UK) Intl Spec Bk.

Very Bumpy Bus Ride. Michaela Muntean. LC 93-13042. (Parents Magazine Read Aloud Original Ser.). (Illus.). (J). 1993. lib. bdg. 17.27 (*0-8368-0980-7*) Gareth Stevens Inc.

Very Bumpy Bus Ride. Michaela Muntean. LC 81-16905. (Illus.). 48p. (J). (ps-3). 1982. 5.95 (*0-8193-1079-4*); 5.95 (*0-8193-1080-8*) Parents.

Very Busy Barbie. Mattel Staff. (Popular Characters/Author Collection). (Illus.). 24p. (J). (ps-2). 1995. bds. 1.59 (*0-307-30121-4*, Golden Books) Western Pub.

Very Busy Spider. Eric Carle. (Illus.). 24p. (J). (ps-2). 1985. 19.95 (*0-399-21166-7*, Philomel Bks) Putnam Pub Group.

Very Busy Spider - Mini. Eric Carle. LC 84-5907. (Illus.). 24p. (J). (ps-2). 1989. 6.95 (*0-399-21592-1*, Philomel Bks) Putnam Pub Group.

Very Busy Spider Board Book. Eric Carle. LC 84-5907. (Illus.). 24p. (J). (ps up). 1995. bds. 9.95 (*0-399-22919-1*, Philomel Bks) Putnam Pub Group.

***Very Busy Spider Plus.** Eric Carle. (J). Date not set. 19.95 (*0-399-23014-9*) Putnam Pub Group.

Very Cagey Lady. Joyce Elbert. 1980. pap. 2.95 (*0-451-09936-2*, E9936, Sig) NAL-Dutton.

Very Civil War: The Swiss Sonderbund War of 1847. Joachim Remak. 221p. 1993. text ed. 35.01 (*0-8133-1529-8*) Westview.

Very Close to Trouble: The Johnny Grant Memoir. Ed. by Lyndel Meikle. (Illus.). 250p. 1996. 35.00 (*0-87422-140-4*); pap. 17.95 (*0-87422-139-0*) Wash St U Pr.

Very Convenient Marriage: (A Family Circle) Dallas Schulze. (Intimate Moments Ser.). 1994. mass mkt. 3.50 (*0-373-07608-8*, 1-07608-2) Silhouette.

***Very Different Age: Americans of the Progressive Era.** Steven J. Diner. LC 97-3801. 1997. 25.00 (*0-8090-2553-1*) Hill & Wang.

Very Dutiful Daughter. Elizabeth Mansfield. 256p. (Orig.). 1986. mass mkt. 4.50 (*0-515-08740-8*) Jove Pubns.

Very Easiest Exercises for Piano, Op. 190. Louis Kohler. (Carl Fischer Music Library: No. 381). 1905. pap. 4.00 (*0-8258-0117-6*, L381) Fischer Inc NY.

Very Easy Death. Simone De Beauvoir. 1985. pap. 11.00 (*0-394-72899-8*) Pantheon.

Very Easy WordPerfect. David Zeigler. 53p. 1992. pap. 6.95 (*0-9633375-0-5*) Creat Sol WA.

Very Efficient Carpenter. Larry Haun. (Illus.). 224p. 1993. pap. 27.95 (*1-56158-049-X*) Taunton.

Very Efficient Carpenter: Basic Framing for Residential Construction. Larry Haun. LC 92-12644. 1992. 27.95 (*1-56158-001-5*) Taunton.

Very Entertaining: Menus for Special Occasions. Diane Morgan et al. Ed. by Lynn Lustburg. LC 89-81843. (Illus.). 174p. (Orig.). 1990. pap. 19.95 (*0-9620937-1-8*) Entertaining People.

Very Far Away. Maurice Sendak. LC 57-5356. (Illus.). (J). (gr. k-3). 1957. 13.00 (*0-06-025514-5*) HarpC Child Bks.

Very Far Away. Maurice Sendak. LC 57-5356. (Illus.). (J). (gr. k-3). 1962. lib. bdg. 13.89 (*0-06-025515-3*) HarpC Child Bks.

Very Favorites of the Very Young. Ed. by Carol Henry. (Illus.). 72p. 1990. 3.00 (*0-944470-02-5*) World Around Songs.

Very Few People Come This Way: Lyrical Episodes from the Year of the Rabbit. Edward G. Seidensticker. 208p. 1996. pap. text ed. 16.00 (*1-873047-31-2*, Pub. by In Print Pubng UK) UH Pr.

***Very Fine Rooster Little Book Level A.** Walker. (J). 1996. ring bd. 4.33 (*0-201-85335-3*) Addison-Wesley.

Very First Americans. Cara Ashrose. LC 92-38076. (All Aboard Bks.). (Illus.). 32p. (J). (ps-3). 1993. pap. 2.95 (*0-448-40168-1*, G&D) Putnam Pub Group.

Very First Christmas: A Child's Story of the Savior's Birth. Jean D. Crowther. 48p. 1991. pap. 5.98 (*0-88290-432-9*) Horizon Utah.

Very First Easter Bunny. Kari Dahlin. 16p. (J). 1995. write for info. (*0-944943-57-8*, 247799) Current Inc.

Very First Flute Duets. Arnold. 1990. 4.95 (*0-685-32135-5*, H606) Hansen Ed Mus.

Very First Flute Method. Arnold. 1990. 4.95 (*0-685-32136-3*, H607) Hansen Ed Mus.

Very First Light. John Mather & John Boslough. 320p. 1996. 25.00 (*0-465-01575-1*) Basic.

***Very First Lord's Supper.** Arch Books Staff. 1997. pap. 1.99 (*0-570-07528-9*) Concordia.

Very First Method. 1990. 4.95 (*0-685-32206-8*, H550) Hansen Ed Mus.

***Very First Night Before Christmas: A Musical Story Based on Isaiah 9:2, 6, 7; 11:1-3 & Luke 2:1-7: PreviewPak.** Nylea L. Butler-Moore. 1995. pap. 6.00 incl. audio (*0-687-06000-1*) Abingdon.

***Very First Night Before Christmas: Intro Pak.** 1995. 19.95 (*0-687-01086-1*) Abingdon.

***Very First Night Before Christmas: Intro Pak.** 1995. audio 29.95 (*0-687-01090-X*) Abingdon.

***Very First Night Before Christmas: Intro Pak.** 1995. audio 10.95 (*0-687-01091-8*) Abingdon.

***Very First Night Before Christmas: Leader/Accompanist Edition.** 1995. spiral bd., pap. 14.95 (*0-687-01088-8*) Abingdon.

***Very First Night Before Christmas: Singer's Edition.** 1995. pap. 2.95 (*0-687-01087-X*) Abingdon.

Very First Poetry Book. Compiled by John Foster. (Illus.). 128p. (J). 1987. pap. 8.00 (*0-19-916050-3*) OUP.

Very First Thanksgiving: Pioneers on the Rio Grande. Bea Bragg. LC 89-15562. (Illus.). 64p. (Orig.). (J). (gr. 3-7). 1989. pap. 7.95 (*0-943173-22-1*, Harbinger CO) R Rinehart.

***Very First Things to Know about Ants.** Patricia Grossman. (Illus.). (J). 1997. write for info. (*0-614-29331-6*) Workman Pub.

***Very First Things to Know about Bears.** Deborah Kovacs. (Illus.). (J). 1997. write for info. (*0-614-29332-4*) Workman Pub.

Very Fragrant Death of Paul Gauguin. Henry Graham. (Illus.). (C). 1988. pap. 32.00 (*0-947612-24-6*, Pub. by Rivelin Grapheme Pr) St Mut.

***Very Funny, Vol. 1.** Biddlecom. 1998. 13.95 (*0-316-07000-9*) Little.

Very Godly Defense, Defending the Marriage of Priests. Philip Melanchthon. Tr. by L. Beuchame. LC 76-25643. (English Experience Ser.: No. 199). 1969. reprint ed. 20.00 (*90-221-0199-1*) Walter J Johnson.

Very Good Fisherman. Y. Ganz. (Middos Ser.). (J). 1991. 7.99 (*0-89906-510-4*) Mesorah Pubns.

Very Good, Jeeves. P. G. Wodehouse. 256p. 1975. pap. 8.95 (*0-14-001173-0*, Penguin Bks) Viking Penguin.

Very Good, Jeeves. P. G. Wodehouse. reprint ed. lib. bdg. 22.95 (*0-89190-295-3*, Rivercity Pr) Amereon Ltd.

Very Good, Jeeves. P. G. Wodehouse. 1990. reprint ed. lib. bdg. 18.95 (*0-89968-561-7*) Buccaneer Bks.

Very Good Land to Fall With: Scenes from the Life of an American Jew, Vol. 3. John Sanford. LC 87-20844. 300p. (Orig.). 1987. 20.00 (*0-87685-714-4*); pap. 12.50 (*0-87685-713-6*) Black Sparrow.

Very Good Land to Fall With: Scenes from the Life of an American Jew, Vol. 3, signed ed. deluxe limited ed. John Sanford. LC 87-20844. 300p. (Orig.). 1987. 30.00 (*0-87685-715-2*) Black Sparrow.

Very Good Place to Start: Approaches to Teaching Writing & Literature in Secondary School. Ed. by Craig Thorn. LC 91-11035. 194p. 1991. pap. text ed. 23.00 (*0-86709-283-1*, 0283) Boynton Cook Pubs.

Very Grammatical Family. Albert Carriere. 26p. 1940. pap. 3.00 (*0-87129-697-7*, V10) Dramatic Pub.

***Very Greedy Drug: Cocaine in Context.** Jason Ditton & Richard Hammersley. 1996. text ed. 38.00 (*3-7186-5903-4*, Harwood Acad Pubs) Gordon & Breach.

Very Happy Day. Joyce Riffe. (Great Big Bk. Ser.). (Illus.). 16p. (J). 1995. pap. 14.95 (*0-687-01448-4*) Abingdon.

Very Healthy Cat Book. Wendell O. Belfield & Martin Zucker. 247p. 1983. write for info. (*0-9629947-0-7*) Orthomolecular.

U V

Very High Angular Resolution Imaging: Proceedings of the 158th Symposium of the International Astronomical Union Held at the Women's College, University of Sydney, Australia, 11-15 January 1993. Ed. by J. G. Robertson & W. J. Tango. LC 93-23649. 524p. (C). 1994. pap. text ed. 88.50 (*0-7923-2633-4*); lib. bdg. 181.00 (*0-7923-2632-6*) Kluwer Ac.

Very High Energy Gamma Ray Astronomy. Ed. by K. E. Turver. 1987. lib. bdg. 146.00 (*90-277-2459-8*) Kluwer Ac.

Very High Speed MOS Devices. Ed. by Susumo Kohyama. (Illus.). 544p. 1991. 175.00 (*0-19-856340-X*) OUP.

Very High Strength Cement-Based Materials, Vol. 42. Ed. by J. F. Young. (Materials Research Society Symposium Proceedings Ser.). 1985. text ed. 17.50 (*0-931837-07-3*) Materials Res.

Very Hot Samosas. Mathieson. (J). 10.95 (*0-7136-3180-5*, 91836, Pub. by A&C Black UK) Talman.

***Very Hungry Cat Plush.** Eric Carle. (J). 1988. pap. 4.00 (*0-399-21659-6*) Putnam Pub Group.

Very Hungry Caterpillar. Eric Carle. LC 70-82764. (Illus.). 26p. (J). (ps-2). 1981. 18.95 (*0-399-20853-4*, Philomel Bks) Putnam Pub Group.

Very Hungry Caterpillar. Eric Carle. (J). Date not set. pap. 2.50 (*0-590-03029-9*) Scholastic Inc.

Very Hungry Caterpillar: Limited Edition. 25th deluxe limited ed. Eric Carle. (Illus.). 26p. (J). (ps up). 1994. 200.00 (*0-399-22804-7*, Philomel Bks) Putnam Pub Group.

Very Hungry Caterpillar: Mini Book & Plush Package. Eric Carle. (Illus.). 26p. (J). (ps-3). 1991. 15.95 (*0-399-22049-6*, Philomel Bks) Putnam Pub Group.

Very Hungry Caterpillar - Mini. Eric Carle. LC 79-13202. (Illus.). 26p. (J). (ps-k). 1986. 5.95 (*0-399-21301-5*, Philomel Bks) Putnam Pub Group.

Very Hungry Caterpillar Board Book. Eric Carle. LC 79-13202. (Illus.). 26p. (J). (ps up). 1994. bds. 9.95 (*0-399-22690-7*, Philomel Bks) Putnam Pub Group.

Very Hungry Lion. Gita Wolf. (Illus.). 24p. (J). (ps-5). 1996. 24.95 (*1-55037-461-3*, Pub. by Annick CN) Firefly Bks Ltd.

***Very Hungry Lion.** deluxe limited ed. Illus. by Indrapramit Roy. 24p. (J). (ps up). 1996. 29.95 (*1-55037-481-8*, Pub. by Annick CN) Firefly Bks Ltd.

***Very Hungry Lions.** John Ryan. (J). 1997. pap. text ed. 5.99 (*0-7459-3723-3*) Lion USA.

Very Idea of Radical Hermeneutics. Ed. by Roy Martinez. 256p. (C). 1997. text ed. 55.00 (*0-391-04008-1*) Humanities.

Very Important Day. Maggie R. Herold. LC 94-16647. (Illus.). 40p. (YA). (gr. 6 up). 1995. 16.00 (*0-688-13065-8*, Morrow Junior); lib. bdg. 15.93 (*0-688-13066-6*, Morrow Junior) Morrow.

Very Ingenious Man: Claude Martin in Early Colonial India. Rosie Llewellyn-Jones. (Illus.). 250p. 1993. 24.00 (*0-19-563131-5*) OUP.

Very Innovative Parties. Linda Loma. pap. 24.99 (*0-8163-1118-5*) Pacific Pr Pub Assn.

Very Inside: An Anthology of Writings by Asian & Pacific Islander Lesbians. Ed. by Sharon Lim-Hing. 1994. per. 19.95 (*0-920813-97-6*, Pub. by Sister Vision CN) LPC InBook.

Very Large Data Bases Conference, 13th, Brighton, England: Proceedings. 500p. (Orig.). (C). 1987. pap. text ed. 40.00 (*0-934613-46-X*) Morgan Kaufmann.

Very Large Data Bases Conference, 1988: Proceedings, Los Angeles. 500p. 1988. pap. 40.00 (*0-934613-75-3*) Morgan Kaufmann.

***Very Large Databases.** Bobak. (ITCP-US Computer Science Ser.). 1997. pap. 44.99 incl. cd-rom (*1-85032-888-9*) ITCP.

Very Large Databases Conference: Proceedings of the Nineteen Ninety International Conference on Very Large Data Bases, Brisbane, Australia. 730p. 1990. pap. 40.00 (*1-55860-149-X*) Morgan Kaufmann.

Very Large Scale Computation in the Twenty-First Century. Jill P. Mesirov. LC 91-20925. (Miscellaneous Bks.: No. 25). xviii, 327p. 1991. 56.75 (*0-89871-279-3*) Soc Indus-Appl Math.

Very Large Scale Integration (VLSI) Fundamentals & Applications. 2nd ed. Ed. by B. F. Barbe. (Electrophysics Ser.: Vol. 5). (Illus.). 302p. 1982. 63.95 (*0-387-11368-1*) Spr-Verlag.

Very Last First Time. Jan Andrews. LC 85-71606. (Illus.). 32p. (J). (gr. k-4). 1986. text ed. 17.00 (*0-689-50388-1*, McElderry) S&S Childrens.

***Very Last First Time: An Inuit Tale.** Andrews. 1998. mass mkt. 5.99 (*0-689-81960-9*) S&S Childrens.

***Very Last Flower.** Kerry O'Rourke. (Illus.). 10p. (Orig.). (J). (gr. 1-3). 1997. mass mkt. 8.99 (*1-55197-979-9*, Pub. by Comnwlth Pub CN) Partners Pubs Grp.

Very Last Gambado. Jonathan Gash. (Crime Monthly Ser.). 288p. 1991. reprint ed. pap. 5.95 (*0-14-014738-1*, Penguin Bks) Viking Penguin.

Very Last Unicorn, Vol. 1. Marita Conlon-McKenna. (J). (ps-3). 1995. 14.95 (*0-316-54781-6*) Little.

Very Like a Star. Dawn L. Watkins. Ed. by Anne Smith. (Light Line Ser.). (Illus.). 30p. (Orig.). (J). (ps). 1990. pap. 5.49 (*0-89084-533-6*, 050526) Bob Jones Univ Pr.

***Very Little - Almost Nothing: Death, Philosophy, Literature.** Simon Critchley. LC 96-39076. (Warwick Studies in European Philosophy). 248p. (C). 1997. pap. write for info. (*0-415-12822-6*); text ed. write for info. (*0-415-12821-8*) Routledge.

Very Little Boy. Phyllis Krasilovsky. (Illus.). 32p. (J). (ps). 1992. pap. 4.95 (*0-590-44762-9*, 030, Cartwheel) Scholastic Inc.

Very Little Child's Book of Stories. Ada M. Skinner & Eleanor L. Skinner. (J). 1990. 12.99 (*0-517-69332-1*) Random Hse Value.

Very Little Duck. Ellen Patrick. (Easter Ornament Bks.). (J). 1996. 2.95 (*0-689-80786-4*) S&S Childrens.

Very Lonely Firefly. Eric Carle. LC 94-27827. 32p. (J). 1995. 19.95 (*0-399-22774-1*, Philomel Bks) Putnam Pub Group.

Very Long Baseline Interferometry. Ed. by Marcello Felli & Ralph E. Spencer. (C). 1989. lib. bdg. 185.00 (*0-7923-0376-8*) Kluwer Ac.

Very Long Engagement. Sebastien Japrisot. Tr. by Linda Coverdale from FRE. LC 94-11290. 336p. 1994. pap. 11.95 (*0-452-27297-1*, Plume) NAL-Dutton.

Very Long Weekend: The National Guard in Korea 1950-1953. William Berebitsky. LC 96-34615. (Illus.). 256p. 1996. 29.95 (*1-57249-022-5*) White Mane Pub.

***Very Merry Christmas Activity Book.** Anita R. Stohs. LC 96-9627. (Marshal Matt, Mysteries with a Value Ser.). (Illus.). (J). 1997. 3.99 (*0-570-04812-5*, 56-1827) Concordia.

Very Merry Mice. Julie Puntch. Ed. by Jeanne Acheson. (Illus.). 26p. (Orig.). (J). (ps-8). 1996. pap. text ed. 3.98 (*0-937739-27-8*) Roman IL.

Very Merry Santa Story. Joanne Barkan. 24p. (J). 1992. 3.95 (*0-590-46020-X*, Cartwheel) Scholastic Inc.

Very Merry Snowman Story. Joanne Barkan. 24p. (J). 1992. 3.95 (*0-590-46021-8*, Cartwheel) Scholastic Inc.

Very Much a Woman's Book. Peggy Warren. LC 93-90411. (Illus.). 75p. 1989. 15.00 (*0-9628710-0-1*) Art After Five.

Very Necessarie & Profitable Book Concerning Navigation. Joannes Taisnier. 1993. 55.00 (*0-8201-1479-0*) Schol Facsimiles.

Very Noisy Girl. Elizabeth Winthrop. LC 90-39175. (Illus.). 32p. (J). (ps-3). 1991. lib. bdg. 14.95 (*0-8234-0858-2*) Holiday.

Very Old Bones. William P. Kennedy. 288p. 1993. pap. 11.95 (*0-14-013898-6*, Penguin Bks) Viking Penguin.

Very Ordinary Murder. large type ed. Alan Sewart. (Linford Mystery Library). 336p. 1992. pap. 15.99 (*0-7089-7268-3*) Ulverscroft.

Very Ordinary Seaman. J. P. W. Mallalieu. 253p. 1984. pap. 7.00 (*0-583-12808-4*, Pub. by Granada UK) Academy Chi Pubs.

Very Parochial Murder. large type ed. John Wainwright. 1990. 25.99 (*0-7089-2343-7*) Ulverscroft.

Very Peculiar History, 3 vols. 43.26 (*0-531-19953-3*) Watts.

Very Personal Computer. Justine Rendal. LC 95-2252. (Joanna Cotler Bks.). 224p. (J). (gr. 5 up). 1995. 14.95 (*0-06-025404-1*); lib. bdg. 14.89 (*0-06-025408-4*) HarpC Child Bks.

***Very Personal Matter.** Charles Templeton. Date not set. write for info. (*0-688-05073-5*) Morrow.

Very Pleasant Evening with Stevie Smith: Selected Shorter Prose. Stevie Smith. LC 95-2273. 96p. 1995. pap. 8.95 (*0-8112-1295-5*, NDP804) New Directions.

Very Poor & of a Lo Make: The Journal of Abner Sanger. Ed. by Lois K. Stabler. (Illus.). 660p. 1986. 30.00 (*0-914339-17-6*) P E Randall Pub.

Very Practical Guide to Discipline with Young Children. Grace Mitchell. LC 82-16951. 160p. (Orig.). (C). 1982. pap. 14.95 (*0-910287-00-7*, HQ770.5.M57) TelShare Pub Co.

Very Present Help: Life Messages of Great Christians. Amy Carmichael. LC 96-26543. (Life Messages of Great Christians Ser.: Vol. 1). 180p. (Orig.). 1996. pap. 10.99 (*0-89283-978-3*, Vine Bks) Servant.

Very Private Plot: A Blackford Oaks Novel. large type ed. William F. Buckley, Jr. LC 94-7063. 1994. lib. bdg. 24.95 (*0-8161-7431-8*) Thorndike Pr.

Very Profitable War. Didier Daeninckx. Tr. by Sarah martin from FRE. 192p. (Orig.). 1995. pap. 11.99 (*1-85242-247-5*) Serpents Tail.

***Very Public Affair.** Sally Wentworth. 1997. mass mkt. 3.50 (*0-373-11912-7*, 1-11912-2) Harlequin Bks.

Very Quick Job Search: Get a Better Job in Half the Time. 2nd ed. J. Michael Farr. LC 91-12593. 501p. (Orig.). 1996. pap. 14.95 (*1-56370-181-2*, J1812) JIST Works.

Very Quick Job Search Activity Book. rev. ed. J. Michael Farr. 128p. (C). 1993. wbk. ed., pap. 7.95 (*1-56370-275-4*, VQAB) JIST Works.

Very Quiet Baltimoreans: A Guide to the Historic Cemeteries & Burial Sites of Baltimore. Jane B. Wilson. LC 91-33699. (Illus.). 144p. 1991. 29.95 (*0-942597-40-0*) White Mane Pub.

Very Quiet Cricket: A Multi-Sensory Book. Eric Carle. LC 89-78317. (Illus.). 32p. (J). (ps-1). 1990. 19.95 (*0-399-21885-8*, Philomel Bks) Putnam Pub Group.

***Very Quiet Cricket Board Book.** Eric Carle. (Illus.). 24p. (J). (ps). 1997. bds. 10.95 (*0-399-22684-2*, Philomel Bks) Putnam Pub Group.

Very Rare Glassware of the Depression Years: Identification & Value Guide, Vol. 5. 5th ed. Gene Florence. (Illus.). 192p. 1996. 24.95 (*0-89145-739-9*, 4732) Collector Bks.

Very Real Ghost Book of Christina Rose. James M. Deem. LC 95-34127. 176p. (J). (gr. 3-7). 1996. 14.95 (*0-395-76128-X*) HM.

Very Rich Hours. Jean McGarry. LC 86-46290. (Johns Hopkins Poetry & Fiction Ser.). 144p. 1987. 16.95 (*0-8018-3504-6*) Johns Hopkins.

Very Rich Hours: Travels in Orkney, Belize, the Everglades, & Greece. Emily Hiestand. LC 92-8153. 240p. 1993. pap. 12.00 (*0-8070-7117-X*) Beacon Pr.

Very Rich Hours of Adrienne Monnier. Adrienne Monnier. Tr. & Intro. by Richard McDougall. xiv, 536p. 1996. pap. 23.00 (*0-8032-8227-3*, Bison Books) U of Nebr Pr.

Very Rich Hours of Count Von Stauffenberg. Paul West. LC 89-8861. 365p. 1989. 22.50 (*0-87951-368-3*) Overlook Pr.

Very Rich Hours of Count Von Stauffenberg. Paul West. 365p. 1991. pap. 9.95 (*0-87951-388-8*) Viking Penguin.

Very Rich Hours of Count Von Stauffenberg. Paul West. 1991. pap. 11.95 (*0-87951-418-3*) Overlook Pr.

Very Rich School. Townsend Brown, 2nd. 184p. (Orig.). pap. text ed. write for info. (*0-9639999-8-2*) Jay St Pubs.

Very Scary. Tony Johnston. LC 94-10938. (Illus.). 32p. (J). (ps-3). 1995. 14.00 (*0-15-293625-4*, HB Juv Bks) HarBrace.

Very Scary Almanac. Eric Elfman. (Illus.). 80p. (Orig.). (J). (gr. 4-7). 1993. pap. 4.99 (*0-679-84401-5*) Random Bks Yng Read.

Very Scary Dictionary: Who's Who in Fright. R. C. Welch. (Illus.). 64p. (J). 1993. pap. 4.95 (*1-56565-072-7*) Lowell Hse.

Very Scary Haunted House. Joanne Barkan. (Illus.). 24p. (J). 1991. pap. 3.95 (*0-590-44497-2*) Scholastic Inc.

Very Scary Witch Story. Joanne Barkan. 24p. (J). (ps-3). 1992. pap. 3.95 (*0-590-45936-8*) Scholastic Inc.

Very Scraggly Christmas Tree. Christie Pippen. (Publish-a-Book Ser.). (J). (gr. 2-4). 1988. lib. bdg. 21.40 (*0-8172-2754-7*) Raintree Steck-V.

Very Scraggly Christmas Tree. Christie Pippen. (J). (ps-3). 1993. pap. 4.95 (*0-8114-5214-X*) Raintree Steck-V.

Very Secret Affair. large type ed. Miranda Lee. 288p. 1995. 21.50 (*0-263-14263-9*, Pub. by M & B UK) Ulverscroft.

Very Serious Thing: Women's Humor & American Culture. Nancy Walker. (American Culture Ser.). xiii, 229p. (Orig.). 1988. pap. text ed. 14.95 (*0-8166-1703-1*) U of Minn Pr.

Very Seventies: A Cultural History of the 1970s from the Pages of Crawdaddy. Ed. by Peter Knobler et al. LC 94-44455. 1995. write for info. (*0-684-80069-1*, Fireside) S&S Trade.

***Very Sexy Adult Dot-to-Dot Book.** Toni Goffe. Ed. by Cliff Carle. 1994. pap. 4.99 (*0-918259-67-3*) CCC Pubns.

Very Short Introduction to Classics. John Henderson & Mary Beard. (Very Short Introductions Ser.). (Illus.). 112p. 1995. pap. 8.95 (*0-19-285313-9*) OUP.

Very Short Introduction to Politics. Kenneth Minogue. (Very Short Introductions Ser.). 112p. 1995. pap. 8.95 (*0-19-285309-0*) OUP.

Very Short Textbook of Surgery. 3rd ed. Peter Ryan. 173p. (gr. 13). 1994. pap. text ed. 18.95 (*0-412-61530-4*) Chapman & Hall.

Very Short War: The Mayaguez & the Battle of Koh Tang. John F. Guilmartin, Jr. LC 95-17325. (Texas A&M University Military History Ser.: No. 46). (Illus.). 264p. (C). 1995. 39.50 (*0-89096-665-6*) Tex A&M Univ Pr.

Very Simple Arabic. James Peters. (Illus.). 120p. (ARA.). 1994. pap. 10.95 (*0-905743-71-7*, Pub. by Stacey Intl UK) Intl Bk Ctr.

Very Simple Arabic/Simple Etiquette. James Peters. 109p. (ARA.). 1994. pap. 10.95 (*0-86685-709-5*, STA3717, Pub. by Librairie du Liban FR) Intl Bk Ctr.

Very Simple Chinese. Caroline Mason & Starr. pap. 8.95 (*0-904404-71-4*, 91456) Talman.

***Very Simple Chinese.** 2nd ed. Don Starr. 1996. pap. 8.95 (*1-86034-027-X*, Pub. by Global Bks UK) Talman.

***Very Simple French.** Marie-Luce Pugh. 1996. pap. 8.95 (*1-86034-007-5*, Pub. by Global Bks UK) Talman.

Very Simple German. Waltraud Coles & Uwe Koreik. (Illus.). 64p. 1991. pap. 8.95 (*1-873411-15-4*, Pub. by A&C Black UK) Talman.

Very Simple Italian. Hugh Shankland. (Illus.). 64p. 1991. pap. 8.95 (*1-873411-25-1*, Pub. by A&C Black UK) Talman.

Very Simple Japanese. Dominic Williams. pap. 8.95 (*0-904404-63-3*, 90810) Talman.

Very Simple Russian. Irene Slater. pap. 8.95 (*0-904404-75-7*, 92000) Talman.

Very Simple Spanish. Victoria McGuiness. (SPA.). pap. 8.95 (*1-86034-002-4*, 92990, Pub. by Global Bks UK) Talman.

Very Small Farm. William P. Winchester. (Illus.). 128p. 1996. pap. 14.95 (*1-57178-021-1*) Coun Oak Bks.

Very Small Farm. William P. Winchester. (Illus.). 128p. 1996. 17.95 (*1-57178-017-3*) Coun Oak Bks.

Very Small Garden. Martin Baxendale. 128p. 1987. 25.95 (*0-285-62736-8*) Intl Spec Bk.

Very Small Insurance Policy: The Politics of Australian Involvement in Vietnam, 1954-1967. Glen S. Barclay. LC 86-27284. 199p. (Orig.). (C). 1988. pap. text ed. 29.95 (*0-7022-2069-8*, Pub. by Univ Queensland Pr AT) Intl Spec Bk.

Very Small Rebellion. Jan Truss. 128p. (Orig.). (J). (gr. 2-4). 1990. pap. 4.95 (*0-7736-7278-8*, Pub. by Stoddart Pubng CN) Genl Dist Srvs.

Very Social Time: Crafting Community in Antebellum New England. Karen V. Hansen. LC 93-39611. (C). 1994. 30.00 (*0-520-08474-8*) U CA Pr.

Very Social Time: Crafting Community in Antebellum New England. Karen V. Hansen. (Illus.). 292p. 1996. pap. text ed. 16.95 (*0-520-20561-8*) U CA Pr.

***Very Special Agents.** James Moore. pap. 6.50 (*0-671-57035-8*) PB.

Very Special Baby. Kenneth N. Taylor. (Bible Treasures Ser.). 24p. (J). (ps-3). 1994. 3.99 (*0-8423-1301-X*) Tyndale.

Very Special Child. Joan Hebden. (Illus.). 159p. 1985. pap. text ed. 16.95 (*0-285-65010-6*) Demos Vermande.

Very Special Cookbook. Susan O. Huey & Jo A. Moody. 206p. 15.95 (*0-9640097-0-6*) A Very Spec Ckbk.

Very Special Critter. Gina Mayer & Mercer Mayer. (Look-Look Bks.). (Illus.). 24p. (J). (ps-3). 1993. pap. 2.25 (*0-307-12763-X*, 12763, Golden Books) Western Pub.

Very Special Favor. Kristin James. (Intimate Moments Ser.). 1991. mass mkt. 3.29 (*0-373-15160-8*) Silhouette.

Very Special Gift. Shifrah Gettinger. (Illus.). 32p. (J). (ps-3). 1993. 8.95 (*0-922613-52-4*); pap. text ed. 6.95 (*0-922613-53-2*) Hachai Pubns.

Very Special Heroes. Jill C. Wheeler. LC 96-7355. (Everyday Heroes Ser.). (J). 1996. lib. bdg. 13.98 (*1-56239-700-1*) Abdo & Dghtrs.

***Very Special House.** Ruth Krauss & Maurice Sendak. (Illus.). (J). (ps-1). 7.66 (*0-06-023455-5*, 532498) HarpC Child Bks.

Very Special House. Ruth Krauss. LC 53-7115. (Illus.). (J). (ps-1). 1953. lib. bdg. 15.89 (*0-06-023456-3*) HarpC Child Bks.

Very Special Kwanzaa. Debbi Chocolate. (J). 1996. pap. 2.99 (*0-590-84862-3*) Scholastic Inc.

Very Special Mother. JerryAnn P. Wronker. 1996. 10.95 (*0-533-11552-3*) Vantage.

***Very Special Night.** Gill Davies. (Christmas Window Bks.). (Illus.). 14p. (J). (ps up). 1997. bds. 4.98 (*1-85854-668-0*) Brimax Bks.

Very Special People. Frederick Drimmer. (Illus.). 360p. reprint ed. pap. 12.95 (*0-8065-1253-9*, Citadel Pr) Carol Pub Group.

Very Special Place. Joseph Shirley. (Daydream Knapsack Adventure Ser.). (Illus.). 32p. (Orig.). (J). (gr. k-4). 1992. pap. 10.95 (*0-9632816-0-7*) NISIS.

Very Special Raspberry Cookbook. Ed. & Intro. by Very Special Cookbook Committee Staff. (Illus.). 286p. 1993. 18.50 (*0-9646119-0-2*) Very Spec Raspberry.

Very Special Sacred Songs. Ed. by John L. Haag. 160p. (Orig.). 1993. pap. 14.95 (*1-56922-025-5*, 07-1039) Creat Cncpts.

Very Special Sister. Dorothy Hoffman Levi. LC 91-25261. (Illus.). 36p. (J). (gr. k-3). 1992. 9.95 (*0-930323-96-3*, Pub. by K Green Pubns) Gallaudet Univ Pr.

Very Special Sister. Dorothy H. Levi. (Awareness & Caring - Sign Language Storybook Ser.). (Illus.). 36p. (J). (gr. k-3). 1992. lib. bdg. 12.95 (*1-56674-033-9*) Forest Hse.

***Very Special World of Eric Carle.** Eric Carle. 1996. 518.20 (*0-399-22988-4*, Putnam) Putnam Pub Group.

Very Special Yarmulka. 1982. pap. 3.95 (*0-87306-186-1*) Feldheim.

Very Spirit of Cordiality: The Literary Uses of Alcohol... in the Tales of Edgar Allan Poe. Benjamin F. Fisher. Ed. by Averil J. Kadis. 1978. pap. 2.75 (*0-910556-10-5*) Enoch Pratt.

Very Strange Dollhouse. Jennifer Dussling. LC 95-46793. (Eek! Stories to Make You Shriek Ser.). (Illus.). 48p. (J). (gr. 1-3). 1996. pap. 3.95 (*0-448-41311-6*, G&D); lib. bdg. 13.99 (*0-448-41346-9*, G&D) Putnam Pub Group.

Very Stuff: Poems on Color, Thread, & the Habits of Women. Stephen Beal. 120p. (Orig.). 1996. pap. 14.95 (*1-883010-16-0*) Interweave.

Very Stylish Affair. Emma Darcy. (Presents Ser.). 1993. mass mkt. 2.99 (*0-373-11579-2*, 1-11579-9) Harlequin Bks.

***Very Stylish Affair.** large type ed. Emma Darcy. (Magna Large Print Ser.). 240p. 1997. 27.50 (*0-7505-1095-1*) Thorndike Pr.

Very Sure of God: Religious Language in the Poetry of Robert Browning. E. Leroy Lawson. LC 73-21617. xiii, 168p. 1974. 14.95 (*0-8265-1195-3*) Vanderbilt U Pr.

Very Surprising Narrative of a Young Woman Discovered in a Rocky Cave after Having Been Taken by the Savage Indians of the Wilderness in the Year 1777. Abraham Panther. 1972. reprint ed. pap. 4.95 (*0-87770-095-8*) Ye Galleon.

***Very Tastefully Yours, Vol. II.** Patsy Gerlinger. (Illus.). 64p. 1997. 14.95 (*0-9642133-1-1*) Gerlingers Catering.

Very Tastefully Yours: Gerlinger's Catering. Patsy Gerlinger. (Illus.). 64p. 1994. text ed. 12.95 (*0-9642133-0-3*) Gerlingers Catering.

Very Teachable Films. Elizabeth A. Mejia et al. 224p. 1994. pap. 15.95 (*0-13-106824-5*) P-H.

Very Thin Electric Layers in MOS-VLSI Circuits. Beck & Jakubowski. 1995. write for info. (*0-8493-7283-6*) CRC Pr.

Very Thing Your Heart Craves. T. J. King. (Illus.). 140p. (Orig.). 1991. pap. 12.50 (*0-9629792-0-1*) One Another.

Very Touching Book. Jan Hindman. (Illus.). 56p. (Orig.). 1983. pap. 11.95 (*0-9611034-1-8*) AlexAndria OR.

Very Truly Yours. Jacob P. Rudin. 1971. 10.00 (*0-8197-0279-X*) Bloch.

Very Truly Yours, M. L. A Visit with Mary Lincoln. Nancy M. Nilsson. (Illus.). 36p. (Orig.). 1992. pap. 6.95 (*0-9629170-3-6*) Twinbrook Comms.

Very Unusual: The Wonderful World of Mr. K. Nakamura. Manly P. Hall. 12.50 (*0-89314-537-8*) Philos Res.

Very, Very, Very Small Horse. Illus. by Marilyn Felix. 20p. (Orig.). (J). (ps-3). 1995. pap. 4.95 (*0-9649897-0-0*) J M Rose.

Very Violent Rebel: The Civil War Diary of Ellen Renshaw House. Ed. by Daniel E. Sutherland. LC 96-4455. (Voices of the Civil War Ser.). (Illus.). 331p. (C). 1996. 34.00 (*0-87049-944-0*) U of Tenn Pr.

Very Virginia: Culinary Traditions with a Twist. Junior League of Hampton Roads Staff. 302p. 1995. 17.95 (*0-9613600-2-X*) Jr Lge Hampton.

Very Worst Monster. Pat Hutchins. LC 84-5928. (Illus.). 32p. (J). (gr. k-3). 1985. lib. bdg. 16.88 (*0-688-04011-X*) Greenwillow.

Very Worst Monster. Pat Hutchins. (Illus.). (J). (gr. k-3). 1992. 22.95 incl. audio (*0-87499-291-5*); pap. 15.95 incl. audio (*0-87499-290-7*) Live Oak Media.

Very Worst Monster. Pat Hutchins. LC 84-5928. (Illus.). 32p. (J). (gr. k up). 1988. pap. 3.95 (*0-688-07816-8*, Mulberry) Morrow.

Very Worst Monster. Pat Hutchins. LC 84-5928. (Read with Me Books & Cassettes). (Illus.). (J). (gr. 1 up). 1989. pap. 7.95 incl. audio (*0-688-09038-9*, Mulberry) Morrow.

Very Worst Monster, 4 bks., Set. Pat Hutchins. (Illus.). (J). (gr. k-3). 1992. pap. 29.95 incl. audio (*0-87499-292-3*) Live Oak Media.

An Asterisk (*) at the beginning of an entry indicates that the title is appearing in BIP for the first time.

Very Worst of Truly Tasteless Jokes. Blanche Knott. 1990. 10.95 (0-312-05185-9) St Martin.

Very Young: Guiding Children from Infancy Through the Early Years. 5th ed. George W. Maxim. LC 96-36068. 1997. 58.00 (0-13-490210-6, Merrill Coll) P-H.

Very Young Children with Special Needs: A Formative Approach for the 21st Century. Howard et al. 560p. (C). 1996. pap. text ed. 54.00 (0-02-357211-6, Macmillan Coll) P-H.

Very Young Circus Flyer. Jill Krementz. LC 78-20546. (Illus.). 1979. 10.95 (0-394-50574-3) Knopf.

Very Young Poets. Gwendolyn Brooks. 32p. 1991. pap. 4.00 (0-88378-046-1) Third World.

Verzeichnis Aller Anonymischen Schriften und Aufsatze in der Vierten Ausgabe des Gelehrten Teutschlands. Johann S. Ersch. xlviii, 622p. 1975. reprint ed. write for info. (3-487-05649-6) G Olms Pubs.

Verzeichnis der althochdeutschen und altsaechsischen Glossenhandschriften: Mit Bibliographie der Glosseneditionen, der Handschriftenbeschreibungen und der Dialektbestimmungen. Rolf Bergmann. LC 72-76056. (Arbeitem zur Fruehmittelalterforschung Ser.: Vol. 6). (GER.). (C). 1973. 79.25 (3-11-003713-0) De Gruyter.

Verzeichnis der Berliner Universitatsschriften, 1810-1885. Wilhelm Erman. ix, 848p. 1973. reprint ed. write for info. (3-487-04922-8) G Olms Pubs.

Verzeichnis der Breslauer Universitatsschriften, 1811-1885. Karl Pretzsch. xv, 387p. 1975. reprint ed. write for info. (3-487-05573-2) G Olms Pubs.

Verzeichnis der Handsschriften der Stiftsbibliothek von St. Gallen. Gustav Schierrer. 650p. 1975. reprint ed. write for info. (3-487-05335-7) G Olms Pubs.

Verzeichnis der Hebraischen Handschriften, 2 Tle. in 1 Band. Moritz Steinschneider. (Handschriften-Verzeichnisse der Koniglichen Bibliothek Zu Berlin Ser.: Bd. II, 1.2). xvi, 321p. (GER.). 1980. write for info. (3-487-06845-1) G Olms Pubs.

Verzeichnis der Hochschulschriften Uber Rainer Maria Rilke. Walter Simon. xxiii, 255p. 1987. write for info. (3-487-06572-X) G Olms Pubs.

Verzeichnis der Lateinischen Handschriften der Koniglichen Bibliothek Zu Berlin, 5 vols. in 3. Valentin Rose & Fritz Schillmann. l, 2035p. 1976. reprint ed. Set. write for info. (3-487-06038-8) G Olms Pubs.

Verzeichnis der Manuskripte und Inkunabeln der Vadianischen Bibliothek Zu St. Gallen. Gustav Scherrer. xiii, 353p. 1976. reprint ed. write for info. (3-487-06058-2) G Olms Pubs.

Verzeichnis der Nobelpreistrager 1901-1987: Mit Preisbegundungen, Kurzkommentaren, Literarischen, Werkbibliographien und einer Biographie Alfred Nobel. 2nd ed. Ed. by Werner Martin. xi, 382p. 1988. lib. bdg. 60.00 (3-598-10721-8) K G Saur.

Verzeichnis Medizinischer und Naturwissenschaftlicher Drucke 1472-1830: Reihe-A-D, 1-14. Ed. by Herzog August Bibliothek Wolfenbuttal. (GER.). 1988. lib. bdg. 660.00 (3-598-31680-1) K G Saur.

Verzeichnis Rechtswissenschaftlicher Zeitschriften und Serien In Ausgewahlten Bibliotheken der Bundesrepublik Deutschland EinschlieBlich Berlin (West) Union List of Legal Serials in Selected Libraries of the Federal Republic of Germany Including Berlin (West), 3 vols. Ed. by Staatsbibliothek Preussischer Kulturbesit Staff. 2628p. (GER.). 1990. Set. pap. 625.00 (3-598-10819-2) K G Saur.

Verzeichnis Rechtswissenschaftlicher Zeitschriften und Serien In Ausgewahlten Bibliotheken der Bundesrepublik Deutschland EinschlieBlich Berlin (West) Union List of Legal Serials in Selected Libraries of the Federal Republic of Germany Including Berlin (West), 3 vols. Ed. by Staatsbibliothek Preussischer Kulturbesitz Staff. 2628p. (GER.). 1990. Band 1. write for info. (3-598-10820-6); Band 2. write for info. (3-598-10821-4); Band 3. write for info. (3-598-10822-2) K G Saur.

Verzeichnis von Programm-Abhandlungen Deutscher, Osterreichischer und Schweizerischer Schulen der Jahre 1825-1918: Alphabetisch Geordnet nach Verfassern, 4 vols. Franz Kossler. 2134p. (GER.). 1987. lib. bdg. 500.00 (3-598-10665-3) K G Saur.

Verzeichniss von Buchern. Karl H. Von Meusebach. (Deutsche Dichter - und Gelehrtenbibliotheken Ser.). 1990. reprint ed. 39.00 (3-262-00202-X) Periodicals Srv.

Vesicles. Ed. by Morton Rosoff. LC 96-15201. (Surfactant Science Ser.: Vol. 62). 768p. 1996. 195.00 (0-8247-9603-9) Dekker.

Vesle Hans: Little Hans Comes to America. Leona H. Wenaas. (Illus.). 96p. (Orig.). 1989. pap. 9.95 (0-911007-14-8) Prairie Hse.

Vespa: The Color Family Album. Andrea Sparrow & David Sparrow. (Illus.). 96p. 1995. 19.95 (1-874105-48-0, Pub. by Veloce Pub UK) Motorbooks Intl.

Vespa Scooters. Eric Brockway. (Haynes-U. K. Ser.). (Illus.). 96p. 1993. 19.95 (0-85429-892-4) Motorbooks Intl.

Vespasiano Memoirs. Vespaniano. 1997. pap. text ed. 22.50 (0-8020-7968-7) U of Toronto Pr.

Vesper & Compline Music for One Principal Voice: Vesper & Compline Psalms & Canticles for One & Two Voices. Jeffrey Kurtzman. Ed. by Anne Schnoebelen. (Seventeenth-Century Italian Sacred Music Ser.: Vol. 11). 328p. 1996. text ed. 99.00 (0-8153-2165-1) Garland.

Vesper Sparrows. Deborah Digges. (Classic Contemporaries Ser.). 51p. (C). 1996. reprint ed. pap. 12.95 (0-88748-228-7) Carnegie-Mellon.

Vespers. Ed McBain. 352p. 1991. mass mkt. 5.99 (0-380-70385-8) Avon.

Vespers. Ed McBain. 288p. 1991. 6.98 (1-56865-122-8, GuildAmerica) Dblday Direct.

Vespers & Matins. Monks of New Skete Staff. Tr. by Laurence Mancuso from GRE. (Liturgical Music Series II: Divine Services: Vol. 2). 220p. (Orig.). 1988. pap. 45.00 (0-935129-10-3) Monks of New Skete.

Vespers & Matins. abr. large type ed. Monks of New Skete Staff. Ed. & Tr. by Laurence Mancuso from GRE. 166p. (Orig.). 1993. pap. 20.00 (0-935129-23-5) Monks of New Skete.

Vespers for Holy Nativity: Complete Texts & Music. Ed. by Timothy Clader. Tr. by Laurence Campbell & Isaac E. Lambertsen from SLA. 45p. 1996. pap. 10.00 (0-912927-67-4, D033) St John Kronstadt.

Vespers Tapes. Albert DeBartolomeo. 250p. 1991. 22.95 (0-8027-1136-7) Walker & Co.

Vessel Inspection & Maintenance. (Rotary Drilling Ser.: Unit V, Lesson 6). (Illus.). 38p. (Orig.). 1977. pap. text ed. 14.00 (0-88698-074-7, 2.50610) PETEX.

Vessel Management Positioning & Mooring Systems for Offshore Production Vessels. Pedro Da Cruz. 1989. 125.00 (90-6314-563-2, Pub. by Lorne & MacLean Marine) St Mut.

Vessel Named Markings on United States Inland & Ocean Waterways 1810-1890. James W. Milgram et al. Ed. by Charless Hahn & Harold M. Stral. (Illus.). 832p. 1984. 99.00 (0-916675-00-9) Collectors Club IL.

Vessel of Honor. Margaret Miller. LC 97-93383. 264p. 1997. 23.00 (0-9657389-5-7) Herit Pub Hse.

Vessel of Sadness. William Woodruff. LC 74-102075. 1969. 14.95 (0-910824-12-6) Kallman.

Vessel of Sadness. William Woodruff. 208p. 1996. reprint ed. pap. 16.95 (1-57488-054-3) Brasseys Inc.

Vessel Traffic Systems. Charles W. Koburger, Jr. LC 86-47713. (Illus.). 183p. (C). 1986. text ed. 20.00 (0-87033-360-7) Cornell Maritime.

Vessel Traffic Systems. Charles W. Koburger. LC 86-47713. 183p. 1986. reprint ed. pap. 52.20 (0-608-02453-8, 2063097) Bks Demand.

Vessel Voyage Data Analysis: A Comparative Study. Kim J. Loroch. LC 65-20766. (Illus.). 160p. reprint ed. 45.60 (0-8357-9075-4, 2016601) Bks Demand.

Vessels. (Journal: Applied Pathology: Vol. 4, No. 4, 1986). (Illus.). iv, 88p. 1987. pap. 46.50 (3-8055-4583-5) S Karger.

Vessels for the Ancestors: Essays on the Neolithic of Britain & Ireland. Ed. by Niall Sharples & Alison Sheridan. (Illus.). 366p. 1992. 80.00 (0-7486-0341-7, Pub. by Edinburgh U Pr UK) Col U Pr.

Vessels of Evil: American Slavery & the Holocaust. Laurence M. Thomas. LC 93-12386. 232p. (C). 1993. pap. 18.95 (1-56639-100-8) Temple U Pr.

Vessels of Meaning: Women's Bodies, Gender Norms, & Class Bias from Richardson to Lawrence. Laura Fasick. LC 96-43943. 248p. 1997. lib. bdg. 32.00 (0-87580-221-4) N Ill U Pr.

Vessels of Rage, Engines of Power: The Secret History of Alcoholism. James Graham. LC 93-70831. xx, 236p. 1994. 21.95 (0-9630242-2-1) Aculeus Pr.

Vessels of Time: An Essay on Temporal Change & Social Transformation. Akos Ostor. 116p. 1994. 15.95 (0-19-563285-0) OUP.

Vessey Family Histories, Vol. 2. Robert L. Wilson. 118p. 1995. 24.00 (0-9622004-1-7) R L Wilson.

Vessey Family Histories, Vol. 1. Robert L. Wilson & Margaret A. Wilson. (Illus.). 256p. 1989. 25.00 (0-9622004-0-9) R L Wilson.

Vessies et Lanternes. Daniel Boulanger. 339p. (FRE.). 1987. pap. 11.95 (0-7859-2076-5, 2070378918) Fr & Eur.

Vest Book. Jacqueline Farrell. 1995. pap. 19.95 (0-8019-8648-6) Chilton.

Vest Busters: How to Make Your Own Body-Armor-Piercing Bullets. Uncle Fester. LC 96-77087. (Illus.). 60p. (Orig.). 1996. pap. 12.00 (1-55950-150-2, 25081) Loompanics.

Vest Pocket Arabic. D. Berberi. 210p. 1996. pap. 6.50 (0-614-21659-1, 1285) Kazi Pubns.

Vest Pocket Arabic. Dilaver Berberi. LC 89-15367. (ARA & ENG.). 1975. pap. 5.95 (0-8489-5109-3) Inst Lang Study.

Vest Pocket Arabic. Cortina Staff. (Cortina Language Ser.). 260p. 1990. pap. 5.95 (0-8050-1514-0) H Holt & Co.

Vest Pocket Bible Dictionary see Boyd's Bible Dictionary

Vest Pocket Calorie Counter. Walden R. Williams. 48p. 1990. pap. 2.99 (0-385-41220-7) Doubleday.

Vest Pocket CEO. Alexander Hiam. pap. 19.95 (0-13-941691-9) P-H.

Vest Pocket CEO: Decision-Making Tools for Executives. Alexander Hiam. (Illus.). 468p. pap. 14.95 (0-13-948209-1, Busn) P-H.

Vest-Pocket CFO. Joel G. Siegel & Jae K. Shim. 1992. 24.95 (0-13-952870-9) P-H.

Vest Pocket Cholesterol Counter. Susan K. Podell. 48p. 1991. pap. 2.99 (0-385-41329-7) Doubleday.

Vest Pocket Companion. R. A. Torrey. 1996. mass mkt. 1.95 (0-87398-876-0) Sword of Lord.

Vest-Pocket CPA. Nicky A. Dauber et al. 516p. 1988. 29.95 (0-13-942293-5) P-H.

Vest Pocket CPA. Joel G. Siegel. 1989. pap. 9.95 (0-13-942137-8) P-H.

Vest-Pocket CPA. 2nd ed. Nicky A. Dauber et al. LC 96-21189. 1997. 39.95 (0-13-462300-2); pap. 15.95 (0-13-462318-5) P-H.

Vest Pocket English: Ingles en el Bolsillo. Bernard Blau. LC 89-15370. (ENG & SPA.). 1989. pap. 4.95 (0-8489-5107-7) Inst Lang Study.

Vest Pocket English Language Phrasebook Dictionary. Cortina Institute of Languages Staff. 188p. 1990. pap. 4.95 (0-8050-1513-2) H Holt & Co.

Vest Pocket Entrepreneur: Everything You Need to Start & Run Your Own Business. David E. Rye. 1995. 17.95 (0-13-158510-X) P-H.

Vest Pocket Fat Counter. Susan K. Podell. 56p. 1992. pap. 2.99 (0-385-42294-6) Doubleday.

Vest Pocket French. Joseph S. Choquette. LC 89-15397. (ENG & FRE.). 1986. pap. 3.95 (0-8489-5102-6) Inst Lang Study.

Vest Pocket French. Cortina Staff. (Cortina Language Ser.). 132p. 1990. pap. 3.95 (0-8050-1507-8) H Holt & Co.

Vest Pocket German. Cortina Staff. (Cortina Language Ser.). 132p. 1990. pap. 3.95 (0-8050-1508-6) H Holt & Co.

Vest Pocket German. Henry Regensteiner. LC 89-15368. (ENG & GER.). 1986. pap. 3.95 (0-8489-5103-4) Inst Lang Study.

Vest Pocket Guide for Builders & Contractors. John E. Traister. (Illus.). 192p. 1988. 12.95 (0-13-941659-5) P-H.

Vest Pocket Guide for Electrical Engineers & Technicians. John E. Traister. (Illus.). 199p. (Orig.). 1996. pap. 14.95 (1-889892-06-8) Builders Bk Inc.

Vest Pocket Guide for Electrical Engineers & Technicians. John E. Traister. (Illus.). 240p. (Orig.). 1986. pap. 17.95 (0-13-941600-5) P-H.

Vest-Pocket Guide to Business Ratios. Michael R. Tyran. 1991. 18.95 (0-13-951948-3, Busn) P-H.

Vest-Pocket Guide to Business Writing. Deborah Dumaine & Better Communications Staff. 452p. 1996. pap. 17.95 (0-13-440348-7) P-H.

Vest-Pocket Guide to Business Writing. Deborah Dumaine & Better Communications Staff. 452p. 1997. 27.95 (0-13-440355-X) P-H.

Vest Pocket Guide to Electrical Estimating. Paul Rosenberg. 1989. pap. 14.95 (0-13-942930-1) P-H.

Vest Pocket Guide to Electrical Testing & Troubleshooting. John E. Traister. (Illus.). 130p. (Orig.). 1996. pap. 13.95 (1-889892-07-6) Builders Bk Inc.

Vest Pocket Guide to Electrical Testing & Troubleshooting. John E. Traister. (Illus.). 144p. (Orig.). 1986. pap. 17.95 (0-13-941584-X) P-H.

Vest Pocket Guide to HVAC Electricity. John E. Traister. 304p. pap. 18.00 (1-57218-012-9) Craftsman.

Vest-Pocket Guide to Information Technology. Jae K. Shim. 1997. pap. text ed. 19.95 (0-13-463506-X) P-H.

Vest-Pocket Guide to Information Technology (Lex Otone) Jae K. Shim. 1997. pap. text ed. 39.95 (0-13-463555-8) P-H.

Vest-Pocket Guide to the National Electrical Code: 1990 Edition. Marvin J. Fischer. LC 90-6887. 1990. pap. 14.95 (0-13-683665-8) P-H.

Vest Pocket Guide to the National Electrical Code, 1996 Edition. Marvin J. Fischer. 448p. 1996. pap. 17.95 (0-13-453549-9) P-H.

Vest Pocket Guide to Value Investing. C. Thomas Howard. 224p. 1996. pap. 19.95 (0-7931-1728-3, 56802901) Dearborn Trade.

Vest Pocket Investor: Everything You Need to Know to Invest Successfully. Joel G. Siegel & Jae K. Shim. 300p. 1995. per. 19.95 (1-55738-813-X) Irwin Prof Pubng.

Vest Pocket Italian. Cortina Staff. (Cortina Language Ser.). 132p. 1990. pap. 3.95 (0-8050-1509-4) H Holt & Co.

Vest Pocket Italian. Nicholas Milella. LC 89-15366. (ENG & ITA.). 1986. pap. 3.95 (0-8489-5104-2) Inst Lang Study.

Vest Pocket Japanese. Cortina Institute of Languages Staff. 188p. 1990. pap. 4.95 (0-8050-1512-4) H Holt & Co.

Vest Pocket Japanese. Takeshi Hattori. LC 89-15384. (ENG & JPN.). 1967. pap. 4.95 (0-8489-5108-5) Inst Lang Study.

Vest-Pocket Marketer: Classic Marketing Tools for Executives. Alexander Hiam. 1991. 19.95 (0-13-932302-3) P-H.

Vest-Pocket MBA. Jae K. Shim et al. 308p. pap. 12.95 (0-13-941709-5); text ed. 39.95 (0-13-941627-7) P-H.

Vest-Pocket MBA. Jae K. Shim. 400p. 1996. pap. 19.95 incl. 3.5 hd (0-13-485178-1) P-H.

Vest-Pocket MBA. 2nd ed. Jae K. Shim et al. LC 96-40269. 1997. write for info. (0-13-460312-5); pap. write for info. (0-13-460304-4) P-H.

Vest Pocket Modern Greek. Cortina Staff. (Cortina Language Ser.). 188p. 1990. pap. 4.95 (0-8050-1510-8) H Holt & Co.

Vest Pocket Modern Greek. George C. Pappageotes. LC 89-15362. (ENG & GRE.). 1989. pap. 4.95 (0-614-14107-9) Inst Lang Study.

Vest Pocket Real Estate Advisor. Martin J. Miles. 544p. 1989. pap. 24.95 (0-13-945064-5) P-H.

Vest-Pocket Real Estate Advisor. Martin J. Miles. 560p. 1990. pap. 12.95 (0-13-964941-7) P-H.

Vest Pocket Russian. Marshal D. Berger. LC 89-15396. (ENG & RUS.). 1989. pap. 4.95 (0-8489-5105-0) Inst Lang Study.

Vest Pocket Russian Language Phrasebook Dictionary. Cortina Institute of Languages Staff. 132p. 1990. pap. 4.95 (0-8050-1511-6) H Holt & Co.

Vest Pocket Spanish. Cortina Staff. (Cortina Language Ser.). 132p. 1990. pap. 3.95 (0-8050-1506-X) H Holt & Co.

Vest Pocket Spanish. Susana Redondo. LC 89-15369. (ENG & SPA.). 1986. pap. 3.95 (0-8489-5101-8) Inst Lang Study.

Vest-Pocket Tax Advisor 1997: Tax Facts at Your Fingertips. Terence M. Myers. 1996. pap. text ed. 49.95 (0-13-493479-2) P-H.

Vest-Pocket Tax Advisor 1998. Joe K. Shim et al. (Vest-Pocket Ser.). 1997. 54.95 (0-13-636721-6) P-H.

Vest Pocket Vietnamese. Cortina. 1993. pap. text ed. 5.95 (0-8050-3375-0) H Holt & Co.

Vest Pocket Vietnamese. Vuong-Gia Thuy. LC 93-46190. Orig. Title: Vietnamese in a Nutshell. (ENG & VIE.). 1994. pap. 5.95 (0-8489-5110-7) Inst Lang Study.

Vest-Pocket Writer's Guide. LC 87-2768. 272p. 1987. pap. 3.95 (0-395-44145-5) HM.

Vesta Mangun Continues. Vesta Mangun. 87p. (Orig.). 1990. pap. 6.00 (0-9619753-1-8) Pentecostals Alexandria.

Vestal & the Fasces: Hegel, Lacan, Property & the Feminine. Jeanne L. Schroeder. LC 97-20523. (Philosophy, Social Theory & the Rule of Law Ser.). 1998. write for info. (0-520-21145-6) U CA Pr.

Vestal Fire: An Environmental History, Told Through Fire, of Europe & Europe's Encounter with the World. Stephen J. Pyne. LC 97-19032. (Weyerhaeuser Environmental Bks.). (Illus.). 704p. 1997. 34.95 (0-295-97596-2) U of Wash Pr.

Vestale. Mercadante Saverio. (Italian Opera II Ser.). 225p. 1986. text ed. 30.00 (0-8240-6571-9) Garland.

Vestalische Ewige Feuer (Il Fuoco Eterno) Lodovico O. Burnacini. LC 68-21208. (Illus.). (GER.). 1972. reprint ed. 38.95 (0-405-08333-5) Ayer.

Vested Angels: Eucharistic Symbolism in Early Dutch Painting. Maurice B. McNamee. (Liturgia Condenda Ser.: Vol. 6). 432p. 1997. 54.00 (90-390-0542-7, Pub. by KOK Pharos NE) Eisenbrauns.

Vested Interests. Ralph A. Raimi. xiv, 209p. 1982. 14.95 (0-9609370-0-5) Raimi.

Vested Interests: Crossdressing & Cultural Anxiety. Margorie Garber. 456p. 1997. pap. 23.00 (0-415-91951-7, Routledge NY) Routledge.

Vested Interests & the Common Man: "The Modern Point of View & the New Order" Thorstein B. Veblen. LC 63-23513. (Reprints of Economic Classics Ser.). 183p. 1964. reprint ed. 29.50 (0-678-00053-0) Kelley.

Vested Rights: Balancing Public & Private Development Expectations. Charles L. Siemon et al. LC 82-50897. 106p. (Orig.). 1982. pap. 59.95 (0-87420-612-X, VO1) Urban Land.

Vestiaire de l'Enfance. Patrick Modiano. (FRE.). 1991. pap. 10.95 (0-7859-2925-8) Fr & Eur.

Vestiaire de l'Enfance. Patrick Modiano. (Folio Ser.: No. 2253). (FRE.). pap. 8.95 (2-07-038364-4) Schoenhof.

Vestibular & Brain Stem Control of Eye, Head & Body Movements. Yoshikazu Shinoda. (Illus.). xii, 466p. 1992. 287.00 (3-8055-5548-2) S Karger.

Vestibular & Neural Front: Proceedings of the 12th International Symposium on Posture & Gait, Matsumoto, 3-7 October 1994. Ed. by Kiichiro Taguchi et al. LC 94-34759. (International Congress Ser.: 1070). 640p. 1994. 272.25 (0-444-81933-9) Elsevier.

Vestibular & Oculomotor Physiology: International Meeting of the Barany Society, Vol. 374. Ed. by Bernard Cohen. LC 81-14230. 892p. 1981. 177.00 (0-89766-137-0); pap. 177.00 (0-89766-138-9) NY Acad Sci.

Vestibular & Visual Control on Posture & Locomotor Equilibrium. M. Igarashi & O. F. Black. (Illus.). x, 366p. 1985. 151.25 (3-8055-3951-7) S Karger.

Vestibular Autonomic Regulation. Bill J. Yates & Alan D. Miller. 266p. 1996. 149.95 (0-8493-7668-8) CRC Pr.

Vestibular Neurotology. Ed. by P. Molina-Negro. (Advances in Oto-Rhino-Laryngology Ser.: Vol. 28). (Illus.). viii, 148p. 1982. 92.00 (3-8055-3490-6) S Karger.

Vestibular Organs: S. E. M. Atlas of the Inner Ear. Yasuo Harada. LC 87-36673. (Illus.). 216p. 1988. lib. bdg. 112.50 (90-6299-043-6, Pub. by Kugler NE) Kugler Pubns.

Vestibular Processing Dysfunction in Children. Ed. by Kenneth J. Ottenbacher & Margaret A. Short. LC 85-8636. (Physical & Occupational Therapy in Pediatrics Ser.: Vol. 5, Nos. 2 & 3). 152p. 1985. text ed. 49.95 (0-86656-431-4); pap. text ed. 14.95 (0-86656-432-2) Haworth Pr.

Vestibular Rehabilitation. Susan J. Herdman. LC 93-23544. (Contemporary Perspectives in Rehabilitation Ser.). 392p. 1994. 60.00 (0-8036-4624-0) Davis Co.

Vestibular Rehabilitation: Protocols & Programs. Richard E. Gans. LC 96-6911. (Illus.). 128p. (Orig.). 1996. pap. 150.00 (1-56593-625-6, 1296) Singular Publishing.

Vestibular Rehabilitation: Protocols & Programs. Richard E. Gans. (Orig.). 1996. write for info. (1-56593-806-2, 1574); 39.95 (1-56593-805-4, 1576) Singular Publishing.

Vestibular System: Function & Morphology. Ed. by T. Gualtierotti. (Illus.). 560p. 1981. 195.00 (0-387-90559-6) Spr-Verlag.

Vestibular System: Neurophysiologic & Clinical Research. Ed. by Malcolm D. Graham & John L. Kemink. LC 85-43519. reprint ed. pap. 180.00 (0-608-04680-9, 2065401) Bks Demand.

Vestibule. Weiss. 1997. pap. 12.00 (0-671-00417-4, PB Trade Paper) PB.

Vestibule. Jess E. Weiss. Ed. by Billie Young. LC 72-78506. 1972. 19.95 (0-87949-004-7) Ashley Bks.

Vestibule Training: Basic Skills for New Hires, Pt. I. Jerome M. Rosow & Robert Zager. Ed. by Jill Casner-Lotto. 97p. 1991. pap. 95.00 (0-89361-049-6) Work in Amer.

Vestibulo-Ocular Reflex & Vertigo. Ed. by James A. Sharpe & Hugh O. Barber. LC 92-21585. 416p. 1992. text ed. 121.00 (0-88167-955-0) Lppncott-Raven.

Vestibulospinal Control of Posture & Locomotion. Ed. by O. Pompeiano & J. H. Allum. (Progress in Brain Research Ser.). 456p. 1988. 260.00 (0-444-80976-7) Elsevier.

Vestiges of Mortality & Remembrance: A Bibliography on the Historical Archaeology of Cemeteries. Edward L. Bell. 419p. 1994. 47.50 (0-8108-2893-6) Scarecrow.

Vestiges of Old Madras, 4 Vols. in 3. Henry D. Love. reprint ed. Set. 310.00 (0-404-04060-8) AMS Pr.

Vestiges of the Natural History of Creation & Other Evolutionary Writings. Robert Chambers. LC 93-48415. 312p. 1994. pap. text ed. 19.95 (0-226-10073-1) U Ch Pr.

Vestiges of the Natural History of Creation & Other Evolutionary Writings. Robert Chambers. LC 93-48415. 304p. 1994. lib. bdg. 45.00 (0-226-10072-3) U Ch Pr.

UV

An Asterisk (*) at the beginning of an entry indicates that the title is appearing in BIP for the first time.

Vestiges of the Venerable City: A Chronicle of Lexington, Kentucky. Clay Lancaster. LC 78-61797. (Illus.). 282p. 1978. 14.95 (*0-912839-01-5*) Lexington-Fayette.

Vestigial Organs Are Fully Functional: A History & Evaluation of the Vestigial Organ Origins Concept. Jerry Bergman & George Howe. Ed. by Emmett L. Williams. (Creation Research Society Monographs: No. 4). (Illus.). 97p. (Orig.). 1990. pap. text ed. 10.95 (*0-940384-09-4*) Creation Research.

Vesting. Jean Wells. (Illus.). (Orig.). 1985. pap. text ed. 9.00 (*0-932946-25-9*) Burdett CA.

Vestry Book of Antrim Parish, Halifax County, Virginia 1752-1817. Marian D. Chiarito. 160p. 1983. 25.00 (*0-945503-07-5*) Clarkton Pr.

Vestry Book of Antrim Parish, Halifax County, Virginia, 1752-1817. Marian D. Chiarito. 160p. 1983. pap. 24.00 (*0-8095-8705-X*); lib. bdg. 54.00 (*0-8095-8251-1*) Borgo Pr.

Vestry Book of Blisland (Blissland) Parish, New Kent & James City Counties, Virginia, 1721-1786. Ed. by C. G. Chamberlayne. LC 79-16401. lxii, 277p. 1979. reprint ed. 15.00 (*0-88490-030-4*) Library of VA.

Vestry Book of Petsworth Parish, Glouster County, Virginia, 1677-1793. Ed. by C. G. Chamberlane. LC 79-13640. xv, 429p. 1979. reprint ed. 15.00 (*0-88490-032-0*) Library of VA.

Vestry Book of St. Paul's Parish. Ed. by C. G. Chamberlayne. xx, 672p. 1989. reprint ed. pap. text ed. 15.00 (*0-88490-162-9*) Library of VA.

Vestry Book of St. Peter's Parish. Ed. by C. G. Chamberlayne. xxvi, 840p. 1989. reprint ed. pap. text ed. 15.00 (*0-88490-140-8*) Library of VA.

Vestry Book of Stratton Major Parish, King & Queen County, Virginia, 1729-1783. Ed. by C. G. Chamberlyne. LC 80-14672. xxi, 257p. 1980. reprint ed. 15.00 (*0-88490-087-8*) Library of VA.

Vestry Book of the Upper Parish, Nansemond County, Virginia, 1793-1943. Ed. by Wilmer L. Hall. LC 50-9492. lxxiv, 328p. 1949. 15.00 (*0-88490-039-8*) Library of VA.

Vestry Handbook. Christopher L. Webber. LC 88-5160. 112p. 1995. pap. 7.95 (*0-8192-1453-1*) Morehouse Pub.

Vestry Member's Guide. rev. ed. Van S. Bowen. 80p. 1984. pap. 8.00 (*0-86683-892-9*) Harper SF.

Vests to Dye For. Marty Lawrence. (Illus.). 8p. 1990. pap. 2.95 (*0-944588-14-X*) K Wood.

Vesuvius & Other Latin Plays. Dick Burnell. (Illus.). 48p. (C). 1991. pap. text ed. 11.95 (*0-521-40959-4*) Cambridge U Pr.

Vet Guide to Parasites of Reptiles Vol. 2: Arthropods. Barnard. 1998. lib. bdg. write for info. (*0-89464-908-6*) Krieger.

***Vet in Africa: John Smith's Diaries & Letters Home, 1913-1933.** Ed. by John B. Smith. (Illus.). 256p. 1997. text ed. 39.50 (*1-86064-132-6*, Pub. by I B Tauris UK) St Martin.

Vet in Charge. large type ed. Mary Bowring. 1993. 17.95 (*0-7505-0473-0*, Pub. by Magna Print Bks UK) Ulverscroft.

Vet in the Vestry. large type ed. Alexander Cameron. LC 90-10793. 451p. 1990. lib. bdg. 17.95 (*0-89621-993-3*) Thorndike Pr.

Vet Pharmacology & Therapeutics. 5th ed. George C. Brander et al. (Illus.). 600p. 1991. text ed. 87.95 (*0-7020-1366-8*, Bailliere-Tindall) Saunders.

***Vet Surfari, Vol. 1.** Kenneth R. Boschert. 304p. (gr. 13). 1997. pap. text ed. 24.95 (*0-8151-2935-1*) Mosby Yr Bk.

Vet Thuong. Son Tung. 180p. 1992. 10.00 (*0-9635574-1-6*) Alpha Bks VA.

***Veteran & Vintage Transit: A Guide to North America's Mass Transit Museums & Tourist Trolley Operators.** Andrew D. Young. (Illus.). 160p. (Orig.). 1997. pap. 17.95 (*0-9647279-2-7*) Archway Pub.

Veteran & Weasel: Two One Act Renaissance Plays, Vol. 17. Angelo Beolco. Tr. by Ronnie Ferguson from ITA. (Studies in Italian Culture). 152p. (C). 1995. text ed. 46.95 (*0-8204-2700-4*) P Lang Pubng.

Veteran Counselor. Jack Rudman. (Career Examination Ser.: C-2690). 1994. pap. 29.95 (*0-8373-2690-7*) Nat Learn.

Veteran Motorcycles. Jeff Clew. 1995. pap. 25.00 (*0-7478-0276-9*, Pub. by Shire UK) St Mut.

Veterans: Index of Problems, Cases & Outcomes - Before, During & After Wars. American Health Research Institute Staff. LC 90-56249. 220p. 1991. 44.50 (*1-55914-260-X*); pap. 39.50 (*1-55914-261-8*) ABBE Pubs Assn.

Veterans' Administration: Its History, Activities & Organization. Gustavus A. Weber & Laurence F. Schmeckebier. LC 72-3083. (Brookings Institution. Institute for Government Research. Service Monographs of the U. S. Government: No. 66). reprint ed. 56.00 (*0-404-57166-2*) AMS Pr.

Veterans Administration Program for Disabled Veterans: An Overview. Cindy Charleston-Pinola & Harold Jordan. 1986. pap. 2.50 (*0-685-23193-3*, 40,900) NCLS Inc.

Veterans & Agent Orange: Health Effects of Herbicides Used in Vietnam. Institute of Medicine, Committee to Review the Health Effects in Vietnam Veterans of Exposure to Herbicides Staff. LC 93-27237. 832p. (Orig.). (C). 1993. text ed. 79.95 (*0-309-04887-7*) Natl Acad Pr.

Veterans & Agent Orange: Update 1996. rev. ed. Institute of Medicine, Committee to Review the Health Effects in Vietnam Veterans of Exposure to Herbicides Staff. 384p. (Orig.). 1996. text ed. 49.00 (*0-309-05487-7*) Natl Acad Pr.

Veterans at Risk: The Health Effects of Mustard Gas & Lewisite. Institute of Medicine, Committee on the Health Effects of Indoor Allergens Staff. Ed. by Constance M. Pechura & David P. Rall. LC 92-40735. 448p. (Orig.). (C). 1993. pap. text ed. 39.95 (*0-309-04832-X*) Natl Res Coun.

Veterans' Benefits: Basing Survivors' Compensation on Veterans' Disability is a Viable Option. (Illus.). 56p. (Orig.). (C). 1995. pap. text ed. 25.00 (*0-7881-2052-2*) DIANE Pub.

***Veterans' Benefits: Effective Interaction Needed Within VA to Address Appeals Backlog.** (Illus.). 53p. (Orig.). (C). 1996. pap. 20.00 (*0-7881-3027-7*) DIANE Pub.

Veterans' Benefits: Lack of Timeliness, Poor Communication Cause Customer Dissatisfaction. (Illus.). 57p. (Orig.). (C). 1995. pap. text ed. 20.00 (*0-7881-1698-3*) DIANE Pub.

Veterans Benefits: The Complete Guide. Keith D. Snyder et al. LC 92-52540. 410p. (Orig.). 1994. pap. 16.00 (*0-06-273146-7*, Harper Ref) HarpC.

***Veterans Benefits Administration: An Organizational History, 1776-1994.** 1996. lib. bdg. 252.99 (*0-8490-6358-2*) Gordon Pr.

***Veterans Benefits Administration: An Organizational History, 1776-1994.** 1997. lib. bdg. 250.75 (*0-8490-7645-5*) Gordon Pr.

***Veterans Benefits Administration: An Organizational History 1776-1994.** Amy W. Knight & Robert L. Worden. (Illus.). 89p. (Orig.). (C). 1996. pap. 25.00 (*0-7881-3032-3*) DIANE Pub.

Veterans' Benefits Handbook. Lee E. Sharff & Eugene Borden. 192p. 1992. pap. 10.00 (*0-13-952896-2*, Arco) Macmillan Gen Ref.

Veterans Claims Examiner. Jack Rudman. (Career Examination Ser.: C-3288). 1994. pap. 27.95 (*0-8373-3288-5*) Nat Learn.

Veterans Day. Lynda Sorensen. LC 94-17721. (Holidays Ser.). (J). 1994. write for info. (*1-57103-070-0*) Rourke Pr.

Veterans Flag List, Spencer & Halsey Valley New York (Tioga County) Laura C. Uhl. 1982. 2.00 (*0-943240-05-0*) UHLs Pub.

Veteran's Guide to Benefits. P. J. Budahn. 272p. 1994. pap. 13.95 (*0-8117-2596-0*) Stackpole.

***Veteran's Guide to Benefits.** 2nd ed. P. J. Budahn. LC 97-17038. (Illus.). 272p. 1997. pap. 14.95 (*0-8117-2975-3*) Stackpole.

Veteran's Guide to Owning Your Own Business. James W. Grant. Ed. by Robert E. Grant. (Illus.). 256p. (Orig.). pap. 9.95 (*0-9620051-5-0*) Grants Guide.

Veterans' Health Care: Implications of Other Countries' Reforms for the U. S. (Illus.). 56p. (Orig.). (C). 1995. pap. text ed. 20.00 (*0-7881-2081-6*) DIANE Pub.

Veteran's Health Care: Veteran's Perceptions of V. A. Services & V. A.'s Role in Health Care Reform. (Illus.). 40p. (Orig.). (C). 1995. pap. text ed. 25.00 (*0-7881-1767-X*) DIANE Pub.

***Veterans' Interview: 101 Questions to Help You Record & Preserve Your Military Memories.** Charles J. Myers & Thomas M. Gaughan. LC 96-61139. 176p. 1997. pap. 17.95 (*0-9655551-1-9*) Timber Creek.

Veterans Law Practice & Procedure, 1st Annual. 74p. 1993. 15.00 (*1-56986-229-X*, VET-93-74) Federal Bar.

Veterans Law Practice & Procedure, 2nd Annual (1994) 150p. 1993. 35.00 (*1-56986-244-3*) Federal Bar.

Veteran's Return to a Battlefield: Where 29th Division Fought near Aachen. Boyd Miller. (Illus.). 36p. 1985. 4.00 (*0-9615971-0-0*) Wordpix Serv.

Veteran's Self-Help Guide to Discharge Upgrading: Suggestions for the Veteran on How to Apply for a Change in Military Discharge. 3rd rev. ed. 8p. 1990. pap. text ed. 5.00 (*0-941486-09-5*) Vets Ed Proj.

Veterans You Are America: History in Photos 1985-1991. Robert A. Jones. (Illus.). 186p. (Orig.). 1992. pap. 17.95 (*0-9632488-0-4*) Vets Voice Am.

Veterens' Health Care: Facilities Resource Allocations Could Be More Equitable. (Illus.). 72p. (Orig.). 1996. pap. text ed. 30.00 (*0-7881-2894-9*) DIANE Pub.

Veterinarian. Jack Rudman. (Career Examination Ser.: C-870). 1994. pap. 49.95 (*0-8373-0870-4*) Nat Learn.

Veterinarian Trainee. Jack Rudman. (Career Examination Ser.: C-1529). 1994. pap. 39.95 (*0-8373-1529-8*) Nat Learn.

Veterinarians. Lee Gutkind. (J). 1997. 25.00 (*0-8050-3321-1*) H Holt & Co.

***Veterinarians.** Dee Ready. (Community Helpers Ser.). (J). 1997. 13.25 (*0-516-20506-4*) Childrens.

***Veterinarians.** Dolores Ready. LC 96-47312. (Community Helpers Ser.). (J). 1997. write for info. (*1-56065-514-3*) Capstone Pr.

Veterinarian's Anatomy & Physiology. Molgaard. (Agriculture Ser.). 1998. teacher ed. 12.00 (*0-8273-7872-6*); lab manual ed., teacher ed. 12.00 (*0-8273-7874-2*) Delmar.

Veterinarian's Anatomy & Physiology. Molgaard. (Agriculture Ser.). 1998. 57.95 (*0-8273-7871-8*) Delmar.

Veterinarian's Anatomy & Physiology Lab Manual. Molgaard. (Agriculture Ser.). 1998. lab manual ed. 21.00 (*0-8273-7873-4*) Delmar.

Veterinarian's Encyclopedia of Animal Behavior. Bonnie V. Beaver. LC 94-27257. (Illus.). 320p. 1994. text ed. 29.95 (*0-8138-2114-2*) Iowa St U Pr.

Veterinarian's Guide to the Laboratory Diagnosis of Infectious Diseases. G. R. Carter. 326p. 1986. 29.95 (*0-935078-37-1*) Veterinary Med.

Veterinarians Help Animals. Carol Greene. LC 96-14017. (Career Bks.). 32p. (J). (gr. k-4). 1996. lib. bdg. 21.36 (*1-56766-310-9*) Childs World.

Veterinarians' New Research Bible: Index of New Information. Max W. Denton. LC 95-19209. 1995. 47.50 (*0-7883-0494-1*); pap. 44.50 (*0-7883-0495-X*) ABBE Pubs Assn.

Veterinarian's Puzzle Book: Continuing Education the Fun Way. Sherman J. Marcus. 140p. (Orig.). 1983. pap. 4.95 (*0-9610444-0-3*) Cambita Bks.

Veterinarian's Treasury of Practice Tips II. Ed. by Seymour Glasofer & Lester Mandelker. 144p. 8.95 (*0-935078-14-2*) Veterinary Med.

Veterinary Acupuncture. Alan M. Klide & Shiu H. Kung. LC 76-53193. (Illus.). 314p. 1977. 67.95 (*0-8122-7721-X*) U of Pa Pr.

Veterinary Acupuncture: Ancient Art to Modern Medicine. Ed. by Allen M. Schoen. LC 93-74075. 500p. 1993. 75.00 (*0-939674-51-3*) Am Vet Pubns.

Veterinary Advice for Greyhound Owners. John Kohnke. (Illus.). 160p. 1994. 24.95 (*0-948955-87-2*, Pub. by Ringpr Bks UK) Seven Hills Bk.

***Veterinary Advice for Gundog Owners.** Gillian Averis. 1997. 27.95 (*0-87605-642-7*) Howell Bk.

Veterinary Anaesthesia. 9th ed. Hall. 1991. text ed. 82.00 (*0-7020-1421-4*) HarBrace.

Veterinary & Plant Health Controls Internal Market: Current Status 1 July 1994, Vol. 5. ECE Staff. 112p. 1994. pap. 40.00 (*92-826-7268-9*, CE-15-93-005ENC, Pub. by Europ Com UK) Bernan Associates.

Veterinary Anesthesia. Sawyer. text ed. write for info. (*0-7216-7942-0*) Saunders.

Veterinary Annual. 26th ed. Ed. by C. S. Grunsell et al. (Illus.). 309p. 1986. 62.95 (*0-85608-041-1*) Buttrwrth-Heinemann.

Veterinary Annual. 31th ed. Ed. by C. S. Grunsell et al. (Illus.). 232p. 1991. text ed. 95.00 (*0-632-03264-2*) Blackwell Sci.

Veterinary Annual, No. 34. Ed. by Mary-Elizabeth Raw & T. J. Parkinson. (Illus.). 256p. 1994. 135.00 (*0-86542-809-3*) Blackwell Sci.

Veterinary Annual Thirty-Two. Ed. by Mary-Elizabeth Raw & T. J. Parkinson. (Illus.). 320p. (C). 1992. 178.95 (*0-8464-4163-2*) Beekman Pubs.

Veterinary Annual 1989. 29th ed. F. Hill et al. 330p. 1989. 95.00 (*0-407-01767-4*) Blackwell Sci.

Veterinary Annual 34: 1994. Ed. by Mary-Elizabeth Raw & T. J. Parkinson. (Illus.). 272p. 1994. 97.95 (*0-632-03878-0*) Blackwell Sci.

Veterinary Annual 36: 1996. Ed. by Mary-Elizabeth Raw & T. J. Parkinson. (Illus.). 400p. 1996. 79.95 (*0-632-04049-1*) Blackwell Sci.

Veterinary Aptitude Test (VAT) Student Guide. rev. ed. David M. Tarlow. (Illus.). 120p. (C). 1993. pap. 16.95 (*0-931572-06-1*) Datar Pub.

Veterinary Aromatherapy. Nelly Grosjean. 130p. 1994. pap. 15.95 (*0-85207-274-0*, Pub. by C W Daniel UK) Natl Bk Netwk.

Veterinary Biology & Medicine of Captive Amphibians & Reptiles. Leonard C. Marcus. LC 80-24859. 251p. reprint ed. pap. 71.60 (*0-685-20937-7*, 2056518) Bks Demand.

Veterinary Book for Dairy Farmers. 2nd ed. R. W. Blowey. (Illus.). 496p. 1988. 38.95 (*0-85236-179-3*, Pub. by Farming Pr UK) Diamond Farm Bk.

Veterinary Book for Sheep Farmers. Dave Brown & Sam Meadowcroft. (Illus.). 240p. 1990. 49.95 (*0-85236-189-0*, Pub. by Farming Pr UK) Diamond Farm Bk.

Veterinary Cancer Medicine. 2nd ed. Ed. by Gordon H. Theilen & Bruce R. Madewell. LC 86-21332. 688p. reprint ed. pap. 180.00 (*0-7837-2751-8*, 2043131) Bks Demand.

Veterinary Care of Pot Bellied Pet Pigs. Lorrie B. Boldrick. 130p. (Orig.). 1993. 20.00 (*0-9624531-2-9*) All Pub.

Veterinary Care of the Horse. Sue Devereux & Liz Morrison. 245p. 1990. 90.00 (*0-85131-543-7*, Pub. by J A Allen & Co UK) St Mut.

Veterinary Clinical Diagnosis. 3rd ed. W. H. Kelly. (Illus.). 430p. 1984. text ed. 69.00 (*0-7216-0947-3*, Bailliere-Tindall) Saunders.

Veterinary Clinical Epidemiology: A Problem Oriented Approach. Ronald D. Smith. 1992. 49.00 (*0-7506-9182-4*, R) CRC Pr.

Veterinary Clinical Epidemiology: A Problem-Oriented Approach. Ronald D. Smith. LC 93-45328. 248p. 1992. 49.95 (*0-8493-8765-5*) CRC Pr.

Veterinary Clinical Epidemiology: A Problem-Oriented Approach. 2nd ed. Ronald D. Smith. 304p. 1995. 57.95 (*0-8493-2445-9*, 2445) CRC Pr.

Veterinary Clinical Immunology. Richard E. Halliwell & Neil T. Gorman. 496p. 1989. text ed. 79.00 (*0-7216-1197-4*) Saunders.

Veterinary Clinical Immunology: From Classroom to Clinics. Robert M. Lewis & Catherine A. Picut. LC 88-22624. 280p. reprint ed. pap. 79.80 (*0-7837-2851-4*, 2057621) Bks Demand.

Veterinary Clinical Laboratory Procedures. Ed. by Margi Sirois. LC 94-30737. (Fundamentals of Veterinary Technology Ser.). 256p. (C). (gr. 13). 1994. pap. text ed. 29.00 (*0-8016-8065-4*) Mosby Yr Bk.

Veterinary Clinical Parasitology. 6th ed. Margaret W. Sloss et al. LC 93-33959. (Illus.). 208p. 1994. pap. text ed. 39.95 (*0-8138-1733-1*) Iowa St U Pr.

Veterinary Clinical Pathology. 4th ed. Embert H. Coles. (Illus.). 486p. 1986. text ed. 64.00 (*0-7216-1828-6*) Saunders.

Veterinary Clinical Pharmacology & Therapeutics. Thomas B. Barragry. Ed. by Carroll C. Cann. (Illus.). 800p. 1993. 79.50 (*0-8121-1447-7*) Williams & Wilkins.

Veterinary College Admission Test (College) (VCAT) Jack Rudman. (Admission Test Ser.: ATS-29). 1994. pap. 23.95 (*0-8373-5029-8*) Nat Learn.

Veterinary College Admission Test (VCAT) - Core Content. David M. Tarlow. (Medical Examinations Ser.). (Illus.). 572p. (Orig.). (C). 1996. pap. 49.95 (*1-57774-004-1*) Educ Tsting Cnslts.

Veterinary Contribution to Public Health Practice: Report of the FAO-WHO Expert Committee on Veterinary Public Health, Geneva, 1974. FAO-WHO Expert Committee on Veterinary Public Health. (Technical Report Ser.: No. 573). 1975. pap. text ed. 8.00 (*92-4-120573-3*, 1100573) World Health.

Veterinary Conversations with Mid-Twentieth Century Leaders. Ole H. Stalheim. LC 95-38586. 328p. 1996. text ed. 34.95 (*0-8138-2995-X*) Iowa St U Pr.

Veterinary Critical Care. Fred P. Sattler. LC 80-27880. (Illus.). 562p. reprint ed. pap. 160.20 (*0-7837-1496-3*, 2057192) Bks Demand.

***Veterinary Demographic Annual Reports, 4 vols.** 5th ed. Center for Info. Management Staff. Incl. Pt. 1 National Distribution of U. S. Veterinarians. 5th ed. (Illus.). 31p. (Orig.). 1996. pap. 25.00 (*1-882691-04-0*); Pt. 2 Distribution of U. S. Veterinarians by Primary Employment. 5th ed. Orig. Title: Veterinary Demographic Data Resource, Chap. 4. (Illus.). 55p. (Orig.). 1996. pap. 25.00 (*1-882691-05-9*); Pt. 3 Distribution of U. S. Veterinarians by Veterinary Medical College. 5th ed. Orig. Title: Veterinary Demographic Data Resource, Chap. 5. (Illus.). 57p. (Orig.). 1996. pap. 125.00 (*1-882691-06-7*); Pt. 4 Distribution of U. S. Veterinarians by State. 5th ed. Orig. Title: Veterinary Demographic Data Resource, Chap. 6. (Illus.). 107p. (Orig.). 1996. pap. 125.00 (*1-882691-07-5*); 295.00 (*1-882691-03-2*) Am Veterinary Med Assn.

Veterinary Dental Techniques. 2nd ed. Holmstrom. 1998. text ed. write for info. (*0-7216-5839-3*) Saunders.

***Veterinary Dental Techniques: For the Small Animal Practitioner.** Steven E. Holmstrom et al. (Illus.). 440p. 1992. write for info. (*0-7216-3234-3*) Saunders.

Veterinary Dentistry. Erich Eisenmenger & Karl Zetner. LC 84-7908. (Illus.). 175p. reprint ed. pap. 49.90 (*0-7837-1487-4*, 2057182) Bks Demand.

Veterinary Diagnostic Ultrasound. Thomas G. Nyland & John S. Mattoon. 512p. 1995. text ed. 83.00 (*0-7216-2745-5*) Saunders.

Veterinary Diagnostic Virology. Castro & Heuschle. 285p. (gr. 13). 1991. text ed. 49.95 (*0-8016-6396-2*) Mosby Yr Bk.

Veterinary Dictionary: Russian-English. Roy Mack. 104p. (ENG & RUS.). 1972. pap. 35.00 (*0-8288-6425-X*, M-9710) Fr & Eur.

Veterinary Drug Handbook. Donald C. Plumb. LC 90-91729. 688p. (Orig.). 1991. pap. 39.95 (*0-9626619-0-2*) Pharmavet Pub.

Veterinary Drug Handbook. 2nd ed. Donald C. Plumb. LC 94-38603. (Illus.). 732p. (Orig.). 1994. pap. 47.95 (*0-8138-2443-5*) Iowa St U Pr.

Veterinary Drug Handbook. 2nd ed. Donald C. Plumb. 800p. (Orig.). 1995. pap. text ed. 47.95 (*0-8138-2352-8*) Iowa St U Pr.

Veterinary Drug Reference. Duran & Lin. 750p. (C). (gr. 13). 1998. pap. text ed. 39.95 (*0-8151-2939-4*) Mosby Yr Bk.

Veterinary Drug Residues: Food Safety, Vol. 636. Ed. by William A. Moats & Marjorie B. Medina. (Symposium Ser.: No. 636). (Illus.). 200p. 1996. 79.95 (*0-8412-3419-1*) Am Chemical.

***Veterinary Emergency & Critical Care.** Douglas MacIntire. 1998. text ed. write for info. (*0-397-58463-6*) Lppncott-Raven.

Veterinary Emergency & Critical Care Medicine. Robert J. Murtaugh & Kaplan. 685p. (gr. 13). 1991. text ed. 84.95 (*0-8016-6399-7*) Mosby Yr Bk.

***Veterinary Emergency Medicine Secrets.** Wayne E. Wingfield. LC 97-13886. (Secrets Ser.). 1997. write for info. (*1-56053-215-7*) Hanley & Belfus.

Veterinary Endocrinology & Reproduction. 4th ed. Ed. by L. E. McDonald. LC 88-9015. (Illus.). 571p. 1989. text ed. 58.00 (*0-8121-1134-6*) Williams & Wilkins.

Veterinary Endoscopy: Small Animal. Jones. 1998. write for info. (*0-7216-3653-5*) Saunders.

***Veterinary Endosurgery.** Freeman. 320p. (gr. 13). 1998. text ed. 110.00 (*0-8151-3321-9*) Mosby Yr Bk.

***Veterinary Entomology.** Wall & Shearer. (Illus.). 304p. (Orig.). 1996. pap. text ed. 45.95 (*0-412-61510-X*, Chap & Hall NY) Chapman & Hall.

Veterinary Entrance Tests: The Betz Guide. Aftab Hassan et al. 279p. 1996. pap. text ed. 27.95 (*0-683-18057-6*) Williams & Wilkins.

***Veterinary Epidemiology.** Ed. by M. V. Thrusfield. 300p. 1991. write for info. (*0-7506-1496-X*) Buttrwrth-Heinemann.

Veterinary Epidemiology. 2nd ed. Michael Thrusfield. (Illus.). 500p. 1996. 89.95 (*0-632-04036-X*) Blackwell Sci.

Veterinary Epidemiology: Principles & Methods. S. Wayne Martin et al. LC 87-3169. 356p. 1987. text ed. 46.95 (*0-8138-1856-7*) Iowa St U Pr.

Veterinary Ethics. Jerrold Tannenbaum. 384p. 1989. pap. 29.00 (*0-683-08102-0*) Williams & Wilkins.

Veterinary Ethics: Animal Welfare, Client Relations, Competition & Collegiality. 2nd ed. Tannenbaum. 650p. (gr. 13). 1995. pap. text ed. 44.00 (*0-8151-8840-4*) Mosby Yr Bk.

Veterinary Eye Surgery. S. W. Petrick. (Illus.). 1983. 45.00 (*0-409-11265-8*) Buttrwrth-Heinemann.

Veterinary Fluid Therapy. Michell. 280p. 1989. 85.00 (*0-632-01407-5*) Blackwell Sci.

Veterinary Gastroenterology. 2nd ed. Neil V. Anderson. (Illus.). 750p. 1992. text ed. 132.00 (*0-8121-1170-2*) Williams & Wilkins.

An Asterisk (*) at the beginning of an entry indicates that the title is appearing in BIP for the first time.

Veterinary Genetics. F. W. Nicholas. (Illus.). 500p. 1987. 69.50 (*0-19-857569-6*) OUP.

Veterinary Guide for Animal Owners. C. E. Spaulding. 1996. 22.95 (*0-87596-384-6*) Rodale Pr Inc.

***Veterinary Guide for Animal Owners: Cattle, Goats, Sheep, Horses, Pigs, Poultry, Rabbits, Dogs, Cats.** C. E. Spaulding & Jackie S. Clay. 1998. pap. 17.95 (*0-87596-967-4*) Rodale Pr Inc.

Veterinary Guide to the Parasites of Reptiles: Protozoa, Vol. 1. Susan M. Barnard & Steve J. Upton. LC 93-20082. 164p. 1994. lib. bdg. 26.50 (*0-89464-832-2*) Krieger.

Veterinary Helmenthology & Entomology. Moning. 1987. 460.00 (*81-7089-041-1*, Pub. by Intl Bk Distr II) St Mut.

***Veterinary Hematology: Atlas of Common Domestic Species.** William J. Reagan et al. LC 97-7678. 1997. write for info. (*0-8138-2664-0*) Iowa St U Pr.

Veterinary Histology: An Outline Text-Atlas. Horst-Dieter Dellmann. LC 78-146030. 316p. reprint ed. pap. 90.10 (*0-685-20929-6*, 2056506) Bks Demand.

Veterinary Immunology. Peter M. Outteridge. 280p. 1986. pap. text ed. 49.00 (*0-12-531131-1*) Acad Pr.

Veterinary Immunology: An Introduction. 5th ed. Ian R. Tizard. Ed. by Ray Kersey. 624p. 1996. pap. text ed. 49.00 (*0-7216-5772-9*) Saunders.

Veterinary Information Management. D. C. Blood. 1989. text ed. 63.00 (*0-7020-1328-5*) Saunders.

Veterinary Laboratory Medicine. 3rd ed. J. Robert Duncan et al. LC 09-415444. (Illus.). 308p. 1994. text ed. 42.95 (*0-8138-1917-2*) Iowa St U Pr.

Veterinary Laboratory Medicine: Clinical Pathology. 2nd ed. J. Robert Duncan & Keith W. Prasse. LC 85-19786. (Illus.). 293p. 1986. reprint ed. pap. 83.60 (*0-608-00014-0*, 2060780) Bks Demand.

***Veterinary Laboratory Medicine: Interpretation & Diagnosis.** D. J. Meyer et al. (Illus.). 360p. 1992. pap. write for info. (*0-7216-2654-8*) Saunders.

Veterinary Laboratory Medicine: Interpretation & Diagnosis. 2nd ed. Dennie J. Meyer & John W. Harvey. Ed. by Ray Kersey. (Illus.). 352p. 1997. pap. text ed. write for info. (*0-7216-6222-6*) Saunders.

Veterinary Laboratory Medicine in Practice. 271p. 1993. pap. 58.00 (*1-884254-01-2*) Vet Lrn Syst.

Veterinary Manual for the Performance Horse. Nancy L. Loving. Ed. by Don M. Wagoner. (Illus.). 608p. (C). 1993. text ed. 75.00 (*0-935842-06-3*) Equine Res.

Veterinary Materia Medica & Clinical Repertory. Macleod. 165p. 1983. pap. 17.95 (*0-85207-257-0*, Pub. by C W Daniel UK) Natl Bk Netwk.

Veterinary Materia Medica Rep. A. Hora. (C). 1986. 200.00 (*0-317-92321-8*, Pub. by Scientific UK) St Mut.

Veterinary Material Medical & Clincial Repertory. George MacLeod. 208p. (Orig.). pap. 17.95 (*0-8464-4309-0*) Beekman Pubs.

Veterinary Medical Mycology. Paul F. Jungerman & Robert M. Schwartzman. LC 78-157469. 207p. reprint ed. pap. 59.00 (*0-317-28598-X*, 2055434) Bks Demand.

Veterinary Medical Officer. Jack Rudman. (Career Examination Ser.: C-875). 1994. pap. 49.95 (*0-8373-0875-5*) Nat Learn.

***Veterinary Medical School Admission Requirements in the United States & Canada: 1997 Edition for 1998 Matriculation.** Association of American Veterinary Medical Colleges. 176p. (Orig.). 1997. pap. 14.95 (*1-55753-107-2*) Purdue U Pr.

***Veterinary Medical School Admissions Requirements.** 12th ed. Jane D. Crawford. 1997. pap. text ed. 14.95 (*0-683-30099-7*) Williams & Wilkins.

Veterinary Medical Terminology. Dawn E. Christenson. Ed. by Selma Kaszczuk. 320p. 1996. pap. text ed. 28.00 (*0-7216-4859-2*) Saunders.

***Veterinary Medicine.** (Illus.). 48p. (YA). (gr. 6-12). 1996. pap. 2.40 (*0-8395-5004-9*, 35004) BSA.

***Veterinary Medicine: A Textbook of the Diseases of Cattle, Sheep, Pigs, Goats & Horses.** 8th ed. Ed. by O. M. Radostits et al. (Illus.). 1787p. 1994. write for info. (*0-7020-1592-X*, Pub. by W B Saunders UK) Saunders.

***Veterinary Medicine: Pocket Companion.** D. C. Blood. (Illus.). 743p. 1994. write for info. (*0-7020-1695-0*, Pub. by W B Saunders UK) Saunders.

Veterinary Medicine: Subject, Reference & Research Guide. Max W. Denton. LC 87-47614. 160p. 1987. 44.50 (*0-88164-532-X*); pap. 39.50 (*0-88164-533-8*) ABBE Pubs Assn.

***Veterinary Medicine in Economic Transition.** Malcolm Getz. LC 96-47012. (Illus.). 288p. (C). 1997. text ed. 44.95 (*0-8138-1814-1*) Iowa St U Pr.

Veterinary Medicine in the West. Ole H. Stalheim. (Illus.). 84p. 1988. pap. text ed. 15.00 (*0-89745-109-0*) Sunflower U Pr.

Veterinary Microbiology. Ed. by R. Pandey. (Progress in Veterinary Microbiology & Immunology Ser.: Vol. 2). (Illus.). x, 222p. 1985. 118.50 (*3-8055-4067-1*) S Karger.

Veterinary Neuroanatomy & Clinical Neurology. 2nd ed. Alexander DeLahunta. LC 76-4246. (Illus.). (C). 1983. text ed. 72.00 (*0-7216-3029-4*) Saunders.

Veterinary Neuropathology. Summers et al. (Illus.). 650p. (gr. 13). 1994. text ed. 141.00 (*0-8016-5063-1*) Mosby Yr Bk.

Veterinary Notes for Dog Breeders. Annette M. Carricato. (Illus.). 256p. 1992. pap. 25.95 (*0-87605-805-5*) Howell Bk.

Veterinary Notes for Horse Owners: An Illustrated Manual of Horse Medicine & Surgery. M. Horace Hayes. 688p. 1988. 35.00 (*0-671-76561-2*) S&S Trade.

***Veterinary Nursing, 2 vols.** Lane. 836p. 1996. pap. 65.00 (*0-7506-3417-0*) Buttrwrth-Heinemann.

Veterinary Parasitology. Omar Barriga. (Illus.). 316p. (C). 1995. pap. text ed. 16.00 (*1-57074-242-1*) Greyden Pr.

Veterinary Parasitology. 2nd rev. ed. G. M. Urquhart et al. LC 95-54099. (Illus.). 350p. (C). 1996. pap. text ed. 62.95 (*0-632-04051-3*) Iowa St U Pr.

***Veterinary Pathology.** 6th ed. Thomas C. Jones et al. LC 96-32932. 1996. write for info. (*0-683-04481-8*) Williams & Wilkins.

Veterinary Pediatrics: Dogs & Cats from Birth to Six Months. 2nd ed. Johnny D. Hoskins. 608p. 1995. text ed. 65.00 (*0-7216-3887-2*) Saunders.

Veterinary Pharmaceutical & Biologicals. Medical Economics Staff. 1995. 59.00 (*0-935078-46-0*) Veterinary Med.

Veterinary Pharmaceuticals & Biologicals. 5th ed. LC 85-647677. 600p. 1986. 32.95 (*0-87489-843-9*) Veterinary Med.

Veterinary Pharmaceuticals & Biologicals. 9th ed. 1995. 75.00 (*0-935078-53-3*) Veterinary Med.

***Veterinary Pharmaceuticals & Biologicals (VPB)** Ed. by Kim Holt. 1312p. 1996. 79.95 (*0-935078-61-4*) Veterinary Med.

Veterinary Pharmacology & Therapeutics. 7th ed. Ed. by H. Richard Adams. LC 95-15276. 1056p. (C). 1995. text ed. 129.95 (*0-8138-1741-2*) Iowa St U Pr.

***Veterinary Practice Management.** J. Bower et al. 288p. 1991. pap. write for info. (*0-632-03391-6*) Blackwell Sci.

Veterinary Practice Management. Dennis M. McCurnin. LC 65-9467. 401p. 1988. text ed. 59.50 (*0-397-50782-8*, Lippncott) Lppncott-Raven.

***Veterinary Practice Management.** 2nd ed. John Bower & Society of Practicing Veterinary Surgeons Staff. LC 96-48694. 1997. 32.95 (*0-632-04129-3*) Iowa St U Pr.

Veterinary Practice Management: Building Profit & Value. Jerry L. Simmons. LC 96-7178. 224p. (C). (gr. 13). 1996. text ed. 38.95 (*0-8151-7555-8*) Mosby Yr Bk.

Veterinary Protozoan & Hemoparasite Vaccines. Ed. by I. G. Wright. 272p. 1989. 217.00 (*0-8493-4757-2*, QR189) CRC Pr.

Veterinary Protozoology. Norman D. Levine. LC 84-27867. (Illus.). 414p. 1985. text ed. 59.95 (*0-8138-1861-3*) Iowa St U Pr.

***Veterinary Receptionist's Handbook.** M. T. McClister & Amy Midgley. LC 95-61831. 264p. 1995. pap. 39.95 (*0-935078-56-8*) Veterinary Med.

Veterinary Reproduction & Obstetrics. 7th ed. David E. Noakes. 1995. text ed. 79.00 (*0-7020-1785-X*) Saunders.

Veterinary Science Officer. Jack Rudman. (Career Examination Ser.: C-871). 1994. pap. 49.95 (*0-8373-0871-2*) Nat Learn.

***Veterinary Therapeutic Diet Reference for Dog & Cat Foods.** Howard D. Coffman. 200p. (Orig.). 1998. spiral bd. write for info. (*0-9645009-8-1*, PDP09) PigDog Pr.

Veterinary Toxicology. 2nd ed. Rudolph D. Radeleff. LC 74-85846. 365p. reprint ed. pap. 104.10 (*0-317-29245-5*, 2055440) Bks Demand.

Veterinary Treatments & Medications for Horsemen. Equine Research, Inc. Research Staff. Ed. by Don M. Wagoner. (Illus.). 612p. (C). 1977. text ed. 75.00 (*0-935842-01-2*) Equine Res.

Veterinary Ultrasonography. Ed. by P. J. Goddard. 346p. 1995. 135.00 (*0-85198-923-3*) CAB Intl.

Veterinary Vaccines. Ed. by R. Pandey et al. (Progress in Vaccinology Ser.: Vol. 4). (Illus.). 376p. 1992. 218.95 (*0-387-97819-4*) Spr-Verlag.

***Veterinary Vaccinology.** Paul-Pierre Pastoret. LC 97-11156. 1997. write for info. (*0-444-81968-1*) Elsevier.

Veterinary Virology. 2nd ed. Frank Fenner et al. (Illus.). 666p. 1993. text ed. 79.00 (*0-12-253056-X*) Acad Pr.

Veterinary Virology. Sashi B. Mohanty & Sukanta K. Dutta. LC 80-26157. 382p. 1981. reprint ed. pap. 108.90 (*0-7837-2849-2*, 2057623) Bks Demand.

Veterinarians' New Research Bible & Index of New Information. Max W. Denton. 150p. 1994. 44.50 (*0-7883-0060-1*); pap. 39.50 (*0-7883-0061-X*) ABBE Pubs Assn.

Vetir Ceux Qui Sont Nus, Comme Avant, Mieux Qu'Avant. Luigi Pirandello. (FRE.). 1982. pap. 10.95 (*0-7859-4176-2*) Fr & Eur.

Vetiver Grass: A Thin Green Line Against Erosion. National Research Council Staff. LC 92-50175. 188p. (Orig.). (C). 1993. pap. text ed. 12.00 (*0-309-04269-0*) Natl Acad Pr.

Vetiver Grass: The Hedge Against Erosion. 88p. 1990. 6.95 (*0-8213-1405-X*, 11405) World Bank.

Vetiver Grass for Soil & Water Conservation, Land Rehabilitation, & Embankment Stabilization: A Collection of Papers & Newsletters. Ed. by Richard Grimshaw & Larisa Helfer. LC 94-23998. (Technical Papers: Vol. 273). 288p. 1996. 16.95 (*0-8213-3144-2*, 13144) World Bank.

Vetluga Memoir: A Turkish Prisoner of War in Russia, 1916-1918. Mehmet A. Olcen. Ed. & Tr. by Gary Leiser from TUR. LC 94-48881. (Illus.). 264p. 1995. 39.95 (*0-8130-1353-4*) U Press Fla.

Vets. Stephen Leather. Ed. by Bill Grose. 512p. 1994. reprint ed. mass mkt. 5.99 (*0-671-74304-X*) PB.

Vets at Variance. large type ed. Mary Bowring. 269p. 1994. 25.99 (*0-7505-0663-6*) Ulverscroft.

Vets in Love. large type ed. Mary Bowring. (Magna Romance Ser.). 284p. 1992. 25.99 (*0-7505-0393-9*) Ulverscroft.

Vets Might Fly. large type ed. James Herriot. LC 92-15293. 289p. 1993. 16.95 (*0-8161-5222-5*) G K Hall.

Vette Vues Factbook of the Nineteen Seventy-Three to Nineteen Seventy-Seven Stingray. (Vette Vues Factbook Ser.). (Illus.). 200p. 1991. 34.95 (*0-9607176-9-2*) M F Dobbins.

Vette Vues Factbook of the Nineteen Sixty-Eight to Nineteen Seventy-Two Stingray. 4th ed. (Vette Vues Factbook Ser.). (Illus.). 291p. 1991. 39.95 (*1-880835-00-2*) M F Dobbins.

Vette Vues Factbook of the Nineteen Sixty-Three to Nineteen Sixty-Seven Stingray. 9th ed. (Vette Vues Factbook Ser.). (Illus.). 378p. 1989. 39.95 (*0-9607176-8-4*) M F Dobbins.

'Vette 'Vues Fact Books: 'Vette 'Vues 1963-67. M.F. Dobbins. (Illus.). 347p. Date not set. pap. 34.95 (*0-614-99677-5*) Motorbooks Intl.

'Vette 'Vues Fact Books: 'Vette 'Vues 1973-77. M.F. Robbins. (Illus.). 200p. Date not set. pap. 34.95 (*0-614-99679-1*) Motorbooks Intl.

Vettius Valens. Ed. by Guilelmus Kroll. xvii, 420p. 1973. write for info. (*3-296-15860-X*) G Olms Pubs.

Vetus Registrum Sarisberiense, Alias Dictum Registrum S. Osmundi Episcopi, Register of St. Osmund, 2 vols. Ed. by W. Rich-Jones. (Rolls Ser.: No. 78). 1974. reprint ed. Set. 140.00 (*0-8115-1148-0*) Periodicals Srv.

***Veuve Noire.** Chrystine Brouillet. (Novels in the Roman Jeunesse Ser.). 96p. (FRE.). (J). (gr. 4-7). 1996. pap. 7.95 (*2-89021-237-8*, Pub. by Les Editions CN) Firefly Bks Ltd.

Vexillophily: A Capsule History of the Stars & Stripes. 2nd rev. ed. Grandpa Blair. (Illus.). 46p. (YA). (gr. 11 up). 1992. pap. 9.95 (*0-930366-74-3*) Northcountry Pub.

Vez Fui Catolico. Tony Coffey. 176p. (SPA.). 1994. pap. 7.99 (*0-8254-1124-6*, Edit Portavoz) Kregel.

Vez Mas. James H. Couch et al. (gr. 4-12). 1982. pap. 13.95 (*0-88334-164-6*); 4.25 (*0-317-02593-7*) Longman.

Vezeichniss einer Auswahl Amerikanischer Grammatiken. Julius Platzmann. 1977. reprint ed. 23.95 (*0-518-19010-2*) Ayer.

VFR Pilot Exam-O-Grams (AP104) FAA Department of Transportation Staff. (Illus.). 124p. (Orig.). 1982. reprint ed. pap. text ed. 5.95 (*0-941272-07-9*) Astro Pubs.

***VGM Business Portraits.** William Gould. LC 97-1795. (J). 1997. write for info. (*0-8442-4780-4*, VGM Career Bks); write for info. (*0-8442-4781-2*, VGM Career Bks) NTC Pub Grp.

***VGM S Careers Encyclopedia.** 4th ed. VGM Career Horizons Editors. LC 96-47289. 1997. write for info. (*0-8442-4525-9*) NTC Pub Grp.

VGM's Careers Encyclopedia. 3rd ed. Craig T. Norback. LC 90-50726. 500p. (YA). (gr. 7 up). 1995. 39.95 (*0-8442-8692-3*, VGM Career Bks) NTC Pub Grp.

VGM's Complete Guide to Career Etiquette: From Job Search Through Career Advancement. Mark Satterfield. 160p. (Orig.). 1995. pap. 12.95 (*0-8442-4471-6*, VGM Career Bks) NTC Pub Grp.

VGM's Guide to Temporary Employment. Lewis Baratz. Ed. by Sarah Kennedy. 176p. (Orig.). 1995. pap. 11.95 (*0-8442-4472-4*, VGM Career Bks) NTC Pub Grp.

VGM's Handbook of Business & Management Careers. Craig T. Norback. 1993. pap. 12.95 (*0-8442-8683-4*, VGM Career Bks) NTC Pub Grp.

VGM's Handbook of Business & Management Careers. Ed. by Annette Selden. LC 92-41818. 130p. 1994. pap. 12.95 (*0-8442-4140-7*, VGM Career Bks) NTC Pub Grp.

VGM's Handbook of Government & Public Service Careers. 2nd ed. Ed. by Annette Selden. LC 93-11255. 130p. 1994. pap. 12.95 (*0-8442-4142-3*, VGM Career Bks) NTC Pub Grp.

VGM's Handbook of Health Care Careers. Ed. by Annette Selden. LC 92-49633. 12p. 1994. pap. 12.95 (*0-8442-4148-2*, VGM Career Bks) NTC Pub Grp.

VGM's Handbook of Scientific & Technical Careers. Craig T. Norback. 1993. pap. 12.95 (*0-8442-8684-2*, VGM Career Bks) NTC Pub Grp.

VGM's Handbook of Scientific & Technical Careers. Ed. by Annette Selden. 128p. 1995. pap. 12.95 (*0-8442-4147-4*) NTC Pub Grp.

VH Amino Acids: Products & Technology. 120p. 1991. 1,750.00 (*0-89336-856-3*, C056R) BCC.

***VH-2000 Hobber.** M. R. Anderson & H. W. Semar. (AGMA Technical Paper). 1966. pap. text ed. 30.00 (*1-55589-162-4*) AGMA.

VHDL. 2nd ed. Douglas L. Perry. LC 93-23153. (Computer Engineering Ser.). 1993. text ed. 52.00 (*0-07-049434-7*) McGraw.

VHDL: A Logic Synthesis Approach. S. Jones. 320p. 1996. 60.50 (*0-412-61650-5*) Chapman & Hall.

VHDL: Analysis Modeling of Digital Systems. Zainalabedin Navabi. 1992. text ed. write for info. (*0-07-046472-3*) McGraw.

***VHDL: Features & Applications, Incl. primer, final exam.** J. Bhasker. Ed. by Paul Menchini. 185p. 1995. student ed. 299.00 (*0-7803-2297-5*, HL5712) Inst Electrical.

VHDL: Hardware Description & Design. Roger Lipsett et al. 320p. (C). 1989. lib. bdg. 96.50 (*0-7923-9030-X*) Kluwer Ac.

VHDL: Techniques, Experiments & Caveats. Joseph R. Pick. 1996. text ed. 50.00 (*0-07-049906-3*) McGraw.

VHDL: The Complete Reference & User's Guide. David R. Coehlo et al. 400p. 1993. text ed. write for info. (*0-13-950684-5*) P-H.

***VHDL Answers to Frequently Asked Questions.** Ben Cohen. LC 96-43190. 320p. (C). 1996. lib. bdg. 100.00 (*0-7923-9791-6*) Kluwer Ac.

***VHDL for Designers.** Stefan Sjoholm. LC 96-29744. 1997. pap. 51.00 (*0-13-473414-9*) P-H.

VHDL for Logic Synthesis: An Introductory Guide for Achieving Design Requirements. Andrew Rushton. LC 95-30321. 1996. text ed. 55.00 (*0-07-709092-6*) McGraw.

VHDL for Programmable Logic. Kevin Skahill. (C). 1996. text ed. 10.00 (*0-201-89586-2*) Addison-Wesley.

VHDL for Programmable Logic. Kevin Skahill. LC 96-16472. 1996. write for info. (*0-8058-9573-6*) Addison-Wesley.

VHDL for Simulation, Synthesis, & Formal Proofs of Hardware. Ed. by Jean P. Mermet. LC 92-16266. (International Series in Engineering & Computer Science, VLSI, Computer Architecture, & Digital Screen Processing: Vol. 183). 316p. (C). 1992. lib. bdg. 128.00 (*0-7923-9253-1*) Kluwer Ac.

VHDL Handbook. David R. Coelho. 416p. (C). 1989. lib. bdg. 109.50 (*0-7923-9031-8*) Kluwer Ac.

VHDL International Users Forum, 1994. LC 94-75466. 200p. 1994. pap. text ed. 40.00 (*0-8186-6215-8*, 6215) IEEE Comp Soc.

***VHDL Made Easy!** David Pellerin & Douglas Taylor. LC 96-26999. 1996. 53.00 (*0-13-650763-8*) P-H.

VHDL Modeling for Digital Design Synthesis. Yu-Chin Hsu. 376p. (C). 1995. lib. bdg. 98.00 (*0-7923-9597-2*) Kluwer Ac.

VHDL Primer. J. Bhasker. LC 94-3450. (IEEE Std 1076-1993). 303p. 1994. text ed. 57.00 (*0-13-181447-8*) P-H.

VHDL Primer. Jayram Bhasker. 1992. text ed. 52.00 (*0-13-952987-X*) P-H.

VHDL Programming: With Advanced Topics. Louis Baker. 384p. 1992. pap. text ed. 49.95 (*0-471-57464-3*) Wiley.

***VHDL Starter's Guide.** Yalamanchili. 1997. pap. text ed. 26.67 (*0-13-519802-X*) P-H.

VHDL Synthesis Primer. J. Bhasker. LC 95-73048. 238p. 1996. 49.95 (*0-9650391-0-2*) Peer-to-Peer Communications.

VHDL 1992: The New Features of the VHDL Hardware Description Language. Jean-Michel Berge. 232p. (C). 1993. lib. bdg. 108.50 (*0-7923-9356-2*) Kluwer Ac.

VHF & UHF Antennas. R. A. Burberry. (Electromagnetic Waves Ser.: No. 35). 320p. 1992. text ed. 98.00 (*0-86341-269-6*, EW035) Inst Elect Eng.

VHF How to Book: A Guide for All Amateurs. Joe Lynch. LC 94-71290. (Illus.). 136p. (Orig.). 1994. pap. 15.95 (*0-943016-07-X*) CQ Commns Inc.

VI - The Flying Bomb. Joachim Engelmann. Tr. by Edward Force from GER. (Illus.). 48p. 1992. pap. 7.95 (*0-88740-408-1*) Schiffer.

Vi Hadde Det Godt Her: We Had It Good Here. Ardis B. Folstad. LC 28-2322. 150p. (Orig.). 1987. pap. 6.50 (*0-9618318-0-4*) Folstad & Co.

Vi Pack: For UNIX Vi Editor. SSC, Inc. Staff. (Orig.). (C). 1989. pap. 9.00 (*0-916151-33-6*, VIP) Specialized Sys.

VI Reference. rev. ed. Cscapes. 10p. 1987. pap. 3.00 (*0-916151-19-0*) Specialized Sys.

Vi Reference Card. 4th ed. Anatole Olczak. (Orig.). 1996. pap. 2.95 (*0-935739-02-5*) ASP.

VI Tutorial. 3rd rev. ed. Specialized Systems Consultants, Inc. Staff & Belinda Frazier. (Illus.). 56p. (Orig.). (C). 1991. reprint ed. pap. text ed. 6.00 (*0-916151-54-9*) Specialized Sys.

VI User's Handbook. AT&T Bell Laboratories Staff & Morris I. Bolsky. 66p. 1985. 29.95 (*0-13-941733-8*) P-H.

Via Airmail, an Aerophilatelic Survey of Events, Routes, & Rates. Tr. & Frwd. by Simine Short. LC 92-53852. (Illus.). 224p. 1992. 20.00 (*0-939429-01-2*) Am Air Mail.

Via Crucis. Francis M. Crawford. (Works of Francis Marion Crawford Ser.). 1990. reprint ed. lib. bdg. 79.00 (*0-7812-2550-7*) Rprt Serv.

***Via Crucis: Con el Papa Juan Pablo II.** Joseph M. Champlin. 40p. (Orig.). (SPA.). 1997. pap. 2.95 (*0-89243-876-2*) Liguori Pubns.

Via Cruis, 2 pts. Emilio Bacardi. Incl. Pt. 1 Paginas De Ayer. LC 77-128478. (*0-318-54344-3*); Pt. 2 Magdalena. LC 77-128478. (*0-318-54345-1*); LC 77-128478. (Cuban Reprint Ser.). 475p. 15.00 (*0-685-58251-5*) Mnemosyne.

***Via de Escape.** Neil T. Anderson. 272p. (SPA.). 1995. write for info. (*1-56063-972-5*) Editorial Unilit.

Via Diaz. Romano Perticarnini. 1989. pap. 10.00 (*0-920717-36-5*) Guernica Editions.

Via Dolorosa. Ernest Laguette. LC 94-61407. 110p. (Orig.). 1994. pap. 4.00 (*1-877678-29-5*) Riehle Found.

Via Focal Problems. Gordon Burnand. 275p. 1982. text ed. 75.00 (*0-907774-00-8*, Pub. by Ldrship Ltd UK) St Mut.

Via Latina Catacomb: Imitation & Discontinuity in Fourth-Century Roman Painting. William Tronzo. LC 84-43089. (College Art Association Monographs: Vol. 38). (Illus.). 160p. 1986. 35.00 (*0-271-00389-8*) Pa St U Pr.

Via Media of the Anglican Church. John H. Newman. 496p. 1990. 110.00 (*0-19-826693-6*) OUP.

Via Nicaragua, a Sketch of Travel. Dora Hort. 6267p. 1987. reprint ed. 25.00 (*0-913129-17-8*) La Tienda.

Via Poetica. Francisco Arrivi. LC 77-25892. 1978. 5.00 (*0-8477-3222-3*); pap. text ed. 4.00 (*0-8477-3223-1*) U of PR Pr.

VIA-U. S. A.'s Living & Working in America, Vol. I. Mary E. McSwain & Bonnie V. Morihara. Tr. by Yuko Higuchi & Kazuko Ikeda. (Illus.). ix, 178p. (Orig.). (ENG & JPN.). (C). 1988. vhs 200.00 (*0-685-21729-9*) VIA Pr.

VIA-U. S. A.'s Living & Working in America, Vol. II. Mary E. McSwain & Bonnie V. Morihara. (Illus.). 150p. (Orig.). (C). 1989. vhs 250.00 (*0-685-21730-2*) VIA Pr.

VIA-U. S. A.'s Living & Working in America, Vol. III. Mary E. McSwain & Bonnie V. Morihara. (Illus.). (Orig.). (C). 1989. vhs 250.00 (*0-685-21728-0*) VIA Pr.

Via Veneto Papers. Ennio Flaiano. Tr. by John Satriano from ITA. LC 92-80360. 288p. 1992. 29.95 (*0-910395-66-7*) Marlboro Pr.

Via Veneto Papers. Ennio Flaiano. Tr. by John Satriano from ITA. LC 92-80360. 288p. 1994. pap. 12.95 (*0-910395-67-5*) Marlboro Pr.

Via, Veritas, Vita: Lectures on "Christianity in Its Most Simple & Intelligible Form" 2nd ed. James Drummond. LC 77-27160. (Hibbert Lectures: 1894). reprint ed. 31.50 (*0-404-60412-9*) AMS Pr.

Via Vertendi: A Latin Unseen Course. B. W. Young. 160p. 1992. pap. 16.95 (*1-85399-327-1*, Pub. by Brstl Class Pr UK) Focus Pub-R Pullins.

U
V

Viability of Seeds. Ed. by E. H. Roberts. LC 73-39736. (Illus.). 448p. (C). 1972. 39.95 (*0-8156-5033-7*) Syracuse U Pr.

Viability Theory. Jean P. Aubin. (Systems & Control: Foundations & Applications Ser.). (Illus.). xxv, 543p. 1991. 99.50 (*0-8176-3571-8*) Birkhauser.

Viable Democracy. Michael Margolis. LC 79-5053. 1979. text ed. 29.95 (*0-312-83886-7*) St Martin.

Viable Polity. Edward W. Lehman. LC 92-9854. 296p. (C). 1992. 49.95 (*0-87722-994-5*) Temple U Pr.

Viable Populations for Conservation. Ed. by Michael E. Soule. (Illus.). 250p. 1987. pap. text ed. 24.95 (*0-521-33657-0*) Cambridge U Pr.

Viable System Model: Concepts, Methodology & Applications. Ed. by Raul Espejo & Roger Harnden. LC 89-8916. 472p. 1989. text ed. 100.00 (*0-471-92288-9*) Wiley.

Viaducs de la Seine et Oise. Marguerite Duras. (Coll. Le Manteau d'Arlequin). pap. 8.95 (*0-685-34112-7*) Fr & Eur.

Viaja con Victor. Tr. by Mary M. Foreman from ENG. (Gus Is Gone Ser.). (Illus.). 24p. (SPA.). (J). 1992. pap. 3.95 (*1-56288-237-6*) Checkerboard.

Viajando. (Illus.). 24p. (SPA.). (J). (ps-3). 1993. pap. 1.95 (*0-307-50057-8*, Golden Books) Western Pub.

***Viajando por la Cuba que Fue Libre.** Josefina Inclan. (SPA.). pap. 15.00 (*0-89729-157-3*) Ediciones.

Viaje. David Scoma. 196p. 1992. pap. 14.95 (*0-9632780-0-2*) Misdemeanor.

***Viaje a Ixtlan.** Carlos Castaneda. 1992. pap. text ed. 12.99 (*968-16-0335-4*) Fondo de Cultura Economica.

Viaje a la Alcarria. Camilo Jose Cela. (Nueva Austral Ser.: Vol. 131). (SPA.). 1991. pap. text ed. 24.95 (*84-239-1931-5*) Elliots Bks.

Viaje a la Habana. Reinaldo Arenas. LC 89-85397. (Coleccion Caniqui). 158p. (Orig.). (SPA.). 1990. pap. 15.00 (*0-89729-544-7*) Ediciones.

Viaje a la Luna. Julio Verne. (SPA.). 9.95 (*84-241-5635-8*) E Torres & Sons.

***Viaje al Casabe.** Ana R. Nunez. (SPA.). pap. 5.00 (*0-89729-056-9*) Ediciones.

Viaje al Centro de la Tierra see Serie Illustrada, "Now Age"

Viaje de Hector Rabinal. Donley Watt. Tr. by Pedro A. Palou & Peggy Watson from ENG. LC 93-30375. 204p. (SPA.). (C). 1995. pap. 12.95 (*0-87565-128-3*) Tex Christian.

Viaje de Jenny. Sheila W. Samton. Tr. by Arshes Anasal. Orig. Title: Jenny's Journey. (Illus.). 32p. (SPA.). (J). (ps-1). 1996. pap. 5.99 (*0-14-055605-2*, Puffin) Puffin Bks.

Viaje de Jenny: Jenny's Journey. Sheila W. Samton. (Illus.). 32p. (J). (ps-3). 1993. pap. 14.99 (*0-670-84843-3*) Viking Child Bks.

Viaje de la Jirafa. Tim Dowley. (Serie Libros de Carton - Board Bks.). 6p. (SPA.). (J). 1992. bds. 2.99 (*1-56063-220-8*, 490386) Editorial Unilit.

***Viaje de los Camellos - The Camel's Journey.** Gordon Stowell. (Serie Pescaditos - Little Fish Ser.). 24p. (SPA.). (J). 1991. write for info. (*1-56063-141-4*) Editorial Unilit.

***Viaje de los "Micronautas" - Voyage of the Micronauts.** (Early Learning Program Ser.). (Illus.). 64p. (SPA.). (J). (gr. k-2). 16.95 (*0-7835-3537-6*) Time-Life.

Viaje de Perico Ligero al Pais de Los Moros: A Critical Edition of Antonio Lopez Matoso's Unpublished Diary, 1816-1820. James C. Tatum. (Publications: No. 36). (Illus.). 114p. 1972. 15.00 (*0-939238-41-1*) Tulane MARI.

Viaje Especial del Burrito. Tim Dowley. (Serie Libros de Carton - Board Bks.). 6p. (SPA.). (J). 1992. bds. 2.99 (*1-56063-225-9*, 490391) Editorial Unilit.

Viaje Extraordinario: El Lengueta. H. Tramp. 25p. (SPA.). (J). 1995. 12.99 (*1-56063-630-0*, 490311) Editorial Unilit.

***Viaje Hacia Adentro.** Gene Edwards. 216p. (SPA.). 1995. pap. write for info. (*1-56063-533-9*) Editorial Unilit.

Viaje Historico de un Pueblo. Mendez Fernandez. 24.95 (*0-87751-003-2*) E Torres & Sons.

Viaje y Escritura: Viajeros Romanticos Chilenos. Lilianet Brintrup. LC 91-45844. (American University Studies: Romance Languages & Literature: Ser. II, Vol. 168). 274p. (C). 1992. text ed. 49.95 (*0-8204-1535-9*) P Lang Pubng.

VIAJEMOS 2001: Repaso y Progreseo. Evelyn F. Brod & Carol J. Brady. 416p. (C). 1989. text ed. 55.00 (*0-13-948670-4*) P-H.

VIAJEMOS 2001 Workbook: Repaso y Progreso. Evelyn F. Brod & Carol J. Brady. 173p. (C). 1990. pap. text ed. 23.80 (*0-13-948688-7*) P-H.

Viajes De Gulliver. (Spanish Children's Classics Ser.: No. 800-9). (SPA.). (J). 1990. boxed 3.50 (*0-7214-1403-6*, Ladybrd) Penguin.

Viajes de Gulliver. Jonathan Swift. (SPA.). 9.95 (*84-241-5631-5*) E Torres & Sons.

Viajes de Marco Polo. (SPA.). 9.95 (*84-241-5627-7*) E Torres & Sons.

Viajes de Orlando Cachumbambe. Elias M. Munoz. LC 83-81356. (Coleccion Caniqui). 143p. (Orig.). (SPA.). 1984. pap. 7.95 (*0-89729-332-0*) Ediciones.

Viajes Fantasticos. Elias M. Munoz. 1994. pap. text ed. write for info. (*0-07-044311-4*) McGraw.

Vial Judgments. Gordon Lindsay. (Revelation Ser.: Vol. 12). 1962. 1.95 (*0-89985-045-6*) Christ for the Nations.

Vial Murders. Marsha Landreth. LC 94-16398. (Doctor Samantha Turner Mystery Ser.). 1994. 19.95 (*0-8027-3199-6*) Walker & Co.

Viandier de Taillevent: Fourteenth Century Cookery. 2nd ed. James Prescott. LC 89-80811. (Illus.). 129p. 1989. 15.00 (*0-9623719-0-4*); pap. 8.00 (*0-9623719-1-2*) Alfarhaugr Pub Soc.

Vias Teoricas a Altazor de Vincete Huidobro. Pedro Lopez-Adorno. (American University Studies: Romance Languages & Literature: Ser. II, Vol. 33). 263p. 1987. text ed. 39.95 (*0-8204-0250-8*) P Lang Pubng.

Viata Familiei Crestine - Christian Family Living. John Coblenz. Ed. & Tr. by Daniel Brinzei from ENG. 272p. (SPA.). (YA). pap. text ed. write for info. (*1-885270-02-X*) Christian Aid.

Viatical Settlements Exposed! A Financial Guide for the Terminally Ill & Their Advisors. Gloria G. Wolk. (Illus.). 224p. (Orig.). Date not set. pap. 22.95 (*0-9652615-2-2*) Bialkin Bks.

Vibes of the Saints. deluxe ed. Paul Grillo. LC 76-48211. (Illus.). 1977. 20.00 (*0-916156-11-7*) Cherry Valley.

Viborita de Cascabel. Lynn Moroney & Te Ata. Tr. by Francisco X. Alarcon. (Illus.). 32p. (ENG & SPA.). (J). (gr. 2-6). 1996. pap. 6.95 (*0-89239-140-5*) Childrens Book Pr.

***Vibrant Ann Arbor.** Doris K. Kraushaar. (Illus.). 1996. pap. 11.95 (*1-886569-05-3*) J W Edwards.

Vibrant Flower Painting. Frances Treanor. (Illus.). 128p. 1995. 24.95 (*0-7153-0247-7*, Pub. by D & C Pub UK) Sterling.

***Vibrant Health from Your Kitchen.** Bernard Jensen. (Illus.). 490p. 1986. 22.00 (*0-932615-01-5*) B Jensen.

Vibrant Life: 1866-1942--Trenton's Italian Americans. Erasmo S. Ciccolella. LC 86-6828. 165p. 1986. pap. 5.00 (*0-934733-00-7*) CMS.

Vibrant Living. James Levin & Natalie Cederquist. (Illus.). 261p. 1993. pap. 14.95 (*0-9628698-2-1*) GLO Inc.

Vibrant Living: Over 250 Heart Healthy Live Food Recipes. James Levin & Natalie Cederquist. (Illus.). 264p. Date not set. pap. 16.95 (*0-89529-683-7*) Avery Pub.

Vibrating Concrete. 2nd ed. 44p. 1981. pap. 11.95 (*0-924659-11-4*, 4405) Aberdeen Group.

Vibrating Systems & Their Equivalent Circuits. Z. Skvor. (Studies in Electrical & Electronic Engineering: No. 40). 244p. 1991. 149.50 (*0-444-98806-8*) Elsevier.

Vibrating Things Make Sound. Virginia King. LC 93-114. (J). 1994. pap. write for info. (*0-383-03724-7*) SRA McGraw.

Vibrating Universe. N. C. Panda. (C). 1995. 18.00 (*81-208-1291-3*, Pub. by Motilal Banarsidass II) S Asia.

Vibration: A System of Numbers As Taught by Pythagoras. L. Dow Balliett. 80p. 1983. pap. 7.00 (*0-89540-138-X*, SB-138) Sun Pub.

Vibration: Friend or Foe? K. V. Frolov. Tr. by Alexander Repyev. 304p. 1990. 95.00 (*0-89116-699-8*) CRC Pr.

Vibration: How to Obtain Success Through the Strength of Vibration. L. Dow Balliett. 81p. 1969. reprint ed. spiral bd. 8.00 (*0-7873-1182-0*) Hlth Research.

Vibration: Non-Standard Methods. I. F. Goncharevich. 1991. 95.00 (*0-89116-957-1*) CRC Pr.

Vibration Analysis. 2nd ed. Robert K. Vierck. (C). 1978. text ed. 85.00 (*0-7002-2525-0*) Addson-Wesley Educ.

Vibration Analysis & Control System Dynamics. 2nd ed. C. F. Beards. LC 92-18183. (Ellis Horwood Series in Mechanical Engineering). 1992. 35.95 (*0-13-953332-X*, Pub. by Tavistock-E Horwood UK) Routledge Chapman & Hall.

Vibration Analysis for Electronic Equipment. 2nd ed. Dave S. Steinberg. LC 00-88. 443p. 1988. text ed. 132.00 (*0-471-63301-1*) Wiley.

Vibration Analysis Handbook. James I. Taylor. (Illus.). 360p. 1994. 125.00 (*0-9640517-0-2*) Vibrat Cnslt.

Vibration Analysis of Rotors. Chong-Won Lee. LC 93-15585. (Solid Mechanics & Its Applications Ser.: Vol. 21). 328p. (C). 1993. lib. bdg. 144.00 (*0-7923-2300-9*) Kluwer Ac.

Vibration & Behavior of Composite Structures: Presented at the Winter Annual Meeting of the American Society of Mechanical Engineers, San Francisco, California, December 10-15, 1989. American Society of Mechanical Engineers Staff. Ed. by C. Mei et al. LC 89-46375. (AD Ser.: Vol. 14). 1989. reprint ed. pap. 25.00 (*0-608-00291-7*, 2059319) Bks Demand.

Vibration & Control of Mechanical Systems. C. A. Tan & L. A. Bergman. LC 93-72637. (DE Ser.: Vol. 61). 272p. 1993. 62.50 (*0-7918-1177-8*, G00822) ASME.

Vibration & Coupling of Continuous Systems. J. Sanchez Hubert & E. Sanchez Palencia. (Illus.). 480p. 1989. 133.95 (*0-387-19384-7*) Spr-Verlag.

Vibration & Damping in Distributed Systems, I. Goong Chen & Jianxin Zhou. LC 93-19888. 464p. 1993. 91.95 (*0-8493-7161-9*) CRC Pr.

Vibration & Damping in Distributed Systems, II. Goong Chen & Jianxin Zhou. LC 93-19888. 400p. 1993. 87.00 (*0-8493-7162-7*, TA355) CRC Pr.

Vibration & Damping in Distributed Systems, Set. Goong Chen. 1993. write for info. (*0-8493-7153-8*) CRC Pr.

Vibration & Shock in Damped Mechanical Systems. John C. Snowdon. LC 68-18630. 502p. reprint ed. pap. 143.10 (*0-685-20940-7*, 2056551) Bks Demand.

Vibration & Shock Mount Handbook. Frank Buchsbaum & Ferdinand Freudenstein. (Illus.). 144p. 1984. pap. 3.75 (*0-318-01513-7*) Stock Drive.

Vibration & Shock Test Fixture Design. Wayne Tustin et al. 1971. text ed. 30.00 (*0-685-10758-2*) Tustin Tech.

Vibration & Sound. Philip M. Morse. LC 81-68618. 468p. 1981. Prepaid. 33.00 (*0-88318-287-4*) Acoustical Soc Am.

Vibration & Wear in High Speed Rotating Machinery: Proceedings of the NATO Advanced Study Institute on Vibration & Wear Damage in High Speed Rotating Machinery, Troia, Sebutal, April 10-22, 1989. Ed. by J. M. Montalvao e Silva & F. A. Pina da Silva. (C). 1990. lib. bdg. 325.50 (*0-7923-0533-7*) Kluwer Ac.

***Vibration Characteristics of Geared Transmission Systems.** N. F. Rieger. (Technical Papers). 1964. pap. text ed. 30.00 (*1-55589-372-4*) AGMA.

Vibration Control, Analysis, & Identification Vol. 19-230: Flow Noise Modeling, Measurement & Control, DE-Vol. 84-3. Ed. by R. M. Lueptow et al. (Proceedings of the 1995 ASME Design Technical Engineering Conferences Ser.: Vol. 3, Pt. C). 1516p. 1995. 420.00 (*0-7918-1720-2*, H1000C) ASME.

***Vibration Control of Active Structures: An Introduction.** Andre Preumont. LC 96-52589. (Solid Mechanics & Its Applications Ser.). 276p. (C). 1997. lib. bdg. 149.00 (*0-7923-4392-1*) Kluwer Ac.

Vibration Control of Flexible Servo Mechanisms. Ed. by J. L. Faillot. (Research Reports ESPRIT, Project 1561). vi, 212p. 1994. 39.95 (*0-387-56142-0*) Spr-Verlag.

Vibration Cooking: Or the Travel Notes of a Geechee Girl. Vertamae Smart-Grosvenor. 256p. 1992. pap. 8.00 (*0-345-37667-6*, Ballantine Trade) Ballantine.

Vibration Damping. Ahid D. Nashif et al. LC 84-17247. 453p. 1985. text ed. 99.95 (*0-471-86772-1*, Wiley-Interscience) Wiley.

Vibration Damping of Structural Elements. C. T. Sun & Y. P. Lu. LC 94-45861. 372p. (C). 1995. text ed. 89.00 (*0-13-079229-2*) P-H.

Vibration, Dynamics & Structural Systems. M. Mukhopadyay. (C). 1989. 20.00 (*81-204-0421-1*) S Asia.

Vibration Isolation, Acoustics, & Damping in Mechanical Systems. Ed. by C. D. Johnson & S. H. Shung. LC 93-72638. (DE Ser.: Vol. 62). 124p. 1993. 37.50 (*0-7918-1178-6*, G00823) ASME.

Vibration Isolators. Richard K. Miller & Marcia E. Rupnow. LC 90-83930. (Survey on Technology & Markets Ser.: No. 135). 50p. 1991. pap. text ed. 200.00 (*1-55865-160-8*) Future Tech Surveys.

***Vibration Isolators.** Richard K. Miller et al. (Market Research Survey Ser.: No. 235). 50p. 1996. 200.00 (*1-55865-266-3*) Future Tech Surveys.

Vibration Measurement. Gh. Buzdugan et al. LC 84-25523. 1986. lib. bdg. 171.00 (*90-247-3111-9*) Kluwer Ac.

Vibration Mechanics: Linear Discrete Systems. M. Del Pedro & P. Pahud. (C). 1991. lib. bdg. 145.00 (*0-7923-1427-1*) Kluwer Ac.

***Vibration Monitoring for Building Services.** Ed. by BSRIA Staff. 1995. pap. 75.00 (*0-86022-398-1*, Pub. by Build Servs Info Assn UK) St Mut.

Vibration of Bearings. K. M. Ragulskis & A. Y. Yurkauskas. (Applications of Vibration Ser.). (Illus.). 120p. 1989. 78.95 (*0-89116-829-X*) Hemisp Pub.

***Vibration of Buildings to Wind.** 1995. text ed. 174.95 (*3-540-19833-4*) Spr-Verlag.

Vibration of Buildings to Wind & Earthquakes. Thambirajah Balendra. LC 93-15460. 1995. 159.00 (*0-387-19833-4*) Spr-Verlag.

Vibration of Discrete & Continuous Systems. 2nd ed. A. A. Shabana. LC 96-12476. (Mechanical Engineering Ser.). 416p. 1996. 69.95 (*0-387-94744-2*) Spr-Verlag.

Vibration of Linear Mechanical Systems. H. McCallion. LC 73-181235. 316p. reprint ed. pap. 90.10 (*0-317-11053-5*, 2006380) Bks Demand.

Vibration of Mechanical & Structural Systems: With Microcomputer Applications. 2nd ed. Merlin L. James et al. LC 93-23119. (C). 1994. text ed. 78.75 (*0-06-501487-1*) Addson-Wesley Educ.

Vibration of Nonlinear, Random, & Time-Varying Systems Vol. 3: Vibration of Nonlinear, Random, & Time-Varying Systems, 3 pts., DE-Vol. 84-1. Ed. by S. C. Sinha et al. LC 95-80402. (Proceedings of the 1995 ASME Design Technical Engineering Conferences Ser.: Vol. 3, Pt. A). 1436p. 1995. 420.00 (*0-7918-1718-0*, H1000A) ASME.

Vibration of Plates, Vol. 1. Arthur W. Leissa. 353p. 1993. text ed. 33.00 (*1-56396-294-2*) Acoustical Soc Am.

Vibration of Rotating Systems. Ed. by K. W. Wang & D. Segalman. LC 93-72636. (DE Ser.: Vol. 60). 372p. 1993. 75.00 (*0-7918-0639-1*, G00821) ASME.

Vibration of Shells. Arthur W. Leissa. 428p. 1993. text ed. 33.00 (*1-56396-293-4*) Acoustical Soc Am.

Vibration of Steel Joist-Concrete Slab Floors. (Technical Digest Ser.: No. 5). 1988. 12.50 (*0-318-04229-0*) Steel Joist Inst.

***Vibration of Structures: Applications in Civil Engineering Design.** Smith. (Illus.). 356p. (C). (gr. 13 up). 1988. text ed. 78.95 (*0-412-28020-5*) Chapman & Hall.

Vibration of Structures & Machines: Practical Aspects. Giancarlo Genta. LC 92-29502. 1992. 83.95 (*0-387-97919-0*) Spr-Verlag.

Vibration of Structures & Machines: Practical Aspects. 2nd ed. Giancarlo Genta. LC 94-35403. 1994. 69.95 (*0-387-94403-6*) Spr-Verlag.

***Vibration Problems in Engineering.** F. C. Rushing. (Technical Papers). (Illus.). (Orig.). 1944. pap. text ed. 30.00 incl. audio compact disk (*1-55589-380-5*) AGMA.

***Vibration Problems in Engineering.** R. D. Rushing. (Technical Papers). 1944. pap. text ed. 30.00 (*1-55589-371-6*) AGMA.

Vibration Problems in Engineering. 5th ed. Stephen P. Timoshenko et al. LC 89-31896. 610p. 1990. text ed. 89.95 (*0-471-63228-7*) Wiley.

***Vibration Problems in Engineering.** 5th ed. W. Weaver et al. 1990. pap. text ed. 27.50 (*0-471-51504-3*) Wiley.

Vibration Problems in Geotechnical Engineering: Proceedings of a Symposium Sponsored by the Geotechnical Engineering Division. Ed. by George Gazetas & Ernest T. Selig. 303p. 1985. 33.00 (*0-87262-492-7*) Am Soc Civil Eng.

Vibration Problems in Structures: Practical Guidelines. Hugo Bachmann et al. LC 94-41548. 1997. 58.00 (*0-8176-5148-9*) Birkhauser.

***Vibration Problems in Structures: Practical Guidelines.** H. Bachmann. xvii, 234p. 1995. reprint ed. 58.00 (*3-7643-5148-9*) Birkhauser.

Vibration Problems Solved in BASIC. 1988. 45.00 (*0-685-24856-9*, 92-1-B); disk 25.00 (*0-685-24857-7*, 92-1-ID) Kern Intl.

Vibration Protecting & Measuring Systems with Quasi-Zero Stiffness. P. Alabuzhev et al. (Applications of Vibration Ser.). 100p. 1989. 68.95 (*0-89116-811-7*) Hemisp Pub.

Vibration Sensors & Analyzers. Richard K. Miller & Terri C. Walker. LC 88-81666. (Survey on Technology & Markets Ser.: No. 75). 50p. 1989. pap. text ed. 200.00 (*1-55865-074-1*) Future Tech Surveys.

Vibration, Shock, Damage, & Identification of Mechanical Systems. Ed. by D. Carne et al. LC 93-72640. (DE Ser.: Vol. 64). 124p. 1993. 37.50 (*0-7918-1180-8*, G00825) ASME.

Vibration Spectrum Analysis: Basic Problem Solving. Steve Goldman. 280p. 1990. 39.95 (*0-8311-3027-X*) Indus Pr.

Vibration Technology. Frolov. 1991. 104.00 (*0-8493-7535-5*, TA535) CRC Pr.

Vibration Testing: Theory & Practice. Kenneth G. McConnell. LC 95-16398. 624p. 1995. text ed. 89.95 (*0-471-30435-2*) Wiley.

Vibration Testing--Instrumentation & Data Analysis: Presented at ASME - DED Vibrations Conference. DED Vibrations Conference Staff ASME. Ed. by Edward B. Magrab & Osman A. Shinaishin. LC 75-8349. (American Society of Mechanical Engineers Handbook: Vol. 12). (Illus.). 148p. reprint ed. pap. 42.20 (*0-317-09976-0*, 2015395) Bks Demand.

Vibration Testing of Machines & Their Maintenance. G. Lipovszky et al. (Studies in Mechanical Engineering: No. 10). 312p. 1990. 189.50 (*0-444-98808-4*) Elsevier.

Vibration the Law of Life. W. H. Williams. 80p. 1959. reprint ed. spiral bd. 10.50 (*0-7873-0971-0*) Hlth Research.

***Vibrational Intensities.** Ed. by B. S. Galabov & T. Dudev. 342p. 1996. 240.75 (*0-444-81497-3*) Elsevier.

Vibrational Medicine: New Choices for Healing Ourselves. rev. ed. Richard Gerber. 600p. (Orig.). 1996. pap. text ed. 18.00 (*1-879181-28-2*) Bear & Co.

***Vibrational Medicine Cards: The Sacred Geometry of the Self.** Rowena P. Kryder. (Illus.). 192p. (Orig.). 1997. boxed, pap. 44.00 (*0-9624716-5-8*) Golden Point Prod.

Vibrational-Rotational Spectroscopy & Molecular Dynamics. Dusan Popousek. (Advanced Series in Physical Chemistry). 500p. 1997. text ed. 95.00 (*981-02-1635-1*) World Scientific Pub.

Vibrational Spectra: Principles, Applications & Molecular Structure. P. L. Polavarapu. (Studies in Physical & Theoretical Chemistry). 1996. text ed. write for info. (*0-444-89599-X*) Elsevier.

Vibrational Spectra & Structure, 21. Ed. by J. R. Durig. 466p. 1995. 294.50 (*0-444-82295-X*) Elsevier.

Vibrational Spectra & Structure, Vol. 1. Ed. by James R. Durig. 208p. reprint ed. pap. 59.30 (*0-317-08365-1*, 2055083) Bks Demand.

Vibrational Spectra & Structure, 2 vols., Vol. 2. Ed. by James R. Durig. LC 72-87850. (Illus.). 431p. reprint ed. pap. 116.40 (*0-7837-0855-6*, 2041164) Bks Demand.

Vibrational Spectra & Structure, 2 vols., Vol. 3. Ed. by James R. Durig. LC 72-87850. (Illus.). 342p. reprint ed. pap. 97.50 (*0-7837-0856-4*) Bks Demand.

Vibrational Spectra & Structure, Vol. 19: A Series of Advances. Ed. by James R. Durig. 522p. 1991. 351.25 (*0-444-89027-0*) Elsevier.

Vibrational Spectra & Structures: A Series of Advances, Vol. 20. Ed. by James R. Durig. 352p. 1992. 272.25 (*0-444-89865-4*) Elsevier.

Vibrational Spectra of Organometallic Compounds. Edward Maslowsky. LC 76-18694. (Illus.). 542p. reprint ed. pap. 154.50 (*0-317-09212-X*, 2013117) Bks Demand.

Vibrational Spectroscopies for Absorbed Species. Ed. by Alexis T. Bell & Michael L. Hair. LC 80-21181. (ACS Symposium Ser.: No. 137). 1980. 37.95 (*0-8412-0585-X*) Am Chemical.

***Vibrational Spectroscopies for Adsorbed Species.** Ed. by Alexis T. Bell & Michael L. Hair. LC 80-21181. (ACS Symposium Ser.: No. 137). (Illus.). 303p. 1980. reprint ed. pap. 86.40 (*0-608-03225-5*, 2063744) Bks Demand.

Vibrational Spectroscopy at Surfaces: Infrared & Raman Spectroscopy in Electrochemistry. Martin Fleischman et al. (Illus.). 363p. (C). 1988. 49.95 (*0-9618927-2-2*) Datatech Systems.

Vibrational Spectroscopy of Adsorbates. Ed. by R. F. Willis. (Chemical Physics Ser.: Vol. 15). (Illus.). 184p. 1980. 38.95 (*0-387-10429-1*) Spr-Verlag.

Vibrational Spectroscopy of Molecules & Macromolecules on Surfaces. Marek W. Urban. LC 93-18560. (Society of Plastics Engineers Monographs). 384p. 1994. Acid-free paper. text ed. 59.95 (*0-471-52815-3*) Wiley.

Vibrational Spectroscopy of Molecules on Surfaces. Ed. by J. T. Yates & T. E. Madey. LC 87-14115. (Methods of Surface Characterization Ser.: Vol. 1). (Illus.). 484p. 1987. 110.00 (*0-306-42505-X*, Plenum Pr) Plenum.

Vibrational Spectroscopy of Polymers. D. I. Bower & W. F. Maddams. (Cambridge Solid State Science Ser.). (Illus.). 300p. 1989. text ed. 120.00 (*0-521-24633-4*) Cambridge U Pr.

Vibrational Spectroscopy of Polymers. D. I. Bower & W. F. Maddams. (Cambridge Solid State Science Ser.). (Illus.). 326p. (C). 1992. pap. text ed. 42.95 (*0-521-42195-0*) Cambridge U Pr.

Vibrational Spectroscopy of Trapped Species: Infrared & Raman Studies of Matrix-Isolated Molecules, Radicals & Ions. Ed. by Harry E. Hallam. LC 72-8601. 442p. reprint ed. pap. 126.00 (*0-317-26652-7*, 2024035) Bks Demand.

Vibrational States. S. Califano. LC 75-19268. 347p. reprint ed. pap. 98.90 (*0-685-20702-1*, 2030486) Bks Demand.

Vibrations: Healing Through Color, Homeopathy & Radionics. Virginia MacIvor & Sandra LaForest. 196p. 1979. pap. 9.95 (*0-87728-393-1*) Weiser.

An Asterisk (*) at the beginning of an entry indicates that the title is appearing in BIP for the first time.

Vibrations: The Adventures & Musical Times of David Amram. David W. Amram. LC 79-24422. (Illus.). 469p. 1980. reprint ed. text ed. 65.00 (*0-313-22230-4*, AMVI, Greenwood Pr) Greenwood.

Vibrations - Poems. Aditya Damodaran. (C). 1992. text ed. 10.00 (*81-220-0267-6*, Pub. by Konark Pubs Pvt Ltd II) Advent Bks Div.

Vibrations & Audible Noise in Alternating Current Machines. Ed. by R. Belmans et al. (C). 1988. lib. bdg. 234.00 (*90-247-3732-X*) Kluwer Ac.

Vibrations & Dynamics of Robotic & Multibody Structures. Mo Shahinpoor. LC 93-72633. (DE Ser.: Vol. 57). 132p. 1993. 45.00 (*0-7918-1174-3*, G00818) ASME.

Vibrations & Impedences of Rectangular Plates with Free Boundaries. P. Hagedorn et al. (Lecture Notes in Engineering Ser.: Vol. 23). 160p. 1986. pap. 23.00 (*0-387-17043-X*) Spr-Verlag.

***Vibrations & Stability: Order & Chaos.** Jon J. Thomsen. LC 97-9509. 1997. pap. write for info. (*0-07-709362-3*) McGraw.

Vibrations & Stability of Multiple Parameter System. Koncay Huseyin. (Mechanics of Elastic Stability Ser.: No. 3). 228p. 1978. lib. bdg. 117.00 (*90-286-0136-8*) Kluwer Ac.

***Vibrations & Waves.** French. (MIT Introductory Physics Ser.). (Illus.). 328p. (Orig.). (C). (gr. 13 up). 1990. pap. text ed. 37.50 (*0-412-38460-4*, Chap & Hall NY) Chapman & Hall.

Vibrations & Waves. A. P. French. (M.I.T. Introductory Physics Ser.). (Illus.). (C). 1971. pap. text ed. 18.95 (*0-393-09936-9*) Norton.

Vibrations & Waves. Gough & Richards. 1991. pap. text ed. write for info. (*0-318-68772-0*) P-H.

***Vibrations & Waves.** S. Kaliski & L. Solarz. (Studies in Applied Mechanics: Vol. 30). 382p. 1992. 413.00 (*0-444-98855-6*) Elsevier.

Vibrations & Waves. 2nd ed. R. P. Williams et al. LC 95-18274. 288p. (C). 1995. pap. text ed. 41.00 (*0-13-451113-1*) P-H.

Vibrations & Waves in Physics. 3rd ed. Iain G. Main. LC 92-33323. (Illus.). 379p. (C). 1993. pap. text ed. 30.95 (*0-521-44701-1*) Cambridge U Pr.

Vibrations & Waves in Physics. 3rd ed. Iain G. Main. LC 92-33323. (Illus.). 379p. (C). 1993. text ed. 85.00 (*0-521-44186-2*) Cambridge U Pr.

Vibrations for Engineers. 2nd ed. Andrew D. Dimarogonas. LC 95-34189. 1996. text ed. 85.00 (*0-13-456229-1*) P-H.

Vibrations from a Gull's Wing. Mary E. Works. 36p. (Orig.). 1990. pap. 6.50 (*0-9623452-3-7*) Oregon Coast Cmnty Col.

Vibrations from Blasting Rock. Lewis D. Leet. LC 60-10037. 150p. reprint ed. 42.80 (*0-8357-9183-1*, 2017747) Bks Demand.

Vibrations in Mechanical Systems. M. Roseau. (Illus.). 530p. 1987. 129.00 (*0-387-17950-X*) Spr-Verlag.

Vibrations in Time. David Watmough. 130p. 19.95 (*0-88962-340-6*); pap. 9.95 (*0-88962-339-2*) Mosaic.

Vibrations of Bladed Disk Assemblies. Ed. by D. J. Ewins & A. V. Srinivasan. 1983. pap. text ed. 10.00 (*0-317-02660-7*, G00235) ASME.

Vibrations of Concrete Structures. Symposium on Vibrations of Concrete Structures Staff. LC 79-84810. (American Concrete Institute Publication Ser.: No. SP-60). (Illus.). 306p. reprint ed. pap. 87.30 (*0-7837-6669-6*, 2046285) Bks Demand.

Vibrations of Elastic Plates: Linear & Nonlinear Dynamical Modeling of Sandwiches, Laminated Composites, & Piezoelectric Layers. Yi-Yuan Yu. Ed. by F. F. Ling. LC 95-8375. (Mechanical Engineering Ser.). (Illus.). 224p. 1996. 59.95 (*0-387-94514-8*) Spr-Verlag.

Vibrations of Mechanical Systems & the History of Mechanical Design. Ed. by R. Echempati et al. LC 93-72639. (DE Ser.: Vol. 63). 156p. 1993. 55.00 (*0-7918-1179-4*, G00824) ASME.

Vibrations of My Life. Dennis Hassell. 128p. (C). 1988. 35.00 (*0-7212-0718-9*, Pub. by Regency Press UK) St Mut.

Vibrations of Shells & Plates. 2nd ed. Soedel. (Mechanical Engineering Ser.: Vol. 86). 496p. 1993. 165.00 (*0-8247-9035-9*) Dekker.

***Vibrations of Tubes in Heat Exchangers.** Vladislavas Katinas & A. A. Zhukauskas. LC 96-45098. 1996. write for info. (*1-56700-077-0*) Begell Hse.

Vibrato. Ed. by P. H. Dejonckere et al. LC 95-24542. 128p. 1995. pap. 34.95 (*1-56593-146-7*, 1242) Singular Publishing.

Vibratory Compacting: Principles & Methods. Ed. by Henry H. Hausner et al. LC 65-24898. (Perspectives in Powder Metallurgy: Fundamentals, Methods, & Applications Ser.: Vol. 2). (Illus.). 312p. reprint ed. pap. 89.00 (*0-317-08350-3*, 2019458) Bks Demand.

Vibrio Cholerae & Cholera: A New Perspective on a Resurgent Disease. Ed. by I. Kaye Wachsmuth et al. LC 93-39024. (Illus.). 400p. 1994. text ed. 72.00 (*1-55581-067-5*) Am Soc Microbio.

Vibro-Acoustic Characterization of Materials & Structures. Ed. by P. K. Raju. (NCA Ser.: Vol. 14). 242p. 1992. 57.50 (*0-7918-1125-5*, G00769) ASME.

Vibroacoustic Condition Monitoring. Czeslaw Cempel. 250p. 1991. text ed. write for info. (*0-13-931718-X*) P-H.

Vibroacoustical Diagnostics for Machines & Structures. M. F. Dimentberg et al. LC 90-29896. (Mechanical Engineering Research Studies: Engineering Dynamics). 148p. 1991. text ed. 128.00 (*0-471-93004-0*) Wiley.

Vibromotors for Precision Microrobots. K. M. Ragulskis et al. (Applications of Vibration Ser.). 400p. 1988. 120.00 (*0-89116-549-5*) Hemisp Pub.

Vibronic Coupling. Gad Fischer. (Theoretical Chemistry Ser.). 1984. text ed. 119.00 (*0-12-257240-8*) Acad Pr.

Vibronic Interactions in Molecules & Crystals. I. B. Bersuker & V. Z. Polinger. (Chemical Physics Ser.: Vol. 49). (Illus.). 435p. 1989. 130.95 (*0-387-19259-X*) Spr-Verlag.

Vibronic Processes in Inorganic Chemistry. Ed. by Colin D. Flint. (C). 1989. lib. bdg. 181.00 (*0-7923-0436-5*) Kluwer Ac.

***Vibroplex Collector's Guide.** 2nd rev. ed. Tom French. LC 96-85882. (Illus.). 130p. 1996. pap. 19.95 (*1-890024-04-X*, VCG) Artifax Bks.

Vibroseis. Ed. by Robert L. Geyer. LC 89-63262. (Geophysics Reprint Ser.: No. 11). 856p. 1989. pap. 44.00 (*0-931830-90-7*, 471) Soc Expl Geophys.

Vibroseis Source. Anton Ziolkowski. (Advances in Exploration Geophysics Ser.: No. 3). 300p. 1990. 150.75 (*0-444-88879-9*) Elsevier.

Vibs & T-Jets, Vol. 1. Kevin Timothy. Ed. by Joanne Collison. (Collector's Quick Reference Ser.: 1). (Illus.). 100p. (Orig.). 1994. pap. text ed. 14.95 (*1-883796-04-0*) What It Is.

Vic & Blood: The Chronicles of a Boy & His Dog. limited ed. Harlan Ellison. Ed. by Jan Strnad. (Illus.). 120p. 1988. 40.00 (*0-89865-605-2*, Starblaze) Donning Co.

***Vic Braden's Laugh & Win at Doubles.** Vic Braden & Bill Bruns. 1997. pap. 13.95 (*0-316-10505-8*) Little.

Vic Braden's Mental Tennis: How to Psyche Yourself to a Winning Team. Vic Braden. 1994. pap. 12.95 (*0-316-10517-1*) Little.

Vic Braden's Quick Fixes: Expert Cures for Common Tennis Problems. Vic Braden & Bill Bruns. LC 87-26099. (Illus.). 224p. 1988. 17.95 (*0-316-10514-7*) Little.

Vic Braden's Quick Fixes: Expert Cures for Common Tennis Problems. Vic Braden. 1990. pap. 14.95 (*0-316-10515-5*) Little.

Vic Braden's Tennis for the Future. Vic Braden & Bill Bruns. 1980. 24.95 (*0-316-10510-4*) Little.

Vic Dunaway's Complete Book of Baits, Rigs & Tackle. Vic Dunaway. 1989. pap. 8.95 (*0-936240-12-1*) Wickstrom.

Vic Dunaway's Complete Book of Baits, Rigs & Tackle. 6th rev. ed. Vic Dunaway. (Illus.). 224p. 1984. reprint ed. pap. 6.95 (*0-936240-02-4*) Wickstrom.

Vic Knight's Florida. Victor M. Knight. LC 93-15569. (Illus.). 240p. 1993. 16.95 (*0-88289-964-3*) Pelican.

Vic the Vampire, No. 1: School Ghoul. Hanya Bloom. 80p. (J). (gr. 4-7). 1990. mass mkt. 2.95 (*0-06-106004-6*, Harp PBks) HarpC.

VIC-20, Vol. 1. Robin Buxton. (Thinking-Learning-Creating: TLC for Growing Minds Ser.). 51p. (J). (gr. 4-12). 1983. pap. text ed. 11.95 (*0-88193-061-X*) Create Learn.

VIC-20, Vol. 2. Robin Buxton. (Thinking-Learning-Creating: TLC for Growing Minds Ser.). 59p. (J). (gr. 4-12). 1983. pap. text ed. 11.95 (*0-88193-062-8*) Create Learn.

VIC-20, Vol. 3. Robin Buxton. (Thinking-Learning-Creating: TLC for Growing Minds Ser.). 59p. (J). (gr. 5-12). 1983. pap. text ed. 11.95 (*0-88193-063-6*) Create Learn.

VIC-20, Vol. 4. Marilyn Buxton & Robin Buxton. (Thinking-Learning-Creating: TLC for Growing Minds Ser.). 63p. (J). (gr. 5-12). 1983. pap. text ed. 11.95 (*0-88193-064-4*) Create Learn.

VIC-20 & Commodore 64 Computer Program Writing Workbook. Howard Adler. 96p. 1983. 4.95 (*0-86668-811-0*) ARCsoft.

VIC-20 BASIC Made Easy. David A. Gardner & Marianne L. Gardner. (Illus.). 256p. 1984. pap. text ed. 23.95 (*0-13-941972-1*) P-H.

VIC-20 Computer Graphics Toolbox. Russell L. Schnapp & Irvin G. Stafford. (Personal Computing Ser.). (Illus.). 176p. 1984. 29.95 (*0-13-942012-6*); pap. text ed. 14.95 (*0-13-941998-5*); audio 14.95 (*0-13-942004-5*) P-H.

Vica Done It. large type ed. Freda Bream. 1990. pap. 15.99 (*0-7089-6904-6*, Trailtree Bookshop) Ulverscroft.

Vicar Investigates. large type ed. Freda Bream. (Linford Mystery Library). 1990. pap. 15.99 (*0-7089-6849-X*) Ulverscroft.

Vicar of Bullhampton. Anthony Trollope. Ed. by David Skilton. (World's Classics Ser.). 574p. 1988. pap. 9.95 (*0-19-282163-6*) OUP.

Vicar of Nibbleswicke. Roald Dahl. (Illus.). 48p. (J). (gr. 5 up). 1994. pap. 4.99 (*0-14-036837-X*) Puffin Bks.

Vicar of Nibbleswicke. Roald Dahl. (Illus.). 24p. (J). 1992. pap. 12.50 (*0-670-84384-9*) Viking Child Bks.

Vicar of Sorrows. A. N. Wilson. 384p. 1994. 23.00 (*0-393-03610-3*) Norton.

Vicar of Sorrows: A Novel. A. N. Wilson. 400p. 1995. pap. 12.00 (*0-393-31294-1*, Norton Paperbks) Norton.

Vicar of Wakefield. Oliver Goldsmith. (Airmont Classics Ser.). (YA). (gr. 10 up). 1964. mass mkt. 1.25 (*0-8049-0052-3*, CL-52) Airmont.

Vicar of Wakefield. Oliver Goldsmith. 1976. 20.95 (*0-8488-0507-0*) Amereon Ltd.

Vicar of Wakefield. Oliver Goldsmith. pap. 2.95 (*0-451-52252-4*, CE1723, Sig Classics) NAL-Dutton.

Vicar of Wakefield. Oliver Goldsmith. Ed. & Intro. by Stephen Coote. 224p. 1982. pap. 6.95 (*0-14-043159-4*, Penguin Classics) Viking Penguin.

Vicar of Wakefield. Oliver Goldsmith. Ed. by Arthur Friedman. (World's Classics Paperback Ser.). 232p. 1982. pap. 5.95 (*0-19-281560-1*) OUP.

Vicar of Wakefield. large type ed. Oliver Goldsmith. (Clear Type Classics Ser.). 176p. 1993. 18.95 (*1-85695-330-0*, Pub. by ISIS UK) Transaction Pubs.

Vicar of Wakefield. Oliver Goldsmith. 1982. reprint ed. lib. bdg. 19.95 (*0-89966-373-7*) Buccaneer Bks.

Vicar of Wrexhill. Frances M. Trollope. (Pocket Classics Ser.). 368p. 1996. pap. 12.95 (*0-7509-1156-5*, Pub. by Sutton Pubng UK) Bks Intl VA.

Vicarious Humanity of Christ & the Reality of Salvation. Christian D. Kettler. 338p. (C). 1991. pap. text ed. 29.50 (*0-8191-8273-7*); lib. bdg. 56.50 (*0-8191-8272-9*) U Pr of Amer.

Vicarious Image. Wanda Castle. Ed. by Steve Ingraham. 108p. (Orig.). 1985. pap. 1.45 (*0-916835-00-6*, 600) C & I Pubns.

Vicarious Liability or Liability for the Acts of Others. J. B. Hodge. 48p. 1986. 68.00 (*0-948691-00-X*, Pub. by Witherby & Co UK) St Mut.

Vicarious Thrills: Reflections on a Championship Season of High School Basketball. Paul E. Bates. LC 94-22660. (Illus.). 225p. (C). 1995. 34.95 (*0-8093-1978-0*); pap. 14.95 (*0-8093-1979-9*) S Ill U Pr.

***Vicar's Daughter.** Betty Neels. (Harlequin Ser.). 1997. 20.95 (*0-263-15008-9*, Pub. by Mills & Boon UK) Thorndike Pr.

Vicar's Daughter. Deborah Simmons. (Historical Ser.). 1995. pap. 4.50 (*0-373-28858-1*, 1-28858-8) Harlequin Bks.

Vicar's Daughter. George MacDonald. (George MacDonald Original Works: Series II). 389p. 1992. reprint ed. 16.00 (*1-881084-09-4*) Johannesen.

Vicar's Girl. 1992. mass mkt. 5.95 (*1-56201-026-3*, 122) Blue Moon Bks.

Vice. Jane Feather. 432p. 1996. mass mkt. 5.99 (*0-553-57249-0*, Fanfare) Bantam.

Vice. Carla Harryman. 104p. (Orig.). 1987. pap. 7.50 (*0-937013-16-1*) Potes Poets.

Vice & Virtue in Everyday Life. 3rd ed. Christina H. Sommers. LC 92-71052. 850p. (C). 1993. pap. text ed. 26.75 (*0-15-500375-5*) HB Coll Pubs.

Vice & Virtue in Everyday Life: Introductory Readings in Ethics. 4th ed. Christina H. Sommers. 944p. (C). 1996. pap. text ed. 35.00 (*0-15-503039-6*) HB Coll Pubs.

Vice Chamberlain Coke's Theatrical Papers, 1706-1715. Ed. by Judith Milhous & Robert D. Hume. LC 81-5616. 319p. 1982. 29.95 (*0-8093-1024-4*) S Ill U Pr.

Vice-Consul. Marguerite Duras. (Imaginaire Ser.). 216p. (FRE.). 1965. 11.95 (*2-07-029844-2*) Schoenhof.

Vice Cop. Bill McCarthy & Mike Mallowe. 352p. 1993. mass mkt. 5.99 (*0-8217-4025-3*, Zebra Kensgtn) Kensgtn Pub Corp.

Vice in Chicago. Walter C. Reckless. LC 69-16243. (Criminology, Law Enforcement, & Social Problems Ser.: No. 84). 1969. reprint ed. 18.00 (*0-87585-084-7*) Patterson Smith.

Vice Lords Fieldwork: Warriors of the Streets, Fieldwork Edition. Keiser. 129p. (C). 1979. pap. write for info. (*0-03-045396-8*) HB Coll Pubs.

Vice of Wedlock: The Theme of Marriage in George Gissing's Novels. Christian Sjoholm. (Studia Anglistica Upsaliensia Ser.: No. 85). 144p. (Orig.). 1994. pap. 38.50 (*91-554-3258-1*) Coronet Bks.

Vice Park Place. (Orig.). 1992. mass mkt. 4.95 (*1-56333-008-3*) Masquerade.

Vice-President As Policy Maker: Rockefeller in the Ford White House. Michael Turner. LC 81-20301. (Contributions in Political Science Ser.: No. 78). xvii, 252p. 1982. text ed. 55.00 (*0-313-23229-6*, TUV/, Greenwood Pr) Greenwood.

Vice-Presidential Power: Advice & Influence in the White House. Paul C. Light. LC 83-48050. 288p. 1983. text ed. 45.00 (*0-8018-3058-3*) Johns Hopkins.

***Vice Presidents: A Biographical Dictionary.** L. Edward Purcell. LC 97-9164. 1997. 50.00 (*0-8160-3109-6*) Facts on File.

Vice Presidents: Biographies of the 45 Men Who Have Held the Second Highest Office in the United States. Carole C. Waldrup. LC 96-30538. (Illus.). 279p. 1996. lib. bdg. 35.00 (*0-7864-0179-6*) McFarland & Co.

Vice-Presidents & Their Wives. George E. Ross & Barbara Novack. 1975. pap. 4.95 (*0-89036-052-9*) Hawkes Pub Inc.

Vice Unmasked: An Essay Being a Consideration of the Influence of Law upon the Moral Essence of Man, with Other Reflections. P. W. Grayson. viii, 168p. 1996. reprint ed. lib. bdg. 32.50 (*0-8377-2215-2*) Rothman.

Vice Versa. Marjorie Garber. (Illus.). 608p. 1996. pap. 18.00 (*0-684-82412-4*, Touchstone Bks) S&S Trade.

Vice-Versa. James E. Reveley. 128p. 7.95 (*0-89015-884-3*) Sunbelt Media.

Vice Versa: Bisexuality & the Eroticism of Everyday Life. Marjorie Garber. (Illus.). 606p. 1995. 30.00 (*0-684-80308-9*) S&S Trade.

Vicente Aleixandre. Kessel Schwartz. LC 79-79209. (Twayne's World Authors Ser.). 1970. pap. text ed. 4.95 (*0-8290-2047-0*); lib. bdg. 17.95 (*0-8057-2024-3*) Irvington.

Vicente Aleixandre: A Critical Appraisal. Ed. by Santiago Daydi-Tolson. LC 81-65036. (Studies in Literary Analysis). 330p. (C). 1981. pap. text ed. 20.00 (*0-916950-20-4*); lib. bdg. 30.00 (*0-916950-21-2*) Biling Rev-Pr.

***Vicente Blasco Ibanez: Color Symbolism in Slected Novels.** Jeffrey Oxford. (American University Studies II: No. 223). 112p. (C). 1997. text ed. 29.95 (*0-8204-3358-6*) P Lang Pubng.

Vicente Espinel & Marcos de Obregon: A Life & Its Literary Representation. George Haley. LC 59-12056. (Brown University Studies). 270p. reprint ed. 77.00 (*0-685-15654-0*, 2027506) Bks Demand.

Vicente Lenero: The Novelist As Critic. Danny J. Anderson. (University of Texas Studies in Contemporary Spanish-American Fiction: Vol. 3). 281p. (C). 1989. text ed. 40.95 (*0-8204-0937-5*) P Lang Pubng.

Viceroyalty of New Spain & Early Independent Mexico: A Guide to Original Manuscripts in the Collections of the Rosenbach Museum & Library. Ed. by David M. Szewczyk. LC 81-180741. (Illus.). 144p. 1981. 15.00 (*0-939084-00-7*, U Pr of Va) R Mus & Lib.

Viceroys & Governors-General of India, 1757-1947. Clive B. Mersey. LC 70-160925. (Biography Index Reprint Ser.). 1977. reprint ed. 21.95 (*0-8369-8088-3*) Ayer.

Vices. Lola Guymon. (Ryall Ser.). 246p. 1991. pap. 8.95 (*0-9633935-1-0*) Rocket Pr WY.

Vices & Virtues, Pt. I. Ed. by F. Holthausen. (EETS, OS Ser.: Vol. 89). 1974. reprint ed. 20.00 (*0-8115-3364-6*) Periodicals Srv.

Vices & Virtues, Pt. 2. Ed. by F. Holthausen. (EETS, OS Ser.: Vol. 159). 1974. reprint ed. pap. 20.00 (*0-8115-3373-5*) Periodicals Srv.

Vices & Virtues Vol. I: Text & Translation from BMMS. Stowe 240, Vol. I. Ed. by F. Holthausen. (EETS Original Ser.: Vol. 89). 1967. reprint ed. 20.00 (*0-19-722260-9*, Pub. by EETS UK) Boydell & Brewer.

Vices & Virtues Vol. II: From British Museum MS. Stowe 240 Notes & Glossary, Vol. II. Ed. by F. Holthausen. (EETS Original Ser.: Vol. 159). 1963. reprint ed. pap. 20.00 (*0-19-722159-9*, Pub. by EETS UK) Boydell & Brewer.

***Vices of Economists: The Virtues of the Bourgeoisie.** Dierdre McCloskey. (C). 1997. 22.95 (*90-5356-244-3*, Pub. by Amsterdam U Pr NE) U of Mich Pr.

Vicharsagar: The Metaphysics of the Upanisads. Lala Shreeram. 448p. 1994. 42.50 (*81-215-0654-9*, Pub. by M Manoharial II) Coronet Bks.

Vichy France: Old Guard & New Order, 1940-1944. Robert O. Paxton. LC 81-15221. (Morningside Bk.). 424p. 1982. reprint ed. text ed. 59.50 (*0-231-05426-2*); reprint ed. pap. text ed. 18.00 (*0-231-05427-0*) Col U Pr.

Vichy France & the Jews. Michael R. Marrus & Robert O. Paxton. 448p. 1995. pap. 17.95 (*0-8047-2499-7*) Stanford U Pr.

Vichy Law & the Holocaust in France. Richard Weisberg. LC 95-25844. 447p. (C). 1996. 45.00 (*0-8147-9302-9*) NYU Pr.

***Vichy Law & the Holocaust in France.** Richard Weisberg. (Studies in Antisemitism: Vol. 3). 472p. 1997. 49.00 (*0-614-26655-6*, ECU41, Harwood Acad Pubs) Gordon & Breach.

***Vichy Law & the Holocaust in France.** Richard Weisberg. (Studies in Antisemitism). 1997. text ed. 49.00 (*3-7186-5892-5*, Harwood Acad Pubs) Gordon & Breach.

Vichy Syndrome: History & Memory in France since 1914. Henry Rousso. 384p. (C). 1994. pap. text ed. 15.95 (*0-674-93539-X*) HUP.

Vichy Syndrome: History & Memory in France since 1944. Henry Rousso. Tr. by Arthur Goldhammer. 384p. (C). 1991. 42.50 (*0-674-93538-1*) HUP.

Vicinal Heteroaromatic Hydroxy, Mercapto & Hydroseleno, Vol. 11. V. Litvinov. (Sulfur Reports). 389p. 1992. pap. text ed. 275.00 (*3-7186-5271-4*, Harwood Acad Pubs) Gordon & Breach.

Vicinal Water. J. A. Schufle. 130p. (C). 1989. 29.95 (*0-945407-01-7*) Meadow Pr NM.

Vicious Circle. large type ed. Alan Evans. (Linford Mystery Library). 280p. 1988. pap. 15.99 (*0-7089-6568-7*, Linford) Ulverscroft.

Vicious Circle of External Debt Servicing. Alvaro Cencini & Bernard Schmitt. 1991. text ed. 59.00 (*0-86187-185-5*) St Martin.

Vicious Circle Phenomenon: Our Battle for Self-Control - How to Win the War. Phyllis D. Brister & David M. Brister. LC 87-15434. (Illus.). 304p. (C). 1987. 19.95 (*0-939977-69-9*) Diadem Pub.

Vicious Circles. Maurice Blanchot. Tr. by Paul Auster from FRE. LC 84-8437. Orig. Title: Le Ressassement Eternel. 80p. (Orig.). 1985. 13.95 (*0-930794-98-2*); pap. 7.95 (*0-930794-97-4*) Station Hill Pr.

Vicious Circles: On the Mathematics of Non-Wellfounded Phenomena. Jon Barwise & Lawrence S. Moss. (Lecture Notes Ser.). 350p. (C). 1996. 64.95 (*1-57586-009-0*); pap. 24.95 (*1-57586-008-2*) CSLI.

Vicious Habits. Arlene S. Skolnick. Date not set. 25.00 (*0-02-929315-4*, Free Press) Free Pr.

Vicious Lies & Heinous Slander. Tami Knight. (Illus.). 32p. 1992. pap. 5.50 (*0-89732-115-4*) Menasha Ridge.

Vicious Modernism: Black Harlem & the Literary Imagination. James L. De Jongh. (Illus.). 256p. (C). 1990. text ed. 44.95 (*0-521-32620-6*) Cambridge U Pr.

Vicissitudes of the I: An Introduction to the Philosophy of the Mind. Hollibert E. Phillips. LC 94-4967. 176p. 1994. pap. text ed. 25.60 (*0-13-108721-5*) P-H.

Vicitrakarnika-Vadanoddhrta: A Collection of Buddhistic Legends. Ed. by Hans Jorgensen. LC 78-70134. reprint ed. 34.50 (*0-404-17404-3*) AMS Pr.

Vicki! The True - Life Adventures of Miss Fireball. Lawrence. 1995. 23.00 (*0-671-89204-5*) S&S Trade.

Vicki! The True-Life Adventures of Miss Fireball. Vicki Lawrence & Marc Eliot. LC 94-46710. (Illus.). 237p. 1995. 23.00 (*0-684-80286-4*) S&S Trade.

Vicki Lansky's Divorce Book for Parents: Helping Your Children Cope with Divorce & Its Aftermath. 3rd rev. ed. Vicki Lansky. 240p. 1996. pap. 5.99 (*0-916773-48-5*) Book Peddlers.

***Vicksburg.** Time Life-Books Staff. LC 97-25385. (Voices of the Civil War Ser.). 1997. write for info. (*0-7835-4713-7*) Time-Life.

Vicksburg: Southern City Under Siege. William L. Foster. Ed. by Kenneth T. Urquhart. LC 80-84685. (Illus.). xxvi, 82p. 1980. pap. text ed. 7.95 (*0-917860-12-8*) Historic New Orleans.

Vicksburg: 47 Days of Siege. Adolph A. Hoehling. (Illus.). 400p. 1995. pap. 16.95 (*0-8117-2980-X*) Stackpole.

***Vicksburg & the Opening of the Mississippi River, 1862-63.** 1997. lib. bdg. 250.95 (*0-8490-6143-1*) Gordon Pr.

Vicksburg Campaign, 3 vols., Set. Edwin C. Bearss. (Illus.). 2219p. 1991. 125.00 (*0-89029-308-2*) Morningside Bkshop.

Vicksburg Campaign, Vol. I. Edwin C. Bearss. (Illus.). 769p. 1991. 42.50 (*0-89029-312-0*) Morningside Bkshop.

Vicksburg Campaign, Vol. II. Edwin C. Bearss. (Illus.). 689p. 1991. 42.50 (*0-89029-313-9*) Morningside Bkshop.

UV

An Asterisk (*) at the beginning of an entry indicates that the title is appearing in BIP for the first time.

Vicksburg Campaign, Vol. III. Edwin C. Bearss. (Illus.). 761p. 1991. 42.50 (0-89029-516-6) Morningside Bkshop.
Vicksburg Campaign: April 1862-July 1863. rev. ed. David G. Martin. (Illus.). 256p. 1994. 22.95 (0-938289-37-3, 7328) Combined Pub.
Vicksburg 1863. Alan Hankinson. (Campaign Ser.). (Illus.). 96p. 1993. pap. 14.95 (1-85532-353-2, 9525, Pub. by Osprey UK) Stackpole.
Vicky: God's Angel in Our Midst. Barbara Dan. Orig. Title: Vicky: The Death of Our Baby. 64p. (Orig.). 1996. reprint ed. per., pap. 5.95 (1-884898-10-6) Eden Pubng NV.
Vicky: The Death of Our Baby see Vicky: God's Angel in Our Midst
Vicky's New Hat. (Tales of Oaktree Wood Ser.). (J). 1989. 2.99 (0-517-69124-8) Random Hse Value.
Vico. Robert Flint. Ed. & Intro. by J. P. Mayer. LC 78-67355. (European Political Thought Ser.). 1980. reprint ed. lib. bdg. 18.95 (0-405-11697-7) Ayer.
Vico: A Bibliography of Works in English from 1884-1994. Ed. by Molly B. Verene. 183p. 1994. 37.00 (0-912632-97-6) Philos Document.
Vico & Humanism: Essays on Vico, Heidegger, & Rhetoric. Ernesto Grassi. LC 89-2350. (Emory Vico Studies: Vol. 3). 217p. (C). 1989. text ed. 44.95 (0-8204-0962-6) P Lang Pubng.
Vico & Joyce. Ed. by Donald P. Verene. LC 86-23106. 241p. 1987. text ed. 21.50 (0-88706-500-7) State U NY Pr.
***Vico & Moral Perception.** David W. Black. (Emory Vico Studies: Vol. 5). 296p. (C). 1997. 49.95 (0-8204-2898-1) P Lang Pubng.
Vico & Providence. Maeve Albano. Ed. by Donald P. Verene. (Emory Vico Studies: Vol. 1). 198p. (Orig.). 1986. text ed. 37.50 (0-8204-0331-8) P Lang Pubng.
Vico in the Tradition of Rhetoric. Michael Mooney. (Illus.). 318p. (C). 1994. pap. 16.95 (1-880393-24-7, Hermagoras) L Erlbaum Assocs.
Vico in the Tradition of Rhetoric. Michael Mooney. LC 84-42569. 343p. reprint ed. pap. 97.80 (0-8357-2930-3, 2039169) Bks Demand.
Vico, Metaphor, & the Origin of Language. Marcel Danesi. LC 92-30604. 212p. 1993. 35.00 (0-253-31607-3) Ind U Pr.
Vico Revisited: Orthodoxy, Naturalism & Science in the Scienza Nuova. Gino Bedani. LC 88-11117. 308p. 1989. 19.95 (0-85496-266-2) Berg Pubs.
Vicomte de Bragelonne. Alexandre Dumas. Ed. & Intro. by David Coward. (World's Classics Ser.). 768p. 1995. pap. 14.95 (0-19-282390-6) OUP.
Vico's Axioms: The Geometry of the Human World. James R. Goetsch. LC 95-7649. 176p. 1995. 25.00 (0-300-06272-9) Yale U Pr.
***Vico's Cultural History: The Production & Transmission of Ideas in Naples, 1685-1750.** Harold S. Stone. LC 96-3080. (Studies in Intellectual History: Vol. 73). (Illus.). 368p. 1997. text ed. 116.00 (90-04-10650-2, NLG180) E J Brill.
Vico's Science of Imagination. Donald P. Verene. LC 80-69828. 232p. 1981. 39.95 (0-8014-1391-5) Cornell U Pr.
Vico's Science of Imagination. Donald P. Verene. LC 80-69828. 232p. 1992. reprint ed. pap. 14.95 (0-8014-9972-0) Cornell U Pr.
Vico's Theory of the Causes of Historical Change. Leon Pompa. 23p. 1971. pap. 6.00 (0-9500029-2-5, Pub. by Octagon Pr UK) ISHK.
VICS EDI Architectural Guide. 1993. 115.00 (0-614-15373-5) Uniform Code.
VICS EDI Ship Notice/Manifest Guidelines. 1993. 30.00 (0-614-15374-3, 856) Uniform Code.
VICS EDI Standards Manual: Version 3030. 1993. 550.00 (0-614-15367-0) Uniform Code.
VICS EDI Standards Manual: Version 3040. 1994. 590.00 (0-614-15368-9) Uniform Code.
VICS EDI Standards Manual: Version 3050. 1995. 590.00 (0-614-15369-7) Uniform Code.
VICS EDI Standards Manual: Version 3060. 1996. 620.00 (0-614-15370-0) Uniform Code.
Victim. Saul Bellow. 264p. 1988. pap. 10.95 (0-14-002493-X, Penguin Bks) Viking Penguin.
Victim. Saul Bellow. 288p. 1996. pap. 11.95 (0-14-018938-6) Viking Penguin.
Victim. Julian Eymard. 1992. 2.95 (1-56036-018-6, 51416) AMI Pr.
Victim: Caught in the Environmental Web. Bruce G. Siminoff. LC 92-71366. 300p. 1993. 19.95 (0-944435-19-X) Glenbridge Pub.
Victim & Its Masks: An Essay on Sacrifice & Masquerade in the Maghreb. Abdellah Hammoudi. Tr. by Paula Wissing. (Illus.). 224p. 1993. pap. text ed. 16.95 (0-226-31526-6); lib. bdg. 39.95 (0-226-31525-8) U Ch Pr.
Victim As Witness: Legal & Psychological Issues. Ed. by Byrgen P. Finkelman. LC 95-753. (Child Abuse: a Multidisciplinary Survey Ser.: Vol. 8). 328p. 1995. text ed. 60.00 (0-8153-1820-0) Garland.
Victim Assistance: Frontiers & Fundamentals. NOVA Staff. 416p. 1993. per. 34.95 (0-8403-8971-X) Kendall-Hunt.
Victim in International Perspective. Hans J. Schneider. LC 82-1436. x, 513p. 1982. 138.50 (3-11-007510-5) De Gruyter.
***Victim Meets Offender: The Impact of Restorative Justice & Mediation.** M. B. Umbreit. 244p. 1994. pap. 25.00 (1-881798-02-X) Willow Tree NY.
Victim No More: Ministry to Survivors of Sexual Abuse. Mollie Brown. LC 93-61501. 80p. (Orig.). 1994. pap. 7.95 (0-89622-592-5) Twenty-Third.
Victim No More: Your Guide to Overcome Revictimization. Jean Carlton. 288p. 1995. pap. 13.95 (0-9639632-7-9) Stonehorse.
Victim of Anonymity. Neil MacGregor. LC 93-60981. (Walter Neurath Memorial Lectures). (Illus.). 48p. 1994. 14.95 (0-500-55026-3) Thames Hudson.
Victim of Circumstance. W. E. Davis. LC 95-10851. (Gil Beckman Mystery Ser.: Bk. 2). 208p. (Orig.). 1995. pap. 8.99 (0-89107-843-6) Crossway Bks.
Victim of Circumstance. large type ed. W. E. Davis. 320p. 1996. 21.95 (0-7838-1701-0, GK Hall) Thorndike Pr.
Victim of Circumstance. large type ed. Michael Underwood. 1993. 39.95 (0-7066-1003-2, Pub. by Remploy Pr CN) St Mut.
Victim of Circumstances, & Other Stories. George R. Gissing. LC 73-169551. (Short Story Index Reprint Ser.). 1977. reprint ed. 19.95 (0-8369-4013-X) Ayer.
Victim of Despotism, Mexico City, 1839, a Translation: Introduction & Footnotes by Roger Borroel. Jose E. De La Pena. Ed. by Roger Borroel. Tr. by Elena Luna from SPA. (Illus.). 51p. (Orig.). (J). (ps-12). 1996. pap. text ed. 9.98 (0-9624727-7-8) LaVillita Pubns.
Victim of Prejudice. Mary Hays. Ed. by Eleanor Ty. 280p. 1994. pap. 12.95 (0-921149-37-9) Broadview Pr.
Victim of Prejudice. Mary Hays. LC 90-43888. 468p. 1990. reprint ed. 75.00 (0-8201-1446-4) Schol Facsimiles.
Victim of Rape: Institutional Reactions. Lynda L. Holmstrom & Ann W. Burgess. LC 83-678. 320p. 1991. pap. 21.95 (0-87855-932-9) Transaction Pubs.
Victim of the Aurora. Thomas Keneally. LC 77-84391. 228p. 1985. pap. 8.95 (0-15-693534-1, Harvest Bks) HarBrace.
***Victim or Hero? Writing Your Own Life Story: A Passage Guide for Life's Transitions.** Lana S. Leonard. (Orig.). 1996. pap. write for info. (0-614-25747-6) Teaching Peace.
Victim, Survivor, Celebrant. Roberta Nobleman. LC 94-72394. 240p. 1994. pap. 12.95 (0-87029-249-8) Abbey.
Victimes du Devoir. Eugene Ionesco. (Folio Ser.: No. 2209). (Orig.). (FRE.). pap. 8.95 (2-07-038299-0) Schoenhof.
Victimes Du Devoir. Eugene Ionesco. (FRE.). 1990. pap. 10.95 (0-8288-3697-3, F109960) Fr & Eur.
Victimes du Devoir see Theatre
Victimization: Examining Christian Complicity. Christine E. Gudorf. LC 92-13671. 128p. 1992. pap. 13.95 (1-56338-044-7) TPI PA.
Victimization & Exploitation of Women & Children: A Study of Physical, Mental & Sexual Maltreatment in the United States. R. Barri Flowers. LC 94-16362. (Illus.). 254p. 1994. lib. bdg. 32.50 (0-89950-978-9) McFarland & Co.
Victimization & Fear of Crime: World Perspectives. Ed. by Richard Block. (Illus.). 102p. (Orig.). (C). 1995. pap. text ed. 25.00 (0-7881-2065-4) DIANE Pub.
Victimization & Survivor Services: A Guide to Victim Assistance. Arlene B. Andrews. LC 91-15488. (Social Work Ser.: Vol. 21). 280p. (C). 1991. text ed. 35.95 (0-8261-7160-5) Springer Pub.
Victimization & the Aged. Peter Yin. (Illus.). 222p. (C). 1985. 39.95 (0-398-05079-1) C C Thomas.
***Victimization & the Aged.** Peter Yin. (Illus.). 222p. 1985. pap. 24.95 (0-398-06653-1) C C Thomas.
Victimization in Schools. Gary D. Gottfredson & Denise C. Gottfredson. (Law, Society, & Policy Ser.: Vol. 2). 262p. 1985. 52.50 (0-306-42023-6, Plenum Pr) Plenum.
Victimization of Women. Ed. by Jane R. Chapman & Margaret Gates. LC 77-93701. (Sage Yearbooks in Women's Policy Studies: No. 3). 282p. 1978. reprint ed. pap. 80.40 (0-608-01516-4, 2059560) Bks Demand.
Victimized Daughters: Incest & the Development of the Female Self. Janet L. Jacobs. LC 93-39239. 256p. (C). 1994. text ed. 49.95 (0-415-90626-1) Routledge.
Victimized Daughters: Incest & the Development of the Female Self. Janet L. Jacobs. LC 93-39239. 256p. (C). (gr. 13). 1994. pap. 16.95 (0-415-90922-8) Routledge.
Victimless Crime? Prostitution, Drugs, Homosexuality, Abortion. Robert F. Meier & Gilbert Geis. LC 96-37333. 210p. (Orig.). (C). 1997. pap. text ed. 18.95 (0-935732-46-2) Roxbury Pub Co.
Victimology. William G. Doerner & Steven P. Lab. LC 94-73267. 268p. (C). 1995. pap. 32.95 (0-87084-200-5) Anderson Pub Co.
***Victimology.** Meadows. 1997. pap. text ed. 36.00 (0-13-452129-3) P-H.
***Victimology.** Wallace. 1997. text ed. 40.00 (0-205-19153-3) P-H.
Victimology: International Library of Criminology & Criminal Justice. Ed. by Paul E. Rock. 324p. 1994. 89.95 (1-85521-405-9, Pub. by Dartmth Pub UK) Ashgate Pub Co.
Victimology: The Victim & the Criminal Justice Process. Sandra Walklate. 208p. 1989. text ed. 49.95 (0-04-445159-8); pap. text ed. 17.95 (0-04-445160-1) Routledge Chapman & Hall.
Victimology Handbook: Research Findings, Treatment, & Public Policy. Ed. by Emilio C. Viano. LC 90-38717. 352p. 1990. text ed. 55.00 (0-8240-4031-7, 605) Garland.
Victimology in India. V. N. Rajan. 136p. 1981. 16.95 (0-940500-86-8, Pub. by Allied Pubs II) Asia Bk Corp.
Victimology in India: Perspectives Beyond Frontiers. V. N. Rajan. vi, 268p. (C). 1995. 32.00 (81-7024-673-3, Pub. by Ashish Pub Hse II) Nataraj Bks.
Victims. James W. Chichetto. LC 87-70891. 52p. (Orig.). (C). 1987. 5.95 (0-9618657-0-9); pap. 3.95 (0-9618657-1-7) CT Poetry Rev Pr.
Victims. Leslie McGuire. LC 91-11041. (Women Today Ser.). 64p. (J). (gr. 5-7). 1991. 12.95 (0-86593-120-8) Rourke Corp.
Victims. Isadore Okpewho. (Longman African Writers Ser.). (C). 1995. pap. text ed. 9.50 (0-582-26520-7) Addison-Wesley.
Victims. Roger Olden. LC 95-68400. 204p. 1995. lib. bdg. 50.00 (0-923687-35-1) Celo Valley Bks.
Victims. large type ed. Shirley Shea. 416p. 1989. 25.99 (0-7089-2048-9) Ulverscroft.
Victims: A Survival Guide for the Age of Crime. Richard L. Bloom. Ed. by Richard W. Eaves. 160p. (Orig.). 1993. pap. 9.95 (0-9632355-1-6) Guardian Pr.
Victims: A True Story of the Civil War. Phillip S. Paludan. LC 81-2578. 160p. 1981. 21.00 (0-87049-316-7); pap. 11.00 (0-87049-442-2) U of Tenn Pr.
Victims: Textual Strategies in Recent American Fiction. Paul Bruss. LC 80-67319. 259p. 1981. 36.50 (0-8387-5006-0) Bucknell U Pr.
Victims: The LDS Church & the Mark Hofmann Case. Richard E. Turley, Jr. (Illus.). 528p. (C). 1992. 27.95 (0-252-01885-0) U of Ill Pr.
***Victims & Heroes: Racial Violence in the African American Novel.** Jerry H. Bryant. LC 96-48656. 384p. 1997. text ed. 60.00 (1-55849-094-9) U of Mass Pr.
***Victims & Heroes: Racial Violence in the African American Novel.** Jerry H. Bryant. LC 96-48656. 384p. 1997. pap. 18.95 (1-55849-095-7) U of Mass Pr.
Victims & Neighbors: A Small Town in Nazi Germany Remembered. Frwd. by Frances Henry & William K. Brandt. LC 83-25722. (Illus.). 216p. 1984. text ed. 37.95 (0-89789-047-7, Bergin & Garvey); pap. text ed. 14.95 (0-89789-048-5, Bergin & Garvey) Greenwood.
Victims & Sinners: Spiritual Roots of Addiction & Recovery. Linda A. Mercadante. LC 96-18498. 256p. (Orig.). 1996. pap. 20.00 (0-664-25508-6) Westminster John Knox.
Victims & Society. Ed. by Emilio C. Viano. LC 76-11949. 1980. pap. text ed. 25.00 (0-916965-46-5) Victimology.
Victims & Survivors: Displaced Persons & Other War Victims in Viet-Nam, 1954-1975. Louis A. Wiesner. LC 88-15494. (Contributions to the Study of World History Ser.: No. 14). 478p. 1988. text ed. 69.50 (0-313-26306-X, WIU/, Greenwood Pr) Greenwood.
***Victims & Survivors 1940-1944.** Moore. LC 97-4209. 1997. text ed. 59.95 (0-340-49563-4); text ed. 19.95 (0-340-69157-3) St Martin.
Victims & the Postmodern Narrative, or, Doing Violence to the Body: An Ethic of Reading & Writing. Mark Ledbetter. LC 95-17626. (Studies in Literature & Religion). 172p. 1996. text ed. 45.00 (0-312-12863-0) St Martin.
Victims & Values: A History & a Theory of Suffering. Joseph A. Amato, II. LC 90-36712. (Contributions in Philosophy Ser.: No. 42). 264p. 1990. text ed. 59.95 (0-313-25903-8, B3690, Greenwood Pr); pap. text ed. 16.95 (0-275-93690-2, Greenwood Pr) Greenwood.
Victims & Victims' Rights. Sara Faherty. Ed. by Austin Sarat. (Crime, Justice, & Punishment Ser.). (YA). 1996. lib. bdg. 19.95 (0-7910-4308-8) Chelsea Hse.
Victims, Authority, & Terror: The Parallel Deaths of D'Orleans, Custine, Bailly, & Malesherbes. fac. ed. George A. Kelly. LC 81-10298. 405p. 1982. reprint ed. pap. 115.50 (0-7837-8059-1, 2047812) Bks Demand.
Victim's Guide to Air Travel. Roland Fiddy. (Victim's Guides Ser.). (Illus.). 80p. 1994. pap. 4.99 (1-85015-430-9) Exley Giftbooks.
Victim's Guide to Christmas. Roland Fiddy. (Victim's Guides Ser.). (Illus.). 80p. (Orig.). 1994. pap. 4.99 (1-85015-504-6) Exley Giftbooks.
Victim's Guide to Middle Age. Roland Fiddy. (Victim's Guides Ser.). (Illus.). 80p. 1993. pap. 4.99 (1-85015-431-7) Exley Giftbooks.
Victim's Guide to the Baby. Roland Fiddy. (Victim's Guides Ser.). (Illus.). 80p. (Orig.). 1994. pap. 4.99 (1-85015-503-8) Exley Giftbooks.
Victim's Guide to the Boss. Roland Fiddy. (Victim's Guides Ser.). (Illus.). 80p. 1995. pap. 4.99 (1-85015-626-3) Exley Giftbooks.
Victim's Guide to the Dentist. Roland Fiddy. (Victim's Guides Ser.). (Illus.). 80p. 1993. pap. 4.99 (1-85015-404-X) Exley Giftbooks.
Victim's Guide to the Doctor. Roland Fiddy. (Victim's Guides Ser.). (Illus.). 80p. 1993. pap. 4.99 (1-85015-429-5) Exley Giftbooks.
***Victims in Context.** Leslie W. Kennedy & Vincent F. Sacco. LC 97-17785. (Illus.). 350p. (Orig.). (C). 1997. pap. text ed. write for info. (0-935732-00-4) Roxbury Pub Co.
Victims in the News: Crime & the American News Media. Steven Chermak. LC 94-46207. (C). 1995. pap. text ed. 20.95 (0-8133-2497-1) Westview.
Victims No Longer: Men Recovering from Incest & Other Childhood Sexual Abuse. Mike Lew. LC 89-45839. 352p. 1990. reprint ed. pap. 17.00 (0-06-097300-5, PL) HarpC.
Victims of a Map: A Bilingual Anthology of Arabic Poetry. Mahmoud Darwish et al. 1989. 25.00 (0-86356-112-8, Pub. by Saqi Bks UK) Interlink Pub.
Victims of a Map: A Bilingual Anthology of Arabic Poetry. Mahmoud Darwish et al. 1989. pap. 12.95 (0-86356-022-9, Pub. by Saqi Books UK) Interlink Pub.
Victims of Abuse: The Emotional Impact of Child & Adult Trauma. Ed. by Alan Sugerman. (Ralph R. Greenson Memorial Library of the San Diego Psychoanalytic Society & Institute: Monograph 3). 250p. 1993. 35.00 (0-8236-6730-8) Intl Univs Pr.
Victims of Change: Juvenile Delinquents in American Society. Harold Finestone. LC 76-5327. (Contributions in Sociology Ser.: No. 20). (Illus.). 235p. 1976. text ed. 55.00 (0-8371-8897-0, FTD/, Greenwood Pr) Greenwood.
***Victims of Child Abuse, Domestic Abuse, Elderly Abuse, Rape, Robbery, Assault & Violent Death: A Manual for Clergy & Congregations.** 4th ed. David Delaplane & Anne Delaplane. (Illus.). 189p. (C). 1996. pap. 30.00 (0-7881-3150-8) DIANE Pub.
***Victims of Choice.** Kevin Sherlock. 200p. (Orig.). 1996. pap. 19.95 (0-9654036-0-2, VCH896) Brennyman Bks.
***Victims of Crime.** 2nd ed. Ed. by Robert C. Davis et al. LC 96-45872. 295p. 1996. 56.00 (0-7619-0154-X); pap. 25.95 (0-7619-0155-8) Sage.
Victims of Crime: A New Deal? Ed. by Mike Maguire & John Pointing. 256p. 1988. 90.00 (0-335-15567-7, Open Univ Pr); pap. 32.00 (0-335-15566-9, Open Univ Pr) Taylor & Francis.
Victims of Crime: Problems, Policies, & Programs. Ed. by Arthur J. Lurigio et al. (Criminal Justice System Annuals Ser.). (Illus.). 320p. (C). 1990. text ed. 54.00 (0-8039-3369-X); pap. text ed. 24.95 (0-8039-3370-3) Sage.
***Victims of Crime: The Search for Justice.** Robert Jerin & Laura Moriarty. (C). 1997. pap. text ed. 25.95 (0-8304-1424-X) Nelson-Hall.
Victims of Crime & Punishment: Interviews with Victims, Convicts, Their Families, & Support Groups. Shirley Dicks. LC 91-52753. 174p. 1991. pap. 24.95 (0-89950-638-0) McFarland & Co.
Victims of Crime & the Victimization Process. Ed. by McShane & Williams. LC 96-39140. (Criminal Justice Ser.: Vol. 6). 400p. 1997. text ed. 77.00 (0-8153-2513-4) Garland.
Victims of Dementia: Services, Support, & Care. William M. Clemmer. LC 91-36172. (Illus.). 172p. 1992. lib. bdg. 29.95 (1-56024-264-7) Haworth Pr.
Victims of Dementia: Services, Support, & Care. William M. Clemmer. LC 91-36172. 161p. 1993. pap. 19.95 (1-56024-265-5) Haworth Pr.
Victims of Democracy: Malcolm X & the Black Revolution. Eugene V. Wolfenstein. LC 93-18017. 422p. 1993. pap. text ed. 19.95 (0-89862-133-X) Guilford Pr.
Victims of Democracy: Malcolm X & the Black Revolution. Eugene V. Wolfenstein. LC 79-63551. 434p. reprint ed. pap. 123.70 (0-7837-4829-9, 2044476) Bks Demand.
Victims of Development: Resistance & Alternatives. Jeremy Seabrook. 200p. (C). 1993. pap. text ed. 19.00 (0-86091-611-1, B2514, Pub. by Vrso UK) Norton.
Victims of Development: Resistance & Alternatives. Jeremy Seabrook. 200p. (C). (gr. 13). 1993. text ed. 60.00 (0-86091-385-6, B2510, Pub. by Vrso UK) Norton.
***Victims of Gang Violence: A New Frontier in Victim Services.** 62p. 1996. pap. text ed. 30.00 (1-57979-234-0) BPI Info Servs.
***Victims of Gravity.** Dayv James-French. 160p. 1990. pap. 10.95 (0-88984-109-8, Pub. by Porcupines Quill CN) Genl Dist Srvs.
Victims of Memory: Incest Accusations & Shattered Lives. Mark Pendergrast. 603p. (Orig.). 1995. pap. 24.95 (0-942679-16-4) Upper Access.
Victims of Memory: Sex Abuse Accusations & Shattered Lives. 2nd ed. Mark Pendergrast. 603p. (Orig.). 1996. pap. 24.95 (0-942679-18-0) Upper Access.
Victims of Mental, Political & Spiritual Adultery: A Psychology of Religion & a Philosophy of Politics in a Dramatic Novel Based on Fact. Al D. Bernstein. 434p. 1991. pap. 20.00 (0-9611682-1-8) Rel Psych.
Victims of Paradox: Photographs by Wallace Wilson. Alison D. Nordstrom. 55p. 1993. pap. text ed. 10.00 (1-887040-03-X) SE Mus Photo.
Victims of Progress. 3rd ed. John H. Bodley. LC 89-33782. 261p. (C). 1990. pap. text ed. 24.95 (0-87484-945-4, 945) Mayfield Pub.
Victims of Sexual Violence: A Handbook for Helpers. Colleen Ward & Fathiah Inserto. 201p. 1990. pap. 27.50 (9971-69-142-6, Pub. by Singapore Univ Pr SI) Intl Spec Bk.
Victims of Soviet Terror: The Story of the Memorial Movement. Nanci D. Adler. LC 92-46164. 200p. 1993. text ed. 52.95 (0-275-94502-2, C4502, Praeger Pubs) Greenwood.
Victims of Teen Violence. Karen Zeinert. LC 95-42133. (Issues in Focus Ser.). (Illus.). 128p. (YA). (gr. 6 up). 1996. lib. bdg. 18.95 (0-89490-737-9) Enslow Pubs.
Victims of the Environment: Loss from Natural Hazards In the United States, 1970-1980. James D. Wright et al. 256p. 1983. 54.50 (0-306-41413-9, Plenum Pr) Plenum.
Victims of the Holocaust see Nazi Holocaust
***Victims of the Latest Dance Craze.** Cornelius Eady. 64p. 1997. reprint ed. pap. 12.95 (0-88748-254-6) Carnegie-Mellon.
Victims of the Latest Dance Craze: Lamont Poetry Selection 1985. Cornelius Eady. (Dialogues on Dance Ser.: No. 5). (Illus.). 52p. 1986. 18.00 (0-941240-02-9) Ommation Pr.
Victims of the Miracle. S. H. Davis. (Illus.). 1977. pap. 18.95 (0-521-29246-8) Cambridge U Pr.
Victims of the System: Crime Victims & Compensation in American Politics & Criminal Justice. Robert Elias. LC 83-383. (Illus.). 352p. 1983. 44.95 (0-87855-470-X); pap. 24.95 (0-88738-600-8) Transaction Pubs.
Victims of Vesuvius. Elizabeth Heimbach. 91p. (Orig.). 1992. spiral bd. 7.90 (0-939507-36-6, B427) Amer Classical.
***Victims of White Collar Crime: The Social & Media Construction of Business Fraud.** Michael Levi & Andrew Pithouse. (Clarendon Studies in Criminology). 300p. 1997. 75.00 (0-19-826254-X, Clarendon Pr) OUP.
Victims or Criminals? A Study of Women in Colonial North-Western Provinces & Oudh, India, 1870-1910. Priyam Singh. 177p. (C). 1996. 35.00 (0-391-03971-7) Humanities.
Victim's Rights. William L. Ginsburg. LC 94-65393. 163p. (Orig.). 1994. pap. 12.95 (0-913825-82-4, Leg Surv Guides) Sourcebks.
Victims Rights. Glenn Leigh. (Contemporary World Issues Ser.). 1997. lib. bdg. 39.50 (0-87436-870-7) ABC-CLIO.
Victim's Rights: The Biblical View of Civil Justice. Gary North. LC 90-44629. 315p. 1990. 14.95 (0-930464-17-6) Inst Christian.

UV

An Asterisk (*) at the beginning of an entry indicates that the title is appearing in BIP for the first time.

Victims' Rights, Restitution, & Retribution. Williamson M. Evers. (Independent Policy Reports Ser.). 52p. (Orig.). 1996. pap. 7.95 (*0-945999-48-8*) Independent Inst.

Victims' Services Coordinator. Jack Rudman. (Career Examination Ser.: C-3537). 1994. pap. 29.95 (*0-8373-3537-X*) Nat Learn.

Victim's Song. Alice Kaminsky. LC 85-42534. 268p. 1985. 28.95 (*0-87975-292-0*) Prometheus Bks.

Victims Still: The Political Manipulation of Crime Victims. Robert Elias. (Illus.). 160p. (C). 1993. text ed. 45.00 (*0-8039-5052-7*); pap. text ed. 19.50 (*0-8039-5053-5*) Sage.

Victor. Leland Feitz. (Illus.). pap. 3.50 (*0-936564-13-X*) Little London.

Victor: Handley Page Victor K Mk2. (Aeroguide Ser.: No. 11). 1985. pap. 5.95 (*0-918805-10-4*) Pac Aero Pr.

Victor & the Spoils: A Life of William L. Marcy. Ivor D. Spencer. LC 59-6898. 450p. reprint ed. 128.30 (*0-685-15780-6*, 2027524) Bks Demand.

Victor Berger & the Promise of Constructive Socialism, 1910-1920. Sally M. Miller. LC 72-175609. (Contributions in American History Ser.: No. 24). 390p. 1973. text ed. 59.95 (*0-8371-6264-5*, MVB/, Greenwood Pr) Greenwood.

Victor Bible Background Commentary: New Testament. Lawrence O. Richards. LC 93-27863. 640p. 1994. 29.99 (*0-89693-507-8*, 6-1507, Victor Bks) Chariot Victor.

***Victor Borge: An Autobiography.** Victor Borge. Date not set. write for info. (*0-688-09910-6*) Morrow.

Victor Burgin: History Painting. Victor Burgin et al. (Illus.). 52p. (Orig.). 1995. 15.00 (*0-9645577-0-3*) U Buff Art Gall.

Victor Burgin: Office at Night & Danaides-Dames. John Howett. Ed. by Henry Barendse et al. LC 87-81371. (Illus.). 34p. (Orig.). 1988. pap. 7.50 (*0-915427-06-0*) Spirit Sq Ctr.

Victor Duruy & French Education: Liberal Reform in the Second Empire. Sandra Horvath-Peterson. LC 83-23896. xv, 273p. 1984. text ed. 37.50 (*0-8071-1157-0*) La State U Pr.

Victor Gollancz: A Biography. Ruth D. Edwards. (Illus.). 782p. 1987. 50.00 (*0-575-03175-1*, Pub. by V Gollancz UK) Trafalgar.

Victor Griffuelhes & French Syndicalism, 1895-1922. Bruce Vandervort. LC 96-16741. (Illus.). 344p. (C). 1996. text ed. 50.00 (*0-8071-2045-6*) La State U Pr.

Victor Herbert. Joseph Kaye. LC 74-109628. (Select Bibliographies Reprint Ser.). 1977. 23.95 (*0-8369-5237-5*) Ayer.

Victor Herbert: A Life in Music. Edward N. Waters. LC 78-9597. (Music Reprint Ser.: 1978). 1978. reprint ed. lib. bdg. 65.00 (*0-306-79502-7*) Da Capo.

Victor Horta. David Dernie. (Illus.). 224p. 1995. 69.00 (*1-85490-418-3*) Academy Ed UK.

***Victor Hugo.** Graham Robb. LC 97-23596. 1998. 35.00 (*0-393-04578-1*) Norton.

Victor Hugo a Guernsey. Michel Le Bris. (Illus.). 180p. (FRE.). 1996. 59.95 (*2-86808-098-7*) Intl Scholars.

Victor Hugo & Golgotha: Two Essays. Edgar E. Saltus. LC 68-54295. reprint ed. 37.50 (*0-404-05551-6*) AMS Pr.

Victor Hugo & His Poetry. William H. Hudson. LC 70-120967. (Poetry & Life Ser.). reprint ed. 16.00 (*0-404-52514-8*) AMS Pr.

Victor Hugo & His Time. Alfred Barbou. 1972. 59.95 (*0-8490-1259-7*) Gordon Pr.

Victor Hugo & the Visionary Novel. Victor Brombert. (Illus.). 320p. 1986. pap. 15.95 (*0-674-93551-9*) HUP.

Victor Hugo's Drama: An Annotated Bibliography, 1900 to 1980. Compiled by Ruth L. Doyle. LC 80-29680. x, 217p. 1981. text ed. 49.95 (*0-313-22884-1*, DVH/, Greenwood Pr) Greenwood.

Victor Hugo's Intellectual Autobiography. Victor Hugo. LC 79-130260. (Studies in French Literature: No. 45). 1970. reprint ed. lib. bdg. 75.00 (*0-8383-1164-4*) M S G Haskell Hse.

Victor Hugo's Les Miserables & the Novels of the Groteque Vol. 12. Karen Masters-Wicks. LC 92-25009. (Currents in Comparative Romance Languages & Literatures Ser.: Vol. 12). 248p. (C). 1994. text ed. 45.95 (*0-8204-2000-X*) P Lang Pubng.

Victor Journey Through the Bible. V. Gilbert Beers. LC 95-48853. 416p. 1996. 34.99 (*1-56476-480-X*, 63480, Victor Bks) Chariot Victor.

Victor-Marie, Comte Hugo. Charles Peguy. pap. 5.95 (*0-685-37047-X*) Fr & Eur.

Victor Mira: You Can't Sleep in Spain. Ed. by Gregory Steinsieck. (Illus.). 40p. (Orig.). 1989. 8.00 (*0-925941-00-X*) Dorsky Gallery.

Victor Moritz Goldschmidt: Father of Modern Geochemistry. Brian Mason. LC 91-78244. (Special Publication: No. 4). (Illus.). xii, 184p. 1992. 40.00 (*0-941809-03-X*) Geochemical Soc.

Victor of Vita: A History of the Vandal Persecution. Tr. & Intro. by John Moorhead. (Translated Texts for Historians Ser.). 136p. (Orig.). (C). 1992. pap. text ed. 15.95 (*0-85323-127-3*, Pub. by Liverpool Univ Pr UK) U of Pa Pr.

Victor Ollnee's Disciple. Hamlin Garland. (Collected Works of Hamlin Garland). 1988. reprint ed. lib. bdg. 59.00 (*0-7812-1242-1*) Rprt Serv.

Victor Ollnee's Disciple see Collected Works of Hamlin Garland

Victor Pasmore. Lawrence Gowing et al. LC 88-51288. (Illus.). 48p. (Orig.). 1989. pap. 10.00 (*0-930606-58-2*) Yale Ctr Brit Art.

Victor Pasmore: Paintings & Graphics 1980-92. Norbert Lynton. (Illus.). 156p. (C). 1992. 95.00 (*0-85331-606-6*, Pub. by Lund Humphries UK) Antique Collect.

Victor Record Labels, Nineteen Hundred to Nineteen Fifty-Eight: A Complete Illustrated Guide. Michael Sherman. (Illus.). 176p. (Orig.). 1992. pap. 29.95 (*0-937612-06-5*) A P M Pr.

Victor Segalen's Literary Encounter with China: Chinese Moulds, Western Thoughts. Yvonne Y. Hsieh. (Romance Ser.: No. 58). 325p. 1988. 45.00 (*0-8020-2668-0*) U of Toronto Pr.

Victor Serge: The Uses of Dissent. Bill Marshall. 240p. 1992. 19.95 (*0-85496-766-4*) Berg Pubs.

Victor Sjostrom. Bengt Forslund. 420p. 1988. reprint ed. 24.95 (*0-918432-82-0*) Baseline Bks.

Victor Story: History of a Bitter Root Valley Town. Jeffrey H. Langton. LC 85-61259. (Illus.). 126p. 1985. 14.95 (*0-933126-62-X*) Pictorial Hist.

Victor Tausk's Suicide. K. R. Eissler. LC 82-12725. vi, 322p. 1982. 42.50 (*0-8236-6735-9*) Intl Univs Pr.

Victor, the Vegetarian: Saving the Little Lambs. Radha Vignola. LC 94-71475. (Illus.). 56p. (Orig.). (J). (gr. k-3). 1994. pap. 6.95 (*0-9640394-2-7*) AVIVA CA.

Victor the Vulture. Grandpa Blair. 7p. (YA). (gr. 9 up). 1991. pap. 4.75 (*0-930366-64-6*) Northcountry Pub.

Victor Turner & the Construction of Cultural Criticism: Between Literature & Anthropology. Ed. by Kathleen M. Ashley. LC 89-46338. (Illus.). 206p. 1990. 31.50 (*0-253-31003-2*); pap. 13.95 (*0-253-20594-8*, MB 594) Ind U Pr.

Victor Turner Revisited: Ritual As Social Change. Bobby C. Alexander. (American Academy of Religion Academy Ser.). 202p. 1991. 24.95 (*1-55540-600-9*, 010174); pap. 15.95 (*1-55540-601-7*, 010174) Scholars Pr GA.

Victor Vampire's Cut-Out Mask Book. (Illus.). 20p. (Orig.). (J). (ps-1). 1991. pap. 3.95 (*0-8249-8348-3*, Ideals Child) Hambleton-Hill.

Victor Vasnetsov. N. Shanina. 132p. 1979. 130.00 (*0-317-14330-1*, Pub. by Collets) St Mut.

Victor W. Page: Automotive & Aviation Pioneer. Frank C. Derato. LC 91-71257. (Illus.). 343p. (Orig.). 1991. pap. 24.95 (*0-9629323-0-2*) Cranbury Pubns.

Victoria. Knut Hamsun. Tr. by Oliver Stallybrass from NOR. LC 94-28581. (Sun & Moon Classics Ser.: No. 69). 162p. 1994. pap. 10.95 (*1-55713-177-5*) Sun & Moon CA.

Victoria: An Intimate Biography. Stanley Weintraub. (Illus.). 688p. 1988. pap. 13.95 (*0-525-48420-5*, Dutton-Truman Talley) NAL-Dutton.

Victoria: An Intimate Biography. Stanley Weintraub. LC 92-31365. 1992. pap. 16.95 (*0-452-26979-2*, Plume-Truman Talley Bks) NAL-Dutton.

Victoria: Dear Friends. Victoria Magazine Editors. 1994. pap. 14.95 (*0-688-13406-8*) Morrow.

Victoria: Father of My Heart. 1996. 18.95 (*0-688-14472-1*) Hearst Bks.

Victoria: On Being a Mother. Victoria Magazine Editors. LC 89-81524. 140p. 1990. 16.95 (*0-688-09735-9*) Hearst Bks.

Victoria: Our Wedding Guests. Victoria Magazine Editors. 1994. pap. 16.95 (*0-688-13405-X*) Morrow.

Victoria: The Heart of Christmas. Victoria Magazine Editors. (Illus.). 144p. 1992. 20.00 (*0-688-09737-5*) Hearst Bks.

***Victoria: The Insider's Guide.** rev. ed. Robert Moyes. LC 97-65297. (Illus.). 128p. 1997. pap. 5.95 (*1-55143-079-7*) Orca Bk Pubs.

Victoria: The Romantic Heart. Ed. by Victoria Magazine Editors. LC 94-30612. (Illus.). 144p. 1995. boxed 18.95 (*0-688-12589-1*) Hearst Bks.

Victoria: The Way of Flowers. Victoria Editors. 1994. 20.50 (*0-688-12591-3*) Hearst Bks.

Victoria: The Young Queen. Monica Charlot. 500p. 1991. 34.95 (*0-631-17437-0*) Blackwell Pubs.

Victoria - A Love Is Born: A New Mother's Keepsake Journal. Victoria Hearst Books Editors. 1993. 17.00 (*0-688-09430-9*) Hearst Bks.

Victoria & Albert. Richard Hough. LC 96-25614. 240p. 1996. 23.95 (*0-312-14822-4*) St Martin.

***Victoria & Albert.** large type ed. Richard Hough. (Large Print Ser.). (Illus.). 464p. 1997. 27.50 (*0-7089-3701-2*) Ulverscroft.

Victoria & Albert Museum. Intro. by Elizabeth Esteve-Coll. (Illus.). 160p. 1991. 30.00 (*1-870248-67-8*) Scala Books.

***Victoria & Albert Museum: Publications & Exhibitions 1852-1996.** Ed. by Elizabeth James. 1997. lib. bdg. 95.00 (*1-884964-95-8*) Fitzroy Dearborn.

***Victoria & Albert Museum's Textile Collection Vol. 1: Design for Printed Textiles in England from 1750 to 1850.** W. Hefford. (Illus.). 1992. pap. 36.00 (*1-85177-115-8*, Pub. by V&A Ent UK) Antique Collect.

***Victoria & Albert Museum's Textile Collection Vol. 2: British Textiles from 1900 to 1937.** V. D. Mendes. (Illus.). 1992. pap. 36.00 (*1-85177-114-X*, Pub. by V&A Ent UK) Antique Collect.

***Victoria & Albert Museum's Textile Collection Vol. 3: Embroidery in Britain from 1200 to 1750.** D. King & S. M. Levey. (Illus.). 1933. pap. 36.00 (*1-85177-126-3*, Pub. by V&A Ent UK) Antique Collect.

***Victoria & Albert Museum's Textile Collection Vol. 4: British Textiles from 1850 to 1900.** L. Parry. (Illus.). 1993. pap. 36.00 (*1-85177-127-1*, Pub. by V&A Ent UK) Antique Collect.

***Victoria & Albert Museum's Textile Collection Vol. 5: Woven Textiles Design in Britain to 1750.** N. Rothstein. (Illus.). 1994. pap. 36.00 (*1-85177-128-X*, Pub. by V&A Ent UK) Antique Collect.

***Victoria & Albert Museum's Textile Collection Vol. 6: Woven & Embroidered Textiles in Britain from 1750 to 1850.** N. Rothstein. (Illus.). 1994. pap. 34.00 (*1-85177-129-8*, Pub. by V&A Ent UK) Antique Collect.

***Victoria & Albert Museum's Textile Collection Vol. 7: British Textiles 1938 to 1993.** (Illus.). 1996. pap. write for info. (*1-85177-130-1*, Pub. by V&A Ent UK) Antique Collect.

Victoria & Fitzmaurice River Systems see Survey of Tidal River Systems in the Northern Territory & Their Crocodile Populations: Monographs

Victoria & Her Times. Jean-Loup Chifflet. LC 96-28394. (W5 Who, What, Where, When, & Why Ser.). (Illus.). 96p. 1996. 19.95 (*0-8050-5084-1*) H Holt & Co.

***Victoria & Vancouver Island: The Almost Perfect Eden.** Kathleen T. Hill & Gerald N. Hill. (Hill Guides Ser.: Vol. 2). 304p. (Orig.). 1997. pap. 14.95 (*0-912133-13-9*) Hilltop Pub Co.

***Victoria at Home with Roses.** Victoria Magazine Editors. LC 96-54305. (Illus.). 144p. 1997. 25.00 (*0-688-14474-8*) Hearst Bks.

Victoria, at Home with White. Text by Jeanine Larmoth. LC 95-41343. 1996. 25.00 (*0-688-14471-3*) Hearst Bks.

Victoria at Table with Family & Friends. Victoria Magazine Editors. LC 94-23779. 1995. 27.00 (*0-688-11662-0*) Hearst Bks.

Victoria At 18. Tim Kelly. 1978. 3.00 (*0-87129-559-8*, V12) Dramatic Pub.

***Victoria Baking.** Victoria Editors. Date not set. write for info. (*0-688-14469-1*) Hearst Bks.

Victoria: Beyond the Island: An Illustrated History. Peter Bakerville. 144p. 1986. 27.95 (*0-89781-192-5*) Am Historical Pr.

Victoria Bridge: The Vital Link. Stanley Triggs et al. (Illus.). 128p. 1992. pap. 32.95 (*0-7735-0964-X*, Pub. by McGill CN) U of Toronto Pr.

Victoria Calling Cards. Victoria Hearst Books Editors. 1992. 13.00 (*0-688-11400-8*) Hearst Bks.

Victoria Charms of Tea. Victoria Magazine Editors. (Illus.). 96p. 1991. 16.00 (*0-688-09432-5*) Hearst Bks.

Victoria Claflin Woodhull. Foner. Date not set. 23.00 (*0-02-910491-2*, Free Press) Free Pr.

Victoria Creek Neighbors. Anselmo Book Committee Staff. 832p. 45.00 (*0-9615586-9-5*) Loup Valley.

Victoria de L A-Bio-Voi. James McCourt. pap. write for info. (*0-679-44150-6*) Random.

Victoria Final del Ano 2.000. 2nd ed. Marvin Byers. 350p. (Orig.). Date not set. pap. 11.95 (*0-9647871-0-5*) Hebron Minist.

Victoria Harbour: A Mill-Town Legacy. Barbaraane Boyer & Michael Boyer. (Illus.). 128p. (Orig.). pap. 15.00 (*0-919783-69-4*, Pub. by Boston Mills Pr CN) Genl Dist Srvs.

Victoria Hats. LC 93-5641. 1994. 14.00 (*0-688-12636-7*) Hearst Bks.

Victoria History of the Counties of England General Introduction: Supplement, 1970-90. Ed. by C. R. Elrington. (Victoria History of the Counties of England Ser.). 80p. 1991. 29.95 (*0-19-722777-5*) OUP.

Victoria Intimate Home: Creating a Private World. Victoria Magazine Editors. (Illus.). 112p. 1992. 16.00 (*0-688-09739-1*) Hearst Bks.

Victoria Mundi. Charles Foster. LC 72-96445. 80p. 1973. 10.00 (*0-912292-29-6*) Smith.

Victoria, No Friend Like a Sister. Ed. by Linda Sunshine. LC 92-27649. (Illus.). 1993. 17.00 (*0-688-10624-2*) Hearst Bks.

Victoria Ocampo: Against the Wind & the Tide. Doris Meyer. (Illus.). 348p. 1989. reprint ed. pap. 13.95 (*0-292-78710-3*) U of Tex Pr.

***Victoria, Off. Heb. San Vol. 31/2: Maunday Thursday.** E. Cramer. (Wissenschaftliche Abhandlungen - Musicological Studies). Date not set. write for info. (*0-931902-05-3*) Inst Mediaeval Mus.

Victoria Officium Hebdomadae Sanctae, I: Introduction, Vol. XXXI. E. Cramer. 1979. lib. bdg. 40.00 (*0-931902-04-5*) Inst Mediaeval Mus.

Victoria Officium Hebdomadae Sanctae, III: Good Friday, Vol. XXXI. E. Cramer. 1979. lib. bdg. 40.00 (*0-931902-06-1*) Inst Mediaeval Mus.

Victoria Officium Hebdomadae Sanctae, IV: Holy Saturday, Vol. XXXI. E. Cramer. 1979. lib. bdg. 40.00 (*0-931902-07-X*) Inst Mediaeval Mus.

Victoria Officium Hebdomadae Sanctae, Two: Maudy Thursday, Vol. XXXI. E. Cramer. write for info. (*0-318-60711-5*) Inst Mediaeval Mus.

Victoria para Mujeres en Crisis. Compiled by Alicia S. De Zorzoli. 96p. (Orig.). (SPA.). 1992. pap. 7.50 (*0-311-12104-7*) Casa Bautista.

Victoria Plaza Revisited: Lessons for the Evaluation of Housing for the Elderly. Ed. by Arza Churchman. (Illus.). (C). 1995. 15.00 (*0-938744-88-7*, R94-7) U of Wis Ctr Arch-Urban.

***Victoria Rose's Tea Party.** Ladybird Staff. 1997. pap. 19.99 (*0-7214-5781-9*) Dutton Child Bks.

***Victoria Sobre la Oscuridad.** Neil T. Anderson. 198p. (SPA.). 1995. write for info. (*1-56063-469-3*) Editorial Unilit.

***Victoria Sobre la Vida Egocentrica.** Caram. 94p. (SPA.). pap. write for info. (*0-7899-0240-0*) Editorial Unilit.

Victoria Walking Guide: Old Town Chinatown, the Waterfront James Bay. Rosemary Neering. 1994. pap. text ed. 4.95 (*1-55110-171-8*) Gr Arts Ctr Pub.

***Victoria Wallpaper.** Victoria Magazine Editors. 1997. 25.00 (*0-688-14475-6*) Hearst Bks.

Victoria Woodhull Reader. Victoria C. Woodhull. Ed. by Madeleine B. Stern. 650p. 1974. 30.00 (*0-87730-009-7*) M&S Pr.

***Victoria y No Derrota.** K. Arthur. (SPA.). 6.95 (*0-8297-1505-3*) Life Pubs Intl.

Victorian: Stained Glass for Today. Bill Hillman. (Illus.). 40p. 1989. pap. 14.95 (*0-935133-26-7*) CKE Pubns.

Victorian Achievement of Sir Henry Maine: A Centennial Reappraisal. Ed. by Alan Diamond. 472p. (C). 1991. text ed. 85.00 (*0-521-40023-6*) Cambridge U Pr.

Victorian Actors & Actresses in Review: A Dictionary of Contemporary Views of Representative British & American Actors & Actresses, 1837-1901. Compiled by Donald Mullin. LC 83-1407. (Illus.). xxxvi, 571p. 1983. text ed. 65.00 (*0-313-23316-0*, MVA/) Greenwood.

Victorian Administrative Law, 3 vols. Emilios J. Kyrou. 1990. Set. ring bd. 245.00 (*0-685-50924-9*, Pub. by Law Bk Co AT) Gaunt.

Victorian Administrative Law, 3 vols., Vol. 1: 1985-1987. Emilios J. Kyrou. 1990. Vol. 1, 1985-1987. 75.00 (*0-685-74368-3*, Pub. by Law Bk Co AT) Gaunt.

Victorian Administrative Law, 3 vols., Vol. 2: 1987-1989. Emilios J. Kyrou. 1990. Vol. 2, 1987-1989. 75.00 (*0-685-74369-1*, Pub. by Law Bk Co AT) Gaunt.

Victorian Administrative Law, 3 vols., Vol. 3: 1987-1989. Emilios J. Kyrou. 1990. Vol. 3, 1987-1989. 75.00 (*0-685-74370-5*, Pub. by Law Bk Co AT) Gaunt.

Victorian Age: Essays in History & in Social & Literary Criticism. Ed. by Robert Langbaum. 320p. (C). 1983. reprint ed. pap. 8.00 (*0-89733-055-2*) Academy Chi Pubs.

Victorian Age of German Literature: Eight Essays. Norbert Fuerst. LC 65-23845. 1966. 30.00 (*0-271-73107-9*) Pa St U Pr.

Victorian Album: Julia Margaret Cameron & Her Circle. Ed. by Graham Ovenden. LC 75-18728. (Photography Ser.). (Illus.). 119p. 1975. lib. bdg. 45.00 (*0-306-70749-7*) Da Capo.

Victorian Allover Patterns for Artists & Designers. Carol B. Grafton. 1990. pap. 5.95 (*0-486-26437-8*) Dover.

Victorian Alphabets, Monograms & Names for Needle Workers. Godey's Lady's Book Staff & Peterson's Magazine Staff. LC 74-79939. 128p. 1974. reprint ed. pap. 4.95 (*0-486-23072-4*) Dover.

Victorian Amateur Astronomer: Independent Astronomical Research in Britain 1820-1920. Allan Chapman. LC 95-48037. (Wiley-Praxis Series in Astronomy & Astrophysics). 1996. text ed. 59.95 (*0-471-96257-0*) Wiley.

Victorian America: Classical Romanticism to Gilded Opulence. Wendell Garrett. (Illus.). 208p. 1996. pap. 25.00 (*0-7893-0025-7*) Universe.

Victorian America: Transformations in Everyday Life, 1876-1915. Thomas J. Schlereth. LC 89-46555. (Illus.). 416p. 1992. reprint ed. pap. 14.00 (*0-06-092160-9*, PL) HarpC.

Victorian America: 1876 to 1913. Crandall A. Shifflett. Ed. by Rick Balkin. LC 95-13553. (Almanacs of Everyday Life Ser.). (Illus.). 416p. (J). (gr. 5-10). 1996. 70.00 (*0-8160-2531-2*) Facts on File.

Victorian America & the Civil War. Anne C. Rose. (Illus.). 272p. (C). 1992. text ed. 54.95 (*0-521-41081-9*) Cambridge U Pr.

Victorian America & the Civil War. Anne C. Rose. (Illus.). 320p. (C). 1994. pap. text ed. 16.95 (*0-521-47883-9*) Cambridge U Pr.

Victorian American, Henry Wadsworth Longfellow. Herbert S. Gorman. (BCL1-PS American Literature Ser.). 363p. 1992. reprint ed. lib. bdg. 89.00 (*0-7812-6780-3*) Rprt Serv.

Victorian American Women, 1840-1880: An Annotated Bibliography. Karen R. Mehaffey. LC 91-22206. 192p. 1991. text ed. 30.00 (*0-8240-7142-5*) Garland.

Victorian & Country Home Designs, No. A102. Ed. by National Plan Service Staff. (Illus.). 32p. reprint ed. 4.95 (*0-934039-33-X*) Natl Plan Serv.

Victorian & Edwardian Country House Life. Anthony J. Lambert. LC 80-26606. (Illus.). 120p. 1981. 29.50 (*0-8419-0684-X*) Holmes & Meier.

Victorian & Edwardian Decor: From the Gothic Revival to Art Nouveau. Jeremy Cooper. (Illus.). 256p. 1987. 60.00 (*0-89659-768-7*) Abbeville Pr.

Victorian & Edwardian Fashion: A Photographic Survey. Alison Gernsheim. (Illus.). 240p. 1982. reprint ed. pap. 6.95 (*0-486-24205-6*) Dover.

Victorian & Edwardian Fashions for Women: 1840-1910. Kristina Harris. LC 95-11839. (Illus.). 466p. (Orig.). 1995. pap. 29.95 (*0-88740-842-7*) Schiffer.

***Victorian & Edwardian Fashions from "La Mode Illustree"** Ed. by Joanne Olian. (Illus.). 256p. (Orig.). 1997. reprint ed. pap. text ed. 16.95 (*0-486-29711-X*) Dover.

Victorian & Edwardian Furniture: Price Guide & Reasons for Values. John Andrews. (Illus.). 456p. 1993. 69.50 (*1-85149-118-X*) Antique Collect.

Victorian & Edwardian Schoolchild. Pamela Horn. (Illus.). 184p. (C). 24.00 (*0-86299-574-4*, Pub. by Sutton Pubng UK) Bks Intl VA.

Victorian & Modern Poetics. Carol T. Christ. LC 83-18200. x, 188p. 1986. pap. text ed. 10.95 (*0-226-10459-1*) U Ch Pr.

Victorian Anthology, 1837-1895, 2 vols. Ed. by Edmund C. Stedman. LC 04-13936. 1969. reprint ed. Set. 59.00 (*0-685-38429-2*) Scholarly.

Victorian Anthology, 1837-1895. Edmund C. Stedman. (BCL1-PR English Literature Ser.). 744p. 1992. reprint ed. lib. bdg. 109.00 (*0-7812-7141-X*) Rprt Serv.

Victorian Anthropology. George W. Stocking, Jr. 1987. pap. 16.95 (*0-02-931151-9*, Free Press) Free Pr.

Victorian Anthropology. George W. Stocking. 1991. pap. 18.95 (*0-02-931551-4*, Free Press) Free Pr.

Victorian Architectural Competitions: An Index to British & Irish Architectural Competitions in The Builder, 1843-1900. R. Harper. 448p. 1983. text ed. 100.00 (*0-7201-1685-6*, Mansell Pub) Cassell.

Victorian Architecture. Roger Dixon & Stefan Muthesius. (World of Art Ser.). (Illus.). 208p. 1985. pap. 14.95 (*0-500-20160-9*) Thames Hudson.

Victorian Architecture in Britain. Julian Orbach. (Blue Guides Ser.). 1988. pap. 24.95 (*0-393-30070-6*) Norton.

UV

An Asterisk (*) at the beginning of an entry indicates that the title is appearing in BIP for the first time.

Victorian Architecture in London & Southwestern Ontario: Symbols of Aspiration. Nancy Z. Tausky & Lynne D. DiStefano. 494p. 1978. 19.95 (0-8020-5698-9) U of Toronto Pr.

Victorian Arkansans: How They Lived, Played & Worked. Louise Bloom et al. Ed. by Mala Daggett. LC 81-67251. (Illus.). 208p. 1981. 17.00 (0-686-30547-7) AR Commemorative.

Victorian Army at Home: The Recruitment & Terms & Conditions of the British Regular, 1859-1899. Alan Skelley. (Illus.). 1977. lib. bdg. 32.95 (0-7735-0304-8, Pub. by McGill CN) U of Toronto Pr.

Victorian Art Reproductions in Modern Sources: A Bibliography. Kristine O. Garrigan. LC 90-22349. 624p. 1991. text ed. 89.00 (0-8240-3335-3, 1225) Garland.

Victorian at Bay. Anne K. Tuell. LC 67-22123. (Essay Index Reprint Ser.). 1977. 18.95 (0-8369-0952-6) Ayer.

Victorian Authority: The Daily Press in Late Nineteenth-Century Canada. Paul Rutherford. LC 82-190489. (Illus.). 305p. reprint ed. pap. 87.00 (0-7837-4288-6, 2043980) Bks Demand.

Victorian Authors & Their Works: Revision Motivations & Modes. Ed. by Judith Kennedy. LC 91-324. 214p. (C). 1991. text ed. 29.95 (0-8214-0976-X) Ohio U Pr.

Victorian Autobiography. Clinton Machann. 160p. (C). 1994. text ed. 39.50 (0-472-10565-5) U of Mich Pr.

Victorian Ballet Girl: The Tragic Story of Clara Webster. Ivor Guest. LC 80-16216. (Series in Dance). 1980. reprint ed. 25.00 (0-306-76043-6) Da Capo.

Victorian Banbury. Barrie Trinder. (C). 1982. 60.00 (0-685-10642-X) St Mut.

Victorian Bathing Costumes. Paula J. Darnell. LC 95-90477. 1995. pap. 19.95 (1-887402-06-3) Fabric Fancies.

Victorian Bibliomania: The Illuminated Book in 19th-Century Britain. Alice Beckwith. Ed. by Janet Phillips. LC 86-62734. (Illus.). 83p. (Orig.). 1987. pap. 18.00 (0-911517-45-6) Mus of Art RI.

Victorian Biography: Intellectuals & the Ordering of Discourse. David Amigoni. LC 93-26875. 207p. 1994. text ed. 45.00 (0-312-10394-8) St Martin.

Victorian Bloomsbury: The Early Literary History of the Bloomsbury Group, Vol. 1. S. P. Rosenbaum. 298p. 1987. text ed. 29.95 (0-312-84051-9) St Martin.

Victorian Board Games. Olivia Bristol. LC 95-25476. 12p. 1995. 17.95 (0-312-13637-4) St Martin.

Victorian Book Illustration. Morna Daniels. 1988. pap. 14.75 (0-7123-0157-7, Pub. by Brit Library UK) U of Toronto Pr.

Victorian Book Lavender & Old Lace. Pamela Westland. 1996. 6.98 (0-7858-0382-3) Bk Sales Inc.

Victorian Book of Flowers: An Inspiring Collection of Delightful Projects & Pastimes. Pamela Westland. 1996. 14.98 (0-8317-7292-1) Smithmark.

Victorian Book of Pressed Flowers & Roses. Pamela Westland. 1996. 6.98 (0-7858-0379-3) Bk Sales Inc.

Victorian Book of Ribbons & Roses. Pamela Westland. 1996. 6.98 (0-7858-0381-5) Bk Sales Inc.

Victorian Book Potions & Perfumes. Pamela Westland. 1996. 6.98 (0-7858-0380-7) Bk Sales Inc.

Victorian Bookbindings: A Pictorial Survey. rev. ed. Sue Allen. LC 76-7420. 58p. 1976. lib. bdg. 34.00 (0-226-68787-2) U Ch Pr.

Victorian Brass Needlecases. Estelle Horowitz & Ruth Mann. LC 90-91493. (Illus.). 160p. 1990. 32.50 (0-9625853-2-7) Needlework Treasures.

Victorian Brick & Terra-Cotta Architecture in Full Color. Pierre Chabat. (Illus.). 168p. 1990. pap. 26.95 (0-486-26164-6) Dover.

Victorian Britain. Ed. by Boris Ford. (Cultural History of Britain Ser.). (Illus.). 352p. (C). 1992. pap. 21.95 (0-521-42887-4) Cambridge U Pr.

***Victorian Britain: An Encyclopedia.** 1990. 136.00 (1-55862-105-9, 00007729) St James Pr.

Victorian Britain: An Encyclopedia. Ed. by Sally Mitchell. LC 87-29947. (Illus.). 1010p. 1988. text ed. 125.00 (0-8240-1513-4, SS438) Garland.

Victorian Britain: An Encyclopedia. Ed. by Sally Mitchell. LC 87-29947. (Illus.). 1010p. 1991. pap. text ed. 32.50 (0-8153-0803-5, SS438) Garland.

Victorian Building Regulations: Summary Tables of the Principal English Building Acts & Model By-Laws, 1840-1914. R. Harper. 176p. 1985. text ed. 85.00 (0-7201-1751-8, Mansell Pub) Cassell.

***Victorian Buildings in South Africa Including Edwardian & Transvaal Republican Styles, 1850-1910.** 424p. 1977. 110.00 (0-86961-083-X, Pub. by A A Balkema NE) Ashgate Pub Co.

Victorian Cabinet Maker: The Memoirs of James Hopkinson, 1819-1894. James Hopkinson. Ed. by Jocelyne B. Goodman. LC 69-17113. (Illus.). xiii, 138p. 1969. 29.50 (0-678-06526-8) Kelley.

Victorian Cabinet-Maker's Assistant. Blackie & Son Staff. (Illus.). 1970. reprint ed. pap. 14.95 (0-486-22353-1) Dover.

Victorian Cakes. Caroline B. King. (Illus.). 240p. 1988. pap. 9.57 (0-201-19184-9) Addison-Wesley.

Victorian Cakes. Caroline B. King. 240p. 1986. reprint ed. pap. 9.95 (0-943186-26-9) Aris Bks.

Victorian Cambridge: Josiah Chater's Diearies, 1844-1883. Enid Porter. (C). 1975. 40.00 (0-85033-213-3) St Mut.

Victorian Card Kit. Michelle Lovric. 1996. pap. text ed. 9.95 (1-55670-477-1) Stewart Tabori & Chang.

Victorian Cat: The Classic Collection for Cat Lovers. Ed. by Sted Mays. LC 95-20824. (Illus.). 64p. 1995. 7.99 (0-517-14727-0) Random Hse Value.

Victorian Catalogue of Household Furnishings. Stephen Calloway. 1995. 12.98 (0-8317-9407-0) Smithmark.

Victorian Catalogue of Household Goods: A Complete Compendium to Furnish & Decorate. Dorothy Bosomworth. 1996. 19.98 (0-8317-3774-3) Smithmark.

Victorian Catalogue of Tools for Trades & Craft. Philip Walker. 1995. 12.98 (0-8317-9411-9) Smithmark.

***Victorian Cats: Decoupage Book with 10 Projects.** Maggie Philo & Michelle Lovric. (Illus.). 48p. 1997. 22.50 (1-85410-462-4, Pub. by Aurum Pr UK) London Brdge.

Victorian Cats: Postbox Collections. Roger Eisinger. 1995. 10.95 (0-8118-1014-3) Chronicle Bks.

Victorian Cat's Journal. Susan Herbert. (Illus.). 64p. 1991. 16.95 (0-8212-1865-4) Bulfinch Pr.

Victorian Chaise Longue. Marghanita Laski. 152p. 1984. pap. 5.00 (0-89733-097-8) Academy Chi Pubs.

Victorian Chemist & Druggist. W. A. Jackson. 1989. pap. 25.00 (0-85263-583-4, Pub. by Shire UK) St Mut.

Victorian Childhood: Themes & Variations. Thomas E. Jordan. LC 86-30184. (Illus.). 391p. 1987. text ed. 64.50 (0-88706-544-9); pap. text ed. 21.95 (0-88706-545-7) State U NY Pr.

Victorian Children. Eleanor Allen. (Junior Reference Ser.). (Illus.). 64p. (J). (gr. 6 up). 1988. 15.95 (0-7136-1324-6) Dufour.

Victorian Christian Socialists. Edward Norman. 210p. 1987. text ed. 54.95 (0-521-32515-3) Cambridge U Pr.

Victorian Christmas. Bobbie Kalman. LC 96-26735. (Historic Communities Ser.). 32p. 1996. pap. 7.95 (0-86505-460-6); lib. bdg. 19.16 (0-86505-430-4) Crabtree Pub Co.

Victorian Christmas. Betina M. Krahn et al. 352p. (Orig.). 1992. pap. 4.99 (0-451-17442-9, Sig) NAL-Dutton.

Victorian Christmas. Bruce Paddock. LC 94-78179. (Traditional Country Life Recipe Ser.). (Illus.). 96p. 1994. pap. 9.95 (1-883283-06-X) Brick Tower.

Victorian Christmas. Robin Petrie. 9.95 (1-56222-889-7, 94816) Mel Bay.

***Victorian Christmas.** Robin Petrie. 10.98 incl. audio (1-56222-519-7, 94816C) Mel Bay.

Victorian Christmas. Maria H. Von Staufer. (Illus.). 48p. 1988. 28.00 (0-88014-074-7) Mosaic Pr OH.

Victorian Christmas Celebration Cookbook. rev. ed. Patricia B. Mitchell. 1991. pap. 4.00 (0-925117-44-7) Mitchells.

***Victorian Christmas Tea.** Catherine Palmer. LC 97-23054. 1997. pap. write for info. (0-8423-7775-1) Tyndale.

Victorian Church. Ed. by Chris Brooks & Andrew Saint. LC 94-26465. 1995. text ed. 79.95 (0-7190-4019-1, Pub. by Manchester Univ Pr UK); text ed. 24.95 (0-7190-4020-5, Pub. by Manchester Univ Pr UK) St Martin.

Victorian Cities. Asa Briggs. LC 92-30443. (Classics in Urban History Ser.: Vol. 2). 1993. 15.00 (0-520-07922-1) U CA Pr.

Victorian City: A Reader in British Urban History, 1820-1914. Ed. by R. J. Morris & Richard Rodger. LC 92-28232. (Readers in Urban History Ser.). (C). 1993. text ed. 55.50 (0-582-05133-9, 79760); pap. text ed. 29.95 (0-582-05132-0, 79759) Longman.

Victorian City & Country Houses: Plans & Designs. George E. Woodward. LC 95-43860. Orig. Title: Woodward's National Architect. (Illus.). 128p. reprint ed. pap. 8.95 (0-486-29080-8) Dover.

Victorian Classics of San Francisco 1887. Ed. by Wayne Bonnett. (Illus.). 120p. 1987. 32.00 (0-915269-05-8) Windgate Pr.

Victorian Clerks. Gregory L. Anderson. (Illus.). 145p. 1976. lib. bdg. 29.50 (0-678-06794-5) Kelley.

***Victorian Clocks.** Richard Good. 1996. 75.00 (0-7141-0578-3) Parkwest Pubns.

Victorian Color Vignettes & Illustrations for Artists & Craftsmen: 344 Antique Chromolithographs. Carol B. Grafton. (Illus.). 48p. (Orig.). 1983. pap. 4.95 (0-486-24477-6) Dover.

Victorian Coloring Book, No. 1: Featuring Ferndale, California. Donna J. Setterlund. (Illus.). 24p. (Orig.). (J). 1990. pap. 4.95 (0-9624342-1-3) Carriage Hse Studio Pubns.

Victorian Connections. Ed. by Jerome J. McGann. LC 89-30993. (Virginia Victorian Studies). 214p. 1989. text ed. 35.00 (0-8139-1218-0) U Pr of Va.

Victorian Conscience. Clarence R. Decker. LC 77-8021. 213p. 1977. reprint ed. text ed. 38.50 (0-8371-9684-1, DEVC, Greenwood Pr) Greenwood.

Victorian Contexts: Literature & the Visual Arts. Murray Roston. LC 96-33091. (Illus.). 246p. (C). 1996. 45.00 (0-8147-7485-7) NYU Pr.

Victorian Controversy Surrounding the Wellington War Memorial: The Archduke of Hyde Park Corner. F. Darrell Munsell. LC 91-22672. (Illus.). 125p. 1991. lib. bdg. 69.95 (0-7734-9735-8) E Mellen.

Victorian Conventions. John R. Reed. LC 73-92908. xiii, 561p. 1975. pap. text ed. 27.95 (0-8214-0828-3) Ohio U Pr.

Victorian Conventions. John R. Reed. LC 73-92908. xiii, 561p. 1975. 40.00 (0-8214-0147-5) Ohio U Pr.

Victorian Cookbook. Michelle Berriedale-Johnson. LC 89-7598. (Illus.). 160p. 1989. Cookery Book. 24.95 (0-940793-38-5) Interlink Pub.

Victorian Cornwall. S. Daniell. (C). 1989. pap. text ed. 24.95 (0-85025-315-2, Pub. by Tor Mark Pr UK) St Mut.

***Victorian Costume & Costume Accessories.** 2nd rev. ed. Anne Buck. (Illus.). 224p. 1997. pap. 22.50 (0-89676-220-3, Costume & Fashion Pr) QSMG Ltd.

Victorian Costuming. Janet Winter. 1991. reprint ed. pap. 10.00 (0-9630220-1-6) Other Times Prods.

Victorian Cottage Residences. Andrew J. Downing. Ed. by George E. Harney. (Illus.). 352p. 1981. reprint ed. pap. 7.95 (0-486-24078-9) Dover.

Victorian Cottage Rugs: How to Hook 16 Traditional Patterns. Pat Hornafius. LC 94-41929. (Illus.). 256p. 1995. pap. 24.95 (0-8117-2593-6) Stackpole.

Victorian Cottages. Andrew Clayton-Payne. (Country Ser.). (Illus.). 160p. 1996. pap. 17.95 (0-297-83563-7, Weidenfeld) Trafalgar.

Victorian Country Child. Pamela Horn. (Illus.). 256p. (C). 1990. text ed. 30.00 (0-86299-776-3, Pub. by Sutton Pubng UK) Bks Intl VA.

***Victorian Country Child.** Pamela Horn. (History Paperback Ser.). (Illus.). 304p. (Orig.). 1997. pap. 19.95 (0-7509-1499-8, Pub. by Sutton Pubng UK) Bks Intl VA.

Victorian Country House. Mark Girouard. LC 79-64077. 1985. pap. 32.50 (0-300-03472-5) Yale U Pr.

Victorian Countryside, 2 vols. Ed. by G. E. Mingay. (Illus.). 1986. Set. pap. 45.00 (0-685-43559-8, 88888); Vol. I, 380 pg. write for info. (0-7102-0884-7); Vol. II, 348 pg. write for info. (0-7102-0886-3) Routledge Chapman & Hall.

Victorian Countrywomen. Pamela Horn. 288p. 1991. 42.95 (0-631-15522-8) Blackwell Pubs.

Victorian Crafts: Over Forty Charming Projects to Make from the Victorian Era. Ed. by Tracy Marsh. (Illus.). 168p. 1993. 29.95 (0-943955-75-0, Trafalgar Sq Pub) Trafalgar.

Victorian Critic & the Idea of History: Carlyle, Arnold, Pater. Peter Dale. 320p. 1977. 34.50 (0-674-93581-0) HUP.

Victorian Criticism of American Writers: A Guide to British Criticism of American Writers in the Leading British Periodicals of the Victorian Period, 1824-1900. Arnella K. Turner. LC 87-807. (Borgo Literary Guide Ser.: No. 6). 456p. (C). 1991. pap. 43.00 (0-89370-916-6); lib. bdg. 53.00 (0-89370-816-X) Borgo Pr.

Victorian Crocheted Christmas Ornaments: 33 Quick-&-Easy Projects. Barbara Christopher. LC 93-13773. (Needlework Ser.). 1993. pap. 3.50 (0-486-27627-9) Dover.

Victorian Cross Stitch. Jane Greenoff. (Illus.). 128p. 1996. pap. 14.95 (0-7153-0373-2, Pub. by D & C Pub UK) Sterling.

Victorian Cross Stitch Samplers. Angela Wainwright. (Illus.). 96p. (Orig.). 1996. pap. 14.95 (0-304-34693-4, Pub. by Cassell UK) Sterling.

Victorian Culture in America, 1865-1914. Ed. by H. Wayne Morgan. LC 72-89722. (Primary Sources in American History Ser.). 1973. pap. text ed. write for info. (0-88295-787-2) Harlan Davidson.

Victorian Cup of Tea: A Guide to Victorian Entertaining. Frances Norton. 90p. (Orig.). 1997. per. 12.95 (0-9632938-0-X) F M Norton.

***Victorian Danville: Fifth-Two Landmarks, Their Architecture & History.** 2nd rev. ed. Mary Cahill & Gary Grant. (Illus.). 130p. 1996. reprint ed. write for info. (0-933571-10-0) Ure Pr.

Victorian Days. Gloria Gaffney. 100p. 1991. pap. text ed. 9.50 (1-56770-240-6) S Scheewe Pubns.

***Victorian Decorative Papers.** Munice Hendler. (Illus.). pap. 5.95 (0-486-23885-7) Dover.

***Victorian Decoupage Source Book.** Michelle Lovric. Date not set. 22.50 (1-85410-355-5, Pub. by Aurum Pr UK) London Brdge.

Victorian Delights: Reflections of Taste in the Nineteenth Century. John Hadfield. (Illus.). 128p. (C). 1987. 24.95 (0-941533-02-6) New Amsterdam Bks.

Victorian Detective Stories: An Oxford Anthology. Ed. by Michael Cox. 608p. (C). 1993. pap. 15.95 (0-19-283150-X, 12242) OUP.

Victorian Devotional Poetry: The Tractarian Mode. G. B. Tennyson. LC 80-14416. 282p. 1981. 29.00 (0-674-93586-1) HUP.

Victorian Discourses on Sexuality & Religion. John Maynard. LC 92-12820. (Illus.). 352p. (C). 1993. text ed. 69.95 (0-521-33254-0) Cambridge U Pr.

Victorian Display Alphabets: One Hundred Complete Fonts. Dan X. Solo. (Pictorial Archive Ser.). (Illus.). 112p. (Orig.). 1976. pap. 5.95 (0-486-23302-2) Dover.

Victorian Divorce. Allen Horstman. LC 85-14491. 208p. 1985. text ed. 32.50 (0-312-84156-6) St Martin.

Victorian Doll House: Coloring Poster. Illus. by Pamela G. Szarek. 1989. 9.95 (0-943114-97-7, PC100) Childbirth Graphics.

Victorian Dollhouse. Herman Lellie & Margaret Bateson. (Illus.). 4p. (J). 1991. bds. 19.95 (0-312-06228-1) St Martin.

***Victorian Dollhouse Book.** N. Furder. 1996. 17.98 (0-7858-0566-4) Bk Sales Inc.

Victorian Domestic Architectural Plans & Details: Seven Hundred Thirty-Four Scale Drawings of Doorways, Windows, Staircases, Moldings, Cornices & Other Elements. William T. Comstock. (Illus.). 96p. 1987. reprint ed. pap. 6.95 (0-486-25442-9) Dover.

Victorian Doubt: Literary & Cultural Discourses. Lance S. Butler. 240p. (C). 1990. text ed. 75.00 (0-389-20938-4) B&N Imports.

Victorian Dream Homes: One Hundred Sixty Victorian & Farmhouse Plans from 3 Master Designers. (Illus.). 192p. 1991. pap. 12.95 (0-918894-90-5) Home Planners.

Victorian Dulcimer. Rosamond Campbell. 1993. 7.95 (1-56222-315-1, 94690) Mel Bay.

***Victorian Dulcimer.** Rosamond Campbell. 1993. audio compact disk 15.98 (0-7866-2862-6, 94690CD) Mel Bay.

Victorian Economy. Francois Crouzet. Tr. by A. S. Forster. LC 82-1292. 400p. 1982. pap. text ed. 24.50 (0-231-05543-9) Col U Pr.

Victorian Elegance: Exquisite Stitches & Crazy Patchwork. Lezette Thomason. Ed. by Melissa Lowe. LC 96-16465. (Illus.). 80p. (Orig.). 1996. pap. 19.95 (1-56477-159-8, B270) That Patchwork.

Victorian Embroidery. Robbyn MacDonald. (Illus.). 128p. 1994. 24.95 (1-86351-110-5, Pub. by S Milner AT) Sterling.

Victorian Encounter with Marx: A Study of Ernest Belfort Bax. John Cowley. 224p. (C). 1993. text ed. 59.50 (1-85043-601-0, Pub. by I B Tauris UK) St Martin.

Victorian England: Aspects of English & Imperial History, 1837-19... L. C. Seaman. 496p. (C). 1973. pap. text ed. 23.75 (0-415-04576-2) Routledge.

Victorian England: Aspects of English & Imperial History 1837-1901. L. C. Seaman. 500p. 1973. pap. 15.95 (0-416-77550-0, NO. 2434) Routledge Chapman & Hall.

Victorian English & American Shop Front Designs & Drawings 1834-1900. limited rev. ed. Ken White & Frank White. Ed. by Joan Gerlacher. (Illus.). 208p. 1994. 125.00 (0-9625457-2-4) St Francis Pr.

Victorian English & American Shop Front Designs & Drawings 1834-1900. rev. ed. Ken White & Frank White. Ed. by Joan Gerlacher. (Illus.). 208p. 1994. 69.00 (0-9625457-3-2) St Francis Pr.

Victorian Erotic Tales. Shelly Klein. 1995. 8.98 (0-7858-0461-7) Bk Sales Inc.

Victorian Eureka & Ferndale. Bob Von Normann. Ed. by George Castaldo. 32p. (Orig.). 1988. 6.95 (0-915687-02-X) FVN Corp.

***Victorian Fairy Painting.** Jeremy Maas. (Illus.). 168p. 1997. 40.00 (1-85894-043-5, Pub. by Merrell Holberton Pubs UK) U of Wash Pr.

Victorian Fairy Tale Book. Michael P. Hearn. LC 87-36039. (Illus.). 416p. 1990. pap. 17.00 (0-679-73258-6) Pantheon.

Victorian Fairy Tales: The Revolt of the Fairies & Elves. Ed. by Jack D. Zipes. 400p. (C). 1989. pap. 15.95 (0-415-90140-5, Routledge NY) Routledge.

Victorian Fairy Tales: The Revolt of the Fairies & Elves. Ed. by Jack D. Zipes. 400p. 1989. 29.50 (0-416-42080-X, Routledge NY) Routledge.

Victorian Faith in Crisis: Essays on Continuity & Change in Nineteenth-Century Religious Belief. Ed. by Bernard V. Lightman & Richard J. Helmstadter. LC 88-63908. 403p. 1991. 49.50 (0-8047-1602-1) Stanford U Pr.

***Victorian Families Fact & Fiction.** Kane. 1997. text ed. 18.95 (0-312-17221-4) St Martin.

Victorian Fancies. 190p. 1988. pap. 4.50 (0-88184-379-2) Carroll & Graf.

Victorian Fantasy Literature: Literary Battles with Church & Empire. Karen Michalson. LC 90-19302. (Studies in British Literature: Vol. 10). 308p. 1990. lib. bdg. 99.95 (0-88946-378-6) E Mellen.

Victorian Farm House. Herman Leslie & Margaret Bateson. (J). 1993. 19.95 (0-312-08931-7) St Martin.

Victorian Farmer. David J. Eveleigh. 1989. pap. 25.00 (0-7478-0106-1, Pub. by Shire UK) St Mut.

Victorian Fashion Paper Dolls from Harper's Bazaar, 1867-1898. Theodore Menten. (Illus.). (J). pap. 4.95 (0-486-23453-3) Dover.

Victorian Fashions: 1880-1890. Hazel Ulseth & Helen Shannon. 130p. 1988. pap. 14.95 (0-87588-309-5, 3591) Hobby Hse.

Victorian Fashions: 1890-1905, Vol. II. Hazel Ulseth & Helen Shannon. (Illus.). 130p. (Orig.). (C). 1989. pap. 14.95 (0-87588-329-X, 3718) Hobby Hse.

Victorian Fashions & Costumes from Harper's Bazar: 1898-1967. Stella Blum. (Illus.). 320p. (Orig.). 1974. pap. 14.95 (0-486-22990-4) Dover.

Victorian Feminism, 1850-1900. Philippa Levine. LC 94-11565. 176p. 1989. 17.95 (0-8130-1321-6) U Press Fla.

Victorian Feminists. Barbara Caine. 304p. (C). 1993. reprint ed. pap. 22.00 (0-19-820433-7, 14328) OUP.

Victorian Fiction: A Guide to Research. fac. ed. Lionel Stevenson. LC 64-21246. 448p. 1980. reprint ed. pap. 127.70 (0-7837-8035-4, 2047791) Bks Demand.

Victorian Fiction: A Second Guide to Research. Ed. by George H. Ford. (Reviews of Research Ser.: No. 3). xxv, 401p. 1978. pap. 19.75 (0-87352-255-9, Z4400) Modern Lang.

Victorian Fiction: A Second Guide to Research. fac. ed. Ed. by George H. Ford. LC 77-83468. 427p. 1978. reprint ed. pap. 121.70 (0-7837-8028-1, 2047784) Bks Demand.

Victorian Fiction: Writers, Publishers, Readers. John Sutherland. LC 94-49074. 1995. text ed. 39.95 (0-312-12614-X) St Martin.

Victorian Floral Designs in Full Color. F. Edward Hulme. LC 93-49490. (Pictorial Archive Ser.). (Illus.). 1994. pap. write for info. (0-486-27950-2) Dover.

Victorian Floral Illustrations: Three Hundred Forty-Four Wood Engravings of Exotic Flowers & Plants. Carol B. Grafton. (Pictorial Archive Ser.). 112p. 1985. pap. 7.95 (0-486-24822-4) Dover.

Victorian Floral Iron-on Transfer Patterns. Claire Bryant. (Transfer Patterns Ser.). (Illus.). 48p. (Orig.). 1991. pap. 2.95 (0-486-26665-6) Dover.

Victorian Flower Garden. Andrew Clayton-Payne & Brent Elliott. (Country Ser.). (Illus.). 160p. 1994. pap. 17.95 (0-297-83017-1) Trafalgar.

Victorian Flower Garden. Jennifer Davies. (Illus.). 160p. 1992. 25.00 (0-393-03100-4) Norton.

Victorian Flower Garden Book of Days. 1992. 15.99 (1-85145-622-8, Pavilion Bks) Viking Penguin.

Victorian Flower Oracle: The Language of Nature. Patricia Telesco. LC 93-49090. (Illus.). 264p. 1994. pap. 12.95 (0-87542-786-3) Llewellyn Pubns.

***Victorian Flowers: Address & Day Book Gift Set, 2 bks.** (Illus.). 128p. 1997. boxed 14.95 (1-85967-581-6, Lorenz Bks) Anness Pub.

***Victorian Flowers & Fairies: A Victorian Photograph Album.** (Illus.). 24p. 1997. 19.95 (1-85967-495-X, Lorenz Bks) Anness Pub.

Victorian Fol Sage: Comparative Readings on Carlyle, Emerson, Melville & Conrad. Camille R. La Bossiere. LC 87-480005. 136p. 1989. 29.50 (0-8387-5145-8) Bucknell U Pr.

Victorian Forerunner: The Later Career of Thomas Hood. John Clubbe. LC 68-28520. 275p. reprint ed. 78.40 (0-8357-9120-3, 2017893) Bks Demand.

Victorian Frame of Mind, 1830-1870. Walter E. Houghton. (C). 1963. pap. 20.00 (0-300-00122-3, Y99) Yale U Pr.

UV

An Asterisk (*) at the beginning of an entry indicates that the title is appearing in BIP for the first time.

Victorian Frames, Borders & Cuts. Bruce's Son & Company Staff. LC 76-3052. (Pictorial Archive Ser.). (Illus.). 128p. (Orig.). 1976. pap. 6.95 (*0-486-23320-0*) Dover.

Victorian Furniture: Our American Heritage. Kathryn McNerney. (Illus.). 252p. 1981. pap. 9.95 (*0-89145-164-1*) Collector Bks.

Victorian Furniture: Our American Heritage. Kathryn McNerney. 1994. pap. 12.95 (*0-89145-598-1*) Collector Bks.

Victorian Furniture: Technology & Design. Clive Edwards. (Studies in Design & Material Culture). 1993. text ed. 22.95 (*0-7190-3783-2*, Pub. by Manchester Univ Pr UK) St Martin.

Victorian Furniture with Prices. David P. Lindquist & Caroline C. Waren. LC 95-10554. 248p. 1995. pap. 22.95 (*0-87069-664-5*, Wallace-Hmestead) Chilton.

Victorian Garden. George Carter. (Illus.). 224p. 1995. 19.98 (*0-8317-9167-5*) Smithmark.

Victorian Garden: A Treasury of 19th-Century Garden Lore. Allison K. Leopold. LC 94-37318. (J). 1995. 40.00 (*0-517-58660-6*, Clarkson Potter) Crown Bks Yng Read.

Victorian Garden Album. Elizabeth Drury & Philippa Lewis. (Illus.). 128p. 1995. 18.95 (*0-926684-12-4*) Eclectic Oregon.

Victorian Gardens at the Molly Brown House. Leigh A. Grinstead & Gueda Gayou. (Illus.). 21p. (Orig.). 1995. pap. 2.95 (*0-914248-19-7*) Hist Denver.

Victorian Gentlewoman in the Far West: The Reminiscences of Mary Hallock Foote. Mary H. Foote. Ed. by Paul Rodman. LC 72-86535. (Illus.). 416p. 1983. pap. 14.95 (*0-87328-057-1*) Huntington Lib.

Victorian Ghost Stories. Ed. by Richard Dalby. 347p. 1989. 18.95 (*0-88184-473-X*) Carroll & Graf.

*__Victorian Ghost Stories.__ Mike Stocks. (Library of Fantasy & Adventure). (Illus.). 96p. (J). (gr. 3 up). 1996. pap. 9.95 (*0-7460-2727-3*, Usborne) EDC.

*__Victorian Ghost Stories.__ Mike Stocks. (Library of Fantasy & Adventure). (Illus.). 96p. (J). (gr. 3 up). 1996. lib. bdg. 17.95 (*0-88110-901-0*, Usborne) EDC.

Victorian Ghost Stories: An Oxford Anthology. Ed. by Michael Cox & R. A. Gilbert. 528p. 1993. reprint ed. pap. 15.95 (*0-19-282999-8*) OUP.

Victorian Ghost Stories by Eminent Women Writers. Ed. by Richard Dalby. 347p. 1990. pap. 9.95 (*0-88184-593-0*) Carroll & Graf.

Victorian Ghosts in the Noontide: Women Writers & the Supernatural. Vanessa D. Dickerson. 192p. (C). 1996. 34.95 (*0-8262-1081-3*) U of Mo Pr.

Victorian Gingerbread: Patterns & Techniques. Patrick Spielman & James Reidle. LC 92-19160. (Illus.). 200p. 1992. pap. 14.95 (*0-8069-7452-4*) Sterling.

*__Victorian Girls: Lord Lyttelton's Daughters.__ Sheila Fletcher. LC 96-29455. 1997. write for info. (*1-85285-150-3*) Hambledon Press.

*__Victorian Goods & Merchandise.__ Ed. by Carol B. Grafton. LC 97-15501. (Illus.). 128p. 1997. pap. 9.95 (*0-486-29698-9*) Dover.

Victorian Gothic & Renaissance Revival Furniture. David Hanks. 1977. 15.00 (*0-916530-06-X*) Athenaeum Phila.

Victorian Gothic Design Book. Ramona Jablonski. (International Design Library). (Illus.). 48p. (Orig.). 1981. pap. 5.95 (*0-916144-82-8*) Stemmer Hse.

Victorian Governess. Kathryn Hughes. LC 92-25847. 274p. 1992. boxed 40.00 (*1-85285-002-7*) Hambledon Press.

Victorian Grimoire. Patricia Telesco. LC 92-20393. (Illus.). 382p. 1992. 14.95 (*0-87542-784-7*) Llewellyn Pubns.

Victorian Hardware, Housewares & Kitchen Tools, 1865-1915: 5,000 Copyright Free Engravings for Artists & Craftsmen with Current Price Guide for Antique Collectors. Ronald S. Barlow & Linda C. Franklin. (Illus.). 376p. (Orig.). 1992. pap. 19.95 (*0-933846-03-7*) Windmill Pub Co.

Victorian Heritage of Virginia Woolf. Janis M. Paul. 225p. 1987. 29.95 (*0-937664-73-1*) Pilgrim Bks OK.

Victorian Heroine: A Changing Ideal, 1837-1873. Patricia Thomson. LC 73-19303. 178p. 1978. reprint ed. text ed. 49.75 (*0-8371-7118-0*, THVH, Greenwood Pr) Greenwood.

Victorian Heroines: Representations of Feminity in Nineteenth-Century Literature & Art. Kimberley Reynolds & Nicola Humble. LC 93-27468. (C). 1993. 45.00 (*0-8147-7361-3*); pap. 18.50 (*0-8147-7362-1*) NYU Pr.

Victorian Home. Bobbie Kalman. LC 96-26733. (Historic Communities Ser.). 32p. 1996. pap. 7.95 (*0-86505-461-4*); lib. bdg. 19.16 (*0-86505-431-2*) Crabtree Pub Co.

Victorian Home. Joni Prittie. (Illus.). 76p. 1990. 11.95 (*0-937769-81-9*) Mark Inc CA.

Victorian Home: The Grandeur & Comforts of the Victorian Era, in Households Past & Present. Ellen M. Plante. (Illus.). 176p. 1995. 24.95 (*1-56138-452-6*) Running Pr.

*__Victorian Home in Cross Stitch.__ Barbara Thompson & Ann Green. (Illus.). 128p. 1997. 24.95 (*0-7153-0430-5*, Pub. by D & C Pub UK) Sterling.

*__Victorian Horror.__ Mike Stocks. (Library of Fear, Fantasy & Adventure). (Illus.). 80p. (Orig.). (YA). (gr. 5 up). 1997. pap. 8.95 (*0-7460-2729-X*, Usborne) EDC.

Victorian House Book. Robin Guild et al. LC 89-6114. (Illus.). 320p. 1989. reprint ed. 50.00 (*0-8478-1095-X*) Rizzoli Intl.

*__Victorian House Designs in Authentic Full Color: 75 Plates from the Scientific American - Architects & Builders Edition, 1886-1894.__ Ed. by Blanche Cirker. LC 96-47807. (Illus.). 80p. (Orig.). 1997. pap. text ed. 12.95 (*0-486-29438-2*) Dover.

Victorian House Style. Linda Osband. (Illus.). 1992. 39.95 (*0-7153-9841-5*, Pub. by D & C Pub UK) Sterling.

Victorian Housebuilder's Guide: Woodward's National Architect, of 1869. George E. Woodward & Edward G. Thompson. (Illus.). 160p. 1988. reprint ed. pap. 7.95 (*0-486-25704-5*) Dover.

Victorian Household. Shirley Nicholson. (Illus.). 224p. 1994. pap. 20.00 (*0-7509-0637-5*, Pub. by Sutton Pubng UK) Bks Intl VA.

Victorian Housekeeping: A Combined Study of Restoration & Photography. Judith M. Johnson. Ed. by Linda H. Smith. 1978. pap. 6.95 (*0-936386-05-3*) Creative Learning.

Victorian Houses: A Treasury of Lesser-Known Examples. Edmund V. Gillon, Jr. & Clay Lancaster. (Illus.). 128p. (Orig.). 1973. pap. 9.95 (*0-486-22966-1*) Dover.

Victorian Houses Coloring Book. Daniel Lewis. (Illus.). (J). (gr. k-3). 1950. pap. 2.95 (*0-486-23908-X*) Dover.

Victorian Identities: Social & Cultural Formations in Nineteenth-Century Literature. Ed. by Ruth Robbins & Julian Wolfreys. LC 95-14915. 256p. 1996. text ed. 49.95 (*0-312-12850-9*) St Martin.

Victorian Illustrated Books: The Heyday of Wood-Engraving, 1850-1870. Paul Goldman. (Illus.). 144p. (C). 1994. 35.00 (*1-56792-014-4*) Godine.

Victorian Illustration: The Pre-Raphaelites, the Idyllic School & the High Victorians. Paul Goldman. (Illus.). 400p. 1996. 99.50 (*0-85967-864-4*, Pub. by Scolar Pr UK) Ashgate Pub Co.

Victorian Imagination: Essays in Aesthetic Exploration. William E. Buckler. (Gotham Library). 384p. (C). 1980. pap. text ed. 16.00 (*0-8147-1033-6*) NYU Pr.

*__Victorian Imprint Kegan Paul: Publishers, Books, & Cultural History.__ Leslie Howsam. 227p. 1996. 45.00 (*0-8020-4126-4*) U of Toronto Pr.

Victorian in the Modern World. Hutchins Hapgood. (American Biography Ser.). 604p. 1991. reprint ed. lib. bdg. 109.00 (*0-7812-8166-0*) Rprt Serv.

Victorian Insolvency: Bankruptcy, Imprisonment for Debt, & Company Winding-up in Nineteenth-Century England. V. Markham Lester. (Oxford Historical Monographs). (Illus.). 368p. 1995. 69.00 (*0-19-820518-X*) OUP.

*__Victorian Interior Decoration, Vol. 1.__ R. Moss. 1986. write for info. (*0-03-007989-6*) St Martin.

Victorian Interior Style. Joanna Banham. 1996. 24.98 (*0-8317-3769-7*) Smithmark.

Victorian Interiors. R. Moss & G. C. Winkler. 25.00 (*0-670-80612-9*) Viking Penguin.

Victorian Interpretation of Racial Conflict: The Maori, the British, & the New Zealand Wars. James Belich. (McGill-Queen's Studies in Ethnic History). 400p. (C). 1989. text ed. 55.00 (*0-7735-0750-7*, Pub. by McGill CN); pap. text ed. 24.95 (*0-7735-0739-6*, Pub. by McGill CN) U of Toronto Pr.

Victorian Inventions. Leonard De Vries. (Illus.). 192p. 1992. pap. 24.95 (*0-7195-5006-8*, Pub. by John Murray UK) Trafalgar.

Victorian Ironmonger. Cecil A. Meadows. 1989. pap. 25.00 (*0-85263-704-7*, Pub. by Shire UK) St Mut.

Victorian Jewelry: A Compendium of over Four Thousand Pieces of Jewelry. Peter Hinks. 1995. 19.98 (*0-8317-2178-2*) Smithmark.

Victorian Jewelry: Unexplored Treasures. Corinne Davidov & Ginny R. Dawes. (Illus.). 156p. 1991. 35.00 (*1-55859-135-4*) Abbeville Pr.

Victorian Kitchen. Jennifer Davies. LC 91-72390. (Illus.). 192p. 1992. reprint ed. pap. 17.95 (*0-563-36281-2*, BBC-Parkwest) Parkwest Pubns.

Victorian Kitchen Garden. Jan Hughes. 128p. 1996. text ed. 17.95 (*0-89815-798-6*) Ten Speed Pr.

*__Victorian Kittens.__ Brownlow Publishing Company Staff. 1997. pap. text ed. 6.99 (*1-57051-101-2*) Brownlow Pub Co.

Victorian Knight-Errant: A Study of the Early Literary Career of James Russell Lowell. Leon Howard. LC 72-136072. 1971. reprint ed. text ed. 69.50 (*0-8371-5222-4*, HOVK, Greenwood Pr) Greenwood.

Victorian Lace. Patricia Wardle. 1984. 21.95 (*0-903585-13-8*) Robin & Russ.

*__Victorian Lady Novelists.__ M. L. Parrish. (Illus.). 173p. 1995. reprint ed. 60.00 (*1-888262-57-5*) Martino Pubng.

Victorian Lady Travellers. Dorothy Middleton. (Illus.). 189p. 1993. reprint ed. pap. 11.00 (*0-89733-063-3*) Academy Chi Pubs.

Victorian Lady's Album. Ed. by Della Stanley. (Illus.). 124p. 1995. 19.95 (*0-88780-231-1*) Formac Dist Ltd.

Victorian Landscape Watercolors. Scott Wilcox & Christopher Newall. LC 92-10149. (Illus.). 196p. (C). 1992. 50.00 (*1-55595-071-X*) Hudson Hills.

Victorian Law Reports: Australia, 138 vols. Council of Law Reporting of Victoria, Australia Staff. Set. 4,279.00 (*0-409-49004-0*) MICHIE.

Victorian Life & Victorian Fiction: A Companion for the American Reader. Jo McMurtry. LC 78-17049. (Illus.). 315p. (C). 1978. lib. bdg. 34.00 (*0-208-01744-5*, Archon Bks) Shoe String.

*__Victorian Life & Victorian Fiction: A Companion for the American Reader.__ Jo McMurtry. LC 78-17049. (Illus.). 315p. (C). 1996. pap. 25.00 (*0-208-02401-8*, Archon Bks) Shoe String.

*__Victorian Literary & Intellectual Culture: An Anthology of Sources & Documents.__ Josephine M. Guy. LC 96-27668. 1997. write for info. (*0-13-355322-1*) P-H.

Victorian Literature & Culture, 1992-1993, Set. rev. ed. Ed. by John Maynard & Adrienne A. Munich. (Illus.). 1992. write for info. (*0-404-64200-4*) AMS Pr.

Victorian Literature & Culture, 1992-1993, Vol. 20. rev. ed. Ed. by John Maynard & Adrienne Auslander Munich. (Illus.). 1993. 57.50 (*0-404-64220-9*) AMS Pr.

Victorian Literature & Culture, 1992-1993, Vol. 21. rev. ed. Ed. by John Maynard & Adrienne Auslander Munich. (Illus.). 1993. Set. 52.25 (*0-404-64221-7*) AMS Pr.

Victorian Literature & Society: Essays Presented to Richard D. Altick. Ed. by James R. Kincaid & Albert J. Kuhn. LC 83-13317. 382p. 1984. 45.00 (*0-8142-0362-0*) Ohio St U Pr.

Victorian Literature & the Victorian Visual Imagination. Ed. by Carol T. Christ & John O. Jordan. LC 94-40328. 400p. 1995. 50.00 (*0-520-08641-4*); pap. 20.00 (*0-520-20022-5*) U CA Pr.

Victorian London Street Life in Historic Photographs. John Thompson. Orig. Title: Street Life in London. (Illus.). 160p. 1994. reprint ed. pap. 12.95 (*0-486-28121-3*) Dover.

*__Victorian Love Stories.__ Ed. by Kate Flint. 520p. 1996. 29.95 (*0-19-212330-0*) OUP.

*__Victorian Love Stories: An Oxford Anthology.__ Ed. by Kate Flint. 528p. 1998. reprint ed. pap. 13.95 (*0-19-288040-3*) OUP.

Victorian Lunacy: Richard M. Bucke & the Practice of Late 19th-Century Psychiatry. S. E. Shortt. (History of Medicine Ser.). (Illus.). 256p. 1986. text ed. 44.95 (*0-521-30999-9*) Cambridge U Pr.

Victorian Lunatics: A Social Epidemiology of Mental Illness in Mid-Nineteenth-Century England. Marlene A. Arieno. LC 88-43163. (Illus.). 144p. 1989. 32.50 (*0-945636-03-2*) Susquehanna U Pr.

Victorian Majolica: With Price Guide. Leslie Bockol. LC 95-45611. (Books for Collectors). (Illus.). 192p. 1996. pap. 39.95 (*0-88740-953-9*) Schiffer.

Victorian Marblehead. Gail P. Hercher. LC 80-50011. (Illus.). 144p. (Orig.). 1980. pap. 10.95 (*0-936230-24-X*) Sometime Pr.

Victorian Masculinities: Manhood & Masculine Poetics in Early Victorian Literature & Art. Herbert Sussman. LC 94-10268. (Studies in Nineteenth-Century Literature & Culture: Vol. 3). (Illus.). 241p. (C). 1995. text ed. 54.95 (*0-521-46571-0*) Cambridge U Pr.

Victorian Millinery: Ladies' Hats 1850-1900. Paula J. Darnell. LC 95-61332. (Illus.). 105p. (Orig.). 1995. pap. 19.95 (*1-887402-08-X*) Fabric Fancies.

Victorian Minds. Gertrude Himmelfarb. LC 94-43053. 480p. 1995. pap. 16.95 (*1-56663-077-0*, Elephant Paperbacks) I R Dee.

Victorian Miniature. Owen Chadwick. (Canto Book Ser.). 192p. (C). 1991. pap. text ed. 10.95 (*0-521-42251-5*) Cambridge U Pr.

Victorian Murderesses: A True History of Thirteen Respectable French & English Women Accused of Unspeakable Crimes. Mary S. Hartman. 318p. 1995. pap. 10.95 (*0-86051-343-2*, Pub. by Robson UK) Parkwest Pubns.

Victorian Music Hall: Culture, Class & Conflict. Dagmar Kift. (Illus.). 255p. (C). 1996. text ed. 54.95 (*0-521-47472-8*) Cambridge U Pr.

Victorian Naturalist: Beatrix Potter's Drawings from the Armitt Collection. Ed. by Anne S. Hobbs & Mary Noble. (Illus.). 192p. (J). 1992. pap. 40.00 (*0-7232-3990-8*) Warne.

Victorian Needle-Craft: Artistic & Practical. enl. ed. Ed. by R. L. Shep. LC 94-13688. (Illus.). 336p. 1994. reprint ed. pap. 24.95 (*0-914046-21-7*) R L Shep.

Victorian Needlepoint. Beth Russell. (Illus.). 112p. 1996. pap. 19.95 (*1-85470-258-0*, Coll & Brown) Trafalgar.

Victorian Needlepoint Designs. Godey's Lady's Book Staff & Peterson's Magazine Staff. LC 74-24489. (Illus.). 48p. 1975. pap. 2.95 (*0-486-23163-1*) Dover.

*__Victorian Noon: English Literature in 1850.__ Carl Dawson. LC 78-13939. 288p. 1979. reprint ed. pap. 82.10 (*0-608-03680-3*, 2064506) Bks Demand.

*__Victorian Novel: An Annotated Bibliography.__ Laurence W. Mazzeno. (Magill Bibliographies Ser.). 222p. 1989. 40.00 (*0-8108-2805-7*) Scarecrow.

Victorian Novelist: Conscience & Social Change. Kate Flint. Ed. by Isobel Armstrong. (World & Word Ser.). 256p. 1987. pap. text ed. 14.95 (*0-685-19167-2*, Pub. by Croom Helm UK); lib. bdg. 65.00 (*0-685-19166-4*, Pub. by Croom Helm UK) Routledge Chapman & Hall.

Victorian Novelists. James Oliphant. LC 02-26320. reprint ed. 29.50 (*0-404-04816-1*) AMS Pr.

Victorian Novelists after Eighteen Eighty-Five, Vol. 18. Ed. by Ira B. Nadel & William E. Fredeman. (Dictionary of Literary Biography Ser.: Vol. 18). (Illus.). 410p. 1983. 140.00 (*0-8103-1143-7*) Gale.

Victorian Novelists Before Eighteen Eighty-Five, Vol. 21. Ed. by Ira B. Nadel et al. LC 83-8848. (Dictionary of Literary Biography Ser.: Vol. 21). 432p. 1983. 140.00 (*0-8103-1701-X*) Gale.

Victorian Novels in Serial. J. Don Vann. LC 84-20538. x, 181p. 1985. lib. bdg. 50.00 (*0-87352-135-8*) Modern Lang.

Victorian Novelties & Figurals: Geo. Duncan & Sons. Neila Bredehoft & Tom Bredehoft. 51p. 1989. pap. 5.95 (*1-885503-01-6*) Cherry H Pubns.

*__Victorian Nude.__ Smith. 1997. text ed. 19.95 (*0-7190-4403-0*); text ed. 59.95 (*0-7190-4402-2*) St Martin.

Victorian Ornaments. Elspeth. 11p. 1988. pap. 10.95 (*0-87588-328-1*) Hobby Hse.

Victorian Ornaments & Pattern Designs. Sue A. Sonesifer. (International Design Library). (Illus.). 48p. 1982. pap. 5.95 (*0-916144-96-8*) Stemmer Hse.

Victorian Oxford. W. Reginald Ward. 431p. 1965. 35.00 (*0-7146-1370-3*, Pub. by F Cass Pubs UK) Intl Spec Bk.

Victorian Painting. Julian Treuherz. LC 92-61580. (World of Art Ser.). (Illus.). 216p. 1993. pap. 14.95 (*0-500-20263-X*) Thames Hudson.

*__Victorian Paintings in Oils & Watercolors.__ Christopher Wood. 69.50 (*1-85149-249-6*) Antique Collect.

Victorian Paper Dolls. (J). Date not set. pap. text ed. 2.95 (*1-57122-079-8*) Nickel Pr.

Victorian Parlors & Tea Parties. Patricia B. Mitchell. 1991. pap. 4.00 (*0-925117-36-6*) Mitchells.

Victorian Parlour Poetry: An Annotated Anthology. Michael R. Turner. Orig. Title: Parlour Poetry: A Casquet of Gems. (Illus.). 352p. 1992. reprint ed. pap. 9.95 (*0-486-27044-0*) Dover.

Victorian Pastoral: Tennyson, Hardy, & the Subversion of Forms. Owen Schur. 240p. 1989. text ed. 42.50 (*0-8142-0483-X*) Ohio St U Pr.

Victorian Patchwork Patterns: Instructions & Full-Size Templates for 12 Quilts. Sandra MacDonagh. (Illus.). 64p. (Orig.). 1988. pap. 5.95 (*0-486-25543-3*) Dover.

Victorian Pattern Glass & China Book. 1990. 29.99 (*0-517-03045-4*) Random Hse Value.

Victorian Patterns & Designs in Full Color. George A. Audsley & Maurice A. Audsley. 112p. 1988. pap. 14.95 (*0-486-25756-8*) Dover.

Victorian Peasant. Richard Heath. Ed. by Keith Dockray. 224p. 1989. text ed. 39.95 (*0-312-02852-0*) St Martin.

Victorian People: A Reassessment of Persons & Themes, 1851-67. rev. ed. Asa Briggs. LC 55-5118. (Chicago Collectors Editions Ser.). (Illus.). x, 368p. 1975. reprint ed. pap. text ed. 16.95 (*0-226-07488-9*, P365) U Ch Pr.

Victorian People & Ideas. Richard D. Altick. (Illus.). 338p. (C). 1974. pap. text ed. 11.95 (*0-393-09376-X*) Norton.

Victorian Period: The Intellectual & Cultural Context of English Literature, 1830-1890. Robin Gilmour. (C). 1994. text ed. 77.95 (*0-582-49346-3*, Pub. by Longman UK); pap. text ed. 31.95 (*0-582-49347-1*, Pub. by Longman UK) Longman.

Victorian Periodical Press: Samplings & Soundings. Ed. by Joanne Shattock & Michael Wolff. LC 82-184551. (Illus.). 420p. reprint ed. pap. 119.70 (*0-8357-3665-2*, 2036391) Bks Demand.

Victorian Periodicals: A Guide to Research, Vol. I. Ed. by J. Don Vann & Rosemary T. VanArsdel. LC 77-94918. (Reviews of Research Ser.: No. 4). xi, 188p. 1978. lib. bdg. 19.75 (*0-87352-256-7*, Z4500) Modern Lang.

Victorian Periodicals: A Guide to Research, Vol. II. Ed. by J. Don Vann & Rosemary T. VanArsdel. LC 77-94918. (Reviews of Research Ser.: No. 7). vii, 177p. 1989. reprint ed. pap. 19.75 (*0-87352-265-6*, Z480P); reprint ed. lib. bdg. 37.50 (*0-87352-264-8*, Z480C) Modern Lang.

Victorian Periodicals & Victorian Society. Ed. by J. Don Vann & Rosemary T. VanArsdel. 416p. 1993. 125.00 (*0-8020-0522-5*) U of Toronto Pr.

Victorian Periodicals & Victorian Society. Ed. by J. Don Vann & Rosemary T. VanArsdel. 382p. 1996. pap. 35.00 (*0-8020-7174-0*) U of Toronto Pr.

Victorian Perspectives. Ed. by John Clubbe & Jerome Meckier. LC 88-40132. 200p. 1989. 35.00 (*0-87413-350-5*) U Delaware Pr.

*__Victorian Photograph Album.__ (Illus.). 22p. 1997. 19.95 (*1-85967-385-6*, Lorenz Bks) Anness Pub.

Victorian Photography, Painting & Poetry: The Enigma of Visibility in Ruskin, Morris & the Pre-Raphaelites. Lindsay Smith. (Studies in Nineteenth-Century Literature & Culture: Vol. 6). (Illus.). 268p. (C). 1995. text ed. 54.95 (*0-521-47288-1*) Cambridge U Pr.

Victorian Pictorial Borders: One Hundred Twenty-Four Full-Page Designs. Carol B. Grafton. 128p. 1984. pap. 6.95 (*0-486-24693-0*) Dover.

Victorian Pictures in the Collection of Her Majesty the Queen. Oliver Millar. (Pictures in the Collection of Her Majesty the Queen). (Illus.). 736p. (C). 1993. text ed. 335.00 (*0-521-26522-3*) Cambridge U Pr.

Victorian Plays: A Record of Significant Productions on the London Stage, 1837-1901. Compiled by Donald Mullin. LC 86-25718. (Bibliographies & Indexes in the Performing Arts Ser.: No. 4). 460p. 1987. text ed. 69.50 (*0-313-24211-9*, MVP/) Greenwood.

Victorian Poet: Poetics & Persona. Joseph Bristow. (World & Word Ser.). 256p. 1987. 65.00 (*0-7099-3925-6*, Pub. by Croom Helm UK) Routledge Chapman & Hall.

Victorian Poet: Poetics & Persona. Joseph Bristow. (World & Word Ser.). 256p. (C). 1987. pap. text ed. 14.95 (*0-7099-3977-9*, Pub. by Croom Helm UK) Routledge Chapman & Hall.

Victorian Poetry. Armstrong. 560p. 1996. pap. 22.95 (*0-415-14425-6*) Routledge.

Victorian Poetry. John Drinkwater. (BCL1-PR English Literature Ser.). 236p. 1992. reprint ed. lib. bdg. 79.00 (*0-7812-7068-5*) Rprt Serv.

Victorian Poetry: An Annotated Bibliography. annot. ed. Laurence W. Mazzeno. LC 95-5328. (Magill Bibliographies Ser.). 261p. 1995. 32.50 (*0-8108-3008-6*) Scarecrow.

Victorian Poetry: Poetry, Poetics, Politics. Isobel Armstrong. LC 92-2451. (Critical History of Victorian Poetry Ser.). 512p. (C). (gr. 13). 1993. text ed. 45.00 (*0-415-03016-1*, B0703, Routledge NY) Routledge.

Victorian Poetry & Poetics, 2 Vols. 2nd ed. Walter E. Houghton & G. Robert Stange. LC 74-370. (C). 1972. text ed. 57.96 (*0-395-04646-7*) HM.

Victorian Poetry & the Romantic Religion. Derek Colville. LC 76-97213. 262p. 1970. pap. text ed. 19.95 (*0-87395-074-7*) State U NY Pr.

Victorian Poets. rev. ed. Edmund C. Stedman. LC 78-148307. reprint ed. 32.50 (*0-404-06237-7*) AMS Pr.

Victorian Poets. Edmund C. Stedman. (BCL1-PR English Literature Ser.). 521p. 1992. reprint ed. lib. bdg. 99.00 (*0-7812-7072-3*) Rprt Serv.

Victorian Poets. Edmund C. Stedman. LC 18-108542. 1970. reprint ed. 14.00 (*0-403-00282-6*) Scholarly.

Victorian Poets: A Guide to Research. Frederic E. Faverty. LC 56-7213. 302p. reprint ed. pap. 86.10 (*0-7837-4144-8*, 2057992) Bks Demand.

Victorian Poets: Critical Heritage, 6 vols., Set. Incl. Algernon Swinburne. Ed. by Hyder. 307p. (C). 1996. text ed. 120.00 (*0-415-13454-4*); Gerard Manley Hopkins. Ed. by Roberts. 414p. (C). 1996. text ed. 130.00 (*0-415-13453-6*); Arthur Hugh Clough. Ed. by Thorpe. 429p. (C). 1996. text ed. 130.00 (*0-415-13452-8*); Robert Browning. Ed. by Litzinger. 568p. (C). 1996. text ed. 150.00 (*0-415-13451-X*); Lord Alfred Tennyson. Ed. by Jump. 474p. (C). 1996. text ed. 130.00 (*0-415-13450-1*); John Clare. 472p. (C). 1996. text ed. 130.00 (*0-415-13449-8*); 2664p. (C). 1996. Set boxed, text ed. 659.00 (*0-415-13448-X*) Routledge.

Victorian Poets after 1850, Vol. 35. Ed. by William E. Fredeman & Ira B. Nadel. (Dictionary of Literary Biography Ser.: Vol. 35). 456p. 1985. 140.00 (*0-8103-1713-3*) Gale.

Victorian Poets & Prose Writers. 2nd ed. Jerome H. Buckley. LC 76-5212. (Goldentree Bibliographies Series in Language & Literature). (C). 1977. pap. text ed. write for info. (*0-88295-560-8*) Harlan Davidson.

Victorian Poets & Romantic Poems: Intertextuality & Ideology. Antony H. Harrison. LC 89-22443. (Virginia Victorian Studies). 235p. 1990. text ed. 35.00 (*0-8139-1253-9*) U Pr of Va.

Victorian Poets & Romantic Poems: Intertextuality & Ideology. Antony H. Harrison. (Victorian Literature & Culture Ser.). 235p. 1992. reprint ed. pap. text ed. 16.50 (*0-8139-1364-0*) U Pr of Va.

Victorian Poets Before 1850, Vol. 32. Ed. by William E. Fredeman & Ira B. Nadel. (Dictionary of Literary Biography Ser.: Vol. 32). 440p. 1984. 140.00 (*0-8103-1710-9*) Gale.

Victorian Portraits. Percy Colson. LC 68-16921. (Essay Index Reprint Ser.). 1977. 18.95 (*0-8369-0328-5*) Ayer.

Victorian Post Office: The Growth of a Bureaucracy. C. R. Perry. (Royal Historical Society: Studies in History: No. 64). 320p. (C). 1992. 79.00 (*0-86193-220-X*, Royal Historical Soc) Boydell & Brewer.

Victorian Posy. Sheila Pickles. 1991. 45.00 (*0-517-58213-9*, Ebury Pr Stationery) Crown Pub Group.

***Victorian Posy.** Sheila Pickles. 1995. 9.99 (*0-517-16554-6*) Random Hse Value.

Victorian Posy: A Treasury of Verse & Prose. Sheila Pickles. (Scented Treasuries of Verse & Prose Ser.). 1994. 6.50 (*0-517-59901-5*, Harmony) Crown Pub Group.

Victorian Posy: Penhaligon's Scented Treasury of Verse & Prose. Sheila Pickles. (Illus.). 112p. 1988. 20.00 (*0-517-56766-0*, Harmony) Crown Pub Group.

Victorian Posy Birthday Book. Sheila Pickles. 1990. 11.00 (*0-517-57854-9*, Harmony) Crown Pub Group.

Victorian Posy Book of Days. Sheila Pickles. 1990. 17.00 (*0-517-57858-1*, Harmony) Crown Pub Group.

Victorian Posy Notebook. Sheila Pickles. 1990. 9.95 (*0-517-57855-7*, Harmony) Crown Pub Group.

Victorian Posy Visitor's Book. Pickles. 1990. 20.00 (*0-517-57856-5*, Ebury Pr Stationery) Crown Pub Group.

Victorian Preserves, Pickles, & Relishes. Allison K. Leopold. (Illus.). 64p. 1992. 10.00 (*0-517-58315-1*, C P Pubs) Crown Pub Group.

Victorian Princess & Battenberg Lace Designs: By Hand Or on the Sewing Machine. 2nd rev. ed. Eunice S. Jurado. Ed. by Edward Lyons. (Illus.). (C). 1988. reprint ed. 10.95 (*0-944488-01-3*) E S Jurado.

***Victorian Printer.** Graham Hudson. 1996. pap. 30.00 (*0-7478-0330-7*) St Mut.

Victorian Prison Lives. Philip Priestly. (Illus.). 250p. 1985. 27.50 (*0-416-34770-3*, 9594) Routledge Chapman & Hall.

Victorian Prose. Frederick W. Roe. LC 47-12149. 773p. reprint ed. pap. 180.00 (*0-317-28653-6*, 2055090) Bks Demand.

Victorian Prose: A Guide to Research. Ed. by David J. DeLaura. LC 73-80586. (Reviews of Research Ser.: No. 1). xvi, 560p. 1973. pap. 25.00 (*0-87352-251-6*, Z4200) Modern Lang.

Victorian Prose & Poetry. Ed. by Lionel Trilling & Harold Bloom. (Oxford Anthology of English Literature: Vol. V). (Illus.). 766p. 1973. pap. 26.95 (*0-19-501616-5*) OUP.

Victorian Prose Masters. William C. Brownell. 1972. 59.95 (*0-8490-1260-0*) Gordon Pr.

Victorian Prose Masters. William C. Brownell. (BCL1-PR English Literature Ser.). 289p. 1992. reprint ed. lib. bdg. 79.00 (*0-7812-7112-6*) Rprt Serv.

Victorian Prose Masters: Thackeray-Carlyle-George Eliot-Matthew Arnold-Ruskin-George Meredith. William C. Brownell. LC 72-108771. (BCL Ser. I). reprint ed. 52.50 (*0-404-01142-X*) AMS Pr.

Victorian Prose Writers after 1867, Vol. 57. Ed. by William B. Thesing. LC 87-336. (Dictionary of Literary Biography Ser.: Vol. 57). 596p. 1987. 140.00 (*0-8103-1735-4*) Gale.

Victorian Prose Writers Before 1867, Vol. 55. Ed. by William B. Thesing. (Dictionary of Literary Biography Ser.: Vol. 55). 379p. 1986. 140.00 (*0-8103-1733-8*) Gale.

Victorian Publisher's Bindings. Douglas Ball. (Illus.). 214p. 1985. 38.50 (*0-916271-01-3*) BkPr Ltd.

Victorian Pubs. Mark Girouard. LC 83-51291. (Illus.). 232p. 1984. pap. 27.50 (*0-300-03201-3*, Y-492) Yale U Pr.

Victorian Quaker Courtship Eighteen Fifty-Three to Eighteen Fifty-Five: Lancashire Love Letters of the 1850's by Dr. John Dilworth Abbott. Sessions, William Ltd., Staff. (C). 1989. 34.00 (*1-85072-043-6*, Pub. by W Sessions UK) St Mut.

Victorian Quilt Block. Jodie Davis. 1996. 24.95 (*1-56799-258-7*, Friedman-Fairfax) M Friedman Pub Grp Inc.

Victorian Quilt Block Design. Jodie Davis. 1996. 24.95 (*0-614-96824-0*, Friedman-Fairfax) M Friedman Pub Grp Inc.

Victorian Quilts, 1875-1900: They Aren't All Crazy. Paul D. Pilgrim. 1995. pap. 14.95 (*0-89145-846-8*) Collector Bks.

Victorian Railroad Stations of L. I. Ron Ziel. 42.95 (*0-8488-0406-6*) Amereon Ltd.

Victorian Railway Atlas: Lancashire & North Cheshire. Village Press Editorial Board Staff. (Village Atlas Ser.). (Illus.). (C). 1989. 95.00 (*1-85540-027-8*, Pub. by Village Pr UK) St Mut.

Victorian Railway Atlas: The West Midlands. Village Press Editorial Board Staff. (Village Atlas Ser.). (Illus.). (C). 1990. 95.00 (*1-85540-028-6*, Pub. by Village Pr UK) St Mut.

Victorian Relief Moulded Jugs. Jill Rumsey. (Illus.). 48p. 1987. pap. 12.95 (*0-903685-20-5*, Pub. by R Dennis UK) Antique Collect.

***Victorian Resource Book.** (Sense of History Ser.). 1993. pap. text ed. write for info. (*0-582-09214-0*, Pub. by Longman UK) Longman.

Victorian Ribbon & Lacecraft Designs. Mary Jo Hiney. (Illus.). 144p. 1994. pap. 14.95 (*0-8069-0403-8*, Chapelle) Sterling.

Victorian Ribbon Embroidery for Dolls. Remona Gibeson. (Illus.). 38p. reprint ed. pap. 11.50 (*0-9631893-3-6*) Sloane Pubns.

Victorian Romance. 2nd ed. Lindsay Welsh. (Orig.). 1995. mass mkt. 5.95 (*1-56333-365-1*, Rosebud) Masquerade.

Victorian Rose Little Book of Love. 1995. 5.00 (*0-687-00138-2*) Abingdon.

Victorian Rotherham: A Pictorial History. Tony Munford. (Illus.). 80p. (C). 1989. pap. 50.00 (*1-85563-003-6*, Pub. by Quoin Pub Ltd UK) St Mut.

Victorian Sages & Cultural Discourse: Renegotiating Gender & Power. Ed. by Thais E. Morgan. LC 90-30977. (Illus.). 320p. (C). 1990. text ed. 45.00 (*0-8135-1600-5*); pap. text ed. 16.95 (*0-8135-1601-3*) Rutgers U Pr.

Victorian Sampler. Ed. by Richard Manton. 1992. mass mkt. 5.95 (*1-56201-019-0*, 118) Blue Moon Bks.

Victorian Scandals: Representations of Gender & Class. Ed. by Kristine O. Garrigan. LC 92-3945. (Illus.). 350p. (C). 1992. text ed. 42.00 (*0-8214-1019-9*) Ohio U Pr.

Victorian Scene. Neil King. (Drama Ser.). 128p. 8500. pap. 13.95 (*0-7175-1235-5*) Dufour.

Victorian Scene. Neil King. 128p. (C). 1985. 49.00 (*0-685-33823-1*, Pub. by S Thornes Pubs UK) St Mut.

Victorian Science & Engineering: Portrayed in the Illustrated London News. Kenneth K. Chew & Anthony Wilson. (Illus.). 160p. 1993. pap. 25.99 (*0-7509-0326-0*, Pub. by Sutton Pubng UK) Bks Intl VA.

Victorian Science & Religion: A Bibliography of Works on Ideas & Institutions with Emphasis on Evolution, Belief & Unbelief, Published from 1900 to 1975. Ed. by Sydney Eisen & Bernard V. Lightman. LC 82-24497. xix, 696p. (C). 1984. lib. bdg. 72.50 (*0-208-02010-1*, Archon Bks) Shoe String.

Victorian Science & Victorian Values: Literary Perspectives. Ed. by Thomas Postlewait & James G. Paradis. LC 80-29513. 362p. 1981. pap. 72.00 (*0-89766-110-9*) NY Acad Sci.

Victorian Science & Victorian Values: Literary Perspectives. Thomas Postlewait. Ed. by James G. Paradis. 375p. (C). 1985. pap. text ed. 15.00 (*0-8135-1107-0*) Rutgers U Pr.

***Victorian Science in Context.** Lightman. LC 97-20789. 1997. lib. bdg. 70.00 (*0-226-48111-5*) U Ch Pr.

***Victorian Science in Context.** Bernard Lightman. LC 97-20789. 1997. pap. text ed. 22.50 (*0-226-48112-3*) U Ch Pr.

Victorian Scrapbook. Cynthia Hart et al. LC 89-40373. (Illus.). 160p. 1989. 27.95 (*0-89480-620-3*, 1620) Workman Pub.

Victorian Scroll Saw Patterns. Patrick Spielman. LC 90-37344. (Illus.). 192p. (Orig.). 1990. pap. 14.95 (*0-8069-7294-7*) Sterling.

Victorian Sculpture. Benedict Read. LC 83-70483. (Paul Mellon Centre for Studies in British Art). (Illus.). 416p. 1984. reprint ed. pap. 35.00 (*0-300-03177-7*) Yale U Pr.

Victorian Self: Autobiography & Biblical Narrative. Heather Henderson. LC 89-7270. 216p. 1989. 35.00 (*0-8014-2294-9*) Cornell U Pr.

Victorian Serial. Linda K. Hughes & Michael Lund. (Victorian Literature & Culture Ser.). (Illus.). 448p. (C). 1991. text ed. 42.50 (*0-8139-1314-4*) U Pr of Va.

Victorian Sewing & Crafts: Program Guide for Public T. V. Series 200. Martha C. Pullen. Ed. by Kathy McMakin. (Illus.). 360p. 1995. 19.95 (*1-878048-04-X*) M Pullen.

Victorian Shadows, No. 1. Jill Morgan. 1996. pap. 4.99 (*0-679-87457-7*) Random.

Victorian Shadows, No. 2. Jill Morgan. 1997. pap. 4.99 (*0-679-87458-5*) Random.

Victorian Shadows, No. 3. Jill Morgan. 3.99 (*0-679-87459-3*) Random.

Victorian Shadows, No. 4. Jill Morgan. write for info. (*0-679-87460-7*) Random.

Victorian Shipping, Business & Imperial Policy: Donald Currie, the Castle Line & Southern Africa. Andrew Porter. LC 86-15619. (Royal Historical Society Studies in History). 352p. 1986. text ed. 39.95 (*0-312-84442-5*) St Martin.

Victorian Short Stories 2: The Trials of Love. Ed. by Harold Orel. 287p. 1991. pap. 8.95 (*0-460-87007-6*, Everyman's Classic Lib) C E Tuttle.

Victorian Short Story: Development & Triumph of a Literary Genre. Harold Orel. (Illus.). 224p. 1986. text ed. 80.00 (*0-521-25899-5*) Cambridge U Pr.

Victorian Snapshots. Paul Martin. LC 72-9219. (Literature of Photography Ser.). 1978. reprint ed. 13.95 (*0-405-04926-9*) Ayer.

Victorian Social Medicine: The Ideas & Methods of William Farr. John M. Eyler. 1979. 42.50 (*0-8018-2246-7*) Johns Hopkins.

Victorian Social Problems: A Novel. Guy. 1996. text ed. 45.00 (*0-312-16139-5*) St Martin.

Victorian Songs. Ed. & Illus. by Edmund H. Garrett. LC 78-116404. (Granger Index Reprint Ser.). 1977. 20.95 (*0-8369-6145-5*) Ayer.

Victorian Sourcebook of Medieval Decoration: With 166 Full-Color Designs. W. Audsley & G. Audsley. (Pictorial Archive Ser.). Orig. Title: Polychromatic Decoration As Applied to Buildings in the Medieval Styles. (Illus.). 64p. reprint ed. pap. 9.95 (*0-486-26834-9*) Dover.

Victorian Souvenir Medals. Daniel Fearon. 1989. pap. 25.00 (*0-85263-837-X*, Pub. by Shire UK) St Mut.

Victorian Spot Illustrations, Alphabets & Ornaments from Porret's Type Catalog. Ed. by Carol B. Grafton. (Illus.). 96p. (J). (gr. 5 up). 1982. pap. 5.95 (*0-486-24271-4*) Dover.

Victorian Stained Glass Pattern Book: 96 Designs for Workable Projects. Ed Sibbett, Jr. 1979. pap. 4.95 (*0-486-23811-3*) Dover.

Victorian Statutes, Annotations. 6th ed. Butterworths Staff. ring bd. 127.00 (*0-409-48827-5*) MICHIE.

Victorian Stencils for Design & Decoration. Edmund V. Gillon, Jr. LC 68-26054. (Illus.). (Orig.). 1968. reprint ed. pap. 4.95 (*0-486-21995-X*) Dover.

***Victorian Style.** Judith Miller & Martin Miller. (Antique Collectors' Club Ser.). (Illus.). 240p. 1993. pap. 29.95 (*1-85732-955-4*, Pub. by M Beazley Pubs Ltd UK) Antique Collect.

Victorian Style: Creating Period Interiors for Contemporary Living. Ed. by Judith Miller & Martin Miller. (Illus.). 240p. 1993. 45.00 (*1-85732-098-0*, Pub. by Millers Pubns UK) Antique Collect.

Victorian Subjects. J. Hillis Miller. LC 90-44885. 336p. 1991. text ed. 54.95 (*0-8223-1110-0*) Duke.

Victorian Suicide: Mad Crimes & Sad Histories. Barbara T. Gates. (Illus.). 192p. 1989. text ed. 37.50 (*0-691-09437-3*) Princeton U Pr.

Victorian Tales of Mystery & Detection. Ed. by Michael Cox. 610p. 1992. 25.00 (*0-19-212308-4*) OUP.

Victorian Tea Time Treasury. Angela Hynes. (Illus.). 101p. 1991. write for info. (*1-879577-01-1*) Bks Two Thousand.

Victorian Temper: A Study in Literary Culture. Jerome H. Buckley. (Illus.). 282p. 1966. 35.00 (*0-7146-2052-1*, Pub. by F Cass Pubs UK) Intl Spec Bk.

Victorian Temper: A Study in Literary Culture. Jerome H. Buckley. LC 74-89967. (Illus.). 306p. reprint ed. pap. 87.30 (*0-7837-3855-2*, 2043677) Bks Demand.

Victorian Thames. D. G. Wilson. (Illus.). 160p. 1993. 30.00 (*0-7509-0183-7*, Pub. by Sutton Pubng UK) Bks Intl VA.

Victorian Theater. Ed. by Russell Jackson. (Illus.). 359p. (C). 1994. pap. text ed. 19.95 (*0-941533-72-7*) New Amsterdam Bks.

Victorian Things. Asa Briggs. LC 88-30633. (Illus.). 464p. 1989. 35.95 (*0-226-07483-8*) U Ch Pr.

Victorian Thinkers, 6 vols., Set. Incl. William Morris. Ed. by Faulkner. 480p. (C). 1996. text ed. 130.00 (*0-415-13474-9*); Vol. 2. Matthew Arnold Vol. 2: The Poetry. Ed. by Dawson. 480p. (C). 1996. text ed. 130.00 (*0-415-13473-0*); Vol. 1. Matthew Arnold Vol. 1: Prose Writings. Ed. by Dawson. 474p. (C). 1996. text ed. 130.00 (*0-415-13472-2*); Vol. 2. John Ruskin. Ed. by Bradley. 452p. 1996. text ed. 130.00 (*0-415-13471-4*); Thomas Carlyle. Ed. by Siegel. 542p. (C). 1996. text ed. 150.00 (*0-415-13470-6*); Walter Pater. Ed. by Seiler. 465p. (C). 1996. text ed. 130.00 (*0-415-13394-7*); 2897p. (C). 1996. Set boxed, text ed. 659.00 (*0-415-13469-2*) Routledge.

***Victorian Times.** (Focus on History Ser.). (J). Date not set. pap. text ed. write for info. (*0-582-18240-9*, Pub. by Longman UK) Longman.

Victorian Toronto, 1850-1900: Pattern & Process of Growth. Peter G. Goheen. LC 76-137736. (Research Papers: No. 127). 278p. 1970. pap. 12.00 (*0-89065-034-9*) U Ch Pr.

***Victorian Town Child.** Pamela Horn. (Illus.). 256p. 1997. 33.95 (*0-7509-1119-0*, Pub. by Sutton Pubng UK) Bks Intl VA.

***Victorian Town Child.** Pamela Horn. LC 97-23642. 1997. write for info. (*0-8147-3575-4*) NYU Pr.

Victorian Trade Cards: Historical Reference & Value Guide. Dave Cheadle. 224p. 1996. pap. 19.95 (*0-89145-706-2*, 4654) Collector Bks.

Victorian Transformations: Fairy Tales, Adolescence, & the Novel of Female Development. Phyllis C. Ralph. (American University Studies: English Language & Literature: Ser. IV, Vol. 96). 176p. (C). 1989. text ed. 31.95 (*0-8204-1039-X*) P Lang Pubng.

Victorian Treasures: An Album & Historical Guide for Collectors. Carol M. Wallace. LC 96-3895. (Illus.). 176p. 1996. pap. 19.98 (*0-8109-8149-1*) Abrams.

***Victorian Undertaker.** Trevor May. 1996. pap. 25.00 (*0-7478-0331-5*, Pub. by Shire UK) St Mut.

Victorian Urban Settings: Essays on the Nineteenth-Century City & Its Contexts. Ed. by Debra N. Mancoff et al. LC 96-12754. (Literature & Society in Victorian Britain Ser.: Vol. 1). (Illus.). 288p. 1996. text ed. 40.00 (*0-8153-1949-5*, H1889) Garland.

Victorian Vacation Recipe Book. Patricia B. Mitchell. 1992. pap. 4.00 (*0-925117-67-6*) Mitchells.

Victorian Values: Personalities & Perspectives in Nineteenth Century Society. Ed. by Gordon Marsden. (Illus.). 248p. (Orig.). (C). 1990. pap. text ed. 26.50 (*0-582-03685-2*, 78418) Longman.

Victorian Values: The Life & Times of Dr. Edwin Lankester, M.D., F.R.S. Mary P. English. (Illus.). 187p. 1990. lib. bdg. 59.00 (*0-948737-14-X*, Pub. by Biopress UK) Balogh.

Victorian Vampires. Jedediah Clauss. 22.95 (*0-8488-0965-3*) Amereon Ltd.

***Victorian Vapours.** Mary Dobson. (Smelly Old History). (Illus.). 32p. 1997. pap. 7.95 (*0-19-910095-0*) OUP.

***Victorian Venetian Travel Guide.** Orig. Title: Venice. (Illus.). 60p. 1998. reprint ed. 22.50 (*0-614-28366-3*) Attic Pr Discoveries.

Victorian Verse: A Critical Anthology. Xenophon. Ed. by George Macbeth. 448p. 1986. pap. 10.95 (*0-14-042110-6*, Penguin Classics) Viking Penguin.

Victorian Viceroy. E. Neill Raymond. 346p. 1984. 39.00 (*0-7212-0599-2*, Pub. by Regency Press UK) St Mut.

Victorian Village. Margaret Bateson & HErman Lelie. LC 95-5315. (J). 1995. 19.95 (*0-312-11485-0*) St Martin.

Victorian Visionary: The Art of Elliott Daingerfield. Estill C. Pennington. (Illus.). 1994. 29.95 (*0-9638753-2-9*) Morris Mus Art.

Victorian Vocal Varieties. Jerry Silverman. 19.95 (*1-56222-421-2*, 94741) Mel Bay.

Victorian Wallflowers. Malcolm Elwin. LC 78-58256. (Essay Index in Reprint Ser.). (Illus.). 1978. 30.00 (*0-8486-3018-1*) Roth Pub Inc.

Victorian Wallpaper Design Book. Ramona Jablonski. (International Design Library). (Illus.). 48p. 1981. pap. 5.95 (*0-916144-89-5*) Stemmer Hse.

Victorian Watercolors. Christopher Newall. (Illus.). 140p. (C). 1993. reprint ed. pap. 24.95 (*0-7148-2811-4*, Pub. by Phaidon Press UK) Chronicle Bks.

Victorian Watercolours & Drawings: In the Collection of Her Majesty the Queen. Delia Millar. (Illus.). 1056p. 1995. 250.00 (*0-85667-436-2*) Sothebys Pubns.

Victorian Watercolours & Drawings: In the Collection of Her Majesty the Queen, 2 vols., Set. Delia Millar. (Illus.). 1056p. 1995. 250.00 (*0-302-00650-8*, Pub. by Zwemmer Bks UK) Sothebys Pubns.

***Victorian Wedding Photograph Album.** BHB International Staff. 1997. 24.95 (*1-85833-653-8*) BHB Intl.

Victorian Wedding Planner. 2nd rev. ed. Eisa Aucot-Yee. (Illus.). 1979. pap. write for info. (*0-9634211-9-0*) Lheure Victorian.

Victorian West: Class & Culture in Kansas Cattle Towns. C. Robert Haywood. LC 90-48972. (Illus.). xiv, 330p. 1991. 29.95 (*0-7006-0477-4*) U Pr of KS.

Victorian West: Class & Culture in Kansas Cattle Towns. C. Robert Haywood. 344p. (C). 1993. pap. 14.95 (*0-7006-0624-6*) U Pr of KS.

Victorian Will. John R. Reed. LC 88-33695. 500p. 1989. lib. bdg. 39.95 (*0-8214-0928-X*) Ohio U Pr.

Victorian Women. Joan Perkin. (Illus.). 273p. (C). 1995. 45.00 (*0-8147-6624-2*); pap. 18.50 (*0-8147-6625-0*) NYU Pr.

Victorian Women: A Documentary Account of Women's Lives in Nineteenth-Century England, France, & the United States. Ed. by Erna O. Hellerstein et al. LC 79-67770. 544p. 1981. 59.50 (*0-8047-1088-0*); pap. 22.50 (*0-8047-1096-1*) Stanford U Pr.

Victorian Women Poets. Ed. by Jennifer Breen. 240p. 1994. pap. 7.50 (*0-460-87457-8*, Everyman's Classic Lib) C E Tuttle.

Victorian Women Poets. Tess Cosslett. LC 96-23025. (C). 1996. text ed. 50.95 (*0-582-27650-0*); pap. text ed. 22.50 (*0-582-27649-7*) Longman.

Victorian Women Poets: A Critical Reader. Ed. by Angela Leighton. (Blackwell Critical Readers in Literature Ser.). 288p. (C). 1996. pap. 24.95 (*0-631-19757-5*) Blackwell Pubs.

Victorian Women Poets: An Anthology. Ed. by Angela Leighton & Margaret Reynolds. (Anthologies Ser.). 800p. 1995. 78.95 (*0-631-17608-X*, Pub. by Polity Pr UK) Blackwell Pubs.

Victorian Women Poets: An Anthology. Ed. by Angela Leighton & Margaret Reynolds. (Anthologies Ser.). 800p. 1995. pap. 29.95 (*0-631-17609-8*, Pub. by Polity Pr UK) Blackwell Pubs.

Victorian Women Poets: Emily Bronte, Elizabeth Barrett Browning, Christina Rossetti. Ed. by Joseph Bristow. LC 95-8581. 1995. text ed. 45.00 (*0-312-12735-9*) St Martin.

Victorian Women Poets: Writing Against the Heart. Angela Leighton. (Victorian Literature & Culture Ser.). 336p. (C). 1992. text ed. 45.00 (*0-8139-1426-4*); pap. text ed. 17.50 (*0-8139-1427-2*) U Pr of Va.

Victorian Women's Fiction: Marriage, Freedom & the Individual. Shirley Foster. LC 84-24367. 248p. 1985. pap. 18.25 (*0-389-20551-6*, 08113) B&N Imports.

Victorian Women's Fiction: Marriage, Freedom & the Individual. Shirley Foster. 248p. 1986. pap. 20.00 (*0-389-20674-1*, N8231) B&N Imports.

Victorian Wooden Molding & Frame Designs: The 1887 Morell Catalog. H. Morell. (Illus.). 208p. 1992. reprint ed. pap. 11.95 (*0-486-26932-9*) Dover.

Victorian Woodturnings & Woodwork. (Illus.). 144p. 1995. reprint ed. pap. 16.95 (*1-879335-67-0*) Astragal Pr.

Victorian Word-Painting & Narrative: Toward the Blending of Genres. Rhoda L. Flaxman. LC 86-30753. 160p. 1991. pap. 19.00 (*0-8357-1957-X*) Univ Rochester Pr.

Victorian Working Class: Selections from the "Morning Chronicle" Peter Razzell. Ed. by R. W. Wainwright. (Illus.). 380p. 1973. 37.50 (*0-7146-2957-X*, Pub. by F Cass Pubs UK) Intl Spec Bk.

Victorian Working Women. Wanda F. Neff. LC 77-181963. reprint ed. 29.50 (*0-404-04676-2*) AMS Pr.

***Victorian World Picture: Perceptions & Introspections in an Age of Change.** David Newsome. LC 97-15588. (Illus.). 320p. 1997. 30.00 (*0-8135-2454-7*) Rutgers U Pr.

Victorian Writers, 1832-1890 see Concise Dictionary of British Literary Biography

U V

An Asterisk (*) at the beginning of an entry indicates that the title is appearing in BIP for the first time.

Victorian Yellow Pages: Resources for Your Victorian Lifestyle. Cheryl Hurd. 102p. 1995. pap. 12.00 (1-887613-04-8) Teapot Pr.

Victorian Yellowbacks & Paperbacks, 1849-1905: George Routledge, Vol. 1. Chester W. Topp. 557p. 1992. 135.00 (0-9633920-0-X) Hermit Antiq Bk.

Victorian Yellowbacks & Paperbacks 1849-1905 Vol. 2: Ward & Lock. Chester W. Topp. (Illus.). 456p. 1994. 135.00 (0-9633920-1-8) Hermit Antiq Bk.

***Victoriana Photo Album.** Illus. by Mullen & Katz. (Photo Albums Ser.). 12p. 1997. 9.99 (0-88088-642-0) Peter Pauper.

Victorianism in the United States: Its Era & Its Legacy. Steve Ickringill. Ed. by Stephen Mills. 200p. 1992. 35.00 (90-5383-117-7, Pub. by VU Univ Pr NE) Paul & Co Pubs.

***Victorians.** Ariel Books Staff. 1996. 3.95 (0-8362-1003-4, Arie Bks) Andrews & McMeel.

Victorians. Ed. by Laurence Lerner. LC 78-15642. (Context of English Literature Ser.). 228p. 1978. 35.95 (0-8419-0419-7) Holmes & Meier.

Victorians. Ed. by Arthur Pollard. LC 87-47750. (New History of Literature Ser.). 580p. 1987. 39.50 (0-87226-130-1) P Bedrick Bks.

Victorians. Jayne Woodhouse. 1996. pap. text ed. 7.95 (0-563-35428-3, BBC-Parkwest) Parkwest Pubns.

Victorians, Vol. 6. Ed. by Arthur Pollard. 592p. 1994. pap. 13.95 (0-14-017756-6, Penguin Bks) Viking Penguin.

Victorians: A Photographic Portrait. Audrey Linkman. (Illus.). 192p. 1993. 39.95 (1-85043-738-6, Pub. by I B Tauris UK) St Martin.

***Victorians: An Anthology of Poetry & Poetics.** Ed. by Valentine Cunningham. (Anthologies Ser.). 1100p. (C). 1998. text ed. 74.95 (0-631-19915-2) Blackwell Pubs.

***Victorians: An Anthology of Poetry & Poetics.** Ed. by Valentine Cunningham. (Anthologies Ser.). 1100p. (C). 1998. pap. text ed. 34.95 (0-631-19916-0) Blackwell Pubs.

***Victorians: British Painting in the Reign of Queen Victoria, 1837-1901.** Malcolm Warner et al. LC 96-27598. 1997. write for info. (0-89468-263-6) Natl Gallery Art.

***Victorians: British Painting, 1837-1901.** Malcolm Warner. (Illus.). 270p. 1997. 49.50 (0-8109-6342-6) Abrams.

Victorians & Ancient Greece. Richard Jenkyns. LC 79-25487. (Harvard Paperbacks Ser.). 397p. 1980. pap. text ed. 11.95 (0-674-93687-6) HUP.

Victorians & Ancient Greece. Richard Jenkyns. (Illus.). 400p. 1990. 37.00 (0-674-93686-8) HUP.

Victorians & Ancient Rome. Norman Vance. LC 96-20982. 296p. (C). 1997. text ed. 59.95 (0-631-18076-1) Blackwell Pubs.

Victorians & Mystery: Crises of Representation. W. David Shaw. LC 89-38545. 360p. 1990. 42.50 (0-8014-2403-8) Cornell U Pr.

***Victorians & Race.** Ed. by Shearer West. LC 96-33140. (Nineteenth Century Ser.). (Illus.). 272p. 1996. 76.95 (1-85928-268-7, Pub. by Scolar Pr UK) Ashgate Pub Co.

Victorians & Renaissance Italy. Hilary Fraser. (Illus.). 1992. 49.95 (0-631-14949-X) Blackwell Pubs.

Victorians & the Machine: Literary Response to Technology. Herbert L. Sussman. LC 68-14274. (Illus.). 273p. reprint ed. 77.90 (0-8357-9184-X, 2016540) Bks Demand.

Victorians & the Stuart Heritage: Interpretations of a Discordant Past. Timothy Lang. 215p. (C). 1995. text ed. 49.95 (0-521-47464-7) Cambridge U Pr.

Victorians in Japan: In & Around the Treaty Ports. Hugh Cortazzi. LC 87-1029. 280p. (C). 1987. text ed. 49.95 (0-485-11312-0, Pub. by Athlone Pr UK) Humanities.

Victorians Unbuttoned: Registered Designs for Clothing, Their Makers & Wearers, 1839-1900. Sarah Levitt. (Illus.). 246p. 1986. 34.95 (0-04-391013-0) Routledge Chapman & Hall.

Victoria's Colonial Governors: 1839-1900. Davis McCaughey et al. (Miegunyah Press Ser.: No. 1:16). (Illus.). 368p. 1993. 49.95 (0-522-84509-6, Pub. by Melbourne Univ Pr AT) Paul & Co Pubs.

Victoria's Conquest. Laurie Paige. (Romance Ser.). 1993. pap. 2.69 (0-373-08933-3, 5-08933-9) Silhouette.

***Victorias Daughters.** Packard. Date not set. write for info. (0-312-18203-1) St Martin.

***Victoria's Emeralds.** large type ed. Rose Boucheron. (Magna Large Print Ser.). 362p. 1997. 27.50 (0-7505-1070-6) Ulverscroft.

Victoria's Enemies, Vol. 3: India. Ian Knight. (Men-at-Arms Ser.: No. 219). (Illus.). 48p. 1990. pap. 11.95 (0-85045-943-5, 9176, Pub. by Osprey UK) Stackpole.

Victoria's Victories. Spellmount Ltd. Publishers Staff. (C). 1986. 120.00 (0-685-60246-X, Pub. by Spellmount UK) St Mut.

Victoria's Victories: Seven Classic Battles of the British Army, 1849-1884. Peter C. Smith. 200p. (C). 1991. 95.00 (0-946771-17-0, Pub. by Spellmount UK) St Mut.

Victoria's World: An Exhibition from the Gernsheim Collection. 3rd ed. Intro. by Roy Flukinger. 1980. 5.00 (0-87959-008-4) U of Tex H Ransom Ctr.

Victoria's Year: English Literature & Culture, 1837-1838. Richard L. Stein. (Illus.). 328p. 1988. 49.95 (0-19-504922-5) OUP.

Victories. George V. Higgins. 1991. mass mkt. 5.99 (0-8217-3566-7, Zebra Kensgtn) Kensgtn Pub Corp.

Victories: Stories of Christian Vietnam Veterans. Wes Keith. 125p. (Orig.). (C). 1995. pap. 7.00 (1-883893-06-2) WinePress Pub.

Victories of the Heart: The Inside Story of a Pioneer Men's Group - How Men Help Each Other Change Their Lives. Robert Mark & Buddy Portugal. 256p. 1996. pap. 14.95 (1-85230-800-1) Element MA.

Victories Without Violence: True Stories of Ordinary People Overcoming Dangers. A. Ruth Fry. Ed. by Liberty Goodwin. LC 85-43527. (Liberty Literary Works: No. 1). 96p. (J). 1986. reprint ed. pap. 6.00 (0-943734-06-1) Ocean Tree Bks.

Victorio & the Mimbres Apaches. Dan L. Thrapp. LC 72-9269. (Civilization of the American Indian Ser.: Vol. 125). (Illus.). 416p. 1991. pap. 14.95 (0-8061-1645-5) U of Okla Pr.

***Victorious Attitude.** Orison S. Marden. 358p. 1997. pap. 32.00 (0-89540-353-6) Sun Pub.

Victorious Christ: A Study of the Book of Revelation. C. Freeman Sleeper. LC 96-18499. 160p. (Orig.). 1996. pap. 10.00 (0-664-25620-1) Westminster John Knox.

Victorious Christian Faith: Lessons in the Higher Christian Life. Alan Redpath. LC 84-4719. (Alan Redpath Library). 192p. (gr. 10). 1994. reprint ed. pap. 11.99 (0-8007-5514-6) Revell.

Victorious Christian Life: A Guide for Spiritual Success. Tony Evans. 1994. 15.99 (0-8407-3448-4) Nelson.

Victorious Christian Life: A Guide to Spiritual Success. Tony Evans. 256p. 1996. pap. text ed. 10.99 (0-7852-7256-9) Nelson.

Victorious Christian Living: Studies in the Book of Joshua. Alan Redpath. (Alan Redpath Library). 256p. (gr. 10). 1993. reprint ed. pap. 11.99 (0-8007-5490-5) Revell.

Victorious Christians You Should Know. Warren W. Wiersbe. 136p. 1954. pap. 7.99 (0-8010-9667-7) Baker Bks.

Victorious Expression: A Study of Four Contemporary Spanish Poets: Miguel de Unamuno, Antonio Machado, Juan Ramon Jimenez, Federico Garcia Lorca. Howard T. Young. LC 64-14508. 247p. 1964. reprint ed. pap. 70.40 (0-608-01874-0, 2062526) Bks Demand.

Victorious Faith. Richard Wurmbrand. 1979. pap. 5.00 (0-88264-120-4) Living Sacrifice Bks.

Victorious Incumbent: A Threat to Democracy? Ed. by Albert Somit et al. 336p. (C). 1994. text ed. 59.95 (1-85521-514-4, Pub. by Dartmth Pub UK) Ashgate Pub Co.

Victorious Life. John A. Coblentz. 1993. pap. 2.25 (0-87813-550-2) Christian Light.

Victorious Living for New Christians. 48p. pap. 2.50 (1-56722-049-5) Word Aflame.

Victorious Overcoming Life. Frederick K. Price. 159p. (Orig.). 1993. pap. 7.99 (1-883798-00-0) Faith One.

Victorious Praying: Studies in the Lord's Prayer. Alan Redpath. (Alan Redpath Library). 152p. 1993. reprint ed. pap. 9.99 (0-8007-5489-1) Revell.

Victorious Present. Ilija Poplasen. (Illus.). 372p. 1983. 20.00 (0-935352-13-9) MIR PA.

Victorious Queen of the World: The Spiritual Diary of Sr. Natalia of Hungary. Natalia. Tr. by Stephen Foglein. 159p. 1992. pap. 7.50 (1-884722-01-6) Two Hrts Bks.

***Victorious Victorian, Vol. 1.** Sinclair. 1985. write for info. (0-03-004063-9) H Holt & Co.

***Victorious Youth.** Carol C. Mattusch. LC 97-6758. (Getty Museum Studies on Art). 1997. write for info. (0-89236-470-X, J P Getty Museum) J P Getty Trust.

***Victors.** 1997. write for info. (1-56476-589-X, Victor Bks) Chariot Victor.

Victor's Adventure in Alphabet Town. Janet McDonnell. LC 92-4036. (Read Around Alphabet Town Ser.). (Illus.). 32p. (J). (ps-2). 1992. lib. bdg. 17.50 (0-516-05422-8) Childrens.

Victors All. Monita I. Syll. Ed. by Renais J. Hill. LC 91-53044. (Illus.). 185p. (Orig.). 1992. pap. 14.95 (1-55666-071-5) Pubs Grp Toluca.

***Victors & Vanquished.** Schwartz. Date not set. pap. text ed. write for info. (0-312-15408-9) St Martin.

Victors & Vanquished: The German Influence on Army & Church in France after 1870. Allan Mitchell. LC 83-25917. xiv, 169p. 1984. 49.95 (0-8078-1603-5) U of NC Pr.

Victors Divided: America & the Allies in Germany, 1918-1923. Keith L. Nelson. LC 72-87203. 463p. reprint ed. pap. 132.00 (0-318-34901-9, 2031308) Bks Demand.

Victors, Not Victims: The Christian's Secret of Overcoming the Power of Sin. Floyd H. Barackman. LC 92-39332. 128p. 1993. pap. 7.99 (0-8254-2273-6) Kregel.

Victor's Picnic: With the Vegetarian Animals. Radha Vignola. LC 96-84666. (Illus.). 56p. (Orig.). (J). (ps-3). 1996. pap. 6.95 (0-9640394-7-8) AVIVA CA.

Victor's Place. Eileen Sherman. (Illus.). 598p. (Orig.). (YA). (gr. 10-12). 1989. pap. write for info. (0-9604382-2-X) Cornerstone Pr.

Victor's Psalm: Words of Wounds, Love, Healing & Growth. Ryan Welwood. 48p. (Orig.). 1996. pap. 7.95 (0-9652053-0-4) Sugar Mtn Pr.

***Victory.** Conrad. 1991. pap. text ed. write for info. (0-17-556579-1) Addison-Wesley.

Victory. Joseph Conrad. 336p. 1991. pap. 5.95 (0-451-52531-0, Sig) NAL-Dutton.

Victory. Joseph Conrad. 416p. pap. 6.95 (0-14-018359-0, Penguin Classics) Viking Penguin.

Victory. Joseph Conrad. 192p. 1995. pap. 8.95 (0-14-018978-5, Viking) Viking Penguin.

Victory. Joseph Conrad. Date not set. pap. 11.95 (0-14-025519-2, Viking) Viking Penguin.

Victory. Joseph Conrad. 464p. 1995. pap. 6.95 (0-460-87478-0, Everyman's Classic Lib) C E Tuttle.

Victory. A.C. Green. 1995. pap. 10.99 (0-88419-417-5) Creation House.

Victory. Henry K. Grynberg. Tr. by Richard Lourie. (Writings from an Unbound Europe). 107p. 1994. 39.95 (0-8101-1106-3); pap. 14.95 (0-8101-1136-5) Northwestern U Pr.

Victory. David Guinn. (Great Race Ser.). 146p. (Orig.). (YA). (gr. 6 up). 1994. pap. 9.95 (1-887002-17-0) Cross Trng.

Victory. D. Sylvester & Karen Dick. 80p. (J). (gr. 4-7). 1995. 8.95 (0-88160-271-X, LW297) Learning Wks.

Victory. LC 72-1874. (Black Heritage Library Collection-Prize Ser.). 1977. reprint ed. 29.95 (0-8369-9051-X) Ayer.

Victory: An Island Tale. Joseph Conrad. Ed. by John Batchelor. (World's Classics Ser.). (Illus.). 464p. (C). 1996. pap. 5.95 (0-19-281708-6) OUP.

***Victory: By Victory Lance, Poet, Philosopher, Private Eye.** Thomas Robbins & Victory Lance. LC 96-30515. (Illus.). 137p. 1996. pap. 9.95 (0-87714-182-7) Denlingers.

Victory: How a Progressive Democratic Party Can Win & Govern. Arthur Sanders. LC 92-13465. (American Political Institutions & Public Policy Ser.). 200p. (gr. 13). 1992. text ed. 56.95 (1-56324-087-4); pap. text ed. 24.95 (1-56324-088-2) M E Sharpe.

Victory: The Reagan Administration's Secret Strategy That Hastened the Collapse of the Soviet Union. Peter Schweizer. 304p. 1996. pap. 13.00 (0-87113-633-3, Atlntc Mnthly) Grove-Atltic.

Victory: The Work of the Spirit. Pieter Potgieter. 42p. 1984. pap. 1.45 (0-85151-430-8) Banner of Truth.

Victory: 50th Year Commemorative Edition of WWII Victory by Allied Forces. Ideals Editorial Staff. 80p. 1996. 9.95 (0-8249-4068-7) Ideals.

Victory see A. C. Green

Victory & Self-Mastery. John H. Tindall. 60p. (Orig.). 1993. per. 5.95 (0-945383-62-2) Teach Servs.

Victory & Success Are Yours: Mini Book. Jerry Savelle. 41p. (Orig.). 1982. pap. text ed. 0.99 (0-89274-236-4, HH-236) Harrison Hse.

Victory at Any Cost: The Genius of Viet Nam's Gen. Vo Nguyen Giap. Cecil B. Currey. (Association of the U. S. Army Book Ser.). (Illus.). 432p. 1997. 25.95 (1-57488-056-X) Brasseys Inc.

Victory at Guadalcanal. Robert E. Lee. (World-at-War Ser.). 1983. mass mkt. 3.50 (0-8217-1198-9, Zebra Kensgtn) Kensgtn Pub Corp.

Victory at High Tide. Robert D. Heinl, Jr. LC 79-90111. (Great War Stories Ser.). (Illus.). 315p. 1979. reprint ed. 28.95 (0-933852-03-7) Nautical & Aviation.

Victory at High Tide: The Inchon-Seoul Campaign. Robert D. Heinl. 1980. 19.95 (0-405-13282-4) Ayer.

Victory at Sea. William S. Sims. (Classics of Naval Literature Ser.). 420p. 1984. reprint ed. 32.95 (0-87021-745-3) Naval Inst Pr.

Victory at Sea: Symphonic Scenario Intermediate. Richard Rodgers. 24p. 1981. pap. 3.95 (0-7935-4728-8, 00312750) H Leonard.

Victory at Sea: World War II in the Pacific. James F. Dunnigan. 1996. pap. 16.00 (0-688-14947-2) Morrow.

Victory at Sebastopol. large type ed. Vivian Stuart. 368p. 1993. 25.99 (0-7089-2995-8) Ulverscroft.

Victory at the Training Table: A Guide to Sports Nutrition. Jim Jordan et al. 160p. (Orig.). 1994. pap. text ed. 19.95 (0-944183-19-0) Prof Reports Corp.

Victory at Video Poker. Frank Scoblete. 281p. 1995. pap. 12.95 (1-56625-043-9) Bonus Books.

Victory Beer: America's Best Homebrew. Frwd. by Pete Slosberg. 228p. (Orig.). 1994. pap. 11.95 (0-937381-41-1) Brewers Pubns.

Victory Beyond the Scoreboard: The Family Guide to Youth Participation in Sports. John Devine & Cliff Gillies. LC 96-83855. 240p. 1997. pap. 14.95 (1-885221-43-6) BookPartners.

Victory Bible Reading Plan. James McKeever. 16p. (C). pap. text ed. 1.25 (0-86694-102-9) Omega Pubns OR.

Victory Book: The Workbook That Will Take You Rapidly Out of Debt. John F. Avanzini & Patrick Ondrey. (Financial Freedom Ser.). 181p. 1991. student ed. 14.95 (1-878605-07-0) HIS Pub Co.

Victory Celebrations, Prisoners, & The Love-Girl & the Innocent. Aleksandr I. Solzhenitsyn. 1986. pap. 12.95 (0-374-51924-2) FS&G.

Victory Christian Church Membership Manual. John-Paul Morgaite. 41p. 1991. pap. 5.00 (1-880322-01-3) Champions Christ.

Victory Denied. Archibald E. Roberts. 300p. 1966. pap. 2.00 (0-318-13714-3, Betsy Ross Pr) Comm Restore Const.

Victory Era in Color! Rare Color Photographs of the World War II Years. Jeff Ethell. Ed. by Mike Beno. LC 94-67301. (Illus.). 164p. 1994. 17.95 (0-89821-127-1, 19521) Reiman Pubns.

Victory Feast: A Worship Celebration of Word, Sacrament & Song. Bruce Becker & Handt Hanson. 10p. 1989. pap. 7.95 (0-933173-19-9) Chging Church Forum.

Victory for Jamie: The Story of Greg Norman & Jamie Hutton. Lawrence Levy & Gordon S. White, Jr. (Illus.). 64p. 1989. 20.00 (0-9615344-4-3) Intl Merc OH.

Victory for Laura Lee. Alice S. Finlay. LC 93-3501. (Laura Lee Ser.: Vol. 2). 48p. (J). (gr. k-2). 1993. pap. 4.99 (0-310-59851-6) Zondervan.

Victory for Progress in Mental Medicine. Lloyd V. Briggs. Ed. by Gerald N. Grob. LC 78-22552. (Historical Issues in Mental Health Ser.). (Illus.). 1980. reprint ed. lib. bdg. 25.95 (0-405-11906-2) Ayer.

***Victory from Defeat: A Collection of History's Greatest Success Stories: Why Winners Win.** 192p. Date not set. 19.95 (1-56315-092-1) Sterling Hse.

Victory Garden Cookbook. Marian Morash. LC 81-48132. (Illus.). 352p. 1982. 35.00 (0-394-50897-1); pap. 35.00 (0-394-70780-X) Knopf.

Victory Garden Kids' Book. Marjorie Waters. LC 93-41043. (Illus.). 160p. (J). 1994. pap. 15.95 (1-56440-361-0) Globe Pequot.

Victory Garden Landscape Guide. Thomas Wirth. (Illus.). 360p. 1984. pap. 24.95 (0-316-94846-2) Little.

Victory Garden Recipes for Vegetable & Fish Dishes. Marian Morash. LC 92-44397. 1993. 35.00 (0-679-42362-1) Knopf.

Victory Garden Vegetable Alphabet Book. Jerry Pallotta & Bob Thomson. LC 92-71580. (Alphabet Book). (Illus.). 32p. (J). (gr. 3-8). 1992. 14.95 (0-88106-469-6); pap. 6.95 (0-88106-468-8); lib. bdg. 15.88 (0-88106-685-0) Charlesbridge Pub.

Victory Gardens & Barrage Balloons: A Collective Memoir. Frank R. Wetzel. (Illus.). 320p. 1995. 30.00 (0-9622337-7-3) Perry Pub WA.

Victory in Adversity. R. Edward Miller. 168p. (Orig.). (YA). (gr. 10). 1988. pap. 6.95 (0-945818-07-6) Peniel Pubns.

Victory in Christ. Charles G. Trumbull. 1992. pap. 4.95 (0-87508-533-4) Chr Lit.

Victory in Europe. Wallace B. Black & Jean F. Blashfield. LC 92-23234. (World War II 50th Anniversary Ser.). (Illus.). 48p. (J). (gr. 5-6). 1993. lib. bdg. 12.95 (0-89686-570-3, Crstwood Hse) Silver Burdett Pr.

Victory in Failure. Alexander Maclaren. Ed. by William J. Petersen. LC 79-88309. (Shepherd Illustrated Classics Ser.). (Illus.). 196p. (Orig.). 1988. pap. 5.95 (0-8254-5311-9) Kregel.

Victory in Faith: Experiences of NSA Members. Ed. by George M. Williams. 100p. (Orig.). 1985. pap. text ed. 5.00 (0-915678-14-4) World Tribune Pr.

Victory in Jesus. Charlie Warren. (Illus.). 224p. (Orig.). 1994. 9.95 (0-9640879-8-7) J I L Ent.

Victory in Jesus: Creative Groups Guide. Jan Johnson. Ed. by Michael C. Mack. 160p. (Orig.). 1996. pap. text ed. 15.99 (0-7847-0424-4, 40314) Standard Pub.

Victory In Jesus: Living Answers for a Dying World. Vincent Longo. LC 96-84794. (Orig.). 1996. pap. 8.95 (0-88270-694-2) Bridge-Logos.

Victory in the East: A Military History of the First Crusade. John France. LC 93-28329. (Illus.). 448p. (C). 1994. text ed. 69.95 (0-521-41969-7) Cambridge U Pr.

***Victory in the East: A Military History of the First Crusade.** John France. 440p. 1997. pap. text ed. 22.95 (0-521-58987-8) Cambridge U Pr.

Victory in the Pacific, 1945 see History of the United States Naval Operations in World War Two

Victory in the Unseen Warfare. Jack N. Sparks. LC 93-32708. 1993. pap. 7.95 (0-9622713-6-5) Conciliar Pr.

Victory in the Valley: A Gil Thorp Collection. Jack Berrill. (Illus.). 256p. (Orig.). 1997. pap. 21.95 (0-930099-11-7) Take Five Pubs.

Victory in the Voting Booth. Beatrice Kay. LC 78-31930. (Illus.). 1981. 19.95 (0-88280-079-5); pap. 12.95 (0-88280-078-7) ETC Pubns.

Victory in the West Vol. I: The Battle for Normandy. L. F. Ellis. (Official Ser.: No. 4). (Illus.). 744p. 1993. reprint ed. 49.95 (0-89839-193-8) Battery Pr.

Victory in the West Vol. II: The Defeat of Germany. L. F. Ellis. (Official History Ser.: No. 6). (Illus.). 608p. 1994. reprint ed. 49.95 (0-89839-197-0) Battery Pr.

***Victory in the Wilderness.** J. Bevere. 1996. pap. 8.99 (0-9633176-0-1) J Bevere Minist.

Victory in Vietnam. William F. Eckbert. LC 93-74762. (Orig.). 1994. pap. 9.95 (0-9639989-0-0) Old Court Pr.

Victory in WWII: The New Mexico Story. Ed. by Gerald W. Thomas et al. (Illus.). 167p. 1994. 32.50 (0-8263-1565-8); pap. 22.95 (0-8263-1566-6) U of NM Pr.

***Victory Is Mine!** Barbara Johnson. (Illus.). 1997. 9.99 (0-8007-7159-1) Revell.

Victory Mountain. Diana DeMato. 50p. 1996. 9.95 (1-887750-19-3) Rutledge Bks.

Victory Must Be Ours: Germany in the Great War. Laurence Moyer. (Illus.). 324p. 1995. 24.95 (0-7818-0370-5) Hippocrene Bks.

Victory Odes: Olympians 2, 7 & 11; Nemean 4; Isthmians 3, 4 & 7. Malcolm M. Willcock. (Cambridge Greek & Latin Classics Ser.). 172p. (C). 1995. text ed. 60.00 (0-521-43055-0) Cambridge U Pr.

Victory Odes: Olympians 2, 7 & 11; Nemean 4; Isthmians 3, 4 & 7. Malcolm M. Willcock. (Cambridge Greek & Latin Classics Ser.). 172p. (C). 1995. pap. text ed. 21.95 (0-521-43636-2) Cambridge U Pr.

Victory of Angels. Isaac C. Brown. LC 91-68354. 217p. 1992. 10.95 (1-55523-508-5) Winston-Derek.

***Victory of Christ's Kingdom: An Introduction to Post Millennialism.** John J. Davis. 96p. (Orig.). 1996. pap. 6.00 (1-885767-22-6) Canon Pr ID.

Victory of Connie Lee. Bess S. Aldrich. 25.95 (0-8488-0160-1) Amereon Ltd.

***Victory of Faith: New Testament Sermons for Lent & Easter.** Mark J. Molldrem. LC 96-37185. 88p. (Orig.). 1997. pap. write for info. (0-7880-1005-0) CSS OH.

Victory of Light. Sam Stern. Ed. by Dorothy Stern. 144p. (Orig.). 1987. pap. 4.95 (0-9619469-0-3) Hebrew Witness.

Victory of Love. Heung Jin Moon. 264p. 12.95 (0-910621-62-4) HSA Pubns.

Victory of Love: A Meditation on Romans 8. Adrienne Von Speyr. Tr. by Sr. Lucia of the Incarnation from GER. LC 90-81773. 109p. 1990. pap. text ed. 9.95 (0-89870-304-2) Ignatius Pr.

Victory of Our Lady: The Age of "One Fold & One Shepherd" Is Coming. Stephen A. Foglein. 232p. 1994. pap. 10.50 (1-884722-00-8) Two Hrts Bks.

Victory of Surrender. Gordon Ferguson. 220p. (Orig.). 1995. pap. 10.99 (1-884553-64-8) Discipleshp.

Victory of Surrender. Gordon Ferguson. 23p. (Orig.). 1995. student ed., wbk. ed., pap. 3.99 (1-884553-73-7) Discipleshp.

***Victory of Surrender.** Gordon Ferguson. (Orig.). 1997. pap. write for info. incl. audio (1-57782-030-4) Discipleshp.

U
V

An Asterisk (*) at the beginning of an entry indicates that the title is appearing in BIP for the first time.

Victory of the Cross. Erskine N. White. 1991. pap. 7.95 (*1-55673-277-5*, 9110) CSS OH.
Victory of the Lamb. Bonnie B. O'Brien. 182p. 1982. pap. 11.50 (*0-311-72280-6*) Casa Bautista.
Victory of the Papacy see Cambridge Medieval History
Victory of the Spirit: Meditations on Black Quotations. Janet C. Bell. 176p. (Orig.). 1996. pap. 8.99 (*0-446-67200-9*) Warner Bks.
Victory on Praise Mountain. Merlin R. Carothers. 175p. 1979. pap. 6.95 (*0-943026-04-0*) Carothers.
Victory over Age. Jerome Ellison. 1980. pap. 7.95 (*0-8159-7103-6*) Devin.
Victory over Death. Rhonda D. Chervin. LC 85-8213. 63p. (Orig.). 1985. pap. 4.95 (*0-932506-43-7*) St Bedes Pubns.
Victory over Debt: Rediscovering Financial Freedom. Larry Burkett. 1992. pap. 10.99 (*1-881273-00-8*) Northfield Pub.
Victory over Deception. Joyce Gill. 107p. (Orig.). 1990. pap. 4.95 (*0-941975-02-9*) Power Hse Pub.
Victory over Depression. Bert Allbritton. 128p. 1981. mass mkt. 4.99 (*0-88368-104-8*) Whitaker Hse.
Victory over Diabetes. Dwight K. Kalita & William Philpott. 275p. 1983. pap. 10.00 (*0-87983-548-6*) Keats.
Victory over Europe: D-Day to VE Day. Max Hastings. (Illus.). 192p. 1985. 25.00 (*0-316-81334-6*) Little.
Victory over Japan: A Book of Stories. Ellen Gilchrist. 256p. 1985. pap. 13.95 (*0-316-31307-6*) Little.
Victory over Life's Challenges. Charles Stanley. 1995. 12.98 (*0-88486-113-9*) Arrowood Pr.
Victory over Migraine: The Breakthrough Study That Explains What Causes It & How It Can Be Completely Prevented Through Diet. Rodolfo Low. LC 86-7708. 208p. 1989. pap. 7.95 (*0-8050-0927-2*, Owl) H Holt & Co.
***Victory over Sickness & Pain.** Chuck Schiappacasse. (Illus.). 128p. Date not set. pap. 7.95 (*0-9635913-3-9*) C Schiappacasse.
Victory over Sin. Billy J. Daugherty. 32p. (Orig.). 1993. pap. 0.50 (*1-56267-072-7*) Victory Ctr OK.
Victory over Sin & Self. David Wilkerson. 80p. (gr. 10). 1994. mass mkt. 3.99 (*0-8007-8434-0*, Spire) Revell.
Victory over the Grand Depression: America & the World Saved from Imminent Economic Collapse. J. R. Estefania. (Victory Ser.). (Illus.). 210p. 1988. 19.95 (*0-945542-00-3*) Park & Park Pub.
Victory over the Impossible. Elbert Willis. 1978. 1.95 (*0-89858-008-0*) Fill the Gap.
Victory over the World. Charles G. Finney. LC 66-24879. (Charles G. Finney Memorial Library). 124p. 1975. pap. 6.99 (*0-8254-2619-7*) Kregel.
Victory Over Trials: Encouragement from the Life of Job. Lottie B. Hobbs. 137p. 1968. pap. 5.95 (*0-913838-09-8*) Harvest TX.
Victory Over Trials: Encouragement from the Life of Job. Lottie B. Hobbs. 134p. 1968. reprint ed. 8.95 (*0-913838-10-1*) Harvest TX.
***Victory Poetry Inspired 40.** William L. Spurloch. 42p. 1996. pap. 5.00 (*1-889463-19-1*) Golden Apple.
***Victory Ride.** Allison Estes. (Short Stirrup Club Ser.: Vol. 8). (YA). 1997. pap. 3.99 (*0-671-00433-6*, Minstrel Bks) PB.
Victory Road. Robert C. Baldridge. LC 95-80653. (World War II Historical Society Monographs). (Illus.). 231p. 1995. 24.95 (*1-57638-043-2*); pap. 19.95 (*1-57638-000-9*) Merriam Pr.
Victory Rode the Rails: The Strategic Place of the Railroads in the Civil War. George E. Turner. LC 73-184842. (Illus.). 419p. 1972. reprint ed. 35.00 (*0-8371-6331-5*, TUVR, Greenwood Pr) Greenwood.
Victory Rode the Rails: The Strategic Place of the Railroads in the Civil War. George E. Turner. LC 92-15147. (Illus.). xii, 433p. 1992. reprint ed. pap. 17.95 (*0-8032-9423-9*, Bison Books) U of Nebr Pr.
Victory Secrets of Attila the Hun. Wess Roberts. 160p. 1994. pap. 11.95 (*0-440-50591-7*) Dell.
Victory Sermon Outlines. Russell E. Spray. (Pulpit Library). 64p. (Orig.). 1990. pap. 4.99 (*0-8010-8299-4*) Baker Bks.
***Victory! The Battle for Europe-Hint & Strategy Guide.** Allen G. Viduka. LC 96-71071. 224p. (Orig.). 1997. pap. 16.95 (*1-57197-056-8*) Pentland Pr.
Victory Through Discipline: First Corinthians 9. ring bd. 15.99 (*0-89957-458-0*) AMG Pubs.
Victory Through Discipline: First Corinthians 9. Spiros Zodhiates. (First Corinthians Commentaries Ser.). pap. 7.99 (*0-89957-457-2*) AMG Pubs.
Victory Through Fire. Tom Crandell. (Illus.). 136p. (Orig.). (J). 1996. pap. text ed. 10.00 (*0-9652105-0-2*) Quintastar.
Victory Through Word Confessions. Wadene C. Ward. 47p. 1985. pap. 1.95 (*0-88144-040-X*) Christian Pub.
Victory to the Mother: The Hindu Goddess of Northwest India in Myth, Ritual, & Symbol. Kathleen M. Erndl. (Illus.). 216p. (C). 1993. pap. text ed. 18.95 (*0-19-507015-1*) OUP.
Victory Turned Sour: Human Rights in Kuwait since Liberation. Ed. by Human Rights Watch Staff. 70p. (Orig.). 1991. pap. 7.00 (*1-56432-041-3*) Hum Rts Watch.
***Victory Week.** Illus. by Tony L. McGregor. 40p. (J). 1997. lib. bdg. 22.95 (*0-9634016-9-6*, Deaf Life Pr) MSM Prods.
Victory Without Triumph: The Wilderness, May 6th & 7th, 1864. John M. Priest. LC 96-30236. (Illus.). 368p. 1996. 34.95 (*1-57249-009-8*) White Mane Pub.
Victrola. Danny Rendleman. 28p. (Orig.). 1994. pap. text ed. 6.00 (*1-56439-033-0*) Ridgeway.
Vid na Nebo. Ina Bliznetsova. LC 91-29079. 90p. (Orig.). (RUS.). 1991. pap. 8.00 (*1-55779-048-5*) Hermitage.
Vida. (Discover My World Ser). (Illus.). 96p. (SPA.). (J). (ps up). 1995. 16.95 (*0-8120-6527-1*) Barron.
Vida. Diego De Torres Villarroel. Ed. by Manuel M. Perez Lopez. (Nueva Austral Ser.: Vol. 90). (SPA.). 1991. pap. text ed. 24.95 (*84-239-1890-4*) Elliots Bks.
Vida. Delacorta, pseud. write for info. (*0-318-59581-8*) S&S Trade.
Vida. Marge Piercy. 480p. 1985. mass mkt. 6.99 (*0-449-20850-8*, Crest) Fawcett.
Vida: Experiencia y Expresion. Albert C. Dawson & Laila M. Dawson. LC 88-32985. 292p. 1989. pap. text ed. 26.00 (*0-471-62402-0*) Wiley.
***Vida: Que Quiere Saber?/Life: Any Questions?** Greg Laurie. 1996. pap. 7.99 (*0-88113-424-4*) Edit Betania.
***VIDA: Thoughts That Empower.** Jorge Espinoza. (ENG & SPA.). 1994. pap. 10.95 (*0-9628722-3-7*) NUVO Ltd.
Vida - Las Moradas. unabridged ed. Santa Teresa de Jesus. (SPA.). pap. 7.95 (*84-410-0048-4*, Pub. by Bookking Intl FR) Distribks Inc.
Vida a Plazos de Don Jacobo Lerner. Isaac Goldemberg. 274p. (SPA.). 1980. pap. 12.00 (*0-910061-00-9*, 1101) Ediciones Norte.
Vida Abundante. Ray E. Baughman. Orig. Title: The Abundant Life. 192p. (SPA.). 1981. pap. 5.25 (*0-8254-1056-8*, Edit Portavoz) Kregel.
Vida & Poesia en Jose Antonio Davila. Mimoso A. Ramos. (UPREX, Estudios Literarios Ser.: No. 71). 409p. 1986. pap. 6.00 (*0-8477-0071-2*) U of PR Pr.
Vida Antes de la Vida. Fay D. De Montes. (Coleccion Aprender). (Illus.). 32p. (Orig.). (SPA.). 1985. pap. 3.00 (*0-89729-359-2*) Ediciones.
Vida Bajo la Tierra. J. M. Parramon & Maria Rius. (Habitats Ser.). 32p. (SPA.). (J). (gr. 3-5). 1987. Span. ed.: La Vida Bajo la Tierra. pap. 6.95 (*0-8120-3866-5*) Barron.
Vida con Dios: Amor en Accion. Helen Johns. Tr. by Arnoldo Casas from ENG. LC 91-71663. 64p. (Orig.). (SPA.). 1991. pap. text ed. 3.95 (*0-916035-45-X*) Evangel Indiana.
Vida con Dios: Elementos Basicos para Los Creyentes Nuevos. Helen Johns. Tr. by Eduardo Llanes from ENG. LC 89-84628. 64p. (Orig.). (SPA.). 1989. pap. 3.95 (*0-916035-30-1*) Evangel Indiana.
Vida Conforme A La Cumbre De La Revelacion De Dios. Witness Lee. 41p. (SPA.). 1.50 (*0-87083-792-3*, 04032002) Living Stream Ministry.
Vida Cristiana Normal. T. S. Nee. Orig. Title: Normal Christian Worker. 128p. (SPA.). 1992. mass mkt. 4.50 (*0-8254-1509-8*, Edit Portavoz) Kregel.
Vida Cristiana Normal De La Iglesia. Watchman Nee. 229p. (SPA.). per. 8.75 (*0-87083-495-9*, 08013002) Living Stream Ministry.
***Vida Cristiana Victoriosa.** T. S. Nee. (SPA.). 8.95 (*0-8297-0399-3*) Life Pubs Intl.
Vida da Celula. OAS, General Secretariat, Department of Scientific & Technological Affairs Staff. (Serie de Biologia: No. 5). (Illus.). 117p. (Orig.). (C). reprint ed. 3.50 (*0-8270-1141-5*) OAS.
Vida de Don Quijote y Sancho, No. 33. Miguel De Unamuno. 230p. (SPA.). 1975. write for info. (*0-8288-8553-2*) Fr & Eur.
Vida de Elias. Arthur W. Pink. 360p. (SPA.). 1992. reprint ed. pap. 10.99 (*0-85151-424-3*) Banner of Truth.
Vida de Gurdzok. Carlos Gonzalez. 1986. write for info. (*1-56491-006-7*) Imagine Pubs.
Vida de Jesucristo. James Stalker. 176p. (SPA.). reprint ed. pap. 5.99 (*0-89922-024-X*) Edit Caribe.
Vida de Jesus. Mary Balchelor. 191p. (SPA.). (J). 1992. 14.99 (*1-56063-544-4*, 490475) Editorial Unilit.
Vida de la Iglesia. Lavonn D. Brown. Tr. by Arnoldo Canclini from ENG. (Biblioteca de Doctrina Cristiana - Layman's Library of Christian Doctrine). 160p. (SPA.). 1989. pap. 7.99 (*0-311-09123-7*) Casa Bautista.
Vida de Lazarillo de Tormes. Jones. 1988. text ed. 15.95 (*0-7190-0210-9*, Pub. by Manchester Univ Pr UK) St Martin.
Vida de Lazarillo de Tormes y de sus Fortunas y Adversidades. rev. ed. Ed. by Everett W. Hesse & Harry F. Williams. 104p. 1961. pap. text ed. 12.95 (*0-299-00545-3*) U of Wis Pr.
Vida De los Animales Salvajes. (SPA.). 9.95 (*84-241-5407-X*) E Torres & Sons.
Vida de Nee-to-Sheng (Watchman Nee) A. I. Kinnear. 232p. (SPA.). 1975. pap. 7.99 (*0-8254-1411-3*, Edit Portavoz) Kregel.
Vida de Novela: Eva Peron, Marilyn Monroe, Grace Kelly. Miami Herald Staff. 160p. 1995. pap. 7.95 (*0-8362-7036-3*) Andrews & McMeel.
Vida de San Millan de la Cogolla Obias Completas II. rev. ed. Bonzalo Berceo. Ed. by Brian Dutton. (Monagrafias A Ser.: Vol. IV). 296p. (SPA.). (C). 1967. pap. 45.00 (*0-7293-0192-3*, Pub. by Tamesis Bks Ltd UK) Boydell & Brewer.
Vida de San Pablo. James Stalker. 160p. (SPA.). 1973. reprint ed. pap. 5.99 (*0-89922-025-8*) Edit Caribe.
Vida de Santo Domingo de Silos: Estudio y Edicion Critica. Gonzalo Berceo. Ed. by Brian Dutton. (Monagrafias A Ser.: Vol. LXXIV). 293p. (Orig.). (SPA.). (C). 1978. pap. 45.00 (*0-7293-0067-6*, Pub. by Tamesis Bks Ltd UK) Boydell & Brewer.
Vida De Santo Domingo De Silos: Poema De Santa Orio. Gonzalo D. Berces. Ed. by Aldo Ruffinatto. (Nueva Austral Ser.: No. 262). (SPA.). 1993. pap. text ed. 24.95 (*84-239-7262-3*) Elliots Bks.
***Vida de Un Salmon.** Tr. by Angelita L. Aguilar. (SPA.). (J). (gr. k-3). 1994. write for info. (*1-57842-053-9*) Delmas Creat.
Vida del Buscon. Francisco Quevedo. Ed. by Thomas Lathrop et al. 310p. 1988. pap. 11.00 (*0-936388-41-2*) Juan de la Cuesta.
Vida Devocional en la Tradicion Wesleyana. Steve Harper. 102p. (SPA.). 1993. pap. 6.95 (*0-8358-0691-X*) Upper Room Bks.
Vida Disciplinada. Richard S. Taylor. 144p. 1979. 3.50 (*0-88113-341-8*) Edit Betania.
Vida Empieza en el Mar. Chelsea House Publishers Staff. 1996. lib. bdg. 15.95 (*0-7910-4027-5*) Chelsea Hse.
Vida en Cristo. James J. Killgallon et al. Tr. by Manuel Pascual from ENG. LC 76-26451. 308p. 1978. pap. 4.95 (*0-914070-12-6*, 103) ACTA Pubns.
Vida en el Aire. J. M. Parramon & Maria Rius. (Habitats Ser.). 32p. (SPA.). (J). (gr. 3-5). 1987. Span. ed.: La Vida en el Aire. pap. 6.95 (*0-8120-3867-3*) Barron.
Vida en el Espiritu: Biblioteca de Doctrina Cristiana - Layman's Library of Christian Doctrine. Earl C. David. Tr. by Edna L. De Gutierrez from ENG. 143p. 1988. pap. 7.99 (*0-311-09121-0*) Casa Bautista.
Vida en el Mar. J. M. Parramon & Maria Rius. (Habitats Ser.). 32p. (J). (gr. 3-5). 1987. Span. ed.: La Vida en el Mar. pap. 6.95 (*0-8120-3869-X*) Barron.
Vida en el Planta Tierra, 20 vols. 2864p. (SPA.). 1979. Set. 695.00 (*0-8288-4840-8*, S50494) Fr & Eur.
Vida en el Reino Romanos. Jack W. Hayford. Date not set. pap. text ed. 5.99 (*0-89922-510-1*) Edit Betania.
Vida Entera. Juan C. Martini. 284p. (SPA.). 1981. pap. 9.50 (*84-02-07874-5*, 3011) Ediciones Norte.
Vida es Sueno No. 31. Cuadros E. Rodriguez. (Nueva Austral Ser.). (SPA.). pap. 10.95 (*84-239-1831-9*) Elliots Bks.
Vida es Sueno - Alcalde de Zalamea. 3rd ed. Pedro Calderon De La Barca. 196p. 1986. pap. 10.95 (*0-7859-5161-X*) Fr & Eur.
***Vida Es Tremenda!** C. Jones. (SPA.). 4.95 (*0-8297-0634-8*) Life Pubs Intl.
Vida Espanola. rev. ed. Diego Marin & Neale H. Tayler. LC 55-7036. (Illus.). (SPA.). 1955. reprint ed. pap. text ed. 7.95 (*0-89197-973-5*) Irvington.
Vida i Sucesos de la Monja Alferez: Autobiografia Atribuida a Dona Catalina de Erauso. Rima Vallbona. LC 92-25926. (Illus.). 236p. (Orig.). (SPA.). (C). 1993. text ed. 30.00 (*0-87918-076-5*); pap. text ed. 25.00 (*0-87918-077-3*) ASU Lat Am St.
***Vida Interior.** A. Murray. (SPA.). 1.50 (*0-8297-1353-0*) Life Pubs Intl.
***Vida Libre de Deudas - Debt Free Living.** Burkett. 297p. (SPA.). 1995. write for info. (*1-56063-504-5*) Editorial Unilit.
Vida (Life) Louise L. Hay. 1996. pap. text ed. 12.00 (*1-56170-294-3*) Hay House.
Vida Llena del Espiritu Santo. Harold Van Brockhoven. 45p. (SPA.). 1970. mass mkt. 2.99 (*0-8254-1800-3*, Edit Portavoz) Kregel.
Vida Loca: El Testimonio de una Pandilla Callejera en Los Angeles. Luis J. Rodriguez. 1996. pap. 10.00 (*0-684-81551-6*, Fireside) S&S Trade.
Vida Maravillosa De los Animales, 2 vols. 6th ed. Cuspinera Jonch & Carlos Antonio y Bas Peired. 960p. (SPA.). 1977. Set. 150.00 (*0-8288-5529-3*, S50487) Fr & Eur.
Vida Maritima: Enciclopedia Ilustrada de los Animales Invertebrados del Mar. D. J. George. Ed. by R. Jordana. 288p. (SPA.). 1979. 125.00 (*0-8288-4841-6*, S37587) Fr & Eur.
***Vida Mas Profunda.** A. W. Tozer. 160p. (SPA.). 1995. pap. write for info. (*0-614-27157-6*) Editorial Unilit.
Vida Mas Profunda. Aiden W. Tozer. (SPA.). 1995. 3.50 (*1-56063-428-6*, 550012) Editorial Unilit.
Vida Matrimonial. (SPA.). 1979. pap. 0.95 (*0-686-32335-1*) Rod & Staff.
***Vida Recta.** James C. Dobson. (Serie Enfoque a la Familia - Focus on the Family Ser.). 23p. (SPA.). 1991. pap. write for info. (*0-614-27158-4*) Editorial Unilit.
***Vida Recta - The Straight Life.** James C. Dobson. (Serie Enfoque a la Familia - Focus on the Family Ser.). 23p. (SPA.). 1991. write for info. (*0-614-24408-0*) Editorial Unilit.
Vida Recta (The Straight Life) James Dobson. (SPA.). 1.79 (*0-685-74986-X*, 497417) Editorial Unilit.
Vida Rimada de Fernan Gonzalez. De Arredondo. Ed. by De Mercedes. (Exeter Hispanic Text Ser.: No. 44). 120p. (SPA.). Date not set. pap. text ed. 19.95 (*0-85989-269-7*, Pub. by Univ Exeter Pr UK) Northwestern U Pr.
Vida Saludable. Pauline Primo. (SPA). 84p. 1990. pap. 9.95 (*0-685-51944-9*) Woodland UT.
Vida Sempiterna. Duane S. Crowther. LC 81-80953. Orig. Title: Life Everlasting. 353p. (SPA.). 1982. pap. 19.98 (*0-88290-185-0*) Horizon Utah.
Vida Set, 4 bks., Set. (Coleccion Mi Mundo Ser.). (Illus.). (Orig.). (SPA.). (J). (gr. 1-3). 1991. pap. 32.00 (*1-56334-113-1*) Hampton-Brown.
***Vida Sin Igual.** Bright. 129p. (SPA.). 1995. write for info. (*0-614-27155-X*) Editorial Unilit.
Vida Sobre la Tierra. J. M. Parramon & Maria Rius. (Habitats Ser.). 32p. (SPA.). (J). (gr. 3-5). 1987. Span. ed.: La Vida Sobre la Tierra. pap. 6.95 (*0-8120-3868-1*) Barron.
***Vida Solitaria.** C. Lloyd Button. Ed. by Richard Meyer. (Adult Sunday School Ser.). 90p. (SPA.). 1991. 3.95 (*1-879892-03-0*) Editorial Bautista.
Vida y Creacion - Life & Creation. Lucia Fox. Ed. by Nueva Cronica Staff. 280p. (Orig.). (ENG & SPA.). 1993. pap. 16.00 (*1-880577-02-X*) La Nueva Cronica.
Vida y Cultura Sefardita en los Poemas de "La Vara" (Del Ladino al Espanol) Berta Savariego & Jose Sanchez-Boudy. LC 87-81595. (Coleccion Polymita). 87p. (Orig.). (SPA.). 1988. pap. 15.00 (*0-89729-447-5*) Ediciones.
Vida y Hechos de Pio V. Antonio de Fuenmayor. Ed. by Lorenzo Riber. 259p. (SPA.). 1968. 100.00 (*0-614-00114-5*) Elliots Bks.
Vida y Memorias de Carlos Montenegro. Enrique J. Pujals. LC 88-80535. (Coleccion Polymita). (Illus.). 81p. (Orig.). (SPA.). 1988. pap. 9.00 (*0-89729-469-6*) Ediciones.
Vida y Milagros de la Farandula de Cuba. 2nd ed. Rosendo Rosell. LC 91-72527. (Coleccion Arte Ser.). (Illus.). 427p. (SPA.). 1992. reprint ed. pap. 19.00 (*0-89729-608-7*) Ediciones.
***Vida y Milagros de la Farandula de Cuba, Tomo IV.** Rosendo Rosell. LC 91-72527. (Coleccion Cuba Sus Jueces Ser.). (Illus.). 430p. (Orig.). (SPA.). 1997. pap. 25.00 (*0-89729-820-9*) Ediciones.
Vida y Milagros de la Farandula de Cuba, Vol. III. Rosendo Rosell. LC 91-72527. (Coleccion Cuba y Sus Jueces Ser.). (Illus.). 468p. (SPA.). 1994. pap. 20.00 (*0-89729-754-7*) Ediciones.
***Vida y Milagros de la Farandula de Cuba, Vol. V.** Rosendo Rosell. (SPA.). Date not set. pap. write for info. (*0-89729-841-1*) Ediciones.
Vida y Ministerio de Cristo. Weldon E. Viertel. Tr. by Ruben O. Zorzoli from SPA. 192p. 1989. pap. text ed. 7.50 (*0-311-04356-9*) Casa Bautista.
Vida y Muerta De Herodes - The Life & Death of Herod: A Christmas Tragedy & Epiphany: Edited with Berse Translation, Introduction, & Notes. Tirso De Molina. Ed. & Tr. by Frederick H. Fornoff from SPA. LC 91-1716. (Iberica Ser.: Vol. 2). 365p. 1992. 37.95 (*0-8204-1617-7*) P Lang Pubng.
Vida y Obra De Luis G. Inclan. Jorge L. Porras-Cruz. LC 76-1829. (Coleccion Mente y Palabra). 230p. (Orig.). (SPA.). 1976. 5.00 (*0-8477-0536-6*); pap. 4.00 (*0-8477-0537-4*) U of PR Pr.
Vida y Obra de Una Maestra. Olga Lorenza. LC 90-84146. (Coleccion Caniqui). 93p. (Orig.). (SPA.). 1990. pap. 9.95 (*0-89729-574-9*) Ediciones.
Vidal Mayor (Vidal de Cannellas), 2 vols., Set. (Illus.). 716p. 1990. 275.00 (*0-89236-175-1*, J P Getty Museum) J P Getty Trust.
Vidas Cubanas (Cuban Lives), 2 vols. Jose I. Lasaga. Tr. by Nelson Duran. LC 84-189243. (Coleccion Cuba y Sus Jueces). (Illus.). (Orig.). (ENG & SPA.). 1988. Vol. 2: Paginas de la Historia de Cuba (Pages from Cuban History), 470p. pap. 12.00 (*0-89729-407-6*) Ediciones.
Vidas Cubanas (Cuban Lives), 2 vols., 1. Jose I. Lasaga. Tr. by Nelson Duran. LC 84-189243. (Coleccion Cuba y Sus Jueces). (Illus.). (Orig.). (ENG & SPA.). 1988. pap. 12.00 (*0-89729-165-4*) Ediciones.
***Vidas de los Santos.** Hugo Hoever. (Illus.). 528p. 1997. 8.25 (*0-89942-373-6*, 370/22S) Catholic Bk Pub.
Vidas Ejemplares. Mempo Giardinelli. 141p. (SPA.). 1982. pap. 9.50 (*0-910061-11-4*, 1110) Ediciones Norte.
Vidas Paralelas: El Teatro Espanol y el Teatro Isabelino, 1580-1686. Ed. by Anita K. Stoll. (Monagrafias A Ser.: No. 153). 144p. (SPA.). (C). 1993. 53.00 (*1-85566-021-0*, Pub. by Tamesis Bks Ltd UK) Boydell & Brewer.
***Vide en los Polos - Arctic & Antarctic.** (Eyewitness in Spanish Ser.). (SPA.). (YA). (gr. 5 up). 1996. 19.95 (*0-614-20249-3*) Santillana.
Video. (Crayola Creativity Ser.). (Illus.). 1988. 30.00 (*0-86696-215-8*) Binney & Smith.
Video. 1991. 12.95 (*0-19-437102-6*) OUP.
Video. 1990. 20.00 (*0-87104-708-X*, Branch Libraries) NY Pub Lib.
Video. Jackie Biel. (Inventors & Inventions Ser.). 64p. (J). (gr. 3-5). 1996. lib. bdg. 17.95 (*0-7614-0048-6*, Benchmark NY) Marshall Cavendish.
Video. George Coulter & Shirley Coulter. LC 96-15474. (You Make It Work Ser.). (J). 1996. write for info. (*0-86625-588-5*) Rourke Pubns.
Video, No. 101. Raymond S. Adams. (Illus.). 116p. 1992. pap. text ed. write for info. (*0-935648-39-9*) Halldin Pub.
Video: A Guide for Lawyers. Ellen Miller. LC 83-80276. 142p. 1983. 29.75 (*0-88238-063-X*) Law Arts.
Video Acquisitions & Cataloging: A Handbook. James C. Scholtz. LC 95-7536. (Library Management Collection). 184p. 1995. text ed. 55.00 (*0-313-29345-7*, Greenwood Pr) Greenwood.
***Video Activist Handbook.** Thomas Harding. 1997. 49.95 (*0-7453-1174-1*); pap. text ed. 15.95 (*0-7453-1169-5*, Pub. by Pluto Pr UK) LPC InBook.
Video Alien Stickers. Irene Astrahan. (Illus.). (J). (gr. k-3). 1993. pap. 1.00 (*0-486-27421-7*) Dover.
Video & Image Processing in Multimedia Systems. Borko Furht et al. LC 95-30423. (International Series in Engineering & Computer Science, Natural Language Processing & Machine Translation). 392p. (C). 1995. lib. bdg. 120.00 (*0-7923-9604-9*) Kluwer Ac.
Video & Movie Guide 1997. Mick Martin & Marsha Porter. 1996. mass mkt. 7.99 (*0-345-40643-5*) Ballantine.
Video & Other Non-Print Resources in the Small Library. Ed. by Alan L. Kaye. LC 91-15682. (LAMA Small Libraries Publications: No. 16). 1991. pap. 5.00 (*0-8389-5734-X*) ALA.
Video Annual, 1990-1991. Jean T. Kreamer. 300p. 1991. lib. bdg. 49.50 (*0-87436-597-X*) ABC-CLIO.
Video Annual, 1992. Jean T. Kreamer. 250p. 1992. lib. bdg. 55.00 (*0-87436-629-1*) ABC-CLIO.
Video Annual 1993. Jean T. Kreamer. 1993. lib. bdg. 55.00 (*0-87436-681-X*) ABC-CLIO.
Video Annual 1994. Jean T. Kreamer. 1994. lib. bdg. 55.00 (*0-87436-741-7*) ABC-CLIO.
Video As a Second Language: How to Make a Video Documentary. rev. ed. Don Harwood. LC 79-63869. (Illus.). 1979. pap. 5.50 (*0-915146-06-1*, V102) VTR Pub.
***Video-Based Information Systems: A Guide for Educational, Business, Library, & Home Use.** William Saffady. LC 84-21567. (Illus.). 251p. 1985. reprint ed. pap. 71.60 (*0-608-02969-6*, 2063437) Bks Demand.
Video-Based Telecommunications in Distance Education. Ed. by Michael G. Moore & Margaret A. Koble. (Readings in Distance Education Ser.: No. 4). 144p. (Orig.). (C). 1995. pap. text ed. 20.00 (*1-877780-12-X*) ACSDE.

An Asterisk (*) at the beginning of an entry indicates that the title is appearing in BIP for the first time.

Video Basics. Herbert Zettl. LC 94-24487. 382p. 1995. pap. 43.95 (*0-534-24786-5*) Wadsworth Pub.
Video Basics. Herbert Zettl. (Radio/TV/Film Ser.). 1995. wbk. ed., pap. 18.95 (*0-534-24788-1*) Wadsworth Pub.
***Video Basics.** 2nd ed. Herbert Zettl. (Radio/TV/Film Ser.). (C). 1997. pap. text ed. 46.95 (*0-534-52686-1*) Wadsworth Pub.
***Video Basics Workbook.** 2nd ed. Zettl. (Radio/TV/Film Ser.). (C). 1998. pap. 19.95 (*0-534-52687-X*) Wadsworth Pub.
***Video Book.** Bruce Clendenin. LC 96-41803. 1997. pap. 37.33 (*0-13-607334-4*) P-H.
Video Book: Creating an Integrated Home Entertainment System with Your TV, VCR, & the Latest Video Components. rev. ed. Gordon McComb. (Illus.). 192p. (C). 1992. reprint ed. pap. 16.95 (*0-7906-1030-2*) Prompt Publns.
Video Burn. Carolee Schneemann. (Illus.). 24p. (Orig.). 1992. pap. 10.00 (*0-930495-14-4*) San Fran Art Inst.
Video Camera Operator's Handbook. Peter Hodges. LC 94-32565. (Illus.). 224p. 1995. 42.95 (*0-240-51314-2*, Focal) Buttrwrth-Heinemann.
Video Camera Techniques: A New Media Manual. 2nd ed. Gerald Millerson. LC 94-18429. (Media Manual Ser.). 160p. 1994. pap. 24.95 (*0-240-51376-2*, Focal) Buttrwrth-Heinemann.
Video Cameras & Camcorders. Marvin Hobbs. 272p. 1989. boxed 40.00 (*0-13-943713-4*) P-H.
Video Cinema: Techniques & Projects for Beginning Filmmakers. John P. Frantz. LC 94-25878. (Illus.). 144p. (Orig.). (YA). (gr. 6 up). 1994. pap. 14.95 (*1-55652-228-2*) Chicago Review.
Video Classics, Vol. 1, Bk. 1: The Adventures of Mighty Mouse. Ed. by Tom Mason. (Illus.). 50p. 1989. pap. 3.50 (*0-944735-22-3*) Malibu Comics Ent.
Video Classics, Vol. 2, Bk. 2: More Adventures of Mighty Mouse. Ed. by Tom Mason. (Illus.). 54p. 1989. pap. 3.50 (*0-944735-06-1*) Malibu Comics Ent.
Video-Clips. Stefano Tamburini et al. Ed. by Bernd Metz. Tr. by Tom Leighton from FRE. (Illus.). 70p. 1985. pap. 10.95 (*0-87416-015-4*) Catalan Communs.
Video Codecs by Example: The Cross-Platform Digital Video Cookbook. Charles Copeland. (C). 1997. pap. text ed. write for info. (*0-201-63491-0*) Addison-Wesley.
Video Coding: The Second Generation Approach. Ed. by Luis Torres & Murat Kunt. LC 95-48430. 448p. (C). 1996. lib. bdg. 140.00 (*0-7923-9680-4*) Kluwer Ac.
Video Collection Development in Multi-Type Libraries: A Handbook. Gary Handman. LC 93-21136. (Library Management Collection). 496p. 1994. text ed. 79.50 (*0-313-27902-0*, Greenwood Pr) Greenwood.
Video Communication: Structuring Content for Maximum Program Effectiveness. David L. Smith. 412p. (C). 1991. pap. 38.95 (*0-534-13146-8*) Wadsworth Pub.
***Video Communications: Forecasts of Markets & Technologies.** Lawrence K. Vanston et al. 111p. 1992. pap. 45.00 (*0-614-18106-2*) Tech Futures.
Video Communications into the Twenty-First Century. 178p. 1992. 1,950.00 (*0-89336-922-5*, G-138) BCC.
Video Compression. Carl Ostrom. 1992. text ed. write for info. (*0-442-01422-8*) Van Nos Reinhold.
Video Compression for Multimedia. Jan Ozer. 387p. 1994. pap. text ed., pap. 39.95 incl. cd-rom (*0-12-531940-1*, AP Prof) Acad Pr.
Video Computers: How to Select, Mix, & Operate Personal Computers & Home Video Equipment. Charles J. Sippl & Fred Dahl. (Illus.). 256p. 1981. 15.95 (*0-13-941856-3*, Spectrum IN) Macmillan Gen Ref.
***Video Conferencing: Usage, Applications, Trends.** 1992. 995.00 (*0-614-18364-2*, IGIC-59) Info Gatekeepers.
Video Connection: Integrating Video into Language Teaching. Charles Altman. (C). 1988. pap. 17.96 (*0-395-48143-0*) HM.
Video Copyright Permissions: A Guide to Securing Permission to Retain, Perform, & Transmit Television Programs Videotaped off the Air. Jerome K. Miller. (Copyright Information Bulletin Ser.: No. 5). 140p. 1989. 29.95 (*0-914143-13-1*, Copy Info Svc) Assn Ed Comm Tech.
Video Courses for the Verbal & Math SAT. Rind & Paul Marasa. 1995. teacher ed. write for info. (*1-57004-024-9*) Lrning NJ.
***Video Data Compression for Multimedia Computing: Statistically Based & Biologically Inspired Techniques.** Hua Harry Li et al. LC 96-47147. (International Series in Engineering & Computer Science, Natural Language Processing & Machine Translation). 440p. (C). 1997. lib. bdg. 130.00 (*0-7923-9790-8*) Kluwer Ac.
***Video Database Systems: Oil Issues, Products, & Applications.** Ahmed K. Elmagarmid. (Advances in Database Systems Ser.). 192p. (C). 1997. lib. bdg. 96.00 (*0-7923-9872-6*) Kluwer Ac.
Video Demo: Sampler. Atkins. (C). 1995. pap. text ed. write for info. (*0-7167-2055-8*) W H Freeman.
Video Demo: 2 Tapes. Atkins. (C). 1995. pap. text ed. write for info. (*0-7167-2039-6*) W H Freeman.
Video Demo Tape: How to Save Money Making a Tape That Gets You Work. Larry Benedict & Susan Benedict. 232p. 1992. pap. 32.95 (*0-240-80140-7*, Focal) Buttrwrth-Heinemann.
Video Democracy: The Vote-from-Home Revolution. Richard Hollander. LC 85-81818. 161p. 1985. 24.95 (*0-912338-51-2*); fiche 9.95 (*0-912338-52-0*) Lomond.
Video Demystified. Keith Jack. 464p. 1995. pap. 39.95 (*1-878707-23-X*) HighText.
***Video Demystified.** 2nd ed. Keith Jack. 1997. 75.00 (*1-878707-36-1*) HighText.
Video Demystified: A Handbook for the Digital Engineer. Keith Jack. 360p. 1993. pap. 29.95 (*1-878707-09-4*) HighText.
Video Detective's Guide to the Top 100 Videos. PFG Staff. 1996. pap. text ed. 4.95 (*0-9649334-0-3*) Palmer Film Group.
***Video Detective's 1997 Guide to the Top 1000 Films of All Time.** Jim Riffel. LC 96-53493. 1997. pap. 5.95 (*0-88001-542-X*) Ecco Pr.
Video Dialtone Technology: Digital Video Services over ADSL, HFC, FTTC, & ATM. Dan Minoli. LC 94-49661. 1995. text ed. 60.00 (*0-07-042724-0*) McGraw.
Video Display Terminals: A Bibliography. 1995. lib. bdg. 252.95 (*0-8490-7531-9*) Gordon Pr.
Video Display Terminals: Health & Safety Update, 1983. Mark Pinsky et al. (Excerpts from Microwave News Ser.). 29p. 1984. pap. 10.00 (*0-9610580-1-3*) Microwave.
Video Display Terminals: Safety & Health (Excerpts from Microwave News) Louis Slesin & Martha Zybko. 84p. (Orig.). 1983. pap. 8.50 (*0-9610580-0-5*) Microwave.
Video Display Terminals & Vision. Howard D. Kahn & Sally M. Corngold. (Illus.). 60p. (Orig.). 1989. pap. text ed. 15.00 (*0-943599-11-3*) OEPF.
Video Displays, Work, & Vision. National Research Council Staff. 273p. 1983. pap. text ed. 19.95 (*0-309-03388-8*) Natl Acad Pr.
Video Economics. Bruce M. Owen & Steven S. Wildman. (Illus.). 364p. (C). 1992. 39.95 (*0-674-93716-3*) HUP.
Video Editing & Post Production. Mavis E. Arthur & James R. Caruso. 400p. 1992. pap. 28.95 (*0-13-946575-8*) P-H.
Video Editing & Post Production: A Professional Guide. 3rd ed. Gary Anderson. LC 83-25124. (Illus.). 218p. 1993. student ed., pap. 36.95 (*0-86729-351-9*, Focal) Buttrwrth-Heinemann.
Video-Endoscopy. Ed. by Harubumi Kato. Tr. by J. Patrick Barron. LC 92-1698. 152, viiip. 1993. text ed. 86.00 (*3-7186-5299-4*) Gordon & Breach.
Video Engineering. 2nd ed. Andrew F. Inglis & Arch C. Luther. (Illus.). 496p. 1996. text ed. 60.00 (*0-07-031791-7*) McGraw.
Video Engineer's Guide to Digital Audio. John Watkinson. 96p. (Orig.). 1995. pap. text ed. 19.95 (*0-9640361-3-4*) NVision.
Video Entepreneurship In Action. 2nd ed. Hutt. (Gb-Basic Business Ser.). 1988. 304.95 (*0-538-04511-6*) S-W Pub.
Video Entrepreneurship in Action. 2nd ed. Hutt. (Gb-Basic Business Ser.). 1988. 304.95 (*0-538-04512-4*) S-W Pub.
Video Family History. Duane Sturm & Pat Sturm. (Illus.). 123p. 1989. pap. 10.95 (*0-916489-44-2*) Ancestry.
Video Field Production. 2nd ed. Ron Whittaker. LC 95-24592. 407p. (C). 1996. text ed. 49.95 (*0-614-17917-3*, 1444) Mayfield Pub.
Video Field Production. 2nd ed. Ron Whittaker. 201p. (C). 1995. teacher ed., pap. text ed. write for info. (*1-55934-445-8*, 1445) Mayfield Pub.
***Video Field Production & Editing.** 4th ed. Ronald J. Compesi & Ronald E. Sherriffs. LC 96-49671. Orig. Title: Small Format Television Production. 452p. 1997. 54.00 (*0-205-26358-5*) Allyn.
***Video for Development: Lessons from Vietnam.** Su Braden & Than Thi Thien Huong. (Development Casebooks Ser.). 128p. 1997. pap. 12.95 (*0-85598-370-1*, Pub. by Oxfam UK) Humanities.
Video for Libraries: Special Interest Video for Small & Medium-Sized Public Libraries. Sally Mason & James C. Scholtz. LC 88-22235. 187p. reprint ed. pap. 53.30 (*0-7837-5921-5*, 2045720) Bks Demand.
Video Forum - A Videography for Libraries: Health Issue. Ed. by William Sloan. 44p. write for info. incl. vhs (*1-884188-03-6*) Nat Video.
Video Forum - A Videography for Libraries: Latino Issue. Ed. by Marie Nethus. 60p. write for info. (*1-884188-02-8*) Nat Video.
Video France - Optiques: La Vie Quotidienne. Jean N. Rey. 80p. 1995. reprint ed. pap. 149.95 (*0-8442-1468-X*, Passport Bks) NTC Pub Grp.
Video France - Panorama de la France. Jean N. Rey. (Illus.). 80p. 1995. reprint ed. pap. 149.95 (*0-8442-1485-X*, Natl Textbk) NTC Pub Grp.
Video France - Profiles des Francaise. Jean N. Rey. 80p. 1995. reprint ed. pap. 149.95 (*0-8442-1471-X*, Natl Textbk) NTC Pub Grp.
Video Game Illustration: Sega Version. Graphic-Sha Staff. (Illus.). 144p. 1994. pap. 44.95 (*4-7661-0772-1*, Pub. by Graphic Sha JA) Bks Nippan.
Video Game Spy. Bob Wright. Tr. by Phyllis Bourne & Eugenia Tusquets. (Tom & Ricky Spanish-English Readers Ser.). (Illus.). 96p. (ENG & SPA.). (J). (gr. 1-5). 1988. pap. 4.95 (*0-87879-662-2*) High Noon Bks.
Video Games. Arlene Erlbach. (J). 1996. pap. text ed. 6.95 (*0-8225-9739-X*) Lerner Group.
Video Games for Virgins: Comprehensive Guide to Gaming. Sean Perkin. (Illus.). 144p. (Orig.). 1996. pap. 1.95 (*1-57787-086-7*) ComEnt Media.
Video Goals: Getting Results with Pictures & Sound. Tom Schroeppel. LC 86-91773. (Illus.). 120p. (Orig.). 1987. pap. 8.95 (*0-9603718-2-6*) Schroeppel.
Video Handbook. 2nd ed. Ru Van Wezel. 456p. 1990. pap. 78.95 (*0-434-92189-0*) Buttrwrth-Heinemann.
Video Icons & Values. Ed. by Alan M. Olson et al. LC 89-49240. (SUNY Series in Speech Communication). 189p. 1990. pap. text ed. 21.95 (*0-7914-0412-9*) State U NY Pr.
Video Icons & Values. Ed. by Alan M. Olson et al. LC 89-49240. (SUNY Series in Speech Communication). 189p. 1991. text ed. 64.50 (*0-7914-0411-0*) State U NY Pr.
Video Imaging Directory Understanding the Earth. Press. write for info. (*0-7167-2667-X*) W H Freeman.
Video in Language Teaching. Jack Lonergan. (New Directions in Language Teaching Ser.). (Illus.). 160p. 1984. pap. text ed. 15.95 (*0-521-27263-7*) Cambridge U Pr.
Video in Second Language Teaching: Using, Selecting, & Producing Video for the Classroom. Ed. by Susan Stempleski & Paul Arcario. LC 92-60523. 183p. 1993. pap. 12.95 (*0-939791-41-2*) Tchrs Eng Spkrs.
Video in the Language Classroom. Gillian Sturtridge. (Practical Language Teaching Ser.: No. 7). (Illus.). 192p. (Orig.). (C). 1982. pap. text ed. 15.00 (*0-435-28971-3*, 28971) Heinemann.
Video Instructor's Manual to Accompany Boone-Kurtz, Contemporary Business. 7th ed. Gayle J. Marco & Anthony J. Lucas. 186p. (C). 1993. pap. text ed. 5.50 (*0-03-076343-6*) Dryden Pr.
Video Kids. Jon Buller & Susan Schade. LC 93-26923. (All Aboard Reading Ser.). (Illus.). 48p. (J). (gr. 2-3). 1994. pap. 3.50 (*0-448-40180-0*, G&D) Putnam Pub Group.
Video Kids: Making Sense of Nintendo. Eugene F. Provenzo, Jr. 192p. 1991. pap. text ed. 10.95 (*0-674-93709-0*) HUP.
***Video Law.** 2nd ed. Bate. 1992. pap. text ed. write for info. (*0-85121-682-X*) Addison-Wesley.
Video Librarian's Guide to Collection Development & Management. Randy Pitman. LC 92-15104. (Professional Librarian Ser.). 280p. 1992. 40.00 (*0-8161-1978-3*, Hall Reference); 25.00 (*0-8161-1979-1*, Hall Reference) Macmillan.
Video Lighting & Special Effects. James R. Caruso. 1990. pap. 28.95 (*0-13-824756-0*) P-H.
Video Made Easy: How to Use & Enjoy Your Home Video Equipment. (Illus.). 224p. (Orig.). 1996. pap. 19.95 (*1-57243-071-0*) Triumph Bks.
Video Making for Kids: Teachers Manual. Donna J. Grisanti & Grace H. Hayes. 100p. 1995. teacher ed., pap. 12.95 (*0-9649693-1-9*) Hot Flash CA.
Video Making for Kids: With the Kids Eye View Club. Donna J. Grisanti & Grace H. Hayes. (Illus.). 203p. (J). (gr. 3-8). 1995. pap. 19.95 (*0-9649693-0-0*) Hot Flash CA.
Video Manual to Accompany Professional Selling. 2nd ed. Mary A. Oberhaus & Sharon Ratliffe. 64p. (C). 1995. pap. text ed. 33.75 (*0-03-010223-5*) Dryden Pr.
Video Media Competition: Regulation, Economics & Technology. Ed. by Eli M. Noam. LC 85-435. (Columbia Studies in Business, Government & Society). 416p. 1985. text ed. 64.00 (*0-231-06134-X*) Col U Pr.
Video-Mediated Communication. Ed. by Kathleen E. Finn et al. LC 96-33431. (Computers, Cognition, & Work Ser.). 576p. 1997. 99.95 (*0-8058-2288-7*) L Erlbaum Assocs.
Video Microscopy. Shinya Inoue. LC 85-2852. 612p. 1986. 85.00 (*0-306-42120-8*, Plenum Pr) Plenum.
***Video Microscopy: The Fundamentals.** (Illus.). 760p. (C). 1997. write for info. (*0-306-45531-5*, Plenum Pr) Plenum.
Video Mind, Earth Mind: Art, Communications, & Ecology. Paul Ryan. LC 92-48540. (Semiotics & the Human Sciences Ser.: Vol. 4). 437p. 1993. 54.95 (*0-8204-1871-4*) P Lang Pubng.
Video Movie Guide 1997. Mick Martin & Marsha Porter. 1664p. 1996. pap. 16.00 (*0-345-40642-7*) Ballantine Trade.
***Video Movie Guide 1998.** Martin & Mick Porter. 1997. mass mkt. 7.99 (*0-345-40793-8*) Ballantine.
***Video Movie Guide 1998.** Martin & Porter. 1997. pap. 18.95 (*0-345-40794-6*) Ballantine.
Video Movies: A Core Collection for Libraries. Randy Pitman & Elliott Swanson. LC 89-48387. 266p. 1990. lib. bdg. 45.00 (*0-87436-577-5*) ABC-CLIO.
Video Night in Kathmandu: And Other Reports from the Not-So-Far East. Pico Iyer. (Departures Ser.). 384p. 1989. pap. 13.00 (*0-679-72216-5*, Vin) Random.
***Video Observations for the Early Childhood Rating Scale: Video Guide & Workbook.** Thelma Harms et al. pap. 4.00 (*0-8077-3249-4*) Tchrs Coll.
***Video Observations for the Family Day Care Rating Scale: Video Guide & Workbook.** Thelma Harms et al. pap. 4.00 (*0-8077-3256-7*) Tchrs Coll.
***Video Observations for the Infant/Toddler Environment Rating Scale: Video Guide & Training Workbook.** Thelma Harms & Debby Cryer. pap. 4.00 (*0-8077-3138-2*) Tchrs Coll.
Video on Demand: Architecture, Performance & Economic Modeling. Winston W. Hodge & Larry Taylor. (Illus.). 68p. 1994. 995.00 (*0-88709-101-6*) Simba Info Inc.
***Video on Demand Systems: Technology, Interoperability & Trials.** Shihfu Chang. LC 97-17632. 1997. write for info. (*0-7923-9949-8*) Kluwer Ac.
Video One Wholesalers, Inc. 2nd ed. 48p. (C). 1992. per. 21.50 (*0-256-10741-6*, 36-3649-02) Irwin.
Video Passport French. Brian Hill. 1995. pap. 39.95 incl. audio, vhs (*0-8442-1566-X*) NTC Pub Grp.
Video Passport Spanish. Phil Batley-Matlas & Brian Hill. 1995. pap. 39.95 incl. audio, vhs (*0-8442-7450-X*) NTC Pub Grp.
Video Pianist, Bk. 1. Walter Noona & Carol Noona. 48p. (Orig.). 1987. pap. 4.95 (*0-89328-100-X*, KM121) Lorenz Corp.
Video Pictures of the Future. Ed. by Jeffrey B. Friedman. (Illus.). 296p. 1983. pap. text ed. 35.00 (*0-940690-07-1*) Soc Motion Pic & TV Engrs.
Video Piracy & the Law. B. V. Gopal. (C). 1990. 85.00 (*0-89771-181-5*) St Mut.
Video Playtime: The Gendering of a Leisure Technology. Ann Gray. LC 92-13309. (Comedia Bk.). 176p. (C). 1992. pap. 17.95 (*0-415-05865-1*, A7932, Comedia) Routledge.
Video Playtime: The Gendering of a Leisure Technology. Ann Gray. LC 92-13309. (Comedia Bk.). 176p. (C). (gr. 13). 1992. text ed. 69.95 (*0-415-05864-3*, A7928, Comedia) Routledge.
Video Poems. Billy Collins. LC 79-50762. 1979. pap. 3.95 (*0-930090-05-5*) Applezaba.
Video Poker. Tony Korfman & David Gerhardt. (Playing to Win Ser.). 76p. (Orig.). 1987. pap. 2.50 (*0-934047-08-1*) Gaming Bks Intl.
Video Poker: The Face of Pain. Shepherd King. 156p. (Orig.). 1992. 4.95 (*1-881362-00-0*) Silv Dollar NV.
Video Poker Mania. Dwight Crevelt & Louise Crevelt. 160p. 1991. pap. 5.99 (*0-914839-20-9*) Gollehon Pr.
Video Policies & Procedures for Libraries. James C. Scholtz. LC 91-21350. 135p. 1991. lib. bdg. 45.00 (*0-87436-582-1*) ABC-CLIO.
Video Power: A Complete Guide to Writing, Planning, & Shooting Videos. Tom Shachtman & Harriet Shelare. LC 87-23681. (Illus.). 96p. (J). (gr. 6-9). 1988. 15.95 (*0-8050-0338-X*, Bks Young Read); pap. 7.95 (*0-8050-0414-9*, Bks Young Read) H Holt & Co.
***Video Production: Disciplines & Techniques.** 7th ed. Thomas D. Burrows & Donald N. Wood. 480p. (C). 1997. per. write for info. (*0-697-32719-1*) Wm C Brown Pubs.
Video Production for Genealogical & Historical Societies - Seminar Teaching Guide: Everything You Need to Conduct This Seminar...Even if You Have Never Given a Seminar Before. Dina C. Carson. LC 91-7344. (Illus.). 130p. (Orig.). 1991. teacher ed., pap. 69.95 (*1-879579-41-3*) Iron Gate Pub.
***Video Production Handbook.** Shyles. (C). Date not set. pap. write for info. (*0-395-71488-5*) HM.
Video Production Handbook. 2nd ed. Gerald Millerson. LC 92-10611. (Illus.). 256p. (Orig.). 1992. pap. 34.95 (*0-240-51321-5*, Focal) Buttrwrth-Heinemann.
Video Production Organizer: A Guide for Businesses, Schools, Government Agencies, & Professional Associations. Aleks Matza. LC 94-44269. (Illus.). 224p. 1995. pap. 29.95 incl. disk (*0-240-80229-2*, Focal) Buttrwrth-Heinemann.
Video Production Seminar Resource Manual & Workbook: Exhibits, Exercises & Examples. Dina C. Carson. (Illus.). 60p. (Orig.). 1991. pap. 10.00 (*1-879579-42-1*) Iron Gate Pub.
Video Projects for Elementary & Middle Schools. Keith Kyker & Christopher Curchy. LC 95-24689. (Illus.). xii, 121p. 1995. pap. text ed. 23.00 (*1-56308-377-9*) Libs Unl.
Video Purchasing Patterns in Schools. Quality Education Data Staff. (School Trend Ser.). 204p. 1988. pap. 49.95 (*0-88747-225-7*, 2257Q) Quality Ed Data.
Video-Read Package, Level 1. Ernest H. Christman. (Illus.). 1991. Set. incl. 2 videotapes, CAT, KITE, BIKE, CAVE, Four Stories, Level One, & Progressive Phonics, Leve. 145.00 incl. vhs (*0-912329-05-X*) Tutorial Press.
Video-Read Package, Level 2. Ernest H. Christman. (Illus.). 1990. 140.00 incl. vhs (*0-912329-02-5*) Tutorial Press.
Video-Read Package, Level 3. Ernest H. Christman. (Illus.). 1990. 90.00 incl. vhs (*0-912329-08-4*) Tutorial Press.
Video-Read Package, Level 4. Ernest H. Christman. (Illus.). 1990. 85.00 incl. vhs (*0-912329-11-4*) Tutorial Press.
Video-Read Package, Level 5. Ernest H. Christman. (Illus.). 1990. 75.00 (*0-912329-14-9*) Tutorial Press.
Video Recording Technology: Its Impact on Media & Home Entertainment. Aaron F. Nmungwun. (Communication Ser.). 304p. (C). 1989. pap. 29.95 (*0-8058-0622-9*); text ed. 59.95 (*0-8058-0360-2*) L Erlbaum Assocs.
Video Renter's Bible: What to Rent Tonight. Seth Godin. 72p. 1993. pap. 2.99 (*0-393-31081-7*) Norton.
***Video Rhetorics: Televised Advertising in American Politics.** John S. Nelson & G. R. Boynton. LC 97-4580. 1997. write for info. (*0-252-02345-5*); pap. text ed. 29.95 (*0-252-06648-0*) U of Ill Pr.
***Video Scrambling & Descrambling for Satellite & Cable TV.** Rudolf F. Graf. 246p. 1986. pap. text ed. 24.95 (*0-7506-9945-0*) Buttrwrth-Heinemann.
Video Scrambling & Descrambling for Satellite & Cable TV. Rudolf F. Graf & William Sheets. 256p. 1986. 24.95 (*0-672-22499-2*) Buttrwrth-Heinemann.
Video Scriptwriting: How to Write for the Four Billion Dollar Commercial Video Market. Barry Hampe. LC 92-29107. 256p. (Orig.). 1993. pap. 15.95 (*0-452-26868-0*, Plume) NAL-Dutton.
Video Segments for Abnormal Psychology. 2nd ed. Comer. Date not set. write for info. (*0-7167-2719-6*) W H Freeman.
***Video Series Training Guide.** Christy Fong. 92p. 1996. teacher ed., spiral bd. 30.00 (*1-886050-16-3*) Egger Pub Inc.
***Video Server: Environments, Applications, & Design.** Asit Dan & Dinkar Sitaram. 500p. 1998. text ed. 64.95 (*1-55860-430-8*) Morgan Kaufmann.
Video Sex: How to Capture Your Lovemaking with a Camcorder. Kevin Campbell. (Illus.). 224p. 1994. pap. 19.95 (*0-936262-25-7*) Amherst Media.
Video-Sig Library: A Collector's Catalog of Affordable Special Interest & Classic Video. Ed. by Bruce R. Kent. (Illus.). 208p. (Orig.). 1989. pap. 4.95 (*0-915835-15-0*) PC Software.
Video Source Book. 10th ed. Ed. by David Weiner. 1988. 199.00 (*0-8103-4258-8*, 70998-02141) Gale.
Video Sourcebook. 11th ed. David Weiner. 1989. 210.00 (*0-8103-4299-5*) Gale.
Video Sourcebook, 2 vols. 12th ed. 1990. Set; incl. suppl. 220.00 (*0-8103-6978-8*) Gale.
Video Sourcebook, 2 vols. & Supplement. 13th ed. Furtaw. 1991. 230.00 (*0-8103-6979-6*) Gale.
Video Sourcebook, 2 vols. & Supplement. 14th ed. Furtaw. 1992. 240.00 (*0-8103-7606-7*) Gale.
Video Sourcebook, 2 vols. & Supplement. 16th ed. Furtaw. 1994. 270.00 (*0-8103-8536-8*) Gale.
Video Sourcebook. 17th ed. Scanlon. 1995. suppl. ed. write for info. (*0-8103-9090-6*) Gale.
Video Sourcebook, 3 Vols. 17th ed. Terri K. Schell. 4000p. 1995. suppl. ed. 275.00 (*0-8103-9087-6*) Gale.

***Video Sourcebook, 2 vols.** 19th ed. 1996. 295.00 (*0-7876-0199-3*, 00108888, Gale Res Intl) Gale.

***Video Sourcebook, 2 vols.** 20th ed. 1997. 295.00 (*0-7876-1157-3*, 00156281, Gale Res Intl) Gale.

Video Sourcebook, Vol. 1. Scanlon. 1996. write for info. (*0-8103-5779-8*) Gale.

Video Sourcebook, Vol. 1. 15th ed. Furtaw. 1993. write for info. (*0-8103-7761-6*) Gale.

Video Sourcebook, Vol. 1. 16th ed. Furtaw. 1994. write for info. (*0-8103-8537-6*) Gale.

Video Sourcebook, Vol. 1. 17th ed. Terri K. Schell. 1995. write for info. (*0-8103-9088-4*) Gale.

Video Sourcebook, Vol. 2. Scanlon. 1996. write for info. (*0-8103-5780-1*) Gale.

Video Sourcebook, Vol. 2. 15th ed. Furtaw. 1993. write for info. (*0-8103-7762-4*) Gale.

Video Sourcebook, Vol. 2. 16th ed. Furtaw. 1994. write for info. (*0-8103-8538-4*) Gale.

Video Sourcebook, Vol. 2. 17th ed. Terri K. Schell. 1995. write for info. (*0-8103-9089-2*) Gale.

Video Sourcebook & Supplement. 18th ed. Scanlon. 1996. 285.00 (*0-8103-5778-X*) Gale.

Video Sourcebook Supp, Pt. 1. 16th ed. Furtaw. 1995. write for info. (*0-8103-8539-2*) Gale.

***Video Sourcebook Supplement.** 10th ed. 1989. 210.00 (*0-8103-7432-3*, 00007499, Gale Res Intl) Gale.

Video Sourcebook Supplement, 2 vols. 15th ed. Furtaw. 1993. 260.00 (*0-8103-5408-X*) Gale.

Video Sourcebook Supplement, Pt. 1. 15th ed. Furtaw. 1994. write for info. (*0-8103-7860-4*) Gale.

Video Spaces: Eight Installations. Barbara London & Samuel R. Delany. (Illus.). 80p. 1995. pap. 22.50 (*0-8109-6146-6*) Abrams.

Video Spaces: Eight Installations. Barbara London. (Illus.). 80p. 1995. pap. 22.50 (*0-87070-646-2*, 0-8109-6146-6) Mus of Modern Art.

Video Stars. Molly Albright. LC 88-15880. (Two of a Kind Ser.). (Illus.). 96p. (J). (gr. 3-6). 1996. pap. 2.95 (*0-8167-1481-9*) Troll Communs.

Video Stereo & Optoelectronics: Eighteen Advanced Electronics Projects. Rudolf F. Graf. (Illus.). 368p. 1990. 28.95 (*0-8306-8358-5*, 3358); pap. 18.95 (*0-8306-3358-8*) McGraw-Hill Prof.

Video, Stereo & Optoelectronics: Eighteen Advanced Electronics Projects. Rudolf F. Graf & William Sheets. 1990. text ed. 28.95 (*0-07-155944-2*) McGraw.

Video Stop: A Computer Applications Simulation. Crippen. (DF - Computer Applications Ser.). 1994. text ed. 28.95 (*0-538-62860-X*) S-W Pub.

Video Studio: A Media Manual. 3rd ed. Alan Bermingham et al. LC 94-3408. (Media Manuals Ser.). 192p. 1994. pap. 24.95 (*0-240-51392-4*, Focal) Buttrwrth-Heinemann.

Video Systems. Badrkhan. 1989. text ed. 71.00 (*0-13-942061-4*) P-H.

Video Systems Engineering Handbook. Gene De Santis. 1500p. 1991. 59.95 (*0-8493-7402-2*, QA, CRC Reprint) Franklin.

Video Techniques. 2nd ed. White. 1988. 55.00 (*0-434-92290-0*) CRC Pr.

Video Techniques in Animal Ecology & Behaviour. Ed. by Stephen D. Wratten. LC 93-32960. 211p. (gr. 13). 1994. text ed. 72.95 (*0-412-46640-6*, Chap & Hall NY) Chapman & Hall.

Video Technology for Computer Graphics. Dean Winkler. (C). 1997. pap. text ed. write for info. (*0-201-53378-2*) Addison-Wesley.

Video Technology for Personal Computers. McGoldrick. 1996. text ed. 50.00 (*0-07-045018-8*) McGraw.

Video Test & Measurement Handbook. Horn. 1995. write for info. (*0-8493-7413-8*) CRC Pr.

Video Texts. (Illus.). 45p. 1983. pap. 5.00 (*0-317-55960-5*) Anthology Film.

Video the Changing World. Ed. by Nancy Thede & Alain Ambrosi. LC 91-72979. (Black Rose Bks.: Vol. 165). 238p. 1991. reprint ed. pap. 67.90 (*0-608-00462-6*, 2061281) Bks Demand.

Video to Online: Reference Service & the New Technology. Ed. by Bill Katz & Ruth A. Fraley. LC 82-23292. (Reference Librarian Ser.: Nos. 5 & 6). 205p. 1983. text ed. 49.95 (*0-86656-202-8*) Haworth Pr.

Video Toaster Companion. Todd Payne & Paul Drust. 450p. 1995. pap. text ed. 49.95 (*1-884474-05-5*) New Era Press.

Video Transformations. Lois Bianchi. LC 85-80971. (Illus.). 24p. 1986. 3.00 (*0-916365-18-2*) Ind Curators.

Video Vengeance. large type ed. Miles Tripp. (General Ser.). 352p. 1993. 25.99 (*0-7089-2852-8*) Ulverscroft.

***Video Verite: Regards et Reflexions sur la Vie.** Elizabeth Joiner et al. 256p. (FRE.). (C). 1993. pap. text ed. 37.16 incl. audio (*0-395-64998-6*) HM.

***Video Verite: Regards et Reflexions sur la Vie.** Elizabeth Joiner et al. (FRE.). (C). 1993. teacher ed., text ed. 5.96 (*0-395-64999-4*) HM.

Video Violence & Children. Ed. by Geoffrey Barlow & Alison Hill. LC 85-14596. 192p. 1986. text ed. 24.95 (*0-312-84571-5*) St Martin.

Video Violence & Values: A Guide to the Use of Video. Dave Pomeroy. 1990. pap. 5.95 (*0-377-00213-5*) Friendship Pr.

Video War & the Diasporic Imagination. Dona Kolar-Panov. (Routledge Research in Cultural & Media Studies). 288p. (C). 1996. text ed. write for info. (*0-415-14880-4*) Routledge.

Video Watchdog Book. Tim Lucas. (Illus.). 416p. (Orig.). 1992. pap. 19.95 (*0-9633756-0-1*) Video Watchdog.

Video Yearbook 1994. Joel Whitburn. 112p. pap. 9.95 (*0-7935-5038-6*, 00330156) H Leonard.

Videocassette Recorders: A Servicing Guide. Beeching. 1988. 44.00 (*0-434-90123-7*) CRC Pr.

Videocassette Recorders: Theory & Servicing. Gerald P. McGinty. (Illus.). 1979. pap. text ed. 24.95 (*0-07-044988-0*) McGraw.

Videocassette Technology in American Education. George N. Gordon & Irving A. Falk. LC 72-81494. 176p. 1972. 34.95 (*0-87778-035-8*) Educ Tech Pubns.

Videocassettes in the NAL Collection Pertaining to Alternative Farming Systems. 25p. (Orig.). (C). 1993. pap. text ed. 20.00 (*1-56806-757-7*) DIANE Pub.

Videoconferencing: The Whole Picture. Toby Trowt-Bayard. 24.95 (*0-936648-48-1*) Flatiron Pubng.

***Videoconferencing: Usage, Applications, Trends.** 495.00 (*0-614-26469-3*) Info Gatekeepers.

***Videoconferencing & Money, Money, Money.** Jeremy Goldstein. 1996. pap. text ed. 14.95 (*1-883527-05-8*) Advert Cnslts.

Videoconferencing & Videotelephony: Technology & Standards. Richard Schaphorst. LC 96-19494. 199p. 1996. 69.00 (*0-89006-844-5*) Artech Hse.

Videoconferencing Hardware & Software Markets. 300p. 1991. pap. 2,495.00 (*1-56851-003-9*, IGIC-55) Info Gatekeepers.

Videodisc & Optical Memory Technologies. Jordan Isailovic. (Illus.). 400p. (C). 1985. text ed. 68.00 (*0-13-942053-3*) P-H.

Videodisc & Related Technologies: A Glossary of Terms. Rockley L. Miller & John H. Sayers. 80p. (Orig.). (C). 1986. pap. 7.95 (*0-938907-02-6*) Future Syst.

Videodisc-Microcomputer Courseware Design. Ed. by Michael L. DeBloois. LC 81-22161. 192p. 1982. 37.95 (*0-87778-183-4*) Educ Tech Pubns.

Videodisc Training: A Cost Analysis: A Guide & Workbook for Choosing your Courseware Delivery System. Richard H. Brandt et al. (Monitor Reports). 150p. 1987. student ed. 15.00 (*0-938907-08-5*) Future Syst.

Videodisc Training: A Cost Analysis: A Guide & Workbook for Choosing your Courseware Delivery System. Richard H. Brandt et al. (Monitor Reports). 150p. (C). 1987. pap. 49.95 (*0-938907-07-7*) Future Syst.

Videodiscs. Edward W. Schneider & Junius L. Bennion. Ed. by James E. Duane. LC 80-23563. (Instructional Media Library: Vol. 16). (Illus.). 128p. 1981. 27.95 (*0-87778-176-1*) Educ Tech Pubns.

Videodiscs for English Classes: Classroom Applications of Videodisc Technology: Secondary English. Martina E. Lewis. 120p. (Orig.). 1989. pap. text ed. 26.95 (*0-933109-02-4*) Probata Pr.

Videodiscs in Museums: A Project & Resource Directory. Robert H. Binder. Ed. by Rockley L. Miller et al. 137p. (C). 1991. spiral bd. 49.95 (*0-938907-09-3*) Future Syst.

Videodiscs in Vocational Educational. William P. Olivier. 35p. 1985. 4.75 (*0-317-01301-7*, IN299) Ctr Educ Trng Employ.

Videodisk Guide with Barcodes - Onyva Videodisk Guide with Barcodes, Level 1. 2nd ed. Bragger. (Secondary French Ser.). 1994. pap. 13.95 (*0-8384-5439-9*) Heinle & Heinle.

Videoendoscopy: From Velopharynx to Larynx. Michael P. Karnell. (Clinical Competence Ser.). (Illus.). 150p. (Orig.). (C). 1994. pap. text ed. 49.95 (*1-879105-97-7*, 0352) Singular Publishing.

Videofluoroscopic Studies of Speech in Patients with Cleft Palate. M. Leon Skolnick & E. R. Cohn. (Illus.). xi, 186p. 1989. 161.00 (*0-387-96958-6*) Spr-Verlag.

***Videogame Characters.** Jeff Rovin & Tim Moriarty. 1997. write for info. (*0-8160-3290-4*) Facts on File.

Videogames. Arlene Erlbach. LC 93-36086. (How It's Made Ser.). (Illus.). 48p. (J). (gr. 4-8). 1995. lib. bdg. 18.95 (*0-8225-2389-2*, Lerner Publctns) Lerner Group.

Videographics: Design for the Small Screen. Hugh Skinner. (Illus.). 96p. 1994. 39.95 (*0-7134-7401-7*, Pub. by Batsford UK) Trafalgar.

Videography: Video Media As Art & Culture. Sean Cubitt. LC 93-25196. 1993. text ed. 45.00 (*0-312-10295-X*); text ed. 18.95 (*0-312-10296-8*) St Martin.

VideoHound & Stargazer All Movie Guide: Profiles of Film Personalities on the Screen & Behind the Scenes. Videohound Staff & AMG Staff. Ed. by Connors et al. (Videohound Ser.). (Illus.). 608p. 1995. 29.95 (*0-7876-0698-7*, 089572) Gale.

Videohound on CD IBM Single (VIP) Ed. by Martin Conners & Julia Furtaw. 1993. 79.95 (*0-8103-4999-X*) Visible Ink Pr.

***VideoHound Soundtracks: Music from the Movies, Television & Broadway.** Ed. by Devra M. Sladics. (VideoHound Ser.). 800p. 1997. 24.95 (*1-57859-025-6*) Visible Ink Pr.

Videohound's Family Video Retriever. 2nd ed. Visible Ink Press Staff. (Illus.). 500p. 1996. 17.95 (*0-7876-0984-6*) Visible Ink Pr.

VideoHound's Golden Bone Awards: Classics, Gems, & Buried Treasures. Les Stone. (VideoHound Ser.). 136p. 1995. pap. 4.95 (*0-7876-0477-1*) Visible Ink Pr.

VideoHound's Golden Movie Retriever, 1992. 1991. pap. 14.95 (*0-8103-9404-9*) Visible Ink Pr.

Videohound's Golden Movie Retriever, 1993. 2nd ed. Videohound Staff. 1400p. 1992. 17.95 (*0-8103-9425-1*, 089401) Visible Ink Pr.

VideoHound's Golden Movie Retriever, 1994. 3rd ed. Connors & Furtan. 1500p. 1993. pap. 17.95 (*0-8103-9131-7*, 089402) Visible Ink Pr.

VideoHound's Golden Movie Retriever 1996. 5th ed. 1600p. 1995. 19.95 (*0-7876-0626-X*) Visible Ink Pr.

VideoHound's Golden Movie Retriever, 1996. 95th ed. Gale Research, Inc., Staff. 1995. 49.95 (*0-7876-0855-6*) Visible Ink Pr.

Videohound's Golden Movie Retriever, 1997. 6th ed. Visible Ink Press Staff & Craddock. 1600p. 1996. 19.95 (*0-7876-0780-0*) Visible Ink Pr.

***VideoHound's Golden Movie Retriever 1998.** 7th ed. Ed. by Jim Craddock. (VideoHound Ser.). 1600p. 1997. 19.95 (*1-57859-024-8*) Visible Ink Pr.

***Videohound's Golden Movie Retriever 94.** 94th ed. 1993. 35.95 (*0-8103-9459-6*, 00100119, Gale Res Intl) Gale.

***Videohound's Golden Movie Retriever '98.** 7th ed. 1997. 19.95 (*0-7876-0781-9*, 00153468) Visible Ink Pr.

Videohound's Golden Movie Retriver 1995. 4th ed. Gale Research, Inc., Staff. 1994. pap. 17.95 (*0-8103-9135-X*) Visible Ink Pr.

***VideoHound's Guide to Three- & Four-Star Movies - 1988 Edition: A Videobuff's Best Friend.** VideoHound Editors. 640p. (Orig.). 1997. pap. 10.99 (*0-7679-0047-2*) Broadway BDD.

***VideoHound's Guide to Three & Four-Star Movies 1997.** 640p. 1996. pap. 9.99 (*0-553-06715-X*) Broadway BDD.

Videohound's Idiot's Delight: The Top 100 Dumbest Movies of All Time. Ed. by Hilary Weber. (Videohound Ser.). (Illus.). 224p. 1995. pap. 9.95 (*0-7876-0617-0*, 089561) Gale.

***VideoHound's Independent Film: Movies Made Outside the System.** Monica Sullivan. Ed. by Carol Schwartz. (VideoHound Ser.). 450p. 1997. 17.95 (*1-57859-018-3*) Visible Ink Pr.

Videohound's Movie Laughlines: Quips, Quotes, & Clever Comebacks. 5th ed. Carol Forget. Ed. by Hilary Weber. (Videohound Ser.). (Illus.). 450p. 1995. 16.95 (*0-7876-0699-5*, 089573) Gale.

Videohound's Pocket Movie Guide. Martin Connors. 1994. 4.95 (*0-8103-9849-4*) Gale.

VideoHounds Pocket Movie Guide, Vol. III. Ed. by Adele Hast. 857p. 1991. 160.00 (*1-55862-059-1*, M88859-200034) St James Pr.

VideoHounds Pocket Movie Guide, Vol. 4. 2nd ed. Connors Martin. 1994. 29.95 (*0-8103-9872-9*, 072444-M99348) Gale.

Videohound's Sci-Fi Experience: Your Quantum Guide to the Video Universe. 5th ed. Visible Ink Press Staff & Fhaner. (Illus.). 520p. 1996. 17.95 (*0-7876-0615-4*) Visible Ink Pr.

Videohound's That's Amore. Martin Conners. Ed. by Christine Tomassini & Dianel Dupuis. 126p. 1994. 4.95 (*0-7876-0086-5*) Visible Ink Pr.

Videohound's That's Amore! Love, Lust, & Longing at the Movies. Gale Research, Inc., Staff. 1994. 29.95 (*0-7876-0148-9*) Visible Ink Pr.

***Videohound's Vampire Film Guide.** LC 97-4010. 1997. 17.95 (*1-57859-002-7*, 00156897) Visible Ink Pr.

***VideoHound's Video Premieres: The Only Guide to Video Originals & Limited Releases.** LC 97-970. (Illus.). 450p. 1997. pap. 17.95 (*0-7876-0825-4*) Visible Ink Pr.

Videohound's Worst Nightmares. Martin Connors. Ed. by Christine Tomassini. 126p. 1994. 4.95 (*0-7876-0085-7*) Visible Ink Pr.

Videohound's Worst Nightmares: Vampires, Werewolves & Other Creatures of the Night. Gale Research, Inc., Staff. 1994. 29.95 (*0-7876-0150-0*) Visible Ink Pr.

***Videojournalism.** Richard Griffiths. (Illus.). 288p. 1997. pap. 47.95 (*0-240-51508-0*, Focal) Buttrwrth-Heinemann.

Videomaker Handbook: A Comprehensive Guide to Making Videos. Ed. by Videomaker Magazine Editors. (Illus.). 384p. 1996. pap. 24.95 (*0-240-80226-8*, Focal) Buttrwrth-Heinemann.

Videomundo. Levy. (C). 1996. teacher ed., pap. text ed. 42.00 incl. trans. (*0-03-017014-1*) HB Coll Pubs.

Videomundo. Levy. (C). 1996. lab manual ed., pap. text ed. 17.00 (*0-03-017017-6*) HB Coll Pubs.

Videos. L. Cridisque. 1977. pap. 1.50 (*0-686-20611-8*) Ghost Dance.

Videos - Uses & Methods for Office, Labs, Research & Personal - Professional Documentations: Index of New Information with Authors, Subjects & References. Warren T. Woodley. 150p. 1994. 47.50 (*1-55914-998-1*); pap. 44.50 (*1-55914-999-X*) ABBE Pubs Assn.

Video's Best: The Easy, Fast, & Fun Way to Choose Tonight's Video. Mark A. Satern. LC 95-5554. 690p. 1995. 49.95 (*1-56024-973-0*) Haworth Pr.

Videos for Business & Training: An Annotated Guide to Approximately 15,000 Titles of Video Programming for Use in Business, Industry, & All Types of Training. David J. Weiner. 700p. 1989. 99.00 (*0-8103-7436-6*) Gale.

Videos for Kids: The Essential, Indispensable Parent's Guide to Children's Movies on Video. Doug Atkinson & Fiona Zippan. LC 94-27680. 432p. 1994. pap. 9.95 (*1-55958-635-4*) Prima Pub.

Videos for Understanding Diversity: A Core Selection & Evaluative Guide. Gregory I. Stevens. LC 93-2662. 1993. pap. 35.00 (*0-8389-0612-5*) ALA.

Videos of African & African-Related Performance: An Annotated Bibliography. annot. ed. Carol Lems-Dworkin. (Illus.). 35300p. 1996. pap. 57.00 (*0-9637048-1-8*) C Lems-Dworkin Pubs.

Videospain. Eugeni Bonet. (Illus.). 16p. (Orig.). 1988. pap. 10.00 (*0-913263-22-2*) Exit Art.

***VideoStore: Catalog Your Videos from A to Z.** Will Limkemann et al. (Software-in-a-Book Ser.: No. 5). (Illus.). 192p. (Orig.). 1997. pap. 39.95 (*1-887155-04-X*) Doubleware Pubns.

Videostroboscopic Examination of the Larynx. Minoru Hirano & Diane M. Bless. LC 93-9421. 260p. (Orig.). (C). 1993. pap. text ed. 65.00 (*1-879105-52-7*, 0232) Singular Publishing.

Videostyle in Senate Campaigns. Dorothy D. Nesbit. LC 88-2166. 192p. 1988. text ed. 26.00 (*0-87049-582-8*) U of Tenn Pr.

Videotape Editing: A Post Production Primer. 3rd ed. Steven E. Browne. (Illus.). 336p. 1996. pap. 34.95 (*0-240-80269-1*, Focal) Buttrwrth-Heinemann.

Videotape Editing: A Postproduction Primer. 2nd ed. Steven E. Browne. LC 92-32379. 336p. 1993. pap. 36.95 (*0-240-80151-2*, Focal) Buttrwrth-Heinemann.

Videotape on Trial: A View from the Jury Box. Norman E. Fontes & Gerald R. Miller. LC 79-18774. (People & Communication Ser.: No. 7). 224p. 1979. reprint ed. pap. 63.90 (*0-608-01517-2*, 2059561) Bks Demand.

Videotape Rental Store: A Step by Step Guide to Setting up & Operating a Videotape Rental Store. 1986. lib. bdg. 250.00 (*0-8490-3814-6*) Gordon Pr.

***Videotape Workbook to Accompany Elementary Algebra: Concepts & Applications.** 5th ed. Janina Udrys. (C). 1998. pap. text ed. write for info. (*0-201-34030-5*) Addison-Wesley.

***Videotape Workbook to Accompany Intermediate Algebra: Concepts & Applications.** 5th ed. Janina Udrys. (C). 1998. pap. text ed. write for info. (*0-201-34031-3*) Addison-Wesley.

Videotex: The New Television-Telephone Information Services. Roger Woolfe. LC 80-40758. (Computing Sciences Ser.). (Illus.). 184p. reprint ed. pap. 52.50 (*0-685-23441-X*, 2032694) Bks Demand.

Videotex & Teletext: New Online Resources for Libraries, Vol. 21. Michael B. Binder. LC 85-5246. (Foundations in Library & Information Science: Vol. 21). 160p. 1985. 73.25 (*0-89232-612-3*) Jai Pr.

Videotex Journalism: Teletext, Viewdata, & the News. David H. Weaver. 160p. 1983. text ed. 36.00 (*0-89859-263-1*) L Erlbaum Assocs.

Videotex-Teleservices Directory, Nineteen Eighty-Five. Ed. by Gary H. Arlen & Richard Adler. 272p. (Orig.). 1985. pap. text ed. 80.00 (*0-9609768-1-7*) Arlen Comm Inc.

Videotexts. Peggy Gale. (Illus.). vi, 154p. (C). 1995. pap. 19.95 (*0-88920-252-4*) Wilfrid Laurier.

Videowalls. Robert Simpson. 208p. 1990. pap. 29.95 (*0-240-51294-4*, Focal) Buttrwrth-Heinemann.

Vidhi Shastra Evem Vidhi Ke Sidhant: (Jurisprudence & Legal Theory in Hindi) G. C. Sbubarao. (HIN.). (C). 1981. 30.00 (*0-685-39662-2*) St Mut.

Vidhik Upchar: (Legal Remedies in Hindi) Ed. by V. M. Shukla. Tr. by Vijay Malik. (HIN.). (C). 1991. 95.00 (*0-685-39633-9*) St Mut.

Vidhik Upchar (Legal Remedies in Hindi) V. M. Shukla. Tr. by Vijay Malik. 281p. 1978. 48.00 (*0-685-17744-0*); pap. 60.00 (*0-317-54762-3*) St Mut.

***Vidhya Vahini (Writings on Knowledge Which Illumines)** Sai B. Sathya. Date not set. pap. 1.75 (*0-614-19047-9*, BA-316) Sathya Sai Bk Ctr.

Vidrieras Modernistas Catalanas. Joan Vila-Grau & Francesc Rodon. (Illus.). 200p. (SPA.). 1993. 150.00 (*84-343-0373-6*) Elliots Bks.

Vidui: Hebrew Version. Aaron Werner. 16p. 1994. pap. text ed. 2.00 (*1-885006-08-X*) Three Beacons.

Vidui, the Confessional for the Day of Atonement: Ashkenazic Community Version. Aaron Werner. 137p. 1994. text ed. 12.95 (*1-885006-04-7*); pap. text ed. 9.95 (*1-885006-05-5*) Three Beacons.

Vidui, the Confessional for the Day of Atonement: Sephardic Community Version. Aaron Werner. 172p. 1994. text ed. 12.95 (*1-885006-02-0*); pap. text ed. 9.95 (*1-885006-03-9*) Three Beacons.

Viduy. 1982. pap. 2.95 (*0-686-76274-6*) Feldheim.

Viduy: Confession. Nosson Scherman. (ArtScroll Mesorah Ser.). 32p. 1986. pap. 2.99 (*0-89906-227-X*) Mesorah Pubns.

Vidya-Vratin: Professor A. M. Ghatage Felicitation Volume. Ed. by V. N. Jha. (Sri Garib Dass Oriental Ser.: No. 160). (C). 1992. 32.00 (*81-7030-349-4*) S Asia.

Vie. Guy De Maupassant. (Folio Ser.: No. 544). (FRE.). 1959. pap. 9.95 (*2-07-036544-1*, 478) Schoenhof.

Vie. Guy De Maupassant. 1959. write for info. (*0-318-63613-1*, 478) Fr & Eur.

Vie. unabridged ed. Guy De Maupassant. (FRE.). pap. 5.95 (*2-87714-134-9*, Pub. by Bookking Intl FR) Distribks Inc.

Vie Americanie de Guillaume Merle d'Aubigne: Avec une Introd et des Notes par Gilbert Chinard. Merle Guillaume. 1979. 18.95 (*0-405-10591-6*) Ayer.

Vie Canoniale en France aux Xe-XIIe Siecles. Jean Becquet. (Collected Studies: No. CS220). 292p. (FRE.). (C). 1985. reprint ed. lib. bdg. 94.95 (*0-86078-168-2*, Pub. by Variorum UK) Ashgate Pub Co.

Vie Chretienne et Culture Dans l'Espagne De VII Au Xe Siecles. Manuel C. Diaz y Diaz. (Collected Studies: Vol. CS377). 304p. 1992. 94.95 (*0-86078-331-6*, Pub. by Variorum UK) Ashgate Pub Co.

Vie Conciliaire et Collections Canoniques en Occident, IVe-XIIe Siecles. Charles Munier. (Collected Studies: No. CS265). 318p. (FRE.). (C). 1987. reprint ed. lib. bdg. 98.95 (*0-86078-213-1*, Pub. by Variorum UK) Ashgate Pub Co.

***Vie d-Etienne le Jeune par Etienne le Diacre.** Marie-France Auzepy. 280p. (FRE.). 1997. text ed. 76.95 (*0-86078-637-4*, Pub. by Ashgate UK) Ashgate Pub Co.

Vie d'Adrian Putney, Poete. Jean-Pierre Remy. (FRE.). 1979. pap. 10.95 (*0-7859-4119-3*) Fr & Eur.

Vie Dangereuse. Blaise Cendrars. (FRE.). 1987. pap. 23.95 (*0-7859-3052-3*) Fr & Eur.

Vie dans les Plis. Henri Michaux. (FRE.). 1989. pap. 16.95 (*0-7859-2822-7*) Fr & Eur.

Vie de Boy. Ferdinand Oyono. (FRE.). 1970. pap. 9.95 (*0-7859-3430-8*) Fr & Eur.

Vie de Chien. Charles M. Schulz. (Peanuts Ser.). (FRE.). (J). 1985. 4.95 (*0-8288-4513-1*) Fr & Eur.

Vie de Disraeli. Andre Maurois. (Coll. Leurs Figures). pap. 32.50 (*0-685-36967-6*) Fr & Eur.

Vie de Disraeli. Andre Maurois. (FRE.). 1978. pap. 11.95 (*0-7859-4494-X*, 207036884X) Fr & Eur.

Vie de Haydn, de Mozart et de Metastase. Stendhal. 48.00 (*0-686-55083-8*) Fr & Eur.

An Asterisk (*) at the beginning of an entry indicates that the title is appearing in BIP for the first time.

Vie De Henri Brulard. Stendhal. (Folio Ser.: No. 447). (FRE.). 1961. pap. 10.95 (*2-07-036447-X*) Schoenhof.
Vie de Henri Brulard, 2 tomes, Set. Stendhal. 150p. (FRE.). 1989. write for info. (*0-318-63614-X*, 2723409228) Fr & Eur.
Vie de Henry Brulard. Stendhal & Beatrice Didier. 544p. (FRE.). 1973. pap. 11.95 (*0-7859-1663-6*, 207036447X) Fr & Eur.
Vie De Jean-Arthur Rimbaud. Paterne Berrichon. LC 77-10252. (Symbolists Ser.). (FRE.). reprint ed. 49.50 (*0-404-16307-6*) AMS Pr.
Vie de Jean Racine: Avec: Le Romancier et ses Personnages, L'Education ces Filles, Mes Grandes Hommes, Recontre avec Barres, Pascal. Francois Mauriac. (Illus.). 12.50 (*0-686-55480-9*) Fr & Eur.
Vie de Jesus. Francois Mauriac. 9.95 (*0-685-34307-3*) Fr & Eur.
Vie de Jesus. Ernest Renan. (FRE.). 1974. pap. 11.95 (*0-7859-4034-0*) Fr & Eur.
Vie de Jesus. Ernest Renan. (Folio Ser.: No. 618). (FRE.). 1974. pap. 9.95 (*2-07-036618-9*) Schoenhof.
Vie de la Princesse d'Angleterre. Marie-Madeleine De La Fayette. 264p. 1967. 29.95 (*0-8288-9925-8*) Fr & Eur.
Vie de Marianne. Pierre C. Marivaux. (FRE.). 1966. pap. 17.95 (*0-7859-0053-5*, M11000) Fr & Eur.
Vie De Mon Pere, 2 vols. in 1. Nicholas E. Restif de la Bretonne. iv, 291p. 1979. reprint ed. write for info. (*3-487-06844-3*) G Olms Pubs.
Vie De Monsieur Descartes, 2 vols., Set. Adrien Baillet. xlii, 1019p. 1972. reprint ed. 240.00 (*3-487-04279-7*) G Olms Pubs.
Vie de Napoleon. Stendhal, pseud. (Petite Bibliotheque Payot Ser.). pap. 5.95 (*0-685-35023-1*) Fr & Eur.
Vie de Porphyre: Le Philosophe Neo-Platonicien. Joseph Bidez. vii, 166p. 1980. reprint ed. lib. bdg. 50.00 (*3-487-07018-9*) G Olms Pubs.
Vie De Pythagore De Diogene Laerce. Laertius Diogenes. Ed. by Gregory Vlastos. LC 78-19342. (Morals & Law in Ancient Greece Ser.). 1979. reprint ed. lib. bdg. 23.95 (*0-405-11537-7*) Ayer.
Vie de Pythagore de Diogene Laerce. Diogenes Laertius. (Memoires de l'Academie Royale de Belgique. Classe des Lettres et des Sciences Morales et Politiques Ser. 2). 272p. (GER.). 1988. reprint ed. write for info. (*3-487-09032-5*) G Olms Pubs.
Vie de Ramakrishna. Romain Rolland. 320p. (FRE.). 1978. pap. 36.95 (*0-7859-5469-4*) Fr & Eur.
Vie de Rance. Rene De Chateaubriand. 379p. (FRE.). 1986. pap. 11.95 (*0-7859-2048-X*, 2070377695) Fr & Eur.
Vie de Rance. Chateaubriand Francois-Rene De & Marius Francois Guyard. (Folio Ser.: No. 1769). (FRE.). 7.95 (*2-07-037769-5*) Schoenhof.
Vie de Rance see Oeuvres Romanesques et Voyages
Vie De Robert Burns. J. Veitch. Tr. by S. Henocque. (C). 1988. 40.00 (*0-907526-26-8*, Pub. by Alloway Pub UK) St Mut.
Vie de Rossini, 2 vols., Ea. Stendhal. Ed. by Ernest Abravanel & Victor Del Litto. (Illus.). 9.95 (*0-318-52318-3*) Fr & Eur.
Vie de Saint Alexis. Ed. by Hemming. (Exeter French Texts Ser.: Vol. 90). 96p. 1995. pap. text ed. 19.95 (*0-85989-462-2*, Pub. by Univ Exeter Pr UK) Northwestern U Pr.
Vie de Saint Alexis - The Old French Text & Its Translation into English & Modern French As The Life of Saint Alexis. Tr. by Guy R. Mermier. LC 93-50730. 108p. 1994. 59.95 (*0-7734-9140-6*) E Mellen.
Vie de Vivekananda. Romain Rolland. 352p. (FRE.). 1978. pap. 36.95 (*0-7859-5470-8*) Fr & Eur.
Vie des Abeilles. Maurice Maeterlinck. 9.95 (*0-686-56293-3*) Fr & Eur.
Vie des Fourmis. Maurice Maeterlinck. 260p. (FRE.). 1969. 39.95 (*0-7859-0021-7*, F66832) Fr & Eur.
Vie des Termites. Maurice Maeterlinck. 210p. (FRE.). 1969. 39.95 (*0-8288-9743-3*, 2246009294) Fr & Eur.
Vie Devant Soi. Romain Gary & Emile Ajar. (Folio Ser.: No. 1362). (FRE.). pap. 8.95 (*2-07-037362-2*) Schoenhof.
Vie Devant Soi. Romain Gary. (FRE.). 1982. pap. 10.95 (*0-7859-2456-6*, 2070373622) Fr & Eur.
Vie Du Langage. Albert Dauzat. 311p. reprint ed. write for info. (*0-318-71336-5*) G Olms Pubs.
Vie du Marquis de Sade. Gilbert Lely. 24.40 (*0-685-34061-9*) Fr & Eur.
Vie d'un Paien. Jacques Perry. (FRE.). 1984. pap. 15.95 (*0-7859-4217-3*) Fr & Eur.
Vie en Angleterre au 18e Siecle. Francois de La Rochefoucauld. 260p. 12.50 (*0-686-54282-7*) Fr & Eur.
Vie en Fleur. Anatole France. 280p. (FRE.). 1966. 15.95 (*0-8288-9766-2*, F101390) Fr & Eur.
Vie en Fleur. Anatole France. 288p. (FRE.). 1983. pap. 11.95 (*0-7859-2473-6*, 2070374653) Fr & Eur.
Vie en Fleur. Anatole France. (Folio Ser.: No. 1465). (FRE.). pap. 9.95 (*2-07-037465-3*) Schoenhof.
Vie est Ailleurs. Milan Kundera. (FRE.). 1976. pap. 13.95 (*0-8288-3703-1*) Fr & Eur.
Vie et Aventures de Salavin. Georges Duhamel. (Illus.). 522p. 1959. write for info. (*0-318-63615-8*) Fr & Eur.
Vie et Aventures de Salavin: Le Journal Salavin. Georges Duhamel. 320p. (FRE.). 1970. pap. 10.95 (*0-7859-0090-X*, M3391) Fr & Eur.
Vie et la Mort d'un Poete. Francois Mauriac. pap. 9.50 (*0-685-34308-1*) Fr & Eur.
Vie et les Oeuvres De Ballanche. Charles Huit. Ed. by J. P. Mayer. LC 78-67358. (European Political Thought Ser.). (FRE.). 1979. reprint ed. lib. bdg. 28.95 (*0-405-11707-8*) Ayer.
Vie et les Oeuvres De Philippe De Monte (1521-1603) Georges V. Doorslaer. (Academie Royale De Belgique Memoires, Cl. Des Beauz Arts Ser.). 309p. 1980. reprint ed. write for info. (*3-487-06919-9*) G Olms Pubs.
Vie et l'Oeuvre de Fragonard. George Grappe. (Illus.). 127p. (FRE.). 1946. lib. bdg. 35.00 (*0-8288-3929-8*) Fr & Eur.
Vie et l'Ouvre de Platon, 2 vols., Set. Charles Huit. ix, 984p. (GER.). 1973. reprint ed. write for info. (*3-487-04527-3*) G Olms Pubs.
Vie et Mort Des Indiens D'Amerique Du Nord. Rene Coulet du Gard. 341p. (Orig.). (FRE.). 1990. pap. 25.00 (*0-685-37828-4*) Edns des Deux Mondes.
Vie Illustre et Libertine de Jean-Baptiste Lully. Henry Prunieres. LC 76-43934. (Music & Theatre in France in the 17th & 18th Centuries Ser.). reprint ed. 52.50 (*0-404-60186-3*) AMS Pr.
Vie Immediate. Paul Eluard. (Poesie Ser.). 256p. (FRE.). 1967. 9.95 (*2-07-030096-X*) Schoenhof.
Vie Immediate, l'Evidence Poetique, la Rose. Paul Eluard. (FRE.). 1967. pap. 10.95 (*0-8288-3859-3*, F100090) Fr & Eur.
Vie Internationale Dans la Grece Des Cites. Victor Martin. Ed. by Gregory Vlastos. LC 78-19368. (Morals & Law in Ancient Greece Ser.). 1979. reprint ed. lib. bdg. 48.95 (*0-405-11559-8*) Ayer.
Vie, La Mort et La Resurrection de Socrate-Marie Gripotard. Pierre Gripari. 384p. (FRE.). 1984. pap. 12.95 (*0-7859-2495-7*, 2070375994) Fr & Eur.
Vie Litteraire. 5th ed. Anatole France. 336p. (FRE.). 1950. 24.95 (*0-8288-9767-0*, F101400) Fr & Eur.
Vie Mode d'Emploi. Georges Perec. (FRE.). 1980. pap. 17.95 (*0-7859-3100-7*) Fr & Eur.
Vie Municipale En Antique. Bernard Hauseculler. Ed. by Gregory Vlastos. LC 78-19358. (Morals & Law in Ancient Greece Ser.). 1979. reprint ed. lib. bdg. 21.95 (*0-405-11550-4*) Ayer.
Vie Parisienne. Richard Manton. 1988. mass mkt. 5.95 (*0-929654-66-8*, 09) Blue Moon Bks.
Vie Politique en France Aujourd'hui. Ed. by Claire Laudet & Richard Cox. LC 94-29770. (Readers in Contemporary French Civilisation Ser.). 1995. text ed. 19.95 (*0-7190-4218-6*, Pub. by Manchester Univ Pr UK); text ed. 59.95 (*0-7190-4217-8*) St Martin.
Vie pour Deux. Marie Cardinal. (FRE.). 1980. pap. 12.95 (*0-7859-3102-3*) Fr & Eur.
Vie Revee. Francois-Regis Bastide. (FRE.). 1982. pap. 12.95 (*0-7859-1945-7*, 2070373428) Fr & Eur.
Vie Royale: Essai sur l'Idee de Peuple dans l'Oeuvre de Michelet. Vialleneix. 24.50 (*0-685-34947-0*) Fr & Eur.
Vie Secrete de Dorothee Gindt. Guy Des Cars. 504p. (FRE.). 1987. 10.95 (*0-7859-1188-X*, 2277222917) Fr & Eur.
Vie Tranquille. Marguerite Duras. (FRE.). 1982. pap. 10.95 (*0-8288-3643-4*, M11315) Fr & Eur.
Vie Tranquille. Marguerite Duras. (Folio Ser.: No. 1341). 222p. (FRE.). 1944. 8.95 (*2-07-037341-X*) Schoenhof.
Vie Tres Honorifique du Grand Gargantua, Vol. 1. Francois Rabelais. 233p. (FRE.). 1973. pap. 180.00 (*0-7859-5379-5*) Fr & Eur.
Vie Tres Horrificque du Grand Gargantua. Francois Rabelais. 248p. 1968. 14.95 (*0-8288-7423-9*) Fr & Eur.
Vieil Homme et la Mer. Ernest Hemingway. (FRE.). 1972. pap. 10.95 (*0-7859-2257-1*, 2070360075) Fr & Eur.
Vieil Homme et la Mer de Hemingway. Genvieve Hily-Mane. 249p. (FRE.). 1991. pap. 15.95 (*0-7859-2609-7*, 2070383561) Fr & Eur.
Vieille. Georges Simenon. (FRE.). 1991. pap. 11.95 (*0-7859-3245-3*, 2266045210) Fr & Eur.
Vieille Fille. Honore De Balzac. 348p. (FRE.). 1990. pap. 11.95 (*0-7859-1154-5*, 2070370240) Fr & Eur.
Vieille Fille. Honore De Balzac. (Folio Ser.: No. 1024). (FRE.). pap. 9.95 (*2-07-037024-0*) Schoenhof.
Vieille France. Roger Martin du Gard. (Folio Ser.: No. 540). 160p. (FRE.). 6.95 (*2-07-036540-9*) Schoenhof.
Vieille Maitresse: Un Pretre Marie: L'Ensorceles. Jules B. D'Aurevilly. (FRE.). 1981. pap. 52.95 (*0-7859-3035-3*) Fr & Eur.
Vieillesse, 2 vols., 1. Simone De Beauvoir. (Idees Ser.). (FRE.). pap. 10.95 (*2-07-035408-3*) Schoenhof.
Vieillesse, 2 vols., 2. Simone De Beauvoir. (Idees Ser.). (FRE.). pap. 9.95 (*2-07-035409-1*) Schoenhof.
Vieillesse, 2 vols., Set. Simone De Beauvoir. (Idees Ser.). (FRE.). 10.95 (*0-685-37193-X*) Schoenhof.
Vieillesse de Prosper Merimee (1854-1870) Pierre Trahard. 26.25 (*0-685-34945-4*) Fr & Eur.
Vieira Da Silva. Jacques Lassaigne & Guy Weelen. (Grandes Monografias). (Illus.). 340p. (SPA.). 1993. 175.00 (*84-343-0303-5*) Elliots Bks.
Vieja Furia de los Fusiles: Cuentos de la Revolucion Cubana. Andres Candelario. LC 90-83327. (Coleccion Caniqui). 96p. (Orig.). (SPA.). 1990. pap. 9.95 (*0-89729-255-3*) Ediciones.
Vieja Letivia y el Monte de los Pesares. Nicholasa Mohr. Orig. Title: Old Letivia & the Mountain of Sorrows. (Illus.). 32p. (SPA.). (J). (ps-3). 1996. pap. 15.99 (*0-670-86324-6*) Viking Child Bks.
Viejecita Que No le Miedo Tenia a Nada. Linda Williams. Tr. by Yolanda Noda from SPA. LC 95-23887. (Trophy Picture Bk.). (Illus.). 32p. (SPA.). (J). (ps-2). 1996. pap. 5.95 (*0-06-443420-6*, HpArco Iris) HarpC Child Bks.
Viejecita Que No le Tenia Miedo a Nada: Spanish Edition of The Little Old Lady Who Was Not Afraid of Anything. Linda Williams. Tr. by Yolanda Noda from SPA. LC 95-23887. (Illus.). 32p. (ENG & SPA.). (J). (ps-2). 1996. 15.95 (*0-06-026238-9*, HpArco Iris) HarpC Child Bks.
Viejo. Maurice Casseus. (B. E. Ser.: No. 45). (FRE.). 1935. 25.00 (*0-8115-2996-7*) Periodicals Srv.
Viejo. Adriano G. Leon. 1995. pap. 14.95 (*0-679-76337-6*, Vin) Random.
Viejos Suenos. Susan Napier. (Harlequin Bianca Ser.: No. 369). 1996. mass mkt. 3.50 (*0-373-33369-2*, 1-33369-9) Harlequin Bks.
Viel: Louisiana's Firstborn Author with Evandre, the First Literary Creation of a Native of the Mississippi Valley. Charles E. O'Neill. LC 90-84994. 96p. (FRE.). (C). 1991. 10.00 (*0-940984-65-2*) U of SW LA Ctr LA Studies.
***Vielfalt & Qualitat des Fernsehprogramms in der Bundesrepublik Deutschland: Bestimmungsfaktoren & Moglichkeiten zu deren Beeinflussung.** Bruno Schmelzer. (Illus.). xvii, 272p. (GER.). 1996. 54.95 (*3-631-30724-1*) P Lang Pubng.
Vielle Fille: Le Cabinet des Antiques. Honore De Balzac. (FRE.). 1990. reprint ed. pap. 13.95 (*0-7859-2990-8*) Fr & Eur.
Vielle France. Roger Martin du Gard. (FRE.). 1974. pap. 8.95 (*0-7859-4025-1*) Fr & Eur.
Vielle Maitresse. Jules Barabey d'Aurevilly. (FRE.). 1979. pap. 16.95 (*0-7859-1893-0*, 2070371158) Fr & Eur.
Viellesse, Vol. 1. Simone de Beauvoir. (FRE.). 1979. pap. 13.95 (*0-8288-9685-2*, 2070354083) Fr & Eur.
Viellesse, Vol. 2. Simone de Beauvoir. (FRE.). 1979. pap. 13.95 (*0-8288-9686-0*, 2070354091) Fr & Eur.
Vien-Easy Waltz. (Ballroom Dance Ser.). 1986. lib. bdg. 79.95 (*0-8490-3435-3*) Gordon Pr.
Vien-Easy Waltz. (Ballroom Dance Ser.). 1985. lib. bdg. 62.00 (*0-87700-759-4*) Revisionist Pr.
Vien Verbiage. Enid Vien. (Illus.). 40p. (Orig.). Date not set. pap. text ed. 10.00 (*0-9648330-3-4*) Dynamism Pubns.
Viene el Asedio. Gladys Zaldivar. LC 87-71298. (Illus.). 92p. (Orig.). (SPA.). (C). 1987. pap. 15.00 (*0-943503-02-7*) ASHAM.
Vienna. LC 94-18210. (Eyewitness Travel Guides Ser.). (Illus.). 288p. 1994. pap. 22.95 (*1-56458-647-2*) DK Pub Inc.
Vienna. (Panorama Bks.). (Illus.). (FRE.). 3.95 (*0-685-11619-0*) Fr & Eur.
Vienna. (Insight Pocket Guides Ser.). (Illus.). 98p. 1994. pap. 12.95 (*0-395-71064-2*) HM.
Vienna. (Baedeker's Ser.). (Illus.). 248p. 1992. pap. 17.00 (*0-13-063660-6*, P-H Travel) P-H Gen Ref & Trav.
Vienna. (Address Bks.). (Illus.). 256p. pap. 9.95 (*2-8315-0636-0*) Berlitz.
Vienna. Berlitz Staff. (Pocket Guides Ser.). (Illus.). 144p. 1993. pap. 7.95 (*2-8315-1467-3*) Berlitz.
Vienna. Louis James. (Illustrated Travel Guides from Thomas Cook Ser.). (Illus.). 192p. 1995. pap. 12.95 (*0-8442-9046-7*, Passport Bks) NTC Pub Grp.
***Vienna.** Louis James. 1997. pap. 14.95 (*0-8442-4844-4*) NTC Pub Grp.
***Vienna.** Nicholas T. Parsons. (Blue Guides Ser.). (Illus.). 224p. (Orig.). 1997. pap. 18.95 (*0-393-31423-5*) Norton.
Vienna: A Bridge Between Cultures. Elisabeth Lichtenberger. Tr. by Dietlinde Muhlgassner & Craig Reisser. LC 93-7361. (World Cities Ser.). 212p. 1993. text ed. 49.95 (*0-470-22008-2*, Belhaven) Halsted Pr.
Vienna: Bridge Between Cultures. Elisabeth Lichtenberger. LC 93-7361. (World Cities Ser.). 212p. 1993. text ed. 75.00 (*0-471-94705-9*) Wiley.
Vienna: City Guide. Mark Honan. (Illus.). 240p. 1995. pap. 9.95 (*0-86442-267-9*) Lonely Planet.
Vienna: The Past in the Present. Inge Lehne & Lonnie Johnson. (Studies in Austrian Literature, Culture & Thought; Translation Ser.). (Illus.). 194p. 1995. pap. 15.95 (*1-57241-018-3*) Ariadne CA.
Vienna: Yesterday & Today. J. Alex Mahan. 1976. lib. bdg. 59.95 (*0-8490-2797-7*) Gordon Pr.
Vienna & Its Jews: The Tragedy of Success 1880s-1980s. George E. Berkley. LC 88-1521. 460p. 1988. 24.95 (*0-8191-6816-5*) Madison Bks UPA.
***Vienna & the Danube Valley.** 12th ed. Fodor's Staff. 1997. pap. 11.00 (*0-679-03592-3*) Fodors Travel.
Vienna & the Jews, 1867-1938: A Cultural History. Steven Beller. 304p. (C). 1991. pap. text ed. 19.95 (*0-521-40727-3*) Cambridge U Pr.
Vienna, Austria: In One Hundred Eleven Color Photographs. (Cities in Color Pictorial Guidebooks Ser.). (Illus.). 80p. (Orig.). 1992. pap. 10.95 (*0-9617959-3-X*) Cities in Color.
Vienna Blood & Other Poems. Jerome Rothenberg. LC 79-24966. (Orig.). 1980. pap. 4.95 (*0-8112-0759-5*, NDP498) New Directions.
Vienna Broadcasts to Slovakia, 1938-1939: A Case Study in Subversion. Henry Delfiner. (East European Monographs: No. 7). 142p. 1974. text ed. 64.00 (*0-914710-00-1*) East Eur Monographs.
Vienna Circle & the Lvov-Warsaw School. Ed. by Klemens Szaniawski. (Nijhoff International Philosophy Ser.: No. 38). 474p. 1988. lib. bdg. 167.00 (*90-247-3798-2*) Kluwer Ac.
Vienna Circle, the Origin of Neo-Positivism. Viktor Kraft. Tr. by Arthur Pap. LC 70-75584. 209p. 1969. reprint ed. text ed. 55.50 (*0-8371-0517-X*, KRVC, Greenwood Pr) Greenwood.
Vienna Coffeehouse Wits, 1890-1938. Ed. & Tr. by Harold B. Segel. LC 92-24804. (Illus.). 404p. 1993. 40.00 (*1-55753-033-5*) Purdue U Pr.
Vienna Coffeehouse Wits, 1890-1938. Ed. & Tr. by Harold B. Segel. LC 92-24804. (Illus.). 404p. 1995. reprint ed. pap. 19.95 (*1-55753-064-5*) Purdue U Pr.
Vienna Demotic Papyrus on Eclipes & Lunar-Omina. Ed. by Richard A. Parker. (Brown Egyptological Studies: No. 2). 76p. reprint ed. pap. 25.00 (*0-317-09427-0*, 2022398) Bks Demand.
***Vienna Green Guide.** 1997. per. 18.00 (*2-06-150901-0*, 1509) Michelin.
Vienna Group: Six Major Austrian Poets. Tr. by Rosmarie Waldrop & Harriett Watts. LC 84-12368. 116p. 1985. 13.95 (*0-88268-005-6*); pap. 6.95 (*0-88268-004-8*) Station Hill Pr.
Vienna Institute for Comparative Economic Studies, Comecon Data 1988. 425p. 1989. text ed. 65.00 (*0-313-27284-0*, VIC88, Greenwood Pr) Greenwood.
***Vienna Masquerade.** large type ed. Lorna McKenzie. (Linford Romance Library). 224p. 1997. pap. 16.99 (*0-7089-5038-8*) Ulverscroft.
***Vienna Medical School of the 19th Century.** Erna Lesky. LC 76-24938. 677p. 1976. reprint ed. pap. 180.00 (*0-608-03715-X*, 2064540) Bks Demand.
Vienna, Minoritenkonvent, Klosterbibliothek und Archiv, MX XIV.714. Alexander Silbiger. (Seventeenth-Century Keyboard Music Ser.). 275p. 1988. text ed. 50.00 (*0-8240-8023-8*) Garland.
Vienna, Oesterreichische Nationalbibothek Musiksammlung Mus. HS. (Poglietti Autograph), No. 19248. Ed. by Alexander Silbiger. (Seventeenth-Century Keyboard Music Ser.). 100p. 1987. text ed. 20.00 (*0-8240-8005-X*) Garland.
Vienna Passage. David Porter. LC 95-16346. 288p. (Orig.). 1995. pap. 9.99 (*0-89107-824-X*) Crossway Bks.
Vienna Prelude. Bodie Thoene. LC 89-30. (Zion Covenant Ser.: Bk. 1). 416p. (Orig.). 1989. pap. 11.99 (*1-55661-066-1*) Bethany Hse.
Vienna Regulator Clocks. Rick Ortenburger. LC 89-64090. (Illus.). 180p. 1990. 39.95 (*0-88740-224-0*) Schiffer.
Vienna Regulators of Lenzkirch & Lorenz Bob. 1981. pap. 7.00 (*0-930476-06-9*) Am Clock & Watch.
Vienna Revisited. Freda Teitelbaum. 208p. (Orig.). 1995. pap. 12.95 (*1-56474-139-7*) Fithian Pr.
Vienna Secession: Dream & Reality. Ed. by Hans Hollein & Catherine Cooke. (Architectural Design Profiles Ser.). 80p. 1987. 21.95 (*0-312-84576-6*) St Martin.
Vienna, the World of Yesterday 1889-1914. Ed. by Stephen E. Bronner & F. Peter Wagner. 279p. (C). 1996. text ed. 49.95 (*0-391-03987-3*) Humanities.
Vienna to Los Angeles: Two Journeys. Esther McCoy. LC 78-54270. (Illus.). 1979. 17.50 (*0-931228-01-8*); pap. 10.95 (*0-931228-02-6*) Arts & Arch.
Vienna up Close. Louis James. (Up Close Ser.). (Illus.). 144p. (Orig.). 1996. pap. text ed. 12.95 (*0-8442-9449-7*, Passport Bks) NTC Pub Grp.
Vienna Urtext Guide to Piano Literature: Compiled & Introduced by Maurice Hinson. Vienna Urtext Edition Editors. 240p. (Orig.). (C). 1995. pap. text ed. 29.95 (*0-913574-97-X*, EA763) Eur-Am Music.
Vienna, 1900. Franco Borsi. 1992. pap. 24.95 (*0-8109-6106-7*) Abrams.
Vienna 1900: Art, Architecture, Design. Kirk Varnedoe. 264p. 1986. 50.00 (*0-87070-618-7*); pap. 24.95 (*0-87070-619-5*, 0-8109-6106-7) Mus of Modern Art.
Vienna 1990. Ed. by Edward Timms & Robertson. 1990. text ed. 60.00 (*0-7486-0169-4*, Pub. by Edinburgh U Pr UK); pap. text ed. 25.00 (*0-7486-0175-9*, Pub. by Edinburgh U Pr UK) Col U Pr.
Vienna's Golden Years of Music, 1850-1900. Eduard Hanslick. Ed. by Henry Pleasants. LC 69-18928. (Essay Index Reprint Ser.). 1977. 23.95 (*0-8369-0043-X*) Ayer.
Viennawalks. rev. ed. J. Sydney Jones. LC 93-30360. (Walks Ser.). (Illus.). 1994. pap. 15.95 (*0-8050-2385-2*, Owl) H Holt & Co.
***Vienne Green Guide.** (FRE.). 1997. per. 18.00 (*2-06-050901-7*, 509) Michelin.
Viennese Concerted Mass of the Early Classic Period. Bruce C. MacIntyre. LC 85-20872. (Studies in Musicology: No. 89). (Illus.). 788p. reprint ed. pap. 180.00 (*0-8357-1673-2*, 2070609) Bks Demand.
Viennese Cooking. Olga Hess & A. Hess. Tr. by Carla Schlesinger. (International Cookbook Ser.). 1985. 15.00 (*0-517-50668-8*, Crown) Crown Pub Group.
Viennese Design & the Wiener Werkstaette. Jane Kallir. (Illus.). 152p. 1986. pap. 18.00 (*0-907611-53-2*) Johannes.
Viennese Design & the Wiener Werkstatte. Jane Kallir. LC 86-915. (Illus.). 152p. (Orig.). 1986. pap. 14.95 (*0-8076-1153-0*) Braziller.
Viennese Enlightenment. Ed. by Mark Francis. LC 84-18385. 192p. 1985. text ed. 32.50 (*0-312-84583-9*) St Martin.
Viennese Harmonic Theory from Albrechtsberger to Schenker & Schoenberg. Robert W. Wason. (Illus.). 216p. 1995. pap. text ed. 24.95 (*1-878822-52-7*) Univ Rochester Pr.
Viennese Harmonic Theory from Albrechtsberger to Schenker & Schoenberg. Robert W. Wason. LC 84-16124. (Studies in Musicology: No. 80). (Illus.). 216p. reprint ed. pap. 61.60 (*0-8357-1586-8*, 2070600) Bks Demand.
Viennese Idylls. Arthur Schnitzler. Tr. by Frederick Eisemann. LC 72-10811. (Short Story Index Reprint Ser.). 1977. reprint ed. 18.95 (*0-8369-4226-4*) Ayer.
Viennese Novelettes. Arthur Schnitzler. LC 71-175578. reprint ed. 37.50 (*0-404-08278-5*) AMS Pr.
***Viennese Pastry Cookbook.** Lilly J. Reich. (Illus.). 336p. 1996. 9.98 (*0-9643600-5-5*) Biscuit Bks.
Viennese Revolution of 1848. Reuben J. Rath. LC 56-11770. 440p. reprint ed. pap. 125.40 (*0-8357-7757-X*, 2036115) Bks Demand.
Viennese Stained Glass Designs in Full Color. Franz C. Renner & Max Seemann. (Illus.). 32p. 1988. reprint ed. pap. 6.95 (*0-486-25590-5*) Dover.
Viennese Waltz. Earl Atkinson. (Ballroom Dance Ser.). 1986. lib. bdg. 250.00 (*0-8490-3636-4*) Gordon Pr.
Viennese Waltz. C. Frost. (Ballroom Dance Ser.). 1986. lib. bdg. 79.95 (*0-8490-3306-3*) Gordon Pr.
Viennese Waltz. C. Frost. (Ballroom Dance Ser.). 1985. lib. bdg. 70.00 (*0-87700-833-7*) Revisionist Pr.
Viennese Waltz. Smith Hampshire. (Ballroom Dance Ser.). 1985. lib. bdg. 77.95 (*0-87700-864-7*) Revisionist Pr.
Viennese Waltz: Origins, Development & Techniques. (Ballroom Dance Ser.). 1991. lib. bdg. 75.00 (*0-8490-5193-2*) Gordon Pr.

Viente Pasos Faciles para Hablar Mejor Ingles. Sharon Elwell. 32p. (SPA.). 1991. pap. text ed. 8.95 (0-9626210-3-X) Rattle Ok Pubns.

Viento En los Sauces. (Spanish Children's Classics Ser.: No. 800-5). (SPA.). (J). 1990. boxed 3.50 (0-7214-1399-4, Ladybrd) Penguin.

Viento para Tu Barco. Benny Hinn. 32p. (SPA.). 1995. pap. 1.99 (1-56063-735-8, 550134) Editorial Unilit.

***Vier Fassungen der "Nibelungenklage" Untersuchungen zur Ueberlieferungsgeschichte & Textkritik der Hoefischen Epik im 13. Jahrhundert.** Joachim Bumke. (Quellen & Forschungen zur Literatur- & Kulturgeschichte Ser.: Vol. 8(242)). (Illus.). xiv, 746p. (GER.). (C). 1996. lib. bdg. 207.40 (3-11-015076-X) De Gruyter.

Vier Juvenal-Kommentare Aus Dem 12. JH. Ed. by Bengt Lofstedt. xx, 492p. (GER.). 1995. lib. bdg. 107.00 (90-5063-306-4, Pub. by Gieben NE) Benjamins North Am.

Vier Plus: Ubungsmaterial Zur Vorbereitung Auf die "Prufung Wirtschaftsdeutsch International" Bettina Cothrun & Hartmut Karottki. 155p. (Orig.). (GER.). (C). 1994. pap. 20.00 (0-942017-15-3) Amer Assn Teach German.

Vier Plus: Ubungsmaterial Zur Vorbereitung Auf die "Prufung Wirtschaftsdeutsch International" Bettina Cothrun & Hartmut Karottki. 155p. (Orig.). (GER.). (C). 1994. pap. 15.00 (0-942017-24-2) Amer Assn Teach German.

Vier Pole expressionistscher Prosa: Kasimir Edschmid, Carl Einstein, Alfred Doeblin August Stramm, Vol. 4. Joseph L. Brockington. (Studies in Modern German Literature). 216p. (Orig.). (C). 1988. text ed. 39.50 (0-8204-0422-5) P Lang Pubng.

Vier und Zwantzigste Schiffahrt. Willem Y. Bontekoe. Ed. by Augustus J. Veenendaal. LC 93-28793. 1993. reprint ed. 75.00 (0-8201-1485-5) Schol Facsimiles.

Viera, Vol. 1. 3rd rev. ed. Vladimir Uhri. 54p. (Orig.). (SLO.). 1995. pap. 3.00 (1-56983-040-1) New Creat WI.

Vierfache Vernunftantinomie: Natur und Freiheit; intelligibler und empirischer Charakter see Transzendentale Dialektik: Ein Kommentar zu Kants Kritik der reinen Vernunft

Vierke's Aquarium Book. Jorg Vierke. (Illus.). 352p. 1986. 29.95 (0-86622-103-4, PS-834) TFH Pubns.

***Vierne & the Organ.** Rollin Smith. (Complete Organ Ser.: Vol. 3). 1998. text ed. 54.00 (1-57647-004-0) Pendragon NY.

***Viernes o la Vida Salvaje (Friday or Life in the Wilderness)** Michel Tournier. 1996. pap. text ed. 7.95 (84-279-3137-9) Lectorum Pubns.

Viersprachiges Enzyklopadisches Worterbuch Der Physischen Geographie: Quadrilingual Encyclopedic Dictionary of Physical Geography. I. S. Spiridonov. 703p. (ENG, FRE, GER & RUS.). 1980. 45.00 (0-8288-1465-1, M15248) Fr & Eur.

Viersprachiges Woerterbuch der Lebensmitteltechnologie: English-German-Spanish-French. Erich Luck. 655p. (ENG, FRE & GER.). 1992. 295.00 (0-7859-7051-7) Fr & Eur.

***Vierzehn Tage in Paris.** Caroline A. Fischer. (Fruhe Frauenliteratur in Deutschland Ser.: Vol. 6). 193p. (GER.). 1997. reprint ed. write for info. (3-487-10023-1) G Olms Pubs.

Vierzig Jahre Deutscher Bundestag. Ed. by Konrad Porzner et al. 309p. (GER.). 1991. pap. 45.00 (3-7890-1962-3, Pub. by Nomos Verlags GW) Intl Bk Import.

Vies des Homme Illustres, 2 vols., Ea. Plutarque. Tr. by D'Amyot. 37.50 (0-318-52319-1) Fr & Eur.

Vies des Hommes Illustres, Vol. 1. Plutarch. (FRE.). 1937. lib. bdg. 95.00 (0-8288-3525-X, F19161) Fr & Eur.

Vies des Hommes Illustres, Vol. 2. Plutarch. (FRE.). 1937. lib. bdg. 95.00 (0-8288-3526-8, F19162) Fr & Eur.

Vies Des Plus Celebres et Anciens Poetes Provencaux. Jehan De Nostredame. 258p. 1971. reprint ed. write for info. (0-318-71384-5) G Olms Pubs.

Vies des Plus Celebres et Anciens Poetes Provencaux. Jehan D. Nostredame. 258p. 1971. reprint ed. write for info. (0-318-71936-3) G Olms Pubs.

Vies Paralleles. Boris Vian. 608p. (FRE.). pap. 18.95 (0-685-72635-5) Fr & Eur.

Viet-Minh Regime. Bernard B. Fall. LC 75-11493. 196p. 1975. reprint ed. text ed. 35.00 (0-8371-8197-6, FAVM, Greenwood Pr) Greenwood.

Viet-Minh Regime: Government & Administration in the Democratic Republic of Vietnam. Bernard B. Fall. LC 54-11255. (Cornell University, Dept. of Far Eastern Studies, Southeast Asia Program, Data Paper: No. 14). (Illus.). 155p. reprint ed. pap. 44.20 (0-8357-3583-4, 2034580) Bks Demand.

Viet Nam: An Anthology. Ed. by Jim Villani. LC 84-61225. (Pig Iron Ser.: No. 12). (Illus.). 96p. 1984. pap. 8.95 (0-917530-20-9) Pig Iron Pr.

Viet Nam Chinh Su. Nguyen Van Chuc. 630p. 1992. 20.00 (0-9635574-0-8) Alpha Bks VA.

Viet Nam War - The American War: Images & Representations in Euro-American & Vietnamese Exile Narratives. Renny Christopher. LC 95-19687. 360p. (C). 1996. pap. 19.95 (1-55849-009-4); text ed. 55.00 (1-55849-008-6) U of Mass Pr.

Vietcong Memoir. Truong N. Tang et al. 1986. pap. 14.00 (0-394-74309-1, Vin) Random.

***Vietnam.** LC 97-5243. (Fiesta! Ser.). 1997. write for info. (0-7172-9115-4) Grolier Educ.

Vietnam. (World Focus Ser.). (Illus.). (J). (gr. 3-7). pap. 3.99 (0-431-07264-7, Pub. by Oxfam UK) Humanities.

***Vietnam.** LC 97-21880. (Major World Nations Ser.). (Illus.). 120p. (YA). (gr. 5 up). 1997. lib. bdg. 19.95 (0-7910-4751-2) Chelsea Hse.

Vietnam. Denise Allard. LC 96-255. (Postcards From Ser.). (J). 1997. lib. bdg. 21.40 (0-8172-4023-3) Raintree Steck-V.

Vietnam. Melanie Beresford. (Marxist Regimes Ser.). 262p. 1988. text ed. 49.00 (0-685-61126-4) St Martin.

Vietnam. Melanie Beresford. (Marxist Regimes Ser.). 220p. 1988. 47.50 (0-86187-448-X); text ed. 17.50 (0-86187-449-8) St Martin.

Vietnam. Stephen Bull. (Guidebook Ser.). 1991. pap. 9.95 (962-217-120-6) L A Michaux.

Vietnam. Wendy M. Cole. (Let's Visit Places & Peoples of the World Ser.). (Illus.). 112p. (J). (gr. 5 up). 1989. lib. bdg. 19.95 (1-55546-800-4) Chelsea Hse.

Vietnam. Joan M. Crouse et al. LC 93-14939. (YA). 1994. pap. text ed. 22.40 (0-8013-0865-8) Longman.

Vietnam. Austin Deuel. (Illus.). 160p. 1988. 28.95 (0-9615217-3-2) Desert Wind Pub.

Vietnam. Ole S. Hansen. LC 96-18314. (Economically Developing Countries Ser.). (J). 1997. lib. bdg. 24.26 (0-8172-4526-X) Raintree Steck-V.

Vietnam. Karen Jacobsen. LC 91-35272. (New True Bks.). (Illus.). 48p. (J). (gr. k-4). 1992. lib. bdg. 19.00 (0-516-01147-2) Childrens.

Vietnam. Stanley Karnow. 1991. pap. 15.95 (0-14-771017-0) NAL-Dutton.

***Vietnam.** Stanley Karnow. 1997. pap. 17.95 (0-14-026547-3) Viking Penguin.

Vietnam. David G. Marr. (World Bibliographical Ser.). 1993. lib. bdg. 110.00 (1-85109-092-4) ABC-CLIO.

***Vietnam.** Susan McKay. LC 97-8266. (Festivals of the World Ser.). 1997. lib. bdg. write for info. (0-8368-1937-3) Gareth Stevens Inc.

Vietnam. Jacques Nespote. (Illus.). 304p. 1995. pap. 15.95 (0-8442-9691-0, Natl Textbk) NTC Pub Grp.

Vietnam. Harry Nickelson. LC 89-13100. (Overview Ser.). (Illus.). 80p. (J). (gr. 5-8). 1989. lib. bdg. 17.96 (1-56006-110-3) Lucent Bks.

Vietnam. Lewis K. Parker. LC 94-7558. (Dropping in On Ser.). (J). 1994. write for info. (1-55916-008-X) Rourke Bk Co.

Vietnam. Ritu Sharma. (Lands & Peoples of the World Ser.). 1988. text ed. 18.95 (81-207-0667-6, Pub. by Sterling Pubs II) Apt Bks.

Vietnam. Pat Simmons. (Worldfocus Ser.). (J). 1996. lib. bdg. write for info. (1-57572-026-4) Rigby Interact Libr.

Vietnam. David K. Wright. LC 88-30486. (Enchantment of the World Ser.). (Illus.). 128p. (J). (gr. 5-9). 1989. lib. bdg. 30.00 (0-516-02712-3) Childrens.

***Vietnam.** 3rd ed. Moss. 1997. pap. text ed. 24.00 (0-13-897083-1) P-H.

***Vietnam.** 4th ed. Robert Storey. (Illus.). 544p. 1997. pap. 16.95 (0-86442-515-5) Lonely Planet.

Vietnam: A Book of Changes. Mitch Epstein. LC 96-22871. 176p. 1996. 35.00 (0-393-04027-5) Norton.

Vietnam: A Casebook. Ed. by Jacob D. Lindy et al. LC 87-15062. (Psychosocial Stress Ser.: No. 10). 384p. 1987. text ed. 53.95 (0-87630-471-4) Brunner-Mazel.

Vietnam: A Country Study. Ed. by Ronald J. Cima. LC 88-600482. (Illus.). 432p. (Orig.). 1990. boxed 18.00 (0-16-018143-7, 008-020-01190-8) USGPO.

Vietnam: A Country Study. Ed. by Ronald J. Cima. (Illus.). 386p. (Orig.). (C). 1995. reprint ed. 45.00 (0-7881-1876-5) DIANE Pub.

Vietnam: A History. Stanley Karnow. LC 84-6270. 768p. 1984. pap. 13.95 (0-14-007324-8, Penguin Bks) Viking Penguin.

Vietnam: A History. Stanley Karnow. LC 91-11088. (Illus.). 816p. 1991. pap. 17.95 (0-14-014533-8, Viking) Viking Penguin.

***Vietnam: A History.** Stanley Karnow. 1997. pap. 17.95 (0-614-27380-3) Penguin.

Vietnam: A History & Anthology. Ed. by James W. Mooney & Thomas R. West. (Illus.). 341p. (Orig.). (C). 1994. pap. text ed. 14.50 (1-881089-28-2) Brandywine Press.

Vietnam: A Kick Start Guide for Business Travelers. Guy Brooks & Victoria Brooks. 160p. (Orig.). 1995. pap. 9.95 (0-88908-843-8) Self-Counsel Pr.

Vietnam: A Portrait. Jacques Bekaert. (Illus.). 200p. 1996. 45.00 (962-7787-02-7, Pub. by O&A Edits HK) Weatherhill.

Vietnam: A Portrait of Its People at War. David Chanoff. 240p. 1996. pap. 16.95 (1-86064-076-1) St Martin.

***Vietnam: A Portrait of Its People at War.** David Chanoff & Doan Van Toai. 240p. 1996. pap. 18.95 (0-614-19280-3) St Martin.

Vietnam: A Reporter's War. Hugh Lunn. LC 85-40967. (Illus.). 272p. 1987. 18.95 (0-8128-3088-1, Scrbrough Hse) Madison Bks UPA.

Vietnam: A Reporter's War. Hugh Lunn. (Illus.). 283p. 1989. reprint ed. pap. 14.95 (0-7022-2018-3, Pub. by Univ Queensland Pr AT) Intl Spec Bk.

Vietnam: A Traveler's Literary Companion. Ed. by John Balaban & Nguyen Q. Duc. (The Traveler's Literary Companion Ser.). (Illus.). 256p. 1996. pap. 12.95 (1-883513-02-2) Whereabouts.

***Vietnam: Anatomy of a Peace.** Gabriel Kolko. 200p. 1997. pap. 15.95 (0-415-15990-3) Routledge.

Vietnam: Beyond the War. Joseph S. Salzburg. LC 75-10622. 250p. 1975. 12.50 (0-682-48258-7); 12.50 (0-317-60908-4) Sovereign MD.

Vietnam: Business Opportunities & Risks. Joseph P. Quinlan. LC 94-67837. 178p. (Orig.). 1994. pap. 19.95 (1-881896-10-2) Pacific View Pr.

Vietnam: Coming All the Way Home. Carl Mumpower. (Illus.). 112p. (Orig.). 1992. pap. 9.95 (1-56664-008-3) WorldComm.

***Vietnam: Conflict & Controversy.** Paul Elliott. (Illus.). 200p. 1997. 24.95 (1-85409-320-7, Pub. by Arms & Armour UK) Sterling.

***Vietnam: Dawn of a New Market.** Murray. Date not set. text ed. 20.00 (0-312-17392-X) St Martin.

***Vietnam: Dawn of a New Market.** Murray. LC 97-23013. 1997. text ed. 55.00 (0-312-17390-3) St Martin.

Vietnam: Four American Perspectives - Lectures by George S. McGovern, William C. Westmoreland, Edward N. Luttwak, & Thomas J. McCormick. G. S. McGovern et al. Ed. by Patrick J. Hearden. LC 89-24267. 128p. 1990. 17.50 (1-55753-002-5); pap. 9.95 (1-55753-003-3) Purdue U Pr.

Vietnam: In Pictures. Geography Department Staff. LC 93-21343. (Visual Geography Ser.). (Illus.). 64p. (J). (gr. 5 up). 1994. lib. bdg. 19.95 (0-8225-1909-7, Lerner Publctns) Lerner Group.

Vietnam: Inside Story of the Guerrilla War. 2nd ed. Wilfred G. Burchett. LC 65-18719. (Illus.). 264p. reprint ed. pap. 75.30 (0-8357-3584-2, 2034249) Bks Demand.

Vietnam: Opening Doors to the World. Rick Graetz. (Illus.). 160p. (Orig.). 1988. pap. 2.95 (0-938314-57-2) Am Wrld Geog.

Vietnam: Our Story, One on One. rev. ed. Compiled by Gary D. Gullickson et al. 531p. 1992. pap. 16.95 (0-9631572-2-1) G D Gullickson.

Vietnam: Peasant Land, Peasant Revolution. Nancy Wiegersma. LC 87-27352. 300p. 1988. text ed. 45.00 (0-312-01358-2) St Martin.

Vietnam: Perspectives & Performance. Chris Ellsbury et al. Ed. by Noel H. Kaylor, Jr. (Northern Iowa Texts Ser.: No. 1). (Illus.). 165p. (Orig.). (C). 1994. pap. 10.95 (0-9641511-0-3) Assn Text Study.

***Vietnam: Perspectives & Performance.** 2nd rev. ed. Chris Ellsbury et al. Ed. by Noel H. Kaylor, Jr. (Northern Iowa Texts Ser.: No. 1). (Illus.). 165p. (Orig.). (C). 1996. pap. 10.95 (0-9641511-3-8) Assn Text Study.

Vietnam: Poetic Words from the Unknowns. Ed. by Allan L. Harrington. LC 92-70823. 120p. (Orig.). 1992. pap. text ed. 19.95 (1-879183-13-7) Bristol Banner.

Vietnam: Rebuilding a Nation. Sherry Garland. LC 89-29212. (Discovering Our Heritage Ser.). (Illus.). 130p. (J). (gr. 5 up). 1990. text ed. 14.95 (0-87518-422-7, Dillon Silver Burdett) Silver Burdett Pr.

Vietnam: Renovation (Doi Moi), the Law & Human Rights in the 1980s. 67p. 1990. pap. 5.00 (0-685-46976-X) Amnesty Intl USA.

Vietnam: Revolution in Transit. 2nd ed. William J. Duiker. (Nations of the Modern World Ser.). (C). 1995. pap. text ed. 19.95 (0-8133-8589-X) Westview.

Vietnam: Socialist Economic Development, 1955-1992. Dang T. Tran. LC 94-8699. (Country Studies: No. 12). 1994. pap. 9.95 (1-55815-316-0) ICS Pr.

Vietnam: Some Basic Issues & Alternatives. Walter Isard. 213p. 1969. pap. 18.95 (0-87073-003-7) Schenkman Bks Inc.

Vietnam: Strategy for a Stalemate. F. Charles Parker, IV. LC 88-25482. 268p. 1988. text ed. 19.95 (0-88702-041-0) Washington Inst Pr.

Vietnam: The Australian Dilemma 1962-1972. Terry Burstall. 1993. pap. 19.95 (0-7022-2470-7, Pub. by Univ Queensland Pr AT) Intl Spec Bk.

Vietnam: The Boat People Search for a Home. Photos by John Isaac. (Illus.). 32p. (J). (gr. 3-7). 1996. lib. bdg. 14. 95 (1-56711-188-2) Blackbirch.

Vietnam: The Culture. Bobbie Kalman. (J). 1996. pap. 7.95 (0-86505-305-7) Crabtree Pub Co.

Vietnam: The Decisive Battles. Marshall Editions Staff. (Illus.). 200p. 1990. text ed. 39.95 (0-02-580171-6) Macmillan.

***Vietnam: The Early Decisions.** Ed. by Lloyd C. Gardner & Ted Gittinger. LC 97-2031. 232p. 1997. 35.00 (0-292-72800-X) U of Tex Pr.

Vietnam: The Endless War: From Monthly Review, 1954-1970. Paul M. Sweezy et al. LC 77-127927. 157p. reprint ed. pap. 44.80 (0-318-34962-0, 2030759) Bks Demand.

Vietnam: The Heartland Remembers. Stanley W. Beesley. 208p. 1987. 21.95 (0-8061-2062-2) U of Okla Pr.

Vietnam: The Heartland Remembers. Stanley W. Beesley. 208p. 1988. pap. 9.95 (0-8061-2162-9) U of Okla Pr.

Vietnam: The Helicopter War. Philip Chinnery. (Illus.). 200p. 1991. 39.95 (1-55750-875-5) Naval Inst Pr.

Vietnam: The Land. Bobbie Kalman. (J). 1996. pap. 7.95 (0-86505-303-0) Crabtree Pub Co.

Vietnam: The Land. Bobbie Kalman. (YA). 1996. lib. bdg. 19.16 (0-86505-223-9) Crabtree Pub Co.

Vietnam: The Naval Story. Ed. by Frank Uhlig, Jr. LC 86-16345. (Illus.). 516p. 1986. 37.95 (0-87021-014-9) Naval Inst Pr.

***Vietnam: The New Investment Frontier in Southeast Asia.** Nguyen X. Oanh & Phillip D. Grub. 148p. 1992. pap. write for info. (981-210-023-7, Pub. by Times Academic SI) Intl Spec Bk.

Vietnam: The No BS Business Guide. Ed. by Thomas M. Timberman. (No BS Business Ser.). (Illus.). 300p. 1994. pap. 28.95 (0-9633925-1-4) LOI.

Vietnam: The Politics of Bureaucratic Socialism. Gareth Porter. LC 92-54976. (Politics & International Relations of Southeast Asia Ser.). (Illus.). 256p. 1993. 29.95 (0-8014-2168-3) Cornell U Pr.

Vietnam: The Price of Peace. Chris Brazier. (Country Profiles Ser.). (Illus.). 64p. (C). 1992. pap. 9.95 (0-85598-152-0, Pub. by Oxfam UK) Humanities.

Vietnam: The Valor & the Sorrow. Thomas D. Boettcher. (Illus.). 384p. 1985. pap. 21.95 (0-316-10081-1) Little.

Vietnam: The War Nobody Won. Stanley Karnow. LC 83-81891. (Headline Ser.: No. 263). (Illus.). 64p. (Orig.). 1983. pap. 5.95 (0-87124-083-1) Foreign Policy.

Vietnam: Transition to a Market Economy. J. R. Dodsworth et al. (Occasional Paper Ser.: Vol. 135). 1996. pap. 15.00 (1-55775-538-8) Intl Monetary.

Vietnam: Travel Survival Kit. 3rd ed. Daniel Robinson & Robert Storey. (Illus.). 544p. 1995. pap. 15.95 (0-86442-316-0) Lonely Planet.

Vietnam: Trial & Triumph. R. S. Chavan. (C). 1988. 32.00 (81-7050-047-8, Pub. by Patriot II) S Asia.

Vietnam: U. S. Uniforms in Colour Photographs. Kevin Lyles. (Europa Militaria Ser.: Vol. 3). (Illus.). 96p. 1992. pap. 19.95 (1-872004-52-0, Pub. by Windrow & Green UK) Motorbooks Intl.

Vietnam see Cultures of the World - Group 7

Vietnam see Exploring Cultures of the World: Group 5

Vietnam, A Business Guide. Neil Ashwood. LC 94-29515. 1995. lib. bdg. 110.00 (1-85966-083-5) G & T Inc.

Vietnam a Comprehensive History: The Most Updated Book on Vietnam. Pham K. Vinh. 650p. 1992. pap. text ed. 28.00 (1-882273-24-9) P K Vinh Res.

Vietnam above the Treetops: A Forward Air Controller Reports. John F. Flanagan. LC 91-23141. 336p. 1992. text ed. 24.95 (0-275-93738-0, C3738, Praeger Pubs) Greenwood.

Vietnam after the War: Peacekeeping & Rehabilitation. Henry F. Haviland, Jr. LC 69-18821. 129p. reprint ed. pap. 36.80 (0-317-08412-7, 2005705) Bks Demand.

Vietnam Airborne. Gordon L. Rottman. (Elite Ser.: No. 29). (Illus.). 64p. 1990. pap. 12.95 (0-85045-941-9, 9429, Pub. by Osprey Pubng Ltd UK) Stackpole.

Vietnam, an American Ordeal. 2nd ed. George D. Moses. LC 92-46988. 454p. (C). 1993. pap. text ed. 30.60 (0-13-221151-3) P-H Gen Ref & Trav.

***Vietnam Anatomy of a Peace.** Gabriel Kolko. 200p. (C). 1997. text ed. 55.00 (0-415-15989-X) Routledge.

Vietnam & America: A Documented History. 2nd enl. rev. ed. Ed. by Marvin E. Gettleman et al. 528p. 1995. pap. 16.95 (0-8021-3362-2, Grove) Grove-Atltic.

Vietnam & China, 1938-1954. King C. Chen. LC 78-83684. 452p. reprint ed. pap. 128.90 (0-8357-3433-1, 2039690) Bks Demand.

Vietnam & International Law: An Analysis of International Law & the Use of Force, & the Precedent of Vietnam for Subsequent Interventions. 3rd ed. Consultative Council of the Lawyers Committee on American Policy Towards Vietnam Staff. Ed. by John H. Fried. LC 90-36599. (Normative International Relations Ser.). 208p. 1990. reprint ed. pap. text ed. 12.50 (0-9623718-0-7); reprint ed. lib. bdg. 27.50 (0-9623718-3-1) Aletheia Pr.

Vietnam & Meta Revolution. Nguyen N. Phach. Ed. by Mac N. Pha. 374p. (C). 1992. 50.00 (0-9636159-0-4) Vietnam & Wrld.

Vietnam & Other Alien Worlds. Joe Haldeman. LC 92-62235. (Boskone Bks.). 1993. 17.00 (0-915368-52-8) New Eng SF Assoc.

Vietnam & the Antiwar Movement. Ed. by John Dumbrell. 190p. 1989. text ed. 63.95 (0-566-05684-4, Pub. by Avebury Pub UK) Ashgate Pub Co.

Vietnam & the Chinese Model: A Comparative Study of Vietnamese & Chinese Government in the First Half of the Nineteenth Century. Alexander B. Woodside. (East Asian Monographs: No. 140). 360p. 1988. reprint ed. pap. 14.00 (0-674-93721-X) Coun East Asian Stud.

Vietnam & the Great Powers: Roosevelt, Ho Chi Minh & De Gaulle in a World at War. Stein Tonnesson. 400p. 1991. 60.00 (0-8039-8521-5) Sage.

Vietnam & the Southern Imagination. Owen W. Gilman, Jr. 248p. 1993. 35.00 (0-87805-591-6) U Pr of Miss.

***Vietnam & the World.** Palmujoki Eero. 1997. text ed. 65. 00 (0-312-17240-0) St Martin.

Vietnam & the World Revolution: A Trotskyist Analysis. Martin McLaughlin. 151p. (Orig.). (C). 1985. pap. 9.95 (0-929087-01-1) Labor Pubns Inc.

***Vietnam & Vietnamese.** Khamchong Luangpraseut. (Illus.). 96p. (Orig.). (VIE.). (J). (gr. 2-5). pap. 13.95 (1-879600-43-9) Pac Asia Pr.

Vietnam Anthology: American War Literature. Ed. by Nancy Anisfield. LC 87-71030. 150p. 1987. 26.95 (0-87972-395-5); pap. 12.95 (0-87972-396-3) Bowling Green Univ Popular Press.

***Vietnam Assessment: Creating a Sound Investment Climate.** Ed. by Suiwah Leung. (Illus.). 140p. (Orig.). (C). 1997. pap. 45.00 (0-7881-3706-9) DIANE Pub.

***Vietnam Asylum Seekers: Refugee Screening Procedures under the Comprehensive Plan of Action.** (Illus.). 52p. (Orig.). (C). 1997. pap. text ed. 30.00 (0-7881-3803-0) DIANE Pub.

Vietnam at War: The History Nineteen Forty-Six to Nineteen Seventy-Five. Phillip B. Davidson. (Illus.). 864p. 1991. pap. 19.95 (0-19-506792-4) OUP.

Vietnam at 24 Frames a Second: A Critical & Thematic Analysis of over 350 Films about the Vietnam War. Jeremy M. Devine. LC 92-56639. (Illus.). 416p. 1995. lib. bdg. 39.95 (0-89950-848-0) McFarland & Co.

Vietnam Battle Chronology: U. S. Army & Marine Corps Combat Operations, 1965-1973. David B. Sigler. LC 91-50941. 200p. 1992. lib. bdg. 46.50 (0-89950-683-6) McFarland & Co.

Vietnam Blues. John B. Carn. 272p. (Orig.). (J). 1988. mass mkt. 3.25 (0-87067-730-6) Holloway.

Vietnam Book List. Compiled by Benjamin R. McDonald. 164p. 1990. 34.95 (0-685-35161-0); ring bd. 19.95 (0-9626437-0-X) Biblio Unlimited.

Vietnam Book List. 2nd ed. Benjamin R. McDonald. LC 89-81201. 180p. 1990. ring bd. 29.95 (0-685-37770-9) Biblio Unlimited.

Vietnam Book List. 3rd ed. Benjamin R. McDonald. 1991. pap. 23.95 (0-9626437-3-4) Biblio Unlimited.

Vietnam Business Yellow Pages: 1994. (Illus.). 500p. 1993. pap. write for info. (1-885345-00-3) Viam Communs.

Vietnam, Cambodia & Laos Handbook. Michael Buckley. (Moon Travel Handbooks Ser.). (Illus.). 650p. (Orig.). 1996. pap. 18.95 (1-56691-029-3) Moon Trvl Hdbks.

Vietnam Coastal & Riverine Forces. Barry Gregory. (Illus.). 128p. (C). 1989. reprint ed. lib. bdg. 29.00 (0-8095-7107-2) Borgo Pr.

Vietnam Connection. Isabel Molyneux. (Illus.). 264p. 1995. pap. 18.95 (1-85756-134-1) Paul & Co Pubs.

Vietnam Debate: A Fresh Look at the Arguments. Ed. by John N. Moore. LC 89-30902. 330p. (Orig.). (C). 1990. pap. text ed. 24.50 (*0-8191-7417-3*, Ctr for Law & Natl Security) U Pr of Amer.

Vietnam Diary. Steven Spetz. (Orig.). 1996. mass mkt. 4.99 (*1-55197-133-X*, Pub. by Comnwlth Pub CN) Partners Pubs Grp.

Vietnam Documents: American & Vietnamese Views of the War. Ed. by George N. Katsiaficas. LC 91-22957. 262p. (C). (gr. 13). 1992. text ed. 63.95 (*0-87332-896-5*); pap. text ed. 25.95 (*0-87332-897-3*) M E Sharpe.

Vietnam Era: A Guide to Teaching Resources. Breakstone et al. (Illus.). 105p. (Orig.). (gr. 9-12). 1978. pap. text ed. 5.00 (*0-9607794-1-8*) Indochina Curriculum Grp.

***Vietnam Experience: A Concise Encyclopedia of American Literature, Songs & Films.** Kevin C. Hillstrom & Laurie Hillstrom. LC 97-21965. 1998. text ed. write for info. (*0-313-30183-2*, Greenwood Pr) Greenwood.

Vietnam Experience: Images of War. Julene Fischer, the Picture Editors of Boston Publishing. 1986. 16.30 (*0-201-11274-4*) Addison-Wesley.

Vietnam Experience: Ten Years of Reflection. James B. Stockdale. (Publication Ser.: No. 315). ix, 147p. 1984. pap. text ed. 9.95 (*0-8179-8152-7*) Hoover Inst Pr.

Vietnam Experience: The Fall of the South, The False Peace 1972-74, The Aftermath 1975-85. Ed. by Robert Manning. write for info. (*0-318-60206-7*) Addison-Wesley.

***"Vietnam" Follow the Money.** H. Danny Williams. LC 97-90049. 324p. (Orig.). 1997. mass mkt. 6.99 (*0-9656998-0-3*) Faro Pub.

Vietnam Forum No. 14: Focus on Contemporary Fiction, the 1920's & Visits Home. Ed. by Dan Duffy. 358p. 1993. pap. 15.00 (*0-614-14929-0*) Yale U SE Asia.

Vietnam Forum Five. Ed. by Huynh Sanh Thong. 259p. 1985. pap. 10.00 (*0-685-63096-X*) Yale U SE Asia.

Vietnam Forum Four. Ed. by Huynh Sanh Thong. 174p. 1984. pap. 10.00 (*0-685-63095-1*) Yale U SE Asia.

Vietnam Forum One. Ed. by Huynh Sanh Thong. (Vietnam Forum Ser.: No. 1). 120p. 1983. pap. 10.00 (*0-317-64466-1*) Yale U SE Asia.

Vietnam Forum Seven. Ed. by O. W. Wolters & Huynh Sanh Thong. 278p. 1986. pap. 10.00 (*0-685-63098-6*) Yale U SE Asia.

Vietnam Forum Six. Ed. by O. W. Wolters & Huynh Sanh Thong. 273p. 1985. pap. 10.00 (*0-685-63097-8*) Yale U SE Asia.

Vietnam Forum Thirteen. Ed. by O. W. Wolters & Huynh Sanh Thong. 233p. 1990. pap. 10.00 (*0-685-63099-4*) Yale U SE Asia.

Vietnam Forum Three. Ed. by Huynh Sanh Thong. 169p. 1984. pap. 10.00 (*0-685-63094-3*) Yale U SE Asia.

Vietnam Forum Two. Ed. by Huynh Sanh Thong. (Vietnam Forum Ser.: No. 2). 161p. 1983. pap. 10.00 (*0-317-64468-8*) Yale U SE Asia.

Vietnam Guide. Judy Moore. (Illus.). 288p. (Orig.). 1996. pap. 14.95 (*1-883323-39-8*) Open Rd Pub.

Vietnam Guidebook. 3rd ed. Barbara M. Cohen. (Eurasia Travel Guides Ser.). (Illus.). 496p. (Orig.). 1993. pap. 19.95 (*0-395-67027-6*, Travl Guides) HM.

***Vietnam Handbook.** John Colet. 1997. 16.95 (*0-8442-4920-3*) NTC Pub Grp.

Vietnam Helicopter Handbook. Barry Gregory. (Illus.). 152p. (C). 1989. reprint ed. lib. bdg. 29.00 (*0-8095-7109-9*) Borgo Pr.

Vietnam Helicopter Pilots. Turner Publishing Company Staff. LC 95-60324. 104p. 1995. 48.00 (*1-56311-190-X*) Turner Pub KY.

Vietnam, Ho Quy Ly, & the Ming (Thirteen Seventy-One to Fourteen Twenty-One) John K. Whitmore. LC 85-51296. (Lac-Viet Ser.: No. 2). 205p. 1985. pap. 10.00 (*0-938692-22-4*) Yale U SE Asia.

Vietnam Images: War & Representation. Ed. by Jeffrey Walsh & James Aulich. LC 88-10117. 256p. 1989. text ed. 39.95 (*0-312-02105-4*) St Martin.

Vietnam in a Changing World. Ed. by Irene Norlund et al. (SIAS Studies in Asian Topics: No. 17). 320p. (C). 1995. text ed. 49.00 (*0-7007-0300-4*, Pub. by Curzon Press UK); pap. text ed. 24.95 (*0-7007-0291-1*, Pub. by Curzon Press UK) UH Pr.

Vietnam in Military Statistics: A History of the Indochina Wars, 1772-1991. Micheal Clodfelter. LC 95-15054. 336p. 1995. lib. bdg. 68.50 (*0-7864-0027-7*) McFarland & Co.

Vietnam in Remission: Published for Texas Committee for the Humanities. Ed. by James F. Veninga & Harry A. Wilmer. LC 84-40560. (Illus.). 160p. 1985. 15.95 (*0-89096-213-8*) Tex A&M Univ Pr.

Vietnam Insights: A Guide to the American Experience in Vietnam 1940 to Present. rev. ed. Robert P. Arnoldt & Jacqueline A. Marx. Ed. by Robert S. Carpenter. LC 89-50664. 232p. (Orig.). 1992. reprint ed. pap. 22.95 (*0-9622776-0-6*) Visions Unlimited.

Vietnam Investment Manual. 210p. 1995. 235.00 (*962-7708-52-6*, Pub. by Euromoney UK) Am Educ Systs.

Vietnam Is My Home. (My Home Country Ser.). (Illus.). 48p. (J). (gr. 2-8). 1992. lib. bdg. 19.93 (*0-8368-0905-X*) Gareth Stevens Inc.

***Vietnam Joins the World.** Ed. by James W. Morley & Masashi Nishihara. LC 96-39809. 232p. (C). (gr. 13). 1997. text ed. 58.95 (*1-56324-974-X*, East Gate Bk); pap. text ed. 23.95 (*1-56324-975-8*, East Gate Bk) M E Sharpe.

Vietnam Journal: Delta to Dak To. Don Lomax. (Vietnam Journal Graphic Story Collection Ser.: Vol. 3). (Illus.). 144p. (Orig.). 1991. pap. 13.95 (*0-927203-07-3*) Apple Pr PA.

Vietnam Journal: Indian Country. Don Lomax. (Vietnam Journal Graphic Story Collection Ser.: Vol. 1). (Illus.). 144p. (Orig.). 1990. pap. 12.95 (*0-927203-02-2*) Apple Pr PA.

Vietnam Journal: The Iron Triangle. Don Lomax. (Vietnam Journal Graphic Story Collection Ser.: Vol. 2). (Illus.). 144p. (Orig.). 1991. pap. 12.95 (*0-927203-06-5*) Apple Pr PA.

Vietnam, Kampuchea, Laos: Bound in Comradeship, 2 vols., Set. H. R. Chakrabartty. (C). 1988. 72.00 (*81-7050-048-6*, Pub. by Patriot II) S Asia.

Vietnam, Laos & Cambodia. (Insider's Guides Ser.). (Illus.). 224p. (Orig.). 1994. pap. 15.95 (*1-55650-625-2*) Hunter NJ.

Vietnam, Laos & Cambodia. (Handbooks of the World Ser.). 1994. 19.95 (*0-8442-8980-9*, Passport Bks) NTC Pub Grp.

Vietnam, Laos & Cambodia Handbook. 2nd ed. Ed. by Joshua Eliot et al. 624p. 1995. 21.95 (*0-8442-8884-5*, Passport Bks) NTC Pub Grp.

Vietnam Law Yearbook 1995. 112p. 1995. 70.00 (*962-7708-66-6*, Pub. by Euromoney UK) Am Educ Systs.

Vietnam Literature Anthology. enl. rev. ed. Peter Hollenbeck et al. LC 89-17695. 188p. 1990. pap. 14.95 (*0-930933-14-1*); text ed. 25.95 (*0-930933-13-3*) Am Poetry & Lit.

Vietnam Literature Anthology. 2nd enl. rev. ed. Peter Hollenbeck et al. LC 89-17695. 188p. 1990. lib. bdg. 25.95 (*0-930933-12-5*) Am Poetry & Lit.

***Vietnam Lobby: The American Friends of Vietnam, 1955-1975.** Joseph G. Morgan. LC 96-32708. 312p. (C). (gr. 13). 1997. 39.95 (*0-8078-2322-8*) U of NC Pr.

Vietnam Marines 1965-73. Charles D. Melson. (Elite Ser.: No. 43). (Illus.). 64p. pap. 12.95 (*1-85532-251-X*, 9458, Pub. by Osprey UK) Stackpole.

Vietnam Mau Lua Que Huong Toi: Bo-Tuc Ho-So Ve Su Sup Do Cua Viet-Nam Cong-Hoa. 2nd ed. Hoanh L. Do Mau. Ed. by Tai H. Do. (Illus.). 1100p. (VIE.). 25.00 (*1-884129-31-5*) Van Nghe.

Vietnam Medic: What Am I Doing Here? Cliff Roberson. (Illus.). 192p. (Orig.). 1996. pap. 6.95 (*0-9647256-0-6*) CSR Indus.

Vietnam Military Lore, 1959-1973: ...Another Way to Remember. Ray Bows. (Illus.). 720p. (Orig.). (C). 1988. pap. 29.95 (*0-929973-00-3*) Bows & Sons.

Vietnam Negotiations, October-December 1972. Allan E. Goodman. (Pew Case Studies in International Affairs). 50p. (C). 1992. pap. text ed. 3.50 (*1-56927-307-3*) Geo U Inst Dplmcy.

***Vietnam Nelles Guide.** 2nd ed. Nelles Staff. (Nelles Guides Ser.). (Illus.). 256p. 1997. pap. 14.95 (*3-88618-116-2*, Pub. by Nelles Verlag GW) Seven Hills Bk.

Vietnam 1945: The Quest for Power. David G. Marr. (Illus.). 587p. 1995. 50.00 (*0-520-07833-0*) U CA Pr.

***Vietnam 1945: The Quest for Power.** David G. Marr. 1997. pap. text ed. 24.95 (*0-520-21228-2*) U CA Pr.

Vietnam North. Wilfred G. Burchett. LC 66-28970. 207p. reprint ed. pap. 59.00 (*0-8357-3585-0*, 2034250) Bks Demand.

Vietnam Notebook. Murray Hiebert. 1995. pap. text ed. 17.95 (*962-7010-55-3*) C E Tuttle.

Vietnam-on-the Potomac. Moya A. Ball. LC 91-31690. (Political Communication Ser.). 206p. 1992. text ed. 55.00 (*0-275-93881-6*, Praeger Pubs) Greenwood.

Vietnam People's Army under Doi Moi. Carlyle A. Thayer. 112p. (Orig.). (C). 1994. pap. 40.00 (*0-7881-1301-1*) DIANE Pub.

***Vietnam People's Army under Doi Moi.** Carlyle A. Thayer. 112p. 1994. pap. text ed. 40.00 (*1-57979-096-8*) BPI Info Servs.

Vietnam-Perkasie. W.D. Ehrhart. 1989. pap. 4.50 (*0-8217-3023-1*) NAL-Dutton.

Vietnam-Perkasie: A Combat Marine Memoir. W. D. Ehrhart. LC 83-9426. (Illus.). 328p. (Orig.). 1983. pap. 18.95 (*0-89950-076-5*) McFarland & Co.

Vietnam-Perkasie: A Combat Marine Memoir. 2nd ed. W. D. Ehrhart. LC 94-36917. 328p. (Orig.). 1995. pap. 17.95 (*0-87023-957-0*) U of Mass Pr.

Vietnam Plays, Vol. 1. David Rabe. LC 92-37145. 177p. 1993. pap. 12.95 (*0-8021-3313-4*, Grove) Grove-Atltic.

Vietnam Plays: Streamers & the Orphan, Vol. 2. David Rabe. LC 92-37145. 1993. pap. 12.95 (*0-8021-3345-2*, Grove) Grove-Atltic.

Vietnam Poems: The War Poems of Today. Jocelyn Hollis. LC 80-65621. 33p. 1991. reprint ed. pap. text ed. 9.95 (*0-933486-10-3*) Am Poetry & Lit.

Vietnam Poems II: The War Poems of Today, A New Collection. Jocelyn Hollis. LC 83-12275. 32p. 1991. reprint ed. pap. text ed. 9.95 (*0-933486-45-6*) Am Poetry & Lit.

Vietnam Population Dynamics & Prospects. Judith Banister. LC 92-32674. (Indochina Research Monograph: No. 6). 1993. 10.00 (*1-55729-038-5*) IEAS.

Vietnam Postwar. Halim Berbar. (Illus.). 202p. 1995. 55.00 (*983-9808-34-6*, Pub. by Delta Edits MY) Weatherhill.

Vietnam Primer. S. L. Marshal & David Hackworth. 58p. 1983. pap. 5.95 (*0-318-36168-X*) Lancer.

Vietnam Protest Theatre: The Television War on Stage. Nora M. Alter. LC 95-32287. (Drama & Performance Studies). 256p. (Orig.). 1996. 29.95 (*0-253-33032-7*) Ind U Pr.

Vietnam Reader. Ed. by Walter H. Capps. (Illus.). 288p. 1991. 45.00 (*0-415-90126-X*, A3261, Routledge NY) Routledge.

Vietnam Reader. Ed. by Walter H. Capps. (Illus.). 288p. (C). (gr. 13). 1991. pap. 18.95 (*0-415-90127-8*, A3265, Routledge NY) Routledge.

***Vietnam Redux.** Carol Brightman. 256p. 1997. 24.00 (*0-465-09035-4*) Basic.

***Vietnam Redux.** Carol Brightman. 256p. 1998. pap. write for info. (*0-465-09036-2*) Basic.

Vietnam Remembered: The Folk Art of Marine Veteran Michael D. Cusino. Varick A. Chittenden. (Folk Art & Artists Ser.). (Illus.). 72p. 1995. 32.50 (*0-87805-715-3*); pap. 16.95 (*0-87805-716-1*) U Pr of Miss.

***Vietnam Shadows: The War, Its Ghosts, & Its Legacy.** Arnold R. Isaacs. LC 97-10823. 1997. write for info. (*0-8018-5605-1*) Johns Hopkins.

Vietnam since the Fall of Saigon. rev. ed. William J. Duiker. LC 85-18912. (Monographs in International Studies, Southeast Asia Ser.: No. 56). 280p. reprint ed. pap. 79.80 (*0-7837-6475-8*, 2046479) Bks Demand.

Vietnam Since the Fall of Saigon. 3rd rev. ed. William Duiker. LC 89-39990. (Monographs in International Studies, Southeast Asia Ser.: No. 56A). 397p. 1989. pap. 20.00 (*0-89680-162-4*, Ohio U Ctr Intl) Ohio U Pr.

***Vietnam Snapshots: Stories of a Conflict.** Craig Etchison. LC 96-78489. 150p. (Orig.). 1996. pap. 12.95 (*0-941092-34-8*) Mtn St Pr.

***Vietnam Stories: A Judge's Memoir.** Jack Crouchet. LC 97-15887. 1997. write for info. (*0-87081-453-2*) Univ Pr Colo.

***Vietnam Studies: An Annotated Bibliography.** Carl Singleton. LC 97-666. (Magill Bibliographies Ser.). 1997. write for info. (*0-8108-3317-4*) Scarecrow.

***Vietnam Syndrome.** Simons. LC 97-18979. 1997. text ed. 45.00 (*0-312-17557-4*) St Martin.

Vietnam, the Culture. Bobbie Kalman. (YA). 1995. lib. bdg. 19.16 (*0-86505-225-5*) Crabtree Pub Co.

Vietnam, the People. David Schimpky & Bobbie Kalman. LC 95-37609. (Lands, Peoples, & Cultures Ser.). (J). 1996. pap. 7.95 (*0-86505-304-9*); lib. bdg. 19.19 (*0-86505-224-7*) Crabtree Pub Co.

Vietnam Theo Duong Nai Vao The'Ky 21C - Which Way Will Vietnam Follow to Enter the 21st Century. Pham K. Vinh. 220p. (Orig.). (VIE.). 1995. 12.00 (*1-882273-26-5*) P K Vinh Res.

Vietnam There & Here. Margot C. Mabie. LC 84-20518. (Illus.). 176p. (J). (gr. 4 up). 1985. 11.95 (*0-8050-0545-5*, Bks Young Read) H Holt & Co.

Vietnam to 2005: Advancing on All Fronts. (Research Reports: No. M611). 1995. 395.00 (*0-85058-840-5*) Economist Intell.

Vietnam Today: Assessing the New Trends. Ed. by Thai Q. Trung. 200p. 1990. 52.00 (*0-8448-1661-2*, Crane Russak) Taylor & Francis.

Vietnam Trauma in American Foreign Policy, 1945-1975. Paul M. Kattenburg. LC 79-702. 354p. 1980. pap. 24.95 (*0-87855-903-5*) Transaction Pubs.

Vietnam Travel Atlas. Contrib. by Robert Storey. (Illus.). 56p. 1996. pap. 9.95 (*0-86442-367-5*) Lonely Planet.

Vietnam Trilogy: And God Died Too! Elizabeth Warner & Edward Young. 126p. 1994. pap. text ed. 22.45 (*1-56226-170-3*) CT Pub.

Vietnam under Communism, 1975-1982. Robert A. Scapalino. LC 83-10754. (Illus.). xvi, 312p. 1983. pap. 9.95 (*0-8179-7852-6*) Hoover Inst Pr.

Vietnam Veteran: A History of Neglect. David E. Bonior et al. LC 84-15154. 208p. 1984. text ed. 55.00 (*0-275-91733-9*, C1733, Praeger Pubs) Greenwood.

Vietnam Veteran: A History of Neglect. David E. Bonior et al. LC 84-15154. 208p. 1985. pap. text ed. 15.95 (*0-275-92026-7*, B2026, Praeger Pubs) Greenwood.

Vietnam Veteran Films. Mark Walker. LC 91-28813. (Illus.). 238p. 1991. 25.00 (*0-8108-2475-2*) Scarecrow.

Vietnam Veteran Redefined: Fact & Fiction. Ed. by Ghislaine Boulanger & Charles Kadushin. 200p. (C). 1986. text ed. 39.95 (*0-89859-761-7*) L Erlbaum Assocs.

Vietnam Veterans: The Road to Recovery. Joel O. Brende & Erwin R. Parson. LC 84-26396. 300p. 1985. 19.95 (*0-306-41966-1*, Plenum Pr) Plenum.

***Vietnam Veterans: The Tuscarawas Valley's Survivors, Vol. IV.** Michael A. Gunther. (Illus.). vi, 175p. 1997. write for info. (*0-9656317-0-2*) Dover HS Adv.

***Vietnam Veterans Memorial.** Patra M. Sevastiades. LC 97-10839. (Library of American Landmarks). (J). 1997. write for info. (*0-8239-5019-0*, PowerKids) Rosen Group.

Vietnam Victory Option. Norborne T. Robinson, III. LC 93-73398. 248p. 1993. 35.00 (*0-9638286-0-6*) Gram Pr.

Vietnam Voices. Peter Ulisse. Ed. by Patricia Schulz. LC 90-6404. (Poetry Ser.: Vol. 11). 64p. 1990. lib. bdg. 12.95 (*0-88946-848-6*) E Mellen.

Vietnam War. Roger Barr. LC 91-23067. (America's Wars Ser.). (Illus.). 112p. (J). (gr. 5-8). 1991. lib. bdg. 20.96 (*1-56006-410-2*) Lucent Bks.

Vietnam War. John Devaney. LC 91-14755. (First Bks.). (Illus.). 64p. (J). (gr. 5-8). 1992. lib. bdg. 21.00 (*0-531-20046-9*) Watts.

Vietnam War. John Devaney. (First Bks.). (Illus.). 64p. (J). (gr. 5-8). 1993. pap. 6.95 (*0-531-15658-3*) Watts.

Vietnam War. David W. Felder. 52p. 1996. pap. text ed. 8.95 (*0-910959-56-0*, B&G 11B) Wellington Pr.

***Vietnam War.** Gay. 1996. write for info. (*0-8050-5283-6*) H Holt & Co.

Vietnam War. Kathlyn Gay & Martin Gay. LC 96-15578. (Voices from the Past Ser.). (J). 1996. write for info. (*0-8050-4101-X*) TFC Bks NY.

Vietnam War. Ken Hills. (Wars That Changed the World Ser.). (Illus.). 32p. (J). (gr. 3-9). 1991. lib. bdg. 10.95 (*1-85435-259-8*) Marshall Cavendish.

Vietnam War. Maurice Isserman et al. (America At War Ser.). 144p. (J). (gr. 5-12). 1992. 17.95 (*0-8160-2508-8*) Facts on File.

***Vietnam War.** Maurice Isserman. Ed. by John Bowman. (America At War Ser.). (Illus.). 128p. 1992. 17.95 (*0-8160-2375-1*) Facts on File.

***Vietnam War.** William C. Westmoreland. 1996. 19.98 (*0-7651-9737-5*) Smithmark.

Vietnam War. David Wright. LC 95-17256. (Causes & Consequences Ser.). (J). 1995. lib. bdg. 25.68 (*0-8172-4053-5*) Raintree Steck-V.

Vietnam War, Reading Level 8. Richard Edwards. LC 86-20295. (Flashpoints Ser.: Set I). (Illus.). 77p. (YA). (gr. 7 up). 1987. lib. bdg. 18.60 (*0-86592-031-1*); lib. bdg. 13.95 (*0-685-58244-2*) Rourke Corp.

Vietnam War: "What Are We Fighting For?" Deborah Kent. LC 93-48471. (American War Ser.). (Illus.). 128p. (YA). (gr. 5 up). 1994. lib. bdg. 18.95 (*0-89490-527-9*) Enslow Pubs.

***Vietnam War: A Short History.** Douglas Kinnard. Date not set. write for info. (*0-688-11841-0*) Morrow.

Vietnam War: A Study in the Making of American Policy. Michael P. Sullivan. LC 85-7497. 206p. reprint ed. pap. 58.80 (*0-7837-5806-5*, 2045472) Bks Demand.

Vietnam War: Handbook of the Literature & Research. James S. Olson. LC 92-25626. 536p. 1993. text ed. 85.00 (*0-313-27422-3*, OVA, Greenwood Pr) Greenwood.

Vietnam War: How the U. S. Became Involved. Ed. by Mitch Yamasaki. (Perspectives on History Ser.: Vol. 29). (Illus.). 64p. (Orig.). 1996. pap. 5.95 (*1-878668-61-7*) Disc Enter Ltd.

Vietnam War: Lessons from Yesterday for Today. rev. ed. George C. Herring & Kevin Simon. Ed. by Jerold M. Starr. (Lessons of the Vietnam War Ser.). (Illus.). 24p. (C). 1991. pap. text ed. 5.00 (*0-945919-12-3*) Ctr Social Studies.

***Vietnam War: Opposing Viewpoints.** William Dudley. LC 97-9448. (Opposing Viewpoints Ser.). (Illus.). (J). (gr. 5-12). 1997. pap. 12.96 (*1-56510-700-4*) Greenhaven.

***Vietnam War: Opposing Viewpoints.** William Dudley. LC 97-9448. (Opposing Viewpoints Ser.). (Illus.). (J). (gr. 5-12). 1997. lib. bdg. 20.96 (*1-56510-701-2*) Greenhaven.

Vietnam War: Teaching Strategies & Resources. Ed. by Marc J. Gilbert. LC 90-20674. (Contributions in Military Studies: No. 109). 312p. 1991. text ed. 55.00 (*0-313-27740-0*, GVM/, Greenwood Pr) Greenwood.

Vietnam War: The History of America's Conflict in Southeast Asia. Bernard C. Nalty. 1996. 14.98 (*0-8317-7157-7*) Smithmark.

Vietnam War: The Story & Photographs. Donald M. Goldstein et al. LC 97-11574. (Illus.). 192p. 1997. 31.95 (*1-57488-075-6*) Brasseys Inc.

Vietnam War: Vietnamese & American Perspectives. Jayne S. Werner. LC 92-30989. 328p. (gr. 13). 1993. text ed. 63.95 (*1-56324-057-2*) M E Sharpe.

Vietnam War: Vietnamese & American Perspectives. Jayne S. Werner. LC 92-30989. 328p. (gr. 13). 1994. pap. text ed. 27.95 (*1-56324-131-5*) M E Sharpe.

Vietnam War Almanac. Harry G. Summers, Jr. (Illus.). 416p. 1987. 27.95 (*0-8160-1017-X*); pap. 14.95 (*0-8160-1813-8*) Facts on File.

Vietnam War & American Culture. Ed. by John C. Rowe & Richard Berg. (Social Foundations of Aesthetic Forms Ser.). 320p. (C). 1992. pap. 16.00 (*0-231-06733-X*) Col U Pr.

Vietnam War & International Law, 4 vols., 2. Ed. by Richard A. Falk. LC 67-31295. 1280p. 1968. pap. 180.00 (*0-8357-7082-6*, 2052290) Bks Demand.

Vietnam War & International Law, 4 vols., 3. Ed. by Richard A. Falk. LC 67-31295. 963p. 1968. pap. 180.00 (*0-8357-7069-9*, 2033381) Bks Demand.

Vietnam War & International Law, 4 vols., 4. Ed. by Richard A. Falk. LC 67-31295. 1065p. 1968. pap. 180.00 (*0-8357-7070-2*, 2033381) Bks Demand.

Vietnam War & International Law Vol. 1, 4 vols. Ed. by Richard A. Falk. LC 67-31295. 643p. 1968. Vol. 1. pap. 180.00 (*0-8357-7068-0*, 2033381) Bks Demand.

Vietnam War & Public Policy. Melvin Sharp. (Illus.). 148p. (Orig.). (YA). (gr. 11-12). 1991. pap. text ed. 16.00 (*0-936826-37-1*) PS Assocs Croton.

Vietnam War As History. Ed. by Elizabeth J. Errington & B. J. McKercher. LC 90-31188. 216p. 1990. text ed. 49.95 (*0-275-93560-4*, C3560, Praeger Pubs) Greenwood.

Vietnam War Choppers, Fighters, & Bombers: Sidelights to Their Fighting Histories. 2nd rev. ed. Ed. by Walter Jacob. (Southfarm Sidelights to History Ser.). (Illus.). 128p. (Orig.). 1996. pap. 14.00 (*0-913337-14-5*) Southfarm Pr.

Vietnam War Diary. Chris Bishop. 1990. 19.99 (*0-517-03556-1*) Random Hse Value.

Vietnam War Facts Quiz: The Truth & Drama of American Involvement. Erhard Konerding. LC 85-63489. (Illus.). 96p. (Orig.). 1986. pap. 9.00 (*0-913337-07-2*) Southfarm Pr.

Vietnam War Films: Over 600 Feature, Made-for-TV, Pilot & Short Movies, 1939-1992, from the United States, Vietnam, France, Belgium, Australia, Hong Kong, South Africa, Great Britain & Other Countries. Ed. by Jean-Jacques Malo & Tony Williams. LC 92-56662. (Illus.). 592p. 1994. lib. bdg. 78.50 (*0-89950-781-6*) McFarland & Co.

Vietnam War in Literature. Philip K. Jason. (Magill Bibliographies Ser.). 175p. 1992. 40.00 (*0-8108-2791-3*) Scarecrow.

Vietnam War in Songs, Poems, & Stories. H. Bruce Franklin. 352p. (Orig.). 1995. pap. text ed. 10.00 (*0-312-11552-0*) St Martin.

Vietnam War Literature: An Annotated Bibliography of Imaginative Works about Americans Fighting in Vietnam. 2nd ed. John Newman & Ann Hilfinger. LC 88-15747. 299p. 1988. 27.50 (*0-8108-2155-9*) Scarecrow.

Vietnam War Literature: An Annotated Bibliography of Imaginative Works about Americans Fighting in Vietnam. 3rd ed. John Newman et al. 1996. 68.00 (*0-8108-3184-8*) Scarecrow.

Vietnam War Memorials: An Illustrated Reference to Veterans Tributes Throughout the United States. Jerry L. Strait & Sandra S. Strait. LC 87-46385. (Illus.). 240p. 1988. lib. bdg. 42.50 (*0-89950-329-2*) McFarland & Co.

U
V

Vietnam War Soldier at Con Thien. (Soldier Ser.). 48p. (J). (gr. 5-6). 1991. lib. bdg. 17.80 (*1-56065-007-9*) Capstone Pr.

Vietnam War Soldiers. Neil Super. (African-American Soldiers Ser.). (Illus.). 80p. (J). (gr. 4-7). 1993. lib. bdg. 14.98 (*0-8050-2307-0*) TFC Bks NY.

Vietnam War Stories: Innocence Lost. Tobey C. Herzog. 224p. 1992. 39.95 (*0-00-302005-3*, A8214); pap. 17.95 (*0-00-302004-5*, A8215) Routledge Chapman & Hall.

Vietnam War Stories: Innocence Lost. Tobey C. Herzog. LC 91-41795. 240p. (C). 1992. pap. 17.95 (*0-415-07631-5*, Pub. by Tavistock UK) Routledge Chapman & Hall.

Vietnam Wars: 1945-1990. Marilyn Young. LC 90-55560. (Illus.). 384p. 1991. reprint ed. pap. 13.50 (*0-06-092107-2*, PL) HarpC.

Vietnam, We've All Been There: Interviews with American Writers. Eric J. Schroeder. LC 92-16557. 240p. 1992. text ed. 29.95 (*0-275-93561-2*, C3561, Praeger Pubs) Greenwood.

Vietnam, What a Soldier Gives. 2nd ed. David L. Hartline. (Illus.). 1996. pap. 12.95 (*1-889368-00-8*) Hartline Ent.

Vietnam Wives: Facing the Challenges of Life with Veterans Suffering Post-Traumatic Stress. 2nd rev. ed. Aphrodite Matsakis. LC 96-67798. viii, 440p. (Orig.). 1996. pap. 19.95 (*1-886968-00-4*, MAVW) Sidran Pr.

Vietnam Women's Memorial. Deborah Kent. LC 94-38019. (Cornerstones of Freedom Ser.). (Illus.). 32p. (J). (gr. 3-6). 1995. lib. bdg. 18.00 (*0-516-06698-6*) Childrens.

Vietnam Women's Memorial. Turner Publishing Company Staff. LC 95-60550. 175p. 1996. 48.00 (*1-56311-206-X*) Turner Pub KY.

Vietnam 1968-1969: A Battalion Surgeon's Journal. Byron E. Holley. (Orig.). 1993. mass mkt. 4.99 (*0-8041-0934-6*) Ivy Books.

Vietnamerica: The War Comes Home. Thomas A. Bass. LC 95-49994. 278p. 1996. 25.00 (*1-56947-050-2*) Soho Press.

***Vietnamerica: The War Comes Home.** Thomas A. Bass. 278p. 1997. pap. 14.00 (*1-56947-088-X*) Soho Press.

***Vietnamese.** Nguyen Dinh-Hoa. LC 97-4965. (London Oriental & African Language Library: Vol. 9). x, 240p. 1997. lib. bdg. 84.00 (*1-55619-733-0*) Benjamins North Am.

Vietnamese - English Picture Dictionary. Claudia Schwalm. (Illus.). 89p. (J). (gr. k-6). 1995. 22.95 incl. audio (*1-57371-011-3*) Cultural Cnnect.

Vietnamese AF - The South Vietnamese AF 1945-1975. (Illus.). 1987. pap. 10.95 (*0-89747-193-8*, 6046) Squad Sig Pubns.

Vietnamese Americans. Susan Auerbach. LC 91-15806. (American Voices Ser.). 104p. (J). (gr. 5-9). 1991. 13.95 (*0-86593-136-4*) Rourke Corp.

Vietnamese Americans. Alexandra Bandon. LC 93-45497. (J). 1994. pap. 7.95 (*0-382-24763-9*, New Dscvry Bks) Silver Burdett Pr.

Vietnamese & Chinese Ceramics Used in the Japanese Tea Ceremony. Hiromu Honda & Noriki Shimazu. LC 92-31993. (Asia Collection). (Illus.). 232p. (C). 1993. pap. 85.00 (*0-19-588607-0*) OUP.

Vietnamese, Basic, Vol. I. Foreign Service Institute Staff. 328p. 1980. pap. 225.00 incl. audio (*0-88432-051-0*, AFV401) Audio-Forum.

Vietnamese, Basic, Vol. II. Foreign Service Institute Staff. 321p. 1967. pap. 195.00 incl. audio (*0-88432-108-8*, AFV450) Audio-Forum.

Vietnamese Catholicism. Jesse W. Nash. LC 93-56459. (Illus.). xix, 184p. (Orig.). (C). 1994. pap. 9.95 (*0-9625762-1-2*) Art Review Pr.

***Vietnamese Ceramics: A Separate Tradition.** Ed. by John Stevenson & John Guy. LC 97-25142. (Illus.). 432p. 1997. 125.00 (*1-878529-22-6*) Art Media Resources.

Vietnamese Communism: A Research Bibliography. Chau Phan Thien. LC 75-16961. 359p. 1975. text ed. 85.00 (*0-8371-7950-5*, CVC/, Greenwood Pr) Greenwood.

Vietnamese Communism, 1925-1945. Huynh K. Khanh. LC 81-70696. (Illus.). 384p. 1982. pap. 16.95 (*0-8014-9397-8*) Cornell U Pr.

***Vietnamese Communists' Relations with China & the Second Indochina Conflict, 1957-1962.** Cheng Guan Ang. 368p. 1997. lib. bdg. 45.00 (*0-7864-0404-3*) McFarland & Co.

Vietnamese Cooking. Tony Lam. 1993. 12.98 (*1-55521-907-1*) Bk Sales Inc.

Vietnamese Culture: An Introduction. Pham K. Vinh. (Illus.). 260p. (Orig.). 1990. pap. text ed. 15.00 (*99912-80-30-8*) P K Vinh Res.

Vietnamese Culture: An Introduction. rev. ed. Pham Kim Vinh. (Illus.). 314p. 1994. pap. 18.00 (*1-882273-25-7*) P K Vinh Res.

***Vietnamese-English Archaeological Glossary.** H. H. Loofs-Wissowa et al. 116p. (ENG & VIE.). 1997. pap. text ed. 25.00 (*0-7315-0665-0*, Pub. by Aust Nat Univ AT) UH Pr.

Vietnamese-English Dictionary. Nguyen Dihn-Hoa. LC 66-17773. 584p. 1991. pap. 21.95 (*0-8048-1712-X*) C E Tuttle.

Vietnamese-English Dictionary Romanized. (ENG & VIE.). 32.50 (*0-87559-014-4*) Shalom.

Vietnamese-English Glossary of Commercial Terms. Tolan Vu et al. LC 94-72455. 183p. 1995. 64.00 (*1-881265-10-2*) Dunwoody Pr.

Vietnamese-English Pocket Dictionary. (ENG & VIE.). pap. 17.50 (*0-87559-165-5*) Shalom.

Vietnamese-English-Vietnamese Dictionary. 9th ed. Le-Ba-Khanh & Le-Ba-Kong. 501p. (ENG & VIE.). 1980. 69.95 (*0-8288-1085-0*, M 9502) Fr & Eur.

Vietnamese Entrepreneurs in the U. S. A. The First Decade. John K. Leba et al. 276p. 1985. 14.50 (*0-936675-00-4*) Zieleks Co.

Vietnamese Experience in America. Paul J. Rutledge. LC 91-26520. (Minorities in Modern America Ser.). (Illus.). 192p. 1992. text ed. 31.50 (*0-253-34997-4*); pap. text ed. 11.95 (*0-253-20711-8*, MB-711) Ind U Pr.

Vietnamese for English. 74p. (ENG & VIE.). 1975. pap. 24.50 incl. audio (*0-88432-419-2*, AFE552) Audio-Forum.

Vietnamese-German Dictionary: Woerterbuch Vietnamesisch-Deutsch. 5th ed. Winfried Boscher. 738p. (GER & VIE.). 1989. 135.00 (*0-8288-1086-9*, F65620) Fr & Eur.

Vietnamese Holdings in the Library of Congress: A Bibliography. Compiled by A. Kohar Rony. LC 81-2847. 236p. 1982. Incls. Supplement, 1979-1985, 1987, 167p. suppl. ed. 13.00 (*0-8444-0564-7*, 030-000-00196-6) Lib Congress.

Vietnamese in a Nutshell see Vest Pocket Vietnamese

Vietnamese in America. Paul Rutledge. (In America Bks.). (Illus.). 64p. (J). (gr. 5 up). 1987. pap. 5.95 (*0-8225-1033-2*, Lerner Publctns) Lerner Group.

Vietnamese in America. Paul Rutledge. (In America Bks.). (Illus.). 64p. (YA). (gr. 5 up). 1987. lib. bdg. 18.95 (*0-8225-0235-6*, Lerner Publctns) Lerner Group.

Vietnamese in Oklahoma City: A Study of Ethnic Change. Charles C. Muzny. LC 88-35115. (Immigrant Communities & Ethnic Minorities in the U. S. & Canada Ser.: No. 37). 1989. 45.00 (*0-404-19447-8*) AMS Pr.

Vietnamese Novel in French: A Literary Response to Colonialism. Jack A. Yeager. LC 86-40110. (Illus.). 251p. 1987. text ed. 35.00 (*0-87451-382-0*) U Pr of New Eng.

Vietnamese Peasants under French Domination 1861-1945. Pham C. Duong. LC 85-7499. (Monographs: No. 24). (Illus.). 240p. (Orig.). 1985. pap. 26.00 (*0-8191-4715-X*) U Pr of Amer.

Vietnamese Phrasebook. 2nd ed. Nguyen Xuan Thu. (Illus.). 176p. 1996. pap. 5.95 (*0-86442-347-0*) Lonely Planet.

Vietnamese Pronunciation. Dang Nguyen. LC 70-128082. (Pali Language Texts : Southeast Asia). 281p. reprint ed. pap. 80.10 (*0-685-17125-6*, 2027029) Bks Demand.

Vietnamese Public Management in Transition: South Vietnam Public Administration, 1955-1975. Hai B. Pho. LC 89-14648. (Illus.). 210p. (C). 1990. lib. bdg. 42.50 (*0-8191-7517-X*) U Pr of Amer.

Vietnamese Reference Grammar. rev. ed. Laurence C. Thompson. Ed. by Stephen D. O'Harrow. (Mon-Khmer Studies: Vol. 13/14). 416p. 1987. pap. text ed. 25.00 (*0-8248-1117-8*) UH Pr.

Vietnamese Refugees in Southeast Asian Camps. Linda Hitchcox. 200p. 1991. text ed. 69.95 (*0-312-05703-2*) St Martin.

Vietnamese Response to French Intervention, 1862-1874. Mark W. McLeod. LC 90-44389. 192p. 1991. text ed. 45.00 (*0-275-93562-0*, C3562, Praeger Pubs) Greenwood.

Vietnamese Revolution: Fundamental Problems & Essential Tasks. Duan Le. LC 71-171528. 159p. reprint ed. pap. 45.40 (*0-317-28060-0*, 2025549) Bks Demand.

Vietnamese Students: Changing Patterns, Changing Needs. Chung H. Chuong. (Illus.). 23p. (Orig.). 1994. pap. 5.00 (*0-936434-71-6*, Many Cultures Pubng) SF Study Ctr.

Vietnamese Tradition of Human Rights. Ta Van Tai. LC 88-80209. (Indochina Research Monograph: No. 4). 320p. (Orig.). 1989. pap. 17.00 (*1-55729-002-4*) IEAS.

Vietnamese Tradition on Trial, 1920-1945. David G. Marr. (Illus.). 450p. 1981. pap. 16.00 (*0-520-05081-9*) U CA Pr.

Vietnamese Word Book. Kim-Anh Nguyen. LC 93-73560. (Illus.). 144p. (ENG & VIE.). (J). (gr. k-6). 1994. 19.95 (*1-880188-70-8*); pap. 11.95 (*1-880188-51-1*) Bess Pr.

***Vietnamese Word Book.** Kim-Anh Nguyen. LC 93-73560. (Illus.). 144p. (ENG & VIE.). (J). (gr. k-6). 1994. pap. 19.95 incl. audio (*1-880188-71-6*) Bess Pr.

***Vietnamien Sans Peine.** (Illus.). (Orig.). (FRE & VIE.). 1997. pap. 75.00 incl. audio (*2-7005-1336-3*, Pub. by ASSIMIL FR) Distribks Inc.

Vietnamization of New Jersey (An American Tragedy) Christopher Durang. 1978. pap. 5.25 (*0-8222-1208-0*) Dramatists Play.

***Vietnam's Reforms & Economic Growth.** Harvie. LC 96-30026. 1997. text ed. 65.00 (*0-312-17411-X*) St Martin.

***Vietnam's Rural Transformation.** Benedict J. Kerkvliet & Doug J. Porter. LC 96-40070. (Transitions: Asia & Asian American Ser.). (C). 1997. pap. text ed. 29.00 (*0-8133-9022-2*) Westview.

Vietnam's Social & Political Development As Seen Through the Modern Novel. Hoang Hgoc Thanh. LC 91-18775. (American University Studies: History: Ser. IX, Vols. 114). 387p. (C). 1992. text ed. 54.95 (*0-8204-1645-2*) P Lang Pubng.

Vietnam's Will to Live: Resistance to Foreign Aggression from Early Times Through the Nineteenth Century. Helen B. Lamb. LC 72-81760. 352p. 1972. reprint ed. pap. 100.40 (*0-7837-9612-9*, 2060369) Bks Demand.

Vietnam's Women in Transition. Ed. by Kathleen L. Barry. (International Political Economy Ser.). 1996. text ed. 49.95 (*0-312-12830-4*) St Martin.

Vieux Carre. Tennessee Williams. LC 78-26621. 1979. pap. 8.95 (*0-8112-0728-5*, NDP482) New Directions.

Vieux de la Vielle. Rene Fallet. 224p. (FRE.). 1973. pap. 10.95 (*0-7859-2317-9*, 2070364372) Fr & Eur.

Vieux Gringo. Carlos Fuentes. 282p. (FRE.). 1990. pap. 11.95 (*0-7859-2584-8*, 2070382133) Fr & Eur.

Vieux Negre et la Medaille. Ferdinand Oyono. (FRE.). 1972. pap. 14.95 (*0-7859-3195-3*, 2264009624) Fr & Eur.

View. 1995. 3.98 (*0-8317-2214-2*) Smithmark.

View: Parade of the Avant-Garde, 1940-1947. Ed. by Charles H. Ford. (Illus.). 304p. 1992. pap. 17.95 (*1-56025-014-3*) Thunders Mouth.

View Askew: Postmodern Investigations. Steve Abbott. (Illus.). 195p. (Orig.). 1989. pap. text ed. 9.95 (*1-879594-13-7*) Androgyne Bks.

View at Your Own Risk. Joe L. Wheeler. LC 93-6809. 1993. pap. 0.89 (*0-8280-0725-X*) Review & Herald.

View by the Sea. Shotaro Yasuoka. Tr. by Karen Wigen from JPN. (Modern Asian Literature Ser.). 196p. (Orig.). (C). 1992. pap. 14.50 (*0-231-05873-X*) Col U Pr.

View Camera. rev. ed. Harvey Shaman. (Illus.). 144p. 1991. pap. 22.50 (*0-8174-6375-5*, Amphoto) Watsn-Guptill.

View Camera Technique. 6th ed. Leslie Stroebel. (Illus.). 320p. 1993. 44.95 (*0-240-80158-X*, Focal) Buttrwrth-Heinemann.

View for Jacob's Ladder: One Hundred Midrashim. David Curzon. 200p. 1996. 27.95 (*0-8276-0568-4*) JPS Phila.

View from a Distance. Lore L. Waller. LC 92-44763. (Studies in Austrian Literature, Culture, & Thought). 1993. pap. 19.50 (*0-929497-61-9*) Ariadne CA.

View from A Mississippi River Cotton Sack. Frances B. Cowden. Ed. by Marcelle B. Zarshenas. (Illus.). 68p. (Orig.). 1993. spiral bd. 10.95 (*1-884289-01-0*) Grandmother Erth.

View from A Mississippi River Cotton Sack. 2nd ed. Frances B. Cowden. Ed. by Marcelle B. Zarshenas. LC 93-80265. (Illus.). 80p. (Orig.). 1994. 18.00 (*1-884289-03-7*) Grandmother Erth.

View from a Ninetieth Birthday: Lyrical Poems of Old Age. Ernest G. Moll. Ed. by Kathleen Iddings. LC 91-77893. 71p. (Orig.). 1992. per. 10.00 (*0-931721-12-1*) La Jolla Poets.

View from a Tower Blind: Reflections of a Texas Whitetail Hunter. Ray Sasser. 240p. 1995. 19.95 (*0-9632969-6-5*) Collect Covey.

View from Above. John E. Fulker. LC 91-77548. 1992. 15.00 (*0-87212-254-9*) Libra.

View from Above. Rachel Noam. 200p. (C). 1993. 14.95 (*1-56062-178-8*) CIS Comm.

View from Abroad. N. Kent. (C). 1990. 40.00 (*0-7487-0493-0*, Pub. by Stanley Thornes UK) Trans-Atl Phila.

View from Afar. Claude Levi-Strauss. 328p. 1992. pap. 16.50 (*0-226-47474-7*) U Ch Pr.

***View from Another Dimension: An Angel Speaks.** rev. ed. Ed. by T. Dean Adams & Daniel T. Rico. LC 97-71221. (Illus.). 180p. 1997. pap. 14.95 (*0-9655288-1-2*) Interdimensional Pubns.

***View from Another Dimension - An Angel Speaks.** Bethany J. O'Halloran. Ed. by T. Dean Adams. 1996. pap. 12.95 (*0-9655288-0-4*) Interdimensional Pubns.

***View from Belmont.** Kevyn A. Arthur. 230p. 1997. pap. 14.95 (*1-900715-02-3*, Pub. by Peepal Tree Pr UK) Paul & Co Pubs.

View from Black Mesa: The Changing Face of Archaeology. George J. Gumerman. LC 84-8581. (Illus.). 184p. 1992. reprint ed. pap. 16.95 (*0-8165-1340-6*) U of Ariz Pr.

View from Building Twenty: Essays in Linguistics in Honor of Sylvain Bromberger. Ed. by Kenneth Hale & Samuel J. Keyser. LC 92-38255. (Current Studies in Linguistics: Vol. 24). (Illus.). 280p. 1993. 39.95 (*0-262-08223-3*); pap. 19.95 (*0-262-58124-8*) MIT Pr.

View from Capitol Hill: Lawmakers on Congressional Reform. Robert T. Braye et al. 78p. (Orig.). (C). 1989. pap. text ed. 10.50 (*0-939715-12-0*) Ctr Politics.

View from Chapultepec: Mexican Writers on the Mexican-American War. Ed. & Tr. by Cecil Robinson from SPA. LC 88-36260. 223p. 1989. 38.50 (*0-8165-1083-0*) U of Ariz Pr.

View from Coyaba. Peter Abrahams. LC 84-28746. 440p. 1985. pap. 8.95 (*0-571-13289-8*) Faber & Faber.

View from Diamond Head: Royal Residence to Urban Resort. Don Hibbard & David Franzen. (Illus.). 233p. 1986. text ed. 24.95 (*0-915013-02-9*) Editions Ltd.

View from Eternity. Vaughan Shelton & Forbes Nichols. 196p. 1982. pap. 8.00 (*1-877712-00-0*) Forbes Nichols.

View from Headquarters: Civil War Letters of Harvey Reid. Ed. by Frank L. Byrne. LC 65-63010. (Illus.). 258p. 1965. 7.50 (*0-87020-004-6*) State Hist Soc Wis.

***View from Here.** Brian K. Jackson. 1997. 22.00 (*0-671-56895-7*, PB Hardcover) PB.

***View from Highway 1: Essays on Television.** Michael J. Arlen. LC 97-1277. (Television Ser.). 283p. 1997. reprint ed. pap. 17.95 (*0-8156-0467-X*) Syracuse U Pr.

View from Hill Cabin. Arnold Perrin. 1979. pap. 2.95 (*0-89002-119-8*) Wings ME.

View from Jerusalem, Eighteen Forty-Nine to Eighteen Fifty-Eight: The Consular Diary of James & Elizabeth Anne Finn. Arnold Blumberg. (Illus.). 352p. 1970. 45.00 (*0-8386-2271-2*) Fairleigh Dickinson.

View from Jerusalem, 1849-1958: The Consular Diaries of James & Elizabeth Anne Finn. Arnold Blumberg. 1990. write for info. (*0-318-66861-0*) Fairleigh Dickinson.

View from Lincoln Hill: Man & the Land in a New England Town. Paul Brooks. (Illus.). 273p. 1986. reprint ed. 14.95 (*0-944856-05-5*) Lincoln Hist Soc.

***View from Local Newspapers: Editorials & National Politics.** Jan P. Vermeer. 176p. 1997. 53.00 (*0-8476-8652-3*) Rowman.

***View from Local Newspapers: Editorials & National Politics.** Jan P. Vermeer. 176p. 1997. pap. 21.95 (*0-8476-8653-1*) Rowman.

View from Minerva's Tower: Learning & Imagination in the Anatomy of Melancholy. E. Patricia Vicari. 264p. 1989. 45.00 (*0-8020-2685-0*) U of Toronto Pr.

View from Mountain Campus: Northern Arizona University in the 1980's. Platt Cline. LC 90-52533. 174p. 1990. 24.94 (*0-87358-506-2*) Northland AZ.

View from Mt. Morris: A Harlem Boyhood. John B. Sanford. LC 94-525440. 231p. 1994. 22.00 (*1-56980-018-9*) Barricade Bks.

***View from My Easel.** Jim Stratton. (Orig.). 1997. pap. write for info. (*1-57553-500-9*) Watermrk Pr.

***View from My Loft: A Collection of Essays about the State of the World: the Political, the Natural, the Familiar.** x, 110p. (Orig.). 1996. pap. text ed. 10.00 (*0-9655528-0-2*) Annakie Pr.

View from My Stump. Charles E. Tomlinsen. 139p. (Orig.). 1992. pap. 9.95 (*0-9633194-0-X*) D R Virtue Pr.

View from Nowhere. Thomas Nagel. 256p. 1989. reprint ed. pap. 17.95 (*0-19-505644-2*) OUP.

View from Officers' Row: Army Perceptions of Western Indians. Sherry L. Smith. LC 89-5216. (Illus.). 263p. 1991. reprint ed. pap. 16.95 (*0-8165-1245-0*) U of Ariz Pr.

View from Olympus. 2nd ed. Maurice Kelly. 1987. pap. text ed. 18.33 (*0-582-68887-6*, 74686) Longman.

View from Olympus: Evolution of Consciousness Through Astrological - Historical Ages. Donna H. Lloyd. (Illus.). 300p. (C). 1992. pap. 13.95 (*0-9627291-1-6*) Deltaran Pub.

View from Plum Lick. David B. Dick. (Illus.). 248p. (Orig.). 1992. pap. 14.95 (*0-9632886-0-1*) Plum Lick Pub.

***View from Plum Lick.** David B. Dick. (Illus.). 256p. 1997. 17.95 (*0-9632886-6-0*) Plum Lick Pub.

View from Pompey's Head. Hamilton Basso. 1994. reprint ed. lib. bdg. 24.95 (*1-56849-557-9*) Buccaneer Bks.

View from Rappahannock, No. II. 2nd ed. Eugene J. McCarthy. LC 89-1640. (Illus.). 96p. 1989. pap. 12.95 (*0-939009-19-6*) EPM Pubns.

View from Rat Lake. John Gierach. 208p. (Orig.). 1989. pap. 11.00 (*0-671-67581-8*, Fireside) S&S Trade.

View from Rat Lake: Essays on the Sport of Fly Fishing. John Gierach. 193p. (Orig.). 1988. 19.95 (*0-87108-743-X*) Pruett.

View from Rome: On the Eve of the Modernist Crisis. David G. Schultenover. LC 92-23892. 283p. 1993. 30.00 (*0-8232-1358-7*); pap. 19.95 (*0-8232-1359-5*) Fordham.

View from Round Hill: Selected Writings of J. Ward Shank. J. Ward Shank. 200p. (Orig.). 1988. pap. 5.95 (*0-685-24091-6*) Sword & Trumpet.

***View from Saturday.** E. L. Konigsburg. (J). 1998. mass mkt. 4.50 (*0-689-81721-5*) S&S Childrens.

View from Saturday. E. L. Konigsburg. (J). (gr. 3-7). 1996. 16.00 (*0-689-80993-X*, Atheneum S&S) S&S Trade.

View from Space: Photographic Exploration of the Planets. Merton Davies & Bruce C. Murray. LC 75-16887. 1973. pap. text ed. 18.00 (*0-231-08330-0*) Col U Pr.

View from Sterling Bluff. Glen McCaskey. LC 88-83080. (Illus.). 56p. 1989. 24.95 (*0-929264-13-4*) Longstreet Pr Inc.

***View from Sunset Towers.** Kent R. Brown. 75p. 1996. pap. 5.25 (*0-87129-739-6*, V26) Dramatic Pub.

View from Tehran: A Diplomatist Looks at the Shah's Regime in June, 1964. 16p. (C). 1985. reprint ed. pap. text ed. 12.00 (*0-8191-5057-6*, Inst Study Diplomacy) U Pr of Amer.

View from the Academy: Liberal Arts Professors on Excellent Teaching. Ed. by Thomas F. Warren. 184p. (Orig.). (C). 1992. pap. text ed. 18.50 (*0-8191-8668-6*); lib. bdg. 34.75 (*0-8191-8667-8*) U Pr of Amer.

View from the Air: Charles Lindbergh's Earth & Sky. Reeve Lindbergh. (Illus.). 32p. 1996. pap. 4.99 (*0-14-054818-1*) Puffin Bks.

View from the Air: Charles Lindbergh's Earth & Sky. Reeve Lindbergh. (Illus.). 32p. (J). 1992. pap. 15.00 (*0-670-84660-0*) Viking Child Bks.

View from the Barrio. Lisa R. Peattie. LC 68-16441. (Illus.). 1968. 23.95 (*0-472-72280-8*); pap. 14.95 (*0-472-06169-0*) U of Mich Pr.

View from the Boys: Sociology of Down-Town Adolescents. Howard Parker. (Modern Revivals in Sociology Ser.). 238p. 1992. 49.95 (*0-7512-0046-8*, Pub. by Gregg Revivals UK) Ashgate Pub Co.

View from the Bridge. Ed. by Geoff Armstrong. 176p. 1993. 75.00 (*0-85292-541-7*, Pub. by IPM Hse UK) St Mut.

***View from the Bridge.** John A. Loftus. 1997. pap. 12.95 (*1-56929-058-X*) Pastoral Pr.

View from the Bridge. Arthur Miller. 1956. pap. 5.25 (*0-8222-1209-9*) Dramatists Play.

View from the Bridge. Arthur Miller. (Plays Ser.). 1977. pap. 7.95 (*0-14-048135-4*, Penguin Bks) Viking Penguin.

View from the Bridge see Best American Plays: Fourth Series, 1952-1957

View from the Cherry Tree. 2nd ed. Willo D. Roberts. LC 93-31170. 192p. (J). (gr. 3-7). 1994. reprint ed. pap. 3.95 (*0-689-71784-9*, Aladdin Paperbacks) S&S Childrens.

***View from the Chinaberry Tree: Coming of Age in Winfield, Texas.** Charles Shafer. (Illus.). 172p. (Orig.). 1996. 25.00 (*0-9642481-2-3*); pap. 14.00 (*0-9642481-3-1*) NE Texas Pub.

View from the Closet: Essays on Gay Life & Liberation, 1973-1977. A. Nolder Gay. LC 78-105579. 1978. pap. 3.00 (*0-9601570-0-X*) Union Park.

***View from the Cockpit.** David Brown. (Illus.). 200p. 1996. 32.95 (*1-85310-302-0*) Specialty Pr.

View from the Cockpit. Len Morgan. 112p. 1985. pap. 7.95 (*0-89745-072-8*) Sunflower U Pr.

View from the Cradle: Children's Emotions in Everyday Life. Otto Weininger. 240p. 1993. pap. text ed. 33.95 (*1-85575-037-6*, Pub. by Karnac Bks UK) Brunner-Mazel.

View from the Edge: The Life & Landscape of Beverly Johnson. Gabriella Zim. LC 96-47242. (Illus.). 296p. (Orig.). 1996. pap. 17.00 (*1-879415-16-X*) Mtn n Air Bks.

View from the End of Blue Rooster Road. Robert P. Herbst. 1986. pap. 6.95 (*0-9617075-0-X*) Blue Rooster Pr.

View from the Fender. large type ed. Tom A. Shaughnessy. 310p. 1993. pap. 17.99 (*1-85389-424-9*, Dales) Ulverscroft.

View from the Gazebo. Marianne Boruch. LC 84-20834. (Wesleyan New Poets Ser.). 63p. 1985. 12.95 (*0-8195-2125-6*, Wesleyan Univ Pr) U Pr of New Eng.

View from the Ground. Martha Gellhorn. LC 87-31837. 432p. 1988. pap. 9.95 (*0-87113-212-5*, Atlntc Mnthly) Grove-Atltic.

View from the Heart: Bayou Country Ecology. June Kennedy. Ed. by Carolyn P. Gorman. (Illus.). 150p. (C). 1991. pap. 16.95 (*0-9621724-4-8*) Blue Heron LA.

View from the Heights Vol. 1: Daily Meditations from God's Word. Frank E. Lasater, Jr. 384p. (Orig.). 1996. pap. 15.95 (*0-9650559-1-4*) Paloma TX.

View from the Heights Vol. 1: Daily Meditations from God's Word, Set. Frank E. Lasater, Jr. (Orig.). 1996. pap. write for info. (*0-9650559-0-6*) Paloma TX.

***View from the Hills.** Gene Cavin. iv, 119p. 1996. 16.95 (*0-9657025-1-0*) Hanover Pub.

***View from the Interior: Women & Design-NE.** Ed. by Judy Attfield & Pat Kirkham. pap. 29.95 (*0-7043-4451-3*, Pub. by Womens Press UK) Trafalgar.

View from the Islands: The Samal of Tawi-tawi. Karen J. Allison. LC 81-85309. (International Museum of Cultures Publications: No. 15). 50p. (Orig.). 1984. fiche 4.00 (*0-88312-253-7*) Summer Instit Ling.

***View from the Litter Box.** Gail Gastfield & Richard Record. (Illus.). 160p. (Orig.). 1997. per., pap. 6.95 (*0-9635176-5-1*) Walrus Prods.

View from the Mountaintop: A Journey into Wholeness: A Contemplative, Inspirational Book of Poems. Lee Ann F. Dzelzkalns. Ed. by Rhonda Foster. LC 95-80180. (Illus.). 110p. (Orig.). 1995. pap. 11.95 (*1-881300-01-3*) Ageless. In this contemplative, inspirational book, Lee Ann offers her powerful expressions of personal expansion as springboards for others' transformation. Through levels of awareness, you decondition from the past, breaking limiting patterns of anxiety & fear. You become aware of your own strength, beauty & inner wisdom, reconditioning to a more fulfilling positive reality. Ultimately, the journey leads you to self-empowerment, spiritual renewal & unconditional love. The delightful poetic meter & thought-provoking illustrations speak to you on many levels. You'll cherish this book as you do a dear friend. "...a sweet meditation designed to allow the feverish mind to rest, relax & enjoy. Read this whenever you need to stop the world..."--Fred Alan Wolf, Ph.D., author. The guided meditation audiotape VIEW FROM THE MOUNTAINTOP: A JOURNEY TO SELF-RENEWAL compliments the book perfectly. $10. 95. 1-881300-00-7. You can't help but relax & rejuvenate as Lee Ann's soothing, soul-filled voice leads you from self-doubt to self-respect. "This tape is for anyone seeking that special feeling of accomplishment & confidence!"--Richard Fuller, Metaphysical Reviews. Order from: Ageless Dominion Publishing, P.O. Box 11546, Milwaukee, WI 53211, 414-332-6775. FAX: 414-332-6566. ***Publisher Provided Annotation.***

View from the Pew. Martha Bolton. 1985. 8.99 (*0-8341-9180-6*, MP-633) Lillenas.

***View from the Press Shack: Indiana Politics from the Notebook of Edward H. Ziegner.** (Illus.). 168p. 1997. pap. 14.95 (*0-9657253-0-8*) M M Ziegner.

View from the Rainbow Balcony. Bill Gillespie. Ed. by Sandy Sheppard. 200p. (Orig.). 1989. pap. 11.00 (*0-940859-07-6*) Snd Dollar Pub.

***View from the Red Tees: The Truth about Women & Golf.** Dorothy Langley. LC 97-17002. 1997. write for info. (*1-55972-440-4*) Carol Pub Group.

View from the Ridge: The Testimony of a Twentieth-Century Christian. Morris West. LC 96-28489. 144p. 1996. 18.00 (*0-06-069062-3*) Harper SF.

***View from the Ridge: The Testimony of a Twentieth-Century Christian.** Morris West. 1996. pap. 12.00 (*0-00-628022-6*) HarperColl Wrld.

***View from the Ridge: The Testimony of a Twentieth-Century Christian.** Morris L. West. LC 96-28489. 1996. pap. 12.00 (*0-06-069381-9*) Harper SF.

***View from the Roof.** David Carley. 1997. pap. text ed. 12. 95 (*0-88754-525-4*, Pub. by Playwrights CN Pr CN) Theatre Comm.

View from the Rough. Mike Klemme. (Illus.). 144p. 1996. 39.95 (*1-886947-06-6*) Sleepng Bear.

View from the Stands - a Season with Bob the Beerman. Bob D. Beerman. LC 94-65390. 139p. 1994. pap. 9.95 (*0-9640341-0-7*) Successful Concepts.

View from the State House: Recollections & Reflections, 1961-1965. Matthew E. Welsh. 290p. 1992. pap. 16.95 (*1-885323-32-8*) IN Hist Bureau.

***View from the Top.** Margaret Jensen. LC 97-2663. 175p. (Orig.). 1997. pap. 8.99 (*1-56507-570-6*) Harvest Hse.

***View from the Top: A Small Town Veteran Trial Lawyer Looks Back on 50 Years of Courtroom Experience.** George S. Keller. (Illus.). 162p. 1996. 22.95 (*1-890103-00-4*) Rowan Tree IN.

View from the Top: Forest Service Research. R. Keith Arnold et al. Ed. by Harold K. Steen. LC 93-46520. xiv, 365p. 1994. pap. 13.00 (*0-89030-049-6*) Forest Hist Soc.

View from the Top: Liberal Arts Presidents on Teacher Education. Ed. by Thomas F. Warren. 176p. (Orig.). (C). 1990. pap. text ed. 22.50 (*0-8191-7981-7*); lib. bdg. 42.00 (*0-8191-7980-9*) U Pr of Amer.

***View from the Top: The Kasparov-Anand PCA Match, New York, 1995.** John Hall & Jan Cartier. Ed. by Lou Hays. 123p. (Orig.). 1996. pap. 14.95 (*1-880673-12-6*) Hays Pub.

View from the Top: The Story of Prospect, Connecticut. John R. Guevin. LC 95-75335. (Illus.). 288p. 1995. 19. 50 (*0-9637240-3-7*) Biograph Pub.

View from the Top of the Mountain. Ed. by Tom Koontz & Thom Tammaro. LC 81-65930. 130p. (Orig.). 1981. pap. 7.95 (*0-935306-12-9*) Barnwood Pr.

View from the Turret. William B. Folkestad. LC 96-2301. (Illus.). 172p. 1996. 24.95 (*1-57249-001-2*, Burd St Pr) White Mane Pub.

View from the Veranda: The History & Architecture of the Summer Cottages on Mackinac Island. Phil Porter. Ed. by David A. Armour. LC 83-198939. (Reports in Mackinac History & Archaeology: No. 8). (Illus.). 76p. (Orig.). 1981. pap. 8.50 (*0-911872-41-8*) Mackinac St Hist Pks.

View from the Weeds. Owen Hernan. 36p. (Orig.). 1993. pap. text ed. 6.00 (*0-9628478-4-4*) North Star Assocs.

View from the West. Eric Segura. LC 90-61817. 89p. 1991. pap. 26.00 (*0-939044-31-5*) Lingua Pr.

View from the Witch's Cave: Folktales of the Pyrenees. Tr. by Linda White. LC 91-21668. (Basque Ser.). (Illus.). 152p. 1991. 21.95 (*0-87417-176-8*) U of Nev Pr.

View from Three Windows. Elain Jagier & Mark Shaw. 215p. (Orig.). 1994. pap. 12.00 (*0-9643696-0-5*) Dreamers Pr.

***View from Within: A Case Study of Chinese Heritage Community Language Schools in the United States.** Xueying Wang. LC 96-35239. (National Foreign Language Center Monographs). 1996. write for info. (*1-880671-05-0*) NFLC Pubns.

View from Within: Japanese American Art from Internment Camps 1942-1945. Karin M. Higa. LC 92-61946. (Illus.). 100p. (C). pap. 24.95 (*0-934052-21-2*) UCLA Asian Am Studies Ctr.

View from Wrightsville Beach. E. T. Malone, Jr. (Illus.). (Orig.). 1988. pap. 8.95 (*0-9621668-0-4*) Lit Lantern.

View from Xanadu: William Randolph Hearst & United States Foreign Policy. Ian Mugridge. 220p. 1995. pap. 17.95 (*0-7735-1295-0*, Pub. by McGill CN) U of Toronto Pr.

***View from Xanadu: William Randolph Hearst & United States Foreign Policy.** Ian Mugridge. 1995. 44.95 (*0-7735-1281-0*, Pub. by McGill CN) U of Toronto Pr.

View from 10 Downing Street. Lord H. Wilson. (Grace A. Tanner Lecture in Human Values Ser.). 17p. 1988. 7.50 (*0-910153-05-1*) E T Woolf.

View in Winter. Margery W. Steer. Ed. by Janice W. Stridick. (Illus.). 60p. 1992. 14.95 (*0-9632494-0-1*); pap. 9.95 (*0-9632494-1-X*) Southbound.

View into Essex. Stan Jarvis. 176p. 1990. pap. 24.00 (*0-86138-053-3*, Pub. by T Dalton UK) St Mut.

View North: A Long Look at Northern England. Frederick Alderson. LC 68-23825. (Illus.). 283p. 1968. 29.95 (*0-678-05577-7*) Kelley.

View of a Universe: A Love Story of Ann Arbor at Middle Age. Milo Ryan. (Illus.). 211p. (Orig.). 1985. pap. 9.95 (*1-882574-02-8*) Ann Arbor Hist.

View of Berg's Lulu Through the Autograph Sources. Patricia Hall. LC 95-40543. (Illus.). 185p. (C). 1996. 42. 00 (*0-520-08819-0*) U CA Pr.

View of Europe, 1932. Paul V. Zeeland. 1979. 17.95 (*0-405-10639-4*) Ayer.

View of Greek Art. R. Ross Holloway. LC 72-187947. 235p. reprint ed. pap. 67.00 (*0-317-55628-2*, 2029250) Bks Demand.

View of Life. Salvador E. Luria et al. 1981. teacher ed. 10. 75 (*0-8053-6649-0*); teacher ed., text ed. 10.75 (*0-8053-6648-2*) Benjamin-Cummings.

View of My Own: Essays on Literature & Society. Elizabeth Hardwick. LC 81-9680. 214p. 1982. reprint ed. pap. 6.95 (*0-912946-91-1*) Ecco Pr.

View of Rome: A Guide to Understanding the Beliefs & Practices of Roman Catholics. John H. Armstrong. 1995. pap. 9.99 (*0-8024-9146-4*) Moody.

View of the Action of the Federal Government in Behalf of Slavery. William Jay. LC 70-83891. (Black Heritage Library Collection). 1977. 21.95 (*0-8369-8612-1*) Ayer.

View of the American Indians: General Character, Customs, Language, Public Festivals, Religious Rite, & Traditions. Israel Worsley. Ed. by Moshe Davis. LC 77-70757. (America & the Holy Land Ser.). 1977. reprint ed. lib. bdg. 21.95 (*0-405-10303-4*) Ayer.

View of the Art of Colonization: With Present Reference to the British Empire. Ed. by Edward G. Wakefield. LC 68-30548. (Reprints of Economic Classics Ser.). xxiv, 513p. 1969. reprint ed. 57.50 (*0-678-00561-3*) Kelley.

View of the Constitution of the United States of America. William Rawle. LC 70-109548. (American Constitutional & Legal History Ser). 1970. reprint ed. lib. bdg. 39.50 (*0-306-71902-9*) Da Capo.

View of the Court of Chancery. William L. Wellesley. 110p. 1980. reprint ed. lib. bdg. 15.00 (*0-8377-1303-X*) Rothman.

View of the Edinburgh Theatre During the Summer Season, 1759. James Boswell. LC 92-543. (Augustan Reprints Ser.: No. 179). 1992. reprint ed. 14.50 (*0-404-70179-5*, PN2605) AMS Pr.

View of the Hebrews: Exhibiting the Destruction of Jerusalem, the Certain Restoration of Judah & Israel, the Present State of Judah & Israel & an Address of the Prophet Isaiah Relative to Their Restoration. Ethan Smith. Ed. by Moshe Davis. LC 77-70742. (America & the Holy Land Ser.). 1977. reprint ed. lib. bdg. 19.95 (*0-405-10288-7*) Ayer.

View of the Holy Land: Its Present Inhabitants, Their Manners & Customs, Polity & Religion. George Thompson et al. Ed. by Moshe Davis. LC 77-70750. (America & the Holy Land Ser.). 1977. reprint ed. lib. bdg. 42.95 (*0-405-10295-X*) Ayer.

View of the Lead Mines of Missouri: Including Some Observations on the Mineralogy, Geology, Geography, Antiquities, Soil, Climate, Population & Productions of Missouri & Arkansas, & Other Sections of the Western Country. Henry R. Schoolcraft. LC 72-2867. (Use & Abuse of America's Natural Resources Ser.). (Illus.). 302p. 1972. reprint ed. 23.95 (*0-405-04534-4*) Ayer.

View of the Life, Travels, & Philanthropic Labours of the Late John Howard, Esquire, LL.D.F.R.S. John Aikin. 180p. 1994. reprint ed. lib. bdg. 37.50 (*0-8377-1912-7*) Rothman.

View of the Nation: 1955-1959. Nation Magazine Staff. Ed. by Henry M. Christman. LC 79-111853. (Essay Index Reprint Ser.). 1977. 21.95 (*0-8369-1620-4*) Ayer.

View of the Nervous Temperament. Thomas Trotter. LC 75-16735. (Classics in Psychiatry Ser.). 1976. reprint ed. 26.95 (*0-405-07456-5*) Ayer.

View of the Present State of Ireland. Edmund Spenser. LC 74-145312. reprint ed. 29.00 (*0-403-01224-4*) Scholarly.

View of the Progress of Political Economy in Europe since the Sixteenth Century. Travers Twiss. LC 68-58035. (Reprints of Economic Classics Ser.). xv, 298p. 1973. reprint ed. 45.00 (*0-678-00850-7*) Kelley.

View of the River. Luna B. Leopold. LC 93-34698. 312p. 1994. 39.95 (*0-674-93732-5*) HUP.

View of the Russian Empire, During the Reign of Catherine the Second, to the Close of the 18th Century, 3 Vols., Set. William Tooke. LC 70-115591. (Russia Observed Ser., No. 1). 1971. reprint ed. 90.95 (*0-405-03068-1*) Ayer.

View of the Russian Empire, During the Reign of Catherine the Second, to the Close of the 18th Century, 3 Vols., Vol. 1. William Tooke. LC 70-115591. (Russia Observed Ser., No. 1). 1970. reprint ed. 44.95 (*0-405-03237-4*) Ayer.

View of the Russian Empire, During the Reign of Catherine the Second, to the Close of the 18th Century, 3 Vols., Vol. 2. William Tooke. LC 70-115591. (Russia Observed Ser., No. 1). 1970. reprint ed. 45.95 (*0-405-03236-6*) Ayer.

View of the Russian Empire, During the Reign of Catherine the Second, to the Close of the 18th Century, 3 Vols., Vol. 3. William Tooke. LC 70-115591. (Russia Observed Ser., No. 1). 1970. reprint ed. 41.00 (*0-685-00520-8*) Ayer.

View of the Sea: A Discussion between a Chief Engineer & an Oceanographer about the Machinery of the Ocean Circulation. Henry Stommel. 184p. 1987. pap. 10.95 (*0-691-02431-6*) Princeton U Pr.

View of the Soil & Climate of the United States of America. Charles B. Brown. (Works of Charles Brockden Brown). 1989. reprint ed. lib. bdg. 79.00 (*0-7812-2073-4*) Rprt Serv.

***View of the State of Ireland by Edmund Spenser.** Edmund Spenser. Ed. by Andrew Hadfield & Willy Maley. 208p. (C). 1997. text ed. 54.95 (*0-631-20534-9*) Blackwell Pubs.

***View of the State of Ireland by Edmund Spenser.** Edmund Spenser. Ed. by Andrew Hadfield & Willy Maley. 208p. (C). 1997. pap. text ed. 21.95 (*0-631-20535-7*) Blackwell Pubs.

View of the United States of America in a Series of Papers Written Between the Years 1787 & 1794. Tench Coxe. LC 64-24342. (Reprints of Economic Classics Ser.). 512p. 1965. reprint ed. 75.00 (*0-678-00070-0*) Kelley.

View of the Universe. David Malin. LC 92-46469. (Illus.). 288p. (C). 1993. text ed. 39.95 (*0-521-44477-2*) Cambridge U Pr.

View of the Universe. David Malin. (Illus.). 292p. 1993. 39. 95 (*0-933346-66-2*) Sky Pub.

View of Tomorrow: The Senior Financial Officer in the Year 2005. International Federation of Accountants Staff. 98p. (Orig.). 1995. pap. text ed. 20.00 (*1-887464-03-4*) Intl Fed Accts.

View of West Florida, Embracing Its Geography, Topography, & C., with an Appendix Treating of Its Antiquities, Land Titles, & Canals, & Containing a Map Exhibiting a Chart of the Coast, a Plan of Pensacola, & the Entrance of the Harbour. John L. Williams. LC 75-45282. (Floridiana Facsimile & Reprint Ser.). (Illus.). 1976. reprint ed. 15.95 (*0-8130-0375-X*) U Press Fla.

View of Women Found in the Deuteronomic Family Laws. Carolyn Pressler. LC 93-27800. (Beiheft zur Zeitschrift fuer die Alttestamentliche Wissenschaft Ser.: Vol. 216). ix, 127p. (C). 1993. lib. bdg. 83.10 (*3-11-013743-7*) De Gruyter.

View Points. David Sattler. (Illus.). 60p. 1995. pap. 12.95 (*1-887498-00-1*) Winterberry Pub.

View the Land: Israel Today. Anne Dexter. LC 86-203335. 245p. 1986. pap. 4.95 (*0-88270-609-8*) Bridge-Logos.

View They Arrange. Dale Going. Ed. by Patricia Dienstfrey. LC 94-215. 80p. (Orig.). (C). 1994. pap. 10. 00 (*0-932716-33-4*) Kelsey St Pr.

View to a Death in the Morning: Hunting & Nature Through History. Matt Cartmill. (Illus.). 347p. (C). 1993. text ed. 29.95 (*0-674-93735-X*) HUP.

View to a Death in the Morning: Hunting & Nature Through History. Matt Cartmill. (Illus.). 352p. 1996. pap. 15.95 (*0-674-93736-8*) HUP.

View to a Thrill. John Vincent. (James Bond, Jr. Ser.: Bk. 1). (Illus.). 128p. (J). (gr. 3-7). 1992. pap. 2.99 (*0-14-036011-5*) Puffin Bks.

View Vertical & Other Essays. Winifred M. Kirkland. LC 79-93350. (Essay Index Reprint Ser.). 1977. 21.95 (*0-8369-1300-0*) Ayer.

View with a Grain of Sand: Selected Poems. Wislawa Szymborska. Tr. by Stanislaw Baranczak & Clare Cavanagh from POL. LC 94-36112. 224p. 1995. pap. 12. 00 (*0-15-600216-7*) HarBrace.

View with a Grain of Sand: Selected Poems. Wislawa Szymborska. Tr. by Stanislaw Baranczak & Clare Cavanagh from POL. LC 94-36112. 224p. 1995. 20.00 (*0-15-100153-7*) HarBrace.

Viewbook Hawaii. Douglas Peebles. (Illus.). 32p. (Orig.). 1991. pap. 6.95 (*0-9627294-6-9*) Hawaiian Resources.

Viewbook Hawaii's Volcanos. Douglas Peebles. (Illus.). 32p. (Orig.). 1994. pap. 6.95 (*0-9627294-9-3*) Hawaiian Resources.

Viewbook Kauai. Douglas Peebles. (Illus.). 32p. (Orig.). 1991. pap. 6.95 (*0-9627294-5-0*) Hawaiian Resources.

Viewbook Maui. Douglas Peebles. (Illus.). 32p. 1988. pap. 6.95 (*0-9627294-7-7*) Hawaiian Resources.

Viewbook Oahu. Douglas Peebles. (Illus.). 32p. (Orig.). 1989. pap. 6.95 (*0-9627294-8-5*) Hawaiian Resources.

***Viewer, Vol. 3.** George Quasha. (Gary Hill's Projective Installations Ser.). 1997. pap. text ed. 15.00 (*1-886449-50-3*) Barrytown Ltd.

Viewer As Poet: The Renaissance Response to Art. Norman E. Land. LC 93-4469. 1994. 40.00 (*0-271-01004-5*) Pa St U Pr.

Viewer's Choice: A Comprehensive Record Keeping. Patton & Labarre. (BB - Record Keeping I Ser.). 1988. pap. 11. 95 (*0-538-02080-6*) S-W Pub.

Viewer's Guide to Film: Arts, Artifices & Issues. Richard M. Gollin. 1992. pap. text ed. write for info. (*0-07-023700-X*) McGraw.

Viewer's Guide to Professional Golf, 1993. Whitney McClelland. 1992. pap. 24.95 (*0-9631259-0-7*) Golfguide.

Viewers Guide to Professional Golf, 1993. Whitney McClelland. (Illus.). 192p. 1993. write for info. (*0-9631259-2-3*) Golfguide.

Viewers Guide to Professional Golf, 1995. Whitney McClelland. 1994. pap. 24.95 (*0-9631259-3-1*) Golfguide.

Viewer's Journal. Education. (C). Date not set. pap. write for info. (*0-395-82883-X*) HM.

Viewfinders: Black Women Photographers. Jeanne Moutoussamy-Ashe. (Illus.). 200p. 1993. 39.95 (*0-86316-159-6*); pap. 19.95 (*0-86316-158-8*) Writers & Readers.

***Viewing America, Vol. 1.** Masur. Date not set. pap. text ed. write for info. (*0-312-11693-4*) St Martin.

Viewing Children Through Television. Ed. by Hope Kelly & Howard Gardner. LC 80-84257. (New Directions for Child Development Ser.: No. 13). 1981. 19.00 (*0-87589-803-3*) Jossey-Bass.

***Viewing Europe from the Outside: Cultural Encounters & Critiques in the Eighteenth-Century Pseudo-Oriental Travelogue & the Nineteenth-Century "Voyage en Orient"** Syrine C. Hout. (Age of Revolution & Romanticism: Vol. 18). 304p. (C). 1997. 53.95 (*0-8204-3113-3*) P Lang Pubng.

***Viewing Olmsted: Photographs by Robert Burley, Lee Friedlander, & Geoffrey James.** Ed. by Phyllis Lambert. (Illus.). 108p. 1997. pap. text ed. 25.00 (*0-262-62116-9*) MIT Pr.

Viewing Positions: Ways of Seeing Film. Ed. by Linda Williams. LC 94-14489. (Depth of Field Ser.). (Illus.). 280p. (C). 1994. text ed. 48.00 (*0-8135-2132-7*); pap. text ed. 17.00 (*0-8135-2133-5*) Rutgers U Pr.

Viewing the Earth: The Social Construction of the Landsat Satellite System. Pamela E. Mack. Ed. by Wiebe E. Bijker et al. (Inside Technology Ser.). 280p. 1990. 30.00 (*0-262-13259-1*) MIT Pr.

***Viewing the Earth from Space: The Complete Guide to Public Domain Radio-Based Imagery & Weather Services.** James R. Buchanan. Ed. by Pamela Buchanan. (Illus.). 152p. (Orig.). 1996. pap. 24.00 (*0-9655390-0-8*) Woodhse Commun.

Viewing the Past: An Interpretive Guidebook. 60p. 1977. pap. 2.00 (*0-910524-03-3*) Eastern Wash.

Viewing Violence: How Media Violence Affects Your Child & Adolescent. Madeline Levine. 304p. 1996. 22.95 (*0-385-47686-8*) Doubleday.

Viewless Winds. Murray Morgan. LC 89-16355. (Northwest Reprints Ser.). 240p. 1990. reprint ed. pap. 13.95 (*0-87071-505-4*); reprint ed. text ed. 24.95 (*0-87071-504-6*) Oreg St U Pr.

Viewpoint. Ben Bova. (Boskone Bks.). (Illus.). 1977. 10.00 (*0-915368-14-5*) New Eng SF Assoc.

Viewpoint. Starr. (C). 1993. pap. 45.96 (*0-395-63791-0*) HM.

***Viewpoint: An Introduction to Travel, Tourism, & Hospitality.** Nona Starr. (C). 1993. teacher ed., text ed. 3.96 (*0-395-63792-9*) HM.

Viewpoint: An Introduction to Travel, Tourism, & Hospitality. 2nd ed. Nona Starr. LC 96-24806. 320p. (C). 1996. 47.00 (*0-13-228669-6*) P-H.

Viewpoint Tips & Tricks. Terry Heiney. Ed. by Jesse Benst. (Illus.). 250p. 1990. pap. 29.95 (*1-878567-04-7*) D A Pub.

***Viewpoints.** O'neill. Date not set. pap. text ed. write for info. (*0-582-55210-9*, Pub. by Longman UK) Longman.

Viewpoints: A Guide to Conflict Resolution & Decision Making for Adolescents. Nancy G. Guerra et al. LC 95-69160. 160p. (Orig.). 1995. teacher ed., pap. text ed. 13.95 (*0-87822-358-4*, 4847) Res Press.

UV

Viewpoints: Exploring the Reformed Vision - Selected Readings. Ed. by James D. Bratt. LC 92-18723. 1992. 10.10 (*1-56212-024-7*) CRC Pubns.

Viewpoints: Nonfiction Selections. Ed. by Fox. 1991. pap. 10.60 (*0-8092-3992-2*) Contemp Bks.

***Viewpoints: Perspectives of Faith & Christian Nurture.** H. Edward Everding, Jr. et al. 160p. (Orig.). 1998. pap. 15.00 (*1-56338-222-9*) TPI PA.

Viewpoints: Reading Worth Thinking & Writing About. W. Royce Adams. 512p. (C). 1993. pap. text ed. 29.56 (*0-669-27366-X*) HM College Div.

***Viewpoints: Readings Worth Thinking & Writing About.** 2nd ed. W. Royce Adams. (C). 1993. teacher ed., text ed. 2.66 (*0-669-27369-4*) HM College Div.

Viewpoints: The Library of Congress Selection of Pictorial Treasures. Ed. by Alan Fern & Milton Kaplan. LC 76-5442. (Illus.). 1976. 15.95 (*0-405-08106-5*) Ayer.

Viewpoints Vol. 2, Vol. 2. Contemporary Book Editors. 1994. pap. 10.60 (*0-8092-3647-8*) Contemp Bks.

Viewpoints in Biology, 4 vols., 1. Ed. by J. D. Carthy & C. L. Duddington. LC 63-4816. pap. 75.00 (*0-317-42212-X*, 2025766) Bks Demand.

Viewpoints in Biology, 4 vols., 2. Ed. by J. D. Carthy & C. L. Duddington. LC 63-4816. pap. 64.50 (*0-317-42213-8*) Bks Demand.

Viewpoints in Biology, 4 vols., 3. Ed. by J. D. Carthy & C. L. Duddington. LC 63-4816. pap. 67.50 (*0-317-42214-6*) Bks Demand.

Viewpoints in Biology, 4 vols., 4. Ed. by J. D. Carthy & C. L. Duddington. LC 63-4816. pap. 66.50 (*0-317-42215-4*) Bks Demand.

***Viewpoints in Geographical Teaching.** Ed. by Walford. Date not set. pap. text ed. write for info. (*0-582-08449-0*, Pub. by Longman UK) Longman.

Viewpoints of a Commodity Trader. Roy W. Longstreet. 160p. 1986. reprint ed. pap. 14.95 (*0-934380-14-7*, 4) Traders Pr.

Viewpoints of Stanley Marcus: A Ten-Year Perspective. Stanley Marcus. LC 95-1451. 261p. 1995. 24.95 (*0-929398-86-6*) UNTX Pr.

Viewpoints on Folklife: Looking at the Overlooked. Warren E. Roberts. Ed. by Simon J. Bronner. LC 87-22710. (American Material Culture & Folklife Ser.). (Illus.). 350p. reprint ed. pap. 94.40 (*0-8357-1849-2*, 2070758) Bks Demand.

Viewpoints on Supply Side Economics. Thomas J. Hailstones. (C). 1983. pap. text ed. 30.00 (*0-8359-8386-2*, Reston) P-H.

***Views.** annuals 24.00 (*0-614-23198-1*) RID Pubns.

Views. Edward Dorn. Ed. by Donald Allen. LC 79-25498. (Writing Ser.: No. 40). 144p. 1980. 12.00 (*0-87704-050-8*) Four Seasons Foun.

Views. Enslin. 1973. 16.00 (*0-685-36866-1*); pap. 8.00 (*0-685-36867-X*) Elizabeth Pr.

Views. 2nd ed. Roger Dean. LC 92-62867. (Illus.). 156p. 1993. pap. 28.95 (*1-56640-448-7*) Pomegranate Calif.

Views About Hamlet & Other Essays. Albert H. Tolman. LC 78-177468. reprint ed. 34.50 (*0-404-06477-9*) AMS Pr.

Views & Interviews on Journalism. Ed. by Charles F. Wingate. LC 78-125724. (American Journalists Ser.). 1977. reprint ed. 26.95 (*0-405-01707-3*) Ayer.

Views & Reviews, 2 Vols in 1. Havelock Ellis. LC 79-111829. (Essay Index Reprint Ser.). 1977. 31.95 (*0-8369-1606-9*) Ayer.

Views & Reviews. Henry James. LC 68-22101. (Essay Index Reprint Ser.). 1977. 18.95 (*0-8369-0566-0*) Ayer.

Views & Reviews. Henry James. LC 79-98026. reprint ed. 24.50 (*0-404-03547-7*) AMS Pr.

Views & Reviews. Henry James. (BCL1-PR English Literature Ser.). 241p. 1992. reprint ed. lib. bdg. 79.00 (*0-7812-7053-7*) Rprt Serv.

Views & Reviews: Golf Clubs in the Trade Press. Peter Georgiady. (Illus.). 172p. (Orig.). 1996. 50.00 (*1-886752-05-2*); pap. 25.00 (*1-886752-06-0*) Airlie Hall Pr.

Views & Values: Diverse Readings on Universal Themes. Ed. by Kari Sayers. LC 95-3686. 244p. 1996. pap. 26.95 (*0-534-23568-9*) Wadsworth Pub.

Views & Varieties of Automaticity. Ed. by Donelson E. Dulany & Gordon D. Logan. (Special Issue of the American Journal of Psychology Ser.: Vol. 105, No. 2). 160p. 1992. pap. text ed. 12.50 (*0-252-06266-3*) U of Ill Pr.

Views & Viewmakers of Urban America: Lithographs of Towns & Cities in the United States & Canada, Notes on the Artists & Publishers, & a Union Catalog of Their Work, 1825-1925. John W. Reps. LC 83-6495. (Illus.). 588p. 1984. text ed. 89.50 (*0-8262-0416-3*) U of Mo Pr.

Views Beyond the Border Country: Raymond Williams & Cultural Politics. Ed. by Dennis L. Dworkin & Leslie G. Roman. LC 92-11709. (Critical Social Thought Ser.). 352p. (C). (gr. 13). 1992. pap. 17.95 (*0-415-90276-2*, A4262, Routledge NY) Routledge.

Views Expressed in This Book. Mark Sonnenfeld. 36p. pap. 3.00 (*1-887379-00-2*) M Sonnenfeld.

Views from a French Farmhouse. Photos by Carey More. (Illus.). 144p. 1992. pap. 13.95 (*0-943955-55-6*, Trafalgar Sq Pub) Trafalgar.

Views from a Mountain...& Other Stories. Janet R. Harrison. (Orig.). 1996. pap. write for info. (*1-57553-286-7*) Watermrk Pr.

Views from a Pier: Visions of Hope, Dreams, Awareness, & Peace. Carol O. Campbell & Griffin O. Campbell. Ed. by Janet Potter. LC 95-74760. (Illus.). 181p. (Orig.). 1995. pap. 16.00 (*1-880439-05-0*) PERQ Pubns.

Views from a Tortured Libido. Robert Williams. 1993. pap. 24.95 (*0-86719-399-9*) Last Gasp.

Views from a Window: Conversations with Gore Vidal. Ed. by Robert J. Stanton & Gore Vidal. 320p. 1980. lib. bdg. 14.95 (*0-8184-0302-0*) Carol Pub Group.

Views from Abroad. Adam D. Weinberg et al. (Illus.). 96p. 1995. pap. 29.95 (*0-8109-6819-3*) Abrams.

Views from Abroad: European Perspectives on American Art I. Rudi Fuchs & Adam D. Weinberg. LC 95-16525. 1995. 27.50 (*0-87427-096-0*) Whitney Mus.

***Views from Abroad: European Perspectives on American Art 3 American Realities.** Nicholas Serota et al. (Illus.). 128p. 1997. pap. 29.95 (*0-8109-6826-6*) Abrams.

Views from Abroad Vol. II: European Perspectives on American Art. (Illus.). 1996. pap. write for info. (*0-87427-101-0*) Whitney Mus.

Views from Abroad 1, 1950-1980: The Spectator Book of Travel Writing. Ed. by Philip Marsden-Smedley & Jeffery Klinke. 387p. 1989. 21.95 (*1-85089-330-6*, Pub. by ISIS UK) Transaction Pubs.

Views from Abroad 2: European Perspectives on American Art. Adam D. Weinberg & Jean-Christophe Ammann. (Illus.). 128p. 1996. pap. 29.95 (*0-8109-6822-3*) Abrams.

Views from Asian California, 1920-1965: An Illustrated History. Michael D. Brown. (Illus.). 80p. (Orig.). 1992. pap. write for info. (*0-9633968-0-3*) M Brown.

Views from Jade Terrace: Chinese Women Artists, 1300-1912. Marsha S. Weidner. LC 88-80498. (Illus.). 231p. 1988. 45.00 (*0-936260-21-1*); pap. 30.00 (*0-936260-22-X*) Ind Mus Art.

Views from the Apache Frontier: Report on the Northern Provinces of New Spain. Jose Cortes. Ed. by Elizabeth A. John. Tr. by John Wheat. LC 88-40543. (Illus.). 184p. 1994. pap. 12.95 (*0-8061-2609-4*) U of Okla Pr.

Views from the Back of the Bus During WWII & Beyond. Dempsey J. Travis. (Illus.). 301p. 1995. 23.75 (*0-941484-24-6*) Urban Res Pr.

Views from the Education Underground. Zach J. Clements. (Illus.). 125p. 1989. 15.00 (*0-9607256-8-7*) Rich Pub Co.

Views from the Heart. Patricia Edwards. 1990. 5.00 (*1-878255-07-X*) Heartfelt Pr.

Views from the Island. deluxe ed. Charles E. Wadsworth. LC 78-52619. (Illus.). 1978. boxed 75.00 (*0-930954-06-8*) Tidal Pr.

Views from the Island. rev. ed. Charles E. Wadsworth. LC 78-52619. (Illus.). 1978. 10.00 (*0-930954-05-X*) Tidal Pr.

Views from the Mother Lode, Vol. I. Kurt House. 47p. 1992. pap. 25.00 (*0-9638947-2-2*) Three Riv Pub.

Views from the Mother Lode, Vol. II. Kurt House. 54p. 1993. pap. 25.00 (*0-9638947-3-0*) Three Riv Pub.

Views from the Mother Lode, Vol. III. Kurt House. 46p. 1994. pap. 25.00 (*0-9638947-4-9*) Three Riv Pub.

Views from the Mother Lode, Vol. IV. Kurt House. 30p. 1995. pap. 25.00 (*0-9638947-5-7*) Three Riv Pub.

Views from the Real World: Early Talks of G. I. Gurdjieff. G. I. Gurdjieff. 288p. 1991. pap. 12.95 (*0-14-019064-3*, Arkana) Viking Penguin.

Views from the Real World: Early Talks, 1918-1934. G. I. Gurdjieff. (C). 1975. pap. 11.95 (*0-525-48251-2*, Dutton) NAL-Dutton.

Views from the Road: A Community Guide for Assessing Rural Historic Landscapes. David H. Copps. (Orig.). 1995. pap. text ed. 25.00 (*1-55963-412-X*) Island Pr.

***Views from the Tightrope: Balancing Your Passion for Life & Your Fear of Change.** Mitch Bobrow. 144p. (Orig.). 1997. pap. 12.95 (*0-943914-84-1*) Larson Pubns.

Views from the Top: Establishing the Foundation for the Future of Business. Jerome M. Rosow. LC 84-10127. 224p. 1985. reprint ed. pap. 63.90 (*0-7837-9913-6*, 2060639) Bks Demand.

Views from the Trade. Chicago Board of Trade, Education Department Staff. (Readings in Futures Markets Ser.: Bk. 3). 1985. pap. 10.00 (*0-317-46967-3*, 52-37) Chicago Bd Trade.

Views from the Weaving Mountain: Selected Essays in Poetics & Anthropology. Nathaniel Tarn. LC 91-13437. (Studies in Twentieth-Century American Poetry & Poetics Ser.). 371p. (Orig.). 1991. pap. 19.95 (*0-9629172-3-0*) U of NM Pr.

Views from Within: Contemporary Views of the Figure Within an Interior. Cheryl Hahn. 31p. 1989. pap. 5.00 (*0-89792-125-9*) Ill St Museum.

Views from Within: The Japanese American Evacuation & Resettlement Study. Intro. by Yuji Ichioka. 300p. (Orig.). 1989. pap. 12.95 (*0-934052-12-3*) UCLA Asian Am Studies Ctr.

Views in Texas, Eighteen Ninety-Five to Ninety-Six. Henry Stark & A. C. Greene. (Illus.). 120p. 1974. 20.00 (*0-88426-039-9*) Encino Pr.

Views of a Vanishing Frontier. John C. Ewers et al. (Illus.). 150p. (Orig.). 1984. 29.95 (*0-936364-12-2*) Joslyn Art.

Views of Alabama in Nineteenth Century Illustrated Newspapers: From Harper's Weekly, Frank Leslie's Illustrated Newspaper, New-York Illustrated News, the Illustrated London News, Ballou's Pictorial Drawing-Room Companion, Demorest's New-York Illustrated News & Gleason's Pictorial Drawing-Room Companion. Joseph J. Forbes. LC 94-42033. (Illus.). 1994. 5.00 (*0-942301-23-4*) Birm Pub Lib.

Views of American Constitutional Law: Its Bearing Upon American Slavery. William Goodell. LC 78-138337. (Black Heritage Library Collection). 1977. 23.95 (*0-8369-8729-2*) Ayer.

Views of American Landscapes. Ed. by Mick Gidley & Robert Lawson-Peebles. (Illus.). 200p. (C). 1990. text ed. 64.95 (*0-521-36435-3*) Cambridge U Pr.

Views of American Slavery, Taken a Century Ago. Anthony Benezet. LC 78-82171. (Anti-Slavery Crusade in America Ser.). 1975. reprint ed. 21.95 (*0-405-00610-1*) Ayer.

Views of an Early Bird. Edmund C. Lynch. Ed. by Ed Eakin. (Illus.). 304p. 1990. 19.95 (*0-89015-730-8*) Sunbelt Media.

Views of Berlin. Ed. by Gerhard Kirchhoff. 310p. 1989. 47.50 (*0-8176-3380-4*) Birkhauser.

Views of Christian Nurture & Subjects Related Thereto. Horace Bushnell. LC 74-23297. 264p. 1975. reprint ed. lib. bdg. 50.00 (*0-8201-1147-3*) Schol Facsimiles.

Views of Clytemnestra, Ancient & Modern. Ed. by Sally MacEwen. LC 89-28420. (Studies in Comparative Literature: Vol. 9). (Illus.). 154p. 1990. lib. bdg. 69.95 (*0-88946-627-0*) E Mellen.

Views of Eighteenth Century Russia. (Eighteeth Century World Ser.). (Illus.). 224p. 1991. 24.99 (*0-517-69949-4*) Random Hse Value.

Views of Jeopardy. Jack Gilbert. LC 72-144762. (Yale Series of Younger Poets: No. 58). reprint ed. 18.00 (*0-404-53858-4*) AMS Pr.

Views of Louisiana. Henry M. Brachenridge. (Works of Henry Marie Brackenridge). 1989. reprint ed. lib. bdg. 79.00 (*0-7812-2027-0*) Rprt Serv.

Views of Mahlathi: Writings of a Black South African. Allison Wessels & George Champion. Ed. by Maynard W. Swanson. Tr. by A. T. Cope & Eric R. Dahle. (Killie Champbell Africana Library Translation Ser.: No. 2). 236p. 1983. 17.95 (*0-86980-312-3*, Pub. by Univ Natal Pr SA) Intl Spec Bk.

Views of Nature. Alexander Von Humboldt. Tr. by E. C. Otte & Henry G. Bohn from GER. LC 74-26302. (History, Philosophy & Sociology of Science Ser.). 1975. reprint ed. 40.95 (*0-405-06626-0*) Ayer.

Views of Our Heavenly Home. Andrew J. Davis. 290p. 1970. reprint ed. spiral bd. 14.00 (*0-7873-0252-X*) Hlth Research.

***Views of Our Historic District - Galena, Illinois.** Susan Pettey. (Illus.). 72p. (Orig.). 1996. pap. 10.95 (*0-9653052-0-1*) Gear Hse.

***Views of Rome: From the Thomas Ashby Collection in the Vatican Library.** Raymond Keaveney. Ed. by Leonard E. Boyle et al. LC 87-63617. (Illus.). 304p. 1988. 67.50 (*1-870248-15-5*) Scala Books.

Views of Rome Then & Now. Giovanni B. Piranesi & Herschel Levit. (Illus.). 96p. (Orig.). 1976. pap. 14.95 (*0-486-23339-1*) Dover.

Views of Salem History. Dale E. Shaffer. (Illus.). 75p. (Orig.). 1985. pap. 4.25 (*0-915060-22-1*) D E Shaffer.

Views of Society & Manner in America. Francis D'Arusmont. 1988. reprint ed. lib. bdg. 75.00 (*0-7812-0290-6*) Rprt Serv.

Views of Society & Manners in America. Frances W. D'Arusmont. Ed. by Paul R. Baker. LC 63-10878. 317p. reprint ed. pap. 90.40 (*0-317-10071-8*, 2002996) Bks Demand.

Views of Society & Manners in the North of Ireland: Letters Written in the Year 1818. John Gamble. LC 77-87688. 1977. reprint ed. 57.50 (*0-404-16487-0*) AMS Pr.

Views of Spaceship Earth. Stan Proper. 1985. 3.00 (*0-932593-02-X*) Black Bear.

***Views of the Future.** unabridged ed. (Next-Generation Manufacturing Project: Vol. IV). 19p. (Orig.). 1997. pap. 20.00 (*1-885166-25-7*, NGM-16) Agility Forum.

Views of the Green: Presentations from New Directions for the Conservation of Parks; An International Working Conference. Ed. by Paul C. Pritchard. 154p. 1985. 14.95 (*0-940091-14-3*); pap. 9.95 (*0-940091-13-5*) Natl Parks & Cons.

Views of the Past: Essays in Old World Prehistory & Paleoanthropology. Ed. by Leslie G. Freeman. (World Anthropology Ser.). (Illus.). xii, 466p. 1978. 58.50 (*90-279-7670-8*) Mouton.

***Views of the Pearl River Delta: Macau, Canton & Hong Kong.** William R. Sargent. (Illus.). 239p. (CHI & ENG.). 1997. pap. 45.00 (*962-215-147-7*, PEMP219) Peabody Essex Mus.

Views of the Present...Visions of the Past. Randy M. Olson. Ed. by William N. Kremer. (Illus.). 225p. (Orig.). 1984. pap. text ed. 22.50 (*0-318-03518-9*) Gazette Print.

Views of the Royal Pavilion. John Nash. (Illus.). 128p. 1992. 9.98 (*1-55859-340-3*, Cross Riv Pr) Abbeville Pr.

Views of Trinidad. Michel J. Cazabon. (Illus.). reprint ed. 80.00 (*0-910938-92-X*) McGilvery.

Views of Venice by Canaletto. Antonio Canaletto. (Illus.). pap. 9.95 (*0-486-22705-7*) Dover.

Views of Windsor: Watercolours by Thomas & Paul Sandby. Jane Roberts. (Illus.). 144p. 1995. 40.00 (*1-85894-020-6*, Pub. by Merrell Holberton Pubs UK) U of Wash Pr.

Views of Women's Lives in Western Tradition: Frontiers of the Past & the Future. Ed. by Frances R. Keller. LC 89-78313. (Women's Studies: Vol. 5). (Illus.). 792p. 1989. lib. bdg. 139.95 (*0-88946-123-6*) E Mellen.

Views on Ericksonian Brief Therapy, Process & Action. Ed. by Stephen R. Lankton et al. LC 91-16001. (Ericksonian Monographs: No. 8). 128p. 1991. text ed. 28.95 (*0-87630-646-6*) Brunner-Mazel.

Views on Individualism: Presentations. Israel M. Kirzner et al. Ed. & Intro. by Donna C. Charron. 92p. (Orig.). 1986. pap. 5.00 (*0-9616369-0-4*) St Louis Human.

Views on Phrase Structure. Katherine Leffel & Denis Bouchard. (Studies in Natural Language & Linguistic Theory). 240p. (C). 1991. lib. bdg. 121.50 (*0-7923-1295-3*) Kluwer Ac.

Views on the News: The Media & Public Opinion. Ed. by Colin Jones et al. LC 93-43679. (Illus.). 288p. (C). 1995. 35.00 (*0-8147-3510-X*) NYU Pr.

Views on U. S. Economic & Business History: Molding the Mixed Enterprise Economy. Ed. by Jack Blicksilver. 559p. 1985. pap. 35.00 (*0-88406-165-5*, RM95) GA St U Busn Pr.

Views Poetic And Other Portraits. Washington. 184p. (C). 1993. pap. text ed. 9.95 (*1-883069-01-7*) NESB Pubs.

Views Without Rooms. Elaine Equi. 52p. (Orig.). 1989. pap. 5.95 (*0-937815-28-4*) Hanuman Bks.

Vig. John Lescroart. 304p. 1992. mass mkt. 4.50 (*0-440-20986-2*) Dell.

Vig & Wild Card. Jack Dolphin & Ted Fitzgerald. Ed. by Gary Lovisi. (Gryphon Double Novel Ser.: No. 1). (Illus.). 50p. (Orig.). 1991. pap. 5.95 (*0-936071-20-6*, Gryp Grap Nov) Gryphon Pubns.

Vigencia Politica & Literaria De Martin Morua Delgado. Aleyda T. Portuondo. (Coleccion Cuba y Sus Jueces). 1978. pap. 2.00 (*0-89729-205-7*) Ediciones.

***Vigil.** Morris Panych. 80p. 1997. pap. 10.95 (*0-88922-365-3*) LPC InBook.

***Vigil.** Alan Shapiro. LC 97-3247. 1997. 19.95 (*0-226-75034-5*) U Ch Pr.

Vigil. M. L. Sullivan. 1995. 15.95 (*0-533-11480-2*) Vantage.

Vigil. Wendy M. Wright. LC 91-67168. 176p. (Orig.). 1992. pap. 9.95 (*0-8358-0661-8*) Upper Room Bks.

Vigil: A Novel. Elisabeth Y. Bruehl. LC 82-17160. 175p. 1983. reprint ed. pap. 49.90 (*0-608-00875-3*, 2061669) Bks Demand.

Vigil: Poems. Margaret Gibson. LC 93-12336. viii, 114p. 1993. pap. 11.95 (*0-8071-1868-0*); text ed. 19.95 (*0-8071-1867-2*) La State U Pr.

Vigil: Poems. C. K. Williams. LC 96-17253. 96p. 1996. 18.00 (*0-374-22653-9*) FS&G.

Vigil for a Stranger. Kitty B. Florey. 224p. (Orig.). 1995. pap. 13.95 (*0-913089-43-5*) Broken Moon.

Vigil in Benicarlo. Manuel Azana. Ed. by Josephine Stewart & Paul Stewart. LC 81-65339. (Illus.). 136p. 1982. 24.50 (*0-8386-3093-6*) Fairleigh Dickinson.

Vigil of Brunhild: A Narrative Poem. Frederic Manning. LC 90-26796. 76p. 1990. reprint ed. lib. bdg. 49.95 (*0-7734-9986-5*) E Mellen.

Vigil of Faith & Other Poems. Charles F. Hoffman. (Notable American Authors Ser.). 1992. reprint ed. lib. bdg. 75.00 (*0-7812-3134-5*) Rprt Serv.

Vigil of Holy Nativity: The Order of Great Compline & Matins, & Music for the Divine Liturgy. Ed. by Timothy Clader. Tr. by Laurence Campbell & Isaac E. Lambertsen from SLA. 185p. 1996. 35.00 (*0-912927-68-2*, D034) St John Kronstadt.

Vigil of the Wounded. Philip Y. Minthorn. Ed. by Maurice Kenny & Josh Gosciak. (Illus.). 60p. (Orig.). (C). 1987. pap. 5.95 (*0-936556-15-3*) Contact Two.

Vigil Service & Evening Prayer: Leaders' Edition. 132p. 1989. pap. 6.95 (*0-8146-1503-1*) Liturgical Pr.

Vigil Service & Evening Prayer: People's Edition. 48p. 1989. pap. 0.95 (*0-8146-1502-3*) Liturgical Pr.

Vigilance: The Problem of Sustained Attention. C. M. Stroh. 1971. 52.00 (*0-08-016711-X*, Pub. by Pergamon Repr UK) Franklin.

***Vigilance & Vengeance: NGOs Preventing Ethnic Conflict in Divided Societies.** World Peace Foundation Staff. Ed. by Robert I. Rotberg. 250p. 1996. 38.95 (*0-8157-7588-1*); pap. 16.95 (*0-8157-7587-3*) Brookings.

Vigilant God: Providence in the Thought of Augustine, Aquinas, Calvin, & Barth. Horton Davies. LC 92-13701. 176p. (C). 1992. text ed. 35.95 (*0-8204-1496-4*) P Lang Pubng.

Vigilant One. Jo Slade. 64p. 9600. pap. 12.95 (*1-897648-32-4*, Pub. by Poolbeg Pr IE) Dufour.

Vigilante Coffin. John Legg. 304p. 1993. mass mkt. 3.50 (*0-8217-4228-0*, Zebra Kensgtn) Kensgtn Pub Corp.

Vigilante Days & Ways. rev. ed. Nathaniel P. Langford. (Sweetgrass Bks.). 352p. 1996. pap. 14.95 (*1-56037-038-6*) Am Wrld Geog.

Vigilante Days & Ways. Nathaniel P. Langford. LC 71-160979. (Select Bibliographies Reprint Ser.). 1977. reprint ed. 42.95 (*0-8369-5847-0*) Ayer.

Vigilante Days & Ways, 2 Vols, Set. Nathaniel P. Langford. LC 76-156021. reprint ed. 95.00 (*0-404-09121-0*) AMS Pr.

Vigilante Days at Virginia City. Fred Lockley. 21p. reprint ed. pap. 2.95 (*0-8466-0146-X*, SJS146) Shorey.

Vigilante Justice. Will Camp. 240p. 1996. mass mkt. 2.50 (*0-06-101119-3*, Harp PBks) HarpC.

Vigilante Viscount. Bess Willingham. 1995. pap. 4.50 (*0-8217-5174-3*) NAL-Dutton.

Vigilantes in Gold Rush San Francisco. Robert M. Senkewicz. LC 83-40284. (Illus.). 288p. 1985. 42.50 (*0-8047-1230-1*) Stanford U Pr.

***Vigilantes of Christendom: History of the Phineas Priesthood.** Richard K. Hoskins. 432p. 1997. pap. 15.00 (*1-881867-05-6*) Virginia Pub.

Vigilantes of Montana. Thomas J. Dimsdale. LC 53-9887. (Western Frontier Library: No. 1). 1977. reprint ed. pap. 12.95 (*0-8061-1379-0*) U of Okla Pr.

Vigilantes Ride in 1882. Herbert Stevens. 20p. 1994. pap. 7.50 (*0-87770-148-2*) Ye Galleon.

Vigilantism: Political History of Private Power in America. William C. Culberson. LC 89-26555. (Contributions in Criminology & Penology Ser.: No. 28). (Illus.). 184p. 1990. text ed. 49.95 (*0-313-27238-7*, CUV/); pap. text ed. 16.95 (*0-275-93548-5*, B3548) Greenwood.

Vigilantism & the State in Latin America: Essays on Extra-Legal Violence. Ed. by Martha D. Huggins. LC 90-28185. 280p. 1991. text ed. 55.00 (*0-275-93476-4*, C3476, Praeger Pubs) Greenwood.

Vigiles of Imperial Rome. P. K. Reynolds. 1996. pap. 15.00 (*0-89005-552-1*) Ares.

Vigils, Selected Poems. Jeff D. Marion. LC 89-17896. 1989. pap. 9.95 (*0-913239-62-3*) Appalach Consortium.

Vigne et le Vin: Eurolexique. 3rd ed. D. Escarpit. 82p. (ENG, FRE, GER, ITA & SPA.). 1985. pap. 17.95 (*0-7859-4853-8*) Fr & Eur.

Vigner Dictionnaire des Chateaux de France. Bernard De Montgolfier. 250p. (FRE.). pap. 135.00 (*0-686-56837-0*, M-6615) Fr & Eur.

Vigneron dans Sa Vigne see Oeuvres

Vigneron Dans Sa Vigne see Oeuvres

Vignette. Ed. by Dawn Baillie & Deborah Clark. 1995. pap. text ed. 9.95 (*1-887236-01-5*) Vignette Pr.

***Vignette.** Valerie King. 320p. 1997. mass mkt. 4.99 (*0-8217-5620-6*, Zebra Kensgtn) Kensgtn Pub Corp.

An Asterisk (*) at the beginning of an entry indicates that the title is appearing in BIP for the first time.

Vignettes. 2nd ed. Herron. (College French Ser.). 1988. teacher ed., pap. 2.95 (*0-8384-3685-4*) Heinle & Heinle.

*__Vignettes: Auto-Biographical Comix of Valentino.__ Jim Valentino. (Illus.). 100p. (Orig.). (YA). 1997. pap. 7.95 (*1-887279-40-7*) Image Comics.

Vignettes from the Shadows: Glimpses of Norfolk's Past. Ed. by Calvert W. Tazewell. LC 90-80457. (Illus.). 124p. (Orig.). 1992. pap. 14.00 (*1-878515-15-2*) W S Dawson.

Vignettes of Legal History: Second Series. Julius J. Marke. (Illus.). xiv, 274p. 1977. lib. bdg. 15.00 (*0-8377-0833-8*) Rothman.

Vignettes of Life: Experiences & Self-Perceptions of New Canadian Women. Catharine E. Warren. 128p. (Orig.). 1986. pap. 10.95 (*0-920490-60-3*) Temeron Bks.

Vignettes of Louisiana History. Louisiana Pen Women Staff. 25.00 (*0-87511-068-1*) Claitors.

Vignettes of Manhattan. Brander Matthews. LC 70-90587. (Short Story Index Reprint Ser.). 1977. 20.95 (*0-8369-3070-3*) Ayer.

Vignettes of Old Hawaii. David Free. (Illus.). 304p. (Orig.). 1993. pap. text ed. 12.95 (*0-9637946-0-4*) Free Advice.

Vignettes of Philosophy: Thirty-Five Vital Subjects. Homer T. Rosenberger. LC 77-71070. (Horizons of the Humanities Ser.: Vol. 3). 258p. 1977. lib. bdg. 9.00 (*0-917264-01-0*) Rose Hill.

Vignettes of the Beam in a Nigger's Eye. Madeleine S. Gary. 126p. (Orig.). 1982. reprint ed. pap. 8.95 (*0-913459-00-3*) New Writers Guild.

Vigny et sa Fortune Litteraire. Flottes. 10.50 (*0-685-37143-3*) Fr & Eur.

Vigorous Spirit of Enterprise: Merchants & Economic Development in Revolutionary Philadelphia. Thomas M. Doerflinger. LC 84-28036. (Institute of Early American History & Culture Ser.). (Illus.). xvi, 414p. 1986. 49.95 (*0-8078-1653-1*) U of NC Pr.

Vigour of Prophecy: A Study of Virgil's Aeneid. Elizabeth Henry. 240p. (C). 1990. 24.95 (*0-8093-1591-2*) S Ill U Pr.

Vihori Sutrasnjice. Milos Acin-Kosta. 105p. (Orig.). (SER.). 1957. pap. 1.00 (*0-317-61885-7*) Ravnogorski.

VIII Olympiad: Paris 1924, St. Moritz 1928. LC 95-52591. (Olympic Century Ser.: Vol. 8). 1996. write for info. (*1-888383-08-9*) Wld Sport Resch.

Viipuri Library: Alvar Aalto (1927-1935) Michael Spens. (Historical Buildings Monographs). (Illus.). 96p. (Orig.). 1994. pap. 25.00 (*1-85490-366-7*) Academy Ed UK.

Vija Celmins. Vija Clemins & Chuck Close. Ed. by William S. Bartman. (Illus.). 64p. (Orig.). 1992. pap. text ed. 25.00 (*0-923183-08-6*) ART Pr CA.

Vija Celmins: A Survey. Vija Celmins. 1991. pap. 20.00 (*0-932499-38-4*) Lapis Pr.

Vija Celmins Vol. 1: A Survey Exhibition. Contrib. by Vija Celmins & Susan C. Larsen. LC 79-92204. (Illus.). 96p. (Orig.). 1980. pap. 16.00 (*0-911291-04-0*) Fellows Cont Art.

Vijaya Lakshmi Pandit. Ed. by Verinder Grover & Ranjana Arora. (C). 1993. text ed. 28.00 (*81-7100-458-X*, Pub. by Deep II) S Asia.

Vijayanagara. Burton Stein. (New Cambridge History of India Ser.: I: 2). (Illus.). 170p. (C). 1990. text ed. 49.95 (*0-521-26693-9*) Cambridge U Pr.

Vijayanagara Courtly Style. George Michell. (C). 1992. 44.00 (*81-85425-29-9*, Pub. by Manohar II) S Asia.

Vijayanagara Origin of the City & the Empire. N. Venkata Ramanayya. (C). 1990. 19.00 (*81-206-0545-4*, Pub. by Asian Educ Servs II) S Asia.

Vijnanabhairava or Divine Consciousness: A Treasury of 112 Types of Yoga. Jaideva Singh. (C). 1990. reprint ed. 16.50 (*81-208-0817-7*, Pub. by Motilal Banarsidass II) S Asia.

Vijnaptimatratasiddhi: Vimsatika with Introdution, Translation & Commentary. T. R. Sharma. vi, 119p. (C). 1993. 12.00 (*81-85133-87-5*, Pub. by Estrn Bk Linkers II) Nataraj Bks.

Viking. Fabio. 416p. (Orig.). 1994. mass mkt. 5.99 (*0-380-77048-2*) Avon.

Viking. Sue Margeson. LC 93-32593. (Eyewitness Bks.). (Illus.). 64p. (J). (gr. 5 up). 1994. 19.00 (*0-679-86002-9*); lib. bdg. 20.99 (*0-679-96002-3*) Knopf Bks Yng Read.

Viking. Margaret Moore. (Historical Ser.). 1993. mass mkt. 3.99 (*0-373-28800-X*, 1-28800-0) Harlequin Bks.

Viking Age, 2 vols, Set. Paul B. Du Chaillu. LC 75-118628. reprint ed. 155.00 (*0-404-02187-5*) AMS Pr.

Viking Age Archaeology in Britain & Ireland. Richard Hall. 1989. pap. 35.00 (*0-7478-0063-4*, Pub. by Shire UK) St Mut.

Viking Age Gold & Silver of Scotland (AD 850-1100) James Graham-Campbell. (Illus.). 274p. 1995. 75.00 (*0-948636-62-9*, 6629, Pub. by Natl Mus Scotland UK) A Schwartz & Co.

Viking-Age Hoards & Late Anglo-Saxon Coins. Kenneth Jonsson. (Illus.). 156p. (Orig.). 1986. pap. 66.50 (*91-7260-638-X*) Coronet Bks.

Viking Age in Caithness, Orkney & the North Atlantic. Ed. by Colleen E. Batey et al. (Illus.). 560p. 1995. pap. 26.00 (*0-7486-0632-7*, Pub. by Edinburgh U Pr UK) Col U Pr.

Viking Age in Caithness, Orkney, & the North Atlantic. Ed. by Christopher D. Morris et al. (Illus.). 528p. 1993. 45.00 (*0-7486-0430-8*, Pub. by Edinburgh U Pr UK) Col U Pr.

Viking America: The Norse Crossings & Their Legacy. James Robert Enterline. LC 76-175370. (Illus.). xix, 217p. 1972. 9.95 (*0-385-02585-8*) J R Enterline.

Viking & the Mars Landing. Gregory Vogt. (Missions in Space Ser.). (Illus.). 112p. (J). (gr. 4-6). 1991. lib. bdg. 16.90 (*1-878841-32-7*) Millbrook Pr.

Viking Art of War. Paddy Griffith. LC 95-15132. (Illus.). 224p. 1995. 34.95 (*1-85367-208-4*, Pub. by Greenhill Bks UK) Stackpole.

Viking Cards Deck/Book Set. Gudrun Bergmann. (Illus.). 148p. 1995. pap. 19.95 (*0-88079-239-6*, VKS99) US Games Syst.

Viking Children's World Atlas. Jacqueline Tivers & Michael Day. LC 84-675391. (Illus.). (J). (ps-7). 1985. pap. 5.99 (*0-14-031874-7*, Puffin) Puffin Bks.

Viking Children's World Atlas: An Introductory Atlas for Young People. Jacqueline Tivers & Michael Day. LC 83-675053. (Illus.). 48p. (J). (gr. 4-6). 1983. pap. 9.95 (*0-670-21791-3*) Viking Child Bks.

Viking Children's World Atlas: An Introductory Atlas for Young People. rev. ed. Jacqueline Tivers & Michael Day. LC 93-41434. (Illus.). 48p. (J). (gr. k-5). 1994. pap. 11.99 (*0-670-85481-6*) Viking Child Bks.

Viking Circus Block Books: Circus Parade Zoo-A Book in-a-Box with a Performing Picture, 3 vols., Set. Intervisional Communications Staff. LC 83-80225. (Viking Block Bks.). (Illus.). (J). (gr. 1-5). 1983. 10.95 (*0-685-42583-5*) Viking Child Bks.

Viking Colouring Book. Joy-Elizabeth Mitchell. 36p. 9600. pap. 9.95 (*0-946005-94-X*) Dufour.

Viking Enterprise. Sven A. Anderson. LC 77-158254. (Columbia University. Studies in the Social Sciences: No. 424). reprint ed. 22.50 (*0-404-51424-3*) AMS Pr.

Viking Explorers. Luigi Prunetti. LC 96-33. (Voyages of Discovery Ser.). (Illus.). 48p. (YA). (gr. 5 up). 1996. lib. bdg. 18.95 (*0-87226-486-6*) P Bedrick Bks.

Viking Explorers. Rebecca Stefoff. Ed. by William H. Goetzmann. (World Explorers Ser.). (Illus.). 112p. (YA). (gr. 5 up). 1993. lib. bdg. 19.95 (*0-7910-1295-6*) Chelsea Hse.

Viking Hersir. Mark Harrison. (Warrior Ser.). (Illus.). 64p. 1993. pap. 12.95 (*1-85532-318-4*, 9602, Pub. by Osprey UK) Stackpole.

Viking Jews. Ib N. Bamberger. (Illus.). 162p. 1990. reprint ed. pap. 9.95 (*1-871055-60-1*) Soncino Pr.

*__Viking Longboat.__ Fred Finney. LC 96-50173. (Mystery History Ser.). (Illus.). 32p. (YA). (gr. 3 up). 1997. lib. bdg. 17.90 (*0-7613-0601-3*, Copper Beech Bks) Millbrook Pr.

*__Viking Longboat.__ Fred Finney. LC 96-50173. (Mystery History Ser.). (Illus.). 32p. (J). (gr. 3 up). 1997. 9.95 (*0-7613-0590-4*, Copper Beech Bks) Millbrook Pr.

Viking Magic. Angela Wells. 1994. mass mkt. 2.99 (*0-373-11691-8*, 1-11691-2) Harlequin Bks.

Viking Marine, Special Journals, Simulation. 5th ed. Kenton E. Ross. (BA-Accounting-First Year Ser.). 1992. pap. 15.95 (*0-538-61277-0*) S-W Pub.

Viking Opera Guide. Ed. by Amanda Holden et al. (Illus.). 1312p. 1994. pap. 69.95 (*0-670-81292-7*, Viking) Viking Penguin.

Viking Poems on War & Peace: A Study in Skaldic Narrative. Russell G. Poole. (Medieval Texts & Translations Ser.: No. 8). 224p. 1991. text ed. 45.00 (*0-8020-5867-1*); pap. text ed. 14.95 (*0-8020-6789-1*) U of Toronto Pr.

Viking Raiders. Civardi Campbell. (Time Travelers Bks.). (J). (gr. 4-9). 1977. pap. 6.95 (*0-86020-085-X*, Usborne); lib. bdg. 14.95 (*0-88110-102-8*, Usborne) EDC.

*__Viking Saga of Harri Bristlebeard.__ Jonathan Stroud. LC 96-45024. (Illus.). (J). 1997. 14.99 (*0-7636-0270-1*) Candlewick Pr.

Viking Settler. Giovanni Caselli. LC 86-3302. (Everyday Life of Ser.). (Illus.). 32p. (J). (gr. 3-6). 1991. lib. bdg. 12.95 (*0-87226-104-2*) P Bedrick Bks.

Viking Ship. (Illus.). (J). (gr. 2-6). 5.95 (*0-7141-1674-2*, Pub. by Brit Mus UK) Parkwest Pubns.

Viking Ships. Ian Atkinson. LC 77-17510. (Cambridge Introduction to World History Topic Bks.). (Illus.). 48p. (YA). (gr. 7 up). 1979. pap. text ed. 10.95 (*0-521-21951-5*) Cambridge U Pr.

Viking Ships. John Lindow. (J). (gr. 1-9). 1992. pap. 5.95 (*0-88388-078-4*) Bellerophon Bks.

Viking Society for Northern Research. (Old-Lore Ser.: Nos. 1-75 in 14 vols.). reprint ed. write for info. (*0-404-60210-X*) AMS Pr.

Viking Street. Tolhurst. (J). 13.95 (*0-7136-3814-1*, 93341, Pub. by A&C Black UK) Talman.

Viking Symbol Mystery. Franklin W. Dixon. (Hardy Boys Ser.: Vol. 42). 180p. (J). (gr. 5-9). 1962. 5.95 (*0-448-08942-4*, G&D) Putnam Pub Group.

Viking Town. Fiona MacDonald. LC 95-1845. (Inside Story Ser.). (Illus.). 48p. (J). (gr. 5 up). 1995. lib. bdg. 18.95 (*0-87226-382-7*) P Bedrick Bks.

*__Viking Treasury of Children's Stories.__ 1997. 19.99 (*0-614-29142-9*) Viking Penguin.

*__Viking Treasury of Children's Stories.__ (J). 1997. pap. 19.99 (*0-670-87303-9*) Viking Penguin.

Viking World. Philippa Wingate. (Illustrated World History Ser.). (Illus.). 96p. (J). (gr. 5 up). 1994. pap. 11.95 (*0-7460-1398-1*, Usborne); lib. bdg. 19.95 (*0-88110-675-5*, Usborne) EDC.

*__Vikings.__ (History Ser.). (Illus.). (J). pap. 6.95 (*0-590-73880-1*) Scholastic Inc.

*__Vikings.__ Denise Allard. LC 96-46231. (Pictures of the Past Ser.). (Illus.). 32p. (J). (gr. 2 up). 1997. lib. bdg. 18.60 (*0-8368-1717-6*) Gareth Stevens Inc.

Vikings. Alaric Birkett. LC 85-72965. 72p. (J). (gr. 5-8). 1985. pap. 12.95 (*0-7175-1321-1*) Dufour.

Vikings. Alaric Birkett. 72p. (C). 1985. 45.00 (*0-685-33815-0*, Pub. by S Thornes Pubs UK) St Mut.

Vikings. Peter Chrisp. 1995. pap. 7.95 (*0-563-35259-0*, BBC-Parkwest) Parkwest Pubns.

Vikings. John D. Clare. LC 91-24146. (Illus.). 64p. (J). (gr. 2-7). 1996. pap. 9.00 (*0-15-201309-1*, Gulliver Bks) HarBrace.

Vikings. Ed. by John D. Clare. (Living History Ser.). (Illus.). 64p. (J). (gr. 2-7). 1992. 17.00 (*0-15-200512-9*, Gulliver Bks) HarBrace.

Vikings. Lee Gold. Ed. by John D. Ruemmler & Kevin Barrett. (Rolemaster Ser.). (Illus.). 112p. (Orig.). (C). 1989. pap. 13.00 (*1-55806-047-2*, 1030) Iron Crown Ent Inc.

Vikings. Ian Heath. (Elite Ser.: No. 3). (Illus.). 64p. pap. 12.95 (*0-85045-565-0*, 9402, Pub. by Osprey Pubng Ltd UK) Stackpole.

*__Vikings.__ Kathryn Hinds. LC 96-31067. (Cultures of the Past Ser.). (Illus.). 80p. (YA). (gr. 5 up). 1997. lib. bdg. 19.95 (*0-7614-0271-3*, Benchmark NY) Marshall Cavendish.

Vikings. Bob Italia. Ed. by Rosemary Walner. LC 90-82625. (Explorers of the Past & Present Ser.). (Illus.). 32p. (J). (gr. 4). 1990. lib. bdg. 11.96 (*0-939179-93-8*) Abdo & Dghtrs.

Vikings. Fiona MacDonald. (Insights Ser.). (Illus.). 60p. (J). (gr. 4 up). 1993. 15.95 (*0-8120-6375-9*) Barron.

Vikings. Marshall Editions Staff. LC 96-40059. (If You Were There Ser.). (J). 1997. 16.95 (*0-689-81198-5*) S&S Childrens.

Vikings. Hazel M. Martell. LC 91-507. (Worlds of the Past Ser.). (Illus.). 64p. (YA). (gr. 6 up). 1992. text ed. 14.95 (*0-02-762427-7*, Mac Bks Young Read) S&S Childrens.

Vikings. Robert Nicholson. LC 93-11956. (Journey into Civilization Ser.). (Illus.). 32p. (J). (gr. 3-7). 1994. 15.95 (*0-7910-2709-0*) Chelsea Hse.

Vikings. Robert Nicholson. LC 93-11956. (Journey into Civilization Ser.). (Illus.). 32p. (J). (gr. 3-7). 1994. pap. 7.95 (*0-7910-2733-3*) Chelsea Hse.

Vikings. Pamela Odijk. Ed. by Emily Easton. (Ancient World Ser.). (Illus.). 48p. (J). (gr. 5-8). 1990. 7.95 (*0-382-24269-6*); teacher ed., pap. 4.50 (*0-382-24283-1*); lib. bdg. 14.95 (*0-382-09893-5*) Silver Burdett Pr.

Vikings. Anne Pearson. (See Through History Ser.). (Illus.). 48p. (J). (gr. 3-7). 1994. pap. 17.99 (*0-670-85834-X*) Viking Child Bks.

Vikings. Tom Stainer & Harry Sutton. (Illus.). 32p. (J). (gr. 4-6). 1992. pap. 5.95 (*0-563-21356-6*, BBC-Parkwest) Parkwest Pubns.

Vikings. Ruth Thomson & Ruth Levy. LC 94-42247. (Footsteps in Time Ser.). (Illus.). 24p. (J). (ps-3). 1995. lib. bdg. 15.00 (*0-516-08059-8*) Childrens.

Vikings. David M. Wilson. (British Museum Activity Bks.). (Illus.). 16p. (J). 1995. pap. 5.95 (*0-500-27789-3*) Thames Hudson.

Vikings. Rachel Wright. LC 92-4618. (Craft Topics Ser.). (Illus.). 32p. (J). (gr. 5-8). 1993. lib. bdg. 19.10 (*0-531-14210-8*) Watts.

Vikings. rev. ed. Johannes Brondsted. 1960. pap. 10.95 (*0-14-020459-8*, Penguin Bks) Viking Penguin.

Vikings. Else Roesdahl. (Illus.). 368p. 1992. reprint ed. pap. 14.95 (*0-14-012561-2*, Penguin Bks) Viking Penguin.

Vikings: Adventures of Young Vikings in Jorvik. Robin Place. (Illus.). 52p. (J). (gr. 2-8). 1987. pap. text ed. 10.95 (*0-521-31572-7*) Cambridge U Pr.

Vikings: Lords of the Seas. Yves Cohat. (Discoveries Ser.). (Illus.). 176p. 1992. pap. 12.95 (*0-8109-2865-5*) Abrams.

Vikings: Raiders from the North. Ed. by Dale Brown. LC 93-14028. (Lost Civilizations Ser.). (Illus.). 168p. 1993. 19.95 (*0-8094-9895-2*); lib. bdg. 25.93 (*0-8094-9896-0*) Time-Life.

Vikings: With Stand-Up Scenes to Cut Out & Glue Together. Deborah Duncan. pap. 7.95 (*0-906212-81-2*, Pub. by Tarquin UK) Parkwest Pubns.

Vikings & Jorvik. Hazel M. Martell. LC 92-25215. (Hidden Worlds Ser.). (Illus.). 32p. (J). (gr. 5 up). 1993. lib. bdg. 13.95 (*0-87518-541-X*, Dillon Silver Burdett) Silver Burdett Pr.

Vikings & Surnames. Ed. by Kay Rogers. (C). 1989. pap. 35.00 (*1-85072-086-X*, Pub. by W Sessions UK) St Mut.

Vikings & Their Origins. David A. Wilson. LC 88-51523. (Illus.). 96p. (Orig.). 1989. pap. 14.95 (*0-500-27542-4*) Thames Hudson.

*__Vikings & Their Predecessors.__ Kate Gordon & Robert McGhee. (Illus.). 68p. 1981. pap. 12.95 (*0-660-10751-1*, Pub. by Can Mus Civil CN) U of Wash Pr.

Vikings Coloring Book. A. G. Smith. (Illus.). (J). (gr. k-3). 1988. pap. 2.95 (*0-486-25653-7*) Dover.

Vikings in Britain. Loyn. Date not set. 36.95 (*0-631-18711-1*) Blackwell Pubs.

Vikings in Britain. Henry Loyn. 1995. pap. 14.95 (*0-631-18712-X*) Blackwell Pubs.

Vikings in History. F. Donald Logan. 1991. pap. 19.95 (*0-04-446040-6*) Routledge Chapman & Hall.

Vikings in History. 2nd ed. F. Donald Logan. 224p. (C). 1992. pap. 17.95 (*0-415-08396-6*, Pub. by Tavistock UK) Routledge Chapman & Hall.

Vikings in Russia: Yngvar's Saga & Eymund's Saga. Ed. by Paul Edwards & S. H. Palsson. Tr. by S. H. Palsson. 176p. 1989. 30.00 (*0-85224-623-4*, Pub. by Edinburgh U Pr UK) Col U Pr.

*__Vikings in Scotland.__ Gordon Jarvie & Frances Jarvie. (Scottie Bks.). (Illus.). 40p. (J). 1998. pap. 8.95 (*0-11-495813-0*, Pub. by Statnry Ofc UK) Seven Hills Bk.

Vikings in the West. LC 82-187044. 86p. 1982. 12.00 (*0-318-17840-0*) Archaeological Inst.

Vikings in the West. Gwyn Jones et al. Ed. by Eleanor Guralnick. (Illus.). 95p. 1982. pap. 12.00 (*0-9609042-0-4*) Archaeol Chi.

Vikings of the Sunrise. Peter H. Buck. LC 84-22482. (Illus.). xiv, 339p. 1985. reprint ed. text ed. 69.50 (*0-313-24522-3*, BUVS, Greenwood Pr) Greenwood.

Viking's Prize. Tanya A. Crosby. 384p. (Orig.). 1994. mass mkt. 4.50 (*0-380-77457-7*) Avon.

Vikings Resource Book. (Sense of History Ser.). 1991. pap. text ed. 13.32 (*0-582-07313-8*) Longman.

*__Viking's Revenge, No. 124.__ Franklin W. Dixon. (YA). (gr. 6 up). 1997. mass mkt. 3.99 (*0-671-56124-3*, Archway) PB.

*__Vikings Treasure Chest.__ Fiona Macdonald. (Treasure Chest Ser.). (Illus.). 32p. (J). (gr. 3-8). 1997. 19.95 (*0-7624-0147-8*) Running Pr.

Viking's Woman. Heather X. Graham. 480p. (Orig.). 1990. mass mkt. 5.99 (*0-440-20670-7*) Dell.

Vikki Vanishes. Peni R. Griffin. LC 94-48340. (J). 1995. 15.00 (*0-689-80028-2*, McElderry) S&S Childrens.

Vikram & the Vampire, or Tales of the Hindu Diety. Vetalapancavimsati. Ed. by Isadel Burton. Tr. by Richard F. Burton. (Illus.). 264p. reprint ed. text ed. 23.00 (*0-685-13813-5*) Coronet Bks.

Vikramorvasiyam of Kalidasa. 11th ed. M. R. Kale. (C). 1991. reprint ed. pap. text ed. 9.00 (*81-208-0865-7*, Pub. by Motilal Banarsidass II) S Asia.

Viktor E. Frankl: Life with Meaning. William B. Gould. 250p. (C). 1993. pap. 26.95 (*0-534-19470-2*) Brooks-Cole.

*__Viktor Frankl-Recollections: An Autobiography.__ Viktor E. Frankl. Tr. by Joseph Fabry & Judith Fabry from GER. LC 96-48056. 138p. (C). 24.95 (*0-306-45410-6*) Plenum.

Viktor Frankl's Logotherapy: Personal Conscience & Global Concern Proceedings of the Fifth World Congress of Logotherapy. Ed. by Frederic Jones et al. 272p. 1986. pap. 12.95 (*0-917867-06-8*) V Frankl Inst.

Viktor Klimenko un Cosaque Lib. Birger Thureson. 288p. (FRE.). 1991. pap. 2.95 (*0-8297-1529-0*) Life Pubs Intl.

Viktor Lowenfeld Speaks on Art & Creativity. Viktor Lowenfeld. Ed. by National Art Education Association Staff. 64p. (C). 1968. pap. 10.00 (*0-937652-26-1*, 061-02244) Natl Art Ed.

Viktor, Vodka, & Raw Fish: The Last Crossing of the U. S. S. R. John M. Proctor. LC 94-60891. (Illus.). 300p. (Orig.). 1994. pap. 14.95 (*0-9639519-4-7*) Whitewing Pr.

Viktors Pupols, American Master. Larry Parr. Ed. by Robert B. Long. (Illus.). 78p. (Orig.). 1983. pap. 6.50 (*0-938650-31-9*) Thinkers Pr.

Vilain & Courtois: Transgressive Parody in French Literature of the Twelfth & Thirteenth Centuries. Kathryn Gravdal. LC 88-27730. (Regents Studies in Medieval Culture). (Illus.). 205p. 1989. reprint ed. pap. 58.50 (*0-7837-8880-0*, 2049591) Bks Demand.

Vile Acts. Dorothy McMillan. 400p. 1995. mass mkt. 4.99 (*0-8217-0100-2*, Zebra Kensgtn); mass mkt. 4.99 (*0-7860-0100-3*, Pinncle Kensgtn) Kensgtn Pub Corp.

Vile & the Holy: A Commentary on the Book of Daniel. Claude E. Ludy. LC 77-94874. (Illus.). 100p. (Orig.). (YA). 1978. pap. 5.00 (*0-9625164-0-6*) C E Ludy.

Vile Bodies. Evelyn Waugh. 1977. pap. 11.95 (*0-316-92611-6*) Little.

Vilfredo Pareto. Jonathan E. Turner. (Matters of Social Theory Ser.: Vol. 5). (Illus.). 160p. (C). 1987. 44.00 (*0-8039-2284-1*); pap. text ed. 18.95 (*0-8039-2285-X*) Sage.

Vilfredo Pareto, 1848-1923. Ed. by Mark Blaug. (Pioneers in Economics Ser.: Vol. 35). 400p. 1992. 135.00 (*1-85278-498-9*) E Elgar.

Vilhelm Hammershoi: And Danish Art at the Turn of the Century. Poul Vad. Tr. by Kenneth Tindall from DAN. (Illus.). 462p. (C). 1992. text ed. 80.00 (*0-300-04956-0*) Yale U Pr.

Vilhon Reach. Jim Butler. 1996. 15.95 (*0-7869-0400-3*) TSR Inc.

Villa. Paul Vangelisti. (Littoral Bks.). (Illus.). 88p. 1991. pap. 8.95 (*1-55713-054-X*) Sun & Moon CA.

Villa: Form & Ideology of Country Houses. James S. Ackerman. (A. W. Mellon Lectures in the Fine Arts, 1989: Vol. XXXV, No. 34). (Illus.). 304p. 1990. pap. text ed. 26.95 (*0-691-00295-9*) Princeton U Pr.

Villa & Cottage Architecture: The Style Book of the Hudson River School. Calvert Vaux. 1991. pap. 7.95 (*0-486-26757-1*) Dover.

Villa Aurore. J. M. Le Clezio. (Folio - Junior Ser.: No. 603). (Illus.). 112p. (FRE.). (J). (gr. 5-10). 1990. pap. 7.95 (*2-07-033603-4*) Schoenhof.

Villa d'Este at Tivoli. David Dernie. (Illus.). 128p. 1996. 50.00 (*1-85490-447-7*) Academy Ed UK.

*__Villa D'este Cookbook.__ Jean G. Salvadore. (Illus.). 136p. 1997. pap. 19.95 (*1-55670-657-X*) Stewart Tabori & Chang.

Villa in France. J. I. Stewart. 1983. 15.50 (*0-393-01646-3*) Norton.

Villa in the Life of Renaissance Rome. David R. Coffin. (Monographs in Art & Archaeology: No. XLII). (Illus.). 408p. 1979. reprint ed. pap. text ed. 29.95 (*0-691-00279-7*) Princeton U Pr.

Villa-Lobos. Lisa M. Peppercorn. (Illustrated Lives of the Great Composers Ser.). (Illus.). 144p. 1996. 14.95 (*0-7119-1688-8*, OP 45061) Omnibus NY.

Villa-Lobos. Simon Wright. (Oxford Studies of Composers). 160p. 1992. 65.00 (*0-19-315476-5*); pap. 26.00 (*0-19-315475-7*) OUP.

Villa-Lobos: Collected Studies by L. M. Peppercorn. Lisa M. Peppercorn. 200p. 1992. 62.95 (*0-85967-906-3*, Pub. by Scolar Pr UK) Ashgate Pub Co.

Villa-Lobos the Music: An Analysis of His Style. Lisa M. Peppercorn. Tr. by Stefan De Haan. 136p. 1992. 21.75 (*0-912483-36-9*) Pro-Am Music.

Villa Mairea. (Architecture in Detail Ser.). (Illus.). 60p. 1993. pap. 29.95 (*0-7148-2768-1*, Pub. by Phaidon Press UK) Chronicle Bks.

*__Villa Marini: A Family Saga.__ Gloria Montero. LC 97-15463. 320p. 1997. 23.00 (*0-88001-577-2*) Ecco Pr.

*__Villa Muller: A Work of Adolf Loos.__ Leslie Van Duzer & Kent Kleinman. (Illus.). 108p. 1997. pap. 19.95 (*1-56898-123-6*) Princeton Arch.

Villa of Flowers. large type ed. Mary Raymond. (Linford Romance Library). 288p. 1985. pap. 15.99 (*0-7089-6056-1*) Ulverscroft.

Villa of Mysteries: Pompeii Initiation Rites of Women. Katherine Bradway. 1982. pap. 5.00 (*0-317-13541-4*) C G Jung Frisco.

UV

Villa of Singing Water. large type ed. Angela Petron. (Linford Romance Library). 280p. 1988. pap. 15.99 (*0-7089-6537-7*, Linford) Ulverscroft.
***Villa Ottolenghi.** Carlo Scarpa. 1997. pap. 19.95 (*1-885254-50-4*) Monacelli Pr.
Villa Rosa. Richard Manton. (Orig.). 1989. mass mkt. 4.50 (*0-929654-13-7*, 47) Blue Moon Bks.
Villa Sara. Mancebo, pseud. LC 90-62235. 240p. (Orig.). 1990. 16.95 (*0-9626993-1-4*) Armadillo Niche.
Villa Taina de Boqueron: Excavation of an Early Taino Site in Puerto Rico. R. Christopher Goodwin & Jefferey B. Walker. LC 74-30903. (Illus.). 144p. 1975. 15.00 (*0-913480-21-5*); pap. 6.50 (*0-913480-33-9*) Inter Am U Pr.
Villa Triste. Patrick Modiano. (FRE.). 1977. pap. 10.95 (*0-7859-2890-1*) Fr & Eur.
Villa Triste. Patrick Modiano. (Folio Ser.: No. 953). (FRE.). pap. 8.95 (*2-07-036953-6*) Schoenhof.
***Villa Tugendhat: Svetovy Meznik Modernism V Brne.** Peter Lizon. LC 97-9220. (Illus.). 80p. (Orig.). 1996. pap. write for info. (*0-9642219-4-2*) U TN Ofc U Relations.
***Villa Tugendhat in Brno: International Landmark of Modernism.** Peter Lizon. LC 97-9220. (Illus.). 80p. (Orig.). 1996. pap. 20.00 (*0-9642219-3-4*) U TN Ofc U Relations.
Villa Vacations Made Easy. rev. ed. Michael F. Thiel. Ed. by Peg Aaronian. (Illus.). (Orig.). 1996. pap. 9.50 (*0-933613-00-8*) Hideaways Intl.
Villa Voglia. Suzanne Carey. (Horizon Ser.). (FRE.). 1994. pap. 3.50 (*0-373-39290-7*, 1-39290-1) Harlequin Bks.
Village. Mulk-Raj Anand. (Orient Paperbacks Ser.). 286p. 1979. pap. 3.00 (*0-86578-090-0*) Ind-US Inc.
Village. Alice Taylor. 160p. 1994. pap. 8.95 (*0-312-10572-X*) St Martin.
Village. Arthur F. Weegee. (Illus.). 96p. 1989. 13.95 (*0-306-80374-7*) Da Capo.
Village. large type ed. Alice Taylor. LC 93-16666. 1993. reprint ed. Alk. paper. lib. bdg. 17.95 (*1-56054-560-7*) Thorndike Pr.
Village. F. J. West. LC 84-40569. (Illus.). 320p. 1985. reprint ed. pap. text ed. 12.95 (*0-299-10234-3*) U of Wis Pr.
Village: A Novel. David Mamet. LC 94-4342. 1996. pap. 11.95 (*0-316-54338-1*) Little.
Village: An Oral Historical & Ethongraphic Study of a Black Community. Wilbur H. Watson. (Illus.). 232p. (C). 1989. 25.95 (*0-9621460-1-3*); pap. text ed. 16.95 (*0-9621460-0-5*) Village Vanguard.
***Village: As It Happened Through a Fifteen Year Period.** Robert McAlmon. Ed. & Intro. by Edward N. Lorusso. LC 89-70638. 196p. 1990. reprint ed. pap. 55.90 (*0-608-04149-1*, 2064882) Bks Demand.
Village: New & Selected Poems. Judson Jerome. Ed. by Richard Byrne et al. 192p. (Orig.). 1987. pap. 8.95 (*0-940475-60-X*); lib. bdg. 15.95 (*0-940475-61-8*) Dolphin-Moon.
Village Affair. Joanna Trollope. 272p. 1994. pap. 10.95 (*0-552-99410-3*) Bantam.
Village & Bureaucracy in Southern Sung China. Brian E. McKnight. LC 72-159834. xii, 232p. 1983. pap. text ed. 8.95 (*0-226-56060-0*) U Ch Pr.
Village & Family in Contemporary China. William L. Parish & Martin K. Whyte. LC 78-3411. (Illus.). 440p. 1980. pap. text ed. 19.50 (*0-226-64591-6*, P899) U Ch Pr.
Village & Household Economies in India's Semi-Arid Tropics. Thomas S. Walker & James G. Ryan. LC 89-19993. (Studies in Development). (Illus.). 416p. 1990. text ed. 60.00 (*0-8018-3886-X*) Johns Hopkins.
Village & Household Economies in India's Semi-Arid Tropics. T. S. Walker & James G. Ryan. LC 89-19993. 416p. 1990. reprint ed. pap. 118.60 (*0-608-00809-5*, 2061597) Bks Demand.
Village & Plantation Life in Northeastern Brazil. Harry W. Hutchinson. LC 84-45525. (American Ethnological Society Monographs: No. 27). 1988. reprint ed. 32.50 (*0-404-62926-1*) AMS Pr.
Village & Seaport: Migration & Society in Eighteenth-Century Massachusetts. Douglas L. Jones. LC 80-54469. 190p. reprint ed. pap. 54.20 (*0-7837-2616-3*, 2042951) Bks Demand.
***Village & the Hill Vol. 1: Growing up in Seal Harbor, Maine, in the 1930's.** Richard W. Billings. (Illus.). 126p. (Orig.). 1996. pap. 10.00 (*0-9654287-0-2*) Day Mtn Pubns.
Village & the Outside World in Golden Age Castile: Mobility & Migration in Everyday Rural Life. David E. Vassberg. (Illus.). 230p. (C). 1996. text ed. 59.95 (*0-521-56325-9*) Cambridge U Pr.
Village & Town Bands. Christopher Weir. 1989. pap. 25.00 (*0-85263-541-9*, Pub. by Shire UK) St Mut.
Village Architecture of Early New England. Ed. by Lisa C. Mullins. (Architectural Treasures of Early America Ser.). 248p. 1987. 19.85 (*0-918678-26-9*) Natl Hist Soc.
Village at Lane's Cove. Barbara H. Erkkila. (Illus.). 212p. (Orig.). 1989. 14.95 (*0-938459-05-8*) Ten Pound Isl Bk.
Village at War: An Account of Conflict in Vietnam. James W. Trullinger. LC 92-85447. 268p. (C). 1993. pap. 14.95 (*0-8047-2135-1*) Stanford U Pr.
Village at War: Chatham, New Jersey, & the American Revolution. Donald W. White. LC 77-74400. (Illus.). 311p. 1979. 32.50 (*0-8386-2103-1*) Fairleigh Dickinson.
Village Atlas: The Growth of Birmingham & the West Midlands. Village Press Editorial Board Staff. (Illus.). (C). 1989. 95.00 (*0-946619-33-6*, Pub. by Village Pr UK) St Mut.
Village Atlas: The Growth of Derbyshire, Nottinghamshire & Leicestershire, 1834-1904. Village Press Editorial Board Staff. (Illus.). (C). 1990. 95.00 (*1-85540-026-X*, Pub. by Village Pr UK) St Mut.
Village Atlas: The Growth of Manchester, Lancashire & North Cheshire, 1840-1912. Village Press Editorial Board Staff. (Illus.). (C). 1989. 95.00 (*0-946619-34-4*, Pub. by Village Pr UK) St Mut.
Village Atlas: The Growth of North & West Yorkshire, 1840-1910. Village Press Editorial Board Staff. (Illus.). (C). 1990. 95.00 (*1-85540-025-1*, Pub. by Village Pr UK) St Mut.
***Village Baker.** Joe Ortiz. (Illus.). 320p. 1997. pap. 19.95 (*0-89815-916-4*) Ten Speed Pr.
***Village Baker.** Joe Ortiz. Date not set. write for info. (*0-688-09845-2*) Morrow.
***Village Baker's Wife.** Joe Ortiz & Gayle C. Ortiz. LC 96-40240. (Illus.). 336p. (Orig.). 1997. 24.95 (*0-89815-869-9*) Ten Speed Pr.
Village Banking: The State of the Practice. 100p. (Orig.). 1996. pap. 12.95 (*0-912917-39-3*) UNIFEM.
Village Basket Weaver. Jonathan London. LC 95-10383. (Illus.). 32p. (J). (ps-3). 1996. pap. 14.99 (*0-525-45314-8*) Dutton Child Bks.
Village by the Sea. Paula Fox. LC 88-60099. 160p. (J). (gr. 5-7). 1988. 15.95 (*0-531-05788-7*) Orchard Bks Watts.
Village by the Sea. Paula Fox. 160p. (J). (gr. k-6). 1990. reprint ed. pap. 3.99 (*0-440-40299-9*) Dell.
Village Camera. Miss Pinnell & the Children of Sapperton School. (Illus.). 128p. 1991. 28.00 (*0-86299-791-7*, Pub. by Sutton Pubng UK) Bks Intl VA.
Village Carpenter. Walter Rose. LC 88-3. (Illus.). 146p. (YA). (gr. 10 up). 1988. reprint ed. pap. 9.95 (*0-941533-18-2*) New Amsterdam Bks.
Village Centenary. large type ed. Miss Read. LC 96-5403. (Illus.). 309p. 1996. 24.95 (*0-7838-1657-X*, GK Hall) Thorndike Pr.
Village Charter: Act 3 of 1985, as Amended. rev. ed. 1989. pap. 12.00 (*0-317-04602-0*) MI Municipal.
Village Christmas & The Christmas Mouse. large type ed. Miss Read. LC 93-16779. (Large Print Bks.). 1993. 23.95 (*0-8161-5501-1*, GK Hall) Thorndike Pr.
Village Christmas & The Christmas Mouse. large type ed. Miss Read. LC 93-16779. (Large Print Bks.). 1994. pap. 17.95 (*0-8161-5502-X*, GK Hall) Thorndike Pr.
***Village Christmases.** Mollie Harris. (Illus.). 128p. 1996. pap. 19.95 (*0-7509-1190-5*, Pub. by Sutton Pubng UK) Bks Intl VA.
Village Church Cookbook. Ed. by Helen M. Stearns. (Illus.). 100p. 1983. reprint ed. pap. 6.95 (*0-9614281-0-4*, 1472, Cricketfld Pr) Picton Pr.
Village Communities & the Authority of the State: Changing Relations in Maka Villages Since 1900. abr. rev. ed. Peter Geschiere. (Monographs from the African Studies Centre, Leiden). 300p. 1983. reprint ed. 65.00 (*0-7103-0015-8*) Routledge Chapman & Hall.
Village Communities in the East & West. 2nd ed. Henry S. Maine. Ed. by Roy M. Mersky & J. Myron Jacobstein. (Classics in Legal History Reprint Ser.: Vol. 15). 444p. 1972. reprint ed. lib. bdg. 45.00 (*0-89941-014-6*, 302780) W S Hein.
Village-Communities in the East & West. Henry S. Maine. LC 73-14169. (Perspectives in Social Inquiry Ser.). 430p. 1974. reprint ed. 25.95 (*0-405-05513-7*) Ayer.
Village Communities of Cape Anne & Salem. (Principle Works of Herbert Baxter Adams). 1989. reprint ed. lib. bdg. 79.00 (*0-7812-1465-3*) Rprt Serv.
Village Concept in the Transformation of Rural Southeast Asia. Ed. by Mason C. Hoadley & Christer Gunnaesson. (NIAS Studies in Asian Topics: No. 20). 250p. (C). 1996. text ed. 45.00 (*0-7007-0350-0*, Pub. by Curzon Press UK) UH Pr.
Village "Contracts" in Tokugawa Japan: Fifty Specimens with English Translations & Comments. Dan F. Henderson. LC 74-31050. (Asian Law Ser.: No. 2). (Illus.). 220p. 1975. 40.00 (*0-295-95405-1*) U of Wash Pr.
Village Coquettes. Ed. by C. Light. LC 92-85578. 1992. pap. 12.95 (*1-877978-43-4*, FLF Pr) Woldt.
Village Creek. Gordon Baxter. 328p. 1981. reprint ed. pap. 7.95 (*0-940672-03-0*) Shearer Pub.
Village Creek: An Architectural & Historical Resources Survey of Ensley, East Birmingham & East Lake. Marjorie L. White & Carter Hudgins. (Illus.). 151p. (Orig.). 1985. pap. 15.00 (*0-943994-05-5*) Birmingham Hist Soc.
***Village Creek: An Explicitly Regional Approach to the Study of Cultural Resources.** Timothy C. Klinger. (Illus.). 397p. 1986. pap. 6.00 (*1-56349-053-6*, RR26) AR Archaeol.
Village Cricket Tour. Vernon Coleman. (C). 1992. pap. 39.00 (*0-9503527-3-X*, Pub. by Chilton Designs UK) St Mut.
Village Defense: Initial Special Forces Operations in Vietnam. Ronald A. Shackleton. LC 75-18573. (Illus.). 1975. 12.95 (*0-685-16409-8*) Omega Grp.
***Village Diary.** Read. Date not set. lib. bdg. 22.95 (*0-8488-1690-0*) Amereon Ltd.
Village Economies: The Design, Estimation, & Use of Villagewide Economic Models. J. Edward Taylor & Irma Adelman. (Illus.). 250p. (C). 1996. text ed. 54.95 (*0-521-55012-2*) Cambridge U Pr.
Village Economy: Land & People of Huecorio. Michael H. Belshaw. LC 66-28489. (Institute of Latin American Studies). (Illus.). 421p. 1967. text ed. 67.00 (*0-231-02928-4*) Col U Pr.
Village Education in India: The Report of a Commission of Enquiry. A. G. Fraser et al. 222p. 1986. reprint ed. 26.00 (*0-8364-1919-7*, Pub. by Mittal II) S Asia.
Village Entrepreneur: Change Agents in India's Rural Development. Wayne G. Broehl, Jr. LC 77-18880. 228p. 1978. 32.00 (*0-674-93915-8*) HUP.
Village Evenings Near Dikanka & Mirgorod. Nikolai V. Gogol. Tr. by Christopher English. LC 93-49548. (World's Classics Ser.). (Illus.). 496p. 1994. pap. 6.95 (*0-19-282880-0*) OUP.
Village Flottante. Jules Verne. (Illus.). 8.95 (*0-686-55959-2*) Fr & Eur.
Village Folk-Tales of Ceylon, 3 Vols., Set. Henry Parker. Ed. by Richard M. Dorson. LC 77-70614. (International Folklore Ser.). 1977. reprint ed. lib. bdg. 108.95 (*0-405-10113-9*) Ayer.
Village Folk-Tales of Ceylon, 3 Vols., Vol. 1. Henry Parker. Ed. by Richard M. Dorson. LC 77-70614. (International Folklore Ser.). 1977. reprint ed. lib. bdg. 36.95 (*0-405-10114-7*) Ayer.
Village Folk-Tales of Ceylon, 3 Vols., Vol. 2. Henry Parker. Ed. by Richard M. Dorson. LC 77-70614. (International Folklore Ser.). 1977. reprint ed. lib. bdg. 36.95 (*0-405-10115-5*) Ayer.
Village Folk-Tales of Ceylon, 3 Vols., Vol. 3. Henry Parker. Ed. by Richard M. Dorson. LC 77-70614. (International Folklore Ser.). 1977. reprint ed. lib. bdg. 36.95 (*0-405-10116-3*) Ayer.
***Village France.** Date not set. pap. write for info. (*0-393-31644-0*) Norton.
***Village France.** Automobile Association of Great Britain Staff. (Illus.). 224p. 1997. pap. 25.95 (*0-393-31666-1*) Norton.
Village Full of Valentines. James Stevenson. LC 94-624. (TrAC Compendium Ser.: Vol. 14). (Illus.). 40p. (J). (gr. k up). 1995. 16.00 (*0-688-13602-8*); lib. bdg. 15.93 (*0-688-13603-6*) Greenwillow.
Village Gods of South India. Henry Whitehead. (Illus.). 175p. 1986. reprint ed. 15.00 (*0-8364-1709-7*, Pub. by Usha II) S Asia.
Village Hamlet & Field: Changing Medieval Settlements. Lewis. LC 96-2689. 1997. text ed. 59.95 (*0-7190-4577-0*) St Martin.
Village Harmony: Traditional Songs of the Balkans. 2nd rev. ed. Ed. & Tr. by Mary C. Brass. (Illus.). 44p. (Orig.). 1995. pap. 8.00 (*0-9627554-5-1*) Nrthn Harmony Pub.
Village Horse Doctor, West of the Pecos. Ben K. Green. LC 79-118716. 1971. 25.00 (*0-394-42922-2*) Knopf.
Village in Court: Arson, Infanticide, & Poaching in the Court Records of Upper Bavaria, 1848-1910. Regina Schulte. 256p. (C). 1994. text ed. 85.00 (*0-521-43186-7*) Cambridge U Pr.
Village in France: Louis Clergeau's Photographic Portrait of Daily Life in Pontlevoy, 1902-1936. Text by Jean-Mary Couderc. (Illus.). 140p. 1996. 45.00 (*0-8109-3747-6*) Abrams.
Village in Malta: Fieldwork Edition. Boissevain. 160p. (C). 1980. pap. text ed. 13.50 (*0-03-053411-9*) HB Coll Pubs.
Village in the Hills: A History of Danville, VT, 1786-1995. Susannah Clifford. LC 95-33654. (Illus.). 288p. 1995. 35.00 (*0-914659-75-8*) Phoenix Pub.
***Village in the Treetops.** Jules Verne. lib. bdg. 22.95 (*0-8488-2067-3*) Amereon Ltd.
Village in the Turkish Novel & Short Story 1920-1955. Carole Rathbun. (Near & Middle East Monographs: No. 2). 192p. 1972. text ed. 56.95 (*90-279-2327-2*) Mouton.
Village in the Vaucluse. 3rd ed. Laurence W. Wylie. (Illus.). 416p. 1974. pap. 15.95 (*0-674-93936-0*) HUP.
Village in the Vineyards. Thomas Matthews. LC 93-17262. 1993. 23.00 (*0-374-28381-8*) FS&G.
Village in Vietnam. Gerald C. Hickey. LC 64-20923. 352p. reprint ed. pap. 100.40 (*0-317-11300-3*, 2016798) Bks Demand.
Village Indians of the Upper Missouri: The Mandans, Hidatsas, & Arikaras. Roy W. Meyer. LC 77-4202. 392p. reprint ed. pap. 111.80 (*0-7837-3034-9*, 2042903) Bks Demand.
Village Industries & Agriculture in Changing Agrarian Situation. G. P. Mishra et al. 1985. 18.50 (*0-317-40626-4*, Pub. by Ashish II) S Asia.
Village Japan: The Four Seasons of Shimukappu. Nicholas DeVore, III. LC 93-29378. (Illus.). 160p. 1994. 29.95 (*0-8348-0312-7*) Weatherhill.
Village Java under the Cultivation System, 1830-1870. R. E. Elson. 560p. 1994. pap. 34.95 (*1-86373-656-5*, Pub. by Allen Unwin AT) Paul & Co Pubs.
Village Journey: The Report of the Alaska Native Review Commission. rev. ed. Thomas R. Berger. 204p. 1995. pap. 10.95 (*0-8090-1579-X*) Hill & Wang.
Village Keeper: Mixing Ages 8-12, a Continuous Progress Multiage Teacher's Method for Success. Barbara Berst. (Educational Division Ser.). 125p. (Orig.). Date not set. pap. 15.00 (*0-9614126-4-X*) Natl Lilac Pub.
Village Labourer: A Study of the Government of England Before the Reform Bill. J. L. Hammond & Barbara Hammond. 432p. 1989. pap. 12.00 (*0-86299-345-8*, Pub. by Sutton Pubng UK) Bks Intl VA.
Village Law, New York State. annuals New York State Legislature Staff. 200p. 1997. Updated annually. ring bd. 13.95 (*0-930137-42-6*) Looseleaf Law.
Village-Level Brickmaking. Anne Beamish & Will Donovan. Ed. by Deutsches Zentrum fur Entwicklungs-technologien-GATE. (GATE Ser.). 124p. 1989. pap. 17.50 (*3-528-02051-2*, Pub. by Vieweg & Sohn GW) Informatica.
Village Life in America, 1852-1872. Caroline C. Richards. 1977. lib. bdg. 59.95 (*0-8490-2798-5*) Gordon Pr.
Village Life in America 1852-1872. Caroline C. Clarke. (American Biography Ser.). 202p. 1991. reprint ed. lib. bdg. 69.00 (*0-7812-8071-0*) Rprt Serv.
Village Life in America, 1852-1872: Diary of a School Girl. Caroline C. Richards. 225p. 1972. reprint ed. 23.95 (*0-87928-029-8*) Corner Hse.
***Village Life in America 1852-1872: Including the Period of the American Civil War As Told by a School-Girl.** 3rd unabridged ed. Caroline C. Richards. Ed. by Anne W. Ackerson. (Illus.). 258p. 1997. reprint ed. pap. 15.95 (*0-87928-115-4*) Corner Hse.
Village Life in China: A Study in Sociology. Arthur Smith. LC 68-25266. (World History Ser.: No. 48). 1969. reprint ed. lib. bdg. 75.00 (*0-8383-0241-6*) M S G Haskell Hse.
Village Life in Colonial Times. James E. Knight. LC 81-23084. (Illus.). 32p. (J). (gr. 5-9). 1995. pap. 2.95 (*0-89375-729-2*) Troll Communs.
Village Life in Egypt, 2 vols. Bayle St. John. LC 73-6298. (Middle East Ser.). 1973. reprint ed. 42.95 (*0-405-05358-4*) Ayer.
Village Life in India. Steve Brace. (Cambridge Primary Geography Ser.). 48p. (C). 1996. pap. text ed. 6.95 (*0-521-55752-6*) Cambridge U Pr.
Village Life in India: Past & Present. Misra Bidyadhar. (C). 1988. 22.50 (*81-202-0194-9*, Pub. by Ajanta II) S Asia.
Village Life in Late Tsarist Russia: An Ethnography. Semyonova Tian-Shanskaia. Ed. & Tr. by David L. Ransel. Tr. by Michael Levine. LC 92-28558. (Indiana-Michigan Series in Russian & East European Studies). 192p. (C). 1993. 31.50 (*0-253-34797-1*); pap. 11.95 (*0-253-20784-3*, MB-784) Ind U Pr.
Village Life in Old China: A Community Study of Kao Yao Yhunnan. Cornelius Osgood. LC 63-19749. 415p. reprint ed. pap. 118.30 (*0-317-11315-1*, 2012390) Bks Demand.
Village Life Under the Soviets. Karl Borders. LC 72-12699. (Select Bibliographies Reprint Ser.). 1977. reprint ed. 18.95 (*0-8369-7131-0*) Ayer.
Village Life Under the Soviets. Karl Borders. 200p. reprint ed. lib. bdg. 15.00 (*0-8290-0812-8*) Irvington.
Village London, Vol. I. Village Press Editorial Board Staff. (London Library). (C). 1989. 95.00 (*0-946619-05-0*, Pub. by Village Pr UK) St Mut.
Village London, Vol. II. Village Press Editorial Board Staff. (London Library). (C). 1989. 95.00 (*0-946619-10-7*, Pub. by Village Pr UK) St Mut.
Village London, Pt. 1: North & West. Village Press Editorial Board Staff. (C). 1989. pap. 50.00 (*0-946619-11-5*, Pub. by Village Pr UK) St Mut.
Village London, Pt. 2: North & East. Village Press Editorial Board Staff. (C). 1989. pap. 50.00 (*0-946619-12-3*, Pub. by Village Pr UK) St Mut.
Village London, Pt. 3: South-East. Village Press Editorial Board Staff. (C). 1989. pap. 50.00 (*0-946619-13-1*, Pub. by Village Pr UK) St Mut.
Village London, Pt. 4: South-West. Village Press Editorial Board Staff. (C). 1989. pap. 50.00 (*0-946619-14-X*, Pub. by Village Pr UK) St Mut.
***Village Matters.** Rebecca Shaw. 256p. 1997. 27.00 (*1-85797-766-1*, Pub. by Orion Bks UK) Trafalgar.
Village Medical Manual - A Layman's Guide to Health Care in Developing Countries: Diagnosis & Treatment, Vol. 2. 4th ed. Mary Vanderkooi. LC 94-22164. 1994. pap. write for info. (*0-87808-252-2*) William Carey Lib.
Village Medical Manual: A Layman's Guide to Health Care in Developing Countries: Principles & Procedures, 2 vols., Set. 1994. pap. text ed. 29.95 (*0-87808-261-1*) William Carey Lib.
Village Medical Manual: A Layman's Guide to Health Care in Developing Countries: Principles & Procedures, Vol. 1. 4th ed. Mary Vanderkooi. 1994. pap. write for info. (*0-87808-251-4*) William Carey Lib.
Village Memories. W. L. Stone. LC 84-72330. (Illus.). 176p. 1986. pap. 8.95 (*0-941216-24-1*) Cay-Bel.
Village Names in Twelve California Mission Records. fac. ed. C. Hart Merriam. Ed. by Robert Heizer. (Reports of the University of California Archaeological Survey: No. 74). 182p. 1968. reprint ed. pap. 16.25 (*1-55567-390-2*) Coyote Press.
Village Notables in Nineteenth-Century France: Priests, Mayors, Schoolmasters. Barnett Singer. LC 82-3195. 199p. (C). 1983. text ed. 64.50 (*0-87395-629-X*); pap. text ed. 21.95 (*0-87395-630-3*) State U NY Pr.
Village of Bom Jesus. Lloyd E. Hill. LC 92-36306. 238p. 1993. 16.95 (*0-945575-88-2*, 71588) Algonquin Bks.
Village of Cannibals: Rage & Murder in France, 1870. Alain Corbin. Tr. by Arthur Goldhammer from FRE. (Illus.). 164p. 1992. text ed. 22.95 (*0-674-93900-X*) HUP.
Village of Cannibals: Rage & Murder in France, 1870. Alain Corbin. 164p. 1993. pap. text ed. 12.95 (*0-674-93901-8*) HUP.
Village of Curers & Assassins: On the Production of Fala Kpelle Cosmological Categories. Beryl L. Bellman. LC 73-76893. (Approaches to Semiotics Ser.: No. 39). 196p. 1975. text ed. 57.70 (*90-279-3042-2*) Mouton.
Village of Hommlet. Gary Gygax. 1980. 5.00 (*0-394-51185-9*) Random.
Village of Monroe: The Celebration of a Century. limited ed. Monroe Historical Society Staff. (Illus.). 400p. 1994. pap. 20.00 (*0-88092-185-4*) Royal Fireworks.
Village of Monroe: The Celebration of a Century. limited ed. Monroe Historical Society Staff. (Illus.). 400p. 1994. 30.00 (*0-88092-186-2*) Royal Fireworks.
Village of My Childhood. Fred Archer. (Illus.). 192p. 1990. 26.00 (*0-86299-557-4*, Pub. by Sutton Pubng UK) Bks Intl VA.
Village of Outcasts: Historical Archaeology & Documentary Research at the Lighthouse Site. Kenneth L. Feder. LC 93-1441. 230p. (Orig.). (C). 1993. pap. 20.95 (*1-55934-255-2*, 1255) Mayfield Pub.
Village of Round & Square Houses. Ann Grifalconi. (Illus.). 32p. (J). (gr. k-3). 1986. lib. bdg. 16.95 (*0-316-32862-6*) Little.

An Asterisk (*) at the beginning of an entry indicates that the title is appearing in BIP for the first time.

Village of Salem 1761-1994. Katharine L. Tomasi. 430p. 1995. 40.00 (*0-9645921-0-X*) Salem Womans Club.

Village of Stepanchikovo. Fyodor Dostoyevsky. Tr. & Intro. by Ignat Avsey. 224p. 1995. pap. 10.95 (*0-14-044658-3*, Penguin Classics) Viking Penguin.

Village of Stepanchikovo & Its Inhabitants. Fyodor Dostoyevsky. Tr. by Ignat Avsey from RUS. LC 86-47995. 256p. 1987. reprint ed. 35.00 (*0-8014-2051-2*) Cornell U Pr.

Village of the Brothers. Compiled by Rivka Guber. LC 78-54568. (Illus.). 1979. 18.95 (*0-88400-059-1*) Shengold.

Village of the Ghost Bells: A Novel. Edla Van Steen. Tr. by David George. (Texas Pan American Ser.). 215p. (Orig.). (C). 1991. text ed. 27.50 (*0-292-73062-4*); pap. text ed. 12.95 (*0-292-73063-2*) U of Tex Pr.

Village of the Great Kivas on the Zuni Reservation, New Mexico. Ed. by Frank Roberts, Jr. (Bureau of American Ethnology Bulletins Ser.). 197p. 1995. lib. bdg. 79.00 (*0-7812-4111-1*) Rprt Serv.

***Village of the Seine: Tradition & Change in Bonnieres.** Evelyn B. Ackerman. LC 78-58071. (Illus.). 187p. reprint ed. pap. 53.30 (*0-608-05314-7*, 2065852) Bks Demand.

Village of the Vampire Cat. Lensey Namioka. 192p. (YA). 1995. pap. 8.95 (*0-936085-29-0*) Blue Heron OR.

Village of Waiting. George Packer. LC 87-45912. (Departures Ser.). 352p. (Orig.). 1988. pap. 12.00 (*0-394-75754-8*, Vin) Random.

Village on the Border: A Social Study of Religion, Politics, & Football in a North Wales Community. enl. ed. Ronald Frankenberg. (Illus.). 223p. (C). 1990. reprint ed. pap. text ed. 11.50 (*0-88133-485-5*) Waveland Pr.

Village on the Seine: Tradition & Change in Bonnieres, 1815-1914. Evelyn B. Ackerman. LC 78-58071. (Illus.). 188p. 1978. 39.95 (*0-8014-1178-5*) Cornell U Pr.

Village Pastor Looks Back: A History of the First Chnshan Church of Freedom, New Hampshire. George T. Davidson, Jr. 1993. pap. 10.00 (*0-945069-02-2*) Freedom Pr Assocs.

Village Pathetique. Andre Dhotel. 320p. (FRE.). 1974. pap. 10.95 (*0-7859-1786-1*, 2070365824) Fr & Eur.

Village Poems. Man M. Singh. (Indian Poetry Ser.: No. 22). 1982. pap. 8.95 (*0-86578-275-X*) Ind-US Inc.

Village Politics 1793: With the Shepherd of Salisbury Plain. Hannah More. (Revolution & Romanticism, 1789-1834, Ser.). 1995. write for info. (*1-85477-187-6*, Pub. by Woodstock Bks UK) Cassell.

***Village Pub.** Roger Protz & Homer Sykes. (Country Ser.). (Illus.). 160p. 1997. pap. 17.95 (*0-297-83561-0*, Pub. by Orion Bks UK) Trafalgar.

Village Republics: Economics Conditions for Collective Action in South India. Robert Wade. LC 94-18516. 1994. pap. 14.95 (*1-55815-387-X*) ICS Pr.

Village Revolts: Social Protest & Popular Disturbances in England, 1509-1640. Roger B. Manning. (Illus.). 368p. 1988. 85.00 (*0-19-820116-8*) OUP.

***Village School.** Read. Date not set. lib. bdg. 21.95 (*0-8488-1689-7*) Amereon Ltd.

Village Schoolmaster. Joanne Hart. 1985. pap. 45.00 (*0-931460-23-9*) Bieler.

Village Show. Peter Bonnici. (What's Inside Ser.). (Illus.). 32p. (J). (gr. k-2). 1990. 11.95 (*0-340-48610-4*, Pub. by H & S UK) Trafalgar.

Village Show. Ursula Buchan. (Illus.). 160p. 1992. pap. 17.95 (*1-85145-885-9*, Pub. by Pavilion UK) Trafalgar.

Village Sings: Poems. Gabriel Fitzmaurice. LC 96-20631. 96p. (Orig.). 1996. pap. 9.00 (*1-885266-29-4*) Story Line.

Village Sins. large type ed. Anne Worboys. 480p. 1995. 25.99 (*0-7089-3386-6*) Ulverscroft.

Village So Small. Maude F. Zimmer. 1965. 8.95 (*0-8315-0006-9*) Speller.

Village Songs of Western India: Translations from Tukaram. Tr. by John S. Hoyland. 1980. reprint ed. pap. 2.50 (*0-932970-15-X*) Prinit Pr.

Village Spaces: Settlement & Society in Northeastern Iran. Lee Horne. LC 93-8589. (Series in Archaeological Inquiry). (Illus.). 208p. (C). 1994. text ed. 59.00 (*1-56098-329-9*) Smithsonian.

Village Spinster. Laura Matthews. 224p. (Orig.). 1993. pap. 3.99 (*0-451-17568-9*, Sig) NAL-Dutton.

Village Spinster. large type ed. Laura Matthews. LC 93-1107. (Orig.). 1993. lib. bdg. 18.95 (*1-56054-742-1*) Thorndike Pr.

Village Square. Linda Eberhardt. 336p. (Orig.). 1995. mass mkt. 4.99 (*0-515-11740-4*) Jove Pubns.

Village Streets. Mary A. McDonnell. 64p. 1991. pap. 10.00 (*0-9632201-0-1*) Zeugpress.

Village Studies in the Third World. Ed. by Biplab Dasgupta. 400p. 1978. 39.95 (*0-87855-303-7*) Transaction Pubs.

Village Tales: The Story of Scalby & Its Residents. Alan Whitworth. LC 93-26402. 1993. 26.00 (*0-7509-0347-3*, Pub. by Sutton Pubng UK) Bks Intl VA.

Village Technology Handbook. rev. ed. Ed. by Margaret Crouch & Leonard Doak. 425p. 1987. 19.95 (*0-86619-275-1*) Vols Tech Asst.

Village That Died for England: The Strange Story of Tyneham. Patrick Wright. (Illus.). 420p. 1996. 35.00 (*0-224-03886-9*, Pub. by Jonathan Cape UK) Trafalgar.

***Village That Disappeared.** Susan G. Erwin. LC 95-81871. (Illus.). 177p. 1996. 25.00 (*0-9624488-6-9*) Laney-Smith.

Village to Village. Alister Kershaw. 152p. 1994. pap. 9.00 (*0-207-17612-4*, Pub. by Angus & Robertson AT) HarpC.

***Village, Town & District Courts in New York.** James E. Morris et al. LC 95-80836. 700p. 1995. text ed. write for info. (*0-7620-0016-3*); pap. text ed. write for info. (*0-7620-0017-1*) Lawyers Cooperative.

Village Voices: Co-existence & Communication in a Rural Community in Central France. Perle Mohl. 200p. 1996. pap. 45.00 (*87-7289-344-3*, Pub. by Mus Tusculanum DK) Paul & Co Pubs.

Village Voices, Forest Choices: Joint Forest Management in India. Ed. by Mark Poffenberger & Betsy McGean. (Illus.). 392p. (C). 1996. 24.95 (*0-19-563683-X*) OUP.

Village Walks in Britain. Automobile Association Staff. 264p. 1997. pap. 25.00 (*0-393-31502-9*) Norton.

***Village Wannabee.** Kim Harris. (Illus.). 24p. (J). (gr. 1-6). 1996. 12.95 (*1-56550-046-6*) Vis Bks Intl.

Village Watch-Tower. Kate D. Wiggin. LC 74-113696. (Short Story Index Reprint Ser.). 1977. 18.95 (*0-8369-3425-3*) Ayer.

Village Water Supply: Economics & Policy in the Developing World. Robert J. Saunders & Jeremy J. Warford. LC 76-11758. 295p. reprint ed. pap. 84.10 (*0-7837-4464-1*, 2043950) Bks Demand.

***Village Water Supply in the Decade: Lessons from Field Experience.** Colin Glennie. LC 82-23749. (Illus.). 164p. reprint ed. pap. 46.80 (*0-608-05282-5*, 2065820) Bks Demand.

Village Witch Doctor & Other Stories. Amos Tutuola. 128p. 1990. pap. 7.95 (*0-571-14215-X*) Faber & Faber.

Village Without Mirrors: Photographs & Essays. Timothy Francisco & Patricia W. Francisco. LC 89-2266. (Seeing Double Collaborative Book). (Illus.). 112p. (Orig.). 1989. pap. 18.95 (*0-915943-37-9*) Milkweed Ed.

Village Without Solidarity: Polish Peasantry in Years of Crisis. C. M. Hann. LC 84-52242. (Illus.). 192p. 1985. 35.00 (*0-300-03353-2*) Yale U Pr.

Villagers. Jack Oleck. 5.95 (*0-8184-0117-6*) Carol Pub Group.

Villagers & Strangers: An English Proletarian Village over Four Centuries. Patricia H. Fleming. 168p. 1979. 22.95 (*0-87073-818-6*); pap. 15.95 (*0-87073-819-4*) Schenkman Bks Inc.

Villagers (Huasipungo) A Novel. Jorge Icaza. Tr. by Bernard M. Dulsey from SPA. LC 73-9551. (Arcturus Books Paperbacks). 238p. 1973. reprint ed. pap. 12.95 (*0-8093-0653-0*) S Ill U Pr.

Villagers of the Maros: A Portrait of an Early Bronze Age Society. John M. O'Shea. LC 96-30205. (Interdisciplinary Contributions to Archaeology Ser.). (Illus.). 385p. (C). 1996. 59.50 (*0-306-45322-3*, Plenum Pr) Plenum.

Villagers of the Sierra de Gredos: Transhumant Cattle-Raisers in Central Spain. William Kavanagh. LC 92-32093. 208p. 1994. 38.95 (*0-85496-320-0*) Berg Pubs.

Villages. Francis Jammes. Tr. by Antony Oldknow. 64p. (FRE.). 1993. pap. text ed. 7.50 (*1-881604-09-8*) Scopcraeft.

Villages. Lynn M. Stone. LC 93-16152. (Old America Ser.). (J). 1993. write for info. (*0-86625-448-X*) Rourke Pubns.

Villages Astir: Community Development, Tradition & Change in Korea. John E. Turner et al. LC 92-28549. 368p. 1993. text ed. 65.00 (*0-275-94372-0*, C4372, Praeger Pubs) Greenwood.

Villages in the Steppe: Later Neolithic Settlement & Subsistence in the Balikh Valley, Northern Syria. Peter M. Akkermans. LC 93-40086. (Archaeological Ser.: No. 5). (Illus.). xvi, 351p. 1993. pap. 37.50 (*1-879621-10-X*); lib. bdg. 50.00 (*1-879621-11-8*) Intl Mono Prehstry.

Villages of Edinburgh: North Edinburgh. Malcolm Cant. 252p. (C). 1989. pap. 27.00 (*0-85976-131-2*, Pub. by J Donald UK) St Mut.

Villages of Edinburgh, Vol. 2: South Edinburgh. Malcolm Cant. 80p. (C). 1989. pap. 27.00 (*0-85976-186-X*, Pub. by J Donald UK) St Mut.

Villages of France. Joanna Sullam & Charlie Waite. (Country Ser.). (Illus.). 160p. 1996. pap. 17.95 (*0-297-79599-6*, Weidenfeld) Trafalgar.

Villages of Glasgow, Vol. 1. Aileen Smart. 224p. (C). 1989. text ed. 50.00 (*0-85976-231-9*, Pub. by J Donald UK) St Mut.

Villages of Glasgow, Vol. 1. Aileen Smart. 226p. (C). 1996. pap. 27.00 (*0-85976-232-7*, Pub. by J Donald UK) St Mut.

Villages of Hispanic New Mexico. Nancy H. Warren. LC 87-12715. (Illus.). 111p. (Orig.). 1987. pap. 14.95 (*0-933452-20-9*) Schol Am Res.

Villages of Northern France. Andrew Sanger. (Shuttle Ser.). (Illus.). 192p. 1995. pap. 16.95 (*1-85793-155-6*, Pub. by Pavilion UK) Trafalgar.

Villages of the Algonquian, Siouan, & Caddoan Tribes West of the Mississippi. Ed. by David I. Bushnell, Jr. (Bureau of American Ethnology Bulletins Ser.). 211p. 1995. lib. bdg. 89.00 (*0-7812-4077-8*) Rprt Serv.

Villages of the Algonquian, Siouan & Caddoan Tribes West of the Mississippi. David I. Bushnell, Jr. (Illus.). 211p. 1991. reprint ed. 59.00 (*1-878592-24-6*); reprint ed. pap. 39.00 (*1-878592-23-8*) Native Amer Bk Pubs.

Villages of the Algonquian, Siouan & Caddoan Tribes West of the Mississippi. David L. Bushnell. 1988. reprint ed. lib. bdg. 39.00 (*0-7812-0742-8*) Rprt Serv.

Villages of the Rio Grande Postcards. Museum of New Mexico Press Staff. 64p. 1994. pap. text ed. 9.95 (*0-89013-268-2*) Museum NM Pr.

Villages Towns Cities. H. Hayes. (Down to Earth Ser.). 1983. 30.00 (*0-09-138631-4*, Pub. by S Thornes Pubs UK) St Mut.

Villain As Hero in Elizabethan Tragedy. Clarence V. Boyer. (BCL1-PR English Literature Ser.). 264p. 1992. reprint ed. lib. bdg. 79.00 (*0-7812-7102-9*) Rprt Serv.

Villain of the Earth. Simon Shaw. LC 95-1757. 1995. 19.95 (*0-312-13201-8*, Thomas Dunne Bks) St Martin.

Villainage in England: Essays in English Medieval History. Paul Vinogradoff. 1988. reprint ed. lib. bdg. 98.00 (*0-7812-0457-7*) Rprt Serv.

Villainous Company. Amlin Gray. 1981. pap. 3.25 (*0-8222-1210-2*) Dramatists Play.

***Villainous Vicar.** Beverly Van Hook. (Supergranny Ser.: No. 7). (Illus.). (J). 1996. pap. write for info. (*0-916761-25-8*); lib. bdg. write for info. (*0-916761-26-6*) Holderby & Bierce.

Villains: Crime & Community in the Inner City. Janet Foster. LC 89-24177. 176p. (C). 1990. pap. text ed. 22.95 (*0-415-02568-0*, A4232) Routledge.

Villains & Vigilantes. Stanton A. Coblentz. 1992. reprint ed. lib. bdg. 75.00 (*0-7812-5015-3*) Rprt Serv.

Villains by Necessity. Eve Forward. 480p. 1996. pap. write for info. (*0-614-05538-5*) Tor Bks.

Villains by Necessity. Eve Forward. 480p. (Orig.). mass mkt. 6.99 (*0-8125-2228-1*) Tor Bks.

Villain's Lady. Charlotte Maclay. (American Romance Ser.). 1993. mass mkt. 3.39 (*0-373-16474-2*, 1-16474-8) Harlequin Bks.

***Villains' Lorebook.** 1997. 25.00 (*0-7869-0723-1*) TSR Inc.

Villains of Volturnus. Jean Blashfield. 1983. 2.00 (*0-394-71547-0*) Random.

Villains Pop-Up: A Pop-up Book. Illus. by Eric Binder. LC 94-68708. 12p. (J). 1995. 12.95 (*0-7868-3056-5*) Disney Pr.

Villains Unlimited. Kevin Siembieda & Kevin Long. Ed. by Alex Marciniszyn et al. (Heroes Unlimited Ser.). (Illus.). 224p. (Orig.). (YA). (gr. 8 up). 1992. pap. 20.00 (*0-916211-49-5*, 501) Palladium Bks.

Villainy Victorius, Vol. 9. L. Ron Hubbard. (Mission Earth Ser.: No. 9). 465p. 1995. mass mkt. 5.99 (*0-88404-290-1*) Bridge Pubns Inc.

Villancico Yaucano. Amaury Veray & Ivan Camilli. (Children's Bks.). (Illus.). (J). 1992. 12.95 (*0-8477-2506-5*) U of PR Pr.

Villano En Su Rincon. Lope De Vega. 208p. 1987. pap. 10.95 (*0-7859-5212-8*) Fr & Eur.

Villano en Su Rincon. Lope De Vega. 111p. (SPA.). 1969. 7.95 (*0-8288-7143-4*) Fr & Eur.

Villanova Law School. Photos by Scott Goldsmith. (Illus.). 112p. 1990. 39.00 (*0-916509-77-X*) Harmony Hse Pub.

Villanova University. Nick Kelsh. (Illus.). 112p. 1987. 37.50 (*0-916509-20-6*) Harmony Hse Pub.

Villanova University, 1842-1992: American-Catholic-Augustinian. David R. Contosta. LC 94-45427. (Illus.). 328p. 1995. 35.00 (*0-271-01459-8*) Pa St U Pr.

Villas & Cottages. 2nd ed. Calvert Vaux. LC 68-29858. (Architecture & Decorative Art Ser.). (Illus.). 1968. reprint ed. lib. bdg. 49.50 (*0-306-71044-7*) Da Capo.

Villas in Italy. L'Archivolto Editorial Staff. (Illus.). 230p. 1996. 59.95 (*88-7685-076-7*, Pub. by LArchivoto IT) Bks Nippan.

Villas of le Corbusier, 1920-1930. Tim Benton. 244p. (Orig.). (C). 1991. reprint ed. pap. 37.50 (*0-300-04935-8*) Yale U Pr.

Villas of Palladio. Photos by Philip Trager. (Illus.). 168p. 1992. pap. 35.00 (*0-8212-1898-0*) Bulfinch Pr.

Villas of Pliny from Antiquity to Posterity. Pierre de la Ruffiniere du Prey. LC 93-44209. 404p. 1994. 65.00 (*0-226-17300-3*) U Ch Pr.

Villas of Tuscany. Carlo Cresti & Massimo Listri. LC 93-11120. (Illus.). 480p. 1994. 85.00 (*0-86565-144-2*) Vendome.

Villas on the Hudson: A Collection of Photo-Lithographs of Thirty-One Country Residences. LC 76-41854. (Architecture & Decorative Art Ser.). 1977. reprint ed. lib. bdg. 95.00 (*0-306-70800-0*) Da Capo.

Villa's Rifles. large type ed. Lewis B. Patten. LC 94-20140. 235p. 1994. pap. 17.95 (*0-8161-7424-5*, GK Hall) Thorndike Pr.

Villasandino y su Hablante Lirico. Yolanda Rosas. (American University Studies: Romance Languages & Literature: Ser. II, Vol. 53). 186p. (C). 1987. text ed. 32.90 (*0-8204-0342-3*) P Lang Pubng.

Villdemslekre Im Griechischen Recht. Richard Maschko. Ed. by Gregory Vlastos. LC 78-19369. (Morals & Law in Ancient Greece Ser.). 1979. reprint ed. lib. bdg. 18.95 (*0-405-11560-1*) Ayer.

Ville. Paul Claudel. (FRE.). 1982. pap. 10.95 (*0-8288-3634-5*, F137830) Fr & Eur.

Ville. Paul Claudel. (Folio Ser.: No. 1345). (FRE.). 1967. 6.95 (*2-07-037345-2*) Schoenhof.

Ville Dont le Prince Est un Enfant. Henry De Montherlant. (Folio Ser.: No. 293). (FRE.). 1963. pap. 9.95 (*2-07-036293-0*) Schoenhof.

Ville Dont le Prince Est un Enfant. Henry De Montherlant. (FRE.). 1973. pap. 11.95 (*0-8288-3757-0*, M3794) Fr & Eur.

***Ville Engloutie.** Sonia Sarfati. (Novels in the Roman Jeunesse Ser.). 96p. (FRE.). (J). (gr. 4-7). 1996. pap. 7.95 (*2-89021-179-7*, Pub. by Les Editions CN) Firefly Bks Ltd.

***Ville Imaginaire.** Jacques Savoie. (Novels in the Roman Jeunesse Ser.). 96p. (FRE.). (J). (gr. 4-7). 1996. pap. 7.95 (*2-89021-254-8*, Pub. by Les Editions CN) Firefly Bks Ltd.

Ville Noire, 1861. George Sand, pseud. 176p. (FRE.). 1989. pap. 24.95 (*0-7859-1580-X*, 2903950326) Fr & Eur.

Ville ou Nul ne Meurt. Bernard B. Dadie. pap. 8.95 (*0-685-35633-7*) Fr & Eur.

Ville sous l'Ancien Regime, 2 Vols, Set. 2nd ed. Albert A. Babeau. reprint ed. 115.00 (*0-404-07516-9*) AMS Pr.

Villeggiatura. Carlo Goldoni. Tr. by Robert Cornthwaite. LC 94-38078. (Young Actors Ser.). 132p. 1995. pap. 14.95 (*1-880399-72-5*) Smith & Kraus.

Villeggiatura Trilogy. Carlo Goldoni. Tr. by Robert Cornthwaite. (Great Translations for Actors Ser.). 288p. 1994. pap. 19.95 (*1-880399-69-5*) Smith & Kraus.

***Villeneuve: My First Season in Formula 1.** Jacques Villeneuve & Gerald Donaldson. (Illus.). 224p. 1997. 32.00 (*0-00-218766-3*) HarperColl Wrld.

Villette. Charlotte Bronte. 512p. 1986. 5.95 (*0-553-21243-5*) Bantam.

Villette. Charlotte Bronte. Ed. by Sandra Kemp. 576p. 1993. pap. 5.95 (*0-460-87247-8*, Everyman's Classic Lib) C E Tuttle.

Villette. Charlotte Bronte. 1992. 20.00 (*0-679-40988-2*) McKay.

Villette. Charlotte Bronte. 1987. pap. 5.95 (*0-451-52083-1*, Sig Classics) NAL-Dutton.

Villette. Charlotte Bronte. Ed. by Herbert Rosengarten & Margaret Smith. (Illus.). 768p. 1985. 160.00 (*0-19-812597-6*) OUP.

Villette. Charlotte Bronte. Ed. by Margaret Smith & Herbert Rosengarten. (World's Classics Ser.). 704p. 1990. pap. 6.95 (*0-19-281836-8*) OUP.

***Villette.** Charlotte Bronte. 1997. 18.50 (*0-679-60274-7*, Modern Lib) Random.

Villette. Charlotte Bronte. Ed. by Mark Lilly. (English Library). 624p. 1980. pap. 9.95 (*0-14-043118-7*, Penguin Classics) Viking Penguin.

Villette. Charlotte Bronte. 1995. pap. 16.95 (*0-14-086076-2*) NAL-Dutton.

Villette. large type ed. Charlotte Bronte. (Isis Clear Type Classic Ser.). 601p. 1992. 24.95 (*1-85089-449-3*, Pub. by ISIS UK) Transaction Pubs.

Villette. Charlotte Bronte. 1992. reprint ed. lib. bdg. 24.95 (*0-89966-998-0*) Buccaneer Bks.

Villette: Charlotte Bronte. Ed. by Pauline Nestor. LC 91-41407. (New Casebooks Ser.). 184p. 1992. text ed. 45.00 (*0-312-07909-5*) St Martin.

Villian or Hero: Sallust's Portrayal of Catiline. Ann T. Wilkins. LC 93-384. (Am. Univ. Studies, XVII: Vol. 15). 171p. (Orig.). (C). 1994. pap. text ed. 44.95 (*0-8204-2034-4*) P Lang Pubng.

Villiers de l'Isle Adam. Stephane Mallarme. Ed. by Jill Raitt. (Exeter French Texts Ser.: No. 78). 84p. (FRE.). Date not set. pap. text ed. 19.95 (*0-85989-360-X*, Pub. by Univ Exeter Pr UK) Northwestern U Pr.

Villiers-Stuart Goes to War. R. M. Maxwell. 349p. (C). 1989. text ed. 69.00 (*0-946270-85-6*, Pub. by Pentland Pr UK) St Mut.

Villiers-Stuart on the Frontier. R. M. Maxwell. 209p. (C). 1989. text ed. 50.00 (*0-946270-57-0*, Pub. by Pentland Pr UK) St Mut.

Villon. Jean Calais. 1981. pap. 4.95 (*0-915008-18-1*) Duende.

Villon's Last Will: Language & Authority in the Testament. Tony Hunt. LC 96-4266. 176p. (C). 1996. 55.00 (*0-19-815914-5*, Clarendon Pr) OUP.

Villy Sadness: A Novella. Rodney Nelson. 114p. 1987. pap. 7.95 (*0-89823-093-4*) New Rivers Pr.

Vilma Martinez. Corinn Codye. (Hispanic Stories Ser.). (Illus.). 32p. (ENG & SPA.). (J). (gr. 3-6). 1990. lib. bdg. 21.40 (*0-8172-3382-2*) Raintree Steck-V.

Vilma Martinez. Corinn Codye. (Hispanic Stories Ser.). (Illus.). 32p. (ENG & SPA.). (J). (gr. 3-6). 1990. pap. 4.95 (*0-8114-6762-7*) Raintree Steck-V.

Vilna: Fascimile Edition. Israel Cohen. LC 92-6162. (Jewish Communities Ser.). (Illus.). 576p. 1992. pap. 24.95 (*0-8276-0416-5*) JPS Phila.

***Vilna Gaon.** Betzalel Landau. 20.99 (*0-89906-441-8*, VILH); pap. 17.99 (*0-89906-442-6*, VILP) Mesorah Pubns.

Vilna Gaon: The Story of Rabbi Eliyahu Kramer. Dovid Shulman. LC 94-6847. 150p. (YA). 1994. write for info. (*1-56062-278-4*); pap. write for info. (*1-56062-279-2*) CIS Comm.

Vilna on the Seine: Jewish Intellectuals in France since 1968. Judith Friedlander. 264p. (C). 1990. 37.00 (*0-300-04703-7*) Yale U Pr.

Vim, a Very Important Mouse. 10th ed. Jane Weinberger. LC 84-50872. (Illus.). 40p. (J). (ps-4). 1989. reprint ed. pap. 4.95 (*0-932433-01-4*) Windswept Hse.

***Vim & Vinegar: Moisten Cakes, Eliminate Grease, Remove Stains, Kill Weeds, Clean Pots & Pans, Soften Laundry, Unclog Drains, Control Dandruff, Season Salads, Make Pies.** Melodie Moore. LC 96-45253. 192p. (Orig.). 1997. pap. 10.00 (*0-06-095223-7*, PL) HarpC.

Vimalakirti Sutra. Tr. by Burton Watson. (Translations from the Asian Classics Ser.). 184p. 1996. 22.50 (*0-231-10656-4*) Col U Pr.

Vimana Aircraft of Ancient India & Atlantis. David H. Childress. (Lost Science Ser.). (Illus.). 284p. (Orig.). 1991. pap. 15.95 (*0-932813-12-7*) Adventures Unltd.

Vimana Stories. Tr. by P. Masefield from PLI. (C). 1988. 68.50 (*0-86013-272-2*, Pub. by Pali Text) Wisdom MA.

Vimanavatthu - Stories of the Mansions & Pettavatthu - Stories of the Departed. Tr. by J. Kennedy et al. from PLI. (Minor Anthologies Ser.: Vol. 4). (C). 1974. 16.00 (*0-86013-073-8*, Pub. by Pali Text) Wisdom MA.

***Vimy Ridge: Arras.** Nigel Cave. (Battleground Europe Ser.). 1996. pap. text ed. 11.95 (*0-85052-399-0*, Pub. by L Cooper Bks UK) Trans-Atl Phila.

Vin Blanc de la Villette. Jules Romains. 224p. (FRE.). 1923. pap. 10.95 (*0-7859-1305-X*, 2070255034) Fr & Eur.

Vin de Paris. Marcel Ayme. (FRE.). 1984. pap. 12.95 (*0-7859-1981-3*, 2070375153) Fr & Eur.

Vin de Paris. Marcel Ayme. (Folio Ser.: No. 1515). (FRE.). 1947. pap. 9.95 (*2-07-037515-3*) Schoenhof.

Vin Est Tire. Robert Desnos. 206p. (FRE.). 1992. 11.95 (*0-7859-1159-6*, 2070725502) Fr & Eur.

Vin et Societe a Bergerac: Du Moyen Age Aux Temps Modernes. Jacques Beauroy. (Stanford French & Italian Studies: No. 4). (Illus.). 294p. (FRE.). 1977. pap. 46.50 (*0-915838-32-X*) Anma Libri.

Vina Del Mar Workshop on Cataclysmic Variable Stars. Ed. by N. Vogt. (ASP Conference Series Proceedings: Vol. 30). 405p. 1992. 28.00 (*0-937707-49-X*) Astron Soc Pacific.

U V

*__Vina del Senor.__ Pablo Lopez Capestany. (SPA.). Date not set. pap. write for info. (0-89729-839-X) Ediciones.

*__Vinagrerito.__ Alberta Hawse. (SPA.). 1.50 (0-8297-1086-8) Life Pubs Intl.

Vinalhaven at Bowdoin: One Press, Multiple Impressions. David P. Becker. (Illus.). 24p. (Orig.). 1992. pap. 10.00 (0-916606-23-6) Bowdoin Coll.

*__Vinalhaven, ME.__ Vinahlhaven Historical Society Staff. (Images of America Ser.). 1997. pap. 16.99 (0-7524-0524-1, Arcdia) Chalford.

Vinatoarea Regala see Royal Hunt

Vinaver: Theatre de Chambre. Ed. by D. Bradby. (French Texts Ser.). 161p. (FRE.). 1995. pap. 16.95 (1-85399-433-2, Pub. by Brstl Class Pr UK) Focus Pub-R Pullins.

Vinaya Chalisa: Forty Prayers. Baba H. Dass. (Essays on the Search for Peace in Daily Life Ser.: Vol. 3). (Illus.). 92p. (Orig.). 1994. pap. 10.95 (0-918100-16-X) Sri Rama.

Vinaya Texts, 3 vols, Set. Rhys Davids. 1972. lib. bdg. 900.00 (0-87968-513-1) Krishna Pr.

Vinca Alkaloids: Botany, Chemistry, & Pharmacology. Ed. by William I. Taylor & Norman Farnsworth. LC 73-83859. 381p. reprint ed. pap. 108.60 (0-317-28688-9, 2055284) Bks Demand.

Vince: A Personal Biography of Vince Lombardi. Michael O'Brien. LC 87-12980. 352p. 1989. pap. 12.95 (0-688-09204-7, Quill) Morrow.

*__Vince Gill.__ Ed. by Colgan Bryan. (Guitar Anthology Ser.). 124p. (Orig.). 1996. pap. text ed. 22.95 (1-57623-588-2, PG9646) Warner Brothers.

*__Vince Gill: High Lonesome Sound.__ Ed. by Jeannette DeLisa. 44p. (Orig.). (YA). 1996. pap. text ed. 18.95 (1-57623-530-0, PF9626) Warner Brothers.

Vince Gill: Souvenirs. Ed. by Jeannette DeLisa. 72p. (Orig.). (YA). 1996. pap. text ed. 18.95 (1-57623-353-7, PF9611) Warner Brothers.

Vince Gill: When Love Finds You. Ed. by Carol Cuellar. 48p. (Orig.). 1994. pap. 16.95 (0-89724-340-4, VF2150) Warner Brothers.

*__Vince Gill - I Still Believe in You.__ Ed. by Carol Cuellar. 56p. (Orig.). (C). 1992. pap. text ed. 16.95 (0-7692-0729-4, VF1873) Warner Brothers.

*__Vince Gill - Selections from Pocket Full of Gold & When I Call Your Name Plus Other Hits.__ Ed. by Carol Cuellar. 72p. (Orig.). (C). 1994. pap. text ed. 16.95 (0-7692-0728-6, VF1742) Warner Brothers.

*__Vince Lombardi.__ John Wukovits. LC 96-52616. (Football Legends Ser.). (Illus.). 64p. (J). (gr. 3-7). 1997. lib. bdg. 15.95 (0-7910-4398-3) Chelsea Hse.

*__Vince Vance Rock & Roll Reader, Vol. 1.__ Vince Vance. Ed. by Carole Pennington. LC 95-83587. (Illus.). viii, 160p. (J). (gr. 3-8). 1996. 12.95 (0-9652918-0-4) Fullerton Bks.

Vincennes: A Pictorial History. Richard Day. (Indiana Pictorial History Ser.). (Illus.). 1994. reprint ed. write for info. (0-943963-03-6) G Bradley.

Vincennes & Sevres Porcelain: Catalogue of the Collections of the J. Paul Getty Museum. Adrian Sassoon. LC 93-9753. 206p. 1992. 85.00 (0-89236-173-5, J P Getty Museum) J P Getty Trust.

U V

Vincent. Tim Burton. (Illus.). 32p. (J). (gr. k up). 1997. 15.95 (0-7868-0295-2) Hyprn Child.

Vincent. Leonard Nimoy. 1985. pap. 5.95 (0-87129-386-2, V17) Dramatic Pub.

Vincent. Duncan Wherrett. (Color Library). (Illus.). 128p. 1994. pap. 15.95 (1-85532-330-3, Pub. by Osprey Pubng Ltd UK) Motorbooks Intl.

*__Vincent: Special Edition.__ limited ed. Tim Burton. (Illus.). (J). (gr. k up). 1998. pap. 19.95 (0-7868-0299-5) Hyprn Child.

*__Vincent: The Complete Self-Portraits.__ Bernard Denvir. 1997. 10.98 (0-7624-0094-3) Courage Bks.

*__Vincent: The Works of Vincent Van Gogh.__ Franco Vedovello. 1996. 39.98 (0-7651-9790-1) Smithmark.

Vincent & Theo Van Gogh: A Dual Biography. Jan Hulsker & Johann Van Gogh. LC 89-28907. (Illus.). 502p. 1990. 39.00 (0-940537-05-2) Fuller Tech.

Vincent by Himself. Bruce Bernard. 1995. 32.98 (0-7858-0428-5) Bk Sales Inc.

Vincent Crummles: His Theatre & His Times. F. J. Darton. LC 79-173157. 1972. reprint ed. 26.95 (0-405-08431-5, Pub. by Blom Pubns UK) Ayer.

Vincent De Paul: Correspondence, Vol. 5. Vincent De Paul. Ed. by Jacqueline Kilar. Tr. by Helen M. Law et al. 1995. 35.00 (1-56548-036-8) New City.

Vincent de Paul & Louise de Marillac: Rules, Conferences, & Writings. Ed. by Frances Ryan & John E. Rybolt. LC 95-3447. (Classics of Western Spirituality Ser.). 1995. 24.95 (0-8091-0471-7); pap. 18.95 (0-8091-3564-7) Paulist Pr.

*__Vincent d'Indy & His World.__ Andrew Thomson. (Illus.). 264p. 1997. text ed. 55.00 (0-19-816220-0) OUP.

Vincent Lombardi-Pele. John N. Fago. (Pendulum Illustrated Biography Ser.). (Illus.). (J). (gr. 4-12). 1979. student ed. 1.25 (0-88301-382-7); text ed. 7.50 (0-88301-370-3); pap. text ed. 2.95 (0-88301-358-4) Pendulum Pr.

Vincent Longo Prints 1954-1955: A Selection. David Acton & Judith Goldman. (Illus.). 40p. 1995. pap. 7.50 (1-885998-07-4) Hunter College.

Vincent Melzac Collection. (Illus.). 1971. 3.75 (0-686-20543-X) Corcoran.

Vincent of Beauvais & Alexander the Great. Edme R. Smits et al. (Mediaevalia Groningana Ser.: Vol. VII). 187p. (Orig.). 1986. pap. 35.00 (90-6980-009-8, Pub. by Egbert Forsten NE) Benjamins North Am.

Vincent of Beauvais' 'De Eruditione Filiorum Nobilium' The Education of Women. Rosemary B. Tobin. LC 84-47531. (American University Studies: Education: Ser. XIV, Vol. 5). 164p. (C). 1984. text ed. 20.85 (0-8204-0105-6) P Lang Pubng.

Vincent P. Gianella: Recollections of Geological Work in the West, the University of Nevada, & Following Western Trails. Ed. by Mary E. Glass. 429p. 1973. lib. bdg. 61.50 (1-56475-127-9); fiche write for info. (1-56475-128-7) U NV Oral Hist.

Vincent Persichetti: A Bio-Bibliography. Donald L. Patterson & Janet L. Patterson. LC 88-25084. (Bio-Bibliographies in Music Ser.: No. 16). 352p. 1988. text ed. 69.50 (0-313-25334-X, PPE/, Greenwood Pr) Greenwood.

Vincent Price: Actor & Art Collector. Alan Curl & Raul A. Lopez. (Illus.). 48p. 1982. pap. 10.00 (0-935661-08-5) Riverside Mus Pr.

Vincent Thomas Bridge: San Pedro's "Golden Gate" Arthur A. Almeida et al. (Illus.). 48p. (Orig.). 1988. pap. 3.00 (0-9611556-2-0) San Pedro Hist.

Vincent Van Gogh. (Prestel Postcard Bks.). (Illus.). 18p. (Orig.). 1995. pap. 8.95 (3-7913-1617-6, Pub. by Prestel GW) te Neues.

Vincent Van Gogh. Osjkar Hagen. 1972. 59.95 (0-8490-1261-9) Gordon Pr.

*__Vincent Van Gogh.__ Eileen Lucas. LC 96-27617. (On My Own Bks.). (Illus.). (J). 1997. lib. bdg. 13.13 (1-57505-038-2, Carolrhoda) Lerner Group.

*__Vincent Van Gogh.__ John Malam. LC 97-8066. (Tell Me about Ser.). (J). 1998. write for info. (1-57505-249-0, Carolrhoda) Lerner Group.

Vincent Van Gogh. Humberto Nagera. (Illus.). 182p. 1990. text ed. 24.95 (0-8236-8326-5, BN 26741) Intl Univs Pr.

Vincent Van Gogh. Meyer Schapiro. LC 94-1477. (Illus.). 136p. 1994. pap. 19.98 (0-8109-8117-3, Abradale Pr) Abrams.

Vincent Van Gogh. Museum of Modern Art Library Staff. Ed. by Alfred H. Barr, Jr. LC 78-109811. (Illus.). 193p. 1971. reprint ed. text ed. 49.75 (0-8371-4302-0, NYVG, Greenwood Pr) Greenwood.

Vincent Van Gogh: A Biographical Study. Julius Meier-Graefe. Tr. by John Holroyd-Reece. LC 76-109788. 239p. 1970. reprint ed. text ed. 35.00 (0-8371-4278-4, MEVG, Greenwood Pr) Greenwood.

Vincent Van Gogh: A Biography. Julius Meier-Graefe. 160p. 1987. reprint ed. pap. 4.95 (0-486-25253-1) Dover.

Vincent Van Gogh: A Life. Philip Callow. (Illus.). 320p. 1990. 24.95 (0-929587-57-5) I R Dee.

Vincent Van Gogh: A Life. Philip Callow. 312p. 1996. pap. 12.95 (1-56663-134-3) I R Dee.

Vincent Van Gogh: A Monograph. Alfred H. Barr, Jr. & Charles M. Brooks, Jr. LC 66-26121. (Museum of Modern Art Publications in Reprint). 1967. reprint ed. 28.95 (0-405-01514-3) Ayer.

Vincent Van Gogh: Chemicals, Crises, & Creativity. Wilfred N. Arnold. LC 92-13130. (Illus.). x, 322p. 1992. 34.50 (0-8176-3616-1) Birkhauser.

Vincent van Gogh: Christianity vs Nature. Tsukasa Kodera. LC 89-18335. (OCULI Studies in the Arts of the Low Countries: Vol. 3). (Illus.). xii, 283p. 1990. 76.00 (1-55619-076-X) Benjamins North Am.

*__Vincent van Gogh: Complete Paintings & Drawings, Vol. 1.__ Sjaar Van Heugten. 1996. 100.00 (0-85331-721-6, Pub. by Lund Humphries UK) Antique Collect.

Vincent Van Gogh: Irises. Ronald Pickvance. (Getty Museum Studies on Art). pap. 15.95 (0-89236-226-X, J P Getty Museum) J P Getty Trust.

Vincent Van Gogh: Painter on Location. Dennis Thomas. 1994. 12.98 (0-7858-0107-3) Bk Sales Inc.

Vincent Van Gogh: Painter, Printmaker, Collector. Lanier Graham. (Illus.). 32p. (Orig.). 1990. pap. 8.95 (0-915776-07-3) NS Mus.

*__Vincent Van Gogh: Paintings: Arles, Saint-Remy & Auvers 1888-90.__ Sjraar Van Heugten. (Illus.). 1999. 100.00 (0-85331-733-X, Pub. by Lund Humphries UK) Antique Collect.

Vincent Van Gogh: The Painter Who Suffered from Depression. Intro. by Jerry Lewis. (Great Achievers). (Illus.). 128p. (YA). (gr. 5 up). 1995. lib. bdg. 19.95 (0-7910-2422-9) Chelsea Hse.

*__Vincent Van Gogh Vol. 1: Paintings: Dutch Period 1881-85.__ Sjraar Van Heugten. (Illus.). 1997. 100.00 (0-85331-742-9, Pub. by Lund Humphries UK) Antique Collect.

*__Vincent Van Gogh Vol. 2: Drawings: Brabant Period 1883-85.__ Sjraar Van Heugten. (Illus.). 1997. 100.00 (0-85331-731-3, Pub. by Lund Humphries UK) Antique Collect.

*__Vincent Van Gogh Vol. 2: Paintings: Antwerp & Paris 1885-88.__ Sjraar Van Heugten. (Illus.). 1998. 100.00 (0-85331-723-2, Pub. by Lund Humphries UK) Antique Collect.

*__Vincent Van Gogh Vol. 3: Drawings: Antwerp & Paris 1885-88.__ Sjraar Van Heugten. (Illus.). 1998. 100.00 (0-85331-740-2, Pub. by Lund Humphries UK) Antique Collect.

*__Vincent Van Gogh Vol. 4: Drawings: Arles, Saint-Remy & Auvers 1888-90.__ Sjraar Van Heugten. (Illus.). 1999. 100.00 (0-85331-741-0, Pub. by Lund Humphries UK) Antique Collect.

*__Vincent Van Gogh Vol. 5: Drawings: Sketchbooks & Appendices.__ Sjraar Van Heugten. (Illus.). 100.00 (0-85331-732-1, Pub. by Lund Humphries UK) Antique Collect.

Vincent Van Gogh - a Portrait. Jean De Beucken. (Illus.). (FRE.). lib. bdg. 14.95 (0-8288-4000-8) Fr & Eur.

Vincent Van Gogh - Dessins, Pastels, Etudes. Werner L. Muensterberger. (Illus.). 106p. (FRE.). 1948. lib. bdg. 14.95 (0-8288-3978-6) Fr & Eur.

Vincent van Gogh - The Works: Catalogue Raisonne. J. B. De La Faille. (Illus.). 704p. 1970. 300.00 (1-55660-811-X) A Wofsy Fine Arts.

Vincent Van Gogh, Eighteen Fifty-Three to Eighteen Ninety. Walter Pach. LC 78-99666. (Select Bibliographies Reprint Ser.). 1977. 21.95 (0-8369-5095-X) Ayer.

Vincent van Gogh's Self-Portrait Dedicated to Paul Gauguin: An Historical & Technical Study. Vojtech Jirat-Wasiuntynski et al. (Illus.). 38p. 1995. pap. 9.00 (0-916724-58-1, 4581) Harvard Art Mus.

Vincente Espinel "Diversas Rimas" Dorothy C. Clark. 204p. 1956. 4.50 (0-318-22353-8) Hispanic Inst.

Vincente Huidobro & Creationism. H. A. Holmes. 1977. lib. bdg. 59.95 (0-8490-2799-3) Gordon Pr.

Vincent's Cookbook. Vincent Guerithault. LC 94-8090. 288p. 1994. text ed. 25.95 (0-89815-566-5) Ten Speed Pr.

*__Vincent's Religion: The Search for Meaning.__ W. W. Meissner. (Reshaping of Psychoanalysis Ser.: Vol. 8). 296p. (C). 1997. 52.95 (0-8204-3390-X) P Lang Pubng.

Vincent's Revenge - Laissez-Faire-Next Ten Miles: A Flurry of Rage & Crows. Gordon R. Marlow. 224p. (Orig.). 1996. pap. 8.00 (1-887500-00-6) Baillie Caymar Pubns.

Vincent's Systems of Cutting All Kinds of Tailor-Made Garments see Tailoring of the Belle Epoque: Vincent's Systems of Cutting All Kinds of Tailor-Made Garments (1903)

*__Vincent's Tale.__ Nolan Dennett. 1998. 21.95 (1-55713-323-9) Sun & Moon CA.

Vincent's Word Studies in the New Testament, 4 vols. M. R. Vincent. 2720p. 1984. 75.00 (0-917006-30-5) Hendrickson MA.

Vincenzo Capirola Lute Book. Vincenzo Capirola. Ed. by Otto Gombosi. (Music Ser.). 236p. (C). 1983. reprint ed. lib. bdg. 75.00 (0-306-76100-9) Da Capo.

Vincenzo Ruffo: Il Primo Livro de Motetti a Cinque Voci (Milan: Castillione, 1542) Motetti a Sei Voci (Venice: Scotto, 1955) Ed. by Richard Sherr. LC 87-753388. (Sixteenth-Century Motet Ser.: Vos. 19-20). 1988. text ed. 100.00 (0-8240-7919-1) Garland.

Vincenzo Ruffo: Il Primo Livro de Motetti a Cinque Voci (Milan: Castillione, 1542) Motetti a Sei Voci (Venice: Scotto, 1955) Ed. by Richard Sherr. LC 87-754636. (Sixteenth-Century Motet Ser.: Vos. 19-20). 1988. text ed. 95.00 (0-8240-7920-5) Garland.

Vincenzo Ruffo (c. 1508-1587) Madrigali a sei, sette e otto voci--Venice: Girolamo Scotto, 1554, Vol. 26. Ed. by Jessie A. Owens. (Italian Madrigal in the Sixteenth Century Ser.). 1988. text ed. 95.00 (0-8240-5528-4) Garland.

Vincenzo Ruffo (c. 1508-1587) Primo Libro di madrigali a cinque voci--Venice: Girolamo Scotto 1533, Vol. 25. Ed. by Jessie A. Owens. (Italian Madrigal in the Sixteenth Century Ser.). 1989. text ed. 100.00 (0-8240-5527-6) Garland.

Vincit Veritas: A Portrait of the Life & Work of Norman Abraham Haskell, 1905-1970. Ed. by Ari Ben-Menahem. 200p. 1990. 25.00 (0-87590-762-8, SP0307628) Am Geophysical.

Vinculo see Aguilas

*__Vindicating the Founders: Race, Sex, Class, & Justice in the Origins of America.__ Thomas West. LC 97-16791. 200p. 1997. 22.95 (0-8476-8516-0) Rowman.

Vindication. Frances Sherwood. LC 92-41934. 1993. 22.00 (0-374-28390-7) FS&G.

Vindication. Frances Sherwood. 448p. 1994. pap. 11.95 (0-14-023668-6, Penguin Bks) Viking Penguin.

Vindication of Absolute Idealism. Timothy L. Sprigge. 291p. 1983. 45.00 (0-85224-455-X, Pub. by Edinburgh U Pr UK) Col U Pr.

*__Vindication of Judaism: The Polemics of the Hertz Pentateuch.__ LC 96-49370. (Moreshet Ser.). 1997. write for info. (0-87334-073-5) Jewish Sem.

Vindication of Natural Diet: A New Edition. Percy Bysshe Shelley. LC 74-30288. (Shelley Society, Second Ser.: No. 4). reprint ed. 22.50 (0-404-11506-3) AMS Pr.

Vindication of Natural Society. Edmund E. Burke. LC 81-84826. (Illus.). 130p. 1982. reprint ed. 12.00 (0-86597-009-2); reprint ed. pap. text ed. 5.00 (0-86597-010-6) Liberty Fund.

Vindication of Political Virtue: The Political Theory of Mary Wollstonecraft. Virginia Sapiro. LC 91-38426. 394p. 1992. pap. text ed. 18.95 (0-226-73491-9) U Ch Pr.

Vindication of Providence: or A True Estimate of Human Life. 2nd ed. Edward Young. LC 92-23742. (Augustan Reprints Ser.: Nos. 225-226). 1984. reprint ed. 21.50 (0-404-70225-2, BX5133) AMS Pr.

Vindication of the Big Bang: Breakthroughs & Barriers. B. Parker. (Illus.). 354p. (C). 1993. 24.95 (0-306-44469-0, Plenum Pr) Plenum.

Vindication of the Captors of Major Andre. Egbert Benson. (American Revolutionary Ser.). reprint ed. lib. bdg. 29.50 (0-8398-0187-4) Irvington.

Vindication of the Government of New-England Churches. John Wise. Ed. by Perry Miller. LC 58-5422. 1979. reprint ed. 50.00 (0-8201-1246-1) Schol Facsimiles.

Vindication of the Rights of Brutes. Thomas Taylor. LC 66-10010. 1966. reprint ed. 50.00 (0-8201-1045-0) Schol Facsimiles.

Vindication of the Rights of Brutes. Thomas Taylor. Ed. by J. D. Holmes. 1994. reprint ed. pap. 8.95 (1-55818-275-6) Holmes Pub.

Vindication of the Rights of Men. Mary Wollstonecraft. LC 93-46503. (Revolution & Romanticism, 1789-1834 Ser.). 1994. 48.00 (1-85477-174-4, Pub. by Woodstock Bks UK) Cassell.

Vindication of the Rights of Men. Mary Wollstonecraft. LC 96-28487. (Great Books in Philosophy). 100p. 1996. pap. 4.95 (1-57392-106-8) Prometheus Bks.

Vindication of the Rights of Men. Mary Wollstonecraft Shelley. LC 60-5073. 192p. 1975. reprint ed. lib. bdg. 50.00 (0-8201-1164-3) Schol Facsimiles.

Vindication of the Rights of Men & a Vindication of the Rights of Woman. Mary Wollstonecraft Shelley. Ed. by Sylvana Tomaselli. (Cambridge Texts in the History of Political Thought Ser.). 280p. (C). 1995. text ed. 44.95 (0-521-43053-4); pap. text ed. 10.95 (0-521-43633-8) Cambridge U Pr.

Vindication of the Rights of Whores: The International Movement for Prostitutes' Rights. Ed. by Gail Pheterson. LC 88-33060. 320p. (Orig.). 1989. pap. 16.95 (0-931188-73-3) Seal Pr WA.

Vindication of the Rights of Woman. Mary Wollstonecraft Shelley. Ed. by Carol H. Poston. (Critical Editions Ser.). (C). 1987. pap. text ed. 9.95 (0-393-95572-9) Norton.

Vindication of the Rights of Woman. Mary Wollstonecraft. Ed. by Miriam Kramnick. (English Library). 320p. pap. 5.95 (0-14-043199-3, Penguin Classics) Viking Penguin.

Vindication of the Rights of Woman. Mary Wollstonecraft. 1992. 15.00 (0-679-41337-5, Everymans Lib) Knopf.

Vindication of the Rights of Woman. Mary Wollstonecraft. 320p. 1993. pap. 9.95 (0-14-043382-1, Penguin Bks) Viking Penguin.

Vindication of the Rights of Woman. Mary Shelley Wollstonecraft. 400p. 1995. pap. 6.50 (0-460-87615-5, Everyman's Classic Lib) C E Tuttle.

Vindication of the Rights of Woman. unabridged ed. Mary Wollstonecraft. 224p. 1996. reprint ed. pap. text ed. 2.00 (0-486-29036-0) Dover.

Vindication of the Rights of Women. Mary Wollstonecraft. (Great Books in Philosophy). 200p. 1989. pap. 6.95 (0-87975-525-3) Prometheus Bks.

Vindication of the Rights of Women. Mary Wollstonecraft. 27.95 (0-8488-1226-3) Amereon Ltd.

Vindication of the Rights of Women. Mary Wollstonecraft. (C). 1992. 24.00 (81-7100-465-2, Pub. by Deep II) S Asia.

Vindication of Tradition. Jaroslav J. Pelikan. LC 84-5132. 94p. 1986. pap. 11.00 (0-300-03638-8) Yale U Pr.

Vindiciae, Contra Tyrannos: Or, Concerning the Legitimate Power of a Prince over the People, & of the People over a Prince. Ed. by George Garnett. (Illus.). 360p. (C). 1994. text ed. 75.00 (0-521-34209-0) Cambridge U Pr.

Vindiciae Epistolarum Sancti Ignatii, 2 Vols, Set. John Pearson. LC 76-173936. (Library of Anglo-Catholic Theology: No. 16). reprint ed. 57.50 (0-404-52140-1) AMS Pr.

Vine & Branches, Vol. 1. Maryann Hakowski. Ed. by Robert P. Stamschror. (Resources for Youth Retreats Ser.). (Illus.). 158p. (YA). (gr. 7-12). 1991. spiral bd. 22.95 (0-88489-255-7) St Marys.

Vine & Branches, Vol. 2. Maryann Hakowski. Ed. by Robert P. Stamschror. (Resources for Youth Retreats Ser.). (Illus.). 166p. (YA). (gr. 7-12). 1991. spiral bd. 22.95 (0-88489-278-6) St Marys.

Vine & Branches, Vol. 3. Robert P. Stamschror. (Resources for Youth Retreats Ser.: Vol. 3). (Illus.). 175p. (J). (gr. 6-7). 1994. pap. 22.95 (0-88489-323-5) St Marys.

Vine & Branches: Chronique des Guerres de Religion, Vol. 2. Monluc. 1640p. 42.95 (0-686-56543-6) Fr & Eur.

Vine & Dandy. Dave Brandl. LC 93-48188. 52p. (Orig.). 1994. pap. 6.00 (0-88734-260-4) Players Pr.

Vine & the Branches. Jerry L. Schmalenberger. 1991. pap. 6.25 (1-55673-403-4, 9216) CSS OH.

Vine & the Branches. Federico Suarez. 128p. 1996. pap. 7.95 (1-85182-266-6, Pub. by Four Cts Pr IE) Intl Spec Bk.

Vine & the Branches: A History of the International Church of the Foursquare Gospel. Nathaniel M. Van Cleave. Ed. & Intro. by Ronald D. Williams. 1992. 28.95 (0-9635581-0-2) Int Church Foursq.

Vine & Wine Economy: Proceedings of the International Symposium held at Kecskemet, Hungary, 25-29 June June, 1990. Ed. by E. P. Botos & A. Kiado. (Developments in Agricultural Economics Ser.: Vol. 8). 336p. 1991. 196.25 (0-444-98711-8) Elsevier.

Vine & Wine Economy: Proceedings of the International Symposium, Kecskemet, Hungary, June 25-29, 1990. E. P. Botos. 333p. 1991. 160.00 (963-05-6039-9, Pub. by Akad Kiado HU) St Mut.

Vine & Wine '95. Richards Lyon. (Yearly Datebook Journals Ser.). 162p. (Orig.). (C). pap. text ed. 14.95 (0-9616004-6-2) Stonecrest Pr.

Vine of the Soul: Medicine Men, Their Plants & Rituals in the Colombian Amazon. Richard E. Schultes & Robert F. Raffauf. (Illus.). 125p. 1992. 22.95 (0-907791-24-7) Synerg AZ.

Vine Patterns: Asian Art Motifs from Korea. Weatherhill Staff. 1994. 40.00 (89-7059-007-2, Pub. by Ahn Graphics KN) Weatherhill.

Vine to Wine. Richards Lyon. LC 85-62333. (Illus.). 120p. (Orig.). 1985. pap. 9.95 (0-9616004-0-3) Stonecrest Pr.

Vinegar Blossom. large type ed. Maureen Peters. (General Fiction Ser.). 1991. 25.99 (0-7089-2436-0) Ulverscroft.

*__Vinegar Book.__ Emily Thacker. 58p. 1996. pap. 9.95 (1-883944-03-1) Tresco.

Vinegar Boy: A Young Boy's Dramatic Encounter with Christ on the Cross. Alberta Hawse. 1970. pap. 9.99 (0-8024-9172-3) Moody.

Vinegar Hill. Ansay A. Manette. Date not set. pap. 9.95 (0-14-023239-7, Viking) Viking Penguin.

Vinegar Jar. Berlie Doherty. 256p. 1996. 21.95 (0-312-14442-3) St Martin.

*__Vinegar on the Cross.__ Terry Stocker. 236p. 1997. 24.00 (0-9654427-0-5) Tula Press.

Vinegar Pancakes & Vanishing Cream. Bonnie Pryor. LC 86-31085. (Illus.). 128p. (J). (gr. 2-5). 1987. 16.00 (0-688-06728-X, Morrow Junior) Morrow.

An Asterisk (*) at the beginning of an entry indicates that the title is appearing in BIP for the first time.

Vinegar Pancakes & Vanishing Cream. Bonnie Pryor. (J). 1996. pap. 4.95 (*0-688-14744-5*) Morrow.

Vinegar Pie & Chicken Bread: A Woman's Diary of Life in the Rural South, 1890-1891. Ed. by Margaret J. Bolsterli. LC 82-4922. 128p. 1983. pap. 10.00 (*0-938626-25-6*) U of Ark Pr.

Vinegar Pie & Other Tales of the Grand Traverse Region. Al Barnes. LC 58-12684. (Illus.). 184p. 1984. 14.50 (*0-915937-00-X*) Hor Bks MI.

Vinegar Seed. large type ed. Maureen Peters. (General Fiction Ser.). 1990. 25.99 (*0-7089-2339-9*) Ulverscroft.

Vinegar Tree. large type ed. Maureen Peters. (General Fiction Ser.). 384p. 1992. 25.99 (*0-7089-2682-7*) Ulverscroft.

Vinegar Use Poetry Pages. Alpha Pyramis Research Division Staff. 30p. 1984. pap. text ed. 6.50 (*0-913597-66-X*) Prosperity & Profits.

Vinegar Year. Lynne Dowell. Ed. by Clarinda H. Lott. (New Poets Ser.: Vol 7). (Illus.). 50p. 1980. pap. 2.95 (*0-932616-05-4*) Brick Hse Bks.

Vinegars. Ann Creber. LC 94-4154. (Williams-Sonoma Essentials Ser.). 1994. 9.95 (*1-875137-20-3*) Weldon Owen.

Vineland. Thomas Pynchon. 400p. 1991. pap. 11.95 (*0-14-014511-7*) Viking Penguin.

***Vineland.** Thomas Pynchon. 1997. pap. 13.95 (*0-14-118063-3*) Viking Penguin.

Vineland Papers: Critical Takes on Pynchon's Novels. Ed. by Geoffrey Green et al. LC 93-27255. 188p. 1994. 29. 95 (*1-56478-038-4*); pap. 14.95 (*1-56478-039-2*) Dalkey Arch.

Vines. Suzanne F. Bales. LC 94-5195. (Burpee American Gardening Ser.). (Illus.). 1995. pap. 8.00 (*0-671-85045-8*, P-H Gardening) P-H Gen Ref & Trav.

Vines. Burpee Staff. 1994. 9.00 (*0-02-860037-1*, P-H Gardening) P-H Gen Ref & Trav.

Vines & Climbers. Random House Value Editors. LC 97-3454. 1997. 9.99 (*0-517-14274-0*) Random Hse Value.

Vines & Climbers. Warren Schultz. LC 95-52702. (For Your Garden Ser.). 72p. 1996. pap. 12.95 (*1-56799-276-5*, Friedman-Fairfax) M Friedman Pub Grp Inc.

***Vine's Complete Expository Dictionary.** Nelson Staff. 1996. 29.99 (*0-7852-1217-5*); 19.97 (*0-7852-6020-X*) Nelson.

Vine's Complete Expository Dictionary of Old & New Testament Words with Topical Index. rev. ed. William E. Vine et al. LC 96-8956. 1128p. 1996. 29.99 (*0-7852-1160-8*) Nelson.

***Vine's Dictionary of Bible Words.** Thomas Nelson Publishers Staff. LC 96-46032. 1997. pap. 9.99 (*0-7852-1169-1*) Nelson.

***Vine's Expository Commentary of Galatians.** Thomas Nelson Publishers Staff. 224p. 1997. 14.99 (*0-7852-1172-1*) Nelson.

***Vine's Expository Commentary of I & II Thessalonian.** Thomas Nelson Publishers Staff. 224p. 1997. 14.99 (*0-7852-1171-3*) Nelson.

***Vine's Expository Commentary on Isaiah.** W. E. Vine. LC 97-8957. 1997. write for info. (*0-7852-1233-7*) Nelson.

***Vine's Expository Commentary on John.** W. E. Vine. LC 97-8958. 1997. write for info. (*0-7852-1234-5*) Nelson.

Vine's Expository Dicionary of Old & New Testament Words. Ed. by William E. Vine et al. 1128p. 1987. 24. 99 (*0-8407-7559-8*) Nelson.

Vine's Expository Dictionary of New Testament Words. William E. Vine. 1376p. 1989. 16.95 (*0-917006-03-8*) Hendrickson MA.

Vine's Expository Dictionary of New Testament Words. William E. Vine. (Barbour Bks.). 351p. 1985. reprint ed. 14.95 (*0-916441-31-8*); reprint ed. pap. 10.95 (*0-916441-34-2*) Barbour & Co.

Vine's Expository Dictionary of Old & New Testament Words. William E. Vine. 1568p. 1982. 24.99 (*0-8007-1282-X*) Revell.

***Vine's Expository Dictionary of Old & New Testament Words.** William E. Vine. LC 97-8955. 912p. 1997. 24. 99 (*0-7852-1181-0*) Nelson.

Vine's Expository Dictionary to Biblical Words. William E. Vine. (Ellis' Bible Study Ser.). 1110p. (C). 1993. 49.95 (*0-933186-55-X*) IBM Corp Pub.

***Vines, Grapes & Wines: The Wine Drinker's Guide to Grape Varieties.** Jancis Robinson. (Illus.). 280p. pap. 27.95 (*1-85732-999-6*, Pub. by M Beazley Pubs Ltd UK) Antique Collect.

***Vine's Learn New Testament Greek.** William E. Vine. LC 96-30029. 128p. 1997. pap. 9.99 (*0-7852-1232-9*) Nelson.

Vines of San Lorenzo: The Making of a Great Wine in the New Tradition. Edward Steinberg. LC 92-26642. 1992. 25.00 (*0-88001-284-6*) Ecco Pr.

Vineyard. Fanny Howe. (Lost Roads Ser.: No. 33). 80p. (Orig.). 1988. pap. 7.95 (*0-918786-37-1*) Lost Roads.

***Vineyard.** Idwal Jones. LC 96-38103. 1997. write for info. (*0-520-21090-5*) U CA Pr.

Vineyard: Scientists in the Church. Eva-Maria Amrhein & Robert A. Brungs. 153p. (Orig.). 1992. pap. 15.95 (*0-9625431-5-2*) ITEST Faith.

Vineyard & the Sea. Charles W. Stork. 1977. pap. 5.00 (*0-916530-07-8*) Athenaeum Phila.

Vineyard & the Wedding: Stories of God's Kingdom. Dina Strong & Liz Riggeman. (Storyteller Ser.). (J). (ps-2). 1996. suppl. ed. 10.95 (*1-889108-12-X*) Liv Good News.

Vineyard & the Wedding: Stories of God's Kingdom. Dina Strong. (Storyteller Ser.). (Illus.). 32p. (J). (ps-2). 1996. pap. 18.95 (*1-889108-09-X*) Liv Good News.

Vineyard & the Wedding: Stories of God's Kingdom, Set. Dina Strong. (Storyteller Ser.). (Illus.). (J). Date not set. 28.50 (*1-889108-02-2*) Liv Good News.

Vineyard Birds. annot. ed. Susan B. Whiting & Barbara B. Pesch. 115p. (Orig.). 1983. pap. 3.00 (*0-932691-05-6*) MA Audubon Soc.

Vineyard Garden: Ideas from the Earth for Growing, Cooking, Decorating, & Entertaining. Molly Chappellet. LC 91-50165. (Illus.). 304p. 1991. pap. 40.00 (*0-670-83436-X*, Viking Studio) Studio Bks.

Vineyard Handbook: Appellation, Maps & Statistics. Ed. & Illus. by Patrick W. Fegan. 150p. 1991. pap. text ed. 35. 00 (*0-9631428-9-5*) Chi Wine Schl.

Vineyard of Liberty. James M. Burns. LC 83-3506. (Illus.). 768p. 1983. pap. 25.00 (*0-394-71629-9*, Vin) Random.

Vineyard Seasons. Susan Branch. (Illus.). 160p. 1988. 23.95 (*0-316-10632-1*) Little.

Vineyard Summer. Photos by Alison Shaw. LC 93-43504. 1994. 24.95 (*0-316-78345-5*) Little.

Vineyard Tales: Reflections on Wine. Gerald Asher. LC 95-47429. 208p. 1996. 22.95 (*0-8118-1267-7*) Chronicle Bks.

Vineyards in the Sky: The Life of Legendary Vintner Martin Ray. Eleanor Ray & Barbara Marinacci. LC 92-74051. (Illus.). 448p. 1993. 28.95 (*0-9623048-4-0*); pap. 18.95 (*0-9623048-5-9*) Heritage West.

Vingettes. Alexander Russo. 100p. (Orig.). 1996. pap. 10.00 (*1-57502-231-1*) Morris Pubng.

Vingt Annees De Missions Dans le Nord-Ouest De L'amerique Par Mgr. Alex. Tache Eveque De Saint-Boniface (Montreal, 1866) Alexandre A. Tache. (Canadiana Avant 1867 Ser.: N0. 21). 1970. 32.30 (*90-279-6343-6*) Mouton.

Vingt Ans Apres. Alexandre Dumas. Ed. by Charles Samaran. (Coll. Prestige). 12.95 (*0-685-34894-6*) Fr & Eur.

Vingt Ans Apres, 2 vols. Alexandre Dumas. 1975. write for info. (*0-318-63616-6*) Fr & Eur.

Vingt Ans Apres. Alexandre Dumas. Ed. by Charles Samaran. (Class. Garnier Ser.). 1989. pap. 20.95 (*0-7859-3150-3*, 2253050520) Fr & Eur.

Vingt Ans Apres, 2 tomes, Set. Alexandre Dumas, Sr. (Coll. GF). 1961. pap. 9.00 (*0-685-11621-2*) Fr & Eur.

Vingt Ans Apres, Tome I. Alexandre Dumas. 544p. (FRE.). 1975. pap. 11.95 (*0-7859-1803-5*, 2070366820) Fr & Eur.

Vingt Ans Apres, Tome II. Alexandre Dumas. 544p. (FRE.). 1975. pap. 12.95 (*0-7859-1804-3*, 2070366839) Fr & Eur.

Vingt Ans Du Jeune Homme Vert. Michel Deon. 608p. (FRE.). 1981. pap. 12.95 (*0-7859-1938-4*, 2070373010) Fr & Eur.

Vingt-Deux Dessins sur le Theme du Desir. Jean-Paul Sartre & Andre Masson. (Illus.). 1,250.00 (*0-686-55006-4*) Fr & Eur.

Vingt Deuxiesme Livre. Ed. by Albert Seay. (Transcriptions Ser.: No. 4). iii, 67p. 1981. pap. 4.00 (*0-933894-07-4*, Attaingnant) Colo Coll Music.

Vingt Mille Lieues sous les Mers. Jules Verne. (FRE.). 1983. pap. 10.95 (*0-7859-1627-X*, 2070332373) Fr & Eur.

Vingt-Mille Lieues sous les Mers. Jules Verne. (FRE.). 1992. pap. 16.95 (*0-7859-3072-8*) Fr & Eur.

Vingt Mille Lieues Sous les Mers, 2 vols., Ea. Jules Verne. 1977. 10.95 (*0-318-52320-5*) Fr & Eur.

Vingt Mille Lieues Sous les Mers, Vol. 1. Jules Verne. (FRE.). 1983. pap. 10.95 (*0-7859-1626-1*, 2070332365) Fr & Eur.

Vingt Mille Lieuses sous les Mers. unabridged ed. Verne. (FRE.). pap. 7.95 (*2-87714-204-3*, Pub. by Bookking Intl FR) Distribks Inc.

Vingt-Neuf Degres a l'Ombre. Eugene Labiche. 9.95 (*0-686-54257-6*) Fr & Eur.

Vingt suites d'orchestre du XVIIe siecle francais, 2 vols. Ed. by Jules Ecorcheville. (Illus.). 384p. (FRE.). 1973. reprint ed. lib. bdg. 175.00 (*0-8450-1005-0*) Broude.

Vingtieme Siecle: La Problematique du Discours. Ed. by Roy Nelson. LC 81-50963. (Michigan Romance Studies: vol. 6). 127p. (Orig.). 1986. pap. 9.00 (*0-939730-05-7*) Mich Romance.

Vingtieme Siecle see Collection Litteraire

Vinifera. Hudson Cattell & Lee S. Miller. (Wines of the East Ser.). (Illus.). 28p. (Orig.). 1979. pap. 2.75 (*0-911301-02-X*) L&H Photojrnl.

Vinisi...I'd Love to Come..., Vol. IV. Antonio Provenzano. Ed. & Tr. by Gaetano Cipolla. (Pueti D'arba Sicula - Poets of ARBA Sicula). 200p. (Orig.). (ITA.). 1995. pap. 16.00 (*1-881901-08-4*) LEGAS.

Vinland. George M. Brown. 256p. 1993. 24.95 (*0-7195-5149-8*, Pub. by John Murray UK) Trafalgar.

Vinland Map & the Tartar Relation. Thomas E. Marston et al. 1995. write for info. (*0-300-06520-5*) Yale U Pr.

Vinland Map & the Tartar Relation. Raleigh A. Skelton & Thomas E. Marston. LC 65-22339. (Illus.). 353p. reprint ed. pap. 100.70 (*0-8357-8365-0*, 2033892) Bks Demand.

Vinland Sagas: The Norse Discovery of America. Pattr Groenlendinga. LC 66-31936. 124p. reprint ed. pap. 35. 40 (*0-317-08208-6*, 2050271) Bks Demand.

Vinland Sagas & the Norse Discovery of America: The Norse Discovery of America. Tr. by Magnus Magnusson & Hermann Palsson. Incl. Graenlendinga Saga. 1965. pap. (*0-318-55115-2*); Eirik's Saga. 1965. pap. (*0-318-55116-0*); (Classics Ser.). 126p. (Orig.). 1965. pap. 9.95 (*0-14-044154-9*, Penguin Classics) Viking Penguin.

Vinland Voyages. Matthias Thordarson. Tr. by Thorstina J. Walters. LC 75-160996. (Select Bibliographies Reprint Ser.). 1977. reprint ed. 18.95 (*0-8369-5864-0*) Ayer.

Vinnie. LC 90-112. 1990. pap. 13.95 (*0-87949-296-1*) Ashley Bks.

Vinnie & Me. Fiorella D. Calce. (Prose Ser.: No. 31). 90p. 1995. 12.00 (*1-55071-017-6*) Guernica Editions.

***Vinnie & the Stardusters: The Girl from Ipanema Wants to Kill Me.** Eric Dregni et al. (Illus.). 24p. (Orig.). 1996. pap. 5.00 (*1-890529-01-X*) Simple Sense.

Vinny's Wide World of Sports. Rich Manning. LC 95-94690. 104p. 1995. pap. 6.95 (*0-9648690-0-4*) Lowdown Bros.

Vinoba Bhave No. 27: Political Thinkers of Modern India. Ed. by Verinder Grover. (C). 1995. 52.00 (*81-7100-573-X*) S Asia.

Vinoba Bhave on Self-Rule & Representative Democracy. Michael W. Sonnleitner. (C). 1988. 24.00 (*81-85002-10-X*, Pub. by Firma KLM II) S Asia.

Vins de Bordeaux. David Peppercorn. 312p. (FRE.). 1993. lib. bdg. 49.95 (*0-7859-3635-1*, 2082005755) Fr & Eur.

Vinson Court Era: The Supreme Court's Conference Votes: Data & Analysis. J. Palmer. LC 89-45875. (Studies in Social History: No. 9). 1990. 57.50 (*0-404-61609-7*) AMS Pr.

Vintage. Evelyn Carlson et al. Ed. by Patricia Traxler. (Illus.). 104p. (Orig.). 1984. pap. 5.00 (*0-932199-00-3*) Smoky Hill.

Vintage: The Story of Wine. Hugh Johnson. (Illus.). 480p. 1992. pap. 25.00 (*0-671-79182-6*, Fireside) S&S Trade.

Vintage - New & Selected Poems. Leonard A. Slade, Jr. LC 95-16137. 72p. 1995. pap. 12.95 (*0-7734-2735-X*, Mellen Poetry Pr) E Mellen.

Vintage Aircraft Nose Art. G. Valant. (Illus.). 208p. 1987. 39.95 (*0-87938-266-X*) Motorbooks Intl.

Vintage Airplane Coloring Book. Illus. by Richard King. 44p. (Orig.). 1996. pap. 5.95 (*1-882663-07-1*) Plymouth MI.

Vintage Airplane Coloring Book, Incl. crayons. Illus. by Richard King. 44p. (Orig.). 1996. pap. 6.95 (*1-882663-06-3*) Plymouth MI.

Vintage Airplane Directory. T. Scott Harnish. 500p. 1993. pap. 29.95 (*1-57087-006-3*) Prof Pr NC.

***Vintage American & Europ. W. W., No. 7.** Roy Ehrhardt & Joe DeMesy. (Illus.). 672p. (Orig.). 1996. pap. text ed. 35.00 (*0-913902-95-0*) Heart Am Pr.

Vintage American & European, Bk. 3. David Mycko et al. (Illus.). 224p. (Orig.). 1989. pap. text ed. 25.00 (*0-913902-57-8*) Heart Am Pr.

Vintage American & European, Bk. 4. Sherry Ehrhardt et al. (Illus.). 624p. (Orig.). 1989. pap. text ed. 25.00 (*0-913902-58-6*) Heart Am Pr.

Vintage American & European Wrist Watch Price Guide, Bk. 5. Sherry Ehrhardt et al. 1990. 25.00 (*0-913902-59-4*) Heart Am Pr.

Vintage American & European Wrist Watch Price Guide, Bk. 1 & '87 Update. rev. ed. Sherry Ehrhardt & Peter Planes. 1987. 25.00 (*0-913902-51-9*) Heart Am Pr.

Vintage American & European Wrist Watch Price Guide, Bk. 2. Sherry Ehrhardt et al. (Illus.). 1988. pap. 25.00 (*0-913902-56-X*) Heart Am Pr.

Vintage American & European Wrist Watch Price Guide, Bk. 6: 1993 Special Edition. Roy Ehrhardt & Joe DeMesy. (Illus.). 672p. 1993. 25.00 (*0-913902-67-5*) Heart Am Pr.

Vintage American & European Wrist Watch Price Update. Sherry Ehrhardt & Peter Planes. (Illus.). 80p. 1987. 12. 00 (*0-913902-55-1*) Heart Am Pr.

***Vintage & Contemporary Purse Accessories: Identification & Value Guide, Featuring Lipsticks, Mirrors & Solid Perfumes.** Roselyn Gerson. (Illus.). 192p. 1997. 24.95 (*0-89145-790-9*, 4878) Collector Bks.

Vintage & Historic Racing Cars. Alex Gabbard. (Illus.). 192p. 1986. 25.00 (*0-89586-405-3*) Gabbard Writing & Photo.

Vintage & Historic Stock Cars. John Craft. (Enthusiast Color Ser.). (Illus.). 96p. 1994. pap. 12.95 (*0-87938-898-6*) Motorbooks Intl.

***Vintage Baby Book Album, Birth-2 Years: Preserving the Precious.** Jeanne English. 60p. 1993. 15.95 (*1-885425-04-X*) Restorat Source.

***Vintage Baby Book Album Kit, 3-5 Years No. 2: Preserving the Precious.** Jeanne English. 15.95p. 1993. 15.95 (*1-885425-05-8*) Restorat Source.

***Vintage Baby Book Album Kit, 6-8 Years No. 3: Preserving the Precious.** Jeanne English. 60p. 1993. 15. 95 (*1-885425-06-6*) Restorat Source.

Vintage Baja: Adventures of a Gringa in Lower California. Marion Smothers. (Illus.). 96p. (Orig.). 1993. pap. 7.99 (*1-881791-03-3*) In One EAR.

***Vintage Bar Ware: Identification & Value Guide.** Stephen Visakay. (Illus.). 208p. 1997. 24.95 (*0-89145-789-5*, 4877) Collector Bks.

***Vintage Book of Classic Crime.** Michael Dibdin. LC 96-9620. (Vintage Crime - Black Lizard Ser.). 1997. pap. 14.00 (*0-679-76855-6*, Vin) Random.

Vintage Book of Contemporary American Poetry. Ed. by J. D. McClatchy. LC 90-50119. 400p. (Orig.). 1990. pap. 16.00 (*0-679-72858-9*, Vin) Random.

Vintage Book of Contemporary American Short Stories. Intro. by Tobias Wolff. LC 94-15007. 1994. pap. 13.00 (*0-679-74513-0*, Vin) Random.

Vintage Book of Contemporary Irish Fiction. Dermot Bolger. LC 95-11104. 1995. pap. 14.00 (*0-679-76546-8*, Vin) Random.

Vintage Book of Contemporary World Poetry. Ed. & Intro. by J. D. McClatchy. 672p. 1996. pap. 15.00 (*0-679-74115-1*, Vin) Random.

Vintage Bradbury. Ray Bradbury. 1990. pap. 12.00 (*0-679-72946-1*, Vin) Random.

Vintage Case Tractors: American Legends. Peter Letourneau. LC 96-35225. (American Legends Ser.). (Illus.). 112p. 1997. 24.95 (*0-89658-335-X*, Town Sq) Voyageur Pr.

Vintage Clothing 1880-1980: Identification & Value Guide. 3rd rev. ed. Maryanne Dolan. (Vintage Clothing 1880-1980 Ser.). (Illus.). 304p. 1995. pap. 22.95 (*0-89689-109-7*) Bks Americana.

***Vintage Colorado Short Stories: Where Past Meets Present.** James B. Hemesath. LC 97-17595. 1997. write for info. (*0-87081-459-1*) Univ Pr Colo.

***Vintage Compacts & Beauty Accessories.** Lynell Schwartz. (Illus.). 176p. 1997. 34.95 (*0-7643-0110-1*) Schiffer.

Vintage Cork. Cork Millner. LC 96-31623. 176p. 1997. 15. 00 (*1-56474-197-4*) Fithian Pr.

Vintage Denim. David Little. LC 95-11531. (Illus.). 160p. 1996. pap. 21.95 (*0-87905-664-9*) Gibbs Smith Pub.

Vintage Excavation Machinery. Michael Irwin. (Illus.). 144p. 1996. 44.95 (*0-85236-333-8*, Pub. by Farming Pr UK) Diamond Farm Bk.

***Vintage Farm Tractors.** Andrew Morland. (Enthusiast Color Ser.). (Illus.). 96p. 1997. pap. 12.95 (*0-7603-0147-6*) Motorbooks Intl.

Vintage Farm Tractors: The Ultimate Tribute to Classic Tractors. Ralph W. Sanders. LC 96-11995. (Illus.). 192p. 1996. 29.95 (*0-89658-280-9*, Town Sq) Voyageur Pr.

Vintage Fashion & Fabrics. Pamela D. Smith. (Instant Expert Ser.). 128p. 1995. pap. 12.00 (*0-9641509-2-1*) Allian Pubng.

Vintage Fashion Collector: Collected Articles by Kristina Harris. Kristina Harris. 190p. 1994. 40.00 (*1-885133-02-2*) Pioneer Prntwrk.

***Vintage Fashions for Women: The 1950s & 60s.** Kristina Harris. LC 97-6979. 1997. pap. write for info. (*0-7643-0197-7*) Schiffer.

Vintage Fashions for Women 1920s-1940s. Kristina Harris. LC 96-2517. 192p. (gr. 10-13). 1996. pap. 29.95 (*0-88740-986-5*) Schiffer.

***Vintage Feasting.** Sterling. 1997. pap. 14.00 (*0-671-52777-0*, PB Trade Paper) PB.

Vintage Feasting. Joy Sterling. 256p. 1996. 24.00 (*0-671-52776-2*) PB.

Vintage Flying Helmets: Aviation Headgear Before the Jet Age. Mich J. Prodger. LC 94-69862. (Illus.). 336p. 1994. 75.00 (*0-88740-776-5*) Schiffer.

***Vintage Ford Tractor.** Robert N. Pripps. LC 97-1858. (American Legends Ser.). (Illus.). 160p. 1997. 29.95 (*0-89658-354-6*, Town Sq) Voyageur Pr.

Vintage Glory: Airline Color Schemes of the '50s and '60s. Adrian M. Balch. (Illus.). 112p. 1995. pap. 19.95 (*1-85310-436-1*) Motorbooks Intl.

Vintage Guide to Classical Music. Jan Swafford. 1993. pap. 17.00 (*0-679-72805-8*, Vin) Random.

Vintage Guide to Drum Collecting. John Aldridge. (Illus.). 180p. 1994. pap. text ed. 24.95 (*0-931759-78-1*) Centerstream Pub.

***Vintage Guide to Drum Collecting.** John Aldridge. (Illus.). 180p. 1994. pap. text ed. 24.95 (*0-931759-79-X*, 00000167) Centerstream Pub.

***Vintage Hats & Bonnets - 1770-1970: 1770-1970, 4955.** Susan Langley. (Illus.). 288p. 1997. 24.95 (*1-57432-028-9*) Collector Bks.

Vintage Illustration: Discovering America's Calendar Artists (1900-1960) Rick Martin & Charlotte Martin. Ed. by Michael Goldberg & Gail Manchur. LC 96-9529. (Illus.). 208p. 1996. 35.00 (*1-888054-00-X*) Collectors Pr.

***Vintage International Black & Red Sticker.** Date not set. write for info. (*0-676-99333-8*) Random.

***Vintage International Harvester Tractors.** Ralph W. Sanders. LC 97-6793. (American Legends Ser.). (Illus.). 160p. 1997. 29.95 (*0-89658-355-4*, Town Sq) Voyageur Pr.

Vintage John Deere: Early History & the Two-Cylinder Years. Dave Arnold. LC 94-31815. (Illus.). 112p. 1995. 24.95 (*0-89658-265-5*) Voyageur Pr.

***Vintage John Deere: Early History & the Two-Cylinder Years.** Dave Arnold. LC 94-31815. (Illus.). 112p. 1997. pap. 17.95 (*0-89658-348-1*, Town Sq) Voyageur Pr.

Vintage Journey: A Guide to Artful Aging. Trish Herbert. LC 94-35082. 184p. (Orig.). 1994. pap. 15.95 (*0-8298-1012-9*) Pilgrim OH.

Vintage Jukeboxes. Christopher Pearce. 1988. 10.98 (*1-55521-323-5*) Bk Sales Inc.

***Vintage Jukeboxes.** Christopher Pearce. 1997. 12.98 (*0-7858-0785-3*) Bk Sales Inc.

Vintage Mencken. Alistair Cooke. 1976. 22.95 (*0-8488-0465-1*) Amereon Ltd.

Vintage Mencken. H. L. Mencken. LC 89-40542. 1990. pap. 12.00 (*0-679-72895-3*, Vin) Random.

Vintage Miniature Racing Cars. deluxe limited ed. Bob Ames. (Illus.). 128p. 1992. 125.00 (*1-55868-121-3*) Gr Arts Ctr Pub.

Vintage Missouri. Robert F. Scheef. (Illus.). 160p. 1991. pap. 8.95 (*0-935284-90-7*) Patrice Pr.

Vintage Monster Movies. Robert G. Marrero. (Illus.). 160p. 1993. pap. 12.95 (*0-9634982-1-5*) Fantasma Bks.

Vintage Motor Cars. Bill Boddy. 1989. pap. 25.00 (*0-85263-776-4*, Pub. by Shire UK) St Mut.

Vintage Motorcycles. Jeff Clew. 1995. pap. 25.00 (*0-7478-0277-7*, Pub. by Shire UK) St Mut.

Vintage Motorcyclists' Workshop. Radco. LC 86-82145. 1986. 31.95 (*0-85429-472-4*, Pub. by G T Foulis Ltd) Haynes Pubns.

Vintage Murder. Janet L. Smith. 1995. mass mkt. 5.99 (*0-8041-1385-8*) Ivy Books.

Vintage NBA Basketball: The Pioneer Era. Neil D. Isaacs. (Illus.). 256p. (Orig.). 1996. pap. 16.95 (*1-57028-069-X*) Masters Pr IN.

***Vintage Peace.** Bobi Dolara. 80p. 1993. pap. 9.50 (*1-56770-270-8*) S Scheewe Pubns.

Vintage Pellegrini: The Collected Wisdom of an American Buongustaio. Angelo Pellegrini. Ed. by Schuyler Ingle. 262p. 1991. pap. 10.95 (*0-912365-44-7*); text ed. 18.95 (*0-912365-45-5*) Sasquatch Bks.

Vintage Police Cars. Edwin J. Sanow. LC 96-13067. (Enthusiast Color Ser.). (Illus.). 96p. 1996. pap. 12.95 (*0-7603-0180-8*) Motorbooks Intl.

Vintage Port: The Wine Spectator's Ultimate Guide for Consumers, Collectors & Investors. James Suckling. (Illus.). 430p. 1990. 29.95 (0-918076-80-3) M Shanken Comm.
Vintage Purses at Their Best: With Price Guide. Lynell K. Schwartz. LC 95-6380. (Illus.). 160p. 1995. 29.95 (0-88740-831-1) Schiffer.
Vintage Racing British Sports Cars. Terry Jackson. (Illus.). 206p. (Orig.). 1990. pap. 29.95 (0-8376-0153-3) Bentley.
Vintage Racing Machine: Cars from the Collection of George Waterman Jr. Daniel Robbins. (Illus.). 1970. pap. 5.00 (0-911517-41-3) Mus of Art RI.
*Vintage Reading: A Choice Crop of the World's Best Books. Robert Kanigel. 300p. (Orig.). 1998. pap. 16.95 (0-9631246-7-6) Bancroft MD.
Vintage Rock 'n' Roll. (Easy Piano Ser.). 64p. 1985. pap. 7.95 (0-7935-2444-X, 00241021) H Leonard.
*Vintage Snowmobiles: Artic Cat, 1974-1979, John Deere, 1972-1977, Kawasaki, 1976-1980. (Illus.). Date not set. reprint ed. pap. 29.95 (0-89287-677-8, S820) Intertec Pub.
*Vintage Snowmobiles Vol. 2: Polaris, 1973-1979, Ski-Doo, 1970-1979, Yamaha, 1975-1980. LC 96-75978. (Illus.). (Orig.). 1996. pap. 29.95 (0-89287-678-6, S821) Intertec Pub.
*Vintage Spot Illustrations of Children. Judy M. Johnson. (Illus.). pap. 7.95 (0-486-26351-7) Dover.
Vintage Station Wagon Shop Service. Ed. by Thomas B. Garrett. LC 76-57074. (Illus.). 160p. 1977. pap. 19.95 (0-911160-85-X) Post Group.
*Vintage Style: 1920-1960. Desire Smith. LC 97-19736. 1997. write for info. (0-7643-0302-3) Schiffer.
Vintage Synthesizers: Groundbreaking Instruments & Pioneering Designers of Electronic Music Synthesizers. Mark Vail. (Illus.). 300p. 1993. pap. 22.95 (0-87930-275-5) Miller Freeman.
Vintage Talk: Conversations with California's New Winemakers. Dennis Schaefer. (Orig.). 1995. lib. bdg. 43.00 (0-8095-4136-X) Borgo Pr.
Vintage Talk: Conversations with California's New Winemakers. Dennis Schaefer. LC 93-43347. (Illus.). 304p. (Orig.). 1994. pap. 15.95 (0-88496-360-8) Capra Pr.
Vintage Texas: Cooking with Lone Star Wines. Frank R. Giordano, Jr. 224p. 1996. 34.95 (0-88415-856-X, 5856) Gulf Pub.
Vintage Theatre Styles, Bk. 1. W. McMains. 56p. Date not set. pap. 7.95 (0-7935-2202-1, 00030601) H Leonard.
Vintage Tractors. Charles L. Cawood. 1989. pap. 25.00 (0-85263-499-4, Pub. by Shire UK) St Mut.
*Vintage Treasures, Traditional Pleasures, Low Fat Measures. Donna Silberhorn. (Orig.). 1997. spiral bd., pap. 15.95 (0-9657147-0-5) D Silberhorn.
Vintage Vanity Bags & Purses. Roselyn Gerson. 1996. 24.95 (0-89145-599-X) Collector Bks.
Vintage Vicksburg. Ed. by Natalie Bailess et al. 464p. 1985. 16.95 (0-9614988-0-3) Jr Aux Vicksburg.
Vintage Views of Adams County, Ohio. Stephen Kelley. LC 85-90092. (Scenes from the Past Ser.: Vol. I). (Illus.). 52p. (Orig.). 1985. pap. 8.50 (0-9614480-4-0) Kelley Pubns.
Vintage Volkswagens. Photos by Flat 4 Project. (Illus.). 120p. 1985. pap. 14.95 (0-87701-357-8) Chronicle Bks.
Vintage Wein: Shaar Press. J. Weiss. 1992. 22.99 (0-89906-598-8); pap. 17.99 (0-89906-599-6) Mesorah Pubns.
*Vintage White Linen. Marsha L. Manchester. LC 97-19734. 1997. write for info. (0-7643-0363-5) Schiffer.
Vintage Wine Book. 2nd ed. Sommelier Executive Council Staff et al. 376p. 1992. 49.95 (1-56022-008-2); pap. 24.95 (1-56022-009-0) Haworth Jrnl Co-Edits.
*Vintage Worcester Post Card Book. Ed. by Jennifer J. Goguen. (Illus.). 6p. (Orig.). 1996. pap. 9.99 (1-886284-01-6, Tatnuck) Databks.
Vintage Year. large type ed. Pat Lacey. (Linford Romance Library). 288p. 1992. pap. 15.99 (0-7089-7282-9, Traitree Bookshop) Ulverscroft.
Vintage Year for Dying. Frank Orenstein. 256p. 1994. 20.95 (0-312-10442-1, Thomas Dunne Bks) St Martin.
Vintage Year for Dying. Frank Orenstein. (WWL Mystery Ser.). 1996. mass mkt. 4.99 (0-373-26196-9, 1-26196-5, Wrldwide Lib) Harlequin Bks.
*Vintage 93: The League of Canadian Poets. Ed. by Sandra Nicholls. 1996. pap. 16.95 (1-55082-122-9, Pub. by Quarry Pr CN) LPC InBook.
*Vintage 95: The League of Canadian Poets. Ed. by Sandra Nicholls. 104p. 1996. pap. 16.95 (1-55082-170-9, Pub. by Quarry Pr CN) LPC InBook.
Vintages & Traditions: An Ethnohistory of Southwest French Wine Cooperatives. Robert C. Ulin. (Smithsonian Series in Ethnographic Inquiry). (Illus.). 352p. 1996. text ed. 56.00 (1-56098-627-1); pap. text ed. 19.95 (1-56098-628-X) Smithsonian.
Vintner's Art: How Great Wines Are Made. Hugh Johnson & James Halliday. LC 92-14386. (Illus.). 224p. 1992. 40.00 (0-671-72888-1) S&S Trade.
Vinton Memorial, Comprising a Genealogy of the Descendants of John Vinton of Lynn, 1648: Also Genealogical Sketches of Several Allied Families. J. A. Vinton. (Illus.). 554p. 1989. reprint ed. pap. 83.00 (0-8328-1203-X); reprint ed. lib. bdg. 91.00 (0-8328-1202-1) Higginson Bk Co.
*Vinus Solamnus. J. Robert King. (Dragonlance Novel Ser.). 1997. pap. 5.99 (0-7869-0787-8) TSR Inc.
Vinyl: A Material for the Future: Regional Technical Conference, the Society of Plastics Engineers, Quebec Section in Cooperation with the Vinyl Division, September 15 & 16, 1988, Delta Hotel, Montreal, Quebec, Canada. Society of Plastics Engineers Staff. 415p. pap. 118.30 (0-8357-7505-4, 2034185) Bks Demand.
*Vinyl & Plastic Lunch Boxes. 2nd rev. ed. Larry Aikins. (Illus.). 159p. 1995. pap. 14.95 (0-89538-015-3) L-W Inc.
Vinyl Closet: Gays in the Music World. Boze Hadleigh. LC 91-70465. 200p. 1991. pap. 9.95 (0-9623497-9-8) Los Hombres.
Vinyl Graphics How-To. Larry Mitchell. (Illus.). 44p. 1995. pap. 14.95 (0-944094-13-9) ST Pubns.
Vinyl in Building & Construction: Regional Technical Conference, Sheraton Naperville Hotel, Naperville Illinois, Sept, 20-22, 1982. Society of Plastics Engineers Staff. 113p. reprint ed. pap. 32.30 (0-317-29842-9, 2019657) Bks Demand.
Vinyl in Packaging: Regional Technical Conference, Ramada Inn, Airport West, Mississauga, Ontario, Canada, September 13 & 14, 1983. Society of Plastics Engineers Staff. 247p. reprint ed. pap. 70.40 (0-317-28107-0, 2022511) Bks Demand.
Vinyl Leaves: Walt Disney World & America. Stephen M. Fjellman. 492p. (C). 1992. pap. text ed. 25.00 (0-8133-1472-0) Westview.
Vinyl Plastics: A World View of the Industry & Market. Robert A. McCarthy. LC 85-20410. (Series of Special Reports: No. 14). (Illus.). 392p. reprint ed. pap. 111.80 (0-7837-0859-9, 2041167) Bks Demand.
Vinyl Polymerization, 2 pts., Pt. 1. Ed. by George E. Ham. LC 70-15571. (Kinetics & Mechanisms of Polymerization Ser.: No. 1). (Illus.). 558p. reprint ed. pap. 150.70 (0-7837-0641-3, 2040983) Bks Demand.
Vinyl Polymerization, 2 pts., Pt. 2. Ed. by George E. Ham. LC 70-15571. (Kinetics & Mechanisms of Polymerization Ser.: No. 1). (Illus.). 432p. reprint ed. pap. 123.20 (0-7837-0642-1) Bks Demand.
Vinyl 101: A Comprehensive Update: Vinyl RETEC '92, Hyatt Regency Hotel, New Brunswick, NJ, September 23, 30 - October 1, 1992. Society of Plastics Engineers Staff. (Illus.). 326p. reprint ed. pap. 93.00 (0-7837-4497-8, 2044274) Bks Demand.
Vinyl 201: A Comprehensive Processing Update: Vinyl RETEC 93, September 22-23, 1993, Swissotell, Atlanta, GA. Society of Plastics Engineers Staff. (Illus.). 312p. 1993. reprint ed. pap. 89.00 (0-7837-9712-5, 2060443) Bks Demand.
Vinylidene Chloride. (Environmental Health Criteria Ser.: No. 100). 187p. 1990. pap. text ed. 32.00 (92-4-154300-0, 1160100) World Health.
*Vinylidene Chloride Health & Safety Guide. WHO Staff. (Health & Safety Guides: No. 36). 28p. 1989. 5.00 (92-4-154357-4) World Health.
*Viola: Complete Guide for Teachers & Students. 2nd ed. Henry Barrett. LC 70-169498. 232p. 1996. pap. text ed. 29.95 (0-8173-0885-7) U of Ala Pr.
Viola d'Amore. 2nd rev. ed. Harry Danks. LC 79-313933. (Illus.). 128p. 1979. 48.00 (0-900998-16-4, Pub. by S Bonner UK) Theodore Front.
Viola E. Bray Renaissance Gallery. Frwd. by G. Stuart Hodge. (Illus.). 35p. 1969. 0.50 (0-939896-17-6) Flint Inst Arts.
*Viola Forum Highlights. Karen Tuttle et al. (Highlights from the American String Teacher Forums Ser.). 25.00 (0-614-25491-4, 1936S) Am String Tchrs.
Viola Frey. Viola Frey. 1991. pap. 22.50 (0-932499-28-7) Lapis Pr.
Viola Making, Plans. rev. ed. Harry S. Wake. 1996. pap. 24.00 (0-9607048-5-X) H S Wake.
Violas & Violettas. Rodney Fuller. 1995. 8.00 (0-00-412959-8, HarpT) HarpC.
Viola's Favorite Recipes. Viola Lampkin. (Illus.). 74p. (Orig.). 1988. pap. write for info. (0-9621378-0-4) B Clagett.
Violated Heart: Tales by Nathaniel Hawthorne. Ed. by Frank Gado. 360p. 1995. pap. 8.95 (0-912756-19-5) Union Coll.
Violated Perfection: The Architectural Fragmentation of Modernism. Aaron Betsky. LC 90-8399. (Illus.). 256p. 1990. 35.00 (0-8478-1269-3) Rizzoli Intl.
Violation & Repair in the English Novel: The Paradigm of Experience from Richardson to Woolf. Steven Cohan. LC 86-1297. 254p. 1986. 34.95 (0-8143-1794-4) Wayne St U Pr.
Violation of Fair Trial Guarantees by the FMLN's Ad Hoc Courts: El Salvador. Americas Watch Staff. 24p. 1990. 5.00 (0-929692-82-9, Am Watch) Hum Rts Watch.
Violation of Medical Neutrality. G. L. Wackers & C. T. Wennekes. 128p. 1992. pap. 20.00 (90-5170-115-2, Pub. by Thesis Pubs NE) IBD Ltd.
Violation of People at Work in Schools. Arthur G. Wirth. (DeGarmo Lectures). 1988. 3.00 (0-685-31371-9) Soc Profs Ed.
Violation of Trust. LC 91-34297. 306p. 1991. 19.50 (0-685-59350-9) Sovereign MD.
Violation of Trust. Joseph S. Salzburg. 400p. 1991. 19.50 (0-685-52388-8) Sovereign MD.
Violation of Trust: Whatever Happened to the Social Security Trust Funds. Steven J. Allen. LC 95-74711. 144p. 1995. mass mkt. 2.95 (0-9648635-0-2) Srs Coalition.
Violations. Susan Wright. (Star Trek Ser.: No. 4). 1995. mass mkt. 5.99 (0-671-52046-6) PB.
Violations de Frontieres. Jules Romains. 288p. (FRE.). 1951. pap. 10.95 (0-7859-1406-4, 2080506277) Fr & Eur.
Violations of Free Speech & Rights of Labor: Proceedings of the Committee on Education & Labor, U. S. Senate, 76th Congress, 3rd Session, 3 Vols. Education & Labor Committee. Ed. by Dan C. McCurry & Richard E. Rubenstein. LC 74-30659. (American Farmers & the Rise of Agribusiness Ser.). 1975. reprint ed. 95.95 (0-405-06836-0) Ayer.
Violators. Gunnard Landers. 250p. 1991. 19.95 (0-8027-1179-0) Walker & Co.
Violence. LC 93-40803. (To the Point Ser.). 96p. (Orig.). 1994. pap. 8.95 (0-687-43769-5) Abingdon.
Violence. (YouthTalk Ser.). 48p. (YA). 1994. pap. 5.25 (0-8066-0267-8, 15-5222); teacher ed., pap. 4.95 (0-8066-0268-6, 15-5223) Augsburg Fortress.
Violence. Scott Barbour. Ed. by Karin L. Swisher. LC 95-35628. (Opposing Viewpoints Ser.). (Illus.). 306p. (Orig.). (J). (gr. 5-12). 1996. pap. text ed. 12.96 (1-56510-354-8); lib. bdg. 20.96 (1-56510-355-6) Greenhaven.
Violence. Fox & Levin. 100p. (C). pap. text ed. 5.00 (0-673-99076-1) Addson-Wesley Educ.
Violence. Jory Post. (Comprehensive Health for Middle Grades Ser.). (J). (gr. 6-9). 1996. 24.00 (1-56071-472-7, H574) ETR Assocs.
*Violence. Naomi Schor. 1997. pap. text ed. 14.95 (0-253-30025-8) Ind U Pr.
Violence: A Reference Handbook. David E. Newton. (Contemporary World Issues Ser.). 228p. 1996. lib. bdg. 39.50 (0-87436-843-X) ABC-CLIO.
Violence: An Integrated Multivariate Study of Human Aggression. Shlomo G. Shoham et al. (Illus.). 248p. 1995. text ed. 62.95 (1-85521-432-6, Pub. by Dartmth Pub UK) Ashgate Pub Co.
Violence: Basic & Clinical Science. Chris Thompson & Philip Cowen. LC 92-48198. (Mental Health Foundation Ser.). (Illus.). 272p. 1993. pap. 90.00 (0-7506-0926-5) Buttrwrth-Heinemann.
*Violence: From Biology to Society: Proceedings of the International Meeting on Biology & Sociology of Violence, Valencia, Spain, 16-18 September, 1996. Grisolia, James International Meeting on Biology & Sociology of Violence Staff. LC 97-10365. (International Congress Ser.). 1997. write for info. (0-444-82572-X) Elsevier.
Violence: Health Facts. Nora J. Krantzler & Kathleen R. Miner. LC 95-3835. 1994. 12.95 (0-614-06657-3, H418) ETR Assocs.
Violence: Health Facts. Nora J. Krantzler et al. LC 95-3835. 1996. 12.95 (1-56071-476-X, H327) ETR Assocs.
Violence: Our Deadly Epidemic & Its Causes. James Gilligan. LC 95-44832. 304p. 1996. 28.95 (0-399-13979-6, Grosset-Putnam) Putnam Pub Group.
Violence: Prevention & Treatment in Groups. Ed. by George S. Getzel. LC 88-19171. (Social Work with Groups Ser.: Vol. 11, No. 3). (Illus.). 108p. 1989. text ed. 29.95 (0-86656-848-4) Haworth Pr.
*Violence: Reflections on a National Epidemic. James Gilligan. LC 96-36854. 1997. pap. 14.00 (0-679-77912-4, Vin) Random.
Violence: The Unrelenting Assault on Human Dignity. Wolfgang Huber. Tr. by Ruth C. Gritsch. 176p. 1996. pap. 16.00 (0-8006-2858-6, 1-2858, Fortress Pr) Augsburg Fortress.
*Violence - The Crisis of American Confidence: Milton S. Eisenhower Symposium. Ed. by Hugh D. Graham et al. LC 79-171554. 212p. 1971. reprint ed. pap. 60.50 (0-608-04042-8, 2064778) Bks Demand.
Violence, Abuse & Neglect: The American Home. Myron R. Utech. LC 91-75938. 320p. 1993. pap. text ed. 24.95 (0-930390-19-9); lib. bdg. 42.95 (0-930390-20-2) Gen Hall.
Violence Against Black Women Vol. 1: A Sociocultural Perspective. unabridged ed. Ed. by LaFrancis Rodgers-Rose. 348p. (Orig.). 1996. pap. text ed. 18.95 (0-934185-02-6) Traces Inst.
Violence Against Children. 52p. (Orig.). (C). 1993. pap. text ed. 20.00 (1-56806-846-8) DIANE Pub.
Violence Against Children: Physical Child Abuse in the United States. David G. Gil. LC 77-130809. (Commonwealth Fund Publications). (Illus.). 230p. 1973. pap. text ed. 7.95 (0-674-93942-5) HUP.
Violence Against Elders. 55p. (Orig.). (C). 1993. pap. text ed. 20.00 (1-56806-845-X) DIANE Pub.
Violence Against Lesbians & Gay Men. Gary D. Comstock. (Between Men - Between Women Ser.). 320p. (C). 1992. pap. 16.50 (0-231-07331-3) Col U Pr.
Violence Against Social Workers. Dan Norris. 144p. 1990. 42.50 (1-85302-041-9) Taylor & Francis.
Violence Against the Press in U. S. History. John Nerone. (Communication & Society Ser.). 320p. (C). 1994. pap. text ed. 18.95 (0-19-508698-8) OUP.
Violence Against Wives. R. Emerson Dobash & Russell P. Dobash. LC 79-7181. 1983. pap. 15.95 (0-02-907810-5, Free Press) Free Pr.
Violence Against Women. Ed. by Pauline B. Bart & Eileen G. Moran. (Gender & Society Readers Ser.: Vol. 1). (Illus.). 320p. (C). 1993. text ed. 52.00 (0-8039-5044-6); pap. text ed. 24.95 (0-8039-5045-4) Sage.
*Violence Against Women. David Frazee et al. LC 97-11012. 1997. write for info. (0-8366-1127-6) Clark Boardman Callaghan.
Violence Against Women. Ed. by Karin L. Swisher et al. LC 93-1807. (Current Controversies Ser.). 320p. (YA). 1994. pap. 12.96 (1-56510-069-7); lib. bdg. 20.96 (1-56510-070-0) Greenhaven.
Violence Against Women: A Bibliography. Ed. by Joan Nordquist. (Contemporary Social Issues: A Bibliographic Ser.: No. 26). 68p. (Orig.). 1992. pap. 15.00 (0-937855-50-2) Ref Rsch Serv.
Violence Against Women: A Critique of the Sociobiology of Rape. Ed. by Ethel Tobach & Suzanne Sunday. (Genes & Gender Ser.). 176p. (Orig.). (C). 1985. pap. 15.00 (0-87752-231-6) Gordian.
Violence Against Women: Law & Practice. David Frazee & Ann Noel. (Civil Rights Ser.). 1997. ring bd. write for info. (0-614-06277-2) Clark Boardman Callaghan.
Violence Against Women: Nursing Research, Education, & Practice Issues. Ed. by Carolyn M. Sampselle. (Health Care for Women International Publication). 350p. 1991. 49.95 (1-56032-217-9) Hemisp Pub.
Violence Against Women - Concilium. Ed. by M. Shawn Copeland & Elisabeth S. Fiorenza. 1994. pap. 15.00 (0-88344-876-9) Orbis Bks.
Violence Against Women & Children: A Christian Theological Sourcebook. Ed. by Carol J. Adams & Marie M. Fortune. 552p. 1995. pap. text ed. 29.95 (0-8264-0830-3) Continuum.
Violence Against Women & Families Resource Handbook. Alvin C. Lin. 175p. 1995. ring bd. 157.00 (0-933544-85-5) Gov Info Srvs.
Violence Against Women & the Ongoing Challenge to Racism. Angela Y. Davis. (Freedom Organizing Pamphlet Ser.). 20p. (Orig.). (C). 1987. pap. 3.95 (0-913175-11-0) Kitchen Table.
Violence Against Women as Bias Motivated Hate Crime: Defining the Issues. Lois Copeland & Leslie R. Wolfe. (Violence Against Women Ser.). 50p. (Orig.). (C). 1991. pap. 15.00 (1-877966-05-3) Ctr Women Policy.
Violence Against Women in South Africa: The State Response to Domestic Violence & Rape. Human Rights Watch Africa Staff & Human Rights Watch Women's Rights Project Staff. 132p. (Orig.). 1995. pap. 10.00 (1-56432-162-2) Hum Rts Watch.
Violence Against Women in the Family. 120p. 1989. 27.00 (92-1-130133-5, E.89.IV.5) UN.
Violence, Aggression, & Coercive Actions. James T. Tedeschi & Richard B. Felson. (Illus.). 480p. 1994. 49.95 (1-55798-257-0) Am Psychol.
Violence & Abuse in the Lives of People with Disabilities: The End of Silent Acceptance? Dick Sobsey. 480p. 1994. pap. 30.00 (1-55766-148-0, 1480) P H Brookes.
Violence & Aggression: A Physiological Perspective. K. E. Moyer. LC 86-4987. 237p. 1987. pap. text ed. 14.95 (0-943852-19-6) Prof World Peace.
*Violence & Childhood in the Inner City. Ed. by Joan McCord. (Criminology Ser.). (Illus.). 368p. (C). 1997. text ed. 59.95 (0-521-58326-8) Cambridge U Pr.
*Violence & Childhood in the Inner City. Ed. by Joan McCord. (Criminology Ser.). (Illus.). 368p. (C). 1997. pap. text ed. 19.95 (0-521-58720-4) Cambridge U Pr.
*Violence & Civilization: An Introduction to the Work of Norbert Elias. Jonathan Fletcher. Date not set. 54.95 (0-7456-1434-5, Pub. by Polity Pr UK) Blackwell Pubs.
*Violence & Civilization: An Introduction to the Work of Norbert Elias. Jonathan Fletcher. Date not set. pap. 22.95 (0-7456-1879-0, Pub. by Polity Pr UK) Blackwell Pubs.
Violence & Communication: Public Reactions to an Attempted Presidential Assassination. C. David Mortensen. (Illus.). 232p. (Orig.). (C). 1988. pap. text ed. 22.00 (0-8191-6688-X) U Pr of Amer.
Violence & Compassion: Dialogues on a World Today. Dalai Lama & Jean-Claude Carriere. LC 95-30694. 304p. 1996. 20.00 (0-385-47960-3) Doubleday.
Violence & Conflict in Modern French Culture. Ed. by Jan Windebank & R. Gunther. 27.50 (1-85075-512-4, Pub. by Sheffield Acad UK) CUP Services.
Violence & Conflict in the Politics & Society of Modern France. Ed. by Jan Windebank & Renate Gunther. LC 95-6142. (Studies in French Civilization: Vol. 5). (Illus.). 256p. (Orig.). 1995. text ed. 89.95 (0-7734-8968-1) E Mellen.
Violence & Crime in Cross-National Perspective. Dane Archer & Rosemary Gartner. LC 83-21700. 342p. 1987. pap. 19.00 (0-300-04023-7) Yale U Pr.
Violence & Daily Life: Reading, Art, & Polemics in the Citeaux Moralia in Job. Conrad Rudolph. LC 96-22197. (Illus.). 196p. 1997. text ed. 39.50 (0-691-02673-4) Princeton U Pr.
Violence & Defiance. Herbert Lust. LC 83-81847. 184p. (Orig.). 1984. 12.95 (0-930794-91-5); pap. 5.95 (0-930794-90-7) Station Hill Pr.
Violence & Democratic Society: The Need for New Approaches to Human Rights. Jamil Salmi. LC 93-20306. 192p. (C). 1993. pap. 19.95 (1-85649-222-2, Pub. by Zed Bks Ltd UK); text ed. 49.95 (1-85649-221-4, Pub. by Zed Bks Ltd UK) Humanities.
Violence & Devotion: A Novel of the Holocaust. Jacob Biber. (Studies in Judaica & the Holocaust: No. 15). pap. write for info. (0-8095-1409-5); lib. bdg. write for info. (0-8095-0409-X) Borgo Pr.
Violence & Difference: Girard, Derrida, & Deconstruction. Andrew J. McKenna. 256p. 1992. text ed. 39.95 (0-252-01837-0); pap. text ed. 15.95 (0-252-06202-7) U of Ill Pr.
Violence & Diplomacy in Lebanon: The Troubled Years, 1982-1988, Vol. 1. Eli Salem. 1995. text ed. 35.00 (1-85043-835-8, Pub. by I B Tauris UK) St Martin.
Violence & Disability: An Annotated Bibliography. Dick Sobsey et al. LC 94-30747. 288p. 1995. pap. 28.00 (1-55766-172-3) P H Brookes.
Violence & Gender Relations: Theories & Interventions. Barbara Fawcett et al. 208p. 1996. 65.00 (0-8039-7649-6); pap. 21.95 (0-8039-7650-X) Sage.
Violence & Glory: Poems, Nineteen Sixty-Two to Nineteen Sixty-Eight. James Schevill. LC 76-75733. 148p. 1969. pap. 9.95 (0-8040-0314-9) Swallow.
Violence & Grace: Poems about the American West. Michael L. Johnson. 58p. (Orig.). 1993. per. 8.95 (0-685-70531-5) Cottonwood KS.
Violence & Great Estates in the South of Italy: Apulia, 1900-1922. Frank M. Snowden. LC 85-11675. (Illus.). 257p. 1986. 59.95 (0-521-30731-7) Cambridge U Pr.
Violence & Health Care Professionals. T. Wykes. 272p. 1994. 41.50 (1-56593-132-7, 0444) Singular Publishing.
Violence & Law in the Modern Age. Antonio Cassese. Tr. by S. J. Greenleaves. LC 88-3642. 200p. 1988. reprint ed. pap. 57.00 (0-7837-9495-9, 2060239) Bks Demand.

UV

An Asterisk (*) at the beginning of an entry indicates that the title is appearing in BIP for the first time.

Violence & Mediation in Contemporary Culture. Ed. by Ronald Bogue et al. LC 95-2451. (SUNY Series, The Margins of Literature). 207p. (C). 1995. text ed. 54.50 (*0-7914-2719-6*); pap. text ed. 17.95 (*0-7914-2720-X*) State U NY Pr.

Violence & Mental Disorder: Developments in Risk Assessment. John Monahan & Henry J. Steadman. (John D. & Catherine T. MacArthur Foundation Series on Mental Health & Development). (Illus.). 324p. 1996. reprint ed. pap. text ed. 16.95 (*0-226-53406-5*) U Ch Pr.

Violence & Miracle in the Fourteenth Century: Private Grief & Public Salvation. Michael E. Goodich. LC 94-39199. 232p. 1995. pap. text ed. 14.95 (*0-226-30295-4*); lib. bdg. 39.95 (*0-226-30294-6*) U Ch Pr.

Violence & Pathos of Verse. Donald J. Surincik. LC 83-91493. 162p. 1984. 7.50 (*0-9613231-0-8*) Don Surincik.

***Violence & Peace: From the Atomic Bomb to Ethnic Cleansing.** Pierre Hassner. Tr. by Jane Brenton. 384p. 1997. 68.00 (*1-85866-075-0*); pap. 29.95 (*1-85866-076-9*) OUP.

Violence & Politics in Nigeria: A Case-Study of the Tiv & Yoruba. F. O. Anifowose. LC 79-88590. 1982. 22.95 (*0-685-03585-9*); pap. 9.95 (*0-88357-084-X*) NOK Pubs.

Violence & Religion: Attitudes Towards Militancy in the French Civil Wars & the English Revolution. Judith Sproxton. LC 94-25049. 112p. (C). 1995. text ed. 49.95 (*0-415-07681-1*, C0168) Routledge.

Violence & Religious Commitment: Implications of Jim Jones's People's Temple Movement. Ed. by Ken Levi. LC 81-83147. (Illus.). 224p. (C). 1982. 28.50 (*0-271-00296-4*) Pa St U Pr.

***Violence & Sexual Abuse at Home: Current Issues, Interventions, & Research in Spousal Battering & Child Maltreatment.** Ed. by Robert Geffner et al. LC 97-2798. (Journal of Aggression, Maltreatment & Trauma Ser.: Vol. 1, No. 1). 447p. 1997. 69.95 (*1-56024-681-2*); pap. 24.95 (*0-7890-0329-5*) Haworth Pr.

Violence & Social Change. (Great Contemporary Issues Ser.). 1979. lib. bdg. 35.00 (*0-686-59849-0*) Ayer.

Violence & Social Order: East Anglia 1422-1442. Philippa C. Maddern. (Oxford Historical Monographs). (Illus.). 280p. 1992. 69.00 (*0-19-820235-0*) OUP.

***Violence & Society in the Early Medieval West.** Ed. by Guy Halsall. LC 97-20526. 256p. 1997. 71.00 (*0-85115-713-0*) Boydell & Brewer.

Violence & Suicidality: Perspectives in Clinical & Psychobiological Research. Ed. by Herman M. Van Praag et al. LC 90-1309. (Einstein Clinical & Experimental Psychiatry Monograph Ser.: No. 3). (Illus.). 332p. 1990. text ed. 49.95 (*0-87630-551-6*) Brunner-Mazel.

Violence & Terror in the Mass Media: An Annotated Bibliography. Compiled by Nancy Signorielli & George Gerbner. LC 87-29556. (Bibliographies & Indexes in Sociology Ser.: No. 13). 264p. 1988. text ed. 75.00 (*0-313-26120-2*, SVC/, Greenwood Pr) Greenwood.

Violence & the Dream People: The Orang Asli in the Malayan Emergency, 1948-1960. John Leary. (Monographs in International Studies Southeast Asia: No. 95). (Illus.). 275p. (Orig.). (C). 1995. pap. 22.00 (*0-89680-186-1*) Ohio U Pr.

Violence & the Family. Ed. by John P. Martin. LC 77-21846. 377p. reprint ed. pap. 107.50 (*0-8357-3110-3*, 2039366) Bks Demand.

Violence & the Labor Movement. Robert Hunter. LC 71-90180. (Mass Violence in America Ser.). 1969. reprint ed. 17.95 (*0-405-01320-5*) Ayer.

Violence & the Latin American Revolutionaries. Ed. by Michael Radu. 246p. 1988. 39.95 (*0-88738-195-2*) Transaction Pubs.

Violence & the Law. Mark Costanzo & Stuart Oskamp. LC 94-19053. (Claremont Symposium on Applied Social Psychology Ser.: Vol. 7). 256p. 1994. 36.00 (*0-8039-5341-0*); pap. 16.95 (*0-8039-5342-9*) Sage.

***Violence & the Oppressed: Insights from Film.** Ed. by John P. Lovell. 1998. text ed. write for info. (*0-275-95972-4*, Praeger Pubs) Greenwood.

Violence & the Politics of Research. Ed. by Willard Gaylin et al. LC 81-15900. (Hastings Center Series in Ethics). 272p. 1981. 45.00 (*0-306-40789-2*, Plenum Pr) Plenum.

Violence & the Prevention of Violence. Ed. by Leonore A. Loeb et al. LC 94-28007. (Illus.). 248p. 1995. text ed. 59.95 (*0-275-94873-0*, Praeger Pubs) Greenwood.

Violence & the Sacred. Rene Girard. Tr. by Patrick Gregory. LC 77-4539. 1977. pap. 14.95 (*0-8018-2218-1*) Johns Hopkins.

Violence & the Sacred in the Modern World. Ed. by Mark Juergensmeyer. 155p. 1992. text ed. 35.00 (*0-7146-3456-5*, Pub. by F Cass Pubs UK) Intl Spec Bk.

Violence & the Schools: A Collection. Ed. by Philip R. Harris. LC 94-78545. 280p. 1994. pap. 22.95 (*0-932935-80-X*) IRI-SkyLght.

Violence & the Violent Individual. Ed. by J. Ray Hays et al. LC 80-24. (Illus.). 544p. 1981. text ed. 40.00 (*0-88331-210-7*) Luce.

Violence & Theft see Crime & Justice in American History

***Violence & Truth: Colonial Authority in Rajasthan.** Denis Vidal. (Illus.). 304p. 1997. 29.95 (*0-19-564105-1*) OUP.

Violence & Truth: On the Work of Rene Girard. Ed. by Paul Dumouchel. LC 87-61959. vi, 289p. 1988. 39.50 (*0-8047-1338-3*) Stanford U Pr.

Violence & Unintentional Injury Prevention: Abstracts of Active Projects, FY 1993. 90p. (Orig.). (C). 1994. pap. text ed. 30.00 (*0-7881-0612-0*) DIANE Pub.

Violence & Utopia: The Work of Jerome Boime. Ed. by Albert Boime. 176p. 1996. pap. text ed. 28.00 (*0-7618-0324-6*); lib. bdg. 48.50 (*0-7618-0323-8*) U Pr of Amer.

Violence As Obscenity: Limiting the Media's First Amendment Protections. Kevin W. Saunders. LC 95-39400. (Constitutional Conflicts Ser.). 256p. 1996. text ed. 49.95 (*0-8223-1758-3*); pap. text ed. 17.95 (*0-8223-1767-2*) Duke.

Violence As Protest: A Study of Riots & Ghettos. Robert M. Fogelson. LC 80-36808. xviii, 265p. 1980. reprint ed. text ed. 38.50 (*0-313-22642-3*, FOVP, Greenwood Pr) Greenwood.

Violence at Work: How to Make Your Company Safer for Employees & Customers. Joseph A. Kinney. 1995. pap. 24.95 (*0-13-312208-5*) P-H.

***Violence at Work: How to Safeguard Your Firm.** Mark F. Murray. LC 97-19713. 128p. 1997. pap. 37.00 (*0-87051-187-4*, 090430) Am Inst CPA.

***Violence Beat.** Eve Sandstrom. 1997. mass mkt. 5.99 (*0-451-19033-5*, Sig) NAL-Dutton.

Violence Behind Bars: An Explosive Report on Prison Riots in the United States. Vernon B. Fox. LC 73-13414. 317p. 1974. reprint ed. text ed. 35.00 (*0-8371-7131-8*, FOVB, Greenwood Pr) Greenwood.

Violence, Blunders, & Fractured Jaws. Marc A. MacYoung. 344p. 1992. pap. 22.95 (*0-87364-671-1*) Paladin Pr.

Violence, Civil Strife, & Revolution in the Classical City. Andrew Lintott. 288p. (C). 1987. pap. text ed. 14.95 (*0-7099-4170-6*, Pub. by Croom Helm UK) Routledge Chapman & Hall.

Violence, Communalism, & Terrorism in India: Towards Criminalisation of Politics. Ed. by Verinder Grover & Ranjana Arora. (C). 1995. 72.00 (*81-7100-546-2*, Pub. by Deep II) S Asia.

***Violence, Culture & Censure.** Ed. by Colin Sumner. 224p. 1997. 69.95 (*0-7484-0554-2*, Pub. by Tay Francis Ltd UK); pap. 24.95 (*0-7484-0555-0*, Pub. by Tay Francis Ltd UK) Taylor & Francis.

Violence Education: Toward a Solution. Ed. by Marybeth K. Hendricks-Matthews. 188p. 1992. 20.00 (*0-685-62730-6*) Soc Tchrs Fam Med.

***Violence Explained.** Burton. 1997. text ed. 59.95 (*0-7190-5047-2*, Pub. by Manchester Univ Pr UK); text ed. 22.50 (*0-7190-5048-0*) St Martin.

Violence for Equality: Inquiries in Political Philosophy. 3rd ed. Ted Honderich. 240p. (C). 1989. pap. text ed. 13.95 (*0-415-02623-7*, A3448) Routledge.

Violence Hits Home: Comprehensive Treatment Approaches to Domestic Violence. Ed. by Sandra M. Stith et al. LC 90-9459. (Social Work Ser.: Vol. 19). 392p. 1990. 44.95 (*0-8261-7270-9*) Springer Pub.

***Violence, Identity & Self-Determination.** Hent DeVries & Samuel Weber. LC 97-13450. 1997. write for info. (*0-8047-2995-6*); pap. write for info. (*0-8047-2996-4*) Stanford U Pr.

***Violence in America.** Robert M. Macneil & Lehrer. Date not set. write for info. (*0-688-01123-3*) Morrow.

Violence in America. Ed. by Annette Zimmern-Reed. (Conference Proceedings Ser.). 256p. 1987. pap. 8.00 (*0-89940-100-7*) LBJ Sch Pub Aff.

Violence in America, 2 vols., Set. 3rd ed. Ed. by Ted R. Gurr. (Violence, Cooperation, & Peace Ser.). (C). 1989. text ed. 72.00 (*0-8039-3231-6*); pap. text ed. 32.20 (*0-8039-3249-9*) Sage.

Violence in America, 2 vols., Vol. 1: The History of Crime. 3rd ed. Ed. by Ted R. Gurr. (Violence, Cooperation, & Peace Ser.). 282p. (C). 1989. Vol. 1, 282p. - The History of Crime. text ed. 55.00 (*0-8039-3227-8*); Vol. 1, 282p. - The History of Crime. pap. text ed. 24.95 (*0-8039-3228-6*) Sage.

Violence in America, 2 vols., Vol. 2: Protest, Rebellion, Reform. 3rd ed. Ed. by Ted R. Gurr. (Violence, Cooperation, & Peace Ser.). 352p. (C). 1989. Vol. 2, 352p. - Protest, Rebellion, Reform. text ed. 55.00 (*0-8039-3229-4*); Vol. 2, 352p. - Protest, Rebellion, Reform. pap. text ed. 24.95 (*0-8039-3230-8*) Sage.

Violence in America: A Public Health Approach. Ed. by Marc L. Rosenberg. (Illus.). 216p. 1991. 37.50 (*0-19-506437-2*) OUP.

***Violence in America: Coping with Drugs, Distressed Families, Inadequate Schooling & Acts of Hate.** Raymond B. Flannery. LC 96-40431. 192p. 1997. 22.95 (*0-8264-1002-2*) Continuum.

Violence in America: Lessons on Understanding the Agression in Our Lives. Arnold P. Goldstein. LC 96-21541. 296p. 1996. pap. 16.95 (*0-89106-092-8*, 7744) Davies-Black.

Violence in America: Patterns, Causes, & Public Policy. Neil A. Weiner et al. 478p. (C). 1990. pap. text ed. 18.75 (*0-15-594915-2*) HB Coll Pubs.

Violence in American Society: A Bibliography. Ed. by Joan Nordquist. (Contemporary Social Issues: A Bibliographic Ser.: No. 33). 72p. (C). 1994. pap. 15.00 (*0-937855-64-2*) Ref Rsch Serv.

Violence in America's Schools. Ronald E. Sharp & Waln K. Brown. 20p. 1992. 2.95 (*1-56456-073-2*, 272) W Gladden Found.

Violence in Argentine Literature: Cultural Responses to Tyranny. David W. Foster. 224p. 1995. 37.50 (*0-8262-0991-2*) U of Mo Pr.

Violence in Canada: Socio-political Perspectives. Ed. by Jeffrey I. Ross. (Illus.). 416p. 1996. pap. 35.00 (*0-19-541058-0*) OUP.

Violence in Children & Adolescents. Kelley H. Varner. Ed. by Ved P. Varma. LC 96-18256. 217p. 1996. pap. 26.95 (*1-85302-344-2*, Pub. by J Kingsley Pubs UK) Taylor & Francis.

Violence in China: Essays in Culture & Counterculture. Ed. by Jonathan N. Lipman & Stevan Harrell. LC 88-32411. (SUNY Series in Chinese Local Studies). 249p. 1990. text ed. 64.50 (*0-7914-0113-8*); pap. text ed. 21.95 (*0-7914-0115-4*) State U NY Pr.

Violence in Cornet City: A Problem-Solving Exercise. Patricia Kelly et al. (Illus.). 38p. (Orig.). (C). 1995. pap. text ed. 20.00 (*0-7881-2433-1*) DIANE Pub.

Violence in Dating Relationships: Emerging Social Issues. Ed. by Maureen A. Pirog-Good & Jan E. Stets. LC 88-31894. 302p. 1989. text ed. 57.95 (*0-275-93004-1*, C3004, Praeger Pubs); pap. text ed. 19.95 (*0-275-93353-9*, B3353, Praeger Pubs) Greenwood.

Violence in Early Renaissance Venice. Guido Ruggiero. LC 79-25650. (Crime, Law, & Deviance Ser.). 250p. reprint ed. pap. 71.30 (*0-8357-7951-3*, 2057026) Bks Demand.

Violence in Families: Assessing Prevention & Treatment Programs. Ed. by Rosemary Chalk et al. 400p. (C). 1997. 39.95 (*0-309-05496-6*) Natl Acad Pr.

Violence in Gay & Lesbian Domestic Partnerships. Ed. by Claire M. Renzetti & Charles H. Miley. LC 95-52579. (Journal of Gay & Lesbian Social Services: Vol. 4, No. 1). 144p. 1995. 24.95 (*1-56024-753-3*) Haworth Pr.

Violence in Gay & Lesbian Domestic Partnerships. Ed. by Claire M. Renzetti & Charles H. Miley. LC 95-52579. (Journal of Gay & Lesbian Social Services: Vol. 4, No. 1). 121p. 1996. pap. 12.95 (*1-56023-074-6*) Haworth Pr.

Violence in Health Care: A Practical Guide for Coping with Violence & Caring for Victims. Ed. by Jonathan Shepherd. LC 93-43592. 208p. 1994. 48.75 (*0-19-262513-6*); pap. 34.50 (*0-19-262157-2*) OUP.

***Violence in Institutions: Understanding, Prevention & Control.** M. E. Rice. 304p. 1997. 39.00 (*0-88937-161-X*) Hogrefe & Huber Pubs.

Violence in Intimate Relationships. Ed. by Gordon Russell. LC 88-318. 312p. 1988. text ed. 45.00 (*0-89335-231-4*) PMA Pub Corp.

Violence in Lincoln County, Eighteen Sixty-Nine to Eighteen Eighty-One: A New Mexico Item. Charles L. Sonnichsen. LC 82-1984. (Illus.). 424p. reprint ed. pap. 120.90 (*0-8357-4642-9*, 2037573) Bks Demand.

Violence in Modern Philosophy. Piotr Hoffman. LC 88-34125. 174p. 1989. 29.95 (*0-226-34795-8*) U Ch Pr.

Violence in Our Schools, Hospitals, & Public Places: A Prevention & Management Guide. Eugene D. Wheeler & S. Anthony Baron. 288p. 1994. lib. bdg. 39.00 (*0-8095-5916-1*) Borgo Pr.

Violence in Recent Southern Fiction. Louise Y. Gossett. LC 65-13656. 219p. reprint ed. pap. 62.50 (*0-317-42186-7*, 2026200) Bks Demand.

Violence in Schools: Learning in Fear. Nancy Day. LC 95-40198. (Issues in Focus Ser.). (Illus.). 128p. (YA). (gr. 6 up). 1996. lib. bdg. 18.95 (*0-89490-734-4*) Enslow Pubs.

Violence in Schools: The Enabling Factor. Carole Remboldt. 48p. 1994. pap. 2.95 (*1-56246-096-X*, P337) Johnsn Inst.

Violence in Schools & Communities: A Special Report by the Pennsylvania House of Representatives. (Illus.). 85p. (Orig.). (C). 1994. pap. text ed. 25.00 (*0-7881-0875-1*) DIANE Pub.

Violence in Schools & Public Places: A Prevention & Management Guide. Eugene D. Wheeler & S. Anthony Baron. 288p. (Orig.). 1994. 22.95 (*0-934793-52-2*); pap. 14.95 (*0-934793-51-4*) Pathfinder CA.

***Violence in Southern Africa.** William F. Gutteridge & J. E. Spence. LC 97-5647. (Cass Series on Political Violence). 1997. write for info. (*0-7146-4665-2*, Pub. by F Cass Pubs UK); pap. write for info. (*0-7146-4200-2*, Pub. by F Cass Pubs UK) Intl Spec Bk.

Violence in the Arts. John Fraser. LC 73-84319. (Illus.). 236p. reprint ed. pap. 67.30 (*0-685-20549-5*, 2030594) Bks Demand.

Violence in the Black Imagination: Essays & Documents. enl. ed. Ronald T. Takaki. LC 92-33493. 368p. 1993. pap. 18.95 (*0-19-508249-4*) OUP.

Violence in the Black Patch of Kentucky & Tennessee. Suzanne Marshall. (Illus.). 232p. 1994. text ed. 34.95 (*0-8262-0971-8*) U of Mo Pr.

Violence in the Family: A Workshop Curriculum for Clergy & Other Helpers. Marie M. Fortune. LC 91-20978. 288p. (Orig.). 1991. pap. 19.95 (*0-8298-0908-2*) Pilgrim OH.

Violence in the Lives of Adolescents. Ed. by Martha B. Straus. 256p. 1994. 27.00 (*0-393-70186-7*) Norton.

Violence in the Media. Ed. by Carol Wekesser. (Current Controversies Ser.). 192p. 1995. pap. text ed. 12.96 (*1-56510-236-3*, 2363); lib. bdg. 20.96 (*1-56510-237-1*, 2371) Greenhaven.

Violence in the Model City: The Cavanaugh Administration, Race Relations, & the Detroit Riot of 1967. Sidney Fine. (Illus.). 656p. 1989. text ed. 47.50 (*0-472-10104-8*) U of Mich Pr.

Violence in the Schools: How America's School Boards Are Safeguarding Your Children. (Illus.). 115p. (Orig.). (C). 1995. pap. text ed. 25.00 (*0-7881-1935-4*) DIANE Pub.

Violence in the Schools: How America's Schools Are Safeguarding Our Children. National School Boards Association Staff. (NSBA Best Practices Ser.). 115p. (Orig.). 1993. pap. 15.00 (*0-88364-180-1*) Natl Sch Boards.

Violence in the Schools: How to Proactively Prevent & Diffuse It. Joan L. Curcio & Patricia F. First. Ed. by Jerry L. Herman & Janice L. Herman. LC 93-22348. (Road Maps to Success Ser.). 64p. 1993. pap. 11.95 (*0-8039-6058-1*) Corwin Pr.

Violence in the Workplace. Raymond B. Flannery, Jr. LC 94-48654. 240p. 1995. 24.95 (*0-8245-1488-2*) Crossroad NY.

Violence in the Workplace. International Facility Management Association Staff. (IFMA Research Report Ser.: Vol. 15). (Illus.). 40p. (Orig.). 1995. pap. 100.00 (*1-883176-10-7*, 145998) Intl Facility Mgmt Assn.

Violence in the Workplace: A Survey of Published Literature 1989-1994. Ed. by American Society for Industrial Security Staff. (Reference Ser.). iv, 52p. (Orig.). 1994. pap. 48.00 (*1-887056-02-5*) Am Soc Indus Secur.

Violence in the Workplace: Managing People in the Age of Rage. Tom K. Puderbaugh. LC 96-85604. (Illus.). 80p. (Orig.). 1996. wbk. ed. 24.95 (*1-889132-00-4*) Develop Dynam.

Violence in the Workplace: Prevention & Management Guide for Business. S. Anthony Baron. LC 93-19114. 176p. (Orig.). 1995. 24.95 (*0-934793-48-4*); pap. 14.95 (*0-934793-49-2*) Pathfinder CA.

Violence in Urban America: Mobilizing a Response. National Research Council Staff & Harvard University, John F. Kennedy School of Government Staff. 118p. (Orig.). (C). 1994. pap. text ed. 12.95 (*0-309-05039-1*) Natl Acad Pr.

***Violence Issues for Health Care Educators & Providers.** Ed. by L. Kevin Hamberger et al. 1997. write for info. (*1-56024-984-6*) Haworth Pr.

***Violence Mythos.** Barbara Whitmer. LC 96-51554. (Margins of Literature Ser.). (Illus.). 224p. (C). 1997. pap. text ed. 18.95 (*0-7914-3518-0*) State U NY Pr.

***Violence Mythos.** Barbara Whitmer. LC 96-51554. (Margins of Literature Ser.). (Illus.). 224p. (C). 1997. text ed. 57.50 (*0-7914-3517-2*) State U NY Pr.

Violence of Language. Jean-Jacques Lecercle. 320p. (C). 1990. pap. 18.95 (*0-415-03431-0*, A4967) Routledge.

Violence of Literacy. J. Elspeth Stuckey. LC 90-41385. 140p. (Orig.). (C). 1990. pap. 16.95 (*0-86709-270-X*, 0270) Boynton Cook Pubs.

Violence of Men: New Techniques for Working with Abusive Families: A Therapy of Social Action. Cloe Madanes et al. LC 95-12239. (Psychology Ser.). 233p. 27.95 (*0-7879-0117-2*) Jossey-Bass.

Violence of Our Lives: Interviews with American Murderers. Tony Parker. 256p. 1996. pap. 12.95 (*0-8050-4957-6*) H Holt & Co.

Violence of Pity in Euripides' Medea. Pietro Pucci. LC 79-52501. (Cornell Studies in Classical Philology: No. 41). (Illus.). 239p. reprint ed. pap. 68.20 (*0-685-44035-4*, 2030231) Bks Demand.

Violence of Representation: Literature & the History of Violence. Ed. by Nancy Armstrong & Leonard Tennenhouse. 240p. 1989. 45.00 (*0-415-01447-6*, A1582); pap. 16.95 (*0-415-01448-4*, A1586) Routledge.

Violence of Silence: The Impossibility of Dialogue. S. Giora Shoman. 300p. 1982. 39.95 (*0-905927-06-0*) Transaction Pubs.

Violence of the Green Revolution: Third World Agriculture, Ecology & Politics. Vandana Shiva. LC 90-39962. (Illus.). 192p. (C). 1991. pap. 17.50 (*0-86232-965-5*, Pub. by Zed Bks Ltd UK) Humanities.

Violence on America's Streets. Gene Brown. (YA). 1992. pap. 5.44 (*0-395-62469-X*) HM.

Violence on America's Streets. Gene Brown. LC 91-28929. 64p. (gr. 5-8). 1992. pap. 6.95 (*1-878841-95-5*) Millbrook Pr.

Violence on America's Streets. Gene Brown. LC 91-28929. (Headliners Ser.). (Illus.). 64p. (J). (gr. 5-8). 1992. lib. bdg. 17.40 (*1-56294-155-0*) Millbrook Pr.

***Violence on Television: An Analysis of Amount, Nature, Location & Origin of Violence in British Programmes.** Barrie Gunter & Jackie Harrison. LC 97-23330. 1998. write for info. (*0-415-17260-8*) Routledge.

***Violence on Television: Congressional Inquiry, Public Criticism & Industry Response: A Policy Analysis.** Cynthia A. Cooper. LC 96-32884. 214p. 1996. pap. text ed. 24.50 (*0-7618-0477-3*); lib. bdg. 44.50 (*0-7618-0476-5*) U Pr of Amer.

Violence on the Job: Identifying Risks & Developing Solutions. Ed. by Gary R. VandenBos & Elizabeth Q. Bulatao. LC 96-9143. 439p. (Orig.). 1996. pap. text ed. 34.95 (*1-55798-389-5*) Am Psychol.

Violence, or Aggressive Nonviolent Resistance. Phillips P. Moulton. LC 76-170019. (Orig.). 1971. pap. 3.00 (*0-87574-178-9*) Pendle Hill.

Violence, Perspectives on Murder & Aggression. Irwin L. Kutash et al. LC 78-62555. (Jossey-Bass Social & Behavioral Science Ser.). 600p. reprint ed. pap. 171.00 (*0-8357-4991-6*, 2037924) Bks Demand.

Violence Potential: In Our Society Today. Ernest F. Pecci. (Illus.). 6p. (Orig.). 1994. pap. 14.95 (*0-9642637-2-6*) Pavior Pubng.

Violence Prediction: Guidelines for the Forensic Practitioner. Harold V. Hall. (Illus.). 234p. 1987. pap. 27.95 (*0-398-06368-0*) C C Thomas.

Violence Prediction: Guidelines for the Forensic Practitioner. Harold V. Hall. (Illus.). 234p. (C). 1987. text ed. 42.95 (*0-398-05363-4*) C C Thomas.

***Violence Prevention: A Vision of Hope: Final Report of the Policy Council on Violence Prevention.** Kathryn Jett & Vicky Elder. (Illus.). 275p. (C). 1996. reprint ed. pap. 40.00 (*0-7881-3518-X*) DIANE Pub.

Violence Prevention: Awesome Me & Violence-Free. Linda B. Meeks et al. LC 95-95035. (Illus.). 157p. (J). (gr. 6-8). 1995. lib. bdg. 14.00 (*0-9630009-7-7*) Meeks Heit.

Violence Prevention: How to Be Hip, Cool, & Violence-Free. Linda B. Meeks. (Illus.). 130p. (YA). (gr. 9-12). 1995. text ed. 14.00 (*0-9630009-6-9*) Meeks Heit.

Violence Prevention: Special Me & Violence-Free. Linda B. Meeks et al. LC 95-95033. (Illus.). 80p. (Orig.). (J). (gr. k-2). 1995. pap. 11.00 (*0-9630009-9-3*) Meeks Heit.

***Violence Prevention: Students Against Violence.** Mae M. Fletcher. 80p. (J). (gr. k-3). 1997. pap. 13.00 (*0-8059-4080-4*) Dorrance.

Violence Prevention: Super Cool & Violence-Free. Linda B. Meeks et al. LC 95-95034. (Illus.). 80p. (Orig.). (J). (gr. 3-5). 1995. pap. 13.00 (*0-9630009-8-5*) Meeks Heit.

An Asterisk (*) at the beginning of an entry indicates that the title is appearing in BIP for the first time.

Violence Prevention: Totally Awesome Teaching Strategies for Safe & Drug-Free Schools. Linda B. Meeks. (Illus.). 654p. (Orig.). (C). 1994. pap. text ed. 50.00 (*0-9630009-4-2*) Meeks Heit.

Violence Prevention Curriculum for Adolescents. Deborah Prothrow-Stith. (Illus.). 80p. (Orig.). 1987. pap. 30.00 (*0-89292-093-9*) Educ Dev Ctr.

Violence, Resistance, & Survival in the Americas: Native Americans & the Legacy of Conquest. Ed. by William B. Taylor & Franklin Pease. (Illus.). 336p. (C). 1993. text ed. 49.00 (*1-56098-260-8*) Smithsonian.

Violence, Silence, & Anger: Women's Writing As Transgression. Ed. by Deirdre Lashgari. 384p. (C). 1995. pap. text ed. 19.95 (*0-8139-1493-0*) U Pr of Va.

Violence, Silence, & Anger: Women's Writing As Transgression. Ed. by Dierdre Lashgari. 384p. (C). 1995. text ed. 55.00 (*0-8139-1492-2*) U Pr of Va.

Violence, Terrorism, & Justice. Ed. by R. G. Frey & Christopher W. Morris. (Studies in Philosophy & Public Policy). 280p. (C). 1991. pap. text ed. 23.95 (*0-521-40950-0*) Cambridge U Pr.

Violence, Terrorism, & Justice. Ed. by R. G. Frey & Christopher W. Morris. (Studies in Philosophy & Public Policy). 280p. (C). 1991. text ed. 80.00 (*0-521-40125-9*) Cambridge U Pr.

Violence to Non-Violence: Individual Perspectives, Communal Voices. Ed. by Bill Kelly. LC 93-24577. 160p. 1994. text ed. 30.00 (*3-7186-5467-9*) Gordon & Breach.

Violence Unveiled: Humanity at the Crossroads. Gil Bailie. 310p. 1995. 24.95 (*0-8245-1464-5*) Crossroad NY.

***Violence Unveiled: Humanity at the Crossroads.** Gil Bailie. 320p. 1997. pap. 17.95 (*0-8245-1645-1*) Crossroad NY.

Violence, Values & Inner-City Children. T. Y. Okosun. (Orig.). 1994. pap. 8.00 (*0-9637979-2-1*) T Y Okosun.

Violence, Valves & the Media. Reginald Dodrill. 157p. (Orig.). 1994. pap. 12.95 (*0-9640418-0-4*) Fnd For Change.

Violence Was No Stranger: A Guide to the Grave Sites of Famous Westerners. James A. Browning. LC 93-36455. (Illus.). 344p. 1993. 29.95 (*0-935269-11-8*) Western Pubns.

Violence Within the Family: Social Psychological. Sharon D. Herzberger. 272p. (C). 1995. per. write for info. (*0-697-15173-5*) Brown & Benchmark.

Violence Within the Family: Social Psychological Perspedtives. Sharon D. Herzberger. LC 96-1278. (Social Psychology Ser.). (C). 1996. pap. text ed. 21.00 (*0-8133-3002-5*) Westview.

Violencia Institucional: Las Patrollas de Autodefensa Civil en Guatemala 1993-1994. Joel A. Solomon. Tr. by P. O. Coj. 50p. (SPA.). 1994. pap. write for info. (*1-881055-05-1*) RFK Mem Ctr HR.

Violencia y Criminalidad En Puerto Rico, 1898-1973: Apuntes para un Estudio De Historia Social. Blanca Silvestrini De Pacheco. LC 79-15801. Orig. Title: Analisis Historico De la Violencia en Puerto Rico. (Illus.). x, 146p. (SPA.). 1979. pap. text ed. 7.20 (*0-8477-2488-3*) U of PR Pr.

Violencia y Ternura. Juan Rof Carballo. (Nueva Austral Ser.: Vol. 19). (SPA.). 1991. pap. text ed. 24.95 (*84-239-1819-X*) Elliots Bks.

Violent Acts: A Study of Violence in Contemporary Latin American Theatre. Severino J. Albuquerque. LC 90-34750. (Latin American Literature & Culture Ser.). 298p. (C). 1990. text ed. 39.95 (*0-8143-2243-3*); pap. text ed. 19.95 (*0-8143-2244-1*) Wayne St U Pr.

Violent Attachments. J. Reid Meloy. LC 92-10469. 384p. 1992. 42.50 (*0-87668-537-8*) Aronson.

***Violent Attachments.** J. Reid Meloy. LC 92-10469. 392p. 1997. pap. 35.00 (*0-7657-0061-1*) Aronson.

Violent Bear It Away. Flannery O'Connor. 256p. 1960. pap. 11.00 (*0-374-50524-1*) FS&G.

Violent Behavior Vol. 2: Intervention in Treatment. Ed. by Leonard Hertzberg et al. 49.95 (*1-56262-004-5*) PMA Pub Corp.

Violent Behavior, Vol. 1: Assessment & Intervention. Ed. by Leonard Hertzberg et al. LC 85-11780. 464p. 1990. text ed. 49.95 (*0-89335-220-9*) PMA Pub Corp.

Violent Betrayal: Partner Abuse in Lesbian Relationships. Claire M. Renzetti. 168p. (C). 1992. text ed. 54.00 (*0-8039-3888-8*); pap. text ed. 24.50 (*0-8039-3889-6*) Sage.

***Violent Cartographies: Mapping Cultures of War.** Michael J. Shapiro. LC 96-31509. 1997. text ed. 49.95 (*0-8166-2920-X*); pap. text ed. 19.95 (*0-8166-2921-8*) U of Minn Pr.

Violent Cases. deluxe limited ed. Neil Gaiman. (Illus.). 48p. 1993. reprint ed. 39.95 (*0-87816-246-1*) Kitchen Sink.

***Violent Cases: 10th Anniversary Edition.** 3rd rev. ed. Neil Gaiman. (Illus.). 48p. 1997. pap. 12.95 (*0-87816-557-6*) Kitchen Sink.

Violent Children: A Research Handbook. Karen L. Kinnear. LC 96-19326. (Contemporary World Issues Ser.). 251p. 1995. 39.50 (*0-87436-786-7*) ABC-CLIO.

Violent Couple. William A. Stacey et al. LC 93-37021. 192p. 1994. text ed. 49.95 (*0-275-94698-3*, Praeger Pubs) Greenwood.

Violent Crime: I Never Thought It Would Happen to Me, but It Did. Diane M. Crandall. LC 94-90566. 44p. (Orig.). 1994. pap. 10.95 (*0-9642965-0-0*) For-giving Pr.

Violent Crime: Is It Out of Control? John Salak. LC 95-9560. (Issues of Our Time Ser.). (Illus.). 64p. (J). (gr. 5-8). 1995. lib. bdg. 15.98 (*0-8050-4239-3*) TFC Bks NY.

Violent Crime & Gun Control. Gerald D. Robin. LC 91-70555. (ACJS - Anderson Monographs). 98p. (C). 1991. pap. text ed. 12.95 (*0-87084-747-3*) Anderson Pub Co.

***Violent Crime Control & Law Enforcement Act of 1994.** 360p. 1994. pap. text ed. 60.00 (*1-57979-053-4*) BPI Info Servs.

Violent Crime Control & Law Enforcement Act of 1994 (Public Law 103-322) 355p. (Orig.). (C). 1994. pap. text ed. 50.00 (*0-7881-1412-3*) DIANE Pub.

Violent Crime, Violent Criminals. Ed. by Neil A. Weiner & Marvin E. Wolfgang. (Focus Editions Ser.: Vol. 101). 280p. (C). 1988. text ed. 54.00 (*0-8039-3341-X*); pap. text ed. 24.95 (*0-8039-3342-8*) Sage.

***Violent Crimes.** Hugh Holton. LC 96-47195. 384p. 1996. 23.95 (*0-312-86281-4*) St Martin.

Violent Crimes & Other Forms of Victimization in Residence Halls. Carolyn J. Palmer. LC 93-18795. (Higher Education Administration Ser.). 128p. 1994. pap. 16.95 (*0-912557-15-X*) Coll Admin Pubns.

Violent Criminal Acts & Actors Revisited. Lonnie H. Athens. LC 96-25235. 1997. text ed. 24.95 (*0-252-02306-4*); pap. text ed. 14.95 (*0-252-06608-1*) U of Ill Pr.

Violent Criminal Attacks. Robert Ferguson. 224p. (C). 1995. per., pap. text ed. 16.25 (*0-7872-1377-2*) Kendall-Hunt.

Violent Criminal Attacks: How to Prevent Or Survive an Encounter. Ferguson. 1994. pap. text ed. 14.00 (*0-697-25672-3*) Wm C Brown Pubs.

Violent Death in the City: Suicide, Accident, & Murder in Nineteenth-Century Philadelphia. Roger Lane. LC 79-11836. (Commonwealth Fund Publications). 202p. 1979. 32.00 (*0-674-93946-8*) HUP.

Violent Deaths in Childhood & Adolescence. Ed. by David W. Kaplan. (Journal: Pediatrician 1985: Vol.12, No. 1). (Illus.). 80p. 1985. pap. 40.00 (*3-8055-4231-3*) S Karger.

Violent Deaths in the United States: An Epidemiologic Study of Suicide, Homicide, & Accidents. Paul C. Holinger. LC 87-10720. 274p. 1987. lib. bdg. 42.00 (*0-89862-672-2*) Guilford Pr.

***Violent E & Other Tricky Sounds: Learning to Spell from Kindergarten Through Grade 6.** Margaret Hughes & Dennis Searle. LC 97-16201. 1997. pap. text ed. write for info. (*1-57110-034-2*) Stenhse Pubs.

***Violent Earth "Lab Pack" (Windows CDRom)** write for info. (*0-8172-4166-3*) Raintree Steck-V.

Violent Emotions: Shame & Rage in Marital Quarrels. Suzanne M. Retzinger. 256p. (C). 1991. 54.00 (*0-8039-4183-8*); pap. 24.50 (*0-8039-4184-6*) Sage.

Violent Evangelism: The Political & Religious Conquest of the Americas. Luis N. Rivera. Tr. by Marina Herrera. 352p. (Orig.). 1992. pap. 20.00 (*0-664-25367-9*) Westminster John Knox.

Violent Eye: Ernst Junger's Visions & Revisions on the European Right. Marcus P. Bullock. LC 91-26476. (Kritik: German Literary Theory & Cultural Studies). 338p. 1991. 36.95 (*0-8143-2334-0*) Wayne St U Pr.

Violent Family: Victimization of Women, Children & Elders. Ed. by Nancy Hutchings. 184p. 1988. 33.95 (*0-89885-383-4*) Human Sci Pr.

Violent Gang. Lewis Yablonsky. 264p. 1984. reprint ed. pap. text ed. 12.95 (*0-685-06824-2*); reprint ed. write for info. (*0-8290-1356-3*) Irvington.

Violent Imagination. Robin Fox. 204p. 1988. 22.95 (*0-8135-1367-7*) Rutgers U Pr.

Violent Justice: How Three Assassins Fought to Free Europe's Jews. Felix Imonti & Miyoko Imonti. (Illus.). 318p. (C). 1994. 26.95 (*0-87975-925-9*) Prometheus Bks.

Violent Land. Jorge Amado. 288p. (Orig.). 1988. pap. 10.00 (*0-380-75475-4*) Avon.

Violent Land. large type ed. Wayne D. Overholser. LC 95-11097. (Nightingale Ser.). 365p. 1995. pap. 17.95 (*0-7838-1385-6*, GK Hall) Thorndike Pr.

Violent Land: Single Men & Social Disorder from the Frontier to the Inner City. David T. Courtwright. LC 96-9277. (Illus.). 416p. 1996. 29.95 (*0-674-27870-4*) HUP.

Violent Land-the Judas Gun, 2 bks. in 1. Wayne D. Overholser. 400p. 1995. mass mkt., pap. text ed. 4.99 (*0-8439-3802-1*) Dorchester Pub Co.

Violent Legacies: Three Cantos. Richard Misrach. (Illus.). 128p. 1992. 50.00 (*0-89381-519-5*) Aperture.

Violent Legacies: Three Cantos. Richard Misrach. 1994. pap. 29.95 (*0-89381-569-1*) Aperture.

***Violent Memoires: Quiche War Widows of Highland Guatemala.** Judith Zur. 8p. (C). 1998. text ed. 58.00 (*0-8133-2799-7*) Westview.

***Violent Men.** large type ed. Wayne D. Overholser & John S. Daniels. LC 96-35469. (Nightingale Ser.). 196p. 1997. pap. 18.95 (*0-7838-2005-4*, GK Hall) Thorndike Pr.

Violent Men: An Inquiry into the Psychology of Violence. rev. ed. Hans Toch. 286p. 1992. reprint ed. pap. 19.95 (*1-55798-172-8*) Am Psychol.

Violent Men, Violent Couples: The Dynamics of Domestic Violence. Anson Shupe et al. LC 86-45571. 152p. 29.95 (*0-669-13706-5*, Lexington) Jossey-Bass.

Violent Mind. Margaret O. Hyde & Elizabeth H. Forsyth. LC 91-18566. 144p. (YA). (gr. 9-12). 1991. lib. bdg. 22.00 (*0-531-11060-5*) Watts.

Violent No More: Helping Men End Domestic Abuse. Michael Paymar. LC 93-18003. 224p. 1993. 21.95 (*0-89793-139-4*); pap. 12.95 (*0-89793-117-3*) Hunter Hse.

Violent Origins: Walter Burkert, Rene Girard, & Jonathan Z. Smith on Ritual Killing & Cultural Formation. Ed. by Robert G. Hamerton-Kelly. LC 86-23009. 291p. 1987. 42.50 (*0-8047-1370-7*); pap. 14.95 (*0-8047-1518-1*) Stanford U Pr.

Violent Peace: Global Security after the Cold War. Malcolm Dando & Paul Rogers. 207p. 1992. 37.00 (*0-08-036694-5*, Pub. by Brasseys UK) Brasseys Inc.

Violent Persuasions: The Politics & Imagery of Terrorism. Ed. by David J. Brown & Robert Merrill. LC 93-26066. (Illus.). 304p. (Orig.). 1994. pap. 18.95 (*0-941920-25-9*) Bay Pr.

Violent Property Crime. David Indermaur. (Australasian Studies in Criminology). 228p. 1995. 49.00 (*1-86287-173-6*, Pub. by Federation Pr AU) Gaunt.

Violent Relationships: Battering & Abuse among Adults. Ed. by Alison Landes. (Information Plus Reference Ser.). (Illus.). 168p. 1995. pap. text ed. 23.95 (*1-878623-96-6*) Info Plus TX.

***Violent Relationships: Battering & Abuse Among Adults.** 9th rev. ed. Ed. by Alison Landes et al. (Reference Ser.). (Illus.). 134p. 1997. pap. text ed. 23.95 (*1-57302-037-0*) Info Plus TX.

Violent Screen: A Critic's 13 Years on the Front Lines of Movie Mayhem. Stephen Hunter. Ed. by Ann Sjoerdsma. 305p. 1995. 19.95 (*0-9635376-4-4*) Bancroft MD.

Violent Screen: A Critic's 13 Years on the Front Lines of Movie Mayhem. Stephen Hunter. 320p. 1997. pap. 12.95 (*0-385-31652-6*, Delta) Dell.

Violent Social World of Black Men. William Oliver. LC 93-48216. 24.95p. 24.95 (*0-669-27952-8*, Lexington) Jossey-Bass.

Violent Society. Ed. by Eric Moonman. 168p. 1987. 35.00 (*0-7146-3309-7*, Pub. by F Cass Pubs UK); pap. 12.50 (*0-7146-4055-7*, Pub. by F Cass Pubs UK) Intl Spec Bk.

Violent Society. Stuart Palmer. 1972. pap. 21.95 (*0-8084-0353-2*) NCUP.

Violent Solutions: Revolutions, Nationalism, & Secret Societies in Europe to 1918. David R. MacKenzie. LC 96-2999. (Illus.). 332p. 1996. pap. text ed. 34.50 (*0-7618-0400-5*); lib. bdg. 62.50 (*0-7618-0399-8*) U Pr of Amer.

Violent Spring. Gary Phillips. 275p. 1994. pap. 9.00 (*1-883303-13-3*) W Coast Crime.

Violent Spring. Gary Phillips. 27p. 1997. reprint ed. mass mkt. 5.99 (*0-425-15625-7*, Prime Crime) Berkley Pub.

Violent Star Formation: From 30 Doradus to QSOs. Ed. by Guillermo Tenorio-Tagle. (Illus.). 444p. (C). 1995. text ed. 69.95 (*0-521-47277-6*) Cambridge U Pr.

Violent Storms. Jon Erickson. 1988. pap. 16.95 (*0-07-156259-1*) McGraw.

Violent Storms. Jon S. Erickson. (Discovering Earth Science Ser.). (Illus.). 288p. 1988. 24.95 (*0-8306-9042-5*); pap. 16.95 (*0-8306-2942-4*) McGraw-Hill Prof.

Violent Victimization see Assessing & Treating Victims of Violence

Violent Voices: Twelve Steps to Freedom from Emotional & Verbal Abuse. Kay Porterfield. 1989. pap. 9.95 (*1-55874-028-7*) Health Comm.

Violent Ward. Len Deighton. 368p. 1994. mass mkt. 6.50 (*0-06-109195-2*, Harp PBks) HarpC.

Violent Wedding. Robert Lowry. LC 76-110831. 255p. 1971. reprint ed. text ed. 55.00 (*0-8371-2566-9*, LOVW, Greenwood Pr) Greenwood.

Violent Years: The Founding of a Kansas Town. J. Mark Alley. LC 92-73893. (Illus.). 108p. (Orig.). 1992. pap. 12.95 (*0-9627947-6-7*) Hearth KS.

Violet. Jane Feather. 480p. 1995. mass mkt. 5.50 (*0-553-56471-4*, Fanfare) Bantam.

Violet. Leigh Greenwood. (Seven Brides Ser.). 448p. (Orig.). 1996. mass mkt. 5.99 (*0-8439-3995-8*) Dorchester Pub Co.

Violet. Kathleen Leverich. LC 96-111. (Flower Girls Ser.: Vol. 1). (Illus.). 96p. (J). (gr. 1-4). 1997. pap. 3.95 (*0-06-442018-3*, Trophy) HarpC Child Bks.

***Violet: The Life & Loves of Violet Gordon Woodhouse.** Jessica Douglas-Home. 320p. 1997. 28.00 (*1-86046-269-3*) Harvill Pr UK.

***Violet: The Life & Loves of Violet Gordon Woodhouse.** Jessica Douglas-Home. 1997. 28.00 (*0-614-28051-6*) HarperColl Wrld.

Violet Archer: A Bio-Bibliography. Linda Hartig. LC 91-26745. (Bio-Bibliographies in Music Ser.: No. 41). 192p. 1991. text ed. 45.00 (*0-313-26408-2*, HVA/, Greenwood Pr) Greenwood.

Violet Clay. Gail Godwin. 339p. 1995. pap. 12.00 (*0-345-38993-X*) Ballantine.

Violet Fairy Book. Ed. by Andrew Lang. (Illus.). (J). (gr. 4-6). pap. 6.95 (*0-486-21675-6*) Dover.

Violet Fairy Book. Andrew Lang. (Illus.). (J). (gr. 2 up). 1990. 20.50 (*0-8446-0757-6*) Peter Smith.

Violet Fire. Brenda Joyce. 368p. (Orig.). 1989. mass mkt. 4.99 (*0-380-75578-5*) Avon.

Violet Flame: Story of Armageddon & After. Fred T. Jane. LC 74-16501. (Science Fiction Ser.). 254p. 1975. reprint ed. 25.95 (*0-405-06300-8*) Ayer.

Violet Flame & Other Meditations. Gillian DeArmond. (Illus.). 62p. (Orig.). 1990. pap. 5.95 (*0-922356-19-X*) Amer West Pubs.

***Violet Hours: Poems.** Thomas R. McKague. LC 96-42394. 68p. 1996. pap. 12.95 (*0-7734-2689-2*, Mellen Poetry Pr) E Mellen.

Violet or The Danseuse: A Portraiture of the Human Passions & Character, 2 vols. in 1. Marianne D. Malet. LC 79-8167. reprint ed. 44.50 (*0-404-62018-3*) AMS Pr.

Violet Quill Reader: The Emergence of Gay Writing after Stonewall. David Bergman. LC 95-15238. 1995. pap. 14.95 (*0-312-13202-6*) St Martin.

Violet Shyness of Their Eyes: Notes from Nepal. Barbara J. Scot. 240p. 1993. 24.95 (*0-934971-36-6*); pap. 14.95 (*0-934971-35-8*) Calyx Bks.

Violet Trefusis: Life & Letters. Philippe Jullian & John Phillips. LC 84-22358. (Illus.). 256p. 1985. pap. 9.95 (*0-15-693555-4*, Harvest Bks) HarBrace.

Violet, Vert et Jaune: Purple, Green & Yellow in French. Robert Munsch. 32p. (J). 1992. pap. 5.95 (*1-55037-272-6*, Pub. by Annick CN) Firefly Bks Ltd.

Violet Ward. (*0-8317-5442-7*) Smithmark.

***Violet 19.** Stuart Wilde. 250p. 1997. write for info. (*1-56170-382-6*, 808) Hay House.

Violeta. Maria V. Queral. LC 91-71263. (Coleccion Espejo de Paciencia). (Illus.). 56p. (Orig.). (SPA.). 1992. pap. 9.95 (*0-89729-602-8*) Ediciones.

Violets. Doretta Klaber. (Illus.). 208p. 1975. 60.00 (*0-8386-7915-3*) Fairleigh Dickinson.

Violets. John F. Prevost. LC 96-10482. (Flowers Ser.). (Illus.). (J). 1996. lib. bdg. 13.98 (*1-56239-613-7*) Abdo & Dghtrs.

Violet's Garden. Launi K. Anderson. LC 96-3443. (Latter-Day Daughters Ser.). (Illus.). 80p. (Orig.). (J). (gr. 3-9). 1996. pap. 4.95 (*1-56236-506-1*) Aspen Bks.

Violetta. Pieke Bierman. Tr. by Ines Reider from GER. (Mask Noir Ser.). 256p. 1996. pap. 13.99 (*1-85242-289-0*) Serpents Tail.

Violetta & Her Sisters: Female Responses to the Lady of the Camellias. Ed. by Nicholas John. (Illus.). 176p. (Orig.). 1993. pap. 13.95 (*0-571-16665-2*) Faber & Faber.

Violette. (Red Stripe Ser.). 1988. pap. 4.50 (*0-8216-5055-6*, Univ Books) Carol Pub Group.

Violette, Je t'Aime. Remo Forlani. 184p. (FRE.). 1986. pap. 10.95 (*0-7859-2519-8*, 2070377490) Fr & Eur.

Violette's Daring Adventure. (Beechwood Bunny Tales Ser.). (Illus.). 32p. (J). (gr. k-3). 1992. lib. bdg. 18.60 (*0-8368-0912-2*) Gareth Stevens Inc.

Violette's Embrace. Michele Zackheim. 256p. 1996. 23.95 (*1-57322-036-1*, Riverhead Books) Putnam Pub Group.

***Violette's Embrace.** Michele Zackheim. 224p. 1997. reprint ed. pap. 12.00 (*1-57322-608-4*, Riverhd Trade) Berkley Pub.

Violin. Lesley Einer. 12p. (Orig.). 1990. pap. 2.50 (*0-9620822-2-8*) Sage Shadow Pr.

Violin. Yehudi Menuhin. (Illus.). 304p. 1996. 50.00 (*2-08-013623-2*, Pub. by Flammarion FR) Abbeville Pr.

Violin. Michael J. Pagliaro. (How Musical Instruments Work Ser.: Vol. I). (Illus.). 60p. (J). (gr. 4-8). 1993. student ed. 6.95 (*1-884417-00-0*) Ardsley Pr.

***Violin.** Anne O. Rice. 1997. 25.95 (*0-679-43302-3*) Knopf.

***Violin.** deluxe limited ed. Anne Rice. 304p. 1997. boxed 150.00 (*1-890885-00-2*) B E Trice.

***Violin.** large type ed. Anne Rice. LC 97-11708. (Large Print Ser.). 1997. pap. 25.95 (*0-679-77444-0*) Random.

Violin: History, Aesthetics, Manufacture, & Acoustics. Emile Leipp. Tr. by Hildegarde W. Parry. LC 79-414278. (Illus.). 126p. reprint ed. pap. 36.00 (*0-317-09906-X*, 2014298) Bks Demand.

Violin: How to Construct from Beginning to Completion: 1893. A. W. White. (Illus.). 44p. 1983. pap. 15.00 (*0-87556-716-9*) Saifer.

Violin: Its Famous Makers & Players. Paul Stoeving. LC 71-109855. (Illus.). 100p. 1970. reprint ed. text ed. 35.00 (*0-8371-4346-2*, STVI, Greenwood Pr) Greenwood.

Violin: Its Famous Makers & Players. Paul Stoeving. 100p. 1990. reprint ed. lib. bdg. 59.00 (*0-685-56143-7*) Rprt Serv.

Violin: Its Famous Makers & Their Imitators. enl. rev. ed. George Hart. LC 74-24266. (Illus.). reprint ed. 69.50 (*0-404-12955-2*) AMS Pr.

Violin: Precepts & Observations of a Luthier. Sourene Arakelian. 88p. pap. 23.95 (*0-933224-36-2*, T/47) Bold Strummer Ltd.

Violin - the Technic of Relaxation & Power. Fred Rosenberg. 1987. 4.75 (*0-89917-504-X*) Am String Tchrs.

Violin, a Lily & You. Victoria B. Demarest. LC 76-42917. 56p. 1976. pap. 9.50 (*0-912760-28-1*) Valkyrie Pub Hse.

Violin & Bowmakers of Minnesota. Thomas J. Wenberg. (Illus.). 88p. 1988. 25.00 (*0-912373-04-0*) Schubert.

Violin & Cello Building & Repairing. Robert Alton. 1988. reprint ed. lib. bdg. 49.00 (*0-7812-0517-4*) Rprt Serv.

Violin & Cello Building & Repairing. Robert Alton. 1976. reprint ed. lib. bdg. 59.00 (*0-403-03758-1*) Scholarly.

Violin & Flamethrower: Poems. Lindsay S. Amoss. LC 95-20574. 68p. 1996. pap. 12.95 (*0-7734-2759-7*, Mellen Poetry Pr) E Mellen.

Violin & Keyboard, Vol. Abram Loft. LC 90-20922. 364p. 1991. reprint ed. 34.00 (*0-931340-36-5*, Amadeus Pr) Timber.

Violin & Keyboard, Vol. 2. Abram Loft. LC 90-20922. 436p. 1991. reprint ed. 34.00 (*0-931340-37-3*, Amadeus Pr) Timber.

Violin & Old Violin Makers. A. Mason Clarke. 1976. lib. bdg. 45.00 (*0-403-03813-8*) Scholarly.

Violin & Old Violin Makers. Mason A. Clarke. 1988. reprint ed. lib. bdg. 49.00 (*0-7812-0486-0*) Rprt Serv.

Violin & Viola. Yehudi Menuhin et al. (Illus.). 1976. write for info. (*0-318-54251-X*); pap. 9.95 (*0-685-03273-6*) Macmillan.

Violin Bow Rehair & Repair. Harry S. Wake. LC 81-186555. (Illus.). 93p. (Orig.). 1975. student ed., pap. 23.00 (*0-9607048-1-7*) H S Wake.

Violin Carol Time. Keyser. 1989. 8.95 (*0-7935-5465-9*, 50488945) H Leonard.

Violin Concerto. Frederic B. Emery. LC 75-93979. (Music Reprint Ser.). 1969. reprint ed. lib. bdg. 75.00 (*0-306-71822-7*) Da Capo.

Violin Concerto. Benjamin Swalin. LC 72-8292. (Music Reprint Ser.). 186p. 1973. reprint ed. lib. bdg. 27.50 (*0-306-70537-0*) Da Capo.

Violin Concerto: Piano Reduction. J. Tower. 40p. 1995. pap. 29.95 (*0-7935-3923-4*, 50482283) H Leonard.

Violin Concerto No. 13 in D Major for Violin & Piano. R. Kreutzer. (Carl Fischer Music Library: No. 699). 1913. pap. 7.00 (*0-8258-0086-2*, L699) Fischer Inc NY.

Violin Duets, EFS135. (Illus.). 80p. 1968. pap. 14.95 (*0-8256-2135-6*, AM40569) Music Sales.

U V

An Asterisk (*) at the beginning of an entry indicates that the title is appearing in BIP for the first time.

***Violin Explained: Components, Mechanism, & Sound.** James Beament. (Illus.). 256p. 1997. text ed. 65.00 (*0-19-816623-0*) OUP.

Violin Family. David D. Boyden. 1989. pap. 14.95 (*0-393-30517-1*) Norton.

Violin Family & Its Makers in the British Isles: An Illustrated History & Directory. Brian W. Harvey. (Illus.). 496p. 1995. 145.00 (*0-19-816259-6*) OUP.

Violin Fingering: Its Theory & Practice. Carl Flesch. (Music Reprint Ser.). 1979. reprint ed. lib. bdg. 45.00 (*0-306-79573-6*) Da Capo.

***Violin Forum Highlights.** Karen Tuttle et al. (Highlights from the American String Teacher Forums Ser.). 25.00 (*0-614-25490-6*, 1935S) Am String Tchrs.

***Violin Fraud: Deception, Forgery & Lawsuits in England & America.** 2nd ed. Brian W. Harvey & Carla J. Shapreau. LC 97-9091. (Illus.). 192p. 1997. 35.00 (*0-19-816655-9*) OUP.

***Violin Guide.** Stefan Krayk. (Illus.). 42p. 11.25 (*0-614-25498-1*, 1912S) Am String Tchrs.

Violin Harmonics. C. E. Jacomb. 75p. 1991. reprint ed. lib. bdg. 59.00 (*0-7812-9357-X*) Rprt Serv.

Violin Iconography of Antonio Stradivari. Herbert K. Goodkind. LC 73-169961. (Illus.). 780p. 1972. 400.00 (*0-9600498-1-9*) Stradivari Iconography.

Violin Identification & Price Guide, Bk. 1. Roy Ehrhardt. (Illus.). 192p. 1977. reprint ed. spiral bd. 35.00 (*0-913902-22-5*) Heart Am Pr.

Violin Identification & Price Guide, Bk. 3. Roy Ehrhardt. (Illus.). 152p. 1978. spiral bd. 35.00 (*0-913902-25-X*) Heart Am Pr.

Violin Identification & Price Guide, No. 2. Roy Ehrhardt. (Illus.). 206p. 1978. 35.00 (*0-913902-24-1*) Heart Am Pr.

***Violin Lesson & the Cross Street Band.** Steven J. Givens. (Illus.). 32p. (Orig.). (J). (gr. 3-5). 1997. pap. 5.75 (*1-889658-06-5*) New Canaan Pub.

Violin-Maker's Gift. large type ed. Donn Kushner. 88p. (J). (gr. 5-6). reprint ed. 22.00 (*0-317-01960-0*, J-27120-00) Am Printing Hse.

Violin Maker's Notebook: A Companion Volume to: Useful Measurements for Violin Makers. 2nd ed. Henry A. Strobel. LC 90-71075. (Illus.). 66p. 1991. pap. 19.50 (*0-9620673-3-4*) H A Strobel.

***Violin Makers of Guarneri Family.** William H. Hill. pap. 16.95 (*0-486-26061-5*) Dover.

Violin Makers of the Guarneri Family, 1626-1762. Alfred Hill et al. (Illus.). 1983. reprint ed. 35.00 (*0-87556-125-X*) Saifer.

***Violin Making: A Guide for the Amateur.** Bruce Ossman. 1997. pap. 14.95 (*1-56523-091-4*) Fox Chapel Pub.

Violin Making, Step by Step. 2nd ed. Henry A. Strobel. LC 94-92156. (Illus.). 78p. 1994. pap. 29.50 (*0-9620673-6-9*) H A Strobel.

Violin Man. Maureen B. Hooper. LC 91-70417. 80p. (J). (gr. 3-7). 1991. 12.95 (*1-878093-79-7*) Boyds Mills Pr.

Violin Market: The Violinist's Guide to Instrument Purchase. John Huber. (Illus.). 184p. (ENG & GER.). 1995. 195.00 (*0-933224-65-6*, Pub. by Das Musikinstrument GW) Bold Strummer Ltd.

Violin Method. Frank Zucco. 1993. 7.95 (*0-87166-870-X*, 93474) Mel Bay.

Violin Method, Bk. 4. M. Bang. (Illus.). 96p. 1922. pap. 12.95 (*0-8258-0252-0*, 0-45) Fischer Inc NY.

Violin Method, Vol. 1. (SPA.). 5.95 (*1-56222-433-6*, 94664SP) Mel Bay.

Violin Music by Women Composers: A Bio-Bibliographical Guide. Compiled by Rose M. Johnson. LC 89-17200. (Music Reference Collection: No. 22). 288p. 1989. text ed. 55.00 (*0-313-26652-2*, JVM/, Greenwood Pr) Greenwood.

Violin Obligato & Other Studies. Margaret Crosby. LC 74-106283. (Short Story Index Reprint Ser.). 1977. 21.95 (*0-8369-3320-6*) Ayer.

Violin of Passing Time. Aristide-Christian Charpentier. (J). (gr. 1-7). 1972. 5.00 (*0-87602-217-4*) Anchorage.

Violin Pieces Country Style. Betty McDermott. (Illus.). 72p. 1977. pap. 11.95 (*0-8256-2164-X*, AM32426) Music Sales.

Violin Pieces the Whole World Plays. (Illus.). 208p. 1916. pap. 21.95 (*0-8256-1001-X*, AM42532) Music Sales.

***Violin Players.** Eileen B. Sherman. 130p. (YA). (gr. 8 up). 1997. 14.95 (*0-8276-0595-1*) JPS Phila.

Violin Playing As I Teach It. Leopold Auer. 99p. 1980. reprint ed. pap. 3.95 (*0-486-23917-9*) Dover.

Violin Playing As I Teach It. Leopold Auer. LC 75-35022. (Illus.). 99p. 1976. reprint ed. text ed. 42.50 (*0-8371-8573-4*, AUVP, Greenwood Pr) Greenwood.

Violin Primer. Frank Zucco. 1993. 4.95 (*0-87166-377-5*, 93408) Mel Bay.

Violin Restoration: A Manual for Violin Makers. Hans Weisshaar & Margaret Shipman. (Illus.). 250p. 1988. text ed. 300.00 (*0-9621861-0-4*) Weisshaar & Shipman.

Violin Solos, EFS66. (Illus.). 128p. pap. 14.95 (*0-8256-2066-X*, AM40262) Music Sales.

Violin Sonata. A. Davis. 32p. 1995. pap. 11.95 (*0-7935-4502-1*, 50482386) H Leonard.

Violin Technique & Performance Practice in the Late-Eighteenth & Early-Nineteenth Centuries. Robin Stowell. (Cambridge Musical Texts & Monographs). 450p. 1985. 94.95 (*0-521-23279-1*) Cambridge U Pr.

Violin Technique & Performance Practice in the Late-Eighteenth & Early-Nineteenth Centuries. Robin Stowell. (Cambridge Musical Texts & Monographs). (Illus.). 412p. (C). 1990. pap. 31.95 (*0-521-39744-8*) Cambridge U Pr.

Violin Time. Campbell. 1996. pap. 13.95 (*0-413-70960-4*, Pub. by Methuen UK) Heinemann.

Violin Virtuosos: From Paganini to the 21st Century. Henry Roth. (Illus.). 400p. (Orig.). 1997. pap. 29.95 (*1-879395-15-0*) CA Classics Bks.

***Violin Virtuosos: From Paganini to the 21st Century.** Henry Roth. (Illus.), 396p. 1997. 44.95 (*1-879395-18-5*) CA Classics Bks.

Violinist's Guide for Exquisite Intonation. Barry Ross. 1988. 9.75 (*0-89917-520-1*) Am String Tchrs.

Violinists of To-Day. Donald Brook. LC 74-38313. (Biography Index Reprint Ser.). 1977. reprint ed. 18.95 (*0-8369-8117-0*) Ayer.

Violinists of Today: Music Book Index. Donald Brook. 192p. 1993. reprint ed. lib. bdg. 69.00 (*0-7812-9583-1*) Rprt Serv.

Viollet. Julia Cunningham. (Illus.). (J). (gr. 4-7). 1966. lib. bdg. 6.99 (*0-394-91821-5*) Pantheon.

Violoncello & Its History. 2nd ed. Wilhelm J. Von Wasielewski. LC 67-30401. (Music Reprint Ser.). 1968. reprint ed. 32.50 (*0-306-70952-X*) Da Capo.

Violons Parfois. Francoise Sagan. 260p. 1966. 8.95 (*0-685-23933-0*, 1617) Fr & Eur.

Viols & Other Bowed Instruments. Gerald R. Hayes. (Illus.). 278p. 1969. reprint ed. lib. bdg. 37.50 (*0-8450-2581-3*) Broude.

***Vionnet.** J. Demorex. (Fashion Memoir Ser.). (Illus.). 1996. 24.00 (*0-500-01722-0*) Thames Hudson.

V.I.P. Address Book Updates. annuals James M. Wiggins. LC 94-30776. 100p. 1997. pap. 24.95 (*0-938731-10-6*) Assoc Media Cos.

VIP Cruising Guide: St. Maarten - St. Martin Area to Antigua & Barbuda. William J. Elman. 258p. 1992. pap. 10.77 (*0-9635048-0-0*) VI Plus Yacht.

VIP Investments: How to Make Big Money from Real Estate's Sleeping Giants. Joan Paskow & Irwin Paskow. 1977. 69.50 (*0-13-942128-9*) Exec Reports.

***Vip, Pacap, & Related Peptides: Second International Symposium.** Akira Arimura & Sami I. Said. LC 96-39419. (Annals of the New York Academy of Sciences Ser.). 1997. 135.00 (*0-89766-983-5*); pap. write for info. (*0-89766-984-3*) NY Acad Sci.

Vip, Pacap & Related Regulatory Peptides. G. Rosselini. 648p. 1994. text ed. 137.00 (*981-02-1788-9*) World Scientific Pub.

VIP 2: Looking Ahead. large type ed. F. N. Hogg. 1995. 40.00 (*0-7089-3494-3*) Ulverscroft.

Vipassana Dipani: or The Manual of Insight. U. Nyana. LC 78-70107. reprint ed. 22.00 (*0-404-17357-8*) AMS Pr.

***Vipassana, Its Relevance to the Present World.** 141p. pap. 6.95 (*81-7414-018-2*) Vipassana Res.

***Vipassana Meditations: Healing the Healer & the Experience of Impermanence.** Paul R. Fleischman. 29p. pap. 2.50 (*81-7414-009-3*) Vipassana Res.

Vipassana, the Buddhist Way: Based on Pali Sources. Ed. by Harcharan S. Sobti. 181p. 1992. 17.00 (*81-85133-52-2*, Pub. by Estrn Bk Linkers II) Nataraj Bks.

***Viper.** Iron Crown Enterprises Staff. 1993. 20.00 (*1-55806-179-7*) Iron Crown Ent Inc.

Viper. Matthew L. Stone. LC 96-14074. (Enthusiast Color Ser.). (Illus.). 96p. 1996. pap. 12.95 (*0-7603-0149-2*) Motorbooks Intl.

Viper: F-16. Lou Drendel. (Modern Military Aircraft Ser.). (Illus.). 64p. 1992. pap. 9.95 (*0-89747-281-0*, 5009) Squad Sig Pubns.

Viper: Pure Performance by Dodge. Consumer Guide Auto Editors. (Illus.). 80p. 1993. 12.98 (*0-7853-0109-7*, 1002900) Pubns Intl Ltd.

Viper of Milan. Marjorie Bowen. LC 65-25494. (J). (gr. 4-8). 6500. 14.95 (*0-8023-1014-1*) Dufour.

***Viper on the Hearth: Mormons, Myths, & the Construction of Heresy.** Terryl Givens. (Religion in America Ser.). (Illus.). 256p. 1997. 35.00 (*0-19-510183-9*) OUP.

Viper Quarry. Dean Feldmeyer. 1994. mass mkt. 4.99 (*0-671-76982-0*) PB.

Vipere. Guy Des Cars. 448p. (FRE.). 1955. pap. 11.95 (*0-7859-4801-5*) Fr & Eur.

Vipere au Poing. Herve Bazin. (FRE.). 1972. pap. 10.95 (*0-7859-3056-6*) Fr & Eur.

Vipers. Eric Ethan. (Fangs! An Imagination Library Ser.). (J). 1995. lib. bdg. 17.27 (*0-8368-1432-0*) Gareth Stevens Inc.

Vipers' Club. John H. Richardson. 320p. 1996. 24.00 (*0-688-12672-3*) Morrow.

***Vipers in the Storm: Diary of a Fighter Pilot.** Keith Rosenkranz. LC 97-14209. 1997. 22.95 (*1-57036-379-X*) Turner Pub GA.

Viper's Tangle. Francois Mauriac. 208p. 1987. pap. 8.95 (*0-88184-305-9*) Carroll & Graf.

VIP's Directory of Giant Scale Plans, Vol. 1. John A. DeVries & Richard D. Phillips. (Illus.). 120p. 1987. pap. 11.95 (*0-934575-02-9*) Vip Pubs.

***VIP's Directory of Giant Scale Plans, Vol. 2.** John A. DeVries & Richard D. Phillips. (Illus.). 120p. 1987. pap. 11.95 (*0-934575-06-1*) Vip Pubs.

***VIP's Directory of Giant Scale Plans, Vol. 3.** John A. DeVries & Richard D. Phillips. (Illus.). 120p. 1987. pap. 11.95 (*0-934575-09-6*) Vip Pubs.

***Vir Trilinguis: A Study in the Biblical Exegesis of Saint Jerome.** Dennis Brown. 229p. 1992. pap. 35.75 (*90-390-0031-X*, Pub. by KOK Pharos NE) Eisenbrauns.

Viracocha. Alberto Vazquez-Figueroa. 336p. (SPA.). 1992. pap. 4.95 (*1-56780-058-0*) La Costa Pr.

Virago! The Story of Anne Newport Royall 1769-1854. Alice S. Maxwell & Marion B. Dunlevy. LC 84-42731. 1991. pap. 19.98 (*0-9629706-0-3*) Dunwell Pr.

Virago Book of Fairy Tales see Old Wives' Fairy Tale Book

Virago Woman's Travel Guide to Amsterdam. Catherine Stebbings. LC 94-70213. 345p. (Orig.). 1994. pap. 16.95 (*1-57143-016-4*, Book Passage Pr) RDR Bks.

Virago Woman's Travel Guide to London. Josie Barnard. LC 94-70038. 389p. (Orig.). 1994. pap. 16.95 (*1-57143-017-2*, Book Passage Pr) RDR Bks.

Virago Woman's Travel Guide to San Francisco. Harriet Swift. LC 94-70040. 403p. (Orig.). 1994. pap. 16.95 (*1-57143-015-6*, Book Passage Pr) RDR Bks.

Viral & Autoimmune Hepatitis: Morphologic & Pathogenetic Aspects of Cell Damage in Hepatitis with Potential Chronicity. Hans P. Dienes. LC 88-38640. (Progress in Pathology Ser.: Vol. 132). 107p. 1989. pap. text ed. 80.00 (*0-89574-280-2*) G F Verlag.

Viral & Other Infections of the Human Respiratory System. Myint. 504p. (gr. 13). 1995. text ed. 102.50 (*0-412-60070-6*) Chapman & Hall.

Viral Chemotherapy. David Shugar. (International Encyclopedia of Pharmacology). 1984. 120.00 (*0-08-030792-2*, Pergamon Pr) Elsevier.

Viral Chemotherapy, Vol 2. David Shugar. (International Encyclopedia of Pharmacology & Therapeutics Ser.). 266p. 1985. 123.00 (*0-08-031985-8*, Pub. by PPL UK) Franklin.

Viral Cytopathology. H. H. Malherbe. 112p. 1980. 98.95 (*0-8493-5567-2*, RC114) CRC Pr.

Viral Diarrhea of Man & Animals. Saif & Thiel. 360p. 1989. 217.00 (*0-8493-6640-2*, QR201) CRC Pr.

Viral Disease see Handbook of Clinical Neurology

Viral Diseases in Pregnancy. Ed. by Bernard Gonik. LC 93-38947. (Clinical Perspectives in Obstetrics & Gynecology Ser.). (Illus.). 300p. 1994. 96.00 (*0-387-94207-6*) Spr-Verlag.

***Viral Diseases International Nomenclature of Diseases Vol. II: Infectious Diseases, 2.** (International Nomenclature of Diseases Ser.: No. 3). 1983. pap. text ed. 20.00 (*92-9036-011-9*) World Health.

Viral Diseases of Cattle. Robert F. Kahrs. LC 81-8222. (Illus.). 300p. (C). 1981. pap. text ed. 29.95 (*0-8138-0860-X*) Iowa St U Pr.

Viral Diseases of the Eye. Ed. by Richard W. Darrell. LC 84-7897. 342p. reprint ed. pap. 97.50 (*0-7837-1485-8*, 2057180) Bks Demand.

Viral Diseases of the Fetus & Newborn. 2nd ed. James B. Hanshaw et al. (Major Problems in Clinical Pediatrics Ser.). (Illus.). 308p. 1985. text ed. 77.50 (*0-7216-4501-1*) Saunders.

Viral DNA Synthesis: HIV-1 Reverse Transcription & DNA Synthesis at the Replication Fork of Bacteriophage T-7. Z. Debyser. No. 77. 218p. (Orig.). 1994. pap. 52.50 (*90-6186-600-6*, Pub. by Leuven Univ BE) Coronet Bks.

Viral Etiology of Cervical Cancer. Ed. by Richard Peto & Harald Z. Hausen. LC 86-2227. (Banbury Reports: No. 21). 362p. 1986. text ed. 68.00 (*0-87969-221-9*) Cold Spring Harbor.

Viral Fusion Mechanisms. Bentz. 544p. 1992. 244.00 (*0-8493-5606-7*, QR454) CRC Pr.

***Viral Gastroenteritis.** Shunzo Chiba. LC 96-29701. (Archives of Virology: Supplement Ser.). 1996. write for info. (*3-211-82875-3*) Spr-Verlag.

***Viral Gastroenteritis, Vol. VII.** Ed. by Shunzo Chiba et al. LC 96-29701. (Archives of Virology Ser.: Supplement 12, 1996). (Illus.). 311p. 1997. 198.00 (*3-211-82947-4*) Spr-Verlag.

Viral Genes & Plant Pathogenesis. Ed. by T. P. Pirone & J. G. Shaw. (Illus.). xvi, 215p. 1990. 71.95 (*0-387-97313-3*) Spr-Verlag.

Viral Genome Methods. Ed. by Kenneth W. Adolph. 320p. 1996. 79.95 (*0-8493-4412-3*) CRC Pr.

Viral Haemorrhagic Fevers. (Technical Report Ser.: No. 721). 126p. 1985. pap. text ed. 10.00 (*92-4-120721-3*, 1100721) World Health.

***Viral Hemorrhagic Fever: Current Bibliographies in Medicine (January 1990-June 1996)** Cynthia B. Love & Peter B. Jahrling. 65p. (Orig.). (C). 1996. pap. 30.00 (*0-7881-3508-2*) DIANE Pub.

Viral Hepatitis: Clinical & Scientific Perspectives. E. A. Fagan & T. J. Harrison. 160p. 1997. pap. 34.95 (*1-85996-025-1*, Pub. by Bios Sci UK) Bks Intl VA.

Viral Hepatitis: Current Status & Issues. Eduard Kurstak. (Illus.). 216p. 1992. 97.95 (*0-387-82387-5*) Spr-Verlag.

***Viral Hepatitis: Diagnosis-Treatment-Prevention.** Ed. by Wilson. (Gastroenterology Ser.: Vol. 4). 552p. 1997. 175.00 (*0-8247-9416-8*) Dekker.

Viral Hepatitis: From A to E. 6th rev. ed. Ed. by Richard Westlund et al. (Illus.). 95p. (Orig.). 1994. pap. text ed. 48.00 (*1-879772-01-9*) Health Studies.

Viral Hepatitis: Practical Evaluation & Treatment. rev. ed. Teddy F. Bader. (Illus.). 264p. 1996. 49.00 (*0-88937-133-4*) Hogrefe & Huber Pubs.

Viral Hepatitis: Proceedings of the WHO Expert Committee, Geneva, 1974. WHO Staff. (Technical Report Ser.: No. 570). 1975. pap. text ed. 7.00 (*92-4-120570-9*, 1100570) World Health.

Viral Hepatitis: Scientific Basis & Clinical Management. Arie J. Zuckerman. (Illus.). 416p. 1994. 150.00 (*0-443-04708-1*) Churchill.

Viral Hepatitis: Second International Max von Pettenkofer Symposium. International Max von Pettenkofer Symposium Ser. Ed. by Lacy R. Overby et al. LC 83-15162. (Infectious Diseases & Antimicrobial Agents Ser.: No. 4). (Illus.). 335p. 1983. reprint ed. pap. 95.50 (*0-7837-0619-7*, 2040964) Bks Demand.

Viral Hepatitis: Standardization in Immunoprophylaxis of Infections by Hepatitis Viruses. Ed. by G. Papaevangelou & W. Hennessen. (Developments in Biological Standardization Ser.: Vol. 54). (Illus.). xviii, 590p. 1983. pap. 108.00 (*3-8055-3826-X*) S Karger.

Viral Hepatitis & Liver Disease. K. Nishioka et al. 824p. 1994. 280.00 (*0-387-70132-X*) Spr-Verlag.

Viral Hepatitis B Infection: Vaccine & Control. Ed. by C. L. Lai et al. 304p. 1984. 85.00 (*9971-950-80-4*) World Scientific Pub.

Viral Hepatitis C, D & E. T. Shikata et al. (International Congress Ser.: Vol. 895). 1991. 203.75 (*0-444-81117-6*) Elsevier.

Viral Hepatitis in China: Problems & Control Strategies. Joseph L. Melnick. (Monographs in Virology: Vol. 19). (Illus.). xii, 160p. 1991. 155.75 (*3-8055-5364-1*) S Karger.

Viral Infections. Richard K. Root & Merle A. Sande. (Contemporary Issues in Infectious Diseases Ser.: Vol. 10). (Illus.). 218p. 1993. text ed. 69.00 (*0-443-08859-4*) Churchill.

Viral Infections of Humans: Epidemiology & Control. 3rd ed. Ed. by A. S. Evans. (Illus.). 870p. 1989. 85.00 (*0-306-42731-1*, Plenum Med Bk) Plenum.

Viral Infections of Humans: Epidemiology & Control. 3rd ed. Ed. by A. S. Evans. (Illus.). 870p. 1991. pap. 44.50 (*0-306-43577-2*, Plenum Med Bk) Plenum.

***Viral Infections of Humans: Epidemiology & Control.** 4th ed. Ed. by Alfred S. Evans & Richard A. Kaslow. LC 97-17146. (Illus.). 1051p. (C). 1997. 110.00 (*0-306-44855-6*, Plenum Med Bk); pap. 59.50 (*0-306-44856-4*, Plenum Med Bk) Plenum.

Viral Infections of the Gastrointestinal Tract. 2nd ed. Albert Z. Kapikian. LC 93-46950. (Infectious Disease & Therapy Ser.: Vol. 10). 816p. 1994. 215.00 (*0-8247-8860-5*) Dekker.

Viral Infections of the Heart. J. E. Banatvala. 304p. 1993. 85.00 (*0-340-55737-0*, Pub. by Ed Arnold UK) OUP.

Viral Infections of the Nervous System. Richard T. Johnson. LC 82-7527. 445p. 1982. reprint ed. pap. 126.90 (*0-608-00426-X*, 2061141) Bks Demand.

Viral Messenger RNA. Ed. by Yechiel Becker. (Developments in Molecular Virology Ser.). 1985. lib. bdg. 138.00 (*0-89838-706-X*) Kluwer Ac.

Viral Pathogenesis. Neal M. Nathanson. LC 96-23106. 1,040p. 1996. text ed. 159.00 (*0-7817-0297-6*) Lppncott-Raven.

Viral Pollution of the Environment. Ed. by Gerald Berg. 248p. 1983. 144.00 (*0-8493-6245-8*, TD427, CRC Reprint) Franklin.

Viral Proteinases As Targets for Chemotherapy. Ed. by Hans-Georg Kraeusslich et al. (Current Communications in Molecular Biology Ser.). (Illus.). 287p. (C). 1989. pap. text ed. 24.00 (*0-87969-335-5*) Cold Spring Harbor.

***Viral Regulatory Structures.** Myers. 1997. write for info. (*0-201-32821-6*); pap. write for info. (*0-201-32822-4*) Addison-Wesley.

***Viral Resistance in Plants/Viral Coat Proteins: Bibliography: January 1991-July 1996.** Raymond Dobert. 64p. (Orig.). (C). 1997. pap. text ed. 35.00 (*0-7881-3872-3*) DIANE Pub.

***Viral Respiratory Diseases: Report of a Scientific Group.** (Technical Report Ser.: No. 642). 63p. 1980. pap. text ed. 4.00 (*92-4-120642-X*, 1100642) World Health.

***Viral Safety & Evaluation of Viral Clearance from Biopharmaceutical Products: National Institute of Health, Bethesda, Md., June 1995.** Ed. by Fred Brown & A. S. Lubiniecki. (Developments in Biological Standardization Ser.: Vol. 88, 1996). (Illus.). x, 350p. 1996. pap. 274.00 (*3-8055-6391-4*) S Karger.

Viral Safety of Plasma-Derived Replacement Factors for Hemophilia: How Safe is Safe? Ed. by P. M. Mannucci et al. (Journal: Vox Sanguinis Ser.: Vol. 67, Supplement 4, 1994). (Illus.). iv, 28p. 1994. pap. 14.00 (*3-8055-6066-4*) S Karger.

***Viral Sex: The Nature of AIDS.** Jaap Goudsmit. (Illus.). 272p. 1997. text ed. 27.50 (*0-19-509728-9*) OUP.

***Viral Superantigens.** Ed. by Kyuhei Tomonari. LC 96-39363. 288p. 1997. 180.00 (*0-8493-7688-2*) CRC Pr.

Viral Vaccines. P. B. Stones. (Essays in Applied Microbiology Ser.: No. 10). 32p. pap. 25.00 (*0-318-34728-8*, 2031942) Bks Demand.

***Viral Vaccines & Antiviral Drugs.** (Technical Report Ser.: No. 693). 72p. 1983. pap. text ed. 6.00 (*92-4-120693-4*) World Health.

Viral Vectors. Ed. by Yakov Gluzman & Stephen H. Hughes. (Current Communications in Molecular Biology Ser.). (Illus.). 189p. (C). 1988. pap. text ed. 20.00 (*0-87969-316-9*) Cold Spring Harbor.

Viral Vectors. Ed. by Yakov Gluzman & Stephen H. Hughes. LC 88-205936. (Current Communications in Molecular Biology Ser.). 199p. reprint ed. pap. 56.80 (*0-7837-2030-0*, 2042286) Bks Demand.

Viral Vectors: Tools for Study & Genetic Manipulation of the Nervous System. Ed. by Michael G. Kaplitt. (Illus.). 486p. 1995. text ed. 95.00 (*0-12-397570-0*) Acad Pr.

Viral Vectors: Tools for Study & Genetic Manipulation of the Nervous System. Ed. by Michael G. Kaplitt. (Illus.). 486p. 1995. pap. text ed. 49.95 (*0-12-397571-9*) Acad Pr.

Viral Warts: Biology & Treatment. 2nd ed. Mary H. Bunney et al. (Illus.). 208p. 1992. 80.00 (*0-19-262062-2*) OUP.

Viral Zoonoses Sect. B, 2 vols., Set. J. Steele & G. Beran. LC 81-4868. (Handbook Series in Zoonoses). 1981. reprint ed. 561.00 (*0-8493-2910-8*, CRC Reprint) Franklin.

***Viramma.** Viramma Racine. Date not set. pap. 19.00 (*1-85984-148-1*, Pub. by Verso UK) Routledge Chapman & Hall.

***Viramma.** Viramma Racine. (C). Date not set. text ed. 65.00 (*1-85984-817-6*, Pub. by Verso UK) Routledge Chapman & Hall.

Viravax. Bill Ransom. LC 92-21148. 320p. 1993. 17.95 (*0-441-86476-7*) Ace Bks.

Viravax. Bill Ransom. 320p. 1994. mass mkt. 4.99 (*0-441-00083-5*) Ace Bks.

Virdins of Delaware & Related Families. Donald O. Virdin. iv, 143p. 1992. reprint ed. pap. 21.50 (*1-55613-546-7*) Heritage Bk.

***Vireyas: A Practical Gardening Guide.** Jacqueline Walker. (Illus.). 96p. (Orig.). 1997. pap. 19.95 (*0-88192-402-4*) Timber.

U V

Virgen de los Sicarios. Fernando Vallejo. 1995. pap. 12.50 (0-679-76321-X, Vin) Random.
***Virgen Maria - The Virgin Mary.** Rogelio Archilla. 101p. (SPA.). 1995. write for info. (1-56063-663-7) Editorial Unilit.
Virgen y Madre. Virgil Elizondo. (Illus.). 117p. (SPA.). 1983. write for info. (0-614-04871-0) Mex Am Cult.
Virgie Goes to School. Howard. (J). Date not set. 17.00 (0-689-80076-2, S&S Bks Young Read) S&S Childrens.
Virgil. Ed. by Ian McAuslan & Peter Walcot. (Greece & Rome Studies: No. I). 208p. 1990. 65.00 (0-19-920166-8) OUP.
Virgil. Plutarch. Tr. by H. J. Rose. 1924. 30.00 (0-8196-0284-1) Biblo.
Virgil. David R. Slavitt. (Hermes Bks.). 224p. (Orig.). 1992. text ed. 14.00 (0-300-05101-8); pap. text ed. 14.00 (0-300-05102-6) Yale U Pr.
Virgil. George E. Woodberry. LC 72-3495. (Studies in European Literature: No. 56). 1972. reprint ed. lib. bdg. 40.95 (0-8383-1564-X) M S G Haskell Hse.
Virgil: "The Aeneid" K. W. Grandsen. (Landmarks of World Literature Ser.). 128p. (C). 1990. text ed. 29.95 (0-521-32329-0); pap. text ed. 11.95 (0-521-31157-8) Cambridge U Pr.
Virgil: A Study in Civilized Poetry. Brooks Otis. LC 95-17062. (Oklahoma Classical Culture Ser.: Vol. 20). 456p. 1995. pap. 17.95 (0-8061-2782-1) U of Okla Pr.
Virgil: Aeneid: A Companion to the Translation of C. Day Lewis. R. D. Williams. (Classics Companions Ser.). 151p. 1985. pap. 14.95 (0-86292-044-2, Pub. by Brstl Class Pr UK) Focus Pub-R Pullins.
Virgil: Aeneid I. Ed. by J. Whiteley & H. Gould. (Bristol Latin Texts Ser.). 185p. (LAT.). 1984. reprint ed. pap. 17.95 (0-86292-167-8, Pub. by Brstl Class Pr UK) Focus Pub-R Pullins.
Virgil: Aeneid II. Ed. by J. Whiteley & H. Gould. (Bristol Latin Texts Ser.). 164p. (LAT.). 1991. reprint ed. pap. 15.95 (0-86292-056-6, Pub. by Brstl Class Pr UK) Focus Pub-R Pullins.
Virgil: Aeneid III. Ed. by R. D. Williams. (Bristol Latin Texts Ser.). 156p. (LAT.). 1981. reprint ed. pap. 25.95 (0-906515-99-8, Pub. by Brstl Class Pr UK) Focus Pub-R Pullins.
Virgil: Aeneid IV. Ed. by H. Gould & J. Whiteley. (Bristol Latin Texts Ser.). 156p. (LAT.). 1981. reprint ed. pap. 15.95 (0-906515-93-9, Pub. by Brstl Class Pr UK) Focus Pub-R Pullins.
Virgil: Aeneid IX. Ed. by J. Whiteley. (Bristol Latin Texts Ser.). 156p. (LAT.). 1978. reprint ed. 14.95 (0-906515-38-6, Pub. by Brstl Class Pr UK) Focus Pub-R Pullins.
Virgil: Aeneid V. Ed. by R. D. Williams. (Bristol Latin Texts Ser.). 252p. (LAT.). 1981. reprint ed. pap. 25.95 (0-86292-000-0, Pub. by Brstl Class Pr UK) Focus Pub-R Pullins.
Virgil: Aeneid VI. J. Whiteley. Ed. by H. Gould. (Bristol Latin Texts Ser.). 208p. (LAT.). 1984. reprint ed. 17.95 (0-86292-146-5, Pub. by Brstl Class Pr UK) Focus Pub-R Pullins.
Virgil: Aeneid VII & VIII. Ed. by C. Fordyce. (Bristol Latin Texts Ser.). 340p. (LAT.). 1985. reprint ed. pap. 25.95 (0-86292-171-6, Pub. by Brstl Class Pr UK) Focus Pub-R Pullins.
Virgil: Aeneid VIII. J. Whiteley. Ed. by H. Gould. (Bristol Latin Texts Ser.). 152p. (LAT.). 1979. reprint ed. 15.95 (0-906515-39-4, Pub. by Brstl Class Pr UK) Focus Pub-R Pullins.
Virgil: Aeneid X. Ed. by R. H. Jordan. (Bristol Latin Texts Ser.). 130p. (LAT.). 1990. pap. 13.95 (1-85399-045-0, Pub. by Brstl Class Pr UK) Focus Pub-R Pullins.
Virgil: Aeneid XII. Ed. by W. S. Maguinness. (Bristol Latin Texts Ser.). 160p. (LAT.). 1992. pap. 14.95 (1-85399-244-5, Pub. by Brstl Class Pr UK) Focus Pub-R Pullins.
***Virgil: Eclogues & Georgics.** Ed. by R. D. Williams. 240p. (Orig.). 1996. pap. text ed. 26.95 (1-85399-508-8, Pub. by Brstl Class Pr UK) Focus Pub-R Pullins.
Virgil: Georgics I & IV. Ed. by H. H. Huxley. (Bristol Latin Texts Ser.). 232p. (LAT.). 1979. reprint ed. 21.95 (0-906515-34-3, Pub. by Brstl Class Pr UK) Focus Pub-R Pullins.
Virgil: Moretum (The Ploughman's Lunch) Ed. by E. J. Kenney. (Bristol Latin Texts Ser.). 128p. (LAT.). 1984. 19.95 (0-86292-084-1, Pub. by Brstl Class Pr UK) Focus Pub-R Pullins.
Virgil Aeneid, Bks. 7-12. Virgil. Ed. by R. D. Williams. (Classical Ser.). 1972. write for info. (0-312-84340-2) St Martin.
***Virgil: Aeneid 10: With Introduction, Translation & Commentary.** Virgil. Ed. & Tr. by S. J. Harrison. 344p. 1997. pap. 35.00 (0-19-815096-2) OUP.
Virgil & Caesar: A Play. Francis Warner. (Illus.). 95p. 9400. 18.95 (0-86140-348-7, Pub. by Colin Smythe Ltd UK) Dufour.
Virgil & Spenser. Merritt Y. Hughes. LC 79-118629. reprint ed. 27.50 (0-404-07809-5) AMS Pr.
Virgil & the Moderns. Theodore J. Ziolkowski. LC 92-41209. 296p. 1993. text ed. 42.50 (0-691-03248-3) Princeton U Pr.
Virgil & the Tempest: The Politics of Imitation. Donna B. Hamilton. 200p. 1990. 40.00 (0-8142-0517-8) Ohio St U Pr.
Virgil As Orpheus: A Study of the Georgics. M. Owen Lee. LC 95-7687. (SUNY Series in Classical Studies). 171p. (C). 1996. text ed. 44.50 (0-7914-2783-8); pap. text ed. 14.95 (0-7914-2784-6) State U NY Pr.
Virgil Earp: Western Peace Officer. Don Chaput. 272p. 1994. 24.50 (1-879915-09-X) Affil Writers America.
Virgil Earp: Western Peace Officer. Donald Chaput. LC 96-17089. (Illus.). 272p. 1996. pap. 14.95 (0-8061-2881-X) U of Okla Pr.
Virgil Finlay: An Astrology Sketch Book. Virgil Finlay. (Illus.). 1975. 15.00 (0-937986-32-1) D M Grant.
Virgil Finlay's Far Beyond. Virgil Finlay. 144p. 1994. 24.95 (1-885611-03-X); pap. 14.95 (1-885611-04-8) C F Miller.
Virgil Hunter: A Novel. James M. Bellarosa. 176p. (Orig.). 1993. pap. 9.95 (1-880284-00-6) J Daniel.
Virgil in English. K. W. Gransden. 384p. 1996. pap. 14.95 (0-14-042386-9, Viking) Viking Penguin.
Virgil in Medieval England: Figuring the Aeneid from the Twelfth Century to Chaucer. Christopher Baswell. (Cambridge Studies in Medieval Literature: No. 24). (Illus.). 483p. (C). 1995. text ed. 64.95 (0-521-46294-0) Cambridge U Pr.
***Virgil Is Still the Frogboy.** Lanford Wilson. 1997. pap. 5.25 (0-8222-1592-6) Dramatists Play.
Virgil Thomson. Koslelanetz. 1997. 28.00 (0-02-864722-X) Mac Lib Ref.
Virgil Thomson: A Bio-Bibliography. Michael Meckna. LC 86-14229. (Bio-Bibliographies in Music Ser.: No. 4). 217p. 1986. text ed. 49.95 (0-313-25010-3, MVN/, Greenwood Pr) Greenwood.
Virgil Thomson: His Life & Music. Kathleen O. Hoover & John Cage. LC 70-119933. (Select Bibliographies Reprint Ser.). 1977. reprint ed. 25.95 (0-8369-5376-2) Ayer.
Virgil Thomson's Musical Portraits. Anthony Tommasini. LC 85-6297. (Thematic Catalogues Ser.: No. 13). 1986. lib. bdg. 55.00 (0-918728-51-7) Pendragon NY.
Virgil's Aeneid. Virgil. Tr. by John Dryden. (Airmont Classics Ser.). (J). (gr. 11 up). 1968. mass mkt. 1.95 (0-8049-0177-5, CL-177) Airmont.
***Virgil's Aeneid: Semantic Relations & Proper Names.** Ed. by Michael Paschalis. 500p. 1997. 110.00 (0-19-814688-4) OUP.
Virgil's Aeneid--Essays in Interpretation & Influence. Michael C. Putnam. LC 94-19891. 420p. 1995. pap. text ed. 16.95 (0-8078-4499-3); lib. bdg. 45.00 (0-8078-2191-8) U of NC Pr.
Virgil's Augustan Epic. Francis Cairns. 300p. (C). 1989. text ed. 65.00 (0-521-35358-0) Cambridge U Pr.
Virgil's Elements: Physics & Poetry in the Georgics. David O. Ross. LC 86-22598. 268p. 1987. reprint ed. pap. 76.40 (0-7837-9435-5, 2060177) Bks Demand.
Virgil's Epic Technique. Richard Heinze. Tr. by Hazel Harvey et al. LC 93-5491. (GER.). 1993. 50.00 (0-520-06444-5) U CA Pr.
Virgil's Iliad: An Essay on Epic Narrative. K. W. Gransden. 232p. 1985. text ed. 59.95 (0-521-24504-4); pap. text ed. 22.95 (0-521-28756-1) Cambridge U Pr.
Virgil's Machines. Joel Sloman. (Orig.). 1966. pap. 1.95 (0-393-04267-7) Norton.
Virgil's Metre. G. Nussbaum. 104p. 1986. 11.95 (0-86292-173-2, Pub. by Brstl Class Pr UK) Focus Pub-R Pullins.
Virgil's Mind at Work: An Analysis of the Symbolism of the Aeneid. Robert W. Cruttwell. LC 78-114505. 182p. 1971. reprint ed. text ed. 35.00 (0-8371-4733-6, CRVM, Greenwood Pr) Greenwood.
***Virgin.** Lisa Jackson. 1998. mass mkt. 5.99 (0-451-40777-6, Onyx) NAL-Dutton.
Virgin. Mary E. Murphy. 352p. (Orig.). 1996. mass mkt. 6.50 (0-425-15124-7) Berkley Pub.
Virgin. Alison Tyler. (Orig.). 1996. mass mkt. 5.95 (1-56333-379-1, Rosebud) Masquerade.
***Virgin: A History of Virgin Records.** Terry Southern. pap. 24.95 (1-899116-00-1, Pub. by Virgin Pub UK) London Brdge.
***Virgin: A History of Virgin Records.** Terry Southern. 1995. pap. 25.00 (0-684-81383-1) S&S Trade.
Virgin - Mother - Crone: Myths & Mysteries of the Triple Goddess. Donna Wilshire. (Illus.). 256p. (Orig.). 1993. pap. 19.95 (0-89281-494-2) Inner Tradit.
Virgin Anchorages. rev. ed. Nancy Scott & Simon Scott. Ed. by Tom Henschel & Barbara Leibling. (Illus.). 88p. 1995. 24.95 (0-944428-29-0) Cruising Guide.
Virgin & Statue Worship: Quizzes to a Street Preacher. Charles M. Carty & Leslie Rumble. (Radio Replies Quizzes to a Street Preacher Ser.). 32p. 1991. reprint ed. pap. 1.00 (0-89555-107-1) TAN Bks Pubs.
***Virgin & the Boy.** Mary O'Donnell. Date not set. pap. 13.95 (1-85371-557-3, Pub. by Poolbeg Pr IE) Dufour.
Virgin & the Bride: Idealized Womanhood in Late Antiquity. Kate Cooper. LC 96-2256. 256p. 1996. 37.50 (0-674-93949-2) HUP.
Virgin & the Dinosaur. R. Garcia & R. Garcia Robertson. 288p. (Orig.). 1996. mass mkt. 5.99 (0-380-77978-1, AvoNova) Avon.
Virgin & the Gipsy. D. H. Lawrence. LC 84-50303. 128p. 1984. pap. 8.00 (0-394-72666-9, Vin) Random.
Virgin & the Gipsy. D. H. Lawrence. 192p. 1992. pap. 10.00 (0-679-74077-5, Vin) Random.
Virgin & the Mousetrap: Essays in Search of the Soul of Science. Chet Raymo. Date not set. pap. 6.95 (0-14-013324-0) Viking Penguin.
Virgin & the Nightingale. Fleur Adcock. 8300. 24.00 (0-906427-55-X, Pub. by Bloodaxe Bks UK); pap. 16.95 (0-906427-56-8, Pub. by Bloodaxe Bks UK) Dufour.
Virgin & the Unicorn. Kelly Street. (Temptation Ser.). 1993. mass mkt. 2.99 (0-373-25541-1, 1-25541-3) Harlequin Bks.
Virgin & the Unicorn. large type ed. Joan Smith. 226p. 1996. pap. 20.95 (0-7838-1637-5, GK Hall) Thorndike Pr.
Virgin & the Unicorn: Four Plays by Oscar Mandel. Oscar Mandel. LC 93-83430. (Orig.). 1993. pap. 15.95 (0-914502-10-7) Spectrum Prods.
Virgin Birth. Theo Todman. 36p. 1991. pap. 3.00 (1-880573-00-8) Grace WI.
Virgin Birth: A Proposal As to the Source of a Gospel Tradition. William H. Scheide. xvi, 159p. (C). 1995. 15.00 (0-9644891-1-2) Princeton Theol Sem.
Virgin Birth: The Famous Debate Between Herbert M. Shelton & George R. Clements. Herbert M. Shelton. 227p. 1994. reprint ed. spiral bd. 17.50 (0-7873-1173-1) Hlth Research.
Virgin Bride. Tamara Leigh. 336p. 1994. mass mkt. 5.50 (0-553-56536-2) Bantam.
Virgin Fire. Elizabeth Chadwick. 448p. (Orig.). 1991. mass mkt., pap. text ed. 4.50 (0-8439-3141-8) Dorchester Pub Co.
Virgin Fish of Babughat. Lokenath Bhattacharya. Tr. by Meenakshi Mukherjee from BEN. (Indian Novels Ser.). 160p. 1975. 5.95 (0-89253-016-2) Ind-US Inc.
Virgin Goddess: Studies in the Pagan & Christian Roots of Mariology. Stephen Benko. LC 92-44596. (Numen Bookseries (Studies in the History of Religions): No. 59). (Illus.). viii, 293p. 1993. 114.00 (90-04-09747-3) E J Brill.
Virgin Guide to Classical Music. Jeremy J. Beadle. 320p. 1995. pap. 12.95 (0-86369-658-9, Pub. by Virgin Pub UK) London Brdge.
Virgin Heat. Shames. 1997. 21.95 (0-7868-6203-3) Hyperion.
***Virgin Heat.** large type ed. Laurence Shames. LC 97-13839. 1997. write for info. (1-57490-084-6, Beeler LP Bks) T T Beeler.
Virgin Homeowner: The Essential Guide to Owning, Maintaining, & Surviving Your First Home. Janice Papolos. LC 96-31304. 288p. 1997. 25.00 (0-393-04035-6) Norton.
Virgin in Flames. Sax Rohmer. 1978. 8.50 (0-685-90567-5) Bookfinger.
Virgin in the Garden. A. S. Byatt. 1992. pap. 13.00 (0-679-73829-0, Vin) Random.
Virgin in the Ice. Ellis Peters. 208p. 1995. mass mkt. 5.99 (0-446-40428-4, Mysterious Paperbk) Warner Bks.
Virgin Island Reports: The Official Law Reports of the U. S. Virgin Islands, 1959-1994, 29 vols., Set. Ed. by Butterworth Staff. 420p. 1959. boxed 1,000.00 (0-88063-542-8) MICHIE.
Virgin Island Reports: The Official Law Reports of the U. S. Virgin Islands, 1959-1994, 27 vols., Vol. 25. 52.00 (0-88063-634-3) MICHIE.
Virgin Island Reports: The Official Law Reports of the U. S. Virgin Islands, 1959-1994, 27 vols., Vol. 26. 56.00 (1-56257-062-5) MICHIE.
Virgin Island Reports: The Official Law Reports of the U. S. Virgin Islands, 1959-1994, 27 vols., Vol. 27. 70.00 (1-56257-147-8) MICHIE.
Virgin Islands. Verna P. Moll. (World Bibliographical Ser.). 1992. lib. bdg. 78.00 (1-85109-165-3) ABC-CLIO.
Virgin Islands. Wilson Ltd. Staff & Imray L. Norie. (C). 1989. 53.00 (0-685-40405-6, Pub. by Imray Laurie Norie & Wilson UK) St Mut.
Virgin Islands. 4th ed. Harry S. Pariser. (Adventure Guides Ser.). 320p. (Orig.). 1996. pap. 16.95 (1-55650-746-1) Hunter NJ.
Virgin Islands Alive. 2nd ed. Harriet Greenberg. 1996. pap. 15.95 (1-55650-711-9) Hunter NJ.
Virgin Islands Alive. 3rd ed. Harriet Greenberg. (Alive Travel Ser.). (Illus.). 1990. pap. 10.95 (0-935572-18-X) Alive Pubns.
Virgin Islands Bays: Modeling of Water Quality & Pollution Susceptibility. Maynard Nichols. (Illus.). 92p. 1979. 12.50 (0-318-14619-3) Isl Resources.
Virgin Islands Code - Interim Annotation Service. 1,993th ed. Butterworths Staff. 60p. 1993. pap. 25.00 (1-56257-092-7) MICHIE.
Virgin Islands Code Annotated, 1964-1993. 1993. suppl. ed. 160.00 (1-56257-550-3) MICHIE.
Virgin Islands Code Annotated, 1964-1993, 14 vols. annot. ed. Ed. by Butterworth Staff. 1993. boxed 675.00 (0-88063-539-8) MICHIE.
Virgin Islands Cookbook. (Orig.). pap. text ed. write for info. (1-56944-011-5) Terrell Missouri.
Virgin Islands Cooking. Carol Bareuther. (Illus.). 184p. (Orig.). 1994. pap. text ed. 20.00 (0-9631060-6-6) Am Paradise.
Virgin Islands Corporation Laws. Ed. by Butterworth Staff. 200p. 1985. pap. 21.00 (0-88063-538-X) MICHIE.
Virgin Islands Court Rules Annotated, 1993. Ed. by Butterworth Staff. 600p. 1993. pap. 65.00 (1-56257-101-X) MICHIE.
Virgin Islands Digest, 6 vols., Set. Ed. by Butterworth Staff. 450p. 1992. boxed 300.00 (1-56257-104-4) MICHIE.
Virgin Islands Election Laws. Ed. by Butterworth Staff. 200p. 1988. pap. 21.00 (0-88063-554-1) MICHIE.
***Virgin Islands Handbook.** Karl Luntta. 1997. pap. text ed. 13.95 (1-56691-093-5) Moon Trvl Hdbks.
Virgin Islands National Park. (Illus.). 1995. 8.99 (1-56695-009-0) Trails Illustrated.
Virgin Islands National Park: The Story Behind the Scenery. Alan H. Robinson. LC 74-81560. (Illus.). 48p. 1974. pap. 7.95 (0-916122-14-X) KC Pubns.
Virgin Islands of the United States Major Political Documents, 1666-1991. Ed. by Paul M. Leary. 450p. (Orig.). (C). 1992. pap. text ed. 19.95 (0-9628909-2-8) U VI CES.
Virgin Islands, Our New Possessions & the British Islands. Theodoor N. De Booy. LC 72-109318. (Illus.). 292p. 1970. reprint ed. text ed. 35.00 (0-8371-3584-2, BVI&, Greenwood Pr) Greenwood.
***Virgin Islands Restaurant Guide & Recipe Book.** unabridged ed. Charles H. Eanes & Susan E. Eanes. (Illus.). 104p. (Orig.). 1994. pap. 14.95 (1-890494-01-1) Espichel Enterp.
Virgin Islands Session Laws, 28 vols., Set. Ed. by Butterworth Staff. 600p. 1958. Price per volume $40.00. boxed 772.00 (0-88063-543-6) MICHIE.
Virgin Islands Sojourn? S. B. Jones-Hendrickson. LC 90-81159. 64p. 1990. pap. 9.95 (0-932831-02-8) Eastern Caribbean Inst.
Virgin Islands-St. Thomas to Virgin Gorda. Wilson Ltd. Staff & Imray L. Norie. (C). 1984. 85.00 (0-685-40404-8, Pub. by Imray Laurie Norie & Wilson UK) St Mut.
Virgin Islands-Tortola to Anegada. Wilson Ltd. Staff & Imray L. Norie. (C). 1986. 53.00 (0-685-40403-X, Pub. by Imray Laurie Norie & Wilson UK) St Mut.
Virgin Kayenta Cultural Relationships. C. Melvin Aikens. (Glen Canyon Ser.: No. 29). reprint ed. 22.50 (0-404-60679-2) AMS Pr.
Virgin Knows. Christine P. Moore. 320p. 1995. 22.95 (0-312-13203-4) St Martin.
Virgin Land. Henry N. Smith. Date not set. pap. 15.00 (0-674-93952-2) HUP.
Virgin Land. Henry N. Smith. LC 50-6230. 305p. 1970. pap. 13.95 (0-674-93955-7) HUP.
Virgin Landscapes, Native Cultures: The Artist-Explorer in North America. William H. Sterling. (Illus.). 57p. (Orig.). (C). 1992. pap. 10.00 (0-942945-03-4) Sordoni Gal.
Virgin Lives & Holy Deaths: Two Exemplary Biographies for Anglo-Norman Women. Jocelyn Wogan-Browne. Ed. by G. Burgess & J. Wogan-Browne. (Everyman Paperback Classics Ser.). 256p. (Orig.). (C). 1996. pap. 6.50 (0-460-87580-9, Everyman's Classic Lib) C E Tuttle.
***Virgin Martyrs: Legends of Sainthood in Late Medieval England.** Karen A. Winstead. LC 97-9318. (Illus.). 216p. 1997. 35.00 (0-8014-3333-9) Cornell U Pr.
Virgin Mary. Dennis Michelis. LC 92-34728. (Illus.). 172p. (Orig.). (YA). (gr. 10 up). 1994. pap. 12.95 (0-917651-94-4) Holy Cross Orthodox.
Virgin Mary & the Priesthood. Pierre P. Philippe & Laurence J. Spiteri. LC 93-6682. 158p. (Orig.). (ENG.). 1993. pap. 9.95 (0-8189-0668-5) Alba.
***Virgin Mary Had a Baby Boy.** 1992. pap. 1.20 (0-8341-9136-9) Lillenas.
Virgin Mary in Art, Renaissance to Reformation: The Development of Christian Symbolism, 4 vols. Lois S. Jones. Ed. by Presto Jones. (Development of Christian Symbolism Ser.: Vol. IV). (Illus.). 52p. 1996. pap. 5.00 (1-882238-08-7) Swan-Jones Prod.
Virgin Mary, Queen of Poland: Historical Essay. Helm M. Pirgo. 33p. 1966. pap. 2.50 (0-940962-44-6) Polish Inst Art & Sci.
Virgin Mother: The Great Sign. Peter Fehlner. 1993. 1.00 (1-56036-075-5, 98790) AMI Pr.
Virgin Mother, Maiden Queen: Elizabeth I & the Cult of the Virgin Mary. Helen Hackett. LC 94-34701. 303p. 1995. text ed. 45.00 (0-312-12481-3) St Martin.
Virgin of Bosnia. Michael B. Trigleth. (Illus.). 65p. (Orig.). 1994. pap. text ed. 7.95 (1-885826-02-8) Mineral King.
Virgin of Chartres: An Intellectual & Psychological History of the Work of Henry Adams. Joseph F. Byrnes. LC 78-75174. 128p. 1970. 28.50 (0-8386-2369-7) Fairleigh Dickinson.
Virgin of the Andes: Art & Ritual in Colonial Cuzco. Carol Damian. LC 94-73217. (Illus.). 112p. 1995. 48.00 (0-9628514-8-5) Grassfield Pr.
Virgin of the Discos: A Book of Tales. Mike Harding. 208p. 1995. 19.95 (0-86051-895-7, Robson-Parkwest) Parkwest Pubns.
Virgin of the Railway & Other Stories. Pere Calders. Ed. by Amanda Bath. 220p. (C). 1991. 49.95 (0-85668-546-1, Pub. by Aris & Phillips UK); pap. 22.00 (0-85668-547-X, Pub. by Aris & Phillips UK) David Brown.
Virgin of the Sun. Ruby D. Mitchell. LC 84-52477. 1986. 13.95 (0-87212-189-5) Libra.
Virgin of the World, Hermes. 2nd ed. Tr. by Anna B. Kingsford & Edward Maitland from GRE. LC 77-73713. (Secret Doctrine Reference Ser.). (Illus.). 272p. 1977. reprint ed. 16.00 (0-913510-23-8) Wizards.
Virgin of the World of Hermes Mercurius Trismegistus. Hermes M. Trismegistus. Tr. by Anna B. Kingsford & Edward Maitland. 154p. 1968. reprint ed. spiral bd. 10.50 (0-7873-0495-6) Hlth Research.
Virgin of the World of Hermes Mercurius Trismegistus (1885) Anna B. Kingsford & Edward Maitland. 190p. 1996. pap. 19.95 (1-56459-672-9) Kessinger Pub.
Virgin of the World, or Apple of the Eye of the World. G. R. Mead. 1990. reprint ed. pap. text ed. 7.95 (1-55818-129-6) Holmes Pub.
Virgin or Vamp: How the Press Covers Sex Crimes. Helen Benedict. 340p. (C). 1993. reprint ed. pap. 11.95 (0-19-508665-1, 7113) OUP.
Virgin or Vamp: Sex Crimes & the Press. Helen Benedict. 256p. 1992. 30.00 (0-19-506680-4) OUP.
Virgin Princess: An Historic Novel of Mewar (Udaipur, India) - The World's Oldest Dynasty. Jane Richardson. LC 90-90395. 434p. (Orig.). 1991. pap. 15.95 (1-879403-09-9) Thistle Pub.
Virgin Rock Yearbook 94-95. Ed. by Tony Horkins. (Illus.). (Orig.). 1995. pap. 14.95 (0-86369-823-9, Pub. by Virgin Pub UK) London Brdge.
Virgin Song. Frances De Talavera Berger. (Critic's Choice Paperbacks Ser.). 1988. pap. 4.50 (1-55547-281-8, Univ Books) Carol Pub Group.
Virgin Star. Jennifer Horsman. 416p. (Orig.). 1993. mass mkt. 4.50 (0-380-76702-3) Avon.
Virgin Suicides. Jeffrey Eugenides. LC 92-33466. 1993. 18.00 (0-374-28438-5) FS&G.
Virgin Suicides. Jeffrey Eugenides. 256p. 1994. pap. 11.99 (0-446-67025-1) Warner Bks.

Virgin Territory. Sara Maitland. LC 85-26737. 224p. 1986. 14.95 (*0-8253-0350-8*) Beaufort Bks NY.

Virgin Territory. Ed. by Shar Rednaur. (Orig.). 1996. pap. 12.95 (*1-56333-457-7*, R Kasak Bks) Masquerade.

***Virgin Territory 2.** Ed. by Shar Rednour. (Orig.). 1997. pap. 12.95 (*1-56333-506-9*, R Kasak Bks) Masquerade.

Virgin Text: Fiction, Sexuality, & Ideology. Jon Stratton. LC 86-40530. (Project for Discourse & Theory Ser.: Vol. 1). 256p. 1987. 32.95 (*0-8061-2054-1*) U of Okla Pr.

Virgin Time. Patricia Hampl. 326p. 1992. 22.00 (*0-374-28440-7*) FS&G.

Virgin Time: In Search of the Contemplative Life. Patricia Hampl. 256p. 1993. pap. 11.00 (*0-345-38424-5*, Ballantine Trade) Ballantine.

Virgin Unmask'd. Bernard Mandeville. LC 75-14288. 256p. 1975. reprint ed. lib. bdg. 50.00 (*0-8201-1155-4*) Schol Facsimiles.

Virgin Whiteness: The Poetry of Kamala Das. Devindra Kohli. (Greybird Ser.). 1975. 8.00 (*0-88253-668-0*) Ind-US Inc.

Virgin Wholly Marvelous. Ed. by David Supple. LC 81-13928. (Illus.). 204p. 1991. reprint ed. 13.95 (*0-911218-18-1*); reprint ed. pap. 7.95 (*0-911218-17-3*) Ravengate Pr.

Virgin Widows. Gu Hua. Tr. by Howard Goldblatt from CHI. LC 95-46066. (Fiction From Modern China Ser.). 178p. 1996. pap. 12.95 (*0-8248-1802-4*); text ed. 24.00 (*0-8248-1770-2*) UH Pr.

Virgin Wife. Elizabeth August. (Romance Ser.). 1993. pap. 2.69 (*0-373-08921-X*, 5-08921-4) Silhouette.

Virgin Wife. Evelyn K. Deel. LC 83-258166. 1987. 13.95 (*0-87949-246-5*) Ashley Bks.

Virgina. Ellen Glasgow. 432p. 1989. pap. 12.95 (*0-14-039072-3*, Penguin Classics) Viking Penguin.

Virginal Conception & Bodily Resurrection of Jesus. Raymond E. Brown. LC 72-97399. 1973. pap. 7.95 (*0-8091-1768-1*) Paulist Pr.

Virginal Sexuality & Textuality in Victorian Literature. Ed. by Lloyd Davis. LC 91-45286. (SUNY Series, The Body in Culture, History, & Religion). (Illus.). 257p. (C). 1992. pap. text ed. 24.95 (*0-7914-1284-9*) State U NY Pr.

Virginal Sexuality & Textuality in Victorian Literature. Ed. by Lloyd Davis. LC 91-45286. (SUNY Series, The Body in Culture, History, & Religion). (Illus.). 257p. (C). 1993. text ed. 74.50 (*0-7914-1283-0*) State U NY Pr.

Virginalia: Or Songs of My Summer Nights. Thomas H. Chivers. (Works of Thomas Holley Chivers Ser.). 1990. reprint ed. lib. bdg. 79.00 (*0-7812-2288-5*) Rprt Serv.

Virginalia: or Songs of My Summer Nights: A Gift of Love for the Beautiful. Thomas H. Chivers. LC 72-4958. (Romantic Tradition in American Literature Ser.). 136p. 1972. reprint ed. 18.95 (*0-405-04630-8*) Ayer.

Virginia. (Picture Memory Ser.). 1993. 8.99 (*0-517-07264-5*) Random Hse Value.

***Virginia.** Capstone Press Staff. LC 96-35113. (One Nation Ser.). (J). 1997. write for info. (*1-56065-503-8*) Capstone Pr.

Virginia. Mark Dunster. (James Ser.: Pt. 4). 79p. (Orig.). 1975. pap. 4.00 (*0-89642-037-X*) Linden Pubs.

Virginia, 7 vols. Arlene H. Eakle. 1989. pap. write for info. (*0-940764-35-0*) Genealog Inst.

Virginia. Robert Fleming. (Road Atlas Ser.). (Illus.). 64p. 1992. pap. 5.95 (*0-13-928268-8*, H M Gousha) P-H Gen Ref & Trav.

Virginia. Dennis B. Fradin. LC 92-6386. (From Sea to Shining Sea Ser.). (Illus.). 64p. (J). (gr. 3-5). 1992. lib. bdg. 24.00 (*0-516-03846-X*) Childrens.

Virginia. Dennis B. Fradin. LC 92-6386. (From Sea to Shining Sea Ser.). (Illus.). 64p. (J). (gr. 3-5). 1992. pap. 5.95 (*0-516-43846-8*) Childrens.

Virginia. Sylvia McNair. LC 88-38203. (America the Beautiful Ser.). (Illus.). 144p. (J). (gr. 5-8). 1989. lib. bdg. 28.30 (*0-516-00492-1*) Childrens.

Virginia. Tim Mulligan. 1986. pap. 12.95 (*0-394-74648-1*) Random.

***Virginia.** Randy Porter. (Mountain Bike! Ser.). 1997. pap. 14.95 (*0-89732-248-7*) Menasha Ridge.

Virginia. Karen Sirvaitis. (Hello U. S. A. Ser.). (Illus.). 72p. (J). (gr. 3-6). 1991. lib. bdg. 18.95 (*0-8225-2702-2*, Lerner Publctns) Lerner Group.

Virginia. Kathleen Thompson. (Portrait of America Library). 48p. (J). (gr. 3 up). 1996. pap. 5.95 (*0-614-10853-5*) Raintree Steck-V.

Virginia. Contrib. by Kathleen Thompson. (Portrait of America Library). 48p. (J). (gr. 3 up). 1996. lib. bdg. 22.83 (*0-8114-7392-9*) Raintree Steck-V.

***Virginia.** Charlotte Wilcox. (One Nation Ser.). (Illus.). (J). 1997. 18.40 (*0-516-20533-1*) Childrens.

***Virginia.** 2nd ed. Compass American Staff. 1996. pap. 18.95 (*1-878867-95-4*, Compass Amrcn) Fodors Travel.

Virginia. 2nd ed. H. M. Gousha Staff. 1991. pap. 2.50 (*0-671-87985-5*, H M Gousha) P-H Gen Ref & Trav.

Virginia. Mark Dunster. (John Brown Ser.: Pt. 3). 34p. (Orig.). 1983. reprint ed. pap. 4.00 (*0-89642-104-X*) Linden Pubs.

Virginia. Jed Hotchkiss. Ed. by Clement A. Evans. (Confederate Military History Extended Edition Ser.: Vol. IV). (Illus.). 1295p. 1987. reprint ed. 50.00 (*1-56837-023-7*) Broadfoot.

Virginia: A Guide to Backcountry Travel & Adventure. James Bannon. LC 96-70792. (Illus.). 372p. (Orig.). 1996. pap. 16.00 (*0-9648584-1-X*) Out There Pr.

Virginia: A Guide to the Old Dominion. Compiled by Workers of the Writers' Program of the Work Projects Administration in the State of Virginia. LC 92-28334. 1992. 35.00 (*0-88490-173-4*) Library of VA.

Virginia: A Guide to the Old Dominion. Federal Writer's Project. LC 72-84513. (American Guidebook Ser.). 1980. reprint ed. lib. bdg. 89.00 (*0-403-02195-2*) Somerset Pub.

Virginia: A Guide to the Old Dominion. Federal Writers' Project Staff & Writers Program-WPA Staff. (American Guide Ser.). 1989. reprint ed. lib. bdg. 89.00 (*0-7812-1045-3*, 1045) Rprt Serv.

Virginia: A History. Louis D. Rubin, Jr. (States & the Nation Ser.). (Illus.). 1984. pap. 7.95 (*0-393-30137-0*) Norton.

Virginia: A History & Guide. Tim Mulligan. 1986. pap. write for info. (*0-394-73321-5*) Random.

Virginia: A History of the People. John E. Cooke. LC 72-3765. (American Commonwealths Ser.: No. 1). reprint ed. 49.50 (*0-404-57201-4*) AMS Pr.

Virginia: A Photographic Journey. Bill Harris. 1990. 15.99 (*0-517-01497-1*) Random Hse Value.

Virginia: A Pictorial Guide to the Old Dominion. Ron Card & Linda Card. 52p. 1992. pap. write for info. (*0-9620127-0-X*) Cards Unltd.

Virginia: A Play. Edna O'Brien. LC 81-7763. 80p. 1985. pap. 4.95 (*0-15-693560-0*, Harvest Bks) HarBrace.

Virginia: An Aerial Portrait. Robert Llewellyn. LC 84-52617. (Illus.). 120p. 1985. 32.00 (*0-934738-12-2*) Lickle Pubng.

Virginia: Bourbonism to Byrd, 1870-1925. Allen W. Moger. LC 68-8538. (Illus.). 414p. reprint ed. pap. 118.00 (*0-7837-4349-1*, 2044059) Bks Demand.

Virginia: Four Personal Narratives. LC 70-141100. (Research Library of Colonial Americana). 148p. 1972. reprint ed. 25.95 (*0-405-03310-9*) Ayer.

Virginia: Hello U. S. A. Karen Sirvaitis. (J). 1996. pap. text ed. 5.95 (*0-8225-9737-3*) Lerner Group.

Virginia: Off the Beaten Path: A Guide to Unique Places. 4th ed. Judy Colbert. LC 95-8851. (Off the Beaten Path Ser.). (Illus.). 176p. 1995. pap. 10.95 (*1-56440-729-2*) Globe Pequot.

Virginia: The New Dominion, a History from 1607 to the Present. Virginius Dabney. LC 78-157580. (Illus.). 629p. 1983. pap. text ed. 22.50 (*0-8139-1015-3*) U Pr of Va.

Virginia: The State & It's Educational System. Harold L. Hodgkinson. 10p. 1990. 7.00 (*0-937846-63-5*) Inst Educ Lead.

Virginia: 1790 Census. 190p. (C). 1990. reprint ed. pap. 22.00 (*0-614-07623-4*); reprint ed. lib. bdg. 52.00 (*0-8095-8163-9*) Borgo Pr.

Virginia: 1870 Census Index, 4 vols. Ed. by Bradley W. Steuart. 3816p. 1989. Set. lib. bdg. 395.00 (*1-877677-02-7*) Precision Indexing.

Virginia see Celebrate the States - Group 1

Virginia - Collected Works of Federal Writers Project, 3 vols. Federal Writers' Project Staff. 1991. reprint ed. Set. lib. bdg. 228.00 (*0-7812-5797-2*) Rprt Serv.

***Virginia - West Virginia Genealogical Data from Revolutionary War Pension & Bounty Land Warrant Records, Vol. 5.** Patrick G. Wardell. vi, 364p. (Orig.). 1996. pap. 29.50 (*0-7884-0551-9*, W071) Heritage Bk.

Virginia - West Virginia Genealogical Data from Revolutionary War Pension & County Land Warrant Records, Vol. 3: Iams Through Myres. Patrick G. Wardell. 390p. (Orig.). 1992. pap. 29.00 (*1-55613-657-9*) Heritage Bk.

Virginia - West Virginia Husbands & Wives, Vol. 1. Patrick G. Wardell. 496p. (Orig.). 1995. text ed. 41.00 (*0-7884-0084-3*) Heritage Bk.

Virginia. A Sermon Preached at Whitechapel in the Presence of the Adventurers & Planters for Virginia, 25 April 1609. William Symonds. LC 68-54666. (English Experience Ser.: No. 52). 54p. 1968. reprint ed. 45.00 (*90-221-0052-9*) Walter J Johnson.

Virginia Accomac County Census Index 1800. Ronald V. Jackson & Gary R. Teeples. LC 77-86061. (Illus.). lib. bdg. 35.00 (*0-89593-146-X*) Accelerated Index.

Virginia Adventure: Roanoke to James Towne: An Archaeological & Historical Odyssey. Ivor N. Hume. LC 93-33213. 1994. 40.00 (*0-394-56446-4*) Knopf.

***Virginia Adventure: Roanoke to James Towne: An Archaeological & Historical Odyssey.** Ivor Noel-Hume. LC 97-16651. (Virginia Bookshelf Ser.). (Illus.). 519p. 1997. pap. 19.95 (*0-8139-1758-1*) U Pr of Va.

Virginia Alternatives for the 1990s: Selected Issues in Public Policy. Ed. by Joseph L. Fisher & Richard T. Mayer. 188p. (Orig.). (C). 1987. text ed. 47.50 (*0-8026-0016-6*, G Mason Univ Pr); pap. text ed. 22.50 (*0-8026-0017-4*, G Mason Univ Pr) Univ Pub Assocs.

Virginia Ancestors & Adventurers, 3 vols. in 1. Charles H. Hamlin. 412p. 1993. reprint ed. pap. 32.50 (*0-685-65696-9*, 2505) Clearfield Co.

Virginia & Maryland: The Complete Guide with Baltimore, Williamsburg & the Chesapeake. 4th ed. Fodor's Travel Staff. 1997. pap. 13.50 (*0-679-03297-5*) Fodors Travel.

Virginia & Other State Greats (Biographies) Carole Marsh. (Carole Marsh Virginia Bks.). (Illus.). (J). 1994. pap. 19.95 (*0-7933-2191-3*); lib. bdg. 29.95 (*0-7933-2190-5*); disk 29.95 (*0-7933-2192-1*) Gallopade Pub Group.

***Virginia & the Capital Region.** Henry Wiencek & Donald Young. (Smithsonian Guide to Historic America Ser.). 1998. write for info. (*1-55670-632-4*) Stewart Tabori & Chang.

Virginia & the Capital Region: Washington, D. C., Virginia, Maryland, Delaware. Henry Wiencek. Ed. by Roger G. Kennedy. LC 88-16152. (Smithsonian Guide to Historic America Ser.). (Illus.). 400p. (Orig.). 1989. 24.95 (*1-55670-058-X*); pap. 18.95 (*1-55670-048-2*) Stewart Tabori & Chang.

Virginia & Truckee: A Story of Virginia City & Comstock Times. 7th ed. Lucius Beebe & Charles Clegg. (Illus.). 72p. 1991. reprint ed. pap. 5.95 (*1-879897-00-8*) NV St Rail Mus.

***Virginia & Virginians, 2 vols.** Virginia A. Lewis & Robert A. Brock. (Illus.). 813p. 1996. reprint ed. pap. 65.00 (*0-614-23491-3*, 9211) Clearfield Co.

Virginia & West Virginia see Atlas of Historical County Boundaries

***Virginia Antiquary Vol. 1: Princess Anne County Loose Papers, 1700-1789.** John H. Creecy. xvi, 221p. 1997. reprint ed. pap. 20.00 (*0-7884-0614-0*, C611) Heritage Bk.

***Virginia Architects, 1835-1955: A Biographical Dictionary.** John E. Wells & Robert E. Dalton. iii, 571p. (C). 1997. 95.00 (*1-882595-02-5*) New So Archit.

Virginia Assembly on Public Policy: Final Report, 1988: The Quest for Community in a National Republic. 1988. (*0-318-69554-5*) U VA Ctr Pub Serv.

Virginia Assembly on Public Policy: Final Report, 1989: The Future of Virginia's Courts. 1989. (*0-318-69553-7*) U VA Ctr Pub Serv.

Virginia Assembly on Public Policy: Final Report, 1990: The Future of Local Government in Virginia. 1990. (*0-318-69552-9*) U VA Ctr Pub Serv.

Virginia Assembly on the Future of the Virginia Environment. Ed. by J. Paxton Marshall & Robert M. De Voursney. 70p. 1986. pap. 8.50 (*0-318-20553-X*) U VA Ctr Pub Serv.

Virginia Atlas & Gazetteer. 2nd ed. DeLorme Staff. (Illus.). 80p. (Orig.). 1995. pap. 16.95 (*0-89933-244-7*, 5303) DeLorme Map.

Virginia, Augusta County: Rev. John Craig, D.D., Baptistmal Records 1740-1749 Scotch-Irish Father-Child Name Lists, Incomplete, Many Came to Ohio. Fay Maxwell. 21p. 1975. 5.00 (*1-885463-28-6*) Ohio Genealogy.

Virginia Bandits, Bushwackers, Outlaws, Crooks, Devils, Ghosts, Desperadoes & Other Assorted & Sundry Characters! Carole Marsh. (Carole Marsh Virginia Bks.). (Illus.). (J). 1994. pap. 19.95 (*0-7933-1153-5*); lib. bdg. 29.95 (*0-7933-1154-3*); disk 29.95 (*0-7933-1155-1*) Gallopade Pub Group.

Virginia Baron: The Story of Thomas, Sixth Lord of Fairfax. Stuart E. Brown, Jr. LC 65-19262. (Illus.). 245p. 1965. 15.00 (*0-685-65062-6*) VA Bk.

Virginia Beach Vibes: More People & Hogs. Ed. by Calvert W. Tazewell. LC 91-70641. 176p. (Orig.). 1991. pap. 19.00 (*1-878515-61-6*) W S Dawson.

Virginia Bill & Nellie. Rea W. Yarnall. Ed. by Gary Yarnall. (Illus.). 172p. 1992. 14.95 (*0-9621821-4-1*) Lil Jewel Enterp.

Virginia Biographical Dictionary. LC 93-38759. 1993. 79.00 (*0-403-09939-0*) Somerset Pub.

Virginia Book. Tulloch. 1993. 12.95 (*0-316-08000-4*) Little.

Virginia Bookstore Book: A Surprising Guide to Our State's Bookstores & Their Specialties for Students, Teachers, Writers & Publishers. Carole Marsh. (Virginia Bks.). (Illus.). 1994. pap. 19.95 (*0-7933-2994-9*); lib. bdg. 29.95 (*0-7933-2993-0*); disk 29.95 (*0-7933-2995-7*) Gallopade Pub Group.

Virginia Born Presidents. LC 79-156728. (Essay Index Reprint Ser.). 1977. reprint ed. 23.95 (*0-8369-2300-6*) Ayer.

Virginia Broderick: Artist Extraordinary. Jack Mahoney. 1983. pap. 1.00 (*0-915866-13-7*) Am Cath Pr.

***Virginia Business Directory 1996-1997.** rev. ed. American Business Directories Staff. 2208p. 1996. boxed 445.00 (*1-56105-866-1*) Am Busn Direct.

Virginia Business Directory 1996-97. rev. ed. American Business Directories Staff. 2016p. 1996. boxed 445.00 (*1-56105-784-3*) Am Busn Direct.

***Virginia Business Directory 1997-1998.** rev. ed. American Business Directories Staff. 2208p. 1997. boxed 445.00 (*1-56105-954-4*) Am Busn Direct.

Virginia Campaign of Eighteen Sixty-Two under Pope. Ed. by T. F. Wright. (Papers of the Military Historical Society of Massachusetts: Vol. 2). (Illus.). 541p. 1989. reprint ed. 40.00 (*1-56837-006-7*) Broadfoot.

Virginia Campaign, 1864-1865. Andrew A. Humphreys. (Campaigns of the Civil War Ser.). (Illus.). 510p. 1995. reprint ed. pap. 15.95 (*0-306-80625-8*) Da Capo.

***Virginia Carolorum: The Colony under the Rule of Charles the First & Second, 1625-1865.** Edward D. Neill. 417p. 1996. pap. 31.00 (*0-7884-0478-4*, N134) Heritage Bk.

Virginia Carroll Crawford Collection: American Decorative Arts, 1825-1917. Donald C. Peirce & David A. Hanks. LC 83-81102. (Illus.). 96p. (Orig.). 1983. pap. 9.95 (*0-939802-16-3*) High Mus Art.

Virginia Celebrates: Recipes & Ideas for Entertaining. Virginia Museum of Fine Arts Council. LC 92-13533. 176p. 29.95 (*1-56566-015-3*) Lickle Pubng.

Virginia Cemeteries: A Guide to Resources. Ed. by Anne M. Hogg. LC 85-22449. 320p. (Orig.). 1986. pap. text ed. 16.50 (*0-8139-1091-9*) U Pr of Va.

Virginia Census Index 1790 Tax List Substitute. Ronald V. Jackson. (Illus.). 1978. lib. bdg. 55.00 (*0-89593-792-1*) Accelerated Index.

Virginia Census Index 1850 Mortality Schedule. (Illus.). lib. bdg. 95.00 (*0-89593-520-1*) Accelerated Index.

Virginia Census Index 1850 Slave Schedule. (Illus.). 1988. lib. bdg. 33.00 (*0-89593-521-X*) Accelerated Index.

Virginia Census Index 1860 Mortality Schedule. (Illus.). lib. bdg. 85.00 (*0-89593-522-8*) Accelerated Index.

Virginia Census Index 1860 Slave Schedule. (Illus.). 1990. lib. bdg. 199.00 (*0-89593-523-6*) Accelerated Index.

Virginia Census Index 1890 Union Vets. (Illus.). lib. bdg. 60.00 (*0-89593-524-4*) Accelerated Index.

Virginia Chronology 1585-1783: "To Pass Away the Time" William W. Abbot. (Illus.). 78p. 1994. pap. 10.00 (*0-614-00899-9*, 9015) Clearfield Co.

Virginia Circuit Court Judges Benchbook - Civil. Supreme Court Of Virginia, Circuit Court Staff. 1991. spiral bd. 105.00 (*0-87473-744-3*) MICHIE.

Virginia Circuit Court Judges Benchbook - Criminal. Supreme Court Of Virginia, Circuit Court Staff. 1991. spiral bd. 105.00 (*0-87473-745-1*) MICHIE.

Virginia Circuit Court Opinions, 30 vols., Set. W. Hamilton Bryson. 1993. 1,150.00 (*1-56257-338-1*) MICHIE.

Virginia City - Its History & Its Ghosts. Phyllis Zauner. (Western Mini-Histories Ser.). (Illus.). 64p. (Orig.). 1989. pap. 7.95 (*0-936914-22-X*) Zanel Pubns.

Virginia City & Alder Gulch. Ken Sievert & Ellen Sievert. LC 93-19257. (Orig.). 1993. pap. 9.95 (*1-56037-041-6*) Am Wrld Geog.

Virginia City & the Silver Region of the Comstock Lode. Douglas McDonald. (Illus.). 128p. 1982. 24.95 (*0-913814-50-4*); pap. 14.95 (*0-913814-47-4*) Nevada Pubns.

Virginia City Mystery. Mary J. Kelso. (Lynne Garrett Adventure Ser.: No. 1). (Illus.). 120p. (Orig.). (YA). (gr. 6 up). 1992. pap. 6.95 (*0-9621406-2-7*) MarKel Pr.

Virginia City Trail Vol. 1. Ralph Compton. 1994. mass mkt. 5.50 (*0-312-95306-2*) St Martin.

Virginia Civil Procedure. T. Munford Boyd et al. 738p. 1982. 80.00 (*0-87215-424-6*) MICHIE.

Virginia Civil Procedure. T. Munford Boyd et al. 738p. 1991. suppl. ed. 30.00 (*0-87215-964-7*) MICHIE.

Virginia Civil Procedure. 2nd ed. Leigh B. Middleditch, Jr. & Kent Sinclair. 1024p. 1992. 90.00 (*1-55834-003-3*) MICHIE.

Virginia Classic Christmas Trivia: Stories, Recipes, Activities, Legends, Lore & More. Carole Marsh. (Carole Marsh Virginia Bks.). (Illus.). (J). 1994. pap. 19.95 (*0-7933-1156-X*); lib. bdg. 29.95 (*0-7933-1157-8*); disk 29.95 (*0-7933-1158-6*) Gallopade Pub Group.

***Virginia Climber's Guide.** Jeff Watson. LC 97-23337. 1998. write for info. (*0-8117-2981-8*) Stackpole.

Virginia Coastales. Carole Marsh. (Carole Marsh Virginia Bks.). (Illus.). (J). 1994. pap. 19.95 (*1-55609-116-8*); disk 29.95 (*0-7933-2186-7*) Gallopade Pub Group.

Virginia Coastales! Carole Marsh. (Virginia Bks.). (J). 1994. lib. bdg. 29.95 (*0-7933-7311-5*) Gallopade Pub Group.

Virginia Code Research Guide. LC 89-84023. 1993. Suppl. 1993. suppl. ed. 110.00 (*0-318-67058-5*) Lawyers Cooperative.

Virginia Colonial Militia, 1651-1776. William A. Crozier. (Virginia County Records Ser.: Vol. II). 144p. 1986. reprint ed. 15.00 (*0-614-10540-4*, 1242) Genealog Pub.

Virginia Colony. Dennis B. Fradin. LC 86-13639. (Thirteen Colonies Ser.). (Illus.). 160p. (J). (gr. 4 up). 1986. lib. bdg. 28.00 (*0-516-00387-9*) Childrens.

Virginia Comedians: Or, Old Days in the Old Dominion, 2 vols. in 1. John E. Cooke. LC 68-23717. (Americans in Fiction Ser.). 625p. reprint ed. lib. bdg. 47.00 (*0-8398-0274-9*) Irvington.

Virginia Comedians: Or, Old Days in the Old Dominion, 2 vol. in 1. John E. Cooke. 625p. (C). 1986. reprint ed. pap. text ed. 9.95 (*0-8290-2048-9*) Irvington.

Virginia Comedians: or Old Days in the Old Dominion, 2 vols. in 1. John E. Cooke. (BCL1-PS American Literature Ser.). 1992. reprint ed. Set. lib. bdg. 99.00 (*0-7812-6691-2*) Rprt Serv.

Virginia Commonwealth University: A Sesquicentennial History. fac. ed. Virginius Dabney. LC 87-1982. (Illus.). 451p. 1987. reprint ed. pap. 128.60 (*0-7837-8113-X*, 2047920) Bks Demand.

Virginia Company of London, 1606-1624. Wesley F. Craven. (Illus.). 70p. 1993. reprint ed. pap. 10.00 (*0-685-69945-5*, 9069) Clearfield Co.

Virginia Company of London 1607-1624, Vol. 3. Lindsay Duvall. (Virginia Company of London 1607-1624, Series 2). 1978. reprint ed. 17.50 (*0-89308-064-0*) Southern Hist Pr.

Virginia Condominium Law, 1990-1991. Douglas S. MacGregor. 250p. 1991. ring bd. 50.00 (*0-409-26579-9*) MICHIE.

Virginia Convention of 1829-1830. Hugh B. Grigsby. LC 79-75321. (American History, Politics & Law Ser.). 1969. reprint ed. lib. bdg. 25.00 (*0-306-71282-2*) Da Capo.

Virginia Corporations. LC 81-85751. (Practice Systems Library Manual). 125.00 (*0-318-11964-1*) Lawyers Cooperative.

Virginia Corporations. (Practice Systems Library Manual). 1993. Suppl. 1993. suppl. ed., ring bd. 65.00 (*0-317-03271-2*) Lawyers Cooperative.

Virginia Counties: Those Resulting from Virginia Legislation. Morgan P. Robinson. (Illus.). 283p. 1992. 25.00 (*0-8063-1335-8*, 4985) Genealog Pub.

Virginia County Records, 11 Vols., Set. Virginia County Records Staff. Ed. by William A. Crozier. LC 79-177870. reprint ed. lib. bdg. 165.00 (*0-404-07610-6*) AMS Pr.

Virginia County Records, Vol. 3. Ed. by William A. Crozier. 77p. 1994. reprint ed. pap. 10.00 (*0-8328-4017-3*) Higginson Bk Co.

Virginia County Records, Vol. VI: Miscellaneous County Records. William A. Crozier. 326p. 1993. reprint ed. pap. 27.50 (*0-685-69942-0*, 1246) Clearfield Co.

Virginia County Records, Vol. VII: Miscellaneous County Records. William A. Crozier. 218p. 1993. reprint ed. pap. 21.00 (*0-685-69963-3*, 1247) Clearfield Co.

Virginia County Supervisors' Manual. 5th rev. ed. Marica S. Mead. 360p. 1988. 25.00 (*0-318-04157-X*) U VA Ctr Pub Serv.

Virginia Cousin & Bar Harbor Tales. Constance C. Harrison. LC 74-96036. (Short Story Index Reprint Ser.). 1977. 18.95 (*0-8369-3110-6*) Ayer.

Virginia Cousins: Selected Goodes. abr. ed. George B. Goode. Ed. by Calvert W. Tazewell. LC 92-71983. (Illus.). 102p. 1993. pap. 13.00 (*1-878515-27-6*) W S Dawson.

Virginia Crime Perspective 1996. Ed. by Kathleen O. Morgan et al. 24p. 1996. pap. 19.00 (*1-56692-545-2*) Morgan Quitno Corp.

UV

***Virginia Crime Perspective 1997.** Ed. by Kathleen O. Morgan & Scott E. Morgan. 24p. 1997. pap. 19.00 (*1-56692-795-1*) Morgan Quitno Corp.

Virginia Criminal & Traffic Law Manual, 1994 Edition. write for info. (*0-614-05992-5*) MICHIE.

Virginia Criminal Law & Motor Vehicle Handbook. annuals Ed. by Gould Staff. 875p. (C). 1996. pap. 21.95 (*1-882476-01-8*) G Pubns FL.

Virginia Criminal Law & Motor Vehicle Handbook: Annual Edition. 875p. Date not set. pap. 21.95 (*0-87526-452-2*) Gould.

Virginia Criminal Law & Procedure. John L. Costello. 866p. 1990. 90.00 (*0-87473-671-4*) MICHIE.

***Virginia Criminal Law & Procedure.** 2nd ed. John L. Costello. 1281p. 1995. 110.00 (*1-55834-308-3*, 61000-11) MICHIE.

Virginia Criminal Law Case Finder. 2nd ed. Joseph M. Clarke, II. 1265p. 1991. 95.00 (*0-87473-763-X*) MICHIE.

***Virginia Criminal Law Case Finder, 2 vols.** 3rd ed. Joseph M. Clarke, II. 1995. 125.00 (*1-55834-233-8*, 60904-11) MICHIE.

***Virginia Criminal Law Case Finder.** 3rd ed. Joseph M. Clarke, II. 1996. suppl. ed. 42.00 (*0-614-25258-X*, 60905-11) MICHIE.

Virginia "Crinkum-Crankum" A Funny Word Book about Our State. Carole Marsh. (Virginia Bks.). (Illus.). (J). (gr. 3-12). 1994. 29.95 (*0-7933-4946-X*); pap. 19.95 (*0-7933-4947-8*); disk 29.95 (*0-7933-4948-6*) Gallopade Pub Group.

Virginia Dare, Stories 1976-1981. Fielding Dawson. LC 84-18573. (Illus.). 178p. (Orig.). 1985. 14.00 (*0-87685-618-0*); pap. 10.00 (*0-87685-617-2*) Black Sparrow.

Virginia Dare, Stories 1976-1981, signed ed. deluxe ed. Fielding Dawson. LC 84-18573. (Illus.). 178p. (Orig.). 1985. 25.00 (*0-87685-619-9*) Black Sparrow.

Virginia Democrats: A Photographic Portrait. Don Patterson. LC 91-61019. (Illus.). 144p. 1991. 34.95 (*0-9629093-0-0*); pap. 24.95 (*0-9629093-1-9*) MyndSeye.

Virginia Dingbats! Bk. 1: A Fun Book of Games, Stories, Activities & More about Our State That's All in Code! for You to Decipher. Carole Marsh. (Virginia Bks.). (Illus.). (J). (gr. 3-12). 1994. pap. 19.95 (*0-7933-3912-X*); lib. bdg. 29.95 (*0-7933-3911-1*); disk 29.95 (*0-7933-3913-8*) Gallopade Pub Group.

Virginia Domestic Relations Case Finder. 2nd ed. Brien A. Roche. 273p. 1991. 75.00 (*0-87473-765-6*) MICHIE.

***Virginia Domestic Relations Case Finder.** 3rd ed. Brien A. Roche. 1996. 90.00 (*1-55834-325-3*, 66607-11) MICHIE.

Virginia Domestic Relations Case Finder with 1992 Supplement. 2nd ed. Brien A. Roche. 273p. 1991. 70.00 (*0-685-59626-5*) MICHIE.

Virginia Domestic Relations Case Finder with 1992 Supplement. 2nd ed. Brien A. Roche. 273p. 1992. suppl. ed. 25.00 (*0-87473-978-0*) MICHIE.

Virginia Domestic Relations Handbook. 2nd ed. Margaret F. Brinig. 472p. 1991. 70.00 (*0-87473-815-6*) MICHIE.

Virginia Dynasties. C. Dowdey. 1976. 36.95 (*0-8488-0212-8*, J M C & Co) Amereon Ltd.

Virginia Early Census Index, Vol. 1. Ronald V. Jackson. (Illus.). lib. bdg. 59.00 (*0-89593-748-4*) Accelerated Index.

Virginia Early Census Index, Vol. 2. 1980. 48.00 (*0-89593-568-6*) Accelerated Index.

Virginia Employer's Guide: A Handbook of Employment Laws & Regulations. Nancy J. Moore. Ed. by Amy Greenspan. 500p. 1997. ring bd. 92.50 (*1-56759-016-0*) Summers Pr.

Virginia Employer's Guide to Labor Law. Michael F. Marino et al. LC 83-171872. (Illus.). 1982. 45.00 (*0-685-08125-7*) VA Chamber Com.

Virginia Entrepreneur's Guide. University MT Staff. 1994. pap. text ed. 19.95 (*0-9624819-2-0*) University MT.

Virginia Environmental Law Handbook. 2nd ed. Mays & Valentine. (State Environmental Law Ser.). 342p. 1992. pap. text ed. 79.00 (*0-86587-315-1*) Gov Insts.

Virginia Facts & Factivities. Carole Marsh. (Carole Marsh State Bks.). (Illus.). 1996. 29.95 (*0-614-11558-2*, C Marsh); teacher ed., pap. 19.95 (*0-7933-7939-3*, C Marsh) Gallopade Pub Group.

Virginia: Family Adventure Guide: Great Things to See & Do for the Entire Family. Candyce H. Stapen. LC 95-13045. (Family Adventure Guide Ser.). (Illus.). 160p. (Orig.). 1995. pap. 9.95 (*1-56440-622-9*) Globe Pequot.

Virginia: Family Adventure Guide see Fun with the Family in Virginia

Virginia Family & Its Plantation Houses. Elizabeth Langhorne et al. LC 86-28072. (Illus.). 176p. 1987. text ed. 28.50 (*0-8139-1127-3*) U Pr of Va.

Virginia Family Law Manual. Anita M. Butler. 360p. 1991. ring bd. 80.00 (*0-409-27224-8*) MICHIE.

Virginia Fare: A Culinary View of the Commonwealth. Junior League of Richmond Staff. LC 94-76194. 1994. 19.95 (*0-9614056-1-9*) Jr Leag Richmond.

Virginia Federal Census Index, 1810. Ronald V. Jackson. LC 77-86062. (Illus.). 1978. lib. bdg. 65.00 (*0-89593-147-8*) Accelerated Index.

Virginia Federal Census Index, 1820. Ronald V. Jackson. LC 77-86063. (Illus.). 1976. lib. bdg. 79.00 (*0-89593-148-6*) Accelerated Index.

Virginia Federal Census Index, 1830. Ronald V. Jackson. LC 77-86065. (Illus.). 1976. lib. bdg. 85.00 (*0-89593-149-4*) Accelerated Index.

Virginia Federal Census Index, 1840. Ronald V. Jackson. LC 77-86066. (Illus.). lib. bdg. 127.00 (*0-89593-150-8*) Accelerated Index.

Virginia Federal Census Index, 1850. Ronald V. Jackson. LC 77-86055. (Illus.). 1981. lib. bdg. 158.00 (*0-89593-151-6*) Accelerated Index.

Virginia Federal Census, 1860 (Excluding Present Day West Virginia) Ronald V. Jackson. 1992. 300.00 (*0-89593-841-3*) Accelerated Index.

Virginia Federal Census, 1870. (Illus.). 1990. 580.00 (*0-89593-613-5*) Accelerated Index.

Virginia Festival Fun for Kids! Carole Marsh. (Virginia Bks.). (Illus.). (YA). (gr. 3-12). 1994. pap. 19.95 (*0-7933-4065-9*); lib. bdg. 29.95 (*0-7933-4064-0*) Gallopade Pub Group.

Virginia Festival Fun for Kids! Carole Marsh. (Virginia Bks.). (Illus.). (J). (gr. 3-12). 1997. disk 29.95 (*0-7933-4066-7*) Gallopade Pub Group.

Virginia Fishing Guide. rev. ed. Bob Gooch. 304p. (Orig.). 1992. reprint ed. pap. 12.95 (*0-8139-1383-7*) U Pr of Va.

Virginia Folk Legends. Intro. by Thomas E. Barden. 348p. 1991. pap. 16.95 (*0-8139-1335-7*); text ed. 39.50 (*0-8139-1331-4*) U Pr of Va.

Virginia Football Mystery. Carole M. Longmeyer. (Sportsmystery Ser.). (Illus.). 80p. (Orig.). (J). (gr. 3 up). 1994. pap. 19.95 (*0-935326-35-9*) Gallopade Pub Group.

Virginia Forms, 5 vols., Set. Frank J. Gallo et al. 1991. 425.00 (*0-87215-816-0*) MICHIE.

Virginia Fossils: An Educational Activity Book. Jasper Burns. (Illus.). 40p. (Orig.). (J). (gr. 4-7). 1996. pap. 2.95 (*1-884549-03-9*) VA Mus Natl Hist.

Virginia Frontier, 1754-1763. Louis K. Koontz. LC 78-64117. (Johns Hopkins University. Studies in the Social Sciences. Thirtieth Ser. 1912: 2). reprint ed. 36.00 (*0-404-61232-6*) AMS Pr.

Virginia Frontier, 1754-1763. Louis K. Koontz. 186p. reprint ed. pap. 17.50 (*1-55613-663-3*) Heritage Bk.

***Virginia Gardener's Guide: The What, Where, When, How & Why of Gardening in Virginia.** Jacqueline Heriteau. LC 97-19411. (Illus.). 400p. 1997. pap. 18.95 (*1-888608-11-0*) Cool Springs Pr.

***Virginia Gardener's Guide: The What, Where, When, How & Why of Gardening in Virginia.** Jacqueline Heriteau. (Illus.). 400p. (Orig.). 1997. pap. write for info. (*0-614-30316-8*) Cool Springs Pr.

Virginia Genealogical Research. 188p. 1994. pap. 15.00 (*0-913857-06-8*) Genealog Sources.

Virginia Genealogies, Vol. 2. Stuart E. Brown, Jr. et al. 351p. 1980. 30.00 (*0-686-64384-4*) VA Bk.

Virginia Genealogies, Vol. III. Stuart E. Brown, Jr. et al. 420p. 1989. 49.50 (*0-685-34656-0*) VA Bk.

Virginia Genealogies: A Genealogy of the Glassell Family of Scotland & Virginia, Also of the Families of Ball, Brown, Bryan, Conway, Daniel, Ewell, Holladay, Lewis, Littlepage, Moncure, Peyton, Robinson, Scott, Taylor, Wallace, & Others of Virginia & Maryland. Horace E. Hayden. 777p. 1996. reprint ed. pap. 49.95 (*0-614-16550-4*, 2630) Clearfield Co.

Virginia Genealogies: A Trial List of Printed Books & Pamphlets. Stuart E. Brown, Jr. LC 67-7956. 310p. 1967. 30.00 (*0-685-65061-8*) VA Bk.

Virginia Genealogist, Vol. 3, 1959. John F. Dorman. 235p. 1992. reprint ed. pap. 18.50 (*1-55613-599-8*) Heritage Bk.

Virginia Genealogist, Vol. 5. John F. Dorman. 234p. reprint ed. pap. 20.00 (*1-55613-714-1*) Heritage Bk.

Virginia Genealogist, Vol. 12, 1968. John F. Dorman. 235p. 1993. reprint ed. pap. text ed. 20.00 (*1-55613-839-3*) Heritage Bk.

Virginia Genealogist, Vol. 15, 1971. Ed. by John F. Dorman. 387p. 1994. reprint ed. pap. text ed. 27.50 (*1-55613-920-9*) Heritage Bk.

Virginia Genealogist, Vol. 16, 1972. Ed. by John F. Dorman. 386p. 1994. reprint ed. pap. text ed. 27.50 (*1-55613-921-7*) Heritage Bk.

Virginia Genealogist, Vol. 17, 1973. John F. Dorman. 399p. 1994. reprint ed. pap. text ed. 26.00 (*1-55613-968-3*) Heritage Bk.

Virginia Genealogist, Vol. 18, 1974. Ed. by John F. Dorman. 386p. 1994. reprint ed. pap. text ed. 26.00 (*1-55613-969-1*) Heritage Bk.

Virginia Genealogist, Vol. 23, 1979. Ed. by John F. Dorman. 397p. 1995. reprint ed. pap. text ed. 26.00 (*0-7884-0086-X*) Heritage Bk.

Virginia Genealogist, Vol. 27, 1983. Ed. by John F. Dorman. 384p. (Orig.). 1995. pap. 28.50 (*0-7884-2129-8*) Heritage Bk.

Virginia Genealogist: Nineteen Sixty-Four, Vol. 8. Ed. by John F. Dorman. 236p. 1993. reprint ed. pap. 20.00 (*1-55613-753-2*) Heritage Bk.

Virginia Genealogist: Nineteen Sixty-Three, Vol. 7. Ed. by John F. Dorman. ii, 243p. 1993. reprint ed. pap. 20.00 (*1-55613-752-4*) Heritage Bk.

Virginia Genealogist Vol. 19: 1975. Ed. by John F. Dorman. 391p. (Orig.). 1994. pap. text ed. 26.00 (*0-7884-0027-4*) Heritage Bk.

Virginia Genealogist Vol. 20: 1976. Ed. by John F. Dorman. 389p. (Orig.). 1994. pap. text ed. 26.00 (*0-7884-0028-2*) Heritage Bk.

Virginia Genealogist Vol. 22: 1978. John F. Dorman. 402p. 1994. reprint ed. pap. text ed. 26.00 (*0-7884-0056-8*) Heritage Bk.

Virginia Genealogist, Vol. 13: 1969. John F. Dorman. 234p. (Orig.). 1993. pap. text ed. 21.00 (*1-55613-882-2*) Heritage Bk.

Virginia Genealogist, Vol. 14: 1970. John F. Dorman. 233p. 1993. reprint ed. pap. text ed. 21.00 (*1-55613-883-0*) Heritage Bk.

Virginia Genealogist, Vol. 6: 1962. Ed. by John F. Dorman. 237p. reprint ed. pap. text ed. 20.00 (*1-55613-715-X*) Heritage Bk.

Virginia Genealogist, 1957, Vol. 1. Ed. by John Frederick Dorman. 235p. 1992. reprint ed. pap. 18.50 (*1-55613-553-X*) Heritage Bk.

Virginia Genealogist, 1965, Vol. 9. Ed. by John F. Dorman. ii, 241p. (Orig.). 1993. reprint ed. pap. text ed. 21.00 (*1-55613-784-2*) Heritage Bk.

Virginia Genealogist, 1966, Vol. 10. Ed. by John F. Dorman. ii, 256p. (Orig.). 1993. reprint ed. pap. text ed. 21.00 (*1-55613-785-0*) Heritage Bk.

Virginia Genealogist, 1967, Vol. 11. John F. Dorman. 240p. 1993. reprint ed. pap. text ed. 20.00 (*1-55613-838-5*) Heritage Bk.

Virginia Genealogist, 1977 Vol. 21: 1977. Ed. by John F. Dorman. 391p. 1994. reprint ed. pap. text ed. 26.00 (*0-7884-0055-X*) Heritage Bk.

Virginia Genealogist, 1980, Vol. 26, 1982. Ed. by John F. Dorman. 398p. (Orig.). reprint ed. pap. 29.00 (*0-7884-0211-0*) Heritage Bk.

Virginia Genealogist, 1981. Ed. by John F. Dorman. 397p. 1995. reprint ed. pap. text ed. 26.00 (*0-7884-0212-9*) Heritage Bk.

Virginia Germans. Klaus Wust. LC 69-17334. 1969. reprint ed. text ed. 35.00 (*0-8139-0256-8*); reprint ed. pap. text ed. 16.50 (*0-8139-1214-8*) U Pr of Va.

Virginia Giving: The Directory of the Commonwealth's Foundations. Anita G. Shirley. Ed. by Sheila Ragland. 1025p. (Orig.). 1994. pap. 99.00 (*0-9624910-2-0*) Capital Consortium.

***Virginia Government! The Cornerstone of Everyday Life in Our State!** Carole Marsh. (Carole Marsh Virginia Bks.). (Illus.). (J). (gr. 3-12). 1996. pap. 19.95 (*0-7933-6320-9*); lib. bdg. 29.95 (*0-7933-6319-5*); disk 29.95 (*0-7933-6321-7*) Gallopade Pub Group.

Virginia Government & Politics: Readings & Comments. 3rd rev. ed. Ed. by Thomas R. Morris & Larry J. Sabato. 231p. 1990. pap. 25.00 (*0-318-04190-1*) U VA Ctr Pub Serv.

Virginia Government & Politics: Readings & Comments. Ed. by Weldon Cooper & Thomas R. Morris. LC 75-44333. 454p. reprint ed. pap. 129.40 (*0-8357-2707-6*, 2039820) Bks Demand.

Virginia Governments Performance Standards, 1990. Ed. by Greg Michels. (Governments Performance Standards Ser.). (Illus.). 150p. 1990. text ed. 125.00 (*1-55507-504-5*) Municipal Analysis.

***Virginia Gun Owner's Guide Vol. 1: Who Can Bear Arms? Where Are Guns Forbidden? When Can You Shoot to Kill?** Alan Korwin & Steve Maniscalco. (Illus.). 208p. (Orig.). 1996. 14.95 (*0-9621958-7-1*) Bloomfield Pr.

Virginia Hamilton. Nina Mikkelsen. LC 94-621. (Twayne's United States Authors Ser.). 200p. 1994. 22.95 (*0-8057-4010-4*, Twayne) Scribnrs Ref.

***Virginia Hamilton.** Jill C. Wheeler. LC 97-3790. (Tribute to the Young at Heart Ser.). (J). 1997. write for info. (*1-56239-790-7*) Abdo & Dghtrs.

Virginia Hamilton #3. Virginia Hamilton. LC 94-33055. (Illus.). (J). (gr. 1-8). write for info. (*0-590-47368-9*, Blue Sky Press) Scholastic Inc.

Virginia Handbook. Blair Howard. 1995. pap. 14.95 (*1-55650-701-1*) Hunter NJ.

Virginia Health Care Perspective 1996. Ed. by Kathleen O. Morgan et al. 24p. 1996. pap. 19.00 (*1-56692-645-9*) Morgan Quitno Corp.

***Virginia Health Care Perspective 1997.** Ed. by Kathleen O. Morgan & Scott E. Morgan. 24p. 1997. pap. 19.00 (*1-56692-745-5*) Morgan Quitno Corp.

Virginia Henderson Reader: Excellence in Nursing. Ed. by Edward J. Halloran. LC 94-42141. 416p. 1995. 48.95 (*0-8261-8830-3*) Springer Pub.

Virginia, Henrico County Federal Census Index, 1870 (Includes City of Richmond) Ronald V. Jackson. 1991. 115.00 (*0-89593-825-1*) Accelerated Index.

Virginia Historical & Biographical Index, Vol. 1. Ronald V. Jackson. LC 78-53722. (Illus.). 1984. lib. bdg. 30.00 (*0-89593-204-0*) Accelerated Index.

Virginia Historical Genealogies. John B. Boddie. (Illus.). 384p. 1996. reprint ed. pap. 32.00 (*0-614-16581-4*, 535) Clearfield Co.

Virginia Historical Index, 2 vols. in 4, Set. Ed. by Earl G. Swem. 1934. 170.00 (*0-8446-1431-9*) Peter Smith.

***Virginia History! Surprising Secrets about Our State's Founding Mothers, Fathers & Kids!** Carole Marsh. (Carole Marsh Virginia Bks.). (Illus.). (J). (gr. 3-12). 1996. pap. 19.95 (*0-7933-6167-2*); lib. bdg. 29.95 (*0-7933-6166-4*); disk 29.95 (*0-7933-6168-0*) Gallopade Pub Group.

Virginia History in Documents. 1621-1788. William H. Gaines, Jr. LC 73-94133. (Illus.). vii, 84p. 1974. pap. 10.00 (*0-88490-000-2*) Library of VA.

***Virginia Homeowners.** Torbet. Date not set. write for info. (*0-688-05077-8*) Morrow.

Virginia Homes of the Lees. rev. ed. Eleanor L. Templeman. LC 73-81139. 1975. 2.50 (*0-911044-03-5*) Templeman.

***Virginia Hospitality.** Wimmer Books Plus Staff. 1975. 14.95 (*0-9613600-1-1*) Wimmer Bks.

***Virginia Hostess: An Entertaining Guide Featuring Traditional & Modern Recipes.** rev. ed. Illus. by Lou W. Harris & Richard Guy. 286p. 1991. text ed. 17.95 (*0-614-30292-7*) Jr Womans Club.

Virginia Hostess: An Entertainment Guide Featuring Traditional & Modern Recipes. Junior Woman's Club of Manassas, Inc. Staff. (Illus.). 286p. 1991. text ed. 16.95 (*0-9630449-0-7*) Jr Womans Club.

Virginia Hot Air Balloon Mystery. Carole Marsh. (Carole Marsh Virginia Bks.). (Illus.). (J). (gr. 2-9). 1994. 29.95 (*0-7933-2732-6*); pap. 19.95 (*0-7933-2733-4*); disk 29.95 (*0-7933-2734-2*) Gallopade Pub Group.

Virginia House: A Home for Three Hundred Years. Anne M. Faulconer. LC 83-51774. (Illus.). 176p. 1984. 25.00 (*0-88740-004-3*) Schiffer.

Virginia House of Burgesses, 1660-1706: The Social, Educational & Economic Bases of Political Power. Martin H. Quitt. (Outstanding Studies in Early American History). 388p. 1989. reprint ed. 25.00 (*0-8240-6194-2*) Garland.

Virginia House-Wife. Mary Randolph. Ed. by Karen Hess. LC 83-19869. 417p. 1984. 24.95 (*0-87249-423-3*) U of SC Pr.

Virginia Housewife: or Methodical Cook: A Facsimile of an Authentic Early American Cookbook. Mary Randolph. LC 93-32924. 192p. 1993. reprint ed. pap. text ed. 4.95 (*0-486-27772-0*) Dover.

Virginia Hunting Guide. Bob Gooch. LC 84-21004. (Illus.). 236p. 1985. pap. 12.95 (*0-8139-1041-2*) U Pr of Va.

Virginia in Foreign Affairs, 1933-1941. Rorin M. Platt. 270p. (C). 1991. lib. bdg. 47.50 (*0-8191-7803-9*) U Pr of Amer.

Virginia in Our Century. Jean Gottmann. LC 68-8541. 670p. reprint ed. pap. 180.00 (*0-317-28909-8*, 2020269) Bks Demand.

Virginia in Perspective 1996. Ed. by Kathleen O. Morgan et al. 26p. 1996. pap. 19.00 (*1-56692-595-9*) Morgan Quitno Corp.

***Virginia in Perspective 1997.** Ed. by Kathleen O. Morgan & Scott E. Morgan. 26p. 1997. pap. 19.00 (*1-56692-695-5*) Morgan Quitno Corp.

Virginia in 1740: A Reconstructed Census. abr. ed. T.L.C. Genealogy Staff. 308p. (Orig.). 1993. spiral bd., pap. 25.00 (*1-886633-39-8*) TLC Genealogy.

Virginia in 1760: A Reconstructed Census. 375p. 1996. spiral bd. 35.00 (*1-57445-020-4*) TLC Genealogy.

Virginia Indian Dictionary for Kids! Carole Marsh. (Carole Marsh State Bks.). (J). (gr. 2-9). 1996. 29.95 (*0-7933-7782-X*, C Marsh); pap. 19.95 (*0-7933-7783-8*, C Marsh) Gallopade Pub Group.

Virginia Indians: An Educational Coloring Book. Jean S. Adams. (Illus.). 24p. (Orig.). (J). (gr. k-3). 1991. pap. 2.95 (*1-884549-05-5*) VA Mus Natl Hist.

Virginia Industrial Directory: 1986-87. 17th ed. 350p. 1986. pap. 60.00 (*0-317-40524-1*) VA Chamber Com.

Virginia Industrial Directory, 1995. 1995. 75.00 (*1-55600-506-7*) Harris InfoSource.

Virginia Insurance Case Finder. Alan B. Rashkind & Gerard P. Rowe. 800p. 1994. 95.00 (*1-55834-146-3*) MICHIE.

***Virginia Invitational 1997: Virginia Photographers.** (Illus.). 21p. (Orig.). 1997. pap. write for info. (*1-890327-00-X*) Longwood Ctr.

***Virginia Invitational 1997: Virginia Photographers.** (Illus.). 21p. (Orig.). 1997. pap. write for info. (*0-614-27213-0*) Longwood Ctr.

Virginia Jeopardy! Answers & Questions about Our State! Carole Marsh. (Virginia Bks.). (Illus.). (J). (gr. 3-12). 1994. pap. 19.95 (*0-7933-4218-X*); lib. bdg. 29.95 (*0-7933-4217-1*); disk 29.95 (*0-7933-4219-8*) Gallopade Pub Group.

Virginia Jobbank, 1997. Adams Publishing Staff. 1996. pap. text ed. 15.95 (*1-55850-667-5*) Adams Media.

Virginia Jography: A Fun Run Through the Old Dominion State. Carole Marsh. (Statemeant Ser.). (Illus.). 50p. (Orig.). (J). (gr. 3-12). 1994. pap. 29.95 (*0-935326-99-5*) Gallopade Pub Group.

Virginia "Jography" A Fun Run Thru Our State. Carole Marsh. (Carole Marsh Virginia Bks.). (Illus.). (J). 1994. pap. 19.95 (*1-55609-057-9*); disk 29.95 (*0-7933-2170-0*) Gallopade Pub Group.

Virginia "Jography" A Fun Run Thru Our State. Carole Marsh. (Carole Marsh Virginia Bks.). (Illus.). (J). 1997. lib. bdg. 29.95 (*0-7933-2169-7*) Gallopade Pub Group.

Virginia Journal of International Law: 1960-1994/95, 35 vols. Bound set. 1,512.50 (*0-8377-9181-2*) Rothman.

Virginia Journals of Benjamin Henry Latrobe, 1795-1798. Benjamin Latrobe. Ed. by Edward C. Carter. LC 77-76301. (Illus.). 1977. Set. 130.00 (*0-300-02198-4*) Yale U Pr.

Virginia Kid's Cookbook: Recipes, How-to, History, Lore & More! Carole Marsh. (Carole Marsh Virginia Bks.). (Illus.). (J). 1994. pap. 19.95 (*0-7933-1165-9*); lib. bdg. 29.95 (*0-7933-1166-7*); disk 29.95 (*0-7933-1167-5*) Gallopade Pub Group.

Virginia Land Surveying Law: Questions & Answers. John E. Keen. 52p. (C). 1995. pap. text ed. 20.00 (*1-56569-042-7*) Land Survey.

Virginia Landlord-Tenant Law. Jerome P. Friedlander, II. 935p. 1992. 85.00 (*0-87473-778-8*) MICHIE.

Virginia Landmarks of Black History: Sites on the Virginia Landmarks Register & the National Register of Historic Places. Ed. by Calder Loth. LC 94-32817. (Carter G. Woodson Institute Series in Black Studies). (Illus.). 224p. (C). 1995. text ed. 40.00 (*0-8139-1600-3*) U Pr of Va.

Virginia Landmarks of Black History: Sites on the Virginia Landmarks Register & the National Register of Historic Places. Ed. by Clader Loth. LC 94-32817. (Carter G. Woodson Institute Series in Black Studies). (Illus.). 224p. (C). 1995. pap. 18.95 (*0-8139-1601-1*) U Pr of Va.

Virginia Lands Grants. Fairfax Harrison. Ed. by Stuart Bruchey. LC 78-56669. (Management of Public Lands in the U. S. Ser.). 1979. reprint ed. lib. bdg. 17.95 (*0-405-11335-8*) Ayer.

Virginia Law Review: 1913-1995, 81 vols. Bound set. 4,362.50 (*0-8377-9182-0*) Rothman.

Virginia Lawyer: A Basic Practice Handbook. Ed. by Joseph R. Mayes. 1991. suppl. ed. 50.00 (*0-87473-907-1*) MICHIE.

Virginia Lawyer: A Basic Practice Handbook, 2 vols., Set. Virginia Bar Association, Virginia Lawyer Committee of Young Lawyers Staff. Ed. by Joseph R. Mayes. 1979. spiral bd. 110.00 (*0-87215-125-5*) MICHIE.

Virginia Legal & Business Forms. Ed. by Thomas L. Bowden. LC 95-14036. 1995. 380.00 (*0-614-05432-X*) Lawyers Cooperative.

An Asterisk (*) at the beginning of an entry indicates that the title is appearing in BIP for the first time.

Virginia Legislative Petitions: Bibliography, Calendar, & Abstracts from Original Sources, 6 May 1776-21 June 1782. Intro. by Randolph W. Church. xv, 508p. 1984. 35.00 (0-88490-114-9) Library of VA.

Virginia Library Book: A Surprising Guide to the Unusual Special Collections in Libraries Across Our State for Students, Teachers, Writers & Publishers - Includes Reproducible Mailing Labels Plus Activities for Young People! Carole Marsh. (Virginia Bks.). (Illus.). 1994. pap. 19.95 (0-7933-3144-7); lib. bdg. 29.95 (0-7933-3143-9); disk 29.95 (0-7933-3145-5) Gallopade Pub Group.

Virginia Limited Liability Company Forms & Practice Manual: Forms & Practice Manual. 2nd rev. ed. Robert B. Webb & James J. Wheaton. 680p. 1996. ring bd. 149.95 (1-57400-009-8) Data Trace Pubng.

Virginia Lineages, Letters & Memories. Alice J. Nelson. (Illus.). x, 302p. 21.50 (0-9614497-0-5) A J Nelson.

Virginia Litigation Forms & Analysis. Laura L. Wagner & Robert J. Wagner. 1994. 285.00 (0-615-00123-8) Lawyers Cooperative.

Virginia Lover & Other Poems. John E. Sturm. Ed. by Jeanne Masson-Douglas. LC 82-81337. (Illus.). 56p. (Orig.). 1982. pap. 4.95 (0-940282-01-1) Outermost Pr.

Virginia Marine: World War, Vol. 2. Robert K. Krick. (Illus.). 99p. 1987. 11.95 (0-930919-38-6) H E Howard.

Virginia Marriages, Early to Eighteen Hundred. Liahona Research, Inc. Staff. Ed. by Jordan Dodd. 1148p. 1991. lib. bdg. 145.00 (1-877677-39-6) Precision Indexing.

Virginia Marriages in Rev. John Cameron's Register & Bath Parish Register, 1827-1897. Virginia Genealogical Society Staff. 56p. 1963. pap. 10.00 (0-89308-264-3, VA 28) Southern Hist Pr.

Virginia, Maryland & the Carolinas see English in America

Virginia Media Book: A Surprising Guide to the Amazing Print, Broadcast & Online Media of Our State for Students, Teachers, Writers & Publishers - Includes Reproducible Mailing Labels Plus Activities for Young People! Carole Marsh. (Virginia Bks.). (Illus.). 1994. pap. 19.95 (0-7933-3300-8); lib. bdg. 29.95 (0-7933-3299-0); disk 29.95 (0-7933-3301-6) Gallopade Pub Group.

Virginia Military Institute Album, 1839-1910. Diane B. Jacob & Judith M. Arnold. LC 82-1865. (Illus.). 112p. 1982. text ed. 16.95 (0-8139-0947-3) U Pr of Va.

Virginia Military Surveys of Clermont & Hamilton Counties, Ohio, 1787-1849. Alma A. Smith. LC 85-90108. (Illus.). x, 253p. 1985. pap. 25.00 (0-9614853-1-7); lib. bdg. 32.00 (0-9614863-0-9) Alma Smith.

Virginia Model Jury Instructions: Civil, 1988 Replacement Edition with 1991 Supplements, 2 vols. 1988. 180.00 (0-87473-423-1) MICHIE.

Virginia Model Jury Instructions - Civil, 1993 Edition, 2 vols., Set. Model Jury Instructions Committee. 1993. spiral bd. 190.00 (1-55834-145-5) MICHIE.

Virginia Model Jury Instructions - Criminal, 1989 Replacement Edition with 1991 Supplements, 2 vols. rev. ed. Model Jury Instructions Committee. 1989. Set. 180.00 (0-87473-482-7) MICHIE.

Virginia Model Jury Instructions - Criminal, 1993 Edition, 2 vols., Set. Model Jury Instructions Committee. 1993. spiral bd. 190.00 (1-55834-137-4) MICHIE.

Virginia Mystery Van Takes Off! Book 1: Handicapped Virginia Kids Sneak Off on a Big Adventure. Carole Marsh. (Virginia Bks.). (Illus.). (J). (gr. 3-12). 1994. 29.95 (0-7933-5099-9); pap. 19.95 (0-7933-5100-6); disk 29.95 (0-7933-5101-4) Gallopade Pub Group.

Virginia Nonagricultural Employment, 1980-1990. 1991. pap. 5.00 (0-318-04164-2) U VA Ctr Pub Serv.

Virginia Northern Neck Land Grants, Vol. III: 1775-1800. Gertrude E. Gray. 293p. 1993. 28.50 (0-8063-1370-6, 2317) Genealog Pub.

Virginia Northern Neck Land Grants, Vol. IV: 1800-1862. Gertrude E. Gray. 311p. 1993. 28.50 (0-8063-1371-4, 2318) Genealog Pub.

Virginia Northern Neck Land Grants, 1742-1775, Vol. II. Gertrude E. Gray. 282p. 1997. 28.50 (0-8063-1229-7, 2316) Genealog Pub.

Virginia Objections at Trial. Ronald L. Carlson et al. LC 93-28249. 280p. 1993. pap. 39.50 (0-250-42767-2) MICHIE.

Virginia Obsolete Paper Money. Ed. by Richard H. Jones & Keith E. Littlefield. (Illus.). 500p. 1991. 50.00 (1-878029-00-2); 45.00 (1-878029-01-0) VA Numismatic Assn.

Virginia Occupational Demand, Supply, & Wage Information. 7th ed. 1988. write for info. (0-318-62799-X) U VA Ctr Pub Serv.

Virginia on Guard: Civilian Defense & the State Militia in the Second World War. Marvin W. Schlegel. LC 49-10538. (Illus.). xxiii, 226p. 1949. 24.95 (0-88490-040-1) Library of VA.

Virginia on My Mind. Intro. by Guy Friddell. (America on My Mind Ser.). (Illus.). 120p. 1995. reprint ed. 29.95 (1-56044-026-0) Falcon Pr MT.

Virginia One-Day Adventures & Weekend Getaways: A Guide to Excursions on the Historic Virginia Peninsula That Both Kids & Grownups Will Enjoy. Mary Eley & Barbara M. Wohlford. (Illus.). 256p. 1994. pap. 8.95 (0-941263-98-3, Tribune) Contemp Bks.

Virginia One-Day Trip Book: From the Mountains to the Sea, Seven Geographic Centers Offer 101 Scenic & Historic Delights. Jane O. Smith. LC 86-13450. 224p. (Orig.). 1986. pap. 8.95 (0-914440-93-4) EPM Pubns.

Virginia One Hundred Years Ago. Compiled by Skip Whitson. (Historical Ser.). (Illus.) (Orig.). 1976. pap. 3.50 (0-89540-024-3, SB-024) Sun Pub.

Virginia Originals. Ellin Gordon et al. 1994. pap. 14.95 (1-885163-00-2) Virginia Beach Ctr.

Virginia OSHA Compliance Handbook. Mays & Valentine Staff. 140p. (Orig.). 1992. pap. text ed. 76.00 (0-86587-304-6) Gov Insts.

Virginia Outdoor Activity Guide. W. Lynn Seldon. (Outdoor Activity Guide Ser.). pap. 9.95 (1-56626-112-0) Country Rds.

Virginia Papers of the Presidency, Vol. V: The White Burkett Miller Center Forums, 1981, Pt. 1. Ed. by Kenneth W. Thompson. 91p. (C). 1981. pap. text ed. 15.00 (0-8191-1503-7); lib. bdg. 36.00 (0-8191-1502-9) U Pr of Amer.

Virginia Papers on the Presidency. Ed. by Kenneth W. Thompson. 140p. (Orig.). (C). 1994. pap. text ed. 22.50 (0-8191-9708-4, Pub. by White Miller Center) U Pr of Amer.

Virginia Papers on the Presidency, Vol. XI. Ed. by Kenneth W. Thompson. LC 79-66241. (White Burkett Miller Center Forums, 1982 Ser.: Pt. II). 102p. (Orig.). (C). 1983. pap. text ed. 14.00 (0-8191-3112-1); lib. bdg. 41.50 (0-8191-3111-3) U Pr of Amer.

Virginia Papers on the Presidency, Vol. XII. Ed. by Kenneth W. Thompson. LC 79-66241. (White Burkett Miller Center Forums, 1983 Ser.: Pt. 1). 110p. (Orig.). (C). 1983. pap. text ed. 15.00 (0-8191-3303-5); lib. bdg. 40.00 (0-8191-3302-7) U Pr of Amer.

Virginia Papers on the Presidency, Vol. XIII. Ed. by Kenneth W. Thompson. LC 79-66241. (White Burkett Miller Center Forums Ser.: Pt. II). 98p. (Orig.). (C). 1984. pap. text ed. 14.00 (0-8191-3623-9); lib. bdg. 37.50 (0-8191-3622-0, Pub. by White Miller Center) U Pr of Amer.

Virginia Papers on the Presidency, Vol. XIV. Ed. by Kenneth W. Thompson. LC 79-66241. (White Burkett Miller Center Forums Ser.: Pt. III). 100p. (Orig.). (C). 1984. lib. bdg. 35.50 (0-8191-3647-6, Pub. by White Miller Center) U Pr of Amer.

Virginia Papers on the Presidency, Vol. XV. Kenneth W. Thompson. (White Burkett Miller Center Forums, 1983 Ser.: Part. 4). 108p. (Orig.). 1984. pap. text ed. 14.50 (0-8191-3867-3) U Pr of Amer.

Virginia Papers on the Presidency, Vol. XVI. Kenneth W. Thompson. LC 79-66241. (White Burkett Miller Center Forums, 1984 Ser.: Pt. I). 140p. (Orig.). (C). 1984. pap. text ed. 13.50 (0-8191-3984-X); lib. bdg. 35.50 (0-8191-3983-1, Pub. by White Miller Center) U Pr of Amer.

Virginia Papers on the Presidency, Vol. XVII. Ed. by Kenneth W. Thompson. LC 79-66241. (White Burkett Miller Center Forums, 1983 Ser.: Pt. II). 110p. (Orig.). 1985. pap. text ed. 15.00 (0-8191-4256-5); lib. bdg. 37.50 (0-8191-4255-7, Pub. by White Miller Center) U Pr of Amer.

Virginia Papers on the Presidency, Vol. XVIII. Ed. by Kenneth W. Thompson. LC 79-66241. (White Burkett Miller Center Forums, 1983 Ser.: Pt. III). 126p. (Orig.). 1985. pap. text ed. 15.00 (0-8191-4316-2) U Pr of Amer.

Virginia Papers on the Presidency, Vol. XIX. Ed. by Kenneth W. Thompson. LC 79-66241. (White Burkett Miller Center Forums, 1983 Ser.: Pt. IV). 122p. (Orig.). 1985. lib. bdg. 40.00 (0-8191-4592-0, Pub. by White Miller Center) U Pr of Amer.

Virginia Papers on the Presidency, Vol. XXI. Ed. by Kenneth W. Thompson. LC 86-66241. (White Burkett Miller Center Forums, 1985 Ser.). 100p. (Orig.). (C). 1986. pap. text ed. 14.50 (0-8191-5490-3, Pub. by White Miller Center); lib. bdg. 39.00 (0-8191-5489-X, Pub. by White Miller Center) U Pr of Amer.

Virginia Papers on the Presidency, Vol. XXII. Ed. by Kenneth W. Thompson. LC 79-66241. (White Burkett Miller Center Forums, 1985 Ser.: Pt. II). 108p. (Orig.). (C). 1986. pap. text ed. 14.50 (0-8191-5523-3); lib. bdg. 40.50 (0-8191-5522-5, Pub. by White Miller Center) U Pr of Amer.

Virginia Papers on the Presidency, Vol. XXIII. Ed. by Kenneth W. Thompson. LC 79-66241. (White Burkett Miller Center Forums, 1983 Ser.: Pt. 1). 112p. (Orig.). 1987. lib. bdg. 29.50 (0-8191-6348-1, Pub. by White Miller Center) U Pr of Amer.

Virginia Papers on the Presidency, Vol. XXV. Ed. by Kenneth W. Thompson. LC 79-66241. (White Burkett Miller Center Forums, 1983 Ser.: Pt. I). 124p. (Orig.). (C). 1989. pap. text ed. 14.00 (0-8191-7272-3, Pub. by White Miller Center); lib. bdg. 34.00 (0-8191-7271-5, Pub. by White Miller Center) U Pr of Amer.

Virginia Papers on the Presidency, Vol. XXVI. Ed. by Kenneth W. Thompson. 162p. (Orig.). (C). 1991. pap. text ed. 22.50 (0-8191-8139-0, Pub. by White Miller Center); lib. bdg. 41.50 (0-8191-8138-2, Pub. by White Miller Center) U Pr of Amer.

Virginia Papers on the Presidency, Vol. XXVII. 220p. 1993. 52.00 (0-8191-8542-6); pap. 23.50 (0-8191-8543-4) U Pr of Amer.

Virginia Papers on the Presidency, Vol. XXVIII. Ed. by Kenneth W. Thompson. 140p. (C). 1994. lib. bdg. 42.50 (0-8191-9707-6, Pub. by White Miller Center) U Pr of Amer.

***Virginia Papers on the Presidency, Vol. XXIX.** Ed. by Kenneth W. Thompson. 198p. (Orig.). 1996. 44.50 (0-7618-0544-3); pap. 22.50 (0-7618-0545-1) U Pr of Amer.

Virginia Papers on the Presidency, Vol. X: The White Burkett Miller Center Forums, 1982, Pt. 1. Ed. by Kenneth W. Thompson. LC 79-66241. 114p. (Orig.). 1983. pap. text ed. 16.50 (0-8191-2824-4); lib. bdg. 47.50 (0-8191-2823-6) U Pr of Amer.

Virginia Papers on the Presidency, Vol. XXIV: The White Burkett Miller Center Forums, 1986-87, Pt. II. Ed. by Kenneth W. Thompson. LC 79-66241. 138p. (Orig.). (C). 1988. lib. bdg. 33.00 (0-8191-6874-2, Pub. by White Miller Center) U Pr of Amer.

Virginia Papers on the Presidency, Vol. 1: The White Burkett Miller Center Forums, 1979. Kenneth W. Thompson. LC 79-66241. 1979. pap. text ed. 16.00 (0-8191-0819-7) U Pr of Amer.

Virginia Papers on the Presidency, Vol. 20: Tenth Anniversary Volume. Ed. by Kenneth W. Thompson. LC 79-66241. (White Burkett Miller Center Forums, 1985 Ser.). 164p. (Orig.). 1986. lib. bdg. 42.00 (0-8191-5002-9, Pub. by White Miller Center) U Pr of Amer.

Virginia Papers on the Presidency, Vol. 3: The White Burkett Miller Center Forums, Pt. 1, 1980. Ed. by Kenneth W. Thompson. LC 79-66241. 133p. 1980. pap. text ed. 16.00 (0-8191-1121-X); lib. bdg. 38.00 (0-8191-1120-1) U Pr of Amer.

Virginia Papers on the Presidency, Vol. 4: The White Burkett Miller Center Forums, 1980, Part II. Ed. by Kenneth W. Thompson. LC 80-5576. 110p. 1980. pap. text ed. 16.00 (0-8191-1202-X); lib. bdg. 38.00 (0-8191-1201-1) U Pr of Amer.

Virginia Papers on the Presidency, Vol. 6: The White Burkett Miller Center Forums, Pt. II. Ed. by Kenneth W. Thompson. LC 79-66241. 128p. 1981. pap. text ed. 15.00 (0-8191-1604-1); lib. bdg. 36.00 (0-8191-1544-4) U Pr of Amer.

Virginia Papers on the Presidency, Vol. 7: The White Burkett Miller Center Forums, 1981, Part III. Ed. by Kenneth W. Thompson. LC 79-66241. 104p. 1982. lib. bdg. 47.00 (0-8191-1901-6) U Pr of Amer.

Virginia Papers on the Presidency, Vol. 8: The White Burkett Miller Center Forums, 1981, Part IV. Ed. by Kenneth W. Thompson. LC 79-66241. 104p. 1982. pap. text ed. 16.50 (0-8191-1952-0); lib. bdg. 47.00 (0-8191-1951-2) U Pr of Amer.

Virginia Papers on the Presidency, Vol. 9: The White Burkett Miller Center Forums, Pt. 5, 1981, Pt. V. Kenneth W. Thompson. LC 79-66241. 90p. (Orig.). 1982. pap. text ed. 16.50 (0-8191-2426-5); lib. bdg. 42.00 (0-8191-2425-7) U Pr of Amer.

Virginia Parks Guide. Margie McCarg. Ed. by Barbara McCarg & Chris Boyer. 100p. (Orig.). 1988. pap. text ed. 5.95 (0-935201-30-0) Affordable Adven.

Virginia Personal Income, 1980-1989: Local Area Personal Income Estimates, New for Most Recent Year & Revisions for Previous Years. (Business & Economics Ser.). 1988. 5.00 (0-318-40063-4) U VA Ctr Pub Serv.

Virginia Personal Injury Forms. John P. Harris, III. 212p. 1994. 95.00 (1-55834-187-0) MICHIE.

***Virginia-Pictorial Souvenir.** Ted Landphair. 1998. write for info. (0-517-18758-2) Random Hse Value.

Virginia Piedmont Blues: The Lives & Art of Two Virginia Bluesmen. Barry L. Pearson. LC 89-28014. (Publications of the American Folklore Society, Bibliographical & Special Ser.). (Illus.). 300p. (C). 1990. text ed. 42.50 (0-8122-8209-4); pap. text ed. 20.95 (0-8122-1300-9) U of Pa Pr.

Virginia Plantation Homes. Photos & Text by David K. Gleason. LC 89-31733. (Illus.). 160p. 1989. 49.95 (0-8071-1570-3) La State U Pr.

Virginia Postmasters & Post Offices, 1789-1832. Edith F. Axelson. 248p. 1991. pap. 20.00 (0-935931-75-9) Borgo Pr.

Virginia Postmasters & Post Offices, 1789-1832. Edith F. Axelson. 248p. 1991. reprint ed. lib. bdg. 49.00 (0-8095-8146-9) Borgo Pr.

Virginia Probate Law, 1991-1993, 2 vols. Elizabeth Hapner. 500p. 1993. suppl. ed. 40.00 (0-685-43797-3) MICHIE.

Virginia Quiz Bowl Crash Courses! Carole Marsh. (Carole Marsh Virginia Bks.). (Illus.). (J). 1994. pap. 19.95 (0-7933-2183-2); lib. bdg. 29.95 (0-7933-2182-4); disk 29.95 (0-7933-2184-0) Gallopade Pub Group.

***Virginia Reader: A Treasury of Writings.** Francis C. Rosenberger. lib. bdg. 33.95 (0-8488-2108-4) Amereon Ltd.

Virginia Real Estate Practice & Law. 4th ed. Maurice A. Boren. LC 96-24742. 1996. write for info. (0-7931-2369-0) Dearborn Trade.

***Virginia Remedies.** John L. Costello. Date not set. write for info. (1-55834-474-8, 67922-10) MICHIE.

Virginia Report of 1799-1800, Touching the Alien & Sedition Laws. James Madison. Bd. with Virginia Resolutions of December 21, 1789. LC 75-107626. LC 75-107626. (Civil Liberties in American History Ser.). 1970. reprint ed. Set lib. bdg. 35.00 (0-306-71860-X) Da Capo.

Virginia Resolutions of December 21, 1789 see Virginia Report of 1799-1800, Touching the Alien & Sedition Laws

***Virginia Review Directory of State & Local Government Officials.** annuals Review Pubns., Inc. Staff. Ed. by Alyson L. Taylor-White. (Illus.). 400p. 1997. ring bd. write for info. (1-883263-06-9) Review Pubns.

Virginia Review of Sociology, Vol. 2. Ed. by Donald Black. 1995. 73.25 (1-55938-903-6) Jai Pr.

Virginia Review of Sociology, Vol. 3. Ed. by Donald Black. 1996. 73.25 (0-7623-0054-X) Jai Pr.

Virginia Review of Sociology: Law & Conflict Management, Vol. 1. Ed. by Donald Black. 191p. 1992. 73.25 (1-55938-413-1) Jai Pr.

Virginia Revolutionary "Publick" Claims, 3 vols., Set. Janice L. Abercrombie & Richard Slatten. 1131p. 1991. lib. bdg. 200.00 (0-8095-8272-4) Borgo Pr.

Virginia Revolutionary War State Pensions. Virginia Genealogical Society Staff. 192p. 1982. reprint ed. 22.50 (0-89308-268-6, VA 33) Southern Hist Pr.

Virginia Rollercoasters! Carole Marsh. (Virginia Bks.). (Illus.). (YA). (gr. 3-12). 1994. pap. 19.95 (0-7933-5363-7); lib. bdg. 29.95 (0-7933-5362-9); disk 29.95 (0-7933-5364-5) Gallopade Pub Group.

Virginia Rules Annotated. Michie Company Editorial Staff. 1461p. 1992. pap. 40.00 (0-87473-875-X) MICHIE.

Virginia Rules Annotated, 1994 Edition. Michie Butterworth Editorial Staff. pap. 45.00 (1-55834-047-5) MICHIE.

Virginia Satir: Foundational Ideas. Barbara J. Brothers. LC 90-26287. (Journal of Couples Therapy). (Illus.). 204p. 1991. text ed. 29.95 (1-56024-104-7) Haworth Pr.

Virginia Satir: The Patterns of Her Magic. Steve Andreas. LC 90-63678. 1991. pap. 14.95 (0-8314-0076-5) Sci & Behavior.

Virginia Satir Photo Calendar, 1988. Jackie Schwartz. 1987. 13.95 (0-9618418-0-X) J Schwartz.

Virginia School Trivia: An Amazing & Fascinating Look at Our State's Teachers, Schools & Students! Carole Marsh. (Carole Marsh Virginia Bks.). (Illus.). (J). 1994. pap. 19.95 (0-7933-1162-4); lib. bdg. 29.95 (0-7933-1163-2); disk 29.95 (0-7933-1164-0) Gallopade Pub Group.

Virginia Seasons. 1984. pap. 16.95 (0-9614056-0-0) Jr Leag Richmond.

Virginia Settlers, Vol. II. A. Maxim Coppage. 1988. 30.00 (0-318-32890-9); pap. 25.00 (0-318-32891-7) A M Coppage.

Virginia Silly Basketball Sportsmysteries, Vol. 1. Carole Marsh. (Carole Marsh Virginia Bks.). (Illus.). (J). 1994. pap. 19.95 (0-7933-1159-4); lib. bdg. 29.95 (0-7933-1160-8) Gallopade Pub Group.

Virginia Silly Basketball Sportsmysteries, Vol. 1. Carole Marsh. (Carole Marsh Virginia Bks.). (Illus.). (J). 1997. disk 29.95 (0-7933-1161-6) Gallopade Pub Group.

Virginia Silly Basketball Sportsmysteries, Vol. 2. Carole Marsh. (Carole Marsh Virginia Bks.). (Illus.). (J). 1994. pap. 19.95 (0-7933-2196-4); lib. bdg. 29.95 (0-7933-2195-6); disk 29.95 (0-7933-2197-2) Gallopade Pub Group.

Virginia Silly Football Sportsmysteries, Vol. 1. Carole Marsh. (Carole Marsh Virginia Bks.). (Illus.). (J). 1994. pap. 19.95 (0-7933-2174-3); disk 29.95 (0-7933-2175-1) Gallopade Pub Group.

Virginia Silly Football Sportsmysteries, Vol. 2. Carole Marsh. (Carole Marsh Virginia Bks.). (Illus.). (J). 1994. pap. 19.95 (0-7933-2177-8); lib. bdg. 29.95 (0-7933-2176-X); disk 29.95 (0-7933-2178-6) Gallopade Pub Group.

Virginia Silly Trivia! Carole Marsh. (Carole Marsh Virginia Bks.). (Illus.). 60p. (Orig.). (J). (gr. 3-12). 1994. pap. 19.95 (0-935326-94-4); lib. bdg. 29.95 (0-7933-2167-0); disk 29.95 (0-7933-2168-9) Gallopade Pub Group.

Virginia Slave-Trade Statistics, 1698-1775. Ed. by Walter Minchinton et al. xvi, 218p. (Orig.). 1984. 45.00 (0-88490-118-1) Library of VA.

Virginia Soldiers in the United States Army, 1800-1815. Stuart L. Butler. 188p. (Orig.). 1986. pap. 17.00 (0-935931-25-2) Borgo Pr.

Virginia Soldiers in the United States Army, 1800-1815. Stuart L. Butler. LC 86-206651. 188p. (Orig.). (C). 1986. reprint ed. lib. bdg. 43.00 (0-8095-8204-X) Borgo Pr.

Virginia Soldiers of Seventeen Seventy-Six: Compiled from Documents in the Virginia Land Office, 3 vols., Set. Louis A. Burgess. 1514p. 1994. reprint ed. pap. 125.00 (0-685-75084-1, 790) Clearfield Co.

Virginia Soldiers of the American Revolution, 2 vols. Hamilton J. Eckenrode. 1989. reprint ed. Set: Vol. 1, 488p.; Vol. 2, 335p. text ed. 25.00 (0-88490-164-5) Library of VA.

Virginia Sorensen. L. L. Lee & Sylvia Lee. LC 78-52559. (Western Writers Ser.: No. 31). 50p. 1978. pap. 4.95 (0-88430-055-2) Boise St U W Writ Ser.

Virginia State Atlas. Gousha, H. H., Editors. 1996. pap. 7.95 (0-671-52253-1, H M Gousha) P-H Gen Ref & Trav.

Virginia State Government: Fun, Frustrating, & Frightening. William E. Porter. LC 92-44977. 1993. 37.50 (0-8191-9031-4); pap. 18.50 (0-8191-9032-2) U Pr of Amer.

Virginia State Line & State Rangers. Jeff Weaver & Randall Osborne. (Virginia Regimental Histories Ser.). (Illus.). 294p. 1994. 25.00 (1-56190-058-3) H E Howard.

Virginia State Parks: A Guide to Virginia State Parks. Bill Bailey. 300p. 1996. pap. 14.95 (1-881139-14-X) Glovebox Guidebks.

Virginia State Rules of Evidence with Objections. Anthony J. Bocchino et al. 249p. 1995. pap. 16.95 (1-55681-396-1) Natl Inst Trial Ad.

Virginia Statistical Abstract. (Statistical Ser.). 1989. 18.00 (0-318-40069-3) U VA Ctr Pub Serv.

Virginia Statistical Abstract, 1987. 1987. 12.54 (0-685-61059-4) U VA Ctr Pub Serv.

Virginia Statistical Abstract, 1992-93. 1992. 36.58 (0-685-61055-1) U VA Ctr Pub Serv.

Virginia Statute for Religious Freedom: Its Evolution & Consequences in American History. Ed. by Merrill D. Peterson & Robert C. Vaughan. LC 87-13786. (Cambridge Studies in Religious & American Public Life: 1). (Illus.). 420p. 1988. text ed. 49.95 (0-521-34329-1) Cambridge U Pr.

Virginia Supreme Court: An Institutional & Political Analysis. Thomas R. Morris. LC 75-1158. 207p. reprint ed. pap. 59.00 (0-8357-2714-9, 2039828) Bks Demand.

Virginia Survival. Betty L. Hall & Frank D. Kizer. 160p. (Orig.). (gr. 10-12). 1979. pap. text ed. 5.84 (0-03-046991-0) Westwood Pr.

Virginia Tech - Then & Now. Photos by Charles Shoffner. (Illus.). 112p. 1991. 39.00 (0-916509-78-8) Harmony Hse Pub.

Virginia, the Gray & the Green. Ned Conquest. LC 90-83455. 160p. 1990. 19.95 (0-9627485-1-X) Apollonian Pr.

Virginia Tidal & Coastal Law. Butler & Livingston. 913p. 1988. 85.00 (0-87473-319-7) MICHIE.

Virginia Tidal & Coastal Law. Lynda L. Butler & Margit Livingston. 913p. 1988. 85.00 (0-614-05993-3) MICHIE.

U V

Virginia Timeline: A Chronology of Virginia History, Mystery, Trivia, Legend, Lore & More. Carole Marsh. (Virginia Bks.). (Illus.). (J). (gr. 3-12). 1994. pap. 19.95 (*0-7933-6014-5*); lib. bdg. 29.95 (*0-7933-6013-7*); disk 29.95 (*0-7933-6015-3*) Gallopade Pub Group.

Virginia Title Examiners' Manual. Sydney F. Parham. 517p. 1977. Nineteen Seventy-Seven suppl. only. suppl. ed. 15.00 (*0-87215-290-1*) MICHIE.

Virginia Title Examiners' Manual. rev. ed. Sydney F. Parham. 517p. 1973. Incl. 1977 cumulative suppl. suppl. ed. 35.00 (*0-87215-151-4*) MICHIE.

Virginia Title Examiner's Manual. 2nd ed. Douglass W. Dewing. 661p. 1992. 75.00 (*0-87473-998-5*) MICHIE.

Virginia Torts Case Finder. 3rd ed. Brien A. Roche. 863p. 1994. 90.00 (*1-55834-161-7*) MICHIE.

Virginia Torts Case Finder: With 1992 Cumulative Supplement. 2nd ed. Brien A. Roche. 792p. 1990. 80.00 (*0-87473-652-8*) MICHIE.

Virginia Torts Case Finder: With 1992 Cumulative Supplement. 2nd ed. Brien A. Roche. 792p. 1992. suppl. ed. 27.50 (*0-87473-979-9*) MICHIE.

Virginia Trivia. rev. ed. Ernie Couch & Jill Couch. LC 91-36309. 192p. (Orig.). 1991. pap. 6.95 (*1-55853-139-4*) Rutledge Hill Pr.

Virginia Trout Streams: A Guide to Fishing the Blue Ridge Watershed. 2nd expanded ed. Harry Slone. (Illus.). 208p. (Orig.). 1994. pap. 15.00 (*0-88150-306-1*, Backcountry) Countryman.

Virginia under Charles I & Cromwell, 1625-1660. Wilcomb E. Washburn. (Illus.). 64p. 1993. reprint ed. pap. 9.50 (*0-685-69947-1*, 9494) Clearfield Co.

Virginia Updikes-Updykes. Robert S. Craig. 1050p. 1985. 40.00 (*0-9615135-0-0*) Craig Pub Hse.

***Virginia Valley Records: Genealogical & Historical Materials of Rockingham County, Virginia & Related Regions.** John W. Wayland. 491p. 1996. reprint ed. pap. 36.50 (*0-614-23604-5*, 6180) Clearfield Co.

Virginia Vets & Widows Census, 1890. Ronald V. Jackson. 1992. 65.00 (*0-89593-862-6*) Accelerated Index.

***Virginia Vineyards & Their Wines.** William Whitman. (Virginia Heritage Ser.: Vol. 5). (Orig.). 1997. pap. 10.95 (*1-885937-05-9*, Virginia Heritage) Casco Commns.

Virginia Votes, 1979-1982. Larry J. Sabato. 205p. 1984. 8.50 (*0-318-04159-6*) U VA Ctr Pub Serv.

Virginia Votes, 1983-1986. Larry J. Sabato. 225p. 1987. pap. 12.00 (*0-317-60300-0*) U VA Ctr Pub Serv.

Virginia Votes, 1987-1990. Larry J. Sabato. 1990. 18.81 (*0-685-61060-8*) U VA Ctr Pub Serv.

Virginia-W. Virginia Automotive Directory. Ed. by T. L. Spelman. 1985. 24.95 (*1-55527-032-8*) Auto Contact Inc.

Virginia-Washington DC Business Directory. CJS, Inc. Staff. 608p. (Orig.). 1995. pap. write for info. (*1-882538-53-6*) CJS.

Virginia, West Virginia, & Maryland. David Emblidge. (Appalachian Trail Companions Ser.). (Illus.). 416p. 1998. pap. 19.95 (*0-8117-2670-3*) Stackpole.

Virginia-West Virginia Genealogical Data from Revolutionary War Pension on Bounty Land Warrant Records, Vol. 4. Patrick G. Wardell. 345p. 1995. pap. text ed. 25.00 (*0-7884-0106-8*) Heritage Bk.

Virginia White Water. H. Roger Corbett, Jr. 1988. pap. text ed. 12.50 (*0-686-22838-3*) Seneca Pr Rockville.

Virginia Wildlife Viewing Guide. Mark D. Duda. LC 94-19271. (Falcon Guides Ser.). (Illus.). 96p. (Orig.). 1994. pap. 8.95 (*1-56044-292-1*) Falcon Pr MT.

Virginia Wills & Administrations, 1632-1800. Clayton Torrence. LC 65-29031. 483p. 1995. reprint ed. 25.00 (*0-8063-0328-X*) Genealog Pub.

Virginia Wills Before Seventeen Ninety-Nine: A Complete Abstract Register of All Names Mentioned in over 600 Recorded Wills. William M. Clemens. 107p. 1986. 10.00 (*0-8063-0461-8*, 1030) Genealog Pub.

Virginia Wolf's Rediscovered Essays: Sources & Allusions. Elizabeth Steele. LC 86-5725. (Library of the Humanities). 256p. 1987. text ed. 20.00 (*0-8240-8527-2*) Garland.

Virginia Women: The First Two Hundred Years. Anne F. Scott & Suzanne Lebsock. (Foundations of America Ser.). (Illus.). 39p. (Orig.). 1988. pap. 9.95 (*0-87935-076-8*) Colonial Williamsburg.

Virginia Woolf. Intro. by Harold Bloom. (Modern Critical Views Series). 274p. 1986. 34.95 (*0-87754-673-8*) Chelsea Hse.

Virginia Woolf. Ed. by Rachel Bowlby. (Critical Readers Ser.). 232p. (C). 1993. pap. text ed. 19.95 (*0-582-06151-2*) Longman.

Virginia Woolf. Susan Dick. 128p. 1989. pap. 9.95 (*0-7131-6561-8*, A3521, Pub. by E Arnold UK) Routledge Chapman & Hall.

Virginia Woolf. Clare Hanson. 1994. text ed. 29.95 (*0-312-06060-2*) St Martin.

Virginia Woolf. James King. (Illus.). 720p. 1995. 35.00 (*0-393-03748-7*) Norton.

***Virginia Woolf.** Hermoine Lee. 893p. 1998. pap. 39.95 (*0-375-70136-2*, Vin) Random.

***Virginia Woolf.** Ed. by Robin Majumdar & Aden McLauren. (Critical Heritage Ser.). 484p. (C). 1997. text ed. 35.00 (*0-415-15914-8*) Routledge.

Virginia Woolf. Laura Marcus. 1990. 50.00 (*0-7463-0721-7*, Pub. by Northcote House UK) St Mut.

Virginia Woolf. Laura Marcus. (Writers & Their Work Ser.). 144p. (Orig.). 1997. pap. 19.00 (*0-7463-0726-8*, Pub. by Nrthcote House UK) U Pr of Miss.

Virginia Woolf. John Mepham. LC 92-22238. (Criticism in Focus Ser.). 1992. text ed. 29.95 (*0-312-08603-2*) St Martin.

Virginia Woolf. Michael Rosenthal. 270p. 1987. pap. text ed. 17.00 (*0-231-04849-1*, King's Crown Paperbacks) Col U Pr.

Virginia Woolf. Carl R. Woodring. LC 66-19554. (Columbia Essays on Modern Writers Ser.: No. 18). (Orig.). (C). 1966. pap. text ed. 10.00 (*0-231-02829-6*) Col U Pr.

Virginia Woolf. David Daiches. LC 78-12655. 169p. 1979. reprint ed. text ed. 35.00 (*0-313-21187-6*, DAVW, Greenwood Pr) Greenwood.

***Virginia Woolf: A Biography.** Hermione Lee. 1997. 39.95 (*0-679-44707-5*) Knopf.

Virginia Woolf: A Biography. Quentin Bell. LC 73-12870. (Illus.). 530p. 1974. reprint ed. pap. 19.95 (*0-15-693580-5*, Harvest Bks) HarBrace.

Virginia Woolf: A Collection of Critical Essays (20th Century Views) Margaret Homans. 256p. 1992. pap. 12.95 (*0-13-953209-9*) P-H.

Virginia Woolf: A Critical Reading. Avrom Fleishman. LC 74-24375. (Illus.). 248p. 1977. pap. 14.95 (*0-8018-1958-X*) Johns Hopkins.

Virginia Woolf: A Feminist Slant. Ed. by Jane Marcus. LC 82-24787. 296p. reprint ed. pap. 84.40 (*0-8357-4129-X*, 2057064) Bks Demand.

Virginia Woolf: A Literary Life. John Mepham. LC 91-9081. (Literary Lives Ser.). 240p. 1991. text ed. 29.95 (*0-312-06204-4*) St Martin.

Virginia Woolf: A Writer's Life. Lyndall Gordon. 360p. 1993. pap. 11.95 (*0-393-31061-2*) Norton.

Virginia Woolf: An Illustrated Anthology. Virginia Woolf. (Illus.). 1995. 2.99 (*0-517-14251-1*) Random Hse Value.

Virginia Woolf: Centennial Papers. Ed. by Elaine Ginsberg & Laura Moss Gottlieb. LC 82-50826. 336p. 1984. 25.00 (*0-87875-242-0*) Whitston Pub.

Virginia Woolf: Critical Assesments, 4 vols., Set. Ed. by Eleanor McNees. (Critical Assessments of Writers in English Ser.). (Illus.). 1900p. (C). (gr. 13 up). 1994. boxed, text ed. 549.95 (*1-873403-06-2*) Routledge Chapman & Hall.

Virginia Woolf: Dramatic Novelist. Jane Wheare. LC 88-18829. 224p. 1989. text ed. 39.95 (*0-312-02449-5*) St Martin.

***Virginia Woolf: Feminism, Creativity & the Unconscious.** John R. Maze. LC 97-5857. (Contributions to the Study of World Literature: Vol. 84). 1997. text ed. write for info. (*0-313-30283-9*, Greenwood Pr) Greenwood.

Virginia Woolf: Four Great Novels. Virginia Woolf. (C). pap. write for info. (*0-19-282287-X*) OUP.

Virginia Woolf: Interviews & Recollections. Ed. by J. H. Stape. LC 94-61439. 216p. 1995. 19.95 (*0-87745-494-9*) U of Iowa Pr.

***Virginia Woolf: Lesbian Readings.** Eileen Barrett & Patricia Cramer. LC 97-4667. (Cutting Edge Ser.). 1997. 55.00 (*0-8147-1263-0*); pap. 18.95 (*0-8147-1264-9*) NYU Pr.

Virginia Woolf: Reflections & Reverberations. Marilyn Kurtz. (American University Studies: English Language & Literature: Ser. IV, Vol. 119). 164p. (C). 1991. text ed. 39.50 (*0-8204-1328-3*) P Lang Pubng.

***Virginia Woolf: Reflexive Frames.** Oddvar Holmesland. 1997. 55.00 (*1-57113-147-7*) Camden Hse.

Virginia Woolf: Strategist of Language. William A. Evans. LC 88-14380. 272p. (Orig.). (C). 1989. pap. text ed. 24.00 (*0-8191-7007-0*) U Pr of Amer.

Virginia Woolf: Texts & Contexts. Ed. by Beth R. Daugherty & Eileen Barrett. LC 96-18435. (Selected Papers from the Fifth Annual Conference). 484p. 1996. pap. 37.50 (*0-944473-28-8*) Pace Univ Pr.

Virginia Woolf: Texts & Contexts. Ed. by Beth R. Daugherty & Eileen Barrett. LC 96-18435. (Selected Papers from the Fifth Annual Conference). 484p. 1996. 69.50 (*0-944473-27-X*) Pace Univ Pr.

***Virginia Woolf: The Common Ground.** Gillian Beer. LC 96-40084. (Orig.). 1997. pap. text ed. 16.95 (*0-472-08463-1*) U of Mich Pr.

Virginia Woolf: The Critical Heritage. Ed. by Robin Majumader & Allen McLaurin. (Critical Heritage Ser.). 1975. 69.50 (*0-7100-8138-3*, RKP) Routledge.

Virginia Woolf: The Frames of Art & Life. C. Ruth Miller. LC 88-4440. 176p. 1988. text ed. 39.95 (*0-312-01914-9*) St Martin.

Virginia Woolf: The Impact of Childhood Sexual Abuse on Her Life & Work. Louise DeSalvo. 400p. 1990. pap. 14.50 (*0-345-36639-5*, Ballantine Trade) Ballantine.

Virginia Woolf see Modern Critical Views Series

***Virginia Woolf A to Z: A Comprehensive Reference for Students, Teachers, & Common Readers to Her Life, Work, & Critical Reception.** Mark Hussey. (Illus.). 464p. 1996. pap. 19.95 (*0-19-511027-7*) OUP.

Virginia Woolf A-Z: A Comprehensive Reference for Students, Teachers, & Common Readers to Her Life, Work & Critical Reception. Mark Hussey. 464p. 1995. 50.00 (*0-8160-3020-0*) Facts on File.

Virginia Woolf Against Empire. Kathy J. Phillips. (Illus.). 312p. (C). 1994. text ed. 34.95 (*0-87049-833-9*) U of Tenn Pr.

Virginia Woolf & Her Circle: Manuscripts, Books, & Images from the Berg Collection. Ed. by Francis O. Mattson. (Illus.). 72p. 1993. pap. 11.95 (*0-87104-434-X*) NY Pub Lib.

Virginia Woolf & London: The Sexual Politics of the City. Susan M. Squier. LC 84-17376. xii, 220p. 1985. text ed. 32.50 (*0-8078-1637-X*) U of NC Pr.

Virginia Woolf & Mrs. Brown: Toward a Realism of Uncertainty. Herta Newman. LC 96-3370. (Origins of Modernism Ser.: Vol. 03). 168p. 1996. text ed. 25.00 (*0-8240-5172-6*, H1328) Garland.

Virginia Woolf & Postmodernism: Literature in Quest & Question of Itself. Pamela L. Caughie. 256p. 1991. text ed. 39.95 (*0-252-01763-3*) U of Ill Pr.

Virginia Woolf & Samuel Johnson: Common Readers. Beth C. Rosenberg. LC 94-27520. 1995. text ed. 39.95 (*0-312-10741-2*) St Martin.

***Virginia Woolf & the Arts: Selected Papers from the Sixth Annual Conference on Virginia Woolf, Clemson University, Clemson, South Carolina, June 13-16, 1996.** Conference on Virginia Woolf Staff et al. LC 97-14185. 1997. write for info. (*0-944473-33-4*); pap. write for info. (*0-944473-34-2*) Pace Univ Pr.

***Virginia Woolf & the Essay.** Beth C. Rosenberg & Jeanne Dubino. LC 97-21442. 1998. write for info. (*0-312-17233-8*) St Martin.

Virginia Woolf & the Fictions of Psychoanalysis. Elizabeth Abel. LC 89-4810. (Women in Culture & Society Ser.). 200p. 1989. 29.95 (*0-226-00079-6*) U Ch Pr.

Virginia Woolf & the Fictions of Psychoanalysis. Elizabeth Abel. LC 89-4810. (Women in Culture & Society Ser.). xviii, 200p. (C). 1992. pap. text ed. 13.95 (*0-226-00081-8*) U Ch Pr.

Virginia Woolf & the "Lust of Creation" A Psychoanalytic Exploration. Shirley Panken. LC 86-29991. 336p. 1987. text ed. 64.50 (*0-88706-200-8*); pap. text ed. 24.95 (*0-88706-201-6*) State U NY Pr.

Virginia Woolf & the Nature of Communion. Betty Kushen. 252p. 1985. 20.00 (*0-9615069-0-3*) Raynor Pr.

Virginia Woolf & the Politics of Style. Pamela J. Transue. LC 85-27952. 222p. (Orig.). (C). 1986. text ed. 64.50 (*0-88706-286-5*); pap. text ed. 21.95 (*0-88706-287-3*) State U NY Pr.

Virginia Woolf & the Problem of the Subject. Makiko Minow-Pinkney. LC 86-26023. 224p. 1987. reprint ed. pap. 63.90 (*0-608-02329-9*, 2062970) Bks Demand.

Virginia Woolf & the Problem of the Subject: Feminine Writing in the Major Novels. Makiko Minow-Pinkney. (Douglass Series on Women's Lives & the Meaning of Gender). 300p. (C). 1987. text ed. 40.00 (*0-8135-1226-3*) Rutgers U Pr.

Virginia Woolf & the Real World. Alex Zwerdling. LC 85-24513. 375p. 1986. pap. 11.00 (*0-520-06184-5*) U CA Pr.

Virginia Woolf & War: Fiction, Reality, & Myth. Intro. by Mark Hussey. LC 91-10235. (Syracuse Studies on Peace & Conflict Resolution). 296p. (C). 1991. text ed. 39.95 (*0-8156-2537-5*) Syracuse U Pr.

Virginia Woolf & War: Fiction, Reality, & Myth. Ed. by Mark Hussey. (Contemporary Issues in the Middle East Ser.). 290p. 1992. pap. text ed. 16.95 (*0-8156-2584-7*) Syracuse U Pr.

Virginia Woolf Chronology. Edward L. Bishop. 192p. 1988. 40.00 (*0-8161-8982-X*, Hall Reference) Macmillan.

Virginia Woolf: Emerging Perspectives: Selected Papers from the Third Annual Conference on Virginia Woolf. Vara Neverow-Turk. Ed. by Mark Hussey. 340p. (Orig.). 1994. lib. bdg. 64.50 (*0-944473-16-4*) Pace Univ Pr.

Virginia Woolf: Emerging Perspectives: Selected Papers from the Third Annual Conference on Virginia Woolf. Ed. by Vara Neverow-Turk & Mark Hussey. 340p. (Orig.). 1994. pap. 34.50 (*0-944473-17-2*) Pace Univ Pr.

Virginia Woolf for Beginners. Aaron Rosenblatt. (Writers & Readers Documentary Comic Bks.). (Illus.). (Orig.). (YA). (gr. 11 up). 1987. pap. 7.95 (*0-86316-133-2*) Writers & Readers.

Virginia Woolf Manuscripts: From the Henry W. & Albert Berg Collection at the New York Public Library. 48p. (C). 1994. 70.00 (*0-89235-154-3*) Primary Srce Media.

Virginia Woolf Miscellanies: Proceedings of the First Annual Conference on Virginia Woolf. Ed. by Mark Hussey & Vara Neverow-Turk. (Illus.). 260p. (Orig.). (C). 1992. pap. text ed. 29.50 (*0-944473-09-1*) Pace Univ Pr.

Virginia Woolf Miscellanies: Proceedings of the First Annual Conference on Virginia Woolf. Ed. by Mark Hussey & Vara Neverow-Turk. (Illus.). 260p. (Orig.). (C). 1992. lib. bdg. 54.50 (*0-944473-08-3*) Pace Univ Pr.

Virginia Woolf Poems. Jackson MacLow. 44p. 1985. pap. 5.00 (*0-930901-28-2*) Burning Deck.

Virginia Woolf Reader. Virginia Woolf. Ed. by Mitchell A. Leaska. LC 84-4478. 384p. 1984. pap. 14.00 (*0-15-693590-2*, Harvest Bks) HarBrace.

***Virginia Woolf, "The Hours" The British Museum Manuscript of Mrs. Dalloway.** Ed. by Helen M. Wussow. LC 96-9653. 528p. (C). 1997. 57.00 (*0-944473-29-6*) Pace Univ Pr.

Virginia Woolf's "Between the Acts" & Jane Harrison's Con-spiracy. Patricia Maika. Ed. by A. Walton Litz. LC 87-13897. (Studies in Modern Literature: No. 78). 102p. reprint ed. 29.10 (*0-8357-1818-2*, 2070736) Bks Demand.

Virginia Woolf's London. Dorothy Brewster. LC 78-26590. 120p. 1979. reprint ed. text ed. 35.00 (*0-313-20788-7*, BRVW, Greenwood Pr) Greenwood.

Virginia Woolf's Quarrel with Grieving. Mark Spilka. LC 80-11792. 154p. reprint ed. pap. 43.90 (*0-7837-4658-X*, 2044382) Bks Demand.

Virginia Woolf's Reading Notebooks. Brenda R. Silver. LC 81-47156. 400p. reprint ed. pap. 114.00 (*0-7837-6498-7*, 2046588) Bks Demand.

***Virginia Woolf's Renaissance: Woman Reader or Common Reader?** Juliet Dusinberre. LC 96-61309. 288p. 1997. 29.95 (*0-87745-576-7*); pap. 14.95 (*0-87745-577-5*) U of Iowa Pr.

Virginia Woolf's Subject & the Subject of Ethics: Notes Toward a Poetics of Persons. Steven Schroeder. LC 95-32134. 256p. 1996. write for info. (*0-7734-8923-1*) E Mellen.

Virginia Woolf's "The Years" The Evolution of a Novel. Grace Radin. LC 80-22590. 212p. 1981. 29.00 (*0-87049-307-8*) U of Tenn Pr.

Virginia Woolf's "To the Lighthouse" Suzanne Raitt. LC 90-46984. (Critical Studies of Key Texts). 143p. 1990. pap. 12.95 (*0-312-05655-9*); text ed. 39.95 (*0-312-05654-0*) St Martin.

Virginia Workers' Compensation: Law & Practice. Lawrence J. Pascal. 1986. 55.00 (*0-87473-256-5*) MICHIE.

Virginia Workers' Compensation: Law & Practice. Lawrence J. Pascal. 1991. suppl. ed. 20.00 (*0-87473-914-4*) MICHIE.

Virginia Workers' Compensation: Law & Practice. 2nd ed. Lawrence J. Pascal. 378p. 1993. 75.00 (*1-55834-027-0*) MICHIE.

Virginia Workers' Compensation Case Finder. Peter M. Sweeny. 354p. 1990. 75.00 (*0-87473-616-1*) MICHIE.

Virginian. Owen Wister. (Airmont Classics Ser.). (J). (gr. 8 up). 1964. mass mkt. 2.95 (*0-8049-0046-9*, CL-46) Airmont.

Virginian. Owen Wister. (J). 1997. pap. 2.95 (*0-8167-0849-5*) Troll Communs.

Virginian. Owen Wister. 505p. 1984. pap. 8.95 (*0-8065-0923-6*, Citadel Pr) Carol Pub Group.

Virginian. Owen Wister. 352p. 1979. pap. 6.95 (*0-451-52325-3*, Sig Classics) NAL-Dutton.

Virginian. Owen Wister. 1983. pap. 3.95 (*0-671-46757-3*, WSP) PB.

Virginian. Owen Wister. 512p. 1988. pap. 10.95 (*0-14-039065-0*, Penguin Classics) Viking Penguin.

***Virginian.** Owen Wister. 30.00 (*0-614-30545-4*) NAVH.

Virginian: A Horseman of the Plains. large type ed. Owen Wister. LC 93-33399. 1993. lib. bdg. 21.95 (*0-8161-5888-6*, GK Hall) Thorndike Pr.

Virginian: A Horseman of the Plains. Owen Wister. LC 92-13728. (Illus.). xxii, 452p. 1992. reprint ed. pap. 12.95 (*0-8032-9736-X*, Bison Books) U of Nebr Pr.

Virginian & Ohio Story. Allen McClelland. (Illus.). 104p. 1983. pap. 19.95 (*0-911868-47-X*, C47) Carstens Pubns.

Virginian at Venncombe. large type ed. Audrey Blanshard. (Historical Romance Ser.). 336p. 1993. 25.99 (*0-7089-2946-X*) Ulverscroft.

***Virginian Era.** Lloyd D. Lewis. (Illus.). 60p. 1996. pap. 14.95 (*0-9622003-9-5*) TLC VA.

Virginian History of African Colonization. Philip Slaughter. LC 71-138346. (Black Heritage Library Collection). 1977. 20.95 (*0-8369-8738-1*) Ayer.

Virginian in Yankeeland Vol. 1: Introduction to the Yankee Tier. Benjamin E. Dean. LC 88-72097. (Illus.). 659p. 1989. pap. text ed. 25.00 (*0-9621451-0-6*) B E Dean Co.

Virginian in Yankeeland Vol. 2: Merriwell Road Through Kangaroo Gate. Benjamin E. Dean. LC 88-72097. (Illus.). 739p. (Orig.). 1989. pap. text ed. 25.00 (*0-9621451-1-4*) B E Dean Co.

Virginian in Yankeeland Vol. 3: Of Monkeys, Quinine, & Magnetos....Linked. Benjamin E. Dean. LC 88-72097. (Illus.). 400p. (Orig.). 1990. pap. text ed. 19.00 (*0-9621451-2-2*) B E Dean Co.

Virginian in Yankeeland Vol. 4: Some Stars & Stripes Voyages. Benjamin E. Dean. LC 88-72097. (Illus.). 950p. (Orig.). 1991. pap. text ed. 29.95 (*0-9621451-3-0*) B E Dean Co.

Virginian in Yankeeland Vol. 5: Quest for Knowledge. Benjamin E. Dean. LC 88-72097. (Illus.). 800p. (Orig.). 1992. pap. text ed. 29.00 (*0-9621451-4-9*) B E Dean Co.

Virginian in Yankeeland Vol. 6: Fishy Political Environment. Benjamin E. Dean. LC 88-72097. (Illus.). 700p. (Orig.). 1994. pap. 28.00 (*0-9621451-5-7*) B E Dean Co.

Virginian in Yankeeland Vol. 7: Treachery at Village Hall. Benjamin E. Dean. LC 88-72097. (Illus.). 700p. (Orig.). 1998. pap. 28.50 (*0-9621451-6-5*) B E Dean Co.

***Virginian Railway Locomotives.** Lloyd D. Lewis. (Illus.). 76p. 1996. pap. 15.95 (*1-883089-05-0*) TLC VA.

Virginian Village, & Other Papers. Ehrman S. Nadal. LC 68-20324. (Essay Index Reprint Ser.). 1977. 20.95 (*0-8369-0733-7*) Ayer.

Virginiana in the Printed Book Collections of the Virginia State Library, 2 vols. Ed. by Donald Haynes. LC 75-622711. 1975. 100.00 (*0-88490-031-2*) Library of VA.

Virginiana in the Printed Book Collections of the Virginia State Library, 2 vols, Vol. 1. Ed. by Donald Haynes. v, 657p. 1975. write for info. (*0-318-56314-2*) Library of VA.

Virginiana in the Printed Book Collections of the Virginia State Library, 2 vols, Vol. 2. Ed. by Donald Haynes. ii, 630p. 1975. write for info. (*0-318-56315-0*) Library of VA.

Virginians All. Carlo Uchello. LC 92-13634. (Illus.). 144p. (YA). (gr. 7-9). 1992. 11.95 (*0-88289-853-1*) Pelican.

Virginians & West Virginians, 1607-1870, Vol. 2. Patrick G. Wardell. vi, 589p. 1988. 30.00 (*1-55613-112-7*) Heritage Bk.

Virginians & West Virginians 1607-1870, Vol. 3. Patrick G. Wardell. 1184p. 1992. pap. 70.00 (*1-55613-564-5*) Heritage Bk.

Virginians at Home: Family Life in the Eighteenth Century. Edmund S. Morgan. LC 52-14250. (America Ser.: Vol. 2). (Illus.). 101p. (Orig.). 1952. 14.95 (*0-910412-52-9*) Colonial Williamsburg.

Virginians' Guide to the Nineteen Ninety Census: Getting, Using, & Understanding Census Data. (Census Analysis Series, 1990: Report No. 1). 1991. 4.18 (*0-685-61072-1*) U VA Ctr Pub Serv.

Virginia's Best Secret Recipes. Young Homemakers of Virginia Staff. LC 88-29220. 1989. pap. 9.95 (*0-87197-244-1*) Favorite Recipes.

Virginia's Blues, Gospel, & Country Records, 1902-1943. Kip Lornell. LC 89-5613. 248p. 1989. 27.00 (*0-8131-1658-9*) U Pr of Ky.

Virginia's Civil War Battlefields. Peter Lockwood. (Virginia Heritage Ser.). 72p. 1995. pap. 7.95 (*1-885937-01-6*) Casco Commns.

Virginia's Constitutional Convention of 1901-1902. Wythe Holt. LC 90-42477. (Distinguished Studies in American Legal & Constitutional History). 282p. 1990. reprint ed. text ed. 15.00 (*0-8240-2570-9*) Garland.

An Asterisk (*) at the beginning of an entry indicates that the title is appearing in BIP for the first time.

*__Virginia's Country Stores - a Quiet Passing.__ Joseph E. Morse. LC 96-47597. (Illus.). 128p. 1997. boxed 24.95 (1-880664-19-4) E M Pr.

Virginia's Eastern Shore: A History of Northampton & Accomack Counties, 2 vols. Ralph T. Whitelaw. LC 89-3883. (Illus.). 1511p. reprint ed. Set. 89.50 (0-929539-47-8, 1147) Picton Pr.

Virginia's Endangered Species. Compiled by Karen Terwilliger. (Illus.). vii, 680p. 1991. 69.95 (0-939923-16-5); pap. 39.95 (0-939923-17-3) M & W Pub Co.

Virginia's Executive Mansion. William Seale. xiv, 206p. 1988. text ed. 25.00 (0-88490-152-1); pap. text ed. 5.95 (0-88490-153-X) Library of VA.

Virginia's General: Robert E. Lee and the Civil War. Albert Marrin. LC 94-13353. (J). 1994. 22.00 (0-689-31838-3, Atheneum Bks Young) S&S Childrens.

Virginia's Ghosts: Haunted Historic House Tours. L. B. Taylor, Jr. (Virginia Heritage Ser.). 72p. 1995. pap. 7.95 (1-885937-02-4) Casco Commns.

Virginia's Historic Courthouses. Margaret T. Peters & John O. Peters. LC 94-41510. (Illus.). 246p. (C). 1995. 39.95 (0-8139-1604-6) U Pr of Va.

Virginia's Historic Restaurants & Their Recipes. 2nd rev. ed. Dawn O'Brien. LC 84-2801. (Illus.). 205p. 1990. 14.95 (0-89587-068-1) Blair.

Virginia's Local Economies. 1990. Set, 30 Reports. 156.75 (0-685-61069-1); Individual Reports. 7.32 (0-318-69549-9) U VA Ctr Pub Serv.

Virginia's Massive Resistance. Benjamin Muse. 1990. 14.50 (0-8446-0816-5) Peter Smith.

Virginia's (Most Devastating!) Disasters & (Most Calamitous!) Catastrophies! Carole Marsh. (Carole Marsh Virginia Bks.). (Illus.). (J). 1994. pap. 19.95 (0-7933-1150-0); lib. bdg. 29.95 (0-7933-2193-X); disk 29.95 (0-7933-2194-8) Gallopade Pub Group.

Virginia's Natural Bridge. Joseph Curreri. (Illus.). 32p. 1984. 18.00 (0-88014-054-2) Mosaic Pr OH.

Virginia's Ninth President: Joseph Jenkins Roberts. Ed. by Calvert W. Tazewell. LC 90-80507. (Illus.). 62p. (Orig.). 1992. pap. 7.00 (1-878515-23-3) W S Dawson.

Virginia's Shenandoah Valley. Greg Mock. LC 90-289. (Illus.). 104p. (Orig.). 1990. pap. 15.95 (0-938314-83-1) Am Wrld Geog.

Virginia's State Government During the Second World War: Its Constitutional, Legislative, & Administrative Adaptations, 1942-1945. Francis H. Heller. LC 50-9206. xvii, 203p. 1949. 24.95 (0-88490-041-X) Library of VA.

Virginia's True Founder: Edward Maria Wingfield & His Times. Jocelyn R. Wingfield. (Illus.). xxiii, 448p. (C). 1993. 50.00 incl. 5.25 hd (0-937543-04-7) Wingfield Family Soc.

Virginia's Unsolved Mysteries (& Their "Solutions") Includes Scientific Information & Other Activities for Students. Carole Marsh. (Virginia Bks.). (Illus.). (J). (gr. 3-12). 1994. pap. 19.95 (0-7933-5861-2); lib. bdg. 29.95 (0-7933-5860-4); disk 29.95 (0-7933-5862-0) Gallopade Pub Group.

*__Virginias/DC Travel Smart Trip Planner.__ Kathleen L. Pond. (Travel Smart Trip Planner Ser.). 240p. (Orig.). 1998. pap. 14.95 (1-56261-316-2) John Muir.

*__Virginia/West Virginia Husbands & Wives, Vol. 2.__ Patrick G. Wardell. x, 466p. 1996. 43.00 (0-7884-0501-2, W070) Heritage Bk.

Virginibus Puerisque, & Other Papers. Robert Louis Stevenson. 1977. text ed. 17.95 (0-8369-7328-3, 8121) Ayer.

*__Virginie: Her Two Lives.__ John Hawkes. 7.95 (0-7867-0054-8) Carroll & Graf.

Virginie: Her Two Lives. John Hawkes. 256p. 1983. pap. 7.95 (0-88184-054-8) Carroll & Graf.

Virginie: Her Two Lives. deluxe limited ed. John Hawkes. LC 81-48054. 256p. 1982. 75.00 (0-8112-0840-0) New Directions.

Virginity: A Positive Approach to Celibacy for the Sake of the Kingdom of Heaven. Raniero Cantalamessa. Tr. by Charles Serignat from ITA. LC 95-32603. 124p. (Orig.). (YA). (gr. 10 up). 1995. pap. 5.50 (0-8189-0745-2) Alba.

Virginius Affair. Richard H. Bradford. LC 20-520000. (Illus.). 198p. reprint ed. pap. 56.50 (0-8357-5509-6, 2035124) Bks Demand.

Virgins & Martyrs. Simon Maginn. 1996. pap. 5.99 (1-56504-923-3, 13302, Borealis) White Wolf.

Virgins & Other Endangered Species: A Memoir. Dorothea Straus. 228p. 1994. pap. 11.95 (1-55921-118-0) Moyer Bell.

Virgins & Viragos: A History of Women in Scotland from 1080-1980. Rosalind K. Marshall. (Illus.). 340p. 1983. pap. 10.00 (0-89733-075-7) Academy Chi Pubs.

Virgin's Children: Life in an Aztec Village Today. William Madsen. LC 74-88900. 248p. 1970. reprint ed. text ed. 65.00 (0-8371-2098-5, MAVC, Greenwood Pr) Greenwood.

Virgins of God: The Making of Asceticism in Late Antiquity. Susanna Elm. (Classical Monographs). 302p. 1994. 79.00 (0-19-814920-4) OUP.

"Virgins of God" The Making of Asceticism in Late Antiquity. Susanna Elm. (Oxford Classical Monographs). (Illus.). 464p. (C). 1996. pap. 24.95 (0-19-815044-X) OUP.

Virgins of Paradise. Barbara Wood. 592p. 1994. mass mkt. 5.99 (0-380-72340-9) Avon.

Virgins of the Sun. Al Ray. 908p. 1992. 24.95 (0-931662-08-7) Photo-Go Pr.

*__Virgin's Triangle.__ (Caribbean Writers Ser.). 1997. pap. 13.95 (0-435-98947-2) Heinemann.

Virgintooth. Mark S. Ivanhoe. (Illus.). 192p. (Orig.). 1991. pap. 7.00 (0-9622937-3-3) III Pub.

Virgo. (Super Horoscopes, 1995 Ser.). 256p. 1994. pap. text ed. 4.99 (0-7865-0031-X) Diamond.

Virgo. (Total Horoscopes, 1995 Ser.). 272p. 1994. pap. text ed. 4.50 (0-515-11416-2) Jove Pubns.

Virgo. (Love Signs Library). 64p. 1996. 8.95 (0-7894-1094-X) DK Pub Inc.

*__Virgo.__ (Parker's Love Signs Ser.). 1996. 8.95 (0-614-20711-8) DK Pub Inc.

*__Virgo.__ (Astrology Journals). (Illus.). 80p. 1997. pap. 6.50 (1-55670-573-5) Stewart Tabori & Chang.

*__Virgo.__ (Fisher-Price Little People Coloring & Activity Ser.). (Illus.). 24p. 1997. pap. write for info. (1-56144-965-2, Honey Bear Bks) Modern Pub NYC.

*__Virgo.__ Ariel Books Staff. (Tiny Tomes Ser.). 128p. 1997. 3.95 (0-8362-2673-9, Arie Bks) Andrews & McMeel.

*__Virgo.__ Berkley Publishing Staff. (Berkley Super Horoscopes Ser.). 256p. 1997. pap. 6.99 (0-425-15891-8) Berkley Pub.

Virgo. Lucille Callard. (Astro-Pups: Your Sign, Your Dogs Ser.). (Illus.). 60p. 1991. pap. 9.95 (1-881038-05-X) Penzance Pr.

*__Virgo.__ Jove Publications Incorporated, Staff. (Total Horoscopes Ser.). 272p. 1997. mass mkt. 5.99 (0-515-12113-4) Jove Pubns.

Virgo. James A. Lely. (Sun Sign Ser.). 40p. (J). (gr. 4). 1989. lib. bdg. 13.95 (0-88682-259-9) Creative Ed.

Virgo. Derek Parker & Julia Parker. LC 92-52789. (Sun & Moon Signs Library). (Illus.). 64p. 1992. 8.95 (1-56458-089-X) DK Pub Inc.

*__Virgo: A Little Book of Zodiac Wisdom, a Pop-Up Book.__ Running Press Staff. (Zodiac Wisdom Ser.). 1997. 4.95 (0-7624-0027-7) Running Pr.

Virgo: Astro-Numerogia. Michael J. Kurban. Tr. by Loretta Hilsher-Kurban from ENG. LC 86-91272. (Illus.). (Orig.). (SPA.). 1992. pap. 8.00 (0-938863-50-9) Libra Press Chi.

Virgo: Astro-Numerology. 2nd ed. Michael J. Kurban. (Illus.). 50p. 1991. pap. 8.00 (0-938863-14-2) Libra Press Chi.

Virgo: Desperately Yours. Jahnna N. Malcolm. (Zodiac Ser.: No. 2). 208p. 1995. mass mkt. 3.99 (0-06-106268-5) HarpC.

Virgo: Little Birth sign. Ariel Books Staff. 1994. 4.95 (0-8362-3080-9) Andrews & McMeel.

*__Virgo: Old Moore's Horoscopes & Astral Diaries.__ W. Foulsham & Co. Staff. 1997. pap. text ed. 5.95 (0-572-02356-1, Pub. by W Foulsham UK) Trans-Atl Phila.

*__Virgo: Your Sun-&-Moon Guide to Love & Life.__ Ariel Books Staff. 374p. (Orig.). 1997. pap. 5.95 (0-8362-3567-3, Arie Bks) Andrews & McMeel.

Virgo Rising. Douglas M. Baker. (Esoteric Astrology: The Rising Signs Ser.). 1978. pap. 7.50 (0-906006-34-1, Pub. by Baker Pubns UK) New Leaf Dist.

Virgo Sun Sign. Douglas M. Baker. (Astrological Sun Sign Ser.). 1972. pap. 5.50 (0-906006-22-8, Pub. by Baker Pubns UK) New Leaf Dist.

Virgo 1994 Purse Book. 1994. mass mkt. 1.25 (0-440-60231-9) Dell.

Virgo 1995 Love Signs. 1995. mass mkt. 1.29 (0-440-22125-0) Dell.

Virgo 1995 Purse Book. 1994. mass mkt. 0.99 (0-440-60236-X) Dell.

Virgo 1996 Purse Book. 1995. mass mkt. 1.19 (0-440-60251-3) Dell.

Virgo's Vengeance No. 8. Ruth Koeppel. 1996. pap. 3.99 (0-679-87968-4) Random.

Virgunga: The Passion of Dian Fossey. Farley Mowat. 448p. 1988. mass mkt. 7.99 (0-7704-2257-8) Bantam.

Virial Theorem in Stellar Astrophysics. George W. Collins, II. (Astronomy & Astrophysics Ser.: Vol. 7). 143p. 1978. pap. text ed. 19.00 (0-912918-13-6, 0013) Pachart Pub Hse.

*__Viridian: Poems by Paul Hoover.__ Paul Hoover. LC 96-31228. (Contemporary Poetry Ser.). 1997. pap. 14.95 (0-8203-1895-7) U of Ga Pr.

Viridiana. Bunnel et al. LC 96-28783. 1996. pap. 12.95 (0-435-07015-0, 07015) Heinemann.

Virile Women. McNamara. Date not set. 19.18 (0-02-920610-3, Free Press) Free Pr.

Virility Factor: Masculinity Through Testosterone, the Male Sex Hormone. rev. ed. Robert Bahr. 213p. 1993. pap. 12.95 (0-9626531-1-X) Factor Pr.

Viroceptors, Virokines & Related Immune Modulators Encoded by DNA Viruses. Ed. by Grant McFadden. LC 94-37913. (Molecular Biology Intelligence Unit Ser.). 210p. 1995. text ed. 89.95 (1-57059-167-9) R G Landes.

Viroids. Ed. by T. O. Diener. LC 87-13017. (Viruses Ser.). (Illus.). 366p. 1987. 95.00 (0-306-42523-8, Plenum Pr) Plenum.

Viroids & Satellites: Molecular Parasites at the Frontier of Life. Karl Maramorosch. 176p. 1991. 123.00 (0-8493-6783-2, QP552) CRC Pr.

Viroids & Viroid-Like Pathogens. Ed. by J. S. Semancik et al. 192p. 1987. 110.00 (0-8493-6060-9, QR500, CRC Reprint) Franklin.

Virological Aspects of the Safety of Biological Products. Ed. by F. Horaud & F. Brwon. (Developments in Biological Standardization Ser.: Vol. 75). (Illus.). x, 280p. 1991. 165.25 (3-8055-5467-2) S Karger.

Virological Safety Aspects of Plasma Derivatives. Ed. by F. Brown. (Developments in Biological Standardization Ser.: Vol. 81). (Illus.). x, 310p. 1994. pap. 235.00 (3-8055-5879-1) S Karger.

Virologie in Deutschland: Die Entwicklung eines Fachgebietes. K. Munk. (Illus.). x, 170p. 1994. 43.50 (3-8055-6004-4) S Karger.

Virologie Medicale. Jacques Maurin. (Collection Traites). (Illus.). 930p. (FRE.). 1985. 150.00 (2-257-10435-8) S M P F Inc.

Virologist. (Career Examination Ser.: C-3759). pap. 27.95 (0-8373-3759-3) Nat Learn.

Virology. Heinz Fraenkel-Conrat & Paul C. Kimball. (Illus.). 432p. (C). 1982. write for info. (0-13-942144-0) P-H.

Virology. Scott. (Biology Ser.). 1998. text ed. 49.95 (0-534-23580-8) Wadsworth Pub.

Virology. 2nd ed. Renato Dulbecco & Harold S. Ginsberg. LC 65-10705. (Illus.). 425p. 1988. text ed. 41.95 (0-397-50905-7, Lippnctt) Lppncott-Raven.

Virology. 2nd ed. Heinz Fraenkel-Conrat et al. (Illus.). 432p. (C). 1988. text ed. 71.00 (0-13-942186-6) P-H.

Virology. 3rd ed. Jay A. Levy et al. LC 93-2450. 480p. 1994. text ed. 84.00 (0-13-953753-8) P-H.

Virology: A Laboratory Manual. Florence G. Burleson et al. (Illus.). 250p. 1992. spiral bd. 19.95 (0-12-144730-8) Acad Pr.

Virology: An Information Profile. R. Nicholas & D. Nicholas. 244p. 1983. text ed. 75.00 (0-7201-1673-2, Mansell Pub) Cassell.

Virology for Medical & Dental Students. Leslie Collier. Ed. by John S. Oxford. 384p. 1993. 32.50 (0-19-261662-5) OUP.

Virology for Medical & Dental Students. Leslie Collier. Ed. by John S. Oxford. 384p. 1993. pap. 75.00 (0-19-262184-X) OUP.

Virology in Agriculture. John A. Romberger. LC 76-42139. (Beltsville Symposia in Agricultural Research Ser.: No. 1). 320p. 1977. text ed. 41.00 (0-916672-14-X) Rowman.

Virology in Medicine. Ed. by Henry R. Rothschild & J. Craig Cohen. (Illus.). 334p. 1986. pap. text ed. 24.95 (0-19-504017-1) OUP.

Virology Labfax. Ed. by D. Harper. (Labfax Ser.). (Illus.). 272p. 1993. 59.95 (0-12-326320-4) Acad Pr.

Virology Methods Manual. Ed. by Brian W. Mahy & Hillar O. Kangro. (Illus.). 384p. 1996. pap. text ed. 69.95 (0-12-465330-8) Acad Pr.

Virology Reviews, Vol. 1. Ed. by V. M. Zhdanov. (Soviet Medical Reviews Ser.: Sect. E, Vol. 1). 332p. 1987. text ed. 413.00 (3-7186-0314-4) Gordon & Breach.

Virology Reviews, Vol. 2. Ed. by V. M. Zhdanov. (Soviet Medical Reviews Ser.: Vol. 2). 378p. (C). 1987. reprint ed. text ed. 438.00 (3-7186-0402-7) Gordon & Breach.

Virology Reviews: Influenza, Vol. 3. A. V. Frolov et al. Ed. by Dmitri K. Lvov. (Soviet Medical Reviews Ser.: Vol. 3, Pt. 3). vi, 178p. 1990. pap. text ed. 133.00 (3-7186-4942-X) Gordon & Breach.

Virology Reviews: Interferon & Its Inducers, Vol. 3. I. G. Balandin et al. Ed. by Dmitri K. Lvov. (Soviet Medical Reviews Ser.: Vol. 3, Pt. 2). vi, 168p. 1989. pap. text ed. 124.00 (3-7186-4921-7) Gordon & Breach.

Virology Reviews Vol. 4, Pt. 1: Chemoprophylaxis & Chemotheraphy of Viral Infections, Vol. 4. E. F. Barinsky. (Soviet Medical Reviews Ser.: Section E). 152p. 1991. pap. text ed. 132.00 (3-7186-5150-5, Harwood Acad Pubs) Gordon & Breach.

Virology Reviews Vol. 4, Pt. 2: Viral Hepatitides A & E Part A, Vol. 4. Yu Kusov. (Soviet Medical Reviews Ser.: Section E). 88p. 1992. pap. text ed. 73.00 (3-7186-5259-5, Harwood Acad Pubs) Gordon & Breach.

Virology Reviews Vol. 4, Pt. 3: Viral Hepatitides A & E Part B, Vol. 4. E. N. Peletskaya. (Soviet Medical Reviews Ser.: Section E). 83p. 1992. pap. text ed. 69.00 (3-7186-5260-9, Harwood Acad Pubs) Gordon & Breach.

Virology Reviews Vol. 4, Pt. 4: Chemoprophylaxis & Chemotherapy of Viral Infections, Vol. 4. M. Balayan. (Soviet Medical Reviews Ser.: Section E). 78p. 1992. pap. text ed. 85.00 (3-7186-5284-6, Harwood Acad Pubs) Gordon & Breach.

Virology Reviews Vol. 5, Pt. 1: Viral Hepatitis, Vol. 5. A. Bluger. (Soviet Medical Reviews Ser.: Section E). 148p. 1992. pap. text ed. 194.00 (3-7186-5356-7, Harwood Acad Pubs) Gordon & Breach.

Virology Two: Proceedings of the International Congress for Virology, 2nd, Budapest, 1971. International Congress for Virology Staff. Ed. by Joseph L. Melnick. 1972. 75.75 (3-8055-1290-2) S Karger.

Viropause: The Male Menopause - Emotional & Physical Changes Midlife Men Experience. Aubrey Hill. 1993. 23.95 (0-88282-084-2); pap. 13.95 (0-88282-080-X) New Horizon NJ.

*__Virtua Fighter 3.__ Prima Publishing Staff. 1997. pap. 12.99 (0-7615-1146-6) Prima Pub.

Virtua Fighter 3 Arcade Secrets. PCS Staff. 144p. 1997. per., pap. 12.99 (0-7615-0797-3) Prima Pub.

Virtua Racing: Official Driver's Strategy Guide. Jason Rich. (Illus.). 96p. (Orig.). 1994. pap. 9.95 (0-614-06069-9) Brady Pub.

*__Virtual Archaeology: Re-Creating Ancient Worlds.__ Ed. by Maurizio Forte & Alberto Siliotti. LC 96-43482. (Illus.). 288p. 1997. 49.50 (0-8109-3943-6) Abrams.

Virtual Architecture. Giuliano Zampi & Conway L. Morgan. LC 95-37204. 1995. text ed. 39.95 (0-07-072722-8) McGraw.

Virtual Attraction. Cheri Connor. 136p. (Orig.). 1996. mass mkt. 4.99 (1-55197-239-5, Pub. by Comnwlth Pub CN) Partners Pubs Grp.

Virtual Auditory Space: Generation & Applications. Ed. by Simon Carlile. LC 96-14117. (Neuroscience Intelligence Unit Ser.). 1996. 89.95 (0-412-10481-4) R G Landes.

Virtual Banality. J. C. Duffy. LC 96-84114. (Fusco Brothers Collection). (Illus.). 128p. (Orig.). 1996. pap. 9.95 (0-8362-2121-4) Andrews & McMeel.

Virtual Bart: Official Game Secrets. Steven A. Schwartz. 1994. pap. 12.95 (1-55958-670-2) Prima Pub.

Virtual Boss. Floyd Kemske. LC 93-8479. 224p. 1993. 19.95 (0-945774-22-2, PS3561.E4226V57) Catbird Pr.

Virtual Charlie No. 2.1: Oda's Web. Charles C. Wehrenberg. (Illus.). 496p. 1997. pap. 20.00 incl. cd-rom (1-886163-08-1) SoloZone.

Virtual Charlie No. 2.1: Ploy of Cooking. Charles C. Wehrenberg. (Illus.). 224p. 1997. pap. 20.00 incl. cd-rom (1-886163-09-X) SoloZone.

Virtual Charlie No. 2.1: Radio-Reactive Apples. Charles C. Wehrenberg. 298p. 1997. pap. 20.00 incl. cd-rom (1-886163-10-3) SoloZone.

Virtual Charlie No. 2.1: Will Ball. Charles C. Wehrenberg. (Illus.). 204p. 1997. pap. 20.00 incl. cd-rom (1-886163-11-1) SoloZone.

Virtual Classroom: Learning Without Limits Via Computer Networks. Starr R. Hiltz. LC 93-13573. (Human-Computer Interaction Ser.). 408p. 1994. pap. 42.50 (1-56750-055-2); text ed. 82.50 (0-89391-928-4) Ablex Pub.

*__Virtual Classrooms: Educational Opportunity Through Two-Way Interactive Television.__ Vicki M. Hobbs & J. Scott Christianson. LC 96-60519. 415p. 1996. text ed. 49.95 (1-56676-312-6) Technomic.

*__Virtual Cody.__ Betsy Duffey. LC 96-47356. (Illus.). (J). 1997. pap. 13.99 (0-670-87470-1) Viking Penguin.

Virtual College: A Quick Guide to How You Can Get the Degree You Want with Computer, TV, Video, Audio, & Other Distance Learning Tools. Pam Dixon. LC 96-41971. 160p. (Orig.). 1996. pap. 9.95 (1-56079-629-4) Petersons.

*__Virtual Combat: A Guide to Distributed Interactive.__ David L. Neyland. 1997. pap. 19.95 (0-8117-3125-1) Stackpole.

Virtual Combat Air Staff: The Promise of Information Technologies. Arthur F. Huber et al. LC 96-9259. 139p. (Orig.). 1996. pap. text ed. 15.00 (0-8330-2415-9, MR-759-AF) Rand Corp.

Virtual Community: Finding Connection in a Computerized World. Howard Rheingold. 1993. 22.95 (0-201-60870-7) Addison-Wesley.

Virtual Community: Homesteading on the Electronic Frontier. Howard Rheingold. LC 94-25495. 352p. 1994. pap. 14.00 (0-06-097641-1, PL) HarpC.

Virtual Connections: Online Activities & Projects for Networking Language Learners. Ed. by Mark Warschauer. (Technical Report Ser.: No. 8). 416p. 1995. pap. text ed. 30.00 (0-8248-1793-1) Sec Lang Tching.

Virtual Corporation: Structuring & Revitalizing the Corporation for the 21st Century. William H. Davidow & Michael S. Malone. LC 92-52569. 304p. 1993. reprint ed. pap. 13.00 (0-88730-657-8) Harper Busn.

*__Virtual Culture: Identity & Communication in Cybersociety.__ Ed. by Steven G. Jones. 272p. 1997. 75.00 (0-7619-5525-9) Sage.

*__Virtual Culture: Identity & Communication in Cybersociety.__ Ed. by Steven G. Jones. 272p. 1997. pap. 26.95 (0-7619-5526-7) Sage.

Virtual Death. Shale Aaron. 304p. 1995. mass mkt. 4.50 (0-06-105430-5, HarperPrism) HarpC.

Virtual Design Studio: A Collaborative Architectural Project. Ed. by Jerzy Wojtowicz. (Illus.). 205p. 1995. pap. 37.50 (962-209-364-7, Pub. by Hong Kong Univ Pr HK) Coronet Bks.

Virtual Destruction. Kevin J. Anderson & Doug Beason. 336p. (Orig.). 1996. mass mkt. 5.99 (0-441-00308-7) Ace Bks.

Virtual Destruction. Nick Baron. 1995. mass mkt. 3.99 (0-8217-5010-0, Z-Fave) Kensgtn Pub Corp.

Virtual Device Driver Book. Michael Conca & Hewlett-Packard Staff. 1994. pap. text ed. 21.75 (0-13-125642-4) P-H.

Virtual Device Drivers, Vol. I. Geoff Chapell & Ralph Shnelvar. (Illus.). 350p. (Orig.). 1996. pap. 32.95 (1-56592-195-X) OReilly & Assocs.

*__Virtual Dimension: Architecture, Representation, & Crash Culture.__ Ed. by John Beckmann. (Illus.). 350p. (Orig.). 1998. pap. 24.95 (1-56898-120-1) Princeton Arch.

Virtual Distortion Method. J. Holnicki-Szulc. (Lecture Notes in Engineering Ser.: Vol. 65). 176p. 1991. pap. 34.00 (0-387-53779-1) Spr-Verlag.

Virtual Doonesbury. Garry B. Trudeau. LC 96-84523. (Doonesbury Bk.). (Illus.). 128p. 1996. pap. 12.95 (0-8362-1032-8) Andrews & McMeel.

*__Virtual Economics.__ Estenson. 1997. text ed. 15.96 incl. cd-rom (0-256-23469-8) McGraw.

Virtual Environments & Advanced Interface Design. Ed. by Woodrow Barfield & Tom Furness, III. (Illus.). 512p. 1995. text ed. 75.00 (0-19-507555-2) OUP.

*__Virtual Environments & Scientific Visualization '96: Proceedings of the Eurographics Workshops in Monte Carlo, Monaco, February 19-20, 1996 & in Prague, Czech Republic, April 23-25, 1996.__ Ed. by M. Gobel et al. (Eurographics Ser.). viii, 324p. 1996. pap. 89.50 (3-211-82886-9) Spr-Verlag.

Virtual Environments '95: Selected Papers of the Eurographics Workshops in Barcelona, Spain, 1993, & Monte Carlo, Monaco, 1995. Ed. by M. Gobel. (Eurographics Ser.). (Illus.). vii, 307p. 1995. pap. 85.00 (3-211-82737-4) Spr-Verlag.

Virtual Equality: The Mainstreaming of Gay & Lesbian Liberation. Urvashi Vaid. 1995. 24.95 (0-614-15450-2) Doubleday.

Virtual Equality: The Mainstreaming of Gay & Lesbian Liberation. Urvashi Vaid. 460p. 1996. pap. 14.95 (0-385-47299-4, Anchor NY) Doubleday.

*__Virtual Field Trips.__ Gail Cooper & Garry Cooper. LC 97-26028. 1997. write for info. (1-56308-557-7) Libs Unl.

Virtual Fred. Courtney Vincent. 1996. pap. 3.99 (0-679-88214-6) McKay.

Virtual Fred. Courtney Vincent. 1996. lib. bdg. 11.99 (0-679-98214-0) McKay.

*__Virtual Fred & the Big Dip.__ Vincent Courtney. LC 97-10968. 1997. pap. 3.99 (0-679-88661-3) Random Bks Yng Read.

*__Virtual Fred & the Big Dip.__ Vincent Courtney. (J). 1997. lib. bdg. 11.99 (0-679-98661-8) Random Bks Yng Read.

***Virtual Futures.** Joan B. Dixon & Eric Cassidy. LC 97-19274. 1998. write for info. (*0-415-13379-3*); pap. write for info. (*0-415-13380-7*) Routledge.

Virtual Geography: Living with Global Media Events. McKenzie Wark. LC 93-48986. (Arts & Politics of the Everday Ser.). 256p. 1994. 29.95 (*0-253-36349-7*); pap. 14.95 (*0-253-20894-7*) Ind U Pr.

Virtual Girl. Amy Thomson. 256p. (Orig.). 1993. mass mkt. 4.99 (*0-441-86500-3*) Ace Bks.

Virtual Girls: The Erotic Gems of Evan Hollander. Evan Hollander. 68p. (Orig.). 1995. pap. 6.95 (*1-885865-04-X*) Circlet Pr.

***Virtual Gods: The Seduction of Power & Pleasure in Cyberspace.** Ed. by Tal Brooke. LC 96-45435. 224p. (Orig.). 1997. pap. 10.99 (*1-56507-620-6*) Harvest Hse.

Virtual Goliath. Richard Crandall & Marvin Levich. 1996. 29.95 (*0-614-14503-1*) Spr-Verlag.

Virtual Goliath: Essays on Mind & Machine. Richard Crandall. 1996. 29.95 (*0-387-94647-0*) Spr-Verlag.

***Virtual Government: C. I. A. Mind Control Operations in America.** Alex Constantine. (Illus.). (Orig.). 1997. pap. 12.95 (*0-614-24067-0*) Feral Hse.

Virtual Government: CIA Mind Control Operations in America. Alex Constantine. 1997. pap. text ed. 12.95 (*0-922915-45-8*) Feral Hse.

***Virtual Grossology.** Sylvia Branzei. 1997. spiral bd. write for info. (*0-201-15417-X*) Addison-Wesley.

Virtual Guitarist. Frederick M. Noad. 1998. 30.00 (*0-02-864584-7*) Macmillan.

***Virtual Health Systems: A Guide to Assessing Organizational Readiness & Strategic Partners.** Richard Coffey. 1997. 34.95 (*0-7879-1078-3*) Jossey-Bass.

Virtual Help Desk: Strategic Management Center. Andrew H. Thomas. (Illus.). 250p. 1996. pap. 29.95 (*1-85032-204-X*) ITCP.

Virtual Humans & Simulated Agents. Norman I. Badler et al. LC 93-12061. 288p. 1993. 65.00 (*0-19-507359-2*) OUP.

Virtual Individuals, Virtual Groups: Human Dimensions of Groupware & Computer Networking. JoAnn Oravec. (Series in Human-Computer Interaction: No. 11). 400p. (C). 1996. text ed. 49.95 (*0-521-45493-X*) Cambridge U Pr.

Virtual Justice: The Flawed Prosecution of Crime in America. H. Richard Uviller. (C). 1996. 30.00 (*0-614-95766-4*) Yale U Pr.

***Virtual LANs: Construction, Implementation, & Management.** Gilbert Held. LC 96-52022. 320p. 1997. pap. 39.99 (*0-471-17732-6*) Wiley.

***Virtual LANs: Construction, Operation, Utilization.** Marina Smith. (Computer Communications Ser.). (Illus.). 300p. 1997. pap. text ed., pap. 44.95 incl. cd-rom (*0-07-913623-0*) McGraw.

Virtual Leadership: Secrets from the Round Table for the Multi-Site Manager. Jaclyn Kostner. 192p. 1996. pap. 11.99 (*0-446-67087-1*) Warner Bks.

Virtual Leadership & ISO 9000. Tom Taormina. 304p. 1996. 34.95 (*0-13-237074-3*) P-H.

***Virtual Learning: A Paradoxical Approach to Building the High Performance Organization.** Roger C. Schank. LC 97-9624. 1997. 24.95 (*0-7863-1148-7*) McGraw.

Virtual Library: An SLA Information Kit. 60p. 1994. 20.00 (*0-87111-428-3*) SLA.

Virtual Library: Visions & Realities. Ed. by Laverna Saunders. (Supplement to Computers in Libraries Ser.: No. 61). 180p. 1993. pap. 37.50 (*0-88736-860-3*) Mecklermedia.

Virtual Light. William Gibson. 368p. 1994. mass mkt. 7.99 (*0-553-56606-7*) Bantam.

Virtual Love. Avodah K. Offit. LC 93-36227. 1994. 22.00 (*0-671-87436-5*) S&S Trade.

***Virtual Macroeconomics.** Estenson. 1997. text ed. 12.76 incl. cd-rom (*0-256-23470-1*) McGraw.

Virtual Marketing: The Battle for the Customer's Mind. Christopher Ryan. Ed. by Sunny Quay. LC 94-33611. 1994. write for info. (*1-882222-08-3*) Libey Pub.

Virtual Memory Management. Richard W. Carr. LC 84-140. (Computer Science: Systems Programming Ser.: No. 20). (Illus.). 175p. reprint ed. pap. 49.90 (*0-8357-1533-7*, 2070367) Bks Demand.

Virtual Memory System Code Secrets Vol. 2: The Virtual Memory System, 2. William F. Joltiz & Lynne G. Joltiz. (Operating System Source Code Secrets Ser.). 200p. (Orig.). 1997. pap. 44.95 (*1-57398-027-7*) Peer-to-Peer Communications.

***Virtual Microeconomics.** Estenson. 1997. text ed. 12.76 incl. cd-rom (*0-256-23471-X*) McGraw.

Virtual Mode. Piers Anthony. 1991. mass mkt. 5.99 (*0-441-86503-8*) Ace Bks.

***Virtual Money: Tailoring Financial Markets to Cyberspace.** Elinor H. Solomon. (Illus.). 368p. 1997. 29.95 (*0-19-509747-5*) OUP.

Virtual Muse: Experiments in Computer Poetry. Charles O. Hartman. LC 96-16074. (Illus.). 164p. 1996. text ed. 35.00 (*0-8195-2238-4*, Wesleyan Univ Pr) U Pr of New Eng.

Virtual Muse: Experiments in Computer Poetry. Charles O. Hartman. LC 96-16074. (Illus.). 164p. 1996. pap. 14.95 (*0-8195-2239-2*, Wesleyan Univ Pr) U Pr of New Eng.

Virtual Musician. Hill. 1996. 30.00 (*0-02-864683-5*) Mac Lib Ref.

Virtual Networks: A Buyer's Guide. Daniel D. Briere. (Artech House Telecom Management Library). 200p. 1990. text ed. write for info. (*0-89006-411-3*) Artech Hse.

Virtual Networks: A Buyer's Guide. Daniel D. Briere. LC 89-48433. (Artech House Materials Science Library). 213p. 1989. reprint ed. pap. 60.80 (*0-608-02078-8*, 2062731) Bks Demand.

***Virtual Nightmare.** S. F. Black. 1997. pap. 3.95 (*0-8167-4343-6*) Troll Communs.

***Virtual Office: Ten Case Studies.** Anita Dennis. LC 97-21467. 100p. 1997. pap. 41.00 (*0-87051-188-2*, 090426) Am Inst CPA.

Virtual Office End-User Markets: Changing Work Habits Create Non-Traditional Office Opportunities. 302p. 1992. 995.00 (*1-56753-014-1*) Frost & Sullivan.

Virtual Office Survival Handbook: What Telecommuters & Entrepreneurs Need to Succeed in Today's Non-Traditional Workplace. Alice Bredin. LC 96-1327. 288p. 1996. text ed. 34.95 (*0-471-12061-8*) Wiley.

Virtual Office Survival Handbook: What Telecommuters & Entrepreneurs Need to Succeed in Today's Non-Traditional Workplace. Alice Bredin. LC 96-1327. 272p. 1996. pap. text ed. 16.95 (*0-471-12059-6*) Wiley.

***Virtual Organizations & Beyond.** Bo Hedberg. LC 97-8658. (Wiley Series in Practical Strategy). 1997. write for info. (*0-471-97493-5*) Wiley.

***Virtual Peril.** 1997. mass mkt. 5.50 (*0-373-61914-6*, 1-61914-7, Wrldwide Lib) Harlequin Bks.

Virtual Political Reality. Graber. 1996. lib. bdg. 34.00 (*0-226-30586-4*) U Ch Pr.

Virtual Political Reality. Graber. 1996. pap. text ed. 13.95 (*0-226-30587-2*) U Ch Pr.

***Virtual Power.** Bunting. 1997. 23.00 (*0-684-81482-X*) S&S Trade.

Virtual Principles in Aircraft Structures, Vol. 1. Analysis. B. E. Gatewood. (C). 1900. lib. bdg. write for info. (*90-247-3754-0*) Kluwer Ac.

Virtual Principles in Aircraft Structures, Vol. 2: Design, Plates, Finite Elements. B. E. Gatewood. (C). 1900. lib. bdg. write for info. (*90-247-3755-9*) Kluwer Ac.

***Virtual Prototyping: Virtual Environments & the Product Design Process.** A. A. Teixeira. (Illus.). 360p. 1995. text ed. 91.00 (*0-412-72160-0*, Chap & Hall NY) Chapman & Hall.

***Virtual Realism.** Michael H. Heim. 216p. 1997. 25.00 (*0-19-510426-9*) OUP.

Virtual Realities & Their Discontents. Ed. by Robert Markley. 197p. 1995. text ed. 38.50 (*0-8018-5225-0*); pap. text ed. 14.95 (*0-8018-5226-9*) Johns Hopkins.

Virtual Realities 2.0: A Shadowrun Sourcebook. 2nd ed. Paul Hume. (Shadowrun Ser.). (Illus.). 128p. 1995. pap. 18.00 (*1-55560-271-1*, 7904) FASA Corp.

Virtual Reality. 118p. 1991. 285.00 (*0-89671-127-7*) SEAI Tech Pubns.

***Virtual Reality.** 214p. 1992. 2,995.00 (*0-614-18365-0*, IGIC-50) Info Gatekeepers.

Virtual Reality. Richard K. Miller & Marcia E. Rupnow. (Survey on Technology & Markets Ser.: No. 201). 50p. 1991. pap. text ed. 200.00 (*1-55865-232-9*) Future Tech Surveys.

Virtual Reality. National Gallery of Australia Staff. LC 94-61763. (Australian National Gallery Ser.). (Illus.). 64p. 1995. pap. 19.95 (*0-500-97419-5*) Thames Hudson.

Virtual Reality. H. P. Newquist. LC 95-9900. (J). 1995. 6.95 (*0-590-48408-7*) Scholastic Inc.

Virtual Reality. Bob Perelman. LC 92-63354. (Roof Bks.). 80p. (Orig.). 1993. pap. 9.95 (*0-937804-49-5*) Segue NYC.

Virtual Reality: A Selected Bibliography. Hilary McLellan. Ed. by William D. Milheim. LC 92-8488. (Educational Technology Selected Bibliography Ser.: Vol. 6). 60p. (Orig.). 1992. pap. 24.95 (*0-87778-246-6*) Educ Tech Pubns.

***Virtual Reality: Beyond the Looking Glass.** Elaine Pascoe. LC 96-42984. (New Explorers Ser.). 48p. (YA). (gr. 5 up). 1997. lib. bdg. 16.95 (*1-56711-228-5*) Blackbirch.

***Virtual Reality: Computers Mimic the Physical World.** Sean M. Grady. LC 97-15813. (Science Sourcebooks Ser.). (J). 1998. write for info. (*0-8160-3605-5*) Facts on File.

Virtual Reality: Practical Applications in Business & Industry. Dimitris N. Chorafas & Heinrich Steinmann. LC 95-7069. (C). 1995. pap. text ed. 49.00 (*0-13-185638-3*) P-H.

Virtual Reality: Scientific & Technological Challenges. National Research Council Staff. Ed. by Anne S. Mavor & Nathaniel I. Durlach. 556p. (C). 1994. text ed. 59.95 (*0-309-05135-5*) Natl Acad Pr.

Virtual Reality: Strategies for Intranet & World Wide Web Applications. Computer Technology Research Corporation Staff. (Illus.). 231p. (Orig.). 1996. 285.00 (*1-56607-971-3*) Comput Tech Res.

Virtual Reality: The Revolutionary Technology of Computer-Generated Artificial Worlds - & How It Promises to Transform Society. Howard Rheingold. 416p. 1992. pap. 12.00 (*0-671-77897-8*, Touchstone Bks) S&S Trade.

Virtual Reality: Theory, Practice & Promise. Sandra K. Helsel & Judith P. Roth. (Illus.). 150p. 1990. pap. text ed. 39.50 (*0-88736-728-3*) Mecklermedia.

Virtual Reality: Theory, Practice, & Promise. Sandra K. Helsel & Judith P. Roth. 1991. pap. 39.50 (*0-685-51984-8*) Mecklermedia.

Virtual Reality: Through the New Looking Glass. Ken Pimentel & Kevin Teixeira. (Illus.). 352p. 1992. 32.95 (*0-8306-4065-7*, 4196, Windcrest); pap. 22.95 (*0-8306-4064-9*, 4196, Windcrest) TAB Bks.

Virtual Reality: Through the New Looking Glass. 2nd ed. Ken Pimental & Kevin Teixeira. LC 94-3440. 1995. text ed. 36.95 (*0-07-050167-X*, Windcrest) TAB Bks.

Virtual Reality: Through the New Looking Glass. 2nd ed. Ken Pimentel & Kevin Teixeira. LC 94-3440. 1994. pap. text ed. 24.95 (*0-07-050168-8*) McGraw-Hill Prof.

***Virtual Reality & Beyond.** Charles A. Jortberg. LC 96-32641. (Kids And Computers Ser.). (J). 1997. lib. bdg. 15.95 (*1-56239-728-1*) Abdo & Dghtrs.

Virtual Reality & Highly Interactive 3-D User Interfaces. Mark Green. 500p. 1998. text ed. 64.95 (*1-55860-389-1*) Morgan Kaufmann.

Virtual Reality Annual International Symposium 1996. 296p. 1996. pap. 60.00 (*0-8186-7295-1*, PRO7295) IEEE Comp Soc.

***Virtual Reality Annual International Symposium 1996 (VRAIS '96)** 300p. 1997. pap. 70.00 (*0-8186-7843-7*, PR07843) IEEE Comp Soc.

Virtual Reality Annual International Symposium, '95 (VRAIS '95) LC 95-75103. 248p. 1995. pap. 50.00 (*0-8186-7084-3*, PR07084) IEEE Comp Soc.

Virtual Reality Applications. Ed. by Rae Earnshaw et al. (Illus.). 304p. 1995. text ed. 44.95 (*0-12-227755-4*) Acad Pr.

Virtual Reality Business. 409p. 1996. 2,650.00 (*0-614-03495-7*, GB175) BCC.

Virtual Reality Casebook. Carl Loeffler & Tim Anderson. Date not set. pap. 29.95 (*0-442-01776-6*) Van Nos Reinhold.

Virtual Reality Construction Kit. Joseph Gradecki. 340p. 1994. pap. text ed. 27.95 (*0-471-00953-9*) Wiley.

Virtual Reality Excursions. Watkins. 1995. pap. text ed. 21.00 (*0-12-784839-8*) Acad Pr.

Virtual Reality Excursions: With Programs in C. Christopher D. Watkins & Stephen R. Marenka. (Illus.). 503p. 1994. text ed., pap. 39.95 incl. disk (*0-12-737865-0*, AP Prof) Acad Pr.

Virtual Reality for Dummies. 1996. pap. 19.99 (*0-7645-0005-8*) IDG Bks.

***Virtual Reality for Training: Proceedings of a Workshop Sponsored by NATO's Defense Research Group Panel 8, Research Study Group 16 on Advanced Technologies Applied to Training Design Held Aboard the HMS Nelson, Portsmouth, England, March 7-9, 1995.** Ed. by Robert J. Seidel & Paul R. Chatelier. LC 96-53454. (Defense Research Ser.: Vol. 6). (Illus.). 232p. (C). 1997. 79.50 (*0-306-45486-6*, Plenum Pr) Plenum.

Virtual Reality Guide to the Internet, With CD-ROM Interactive Internet Tutorial. Dennis R. Neill. 1996. pap. text ed. 26.99 (*1-57613-006-1*) Sulzburger & Graham Pub.

Virtual Reality Handbook: Products, Services & Resources. David Gump. 1993. 248.00 (*0-935453-56-3*) Pasha Pubns.

Virtual Reality Homebrewer's Handbook W/CD-ROM. Robin Hollands. LC 96-26760. 350p. 1996. pap. 50.00 (*0-471-95871-9*) Wiley.

Virtual Reality in Engineering. Ed. by Kevin Warwick et al. (Computing Ser.: No. 20). 196p. 1993. boxed 72.00 (*0-85296-803-5*, CM020) Inst Elect Eng.

Virtual Reality Madness! 1996. Ron Wodaski. (Illus.). 896p. (Orig.). 1995. pap. 49.99 incl. cd-rom (*0-672-30865-7*) Sams.

Virtual Reality Markets: Hardware, Software, Systems & Services. Market Intelligence Staff. 320p. 2,795.00 (*1-56753-593-3*) Frost & Sullivan.

Virtual Reality Programmer's Kit. Joe Gradecki. 488p. 1994. pap. text ed. 29.95 (*0-471-05253-1*) Wiley.

***Virtual Reality Programming with World Tool Kit.** Larry W. Smith. 711p. 1996. pap. 21.95 (*1-57914-004-1*) Campbell-Smith.

Virtual Reality Real World. Heller & Embleton. (C). 1996. pap. text ed. 53.27 (*0-13-487118-9*) P-H.

Virtual Reality Research & Development: An International Directory of Projects. Ed. by Jeremy Thompson. 350p. 1993. pap. text ed. 60.00 (*0-88736-862-X*) Mecklermedia.

Virtual Reality Software & Technology: Proceedings of the Conference. Daniel Thalmann et al. 356p. 1994. text ed. 86.00 (*981-02-1867-2*) World Scientific Pub.

Virtual Reality Systems. Rae Earnshaw et al. (Illus.). 327p. 1993. text ed. 51.00 (*0-12-227748-1*) Acad Pr.

Virtual Reality Systems. John Vince. LC 95-2741. (C). 1995. text ed. 44.95 (*0-201-87687-6*) Addison-Wesley.

Virtual Reality Systems for Business. Robert J. Thierauf. LC 95-3779. 304p. 1995. text ed. 65.00 (*0-89930-946-1*, Quorum Bks) Greenwood.

***Virtual Reality Therapy: An Innovative Paradigm.** Max M. North et al. Ed. by Trussell Pyle & Anne Wilson. (Illus.). 232p. (Orig.). (C). 1996. pap. 26.00 (*1-880930-08-0*) IPI Pr.

Virtual Reality '94. 1994. 71.95 (*0-387-57768-8*) Spr-Verlag.

***Virtual Realty: A Guide to the Internet for Real Estate & Ancillary Professionals.** Lori Robertson & Brian C. Wadell. LC 96-47851. (Orig.). 1996. pap. 34.00 (*1-884186-04-1*, Hollis Pubng) Puritan Pr.

Virtual Realty Technology. Grigore Burdea & Philippe Copiffet. 400p. 1994. text ed. 59.95 (*0-471-08632-0*) Wiley.

***Virtual Roots: A Guide to Genealogy & Local History on the World Wide Web.** Thomas J. Kemp. LC 97-18954. 304p. 1997. 65.00 (*0-8420-2718-1*, SR Bks) Scholarly Res Inc.

***Virtual Roots: A Guide to Genealogy & Local History on the World Wide Web.** Thomas J. Kemp. LC 97-18954. 304p. 1997. pap. 21.95 (*0-8420-2720-3*, SR Bks) Scholarly Res Inc.

Virtual School Library: Gateways to the Information Highway. Ed. by M. Elspeth Goodin et al. 225p. 1996. lib. bdg. 24.00 (*1-56308-336-1*) Libs Unl.

Virtual Selling: Going Beyond the Automated Sales Force to Achieve Total Sales Quality. Thomas M. Siebel & Michael S. Malone. (Illus.). 224p. 1996. 26.00 (*0-684-82287-3*) Free Pr.

Virtual Silence. Joan Schwighardt. LC 94-29232. 176p. 1995. 22.00 (*1-877946-61-3*) Permanent Pr.

***Virtual Spaces: Sex & the Cyber Citizen.** Cleo Odzer. 192p. 1997. pap. 14.00 (*0-425-15986-8*, Berkley Trade) Berkley Pub.

Virtual Terror No. 3: Freddy Krueger's Tales of Terror. David Bergantino & Bruce Richards. (New Elm Street Novel Ser.: No. 3). 160p. (Orig.). (YA). (gr. 6 up). 1995. 3.99 (*0-8125-5190-7*) Tor Bks.

Virtual Theatre from Diderot to Mallarme. Evlyn Gould. LC 89-1794. 256p. 1989. text ed. 39.95 (*0-8018-3822-3*) Johns Hopkins.

Virtual Trading: How Any Trader with a PC Can Use the Power of Neural Nets & Expert Systems. Jess Lederman. 1994. text ed. 45.00 (*1-55738-812-1*) Irwin Prof Pubng.

Virtual Unreality. Exene Cervenka. (Illus.). 128p. (Orig.). (C). 1993. pap. 10.00 (*1-880985-15-2*) Two Thirteen Sixty-one.

***Virtual Utility: Accounting, Technology & Competitive Aspects of the Emerging Industry.** Shimon Awerbuch & Alistair Preston. LC 97-6293. (Topics in Regulatory Economics & Policy Ser.). 1997. lib. bdg. 200.00 (*0-7923-9902-1*) Kluwer Ac.

Virtual Villainy. Franklin W. Dixon. (Hardy Boys Ser.: No. 86). (YA). (gr. 6 up). 1994. mass mkt. 3.99 (*0-671-79470-1*, Archway) PB.

***Virtual War.** Gloria Skurzynski. LC 96-35346. (J). 1997. 16.00 (*0-689-81374-0*) S&S Childrens.

Virtual Work in Structural Analysis. Glyn A. Davies. LC 81-15926. 341p. reprint ed. pap. 97.20 (*0-7837-0192-6*, 2040488) Bks Demand.

***Virtual Workplace: One Size Doesn't Fit All.** 177p. (Orig.). 1997. pap. 31.25 (*0-87111-463-1*) SLA.

***Virtual World.** Chris Westwood. LC 97-9388. (J). 1997. pap. 14.99 (*0-670-87546-5*) Viking Penguin.

Virtual Worlds. Benjamin Woolley. (Illus.). 288p. 1994. pap. 12.00 (*0-14-015439-6*, Penguin Bks) Viking Penguin.

***Virtual Worlds & Multimedia.** Ed. by Nadia M. Thalmann & Daniel Thalmann. LC 93-14588. (Illus.). 248p. reprint ed. pap. 70.70 (*0-608-05303-1*, 2065841) Bks Demand.

Virtual Zen. Ray Nelson. 224p. (Orig.). 1996. mass mkt. 5.50 (*0-380-78185-9*, AvoNova) Avon.

VirtualEscapes. Protologik Computer Systems Staff. (Illus.). 1995. 49.95 (*1-888410-00-0*, SS4101) Elgin Intractve.

VirtualFront. Edward Bolme et al. (Cyberpunk Ser.). (Illus.). 88p. (Orig.). 1995. pap. 12.00 (*0-937279-75-7*, CP3441) R Talsorian.

***Virtualisation of Financial Services.** 1997. write for info. (*0-614-25482-5*, N282) Econ Intel.

Virtually Eliminated. Jefferson Scott. 336p. 1996. pap. 9.99 (*0-88070-885-9*, Multnomah Bks) Multnomah Pubs.

***Virtually Fat Free Cookbook.** Christine McFadden. 1997. 12.98 (*0-7624-0004-8*) Courage Bks.

Virtually Normal. Andrew Sullivan. 1996. pap. 12.00 (*0-679-74614-5*) Knopf.

Virtually Normal: An Argument about Homosexuality. Andrew Sullivan. LC 95-9584. 224p. 1995. 22.00 (*0-679-42382-6*) Knopf.

***Virtually Normal: An Argument about Homosexuality.** Andrew Sullivan. Date not set. pap. 12.00 (*0-614-21933-7*, Vin) Random.

Virtually Now: Stories of Science, Technology, & Power. Ed. by Jeanne Schinto. LC 96-14745. 272p. 1996. pap. 12.95 (*0-89255-220-4*) Persea Bks.

Virtually Vegetarian: Imaginative Vegetarian Recipes. Paul Gayler. (Illus.). 160p. 1996. 30.00 (*0-00-412737-4*, Pub. by HarpC UK) HarpC.

Virtue. Jane Feather. 448p. 1993. mass mkt. 5.99 (*0-553-56054-9*) Bantam.

Virtue. large type ed. Jane Feather. LC 93-32759. 1993. lib. bdg. 21.95 (*0-8161-5871-1*, GK Hall) Thorndike Pr.

Virtue: Nomos XXXIV. Ed. by John W. Chapman & William A. Galston. LC 92-17749. (American Society of Legal & Political Philosophy Ser.: Vol. 34). 416p. (C). 1992. 45.00 (*0-8147-1484-6*) NYU Pr.

Virtue: Nomos XXXIV. Ed. by John W. Chapman & William A. Galston. LC 92-17749. (American Society of Legal & Political Philosophy Ser.: Vol. 34). 416p. (C). 1993. pap. 17.50 (*0-8147-1499-4*) NYU Pr.

***Virtue & Affluence: The Challenge of Wealth.** John Haughey. LC 97-2388. 136p. (Orig.). 1997. pap. 14.95 (*1-55612-811-8*, LL1811) Sheed & Ward MO.

Virtue & Magnificence. Alison Cole. 192p. 1995. pap. text ed. 15.60 (*0-13-433673-9*) P-H.

Virtue & Magnificence: Art of the Italian Renaissance Courts. Alison Cole. LC 94-34268. (The Perspectives Ser.). (Illus.). 176p. 1995. 16.95 (*0-8109-2733-0*) Abrams.

Virtue & Medicine: Explorations in the Character of Medicine. Ed. by Earl E. Shelp. (Philosophy & Medicine Ser.: No. 17). 383p. 1985. lib. bdg. 138.00 (*90-277-1808-3*) Kluwer Ac.

Virtue & Modern Shadows of Turning: Preliminary Agitations. Marion Montgomery. 186p. (C). 1989. pap. text ed. 22.50 (*0-8191-7656-7*); lib. bdg. 45.00 (*0-8191-7655-9*) U Pr of Amer.

Virtue & Taste: Essays on Politics, Ethics, & Aesthetics, in Memory of Flint Schier. Ed. by Dudley Knowles & John Skorupski. LC 92-36844. (Philosophical Quarterly Supplementary Ser.: Vol. 2). 1993. 55.95 (*0-631-18863-0*) Blackwell Pubs.

Virtue & the Promise of Conservatism: The Legacy of Burke & Tocqueville. Bruce Frohnen. LC 92-13803. x, 254p. 1993. 25.00 (*0-7006-0558-4*) U Pr of KS.

Virtue & the Veil of Illusion: Generic Innovation & the Pedagogical Project in Eighteenth-Century Literature. Dorothea E. Von Mucke. (Illus.). 352p. 1991. 39.50 (*0-8047-1865-2*) Stanford U Pr.

Virtue & Venom: Catalogs of Women from Antiquity to the Renaissance. Glenda McLeod. (Women & Culture Ser.). 184p. (C). 1991. text ed. 42.50 (*0-472-10206-0*) U of Mich Pr.

An Asterisk (*) at the beginning of an entry indicates that the title is appearing in BIP for the first time.

Virtue & Vice in the Middle Time. Svend A. Madsen. Tr. by James M. Ogier. LC 92-10596. (Library of World Literature in Translation: Vol. 29). 584p. (DAN & ENG.). 1992. text ed. 20.00 (0-8153-0606-7) Garland.

Virtue, Commerce & History: Essays on Political Thought & History, Chiefly in the Eighteenth Century. J. G. Pocock. (Ideas in Context Ser.). 400p. 1985. text ed. 85.00 (0-521-25701-8); pap. text ed. 23.95 (0-521-27660-8) Cambridge U Pr.

Virtue, Corruption, & Self-Interest: Political Values in the Eighteenth Century. Ed. by Richard K. Matthews. LC 93-55063. 1994. 48.50 (0-934223-26-2) Lehigh Univ Pr.

***Virtue Ethics.** Ed. by Roger Crisp & Michael Slote. (Oxford Readings in Philosophy Ser.). 290p. 1997. pap. 17.95 (0-19-875188-5) OUP.

***Virtue Ethics.** Ed. by Roger Crisp & Michael Slote. (Oxford Readings in Philosophy). 296p. 1997. 65.00 (0-19-875189-3) OUP.

***Virtue Ethics: A Critical Reader.** Ed. by Daniel Statman. LC 97-13008. 320p. 1997. 50.00 (0-87840-220-9); pap. 24.95 (0-87840-221-7) Georgetown U Pr.

Virtue, Happiness & Duclos' 'Histoire de Madame de Luz' L. R. Free. (Archives Internationales D'Histoire des Idees Ser.: No. 15). 102p. 1974. pap. text ed. 41.50 (90-247-1669-1, Pub. by M Nijhoff NE) Kluwer Ac.

Virtue in the Unseen Warfare. Jack N. Sparks. LC 95-531. 188p. (Orig.). 1995. pap. 9.95 (0-9622713-8-1) Conciliar Pr.

Virtue Is More Important Than Riches. Aleksandr Duknovych. Ed. & Tr. by Elaine Rusinko. 85p. 1995. 32.00 (0-88033-290-5) East Eur Monographs.

Virtue, Learning & the Enlightened Historian: Ideas of Scholarship & Society in Early Modern Scotland. David Allan. 256p. 1993. pap. 25.00 (0-7486-0438-3, Pub. by Edinburgh U Pr UK) Col U Pr.

***Virtue of Civility: Selected Essays on Liberalism, Tradition, & Civil Society.** Edward A. Shils. Ed. by Steven Grosby. LC 96-31391. 400p. 1997. write for info. (0-86597-147-1); pap. write for info. (0-86597-148-X) Liberty Fund.

Virtue of Necessity: English Women's Writing 1649-88. Elaine Hobby. 1989. pap. 16.95 (0-472-08098-9); text ed. 44.50 (0-472-10125-0) U of Mich Pr.

Virtue of Necessity: Inconclusiveness & Narrative Form in Chaucer's Poetry. Larry Sklute. LC 84-22825. 160p. 1985. 40.00 (0-8142-0376-0); pap. 27.50 (0-8142-0404-X) Ohio St U Pr.

Virtue of Prudence. Douglas J. Den Uyl. LC 90-25008. (Studies in Moral Philosophy: Vol. 5). 350p. (C). 1991. text ed. 61.95 (0-8204-1504-9) P Lang Pubng.

Virtue of Selfishness. Ayn Rand. 1964. pap. 4.50 (0-451-15699-4, Sig) NAL-Dutton.

Virtue of Selfishness. Ayn Rand. 1964. pap. 5.99 (0-451-16393-1) NAL-Dutton.

Virtue of Sex. Jose M. De Vinck. LC 66-15236. 256p. 1966. 15.75 (0-911726-14-4, CODE VOS) Alleluia Pr.

Virtue of Yin: Essays on Chinese Women. Lily S. Lee. 128p. (C). 1994. pap. text ed. 14.00 (0-646-14925-3, Pub. by Wild Peony Pty AT) UH Pr.

Virtue, Order, Mind: Ancient, Modern & Post-Modern Perspectives. Ed. by Peter V. Amato. (Oneonta Philosophy Studies). 199p. (Orig.). (C). 1994. pap. 12.00 (1-883058-16-3) Inst Global Cultl.

Virtue, Success, Pleasure, & Liberation: Four Aims of Life in the Tradition of Ancient India. Alain Danielou. 1993. pap. 14.95 (0-89281-218-4) Inner Tradit.

Virtue Transformed: Political Argument in England, 1688-1740. Shelley Burtt. 256p. (C). 1992. text ed. 49.95 (0-521-37528-2) Cambridge U Pr.

Virtue Under Fire: How World War II Changed Our Social & Sexual Attitudes. John Costello. 1986. 17.95 (0-316-73968-5) Little.

Virtue under Fire: How World War II Changed Our Social & Sexual Attitudes. John Costello. LC 87-335. (Illus.). 309p. 1987. reprint ed. pap. 9.95 (0-88064-070-7) Fromm Intl Pub.

Virtue Victorious. Tim Kelly. 1974. pap. 5.00 (0-87129-219-X, V15) Dramatic Pub.

Virtues: Contemporary Essays on Moral Character. Ed. by Robert B. Kruschwitz & Robert C. Roberts. 263p. (C). 1987. pap. 31.95 (0-534-06720-4) Wadsworth Pub.

Virtues: Die TuGenden. Herbert Witzenman. Tr. by Daisy Aldan. 1975. 10.95 (0-913152-54-4) Folder Edns.

***Virtues: Die TuGenden.** Herbert Witzenman. Tr. by Daisy Aldan. 1975. 10.95 (0-913152-80-3) Folder Edns.

***Virtues & Practices in the Christian Tradition: Christian Ethics after MacIntyre.** Ed. by Nancey Murphy et al. 304p. (Orig.). 1997. pap. 25.00 (1-56338-215-6) TPI PA.

Virtues & Reasons: Philippa Foot & Moral Theory. Ed. by Rosalind Hursthouse et al. 336p. 1995. 39.95 (0-19-824046-5) OUP.

Virtues & Vices see Athenian Constitution

Virtues & Vices & Other Essays in Moral Philosophy. Philippa Foot. LC 78-54794. 222p. reprint ed. pap. 63.30 (0-7837-4816-7, 2044463) Bks Demand.

***Virtues Collection, 2 vol., Set.** William J. Bennett. 1996. boxed, pap. text ed. 32.00 (0-684-00457-7, Touchstone Bks) S&S Trade.

Virtue's Faults, or, Women's Correspondences in Eighteenth-Century Fiction. April Alliston. 1996. 39.50 (0-8047-2660-4) Stanford U Pr.

Virtues Guide: A Family Handbook. Linda K. Popov et al. (Illus.). 280p. 1993. pap. 24.95 (0-9697634-0-9) Virtues Comm.

Virtue's Hero: Emerson, Antislavery & Reform. Len Gougeon. LC 89-37662. 416p. 1990. 50.00 (0-8203-1193-6) U of Ga Pr.

Virtues in Conflict: Tradition & the Korean Woman Today. Ed. by Sandra Mattielli. 214p. Date not set. pap. 22.00 (0-614-12688-6) E Rock Pr.

Virtues in Medical Practice. Edmund D. Pellegrino & David C. Thomasma. LC 92-49073. 224p. 1993. 39.50 (0-19-508289-3) OUP.

Virtues, Laws & Powers: Universal, Spiritual Principles That Govern Our Destiny. LC 94-79503. (Illus.). 152p. (Orig.). 1995. pap. text ed. 14.95 (1-885186-82-7) Amber Pr OK.

Virtues, Laws & Powers: Universal Spiritual Principles that Govern Our Destiny. (Illus.). 160p. (Orig.). 1995. per., pap. text ed. 15.95 (1-885186-83-5) Amber Pr OK.

***Virtues of an Authentic Life: A Celebration of Spiritual Maturity.** Bernard Haring. LC 97-12992. 192p. (Orig.). 1997. 15.00 (0-7648-0120-1) Liguori Pubns.

Virtues of Aristotle. D. S. Hutchinson. 128p. 1986. 35.00 (0-7102-0858-8, 08588, RKP) Routledge.

***Virtues of Ordinary Christians.** James F. Keenan. 128p. (Orig.). 1996. pap. 12.95 (1-55612-908-4, LL1908) Sheed & Ward MO.

Virtues of the Family. Jacob J. Ross. LC 93-42425. 1994. 27.95 (0-02-927385-4, Free Press) Free Pr.

Virtues of the Mind: An Inquiry into the Nature of Virtue & the Ethical Foundations of Knowledge. Linda T. Zagaebski. 400p. (C). 1996. pap. text ed. 19.95 (0-521-57826-4) Cambridge U Pr.

Virtues of the Mind: An Inquiry into the Nature of Virtue & the Ethical Foundations of Knowledge. Linda T. Zagzebski. 400p. (C). 1996. text ed. 64.95 (0-521-57060-3) Cambridge U Pr.

Virtues of the Solitary Bird. Juan Goytisolo. Tr. by Helen Lane. 160p. (Orig.). 1993. pap. 16.95 (1-85242-175-4) Serpents Tail.

***Virtues of the Vicious: Jacob Riis, Stephen Crane & the Spectacle of the Slum.** Keith Gandal. 224p. 1997. 45.00 (0-19-511063-3) OUP.

Virtues of the Way. Paul Ferrini. (Illus.). (Orig.). 1990. pap. 7.50 (1-879159-04-X) Heartways Pr.

Virtues of the Will: The Transformation of Ethics in the Late Thirteenth Century. Bonnie Kent. LC 95-3087. 272p. 1995. 44.95 (0-8132-0829-7) Cath U Pr.

Virtue's Own Feature: Shakespeare & the Virtue Ethics Tradition. David N. Beauregard. LC 95-5838. 264p. 1995. 41.50 (0-87413-578-8) U Delaware Pr.

Virtue's Reward. Jean R. Ewing. 256p. 1995. mass mkt. 3.99 (0-8217-4847-5, Zebra Kensgtn) Kensgtn Pub Corp.

Virtue's Rewards. Wilma Kauffen. (New Tempo Ser.). 1993. mass mkt. 5.95 (0-929654-84-6, 101) Blue Moon Bks.

Virtues Spiritual Growth Guide. Christine M. Carpenter. LC 96-84478. (Illus.). 200p. (Orig.). 1997. pap. 16.95 (1-887999-50-7) CMC Pr OR.

Virtuleze Begins His Journey. Joleen Tropp. (Illus.). 32p. (Orig.). (J). (ps). 1995. pap. 2.95 (0-9646387-0-3) Virtibilis Vent.

***Virtuosa.** Robert Jacobson. Date not set. write for info. (0-688-04895-1) Morrow.

Virtuosity. Terry Bisson. 1995. mass mkt. 5.99 (0-671-53752-0) PB.

Virtuosity, Charisma & Social Order: A Comparative Sociological Study of Monasticism in Theravada Buddhism & Medieval Catholicism. Ilana F. Silber. (Cambridge Cultural & Social Studies). 265p. (C). 1995. text ed. 54.95 (0-521-41397-4) Cambridge U Pr.

Virtuoso. Katrina Vincenzi. (Black Lace Ser.). 1995. mass mkt. 5.95 (0-352-32907-6, Pub. by Virgin Pub UK) London Brdge.

Virtuoso. Thomas Shadwell. Ed. by Marjorie H. Nicolson & David S. Rodes. LC 65-19466. (Regents Restoration Drama Ser.). 179p. 1966. reprint ed. pap. 51.10 (0-7837-1471-8, 2057166) Bks Demand.

Virtuoso. Thomas Shadwell. Ed. by Marjorie H. Nicolson & David S. Rodes. LC 65-19466. (Regents Restoration Drama Ser.). xxvi, 154p. 1966. reprint ed. pap. text ed. 8.95 (0-8032-5368-0, Bison Books) U of Nebr Pr.

Virtuoso Flute-Player: By Johann George Tromlitz. Johann G. Tromlitz. Ed. by Ardal Powell. (Musical Texts & Monographs). (Illus.). 350p. (C). 1991. text ed. 85.00 (0-521-39067-2); pap. text ed. 29.95 (0-521-39977-7) Cambridge U Pr.

Virtuoso Goldsmiths & the Triumph of Mannerism, 1540-1620. J. F. Hayward. (Illus.). 796p. 1976. 95.00 (0-85667-005-7) Sothebys Pubns.

***Virtuoso Microsoft Word 6.0 for Windows.** Cheryl L. Dukarich. 528p. (C). 1995. spiral bd. 39.56 incl. 3.5 hd (0-395-73788-5) HM.

***Virtuoso Microsoft Word 6.0 for Windows.** Cheryl L. Dukarich. (C). 1996. teacher ed., text ed. 11.96 (0-395-75938-2) HM.

***Virtuoso Microsoft Word 6.0 for Windows: Assistant Tutorial.** Cheryl L. Dukarich. (C). 1996. text ed. 10.47 (0-395-75939-0) HM.

Virtuoso Music for Piano: Centennial Edition. R. Schumann. 200p. 1994. otabind 12.95 (0-7935-3069-5, 50482108) H Leonard.

Virtuoso Pianist Book 1 60 Exercises: Nos. 1-20. C. Hanon. 24p. 1986. pap. 3.95 (0-7935-5121-8) H Leonard.

Virtuoso Tribe of Arts & Sciences: Studies in the Eighteenth-Century Work & Membership of the London Society of Arts. Ed. by D. G. Allan & John L. Abbott. LC 90-11318. (Illus.). 512p. 1992. 65.00 (0-8203-1326-2) U of Ga Pr.

Virtuoso WordPerfect 6.1. Dukarich. (C). 1995. pap. 35.56 (0-395-74880-1) HM.

***Virtuoso WordPerfect 6.1 for Windows.** Cheryl L. Dukarich. 560p. (C). 1995. spiral bd. 39.56 incl. 3.5 hd (0-395-73789-3) HM.

***Virtuoso WordPerfect 6.1 for Windows.** Cheryl L. Dukarich. (C). 1996. teacher ed., text ed. 11.96 (0-395-77447-0) HM.

***Virtuoso WordPerfect 6.1 for Windows: Assistant Tutorial.** Cheryl L. Dukarich. (C). 1996. text ed. 10.47 (0-395-75940-4) HM.

Virtuous Citizens, Disruptive Subjects: The Poetics of Complaint in a New England Court. Barbara Yngvesson. (After the Law Ser.). 288p. (C). (gr. 13). 1993. pap. 16.95 (0-415-90767-5, B0556, Routledge NY) Routledge.

Virtuous Desserts see Naturally Sweet

Virtuous Giving: Philanthropy, Voluntary Service, & Caring. Mike W. Martin. LC 93-8027. (Philanthropic Studies). 244p. (C). 1994. 24.95 (0-253-33677-5) Ind U Pr.

Virtuous Intentions: The Religious Dimension of Narrative. Mark Ledbetter. 100p. 1989. 20.95 (1-55540-394-8, 01 01 66); pap. 13.95 (1-55540-395-6, 01 01 66) Scholars Pr GA.

Virtuous Journalist. Stephen Klaidman & Tom L. Beauchamp. 256p. (C). 1988. pap. text ed. 17.95 (0-19-505688-4) OUP.

Virtuous Life in Business: Stories of Courage & Integrity in the Corporate World. Ed. by Oliver F. Williams & John W. Houck. LC 92-5513. 204p. (C). 1992. text ed. 58.95 (0-8476-7746-X); pap. text ed. 23.95 (0-8476-7747-8) Rowman.

Virtuous Lives: Four Quaker Sisters Remember Family Life, Abolitionism, & Women's Suffrage. Lucille Salitan & Eve L. Perera. (Illus.). 180p. (C). 1994. pap. text ed. 15.95 (0-8264-0687-4) Continuum.

Virtuous Octavia. Samuel Brandon. LC 73-133641. (Tudor Facsimile Texts. Old English Plays Ser.: No. 81). reprint ed. 59.50 (0-404-53381-7) AMS Pr.

Virtuous Pagan in Middle English Literature. Cindy L. Vitto. LC 89-84934. (Transactions Ser.: Vol. 79, Pt. 5). 97p. (C). 1989. pap. 15.00 (0-87169-795-5, T795-VIC) Am Philos.

Virtuous Painter. Eric Felderman. LC 91-27136. 103p. 1992. 38.95 (0-945942-21-4); pap. text ed. 27.95 (0-945942-22-2) Portmanteau Editions.

Virtuous Passions: The Formation of Christian Character. G. Simon Harak. LC 93-23503. 192p. (C). 1994. pap. 11.95 (0-8091-3436-5) Paulist Pr.

Virtuous Reality: How America Surrendered Discussion of Moral Values to Opportunists, Nitwits & Blockheads Like William Bennet. Jon Katz. 1997. 21.00 (0-679-44913-2) McKay.

Virtuous Woman. Kaye Gibbons. LC 88-22026. 168p. 1989. 13.95 (0-945575-09-2) Algonquin Bks.

Virtuous Woman. Kaye Gibbons. LC 89-40513. (Vintage Contemporaries Ser.). 176p. 1990. pap. 9.00 (0-679-72844-9, Vin) Random.

Virtuous Woman. Pat Strickland. LC 86-71360. 165p. 1986. 10.95 (0-86690-321-6, S2360-014) Am Fed Astrologers.

Virtuous Woman: And the Answer to the Submission Question. Marion E. Wade. 73p. 1990. pap. 4.95 (0-88144-149-X) Christian Pub.

Virtuous Woman: Reflections on Christian Feminist Ethics. Denise L. Carmody. LC 92-17952. 180p. (Orig.). 1992. pap. 17.50 (0-88344-817-3) Orbis Bks.

Virtus VRML Toolkit for Macintosh. David Smith et al. (Illus.). (Orig.). 1995. pap. 40.00 (1-56830-246-0) Hayden.

Virtus VRML Toolkit for Windows. (Illus.). 283p. (Orig.). 1995. 40.00 (1-56830-247-9) Hayden.

Virulence Mechanisms. 2nd ed. Ed. by James Roth. 500p. 1995. write for info. (1-55581-085-3) Am Soc Microbio.

Virulence Mechanisms of Bacterial Pathogens. Ed. by James A. Roth. (Illus.). 390p. 1988. text ed. 83.00 (0-914826-99-9) Am Soc Microbio.

Virus. Diane Hoh. (Med Center Ser.: No. 1). (J). (gr. 4-7). 1996. mass mkt. 3.99 (0-590-54322-9) Scholastic Inc.

Virus. Chuck Pfarrer. (Illus.). 136p. 1995. pap. 16.95 (1-56971-104-6) Dark Horse Comics.

Virus. Graham Watkins. 413p. (YA). 1995. 25.00 (0-7867-0194-3) Carroll & Graf.

Virus. Graham Watkins. 1996. mass mkt. 5.99 (0-312-96003-4) St Martin.

Virus. Oas General Secretariat Staff. (Serie de Biologia: No. 8). 72p. (Orig.). (C). 1980. reprint ed. pap. text ed. 3.50 (0-8270-1169-5) OAS.

***Virus: A Novel.** Bill Buchanan. 432p. 1997. mass mkt. 6.50 (0-515-12011-1) Jove Pubns.

Virus: Detection & Elimination. Rune Skardhamar. (Illus.). 290p. 1995. pap. 34.95 (0-12-647690-X) Acad Pr.

Virus & Virus-Like Diseases of Bulb & Flower Crops. Ed. by Gad Loebenstein et al. LC 95-18716. 1995. text ed. 99.95 (0-471-95293-1) Wiley.

***Virus & Virus-Like Diseases of Citrus in the Near East.** Joseph M. Bove. 538p. 1995. 120.00 (92-5-103827-9, F38279, Pub. by FAO IT) Bernan Associates.

Virus Attachment & Entry into Cells: Proceedings of an ASM Conference Held in Philadelphia, Pennsylvania, 10-13 April 1985. American Society for Microbiology Staff. Ed. by Richard L. Crowell & Karl Lonberg-Holm. LC 85-28731. 224p. reprint ed. pap. 63.90 (0-7837-4039-5, 2043869) Bks Demand.

Virus Chemotherapy. Ed. by F. E. Hahn. (Antibiotics & Chemotherapy Ser.: Vol. 27). (Illus.). vi, 310p. 1980. 152.00 (3-8055-0263-X) S Karger.

Virus Creation Labs: A Journey into the Underground. George C. Smith. (Illus.). 176p. (Orig.). 1994. pap. 12.95 (0-929408-09-8) Amer Eagle Pubns Inc.

Virus Defense for Dummies. Wallace Wang. 1996. pap. 19.99 (1-56884-864-1) IDG Bks.

Virus Diseases: Directory of Authors of New Medical & Scientific Reviews with Subject Index. Science & Life Consultants Association Staff. 160p. 1995. 47.50 (0-7883-0620-0); pap. 44.50 (0-7883-0621-9) ABBE Pubs Assn.

Virus Diseases in Laboratory & Captive Animals. Ed. by Gholamreza Darai. (Developments in Veterinary Virology Ser.). (C). 1987. lib. bdg. 242.50 (0-89838-988-7) Kluwer Ac.

Virus Diseases of Food Animals: A World Geography of Epidemiology & Control, Vol. 1. Ed. by E. Paul Gibbs. LC 81-521. (International Perspectives Ser.). 1982. text ed. 199.00 (0-12-282201-3) Acad Pr.

Virus Diseases of Small Fruits & Grapevines. Ed. by N. W. Frazier. 290p. 1970. 20.00 (0-931876-21-4, 4056) ANR Pubns CA.

Virus Diseases of Trees & Shrubs. 2nd ed. J. I. Cooper. LC 92-46392. 224p. (gr. 13). 1993. text ed. 55.95 (0-412-47220-1) Chapman & Hall.

Virus Ground Zero: Stalking the Killer Viruses with the Centers for Disease Control. Ed Regis. 244p. 1996. 23.00 (0-671-55361-5, PB Hardcover) PB.

Virus Hepatitis & Kidney. Ed. by V. A. Mioli. (Journal: Nephron: Vol. 61, No. 3, 1992). (Illus.). 128p. 1992. pap. 56.75 (3-8055-5621-7) S Karger.

***Virus Hunter: Thirty Years of Battling Hot Viruses Around the World.** C. J. Peters & Mark Olshaker. LC 97-977. (Illus.). 323p. 1997. 23.95 (0-385-48557-3, Anchor NY); pap. write for info. (0-385-48558-1, Anchor NY) Doubleday.

Virus Hunters: A Dual Memoir from the Frontiers of Disease. Joseph McCormick & Carl Johnson. 1996. 22.95 (0-614-97001-6) Turner Pub GA.

Virus Hunting: AIDS, Cancer, & the Human Retrovirus: A Story of Scientific Discovery. abr. ed. Robert C. Gallo. LC 90-55600. (Illus.). 368p. 1993. pap. 16.00 (0-465-09815-0) Basic.

Virus Inactivation in Plasma Products. Ed. by J. J. Morgenthaler. (Current Studies in Hematology & Blood Transfusion: No. 56). (Illus.). x, 158p. 1988. 113.75 (3-8055-4836-2) S Karger.

Virus Induced Enzymes. J. M. Morrison. LC 90-13137. 655p. 1991. text ed. 298.00 (0-471-92339-7, Wiley-L) Wiley.

Virus-Induced Immunosuppression. Steven C. Specter. LC 88-31629. (Infectious Agents & Pathogenesis Ser.). 500p. 1989. 110.00 (0-306-43040-1, Plenum Pr) Plenum.

Virus Infection & the Cell Surface. Ed. by George H. Poste & G. Nicholson. (Cell Surface Reviews Ser.: Vol. 2). 342p. 1980. 239.50 (0-7204-0598-X) Elsevier.

Virus Infection & the Developing Nervous System. Ed. by G. Lyon. (C). 1988. lib. bdg. 110.00 (0-7462-0053-6) Kluwer Ac.

Virus Infections: Modern Concepts & Status. Ed. by Lloyd C. Olson. LC 82-5097. (Microbiology Ser.: No. 6). 303p. 1982. reprint ed. pap. 86.40 (0-608-01308-0, 2062053) Bks Demand.

Virus Infections & Diabetes Mellitus. Ed. by Yechiel Becker. (Developments in Medical Virology Ser.). (C). 1987. lib. bdg. 131.50 (0-89838-970-4) Kluwer Ac.

Virus Infections in Bats. S. E. Sulkin. Ed. by Rae Allen. (Monographs in Virology: Vol. 8). 100p. 1974. 55.25 (3-8055-1696-7) S Karger.

Virus Infections of Birds. Ed. by J. B. McFerran & M. S. McNulty. (Virus Infections of Vertebrates Ser.: Vol. 4). 640p. 1993. 289.00 (0-444-89899-9) Elsevier.

Virus Infections of Carnivores. Ed. by M. J. Appel. (Virus Infections of Vertabrates Ser.: Vol. 1). 500p. 1988. 324.25 (0-444-42709-0) Elsevier.

***Virus Infections of Equines.** Ed. by M. J. Studdert. 380p. 1996. 268.75 (0-444-82527-4) Elsevier.

***Virus Infections of Equines.** Michael J. Studdert. LC 96-33479. (Virus Infections of Vertebrates Ser.). 1996. write for info. (0-04-448257-4) Elsevier.

Virus Infections of Porcines. Ed. by M. B. Pensaert & M. C. Horzink. (Virus Infections of Vertebrates Ser.: No. 2). 284p. 1989. 223.50 (0-444-42909-3) Elsevier.

Virus Infections of Rodents & Lagomorphs. Ed. by A. D. Osterhaus. LC 94-21040. (Virus Infections of Vertebrates Ser.: Vol. 5). 432p. 1994. 256.25 (0-444-81909-6) Elsevier.

Virus Infections of Ruminants. Ed. by Z. Dinter & B. Morein. (Virus Infections of Vertebrates Ser.: No. 3). 592p. 1990. 299.50 (0-444-87312-0) Elsevier.

Virus Infections of the Gastrointestinal Tract. Ed. by David A. Tyrrell & Albert Z. Kapikian. LC 82-2383. (Infectious Diseases & Antimicrobial Agents Ser.: No. 3). 486p. reprint ed. pap. 138.60 (0-7837-7017-0, 2046833) Bks Demand.

Virus Invaders. Alan E. Nourse. Ed. by V. Mathews. LC 91-36650. (Venture Bks.). (Illus.). 112p. (YA). (gr. 9-12). 1992. lib. bdg. 22.00 (0-531-12511-4) Watts.

Virus, Mycoplasm & Rickettsia Diseases of Fruit Trees. M. Nemeth. (Forestry Sciences Ser.). 1987. lib. bdg. 323.50 (90-247-2868-1) Kluwer Ac.

Virus of Fear: Demise of the Carolinas Ku Klux Klan. W. Horace Carter. (Illus.). 256p. 1991. 19.95 (0-937866-33-4) Atlantic Pub Co.

Virus of the Mind: The New Science of the Meme. Richard Brodie. LC 95-79421. (Illus.). 1996. 22.00 (0-9636001-1-7) Integral Pr.

Virus Protection. Pamela Kane. 1993. pap. 39.95 (0-679-79021-7) Random.

Virus Separation & Purification Methods. Ed. by Alfred Polson. LC 93-22933. 308p. 1993. 115.00 (0-8247-9149-5) Dekker.

***Virus Strategies: Molecular Biology & Pathogenesis.** Ed. by W. Doerfler & P. Bohm. (Illus.). xxiii, 543p. 1993. 175.00 (3-527-30027-9, VCH) Wiley.

Virus Structure & Assembly. Sherwood Casjens. 290p. (C). 1985. 100.00 (0-86720-044-8) Jones & Bartlett.

Virus Taxonomy. Ed. by Arun Misra. 211p. 1985. 25.00 (1-55528-058-7, Messers Today & Tomorrow) Scholarly Pubns.

Virus Taxonomy: Classification & Nomenclature of Viruses: Sixth Report of the International Committee on Taxonomy of Viruses. International Committee on Taxonomy of Viruses & Frederick A. Murphy. LC 95-10557. (Archives of Virology: Supplementum Ser.: Vol. 10). 1995. 107.95 (3-211-82594-0) Spr-Verlag.

Virus Taxonomy: Classification & Nomenclature of Viruses, Sixth Report of the International Committee on Taxonomy of Viruses. Ed. by Frederick A. Murphy et al. (Archives of Virology Ser.: Suppl. No. 10). (Illus.). 595p. 1995. pap. 98.00 (*0-387-82594-0*) Spr-Verlag.

Virus Vaccines in Asian Countries. International Symposium "Virus Vaccines in Asian Countries" Staff. Ed. by Konosuke Fukai. LC 86-193028. (Japan Intractable Diseases Research Foundation Publication Ser.: No. 25). 233p. 1986. reprint ed. pap. 66.50 (*0-608-01201-7*, 2061890) Bks Demand.

***Virus-X: Tracking the New Killer Plagues Out of the Present & into the Future.** Frank Ryan. (Illus.). 430p. 1997. 24.95 (*0-316-76383-7*) Little.

Viruses. Howard Facklam & Margery Facklam. (Invaders Ser.). (Illus.). 64p. (J). (gr. 5-8). 1994. lib. bdg. 15.98 (*0-8050-2856-0*) TFC Bks NY.

Viruses. S. Jane Flint. Ed. by J. J. Head. LC 87-70987. (Carolina Biology Readers Ser.: No. 194). (Illus.). 16p. (Orig.). (YA). (gr. 10 up). 1988. pap. text ed. 2.75 (*0-89278-094-0*, 45-9794) Carolina Biological.

Viruses. Arnold J. Levine. (Scientific American Library). 1995. text ed. 32.95 (*0-7167-5031-7*) W H Freeman.

Viruses. Cold Spring Harbor Symposia on Quantitative Biology Staff. (Cold Spring Harbor Symposia on Quantitative Biology Ser.: Vol. 18). 317p. 1953. reprint ed. pap. 90.40 (*0-608-00716-1*, 2061490) Bks Demand.

Viruses: Catalogue, Characterization & Classification. Heinz Fraenkel-Conrat. LC 84-1984. 276p. 1985. 85.00 (*0-306-41766-9*, Plenum Pr) Plenum.

Viruses Affecting Man & Animals. Murry Sanders & Morris Schaeffer. LC 75-117612. (Illus.). 478p. 1971. 23.30 (*0-87527-070-0*) Green.

Viruses, Allergies & the Immune System. Jan De Vries. (By Appointment Only Ser.). 128p. 1988. pap. 11.95 (*1-85158-176-6*, Pub. by Mnstream UK) Trafalgar.

Viruses & Bone Marrow: Basic Research & Clinical Practice. Young. (Hematology Ser.: Vol. 16). 464p. 1993. 195.00 (*0-8247-8833-8*) Dekker.

Viruses & Cancer: Fifty-First Symposium for the Society for General Microbiology, Held at the University of Cambridge, March 1994. Ed. by A. C. Minson et al. LC 93-46636. (Society for General Microbiology Symposium Ser.: No. 51). (Illus.). 330p. (C). 1994. text ed. 115.00 (*0-521-45472-7*) Cambridge U Pr.

Viruses & Cancer: Proceedings of the WHO Scientific Group, Geneva, 1964. WHO Staff. (Technical Report Ser.: No. 295). 60p. (ENG, FRE, RUS & SPA.). 1965. pap. text ed. 5.00 (*92-4-120295-5*, 1100295) World Health.

Viruses & Human Cancer. Ed. by J. R. Arrand & D. R. Harper. (Illus.). 256p. (Orig.). 1997. pap. 70.00 (*1-872748-44-9*, Pub. by Bios Sci UK) Bks Intl VA.

Viruses & Human Cancer. Ed. by Yohei Ito. (Progress in Experimental Tumor Research Ser.: Vol. 21). (Illus.). 1977. 89.75 (*3-8055-2701-2*) S Karger.

Viruses & Parasites: Immunodiagnosis & Prevention of Infectious Disease see Immunology of Human Infection

Viruses & Reproduction: A Bibliography. Compiled by Ernest L. Abel. LC 88-16575. 329p. 1988. text ed. 65.00 (*0-313-26439-2*, AVR/, Greenwood Pr) Greenwood.

Viruses & the Cellular Immune Response. Thomas. 544p. 1993. 225.00 (*0-8247-9053-7*) Dekker.

Viruses & Virus-Like Agents in Disease: A Karger Symposium, Basel, March 1993. Ed. by R. M. Zinkernagel & W. Stauffacher. (Journal: Intervirology: Vol. 35, Nos. 1-4). (Illus.). 220p. 1993. reprint ed. 155.75 (*3-8055-5785-X*) S Karger.

U
V

Viruses As the Causative Agents of Naturally Occurring Tumors. Ed. by George Klein. LC 84-24957. (Advances in Viral Oncology Ser.: No. 5). (Illus.). 279p. 1985. reprint ed. pap. 79.60 (*0-7837-9560-2*, 2060309) Bks Demand.

Viruses Associated with Human Cancer. Ed. by Leo A. Phillips. LC 82-25240. (Illus.). 668p. reprint ed. pap. 180.00 (*0-7837-3354-2*, 2043312) Bks Demand.

Viruses, Immunity, & Immunodeficiency. Ed. by Andor Szentivanyi & Herman Friedman. LC 86-3263. (University of South Florida International Biomedical Symposia Ser.). 380p. 1986. 75.00 (*0-306-42235-2*, Plenum Pr) Plenum.

Viruses, Immunity, & Mental Disorders. Eduard Kurstak et al. 470p. 1987. 110.00 (*0-306-42337-5*, Plenum Med Bk) Plenum.

Viruses in Human Gene Therapy. Ed. by Jean-Michel H. Vos. LC 93-73564. (Illus.). 216p. (C). 1995. lib. bdg. 65.00 (*0-89089-559-7*) Carolina Acad Pr.

Viruses in Human Tumors. P. H. Hofschneider. Ed. by K. Munk. (Beitraege zur Onkologie, Contributions to Oncology Ser.: Vol. 24). (Illus.). viii, 216p. 1987. 53.75 (*3-8055-4354-9*) S Karger.

Viruses in Naturally Occurring Cancers, Bk. A. H. Zur Hausen. LC 80-67166. (Cold Spring Harbor Conferences on Cell Proliferation Ser.: Vol. 7). 732p. 1980. reprint ed. pap. 180.00 (*0-608-01805-8*, 2062458) Bks Demand.

Viruses in Naturally Occurring Cancers, Vol. BKB. H. Zur Hausen. LC 80-67166. (Cold Spring Harbor Conferences on Cell Proliferation Ser.: Vol. 7). 595p. 1980. reprint ed. pap. 169.60 (*0-608-01806-6*, 2062458) Bks Demand.

Viruses in Plant Hosts: Form, Distribution, & Pathologic Effects. Katherine Esau. LC 68-9831. (Illus.). 236p. 1968. 25.00 (*0-299-05110-2*) U of Wis Pr.

Viruses in Plant Hosts: Form, Distribution, & Pathologic Effects. Katherine Esau. LC 68-9831. (John Charles Walker Lectures: 1968). 235p. reprint ed. pap. 67.00 (*0-317-27779-0*, 2015359) Bks Demand.

Viruses in Vectors: Transovarial Passage & Retention. H. Ando et al. 53p. 1986. 15.00 (*0-89054-072-1*) Am Phytopathol Soc.

Viruses in Water Systems: Detection & Identification. Jean-Claude Block & Louis Schwartzbrod. LC 88-26124. 136p. 1989. lib. bdg. 55.00 (*0-89573-274-2*, VCH) Wiley.

Viruses of Invertebrates. Ed. by Edouard Kurstak. 360p. 1991. 160.00 (*0-8247-8469-3*) Dekker.

Viruses of Legumes. John R. Edwardson & Richard G. Christie. 680p. 1991. 364.00 (*0-8493-4729-7*, SB608) CRC Pr.

Viruses of Lower Vertebrates. Ed. by W. Ahne & Eduard Kurstak. (Illus.). xiii, 518p. 1989. 139.00 (*0-387-50859-7*) Spr-Verlag.

Viruses of Plants, 2 vols. A. Brunt et al. (CAB International Publication Ser.). 1488p. 1996. Set. 175.00 (*0-85198-794-X*) CAB Intl.

Viruses of Prokaryotes, 2 vols. Ed. by Hans-W. Ackermann & Michael S. Dubow. 1987. Set. 268.00 (*0-8493-6054-4*, QR342, CRC Reprint) Franklin.

Viruses of Prokaryotes, 2 vols., Vol. I. Ed. by Hans-W. Ackermann & Michael S. Dubow. 224p. 1987. write for info. (*0-318-62593-8*, CRC Reprint) Franklin.

Viruses of Prokaryotes, 2 vols., Vol. II. Ed. by Hans-W. Ackermann & Michael S. Dubow. 256p. 1987. write for info. (*0-318-62594-6*, CRC Reprint) Franklin.

Viruses of Prokaryotes, Vol. 1: General Properties of Bacteriophages. H. Ackermann & M. Dubow. LC 87-9407. 216p. 1987. reprint ed. 123.00 (*0-8493-6056-0*, CRC Reprint) Franklin.

Viruses of Prokaryotes, Vol. 2: General Properties of Bacteriophages. H. Ackermann & M. Dubow. LC 87-9407. 256p. 1987. reprint ed. 145.00 (*0-8493-6057-9*, CRC Reprint) Franklin.

Viruses, Oncogenes & Cancer. Joseph L. Melnick. (Progress in Medical Virology Ser.: Vol. 32). (Illus.). viii, 224p. 1985. 134.50 (*3-8055-3976-2*) S Karger.

***Viruses, Plagues & History.** Michael B. Oldstone. LC 97-9545. 1997. 25.00 (*0-19-511723-9*) OUP.

Viruses That Affect the Immune System. Ed. by Hung Y. Fan et al. (Illus.). 264p. 1991. 62.00 (*1-55581-032-2*) Am Soc Microbio.

Vis-a-Vis: Beginning French. Evelyne Amon et al. LC 95-45823. 1995. student ed. write for info. (*0-07-001700-X*) McGraw.

Vis-a-Vis: Beginning French. Evelyne Amon & Judity A. Muyskens. 1996. lab manual ed., wbk. ed., pap. text ed. write for info. (*0-07-001702-6*) McGraw.

Vis-a-Vis: Beginning French. Judith A. Muyskens et al. 1996. student ed., text ed. write for info. incl. audio (*0-07-912278-7*) McGraw.

Visa & Work Permits for the U. S. - Visa und Arbeitserlaubnis Fuer die U. S. A. J. Hayes Kavanagh. 238p. (ENG & GER.). 1993. 30.00 (*0-86640-033-8*) German Am Chamber.

***Visa est Vox: Sprache und Bild in der Spatantiken Literatur.** Maria Boeder. (Europaische Hochschulschriften, Reihe 28: Bd. 268). 200p. (GER.). 1996. 42.95 (*3-631-30402-1*) P Lang Pubng.

Visa for a Dream: Dominicans in the United States. Patricia R. Pessar. Ed. by Nancy Foner. (Immigrants Ser.). 128p. (C). 1996. pap. text ed. 11.25 (*0-205-16675-X*) Allyn.

Visa Qualifying Examination (VQE) Jack Rudman. (Admission Test Ser.: ATS-48). 1994. pap. 69.95 (*0-8373-5048-4*) Nat Learn.

Visage du Passe. Carole Mortimer. (Azur Ser.). (FRE.). 1994. pap. 3.50 (*0-373-34433-3*, 1-34433-2) Harlequin Bks.

Visage of Muhammad. Ali Shariati. 28p. (Orig.). 1979. pap. 2.00 (*0-318-03828-5*) Book Dist Ctr.

Visages de la Mort Dans L'Oeuvre de Marguerite Yourcenar: Actes d'Un Colloque International Tenu a L'Universite du Minnesota, Morris. Ed. by C. Frederick Farrell, Jr. et al. 232p. (Orig.). (FRE.). 1994. pap. text ed. 20.00 (*0-918032-25-3*) U of Minn Morris.

Visages De l'Amour et De la Haine. Sebastien Japrisot. 120p. (FRE.). 1989. pap. 10.95 (*0-7859-2658-5*, 207038179X) Fr & Eur.

Visages de l'Autre: Alibis, Masques et Identite dans Alexis ou le Traite du vain Combat, Denier du reve et Memoires d'Hadrien de Marguerite Yourcenar. Ana M. De Medeiros. (Currents in Comparative Romance Languages & Literatures Ser.: Vol. 37). 144p. (FRE.). (C). 1996. text ed. 41.95 (*0-8204-2892-2*) P Lang Pubng.

Visages De l'Ombre. Boileau-Narcejac. 214p. (FRE.). 1985. pap. 11.95 (*0-7859-2013-7*, 2070376532) Fr & Eur.

Visages d'un Autoportrait. Zoe Oldenbourg. 409p. (FRE.). 1988. pap. 17.95 (*0-7859-4284-X*, 2070379167) Fr & Eur.

Visages Radieux. Paul Claudel. 144p. (FRE.). 1959. 10.95 (*0-7859-1121-9*, 2070215113) Fr & Eur.

Visaladeuarasa: A Restoration of the Text. John D. Smith. LC 75-30441. (University of Cambridge Oriental Publications: No. 26). 260p. 1977. text ed. 69.95 (*0-521-20815-7*) Cambridge U Pr.

Visalia's Heritage: Buildings, People, History. 1986. 30.00 (*0-614-08603-5*) Visalia Heritage.

Visalia's Heritage: Buildings, People, History. rev. ed. LC 90-191041. 1989. write for info. (*0-9626635-0-6*) Visalia Heritage.

Visas for Life. Yukiko Sugihara. Tr. by Hiroki Sugihara. 260p. 1995. pap. write for info. (*0-9649674-0-5*) Edu-Comm.

Visas for Life: The Remarkable Story of Chiune & Yakiko Sugihara & the Rescue of More Than 6,000 Jews. Holocaust Oral History Project of San Francisco Staff. 64p. (Orig.). 1995. pap. text ed. write for info. (*0-9648999-0-6*) Holocaust Oral.

***Visual C++ 5: No Experience Required.** Steven Holzner. 1997. pap. text ed. 29.99 (*0-7821-2120-9*) Sybex.

Visayan Vignettes: Ethnographic Traces of a Philippine Island. Jean-Paul Dumont. LC 91-37573. (Illus.). 246p. 1992. pap. text ed. 19.95 (*0-226-16955-3*); lib. bdg. 46.00 (*0-226-16954-5*) U Ch Pr.

Visceral Manipulation. Jean-Pierre Barral & Pierre Mercier. LC 87-82743. (Illus.). 278p. 1988. text ed. 50.00 (*0-939616-06-8*) Eastland.

Visceral Manipulation II. Jean-Pierre Barral. LC 87-82743. (Illus.). 264p. (C). 1989. text ed. 48.00 (*0-939616-09-2*) Eastland.

Visceral Pain. Ed. by Gerald F. Gebhart. LC 95-7922. (Progress in Pain Research & Management Ser.: Vol. 5). (Illus.). 528p. 1995. 69.00 (*0-931092-10-8*, PPRM5) Intl Assn Study Pain.

Visceral Vascular Surgery. fac. ed. Ed. by Alfred V. Persson & Paul A. Skudder, Jr. LC 87-6882. (Science & Practice of Surgery Ser.: No. 13). 303p. 1987. reprint ed. pap. 86.40 (*0-7837-8326-4*, 2049113) Bks Demand.

Visco-Plastic Behaviour of Geomaterials. Ed. by N. D. Cristescu & G. Gioda. (CISM International Centre for Mechanical Sciences: Vol. 350). 317p. 1994. 86.95 (*0-387-82586-X*) Spr-Verlag.

Viscoelastic Machine Elements: Elastomers & Lubricants in Machine Systems. Desmond F. Moore. 341p. 1993. 120.00 (*0-7506-1305-X*) Buttrwrth-Heinemann.

Viscoelastic Properties of Polymers. 3rd ed. John D. Ferry. LC 79-28666. 641p. 1980. text ed. 145.00 (*0-471-04894-1*) Wiley.

Viscoelasticity of Biomaterials. Ed. by Wolfgang G. Glasser & Hyoe Hatakeyama. LC 92-10653. (ACS Symposium Ser.: No. 489). (Illus.). 394p. 1992. 84.95 (*0-8412-2221-5*) Am Chemical.

***Viscoelasticity of Engineering Materials.** Haddad. (Illus.). 416p. 1994. text ed. 124.95 (*0-412-59030-1*, Chap & Hall NY) Chapman & Hall.

Viscoelasticity of Paper Coatings & Its Significance in Blade Coating. Technical Association of the Pulp & Paper Industry Staff & Nick G. Triantafillopoulos. LC 96-17236. 1996. 59.00 (*0-89852-328-1*) TAPPI.

Visconti Hours. Intro. by Edith W. Kirsch & Millard Meiss. LC 75-75371. (Illus.). 264p. 1972. boxed 100.00 (*0-8076-0651-0*) Braziller.

Visconti Hours. Intro. by Edith W. Kirsch & Millard Meiss. LC 75-75371. (Illus.). 264p. 1995. 65.00 (*0-8076-1359-2*) Braziller.

Visconti-Sforza Tarocchi. Stuart R. Kaplan. (Illus.). 38p. 1975. pap. 40.00 (*0-913866-06-7*) US Games Syst.

Viscoplasticity. N. Critescu & I. Suliciu. 1982. lib. bdg. 64.40 (*90-247-2592-5*) Kluwer Ac.

Viscosities of Natural Gas Components & Mixtures. N. L. Carr. (Research Bulletin Ser.: No. 23). iv, 59p. 1953. pap. 5.00 (*0-685-43366-8*) Inst Gas Tech.

Viscosity see Thermophysical Properties of Matter: The TPRC Data Series

Viscosity & Density of Light Parafins, Nitrogen & Carbon Dioxide. Ed. by Editions Technip Staff. (Illus.). 120p. (C). 1970. ring bd. 390.00 (*2-7108-0123-X*, Pub. by Edits Technip FR) St Mut.

Viscosity & Density of Liquid Copper & Copper Alloys. Denver Research Institute Staff. 86p. 1974. 13.35 (*0-317-34555-9*, 176) Intl Copper.

Viscosity Index Tables for Celsius Temperatures - DS39-B. 958p. 1996. 75.00 (*0-8031-0817-6*, 05-039020-12) ASTM.

Viscosity Induction. Chris Winkler. (Illus.). 26p. (Orig.). 1989. pap. 3.00 (*0-926935-10-0*) Runaway Spoon.

***Viscosity of the Earth's Mantle.** Lawrence M. Cathles. LC 74-16162. 362p. 1975. reprint ed. pap. 103.20 (*0-608-03321-9*, 2064033) Bks Demand.

***Viscosity Solutions & Applications: Lectures Given at the 2nd Session of the Centro Internazionale Matematico Estivo C.I.M.E. Held in Montecatini Terme, Italy, June 12-20, 1995, Vol. 166.** M. Bardi et al. LC 97-16479. (Lecture Notes in Mathematics Ser.). 1997. pap. write for info. (*3-540-62910-6*) Spr-Verlag.

Viscosity Test Standards for Engine Oils. ASTM Staff. LC 89-120. 75p. 1989. pap. 26.00 (*0-8031-1216-5*, 03-402089-12) ASTM.

Viscosity Testing of Asphalt & Experience with Viscosity Graded Specifications - STP 532. 128p. 1981. 8.75 (*0-8031-0777-3*, 04-532000-08) ASTM.

Viscott Method. David Viscott. 1990. mass mkt. 5.99 (*0-671-72994-2*) PB.

Viscount, Comet & Concorde: Legends of the Air 3. Stewart Wilson & Australian Aviation Staff. (Legends of the Air Ser.: No. 3). (Illus.). 200p. 1996. pap. 22.95 (*1-875671-21-8*, Pub. by Aerospace Pubns AT) Motorbooks Intl.

Viscount Henry St. John Bolingbroke: The Works, 5 vols. Ed. by D. Mallet. (Anglistica & Americana Ser.: No. 13). 1968. reprint ed. Set. 637.00 (*0-685-66435-X*, 05102021) G Olms Pubs.

***Viscount Takes a Wife.** Marcy Stewart. 256p. 1997. mass mkt. 4.99 (*0-8217-5647-8*, Zebra Kensgtn) Kensgtn Pub Corp.

Viscount Vagabond. Loretta Chase. 240p. 1990. mass mkt. 2.95 (*0-380-70836-1*) Avon.

Viscount Vagabond. Loretta Chase. 192p. 1988. 18.95 (*0-8027-1046-8*) Walker & Co.

Viscountess Rhondda, Equalitarian Feminist. Shirley Eoff. 240p. 1991. 42.50 (*0-8142-0539-9*) Ohio St U Pr.

Viscount's Revenge. large type ed. Marion Chesney. 287p. 1992. 25.99 (*0-7505-0157-X*) Ulverscroft.

Viscount's Revenge. Marion Chesney. 1991. reprint ed. 18.00 (*0-7278-4184-X*) Severn Hse.

Viscount's Vixen. Joan E. Overfield. 224p. (Orig.). 1992. mass mkt. 3.99 (*0-380-76922-0*) Avon.

Viscous Circle. Piers Anthony. (Cluster Ser.: No. 5). 272p. 1982. mass mkt. 4.50 (*0-380-79897-2*) Avon.

Viscous Flow. Hilary Ockendon & John Ockendon. (Texts in Applied Mathematics Ser.: No. 13). (Illus.). 130p. (C). 1995. text ed. 59.95 (*0-521-45244-9*); pap. text ed. 20.95 (*0-521-45881-1*) Cambridge U Pr.

Viscous Flow. Frederick S. Sherman. 1990. text ed. write for info. (*0-07-056579-1*) McGraw.

Viscous Flow Applications. Ed. by C. A. Brebbia. (Topics in Boundary Elements Ser.: Vol. 5). 196p. 1989. 54.00 (*1-56252-140-3*) Computational Mech MA.

Viscous Flow Applications. Carlos A. Brebbia. (Topics in Boundary Element Research Ser.: Vol. 5). (Illus.). 200p. 1989. 120.95 (*0-387-50609-8*) Spr-Verlag.

Viscous Flows: The Practical Use of Theory. Stuart W. Churchill. (Illus.). 624p. 1988. 79.95 (*0-409-95185-4*) Buttrwrth-Heinemann.

Viscous Fluid Flow. 2nd ed. Frank M. White. 768p. 1991. text ed. write for info. (*0-07-069712-4*) McGraw.

Viscous Profiles & Numerical Methods for Shock Waves. M. Shearer. LC 91-40934. (Proceedings in Applied Mathematics Ser.: No. 56). x, 252p. 1991. pap. text ed. 56.75 (*0-89871-283-1*) Soc Indus-Appl Math.

Viscous Vortical Flows. L. Ting & R. Klein. Ed. by W. Beiglbock et al. (Lecture Notes in Physics Ser.: Vol. 374). (Illus.). v, 222p. 1991. 17.95 (*0-387-53713-9*) Spr-Verlag.

Visejesicki Medicinski Recnik, Vol. 2: German, French, Italian, Russian. Aleksandar Kostic. 975p. (FRE, GER, ITA & RUS.). 1987. 95.00 (*0-8288-0582-2*, M2041) Fr & Eur.

Visejezicki Medicinski Recnik, Vol. 1: English, Latin, Serbocroatian. Aleksandar Kostic. 1029p. (ENG, LAT & SER.). 1987. 95.00 (*0-8288-0583-0*, M2040) Fr & Eur.

Vishishtadvaita: Philosophy & Religion. Ramanuja Research Society Staff. 273p. 1975. 10.75 (*0-88253-683-4*) Ind-US Inc.

Vishnevi Saad: The Cherry Orchard. Anton P. Chekhov. 175p. (RUS.). 1946. 29.95 (*0-8236-0720-8*) Intl Univs Pr.

Vishnu & His Incarnations. Shakti M. Gupta. (Illus.). xix, 120p. (C). 1993. reprint ed. 16.00 (*81-7039-201-2*, Pub. by Somaiya Publns II) Nataraj Bks.

Vishnu Sahasranamam. Panduranga R. Malyala. (Illus.). 18p. (Orig.). 1986. pap. text ed. 5.00 (*0-938924-28-1*) Sri Shirdi Sai.

Visi Neural Network Systems, Vol. 2. Yuzo A. Hirai. (Japanese Technology Reviews Ser.). 116p. 1992. pap. text ed. 48.00 (*2-88124-868-3*) Gordon & Breach.

VISI Physical Design Automation: Theory & Practice. Sadiq M. Sait & Habib Youssef. 1994. 21.95 (*0-07-707742-3*) McGraw.

Visibility & Power: Essays on Women in Society & Development. Ed. by Leela Dube et al. (Illus.). 416p. 1987. 35.00 (*0-19-561682-0*) OUP.

Visibility Criteria for Signs, Signals, & Roadway Lighting. (Transportation Research Record Ser.: No. 1247). 101p. 1989. 15.50 (*0-309-04972-5*) Transport Res Bd.

Visibility Good. Edward V. Lucas. LC 68-54356. (Essay Index Reprint Ser.). 1977. 18.95 (*0-8369-0632-2*) Ayer.

Visibility of Deep-Sky Objects, 5 Vols. Fred Klein. (Illus.). 283p. (Orig.). 1983. pap. 27.95 (*0-913051-02-0*) F Klein Pubns.

Visibility of Deep-Sky Objects, Vol. 1. Fred Klein. (Illus.). 59p. (Orig.). 1983. pap. 6.95 (*0-913051-03-9*) F Klein Pubns.

Visible Analyst. Thommes. (C). 1994. lab manual ed., pap. text ed. 35.00 (*0-03-004397-2*) HB Coll Pubs.

Visible & Apostolic: The Constitution of the Church in High Church Anglican & Non-Juror Thought. Robert D. Cornwall. LC 92-56626. (C). 1993. 36.50 (*0-87413-466-8*) U Delaware Pr.

Visible & Invisible Group: Two Perspectives on Group Psychotherapy & Group Process. Yvonne Agazarian & Richard Peters. (Karnac Bks.). 302p. 1995. pap. text ed. 36.95 (*1-85575-119-4*, Pub. by Karnac Bks UK) Brunner-Mazel.

Visible & Invisible Group: Two Perspectives on Group Psychotherapy & Group Process. Yvonne Agazarian & Richard Peters. 304p. 1989. pap. 17.95 (*0-415-03770-0*) Routledge.

Visible & Invisible Realms: Power, Magic & Colonial Conquest in Bali. Margaret J. Wiener. (Illus.). 460p. 1995. pap. text ed. 25.95 (*0-226-88582-8*); lib. bdg. 69.95 (*0-226-88580-1*) U Ch Pr.

***Visible & the Invisible.** 300p. 1997. text ed. 33.00 (*981-02-3100-8*) World Scientific Pub.

Visible & the Invisible. Maurice Merleau-Ponty. Tr. by Alphonso Lingis. LC 68-30125. (Studies in Phenomenology & Existential Philosophy). 282p. 1969. 26.95 (*0-8101-0026-6*); pap. 22.50 (*0-8101-0457-1*) Northwestern U Pr.

Visible & Vital: A Handbook for the Aging Congregation. Harriet K. Swenson. LC 93-38870. 160p. (Orig.). 1994. pap. 9.95 (*0-8091-3449-7*) Paulist Pr.

Visible Atomic Spectrum of Hydrogen. S. R. Johnson & Marcia L. Gillette. Ed. by H. Anthony Neidig. (Modular Laboratory Program in Chemistry Ser.). 12p. (C). 1988. pap. text ed. 1.35 (*0-87540-345-X*, STRC 345-X) Chem Educ Res.

Visible Computer: 80286: Assembly Language Teaching System. Software Masters, Inc. Staff. 450p. 1988. 99.95 (*0-927036-04-5*) Soft Mast TX.

Visible Ellison: A Study of Ralph Ellison's Fiction. Edith Schor. LC 92-31758. (Contributions in Afro-American & African Studies: No. 160). 176p. 1993. text ed. 49.95 (*0-313-27492-4*, SUY, Greenwood Pr) Greenwood.

Visible et l'Invisible. Maurice Merleau-Ponty. (Tel Ser.). 360p. (FRE.). 1964. pap. 17.95 (*2-07-028625-8*) Schoenhof.

An Asterisk (*) at the beginning of an entry indicates that the title is appearing in BIP for the first time.

Visible et l'Invisible: Notes de Travail. Maurice Merleau-Ponty. (FRE.). 1979. pap. 22.95 (*0-7859-2744-1*) Fr & Eur.

Visible Fictions. John A. Ellis. (Illus.). 232p. 1983. pap. 13.95 (*0-7100-9304-7*, RKP) Routledge.

Visible Fictions: Cinema, Television, Video. 2nd ed. John A. Ellis. 304p. (C). 1992. pap. 16.95 (*0-415-07513-0*, A7136) Routledge.

Visible Hand: Synergetic Microfoundation of Macroeconomic Dynamics. R. B. Koblo. Ed. by Martin J. Beckmann & W. Krelle. (Lecture Notes in Economics & Mathematical Systems Ser.: Vol. 369). (Illus.). viii, 131p. 1991. 49.95 (*0-387-54595-6*) Spr-Verlag.

Visible Hand: The Managerial Revolution in American Business. Alfred D. Chandler, Jr. 624p. 1977. 48.00 (*0-674-94051-2*) Belknap Pr.

Visible Hand: The Managerial Revolution in American Business. Alfred D. Chandler, Jr. 624p. 1980. pap. text ed. 16.95 (*0-674-94052-0*) Belknap Pr.

Visible Hand & the Fortune of Cities: Economic Planning in Europe Since the Late Middle Ages. Ed. by Herman Diederiks et al. (Illus.). 300p. 1992. text ed. 55.00 (*0-7185-1347-9*) St Martin.

Visible Heritage: Columbia County, New York: A History in Art & Architecture. 2nd ed. Ruth Piwonka & Roderic H. Blackburn. LC 96-20746. (Illus.). 160p. 1996. reprint ed. pap. 24.95 (*1-883789-08-7*) Blk Dome Pr.

***Visible Heritage: Columbia County, New York: A History in Art & Architecture.** 2nd ed. Ruth Piwonka & Roderic H. Blackburn. (Illus.). 160p. 1996. reprint ed. 35.95 (*1-883789-10-9*) Blk Dome Pr.

Visible Histories: Women & Environments in a Post-War British City. Suzanne Mackenzie. 240p. (C). 1989. text ed. 49.95 (*0-7735-0712-4*, Pub. by McGill CN) U of Toronto Pr.

Visible Human Body: An Atlas of Sectional Anatomy. Gunther VonHagens et al. LC 89-13836. (Illus.). 151p. 1991. text ed. 55.00 (*0-8121-1269-5*) Williams & Wilkins.

Visible Library: Practical Public Relations for Public Librarians. Bob Usherwood. LC 81-161278. (Illus.). 221p. reprint ed. pap. 63.00 (*0-7837-5329-2*, 2045069) Bks Demand.

Visible Light. C. J. Cherryh. 230p. (Orig.). 1986. 17.00 (*0-932096-40-9*) Phantasia Pr.

Visible Man. Chukwudi Okpala. 124p. 1995. pap. 10.95 (*1-885392-25-7*) Allied Publishers.

Visible Man: A True Story of Post Racist America. George Gilder. LC 95-8587. 240p. 1995. pap. 19.95 (*1-55815-465-5*) ICS Pr.

Visible Now: Blacks in Private Schools. Ed. by Diana T. Slaughter & Deborah J. Johnson. LC 88-10236. (Contributions in Afro-American & African Studies: No. 116). 360p. 1988. text ed. 59.95 (*0-313-25926-7*, SVN/, Greenwood Pr) Greenwood.

Visible Past: An Archaeological Reinterpretation of the Ancient World. Michael Grant. (Illus.). 416p. 1992. reprint ed. pap. 14.95 (*0-02-080041-X*) Macmillan.

Visible Poor: Homelessness in the United States. Joel Blau. 272p. 1992. 25.00 (*0-19-505743-0*) OUP.

Visible Poor: Homelessness in the United States. Joel Blau. 256p. (C). 1993. reprint ed. pap. 10.95 (*0-19-508353-9*, 6311) OUP.

Visible Record Computers. P. W. Mace. 216p. 1974. 29.00 (*0-8464-0957-7*) Beekman Pubs.

Visible Saints: The History of a Puritan Idea. Edmund S. Morgan. LC 63-9999. 168p. 1965. pap. 10.95 (*0-8014-9041-3*) Cornell U Pr.

Visible Shivers. Tom Raworth. LC 87-90687. 88p. 1987. 8.00 (*0-917585-15-1*) O Bks.

Visible Song: Transitional Literacy in Old English Verse. Katherine O. O'Keefe. (Cambridge Studies in Anglo-Saxon England: No. 4). (Illus.). 220p. (C). 1990. text ed. 69.95 (*0-521-37550-9*) Cambridge U Pr.

Visible Spaces: Hannah Arendt & the German-Jewish Experience. Dagmar Barnouw. LC 89-38885. (Jewish Studies). 320p. 1990. text ed. 48.50 (*0-8018-3923-8*) Johns Hopkins.

Visible Spectrum Researcher. Dinshah P. Ghadiali et al. 708p. 1993. 20.00 (*0-933917-11-2*) Dinshah Hlth Soc.

Visible Speech: The Diverse Oneness of Writing Systems. John DeFrancis. LC 89-4708. 336p. 1989. text ed. 32.00 (*0-8248-1207-7*) UH Pr.

Visible Speech the Science of Universal Alphabetics. Alexander M. Bell. 1976. reprint ed. 69.00 (*0-403-06591-7*, Regency) Scholarly.

Visible Tangible Woman: Conscious Connection among Women. Ralene Friend. Ed. by Karen Smith. 200p. (Orig.). 1996. pap. 14.95 (*0-9649590-1-1*) Creating Futures.

Visible Universe. 2nd ed. (Voyage Through the Universe Ser.). 1991. write for info. (*0-8094-9050-1*); lib. bdg. write for info. (*0-8094-9051-X*) Time-Life.

***Visible Wall: Jews & Other Ethnic Outsiders in Swedish Film.** Rochelle Wright. LC 97-22932. 1998. write for info. (*0-8093-2164-5*); pap. write for info. (*0-8093-2165-3*) S Ill U Pr.

Visible Witness. Wilmer J. Young. (C). 1961. pap. 3.00 (*0-87574-118-5*) Pendle Hill.

***Visible Woman.** Treichler. 1998. 55.00 (*0-8147-1556-7*); pap. 18.95 (*0-8147-1568-0*) NYU Pr.

Visible Women: New Essays on American Activism. Ed. by Nancy A. Hewitt & Suzanne Lebsock. LC 93-18538. (Women in American History Ser.). 432p. 1993. text ed. 47.50 (*0-252-01771-4*); pap. text ed. 18.95 (*0-252-06333-3*) U of Ill Pr.

Visible Women in East Coast Malay Society: On the Reproduction of Gender in Ceremonial, School & Market. Ingrid Rudie. (Contemporary Studies in Social Anthropology; A Scandinavian University Press Publication). 337p. 1994. 39.50 (*82-00-21919-4*) Scandnvan Univ Pr.

Visible Word: Experimental Typography & Modern Art, 1909-1923. Johanna Drucker. LC 93-39657. 306p. 1994. 35.00 (*0-226-16501-9*) U Ch Pr.

Visible Word: Experimental Typography & Modern Art, 1909-1923. Johanna Drucker. vii, 298p. 1996. pap. text ed. 15.95 (*0-226-16502-7*) U Ch Pr.

Visible Wound: A Healing Journey Through Breast Cancer. Julie Friedeberger. 1996. pap. 12.95 (*1-85230-808-7*) Element MA.

***Visibly Different: Coping with Disfigurement.** Richard Lansdown. LC 97-23638. 1997. write for info. (*0-7506-3424-3*) Buttrwrth-Heinemann.

***Visibly Vera.** Cath Jackson. (Illus.). 64p. pap. 5.95 (*0-7043-4908-6*, Pub. by Womens Press UK) Trafalgar.

VisiCalc: Apple. Brandt R. Allen. (C). 1984. pap. text ed. 17.00 (*0-8359-8410-9*, Reston) P-H.

VisiCalc: TRS-80. Brandt R. Allen. 1984. pap. text ed. 17.00 (*0-8359-8409-5*, Reston) P-H.

VisiCalc Book: The Apple Edition. Donald H. Beil. 1983. 30.00 (*0-8359-8398-6*, Reston); 22.95 (*0-8359-8397-8*, Reston) P-H.

VisiCalc Made Simple. Thomas M. O'Donovan. LC 84-3680. 165p. reprint ed. pap. 47.10 (*0-685-23443-6*, 2032696) Bks Demand.

Visigoda: La Monarquia, la Cultura, las Artes. Ramon Menendez Pidal. Ed. by J. M. Prendes. (Historia de Espana Ser.: Vol. 7). 510p. (SPA.). 1992. 195.00 (*0-7859-0545-6*, 9423949966) Fr & Eur.

Visigothic Code: (Forum Judicum) Ed. by S. Scott. Tr. by S. P. Scott. xxiv, 419p. 1982. reprint ed. lib. bdg. 37.50 (*0-8377-1233-5*) Rothman.

Visigoths in Gaul & Spain, A. D. 418-711: A Bibliography. Alberto Ferreiro. lxii, 822p. (C). 1988. text ed. 149.50 (*90-04-08793-1*) E J Brill.

Visio Tnugdali. Ed. by Albrecht Wagner. lxxxii, 186p. 1989. reprint ed. write for info. (*3-487-09193-3*) G Olms Pubs.

Visio 4: Drawing for the Artistically Challenged. Barrie Sosinsky & Christopher Goddard. 1995. pap. text ed. 19.95 (*0-7615-0092-8*) Prima Pub.

Visio 4 for Everyone. Ralph Grabowski. 350p. 1996. pap. 24.95 incl. disk (*1-55622-496-6*) Wordware Pub.

Vision. James W. Bovinet. (Illus.). 75p. (Orig.). (C). 1995. pap. text ed. 14.00 (*0-9650629-0-2*) Coulee Region.

Vision. Tom Brown, Jr. 256p. (Orig.). 1991. pap. 5.99 (*0-425-12911-X*, Berkley Trade) Berkley Pub.

Vision. Pierre Buser & Michel Imbert. Tr. by Roy H. Kay from FRE. (Illus.). 576p. 1992. 47.50 (*0-262-02336-9*, Bradford Bks) MIT Pr.

Vision. Richard Israel & Julianne Crane. 200p. 1996. text ed. 28.95 (*0-566-07797-3*, Pub. by Gower UK) Ashgate Pub Co.

Vision. Dean R. Koontz. LC 77-7079. 368p. 1986. mass mkt. 7.50 (*0-425-09860-5*) Berkley Pub.

Vision. David Marr. 397p. (C). 1995. pap. text ed. 30.95 (*0-7167-1567-8*) W H Freeman.

Vision, 7 vols. Ed. by Joe Oakley. (First Principles Ser.: Vol. 1). 1989. Set. 28.00 (*0-923968-00-8*); student ed. 6.00 (*0-923968-01-6*) Shady Grove Ch Pubns.

Vision. Leonard E. Read. 148p. 1978. 12.95 (*0-910614-59-8*) Foun Econ Ed.

Vision. Jane Samz. (Encyclopedia of Health Ser.). (Illus.). 104p. (YA). (gr. 7 up). 1990. lib. bdg. 19.95 (*0-7910-0031-1*) Chelsea Hse.

Vision. Ronald D. Tucker. (Illus.). 24p. (Orig.). 1983. pap. 3.00 (*0-933643-12-8*) Grace Ch-St Louis.

Vision. Hildegard Von Bingen. 1995. pap. write for info. (*0-670-86655-5*) Viking Penguin.

***Vision.** D. Wilkerson. (SPA.). pap. 5.95 (*0-8297-0608-9*) Life Pubs Intl.

Vision: A Holistic Guide to Healing the Eyesight. Joanna Rotte & Koji Yamamoto. LC 84-80538. 152p. (Orig.). 1986. pap. 18.00 (*0-87040-622-1*) Japan Pubns USA.

Vision: A Personal Call to Create a New World. Ken Carey. LC 91-58901. 95p. 1992. pap. 11.00 (*0-06-250179-8*) Harper SF.

Vision: A Saga of the Sky. Harold Mansfield. Ed. by James B. Gilbert. LC 79-7284. (Flight: Its First Seventy-Five Years Ser.). (Illus.). 1980. reprint ed. lib. bdg. 37.95 (*0-405-12193-8*) Ayer.

Vision: A Thrilling Prophecy of the Coming Armageddon. David Wilkerson. 144p. 1993. mass mkt. 5.99 (*0-8007-8150-3*) Revell.

Vision: Coding & Efficiency. Ed. by Colin Blakemore. (Illus.). 464p. (C). 1993. pap. text ed. 42.95 (*0-521-44769-0*) Cambridge U Pr.

Vision: God's Gift to Joseph & You. Isiah McKinnon. 140p. (Orig.). 1994. pap. 6.95 (*1-56043-771-5*) Destiny Image.

Vision: Harvard Students Look Ahead. Isaac Devash et al. 1993. pap. 11.95 (*0-87584-479-0*) Harvard Busn.

Vision: How Leaders Develop It, Share It, & Sustain It. Joseph V. Quigely. LC 93-9582. 1993. text ed. 24.95 (*0-07-051084-9*) McGraw.

Vision: How Leaders Develop It, Share It, & Sustain It. Joseph V. Quigley. 1994. pap. text ed. 14.95 (*0-07-051766-5*) McGraw.

Vision: In the Eye of the Beholder. K. Cole. (Illus.). 106p. (Orig.). 1979. pap. 8.50 (*0-943451-04-3*) Explorator.

Vision: Reflections on the Way of the Soul. Kahlil Gibran. Tr. by Juan R. Cole from ARA. (Illus.). 144p. 1994. 17.00 (*1-883991-02-1*) Whte Cloud Pr.

Vision: Selections from the Holy Quran (Urdu - English - Arabic) Shaikh Abdul Rauf. 340p. (C). 1987. 25.00 (*1-56744-411-3*) Kazi Pubns.

Vision: Structure & Function. K. L. Chow et al. 624p. (C). 1988. text ed. 90.00 (*9971-5-0365-4*) World Scientific Pub.

Vision: The Dramatic True Story of One Man's Search For. Tom Brown. 1988. pap. 12.00 (*0-425-10703-5*) Berkley Pub.

Vision: The Life & Music of Hildegard von Bingen. Jane Bobko. LC 95-22551. (Illus.). 128p. 1995. pap. 24.95 incl. audio compact disk (*0-670-86405-6*) Penguin.

Vision: Variations on Some Berkeleian Themes. Robert Schwartz. 208p. 1994. pap. 24.95 (*1-55786-536-1*) Blackwell Pubs.

Vision Vol. 3: Harvard Students Look Ahead. Ed. by David Kotchen. 160p. (Orig.). 1995. pap. 10.95 (*0-9641866-1-6*) Dipylon Pr.

Vision - TEST Final Report: Recommendations for American Educational Decision Makers. Ludwig Braun. 50p. 1990. 10.00 (*0-924667-77-X*) Intl Society Tech Educ.

Vision & Action: The Control of Grasping. Melvyn A. Goodale. Ed. by Zenon W. Pylyshyn. LC 89-17509. (Canadian Institute for Advanced Research in Artificial Intelligence & Robotics Ser.: Vol. 2). 380p. (C). 1990. text ed. 82.50 (*0-89391-554-8*) Ablex Pub.

Vision & Aging. 2nd ed. Ed. by Alfred J. Rosenbloom & Meredith W. Morgan. (Illus.). 460p. 1993. text ed. 75.00 (*0-7506-9311-8*) Buttrwrth-Heinemann.

Vision & Aging: Crossroads for Service Delivery. Alberta L. Orr. LC 92-5088. 392p. 1992. pap. 47.95 (*0-89128-216-5*) Am Foun Blind.

Vision & Aging: Issues in Social Work Practice. Ed. by Nancy D. Weber. LC 91-24842. (Journal of Gerontological Social Work). (Illus.). 207p. 1991. lib. bdg. 39.95 (*1-56024-199-3*) Haworth Pr.

***Vision & Aging: Issues in Social Work Practice.** Ed. by Nancy D. Weber. 196p. 1992. pap. 19.95 (*1-56024-251-5*) Haworth Pr.

Vision & Certitude in the Age of Ockham: Optics, Epistemology & the Foundations of Semantics. Katherine H. Tachau. LC 87-24087. (Studien und Texte zur Geistesgeschichte des Mittelalters Ser.: No. 22). xix, 428p. (Orig.). 1988. pap. 113.00 (*90-04-08552-1*) E J Brill.

Vision & Change: Elements of Intuition & the I Ching As Inner Teachers. Allen D. Young. LC 92-91049. (Illus.). 245p. (Orig.). 1993. pap. 19.95 (*0-9633319-1-4*) A Young Bks.

Vision & Difference: Femininity, Feminism & the Histories of Art. Griselda Pollock. 256p. (C). 1988. pap. 14.95 (*0-415-00722-4*) Routledge.

Vision & Difference: Femininity, Feminism & the Histories of Art. Griselda Pollock. (Illus.). 272p. 1988. pap. text ed. 14.95 (*0-317-67353-X*) Routledge Chapman & Hall.

Vision & Discernment: An Orientation in Theological Study. Charles M. Wood. (Studies in Religious & Theological Scholarship). (C). 1985. pap. 19.95 (*0-89130-923-3*) Scholars Pr GA.

***Vision & Discernment: An Orientation in Theological Study.** Charles M. Wood. LC 85-18431. (Scholars Press Studies in Religious & Theological Scholarship). 108p. 1985. reprint ed. pap. 30.80 (*0-608-02837-1*, 2063904) Bks Demand.

Vision & Information Processing for Automation. Arthur Browne & Leonard Norton-Wayne. 480p. 1986. 95.00 (*0-306-42245-X*, Plenum Pr) Plenum.

Vision & Method in Historical Sociology. Ed. by Theda Skocpol. (Illus.). 448p. 1984. pap. text ed. 19.95 (*0-521-29724-9*) Cambridge U Pr.

Vision & Mind: Modeling Mental Functions. Vadim D. Glezer. 288p. 1995. text ed. 59.95 (*0-8058-1668-2*) L Erlbaum Assocs.

***Vision & Motor Control.** L. Proteau & D. Elliott. (Advances in Psychology Ser.: Vol. 85). 478p. 1992. 160.50 (*0-444-88816-0*, North Holland) Elsevier.

Vision & Navigation: The Carnegie Mellon NAVLAB. Ed. by Charles E. Thorpe. (C). 1990. lib. bdg. 117.00 (*0-7923-9068-7*) Kluwer Ac.

Vision & Painting: The Logic of the Gaze. Norman Bryson. LC 82-10901. (Illus.). 208p. 1983. 42.50 (*0-300-02855-5*) Yale U Pr.

Vision & Painting: The Logic of the Gaze. Norman Bryson. LC 82-10901. (Illus.). 208p. 1986. pap. 15.00 (*0-300-03583-7*, Y-556) Yale U Pr.

***Vision & Prophecy in Amos.** John D. Watts. 128p. (Orig.). 1997. pap. text ed. 18.95 (*0-86554-534-0*) Mercer Univ Pr.

Vision & Re-Vision in Alexander Pope. Wallace Jackson. LC 82-20179. 205p. reprint ed. pap. 58.50 (*0-7837-3619-3*, 2043485) Bks Demand.

Vision & Reading. Ed. by Ralph P. Garzia. LC 95-24996. (Mosby's Optometric Problem Solving Ser.). 320p. (C). (gr. 13). 1995. pap. text ed. 36.95 (*0-8151-3438-X*) Mosby Yr Bk.

Vision & Reality, Market & State: Contradictions & Dilemmas Revisited. Janos Kornai. 224p. (C). (gr. 13). 1990. 29.95 (*0-415-90285-1*, A4355, Routledge NY) Routledge.

Vision & Refuge: Essays on the Literature of the Great Plains. Ed. by Virginia Faulkner & Frederick C. Luebke. LC 81-10418. 160p. 1982. reprint ed. pap. 45.60 (*0-608-01834-1*, 2062483) Bks Demand.

Vision & Revision. Karen S. Uehling. (C). 1994. text ed. 17.75 (*0-673-99150-4*) Addson-Wesley Educ.

Vision & Revision: Recent Art from the Netherlands. Janie Cohen. LC 89-85769. (Illus.). 50p. (Orig.). 1989. 12.00 (*1-878248-00-6*) Danforth Mus.

Vision & Revision: The Concept of Inspiration in Thomas Mann's Fiction. Karen D. Vogt. (Germanic Studies in America: Vol. 55). 168p. (C). 1987. text ed. 28.50 (*0-8204-0512-4*) P Lang Pubng.

Vision & Revisions: Essays on Faulkner. John E. Bassett. LC 89-14046. (Locust Hill Literary Studies: No. 4). 255p. (C). 1989. lib. bdg. 30.00 (*0-933951-32-9*) Locust Hill Pr.

Vision & School Success. G. B. Spache et al. Ed. by Sally M. Corngold. (Illus.). 53p. 1992. lib. bdg. 9.95 (*0-929780-04-3*) VisionExtension.

Vision & Separation. Kenneth Wright. 370p. (C). 1991. 45.00 (*1-85343-157-5*) NYU Pr.

Vision & Separation: Between Mother & Baby. Kenneth Wright. LC 90-14553. 392p. 1991. 47.50 (*0-87668-559-9*) Aronson.

Vision & Struggle: Meditations on Feminist Spirituality & Politics. Eleanor H. Haney. LC 89-82511. (Orig.). 1989. pap. 4.95 (*0-9624626-0-8*) Astarte Shell Pr.

Vision & Style in Patrick White: A Study of Five Novels. Rodney S. Edgecombe. LC 88-1382. 184p. 1989. text ed. 29.95 (*0-8173-0407-X*) U of Ala Pr.

Vision & Tactics: Towards an Adult Church. Gabriel Moran. 158p. 1994. pap. 20.00 (*0-85532-018-4*, Pub. by Srch Pr UK) St Mut.

Vision & Textuality. Ed. by Stephen Melville & Bill Readings. LC 94-39995. (Illus.). 288p. 1995. text ed. 49.95 (*0-8223-1630-7*); pap. text ed. 17.95 (*0-8223-1644-7*) Duke.

Vision & the Art of Drawing. Howard S. Hoffman. (Illus.). 256p. 1988. 14.95 (*0-13-942285-4*) P-H.

Vision & the Emergence of Meaning: Blind & Sighted Children's Early Language. Anne Dunlea. (Illus.). 216p. (C). 1990. text ed. 59.95 (*0-521-30496-2*) Cambridge U Pr.

Vision & the Game: Making the Canadian Constitution. Lenard Cohen et al. 197p. (Orig.). (C). 1987. pap. text ed. 14.95 (*0-920490-67-0*) Temeron Bks.

***Vision & the Mission: Selected Papers Presented at the 11th Annual Middle Atlantic Regional Gospel Ministries Conference in Nassau, Bahamas (1997)** E. Myron Noble. Ed. by Shiren T. Noble. 102p. (Orig.). 1997. pap. 11.95 (*1-877971-19-7*) Mid Atl Reg Pr.

Vision & the Voice with Commentary & Other Papers Vol. 4, No. 2: The Equinox. Aleister Crowley. (Illus.). 304p. 1998. 30.00 (*0-87728-887-9*) Weiser.

Vision & Transformation: An Introduction to the Buddha's Noble Eightfold Path. Sangharakshita. 169p. (Orig.). 1996. pap. 13.95 (*0-904766-44-6*) Windhorse Pubns.

Vision & Violence. Arthur Mendel. 350p. (C). 1992. text ed. 34.50 (*0-472-10275-3*) U of Mich Pr.

Vision & Visual Dysfunction, 17 vols. Cronly-Dillon. 1991. Set. 2,125.00 (*0-8493-7500-2*) CRC Pr.

Vision & Visual Dysfunction Index. Cronly-Dillon. 1991. 137.00 (*0-8493-7517-7*) CRC Pr.

Vision & Visuality. Ed. by Hal Foster. LC 89-650815. (Discussions in Contemporary Culture Ser.: No. 2). (Illus.). 152p. (Orig.). (C). 1988. pap. 10.95 (*0-941920-10-0*) Bay Pr.

Vision As Process: Basic Research on Computer Vision Systems. Ed. by J. L. Crowley. (ESPRIT Basic Research Ser.). 464p. 1994. 93.95 (*0-387-58143-X*) Spr-Verlag.

***Vision Assistant Software: A Practical Introduction to Image Processing & Pattern Classifiers.** Allen & Yung. (Optical & Quantum Electronics Ser.). (Illus.). 160p. 1994. text ed. 315.95 (*0-412-59220-7*, Chap & Hall NY) Chapman & Hall.

Vision at Patmos. Catherine G. Gonzalez & Justo L. Gonzalez. LC 90-37147. 128p. 1991. pap. 6.95 (*0-687-43774-1*) Abingdon.

Vision-Bearers: Dynamic Evangelism into the Twenty-First Century. Richard Kew & Cyril C. Okorocha. 144p. (Orig.). 1996. pap. 11.95 (*0-8192-1656-9*) Morehouse Pub.

Vision Betrayed: The Jesuits in Japan & China 1542-1742. Andrew C. Ross. LC 94-10623. 225p. 1994. 35.00 (*0-88344-991-9*) Orbis Bks.

Vision, Brain & Behavior in Birds. Ed. by H. Philip Zeigler & Hans-Joachim Bischof. LC 93-22353. 460p. 1993. 75.00 (*0-262-24036-X*, Bradford Bks) MIT Pr.

Vision, Brain & Cooperative Computation. Allen R. Hanson. Ed. by Michael A. Arbib. 744p. 1990. reprint ed. pap. 30.00 (*0-262-51049-9*, Bradford Bks) MIT Pr.

Vision Care Assistant: An Introductory Handbook. Pamela Miller. Ed. by Sally M. Corngold. 112p. (Orig.). 1990. lib. bdg. 15.00 (*0-929780-01-9*) VisionExtension.

Vision Catcher. Larsen. pap. 10.00 (*0-06-250978-0*, PL) HarpC.

Vision Chips: Implementing Vision Algorithms with Analog VLSI Circuits. Ed. by Christof Koch & Hua Li. LC 94-2715. 520p. 1994. 58.00 (*0-8186-6492-4*, BP06492) IEEE Comp Soc.

Vision Completa Del Cuerpo De Cristo. Witness Lee. 62p. (SPA.). per. 2.25 (*0-87083-531-9*, 08030002) Living Stream Ministry.

Vision Confronts Reality: Historical Perspectives on the Contemporary Jewish Agenda. Ed. by Ruth Kozodoy et al. LC 87-46236. 368p. 1989. 30.00 (*0-8386-3333-1*) Fairleigh Dickinson.

***Vision Cristiana del Hombre.** J. Gresham Machen. 257p. (SPA.). 1996. reprint ed. pap. 6.25 (*0-85151-709-9*) Banner of Truth.

Vision Critica de la Historia de la Conquista de Mexico-Tenochtitlan. Eulalia Guzman. 206p. 1989. pap. 5.70 (*968-36-1379-9*, UN039) UPLAAP.

Vision Day. Elmer L. Towns. 80p. 1994. ring bd. 119.95 incl. vhs (*1-57052-002-X*) Chrch Grwth VA.

Vision de Espana de Julian Marias. Maria-Rosario Castro. LC 90-34651. (American University Studies: Romance Languages & Literature: Ser. II, Vol. 152). 161p. (C). 1991. text ed. 33.95 (*0-8204-1364-X*) P Lang Pubng.

UV

An Asterisk (*) at the beginning of an entry indicates that the title is appearing in BIP for the first time.

***Vision de la Mujer en la Obra de Elena Garro: El Arbol, los Perros, los Recuerdos del Porvenir, Testimonios Sobre Mariana y la Casa Junto Al Rio.** Maria A. Umanzor. LC 96-84333. (Coleccion Polymita Ser.). 158p. (Orig.). (SPA.). 1996. pap. 14.95 (0-89729-806-3) Ediciones.
Vision del Mundo en la Novela: Tiempo de silencio, de Luis Martin-Santos. Emilio Diaz-Valcarcel. 98p. (Orig.). (SPA.). (C). 1982. pap. 5.00 (0-8477-3506-0) U of PR Pr.
Vision, Doctrine, War: Mennonite Identity & Organization in America. James C. Juhnke. LC 89-34243. (Mennonite Experience in America Ser.). (Illus.). 384p. (Orig.). 1989. pap. 19.99 (0-8361-3104-5) Herald Pr.
Vision Enhancement Training. Albert L. Shankman. Ed. by Sally M. Corngold. (Illus.). 156p. (Orig.). 1988. pap. text ed. 12.00 (0-943599-02-4) OEPF.
Vision, Etheric: And What It Reveals. 2nd ed. Ed. by Rosicrucian Fellowship Staff. 110p. (C). 1989. reprint ed. pap. text ed. 3.50 (0-911274-59-6) Rosicrucian.
***Vision for a World Gone Blind.** Robert G. Tuttle, Sr. 1996. 10.95 (1-55673-955-9) CSS OH.
***Vision for a 21st Century Information Infrastructure.** iv, 25p. (Orig.). 1993. pap. 15.00 (1-889866-06-7) Coun on Competitiveness.
***Vision for Arts Education in the 21st Century: The Ideas & Ideals Behind the Development of the National Standards for Education in the Arts.** Intro. by A. Graham Down & John J. Mahlmann. (Music Educators National Conference Ser.). 104p. (C). 1993. pap. 18.25 (1-56545-025-6, 1617) Music Ed Natl.
Vision for Lake Superior. Mary Durfee. (Pew Case Studies in International Affairs). 50p. (C). 1995. pap. text ed. 3.50 (1-56927-164-X, GU Schl Foreign) Geo U Inst Dplmcy.
Vision for London 1889-1914: Labour, Everyday Life & the LCC Experiment. Susan D. Pennybacker. LC 94-41561. 336p. (C). (gr. 13). 1995. text ed. 79.95 (0-415-03588-0) Routledge.
Vision for Missions. Tom Wells. 157p. 1985. pap. 6.99 (0-85151-433-2) Banner of Truth.
Vision for Robots Workshop, 1995. LC 95-76068. 160p. 1995. pap. 50.00 (0-8186-7114-9, PR07114) IEEE Comp Soc.
Vision for the Catechetical Ministry: An Instrument for Diocesan & Parish Planning. 1985. 5.30 (0-318-18576-8); 4.00 (0-685-11854-1) Natl Cath Educ.
Vision for the Church. Mike Phillips. 110p. 1981. pap. 3.95 (0-940652-02-1) Sunrise Bks.
Vision for the College Placement Center: Systems, Paradigms, Processes, People. Joey Freeman. LC 94-13732. 208p. 1994. text ed. 49.95 (0-275-94805-6, Praeger Pubs) Greenwood.
Vision for the Future. Ann R. Colton. LC 96-83732. 124p. 1960. pap. 9.95 (0-917189-17-5) A R Colton Fnd.
Vision for the Future: Jules Stein Eye Institute 1966-1991. Compiled by Twenty-fifth Anniversary Book Committee Staff. LC 91-66445. (Illus.). 200p. 1992. write for info. (0-9630545-1-1) J S Eye Inst.
Vision for the Future: Meeting the Challenge of Sight Loss. Maria Conyers. 1992. 42.50 (1-85302-110-5) Taylor & Francis.
***Vision for the Local Congregation: God's People on Mission Through Ministry.** Gerald G. Nevitt. 210p. 1995. pap. write for info. (1-887998-01-2) Ch of God in MI.
***Vision for the World.** 96p. 1996. pap. 13.00 (981-02-2508-3); lib. bdg. 27.00 (981-02-2848-1) World Scientific Pub.
Vision for the World Economy: Openness, Diversity, & Cohesion. Robert Z. Lawrence et al. LC 95-21051. (Integrating National Economies Ser.). 124p. (C). 1996. 34.95 (0-8157-5184-2); pap. 14.95 (0-8157-5183-4) Brookings.
***Vision for Victory: A Pictorial History of Voorhees College, 1897-1997.** LC 96-40189. (Illus.). 1997. write for info. (0-89865-985-X) Donning Co.
***Vision for Virginia.** 2nd ed. Virginia F. McInturff. LC 95-70998. 234p. (Orig.). 1995. spiral bd., pap. 20.00 (0-9625315-2-9) New Faith Pub.
***Vision from the Hill.** Beardslee. 1984. pap. 10.00 (0-8028-0035-1) Eerdmans.
Vision Fulfilled. 1991. write for info. (1-879605-12-0) U Sci & Philos.
***Vision Fulfilling: The Story of Rural & Small Church Community Work of the Episcopal Church in the 20th Century.** William Davidson & Leo M. Brown. 320p. 1997. 25.95 (0-8192-1732-8) Morehouse Pub.
***Vision Fulfilling: The Story of Rural & Small Church Community Work of the Episcopal Church in the 20th Century.** William Davidson & Leo M. Brown. 320p. 1997. pap. 19.95 (0-8192-1733-6) Morehouse Pub.
Vision Geometry. R. A. Melter et al. LC 91-2408. (Contemporary Mathematics Ser.). 237p. 1991. 90.00 (0-8218-5125-X, CONM/119) Am Math.
Vision Glorious: Themes & Personalities of the Catholic Revival in Anglicanism. Geoffrey Rowell. (Illus.). 296p. 1992. reprint ed. pap. 32.00 (0-19-826332-5) OUP.
Vision Guest. Louis Hooban. 50p. 1981. pap. 13.00 (1-884710-04-2) Indian Heritage.
Vision, Identity & Time. C. Tsehloane Keto. 176p. (C). 1995. per., pap. text ed. 19.89 (0-8403-9614-7) Kendall-Hunt.
Vision in Action. Tregoe. 1994. 23.99 (0-02-932632-X) S&S Trade.
Vision in Action: Working with Soul & Spirit in Small Organizations. 2nd ed. Christopher Schaefer & Tijno Voors. LC 96-28323. 272p. 1996. pap. 16.95 (0-940262-74-6) Lindisfarne Bks.
Vision in Context: Historical & Contemporary Perspectives on Sight. Teresa Brennan. 256p. 1996. pap. 17.95 (0-415-91475-2) Routledge.
Vision in Context: Historical & Contemporary Perspectives on Sight. Ed. by Teresa Brennan. 256p. (C). (gr. 13 up). 1996. text ed. 59.95 (0-415-91474-4, Routledge NY) Routledge.
Vision in Spring. William Faulkner. (Illus.). 134p. (C). 1984. 22.95 (0-292-78712-X) U of Tex Pr.
Vision in the Christian Life. Bill Freeman. LC 90-92289. 74p. (Orig.). 1991. pap. 3.00 (0-914271-12-1) Mnstry Wrd.
Vision in the Sky: New Haven's Early Years, 1638-1783. Myrna Kagan. LC 89-2762. (Illus.). 152p. (J). (gr. 4-8). 1989. lib. bdg. 17.50 (0-208-02246-5, Linnet Bks) Shoe String.
Vision in Vehicles: Proceedings of the Conference, Nottingham, U. K., 9-13 September 1985. Ed. by A. G. Gale et al. 465p. 1986. 183.75 (0-444-87983-8) Elsevier.
***Vision in Vehicles II.** A. G. Gale et al. 428p. 1988. 195.75 (0-444-70423-X, North Holland) Elsevier.
Vision in Vehicles, No. 3: Proceedings of the 3rd International Conference, Aachen, Germany, 11-15 Sept., 1989. Ed. by A. G. Gale et al. 498p. 1991. 196.50 (0-444-88601-X, North Holland) Elsevier.
Vision in Vehicles V. Ed. by A. G. Gale & D. H. Foster. 1996. write for info. (0-614-17891-6, North Holland) Elsevier.
***Vision in Vehicles V: Selected/Edited Proceedings of the Fifth International Conference, Glasgow, Scotland, Autumn, 1993.** Ed. by A. G. Gale et al. 422p. 1996. 145.25 (0-444-81477-9) Elsevier.
Vision in Vehicles 4: Selected-Edited Proceedings of the 4th International Conference, Leiden, the Netherlands, August 1991. Ed. by A. G. Gale. 364p. 1993. 153.25 (0-444-89362-8) Elsevier.
Vision in Vertebrates. M. A. Ali & M. A. Klyne. LC 85-12191. 282p. 1985. 79.50 (0-306-42065-1, Plenum Pr) Plenum.
Vision, Instruction & Action. David Chapman. (Artificial Intelligence - Bobrow, Brady & Davis Ser.). (Illus.). 310p. 1991. 42.00 (0-262-03181-7) MIT Pr.
Vision Into Action: The Leader's Guide to Driving Change in Turbulent Times. Tero Kauppinen et al. 200p. 1994. text ed. 29.95 (0-9640787-0-8) Ldrship Studies.
Vision into the Future - Toward a Low-Vision Research Agenda: Pisart Tenth-Anniversary Scientific Symposium. Ed. by Aries Arditi et al. 68p. (Orig.). 1991. pap. 10.00 (0-9603444-9-7) Lighthouse NYC.
Vision Is Fulfilled. Kay L. McDonald. 383p. 1995. reprint ed. pap. 9.95 (1-883273-05-6) Trilogy OR.
Vision Machine. Paul Virillio. (Perspectives Ser.). 96p. 1994. pap. 14.95 (0-253-20901-3); text ed. 35.00 (0-253-32574-9) Ind U Pr.
Vision Machines: Cinema, Literature & Sexuality in Spain & Cuba, 1983-1993. Paul J. Smith. (Illus.). 192p. 1996. pap. 19.00 (1-85984-079-5, Pub. by Vrso UK) Norton.
Vision Machines: Cinema, Literature, & Sexuality in Spain & Cuba, 1983-93. Paul J. Smith. (Critical Studies in Latin American & Iberian Culture). (Illus.). 192p. (C). 1996. text ed. 60.00 (1-85984-944-X, Pub. by Vrso UK) Norton.
Vision, Memory & the Temporal Lobe. Ed. by E. Iwai & M. Mishkin. 470p. 1990. 95.00 (0-444-01531-0) P-H.
Vision, Memory & the Temporal Lobe. E. Iwai. 1990. text ed. 140.00 (0-13-500695-3) P-H.
Vision Models for Target Detection & Recognition - In Memory of Arthur Menedez. Eli Peli. (World Scientific Series on Information Display). 432p. 1995. text ed. 69.00 (981-02-2149-5) World Scientific Pub.
Vision Narratives of Women in Prison. Carol Burke. LC 91-3516. 208p. (C). 1992. text ed. 28.00 (0-87049-727-8) U of Tenn Pr.
Vision of a Contemporary University: A Case Study of Expansion & Development in American Higher Education, 1950-75. Russell M. Cooper & Margaret B. Fisher. LC 80-29022. 332p. reprint ed. pap. 94.70 (0-7837-5088-9, 2044786) Bks Demand.
***Vision of a New Liberalism? Critical Essays on Murakami's Anticlassical Analysis.** Kozo Yamamura. LC 97-21409. 1998. write for info. (0-8047-3150-0) Stanford U Pr.
Vision of a Storm Cloud. William Olsen. LC 96-1876. (Illus.). 136p. 1996. 29.95 (0-8101-5043-3) TriQuarterly.
Vision of a Storm Cloud. William Olsen. LC 96-1876. (Illus.). 136p. 1996. pap. 12.95 (0-8101-5044-1) TriQuarterly.
***Vision of American Law: Judging Law, Literature & the Stories We Tell.** Barry R. Schaller. LC 96-44683. 200p. 1997. text ed. 55.00 (0-275-95111-1, Praeger Pubs) Greenwood.
Vision of Anglo-America. H. B. Ryan. 240p. 1987. text ed. 59.95 (0-521-32928-0) Cambridge U Pr.
Vision of Apartheid's Death. Ayotunde A. Babatumji. LC 94-75278. (Illus.). 176p. (Orig.). 1994. pap. 16.95 (0-9640639-0-5) GTNN Pr.
Vision of Aridaeus. G. R. Mead. 74p. 1996. reprint ed. pap. 12.95 (1-56459-614-1) Kessinger Pub.
Vision of Benjamin One Feather. Paul A. Hawkins. (Ben Tree Saga Ser.: Vol. II). 352p. (Orig.). 1993. pap. 4.50 (0-451-17705-3, Sig) NAL-Dutton.
Vision of Buddhism. Roger J. Corless. 362p. 1992. pap. 14.95 (1-55778-200-8) Paragon Hse.
Vision of Change for America: President Clinton's Economic Proposal. (Illus.). 145p. (Orig.). (C). 1994. pap. text ed. 35.00 (1-56806-653-8) DIANE Pub.
***Vision of Christian College.** (Reformed Ser.: Vol. 18). 1988. 13.00 (0-8028-0441-1) Eerdmans.
Vision of Color & Pattern. Gordon E. Legge & Fergus W. Campbell. Ed. by J. J. Head. LC 84-45835. (Carolina Biology Readers Ser.: No. 165). (Illus.). 16p. (Orig.). (YA). (gr. 10 up). 1987. pap. text ed. 2.75 (0-89278-365-6, 45-9765) Carolina Biological.
***Vision of Comets.** James Harpur. 86p. 1993. pap. 17.95 (0-85646-257-8, Pub. by Anvil Press UK) Dufour.
Vision of Corrected History with Breakfast. Al Hellus. 24p. (Orig.). 1995. pap. 5.00 (0-932412-08-4) Mayapple Pr.
Vision of Daniel Eight: Interpretations from 1700-1800. Samuel Nunez. (Andrews University Seminary Doctoral Dissertation Ser.: Vol. 14). 462p. (Orig.). 1989. pap. 19.99 (0-943872-95-2) Andrews Univ Pr.
Vision of Death. Patricia Matthews & Clayton Matthews. 256p. 1993. lib. bdg. 19.00 (0-7278-4397-4) Severn Hse.
Vision of Death. large type ed. Patricia Matthews & Clayton Matthews. LC 93-21868. (Basic Ser.). 353p. 1993. reprint ed. lib. bdg. 21.95 (1-56054-333-7) Thorndike Pr.
Vision of Destiny: A Warrior's Guide to Political Economics. Jerry L. Aiello. Ed. by Dina M. Baganz. (Warrior Ser.). 200p. (Orig.). 1993. pap. text ed. 15.00 (1-883702-00-3) Aiello Grp.
Vision of Dhamma: The Buddhist Writings of Nyanaponika Thera. Nyanaponika Thera. Ed. by Bhikkhu Bodhi. 196p. (Orig.). 1987. pap. 12.50 (0-87728-669-8) Weiser.
Vision of Emerson. Richard Geldard. (Element Masters of Philosophy Ser.). 1995. pap. 10.95 (1-85230-626-2) Element MA.
Vision of Excellence: Organizing Principles for Middle Grades Teacher Preparation. C. Kenneth McEwin et al. 46p. (Orig.). 1995. pap. 12.00 (1-57482-707-3) Search Inst.
Vision of God. Vladimir Lossky. 139p. 1963. 8.95 (0-913836-19-2) St Vladimirs.
Vision of God. abr. ed. Kenneth E. Kirk. LC 90-22764. 207p. (Orig.). 1991. pap. 10.95 (0-8192-2087-6) Morehouse Pub.
Vision of God & Man. rev. ed. Inayat Khan. LC 79-67754. (Sufi Message of Hazrat Inayat Khan Ser.: Vol. 12). 274p. 1982. 19.00 (90-6325-100-9, Pub. by Sufi Mvemnt NE) Omega Pubns NY.
Vision of God's Building. Witness Lee. 227p. per. 8.75 (0-87083-025-2, 08027001) Living Stream Ministry.
***Vision of His Glory.** Anne G. Lotz. 304p. 1997. pap. 12.99 (0-8499-4016-8) Word Pub.
Vision of His Glory: Finding Hope Through the Revelation of Jesus Christ. Anne Graham-Lotz. LC 95-43760. 240p. 1996. 17.99 (0-8499-1216-4) Word Pub.
Vision of His Own: The Mind & Art of William Gaddis. Peter Wolfe. LC 96-15940. 312p. 1996. 45.00 (0-8386-3694-2) Fairleigh Dickinson.
Vision of Hume. David Applebaum. 1996. pap. 10.95 (1-85230-850-8) Element MA.
***Vision of Islam.** William C. Chittick. 370p. 1996. pap. 24.95 (0-614-21477-7, 1286) Kazi Pubns.
Vision of Islam: Reflecting on the Hadith of Gabriel. Sachiko Murata & William C. Chittick. LC 94-16064. (Visions of Reality Ser.). (Illus.). 352p. (Orig.). (C). 1994. pap. text ed. 18.95 (1-55778-516-3) Paragon Hse.
Vision of James. Stephen C. Rowe. (Spirit of Philosophy Ser.). 144p. 1996. pap. 10.95 (1-85230-895-8) Element MA.
Vision of Kant. David Applebaum. (Element Masters of Philosophy Ser.). 1995. pap. 10.95 (1-85230-624-6) Element MA.
Vision of Krishnamurti. R. K. Shringy. 140p. 1979. 8.95 (0-318-37040-9) Asia Bk Corp.
Vision of Life: Balance in Life &-- Tahirih Foroughi. LC 94-29218. 1994. pap. write for info. (0-89865-894-2) Donning Co.
Vision of Love. Rebecca Bennett. (Rainbow Romances Ser.: No. 898). 160p. 1994. 14.95 (0-7090-4970-6, Hale-Parkwest) Parkwest Pubns.
Vision of Love. large type ed. Rebecca Bennett. LC 93-48429. 1994. lib. bdg. 16.95 (0-8161-5953-X, GK Hall) Thorndike Pr.
Vision of "Love's Rare Universe" A Study of Shelley's EPIPSYCHIDION. K. D. Verma. 132p. (Orig.). (C). 1995. pap. text ed. 28.50 (0-7618-0111-1); lib. bdg. 48.00 (0-7618-0110-3) U Pr of Amer.
***Vision of Modern Dance: In the Words of Its Creators.** 2nd ed. Ed. by Jean Brown & Charles H. Woodford. 230p. 1997. pap. 16.95 (0-87127-205-9) Princeton Bk Co.
Vision of Multicultural Education for the Year 2000. Ed. by Rose M. Duhon-Sells & Emma T. Pitts. LC 93-44824. 1994. text ed. 79.95 (0-7734-9427-8) E Mellen.
Vision of Nature: Traces of the Original World. Michael Tobias. LC 94-28922. (Illus.). 312p. 1995. 39.00 (0-87338-483-0) Kent St U Pr.
Vision of New England: Selected Writings see Library of American Puritan Writings. The Seventeenth Century: The Seventeenth Century
Vision of Nietzsche. Philip Novak. (Spirit of Philosophy Ser.). 176p. 1996. pap. 10.95 (1-85230-896-6) Element MA.
Vision of Order: A Study of Black South African Literature in English, 1914-1980. Ursula A. Barnett. LC 83-9296. 336p. 1983. lib. bdg. 35.00 (0-87023-406-4) U of Mass Pr.
Vision of Perfection. Grant Von Harrison. (Personal Enrichment Ser.). 65p. (Orig.). 1991. pap. write for info. (0-929985-72-9) Jackman Pubng.
Vision of Piers Plowman. William Langland. 352p. 1991. pap. 8.50 (0-460-87094-7, Everyman's Classic Lib) C E Tuttle.
Vision of Piers Plowman. William Langland. 352p. 1994. pap. 10.50 (0-460-87509-4, Everyman's Classic Lib) C E Tuttle.
Vision of Piers Plowman. William Langland. Tr. by Henry W. Wells. LC 68-55324. 304p. 1969. reprint ed. text ed. 38.50 (0-8371-0525-0, LAPP, Greenwood Pr) Greenwood.
Vision of Piers Plowman: Text C, Pt. III. Walter W. Skeat. (EETS, OS Ser.: Vol. 54). 1974. reprint ed. 30.00 (0-8115-3352-2) Periodicals Srv.
Vision of Piers the Plowman. William Langland. Ed. by Walter W. Skeat. LC 66-26827. (Medieval Library). reprint ed. 45.00 (0-8154-0134-5) Cooper Sq.
Vision of Ramala. 356p. (Orig.). pap. 26.95 (0-8464-4310-4) Beekman Pubs.
Vision of Ramala. Centre. (Ramala Trilogy Ser.). 191p. 1991. pap. 17.95 (0-85207-231-7, Pub. by C W Daniel UK) Natl Bk Netwk.
Vision of Richard Weaver. Ed. by Joseph Scotchie. LC 95-3273. 245p. 1995. 39.95 (1-56000-212-3) Transaction Pubs.
Vision of Robert Flaherty: The Artist As Myth & Filmmaker. Richard M. Barsam. LC 87-45245. (Illus.). 160p. 1988. pap. 11.95 (0-253-20460-7, MB 460) Ind U Pr.
Vision of Sai, Bk. 1. Rita Bruce. LC 95-1937. (Illus.). 320p. (Orig.). 1995. pap. 12.95 (0-87728-833-X) Weiser.
Vision of Sai, Bk. 2. Rita Bruce. LC 95-1937. (Illus.). 320p. (Orig.). 1995. pap. 12.95 (0-87728-834-8) Weiser.
***Vision of Service: Celebrating the Sisters of Charity.** Geraldine Anthony. LC 97-20334. 1997. write for info. (1-55612-972-6) Sheed & Ward MO.
Vision of Simeon Solomon. Simon Reynolds. 183p. 1984. 45.00 (0-904995-07-0, Pub. by Catalpa Pr Ltd UK) Oak Knoll.
Vision of the Anointed: Self-Congratulation As Basis for Social Policy. Thomas Sowell. 320p. 1996. pap. 14.00 (0-465-08995-X) Basic.
Vision of the Aquarian Age: The Emerging Spiritual World View. George M. Trevelyan. 1991. pap. 8.95 (0-904576-52-3, Coventure Ltd) Sigo Pr.
***Vision of the Aquarian Age: The Emerging Spiritual World View.** 3rd ed. George Trevelyan. 180p. 1994. pap. 11.95 (0-946551-83-9, Pub. by Gateway Books UK) ACCESS Pubs Network.
Vision of the Brain. Semir Zeki. LC 92-48866. (Illus.). 380p. 1993. pap. 44.95 (0-632-03054-2) Blackwell Sci.
Vision of the Buddha. Tom Lowenstein. (Living Wisdom Ser.). 1996. pap. 14.95 (0-316-53431-5) Little.
Vision of the Disinherited: The Making of American Pentecostalism. Robert M. Anderson. LC 92-30434. 344p. 1992. reprint ed. pap. 14.95 (1-56563-000-9) Hendrickson MA.
Vision Of The Divine Dispensing And Guidelines For The Practice Of The New Way. Witness Lee. 94p. per. 3.50 (0-87083-559-9, 12031001) Living Stream Ministry.
***Vision of the Fool & Other Writings.** Cecil Collins. Ed. & Intro. by Brian Keeble. (Illus.). 192p. (Orig.). 1994. pap. 32.95 (0-903880-64-4, Pub. by Golgonooza Pr UK) S Perennis.
***Vision of the Grail: A Spiritual Adventure at the Dawn of the 21st Century.** Kathleen Jacoby. 288p. (Orig.). 1997. pap. 17.95 (0-9650576-1-5) Mouse the Pub.
Vision of the Hunter. John Tempest. Ed. by Julie Rubenstein. 288p. 1991. reprint ed. mass mkt. 4.95 (0-671-69409-X) PB.
Vision of the New Community: Public Ethics in the Light of Christian Eschatology. Lynn E. Mitchell. (American University Studies: Theology & Religion: Ser. VII, Vol. 29). 213p. (C). 1988. text ed. 37.00 (0-8204-0450-0) P Lang Pubng.
Vision of the Public Junior College, 1900-1940: Professional Goals & Popular Aspirations. John H. Frye. LC 91-825. (Contributions to the Study of Education Ser.: No. 51). 176p. 1991. text ed. 42.95 (0-313-28001-0, FVP, Greenwood Pr) Greenwood.
Vision of the Spokane Prophet. Rebecca A. Egbert. Ed. by Hap Gilliland. (Indian Culture Ser.). (Illus.). 36p. (Orig.). (J). (gr. 5-10). 1989. pap. 5.95 (0-89992-118-3) Coun India Ed.
Vision of the Trinity. George H. Tavard. LC 80-5845. 166p. (Orig.). (C). 1981. pap. text ed. 20.00 (0-8191-1413-8) U Pr of Amer.
Vision of the Vedic Poets. Jan Gonda. (Disputationes Rheno-Trajectinae Ser.: No. 8). (Orig.). 1963. pap. text ed. 48.00 (90-279-0034-5) Mouton.
Vision of the World see Elie Wiesel: God, the Holocaust, & the Children of Israel
Vision of This Land: Studies of Vachel Lindsay, Edgar Lee Masters, & Carl Sandburg. Ed. by John E. Hallwas & Dennis J. Reader. LC 76-4350. 1976. pap. 5.00 (0-934312-00-1) WIU Essays Lit.
Vision of Tnugdal. J. M. Picard & Y. De Pontfarcy. (Illus.). 192p. 1989. 35.00 (1-85182-039-6, Pub. by Four Cts Pr IE) Intl Spec Bk.
Vision of Tnugdal. Jean-Michel Picard & Y. De Pontfarcy. 160p. 1990. 35.00 (1-85182-038-8, Pub. by Four Cts Pr IE) Intl Spec Bk.
Vision of Tragedy. enl. ed. Richard B. Sewall. LC 79-24203. 221p. reprint ed. pap. 63.00 (0-8357-8366-9, 2032142) Bks Demand.
Vision of Tragedy: Tragic Themes in Literature from the Book of Job to O'Neill & Miller. Richard B. Sewall. 1994. pap. 12.95 (1-56924-906-7) Marlowe & Co.
Vision of Transformation: The Territorial Rhetoric of Ezekiel 40-48. Kalinda R. Stevenson. LC 96-7000. (SBL Dissertation Ser.: No. 154). 192p. 1996. 39.95 (0-7885-0242-5, 062154) Scholars Pr GA.
Vision of Unity. John Meyendorff. LC 87-23495. 192p. (Orig.). 1987. pap. 8.95 (0-88141-068-3) St Vladimirs.
Vision of Unity: The Bland Family in England & America, 1555-1900. Charles Bland. 610p. (Orig.). 1982. 74.95 (0-9610804-0-X) C L Bland.

An Asterisk (*) at the beginning of an entry indicates that the title is appearing in BIP for the first time.

*Vision of Wholeness. John Gaden. Date not set. pap. 14.95 (0-85574-397-2, Pub. by E J Dwyer AT) Morehouse Pub.

Vision of William Concerning Piers Plowman, Pt. 4. William Langland. Ed. by Walter W. Skeat. (EETS, OS Ser.: No. 67). 1974. reprint ed. 72.00 (0-527-00059-0) Periodicals Srv.

Vision of William Concerning Piers the Plowman. William Langland. (BCL1-PR English Literature Ser.). 216p. 1992. reprint ed. lib. bdg. 79.00 (0-7812-7183-5) Rprt Serv.

Vision of William Concerning Piers the Plowman, in Three Parallel Texts, Together with Richard the Redeless, 2 Vols. William Langland. Ed. by Walter W. Skeat. 1314p. 1986. 140.00 (0-19-811366-8) OUP.

Vision of Wittgenstein. Henry L. Finch. (Element Masters of Philosophy Ser.). 1995. pap. 10.95 (1-85230-625-4) Element MA.

Vision of Words: Poetry by Southeast Michigan Poets. Ed. by M. L. Liebler. (Illus.). 80p. (Orig.). 1992. per. 19.95 (1-56439-022-5) Ridgeway.

Vision of Youth Ministry: Bilingual Edition. 40p. (ENG & SPA.). 1986. pap. text ed. 3.95 (1-55586-107-5) US Catholic.

Vision on Fire: Emma Goldman on the Spanish Revolution. Ed. by David Porter. LC 82-74015. (Illus.). 383p. (Orig.). 1983. pap. 7.50 (0-9610348-2-3) Commonground Pr.

Vision or Villainy: Origins of the Owens Valley - Los Angeles Water Controversy. Abraham Hoffman. LC 80-6111. (Environmental History Ser.: No. 3). (Illus.). 352p. 1992. pap. 15.95 (0-89096-509-9) Tex A&M Univ Pr.

*Vision Partners with God. Ralph W. Hershberger. LC 95-95145. 248p. (Orig.). 1996. pap. 9.95 (0-7880-0645-2) CSS OH.

Vision, Passion, & the Pursuit of God. Mike Francen. (Illus.). 70p. 1995. pap. 6.00 (0-9634878-9-2) Francen Wrld.

Vision, Perception & Cognition: A Manual for the Evaluation & Treatment of the Neurologically Impaired Adult. 3rd ed. Barbara B. Zoltan. 232p. 1996. pap. text ed. 29.00 (1-55642-265-2, 32652) SLACK Inc.

Vision Problems in the United States. rev. ed. 20p. 1994. 21.95 (0-318-15871-X, P10) Prevent Blindness.

*Vision Professional for Dummies. Dummies Technology Press Staff. 1997. pap. 29.99 (0-7645-0268-9) IDG Bks.

Vision Profetica - Prophetic Vision: Pastoral Reflections on the National Pastoral Plan for Hispanic Ministry. Ed. by Soledad Galeron et al. Tr. by Mexican American Cultural Center Staff. LC 92-19356. 390p. (Orig.). (ENG & SPA.). 1992. pap. 19.95 (1-55612-453-8, LL1453) Sheed & Ward MO.

Vision Quest. Judd Cole. (Cheyenne Ser.: No. 4). 176p. (Orig.). 1993. mass mkt., pap. text ed. 3.50 (0-8439-3411-5) Dorchester Pub Co.

Vision Quest. Terry Davvis. 224p. (YA). 1991. mass mkt. 3.99 (0-440-21026-7) Dell.

Vision Quest. Doll S. Don. 1995. 19.99 (0-517-15873-6) Random Hse Value.

Vision Quest. Pamela F. Service. 128p. 1990. mass mkt. 3.99 (0-449-70372-X, Juniper) Fawcett.

Vision Quest: A Young Man's Journey. Kathy S. Adams. (J). (gr. 6-9). 1995. pap. 10.95 (0-9649555-0-4) Eagles Path.

*Vision Quest: Journey to Manhood. Joe D. Haines. LC 96-96809. 64p. (Orig.). (YA). (gr. 7-12). 1997. pap. 12.95 (0-9653119-0-2) Arrowsmith Pub.

Vision Quest: Journeys Through Visual Literacy. Ed. by Robert E. Griffin. (Illus.). (Orig.). 1997. pap. 25.00 (0-614-14377-2) Intl Visual.

Vision Quest: Men, Women, & Sacred Sites of the Sioux Nation. Intro. by Don Doll & Vine Deloria, Jr. LC 94-7642. 1994. 60.00 (0-517-59904-X) Crown Pub Group.

Vision Quest of the Plains Indians: Its Spiritual Significance. Kathleen M. Dugan. LC 85-18768. (Studies in American Religion: Vol. 13). 272p. 1985. lib. bdg. 89.95 (0-88946-659-9) E Mellen.

Vision Quests: A Guide to Adventures with Horses. Dan Aadland. LC 94-48909. 1995. pap. 30.00 (0-87605-990-6) Howell Bk.

Vision Quests: Science Fiction & Fantasy Tales of Shamanism. Ed. by Dawn Albright & Sandra J. Hutchinson. 128p. 1995. pap. 9.95 (0-9648653-1-9) Avesta Blue.

*Vision, Race & Modernity: A Visual Economy of the Andean Image World. Deborah Poole. LC 96-45561. (Princeton Studies in Culture, Power & Modernity). 272p. 1997. text ed. 69.50 (0-691-00646-6); pap. text ed. 19.95 (0-691-00645-8) Princeton U Pr.

Vision Research for Flight Simulation: A Report on a Workshop on Simulation of Low-Level Flight. Whitman Richards. 109p. reprint ed. pap. 31.10 (0-8357-7689-1, 2036040) Bks Demand.

Vision Retreat: A Participant's Workbook. Burt Nanus. (Business & Management Ser.). 80p. (Orig.). 1995. 11.95 (0-7879-0176-8) Jossey-Bass.

Vision Retreat: Facilitator's Guide. Nanus Burt. (Management Ser.). 48p. pap. 19.95 (0-7879-0175-X) Jossey-Bass.

Vision Retreat Complete Package. Burt Nanus. 1995. 64.95 (0-7879-0188-1) S&S Trade.

Vision Retreat Package 5 Workbooks 1 Guide. Burt Nanus. 1995. 49.95 (0-7879-0186-5) S&S Trade.

*Vision Science & Its Applications. LC 95-7240. (Technical Digest Ser.). 292p. (Orig.). 1996. pap. 92.00 (1-55752-421-1) Optical Soc.

Vision Science & Its Applications, 1994. LC 93-87351. (Technical Digest Ser.: Vol. 2). 300p. (Orig.). 1994. pap. 92.00 (1-55752-327-4) Optical Soc.

Vision Science & Its Applications, 1994. LC 94-80083. (1995 Technical Digest Ser.: Vol. 2). 356p. (Orig.). 1995. pap. 92.00 (1-55752-372-X) Optical Soc.

*Vision Seeker. unabridged ed. James Whetung. (Illus.). 32p. (J). (gr. 2 up). 1996. 14.95 (0-7737-2966-6, Pub. by Stoddart Kids CN) Genl Dist Srvs.

Vision, Speech, Language, & Motor Control see Adaptive Brain

Vision Systems. 87.00 (0-686-40543-9) C I M Systems.

Vision Tennis: A Story That Teaches the Secrets of Mental Toughness. Michael Zosel. LC 95-52001. 150p. 1996. pap. 15.95 (0-912083-97-2) Diamond Communications.

*Vision Therapist Vol. 34-2: COVTT Study Guide. Sarah Cobb et al. (Illus.). 131p. (Orig.). 1992. pap. text ed. 18.00 (0-943599-53-9) OEPF.

*Vision Therapist Vol. 34-3: Amblyopia. Anne Barber et al. (Illus.). 120p. (Orig.). 1992. pap. text ed. 18.00 (0-943599-52-0) OEPF.

*Vision Therapist Vol. 34-4: Infant & Toddler Vision. Carol L. Scott et al. (Illus.). 65p. (Orig.). 1992. pap. text ed. 18.00 (0-943599-54-7) OEPF.

*Vision Therapist Vol. 35-1: Working with the Brain Injured. (Illus.). 100p. (Orig.). 1993. pap. text ed. 18.00 (0-943599-60-1) OEPF.

*Vision Therapist Vol. 35-2: Communicating Effectively. Robert Williams et al. (Illus.). 122p. (Orig.). 1993. pap. text ed. 18.00 (0-943599-61-X) OEPF.

*Vision Therapist Vol. 35-3: Hot Topics. Diann Geisert et al. (Illus.). 101p. (Orig.). 1993. pap. text ed. 18.00 (0-943599-62-8) OEPF.

*Vision Therapist Vol. 35-4: Focusing on Accommodation. Cathe Kennedy et al. (Illus.). 89p. (Orig.). 1994. pap. text ed. 18.00 (0-943599-63-6) OEPF.

*Vision Therapist Vol. 36-1: Behavioral Issues. Anne Barber et al. (Illus.). 70p. (Orig.). 1994. pap. text ed. 18.00 (0-943599-68-7) OEPF.

*Vision Therapist Vol. 36-2: Vision Screenings. Bobby Mansfield et al. (Illus.). 90p. (Orig.). 1994. pap. text ed. 18.00 (0-943599-69-5) OEPF.

*Vision Therapy Vol. 37-1: Training Laterality & Directionality. Anne Barber et al. (Illus.). 87p. (Orig.). 1994. pap. text ed. 18.00 (0-943599-75-X) OEPF.

*Vision Therapy Vol. 37-2: Pursuits & Saccades Theories & Testing. Marisa A. Atria et al. (Illus.). 116p. (Orig.). 1995. pap. text ed. 18.00 (0-943599-76-8) OEPF.

*Vision Therapy Vol. 37-3: Pursuits & Saccades Testing & Training. Ellen Severtson et al. (Illus.). 90p. (Orig.). 1995. pap. text ed. 18.00 (0-943599-77-6) OEPF.

*Vision Therapy Vol. 37-4: Tools of Behavioral Vision Care: Prisms. Paul Harris et al. (Illus.). 127p. (Orig.). 1996. pap. text ed. 18.00 (0-943599-78-4) OEPF.

*Vision Therapy Vol. 38-1: Tools of Behavioral Vision Care: Lenses Occluders & Filters. Homer Hendrickson et al. (Illus.). 89p. (Orig.). 1996. pap. text ed. 20.00 (0-943599-83-0) OEPF.

Vision Therapy in a Primary Care Practice. Jerome Rosner & Joy Rosner. (Illus.). 148p. 1988. Text & manual. 55.00 (0-87873-077-X); Manual only. pap. 27.50 (0-87873-082-6) Buttrwrth-Heinemann.

*Vision Thing: Making Sense of Life. Roger Nelson. (Life Wise Ser.). 36p. (Orig.). (YA). 1996. teacher ed., pap. 7.35 (1-56212-188-X, 1210-4016) CRC Pubns.

Vision Through the Atmosphere. William E. Middleton. 264p. reprint ed. pap. 75.30 (0-317-08955-2, 2014366) Bks Demand.

Vision to Pursue. Keith Ward. 240p. 1992. pap. 17.50 (0-334-02411-0, SCM Pr) TPI PA.

Vision to Reality: Critical Dimensions in Science Center Development, 3 vols. Mark St. John & Sheila Grinell. 1993. pap. 10.00 (0-944040-35-5); pap. 20.00 (0-944040-36-5); pap. 25.00 (0-944040-37-3) AST Ctrs.

Vision to Reality: Critical Dimensions in Science Center Development, 3 vols., Set. Mark St. John & Sheila Grinell. 1993. pap. 45.00 (0-944040-34-9) AST Ctrs.

Vision Twenty-Twenty: Una Mirada Clara al Reino de Dios. Earl Paulk. 50p. 1989. mass mkt. 2.50 (0-917595-26-2) Kingdom Pubs.

*Vision 2000: Planeando el Ministerio para el Proximo Siglo. Joe A. Harding & Ralph W. Mohney. Tr. by Lia Icaza-Willets & Reinaldo Toledo. 104p. (SPA.). pap. 5.95 (0-88177-142-2, DR142) Discipleship Res.

Vision Unfolding: The Scalabrinians in North America (1888-1988) Alba Zizzamia. (Pastoral Ser.). 150p. 1989. pap. 10.00 (0-934733-11-2, 8.06) CMS.

*Vision Unfulfilled: Russia & the Soviet Union in the Twentieth Century. John M. Thompson. 612p. (C). 1996. pap. text ed. 31.16 (0-669-28291-X) HM College Div.

Vision Unveiled: Women on Television. Ed. by Nandini Prasad. (C). 1994. 28.00 (81-241-0243-0, Pub. by Har-Anand Pubns II) S Asia.

Vision, Values & Courage: Leadership for Quality Management. Neil H. Snyder et al. LC 93-23935. 288p. 1993. 29.95 (0-02-929755-9, Free Press) Free Pr.

Vision, Vitality, Virtue. Judy G. Smith. LC 91-78395. 80p. 1992. wbk. ed., pap. 5.95 (0-88177-114-7, DR114) Discipleship Res.

Vision Voiced: Narrative Viewpoint in Autobiographical Writing. Edward R. Heidt. LC 90-6094. (American University Studies: Comparative Literature: Ser. III, Vol. 34). 268p. (C). 1990. text ed. 42.95 (0-8204-1245-7) P Lang Pubng.

Vision with a Task: Christian Schooling for Responsive Discipleship. Ed. by Gloria G. Stronks & Doug Blomberg. LC 93-30275. 384p. (Orig.). (C). 1993. pap. 19.99 (0-8010-8360-5) Baker Bks.

Vision within Extrageniculo-Striate Systems. Ed. by T. P. Hicks & G. Benedek. (Progress in Brain Research Ser.: Vol. 75). 344p. 1988. 196.25 (0-444-80972-4) Elsevier.

Vision y Ceguera. Paul De Man. 460p. 1991. pap. 30.50 (0-8477-3614-8) U of PR Pr.

Vision y Vos. Angela Labarca. (College Spanish Ser.). 1993. suppl. ed., teacher ed. 4.95 incl. audio (0-8384-3454-1) Heinle & Heinle.

Vision y Vos. Angela Labarca. (College Spanish Ser.). 1993. student ed., wbk. ed., pap. 7.95 (0-8384-3456-8) Heinle & Heinle.

Vision y Voz. Vicki Galloway & Angela Labarca. LC 92-38488. 1993. student ed., text ed. 58.95 (0-8384-3453-3) Heinle & Heinle.

Vision y Voz. Vicki Galloway & Angela Labarca. LC 92-38488. 1993. student ed., pap. 36.95 (0-8384-3457-6) Heinle & Heinle.

Vision 1990: Conference Proceedings. Intro. by Ken W. White. (Illus.). 741p. 1990. pap. 80.00 (0-87263-391-8) SME.

Vision, 1994, Vol. 2: Harvard Students Look Ahead. Ed. by Gary Mueller & Allison Hughes. xiv, 137p. (Orig.). 1994. pap. 10.95 (0-9641866-0-8) Dipylon Pr.

*Vision 2000. Ed. by Silvio Vietta. 204p. (GER.). 1995. write for info. (3-487-09998-5) G Olms Pubs.

Vision 2000: Daily Meditations Based on the Lectionary, Cycle A. Mark Link. (Mark Link, S. J., Library). 407p. 1992. pap. 8.95 (0-7829-0103-4, 22043) Tabor Pub.

Vision 2000: Planning for Ministry into the Next Century. Joe A. Harding & Ralph W. Mohney. LC 90-62153. 112p. 1991. pap. 8.95 (0-88177-098-1, DR098) Discipleship Res.

Vision 2001. Jana R. Flanagan. 638p. (C). 1995. pap. text ed. 95.00 (0-13-244633-2) P-H.

*Vision 2001: Energy & Environmental Engineering. Ed. by Jana R. Flanagan. 624p. 1996. pap. 95.00 (0-88173-236-2, 68814) Fairmont Pr.

*Vision 20/20. Galloway. 188p. (SPA.). pap. write for info. (1-56063-919-9) Editorial Unilit.

Vision 2020: Reordering Chaos for Global Survival. Ervin Laszlo. LC 93-30959. 134p. 1994. pap. text ed. 12.95 (2-88124-612-5) Gordon & Breach.

Vision '85: Conference Proceedings, March 25-28, 1985, Detroit, MI. Society of Manufacturing Engineers Staff. LC 84-52599. (Illus.). 716p. reprint ed. pap. 180.00 (0-8357-6468-0, 2035839) Bks Demand.

Vision '87 Conference Proceedings. Machine-Vision Association of the Society of Manufacturing Engineers. (Illus.). 981p. (Orig.). 1987. pap. 87.00 (0-87263-278-4) SME.

Vision '89: Conference Proceedings, April 24-27, 1989, Chicago, IL. Society of Manufacturing Engineers Staff. LC 89-60088. (Illus.). 556p. reprint ed. pap. 158.50 (0-8357-6506-7, 2035877) Bks Demand.

*Visionaire's Fashion 2000. Stephan Gan. 1997. 35.00 (0-7893-0102-4) Universe.

Visionaries. James G. Huneker. LC 78-116979. (Short Story Index Reprint Ser.). 1977. 18.95 (0-8369-3459-8) Ayer.

Visionaries. Bill Mosher. LC 95-17030. 200p. 1995. 17.95 (1-57075-024-6) Orbis Bks.

Visionaries: The Spanish Republic & the Reign of Christ. William A. Christian, Jr. LC 95-16729. (Illus.). 544p. (C). 1996. 39.95 (0-520-20040-3) U CA Pr.

Visionaries & Planners: The Garden City Movement & the Modern Community. Stanley Buder. (Illus.). 288p. 1990. 55.00 (0-19-506174-8) OUP.

Visionaries & Seers: The People Who Saw Tomorrow. Charles Gattey. 288p. (Orig.). pap. 10.95 (1-85327-020-2, Pub. by Prism Pr UK) Assoc Pubs Grp.

*Visionaries, Mystics & Stigmatists. Bob Lord & Penny Lord. (Illus.). 448p. 1995. pap. 12.95 (0-926143-57-3, BVMS) Journeys Faith.

Visionaries of Our Times: An Introduction to Their Creative Legacy. Miriam T. Sajkovic. (Illus.). 280p. 1993. 24.95 (0-8059-3507-X) Dorrance.

Visionary, 2 vols. in 1. Ursula K. Leguin. Bd. with Wonders Hidden. (Back-to-Back Ser.: Vol. 1). (YA). 7.50 (0-685-10479-6) McGraw.

*Visionary. Donald Passman. 1998. write for info. (0-446-52159-0) Warner Bks.

Visionary. rev. ed. Michael J. Bugeja. LC 94-42460. 64p. 1995. reprint ed. pap. 10.00 (0-914061-50-X) Orchises Pr.

Visionary & Dreamer: Two Poetic Painters, Samuel Palmer & Edward Burne-Jones. David Cecil. LC 68-57088. (Bollingen Ser.: No. 35). (Illus.). 177p. 1970. pap. text ed. 21.95 (0-691-01858-8) Princeton U Pr.

Visionary Architects: Boullee, Ledoux, Lequeu. Intro. by Jean-Claude Lemagny. (Illus.). 240p. 1968. pap. 24.95 (0-914412-21-3) Inst for the Arts.

Visionary Architecture: From Babylon to Virtual Reality. Christian W. Thomsen et al. (Illus.). 192p. 1995. 60.00 (3-7913-1425-4, Pub. by Prestel GW) te Neues.

Visionary Betrayed: Aesthetic Discontinuity in Henry James's The American Scene. David L. Furth. (LeBaron Russell Briggs Prize Honors Essays in English Ser.). 67p. 1980. pap. 3.95 (0-674-94085-7) HUP.

Visionary Business: An Entrepreneur's Guide to Success. Marc Allen. 192p. 1996. 16.95 (1-880032-46-5) New Wrld Lib.

*Visionary Business: An Entrepreneur's Guide to Success. Marc Allen. 192p. 1997. pap. 12.95 (1-57731-019-5) New Wrld Lib.

Visionary Capitalism: Financial Markets & the American Dream in the Twentieth Century. Charles R. Geisst. LC 90-37789. 216p. 1990. text ed. 49.95 (0-275-93283-4, C3283, Praeger Pubs) Greenwood.

Visionary Christian. C. S. Lewis. 288p. 1996. pap. 11.00 (0-684-82386-1, Touchstone Bks) S&S Trade.

Visionary Closure in the Modern Novel. William R. Thickstun. 305p. 1988. text ed. 39.95 (0-312-01339-6) St Martin.

Visionary Compacts: American Renaissance Writings in Cultural Context. Ed. by Donald E. Pease. LC 86-23371. (Wisconsin Project on American Writers Ser.). 320p. 1987. pap. 17.50 (0-299-11004-4) U of Wis Pr.

Visionary Company: A Reading of English Romantic Poetry. rev. ed. Harold Bloom. LC 73-144032. 506p. 1971. pap. 16.95 (0-8014-9117-7) Cornell U Pr.

*Visionary Cosmos: Peter Russell's & Edith Sitwell's Poetry & Poetic Theory. Wilfried Steiner. 1996. pap. 14.95 (0-614-29766-4, Pub. by Univ of Salzburg AT) Intl Spec Bk.

Visionary D. H. Lawrence: Beyond Philosophy & Art. Robert E. Montgomery. 256p. (C). 1994. text ed. 59.95 (0-521-45213-9) Cambridge U Pr.

Visionary Experience in the Golden Age of Spanish Art. Victor I. Stoichita. (Illus.). 224p. 1996. pap. 25.00 (0-948462-75-2, Pub. by Reaktion Bks UK) Consort Bk Sales.

Visionary Eye: Essays in the Arts, Literature, & Science. Jacob Bronowski. Ed. by Piero Ariotti & Rita Bronowski. 1981. pap. 11.95 (0-262-52068-0) MIT Pr.

Visionary Fictions: Apocalyptic Writing from Blake to the Modern Age. Edward J. Ahearn. LC 95-46640. (Illus.). 224p. 1997. 27.50 (0-300-06536-1) Yale U Pr.

Visionary Film: The American Avant-Garde 1943-1978. 2nd ed. P. Adams Sitney. (Illus.). 480p. 1979. pap. 16.95 (0-19-502486-9) OUP.

Visionary Gleam: Forty Books from the Romantic Period. Jonathan Wordsworth. LC 96-5340. 256p. 1993. pap. 55.00 (1-85477-126-4, Pub. by Woodstock Bks UK) Cassell.

Visionary Gleam: Forty Books from the Romantic Period. Jonathan Wordsworth. LC 96-5340. 243p. 1996. pap. 21.95 (1-85477-214-7, Pub. by Woodstock Bks UK) Cassell.

Visionary Gleam: Texts & Transformations. Elise Asher. LC 94-19190. (Illus.). 1994. pap. 30.00 (1-878818-33-3) Sheep Meadow.

Visionary Human: Mystical Consciousness & Paranormal Perspectives. Nevill Drury. 144p. 1993. pap. 14.95 (1-85230-206-2) Element MA.

Visionary Human: Mystical Consciousness & Paranormal Perspectives. Nevill Drury. 40p. (C). 1996. reprint ed. pap. 12.95 (1-85327-102-0, Pub. by Prism Pr UK) Assoc Pubs Grp.

Visionary Leader: From Mission Statement to a Thriving Organization, Here's Your Blueprint. Bob Wall. 1994. pap. 12.95 (1-55958-494-7) Prima Pub.

Visionary Leader: How Anyone Can Learn to Lead Better. Joseph M. Champlin & Charles Champlin. 224p. (Orig.). 1993. pap. 14.95 (0-8245-1235-9) Crossroad NY.

Visionary Leader: How to Build Leadership, Trust, & Participation in Your Company. Bob Wall et al. 256p. 1992. 22.95 (1-55958-163-8) Prima Pub.

Visionary Leadership. Robert Dilts. LC 96-75856. 1996. 25.95 (0-916990-38-9) META Pubns.

Visionary Leadership: Creating a Compelling Sense of Direction for Your Organization. Burt Nanus. LC 92-18435. (Management Ser.). 267p. pap. 18.50 (0-7879-0114-8) Jossey-Bass.

Visionary Leadership: Creating a Compelling Sense of Direction for Your Organization. Burt Nanus. LC 92-18435. (Management Ser.). 263p. 28.50 (1-55542-460-0) Jossey-Bass.

Visionary Leadership in Schools: Successful Strategies for Developing & Implementing an Educational Vision. Edward W. Chance. (Illus.). 136p. 1992. pap. 19.95 (0-398-06049-5); text ed. 29.95 (0-398-05784-2) C C Thomas.

Visionary Mode: Biblical Prophecy, Hermeneutics & Cultural Change. Michael Lieb. LC 91-9439. 352p. 1991. 39.95 (0-8014-2273-6) Cornell U Pr.

Visionary Physics: Blake's Response to Newton. Donald D. Ault. LC 73-77128. (Midway Reprint Ser.). 245p. reprint ed. pap. 69.90 (0-685-15646-X, 2026762) Bks Demand.

Visionary Poetics: Essays on Northrop Frye's Criticism. Ed. by Robert D. Denham & Thomas Willard. 359p. 1991. 37.95 (0-8204-1216-3) P Lang Pubng.

*Visionary Poetics: Milton's Tradition & His Legacy. Joseph A. Wittreich. LC 78-52569. (Illus.). 358p. 1979. reprint ed. pap. 99.20 (0-608-03176-3, 2063629) Bks Demand.

Visionary Republic: Millennial Themes in American Thought, 1756-1800. Ruth H. Bloch. 320p. 1985. text ed. 59.95 (0-521-26811-7) Cambridge U Pr.

Visionary Republic: Millennial Themes in American Thought, 1756-1800. Ruth H. Bloch. 320p. 1988. pap. text ed. 18.95 (0-521-35764-0) Cambridge U Pr.

Visionary Science: A Translation of Tillich's "On the Idea of a Theology of Culture" with an Interpretive Essay. Victor Nuovo. LC 87-26352. 196p. 1987. 29.95 (0-8143-1940-8) Wayne St U Pr.

Visionary States: Surrealist Prints from the Gilbert Kaplan Collection. Grunwald Center for the Graphic Arts Staff. LC 96-28625. 1996. pap. write for info. (0-9628162-5-6) Grunwald Arts.

Visionary Thinking. George J. Nosis. LC 86-70664. 120p. 6.95 (0-910977-02-X) Avenue Pub.

Visionary Universe: A Prophecy. Raymond L. Neubauer. (Illus.). 273p. (Orig.). 1995. pap. 8.95 (0-914220-00-4, A441941) Bay Rainbows Pr.

Visionary Vine: Hallucinogenic Healing in the Peruvian Amazon. Marlene Dobkin de Rios. (Illus.). 161p. (C). 1984. reprint ed. pap. text ed. 10.50 (0-88133-093-0) Waveland Pr.

Visionary Voices: Women on Power: Conversations with Shaman, Activists, Teachers, Artists & Healers. Ed. by Penny Rosenwasser. LC 92-5113. 204p. (Orig.). 1992. pap. 9.95 (1-879960-20-6) Aunt Lute Bks.

Visionary Women: Ecstatic Prophecy in Seventeenth-Century England. Phyllis Mack. 1992. pap. 16.00 (0-520-08937-5) U CA Pr.

Visionary; Wonders Hidden. Ursula K. Le Guin & Scott R. Sanders. (Capra Back-to-Back Ser.: No. 1). 133p. (C). 1988. reprint ed. lib. bdg. 27.00 (0-8095-4100-9) Borgo Pr.

U V

Visionary Worlds: The Making & Unmaking of Reality. Lee Irwin. LC 95-16633. (SUNY Series in Western Esoteric Traditions). 214p. (C). 1996. text ed. 49.50 (*0-7914-2861-3*); pap. text ed. 16.95 (*0-7914-2862-1*) State U NY Pr.

Visiones De Don Quevedo, 2 vols. in 1. Johann M. Moscherosch, pseud. xliv, 976p. 1974. reprint ed. write for info. (*3-487-05288-1*) G Olms Pubs.

Visiones de Thomas Mann. Esteban Tollinchi. (UPREX, Estudios Literarios Ser.: No. 16). 239p. (C). 1973. pap. 1.50 (*0-8477-0016-X*) U of PR Pr.

Visiones Profecticas de Daniel. Abraao De Almeida. 224p. (SPA.). 1986. pap. 5.95 (*0-8297-0497-3*) Life Pubs Intl.

Visiones y Visitas Con Don Francisco de Quevedo. Diego De Torres Villarroel. Ed. by Russell P. Sebold. (Nueva Austral Ser.: Vol. 204). (SPA.). 1991. pap. text ed. 24.95 (*84-239-7204-6*) Elliots Bks.

Visioning. Strange De Jim. LC 79-66208. (Illus.). 112p. (Orig.). 1979. pap. 5.95 (*0-9605308-0-0*) Ash-Kar Pr.

***Visioning for Success! Using Probability-Based Thinking to 'Create' Your Life.** rev. ed. Lisa L. Osen. LC 96-93061. (Illus.). 106p. 1996. spiral bd., pap. 14.00 (*1-890282-19-7*, Aevi Vision) AeviVision.

***Visioning for Success! Using Probability-Based Thinking to 'Create' Your Life.** 2nd ed. Lisa L. Osen. LC 96-93061. (Illus.). 160p. 1997. pap. 14.00 (*1-890282-21-9*, Aevi Vision) AeviVision.

Visionizing. Sidney J. Parnes. 1992. reprint ed. 24.95 (*0-930222-88-1*) Creat Educ Found.

Visionnaire. Julien Green. (FRE.). 1986. pap. 14.95 (*0-7859-2709-3*) Fr & Eur.

Vision/Re-Vision: Adapting Contemporary American Fiction by Women to Film. Ed. by Barbara T. Lupack. (Illus.). 250p. 1996. 45.95 (*0-87972-713-6*); pap. 24.95 (*0-87972-714-4*) Bowling Green Univ Popular Press.

***Visions.** Anne F. Doyle. (Orig.). 1997. pap. write for info. (*1-57553-486-X*) Watermrk Pr.

***Visions.** Michio Kaku. 400p. 1997. 24.95 (*0-385-48498-4*, Anchor NY) Doubleday.

Visions. Lehman & Emily Lites. 1990. teacher ed., pap. text ed. 18.75 (*0-13-328824-2*) P-H.

Visions. Jessica March. 1999. pap. 5.99 (*0-451-40485-8*, Onyx) NAL-Dutton.

Visions. Mark A. Patton. LC 90-70313. 49p. 1990. 5.95 (*1-55523-335-X*) Winston-Derek.

Visions. Alison Tartt. (Pathways to Poetry Ser.). 104p. 1985. pap. 17.95 (*0-86617-032-4*) Multi Media TX.

Visions. Ed. by William C. Wyles & Terri Whalen. (Illus.). 136p. 1991. write for info. (*0-9630997-0-1*) NM Military.

Visions. 3rd ed. Warner. (C). 1997. teacher ed., pap. text ed. 28.00 (*0-15-505225-X*) HarBrace.

Visions: A Low Intermediate Grammar. Emily Lites & Lehman. 256p. (C). 1990. pap. text ed. 20.10 (*0-13-328816-1*) P-H.

***Visions: African-American Experiences, 40 vols.** Patricia T. Cousin et al. (Young Readers Ser.). (Illus.). (Orig.). (J). (gr. k-1). 1995. pap. text ed. 125.00 (*1-57518-040-5*) Arborlake.

Visions: Cape Cod & the Vineyard. Harold Wilson. 100p. 1994. pap. 9.95 (*0-924771-42-9*, Covered Brdge Pr) D C Press.

***Visions: Early Emergent Teacher's Resource Guide.** Patricia T. Cousin et al. (Visions: African-American Experiences). (Illus.). (Orig.). 1995. pap. text ed. 14.50 (*1-57518-041-3*) Arborlake.

Visions: From the Leaders of Today for the Leaders of Tomorrow. Ty Boyd. 176p. (C). Date not set. pap. 10.00 (*0-937539-16-3*) Executive Bks.

Visions: Nineteen Short Stories by Outstanding Writers for Young Adults. Ed. by Donald R. Gallo. 240p. (J). (gr. k-12). 1988. mass mkt. 3.99 (*0-440-20208-6*, LLL BDD) BDD Bks Young Read.

Visions: Notes of the Seminar Given in 1930-1934. C. G. Jung & Claire Douglas. LC 96-25402. (Bollingen Ser.). 1997. write for info. (*0-691-09971-5*) Princeton U Pr.

Visions: QuiltArt. Ed. by Janet E. Rogers. LC 96-28178. (Illus.). 88p. (Orig.). 1996. pap. 21.95 (*1-57120-021-5*, 10145) C & T Pub.

Visions: Stories about Women Artists. Leslie Sills. Ed. by Abby Levine. LC 92-32909. (Illus.). 64p. (J). (gr. 4 up). 1993. lib. bdg. 18.95 (*0-8075-8491-6*) A Whitman.

Visions: The Art of Arthur Suydam. Arthur Suydam. (Illus.). 128p. 1995. pap. 29.95 (*1-56971-043-0*) Dark Horse Comics.

Visions: The Window to the Supernatural. Norvel Hayes. 96p. (Orig.). 1992. pap. 6.99 (*0-89274-878-8*, HH878) Harrison Hse.

Visions: Writing One. Emily Lites & Lehman. 164p. (C). 1989. pap. text ed. 16.50 (*0-13-946070-5*) P-H.

Visions: 50 Years of United Nations 1945-1995. Intro. by Boutros Boutros-Ghali. LC 95-7891. (Illus.). 1995. 50.00 (*0-688-14313-X*) Hearst Bks.

Visions Across the Americas. 2nd ed. Warner. (C). 1994. teacher ed., pap. text ed. 33.75 (*0-15-501231-2*) HB Coll Pubs.

Visions Across the Americas. 3rd ed. Warner. (C). 1997. text ed. 21.00 (*0-15-505226-8*) HarBrace.

Visions Across the Americas, No. 2. 2nd ed. Warner. (C). 1994. pap. text ed. 32.00 (*0-15-501227-4*) HB Coll Pubs.

Visions Across the Americas: Short Essays for Composition. J. Sterling Warner et al. 416p. (C). 1993. pap. text ed. 20.00 (*0-03-073594-7*) HB Coll Pubs.

***Visions along the Poudre.** Phil Walker. 1996. write for info. (*1-887982-00-0*) Walker Commun.

Visions & Actions for Medium-Sized Cities: Reports from the European Workshop. European Communities Staff. 310p. 1994. pap. 45.00 (*92-826-9293-0*, SY-86-94-521ENC, Pub. by Europ Com UK) Bernan Associates.

Visions & Beliefs in the West of Ireland. Isabella A. Gregory. 1970. pap. 10.95 (*0-7705-1412-X*, Pub. by Colin Smythe Ltd UK) Dufour.

Visions & Beliefs in the West of Ireland. Isabella A. Gregory. 365p. 7000. 45.00 (*0-900675-25-X*, Pub. by Colin Smythe Ltd UK) Dufour.

Visions & Beliefs in the West of Ireland. Isabella A. Gregory. 365p. 7000. pap. 15.95 (*0-901072-36-2*, Pub. by Colin Smythe Ltd UK) Dufour.

Visions & Beyond. Charles J. Palmer & Jacqueline Palmer. LC 92-73144. (Illus.). 300p. 1992. 48.00 (*1-881808-00-9*) Creat Arts & Sci.

Visions & Blueprints: Avant-Garde Culture & Radical Politics in Early Twentieth-Century Europe. Ed. by Edward Timms & Peter Collier. LC 87-31943. (Illus.). 340p. 1989. reprint ed. text ed. 29.95 (*0-7190-2261-4*, Pub. by Manchester Univ Pr UK) St Martin.

Visions & Chimeras. Prosser H. Frye. LC 66-23517. 1929. 30.00 (*0-8196-0179-9*) Biblo.

Visions & Imaginings. Robert H. Boyer. 375p. 1992. pap. 13.95 (*0-89733-361-6*) Academy Chi Pubs.

***Visions & Longings: Medieval Women Mystics.** Monica Furlong. 254p. 1997. pap. 14.00 (*1-57062-314-7*) Shambhala Pubns.

Visions & Memories. Henry W. Nevinson. 1972. 69.95 (*0-8490-1262-7*) Gordon Pr.

Visions & Metaphysical Experiences. Manly P. Hall. pap. 4.95 (*0-89314-378-2*) Philos Res.

Visions & Mirages: The Middle East in a New Era. John Roberts. (Illus.). 322p. 1996. 35.00 (*1-85158-429-3*, Pub. by Mnstream UK) Trafalgar.

Visions & Opportunities in Electronic Publishing: Proceedings of the Second Symposium. 175p. 1993. pap. 20.00 (*0-918006-61-9*) ARL.

Visions & Prophecies. Time-Life Books Editors. (Mysteries of the Unknown Ser.). (Illus.). 144p. (Orig.). 1988. 14.95 (*0-8094-6320-2*); pap. write for info. (*0-8094-6323-7*); text ed. write for info. (*0-8094-6322-9*); lib. bdg. 23.27 (*0-8094-6321-0*) Time-Life.

Visions & Reveries. George Chrissos. LC 96-90170. (Orig.). 1996. pap. 8.95 (*0-533-11945-6*) Vantage.

***Visions & Revisions.** Terrie Brookins. 70p. (Orig.). 1997. pap. 5.00 (*1-57502-474-8*, P01419) Morris Pubng.

Visions & Revisions. Ed. by Stephen E. Ostrow. LC 68-56466. (Illus.). 1968. pap. 2.00 (*0-911517-42-1*) Mus of Art RI.

Visions & Revisions. John Cowper Powys. 221p. text ed. 29.95 (*0-912568-13-5*) Colgate U Pr.

Visions & Revisions: A Book of Literary Devotions. John Cowper Powys. LC 78-58263. (Essay Index in Reprint Ser.). 1978. reprint ed. 28.00 (*0-8486-3025-4*) Roth Pub Inc.

Visions & Revisions: A Guide for Creative Writing. 2nd ed. Marilyn H. Walker. 240p. 1989. pap. text ed. 17.95 (*0-917962-94-X*) T H Peek.

Visions & Revisions: Critical Reading & Writing. Harvey Minkoff & Evelyn B. Melamed. 480p. (C). 1989. pap. text ed. 19.65 (*0-13-949884-2*) P-H.

Visions & Revisions: Essays on African Literature & Criticism. Oyekan Owomoyela. LC 91-6763. (American University Studies: African Literature: Ser. XVIII, Vol. 3). 239p. (C). 1991. text ed. 41.95 (*0-8204-1471-9*) P Lang Pubng.

Visions & Revisions: Reflections on Culture & Democracy at the End of the Century. Marcus G. Raskin. LC 94-25203. (Voices & Visions). 360p. 1995. pap. 18.95 (*1-56656-172-8*, Olive Branch Pr) Interlink Pub.

Visions & Revisions: Reflections on Culture & Democracy at the End of the Century. Marcus G. Raskin. LC 94-25203. (Voices & Visions Ser.). 360p. 1996. XOlive Branch Pr. 40.00 (*1-56656-171-X*, Olive Branch Pr) Interlink Pub.

Visions & Revisions: Women in Italian Culture. Ed. by Mirna Cicioni & Nicole Prunster. LC 92-16782. (European Studies Ser.). 224p. 1993. 38.95 (*0-85496-710-9*) Berg Pubs.

Visions & Revisions of American Poetry. Lewis Turco. LC 85-1056. 190p. 1986. pap. 14.00 (*0-938626-50-7*) U of Ark Pr.

***Visions & Revisions of Eighteenth-Century France.** Christine Adams et al. LC 96-31048. 1997. 45.00 (*0-271-01636-1*); pap. 16.95 (*0-271-01637-X*) Pa St U Pr.

Visions & Strategies in European Integration: A Northern European Perspective. Lars Lundgvist & Lars O. Persson. LC 93-1585. 1993. 111.95 (*0-387-56615-5*) Spr-Verlag.

Visions & Values in Catholic Higher Education. J. Patrick Murphy. LC 90-64033. 300p. (Orig.). (C). 1991. pap. 14.95 (*1-55612-421-X*) Sheed & Ward MO.

Visions & Verities. George G. Benedict. LC 57-14845. 1957. 18.95 (*0-87015-077-4*) Pacific Bks.

Visions & Verses of the American Cowboy: An Assemblage of Authentic Cowboy Poetry. Photos by Barbara Van Cleve. 28p. 1994. 12.95 (*1-884374-02-6*) Border Bks.

Visions & Views: Fort Lauderdale, Venice of America. Ed. by Eleanor C. Goldstein. (Social Issues Resources Ser.). 1992. 20.00 (*0-89777-142-7*) Sirs Inc.

Visions & Voices. Yog D. Ahuja. 108p. (Orig.). (YA). 1996. pap. 9.95 (*0-9637230-2-2*) Y D Ahuja.

***Visions & Voices: Native American Painting from the Philbrook Museum of Art.** Lydia Wyckoff & Ruthe B. Jones. (Illus.). 304p. 1996. 70.00 (*0-86659-012-9*); pap. 37.00 (*0-86659-013-7*) Philbrook Mus Art.

Visions at Work: Decision-Making Strategy for the Business Leader. John F. Mitchell. LC 95-37230. 1995. pap. write for info. (*0-07-709085-3*) McGraw.

Visions by Briggs. Kevin Briggs. 104p. (Orig.). 1994. pap. 11.95 (*0-9643810-0-1*) Culture Cards.

Visions et Propheties: Piano Solo. E. Bloch. 16p. 1992. pap. 7.95 (*0-7935-1587-4*, 50328750) H Leonard.

Visions et Revisions. Ruth P. Weinreb. (gr. 11-12). 1983. pap. text ed. 14.95 (*0-88334-172-7*) Longman.

Visions for a New American Dream: Process, Principles, & an Ordinance to Plan & Design Small Communities. 2nd ed. Anton C. Nelessen. LC 94-71145. (Illus.). 374p. 1994. reprint ed. pap. 55.95 (*1-884829-00-7*); reprint ed. lib. bdg. 70.00 (*1-884829-01-5*) Planners Pr.

Visions for Black Men. Na'im Akbar. LC 91-65248. 71p. 1991. pap. 7.95 (*1-55523-428-3*) Winston-Derek.

Visions for Black Men. Na'im Akbar. LC 91-65248. 95p. 1992. reprint ed. pap. 10.00 (*0-935257-01-2*) Mind Prods Assocs.

Visions for Change: Crime & Justice in the Twenty-First Century. Roslyn Muraskin & Albert R. Roberts. LC 95-36550. 364p. 1995. pap. text ed. 36.60 (*0-13-294604-1*) Macmillan.

Visions for Infant-Toddler Care: Guidelines for Professional Caregiving. Center for Child & Family Studies Staff. (Program for Infant - Toddler Caregivers Ser.). (Illus.). 48p. 1988. pap. 6.50 (*0-8011-0758-X*) Calif Education.

Visions for the Future. Ed. by Richard Economakis. (Architectural Design Ser.: No. 104). (Illus.). 120p. (Orig.). 1993. pap. 26.95 (*1-85490-197-4*) Academy Ed UK.

Visions for the Future of Continuing Professional Education. Ronald M. Cervero et al. (Illus.). (Orig.). (C). 1990. pap. text ed. 14.95 (*0-9619031-2-0*) U GA GA Ctr Cnt Educ.

Visions for the Twenty-First Century. Ed. by Sheila M. Moorcroft. LC 92-35824. (Praeger Studies on the 21st Century). 1993. text ed. 55.00 (*0-275-94571-5*, C4571, Praeger Pubs) Greenwood.

Visions for the Twenty-First Century. Ed. by Sheila M. Moorcroft. LC 92-35824. (Praeger Studies on the 21st Century). 1993. pap. text ed. 17.95 (*0-275-94572-3*, B4572, Praeger Pubs) Greenwood.

Visions from Grymes Hill. Antonio Gomes. Ed. by Ralph Nazareth. LC 94-61436. (Orig.). 1994. pap. 19.95 (*0-938999-06-0*) Turn of River.

Visions from San Francisco Bay. Czeslaw Milosz. Tr. by Richard Lourie from POL. 226p. 1982. 14.95 (*0-374-28488-1*) FS&G.

Visions from the Heart. Jennifer James. (Illus.). (Orig.). 1991. pap. 8.95 (*0-915423-59-6*); pap. 9.95 (*1-55704-141-5*) Jennifer J.

Visions from the Left Coast: California Self-Taught Artists. Roger Cardinal et al. (Orig.). 1995. pap. write for info. (*1-880658-08-9*) San Barb CAF.

Visions, Images & Dreams: Yiddish Film--Past & Present. rev. ed. Eric A. Goldman. LC 88-82683. (Illus.). 243p. (C). 1988. reprint ed. pap. text ed. 16.95 (*0-9622024-0-1*) Ergo Media Inc.

Visions in Exile: The Body in Spanish Literature & Linguistics. Malcom K. Read. LC 89-17736. xii, 211p. 1990. 65.00 (*1-55619-071-9*); pap. 27.95 (*1-55619-072-7*) Benjamins North Am.

Visions in Ink. Kahionhes, pseud. 60p. (Orig.). 1983. pap. 19.95 (*0-936574-10-0*) Strawberry Pr NY.

Visions in Poetry. Geoffrey Bradley. (Orig.). 1996. pap. write for info. (*1-57553-225-5*) Watermrk Pr.

Visions in the Stone: Journey to the Source of Hidden Knowledge. E. J. Gold. LC 89-1440. (Illus.). 220p. (Orig.). 1989. pap. 14.50 (*0-89556-057-7*) Gateways Bks & Tapes.

Visions in Verse. Pennsylvania Poetry Society, Inc. Wallace Stevens Chapter Staff. Ed. & Illus. by Ann Gasser. 72p. (Orig.). 1995. pap. 3.00 (*1-884257-09-7*) AGEE Keyboard.

***Visions of a Better City: Selected Papers: 1984-1990.** Edward A. Schwartz. (Illus.). 103p. 1997. reprint ed. pap. 15.00 (*0-7881-3696-8*) DIANE Pub.

Visions of a Better Way: A Black Appraisal of Public Schooling. Committee on Policy for Racial Justice Staff. 64p. (Orig.). (C). 1989. pap. text ed. 13.50 (*0-941410-76-5*) Jt Ctr Pol Studies.

Visions of a Better World. Ed. by Brahma Kumaris World Spiritual University Staff. (Illus.). 232p. 1993. 24.95 (*0-9637396-9-7*); pap. 19.95 (*0-9637396-8-9*) Brahma Kumaris.

Visions of a Daughter, Foretold. Jessica Hagedorn & Paloma H. Woo. (Light & Dust Bks.). 1994. pap. 6.00 (*0-87924-061-X*) Membrane Pr.

Visions of a Dream: History Makers - Contributions of African & African Americans in Science & Mathematics. (Illus.). 40p. (YA). (gr. 7-12). student ed. write for info. (*0-9628233-3-3*) M E Harmon.

***Visions of a Flying Machine: The Wright Brothers & the Process of Invention.** Peter L. Jakab. (History of Aviation Ser.). (Illus.). 272p. 1997. pap. 15.95 (*1-56098-748-0*) Smithsonian.

Visions of a Future: The Study of Christian Eschatology. Zachary Hayes. LC 92-13827. (New Theology Studies). 213p. (Orig.). 1992. pap. 15.95 (*0-8146-5742-7*) Liturgical Pr.

Visions of a New Industrial Order: Social Science & Labor Theory in America's Progressive Era. Clarence E. Wunderlin, Jr. 320p. 1992. text ed. 49.50 (*0-231-07698-3*) Col U Pr.

Visions of a Rainforest: A Year in Australia's Tropical Rainforest. Illus. by William T. Cooper. LC 92-34167. 208p. 1992. pap. 24.95 (*0-89815-523-1*) Ten Speed Pr.

Visions of a Vanishing Race. Florence C. Graybill. 1994. 22.98 (*0-88394-089-2*) Promntory Pr.

Visions of a Wild America: Pioneers of Preservation. 200p. 1996. 16.00 (*0-7922-2944-4*) Natl Geog.

Visions of a Wild America: Pioneers of Preservation. Kim Heacox & National Geographic Society Staff. LC 96-18715. 1996. write for info. (*0-7922-2974-6*) Natl Geog.

Visions of Addiction: Major Contemporary Perspectives on Addiction & Alcoholism. Stanton Peele. LC 86-45054. 244p. 35.00 (*0-669-13092-3*, Lexington) Jossey-Bass.

Visions of Aesthetics, the Environment, & Development: The Legacy of Joachim F. Wohlwill. Ed. by Roger M. Downs et al. 352p. 1991. text ed. 69.95 (*0-8058-1000-5*) L Erlbaum Assocs.

Visions of Africa: The Jerome L. Joss Collection of African Art at UCLA. Doran H. Ross. (Exhibition Ser.). (Illus.). 164p. 1994. 40.00 (*0-930741-33-1*) UCLA Fowler Mus.

Visions of Africa: The Jerome L. Joss Collection of African Art at UCLA. Doran K. Ross. (Exhibition Ser.). (Illus.). 164p. 1994. pap. 24.00 (*0-930741-34-X*) UCLA Fowler Mus.

Visions of America. Miller. Date not set. pap. text ed. 41.00 (*0-314-60974-1*) West Pub.

Visions of America. limited ed. Jack Kerouac. (Illus.). 1991. 125.00 (*0-934953-30-9*) Water Row Pr.

Visions of America: Landscape As Metaphor in the Twentieth Century. Albert J. Solnit et al. (Illus.). 1993. pap. write for info. (*0-914738-43-7*) Denver Art Mus.

Visions of America: Landscapes As Metaphor in the Twentieth-Century. Contrib. by John Beardsley et al. LC 93-45015. 1994. 60.00 (*0-8109-3925-8*) Abrams.

Visions of America: Personal Narratives from the Promised Land. Ed. by Wesley Brown & Amy Ling. LC 92-11725. 384p. 1992. 29.95 (*0-89255-173-9*); pap. 11.95 (*0-89255-174-7*) Persea Bks.

Visions of America since 1492. Ed. by Deborah L. Madsen. LC 94-12856. 1994. text ed. 45.00 (*0-312-12281-0*) St Martin.

***Visions of American Agriculture.** William Lockeretz. LC 97-5083. 1997. 39.95 (*0-8138-2044-8*) Iowa St U Pr.

Visions of Antiquity: Neoclassical Figure Drawings. Richard J. Campbell & Victor Carlson. LC 93-15097. (Illus.). 368p. 1993. 75.00 (*0-295-97309-9*) U of Wash Pr.

Visions of Apocalypse: End or Rebirth? Ed. by Saul Friedlander et al. LC 84-19246. 272p. (C). 1985. 32.95 (*0-8419-0673-4*); pap. 18.50 (*0-8419-0755-2*) Holmes & Meier.

***Visions of Ararat.** Walker. 1997. text ed. 29.95 (*1-86064-111-3*, Pub. by I B Tauris UK) St Martin.

***Visions of Arcadia: European Gardens from Renaissance to Rococo.** May Woods. (Illus.). 224p. 1996. 39.95 (*1-85410-429-2*, Pub. by Aurum Pr UK) London Brdge.

Visions of Arzach. Ed. by Randy L'Officier & Jean-Marc L'Officier. (Illus.). 64p. (YA). (gr. 6 up). 1993. reprint ed. 14.95 (*0-87816-233-X*) Kitchen Sink.

Visions of Caliban: On Chimpanzees & People. Dale E. Peterson. 1994. pap. 12.95 (*0-395-70100-7*) HM.

Visions of Childhood: Influential Models from Locke to Spock. John F. Cleverley & D. C. Phillips. (Early Childhood Education Ser.). 176p. 1986. pap. text ed. 17.95 (*0-8077-2800-4*) Tchrs Coll.

Visions of Children. Connell. 1993. write for info. (*0-312-92968-4*) St Martin.

***Visions of Children Apparition.** Connell. Date not set. pap. write for info. (*0-312-18204-X*) St Martin.

***Visions of Christmas: With Renaissance Triptychs.** LC 96-31506. (J). 1997. 18.00 (*0-689-81359-7*) S&S Trade.

Visions of Cody. Jack Kerouac. 414p. 1993. pap. 12.95 (*0-14-017907-0*, Penguin Bks) Viking Penguin.

***Visions of Culture: An Introduction to Anthropological Theories & Theorists.** Jerry D. Moore. 320p. 1996. 48.00 (*0-7619-7096-7*); pap. 24.95 (*0-7619-7097-5*) AltaMira Pr.

***Visions of Culture: Anthropological Theories & Theorists.** Jerry D. Moore. LC 96-25386. 286p. 1996. 19.95 (*0-8039-7097-8*); pap. 42.00 (*0-8039-7096-X*) AltaMira Pr.

Visions of Cycling. Watson. 1991. 34.95 (*0-9622630-0-1*) VeloPress.

Visions of Cycling. Graham Watson. (Illus.). 128p. 1989. 34.95 (*0-317-93750-2*) VeloPress.

***Visions of Dame Kind.** Jeffery Beam. (Illus.). 84p. 1995. 20.00 (*0-912330-78-3*) Jargon Soc.

***Visions of Dame Kind.** Jeffery Beam. (Illus.). 84p. 1995. pap. 12.50 (*0-912330-80-5*) Jargon Soc.

Visions of Desirable Societies. Ed. by E. Masini. LC 82-18069. (Systems Science & World Order Library, Explorations of World Order Ser.). (Illus.). 260p. 1983. text ed. 130.00 (*0-08-026089-6*, Pub. by Pergamon Repr UK) Franklin.

Visions of Desire: Tanizaki's Fictional Worlds. Ken K. Ito. 320p. 1991. 42.50 (*0-8047-1869-5*) Stanford U Pr.

Visions of Diana. 1993. pap. 9.98 (*1-879496-96-8*) Lightyear Entrtnmnt.

***Visions of Eden: Environmentalism, Urban Planning & City Building in St. Petersburg, Florida, 1900-1995.** LC 96-39627. (Urban Life & Urban Landscape Ser.). 1997. write for info. (*0-8142-0725-1*) Ohio St U Pr.

***Visions of Eden: Environmentalism, Urban Planning & City Building in St. Petersburg, Florida, 1900-1995.** LC 96-39627. (Urban Life & Urban Landscape Ser.). 1997. pap. write for info. (*0-8142-0726-X*) Ohio St U Pr.

Visions of Emancipation: The Italian Workers' Movement since 1945. Joanne Barkan. LC 82-22763. 288p. 1984. text ed. 49.95 (*0-275-91123-3*, C1123, Praeger Pubs) Greenwood.

Visions of Emancipation: The Italian Workers' Movement since 1945. Joanne Barkan. LC 84-6762. 288p. 1986. pap. text ed. 13.95 (*0-275-92597-8*, B2597, Praeger Pubs) Greenwood.

Visions of Empire: Political Imagery in Contemporary American Film. Stephen Prince. LC 91-44449. (Political Communication Ser.). 232p. 1992. text ed. 55.00 (*0-275-93661-9*, C3661, Praeger Pubs); pap. text ed. 17.95 (*0-275-93662-7*, B3662, Praeger Pubs) Greenwood.

Visions of Empire: Voyages, Botany, & Representations of Nature. Ed. by David P. Miller & Peter H. Reill. (Illus.). 358p. (C). 1996. text ed. 59.95 (*0-521-48303-4*) Cambridge U Pr.

U V

Visions of Enchantment. Diana K. Rubin. LC 91-90088. (Illus.). 80p. 1991. pap. 6.95 (*1-878116-09-6*) JVC Bks.
Visions of Entitlement: The Care & Education of America's Children. Ed. by Mary A. Jensen & Stacie G. Goffin. LC 92-40884. (SUNY Series, Early Childhood Education: Inquiries & Insights). 303p. (C). 1993. text ed. 64.50 (*0-7914-1675-5*); pap. text ed. 24.95 (*0-7914-1676-3*) State U NY Pr.
Visions of Europe. 244p. 1993. 35.95 (*0-7156-2496-2*, Pub. by Duckworth UK) Focus Pub-R Pullins.
Visions of European Unity. Ed. by Philomena B. Murray & Paul B. Rich. LC 95-42498. 232p. (C). 1996. text ed. 51. 50 (*0-8133-8965-8*) Westview.
***Visions of Eventing.** Elizabeth Furth. (Illus.). 176p. 1997. 40.00 (*0-85131-662-X*, Pub. by J A Allen & Co UK) Lyons & Burford.
Visions of Ezekiel. Witness Lee. 242p. per. 9.25 (*0-87083-035-X*, 10044001) Living Stream Ministry.
Visions of Fear. Ed. by David G. Hartwell. (Foundations of Fear Ser.: No. 3). 448p. 1994. pap. 5.99 (*0-8125-5001-3*) Tor Bks.
Visions of Florida. Woody Walters. LC 94-389. (Illus.). 80p. 1994. 35.00 (*0-8130-1289-9*) U Press Fla.
Visions of Gerard. Jack Kerouac. 160p. 1991. pap. 10.95 (*0-14-014452-8*, Penguin Bks) Viking Penguin.
Visions of Global Unity: Inspired Images from the Global Art Project. (Illus.). 64p. (Orig.). 1996. pap. 12.95 (*0-9629097-1-8*) Artifact Pr.
Visions of Glory: Studies in the Book of Revelation. David J. Wieand. LC 79-9294. 144p. 1979. reprint ed. pap. 41. 10 (*0-608-02170-9*, 2062839) Bks Demand.
Visions of God: Four Medieval Mystics & Their Writings. Karen Armstrong. LC 94-20217. 256p. 1994. pap. 10.95 (*0-553-35199-0*) Bantam.
Visions of God: From the Near Death Experience. Ken R. Vincent. (Illus.). 160p. 1994. 18.95 (*0-943914-66-3*); pap. 11.95 (*0-943914-67-1*) Larson Pubns.
Visions of Golf. Kensington West Productions Ltd. Staff. 1996. 26.95 (*1-871349-37-0*, Pub. by Kensington West UK) BookWorld Dist.
Visions of Greatness. Yosef Weiss. LC 93-72597. 130p. 1993. 12.95 (*1-56062-228-8*) CIS Comm.
Visions of Handy Hopper, 7 vols. William Hull. 1975. Set. 100.00 (*0-88253-813-6*); Set. pap. 50.00 (*0-88253-812-8*) Ind-US Inc.
Visions of Health: Understanding Iridology. Bernard Jensen & Donald V. Bodeen. LC 91-21992. 192p. pap. 12.95 (*0-89529-433-8*) Avery Pub.
Visions of Heaven. H. A. Baker. 139p. 1973. mass mkt. 4.99 (*0-88368-401-2*) Whitaker Hse.
Visions of Heaven & Hell Before Dante. Ed. by Eileen Gardiner. LC 88-45731. (Illus.). 318p. 1989. pap. 17.50 (*0-934977-14-3*) Italica Pr.
***Visions of Heaven, Hell & Purgatory.** Bob Lord & Penny Lord. (Illus.). 336p. (Orig.). 1996. pap. 12.95 (*0-926143-84-0*, BHHP) Journeys Faith.
***Visions of Home: American Impressionist Images of Suburban Leisure & Country Comfort.** Lisa N. Peters. LC 96-61734. (Illus.). 148p. 1997. pap. 29.95 (*0-87451-970-5*) U Pr of New Eng.
Visions of Infamy: The Untold Story of How Journalist Hector C. Bywater Devised the Plans That Led to Pearl Harbor. William H. Honan. (Illus.). 368p. 1992. pap. 14.95 (*0-312-08332-7*) St Martin.
***Visions of Inspiration.** Mary F. Nicholson-Ware. (Orig.). 1997. pap. write for info. (*1-57553-429-0*) Watermrk Pr.
***Visions of Jesus.** Philip H. Wiebe. LC 96-39445. 304p. 1997. 30.00 (*0-19-509750-5*) OUP.
***Visions of Joe Smith.** Louis V. Rohr. 226p. (Orig.). 1997. mass mkt. 4.99 (*1-55197-806-7*, Pub. by Comnwlth Pub CN) Partners Pubs Grp.
Visions of Kerouac: The Life of Jack Kerouac. Charles E. Jarvis. LC 75-24815. (Illus.). (C). 1975. pap. 7.95 (*0-915940-00-0*) Ithaca Pr MA.
Visions of Kings. Michael Brand. (Illus.). 192p. 1996. pap. 24.95 (*0-500-97438-1*) Thames Hudson.
Visions of Knowledge: Liberation of the Modern Mind. Tarthang Tulku. LC 93-42772. (Time, Space, & Knowledge Ser.). 284p. 1994. pap. 14.95 (*0-89800-258-3*) Dharma Pub.
Visions of Lent. Betty L. Schwab. 1994. pap. 5.00 (*1-55673-521-9*, 9408) CSS OH.
Visions of Lent: Lenten Congregational Resources, Vol. 2. Betty L. Schwab. (Illus.). 32p. (Orig.). 1995. pap. 4.75 (*0-7880-0291-0*) CSS OH.
Visions of Lent Vol. 3: Lenten Congregational Resources, Vol. 3. Betty L. Schwab. (Illus.). 51p. (Orig.). 1996. pap. 5.95 (*0-7880-0227-9*) CSS OH.
Visions of Liberty: The Bill of Rights for All Americans. Ira Glasser. (Illus.). 288p. 1993. pap. 14.95 (*1-55970-198-6*) Arcade Pub Inc.
Visions of Light & Air: Canadian Impressionism, 1885-1920. Carol Lowrey. LC 95-78255. (Illus.). 152p. 1995. pap. 25.00 (*1-879128-12-8*) Americas Soc.
Visions of Liturgy & Music for a New Century. Lucien Deiss. LC 96-17693. 280p. (Orig.). 1996. pap. 24.95 (*0-8146-2298-4*) Liturgical Pr.
Visions of Love. Sandy A. Stein. (Illus.). 25p. (Orig.). 1993. pap. 8.95 (*1-56550-017-2*) Vis Bks Intl.
Visions of Love & Life: Pre-Raphaelite Art from the Birmingham Collection, England. Stephen Widman. LC 94-49716. 1995. pap. 34.95 (*0-88397-113-5*) Art Srvc Intl.
Visions of Luscombe: The Early Years. James B. Zazas. (Illus.). 330p. 1993. pap. text ed. 26.95 (*0-943691-09-5*) Aviation Heritage.
Visions of Luscombe: The Early Years. James B. Zazas. (Illus.). 320p. 26.95 (*0-614-13192-8*, 21-85076) EAA Aviation.
Visions of Mary. Peter Eicher. 240p. (Orig.). 1996. mass mkt. 5.50 (*0-380-78270-7*) Avon.
Visions of Moving Crucifixes in Modern Spain. William A. Christian, Jr. 232p. 1992. text ed. 35.00 (*0-691-07387-2*) Princeton U Pr.
Visions of Murder. Florence W. McClain. LC 95-45090. 336p. 1996. mass mkt. 5.99 (*1-56718-452-9*) Llewellyn Pubns.
Visions of New York State: The Historical Paintings of L. F. Tantillo. L. F. Tantillo. 37p. 1996. pap. text ed. 37. 50 (*1-885482-05-1*) Shawangunk Pr.
Visions of One World: Legacy of Alexander. John H. Marks. LC 85-4441. iv, 257p. (Orig.). (C). 1985. 25.00 (*0-931500-10-9*); pap. 16.95 (*0-931500-09-5*) Eisenbrauns.
Visions of Our Lady. Therese Johnson. Ed. by Grace Dumelle. (Illus.). 56p. 1996. 25.00 (*0-937739-26-X*) Roman IL.
Visions of Our Native American Heritage. Jay Stock. LC 94-68513. (Illus.). 192p. 1994. 79.95 (*1-888003-01-4*) Jays Inc.
Visions of Paradise: Installations by Vito Acconci, James Surls & David Ireland. Gary Garrels. (Illus.). 56p. (Orig.). 1984. pap. 5.00 (*0-938437-09-7*) MIT List Visual Arts.
Visions of Paradise: Themes & Variations on the Garden. Marina Schinz & Susan Littlefield. LC 85-2826. (Illus.). 272p. 1985. 50.00 (*0-941434-66-4*) Stewart Tabori & Chang.
Visions of Peace. Ed. by Vito Perrone. (Illus.). 90p. 1988. pap. 5.00 (*0-940237-02-4*) ND Qtr Pr.
Visions of Peace. fac. ed. Ed. by Shirley J. Heckman. LC 83-16522. (Illus.). 87p. 1984. pap. 25.00 (*0-7837-7711-6*, 2047471) Bks Demand.
Visions of Peace: The Story of the Messianic Expectation. Aaron H. Shovers. LC 81-86206. 237p. (Orig.). 1985. student ed. 8.75 (*0-9613613-1-X*); pap. 18.00 (*0-9613613-0-1*) Three Dimensional.
Visions of Post-Compulsory Education. Ian McNay. 176p. 1992. 85.00 (*0-335-09779-0*, Open Univ Pr); pap. 32.00 (*0-335-09778-2*, Open Univ Pr) Taylor & Francis.
Visions of Power: Imaging Medieval Buddhism. Bernard Faure. Tr. by Phyllis Brooks. 336p. 1996. text ed. 45.00 (*0-691-03758-2*) Princeton U Pr.
Visions of Presence in Modern American Poetry. Nathan A. Scott, Jr. LC 92-27648. 312p. 1993. 39.95 (*0-8018-4537-8*) Johns Hopkins.
***Visions of Reality.** Haynesly R. Blake. 53p. (Orig.). 1996. mass mkt. 9.95 (*0-9655656-0-2*) Rhythmic Images.
Visions of Reality: What Fundamentalist Schools Teach. Albert J. Menendez. LC 92-33260. 152p. (Orig.). (C). 1993. pap. 16.95 (*0-87975-802-3*) Prometheus Bks.
Visions of Reform: Implications for the Education Profession. John Sikula. (Blue Ribbon Task Force Reports). 1986. pap. 6.25 (*0-317-60474-0*) Assn Tchr Ed.
Visions of Rogers's Science-Based Nursing. Ed. by Elizabeth A. Barrett. 432p. 1990. 36.95 (*0-88737-447-6*) Natl League Nurse.
Visions of Ron Herron. Reynor Banham. (Architectural Monographs: No. 35). (Illus.). 144p. 1995. pap. 38.00 (*1-85490-268-7*) Academy Ed UK.
Visions of Roses: Using Roses in Over 30 Beautiful Gardens. Peter Beales. 1996. 40.00 (*0-8212-2318-6*) Little.
Visions of Show Jumping. Elizabeth Furth. (Illus.). 128p. 1995. 32.95 (*1-85688-038-9*) Lyons & Burford.
Visions of Social Control: Crime, Punishment & Classification. Stanley Cohen. 336p. 1985. pap. 24.95 (*0-7456-0021-2*) Blackwell Pubs.
Visions of Sor Maria de Agreda: Writing Knowledge & Power. Clark Colahan. LC 94-9569. 194p. 1994. 36.00 (*0-8165-1419-4*) U of Ariz Pr.
Visions of Sound: Musical Instruments of First Nations Communities in Northeastern America. Beverley Diamond et al. 1994. cd-rom 60.00 (*0-88920-246-X*) W Laurier Pr.
Visions of Sound: Musical Instruments of First Nations Communities in Northeastern America. Beverley Diamond et al. 222p. 1994. 24.95 (*0-88920-228-1*) Wilfrid Laurier.
Visions of Sound: Musical Instruments of First Nations Communities in Northeastern America. Beverly Diamond et al. LC 94-10337. (Chicago Studies in Ethnomusicology). (Illus.). 240p. 1995. pap. 19.95 (*0-226-14476-3*); lib. bdg. 47.50 (*0-226-14475-5*) U Ch Pr.
Visions of Spiritual Unity & Peace. Rajinder Singh. 86p. 1994. pap. 5.00 (*0-918224-33-0*) S K Pubns.
Visions of Sri Ramakrishna. Compiled by Swami Yogeshananda. 150p. 1974. 3.95 (*0-87481-455-3*) Vedanta Pr.
Visions of Suburbia. Roger Silverstone. LC 96-6379. 264p. (C). 1996. pap. 18.95 (*0-415-10717-2*); text ed. 69.95 (*0-415-10716-4*) Routledge.
Visions of Sukhavati: Shan-tao's Commentary on the Kuan Wu-liang-shou-Fo Ching. Julian F. Pas. LC 94-31689. (SUNY Series in Buddhist Studies). 452p. (C). 1995. text ed. 74.50 (*0-7914-2519-3*); pap. text ed. 24.95 (*0-7914-2520-7*) State U NY Pr.
Visions of Sunsets. rev. ed. Thea M. Kellogg. LC 95-90025. 192p. 1996. pap. 12.00 (*0-9645035-3-0*) WynnHart Pr.
Visions of Symmetry: Notebooks, Periodic Drawings, & Related Work of M. C. Escher. Doris S. Schattschneider. LC 90-3411. 1995. pap. text ed. write for info. (*0-7167-2352-2*) W H Freeman.
Visions of Teaching & Learning: Eighty Exemplary Middle Level Projects. Ed. by John Arnold. 150p. (Orig.). (C). 1990. pap. text ed. 14.00 (*1-56090-048-2*) Natl Middle Schl.
Visions of Technology: Social Institutional Factors Shaping the Development of New Technologies. Meinolf Dierkes et al. LC 96-7155. 140p. 1996. text ed. 59.95 (*0-312-16053-4*) St Martin.
***Visions of Tennis.** Allsport Staff. 1996. 24.95 (*1-899163-25-5*) Cimino Pub Grp.
Visions of the American West. Gerald F. Kreyche. LC 88-26176. 312p. 1989. pap. 16.00 (*0-8131-0197-2*); text ed. 34.00 (*0-8131-1642-2*) U Pr of Ky.
***Visions of the Beast: A Pictorial History of Iron Maiden (& Eddie 1979-1997)** Compiled by S. Harris & R. Smallwood. 180p. pap. 29.95 (*1-86074-333-1*, Pub. by Sanctuary Pr UK) Music Sales.
Visions of the Children: The Apparitions of the Blessed Mother at Medjugorje. Janet T. Connell. (Illus.). 256p. 1992. 19.95 (*0-312-07879-X*) St Martin.
Visions of the Children: The Apparitions of the Blessed Mother at Medjugorje. Janice T. Connell. (Illus.). 304p. 1993. pap. 10.95 (*0-312-09933-9*) St Martin.
Visions of the Dusk. Fenton Johnson. LC 73-161265. (Black Heritage Library Collection). 1977. reprint ed. 15. 95 (*0-8369-8824-8*) Ayer.
Visions of the East: Orientalism in Film. Ed. by Matthew Bernstein & Gaylyn Studlar. LC 96-18112. (Illus.). 325p. (C). 1997. text ed. 50.00 (*0-8135-2294-3*); pap. text ed. 18.95 (*0-8135-2295-1*) Rutgers U Pr.
Visions of the Fantastic: Selected Essays from the Fifteenth International Conference on the Fantastic in the Arts. Ed. by Allienne R. Becker. LC 95-39493. (Contributions to the Study of Science Fiction & Fantasy Ser.: Vol. 68). 240p. 1996. text ed. 55.00 (*0-313-29725-8*, Greenwood Pr) Greenwood.
Visions of the Fathers of Lascaux. Intro. by Clayton Eshleman. 44p. (Orig.). (C). 1983. pap. 5.00 (*0-915572-70-2*) Panjandrum.
Visions of the Future: Almanacs, Time, & Cultural Change 1775-1870. Maureen Perkins. LC 96-16985. 304p. 1996. 75.00 (*0-19-812178-4*, Clarendon Pr) OUP.
Visions of the Future: Proceedings of the Third National Irrigation Symposium. 761p. 1990. 65.00 (*0-929355-09-1*) Am Soc Ag Eng.
Visions of the Future: The Distant Past, Yesterday, Today, Tomorrow. Robert Heilbroner. 220p. 1995. 19.95 (*0-19-509074-8*) OUP.
Visions of the Future: The Distant Past, Yesterday, Today, Tomorrow. Robert Heilbroner. (Oxford American Lectures). 144p. 1996. pap. 10.95 (*0-19-510286-X*) OUP.
Visions of the Great Rememberer. Allen Ginsberg. LC 74-77758. (Haystack Bks.). (Illus.). 72p. 1974. pap. 3.50 (*0-913142-03-4*) Mulch Pr.
***Visions of the Harvest.** Rick Joyner. 112p. 1996. pap. 5.00 (*1-878327-36-4*, RJI-007) Morning NC.
Visions of the Harvest. Rick Joyner. 116p. 1995. mass mkt. 4.99 (*0-88368-374-1*) Whitaker Hse.
Visions of the Heavenly Sphere: A Study in Shaker Religious Art. Edward D. Andrews & Faith Andrews. LC 79-83652. (Illus.). 155p. reprint ed. pap. 44.20 (*0-317-10386-5*, 2017650) Bks Demand.
Visions of the King. Calliope Doxiadis. 1966. pap. 6.00 (*0-685-62614-8*) Atlantis Edns.
Visions of the Last Prophet. Terence De Malaherre. 1994. 10.95 (*0-533-10843-8*) Vantage.
Visions Of the Modern. John Golding. LC 93-41275. 1994. 35.00 (*0-520-08791-7*); pap. 18.00 (*0-520-08792-5*) U CA Pr.
Visions of the Modern City: Essays in History, Art, & Literature. Ed. by William Sharpe & Leonard Wallock. LC 87-2764. 280p. (Orig.). 1987. pap. text ed. 13.95 (*0-8018-3540-2*) Johns Hopkins.
Visions of the "Neue Frau" Women & the Visual Arts in Weimar Germany. Ed. by Marsha Meskimmon & Sherer West. (Illus.). 235p. (C). 1995. 64.95 (*1-85928-157-5*, Pub. by Scolar Pr UK) Ashgate Pub Co.
Visions of the New World in the Drama of Lope de Vega. Robert M. Shannon. (American University Studies: Romance Languages & Literature: Ser. II, Vol. 67). 212p. (C). 1989. text ed. 32.95 (*0-8204-0574-4*) P Lang Pubng.
Visions of the North: Native Arts of the Northwest Coast. Don McQuiston & Debra McQuiston. (Illus.). 120p. 1995. 35.00 (*0-8118-0881-5*); pap. 19.95 (*0-8118-0859-9*) Chronicle Bks.
Visions of the Other: Jewish & Christian Theologians Assess the Dialogue. Frank De Siano. Ed. by Eugene J. Fisher. LC 94-18416. (Stimulus Bks.). 175p. 1994. pap. 7.95 (*0-8091-3477-2*) Paulist Pr.
Visions of the Past: The Challenge of Film to Our Idea of History. Robert A. Rosenstone. LC 95-6720. 288p. (C). 1995. text ed. 35.00 (*0-674-94097-0*); pap. text ed. 16.95 (*0-674-94098-9*) HUP.
Visions of the People: Industrial England & the Question of Class, c. 1848-1914. Patrick W. Joyce. 320p. (C). 1991. text ed. 74.95 (*0-521-37152-X*) Cambridge U Pr.
Visions of the People: Industrial England & the Question of Class, c. 1848-1914. Patrick W. Joyce. (Illus.). 463p. (C). 1993. pap. text ed. 24.95 (*0-521-44797-6*) Cambridge U Pr.
***Visions of the Prophet.** Kahlil Gibran. Tr. by Margaret Crosland from FRE. LC 96-39837. 160p. 1997. 12.95 (*1-883319-60-9*) Frog Ltd CA.
Visions of the Self in the Novel of Camilo Castelo Branco (1850-1870) David G. Frier. LC 95-34698. (Hispanic Literature Ser.: Vol. 29). 474p. 1996. text ed. 109.95 (*0-7734-8836-7*) E Mellen.
Visions of the Sharma: Japanese Buddhist Paintings & Prints in the Honolulu Academy of Arts. Stephen Little. (Illus.). 200p. (Orig.). (C). 1991. pap. 35.00 (*0-937426-14-8*, Woodstocker Bks) A Schwartz & Co.
Visions of the Sky, Vol. 16. Edwin C. Krupp et al. (Archives of California Prehistory Ser.: Vol. 16). (Illus.). 186p. (Orig.). (C). 1988. pap. text ed. 18.05 (*1-55567-050-4*) Coyote Press.
Visions of the Sociological Tradition. Donald N. Levine. LC 95-3389. 381p. 1995. pap. text ed. 15.95 (*0-226-47547-6*) U Ch Pr.
Visions of the Sociological Tradition. Donald N. Levine. LC 95-3389. 380p. 1995. lib. bdg. 47.50 (*0-226-47546-8*) U Ch Pr.
Visions of the Universe. Michigan State University Staff. (C). 1993. student ed. 13.00 (*1-881592-08-1*) Hayden-McNeil.
***Visions of the Valley.** Carol Defrank & Marietta Brzeczek. LC 96-26890. (Illus.). 256p. 1996. 39.00 (*1-885352-38-7*) Community Comm.
***Visions of the Valley: Flowers & Pumpkins.** Carol Defrank & Marietta Brzeczek. LC 96-26890. 1996. write for info. (*1-885352-39-5*) Community Comm.
Visions of the West: American Art from Dallas Private Collections. Rick Stewart. 200p. 1986. write for info. (*0-936227-01-X*) Dallas Mus.
Visions of the Wild. John Shaw. LC 80-83734. (Illus.). 128p. 1980. 24.95 (*0-941912-00-0*) Mich Nat Res.
Visions of Tomorrow: A Focus on National Space Transportation Issues. Ed. by Gerald A. Soffen. (Science & Technology Ser.: Vol. 69). (Illus.). 338p. 1988. pap. text ed. 45.00 (*0-87703-275-0*); lib. bdg. 55. 00 (*0-87703-274-2*) Univelt Inc.
Visions of Tomorrow: Six Journeys from Outer to Inner Space. David W. Samuelson. (Science Fiction Ser.). 433p. 1977. 36.95 (*0-405-06334-2*) Ayer.

***Visions of Tomorrow: The War Against the Power of Fear. Dean Steeves. 132p. (Orig.). 1997. pap. 16.95 (*0-9657073-1-8*) Three-D Mktg.**
The paralytic or panicked feeling/ Of danger in the air/ Or perhaps a healthy signal to the self/ That it should be attentive & aware/ What makes fear a formidable opponent/ Or your worst nightmare/ Who left unaddressed/ Will bring you to your knees/ And leave you wallowing in despair?/ What great benefit can be derived/ When the vision of who he is/ Becomes very, very clear? Fear is the self-created energy that acts in opposition to what love desires for the self--The Feeling of Power. It is therefore SOMETHING THAT MUST BE OVERCOME. One's very Growth depends on it. Fear reveals itself in its multiple tones such as greed, hatred, anger, pity, envy, guilt & its most powerful tone of all, the debilitating feeling of one's own self-doubt. Acquiescence to fear, via avoidance &/or acceptance authorizes it to take control which results in subjugation to its will. In today's world the lives of the overwhelming majority of people are controlled by the power of fear for just this very reason. The energy in VISIONS OF TOMORROW combats this fear by rejuvenating the POWER OF LOVE which then ignites a Desire for one to engage in their own personal WAR Against The POWER OF FEAR so that as Steeves so conclusively says in the final line of his stirring piece, "FEAR"... "And growth will be the result of my days." To order call 3-D Marketing LLC - USA call Toll Free: 1-888-809-6105, International call: 516-262-0157, International FAX: 516-262-0172.
Publisher Provided Annotation.

Visions of Tondal from the Library of Margaret of York. Thomas Kren & Roger Wieck. LC 89-48423. (Illus.). 64p. 1990. pap. 14.95 (*0-89236-169-7*, J P Getty Museum) J P Getty Trust.
Visions of Utopia: Nashoba, Rugby, Ruskin, & the "New Communities" in Tennessee's Past. John Egerton. LC 77-1509. (Tennessee Three Star Ser.). (Illus.). 104p. 1977. 11.00 (*0-87049-294-2*); pap. 5.50 (*0-87049-213-6*) U of Tenn Pr.
***Visions of Virtue in Tokugawa Japan: The Kaitokudo Merchant Academy of Osaka.** Tetsuo Najita. LC 97-15881. 1997. pap. write for info. (*0-8248-1991-8*) UH Pr.
Visions of War: Hollywood Combat Films of World War Two. Kathryn R. Kane. LC 81-21864. (Studies in Cinema: No. 9). (Illus.). 186p. reprint ed. pap. 53.10 (*0-8357-1286-9*, 2070220) Bks Demand.
Visions of War: World War II in Popular Literature & Culture. Ed. by M. Paul Holsinger & Mary A. Schofield. 1992. pap. 15.95 (*0-87972-556-7*) Bowling Green Univ Popular Press.
***Visions of War: World War II in Popular Literature & Culture.** Ed. by M. Paul Holsinger & Mary A. Schofield. 1992. 39.95 (*0-87972-555-9*) Bowling Green Univ Popular Press.
Visions of War, Dreams of Peace. Lynda Van Devanter & Joan Furie. 1991. pap. 9.95 (*0-446-39251-0*) Warner Bks.
Visions of Washington: Composite Plan of Urban Interventions. Iris Miller. 1992. 68.00 (*0-9635710-0-1*) Iris Miller.
Visions of Washington Irving: Selected Works from the Collections of Historic Hudson Valley. Fordham University Press Staff. 1995. pap. 19.95 (*0-912882-99-9*) Sleepy Hollow.

U V

Visions of Wisdom. limited ed. Helene Smith & Lloyd M. Coyote. LC 93-81241. (Illus.). 180p. (Orig.). 1997. write for info. (*0-945437-13-7*) MacDonald-Sward.

Visions of Women. Ed. by Linda Bell. LC 82-4866. (Contemporary Issues in Biomedicine, Ethics, & Society Ser.). 512p. 1983. 44.50 (*0-89603-044-X*); pap. 22.95 (*0-89603-054-7*) Humana.

Visions of Wonder. David G. Hartwell. 1996. 35.00 (*0-312-86224-5*); pap. 24.95 (*0-312-85287-8*) St Martin.

Visions of World Order: Between State Power & Human Justice. Julius Stone. LC 84-5749. 280p. (C). 1984. text ed. 39.50 (*0-8018-3174-1*) Johns Hopkins.

Visions of Yesterday Are the Realities of Today: 1988 Proceedings. 34th Annual Technical Meeting. LC 62-38584. 543p. (Orig.). 1988. pap. text ed. 125.00 (*0-915414-28-7*) Inst Environ Sci.

Visions of Zion. Alexander B. Morrison. LC 93-36628. vii, 139p. 1993. 12.95 (*0-87579-788-1*) Deseret Bk.

***Visions Revealed: A Review of the Visions Edition of Magic: The Gathering.** Sol Malka. 152p. 1997. pap. 12.95 (*1-55622-563-6*) Wordware Pub.

Visions to Keep. Sandra S. Michel. Ed. by Steven Syrja. 320p. (Orig.). 1990. pap. 14.95 (*0-917178-20-3*) Lenape Pub.

Visions Toward Tomorrow: A History of the East Bay Afro-American Community, 1852-Present. Lawrence P. Crouchett et al. LC 89-141462. (Illus.). 76p. (Orig.). 1989. pap. 10.00 (*0-9622334-0-4*) N CA Afro-Am Hist.

***Visions Unveiled or the Revulation Explained.** N. W. Allphin. 298p. 1985. 8.95 (*0-933672-89-6*, C-2098) Star Bible.

Visions upon the Land: Man & Nature on the Western Range. Karl Hess, Jr. LC 92-14446. 278p. 1992. 22.00 (*1-55963-183-X*) Island Pr.

Visit. Friedrich Durrenmatt. Tr. by Patrick Bowles from GER. LC 62-16341. 112p. 1987. pap. 9.00 (*0-8021-3066-6*, Grove) Grove-Atltic.

Visit. S. Latisha Herbert. (Illus.). 20p. (J). 1991. 12.95 (*0-87868-477-8*) Child Welfare.

Visit. Dee Shulman. (Illus.). 32p. (J). (ps-1). 1993. 15.95 (*0-370-31584-7*, Pub. by Bodley Head UK) Trafalgar.

Visit. Penny Strawser. (Orig.). 1983. pap. text ed. 4.25 (*0-687-43795-4*) Abingdon.

***Visit by Farrakhan: Role Play Peacegame.** David W. Felder. 58p. 1997. pap. text ed. 8.95 (*1-57501-110-7*, 22E) Wellington Pr.

Visit down Dogwood Lane. Jasper Pickens. 240p. 1995. write for info. (*0-614-06925-4*) Rountree Pub NC.

Visit for Lollypop. Mecheline Chartrand. (Kite Collection). (Illus.). 12p. (J). 1990. bds. 4.50 (*2-921198-10-X*, Pub. by Edits Chouette CN) Orca Bk Pubs.

Visit from Ellsworth. Russell K. Hooker. (Dunsworth P. Dragon Coloring Storybooks Ser.). (Illus.). 34p. (J). (ps-6). 1993. pap. 4.95 (*1-884534-02-3*) Duzall Toys.

Visit from Father & Other Tales of the Mojave. Donald E. Worcester. LC 89-5103. (Illus.). 112p. 1990. 16.95 (*0-89096-429-7*) Tex A&M Univ Pr.

Visit from St. Nicholas. Clement C. Moore. LC 93-33703. (Little Activity Bks.). (Illus.). (J). (gr. 2 up). 1994. pap. write for info. (*0-486-27978-2*) Dover.

Visit from St. Nicholas: The Night Before Christmas. Lowell Swortzell. 1991. pap. 3.00 (*0-87129-134-7*, V22) Dramatic Pub.

Visit from the Footbinder. Emily Prager. LC 87-40110. (Contemporaries Ser.). 208p. 1987. pap. 10.00 (*0-394-75592-8*, Vin) Random.

Visit from the Leopard. Catherine Mudibo-Piwang & Edward Frascino. (Illus.). 64p. (J). (gr. 2-5). Date not set. lib. bdg. 15.95 (*0-945912-27-7*) Pippin Pr.

Visit Home. Elaine Erickson. 28p. 1990. pap. 3.95 (*0-932616-30-5*) Brick Hse Bks.

Visit of His Holiness Pope John Paul II to the United Nations. Ed. by Carl J. Marucci. 80p. (Orig.). (C). 1996. pap. text ed. 20.00 (*0-9651613-0-7*) Path to Peace.

Visit of Nicholas. James G. Cobb. (Orig.). 1988. pap. 2.00 (*1-55673-073-X*, 8870) CSS OH.

Visit of Teshoo Lama to Peking. Ernest Ludwig. LC 78-70096. reprint ed. 18.50 (*0-404-17345-4*) AMS Pr.

***Visit of the Tomten.** Johnson. 10.35 (*0-687-61264-0*) Abingdon.

Visit of the Wisemen: Matthew 2:1-12. Martha Jander. (Illus.). 24p. 1987. pap. 1.99 (*0-570-09012-1*, 59-1439) Concordia.

Visit the Fatherless. Ruth Strange. 64p. (Orig.). 1988. pap. text ed. 1.95 (*0-937580-10-4*) LeSEA Pub Co.

Visit to a Gnani. Edward Carpenter. 65p. 1971. reprint ed. 10.00 (*0-911662-44-8*) Yoga.

Visit to a Small Planet. Gore Vidal. 1958. pap. 5.25 (*0-8222-1211-0*) Dramatists Play.

***Visit to a Small Planet.** Gore Vidal. lib. bdg. 17.95 (*0-8488-2040-1*) Amereon Ltd.

Visit to a Small Universe. Virginia Trimble. (Masters of Modern Physics Ser.). 320p. 1992. 24.95 (*0-88318-792-2*) Am Inst Physics.

Visit to Amish Country. Raymond Bial. (Illus.). 112p. 1995. 29.95 (*1-886154-02-3*) Phoenix IL.

Visit to Amy-Claire. Claudia Mills. LC 91-280. (Illus.). 32p. (J). (gr. k-3). 1992. text ed. 14.95 (*0-02-766991-2*, Mac Bks Young Read) S&S Childrens.

Visit to B. B.'s Planet. Sidney J. Rauch. (Barnaby Brown Bks.: Bk. 3). (Illus.). 64p. (Orig.). (J). (gr. 2-4). 1989. pap. 4.95 (*1-55743-156-6*) Berrent Pubns.

***Visit to Ceylon.** Ernst Haeckel. Tr. by Clara Bell. (C). 1995. reprint ed. 36.00 (*81-206-1042-3*, Pub. by Asian Educ Servs II) S Asia.

Visit to Christmasland: A Storybook with a Real Charm Bracelet. Armand Eisen. (Illus.). 32p. (J). 1993. 12.95 (*0-8362-4506-7*) Andrews & McMeel.

***Visit to Crinkle Cave.** Arnosky. (J). Date not set. mass mkt. 5.99 (*0-689-81603-0*) S&S Childrens.

Visit to Europe in Eighteen Fifty-One, 2 Vols. Benjamin Silliman, Jr. Ed. by I. Bernard Cohen. LC 79-8406. (Three Centuries of Science in America Ser.). (Illus.). 1980. reprint ed. lib. bdg. 82.95 (*0-405-12574-7*) Ayer.

Visit to Europe in Eighteen Fifty-One, 2 Vols., Vol. 1. Benjamin Silliman, Jr. Ed. by I. Bernard Cohen. LC 79-8406. (Three Centuries of Science in America Ser.). (Illus.). 1980. reprint ed. lib. bdg. 41.95 (*0-405-12684-0*) Ayer.

Visit to Europe in Eighteen Fifty-One, 2 Vols., Vol. 2. Benjamin Silliman, Jr. Ed. by I. Bernard Cohen. LC 79-8406. (Three Centuries of Science in America Ser.). (Illus.). 1980. reprint ed. lib. bdg. 41.95 (*0-405-12575-5*) Ayer.

Visit to Fairyland. Lucy B. Nuttall. (Illus.). 24p. (J). (gr. k-2). 1996. pap. 14.00 (*0-8059-3937-7*) Dorrance.

***Visit to Fairyland: Glitter Sticker Book.** Jane E. Gerver. (J). 1997. pap. 4.99 (*0-689-81735-5*, Litl Simon S&S) S&S Childrens.

***Visit to Forest Lawn: Educator's Handbook.** Donna S. Percy. (Illus.). 54p. (Orig.). 1996. pap. text ed. 5.00 (*0-9652756-2-0*) Forest Lawn.

Visit to Galapagos. Katie Lee. 1994. pap. 16.95 (*0-8109-2597-4*) Abrams.

Visit to Germany, Italy & Malta, 1840-1841. Hans Christian Andersen. (Illus.). 182p. 1986. 30.00 (*0-7206-0636-5*, Pub. by P Owen Ltd UK) Dufour.

***Visit to Grandma.** Berlitz Publishing Staff. (Berlitz Kids: Adventures with Nicholas Ser.). (J). 1997. pap. text ed. 16.95 (*2-8315-6248-1*); pap. text ed. 16.95 (*2-8315-6249-X*); pap. text ed. 16.95 (*2-8315-6250-3*); pap. text ed. 16.95 (*2-8315-6251-1*); pap. text ed. 16.95 (*2-8315-6252-X*) Berlitz.

Visit to Grandma's. Nancy Carlson. (J). (ps-3). 1991. pap. 13.95 (*0-670-83288-X*) Viking Child Bks.

Visit to Grandma's. Nancy Carlson. LC 93-18607. (Illus.). 32p. (J). (ps-3). 1993. pap. 4.99 (*0-14-054243-4*, Puffin) Puffin Bks.

Visit to Grandpa's Garden. Sunny Griffin. (Little Landoll Bunny Bunch Ser.). (Illus.). 32p. (J). (ps-3). Date not set. 1.25 (*1-56987-079-9*) Landoll.

***Visit to Great West.** Laura L. Hope. 1966. pap. 4.50 (*0-448-08013-3*) Putnam Pub Group.

***Visit to Louisiana's Jean Lafitte National Historical Park & Preserve.** Linda B. Montgomery. (Illus.). 20p. (Orig.). (J). (gr. 1-6). 1996. pap. text ed. 3.00 (*1-890113-00-X*) LB Collection.

Visit to Marchmont. large type ed. Frances Turk. 1977. 25.99 (*0-7089-0046-1*) Ulverscroft.

Visit to Montgomery Place. Andrew J. Downing. (Illus.). 16p. 1988. pap. 4.95 (*0-912882-75-1*) Sleepy Hollow.

Visit to New Orleans: With Pictures to Color & Verses to Read. rev. ed. Ruth Carvin. (Illus.). 32p. (J). (gr. k-4). 1988. ring bd. 3.50 (*0-9616390-2-4*) Carvin Pub.

Visit to New Orleans Coloring Book. Ruth Carvin. 28p. (J). (gr. k-4). 1986. 3.50 (*0-9616390-0-8*) Carvin Pub.

Visit to Oma. Marisabina Russo. LC 89-77716. (Illus.). 32p. (J). (ps up). 1991. lib. bdg. 13.88 (*0-688-09624-7*) Greenwillow.

Visit to Pinky Ryder's. deluxe ed. Marshall Brooks. (Illus.). 20p. (Orig.). 1991. 35.00 (*0-933292-19-8*) Arts End.

Visit to Pinky Ryder's: A Book to Read Inside a Whale. Marshall Brooks. LC 94-66399. 48p. 1995. bds. 15.00 (*1-882986-18-0*) Smith.

Visit to Portland. David Lipton. 39p. (J). 1990. 3.50 (*0-9643034-0-X*) White Truffle Bks.

Visit to Sesame Street Zoo. Outlet Book Co. Staff. (J). pap. 3.99 (*0-517-11124-1*) Random Hse Value.

Visit to Storybook Ranch. Storybook Heirlooms Staff. (Sticker Paperdolls Ser.). (Illus.). 10p. (Orig.). (J). 1993. 9.00 (*0-9638614-0-9*) Strybook Heirlooms.

Visit to Strangers: Stories. Gladys Swan. LC 95-42679. 184p. (C). 1996. pap. 16.95 (*0-8262-1051-1*) U of Mo Pr.

Visit to the Art Galaxy. Annie Reiner. LC 91-16989. (Illus.). (J). (gr. 1 up). 1991. 15.95 (*0-671-74957-9*, Green Tiger S&S) S&S Childrens.

Visit to the Attic. Harry R. Welty. LC 92-90838. (Illus.). 250p. (Orig.). (YA). (gr. 6-8). 1992. pap. 6.95 (*0-9632953-0-6*) Welty Pr.

Visit to the Barbary Regencies. R. Grosvenor. 112p. 1986. 200.00 (*1-85077-102-2*, Pub. by Darf Pubs Ltd UK) St Mut.

Visit to the Big House. Oliver Butterworth. LC 92-9787. (Illus.). 48p. (J). (gr. 2-5). 1993. 13.95 (*0-395-52805-4*) HM.

Visit to the Big House see Visitng the Big House

Visit to the Circus. (Crayon Kids Coloring Bks.). (Illus.). 16p. (J). 1993. pap. 1.49 (*0-7847-0009-5*, 02413) Standard Pub.

Visit to the Cities of Cheese. deluxe ed. Margaret Johnson. (Burning Deck Poetry Chapbooks Ser.). 40p. (Orig.). 1985. pap. 15.00 (*0-930901-37-1*) Burning Deck.

***Visit to the Dr. Pepper Museum, Waco, Texas.** Linda B. Montgomery et al. 20p. (J). (gr. 1-6). 1996. pap. text ed. write for info. (*1-890113-01-8*) LB Collection.

***Visit to the Gallery.** Ed. by Richard Tillinghast. (C). 1997. 39.95 (*0-912303-50-6*) U of Mich Pr.

Visit to the Logos of Earth. George King. LC 86-198490. (Illus.). 125p. (C). 1986. pap. 24.95 (*0-937249-11-4*) Aetherius Soc.

Visit to the Missions of Southern California in February & March 1874. Henry L. Oak. Ed. by Ruth F. Axe et al. LC 81-52830. (Frederick Webb Hodge Publications: No. 11). (Illus.). 87p. 1981. 20.00 (*0-916561-66-6*) Southwest Mus.

Visit to the North Pole. Tracy Sabin. (Illus.). 12p. (J). (ps up). 1996. pap. 15.95 (*0-8167-3137-3*) BrdgeWater.

Visit to the People Zoo. David C. Schneider. Ed. by Cheryl V. Scallon. (Illus.). 16p. (Orig.). (J). (ps-1). 1989. pap. write for info. (*0-318-65792-9*) Early Childhood.

***Visit to the Ranquel Indians.** Lucio V. Mansilla. Tr. by Eva Gillies from SPA. LC 96-49173. (Illus.). 448p. 1997. text ed. 50.00 (*0-8032-3183-0*); pap. text ed. 20.00 (*0-8032-8235-4*) U of Nebr Pr.

***Visit to the Sesame Street Aquarium.** Rebecca Gold. (Pictureback Ser.). (J). 1998. lib. bdg. 8.99 (*0-679-98698-7*) Random Bks Yng Read.

Visit to the Sesame Street Aquarium. Rebecca Gold. LC 97-25471. (Pictureback Ser.). (J). 1998. pap. 3.25 (*0-679-88698-2*) Random Bks Yng Read.

Visit to the Sesame Street Firehouse. Dan Elliott. LC 83-4606. (Pictureback Ser.). (Illus.). 32p. (J). (ps-3). 1983. lib. bdg. 6.99 (*0-394-96029-7*) Random Bks Yng Read.

Visit to the Sesame Street Firehouse. Dan Elliott. LC 83-4606. (Pictureback Ser.). (Illus.). 32p. (J). (ps-3). 1983. pap. 3.25 (*0-394-86029-2*) Random Bks Yng Read.

Visit to the Sesame Street Hospital. Deborah Hautzig. LC 84-17852. (Pictureback Ser.). (Illus.). 32p. (J). (ps-4). 1985. pap. 3.25 (*0-394-87062-X*) Random Bks Yng Read.

Visit to the Sesame Street Library. Deborah Hautzig. LC 85-18312. (Pictureback Ser.). (Illus.). 32p. (J). (ps-1). 1986. pap. 3.25 (*0-394-87744-6*) Random Bks Yng Read.

Visit to the Sesame Street Museum. Liza Alexander. LC 87-1685. (Pictureback Bks.). (Illus.). 32p. (J). (gr. 3-6). 1987. lib. bdg. 5.99 (*0-394-98715-2*) Random Bks Yng Read.

Visit to the Sesame Street Museum. Liza Alexander. LC 87-1685. (Pictureback Bks.). (Illus.). 32p. (J). (gr. 3-6). 1987. pap. 3.25 (*0-394-88715-8*) Random Bks Yng Read.

Visit to the Sesame Street Zoo. Ellen Weiss. LC 88-3201. (Pictureback Ser.). (Illus.). 32p. (Orig.). (J). (ps-1). 1988. pap. 3.25 (*0-394-80447-3*) Random Bks Yng Read.

***Visit to the Texas Capitol.** Linda B. Montgomery. LC 96-95443. (Illus.). 20p. (J). (gr. 1-6). 1997. pap. text ed. 3.00 (*1-890113-04-2*) LB Collection.

Visit to the United States in Eighteen Forty-One. Joseph Sturge. LC 68-58023. 1969. reprint ed. 45.00 (*0-678-00583-4*) Kelley.

***Visit to the University of Texas at Austin McDonald Observatory & the W. L. Moody, Jr. Visitor's Information Center, Fort Davis, Texas.** Linda B. Montgomery. LC 96-95249. (Illus.). 20p. (J). (gr. 1-6). 1996. pap. text ed. 3.00 (*1-890113-03-4*) LB Collection.

***Visit to Transurania.** Date not set. 12.00 (*0-8464-4429-1*) Beekman Pubs.

Visit to Washington, D.C. Jill Krementz. 48p. (J). (gr. 1-3). 1989. pap. 5.95 (*0-590-40583-7*) Scholastic Inc.

Visit to William Blake's Inn: Poems for Innocent & Experienced Travelers. Nancy Willard. LC 80-27403. (Illus.). 48p. (J). (ps up). 1981. 16.00 (*0-15-293822-2*, HB Juv Bks) HarBrace.

Visit to William Blake's Inn: Poems for Innocent & Experienced Travelers. Nancy Willard. LC 80-27403. (Voyager Picture Bks.). (Illus.). 48p. (J). (ps up). 1982. pap. 7.00 (*0-15-293823-0*, Voyager Bks) HarBrace.

Visit with Great-Grandma. Sharon H. Addy. Ed. by Ann Fay. LC 88-20867. (Illus.). 32p. (J). (gr. 1-3). 1989. lib. bdg. 14.95 (*0-8075-8497-5*) A Whitman.

***Visit with Harlan Hubbard.** Wade Hall. (Occasional Papers). (Illus.). 60p. (Orig.). 1996. pap. text ed. 15.00 (*0-917519-04-3*) U of KY Libs.

Visit with K'tonton. Sadie R. Weilerstein. 1986. pap. 10.95 incl. audio (*0-944633-11-0*); pap. 2.95 (*0-944633-21-8*); audio 8.95 (*0-944633-01-3*) J Chernak.

Visit with Mr. Mantis see Hewitt Early Readers: Level I

Visit with Myself. Peggy Warren & Michael Ebeling. 20p. (Orig.). 1994. spiral bd. 9.95 (*0-9628710-5-2*) Art After Five.

***Visit with the Fairies.** Mary Seat. 1995. pap. text ed. write for info. (*1-56226-264-5*) CT Pub.

***Visita a low Indigenas Kagaba de la Sierra Nevada de Santa Marta, 2 vols.** Konrad T. Preuss. 316p. (SPA.). 1993. pap. 16.00 (*958-612-080-5*, IC003) UPLAAP.

Visita a Mexico. Laura Conlon. Tr. by Aida E. Marcuse. LC 94-18335. (Al Sur de Nuestra Frontera Ser.). (SPA.). (J). 1994. write for info. (*1-55916-078-0*) Rourke Bk Co.

Visita de Osito: (La Visita de Osito) Else H. Minarik. (SPA.). (J). (gr. 1-6). pap. 9.50 (*84-204-3051-X*) Santillana.

Visita Que No Toco el Timbre. J. Calvo Sotelo. 146p. (SPA.). 1954. 9.95 (*0-8288-7031-4*) Fr & Eur.

Visitable Past: Views of Venice by American Artists, 1860-1915. Margaretta M. Lovell. (Illus.). 152p. 1988. 47.95 (*0-226-49412-8*) U Ch Pr.

Visitandines: Comedie Melee D'Ariettes. Francois Devienne. Ed. by Sherwood Dudley. LC 92-756190. (French Opera in the 17th & 18th Centuries Ser.: No. 9, Vol. LXXIIa). (Illus.). 1992. lib. bdg. 86.00 (*0-945193-22-X*) Pendragon NY.

Visitas al Santismo. St. Alphonsus De Liguori. LC 94-78484. 64p. (Orig.). (SPA.). 1994. pap. 2.95 (*0-89243-771-5*) Liguori Pubns.

Visitation. Don Cushman. LC 95-41356. 208p. 1996. 22.95 (*0-312-14062-2*, Wyatt Bk) St Martin.

***Visitation.** Mary S. Rain. 1997. pap. 12.95 (*0-614-27441-9*) Hampton Roads Pub Co.

***Visitation.** Sue Reidy. LC 97-16819. 1997. pap. 11.00 (*0-684-83954-7*) S&S Trade.

Visitation. Michele Roberts. 192p. 1997. pap. 13.95 (*0-7043-3903-X*, Pub. by Womens Press UK) Trafalgar.

Visitation. Kathryn Walters & Faith Walters. (Illus.). 64p. 1995. lib. bdg. write for info. (*0-9629559-8-1*) Good News Min.

***Visitation: An Archangel's Prophecy.** Mary Summer Rain. 224p. (Orig.). 1997. pap. 12.95 (*1-57174-062-7*) Hampton Roads Pub Co.

Visitation: Key to Church Growth. Gordon Lindsay. 1966. 2.95 (*0-89985-119-3*) Christ for the Nations.

Visitation: Modern Miracles & Signs. Timothy G. Beckley. 14p. 1981. spiral bd. 7.00 (*0-7873-1207-X*) Hlth Research.

Visitation Articles & Injunctions of the Early Stuart Church, Vol. I. Ed. by Kenneth Fincham. (Church of England Record Society Ser.: Vol. 1). 253p. (C). 1994. 63.00 (*0-85115-353-4*) Boydell & Brewer.

Visitation (La Llave Al Crecimiento De Su Iglesia) Gordon Lindsay. (Literature Crusade Ser.). (SPA.). 1965. pap. 0.95 (*0-89985-375-7*) Christ for the Nations.

Visitation Made Easy. C. S. Lovett. 1959. pap. 4.95 (*0-938148-15-X*) Prsnl Christianity.

***Visitation of England & Wales, Vol. 13.** Joseph J. Howard. (Illus.). 217p. 1996. pap. 35.00 (*0-7884-0476-8*, H013) Heritage Bk.

***Visitation of England & Wales, Vol. 14.** Joseph J. Howard. (Illus.). 220p. 1996. pap. 35.00 (*0-7884-0477-6*, H014) Heritage Bk.

***Visitation of England & Wales, Vol. 15.** Joseph J. Howard & Frederick A. Crisp. (Illus.). 268p. 1996. pap. 35.50 (*0-7884-0519-5*, H015) Heritage Bk.

***Visitation of England & Wales, Vol. 16.** Joseph J. Howard & Frederick A. Crisp. (Illus.). 280p. 1996. pap. 37.00 (*0-7884-0520-9*, H016) Heritage Bk.

Visitation of England & Wales: 1895, Vol. 3. J. J. Howard & Mallravers Herald. Ed. by Extraordinary Crisp & F. A. Crisp. (Illus.). 238p. 1995. reprint ed. pap. 26.00 (*0-7884-0286-2*) Heritage Bk.

Visitation of England & Wales: 1901. (Illus.). 200p. 1996. pap. 32.00 (*0-7884-0404-0*, H009) Heritage Bk.

***Visitation of England & Wales Vol. 1: Notes, 1896.** Joseph J. Howard. Ed. by Frederick A. Crisp. (Illus.). 130p. 1997. reprint ed. pap. 25.00 (*0-7884-0622-1*, HN01) Heritage Bk.

Visitation of England & Wales Vol. 1: 1893. Ed. by Joseph J. Howard et al. (Illus.). 320p. (Orig.). 1995. reprint ed. pap. text ed. 33.00 (*0-7884-0221-8*) Heritage Bk.

***Visitation of England & Wales Vol. 2: Notes, 1897.** Joseph J. Howard. Ed. by Frederick A. Crisp. (Illus.). 132p. 1997. pap. 25.00 (*0-7884-0623-X*, HN02) Heritage Bk.

Visitation of England & Wales Vol. 2: 1894. Ed. by Joseph J. Howard et al. (Illus.). 200p. (Orig.). 1995. reprint ed. pap. text ed. 26.50 (*0-7884-0222-6*) Heritage Bk.

Visitation of England & Wales Vol. 5: 1897. Joseph J. Howard & Maltravers Herald. Ed. by Extraordinary Crisp & Frederick A. Crisp. (Illus.). 235p. 1995. reprint ed. pap. 29.00 (*0-7884-0323-0*) Heritage Bk.

Visitation of England & Wales Vol. 6: 1898. Joseph J. Howard & Maltravers Herald. Ed. by Extraordinary Crisp & Frederick A. Crisp. (Illus.). 243p. 1995. reprint ed. pap. 29.00 (*0-7884-0324-9*) Heritage Bk.

Visitation of England & Wales Vol. 7: 1899. Joseph J. Howard & Frederich A. Crisp. (Illus.). 232p. 1995. reprint ed. pap. 30.00 (*0-7884-0358-3*, H007) Heritage Bk.

Visitation of England & Wales Vol. 8: 1900. Joseph J. Howard & Frederick A. Crisp. (Illus.). 229p. 1995. pap. 30.00 (*0-7884-0359-1*, H008) Heritage Bk.

Visitation of England & Wales Vol. 10: 1902. (Illus.). 227p. 1996. pap. 32.00 (*0-7884-0405-9*, H010) Heritage Bk.

Visitation of England & Wales Vol. 11: 1903. Joseph J. Howard. (Illus.). 245p. 1996. pap. 33.00 (*0-7884-0435-0*) Heritage Bk.

Visitation of England & Wales Vol. 12: 1904. Joseph J. Howard. (Illus.). 289p. 1996. pap. 38.00 (*0-7884-0436-9*, H012) Heritage Bk.

***Visitation of England & Wales Vol. 19: 1917.** Ed. by Joseph J. Howard et al. (Illus.). lxxix, 226p. 1996. reprint ed. pap. 40.00 (*0-7884-0591-8*, H019) Heritage Bk.

***Visitation of England & Wales Vol. 20: 1919.** Ed. by Joseph J. Howard et al. (Illus.). xlii, 224p. 1996. reprint ed. pap. 35.00 (*0-7884-0592-6*, H020) Heritage Bk.

***Visitation of England & Wales Vol. 21: 1921.** Ed. by Joseph J. Howard et al. (Illus.). xvi, 214p. 1996. reprint ed. pap. 35.00 (*0-7884-0593-4*, H021) Heritage Bk.

***Visitation of England & Wales, 1911, Vol. 17.** Ed. by Joseph J. Howard & Frederick A. Crisp. (Illus.). 272p. 1996. reprint ed. pap. 33.50 (*0-7884-0556-X*, H017) Heritage Bk.

***Visitation of England & Wales, 1914, Vol. 18.** Ed. by Joseph J. Howard & Frederick A. Crisp. (Illus.). 324p. 1996. reprint ed. pap. 40.00 (*0-7884-0557-8*, H018) Heritage Bk.

***Visitation of God? The Potato & the Great Irish Famine.** Austin Bourke. 1996. 39.95 (*0-946640-93-9*, Pub. by Lilliput Pr Ltd IE) Irish Bks Media.

Visitation of Spirits. Randall Kenan. 272p. 1996. pap. 11.00 (*0-385-41505-2*, Anchor NY) Doubleday.

Visitation of the County of Huntingdon, Under the Authority of William Camden. Nicholas Charles. Ed. by Henry Ellis. LC 17-1223. (Camden Society, London. Publications, First Ser.: No. 43). reprint ed. 39.00 (*0-404-50143-5*) AMS Pr.

***Visitation Unimplor'd: John Milton & the Authorship of De Doctrina Christiana.** William B. Hunter. (Medieval & Renaissance Literary Studies). 175p. (C). 1998. 45.00 (*0-8207-0289-7*) Duquesne.

Visitations. Jean Giraudoux. (Coll. Le Fleuron). pap. 14.95 (*0-685-33932-7*) Fr & Eur.

Visitations. Munibur Rahman. Ed. by Thomas Fitzsimmons. 208p. (Orig.). 1988. 19.95 (*0-942668-16-2*); pap. 14.95 (*0-942668-17-0*) Katydid Bks.

Visitations: A Saga of Gods & Men, Vol. I. Ruth E. Norman. (Illus.). 572p. 1987. 80.00 (*0-932642-84-5*) Unarius Acad Sci.

Visite Guide E. Sophie Calle. 48p. 1996. 35.00 (*90-6918-158-4*, Pub. by Museum Boymans-van NE) Dist Art Pubs.

Visiterm for Apple. 1991. 150.00 (*0-8306-6212-X*) McGraw-Hill Prof.

An Asterisk (*) at the beginning of an entry indicates that the title is appearing in BIP for the first time.

Visiteurs du Soir. Jacques Prevert & Marcel Carne. (Illus.). 256p. 1974. 25.00 (0-686-54920-1) Fr & Eur.

Visiting: A Pastoral Care Ministry. Pastoral Care Office, Reorganized Church of Jesus Christ of Latter Day Saints Staff. 186p. (Orig.). 1985. pap. 13.00 (0-8309-0429-8) Herald Hse.

Visiting a Farm? "Be Safe & Sound" Says Safety Hound: A Guide to Teaching & Learning about Farm Visit Safety. Betty A. Lockhart. Ed. by Donald G. Lockhart. (Illus.). 1994. teacher ed. 2.50 (1-880327-32-5) Perceptions.

Visiting a Village. Bobbie Kalman. (Historic Communities Ser.). (Illus.). 32p. (J). (gr. 3-4). 1990. pap. 7.95 (0-86505-507-6); lib. bdg. 19.16 (0-86505-487-8) Crabtree Pub Co.

Visiting Art Museums. Laurene Krasny Brown. 1992. pap. 5.99 (0-14-054820-3) NAL-Dutton.

Visiting Britain: The English You Need. Frank Candlin. 64p. (C). 1984. 35.00 (0-7175-1269-X, Pub. by S Thornes Pubs UK) St Mut.

Visiting Canada. Lynda Sorensen. LC 94-46852. (North of the Border Ser.). 24p. (J). (gr. 2-6). 1995. lib. bdg. 13.27 (1-55916-107-8) Rourke Bk Co.

Visiting Card: Ancient & Modern History of Script & Money. Ezra Pound. 1983. lib. bdg. 250.00 (0-87700-458-7) Revisionist Pr.

Visiting Cards of Pianists. F. C. Schang. LC 79-88628. (Illus.). 1979. pap. 7.50 (0-915282-06-2) J Patelson Mus.

Visiting Cards of Violinists. F. C. Schang. LC 79-63411. (Illus.). 1979. reprint ed. pap. 6.50 (0-915282-05-4) J Patelson Mus.

***Visiting College Campuses 1997.** J. Spencer & Sandra Maleson. 1997. pap. 20.00 (0-679-77852-7) Random.

Visiting Day on the Psychiatric Ward. Alan Catlin. 1983. pap. 5.00 (0-318-04451-X) Pudding Hse Pubns.

Visiting Gig Harbor. Tanya Braumiller. (Color-A-Story Ser.). (Illus.). (Orig.). (J). (gr. 1-4). 1983. pap. 2.75 (0-933992-28-9) Coffee Break.

Visiting Grandma: A Miniature Pop-Up & Pull-the-Tab Book. Ernest Nister. LC 88-25497. (Illus.). 10p. (J). (gr. k up). 1989. 6.95 (0-399-21695-2, Philomel Bks) Putnam Pub Group.

Visiting Granny. Kim Fernandes. (Illus.). 24p. (J). (ps). 1990. 12.95 (1-55037-077-4, Pub. by Annick CN); pap. 4.95 (1-55037-084-7, Pub. by Annick CN) Firefly Bks Ltd.

***Visiting Home in Poland after 33 Years: And World War II True Stories.** Marian S. Mazgaj. 1996. pap. 14.95 (0-87012-561-3) McClain.

Visiting in Age of Mission. Callahan. LC 92-53918. pap. 15.00 (0-06-061359-9, HarpT) HarpC.

Visiting in an Age of Mission: A Handbook for Person-to-Person Ministry. Kennon L. Callahan. 176p. 1994. 16.00 (0-06-061287-8) Harper SF.

***Visiting in an Age of Mission: A Handbook for Person-to-Person Ministry.** Kennon L. Callahan. LC 97-24759. 1997. write for info. (0-7879-3868-8) Jossey-Bass.

Visiting Judges in Federal District Courts. Federal Judicial Center Staff & Donna Stienstra. 1985. write for info. (0-318-61040-X) Bates Info Serv.

Visiting Junjun & Meimei in China. Janet Whitaker. (Illus.). 32p. (J). (gr. 3-7). 1988. 10.95 (0-521-34575-8) Cambridge U Pr.

Visiting Mexico. Laura Conlon. (J). 1994. 15.00 (1-55916-057-8) Rourke Bk Co.

Visiting Miss Pierce. Pat Derby. LC 86-7559. 144p. (J). (gr. 6 up). 1986. 11.95 (0-374-38162-3) FS&G.

Visiting Miss Pierce. Pat Derby. 144p. (J). (gr. 3 up). 1989. pap. 3.50 (0-374-48156-3, Sunburst Bks) FS&G.

Visiting Mother Series, 3 vols., Set. Louise Wallace. 300p. (Orig.). pap. 28.00 (1-885800-03-7) PineTree Pr.

Visiting Mother's Dictionary: Civil Law Was Never Like This! Louise Wallace. LC 94-69178. (Visiting Mother Ser.: Vol. II). 64p. 1996. pap. 8.00 (1-885800-01-0) PineTree Pr.

Visiting Mrs. Nabokov: And Other Excursions. Martin Amis. 1995. pap. 13.00 (0-679-75793-7, Vin) Random.

Visiting Mt. Rainier. David C. Helstrom. (Color-A-Story Ser.). (Illus.). 28p. (Orig.). (J). (gr. 1-4). 1984. pap. 2.75 (0-933992-37-8) Coffee Break.

Visiting Olympia. Val Dumond. (Color-A-Story Ser.). (Illus.). 24p. (Orig.). (J). (gr. 1-4). 1983. pap. 2.75 (0-933992-39-4) Coffee Break.

Visiting Our Past: America's Historylands. rev. ed. Ed. by Ross Bennett. (Illus.). 400p. 1986. 27.95 (0-87044-647-9) Natl Geog.

Visiting Physician. Susan R. Shreve. 304p. 1996. 23.95 (0-385-47701-5, N A Talese) Doubleday.

***Visiting Physician.** large type ed. Susan R. Shreve. LC 96-34280. (Large Print Bks.). 1996. 25.95 (1-56895-369-0, Compass) Wheeler Pub.

Visiting Rites. Phyllis Janowitz. (Contemporary Poets Ser.). 84p. 1982. pap. 9.95 (0-691-01398-5) Princeton U Pr.

Visiting Santa's Workshop. Paul Stickland. 1994. pap. 6.99 (0-525-45170-6) NAL-Dutton.

***Visiting Small-Town Florida.** Bruce Hunt. LC 96-52986. (Illus.). 240p. (Orig.). 1997. pap. 14.95 (1-56164-128-6) Pineapple Pr.

Visiting Tacoma. Carole Parkhurst. (Color-A-Story Ser.). (Illus.). 24p. (Orig.). (J). (gr. 1-4). 1983. pap. 2.75 (0-933992-38-6) Coffee Break.

Visiting Teacher. Jack Rudman. (National Teacher Examination Ser.: NT-21). 1994. pap. 23.95 (0-8373-8431-1) Nat Learn.

Visiting Teaching: A Call to Serve. Johanna Flynn & Anita Canfield. 62p. (Orig.). 1989. reprint ed. pap. 7.95 (0-87579-288-X) Deseret Bk.

Visiting the Father. David R. Pichaske. 1987. 2.50 (0-941127-02-8) Dacotah Terr Pr.

Visiting the Midwest's Historic Preservation Sites. Majory Grannis et al. 280p. 1991. pap. 14.95 (0-915463-53-9) Jameson Bks.

Visiting the Mino Kilns: With a Translation of Arakawa Toyozo's "The Traditions & Techniques of Mino Pottery" Janet Barriskill. (University of Sydney East Asian Ser.: No. 9). (Illus.). 156p. (C). 1995. text ed. 48.00 (0-646-20424-6, Pub. by Wild Peony Pty AT) UH Pr.

Visiting the Nicelies: A Lil'l Charmers Book. rev. ed. Sandra J. Ross. LC 92-70147. (Nicelies Ser.). (Illus.). 60p. (J). (ps-2). 1994. pap. 5.95 (1-881235-00-9) Creat Opport.

Visiting the Sick: A Guide for Parish Ministers. Patti Normile. 139p. 1992. pap. 6.95 (0-86716-150-7) St Anthony Mess Pr.

Visiting the Virgin Islands with the Kids: A Complete Guide to Enjoyable Travel with Kids in the British & U. S. Virgin Islands. Richard B. Myers. LC 96-2165. (Illus.). 128p. (Orig.). 1996. pap. 13.95 (0-9639905-6-X) Two Thous-Three Assocs.

***Visiting with the Angels.** Curt H. Von Dornheim. 128p. (Orig.). 1997. pap. 12.95 (0-89404-224-6) Aztex.

Visitng the Big House. Oliver Butterworth. Ed. by Amy Cohn. LC 94-20844. Orig. Title: A Visit to the Big House. (Illus.). 48p. (J). 1999. reprint ed. pap. 3.95 (0-688-13303-7) Morrow.

***Visitor.** Patrice Aggs. LC 97-8195. (J). 1998. write for info. (0-531-30059-5) Orchard Bks Watts.

Visitor. K. A. Applegate. (Animorphs Ser.: No. 2). 144p. (J). (gr. 4-7). 1996. pap. 3.99 (0-590-62978-6) Scholastic Inc.

Visitor. Ev Miller. 33p. 1995. pap. 4.00 (1-57514-137-X, 1096) Encore Perform Pub.

Visitor. Christopher Pike. (J). 1995. mass mkt. 3.99 (0-671-87270-2, Archway) PB.

Visitor. Jenna Ryan. (Intrigue Ser.). 1993. mass mkt. 2.99 (0-373-22239-4, 1-22239-7) Harlequin Bks.

Visitor. 2nd rev. ed. Date not set. 32.00 (0-614-14704-2) Jones.

Visitor. 2nd rev. ed. Date not set. pap. 28.00 (0-614-14705-0) Jones.

Visitor: A Play in Three Acts. Lisa Kirazian. (Orig.). pap. 6.95 (0-9644485-0-5) Laurel Co.

Visitor Centres at Nuclear Facility Sites. OECD Staff. 250p. (Orig.). 1993. pap. text ed. 41.00 (92-64-03972-4, 66-93-12-3) OECD.

***Visitor from Beyond.** S. F. Black. 1997. pap. 3.95 (0-8167-4428-9) Troll Communs.

***Visitor from Beyond.** Troll Communs Staff. 1997. pap. 47.40 (0-8167-4420-3) Troll Communs.

Visitor from Orion. Eldon Patterson. 165p. (Orig.). 1988. pap. 12.75 (0-9623403-0-8) Human Possibilities.

Visitor from Outer Space. Sidney J. Rauch. (Barnaby Brown Bks.: Bk. 1). (Illus.). 48p. (Orig.). (J). (gr. 2-4). 1989. pap. 4.95 (1-55743-150-7) Berrent Pubns.

Visitor from the Past: An Audio Adventure in Ten Thrilling Episodes, 5 cass., Set. Joe McHugh. (Illus.). 40p. (YA). (gr. 6-11). 1993. teacher ed. 55.00 incl. audio (0-9619943-2-0) Catalpa Pr.

Visitor Guide: Mid Wales. Roger Thomas. (Illus.). 64p. (Orig.). 1994. pap. 7.95 (0-7117-0537-2, Pub. by Jarrold Pub UK) Seven Hills Bk.

Visitor Guide: North Wales. Roger Thomas. (Illus.). 64p. (Orig.). 1994. pap. 7.95 (0-7117-0536-4, Pub. by Jarrold Pub UK) Seven Hills Bk.

Visitor Guide: South Wales. Roger Thomas. (Illus.). 64p. (Orig.). 1994. pap. 7.95 (0-7117-0538-0, Pub. by Jarrold Pub UK) Seven Hills Bk.

Visitor Impact Management, Vol. 1: A Review of Research. Fred R. Kuss et al. LC 90-61819. (Illus.). 256p. 1990. pap. 12.95 (0-940091-31-3) Natl Parks & Cons.

Visitor Impact Management, Vol. 2: The Planning Framework. Fred R. Kuss et al. LC 90-61821. 105p. (C). 1990. pap. 9.95 (0-940091-32-1) Natl Parks & Cons.

***Visitors.** Anita Brookner. LC 97-10494. 1998. 22.00 (0-679-45785-2) Random.

Visitors. Walter J. De La Mare. LC 86-6244. (Creative's Classic Short Stories Ser.). 40p. (J). (gr. 4 up). 1986. lib. bdg. 13.95 (0-88682-070-7) Creative Ed.

Visitor's Book. Helen Exley. (Record Bks.). (Illus.). 80p. 1995. 12.00 (1-85015-605-0) Exley Giftbooks.

***Visitor's Companion to the Appalachian Trail.** Leonard M. Adkins. LC 97-8059. 1997. write for info. (0-89732-241-X) Menasha Ridge.

***Visitors' Day.** Anne F. Rockwell. LC 97-20999. (Illus.). (J). 1998. write for info. (0-06-027565-0); lib. bdg. write for info. (0-06-027566-9) HarpC.

Visitors from Other Planets. Nada-Yolanda. LC 73-90880. 334p. 1974. 15.00 (0-912322-04-7) Mark-Age.

Visitors from Time: The Secret of the UFO's. rev. ed. Marc Davenport. LC 94-36813. 266p. 1994. reprint ed. pap. 16.95 (1-883729-02-5) Greenleaf Tenn.

Visitors from Within. Lyssa Royal & Keith Priest. 167p. 1992. pap. 12.95 (0-9631320-1-6) Royal Priest.

Visitor's Guide to Ancient Forests of Washington. 2nd ed. Charlie Raines & Wilderness Society Staff. LC 96-27000. 1996. pap. 7.95 (0-89886-473-9) Mountaineers.

Visitors Guide to Cape Cod National Seashore. Margaret H. Koehler. LC 72-92014. (Illus.). 80p. (Orig.). 1973. pap. 6.95 (0-85699-066-3) Chatham Pr.

Visitor's Guide to Charleston. Ed. by Charles L. Wyrick, Jr. (Coastal Cities Guidebook Ser.). (Illus.). (Orig.). 1997. pap. 12.95 (0-941711-28-5) Wyrick & Co.

Visitor's Guide to Dealey Plaza National Historic Landmark Including the Sixth Floor Museum. Conover Hunt. 92p. 1995. pap. 4.95 (0-9648131-0-6) Dallas Cty Hist Foun.

***Visitor's Guide to Dealey Plaza National Historic Landmark Including the Sixth Floor Museum: Your Country in Context: U. S. - Japan 1963.** Conover Hunt. Ed. by Marian A. Montgomery. Tr. by Kazuo Kimura. (Illus.). 96p. (Orig.). (JPN.). 1996. pap. write for info. (0-9648131-1-4, Sixth Flr Mus) Dallas Cty Hist Foun.

Visitor's Guide to Florida's Suncoast. PKM Publications Staff. 396p. 1993. pap. 17.95 (0-9633219-0-0) PKM Pubns.

Visitor's Guide to Hawaii see Hawaii to Da Max

Visitors Guide to Hilo. Marlene Werner. 32p. 1991. pap. text ed. 5.50 (0-930081-02-1) Molokai Bk Pubs.

Visitors Guide to Kaibab National Forest: Chalender, Williams & Tusayan Ranger Districts. Ed. by Stephen G. Maurer. (National Forest Visitors Guide Ser.). (Illus.). 128p. (Orig.). 1990. pap. 6.95 (1-879343-00-2) SW NCH Assn.

Visitor's Guide to Mount Rainier Glaciers. Carolyn L. Driedger. Ed. by Shirley T. Moore. (Illus.). 80p. (Orig.). 1986. pap. text ed. 4.95 (0-914019-11-2) NW Interpretive.

Visitor's Guide to Myrtle Beach & the Grand Strand. Trip Dubard. (Illus.). (Orig.). 1995. pap. 12.95 (0-941711-22-6) Wyrick & Co.

Visitor's Guide to Nicolet National Forest. Gary Kuilbert. (Visitor's Guide to National Forest Ser.). (Illus.). 160p. Date not set. pap. 12.95 (1-879432-18-8) Explorers Guide Pub.

Visitor's Guide to Planet Earth: An Astrological Primer. Celeste Longacre. (Orig.). 1984. pap. 6.95 (0-930043-00-6) Sweet Fern.

Visitor's Guide to Point Reyes National Seashore. Alice F. Dalbey. LC 73-89770. (Orig.). 1974. pap. 5.95 (0-85699-098-1) Chatham Pr.

Visitor's Guide to Savannah. Emmeline Cooper & Polly Cooper. (Illus.). (Orig.). 1995. pap. 12.95 (0-941711-27-7) Wyrick & Co.

Visitor's Guide to the Americas: Say It in 5 Languages. Khalil El-Sayed & Luis A. Tafur. LC 89-92190. (Illus.). 260p. (Orig.). (ENG, FRE, GER, POR & SPA.). 1990. pap. 9.95 (0-9624579-0-6) K El-Sayed.

Visitor's Guide to the Birds of the Central National Parks: United States & Canada. Roland H. Wauer. (Illus.). 432p. (Orig.). 1994. pap. 15.95 (1-56261-140-2) John Muir.

Visitor's Guide to the Birds of the Eastern National Parks: United States & Canada. Roland H. Wauer. LC 92-19638. (Illus.). 432p. (Orig.). 1992. pap. 15.95 (1-56261-039-2) John Muir.

Visitor's Guide to the Birds of the Rocky Mountain National Parks: United States & Canada. Roland H. Wauer. LC 93-1773. 432p. (Orig.). 1993. pap. 15.95 (1-56261-101-1) John Muir.

Visitors Guide to the Chequamegon National Forest: Exploring America's Great Outdoors. Gary F. Kulibert. LC 94-72154. (Illus.). 160p. (Orig.). 1995. pap. 12.95 (1-879432-10-2) Explorers Guide Pub.

Visitor's Guide to the Everglades. Jeff Weber. LC 86-82931. (Illus.). 64p. 1986. pap. 4.95 (0-9613236-7-1) Florida Flair Bks.

***Visitor's Guide, Whitehouse Is Our House.** Auto Desk Press Staff. (Cord Communications Ser.). 1997. pap. 7.95 (0-538-67180-7) S-W Pub.

Visitors to Monticello. Intro. by Merrill D. Peterson. LC 89-5778. (Illus.). 212p. 1989. text ed. 32.50 (0-8139-1231-8); pap. text ed. 16.50 (0-8139-1232-6) U Pr of Va.

Visitors to the City: Readers of Christine De Pizan. Intro. by Glenda McLeod. 225p. (Orig.). (C). 1989. pap. 20.00 (0-941107-04-3) MARC Pub Co.

Visitors Who Never Left: The Origin of the People of Damelahamid. Kenneth B. Harris & Frances M. Robinson. (Illus.). 171p. 1974. pap. 13.95 (0-7748-0034-8) U of Wash Pr.

Visits: On the Road to Things Past. Dave McIntosh. 240p. 1990. 24.95 (0-7737-2428-1) Genl Dist Srvs.

***Visits & Customs: The Visit to the Tomb of Propher Hud.** Tr. & Intro. by Linda Boxberger. Date not set. write for info. (1-882557-06-9) Am Inst Yemeni.

Visits of Love. Alfred Jarry. Tr. by Iain White from FRE. 120p. 1993. reprint ed. pap. 13.99 (0-947757-63-5, Pub. by Atlas Pr UK) Serpents Tail.

Visits of Shakespeare's Company of Actors to the Provincial Cities & Towns of England. James O. Halliwell-Phillipps. LC 72-144632. reprint ed. 29.50 (0-404-03087-4) AMS Pr.

Visits to Monasteries in the Levant. Robert Curzon. Ed. by James Hogg. LC 96-129588. 496p. 1996. reprint ed. text ed. 109.95 (0-7734-4198-0) E Mellen.

Visits to Sufi Centers. 35p. 1980. pap. 7.00 (0-86304-005-5, Pub. by Octagon Pr UK) ISHK.

***Visits to the Manger: Enlightening Parables of Spiritual Wonder.** Robert G. Chaney. 140p. Date not set. pap. 9.95 (0-918936-32-2) Astara.

Visits to the Monasteries in the Levant. Robert Curzon. (Curzon Travellers Ser.). (Illus.). 288p. (C). 1996. reprint ed. 70.00 (0-7007-0346-2, Pub. by Curzon Pr UK) Paul & Co Pubs.

Visits to the Most Blessed Sacrament & the Blessed Virgin Mary. rev. ed. St. Alphonsus De Liguori. LC 94-78485. (Classic Ser.). 64p. 1994. pap. 2.95 (0-89243-770-7) Liguori Pubns.

Visits to Walt Whitman. J. Johnston & J. W. Wallace. LC 77-129195. (Studies in Whitman: No. 28). 1970. reprint ed. lib. bdg. 59.95 (0-8383-1159-8) M S G Haskell Hse.

VISITT: Vendor Information System for Innovative Treatment Technologies. (Illus.). 35p. (Orig.). (C). 1993. pap. text ed. 35.00 incl. disk (1-56806-756-9) DIANE Pub.

***Vislumbrar la Otredad: Los Pasajes en la Narrativa de Julio Cortazar.** Lauri H. Kahn. (Wor(l)ds of Change Ser.: Vol. 15). 232p. (SPA.). (C). 1996. text ed. 45.95 (0-8204-2754-3) P Lang Pubng.

***Vislumbre de Gloria.** Kuhlman. (SPA.). write for info. (0-614-27159-2) Editorial Unilit.

***Vislumbre de Gloria - A Glimpse into Glory.** Kathryn Kuhlman. (SPA.). write for info. (0-614-24409-9) Editorial Unilit.

Vislumbre de Gloria (A Glimpse into Glory) Kathryn Kuhlman. (SPA.). 1994. 5.99 (987-99427-2-8, 550123) Editorial Unilit.

***Vislumbres de Dios.** Steven R. Mosley. (SPA.). 1.50 (0-8297-0340-3) Life Pubs Intl.

Visnu Sahasranamam, Sri. Tr. by Tapasyananda from SAN. 216p. (Orig.). 1988. pap. 5.95 (0-87481-548-7, Pub. by Ramakrishna Math II) Vedanta Pr.

Visnu the Ever Free: A Study of the Madhva Concept of God. (C). 1985. 7.00 (0-8364-2335-6, Pub. by Usha II) S Asia.

Visnuism & Sivaism: A Comparison. Jan Gonda. (Jordan Lectures in Comparative Religion: No. 9). 228p. (C). 1970. text ed. 38.50 (0-485-17409-X, Pub. by Athlone Pr UK) Humanities.

Visoko-Dechanskaja Lavra na Kosovje Polje (v Serbii) P. N. Paganuzzi. 1976. pap. 1.00 (0-317-30331-7) Holy Trinity.

Visokopreosvjashennij Theofan, Arkhiepiskop Poltavsky i Perejaslavsky. Archbishop Averky Taushev. 88p. 1974. pap. 5.00 (0-317-29284-6) Holy Trinity.

Visons of Sunsets. Thea M. Kellogg. 176p. 1995. pap. text ed. write for info. (0-9645035-0-6) WynnHart Pr.

VISPO: O!!Zone Looks at Visual Poetry. 1996. pap. 10.00 (1-884185-13-4) O Zone.

Vispo Auf Deutsch: An Anthology of Verbo-Visual Art in German. Ed. by Bob Grumman & Crag Hill. 58p. (Orig.). (GER.). 1995. pap. 10.00 (1-57141-018-X) Runaway Spoon.

Vista. Chelsea House Publishers Staff. 1996. lib. bdg. 14.95 (0-7910-4003-8) Chelsea Hse.

***Vista del Amanecer.** Guillermo C. Infante. 1997. pap. 11.95 (0-14-026286-5) Viking Penguin.

Vista del Amanecer en el Tropico. Guillermo C. Infante. (Coleccion Clasicos Cubanos). 138p. (SPA.). 1994. pap. 16.00 (0-89729-722-9) Ediciones.

Vista of English Verse. Ed. by Henry S. Pancoast. LC 76-149108. (Granger Index Reprint Ser.). 1977. 40.95 (0-8369-6233-8) Ayer.

Vista Ridge Mall: A Keyboarding Simulation. 3rd ed. Jones. (TA - Typing/Keyboarding Ser.). 1992. pap. 13.95 (0-538-60813-7) S-W Pub.

Vistas: Poems from Hollywood. Mark Dunster. 17p. (Orig.). (YA). (gr. 9-12). 1997. pap. 5.00 (0-89642-345-X) Linden Pubs.

Vistas: Voces del Mundo Hispanico. 2nd ed. Constance M. Montross & Levine. (Illus.). 224p. (C). 1994. pap. text ed. 30.00 (0-13-181686-1) P-H.

Vistas & Mazes. Edward DeZurko. LC 95-71266. 80p. 1996. 11.95 (1-887750-07-X) Rutledge Bks.

Vistas & Vectors: Essays Honoring the Memory of Helmut Rehder. Ed. by Lee B. Jennings & George Schulz-Behrend. 214p. 1979. lib. bdg. 18.00 (0-917324-08-0) German Bk Ctr.

Vistas Hispanicas: Introduccion a la Lengua y la Cultura. 2nd ed. Clay B. Christensen et al. 1981. 2.75 (0-685-05580-9) HM.

Vistas in Applied Mathematics. J. L. Lions. Ed. by A. V. Balakrishnan et al. xii, 384p. 1986. 160.95 (0-387-96376-6) Spr-Verlag.

Vistas in Applied Mathematics: Numerical Analysis, Atmospheric Sciences, Immunology. Ed. by A. V. Balakrishnan et al. LC 86-8340. (Translations Series in Mathematics & Engineering). 396p. 1986. text ed. 98.00 (0-911575-38-3) Optimization Soft.

Vistas in Astronomy, 22 vols., Vol. 4. Albert C. Beer. 1979. pap. 39.00 (0-08-023071-7, Pergamon Pr) Elsevier.

Vistas in Astronomy, Vol. 17. A. Beer. 1975. 115.00 (0-08-017878-2, Pergamon Pr) Elsevier.

Vistas in Astronomy, Vol. 23. P. Beer & Albert C. Beer. 1980. 140.00 (0-08-026046-2, Pergamon Pr) Elsevier.

Vistas in Astronomy, Vol. 25. Ed. by P. Beer & K. Pounds. (Illus.). 436p. 1984. 160.00 (0-08-031042-7, Pergamon Pr) Elsevier.

Vistas in Astronomy, Vol. 26. Ed. by P. Beer. (Illus.). 426p. 1985. 180.00 (0-08-032314-6, Pergamon Pr) Elsevier.

Vistas in Astronomy, Vol. 27. Ed. by P. Beer et al. (Illus.). 486p. 1986. 162.00 (0-08-033235-8, C150, Pub. by PPL UK); write for info. (0-685-01782-6) Elsevier.

Vistas in Astronomy, Vol. 28. Ed. by P. Beer et al. (Illus.). 650p. 1986. 162.00 (0-08-034129-2, Pub. by PPL UK) Elsevier.

Vistas in Insect Pest & Disease of Soybean in India. O. P. Singh. 600p. 1993. 375.00 (0-685-69783-5, Pub. by Intl Bk Distr II) St Mut.

Vistas in Insect Pest & Disease of Soybeans in India. O. P. Singh. 600p. (C). 1991. text ed. 500.00 (0-89771-651-5, Pub. by Intl Bk Distr II) St Mut.

Vistas in Plant Sciences, Vol. 6. Ed. by T. M. Varghese. (Illus.). 117p. (C). 1983. 14.00 (0-88065-232-2, Pub. by Today & Tomorrows P & P II) Scholarly Pubns.

Vistas in Plant Sciences: Special Volume in Genetics & Plant Breeding, Vol. III. Ed. by T. M. Verghese. 166p. 1978. 14.00 (0-88065-203-9, Messers Today & Tomorrow) Scholarly Pubns.

Vistas in Plant Sciences: Special Volume in Plant Morphology, Vol. V. Ed. by T. M. Verghese. 146p. 1979. 14.00 (0-88065-205-5, Messers Today & Tomorrow) Scholarly Pubns.

Vistas in Plant Sciences: Special Volume on Plant Pathogens, Vol. IV. Ed. by T. M. Verghese. 153p. 1978. 14.00 (0-88065-204-7, Messers Today & Tomorrow) Scholarly Pubns.

Vistas, No. Two: An Interactive Course in English. Douglas H. Brown. 144p. (C). 1991. pap. text ed. 8.50 (0-13-650334-9, 640802) P-H.

***Vistas of Challenge.** 16.99 (0-89906-585-6, TIMH) Mesorah Pubns.

UV

***Vistas of Challenge.** pap. 13.99 (0-89906-586-4, TIMP) Mesorah Pubns.

Vistas of Inner Stillness. Richard Walker. LC 91-62760. 32p. (Orig.). 1991. pap. 3.00 (0-87574-299-8) Pendle Hill.

Vistas of New York. Brander Matthews. LC 70-37279. (Short Story Index Reprint Ser.). 1977. reprint ed. 20.95 (0-8369-4090-3) Ayer.

Vistas One: An Interactive Course in English. Douglas H. Brown. 144p. (C). 1991. pap. text ed. 8.50 (0-13-650326-8) P-H.

Vistas, the Gypsy Christ, & Other Prose Imaginings. William Sharp. 1977. 26.95 (0-8369-4228-0, 6039) Ayer.

Vistas Three: An Interactive Course in English. Douglas H. Brown. 144p. (C). 1992. pap. text ed. 8.50 (0-13-471160-2) P-H.

Vistazos 1. Teresa Carrera-Hanley et al. 158p. (C). 1986. pap. text ed. 18.16 (0-669-10290-3) McDougal-Littell.

Vistazos 2. Teresa Carrera-Hanley et al. 197p. (SPA.). (C). 1986. pap. text ed. 18.16 (0-669-10291-1) HM College Div.

Visual Addiction. Robert Williams. 1993. pap. text ed. 24.95 (0-86719-377-8) Last Gasp.

Visual Addiction: The Art Of... Robert Williams. 1991. pap. 19.95 (0-86719-369-7) Last Gasp.

Visual Age Smalltalk Distributed: Developing Distributed Object Applications. Walter Fang et al. 1996. pap. text ed. 40.00 (0-13-570805-2) P-H.

Visual Age Version 2.0 & Transaction Processing in a Client/Server Environment. Andi Bitter. 384p. (C). 1995. pap. text ed. 44.00 (0-13-460874-7) P-H.

Visual Agnosia: Disorders of Object Recognition & What They Tell Us About Normal Vision. Martha J. Farah. (Issues in the Biology of Language & Cognition). 208p. 1995. pap. 15.95 (0-262-56082-8, Bradford Bks) MIT Pr.

Visual Agnosias. Cronly-Dillon. 1991. 137.00 (0-8493-7512-6) CRC Pr.

Visual Aid Calorie Counter. Arlene F. Cottrell. 246p. 1993. ring bd. write for info. (0-9642419-0-0) Seven-Shooter.

***Visual Aid Packet.** (J). teacher ed., pap. 15.00 (0-614-18240-9) Let Us Tch Kids.

Visual Aid to Electronics. Barry L. Cole. pap. 1.25 (0-89741-011-4) Gila River.

Visual Aids for Nonformal Education. Jane K. Vella. 43p. 1979. pap. 4.00 (0-932288-53-7) Ctr Intl Ed U of MA.

Visual Aids to the MRCP Examination. N. K. Chakravorty. LC 94-40907. 1900. lib. bdg. write for info. (0-7923-8873-9) Kluwer Ac.

Visual Aircraft Recognition. 1995. lib. bdg. 259.95 (0-8490-6609-3) Gordon Pr.

Visual Amenity Aspects of High Voltage Transmission. George A. Goulty. LC 89-10925. (Lines & Cables for Power Transmission Research Ser.). 290p. 1990. text ed. 175.00 (0-471-92588-8) Wiley.

***Visual Analyst Workbench for Windows (Version 6.0)** 4th ed. Visible Systems Staff. (C). 1996. text ed. 102.50 incl. 3.5 hd (0-256-24551-7) Irwin.

Visual & Active Supervision: Roles, Focus, Technique. Antony Williams. (C). 1995. 30.00 (0-393-70185-9) Norton.

***Visual & Attentional Processes in Reading & Dyslexia.** 192p. (C). 1999. text ed. 59.95 (0-415-12327-5) Routledge.

Visual & Auditory Perception. Gerald M. Murch. LC 74-172349. (Illus.). (C). 1973. pap. write for info. (0-672-60779-4, Bobbs) Macmillan.

Visual & Hearing Information Science. Habara. LC 94-73405. (gr. 12). 1995. 79.00 (90-5199-207-6) IOS Press.

Visual & Oculomotor Functions: Advances in Eye Movement Research. Ed. by Gery D'Ydewalle & Johan Van Rensbergen. LC 94-3974. (Studies in Visual Information Processing: Vol. 5). 474p. 1994. 155.75 (0-444-81808-1, North Holland) Elsevier.

Visual & Other Pleasures. Laura Mulvey. LC 88-9627. (Theories of Representation & Difference Ser.). 218p. (Orig.). 1989. 35.00 (0-253-36226-1); pap. 13.95 (0-253-20494-1, MB-494) Ind U Pr.

Visual & Performing Arts Framework for California Public Schools, K-12. California Department of Education Staff. (Illus.). 176p. 1996. pap. 15.00 (0-8011-1261-3) Calif Education.

Visual & Technical Aspects of Type. Ed. by Roger D. Hersch. (Illus.). 224p. (C). 1993. text ed. 74.95 (0-521-44026-2) Cambridge U Pr.

***Visual & the Visionary: Art & Female Spirituality in Late Medieval Germany.** Jeffrey F. Hamburger. LC 97-19662. 1998. write for info. (0-942299-45-0) Zone Bks.

Visual & Transient Love: An Anthology of Rococo Poetry in English, French, German, Italian. Patrick Brady. 216p. (Orig.). (ENG, FRE & GER.). 1995. pap. text ed. 29.95 (1-886935-01-7) New Prdigm Pr.

Visual Anthropology: Photography As a Research Method. enl. rev. ed. John Collier, Jr. & Malcolm Collier. LC 86-6926. (Illus.). 266p. 1986. pap. 24.95 (0-8263-0899-6) U of NM Pr.

***Visual Approach to Algebra.** Frances Van Dyke. (J). (gr. 6-12). 1997. pap. text ed. 18.95 (1-57232-441-4) Seymour Pubns.

Visual Art: A Critical Introduction. James M. Carpenter. 289p. (C). 1982. pap. text ed. 26.75 (0-15-594935-7) HB Coll Pubs.

Visual Art As Theology. Barbara D. Baumgarten. LC 93-46854. (New Studies in Aesthetics: Vol. 21). 272p. (C). 1994. text ed. 57.95 (0-8204-2462-5) P Lang Pubng.

***Visual Art Introductory Unit.** Project Success Enrichment Staff. 244p. 1996. pap. text ed., spiral bd. 50.00 (0-7872-2642-4) Kendall-Hunt.

Visual Art, Mathematics & Computers: Selections from the Journal Leonardo. Ed. by Frank J. Malina. 1979. 151.00 (0-08-021854-7, Pub. by Pergamon Repr UK) Franklin.

Visual Artist & the Law. 2nd ed. Shane Simpson. xix, 311p. 1989. pap. 39.50 (0-455-20809-3, Pub. by Law Bk Co AT) Gaunt.

***Visual Artists & the Puerto Rican Performing Arts, 1950-1990: The Works of Jack & Irene Delano, Antonio Martorell, Jaime Suarez, & Oscar Mestey-Villamil.** Nelson Rivera. (Wor(l)ds of Change: No. 9). 256p. (C). 1997. text ed. 47.95 (0-8204-2620-2) P Lang Pubng.

Visual Artist's Business & Legal Guide. 1994. pap. 35.95 (0-13-304593-5) P-H.

Visual Arts. Ed. & Compiled by Jackie Mallis. (Ideas for Teaching Gifted Students Ser.). spiral bd., pap. 29.95 (0-86617-016-2) Multi Media TX.

Visual Arts. 4th ed. Rigby. 1994. student ed., pap. text ed. 19.40 (0-13-180738-2) P-H.

Visual Arts: A History. 2nd ed. Hugh Honour & John Fleming. (Illus.). 688p. 1986. 46.50 (0-13-942533-0) P-H.

Visual Arts: A History. 3rd ed. Hugh Honour. 1991. 60.00 (0-8109-3913-4) Abrams.

Visual Arts: A History. 4th ed. John Fleming & Hugh Honour. LC 94-13937. 1995. 65.00 (0-8109-3928-2) Abrams.

Visual Arts: A History. 4th ed. Honour & Fleming. (Illus.). 864p. 1994. pap. text ed. 62.67 (0-13-104662-4) P-H.

Visual Arts: Plastic & Graphic. Ed. by Justine Cordwell. (World Anthropology Ser.). (Illus.). xii, 818p. 1979. text ed. 107.70 (90-279-7820-4) Mouton.

Visual Arts see Ideas for Teaching Gifted Students

Visual Arts & Christianity in America: The Colonial Period Through the Nineteenth Century. John Dillenberger. LC 84-3897. (Studies in Humanities). 357p. 1984. pap. 22.95 (0-89130-761-3, 00 01 05) Scholars Pr GA.

Visual Arts & Early Childhood Learning. Ed. by Christine Thompson. 118p. (Orig.). 1995. pap. text ed. 22.00 (0-937652-80-6, 238) Natl Art Ed.

***Visual Arts As Critical Practice.** Richard Cary & Shirley R. Steinberg. Ed. by Joe Kincheloe. (Critical Education Practice Ser.). 200p. Date not set. text ed. 30.00 (0-8153-0915-5) Garland.

***Visual Arts As Critical Practice.** Richard Cary. Ed. by Joe Kincheloe & Shirley R. Steinberg. 200p. Date not set. pap. text ed. 18.95 (0-8153-2314-X) Garland.

Visual Arts Companion. Larry Smolucha. LC 94-31193. 368p. (C). 1995. pap. text ed. 38.67 (0-13-042987-2) P-H.

Visual Arts in Education. Rod Taylor. (Falmer Press Library on Aesthetic Education). 224p. 1992. 80.00 (1-85000-769-1, Falmer Pr); pap. 29.00 (1-85000-770-5, Falmer Pr) Taylor & Francis.

Visual Arts in Poland: An Annotated Bibliography. 1994. lib. bdg. 250.00 (0-8490-5709-4) Gordon Pr.

Visual Arts in Poland: An Annotated Bibliography of Selected Holdings in the Library of Congress. Janina W. Hoskins. LC 92-27991. 1992. 28.00 (0-8444-0741-0) Lib Congress.

Visual Arts in Puerto Rico. Ed. by Raoul Gordon. 1976. lib. bdg. 59.95 (0-8490-1264-3) Gordon Pr.

Visual Arts in the Twentieth Century. Edward Lucie-Smith. (Illus.). 400p. 1997. 60.00 (0-8109-3934-7) Abrams.

Visual Arts in the United States. Ed. by Emma L. Fundaburk & Mary D. Foreman. 455p. 1976. 12.00 (0-910642-03-6) Am Bicent Mus.

***Visual Arts in the 20th Century.** Edward Lucie-Smith. (Illus.). 4002p. (C). 1996. pap. text ed. 54.00 (0-13-494436-4) P-H.

Visual Arts Major's College Guide. Brown & Linda Sweetow. 1996. pap. 20.00 (0-671-51731-7) S&S Trade.

***Visual Arts of Africa.** Perani & Smith. 1997. pap. text ed. 42.67 (0-13-442328-3) P-H.

Visual Arts on the U. S. - Mexico Border. Ed. by Harry Polkinhorn et al. (Binational Press Ser.: No. 3). 96p. (ENG & SPA.). 1991. pap. 12.50 (0-916304-93-0) SDSU Press.

Visual Arts, Pictorialism & the Novel: James, Lawrence, & Woolf. Marianna Torgovnick. LC 84-26617. (Illus.). 280p. 1985. text ed. 45.00 (0-691-06644-2) Princeton U Pr.

***Visual Arts, Pictorialism, & the Novel: James, Lawrence, & Woolf.** Marianna Torgovnick. LC 84-26617. (Illus.). 275p. 1985. reprint ed. pap. 78.40 (0-608-02539-9, 2063183) Bks Demand.

Visual Arts Research: A Handbook. Elizabeth B. Pollard. LC 86-375. 180p. 1986. text ed. 49.95 (0-313-24186-4, PVA/, Greenwood Pr) Greenwood.

Visual Arts Teacher Resource Handbook: A Practical Guide for Teaching K-12 Visual Arts. John A. Michael. LC 93-15855. (Teacher Resource Handbook Ser.). (Illus.). 410p. 1993. pap. 29.95 (0-8039-6375-0) Corwin Pr.

Visual Arts Today. Gyorgy Kepes. LC 60-13159. 278p. reprint ed. pap. 79.30 (0-317-10377-6, 2001953) Bks Demand.

Visual Astronomy of the Deep Sky. Roger Clark. (Illus.). 376p. 1991. 39.95 (0-933346-54-9) Sky Pub.

Visual Astronomy of the Deep Sky. Roger N. Clark. (Illus.). 416p. (C). 1991. text ed. 39.95 (0-521-36155-9) Cambridge U Pr.

Visual Attention & Cognition. Ed. by W. H. Zangemeister et al. LC 96-27978. (Advances in Psychology Ser.: Vol. 116). 412p. 1996. text ed. 160.50 (0-444-82291-7, North Holland) Elsevier.

Visual Aural Discrimination Series: Student Test Booklet. 1lizabeth M. Henzl. (gr. 1-12). 1973. 5.00 (0-87879-764-5, Ann Arbor Div) Acad Therapy.

Visual Aural Discriminations: A Self-Instructional Workbook for Initial Two-Letter Blends, 5 bks. Elizabeth M. Henzl. (gr. 1-12). 1973. student ed. 10.00 (0-685-73164-2, Ann Arbor Div) Acad Therapy.

Visual Aural Discriminations: A Self-Instructional Workbook for Initial Two-Letter Blends, 5 bks., Bk. 1. Elizabeth M. Henzl. (gr. 1-12). 1973. 10.00 (0-87879-759-9, Ann Arbor Div) Acad Therapy.

Visual Aural Discriminations: A Self-Instructional Workbook for Initial Two-Letter Blends, 5 bks., Bk. 2. Elizabeth M. Henzl. (gr. 1-12). 1973. 10.00 (0-87879-760-2, Ann Arbor Div) Acad Therapy.

Visual Aural Discriminations: A Self-Instructional Workbook for Initial Two-Letter Blends, 5 bks., Bk. 3. Elizabeth M. Henzl. (gr. 1-12). 1973. 10.00 (0-87879-761-0, Ann Arbor Div) Acad Therapy.

Visual Aural Discriminations: A Self-Instructional Workbook for Initial Two-Letter Blends, 5 bks., Bk. 4. Elizabeth M. Henzl. (gr. 1-12). 1973. 10.00 (0-87879-762-9, Ann Arbor Div) Acad Therapy.

Visual Aural Discriminations: A Self-Instructional Workbook for Initial Two-Letter Blends, 5 bks., Bk. 5. Elizabeth M. Henzl. (gr. 1-12). 1973. 10.00 (0-87879-763-7, Ann Arbor Div) Acad Therapy.

Visual Awareness & Design: An Introductory Program in Perceptual Sensitivity, Conceptual Awareness, & Basic Design Skills. Philip Thiel. LC 80-51079. (Illus.). 288p. 1981. pap. 19.50 (0-295-95786-7) U of Wash Pr.

Visual BASIC. Buck. 1994. write for info. (0-201-41866-5) Addison-Wesley.

Visual BASIC. Cassel. 1996. pap. text ed. write for info. (0-13-657462-9) P-H.

***Visual Basic.** Eaton & Grauer. 1997. pap. text ed. write for info. (0-13-657594-3) P-H.

Visual Basic: A Beginner's Approach. Emilio Ramos et al. Ed. by Lynne D. Cote. LC 95-8094. (Illus.). 350p. (C). 1995. pap. text ed. 24.95 (0-201-80884-6) Addison-Wesley.

Visual Basic: A Programmer's Guide to Managing Component Based Development. Eron Marom. LC 96-36077. 289p. 1996. 29.95 (0-13-591504-X) P-H.

Visual BASIC: Easy Windows Programming. Namir C. Shammas. 488p. 1992. pap. 29.95 (0-8306-3733-8, Windcrest) TAB Bks.

Visual BASIC: Easy Windows Programming. 2nd ed. Namir C. Shammas. LC 92-40056. 1993. pap. write for info. (0-8306-4450-4, Windcrest) TAB Bks.

Visual BASIC - SQL Server Primer. Heng Tan. 1994. pap. 59.90 (1-881679-10-1) ETN.

Visual Basic Algorithms: A Developers Sourcebook of Ready-to-Run Code. Kenneth R. Stephens. LC 95-45546. 1996. pap. 39.95 (0-471-13418-X) Wiley.

Visual BASIC Animation Graphic Programming. Lee Adams. 1993. pap. text ed. 39.95 (0-07-000452-8) McGraw-Hill Prof.

Visual BASIC Animation Programming. Lee Adams. (Illus.). 736p. 1992. pap. 39.95 (0-8306-4120-3, 4224, Windcrest) TAB Bks.

Visual BASIC Book. Steven Holzner. (Illus.). (Orig.). 1991. pap. 39.95 (0-13-489287-9); pap. 26.95 (0-13-489295-X) Brady Pub.

Visual Basic by Example: New Edition. R. Jacobs et al. (Illus.). 598p. (Orig.). 1995. 29.99 (0-7897-0000-X) Que.

Visual Basic Client - Server Development. Michael Meyers. (Illus.). 900p. (Orig.). 1995. 59.99 (0-7897-0099-9) Que.

***Visual Basic Control Creation Starter Kit.** Clayton Walnum. 430p. 1997. 39.99 (0-7897-1172-9) Mac Comp Pub.

Visual Basic Controls Desk Reference. C. Woody Butler et al. 750p. 1995. pap. 44.95 (1-878739-87-5, Waite Grp Pr) Sams.

Visual Basic Coursebook. Forest Lin. 856p. (C). 1994. pap. text ed. 38.00 (1-881991-37-7) Scott Jones Pubng.

Visual BASIC Database Programming. Karen Watterson. LC 93-33261. 1993. write for info. (0-201-62661-6) Addison-Wesley.

Visual Basic Database Programming. 2nd ed. Karen Watterson & Ibrahim Malluf. 448p. (C). 1997. pap. text ed., pap. 39.95 incl. audio compact disk (0-201-48919-8) Addison-Wesley.

***Visual Basic Developers Reference.** Sams Publishing Staff. 1400p. 1997. 59.99 (0-672-31042-2) Sams.

Visual Basic Developer's Toolkit: Performance Optimization, Rapid Application Development, Debugging & Distribution. Martin A. Nemzow. (Illus.). 464p. 1996. pap. text ed., pap. 44.95 incl. cd-rom (0-07-912309-0) McGraw.

Visual Basic Enterprise Development. Craig Goren. 1100p. 1997. 59.99 (0-7897-0920-1) Mac Comp Pub.

Visual Basic Example Book. Larry W. Smith et al. (Programmer's Example Ser.). 1995. pap. 24.95 incl. disk (1-55622-474-5) Wordware Pub.

Visual Basic Expert Solutions. 2nd ed. Ron Schwarz. 1000p. 1997. 49.99 (0-7897-0923-6) Mac Comp Pub.

***Visual Basic Fat Faqs.** Jan Haugland. 1997. pap. text ed. 39.95 incl. cd-rom (0-07-913681-8) McGraw.

***Visual Basic 5 Developer's Guide.** Anthony T. Mann. 1200p. 1997. 49.99 (0-672-31048-1) Sams.

***Visual Basic for Application Unleashed.** Paul McFedries. 800p. 1997. 49.99 (0-672-31046-5) Mac Comp Pub.

Visual BASIC for Applications Database Solutions. John Lacher. 1996. pap. text ed. 59.99 incl. cd-rom (0-7897-0802-7) Que.

Visual BASIC for Applications Revealed! Creating Time Saving Macros for Microsoft Applications. Karen Kenworthy. 1994. pap. 27.95 (1-55958-517-X) Prima Pub.

Visual Basic for Beginners: A Project Approach to Object-Oriented Programming. Alfred J. Bruey. LC 95-94248. 128p. (C). 1995. pap. text ed. 12.95 (0-9646968-0-0) Comp Systs Consult.

Visual BASIC for DOS. Namir C. Shammas. 1993. pap. text ed. 29.95 (0-07-056860-X) McGraw.

Visual BASIC for DOS. Namir C. Shammas. (Illus.). 400p. 1992. pap. 29.95 (0-8306-4375-3, Windcrest) TAB Bks.

Visual BASIC for DOS: Building Scientific & Technical Applications. James W. Cooper. LC 93-16839. 424p. (Orig.). 1993. pap. text ed. 37.95 (0-471-59772-4) Wiley.

Visual Basic for Kids. Nancy Nicholaisen. 1996. pap. write for info. (0-201-68802-6) Addison-Wesley.

Visual Basic for Thinkers. J. D. Evans, Jr. 1000p. (Orig.). 1996. pap. 49.95 (1-881679-33-0) ETN.

Visual BASIC for Windows Interactive Graphics Programming. Lee Adams. 1994. pap. 39.95 (0-8306-4126-2, Windcrest) TAB Bks.

Visual BASIC for Windows 95 Insider: Guide to Hard-to-Find & Undocumented Features. Peter G. Aiken. LC 96-13217. 560p. 1996. pap. text ed. 44.95 (0-471-06483-1) Wiley.

Visual Basic Graphics Programming. Rod Stephens. LC 96-26965. 720p. 1996. pap. text ed. 49.99 incl. cd-rom (0-471-15533-0) Wiley.

Visual BASIC Handbook. Douglas Hergert. 1995. pap. 39.95 (1-56884-312-7) IDG Bks.

***Visual Basic in a Nutshell.** Doug Hergert. Ed. by Ronald Petrusha. (Nutshell Handbook Ser.). (Orig.). 1997. pap. 27.95 (1-56592-294-8) OReilly & Assocs.

Visual Basic in the Classroom. Jennings. (DF - Computer Applications Ser.). 1997. wbk. ed., pap. 16.95 (0-538-65186-5) S-W Pub.

Visual BASIC Made Easy. Edward J. Coburn. LC 94-30576. 560p. 1995. pap. 56.95 (0-534-22206-4) PWS Pubs.

***Visual Basic Made Easy.** 11th ed. Coburn. 1997. suppl. ed., text ed. 59.95 (0-534-95381-6) Brooks-Cole.

Visual BASIC Numeric Compression: Bring Back the MKL Dollars, CVL, etc. Functions. 102p. 1993. 29.95 incl. disk (0-89496-056-3) Ross Bks.

Visual Basic Power Guides, 4 vols., Set. 693p. 1995. pap. 199.00 (1-886213-05-4) Bldg Blocks.

Visual BASIC Power Guides, Set. Paul Sheriff. 1994. spiral bd. 149.00 (1-886213-03-8) Bldg Blocks.

Visual BASIC Power Programming. Namir C. Shammas. 392p. 1992. 39.95 (0-8306-3962-4, 4149, Windcrest); pap. 29.95 (0-8306-3963-2, 4149, Windcrest) TAB Bks.

Visual BASIC Professional 3.0 Programming. Thomas W. Torgerson. 304p. 1994. Incl. diskette. pap. text ed. 29.95 incl. disk (0-471-60693-6) Wiley.

Visual BASIC Professional 3.0 Programming with Disk. Thomas W. Torgerson. (Orig.). 1993. pap. 39.95 (0-89435-470-1) Wiley.

***Visual Basic Programmers Guide to Java.** James W. Cooper. 450p. 1997. 39.99 (1-56604-527-4) Ventana Communs.

***Visual Basic Programmer's Guide to Serial Communications.** Richard Grier. Ed. by Zane Thomas & James Shields. (Illus.). 300p. (Orig.). 1997. pap. 34.95 (1-890422-25-8) Mabry Sftware.

***Visual Basic Programmer's Guide to Web Development.** William Martiner. LC 97-20877. 400p. 1997. pap. 34.99 (0-471-19382-8) Wiley.

***Visual Basic Programmer's Library.** Kris Jamsa & Jamsa Press Staff. (Orig.). 1997. pap. 54.95 (1-884133-57-6) Jamsa Pr.

Visual BASIC Programming. Judith L. Gersting. (C). Date not set. teacher ed., text ed. write for info. (0-7167-8319-3) W H Freeman.

Visual Basic Programming. Forest Lin. (Illus.). 600p. (Orig.). (C). 1996. pap. text ed. 35.00 (1-881991-43-1) Scott Jones Pubng.

Visual BASIC Programming in 12 Easy Lessons. Greg M. Perry. (Illus.). 672p. (Orig.). 1995. 39.99 (0-672-30728-6) Sams.

Visual Basic Programming Pearls. Keith Pleas. (C). 1997. pap. text ed. 24.95 (0-201-56070-4) Addison-Wesley.

Visual BASIC Quick Tutor. Smythe. (DF - Computer Applications Ser.). 1996. pap. 33.95 (0-7895-0016-7) Course Tech.

***Visual Basic Script & ActiveX Wizardry.** Scott Palmer. 1996. pap. text ed. 39.99 incl. cd-rom (1-57610-052-9) Coriolis Grp.

Visual BASIC Script by Example. Jerry Honeycutt. 368p. 1996. pap. text ed. 34.99 incl. cd-rom (0-7897-0815-9) Que.

Visual Basic Script for Dummies. Dummies Press Staff. 1996. pap. 24.99 (0-7645-0030-9) IDG Bks.

Visual Basic Script Unleashed. Brian Johnson. 650p. 1996. pap. text ed. 39.99 incl. cd-rom (1-57521-124-6, SamsNet Bks) Sams.

***Visual Basic Scripting Edition SuperBible.** Jinjer L. Simon. LC 96-45240. 700p. 1997. 49.99 (1-57169-081-6, Waite Grp Pr) Mac Comp Pub.

Visual Basic SuperBible. 2nd ed. William Potter et al. (Illus.). 1600p. 1994. pap. 49.95 (1-878739-50-6, Waite Grp Pr) Sams.

Visual Basic Telephony. Kristina Holly & Chris Brookins. write for info. (0-614-17422-8) Flatiron Pubng.

***Visual Basic Training Guide.** William Murray. (Training Guides Ser.). (Illus.). 525p. 1997. pap. 49.95 incl. cd-rom (0-12-511905-4, AP Prof) Acad Pr.

Visual Basic Unleashed. 2nd ed. Sams Development Group Staff. 1100p. Date not set. 55.00 (0-672-30979-3) Mac Comp Pub.

Visual Basic Using Modular Structure. Julia C. Bradley & Anita Millspaugh. 400p. (C). 1996. per. 39.95 (0-697-20273-9) Irwin.

***Visual Basic WIN 32 API Quick Reference.** Dan Appleman. 400p. Date not set. 19.99 (1-56276-509-4) Mac Comp Pub.

Visual BASIC with Applications. Mark G. Simkin. 484p. (Orig.). (C). 1996. pap. text ed. 35.00 (1-881991-33-4) Scott Jones Pubng.

***Visual Basic "X" Bible.** Douglas Hergert. 800p. (Orig.). 1997. pap. write for info. (0-614-26293-3) IDG Bks.

***Visual Basic X Bible.** Douglas Hergert. 1997. pap. 49.99 (0-7645-8020-5) IDG Bks.

UV

An Asterisk (*) at the beginning of an entry indicates that the title is appearing in BIP for the first time.

***Visual Basic X Internet Secrets.** Kenneth Spencer. 1997. pap. text ed. 49.99 incl. cd-rom (*0-7645-8012-4*) IDG Bks.

***Visual Basic "X" Intranet SECRETS.** Kenneth L. Spencer & Kenneth C. Miller. 800p. (Orig.). 1997. pap. write for info. (*0-614-26338-7*) IDG Bks.

Visual Basic X Night School. Greg Perry. 900p. 1997. 34.99 (*0-7897-0921-X*) Mac Comp Pub.

***Visual Basic X Night School.** Greg Perry. 1997. pap. 39.99 (*0-614-28482-1*) Que.

***Visual Basic "X" Object-Oriented Programming.** Rinehart. pap. 49.99 (*0-7645-3029-1*) IDG Bks.

***Visual Basic "X" Object-Oriented Programming.** Martin L. Rinehart. 912p. (Orig.). 1997. pap. write for info. (*0-614-26303-4*) IDG Bks.

***Visual Basic "X" Professional Trainer.** Michelle Moore. 704p. (Orig.). 1997. pap. write for info. (*0-614-26349-2*) IDG Bks.

***Visual Basic "X" SECRETS.** Harold Davis. 912p. (Orig.). 1997. pap. write for info. (*0-614-26282-8*) IDG Bks.

***Visual Basic X Secrets.** Harold Davis. 1997. pap. 49.99 (*0-7645-8019-1*) IDG Bks.

Visual Basic X.0 Programming with Windows X.0 Applications. 3rd ed. Douglas A. Hergert. 512p. 1995. pap. 39.00 (*0-679-75801-1*) Random.

Visual Basic 3 for Dummies. Wallace Wang. (For Dummies Ser.). (Illus.). 1994. pap. 19.95 (*1-56884-076-4*) IDG Bks.

***Visual BASIC 3 for Dummies, 2 vols.** large type ed. Wallace Wang. (For Dummies Ser.). (Illus.). 540p. 135.00 (*0-614-20552-2*, L-39083-00 APHB) Am Printing Hse.

***Visual Basic 3.0: A Brief Introduction.** Timothy M. Spear. 62p. (C). 1996. pap. text ed. 24.00 (*0-03-019779-1*) Dryden Pr.

Visual BASIC 3.0 for Windows. (Prisma Computer Courses Ser.). (Illus.). 200p. (Orig.). 1995. pap. 12.95 (*1-85365-371-3*, Pub. by Spectrum UK) Seven Hills Bk.

Visual Basic 3.0 Windows Advanced. 160p. 1995. 55.00 (*1-57533-051-2*) Comput Confidence.

Visual Basic 3.0 Windows Introduction. 160p. 1995. 55.00 (*1-57533-050-4*) Comput Confidence.

Visual BASIC 4 API How-To. Noel Jerke & Eric Brierly. 930p. (Orig.). 1996. pap. 49.99 incl. cd-rom (*1-57169-072-7*, Waite Grp Pr) Sams.

Visual BASIC 4 CD Tutor: Interactive Multimedia Seminar in a Box. Clint Hicks. 1996. pap. text ed. 49.99 incl. cd-rom (*0-7897-0733-0*) Que.

Visual Basic 4 Coursebook. Forest Lin. (Illus.). 900p. (C). 1996. pap. text ed. 38.00 (*1-881991-46-6*) Scott Jones Pubng.

Visual Basic 4 Developer's Guide. Boyle et al. (Illus.). 1032p. (Orig.). 1996. 55.00 (*0-672-30783-9*) Sams.

Visual Basic 4 Developer's Handbook. Michael Meyer. 1996. pap. 34.99 (*0-7821-1605-1*) Sybex.

Visual BASIC 4 for Windows 95 for Dummies. 2nd ed. Wallace Wang. 400p. 1995. pap. 19.99 (*1-56884-230-9*) IDG Bks.

Visual Basic 4 for Windows 95 Handbook. 4th ed. Gary Cornell & Joanne Cuthbertson. 982p. 1995. pap. text ed. 34.95 (*0-07-882091-X*) Osborne-McGraw.

Visual Basic 4 in 12 Easy Lessons. 2nd ed. Greg M. Perry. 662p. 1996. pap. text ed. 45.00 incl. cd-rom (*0-672-30947-5*) Sams.

Visual Basic 4 Interactive Course: Master Visual Basic & Earn a Certificate of Achievement. Cliff Diamond et al. 650p. (Orig.). 1996. 39.99 (*1-57169-065-4*) Mac Comp Pub.

Visual BASIC 4 Multimedia Adventure Set. Coriolis Media Staff. 1995. boxed 44.99 incl. cd-rom (*1-883577-46-2*) Coriolis Grp.

Visual BASIC 4 Multimedia Adventure Set. Scott Jarol. 1995. pap. 39.99 incl. cd-rom (*1-883577-45-4*) Coriolis Grp.

Visual Basic 4 Nuts & Bolts: For Experienced Programmers. Gary Cornell & Troy Strain. 256p. 1995. pap. text ed. 24.95 (*0-07-882141-X*) McGraw.

Visual Basic 4 Objects & Classes SuperBible, Bk. 1. Bill Potter et al. (Illus.). 900p. 1995. pap. 44.95 (*1-57169-006-9*, Waite Grp Pr) Sams.

Visual BASIC 4 Performance Tuning & Optimization. Keith Brophy & Tim Koets. (Illus.). 784p. (Orig.). 1995. 49.99 (*0-672-30796-0*) Sams.

Visual BASIC 4 Programming Explorer. Peter Aitken. 1995. pap. 39.99 (*1-883577-21-7*) Coriolis Grp.

Visual BASIC 4 Secrets. Harold Davis. 1996. pap. 44.99 incl. cd-rom (*1-56884-872-2*) IDG Bks.

Visual Basic 4 Smartstart. Que Education & Training Staff. 1996. pap. text ed. 29.99 (*1-57576-010-X*) Que Educ & Trng.

Visual BASIC 4 Unleashed. Sams Development Group Staff. (Illus.). 1224p. (Orig.). 1995. 45.00 (*0-672-30837-1*) Sams.

***Visual Basic 4.D.** Alan Eliason. 1996. 72.00 (*1-57576-260-9*) Sams.

Visual BASIC 4.0 Ole, Databases, & Controls SuperBible, Bk. 2. Bill Potter et al. (Illus.). 1000p. 1995. pap. 44.95 (*1-57169-007-7*, Waite Grp Pr) Sams.

***Visual Basic 4.0.** Spear. (C). 1996. teacher ed., pap. text ed. 28.00 (*0-03-019778-3*) HB Coll Pubs.

***Visual Basic 4.0: A Brief Introduction.** Robert J. Spear & Timothy M. Spear. 64p. (C). 1996. pap. text ed. 24.00 (*0-03-019777-5*) Dryden Pr.

Visual Basic 4.0 Exam Guide. Howard Hawhee & Peg Toomey. 900p. 1996. 99.99 (*0-7897-0864-7*) Mac Comp Pub.

Visual BASIC 4.0 Internet Programming. Carl Franklin. LC 96-14111. 352p. 1996. pap. 39.95 (*0-471-13420-1*) Wiley.

Visual Basic 4.0 Power Toolkit: Cutting-Edge Tools & Techniques for Programmers. 2nd ed. Richard Mansfield & Evangelos Petroutsos. 1098p. 1995. pap. 49.95 incl. cd-rom (*1-56604-263-1*) Ventana Communs.

***Visual Basic 5.** Eric A. Smith. (New Tutorial Ser.). 1997. pap. 39.99 (*0-7645-3054-2*) IDG Bks.

***Visual Basic 5: No Experience Required.** Steve Brown. 1997. pap. text ed. 29.99 (*0-7821-2074-1*) Sybex.

***Visual Basic 5 Advanced.** Forest Lin. (Illus.). 420p. (Orig.). (C). Date not set. pap. text ed. 36.00 (*1-57676-007-3*) Scott Jones Pubng.

***Visual Basic 5 Bootcamp: Everything You Need to Pass Microsoft's Visual Basic 5 Certification.** Dan Mezick. 1997. 54.95 incl. cd-rom (*0-07-913671-0*) Osborne-McGraw.

***Visual Basic 5 Client/Server How-To.** George Szabo et al. LC 97-5116. 900p. 1996. 49.99 (*1-57169-078-6*) Mac Comp Pub.

***Visual Basic 5 Coursebook.** Forest Lin. (Illus.). 1020p. (Orig.). (C). Date not set. pap. text ed. 41.00 (*1-57676-004-9*) Scott Jones Pubng.

***Visual Basic 5 Database: How-to.** Don Kiely. 1000p. 1997. pap. text ed. 49.99 incl. cd-rom (*1-57169-104-9*, Waite Grp Pr) Sams.

***Visual Basic 5 Development Unleashed, Vol. 2.** Sams Publishing Staff. 1997. 39.99 (*0-672-31072-4*) Sams.

***Visual Basic 5 for the Enterprise.** Ron Schwarz. (C). 1998. pap. text ed. write for info. (*0-201-30948-3*) Addison-Wesley.

***Visual Basic 5 for Windows for Dummies.** Wallace Wang. (Illus.). 400p. (Orig.). 1997. pap. 24.99 (*0-7645-0122-4*) IDG Bks.

***Visual Basic 5 from the Ground Up.** Gary Cornell. 1997. pap. text ed. 34.99 (*0-07-882349-8*) Osborne-McGraw.

***Visual Basic 5 Fundamentals Unleashed, Vol. 1.** Sams Publishing Staff. 1997. 29.99 (*0-672-31073-2*) Sams.

***Visual Basic 5 Interactive Course.** Mark Spenik et al. LC 97-1819. 1000p. 1997. 49.99 (*1-57169-077-8*) Mac Comp Pub.

***Visual Basic 5 Made Easy.** 2nd ed. Coburn. (Computer Science Ser.). (C). 1998. pap. 57.95 (*0-534-95044-2*) PWS Pubs.

***Visual Basic 5 Object Oriented Programming.** Swartfager. 1997. pap. text ed. 49.99 (*1-57610-106-1*) Coriolis Grp.

***Visual Basic 5 Programmer's Reference.** Wayne S. Freeze. 1997. 59.99 (*1-56604-714-5*) Ventana Communs.

***Visual Basic 5 Programming Explorer.** Aitken. 1997. pap. text ed. 49.99 (*1-57610-065-0*) Coriolis Grp.

***Visual Basic 5 Training Guide.** William H. Murray & Chris H. Pappas. LC 97-10938. 1997. 1.95 (*0-12-511906-2*) Acad Pr.

***Visual BASIC 5 Web & Multimedia Adventure.** Potts. 1997. pap. text ed. 49.99 incl. cd-rom (*1-57610-105-3*) Coriolis Grp.

***Visual Basic 5 with Applications.** Mark Simkin. 754p. 1998. pap. text ed. write for info. (*1-57676-006-5*) Scott Jones Pubng.

***Visual Basic 5.0.** Stephen Solosky. (Select Ser.). (C). 1998. pap. text ed. 31.50 (*0-201-31115-1*) Addison-Wesley.

Visual Basic/Multimedia Primer. Heng Tan. (Heng Tan Visual Basic Primer Ser.: Vol. 2). 1000p. (Orig.). 1996. pap. 59.95 (*1-881679-77-2*) ETN.

Visual Basic/SQL Server Primer. 3rd ed. Heng Tan. (Heng Tan Visual Basic Primer Ser.: Vol. 1). 800p. 1996. pap. 59.95 (*1-881679-12-8*) ETN.

Visual Behavior. Beverly Jones. LC 95-75986. 228p. (Orig.). 1995. pap. 17.95 (*0-9627939-1-4*) Lockwood Pr.

Visual Behaviors, 1994 Workshop. LC 94-75385. 136p. 1994. pap. text ed. 40.00 (*0-8186-5805-3*) IEEE Comp Soc.

***Visual Brain in Action.** A. David Milner & Melvyn A. Goodale. (Oxford Psychology Ser.: No. 27). (Illus.). 272p. 1996. reprint ed. pap. 35.00 (*0-19-852408-0*) OUP.

Visual C++ Developer's Guide. 3rd ed. 1996. 49.99 (*0-672-30809-6*) Macmillan.

***Visual C++ from the Ground Up.** John P. Mueller. 1997. pap. 34.99 incl. cd-rom (*0-07-882307-2*) Osborne-McGraw.

Visual C++ Handbook. 2nd ed. William H. Murray, 3rd & Chris H. Pappas. 1136p. 1995. pap. text ed. 36.95 (*0-07-882125-8*) McGraw.

Visual C++ How-To: The Definitive VC++ Problem Solver. Scott Stanfield et al. 550p. 1995. pap. 39.95 (*1-878739-82-4*, Waite Grp Pr) Sams.

***Visual C++ Master Class.** Ramirez. 1996. pap. 49.95 (*1-874416-44-3*) Wrox Pr Inc.

***Visual C++ Bible.** Paul Yao. 1997. pap. 49.99 (*0-7645-8022-1*) IDG Bks.

Visual C Plus Plus Construction Kit: A Programmer's Resource. Keith E. Bugg & Jack Tackett, Jr. 333p. 1994. pap. text ed. 39.95 (*0-471-00961-X*) Wiley.

***Visual C++ Developer's Guide.** David Bennett. 1000p. 1997. 55.00 (*0-672-31031-7*) Mac Comp Pub.

Visual C Plus Plus Generic Programming. Namir C. Shammas. 1993. pap. text ed. 47.00 (*0-07-056883-9*) McGraw.

Visual C Plus Plus Generic Programming. Namir C. Shammas. LC 93-13132. 1993. pap. text ed. 34.95 (*0-8306-4504-7*, Windcrest) TAB Bks.

Visual C Plus Plus in 12 Easy Lessons. Ian Spencer & Greg M. Perry. (Illus.). 784p. (Orig.). 1995. 45.00 (*0-672-30637-9*) Sams.

Visual C Plus Plus Multimedia Adventure Set. Coriolis Media Staff. 1995. boxed 39.99 incl. cd-rom (*1-883577-38-1*) Coriolis Grp.

Visual C Plus Plus Multimedia Adventure Set. Scott Jarol. 1995. pap. 39.99 incl. cd-rom (*1-883577-19-5*) Coriolis Grp.

***Visual C++ Unleashed.** 2nd ed. Viktor Toth. 1000p. 1997. 55.00 (*0-672-31013-9*) Mac Comp Pub.

Visual C Plus Plus X Insider. Scott R. Ladd. 448p. 1995. pap. text ed. 26.95 (*0-471-00777-3*) Wiley.

Visual C Plus Plus 2.0: A Developer's Guide. Alex Leavens. 1995. pap. 39.95 incl. disk (*1-55851-416-3*, M&T Books) H Holt & Co.

Visual C Plus Plus 4 Unleashed. Victor Toth. (Illus.). 912p. (Orig.). 1996. 49.99 (*0-672-30874-6*) Sams.

***Visual C++ Power Toolkit.** 2nd ed. Rick Leinecker. LC 97-3503. 800p. 1997. 49.99 (*1-56604-528-2*) Ventana Communs.

Visual C++ Power Toolkit: Cutting-Edge Tools & Techniques for Programmers. Richard C. Leinecker & Jamie Nye. (Illus.). 832p. 1995. 49.95 (*1-56604-191-0*) Ventana Communs.

Visual C++ 2: Developing Professional Applications in Windows 95 & NT Using MFC. Marshall Brain. 848p. 1995. pap. 42.95 (*0-13-305145-5*) P-H.

Visual C++ 2 for Dummies. Michael Hyman & Bob Arnson. 400p. 1995. pap. 19.99 (*1-56884-328-3*) IDG Bks.

Visual C++ 4 How-To. Scott Stanfield & Ralph Arvesen. 600p. (Orig.). 1996. pap. 44.99 incl. cd-rom (*1-57169-069-7*, Waite Grp Pr) Sams.

Visual C++ 5 for Dummies. 2nd ed. Michael Hyman & Robert Arnson. (Illus.). 400p. (Orig.). 1997. pap. 24.99 (*0-7645-0059-7*) IDG Bks.

***Visual C++ 5 Programmer's Reference.** Richard Leinecker. 1997. pap. text ed. 59.95 (*1-56604-735-8*) Ventana Communs.

***Visual C++ 5 Unleashed.** 1997. 69.99 (*0-672-31196-8*) Mac Comp Pub.

***Visual C++ 6 How-To.** Scott Stanfield. 1997. 49.99 (*1-57169-127-8*) Sams.

***Visual Cafe.** Thomas A. Lockwood. (New Tutorial Ser.). 1997. pap. 29.99 (*0-7645-3089-5*) IDG Bks.

***Visual Cafe for Dummies.** Ed Tittel. (Illus.). 400p. (Orig.). 1997. pap. 29.99 (*0-7645-0077-5*) IDG Bks.

***Visual Cafe Personal Trainer.** Thomas A. Lockwood & Charles J. Kremer. 550p. (Orig.). 1997. pap. write for info. (*0-614-26325-5*) IDG Bks.

***Visual Cafe Programming Frontrunner for Macintosh.** Dan Shafer. 1996. pap. text ed. 29.99 (*1-57610-059-6*) Coriolis Grp.

Visual Calculus Book IBM 3.5. 6th ed. David I. Schneider. 60p. 1993. pap. 13.33 (*0-13-042177-4*) P-H.

Visual Calorie Counter. 2nd ed. Arlene F. Cottrell. (Illus.). 246p. spiral bd. 35.95 (*0-9642419-1-9*) Seven-Shooter.

Visual Cells in Evolution. Ed. by Jane A. Westfall. LC 81-19903. 172p. 1982. reprint ed. pap. 49.10 (*0-608-00298-4*, 2059328) Bks Demand.

***Visual CH5: The Complete Reference.** William H. Murray, III & Chris H. Pappas. (Illus.). 1008p. (Orig.). 1997. pap. 39.99 (*0-07-882391-9*, Oracle Press) Osborne-McGraw.

Visual Coding & Adaptability. Ed. by Charles S. Harris. LC 79-26604. (Illus.). 400p. 1980. text ed. 79.95 (*0-89859-016-7*) L Erlbaum Assocs.

Visual Communicating. Ralph E. Wileman. LC 92-23771. (Illus.). 160p. 1993. pap. 37.95 (*0-87778-248-2*) Educ Tech Pubns.

Visual Communication: Images with Messages. Paul M. Lester. LC 94-19173. 450p. 1995. pap. 41.95 (*0-534-19530-X*) Wadsworth Pub.

Visual Communication: Studies in Mass Media Resources I & II, Vol. 13, Nos. 2-3. Michael Griffin. 152p. 1992. pap. text ed. 36.00 (*2-88124-614-1*) Gordon & Breach.

***Visual Communication & the Graphic Arts.** Estelle Jussim. 17.50 (*0-614-18202-6*) Visual Studies.

Visual Communications Media Handbook. Harry Eggink & Paul Laseau. (Illus.). 31p. (Orig.). 1982. pap. 3.00 (*0-912431-02-4*) Ctr Env Des Res.

Visual Communications Systems. Ed. by Arun N. Netravali. LC 88-34726. (Illus.). 552p. 1989. text ed. 79.95 (*0-87942-250-5*, PC02410) Inst Electrical.

***Visual Communicatonan Information Theory Approach.** LC 97-14735. 1997. text ed. 220.00 (*0-7923-9956-0*) Kluwer Ac.

***Visual Complex Analysis.** Tristan Needham. (Illus.). 624p. 1997. 55.00 (*0-19-853447-7*) OUP.

Visual Computing: Integrating Computer Graphics with Computer Vision. Ed. by Toshiyasu L. Kunii. LC 92-32343. (CGS CG International Ser.). 1992. 198.00 (*0-387-70103-6*) Spr-Verlag.

Visual Computing: The Integration of Computer Graphics, Visual Perception & Imaging. Markus Grogbs. LC 94-21762. 1994. 69.95 (*0-387-57222-8*) Spr-Verlag.

***Visual Control of Robots: High-Performance Visual Servoing.** Peter I. Corke. LC 96-41151. (Robotics & Mechatronics Ser.). 1997. text ed. 95.00 (*0-471-96937-0*) Wiley.

***Visual Controls Systems.** Nikkan K. Shimbun. (Factory Management Ser.). (Illus.). 189p. 1996. pap. 30.00 (*1-56327-143-5*) Prod Press.

Visual Cues: Practical Data Visualization. Peter Keller & Mary Keller. 350p. 1993. 59.00 (*0-8186-3102-3*, 3102) IEEE Comp Soc.

Visual Culture. Ed. by Chris Jenks. LC 94-42069. (Illus.). 256p. (gr. 13). 1995. pap. 17.95 (*0-415-10623-0*, C0401) Routledge.

Visual Culture. Ed. by Chris Jenks. LC 94-42069. (Illus.). 256p. (C). (gr. 13). 1995. text ed. 69.95 (*0-415-10622-2*, C0404) Routledge.

***Visual Culture: An Introduction.** John W. Walker & Sarah Chaplin. LC 97-12983. 1997. text ed. write for info. (*0-7190-5019-7*, Pub. by Manchester Univ Pr UK); text ed. write for info. (*0-7190-5020-0*, Pub. by Manchester Univ Pr UK) St Martin.

Visual Culture: Images & Interpretations. Ed. by Norman Bryson et al. LC 93-13614. (Illus.). 461p. 1994. pap. 21.00 (*0-8195-6267-X*, Wesleyan Univ Pr) U Pr of New Eng.

Visual Dance: Creating Spectacular Quilts. Joen Wolfrom. LC 94-4461. (Illus.). 144p. 1995. pap. 24.95 (*0-914881-93-0*, 10111) C & T Pub.

Visual Data Interpretation. Ed. by J. R. Alexander. 1992. 20.00 (*0-8194-0822-0*, 1668) SPIE.

Visual Database Systems: Proceedings of the IFIP TC2 WG2.6 Working Conference, Tokyo, Japan, 3-7 April, 1989. Ed. by Toshiyasu L. Kunii. 546p. 1989. 175.75 (*0-444-87334-1*, North Holland) Elsevier.

***Visual Database Systems 3: Visual Information Management.** Ed. by S. Spaccapietra & R. Jain. (Illus.). 448p. 1995. text ed. 89.95 (*0-412-72170-8*, Chap & Hall NY) Chapman & Hall.

Visual Database 5/5.5 for Windows. Gary B. Shelly. (Double Diamond Ser.). 1996. pap. 19.95 (*0-7895-0559-2*) S-W Pub.

Visual Databases in Architecture: Recent Advances in Design & Decision Making. Ed. by Alexander Koutamanis et al. 282p. 1995. 63.95 (*1-85628-994-X*, Pub. by Avebury Pub UK) Ashgate Pub Co.

Visual dBase 5.5 for Windows. Richard A. Biegel & Sumant S. Pendharkar. LC 95-48342. 1996. text ed. write for info. (*0-02-802618-7*) Glencoe.

Visual DBase 5.5 Programming. Michael Irwin. 720p. 1996. 44.95 (*0-13-239922-9*) P-H.

Visual Delights. Nathalie Hambro. 1986. 19.95 (*0-316-34097-9*) Little.

Visual Design in Dress. 3rd ed. Marian Davis. 386p. (C). 1996. text ed. 58.00 (*0-13-112129-4*) P-H.

Visual Design on the Computer. Wucious Wong & Benjamin Wong. (Illus.). 288p. 1994. pap. 24.95 (*1-55821-298-1*) Lyons & Burford.

Visual Design with OSF Motif. Shiz Kobrar. 1991. pap. 45.95 (*0-201-56320-7*) Addison-Wesley.

Visual Detection: Collected Works in Optics, Vol. 3. Ed. by Theodore E. Cohn. 470p. (Orig.). 1993. pap. 74.00 (*1-55752-265-0*) Optical Soc.

Visual Detection of Motion. Ed. by Andrew T. Smith & Robert J. Snowden. (Illus.). 480p. 1994. text ed. 90.00 (*0-12-651660-X*) Acad Pr.

***Visual Developer Creating NT 4 Web Servers: Support the Web & Corporate Intranets.** Jeff Bankston. 1997. pap. text ed. 49.99 (*1-57610-165-7*) Coriolis Grp.

Visual Development. Nigel W. Daw. (Perspectives in Vision Research Ser.). 225p. 1995. 45.00 (*0-306-45023-2*) Plenum.

Visual Diagnosis of Child Physical Abuse. American Academy of Pediatrics Staff & C. Henry Kempe National Center on Child Abuse & Neglect Staff. 1994. student ed., ring bd. 149.95 (*0-910761-46-9*) Am Acad Pediat.

***Visual Diagnosis Self-Tests on HIV Medicine.** Marc Lipman & Paul Thomas. (Visual Diagnosis Self-Tests Ser.). (Illus.). 86p. (Orig.). 1997. pap. 34.95 (*1-873413-41-6*) Merit Pub Intl.

***Visual Diagnosis Self-Tests on Respiratory Tract Infections.** rev. ed. Paul Thomas. (Visual Diagnosis Self-Tests Ser.). (Illus.). 100p. 1997. pap. 34.95 (*0-614-25414-0*) Merit Pub Intl.

***Visual Diagnosis Self-Tests on Respiratory Tract Infections.** 2nd ed. Paul Thomas. (Illus.). 88p. (Orig.). 1997. pap. 34.95 (*1-873413-61-0*) Merit Pub Intl.

Visual Diagnosis Self-Tests on Rheumatology: Questions & Answers. Emery & E. C. Huskisson. (Visual Diagnosis Self-Tests Ser.). (Illus.). 86p. (Orig.). 1996. pap. 34.95 (*1-873413-06-8*) Merit Pub Intl.

Visual Diagnosis Self-Tests on the Menopause & Hormone Replacement Therapy. Goran Samsioe. (Illus.). 100p. 1996. pap. 34.95 (*1-873413-11-4*) Merit Pub Intl.

***Visual Diagnosis Self-Tests on the Menopause & HRT: Spanish Edition.** Goran Samsioe. (Visual Diagnosis Self-Tests Ser.). (Illus.). 96p. (Orig.). (SPA.). 1996. pap. text ed. 34.95 (*1-873413-65-3*) Merit Pub Intl.

Visual Dialogue: An Introduction to the Appreciation of Art, 1980. 3rd ed. Nathan Knobler. 324p. (C). 1980. pap. text ed. 37.25 (*0-03-049316-1*) HB Coll Pubs.

Visual Dictionary Botany: English-Arabic. Lordys Labaky. (Large Bks.). (Illus.). (ARA.). 19.95 (*0-86685-605-6*, LDL6056, Pub. by Librairie du Liban FR) Intl Bk Ctr.

Visual Dictionary, Four Languages. Macmillan Publishing Co. Staff. 928p. 1993. 60.00 (*0-685-70478-5*) Macmillan.

***Visual Dictionary in English & Danish.** Jean-Claude Corbeil. (DAN & ENG.). 1993. 150.00 (*0-7859-9373-8*) Fr & Eur.

***Visual Dictionary in English & German.** Jean-Claude Corbeil. (ENG & GER.). 1993. 150.00 (*0-7859-9378-9*) Fr & Eur.

***Visual Dictionary in English & Italian.** Jean-Claude Corbeil. 896p. (ENG & ITA.). 1993. 150.00 (*0-7859-9371-1*) Fr & Eur.

***Visual Dictionary in English & Japanese.** Jean-Claude Corbell. (ENG & JPN.). 1993. 195.00 (*0-7859-9372-X*) Fr & Eur.

***Visual Dictionary in English & Korean.** Jean-Claude Corbeil. (ENG & KOR.). 1993. 150.00 (*0-7859-9380-0*) Fr & Eur.

***Visual Dictionary in English & Norwegian.** Jean-Claude Corbeil. (ENG & NOR.). 1993. 150.00 (*0-7859-9376-2*) Fr & Eur.

***Visual Dictionary in English & Polish.** Jean-Claude Corbeil. (ENG & POL.). 1993. 150.00 (*0-7859-9379-7*) Fr & Eur.

***Visual Dictionary in English & Portuguese.** Jean-Claude Corbeil. (ENG & POR.). 1993. 150.00 (*0-7859-9374-6*) Fr & Eur.

***Visual Dictionary in English & Slovenian.** Jean-Claude Corbeil. (ENG & SLO.). 1993. 150.00 (*0-7859-9377-0*) Fr & Eur.

***Visual Dictionary in English, French, German & Spanish.** Jean-Claude Corbeil. 964p. (ENG, FRE, GER & SPA.). 1992. 150.00 (*0-7859-9370-3*) Fr & Eur.

Visual Dictionary of American Domestic Architecture. Rachel Carley. LC 94-20071. (Illus.). 272p. 1995. 40.00 (0-8050-2646-0) H Holt & Co.

Visual Dictionary of American Domestic Architecture. Rachel Carley. (Illus.). 272p. 1997. pap. 18.95 (0-8050-4563-5, Owl) H Holt & Co.

***Visual Dictionary of American Domestic Architecture.** Rachel Carley. (Illus.). 1997. pap. 18.95 (0-614-28153-9, Owl) H Holt & Co.

Visual Dictionary of Ancient Civilizations. LC 94-8395. (Eyewitness Visual Dictionaries Ser.). (Illus.). 64p. (J). (gr. 4 up). 1994. 15.95 (1-56458-701-0) DK Pub Inc.

Visual Dictionary of Animals. (Eyewitness Visual Dictionaries Ser.). (Illus.). 64p. (J). (gr. 4 up). 1991. 16.95 (1-879431-19-X) DK Pub Inc.

***Visual Dictionary of Architecture.** Ching. (Architecture Ser.). 1997. pap. 29.95 (0-442-02462-2) Van Nos Reinhold.

Visual Dictionary of Architecture. Francis D. Ching. (Architecture Ser.). 448p. 1995. text ed. 44.95 (0-442-00904-6) Van Nos Reinhold.

Visual Dictionary of Buildings. LC 92-7673. (Eyewitness Visual Dictionaries Ser.). (Illus.). 64p. (J). (gr. 4 up). 1993. 15.95 (1-56458-102-0) DK Pub Inc.

Visual Dictionary of Cars. LC 91-58205. (Eyewitness Visual Dictionaries Ser.). (Illus.). 64p. (J). (gr. 4 up). 1992. 16.95 (1-56458-007-5); 15.99 (1-56458-008-3) DK Pub Inc.

Visual Dictionary of Dinosaurs. LC 72-91418. (Eyewitness Visual Dictionaries Ser.). (Illus.). 64p. (J). (gr. 4 up). 1993. 16.95 (1-56458-188-8) DK Pub Inc.

Visual Dictionary of Everyday Things. LC 92-52830. (Eyewitness Visual Dictionaries Ser.). (Illus.). 64p. (J). (gr. 4 up). 1991. 15.99 (1-879431-32-7) DK Pub Inc.

Visual Dictionary of Flight. (Illus.). 64p. 14.95 (0-614-13203-7, 21-36034) EAA Aviation.

Visual Dictionary of Flight. Ed. by David Learmont. (Eyewitness Visual Dictionaries Ser.). (Illus.). 64p. (J). (gr. 4 up). 1993. 16.95 (1-56458-101-2) DK Pub Inc.

Visual Dictionary of Military Uniforms. LC 91-58206. (Eyewitness Visual Dictionaries Ser.). (Illus.). 64p. (J). (gr. 4 up). 1992. 16.95 (1-56458-010-5); 15.99 (1-56458-011-3) DK Pub Inc.

Visual Dictionary of Physics. Jack Challoner. LC 95-11937. (Eyewitness Visual Dictionaries Ser.). (Illus.). 64p. (J). (gr. 4 up). 1995. 16.95 (0-7894-0239-4, 5-70647) DK Pub Inc.

Visual Dictionary of Plants. LC 91-58208. (Eyewitness Visual Dictionaries Ser.). (Illus.). 64p. (J). (gr. 4 up). 1992. 15.95 (1-56458-016-4) DK Pub Inc.

Visual Dictionary of Prehistoric Life. LC 94-30705. (Eyewitness Visual Dictionaries Ser.). (Illus.). 64p. (J). (gr. 4 up). 1995. 15.95 (1-56458-859-9) DK Pub Inc.

Visual Dictionary of Ships & Sailing. LC 91-60900. (Eyewitness Visual Dictionaries Ser.). (Illus.). 64p. (J). (gr. 4 up). 1991. 15.95 (1-879431-20-3) DK Pub Inc.

Visual Dictionary of Special Military Forces. LC 92-53448. (Eyewitness Visual Dictionaries Ser.). (Illus.). 64p. (J). (gr. 4 up). 1993. 15.95 (1-56458-189-6) DK Pub Inc.

Visual Dictionary of the Earth. (Eyewitness Visual Dictionaries Ser.). (Illus.). 64p. (J). (gr. 4 up). 1993. 16.95 (1-56458-335-X) DK Pub Inc.

Visual Dictionary of the Horse. LC 93-20819. (Eyewitness Visual Dictionaries Ser.). (Illus.). 64p. (J). (gr. 4 up). 1993. 16.95 (1-56458-504-2) DK Pub Inc.

Visual Dictionary of the Skeleton. Richard Walker. (Eyewitness Visual Dictionaries Ser.). (Illus.). 64p. (J). (gr. 5-10). 1995. 16.95 (0-7894-0135-5, 5-70593) DK Pub Inc.

Visual Dictionary of the Universe. (Eyewitness Visual Dictionaries Ser.). (Illus.). (J). (gr. 4 up). 1993. 16.95 (1-56458-336-8) DK Pub Inc.

Visual Diplomacy: The Art of the Cameroon Grassfields. Marcilene Wittmer. (Illus.). 1991. pap. 15.00 (0-9628074-1-9) Hurst Gal.

Visual Discrimination. Fred Justus. (Language Arts Ser.). 24p. (gr. 1-2). 1979. student ed. 5.00 (0-8209-0319-1, LA-5) ESP.

Visual Display: Culture Beyond Appearances. Ed. by Lynne Cooke & Peter Wollen. (Discussions in Contemporary Culture Ser.: No. 10). (Illus.). 240p. 1995. pap. 16.95 (0-941920-32-1) Bay Pr.

Visual Display Equipment. Neville Williams. (Safety Instruction Booklet Ser.). (Illus.). 16p. 1994. pap. 6.00 (1-85573-169-X, Pub. by Woodhead Pubng UK) Am Educ Systs.

Visual Display of Biological Information. Clifford A. Pickover. 300p. 1995. text ed. 74.00 (981-02-1427-8) World Scientific Pub.

Visual Display of Quantitative Information. Edward R. Tufte. (Illus.). 197p. 1983. 40.00 (0-9613921-0-X) Graphics Pr.

Visual Display Terminals: A Manual Covering Ergonomics, Workplace Design, Health & Safety, Task Organization. A. Cakir et al. LC 80-40070. (Illus.). 335p. reprint ed. pap. 95.50 (0-685-20635-1, 2030420) Bks Demand.

***Visual Display Terminals & Workers' Health: With Update 1990.** WHO Staff. (WHO Offset Publications: No. 99). 212p. 1987. 32.00 (92-4-170099-8) World Health.

Visual Dynamics in Jackson Pollock's Abstractions. Matthew Rohn. LC 86-30746. (Studies in the Fine Arts - Art Theory: No. 14). 190p. reprint ed. pap. 54.20 (0-8357-1790-9, 2070662) Bks Demand.

Visual Editing on Unix. Ed. by K. Ranai & B. Srinivasan. 200p. (C). 1989. text ed. 55.00 (9971-5-0770-6) World Scientific Pub.

Visual Education Medical Terminology. Alan Cohen. 1987. pap. 9.95 (1-55637-020-2) Visual Educ.

Visual Electrodiagnosis. Harding & Drasdo. Date not set. write for info. (0-7506-1459-5) Buttrwrth-Heinemann.

Visual Electrodiagnosis in Systematic Diseases. Ed. by E. Schmoger & J. H. Kelsey. (Documenta Ophthalmologica Proceedings Ser.: No. 23). 290p. 1980. lib. bdg. 152.00 (90-6193-163-0) Kluwer Ac.

Visual Elements Four: World Folk Patterns. Ed. by Blount & Co. Staff. (Design Sourcebook Ser.). (Illus.). 120p. 1989. pap. 19.99 (0-935603-12-3, 30143) Rockport Pubs.

Visual Elements of Landscape. John A. Jakle. LC 86-25078. (Illus.). 216p. 1987. pap. text ed. 15.95 (0-87023-567-2); lib. bdg. 35.00 (0-87023-566-4) U of Mass Pr.

Visual Elements Three: Marks & Patterns. Ed. by Mike Milgroom. (Design Sourcebook Ser.). (Illus.). 1990. pap. 19.99 (0-935603-40-9, 30212) Rockport Pubs.

Visual Elements Two: Sports. (Design Sourcebook Ser.). (Illus.). 120p. 1989. pap. 19.99 (0-935603-33-6, 30174) Rockport Pubs.

Visual Encounters with Chance, Unit VIII. Michael Shaughnessy & Michael J. Arcidiacono. (Math & the Mind's Eye Ser.). (Illus.). 96p. (C). 1993. teacher ed., ring bd. 14.50 (1-886131-20-1, ME8) Math Lrning.

Visual Encyclopedia of Natural Healing. Prevention Magazine Health Book Editors. 1996. pap. 15.95 (0-87596-273-4) Rodale Pr Inc.

Visual Encyclopedia of Natural Healing: A Step-by-Step Pictorial Guide to Solving 100 Everyday Health Problems. LC 90-45937. 432p. 1991. 27.95 (0-87857-928-1, 05-998-0) Rodale Pr Inc.

Visual Encyclopedia of Science: Stars & Planets, Planet Earth, the Living World, Science & Technology, World History, Countries of the World. LC 93-43118. (Visual Factfinders Ser.). 320p. (YA). (gr. 5 up). 1994. 22.95 (1-85697-998-9, Kingfisher LKC) LKC.

Visual Evoked Potentials. J. E. Desmedt. (Clinical Neurophysiology Updates Ser.: Vol. 3). 1990. 192.00 (0-444-81240-7, CNU 3) Elsevier.

Visual Experience. Jack A. Hobbs & Richard Salome. 1995. teacher ed., text ed. 51.50 (0-87192-292-4) Davis Mass.

Visual Experience. 2nd ed. Jack Hobbs & Richard Salome. (Illus.). 352p. 1995. text ed. 39.70 (0-87192-291-6) Davis Mass.

***Visual Explanations: Images & Quantities, Evidence & Narrative.** Edward R. Tufte. (Illus.). 160p. 1997. 45.00 (0-9613921-2-6) Graphics Pr.

Visual Eyes. Toadhouse. (Illus.). 116p. (Orig.). 1991. pap. 25.00 (0-9623420-1-7) E J Wagner.

Visual Fact over Verbal Fiction: A Study of the Carracci & the Criticism, Theory & Practice of Art in Renaissance & Baroque Italy. Carl Goldstein. (Illus.). 304p. 1988. text ed. 90.00 (0-521-34331-3) Cambridge U Pr.

Visual Factory: Building Participation Through Shared Information. Michel Greif. LC 90-48170. (Illus.). 305p. 1991. 55.00 (0-915299-67-4) Prod Press.

Visual Feast: The Detroit Institute of Arts Cookbook. (Illus.). 168p. 1985. pap. 17.95 (0-89558-114-0) Det Inst Arts.

Visual Feast Recipe Journal. Woodleigh Hubbard. 200p. 1995. 18.95 (0-8118-0747-9) Chronicle Bks.

***Visual Feedback Photography: Making Your 5S Implementation Click.** Ken I. Ono & Tomoo Sugiyama. LC 96-45256. (Shopfloor Ser.). 1996. teacher ed., ring bd. 150.00 (1-56327-090-0) Prod Press.

***Visual Field.** Marcilio R. Farias. (Orig.). 1996. pap. write for info. (1-57553-361-8) Watermrk Pr.

Visual Field Examination. rev. ed. Norma R. Garber. Ed. by Susan Benes. LC 90-53184. (Ophthalmic Technical Skills Ser.: Vol. I). 180p. 1991. pap. 40.00 (1-55642-172-9) SLACK Inc.

Visual Field Guide for Microsoft Powerpoint 7 Projects for Windows 95. 2nd ed. Marianne B. Fox. (C). 1997. pap. text ed. write for info. (0-8053-1308-7) Addison-Wesley.

Visual Field in Glaucoma: Cellular Proliferation. Ed. by W. Straub. (Developments in Ophthalmology Ser.: Vol. 12). (Illus.). vi, 134p. 1985. 74.50 (3-8055-4022-1) S Karger.

Visual Field Symposium, Fifth International: Documenta Ophthalmoligica Proceedings. Ed. by Erik L. Greve & A. Heijl. 1983. lib. bdg. 253.00 (90-6193-731-0) Kluwer Ac.

Visual Field Testing with the Humphrey Field Analyzer. Neil T. Choplin & Russell P. Edwards. LC 94-24450. 216p. 1994. pap. 45.00 (1-55642-247-4, 62474) SLACK Inc.

Visual Fields. David B. Henson. LC 92-49925. (Oxford Medical Publications). (C). 1993. 38.50 (0-19-261887-3); pap. 36.95 (0-19-262361-3) OUP.

Visual Fields: Clinical Case Presentations. John R. Griffin et al. (Illus.). 512p. 1991. text ed. 95.00 (0-409-90159-8) Buttrwrth-Heinemann.

Visual Fields: Examination & Interpretation. 2nd ed. Thomas J. Walsh. LC 96-20818. (Ophthalmology Monographs Ser.). 1996. write for info. (1-56055-035-X) Am Acad Ophthal.

Visual Fields: Text & Atlas of Clinical Perimetry. 6th ed. Harrington & Drake. (Illus.). 408p. (C). (gr. 13). 1989. text ed. 64.95 (0-8016-2073-2) Mosby Yr Bk.

Visual Food Encyclopedia. 688p. 1997. 45.00 (0-02-861006-7) Macmillan.

Visual Foolery. Dispezio. 1995. pap. 18.50 (0-201-41040-0) Addison-Wesley.

Visual Forces: An Introduction to Design. 2nd ed. Benjamin Martinez & Jacqueline Block. LC 93-29027. 228p. 1994. pap. text ed. 52.00 (0-13-948290-3) P-H.

Visual Form: Analysis & Recognition. Ed. by C. Arcelli et al. (Illus.). 632p. (C). 1992. 125.00 (0-306-44185-3, Plenum Pr) Plenum.

Visual Form Detection in Three Dimensional Space. William R. Uttal. (MacEachram Lectures). 176p. 1983. text ed. 29.95 (0-89859-289-5) L Erlbaum Assocs.

Visual FoxPro Client - Server Development. D. Jurden. (Illus.). 800p. (Orig.). 1996. 49.99 (0-7897-0347-5) Que.

Visual FoxPro Data Dictionary: Special Report. Doug Hennig. LC 96-624. 1996. write for info. (1-880935-41-4) Pinnacle WA.

Visual FoxPro Form Designer: Special Report. Stephen Sawyer. LC 96-3178. 1996. write for info. (1-880935-43-0) Pinnacle WA.

Visual FoxPro Programming Basics. Tom Stearns & Leonard Stearns. 448p. 1996. pap. text ed. 27.95 (0-07-882092-8) Osborne-McGraw.

Visual FoxPro 3 Codebook. Yair A. Griver. 548p. 1995. 39.99 (0-7821-1648-5) Sybex.

Visual Foxpro 3 for Dummies. 2nd ed. John Kaufeld. 1996. pap. 24.99 (1-56884-372-0) IDG Bks.

Visual FoxPro 3 for Windows Developer's Guide. 3rd ed. Jeb J. Long. (Illus.). 1504p. (Orig.). 1995. 49.99 (0-672-30653-0) Sams.

Visual FoxPro 3 Unleashed. 2nd ed. Edward Jones & Sutton. (Illus.). 1056p. (Orig.). 1995. 45.00 (0-672-30758-8) Sams.

***Visual FoxPro 5 Enterprise Development Professional Programming.** Ron Paddock. 576p. 1996. per., pap. 45.00 (0-7615-0903-8) Prima Pub.

***Visual FoxPro 5 for Dummies.** Jim Keogh. (Illus.). 400p. (Orig.). 1997. pap. 24.99 (0-7645-0123-2) IDG Bks.

***Visual French Adjectives & Adverbs.** Barry J. DeMillion & Yumiko Yoshitake. (Illus.). 100p. (ENG & FRE.). 1997. ring bd. 10.95 (1-889950-09-2) Lang Express.

***Visual French Verbs.** Barry J. DeMillion & Yumiko Yoshitake. (Illus.). 100p. (ENG & FRE.). 1997. ring bd. 10.95 (1-889950-08-4) Lang Express.

***Visual French Vocabulary Connections.** Barry J. DeMillion & Yumiko Yoshitake. (Illus.). 100p. (ENG & FRE.). 1997. ring bd. 10.95 (1-889950-10-6) Lang Express.

***Visual Function: An Introduction to Information Design.** Paul Mijksenaar. (Illus.). 56p. (Orig.). 1997. pap. 14.95 (1-56898-118-X) Princeton Arch.

***Visual Genetics Basic.** Day & Dean. 1996. student ed. 32.00 (0-7637-0148-3) Jones & Bartlett.

***Visual Genetics Enhanced.** Day & Dean. 1996. student ed. 48.00 (0-7637-0149-1) Jones & Bartlett.

***Visual Genetics Faculty Version.** Day & Dean. 1996. 395.00 (0-7637-0150-5) Jones & Bartlett.

Visual Geometry & Topology. Anatolij Fomenko. Tr. by Marianna Tsaplina. LC 92-39676. 1994. 89.00 (0-387-53361-3) Spr-Verlag.

Visual Golf: Mental Images & the Flight from Tee to Green. Kenneth Van Kampen. (Illus.). 176p. 1993. pap. 12.00 (0-671-73731-7, Fireside) S&S Trade.

Visual Guide to dBase for Windows: The Pictorial Companion to Windows Database Management & Programming. Carl Townsend. (Illus.). 576p. 1994. 29.95 (1-56604-178-3) Ventana Communs.

Visual Guide to Handwriting Analysis with Encyclopedic Dictionary. Ilyas M. Zeshan. (Illus.). 196p. (Orig.). 1988. pap. 14.95 (0-9619922-3-9) Intl Inst Handwrit.

Visual Guide to Paradox for Windows: The Pictorial Companion to Windows Database Management & Programming. Patrick J. Burns et al. (Illus.). 692p. 1994. 29.95 (1-56604-150-3) Ventana Communs.

Visual Guide to the Ancient Maya. Robert Eckhardt. 1996. 40.00 (0-8050-4959-2) H Holt & Co.

Visual Guide to Visual Basic for Windows: The Illustrated Plain-English Encyclopedia to the Windows Programming Language. 2nd ed. Richard Mansfield. (Illus.). 1300p. 1993. 29.95 (1-56604-063-9) Ventana Communs.

Visual Guide to Visual Basic 4.0 for Windows: The Illustrated, Plain-English Encyclopedia to the Windows Programming Language. Richard Mansfield. (Illus.). 1456p. 1995. pap. 34.95 incl. disk (1-56604-192-9) Ventana Communs.

Visual Guide to Visual C++ The Pictorial Encyclopedia to the Windows Programming Language. Nancy Nicolaison. (Illus.). 888p. 1994. 29.95 (1-56604-079-5) Ventana Communs.

Visual Handbook of Building & Remodeling: The Only Guide to Choosing the Right Materials & Systems for Every Part of Your Home. Charlie Wing. LC 90-8121. 512p. 1991. pap. 19.95 (0-87857-969-9, 14-167-1) Rodale Pr Inc.

Visual Handicaps & Learning. 3rd ed. Natalie C. Barraga & Jane N. Erin. LC 91-27820. 213p. (Orig.). 1992. pap. text ed. 28.00 (0-89079-515-0, 0387) PRO-ED.

Visual Histology. David T. Moran & J. Carter Rowley. LC 87-3835. 299p. reprint ed. pap. 85.30 (0-7837-2730-5, 2043110) Bks Demand.

***Visual History of Costume.** Valerie Cumming & Aileen Ribeiro. (Illus.). 240p. 1997. reprint ed. pap. write for info. (0-89676-221-1, Costume & Fashion Pr) QSMG Ltd.

***Visual I Ching: A New Approach to the Ancient Chinese Oracle Cards & Commentary.** Oliver Perottet. 1997. pap. 18.95 (0-8048-3102-5) Tuttle Pr.

Visual IFPS/Plus for Business. Paul Gray. LC 95-22212. (Series in Information Management). 384p. (C). 1995. pap. text ed. 44.00 (0-13-185604-9) P-H.

Visual Illusion of Motion During Eye Closure see Yale Psychological Studies, N.S.

Visual Illusions: Their Causes, Characteristics & Applications. M. Luckiesh. (Illus.). 1990. 20.00 (0-8446-0780-0) Peter Smith.

Visual Illusions: Their Causes, Characteristics & Applications. Matthew Luckiesh. (Illus.). 252p. 1965. pap. 5.95 (0-486-21530-X) Dover.

Visual Illusions Quilts. Pat Gaska. (Illus.). 64p. 1990. pap. 4.95 (0-486-26159-X) Dover.

Visual Imagination: An Introduction to Art. Bruce D. Kurtz. (Illus.). 448p. (C). 1987. pap. text ed. 72.00 (0-13-942517-9) P-H.

Visual Impact: Creative Language Learning Through Pictures. David A. Hill. (Pilgrims Resource Bks.). 67p. 1990. pap. text ed. 21.32 (0-582-03765-4, 78672) Longman.

Visual Impairment: An Overview. Ian L. Bailey & Amanda Hall. LC 90-1099. 56p. 1990. pap. 17.95 (0-89128-174-6) Am Foun Blind.

Visual Impairment: Perspectives on Practice. J. Hutchinson. (Illus.). 200p. (Orig.). 1997. pap. 41.50 (1-56593-133-5, 0445) Singular Publishing.

Visual Impairment: Social Support: Recent Research in Context. Robin Lovelock. 309p. 1995. 72.50 (1-85628-391-7, Pub. by Avebury Pub UK) Ashgate Pub Co.

Visual Impairment in the Schools. 2nd ed. Randall K. Harley & G. Allen Lawrence. (Illus.). 204p. 1984. 34.95 (0-398-05026-0); pap. 21.95 (0-398-06374-5) C C Thomas.

Visual Impairments & Business Administration. Kenneth Lysons. (Special Needs & Business Administration Ser.). 76p. 1993. pap. 36.00 (1-85302-197-0) Taylor & Francis.

Visual Index of Artists' Signatures & Monograms. Radway Jackson. (Illus.). 240p. 1991. 59.50 (0-572-01649-2, Pub. by W Foulsham UK) Trans-Atl Phila.

Visual Index of Creative Services 1997. Lanre. 1993. pap. 150.00 (0-9518494-2-5, Pub. by Janvier Pubng Ltd UK) St Mut.

Visual Information. 2nd ed. Rune Pettersson. (Illus.). 400p. 1993. 49.95 (0-87778-262-8) Educ Tech Pubns.

***Visual Information Processing VI.** Ed. by Stephen K. Park. 41p. 1997. pap. 80.00 (0-8194-2489-7) SPIE.

Visual Information Systems: The Power of Graphics & Video. Richard H. Veith. (Professinal Librarian Ser.). 354p. (C). 1988. 40.00 (0-8161-1861-2, Hall Reference); 30.00 (0-8161-1881-7, Hall Reference) Macmillan.

***Visual Intelligence: Perception, Image, & Manipulation in Visual Communication.** Anne M. Barry. LC 96-42465. 425p. (C). 1997. pap. text ed. 19.95 (0-7914-3436-2) State U NY Pr.

***Visual Intelligence: Perception, Image, & Manipulation in Visual Communication.** Anne Marie Barry. LC 96-42465. 425p. (C). 1997. text ed. 59.50 (0-7914-3435-4) State U NY Pr.

***Visual Interdev Database Applications Development for the Web.** 1997. pap. text ed. 49.95 incl. cd-rom (0-07-912313-9) McGraw.

***Visual InterDev Handbook.** Brian Maso. 1997. pap. text ed., pap. 29.99 incl. cd-rom (0-07-882330-7) Osborne-McGraw.

Visual Interdevelopment for Dummies. Aaron E. Walsh. 1997. pap. 29.99 (0-7645-0010-4) IDG Bks.

Visual Interface Design for Windows: Effective User Interfaces for Windows 95. Virginia Howlett. LC 95-48046. 256p. 1996. pap. text ed. 39.95 (0-471-13419-8) Wiley.

***Visual Introduction to AutoCAD & 3D Designing.** Bethune. (C). 1997. pap. text ed. 46.67 (0-13-207275-0) P-H.

Visual Introduction to Bucks Point Lace. Geraldine Stott. (Illus.). 96p. 1996. pap. 35.00 (0-7134-4372-3, Pub. by Batsford UK) Trafalgar.

Visual Introduction to Dynamical Systems Theory for Psychology. Frederick D. Abraham et al. (Science Frontier Express Ser.). (Illus.). 290p. 1990. spiral bd. 25.00 (0-942344-09-X) Dakota Bks.

Visual Introduction to SQL. J. Harvey Trimble & David M. Chappell. LC 88-32126. 254p. 1989. pap. text ed. 46.95 (0-471-61684-2) Wiley.

Visual Investor: How to Spot Market Trends. John L. Murphy. 1996. text ed. 29.95 (0-471-14447-9) Wiley.

***Visual J++** Brian Maso. 1996. pap. text ed. 29.99 (0-07-882266-1) Osborne-McGraw.

***Visual J++** Namir C. Shammas. (New Tutorial Ser.). 1997. pap. 39.99 (0-7645-3051-8) IDG Bks.

Visual J++ Charles A. Wood. 624p. 1996. per. 35.00 incl. cd-rom (0-7615-0814-7) Prima Pub.

***Visual J++ No Experience Required.** Steven Holzner. 1997. pap. text ed. 29.99 (0-7821-2078-4) Sybex.

***Visual J++ Bible.** Richard Leinecker. 912p. (Orig.). 1997. pap. write for info. (0-614-26288-7) IDG Bks.

***Visual J++ Handbook.** Ed. by William H. Murray & Chris H. Pappas. LC 96-35323. (Illus.). 574p. 1996. pap. text ed. 39.95 (0-12-511915-1, AP Prof) Acad Pr.

Visual J++ Java Programming. Jim Flynn. 688p. 1996. 45.00 (1-56205-602-6) New Riders Pub.

***Visual J++ Bible.** Richard C. Leinecker. 1997. pap. 49.99 (0-7645-8021-3) IDG Bks.

***Visual J++ Developer's Guide.** Samsnet Publishing Staff. 1200p. 1997. 55.00 (1-57521-266-8) Mac Comp Pub.

***Visual J++ for Dummies.** Michael Hyman & Dummies Technical Press Staff. (Illus.). 384p. (Orig.). 1997. pap. 24.99 (0-7645-0079-1) IDG Bks.

***Visual J++ Starter Kit.** Gregg Perry. 416p. 1997. 34.99 (0-7897-1282-2) Que.

***Visual J++ Professional Trainer.** Namir C. Shammas. 704p. (Orig.). 1997. pap. write for info. (0-614-26295-X) IDG Bks.

***Visual J++ Programming Frontrunner.** Peter Aitken. 1996. pap. text ed. 34.99 (1-57610-064-2) Coriolis Grp.

Visual J++ Unleashed. Sams Publishing Staff. 1000p. 1996. pap. text ed. 49.99 incl. cd-rom (1-57521-161-0, SamsNet Bks) Sams.

***Visual J++ X Secrets.** Michael Farr. 1997. pap. 59.99 (0-7645-3138-7) IDG Bks.

***Visual J++ 1.1 Unleashed.** 2nd ed. Bryan Morgan. 1997. 49.99 (1-57521-356-7) Sams.

***Visual Japanese Adjectives & Adverbs.** Barry J. DeMillion & Yumiko Yoshitake. (Illus.). 100p. (ENG, JPN & LAT.). 1994. ring bd. 11.95 (1-889950-02-5) Lang Express.

An Asterisk (*) at the beginning of an entry indicates that the title is appearing in BIP for the first time.

***Visual Japanese Verbs.** Barry J. DeMillion & Yumiko Yoshitake. (Illus.). 100p. (ENG, JPN & LAT.). 1993. ring bd. 11.95 (1-889950-01-7) Lang Express.

***Visual Japanese Vocabulary Connections.** Barry J. DeMillion & Yumiko Yoshitake. (Illus.). (ENG & JPN.). 1997. ring bd. 11.95 (1-889950-04-1) Lang Express.

Visual Journal: Harlem & D.C. in the Thirties & Forties. Ed. by Deborah Willis & Jane Lusaka. (Illus.). 208p. 1996. pap. 39.95 (1-56098-691-3) Smithsonian.

Visual Journeys. Mitchell Crites. LC 94-60283. (Illus.). 256p. 1994. 50.00 (0-500-97414-4) Thames Hudson.

***Visual Junior Dictionary in English & French.** Jean-Claude Corbeil. 232p. (ENG & FRE.). 1993. 39.95 (0-7859-9375-4) Fr & Eur.

Visual Keyboard Chord Progressions, Bk. I. William L. Fowler. LC 83-81908. (Illus.). 75p. 1983. pap. text ed. 10.00 (0-943894-02-6) Fowler Music.

Visual Keyboard Chord Progressions, Bk. II. William L. Fowler. (Illus.). 76p. 1984. pap. text ed. 10.00 (0-943894-03-4) Fowler Music.

Visual Keyboard Chord Progressions, Bk. III. William L. Fowler. LC 83-81908. (Illus.). 84p. 1985. pap. text ed. 10.00 (0-943894-08-5) Fowler Music.

Visual Keyboard Chord Progressions, Bk. IV. William L. Fowler. LC 83-81908. (Illus.). 84p. 1986. pap. text ed. 10.00 (0-943894-10-7) Fowler Music.

Visual Language Cookbook. Gayle Joyce & Laurene Gallimore. LC 79-92053. (Illus.). 60p. (gr. 6-12). 1979. 24.00 (0-917002-41-5) Joyce Media.

Visual Languages. Ed. by Shi-Kuo Chang. (Management & Information Systems Ser.). 452p. 1987. 105.00 (0-306-42350-2, Plenum Pr) Plenum.

Visual Languages & Applications. Ed. by T. Ichikawa et al. (Management & Information Systems Ser.). (Illus.). 345p. 1990. 89.50 (0-306-43427-X, Plenum Pr) Plenum.

Visual Languages & Visual Programming. Ed. by S. K. Chang. (Management & Information Systems Ser.). (Illus.). 352p. 1990. 75.00 (0-306-43428-8, Plenum Pr) Plenum.

Visual Languages, 1994 IEEE Symposium On. LC 90-640177. 336p. 1994. pap. 70.00 (0-8186-6660-9) IEEE Comp Soc.

Visual Languages, 1995 IEEE Symposium On. LC 10-492615. 368p. 1995. pap. text ed. 70.00 (0-8186-7045-2, PR07045) IEEE Comp Soc.

Visual Languages, 1996 IEEE Symposium On. LC 10-492615. 368p. 1996. pap. 70.00 (0-8186-7508-X, PR07508) IEEE Comp Soc.

***Visual Literacy.** Ed. by Peter B. Mosenthal. (Advances in Reading/Language Research Ser.: Vol. 7). 1998. 78.50 (0-7623-0264-X) Jai Pr.

Visual Literacy: A Conceptual Approach to Solving Graphic Problems. Richard Wilde & Judith Wilde. (Illus.). 192p. 1991. 45.00 (0-8230-5619-8, Watsn-Guptill) Watsn-Guptill.

Visual Literacy: A Selected Bibliography. Rebecca Clemente & Roy M. Bohlin. Ed. by William D. Milheim. LC 90-41870. (Educational Technology Selected Bibliography Ser.: Vol. 2). 50p. 1990. pap. 24.95 (0-87778-227-X) Educ Tech Pubns.

Visual Literacy: A Spectrum of Visual Learning. Ed. by David M. Moore & Francis M. Dwyer. LC 93-2437. 450p. 1994. 49.95 (0-87778-264-4) Educ Tech Pubns.

Visual "Literacy" Image, Mind, & Reality. Paul Messaris. LC 93-26069. 208p. (C). 1994. pap. text ed. 22.00 (0-8133-1937-4) Westview.

Visual Literacy in the Digital Age: Selected Readings from the 25th Annual Conference of the International Visual Literacy Association. Ed. by Darrell G. Beauchamp et al. (Illus.). 480p. (Orig.). (C). 1994. pap. text ed. 25.00 (0-945829-08-6) Intl Visual.

Visual Literature Criticism. Richard Kostelanetz. (Precisely: 3 4 5 Ser.). 192p. (Orig.). 1979. reprint ed. pap. 6.00 (0-932360-44-0) Archae Edns.

Visual Masking: An Integrative Approach. Bruno G. Breitmeyer. (Oxford Psychology Ser.). (Illus.). 500p. 1984. 45.00 (0-19-852105-7) OUP.

Visual Mathematics: Course I. Linda C. Foreman & Albert B. Bennett, Jr. (Illus.). 566p. 1995. teacher ed., spiral bd. 145.00 (1-886131-27-9, VMC1) Math Lrning.

Visual Mathematics: Course II. Linda C. Foreman & Albert B. Bennett, Jr. (Illus.). 1996. teacher ed., spiral bd. 145.00 (1-886131-42-2, VMC2) Math Lrning.

Visual Meditations on the Universe. James S. Perkins. LC 83-40233. (Illus.). 136p. 1984. 16.95 (0-8356-0233-8, Quest) Theos Pub Hse.

***Visual Merchandising.** Date not set. 35.00 (0-688-15361-5); pap. 29.95 (0-688-15782-3) Morrow.

Visual Merchandising. Bonanno. (C). 1998. 26.95 (1-56253-351-7) Milady Pub.

Visual Merchandising. Colborne. (SV-Fashion Merchandising). 64p. 1995. teacher ed. 10.00 (0-8273-5760-5) Delmar.

***Visual Merchandising: From the Editors of VM+SD Magazine.** Hearst Books International Staff. 1997. pap. text ed. 34.95 (0-8230-5621-X) Watsn-Guptill.

Visual Merchandising: Planning & Techniques. 2nd ed. Samson. (SB - Marketing Education Ser.). 1985. pap. 19.95 (0-538-04210-9) S-W Pub.

Visual Merchandising: The Business of Merchandise Presentation. Robert Colborne. LC 95-10179. 352p. 1996. pap. 31.95 (0-8273-5759-1) Delmar.

Visual Merchandising & Display. 3rd ed. Martin M. Pegler. (Illus.). 375p. (C). 1995. 45.00 (1-56367-043-7, AAF6) Fairchild.

Visual Merchandising & Store Design Workbook. Greg M. Gorman. (Illus.). 112p. 1996. wbk. ed., pap. 24.95 (0-944094-20-1) ST Pubns.

Visual Merchandising for the Retail Florist. Redbook Florist Services Educational Advisory Committee. LC 91-67527. (Encycloflora Ser.). (Illus.). 246p. (Orig.). 1992. pap. text ed. 34.95 (1-56963-017-8) Redbk Florist.

Visual Messages: Integrating Imagery into Instruction. David M. Considine & Gail E. Haley. (Illus.). xv, 269p. 1992. pap. text ed. 26.50 (0-87287-912-7) Teacher Ideas Pr.

Visual Mind: Art & Mathematics. Ed. by Michele Emmer. (Leonardo Book Ser.). (Illus.). 294p. 1993. 47.50 (0-262-05048-X) MIT Pr.

Visual Modelling Technique: Object Technology Using Visual Programming. Daniel Tkach et al. 426p. (C). 1997. pap. text ed. 45.95 (0-8053-2574-3) Addison-Wesley.

Visual Motion & Its Role in the Stabilization of Gaze. Ed. by F. A. Miles & J. Wallman. LC 92-32805. (Reviews of Oculomotor Research Ser.: Vol. 5). 418p. 1992. 296.50 (0-444-81195-8) Elsevier.

Visual-Motor Development Remedial Activities. Karen G. Codding & Morrison F. Gardner. 1988. pap. 7.95 (0-931421-16-0); 8.95 (0-931421-12-8); 8.95 (0-931421-17-9); 8.95 (0-931421-25-X); 8.95 (0-931421-26-8); 8.95 (0-931421-28-4) Psychol Educ Pubns.

Visual-Motor Upper Level Remedial Activities. Morrison F. Gardner. 1993. pap. 9.95 (0-931421-43-8) Psychol Educ Pubns.

Visual Narratives: Storytelling in Etruscan & Roman Art. Richard Brilliant. LC 83-18869. (Illus.). 208p. 1984. 47.50 (0-8014-1558-6) Cornell U Pr.

***Visual Narratives: Storytelling in Etruscan & Roman Art.** Richard Brilliant. LC 83-18869. (Illus.). 202p. reprint ed. pap. 57.60 (0-608-05315-5, 2065853) Bks Demand.

Visual Nature of Color. Patricia Sloane. (Illus.). 288p. (Orig.). (C). 1989. 29.95 (0-8306-5500-X) TAB Bks.

Visual Navigation: From Biological Systems to Unmanned Ground Vehicles. Ed. by Yiannis Aloimonos. LC 96-18717. (Computer Vision Ser.). 432p. (C). 1996. text ed. 69.95 (0-8058-2050-7) L Erlbaum Assocs.

Visual Notes for Architects & Designers. Norman Crowe & Paul Laseau. (Illus.). 224p. 1984. pap. 34.95 (0-442-29334-8) Van Nos Reinhold.

Visual Novel: Emile Zola & the Art of His Times. William J. Berg. 304p. 1992. 39.50 (0-271-00826-1) Pa St U Pr.

Visual Novel of the War of Tomorrow: Armor at Fulda Gap, Vol. 2. John L. Cook. (Illus.). 224p. 1990. pap. 6.95 (0-380-75843-1) Avon.

Visual Novel of the War of Tomorrow: Helicopter Aces. James W. Bradin. 224p. (Orig.). 1990. pap. 6.95 (0-380-75847-4) Avon.

Visual Novel of the War of Tomorrow, Vol. 1: Strike Eagles. James P. Coyne. 224p. 1990. pap. 6.95 (0-380-75845-8) Avon.

Visual Object-Oriented Programming: Concepts & Environments. Margaret Burnett. 300p. 1994. text ed. 43.00 (0-13-172397-9) P-H.

***Visual Object-Oriented Programming Using Delphi.** Richard S. Wiener & Claude Wiatrowski. 400p. (C). 1996. pap. text ed. 50.00 (0-13-618638-6) P-H.

***Visual Object-Oriented Programming Using Delphi.** Richard S. Wiener & Claude A. Wiatrowski. LC 96-42363. (Advances in Object Technology Ser.). 1996. write for info. (1-884842-60-7) SIGS Bks & Multimedia.

Visual Object-Oriented Programming with Prograph CPX. Scott B. Steinman. 1995. pap. text ed. 32.00 (0-13-441163-3) P-H.

Visual Objects: A Developer's Guide. Joseph D. Booth. 1995. pap. 39.95 incl. disk (1-55851-410-4, M&T Books) H Holt & Co.

***Visual Objects 2.0 Encyclopedia: Box Set, 3 vols.** Stephen J. Straley. Incl. Bk. 1 Fundamentals. (Illus.). 980p. (Orig.). 1997. pap. 70.00 (1-890726-02-8); Bk. 2 Building an Application. (Illus.). 700p. (Orig.). 1997. pap. 70.00 (1-890726-03-6); Bk. 3 Advanced Programming. (Orig.). 1997. pap. 70.00 (1-890726-04-4); 150.00 (1-890726-00-1, ENCY01) Sirius Pr.

Visual Optics: Diamond & Gem Identification Without Instruments. Alan Hodgkinson. (Illus.). 50p. 1995. spiral bd. 25.00 (0-9641733-1-X) Gemwrld Intl.

Visual Optics & Instrumentation. Charman. 1991. 137.00 (0-8493-7501-0) CRC Pr.

Visual Order: The Nature & Development of Pictorial Representation. Ed. by N. H. Freeman & M. V. Cox. (Illus.). 409p. 1985. 74.95 (0-521-26668-8) Cambridge U Pr.

***Visual Parables Vol. 1: Engaging the Spiritual Elements of Film - a Text for Christian Parents, Educators & Clergy.** Janet L. Meyer. LC 97-72830. 160p. (Orig.). 1997. pap. write for info. (1-890852-02-3) Inst SW Pub.

Visual Paradox: Truth & Fiction in the Photographic Image. Contrib. by Joanne Cubbs. (Illus.). 80p. 1988. pap. 21.95 (0-932718-24-8) Kohler Arts.

Visual Paraphrasing of Poetry: A Sourcebook for Teachers & Readers. Donna Richardson. 222p. (Orig.). (C). 1992. pap. text ed. 26.50 (0-8191-8820-4); lib. bdg. 52.00 (0-8191-8819-0) U Pr of Amer.

Visual Pathways. Ed. by H. Spekreijse & P. A. Apkarian. (Documenta Ophthalmologica Proceedings Ser.: No. 27). 472p. 1981. lib. bdg. 230.00 (90-6193-723-X) Kluwer Ac.

Visual Pathways to the Inner Self. Keith Armstrong. (Illus.). 295p. (C). 1996. text ed. 35.00 (1-879528-17-7); pap. text ed. 19.95 (1-879528-16-9) LEPS Pr.

Visual Pattern Analyzers. Norma V. Graham. (Oxford University South Asian Studies Ser.: No. 16). (Illus.). 670p. 1989. 75.00 (0-19-505154-8) OUP.

Visual Perception. Tom N. Cornsweet. 475p. (C). 1970. text ed. 42.75 (0-15-594936-5, CORN) HB Coll Pubs.

Visual Perception: A Clinical Orientation. Steven H. Schwartz. (Illus.). 368p. 1994. text ed. 59.95 (0-8385-9473-5, A9473-8) Appleton & Lange.

Visual Perception: An Introduction. Nicholas J. Wade & Michael Swanston. (Introductions to Modern Psychology Ser.). (Illus.). 224p. (C). 1991. pap. text ed. 17.95 (0-415-01043-8, A5424) Routledge.

***Visual Perception: Physiology, Psychology, & Ecology.** 3rd ed. Bruce et al. 1997. 59.95 (0-86377-450-4) L Erlbaum Assocs.

***Visual Perception: Physiology, Psychology & Ecology.** 3rd ed. Vicki Bruce et al. 448p. 1997. pap. 26.00 (0-86377-451-2) L Erlbaum Assocs.

Visual Perception: The Neurophysiological Foundations. Ed. by Lothar Spillman & John S. Werner. 531p. 1989. text ed. 59.00 (0-12-657675-0) Acad Pr.

Visual Perception & Cognition in Infancy. Ed. by Carl Granrud. (Carnegie-Mellon Symposia on Cognition (David Klahr) Ser.). 368p. 1993. pap. 39.95 (0-8058-0706-3); text ed. 79.95 (0-8058-0705-5) L Erlbaum Assocs.

Visual Perceptions: Twenty-One African American Designers Challenge Modern Stereotypes. Michele Washington. 48p. 1992. 10.95 (0-9635695-1-1) M Washington.

Visual-Perceptual Upper Level Remedial Activities. Karen G. Codding & Morrison F. Gardner. 1993. pap. 9.95 (0-931421-81-0) Psychol Educ Pubns.

Visual Persuasion: The Role of Images in Advertising. Paul Messaris. LC 96-25184. 328p. 1996. 54.00 (0-8039-7245-8); pap. 24.95 (0-8039-7246-6) Sage.

Visual Phonetic Map Method & Consonant Review. 380p. 1992. pap. text ed. 24.95 (0-9631423-4-8); 24.95 (0-9631423-5-6); 24.95 (0-9631423-6-4) AZ Learn Mats.

***Visual Piety: A History & Theory of Popular Religious Images.** David Morgan. LC 97-14354. 1998. write for info. (0-520-20978-8) U CA Pr.

Visual Play: A Green Dance in Three Acts. Elizabeth Cook. (Illus.). 30p. 1983. ring bd. 15.00 (0-915066-53-X) Assembling Pr.

Visual Polemics in Ninth Century Byzantine Psalters. Kathleen Corrigan. 344p. (C). 1992. text ed. 110.00 (0-521-40050-3) Cambridge U Pr.

Visual Precalculus. David I. Schneider. LC 93-37674. (C). 1993. 15.00 (0-673-99245-4) Addson-Wesley Educ.

Visual Preferences of Travelers along the Blue Ridge Parkway. Ed. by Francis P. Noe & William E. Hammitt. LC 88-600093. (Scientific Monograph Ser.: No. 18). (Illus.). (Orig.). (C). 1988. pap. write for info. (0-943475-00-7) Natl Park GA.

Visual Principles. Neil Watson. Date not set. write for info. (0-393-73011-5) Norton.

Visual Problems in Childhood. Ed. by Terry Buckingham. (Illus.). 376p. 1993. text ed. 95.00 (0-7506-1061-1) Buttrwrth-Heinemann.

Visual Processes in Reading & Reading Disabilities. Ed. by Dale M. Willows et al. LC 93-26065. 504p. 1993. pap. 45.00 (0-8058-1332-2); text ed. 89.95 (0-8058-0900-7) L Erlbaum Assocs.

***Visual Programming for HP-VEE.** 2nd ed. Robert Helsel. 480p. (C). 1997. pap. text ed. 46.00 (0-13-631797-9) P-H.

Visual Programming Plus Plus: Cool Ways to Master Visual C Plus Plus & Mfc. Richard H. Shaw. 1994. pap. 34.95 (0-201-62662-4) Addison-Wesley.

Visual Programming Technology. Dimitris N. Chorafas. (Illus.). 352p. 1996. pap. text ed. 49.00 (0-07-011685-7) McGraw.

Visual Programming Tools for X. Steven Mikes. 1994. pap. 34.00 (0-13-954132-2) P-H.

Visual Programming with Hp VEE. 2nd ed. Robert Helsel. 384p. (C). 1996. pap. text ed. 51.00 incl. audio compact disk (0-13-533548-5) P-H.

Visual Programming with Prograph CPX. Scott B. Steinman & Kevin G. Carver. 1995. write for info. (1-884777-05-8) Manning Pubns.

Visual Project Management. Kevin Forsberg et al. LC 95-52250. 320p. 1996. text ed. 29.95 (0-471-57779-0) Wiley.

Visual Psychophysics see Handbook of Sensory Physiology

Visual Quality in the Coastal Zone: Proceedings. 1975. 4.00 (0-686-20723-8) SUNY Environ.

Visual Reading & Braille Reading: An Experimental Investigation of the Physiology & Psychology of Visual & Tactual Reading. Tokisuke Kusajima. Ed. by Leslie L. Clark & Zofia S. Jastrzembska. LC 75-329731. 70p. 1974. reprint ed. pap. 25.00 (0-7837-0142-X, 2040431) Bks Demand.

Visual Representations of Speech Signals. M. Cooke & S. W. Beet. LC 92-40219. 385p. 1993. text ed. 115.00 (0-471-93537-9) Wiley.

Visual Resources Directory: Art Slide & Photograph Collections in the United States & Canada. Ed. by Carla C. Freeman & Barbara Stevenson. (Illus.). xvii, 174p. 1995. pap. text ed. 45.00 (1-56308-196-2) Libs Unl.

Visual Resources, Vol. IV, No. 3: A Special Issue of the Journal Visual Resources. Ed. by H. E. Roberts et al. viii, 90p. 1987. text ed. 37.00 (2-88124-370-3) Gordon & Breach.

***Visual Revelations: Graphical Tales of Fate & Deception from Napoleon Bonaparte to Ross Perot.** Howard Wainer. LC 96-44235. (Copernicus Ser.). 250p. 1997. 29.95 (0-387-94902-X) Spr-Verlag.

Visual Sampling Scanning Processes. John W. Senders. 160p. (C). 1983. pap. text ed. 24.95 (0-89859-516-9) L Erlbaum Assocs.

Visual Science: Proceedings of the International Symposium, Indiana University, 1968. International Symposium on Visual Science Staff. Ed. by John R. Pierce & John R. Levene. LC 78-150216. 428p. reprint ed. pap. 122.00 (0-317-28585-8, 2055236) Bks Demand.

Visual Science & Engineering: Models & Applications. Ed. by D. Kelly. LC 93-46484. (Optical Engineering Ser.: Vol. 43). 448p. 1994. 165.00 (0-8247-9185-1) Dekker.

Visual Search Proceedings of the First International Conference on Visual Search. Ed. by David Brogan. 500p. 1990. 145.00 (0-85066-773-9) Taylor & Francis.

Visual Search Two. Ed. by David Brogan et al. 448p. 1993. 125.00 (0-7484-0010-9, Pub. by Tay Francis Ltd UK) Taylor & Francis.

***Visual Select: Office 97.** Toliver Johnson. (C). 1997. pap. text ed. 48.95 (0-201-30321-3) Addison-Wesley.

***Visual Select: Windows 97.** Gary R. Brent. (C). 1997. pap. text ed. write for info. (0-8053-1637-X) Benjamin-Cummings.

***Visual Select: Word for Windows 97.** James Folts. (C). 1997. pap. text ed. write for info. (0-8053-1636-1) Benjamin-Cummings.

***Visual Selling Design.** PBC International Staff. 1990. 47.50 (0-688-09793-6) Morrow.

Visual Serving: Real Time Control of Robot Manipulators Based on Visual Sensory Feedback. K. Hashimoto. (Old Series in Robotics & Automated Systems). 300p. 1993. text ed. 95.00 (981-02-1364-6) World Scientific Pub.

Visual Skills. Shirley Ross. (Rainbow Skill Builders Ser.: Level 3). 80p. (J). (ps-3). 1989. 2.95 (0-8431-2516-0) Price Stern Sloan.

Visual Skills Appraisal (VSA) Regina Richards & Gary S. Oppenheim. 80p. 1984. 60.00 (0-685-42805-2, 453-0A); teacher ed. 19.00 (0-87879-453-0); 15.00 (0-685-42807-9); 8.00 (0-87879-454-9); 9.00 (0-87879-455-7); 9.00 (0-87879-456-5); 9.00 (0-87879-457-3); 8.00 (0-87879-458-1); 10.00 (0-685-42806-0) Acad Therapy.

***Visual Spanish Adjectives & Adverbs.** Barry J. DeMillion & Yumiko Yoshitake. (Illus.). 100p. (ENG & SPA.). 1996. ring bd. 10.95 (1-889950-06-8) Lang Express.

***Visual Spanish Verbs.** Barry J. DeMillion & Yumiko Yoshitake. (Illus.). 100p. (ENG & SPA.). 1996. ring bd. 10.95 (1-889950-05-X) Lang Express.

***Visual Spanish Vocabulary Connections.** Barry J. DeMillion & Yumiko Yoshitake. (Illus.). 100p. (ENG & SPA.). 1996. ring bd. 10.95 (1-889950-07-6) Lang Express.

***Visual Special Effects Toolkit in C++** Tim Wittenburg. LC 96-48158. 416p. 1997. pap. 49.99 incl. cd-rom (0-471-13220-9) Wiley.

***Visual Statistics.** David P. Doane et al. LC 96-35867. 1996. write for info. (0-256-20876-X) Irwin Prof Pubng.

Visual Strategies for Improving Communication: Practical Supports for School & Home. Linda A. Hodgdon. (Illus.). 232p. (Orig.). 1995. pap. text ed. 39.95 (0-9616786-1-5) Quirk Roberts.

***Visual Strategies for Improving Communication: Solving Behavior Problems.** Linda A. Hodgdon. (Visual Strategies Ser.: No. 2). (Illus.). (Orig.). 1997. pap. text ed. write for info. (0-9616786-2-3) Quirk Roberts.

Visual Stress. A. Wilkins. (Oxford Psychology Ser.: No. 24). (Illus.). 216p. 1995. text ed. 59.00 (0-19-852174-X) OUP.

Visual Structures & Integrated Functions. Ed. by Michael A. Arbib et al. (Research Notes in Neural Computing Ser.: Vol. 3). (Illus.). xii, 441p. 1991. pap. 53.00 (0-387-54241-8) Spr-Verlag.

Visual Studies: A Foundation for Artists & Designers. Frank M. Young. (Illus.). 300p. (C). 1985. pap. text ed. write for info. (0-13-942508-X) P-H.

***Visual Studio 97 6-in-1.** Kate Gregory. Date not set. 39.99 (0-7897-1413-2) Que.

Visual System from Genesis to Maturity. Ed. by Roberto Lent. LC 92-21738. xii, 285p. 1992. 108.00 (0-8176-3598-X) Birkhauser.

Visual System in Evolution in Vertebrates. A. Hughes. LC 77-4371. (Handbook of Sensory Physiology Ser.: Vol. 7, Pt. 5). 1977. 299.00 (0-387-07908-4) Spr-Verlag.

***Visual System of Fish.** Ed. by Douglas & Djamgoz. (Illus.). 548p. (C). (gr. 13 up). 1992. text ed. 97.95 (0-412-33050-4) Chapman & Hall.

Visual System of Fish. Ed. by Ron H. Douglas & Mustafa B. Djamgoz. 1990. 69.95 (0-685-45312-X) Chapman & Hall.

Visual Systems: Harnessing the Power of a Visual Workplace. Gwendolyn D. Galsworth. Ed. by Anthony Vlamis. LC 96-46034. 350p. 1996. 65.00 (0-8144-0320-4) AMACOM.

Visual TCL Handbook. David Young. LC 96-17226. 1996. pap. text ed. 45.00 (0-13-461674-X) P-H.

Visual Technology: Computer Art & Design Basics. Mark Jurey. 225p. (C). 1996. pap. text ed. 20.94 (0-7872-2503-7) Kendall-Hunt.

***Visual Terms: Reaching Across Space, Time & Organizations with Technology.** Jessica Lipnack & Jeffrey Stamps. LC 96-40505. 288p. 1997. 28.00 (0-471-16553-0) Wiley.

Visual Text of William Carlos Williams. Henry M. Sayre. LC 83-1395. (Illus.). 168p. 1983. text ed. 24.95 (0-252-01059-0) U of Ill Pr.

Visual Thalamocortical System & Its Modulation by the Brain Stem Core. Mircea Steriade et al. (Progress in Sensory Physiology Ser.: Vol. 10). (Illus.). 148p. 1990. 100.00 (0-387-51380-9) Spr-Verlag.

Visual Thinking. Rudolf Arnheim. LC 71-76335. (Illus.). 1980. reprint ed. pap. 14.00 (0-520-01871-0) U CA Pr.

Visual Thinking for Architecture & Design. Ronald J. Kasprisin. 1996. pap. 39.95 (0-442-01641-7) Van Nos Reinhold.

UV

***Visual Thinking Puzzles.** Michael DiSpezio. Date not set. write for info. (*0-8069-9975-6*) Sterling.

Visual Tools for Constructing Knowledge. David Hyerle. 133p. (Orig.). 1996. pap. 22.95 (*0-87120-266-2*) Assn Supervision.

Visual Training: The Joy of Optometry. rev. ed. Coleman Hatfield. Ed. by Sally M. Corngold. (Introduction to Behavioral Optometry Ser.). (Illus.). 64p. 1990. reprint ed. pap. text ed. 150.00 (*0-943599-09-1*) OEPF.

***Visual Turn & the Transformation of the Textbook.** James A. LaSpina. 180p. 1998. write for info. (*0-8058-2701-3*) L Erlbaum Assocs.

***Visual Turn & the Transformation of the Textbook.** James A. LaSpina. 180p. 1998. pap. write for info. (*0-8058-2702-1*) L Erlbaum Assocs.

Visual Values for the Highway User. 118p. 5.00 (*0-318-17834-6*, Landscape Architecture) Am Landscape Arch.

Visual Voices: Between Mountains & Me. George L. Bristol. LC 91-614915. (Illus.). 96p. 1991. 34.95 (*1-879234-24-6*) State House Pr.

Visual Voices: The Poem As a Print Object. Irving Weiss. 145p. (Orig.). 1994. pap. 20.00 (*0-926935-95-X*) Runaway Spoon.

Visual World of the Child. Eliane Vurpillot. LC 75-790. 372p. 1976. 47.50 (*0-8236-6749-9*) Intl Univs Pr.

VisualAge Smalltalk & SOMobjects: Developing Distributed Object Applications with VisualAge Smalltalk & SOMobjects. Walter Fang et al. LC 96-13239. 1996. pap. text ed. 44.67 (*0-13-570813-3*) P-H.

VisualDsolve: New Frontiers in the Visualization of Differential Equations. Dan Schwalbe. 1997. pap. text ed. 34.95 (*0-387-94721-3*) Spr-Verlag.

***VisualEyes Curriculum.** (Aging & Vision Ser.). 1996. 49.95 (*1-888504-00-5*, 990) Lighthouse NYC.

***VisualEyes Workbook.** (Aging & Vision Ser.). 1996. 2.49 (*1-888504-01-3*, P1000) Lighthouse NYC.

Visualizacion Creativa: Como Usar la Imaginacion para Producir Cambios Positivos. Shakti Gawain. Tr. by Editorial Planeta Staff. 208p. (Orig.). (SPA.). 1995. pap. 10.95 (*1-880032-69-4*) New Wrld Lib.

Visualization. Pauline Wills. (Headway Lifeguides Ser.). (Illus.). 128p. 1995. pap. 15.95 (*0-340-61107-3*, Pub. by Headway UK) Trafalgar.

Visualization: Breaking Through the Illusion of Problems. Stephen R. Schwartz. 64p. (Orig.). 1985. pap. 12.00 (*0-936415-00-2*) Riverrun Piermont.

Visualization: The Master Skill in Mental Training. Marie Dalloway. 67p. 1992. pap. text ed. 14.95 (*0-9634933-0-2*) Optimal Perf.

Visualization: The Second Computer Revolution. Richard M. Friedhoff & En. 1995. pap. text ed. 25.95 (*0-7167-2231-3*) W H Freeman.

Visualization: Using Computer Graphics to Explore Data & Present Information. Judith R. Brown et al. LC 95-15663. 320p. 1995. pap. 49.95 (*0-471-12991-7*) Wiley.

Visualization & Concentration. Fenwicke L. Holmes. 62p. 1993. pap. 5.00 (*0-89540-214-9*, SB-214) Sun Pub.

Visualization & Intelligent Design in Engineering & Architecture. Ed. by J. J. Connor et al. LC 92-75800. (VIDEA Ser.: Vol. 1). 672p. 1993. 295.00 (*1-56252-151-9*) Computational Mech MA.

Visualization & Intelligent Design in Engineering & Architecture II: Proceedings of the Second International Conference. Ed. by S. Hernandez & C. A. Brebbia. LC 95-67476. (VIDEA Ser.: Vol. 2). 288p. 1995. 133.00 (*1-56252-243-4*) Computational Mech MA.

Visualization & Machine Vision, 1994 Workshop On: Proceedings. LC 94-75260. 120p. 1994. pap. text ed. 30.00 (*0-8186-5875-4*) IEEE Comp Soc.

***Visualization & Mathematics: Experiments, Simulations & Environments.** Ed. by H. C. Hege & K. Polthier. 380p. 1997. 99.00 (*3-540-61269-6*) Spr-Verlag.

***Visualization & Modeling.** Ed. by Rae Earnshaw et al. LC 97-7557. (Illus.). 496p. 1997. pap. 49.95 (*0-12-227738-4*, AP Prof) Acad Pr.

Visualization & Virtual Reality: Programming with Visual Basic for Windows. Lee Adams. 1993. pap. 49.95 (*0-8306-4121-1*, Windcrest); pap. 39.45 (*0-8306-4124-6*, Windcrest) TAB Bks.

Visualization & Virtual Reality: Three-D Programming with Visual BASIC for Windows. Lee Adams. 1994. text ed. 49.95 (*0-07-000462-5*); pap. text ed. 39.95 (*0-07-000463-3*) McGraw-Hill Prof.

Visualization Directing. Adelaide Bry. 1979. pap. 10.00 (*0-06-092249-4*, PL) HarpC.

Visualization for Beginners. Pauline Wills. (Headway Guide for Beginners Ser.). (Illus.). 128p. 1996. pap. 11.95 (*0-340-65495-3*, Pub. by Headway UK) Trafalgar.

Visualization for Better Health & Mind Expansion. 1991. lib. bdg. 76.95 (*0-8490-4710-2*) Gordon Pr.

Visualization for Change. 2nd ed. Patrick Fanning. LC 94-67044. 338p. 1996. pap. 13.95 (*1-879237-84-9*) New Harbinger.

Visualization for Change. 2nd ed. Patrick Fanning. LC 94-67044. 338p. 1994. 15.95 (*1-879237-85-7*) New Harbinger.

Visualization Graphics in C. Lee Adams. (Applied C Graphics Ser.). (Illus.). 496p. 1990. pap. 26.95 (*0-8306-3487-8*, 3487, Windcrest) TAB Bks.

***Visualization in Biomedical Computing: 4th International Conference, VBC 96, Hamburg, Germany, September 1996: Proceedings.** K. H. Hohne & Ron Kikinis. LC 96-35786. (Lecture Notes in Computer Science Ser.: Vol. 1131). 610p. 1996. 99.00 (*3-540-61649-7*) Spr-Verlag.

Visualization in Biomedical Microscopies: 3-D Imaging & Computer Applications. Ed. by Andres Kriete. LC 92-16841. 404p. 1992. 175.00 (*3-527-28445-1*, VCH) Wiley.

Visualization in Geographic Information Systems. Unwin & Hernshaw. 1994. 99.00 (*1-85293-283-X*, Belhaven) Halsted Pr.

Visualization in Geographical Information Systems. Ed. by Hilary M. Hearnshaw & David J. Unwin. 243p. 1994. text ed. 130.00 (*0-471-94435-1*) Wiley.

Visualization in Human-Computer Interaction: Seventh Interdisciplinary Workshop on Informatics & Psychology Scharding, Austria, May 24-17, 1988 Selected Contributions. Ed. by P. Gorny et al. (Lecture Notes in Computer Science Ser.: Vol. 439). vi, 274p. 1990. 33.00 (*0-387-52698-6*) Spr-Verlag.

Visualization in Modern Cartography. LC 94-19075. (Modern Cell Biology Ser.: No. 2). 368p. 1994. text ed. 127.25 (*0-08-042416-3*, Pergamon Pr) Elsevier.

Visualization in Modern Cartography. Alan M. MacEachren. LC 94-19075. (Modern Cartography Ser.: No. 2). 368p. 1994. pap. text ed. 50.00 (*0-08-042415-5*, Pergamon Pr) Elsevier.

Visualization in Programming. Ed. by P. Gorny & Michael J. Tauber. (Lecture Notes in Computer Science Ser.: Vol. 282). vii, 210p. 1987. 33.00 (*0-387-18507-0*) Spr-Verlag.

Visualization in Scientific Computing. Ed. by M. Gobel et al. LC 94-25235. 1995. 85.00 (*3-211-82633-5*) Spr-Verlag.

Visualization in Scientific Computing. Ed. by M. Grave et al. (Focus on Computer Graphics Ser.). xi, 200p. 1994. 109.00 (*0-387-56147-1*) Spr-Verlag.

Visualization in Supercomputing. Ed. by Raul H. Mendez. (Illus.). 224p. 1990. 54.95 (*0-387-97149-1*) Spr-Verlag.

Visualization in Teaching & Learning Mathematics. Ed. by Walter Zimmermann & Steve Cunningham. LC 90-63690. (MAA Notes Ser.). 230p. (C). 1991. pap. text ed. 34.95 (*0-88385-071-0*, NTE-19) Math Assn.

***Visualization Methods in High Performance Computing & Flow Simulation: Proceedings of the International Workshop on Visualization, Paderborn.** Ed. by W. Borchers et al. (Illus.). 190p. 1996. 162.50 (*90-6764-214-2*, Pub. by VSP NE) Coronet Bks.

Visualization of Climate. Joe R. Eagleman. LC 75-36988. (Illus.). 227p. (C). 1989. reprint ed. text ed. 24.95 (*1-877696-02-1*) Trimedia Pub.

***Visualization of Foreign Language Vocabulary in CALL.** Angela Heidemann. (Duisburg Papers on Research in Language & Culture: Vol. 28). (Illus.). 128p. 1996. pap. 32.95 (*3-631-30685-7*) P Lang Pubng.

Visualization of Heat Transfer Processes. Ed. by R. J. Simoneau & B. F. Armaly. (HTD Ser.: Vol. 252). 108p. 1993. 35.00 (*0-7918-1165-4*, G00809) ASME.

***Visualization of Information Processing in the Human Brain: Recent Advances in MEG & Functional MRI.** I. Hashimoto et al. LC 96-35299. (Electroencephalography & Clinical Neurophysiology Ser. Supplement). 478p. 1996. 262.50 (*0-444-82361-1*) Elsevier.

Visualization of Natural Phenomena. Robert S. Wolff & Larry Yaeger. LC 93-28334. 1993. 72.95 (*0-387-97809-7*); write for info. (*3-540-97809-7*) Spr-Verlag.

Visualization of Nucleic Acids. Gerard Morel. LC 94-22190. 384p. 1995. 131.95 (*0-8493-4781-5*) CRC Pr.

***Visualization of Receptors: Methods in Light & Electron Microscopy.** Ed. by Gerard Morel. LC 96-54597. 512p. 1997. 110.00 (*0-8493-2644-3*) CRC Pr.

Visualization of Scientific Parallel Programs. Gerald Tomas & Christopher W. Ueberhuber. LC 94-2106. (Lecture Notes in Computer Science Ser.: Vol. 771). xi, 310p. 1994. 50.95 (*0-387-57738-6*) Spr-Verlag.

Visualization Quest: A History of Computer Animation. Valliere R. Auzenne. LC 90-56229. 1994. 32.50 (*0-8386-3440-0*) Fairleigh Dickinson.

Visualization Techniques. 2nd ed. Leinbach. 1990. pap. text ed. 63.00 (*0-13-946518-9*) P-H.

Visualization Toolkit. Ken Martin et al. 1996. 59.95 (*0-614-14485-X*) P-H Pro Soft.

***Visualization Toolkit: An Object-Oriented Approach to 3D Graphics.** 2nd ed. Will Schroeder & Ken Martin. 1997. 69.95 (*0-13-954694-4*) P-H.

Visualization 1996 Conference, 7th IEEE. IEEE Staff. 500p. 1996. pap. text ed. 100.00 (*0-8186-7665-5*, PR07665) IEEE Comp Soc.

Visualization '95 Conference, 6th IEEE. LC 10-702385. 512p. 1995. 100.00 (*0-8186-7187-4*, PR07187) IEEE Comp Soc.

Visualize. Bobby G. Price. 58p. (Orig.). 1986. pap. 10.00 (*0-932662-60-9*) St Andrews NC.

Visualized Flight Maneuvers: For Low Wing Aircraft, for Instructors & Students. 2nd rev. ed. Ed. by ASA Staff. (Illus.). 58p. 1996. spiral bd. 16.95 (*1-56027-249-X*, ASA-VFM-LO) Av Suppl & Acad.

Visualized Flight Maneuvers Handbook. rev. ed. Harold J. Holmes. (Illus.). 192p. 1985. spiral bd. 20.00 (*0-940766-05-1*) Haldon Bks.

Visualized Flight Maneuvers Handbook: For High Wing Aircraft, for Instructors & Students. 2nd rev. ed. Ed. by ASA Staff. (Illus.). 58p. 1996. spiral bd. 16.95 (*1-56027-248-1*) Av Suppl & Acad.

Visualized Flight Maneuvers (High Wing) (Illus.). reprint ed. 20.00 (*0-614-13204-5*, 21-15810) EAA Aviation.

Visualized Flow. Japanese Society of Mechanical Engineering Staff. 1988. 78.95 (*0-08-034065-2*, Prgamon Press) Buttrwrth-Heinemann.

Visualizing Abstract Objects & Relations. Ed. by Tomihisa Kamada. (Series in Computer Science: Vol. 5). 176p. (C). 1989. text ed. 48.00 (*981-02-0009-9*) World Scientific Pub.

Visualizing & Verbalizing for Language Comprehension & Thinking. 2nd ed. Nanci Bell. (Illus.). 225p. 1991. pap. 29.95 (*0-945856-02-4*); lib. bdg. 29.95 (*0-945856-01-6*) Nancibell Inc.

***Visualizing Boccaccio.** Jill M. Ricketts. (Cambridge Studies in New Art History & Criticism). (Illus.). 256p. (C). 1997. text ed. 60.00 (*0-521-49600-4*) Cambridge U Pr.

***Visualizing Calculus: Powerful Programs for Graphing Calculators.** Clarence Hopper. 1997. pap. text ed. 17.95 (*1-57232-442-2*) Seymour Pubns.

Visualizing Chemistry: Investigations for Teachers. Julie B. Ealy & James L. Ealy, Jr. (Professional Reference Book Ser.). (Illus.). 434p. 1995. pap. text ed. 24.95 (*0-8412-2919-8*) Am Chemical.

Visualizing Data. William S. Cleveland. LC 92-75077. (Illus.). 360p. 1993. 45.00 (*0-9634884-0-6*) Hobart Pr.

***Visualizing Deviance: A Study of News Organization.** R. V. Ericson et al. 400p. 1987. 45.00 (*0-335-15515-4*, Open Univ Pr) Taylor & Francis.

***Visualizing Deviance: A Study of News Organization.** R. V. Ericson et al. 400p. 1987. pap. 16.99 (*0-335-15514-6*, Open Univ Pr) Taylor & Francis.

Visualizing Deviance: A Study of News Organizations. Richard V. Ericson et al. 390p. 1987. pap. 21.95 (*0-8020-6640-2*) U of Toronto Pr.

Visualizing Economics: The Art of Investing Without Statistics. Curtis McKallip. (Illus.). 146p. 1991. write for info. (*1-878353-22-5*) Silent Partners.

Visualizing Ireland: National Identity & the Pictorial Tradition. Ed. by Adele M. Dalsimer. 176p. (Orig.). 1993. pap. 16.95 (*0-571-19813-9*) Faber & Faber.

Visualizing Muscles: A New Ecorche Approach to Surface Anatomy. John Cody. LC 90-50112. (Illus.). xiv, 242p. 1991. pap. 25.00 (*0-7006-0426-X*) U Pr of KS.

Visualizing Number Concepts, Unit II. Albert Bennett et al. (Math & the Mind's Eye Ser.). (Illus.). 49p. (C). 1988. teacher ed., ring bd. 8.00 (*1-886131-14-7*, ME2) Math Lrning.

Visualizing Software: A Graphic Notation for Analysis, Design, & Discussion. Bennett. 208p. 1992. 99.75 (*0-8247-8714-5*) Dekker.

Visualizing the Moral Life. Clifford Davidson. LC 88-47809. (AMS Studies in the Middle Ages: No. 16). 1989. 39.50 (*0-404-61446-9*) AMS Pr.

Visualizing Theory: Selected Essays from V.A.R., 1990-1993. Ed. by Lucien Taylor. LC 93-31997. 500p. (C). 1994. text ed. 74.95 (*0-415-90842-6*, Pub. by Tavistock UK) Routledge Chapman & Hall.

Visualizing Theory: Selected Essays from V.A.R., 1990-1993. Ed. by Lucien Taylor. LC 93-31997. 500p. (C). (gr. 13). 1994. pap. 24.95 (*0-415-90843-4*, Pub. by Tavistock UK) Routledge Chapman & Hall.

Visualizing with CAD: Why & How to Generate Forms from Geometry to Architecture Using AutoCAD. Daniela Bertol. LC 94-17611. 384p. 1994. pap. 49.95 (*0-387-94275-0*) Spr-Verlag.

Visually Impaired: Curricular Access & Entitlemennt in Further Education. Ed. by David T. Etheridge & Heather L. Mason. 144p. 1994. pap. 27.50 (*1-85346-248-9*, Pub. by D Fulton UK) Taylor & Francis.

Visually Impaired Seniors As Senior Companions: A Reference Guide for Program Development. 108p. 1992. pap. 20.00 (*0-89128-238-6*) Am Foun Blind.

Visually Limited Child. R. Bonner et al. 1970. pap. text ed. 12.95 (*0-8422-0061-4*) Irvington.

Visually Programming with Os-2. Williams. 1996. pap. 36.95 (*0-442-01837-1*) Van Nos Reinhold.

Visually Responsive Neuron: From Basic Neurophysiology to Behavior. Ed. by T. P. Hicks et al. LC 92-48461. (Progress in Brain Research Ser.: Vol. 95). 488p. 1993. 296.50 (*0-444-89492-6*) Elsevier.

Visuals for the Language Classroom. A. Wright & S. Haleem. (C). 1991. pap. text ed. 20.67 (*0-582-04781-1*, 79113) Longman.

Visuals of the Clinical Histocompatibility Workshop: Palm Springs Invitational. Compiled by Paul I. Terasaki. LC 88-60350. (Illus.). 173p. (Orig.). 1988. pap. 10.00 (*0-945756-00-3*, VIS88) One Lambda.

Visuals of the Clinical Histocompatibility Workshop: Palm Springs Invitational, February 1989. Compiled by Paul I. Terasaki. (Illus.). 200p. (Orig.). 1989. pap. 10.00 (*0-945756-01-1*, VIS89) One Lambda.

Visuddhimagga of Buddhaghosacariya. Henry C. Warren & Dharmananda D. Kosambi. (C). 1989. reprint ed. 67.50 (*81-208-0653-0*, Pub. by Motilal Banarsidass II) S Asia.

Visuel: Dictionnaire Thematique: French & English. Jean-Claude Corbeil. 928p. (ENG & FRE.). 1992. 115.00 (*0-7859-8025-3*, 2761910834) Fr & Eur.

Visuo-Spatial Working Memory. Logie. 176p. 1995. 34.50 (*0-86377-107-6*) L Erlbaum Assocs.

Visuomotor Coordination: Amphibians, Comparisons, Models, & Robots. Ed. by J. P. Ewert & Michael A. Arbib. (Illus.). 954p. 1989. 165.00 (*0-306-43230-7*, Plenum Pr) Plenum.

Visvakarmiya Rathalaksanam: Study of Ancient Indian Chariots. R. P. Kulkarni. (C). 1994. 34.00 (*81-7391-004-9*, Pub. by Kanishka) S Asia.

Visvambhara: Probings in Orientology, 2 vols., Set. Ed. by Ajay M. Shastri et al. (C). 1995. 200.00 (*81-85151-76-8*, Pub. by Harman II) S Asia.

Visvarupa. T. S. Maxwell. (Illus.). 382p. 1989. 29.95 (*0-19-562117-4*) OUP.

Viswambhara. C. Narayana Reddy. 66p. 1987. text ed. 15.95 (*81-207-0578-5*, Pub. by Sterling Pubs II) Apt Bks.

Vita: A Grandfather's Story. Nicholas Romanelli. Ed. by Dorothy H. Romanelli. (Illus.). 185p. (Orig.). 1981. pap. 6.50 (*0-9606104-0-5*) Port Pr.

Vita Craft: Los Fundamentos. Ed. by Cheri Sparks. 208p. (SPA.). 1995. 24.95 (*0-9648421-2-2*) Vita Craft.

Vita Craft: The Basics. Ed. by Cheri Sparks. 208p. 1995. 24.95 (*0-9648421-0-6*) Vita Craft.

Vita Haroldi: The Romance of the Life of Harold, King of England. Ed. by William D. Birch. Tr. by William D. Birch. LC 80-2232. reprint ed. 36.00 (*0-404-18753-6*) AMS Pr.

Vita Italiana. G. Dekovic. (C). 1985. 85.00 (*0-8442-8039-9*, Pub. by S Thornes Pubs UK) St Mut.

Vita Leonis IX. Wibertus of Toul. Tr. by Richard Hamilton from LAT. 1996. lib. bdg. 40.00 (*0-89241-560-6*) Caratzas.

Vita Mathematics: Historical Research & Integration with Teaching. Ed. by Ronald Calinger. LC 96-75298. (MAA Notes Ser.: No. 40). 350p. (Orig.). 1996. pap. text ed. 35.95 (*0-88385-097-4*, NTE-40) Math Assn.

Vita Nuoja: A Book of Poems Written in English & Translated from Russian by the Author. Jan Probstein. Ed. by Michael Graves. 64p. (Orig.). 1993. pap. 4.00 (*0-9635200-3-2*) R E M Pr.

Vita Nuova. Dante Alighieri. Tr. by Barbara Reynolds from ITA. (Classics Ser.). 128p. 1969. pap. 8.95 (*0-14-044216-2*, Penguin Classics) Viking Penguin.

Vita Nuova. Dante Alighieri. Ed. by Mark Musa. (World's Classics Ser.). 128p. 1992. pap. 5.95 (*0-19-282877-0*, Penguin Classics) Viking Penguin.

Vita Nuova. Dante Alighieri. Tr. by Dino S. Cervigni & Edward Vasta from ITA. LC 95-2300. 339p. 1996. pap. text ed. 16.95 (*0-268-01926-6*) U of Notre Dame Pr.

Vita Nuova. Dante Alighieri. Tr. & Intro. by Theodore Martin. (Select Bibliographies Reprint Ser.). 1977. reprint ed. 18.95 (*0-8369-6797-6*, Penguin Classics) Viking Penguin.

Vita Nuova: Italian Text with Facing English Translation. Dante Alighieri. Tr. by Dino S. Cervigni & Edward Vasta. LC 95-2300. 339p. (ENG & ITA.). (C). 1995. text ed. 34.95 (*0-268-01925-8*) U of Notre Dame Pr.

Vita Patrum: The Life of the Fathers. St. Gregory of Tours. Ed. & Tr. by Seraphim Rose. LC 88-60562. (Illus.). 330p. (Orig.). 1988. pap. 15.00 (*0-938635-23-9*) St Herman Pr.

Vita S. Remigii see Giraldi Cambrensis Opera

Vita Sancti Columbae. Saint Adamnan. Ed. by William Reeves. LC 79-174801. (Bannatyne Club, Edinburgh. Publications: No. 103). reprint ed. 94.50 (*0-404-52858-9*) AMS Pr.

Vita Sexualis. Ogai Mori. Tr. by Sanford Goldstein & Kazuji Ninomiya. LC 72-79020. 156p. 1972. pap. 8.95 (*0-8048-1048-6*) C E Tuttle.

Vita Viri Clarissimi et Famosissimi Kyriaci Anconitani. Ed. by Edward W. Bodnar & Charles Mitchell. LC 94-78512. (Transactions of the American Philosophical Society Ser.: Vol. 86, Pt. 4). 278p. (Orig.). 1996. pap. 25.00 (*0-87169-864-1*, T864-boe) Am Philos.

Vitae Dunkeldensis Ecclesiae Episcoporum, a Prima Sedis Foundatione, Ad Annum MDXV Ab Alexandro Myln, Eiusdem Ecclesiae Canonica Conscriptae, Repr. Of 1823 Ed. Alexander Mylne. Ed. by Thomas Thomson. Bd. with Compotum Magistri Fabrice Pontis Dunkeldensis, MDXIII-MDXVI. LC 78-173008. LC 78-173008. 20.00 (*0-404-52701-9*) AMS Pr.

Vitae Sanctorum Hiberniae, Vol. I. Ed. by Charles Plummer. (Celtic Studies). 463p. 1997. 65.00 (*1-85182-225-9*, Pub. by Four Cts Pr IE) Intl Spec Bk.

Vitae Sanctorum Hiberniae, Vol. II. Ed. by Charles Plummer. (Celtic Studies). 463p. 1997. 65.00 (*1-85182-226-7*, Pub. by Four Cts Pr IE) Intl Spec Bk.

Vitae Sophistarum. Flavius Philostratus. xlii, 416p. 1971. reprint ed. write for info. (*3-487-04155-3*) G Olms Pubs.

Vital: Three Contemporary African Artists. Intro. by Abdelwahab Meddeb. (Illus.). 48p. (C). 1996. pap. 20.00 (*1-85437-170-3*, Pub. by Tate Gallery UK) U of Wash Pr.

Vital Adult Learning: Choices to Fit Your Church. R. Wade Paschal, Jr. LC 93-28212. (Choices to Fit Your Church Ser.). 144p. (Orig.). 1994. pap. 7.77 (*0-687-00773-9*) Abingdon.

Vital & Health Statistics of the U. S. Natality & Mortality, 2 vols., Set. 1994. lib. bdg. 1,795.95 (*0-8490-5817-1*) Gordon Pr.

Vital & Health Statistics Series: An Annotated Checklist & Index to the Publications of the "Rainbow Series" Jim Walsh & A. James Bothmer. LC 91-18077. (Bibliographies & Indexes in Medical Studies: No. 7). 408p. 1991. text ed. 79.50 (*0-313-27260-3*, WVH, Greenwood Pr) Greenwood.

Vital & Important Appeal to the United Nations. Marie B. Hall. 1974. pap. 6.50 (*0-938760-05-X*) Veritat Found.

Vital Apologetics Issues: Examining Reason & Revelation in Biblical Perspective. Roy B. Zuck. 264p. 1995. pap. 12.99 (*0-8254-4070-X*, 95-002) Kregel.

Vital Balance: The Life Process in Mental Health & Illness. Karl A. Menninger. 1983. 21.55 (*0-8446-6077-9*) Peter Smith.

***Vital Balance: The Life Process in Mental Health & Illness.** Karl A. Menninger. 1983. 21.75 (*0-8446-6125-2*) Peter Smith.

Vital Biblical Issues: Examining Problem Passages of the Bible. Roy B. Zuck. LC 94-31339. 280p. 1994. pap. 12.99 (*0-8254-4072-6*) Kregel.

***Vital Center: The Politics of Freedom.** Arthur M. Schlesinger. LC 97-23127. 1997. pap. write for info. (*1-56000-989-6*) Transaction Pubs.

Vital Center: The Politics of Freedom. Arthur M. Schlesinger. (Quality Paperbacks Ser.). 300p. 1988. reprint ed. pap. 10.95 (*0-306-80323-2*) Da Capo.

***Vital Century.** Rule. 1992. text ed. write for info. (*0-582-49424-9*, Pub. by Longman UK) Longman.

Vital Century, 1714-1815. John Rule. (Social & Economic History of England Ser.). 334p. (C). 1991. pap. text ed. 30.50 (*0-582-49425-7*, 79211) Longman.

***Vital Christian Living Issues: Examining Crucial Concerns in the Spiritual Life.** Ed. by Roy B. Zuck. (Vital Issues Ser.). 256p. (Orig.). 1997. pap. 12.99 (*0-8254-4097-1*) Kregel.

***Vital Christology Issues: Examining Contemporary & Classic Concerns.** Ed. by Roy B. Zuck. (Vital Issues Ser.). 256p. (Orig.). 1997. pap. 12.99 (*0-8254-4096-3*) Kregel.

An Asterisk (*) at the beginning of an entry indicates that the title is appearing in BIP for the first time.

Vital Church Leader. Robert Cueni. Ed. by Herb Miller. (Effective Church Ser.). 128p. 1991. pap. 7.77 (*0-687-43793-8*) Abingdon.

Vital Circuits: On Pumps, Pipes, & the Workings of Circulatory Systems. Steven Vogel. (Illus.). 336p. 1993. reprint ed. pap. 12.95 (*0-19-508269-9*) OUP.

Vital Concept of Personal Growth. Manly P. Hall. pap. 4.95 (*0-89314-367-7*) Philos Res.

Vital Congregation: Ten Basic Measurements. Herb Miller. LC 90-31095. (Effective Church Ser.). 1990. pap. 12.95 (*0-687-43796-2*) Abingdon.

Vital Connections: Children, Science, & Books. Ed. by Wendy Saul & Sybille A. Jagusch. LC 91-46814. (Illus.). 165p. 1992. pap. 15.95 (*0-435-08332-5*, 08332) Heinemann.

Vital Connections: Children, Science, & Books. Ed. by Wendy Saul & Sybille A. Jagusch. LC 90-27430. 165p. 1991. 13.00 (*0-8444-0714-3*) Lib Congress.

Vital Contemporary Issues: Examining Current Questions & Controversies. Roy B. Zuck. LC 94-6931. 272p. 1994. pap. 12.99 (*0-8254-4071-8*) Kregel.

Vital Continuum. rev. ed. Ed. by Eugene D. Fleharty & Gary K. Hulett. LC 80-50300. (Illus.). 500p. 1980. pap. 5.00 (*0-936352-00-0*, B511) U of KS Cont Ed.

Vital Control: Forest Essays, First Series. Lynn H. Hough. LC 70-117809. (Essay Index Reprint Ser.). 1977. 21.95 (*0-8369-1756-1*) Ayer.

Vital Corporation. Garry Jacobs. 1990. 19.95 (*0-13-946450-6*) P-H.

Vital Crises in Italian Cinema: Iconography, Stylistics, Politics. P. Adam Sitney. (Illus.). 288p. (C). 1995. pap. 17.95 (*0-292-77688-8*); text ed. 45.00 (*0-292-77687-X*) U of Tex Pr.

Vital Dust: Life As a Cosmic Imperative. Christian De Duve. (Illus.). 384p. 1996. pap. 14.00 (*0-465-09045-1*) Basic.

***Vital Dye Staining of Giardia & Cryptosporidium.** Miodrag Belosevic. LC 97-22877. 1997. write for info. (*0-89867-913-3*) Am Water Wks Assn.

Vital Energy Easy Oriental Exercises for Health & Wellbeing. J. Young. (Illus.). 128p. 1991. text ed. 15.95 (*0-340-54549-6*, Pub. by Hodder & Stoughton Ltd UK) Lubrecht & Cramer.

Vital Enthusiasm. James E. Melton. LC 82-81903. 232p. 1983. 12.95 (*0-9604752-1-4*) Global Pubns CA.

Vital Factors For The Recovery Of The Church Life. Witness Lee. 85p. per. 3.50 (*0-87083-228-X*, 08028001) Living Stream Ministry.

Vital Facts about Foods: A Guide to Health & Longevity. Otto Carque. 208p. 1974. reprint ed. spiral bd. 12.50 (*0-7873-0148-5*) Hlth Research.

Vital Few: The Entrepreneur & American Economic Progress. Jonathan Hughes. 576p. 1986. pap. 15.95 (*0-19-504038-4*) OUP.

Vital Force. Franlin M. Harold. 1995. pap. text ed. write for info. (*0-7167-1736-0*) W H Freeman.

***Vital Force: A Proposal for the Overhaul of the U. N. Peace Operating System & for the Creation of a U. N. Legion.** Carl Conetta & Charles Knight. 141p. 1995. pap. write for info. (*1-881677-05-2*) Commonwlth Inst.

Vital Force: A Study of Bioenergetics. Franklin M. Harold. LC 85-13640. (Illus.). 577p. (C). 1995. text ed. write for info. (*0-7167-1734-4*) W H Freeman.

Vital Force: Physico-Physiological Researches on the Dynamics of Magnetism, Electricity, Heat, Light, Crystalization & Chemism in Their Relations to Vital Force. Charles Von Reichenbach. (Alternative Energy Ser.). 1991. lib. bdg. 88.00 (*0-8490-4262-3*) Gordon Pr.

Vital Force: Physico-Physiological Researches on the Dynamics of Magnetism, Electricity, Heat, Light, Crystalization & Chemism in Their Relations to Vital Force. Charles Von Reichenbach. 1991. lib. bdg. 79.95 (*0-87700-995-3*) Revisionist Pr.

***Vital Guide to Combat Guns & Infantry Weapons.** Ed. by Chris Bishop. (Illus.). 128p. 1996. 14.95 (*1-85310-539-2*) Specialty Pr.

Vital Guide to Commercial Aircraft & Airliners. Voyageur Press Staff. Ed. by Robert Hewson. (Illus.). 128p. 14.95 (*1-85310-538-4*) Specialty Pr.

***Vital Guide to Major Airlines of the World: Voices of October.** Bobeit Hewson. (Illus.). 128p. 1997. 14.95 (*1-85310-581-3*) Voyageur Pr.

Vital Guide to Military Aircraft. Ed. by Sophearith Moeng. (Illus.). 128p. 14.95 (*1-85310-537-6*) Specialty Pr.

Vital Health Facts & Composition of Foods. Patricia Krimmel & Edward A. Krimmel. (Illus.). 96p. (Orig.). 1994. pap. 4.50 (*0-916503-06-2*) Franklin Pubs.

Vital Information for My Heirs. Robert Berko & Frank Jarvie. 96p. pap. write for info. (*0-934873-18-6*) Consumer Ed Res.

Vital Interests: The Soviet Issue in U. S. Central American Policy. Ed. by Bruce D. Larkin. LC 87-39458. 512p. (C). 1988. pap. text ed. 16.95 (*1-55587-112-7*); lib. bdg. 42.00 (*1-55587-111-9*) Lynne Rienner.

Vital Involvement in Old Age: The Experience of Old Age in Our Time. Erik H. Erikson et al. 352p. 1994. pap. 12.00 (*0-393-31216-X*, Norton Paperbks) Norton.

Vital Issues in Christian Science: A Record of Unsettled Questions... Augusta E. Stetson. LC 91-71097. vii, 405p. 1991. reprint ed. 20.00 (*1-879135-08-6*) Emma Pub Soc.

Vital Issues of the Constitution. 1988. teacher ed., pap. 8.68 (*0-395-48341-7*) HM.

Vital Issues of the Constitution. 1988. pap. 18.68 (*0-395-48340-9*) HM.

Vital Judo: Grappling Techniques. Isai Okano. pap. 14.95 (*0-685-70712-1*) Wehman.

Vital Judo: Throwing Techniques. T. Sato & Isai Okano. pap. 14.95 (*0-685-38458-6*) Wehman.

Vital Lies. Ellen Hart. 256p. (Orig.). 1994. reprint ed. mass mkt. 4.99 (*0-345-38141-6*) Ballantine.

Vital Lies, Simple Truths. Daniel Goleman. 1996. pap. 12.00 (*0-684-83107-4*) S&S Trade.

Vital Link. 2nd ed. American College of Emergency Physicians Staff. 99p. (gr. 13). 1994. 65.00 (*0-8151-0064-7*) Mosby Yr Bk.

Vital Link Vol. 1: With CEH Packet. American College of Emergency Physicians Staff. 1993. suppl. ed., text ed. 65.00 (*0-07-000211-8*) McGraw.

Vital Link Vol. 2: With CEH Packet, Vol. 2. American College of Emergency Physicians Staff. 1994. suppl. ed., text ed. 65.00 (*0-07-000212-6*) McGraw.

Vital Link I. American College of Emergency Physicians Staff. (gr. 13). 1994. 65.00 (*0-8151-0063-9*) Mosby Yr Bk.

Vital Machine: A Study of Technology & Organic Life. David F. Channell. (Illus.). 216p. 1991. 25.00 (*0-19-506040-7*) OUP.

Vital Magnetic Cure: An Exposition of Vital Magnetism & Its Application to the Treatment of Mental & Physical Disease. 4th ed. 216p. 1975. reprint ed. spiral bd. 13.50 (*0-7873-0011-X*) Hlth Research.

Vital Magnetic Power: Mesmerism, Hopnotism, & Thought Reading. Frank H. Handall. 57p. 1959. reprint ed. spiral bd. 7.00 (*0-7873-0366-6*) Hlth Research.

Vital Message. Arthur Conan Doyle. 164p. 1994. pap. 14.95 (*1-56459-450-5*) Kessinger Pub.

Vital Ministry Issues: Examining Concerns & Conflicts in Ministry. Roy B. Zuck. LC 94-6932. 288p. 1994. pap. 12.99 (*0-8254-4068-8*) Kregel.

***Vital Minute.** Roger Ormerod. 224p. 1996. 22.00 (*0-7278-5152-7*) Severn Hse.

Vital Mummies: Performance Design for the Show-Window Mannequin. Sara K. Schneider. LC 94-40233. 1995. 35.00 (*0-300-06039-4*) Yale U Pr.

Vital New Testament Issues: Examining New Testament Passages & Problems. Ed. by Roy B. Zuck. 256p. 1996. pap. 12.99 (*0-8254-4074-2*) Kregel.

Vital Oils. Liz Earle. (Illus.). 186p. 1993. pap. 13.95 (*0-09-174974-3*, Pub. by Ebury Pr UK) Trafalgar.

Vital Old Testament Issues: Examining Textual & Topical Questions. Ed. by Roy B. Zuck. 256p. 1996. pap. 12.99 (*0-8254-4073-4*) Kregel.

Vital Parts. Nancy Fisher. 384p. (Orig.). 1993. mass mkt. 4.99 (*0-451-17498-4*, Sig) NAL-Dutton.

Vital Past: Writings on the Uses of History. Ed. by Stephen Vaughn. LC 84-16204. 424p. 1985. pap. 20.00 (*0-8203-0754-8*) U of Ga Pr.

Vital Problems in Social Evolution: An Introduction to the Materialist Conception of History. Arthur M. Lewis. (Science for the Workers Ser.). 192p. 1984. 17.95 (*0-88286-089-5*) C H Kerr.

Vital Prophetic Issues: Examining Promises & Problems in Eschatology. Ed. by Roy B. Zuck. LC 95-35768. (Vital Issues Ser.: Vol. 3). 296p. 1995. pap. 12.99 (*0-8254-4067-X*, 95-034) Kregel.

Vital Rationalist: Selected Writings from Georges Canguilhem. Georges Canguilhem. Ed. by Francois Delaporte. Tr. by Arthur Goldhammer. LC 93-8613. 481p. 1994. 27.95 (*0-942299-72-8*) Zone Bks.

Vital Record of Cranston, Johnston & North Providence, Rhode Island. James N. Arnold. (Vital Record of Rhode Island Ser.: Vol. 2, Pts. 2, 3 & 4). 138p. 1983. reprint ed. lib. bdg. 14.00 (*0-912606-12-6*) Hunterdon Hse.

Vital Record of Providence, Rhode Island. James N. Arnold. (Vital Record of Rhode Island Ser.: Vol. 2, Pt. 1). 304p. 1988. lib. bdg. 21.00 (*0-912606-31-2*) Hunterdon Hse.

Vital Record of Warwick, Rhode Island. James N. Arnold. (Vital Record of Rhode Island Ser.: Vol. 1, Pt. 1). 234p. 1983. reprint ed. lib. bdg. 16.00 (*0-912606-11-8*) Hunterdon Hse.

***Vital Record of (West Greenwich), 1636-1850: Births, Marriages & Deaths.** James N. Arnold. 109p. 1997. reprint ed. pap. 15.00 (*0-8328-6491-9*) Higginson Bk Co.

Vital Records: A Guideline. 2nd ed. 29p. 1993. pap. 18.00 (*0-933887-14-0*, A4543) ARMA Intl.

Vital Records: Town of Chatham, 1851-1900. Ed. by Anna-Lowell Tomlinson. 576p. 1993. write for info. (*0-9615051-4-1*) Chatham His Soc.

Vital Records from Chicago Newspapers 1833-1839. 64p. 1971. pap. 6.00 (*1-881125-01-7*) Chi Geneal Soc.

Vital Records from Chicago Newspapers 1840-1842. 102p. 1972. pap. 7.00 (*1-881125-02-5*) Chi Geneal Soc.

Vital Records from Chicago Newspapers 1843-1844. 57p. 1974. pap. 6.00 (*1-881125-03-3*) Chi Geneal Soc.

Vital Records from Chicago Newspapers 1845. 72p. 1975. pap. 6.00 (*1-881125-04-1*) Chi Geneal Soc.

Vital Records from Chicago Newspapers 1846. 95p. 1976. pap. 6.00 (*1-881125-05-X*) Chi Geneal Soc.

Vital Records from Chicago Newspapers 1847. 102p. 1979. pap. 7.00 (*1-881125-06-8*) Chi Geneal Soc.

Vital Records from Chicago Newspapers 1848. 107p. 1980. pap. 7.00 (*1-881125-07-6*) Chi Geneal Soc.

Vital Records from Dover, New Hampshire's First Newspaper 1790-1829. William E. Wentworth. (New Hampshire Society of Genealogists Special Publication Ser.: No. 6). 411p. 1995. 37.50 (*0-89725-217-9*, 1593) Picton Pr.

***Vital Records from the Eastport Sentinel of Eastport Maine 1818-1900.** Ed. by Kenneth L. Willey. LC 95-73100. 884p. 1996. 54.50 (*0-89725-249-7*, 1678) Picton Pr.

Vital Records from the Thomaston Recorder of Thomaston, Maine 1837-1846. Tr. by Steven E. Sullivan. (Maine Genealogical Society Special Publication: No. 23). 128p. 1995. 20.00 (*0-89725-237-3*, 1610) Picton Pr.

Vital Records of Appleton - Knox County, ME Prior to 1892. 246p. 1993. 65.00 (*0-929539-65-6*, 1165) Picton Pr.

***Vital Records of Appleton - Knox County, ME Prior to 1892: Facsimile Edition.** (Illus.). 603p. 1993. 79.50 (*0-89725-162-8*, 1510) Picton Pr.

***Vital Records of Barrington, 1720-1851.** Priscilla Hammond. 110p. 1997. reprint ed. pap. 15.00 (*0-8328-5974-5*) Higginson Bk Co.

Vital Records of Berwick, South Berwick & North Berwick, Maine Prior to 1892. Ed. by John E. Frost & Joseph C. Anderson, II. LC 92-62229. 864p. 1993. 62.50 (*0-929539-79-6*, 1337) Picton Pr.

***Vital Records of Bowdoin to the Year 1892: Volume I, Births; Volume II, Births & Deaths; Volume III, Marriages.** Ed. by Rachel T. Cox. (Illus.). 583p. 1997. reprint ed. lib. bdg. 57.50 (*0-8328-5814-5*) Higginson Bk Co.

Vital Records of Charlestown, Massachusetts, to the Year 1850, Vol. 1. Ed. by Roger D. Joslyn. LC 84-25427. 919p. 1984. lib. bdg. 30.00 (*0-88082-009-8*) New Eng Hist.

Vital Records of Cortlandtown Reformed Church, Montrose NY, 1741-1894. Arthur C. Kelly. LC 80-123822. (Palatine Transcripts Ser.). 106p. 1980. lib. bdg. 23.00 (*1-56012-047-9*, 46) Kinship Rhinebeck.

Vital Records of Falmouth, Massachusetts to the Year 1850. Ed. by Oliver B. Brown. LC 76-3955. 272p. 1993. reprint ed. 22.50 (*0-89725-108-3*, 1403) Picton Pr.

***Vital Records of Farmingdale Maine to the Year 1892.** Ed. by Henry S. Webster. 96p. 1996. reprint ed. pap. 17.50 (*0-8328-5199-X*) Higginson Bk Co.

Vital Records of Farmingdale, Maine to Year 1892. Ed. by Henry S. Webster. 96p. 1993. reprint ed. lib. bdg. 18.00 (*0-8328-3190-5*) Higginson Bk Co.

Vital Records of First Lutheran Church, Albany, NY, 1774-1842: (ALbany Evangelical Lutheran Church Called Ebenezer) (Baptismal Register 1774-1843, Marriage Register 1794-1842 Index Ser.). 345p. 1993. pap. 52.00 (*1-56012-129-7*, 84D) Kinship Rhinebeck.

Vital Records of Freedom, Waldo County, Maine Prior to 1892. Tr. by Elizabeth M. Mosher. (Illus.). 194p. 1991. lib. bdg. 65.00 (*0-929539-81-8*, 1181) Picton Pr.

***Vital Records of Gardiner Maine to the Year 1892 Pt. II: Marriages & Deaths.** Ed. by Henry S. Webster. 675p. 1996. reprint ed. lib. bdg. 69.50 (*0-8328-5200-7*) Higginson Bk Co.

***Vital Records of Greenland, 1710-1851.** Priscilla Hammond. 172p. 1997. reprint ed. pap. 22.50 (*0-8328-5992-3*) Higginson Bk Co.

***Vital Records of Hallowell, to the Year 1892, 6 vols. in 3.** Ed. by Mabel G. Hall. (Illus.). 1997. reprint ed. lib. bdg. 110.00 (*0-8328-5850-1*) Higginson Bk Co.

Vital Records of Hamilton, Massachusetts to 1849. 1908. 15.00 (*0-88389-075-5*, Essx Institute) Peabody Essex Mus.

***Vital Records of Hampstead, 1731-1870. With Supplement, Abstracts from the Church Records, 1752-1866.** Priscilla Hammond. 467p. 1997. reprint ed. lib. bdg. 47.00 (*0-8328-5993-1*) Higginson Bk Co.

Vital Records of Hampton, New Hampshire to the End of the Year 1900, Vol. 1. Ed. by George F. Sanborn, Jr. & Melinde L. Sanborn. xii, 665p. 1992. 40.00 (*0-88082-032-2*) New Eng Hist.

Vital Records of Jackson Maine Pror to 1892. LC 89-61082. 249p. 1989. lib. bdg. 110.00 (*0-929539-28-1*, 1128) Picton Pr.

Vital Records of Jerusalem Reformed Church: Baptisms, 1792-1886; Marriages, 1822-1885; Deaths, 1851-1890; Feura Bush, Albany County, NY. Florence Christoph. Ed. by Arthur C. Kelly. (Palatine Transcripts Ser.). 140p. 1987. lib. bdg. 28.00 (*1-56012-082-7*, 81) Kinship Rhinebeck.

Vital Records of Kingston, New Hampshire 1694-1994. Judith A. Arseneault. 315p. 1995. pap. 27.50 (*0-614-09966-8*) Clearfield Co.

Vital Records of Kittery, Maine: To the Year 1892. Joseph C. Anderson & Lois W. Thurston. LC 91-62157. 640p. 1991. 49.50 (*0-929539-73-7*, 1173) Picton Pr.

Vital Records of Lawyersville Reformed Church, Lawyersville, Schoharie County, New York: Baptisms 1790-1876, Marriages 1790-1882. Ed. by Lawrence V. Rickard. 1995. lib. bdg. 30.00 (*1-56012-142-4*, 140) Kinship Rhinebeck.

Vital Records of Lebanon, Maine to the Year 1892, Vol. 1 - Births. Ed. by George W. Chamberlain. 1986. reprint ed. pap. 6.00 (*0-935207-51-1*) Danbury Hse Bks.

Vital Records of Lincolnville, Maine. Elizabeth M. Mosher. (Illus.). 394p. 1993. lib. bdg. 85.00 (*0-89725-098-2*, 1130) Picton Pr.

Vital Records of Lisbon, Maine Prior to 1892. Marlene Groves. (Maine Genealogical Society Special Publication: No. 19). 509p. 1995. 39.95 (*0-89725-213-6*, 1562) Picton Pr.

Vital Records of Londonderry, New Hampshire 1719-1910. Daniel G. Annis. 328p. 1994. reprint ed. 25.00 (*0-8063-1415-X*) Genealog Pub.

Vital Records of Low Dutch Church of Klyn Esopus, Ulster Park NY, 1791-1899. Arthur C. Kelly. (Palatine Transcripts Ser.). 151p. 1980. lib. bdg. 29.00 (*1-56012-049-5*, 48) Kinship Rhinebeck.

***Vital Records of Lubec, Maine Prior to 1892.** Ed. by Patricia M. Townsend. LC 96-67592. 338p. 1996. 39.50 (*0-89725-258-6*, 1738) Picton Pr.

Vital Records of Lynnfield, Massachusetts to 1849. 1907. 15.00 (*0-88389-077-1*, Essx Institute) Peabody Essex Mus.

Vital Records of Manchester, Massachusetts, to the End of the Year 1849. LC 04-9195. 298p. 1903. 15.00 (*0-88389-035-6*, Essx Institute) Peabody Essex Mus.

Vital Records of Marshfield, Massachusetts to the Year 1850. Ed. by Robert M. Sherman. LC 71-4447. 512p. 1993. reprint ed. 39.50 (*0-89725-106-7*, 1401) Picton Pr.

Vital Records of Mount Desert Island, Maine, 1776-1820: And Other Nearby Islands. Ed. by Maine Genealogical Society Staff et al. LC 90-60973. (Illus.). 96p. 1990. text ed. 20.00 (*0-929539-68-0*, 1168) Picton Pr.

Vital Records of Natick, Massachusetts, to 1850. Thomas W. Baldwin. 249p. 1991. reprint ed. pap. 19.00 (*1-55613-457-6*) Heritage Bk.

***Vital Records of Newington, 1703-1853.** Priscilla Hammond. 29p. 1997. reprint ed. pap. 6.00 (*0-8328-6016-6*) Higginson Bk Co.

Vital Records of Niskayuna Reformed Church, Schenectady, NY, 1783-1861. Arthur C. Kelly. LC 85-102252. (Palatine Transcripts Ser.). 85p. 1984. lib. bdg. 20.00 (*1-56012-069-X*, 68) Kinship Rhinebeck.

Vital Records of North Yarmouth, Maine to the Year 1850. 2nd ed. Society of Mayflower Descendants in the State of Rhode Island Staff. LC 80-3220. 480p. 1993. reprint ed. 39.50 (*0-89725-109-1*, 1405) Picton Pr.

***Vital Records of Old Town Maine Prior to 1892.** Ed. by Ruth Gray. (Illus.). 593p. 1997. 47.50 (*0-89725-289-6*, 1451) Picton Pr.

Vital Records of Pepperell, Massachusetts, to the Year 1850. Compiled by George A. Rice. LC 84-16660. 323p. 1985. 20.00 (*0-88082-008-X*) New Eng Hist.

***Vital Records of Phippsburg, to the Year 1892: Births, Marriages & Deaths.** Ed. by Mary P. Hill. (Illus.). 431p. 1997. reprint ed. lib. bdg. 47.00 (*0-8328-5894-3*) Higginson Bk Co.

Vital Records of Plymouth, Massachusetts to the Year 1850. Ed. by Ruth W. Sherman. LC 93-84753. 640p. 1993. 59.50 (*0-89725-110-5*, 1406) Picton Pr.

Vital Records of Princetown Reformed Church, Duanesburg, NY, 1824-1899: Also Known As: South Princetown Reformed Church; Dutch Church of Princetown; Gifford's Reformed Church at Giffords NY. Arthur C. Kelly. LC 84-151995. (Palatine Transcripts Ser.). 59p. 1984. lib. bdg. 11.50 (*1-56012-065-7*, 64) Kinship Rhinebeck.

***Vital Records of Randolph, Maine, to the Year 1892.** Ed. by Henry S. Webster. 144p. 1996. reprint ed. pap. 19.00 (*0-8328-5203-1*) Higginson Bk Co.

Vital Records of Randolph, Maine to Year 1892. Ed. by Henry S. Webster. 144p. 1993. reprint ed. lib. bdg. 22.50 (*0-8328-3189-1*) Higginson Bk Co.

Vital Records of Reformed Church, Middleburgh, NY, 1797-1899. Arthur C. Kelly. LC 85-158781. (Palatine Transcripts Ser.). 146p. 1984. lib. bdg. 29.00 (*1-56012-071-1*, 70) Kinship Rhinebeck.

Vital Records of Reformed Church Wynantskill NY, 1794-1889: Baptisms, 1794-1889; Marriages, 1794-1889; Members, 1794-1838. Arthur C. Kelly. LC 89-119377. (Palatine Transcripts Ser.). 136p. 1988. lib. bdg. 27.00 (*1-56012-086-X*, 86) Kinship Rhinebeck.

Vital Records of Reformed Dutch Church, Hyde Park, NY, 1810-1899. Arthur C. Kelly. LC 79-117954. (Palatine Transcripts Ser.). 114p. 1979. lib. bdg. 24.00 (*1-56012-044-4*, 43) Kinship Rhinebeck.

Vital Records of Reformed Dutch Church Prattsville NY, 1798-1899: Also Called: Schoharie Kill Reformed Church Windham Reformed Church; Windham Reformed Church. Arthur C. Kelly. (Palatine Transcripts Ser.). 111p. 1981. lib. bdg. 22.50 (*1-56012-053-3*, 52) Kinship Rhinebeck.

Vital Records of Sandwich, Massachusetts. Compiled by Caroline L. Kardell & Russell A. Lovell, Jr. LC 96-7775. 1996. write for info. (*0-88082-048-9*) New Eng Hist.

Vital Records of Saugus, Massachusetts to 1849. 1907. 15.00 (*0-88389-078-X*, Essx Institute) Peabody Essex Mus.

Vital Records of St. James Episcopal Church, Great Barrington, Mass., 1827-1899. Arthur C. Kelly. (Palatine Transcripts Ser.). 114p. 1992. lib. bdg. 25.00 (*1-56012-125-4*, 121) Kinship Rhinebeck.

Vital Records of St. John's Episcopal Church, Johnstown, NY, 1815-1899. Arthur C. Kelly. LC 85-158030. (Palatine Transcripts Ser.). 133p. 1984. lib. bdg. 27.00 (*1-56012-070-3*, 69) Kinship Rhinebeck.

Vital Records of Swansea, Massachusetts to 1850. Peter Rounds. 600p. 1992. 40.00 (*0-88082-031-4*) New Eng Hist.

Vital Records of the Christ Lutheran Church Ghent, Columbia County, New York: 1801-1901. Arthur C. Kelly. 234p. 1993. lib. bdg. 42.00 (*1-56012-128-9*, 123) Kinship Rhinebeck.

Vital Records of the Greenbush Reformed Church: East Greenbush, Rensselaer County, New York 1788-1899. Arthur C. Kelly. 145p. 1994. lib. bdg. 29.00 (*1-56012-135-1*, 133) Kinship Rhinebeck.

Vital Records of the Protestant Dutch Reformed Church at Acquackanonk (Passaic NJ), 1727-1816 (Including Some Births, 1692-1726) Acquackanonk & Reformed Church Graveyard. Arthur C. Kelly. LC 77-155014. 381p. 1977. reprint ed. lib. bdg. 49.00 (*1-56012-037-1*, 36) Kinship Rhinebeck.

Vital Records of the Town of Fairhaven, Massachusetts to 1850. Leonard H. Smith, Jr. & Dorothy M. Boyer. 175p. 1993. reprint ed. pap. 24.95 (*0-685-69926-9*, 9484) Clearfield Co.

Vital Records of the Town of Freetown, MA 1686 Through 1890. Helen G. Thomas. 484p. (Orig.). 1988. pap. 30.00 (*1-55613-136-4*) Heritage Bk.

Vital Records of the Town of Lebanon (ME), Vol. 1: Births. 168p. 1986. reprint ed. pap. 18.50 (*0-935207-40-6*) Danbury Hse Bks.

Vital Records of the Towns of Barnstable & Sandwich: An Authorized Facsimile Reproduction of Records Published Serially 1901-1937 in "The Mayflower Descendant" with an Added Index of Persons. Leonard H. Smith, Jr. & Norma H. Smith. 238p. 1996. reprint ed. pap. 31.00 (*0-685-62569-9*, 9560) Clearfield Co.

U
V

Vital Records of the Towns of Eastham & Orleans (Massachusetts) An Authorized Facsimile Reproduction of Records Published Serially 1901-1935 in "The Mayflower Descendant," with an Added Index of Persons. Leonard H. Smith, Jr. & Norma H. Smith. 250p. 1993. reprint ed. pap. 31.50 (*0-685-65701-9*, 9476) Clearfield Co.

Vital Records of Three Burned Counties: Births, Marriages, & Deaths of King & Queen, King William, & New Kent Counties, VA 1680-1860. Therese A. Fisher. 153p. (Orig.). 1995. pap. write for info. (*0-7884-0336-2*) Heritage Bk.

Vital Records of Tisbury, Massachusetts, to the Year Eighteen Fifty. New England Historical & Genealogical Society Staff. ii, 244p. reprint ed. pap. 19.00 (*1-55613-555-6*) Heritage Bk.

***Vital Records of Topsham, Maine, to the Year 1892, 2 vols., Set.** Ed. by Mary P. Hill. 1996. reprint ed. lib. bdg. 77.00 (*0-8328-5204-X*) Higginson Bk Co.

Vital Records of Townsend, Massachusetts. Henry Hallowell. 600p. 1992. 40.00 (*0-88082-030-6*) New Eng Hist.

Vital Records of Trinity Lutheran Church, West Sand Lake, NY, 1784-1899: Formed from the Merger of Zion Lutheran Church, West Sand Lake & Second Evangelical Lutheran Church, West Sand Lake. Arthur C. Kelly. LC 84-151650. (Palatine Transcripts Ser.). 163p. 1984. lib. bdg. 32.00 (*1-56012-064-9*, 63) Kinship Rhinebeck.

Vital Records of Troy, Maine Prior to 1892. Ralph E. Hillman. (Maine Genealogical Society Special Publication Ser.: No. 21). 224p. 1995. 24.95 (*0-89725-178-4*, 1525) Picton Pr.

Vital Records of Vinalhaven, Maine Prior to 1892. Elizabeth M. Mosher. 328p. 1994. lib. bdg. 75.00 (*0-89725-212-8*, 1465) Picton Pr.

Vital Records of Wenham, Massachusetts, to the End of the Year 1849. LC 06-13929. 227p. 1904. 15.00 (*0-88389-045-3*, Essx Institute) Peabody Essex Mus.

***Vital Records of West Gardiner, to the Year 1892.** Ed. by Henry S. Webster. (Illus.). 109p. 1997. reprint ed. pap. 15.00 (*0-8328-5926-5*) Higginson Bk Co.

***Vital Records of West Gardiner, to the Year 1892: Volume I, Births & Marriages (A-B); Volume II, Marriages (C-Z), 2 vols. in 1.** Ed. by Mary P. Hill. (Illus.). 406p. 1997. reprint ed. lib. bdg. 43.00 (*0-8328-5843-9*) Higginson Bk Co.

***Vital Records of (Westerly), 1636-1850: Births, Marriages & Deaths.** James N. Arnold. 152p. 1997. reprint ed. pap. 21.00 (*0-8328-6492-7*) Higginson Bk Co.

***Vital Records of Wilton, 1718-1853.** Priscilla Hammond. 170p. 1997. reprint ed. pap. 21.50 (*0-8328-6029-8*) Higginson Bk Co.

Vital Records of Woestina Reformed Church (Rotterdam NY) & Glenville Reformed Church, 1800-1899. Arthur C. Kelly. LC 84-196186. (Palatine Transcripts Ser.). 119p. 1984. lib. bdg. 25.00 (*1-56012-068-1*, 67) Kinship Rhinebeck.

***Vital Records of Woodstock, 1686-1854.** (Illus.). 622p. 1997. reprint ed. lib. bdg. 65.00 (*0-8328-5703-3*) Higginson Bk Co.

Vital Records of Yarmouth, Massachusetts to the Year 1850, 2 vols. in 1. Ed. by Robert M. Sherman & Ruth W. Sherman. LC 75-40870. 976p. 1993. reprint ed. 59.50 (*0-89725-107-5*, 1402) Picton Pr.

Vital Records of York Maine. Ed. by Lester M. Bragdon. LC 91-60426. 640p. 1991. 59.50 (*0-929539-84-2*, 1187) Picton Pr.

Vital Records, Town of Chatham, Massachusetts, 1696-1850. Ed. by Anna-Lowell Tomlinson & Sheila Westgate. 500p. 1991. text ed. 60.00 (*0-9615051-2-5*) Chatham His Soc.

Vital Records, Town of Harwich Masschusetts, 1694 to 1850. Ed. by Louise H. Kelley & Dorothy Straw. 616p. 1982. write for info. (*0-88492-040-2*) W S Sullwold.

Vital Response: A First Responder Training Manual. C. Mark Vasu. (Illus.). 240p. (Orig.). 1991. pap. text ed. 22.95 (*0-9629479-4-6*) Cordith.

Vital Role for Fungicides in Cereal Production. Ed. by H. G. Hewitt et al. 258p. (Orig.). 1995. pap. 87.50 (*1-85996-140-1*, Pub. by Bios Scientific UK) Coronet Bks.

Vital Role of Potassium Fertilizers in Tropical Agriculture: The Present Position, Future Potential & Constraints to Progress. T. Kaddar et al. Ed. by E. N. Roth & E. D. Frederick. LC 84-12971. (Technical Bulletin Ser.: No. T-29). (Illus.). 15p. (Orig.). 1984. pap. text ed. 4.00 (*0-88090-051-2*) Intl Fertilizer.

Vital Signs. Dennis L. Breo. (Illus.). 306p. 1995. 19.95 (*1-56625-034-X*) Bonus Books.

Vital Signs. Robin Cook. 1992. mass mkt. 6.99 (*0-425-13176-9*) Berkley Pub.

Vital Signs. large type ed. Robin Cook. 560p. 1991. pap. 16.95 (*0-8161-5304-3*, GK Hall) Thorndike Pr.

Vital Signs. Robin Cook. 1994. reprint ed. lib. bdg. 32.95 (*1-56849-267-7*) Buccaneer Bks.

Vital Signs: A Mission of the Heart. Janet Bergera. LC 95-1145. (J). 1995. pap. 9.95 (*1-55503-773-9*) Covenant Comms.

Vital Signs: Contemporary American Poetry from the University Presses. Ed. by Ronald Wallace. LC 89-40271. 592p. (C). 1989. 29.95 (*0-299-12160-7*); pap. 14.95 (*0-299-12164-X*) U of Wis Pr.

Vital Signs: Essays on American Literature & Criticism. James W. Tuttleton. 382p. 1996. 27.50 (*1-56663-100-9*) I R Dee.

Vital Signs: International Stories on Aging. Ed. by Dorothy Sennett & Anne Czarniecki. 256p. 1991. pap. 12.95 (*1-55597-143-1*) Graywolf.

Vital Signs: Mainstream Protestantism's Past & Prospects. Ed. by Milton J. Coalter et al. 168p. (Orig.). 1996. pap. 12.00 (*0-8028-0855-7*) Eerdmans.

Vital Signs: Mathematics in Everyday Life. Tina Levy. 326p. (C). 1991. pap. text ed. 23.95 (*0-89863-144-0*) Star Pub CA.

Vital Signs: Medical Realism in Nineteenth-Century Fiction. Lawrence Rothfield. (Literature in History Ser.). 250p. 1992. text ed. 37.50 (*0-691-06896-8*); pap. text ed. 15.95 (*0-691-02954-7*) Princeton U Pr.

Vital Signs: Using Quality, Time, & Cost Performance Measurements to Chart Your Company's Future. Steven M. Hronec. 256p. 1992. 27.95 (*0-8144-5073-3*) AMACOM.

Vital Signs: Working Doctors Tell the Real Story Behind Medical School & Practice. Deborah Bernal et al. LC 94-28687. 219p. (Orig.). 1994. pap. 12.95 (*1-56079-376-7*) Petersons.

Vital Signs of Christ's Return. Ray W. Yerbury. 192p. (Orig.). 1995. pap. 9.95 (*0-89221-293-4*) New Leaf.

Vital Signs 1: Bringing Together Reading & Writing. Ed. by James L. Collins. 170p. (Orig.). 1989. pap. text ed. 21.50 (*0-86709-253-X*, 0253) Boynton Cook Pubs.

Vital Signs, 1994: The Trends That Are Shaping Our Future. Lester R. Brown. 1994. 22.00 (*0-393-03637-5*) Norton.

Vital Signs, 1995: The Trends That Are Shaping Our Future. Lester R. Brown et al. (Illus.). 160p. 1995. 19.95 (*0-393-03781-9*, Norton Paperbks); pap. 10.95 (*0-393-31279-8*, Norton Paperbks) Norton.

Vital Signs 1996: The Trends That Are Shaping Our Future. Lester Brown. (Illus.). 160p. 1996. 24.00 (*0-393-03928-5*); pap. 12.00 (*0-393-31426-X*) Norton.

***Vital Signs 1997: The Trends That Are Shaping Our Future.** 6th ed. Lester R. Brown et al. (Illus.). 160p. (C). 1997. 24.95 (*0-393-04067-4*); pap. 12.00 (*0-393-31637-8*) Norton.

Vital Signs 2: Teaching & Learning Language Collaboratively. Ed. by James L. Collins. 149p. 1990. pap. text ed. 21.50 (*0-86709-269-6*, 0269) Boynton Cook Pubs.

Vital Signs 3: Restructuring the English Classroom. Ed. by James L. Collins. 197p. 1992. pap. text ed. 22.50 (*0-86709-297-1*, 0297) Boynton Cook Pubs.

Vital Singles Ministry. Harry Odum. (Effective Church Ser.). 144p. 1992. pap. 3.15 (*0-687-43800-4*) Abingdon.

Vital South: How Presidents Are Elected. Earl Black & Merle Black. (Illus.). 400p. (C). 1993. pap. 16.95 (*0-674-94131-4*) HUP.

Vital Statistics. Ed. by Glenda J. Beal. 88p. 1994. pap. 19.95 (*1-56991-009-X*, 158) Am Correctional.

Vital Statistics, Vol. 1. Ed. by Sandra Braman & Douglas Woolf. 1978. pap. 3.00 (*0-942296-04-4*) Wolf Run Bks.

Vital Statistics, Vol. 2. Ed. by Sandra Braman & Douglas Woolf. 1978. pap. 3.00 (*0-942296-05-2*) Wolf Run Bks.

Vital Statistics, Vol. 3. Ed. by Sandra Braman & Douglas Woolf. 1980. pap. 3.00 (*0-942296-06-0*) Wolf Run Bks.

Vital Statistics: A Memorial Volume of Selections from the Reports & Writings of William Farr. William Farr. Ed. by Noel A. Humphreys & Sanitary Institute of Great Britain Staff. LC 75-38128. (Demography Ser.). (Illus.). 1976. reprint ed. 46.95 (*0-405-18600-2*) Ayer.

Vital Statistics: American Folk Drawings & Watercolors from a Private Collection. Intro. by Phillip M. Isaacson. LC 86-61948. (Illus.). 16p. (Orig.). 1986. pap. 5.00 (*0-916606-13-9*) Bowdoin Coll.

Vital Statistics for the Public Health Educator. Mark J. Kittleson. LC 94-7915. (Illus.). 184p. (C). 1995. pap. 15.95 (*0-8093-1950-0*) S Ill U Pr.

***Vital Statistics from Town Records, Penobscot, 1787 to 1875.** Compiled by Brooksville Historical Society Staff. (Illus.). 217p. 1997. reprint ed. lib. bdg. 29.00 (*0-8328-5892-7*) Higginson Bk Co.

Vital Statistics of Japan, 3 vols. 1991. Set. lib. bdg. 1,500.00 (*0-87700-922-8*) Revisionist Pr.

***Vital Statistics of Seymour, Connecticut.** Compiled by W. C. Sharpe. (Illus.). 136p. 1997. reprint ed. pap. 18.00 (*0-8328-5685-1*) Higginson Bk Co.

***Vital Statistics of Stewartstown, from Dec., 1770 to Jan. 1, 1888. With Names & Dates of the Original Grant, Incorporation, Settlement, Marriages, Births & Deaths.** C. E. Tewksbury. (Illus.). 51p. 1997. reprint ed. pap. 11.00 (*0-8328-6026-3*) Higginson Bk Co.

***Vital Statistics of the Town of Keene, Compiled from the Town Records, First Church & Family Records, the Original Fisher Record & the Newspapers.** Frank H. Whitcomb. (Illus.). 268p. 1997. reprint ed. lib. bdg. 32.00 (*0-8328-6001-8*) Higginson Bk Co.

Vital Statistics of the United States, Vol. 1: Natality, 1988 PHS 90-1100. 31.00 (*0-685-61591-X*, 017-022-01120-4) Natl Ctr Health Stats.

Vital Statistics of the United States, Vol. 2: Mortality, 1987 PHS 90-1101, Pt. A. 652p. 44.00 (*0-685-61593-6*, 017-022-01102-6) Natl Ctr Health Stats.

Vital Statistics of the United States, Vol. 2: Mortality, 1988 PHS 90-1102, Pt. B. 756p. 39.00 (*0-685-61592-8*, 017-022-01121-2) Natl Ctr Health Stats.

Vital Statistics of the United States, Vol. 3: Marriage & Divorce, 1986 PHS 90-1103. 187p. 16.00 (*0-685-61594-4*, 017-022-01124-7) Natl Ctr Health Stats.

Vital Statistics of the United States, 1986, Vol. 1: Natality. 404p. 1991. 31.00 (*0-685-61568-5*, 017-022-01120-4) Natl Ctr Health Stats.

Vital Statistics of the United States, 1986, Vol. 2: Mortality, Pt. B. 713p. 1991. 39.00 (*0-685-61569-3*, 017-022-01121-2) Natl Ctr Health Stats.

Vital Statistics of the United States, 1987 Life Tables: PHS 90-1104, Vol. II, Section 6. (Reports from the National Medical Care Utilization & Expenditure Survey, Analytical Report Ser. C). 19p. 1.50 (*0-685-61596-0*, 017-022-01103-4) Natl Ctr Health Stats.

Vital Statistics of the United States, 1987, Vol. 3: Marriage & Divorce. 196p. 1991. 12.00 (*0-685-61577-4*, 017-022-01137-9) Natl Ctr Health Stats.

Vital Statistics of the United States, 1988, Vol. 1: Natality. 464p. 1991. 31.00 (*0-685-61576-6*, 017-022-01120-4) Natl Ctr Health Stats.

Vital Statistics of the United States, 1988, Vol. 2: Mortality, Pt. A. 652p. 1991. write for info. (*0-318-69611-8*) Natl Ctr Health Stats.

Vital Statistics of the United States, 1990 Life Tables Vol. II, Sect. 6. National Center for Health Statistics Staff. LC 94-1104. 20p. 2.25 (*0-614-02951-1*, 017-022-01266-9) Natl Ctr Health Stats.

Vital Statistics on American Politics. Harold W. Stanley & Richard G. Niemi. LC 93-8925. 1993. pap. text ed. 23.95 (*0-87187-782-1*) Congr Quarterly.

Vital Statistics on American Politics. 4th ed. Harold W. Stanley & Richard G. Niemi. LC 93-8925. 465p. 1993. 36.95 (*0-87187-781-3*) Congr Quarterly.

Vital Statistics on American Politics. 5th ed. Harold W. Stanley & Richard G. Niemi. LC 95-35053. 440p. 1995. 39.95 (*0-87187-793-7*) Congr Quarterly.

Vital Statistics on Congress, 1989-1990. Norman J. Ornstein. 275p. 1989. 44.95 (*0-87187-526-8*); pap. 30.95 (*0-87187-528-4*) Congr Quarterly.

Vital Statistics on Congress 1990-1991. Norman J. Ornstein. 1991. 46.95 (*0-87187-620-5*); pap. 32.95 (*0-87187-621-3*) Congr Quarterly.

Vital Statistics on Congress, 1993-94. Norman J. Ornstein. 275p. 1993. 42.95 (*0-87187-778-3*); pap. 30.95 (*0-87187-779-1*) Congr Quarterly.

Vital Statistics on Congress, 1995-1996. Norman J. Ornstein et al. LC 87-65932. 291p. 1995. 46.95 (*0-87187-845-3*) Congr Quarterly.

Vital Statistics on the Presidency: Washington to Clinton. Lyn Ragsdale. (Illus.). 455p. 1995. 46.95 (*1-56802-050-3*) Congr Quarterly.

Vital Statistics on the Presidency: Washington to Clinton. Lyn Ragsdale. LC 95-33031. (Illus.). 455p. 1995. pap. 32.95 (*1-56802-049-X*) Congr Quarterly.

Vital Statistics Rates in the United States: 1900-1940. U. S. Public Health Service, National Office of Vital Statistics Staff & Federal Security Agency Staff. LC 75-38136. (Demography Ser.). (Illus.). 1976. reprint ed. 84.95 (*0-405-07989-3*) Ayer.

Vital Statistics Rates in the United States: 1940-1960. U. S. Department of Health, Education & Welfare, Washington, D. C. Staff et al. LC 75-37269. (Demography Ser.). (Illus.). 1976. reprint ed. 71.95 (*0-405-08001-8*) Ayer.

Vital Theological Issues: Examining Enduring Issues of Theology. Roy B. Zuck. LC 94-37863. 232p. 1994. pap. 12.99 (*0-8254-4069-6*) Kregel.

Vital Ties. Karen Kringle. LC 92-26958. 280p. (Orig.). 1992. pap. 10.95 (*0-933216-90-4*) Spinsters Ink.

Vital Tooth Bleaching: Putting It All Together. Thomas E. Huntzinger. LC 92-24901. 152p. 1992. 29.95 (*1-881350-00-2*) Moontree Pub.

Vital Touch. Sharon Heller. 1997. 25.00 (*0-8050-4827-8*) H Holt & Co.

***Vital Touch: How Intimate Contact with Your Baby Leads to Happier, Healthier Development.** Sharon Heller. LC 97-9434. 1997. pap. 14.95 (*0-8050-5354-9*, Owl) H Holt & Co.

Vitale: Just Your Average Bald, One-Eyed Basketball Wacko Who Beat the Ziggy & Become a PTP'er. Dick Vitale & Curry Kirkpatrick. 320p. 1989. mass mkt. 4.50 (*0-671-67730-6*) PB.

Vitalic Breathing: The Miracle Air Discovery. Thomas Gaines. 215p. 1978. reprint ed. spiral bd. 12.00 (*0-7873-0339-9*) Hlth Research.

Vitalistic Thought in India: (A Study of the 'Prana' Concept in Vedic Literature & Its Development in the Vedanta, Samkhya & Pancaratra Traditions) Peter Connolly. (C). 1992. 19.00 (*81-7030-348-6*) S Asia.

Vitality & Civilization. Griscom Morgan. 1947. pap. 1.00 (*0-910420-06-8*) Comm Serv OH.

Vitality & Renewal: A Manager's Guide for the 21st Century. Colin Hutchinson. LC 95-3338. (Praeger Studies on the 21st Century). 344p. 1995. text ed. 69.50 (*0-275-95233-9*, Praeger Pubs); pap. text ed. 29.95 (*0-275-95234-7*, Praeger Pubs) Greenwood.

Vitality, Energy, Spirit: A Taoist Sourcebook. Ed. & Tr. by Thomas Cleary from CHI. LC 90-53387. (Dragon Editions Ser.). 264p. (Orig.). 1991. pap. 19.00 (*0-87773-519-0*) Shambhala Pubns.

***Vitality Factor.** Elizabeth Somer. Date not set. write for info. (*0-688-15151-5*) Morrow.

Vitality, Fasting & Nutrition. Hereward Carrington. 690p. 1996. pap. 36.00 (*1-56459-915-9*) Kessinger Pub.

Vitality, Fasting & Nutrition. Hereward Carrington. 648p. 1963. reprint ed. spiral bd. 34.50 (*0-7873-0151-5*) Hlth Research.

Vitality of Death: Essays in Existential Psychology & Philosophy. Peter Koestenbaum. LC 72-105989. (Contributions in Philosophy Ser.: No. 5). 589p. 1971. text ed. 29.95 (*0-8371-3319-X*, KOV/, Greenwood Pr) Greenwood.

***Vitality of Japan.** Clesse. LC 96-37768. 1997. text ed. 59.95 (*0-312-17313-X*) St Martin.

Vitality of Old Testament Traditions. 2nd ed. Walter Brueggemann & Hans W. Wolff. LC 82-7141. (Orig.). 1985. pap. 11.00 (*0-8042-0112-9*, John Knox) Westminster John Knox.

Vitality of the Christian Tradition. Ed. by George F. Thomas. LC 70-134143. (Essay Index Reprint Ser.). 1977. reprint ed. 24.95 (*0-8369-2378-2*) Ayer.

Vitalizing African Public Administration for Recovery & Development. Mohamed Alfani. Ed. by Gelase Mutahaba et al. LC 91-46723. (Library of Management for Development). xiii, 119p. 1993. 30.00 (*1-56549-012-6*); pap. 9.95 (*1-56549-011-8*) Kumarian Pr.

Vitalogy. E. H. Ruddock. (Illus.). 128p. 1995. reprint ed. pap. 8.95 (*1-55709-404-7*) Applewood.

Vitals of Faith. S. Abul Ala Maududi. 54p. (Orig.). 1987. pap. 3.00 (*1-56744-412-1*) Kazi Pubns.

Vitamania: Vitamins in American Culture. Rima D. Apple. LC 95-43281. (Health & Medicine Ser.). (Illus.). 280p. (C). 1996. text ed. 48.00 (*0-8135-2277-3*); pap. text ed. 18.95 (*0-8135-2278-1*) Rutgers U Pr.

Vitamin A & the Immune Function: A Symposium. Ed. by Chris Kjohhede & William R. Beisel. LC 95-45330. (Journal of Nutritional Immunology: Vol. 4, Nos. 1/2). 177p. 1996. 29.95 (*1-56024-757-6*, Hawrth Medical) Haworth Pr.

Vitamin A Deficiency: Health, Survival, & Vision. Alfred Sommer & Keith P. West. (Illus.). 464p. (C). 1996. 75.00 (*0-19-508824-7*) OUP.

Vitamin A Deficiency & Its Consequences: A Field Guide to Detection & Control. 3rd ed. A. Sommer. (Illus.). vii, 69p. (FRE & SPA.). (C). 1995. pap. text ed. 17.00 (*92-4-154478-3*, 1153050) World Health.

***Vitamin A Deficiency & Xerophthalmia: Report of a Joint WHO/USAID Meeting, 1976.** (Technical Report Ser.: No. 590). 0088p. 1976. pap. text ed. 10.00 (*92-4-120590-3*, 1100590) World Health.

Vitamin A in Health & Disease. Blomhoff. (Antioxidants in Health & Disease Ser.: Vol. 1). 704p. 1994. 190.00 (*0-8247-9120-7*) Dekker.

***Vitamin A Supplements: A Guide to Their Use in the Treatment & Prevention of Vitamin A Deficiency & Xerophthalmia: Prepared by a WHO/UNICEF/IVACG Task Force.** WHO Staff. 24p. 1988. 8.00 (*92-4-154236-5*) World Health.

Vitamin A Through Zinc: An Alphabet of Good Health. S. Ifetayo Muhammad. 16p. (Orig.). (J). 1985. pap. 1.00 (*0-916157-13-X*) African Islam Miss Pubns.

Vitamin A Training activities for community Health & Development. Helen Keller International Staff. LC 93-395669. (Illus.). 72p. (Orig.). 1993. pap. 10.00 (*0-915173-26-3*) Helen Keller Intl.

Vitamin & Carrier Functions of Polyprenoids. Ed. by G. H. Bourne & H. R. Cama. (World Review of Nutrition & Dietetics Ser.: Vol. 31). (Illus.). 1978. 110.50 (*3-8055-2801-9*) S Karger.

Vitamin & Health Encyclopedia. Jack Ritchason. 129p. 1986. pap. 7.95 (*0-913923-92-3*) Woodland UT.

***Vitamin & Herb Guide.** Global Health Research Staff. 96p. 1997. pap. 6.95 (*0-921202-00-8*, Pub. by Global Hlth CN) BookWorld Dist.

Vitamin & Herbal Digest. LC 96-92151. 372p. Date not set. pap. 7.95 (*0-9624780-7-5*) HealthWorld.

Vitamin & Mineral Deficiencies. Robert E. Cornish. 150p. 1973. reprint ed. spiral bd. 12.00 (*0-7873-0224-4*) Hlth Research.

Vitamin & Mineral Requirements in Preterm Infants. Ed. by Reginald C. Tsang. LC 84-22999. (Clinical Disorders in Pediatric Nutrition Ser.: No. 3). 232p. 1985. reprint ed. pap. 66.20 (*0-608-01306-4*, 2062051) Bks Demand.

Vitamin B Six Catalysis. Ed. by T. Korpela & P. Christen. (Congress Reports: No. 1). 500p. 1987. 106.50 (*0-8176-1942-9*) Birkhauser.

***Vitamin B-3 & Schizophrenia: Discovery, Recovery, Controversy.** Abram Hoffer. 160p. 1997. pap. text ed. 16.95 (*1-55082-079-6*, Pub. by Quarry Pr CN) LPC InBook.

Vitamin B-6 Metabolism in Pregnancy, Lactation & Infancy. Ed. by Daniel J. Raiten. LC 94-32693. 212p. 1995. 178.00 (*0-8493-4594-4*) CRC Pr.

Vitamin Bible for Kids see Parents' Nutrition Bible: A Guide to Raising Healthy Children

Vitamin Book. Consumer Guide Editors. 1979. pap. 5.95 (*0-671-24819-7*, Fireside) S&S Trade.

Vitamin Book. Harold Silerman. 368p. 1985. mass mkt. 6.50 (*0-553-27435-X*) Bantam.

***Vitamin B1 for Dentistry! Medicine! Research!** Sam Ziff & Michael F. Ziff. 120p. (Orig.). 1996. pap. 19.95 (*0-941011-15-1*) Bio-Probe.

Vitamin B3 (Niacin) Update. rev. ed. Abram Hoffer. 32p. (Orig.). 1990. pap. 2.25 (*0-87983-513-3*) Keats.

Vitamin B6: Metabolism & Role in Growth. George P. Tryfiates. 377p. 1980. 71.00 (*0-917678-10-9*) Food & Nut Pr.

Vitamin C, 3 vols., Vol. I. C. Alan Clemetson. 368p. 1989. 165.00 (*0-8493-4841-2*, RC627) CRC Pr.

Vitamin C, 3 vols., Vol. II. C. Alan Clemetson. 304p. 1989. 165.00 (*0-8493-4842-0*, RC627) CRC Pr.

Vitamin C, 3 vols., Vol. III. C. Alan Clemetson. 320p. 1989. 165.00 (*0-8493-4843-9*, RC627) CRC Pr.

Vitamin C: Its Chemistry & Biochemistry. Davies & Austin. 1991. 39.00 (*0-85186-333-7*) CRC Pr.

Vitamin C: The Future is Now. Jeffrey S. Bland. Ed. by Don R. Bensen. 1995. 3.95 (*0-87983-685-7*) Keats.

Vitamin C: The Master Nutrient. Sandra Goodman. 1991. pap. 9.95 (*0-87983-571-0*) Keats.

***Vitamin C & Cancer: Discovery, Recovery, Controversy.** Abram Hoffer. 160p. 1997. pap. text ed. 16.95 (*1-55082-078-8*, Pub. by Quarry Pr CN) LPC InBook.

Vitamin C & the Common Cold. Linus Pauling. 1995. reprint ed. lib. bdg. 18.95 (*1-56849-669-9*) Buccaneer Bks.

Vitamin C Controversy: Questions & Answers. Emanuel Cheraskin. LC 87-71003. (Illus.). 221p. (Orig.). 1988. pap. 12.95 (*0-942333-01-2*) Bio-Comns Pr.

***Vitamin C in Health & Disease.** Ed. by Packer & Fuchs. LC 97-7703. (Antioxidants in Health & Disease Ser.: Vol. 5). 560p. 1997. 150.00 (*0-8247-9313-7*) Dekker.

Vitamin C Testing. rev. ed. Jacqueline Barber. Ed. by Lincoln Bergman & Kay Fairwell. (Great Explorations in Math & Science (GEMS) Ser.). (Illus.). 64p. (Orig.). (J). (gr. 4-8). 1990. reprint ed. teacher ed., pap. 9.00 (*0-912511-70-2*) Lawrence Science.

Vitamin C Updated. Jack J. Challem. Ed. by Richard A. Passwater & Earl R. Mindell. (Good Health Guide Ser.). 32p. 1983. pap. text ed. 2.95 (*0-87983-285-1*) Keats.

Vitamin Contents of Arterial Tissue. J. E. Kirk. (Monographs on Atherosclerosis: Vol. 3). 1973. 40.00 (*3-8055-1466-2*) S Karger.

***Vitamin D.** David Feldman. 1997. 159.95 (*0-12-252685-6*) Acad Pr.

Vitamin D: Basic & Clinical Aspects. Rajiv Kumar. 1984. lib. bdg. 209.50 (*0-89838-620-9*) Kluwer Ac.

Vitamin D: Chemical, Biochemical & Clinical Endocrinology of Calcium Metabolism. Ed. by A. W. Norman et al. (Illus.). 1288p. 1982. text ed. 257.70 (*3-11-008864-9*) De Gruyter.

Vitamin D: Gene Regulation, Structure-Function Analysis & Clinical Application Proceedings of the 8th Workshop on Vitamin D, Paris, France, July 5-10, 1991. Ed. by A. W. Norman et al. (Illus.). xxxviii, 995p. (C). 1991. lib. bdg. 300.00 (*3-11-012638-9*, 261-91) De Gruyter.

Vitamin D: Molecular Biology & Clinical Nutrition. Ed. by Anthony W. Norman. LC 80-14327. (Basic & Clinical Nutrition Ser.: No. 2). 818p. reprint ed. pap. 180.00 (*0-7837-3342-9*, 2043300) Bks Demand.

Vitamin D - A Pluripotent Steroid Hormone: Structional Studies, Molecular Endocrinology & Clinical Applications: Proceedings of the Ninth Workshop on Vitamin D, Orlando, Florida (U. S. A.), May 28-June 2, 1994. Anthony W. Norman. LC 94-35262. (Proceedings of the 9th Workshop on Vitamin D, Orlando, Florida, May 28-June 2, 1994 Ser.). 1007p. (C). 1994. lib. bdg. 361.55 (*3-11-014157-4*) De Gruyter.

Vitamin D - Chemical, Biochemical & Clinical Update: Proceedings of the 6th Workshop on Vitamin D, Italy, March 1985. Ed. by A. W. Norman et al. (Illus.). xxxxiii, 1249p. 1985. 307.70 (*0-89925-066-1*); 307.70 (*3-11-010181-5*) De Gruyter.

Vitamin D - Molecular, Cellular, & Clinical Endocrinology: Proceedings of the Seventh Workshop on Vitamin D, Rancho Mirage, CA, U. S. A., April 1988. Ed. by A. W. Norman et al. xl, 1072p. (C). 1988. lib. bdg. 300.00 (*3-11-011477-1*) De Gruyter.

Vitamin D & Calcium Metabolism in the Renal Diseases. Ed. by K. Maeda et al. (Contributions to Nephrology Ser.: Vol. 22). (Illus.). vi, 122p. 1980. 56.00 (*3-8055-0389-X*) S Karger.

Vitamin Deficiencies: Index of Modern Information with Bibliography. Michael J. Lichtenstein. LC 88-47794. 150p. 1988. 44.50 (*0-88164-888-4*); pap. 39.50 (*0-88164-889-2*) ABBE Pubs Assn.

Vitamin Deficiencies: Symptoms. 1996. lib. bdg. 251.75 (*0-8490-5915-1*) Gordon Pr.

***Vitamin E.** Ruth Winter. LC 97-15955. 1998. pap. write for info. (*0-609-80132-5*, Crown) Crown Pub Group.

Vitamin E: (For a Healthy Heart & Long Life) Herb Bailey. 256p. (Orig.). 1993. pap. 4.95 (*0-7867-0053-X*) Carroll & Graf.

Vitamin E: Biochemical, Hematological, Clinical Aspects, Annals Nov. 11-13, 1981, Vol. 393. New York Academy of Sciences Staff. Ed. by Bertram Lubin & Lawrence J. Machlin. 506p. 1982. 95.00 (*0-89766-176-1*); pap. write for info. (*0-89766-177-X*) NY Acad Sci.

Vitamin E: Is It Safe? H. J. Roberts. LC 93-85653. (Illus.). 130p. 1994. pap. 17.95 (*0-9633260-8-2*) Sunshine Sentinel.

Vitamin E: Its Usefulness in Health & in Curing Diseases. Ed. by M. Mino et al. (Illus.). xiv, 368p. 1993. 215.75 (*3-8055-5753-1*) S Karger.

***Vitamin E & Disease Prevention Including Cancer: Index of New Information with Authors, Subjects & References.** Gus J. Torelli. (Illus.). 150p. 1997. 47.50 (*0-7883-1342-8*); pap. 44.50 (*0-7883-1343-6*) ABBE Pubs Assn.

Vitamin E & Its Uses. 1996. lib. bdg. 250.75 (*0-8490-5913-5*) Gordon Pr.

Vitamin E in Health & Disease: Biochemistry & Clinical Applications. Ed. by Lester Packer & Jurgen Fuchs. LC 92-49976. 1024p. 1992. 235.00 (*0-8247-8692-0*) Dekker.

Vitamin E Updated. Len Mervyn. Ed. by Richard A. Passwater & Earl R. Mindell. (Good Health Guide Ser.). 32p. (Orig.). 1983. pap. 3.95 (*0-87983-274-6*) Keats.

Vitamin Intake & Health: A Scientific Review. Gaby et al. 232p. 1990. 125.00 (*0-8247-8382-4*) Dekker.

Vitamin K & Vitamin K-Dependent Proteins. Shearer. 368p. 1993. 218.00 (*0-8493-6423-X*) CRC Pr.

Vitamin K-Dependent Biological Processes. Ed. by Maria B. Donati. (Journal: Haemostasis: Vol. 16, No. 2, 1986). (Illus.). 132p. 1986. pap. 66.50 (*3-8055-4270-4*) S Karger.

Vitamin-Lexikon: Fur Artze, Apotheker und Ernahrungswissenschaftler. Karl-Heinz Bassler. 432p. (GER.). 1992. 105.00 (*0-7859-8360-0*, 3437006606) Fr & Eur.

Vitamin P Complex (Bioflavanoids) Index of New Information. Wally V. Ullman. 155p. 1995. 44.50 (*0-7883-0628-6*); pap. 39.50 (*0-7883-0629-4*) ABBE Pubs Assn.

Vitamin Parade. Marsha L. Love. LC 89-51346. (Illus.). 44p. (J). (gr. k-3). 1989. 5.95 (*1-55523-264-7*) Winston-Derek.

Vitamin Politics. John J. Fried. LC 83-62187. 238p. 1984. pap. 19.95 (*0-87975-222-X*) Prometheus Bks.

Vitamin Pushers: How the "Health Food" Industry Is Selling America a Bill of Goods. Stephen J. Barrett & Victor Herbert. (Illus.). 536p. (C). 1994. 26.95 (*0-87975-909-7*) Prometheus Bks.

Vitamin Receptors: Vitamins As Ligands in Cell Communication-Metabolic Indicators. Ed. by Krishnamurti Dakshinamurti. (Intercellular & Intracellular Communications Ser.: No. 6). (Illus.). 350p. (C). 1994. text ed. 80.00 (*0-521-39280-2*) Cambridge U Pr.

Vitamin Revolution in Health Care. Julian M. Whitaker. LC 95-81032. 236p. Date not set. pap. 12.95 (*0-9649236-9-6*) Arcadia Pr NH.

Vitamin Revolution in Health Care. Julian M. Whitaker. LC 95-81032. 236p. 1996. 22.95 (*0-9649236-8-8*) Arcadia Pr NH.

Vitamin Robbers. Earl R. Mindell. Ed. by Richard A. Passwater. (Good Health Guide Ser.). (Illus.). (C). 1983. pap. 10.00 (*0-87983-275-4*) Keats.

***Vitamin Strategy: A Personalized Plan.** Art Ulene & Val Ulene. 286p. 1997. 29.98 (*0-941683-37-0*) Instant Improve.

***Vitamin Supplements: Real Information You Can Use.** Randy Shields. LC 96-70827. 118p. (Orig.). 1996. mass mkt. 4.99 (*1-888886-36-6*) CEPI.

***Vitamin Vitality: Use Nature's Powers to Obtain Optimal Health.** Raskin. Ed. by Men's Health Books Editors. 176p. 1997. pap. 14.95 (*0-87596-408-7*) Rodale Pr Inc.

Vitamin-Zone Refining see Encyclopedia of Chemical Technology

Vitaminas y Otros Complementos Alimentarios y Su Salud. Carlson Wade. Orig. Title: Fact Book on Vitamins & Other Supplements. (Orig.). (SPA.). 1980. pap. 4.95 (*0-87983-175-8*) Keats.

Vitamins. Wihelm Friedrich. 1060p. (C). 1988. lib. bdg. 307.70 (*3-11-010244-7*) De Gruyter.

Vitamins. Rhoda Nottridge. LC 92-21415. (J). (gr. 2-5). 1993. lib. bdg. 14.21 (*0-87614-795-3*, Carolrhoda) Lerner Group.

Vitamins: Fundamental Aspects in Nutrition & Health. Gerald F. Combs, Jr. (Illus.). 528p. 1991. text ed. 65.00 (*0-12-183490-5*) Acad Pr.

Vitamins: Index of Modern Information. Vincent A. Spedding. LC 88-47631. 150p. 1988. 44.50 (*0-88164-792-6*); pap. 39.50 (*0-88164-793-4*) ABBE Pubs Assn.

Vitamins: Their Use & Abuse. Joseph V. Levy & Paul Bach-Y-Rita. 155p. 1976. 8.95 (*0-87140-616-0*) Liveright.

Vitamins & Cancer: Human Cancer Prevention by Vitamins & Micronutrients. Ed. by Frank L. Meyskens, Jr. & Kedar Prasad. LC 85-27134. (Experimental Biology & Medicine Ser.: Vol. 10). 504p. 1986. 109.50 (*0-89603-094-6*) Humana.

Vitamins & Cancer Prevention. Ed. by George A. Bray & Donna H. Ryan. LC 92-19677. (Pennington Center Nutrition Ser.: Vol. 3). (Illus.). 456p. (C). 1992. text ed. 55.00 (*0-8071-1789-7*) La State U Pr.

Vitamins & Cancer Prevention Contemporary Issues in Clinical Nutrition, Vol. 14. Toni A. Laidlaw. LC 90-44657. (Contemporary Issues in Clinical Nutrition Ser.). 145p. 1991. text ed. 102.95 (*0-471-56066-9*) Wiley.

Vitamins & Coenzymes see Methods in Enzymology

Vitamins & Coenzymes, Pt. D see Methods in Enzymology

Vitamins & Hormones, Vol. 38. Ed. by Paul L. Munson et al. (Serial Publication Ser.). 1981. text ed. 159.00 (*0-12-709838-0*) Acad Pr.

Vitamins & Hormones, Vol. 39. 1982. text ed. 159.00 (*0-12-709839-9*) Acad Pr.

Vitamins & Hormones, Vol. 40. Ed. by Donald D. McCormick. (Serial Publication Ser.). 1983. text ed. 159.00 (*0-12-709840-2*) Acad Pr.

Vitamins & Hormones, Vol. 41. Ed. by Robert S. Harris & Kenneth V. Thimann. 1984. text ed. 159.00 (*0-12-709841-0*) Acad Pr.

Vitamins & Hormones, Vol. 42. Ed. by Donald B. McCormick. 372p. 1985. text ed. 159.00 (*0-12-709842-9*) Acad Pr.

Vitamins & Hormones, Vol. 45. Ed. by Gerald D. Aurbach & Donald B. McCormick. 375p. 1989. text ed. 129.00 (*0-12-709845-3*) Acad Pr.

Vitamins & Hormones, Vol. 48. Ed. by Gerald Litwack. (Illus.). 306p. 1994. text ed. 99.00 (*0-12-709848-8*) Acad Pr.

Vitamins & Hormones, Vol. 51. Ed. by Gerald Litwack. (Illus.). 468p. 1995. boxed 85.00 (*0-12-709851-8*) Acad Pr.

Vitamins & Hormones, Vol. 52. Ed. by Gerald Litwack. (Illus.). 202p. 1996. text ed. 74.95 (*0-12-709852-6*) Acad Pr.

Vitamins & Hormones: Advances in Research & Applications, Vol. 43. Ed. by Gerald D. Aurbach & Donald M. McCormick. 316p. 1986. text ed. 129.00 (*0-12-709843-7*) Acad Pr.

Vitamins & Hormones Vol. 49: Steroids. Ed. by Gerald Litwack. (Illus.). 512p. 1994. text ed. 89.00 (*0-12-709849-6*) Acad Pr.

Vitamins & Hormones Vol. 50, Vol. 50. Ed. by Gerald Litwack. (Illus.). 496p. 1995. boxed 85.00 (*0-12-709850-X*) Acad Pr.

***Vitamins & Hormones Vol. 53: Cell Death Proteins, Vol. 53.** Gerald Litwack. (Illus.). 250p. 1997. text ed. 89.95 (*0-12-709853-4*, AP Prof) Acad Pr.

Vitamins & Memory: Niacin & Vitamin B-6 in Age-Related Cognitive Decline. Jan B. Deijen. 175p. 1993. pap. 26.50 (*90-5170-229-9*, Pub. by Thesis Pubs NE) IBD Ltd.

***Vitamins & Minerals.** Joan Kalbacken. LC 97-8231. (True Book Ser.). (J). 1998. write for info. (*0-516-20758-X*) Childrens.

Vitamins & Minerals. Don Nardo. (Encyclopedia of Health Ser.). (Illus.). (YA). (gr. 7 up). 1994. lib. bdg. 19.95 (*0-7910-0032-X*) Chelsea Hse.

***Vitamins & Minerals.** Andrew Weil. 1997. mass mkt. 2.99 (*0-8041-1672-5*) Ivy Books.

Vitamins & Minerals: Hazardous to Your Health? Mark J. Sweet & Stanley H. Freeman. 162p. 1992. pap. 8.95 (*0-930753-15-1*) Spect Ln Pr.

Vitamins & Minerals: Help or Harm. Charles W. Marshall. 206p. 1985. text ed. 11.95 (*0-397-53060-9*) Lppncott-Raven.

Vitamins & Minerals: Questions You Have - Answers You Need. Ellen Moyer. 1993. pap. 10.95 (*1-882606-05-1*) Peoples Med Soc.

Vitamins & Minerals: The Health Connection. Anni M. Lines. LC 85-7638. 188p. 1985. pap. 6.95 (*0-932090-14-1*) Health Plus.

Vitamins & Minerals from A to Z. Jewel Pookrum. 138p. 1993. pap. text ed. 9.95 (*1-881316-66-1*) A&B Bks.

***Vitamins & Minerals in Health & Nutrition.** Tolonen. (Ellis Horwood Series in Food Science & Technology). (Illus.). 256p. (Orig.). (C). pap. text ed. 41.95 (*0-7476-0068-6*) Van Nos Reinhold.

***Vitamins & Minerals in Pregnancy & Lactation.** Ed. by Heribert Berger. LC 88-3221. (Nestle Nutrition Workshop Ser.: Vol. 16). reprint ed. pap. 136.30 (*0-608-04717-1*, 2065438) Bks Demand.

Vitamins & Minerals in the Prevention & Treatment of Cancer. Maryce M. Jacobs. 312p. 1991. 121.95 (*0-8493-4259-7*, RC271) CRC Pr.

Vitamins & Minerals Library. Ed. by Janet R. Nagy. (Good Health Guides Library: Vol. 4). (Illus.). 1990. lib. bdg. 60.00 (*0-931013-84-4*) Moonbeam Pubns.

Vitamins & Nutrient Market. 220p. 1990. 950.00 (*0-318-00514-X*) Busn Trend.

Vitamins & Over-the-Counter Nutritional Supplements. Business Communications Co., Inc. Staff. 129p. 1987. pap. 1,750.00 (*0-89336-523-8*, GA-060) BCC.

Vitamins & Tonics: The International Market. Euromonitor Staff. 120p. (C). 1988. 2,925.00 (*0-685-30321-7*, Pub. by Euromonitor Pubns UK) Gale.

***Vitamins for the Soul.** Ann Spangler. LC 97-9324. 1997. 15.95 (*0-385-48738-X*) Doubleday.

Vitamins in Animal Nutrition: Comparative Aspects to Human Nutrition. Lee R. McDowell. Ed. by Tony J. Cunha. (Animal Feeding & Nutrition Ser.). 486p. 1989. text ed. 95.00 (*0-12-483372-1*) Acad Pr.

Vitamins in Cancer Prevention & Treatment: A Practical Guide. rev. ed. Kedar N. Prasad. 128p. 1993. pap. 9.95 (*0-89281-483-7*, Heal Arts VT) Inner Tradit.

Vitamins in Human Biology & Medicine. M. H. Briggs. 272p. 1981. 152.00 (*0-8493-5673-3*, QP771, CRC Reprint) Franklin.

Vitamins in Human Health & Disease. Tapan K. Basu & John W. Dikerson. (A CAB International Publication). 350p. 1996. pap. 50.00 (*0-85198-986-1*, Pub. by CAB Intntl UK) OUP.

Vitamins, Minerals, & Dietary Supplements: A Definitive Guide to Healthy Eating. Hasnain Walji. 144p. 1995. pap. 11.95 (*0-340-61905-8*, Pub. by H & S UK) Trafalgar.

Vitamins, Minerals, & Food Supplements Nutrition. American Dietetic Association Staff. 1996. pap. text ed. 5.95 (*1-56561-092-X*) Chronimed.

Vitamins, Minerals & Other Supplements. Carlson Wade. 148p. (Orig.). 1983. pap. 2.95 (*0-87983-333-5*) Keats.

Vitamins, Minerals, & Protein-Amino Acids Used for Animal Health. (Illus.). 112p. 1993. 1,500.00 (*0-89336-986-1*, GA-080B) BCC.

Vitamins, Minerals, & Protein-Amino Acids Used for Human Health. 176p. 1993. 1,500.00 (*0-89336-985-3*, GA-080A) BCC.

Vitamins, Nutrition & Cancer. Ed. by K. N. Prasad. (Illus.). xii, 320p. 1984. 158.50 (*3-8055-3846-4*) S Karger.

Vitas Patrum. Henri D'Arci. Ed. by Basilides A. O'Connor. (Catholic University of America. Studies in Romance Languages & Literatures: No. 29). reprint ed. 37.50 (*0-404-50329-2*) AMS Pr.

Vitas Patrum: The Lyff of the Olde Auncyent Fathers Hermytes. Saint Jerome. Tr. by William Caxton. LC 77-7409. (English Experience Ser.: No. 874). 1977. reprint ed. lib. bdg. 99.00 (*90-221-0874-0*) Walter J Johnson.

Vitazstvo. Vladimir Uhri. 60p. (Orig.). (SLO.). 1996. pap. 3.00 (*1-56983-042-8*) New Creat WI.

Vite De' Pittori, Scvltori et Architetti Moderni. fac. ed. Giovanni P. Bellori. (Documents of Art & Architectural History Ser. 1: Vol. 4). (Illus.). (ITA.). 1980. lib. bdg. 50.00 (*0-89371-104-7*) Broude Intl Edns.

Vite De' Piu Eccellenti Pittori see Lives of the Most Eminent Painters, Sculptors & Architects

Vite De Piv Eccellenti Architetti, Pittori, et Scvltori Italiani, 2 Vols. fac. ed. Giorgio Vasari. (Documents of Art & Architectural History Ser.: Ser. I; Vol. 1). (Illus.). (ITA.). 1980. Set. lib. bdg. 150.00 (*0-89371-101-2*) Broude Intl Edns.

Viterbo: Profile of a Thirteenth-Century Papal Palace. Gary M. Radke. LC 95-47503. (Illus.). 336p. (C). 1996. text ed. 85.00 (*0-521-48200-3*) Cambridge U Pr.

Vitex: The Women's Herb. Christopher Hobbs. Ed. by Michael Miovic & Beth Baugh. (Illus.). 53p. 1990. pap. text ed. 3.95 (*0-9618470-2-6*) Botanica CA.

***Vitex: The Women's Herb.** Christopher Hobbs. 1993. pap. text ed. 5.95 (*1-884360-07-6*) Botanica CA.

Vitez Voros Janos M. kir Vezerezredes Vezerkari Fonok Naploja see War Diary of the Chief of the General Staff, Janos Voros: From April 17 to October 15, 1944

Vitiligo & Other Hypomelanoses of Hair & Skin. Jean-Paul Ortonne et al. LC 82-16490. (Topics in Dermatology Ser.). 700p. 1983. 145.00 (*0-306-40974-7*, Plenum Med Bk) Plenum.

Vito Acconci. Kate Linker. LC 92-37681. (Illus.). 224p. 1994. 50.00 (*0-8478-1645-1*) Rizzoli Intl.

Vito Acconci: Dal Testo-Azione Al Corpo Come Testo. Mario Diacono. LC 75-22995. (Illus.). 245p. (ITA.). 1975. 9.95 (*0-915570-03-3*) Oolp Pr.

Vito & Zona. Wilma E. McDaniel. (Dog River Review Poetry Ser.). 40p. (Orig.). 1993. pap. 4.00 (*0-916155-21-8*) Trout Creek.

Vito Loves Geraldine: A Collection of Stories. Janice Eidus. 169p. (Orig.). 1990. pap. 7.95 (*0-87286-247-X*) City Lights.

Vito Marcantonio: Radical Politician, 1902-1954. Gerald Meyer. LC 88-31669. (SUNY Series in American Labor History). 303p. 1989. text ed. 64.50 (*0-7914-0082-4*); pap. text ed. 21.95 (*0-7914-0083-2*) State U NY Pr.

Vito Marcantonio: Selected Debates, Speeches & Writings 1935-1950. Ed. by Annette T. Rubinstein et al. LC 73-12402. (Illus.). xii, 494p. 1973. reprint ed. 49.50 (*0-678-01365-9*) Kelley.

Vito Marcantonio, Radical in Congress. Alan Schaffer. LC 66-29201. (Men & Movements Ser.). 272p. reprint ed. pap. 77.60 (*0-317-52021-0*, 2027415) Bks Demand.

Vito Marcantonio y Puerto Rico. Ed. by Felix Ojeda. 156p. 1978. pap. 6.95 (*0-940238-40-3*) Ediciones Huracan.

Vitoria Final: O Ano 2000. Marvin Byers. (Orig.). (POR.). 1996. pap. 11.95 (*0-9647871-2-1*, Hope of Israel) Hebron Minist.

***Vitreoretinal Surgery.** Zivojnovic. 1996. lib. bdg. 98.00 (*0-7923-3311-X*); lib. bdg. 98.00 (*0-7923-3312-8*); lib. bdg. 98.00 (*0-7923-3313-6*); lib. bdg. 98.00 (*0-7923-3314-4*); lib. bdg. 98.00 (*0-7923-4331-X*); lib. bdg. 98.00 (*0-7923-4332-8*) Kluwer Ac.

Vitreous & Retinal Laser Investigation. Marie-Jose Tassignon. (Illus.). 187p. 1994. pap. 25.00 (*90-70289-76-8*) Paul & Co Pubs.

Vitreous & Vitreoretinal Interface. Ed. by Charles L. Schepens et al. (Illus.). 195p. 1987. 96.00 (*0-387-96553-X*) Spr-Verlag.

Vitreous State. I. Gutzow & J. Schmelzer. 470p. 1995. 173.95 (*3-540-59087-0*) Spr-Verlag.

Vitreous State: Thermodynamic & Kinetic Aspects. Nemilov. 224p. 1994. 104.95 (*0-8493-3782-8*) CRC Pr.

Vitreous Substitutes. Gholam A. Peyman & Joel A. Schulman. LC 94-39562. 1995. text ed. 95.00 (*0-8385-9484-0*) Appleton & Lange.

Vitreous Surgery. Ronald G. Michels. (Illus.). 126p. 1982. 25.00 (*0-317-94081-3*) Am Acad Ophthal.

Vitrines. Joseph Beuys. 1994. 50.00 (*3-88375-168-5*, Pub. by Walther Konig GW) Dist Art Pubs.

Vitrinite Reflectance As a Maturity Parameter: Applications & Limitations. Prasanta K. Mukhopadhyay & Wallace G. Dow. LC 94-34670. (Symposium Ser.: No. 570). (Illus.). 306p. 1994. 79.95 (*0-8412-2994-5*) Am Chemical.

Vitruvius: Architect & Engineer. Vitruvius. Ed. by A. MacKay. 88p. 1985. reprint ed. pap. 14.95 (*0-86292-157-0*, Pub. by Brstl Class Pr UK) Focus Pub-R Pullins.

***Vitruvius: Dictionnaire des Termes Techniques du De Architectura de Vitruve.** Ed. by Louis Callebat & Philippe Fleury. (GER.). 1995. write for info. (*3-487-09398-7*) G Olms Pubs.

Vitruvius - Vitruve, de Architectura: Concordance. Documentation Bibliographique, Lexicale Et Grammaticale, 2 vols. Vitruvius. Ed. by L. Callebat et al. (Alpha-Omega, Reihe A Ser.: Bd. XLIII). lxxxi, 1401p. 1984. Set. write for info. (*3-487-07471-0*) G Olms Pubs.

Vitruvius & Later Roman Building Manuals. William H. Plommer. LC 72-90487. (Cambridge Classical Studies). 125p. reprint ed. pap. 35.70 (*0-317-27568-2*, 2024512) Bks Demand.

Vitruvius Britannicus, 3 Vols. Incl. Vol. 1. 1715-25 Ed. Colin Campbell. LC 67-18052. 47.50 (*0-685-73174-X*); Vol. 2. 1739 & 1767-71 Eds. J. Badeslade et al. LC 67-18052. 600.95 (*0-405-09045-5*); Vol. 3. 1802-08 Ed. George Richardson. LC 67-18052. 47.50 (*0-685-73176-6*); LC 67-18052. write for info. (*0-318-50911-3*) Ayer.

Vitruvius Scoticus: A Facsimile of a Rare & Important Book. William Adam. reprint ed. 360.00 (*0-404-18136-8*) AMS Pr.

Vitruvius Teutsch (De Architectura Libri X, Deutsch) Vitruvius Pollio. 641p. 1973. reprint ed. write for info. (*3-487-05010-2*) G Olms Pubs.

Vittles & Verse: A Unique Cookbook of Delicious Verse & Poetic Food. Selma Raskin. 128p. 1989. pap. 9.95 (*0-938509-02-0*) Pretty Penny Pr.

Vittoria. large type ed. Robert Merle. LC 90-29258. 724p. 1991. reprint ed. lib. bdg. 21.95 (*1-56054-122-9*) Thorndike Pr.

Vittoria Colonna. Maud F. Jerrold. (Select Bibliographies Reprint Ser.). 1977. 30.95 (*0-8369-5153-0*) Ayer.

Vittoria Cottage. D. E. Stevenson. 17.95 (*0-8488-1473-8*) Amereon Ltd.

Vittoria Cottage. D. E. Stevenson. 350p. 1983. reprint ed. lib. bdg. 16.95 (*0-89966-163-7*) Buccaneer Bks.

Vittorini Omnibus: The Twilight of the Elephant in Sicily, La Garibaldina. Elio Vittorini. Tr. by Cinina Brescia et al. from ITA. LC 73-78790. 320p. 1973. pap. 8.95 (*0-8112-0499-5*, NDP366) New Directions.

***Vittorino da Feltre & Other Humanist Educators.** William H. Woodward. (Renaissance Society of America Reprint Texts Ser.: No. 5). 261p. 1996. reprint ed. pap. text ed. 17.95 (*0-8020-7157-0*) U of Toronto Pr.

Vittorio Gregotti. Vittorio Gregotti et al. (Illus.). 288p. 1997. 65.00 (*0-8478-1951-5*) Rizzoli Intl.

Vittorio Sainati, die Geschichte des Aristotelischen Organons, I, Band VI. (GER.). write for info. (*0-318-70429-3*) G Olms Pubs.

Vitus Bering. Peter Lauridsen. LC 70-94274. (Select Bibliographies Reprint Ser.). 1977. 23.95 (*0-8369-5048-8*) Ayer.

UV

An Asterisk (*) at the beginning of an entry indicates that the title is appearing in BIP for the first time.

***Viudo en Apuros.** Leslie D. Guccione. (Deseo Ser.: No. 35181). (SPA.). 1997. mass mkt. 3.50 (*0-373-35181-X*, 1-35181-6) Harlequin Bks.

Vi's Night Book. William Rowe. (Illus.). 56p. (J). (gr. 3-6). 1995. pap. 7.95 (*0-9641330-0-8*) Portunus Pubng.

Viva. Incl. . Ed. by S. Moodie et al. 1991. 17.00 (*0-582-07751-6*); . Ed. by S. Moodie et al. 1991. 7.67 (*0-582-05391-9*); . Ed. by S. Moodie et al. 1991. vhs 22.61 (*0-582-06300-0*); . Ed. by S. Moodie et al. 1991. 17.00 (*0-582-07754-0*); . Ed. by S. Moodie et al. 1991. 7.67 (*0-582-05390-0*); . Ed. by S. Moodie et al. 1991. audio 22.61 (*0-582-08689-2*); . Ed. by S. Moodie et al. 1991. 18.60 (*0-582-07755-9*); . Ed. by S. Moodie et al. 1991. 7.67 (*0-582-05392-7*); . Ed. by S. Moodie et al. 1991. audio 22.61 (*0-582-09829-7*); 1991. write for info. (*0-318-70411-0*) Longman.

Viva: Women & Popular Protest in Latin America. Ed. by Sarah A. Radcliffe & Sallie Westwood. LC 92-20274. (International Studies of Women & Places). 288p. (C). 1993. pap. 17.95 (*0-415-07313-8*, A7383, Routledge NY) Routledge.

***Viva Baseball! Latin Major Leaguers & Their Special Hunger.** Samuel O. Regalado. LC 97-21066. (Sports & Society Ser.). 1998. write for info. (*0-252-02372-2*) U of Ill Pr.

Viva California! Three Accounts of Life in Early California. Benjamin D. Wilson et al. (West Coast Studies: No. 1). 80p. lib. bdg. write for info. (*0-8095-2801-0*, Sidewinder Press) Borgo Pr.

Viva Cristo Rey: The Cristero Rebellion & the Church-State Conflict in Mexico. David C. Bailey. LC 73-17119. (Texas Pan-American Ser.). 368p. reprint ed. pap. 104.90 (*0-8357-7722-7*, 2036079) Bks Demand.

***Viva Guadalupe! The Virgin in New Mexican Art.** Jacqueline Dunnington. (Illus.). 96p. (Orig.). 1997. pap. 19.95 (*0-89013-321-2*) Museum NM Pr.

Viva Heather! Sheri C. Sinykin. (Magic Attic Club Ser.). (Illus.). 80p. (J). (gr. 2-6). 1996. 12.95 (*1-57513-067-X*); pap. 5.95 (*1-57513-068-8*) Magic Attic.

Viva la Accion! Live Action Spanish. Contee Seely & Elizabeth Romijn. (Live Action Ser.). (Illus.). 192p. (Orig.). (SPA.). 1989. pap. 11.95 (*0-929724-01-1*) Command Performance.

Viva la Lengua. 2nd ed. Francisco Jimenez et al. 144p. (C). 1987. pap. text ed. 18.00 (*0-15-594939-X*) HB Coll Pubs.

Viva La Liberta! Politics in Opera. Anthony Arblaster. LC 92-27541. 340p. (C). (gr. 13). 1992. text ed. 35.00 (*0-86091-391-0*, A9738, Pub. by Vrso UK) Norton.

***Viva La Liberta: Politics in Opera.** Anthony Arrlaster. 1997. pap. text ed. 18.00 (*0-86091-618-9*, Pub. by Verso UK) Routledge Chapman & Hall.

Viva la Mediterranean: A Cultural Feast from Healthmark. Jean Oliva-Rasbich. 1994. 21.95 (*0-9624784-2-3*) HealthMark.

Viva la Muerta (Baal Babylone) Fernando Arrabal. 9.95 (*0-686-54477-3*) Fr & Eur.

Viva la Musica. Pete Escovito. (J). (gr. 4-7). 1991. pap. 9.95 (*0-930647-09-2*) Lancaster Prodns.

Viva la Vida-Un Hijo Prodigo (Live it Up-Prodigal Son) A. Hartley. (SPA.). 0.49 (*0-685-74987-8*, 496011); 0.59 (*0-8423-6511-7*, 496001) Editorial Unilit.

Viva la Virgen de Guadalupe! Photos & Intro. by Mary-Ann S. Bruni. (Illus.). 64p. 1989. 24.95 (*0-935857-18-4*); pap. 14.95 (*0-935857-19-2*) Texart.

Viva Las Elvis. Ed. by Peg Thompson. 1995. pap. 4.95 (*1-55152-010-9*) LPC InBook.

Viva Las Vegas: After-Hours Architecture. Alan Hess. LC 92-39642. (Illus.). 128p. 1993. pap. 18.95 (*0-8118-0111-X*) Chronicle Bks.

Viva Las Vegas: Nightclub Greats. Friedman-Fairfax & Sony Music Staff. (Life, Times & Music Book/CD Ser.). 1995. pap. 16.98 incl. audio compact disk (*1-56799-234-X*, Friedman-Fairfax) M Friedman Pub Grp Inc.

Viva l'Azione! Live Action Italian. Contee Seely & Elizabeth Romijn. Tr. by Donatella Carta & Julia L. Montrond from ENG. (Live Action Ser.). (Illus.). 192p. (Orig.). (ITA.). 1993. pap. text ed. 11.95 (*0-929724-04-6*) Command Performance.

Viva Mexico! The Story of Benito Juarez & Cinco de Mayo. Ruiz. LC 92-18071. (Stories of America Ser.). (Illus.). 32p. (J). (gr. 2-5). 1992. lib. bdg. 22.83 (*0-8114-7214-0*) Raintree Steck-V.

Viva Mi Dueno. Ramon Del Valle-Inclan. (Nueva Austral Ser.: Vol. 193). (SPA.). 1993. pap. text ed. 34.95 (*84-239-1993-5*) Elliots Bks.

Viva Nippon!? T. Ichikawa. Tr. by M. McDonald & S. McDonald. 300p. (C). 1990. text ed. 46.00 (*9971-5-0591-6*); pap. text ed. 18.00 (*981-02-0284-9*) World Scientific Pub.

Viva Tejas: The Story of the Tejanos, the Mexican-Born Patriots of the Texas Revolution. Ruben R. Lozano. (Illus.). 82p. (Orig.). 1991. pap. 8.95 (*0-943260-02-7*) Alamo Pr TX.

***Viva! Tradiciones: South Texas Cooks from Brushto Bay.** Junior League of Corpus Christ Staff. 1996. 19.95 (*0-9609144-2-0*) Jr League Corpus Christi.

Viva Villa: A Recovery of the Real Pancho Villa, Peon, Bandit, Soldier, Patriot. Edgcumb Pinchon. LC 70-111729. (American Imperialism: Viewpoints of United States Foreign Policy, 1898-1941 Ser.). 1980. reprint ed. 26.95 (*0-405-02045-7*) Ayer.

Viva Vocab. Lucy E. Haagen. 1983. teacher ed. 6.96 (*0-88334-168-9*, 76135); student ed. 12.00 (*0-8013-0105-X*, 75769) Longman.

Viva Zapata! Generation, Gender, & Historical Consciousness in the Reception of the Ejido Reform in Mexico. Lynn Stephen. (Transformation of Rural Mexico Ser.: No. 6). 36p. 1994. pap. 7.00 (*1-878367-24-2*) UCSD Ctr US-Mex.

Vivacious Daughter: Seven Lectures on the Religious Situation among Norwegians in the United States. Herman A. Preus. Ed. by Todd W. Nichol. LC 90-212645. (Publications of the Norwegian-American Historical Association: No. 11). 246p. reprint ed. pap. 70.20 (*0-7837-0109-8*, 2040386) Bks Demand.

Vivacites du Capitaine Tic. Eugene Labiche. 9.95 (*0-686-54258-4*) Fr & Eur.

Vivaha: The Hindu Marriage Samskaras. Tr. by R. C. Prasad. (C). 1993. pap. 11.50 (*81-208-1132-1*, Pub. by Motilal Banarsidass II) S Asia.

Vivaldi. (Dent Master Musicians Ser.). (Illus.). (C). pap. write for info. (*0-19-816497-1*) OUP.

Vivaldi. John Booth. (Illustrated Lives of the Great Composers Ser.). (Illus.). 128p. 1996. 14.95 (*0-7119-1727-2*, OP 45202) Omnibus NY.

Vivaldi. H. C. Landon. LC 93-60428. (Illus.). 240p. 1993. 24.95 (*0-500-01576-7*) Thames Hudson.

***Vivaldi.** Michael Talbot. (BBC Music Guides Ser.). 112p. 1996. 4.95 (*0-563-12856-9*, BB 11137, Pub. by BBC UK) Parkwest Pubns.

Vivaldi. Michael Talbot. LC 93-15281. (Master Musicians Ser.). 237p. 1993. 30.00 (*0-02-872665-0*) Schirmer Bks.

Vivaldi. Tutti Staff. (TuTTi Ser.: No. 10). 176p. pap. 16.95 incl. disk (*1-57301-024-3*) TuTTi USA.

Vivaldi: Voice of the Baroque. H. C. Landon. (Illus.). 224p. 1996. pap. 15.95 (*0-226-46842-9*) U Ch Pr.

Vivaldi No. 8: The Four Seasons & Other Concertos Op. 8. Paul Everett. (Music Handbooks Ser.). (Illus.). 128p. (C). 1996. text ed. 34.95 (*0-521-40499-1*); pap. text ed. 11.95 (*0-521-40692-7*) Cambridge U Pr.

Vivaldi Violin Concertos: A Handbook. Arlan S. Martin. LC 76-169698. 278p. 1972. 20.00 (*0-8108-0432-8*) Scarecrow.

Vivan los Colores. Jill Slynne. 1992. pap. 1.50 (*0-8167-2650-7*) Troll Communs.

Vivan los Numeros. Watermill Press Staff. (J). (gr. 4-7). 1997. pap. 1.50 (*0-8167-2651-5*) Troll Communs.

Vivan los Titeres! Judy B. Graner & Sara Segura. 120p. (SPA.). 1990. pap. 6.95 (*0-8297-0426-4*) Life Pubs Intl.

Vivandiere Pas de Six. Text by Ann H. Guest. (Language of Dance Ser.: Vol. 6). 163p. (FRE.). 1995. text ed. 58.00 (*2-88124-989-2*, ECU49) Gordon & Breach.

Vivandiere Pas de Six, Vol. 6. Text by Ann H. Guest. (Language of Dance Ser.: Vol. 6). 163p. 1995. pap. text ed. 34.00 (*2-88124-990-6*, ECU29) Gordon & Breach.

Vivaranaprameyasangraha of Vidyaranya: Summary of the Tropics of the Elucidation. Tr. by G. Thibaut. (C). 1994. reprint ed. text ed. 20.00 (*81-7030-391-5*, Pub. by Sri Satguru Pubns II) S Asia.

Vivas As Critic Essays in Poetics & Criticism by Eliseo Vivas. Hugh Curtler. LC 82-50419. 271p. (C). 1982. 22.50 (*0-87875-224-2*) Whitston Pub.

***Vivas in General Surgery.** F. G. Smiddy. (Illus.). 336p. 1987. pap. write for info. (*0-632-01656-6*) Blackwell Sci.

Vivation: The Science of Enjoying All of Your Life. Jim Leonard & Phil Laut. Orig. Title: Rebirthing: The Science of Enjoying all of Your Life. 320p. 1991. pap. 12.95 (*0-9610132-4-9*) Vivation Pub.

Viva!...Una Pinata! Elisa Kleven. Orig. Title: Hooray, a Pinata!. (Illus.). 32p. (J). (ps-3). 1996. pap. 15.99 (*0-525-45606-6*) NAL-Dutton.

Vive la Difference: A Celebration of the Sexes. Anthony Walsh & Grace J. Walsh. (Skeptic's Bookshelf Ser.). (Illus.). 140p. 1993. 23.95 (*0-87975-852-X*) Prometheus Bks.

Vive la French Toast: Gail Greco's Little Bed & Breakfast Cookbooks. Gail Greco. LC 96-30490. 1996. 12.95 (*1-55853-435-0*) Rutledge Hill Pr.

Vive la Pologne! The Henryk Gierszynski Collection. Ed. by Eugene J. Kisluk & Eugene Beshenkovsky. LC 85-61817. (Russica Bibliography Ser.: No. 6). 500p. 1987. 92.50 (*0-89830-101-7*) Russica Pubs.

Vive l'Action! Live Action French. Contee Seely & Elizabeth Romijn. Tr. by Lia Raileanu & Jean-Paul Raffinot from ENG. (Live Action Ser.). (Illus.). 192p. (Orig.). (FRE.). 1989. pap. text ed. 11.95 (*0-929724-02-X*) Command Performance.

Vive le Francais, Level 1. G. McConnell. 1978. pap. text ed. 22.20 (*0-201-14700-9*) Addison-Wesley.

Vive le Francais: Cahier D'Activites, Level 2. James V. McConnell. 1978. pap. text ed. 10.04 (*0-201-14708-4*) Addison-Wesley.

Vive Le Francais Level 1: Cahier D'Activities. G. McConnell. (FRE.). 1978. pap. text ed. 10.04 (*0-201-14701-7*) Addison-Wesley.

Vive le Francais Level 2. G. McConnell. 1978. pap. text ed. 22.20 (*0-201-14707-6*) Addison-Wesley.

Vive Le Francais Level 3. G. McConnell. (FRE.). 1979. pap. text ed. 12.16 (*0-201-14715-7*) Addison-Wesley.

Vive le Roi! A History of the French Coronation from Charles V to Charles X. Richard A. Jackson. LC 83-25896. xvi, 310p. 1984. 39.95 (*0-8078-1602-7*) U of NC Pr.

Vive le Roi Babar. Jean de Brunhoff. 20p. (J). 1976. 4.95 (*0-7859-0675-4*, FC253) Fr & Eur.

Vive le Roi Babar. Laurent De Brunhoff. (FRE.). (J). (gr. 2-3). 4.95 (*0-685-28423-9*) Fr & Eur.

Vive Lo Que Crees! - Live What You Believe! Floreal Ureta & Eduardo Malve. 96p. (SPA.). (YA). 1990. pap. 4.99 (*0-311-12349-X*) Casa Bautista.

***Vive Mon Corps!** Marie-Francine Hebert. (Gout De Savoir Ser.). (Illus.). 24p. (FRE.). (J). (ps up). 1996. pap. 4.95 (*2-89021-226-2*, Pub. by Les Editions CN) Firefly Bks Ltd.

Vive Napoleon, Vol. 13. Betty Y. Ho. LC 92-26675. (System of Government in the Living Body Ser.). (Illus.). 300p. (Orig.). (YA). (gr. 5 up). 1993. reprint ed. pap. write for info. (*0-9600148-7-X*) Juvenescent.

Viveka-Cudamani or the Crest Jewel of Wisdom. Mohini M. Chatterji. 1983. 6.25 (*0-8356-7091-0*) Theos Pub Hse.

Vivekachudamani. Shankara. Tr. by Swami Madhavananda. 1921. Bilingual ed. pap. 4.95 (*0-87481-147-3*, Pub. by Advaita Ashrama II) Vedanta Pr.

Vivekananda: A Biography. Swami Nikhilananda. LC 53-7851. (Illus.). 227p. (C). 1989. pap. 12.50 (*0-911206-25-6*) Ramakrishna.

Vivekananda: A Biography in Pictures. 2nd ed. Swami Vivekananda. Ed. by Advaita Ashrama Staff. (Illus.). 1974. 10.95 (*0-87481-136-8*, Pub. by Advaita Ashrama II) Vedanta Pr.

Vivekananda: East Meets West, a Pictorial Biography. Swami Chetanananda. LC 94-45710. (Illus.). 175p. 1996. 35.00 (*0-916356-78-7*) Vedanta Soc St Louis.

Vivekananda: The Great Spiritual Teacher. 587p. 1996. 10.95 (*81-7505-147-7*, Pub. by Advaita Ashrama II) Vedanta Pr.

Vivekananda: The Man & His Message by Eastern & Western Disciples. 192p. pap. 4.50 (*81-7505-000-4*) Vedanta Pr.

Vivekananda: The Yogas & Other Works. Ed. by Swami Nikhilananda. LC 53-7534. (Illus.). 1018p. 1953. 29.50 (*0-911206-04-3*) Ramakrishna.

Vivencias Hispanicas: Cuentos Del Siglo XX. James H. Hoddie. 248p. (C). 1988. pap. text ed. 20.75 (*0-15-594943-8*) HB Coll Pubs.

Vivendo Sob Pressao. Gene A. Getz. Orig. Title: When the Pressure Is on. 176p. (POR.). 1986. pap. 4.95 (*0-8297-0897-9*) Life Pubs Intl.

Vivere All Italiana. Antonella Pease & Daniela B. Carter. (C). 1985. pap. text ed. write for info. (*0-07-554713-9*) McGraw.

Vives & Phillips Lexicon. Miguel Vives & Joan Phillips. 440p. 1987. pap. 14.95 (*0-945933-00-2*) Intechnos.

Vives & Phillips Subject Lexicon. 2nd ed. 1989. 14.95 (*0-945933-01-0*) Intechnos.

Vives Bibliography. Carlos G. Norena. LC 89-78313. (Studies in Renaissance Literature: Vol. 5). 88p. 1990. lib. bdg. 49.95 (*0-88946-148-1*) E Mellen.

Vivet Sesh. Ed. by Nicholas M. Edgerton. LC 90-71994. 61p. (Orig.). 1991. pap. 7.00 (*1-56002-094-6*) Aegina Pr.

***Vivi.** E. E. Cummings. Ed. by George J. Firmage. 80p. 1997. pap. 12.00 (*0-87140-169-X*) Liveright.

Vivian: Growing up Abused. Vivian Harvest & Kristen J. Ingram. LC 88-88167. 147p. 1988. pap. 8.95 (*0-935435-02-6*) High Impact Pr.

Vivian Grey: A Romance of Youth see Works of Benjamin Disraeli

Vivid. Beverly Jenkins. 400p. (Orig.). 1995. mass mkt. 4.99 (*0-380-78085-2*) Avon.

Vivid Flavors Cookbook: International Recipes from Hot & Spicy to Smoky & Sweet. Robert Wemischner. 320p. 1994. 25.00 (*1-56565-152-9*) Lowell Hse.

Vivid Flavors Cookbook: International Recipes from Hot & Spicy to Smoky & Sweet. Robert Wemischner. 320p. 1995. pap. 16.00 (*1-56565-340-8*) Lowell Hse.

Vivid Logic: Knowledge-Based Reasoning with Two Kinds of Negation. Gerd Wagner. LC 93-46747. (Lecture Notes in Computer Science, Lecture Notes in Artificial Intelligence Ser.: Vol. 764). 1994. 34.95 (*0-387-57604-5*) Spr-Verlag.

Vivid Steady State: Les Murray & Australian Poetry. Lawrence Bourke. 174p. 1992. pap. 22.95 (*0-86840-045-9*, Pub. by New South Wales Univ Pr AT) Intl Spec Bk.

Vividness of Visual Imagery: Measurement, Nature, Function & Dynamics. Stuart J. McKelvie. 275p. (Orig.). (C). 1995. pap. text ed. 30.00 (*0-913412-72-4*) Brandon Hse.

Vivien: Life of Vivien Leigh. Alexander Walker. LC 87-20966. 1989. pap. 12.95 (*0-8021-3259-6*, Grove) Grove-Atltic.

Vivien Alone. large type ed. Lucy Lilley. 1990. 25.99 (*0-7089-2237-6*) Ulverscroft.

Vivien Greene's Doll House Collection: The Complete Rotunda Collection. Vivien Greene & Margaret Towner. (Illus.). 192p. 1995. 60.00 (*0-87951-632-1*) Overlook Pr.

Vivien Leigh: A Bio-Bibliography. Cynthia M. Molt. LC 92-23785. (Bio-Bibliographies in the Performing Arts Ser.: No. 35). 352p. 1992. text ed. 49.95 (*0-313-27578-5*, MVL, Greenwood Pr) Greenwood.

Vivien Leigh: A Biography. Hugo Vickers. (Illus.). 384p. 1989. 22.95 (*0-316-90245-4*) Little.

Vivien Leigh Paper Dolls in Full Color. Tom Tierney. (J). pap. 3.95 (*0-486-24207-2*) Dover.

Vivienda Precolombina e Indigena Actual en Tierradentro. Alvaro Chaves & Mauricio Puerta. (Illus.). 284p. (SPA.). 1988. pap. 8.50 (*1-877812-33-1*) UPLAAP.

Viviendas: Spanish Take-Home Parent Pack, Set. (Take-Home Parent Packs Ser.). (Illus.). (Orig.). (SPA.). 1993. pap. 11.95 (*1-56334-386-X*) Hampton-Brown.

Viviendas: Teacher's Theme Guide. (Que Maravilla! Ser.). (Illus.). (Orig.). (SPA.). 1992. pap. 29.95 (*1-56334-161-1*) Hampton-Brown.

Viviendo el Evangelio see Living the Gospel with the Mother

***Viviendo Libre en Cristo - Living Free in Christ.** Anderson. 292p. (SPA.). write for info. (*1-56063-497-9*) Editorial Unilit.

Viviendo Sobrio. 126p. (SPA.). 1981. pap. 1.50 (*0-916856-08-9*) AAWS.

***Vivienne Westwood.** Molyneux. Date not set. 18.95 (*0-7893-0115-6*) Universe.

***Vivienne Westwood: Fashion, Perversity & the Sixties Laid Bare.** Fred Vermorel. (Illus.). 256p. 1997. pap. 14.95 (*0-87951-795-6*) Overlook Pr.

Vivienne Westwood: Fashion, Perversity & the Sixties Laid Bare. Fred Vermorel. LC 96-19535. (Illus.). 256p. 1996. reprint ed. 23.95 (*0-87951-691-7*) Overlook Pr.

Vivir a Hostos. Comite Del Sesquicentenario Eugenio Maria de Hostos Staff & Jose E. Gonzalez. 165p. 1989. pap. 10.00 (*0-685-51575-3*) U of PR Pr.

Vivir Despues de la Perdida. Bob Deits. LC 94-30395. 240p. (SPA.). 1994. pap. 12.95 (*1-55561-062-5*) Fisher Bks.

Vivir en Caimito. Fernando Pico. LC 88-83372. 185p. 1989. pap. 7.25 (*0-940238-74-8*) Ediciones Huracan.

Vivir en Madrid. Silverio Munoz. 140p. (Orig.). (SPA.). 1991. text ed. 13.50 (*0-937985-05-8*) Ediciones Arauco.

Vivir Hoy. 2nd ed. Gloria Duran & Manuel Duran. 224p. (C). 1981. pap. text ed. 20.00 (*0-15-594948-9*) HB Coll Pubs.

Vivir la Misa. (SPA.). (J). (gr. 6). 1986. pap. text ed. 4.00 (*0-8198-8007-8*) Pauline Bks.

Vivir la Muerte: Rituals of Death in Latin America. Hans-Georg Pospischil & Andrian Kreye. 148p. 1996. 39.95 (*3-905514-73-7*) Dist Art Pubs.

Vivir Necesario Para La Edificacion De Las Reuniones De Grupos Pequenos. Witness Lee. 132p. (SPA.). per. 4.50 (*0-87083-251-4*, 12010002) Living Stream Ministry.

Vivir por Fe: Encuentro Biblicos. Catherine Schell & Marilyn Kunz. (Encuentros Biblicos Ser.). 72p. (SPA.). 1989. pap. 1.50 (*0-945792-54-9*, 490452) Editorial Unilit.

***Viviremos! On the Road to Healthy Living.** Gay Callaway Villarreal et al. Tr. by Maria C. Saiz. (Illus.). 312p. (ENG & SPA.). 1996. pap. 19.95 (*1-880002-12-4*) Natl Coal Advocates.

Vivisection & Dissection in the Classroom: A Guide to Conscientious Objection. Gary L. Francione & Anna E. Charlton. (Illus.). xiv, 136p. (Orig.). 1992. pap. 7.95 (*1-881699-00-5*) Am Anti-Viv Soc.

Vivisection & the True Aims of Education in Biology. 3rd ed. George K. Russell. 14p. (gr. 8-12). pap. 0.75 (*0-913098-30-2*) Myrin Institute.

Vivisection Controversy in Britain. C. W. Hume. 1960. 40.00 (*0-317-43892-1*) St Mut.

Vivisection in Historical Perspective. Ed. by Nicolaas A. Rupke. 384p. (C). 1990. pap. text ed. 27.95 (*0-415-05021-9*, A4489) Routledge.

Vivisection in Historical Perspective. Ed. by Nicolaas A. Rupke. LC 87-8992. 373p. 1987. 85.00 (*0-7099-4236-2*, Pub. by Croom Helm UK) Routledge Chapman & Hall.

Vivisector. Patrick White. 1,624p. 1992. pap. 11.95 (*0-14-018527-5*, Penguin Classics) Viking Penguin.

Vivo en El Espiritu. (ENG & SPA.). (J). (gr. 5). 1985. pap. text ed. 4.00 (*0-8198-8006-X*) Pauline Bks.

Vivolo & His Wooden Children. Ken Laffal. LC 76-11492. (Illus.). 144p. 1976. 19.95 (*0-913622-04-4*) Gallery Pr.

Vivre les Actes des Apotres Aujourd'hui see Experiencing the Acts of the Apostle Today

Vivvs per Ora. E. O. Furber. (C). 1982. pap. text ed. 60.00 (*0-900269-04-9*, Pub. by Old Vicarage UK) St Mut.

Vixen. Mary E. Braddon. LC 93-33711. (Pocket Classics Ser.). 1993. 8.00 (*0-7509-0445-3*, Pub. by Sutton Pubng UK) Bks Intl VA.

Vixen. Jane Feather. 432p. 1994. 5.99 (*0-553-56055-7*, Fanfare) Bantam.

***Vixen.** W. S. Merwin. 1997. pap. 14.00 (*0-679-76601-4*) Knopf.

Vixen: Poems. W. S. Merwin. LC 95-30283. 88p. 1996. 21.00 (*0-679-44477-7*) Knopf.

Vixen & Her Pups see Hewitt Early Readers: Level II

Vixen in Velvet. Fern Michaels. 224p. 1986. mass mkt. 3.50 (*0-345-34014-0*) Ballantine.

Vixen 03. Clive Cussler. 1976. 23.95 (*0-8488-0470-8*) Amereon Ltd.

***Vixen 03.** Clive Cussler. 384p. 1984. mass mkt. 6.99 (*0-553-27390-6*) Bantam.

***Vixen 03.** Clive Cussler. 1994. reprint ed. lib. bdg. 32.95 (*1-56849-272-3*) Buccaneer Bks.

Vixens. large type ed. Frank Yerby. 535p. 1981. 25.99 (*0-7089-0628-1*) Ulverscroft.

Vixens' Keep. Mark Wallace. 88p. 1995. pap. 5.95 (*1-883847-18-4*) MU Press.

Vizability Handbook. Woolsey & Curtis. (General Engineering Ser.). 1996. pap. 43.95 (*0-534-95112-0*) PWS Pubs.

Vizability Sketchbook. Woolsey & Curtis. (General Engineering Ser.). 1996. pap. 7.95 (*0-534-95118-X*) PWS Pubs.

Vizagapatam District Gazetteer. W. Francis. (C). 1992. reprint ed. 48.00 (*81-206-0811-9*, Pub. by Asian Educ Servs II) S Asia.

Vizcaya on the Eve of Carlism: Politics & Society, 1800-1833. Renato Barahona. (Basque Ser.). (Illus.). 352p. 1989. 44.95 (*0-87417-122-9*) U of Nev Pr.

Vizi's Book: Visual Puns in a Frame for You to Figure Out. Richard M. Greene, Jr. (Illus.). 1990. pap. 19.95 (*0-934487-59-6*) R M Greene.

Vizje de Hierusalem. Guerrero. Ed. by Calcraft. (Exeter Hispanic Text Ser.: No. 37). 119p. (SPA.). Date not set. pap. text ed. 19.95 (*0-85989-235-2*, Pub. by Univ Exeter Pr UK) Northwestern U Pr.

Vizsla Champions, 1960-1984. Jan L. Freund. (Illus.). 131p. 1986. pap. 36.95 (*0-940808-06-4*) Camino E E & Bk.

Vizsla Champions, 1985-1994. Camino E. E. & Bk. Co. Staff. (Illus.). 65p. 1997. pap. 32.95 (*0-940808-63-3*) Camino E E & Bk.

Vizslas. Ernest H. Hart. (Illus.). 160p. 1989. 9.95 (*0-86622-685-0*, KW-178) TFH Pubns.

VJ Day in Photographs. Tony Hall. (Illus.). 64p. 1995. 1.50 (*0-517-12157-3*) Random Hse Value.

VLA Membership Directory, 1995. 57p. 1995. pap. 15.00 (*0-614-05461-3*) Vol Lawyers Arts.

UV

An Asterisk (*) at the beginning of an entry indicates that the title is appearing in BIP for the first time.

Vlachs: The History of a Balkan People. T. Winnifrith. 65. 95 (*0-7156-2135-1*, Pub. by Duckworth UK) Focus Pub-R Pullins.

Vlachs of the Balkans: A Submerged Nation Existing Throughout the Millennia. Vatro Murvar. 155p. 30.00 (*0-931635-02-0*); pap. 16.00 (*0-931635-03-9*) Fnd Soc Stdy.

Vlad Dracula, the Impaler: A Play. Marin Sorescu. Tr. by Dennis Deletant. LC 86-82941. (Illus.). 111p. 1990. reprint ed. pap. 19.95 (*0-948259-98-1*, Pub. by Forest Bks UK) Dufour.

***Vlad the Drac Superstar.** large type ed. Ann Jungman. (J). 1997. 16.95 (*0-7451-6970-8*, Galaxy Child Lrg Print) Chivers N Amer.

Vladimar Nabokov. L. L. Lee. Ed. by Sylvia E. Bowman. LC 76-128. (Twayne's United States Authors Ser.). 166p. (C). 1976. lib. bdg. 17.95 (*0-8057-7166-2*) Irvington.

Vladimir & Nadya. Original Work. Mary H. Dann. LC 97-5843. (Illus.). 400p. 1997. pap. 9.95 (*0-7178-0712-6*) Intl Pubs Co.

Vladimir Ivanovicdal As a Belletrist. Joachim T. Baer. LC 72-88190. (Slavistic Printings & Reprintings Ser.: No. 276). 204p. 1972. text ed. 46.15 (*90-279-2334-5*) Mouton.

Vladimir Lenin. John Haney. (World Leaders - Past & Present Ser.). (Illus.). 112p. (J). (gr. 5 up). 1988. lib. bdg. 19.95 (*0-87754-570-7*) Chelsea Hse.

Vladimir Nabokov. G. M. Hyde. LC 78-307708. 240p. 1979. pap. 7.95 (*0-7145-2574-X*) M Boyars Pubs.

***Vladimir Nabokov.** Ed. by Norman Page. (Critical Heritage Ser.). 264p. (C). 1997. text ed. 15.00 (*0-415-15916-4*) Routledge.

Vladimir Nabokov. David Rampton. LC 93-16140. (Modern Novelists Ser.). 160p. 1993. text ed. 29.95 (*0-312-09629-1*) St Martin.

Vladimir Nabokov. Tony Sharpe. LC 91-33907. (Modern Fiction Ser.). 128p. (Orig.). 1995. text ed. 12.95 (*0-7131-6575-8*, A6113, Pub. by E Arnld UK) St Martin.

Vladimir Nabokov. Michael Wood. (Contemporary Writers Ser.). 96p. 1988. pap. text ed. 8.95 (*0-415-00659-7*) Routledge.

Vladimir Nabokov. Julian Moynahan. LC 71-633325. (University of Minnesota Pamphlets on American Writers Ser.: No. 96). 47p. (Orig.). reprint ed. pap. 25.00 (*0-7837-2871-9*, 2057584) Bks Demand.

Vladimir Nabokov: Selected Letters, 1940-1977. Ed. by Dmitri Nabokov & Matthew J. Bruccoli. (Illus.). 608p. 1990. pap. 14.95 (*0-15-693610-0*, Harvest Bks) HarBrace.

Vladimir Nabokov: The American Years. Brian Boyd. (Illus.). 783p. 1991. text ed. 69.50 (*0-691-06797-X*); pap. text ed. 19.95 (*0-691-02471-5*) Princeton U Pr.

Vladimir Nabokov: The Russian Years. Brian Boyd. (Illus.). 619p. 1990. pap. text ed. 19.95 (*0-691-02470-7*) Princeton U Pr.

Vladimir Nabokov: The Russian Years. Brian Boyd. (Illus.). 598p. (C). 1990. text ed. 59.50 (*0-691-06794-5*) Princeton U Pr.

Vladimir Nabokov: The Velvet Butterfly. Alan Levy. LC 83-63247. (Illus.). 164p. (C). 1984. pap. 16.00 (*0-932966-41-1*) Permanent Pr.

***Vladimir Oblast: Economy, Industry, Government, Business.** 2nd rev. ed. Russian Information & Business Center, Inc. Staff. (Russian Regional Business Directories Ser.). (Illus.). 200p. 1997. pap. 99.00 (*1-57751-423-8*) Russ Info & Busn Ctr.

***Vladimir Odoesvsky.** Cornwell. 224p. 1997. 54.00 (*1-57181-907-X*) Berghahn Bks.

Vladimir Soloviev: Russian Mystic, Vol. 9. Paul M. Allen. LC 72-81592. (Illus.). 544p. 1978. lib. bdg. 15.95 (*0-8334-0709-0*, Spir Sci Lib) Garber Comm.

Vladimir Stasov & Russian National Culture. Yuri Olkhovsky. LC 83-3528. (Russian Music Studies: No. 6). (Illus.). 207p. reprint ed. pap. 59.00 (*0-8357-1412-8*, 2070515) Bks Demand.

Vladimir Tatlin & the Russian Avant-Garde. John Milner. LC 82-25923. (Illus.). 262p. reprint ed. pap. 74.70 (*0-7837-6219-4*, 2080229) Bks Demand.

Vladimir the Russian Viking. Vladimir Volkoff. LC 84-22741. (Illus.). 400p. 1985. 23.95 (*0-87951-993-2*) Overlook Pr.

Vladimir, the Russian Viking. Vladimir Volkoff. 400p. 1988. Tusk. pap. 13.95 (*0-87951-234-2*) Overlook Pr.

Vladimir Zhirinovskiy: An Assessment of a Russian Ultra-Nationalist. (Illus.). 156p. (Orig.). (C). 1995. pap. text ed. 40.00 (*0-7881-1633-9*) DIANE Pub.

Vladimir Zhirinovsky: An Assessment of a Russian Ultranationalist. 1996. lib. bdg. 252.95 (*0-8490-6017-6*) Gordon Pr.

Vladimir Zhirinovsky: The Man Who Would Be God. Scot Overbey. (Illus.). 150p. (Orig.). 1994. pap. 9.95 (*1-879366-74-6*) Hearthstone OK.

Vladimir's Carrot: Modern Drama & the Modern Imagination. John Peter. LC 87-5838. xii, 384p. 1987. 29.95 (*0-226-66265-9*) U Ch Pr.

Vlasi U Hrvatskoj Nisu Raci. Ivo Omrcanin. 72p. (Orig.). (CRO.). 1995. pap. 7.00 (*0-614-10152-2*) Ivor Pr.

Vlasov & the Russian Liberation Movement: 1941-1945. Catherine Andreyev. (Cambridge Russian, Soviet & Post-Soviet Studies: No. 51). (Illus.). 233p. 1987. text ed. 54.95 (*0-521-30545-4*) Cambridge U Pr.

Vlasov & the Russian Liberation Movement 1941-1945. Catherine Andreyev. (Cambridge Russian, Soviet & Post-Soviet Studies: No. 51). 268p. (C). 1990. pap. text ed. 19.95 (*0-521-38960-7*) Cambridge U Pr.

VLBI & Compact Radio Sources. Ed. by Roberto Fanti et al. 1984. pap. text ed. 75.00 (*90-277-1740-0*); lib. bdg. 149.00 (*90-277-1739-7*) Kluwer Ac.

VLDB '89: Proceedings of the 1989 International Conference on Very Large Data Bases. 1989. 40.00 (*1-55860-101-5*) Morgan Kaufmann.

VLDB '94. VLDB Staff. 600p. 1994. 40.00 (*1-55860-153-8*) Morgan Kaufmann.

Vlemk the Box-Painter. John Gardner. LC 79-91630. (Illus.). 1979. 15.00 (*0-935716-01-7*) Lord John.

VLF Radio Engineering. A. Watt & A. Cullen. LC 67-18166. (International Series of Monographs in Electromagnetic Waves: Vol. 14). 1967. 310.00 (*0-08-012313-9*, Pub. by Pergamon Repr UK) Franklin.

VLISP: A Verified Implementation of Scheme. Ed. by Joshua D. Guttman. 192p. (C). 1995. lib. bdg. 105.00 (*0-7923-9566-2*) Kluwer Ac.

VLS Reader. Susan Daitch et al. Ed. by M. Mark. 272p. (Orig.). 1991. pap. 12.95 (*1-85242-245-9*) Serpents Tail.

VLSI Algorithms & Architecture. Kurt Mehlhorn. (Lecture Notes in Computer Science Ser.: Vol. 227). viii, 328p. 1986. 39.00 (*0-387-16766-8*) Spr-Verlag.

VLSI Algorithms & Architectures. Ed. by J. H. Reif. (Lecture Notes in Computer Science Ser.: Vol. 319). x, 476p. 1988. 71.95 (*0-387-96818-0*) Spr-Verlag.

VLSI & Parallel Computation. Ed. by Robert Suaya & Graham Birtwistle. 400p. (C). 1990. text ed. 49.95 (*0-934613-99-0*) Morgan Kaufmann.

VLSI & Parallel Computing for Pattern Recognition & Artificial Intelligence, Vol. 18. N. Ranganathan. (Series in Machine Perception & Artificial: Vol. 18). 250p. 1995. text ed. 64.00 (*981-02-2312-9*) World Scientific Pub.

VLSI Architecture for Concurrent Data Structures. William J. Dally. (C). 1987. lib. bdg. 76.50 (*0-89838-235-1*) Kluwer Ac.

VLSI Artificial Neural Networks Engineering. Ed. by Mohamed I. Elmasry. LC 94-26768. 344p. (C). 1994. lib. bdg. 114.00 (*0-7923-9493-3*) Kluwer Ac.

VLSI Chip Design with the Hardware Description Language VERILOG: An Introduction Based on a Large RISC Processor Design. Ulrich Golze. LC 95-51357. 1996. 49.95 incl. 3.5 hd (*3-540-60032-9*) Spr-Verlag.

VLSI Circuit Layout: Theory & Design. Ed. by T. C. Hu & E. S. Kuh. LC 85-14313. (Reprint Ser.: PC01875). 280p. 1985. reprint ed. 69.95 (*0-87942-193-2*, PC01875) Inst Electrical.

VLSI Circuit Simulation & Optimisation. Litovski. 1995. 85.95 (*0-412-63860-6*) Chapman & Hall.

***VLSI-Compatible Implementations for Artificial Neural Networks.** Sied M. Fakhraie. LC 96-43999. (The Kluwer International Series in Engineering & Computer Science). 224p. (C). 1996. lib. bdg. 87.50 (*0-7923-9825-4*) Kluwer Ac.

VLSI Design: From System to Silicon. Tim Pagden. 400p. 1992. pap. text ed. 42.00 (*0-13-950940-2*) P-H.

VLSI Design: Proceedings of the International Conference on FLSI Design (8th: 1995: New Delhi, India) 456p. 1995. pap. 90.00 (*0-8186-6905-5*, PR06905) IEEE Comp Soc.

VLSI Design Environments. Ed. by George W. Zobrist. LC 96-8852. (Computer Engineering & Computer Science Ser.). (Illus.). 190p. 1997. text ed. 65.00 (*1-56750-284-9*) Ablex Pub.

VLSI Design Environments & Silicon Compilation. Walling Cyre. Ed. by George W. Zobrist. (VLSI Design Automation Ser.). (Illus.). 400p. (C). 1996. 65.00 (*0-89391-783-4*) Ablex Pub.

VLSI Design for Manufacturing: Yield Enhancement. Stephen W. Director et al. (C). 1989. lib. bdg. 97.50 (*0-7923-9054-7*) Kluwer Ac.

VLSI Design Methodologies for Digital Signal Processing Architectures. Ed. by Magdy A. Boyoumi. LC 93-39842. (International Series in Engineering & Computer Science, VLSI, Computer Architecture, & Digital Screen Processing). 416p. (C). 1994. lib. bdg. 122.50 (*0-7923-9428-3*) Kluwer Ac.

VLSI Design Methods, Vol. I: Formal VLSI Specification & Synthesis; Vol. II: Formal VLSI Correctness Verification: Proceedings of the IFIP WG10.2 WG10.5 International Workshop on Applied Formal Methods for Correct VLSI Design. Ed. by Luc J. Claesen. 1990. Set. 228.00 (*0-444-88689-3*, North Holland) Elsevier.

VLSI Design Nineteen Ninety-Four, 7th International Conference. LC 93-61327. 448p. 1994. pap. 80.00 (*0-8186-4990-9*, 4990) IEEE Comp Soc.

VLSI Design Principles & Practices. Joseph DiGiacomo. (Illus.). 1990. 159.00 (*0-87942-489-3*, HL4382) Inst Electrical.

VLSI Design Techniques for Analog & Digital Circuits. R. L. Geiger et al. 992p. (C). 1990. text ed. write for info. (*0-07-023253-9*) McGraw.

VLSI Design 1996, 9th International Conference On. LC 10-639667. 480p. 1996. pap. 100.00 (*0-8186-7228-5*, PRO7228) IEEE Comp Soc.

VLSI Digital Signal Processors: An Introduction to Rapid Prototyping & Design Synthesis. Vijay Madisetti. 412p. 1995. 74.95 (*0-7506-9406-8*) Buttrwrth-Heinemann.

VLSI Digital Systems: Architecture, Organization, & Implementation. Ramautar Sharma. (Illus.). 512p. 1996. text ed. 41.50 (*0-07-056445-0*) McGraw.

VLSI 'Eighty-Seven: VLSI Design of Digital Systems. Ed. by Carlo H. Sequin. 420p. 1988. 134.50 (*0-444-70370-5*, North Holland) Elsevier.

VLSI Electronics Vol. 22: Microstructure Science: VLSI Reliability. Anant G. Sabnis. Ed. by Norman G. Einspruch. 207p. 1990. text ed. 116.00 (*0-12-234122-8*) Acad Pr.

VLSI Engineering. Thomas E. Dillinger. (Illus.). 832p. 1987. text ed. 105.00 (*0-13-942731-7*) P-H.

VLSI Fabrication Principles: Silicon & Gallium Arsenide. 2nd ed. Sorab K. Ghandhi. 834p. 1994. text ed. 79.95 (*0-471-58005-8*) Wiley.

VLSI Fault Modeling & Testing Techniques. Ed. by George W. Zobrist. (Computer Engineering & Computer Science Ser.). 208p. (C). 1993. text ed. 78.50 (*0-89391-781-8*) Ablex Pub.

VLSI for Artificial Intelligence. Ed. by Jose G. Delgado-Frias & Will R. Moore. (C). 1989. lib. bdg. 86.50 (*0-7923-9000-8*) Kluwer Ac.

VLSI for Artificial Intelligence & Neural Networks. Ed. by Jose G. Delgado-Frias & W. R. Moore. (Illus.). 408p. 1991. 110.00 (*0-306-44029-6*, Plenum Pr) Plenum.

VLSI for Neural Networks & Artificial Intelligence. Ed. by J. G. Delgado-Frias & W. R. Moore. (Illus.). 320p. (C). 1994. 85.00 (*0-306-44722-3*, Plenum Pr) Plenum.

VLSI for Pattern Recognition & Image Processing. Ed. by K. S. Fu. (Information Sciences Ser: Vol. 13). (Illus.). 255p. 1984. 56.95 (*0-387-13268-6*) Spr-Verlag.

VLSI Implementations for Image Communications. Ed. by P. Pirsch. LC 93-30175. (Advances in Image Communication Ser.: Vol. 2). 412p. 1993. 184.00 (*0-444-88790-3*) Elsevier.

VLSI Logic Synthesis & Design. Ed. by Robert W. Dutton. 326p. (gr. 12). 1991. 120.00 (*90-5199-046-4*, Pub. by IOS Pr NE) IOS Press.

VLSI Metallization Technologies. Ed. by Krishna Shenai. (Artech House Materials Library). 505p. 1991. text ed. 24.00 (*0-89006-501-2*) Artech Hse.

VLSI Neural Networks Learning Chips. Jardi. 224p. (gr. 13). 1995. pap. text ed. 55.00 (*0-412-61630-0*) Chapman & Hall.

VLSI Ninety-Three: Proceedings of the IFIP TC10 - WG10.5 International Conference on Very Large Scale Integration, Grenoble, France, 7-10 September 1993. Ed. by Takayuki Yanagawa & Peter A. Ivey. LC 93-48195. (IFIP Transactions A: Computer Science & Technology Ser.: Vol. A-42). 374p. 1994. 139.50 (*0-444-89911-1*, North Holland) Elsevier.

***VLSI Physical Design Automation: Theory & Practice.** Sadiq M. Sait & Habib Youssef. 448p. 1995. 69.95 (*0-7803-1141-8*, PC5609) Inst Electrical.

VLSI Placement & Routing: The PI Project. A. T. Sherman. (Texts & Monographs in Computer Science). (Illus.). xii, 189p. 1989. 72.95 (*0-387-97077-0*) Spr-Verlag.

***VLSI Planarization Methods, Models, Implementation.** 1997. lib. bdg. 109.00 (*0-7923-4510-X*) Kluwer Ac.

VLSI Process Development. Agricola & Bastae. 1995. write for info. (*0-8493-7282-8*) CRC Pr.

VLSI Prolong Processor, Design & Methodology: A Case Study in High Level Language Processor Design. Ed. by Pierluigi Civera. LC 94-6831. 264p. 1994. 145.75 (*0-444-89976-6*, North Holland) Elsevier.

VLSI RISC Architecture & Organization. Furber. (Electrical Engineering & Electronics Ser.: Vol. 56). 392p. 1989. 140.00 (*0-8247-8151-1*) Dekker.

VLSI, Signal Processing, No. V. Ed. by King Yao et al. LC 92-31626. 1992. write for info. (*0-7803-0811-5*) Inst Electrical.

VLSI Signal Processing Systems. Earl E. Swartzlander, Jr. 1985. lib. bdg. 86.50 (*0-89838-207-6*) Kluwer Ac.

VLSI Signal Processing Technology. Ed. by Magdy A. Bayoumi. 248p. (C). 1994. lib. bdg. 103.00 (*0-7923-9490-9*) Kluwer Ac.

VLSI Technology. 2nd ed. Simon M. Sze. LC 87-22803. 1988. text ed. write for info. (*0-07-062735-5*) McGraw.

VLSI Technology & Design. J. V. McCanny & John White. (Microelectronics & Signal Processing Ser.). 388p. 1987. text ed. 130.00 (*0-12-481840-4*) Acad Pr.

VLSI Test Symposium, 12th IEEE. LC 94-75000. 488p. 1994. pap. text ed. 90.00 (*0-8186-5440-6*, 5440) IEEE Comp Soc.

VLSI Test Symposium, 14th IEEE (VTS '96) LC 96-75502. 500p. 1996. pap. 100.00 (*0-8186-7304-4*, PRO7304) IEEE Comp Soc.

***VLSI Test Symposium, 15th IEEE (VTS '97) Innovations in Test & Diagnosis: From Embedded Cores to Systems.** 175p. 1997. pap. 100.00 (*0-8186-7810-0*, PRO7810) IEEE Comp Soc.

VLSI Test Symposium, 1995 IEEE. 520p. 1995. pap. 100. 00 (*0-8186-7000-2*, PRO7000) IEEE Comp Soc.

VLSI Testing. Ed. by T. W. Williams. (Advances in CAD for VLSI Ser.: Vol. 5). 278p. 1986. 69.25 (*0-444-87895-5*, North Holland) Elsevier.

VLSI Video - Image Signal Processing. Ed. by Takao Nishitani et al. LC 93-12673. 176p. (C). 1993. lib. bdg. 130.00 (*0-7923-9342-2*) Kluwer Ac.

***VLSI 91.** A. Halaas & P. B. Denyer. (IFIP Transactions A: Vol. 1). 500p. 1992. pap. 166.25 (*0-444-89019-X*, North Holland) Elsevier.

VL02 Achieving Quality. CUNA (Ewing) Staff. 160p. 1995. per., pap. text ed. 25.70 (*0-7872-1023-4*) Kendall-Hunt.

VL03 Leadership. CUNA (Ewing) Staff. 128p. 1995. per., pap. text ed. 25.70 (*0-7872-1112-5*) Kendall-Hunt.

VL04 Strategic Planning. CUNA (Ewing) Staff. 128p. 1995. per., pap. text ed. 25.70 (*0-7872-1401-9*) Kendall-Hunt.

VL06 Diversity. CUNA (Ewing) Staff. 160p. 1995. per., pap. text ed. 25.70 (*0-7872-1404-3*) Kendall-Hunt.

***VL08 A Director's Guide to Asset-Liability Management.** Rees. 160p. 1996. per., pap. text ed. 25.70 (*0-7872-2687-4*) Kendall-Hunt.

VL09 Recruiting, Developing & Retaining Board Members & Volunteers. CUNA Staff. 176p. 1996. per., pap. text ed. 25.70 (*0-7872-2429-4*) Kendall-Hunt.

VL10 Effective Credit Union Boards. CUNA (Rees) Staff. 128p. 1996. per. 25.70 (*0-7872-2458-8*) Kendall-Hunt.

VL12 Developing Compensation Systems. Ewing. 128p. 1996. per., pap. text ed. 25.70 (*0-7872-2236-4*) Kendall-Hunt.

VL86C010 32-Bit RISC MPU & Peripherals User's Manual. VLSI Technology, Inc. Staff. 224p. 1989. 21. 95 (*0-13-944968-X*) P-H.

VM - CMS: A Survival Guide. James E. Potter. (Orig.). (C). 1993. pap. text ed. 39.95 (*0-9632069-2-3*) Bridge Lrn Systs.

VM-CMS: A User's Guide. Paul Chase. LC 88-26069. 466p. 1989. pap. text ed. 51.95 (*0-471-50170-0*) Wiley.

VM-CMS: XEDIT Commands & Features. Steve Eckols. LC 88-60889. 225p. 1988. pap. 25.00 (*0-911625-47-X*) M Murach & Assoc.

VMEbus: A Practical Companion. 2nd ed. Steve Heath. LC 93-38306. (Illus.). 384p. 1994. pap. 44.95 (*0-7506-1750-0*) Buttrwrth-Heinemann.

VMEbus Handbook. Wade D. Peterson. 332p. 1993. pap. 53.00 (*1-885731-01-9*) VFEA Int Trade.

VMEBUS User's Handbook. Heath. 1989. 58.00 (*0-8493-7130-9*, TK7895) CRC Pr.

***VMR Standard New Car Prices.** Vehicle Market Research Staff. 1997. pap. text ed. 4.99 (*1-883899-21-4*) VMR Intl.

***VMR Standard New Van, Truck & Sport Utility Prices.** Vechicle Market Research Staff. 1997. pap. text ed. 4.99 (*1-883899-22-2*) VMR Intl.

***VMR Standard Used Car Prices: Now Covers 14 Years of Prices!, 1983-1996.** Vehicle Market Research Staff. 1997. pap. text ed. 4.99 (*1-883899-14-1*) VMR Intl.

VMR Standard Used Car Prices April, 1996. (VMR Used Car Prices Ser.). (Orig.). 1996. pap. 4.99 (*1-883899-09-5*) VMR Intl.

VMR Standard Used Car Prices January 1996. (VMR Used Car Prices Ser.). (Orig.). 1995. pap. 4.99 (*1-883899-08-7*) VMR Intl.

VMR Theory. Robert Frezza. 1996. mass mkt. 5.99 (*0-345-39026-1*, Del Rey) Ballantine.

VMS Files Systems Internals. Kirby McCoy. (VAX-VMS Ser.). (Illus.). 460p. (Orig.). 1990. 59.95 (*1-55558-056-4*, Digital DEC) Buttrwrth-Heinemann.

VMS for Alpha Platforms Internals & Data Structures: Preliminary Edition. Ruth E. Goldenberg & Saro Saravanan. (Alpha Ser.: Vol. 2). (Illus.). 300p. 1992. 51. 95 (*1-55558-105-6*, EYL466EP2, Digital DEC) Buttrwrth-Heinemann.

VMS for Alpha Platforms Internals & Data Structures: Preliminary Edition. Ruth E. Goldenberg & Saro Saravanan. (Alpha Ser.: Vol. 3). (Illus.). 300p. 1993. 51. 95 (*1-55558-109-9*, EYL466EP3, Digital DEC) Buttrwrth-Heinemann.

VMS for Alpha Platforms Internals & Data Structures, Vol. 1: Preliminary Edition. Ruth E. Goldenberg & Saro Saravanan. (Alpha Ser.). (Illus.). 416p. (Orig.). 1992. 51. 95 (*1-55558-095-5*, EY-L466E-DP, Digital DEC) Buttrwrth-Heinemann.

VMS Systems Management. Lesley O. Rice. 352p. 1994. pap. text ed. 56.00 (*0-13-948456-6*) P-H.

VNR Dictionary of Business & Finance. David M. Brownstone et al. 288p. 1980. 35.00 (*0-8288-4715-0*, M9376) Fr & Eur.

VNR Investor's Dictionary. David M. Brownstone & I. M. Frack. 326p. 1981. 29.95 (*0-8288-4682-0*, M9374) Fr & Eur.

VNR's Encyclopedia of Hospitality & Tourism. Ed. by Mahmood A. Khan et al. LC 92-40238. 1008p. 1993. text ed. 108.95 (*0-442-00346-3*) Van Nos Reinhold.

VOC Calculation Manual. Pollution Engineering Staff. 238p. 1994. 39.95 (*0-934165-36-X*) Gulf Pub.

***VOC Control Equipment.** Richard K. Miller & Christy H. Gunter. (Market Research Survey Ser.: No. 294). 50p. 1996. 200.00 (*1-55865-318-X*) Future Tech Surveys.

***VOC Emissions Control.** Frost & Sullivan Staff. Date not set. write for info. (*0-7889-0542-2*, 3178) Frost & Sullivan.

Voc-Tech Quick Screener. CFKR Career Materials Staff. 6p. (YA). (gr. 9 up). 1995. reprint ed. 0.75 (*0-934783-18-7*) CFKR Career.

Vocabolarietto della Lingua Italiana. C. Grassi. (ITA.). write for info. (*0-318-56660-5*) Fr & Eur.

Vocabolario Nomenclatorio. P. Premoli. 1991. 250.00 (*0-8288-3919-0*, F83910) Fr & Eur.

Vocabolario Toscano Dell'arte Del Disegno. fac. ed. Filippo Baldinucci. (Documents of Art & Architectural History Ser. 1: Vol. 5). (Illus.). (ITA.). 1980. lib. bdg. 45.00 (*0-89371-105-5*) Broude Intl Edns.

Vocabula Et Sermones - Basic Vocabulary & Sample Conversations. Philip E. Lebet & David J. Perry. 25p. (LAT.). (YA). (gr. 6-12). 1991. spiral bd. 1.70 (*0-939507-19-6*, B4) Amer Classical.

Vocabulaire: Plain-Chant et Autre Poemes. Jean Cocteau. (FRE.). 1983. pap. 14.95 (*0-7859-2787-5*) Fr & Eur.

Vocabulaire Allemand de Base. Bock & Heiko. 420p. 1992. Vocabulaire allemande de base. 20.00 (*3-468-49402-5*) Langenscheidt.

Vocabulaire Allemand de Base. Bock & Muller. 328p. 1992. Activites ecrites. student ed. 17.50 (*3-468-49403-3*) Langenscheidt.

Vocabulaire Anglais et Americain Robert & Collins. Peter Atkins. 394p. 1994. 59.95 (*0-7859-9198-0*) Fr & Eur.

Vocabulaire Barometre Dans le Langage Economique. 3rd ed. J. Delattre & G. DeVernisy. 155p. (ENG & FRE.). 1978. pap. 29.95 (*0-8288-6695-3*, M-6109) Fr & Eur.

Vocabulaire Biblique. Ed. by Jean-Jacques Von Allmen. 320p. (FRE.). 1964. pap. 39.95 (*0-7859-0407-7*, M6759) Fr & Eur.

Vocabulaire d'Ancien Francais. Magali Rouquier. 127p. (FRE.). 1992. pap. 22.95 (*0-7859-0969-9*, 2091906549) Fr & Eur.

Vocabulaire d'Astronomie. CILF Staff. 320p. (DUT, ENG, FRE, GER & ITA.). 1980. pap. 49.95 (*0-8288-0773-6*, M6555) Fr & Eur.

Vocabulaire de Base Allemand-Francais. Charles Chatelant. 211p. (FRE & GER.). 1984. pap. 20.95 (*0-7859-4848-1*) Fr & Eur.

An Asterisk (*) at the beginning of an entry indicates that the title is appearing in BIP for the first time.

Vocabulaire de la Fonderie, Francais-Anglais. (ENG & FRE.). pap. 19.95 (0-686-56719-6, M-6557); pap. 19.95 (0-686-56720-X, M-6556) Fr & Eur.

Vocabulaire de la Mechatronique Automobile, Vol. 2 La Transmission: Vocabulary of Automobile Mechatronics, English - French. Normand Cote. 32p. (ENG & FRE.). 1993. pap. 19.95 (0-7859-3640-8, 2551155150) Fr & Eur.

Vocabulaire de la Micrographie. CILF Staff. 230p. (ENG, FRE & GER.). 1980. pap. 49.95 (0-8288-0187-8, M 14590) Fr & Eur.

Vocabulaire de la Psychanalyse. 5th ed. Jean-Baptiste Pontalis. Ed. by Jean Laplanche. (FRE.). 1976. 85.00 (0-8288-5759-8, M6558) Fr & Eur.

Vocabulaire de la Psychologie. 8th ed. Henri Pieron. 608p. (FRE.). 1990. 115.00 (0-7859-4835-X) Fr & Eur.

Vocabulaire de la Publicite. Ed. by Conseil International de la Langue Francaise Staff. (FRE.). 1976. pap. 19.95 (0-8288-5760-1, M6559) Fr & Eur.

Vocabulaire de la Radio & de la Television. 30p. (FRE.). 1977. pap. 9.95 (0-7859-0819-6, M-9022) Fr & Eur.

Vocabulaire de la Vente Promotionelle: Anglais-Francais. M. Villiers et al. 30p. (ENG & FRE.). 1975. pap. 7.95 (0-8288-5950-7, M9242) Fr & Eur.

Vocabulaire de L'astronautique. Louis Guilbert. 361p. (FRE.). pap. 45.00 (0-686-57265-3, F-137130) Fr & Eur.

Vocabulaire de l'Astronautique: Enquete Linguistique a l'Occasion de 5 Exploits de Cosmonautes. Louis Guilbert. (FRE.). 33.95 (0-8288-7795-5, F135670) Fr & Eur.

Vocabulaire de L'astronautique: Enquete Linguistique a travers la Presse d'information a L'occasion De Cinq Exploits de Cosmonautes. Louis Guilbert. (Publ. de l'Univ. de Rouen Fac. des Lettres et Sc. Hum.). (FRE.). 15.95 (0-685-36683-9) Fr & Eur.

Vocabulaire de L'economie. Gilbert Mathieu. (FRE.). pap. 35.00 (0-686-57041-3, M-6401) Fr & Eur.

Vocabulaire de l'Economie. Gilbert Mathieu. (FRE.). 35.00 (0-8288-7890-0, M6401) Fr & Eur.

Vocabulaire de L'Education: Vocabulary of Education. Gaston Mialaret. 488p. (FRE.). 1979. 125.00 (0-8288-4842-4, M6410) Fr & Eur.

Vocabulaire de l'Environnement. 3rd ed. Ed. by Conseil International de la Langue Francaise Staff. 351p. (ENG & FRE.). 1992. 135.00 (0-7859-4780-9, M4648) Fr & Eur.

Vocabulaire de L'equitation et des Courses. CILF Staff. (FRE.). 1984. pap. 22.50 (0-8288-2338-3, M14596) Fr & Eur.

Vocabulaire de l'Informatique de Gestion: English - French. Marie-Eva De Villers. 33p. (ENG & FRE.). 1990. pap. 19.95 (0-8288-9413-2) Fr & Eur.

Vocabulaire de L'Informatique de Gestion Anglais-Francais. M. Villiers. 31p. (ENG & FRE.). 1980. pap. 7.95 (0-8288-0237-8, M9228) Fr & Eur.

Vocabulaire de L'oceanologie. Ed. by Agence de Cooperation Culturelle et Technique. 431p. (FRE.). 1976. pap. 49.95 (0-8288-5758-X, M6560) Fr & Eur.

Vocabulaire de Medecine et des Sciences Connexes: Francais-Anglais, Anglais-Francais. W. J. Gladstone. 298p. (ENG & FRE.). 1971. 75.00 (0-7859-5542-9) Fr & Eur.

Vocabulaire de Psychopedagogie et de Psychiatrie de L'enfant: Vocabulary of Child Psychiatry & Educational Psychology. 3rd ed. Robert Lafon. 868p. (FRE.). 1973. 95.00 (0-8288-6335-0, F-19440) Fr & Eur.

Vocabulaire d'Ecologie: Ecological Vocabulary. Ed. by Conseil International de la Langue Francaise Staff. (FRE.). 1974. pap. 39.95 (0-8288-6218-4, M-4641) Fr & Eur.

Vocabulaire des Assurances Sociales. Georges Desrosier & Jacques Boulay. 21p. (FRE.). 1980. pap. 19.95 (0-8288-9393-4) Fr & Eur.

Vocabulaire des Assurances Sociales. G. Desrosiers & Jacques Boulay. 21p. (FRE.). 1971. pap. 9.95 (0-8288-6486-1, M-9231) Fr & Eur.

Vocabulaire des assurances sur la vie: Life Insurance Vocabulary. V. P. Grandpre. 14p. 1973. pap. 5.95 (0-8288-6336-9, M-9230) Fr & Eur.

Vocabulaire des Scieries: French - English. Theresa Sicard. 123p. (ENG & FRE.). 1992. pap. 39.95 (0-8288-9418-3) Fr & Eur.

Vocabulaire des Travaux Publiques: Anglais-Francais, Francais-Anglais. Fabrice Antoine. 55p. (ENG & FRE.). 1988. pap. 35.00 (0-7859-3913-X, 2856080278) Fr & Eur.

Vocabulaire du Breton. Ed. by Conseil International de la Langue Francaise Staff. 192p. (FRE.). 1976. pap. 45.00 (0-8288-5761-X, M6084) Fr & Eur.

Vocabulaire Economique et Financier: Coll. Points Economie. 6th ed. Yves Bernard & Jean-Claude Colli. 634p. (FRE.). 1990. pap. 14.95 (0-7859-4807-4, M6031) Fr & Eur.

Vocabulaire Ethnologique. Armin Heymer. 237p. (ENG, FRE & GER.). 1977. 75.00 (0-8288-5531-5, F16361) Fr & Eur.

Vocabulaire Fondamental de Technologie: Fundamental Vocabulary of Technology. Jacques Deweerdt. 272p. (FRE.). 1974. pap. 49.95 (0-7859-0773-4, M-4654) Fr & Eur.

Vocabulaire Francais-Anglais, Anglais-Francais D'archeologie Prehistorique: French - English, English - French Vocabulary of Prehistoric Archaeology. Roger Marois. 116p. (ENG & FRE.). 1972. pap. 29.95 (0-8288-6427-6, M-6399) Fr & Eur.

Vocabulaire Francais-Anglais des Relations Professionnelles. Ed. by Ministre du Travail et de la Main d'Oeuvre Staff. 302p. (ENG & FRE.). 1972. pap. 37.50 (0-686-57279-3, M-4655) Fr & Eur.

Vocabulaire Francais-Anglais des Relations Professionnelles. 2nd ed. Gerard Dion. 350p. (ENG & FRE.). 1975. 39.95 (0-8288-5951-5, M4655) Fr & Eur.

Vocabulaire Francais-Arabe de L'ingenieur et du Technicien, 1: Eletricite: French - Arab Vocabulary of Engineers & Technicians, Vol. 1: Electricity. J. J. Schmidt. 136p. (ARA & FRE.). 1973. pap. 39.95 (0-8288-6339-3, M-6504) Fr & Eur.

Vocabulaire Franco-Anglo-Allemand de Geomorphologie. (ENG, FRE & GER.). 1970. pap. 49.95 (0-8288-6559-0, F-136940) Fr & Eur.

Vocabulaire Juridique. 2nd ed. Gerard Cornu. 880p. (FRE.). 1990. 295.00 (0-7859-4658-6) Fr & Eur.

Vocabulaire Latin des Relations et des Partis Politiques Sous la Republique. Jean Hellegouarc'h. (FRE.). 69.95 (0-686-57327-7) Fr & Eur.

Vocabulaire Latin des Relations et des Partis Politiques Sous la Republique. Jean Hellegouarc'h. 1972. 95.00 (0-7859-4567-9) Fr & Eur.

Vocabulaire Maritime. Bernard Rosselot. 95p. (FRE.). 1980. pap. 19.95 (0-8288-1581-X, F136860) Fr & Eur.

Vocabulaire Medical de Base, 2 vols., Set. Marie Bonvalot. 447p. (FRE.). 1989. pap. 59.95 (0-7859-4808-2) Fr & Eur.

Vocabulaire Oecumenique. Yves Congar & Gerard Siegwalt. 39.95 (0-8288-7665-7, M6083); pap. 39.95 (0-686-56960-1, M-6083) Fr & Eur.

Vocabulaire Pratique de la Philosophie: Practical Vocabulary of Philosophy. Jean Miquel. 260p. (FRE.). 1974. pap. 12.95 (0-8288-6220-6, M-6412) Fr & Eur.

Vocabulaire Pratique des Sciences Sociales. Alain Birou. 384p. (FRE.). 49.95 (0-686-57277-7, F136960); 49.95 (0-8288-7617-7, F136960) Fr & Eur.

Vocabulaire Psychologique et Psychiatrique. Michel Godfryd. 128p. (FRE.). 1993. pap. 16.50 (0-7859-0977-X, 2130452450) Fr & Eur.

Vocabulaire Technique Allemand-Francais, Francais-Allemand. 8th ed. Francis Cusset. 474p. (FRE & GER.). 1977. 49.95 (0-8288-5532-3, M6097) Fr & Eur.

Vocabulaire Technique Anglais-Francais, Francais-Anglais. 9th ed. Francis Cusset. 434p. (FRE & GER.). 1977. 69.95 (0-8288-5533-1, M6098) Fr & Eur.

Vocabulaires des Engins et Materials de Chantiers: Anglais-Francais, Francais-Anglais. Fabrice Antoine. 64p. (ENG & FRE.). 1989. pap. 35.00 (0-7859-3916-4) Fr & Eur.

Vocabulari Castella-Catala. Eduard A. Bover. 465p. (CAT & SPA.). 1961. pap. 9.95 (0-7859-5128-8, S50355) Fr & Eur.

Vocabulari Catala de Matematica Basica. 4th ed. Claudi Alsina. 48p. (CAT.). 1976. pap. 8.95 (0-7859-5081-8) Fr & Eur.

Vocabularie du Roman Francais 1962-68: Dictionnaire des Frequences. Gunnel Engwall. 427p. (FRE.). 1984. 295.00 (0-7859-8711-8, 912200629x) Fr & Eur.

Vocabulario Andaluz. Antonio A. Venecesiao. 676p. (SPA.). 1980. pap. 69.95 (0-8288-2028-7, S32726) Fr & Eur.

Vocabulario Basico de la Arquitectura: Basic Architecture Vocabulary. 5th ed. Jose R. Paniaqua Soto. 408p. (SPA.). 1987. pap. 24.00 (0-7859-5059-1) Fr & Eur.

Vocabulario Basico en la E.G.B. Ministerio de Educacion Y Ciencia, 3 vols. Ed. by Maria A. Casanova. 1940p. (SPA.). 1990. 295.00 (84-239-5632-6) Elliots Bks.

Vocabulario Cientifico Y Tecnico: Real Academia de Ciencias Exactas, Fisicas y Naturales. 2nd ed. 773p. (SPA.). 1991. 249.50 (84-239-5987-2) Elliots Bks.

Vocabulario Culto. 2nd ed. Gladys Neggers. 168p. (SPA.). 1977. pap. 17.95 (0-8288-5535-8, S50023) Fr & Eur.

Vocabulario de Artes de la Madera, Arquitectura y Decoracion. Don Bosco Staff. 152p. (SPA.). 1975. pap. 29.95 (0-8288-5952-3, S50084) Fr & Eur.

Vocabulario de Cervantes. Carlos Fernandez Gomez. 1136p. (SPA.). 1968. pap. 200.00 (0-614-00133-1) Elliots Bks.

Vocabulario de Cine y Television en Espana. Maria V. Romero Gualda. 400p. (SPA.). 1976. pap. 29.95 (0-8288-5763-6, S50002) Fr & Eur.

Vocabulario de la Obra Poetica de Herrera. David Kossoff. 363p. (SPA.). 1968. 125.00 (0-614-00124-2) Elliots Bks.

Vocabulario de las Dos Lenguas Toscana y Castellana. Cristobal De Las Casas. 500p. reprint ed. write for info. (0-318-71602-X) G Olms Pubs.

Vocabulario de Lope de Vega, 3 vols. Carlos Fernandez Gomez. (SPA.). 1968. 450.00 (0-614-00125-0) Elliots Bks.

Vocabulario De Romance En Latin: Antonio De Nebrija. Ed. by Gerald MacDonald. LC 72-96003. 214p. (LAT & SPA.). 1973. 19.95 (0-87722-018-2) Temple U Pr.

Vocabulario de Teologia Biblica. 9th ed. Leon Dufour. 976p. (SPA.). 1977. 49.95 (0-8288-5536-6, S50205); pap. 49.95 (0-8288-5539-0, S50204) Fr & Eur.

Vocabulario del Comercio Medieval. 2nd ed. Miguel Gual Camarena. 532p. (SPA.). 1976. 75.00 (0-8288-5764-4, S50115) Fr & Eur.

Vocabulario des las Dos Lenguas Toscana y Castellana. Cristobal De Las Casas. 500p. reprint ed. write for info. (0-318-71623-2) G Olms Pubs.

Vocabulario Economico y Financiero. Yves Bernard & Jean-Claude Colli. 488p. (SPA.). 1981. pap. 36.00 (0-7859-4916-X) Fr & Eur.

Vocabulario Galego-Castelan. Xose L. Grande. 320p. (SPA.). 1983. 9.80 (0-7859-5114-8) Fr & Eur.

Vocabulario General de Orientacion Cientifica y Sus Estratos. Victor Garcia Hoz. 432p. (SPA.). 1976. pap. 45.00 (0-8288-5765-2, S50108) Fr & Eur.

***Vocabulario Ilustrador.** (SPA.). 1975. pap. text ed. 18.13 (0-673-03552-2) Addison-Wesley.

Vocabulario Ingles. Harraps Staff. 1995. 6.00 (0-02-860094-0, Harraps IN) Macmillan Gen Ref.

Vocabulario Ingles-Espanol de Electronica y Tecnica Nuclear. 2nd ed. John Markus. 196p. (ENG & SPA.). pap. 39.95 (84-267-0247-3, S-30684) Fr & Eur.

Vocabulario Ingles-Espanol, Espanol-Ingles. 8th ed. Jose Merino-Bustamante. 192p. (ENG & SPA.). 1990. pap. write for info. (0-7859-5082-6) Fr & Eur.

Vocabulario Maritimo Ingles-Espanol y Espanol-Ingles. 5th ed. Dagnino J. Navarro. 151p. (ENG & SPA.). 1976. pap. 19.95 (0-8288-5766-0, S12239) Fr & Eur.

Vocabulario Medico Portugues - Ingles, Ingles - Portugues. R. da Graca Veiga. (ENG & POR.). 1979. pap. 39.95 (0-7859-0907-9, F99490) Fr & Eur.

Vocabulario Politico Republicano y Franquista: Republican & Franco-ite Political Vocabulary, 1931-1971. Miguel A. Rebollo Torio. 184p. (SPA.). 1978. 24.95 (0-8288-5277-4, S50122) Fr & Eur.

Vocabulario Portuguez e Latino, 5 vols. Ralphael Bluteau. cclxiv, 7085p. Set. write for info. (0-318-71076-5) G Olms Pubs.

Vocabulario Practico De la Biblia. Anton Grabner Haider. 892p. (SPA.). 1975. 59.95 (0-8288-5953-1, S50206) Fr & Eur.

Vocabulario Puertorriqueno. De Rosario. (SPA.). 1966. 10.95 (0-87751-010-5) E Torres & Sons.

Vocabulario Sonorense. Horacio Sobrrzo. (SPA.). write for info. (0-8288-7997-4, S-12361) Fr & Eur.

Vocabulario Superior. Gaston Fernandez De La Torriente. 176p. (SPA.). 1975. pap. 24.95 (0-8288-5954-X, S33274) Fr & Eur.

Vocabulario Tecnico: Portuguese-English-French-German. 5th ed. F. J. Buecken. 600p. (FRE, GER & POR.). 1976. 105.00 (0-7859-7144-0) Fr & Eur.

Vocabulario Tecnico de Contabilidad Moderna. Abiud R. Ramos. 159p. 1992. pap. 8.95 (0-8477-2645-2) U of PR Pr.

Vocabulario Teologico del Evangelio de San Juan. Alvarez J. Mateos. 310p. (SPA.). 1980. pap. 29.95 (0-8288-2318-9, S33107) Fr & Eur.

Vocabulario Vial. Oas General Secretariat Staff. 368p. (ENG, FRE, POR & SPA.). 1979. text ed. 15.00 (0-8270-1332-9) OAS.

Vocabulario y Refranero Criollo. Tito Saubidet. (SPA.). 95.00 (0-8288-7979-6, S33072) Fr & Eur.

Vocabulario Zapoteco Castellano. Joseph W. Whitecotton & Judith Bradley-Whitecotton. (Publications in Anthropology: No. 45). 455p. (Orig.). 1993. pap. 24.50 (0-934562-36-9) VUPA.

Vocabularium Codicis Justiniani, 2 vols. Robert Mayr. 1965. reprint ed. Set. write for info. (0-318-72048-5) G Olms Pubs.

Vocabularium Codicis Justiniani, 2 vols. Robert Mayr. 1552p. 1986. reprint ed. Set. write for info. (3-487-00835-1); reprint ed. Bd. I: Pars Latina. write for info. (0-318-70781-0); reprint ed. Bd. II: Pars Graeca. write for info. (0-318-70782-9) G Olms Pubs.

Vocabularium Polyglottum Vitae Silvarum. R. Litschauer. 126p. (ENG, FRE, GER, LAT, RUM & SPA.). 1955. 55.00 (0-8288-6869-7, M-7679) Fr & Eur.

Vocabulary. 1987. 12.95 (0-19-437091-7) OUP.

Vocabulary. 1990. 14.50 (0-19-437136-0) OUP.

***Vocabulary.** McClanahan Book Co., Inc. Staff. 1997. wbk. ed., pap. 2.25 (1-56293-918-1) McClanahan Bk.

Vocabulary. Jack Rudman. (Teachers License Examination Ser.: G-5). 1994. pap. 27.95 (0-8373-8195-9) Nat Learn.

Vocabulary. 3rd ed. Patricia Dunn-Rankin. 1990. pap. text ed. write for info. (0-07-018319-8) McGraw.

Vocabulary. 3rd ed. Patricia Dunn-Rankin. 1990. teacher ed., pap. text ed. 7.50 (0-07-018320-1) McGraw.

Vocabulary: Applied Linguistic Perspectives. Ronald A. Carter. (Aspects of English Ser.). 272p. 1987. text ed. 49.95 (0-04-418007-1); pap. text ed. 19.95 (0-04-418008-X) Routledge Chapman & Hall.

***Vocabulary: Sifreinu, Pt. 2.** (Orig.). (J). (gr. 3 up). Date not set. pap. text ed. 1.00 (0-8266-0206-1) Kehot Pubn Soc.

Vocabulary Analysis of Gadda's "Pasticciaccio" Joan McConnell. LC 73-81570. (Romance Monographs: No. 2). 1973. 24.00 (84-399-0685-4); pap. 19.00 (0-686-31729-7) Romance.

Vocabulary & Grammar for "The Learnables & Basic Structures, Bk. 2. Andres M. Trimino. 30p. (Orig.). (SPA.). (YA). (gr. 7 up). 1994. pap. text ed. 15.00 (0-939990-91-1) Intl Linguistics.

Vocabulary & Notes to Ba Jin's Jia: An Aid for Reading the Novel. Cornelius C. Kubler. LC 76-369994. (Cornell East Asia Ser.: No. 8). 304p. 1976. pap. 15.00 (0-939657-08-2) Cornell East Asia Pgm.

Vocabulary & Reading Skills Builder. Linford Lougheed. (Regents Prep Series for the TOEFL Test). (Illus.). 80p. 1994. pap. text ed. 8.40 (0-13-100660-6) P-H.

Vocabulary & Spelling in 20 Minutes a Day. LC 96-17814. 1996. pap. 16.00 (1-57685-041-2) LrningExprss.

Vocabulary & Style of the Soliloquies & Dialogues of St. Augustine, Vol. 42. Mary Inez Bogan. (Patristic Studies). 238p. 1984. reprint ed. 28.00 (0-939738-27-9) Zubal Inc.

Vocabulary Arranged for the Instruction of the Deaf & Dumb. Wm. Vaughan. 1973. 69.95 (0-8490-1265-1) Gordon Pr.

Vocabulary Basics. Barbara Cox. 160p. (C). 1993. pap. text ed. 13.95 (1-56118-175-7) Paradigm MN.

Vocabulary Basics. Barbara Cox. 160p. (C). 1993. teacher ed., pap. text ed. 8.00 (1-56118-176-5) Paradigm MN.

***Vocabulary Book.** Mary A. De Vries. 1998. mass mkt. 6.99 (0-451-19268-0, Sig) NAL-Dutton.

Vocabulary Boosters I. Nancy Gill. (J). (gr. 3-6). 1985. pap. 8.99 (0-8224-7280-5) Fearon Teach Aids.

Vocabulary Boosters II. Nancy Gill. (J). (gr. 3-6). 1985. pap. 8.99 (0-8224-7281-3) Fearon Teach Aids.

Vocabulary Boosters Set, 2 bks., Set. Nancy Gill. (YA). (gr. 4 up). 16.99 (1-56417-734-3, FE0010) Fearon Teach Aids.

Vocabulary Builder. Samuel C. Brownstein. 1984. pap. 8.95 (0-8120-2449-4) Barron.

Vocabulary Builder: The Practicallly Painless Way to a Larger Vocabulary. Judi Kesselman-Turkel & Franklynn Peterson. 168p. 1982. pap. 8.86 (0-8092-5650-9) Contemp Bks.

Vocabulary Builder Game Pack for Levels 1-3: Introductory Sequence. Barbara D. DiBenedetto. (Linguistic Pattern Ser.). 21p. (Orig.). 1993. 15.00 (1-56775-049-4) ISM Teach Systs.

Vocabulary Builder Game Pack for Levels 12-15: Long Vowel Sequence. Barbara DiBenedetto. (Linguistic Pattern Ser.). 71p. (Orig.). 1993. 20.00 (1-56775-052-4) ISM Teach Systs.

Vocabulary Builder Game Pack for Levels 4-7: Short Vowel I Sequence. Barbara D. DiBenedetto. (Linguistic Pattern Ser.). 29p. (Orig.). 1993. 15.00 (1-56775-050-8) ISM Teach Systs.

Vocabulary Builder Game Pack for Levels 8-11: Short Vowel II Sequence. Barbara DiBenedetto. (Linguistic Pattern Ser.). 49p. (Orig.). 1993. 20.00 (1-56775-051-6) ISM Teach Systs.

Vocabulary Building: A Process Approach. Edgar Dale & Joseph O'Rourke. Ed. by Walter B. Barbe. 1986. 14.95 (0-88309-122-4, 280199) Zaner-Bloser.

Vocabulary Building: Syllabus, Level III. Diana C. Watson & Hernan Hurtado. 1973. pap. text ed. 6.85 (0-89420-007-0, 270043); audio 70.20 (0-89420-194-8, 270000) Natl Book.

Vocabulary Building: Syllabus, Level IV. Diana C. Watson & Malcom Watson. 1975. pap. text ed. 7.95 (0-89420-039-9, 270053); audio 69.80 (0-89420-195-6, 270200) Natl Book.

Vocabulary Building in Indonesian: An Advanced Reader. Soenjono Dardjowidjojo. LC 82-90652. (Monographs in International Studies, Southeast Asia Ser.: No. 64). 660p. 1984. pap. text ed. 30.00 (0-89680-118-7, Ohio U Ctr Intl) Ohio U Pr.

Vocabulary College. Atkinson. Date not set. teacher ed., pap. text ed. write for info. (0-314-70531-7) West Pub.

Vocabulary Control & Search Strategies in Online Searching. Alice Y. Chamis. LC 90-25224. (New Directions in Information Management Ser.: No. 27). 136p. 1991. text ed. 45.00 (0-313-25490-7, CVY/, Greenwood Pr) Greenwood.

Vocabulary Control for Information Retrieval. 2nd ed. F. Wilfrid Lancaster. LC 84-82260. (Illus.). xvii, 270p. 1992. reprint ed. text ed. 27.50 (0-87815-053-6) Info Resources.

Vocabulary Development. Carson & Dellosa. (Home Workbooks Ser.). (Illus.). 64p. (Orig.). (J). (gr. 3-4). 1995. wbk. ed., pap. 2.49 (0-88724-337-1, CD6834) Carson-Dellos.

Vocabulary Development. Dale McMaster. (Language Arts Ser.). 24p. (gr. 6-9). 1976. student ed. 5.00 (0-8209-0312-4, VD-4) ESP.

Vocabulary Development: A Morphological Analysis. Jeremy M. Anglin. (Monographs of the Society for Research in Child Development: No. 238). 200p. 1993. pap. text ed. 15.00 (0-226-02091-6) U Ch Pr.

Vocabulary Development: Using Roots & Riddles. Frank Schaffer Publications, Inc. Staff. (Middle School Bks.). (Illus.). 1996. wbk. ed. 10.95 (0-7647-0052-9, 10204) Schaffer Pubns.

Vocabulary Development Vol. II. rev. ed. Beverly L. Ritter & Kim C. Davis. (Realtime Machine Shorthand Ser.). 73p. (C). 1991. teacher ed., pap. text ed. 13.25 (0-938643-08-8) Stenotype Educ.

Vocabulary Development Vol. II. rev. ed. Beverly L. Ritter & Kim C. Davis. (Realtime Machine Shorthand Ser.). 176p. (C). 1992. pap. text ed. 25.00 (0-938643-06-1) Stenotype Educ.

Vocabulary Development for Science & Technology. Osborne Robinson. 112p. 1989. spiral bd. 13.59 (0-8403-5292-1) Kendall-Hunt.

Vocabulary Drills, Advanced Level. Edward Fry. (Illus.). 224p. 1989. pap. text ed. 13.97 (0-89061-447-4) Jamestown Pubs.

Vocabulary Drills, Intermediate Level. Edward Fry. (Illus.). 224p. 1989. pap. text ed. 13.23 (0-89061-448-2) Jamestown Pubs.

Vocabulary Dynamics. Gwen Harrison. 384p. (Orig.). 1992. mass mkt. 5.99 (0-446-36350-2) Warner Bks.

Vocabulary Energizers: Stories of Word Origins. David Popkin. 143p. (Orig.). (C). 1988. pap. text ed. 9.95 (0-929166-01-9) Hada Pubns.

Vocabulary Energizers II: Stories of Word Origins. David Popkin. 149p. (Orig.). (C). 1990. pap. text ed. 9.95 (0-929166-02-7) Hada Pubns.

Vocabulary Exercises: Analyzing Word Parts. Roderman. 1994. pap. 2.50 (0-8092-3580-3) Contemp Bks.

Vocabulary Exercises: GED Vocabulary Crosswords. Echaore-Yoon. 1994. pap. 2.50 (0-8092-3578-1) Contemp Bks.

Vocabulary Exercises: Getting the Meaning & Context. Echaore-Yoon. 1994. pap. 2.50 (0-8092-3584-6) Contemp Bks.

Vocabulary Exercises: Getting the Most from Your Dictionary. Roderman. 1994. pap. 2.50 (0-8092-3581-1) Contemp Bks.

Vocabulary Exercises: More Vocabulary For Everyday. Echaore-Yoon. 1994. pap. 2.50 (0-8092-3583-8) Contemp Bks.

Vocabulary Exercises: Understanding Language. Roderman. 1994. pap. 2.50 (0-8092-3587-0) Contemp Bks.

Vocabulary Exercises: Using a Dictionary. Roderman. 1994. pap. 2.50 (0-8092-3585-4) Contemp Bks.

UV

An Asterisk (*) at the beginning of an entry indicates that the title is appearing in BIP for the first time.

Vocabulary Exercises: Vocabulary for Everyday. Echaore-Yoon. 1994. pap. 2.50 (*0-8092-3586-2*) Contemp Bks.

Vocabulary Expansion. 2nd ed. Dorothy Rubin. 352p. (C). 1990. pap. text ed. 39.00 (*0-02-404245-5*, Macmillan Coll) P-H.

Vocabulary for a New World. Linda J. Palumbo & Frank J. Gaik. (Illus.). 384p. (Orig.). (C). 1991. pap. text ed. 38.00 (*0-02-390567-0*, Macmillan Coll) P-H.

Vocabulary for Advanced Reading Comprehension: The Keyword Approach. John T. Crow. (Illus.). 288p. (C). 1985. pap. text ed. 18.00 (*0-13-942988-3*) P-H.

Vocabulary for College (A) Diederich. (C). 1981. pap. 15.25 (*0-15-329700-X*) HR&W Schl Div.

Vocabulary for College (A) Diederich. 1989. teacher ed., pap. text ed. 6.25 (*0-15-329688-7*) HR&W Schl Div.

Vocabulary for College (A) Diederich. (C). 1989. pap. text ed. 15.25 (*0-15-329684-4*) HR&W Schl Div.

Vocabulary for College (B) Diederich. 1989. teacher ed., pap. text ed. 6.25 (*0-15-329689-5*) HR&W Schl Div.

Vocabulary for College (B) Diederich. (C). 1989. pap. text ed. 15.25 (*0-15-329685-2*) HR&W Schl Div.

Vocabulary for College (C) Diederich. 1989. teacher ed., pap. text ed. 6.25 (*0-15-329690-9*) HR&W Schl Div.

Vocabulary for College (C) Diederich. (C). 1989. pap. text ed. 15.25 (*0-15-329686-0*) HR&W Schl Div.

Vocabulary for College (D) Diederich. 1989. teacher ed., pap. text ed. 6.25 (*0-15-329691-7*) HR&W Schl Div.

Vocabulary for College (D) Diederich. (C). 1989. pap. text ed. 15.25 (*0-15-329687-9*) HR&W Schl Div.

Vocabulary Growth in the First Two Years see Speech Development of a Bilingual Child

***Vocabulary I.** Patricia K. Duffie. 861p. (C). 1996. student ed., pap. text ed., spiral bd. write for info. (*1-890601-02-0*) P L Duffy.

***Vocabulary I.** Patricia K. Duffie. 251p. (C). 1996. teacher ed., pap. text ed., spiral bd. write for info. (*1-890601-03-9*) P L Duffy.

***Vocabulary II.** Patricia K. Duffie. 250p. (C). 1996. student ed., pap. text ed., spiral bd. write for info. (*1-890601-04-7*) P L Duffy.

***Vocabulary II.** Patricia K. Duffie. 837p. (C). 1996. teacher ed., pap. text ed., spiral bd. write for info. (*1-890601-05-5*) P L Duffy.

Vocabulary Improvement. (J). pap. 3.00 (*0-590-30043-1*) Scholastic Inc.

Vocabulary Improvement. (J). pap. 0.67 (*0-590-30044-X*) Scholastic Inc.

Vocabulary Improvement. Diana Bonet. Ed. by W. Philip Gerould. LC 91-76246. (Fifty-Minute Ser.). 134p. (Orig.). 1992. pap. 10.95 (*1-56052-124-4*) Crisp Pubns.

Vocabulary in Action. Linda L. Taylor. 198p. 1992. pap. 13.95 (*0-13-950916-X*) P-H.

Vocabulary in Context. English Language Institute Staff. (Intensive Course in English Ser.). 1964. pap. 13.95 (*0-472-08305-8*) U of Mich Pr.

Vocabulary in Context: Reading Level 10-J. (Single Skills Ser.). Date not set. pap. 5.65 (*0-89061-386-9*) Jamestown Pubs.

Vocabulary In Context: Reading Level 11-K. (Single Skills Ser.). Date not set. pap. 5.65 (*0-89061-392-3*) Jamestown Pubs.

Vocabulary in Context: Reading Level 12-L. (Single Skills Series). Date not set. pap. 5.65 (*0-89061-398-2*) Jamestown Pubs.

Vocabulary in Context: Reading Level 3-C. (Single Skills Series). Date not set. pap. 5.65 (*0-89061-369-9*) Jamestown Pubs.

Vocabulary in Context: Reading Level 4-D. (Single Skills Ser.). Date not set. pap. 5.65 (*0-89061-325-7*) Jamestown Pubs.

Vocabulary in Context: Reading Level 5-E. (Single Skills Series). Date not set. pap. 5.65 (*0-89061-331-1*) Jamestown Pubs.

Vocabulary in Context: Reading Level 6-F. (Single Skills Series). Date not set. pap. 5.65 (*0-89061-337-0*) Jamestown Pubs.

Vocabulary in Context: Reading Level 7-G. (Single Skills Ser.). Date not set. pap. 5.65 (*0-89061-343-5*) Jamestown Pubs.

Vocabulary in Context: Reading Level 8-H. (Single Skills Series). Date not set. pap. 5.65 (*0-89061-349-4*) Jamestown Pubs.

Vocabulary in Context: Reading Level 9-I. (Single Skills Ser.). Date not set. pap. 5.65 (*0-89070-380-9*) Jamestown Pubs.

***Vocabulary in Use: Vocabulary Reference & Practice for Intermediate to Advanced Students.** Michael McCarthy & Felicity A. O'Dell. LC 96-44820. 304p. (C). 1997. student ed., pap. 19.95 (*0-521-57768-3*) Cambridge U Pr.

***Vocabulary in Use: Vocabulary Reference & Practice for Intermediate to Advanced Students.** Michael McCarthy & Felicity A. O'Dell. LC 96-44820. 240p. (C). 1997. student ed., pap. 16.95 (*0-521-57700-4*) Cambridge U Pr.

Vocabulary Made Easy. Visual Education Corporation Staff. (Illus.). 136p. (gr. 9 up). 1984. student ed. 9.36 (*0-07-039665-5*) McGraw.

Vocabulary Made Easy for Spanish Speakers. Muriel Hernandez de Prieto. LC 76-3732. 112p. (Orig.). 1978. pap. text ed. 3.00 (*0-8477-2622-3*) U of PR Pr.

Vocabulary Made Easy for Spanish Speakers: Teacher's Guide. Muriel H. Prieto. LC 76-3732. 49p. 1978. pap. text ed. 2.50 (*0-8477-2635-5*) U of PR Pr.

Vocabulary Maps: Strategies for Developing Word Meanings. Jean Hamersky. LC 92-37290. 1993. pap. 29.00 (*0-930599-81-0*) Thinking Pubns.

Vocabulary Mastery. Scott Bornstein. (Illus.). 272p. (YA). (gr. 9-12). 1982. 22.50 (*0-9602610-1-X*); pap. 14.95 (*0-9602610-2-8*) Bornstein Memory.

Vocabulary Norms for Deaf Children. Toby R. Silverman-Dresner. LC 72-83498. (Lexington School Ser.: Book 7). 1972. pap. 8.00 (*0-88200-060-8*, C2344) Alexander Graham.

Vocabulary of Banking & Currency. Office de la Langue Francaise Staff. 39p. (ENG & FRE.). 1974. pap. 14.95 (*0-8288-9388-8*) Fr & Eur.

Vocabulary of Common Japanese Words. A. Rose-Innes. (JPN.). 1945. 8.95 (*0-88710-123-2*) Yale Far Eastern Pubns.

Vocabulary of Cooking Utensils. France Michel. 39p. (ENG & FRE.). 1990. pap. 29.95 (*0-8288-9379-9*) Fr & Eur.

Vocabulary of Dialects Spoken in the Nicobar & Andaman Isles with a Short Account of the Natives, Their Customs & Habits, & of Previous Attempts at Colonisation. A. De Roepstorff. (C). 1987. reprint ed. 19.00 (*81-206-0274-9*, Pub. by Asian Educ Servs II) S Asia.

Vocabulary of Education. 2nd ed. Joce-Lyne Biron. 229p. (ENG & FRE.). 1988. pap. 39.95 (*0-8288-9390-X*) Fr & Eur.

Vocabulary of Educational Technology & Training. Canada Communication Group Staff. (Vocabulary Ser.: No. 196). (ENG & FRE.). 1992. 95.00 (*0-8288-7368-2*, 660557932) Fr & Eur.

Vocabulary of Enzyme Engineering. Edgard Delvin. (Terminology Bulletin Ser.: No. 217). 529p. (Orig.). 1993. pap. 50.65 (*0-660-58874-9*, Pub. by Canada Commun Grp CN) Accents Pubns.

Vocabulary of Family Violence. Marisa Rondina. (Terminology Bulletin Ser.: No. 222). 209p. (Orig.). 1994. pap. 25.95 (*0-660-59106-5*, Pub. by Canada Commun Grp CN) Accents Pubns.

Vocabulary of Hazardous Materials in the Workplace. Ed. by Helene Jacob. (Terminology Bulletin Ser.: No. 215). 1038p. (Orig.). 1993. pap. 51.95 (*0-660-57958-8*, Pub. by Canada Commun Grp CN) Accents Pubns.

Vocabulary of High School Latin. Gonzalez Lodge. LC 73-177003. (Columbia University. Teachers College. Contributions to Education Ser.: No. 9). (LAT.). reprint ed. 37.50 (*0-404-55009-6*) AMS Pr.

Vocabulary of Iberian Languages: Vocabulario de las Lenguas Ibericas. M. Regueiro. 169p. (BAQ & SPA.). 1982. pap. 11.95 (*0-8288-1455-4*, S39893) Fr & Eur.

Vocabulary of Marble Playing; More Marble Words; the Position of the Charleston Dialect; Gritted & Gritter. K. B. Harder & R. I. McDavid. (Publications of the American Dialect Society: No. 23). 61p. 1955. pap. text ed. 7.15 (*0-8173-0623-4*) U of Ala Pr.

Vocabulary of Marxism: Vocabulaire du Marxisme. Gerard Bekerman. 360p. (FRE & GER.). 1981. 65.00 (*0-8288-2254-9*, F70762) Fr & Eur.

Vocabulary of Mechanics in Five Languages, Vol. 2: Mechanics of Fluids. A. T. Troskolanski. LC 62-11559. 1967. 208.00 (*0-08-012237-X*, Pub. by Pergamon Repr UK) Franklin.

Vocabulary of Mental Aberration in Roman Comedy & Petronius. Dorothy M. Paschall. (Language Dissertations Ser.: No. 27). 1939. pap. 25.00 (*0-527-00773-0*) Periodicals Srv.

Vocabulary of Metal Working: Vocabulaire du Travail des Metaux en Fauilles, Barres, Tubes et Profils. Jean Mercier & Francine Belanger. 99p. (ENG & FRE.). 1984. pap. 9.95 (*0-8288-1916-5*, M4663) Fr & Eur.

Vocabulary of Modern Chinese. Urs Bucher. 815p. (CHI & ENG.). 1986. 49.95 (*0-8288-1603-4*, M4200) Fr & Eur.

Vocabulary of Modern Chinese: English Translation of Illustrative Sentences. Urs Bucher. 250p. (CHI & ENG.). 1986. 49.95 (*0-8288-1604-2*, M4240) Fr & Eur.

***Vocabulary of Modern French: Origins Structure & Function.** Hilary Wise. 272p. (C). 1997. pap. 19.95 (*0-415-11739-9*); text ed. 65.00 (*0-415-11738-0*) Routledge.

Vocabulary of Modern Spoken Greek (English-Greek & Greek-English) Donald C. Swanson. Ed. by Theofanis G. Stavrou. (Modern Greek History & Culture Ser.). 1982. 15.00 (*0-935476-11-3*) Nostos Bks.

Vocabulary of Modern Standard Arabic. Urs Bucher. 458p. (ARA & ENG.). 1984. 49.95 (*0-8288-1584-4*, M3515) Fr & Eur.

Vocabulary of Paper Industry Materials: Vocabulaire du Materiel Papetier. Office de la Langue Francaise Staff. 144p. (ENG & FRE.). 1983. 75.00 (*0-8288-4419-4*, M7573) Fr & Eur.

Vocabulary of Peace: Life, Culture, & Politics in the Middle East. Shulamith Hareven. Tr. by Marsha Weinstein. LC 94-23851. 256p. 1995. pap. 14.95 (*1-56279-072-2*) Mercury Hse Inc.

Vocabulary of Philosophy & Humanist Sciences: Vocabulaire de la Philosophie et des Sciences Humanies. L. M. Morfaux. 392p. (FRE.). 1979. reprint ed. 34.95 (*0-7859-4857-0*) Fr & Eur.

Vocabulary of Physics. William S. Rothwell. 188p. (Orig.). 1988. pap. text ed. 13.95 (*0-89420-250-2*, 230500) Natl Book.

Vocabulary of Psychoanalysis (Vocabulaire de la Psychanalyse) 10th ed. Jean-Baptiste Pontalis & Jean Laplanche. 544p. (FRE.). 1990. 105.00 (*0-7859-4741-8*, M14530) Fr & Eur.

Vocabulary of Public Life. Ed. by Robert Wuthnow. 288p. (C). 1992. pap. text ed. 17.95 (*0-415-07637-4*, Routledge NY) Routledge.

Vocabulary of Radio & Television: Vocabulaire de la Radio et de la Television. F. P. Cormier et al. 31p. (ENG & FRE.). 1983. 14.95 (*0-8288-1315-9*, F134401) Fr & Eur.

Vocabulary of Soviet Society & Culture: A Selected Guide to Russian Words, Idioms, & Expressions of the Post-Stalin Era, 1953-1991. Irina H. Corten. LC 91-31876. 197p. 1992. text ed. 29.95 (*0-8223-1213-1*) Duke.

Vocabulary of the Automobile, Vol. 1: The MotorEnglish Vocabulary of the Automobile: The Motor. Anne-Marie Baudoin. 106p. (ENG & FRE.). 1992. pap. 24.95 (*0-8288-6337-7*, M-6025) Fr & Eur.

Vocabulary of the Automobile, Vol. 2: Maintenance & Repairs. Anne-Marie Baudoin. 90p. (ENG & FRE.). 1990. pap. 24.95 (*0-8288-9378-0*) Fr & Eur.

Vocabulary of the Automobile, Vol. 3: The Transmission. Anne-Marie Baudoin et al. 87p. (ENG & FRE.). 1992. pap. 24.95 (*0-8288-0763-9*, M9036) Fr & Eur.

Vocabulary of the Automobile, Vol. 4: The Chassis & Body. Anne-Marie Baudoin. 101p. (ENG & FRE.). 1980. pap. 24.95 (*0-8288-9377-2*) Fr & Eur.

***Vocabulary of the Greek Testament.** G. Milligan & James H. Moulton. 736p. 1997. reprint ed. 39.95 (*1-56563-271-0*) Hendrickson MA.

Vocabulary of the Greek Testament: Illustrated from the Papyri & Other Non-Literary Sources, 2 vols. G. Milligan & James H. Moulton. 1977. lib. bdg. 250.00 (*0-8490-2800-0*) Gordon Pr.

***Vocabulary of the Holy Qur'an.** 2nd ed. Ed. by Abidullah Ghazi & Tasneema Ghazi. 894p. 1986. reprint ed. lib. bdg. 24.00 (*1-56316-014-5*) Iqra Intl Ed Fdtn.

Vocabulary of the Institutiones of Cassiodorus with Special Advertence to the Technical Terminology & Its Sources, No. 9. Mary Gratia Ennis. (Studies in Medieval & Renaissance Latin Language & Literature). 186p. 1983. reprint ed. 38.00 (*0-939738-24-4*) Zubal Inc.

Vocabulary of the Kiowa Language. John P. Harrington. (Bureau of American Ethnology Bulletins Ser.). 255p. 1995. lib. bdg. 89.00 (*0-7812-4084-0*) Rprt Serv.

Vocabulary of the Language of San Antonio Mission, California. fac. ed. Bonaventure Sitjar. (Shea's Library of American Linguistics: No. VII). 64p. (C). 1961. reprint ed. pap. text ed. 5.90 (*1-55567-509-3*) Coyote Press.

Vocabulary of the Language of San Antonio Mission, California. Buenaventura Sitjar. LC 10-26367. (Library of American Linguistics: No. 7). (SPA.). reprint ed. 42.75 (*0-404-50987-8*) AMS Pr.

Vocabulary of the Lau Language, Big Mala, Solomon Islands. Walter G. Ivens. LC 75-35127. (LAO.). reprint ed. 29.50 (*0-404-14143-9*) AMS Pr.

Vocabulary of the Limbu Language. W. H. Senior. (C). 1977. reprint ed. 65.00 (*0-89771-115-7*, Pub. by Ratna Pustak Bhandar) St Mut.

Vocabulary of the Limbu Language of Eastern Nepal. W. H. Senior. 1977. 50.00 (*0-7855-0291-2*, Pub. by Ratna Pustak Bhandar); 50.00 (*0-7855-0324-2*, Pub. by Ratna Pustak Bhandar) St Mut.

Vocabulary of the Mangaian Language. F. W. Christian. (BMB Ser.). 1974. reprint ed. pap. 25.00 (*0-527-02114-8*) Periodicals Srv.

Vocabulary of the Micro-Computer. Marie-Eva De Villers. 67p. (FRE.). 1990. pap. 29.95 (*0-8288-9403-5*) Fr & Eur.

Vocabulary of the Nanticoke Dialect. Daniel G. Brinton et al. 58p. 1996. reprint ed. 24.95 (*0-9644234-3-X*) Evol Pubng & Manuf.

Vocabulary of the Navaho Language, 2 vols. Franciscans, Saint Michaels, Arizona. LC 76-43711. (NAV.). reprint ed. Set. write for info. (*0-404-15770-X*) AMS Pr.

***Vocabulary of the Quran.** A. Abbas Nadvi. 846p. 1996. 22.50 (*0-614-21076-3*, 1289) Kazi Pubns.

Vocabulary of the Shoe: Vocabulaire de la Chaussure. Celine Dupre. 48p. (ENG & FRE.). 1982. pap. 19.95 (*0-8288-0741-8*, F37380) Fr & Eur.

Vocabulary of the Shoshone Language. 2nd ed. George W. Hill. 40p. reprint ed. pap. 11.75 (*0-933046-05-7*) Little Red Hen.

Vocabulary of the Telephone. Helene Martin & Claire Pelletier. 39p. (ENG & FRE.). 1984. pap. 14.95 (*0-8288-9402-7*) Fr & Eur.

Vocabulary of the Transportation of Dangerous Goods. Jacques Simond. 481p. (ENG & FRE.). 1988. pap. 65.00 (*0-8288-7994-X*) Fr & Eur.

***Vocabulary of the Unami Jargon.** Thomas C. Holm. Tr. by Peter S. Duponceau. LC 97-14272. (American Language Reprints Ser.: Vol. 3). 62p. 1997. reprint ed. lib. bdg. 12.00 (*0-9644234-6-4*) Evol Pubng & Manuf.

Vocabulary One Thousand: With Words in Context. 2nd ed. Morton J. Cronin. 180p. (C). 1981. pap. text ed. 21.50 (*0-15-594987-X*) HB Coll Pubs.

Vocabulary or Phrase Book of the Mutsun Language of Alta California. fac. ed. Felipe A. De La Cuesta. (Shea's Library of American Linguistics: No. IV). 48p. (C). 1961. reprint ed. pap. text ed. 4.35 (*1-55567-508-5*) Coyote Press.

Vocabulary or Phrase Book of the Mutsun Language of Alta California. Felipe Arroyo de la Cuesta. (Library of American Linguistics: Vol. 8). (CAT.). reprint ed. 42.75 (*0-404-50988-6*) AMS Pr.

Vocabulary, Reading, & Reasoning. Martha Efurd & Margaret Newell. 101p. 1984. pap. text ed. 18.95 (*0-913507-03-2*) New Forums.

Vocabulary, Semantics, & Language Education. Evelyn Hatch & Cheryl Brown. (Cambridge Language Teaching Library). (Illus.). 416p. (C). 1995. text ed. 49.95 (*0-521-47409-4*); pap. text ed. 22.95 (*0-521-47942-8*) Cambridge U Pr.

***Vocabulary Start-Ups.** Murray Suid. (Start-Ups Ser.). (Illus.). 96p. (Orig.). (J). (gr. 3-6). 1997. pap. 9.95 (*1-57612-003-1*, MM2031) Monday Morning Bks.

Vocabulary Strategies. Beau F. Jones et al. (Orig.). (J). (gr. 1-6). 1989. student ed. 5.00 (*0-88106-087-9*); teacher ed. 15.00 (*0-88106-088-7*) Charlesbridge Pub.

Vocabulary Strategies for Success. Lee A. Rinsky. (C). 1995. pap. text ed. 34.25 (*0-15-502134-6*) HB Coll Pubs.

Vocabulary Strategies for Success. Lee A. Rinsky. (C). 1996. teacher ed., pap. text ed. 28.00 (*0-15-502137-0*) HB Coll Pubs.

Vocabulary Study. Dale McMasters. (Language Arts Ser.). 24p. (gr. 5-7). 1976. student ed. 5.00 (*0-8209-0311-6*, VD-3) ESP.

Vocabulary to Go: Ready to Go, Ready to Teach Worksheets for Vocabulary Skills. Jan Danielson. 1987. 31.95 (*1-55999-080-5*) LinguiSystems.

***Vocabulary Unlimited: For a More Powerful Vocabulary: The Unlimited Power for Success with Words--On the SAT, GRE & Other Standardized Tests--For Communication in School or Business.** Sandi A. Sirotowitz & Lesli I. Davis. LC 96-31721. (Illus.). 189p. 1996. 16.00 (*1-886941-14-9*) Spec Pr FL.

Vocabulary Workbook: Prefixes, Roots & Suffixes for ESL Students. Anne Farid. 240p. (C). 1984. pap. text ed. 16.65 (*0-13-942913-1*) P-H.

Vocabulary 4000: The 4000 Words Essential for Educated Vocabulary. Jeff Kolby. 150p. (Orig.). 1996. pap. 9.95 (*0-9637371-3-9*) Nova Pr.

Vocabutoons - Vocabulary Cartoons: The New Way to Build a More Powerful Vocabulary. Samuel Burchers et al. LC 96-96399. (Illus.). 344p. (Orig.). (YA). (gr. 7 up). 1996. pap. 10.95 (*0-9652422-9-3*) New Monic Bks.

***Vocabutoons, Vocabulary Cartoons: Learn Hundreds of New SAT Words Fast with Easy Memory Techniques.** 2nd rev. ed. Bryan Burchers et al. (YA). (gr. 7-12). Date not set. pap. 12.95 (*0-9652422-8-5*) New Monic Bks.

Vocacyon of Johan Bale. Ed. by Peter Happe & John N. King. (Renaissance English Text Society Series, Medieval & Renaissance Texts & Studies: Vol. 70). 160p. 1990. 24.00 (*0-86698-079-2*, MR70) MRTS.

Vocal Advantage. Jeffrey Jacobi. 224p. 1996. pap. 12.95 (*0-13-103656-4*) P-H.

Vocal Advantage. Jeffrey Jacobi. 224p. 1996. 29.95 incl. Apple II (*0-13-103664-5*) P-H.

***Vocal Arts: The Hermeneutic Dimension.** Michael Besack. LC 96-52358. (Vocal Arts Ser.: Vol. 1). (Illus.). 287p. (Orig.). 1997. pap. 20.00 (*1-889059-05-6*) Regent Pr.

Vocal Arts Medicine: The Care & Prevention of Professional Voice Disorders. Ed. by Michael Benninger et al. LC 93-5013. (Illus.). 374p. 1993. text ed. 69.00 (*0-86577-439-0*) Thieme Med Pubs.

Vocal Cord Paralysis: Diagnosis & Management. Michael E. Johns & Stewart R. Rood. (Self-Instructional Package Ser.). (Illus.). 86p. (Orig.). (C). 1993. pap. text ed. 25.00 (*1-56772-011-0*) AAO-HNS.

Vocal Development Through Organic Imagery. 2nd enl. rev. ed. William D. Leyerle. LC 78-103579. (Illus.). 189p. (C). 1986. pap. 14.95 (*0-9602296-6-3*) Leyerle Pubns.

Vocal Direction for the Theatre: From Script Analysis to Opening Night. Nan Withers-Wilson. 192p. (C). 1993. pap. 19.95 (*0-89676-122-3*, Drama Pubs) QSMG Ltd.

Vocal Exercise Physiology. Keith G. Saxon & Carole M. Schneider. (Illus.). 166p. (C). 1995. 39.95 (*1-56593-159-9*, 0467) Singular Publishing.

Vocal Fold Physiology: Acoustic, Perceptual, & Physiological Aspects of Voice Mechanisms. Ed. by Jan Gauffin & Britta Hammarberg. (Vocal Fold Physiology Ser.). (Illus.). 304p. (Orig.). (C). 1991. pap. text ed. 57.50 (*1-879105-51-9*, 0219) Singular Publishing.

Vocal Fold Physiology: Biomechanics, Acoustics & Phonatory Control. Ronald C. Scherer. 327p. 1985. 39.50 (*0-936947-53-5*) Denver Ctr Performing Arts.

Vocal Fold Physiology: Controlling Complexity & Chaos. Pamela J. Davis & Neville H. Fletcher. (Vocal Fold Physiology Ser.). (Illus.). 288p. (Orig.). 1996. pap. 57.50 (*1-56593-714-7*, 1404) Singular Publishing.

Vocal Fold Physiology: Frontiers in Basic Science. Ed. by Ingo R. Titze. LC 92-26498. (Vocal Fold Physiology Ser.). (Illus.). 416p. (Orig.). (C). 1992. pap. text ed. 57.50 (*1-879105-86-1*, 0349) Singular Publishing.

Vocal Fold Physiology: Proceedings of the Vocal Fold Physiology Conference Held in Kurume in January 15-19, 1980 As a Project of the Voice Foundation, New York. Vocal Fold Physiology Conference Staff. Ed. by Kenneth N. Stevens & Minoru Hirano. LC 81-188864. 435p. 1981. reprint ed. pap. 124.00 (*0-608-01555-5*, 2061966) Bks Demand.

Vocal Fold Physiology: Voice Production, Mechanisms & Functions. Ed. by Osamu Fujimura. (Vocal Fold Physiology Ser.: Vol. 2). (Illus.). 508p. (C). 1988. 65.00 (*1-56593-456-3*, 1130) Singular Publishing.

Vocal Fold Physiology: Voice Quality Control. Ed. by Osamu Fujimura & Minoru Hirano. (Vocal Fold Physiology Ser.). (Illus.). 320p. (C). 1995. pap. text ed. 57.50 (*1-56593-379-6*, 0766) Singular Publishing.

***Vocal Harmony Course Book.** (Illus.). 88p. 1989. pap. text ed. 29.95 incl. audio (*0-934419-24-8*) Vocal Power.

Vocal Melodies. Bartok. (Rumanian Folk Music Ser: Vol. 2). 1967. lib. bdg. 185.00 (*90-247-0624-6*) Kluwer Ac.

Vocal Music, Vol. 2. Philip L. Miller. LC 78-94. (Guide to Long-Playing Records Ser.: Vol. 2). 381p. 1978. reprint ed. text ed. 55.00 (*0-313-20295-8*, GULP02, Greenwood Pr) Greenwood.

Vocal or Instrumental Music - Which? Richard E. Stephens. 1972. pap. 2.95 (*0-89137-208-3*) Quality Pubns.

***Vocal Pathologies: Diagnosis, Treatment & Case Studies.** James P. Dworkin & Robert J. Meleca. LC 96-24941. 336p. 1996. 55.00 incl. cd-rom (*1-56593-623-X*, 1292) Singular Publishing.

Vocal Re-Education Therapy: A Clinician's Guide to the Hyperkinetic Voice. P. B. Mueller. 50p. 1989. ring bd. 35.00 (*0-930599-53-5*) Thinking Pubns.

Vocal Rehabilitation: A Practice Book for Voice Improvement. 3rd ed. Virginia Agnello & Cindy Garcia. 1990. spiral bd. 24.00 (*0-89079-233-X*, 3652) PRO-ED.

Vocal Rehabilitation: Let's Talk Voice. Virginia L. Agnello. LC 93-5981. 1993. spiral bd. 11.00 (*0-89079-591-6*, 3659) PRO-ED.

UV

Vocal Science & Art. Charles Gib. 118p. 1991. reprint ed. lib. bdg. 69.00 (*0-7812-9342-1*) Rprt Serv.

Vocal Selections from She Loves Me. Ed. by Sy Feldman. (Classic Broadway Shows Ser.). 24p. (Orig.). 1994. pap. 9.95 (*0-89724-266-1*, VF1788) Warner Brothers.

Vocal Songs in the Plays of Shakespeare: A Critical History. Peter J. Seng. LC 66-18256. 336p. reprint ed. pap. 95.80 (*0-7837-4128-6*, 2057951) Bks Demand.

***Vocal Vision: Voice in Tomorrow's Theatre.** Barbara Acker. LC 97-13927. 1997. pap. text ed. 18.95 (*1-55783-282-X*) Applause Theatre Bk Pubs.

Vocal Wisdom. William E. Brown & Giovanni B. Lamperti. Ed. by Lillian Strongin. 1957. pap. 9.95 (*0-8008-8023-4*, Crescendo) Taplinger.

Vocalcontraction Bei Homer. Friedrich Bechtel. xi, 314p. 1976. reprint ed. 80.00 (*3-487-05837-5*) G Olms Pubs.

Vocalian Organ. New York Organ Co. Staff. (Illus.). 25p. 1981. pap. 6.00 (*0-913746-16-9*) Organ Lit.

Vocalised Talmudic Manuscripts in the Cambridge Genizah Collections: Taylor-Schnechter Old Series, Vol. I: Taylor-Schechter Old Series. Shelomo Morag. (Cambridge University Library Genizan Ser.: No. 4). 60p. 1988. text ed. 89.95 (*0-521-26863-X*) Cambridge U Pr.

Vocalisme et le Consonantisme Francais. Donahue-Gaudet. 26.15 (*0-685-36654-5*) Fr & Eur.

Vocalisme et le Consonantisme Francais. Donahue-Gaudet. 26.15 (*0-8288-7703-3*, F135030) Fr & Eur.

Vocalitos: Vowels. (Illus.). 56p. (SPA.). (J). (ps-2). 1991. 6.95 (*0-935303-05-7*) Victory Pub.

Vocalizacion Aguda: Coloratura Vocalise for Flute & Piano. C. Chavez. 1992. pap. 9.95 (*0-7935-1993-4*) H Leonard.

Vocalization Systems of Arabic, Hebrew & Aramaic: Their Phonetic & Phonemic Principles. Shelomo Morag. (Janua Linguarum, Ser. Minor: No. 13). 1972. pap. text ed. 16.95 (*90-279-1965-8*) Mouton.

Vocation & a Voice. Kate Chopin. 1993. 20.75 (*0-8446-6708-0*) Peter Smith.

Vocation & a Voice: Stories. Kate Chopin. Ed. & Intro. by Emily Toth. 1991. pap. 10.95 (*0-14-039078-2*, Penguin Classics) Viking Penguin.

Vocation & Desire: George Eliot's Heroines. Dorothea Barrett. 208p. 1989. 35.00 (*0-415-00979-0*, A3453) Routledge.

Vocation & Identity in the Fiction of Muriel Spark. Rodney S. Edgecombe. 184p. 1990. text ed. 27.50 (*0-8262-0750-2*) U of Mo Pr.

Vocation & Mission of Joseph & Mary. Paul Molinary & Anne Hennessy. 60p. 1992. 5.95 (*1-85390-149-0*) Ignatius Pr.

Vocation & Mission of the Laity. Veritas Publications Staff. 1989. pap. 22.00 (*1-85390-009-5*, Pub. by Veritas IE) St Mut.

Vocation Counselling. Ny. 1989. pap. text ed. 21.40 (*0-13-945676-7*) P-H.

Vocation of a Teacher: Rhetorical Occasions, 1967-1988. Wayne C. Booth. LC 88-14297. 372p. 1989. 29.95 (*0-226-06581-2*) U Ch Pr.

Vocation of a Teacher: Rhetorical Occasions, 1967-1988. Wayne C. Booth. LC 88-14297. 384p. 1990. pap. 17.95 (*0-226-06582-0*) U Ch Pr.

Vocation of Man. Johann G. Fichte. Tr. by Peter Preuss from GER. LC 87-3610. (HPC Classics Ser.). (C). 1987. pap. text ed. 7.95 (*0-87220-037-X*); lib. bdg. 27.95 (*0-87220-038-8*) Hackett Pub.

Vocation of Man: Fichte. Ed. by Roderick M. Chisholm. (C). 1956. pap. write for info. (*0-02-322530-0*, Macmillan Coll) P-H.

Vocation of Peace. Gordon C. Zahn. 172p. (Orig.). 1993. pap. 15.95 (*1-879175-12-6*) Fortkamp.

***Vocation of the Artist.** Deborah J. Haynes. LC 96-46114. (Illus.). 300p. (C). 1997. text ed. 80.00 (*0-521-58040-4*); pap. text ed. 24.95 (*0-521-58969-X*) Cambridge U Pr.

***Vocation of the Catholic Educator.** Richard M. Jacobs. (Educational Monography Ser.). 79p. (Orig.). 1996. pap. 13.00 (*1-55833-174-3*) Natl Cath Educ.

Vocational & Personal Adjustments in Practical Nursing. 7th ed. Betty G. Becker & Dolores T. Fendler. LC 93-8185. 194p. (C). (gr. 13). 1993. pap. text ed. 23.95 (*0-8016-6839-5*) Mosby Yr Bk.

Vocational & Technical Education & Training. (Policy Paper Ser.). 84p. 1991. 7.95 (*0-8213-1780-6*, 11780) World Bank.

Vocational & Technical Resources for Community College Libraries. Ed. by Mary A. Laun. 622p. (Orig.). (C). 1995. pap. 95.00 (*0-8389-7775-8*) Assn Coll & Res Libs.

Vocational & Technical Resources for Community College Libraries: Selected Materials. Ed. by Mary Ann Laun. LC 94-46648. 1995. pap. 85.00 (*0-8389-7758-8*) ALA.

Vocational Assessment of Special Needs Students for Vocational Education: A State-of-the-Art Review. Michael Peterson. 1988. 8.00 (*0-318-40005-7*, IN 327) Ctr Educ Trng Employ.

***Vocational Biographies Career Finder.** (Expanded Career Library). 1994. ring bd. 454.00 incl. 5.25 hd (*0-87063-642-1*) Vocational Biographies.

***Vocational Biographies Career Finder.** (Expanded Career Library). 1994. ring bd. 454.00 incl. 3.5 hd (*0-87063-643-X*) Vocational Biographies.

***Vocational Biographies Career Finder.** (Expanded Career Library). 1994. ring bd. 454.00 incl. Apple II (*0-87063-644-8*) Vocational Biographies.

***Vocational Biographies Career Finder.** (Expanded Career Library). 1994. ring bd. 454.00 incl. mac hd (*0-87063-645-6*) Vocational Biographies.

Vocational Careers in the Twenty First Century. Norman C. Tognazzini. (Illus.). 16p. 1994. pap. 2.50 (*1-884241-28-X*, SPSO) Energeia Pub.

Vocational Careers Sourcebook. Karen Hill. 1992. 79.00 (*0-8103-8405-1*) Gale.

***Vocational Careers Sourcebook.** 3rd ed. 1997. 79.00 (*0-8103-6470-0*, 00000349, Gale Res Intl) Gale.

Vocational Careers Sourcebook, Vol. 1. 2nd ed. Bernstein. 1995. 79.00 (*0-8103-8812-X*) Gale.

Vocational Counseling for Special Populations. Chrisann Schiro-Geist. 172p. (C). 1990. pap. text ed. 32.95 (*0-398-05650-1*) C C Thomas.

***Vocational Counseling Models for Diverse.** Peterson. (Counseling Ser.). (C). Date not set. pap. 27.95 (*0-534-34972-2*) Brooks-Cole.

Vocational Counselling & Guidance in the Federal Republic of Germany. rev. ed. FESC. 1983. 35.00 (*0-907659-23-3*) St Mut.

Vocational Counselor. Jack Rudman. (Career Examination Ser.: C-1530). 1994. pap. 29.95 (*0-8373-1530-1*) Nat Learn.

Vocational Counselor Trainee. Jack Rudman. (Career Examination Ser.: C-1531). 1994. pap. 27.95 (*0-8373-1531-X*) Nat Learn.

Vocational Curriculum for Developmentally Disabled Persons. Paul Wehman & Philip J. McLaughlin. LC 79-16433. (Illus.). 253p. 1980. pap. 27.00 (*0-89079-118-X*, 1156) PRO-ED.

Vocational Decision Workbook. Richard Z. Glerum & Donna J. Blake. 1977. 4.50 (*0-910328-14-5*); 2.50 (*0-910328-15-3*) Sulzburger & Graham Pub.

Vocational Development & Guidance. W. Wesley Tennyson et al. 1974. 29.50 (*0-8422-7160-0*) Irvington.

***Vocational Education: Changes at High School Level after Amendments to Perkins Act.** Ed. by Henry Felder & Sarah L. Glavin. (Illus.). 69p. 1997. reprint ed. pap. text ed. 30.00 (*0-7881-4104-X*) DIANE Pub.

Vocational Education: Concepts & Operations. 2nd ed. Calfrey C. Calhoun & Alton V. Finch. 352p. (C). 1982. text ed. 53.95 (*0-534-00996-4*) Wadsworth Pub.

Vocational Education: Status in School Year 1990-91 & Early Signs of Change at Secondary Level. (Illus.). 88p. (Orig.). (C). 1995. pap. text ed. 20.00 (*0-7881-1792-0*) DIANE Pub.

Vocational Education: Status in 2-Year Colleges & Early Signs of Change. (Illus.). 68p. (Orig.). (C). 1994. pap. text ed. 20.00 (*0-7881-0363-6*) DIANE Pub.

Vocational Education & Economic Growth: Connections & Conundrums. Stuart Rosefeld. 22p. 1986. 3.00 (*0-318-22232-9*, OC 112) Ctr Educ Trng Employ.

Vocational Education & the Public Schools: A Chief State School Officer's Perspective. Franklin B. Walter. 12p. 2.75 (*0-318-22233-7*, OC117) Ctr Educ Trng Employ.

Vocational Education & Training. Pat Ainley. Ed. by C. E. Wragg. (Education Matters Ser.). 144p. 1990. text ed. 50.00 (*0-304-31942-2*); pap. text ed. 17.95 (*0-304-31948-1*) Cassell.

Vocational Education & Training for Youth: Towards Coherent Policy & Practice. OECD Staff. 180p. (Orig.). 1994. pap. 41.00 (*92-64-14285-1*) OECD.

***Vocational Education & Training in Belgium.** 128p. 1996. pap. 25.00 (*92-826-8775-9*, HX78-93-265-ENC, Pub. by Europ Com UK) Bernan Associates.

Vocational Education & Training in Denmark. FESC. 1985. 25.00 (*0-907659-28-4*) St Mut.

Vocational Education & Training in Greece. CEDEFOP Staff. 102p. 1995. pap. text ed. 19.00 (*92-826-8208-0*, HX-81-93-793ENC, Pub. by Europ Com UK) Bernan Associates.

***Vocational Education & Training in Portugal.** 94p. 1996. pap. 25.00 (*92-826-9503-4*, HX81-93-810-ENC, Pub. by Europ Com UK) Bernan Associates.

Vocational Education & Training in Sweden. FESC. 1984. 25.00 (*0-907659-03-9*) St Mut.

Vocational Education & Training in the Developed World: A Comparative Study. Leonard Cantor. 192p. 1989. 49.95 (*0-415-02541-9*, A3449) Routledge.

Vocational Education & Training in the Federal Republic of Germany. FESC. 1985. 25.00 (*0-907659-04-7*) St Mut.

Vocational Education & Training in the Federal Republic of Germany CEDEFOP. European Communities Staff. 119p. 1995. pap. 19.00 (*92-826-8756-2*, HX-81-93-826ENC, Pub. by Europ Com UK) Bernan Associates.

Vocational Education & Training in the German Democratic Republic. FESC. 1985. 25.00 (*0-907659-21-7*) St Mut.

Vocational Education & Training in the Republic of Ireland. FESC. 1984. 55.00 (*0-907659-02-0*) St Mut.

Vocational Education & Youth Employment. George H. Copa. 73p. 1984. 7.25 (*0-318-22236-1*, IN274) Ctr Educ Trng Employ.

Vocational Education for Immigrant & Minority Youth. Peggy Reubens. 42p. 1983. 4.25 (*0-318-22240-X*, IN257) Ctr Educ Trng Employ.

Vocational Education for Youth & Adults. Michael N. Sugarman & Albert J. Pautler. 147p. 1974. pap. text ed. 7.95 (*0-8422-0459-8*) Irvington.

Vocational Education in Agriculture in Federally-Aided Secondary Schools: A Study of Its Instructional & Training Phases. Gustavus A. Schmidt. LC 75-177802. (Columbia University. Teachers College. Contributions to Education Ser.: No. 534). reprint ed. 37.50 (*0-404-55534-9*) AMS Pr.

Vocational Education in an Information Age: Society at Risk? Anne Campbell. 20p. 1984. 3.00 (*0-318-22242-6*, OC99) Ctr Educ Trng Employ.

Vocational Education in Japan & Texas. Laura Lein & Robert C. Rickards. (Policy Research Project Report: No. 100). 123p. 1992. pap. 12.50 (*0-89940-708-0*) LBJ Sch Pub Aff.

Vocational Education in the Industrialization of Japan. 267p. 1988. pap. 30.00 (*92-808-0584-3*, E.87.III.A.1) UN.

Vocational Education in the Nineteen Nineties II: A Sourcebook for Strategies, Methods, & Materials. Craig Anderson & Lary C. Rampp. 294p. (Orig.). 1993. pap. text ed. 19.50 (*0-911168-87-7*) Prakken.

Vocational Education in the United States: Retrospect & Prospect. Robert M. Worthington. 26p. 1984. 3.00 (*0-318-22244-2*, OC101) Ctr Educ Trng Employ.

Vocational Education in the 1990's: Major Issues. Ed. by Albert J. Pautler, Jr. 302p. (Orig.). (C). 1990. pap. text ed. 16.95 (*0-911168-78-8*) Prakken.

Vocational Education Programs for the Disadvantaged. Lynda L. West et al. 1988. 5.25 (*0-318-40007-3*, IN 329) Ctr Educ Trng Employ.

Vocational Entry-Skills for Secondary & Adult Students with Learning Disabilities. Winifred Washburn. 1993. student ed. 10.00 (*0-87879-129-9*) Acad Therapy.

Vocational Entry-Skills for Secondary & Adult Students with Learning Disabilities. Winifred V. Washburn. 1993. 18.00 (*0-87879-128-0*) Acad Therapy.

Vocational Evaluation & Traumatic Brain Injury: A Procedural Manual. Stephen W. Thomas. 61p. (Orig.). (C). 1991. pap. 14.75 (*0-916671-94-1*) TRR.

Vocational Evaluation in Private Sector Rehabilitation. Anthony J. Choppa et al. 201p. (Orig.). (C). 1992. pap. 24.00 (*0-916671-96-8*) TRR.

Vocational Evaluation Systems & Software: A Consumer's Guide. Clarence D. Brown et al. 180p. (C). 1993. pap. 24.00 (*0-916671-99-2*) TRR.

Vocational General Knowledge. (National Teacher Examination Ser.: NT-64). pap. 23.95 (*0-8373-8484-2*) Nat Learn.

Vocational Guidance: Theory & Practice. W. P. Gothard. LC 84-23780. 198p. 1987. pap. text ed. 19.95 (*0-7099-1195-5*, Pub. by Croom Helm UK) Routledge Chapman & Hall.

Vocational Guidance & Human Development. Ed. by Edwin L. Herr. LC 81-40850. 608p. 1982. reprint ed. pap. text ed. 38.00 (*0-8191-1956-3*) U Pr of Amer.

Vocational Guidance Counselor. Jack Rudman. (Career Examination Ser.: C-1532). 1994. pap. 29.95 (*0-8373-1532-8*) Nat Learn.

Vocational Guidance in Catholic Secondary Schools: A Study of Developments & Present Status. Teresa G. Murray, Sr. LC 77-177098. (Columbia University. Teachers College. Contributions to Education Ser.: No. 754). reprint ed. 37.50 (*0-404-55754-6*) AMS Pr.

Vocational Guidance of Youth. Meyer Bloomfield. LC 70-89151. (American Education: Its Men, Institutions, & Ideas. Series 1). 1975. reprint ed. 16.95 (*0-405-01389-2*) Ayer.

Vocational Integration Index. Wendy S. Parent et al. 112p. 1992. pap. 48.00 (*0-9626521-9-9*) PRO-ED.

Vocational Integration Index: Measuring Integration of Workers with Disabilities. Wendy S. Parent et al. LC 94-40055. 1995. write for info. (*0-89079-659-9*) PRO-ED.

Vocational Interests of High School Girls As Inventoried by the Strong & Manson Blanks. Grace E. Laleger. LC 76-176970. (Columbia University. Teachers College. Contributions to Education Ser.: No. 857). reprint ed. 37.50 (*0-404-55857-7*) AMS Pr.

Vocational Interests of Men & Women. Edward K. Strong, Jr. xxix, 746p. 1943. 75.00 (*0-8047-0375-2*) Stanford U Pr.

Vocational Math for Business. 4th ed. James L. Southam. (MB - Business/Vocational Math Ser.). 1990. pap. 33.95 (*0-538-60219-8*) S-W Pub.

Vocational Mathematics. 4th ed. James L. Southam. (MB - Business/Vocational Math Ser.). 1990. pap. 27.95 (*0-538-60218-X*) S-W Pub.

Vocational Mathematics for Business. 3rd ed. Martinka. (MB - Business/Vocational Math Ser.). 1984. pap. 31.95 (*0-538-13180-2*) S-W Pub.

Vocational Objectives Within the U. S. Education System. FESC. 1985. 25.00 (*0-907659-00-4*) St Mut.

Vocational Preparation & Employment of Students with Physical & Multiple Disabilities. Sowers & Powers. 224p. 1991. pap. 30.00 (*1-55766-066-2*) P H Brookes.

Vocational Quest: New Directions for Education & Training. Malcolm Skilbeck et al. LC 93-40797. (Key Issues in Education Ser.). 288p. (C). (gr. 13). 1994. text ed. 69.95 (*0-415-10915-9*, B3928) Routledge.

***Vocational Readiness in American Indian Learning Disabled Adolescents.** J. M. Dodd et al. 89p. 1992. pap. text ed. write for info. (*1-888557-14-1*, 100108) No Ariz Univ.

Vocational Rehabilitation: Effectiveness of Federal Programs. (Illus.). 104p. (Orig.). (C). 1994. pap. text ed. 30.00 (*0-7881-0456-X*) DIANE Pub.

Vocational Rehabilitation: Its Relationship to Vocational Education. Richard P. Melia. 16p. 1986. 2.75 (*0-318-22246-9*, OC 120) Ctr Educ Trng Employ.

Vocational Rehabilitation & Employment of the Disabled: A Glossary. 182p. 1989. pap. 13.50 (*92-2-002571-X*) Intl Labour Office.

***Vocational Rehabilitation & Europe.** Michael Floyd. LC 96-3423. (Disability & Rehabilitation Ser.). 1996. pap. write for info. (*1-85302-235-7*, Pub. by J Kingsley Pubs UK) Taylor & Francis.

Vocational Rehabilitation Business: A Case-Management & Business Start-up Manual. Monty Campbell. 136p. (Orig.). 1992. pap. 17.50 (*1-877718-04-1*) Archangel Pr.

Vocational Rehabilitation Counselor. Jack Rudman. (Career Examination Ser.: C-2425). 1994. pap. 29.95 (*0-8373-2425-4*) Nat Learn.

Vocational Rehabilitation Counselor Assistant. Jack Rudman. (Career Examination Ser.: C-3040). 1994. Cloth bdg. avail. pap. 27.95 (*0-8373-3040-8*) Nat Learn.

Vocational Rehabilitation Counselor Trainee. Jack Rudman. (Career Examination Ser.: C-858). 1994. pap. 27.95 (*0-8373-0858-5*) Nat Learn.

Vocational Rehabilitation for Persons with Traumatic Brain Injury. Paul Wehman & Jeffrey Kreutzer. 372p. 1990. 66.00 (*0-8342-0135-6*) Aspen Pub.

Vocational Rehabilitation for Women with Disabilities. Sheila Stace. viii, 38p. (Orig.). 1987. pap. 11.25 (*92-2-105723-2*) Intl Labour Office.

Vocational Rehabilitation in Employment Training. Pamela Finnerty-Fried & Robert N. Ianacone. 63p. 1984. 5.75 (*0-318-22245-0*, IN272) Ctr Educ Trng Employ.

Vocational Rehabilitation in Florida Workers' Compensation: Rehabilitants, Services, Costs, & Outcomes. John A. Gardner. LC 87-37119. 1988. 25.00 (*0-935149-11-2*, WC-88-1) Workers Comp Res Inst.

Vocational Rehabilitation in Workers' Compensation: Issues & Evidence. John A. Gardner. 1985. 25.00 (*0-935149-05-8*, S-85-1) Workers Comp Res Inst.

***Vocational Rehabilitation of American Indians & Alaska Natives Who Have Alcohol & Substance Abuse Disorders: Treatment Center Survey.** R. M. Schacht et al. 45p. 1994. pap. text ed. write for info. (*1-888557-49-4*) No Ariz Univ.

***Vocational Rehabilitation of American Indians Who Have Alcohol or Other Substance Abuse Disorders.** R. M. Schacht & L. Gaseoma. 45p. 1993. pap. text ed. write for info. (*1-888557-23-0*, 100030) No Ariz Univ.

Vocational Rehabilitation of Persons with Prolonged Psychiatric Disorders. Ed. by Jean A. Ciardiello & Morris D. Bell. LC 87-26082. (Contemporary Medicine & Public Health Ser.). 320p. 1988. text ed. 45.00 (*0-8018-3635-2*) Johns Hopkins.

Vocational Rehabilitation Outcomes: Evidence from New York. John A. Gardner. LC 86-28144. 120p. (Orig.). 1986. 25.00 (*0-935149-03-1*, WC-86-1) Workers Comp Res Inst.

Vocational Selection & Counseling, 2 vols., Vol. 1. Doris C. Doane. LC 81-71851. 158p. 16.00 (*0-86690-011-X*, D1073-014) Am Fed Astrologers.

Vocational Selection & Counseling, 2 vols., Vol. 2. Doris C. Doane. LC 81-71851. 176p. 16.00 (*0-86690-012-8*, D1074-014) Am Fed Astrologers.

Vocational Special Needs. Michelle D. Sarkees. (Illus.). 433p. 1995. 74.96 (*0-8269-4006-4*) Am Technical.

Vocational Specialist. Jack Rudman. (Career Examination Ser.: C-3293). 1994. pap. 29.95 (*0-8373-3293-1*) Nat Learn.

Vocational-Technical Core Collection: Vol. I, Books. Jack Hall & Victoria C. Lessard. LC 81-11048. 394p. 1981. 39.95 (*0-918212-46-4*) Neal-Schuman.

Vocational-Technical Core Collection: Vol. II, Films & Video. Jack Hall & Victoria C. Lessard. LC 81-11048. 250p. 1984. 39.95 (*0-918212-47-2*) Neal-Schuman.

Vocational-Technical Mathematics. 2nd ed. Robert D. Smith. 640p. (Orig.). 1991. text ed. 46.95 (*0-8273-3314-5*) Delmar.

Vocational-Technical Mathematics. 2nd ed. Robert D. Smith. 640p. (Orig.). 1991. teacher ed., pap. 16.00 (*0-8273-3315-3*) Delmar.

Vocational Technical Mathematics. 3rd ed. Smith. (Trade/Tech Math Ser.). 1996. teacher ed. 69.95 (*0-8273-6811-9*) Delmar.

Vocational Technical Mathematics. 3rd ed. Smith. (Trade/Tech Math Ser.). 208p. 1996. teacher ed., text ed. 20.00 (*0-8273-6812-7*) Van Nos Reinhold.

Vocational-Technical Mathematics Simplified. Cheryl Cleaves et al. (Illus.). 368p. 1987. pap. text ed. 66.00 (*0-13-943093-8*) P-H.

Vocational Technical Mathematics TRB. 3rd ed. Smith. (Trade/Tech Math Ser.). 1996. 59.95 (*0-8273-6809-7*) Van Nos Reinhold.

Vocational Tests & Reviews. Ed. by Oscar K. Buros. LC 75-8116. xxvi, 1087p. 1975. 75.00 (*0-8032-4650-1*) U of Nebr Pr.

Vocational Training & Employment of the Moderately & Severely Handicapped & Autistic Adolescent with Particular Emphasis to Bilingual Special Education. Elva Duran. (Illus.). 182p. 1992. pap. 25.95 (*0-398-06101-7*) C C Thomas.

Vocational Training & Employment of the Moderately & Severely Handicapped & Autistic Adolescent with Particular Emphasis to Bilingual Special Education. Elva Duran. (Illus.). 182p. (C). 1992. text ed. 39.95 (*0-398-05801-6*) C C Thomas.

Vocational Training & Employment of Youth. Selden C. Menefee. LC 70-166953. (Research Monographs: Vol. 25). 1971. reprint ed. lib. bdg. 22.50 (*0-306-70357-2*) Da Capo.

Vocational Training for Persons with Severe Handicaps. H. D. Fredericks et al. 200p. (Orig.). 1987. pap. 13.00 (*0-944232-01-9*) Teaching Res.

Vocational Training in Germany: Modernisation & Responsiveness. OECD Staff. 120p. (Orig.). 1994. pap. 29.00 (*92-64-14301-7*) OECD.

Vocational Training Supervisor. Jack Rudman. (Career Examination Ser.: C-2673). 1994. pap. 34.95 (*0-8373-2673-7*) Nat Learn.

Vocations in Fiction: An Annotated Bibliography. Mary R. Lingenfelter. LC 74-3102. (Studies in Fiction: No. 34). 1974. lib. bdg. 75.00 (*0-8383-2052-X*) M S G Haskell Hse.

Vocative Figure. 2nd rev. ed. Anne-Marie Albiach. Tr. by Anthony Barnett & Joseph Simas from FRE. 48p. 1992. reprint ed. pap. 12.00 (*0-907954-18-9*, Pub. by Allardyce Barnett UK) SPD-Small Pr Dist.

Vocabulaire du Cirque et Music Hall. Hughes Hotier. 270p. (FRE.). 1981. pap. 42.95 (*0-8288-2168-2*, M12412) Fr & Eur.

Voces: An Anthology of Nuevo Mexicano Writers. Ed. by Rudolfo A. Anaya. LC 88-22705. 241p. (Orig.). (ENG & SPA.). 1987. pap. 15.95 (*0-8263-1040-0*) U of NM Pr.

Voces: Eine Bibliographie zu Woertern und Begriffen aus der Patristik (1918-1978) Hermann J. Sieben. (Bibliographia Patristica Ser.). 461p. (C). 1979. text ed. 126.95 (*3-11-007966-6*) De Gruyter.

An Asterisk (*) at the beginning of an entry indicates that the title is appearing in BIP for the first time.

Voces: Voices from the Hispanic Church. Justo L. Gonzalez. 172p. (Orig.). 1992. pap. 9.95 (*0-687-43810-1*) Abingdon.

Voces de Hispanoamerica. Ragucci. 49.95 (*0-686-56674-2*, S-33067); 55.00 (*0-8288-7948-6*, S33067) Fr & Eur.

Voces de Hispanoamerica. 2nd ed. Raquel Chang-Rodriguez & Malva E. Filer. (College Spanish Ser.). (SPA.). 1995. text ed. 48.95 (*0-8384-5186-1*) Heinle & Heinle.

Voces de Hispanoamerica: Antologia Literaria. Rodriguez R. Chang & Malva Filer. 1988. text ed. 37.25 (*0-8384-1603-9*) Heinle & Heinle.

Voces del Pulpito Hispano. Ed. by Angel L. Gutierrez. 112p. (SPA.). 1988. pap. 11.00 (*0-8170-1145-5*) Judson.

Voces en el Desierto. Luis Zalamea. LC 83-81726. (Coleccion Espejo de Paciencia). 77p. (Orig.). (SPA.). 1984. pap. 6.00 (*0-89729-339-8*) Ediciones.

Voces Femeninas de Hispanoamerica. Ed. by Gloria Bautista. (Latin American Ser.). 336p. (SPA.). (C). 1997. 55.00 (*0-8229-3877-4*); pap. 22.95 (*0-8229-5558-X*) U of Pittsburgh Pr.

***Voces Fronterizas: The Border Voices Literary Festival Anthology.** Ed. by Belinda Subraman. (Illus.). 80p. (Orig.). Date not set. pap. 5.00 (*0-935839-20-8*) Vergin Pr.

Voces Por Independencia: Retrados de Personas Notables Gyudando la Independencia de Puerto Rico. Jean W. Zwickel. Tr. by J. M. Monsanto from ENG. (Illus.). 141p. (Orig.). (SPA.). 1990. pap. 8.50 (*0-9620448-1-4*) White Star Pr.

"Voces Super Speciosa Facta Est" for ATB Chorus. Brian Banks. (University Choral Ser.: No. 4). 4p. 1994. pap. text ed. 1.50 (*1-56571-101-7*) PRB Prods.

Voces y Costumbres de Catamarca, 2 vols. Carlos Villafuerte. Set. 75.00 (*0-8288-8026-3*, S33071) Fr & Eur.

Voces y Ecos en la Poesia de Jose Angel Valente. Santiago Daydi-Tolson. LC 83-51783. 182p. 1984. pap. 25.00 (*0-89295-034-X*) Society Sp & Sp-Am.

***Voci: Encounters with Italian.** Nina D. Glassman & Frederick J. Bosco. (Toronto Italian Studies). 272p. 1996. pap. 24.95 (*0-8020-7824-9*) U of Toronto Pr.

Voci d'Italia: An Anthology of Contemporary Italian Writing. Ed. by Marisa Katis et al. (Illus.). 224p. 1984. pap. text ed. 21.00 (*0-08-029832-X*, Pergamon Pr) Elsevier.

Vocrescends. Bern Porter & Malok. 32p. (Orig.). 1991. pap. 3.00 (*0-926935-42-9*) Runaway Spoon.

***Vodka, Tears & Lenin's Angel: My Adventures in the Wild & Woolly F. S. U. (Former Soviet Union)** Jennifer Gould. LC 96-3252. 1997. 25.95 (*0-312-15241-8*) St Martin.

Vodnik. Stepan Zavrel. LC 72-121796. (Illus.). 32p. (J). (ps-3). 8.95 (*0-87592-058-6*) Scroll Pr.

Vodopad: A Soviet Torpedo. Leonid Zeliger. (Illus.). 127p. (Orig.). 1989. pap. text ed. 75.00 (*1-55831-102-5*) Delphic Associates.

***Vodou Things: The Art of Pierrot Barra & Marie Cassaise.** Donald J. Cosentino. LC 97-17175. (Folk Art & Artists Ser.). (Illus.). 72p. 1998. 22.50 (*1-57806-014-1*) U Pr of Miss.

Voegel der Palaearkischen Fauna, 4 vols., Set. E. Hartert. 1970. 480.00 (*3-7682-0604-1*) Lubrecht & Cramer.

Voegelin & the Theologian: Ten Studies in Interpretation. Ed. by John Kirby & William M. Thompson. LC 82-22914. (Toronto Studies in Theology: Vol. 10). 392p. 1983. lib. bdg. 99.95 (*0-88946-751-X*) E Mellen.

Voegelin on the Idea of Race: An Analysis of Modern European Racism. Thomas W. Heilke. LC 89-28160. 192p. 1990. text ed. 27.50 (*0-8071-1563-0*) La State U Pr.

Voge Patterns. Carol Stetser. (Illus.). 16p. (Orig.). 1992. reprint ed. pap. 49.00 (*0-917960-04-1*) Padma.

Vogel. (Meyers Klien Kinderbibliothek). 24p. (GER.). (J). 13.75 (*3-411-08531-2*) Langenscheidt.

Vogel Atmungs-und Nahrungswelt, Gesehlecht und Fortoflanzung. F. Groebbels. 1969. 350.00 (*3-7682-0241-0*) Lubrecht & Cramer.

Vogel und Sein Leben. Bernard Altum. Ed. by Keir B. Sterling. LC 77-81082. (Biologists & Their World Ser.). (GER.). 1978. reprint ed. lib. bdg. 19.95 (*0-405-10652-1*) Ayer.

Vogel's Cross-Reference & Index to the Contents of Luther's Works. Heinrich J. Vogel. LC 82-63053. 281p. (Orig.). 1983. pap. 7.99 (*0-8100-0168-3*, 15N0401) Northwest Pub.

Vogel's Elementary Practical Organic Chemistry 1 - Preparations. rev. ed. B. V. Smith & N. M. Waldron. (Illus.). 416p. 1979. text ed. 27.00 (*0-582-47009-9*) Longman.

Vogel's Qualitative Inorganic Analysis. 7th ed. G. Suehla. 1996. 54.50 (*0-582-21866-7*) Addison-Wesley.

***Vogel's Textbook of Practical Organic Chemistry.** 5th ed. B. S. Furniss. (C). 1989. text ed. 133.50 (*0-582-46236-3*, Pub. by Longman UK) Longman.

***Vogel's Textbook of Quantitative Chemical Analysis.** 5th ed. G. H. Jeffery. (C). 1989. text ed. 127.50 (*0-582-44693-7*, Pub. by Longman UK) Longman.

Vogt for the Environment. John Sailer. LC 93-15313. (Illus.). 96p. (YA). (gr. 7-12). 1993. 6.95 (*0-913990-34-5*) Book Pub Co.

Vogue & Butterick's Designer Sewing. Nancy Fleming. (Illus.). 128p. 1994. pap. 17.00 (*0-671-88878-1*, Fireside) S&S Trade.

Vogue Beauty for Life. Hutton. 18.00 (*0-517-88452-6*) Random Hse Value.

Vogue Beauty for Life: Health, Fitness, Looks, & Style for Women in Their 30s, 40s, 50s. Deborah Hutton. LC 94-2592. 1994. reprint ed. 30.00 (*0-517-59224-X*, Crown) Crown Pub Group.

Vogue Cocktails, Vol. 1. Henry McNulty. (Illus.). 80p. 1993. 9.95 (*0-8212-2013-6*) Bulfinch Pr.

Vogue Knitting: The Ultimate Knitting Book. LC 89-42555. (Illus.). 288p. 1989. 35.00 (*0-394-57186-X*) Pantheon.

Vogue la Galere. Marcel Ayme. 176p. 1944. pap. 11.95 (*0-7859-0372-0*, F84060) Fr & Eur.

Vogue of Revolution in Poor Countries. Forrest D. Colburn. LC 94-10318. 152p. 1994. text ed. 24.95 (*0-691-03676-4*) Princeton U Pr.

Vogul Folklore. Munkacsi et al. Ed. by E. Schmidt. (ISTOR Bks.: Vol. 4). (Illus.). 215p. 1995. 38.00 (*963-05-6629-X*, Pub. by A K HU) Intl Spec Bk.

Vogul Suffixes & Pronouns. Wolfgang Veenker. LC 77-625112. (Uralic & Altaic Ser.: Vol. 110). 65p. (Orig.). 1969. pap. text ed. 9.00 (*0-87750-044-4*) Res Inst Inner Asian Studies.

Voi Altri Pochi: Ezra Pound & His Audience, 1908-1925. Mark Kyburz. LC 96-17020. (ICSELL Ser.). 200p. 1996. pap. 44.95 (*0-8176-5405-4*) Birkhauser.

Voice. David Appelbaum. LC 89-35228. 155p. 1990. text ed. 59.50 (*0-7914-0287-8*); pap. text ed. 19.95 (*0-7914-0288-6*) State U NY Pr.

Voice. Colm Connolly. 256p. 1986. 15.95 (*0-8253-0347-8*) Beaufort Bks NY.

***Voice.** Anne Szumigalski. (Illus.). 9.95 (*1-55050-089-9*, Pub. by Coteau CN) Genl Dist Srvs.

Voice: A Dramatic New Concept. Denton Rossell. Ed. by Delorez Westman. (Illus.). 227p. 1984. 28.50 (*0-913145-00-9*) Clark & Westman-Magnolia.

Voice: An Introduction to Practical Phonology. W. A. Aikin. Ed. by H. St. John Rumsey. LC 51-13505. 175p. reprint ed. pap. 49.90 (*0-317-09971-X*, 2051248) Bks Demand.

Voice: Form & Function. Ed. by Barbara Fox & Paul J. Hopper. LC 93-37185. (Typological Studies in Language: No. 27). xiii, 377p. 1994. pap. 32.95 (*1-55619-419-6*); lib. bdg. 98.00 (*1-55619-418-8*) Benjamins North Am.

Voice: Onstage & Off. Robert Barton & Rocco DalVera. 350p. (Orig.). (C). 1994. text ed. 44.25 (*0-15-500120-5*) HB Coll Pubs.

Voice: Psyche & Soma. Cornelius L. Reid. LC 74-30987. (Orig.). 1975. pap. 6.95 (*0-915282-00-3*) J Patelson Mus.

Voice - Data Telecommunications for Business. Stanley Schatt & Steven Fox. 356p. 1989. text ed. 60.00 (*0-13-107889-5*) P-H.

Voice - Over: Collected Poems. Olga Cabral. 122p. (Orig.). 1993. pap. 9.95 (*0-931122-73-2*) West End.

Voice Advantage. Deborah Ross-Swain. (Illus.). 52p. (Orig.). (C). 1990. student ed., pap. text ed. 49.95 (*1-879105-09-8*, 0073) Singular Publishing.

Voice Against the Wind: John G. Neihardt as Critic & Reviewer. John T. Richards. (Illus.). 161p. (Orig.). 1986. pap. 6.00 (*0-9605980-1-4*) J T Richards.

Voice & Articulation. 2nd ed. Kenneth C. Crannell. 428p. (C). 1991. pap. 27.25 (*0-534-14112-9*) Wadsworth Pub.

Voice & Articulation. 3rd ed. Kenneth C. Crannell. LC 96-8347. (Communications Studies). (Illus.). 465p. (C). 1997. pap. 37.95 (*0-534-50899-5*) Wadsworth Pub.

Voice & Articulation: A Handbook. Donald H. Ecroyd et al. LC 66-20352. 152p. reprint ed. pap. 43.40 (*0-7837-3013-6*, 2042927) Bks Demand.

Voice & Crisis: Invocation in Milton's Poetry. Walter L. Schindler. LC 84-2897. x, 130p. (C). 1984. lib. bdg. 27.50 (*0-208-02046-2*, Archon Bks) Shoe String.

Voice & Data Communications Handbook. Bud Bates & Donald Gregory. LC 95-22058. 1996. text ed. 65.00 (*0-07-005147-X*) McGraw.

Voice & Diction. Carla Bennett. (C). 1995. 5.46 (*1-56870-167-5*) RonJon Pub.

Voice & Diction. 2nd ed. P. Judson Newcombe. (Illus.). 317p. (C). 1991. pap. text ed. 34.95 (*0-89892-063-9*) Contemp Pub Co of Raleigh.

Voice & Diction. 7th ed. Eisenson. 424p. 1996. pap. 50.00 (*0-205-19869-4*) Allyn.

Voice & Diction Handbook. Robert King & Eleanor DiMichael. (Illus.). 498p. (Orig.). (C). 1991. pap. text ed. 27.95 (*0-88133-585-1*) Waveland Pr.

Voice & Equality: Civic Voluntarism in American Politics. Kay L. Schlozman et al. LC 95-16501. (Illus.). 512p. (C). 1996. 39.95 (*0-674-94292-2*); pap. 17.95 (*0-674-94293-0*) HUP.

Voice & Fax Processing Printed Circuit Cards: A Sourcebook of Suppliers & Products. Marc Robins. 188p. (Orig.). 1996. pap. 85.00 (*0-9624360-8-9*) Robins Pr.

Voice & Fax Processing System Application Generators. Marc Robins. 247p. (Orig.). 1996. pap. 85.00 (*0-9624360-6-2*, SR302) Robins Pr.

Voice & Inversion. Ed. by T. Givon. LC 94-14762. (Typological Studies in Language: No. 28). viii, 402p. 1994. pap. 32.95 (*1-55619-421-8*); lib. bdg. 95.00 (*1-55619-420-X*) Benjamins North Am.

Voice & Its Disorders. 5th ed. Greene. 444p. 1991. pap. 54.99 (*1-879105-08-X*, A028) Singular Publishing.

Voice & Other Stories. Seicho Matsumoto. Tr. by Adam Kabat. 180p. 1989. 17.95 (*0-87011-895-1*) Kodansha.

Voice & Other Stories. Seicho Matsumoto. Tr. by Adam Kabat. 180p. 1995. pap. 9.00 (*4-7700-1949-1*) Kodansha.

Voice & Speech Processing. Richard K. Miller & Terri C. Walker. 293p. 1991. 285.00 (*0-89671-126-9*) SEAI Tech Pubns.

Voice & Speech Processing. T. Parsons. (Electrical Engineering Ser.). 448p. 1987. text ed. write for info. (*0-07-048541-0*) McGraw.

Voice & Style. Johnny Payne. 176p. 1995. 15.99 (*0-89879-693-8*, Wrtrs Digest Bks) F & W Pubns Inc.

Voice & the Actor. Cicely Berry. 160p. 1991. pap. 8.95 (*0-02-041555-9*) Macmillan.

Voice & Vision in Ronsard's Les Sonnets por Helene. Jean M. Fallon. LC 93-22220. (Renaissance & Baroque Studies & Texts: Vol. 10). 142p. (C). 1994. text ed. 48.95 (*0-8204-2159-6*) P Lang Pubng.

Voice & Vision of Anita Desai. Seema Jena. (C). 1988. 14.00 (*81-7024-227-4*, Pub. by Ashish II) S Asia.

Voice & Vocabulary of the Wild Turkey. Lovett E. Williams, Jr. (Illus.). 85p. 1984. 14.95 (*0-685-62742-X*) Real Turkeys Pubs.

Voice & Voice Therapy. 3rd ed. Daniel R. Boone. (Illus.). 320p. 1983. text ed. write for info. (*0-13-943118-7*) P-H.

Voice & Voice Therapy. 5th ed. Daniel R. Boone & Stephen C. McFarlane. LC 93-32168. 1993. text ed. 64.00 (*0-13-030677-0*) P-H.

Voice As a Bridge: A Quartet of Contemporary German Poets. Lioba Happel et al. Ed. by Dieta Sixt & William Gilcher. Tr. by Lane Jennings & Rick Bolling. 100p. (Orig.). (GER.). (C). 1996. pap. text ed. 15.00 (*0-938572-15-6*) Bunny Crocodile.

Voice at the Back Door. Elizabeth Spencer. LC 81-18421. (Voices of the South Ser.). vii, 392p. 1994. pap. 12.95 (*0-8071-1927-X*) La State U Pr.

Voice at the Workplace: Reflections on Colonialism and the Jamaican Worker. Michael Manley. 1991. pap. 16.95 (*0-88258-068-X*) Howard U Pr.

Voice At the Workplace: Reflections on Colonialism and the Jamaican Worker. Micheal Manley. 1991. 29.95 (*0-88258-067-1*) Howard U Pr.

Voice at Twilight: Diary of a Dying Man. Tessa L. Warburg. LC 88-61444. 252p. 8800. 30.00 (*0-7206-0706-X*, Pub. by P Owen Ltd UK) Dufour.

Voice Behind the Screen. unabridged ed. Gottfried Benn. Ed. & Tr. by Simona Draghici from GER. LC 96-14104. 56p. (Orig.). 1996. pap. text ed. 4.95 (*0-943045-10-X*) Plutarch Pr DC.

Voice Book: For Actors, Public Speakers, & Everyone Who Wants to Make Best Use of Their Voice. Michael McCallion. 256p. 1988. 45.00 (*0-87830-986-1*, Thtre Arts Bks); pap. 15.95 (*0-87830-987-X*, Thtre Arts Bks) Routledge.

Voice Building for Choirs. rev. ed. Wilhelm Ehmann & Frauke Haasemann. Tr. by Brenda Smith from GER. 141p. (C). 1981. pap. 9.95 (*0-937276-02-2*) Hinshaw Mus.

Voice Communication Between Humans & Machines. David B. Roe & Jay G. Wilpon. 560p. (C). 1994. text ed. 79.95 (*0-309-04988-1*) Natl Acad Pr.

Voice Communication in Business. Lee F. Goeller. LC 73-85629. (Specialized Ser.). (Illus.). 140p. (Orig.). (C). 1982. pap. 20.95 (*1-56016-019-5*) ABC TeleTraining.

Voice Communication with Computers. Christopher Schmandt. (C). 1994. pap. 39.95 (*1-85032-844-7*) ITCP.

Voice Communications with Computers. Christopher Schmandt. 1994. pap. 39.95 (*0-442-23935-1*) Van Nos Reinhold.

Voice Compression Technology. Business Communications Co., Inc. Staff. 146p. 1985. pap. 1,750.00 (*0-89336-430-4*, G-092) BCC.

Voice Crying in the Wilderness. Edward Abbey. 1990. 14.95 (*0-312-04147-0*) St Martin.

Voice Crying in the Wilderness (Vox Clamantis in Deserto) Notes from a Secret Journal. Edward Abbey. (Illus.). 112p. 1991. pap. 7.95 (*0-312-06488-8*) St Martin.

Voice Crying Out in the Desert: Preparing for Vatican II with Barnabas M. Ahern, C. P. Ed. by Carroll Stuhlmueller & Sebastian MacDonald. 384p. (Orig.). 1996. pap. 24.95 (*0-8146-2354-9*, Liturg Pr Bks) Liturgical Pr.

Voice-Data Telecommunications Systems: An Introduction to Technology. Michael Gurrie & Patrick J. O'Connor. (Illus.). 416p. (C). 1985. text ed. 98.00 (*0-13-943283-3*) P-H.

Voice Disorders: Current Therapy of Communication Disorders, Vol. 4. Ed. by William H. Perkins. 160p. 1983. 24.00 (*0-86577-407-2*) Thieme Med Pubs.

Voice Disorders & Their Management. Ed. by Margaret Fawcus. (Illus.). 400p. (Orig.). (C). 1991. pap. 51.95 (*1-879105-57-8*, 0256) Singular Publishing.

Voice For Achievement. (C). 1993. pap. 11.93 (*0-395-67504-9*) HM.

Voice for Children. Malfrid G. Flekkoy. 280p. 1991. 45.00 (*1-85302-119-9*); pap. 23.00 (*1-85302-118-0*) Taylor & Francis.

Voice for the Excluded: Popular Participation in Development. Matthias Stiefel & Marshall Wolfe. LC 94-10688. 304p. (C). 1994. pap. 25.00 (*1-85649-248-6*, Pub. by Zed Bks Ltd UK); text ed. 59.95 (*1-85649-247-8*, Pub. by Zed Bks Ltd UK) Humanities.

Voice for the Future. Nikias Livadas. Tr. by Rhea Frangofinou. LC 94-90530. 176p. (Orig.). 1996. pap. 8.00 (*1-56002-501-8*, Univ Edtns) Aegina Pr.

Voice for the Mad: A Life of Dorothea Dix. David Gollaher. (Illus.). 352p. 1995. 28.00 (*0-02-912399-2*, Free Press) Free Pr.

Voice for the People: The Life & Work of Harold Courlander. Nina Jaffe. LC 96-32513. (J). 1996. 16.95 (*0-8050-3444-7*) H Holt & Co.

Voice for the Planet a Voice for Humanity. Anna M. Gallo. Ed. by Rodney Charles & Elizabeth Pasco. LC 95-71070. (Illus.). 90p. (Orig.). (C). 1995. pap. 10.95 (*1-887472-00-2*) Sunstar Pubng.

Voice from Harper's Ferry. Osborne P. Anderson. LC 72-8569. (Black Heritage Library Collection). 1977. reprint ed. 19.95 (*0-8369-9182-6*) Ayer.

Voice from Inner Space: Answers Who Am I? Why Am I Here? Marilyn Lindstrom. Ed. by Jean Beckman. LC 90-35087. 112p. (Orig.). (J). 1990. pap. 7.95 (*0-941992-20-9*) Los Arboles Pub.

Voice from Japan: An Outsider Looks In. Carolyn Meyer. 240p. (YA). (gr. 7 up). 1992. pap. 10.00 (*0-15-200634-6*, Gulliver Bks) HarBrace.

Voice from Nowhere. Jane Norman & Frank Beazley. 24p. (J). (ps-3). 1993. pap. write for info. (*1-883585-10-4*) Pixanne Ent.

Voice from South Carolina. John Leland. LC 72-37310. (Black Heritage Library Collection). 1977. reprint ed. 20.95 (*0-8369-8947-3*) Ayer.

Voice from the Attic: Essays on the Art of Reading. rev. ed. Robertson Davies. 384p. 1990. pap. 9.95 (*0-14-012081-5*, Penguin Bks) Viking Penguin.

Voice from the Byzantine East. Elias Zoghby. Tr. by R. Bernard. LC 92-13838. 178p. (Orig.). 1992. pap. text ed. 7.95 (*1-56125-018-X*) Educ Services.

***Voice from the Chorus.** Abram Terts. LC 94-61487. 328p. Date not set. pap. 14.00 (*0-300-06119-6*, PG3476) Yale U Pr.

***Voice from the Cloud: A Fresh Look at the Gospel of Mark.** Nick Overduin. LC 96-28194. (Fresh Look Ser.). 100p. (Orig.). 1996. student ed., pap. 11.10 (*1-56212-192-8*, 1315-2020) CRC Pubns.

Voice from the Desert. Jacques Gaillot. LC 96-23244. 144p. (Orig.). 1996. pap. text ed. 15.95 (*0-8245-1584-6*) Crossroad NY.

Voice from the Dumb: A Memoir of John William Lashford. W. Sleight. 1972. 59.95 (*0-8490-1266-X*) Gordon Pr.

Voice from the Factories. Caroline Norton. LC 93-46507. (Revolution & Romanticism, 1789-1834 Ser.). 1994. 40.00 (*1-85477-169-8*, Pub. by Woodstock Bks UK) Cassell.

Voice from the Forest. Nahum Kohn & Howard Roiter. LC 80-81685. (Illus.). 256p. (Orig.). 1985. 12.95 (*0-89604-020-8*, Holocaust Library); pap. 5.95 (*0-89604-021-6*, Holocaust Library) US Holocaust.

Voice from the Grave. Carol Mercado. 1996. mass mkt. 5.99 (*0-425-15511-0*) Berkley Pub.

Voice from the Heart. Ruth Zakutinsky. 429p. 1992. 18.95 (*0-911643-16-8*) Aura Bklyn.

Voice from the Hump. John Wheatcroft. 8.95 (*0-8453-1909-4*, Cornwall Bks) Assoc Univ Prs.

Voice from the Loess Hills. Cran K. Shaw. 1996. 12.95 (*0-533-11688-0*) Vantage.

Voice from the Mendelsohns Maple. Mary C. Ryan. LC 89-31569. (Illus.). 132p. (J). (gr. 5-7). 1990. 13.95 (*0-316-76360-8*) Little.

Voice from the Mendelsohns' Maple. Mary C. Ryan. 144p. (J). (gr. 5). 1992. pap. 3.50 (*0-380-71140-0*, Camelot) Avon.

Voice from the River. Dan Gerber. LC 89-82472. 212p. 1990. pap. 12.95 (*0-944439-20-9*) Clark City Pr.

Voice from the South. Anna J. Cooper. LC 77-78762. 304p. 1969. reprint ed. text ed. 59.75 (*0-8371-1384-9*, COV&, Greenwood Pr) Greenwood.

Voice from the South. Anna J. Cooper. (Schomburg Library of Nineteenth-Century Black Women Writers). 368p. 1988. reprint ed. 32.00 (*0-19-505246-3*) OUP.

Voice from the South. Anna J. Cooper. (Schomburg Library of Nineteenth-Century Black Women Writers). 368p. 1990. reprint ed. pap. 12.95 (*0-19-506323-6*) OUP.

Voice from Waterloo. Edward Cotton. (Illus.). 1977. reprint ed. 15.95 (*0-85409-957-3*) Charles River Bks.

***Voice from Within.** Robert W. Crary. LC 95-70819. 336p. (Orig.). 1996. pap. 12.95 (*0-914711-12-1*) Rishis Inst.

Voice-Haunted Journey. Eliud Martinez. LC 89-81825. 264p. 1990. 27.00 (*0-927534-03-7*); pap. 17.00 (*0-927534-04-5*) Biling Rev-Pr.

Voice He Loved. Laurel Schunk. LC 94-36603. 1995. pap. text ed. 11.99 (*0-7852-8082-0*) Nelson.

***Voice Imitator.** Bernhard. LC 97-14412. 1996. pap. 17.95 (*0-226-04401-7*) U Ch Pr.

Voice in Her Tribe: A Navajo Woman's Own Story. Irene Stewart. (Anthropological Papers: No. 17). (Illus.). 91p. (Orig.). 1980. pap. 8.95 (*0-87919-088-4*) Ballena Pr.

Voice in Social Interaction: An Interdisciplinary Approach to Vocal Communication. Jeffery Pittam. (Language & Language Behaviors Ser.: Vol. 5). 200p. 1994. 44.00 (*0-8039-5750-5*); pap. 19.50 (*0-8039-5751-3*) Sage.

Voice in Speech. Albert Haberstro. 100p. 1969. reprint ed. spiral bd. 10.00 (*0-7873-0365-8*) Hlth Research.

Voice in Speech & Song. Ellen G. White. (Christian Home Library). 480p. 1988. 12.99 (*0-8163-0746-6*) Pacific Pr Pub Assn.

Voice in the Basement. T. Chris Martindale. Ed. by Claire Zion. 288p. (Orig.). 1993. mass mkt. 4.99 (*0-671-76012-2*) PB.

Voice in the Chorus: Life As a Teenager in the Holocaust. Abraham Zuckerman. (Illus.). 160p. 1990. 19.95 (*0-9627413-0-2*) AMZ Pub.

Voice in the Chorus: Life As a Teenager in the Holocaust. Abraham Zuckerman. 176p. 1991. 17.95 (*0-88125-369-3*) Ktav.

Voice in the Closet. Raymond Federman. 80p. 1986. pap. 6.95 (*0-930956-05-2*) Station Hill Pr.

Voice in the Dark. large type ed. Claire Lorrimer. 1991. 25.99 (*0-7089-2410-7*) Ulverscroft.

Voice in the Desert: A History of First Presbyterian Church, Las Vegas, Nevada. Zelvin D. Lowman. (Illus.). 168p. 1992. 19.95 (*1-881576-03-5*) Providence Hse.

Voice in the Fog. large type ed. Mary Mackie. (Romance Ser.). 288p. 1992. 25.99 (*0-7089-2695-9*) Ulverscroft.

Voice in the Margin: Native American Literature & the Canon. Arnold Krupat. 1989. pap. 12.00 (*0-520-06827-0*) U CA Pr.

Voice in the Mirror. Diane Hoh. (Nightmare Hall Ser.: No. 29). (J). 1995. pap. 3.50 (*0-590-56869-8*) Scholastic Inc.

***Voice in the Mirror: Will the Final Apocalypse Be Averted?** Lee Shargel. Ed. by Tony Stubbs. LC 96-49398. (Chulosian Chronicles Ser.). 240p. 1997. 23.95 (*1-880666-54-5*, Inner Eye Bks) Oughten Hse.

Voice in the Wilderness. Grace L. Hill. (Grace Livingston Hill Ser.: Vol. 91). 320p. 1995. pap. 5.99 (*0-8423-7908-8*) Tyndale.

Voice in the Wilderness: An Autobiography. large type ed. Phil Drabble. (Illus.). 301p. 1992. 21.95 (*1-85089-548-1*, Pub. by ISIS UK) Transaction Pubs.

UV

Voice in the Wilderness: Clear Preaching in a Complicated World. Haddon W. Robinson et al. (Pressure Points Ser.). 156p. 1993. 15.99 (*0-88070-589-2*, Multnomah Bks) Multnomah Pubs.

Voice in the Wind. Henry B. Isensee. LC 90-71990. 126p. (Orig.). 1992. pap. 7.95 (*1-56002-075-X*) Aegina Pr.

Voice in the Wind. Francine Rivers. LC 93-16608. (Mark of the Lion Ser.: Vol. 1). 514p. 1993. pap. 11.99 (*0-8423-7750-6*) Tyndale.

Voice in the Wind: A Starbuck Family Adventure. Kathryn Lasky. 224p. (J). (gr. 3-7). 1993. 11.00 (*0-15-294102-9*, HB Juv Bks); pap. 4.00 (*0-15-294103-7*, HB Juv Bks) HarBrace.

Voice in the Wind: Discussion Guide. Francine Rivers. 1995. pap. 4.99 (*0-8423-1638-8*) Tyndale.

Voice in Three Mirrors: Poems. Mary Low. 48p. 1983. pap. 12.00 (*0-941194-21-3*) Black Swan Pr.

Voice into Text: Orality & Literacy in Ancient Greece. Ed. by Ian Worthington. (Mnemosyne, Bibliotheca Classica Batava Ser.: Vol. 153). 1995. suppl. ed. 88.50 (*90-04-10431-3*) E J Brill.

Voice Is the Mirror of the Soul: An Historic Perspective on Great Voices Through History & How You Can Achieve Vocal Greatness. Bettye P. Zoller & Hugh Lampman. Ed. by Michael Smith. (Illus.). 250p. (Orig.). 1997. pap. 19.95 (*1-884643-09-4*, VMS95) ZWL Pubng.

Voice Lessons: On Becoming a (Woman) Writer. Nancy Mairs. LC 93-31513. 176p. 1994. 15.00 (*0-8070-6006-2*) Beacon Pr.

Voice Lessons: On Becoming a (Woman) Writer. Nancy Mairs. 176p. 1997. pap. 10.00 (*0-8070-6007-0*) Beacon Pr.

Voice Magic: Secrets of Ventriloquism & Voice Conjuring. Ormond McGill. LC 91-21000. (Illus.). 64p. (J). (gr. 4-6). 1992. lib. bdg. 14.90 (*1-56294-137-2*) Millbrook Pr.

Voice Mail Box Hacking. John J. Williams & Shark. 40p. 1997. pap. 29.00 (*0-934274-37-1*) Consumertronics.

Voice Mail Reference Manual & Buyer's Guide. 6th ed. Marc Robins. 465p. (C). 1996. pap. 75.00 (*0-9624360-0-3*) Robins Pr.

Voice Messaging Industry Review, 1991. MultiMedia Telecommunications Association Staff et al. (Illus.). 60p. (Orig.). 1991. pap. 253.00 (*0-940919-23-0*) MultiMedia Telecomm.

Voice Messaging Service Markets. Market Intelligence Staff. 220p. 1993. 1,695.00 (*1-56753-431-7*) Frost & Sullivan.

Voice of a Christian Heart: A Poetic Anthology by Jacqueline M. Gines. Lady J, pseud. 68p. (Orig.). 1993. pap. 6.25 (*1-889133-00-0*) Rising Son Media.

Voice of a Nation? Rowland Lucas. 233p. (C). 1990. text ed. 59.00 (*0-85088-745-3*, Pub. by Gomer Pr UK) St Mut.

Voice of a Native Son: The Poetics of Richard Wright. Eugene E. Miller. LC 89-37374. 275p. 1990. 35.00 (*0-87805-399-9*) U Pr of Miss.

Voice of a Stranger: On the Lay Origin of Anglican Liturgies. Paul V. Marshall. 269p. 1993. 24.95 (*0-89869-236-9*) Church Pub Inc.

Voice of Africa, 2 vols. Leo Frobenius. LC 68-56516. (Illus.). 1972. reprint ed. 46.95 (*0-405-08536-2*, Pub. by Blom Pubns UK) Ayer.

Voice of Africa, 2 vols., I. Leo Frobenius. LC 68-56516. (Illus.). 1972. reprint ed. 57.95 (*0-405-08537-0*, Pub. by Blom Pubns UK) Ayer.

Voice of Africa, 2 vols., II. Leo Frobenius. LC 68-56516. (Illus.). 1972. reprint ed. 30.95 (*0-405-08538-9*, Pub. by Blom Pubns UK) Ayer.

***Voice of All Things, Singing.** Larry Ollivier. 90p. (Orig.). 1997. pap. 12.00 (*0-944920-27-6*) Bellowing Ark Pr.

Voice of America. Robert W. Pirsein. Ed. by Christopher H. Sterling. LC 78-21733. (Dissertations in Broadcasting Ser.). 1980. lib. bdg. 44.95 (*0-405-11770-1*) Ayer.

Voice of America: From Detente to Reagan Doctrine. Laurien Alexandre. Ed. by Brenda Dervin. LC 88-10449. (Communication & Information Science Ser.). 224p. 1988. text ed. 73.25 (*0-89391-465-7*) Ablex Pub.

Voice of America: Management Actions Needed to Adjust to a Changing Environment. (Illus.). 58p. (Orig.). (C). 1993. pap. text ed. 20.00 (*1-56806-541-8*) DIANE Pub.

Voice of America: Propaganda & Democracy, 1941-1945. Holly C. Shulman. LC 90-50098. (History of American Thought & Culture Ser.). 256p. (Orig.). (C). 1991. pap. text ed. 14.95 (*0-299-12624-2*) U of Wis Pr.

***Voice of Anna Julia Cooper: Including "A Voice from the South"** Ed. by Charles Lemert & Esme Bhan. 265p. (Orig.). 1997. pap. 15.95 (*0-8476-8408-3*); text ed. 55.00 (*0-8476-8407-5*) Rowman.

Voice of Asia: Two Leaders Discuss the Coming Century. Mahathir Mohamad & Shintaro Ishihara. Tr. by Frank Baldwin. (International Ser.). 160p. 1996. 25.00 (*4-7700-2043-0*) Kodansha.

Voice of Beech Oracle. Will Inman. 1988. 1.00 (*0-318-41312-4*) Man-Root.

Voice of Beech Oracle. deluxe ed. Will Inman. 1988. 3.00 (*0-318-41313-2*) Man-Root.

***Voice of Bethel.** James Douse. 96p. 1997. pap. 10.00 (*0-8059-4046-4*) Dorrance.

Voice of Black Theology in South Africa. Louise Kretzschmar. 136p. 1986. pap. text ed. 10.95 (*0-86975-269-3*, Pub. by Ravan Pr ZA) Ohio U Pr.

Voice of Bliss: Spreading the Voice of Buddha's Teachings - The Synopsis of Dharma Lecture, Vols. I, II, III & IV. Shen Kai. LC 93-77727. 250p. (Orig.). (CHI.). 1993. write for info. (*1-56369-015-2*); pap. write for info. (*1-56369-010-1*) Jen Chen Buddhism.

Voice of Bliss, Vol. I: Spreading the Voice of Buddha's Teachings. Shen Kai, pseud. LC 93-77726. 250p. (Orig.). (CHI.). 1993. write for info. (*1-56369-016-0*); pap. write for info. (*1-56369-011-X*) Jen Chen Buddhism.

Voice of Bliss, Vol. II: Spreading the Voice of Buddhism Teachings. Shen Kai, pseud. LC 93-77725. 250p. (Orig.). (CHI.). 1993. write for info. (*1-56369-017-9*); pap. write for info. (*1-56369-012-8*) Jen Chen Buddhism.

Voice of Bliss, Vol. III: Spreading the Voice of Buddhism Teachings. Shen Kai, pseud. LC 93-77728. 250p. (Orig.). (CHI.). 1993. write for info. (*1-56369-018-7*); pap. write for info. (*1-56369-013-6*) Jen Chen Buddhism.

Voice of Bliss, Vol. IV: The Synopsis of Dharma Lectures. Shen Kai, pseud. LC 93-77729. 250p. (Orig.). (CHI.). 1993. write for info. (*1-56369-019-5*); pap. write for info. (*1-56369-014-4*) Jen Chen Buddhism.

Voice of Books. Julius Moldenhawer. LC 70-121491. (Essay Index Reprint Ser.). 1977. 19.95 (*0-8369-1766-9*) Ayer.

Voice of Bugle Ann & the Romance of Rosy Ridge. MacKinlay Kantor. 1994. lib. bdg. 18.95 (*1-56849-379-7*) Buccaneer Bks.

Voice of Cecil Harwood: A Miscellany. A. C. Harwood. Ed. by Owen Barfield. (Illus.). 320p. 1979. 16.95 (*0-85440-329-9*) Anthroposophic.

Voice of Christian & Jewish Dissenters in America: U. S. Internal Revenue Service Hearings, December 1978. Martin P. Claussen & Evelyn B. Claussen. xv, 591p. 1982. pap. 25.00 (*0-685-05732-1*) Piedmont.

Voice of Citizenry: Artists & Communities in Collaboration. Lydia Matthews. (Illus.). 36p. (Orig.). 1993. pap. write for info. (*0-930495-22-5*) San Fran Art Inst.

Voice of Conscience. Krikor Zohrab. Tr. by Jack Antreassian & Michael Kermian from ARM. 164p. 1983. 10.00 (*0-934728-09-7*) D O A C.

Voice of Cyprus. Ed. by Adonis Decavalles et al. 1966. 8.50 (*0-8079-0132-6*) October.

***Voice of Democracy.** Maynard H. Harper. LC 96-86071. 180p. (Orig.). 1996. 10.95 (*1-56883-066-1*); pap. 10.95 (*0-614-24430-7*) Colonial Pr AL.

Voice of Dissent: Theophilus Gould Steward (1843-1924) & Black America. William Seraile. LC 91-38540. 266p. 1991. 50.00 (*0-926019-58-9*) Carlson Pub.

Voice of Doom. Steve Perrin. 32p. (Orig.). (YA). (gr. 10-12). 1987. pap. 6.00 (*0-915795-80-9*, 38) Iron Crown Ent Inc.

***Voice of Egypt: Umm Kulth Um, Arabic Song, & Egyptian Society in the Twentieth Century.** LC 96-45394. (Studies in Ethnomusicology). 1997. pap. 17.95 (*0-226-13612-4*) U Ch Pr.

***Voice of Egypt: Umm Kulthum, Arabic Song, & Egyptian Society in the Twentieth Century.** Virginia Danielson. LC 96-45394. (Studies in Ethnomusicology). 1997. lib. bdg. 45.00 (*0-226-13611-6*) U Ch Pr.

Voice of Empire: A Centennial Sketch of "The Denver Post" William H. Hornby. LC 92-2236. 1992. 7.95 (*0-942576-32-2*) CO Hist Soc.

Voice of Eros, Vol. 2. 2nd ed. Ernest L. Norman. (Pulse of Creation Ser.). (Illus.). 260p. 1962. 17.00 (*0-932642-01-2*) Unarius Acad Sci.

***Voice of Fashion: 79 Turn-of-the-Century Patterns with Instructions & Fashion Plates.** Ed. by Frances Grimble. (Illus.). 450p. (Orig.). 1997. pap. 42.00 (*0-9636517-2-2*) Lavolta Pr.

Voice of Fire: Communiques & Interviews from the Zapatista National Liberation Army. Zapatista National Liberation Army Staff. Ed. by Ben Clarke & Clifton Ross. Tr. by Clifton Ross from SPA. 128p. (Orig.). 1994. pap. 7.95 (*0-915117-03-7*) New Earth Pubns.

Voice of Free Earth. Michael Klein. Ed. by Kyra B. Hughes. 285p. 1996. pap. 11.95 (*0-9637981-0-3*) One Horse Rhino.

***Voice of Free Earth, Vol. 2.** 2nd ed. Michael Klein. 285p. (Orig.). 1996. pap. 11.95 (*0-614-28605-0*) One Horse Rhino.

Voice of God, 2 bks., Bk. 2. Mona Johnian. 50p. 1991. pap. 1.25 (*0-929685-35-0*) Superior Bks.

Voice of God: How God Speaks Personally & Corporately to His Children Today. Cindy Jacobs. Ed. by Virginia Woodard. 276p. 1995. 15.99 (*0-8307-1741-2*, 5112553) Regal.

Voice of Greece: The First Great Literature & Its Living Context. rev. ed. H. C. Baldry. (Illus.). 64p. (C). 1991. pap. text ed. 1.75 (*1-877891-25-8*) Paperbook Pr Inc.

Voice of Her Own: Women & the Journal Writing Experience. Marlene Schiwy. 320p. 1996. pap. 14.00 (*0-684-80342-9*, Fireside) S&S Trade.

Voice of Her Own: Women, Literature, & Transformation. Nancy M. Tischler. 159p. (Orig.). (C). 1987. pap. 10.99 (*0-310-33951-0*, 11330P) Probe Bks.

Voice of Hermes. 2nd ed. Ernest L. Norman. (Pulse of Creation Ser.: Vol. 3). (Illus.). 259p. 1962. 17.00 (*0-932642-02-0*) Unarius Acad Sci.

Voice of History: An Exegesis of Selected Short Stories from Ingeborg Bachmann's Das Dreissigste Jahr & Simultan from the Perspective of Austrian History. Lisa De Serbine Bahrawy. (American University Studies: Germanic Languages & Literature: Ser. I, Vol. 78). 200p. (C). 1989. text ed. 37.50 (*0-8204-1027-6*) P Lang Pubng.

Voice of Hope. Thomas Flynn. 192p. (Orig.). 1994. pap. write for info. (*1-56167-133-9*) Am Literary Pr.

Voice of Hope: Heard Across the Heart of Life. Ronna F. Jevne. LC 93-46491. 160p. (Orig.). 1994. pap. 13.95 (*1-880913-09-7*) Innisfree Pr.

Voice of Human Justice (Sautu'l Adalatil Insaniyah) rev. ed. George Jordac. Ed. by Amirali Aini. Tr. by Fazal Haq from ARA. 508p. (C). 1984. reprint ed. text ed. 12.00 (*0-941724-24-7*) Islamic Seminary.

Voice of Illness: A Study of Therapy and Prophecy. Aarne Siirala. LC 81-38338. 225p. 1981. reprint ed. 89.95 (*0-88946-995-4*) E Mellen.

Voice of Indigenous Peoples: A Plea to the World: Native People Address the United Nations. Tonya Frichner. LC 93-36081. (Illus.). 120p. 1993. pap. 12.95 (*0-940666-31-6*) Clear Light.

Voice of Isis. Harriette A. Curtiss & F. Homer Curtiss. 472p. 1992. pap. 35.00 (*0-89540-130-4*, SB-130) Sun Pub.

Voice of Isis. 9th rev. ed. Harriette A. Curtiss & F. Homer Curtiss. 440p. 1978. reprint ed. spiral bd. 21.00 (*0-7873-0233-3*) Hlth Research.

Voice of Isis (1913) Harriette A. Curtiss & F. Homer Curtiss. 442p. 1996. pap. 29.95 (*1-56459-699-0*) Kessinger Pub.

Voice of Jacob: On the Composition of Genesis. Leslie Brisman. LC 89-45194. (Indiana Studies in Biblical Literature). 144p. 1990. 27.50 (*0-253-31264-7*) Ind U Pr.

Voice of Jerusalem. Israel Zangwill. 1976. lib. bdg. 250.00 (*0-8490-2801-9*) Gordon Pr.

Voice of Jupiter Pluvius. Robert H. Neill. 1990. 17.95 (*0-9617591-8-6*) MS River Pub.

Voice of Labor. Symmes M. Jelley. LC 78-89740. (American Labor, from Conspiracy to Collective Bargaining Ser., No. 1). 401p. 1974. reprint ed. 26.95 (*0-405-02129-1*) Ayer.

Voice of Love. large type ed. D. H. Thomson. 247p. 1980. 25.99 (*0-7089-0483-1*) Ulverscroft.

Voice of Manush. Victor Walter. 264p. (Orig.). 1996. pap. 14.00 (*1-877727-60-1*) White Pine.

Voice of Muse, Unarius, Elysium, Vol. 5. Ernest L. Norman. (Pulse of Creation Ser.). (Illus.). 265p. 1964. 17.00 (*0-932642-04-7*) Unarius Acad Sci.

Voice of My Beloved: The Song of Songs in Western Medieval Christianity. E. Ann Matter. LC 89-28621. (Middle Ages Ser.). 268p. (C). 1990. pap. 16.95 (*0-8122-1420-X*) U of Pa Pr.

Voice of My Own. Elinor Jones. 1979. pap. 5.25 (*0-8222-1212-9*) Dramatists Play.

Voice of My Own: A Verbal Box of Chocolates. Sue Chance. LC 93-91044. 260p. 1993. 19.95 (*0-9638398-0-2*) Bonne Chance.

Voice of Nations: European National Anthems & Their Authors. F. Gunther Eyck. LC 94-13235. (Contributions to the Study of Music & Dance Ser.: Vol. 34). 264p. 1995. text ed. 59.95 (*0-313-29320-1*, Greenwood Pr) Greenwood.

Voice of Norway. Halvdan Koht & Sigmund Skard. LC 75-181941. reprint ed. 37.50 (*0-404-03769-0*) AMS Pr.

Voice of One's Own: Conversations with America's Writing Women. Mickey Pearlman. 1992. pap. 9.95 (*0-395-59972-5*) HM.

Voice of Orion, Vol. 4. Ernest L. Norman. (Pulse of Creation Ser.). (Illus.). 232p. 1961. 17.00 (*0-932642-03-9*) Unarius Acad Sci.

Voice of Our Own Leading American Women Celebrate the Right to Vote. Ed. by Nancy M. Neuman. (Public Administration Ser.). (Illus.). 304p. 1996. 20.00 (*0-7879-0231-4*, 1045) LWVUS.

Voice of Rapture: A Symbolist System of Ecstatic Speech in Oscar Wilde's Salome. Karl Toepfer. LC 91-9857. (American University Studies: Theatre Arts: Ser. XXVI, Vol. 7). 182p. (C). 1991. text ed. 37.95 (*0-8204-1491-3*) P Lang Pubng.

Voice of Reason: Essays in Objectivist Thought. Ayn Rand & Leonard Peikoff. (Ayn Rand Library Ser.: Vol. V). 372p. 1990. pap. 14.95 (*0-452-01046-2*, Mer) NAL-Dutton.

Voice of Reason: Hanan Ashrawi & Peace in the Middle East. Barbara Victor. 1994. 24.95 (*0-15-103968-2*) HarBrace.

Voice of Reflection: A Writer's Reader. Ed. by Janet Marting. LC 94-1385. (C). 1995. text ed. 26.50 (*0-673-46934-4*) Addson-Wesley Educ.

Voice of Reform: Tat'iana I. Zaslavskaia. Ed. by Murray Yanowitch. LC 88-23802. 216p. (gr. 13). 1989. text ed. 59.95 (*0-87332-505-2*) M E Sharpe.

Voice of Sarah: Feminine Spirituality & Traditional Judaism. Tamar Frankiel. 148p. 1995. reprint ed. pap. 9.95 (*0-930395-22-0*) Biblio NY.

Voice of Shame: Silence & Connection in Psychotherapy. Ed. by Robert G. Lee & Gordon Wheeler. LC 95-44296. (Psychology Ser.). 496p. 1996. 38.95 (*0-7879-0201-2*) Jossey-Bass.

Voice of Silence. 5th ed. Starr Farish. (Illus.). 119p. 1983. reprint ed. pap. 8.95 (*0-9605492-2-6*) Touch Heart.

Voice of Singing. Timothy Dudley-Smith. LC 92-74551. 65p. (Orig.). (C). 1993. pap. 6.95 (*0-916642-50-X*, 780) Hope Pub.

Voice of Terror: A Biography of Johann Most. Frederic Trautmann. LC 79-8279. (Contributions in Political Science Ser.: No. 42). (Illus.). xxv, 288p. 1980. text ed. 55.00 (*0-313-22053-0*, TVT/, Greenwood Pr) Greenwood.

***Voice of the Avatar.** Sai B. Sathya. Date not set. pap. write for info. (*0-614-19098-3*, BW-220) Sathya Sai Bk Ctr.

Voice of the Buddha: The Beauty of Compassion, 2 vols. Lalitavistara Sutra. Tr. by Gwendolyn Bays from FRE. LC 83-15024. (Translation Ser.). (Illus.). 726p. 1983. Set. pap. 44.00 (*0-913546-86-0*) Dharma Pub.

Voice of the Buddha: The Beauty of Compassion, 2 vols., Set. Lalitavistara Sutra. Tr. by Gwendolyn Bays from FRE. LC 83-15024. (Translation Ser.). (Illus.). 704p. 1983. Slipcased set. boxed 108.00 (*0-913546-84-4*) Dharma Pub.

Voice of the Child: A Handbook for Professionals. Ed. by Graham Upton et al. LC 95-50706. 240p. 1996. 69.95 (*0-7507-0459-4*, Falmer Pr); pap. 24.95 (*0-7507-0460-8*, Falmer Pr) Taylor & Francis.

Voice of the Child in American Literature: Linguistic Approaches to Fictional Child Language. Mary J. Hurst. LC 90-33190. 200p. 1990. text ed. 25.00 (*0-8131-1723-2*) U Pr of Ky.

Voice of the Coyote. J. Frank Dobie. LC 49-8879. xx, 386p. 1961. pap. 12.95 (*0-8032-5050-9*, Bison Books) U of Nebr Pr.

***Voice of the Customer Application Report.** 56p. 1995. pap. write for info. (*1-879364-75-1*) GOAL-QPC.

Voice of the Deep - Chinese Edition. Moody Institute of Science Staff. Tr. by CRM Staff. 15p. (CHI.). 1982. 0.40 (*1-56582-063-0*) Christ Renew Min.

Voice of the Dolphins: And Other Stories. Leo Szilard. LC 89-61007. (Nuclear Age Ser.). 200p. 1992. reprint ed. 29.50 (*0-8047-1753-2*); reprint ed. pap. 11.95 (*0-8047-1754-0*) Stanford U Pr.

Voice of the Eagle. Linda L. Shuler. 1993. pap. 6.99 (*0-451-17681-2*, Sig) NAL-Dutton.

Voice of the Earth. Theodore Roszak. (Illus.). 368p. 1993. pap. 13.00 (*0-671-86753-9*, Touchstone Bks) S&S Trade.

Voice of the Frontier: John Bradford's Notes on Kentucky. Ed. by Thomas D. Clark. LC 92-28767. 424p. (C). 1993. text ed. 36.00 (*0-8131-1801-8*) U Pr of Ky.

Voice of the Gawain Poet. Lynn S. Johnson. LC 83-12401. 256p. 1983. text ed. 32.50 (*0-299-09540-1*) U of Wis Pr.

***Voice of the Hare.** Padraig Daly. 80p. 1997. 19.95 (*1-873790-97-X*, Pub. by Dedalus IE); pap. 12.95 (*1-873790-96-1*, Pub. by Dedalus IE) Dufour.

Voice of the Heart. Barbara Taylor Bradford. 912p. 1994. mass mkt. 6.50 (*0-06-100810-9*, Harp PBks) HarpC.

Voice of the Hidden Waterfall. Kevin Nichols. (C). 1988. 39.00 (*0-85439-178-9*, Pub. by St Paul Pubns UK) St Mut.

Voice of the Hive. rev. ed. Ric Masten. LC 78-59786. (Orig.). 1978. pap. 6.00 (*0-931104-02-5*) Sunflower Ink.

Voice of the Image. Laura Qa. LC 92-61605. 64p. (Orig.). 1992. pap. 10.95 (*0-9633497-0-8*) Red Dragon VA.

***Voice of the Last Frontier.** Gene Hendryx. (Illus.). 224p. 19.95 (*0-9636577-4-7*) Trego-Hill.

Voice of the Master. Kahlil Gibran. 1963. pap. 5.95 (*0-8065-0022-0*, 150, Citadel Pr) Carol Pub Group.

Voice of the Master. 2nd ed. Eva B. Werber. 1970. pap. 6.95 (*0-87516-105-7*) DeVorss.

Voice of the Masters: Writing & Authority in Modern Latin American Literature. Roberto Gonzalez Echevarria. 207p. 1985. reprint ed. pap. 10.95 (*0-292-78709-X*) U of Tex Pr.

Voice of the Middle Ages: In Personal Letters 1100-1500. Ed. by Catherine Moriarty. (Illus.). 352p. 1991. 29.95 (*0-87226-343-6*) P Bedrick Bks.

Voice of the Middle Ages: In Personal Letters, 1100-1500. Ed. by Catherine Moriarty. (Illus.). 352p. 1991. pap. 12.95 (*0-87226-252-9*) P Bedrick Bks.

Voice of the Moon. Ermanno Cavazzoni. Tr. by Ed Emery from ITA. LC 90-60279. 320p. (Orig.). 1990. 14.95 (*1-85242-164-9*) Serpents Tail.

Voice of the Narrator in Children's Literature: Insights from Writers & Critics. Ed. by Charlotte F. Otten & Gary D. Schmidt. LC 88-7709. (Contributions to the Study of World Literature Ser.). 432p. 1989. text ed. 59.95 (*0-313-26370-1*, OVN) Greenwood.

Voice of the Negro, Nineteen Nineteen. Robert T. Kerlin. LC 68-54163. (American Negro: His History & Literature. Series 1). 1969. reprint ed. 19.95 (*0-405-01825-8*) Ayer.

Voice of the Night. Dean R. Koontz. 352p. 1991. reprint ed. mass mkt. 7.50 (*0-425-12816-4*) Berkley Pub.

Voice of the Night: Complete Poetry & Prose of Chairil Anwar. Chairil Anwar. Tr. by Burton Raffel from IND. (Monographs in International Studies, Southeast Asia Ser.: No. 89). xxvi, 176p. (Orig.). (C). 1993. pap. text ed. 20.00 (*0-89680-170-5*) Ohio U Pr.

***Voice of the Nightingale: A Personal Account of the Wakhi Culture in Hunza.** Sabine Felmy. (Illus.). 120p. 1997. text ed. 29.95 (*0-19-577599-6*) OUP.

Voice of the Nightingale in Middle English Poems & Bird Debates. Josepha E. Gellinek-Schellekens. LC 84-47905. 191p. (Orig.). (C). 1984. pap. text ed. 19.00 (*0-8204-0161-7*) P Lang Pubng.

Voice of the Old Wolf: Lucullus V. McWhorter & the Nez Perce Indians. Steven R. Evans. (Illus.). 250p. 1996. 32.00 (*0-87422-129-3*); pap. 19.95 (*0-87422-128-5*) Wash St U Pr.

Voice of the Other: Language As Illusion in the Formation of the Self. Stanley W. Rothstein. LC 92-23059. 192p. 1992. text ed. 45.00 (*0-275-94358-5*, C4358, Praeger Pubs) Greenwood.

Voice of the Past: Oral History. 2nd ed. Paul Thompson. 336p. 1988. pap. text ed. 19.95 (*0-19-289216-9*) OUP.

Voice of the People. Ellen Glasgow. Ed. by W. L. Godshalk. (Masterworks of Literature Ser.). 1972. 19.95 (*0-8084-0030-4*); pap. 15.95 (*0-8084-0031-2*) NCUP.

Voice of the People. Ellen Glasgow. reprint ed. lib. bdg. 29.95 (*0-89190-151-5*, Rivercity Pr) Amereon Ltd.

Voice of the People. Ellen Glasgow. LC 71-96882. 444p. reprint ed. lib. bdg. 19.50 (*0-8398-0662-0*) Irvington.

Voice of the People: American Democracy In Action. Betsy C. Maestro. LC 95-12672. (Illus.). 48p. (J). (gr. 3-5). 1996. lib. bdg. 15.93 (*0-688-10679-X*) Lothrop.

Voice of the People: American Democracy in Action. Betsy C. Maestro. LC 95-12672. (Illus.). 48p. (J). (gr. 3-5). 1996. 16.00 (*0-688-10678-1*) Lothrop.

Voice of the People: Public Opinion & Democracy. James S. Fishkin. LC 95-34620. 195p. 1995. 20.00 (*0-300-06556-6*) Yale U Pr.

***Voice of the People: Public Opinion & Democracy.** James S. Fishkin. 1997. pap. text ed. 15.00 (*0-300-07255-4*) Yale U Pr.

Voice of the People: The European Parliament in the 1990s. Julie Smith. 116p. 1995. pap. 14.95 (*0-905031-88-1*, Pub. by Royal Inst Intl Affairs UK) Brookings.

***Voice of the Pioneer.** large type ed. Bill McNeil. 1997. pap. 21.95 (*1-55041-320-1*, Pub. by Fitzhenry & Whiteside CN) Iowa St U Pr.

Voice of the Plains: Selected Radio Commentaries. John Cogswell. (Illus.). (Orig.). 1987. pap. 9.95 (*0-944720-01-3*) Greenridge Pr.

An Asterisk (*) at the beginning of an entry indicates that the title is appearing in BIP for the first time.

Voice of the Poet: The Shape & Sound of Southern Poetry Today. Adrienne Bond. (Georgia Humanities Council Publications). (Illus.). 60p. 1991. pap. 9.95 (0-8203-1318-1) U of Ga Pr.

Voice of the Poor: Essays in Economic & Political Persuasion. John Kenneth Galbraith. 96p. 1983. 12.95 (0-674-94295-7) HUP.

Voice of the Poor: Essays in Economic & Political Persuasion. John Kenneth Galbraith. LC 82-18732. 96p. 1984. pap. text ed. 5.95 (0-674-94296-5) HUP.

Voice of the Print. Paul Caponigro. LC 94-75829. 48p. (Orig.). 1994. pap. 32.50 (1-882265-02-5) Tandem Alley.

Voice of the Saints. Ed. by Francis W. Johnston. LC 86-50851. 150p. 1993. reprint ed. pap. 6.00 (0-89555-304-X) TAN Bks Pubs.

***Voice of the Seas & Hills.** Nan McCurdy. 65p. (Orig.). 1983. pap. 10.00 (0-9655169-0-3) Bard Pub Co.

***Voice of the Seasons.** Nan McCurdy. 160p. (Orig.). 1996. pap. 12.00 (0-9655169-1-1) Bard Pub Co.

Voice of the Shepherdess. Ed. by Peter J. McCord. LC 96-6982. 94p. (Orig.). 1996. pap. 10.95 (1-55612-819-3) Sheed & Ward MO.

Voice of the Silence. Blavatsky. 1995. 5.50 (81-7059-116-3) Theos Pub Hse.

Voice of the Silence. H. P. Blavatsky. 1989. pap. 12.95 (0-88695-046-5) Concord Grove.

Voice of the Silence. H. P. Blavatsky. LC 91-50978. 178p. 1992. 15.95 (0-8356-0681-3, Quest); pap. text ed. 5.95 (0-8356-0680-5, Quest) Theos Pub Hse.

Voice of the Silence. Helena P. Blavatsky. LC 76-25345. 1993. audio 12.00 (0-911500-24-3) Theos U Pr.

Voice of the Silence. Helena P. Blavatsky. LC 76-25345. 112p. 1992. reprint ed. 10.00 (0-911500-04-9) Theos U Pr.

Voice of the Silence. Helena P. Blavatsky. LC 76-25345. 112p. 1992. reprint ed. pap. 6.00 (0-911500-05-7) Theos U Pr.

Voice of the Silence: Chosen Fragments from the Book of the Golden Precepts. Tr. & Intro. by Helena P. Blavatsky. iv, 110p. 1928. reprint ed. 4.00 (0-938998-06-4) Theosophy.

Voice of the Stranger. Madge Reinhardt. LC 81-65402. (Illus.). 477p. 1982. pap. 11.00 (0-917162-06-4) Back Row Pr.

Voice of the Titans: And Other Stories. Spiro Athanas. (Illus.). 84p. (Orig.). 1996. pap. 7.95 (0-9652078-0-3) St Spyridon.

***Voice of the Tree.** Robert Holland. (Illus.). 165p. (Orig.). (J). (gr. 5-10). 1997. pap. 9.95 (0-9658523-1-8, C-0001) Frost Hollow.

Voice of the Trobairitz: Perspectives on the Women Troubadours. Ed. by William D. Paden. LC 89-4920. (Middle Ages Ser.). (Illus.). 274p. (C). 1989. text ed. 36.50 (0-8122-8167-5) U of Pa Pr.

Voice of the Turtle. Harold A. Lawrence. (Illus.). 97p. (Orig.). 1995. pap. 12.95 (0-9644858-4-2) Boyd Pub Co.

Voice of the Turtle. John Van Druten. 1945. pap. 5.25 (0-8222-1213-7) Dramatists Play.

Voice of the Turtle: American Indian Literature 1900-1970. Ed. by Paula G. Allen. 336p. 1995. pap. 12.50 (0-345-39505-0) Ballantine.

Voice of the Turtle & Other Poems. Bernedette K. Cole. Ed. by Almus D. Cole. Tr. by Jean Cushing. LC 89-85217. 104p. 1989. 12.95 (0-9623488-0-5) Hse Kim Pub.

Voice of the Turtledove: New Catholic Women in Europe. Ed. by Anne Brotherton. LC 92-9442. 240p. 1992. pap. 12.95 (0-8091-3307-5) Paulist Pr.

Voice of the Universe: Building the Jodrell Bank Telescope. rev. ed. Bernard Lovell. LC 87-9322. 336p. 1987. text ed. 55.00 (0-275-92678-8, C2678, Praeger Pubs); pap. text ed. 14.95 (0-275-92679-6, B2679, Praeger Pubs) Greenwood.

Voice of the Vanquished: The Story of the Slave Marina & Herna'n Corte's. LC 94-90752. 488p. (Orig.). 1996. pap. 15.00 (1-56002-530-1, Univ Edtns) Aegina Pr.

Voice of the Voiceless: The Four Pastoral Letters & Other Statements. Oscar Romero. Tr. by Michael J. Walsh from SPA. LC 84-14722. 208p. (Orig.). 1985. pap. 18.00 (0-88344-525-5) Orbis Bks.

Voice of the Whaleman: With an Account of the Nicholson Whaling Collection. Stuart C. Sherman. LC 65-18564. 216p. reprint ed. pap. 61.60 (0-317-28766-4, 2020627) Bks Demand.

Voice of the Whirlwind. Walter J. Williams. 1992. mass mkt. 3.99 (0-8125-1924-8) Tor Bks.

Voice of the Wild: An Anthology of Animal Stories. Ed. by Patricia Beard. LC 92-53780. 384p. 1992. pap. 22.00 (0-670-84293-1, Viking) Viking Penguin.

Voice of the Wilderness. Grace L. Hill. reprint ed. lib. bdg. 27.95 (0-89190-031-4, Rivercity Pr) Amereon Ltd.

Voice of Their Own: The Woman Suffrage Press, 1840-1910. Ed. by Martha M. Solomon. LC 90-23922. (Studies in Rhetoric & Communication). 248p. 1991. text ed. 34.95 (0-8173-0526-2) U of Ala Pr.

Voice of Thunder: The Civil War Letters of George E. Stephens. Ed. by Donald Yacovone. 320p. 1995. 26.95 (0-252-02245-9) U of Ill Pr.

Voice of Truth: Challenges & Struggles of a Nepalese Woman. Shanti Mishra. (C). 1994. 44.00 (81-7303-022-7, Pub. by Book Faith II) S Asia.

Voice of Truth: The Challenges & Struggles of a Nepalese Woman. S. Mishra. 1994. pap. 130.00 (0-7855-0490-7, Pub. by Ratna Pustak Bhandar) St Mut.

Voice of Venus. 7th ed. Ernest L. Norman. (Pulse of Creation Ser.: Vol. 1). (Illus.). 197p. 1995. 20.00 (0-932642-00-4) Unarius Acad Sci.

Voice of Venus. 7th ed. Ed. by Ernest L. Norman. (Pulse of Creation Ser.: Vol. 1). (Illus.). 197p. 1995. pap. 15.00 (0-935097-33-3) Unarius Acad Sci.

Voice of Young Burma. Aye Kyaw. (Southeast Asia Program Ser.: No. 12). 98p. (Orig.). 1993. pap. text ed. 10.00 (0-87727-129-1) Cornell SE Asia.

Voice on an Anthill. Jonas Zdanys. 1981. pap. 4.00 (0-87141-063-X) Manyland.

Voice on the Radio. Caroline B. Cooney. 192p. (J). 1996. 13.45 (0-385-32213-5) Delacorte.

***Voice on the Wind: Poems.** Robert Richman. LC 96-47669. 60p. 1997. pap. 10.00 (0-914278-72-X) Copper Beech.

Voice over the Water. (Illus.). 1993. reprint ed. pap. 8.00 (0-910845-50-6, 595) Landmark Ent.

Voice-Overs: Putting Your Mouth Where the Money Is. Chris Douthitt. Ed. by Tom Wiecks. (Illus.). 240p. (Orig.). 1996. pap. 19.95 (0-935566-21-X) Grey Heron.

Voice Placing & Training Exercise, 2 vols. George Dodds. Incl. Contralto & Baritone. 1927. 10.95 (0-19-322141-1); Soprano & Tenor. 1927. 10.95 (0-19-322140-3); (YA). (gr. 9 up). 1927. write for info. (0-318-54901-8) OUP.

Voice Power. Evelyn Bowling. (Illus.). 219p. (Orig.). 1988. pap. 15.00 (0-923834-04-4) Shenandoah Val Bk.

Voice Privacy: A Guide to the Equipment for Communication Systems. Ed. & Frwd. by Michael P. Jones. (Illus.). 52p. (Orig.). 1985. text ed. 11.00 (0-89904-175-2); pap. text ed. 7.00 (0-89904-086-1) Crumb Elbow Pub.

Voice Problems of Children. 3rd ed. D. Kenneth Wilson. (Illus.). 416p. 1986. text ed. 40.00 (0-683-09194-8) Williams & Wilkins.

Voice Processing. Richard K. Miller & Terri C. Walker. LC 88-81660. (Survey on Technology & Markets Ser.: No. 69). 50p. 1989. pap. text ed. 200.00 (1-55865-068-7) Future Tech Surveys.

Voice Processing. Gordon E. Pelton. (Computer Communications Ser.). 389p. 1993. text ed. 45.00i (0-07-049309-X) McGraw.

Voice Processing. 2nd ed. Walt Tetschner. LC 92-21881. (Telecommunications Ser.). 425p. (C). 1992. text ed. 79.00 (0-89006-637-X) Artech Hse.

Voice Processing Primer. Marc Robins. 210p. (Orig.). 1996. pap. 24.95 (0-9624360-2-X) Robins Pr.

Voice Quality: A Classified Research Bibliography. John Laver. (Library & Information Sources in Linguistics: No. 5). viii, 225p. 1979. 52.00 (90-272-0996-0) Benjamins North Am.

Voice Recognition, Response & Synthesis Markets: Explosive Growth Across All Segments. Market Intelligence Staff. 284p. 1992. 1,695.00 (1-56753-410-4) Frost & Sullivan.

Voice Response Reference Manual & Buyer's Guide. 5th ed. Marc Robins. (Illus.). 375p. (C). 1996. pap. 85.00 (0-9624360-1-1) Robins Pr.

Voice Speaks: Addresses & Prologues. Charles L. Anspach. LC 77-353338. (Illus.). xix, 394p. 1976. 10.00 (0-916699-07-2) CMU Clarke Hist Lib.

Voice Speech & Gesture. Hugh Campbell et al. LC 72-5589. (Granger Index Reprint Ser.). 1977. reprint ed. 57.95 (0-8369-6381-4) Ayer.

Voice, Speech, & Language in the Child: Development & Disorder. J. A. Martin. (Disorders of Human Communication Ser.: Vol. 4). (Illus.). 230p. 1981. 56.95 (0-387-81629-1) Spr-Verlag.

Voice Studio Manual: Introduction to the Deva Method. 8th ed. Jeannie Deva. Ed. by Joe Scoglio. (Illus.). 80p. 1996. pap. 12.95 (1-882224-12-4) Voice Studio.

Voice Surgery. Ed. by Robert T. Sataloff & Wilbur J. Gould. LC 92-49947. 1992. write for info. (0-8016-1988-2) Mosby Yr Bk.

Voice Synthesis. Heath Company Staff. (Illus.). 376p. 1983. 129.95 (0-87119-091-5, EE-3403A) Heathkit-Zenith Ed.

Voice Synthesis Recognition. Business Communications Co., Inc. Staff. (Illus.). 201p. 1986. pap. 1,750.00 (0-89336-450-9, G-O56R) BCC.

Voice Teletraffic System Engineering. James R. Boucher. (Telecommunications Engineering Library). 165p. 1988. text ed. write for info. (0-89006-335-4) Artech Hse.

Voice Teletraffic Systems Engineering. James R. Boucher. LC 88-24226. (Artech House Telecommunications Library). 179p. 1988. reprint ed. pap. 51.10 (0-608-02366-3, 2063008) Bks Demand.

Voice Terminal Echo: Postmodernism & English Renaissance Texts. Jonathan Goldberg. 208p. (C). 1986. pap. text ed. 14.95 (0-416-42200-4, 9698) Routledge Chapman & Hall.

Voice That Is Great Within Us. Hayden Carruth. 768p. 1983. mass mkt. 7.99 (0-553-26263-7) Bantam.

Voice That Spoke for Justice: The Life & Times of Stephen S. Wise. Melvin I. Urofsky. LC 81-5676. 439p. 1981. text ed. 59.50 (0-87395-538-2) State U NY Pr.

***Voice That Thinks: Heidegger Studies & Translations with an Historical Bibliography of Heidegger in English Translation 1949-1996.** LC 96-42255. 200p. (C). 1996. 45.00 (0-929914-21-X) Eadmer Pr.

Voice Therapy: Clinical Studies. Joseph C. Stemple. LC 92-49999. 186p. (gr. 13). 1992. text ed. 36.00 (0-8016-4763-0) Mosby Yr Bk.

Voice Therapy for Adolescents. Moya L. Andrews & Anne C. Sommers. (Illus.). 220p. (Orig.). (C). 1991. reprint ed. pap. 32.50 (1-879105-21-7, A001) Singular Publishing.

Voice Therapy for Children. Moya L. Andrews. (Illus.). (C). 1991. reprint ed. pap. text ed. 34.95 (1-879105-48-9, 0231) Singular Publishing.

Voice Through a Cloud. Denton Welch. 256p. 1996. pap. 13.95 (1-878972-15-4) Exact Change.

Voice to the Voiceless: The Power of People's Theatre in India. Jacob Srampickal. LC 93-32576. 207p. 1995. text ed. 45.00 (0-312-10359-X) St Martin.

Voice to the Voiceless: The Power of People's Theatre in India. Jacob Strampickal. (C). 1995. 27.00 (81-7304-055-9, Pub. by Manohar II) S Asia.

Voice to Voice, Heart to Heart: The Story of an Interim Ministry. Sarah Voss. 104p. (Orig.). 1995. pap. 7.00 (1-55896-338-3, 5318, Skinner Hse Bks) Unitarian Univ.

Voice Underneath the Pillow. Tommy Hawkins. LC 91-41233. (Illus.). 80p. (J). (ps-3). 1992. 12.00 (1-880691-17-5) Blackbird MI.

***Voice Update: Proceedings of the 1st World Congress, Oporto, Portugal, April 9-13, 1995, Vol. 109.** M. Pais Clemente. LC 96-29317. (International Congress Ser.). 428p. 1996. 203.75 (0-444-82230-5) Elsevier.

Voice Wedding Classics: Low. 1992. pap. 16.95 incl. audio (0-7935-0928-9, 00747016) H Leonard.

Voice Within. Ed. by Cynthia Stevens. 1996. 69.95 (1-57553-008-2) Watermrk Pr.

Voice Within: A Workbook for Achieving Higher Consciousness. Lisa Hays. 221p. (Orig.). 1996. pap. 19.95 (0-9648095-0-8) Star NC.

Voice Within: Three Women Poets. Elizabeth Barrett Browning et al. 176p. 1995. 14.95 (1-85410-262-1, Pub. by Aurum Pr UK) London Brdge.

Voiced Connections of James Dickey: Interviews & Conversations. Ed. by Ronald Baughman. 294p. (C). 1989. text ed. 21.95 (0-87249-670-8) U of SC Pr.

Voiceless India. Gertrude E. Sen. LC 74-109975. (Illus.). 1971. reprint ed. text ed. 65.00 (0-8371-4481-7, SEVI, Greenwood Pr) Greenwood.

Voiceless People. Chuck Shelton. Ed. by Stephen Hayner & Gordon Aeschliman. (Global Issues Bible Study Ser.). 48p. (Orig.). 1990. wbk. ed., pap. 4.99 (0-8308-4912-2, 4912) InterVarsity.

Voicelust: Eight Contemporary Fiction Writers on Style. Ed. by Allen Wier & Don Hendrie, Jr. LC 84-25721. 139p. reprint ed. pap. 39.70 (0-7837-6168-6, 2045890) Bks Demand.

Voiceprints. David Walker. (Illus.). 48p. (Orig.). 1989. 400.00 (0-913341-09-6); pap. 8.95 (0-913341-08-8) Coyote Love.

Voiceprints of Lincoln: Memories of an Old Massachusetts Town & Its Unique Response to Industrial America. Ruth M. Ragan. 292p. 1991. text ed. 29.95 (0-944856-03-9) Lincoln Hist Soc.

Voices. Ed. by Case & Lawrence. 450p. (Orig.). 1995. 45.00 (1-885206-25-9, Iliad Pr) Cader Pubng.

Voices. Judy Collins. LC 94-47948. 1995. 25.00 (0-517-70092-1) Crown Bks Yng Read.

Voices. Judy Collins. 1995. 25.00 incl. cd-rom (0-614-15424-3, C P Pubs) Crown Pub Group.

Voices. Ed. & Intro. by Lydia Cosentino. LC 95-45223. 96p. (Orig.). 1995. pap. 9.95 (0-940669-32-3, D-38) Dramaline Pubns.

Voices. Soleiman Fayyad. Tr. by Hosam Abou-Ela from ARA. 128p. 1993. 21.00 (0-7145-2945-1) M Boyars Pubs.

Voices. Dacia Maraini. Tr. by Dick Kilto & Elspeth Spottiswood from ITA. LC 96-69699. 248p. (Orig.). (C). 1997. pap. 14.99 (1-85242-527-X) Serpents Tail.

Voices. John Vornholt. (Babylon 5 Ser.: No. 1). 256p. 1995. mass mkt. 5.50 (0-440-22057-2) Dell.

Voices: A Woman's Journal of Self-Expression. (Illus.). 144p. 1993. 14.95 (1-56138-316-3) Running Pr.

Voices: An Anthropologist's Dialogue with an Italian-American Festival. Richard M. Swiderski. 146p. 1987. 20.95 (0-87972-364-5); pap. 9.95 (0-87972-365-3) Bowling Green Univ Popular Press.

Voices: Native American Hymns & Worship Resources. Compiled by Marilyn Hofstra. 112p. 1992. pap. 9.95 (0-88177-095-7, DR095) Discipleship Res.

***Voices: Poems from the Missouri Heartland.** Ed. by Edward J. Steinhardt & Charles J. Guenther. 113p. 1994. pap. 10.00 (0-9641235-0-9) Dormer Window.

Voices: Singers & Critics. J. B. Steane. (Illus.). 304p. 1992. 32.95 (0-931340-54-3, Amadeus Pr) Timber.

Voices: Six Dialogues & Orders of Service for Lent. J. B. Quisenberry. LC 92-34836. 1992. pap. 5.75 (1-55673-572-3, 9318) CSS OH.

Voices - Circles - Echoes: A Ten Year Journey. Geo. B. Drennan. LC 95-92857. (Illus.). 115p. 1996. 60.00 (0-9651159-0-9) Printing Corner.

Voices Across the Water: An Anglo-Canadian Boyhood. Sydney G. Checkland. (Illus.). 154p. 1990. pap. 19.95 (0-08-037972-9, Pub. by Aberdeen U Pr) Macmillan.

Voices after Midnight. Richard Peck. 192p. (YA). 1990. reprint ed. pap. 4.50 (0-440-40378-2) Dell.

***Voices & Echoes: Canadian Women's Spirituality.** Ed. by Jo-Anne Elder & Colin O'Connell. (Studies in Women & Religion: Vol. 4). 264p. (Orig.). 1997. pap. 24.95 (0-88920-286-9) Wilfrid Laurier.

Voices & Messages. (YouthTalk Ser.). 32p. (YA). 1994. teacher ed., pap. 4.95 (0-8066-0266-X, 15-5221) Augsburg Fortress.

Voices & Messages. (YouthTalk Ser.). 48p. (YA). 1994. pap. 5.95 (0-8066-0265-1, 15-5220) Augsburg Fortress.

Voices & Silences. James E. Jones & Penelope Niven. LC 93-19021. (Illus.). 368p. 1993. text ed. 24.00 (0-684-19513-5) S&S Trade.

***Voices & Vision.** 29.95 (1-56176-928-2) Mystic Fire.

***Voices & Vision, Vol 2.** 29.95 (1-56176-929-0) Mystic Fire.

***Voices & Vision, Vol. 3.** 39.95 (1-56176-930-4) Mystic Fire.

***Voices & Vision - Wallace Stevens.** 10.95 (1-56176-927-4) Mystic Fire.

***Voices & Vision - Walt Whitman.** 10.95 (1-56176-916-9) Mystic Fire.

***Voices & Vision - William Carlos Williams.** 10.95 (1-56176-918-5) Mystic Fire.

Voices & Visions. Meyer. 1995. teacher ed., pap. text ed. 27.50 (0-312-08383-1) St Martin.

Voices & Visions. Meyer. 1995. teacher ed., pap. text ed. 0.26 (0-312-08384-X) St Martin.

Voices & Visions. Carolyn Visser. 1994. 23.75 (0-87364-761-0) Paladin Pr.

***Voices & Visions: A Collection of Primary Sources.** William L. Shulman. LC 97-2578. (Holocaust Ser.). 1997. write for info. (1-56711-207-2) Blackbirch.

Voices & Visions: An Integrated Approach to Reading & Writing. Russell Meyer & Sheryl Mylan. 450p. 1995. pap. text ed. 29.00 (0-312-08385-8) St Martin.

Voices & Visions: The Poet in America. Ed. by Helen H. Vendler. LC 86-40154. (Illus.). 560p. 1987. 29.95 (0-394-53520-0) Random.

***Voices & Visions - Elizabeth Bishop.** 10.95 (1-56176-921-5) Mystic Fire.

***Voices & Visions - Emily Dickinson.** 10.95 (1-56176-919-3) Mystic Fire.

***Voices & Visions - Ezra Pound.** 10.95 (1-56176-917-7) Mystic Fire.

***Voices & Visions - Hart Crane.** 10.95 (1-56176-915-0) Mystic Fire.

***Voices & Visions - Langston Hughes.** 10.95 (1-56176-925-8) Mystic Fire.

***Voices & Visions - Marianne Moore.** 10.95 (1-56176-920-7) Mystic Fire.

***Voices & Visions - Robert Frost.** 10.95 (1-56176-926-6) Mystic Fire.

***Voices & Visions - Robert Lowell.** 10.95 (1-56176-924-X) Mystic Fire.

***Voices & Visions - Sylvia Plath.** 10.95 (1-56176-922-3) Mystic Fire.

***Voices & Visions - T. S. Eliot.** 10.95 (1-56176-923-1) Mystic Fire.

Voices & Visions of Aging: Toward a Critical Gerontology. Ed. by Thomas R. Cole et al. LC 92-10680. 368p. 1992. 41.95 (0-8261-8020-5) Springer Pub.

Voices & Words of Women & Men. Ed. by Cheris Kramarae. 195p. 1981. 46.00 (0-08-026106-X, Pergamon Pr) Elsevier.

Voices at Dawn: New Work for the Institute of American Indian Arts. Ed. by Eddie Chuculate et al. 139p. (Orig.). (C). 1996. pap. text ed. 8.00 (1-881396-11-8) IOA Indian Arts.

Voices at Serendipity. Buck et al. 35p. (Orig.). 1986. pap. 2.00 (0-9618011-0-7) Daisy Pr.

Voices at the Door: An Anthology of Favorite Poems. Ed. by Christine Jones & Owen Burt. (Illus.). 274p. 1996. pap. 19.95 (0-7083-1316-7, Pub. by Univ Wales Pr UK) Paul & Co Pubs.

Voices Cast Out to Talk Us In. Ed Roberson. LC 95-1031. (Iowa Poetry Prize Ser.). 166p. (Orig.). 1995. pap. 10.95 (0-87745-510-4) U of Iowa Pr.

Voices for Change: South Africa's Other Whites. Robert S. Jaster & Shirley K. Jaster. LC 92-25572. 1993. text ed. 45.00 (0-312-08947-3) St Martin.

Voices for Evolution. Ed. by Molleen Matsumura. 176p. 1995. pap. 10.00 (0-939873-53-2) Natl Ctr Sci Educ.

Voices for Freedom. Amnesty International Staff. (Illus.). 208p. (Orig.). 1986. pap. 15.00 (0-939994-20-8, Pub. by Amnesty Intl Pubns UK) Amnesty Intl USA.

Voices for the Earth: Vital Ideas from America's Best Environmental Books. Sustainable Futures Society Staff & Daniel D. Chiras. LC 95-11887. 256p. (Orig.). 1995. pap. 16.95 (1-55566-146-7) Johnson Bks.

Voices for the Future: Essays on Major Science Fiction Writers. Ed. by Thomas D. Clareson. 1976. pap. 8.95 (0-87972-120-0) Bowling Green Univ Popular Press.

Voices for the Future: Essays on Major Science Fiction Writers, Vol. 2. Ed. by Thomas Clareson. LC 76-61202. 1979. 14.95 (0-87972-135-9); pap. 8.95 (0-87972-136-7) Bowling Green Univ Popular Press.

Voices for the Future: Essays on Major Science Fiction Writers, Vol. 3. Ed. by Thomas Clareson & Thomas Wymer. LC 76-10939. 1983. 20.95 (0-87972-251-7); pap. 9.95 (0-87972-252-5) Bowling Green Univ Popular Press.

Voices from a Black Mask. Anthony K. Alfred. (Orig.). 1996. pap. write for info. (1-57553-144-5) Watermrk Pr.

Voices from a Borrowed Garden: A Collection of Poetry. Ed. by Duane L. Herrmann. 107p. 1990. pap. 5.00 (1-879448-03-3) Buffalo Pr KS.

***Voices from a Drum.** Earl Long. (Longman Caribbean Writers Ser.). (C). 1996. pap. text ed. 11.95 (0-582-28709-X) Addison-Wesley.

Voices From a Far Country. Hugh Carr. 304p. 9600. pap. 18.95 (0-85640-545-0, Pub. by Blackstaff Pr IE) Dufour.

Voices from a Promised Land: Palestinian & Israeli Peace Activists Speak Their Hearts. Penny Rosenwasser. LC 91-55411. (Illus.). 270p. (Orig.). 1992. pap. 12.95 (0-915306-57-3) Curbstone.

Voices from Afar: Modern Chinese Writers on Oppressed Peoples & Their Literature. Irene Eber. LC 80-10411. (Michigan Monographs in Chinese Studies: No. 38). 162p. (Orig.). 1980. pap. text ed. 15.00 (0-89264-038-3) Ctr Chinese Studies.

Voices from Africa: Local Perspectives on Conservation. Dale Lewis & Nick Carter. LC 93-4758. 216p. (Orig.). 1993. pap. 19.95 (0-89164-124-6) World Wildlife Fund.

Voices from Alabama: A Twentieth-Century Mosaic. J. Mack Lofton, Jr. LC 92-36110. (Illus.). 368p. (Orig.). 1993. pap. 24.95 (0-8173-0684-6) U of Ala Pr.

Voices from Amsterdam: A Modern Tradition of Reading Biblical Narrative. Martin Kessler. LC 93-5716. (Society of Biblical Literature Semeia Studies). 240p. 1994. 44.95 (1-55540-896-6, 060626); pap. 29.95 (1-55540-897-4, 060626) Scholars Pr GA.

Voices from an Empire: A History of Afro-Portuguese Literature. Russell G. Hamilton. LC 74-24416. (Minnesota Monographs in the Humanities: No. 8). 460p. 1975. reprint ed. pap. 131.70 (0-7837-2951-0, 2057503) Bks Demand.

Voices from an Evil God. Barbara Jones. 1996. mass mkt. 4.99 (*1-85782-065-7*, Pub. by Blake Publng UK) Seven Hills Bk.

Voices from an Island. Marguerite Bouvard. LC 85-3831. 70p. 1985. 14.95 (*0-932576-25-7*); pap. 6.95 (*0-932576-26-5*) Breitenbush Bks.

Voices from Ancient Egypt: An Anthology of Middle Kingdom Writings. R. B. Parkinson. LC 91-7250. (Oklahoma Series in Classical Culture: Vol. 9). (Illus.). 160p. 1991. pap. 22.95 (*0-8061-2362-1*) U of Okla Pr.

Voices from Around the World: Selections from the Annual Proceedings of the International Association of School Librarianship. Ed. by Philomena Hauck. LC 89-10568. (Illus.). 331p. 1989. 35.00 (*0-8108-2231-8*) Scarecrow.

Voices from Beyond. Canevari. 1995. pap. write for info. (*0-312-95581-2*) St Martin.

Voices from Captivity: Interpreting the American POW Narrative. Robert C. Doyle. LC 93-41111. (Modern War Studies). (Illus.). 392p. 1994. 35.00 (*0-7006-0663-7*) U Pr of KS.

Voices from Cemetery Hill: The Civil War Diary, Reports, & Letters of Colonel William Henry Asbury Speer (1861-1864) Allen P. Spper & V. N. Phillips. (Illus.). 221p. (Orig.). (YA). Date not set. pap. text ed. 19.95 (*1-57072-050-9*) Overmountain Pr.

Voices from Connecticut Hill: Recollections of Cornell Wildlife Students, 1930-1942. Harlan B. Brumsted et al. LC 94-72544. 132p. 1994. 30.00 (*0-9605314-7-5*) NY St Coll Ag.

***Voices from Fatherhood.** Patrick Kilcarr. 1997. 17.95 (*0-87630-858-2*) Brunner-Mazel.

***Voices from Fatherhood: Fathers, Sons, & ADHD.** Patrick Kilcarr & Patricia O. Quinn. 154p. (J). 1997. 17.95 (*0-945354-77-0*) Magination Pr.

Voices from French Ontario. Sheila M. Arnopoulos. 216p. 1982. 44.95 (*0-7735-0405-2*, Pub. by McGill CN); pap. 22.95 (*0-7735-0406-0*, Pub. by McGill CN) U of Toronto Pr.

Voices from French Ontario. Sheila M. Arnopoulos. LC 83-185309. 215p. reprint ed. pap. 61.30 (*0-7837-6898-2*, 2046728) Bks Demand.

Voices from Great Black Baseball Leagues. John B. Holway. 1976. 31.95 (*0-8488-1566-1*) Amereon Ltd.

Voices from Ground Zero: Recollections & Feelings of Nuclear Test Veterans. F. Lincoln Grahlfs. 216p. 1996. pap. text ed. 27.50 (*0-7618-0396-3*); lib. bdg. 47.00 (*0-7618-0395-5*) U Pr of Amer.

***Voices from Hudson Bay: Cree Stories from York Factory.** Ed. by Flora Beardy & Robert Coutts. (Rupert's Land Record Society Ser.). (Illus.). 208p. 1996. pap. 18.95 (*0-7735-1441-4*, Pub. by McGill CN) U of Toronto Pr.

***Voices from Hudson Bay: Cree Stories from York Factory.** Ed. by Flora Beardy & Robert Coutts. (Rupert's Land Record Society Ser.). (Illus.). 208p. 1996. 44.95 (*0-7735-1440-6*, Pub. by McGill CN) U of Toronto Pr.

Voices from Indenture: Experiences of Indian Migrants in the British Empire. Marina Carter. LC 95-43296. (New Historical Perspectives on Migration Ser.). (Illus.). 224p. (C). 1996. 75.00 (*0-7185-0031-8*, Pub. by Leicester Univ Pr) Bks Intl VA.

Voices from Israel: Understanding the Israeli Mind. Ed. by Etan Levine. LC 85-47911. 288p. 1986. 19.95 (*0-8453-4825-6*, Cornwall Bks) Assoc Univ Prs.

Voices from Jerusalem: Jews & Christians Reflect on the Holy Land. Ed. by David Burrell & Yehezkel Landau. 1991. pap. 9.95 (*0-8091-3270-2*) Paulist Pr.

Voices from Marshall Street: Jewish Life in a Philadelphia Neighborhood, 1920-1960. Elaine K. Ellison & Elaine M. Jaffe. LC 93-26123. (Illus.). 152p. (Orig.). 1994. pap. 10.00 (*0-940159-25-2*) Camino Bks.

Voices from Mutira: Change in the Lives of Rural Gikuyu Women, 1910-1995. 2nd ed. Jean Davison. 271p. 1995. pap. text ed. 19.95 (*1-55587-602-1*) Lynne Rienner.

Voices from Mutira: Lives of Rural Gikuyu Women. Jean Davison. LC 89-31703. 238p. 1989. pap. text ed. 18.95 (*1-55587-158-5*); lib. bdg. 40.00 (*1-55587-157-7*) Lynne Rienner.

Voices from My Female Journey, Vol. 1. Sophia C. Litman. LC 95-95289. (Illus.). 88p. (Orig.). 1996. pap. 7.99 (*0-9650281-0-0*, 0001) Poetic Voices.

Voices from Our World. Joan Ferrante. (Sociology Ser.). Date not set. pap. 19.95 (*0-534-23940-4*) Wadsworth Pub.

Voices from Paradise. Ed. by Edgar C. Alward & Kathleen Murphy. (Illus.). 116p. (Orig.). 1990. 35.00 (*0-9620092-2-9*); pap. 15.00 (*0-685-47512-3*) Pine Isl Pr.

Voices from Robben Island. Jurgen Schadeberg. (Illus.). 124p. (Orig.). 1994. pap. text ed. 21.95 (*0-86975-454-8*, Pub. by Ravan Pr ZA) Ohio U Pr.

Voices from Russia & America. Compiled by Steven Porter. LC 93-83376. (Illus.). 340p. (Orig.). 1994. pap. write for info. (*0-9625372-4-1*) Phantom Pubns.

Voices from School & Home: Arkansas Parents & Students Talk about Preparing for the World of Work & the Potential for Youth Apprenticeship. 57p. 1991. pap. 5.00 (*1-887410-67-8*) Jobs for Future.

Voices from School & Home: Pennsylvania Students & Parents Talk about Preparing for the World of Work & a Youth Apprenticeship Program. Judy Kallick. 35p. 1990. pap. 5.00 (*1-887410-68-6*) Jobs for Future.

Voices from School & Home: Wisconsin Parents & Students Focus on Youth Apprenticeship. 28p. 1992. pap. 5.00 (*1-887410-57-0*) Jobs for Future.

Voices from Scripture. Robert Whitelaw. pap. 1.49 (*0-87377-117-6*) GAM Pubns.

Voices from Silence. Douglas Unger. 304p. 1995. 21.95 (*0-312-13204-2*) St Martin.

Voices from State: An Oral History of Arkansas State University. Larry D. Ball & William M. Clements. Ed. by Ruth Hawkins. 208p. 1985. 19.95 (*0-930677-00-5*) Ark St Univ.

Voices from Summerland: An Anthology of Jamaican Poetry. Ed. by John E. McFarlane. 1977. lib. bdg. 59.95 (*0-8490-2802-7*) Gordon Pr.

Voices from the Amazon. Binka Le Breton. LC 93-16349. (Books for a World That Works). (Illus.). xiv, 165p. 1993. pap. 14.95 (*1-56549-021-5*) Kumarian Pr.

Voices from the Battlefront: Achieving Cultural Equity. Ed. by Marta M. Vega & Cheryl Y. Greene. LC 93-24658. 210p. 1993. 49.95 (*0-86543-393-3*); pap. 49.95 (*0-86543-394-1*) Africa World.

Voices from the Big House. Ed. by Earl Andrews & Albert Dickens. LC 72-86910. 192p. 1972. 7.00 (*0-8187-0009-2*) Harlo Press.

Voices from the Big Thicket, Vol. II. Ed. by J. Richards. 152p. (Orig.). (YA). (gr. 9). 1995. pap. 8.00 (*1-887303-03-0*) Blu Lantern Pub.

Voices from the Black Experience. Turner. 1991. 19.00 (*0-536-57551-7*) Ginn Pr.

Voices from the Camps: Japanese Americans during World War II. Larry D. Brimner. LC 93-31956. (International Affairs Ser.). (Illus.). 144p. (YA). (gr. 9-12). 1994. lib. bdg. 22.70 (*0-531-11179-2*) Watts.

Voices from the Catholic Worker. Compiled by Rosalie R. Troester. LC 92-33411. (Illus.). 632p. 1993. pap. 22.95 (*1-56639-059-1*) Temple U Pr.

Voices from the Catholic Worker. Compiled by Rosalie R. Troester. LC 92-33411. (Illus.). 632p. 1993. 59.95 (*1-56639-058-3*) Temple U Pr.

Voices from the Century Before: The Odyssey of a Nineteenth-Century Kentucky Family. Mary Clay Berry. 560p. 1996. 35.00 (*1-55970-342-3*) Arcade Pub Inc.

Voices from the Civil War: A Documentary History of the Great American Conflict. large type ed. Ed. by Milton Meltzer. 1995. 61.50 (*0-614-09614-6*, L-81913-00) Am Printing Hse.

Voices from the Classroom: Educational Practice Can Inform Policy. David J. Flinders. LC 89-35176. x, 82p. (Orig.). 1989. pap. 9.50 (*0-86552-093-3*) U of Oreg ERIC.

Voices from the Clay: The Development of Assyro-Babylonian Literature. Silvestro Fiore. LC 65-11233. 304p. reprint ed. pap. 86.70 (*0-317-09922-1*, 2010092) Bks Demand.

Voices from the Crowd, Against the H Bomb. Ed. by David Boulton. LC 65-25493. 6400. 15.95 (*0-8023-1012-5*) Dufour.

Voices from the Deep: The Scuba Diving Experience in Contemporary Poetry. Illus. by Nancy V. Velde et al. LC 86-27044. 200p. (Orig.). 1988. pap. 12.50 (*0-915180-30-8*) Harrowood Bks.

Voices from the Desert. Joy Short. 250p. Date not set. text ed. 25.00 (*1-888521-05-8*) Brunswick Pr.

***Voices from the Dust.** Susan E. McCloud. 1996. pap. 10.95 (*1-57008-226-X*) Bookcraft Inc.

Voices from the Earth/Voces de la Tierra: A Bilingual Anthology of Poetry. unabridged ed. Andres Berger-Kiss. 203p. (ENG & SPA.). 1996. 14.95 (*958-648-105-0*) Condor Bks OR.

Voices from the East: Documents of the Present State & Working of the Oriental Church. John M. Neale. LC 75-173069. reprint ed. 34.50 (*0-404-04659-2*) AMS Pr.

Voices from the Edge: More Conversations for the New Millenium. (Illus.). 420p. 1995. pap. 14.95 (*0-89594-732-3*) Crossing Pr.

Voices from the Edge of Eternity. John Myers. 1994. 9.97 (*1-55748-548-8*) Barbour & Co.

Voices from the Environmental Movement: Perspectives for a New Era. Ed. by Donald Snow. LC 91-39067. 237p. (Orig.). 1992. 34.95 (*1-55963-133-3*); pap. 19.95 (*1-55963-132-5*) Island Pr.

***Voices from the Field: Group Work Responds.** Albert S. Alissi & Catherine G. Mergins. LC 96-52244. (Illus.). 181p. 1997. 49.95 (*0-7890-0138-1*) Haworth Pr.

Voices from the Field: Lessons from the Family Academy. Kathryn E. Nelson et al. LC 94-18656. 1994. 16.95 (*0-934842-30-2*) CSPA.

Voices from the Fields. Ed. by Russell Lord. LC 78-76945. (Granger Index Reprint Ser.). 1977. 18.95 (*0-8369-6026-2*) Ayer.

Voices from the Fields: America's Migrant Children. S. Beth Atkin. LC 92-32248. 96p. (J). 1993. 16.95 (*0-316-05633-2*) Little.

Voices from the Forest. Lisel Mueller. (W.N.J. Ser.: No. 7). 1977. pap. 8.00 (*1-55780-056-1*) Juniper Pr WI.

Voices from the Future: Children Speak About Violence in America. Children's Express. Ed. by Susan Goodwillie. LC 93-20332. 1993. 20.00 (*0-517-59494-3*, Crown) Crown Pub Group.

Voices from the Future: Children Speak Out about violence in America. 2nd ed. Ed. by Susan Goodwillie. (Illus.). 254p. 1996. reprint ed. pap. 14.95 (*0-9621641-3-5*) CEF Inc.

Voices from the Great Black Baseball Leagues. rev. ed. John B. Holway. (Illus.). 404p. 1992. reprint ed. pap. 13.95 (*0-306-80470-0*) Da Capo.

Voices from the Harlem Renaissance. Ed. by Nathan I. Huggins. (Illus.). 448p. 1995. reprint ed. pap. 17.95 (*0-19-509360-7*) OUP.

Voices from the Heart: Four Centuries of American Piety. Ed. by Roger Lundin & Mark A. Noll. LC 87-441. 414p. reprint ed. pap. 118.00 (*0-7837-3183-3*, 2042787) Bks Demand.

***Voices from the Hills: Readings of Southern Appalachia.** 2nd ed. Robert Higgs & Ambrose N. Manning. 540p. (C). 1996. per., pap. text ed. 37.74 (*0-7872-2849-4*) Kendall-Hunt.

Voices from the Ho Chi Minh Trail. Larry Rottmann. LC 93-71258. (Illus.). 224p. (Orig.). 1993. pap. 19.95 (*1-880391-06-6*) Event Horizon.

Voices from the Holocaust. Harry J. Cargas. LC 92-20178. 184p. (C). 1993. 24.00 (*0-8131-1802-6*) U Pr of Ky.

Voices from the Holocaust. Harry J. Cargas. LC 92-20178. 184p. 1993. pap. 14.95 (*0-8131-0825-X*) U Pr of Ky.

Voices from the House Divided: The United States Civil War as Personal Experience. Glenn M. Linden & Thomas J. Pressly. LC 94-26795. 1995. pap. text ed. write for info. (*0-07-037934-3*) McGraw.

***Voices from the Hunger Marches, Vol. II.** Ian MacDougall. write for info. (*0-7486-6101-8*, Pub. by Polygon UK) Subterranean Co.

Voices from the Ice. John L. Peyton. (Illus.). 56p. (J). (gr. k-4). 1990. pap. 9.95 (*0-939923-15-7*) M & W Pub Co.

Voices from the Iron House: A Study of Lu Xun. Leo O. Lee. LC 85-46049. (Studies in Chinese Literature & Society). 266p. 1987. 34.95 (*0-253-36263-6*) Ind U Pr.

Voices from the Japanese Women's Movement. Ed. by AMPO, Japan Asia Quarterly Review Staff. LC 95-43512. (Japan in the Modern World Ser.). 208p. (C). (gr. 13). 1996. text ed. 57.95 (*1-56324-725-9*); pap. text ed. 18.95 (*1-56324-726-7*) M E Sharpe.

Voices from the Land. Ed. & Frwd. by Robert Wolf. (Folk Literature Ser.). 67p. (Orig.). 1992. pap. 5.95 (*1-878781-05-7*) Free River Pr.

***Voices from the Landwash: 10 Plays from "The Rock"** Theatre Communications Group Staff. 1997. pap. text ed. 29.95 (*0-88754-527-0*, Pub. by Playwrights CN Pr CN) Theatre Comm.

Voices from the Language Classroom: Qualitative Research in Second Language Education. Ed. by Kathleen M. Bailey & David Nunan. (Language Teaching Library). (Illus.). 472p. (C). 1996. text ed. 54.95 (*0-521-55127-7*); pap. text ed. 24.95 (*0-521-55904-9*) Cambridge U Pr.

Voices from the Literacy Field. James A. Draper & Maurice C. Taylor. LC 93-21016. 432p. (C). 1994. reprint ed. text ed. 39.95 (*0-89464-861-6*) Krieger.

Voices from the Margin: Interpreting the Bible in the Third World. rev. ed. R. S. Sugirtharajah. 464p. 1995. pap. 19.95 (*1-57075-046-7*) Orbis Bks.

Voices from the Ming-Qing Cataclysm: China in Tigers' Jaws. Ed. & Tr. by Lynn Struve. (Illus.). 352p. (C). 1993. text ed. 45.00 (*0-300-05679-6*) Yale U Pr.

***Voices from the Mist, Vol. 2.** Bea Carlton. (SonLight Mysteries Ser.: Vol. 3). 207p. (Orig.). 1997. pap. 8.99 (*0-9658103-9-9*) SonLife Pub.

Voices from the Moon: A Novel. Andre Dubus. LC 84-47652. 160p. 1984. 12.95 (*0-87923-532-2*) Godine.

Voices from the Mountains. Guy Carawan & Candie Carawan. LC 96-19867. 1996. pap. 24.95 (*0-8203-1882-5*) U of Ga Pr.

***Voices from the Negro Leagues: Conversations with 52 Baseball Standouts of the Period 1924-1960.** Brent Kelley. (Illus.). 304p. 1997. boxed 45.00 (*0-7864-0369-1*) McFarland & Co.

Voices from the Nettle-Way. Brian Lynch. 60p. 1990. pap. 10.95 (*1-85186-055-X*) Dufour.

Voices from the Night. deluxe limited ed. Intro. by John Maclay. LC 93-80782. 320p. 1994. 60.00 (*0-940776-29-4*) Maclay Assoc.

Voices from the North Edge. St. Croix Writers Staff. 1992. pap. 9.95 (*1-886028-10-9*) Savage Pr.

Voices from the Oil Fields. Ed. by Paul F. Lambert & Kenny A. Franks. LC 84-7327. (Illus.). 288p. 1984. 26.95 (*0-8061-1799-0*) U of Okla Pr.

Voices from the Old Firm. Steven Walsh. (Illus.). 208p. 1996. 29.95 (*1-85158-713-6*, Pub. by Mnstream UK) Trafalgar.

Voices from the Past. Michael J. Groothuis. 64p. 1987. 17.95 (*0-9617745-0-9*) Chinhinta Prodns.

***Voices from the Past: Reformed Educators.** Ed. by Donald Oppewal. 352p. 1997. pap. 37.50 (*0-7618-0767-5*) U Pr of Amer.

Voices from the Past: The Cycle of Life in Indo-European Folktale. 2nd ed. D. L. Ashliman. 508p. (C). 1996. per., pap. text ed. 35.64 (*0-7872-1503-1*) Kendall-Hunt.

Voices from the Past Ser., 6 Vol., Set. Kathlyn Gay & Martin Gay. (Illus.). 64p. (J). (gr. 5-8). 1995. lib. bdg. 95.88 (*0-8050-4279-2*) TFC Bks NY.

Voices from the Plains. Gianni Celati. 1990. pap. 10.95 (*1-85242-143-6*) Serpents Tail.

Voices from the Rapids: An Underwater Search for Fur Trade Artifacts, 1960-73. Robert C. Wheeler et al. LC 75-1194. (Minnesota Historical Archaeology Ser.). 132p. reprint ed. pap. 37.70 (*0-8357-3313-0*, 2039537) Bks Demand.

Voices from the River. Victor Kelleher. 213p. 1994. pap. 14.95 (*0-7022-2358-1*, Pub. by Univ Queensland Pr AT) Intl Spec Bk.

Voices from the River. Ed. by Margo Stever & Patricia Farewell. 36p. (Orig.). 1990. pap. 8.00 (*0-9624178-3-1*, HVWC) Slapering Hol.

***Voices from the San Antonio Missions.** Luis Torres. LC 97-709. (Illus.). 256p. 1997. 24.95 (*0-89672-378-X*) Tex Tech Univ Pr.

***Voices from the Shadows: Women with Disabilities Speak Out.** Gwenyth F. Matthews. 200p. pap. 8.95 (*0-88961-080-0*, Pub. by Wmns Pr CN) LPC InBook.

Voices from the Silence. Catharine Berliner. Ed. by Lucille B. Smeeth. 44p. (Orig.). 1985. pap. 10.00 (*0-9612592-2-1*) StarRays Pubs.

Voices from the Snowy: Personal Recollections of the Snowy Mountains Scheme. Margaret Unger. (Illus.). 244p. 1989. 39.95 (*0-86840-315-6*, Pub. by New South Wales Univ Pr AT) Intl Spec Bk.

Voices from the Streets: Young Former Gang Members Tell Their Stories. Photos & Told to S. Beth Atkin. LC 95-26757. (Illus.). 144p. (YA). (gr. 5 up). 1996. 17.95 (*0-316-05634-0*) Little.

Voices from the Thai Countryside: The Short Stories of Samruam Singh. Katherine A. Bowie & Samruam Singh. LC 90-71960. (Monographs: No. 6). (Illus.). 130p. (Orig.). (C). pap. 11.95 (*1-881261-01-8*) U Wisc Ctr SE Asian.

Voices from the Third Reich: An Oral History. Johannes Steinhoff et al. LC 88-32195. 512p. 1989. 24.95 (*0-89526-766-7*) Regnery Pub.

Voices from the Third Reich: An Oral History. Ed. by Dennis Showalter et al. 590p. 1994. reprint ed. pap. 17.95 (*0-306-80594-4*) Da Capo.

Voices from the Underground, 2 vols. Intro. by Ken Wachsberger et al. LC 92-82780. (Illus.). (Orig.). (C). 1993. Set. pap. text ed. 74.50 (*1-879461-03-X*) Incredible Librn.

Voices from the Underground: A Directory of Resources & Sources on the Vietnam Era Underground Press, Vol. 2. Intro. by Ken Wachsberger. LC 92-82780. 144p. (Orig.). (C). 1993. Smythe sewn. pap. text ed. 45.00 (*1-879461-02-1*) Incredible Librn.

Voices from the Underground: Insider Histories of the Vietnam Era Underground Press, Vol. 1. Intro. by Ken Wachsberger. LC 92-82780. (Illus.). 640p. (Orig.). (C). 1993. Smyth sewn. pap. text ed. 29.50 (*1-879461-01-3*) Incredible Librn.

Voices from the Universe: Poems by Karl Isaacs. Karl Isaacs. 171p. (Orig.). 1994. pap. text ed. 6.95 (*1-885066-00-7*) Four-G Pubs.

Voices from the Valley: Selections from the Knoxville Writers' Guild. Ed. by Jeanne P. McDonald. 239p. (Orig.). 1994. pap. text ed. 14.95 (*0-9643178-0-X*) Knoxville Writ.

Voices from the Void. Hester T. Smith. 107p. 1972. reprint ed. spiral bd. 5.50 (*0-7873-0802-1*) Hlth Research.

***Voices from the Waterways.** Jean Stone. (Illus.). 192p. 1997. 30.95 (*0-7509-1351-7*, Pub. by Sutton Pubng UK) Bks Intl VA.

Voices from the Well. Terre Ouwehand. (Illus.). 1986. pap. 8.95 (*0-914598-44-9*) Pr MacDonald & Reinecke.

Voices from the Well. deluxe ed. Terre Ouwehand. (Illus.). 1986. 12.95 (*0-914598-41-4*) Pr MacDonald & Reinecke.

Voices from the West: Life along the Trail. Katharine N. Emsden. LC 92-74781. (Perspectives on History Ser.). (Illus.). 60p. (Orig.). (YA). (gr. 5-12). 1992. pap. 4.95 (*1-878668-18-8*) Disc Enter Ltd.

Voices from the Whirlwind: Interpreting the Book of Job. Ed. by Leo G. Perdue & W. Clark Gilpin. 224p. 1992. pap. 19.95 (*0-687-43812-8*) Abingdon.

Voices from the Wild: Animal Sensagoria. David Bouchard. LC 96-11519. (Illus.). 72p. (J). (gr. 1 up). 1996. 17.95 (*0-8118-1462-9*) Chronicle Bks.

***Voices from the Wild Horse Desert: The Vaquero Families of the King & Kenedy Ranches.** Jane C. Monday & Betty B. Colley. LC 96-45639. (Illus.). 288p. 1997. pap. 15.95 (*0-292-75205-9*) U of Tex Pr.

Voices from the Wilderness: The Frontiersman's Own Story. Ed. by Thomas Froncek. 1983. 14.75 (*0-8446-6040-X*) Peter Smith.

Voices from Tiananmen Square: Beijing Spring & the Democracy Movement. Ed. by Mok C. Yu & J. Fran Harrison. 201p. (Orig.). (C). 1990. 38.95 (*0-921689-59-4*, Pub. by Black Rose Bks CN); pap. 19.95 (*0-921689-58-6*, Pub. by Black Rose Bks CN) Consort Bk Sales.

Voices from Under: Black Narrative in Latin America & the Caribbean. Ed. by William Luis. LC 83-22792. (Contributions in Afro-American & African Studies: No. 76). xii, 263p. 1984. text ed. 59.95 (*0-313-23826-X*, LUV/, Greenwood Pr) Greenwood.

Voices from Vietnam. Barry Denenberg. LC 93-44886. 272p. (J). (gr. 7-9). 1995. 16.95 (*0-590-44267-8*) Scholastic Inc.

***Voices from Vietnam.** Barry Denenberg. (J). 1997. mass mkt. 4.99 (*0-590-43530-2*) Scholastic Inc.

Voices from Vietnam. Ed. by Michael E. Stevens et al. (Illus.). 255p. 1996. 24.95 (*0-87020-285-5*) State Hist Soc Wis.

***Voices from Vietnam, 3 vol. set.** Ed. by Michael E. Stevens et al. (Voices of the Wisconsin Past Ser.). (Illus.). 255p. 1996. pap. 12.95 (*0-87020-287-1*) State Hist Soc Wis.

Voices from Washington High. Craig Sodaro. 1993. pap. 5.00 (*0-87129-285-8*, V23) Dramatic Pub.

***Voices from Wild Horse Desert: The Vaquero Families of the King & Kennedy Ranches.** Jane C. Monday & Betty B. Colley. (Illus.). 288p. 1997. 35.00 (*0-292-75204-0*) U of Tex Pr.

Voices from Within. Ed. by Nancy Jones. LC 91-47629. 108p. (Orig.). 1992. pap. text ed. 9.95 (*0-929398-37-8*) UNTX Pr.

Voices from Within: Faith-life Stories of Women in the Church. Patricia Gillespie & Mary Mathews. LC 94-10733. 248p. 1994. pap. 11.95 (*0-932727-75-1*); lib. bdg. 19.95 (*0-932727-76-X*) Hope Pub Hse.

Voices from Within: Women in Bengal Through Early Personal Narratives. Malavika Karlekar. (Oxford India Paperbacks Ser.). (Illus.). 264p. (C). 1993. reprint ed. pap. 10.95 (*0-19-563089-0*, 14333) OUP.

Voices from Within: Women in Conflict with the Law. Evelyn K. Sommers. 216p. 1995. 50.00 (*0-8020-2998-1*); pap. 16.95 (*0-8020-7449-9*) U of Toronto Pr.

Voices Heard by the Master. James R. Adams. Ed. by Patricia Adams. (Illus.). 152p. (Orig.). 1991. pap. 9.95 (*0-9618060-5-2*) Sheer Joy Pr.

Voices in a Revolution: The Collapse of East German Communism. Melvin J. Lasky & Michael S. Lasky. 188p. (C). 1992. 34.95 (*1-56000-030-9*) Transaction Pubs.

Voices in a Roar: An Independent Voter Speaks Out. Greg K. Gideon. (Illus.). 183p. (Orig.). 1996. pap. 10.00 (*0-9652098-0-6*) G K Gideon.

An Asterisk (*) at the beginning of an entry indicates that the title is appearing in BIP for the first time.

Voices in America: Bicentennial Conversations. Bernard Murchland. LC 86-63412. 250p. 1987. pap. 14.95 (*0-911168-70-2*) Prakken.

Voices in American Education: Conversations with Fourteen Major Educators & Public Figures. Compiled by Bernard Murchland. 219p. (Orig.). 1990. pap. 11.95 (*0-911168-77-X*) Prakken.

Voices in Architectural Education: Cultural Politics & Pedagogy. Ed. by Thomas A. Dutton. LC 91-9593. (Critical Studies in Education & Culture). 328p. 1991. text ed. 59.95 (*0-89789-253-4*, H253, Bergin & Garvey) Greenwood.

***Voices in Bali: Energies & Perceptions in Vocal Music & Dance Theater.** Edward Herbst. LC 97-19855. (Illus.). 224p. 1997. 45.00 incl. cd-rom (*0-8195-6316-1*, Wesleyan Univ Pr) U Pr of New Eng.

***Voices in Bali: Energies & Perceptions in Vocal Music & Dance Theater.** Edward Herbst. (Illus.). 224p. 1997. pap. 19.95 incl. cd-rom (*0-8195-6319-6*, Wesleyan Univ Pr) U Pr of New Eng.

Voices in Black & White: Writings on Race in America from Harper's Magazine, 1850-1992. Ed. by Katharine Whittemore & Gerald Marzorati. (American Retrospective Ser.). 288p. 1992. pap. 14.95 (*1-879957-06-X*, Franklin Sq Pr); lib. bdg. 21.95 (*1-879957-07-8*, Franklin Sq Pr) Harpers Mag Found.

Voices in Dissent. Ed. by Arthur A. Ekirch, Jr. 1964. 6.50 (*0-685-08137-0*, Citadel Pr); pap. 2.45 (*0-8065-0023-9*, 146, Citadel Pr) Carol Pub Group.

Voices in Exile: A Study in Sephardic Intellectual History. Marc D. Angel. 1993. 25.00 (*0-88125-370-7*) Ktav.

Voices in Exile: Jamaican Texts of the 18th & 19th Centuries, Vol. 1. Ed. by Jean D'Costa & Barbara Lalla. LC 87-13267. (Illus.). 176p. 1989. text ed. 32.50 (*0-8173-0382-0*) U of Ala Pr.

Voices in Exile: The Decembrist Memoirs. Glynn R. Barratt. LC 75-310670. 403p. reprint ed. pap. 114.90 (*0-317-26443-5*, 2023852) Bks Demand.

Voices in Family Psychology, Vol. 1. Ed. by Florence W. Kaslow. 456p. (C). 1990. text ed. 55.00 (*0-8039-3336-3*); pap. text ed. 26.95 (*0-8039-3855-1*) Sage.

Voices in Family Psychology, Vol. 2. Ed. by Florence W. Kaslow. 304p. (C). 1990. text ed. 52.00 (*0-8039-3794-6*); pap. text ed. 24.00 (*0-8039-3856-X*) Sage.

***Voices in Ferment.** Leonor Kobler. (Orig.). 1996. pap. 12.95 (*0-9654718-0-2*) Brook Press.

Voices in Ireland: A Traveller's Literary Companion. P. J. Kavanagh. (Illus.). 345p. 1994. 39.95 (*0-7195-4974-4*, Pub. by John Murray UK) Trafalgar.

Voices in Ireland: A Traveller's Literary Companion. P. J. Kavanagh. (Illus.). 368p. 1995. pap. 24.95 (*0-7195-5389-X*, Pub. by John Murray UK) Trafalgar.

Voices in Literature, Bk. 1. Lydia Stack. 1993. teacher ed., pap. 15.95 (*0-8384-2260-8*); text ed. 27.25 (*0-8384-2258-6*) Heinle & Heinle.

Voices in Literature, Bk. 2. Lydia Stack. 1995. text ed. 27.25 (*0-8384-2259-4*) Heinle & Heinle.

Voices in Literature, Bk. 2. Lydia Stack. 1996. teacher ed., pap. 11.25 (*0-8384-2261-6*) Heinle & Heinle.

Voices in Literature, Bk. 2. Lydia Stack. 1997. pap. 25.95 (*0-8384-2265-9*) Heinle & Heinle.

Voices in Literature: Integrated Language & Literature for ESL, Gold, Silver, & Bronze. Mary L. McCloskey & Lydia Stack. 1997. text ed. 32.95 (*0-8384-2283-7*) Heinle & Heinle.

Voices in Literature Book 3-Bronze. McCloskey. (Global ESL/ELT Ser.). 1997. suppl. ed., pap. 25.95 (*0-8384-2284-5*) Heinle & Heinle.

Voices in Literature Book 3-Bronze. McCloskey. (Global ESL/ELT Ser.). 1997. teacher ed., pap. 15.95 (*0-8384-2285-3*) Heinle & Heinle.

Voices in Literature Bronze. McCloskey. (Adult ESL Ser.). 1996. student ed., pap. 27.95 (*0-8384-7029-7*) Heinle & Heinle.

Voices in Literature Bronze. St. John. (Global ESL/ELT Ser.). 1996. pap. 8.95 (*0-8384-6383-5*); suppl. ed., pap. 65.95 (*0-8384-6390-8*) Heinle & Heinle.

Voices in Literature Gold. McCloskey. (Adult ESL Ser.). 1996. student ed., pap. 28.95 (*0-8384-7025-4*) Heinle & Heinle.

Voices in Literature Gold. St. John. (Global ESL/ELT Ser.). 1996. wbk. ed., pap. 8.95 (*0-8384-6381-9*); suppl. ed., pap. 65.95 (*0-8384-6384-3*) Heinle & Heinle.

Voices in Literature Gold: 1996 Version. McCloskey. (Adult ESL Ser.). 1997. teacher ed., pap. 15.95 (*0-8384-7033-5*) Heinle & Heinle.

Voices in Literature Gold: 1996 Version. McCloskey. (Adult ESL Ser.). (C). 1997. student ed., text ed. 32.95 (*0-8384-7035-1*) Heinle & Heinle.

Voices in Literature Silver. McCloskey. (Adult ESL Ser.). 1997. pap. 25.95 (*0-8384-7023-8*) Heinle & Heinle.

Voices in Literature Silver. St. John. (Global ESL/ELT Ser.). 1996. pap. 8.95 (*0-8384-6382-7*); suppl. ed., pap. 65.95 (*0-8384-6385-1*) Heinle & Heinle.

Voices in Literature Silver: 1996 Version. McCloskey. (Adult ESL Ser.). 1996. student ed., pap. 32.95 (*0-8384-7018-1*) Heinle & Heinle.

Voices in Literature Silver: 1996 Version. McCloskey. (Adult ESL Ser.). 1997. teacher ed., pap. 15.95 (*0-8384-7020-3*) Heinle & Heinle.

Voices in Literature Silver: 1996 Version. McCloskey. (Adult ESL Ser.). (C). 1997. student ed., text ed. 32.95 (*0-8384-7019-X*) Heinle & Heinle.

Voices in Summer. Rosamunde Pilcher. 1990. mass mkt. 5.99 (*0-312-92527-1*) St Martin.

Voices in Summer. large type ed. Rosamunde Pilcher. LC 92-6493. 396p. 1992. reprint ed. lib. bdg. 19.95 (*1-56054-150-4*) Thorndike Pr.

Voices in the Air: French Dramatists & the Resources of Language. J. Dunkley & W. Kirton. 200p. 1993. 75.00 (*0-85261-340-7*, Pub. by Univ of Glasgow UK) St Mut.

***Voices in the Air: The Fascination of Radio.** unabridged ed. Robert Bonebrake. LC 97-91675. (Illus.). 150p. (Orig.). 1997. pap. 12.95 (*0-9656902-2-9*) RAD Pub IL.

Voices in the Big Sky! The History of Montana Broadcasting. Howard McDonald. 160p. (Orig.). 1996. pap. 12.95 (*1-57502-109-9*) Morris Pubng.

Voices in the City. 2nd ed. Anita Desai. 257p. 1982. reprint ed. pap. 5.95 (*0-88253-250-2*) Ind-US Inc.

Voices in the Dark: The Narrative Patterns of Film Noir. J. P. Telotte. LC 88-17525. (Illus.). 272p. 1989. pap. text ed. 13.95 (*0-252-06056-3*) U of Ill Pr.

Voices in the Desert: Writings & Photographs. Ed. & Selected by Lawrence W. Cheek. LC 95-12539. (Wilderness Experience Ser.). (Illus.). 108p. (Orig.). (YA). 1995. pap. 16.95 (*0-15-600225-6*, Harvest Bks) HarBrace.

***Voices in the Dreamtime: A Journey into the Self.** H. Sydney Salt. (Illus.). 196p. (Orig.). 1997. pap. 14.95 (*0-9652596-2-5*, 00009) Inner Wrks Pr.

Voices in the Evening. N. Ginzburg. 1989. 15.95 (*0-8050-0854-3*) H Holt & Co.

Voices in the Evening. Natalia Ginzburg. Tr. by D. M. Low from ITA. 176p. 1989. 16.95 (*1-55970-016-5*) Arcade Pub Inc.

Voices in the Family: Healing in the Heart of the Family. Daniel Gottlieb & Edward Claflin. 272p. 1993. mass mkt. 5.99 (*0-451-17592-1*, Sig) NAL-Dutton.

Voices in the House. Susan Snively. LC 87-25471. (Alabama Poetry Ser.). (Illus.). 88p. 1988. text ed. 15.95 (*0-8173-0393-6*) U of Ala Pr.

***Voices in the Light: Book One of Greatwinter.** Sean McMullen. (Greatwinter Ser.: Vol. 1). 306p. (Orig.). pap. 10.00 (*1-875346-10-4*, Pub. by Aphelion AT) Firebird Dist.

Voices in the Night: Women Speaking about Incest. Ed. by Toni A. McNaron & Yarrow Morgan. LC 82-71369. 187p. (Orig.). (C). 1982. pap. 9.95 (*0-939416-02-6*) Cleis Pr.

***Voices in the Purple Haze: Underground Radio & the Sixties.** Michael C. Keith. LC 96-37117. (Media & Society Ser.). 216p. 1997. text ed. 22.95 (*0-275-95266-5*, Praeger Pubs) Greenwood.

Voices in the Room. Richard Wilmarth. LC 93-70428. 60p. (Orig.). 1993. pap. 4.95 (*1-880743-03-5*) Dead Metaphor.

Voices in the Solemn Wind. Patricia A. Daniels. Ed. by Rosella Mackey. 96p. (Orig.). (J). pap. text ed. 10.00 (*0-9628081-1-3*) Daw Enter.

Voices in the Street: Explorations in Gender, Media & Public Space. Ed. by Susan J. Drucker & Gary Gumpert. LC 96-44098. (The Hampton Press Communication Ser.). 320p. (Orig.). (C). 1996. text ed. 27.50 (*1-57273-017-X*) Hampton Pr NJ.

Voices in the Street: Explorations in Gender, Media & Public Space. Ed. by Susan J. Drucker & Gary Gumpert. LC 96-44098. (Communication Ser.). 320p. (Orig.). (C). 1996. text ed. 69.50 (*1-57273-016-1*) Hampton Pr NJ.

Voices in the Wilderness. John Ressich. LC 79-152954. (Short Story Index Reprint Ser.). 1977. reprint ed. 19.95 (*0-8369-3869-0*) Ayer.

Voices in the Wilderness: American Nature Writing & Environmental Politics. Daniel G. Payne. LC 95-39422. 200p. 1996. pap. 15.95 (*0-87451-752-4*) U Pr of New Eng.

Voices in the Wilderness: American Nature Writing & Environmental Politics. Daniel G. Payne. LC 95-39422. 195p. (C). 1996. text ed. 42.00 (*0-87451-751-6*) U Pr of New Eng.

Voices in the Wilderness: An Anthology of Patristic Prayers. Nikolaos S. Hatzinikolaou. (Illus.). 260p. 1988. 17.95 (*0-917651-47-2*) Holy Cross Orthodox.

Voices in the Wind: Eddie, Stronger Than I'll Ever Be. Belinda A. Dalton. LC 94-90781. (Orig.). 1995. pap. 8.95 (*0-533-11361-X*) Vantage.

Voices in Translation: The Authority of "Olde Bookes" in Medieval Literature: Essays in Honor of Helaine Newstead. Ed. by Deborah M. Sinnreich-Levi & Gale Sigal. LC 89-45929. (Studies in the Middle Ages: No. 17). 1992. 39.50 (*0-404-61447-7*) AMS Pr.

Voices in Your Blood: Discovering Identity Through Family History. G. G. Vandagriff. 224p. 1993. pap. 9.95 (*0-8362-8020-2*) Andrews & McMeel.

***Voices into Choices: Acting on the Voice of the Customer.** Center for Quality of Management Staff et al. Date not set. write for info. (*1-884731-13-9*) Joiner Assoc.

Voices Louder Than Words: A Second Collection. Ed. by William Shore. LC 89-40138. (Vintage Original Ser.). 352p. 1991. pap. 11.00 (*0-679-73429-5*, Vin) Random.

Voices Made Night. Mia Couto. (African Writers Ser.). 115p. (Orig.). (C). 1990. pap. 9.95 (*0-435-90570-8*, 90570) Heinemann.

Voices of a Black Nation: Political Journalism in the Harlem Renaissance. Theodore G. Vincent. LC 90-64140. 1991. 35.00 (*0-86543-202-3*); pap. 14.95 (*0-86543-203-1*) Africa World.

***Voices of a Nation.** 3rd ed. Folkerts & Teeter. 1997. pap. text ed. 51.00 (*0-205-27789-6*) P-H.

Voices of a Nation: A History of Media in the United States. Jean Folkerts & Dwight L. Teeter, Jr. 747p. (C). 1988. pap. write for info. (*0-02-419030-6*, Macmillan Coll) P-H.

Voices of a Nation: A History of Media in the United States. 2nd ed. Jean Folkerts & Dwight L. Teeter, Jr. LC 93-16245. 592p. (C). 1993. pap. text ed. 54.00 (*0-02-338651-7*, Macmillan Coll) P-H.

Voices of a People: The Story of Yiddish Folksong. Ruth Rubin. LC 79-84679. 558p. 1979. reprint ed. pap. 13.95 (*0-8276-0121-2*) JPS Phila.

Voices of a Wanderer. E. B. Bortz. LC 93-93717. 61p. (Orig.). 1993. pap. 7.00 (*0-9639226-0-2*) Out There Pubs.

Voices of AIDS. Michael T. Ford. LC 95-10629. (Illus.). 208p. (YA). (gr. 7 up). 1995. 15.00 (*0-688-05322-X*, Morrow Junior) Morrow.

Voices of Aids. Michael T. Ford. 1995. 15.00 (*0-688-15322-4*, Morrow Junior) Morrow.

Voices of Aids. Michael T. Ford. 208p. (J). (gr. 7 up). 1995. pap. 4.95 (*0-688-05323-8*, Morrow Junior) Morrow.

Voices of American History Vol. I: Pre-Colonial Times Through the Revolutionary War. Steven Traugh. Ed. by June Hetzel. (Illus.). 38p. (Orig.). (J). (gr. 4-8). 1994. wbk. ed., pap. 15.98 (*1-57471-069-9*) Creat Teach Pr.

Voices of American History Vol. II: The Young Nation Through the Civil War. Steven Traugh. Ed. by June Hetzel. (Illus.). 36p. (Orig.). (J). (gr. 4-8). 1994. wbk. ed., pap. 15.98 (*1-57471-079-6*) Creat Teach Pr.

Voices of American History Vol. III: The Westward Expansion of the United States. Steven Traugh. Ed. by June Hetzel. (Illus.). 40p. (Orig.). (J). (gr. 4-8). 1994. wbk. ed., pap. 15.98 (*1-57471-084-2*) Creat Teach Pr.

Voices of American Homemakers. Ed. by Eleanor Arnold. LC 92-21509. (Illus.). 304p. (Orig.). (C). 1993. 26.50 (*0-253-12986-9*); pap. 11.95 (*0-253-20799-1*) Ind U Pr.

Voices of Angels, Vol. I. Ariel Roshelle. (Illus.). 32p. (Orig.). 1995. pap. write for info. (*0-9644530-1-0*) AR-L Pubns.

Voices of Arden. Karl Kempton. 20p. (Orig.). 1993. pap. 5.00 (*0-926935-85-2*) Runaway Spoon.

Voices of Authority: The Criminal Obsession in Guy de Maupassant's Short Works. Mary L. Poteau-Tralie. LC 94-902. (Currents in Comparative Romance Languages & Literatures Ser.: Vol. 30). 146p. (C). 1995. text ed. 44.95 (*0-8204-2479-X*) P Lang Pubng.

Voices of Beginning Teachers: Visions & Realities. Richard Dollase. LC 92-13409. 192p. (C). 1992. pap. text ed. 18.95 (*0-8077-3192-7*) Tchrs Coll.

Voices of Brooklyn: An Anthology. Ed. by Sol Yurick. LC 73-6791. 302p. reprint ed. pap. 86.10 (*0-317-26354-4*, 2024226) Bks Demand.

Voices of Change: A Report of the Clinical Schools Project. 1993. 15.00 (*0-89333-100-7*) AACTE.

Voices of Change: Participatory Research in the United States & Canada. Ed. by Peter Park et al. LC 92-42898. 232p. 1993. text ed. 55.00 (*0-89789-334-4*, H334, Bergin & Garvey) Greenwood.

***Voices of Change: Short Stories by Saudi Arabian Women Writers.** Ed. by Abubaker Bagader et al. (Three Continents Ser.). 118p. 1997. 25.00 (*1-55587-750-8*) Lynne Rienner.

***Voices of Change: Short Stories by Saudi Arabian Women Writers.** Ed. by Abubaker Bagader et al. (Three Continents Ser.). 118p. 1997. pap. 11.95 (*1-55587-775-3*) Lynne Rienner.

Voices of Change in the Spanish American Theater: An Anthology. Ed. & Tr. by William I. Oliver. (Texas Pan American Ser.). 312p. 1971. 20.00 (*0-292-70123-3*) U of Tex Pr.

Voices of China: The Interplay of Politics & Journalism. Ed. by Chin-Chuan Lee. LC 90-14003. (Guilford Communication Ser.). 353p. 1990. pap. text ed. 21.95 (*0-89862-288-3*); lib. bdg. 47.95 (*0-89862-310-3*) Guilford Pr.

Voices of Choice: The Education Reform Debate. Ed. by K. L. Billingsley. LC 93-36884. 1993. write for info. (*0-936488-75-1*) PRIPP.

Voices of Christmas: Readers' Theater for Advent. Jerry Nordstrom. (Orig.). 1996. pap. write for info. (*0-7880-0837-4*) CSS OH.

Voices of Cleveland. Ed. by T. Lardner & Leonard M. Trawick. (Illus.). 170p. (Orig.). 1996. pap. 17.50 (*1-880834-21-9*) Cleveland St Univ Poetry Ctr.

Voices of Color: Art & Society in the Americas. Ed. by Dufrene F. Farris. LC 96-18039. (Illus.). 224p. (C). 1997. text ed. 45.00 (*0-391-03991-1*) Humanities.

Voices of Color: Art & Society in the Americas. Ed. by Phoebe Farris-Dufrene. LC 96-18039. 224p. (C). 1997. pap. 15.00 (*0-391-03992-X*) Humanities.

Voices of Color: Fifty Scenes & Monologues by African American Playwrights. Ed. by Woodie King, Jr. (Acting Ser.). 224p. 1994. pap. 9.95 (*1-55783-174-2*) Applause Theatre Bk Pubs.

Voices of Combat: A Century of Liberty & War Songs, 1765-1865. Kent A. Bowman. LC 86-25724. (Contributions to the Study of Music & Dance Ser.: No. 10). 181p. 1987. text ed. 45.00 (*0-313-25408-7*, BVC/, Greenwood Pr) Greenwood.

Voices of Conflict, No. 14. Andrew Strathern. LC 93-73275. (Illus.). x, 265p. (Orig.). (C). 1993. pap. text ed. 11.50 (*0-945428-07-3*) Ethnology Monographs.

Voices of Conflict: Teenagers Themselves. Ed. by Howard Spanogle. 272p. 1987. 16.95 (*0-915361-94-9*) Hemed Bks.

***Voices of Costa Rican Birds - Caribbean Slope.** David Ross & Bret Whitney. 1996. pap. 24.95 incl. audio compact disk (*0-938027-22-0*) Crows Nest Bird.

Voices of D-Day: The Story of the Allied Invasion, Told by Those Who Were There. Ed. by Ronald E. Drez. LC 93-41311. (Eisenhower Center Studies on War & Peace). (Illus.). 312p. (C). 1996. pap. 12.95 (*0-8071-2081-2*) La State U Pr.

Voices of D-Day: The Story of the Allied Invasion, Told by Those Who Were There. Ed. by Ronald J. Drez. LC 93-41311. (Eisenhower Center Studies on War & Peace). (Illus.). 312p. 1994. 24.95 (*0-8071-1902-4*) La State U Pr.

Voices of Death: Letters & Diaries of People Facing Death--Comfort & Guidance for Us All. Edwin S. Shneidman. (Kodansha Globe Ser.). 224p. 1995. pap. 12.00 (*1-56836-112-2*, Kodansha Globe) Kodansha.

Voices of Decline: The Post-War Fate of U. S. Cities. Robert A. Beauregard. LC 93-22616. 256p. (Orig.). 1994. pap. text ed. 23.95 (*1-55786-442-X*) Blackwell Pubs.

Voices of Deliverance: Interviews with Quebec & Acadian Writers. Donald Smith. Tr. by Larry Shouldice. (Illus.). 365p. (Orig.). 1986. pap. 12.95 (*0-88784-148-1*, Pub. by Hse of Anansi Pr CN) Genl Dist Srvs.

Voices of Despair: Four Motifs in American Literature. fac. ed. Edward Stone. LC 65-24646. 252p. pap. 71.90 (*0-7837-7442-7*, 2007509) Bks Demand.

Voices of Difference: Studies in Critical Philosophy & Mass Communication. Thomas S. McCoy. Ed. by Leslie T. Good. LC 93-357. (Communication Series: Critical Studies in Communication). 288p. (C). 1993. text ed. 55.00 (*1-881303-55-1*); pap. text ed. 23.95 (*1-881303-56-X*) Hampton Pr NJ.

Voices of Dissent. Dissent (Periodical). LC 77-99630. (Essay Index Reprint Ser.). 1977. 30.95 (*0-8369-1405-8*) Ayer.

Voices of Dissent. 2nd ed. Grover & Joseph G. Peschek. 320p. (C). 1996. text ed. 26.95 (*0-673-99742-1*) Addson-Wesley Educ.

Voices of Dissent: Critical Readings in American Politics. Ed. by William F. Grover & Joseph G. Peschek. LC 92-19625. (C). 1992. 26.00 (*0-06-501144-9*) Addson-Wesley Educ.

Voices of Dissent: Two Plays by Arpad Goncz. Tr. by Katharina M. Wilson & Christopher C. Wilson. LC 87-46438. 120p. 1989. 29.50 (*0-8387-5142-3*) Bucknell U Pr.

Voices of Diversity: Perspectives on American Political Ideals & Institutions. Patricia Andrews. 287p. (C). 1995. per. 18.77 (*1-56134-251-3*) Dushkin Pub.

Voices of Diversity: Real People Talk about Problems & Solutions in a Workplace Where Everyone Is Not Alike. Renee Blank & Sandra Slipp. 224p. 1994. 22.95 (*0-8144-0217-8*) AMACOM.

Voices of Earth & Sky: The Vision Life of the Native Americans. Vinson Brown. LC 76-41761. (Illus.). 177p. (C). 1976. pap. 8.95 (*0-87961-060-3*) Naturegraph.

Voices of Eden: A History of Hawaiian Language Studies. Albert J. Schutz. LC 94-30968. 520p. (C). 1994. pap. text ed. 28.00 (*0-8248-1637-4*) UH Pr.

Voices of Emergency: An All India Anthology of Protest Poetry of the 1975-77 Emergency, India. Ed. by John O. Perry. 1983. 28.50 (*0-317-05076-1*, Pub. by Popular Prakashan II) S Asia.

Voices of Experience: Fifteen Hundred Retired People Talk about Retirement. rev. ed. Mario A. Milletti. 208p. 1987. pap. 3.00 (*0-9613704-0-8*) Tchrs Insurance.

***Voices of Feminism: Elizabeth Cady Stanton Biography & 4 of Her Hard-to-Find Speeches, 5 vols.** 1994. pap. 5.00 (*1-880589-60-5*) Sky Carrier Pr.

Voices of Feminism: Past, Present, & Future. JoAnn B. Guernsey. LC 95-12683. (Frontline Ser.). (Illus.). (YA). (gr. 6 up). 1996. lib. bdg. 14.25 (*0-8225-2626-3*, Lerner Publctns) Lerner Group.

***Voices of Feminism Vol. 1: Elizabeth Cady Stanton Through Her Stories.** 15p. 1994. pap. 1.50 (*1-880589-50-8*) Sky Carrier Pr.

***Voices of Feminism Vol. 2: Matilda Joslyn Gage: Forgotten Feminist.** 18p. 1994. pap. 1.50 (*1-880589-51-6*) Sky Carrier Pr.

***Voices of Feminism Vol. 3: Elizabeth Cady Stanton on Prisons & Capital Punishment.** 11p. 1994. pap. 1.50 (*1-880589-52-4*) Sky Carrier Pr.

***Voices of Feminism Vol. 4: Elizabeth Cady Stanton on the Matriarchate or Mother-Age.** 33p. 1994. pap. 1.50 (*1-880589-53-2*) Sky Carrier Pr.

***Voices of Feminism Vol. 5: Elizabeth Cady Stanton on Socialism.** 17p. 1994. pap. 1.50 (*1-880589-54-0*) Sky Carrier Pr.

***Voices of Feminism Vol. 6: Elizabeth Cady Stanton on Her 80th Birthday.** 36p. 1994. pap. 1.50 (*1-880589-55-9*) Sky Carrier Pr.

Voices of Feminist Therapy. Ed. by Elizabeth F. Williams. 144p. 1995. text ed. 35.00 (*3-7186-0603-8*, Harwood Acad Pubs); pap. text ed. 19.00 (*3-7186-0604-6*, Harwood Acad Pubs) Gordon & Breach.

Voices of Fire: Art, Rage, Power & the State. Ed. by Bruce Barber et al. (Theory/Culture Ser.). (Illus.). 224p. 1996. 55.00 (*0-8020-0754-6*); pap. 24.95 (*0-8020-7803-6*) U of Toronto Pr.

Voices of Forgotten Worlds: Traditional Music of Indigenous People. (Illus.). 64p. 1993. 34.95 incl. audio compact disk (*1-55961-221-5*); Incl. cassette. 29.95 incl. digital audio (*1-55961-220-7*) Relaxtn Co.

***Voices of Forgotten Worlds: Traditional Music of Indigenous People.** Ellipsis Arts Staff. 1996. pap. text ed. 29.95 incl. cd-rom (*1-55961-406-4*, Ellipsis Arts) Relaxtn Co.

***Voices of France: Social, Political & Cultural Identity.** Maire Cross & Sheila Perry. LC 96-38316. 192p. 1997. 80.00 (*1-85567-394-0*, Pub. by Pntr Pubs UK) Bks Intl VA.

Voices of Freedom: An Oral History of the Civil Rights Movement from the 1950s-1980s. Henry Hampton & Steve Fayer. 720p. 1991. pap. 18.95 (*0-553-35232-6*) Bantam.

Voices of Freedom: English & Civics for the U. S. Citizenship Exam. 2nd ed. Bill Bliss & Steven J. Molinsky. LC 93-7091. 192p. 1993. pap. text ed. 10.60 (*0-13-035684-0*) P-H.

Voices of Freedom: Polish Women Artists & the Avant-Garde. Agnieszka Morawinska. LC 91-34492. (Illus.). 56p. 1991. pap. 18.95 (*0-940979-19-5*) Natl Museum Women.

Voices of Glasnost. Stephen F. Cohen. 1991. pap. 12.95 (*0-393-30735-2*) Norton.

U
V

Voices of Heaven. Frederik Pohl. 352p. 1995. 5.99 (0-8125-3518-9) Tor Bks.

Voices of Hope. David Feintuch. 544p. (Orig.). 1996. pap. 5.99 (0-446-60333-3, Aspect) Warner Bks.

Voices of Hope. Ed. by Caroline Smith. 1992. 8.95 (0-87162-626-8, D8600) Warner Pr.

Voices of Hope: A Collection of Positive Catholic Writings on Gay & Lesbian Issues. Ed. by Jeannine Gramick & Robert Nugent. LC 95-69521. 238p. (Orig.). 1995. pap. 14.95 (0-935877-01-0) Ctr Homophobia Ed.

Voices of Hope: Teenagers Themselves, Pt. III. Ed. by Howard Spanogle. (Illus.). (YA). (gr. 7 up). 1988. 16.95 (1-55774-012-7, Watts) Hemed Bks.

***Voices of Inquiry in Teacher Education.** Thomas S. Poetter. LC 96-54813. 1997. 45.00 (0-8058-2689-0) L Erlbaum Assocs.

***Voices of Inquiry in Teacher Education.** Thomas S. Potter et al. LC 96-54813. 224p. 1997. pap. write for info. (0-8058-2378-6) L Erlbaum Assocs.

***Voices of Islam.** John Bowker. 220p. 1996. pap. 14.95 (0-614-21453-X, 1290) Kazi Pubns.

Voices of Islam. John Bowker. 220p. 1995. pap. 14.95 (1-85168-095-0) Onewrld Pubns.

Voices of Israel: Essays on & Interviews with Yehuda Amichai, A. B. Yehoshua, T. Carmi, Aharon Appelfeld, & Amos Oz. Joseph Cohen. LC 89-11512. (SUNY Series in Modern Jewish Literature & Culture). 231p. 1990. text ed. 21.50 (0-7914-0243-6) State U NY Pr.

Voices of Jacob, Hands of Esau: Jews in American Life & Thought. Stephen J. Whitfield. LC 83-25720. x, 322p. (C). 1984. lib. bdg. 36.00 (0-208-02024-1, Archon Bks) Shoe String.

Voices of Kensington: Vanishing Mills, Vanishing Neighborhoods. 2nd enl. ed. Jean Seder. LC 90-2990. (Illus.). 96p. 1990. pap. 9.95 (0-939009-37-4) EPM Pubns.

Voices of Latino Culture: Reading from Spain, Latin America, & the United States. Dan Whitaker. 200p. (C). 1996. per. write for info. (0-7872-2591-6) Kendall-Hunt.

Voices of Liberty Storybooks Complete Package: Magic Crossbow (Vietnam), Four Champa Trees (Laos), Mountain of Men (Cambodia) Alice Lucas. (Illus.). 1990. Complete Package incls. 3 story bks., 3 tchr. discussion guides & 3 audio tapes. pap. text ed. 40.00 incl. audio (0-936434-49-X, Pub. by Zellerbach Fam Fund) SF Study Ctr.

Voices of Light & Grace. Laura Hedin. Ed. by Karen K. Singer. (Chapbook Ser.: No. 19). 47p. 1991. pap. 5.00 (0-932884-19-9) Red Herring.

Voices of Loss. Charles W. Ginn. LC 93-46939. 56p. 1994. pap. 8.00 (0-935652-21-3) Ctr Applications Psych.

***Voices of Madness: 1683-1796.** Allan Ingram. 224p. 1997. 33.95 (0-7509-1210-3, Pub. by Sutton Pubng UK) Bks Intl VA.

Voices of Man. Mario A. Pei. LC 71-173940. reprint ed. 20.00 (0-404-07928-8) AMS Pr.

Voices of Many Lands. Ed. by Charles J. Palmer & Jacqueline Palmer. LC 95-74715. (Illus.). 240p. 1995. 49.95 (1-881808-21-1) Creat Arts & Sci.

***Voices of Matter.** Arthur G. Gibson. Ed. by Lorine M. Getz. LC 96-44900. 262p. 1996. text ed. 89.95 (0-7734-8769-7) E Mellen.

Voices of Matthew Arnold. W. Stacy Johnson. LC 72-12313. 146p. 1973. reprint ed. text ed. 49.75 (0-8371-6693-4, JOMA, Greenwood Pr) Greenwood.

Voices of Migrants: Rural-Urban Migration in Costa Rica. Paul Kutsche. LC 93-36887. (Illus.). 248p. (C). 1994. pap. text ed. 19.95 (0-8130-1267-8); bds. 39.95 (0-8130-1266-X) U Press Fla.

Voices of Modern Greece: Cavafy, Sikelianos, Seferis, Elytis & Gatsos. rev. ed. Ed. by Edmund Keeley & Phillip Sherrard. LC 81-47282. (Lockert Library of Poetry in Translation). 210p. 1981. reprint ed. pap. 14.95 (0-691-01382-9) Princeton U Pr.

Voices of Multicultural America: Notable Speeches Delivered by Asian Americans, Black Americans, Hispanic Americans, & Native Americans, 1776-1994. Deborah A. Straub. 1372p. 1995. 95.00 (0-8103-9378-6) Gale.

***Voices of Native America.** Hap Gilliland. 176p. 1997. per. 16.95 (0-7872-3881-3) Kendall-Hunt.

***Voices of Native America: Native American Music.** Douglas Spotted-Eagle. Ed. by Monte Smith. LC 97-60768. (Illus.). 64p. (Orig.). 1997. per. 15.95 (0-943604-56-7, BOO/29) Eagles View.

Voices of Nature. William C. Bryant. (Works of William Cullen Bryant). 1989. reprint ed. lib. bdg. 79.00 (0-7812-2132-3) Rprt Serv.

Voices of Negritude: The Expression of Black Experience in the Poetry of Senghor, Cesaire & Dramas. Edward A. Jones. LC 75-152062. 125p. reprint ed. pap. 35.70 (0-8357-9357-5, 2012606) Bks Demand.

Voices of Negro Protest in Amercia. William H. Burns. LC 80-21197. 88p. 1980. reprint ed. text ed. 49.75 (0-313-22219-3, BUVN, Greenwood Pr) Greenwood.

Voices of Northern Ireland: Growing up in a Troubled Land. Carolyn Meyer. LC 87-199. (Illus.). 224p. (YA). (gr. 7 up). 1987. 16.00 (0-15-200635-4, Gulliver Bks) HarBrace.

Voices of Northern Ireland: Growing up in a Troubled Land. Carolyn Meyer. (YA). 1992. pap. 9.95 (0-15-200636-2) HarBrace.

Voices of Our Ancestors: Cherokee Teachings from the Wisdom Fire. Dhyani Ywahoo. LC 87-9711. (Illus.). 294p. (Orig.). 1987. pap. 13.00 (0-87773-410-0, Random) Shambhala Pubns.

Voices of Our Kind. rev. ed. Ed. by Alexander Scott. 128p. 1986. 25.00 (0-550-20495-4, Pub. by Saltire Soc) St Mut.

Voices of Our Kind: An Anthology of Contemporary Scottish Verse. Ed. by Moven Cameron. 80p. 1975. 25.00 (0-85411-000-3, Pub. by Saltire Soc) St Mut.

Voices of Our Sisters: Mourning Songs. Kathryne M. Findley. LC 96-20272. 96p. 1996. pap. 9.95 (1-57312-056-1, Peake Road) Smyth & Helwys.

Voices of Persuasion: The Politics of Representation in 1930's America. Michael E. Staub. LC 93-30372. (Studies in American Literature & Culture: No. 78). 200p. (C). 1994. text ed. 54.95 (0-521-45390-9) Cambridge U Pr.

Voices of Power: Leaders Speak to Followers. Henry Bienen. 1995. 30.00 (0-88001-384-2) Ecco Pr.

***Voices of Protest: Huey Long, Father Coughlin, & the Great Depression.** Alan Brinkley. 1983. pap. text ed. write for info. (0-07-544450-X) McGraw.

Voices of Protest: Huey Long, Father Coughlin & the Great Depression. Alan Brinkley. LC 83-3496. 1983. pap. 14.00 (0-394-71628-0, Vin) Random.

Voices of Rape. Janet Bode. (Teen Issues Ser.). 112p. (YA). (gr. 9-12). 1990. lib. bdg. 22.70 (0-531-10959-3) Watts.

***Voices of Resistance: Oral Histories of Moroccan Women.** Alison Baker. LC 97-2649. (SUNY Series in Oral & Public History). (Illus.). 352p. (C). 1998. text ed. 74.50 (0-7914-3621-7) State Univ of New York.

***Voices of Resistance: Oral Histories of Moroccan Women.** Alison Baker. (SUNY Series in Oral & Public History). (Illus.). 352p. (C). 1998. pap. text ed. 24.95 (0-7914-3622-5) State Univ of New York.

Voices of Resurgent Islam. Ed. by John L. Esposito. 304p. 1983. pap. 19.95 (0-19-503340-X) OUP.

Voices of Robby Wilde. Elizabeth Kytle. LC 94-33591. 344p. 1995. pap. 14.95 (0-8203-1715-2) U of Ga Pr.

Voices of Romance: Studies in Dialogue & Character. Ann Dobyns. 1989. 27.50 (0-87413-351-3) U Delaware Pr.

Voices of Seventeen Seventy-Six: The Story of the American Revolution in the Words of Those Who Were There. Richard Wheeler. 448p. 1991. pap. 12.95 (0-452-01078-0, Mer) NAL-Dutton.

Voices of Sibyls - Three Bulgarian Poets: Elisaveta Bagryana, Nevena Stefanova, Snezhina Slavova. Yuri M. Vidov Karageorge. 76p. (Orig.). 1996. pap. 8.50 (1-57502-123-4) Morris Pubng.

Voices of Silence. Bel Mooney. LC 96-23006. 144p. (J). 1997. 14.95 (0-385-32326-3, Delacorte Pr Bks) BDD Bks Young Read.

Voices of Silence. Andre Malraux. Tr. by Stuart Gilbert from FRE. LC 77-92101. (Bollingen Ser.: Vol. XXIV: A). (Illus.). 661p. 1978. reprint ed. pap. text ed. 29.95 (0-691-01821-9) Princeton U Pr.

Voices of Silence: Lives of the Trappists Today. Frank Bianco. 256p. 1992. pap. 11.00 (0-385-42430-2, Anchor NY) Doubleday.

Voices of Silence: Lives of the Trappists Today. Frank Bianco. (Illus.). 220p. 1991. 18.95 (1-55778-305-5) Paragon Hse.

Voices of Silent: English Translation of Hali's Majalis Un-Nissa & Chup Di Dad. Ed. by Gail Minault. 1986. 18.50 (81-7001-018-7, Pub. by Chanakya II) S Asia.

Voices of Social Education, Nineteen Thirty-Seven to Nineteen Eighty-Seven. Ed. by Daniel Roselle. 528p. (C). 1987. 34.95 (0-02-922380-6, Free Press) Free Pr.

***Voices of Song.** large type ed. Kate Alexander. (Ulverscroft Large Print Ser.). 624p. 1997. 27.50 (0-7089-3584-2) Ulverscroft.

***Voices of South Dakota, Vol. III.** Ed. by Barbara Stevens. 131p. 1989. 4.00 (0-614-24780-2); per. 2.00 (0-614-24781-0) Tesseract SD.

Voices of Spirit. Charles Hapgood. 340p. 1992. reprint ed. pap. 13.00 (1-881343-00-6) Channel One.

Voices of Strength & Hope for a Friend with AIDS. Joseph Gallagher. LC 87-61464. (Illus.). 62p. (Orig.). 1987. pap. 3.95 (1-55612-073-7) Sheed & Ward MO.

Voices of Struggle, Voices of Pride: Quotes by Great African-Americans. Ed. by John P. Beilenson. (Illus.). 64p. 1992. 7.99 (0-88088-563-7) Peter Pauper.

Voices of Summer. large type ed. Diane Pearson. 524p. 1993. 25.99 (0-7505-0455-2) Ulverscroft.

Voices of Survival in the Nuclear Age. Dennis Paulson. 1986. pap. text ed. 12.95 (0-86171-051-7) Wisdom MA.

Voices of the American Past, Vol. I. Raymond Hyser & Chris Arndt. (Illus.). 288p. (Orig.). (C). 1994. pap. text ed. 25.50 (0-15-501963-5) HB Coll Pubs.

Voices of the American Past, Vol. II. Raymond Hyser & Chris Arndt. (Illus.). 320p. (Orig.). (C). 1994. pap. text ed. 25.50 (0-15-501964-3) HB Coll Pubs.

Voices of the Americas: Traditional Music & Dance from North, South, & Central America, & the Caribbean. R. Allen et al. Ed. by Ray Allen. LC 87-51358. (Orig.). (C). 1988. pap. 5.00 (0-945017-00-6) World Mus Inst.

***Voices of the Battle Road: A Performance, Student Activity & Resource Kit for Teachers.** John C. MacLean & Palmer Faran. 42p. (J). (gr. 4-12). 1996. 29.95 (1-882063-40-6) Cottage Pr MA.

Voices of the Civil War. Richard Wheeler. 492p. 1990. pap. 16.95 (0-452-01066-7, Mer) NAL-Dutton.

Voices of the Daughters. Connie A. Maglione & Carmen A. Fiore. LC 89-5031. (Illus.). 335p. 1989. 18.95 (0-939219-05-0) Townhouse Pub.

Voices of the Dead. Autran Dourado. 248p. 1980. 28.00 (0-7206-0558-X, Pub. by P Owen Ltd UK) Dufour.

Voices of the Dream: African-American Women Speak. Ed. by Venice Johnson. (Illus.). 108p. 1996. 12.95 (0-8118-1113-1) Chronicle Bks.

Voices of the Earth: An Anthology of Ideas & Arguments. Ed. by John Clarke. 198p. 1994. pap. 14.95 (0-8076-1349-5) Braziller.

Voices of the Earth: Florida's Environmental Storybook, Vol. 1: Coastal Creatures. Kristin Farquhar. Ed. by Betty Wright & Kimbra Griffin. (Illus.). 48p. (Orig.). (J). (gr. 2-3). 1992. pap. 7.95 (0-9632864-0-4) ECO-ALERT Pubns.

***Voices of the Earth: Indigenous Peoples, New Partners & the Right to Self-Determination.** Leo Van Der Vlist. 1995. pap. text ed. 26.00 (90-6224-983-3, Pub. by Uitgeverij Arkel NE) LPC InBook.

Voices of the Emerging Generation. Patricia Webb. (Illus.). 64p. 1994. teacher ed., pap. 15.00 (0-9611552-4-8) Realistic Living.

Voices of the Emerging Generation. Patricia Webb. (Illus.). 54p. (J). (gr. 3-12). 1994. student ed., pap. 10.00 (0-9611552-5-6) Realistic Living.

***Voices of the 55th: Letters from the 55th Massachusetts Volunteers 1861-1865.** unabridged ed. Ed. by Noah A. Trudeau. (Illus.). 258p. 1996. text ed. 24.95 (0-89029-327-9) Morningside Bkshop.

Voices of the First Day: Awakening in the Aboriginal Dreamtime. Robert Lawlor. (Illus.). 352p. (Orig.). 1991. pap. 29.95 (0-89281-355-5) Inner Tradit.

***Voices of the Forest.** Daveed Forrest. 272p. Date not set. 20.00 (0-06-018248-2) HarpC.

Voices of the Grieving Heart. Mike Bernhardt. LC 94-68210. 144p. 1994. pap. 11.95 (0-9642810-0-7) Cypress Point.

Voices of the Heart. Ed Young. LC 96-7595. 1997. 17.95 (0-590-50199-2) Scholastic Inc.

Voices of the Industrial Revolution: Selected Readings from the Liberal Economists & Their Critics. Ed. by John Bowditch & Clement Ramsland. 1961. pap. 15.95 (0-472-06053-8, 53, Ann Arbor Bks) U of Mich Pr.

Voices of the Jazz Age: Profiles of Eight Vintage Jazz Men. Chip Deffaa. (Music in American Life Ser.). (Illus.). 312p. 1992. 14.95 (0-252-06258-2) U of Ill Pr.

Voices of the Jazz Age: Profiles of Eight Vintage Jazzmen. Chip Deffaa. (Bayou Press Ser.). 278p. 1990. write for info. (1-871478-85-5) Cassell.

Voices of the Jazz Age: Profiles of Eight Vintage Jazzmen. Chip Deffaa. (Music in American Life Ser.). (Illus.). 312p. 1990. 29.95 (0-252-01681-5) U of Ill Pr.

***Voices of the Lakes.** Steve Harrington. 128p. 1996. pap. 12.95 (0-9624629-4-2) Maritime Pr.

Voices of the Marketplace: American Thought & Culture, 1830-1860. Anne C. Rose. (American Thought & Culture Ser.). (Illus.). 272p. 1994. 27.95 (0-8057-9065-9, Twayne); pap. 15.95 (0-8057-9075-6, Twayne) Scribnrs Ref.

Voices of the Mind: A Sociocultural Approach to Mediated Action. James V. Wertsch. LC 90-47211. 169p. 1991. 29.95 (0-674-94303-1, WERVOI) HUP.

Voices of the Mind: A Sociocultural Approach to Mediated Action. James V. Wertsch. 169p. (C). 1993. pap. 16.00 (0-674-94304-X) HUP.

Voices of the Old Sea. Norman Lewis. 208p. 1986. mass mkt. 5.95 (0-14-007780-4, Penguin Bks) Viking Penguin.

Voices of the Old South: Eyewitness Accounts, 1528-1861. Ed. by Alan Gallay. LC 93-12345. 448p. (C). 1994. pap. 19.95 (0-8203-1566-4) U of Ga Pr.

Voices of the Past. Kaye England. (Illus.). (Orig.). pap. 21.95 (0-929950-17-8) ME Pubns.

Voices of the Past: The Status of Language in Eighteenth-Century Japanese Discourse. Naoki Sakai. LC 91-55053. (Illus.). 368p. 1992. 39.95 (0-8014-2580-8) Cornell U Pr.

Voices of the People: The Politics & Life of "La Sociale" at the End of the Second Empire. John Moore et al. (History Workshop Ser.). 376p. 1988. text ed. 65.00 (0-7102-1308-5, RKP) Routledge.

Voices of the Poor: Selections from the "Morning Chronicle" & "Labour & the Poor", 1849-1950. Henry Mayhew. Ed. by Anne Humphreys. (Illus.). 280p. 1971. 37.50 (0-7146-2929-4, Pub. by F Cass Pubs UK) Intl Spec Bk.

Voices of the Prairie. Angela Riggs. (Orig.). pap. 12.00 (0-9634190-0-5) Cottonwood OR.

Voices of the Rainbow: Contemporary Poetry by Native Americans. Ed. by Kenneth H. Rosen. 256p. 1993. pap. 11.95 (1-55970-224-9) Arcade Pub Inc.

Voices of the River: Adventures on the Delaware. Jan Cheripko. LC 93-71611. (Illus.). 48p. (YA). (gr. 7 up). 1996. pap. 9.95 (1-56397-622-6) Boyds Mills Pr.

Voices of the River Plate: Interviews with Writers of Argentina & Uruguay. Clark M. Zlotchew. Ed. by Paul D. Seldis. LC 93-6560. (I. O. Evans Studies in the Philosophy & Criticism of Literature: No. 6). 200p. 1995. pap. 23.00 (0-89370-417-2); lib. bdg. 33.00 (0-89370-317-6) Borgo Pr.

Voices of the Self: A Study of Language Competence. Keith Gilyard. LC 90-24737. (African American Life Ser.). 178p. (C). 1991. pap. text ed. 19.95 (0-8143-2225-5) Wayne St U Pr.

Voices of the Silenced: The Responsible Self in a Marginalized Community. Darryl M. Trimiew. LC 93-19178. 160p. (Orig.). 1993. 22.95 (0-8298-0962-7); pap. 12.95 (0-8298-0967-8) Pilgrim OH.

Voices of the Song Lyric in China. Ed. by Pauline Yu. LC 92-32825. (Studies on China: Vol. 16). (C). 1993. 45.00 (0-520-08056-4) U CA Pr.

Voices of the Southwest: (Verse) Hilton R. Greer. 1993. reprint ed. lib. bdg. 75.00 (0-7812-5931-2) Rprt Serv.

Voices of the Spirit: Sources for Interpreting the African American Experience. Denise M. Glover. LC 94-29139. 211p. (Orig.). 1995. pap. 27.00 (0-8389-0639-7, 06397-7-2045) ALA.

Voices of the Storyteller: Cuba's Lino Novas Calvo. Lorraine E. Roses. LC 85-27148. (Contributions to the Study of World Literature Ser.: No. 14). 170p. 1986. text ed. 49.95 (0-313-25077-4, RVS, Greenwood Pr) Greenwood.

***Voices of the Survivors: Testimony, Mouring, & Memory in Post-Dictatorship.** Liria Evangelista & David W. Foster. 300p. 1998. text ed. 60.00 (0-8153-2917-2) Garland.

Voices of the Twentieth Century: Our Foremothers Speak. Social Thought & Political Economy Junior Seminar II Staff. (Illus.). 85p. (C). 1988. pap. 3.00 (0-924120-00-2) Intl Oil Work.

***Voices of the Voiceless: Women, Justice, & Human Rights in Guatemala.** Michelle Tooley. LC 96-53278. 232p. (Orig.). 1997. pap. 14.99 (0-8361-9057-2) Herald Pr.

Voices of the Wild. Jonathan London. LC 92-27651. (Illus.). 32p. (J). (ps up). 1993. 15.00 (0-517-59217-7) Crown Bks Yng Read.

Voices of the Winds: Native American Legends. Margot Edmonds & Ella E. Clark. (Illus.). 384p. 1989. 27.95 (0-8160-2067-1) Facts on File.

Voices of the Winds: Native American Legends. Margot Edwards & Ella E. Clark. (Illus.). 384p. 1992. reprint ed. pap. 14.95 (0-8160-2749-8) Facts on File.

Voices of the Xiled: A Generation Speaks for Itself. Michael Wexler. 1994. pap. 14.95 (0-385-47449-0) Doubleday.

Voices of Their Own: Contemporary Spanish Narrative by Women. Elizabeth J. Ordonez. LC 90-55690. 256p. 1991. 42.50 (0-8387-5203-9) Bucknell U Pr.

Voices of Thunder: New Work from the Institute of American Indian Arts. Ed. by Heather Ahtone et al. (IAIA Anthology Ser.: No. 4). 184p. 1992. pap. text ed. 8.00 (1-881396-03-7) IOA Indian Arts.

Voices of Time: A Cooperative Survey of Man's Views of Time As Expressed by the Sciences & by the Humanities. 2nd ed. Ed. by J. T. Fraser. LC 81-3025. (Illus.). 772p. 1981. pap. text ed. 29.95 (0-87023-337-8) U of Mass Pr.

***Voices of Tomorrow: An Introduction to English, Bk. 2.** Edna Diolata. 1997. wbk. ed., pap. text ed. write for info. (0-07-044359-9) McGraw.

***Voices of Tomorrow: An Introduction to English, Bk. 2.** Edna Diolata. 1997. pap. text ed. write for info. (0-07-044355-6) McGraw.

Voices of Tomorrow: Critical Studies of the New Spirit in Literature. Edwin A. Bjorkman. LC 74-98818. 328p. 1970. reprint ed. text ed. 59.75 (0-8371-2962-1, BJVT, Greenwood Pr) Greenwood.

Voices of Toni Morrison. Barbara Rigney. 192p. 1991. 45.00 (0-8142-0554-2) Ohio St U Pr.

Voices of Toni Morrison. Barbara Rigney. 192p. (C). 1994. pap. 13.50 (0-8142-0555-0) Ohio St U Pr.

Voices of Two Women. Florence J. Goodman & Shelley Adler. 88p. 1974. pap. 10.00 (0-917232-01-1) Gee Tee Bee.

***Voices of Western World I.** Ed. by Kuzirian. (C). 1991. write for info. (0-673-38036-X) Addison-Wesley.

***Voices of Western World II.** Ed. by Kuzirian. (C). 1991. write for info. (0-673-38037-8) Addison-Wesley.

Voices of Wisdom. Francine Klagsbrun. 594p. 1986. 22.95 (0-8246-0320-6) Jonathan David.

***Voices of Wisdom.** 3rd ed. Kessler. 1998. pap. 9.95 (0-534-52544-X) Brooks-Cole.

Voices of Wisdom: A Multicultural Philosophy Reader. Gary E. Kessler. 515p. (C). 1992. pap. 35.95 (0-534-16296-7) Wadsworth Pub.

Voices of Wisdom: A Multicultural Philosophy Reader. 2nd ed. Gary E. Kessler. LC 94-542. 540p. 1995. pap. 44.95 (0-534-21630-7) Wadsworth Pub.

***Voices of Wisdom: A Multicultural Philosophy Reader.** 3rd ed. Gary Kessler. (C). 1997. pap. text ed. 44.95 (0-534-52542-3) Wadsworth Pub.

Voices of Women: Oral Histories of Six American School Teachers. Rasjidah Franklin. (Illus.). 266p. (Orig.). 1996. pap. 19.95 (1-884690-06-8) Owl Press.

Voices of Women: Three Critics on Three Poets on Three Artist-Heroines. 2nd rev. ed. Intro. by Lucy R. Lippard. LC 80-80281. (Illus.). 1990. pap. text ed. 8.00 (0-9602476-1-0) Midmarch Arts-WAN.

Voices of Women Artists. Wendy Slatkin. LC 92-19849. 320p. (C). 1992. pap. text ed. 34.67 (0-13-951427-9) P-H Gen Ref & Trav.

Voices of Women Aspiring to the Superintendency. Margaret Grogan. LC 95-42348. (SUNY Series, Educational Leadership). 222p. 1996. text ed. 44.50 (0-7914-2939-3); pap. text ed. 14.95 (0-7914-2940-7) State U NY Pr.

Voices of Zaire: Rhetoric or Reality. Jeffrey M. Elliot & Mervyn M. Dymally. LC 89-70696. 175p. 1990. pap. text ed. 12.95 (0-88702-045-3) Washington Inst Pr.

Voices Off: Texts, Contexts & Readers. Ed. by Morag Styles et al. (Education Ser.). (Illus.). 320p. 1996. 90.00 (0-304-33578-9); pap. 19.95 (0-304-33579-7) Cassell.

Voices on a Cold Day: Collected Columns. Bill Easterling. Ed. by Mike Kaylor. LC 86-82553. 220p. (Orig.). 1986. pap. text ed. 5.00 (0-916039-02-1) Kaylor & Kaylor.

Voices on the Landscape: Contemporary Iowa Poets. Ed. by Michael Carey. 193p. 1996. 25.00 (0-931209-64-1, Loess Hills Bks); pap. 14.00 (0-931209-65-X, Loess Hills Bks) Mid-Prairie Bks.

Voices on the Threshold of Tomorrow: One-Hundred Forty-Five Views of the New Millennium. Georg Feuerstein & Trisha L. Feuerstein. LC 93-22751. (Orig.). 1993. pap. 14.00 (0-8356-0692-9, Quest) Theos Pub Hse.

Voices on the Wind. Elisabeth MacDonald. 352p. (Orig.). 1994. mass mkt. 4.99 (0-380-77376-7) Avon.

Voices on the Wind: Polynesian Myths & Chants. Katharine Luomala. (Illus.). 209p. 1986. reprint ed. pap. 15.95 (0-930897-83-8) Bishop Mus.

Voices on the Wind: Women Poets of the Celtic Twilight. Ed. by Ellis Ni Dhuibhne. 144p. (Orig.). 1995. pap. 13.95 (1-874597-23-5, Pub. by New Island Bks IE) Irish Bks Media.

An Asterisk (*) at the beginning of an entry indicates that the title is appearing in BIP for the first time.

Voices on Voice: Perspectives, Definitions, Inquiry. Ed. by Kathleen B. Yancey. LC 94-21168. 363p. 1994. 29.95 (*0-8141-5634-7*) NCTE.

***Voices over Water.** D. Nurkse. LC 96-86009. (Encore Ser.). 100p. 1996. pap. 12.95 (*1-884800-18-1*) Four Way Bks.

Voices Prophesying War, Future Wars, 1763-3749. 2nd ed. I. F. Clarke. LC 92-8583. (Illus.). 272p. 1993. 30.00 (*0-19-212302-5*) OUP.

Voices, Silences & Echoes: A Theory of the Essay & the Critical Reception of Naturalism in Spain. Mary L. Bretz. 148p. (C). 1992. 53.00 (*1-85566-014-8*, Pub. by Tamesis Bks Ltd UK) Boydell & Brewer.

Voices That Are Gone: Themes in Nineteenth-Century American Popular Song. Jon W. Finson. LC 93-28889. 368p. 1994. 45.00 (*0-19-505750-3*) OUP.

***Voices That Are Gone: Themes in Nineteenth-Century American Popular Song.** Jon W. Finson. LC 96-38118. (Illus.). 368p. 1997. reprint ed. pap. text ed. 19.95 (*0-19-511382-9*) OUP.

Voices That Care: Stories & Encouragements for People with Aids/HIV & Those That Love Them. Neal Hitchens. 288p. 1994. pap. 11.00 (*0-671-88230-9*, Fireside) S&S Trade.

Voices-The Walls. M. Basheer. 1977. 4.00 (*0-88386-211-5*) S Asia.

Voices Through Time & Distant Places. D. L. Rudy. 36p. (Orig.). 1993. pap. 6.00 (*0-9637386-0-7*) Willdor Pr.

Voices under One Sky: Contemporary Native Literature. Trish F. Roman. LC 94-12477. 224p. 1994. pap. 12.95 (*0-89594-720-X*) Crossing Pr.

Voices Under the Ground: Themes & Images in the Early Poetry of Gunnar Ekelof. Ross Shideler. LC 70-171620. (U. C. Publ. in Modern Philology Ser.: Vol. 104). 165p. reprint ed. 47.10 (*0-8357-9640-X*, 2013809) Bks Demand.

***Voices under the Yellow Kite.** Rose M. Colucci. 314p. (Orig.). 1998. mass mkt. 8.99 (*1-889501-88-3*, Appaloosa) Sovereign.

***Voices under Water.** Virginia C. McGuire. 40p. (Orig.). 1997. pap. 8.00 (*1-886361-02-9*) Blue Light Pr.

Voices, Vision & Vitality: Redesigning Small Schools. Earle Newton & Patti Newton. 143p. (Orig.). (C). 1992. pap. text ed. 18.95 (*1-55059-047-2*) Temeron Bks.

Voices, Visions, & a New Reality: Mexican Fiction Since 1970. J. Ann Duncan. LC 85-40853. (Latin American Ser.). 280p. 1986. 49.95 (*0-8229-3815-4*) U of Pittsburgh Pr.

Voices, Visions & Apparitions. Michael Freze. LC 93-83239. 368p. (Orig.). 1993. pap. 14.95 (*0-87973-454-X*, 454) Our Sunday Visitor.

Voices We Carry: Recent Italian-American Women's Fiction. Ed. by Mary Jo Bona. 376p. 1994. pap. 18.00 (*0-920717-84-5*) Guernica Editions.

Voices Within the Ark. Ed. by Howard Schwartz & Anthony Rudolf. 1248p. 1980. pap. 15.95 (*0-380-76109-2*) Avon.

Voicing. Julio Cortazar et al. Ed. by Don Wellman. Tr. by Cola Franzen et al. 184p. (Orig.). 1989. pap. 8.00 (*0-942030-08-7*) O ARS.

Voicing a Thought on Sunday: Homilies & Prayer of the Faithful for the Three Year Cycle. Desmond Knowles. 394p. 1991. pap. text ed. 19.95 (*0-89622-690-5*) Twenty-Third.

Voicing America: Language, Literary Form, & the Origins of the United States. Christopher Looby. (Illus.). 280p. 1996. 29.95 (*0-226-49282-6*) U Ch Pr.

Voicing Creation's Praise: Towards a Theology of the Arts. Jeremy S. Begbie. 286p. 1991. pap. 29.95 (*0-567-29188-X*, Pub. by T & T Clark UK) Bks Intl VA.

***Voicing Power.** Ed. by Gail Hanlon. LC 97-1291. 1997. text ed. 52.00 (*0-8133-3203-6*) Westview.

***Voicing Power.** Ed. by Gail Hanlon. LC 97-1291. (C). 1997. pap. text ed. 16.00 (*0-8133-3204-4*) Westview.

Voicing Social Concern: The Mass Media, Violence, Pornography, Censorship, Organization, Social Science, the Ultramultiversity. Otto N. Larsen. 318p. lib. bdg. 39.00 (*0-8191-9437-9*) U Pr of Amer.

Voicing the Void: Muteness & Memory in Holocaust Fiction. Sara R. Horowitz. LC 95-51818. (SUNY Series in Modern Jewish Literature & Culture). 276p. (C). 1997. text ed. 54.50 (*0-7914-3129-0*); pap. text ed. 17.95 (*0-7914-3130-4*) State U NY Pr.

Voicing Today's Visions: Writings by Contemporary Women Artists. Ed. by Mara Witzling. (Illus.). 352p. (Orig.). 1994. pap. 19.50 (*0-87663-640-7*) Universe.

***Voicing Women: Gender & Sexuality in Early Modern Writing.** Kate Chedgzoy et al. LC 97-15999. 208p. (C). 1997. 50.00 (*0-8207-0288-9*) Duquesne.

Voicings: Ten Plays & a Scenario from the Documentary Theatre. Arrilio Favorini. 1995. 30.00 (*0-88001-397-4*) Ecco Pr.

Voicings for Jazz Keyboard. 64p. 1986. spiral bd. 12.95 (*0-7935-3485-2*, 00855475) H Leonard.

Void. Georges Perec. 302p. 1995. pap. 12.00 (*1-86046-098-4*) Harper SF.

Void: A Psychodynamic Investigation of the Relationship Between Mind & Space. A. H. Almaas. LC 85-82559. (Diamond Mind Ser.: Bk. 1). 175p. (Orig.). 1986. pap. 8.00 (*0-936713-00-3*) Diamond Bks CA.

Void: Inner Spaciousness & Ego Structure. 2nd ed. A. H. Almaas. 157p. 1986. pap. 14.00 (*0-936713-06-2*) Diamond Bks CA.

Void & Voice: Questioning Narrative Conventions in Andre Gide's Major First-Person Narratives. Charles O'Keefe. LC 95-21311. (University of North Carolina Studies in the Romance Languages and Literature Sero: Vol. 251). 425p. (C). 1996. pap. text ed. 30.00 (*0-8078-9255-6*) U of NC Pr.

Void Captain's Tale. Norman Spinrad. LC 81-21334. 250p. 1983. 25.00 (*0-671-43483-7*) Ultramarine Pub.

Void If Detached: Jewels of Kesatchie. Walter B. Fielder. (Illus.). Date not set. write for info. (*0-9649366-2-3*) W B Fielder.

Void in Hearts. large type ed. William G. Tapply. (General Ser.). 427p. 1990. lib. bdg. 18.95 (*0-8161-4822-8*, GK Hall) Thorndike Pr.

Void Indigo. Steve Gerber & Val Mayerik. 48p. 1984. 4.95 (*0-87135-059-9*) Marvel Entmnt.

***Void Where Prohibited: Rest Breaks & the Right to Urinate on Company Time.** Marc Linder & Ingrid Nygaard. 192p. 1997. 25.00 (*0-8014-3390-8*) Cornell U Pr.

***Voidoid.** Richard Hell. (Illus.). 79p. (YA). (gr. 12). 1996. pap. 12.95 (*1-899598-02-2*, Pub. by Codex UK) AK Pr Dist.

Voie d'Enfer et de Paradis. Jean de la Mote. Ed. by M. Aquiline Pety. (Catholic University of America. Studies in Romance Languages & Literatures: No. 20). reprint ed. 37.50 (*0-404-50320-9*) AMS Pr.

Voie Royale. Andre Malraux. (Coll. Soleil). 1954. 12.50 (*0-7859-0612-6*) Fr & Eur.

Voie Royale, La Condition Humaine see Oeuvres

Voies de la Pragmatique. Sandra Golopentia. (Stanford French & Italian Studies: No. 51). 252p. (Orig.). (FRE.). 1988. pap. 46.50 (*0-915838-67-2*) Anma Libri.

Voies Du Seigneur. Erskine Caldwell. 224p. (FRE.). 1981. pap. 10.95 (*0-7859-1942-2*, 2070373304) Fr & Eur.

Voies du Vengeance. Isak Dinesen. 440p. (FRE.). 1990. pap. 13.95 (*0-7859-2153-2*, 2070383202) Fr & Eur.

Voight: Precision Training for Body & Mind. Karen Voight. LC 95-41282. (Illus.). 144p. (Orig.). 1996. pap. 19.95 (*0-7868-8159-3*) Hyperion.

Voightlander & I. James F. Ryder. LC 72-9235. (Literature of Photography Ser.). 1973. reprint ed. 23.95 (*0-405-04940-4*) Ayer.

***Voila.** Jacqueline Gonthier. (J). 1997. pap. text ed. 29.95 incl. audio (*0-7641-7015-5*) Barron.

Voila. 2nd annot. ed. Heilenman. (College French Ser.). 1992. suppl. ed., teacher ed. 62.95 incl. audio (*0-8384-3637-4*) Heinle & Heinle.

Voila! 2nd ed. Heilenman et al. 1992. text ed. 58.95 (*0-8384-3626-9*) Heinle & Heinle.

Voila! 2nd ed. Heilenman et al. 1992. student ed., pap. 36. 95 (*0-8384-3640-4*) Heinle & Heinle.

Voila. 2nd ed. Heilenman. (College French Ser.). 1992. suppl. ed., teacher ed. 19.95 incl. audio (*0-8384-3639-0*) Heinle & Heinle.

Voila. 2nd ed. Heilenman. (College French Ser.). 1992. suppl. ed., pap. 21.95 (*0-8384-3647-1*) Heinle & Heinle.

***Voila!** 3rd ed. Heilenman & Kaplan. (College French Ser.). 1996. text ed. 0.95 (*0-8384-7593-0*) Heinle & Heinle.

Voila. 3rd ed. Heinleman & Kaplan. (Miscellaneous/Catalogs). 1997. teacher ed., text ed. 6.95 (*0-8384-7221-4*) Wadsworth Pub.

***Voila.** 3rd ed. Kaplan. (College French Ser.). 1997. lab manual ed., wbk. ed., pap. 33.95 (*0-8384-6604-4*) Heinle & Heinle.

Voila: Glanzstucke Historischer Moden 1750-1960 (Masterpieces of Fashion 1750-1960) Angelika Reschke et al. Ed. by Wilhelm Hornsbostel. (Illus.). 192p. (GER.). 1991. 80.25 (*3-7913-1117-4*, Pub. by Prestel GW) te Neues.

Voima. C. Dale Brittain. 416p. (Orig.). 1995. mass mkt. 5.99 (*0-671-87637-6*) Baen Bks.

Voinovich: By Means of Mutual Correspondence - Putem Vzaimnoi Perepiski. Ed. by R. Porter. (Russian Texts Ser.). 104p. (RUS.). 1996. pap. 16.95 (*1-85399-474-X*, Pub. by Brstl Class Pr UK) Focus Pub-R Pullins.

Voir Dire. Joe Sutton. 1996. pap. 5.25 (*0-8222-1524-1*) Dramatists Play.

Voir Dire 1996. Starr. 1995. 55.00 (*0-316-81043-6*) Little.

Voir Dire '95. Starr. 1994. 45.00 (*0-316-81113-0*) Little.

Vois la Vie en Rose, Snoopy. Charles M. Schulz. (Peanuts Ser.). (FRE.). (J). 1985. 4.95 (*0-8288-4516-6*) Fr & Eur.

***Voisin.** Mary O'Ferrall. 240p. 1998. mass mkt. 7.99 (*1-58006-023-4*, Appaloosa) Sovereign.

Voix dans la Foule. Stuart Merrill. 1972. 250.00 (*0-8490-1267-8*) Gordon Pr.

Voix Des Choses. Marguerite Yourcenar. 111p. (FRE.). 1987. 69.95 (*0-7859-0448-4*, 2070111229) Fr & Eur.

Voix du Siecle. Eunice C. Smith & John K. Savacool. 276p. (Orig.). (FRE.). (C). 1960. pap. text ed. 20.75 (*0-15-595006-1*) HB Coll Pubs.

Voix et Silences: Les Meilleures Pieces Radiophoniques Francaises. Incl. Silences de Paris. Albert Camus & V. Vedres. LC 68-11212. (FRE.). 1968. pap. text ed. (*0-318-53728-1*); Une l'Arme. Jean Forest & Rene Clair. LC 68-11212. (FRE.). 1968. pap. text ed. (*0-318-53729-X*); C'Est Vrai mais Il Ne Faut Pas le Croire. Claude Aveline. LC 68-11212. (FRE.). 1968. pap. text ed. (*0-318-53730-3*); Frederic General. Jacques Constant. LC 68-11212. (FRE.). 1968. pap. text ed. (*0-318-53731-1*); Interview. Robert Pinget. LC 68-11212. (FRE.). 1968. pap. text ed. (*0-318-53732-X*); LC 68-11212. Illus.). (FRE.). 1968. pap. text ed. 8.95 (*0-89197-466-0*) Irvington.

Voix Franco. Kulick. (College French Ser.). (FRE.). 1994. teacher ed., pap. 36.95 (*0-8384-4623-X*) Heinle & Heinle.

Voix Francophones: Discuter le Monde Contemporain. Kulick. (Bridging the Gap Ser.). 1994. pap. 36.95 (*0-8384-4622-1*) Heinle & Heinle.

Voix Francophones: Le Monde Francophone en Textes. Derakhshani. (Bridging the Gap Ser.). 1994. pap. 36.95 (*0-8384-4626-4*) Heinle & Heinle.

Voix Humaine. Jean Cocteau. pap. 18.95 (*0-685-37277-4*) Fr & Eur.

Voix sur Israel. Paul Claudel. 96p. (FRE.). 1950. 10.95 (*0-7859-1123-5*, 2070215199) Fr & Eur.

***Voix Truquees.** Sonia Sarfati. (Novels in the Roman Jeunesse Ser.). 96p. (FRE.). (J). (gr. 4-7). 1996. pap. 7.95 (*2-89021-187-8*, Pub. by Les Editions CN) Firefly Bks Ltd.

Vokabular der Psychoanalyse: The Vocabulary of Psychoanalysis, 2 vols. Jean Laplanche. (GER.). 1973. pap. 49.95 (*0-8288-6340-7*, M-7680, Suhrkamp) Fr & Eur.

Vokalismus des Vulgarlateins, 3 vols. in 1. Hugo E. Schuchardt. (Documenta Semiotica, Series Linguistica). xii, 1362p. 1975. reprint ed. write for info. (*3-487-05575-9*) G Olms Pubs.

Vol# see Cumulative Index to Nursing Literature

Vol de Nuit. Antoine de Saint-Exupery. 1972. write for info. (*0-318-63617-4*) Fr & Eur.

Vol de Nuit. Antoine de Saint-Exupery. (FRE.). 1982. pap. 10.95 (*0-8288-3734-1*, F123571) Fr & Eur.

Vol de Nuit. Antoine de Saint-Exupery. (Folio Ser.: No. 4). (FRE.). 1972. 6.95 (*2-07-036004-0*) Schoenhof.

Vol d'Icare. Raymond Queneau. 260p. (FRE.). 1968. pap. 17.95 (*0-7859-1277-0*, 2070104699) Fr & Eur.

Vol d'Icare. Raymond Queneau. (Gallimard Ser.). (FRE.). pap. 29.95 (*2-07-027298-2*) Schoenhof.

Vol D'Icare see Flight of Icarus

***Vol du Siecle.** Chrystine Brouillet. (Novels in the Roman Jeunesse Ser.). 96p. (FRE.). (J). (gr. 4-7). 1996. pap. 7.95 (*2-89021-160-6*, Pub. by Les Editions CN) Firefly Bks Ltd.

Vol du Vampire. Michel Tournier. (FRE.). 1983. pap. 12.95 (*0-7859-2853-7*) Fr & Eur.

Vol. I Behavioral Medicine - Behavior Modification see Guide to Alcoholism Treatment Research

Vol. I, 1788-1822, The Texas Association see Papers Concerning Robertson's Colony in Texas

Vol. II, 1823 Through September, 1826, Leftwich's Grant see Papers Concerning Robertson's Colony in Texas

Vol. III, Alcoholics Anonymous & Counseling see Guide to Alcoholism Treatment Research

Vol. III, October, 1826, Through April, 1830, The Nashville Colony see Papers Concerning Robertson's Colony in Texas

Vol. IV, May Through October 10, 1830, Tenoxtitlan, Dream Capital of Texas see Papers Concerning Robertson's Colony in Texas

Vol. IX, October, 1834, Through March 20, 1835, Sarahville de Viesca see Papers Concerning Robertson's Colony in Texas

Vol. V, October 11, 1830, Through March 5, 1831, The Upper Colony see Papers Concerning Robertson's Colony in Texas

Vol. VI, March 6 Through December 5, 1831, The Campaigns Against the Tawakoni, Waco, Towash & Comanche Indians see Papers Concerning Robertson's Colony in Texas

Vol. VII, December 6, 1831, Through October, 1833, Those Eleven-League Grants see Papers Concerning Robertson's Colony in Texas

Vol. VIII, November, 1833, Through September, 1834, Robertson's Colony see Papers Concerning Robertson's Colony in Texas

Vol. X, March 21 Through July 25, 1835, The Ranger Rendezvous see Papers Concerning Robertson's Colony in Texas

Vol. XI, July 26 Through October 14, 1835, Nashville-on-the-Brazos see Papers Concerning Robertson's Colony in Texas

Vol. XII, October 15, 1835, Through January 14, 1836, the Municipality of Milam see Papers Concerning Robertson's Colony in Texas

Vol. XIII, January 15 Through March 17, 1936, The Convention at Washington-on-the-Brazos see Papers Concerning Robertson's Colony in Texas

Vol. XIV, March 18 Through July 22, 1836, The Battle of San Jacinto & the Fall of Fort Parker see Papers Concerning Robertson's Colony in Texas

Vol. XV, July 23, 1836, through August 9, 1837, The Gentleman from Milam see Papers Concerning Robertson's Colony in Texas

Vol. XVI, August 10, 1837, through November, 1838, The Creation of Robertson County see Papers Concerning Robertson's Colony in Texas

Vol. 1. G. Hayman et al. 403p. 1973. 35.00 (*0-8218-1901-1*, TABLES-1) Am Math.

***Close ups of the Past.** Lewis. (C). 1997. pap. text ed. 21.00 (*0-15-505398-1*) HB Coll Pubs.

Vol. 1. A-B (fasc. 1-22) repr. 1986 see Encyclopaedia of Islam: New Edition

Vol. 1-Creativity through Calculator Harmonic Braiding see Psycho-Mathematics: The Key to the Universe

Vol. 1, Projective Assessment see Methods in Clinical Psychology

Vol. 1, Songs of Jamaica see Dialect Poetry of Claude McKay

Vol. 1, Student Edition see Performing Arts Management & Law

Vol. 1, The South Atlantic see Ocean Basins & Margins

Vol. 1, 1764-1789 see John Gray Blount Papers

Vol. 1, 1807-1832 see Papers of Willie Person Mangum

Vol. 1, 1825-1837 see Papers of William Alexander Graham

Vol. 1, 1841-1859 see Papers of John Willis Ellis

Vol. 1, 1903 see Edison Phonograph Monthly, 1903-1916

Vol. 10, 1986 see Popular Music: An Annotated Index of Popular Songs

Vol. 11 see Screen World: Volumes 11-20, 1960 to 1969, The Complete Pictorial & Statistical Record of the Movies

Vol. 12 see Growth of Crystals

Vol. 12 see Screen World: Volumes 11-20, 1960 to 1969, The Complete Pictorial & Statistical Record of the Movies

Vol. 12, 1895-1897 see Library of the Palestine Pilgrims' Text Society: Circa 1480-1483 A.D.

Vol. 13 see Screen World: Volumes 11-20, 1960 to 1969, The Complete Pictorial & Statistical Record of the Movies

Vol. 14 see Screen World: Volumes 11-20, 1960 to 1969, The Complete Pictorial & Statistical Record of the Movies

Vol. 15 see Screen World: Volumes 11-20, 1960 to 1969, The Complete Pictorial & Statistical Record of the Movies

Vol. 16 see Screen World: Volumes 11-20, 1960 to 1969, The Complete Pictorial & Statistical Record of the Movies

Vol. 17 see Screen World: Volumes 11-20, 1960 to 1969, The Complete Pictorial & Statistical Record of the Movies

Vol. 18 see Screen World: Volumes 11-20, 1960 to 1969, The Complete Pictorial & Statistical Record of the Movies

Vol. 19 see Screen World: Volumes 11-20, 1960 to 1969, The Complete Pictorial & Statistical Record of the Movies

Vol. 2. W. G. Bulgren et al. Ed. by Institute of Mathematical Statistics. 388p. 1974. 42.00 (*0-8218-1902-X*, TABLES-2) Am Math.

Vol. 2 see DragonLance: The Cataclysm

Vol. 2, Constab Ballads see Dialect Poetry of Claude McKay

Vol. 2-Creativity through Keyboard Harmonic Braiding see Psycho-Mathematics: The Key to the Universe

Vol. 2-Physical Science see Mathematics & Physical Science

Vol. 2, Student Edition see Performing Arts Management & Law

Vol. 2, The North Atlantic see Ocean Basins & Margins

Vol. 2, 1790-1795 see John Gray Blount Papers

Vol. 2, 1833-1838 see Papers of Willie Person Mangum

Vol. 2, 1838-1844 see Papers of William Alexander Graham

Vol. 2, 1860-1861 see Papers of John Willis Ellis

Vol. 2, 1904 see Edison Phonograph Monthly, 1903-1916

Vol. 2: 1925-1927: Essays, Reviews, Miscellany, & "The Public & Its Problems" see Later Works of John Dewey, 1925-1953

Vol. 20 see Screen World: Volumes 11-20, 1960 to 1969, The Complete Pictorial & Statistical Record of the Movies

Vol. 3, The Gulf of Mexico & The Caribbean see Ocean Basins & Margins

Vol. 3, 1796-1802 see John Gray Blount Papers

Vol. 3, 1839-1843 see Papers of Willie Person Mangum

Vol. 3, 1845-1850 see Papers of William Alexander Graham

Vol. 3, 1905 see Edison Phonograph Monthly, 1903-1916

Vol. 3: 1927-1928: Essays, Reviews, Miscellany, & "Impressions of Soviet Russia" see Later Works of John Dewey, 1925-1953

Vol. 4, 1844-1846 see Papers of Willie Person Mangum

Vol. 4, 1851-1856 see Papers of William Alexander Graham

Vol. 4, 1893-1897 see Library of the Palestine Pilgrims' Text Society: Circa 1480-1483 A.D.

Vol. 4, 1906 see Edison Phonograph Monthly, 1903-1916

Vol. 4A, The Eastern Mediterranean see Ocean Basins & Margins

Vol. 4B, The Western Mediterranean see Ocean Basins & Margins

Vol. 5, The Arctic Ocean see Ocean Basins & Margins

Vol. 5, 1847-1894 see Papers of Willie Person Mangum

Vol. 5, 1857-1863 see Papers of William Alexander Graham

Vol. 5, 1907 see Edison Phonograph Monthly, 1903-1916

Vol. 6, 1864-1865 see Papers of William Alexander Graham

Vol. 6, 1908 see Edison Phonograph Monthly, 1903-1916

Vol. 7, 1866-1868 see Papers of William Alexander Graham

Vol. 7, 1909 see Edison Phonograph Monthly, 1903-1916

Vol. 8, 1869-1875 see Papers of William Alexander Graham

Vol. 8, 1910 see Edison Phonograph Monthly, 1903-1916

Vol. 8, 1975-1979 see Popular Music: An Annotated Index of Popular Songs

Vol. 9, 1980-1984 see Popular Music: An Annotated Index of Popular Songs

Volaties in Magmas. Ed. by M. R. Carroll & J. R. Holloway. (Reviews in Mineralogy Ser.: Vol. 30). 500p. 1994. per. 28.00 (*0-939950-36-7*) Mineralogical Soc.

Volatile Bodies: Toward a Corporeal Feminism. Elizabeth Grosz. LC 93-28611. (Theories of Representation & Difference Ser.). 272p. (C). 1994. 35.00 (*0-253-32686-9*); pap. 15.95 (*0-253-20862-9*) Ind U Pr.

Volatile Capital Flows: Taming Their Impact on Latin America. Ed. by Ricardo Hausmann & Liliana R. Suarez. (Inter-American Development Bank Ser.). 107p. (Orig.). (C). 1996. pap. text ed. 14.95 (*1-886938-04-0*) IADB.

Volatile Compounds in Foods & Beverages. Ed. by Henk Maarse. (Food Science & Technology Ser.: Vol. 44). 784p. 1991. 220.00 (*0-8247-8390-5*) Dekker.

***Volatile Oil Crops.** Hay & Waterman. 1993. text ed. write for info. (*0-582-07867-9*, Pub. by Longman UK) Longman.

Volatile Oil Crops: Their Biology, Biochemistry & Production. Robert K. Hay. LC 93-28153. 185p. 1993. text ed. 135.00 (*0-470-22087-2*) Halsted Pr.

Volatile Organic Compounds in the Atmosphere. Ed. by R. E. Hester & R. M. Harrison. (Issues in Environmental Science & Technology Ser.: No. 4). 140p. 1995. 27.00 (*0-85404-215-6*) CRC Pr.

Volatile Organic Compounds (VOCs) in the Environment. Ed. by W. Wang et al. LC 96-13347. (Special Technical Publication Ser.: No. 1261). (Illus.). 300p. 1996. 95.00 (*0-8031-2048-6*, 0401261016) ASTM.

Volatile Powder Keg: Balkan Security after the Cold War. Ed. by F. Stephen Larrabee. 346p. (Orig.). (C). 1994. pap. text ed. 27.50 (*1-879383-23-3*) Am Univ Pr.

Volatile Powder Keg: Balkan Security after the Cold War. Ed. by F. Stephen Larrabee. 346p. (Orig.). (C). 1994. lib. bdg. 62.50 (1-879383-22-5) Am Univ Pr.

Volatiles in the Earth & Solar Systems. Kenneth Farley. (Illus.). 304p. 1995. boxed 110.00 (1-56396-409-0, Vol. CP 341) Am Inst Physics.

*Volatilidad de los Flujos de Capital: Como Controlar su Impacto en America Latina. Ed. by Ricardo Hausmann & Liliana Rojas-Suarez. 112p. (SPA.). 1996. pap. text ed. 14.95 (1-886938-09-1) IADB.

Volatility & Credit Risk in the Capital Markets: Assessing & Managing the Risk of Financial Instruments & Off-Balance Sheet Operations. Erik Banks. 300p. 1993. text ed. 70.00 (1-55738-509-2) Irwin Prof Pubng.

*Volatility in the Capital Markets: State-of-the-Art Techniques for Modeling, Managing, & Trading Volatility. Ed. by Israel Nelken. (Finance Editions Ser.). 224p. 1997. 55.00 (1-888998-05-9) Glenlake Pub.

Volatilization Technologies for Removing Organics from Water. J. L. Fleming. LC 88-37154. (Pollution Technology Review Ser.: No. 164). (Illus.). 120p. 1989. 39.00 (0-8155-1189-2) Noyes.

Volcan: Poems from Central America. Ed. by Alejandro Murguia & Barbara Paschke. LC 83-20936. 159p. 1984. pap. 6.95 (0-87286-153-8) City Lights.

Volcan d'Or. Jules Verne. 442p. (FRE.). 1980. pap. 18.95 (0-7859-1225-8, 2010059352) Fr & Eur.

Volcanes. Norman S. Barrett. LC 90-70893. (Picture Library). (Illus.). 32p. (SPA.). (J). (gr. k-4). 1990. lib. bdg. 18.60 (0-531-07911-2) Watts.

Volcanic Activity & Climate. Kirill Y. Kondratyev & Ignacio Galindo. LC 97-9780. 450p. 1997. 68.00 (0-937194-37-9) A Deepak Pub.

*Volcanic Affair. Xantha Rhodes. (Orig.). 1997. mass mkt. 5.95 (0-352-33184-4, Pub. by Black Lace UK) London Brdge.

Volcanic & Seismic Hazards on the Islands of Hawaii. Christina Heliker. (Illus.). 52p. (Orig.). (C). 1993. pap. text ed. 20.00 (1-56806-552-3) DIANE Pub.

Volcanic Ash. Grant Heiken & Kenneth Wohletz. (Los Alamos Series in Basic & Applied Sciences: No. 6). 1985. 55.00 (0-520-05241-2) U CA Pr.

Volcanic Ash & Aviation Safety: Proceedings of the First International Symposium on Volcanic Ash & Aviation Safety. Ed. by T. J. Casadevall. (Illus.). 450p. (Orig.). (C). 1995. pap. text ed. 75.00 (0-7881-1650-9) DIANE Pub.

Volcanic Ash Soils: Genesis, Properties & Utilization. Sadao Shoji et al. LC 93-4551. (Developments in Soil Science Ser.: Vol. 21). 312p. 1994. 191.50 (0-444-89799-2) Elsevier.

Volcanic Earth: Volcanoes & Plate Tectonics, Past, Present & Future. Lin Sutherland. (Illus.). 248p. 1995. 49.95 (0-86840-071-8, Pub. by New South Wales Univ Pr AT) Intl Spec Bk.

Volcanic Firearms & Their Successors. James Edsall. 1974. 3.50 (0-913150-28-2) Pioneer Pr.

Volcanic Hazards. Ed. by R. I. Tilling. (Short Course Ser.: Vol. 1). 123p. 1989. 23.00 (0-87590-705-9) Am Geophysical.

Volcanic Hazards: A Sourcebook on the Effects of Eruptions. R. J. Blong. 440p. 1984. text ed. 154.00 (0-12-107180-4) Acad Pr.

Volcanic Hazards: Assessment & Monitoring. Ed. by J. H. Latter. (IAVECI Proceedings in Volcanology Ser.: Vol. 1). (Illus.). 625p. 1989. 162.95 (0-387-19337-5) Spr-Verlag.

Volcanic Heaven: Essays on Wyndham Lewis. Ed. by Paul Edwards. LC 96-4671. (Illus.). 200p. (C). 1996. 27.50 (1-57423-011-5); pap. 17.50 (1-57423-010-7) Black Sparrow.

Volcanic Heaven: Essays on Wyndham Lewis. deluxe ed. Ed. by Paul Edwards. LC 96-4671. (Illus.). 200p. (C). 1996. 35.00 (1-57423-012-3) Black Sparrow.

Volcanic History of Honduras. Alexander R. McBirney & Howel Williams. LC 79-627247. (University of California Publications in Social Welfare: vol. 85). 111p. reprint ed. pap. 31.70 (0-685-15301-0, 2015001) Bks Demand.

*Volcanic Plumes. R. S. Sparks. LC 96-39034. 1997. text ed. 95.00 (0-471-93901-3) Wiley.

Volcanic Regimes in Canada: The Proceedings of a Symposium Sponsored by the Volcanology Division of the Geological Association of Canada & Held at the University of Waterloo in Waterloo, Ontario, May 16-17. 1975. Ed. by W. R. Baragar et al. LC 79-305269. (Geological Association of Canada. Special Paper Ser.: No. 16). 482p. reprint ed. pap. 137.40 (0-685-17086-1, 2027845) Bks Demand.

Volcanic Rocks. Robert Bell. (Science Close-up Ser.). (Illus.). 24p. (J). 1994. 6.50 (0-307-12857-1, Golden Pr) Western Pub.

Volcanic Seismology. Roberto Scarpa. LC 92-13939. (IAVCEI Proceedings in Volcanology Ser.: Vol. 3). (Illus.). 592p. 1992. 152.95 (0-387-54651-0) Spr-Verlag.

Volcanic Successions: Modern & Ancient: A Geological Approach to Processes, Products & Successions. R. A. Cas & J. V. Wright. (Illus.). 320p. 1987. pap. text ed. 49.95 (0-04-552022-4) Routledge Chapman & Hall.

*Volcanic Sucessions, Modern & Ancient: A Geological Approach to Processes, Products, & Successions. Cas & Wright. (Illus.). 544p. (Orig.). (C). (gr. 13 up). 1987. pap. text ed. 60.95 (0-412-44640-5, Chap & Hall NY) Chapman & Hall.

Volcanism: Radhakrishna Volume. K. V. Subbarao. 1994. write for info. (81-224-0626-2, Pub. by Wiley Estrn II) Franklin.

Volcanism & Fossil Biotas. Ed. by M. Lockley & A. Rice. (Special Papers: No. 244). (Illus.). 136p. 1990. 14.00 (0-8137-2244-6) Geol Soc.

Volcanism & Tectonism in the Columbia River Flood-Basalt Province. Ed. by S. P. Reidel & P. R. Hooper. (Special Papers: No. 239). 400p. 1990. 26.00 (0-8137-2239-X) Geol Soc.

Volcanism Associated with Extention at Consuming Plate Margins. Ed. by J. L. Smellie. (Geological Society Special Publication: No. 81). 272p. (C). 1995. 100.00 (1-897799-17-9, 201, Pub. by Geol Soc Pub Hse UK) AAPG.

*Volcano. Cullinan. (J). 1994. 23.25 (0-15-302224-8, HB Juv Bks); pap. 11.00 (0-15-302404-6, HB Juv Bks) HarBrace.

Volcano. Brian Knapp. LC 89-11584. (World Disasters Ser.). (Illus.). 48p. (J). (gr. 5-9). 1990. lib. bdg. 24.26 (0-8114-2373-5) Raintree Steck-V.

Volcano! Maurice Krafft. (Young Discovery Library). (Illus.). 40p. (J). (gr. k-5). 1993. lib. bdg. 9.95 (1-56674-074-6, HTS Bks) Forest Hse.

Volcano! Maurice Krafft. Tr. by Vicki Bogard from FRE. LC 92-968. (Illus.). 38p. (J). (gr. k-5). 1992. 5.95 (0-944589-41-3) Young Discovery Lib.

Volcano. Christopher Lampton. (Disaster! Ser.). (Illus.). 64p. (J). (gr. 4-6). 1991. pap. 5.95 (1-56294-786-9); lib. bdg. 14.90 (1-56294-028-7) Millbrook Pr.

Volcano. Fred Martin. LC 95-38352. (J). 1996. lib. bdg. write for info. (1-57572-023-X) Rigby Interact Libr.

*Volcano. Al Newman. 859p. (Orig.). 1997. mass mkt. 5.99 (1-55237-183-2, Pub. by Comnwlth Pub CN) Partners Pubs Grp.

Volcano! Margaret Thomas. LC 90-45372. (Nature's Disasters Ser.). (Illus.). 48p. (J). (gr. 5-6). 1991. lib. bdg. 12.95 (0-89686-595-9, Crstwood Hse) Silver Burdett Pr.

*Volcano. Richard Woodley. 1997. mass mkt. 6.99 (0-06-101165-7, Harp PBks) HarpC.

Volcano! Russell Wright. Ed. by Cathy Anderson et al. (Event-Based Science Ser.). (Illus.). (Orig.). (J). (gr. 6-9). 1996. wbk. ed., pap. 7.95 (0-201-49590-2) Supplementary Div.

Volcano! Russell Wright. Ed. by Cathy Anderson et al. (Event-Based Science Ser.). (Illus.). (Orig.). (YA). (gr. 6-9). 1996. teacher ed., pap. 19.95 incl. vhs (0-201-49594-5) Supplementary Div.

Volcano! Russell Wright. Ed. by Cathy Anderson et al. (Event-Based Science Ser.). (Illus.). (Orig.). (YA). (gr. 6-9). 1996. pap. 115.00 incl. vhs (0-201-49603-8) Supplementary Div.

Volcano: A Disaster Book. Christopher Lampton. (J). (gr. 4-7). 1992. pap. 6.56 (0-395-63645-0) HM.

Volcano: A Memoir of Hawaii. Garrett Hango. 1996. pap. 14.00 (0-679-76748-7) McKay.

Volcano: A Memoir of Hawaii. Garrett Hongo. 1995. 24.00 (0-394-57167-3) Knopf.

*Volcano: Movie Tie-In. Jerome Armstrong. 1997. mass mkt. 4.50 (0-06-440690-3) HarpC.

*Volcano: The Eruption & Healing of Mount St. Helens. Patricia Lauber. (J). (gr. 5). 1995. 8.20 (0-395-73257-3) HM.

Volcano: The Eruption & Healing of Mount St. Helens. Patricia Lauber. LC 85-22442. (Illus.). 64p. (J). (gr. 3-5). 1986. text ed. 16.95 (0-02-754500-8, Bradbury S&S) S&S Childrens.

*Volcano: The Eruption & Healing of Mount St. Helens. large type ed. Patricia Lauber. 86p. (J). (gr. 5). 21.50 (0-614-20626-X, L-38197-00 APHB) Am Printing Hse.

Volcano: The Eruption & Healing of Mount St. Helens. Patricia Lauber. LC 92-23791. (Illus.). 64p. (J). (gr. 2-5). 1993. reprint ed. pap. 7.95 (0-689-71679-6, Aladdin Paperbacks) S&S Childrens.

Volcano & Earthquake. Susanna Van Rose. LC 92-4710. (Eyewitness Bks.). (Illus.). 64p. (J). (gr. 5 up). 1992. 19.00 (0-679-81685-2); lib. bdg. 20.99 (0-679-91685-7) Knopf Bks Yng Read.

*Volcano & Miracle. Gustaw Herling-Grudzinski. 1997. pap. 12.95 (0-14-023615-5) Viking Penguin.

Volcano & Miracle: A Selection from the Journal Written at Night. Gustaw Herling-Grudzinski. Tr. by Ronald Strom from POL. LC 95-21207. 277p. 1996. pap. 24.95 (0-670-85482-4) Viking Penguin.

*Volcano, Earthquake & Hurricane. Nick Arnold. LC 96-32760. (Remarkable World Ser.). (J). 1997. lib. bdg. 24.26 (0-8172-4540-5) Raintree Steck-V.

*Volcano Goddess Will See You Now, Vol. 9. Dan Greenburg. LC 97-16742. (Zack Files Ser.). (Illus.). 64p. (J). (gr. 1-5). 1997. pap. 3.95 (0-448-41559-3, G&D) Putnam Pub Group.

Volcano in My Tummy: Helping Children to Handle Anger. Eliane Whitehouse & Warwick Pudney. (Illus.). 80p. (Orig.). 1996. pap. 12.95 (0-86571-349-9); lib. bdg. 39.95 (0-86571-348-0) New Soc Pubs.

Volcano in Our Yard. John Taylor. (Illus.). (J). (gr. 2-5). 1975. 4.95 (0-686-11663-1) Thompson's.

Volcano Inside. David Dooley. LC 88-60849. (Roerich Poetry Prize Winner Ser.). 64p. (Orig.). 1988. pap. 8.00 (0-934257-15-9) Story Line.

Volcano Instability on the Earth & Other Planets. Ed. by W. C. McGuire et al. (Geological Society Special Publications Classics Ser.: No. 110). (Illus.). viii, 390p. 1996. 125.00 (1-897799-60-8, 349, Pub. by Geol Soc Pub Hse UK) AAPG.

Volcano Lover: A Romance. Susan Sontag. 320p. 1992. 22.00 (0-374-28516-0) FS&G.

Volcano Management in the United States & Japan, Vol. 7. Ronald W. Perry & Hirotada Hirose. Ed. by Judith A. Levy. LC 91-15558. (Contemporary Studies in Applied Behavioral Science). 230p. 1985. 73.25 (1-55938-275-9) Jai Pr.

*Volcano, Mount St. Helena. (Illus.). 32p. (Orig.). 1996. pap. 7.95 (1-884958-25-7) Am Prods.

Volcano Ogre. Lin Carter. LC 75-21217. 177p. 1976. 25.00 (0-385-08807-8) Ultramarine Pub.

*Volcano Watching. 5th rev. ed. Robert Decker & Barbara Decker. (Illus.). 84p. 1997. reprint ed. pap. text ed. 9.95 (0-940295-16-4) HI Natural Hist.

*Volcanoes. Eric Arnold. 1997. pap. 3.99 (0-679-88641-9); lib. bdg. 11.99 (0-679-98641-3) Random.

Volcanoes. Norman S. Barrett. LC 89-5644. (Picture Library). 32p. 1990. lib. bdg. 20.00 (0-531-10841-4) Watts.

Volcanoes. Helen J. Challand. LC 82-17888. (New True Bks.). (Illus.). 48p. (J). (gr. k-4). 1983. pap. 5.50 (0-516-41690-1); lib. bdg. 19.00 (0-516-01690-3) Childrens.

*Volcanoes. Penny Clarke. LC 97-5965. (Worldwise Ser.). (J). 1998. write for info. (0-531-14462-3) Watts.

Volcanoes. Michael George. LC 90-22064. (Images Ser.). (Illus.). 40p. (J). (gr. 3-5). 1992. lib. bdg. 16.95 (0-88682-403-6) Creative Ed.

Volcanoes. Merrilee Hooker. LC 92-43121. (Discovery Library of Disasters). (J). 1993. 12.67 (0-86593-244-1); 9.50 (0-685-66351-5) Rourke Corp.

Volcanoes. Keith Lye. LC 92-32016. (What About...? Ser.). (Illus.). 32p. (J). (gr. 2-3). 1992. lib. bdg. 21.40 (0-8114-3412-5) Raintree Steck-V.

Volcanoes. Keith Lye. (J). 1996. pap. text ed. 4.95 (0-8114-9665-1) Raintree Steck-V.

Volcanoes. Neil Morris. (Wonders of Our World Ser.). (Illus.). 32p. (J). (gr. 2-9). 1995. lib. bdg. 19.16 (0-86505-826-1) Crabtree Pub Co.

Volcanoes. Neil Morris. (Wonders of Our World Ser.). (Illus.). 32p. (J). (gr. 2-9). 1995. pap. 6.95 (0-86505-838-5) Crabtree Pub Co.

Volcanoes. Seymour Simon. LC 87-33316. (Illus.). 32p. (J). (gr. k-3). 1988. 16.00 (0-688-07411-1, Morrow Junior); lib. bdg. 15.88 (0-688-07412-X, Morrow Junior) Morrow.

Volcanoes. Seymour Simon. LC 87-3316. (Illus.). 32p. (J). (gr. k up). 1995. pap. 5.95 (0-688-14029-7, Mulberry) Morrow.

Volcanoes. Gregory Vogt. (First Bks.). (Illus.). 64p. (J). (gr. 5-8). 1993. pap. 6.95 (0-531-15667-2) Watts.

Volcanoes. Gregory Vogt. LC 92-23292. (First Bks.). 64p. (J). 1993. lib. bdg. 21.00 (0-531-20151-1) Watts.

Volcanoes. Jane Walker. (Fascinating Facts Ser.). (Illus.). 32p. (J). (gr. 2-4). 1995. pap. 5.95 (1-56294-898-9) Millbrook Pr.

Volcanoes. Jane Walker. (Fascinating Facts Ser.). (Illus.). 32p. (J). (gr. 2-4). 1995. lib. bdg. 14.90 (1-56294-608-0) Millbrook Pr.

Volcanoes. 2nd ed. Robert Decker & Barbara Decker. 288p. (C). 1995. pap. text ed. write for info. (0-7167-1851-0) W H Freeman.

Volcanoes. 2nd ed. Susanna Van Rose & Ian Mercer. (British Museum of Natural History Ser.). (Illus.). 60p. 1991. pap. text ed. 9.95 (0-674-94307-4, VANVOX) HUP.

*Volcanoes. 3rd ed. Robert W. Decker & Barbara Decker. LC 97-17746. 1997. write for info. (0-7167-3174-6) W H Freeman.

Volcanoes. Franklyn M. Branley. LC 84-45344. (Trophy Let's-Read-&-Find-Out Bk.). (Illus.). 32p. (J). (ps-3). 1986. reprint ed. pap. 4.95 (0-06-445059-7, Trophy) HarpC Child Bks.

*Volcanoes, Vol. 1. Decker. 1997. write for info. (0-7167-2440-5) St Martin.

Volcanoes: A Planetary Perspective. Peter Francis. LC 92-29756. (Illus.). 450p. 1993. pap. 45.00 (0-19-854033-7, Clarendon Pr) OUP.

Volcanoes: A Source Guide. 1991. lib. bdg. 250.00 (0-8490-4829-X) Gordon Pr.

Volcanoes: An Introduction. Alwyn Scarth. LC 94-16258. (Louise Lindsey Merrick Natural Environment Ser.: No. 19). (Illus.). 288p. 1994. 45.00 (0-89096-635-4); pap. 19.95 (0-89096-636-2) Tex A&M Univ Pr.

Volcanoes: Earth's Inner Fire. Sally M. Walker. LC 93-23172. (J). (gr. 1-4). 1994. lib. bdg. 14.96 (0-87614-812-7, Carolrhoda) Lerner Group.

Volcanoes: Fire from Below. Jenny Wood. LC 90-55460. (Wonderworks of Nature Ser.). (Illus.). 32p. (J). (gr. 3-4). 1991. lib. bdg. 19.93 (0-8368-0472-4) Gareth Stevens Inc.

Volcanoes: Fire from the Earth. Maurice Krafft. (Discoveries Ser.). (Illus.). 208p. 1993. pap. 12.95 (0-8109-2844-2) Abrams.

Volcanoes: Mountains That Blow Their Tops. Nicholas Nirgiotis. LC 95-22045. (All Aboard Reading Ser.: Level 2). (Illus.). (J). (gr. 1-3). 1996. pap. 3.95 (0-448-41143-1, G&D) Putnam Pub Group.

Volcanoes! Mountains with a Tummyache!! Carole Marsh. (Interactive Multimedia Titles Ser.). (J). (gr. 2-9). 29.95 (0-7933-7607-6, C Marsh); pap. 19.95 (0-7933-7606-8, C Marsh); teacher ed., pap. 19.95 (0-7933-7835-4, C Marsh) Gallopade Pub Group.

Volcanoes: Passion & Fury. Stephen J. O'Meara & Donna D. O'Meara. LC 93-47387. (Illus.). 96p. (J). 1994. pap. 16.95 (0-933346-70-0) Sky Pub.

Volcanoes & Earthquakes. (Discover Ser.). (Illus.). 48p. (J). 1993. 9.98 (1-56173-423-3) Pubns Intl Ltd.

Volcanoes & Earthquakes. (Information Ser.). 32p. (J). 3.50 (0-7214-1744-2, Ladybrd) Penguin.

Volcanoes & Earthquakes. (Explorers Ser.). (Illus.). 40p. (J). (gr. 2-6). 1996. pap. 4.99 (0-7214-5605-7, Ladybrd) Penguin.

Volcanoes & Earthquakes. Basil Booth. (Our World Ser.). (Illus.). 48p. (J). (gr. 5-8). 1991. lib. bdg. 12.95 (0-382-24227-0) Silver Burdett Pr.

Volcanoes & Earthquakes. Martyn Bramwell. (Earth Science Library). (Illus.). 32p. (J). (gr. 5-8). 1994. lib. bdg. 18.60 (0-531-14337-6) Watts.

Volcanoes & Earthquakes. Mary Elting. LC 89-37107. (Illus.). 48p. (J). (gr. 3-7). 1990. pap. 9.95 (0-671-67217-7, S&S Bks Young Read) S&S Childrens.

Volcanoes & Earthquakes. Jon S. Erickson. (Illus.). 352p. 1987. 22.95 (0-8306-1942-9, 2842); pap. 15.95 (0-8306-2842-8, 2842P) McGraw-Hill Prof.

Volcanoes & Earthquakes. Patricia Lauber. 80p. (J). (gr. 4-7). 1991. pap. 2.95 (0-590-42592-7) Scholastic Inc.

Volcanoes & Earthquakes. Ed. by Eldridge M. Moores. LC 95-12939. (Discoveries Ser.). (Illus.). 64p. (J). (gr. 3 up). 1995. lib. bdg. 15.00 (0-7835-4764-1) Time-Life.

Volcanoes & Earthquakes. Zuza Vrbova. LC 89-20334. (Our Planet Ser.). (Illus.). 32p. (J). (gr. 4-6). 1990. pap. 4.95 (0-8167-1978-0); lib. bdg. 12.95 (0-8167-1977-2) Troll Communs.

*Volcanoes & Earthquakes: God's Power Beneath Our Feet. Michael Carroll. (J). 1997. 12.99 (1-56476-602-0, Chariot Bks) Chariot Victor.

Volcanoes & Earthquakes in Action: An Early Reader Pop-up Book. Marianne Borgardt. (Illus.). 16p. (Orig.). (J). (ps-3). 1993. bds. 8.95 (0-689-71720-2, Aladdin Paperbacks) S&S Childrens.

Volcanoes & Pearl Divers: Essays in Lesbian Feminist Studies. Ed. by Suzanne Raitt. 292p. 1996. pap. text ed. 22.95 (1-56023-880-1) Haworth Pr.

Volcanoes & Society. David Chester. LC 93-1620. (Illus.). 288p. 1993. pap. 25.00 (0-340-51761-1, A9530, Pub. by E Arnold UK) Routledge Chapman & Hall.

Volcanoes & Society. David Chester. 350p. 1995. pap. text ed. 39.95 (0-470-24979-X) Wiley.

Volcanoes, Betjaks, & Dragons: Let's Travel to Indonesia Together see Windows on the World Series

*Volcanoes, Crucibles of Change. Richard V. Fisher et al. LC 96-49516. 344p. 1997. text ed. 35.00 (0-691-01213-X) Princeton U Pr.

Volcanoes from Puebla. Kenneth Gangemi. 192p. 1979. 11.95 (0-7145-2577-4) M Boyars Pubs.

Volcanoes from Puebla. Kenneth Gangemi. 192p. 1989. reprint ed. pap. 9.95 (0-7145-2578-2) M Boyars Pubs.

Volcanoes in the Sea: The Geology of Hawaii. 2nd ed. Gordon A. Macdonald et al. LC 82-23685. (Illus.). 528p. 1983. 34.95 (0-8248-0832-0) UH Pr.

Volcanoes of North America: The United States & Canada. Ed. by Charles A. Wood & Jurgen Kienle. (Illus.). 500p. (C). 1990. text ed. 90.00 (0-521-36469-8) Cambridge U Pr.

Volcanoes of North America: The United States & Canada. Ed. by Charles A. Wood & Jurgen Kienle. (Illus.). 354p. (C). 1992. pap. text ed. 36.95 (0-521-43811-X) Cambridge U Pr.

Volcanoes of the Antarctic Plate & Southern Oceans. Ed. by W. E. LeMasurier & J. W. Thomson. (Antarctic Research Ser.: Vol. 48). 512p. 1990. 55.00 (0-87590-172-7) Am Geophysical.

Volcanoes of the Central Andes. S. L. DeSilva & Peter Francis. (Illus.). viii, 216p. 1991. 135.95 (0-387-53706-6) Spr-Verlag.

Volcanoes of the National Parks in Hawaii. rev. ed. Gordon Macdonald & Douglass Hubbard. (Illus.). 64p. (C). 1989. pap. text ed. 5.95 (0-940295-01-6) HI Natural Hist.

Volcanoes of the Solar System. Charles Frankel. (Illus.). 288p. (C). 1996. text ed. 69.95 (0-521-47201-6); pap. text ed. 24.95 (0-521-47770-0) Cambridge U Pr.

Volcanoes of the United States. Ellen Thro. LC 91-36002. (Venture Bks.). (Illus.). 112p. (YA). (gr. 9-12). 1992. lib. bdg. 22.00 (0-531-12522-X) Watts.

*Volcanoes of the World. John Cleare. 1997. 17.98 (1-57145-079-3) Advan Mktg Servs.

Volcanoes to Zany Zebras. Christopher Carrie. (Crayola Encyclopedia of Coloring Fun Bks.). (Illus.). 40p. (Orig.). (J). (gr. k up). 1989. pap. 1.49 (0-86696-230-1) Binney & Smith.

Volcanogenic Gold Deposits. 1982. 82.60 (0-942218-19-1) Minobras.

Volcanogenic Sulfide & Precious Metal Mineralization in the Southern Appalachians. Ed. by K. C. Misra. (Studies in Geology). (Illus.). ii, 236p. 1986. pap. 10.00 (0-910249-15-6) U of Tenn Geo.

Volcanological & Environmental Studies of Mount Erebus, Antarctica. Ed. by Philip R. Kyle. LC 94-41067. (Antarctic Research Ser.: Vol. 66). 162p. 1995. 60.00 (0-87590-875-6) Am Geophysical.

Volcanology: Reading Earth's Explosive Messages. rev. ed. Bonnie Rassmusen. (Learning Packets - Science Ser.). (Illus.). 92p. (J). (gr. k-8). 1983. pap. 19.95 (0-913705-07-1) Zephyr Pr AZ.

Volcanos. Peter Murray. LC 95-3515. (Nature Bks.). (Illus.). 32p. (J). (gr. 2-6). 1995. lib. bdg. 22.79 (1-56766-197-1) Childs World.

*Volcanos & Earthquakes. Andres L. Ruiz. LC 96-37981. (Sequences of Earth & Space Ser.). (Illus.). (J). 1997. 12.95 (0-8069-9745-1) Sterling.

Voldro's Nest. Margaret Headley. (C). 1986. 30.00 (0-907618-13-8, Pub. by Orkney Pr UK) St Mut.

Volens S Nolens Vol. 1: And Their Amusing Journey Through Times & Lands. (Illus.). 104p. (Orig.). 1995. pap. write for info. (0-9651732-0-8) Borin B M Pub.

Voles, Mice & Lemmings. Charles Elton. 1971. reprint ed. 70.00 (3-7682-0275-5) Lubrecht & Cramer.

Voles (Microtinae) I. M. Gromov & I. Y. Polyakov. (Fauna of the U. S. S. R. - Mammals of the Soviet Union Ser.: No. 3/8). xxvi, 726p. 1992. 132.00 (90-04-09255-2) E J Brill.

Voleur de Maigret. Georges Simenon. pap. 3.95 (0-685-36572-7) Fr & Eur.

Voleur de Talan. Pierre Reverdy. 181p. 1967. 8.95 (0-686-54733-0) Fr & Eur.

Voleur d'Enfants. Jules Supervielle. (Folio Ser.: No. 357). (FRE.). 1973. 6.95 (2-07-036357-0) Schoenhof.

Volga Boatman. Konrad Bercovici. LC 72-131628. 1970. reprint ed. 15.00 (0-403-00515-9) Scholarly.

Volga Falls to the Caspian Sea. Boris Pilnyak, pseud. LC 71-110428. reprint ed. 37.50 (0-404-05047-6) AMS Pr.

An Asterisk (*) at the beginning of an entry indicates that the title is appearing in BIP for the first time.

Volga Germans: In Russia & the Americas, 1763 to the Present. Fred C. Koch. LC 76-41155. 1977. 30.00 (*0-271-01236-6*) Pa St U Pr.
Volga Germans in Old Russia & in Western North America: Their Changing World View. Timothy J. Kloberdanz. 14p. 1979. reprint ed. 6.00 (*0-914222-11-2*) Am Hist Soc Ger.
Volga Tatars: A Profile in National Resilience. Azade-Ayse Rorlich. (Publication Series: Studies of Nationalities in the U. S. S. R.). 288p. (C). 1986. pap. 19.95 (*0-8179-8392-9*); text ed. 31.95 (*0-8179-8391-0*) Hoover Inst Pr.
***Volga, Volga: A Voyage down the Great River.** Lesley Chamberlain. 274p. 1995. 36.50 (*0-330-33345-3*, Pub. by Picador UK) Trans-Atl Phila.
***Volgograd Oblast: Economy, Industry, Government, Business.** 2nd rev. ed. Russian Information & Business Center, Inc. Staff. (Russian Regional Business Directories Ser.). (Illus.). 200p. 1997. pap. 99.00 (*1-57751-418-1*) Russ Info & Busn Ctr.
Vol.III, Reaction Modes & Products-Part II see Singlet 02 Series
Volistaendiges Woerterbuch Ueber die Gedichte des Homeros und der Homeriden. 9th ed. Carl Capelle. (GER.). 1968. 55.00 (*0-8288-6667-8*, M7681) Fr & Eur.
Volition & Personality: Action Versus State Orientation. rev. ed. Ed. by Julius Kuhl & Jurgen Beckmann. LC 93-38609. (Illus.). 512p. 1994. text ed. 98.00 (*0-88937-029-X*) Hogrefe & Huber Pubs.
Volitional Action. Ed. by W. A. Hershberger. (Advances in Psychology Ser.: No. 62). 572p. 1990. 183.75 (*0-444-88318-5*, North Holland) Elsevier.
Volker Barriers to Trade. 1993. pap. text ed. 78.00 (*90-6544-704-0*) Kluwer Ac.
Volker Braun. Ed. by Rolf Jucker. (Contemporary German Writers Ser.: Vol. 2). 136p. 1996. pap. 14.95 (*0-7083-1313-2*, Pub. by Univ Wales Pr UK) Paul & Co Pubs.
Volkereg - en sy Verhouding tot die Suid-Africaanse Reg. H. Booysen. 612p. 1989. pap. write for info. (*0-7021-1057-4*, Pub. by Juta SA) Gaunt.
Volkomer Passionate Liberal. 1970. pap. text ed. 64.50 (*90-247-0561-4*, Pub. by M Nijhoff NE) Kluwer Ac.
***Volks-Und Gesellschaftslieder des 15. und 16. Jahrhunderts.** Deutschen Akademie der Wissenschaften Staff & Arthur Kopp. (Deutsche Texte des Mittelalters Ser.: Band V). xviii, 254p. (GER.). 1970. write for info. (*3-296-17250-5*, Pub. by Weidmann GW) Lubrecht & Cramer.
Volksbuch der Wadsehagga. Bruno Guttmann. (B. E. Ser.: No. 122). (GER.). 1914. 30.00 (*0-8115-3050-7*) Periodicals Srv.
Volksgeist As Method & Ethic: Essays on Boasian Ethnography & the German Anthropological Tradition. Ed. by George W. Stocking, Jr. LC 95-25272. (History of Anthropology Ser.: Vol. 8). 358p. 1996. 27.50 (*0-299-14550-6*) U of Wis Pr.
Volksgesang und Volkslied: Proben und Probleme. Leopole Schmidt. (Illus.). 587p. 1970. 29.50 (*0-614-16456-7*) Theodore Front.
Volksgesundheit Im Krieg, 2 Vols. Clemens Pirquet. (Wirtschafts-Und Sozialgeschichte des Weltkrieges (Osterreichische Und Ungarische Serie)). (GER.). 1926. Set. 235.00 (*0-317-27641-7*) Elliots Bks.
Volkskapitalisme: Class, Capital & Ideology in the Development of Afrikaner Nationalism, 1934-1948. Dan O'Meara. LC 82-9504. (African Studies: No. 34). (Illus.). 352p. 1983. text ed. 85.00 (*0-521-24285-1*) Cambridge U Pr.
Volkswagen: A Week at the Factory. Photos by Peter Keetman. LC 92-14736. (Illus.). 96p. 1992. pap. 12.95 (*0-8118-0268-X*) Chronicle Bks.
Volkswagen: Nine Lives Later. 2nd ed. Dan R. Post. LC 82-173212. (Illus.). 320p. 1982. pap. 19.95 (*0-911160-42-6*) Post Group.
Volkswagen: Then, Now & Forever. Terry Schuler. (Illus.). 200p. 1996. 29.95 (*0-929758-12-9*) Beeman Jorgensen.
***Volkswagen Beetle.** 1997. 6.99 (*0-517-18474-5*) Random Hse Value.
Volkswagen Beetle. Marco Batazzi. (Illus.). 96p. 24.95 (*88-7911-056-X*, Pub. by Giorgio Nada Editore IT) Howell Pr VA.
Volkswagen Beetle. Negel Grimshaw. (Illus.). 144p. 1995. 24.95 (*0-8317-9119-5*) Smithmark.
Volkswagen Beetle. Jonathan Wood. 1989. pap. 25.00 (*0-85263-974-0*, Pub. by Shire UK) St Mut.
Volkswagen Beetle: Cabriolets & Coachbuilts. Keith Seume & Bob Shaill. (Illus.). 128p. 1993. pap. 19.95 (*1-870979-33-8*, Pub. by Bay View Bks UK) Motorbooks Intl.
Volkswagen Beetle: Rise from the Ashes War. Simon Parkinson. (Illus.). 128p. 1996. 19.95 (*1-874105-47-2*, Pub. by Veloce Pub UK) Motorbooks Intl.
Volkswagen Beetle & Karmann Ghia Convertibles, 1949-1980. Walter Zeichner. Tr. by Edward Force from GER. LC 88-63997. (Illus.). 96p. 1989. 19.95 (*0-88740-168-6*) Schiffer.
Volkswagen Beetle & Karmann Ghia Official Service Manual Type 1, 1966-1969. Volkswagen of America, Inc. Staff. LC 70-189047. (Illus.). 512p. (Orig.). 1972. pap. 39.95 (*0-8376-0416-8*) Bentley.
Volkswagen Beetle, Super Beetle, & Karmann Ghia Official Service Manual Type 1, 1970-1979. Volkswagen of America, Inc. Staff. LC 78-75039. (Illus.). 448p. (Orig.). 1979. pap. 34.95 (*0-8376-0096-0*) Bentley.
Volkswagen Bug! The People's Car. Ray Miller. (Autobahn Ser.: Vol. 1). (Illus.). 320p. 1984. 44.95 (*0-913056-12-X*) Evergreen Pr.
Volkswagen Cabriolet, Scirocco Service Manual: 1985-1993, Including 16V. Robert Bentley, Inc. Staff. 49.95 (*0-8376-0362-5*) Bentley.
Volkswagen Corrado Official Factory Repair Manual: 1989-1993. Volkswagen United States Inc. Staff. 1993. write for info. (*0-8376-0387-0*) Bentley.
Volkswagen Customs & Classics. David Fetherston. (Enthusiast Color Ser.). (Illus.). 96p. 1995. pap. 12.95 (*0-87938-984-2*) Motorbooks Intl.
Volkswagen Dasher Service Manual, 1974-1981, Including Diesel. rev. ed. Bentley, Robert, Inc. Staff. LC 81-66944. (Illus.). 692p. (Orig.). 1981. pap. 44.95 (*0-8376-0083-9*) Bentley.
Volkswagen Fastback & Squareback Official Service Manual, Type 3, 1968-1973. Volkswagen of America, Inc. Staff. LC 73-85200. (Illus.). 424p. (Orig.). 1974. pap. 39.95 (*0-8376-0057-X*) Bentley.
Volkswagen for the Wehrmacht. Ed. by U. S. War Department Staff & Dan R. Post. LC 72-84803. 160p. 1972. pap. 14.95 (*0-911160-43-4*) Post Group.
Volkswagen Fox Service Manual: 1987-1992, Including Wagon & Sport. Bentley, Robert, Inc. Staff. (Illus.). 440p. 39.95 (*0-8376-0340-4*) Bentley.
Volkswagen Fox Service Manual, 1987-1993: Including GL, GL Sport, & Wagon. Robert Bentley Publishers Staff. 1993. pap. 39.95 (*0-8376-0363-3*) Bentley.
***Volkswagen Fuel Injection & Emission Control Handbook, 1980-1997: Inspection & Maintenance (IM) Troubleshooting & Service for Volkswagen Cars, Vans & Pickups.** LC 97-16347. 1997. write for info. (*0-8376-0394-3*) Bentley.
Volkswagen Golf, GTI, Jetta, Cabrio: Service Manual, Including Jetta III & Golf III, 1993, 1994, 1995, 1996. Robert Bentley, Inc. Staff. LC 96-23050. 1996. write for info. (*0-8376-0364-1*) Bentley.
Volkswagen GTI Golf-Jetta Service Manual, 1985-1992. Bentley Staff. (Illus.). 846p. 1990. pap. 44.95 (*0-8376-0342-0*) Bentley.
Volkswagen Karmann Ghia. Malcolm Bobbitt. (Illus.). 160p. 1995. 41.95 (*1-874105-54-5*, Pub. by Veloce Pub UK) Motorbooks Intl.
Volkswagen "Kubelwagen" in the War. Reinhard Frank. Tr. by Edward Force from GER. LC 88-64004. (Illus.). 52p. 1989. pap. 9.95 (*0-88740-162-7*) Schiffer.
***Volkswagen Passat: Official Factory Repair Manual, 1995, 1996, 1997:Gasoline, Turbo Diesel & TDI, Including Wagon.** Robert Bentley, Inc. Staff. LC 97-24306. 1997. write for info. (*0-8376-0380-3*) Bentley.
***Volkswagen Passat: Service Maual 1990, 1991, 1992, 1993 - 4-Cylinder Gasoline Models Including Gl & Wagon.** Robert Bentley. LC 96-36416. 1996. pap. write for info. (*0-8376-0378-1*) Bentley.
Volkswagen Passat Service Manual: 1990-1992. Volkswagen United States Inc. Staff. (Illus.). 582p. 1992. 49.95 (*0-8376-0377-3*) Bentley.
Volkswagen Quantum Official Factory Repair Manual: 1982-1988, Gasoline & Turbo Diesel, including Wagon & Syncro. Volkswagen United States Inc. Staff. (Orig.). 89.95 (*0-8376-0341-2*) Bentley.
Volkswagen Rabbit, Jetta Diesel Service Manual: 1977-84 Diesel Models, Including Pickup Truck & Turbo-Diesel. 4th rev. ed. Bentley, Robert, Inc. Staff. LC 84-70138. (Illus.). 624p. (Orig.). 1984. pap. 39.95 (*0-8376-0184-3*) Bentley.
Volkswagen Rabbit, Scirocco, Jetta Service Manual: 1980-1984 Gasoline Models, Including Pickup Truck, Convertible, & GTI. Bentley, Robert, Inc. Staff. LC 84-70139. (Illus.). 715p. (Orig.). 1984. pap. 39.95 (*0-8376-0183-5*) Bentley.
Volkswagen Rabbit, Scirocco Service Manual, Gasoline Models, 1975-1979. rev. ed. Bentley, Robert, Inc. Staff. LC 79-57170. (Illus.). 628p. (Orig.). 1986. pap. 39.95 (*0-8376-0107-X*) Bentley.
Volkswagen Station Wagon Bus Official Service Manual Type 2, 1968-1979. 4th rev. ed. Volkswagen of America, Inc. Staff. LC 78-75038. (Illus.). 464p. (Orig.). 1979. pap. 34.95 (*0-8376-0094-4*) Bentley.
Volkswagen Transporter Workshop Manual: 1963-1967 Type 2. Volkswagen of America, Inc. Staff. (Illus.). 918p. 1992. 94.95 (*0-8376-0391-9*) Bentley.
Volkswagen Vanagon Official Factory Repair Manual: 1980-1991, Including Air-Cooled & Water-Cooled Gasoline Engines, Diesel Engine, Syncro, & Camper. Volkswagen United States Inc. Staff. 84.95 (*0-8376-0336-6*) Bentley.
Volkswagen 1200 Workshop Manual: 1961-1965, Types 11, 14 & 15. Volkswagen of America, Inc. Staff. (Illus.). 1364p. (Orig.). 1990. pap. 94.95 (*0-8376-0390-0*) Bentley.
***Volkswagen, 1949-1969: Air Cooled.** Chilton Book Co. Staff. (New Total Car Care Ser.). 1997. pap. text ed. write for info. (*0-8019-9073-4*) Chilton.
Volkswagen, 1970-81. Chilton Automotives Editorial Staff. LC 78-20249. (Chilton's Repair & Tune-up Guides Ser.). (Illus.). 304p. 1979. pap. 16.95 (*0-8019-6837-2*) Chilton.
Volkswagon: Beetles, Buses & Beyond. James M. Flammang. 256p. 1996. pap. text ed. 19.95 (*0-87341-419-5*) Krause Pubns.
***Volkswagon Jetta, Golf, GTI, Cabrio Service Manual: Including Jetta III & Golf III, 1993, 1994, 1995, 1996, 1997.** Robert Bentley. LC 97-99. 1997. pap. write for info. (*0-8376-0365-X*) Bentley.
Volkszahlung: Birth Census 1856-1878, Evangelical Kirchengemeinde Mrotschen, Kreis Wiristz, Provinz Posen German Kaiser Reich. Marilyn Lind. LC 94-79225. (Illus.). 103p. (Orig.). 1995. pap. 14.95 (*0-937463-14-0*) Linden Tree.
Vollands. large type ed. Pamela Hill. 336p. 1992. 25.99 (*0-7089-2577-4*) Ulverscroft.
Vollendende Mimesis: Wirklichkeitsdarstellung & Selbsbezueglichkeit in Theorie & Literarischer Praxis. Andreas Boehn. (Quellen und Forschungen zur Sprach und Kulturgeschichte der Germanischen Voelker Ser.: NF Bd. 101). xii, 215p. (GER.). (C). 1992. lib. bdg. 84.65 (*3-11-013685-6*) De Gruyter.
Vollenhoven: His Early Development. John H. Kok. 393p. (Orig.). 1992. pap. 15.95 (*0-932914-23-3*) Dordt Coll Pr.
Volley & Bayonet. Frank Chadwick & Greg Novak. (Illus.). 96p. (Orig.). 1994. pap. 14.00 (*1-55878-179-X*) Game Designers.
Volley Ball see Sport Signs
Volleyball. Steven Boga. LC 96-21976. (Illus.). 112p. 1997. pap. 10.00 (*0-8117-2491-3*) Stackpole.
***Volleyball.** Brown & Benchmark Staff. LC 97-6709. (Elements of Learning Ser.). 120p. (C). 1997. per. write for info. (*0-697-29451-X*) Brown & Benchmark.
Volleyball. George Bulman. LC 96-12405. (Know the Sport Ser.). 48p. 1996. pap. 5.95 (*0-8117-2829-3*) Stackpole.
Volleyball. Christie Costanzo. LC 93-27153. (J). 1993. write for info. (*0-86593-344-8*) Rourke Corp.
Volleyball. M. L. Johnson & Dewayne J. Johnson. (Illus.). 51p. 1981. pap. text ed. 8.95 (*0-89641-057-9*) American Pr.
Volleyball. Barrie MacGregor. (EP Sports Ser.). (Illus.). 1978. 8.95 (*0-685-42064-7*) Charles River Bks.
Volleyball. Keith Nicholls. (Skills of the Game Ser.). (Illus.). 120p. 1995. pap. 19.95 (*1-85223-831-3*, Pub. by Crowood UK) Trafalgar.
Volleyball. David Smale. (The Summer Olympics Ser.). 32p. (J). (gr. 4-8). 1995. 14.79 (*1-887068-03-1*) Smart Apple.
Volleyball. 2nd ed. Darlene A. Kluka & Peter J. Dunn. 128p. (C). 1991. per. write for info. (*0-697-10119-3*) Brown & Benchmark.
Volleyball. 3rd ed. Kathryn Davis. 144p. (C). 1996. pap. text ed. 13.59 (*0-7872-2334-4*) Kendall-Hunt.
Volleyball. 3rd ed. Darlene A. Kluka & Peter J. Dunn. 128p. (C). 1996. per. write for info. (*0-697-25616-2*) Brown & Benchmark.
Volleyball: A Step-by-Step Guide. Charles Bracken. LC 89-27352. (Be the Best! Ser.). (Illus.). 64p. (J). (gr. 4-8). 1997. pap. 3.95 (*0-8167-1952-7*) Troll Communs.
Volleyball: Steps to Success. 2nd ed. Barbara L. Viera & Bonnie J. Ferguson. LC 95-42643. (Steps to Success Activity Ser.). (Illus.). 168p. (Orig.). 1996. pap. 14.95 (*0-87322-646-1*, PVIE0646) Human Kinetics.
Volleyball, A Step-by-Step Guide. Charles Bracken. LC 89-27352. (Be the Best! Ser.). (Illus.). 64p. (J). (gr. 4-8). 1990. lib. bdg. 11.89 (*0-8167-1951-9*) Troll Communs.
Volleyball Centennial the First 100 years. Byron Shewman. (Illus.). 320p. 1994. pap. 19.95 (*1-57028-009-6*) Masters Pr IN.
***Volleyball Cybernetics.** Stan Kellner & Dave Cross. (Illus.). 188p. (Orig.). 1997. per., pap. 14.95 (*0-9656175-0-5*) Yes I Can Pubn.
Volleyball Drill Book: Game Action Drills. Bob Bertucci & James Peterson. (Illus.). 224p. 1992. pap. 14.95 (*0-940279-42-8*) Masters Pr IN.
Volleyball Drill Book: Individual Skills. Bob Bertucci & James Peterson. (Illus.). 1992. pap. 14.95 (*0-940279-28-2*) Masters Pr IN.
Volleyball Everyone. 2nd ed. Stokes & Haley. 154p. (Orig.). 1992. pap. text ed. 14.95 (*0-88725-169-2*) Hunter Textbks.
Volleyball Inside Out: Fundamentals, Tactics, & Strategy. 3rd ed. David J. Schakel. (Illus.). 147p. (Orig.). (C). 1997. pap. text ed. 13.95 (*0-89641-301-2*) American Pr.
***Volleyball Rules: A Player's Guide.** Bernard Kilkenny. (Illus.). 80p. 1997. pap. 9.95 (*0-7063-7525-4*, Pub. by Ward Lock UK) Sterling.
Volleyball Scorebook. American Alliance for Health, Physical Education, Recreation & Dance Staff. 1979. pap. 6.00 (*0-88314-169-8*) AAHPERD.
Volleyball Today. Dunphy. Date not set. teacher ed., pap. text ed. write for info. (*0-314-91108-1*) West Pub.
Volleyball Today. Marv Dunphy & Rod Wilde. Ed. by Clyde Perlee. 223p. (C). 1991. pap. text ed. 21.75 (*0-314-83711-6*) West Pub.
Volleyball Training. Rob Youngs et al. (Illus.). 128p. 1995. pap. 22.95 (*1-85223-880-1*, Pub. by Crowood Pr UK) Trafalgar.
***Volleys.** Ed. by J. R. Struthers. 96p. 1990. pap. 9.95 (*0-88984-113-6*, Pub. by Porcupines Quill CN) Genl Dist Srvs.
***Vollkommenes Stimmideal? Eine Suche durch die Jahrhunderte: Wie sich die Ansichten uber den Kunstgesang Anderten.** Beate Hiltner. 130p. (GER.). 1996. 32.95 (*3-631-31017-X*) P Lang Pubng.
Vollstaendige Fuehrer des Yosemite National Parkes - Complete Guidebook to Yosemite National Park. Steven P. Medley. (Illus.). 112p. (GER.). 1993. pap. 10.95 (*0-939666-64-2*) Yosemite Assn.
Vollstaendige Grammatik der neuhochdeutschen Sprache, 5 vols. Heinrich Bauer. (C). 1967. reprint ed. Set. 615.40 (*3-11-000365-1*) De Gruyter.
Vollstaendige Konkordanz zum griechischen Neuen Testament, 2 pts., Vol. 1. Ed. by Institut fuer Neutestamentliche Textforschung, Muenster-Westf Staff & Kurt Aland. viii, 96p. (C). 1983. 1,657.70 (*3-11-009698-6*) De Gruyter.
Vollstaendige Konkordanz zum griechischen Neuen Testament, 2 vols., Vol. 2. Ed. by Institut fuer Neutestamentliche Textforschung, Muenster-Westf Staff & Kurt Aland. viii, 96p. (C). 1978. 188.50 (*3-11-007349-8*) De Gruyter.
Vollstaendiges Woerterbuch Zur Sogenannten Caedmonschen Genesis. Theodor Braasch. (GER.). 1933. 75.00 (*0-685-57725-2*, M7682) Fr & Eur.
Vollstandige Beschreibung der Offentlichen Bibliothek Zu Bamberg, 4 vols. in 1. Heinrich J. Jaeck. clxix, 543p. reprint ed. write for info. (*0-318-71808-1*) G Olms Pubs.
Vollstandiges Bucher-Lexikon, Enthaltend Alle Von 1750 in Deutschland und den Angrenzenden Landern Gedruckten Bucher, 38 vols. Christian G. Kayser. reprint ed. Set. write for info. (*0-318-71832-4*) G Olms Pubs.
Vollstandiges Deutsches Worter-Buch, 2 vols. Christoph E. Steinbach. Ed. by Walther Schroter. (Documenta Linguistica Ser.: Reihe II). xiii, 2220p. 1973. reprint ed. Set. write for info. (*3-487-04606-7*) G Olms Pubs.
Vollstandiges Griechisch-Deutsches Worterbuch Uber die Gedichte des Homeros und der Homeriden. Ernst E. Seiler. xvi, 605p. reprint ed. write for info. (*0-318-72077-9*) G Olms Pubs.
Vollstandiges Heiligen - Lexikon, 5 vols. Ed. by Joh Evang. 1975. reprint ed. Set. write for info. (*3-487-05596-1*) G Olms Pubs.
Vollstandiges Lexikon Zu Den Pseudo-Casarianischen. Siegmund Preuss. 433p. 1964. reprint ed. write for info. (*0-318-71204-0*) G Olms Pubs.
Vollstandiges Lexikon Zu Den Pseudo-Casarianischen Schriftwerkern. Siegmund Preuss. 433p. 1964. reprint ed. write for info. (*0-318-72068-X*) G Olms Pubs.
Vollstandiges Worterbuch Zu dem Geschichtswerk des Q. Curtius Rufus. Otto Eichert. 288p. 1967. reprint ed. write for info. (*0-318-72013-2*) G Olms Pubs.
Vollstandiges Worterbuch Zu dem Geschichtswerk des Q. Curtius Rufus Uber die Taten Alexanders des Grossen. Otto Eichert. 288p. 1967. reprint ed. write for info. (*0-318-71115-X*) G Olms Pubs.
Vollstandiges Worterbuch Zu den Gedichten des P. Vergilius Maro. Georg A. Koch. iv, 588p. 1972. reprint ed. write for info. (*3-487-04359-9*) G Olms Pubs.
Vollstandiges Worterbuch Zu den Geschichtswerken des C. Sallustius Crispus. Otto Eichert. 194p. 1973. reprint ed. write for info. (*3-487-04592-3*) G Olms Pubs.
Vollstandiges Worterbuch Zu den Verwandlungen des Publius Ovidius Naso. Otto Eichert. 292p. 1972. reprint ed. write for info. (*3-487-04507-9*) G Olms Pubs.
Vollstandiges Worterbuch Zum Geschichtswerke des M. Velleius Paterculus. Georg A. Koch. viii, 217p. reprint ed. write for info. (*0-318-72036-1*) G Olms Pubs.
Vollstandiges Worterbuch Zur Philippischen Geschichte des Justinus. Otto Eichert. 200p. 1967. reprint ed. write for info. (*0-318-71116-8*) G Olms Pubs.
Vollstandigste Naturgeschicte der Affen. Heinrich G. Reichenbach. LC 78-72725. reprint ed. 72.50 (*0-404-18298-4*) AMS Pr.
***Vologda Oblast: Economy, Industry, Government, Business.** 2nd rev. ed. Russian Information & Business Center, Inc. Staff. (Russian Regional Business Directories Ser.). (Illus.). 200p. 1997. pap. 99.00 (*1-57751-424-6*) Russ Info & Busn Ctr.
Volontaires Nationaux Pendant la Revolution, 3 vols. Charles L. Chassin. LC 70-38040. reprint ed. 405.00 (*0-404-52600-4*) AMS Pr.
Volo's Cormyr Access. 1995. 12.95 (*0-7869-0151-9*) TSR Inc.
Volo's Guide to the Dalelands. Ed Greenwood. 1996. 14.95 (*0-7869-0406-2*) TSR Inc.
Volo's Guide to Things Magic. Ed Greenwood. 1996. 20.00 (*0-7869-0446-1*) TSR Inc.
Volpone. J. Creaser. (C). 1978. text ed. 14.40 (*0-8147-1374-2*) NYU Pr.
***Volpone.** Jonson. 1995. pap. text ed. write for info. (*0-582-25408-6*, Pub. by Longman UK) Longman.
Volpone. Ben Jonson. Ed. by Philip Brockbank. (New Mermaid Ser.). (C). 1976. pap. text ed. 5.95 (*0-393-90010-X*) Norton.
Volpone. Ben Jonson. Ed. by Alvin B. Kernan. (Ben Jonson Ser.: No. 1). 1963. pap. 15.00 (*0-300-00139-8*, Y80) Yale U Pr.
Volpone. Ben Jonson. 1996. pap. text ed. 6.95 (*1-85459-194-0*, Pub. by N Hern Bks UK) Theatre Comm.
Volpone. Ben Jonson. LC 93-42273. 112p. 1994. reprint ed. pap. 1.00 (*0-486-28049-7*) Dover.
Volpone or the Fox. Ben Jonson. Ed. by David Cook. 312p. (C). 1981. pap. text ed. 8.50 (*0-415-04008-6*, NO. 2256) Routledge.
Volpone, or The Fox. Ben Jonson. Ed. by Jonas A. Barish. (Crofts Classics Ser.). 128p. 1958. pap. text ed. write for info. (*0-88295-049-5*) Harlan Davidson.
Volshebnii Uzori: Poems. Elena Kluyeva. 1982. 6.95 (*0-685-44310-8*) RWCPH.
Voltage. Easton Royce. (X-Files Ser.: Vol. 8). 112p. (J). (gr. 5 up). 1996. pap. 3.95 (*0-06-440643-1*, Trophy) HarpC Child Bks.
Voltage-Sensitive Ion Channels: Modulation by Neurotransmitters & Drugs. Pier F. Spano. (FIDIA Research Ser.: Vol. 6). viii, 189p. 1988. 81.00 (*0-387-96737-0*) Spr-Verlag.
Voltaire. Wayne Andrews. LC 80-29565. (Illus.). (C). 1981. 7.95 (*0-8112-0800-1*) New Directions.
***Voltaire.** Knapp. Date not set. 28.95 (*0-8057-1634-3*) Mac Lib Ref.
Voltaire. A. Meyer. 1972. 59.95 (*0-8490-1268-6*) Gordon Pr.
Voltaire: Candide. Ed. by H. Mason. (French Texts Ser.). 138p. (FRE.). 1995. pap. 14.95 (*1-85399-369-7*, Pub. by Brstl Class Pr UK) Focus Pub-R Pullins.
Voltaire: Lettres Philosophiques. Ed. by F. A. Taylor. (Bristol French Texts Ser.). 246p. (FRE.). 1992. pap. 19.95 (*1-85399-285-2*, Pub. by Brstl Class Pr UK) Focus Pub-R Pullins.
Voltaire: L'Ingenu & Histoire de Jenni. Ed. by J. H. Brumfitt & M. I. Davis. (Bristol French Texts Ser.). 227p. (FRE.). 1992. pap. 19.95 (*1-85399-286-0*, Pub. by Brstl Class Pr UK) Focus Pub-R Pullins.

Voltaire & Catherine the Great: Selected Correspondence. Ed. by A. Lentin. (Illus.). 196p. 1974. 16.00 (*0-89250-099-9*) Orient Res Partners.

Voltaire & Sensibility. Ronald S. Ridgway. LC 72-94539. 308p. reprint ed. pap. 87.80 (*0-317-29412-1*, 2023845) Bks Demand.

***Voltaire & the Century of Light.** Alfred O. Aldridge. LC 75-2978. 456p. 1975. reprint ed. pap. 130.00 (*0-608-02502-X*, 2063146) Bks Demand.

Voltaire & the Cowboy: The Letters of Thurman Arnold. Thurman W. Arnold. Ed. by Gene M. Gressley. LC 76-15772. (Illus.). 576p. reprint ed. pap. 164.20 (*0-8357-5519-3*, 2035135) Bks Demand.

Voltaire & Tragedy. Eva Jacobs. (Theatre in Focus Ser.). 1987. pap. 105.00 incl. sl. (*0-85964-192-9*) Chadwyck-Healey.

Voltaire Bibliographie de ses Oeuvres: Paris, 1882-1890, 4 Vols. G. Bengesco. 1974. 280.00 (*0-318-23472-6*) Periodicals Srv.

Voltaire dans ses contes. Jacques Van Den Heuvel, pseud. 27.95 (*0-685-34066-X*) Fr & Eur.

Voltaire, Dryden & Heroic Tragedy. Trusten W. Russell. LC 46-5389. reprint ed. 20.00 (*0-404-05467-6*) AMS Pr.

Voltaire Essays, & Another. Theodore Besterman. LC 80-17075. (Illus.). 181p. 1980. reprint ed. text ed. 49.75 (*0-313-22527-3*, BEVO, Greenwood Pr) Greenwood.

Voltaire, Historian. J. H. Brumfitt. LC 84-29037. 178p. 1985. reprint ed. text ed. 41.50 (*0-313-24734-X*, BRVO, Greenwood Pr) Greenwood.

Voltaire in His Letters. Tr. by S. G. Tallentyre. LC 77-150205. (Select Bibliographies Reprint Ser.). 1977. reprint ed. 23.95 (*0-8369-5718-0*) Ayer.

Voltaire Musicien. Edmond V. Straeten. LC 76-43943. (Music & Theatre in France in the 17th & 18th Centuries Ser.). reprint ed. 46.50 (*0-404-60197-9*) AMS Pr.

Voltaire Selections. Paul Edwards. (Great Philosophers Ser.). 391p. (C). 1989. pap. write for info. (*0-02-331610-1*, Macmillan Coll) P-H.

Voltaire, the Enlightenment & the Comic Mode: Essays in Honor of Jean Sareil. Maxine Cutler. 284p. (C). 1990. text ed. 29.95 (*0-8204-1289-9*) P Lang Pubng.

Voltaire's Bastards: The Dictatorship of Reason in the West. John R. Saul. 450p. 1992. text ed. 32.95 (*0-02-927725-6*, Free Press) Free Pr.

Voltaire's Bastards: The Dictatorship of Reason in the West. John R. Saul. LC 93-1296. 1993. pap. 16.00 (*0-679-74819-9*, Vin) Random.

Voltaire's Correspondence: An Epistolary Novel. Deidre Dawson. LC 92-35301. (Age of Revolution & Romanticism Ser.: Vol. 5). 190p. (C). 1994. text ed. 52.95 (*0-8204-2116-2*) P Lang Pubng.

Voltaire's Essay on Epic Poetry: A Study & Edition. Ed. by Florence White. LC 74-90363. 167p. 1970. reprint ed. 40.00 (*0-87753-044-0*) Phaeton.

Voltaire's Marginalia on the Pages of Rousseau: A Comparative Study of Ideas. George R. Havens. LC 68-762. (Studies in French Literature: No. 45). 1969. reprint ed. lib. bdg. 75.00 (*0-8383-0695-0*) M S G Haskell Hse.

Voltaire's Politics: The Poet As Realist. Peter Gay. LC 87-51375. 448p. (C). 1988. pap. 21.00 (*0-300-04095-4*) Yale U Pr.

Voltaire's Stylistic Transformation of Rabelaisian Satirical Devices. Ruth C. Flowers. LC 72-94182. (Catholic University of America. Studies in Romance Languages & Literatures: No. 41). 1969. reprint ed. 37.50 (*0-404-50341-1*) AMS Pr.

Voltaire's Visit to England, Seventeen Twenty-Six to Seventeen Twenty-Nine. Archibald Ballantyne. (Works of Archibald Ballantyne). 338p. 1985. reprint ed. lib. bdg. 49.00 (*0-685-10498-2*) Rprt Serv.

Voltairine de Cleyre: A Chronology. V. Munoz. Tr. by W. Scott Johnson. (Libertarian & Anarchist Chronology Ser.). 1979. lib. bdg. 59.95 (*0-8490-3036-6*) Gordon Pr.

Voltairomanie. Desfontaines. Ed. by M. H. Waddicor. (Exeter French Texts Ser.: No. 50). 127p. (FRE.). Date not set. pap. text ed. 19.95 (*0-85989-149-6*, Pub. by Univ Exeter Pr UK) Northwestern U Pr.

Voltammetric Determination of Molecules of Biological Significance. W. Franklin Smyth. LC 91-36594. 133p. 1992. text ed. 120.00 (*0-471-93345-7*) Wiley.

Voltammetric Methods in Brain Systems. Ed. by Alan A. Boulton et al. (Neuromethods Ser.: No. 27). (Illus.). 349p. 1995. 99.50 (*0-89603-312-0*) Humana.

***Voltammetric Sensors: Fundamentals & Applications in Environmental Chemistry.** 350p. 1997. 41.00 (*981-02-3002-8*) World Scientific Pub.

Voltammetry in the Neurosciences. Ed. by Joseph B. Justice, Jr. LC 86-20105. (Contemporary Neuroscience Ser.). 416p. 1987. 79.50 (*0-89603-103-9*) Humana.

Volterra & Functional Differential Equations. Ed. by Kenneth B. Hannsgen et al. (Lecture Notes in Pure & Applied Mathematics Ser.: Vol. 81). (Illus.). 352p. 1982. 140.00 (*0-8247-1721-X*) Dekker.

Volterra & Wiener Theories of Nonlinear Systems. Martin Schetzen. LC 88-31433. 592p. (C). 1989. reprint ed. lib. bdg. 67.50 (*0-89464-356-8*) Krieger.

Volterra-Hamilton Models in the Ecology & Evolution of Colonial Organisms. P. L. Antonelli & R. H. Bradbury. (Series in Mathematical Biology & Medicine: Vol. 2). 250p. 1996. text ed. 38.00 (*981-02-2450-8*, BMBae-B2922) World Scientific Pub.

Volterra Integral & Functional Equations. O. J. Staffans et al. (Encyclopedia of Mathematics & Its Applications Ser.: No. 34). 701p. (C). 1990. text ed. 130.00 (*0-521-37289-5*) Cambridge U Pr.

Volterra Integral Equations & Topological Dynamics. Richard K. Miller & George R. Sell. (Memoirs Ser.: No. 1/102). 67p. 1979. reprint ed. pap. 19.00 (*0-8218-1802-3*, MEMO/1/102) Am Math.

Volts to Hertz: The Rise of Electricity. Sanford P. Bordeau. LC 82-17702. (Illus.). 308p. 1982. write for info. (*0-8087-4908-0*) Burgess MN Intl.

Volume Analysis. Christopher Chaitow. 192p. 1996. 115.00 (*1-85573-192-4*, Pub. by Woodhead Pubng UK) Am Educ Systs.

Volume & File Structure of CD-ROM for Information Exchange: ANSI-NISO-ISO 9660. National Information Standards Organization Staff. LC 93-3113. 64p. (C). 1993. pap. 48.00 (*0-88738-936-8*) Transaction Pubs.

Volume & Open Interest: Classic Trading Strategies for 24-Hour Markets. 2nd rev. ed. Kenneth H. Shaleen. LC 96-22373. 304p. 1996. text ed. 50.00 (*0-7863-0988-1*) Irwin Prof Pubng.

Volume & Open Interest: Cutting Edge Trading Strategies in the Futures Markets. Kenneth H. Shaleen. 1991. text ed. 47.50 (*1-55738-114-3*) Irwin Prof Pubng.

Volume Cycles in the Stock Market: Market Timing Through Equivolume Charting. rev. ed. Richard W. Arms, Jr. (University Ser.). (Illus.). 148p. reprint ed. 39.95 (*1-885439-00-8*) Equis International.

Volume di Tutta L'Arte della Trombetta see Entire Art of Trumpet Playing

Volume Holography & Volume Gratings. L. Solymar & D. J. Cooke. LC 81-66394. 1981. text ed. 142.00 (*0-12-654580-4*) Acad Pr.

Volume Inequalities in the Geometry of Banach Spaces. Gilles Pisier. (Cambridge Tracts in Mathematics Ser.: No. 93). (Illus.). 224p. (C). 1989. text ed. 64.95 (*0-521-36465-5*) Cambridge U Pr.

Volume International Discography of the New Wave, Vol. 1. Ed. by B. George. (Illus.). 264p. (Orig.). (YA). (gr. 8 up). 1980. pap. 7.95 (*0-9605778-0-7*) One Ten Records.

Volume-International Discography of the New Wave, Vol. 2. Ed. by B. George & Martha DeFoe. (Illus.). 736p. 1982. pap. 12.95 (*0-7119-0050-7*) Omnibus Pr.

Volume of Consumer Instalment Credit, 1929-1938. Duncan M. Holthausen et al. (NBER Bulletin Ser.: No. 79). 1940. reprint ed. 20.00 (*0-685-61215-5*) Natl Bur Econ Res.

Volume of Consumer Instalment Credit, 1929-38. Duncan M. Holthausen et al. (Financial Research Program II: Studies in Consumer Installment Financing: No. 7). 157p. 1940. reprint ed. 40.90 (*0-87014-123-6*); reprint ed. mic. film 20.50 (*0-685-61213-9*) Natl Bur Econ Res.

Volume of Corporate Bond Financing since 1900. W. Braddock Hickman. (Financial Research Program V: Studies in Corporate Bond Financing: No. 1). 468p. 1953. reprint ed. 121.70 (*0-87014-145-7*) Natl Bur Econ Res.

Volume of Mortgage Debt in the Postwar Decade. Saul B. Klaman. (Technical Papers: No. 13). 159p. 1958. reprint ed. 41.40 (*0-87014-419-7*); reprint ed. mic. film 20.70 (*0-685-61318-6*) Natl Bur Econ Res.

Volume of Payments & the Informal Economy in the Netherlands 1965-82. W. C. Boeschoten & M. M. G. Fase. 1984. pap. text ed. 40.00 (*90-247-3095-3*) Kluwer Ac.

Volume of Residential Construction, 1889-1950. David M. Blank. (Technical Papers: No. 9). 111p. 1954. reprint ed. 28.90 (*0-87014-454-5*); reprint ed. mic. film 20.00 (*0-685-61298-8*) Natl Bur Econ Res.

Volume Reduction of Low-Activity Solid Wastes. (Technical Reports: No. 106). (Illus.). (Orig.). 1970. pap. 12.00 (*92-0-125170-X*, IDC106, Pub. by IAEA AU) Bernan Associates.

***Volume Transmission in the Brain: Novel Mechanisms for Neural Transmission.** Ed. by Kjell Fuxe & Luigi F. Agnati. LC 90-9171. (Advances in Neuroscience Ser.). reprint ed. pap. 177.90 (*0-608-04673-6*, 2065394) Bks Demand.

Volume 1 see Modern Chinese Medicine

Volume 1113 see United Nations Treaty Series

Volume 1119 see United Nations Treaty Series

Volume 1125 see United Nations Treaty Series

Volume 1126 see United Nations Treaty Series

Volume 1129 see United Nations Treaty Series

Volume 1137 see United Nations Treaty Series

Volume 1143 see United Nations Treaty Series

Volume 1144 see United Nations Treaty Series

Volume 1163 see United Nations Treaty Series

Volume 1187 see United Nations Treaty Series

Volume 1191 see United Nations Treaty Series

Volume 2 see Modern Chinese Medicine

Volume 3 see Modern Chinese Medicine

Volume 9. 1997. 561.00 (*90-04-10422-4*) E J Brill.

Volumen Quintum, Scholia ad Libros y Continens see Scholia Graeca in Homeri Iliadem: Scholia Vetera

Volumetric & Phase Behavior of Oil Field Hydrocarbon Systems. M. B. Standing. 150p. 1977. 30.00 (*0-89520-300-6*, 31606) Soc Petrol Engineers.

***Volumetric Image Analysis.** Gabriele Lohmann. text ed. write for info. (*0-471-97034-4*) Wiley.

Volumetric Leak Detection Methods for Underground Fuel Storage Tanks. Joseph W. Maresca, Jr. et al. LC 89-71008. (Pollution Technology Review Ser.: No. 180). (Illus.). 356p. 1990. 57.00 (*0-8155-1230-9*) Noyes.

***Volumetric Properties of Electrolyte Solutions: Estimation Methods & Experimental Data.** Georgiy G. Aseyev & Ivan D. Zaitsev. LC 96-27714. 1996. write for info. (*1-56700-072-X*) Begell Hse.

Volumezero. Ed. by David H. Bell. (Illus.). 76p. (Orig.). 1986. pap. 15.00 (*0-937919-00-4*) RPI Schl Arch.

Volumina Legum, 11 vols. reprint ed. Set. 1,100.00 (*0-318-23366-5*) Szwede Slavic.

Voluntad de Dios: Viviendo Vida Cristiana. Charles R. Swindoll. (Serie Realidades - Realities Ser.). 36p. (SPA.). 1989. pap. 1.79 (*0-945792-47-6*, 498104) Editorial Unilit.

Voluntad de Dios es Prosperidad. Gloria Copeland. Tr. by Copeland, Kenneth, Publications Staff. 123p. (Orig.). (SPA.). 1984. pap. 5.95 (*0-88114-314-6*) K Copeland Pubns.

Voluntad de Dios Para Usted. Gloria Copeland. Tr. by Copeland, Kenneth, Publications Staff. 170p. (Orig.). (SPA.). 1985. pap. 5.95 (*0-88114-312-X*) K Copeland Pubns.

Voluntarism in Organized Labor in the United States, 1930-40. George C. Higgins. LC 76-89737. (American Labor, from Conspiracy to Collective Bargaining Ser., No. 1: No. 1). 1971. reprint ed. 16.95 (*0-405-02126-7*) Ayer.

Voluntarism, Planning, & the State: The American Planning Experience, 1914-1946. Ed. by Jerold E. Brown & Patrick D. Reagan. LC 88-15462. (Contributions in American History Ser.: No. 130). 188p. 1988. text ed. 45.00 (*0-313-26177-6*, BVM/) Greenwood.

Voluntary Action & Development: Towards a Praxis for Non-Government Agencies. Rudolf C. Heredia. (C). 1988. 12.50 (*81-7022-164-1*, Pub. by Concept II) S Asia.

Voluntary Action & Social Policy in Northern Ireland. Ed. by Nicholas Acheson & Arthur Williamson. 224p. 1995. 55.95 (*1-85628-669-X*, Pub. by Avebury Pub UK) Ashgate Pub Co.

Voluntary Action in Education. Ed. by M. A. Muttalib. 256p. 1989. text ed. 27.50 (*81-207-0956-X*, Pub. by Sterling Pubs II) Apt Bks.

Voluntary Actions for Energy-Related CO2 Abatement. IEA Staff. (Energy & Environmental Policy Analysis Ser.). 160p. 1997. pap. 43.00 (*92-64-14657-1*, 61-97-11-1, Pub. by Org for Econ FR) OECD.

Voluntary & Detachments in Peace & War. Rupert Goodman. 231p. (C). 1990. 120.00 (*0-86439-117-X*, Pub. by Boolarong Pubns AT) St Mut.

***Voluntary Annual Report Disclosure by Listed Dutch Companies 1945-1983.** Kees Camfferman. LC 97-17768. (New Works in Accounting History Ser.). (Illus.). 392p. 1997. 68.00 (*0-8153-3011-1*) Garland.

Voluntary Approaches to Debt Relief. rev. ed. John Williamson. LC 88-8397. (Policy Analyses in International Economics Ser.: No. 25). 80p. (Orig.). 1989. pap. 10.95 (*0-88132-098-6*) Inst Intl Eco.

Voluntary Associations. Ed. by J. Roland Pennock & John W. Chapman. (Nomos Ser.: No. XI). 291p. 1969. text ed. 35.00 (*0-685-37877-2*) Lieber-Atherton.

Voluntary Associations: Perspectives on the Literature. Constance Smith & Anne Freedman. LC 72-75404. 264p. 1972. pap. 17.95 (*0-674-94310-4*) HUP.

Voluntary Associations: Socio-cultural Analyses & Theological Interpretation. James L. Adams. Ed. by J. Ronald Engel. LC 86-80304. 410p. 1986. text ed. 34.95 (*0-913552-34-8*); pap. text ed. 20.95 (*0-913552-35-6*) Exploration Pr.

Voluntary Associations among Mexican Americans in San Antonio, Texas: Organizational & Leadership Characteristics. John H. Lane, Jr. Ed. by Carlos E. Cortes. LC 76-1292. (Chicano Heritage Ser.). 1977. 20.95 (*0-405-09510-4*) Ayer.

Voluntary Associations & the Urban Public Life in Bengal. Sanyal Rajat. 1983. 16.50 (*0-8364-0980-9*, Pub. by Rddhi IA) S Asia.

***Voluntary Associations in the Ancient World.** John Kloppenborg & Stephen Wilson. 368p. (C). 1996. text ed. 74.95 (*0-415-13593-1*) Routledge.

Voluntary Compliance Resolution Program. 40p. 1992. pap. 10.00 (*0-685-67055-4*, 5486) Commerce.

Voluntary Controls. Jack Schwarz. pap. 8.95 (*0-525-48321-7*, Dutton) NAL-Dutton.

Voluntary Controls: Exercises for Creative Meditation & for Activating the Potential of the Chakras. Jack Schwarz. 1978. pap. 7.95 (*0-525-47494-3*, Dutton) NAL-Dutton.

Voluntary Corporate Liquidations. Ronald J. Kudla. LC 87-32282. 152p. 1988. text ed. 45.00 (*0-89930-275-0*, KCR/, Quorum Bks) Greenwood.

Voluntary Death in Japan. Maurice Pinguet. Tr. by Rosemary Morris from FRE. (Illus.). 360p. 1993. 30.95 (*0-7456-0870-1*) Blackwell Pubs.

Voluntary Disclosure. 300p. 1994. pap. 40.00 (*0-89707-344-4*, 539-0131) Amer Bar Assn.

Voluntary Euthanasia: A Comprehensive Bibliography. Gretchen Johnson. 318p. 1987. text ed. 10.00 (*0-9606030-6-9*) Hemlock Soc.

***Voluntary Euthenasia & the Common Law.** Margaret Otlowski. 650p. 1997. 135.00 (*0-19-825996-4*) OUP.

Voluntary Food Intake & Diet Selection in Farm Animals. J. M. Forbes. 544p. 1995. 115.00 (*0-85198-908-X*, Pub. by CAB Intntl UK) OUP.

Voluntary HIV Counseling & Testing: Facts, Issues & Answers. (Illus.). 33p. (Orig.). 1993. pap. text ed. 15.00 (*0-7881-0180-3*) DIANE Pub.

Voluntary Isolation of Control in a Natural Muscle Group. J. C. Barnes. Bd. with Psycho-Motor Norms for Practical Diagnosis. J. E. Wallin. ; Apparatus & Experiments on Sound Intensity. A. P. Weiss. ; No. 2. Wellesley College Studies in Psychology. Ed. by E. A. Gamble. ; Children's Association Frequency Tables. H. Woodrow. (Psychology Monographs General & Applied: Vol. 22). reprint ed. Set pap. 55.00 (*0-8115-1421-8*) Periodicals Srv.

Voluntary Mortification for Today. Alberto C. DoAmaral. 1988. 1.50 (*0-911988-91-2*, 51425) AMI Pr.

Voluntary Nonprofit Enterprise Management. David E. Mason. (Nonprofit Management & Finance Ser.). 206p. 1985. 52.50 (*0-306-41582-8*, Plenum Pr) Plenum.

Voluntary Political Government: Letters from Charles Lane. Charles Lane. LC 82-19787. 104p. (Orig.). 1982. pap. 5.95 (*0-9602574-3-8*) M E Coughlin.

Voluntary Principles in Conservation. Graham Cox et al. 180p. (C). 1991. text ed. 129.00 (*1-85341-041-1*, Pub. by Surrey Beatty & Sons AT) St Mut.

Voluntary Religion, Vol. 23. Ed. by W. J. Sheils & Diana Wood. (Ecclesiastical History Ser.: Vol. 23). 544p. 67.50 (*0-631-15054-4*) Boydell & Brewer.

***Voluntary Reporting of Greenhouse Gases.** 1997. lib. bdg. 250.95 (*0-8490-7719-2*) Gordon Pr.

***Voluntary Reporting of Greenhouse Gases (1995)** Arthur Rypinski. (Illus.). 75p. (Orig.). (C). 1997. pap. text ed. 30.00 (*0-7881-3730-1*) DIANE Pub.

Voluntary Sector in British Social Services. Maria Brenton. LC 85-4285. (Social Policy in Modern Britain Ser.). 278p. reprint ed. pap. 79.30 (*0-7837-1604-4*, 2041896) Bks Demand.

***Voluntary Sector in the U. K.** Jeremy Kendall. 1996. pap. 24.95 (*0-7190-5038-3*, Pub. by Manchester Univ Pr UK) St Martin.

***Voluntary Sector in the U. K.** Jeremy Kendall & Martin Knapp. 320p. 1996. 59.95 (*0-7190-5037-5*, Pub. by Manchester Univ Pr UK) St Martin.

Voluntary Sector, the State & Social Work in Britain: The Charity Organisation Society-Family Welfare Association since 1869. Jane Lewis. 200p. 1995. text ed. 70.00 (*1-85898-188-3*) E Elgar.

Voluntary Simplicity: A Lifestyle Option. Ruth Pestle. 1984. 4.00 (*0-911365-23-0*, A261-08460) Family & Consumer Sci Educ.

Voluntary Simplicity: Toward A Way of Life That Is Outwardly Simple, Inwardly Rich. Duane Elgin. LC 81-643. 1981. pap. 10.00 (*0-688-00322-2*, Quill) Morrow.

Voluntary Simplicity: Toward a Way of Life That Is Outwardly Simple, Inwardly Rich. rev. ed. Duane Elgin. LC 92-23740. 1993. pap. 10.00 (*0-688-12119-5*, Quill) Morrow.

Voluntary Social Service: Manpower Resources Research Paper. Adrian Webb et al. 1976. 22.00 (*0-317-05784-7*, Pub. by Natl Inst Soc Work) St Mut.

Voluntary Social Services: Financial Resources. Judith Unell. 1979. 22.00 (*0-317-05783-9*, Pub. by Natl Inst Soc Work) St Mut.

Voluntary Socialism. F. D. Tandy. 1973. 250.00 (*0-87700-083-2*) Revisionist Pr.

Voluntary Standard for Sliced Decorative Wood Face Veneer, DFV-1. 10p. 1988. 8.00 (*0-318-39802-8*) Hardwd Ply.

Voluntary Standard HPMA FE-86 - Voluntary Standard for Formaldehyde Emission from Hardwood Plywood Paneling, Wood Composition Board Wall Paneling & Industrial Panels Having Face Veneers. 3p. 1988. 5.00 (*0-318-23063-1*) Hardwd Ply.

Voluntary Tax? New Perspectives on Sophisticated Estate Tax Avoidance. George Cooper. LC 78-20853. (Studies of Government Finance). 115p. 1979. pap. 8.95 (*0-8157-1551-X*) Brookings.

Voluntary Tax Collections Process. Gregory A. Diggins. 132p. (Orig.). 1995. pap. text ed. 34.95 (*0-7811-0120-4*) Res Inst Am.

***Voluntary Temporary Relocation of Rural Disabled American Indians: An Investigation of Factors Contributing to Vocational Rehabilitation Outcome.** R. M. Schacht & S. A. Minkler. 109p. 1991. pap. text ed. write for info. (*1-888557-16-8*, 100105) No Ariz Univ.

***Voluntary Termination of Parental Rights (TPR) & Adoption: A Practical Handbook for Judges, Lawyers, & Human Services Providers.** Judith S. Newton. 275p. 1990. ring bd. 75.00 (*0-945574-28-2*) State Bar WI CLE Bk Div.

Voluntary Tutors in Adult Literacy: A Survey of Adult Literacy Volunteers in the Nottingham Area. Ed. by B. Elsey & M. Gibbs. (C). 1981. 35.00 (*0-902031-56-2*, Pub. by Univ Nottingham UK) St Mut.

Voluntary Tutors in Adult Literacy: A Survey of Adult Literacy Volunteers in the Nottingham Area. M. Gibbs. 67p. (C). 1981. text ed. 30.00 (*0-685-44256-X*, Pub. by Univ Nottingham UK) St Mut.

Voluntaryist Creed. Auberon Herbert. 1976. lib. bdg. 59.95 (*0-8490-2803-5*) Gordon Pr.

***Volunteer.** Carter Coleman. 1998. 24.00 (*0-446-52203-1*) Warner Bks.

Volunteer. Virginia B. Ricard. LC 84-90642. (Illus.). 107p. 1985. pap. 12.95 (*0-9613508-0-6*) V B Ricard.

Volunteer. Julie A. Waterman. 6p. (Orig.). 1984. pap. 1.25 (*0-943334-09-8*) Carmonelle Pubns.

Volunteer! The Comprehensive Guide to Voluntary Service in the U. S. & Abroad. rev. ed. 190p. 1995. pap. 12.95 (*1-882036-19-0*) Coun Intl Ed.

Volunteer America. 4th rev. ed. Harriet C. Kipps. LC 96-37431. 600p. pap. 39.95 (*0-89434-169-3*, F619) Ferguson.

Volunteer Army & Allied Intervention in South Russia, 1917-1921: A Study in the Politics & Diplomacy of the Russian Civil War. George A. Brinkley. LC 66-15501. (International Studies of the Committee on International Relations, University of Notre Dame). 464p. reprint ed. pap. 132.30 (*0-317-28870-9*, 2022077) Bks Demand.

Volunteer Choir. Samuel C. Brownstead & McCollam. 1987. 6.95 (*0-912405-37-6*) Pastoral Pr.

Volunteer Development Tool Box. Gail Moore & Marilyn MacKenzie. 1993. pap. 20.00 (*0-911029-41-9*) Heritage Arts.

Volunteer Fire Service Management. 198p. 1995. student ed., teacher ed. 155.00 incl. trans. (*0-614-09676-6*, AVA07338SS00CDL) Natl Tech Info.

Volunteer Fire Service Management, 10 bks., Set. 104p. 1995. student ed. 31.00 (*0-614-09677-4*, AVA07339BB00CDL) Natl Tech Info.

Volunteer Firefighter. Kenneth P. Marion. (Illus.). 32p. (J). (ps-2). 1990. pap. 4.00 (*0-945878-00-1*) JK Pub.

***Volunteer Forty-Niners: Tennesseans & the California Gold Rush.** Walter T. Durham. LC 97-21090. 1997. write for info. (*0-8265-1298-4*) Vanderbilt Univ Gean & Alexander.

Volunteer Handbook. 200p. 1991. 25.00 (0-317-05768-5, PB06) Natl Attys General.

Volunteer Handbook: How to Organize & Manage a Successful Organization. Richard V. Battle. LC 88-50078. 204p. 1992. pap. 12.95 (0-929174-01-1) Vol Concepts.

Volunteer Health Agencies & Volunteer Workers: Index of Modern Conditions & Progress. Garry D. Washburn. LC 94-34026. 1994. 44.50 (0-7883-0380-5); pap. 39.50 (0-7883-0381-3) ABBE Pubs Assn.

Volunteer Industry Involvement in Public Education. Samuel M. Burt & Leon Lessinger. LC 73-132557. 1970. 29.50 (0-89197-974-3) Irvington.

Volunteer Lawyers for the Poor: A Guide to Model Action Program. 68p. 1980. pap. 2.50 (0-317-03747-1, 32,493) NCLS Inc.

Volunteer Leader: Essays on the Role of Trustees of Nonprofit Facilities & Services for the Aging. Ed. by Deborah A. Cloud. LC 84-73168. 146p. 1985. pap. text ed. 15.00 (0-943774-24-1) Am Assn Homes.

***Volunteer Level.** 1993. teacher ed., ring bd. 70.00 (0-87322-413-2, ACEP0450) Human Kinetics.

***Volunteer Liability & Risk Management.** Ed. by Jill Muehreke. 104p. 1997. pap. 20.00 (0-614-30651-5) Soc Nonprofit Org.

Volunteer Management. Ed. by Jill Muehrcke. (Leadership Ser.). 75p. 1993. spiral bd. 20.00 (0-614-07107-0) Soc Nonprofit Org.

Volunteer Management: Mobilizing All the Resources of the Community. Steve McCurley & Rick Lynch. 236p. (Orig.). 1996. pap. 20.00 (0-911029-45-1) Heritage Arts.

Volunteer Management: Workshop Leader's Guide. Margie Morris & Jessie G. Stephens. 65p. (Orig.). 1991. ring bd. 14.95 (0-9620898-5-0) Newton-Cline.

Volunteer Management Handbook. Ed. by Tracy D. Connors. LC 95-12108. (Nonprofit Law, Finance & Management Ser.). 432p. 1995. text ed. 67.95 (0-471-10637-2) Wiley.

Volunteer Mentor: Training Program. Janet L. Walters et al. (Illus.). 96p. 1990. pap. text ed. 10.00 (1-878848-05-4); ring bd. 70.00 (1-878848-04-6) Natl Res Ctr.

Volunteer Mentor Training Program: To Promote Independent Living Skills in Young Adults Preparing to Leave Foster Care. Janet L. Walters et al. (Illus.). 296p. 1990. 75.00 (1-878848-03-8) Natl Res Ctr.

Volunteer Ministries: New Strategies for Today's Church. Margie Morris. 156p. (Orig.) 1990. pap. 15.95 (0-9620898-1-8) Newton-Cline.

Volunteer Ministries: New Strategies for Today's Church. Margie Morris. 152p. (Orig.) 1991. reprint ed. pap. 12.95 (0-9620898-7-7) Newton-Cline.

Volunteer Missions Opportunities for Senior Adults. Naomi R. Hunke. Ed. by Susan Hansen. 104p. (Orig.). 1994. pap. text ed. 6.95 (1-56309-105-4) Womans Mission Union.

Volunteer Moments: Vignettes of the History of the University of Tennessee. Milton M. Klein et al. xii, 231p. 1994. pap. 14.98 (0-9642219-0-X) U TN Ofc U Relations.

Volunteer Moments: Vignettes of the History of the University of Tennessee, 1794-1994. 2nd ed. Milton M. Klein. LC 96-18651. 1996. write for info. (0-9642219-2-6) U TN Ofc U Relations.

Volunteer Program Administration: A Handbook for Museums & Other Cultural Institutions. Joan Kuyper. LC 93-8177. 160p. (Orig.). 1993. pap. 16.95 (0-915400-95-2, ACA Bks) Am Council Arts.

Volunteer Programs That Work. Margie Morris. (Orig.). 1992. pap. write for info. (0-9620898-3-4) Newton-Cline.

Volunteer Recognition Skit Kit. Arlene Grubbs & Evelyn Levine. Ed. by Susan J. Ellis. LC 92-82928. (Volunteer Energy Ser.). (Illus.). 124p. 1992. ring bd. 24.75 (0-940576-13-9) Energize.

Volunteer Recruiting & Retention: A Marketing Approach. rev. ed. Nancy Macduff. Ed. by Janie Millgard. (Illus.). 196p. (C). 1995. pap. 33.00 (0-945795-00-9) MBA Pub.

***Volunteer Recruitment Book.** 2nd ed. Susan J. Ellis. (Illus.). 144p. (Orig.). 1996. pap. 18.75 (0-940576-18-X) Energize.

Volunteer Screening: An Audio Workbook. Nancy Macduff. 24p. 1996. wbk. ed., pap. 12.00 incl. audio (0-945795-11-4) MBA Pub.

Volunteer Services Department in a Health Care Institution. 2nd rev. ed. American Hospital Association Staff. LC 88-37456. 56p. 1988. pap. 14.00 (0-87258-493-3, 202166) Am Hospital.

Volunteer Slavery. Jill Nelson. 1994. 15.00 (1-57042-207-9) Warner Bks.

Volunteer Slavery: My Authentic Negro Experience. Jill Nelson. LC 92-51078. 243p. 1993. 21.95 (1-879360-24-1) Noble Pr.

Volunteer Slavery: My Authentic Negro Experience. Jill Nelson. 256p. 1994. pap. 9.95 (0-14-023716-X, Penguin Bks) Viking Penguin.

Volunteer Soldier of America, with Memoir of the Author & Military Reminiscences from General Logan's Private Journal. John A. Logan. Ed. by Richard H. Kohn. LC 78-22385. (American Military Experience Ser.). (Illus.). 1980. reprint ed. lib. bdg. 55.95 (0-405-11861-9) Ayer.

Volunteer State Battlewagon: USS Tennessee, BB-43. Myron J. Smith, Jr. LC 91-60427. (Illus.). 56p. (Orig.). 1992. pap. 7.95 (0-929521-27-7) Pictorial Hist.

Volunteer Trails: A Program of Visual Aids for the Study of Tennessee. William R. Majors. (Illus.). 80p. 1980. 20.00 (0-939710-06-4) Meridional Pubns.

Volunteer Training Curriculum. National Hospice Organization Staff. Ed. by Ira J. Bates & Katherine E. Brandt. 147p. 1990. ring bd. 45.00 (0-931207-06-1) Natl Hospice.

Volunteer Tutor's Toolbox. Ed. by Beth Ann Herrmann. 156p. 1994. pap. 15.75 (0-87207-394-7) Intl Reading.

***Volunteer Vacations: Short-Term Adventures That Will Benefit You & Others.** 6th rev. ed. Bill McMillon. (Illus.). 480p. 1997. pap. 16.95 (1-55652-314-9) Chicago Review.

Volunteer Youth Workers: Recruiting & Developing Leaders for Youth Ministry. J. David Stone & Rose M. Miller. 75p. (Orig.). 1992. reprint ed. pap. text ed. 6.95 (1-882745-02-7) YMTN-Stone.

Volunteering in Ethiopia: A Peace Corps Odyssey. James W. Skelton, Jr. LC 91-72041. (Illus.). 352p. (Orig.). 1991. pap. 7.95 (0-9616108-6-7) Beaumont Bks.

Volunteering in New York City: Your Guide to Working Small Miracles in the Big Apple. Richard Mintzer. LC 95-43161. 176p. (Orig.). 1996. pap. 10.95 (0-8027-7481-4) Walker & Co.

Volunteering with Your Pet: How to Get Involved in Animal-Assisted Therapy with Any Kind of Pet. Mary R. Burch. LC 95-38944. (Illus.). 224p. 1996. 19.95 (0-87605-791-1) Howell Bk.

Volunteerism: The Directory of Organizations, Training, Programs & Publications, 1990-91. 3rd ed. Ed. by Harriet C. Kipps. 1164p. 1991. 119.00 (0-8352-2739-1) Bowker.

Volunteerism & the Older Adult. Mary Kouri. LC 90-43056. (Choices & Challenges Ser.). 197p. 1990. lib. bdg. 45.00 (0-87436-562-7) ABC-CLIO.

Volunteerism & World Development: Pathway to a New World. Allen Jedlicka. LC 89-49173. 192p. 1990. text ed. 45.00 (0-275-93241-9, C3241, Praeger Pubs) Greenwood.

Volunteerism in Geriatric Settings. Ed. by Vera R. Jackson. LC 95-51301. 106p. 1996. 29.95 (1-56024-790-8) Haworth Pr.

Volunteers. Armand Lauffer & Sarah Gorodezky. LC 77-9003. (Sage Human Services Guides Ser.: No. 5). 87p. 1977. reprint ed. pap. 25.00 (0-608-01518-0, 2059562) Bks Demand.

Volunteers: America's Hidden Resource. Rosalie R. King & Jacquelyn Fluke. LC 89-35500. 152p. (Orig.). (C). 1990. pap. text ed. 16.00 (0-8191-7538-2); lib. bdg. 37.00 (0-8191-7537-4) U Pr of Amer.

***Volunteers: Firefighters.** unabridged ed. Jack Hedger, pseud. (Illus.). (J). 1994. 19.95 (1-882416-01-5) Akela West Pubs.

Volunteers: Means & Ends in a National Organization. David L. Sills. Ed. by Harriet Zuckerman & Robert K. Merton. LC 79-9027. (Dissertations on Sociology Ser.). 1980. reprint ed. lib. bdg. 31.95 (0-405-12994-7) Ayer.

Volunteers: The Organizational Behavior of Unpaid Workers. Jone L. Pearce. LC 92-36057. (People & Organizations Ser.). 256p. (C). (gr. 13). 1993. text ed. 45.00 (0-415-09427-5, Routledge NY) Routledge.

Volunteers: The Organizational Behaviour of Unpaid Workers. Jone L. Pearce. (People & Organizations Ser.). 288p. 1993. 39.95 (0-04-445098-2, A8219) Routledge.

Volunteer's Adventures: A Union Captain's Record of the Civil War. John W. De Forest. Ed. by James H. Croushore. LC 95-50684. (Illus.). 256p. (C). 1996. reprint ed. pap. 11.95 (0-8071-2084-7) La State U Pr.

Volunteers & Voc Ed. Douglas S. Katz. 38p. 1984. 4.25 (0-318-22247-7, IN271) Ctr Educ Trng Employ.

Volunteers for Mental Health. Ed. by Philip Ash. LC 73-10368. 1973. 28.00 (0-8422-5121-9) Irvington.

Volunteer's for Union & Liberty: History of the 5th Tennessee Infantry, U. S. A. 1862-1865. Robert K. Cannon. LC 95-75454. (Illus.). 428p. 1995. 39.95 (1-877791-06-7) Bohemian Brigade.

***Volunteers Handbook: Stories, Stats & Stuff about Tennessee Football.** Ward Gossett. (Illus.). 160p. (Orig.). 1996. pap. 9.95 (1-880652-76-5) Wichita Eagle.

Volunteers in Action. Brian O'Connell & Ann B. O'Connell. LC 89-1472. 1989. 24.95 (0-87954-291-8); pap. 19.95 (0-87954-292-6) Foundation Ctr.

Volunteers in Catholic Schools: An Administrator's Guide to Legal Considerations. Mary A. Shaughnessy. 49p. (Orig.). 1993. pap. 6.50 (1-55833-093-3) Natl Cath Educ.

Volunteers in Child Health: Management, Selection, Training & Supervision. Arlene Keily. 225p. 1992. pap. 27.50 (0-937821-72-1) Assn Care Child.

Volunteers in Leisure: A Management Perspective. Ted Tedrick & Karla Henderson. (Illus.). 167p. (Orig.). 1989. pap. 15.00 (0-88314-436-0, A4360) AAHPERD.

Volunteers in Museums & Heritage Organisations. 96p. 1991. pap. 18.00 (0-11-290491-2, HM2777, Pub. by Stationery Ofc UK) Bernan Associates.

Volunteers in Public Schools. Committee on the Use of Volunteers in Schools, National Research Council Staff. 160p. 1990. pap. text ed. 14.95 (0-309-04149-X) Natl Acad Pr.

Volunteers in Research & Testing. Ed. by Raid Ayesh & Anthony Hubbard. 256p. 1996. 89.95 (0-7484-0397-3) Taylor & Francis.

Volunteers in the Criminal Justice System. Gill & R. I. Mawby. 1990. 90.00 (0-335-15880-3, Open Univ Pr); pap. 32.00 (0-335-15879-X, Open Univ Pr) Taylor & Francis.

Volunteers in the Small Library. Rashelle S. Karp. LC 93-10823. (Small Libraries Publications: No. 20). 1993. 5.00 (0-8389-5756-0) ALA.

Volunteers of Geva. Laurence Vershel. 37p. 1986. 21.00 (0-7223-1969-X, Pub. by A H S Ltd UK) St Mut.

Volunteers Plus Votes Equal Victory: A Resource Manual for Volunteer Program Management of Election Campaigns. Midge Cullis. 150p. 1989. pap. 10.00 (0-9624539-0-0) Diakonos Pubns.

Volunteer's Survival Manual: The Only Practical Guide to Giving Your Time & Money. Darcy C. Devney. (Illus.). 192p. (Orig.). 1992. pap. 15.95 (0-9630686-9-5) Prctcl Pr MA.

Volunteers Teaching Children: A Guide for Establishing VINE Ecology Education Programs. rev. ed. Karen S. Hollweg. (Illus.). 232p. 1995. pap. 17.00 (1-884008-18-6) NAAEE.

***Voluptatem Spectandi Non Perdat Sed Mutet.** J. W. Salomonson. (Verhandelingen der Koninklijke Nederlandse Akademie van Wetenschappen, Afd. Letterkunde, Nieuwe Reeks Ser.: No. 98). 104p. 1979. pap. text ed. 37.50 (0-7204-8458-8) Elsevier.

Volupte. Charles-Augustin Sainte-Beuve. (Folio Ser.: No. 1755). 384p. (FRE.). 1969. 15.95 (2-07-037755-5) Schoenhof.

Volupte: The Sensual Man. Charles-Augustin Sainte-Beuve. Tr. by Marilyn G. Rose. LC 94-38657. 288p. 1995. text ed. 59.50 (0-7914-2451-0); pap. text ed. 19.95 (0-7914-2452-9) State U NY Pr.

Voluptuario. Illus. by Brian Nissen. LC 95-40907. 128p. (ENG & SPA.). 1996. 50.00 (0-312-14063-0) St Martin.

Voluptuous Yearnings: A Feminist Theory of the Obscene. Mary Caputi. (New Feminist Perspectives Ser.). 144p. (Orig.). (C). 1994. pap. text ed. 19.95 (0-8476-7886-5); lib. bdg. 49.50 (0-8476-7885-7) Rowman.

Volver. Maria G. Carbonell. (Coleccion Espejo de Paciencia). (Illus.). 122p. (Orig.). (SPA.). 1980. pap. 5.95 (0-89729-290-1) Ediciones.

***Volver a Empezar - To Begin Again, Vol. 422.** Stephanie Howard. (Harlequin Bianca Ser.). (SPA.). 1997. mass mkt. 3.50 (0-373-33422-2, 1-33422-6) Harlequin Bks.

***Volver a Tus Brazos - To Come Back to Your Arms.** Lynsey Stevens. (SPA.). 1997. mass mkt. 3.50 (0-373-33416-8, 1-33416-8) Harlequin Bks.

***Volver Al Ser: Un Acercamiento a la Poetica de Octavio Paz.** Mario V. Pinho. (Wor(l)ds of Change Ser.: Vol. 5). 144p. (SPA.). (C). 1997. text ed. 36.95 (0-8204-2458-7) P Lang Pubng.

Volvo Gothenburg Sweden. Christer Olsson. (Illus.). 256p. 1995. 59.95 (3-907150-58-9, Pub. by Norden SZ) Motorbooks Intl.

Volvo Guide to Halls of Fame: The Traveler's Handbook of North America's Most Inspiring & Entertaining Attractions. Paul Dickson & Robert Skole. (Illus.). 256p. (Orig.). 1995. pap. 12.95 (1-879326-26-4) Living Planet Pr.

Volvo Stern Drives 1968-1993. 7th ed. (Illus.). 1994. reprint ed. pap. 34.95 (0-89287-638-7, B770) Clymer Pub.

***Volvo Stern Drives 1994-1996.** (Illus.). Date not set. reprint ed. pap. 34.95 (0-89287-684-0, B771) Intertec Pub.

Volvo 1970-89. Chilton Staff. (Total Car Care Ser.). 1996. pap. 22.95 (0-8019-8786-5) Chilton.

Volvo 1970-89: Repair & Tune-Up Guide. Chilton Automotives Editorial Staff. LC 88-43188. (Illus.). 512p. 1989. pap. text ed. 16.95 (0-8019-7944-7) Chilton.

Volvo, 1990-93. Chilton Automotives Editorial Staff. 432p. 1994. pap. 21.95 (0-8019-8428-9) Chilton.

***Volvo 240 Series 1976-93.** (Automobile Repair Manuals Ser.). (Illus.). pap. 16.95 (1-56392-136-7, MBI 105097AM) Haynes Pubns.

Volvo 240 Service Manual 1983 Through 1993. Bently Robert. 1993. 49.95 (0-8376-0285-8) Bentley.

***Volvox: Molecular Genetic Origins of Multicellularity & Cellular Differentiation.** David L. Kirk. (Developmental & Cell Biology Ser.: Vol. 33). (Illus.). 384p. (C). 1997. text ed. 80.00 (0-521-45207-4) Cambridge U Pr.

VOM & DVM Multitesters for the Hobbyist & Technician. Alvis J. Evans. (Illus.). 144p. 1992. pap. 14.95 (0-7906-1031-0) Prompt Publns.

Vom Attischen Menschenbild & Arete und Tragisches Bewusstheit Bei Sophokles und Herodot, 2 Vols. Franz Egermann. Ed. by Gregory Vlastos. LC 78-14613. (Morals & Law in Ancient Greece Ser.). (GER & GRE.). 1979. reprint ed. lib. bdg. 23.95 (0-405-11588-1) Ayer.

Vom Aussern Proletariat Zum Kulturtrager Ein Aspekt Zur Rolle der Germanen in der Spantantike. Gerhard Dobesch. 141p. (GER.). 1994. pap. 54.00 (90-256-1039-0, Pub. by A M Hakkert NE) Benjamins North Am.

Vom Baum Zum Tisch see From Tree to Table

Vom Bilde des Absoluten: Grundzuege der Phaenomenologie Fichtes. Wolfgang Janke. xi, 569p. (GER.). (C). 1993. lib. bdg. 175.40 (3-11-013994-2) De Gruyter.

Vom Bilde Zum Buchstaben: Die Entstehungsgeschichte der Schrift. Kurt Sethe. (Untersuchungen Zur Geschichte und Altertumskunde Agyptens Ser.: Vol. XII). vi, 83p. 1964. reprint ed. write for info. (3-487-05405-1) G Olms Pubs.

***Vom Christentum Aus: Aufsatze und Vortrage Zur Religionsphilosophie.** Ed. by H. J. Adriaanse. (Studies in Philosophical Theology: Vol. 13). 322p. 1995. pap. 43.00 (90-390-0207-X, Pub. by KOK Pharos NE) Eisenbrauns.

Vom Einheitsstaat zum Driegliedrigen Sozialen Organismus see Social Issues: Meditative Thinking & the Threefold Social Order

Vom Eis Zum Regen see From Ice to Rain

***Vom Elend des Menschlichen Daseins.** Lotario De Segni. (Philosophische Texte und Studien: Vol. 24). x, 108p. (GER.). 1990. write for info. (3-487-09232-8) G Olms Pubs.

Vom Erdol Zum Benzin see From Oil to Gasoline

Vom Erz Zum Loffel see From Ore to Spoon

Vom Gesichtspunkt der Phanomenologie, No. II. Rudolph Boehm. (Phaenomenologica Ser.: No. 83). vii, 262p. 1981. lib. bdg. 112.00 (90-247-2415-5, Pub. by M Nijhoff NE) Kluwer Ac.

Vom Gesichtspunkt der Phanomenologie Husserl - Studien. Rudolph Boehm. (Phaenomenologica Ser.: No. 26). 1968. pap. text ed. 55.00 (90-247-0258-5) Kluwer Ac.

Vom Gras Zur Butter see From Grass to Butter

***Vom Halys Zum Euphrat.** Ed. by Ursula Magen & Mahmoud Rashad. 311p. 1996. 92.00 (3-927120-41-3, Pub. by Ugarit-Verlag GW) Eisenbrauns.

Vom Judischen Kriege, Buch 1-4. Josephus Flavius. 512p. 1979. reprint ed. write for info. (3-487-06712-9) G Olms Pubs.

Vom Kern Zur Birne see From Seed to Pear

Vom Korn Zum Brot see From Grain to Bread

Vom Lebendigen Gott see Living God

Vom Lehm Zum Ziegel see From Clay to Bricks

Vom Leiden Zur Lehre: Der Dritte Redegang (Hiob 21-27) und die Redaktionsgeschichte des Hiobbuches. Markus Witte. (Beihefte zur Zeitschrift fuer die Alttestamentliche Wissenschaft Ser.: Vol. 230). xi, 333p. (GER.). (C). 1994. lib. bdg. 126.15 (3-11-014375-5) De Gruyter.

Vom Losen Mathematischer Aufgaben-Einsicht und Entdeckung, Lernen und Lehren, Vol. I. 2nd ed. George Polya. (Science & Civilization Ser.: No. 20). (Illus.). 315p. (GER.). 1980. 84.00 (0-8176-1101-0) Birkhauser.

Vom Losen Mathematischer Aufgaben-Einsicht und Entdeckung, Lernen und Lehren, Vol. II. George Polya. (Science & Civilization Ser.: No. 21). (Illus.). 286p. (GER.). 1980. 76.00 (0-8176-0298-4) Birkhauser.

***Vom Mesopotamischen Menschen der Altbabylonischen Zeit & Seiner Welt.** F. R. Kraus. (Mededelingen der Koninklijke Nederlandse Akademie van Wetenschappen, Afd. Letterkunde Ser.: No. 36(6)). 106p. 1973. pap. text ed. 45.00 (0-7204-8249-6) Elsevier.

Vom Mittelmeer Zum Persischen Golf Durch Den Hauran, die Syrische Wuste und Mesopotamien, 2 vols. Max F. Von Oppenheim. (Illus.). 768p. reprint ed. write for info. (0-318-71547-3) G Olms Pubs.

Vom Modernen Roman zur Antiken Tragodie: Interpretation von Max Frischs "HomoFaber" Manfred Leber. (Quellen und Forschungen zur Sprach und Kulturgeschichte der Germanischen Voelker Ser.). xii, 201p. (C). 1990. lib. bdg. 80.00 (3-11-012240-5) De Gruyter.

Vom Morphem Zum Textem - From Morpheme to Texteme: Essays to Structural Text Analysis & Literary Scholarship. Walter A. Koch. (Studia Semiotica, Series Practica: Vol. 1). 258p. (Orig.). 1969. pap. 12.87 (0-685-66487-2, 05102476) G Olms Pubs.

Vom Mythos Zum Logos: Die Selbstentfaltung Des Griechischen Denkens Von Homer Bis Auf Die Sophistik und Sokrates. Wilhelm Nestle. Ed. by Kees W. Bolle. LC 77-79147. (Mythology Ser.). (GER.). 1978. reprint ed. lib. bdg. 50.95 (0-405-10556-8) Ayer.

Vom Obst Zur Marmelade see From Fruit to Jam

***Vom Orthodoxen Judentum in Deutschland Zwischen Zwei Weltkriegen.** Yehuda Ben-Avner. vi, 100p. (GER.). 1987. write for info. (3-487-07969-0) G Olms Pubs.

Vom Sand Zum Glas see From Sand to Glass

Vom Schaf Zum Schal see From Sheep to Scarf

Vom Sofakissen Zum Stadtebau. K. P. Arnold. 516p. 1992. text ed. 148.00 (3-364-00252-5) Gordon & Breach.

***Vom Stadtforum Zum Forum der Stadt: Entwicklung und Perspektiven des Stadtforums Berlin.** Ed. by Heinz Kleger et al. (Europaische Urbanitat-Politik der Stadte Ser.). (GER.). 1996. text ed. 56.00 (90-5708-009-5); pap. text ed. 25.00 (90-5708-010-9) Gordon & Breach.

Vom Symptom zur Diagnose. 8th ed. Ed. by N. Zoellner & W. Hadorn. (Illus.). x, 682p. 1986. 99.25 (3-8055-4030-2) S Karger.

Vom Trummerfilm Zur Traumfabrik. Peter Stettner. (Studien Zur Filmageschichte Ser.: Bd. 8). 231p. (GER.). 1992. write for info. (3-487-09675-7) G Olms Pubs.

Vom Umgang mit der Anthroposophie see Working with Anthroposophy

***Vom Willen zur Macht: Anthropologie und Metaphysik der Macht am Exemplarischen Fall Friedrich Nietzsches.** Volker Gerhardt. (Monographien und Texte Zur Nietzsche-Forschung Ser.: Vol. 34). xiv, 372p. (GER.). (C). 1996. lib. bdg. 146.70 (3-11-012801-2) De Gruyter.

Von Agedal Bis Malt: Die Skandinavischen Runeninschriften Vom Ende Des 5. Bis Ende Des 9. Jahrhunderts, Bd. 11. Thomas Birkmann. (Ergaenzungsbaende zum Reallexikon der Germanischen Alterrumskunde: Vol. 12). xi, 418p. (GER.). 1995. lib. bdg. 176.95 (3-11-014510-3) De Gruyter.

Von Babel zum Zion. Juergen Van Oorschot. (Beihefte zur Zeitschrift fuer die Alttestamentliche Wissenschaft Ser.: Bd 206). x, 360p. (GER.). (C). 1993. lib. bdg. 121.55 (3-11-013606-6) De Gruyter.

***Von Balthasar Reader.** Kehl & Loser. 49.95 (0-567-09343-3, Pub. by T & T Clark UK) Bks Intl VA.

***Von Balthasar Reader.** Ed. by Medard Kehl & Werner Loser. 456p. 1997. pap. 24.95 (0-8245-1652-4) Crossroad NY.

Von Balthasar Reader. rev. ed. Hans U. Von Balthasar. Ed. by Medard Kehl & Werner Loser. 456p. 1997. reprint ed. pap. 24.95 (0-8245-0720-7, Crossrd Herd) Crossroad NY.

Von Bek. Michael Moorcock. (Eternal Champion Ser.: Vol. 2). 1995. 19.99 (1-56504-177-1, 12503) White Wolf.

Von Bek Vol. 2: The Eternal Champion, 15 vols., Set. Michael Moorcock. (Eternal Champion Ser.). (Illus.). 600p. (YA). 1996. reprint ed. pap. 14.99 (1-56504-192-5, 12518, Borealis) White Wolf.

Von Bismarck zu Hitler see Ailing Empire: Germany from Bismarck to Hitler

U V

Von Bruning Zu Hitler: Der Wandel Des Politischen Systems in Deutschland. Gerhard Schulz. (Zwischen Demokratie und Diktatur Ser.: Bd. 111). xvi, 1102p. (GER.). (C). 1992. lib. bdg. 306.15 (*3-11-013525-6*) De Gruyter.

Von Cassiodor zu Dante: Ausgewaehlte Aufsaetze Zur Geschichtsschreibung und Politischen Ideenwelt des Mittelalters. Heinz Loewe. LC 73-75491. 342p. (C). 1973. 142.30 (*3-11-003739-4*) De Gruyter.

Von Cinggis Khan zur Sowjetrepublik: Eine kurze Geschichte der Mongolei unter besonderer Beruecksichtigung der neuesten Zeit. Iwan J. Korostovetz & Erich Hauer. (Illus.). 351p. (C). 1974. reprint ed. 223.10 (*3-11-002497-7*) De Gruyter.

*__Von Demokrit Bis Dante.__ Gotthard Strohmaier. (Olms Studien: Vol. 43). 400p. (GER.). 1995. write for info. (*3-487-10030-4*) G Olms Pubs.

Von Den Deutschen Tugenden: Zwei Vortrage am AICGS. Peter Wapnewski & Manfred Stassen. 21p. (Orig.). (GER.). 1994. pap. text ed. 7.00 (*0-942017-17-X*) Amer Assn Teach German.

Von Den ersten und letzten Dingen: Studien und Kommentar zu einer Aphorismenreihe von Friedrich Nietzsche. Peter Heller. (Monographien und Texte zur Nietzscge-Forschung Ser.: Vol. 1). (C). 1972. 146.15 (*3-11-003943-5*) De Gruyter.

Von Den Kirchenvatern Zu Karl Barth: Das Altkirkliche Dogma in der "Kerchlichen Dogmatik" E. P. Meijering. 513p. (GER.). 1993. pap. 80.00 (*90-5063-126-6*, Pub. by Gieben NE) Benjamins North Am.

Von den Staufern zu den Habsburgern: Aufloesung des Reiches und Emporkommen der Landesstaaten (1250 bis 1519) 3rd ed. Johannes Haller & Heinrich Dannenbauer. (Sammlung Goeschen Ser.: No. 1077). (C). 1970. 6.00 (*3-11-002892-1*) De Gruyter.

Von der Baumwolle Zur Hose see From Cotton to Pants

*__Von der Koppel Bis Zur Kapriole.__ Waldemar Seunig. (Documenta Hippologica Ser.). 368p. (GER.). 1996. reprint ed. write for info. (*3-487-08348-5*) G Olms Pubs.

Von der Mannigfachen Bedeutung des Seienden Nach Aristoteles. Franz Brentano. x, 220p. 1983. reprint ed. 40.00 (*3-487-00010-5*) G Olms Pubs.

Von der Milch zum Speiseeis see From Milk to Ice Cream

Von der Narration zur Deskription: Generative Textkonstitution bei Jean Ricardou, Claude Simon und Philippe Sollers. Beeke Dummer. (B. A. S. L. Ser.: Vol. 14). 219p. (GER.). 1988. 38.00 (*90-6032-220-7*, Pub. by B R Gruener NE) Benjamins North Am.

Von der Natur Nicht Vorgesehen. Autobiographisches. Hilde Domin. 192p. (GER.). 1993. pap. 11.75 (*3-596-12203-1*, Pub. by Fischer Taschbch Verlag GW) Intl Bk Import.

Von der Raupe Zum Schmetterling see From Egg to Butterfly

Von der RingstraBe zur 72nd Street. Jimmy Bergs Chansons aus dem Wien der dreiBiger Jahre und dem New Yorker Exil, Vol. 17. Jimmy Berg. Ed. by Horst Jarka. (Austrian Culture Ser.). 336p. (C). 1995. 59.95 (*0-8204-2694-6*) P Lang Pubng.

Von der "Store Front Church" Zum "American Dream" James Baldwin und der Amerikanische Rassenkonflikt. Peter Bruck. (Bochum Studies in English: No. 2). (Illus.). viii, 147p. (Orig.). (GER.). 1975. pap. 26.00 (*90-6032-056-5*, Pub. by B R Gruener NE) Benjamins North Am.

Von Dresden Nach Dresden. R. Gilsenbach. 24p. (GER.). 1992. text ed. 30.00 (*3-364-00219-3*) Gordon & Breach.

Von Eudoxos zu Aristoteles: Das Fortwirken der Eudoxischen Proportionentheorie in der Aristotelischen vom Kontinuum. Hans-Joachim Waschkies. 454p. (GER.). 1977. 50.00 (*90-6032-086-7*, Pub. by B R Gruener NE) Benjamins North Am.

Von Frueh an Fit Mit Nico's Kinderkueche. 2nd ed. Olli Leeb. (Illus.). 77p. (GER.). (J). 1990. 17.25 (*3-921799-87-2*, Pub. by Olli Leeb GW) Lubrecht & Cramer.

*__Von Gerkan, Marg & Partner: Architecture for Transportation.__ Meinhard Von Gerkan. (Illus.). 264p. 1997. pap. 69.00 (*3-7643-5611-1*) Birkhauser.

*__Von Gerkan, Marg & Partner: New Leipzig Fair.__ Volkwin Marg. LC 96-46683. (Illus.). 192p. 1997. 56.00 (*3-7643-5429-1*) Birkhauser.

Von Gerkan, Marg & Partners. Academy Editions Staff. 1993. 65.00 (*1-85490-166-4*) Academy Ed UK.

Von Gerkan, Marg und Partner: Architecture, 1991-1995. Meinhard Von Gerkan. (GER.). 1995. write for info. (*0-8176-5222-1*); write for info. (*3-7643-5222-1*) Birkhauser.

Von Guten und Boesen Nachbaurn see Saemtliche Werke

Von Hennig-Schara Gambit. Eric Schiller. 103p. (Orig.). 1992. pap. 8.95 (*0-945470-20-7*) Chess Ent.

*__Von Horaz Bis Hrotsvith von Gandersheim.__ Paul Von Winterfeld. (Spolia Berolinensia Ser.: Bd. 6). (GER.). 1996. write for info. (*3-615-00148-6*) G Olms Pubs.

Von Hyder Faction. Richard J. Johnson. LC 93-92779. 184p. (Orig.). 1994. pap. 7.95 (*1-56002-378-3*, Univ Edtns) Aegina Pr.

Von Kleist: From Hussar to Panzer Marshal. C. R. Davis. LC 79-90615. (Illus.). 112p. 1979. pap. 9.95 (*0-935856-00-5*) Lancer.

Von Kuerenberg: Edition, Notes, & Commentary. Gayle Agler-Beck. (German Language & Literature Monographs: No. 4). xix, 230p. 1978. 52.00 (*90-272-0964-2*) Benjamins North Am.

Von Manstein's Winter Campaign in Southern Russia: Between the Don & the Donets, November 1942 - March 1943. Dana V. Sadarananda. LC 89-16261. 192p. 1990. text ed. 55.00 (*0-275-93440-3*, C3440, Praeger Pubs) Greenwood.

Von Neumann Regular Rings. 2nd ed. K. R. Goodearl. LC 91-19765. 430p. (C). 1991. lib. bdg. 51.50 (*0-89464-632-X*) Krieger.

Von Pope zu Pop, Kunst im Zeitalter von Xerox. Hugh Kenner. 222p. 1995. text ed. 15.00 (*3-364-00310-6*) Gordon & Breach.

Von Reck's Voyage: Drawings & Journal of Philip Georg Friedrich Von Reck. Ed. by Kristian Hvidt. (Illus.). 144p. 1990. 40.00 (*0-88322-002-4*) Beehive GA.

*__Von Richthofen: The Legend Evaluated.__ Richard T. Bickers. (Illus.). 200p. 1997. 27.95 (*1-55750-571-3*) Naval Inst Pr.

*__Von Schneckenhaus bis Adlerhorst: Interdependenzen Zwischen Lebensstil und Wohnungseinrichtung.__ Monika Kritzmoller. (Europaische Hochschulschriften, Reihe 6: Bd. 559). 356p. (GER.). 1996. 57.95 (*3-631-30667-9*) P Lang Pubng.

Von Serbien: Kroatien und das Skandinavische Modell. 2nd ed. Margaret S. Omrcanin. Tr. by Hans P. Rullman. 100p. (GER.). 1990. pap. 7.00 (*1-878716-02-6*) Ivor Pr.

*__Von Taras Sevcenko Bis Joseph Roth: Ukrainisch-Osterreichische Literaturbeziehungen.__ Wolfgang Kraus & Dmytro Zatons'kyi. (GER.). 1995. 62.95 (*3-906753-87-5*) P Lang Pubng.

*__Von Wegener Skull 1980.__ Mozelle Richardson. 303p. (Orig.). 1997. mass mkt. 4.99 (*1-55197-764-8*, Pub. by Comnwlth Pub CN) Partners Pubs Grp.

Von Welanetz Guide to Ethnic Ingredients. Diana Von Welanetz & Paul Von Welanetz. 736p. 1987. pap. 10.95 (*0-446-38420-8*) Warner Bks.

*__Von Weltengagement Zur Weltuberwidung: Theologische Positionen Im Danielbuch.__ Rainer Stahl. (Contributions to Biblical Exegesis & Theology Ser.: Vol. 4). 215p. 1994. pap. 37.50 (*90-390-0013-1*, Pub. by KOK Pharos NE) Eisenbrauns.

*__Von Willebrand Factor & the Mechanisms of Platelet Function.__ Zaverio M. Ruggerl. (Medical Intelligence Unit Ser.). 250p. 89.95 (*0-412-11571-9*) Chapman & Hall.

Von Willebrand's Disease & Hemophilia: Clinical & Genetic Aspects. K. Peerlinck. No. 74. 95p. (Orig.). 1994. pap. 30.00 (*90-6186-593-X*, Pub. by Leuven Univ BE) Coronet Bks.

Vonken der Liefde Jesu. Jan Luyken. xvi, 232p. (GER.). 1982. reprint ed. write for info. (*3-487-06955-5*) G Olms Pubs.

Vonnegut Chronicles: Interviews & Essays. Ed. by Peter Reed & Marc Leeds. LC 95-4670. (Contributions to the Study of World Literature Ser.: Vol. 65). 240p. 1996. text ed. 55.00 (*0-313-29719-3*, Greenwood Pr) Greenwood.

Vonnegut Encyclopedia: An Authorized Compendium. Marc Leeds. LC 94-16122. 712p. 1994. text ed. 85.00 (*0-313-29230-2*, Greenwood Pr) Greenwood.

Vonnegut's Major Works Notes. Thomas R. Holland. 58p. (Orig.). 1973. pap. 3.95 (*0-8220-1352-5*) Cliffs.

Vonu: The Search for Personal Freedom. Rayo. Ed. by Jon Fisher. (Illus.). 1983. pap. 10.00 (*0-915179-96-2*) Loompanics.

*__Voodoo.__ Jeans Favors. 224p. mass mkt. write for info. (*0-06-106191-3*, Harp PBks) HarpC.

*__Voodoo.__ Mayfair Games Staff. 1992. 12.00 (*0-923763-57-0*) Mayfair Games.

Voodoo: Postcardbook. Henning Christoph. 1996. pap. text ed. 39.99 (*3-8228-8649-1*) Taschen Amer.

VooDoo: Search for the Spirit. Laennec Hurbon. Tr. by Lory Frankel. (Discoveries Ser.). (Illus.). 176p. 1995. pap. 12.95 (*0-8109-2857-4*) Abrams.

Voodoo: Treasure in Bootle Bay, Vol. 1. Allan Campbell. (Illus.). 200p. 1985. 14.95 (*0-9613326-0-3*) C I L Inc.

Voodoo & Hoodoo. James Haskins. 226p. 1989. pap. 8.95 (*0-942272-18-8*) Original Pubns.

Voodoo & Hoodoo. James Haskins. LC 77-17213. (Illus.). 226p. (C). 1990. reprint ed. pap. 11.95 (*0-8128-6085-3*, Scrbrough Hse) Madison Bks UPA.

Voodoo & Politics in Haiti. Michel S. Laguerre. LC 88-18181. 160p. 1989. text ed. 35.00 (*0-312-02066-X*) St Martin.

Voodoo Child. Martin I. Green. 1996. pap. write for info. (*0-670-78032-4*) Viking Penguin.

Voodoo Child: The Illustrated Legend of Jimi Hendrix. Martin I. Green. (Illus.). 1995. 35.00 (*0-87816-386-7*) Kitchen Sink.

Voodoo Child: The Illustrated Legend of Jimi Hendrix. Martin I. Green. (Illus.). 1995. boxed 60.00 (*0-87816-387-5*) Kitchen Sink.

Voodoo Child: The Illustrated Legend of Jimi Hendrix. Martin I. Green. (Illus.). 128p. 1995. 34.95 (*0-9648994-1-8*) Berkshire Studio.

Voodoo Child: The Illustrated Legend of Jimi Hendrix. Illus. by Bill Sienkiewicz. 128p. 1995. pap. 34.95 incl. audio compact disk (*0-670-86789-6*) Viking Penguin.

Voodoo Dreams: A Novel of Marie Laveau. Jewell P. Rhodes. 1995. pap. 13.00 (*0-312-11931-3*) St Martin.

Voodoo for the President. Hugo Pratt. Tr. by Terry Nantier from FRE. (Corto Maltese Ser.). 96p. 1986. pap. 8.95 (*0-918348-25-0*, Comics Lit) NBM.

Voodoo Handbook of Cult Secrets. Anna Riva. (Illus.). 48p. 1974. pap. 3.95 (*0-943832-01-2*) Intl Imports.

Voodoo in Haiti. Alfred Metraux. 1989. pap. 11.96 (*0-8052-0894-1*) Schocken.

Voodoo in New Orleans. Robert Tallant. LC 83-8261. 248p. 1983. reprint ed. pap. 4.25 (*0-88289-336-X*) Pelican.

Voodoo Island. 1989. pap. 5.25 (*0-19-421635-7*) OUP.

*__Voodoo Kit.__ N. E. Genge. (Illus.). 64p. 1997. 9.95 (*0-7624-0051-X*) Running Pr.

Voodoo Lost Arts & Sciences. abr. ed. Intro. by Luanna C. Blagrove. (Illus.). 250p. 1988. 24.95 (*0-939776-22-7*) Blagrove Pubns.

Voodoo, Ltd. Ross Thomas. 288p. 1992. 19.95 (*0-89296-451-0*) Mysterious Pr.

Voodoo, Ltd. Ross Thomas. 320p. 1993. mass mkt. 5.99 (*0-446-40030-0*, Mysterious Paperbk) Warner Bks.

Voodoo, Ltd. large type ed. Ross Thomas. LC 92-40635. (General Ser.). 1993. lib. bdg. 21.95 (*0-8161-5679-4*, GK Hall) Thorndike Pr.

Voodoo Mac: Mastery Tips & Masterful Tricks. 2nd ed. Kay Y. Nelson. (Illus.). 472p. 1994. 24.95 (*1-56604-177-5*) Ventana Communs.

Voodoo, Past & Present. Ron Bodin. LC 90-82516. (Louisiana Life Ser.: No. 5). 101p. 1990. pap. 5.00 (*0-940984-60-1*) U of SW LA Ctr LA Studies.

Voodoo Plot. Franklin W. Dixon. (Hardy Boys Ser.: No. 72). (J). (gr. 3-6). 1987. pap. 3.99 (*0-671-64287-1*) PB.

Voodoo Queen. Robert Tallant. LC 83-8160. 314p. 1983. reprint ed. pap. 4.25 (*0-88289-332-7*) Pelican.

Voodoo River. Robert Crais. 304p. 1995. 21.95 (*0-7868-6076-6*) Hyperion.

Voodoo River. Robert Crais. LC 94-32389. (Elvis Cole Ser.). 416p. 1996. mass mkt. 5.99 (*0-7868-8905-5*) Hyperion.

Voodoo Tales As Told among the Negroes of the Southwest. Mary A. Owen. LC 70-149874. (Black Heritage Library Collection). (Illus.). 1977. 30.95 (*0-8369-8754-3*) Ayer.

Voodoo Windows 95: Mastery Tips & Masterful Tricks. Kay Y. Nelson. (Illus.). 504p. 1995. pap. 24.95 incl. disk (*1-56604-145-7*) Ventana Communs.

Voodooism in Music, & Other Essays. Richard R. Terry. LC 68-16978. (Essay Index Reprint Ser.). 1977. 19.95 (*0-8369-0930-5*) Ayer.

Voodoos & Obeahs. Joseph J. Williams. LC 74-11170. 1970. reprint ed. 39.50 (*0-404-06986-X*) AMS Pr.

Voorheesville, New York: A Sketch of the Beginnings of a Nineteenth Century Railroad Town. Dennis Sullivan. (Illus.). 200p. (Orig.). 1989. pap. 15.00 (*0-9622282-0-6*) Village Voorheesville.

Voorslag 1-3 (1926) A Magazine of South African Life & Art. Roy Campbell et al. No. 5. (Illus.). 1985. reprint ed. 24.95 (*0-86980-423-5*, Pub. by Univ Natal Pr SA) Intl Spec Bk.

Voprosy Literatury Za 30 Let, 1957-1986 - Printed Index 1957-1986. Ed. by E. A. Katseva. 456p. (RUS.). 1988. text ed. 50.00 (*0-88354-366-4*) N Ross.

Vor Game. Lois M. Bujold. 352p. 1990. mass mkt. 5.99 (*0-671-72014-7*) Baen Bks.

Voracious Idols & Violent Hands: Iconoclasm in Reformation Zurich, Strasbourg, & Basel. Lee P. Wandel. (Illus.). 217p. (C). 1994. text ed. 42.95 (*0-521-47222-9*) Cambridge U Pr.

*__Vorbild Und Vernunft, Band 5.__ Ludwig Amman. xii, 287p. (GER.). 1993. 49.80 (*3-487-09773-7*) G Olms Pubs.

Vorce: Genealogical & Historical Record of the Vorce Family in America, with Notes of Allied Families. C. M. Vorce. 110p. 1993. reprint ed. pap. 22.00 (*0-8328-3755-5*); reprint ed. lib. bdg. 32.00 (*0-8328-3754-7*) Higginson Bk Co.

*__Vorelektrifizierung Landlicher Gebiete mit Hilfe der Photovoltaik: Technische und Institutionelle Ansatze fur die Wirtschaftlichkeit von Inselnetzen als eine Ubergangslosung.__ Aloisio L. Schmid. (Europaische Hochschulschriften: Reihe 5: Bd. 2024). 266p. (GER.). 1997. pap. 51.95 (*3-631-31212-1*) P Lang Pubng.

Vorformen der Schriftexegese innerhalb des Alten Testaments. Ina Willi-Plein. 286p. (C). 1971. 113.85 (*3-11-001897-7*) De Gruyter.

Vorgeschichtlichen Goldfund der Iberischen Halbinsel: Eine Archaeologische Untersuchung zur Auswertung der Spektralanalysen. Volker Pingel. (Madrider Forschungen Ser.: Bd. 17). (Illus.). xxi, 321p. (GER.). (C). 1992. lib. bdg. 270.80 (*3-11-012337-1*) De Gruyter.

Vorkosigan's Game, 2 vols. in 1. Lois M. Bujold. 492p. 1990. 10.98 (*1-56865-076-0*, GuildAmerica) Dblday Direct.

Vorlesungen I: Schrift Fuer die Kandidatur Am College de France: Lob der Philosophie; Vorlesungszusammenfassungen (College De France 1952-1960) Die Humanwissenschaften und die Phaenomenologie. Maurice Merleau-Ponty. Tr. by Alexandre Metraux from FRE. (Phaenomenologisch-Psychologische Forschungen Ser.: No. 9). (GER.). (C). 1972. 115.40 (*3-11-001823-3*) De Gruyter.

Vorlesungen uber Bedeutungslehre: Sommersemester 1908. Edmund Husserl. Ed. by Ursula Panzer. (Husserliana Collected Works: No. 26). 300p. 1986. lib. bdg. 194.00 (*90-247-3383-9*, Pub. by M Nijhoff NE) Kluwer Ac.

Vorlesungen Uber Continuierliche Gruppen Mit Geometrischen und Anderen Anwendungen. 2nd ed. Sophus Lie. LC 66-12879. 1971. text ed. 59.95 (*0-8284-0199-3*) Chelsea Pub.

Vorlesungen Uber Differential und Integralrechnung, 3 vols. Alexander Ostrowski. Incl. Vol. 3. Integralrechnung auf dem Gebiete Mehrerer Variablen. 396p. 1980. 68.50 (*0-8176-0289-5*); (Mathematische Reihe Ser.: Nos. 4, 5 & 7). (Illus.). write for info. (*0-318-51089-8*) Birkhauser.

Vorlesungen uber Ethik und Wertlehre, 1908-1914. Edmund Husserl. Ed. by Ullrich Melle. (Husserliana Collected Works: No. 28). 576p. (C). 1988. lib. bdg. 346.50 (*90-247-3708-7*, Pub. by Klwr Acad Pubs NE) Kluwer Ac.

Vorlesungen Uber Numerische Mathematik, 2 vols. Ed. by Heinz Rutishauser et al. Incl. Vol. 2. Differentialgleichungen und Eigenwertprobleme. 228p. 1980. 78.00 (*0-8176-0850-8*); (Mathematische Reihe Ser.: Nos. 50 & 57). write for info. (*0-318-51090-1*) Birkhauser.

Vorlesungen uber Partielle und pfaffsche Diggerentialgleichungen. W. Haack & W. L. Wendland. (Mathematische Reihe Ser.: No. 3). (Illus.). 555p. (GER.). 1980. 140.50 (*0-8176-0159-7*) Birkhauser.

Vorlesungen Ueber Hegel: Frankfurt 1931-32. Ed. by Erdmann Strum. (Ergaenzungs - Und Nachlassbaende Zu Den Gesammelten Werken Ser.: Bd. 8). xxii, 621p. (GER.). (C). 1995. 190.75 (*3-11-014421-2*) De Gruyter.

Vorlesungen Ueber Hoehere Geometrie. 3rd ed. Felix Klein. LC 51-3040. 1976. text ed. 19.95 (*0-8284-0065-2*) Chelsea Pub.

Vorlesungen Ueber Reelle Funktionen. 3rd ed. Constantin Caratheodory. LC 63-11321. 1968. 29.50 (*0-8284-0038-5*) Chelsea Pub.

Vorlesungen Ueber Variationsrechnung. Oskar Bolza. LC 62-8228. ix, 715p. (GER.). (C). reprint ed. text ed. 29.50 (*0-8284-0160-8*, 160) Chelsea Pub.

Vormundschaft Mach Attischem Recht. Otto Schulthess. Ed. by Gregory Vlastos. LC 78-19379. (Morals & Law in Ancient Greece Ser.). 1979. reprint ed. lib. bdg. 23.95 (*0-405-11573-3*) Ayer.

Voronezh Notebooks: Poems 1935-1937. Osip Mandelstam. Tr. by Richard McKane & Elizabeth McKane. 128p. 9600. pap. 16.95 (*1-85224-205-1*, Pub. by Bloodaxe Bks UK) Dufour.

*__Voronezh Oblast: Economy, Industry, Government, Business.__ 2nd rev. ed. Russian Information & Business Center, Inc. Staff. (Russian Regional Business Directories Ser.). (Illus.). 200p. 1997. pap. 99.00 (*1-57751-425-4*) Russ Info & Busn Ctr.

Voroshilov Lectures: Materials from the Soviet General Staff Academy, Issues of Soviet Military Strategy, Vol. I. Ed. by Ghulam D. Wardak & Ed G. Turbiville, Jr. (Illus.). 411p. (Orig.). (C). 1994. pap. text ed. 50.00 (*0-7881-1119-1*) DIANE Pub.

Voroshilov Lectures Vol. III: Materials from the Soviet General Staff Academy: Issues of Operational Art. Ghulam D. Wardak et al. 586p. (Orig.). (C). 1995. pap. text ed. 50.00 (*0-7881-2574-5*) DIANE Pub.

Vorsicht! Deutsch macht Spass! The Complete Sourcebook to Create Engaging Cultural Experiences for Beginning German Students. Christine Dunne. (Illus.). 109p. (Orig.). 1994. teacher ed., pap. 19.95 (*1-885126-00-X*) Laurelwood NY.

Vorsicht Fehler! Deutsch. Mentor Lernhilfen. (GER.). 1993. 21.95 (*3-580-64070-4*) Langenscheidt.

Vorsokratische Denker. Walther Kranz. 240p. 1974. write for info. (*3-296-14000-X*) G Olms Pubs.

*__Vorsprung: An Introduction to German Language & Culture for Communication.__ Thomas Lovik et al. 576p. (GER.). (C). 1996. text ed. 56.76 (*0-395-74557-8*) HM.

*__Vorsprung: An Introduction to German Language & Culture for Communication.__ Thomas Lovik et al. (GER.). (C). 1996. lab manual ed., wbk. ed., text ed. 27.96 (*0-395-74560-8*) HM.

*__Vorsprung: An Introduction to German Language & Culture for Communication.__ annot. ed. Thomas Lovik et al. (GER.). (C). 1996. teacher ed., text ed. 51.96 (*0-395-74559-4*) HM.

Vortenwuerfe Von Moderne: Antike Melancholie Und Die Acedia Des Mittelalters. Michael Theunissen. viii, 56p. (Orig.). (GER.). 1996. pap. text ed. 17.80 (*3-11-015216-9*) De Gruyter.

Vortex. (Stony Man Ser.). 1995. mass mkt. 4.99 (*0-373-61901-4*, 1-61901-4) Harlequin Bks.

Vortex. 5.98 (*0-8317-4146-5*) Smithmark.

Vortex. Larry Bond. 944p. 1992. mass mkt. 6.99 (*0-446-36304-9*) Warner Bks.

Vortex. A. Cole & Chris Bunch. 1992. mass mkt. 4.99 (*0-345-37151-8*) Ballantine.

Vortex: Key to Future Science. 4th ed. David Ash. (Illus.). 192p. 1990. pap. 11.95 (*1-85860-019-7*, Pub. by Gateway Books UK) ACCESS Pubs Network.

Vortex Assignment. large type ed. Alfred Handley. 1990. 25.99 (*0-7089-2155-8*) Ulverscroft.

Vortex Dynamics. P. G. Saffman. (Monographs on Mechanics & Applied Mathematics). (Illus.). 400p. (C). 1993. 79.95 (*0-521-42058-X*) Cambridge U Pr.

Vortex Dynamics. P. G. Saffman. (Monographs on Mechanics). 325p. 1995. pap. text ed. 28.95 (*0-521-47739-5*) Cambridge U Pr.

Vortex Dynamics & Chaotic Phenomena. V. V. Meleshko & M. Yu Konstantinov. 300p. 1997. text ed. 61.00 (*981-02-0871-5*) World Scientific Pub.

Vortex Dynamics & Vortex Methods. C. Anderson & C. Greengard. LC 91-29692. (Lectures in Applied Mathematics: Vol. 28). 751p. 1991. pap. 149.00 (*0-8218-1135-5*, LAM/28) Am Math.

Vortex Element Methods for Fluid Dynamic Analysis of Engineering Systems. R. I. Lewis. (Engine Technology Ser.). (Illus.). 450p. (C). 1991. text ed. 155.00 (*0-521-36010-2*) Cambridge U Pr.

Vortex Family: A Family Saga Set in Haiti. Jean Metellus. 235p. 9600. 30.00 (*0-7206-0948-8*, Pub. by P Owen Ltd UK) Dufour.

Vortex Flow. Ogawa. 336p. 1992. 229.95 (*0-8493-5782-9*, QA925) CRC Pr.

Vortex Flow in Nature & Technology. Hans J. Lugt. 316p. (C). 1994. lib. bdg. 64.50 (*0-89464-916-7*) Krieger.

*__Vortex Fluid Mechanics: Numerical Experiments Based on the Method of Discrete Vortices.__ Belo T. Serkovski & Sergei Mikhailovich. LC 92-5067. (Method of Discrete Vortices Ser.). 1993. write for info. (*2-88124-844-6*) Gordon & Breach.

*__Vortex Methods.__ Lung-An Ying. LC 96-45986. (Mathematics & Its Applications Ser.). 340p. (C). 1996. lib. bdg. 149.00 (*0-7923-4276-3*) Kluwer Ac.

Vortex Methods. rev. ed. Ed. by C. R. Anderson & C. Greengard. (Lecture Notes in Mathematics Ser.: Vol. 1360). (Illus.). 141p. 1988. 36.10 (*0-387-50526-1*) Spr-Verlag.

Vortex Methods in Two-Dimensional Fluid Dynamics. Carlo Marchioro et al. (Lecture Notes in Physics Ser.: Vol. 203). iii, 137p. 1984. 18.95 (*0-387-13352-6*) Spr-Verlag.

U V

An Asterisk (*) at the beginning of an entry indicates that the title is appearing in BIP for the first time.

Vortex of Fear. Al Benson. 448p. (Orig.). 1995. 19.95 (*1-880396-43-2*, JP 9643-2) Jalmar Pr.

Vortex of Indian Fevers. Adrian C. Louis. LC 94-45837. 1995. 29.95 (*0-8101-5017-4*); pap. 11.95 (*0-8101-5042-5*) TriQuarterly.

Vortex Points: A Complete Muscular Relaxation. Oscar Ichazo. (Illus.). 32p. 1978. ring bd. 20.00 (*0-916554-10-4*) Arica Inst Pr.

Vortex Processes & Solid Body Dynamics: Spacecraft & Magnetic Levitation Systems Dynamics Problems. Boris I. Rabinovich et al. LC 94-30833. 1994. lib. bdg. 155.00 (*0-7923-3092-7*) Kluwer Ac.

Vortex State: Proceedings of the NATO ASI Vortices in Superfluids, Cargese, Corsica (France, July 19-31 1993) Ed. by Nicole Bontemp. LC 94-21076. (NATO ASI Series, Series C, Mathematical & Physical Science: 438). 1994. lib. bdg. 183.00 (*0-7923-2971-6*) Kluwer Ac.

Vortex Structures in a Stratified Fluid: Order from Chaos. Sergey I. Voropayev & Yakov D. Afanasyev. LC 93-32961. (Applied Mathematics & Mathematical Computation Ser.: Vol. 6). 240p. (gr. 13). 1994. text ed. 62.95 (*0-412-40560-1*, Chap & Hall NY) Chapman & Hall.

Vortex-t: The Poetics of Turbulence. Charles D. Minahen. 200p. 1992. text ed. 30.00 (*0-271-00774-5*) Pa St U Pr.

Vortical Solutions of the Conical Euler Equations. Kenneth G. Powell. (Notes on Numerical Fluid Mechanics Ser.: Vol. 28). x, 285p. (C). 1990. 80.00 (*3-528-07627-5*, Pub. by Vieweg & Sohn GW) Informatica.

Vorticism & the English Avant-Garde. William C. Wees. LC 73-185744. (Illus.). 311p. reprint ed. pap. 88.70 (*0-317-10209-5*, 2014454) Bks Demand.

Vorticity & Turbulence. Alexandre Chorin. LC 93-43311. (Applied Mathematical Sciences Ser.: Vol. 103). (Illus.). 192p. 1994. 42.95 (*0-387-94197-5*) Spr-Verlag.

VOS Story Bible, 3 vols. 1986. Set. pap. 39.99 (*0-85151-442-1*) Banner of Truth.

VOS Story Bible: New Testament. 1984. pap. 14.50 (*0-85151-237-2*) Banner of Truth.

VOS Story Bible: Old Testament (Genesis-Ruth) 1986. pap. 14.50 (*0-85151-250-X*) Banner of Truth.

VOS Story Bible: Old Testament (Samuel-Malachi) 1986. pap. 14.50 (*0-85151-251-8*) Banner of Truth.

Vose: Robert Vose & His Descendants. Eleanor F. Vose. (Illus.). 725p. 1993. reprint ed. pap. 99.50 (*0-8328-3253-7*); reprint ed. lib. bdg. 109.50 (*0-8328-3252-9*) Higginson Bk Co.

Vosges: French Edition-Regions of France. (Green Guides). pap. 12.95 (*0-686-56428-6*) Fr & Eur.

***Vosges/Alsace Map.** 1996. 6.95 (*2-06-700087-X*, 87) Michelin.

Voskhishchenie: Roman. Ilia M. Zdanevich. 252p. (RUS.). 1984. reprint ed. pap. 8.00 (*0-933884-36-2*) Berkeley Slavic.

Vos'migrannik. Vadim Kreyd. LC 85-81524. 90p. (RUS.). 1986. 7.00 (*0-911971-19-X*) Effect Pub.

Vospominanija: Memoirs. M. F. Meyendorff. (Illus.). 432p. 1990. 18.00 (*0-9616413-6-3*) Multilingual.

Voss. Patrick White. 448p. 1984. pap. 9.95 (*0-14-001438-1*, Penguin Bks) Viking Penguin.

Vostaas: White Buffalo's Story of the Plains Indians. Maxine Ruppel. (Indian Culture Ser.). (J). (gr. 3-11). 1995. pap. 6.95 (*0-89992-001-2*) Coun India Ed.

Vostok 1: First Human in Space. Michael D. Cole. LC 94-41180. (Countdown to Space Ser.). (Illus.). 48p. (J). (gr. 4-10). 1995. lib. bdg. 17.95 (*0-89490-541-4*) Enslow Pubs.

Votan Treasure. Jackson Collins. 288p. (Orig.). 1989. mass mkt. 3.95 (*0-380-75509-2*) Avon.

Votary in the Face of God. Bill Panko & Margaret Panko. 100p. (Orig.). Date not set. pap. 9.95 (*1-885342-26-8*) Creative Ways.

Vote. R. L. Singleton. 1996. 12.95 (*0-533-11590-6*) Vantage.

Vote! Harold W. Wilson. 159p. (C). 1988. 35.00 (*0-7223-2321-2*, Pub. by A H S Ltd UK) St Mut.

Vote: Making Your Voice Heard. Linda Scher. LC 92-14474. (Good Citizenship Ser.). (Illus.). 48p. (J). (gr. 5-6). 1992. lib. bdg. 24.26 (*0-8114-7357-0*) Raintree Steck-V.

***Vote: Making Your Voice Heard.** Linda Scher. 1996. pap. text ed. 5.95 (*0-8114-5585-8*) Raintree Steck-V.

***Vote of Intolerance.** Josh McDowell & Ed Stewart. LC 97-11014. 1997. write for info. (*0-8423-3905-1*) Tyndale.

***Vote of Intolerance.** Josh McDowell. 1998. pap. write for info. (*0-8423-7816-2*) Tyndale.

Vote Out Incumbents: Action Plan. Byron C. Diehl & D. Park Teter. 29p. 1992. 1.95 (*0-9634647-0-1*) Polis Pr CO.

Vote to Kill: The Humor, Fraud & Tragedy in Government. George E. Young. Ed. by Cherie L. Hirsch. (Illus.). 300p. 1992. 24.95 (*0-9621037-4-8*) Young Interests.

Voter Behavior in Economic Perspective. A. J. Schram. (Studies in Contemporary Economics). x, 274p. 1991. 48.00 (*0-387-53650-7*) Spr-Verlag.

***Voter Choice '96: A 50-State Report Card on Choice in the Presidential Elections.** E. Joshua Rosenkranz. LC 96-86145. (Illus.). 200p. (Orig.). 1996. pap. write for info. (*0-9654063-0-X*) Brennan Ctr.

Voter Decides. Angus Campbell et al. LC 73-138211. 242p. 1971. reprint ed. text ed. 79.50 (*0-8371-5566-5*, CAVD, Greenwood Pr) Greenwood.

Voter Mobilization & the Politics of Race: The South & Universal Suffrage, 1952-1984. Harold W. Stanley. LC 87-15080. 208p. 1987. text ed. 55.00 (*0-275-92673-7*, C2673, Praeger Pubs) Greenwood.

Voter Purging: The Perils & the Promise. Kim Mangum et al. 50p. 1990. 15.00 (*0-685-56594-7*) CPA Washington.

Voter Registration & the States: Effective Policy Approaches to Increase Registration. Jamie Cooper et al. 100p. 1991. 15.00 (*0-685-56593-9*) CPA Washington.

Voters & School Finance: The Impact of Public Opinion. Terry N. Whitney. 60p. 1993. pap. text ed. 15.00 (*1-55516-329-7*, 3120) Natl Conf State Legis.

***Voters & Tax-Payers of Bureau County, Illinois: Containing Also a Biographical Directory of Its Tax-Payers & Voters; History of the County & State; Etc.** (Illus.). 411p. 1997. reprint ed. lib. bdg. 45.00 (*0-8328-5717-3*) Higginson Bk Co.

Voters Begin to Choose: From Closed-Class to Open Elections in Britain. Richard Rose & Ian McAllister. 192p. (Orig.). 1986. text ed. 45.00 (*0-8039-9743-4*); pap. text ed. 17.50 (*0-8039-9744-2*) Sage.

Voters' Choice: Varieties of American Electoral Behavior. Gerald M. Pomper. (Illus.). 276p. (C). 1983. reprint ed. pap. text ed. 22.00 (*0-8191-3188-1*) U Pr of Amer.

Voters, Elections & Parties: The Practice of Democratic Theory. Gerald M. Pomper. 320p. 1988. 44.95 (*0-88738-160-X*) Transaction Pubs.

Voters, Elections, & Parties: The Practice of Democratic Theory. Gerald M. Pomper. 424p. (C). 1992. pap. text ed. 24.95 (*1-56000-561-0*) Transaction Pubs.

Voters Guide to American Government. Mtv Staff. 1996. pap. text ed. 4.00 (*0-205-26497-2*) Allyn.

Voter's Guide to Election Polls. Michael W. Traugott & Paul J. Lavrakas. LC 96-10014. (Illus.). 208p. (Orig.). (C). 1996. pap. text ed. 19.95 (*1-56643-046-1*) Chatham Hse Pubs.

Voter's Guide to the Sixty-Ninth Legislature. Tom Whatley. xviii, 133p. write for info. (*0-318-60761-1*) Tex Gov.

Voters' Vengeance: The 1990 Election & the Fate of the Fourth Labour Government. Peter Aimer & Jack Vowles. (Auckland University Press Book). (Illus.). 336p. (C). 1993. pap. 32.00 (*1-86940-078-X*, 14487) OUP.

Votes & More for Women: Suffrage & After in Connecticut. Carole Nichols. LC 83-8405. (Women & History Ser.: No. 5). 92p. 1983. text ed. 29.95 (*0-86656-192-7*) Haworth Pr.

Votes & Vetoes in the U. N. General Assembly. Miguel M. Bosch. 544p. Date not set. 150.00 (*0-7201-2317-8*, Mansell Pub) Cassell.

Votes, Budgets & Development: Comparative Studies in Accountable Governance in the South. Ed. by John Healey & William Tordoff. LC 95-5718. (International Political Economy Ser.). 1995. text ed. 59.95 (*0-312-12709-X*) St Martin.

Votes for Women?! A Resouce Guide. Jocelyn Riley. 114p. 1995. 20.00 (*1-877933-10-4*) Her Own Words.

Votes for Women: A 75th Anniversary Album. Ellen Dubois & Karen Kerns. (Illus.). 48p. (Orig.). 1995. pap. 9.50 (*0-87328-157-8*) Huntington Lib.

Votes for Women: Living History. Michael Ryan. (C). 1990. 65.00 (*0-946139-91-1*, Pub. by Elm Pubns UK) St Mut.

Votes for Women: The Australian Story. Kirsten Lees. (Illus.). 224p. 1996. pap. 24.95 (*1-86373-630-1*, Pub. by Allen & Unwin Aust Pty AT) Paul & Co Pubs.

Votes for Women: The Fight for Suffrage. Christine Scriabine. (Illus.). 1992. student ed. 35.00 (*0-614-03228-8*); 27.95 (*1-56696-001-0*) Golden Owl NY.

Votes for Women! The Woman Suffrage Movement in Tennessee, the South, & the Nation. Marjorie S. Wheeler. LC 94-18768. (Illus.). 384p. 1995. text ed. 38.00 (*0-87049-836-3*); pap. text ed. 17.00 (*0-87049-837-1*) U of Tenn Pr.

Votes for Women: Women & the Suffrage Movement. Diane Atkinson. (Women in History Ser.). (Illus.). 48p. (C). 1989. pap. text ed. 11.95 (*0-521-31044-X*) Cambridge U Pr.

Votes Without Power: The Hong Kong Legislative Council Elections, 1991. Ed. by Rowena Y. Kwok et al. 300p. (Orig.). 1992. pap. 42.50 (*962-209-317-5*, Pub. by Hong Kong Univ Pr HK) Coronet Bks.

Votescam: The Stealing of America. 2nd ed. James M. Collier & Kenneth F. Collier. Ed. by Phyllis J. Vernick. 250p. (Orig.). 1993. pap. 9.95 (*0-9634163-0-8*) Victoria House.

Voting: A Study of Opinion Formation in a Presidential Campaign. Bernard R. Berelson et al. LC 54-11205. (Midway Reprint Ser.). (Illus.). 416p. 1986. pap. text ed. 30.00 (*0-226-04350-9*) U Ch Pr.

Voting & Elections. Dennis B. Fradin. LC 85-7715. (New True Bks.). (Illus.). 48p. (J). (gr. k-4). 1985. pap. 5.50 (*0-516-41274-4*); lib. bdg. 19.00 (*0-516-01274-6*) Childrens.

***Voting & Political Attidues in Denmark: A Study of the 1994 Election.** Ole Borre & Jorgen G. Andersen. 352p. 1997. 33.00 (*87-7288-542-4*, Pub. by Aarhus Univ Pr DK) David Brown.

Voting & the Handling of Disputes in the Security Council, Vol. 5. Eduardo Jimenez de Arechaga. LC 78-3780. (Carnegie Endowment for International Peace, United Nations Studies: No. 5). 189p. 1978. reprint ed. text ed. 45.00 (*0-313-20332-6*, ARVH, Greenwood Pr) Greenwood.

Voting & the Spirit of American Democracy: Essays on the History of Voting & Voting Rights in America. Ed. by Donald W. Rogers. 136p. 1992. text ed. 17.50 (*0-252-01918-0*); pap. text ed. 7.95 (*0-252-06247-7*) U of Ill Pr.

Voting Authority Card: Innovations in Election Administration. Marie Garber. Ed. by William C. Kimberling. (Illus.). 49p. (Orig.). (C). 1995. pap. text ed. 25.00 (*0-7881-2104-9*) DIANE Pub.

Voting Behavior. Ed. by Paul A. Winters. (At Issue Ser.). 80p. (J). (gr. 5-12). 1996. pap. text ed. 8.96 (*1-56510-412-9*); lib. bdg. 14.96 (*1-56510-413-7*) Greenhaven.

Voting Behavior: The Nineteen Eighty-Eight Election. Charles Prysby & Carmine Scavo. (SETUPS Ser. - Supplementary Empirical Teaching Units in Political Science). 70p. (Orig.). (C). 1989. pap. text ed. 8.00 (*0-915654-87-3*) Am Political.

Voting Behavior: The 1992 Election. Charles Prysby & Carmine Scavo. (Setups Ser.). 87p. (Orig.). (C). 1993. pap. 8.75 (*1-878147-11-0*) Am Political.

Voting Behavior in the South Dakota Legislature: An Exploratory Investigation into Divisible Roll Calls. Alan L. Clem. 1966. 1.00 (*1-55614-014-2*) U of SD Gov Res Bur.

Voting Behaviour: A Radical Critique. Helena Catt. (Critical Political Studies). 192p. (C). 1997. pap. 21.95 (*0-7185-2232-X*, Pub. by Leicester Univ Pr); text ed. 60.00 (*0-7185-1473-4*, Pub. by Leicester Univ Pr) Bks Intl VA.

Voting Behaviour in the Republic of Ireland: A Geographical Perspective. M. A. Busteed. (Illus.). 264p. 1991. 75.00 (*0-19-823276-4*) OUP.

Voting by Institutional Investors on Corporate Governance Issues - 1992. Sharon Light. Ed. by Peg O'Hara. 69p. (Orig.). 1992. pap. 25.00 (*1-879775-03-4*) IRRC Inc DC.

Voting by Institutional Investors on Corporate Governance Issues in the 1990 Proxy Season. 6th ed. Jeffrey W. Biersach. (Annual Ser.). 118p. 1990. pap. 25.00 (*0-931035-74-0*) IRRC Inc DC.

Voting by Institutional Investors on Corporate Governance Issues in the 1991 Proxy Season. Ann L. Yerger. 112p. 1991. pap. 25.00 (*0-931035-81-3*) IRRC Inc DC.

Voting by Institutional Investors on Corporate Governarle Issues in the 1992 Proxy Season. Amy J. Baker. Ed. by Peg O'Hara. (Illus.). (Orig.). 1993. pap. text ed. 25.00 (*1-879775-16-6*) IRRC Inc DC.

Voting Districts of the Roman Republic: The Thirty-Five Urban & Rural Tribes. Lily R. Taylor. LC 62-2896. (American Academy in Rome. Papers & Monographs: Vol. 20). 390p. reprint ed. pap. 111.20 (*0-685-15624-9*, 2026732) Bks Demand.

Voting for Greater Pluralism: The May 26, 1991 Municipal Elections in Paraguay. National Democratic Institute for International Affairs Staff. 97p. 1992. pap. 8.95 (*1-880134-13-6*) Natl Demo Inst.

Voting for President: The Electoral College & the American Political System. Wallace S. Sayre & Judith H. Parris. LC 78-139815. (Studies in Presidential Selection). 169p. 1970. pap. 9.95 (*0-8157-7719-1*) Brookings.

Voting for Reform: Democracy, Political Liberalization, & Economic Adjustment. Ed. by Stephan Haggard & Steven B. Webb. (World Bank Publication). 536p. (C). 1994. pap. text ed. 19.95 (*0-19-520987-7*) OUP.

***Voting Hopes or Fears? White Voters, Black Candidates, & Racial Politics in America.** Keith Reeves. (Illus.). 200p. 1997. pap. 15.95 (*0-19-510162-6*) OUP.

***Voting Hopes or Fears? White Voters, Black Candidates, & Racial Politics in America.** Keith Reeves. (Illus.). 200p. 1997. 39.95 (*0-19-510161-8*) OUP.

Voting in Provincial America: A Study of Elections in the Thirteen Colonies, 1689-1776. Robert J. Dinkin. LC 77-71861. (Contributions in American History Ser.: No. 64). (Illus.). 284p. 1977. text ed. 55.00 (*0-8371-9543-8*, DIV/, Greenwood Pr) Greenwood.

Voting in Revolutionary America: A Study of Elections in the Original Thirteen States, 1776-1789. Robert J. Dinkin. LC 81-13266. (Contributions in American History Ser.: No. 99). (Illus.). x, 184p. 1982. text ed. 49.95 (*0-313-23091-9*, DVR/) Greenwood.

Voting in the Security Council. Sydney D. Bailey. LC 69-15990. 285p. reprint ed. 81.30 (*0-8357-9252-8*, 2013017) Bks Demand.

Voting Patterns of the United States Supreme Court: Cases in Federalism, 1889-1959. LC 68-18392. 1968. 9.25 (*0-672-51175-4*, Bobbs) Macmillan.

Voting Procedure in International Political Organizations. Wellington Koo, Jr. LC 79-137253. reprint ed. 32.50 (*0-404-03774-7*) AMS Pr.

Voting Procedures. Michael Dummett. (Illus.). 318p. 1985. 75.00 (*0-19-876188-0*) OUP.

Voting Records of the British House of Commons, 1761-1820. Ed. by Donald E. Ginter. LC 95-1207. 1995. 550.00 (*1-85285-107-4*) Hambledon Press.

Voting Reform: Democracy, Political Liberalization & Economic Adjustment: an Overview. Stephan Haggard & Steven B. Webb. LC 94-37743. (ICEG Sector Studies: No. 12). 1994. pap. 9.95 (*1-55815-353-5*) ICS Pr.

Voting Rights. Ed. by Michal R. Belknap. LC 91-3613. (Civil Rights, White House & Justice Dept. Ser.: Vol. 15). 296p. 1991. text ed. 79.00 (*0-8240-3388-4*) Garland.

Voting Rights Act: Consequences & Implications. Lorn S. Foster. LC 85-6600. 224p. 1985. text ed. 55.00 (*0-275-90101-7*, C0101, Praeger Pubs) Greenwood.

Voting Rights Act & Black Electoral Participation. Kenneth H. Thompson. (Illus.). 50p. (Orig.). 1982. pap. 12.25 (*0-941410-24-2*) Jt Ctr Pol Studies.

Voting Rights & Democracy: The Law & Politics of Districting. Richard K. Scher et al. 200p. (Orig.). (C). 1996. pap. text ed. 23.95 (*0-8304-1442-8*) Nelson-Hall.

Voting Rights in America: Continuing the Quest for Full Participation. Ed. by Karen M. Arlington & William L. Taylor. 180p. (C). 1993. pap. text ed. 22.50 (*0-941410-55-2*); lib. bdg. 52.00 (*0-941410-52-8*) Jt Ctr Pol Studies.

Voting Rights, Voting Wrongs: The Legacy of Baker v. Carr. Bernard N. Grofman. (Twentieth Century Fund Papers). 52p. (Orig.). (C). 1990. pap. 8.95 (*0-87078-295-9*) TCFP-PPP.

Votive & Historical Texts from Babylonia & Assyria. Ferris J. Stephens. LC 78-63538. (Yale Oriental Series: Babylonian Texts: No. 9). (Illus.). 160p. reprint ed. 31.00 (*0-404-60259-2*) AMS Pr.

Votive Offerings Among Greek-Philadelphians: A Ritual Perspective. Robert T. Teske. Ed. by Richard M. Dorson. LC 80-735. (Folklore of the World Ser.). 1981. lib. bdg. 36.95 (*0-405-13325-1*) Ayer.

Votive Offerings to Hathor. Pinch. (Griffith Institute Ser.). 1992. 91.50 (*0-900416-54-8*, Pub. by Aris & Phillips UK) David Brown.

Votive Sculpture of Hellenistic Cyprus. Joan B. Connelly. (Illus.). 170p. (C). 1988. text ed. 40.00 (*0-8147-1416-1*) NYU Pr.

Votive Tablets: Studies Chiefly Appreciative of English Authors & Books. Edmund C. Blunden. LC 67-26716. (Essay Index Reprint Ser.). 1977. 23.95 (*0-8369-0219-X*) Ayer.

***Votos de Matrimonio.** Ash. 1997. mass mkt. 3.50 (*0-373-33429-X*) Harlequin Bks.

Votre Force Spirituelle et Emotionnelle. Richard D. Dobbins. Ed. by Annie L. Cosson. Tr. by Valerie Chardenal from ENG. 192p. (FRE.). 1985. 2.95 (*0-8297-0703-4*) Life Pubs Intl.

Votre Livre du Bord, 2 vols., Vol. 1. Bloc Marin. (C). 1989. 105.00 (*0-685-74324-1*, Pub. by Imray Laurie Norie & Wilson UK) St Mut.

Votre Livre du Bord, 2 vols., Vol. 2. Bloc Marin. (C). 1989. 105.00 (*0-685-74325-X*, Pub. by Imray Laurie Norie & Wilson UK) St Mut.

Votre Portee. Eliane McKee & Melissa Gruzs. Ed. by Vincent Duggan et al. (Illus.). 208p. (Orig.). (FRE.). (C). 1988. pap. text ed. 23.50 (*0-03-006643-3*) HB Coll Pubs.

***Votre Tour!** Jean-Paul Valette & Rebecca M. Valette. (FRE.). (C). 1995. lab manual ed., wbk. ed., text ed. 32.76 (*0-669-35559-3*); teacher ed., text ed. 7.16 (*0-669-39317-7*) HM College Div.

***Votre Tour!** annot. ed. Jean-Paul Valette & Rebecca M. Valette. (FRE.). (C). 1995. teacher ed., text ed. 44.36 (*0-669-35558-5*) HM College Div.

Votyak Folksongs. Laszlo Vikar & Gabor Bereczki. Tr. by Imre Gombos from HUN. (Illus.). 521p. (C). 1989. 170.00 (*963-05-4979-4*, Pub. by Akad Kiado HU) St Mut.

Voucher Examiner. Jack Rudman. (Career Examination Ser.: C-3265). 1994. pap. 23.95 (*0-8373-3265-6*) Nat Learn.

Voudon Gnostic Workbook. Michael Bertiaux. 650p. 1988. pap. 29.95 (*0-939708-12-4*) Magickal Childe.

Vought F4U Corsair. Barrett Tillman. (Warbird Tech Ser.: Vol. 4). (Illus.). 100p. (Orig.). 1996. pap. 16.95 (*0-933424-67-1*) Specialty Pr.

Voughts F-8 Crusader, Pt. 1: Development & Testing Foreign Users & F8U-3. Steve Pace. (Naval Fighters Ser.: No. 16). 114p. 1988. pap. 17.95 (*0-942612-16-7*) Naval Fighters.

Vought's F-8 Crusader, Pt. 2: Navy & Marine RF-8 Photo-Recon Squadrons. Steven J. Ginter. (Naval Fighters Ser.: No. 17). (Illus.). 66p. (Orig.). 1988. pap. text ed. 12.95 (*0-942612-17-5*) Naval Fighters.

Vought's F-8 Crusader, Pt. 3: Marine Fighter Squadrons. Steven J. Ginter. (Naval Fighters Ser.: No. 18). (Illus.). 66p. (Orig.). 1989. pap. text ed. 12.95 (*0-942612-18-3*) Naval Fighters.

Vought's F-8 Crusader, Pt. 4: Navy Fighter Squadrons. Steven J. Ginter. (Naval Fighters Ser.: No. 19). (Illus.). 218p. (Orig.). 1990. pap. text ed. 25.95 (*0-942612-19-1*) Naval Fighters.

Vouivre. Marcel Ayme. 256p. (FRE.). 1972. pap. 10.95 (*0-7859-3467-7*, 2070361675) Fr & Eur.

Vouivre. Marcel Ayme. (Folio Ser.: No. 167). (FRE.). pap. 8.95 (*2-07-036167-5*) Schoenhof.

Vous D'Ecrire: Atelier de Francais. Gisele Loriot-Raymer & Michele E. Vialet. 1996. pap. text ed. write for info. (*0-07-044242-8*) McGraw.

Vous D'Ecrire: Atelier de Francais. Gisele Loriot-Raymer & Michele E. Vialet. 1996. wbk. ed., pap. text ed. write for info. (*0-07-044243-6*) McGraw.

Vous D'Ecrire for Advanced French. Lutz. 1986. student ed., pap. 11.00 (*0-15-381925-1*) H Holt & Co.

Vous et Moi: En Avant. Remunda Cadoux. (FRE.). 1970. write for info. (*0-02-268400-X*) Macmillan.

Vous et Moi: Premier Pas. Remunda Cadoux. (FRE.). 1970. write for info. (*0-02-268300-3*) Macmillan.

Vous les Entendez? Nathalie Sarraute. 185p. 1976. 6.95 (*2-07-036839-4*) Schoenhof.

Vous les Entendez. Nathalie Sarraute. (FRE.). 1976. pap. 10.95 (*0-8288-3743-0*, M5976) Fr & Eur.

Vous y Etes. 2nd annot. ed. Susan St. Onge & Robert Terry. 428p. 1990. teacher ed., pap. 57.95 (*0-8384-1910-0*) Heinle & Heinle.

Vous y Etes. 2nd ed. Susan St. Onge & Robert Terry. 428p. 1990. text ed. 52.95 (*0-8384-1909-7*) Heinle & Heinle.

Vous y Etes. 2nd ed. Susan St. Onge & Robert Terry. 428p. 1990. student ed., pap. 34.95 (*0-8384-1911-9*) Heinle & Heinle.

Vous y Etes. 2nd ed. Susan St. Onge & Robert Terry. 428p. 1990. 27.95 (*0-8384-1917-8*) Heinle & Heinle.

Vous Y Etes: Answer Key. 2nd ed. Stonge. (College French Ser.). 1990. wbk. ed., pap. 6.95 (*0-8384-1916-X*) Heinle & Heinle.

Vovlesungen Veber Approximation Im Komplexen. Dieter Gaier. 180p. (GER.). 1980. 34.50 (*0-8176-1161-4*) Birkhauser.

***Vow.** Schulze. 1997. mass mkt. 5.50 (*1-55166-295-7*) Harlequin Bks.

Vow. Dallas Schulze. (Silhouette Intimate Moments Ser.: No. 318). 1990. pap. 2.95 (*0-373-07318-6*) Harlequin Bks.

Vow. Mark Spencer. 464p. 1994. mass mkt. 4.50 (*0-06-108187-6*, Harp PBks) HarpC.

Vow: One Man's Determination to Obey God. Hal Donaldson & Kenneth M. Dobson. 192p. 1991. pap. 7.95 (*1-880689-00-6*) Onward Bks.

UV

Vow & the 'Popular Religious Groups' of Ancient Israel: A Philogical & Sociological Inquiry. Jacques Berlinerlau. (Journal For The Study Of The old Testament Supplement Ser.: No. 210). 305p. 1996. 58.50 (*1-85075-578-7*, Pub. by Sheffield Acad UK) CUP Services.

Vow Keepers, Vow Breakers. Simon Schrock. (Biblical Heritage Ser.: No. 5). 78p. (Orig.). 1989. pap. 3.95 (*0-940883-02-3*) Calvary Pubns.

***Vow of Chastity.** Marcia J. Greenshields. 1996. mass mkt. 4.99 (*1-55197-106-2*, Pub. by Comnwlth Pub CN) Partners Pubs Grp.

Vow of Chastity. large type ed. Veronica Black. (Linford Mystery Library). 400p. 1992. pap. 15.99 (*0-7089-7262-4*, Linford) Ulverscroft.

Vow of Conversation. Thomas Merton. 256p. 1988. 17.95 (*0-374-28535-7*) FS&G.

Vow of Devotion. Veronica Black. LC 95-16054. 186p. (YA). 1995. 20.95 (*0-312-13206-9*) St Martin.

***Vow of Devotion.** Veronica Black. (A Dead Letter Mystery Ser.). 1997. mass mkt. 5.50 (*0-312-96005-0*) St Martin.

Vow of Fidelity. Veronica Black. 208p. 1996. 19.95 (*0-312-14064-9*) St Martin.

***Vow of Fidelity.** Veronica Black. 1997. mass mkt. 5.99 (*0-614-27788-4*) St Martin.

***Vow of Fidelity.** large type ed. Veronica Black. (Large Print Ser.). 352p. 1997. 27.50 (*0-7089-3697-0*) Ulverscroft.

***Vow of Fidelity, Vol. 1.** Black. 1997. mass mkt. 5.50 (*0-312-96259-2*) St Martin.

Vow of Love. (Illus.). 96p. 1992. 15.00 (*0-8362-7992-1*) Andrews & McMeel.

Vow of Love. large type ed. Frances Y. McHugh. (Dales Romance Ser.). 211p. 1992. pap. 17.99 (*1-85389-331-5*) Ulverscroft.

Vow of Obedience. Black. 1996. pap. 143.76 (*0-312-95718-1*) St Martin.

Vow of Obedience. Veronica Black. 192p. 1994. 18.95 (*0-312-10573-8*) St Martin.

Vow of Obedience. Veronica Black. 1995. mass mkt. 5.50 (*0-8041-1245-2*) Ivy Books.

Vow of Obedience. large type ed. Veronica Black. LC 94-28137. 298p. 1994. pap. 19.95 (*0-8161-7472-5*, GK Hall) Thorndike Pr.

Vow of Penance. Veronica Black. 1996. mass mkt. 5.50 (*0-312-95850-1*) Tor Bks.

Vow of Penance. large type ed. Veronica Black. 352p. 1995. 25.99 (*0-7089-3326-2*) Ulverscroft.

Vow of Poverty. Veronica Black. LC 96-25531. 208p. 1996. 20.95 (*0-312-14756-2*) St Martin.

***Vow of Poverty.** large type ed. Veronica Black. (Ulverscroft Large Print Ser.). 388p. 1997. 27.50 (*0-7089-3733-0*) Ulverscroft.

Vow of Sanctity. Veronica Black. 192p. 1993. 16.95 (*0-312-09408-6*) St Martin.

Vow of Sanctity. large type ed. Veronica Black. 1994. 25.99 (*0-7089-3197-9*) Ulverscroft.

Vow of Silence. Veronica Black. 1992. mass mkt. 4.99 (*0-8041-0814-5*) Ivy Books.

***Vow of Silence.** B. J. Hoff. LC 96-43753. (Daybreak Mysteries Ser.: No. 4). 1997. pap. 8.99 (*0-8423-7195-8*) Tyndale.

Vow of Silence. large type ed. Veronica Black. 1991. 25.99 (*0-7089-2529-4*) Ulverscroft.

Vow of Silence. large type ed. B. J. Hoff. 1990. pap. 15.99 (*0-7089-6902-X*, Trailtree Bookshop) Ulverscroft.

***Vow of the Peacock: A Facsimile Reproduction.** LC 97-14800. (Scholars' Facsimiles & Reprints Ser.). 1997. write for info. (*0-8201-1505-3*) Schol Facsimiles.

***Vow of Vengence.** Thomas Sharp. (Orig.). 1997. mass mkt. 4.99 (*1-55237-331-2*, Pub. by Comnwlth Pub CN) Partners Pubs Grp.

Vow to Cherish. Deborah Raney. LC 95-45105. 240p. 1996. pap. 8.99 (*1-55661-666-X*) Bethany Hse.

***Vow to Cherish.** Deborah Raney. LC 96-49226. 1997. 22.95 (*0-7862-0984-4*) Thorndike Pr.

Vow to Keep. Elizabeth Bonner. 1993. mass mkt. 4.99 (*1-55773-957-9*) Diamond.

Vow to Love. Sherryl Woods. 1994. 3.50 (*0-373-09885-5*) Silhouette.

Vowel & Dipthong Tones. 1977. pap. 1.95 (*0-934982-07-4*) Primary Pr.

Vowel Category Individual Spelling Set, Pt. 1. Raymond E. Laurita. 112p. (Orig.). (J). (gr. 1-6). 1980. pap. 28.95 (*0-914051-08-3*) Leonardo Pr.

Vowel Category Individual Spelling Set, Pt. 2. Raymond E. Laurita. 305p. (Orig.). (J). (gr. 6 up). 1982. pap. 34.95 (*0-914051-09-1*) Leonardo Pr.

Vowel Category Resource Lists, Pt. 1. Raymond E. Laurita. 112p. (Orig.). (J). (ps-8). 1980. pap. 13.95 (*0-914051-04-0*) Leonardo Pr.

Vowel Category Resource Lists, Pt. II. Raymond E. Laurita. 305p. (Orig.). (YA). (gr. 6 up). 1989. pap. 17.95 (*0-914051-06-7*) Leonardo Pr.

***Vowel Digraphs.** Scholastic, Inc. Staff. (Fun with Phonics Ser.). (J). 1997. pap. text ed. 6.95 (*0-590-76496-9*) Scholastic Inc.

***Vowel Dipthongs.** Scholastic, Inc. Staff. (Fun with Phonics Ser.). (J). 1997. pap. text ed. 6.95 (*0-590-76497-7*) Scholastic Inc.

Vowel Fun. Betty Jenkins. (Illus.). 96p. (J). (gr. 1-3). 1983. student ed. 11.99 (*0-86653-107-6*, GA 465) Good Apple.

Vowel Perception & Production. B. S. Rosner & J. B. Pickering. LC 93-47078. (Psychology Ser.: No. 23). (Illus.). 416p. (C). 1994. 110.00 (*0-19-852138-3*) OUP.

Vowel Puzzles. Carson & Dellosa. (Home Workbooks Ser.). (Illus.). 64p. (Orig.). (J). (gr. 1-2). 1995. wbk. ed., pap. 2.49 (*0-88724-317-7*, CD6814) Carson-Dellos.

Vowel Sounds & Easy Words. Dennis Graham. Ed. by Livian Perez. (Reading Safari Ser.: Vol. 2). (Illus.). 12p. (Orig.). (J). (gr. k-2). 1996. pap. 19.95 (*1-56767-155-1*) Educ Insights.

Vowel Sounds & Silent Letters: Syllabus. Joanne Piper. 1975. pap. text ed. 6.45 (*0-89420-023-2*, 240008); audio 22.45 (*0-89420-196-4*, 240000) Natl Book.

Vowel System of American English. Lorna D. Sikorski. (Mastering Effective English Communication Ser.). 94p. (YA). (gr. 7 up). 1989. student ed. 70.00 incl. digital audio (*1-883574-09-9*, 5310) L D Sikorski.

Vowel System of American English. 2nd ed. Lorna D. Sikorski. (Mastering Effective English Communication Ser.). 94p. (YA). (gr. 7 up). 1989. pap. 22.00 (*1-883574-03-X*, 3602) L D Sikorski.

***Vowel/Glide Alternation in a Theory of Constraint Interaction.** Samuel Rosenthall. LC 97-12241. (Outstanding Dissertations in Linguistics Ser.). 302p. 1997. 64.00 (*0-8153-2884-2*) Garland.

Vowels & Stories: A Vowel-Centered Approach to Reading Proficiency. Marcia Weinstein. (Illus.). 96p. (gr. 2-6). 1975. pap. text ed. 9.95 (*0-87594-120-6*, 2300); teacher ed., pap. text ed. 9.95 (*0-87594-121-4*, 2301) Book-Lab.

***Vowels with R.** Scholastic, Inc. Staff. (Fun with Phonics Ser.). (J). 1997. pap. text ed. 6.95 (*0-590-76498-5*) Scholastic Inc.

Vows. 1990. 13.95 (*0-87949-318-6*) Ashley Bks.

***Vows.** Rochelle Alers. 288p. 1997. mass mkt. 4.99 (*0-7860-0463-0*, Pinncle Kensgtn) Kensgtn Pub Corp.

Vows. Rebecca Forster. 384p. 1994. mass mkt. 4.50 (*0-8217-4522-0*, Zebra Kensgtn) Kensgtn Pub Corp.

Vows. LaVyrle Spencer. 448p. 1988. mass mkt. 6.99 (*0-515-09477-3*) Jove Pubns.

Vows: (Weddings, Inc.) Margaret Moore. (Historical Ser.). 1994. mass mkt. 3.99 (*0-373-28848-4*, 1-28848-9) Harlequin Bks.

Vows: The New York Times Wedding Column. Lois S. Brady. LC 96-22843. 256p. 1997. 23.00 (*0-688-15052-7*) Morrow.

***Vows & Honor.** Mercedes Lackey. 1998. pap. 5.99 (*0-88677-773-9*) DAW Bks.

Vows & Honor, 2 vols. in 1. Mercedes Lackey. 480p. 1993. 8.98 (*1-56865-083-3*, GuildAmerica) Dblday Direct.

Vows in the Hebrew Bible & the Ancient Near East. Tony W. Cartledge. (Journal for the Study of the Old Testamnet Supplament Ser.: No. 147). 221p. 1992. 50.00 (*1-85075-298-2*, Pub. by Sheffield Acad UK) CUP Services.

Vows Made in Wine. Susan Wiggs. 400p. 1995. mass mkt. 5.50 (*0-06-108144-2*, Harp PBks) HarpC.

Vows Made in Wine. large type ed. Susan Wiggs. (Niagara Large Print Ser.). 486p. 1995. 27.99 (*0-7089-5815-X*) Ulverscroft.

Vows of Silence. Diana L. Michael. 208p. 1993. pap. 12.95 (*0-9634910-4-0*) Sharp Sallys Pr.

Vows of the Heron (Les Voeux du Heron) A Middle French Vowing Poem. Ed. by John Grigsby. Tr. by Norris J. Lacy. LC 91-27788. (Library of Medieval Literature: No. 86A). 112p. (FRE.). 1991. text ed. 10.00 (*0-8153-0724-1*) Garland.

Vows, Virgins, Oaths & Origins: Religious Origins of Vows & Oaths. Arthur F. Ide. LC 88-24999. (Illus.). vi, 170p. (Orig.). 1988. pap. 12.00 (*0-935175-24-5*) Monument Pr.

VOX. Hale Chatfield. (Illus.). 62p. (Orig.). 1995. pap. 13.00 (*0-9628478-5-2*) North Star Assocs.

Vox: A Novel. Nicholson Baker. LC 92-56365. 1993. pap. 10.00 (*0-679-74211-5*) Random.

***Vox: Record Hunter, a Collector's Guide to Rock & Pop.** Tony Rees. 1996. pap. text ed. 18.99 (*1-886894-50-7*) Mus Bk Servs.

Vox--Diccionari Fonamental de la Llengua Catalana: Vox Fundamental Dictionary of the Catalan Language. Vox Staff. 448p. (CAT.). 1979. 17.95 (*0-8288-4846-7*, S50218) Fr & Eur.

Vox--Diccionari Manual Castella-Catala, Catala-Castella: Vox Castilian (Spanish)-Catalan, Catalan-Castilian (Spanish) Dictionary. 3rd ed. Vox Staff. 680p. (CAT & SPA.). 1979. 24.95 (*0-8288-4847-5*, S31578) Fr & Eur.

Vox--Diccionario Abreviado Ingles-Espanol, Espanol-Ingles: Vox Shorter English-Spanish, Spanish-English Dictionary. 4th ed. Vox Staff. 792p. (ENG & SPA.). 1978. 19.95 (*0-7859-0957-5*, S12415) Fr & Eur.

Vox--Diccionario Abreviado Ortografico de la Lengua Espanola: Vox Shorter Orthographic Dictionary of the Spanish Language. 2nd ed. Joaquin C. Sotelo. 416p. (SPA.). 1978. 9.95 (*0-8288-5279-0*, S12372) Fr & Eur.

Vox--Diccionario Conciso de la Lengua Espanola. 2nd ed. Vox Staff. 464p. (SPA.). 1977. pap. 9.95 (*0-7859-0427-1*, S26963) Fr & Eur.

Vox--Diccionario de Sinonimos: Vox Dictionary of Synonyms. Samuel D. Gili Gaya. 376p. (SPA.). 1979. 24.95 (*0-8288-4848-3*, S12324) Fr & Eur.

Vox--Diccionario Fundamental de la Lengua Espanola. Vox Staff. 604p. (SPA.). 1977. pap. 14.95 (*0-8288-5540-4*, S50220) Fr & Eur.

Vox--Enciclopedia Cultural, 12 vols. Vox Staff. 2520p. (SPA.). 1977. Set. 695.00 (*0-8288-5541-2*, S50496) Fr & Eur.

Vox--Enciclopedia Cultural, Tomo 1: La Vida. Dietmar Todt. 210p. (SPA.). 1977. 39.95 (*0-8288-5545-5*, S50510) Fr & Eur.

Vox--Enciclopedia Cultural, Tomo 10: Tecnica. Ulrich Kirschner. 210p. (SPA.). 1977. 49.95 (*0-8288-5542-0*, S50499) Fr & Eur.

Vox--Enciclopedia Cultural, Tomo 11: Ideas. Peter H. Waldeck. 210p. (SPA.). 1977. 39.95 (*0-8288-5543-9*, S50498) Fr & Eur.

Vox--Enciclopedia Cultural, Tomo 12: Futuro. Ulrich Schippke. 210p. (SPA.). 1977. 49.95 (*0-8288-5544-7*, S50497) Fr & Eur.

Vox--Enciclopedia Cultural, Tomo 2: El Hombre. Markus Plessner. 210p. (SPA.). 1977. 29.95 (*0-8288-5546-3*, S50509) Fr & Eur.

Vox--Enciclopedia Cultural, Tomo 3: El Mundo. Ulrich Kirschner. 210p. (SPA.). 1977. 49.95 (*0-8288-5547-1*, S50507) Fr & Eur.

Vox--Enciclopedia Cultural, Tomo 4: La Tierra. Hanns Kneifel. 210p. (SPA.). 1977. 49.95 (*0-8288-5548-X*, S50506) Fr & Eur.

Vox--Enciclopedia Cultural, Tomo 5: Continentes. Margaret Lau-Uhle. 210p. (SPA.). 1977. 49.95 (*0-8288-5549-8*, S50504) Fr & Eur.

Vox--Enciclopedia Cultural, Tomo 6: Pueblos. Paul Gnuva. 210p. (SPA.). 1977. 49.95 (*0-8288-5550-1*, S50503) Fr & Eur.

Vox--Enciclopedia Cultural, Tomo 7: Culturas. Ernst von Khoun. 210p. (SPA.). 1977. 29.50 (*0-8288-5551-X*, S50502) Fr & Eur.

Vox--Enciclopedia Cultural, Tomo 8: Plantas. Herbert Lange. 210p. (SPA.). 1977. 49.95 (*0-7859-0903-6*, S-50501) Fr & Eur.

Vox--Enciclopedia Cultural, Tomo 9: Los Animales. Dietmar Todt. 210p. (SPA.). 1977. 39.95 (*0-7859-0904-4*, S-50500) Fr & Eur.

Vox--Lexis-22, Diccionario Enciclopedia, 23 vols. Vox Staff. 6704p. (SPA.). 1977. Set. 495.00 (*0-8288-5554-4*, S31569) Fr & Eur.

Vox--Vocabulari Basic Infantil i d'Adults. Vox Staff. 112p. (CAT.). 1977. pap. 9.95 (*0-8288-5555-2*, S50216) Fr & Eur.

Vox Angelica. Timothy Liu. LC 92-10732. 72p. (Orig.). 1992. pap. 9.95 (*0-914086-97-9*) Alicejamesbooks.

Vox Civitatis, or Londons Complaint Against Her Children in the Country. Benjamin Spenser. LC 79-84137. (English Experience Ser.: No. 954). 52p. 1979. reprint ed. lib. bdg. 15.00 (*90-221-0954-2*) Walter J Johnson.

Vox Compact English-Spanish-English Dictionary: Diccionario vox Compacto Ingles-Espanol-Ingles. Ed. by Vox Staff. 608p. (ENG & SPA.). 1982. pap. 17.95 (*0-8288-2332-4*, S39218) Fr & Eur.

Vox Compact Spanish & English Dictionary. 2nd ed. National Textbook Company Staff. 662p. 1995. 12.95 (*0-8442-7985-4*); pap. 8.95 (*0-8442-7986-2*) NTC Pub Grp.

Vox Compact Spanish-English Dictionary. 672p. 1994. 9.95 (*0-8442-7997-8*, Natl Textbk); pap. 7.95 (*0-8442-7993-5*, Natl Textbk) NTC Pub Grp.

Vox Compacto Diccionario de la Lengua Espanola. Vox Staff. 446p. (SPA.). 1982. pap. 12.95 (*0-8288-2069-4*, S39219) Fr & Eur.

Vox Concise Spanish-English-Spanish Dictionary: Diccionario vox Concise Espanol-Ingles-Espanol. Ed. by Vox Staff. 316p. (ENG & SPA.). 1982. pap. 12.95 (*0-8288-2333-2*, S39217) Fr & Eur.

Vox Dei: Communications in the Middle Ages. Sophia Menache. (Communication & Society Ser.). (Illus.). 368p. 1990. 49.95 (*0-19-504916-0*) OUP.

Vox-Diccionari Manual Ortografic. Vox Staff. 552p. (CAT.). 1975. 24.95 (*0-8288-5955-8*, S31579) Fr & Eur.

Vox-Diccionario Abreviado de la Lengua Espanola. 9th ed. Vox Staff. 512p. (SPA.). 1979. 4.75 (*0-8288-4851-3*, S12371) Fr & Eur.

Vox-Diccionario Abreviado de Sinonimos: Shorter Vox Synonyms Dictionary. 3rd ed. Vox Staff. 352p. (SPA.). 1978. 13.95 (*0-8288-5280-4*, S12370) Fr & Eur.

Vox-Diccionario Abreviado Frances-Espanol, Espanol-Frances: Vox Shorter French-Spanish, Spanish-French Dictionary. 8th ed. Vox Staff. 672p. (FRE & SPA.). 1978. 22.95 (*0-8288-5281-2*, S12414) Fr & Eur.

Vox Diccionario Actual de la Lengua Espanola. 1681p. (SPA.). 1996. 50.00 (*0-8442-7952-8*) NTC Pub Grp.

Vox-Diccionario Basico Latino-Espanol, Espanol-Latino: Vox Basic Latin-Spanish, Spanish-Latin Dictionary. 8th ed. Eustaquio Echuari. 830p. (LAT & SPA.). 1978. 35.00 (*0-8288-5282-0*, S12396) Fr & Eur.

Vox Diccionario Compacto Espanol & Ingles. 2nd ed. NTC Publishing Staff. 302p. (ENG & SPA.). 1996. pap. text ed. 8.95 (*0-8442-7991-9*) NTC Pub Grp.

Vox-Diccionario Compendiado de la Lengua Espanola: Compendious Dictionary of the Spanish Language. 2nd ed. Vox Staff. 646p. (SPA.). 1979. 9.95 (*0-8288-4852-1*, S12373) Fr & Eur.

Vox Diccionario Escolar de la Lengua Espanola. (Illus.). 336p. (ENG & SPA.). 1995. 9.95 (*0-8442-7980-3*, Natl Textbk); pap. 6.95 (*0-8442-7981-1*, Natl Textbk) NTC Pub Grp.

Vox-Diccionario Escolar de la Lengua Espanola. 5th ed. Vox Staff. 884p. (SPA.). 1978. 35.00 (*0-7859-0425-5*, S12376) Fr & Eur.

Vox-Diccionario Ingles-Espanol, Espanol-Ingles: Vox Spanish-English, English-Spanish Dictionary. 4th ed. Vox Staff. 1450p. (ENG & SPA.). 1978. 49.95 (*0-8288-5284-7*, S12417) Fr & Eur.

Vox-Diccionario Inicial de la Lengua Espanola. Vox Staff. 340p. (SPA.). 1975. 24.95 (*0-8288-5956-6*, S26962) Fr & Eur.

Vox-Diccionario Manual Griego-Espanol: Greek-Spanish. 11th ed. Jose M. Pabon. 724p. (GRE & SPA.). 1979. 39.95 (*0-8288-4854-8*, S12136) Fr & Eur.

Vox-Diccionario Manual Ingles-Espanol, Espanol-Ingles. 8th ed. Vox Staff. 1008p. (ENG & SPA.). 1979. 15.95 (*0-7859-0956-7*, S-12491) Fr & Eur.

Vox-Diccionario Superior Frances-Espanol, Espanol-Frances. Vox Staff. 1224p. (FRE & SPA.). 1977. 29.95 (*0-8288-5556-0*, S31577) Fr & Eur.

Vox-Diccionario Tematico de la Lengua Espanola. Vox Staff. 496p. (SPA.). 1975. 39.95 (*0-8288-5957-4*, S50219) Fr & Eur.

Vox Dictionary of the Catalan Language: Diccionari Vox de la Llengua Catalana. Vox Staff. 496p. (CAT.). 1982. 22.95 (*0-8288-2078-3*, S25645) Fr & Eur.

Vox Encyclopedic Dictionary: Vox--Diccionario Enciclopedia: 6 Tomos y un Atlas Geografico, 7 vols. 3rd ed. Vox Staff. 4868p. (SPA.). 1979. 295.00 (*0-8288-4849-1*, S12374) Fr & Eur.

Vox Everyday Spanish & English Dictionary. 706p. 1994. 8.95 (*0-8442-7983-8*, Natl Textbk) NTC Pub Grp.

Vox Everyday Spanish & English Dictionary. 706p. 1995. pap. 6.95 (*0-8442-7984-6*, Natl Textbk) NTC Pub Grp.

Vox Feminae: Studies in Medieval Woman's Songs. Ed. by John F. Plummer. (Studies in Medieval Culture: No. 25). 1989. pap. 10.95 (*0-918729-12-2*) Medieval Inst.

Vox Graeca: The Pronunciation of Classical Greek. 3rd ed. W. S. Allen. (Illus.). 200p. 1987. pap. text ed. 21.95 (*0-521-33555-8*) Cambridge U Pr.

Vox Illustrated General Dictionary of the Spanish Language: Diccionario Vox General Ilustrado de la Lengua Espanola. 5th ed. Vox Staff. (Illus.). 1711p. (SPA.). 1982. 195.00 (*0-8288-2070-8*, S12377) Fr & Eur.

Vox Intexta: Orality & Textuality in the Middle Ages. Ed. by A. N. Doane & Carol B. Pasternack. LC 91-3573. (Illus.). 304p. (Orig.). (C). 1991. pap. 23.50 (*0-299-13094-0*); lib. bdg. 45.00 (*0-299-13090-8*) U of Wis Pr.

Vox Latina: A Guide to the Pronunciation of Classical Latin. W. Sidney Allen. (Illus.). 124p. (C). 1989. pap. text ed. 16.95 (*0-521-37936-9*) Cambridge U Pr.

Vox Lengua Espanola Sinonimos y Antonimos. 671p. (SPA.). 1996. 27.95 (*0-8442-7950-1*) NTC Pub Grp.

Vox Manual Dictionnaire Francais-Espagnol, Espagnol-Francais. 3rd ed. Jean-Paul Vidal. 626p. (FRE & SPA.). 1977. 45.00 (*0-7859-7697-3*, 2040000860) Fr & Eur.

Vox Modern English-Spanish Dictionary. 1072p. 1995. 16.95 (*0-8442-7990-0*, Natl Textbk) NTC Pub Grp.

Vox Modern Spanish & English Dictionary. Vox Staff. 1995. vinyl bd. 16.95 (*0-8442-7988-9*, Natl Textbk) NTC Pub Grp.

Vox Mystica: Essays on Medieval Mysticism in Honor of Professor Valerie M. Lagorio. Ed. by Anne C. Bartlett et al. (Illus.). 250p. 1995. 71.00 (*0-85991-439-9*) Boydell & Brewer.

Vox New College Spanish-English Dictionary. 1526p. 22.95 (*0-8442-7999-4*, Natl Textbk) NTC Pub Grp.

Vox New College Spanish-English Dictionary. 1536p. 1995. 17.95 (*0-8442-7998-6*, Natl Textbk) NTC Pub Grp.

Vox Populi. 40p. 1992. pap. text ed. 3.00 (*1-881168-02-6*) Red Danceflr.

Vox Populi: Essays in the History of an Idea. George Boas. LC 69-13538. (Seminars in the History of Ideas Ser.). (Illus.). 308p. reprint ed. pap. 87.80 (*0-317-41626-X*, 2025833) Bks Demand.

Vox Populi, Loco Citato: Voice of the People of the Virgin Islands. Robert V. Vaughn. 285p. (Orig.). 1994. pap. text ed. 12.95 (*0-9627257-3-0*) Aye-Aye Pr.

Vox Story: The History of the Vox Amplifier. David Peterson & Dick Denney. Ed. by Angela Marcinello. (Guitar History Ser.). (Illus.). 150p. pap. 19.95 (*0-933224-70-2*) Bold Strummer Ltd.

Vox Super-Mini Spanish & English Dictionary. 384p. 1994. pap. 3.95 (*0-8442-7992-7*, Natl Textbk) NTC Pub Grp.

Vox Traveler's Spanish & English Dictionary. 510p. 1994. vinyl bd. 4.95 (*0-8442-7987-0*, Natl Textbk) NTC Pub Grp.

***Voxel-Man Pt. 1: Brain & Skull, Version 1.1.** 2nd ed. K. H. Hohne. 50p. 1997. pap. 995.00 incl. cd-rom (*3-540-14584-2*) Spr-Verlag.

VOYA Reader. Ed. by Dorothy M. Broderick. LC 90-37812. 320p. 1990. 32.50 (*0-8108-2331-4*) Scarecrow.

Voyage. Charles P. Baudelaire. (C). 1990. pap. 40.00 (*0-906887-47-X*, Pub. by Greville Pr UK) St Mut.

***Voyage.** Stephen Baxter. mass mkt. write for info. (*0-06-105292-2*, Harp PBks) HarpC.

***Voyage.** Stephen Baxter. LC 96-29464. 528p. 1997. 23.00 (*0-06-105258-2*, HarperPrism) HarpC.

***Voyage.** Stephen Baxter. 1997. pap. write for info. (*0-06-105708-8*, HarperPrism) HarpC.

Voyage. David Drake. 416p. 1995. 5.99 (*0-8125-1340-1*) Tor Bks.

Voyage. Dottie Henneberry. (Orig.). Date not set. pap. write for info. (*1-882825-20-9*) Hse of Prayer.

Voyage. Robert MacNeil. LC 95-22795. 304p. 1995. 23.95 (*0-385-46952-7*, N A Talese) Doubleday.

Voyage. Robert MacNeil. 1995. 23.95 (*0-614-15473-1*, N A Talese) Doubleday.

Voyage. Elaine L. Schulte. 256p. 1996. pap. 8.99 (*1-57673-011-5*, Palisades OR) Multnomah Pubs.

Voyage. large type ed. Robert MacNeil. 502p. 1996. 23.95 (*0-7862-0616-0*, Thorndike Lrg Prnt) Thorndike Pr.

Voyage. large type ed. Robert MacNeil. LC 96-28001. (Harvest Bks.). 304p. 1996. pap. 12.00 (*0-15-600463-1*) HarBrace.

Voyage: A Chartbook for Career Life Planning. Margaret G. Anstin. 192p. (C). 1996. per., pap. text ed. 19.42 (*0-8403-2204-6*) Kendall-Hunt.

Voyage: Visions in Color & Form. Claude Sieber. LC 94-33059. 1994. text ed. 148.00 (*0-86715-296-6*) Quint Pub Co.

Voyage a Lyon. Stendahl. (Illus.). 160p. (FRE.). 1995. 54.95 (*2-86808-088-X*) Intl Scholars.

Voyage a Naucratis. Jacques Almira. 552p. (FRE.). 1990. pap. 21.95 (*0-7859-2148-6*, 2070382834) Fr & Eur.

Voyage a Paris. Richard Leeson. (Illus.). 1971. pap. text ed. 5.25 (*0-582-36036-6*); audio 12.50 (*0-582-37175-9*) Longman.

Voyage along the Western Coast or Newest Africa, a Description of Newest Africa: or the Africa of Today & the Immediate Future. Joseph H. Reading. LC 72-5528. (Black Heritage Library Collection). 1977. reprint ed. 25.95 (*0-8369-9147-8*) Ayer.

An Asterisk (*) at the beginning of an entry indicates that the title is appearing in BIP for the first time.

Voyage & Travaile of M. C. Frederick into the East India. Cesare Federici. Tr. by T. Hickock. LC 70-171758. (English Experience Ser.: No. 340). 84p. 1971. reprint ed. 20.00 (*90-221-0340-4*) Walter J Johnson.

Voyage Around My Room: Selected Works of Xavier de Maistre. Xavier De Maistre. Tr. by Stephen Sartarelli from FRE. LC 94-17834. 192p. (Orig.). 1994. pap. 14.00 (*0-8112-1280-7*, NDP791) New Directions.

***Voyage Around the World with the Romanzov Exploring Expedition in the Years 1815-1818 in the Brig Rurik, Captain Otto von Kotzebue.** Adelbert Von Chamisso. Ed. & Tr. by Henry Kratz. LC 86-11255. (Illus.). 400p. 1986. reprint ed. pap. 114.00 (*0-608-04384-2*, 2065165) Bks Demand.

Voyage Around the World, 1816-1819. Camille de Roquefeuil. 143p. 1983. 14.95 (*0-87770-258-6*) Ye Galleon.

Voyage Around the World, 1826-1829, Vol. 1: To Russian America & Siberia. Frederick Luetke. Ed. by Richard A. Pierce. Tr. by Renee Marshall from FRE. (Alaska History Ser.: No. 29). (Illus.). 1986. 26.50 (*0-919642-97-7*) Limestone Pr.

Voyage au Bout de la Nuit. Louis-Ferdinand Celine. (FRE.). 1972. pap. 16.95 (*0-8288-3627-2*, F92100) Fr & Eur.

Voyage au Bout de la Nuit. Louis-Ferdinand Celine. (Folio Ser.: No. 28). (FRE.). pap. 13.95 (*2-07-036028-8*) Schoenhof.

Voyage au bout de Nuit de Celine. Henri Godard. 211p. (FRE.). 1991. pap. 12.95 (*0-7859-2608-9*, 2070383504) Fr & Eur.

Voyage au Centre de la Terre. Jules Verne. 1988. pap. 10.95 (*0-7859-3082-5*) Fr & Eur.

Voyage au Centre de la Terre: Avec: Une Ville Flottante. Jules Verne. 500p. 9.95 (*0-686-55961-4*) Fr & Eur.

Voyage au Congo: Le Retour du Tchad. Andre Gide. (FRE.). 1981. pap. 14.95 (*0-7859-2852-9*) Fr & Eur.

Voyage au Congo - Le Retour du Tchad. Andre Gide. (Idees Ser.). (FRE.). pap. 11.95 (*2-07-035443-1*) Schoenhof.

Voyage au Pays des Arbres. J. M. Le Clezio. (Folio - Cadet Rouge Ser.: No. 187). (Illus.). 48p. (FRE.). (J). (gr. 3-7). 1990. pap. 8.95 (*2-07-031187-2*) Schoenhof.

Voyage Au Tour Du Monde Par le Fregate Du Roi la Boudeuse. Louis-Antoine De Bougainville. (FRE.). 1982. pap. 16.95 (*0-7859-1958-9*, 2070373851) Fr & Eur.

Voyage Autour de Ma Marmite. Eugene Labiche. 9.95 (*0-686-54259-2*) Fr & Eur.

Voyage Autour du Monde par les Mers de l'Indeet de Chine, Tome 1. Cyrille P. Laplace. (Discovery of the Pacific & Australia Ser.). (Illus.). 602p. (FRE.). (C). 1989. reprint ed. 135.00 (*1-85297-001-4*, Pub. by Archival Facs UK) St Mut.

Voyage Autour du Monde...Sur la Covette Tome 1: La Coquille. Rene P. Lesson. (Discovery of the Pacific & Australia Ser.). (Illus.). 518p. (FRE.). (C). 1989. reprint ed. 135.00 (*1-85297-006-5*, Pub. by Archival Facs UK) St Mut.

Voyage Beyond Belief. large type ed. Terence Kelly. (General Ser.). 464p. 1993. 25.99 (*0-7089-2844-7*) Ulverscroft.

Voyage Charters. J. Cooke et al. 930p. 1993. 260.00 (*1-85044-263-0*) LLP.

Voyage Chez les Morts. Eugene Ionesco. (Gallimard Ser.). 133p. (FRE.). 1981. pap. 13.95 (*2-07-024660-4*) Schoenhof.

Voyage d'Alice ou Comment Sont Nes les Droits de l'Enfant. Jean O. Heron. (Folio - Cadet Rouge Ser.: No. 245). (Illus.). 151p. (FRE.). (J). (gr. 3-7). 1990. pap. 11.95 (*2-07-031245-3*) Schoenhof.

Voyage dans la Haute Pennsylvanie et dans l'Etat de New York. Michel-Guillaume Jean De Crevecoeur. (Works of Michel-Guillaume Jean De Crevecoeur Ser.). 1990. reprint ed. lib. bdg. 79.00 (*0-7812-2455-1*) Rprt Serv.

Voyage dans le Midi de la France. Stendhal. 1930. 48.00 (*0-686-55084-6*) Fr & Eur.

***Voyage dans le Temps.** Denis Cote. (Novels in the Roman Jeunesse Ser.). 96p. (FRE.). (J). (gr. 4-7). 1996. pap. 7.95 (*2-89021-095-2*, Pub. by Les Editions CN) Firefly Bks Ltd.

Voyage dans les Tenebres. Jean Rhys. (FRE.). 1978. pap. 10.95 (*0-7859-4108-8*) Fr & Eur.

Voyage dans l'Interieur des Etats-Unis et au Canada. Edouard C. Colbert & Gilbert Chinard. 1979. 17.95 (*0-405-10596-7*) Ayer.

Voyage de Babar. Jean de Brunhoff. 27p. (J). 1975. 15.95 (*0-7859-0676-2*, FC581) Fr & Eur.

Voyage de Babar. Jean De Brunhoff. (Illus.). (FRE & SPA.). (J). bds. 15.95 (*0-685-11626-3*) Fr & Eur.

Voyage de Candide. Georges Duhamel. 15.00 (*0-686-55201-6*) Fr & Eur.

***Voyage de la Vie.** Marie-Francine Hebert. (Monts En Images Ser.). (Illus.). 12p. (FRE.). (J). (ps up). 1996. bds. 4.95 (*2-89021-045-6*, Pub. by Les Editions CN) Firefly Bks Ltd.

Voyage de Laperouse sur les Cotes de l'Alaska et de la California (1786) Jean F. Laperouse & Gilbert Chinard. 1979. 21.95 (*0-405-10592-4*) Ayer.

Voyage de M. Perrichon. Eugene Labiche. Ed. by Andre Barsacq. (FRE.). 1954. 7.95 (*0-7859-0011-X*, F65490); pap. 5.95 (*0-686-54261-4*) Fr & Eur.

Voyage de Monsieur Perrichon. Eugene Labiche. (Coll. Mises en Scene). pap. 9.50 (*0-685-34925-X*) Fr & Eur.

Voyage de Noces. Patrick Modiano. (Folio Ser.: No. 2330). (FRE.). pap. 8.95 (*2-07-038454-3*) Schoenhof.

Voyage de Patrice Periot. Georges Duhamel. 256p. (FRE.). 1983. pap. 12.95 (*0-7859-4724-8*) Fr & Eur.

Voyage de Plume. Hans De Beer. (Illus.). 32p. (FRE.). (J). (gr. k-3). 1992. 14.95 (*3-314-20619-4*) North-South Bks NYC.

Voyage De Shakespeare. Leon Daudet. 384p. (FRE.). 1969. pap. 10.95 (*0-7859-1776-4*, 2070365387) Fr & Eur.

Voyage d'Outremer of Bertrandon de la Broquiere. Galen R. Kline. (American University Studies: Romance Languages & Literature: Ser. II, Vol. 83). 183p. (C). 1988. text ed. 32.50 (*0-8204-0659-7*) P Lang Pubng.

Voyage Egoiste: Quatre Saisons. Sidonie-Gabrielle Colette. (FRE.). 1989. pap. 10.95 (*0-7859-3124-4*) Fr & Eur.

Voyage en Amerique see Oeuvres Romanesques et Voyages

Voyage en Angleterre & en France: Dans les Annees 1831, 1832 & 1833. Francois-Xavier Garneau. LC 76-369264. (Collection Presence, Serie A). 379p. 1968. reprint ed. pap. 108.10 (*0-608-01990-9*, 2062646) Bks Demand.

Voyage en Bretagne. Par les Champs et par les Greves. Gustave Flaubert. (FRE.). 1991. pap. 24.95 (*0-7859-3315-8*, 2870272944) Fr & Eur.

Voyage en Calabre. Alexandre Dumas. (FRE.). 1989. pap. 24.95 (*0-7859-3316-6*, 2870272979) Fr & Eur.

Voyage en Espagne. Theophile Gautier. 400p. 1976. write for info. (*0-318-63618-2*) Fr & Eur.

Voyage en Espana Suivi D'Espana. Theophile Gautier. 608p. (FRE.). 1981. pap. 12.95 (*0-7859-2444-2*, 2070372952) Fr & Eur.

Voyage en Icarie. Etienne Cabet. LC 69-16857. viii, 600p. 1973. reprint ed. 65.00 (*0-678-01022-6*) Kelley.

Voyage en Italie. Jean Giono. 224p. (FRE.). 1979. pap. 10.95 (*0-7859-2425-6*, 2070371433) Fr & Eur.

Voyage en Italie. Jean Giono. (Folio Ser.: No. 1143). 264p. (FRE.). 1954. 8.95 (*2-07-037143-3*) Schoenhof.

Voyage en Orient, 2 vols. Gerard De Nerval. (FRE.). 1980. pap. 12.95 (*0-7859-2976-2*) Fr & Eur.

Voyage en Orient, 2 vols., 1. Gerard De Nerval. (FRE.). 1980. pap. 12.95 (*0-7859-2975-4*) Fr & Eur.

Voyage en Orient see Oeuvres

Voyage from the Past. Julie S. William. (Kamehameha Schools Intermediate Reading Program Ser.). (Illus.). 98p. (Orig.). (J). (gr. 3-7). 1992. pap. 7.95 (*0-87336-044-3*) Kamehameha Schools.

Voyage from Yesteryear. James P. Hogan. 1986. mass mkt. 4.99 (*0-345-34246-1*, Del Rey) Ballantine.

Voyage Home. Vonda N. McIntyre. (Star Trek Ser.: Vol. 4). 1986. mass mkt. 5.50 (*0-671-70283-1*) PB.

Voyage In: Fictions of Female Development. Ed. by Elizabeth Abel et al. LC 82-40473. 374p. 1983. reprint ed. pap. 106.60 (*0-608-02315-9*, 2062956) Bks Demand.

Voyage in a Bowler Hat. Hugh Malet. 272p. (C). 1989. 50.00 (*0-947712-02-X*, Pub. by S A Baldwin UK) St Mut.

Voyage in Search of La Perouse, Performed by Order of the Constituent Assembly, During the Years 1701-1704. Jacques-Julien H. De Labillardiere. (Bibliotheca Australiana Ser.: No. 67). (Illus.). 560p. 1971. reprint ed. lib. bdg. 87.50 (*90-6072-086-5*, Pub. by Nico Israel NE) Lubrecht & Cramer.

Voyage in the Dark. Jean Rhys. 1994. pap. 8.95 (*0-393-31146-5*) Norton.

Voyage in the Indian Ocean & to Bengal, 1789-1790, 2 vols., Set. L. De Grandpre. (C). 1995. reprint ed. 64.00 (*81-206-1031-8*, Pub. by Asian Educ Servs II) S Asia.

Voyage into Creativity: The Modern Kunstlerroman. Roberta Seret. LC 91-35884. (Studies in European Thought: Vol. 4). 168p. (C). 1992. text ed. 39.95 (*0-8204-1812-9*) P Lang Pubng.

Voyage into Levant. Henry Blount. LC 77-6850. (English Experience Ser.: No. 850). 1977. reprint ed. lib. bdg. 25.00 (*90-221-0850-3*) Walter J Johnson.

Voyage into Violence. Frances Lockridge & Richard Lockridge. 1975. reprint ed. lib. bdg. 21.95 (*0-89190-908-7*, Rivercity Pr) Amereon Ltd.

Voyage Into Violence: A Mr. & Mrs. North Mystery. large type ed. Frances Lockridge & Richard Lockridge. LC 93-12738. 1993. Alk. paper. 17.95 (*1-56054-300-0*) Thorndike Pr.

Voyage Journal. Cavallini & Company Staff. 1995. 16.00 (*1-57489-003-4*); 24.00 (*1-57489-004-2*) Cavallini.

Voyage Musical Aux Pays du Passe. Romain Rolland. (Illus.). 271p. (FRE.). 1976. pap. 49.95 (*0-7859-5471-6*) Fr & Eur.

Voyage of a Summer Sun: Canoeing the Columbia River. Robin Cody. LC 96-19995. 320p. 1996. reprint ed. pap. 14.95 (*1-57061-083-5*) Sasquatch Bks.

Voyage of Alexander Mackenzie. 42p. reprint ed. pap. 5.75 (*0-8466-0182-6*, S182) Shorey.

Voyage of Bran, Son of Febal, to the Land of the Living, 2 Vols. Imran Brain. Tr. by Kuno Meyer. LC 70-144520. (Grimm Library: Nos. 4, 6). reprint ed. Set. 84.50 (*0-404-53580-1*) AMS Pr.

Voyage of Brendan. Daniel De'Agnelli & J. J. O'Meara. 96p. 1994. 39.50 (*1-85182-165-1*, Pub. by Four Cts Pr IE); boxed 225.00 (*1-85182-166-X*, Pub. by Four Cts Pr IE) Intl Spec Bk.

Voyage of Captain Don Felipe Gonzalez to Easter Island. Ed. by Bolton G. Corney. (Hakluyt Society Second Ser.: Vol. 13). (Illus.). 254p. 1996. 56.00 (*0-85115-960-5*, Pub. by Hakluyt Soc UK) Boydell & Brewer.

Voyage of Captain John Saris to Japan, 1613. Ed. by Ernest M. Satow. (Hakluyt Society Second Ser.: Vol. 5). (Illus.). 331p. 1996. 63.00 (*0-85115-954-0*, Pub. by Hakluyt Soc UK) Boydell & Brewer.

Voyage of Contemporary Japanese Theatre. Senda Akihiko. Tr. by J. Thomas Rimer. LC 96-22961. (Illus.). 320p. 1997. text ed. 45.00 (*0-8248-1722-2*) UH Pr.

Voyage of Death. write for info. (*0-318-58995-8*) Sri Shirdi Sai.

Voyage of Destiny. large type ed. Janetta Jackson. (Linford Romance Library). 320p. 1993. pap. 15.99 (*0-7089-7464-3*, Traitree Bookshop) Ulverscroft.

Voyage of Destiny. large type ed. Ivy Preston. (Linford Romance Library). 1990. pap. 15.99 (*0-7089-6827-9*, Traitree Bookshop) Ulverscroft.

Voyage of Discovery. J. R. Heavens. (C). 1988. 35.00 (*0-7212-0725-1*, Pub. by Regency Press UK) St Mut.

Voyage of Discovery: A History of Western Philosophy. William F. Lawhead. LC 95-30240. 614p. (C). 1996. text ed. 48.95 (*0-534-23346-5*) Wadsworth Pub.

***Voyage of Discovery from the Big Bang to the Ice Age.** Marc J. Defant. LC 97-14907. 288p. 1997. 34.50 (*0-931541-61-1*) Mancorp Pub.

Voyage of Discovery to the North Pacific Ocean, & Round the World in the Years 1790-95, 3 vols. George Vancouver. 1992. reprint ed. lib. bdg. 225.00 (*0-7812-5100-1*) Rprt Serv.

Voyage of Doctor Dolittle. Hugh Lofting. 336p. (J). (gr. 4-7). 1988. mass mkt. 4.99 (*0-440-40002-3*, YB BDD) BDD Bks Young Read.

Voyage of HMS Herald 1852-1861. Andrew David. (The Miegunyah Press Ser.: No. 2:3). (Illus.). 576p. 1995. 69.95 (*0-522-84390-5*, Pub. by Melbourne Univ Pr AT) Paul & Co Pubs.

Voyage of John Huyghen Van Linschoten to the East Indies: From the Old English Translation of 1598, 2 vols. Ed. by Arthur C. Burnall & P. A. Tiale. (C). 1988. Set. 50.00 (*81-206-0420-2*, Pub. by Asian Educ Servs II) S Asia.

Voyage of King Njoya's Gift: A Beaded Sculpture from the Bamum Kingdon, Cameroon, in the National Museum of African Art. Christraud M. Geary. LC 94-38694. (Illus.). 64p. 1994. pap. 9.95 (*0-295-97428-1*) U of Wash Pr.

Voyage of Life on a Paper Boat, No. 12. Arnold C. Westphal. pap. 4.95 (*0-915398-22-2*) Visual Evangels.

Voyage of Ludgate Hill: Travels with Robert Louis Stevenson. Nancy Willard et al. LC 86-19502. (Illus.). 32p. (J). (gr. k-3). 1994. pap. 5.00 (*0-15-200119-0*) HarBrace.

Voyage of Mael Duin's Curragh. 2nd ed. Patricia Aakhus. 236p. 1989. pap. 12.95 (*0-934257-31-0*) Story Line.

Voyage of Osiris: A Myth of Ancient Egypt. As told by Gerald McDermott. LC 94-7067. (Illus.). (J). 1995. write for info. (*0-15-200216-2*) HarBrace.

Voyage of Osiris: A Myth of Ancient Egypt. Illus. & As told by Gerald McDermott. LC 94-7067. (J). 1995. pap. write for info. (*0-15-294446-X*) HarBrace.

***Voyage of Pedro Alvares Cabral to Brazil & India: From Contemporary Documents & Narratives.** Tr. by William B. Greenlee. (C). 1995. 42.00 (*81-206-1040-7*, Pub. by Asian Educ Servs II) S Asia.

Voyage of Rediscovery: A Cultural Odyssey Through Polynesia. Ben R. Finney. LC 94-3998. (Illus.). 401p. 1994. 30.00 (*0-520-08002-5*) U CA Pr.

Voyage of Robert Dudley to the West Indies 1594-1595. Ed. by George F. Warner. (Hakluyt Society Second Ser.: Vol. 3). 162p. 1996. 45.00 (*0-85115-952-4*, Pub. by Hakluyt Soc UK) Boydell & Brewer.

Voyage of Sir Henry Middleton to the Moluccas 1604-1606. Ed. by William Foster. (Hakluyt Society Second Ser.: Vol. 88). (Illus.). 253p. 1996. 45.00 (*0-85115-985-0*, Pub. by Hakluyt Soc UK) Boydell & Brewer.

Voyage of St. Brendan. Tr. by John J. O'Meara. 1981. pap. 9.95 (*0-85105-384-X*, Pub. by Colin Smythe Ltd UK) Dufour.

Voyage of Sutil & Mexicana, 1792: The Last Spanish Exploration of the Northwest Coast of America. Josef E. Tello. Ed. & Tr. by John Kendrick. LC 90-52753. (Northwest Historical Ser.: No. XVI). (Illus.). 260p. 1991. 32.50 (*0-87062-203-X*) A H Clark.

Voyage of the Argo. Appollonius. Tr. & Intro. by Emil V. Rieu. (Classics Ser.). 224p. (Orig.). 1959. pap. 9.95 (*0-14-044085-2*, Penguin Classics) Viking Penguin.

Voyage of the Basset. James C. Christensen et al. 168p. (J). 1996. 29.95 (*1-885183-58-5*) Artisan IL.

Voyage of the Beagle. Charles Darwin. 1996. pap. 11.95 (*0-452-01163-9*, Mer) NAL-Dutton.

Voyage of the Beagle: Charles Darwin's Journal of Researches. Charles Darwin. Ed. by Janet Browne & Michael Neue. 448p. 1989. pap. 11.95 (*0-14-043268-X*, Penguin Classics) Viking Penguin.

Voyage of the Cap Pilar. Adrian Seligman. (Illus.). 360p. 1993. pap. 14.95 (*0-924486-62-7*) Sheridan.

Voyage of the Chianti. B. J. Morison. LC 87-24888. 300p. 1987. 15.95 (*0-89621-110-X*); pap. 8.95 (*0-89621-112-6*) Nrth Country Pr.

***Voyage of the Damned.** 24.95 (*1-56723-094-6*) Yestermorrow.

Voyage of the Damned. Gordon Thomas & Max Morgan-Witts. LC 73-91845. (Illus.). 287p. 1994. 9.98 (*0-87938-909-5*) Motorbooks Intl.

Voyage of the Dawn Treader. C. S. Lewis. LC 93-11515. (Chronicles of Narnia Ser.). (Illus.). 208p. (J). (gr. 3 up). 1994. pap. 3.95 (*0-06-447107-1*) HarpC Child Bks.

Voyage of the Dawn Treader. C. S. Lewis. LC 93-11515. (Chronicles of Narnia Ser.: Bk. 3). (Illus.). 208p. (J). (gr. 3 up). 1994. 15.00 (*0-06-023486-5*) HarpC Child Bks.

Voyage of the Dawn Treader. C. S. Lewis. LC 93-11515. (Chronicles of Narnia Ser.: Bk. 5). (Illus.). 256p. (J). (gr. 3 up). 1994. lib. bdg. 14.89 (*0-06-023487-3*) HarpC Child Bks.

Voyage of the Devilfish. M. Dimercurio. pap. 4.98 (*0-8317-3439-6*) Smithmark.

Voyage of the Devilfish. Michael DiMercurio. 400p. 1993. pap. 4.99 (*0-451-40392-4*, Onyx) NAL-Dutton.

Voyage of the Dolphin. Gilbert Morris. (Seven Sleepers Ser.: No. 7). 1996. pap. 5.99 (*0-8024-3687-0*) Moody.

Voyage of the Dragonfly. Max Bush. (J). 1990. Playscript. 5.00 (*0-87602-287-5*) Anchorage.

Voyage of the Exiles. Patricia Hickman. LC 94-24234. (Land of the Far Horizons Ser.: Bk. 1). 320p. 1995. pap. 9.99 (*1-55661-541-8*) Bethany Hse.

***Voyage of the Exiles, Angel of the Outback & the Emerald Frame, Vols. 1-3.** Patricia Hickman. (Land of the Far Horizons Ser.). 1997. pap. text ed. 29.99 (*0-7642-8151-8*) Bethany Hse.

Voyage of the Eye. Brett Weston. (Illus.). 128p. 1992. 39.95 (*0-89381-506-3*) Aperture.

Voyage of the Fox Rider. Dennis L. McKiernan. 592p. (Orig.). 1994. pap. 5.99 (*0-451-45411-1*, ROC) NAL-Dutton.

Voyage of the Frog. Gary Paulsen. LC 88-15261. (Illus.). 160p. (J). (gr. 6-8). 1989. 15.95 (*0-531-05805-0*) Orchard Bks Watts.

Voyage of the Frog. large type ed. Gary Paulsen. LC 93-30238. (YA). (gr. 9-12). 1993. pap. 16.95 (*0-7862-0060-X*) Thorndike Pr.

Voyage of the Frog. Gary Paulsen. 160p. (J). 1990. reprint ed. pap. 4.50 (*0-440-40364-2*) Dell.

***Voyage of the Frolic: New England Merchants & the Opium Trade.** Thomas N. Layton. 1997. 24.95 (*0-8047-2909-3*) Stanford U Pr.

Voyage of the Half Moon. Tracey West. LC 93-16462. (Stories of the States Ser.). 64p. (Orig.). (J). (gr. 4-6). 1993. lib. bdg. 13.95 (*1-881889-18-1*) Silver Moon.

Voyage of the Half Moon. Tracey West. (Stories of the States Ser.). 96p. (Orig.). (J). (gr. 4-6). 1995. pap. 4.95 (*1-881889-76-9*) Silver Moon.

Voyage of the Iceberg. Richard Brown. (Illus.). 160p. 1995. 17.95 (*0-88862-656-8*) Formac Dist Ltd.

Voyage of the Iceberg: The Story of the Iceberg That Sank the Titanic. Richard Brown. (Illus.). 1984. 13.95 (*0-8253-0187-4*) Beaufort Bks NY.

***Voyage of the Komagata Maru: The Sikh Challenge to Canada's Colour Bar.** Hugh Johnston. 1989. 19.95 (*0-7748-0340-1*, Pub. by U BC Pr) U of Wash Pr.

Voyage of the Ludgate Hill: A Journey with Robert Louis Stevenson. Nancy Willard et al. LC 86-19502. (Illus.). 32p. (J). (gr. k-3). 1987. 15.00 (*0-15-294464-8*) HarBrace.

***Voyage of the Matthew: John Cabot & the Discovery of North America.** Peter L. Firstbrook. LC 97-11475. (Illus.). 192p. (Orig.). 1997. pap. 18.95 (*0-912333-22-7*) BB&T Inc.

Voyage of the Mayflower: A Teacher's Guide. Cherie Rayburn. Ed. by Sharon Krall. (Illus.). 16p. 1994. pap. text ed. 10.95 (*0-944943-52-7*, CODE 23831-7) Current Inc.

Voyage of the Micronauts: A Book about the Human Body. Time-Life Books Editors. Ed. by Allan Fallow. (Early Learning Program Ser.). (Illus.). 64p. (J). (ps-2). 1992. write for info. (*0-8094-9295-4*); lib. bdg. write for info. (*0-8094-9296-2*) Time-Life.

Voyage of the New Hazard to the Northwest Coast, Hawaii & China, 1810-1813. Stephen Reynolds. 1970. 24.95 (*0-87770-076-1*) Ye Galleon.

Voyage of the Nina II. Robert F. Marx. (Illus.). 264p. 1991. 24.95 (*0-88415-003-8*, 5003) Gulf Pub.

Voyage of the Peregrin: Learning to Ask the Right Questions about Life, Death & Suffering. Steve Chappell. LC 95-40438. 100p. (Orig.). 1996. pap. 8.95 (*0-7880-0723-8*) CSS OH.

Voyage of the Sanderling: Exploring the Ecology of the Atlantic Coast from Maine to Rio. Roger D. Stone. LC 90-55668. 320p. 1991. pap. 12.00 (*0-679-73178-4*, Vin) Random.

Voyage of the Sonora in 1775. Don F. Mourelle. 150p. 1988. 32.50 (*0-87770-402-3*) Ye Galleon.

Voyage of the Space Beagle. A. E. Van Vogt. 192p. 1992. pap. 8.00 (*0-02-025990-5*) Macmillan.

Voyage of the SS Jeremiah O'Brien from San Francisco to Normandy. Coleman Schneider. (Illus.). 140p. 1994. pap. 14.95 (*0-9601662-5-4*) C Schneider.

Voyage of the Storm. Bart Davis. 1995. mass mkt. 5.99 (*0-671-76905-7*) PB.

Voyage of the Tradewind: Norway to America. 180p. 1994. pap. 8.95 (*0-941016-66-8*) Penfield.

Voyage of the Venus: Sojourn in California. Abel De Petit-Thouars. Tr. by Charles N. Rudkin. LC 95-34789. 115p. 1995. pap. 9.95 (*0-87770-553-4*) Ye Galleon.

Voyage of the Vulcania... Coming to America. Richard L. Bencriscutto & Karl Ebenhoch. 150p. (Orig.). 1995. pap. 12.95 (*0-9649345-3-1*) Bencriscutto.

Voyage of the Water Witch: A Scientific Expedition to Paraguay & the La Plata Region (1853-1856) Robert D. Wood. LC 85-50095. (Illus.). 114p. 1985. pap. 15.00 (*0-911437-15-0*) Labyrinthos.

Voyage of Thomas Best to the East Indies 1612-14. Ed. by William Foster. (C). 1995. reprint ed. 44.00 (*81-206-1039-3*, Pub. by Asian Educ Servs II) S Asia.

Voyage of Vengeance, Vol. 7. L. Ron Hubbard. (Mission Earth Ser.: No. 7). 1995. mass mkt. 5.99 (*0-88404-288-X*) Bridge Pubns Inc.

Voyage of Verrazzano. Henry C. Murphy. LC 72-126244. (Select Bibliographies Reprint Ser.). 1977. 25.95 (*0-8369-5471-8*) Ayer.

***Voyage of Wood Duck: In English & Mi'kmaq.** Maxine Trottier. (Illus.). 32p. (J). (gr. k-2). pap. 9.95 (*0-920336-70-1*, Pub. by U Coll Cape Breton CN) Genl Dist Srvs.

Voyage Out. Virginia Woolf. 432p. 1991. pap. 4.95 (*0-451-52555-8*, Sig Classics) NAL-Dutton.

Voyage Out. Virginia Woolf. 432p. 1992. pap. 10.95 (*0-14-018563-1*, Penguin Classics) Viking Penguin.

Voyage Out. Virginia Woolf. Ed. by Lorna Sage. (World's Classics Ser.). 482p. (C). 1996. pap. 8.95 (*0-19-281834-1*) OUP.

Voyage Out. Virginia Woolf. LC 31-141. 375p. 1968. reprint ed. pap. 10.00 (*0-15-693625-9*, Harvest Bks) HarBrace.

Voyage Perilous: Willa Cather's Romanticism. Susan J. Rosowski. LC 86-4341. xviii, 284p. 1986. text ed. 30.00 (*0-8032-3874-6*) U of Nebr Pr.

Voyage Pittoresque en Algerie, 1845. Theophile Gautier. 302p. (FRE.). 1973. 79.95 (*0-7859-0072-1*, M2351) Fr & Eur.

***Voyage Pour Deux - Travels for Two.** Stephane Poulin. (Picture Bks.). (Illus.). 32p. (J). 1996. pap. 6.95 (1-55037-206-8, Pub. by Les Editions CN); lib. bdg. 15.95 (1-55037-207-6, Pub. by Les Editions CN) Firefly Bks Ltd.

Voyage Round the World in the Years 1785, 1786, 1787, & 1788. William C. Lauder. 150p. 1985. reprint ed. 14.95 (0-87770-325-6) Ye Galleon.

Voyage That Never Ends see Malcolm Lowry

Voyage Through Childhood into the Adult World: A Guide to Child Development. Eva A. Frommer. (Illus.). 152p. 1995. pap. 18.95 (1-869890-59-0, Pub. by Hawthorn Press UK) Anthroposophic.

Voyage Through Space: Poems. Vera Flandorf. Ed. by M. A. Myers. LC 91-75905. 64p. (Orig.). 1991. pap. 7.95 (1-879183-12-9) Bristol Banner.

Voyage to Abyssinia. Samuel Johnson. Ed. by Joel J. Gold. LC 57-11918. (Works of Samuel Johnson Ser.: Vol. XV). 400p. 1985. text ed. 60.00 (0-300-03003-7) Yale U Pr.

Voyage to Abyssinia. Jeronymo Lobo. Tr. by Samuel Johnson. LC 74-15064. reprint ed. 55.00 (0-404-12105-5) AMS Pr.

Voyage to Abyssinia & Travels into the Interior of That Country. H. Salt. (Illus.). 600p. 1967. 95.00 (0-7146-1015-1, Pub. by F Cass Pubs UK) Intl Spec Bk.

Voyage to America Ninety Years Ago: The Diary of a Bohemian Jew on His Voyage from Hamburg to New York in 1847. S. E. Rosenbaum. Tr. by Nathan Kravetz. LC 93-2898. (Studies in Judaica & the Holocaust: No. 3). 120p. 1995. reprint ed. pap. 17.00 (0-89370-471-7); reprint ed. lib. bdg. 27.00 (0-89370-371-0) Borgo Pr.

Voyage to America, 1783-1786. Grigorii I. Shelikhov. Ed. by Richard A. Pierce. Tr. by Marina Ramsay from RUS. (Alaska History Ser.: No. 19). (Illus.). 1981. 20.00 (0-919642-67-5) Limestone Pr.

Voyage To Arcturus. David Lindsay. 248p. 1985. pap. 5.95 (0-8065-0944-9, Citadel Pr) Carol Pub Group.

Voyage to Arcturus. David Lindsay. 1993. reprint ed. lib. bdg. 18.95 (0-89968-406-8, Lghtyr Pr) Buccaneer Bks.

Voyage to Atlantis: The Discovery of a Legendary Land. rev. ed. James W. Mavor, Jr. (Illus.). 320p. 1996. reprint ed. pap. 16.95 (0-89281-634-1) Inner Tradit.

Voyage to Dauphin Island in 1720: The Journal of Bertet De la Clue. Ed. by Francis Escoffier & Jay Higginbotham. Tr. by Jay Higginbotham. LC 73-91909. (Illus.). (FRE.). 1974. 7.95 (0-914334-02-6) Museum Mobile.

Voyage to Destiny. Alfred J. Rickey. 226p. (Orig.). 1989. pap. 8.95 (0-9623077-0-X) Aldarob Enterprises.

Voyage to Disaster. Henrietta Drake-Brockman. 324p. (C). 1995. pap. 26.95 (1-875560-32-7, Pub. by Univ of West Aust Pr AT) Intl Spec Bk.

Voyage to Discovery: An Activity Guide to the Age of Exploration. Diane P. Ramsay. (Illus.). xiii, 346p. (Orig.). 1992. pap. text ed. 25.00 (1-56308-063-X) Teacher Ideas Pr.

Voyage to Enchantment. large type unabridged ed. (Harlequin Ser.). 1994. lib. bdg. 19.95 (0-263-13895-X, Pub. by Mills & Boon UK) Thorndike Pr.

Voyage to Freedom: Story of the Pilgrim Fathers. David Gay. 149p. (J). 1984. pap. 8.99 (0-85151-384-0) Banner of Truth.

Voyage to Greenland: A Personal Initiation into Anthropology. Frederica De Laguna. (Illus.). 285p. (C). 1995. reprint ed. pap. text ed. 11.95 (0-88133-854-0) Waveland Pr.

Voyage to Honor. Robert H. Fowler. 576p. 1996. 29.95 (0-8117-0913-2) Stackpole.

Voyage to Illyria: A New Study of Shakespeare. Kenneth Muir & Sean O'Loughlin. LC 79-128891. (Select Bibliographies Reprint Ser.). 1977. reprint ed. 19.95 (0-8369-5511-0) Ayer.

Voyage to Inner Mongolia & Tibet: 1985-86. Christine De Weck. 1988. 10.95 (0-533-07379-0) Vantage.

Voyage to Insight. Rhonda D. Chervin & Lois A. Janis. 116p. (C). 1994. teacher ed., pap. 13.95 (1-887582-02-9) Chiaro Oscuro Pr.

Voyage to Jupiter: The Voyager Mission. 1994. lib. bdg. 260.95 (0-8490-6451-1) Gordon Pr.

Voyage to Maryland 1633: Relatio Itineris in Marilandiam. Andrew White & Jozef Ijsewijn. Ed. by Barbara Lawatsch-Boomgaarden. (Illus.). 119p. (ENG & LAT.). 1995. 50.00 (0-86516-279-4); pap. 25.00 (0-86516-280-8) Bolchazy-Carducci.

Voyage to Pagany. William C. Williams. LC 76-122108. 1970. pap. 8.25 (0-8112-0237-2, NDP307) New Directions.

Voyage to Pagany. William C. Williams. 1988. reprint ed. lib. bdg. 49.00 (0-7812-0459-3) Rprt Serv.

Voyage to Pagany. William C. Williams. LC 71-145373. 338p. 1972. reprint ed. 39.00 (0-403-01278-3) Scholarly.

Voyage to Quiburio Vol. 1: Dawn at Galistea. William R. Lyne. (Illus.). 264p. (Orig.). (YA). 1997. pap. 18.00 (0-9637467-4-X) Creatopia Prods.

Voyage to Remember. Ed. by Rick Schaub. 1996. 69.95 (1-57553-004-X) Watermrk Pr.

Voyage to Rome in French Renaissance Literature. Eric MacPhail. (Stanford French & Italian Studies: Vol. 68). 224p. 1991. pap. 46.50 (0-915838-84-2) Anma Libri.

Voyage to South America, 2 vols. H. M. Brackenridge. 1972. 450.00 (0-8490-1269-4) Gordon Pr.

Voyage to South America, 2 vols. in 1. Henry M. Brackenridge. LC 70-128425. reprint ed. 62.50 (0-404-00922-0) AMS Pr.

Voyage to St. Kilda Sixteen Ninety-Seven. Martin Martin. 63p. (C). 1985. 50.00 (0-685-30235-0, Pub. by Mercat Pr Bks UK) St Mut.

Voyage to Terra Australia, 2 vols. Matthew Flinders. 928p. (C). 1989. Set. 910.00 (0-7855-0332-3, Pub. by Royal Geograp Soc AT) St Mut.

Voyage to the Bunny Planet: First Tomato, Moss Pillows, The Island Light, 3 bks., Set. Rosemary Wells. (Illus.). 32p ea.p. (J). (ps-3). 1992. pap. 14.99 (0-8037-1174-3) Dial Bks Young.

Voyage to the East Indies (1798), 2 vols., Set. John S. Staorinus. Tr. by Samuel H. Wilcooke from DUT. 1110p. 1969. 200.00 (0-614-01796-3) Elliots Bks.

Voyage to the Edge of the World. L. Sims. (Puzzle Adventures Ser.). (Illus.). 48p. (J). 1995. pap. 5.50 (0-7460-1690-5, Usborne); lib. bdg. 13.95 (0-88110-749-2, Usborne) EDC.

Voyage to the Great Attractor: A Journey Through Intergalactic Space. Alan Dressler. LC 93-48580. 1994. 25.00 (0-394-58899-1) Knopf.

Voyage to the Great Attractor: Exploring Intergalactic Space. Alan Dressler. 1995. pap. 13.00 (0-679-73298-5, Vin) Random.

Voyage to the Island. Raija Nieminen. LC 90-19178. 272p. 1990. 17.95 (0-930323-62-9) Gallaudet Univ Pr.

Voyage to the North Pacific. John D'Wolf. LC 93-39255. 19.95 (0-87770-526-7) Ye Galleon.

Voyage to the North Pacific. 2nd ed. John D'Wolf. Date not set. pap. 12.95 (0-87770-560-7) Ye Galleon.

Voyage to the North Pacific. 2nd ed. John D'Wolf. Date not set. 19.95 (0-87770-559-3) Ye Galleon.

Voyage to the Other World: The Legacy of Sutton Hoo. Ed. by Calvin B. Kendall & Peter S. Wells. (Medieval Studies at Minnesota: Vol. 5). (Illus.). 240p. (C). 1992. pap. text ed. 16.95 (0-8166-2024-5) U of Minn Pr.

***Voyage to the Planets.** Richard B. Bliss. 128p. pap. 11.95 (0-932766-32-3, VOYPLA, Inst Creation) Master Bks.

Voyage to the Planets: Proceedings of the Goddard Memorial Symposium, 5th, 1967. Ed. by S. Fred Singer. (Science & Technology Ser.: Vol. 16). 1968. 20.00 (0-87703-044-8) Univelt Inc.

Voyage to the Red Planet. Terry Bisson. 240p. 1991. mass mkt. 3.50 (0-380-75574-2) Avon.

Voyage to the Sonorous Land, or, The Art of Asking & the Hour We Knew Nothing of Each Other. Peter Handke. Tr. by Gitta Honneger. LC 95-47496. 160p. (C). 1996. pap. 12.00 (0-300-06274-5) Yale U Pr.

Voyage to the Sonorous Land, or, the Art of Asking & the Hour We Knew Nothing of Each Other. Peter Handke. Tr. by Gitta Honneger. LC 95-47496. 160p. (C). 1996. text ed. 25.00 (0-300-06273-7) Yale U Pr.

Voyage to the Southern Ocean: The Letters of Lieutenant William Reynolds from the U. S. Exploring Expedition, 1838-1842. Ed. by Anne H. Cleaver & E. Jeffrey Stann. LC 88-10156. (Illus.). 384p. 1988. 34.95 (0-87021-300-8) Naval Inst Pr.

***Voyage to the Stars.** Richard B. Bliss. 111p. pap. 9.95 (0-932766-21-8, VOYSTA, Inst Creation) Master Bks.

Voyager. 56p. (Orig.). 1993. pap. 20.00 (0-9639599-0-5) Candice.

Voyager. Diana Gabaldon. 880p. 1994. 21.95 (0-385-30232-0) Delacorte.

Voyager. Diana Gabaldon. 1072p. 1994. mass mkt. 6.99 (0-440-21756-3) Dell.

Voyager. Jeana Yeager et al. LC 86-46163. (Illus.). 256p. 1987. 19.95 (0-394-55266-0) Knopf.

Voyager. Charles Mills. LC 89-32337. 157p. reprint ed. pap. 44.80 (0-7837-6401-4, 2046117) Bks Demand.

Voyager: A Life of Hart Crane. John Unterecker. (Illus.). 864p. 1987. reprint ed. pap. 14.95 (0-87140-143-6) Liveright.

Voyager: An Adventure to the Edge of the Solar System. Sally K. Ride. LC 91-32495. (Face to Face with Science Ser.). (Illus.). 36p. (J). (gr. 2-6). 1992. 17.00 (0-517-58157-4); lib. bdg. 14.99 (0-517-58158-2) Crown Bks Yng Read.

Voyager: Exploring the Outer Planets. Joan M. Verba. (Space & Aviation Ser.). 64p. (J). (gr. 5 up). 1991. lib. bdg. 19.95 (0-8225-1597-0, Lerner Publctns) Lerner Group.

***Voyager: Mosaic.** Jeri Taylor. (Star Trek Ser.). 1996. 22.00 (0-614-20655-3, PB Hardcover) PB.

Voyager - the World Flight: The Official Log, Flight Analysis & Narrative Explanation of the Record Around the World Flight of the Voyager Aircraft. Jack Norris. LC 88-90609. (Illus.). 72p. (Orig.). 1988. pap. 12.95 (0-9620239-0-6) J Norris.

Voyager from Xanadu: Rabban Sauma & the First Journey from China to the West. Morris Rossabi. (Illus.). 240p. 1992. 22.00 (4-7700-1650-6) Kodansha.

Voyager, II. Charles Mills. Ed. by Richard Coffen. 192p. (Orig.). (J). (gr. 5-8). 1991. pap. 7.99 (0-8280-0595-8) Review & Herald.

Voyager Neptune Travel Guide. 1994. lib. bdg. 260.75 (0-8490-6450-3) Gordon Pr.

Voyager Out: The Life of Mary Kingsley. Katherine Frank. LC 86-10656. (Illus.). 333p. 1986. 18.95 (0-317-53370-3) HM.

Voyager Season Premier: Star Trek. Carey. 1995. pap. 5.99 (0-671-55193-0) PB.

Voyager Solitaire est un Diable. Henry De Montherlant. 212p. (FRE.). 1961. pap. 11.95 (0-685-74010-2, 207024590X) Fr & Eur.

Voyager Tarot Deck, Vol. 1. 2nd ed. James Wanless. 98p. Date not set. boxed 5.00 (0-9615079-0-X) Merrill-West Pub.

Voyager Tarot, Way of the Great Oracle. 3rd ed. James Wanless. 330p. Date not set. pap. 4.95 (0-9615079-3-4) Merrill-West Pub.

Voyager to the Planets. Necia H. Apfel. (J). (gr. 4-7). 1994. pap. 6.95 (0-395-69622-4, Clarion Bks) HM.

Voyagers. Ben Bova. 1989. mass mkt. 4.95 (0-8125-0076-8) Tor Bks.

Voyagers: A Collection of Words & Images. Herb K. Kane. Ed. by Paul Berry. LC 91-66341. (Illus.). 176p. (Orig.). 1991. pap. write for info. (0-9627095-1-4) WhaleSong.

Voyagers: A Collection of Words & Images by Herb Kawainui Kane. Herb K. Kane. Ed. by Paul Berry. LC 91-66341. (Illus.). 176p. 1991. reprint ed. 39.95 (0-9627095-2-2) WhaleSong.

***Voyager's Handbook: The Essential Guide To Blue Water Cruising.** Beth A. Leonard. 1998. 34.95 (0-07-038143-7) McGraw.

Voyagers, II: The Alien Within. Ben Bova. 1991. mass mkt. 4.95 (0-8125-1337-1) Tor Bks.

Voyagers III: Star Brothers. Ben Bova. 1991. mass mkt. 4.95 (0-8125-3236-8) Tor Bks.

Voyagers in Space. Alain Dupas. (J). (ps-3). Date not set. 5.95 (0-944589-47-2) Young Discovery Lib.

Voyager's Notebook: Selected Poetry of Robin Gajdusek. Robin Gajdusek. 175p. (Orig.). 1989. 20.00 (0-9621858-0-9); pap. 11.95 (0-9621858-1-7) Tintagel Assocs.

Voyagers of the Chilcotin. (Illus.). vii, 267p. (Orig.). 1996. pap. 14.95 (0-9650963-0-0) Carolyn Foltz.

Voyagers of the Vitiaz Strait. Thomas G. Harding. LC 84-45537. (American Ethnological Society Monographs: No. 44). 1988. reprint ed. 35.00 (0-404-62942-3) AMS Pr.

Voyagers One & Two. Bob Italia. Ed. by Rosemary Walner. LC 90-82622. (Explorers of the Past & Present Ser.). (Illus.). 32p. (J). (gr. 4). 1990. lib. bdg. 11.96 (0-939179-96-2) Abdo & Dghtrs.

Voyager's Stone: The Adventures of a Message-Carrying Bottle Adrift on the Ocean Sea. Robert Kraske. LC 94-21049. (Illus.). 96p. (J). (gr. 4-6). 1995. 15.95 (0-531-06890-0); lib. bdg. 16.99 (0-531-08740-9) Orchard Bks Watts.

Voyagers to California. Del Wilcox. 1991. pap. 11.95 (0-9630091-4-1) Sea Rock Pr.

Voyagers to California: Teacher's Guide. Del Wilcox. 62p. 1991. student ed. 5.95 (0-9630091-7-6) Sea Rock Pr.

***Voyagers to Freedom.** Gilbert Morris. (The House of Winslow Ser.). 1997. 12.99 (0-88486-167-8) Arrowood Pr.

Voyagers to the West: A Passage in the Peopling of America on the Eve of the Revolution. Bernard Bailyn. LC 86-45358. 704p. 1986. 35.00 (0-394-51569-2) Knopf.

Voyagers to the West: A Passage in the Peopling of America on the Eve of the Revolution. Bernard Bailyn. LC 87-45917. 736p. 1988. reprint ed. pap. 25.00 (0-394-75778-5, Vin) Random.

Voyages. Terri R. Hoyland & Innersources Staff. (Illus.). 32p. 1993. pap. 4.50 (1-883794-16-1) InnerSources.

Voyages. Terri R. Hoyland. (Illus.). 60p. 1993. 14.00 (1-883794-20-X) InnerSources.

Voyages. Peter Najarian. LC 79-23722. 1980. 8.95 (0-933706-12-X); pap. 4.95 (0-933706-13-8) Ararat Pr.

Voyages. Richard O'Connell. 1995. pap. 25.00 (3-7052-0445-9) Atlantis Edns.

Voyages. Eva Wich. (Orig.). 1996. pap. write for info. (1-57553-167-4) Watermrk Pr.

Voyages: Expanding Horizons. Jerry D. Flack. (Journeys: an Individualized Reading, Writing, & Thinking Program Ser.). 112p. 1993. pap. text ed. 13.95 (0-944459-66-8) ECS Lrn Systs.

***Voyages: From Tongan Villages to American Suburbs.** Cathy A. Small. LC 97-20598. 248p. 1997. 45.00 (0-8014-3412-2) Cornell U Pr.

***Voyages: From Tongan Villages to American Suburbs.** Cathy A. Small. LC 97-20598. 248p. 1997. pap. 15.95 (0-8014-8436-7) Cornell U Pr.

***Voyages: Poems by Walt Whitman.** Walt Whitman. Ed. by Lee B. Hopkins. (Illus.). 96p. 1992. pap. 9.00 (0-15-294496-6, HB Juv Bks) HarBrace.

Voyages: Short Narratives of Susanna Moodie. Ed. by John Thurston. 288p. 1991. pap. 15.00 (0-7766-0326-4, Pub. by Univ Ottawa Pr CN) Paul & Co Pubs.

Voyages & Discoveries. Richard Hakluyt. Ed. & Abr. by Jack Beeching. (English Library). 442p. 1972. pap. 10.95 (0-14-043073-3, Penguin Classics) Viking Penguin.

***Voyages & Discoveries in the South Seas.** Fanning. pap. 8.95 (0-486-25960-9) Dover.

Voyages & Explorations of Samuel De Champlain, Sixteen Four to Sixteen Sixteen, 2 vols. Samuel De Champlain. LC 72-2825. (American Explorers Ser.). (Illus.). reprint ed. Set. 79.50 (0-404-54905-5) AMS Pr.

Voyages & Travels to India, Ceylon, the Red Sea, Abyssinia, & Egypt in the Years 1802-1806, 4 vols., Set. George Valentia. (C). 1994. 125.00 (81-206-0870-4, Pub. by Asian Educ Servs II) S Asia.

Voyages & Visions: Nineteenth-Century European Images of the Middle East from the Victoria & Albert Museum. Charles Newton et al. (Illus.). 128p. (C). 1995. 40.00 (0-295-97490-7) U of Wash Pr.

Voyages Aux Equinoxiales du Nouveau Continent, 30 vols. with 9 vols. bound in 5 in English. Alexander Von Humboldt. (Illus.). 10200p. (ENG & FRE.). reprint ed. lib. bdg. write for info. (90-221-1159-8, Pub. by Nico Israel NE) Lubrecht & Cramer.

Voyages by Starlight. Ian R. MacLeod. LC 96-24237. 288p. 1997. 21.95 (0-87054-171-4, Arkham Hse) Arkham.

***Voyages de Gulliver.** unabridged ed. Jonathan Swift. (FRE.). Date not set. reprint ed. pap. 8.95 (2-87714-359-7, Pub. by Bookking Intl FR) Distribks Inc.

Voyages des francais sur les Grands Lacs et Decouverte de l'Ohio et du Mississippi (1614-1684) see Decouvertes et Establissements des francais dans l'ouest et dans le sud de l'Amerique septentrional: 1614-1754

Voyages d'ibn Batoutah, 4 vols. Ibn Batoutah. Tr. by G. Defremery & B. R. Sanguinetti. 2047p. (FRE.). reprint ed. Set. lib. bdg. 325.00 (0-89241-177-5) Caratzas.

Voyages en Frances. Stendhal. Ed. by Vittorio Del Litto. (FRE.). 1992. lib. bdg. 195.00 (0-685-67909-8) Fr & Eur.

Voyages en Italia: Rome, Naples et Florence (1817 et 1826), L'Italie en 1818, Promenades dans Rome, etc. Stendhal. (Pleiade Ser.). 1920p. (FRE.). 85.95 (2-07-010697-7) Schoenhof.

Voyages en Italie. Stendhal. 1920p. (FRE.). 1973. 105.00 (0-7859-1279-7, 2070106977) Fr & Eur.

Voyages et les Proprietes d'Henri Michaux. Lajos Elkan. (American University Studies: Romance Languages & Literature: Ser. II, Vol. 65). 206p. (C). 1988. text ed. 37.95 (0-8204-0514-0) P Lang Pubng.

Voyages from Montreal Through the Continent of North America to the Frozen & Pacific Oceans in 1789 & 1793, with an Account of the Rise & State of the Fur Trade, 2 vols. Alexander Mackenzie. LC 72-2721. (American Explorers Ser.). reprint ed. 115.00 (0-404-54912-8) AMS Pr.

Voyages in Cassical Mythology. Mary E. Snodgrass. LC 94-21167. 472p. 1994. lib. bdg. 55.00 (0-87436-734-4) ABC-CLIO.

***Voyages in Conceptual Chemistry.** Barouch. 1997. 13.00 (0-7637-0308-7) Jones & Bartlett.

Voyages in Print: English Travel to America, 1576-1624. Mary C. Fuller. (Cambridge Studies in Renaissance Literature & Culture: No. 7). (Illus.). 222p. (C). 1995. text ed. 49.95 (0-521-48161-9) Cambridge U Pr.

Voyages into Michigan's Past. 6th ed. Larry B. Massie. LC 88-70890. (Illus.). 1988. pap. 11.95 (0-932212-58-1) Avery Color.

***Voyages into the Unknown: Exploring the Afterlife.** Bruce A. Moen. 256p. (Orig.). 1997. pap. 12.95 (0-614-29816-4) Hampton Roads Pub Co.

Voyages of American Ships to China, 1784-1844. Kenneth S. Latourette. (Connecticut Academy of Arts & Sciences Ser., Trans.: Vol. 28). 1927. pap. 49.50 (0-685-22810-X) Elliots Bks.

Voyages of Christopher Columbus. Bernard Beacroft. Ed. by Marjorie Reeves. (Then & There Ser.). (Illus.). 96p. (Orig.). (gr. 7-12). 1978. pap. text ed. 4.95 (0-582-21727-X) Longman.

Voyages of Christopher Columbus. Ed. by John D. Clare. (Living History Ser.). (Illus.). 64p. (J). (gr. 2-7). 1992. 17.00 (0-15-200507-2, Gulliver Bks) HarBrace.

Voyages of Columbia. Richard S. Lewis. 1984. text ed. 41.00 (0-231-05924-8) Col U Pr.

Voyages of Columbus. Rex Rienits & Thea Rienits. (Illus.). 152p. 1990. 12.99 (0-517-69039-X) Random Hse Value.

Voyages of Discovery. Captain Cook. (Illus.). 555p. 1993. pap. 16.95 (0-89733-316-0) Academy Chi Pubs.

Voyages of Discovery: Captain Cook & the Exploration of the Pacific. Lynne Withey. 1989. pap. 15.00 (0-520-06564-6) U CA Pr.

Voyages of Discovery: Essays on the Lewis & Clark Expedition. Ed. by James P. Ronda. (Illus.). 300p. Date not set. write for info. (0-917298-44-6); pap. write for info. (0-917298-45-4) MT Hist Soc.

Voyages of Discovery: The Cinema of Frederick Wiseman. Barry K. Grant. (Illus.). 280p. 1992. text ed. 39.95 (0-252-01844-3); pap. text ed. 15.95 (0-252-06208-6) U of Ill Pr.

Voyages of Discovery, (1400-1500 AD) (Time Frame Ser.). (Illus.). 176p. 1989. lib. bdg. 25.93 (0-8094-6446-2) Time-Life.

***Voyages of Doctor Dolittle.** abr. ed. Hugh Lofting. (Illus.). 160p. (J). 1997. pap. 3.99 (0-440-41240-4, YB BDD) BDD Bks Young Read.

Voyages of Enlightenment: Malaspina on the Northwest Coast, 1791-1792. Thomas Vaughan et al. LC 77-88147. (North Pacific Studies: No. 3). (Illus.). 72p. 1977. pap. 6.95 (0-87595-058-2) Oregon Hist.

Voyages of Giovanni da Verrazzano, 1524-1528. Lawrence W. Wroth. 1970. 200.00 (0-685-26710-5) Elliots Bks.

Voyages of Jacques Cartier. LC 92-95268. 177p. 1993. 50.00 (0-8020-5015-8); pap. 16.95 (0-8020-6000-5) U of Toronto Pr.

Voyages of Joshua Slocum. Ed. by Walter M. Teller. (Illus.). 406p. 1995. reprint ed. 29.95 (0-911378-55-3) Sheridan.

Voyages of Paul. (Children's Bible Stories Ser.). (Illus.). 24p. (J). 1993. 4.98 (0-7853-0264-6) Pubns Intl Ltd.

Voyages of Pedro Fernandez de Quiros 1595-1606. Ed. by Clements R. Markham. (Hakluyt Society Second Ser.: Vol. 14). (Illus.). 604p. 1996. 63.00 (0-85115-961-3, Pub. by Hakluyt Soc UK) Boydell & Brewer.

Voyages of Pegleg. H. L. Wehrle & Mary E. Wehrle. LC 95-92201. (Illus.). x, 156p. (Orig.). (J). (gr. 3 up). 1996. pap. 12.95 (1-887285-02-4) Noggleman Pr.

Voyages of Peter Esprit Radisson, Being an Account of His Travels & Experiences among the North American Indians, from 1652 to 1684: Transcribed from Original Messages in the Bodleian Library & British Museum. Pierre E. Radisson. (American Biography Ser.). 385p. 1991. reprint ed. lib. bdg. 79.00 (0-7812-8320-5) Rprt Serv.

Voyages of Samuel de Champlain, 1604-1618. Samuel De Champlain. (BCL1 - History - Canada Ser.). 374p. 1991. reprint ed. lib. bdg. 89.00 (0-7812-6351-4) Rprt Serv.

Voyages of Sindbad. Tr. by Denys Johnson-Davies from ARA. (Tales from Egypt & the Arab World Ser.). (Illus.). 48p. (Orig.). (J). (gr. 3-8). 1994. pap. 6.50 (977-5325-31-5, Pub. by Hoopoe Bks UA) AMIDEAST.

Voyages of St. Brendan: The Navigator & Stories of the Saints of Ireland. Lady Gregory. pap. 4.95 (0-89979-092-5) British Am Bks.

Voyages of the Columbia to the Northwest Coast, 1787-1790 & 1790-1793. rev. ed. Ed. by Frederic W. Howay. (North Pacific Studies). (Illus.). 576p. 1990. reprint ed. 40.00 (0-87595-250-X) Oregon Hist.

***Voyages of the Damn Foole.** Tom McGrath. LC 96-52300. (Illus.). 192p. 1997. text ed. 17.95 (0-07-045089-7) McGraw.

UV

***Voyages of the Discovery.** Ann Savours. pap. 24.95 (*0-86369-811-5*, Pub. by Virgin Pub UK) London Brdge.

Voyages of the Discovery: The Illustrated History of Scott's Ship. Ann Savours. (Illus.). 400p. 1995. pap. 24.95 (*1-86369-811-6*, Pub. by Virgin Pub UK) London Brdge.

Voyages of the Heart: Living an Emotionally Creative Life. James R. Averill & Elma P. Nunley. 1992. 27.95 (*0-02-901108-6*, Free Press) Free Pr.

Voyages of the Ship Revere, 1849-1883. Madeleine R. Gleason. LC 94-75378. (Pacific Maritime History Ser.). 1995. pap. 15.95 (*0-9637586-2-4*) Glencannon Pr.

Voyages of the Steamboat Yellow Stone. Donald Jackson. LC 86-40533. (Illus.). 208p. 1987. reprint ed. pap. 9.95 (*0-8061-2036-3*) U of Okla Pr.

Voyages Through Space & Time: Projects for Voyager II. Jon K. Wooley. LC 94-20065. 284p. 1995. pap. 26.95 (*0-534-25002-5*) Wadsworth Pub.

Voyages Through Space & Time: Projects for Voyager, the Interactive Desktop Planetarium for Macintosh. Jon K. Wooley. 249p. 1992. pap. 25.95 (*0-534-17226-1*) Wadsworth Pub.

***Voyages Through the Universe.** Fraknoi. (C). 1996. pap. text ed. 20.00 (*0-03-020039-3*) HB Coll Pubs.

***Voyages Through the Universe 1.** Fraknoi. (C). 1996. pap. text ed. 53.25 (*0-03-020053-9*) HarBrace.

***Voyages Thru Universe, Vol. 2.** Fraknoi. (C). 1997. pap. write for info. (*0-15-504534-2*) HB Coll Pubs.

Voyages to Paradise: Exploring in the Wake of Captain Cook. William R. Gray. Ed. by Donald J. Crump. (Special Publications Series 15: No. 4). (Illus.). 216p. 1981. lib. bdg. 12.95 (*0-87044-289-9*) Natl Geog.

Voyages to Saturn. 1994. lib. bdg. 260.95 (*0-8490-6449-X*) Gordon Pr.

Voyages to the Inland Sea, Vol 3. Thomas McGrath et al. Ed. by John Judson. LC 73-78705. 83p. 1973. 10.00 (*0-917540-03-4*); pap. 7.00 (*0-917540-12-3*) Ctr Cont Poetry.

Voyages to the Inland Sea, Vol. 4. Ed. by John Judson. 1974. 10.00 (*0-917540-04-2*) Ctr Cont Poetry.

Voyages to the Inland Sea, Vol. 5. Ed. by John Judson et al. 1975. 10.00 (*0-917540-05-0*) Ctr Cont Poetry.

Voyages to the Inland Sea, Vol. 6. Ed. by Jonn Judson et al. 1976. 10.00 (*0-917540-06-9*) Ctr Cont Poetry.

Voyages to the Inland Sea, Vol. 7. William Kloefkorn et al. 1977. 10.00 (*0-917540-08-5*) Ctr Cont Poetry.

Voyages to the Inland Sea, Vol. 7. deluxe ed. William Kloefkorn et al. 1977. 15.00 (*0-917540-09-3*) Ctr Cont Poetry.

Voyages to the Inland Sea, Vol. 8. Felix Stefanile & James Hazard. 1979. 10.00 (*0-917540-10-7*) Ctr Cont Poetry.

Voyages to the Inland Sea, Vol. 8. deluxe ed. Felix Stefanile & James Hazard. 1979. 15.00 (*0-917540-11-5*) Ctr Cont Poetry.

Voyages to the South Seas & to the Northwest Coast of America. enl. ed. Edmund Fanning. 321p. 1970. reprint ed. 24.95 (*0-87770-012-5*) Ye Galleon.

Voyageur. Grace L. Nute. LC 55-12180. xi, 289p. 1987. reprint ed. pap. 8.95 (*0-87351-213-8*) Minn Hist.

Voyageur: Northeast Wisconsin's Historical Review Index to Volumes 1-10: Spring 1984 - Winter/Spring 1994. Compiled by Debra Anderson. LC 95-77399. (Illus.). 102p. (Orig.). 1996. pap. 10.00 (*0-9641499-2-3*) Brown County Hist.

Voyageur Country: A Park in the Wilderness. Robert Treuer. LC 78-23339. (Illus.). 195p. reprint ed. pap. 55.60 (*0-318-39670-X*, 2033240) Bks Demand.

Voyageur de la Toussaint. Georges Simenon. (Folio Ser.: No. 932). 360p. (FRE.). 1941. pap. 9.95 (*2-07-036932-3*) Schoenhof.

Voyageur Imprudent. Rene Barjavel. 256p. (FRE.). 1973. pap. 10.95 (*0-7859-1764-0*, 2070364852) Fr & Eur.

Voyageur sans Bagage. Jean Anouilh et al. Ed. by Diane W. Birckbichler et al. 184p. (FRE.). (C). 1973. pap. text ed. 23.50 (*0-03-088529-9*) HB Coll Pubs.

Voyageur sans Bagage see Pieces Noires

Voyageur sans Bagages. Jean Anouilh. Bd. with Bal des Voleurs. (Folio Ser.: No. 759). (FRE.). 1961. Set pap. 9.25 (*2-07-036759-2*) Schoenhof.

Voyageur Suivi De le Bal Des Voleurs. Jean Anouilh. 219p. (FRE.). 1976. pap. 10.95 (*0-7859-1817-5*, 2070367592) Fr & Eur.

Voyageur the Moose. Ted Leagjeld. (Illus.). (Orig.). (J). (gr. 4-8). pap. write for info. (*0-9616127-0-3*) T Leagjeld.

Voyageur's Highway: Minnesota's Border Lake Land. Grace L. Nute. LC 65-63529. (Illus.). xv, 113p. 1941. pap. 7.95 (*0-87351-006-2*) Minn Hist.

Voyageurs of the Midnight Sun. Dan Cushman. (Orig.). 1994. lib. bdg. 31.00 (*0-8095-4129-7*) Borgo Pr.

***Voyageurs of the Midnight Sun.** large type ed. Dan Cushman. LC 96-43604. (Orig.). 1996. lib. bdg. 18.95 (*1-57490-049-8*, Sagebrush LP West) T T Beeler.

Voyageuse du Soir. Annick Geille. 248p. (FRE.). 1988. pap. 11.95 (*0-7859-2560-0*, 2070380734) Fr & Eur.

Voyaging Chiefs of Havai'i. Teuira Henry. Ed. by Dennis Kawaharada. LC 94-78788. (Illus.). 192p. (Orig.). 1995. pap. 10.95 (*0-9623102-5-5*) Kalamaku Pr.

***Voyaging on a Small Income.** Annie Hill. 1996. pap. text ed. 20.00 (*0-07-028894-1*) McGraw.

Voyaging Portraits: Poems. Gustaf Sobin. LC 87-22100. 128p. 1988. pap. 9.95 (*0-8112-1061-8*, NDP651) New Directions.

Voyaging under Power. Robert P. Beebe. 22.95 (*0-8488-0913-0*) Amereon Ltd.

Voyaging under Power. 3rd ed. James Leishman. 1994. text ed. 29.95 (*0-07-158019-0*) Intl Marine.

Voyeur. Alberto Moravia. Tr. by Tim Parks from ITA. 280p. 1987. 18.95 (*0-374-28544-6*) FS&G.

Voyeur. Moriarty. 1998. 20.50 (*0-684-80426-3*) S&S Trade.

***Voyeur.** Michael Moriarty. 1997. 22.00 (*0-684-80425-5*) S&S Trade.

Voyeur. Alain Robbe-Grillet. Tr. by Richard Howard from FRE. LC 58-9912. 224p. 1989. pap. 9.95 (*0-8021-3165-4*, Grove) Grove-Atltic.

Voyeur: (Selected & New Poems: 1972-1991) Marco Fraticelli. (Essential Poets Ser.). 96p. 1993. pap. 8.00 (*0-920717-14-4*) Guernica Editions.

Voyeur: Roman. Alain Robbe-Grillet. 256p. (FRE.). 1955. pap. 24.95 (*0-7859-1510-9*, 2707302430) Fr & Eur.

***Voyeur Video Guide: A Special-Interest Nudist Video Directory for Adults.** Ed. by Steve Stewart. (Illus.). 124p. 1997. pap. 12.95 (*1-889138-05-3*) Companion Press.

Voyeur's Guide to Men-Women in the Movies - The Voyeur's Guide to Women in the Movies. Mart Martin. (Illus.). 528p. 1994. pap. 15.95 (*0-8092-3642-7*) Contemp Bks.

Voyez de Vos Yeux: Etude Structurelle de Vingt Psaumes, dont le Psaume 119. P. Auffret. LC 92-34557. (Supplements to Vetus Testamentum Ser.: Vol. 48). 1993. 164.00 (*90-04-09707-4*) E J Brill.

***Voynich Manuscript: An Elegant Enigma.** M. E. D'Imperio. ix, 140p. 18.80 (*0-89412-038-7*) Aegean Park Pr.

Voz de la Mujer Que Llevo Dentro. Alfredo Villanueva-Collado. (Illus.). 48p. (Orig.). (SPA.). 1990. pap. text ed. 6.00 (*0-9623552-1-6*, Border Pr) Ed Arcas.

Voz de la Torah, Vol. 1: Genesis I. R. Amram Amselem. 790p. (SPA.). 1987. write for info. (*1-883932-04-1*); write for info. (*1-883932-03-3*) A Amselem.

Voz de la Torah, Vol. 2: Genesis II. R. Amram Amselem. 740p. (SPA.). 1987. write for info. (*1-883932-06-8*); write for info. (*1-883932-05-X*) A Amselem.

Voz de la Torah, Vol. 3: Exodo I. R. Amram Amselem. 715p. (SPA.). 1993. write for info. (*1-883932-08-4*); write for info. (*1-883932-07-6*) A Amselem.

Voz de la Torah, Vol. 4: Exodo II. R. Amram Amselem. 710p. (SPA.). 1993. write for info. (*1-883932-10-6*); write for info. (*1-883932-09-2*) A Amselem.

Voz de la Torah, Vol. 5: Levitico. Amram R. Amselem. 840p. (SPA.). 1993. write for info. (*1-883932-12-2*); write for info. (*1-883932-11-4*) A Amselem.

Voz de la Torah, Vol. 6: Numeros I. R. Amram Amselem. 680p. (SPA.). 1993. write for info. (*1-883932-14-9*); write for info. (*1-883932-02-5*) A Amselem.

Voz de la Torah, Vol. 7: Numeros II. Amram R. Amselem. 480p. (SPA.). 1993. write for info. (*1-883932-16-5*); write for info. (*1-883932-15-7*) A Amselem.

Voz de la Torah, Vol. 8: Deuteronomio I. Amram R. Amselem. 600p. (SPA.). 1993. write for info. (*1-883932-18-1*); write for info. (*1-883932-17-3*) A Amselem.

Voz de la Torah, Vol. 9: Deuteronomio II. R. Amram Amselem. 560p. (SPA.). 1993. write for info. (*1-883932-20-3*); write for info. (*1-883932-19-X*) A Amselem.

***Voz en el Viento - Mark of the Lion No. 1: A Voice in the Wind.** Rivers. 526p. (SPA.). write for info. (*0-7899-0087-4*) Editorial Unilit.

Voz Folklorica de Puerto Rico. Rosa-Nieves. 1967. 16.95 (*0-87751-009-1*) E Torres & Sons.

Voz Inevitable. Angel Cuadra. LC 94-70870. (Coleccion Espejo de Paciencia). 93p. (Orig.). (SPA.). 1994. pap. 9.95 (*0-89729-732-6*) Ediciones.

Voz Poetica de America del Sur. Carlos A. Trujillo. 125p. 39.50 (*0-916379-88-4*) Scripta.

Voz Poetica y Mascaras Femeninas en la Obra de Delmira Agustini, Vol. 13. Jacqueline Giron Alvarado. (Wor(l)ds of Change Ser.). 240p. (SPA.). (C). 1995. text ed. 48.95 (*0-8204-2693-8*) P Lang Pubng.

Vozdvizhenije Tchestnago Krjesta Gospodnja. M. Skaballanovitch. 173p. reprint ed. pap. 6.00 (*0-317-29152-1*) Holy Trinity.

Vozvrashchenie Mendelia Marantsa. David Fridman. LC 85-61781. 150p. (Orig.). 1987. reprint ed. pap. 9.50 (*0-89830-086-X*) Russica Pubs.

VP - Expert for Business Application. Richard Hicks & Ronald Lee. (Orig.). (C). 1989. pap. text ed. 39.95 (*0-8162-3777-8*) Holden-Day.

VP Italian Dictionary. Vieri Samek-Lodovici. (ITA.). 1996. write for info. (*0-679-44910-8*) McKay.

Vpered, Eighteen Seventy-Three to Eighteen Seventy-Seven, 2 vols, Set. Incl. 1. On the History of Vpered. Ed. by Boris Sapir. 403p. 1970. (*90-277-0163-6*); 2. Documents. 556p. (*90-277-0164-4*); (Russian Series on Social History). 1970. lib. bdg. 146.00 (*90-277-0516-X*) Kluwer Ac.

Vplotnuyu. Mikhail Armalinsky. LC 94-18382. 100p. (Orig.). (RUS.). 1994. pap. 9.00 (*0-916201-16-3*) M I P Co.

Vprok (To Profit From) 2nd ed. Andrei Platonov. Ed. by Gregory Poliak. (Illus.). 100p. (Orig.). (RUS.). pap. 8.00 (*0-686-88508-2*) Silver Age Pub.

VR Madness & More. 1998. 44.95 (*0-672-30769-3*) Sams.

***Vraie Guitare Blues.** Ed. by Aaron Stang. 84p. (Orig.). (C). 1994. pap. text ed. 19.95 (*0-7692-0961-0*, F3267GTFCD) Warner Brothers.

Vraies Richesses. Jean Giono. 240p. (FRE.). 1936. 11.95 (*0-8288-9747-6*, 2253060291) Fr & Eur.

Vrais Pourtraits et Vies Des Hommes Illustres, 2 vols. Andre Thevet. LC 72-14359. 1400p. (FRE.). 1973. reprint ed. Set. lib. bdg. 150.00 (*0-8201-1112-0*) Schol Facsimiles.

VremePlov. Milos Acin-Kosta. LC 84-60796. 140p. (SER.). 1984. pap. 10.00 (*0-931931-14-2*) Ravnogorski.

Vremion Naskvozniake: A Book of Poems. Jan E. Probstein. (Illus.). 112p. (Orig.). (RUS.). 1993. pap. text ed. 8.00 (*0-911971-85-8*) Effect Pub.

Vril: Vital Magnetism. 123p. 1970. reprint ed. spiral bd. 7.00 (*0-7873-0007-1*) Hlth Research.

Vrilles De la Vigne see Sido

Vrindaban Days: An Exciting Chronicle of Srila Prabhu Pada in the land of Krishna. Hayagriva Dasa. (Illus.). 300p. 1988. 10.95 (*0-932215-20-3*) Palace Pub.

***Vrksayurveda of Parasara: A Treatise on Plant Science.** Ed. by N. N. Sircar & Roma Sarkar. (C). 1996. 32.00 (*81-7030-441-5*, Pub. by Sri Satguru Pubns II) S Asia.

VRML. Walter Goralski et al. 1996. 39.95 incl. cd-rom (*0-614-14500-7*) P-H.

VRML: Bringing Virtual Reality to the Internet. John R. Vacca. LC 96-3546. (Illus.). 552p. 1996. pap. text ed., pap. 34.95 incl. cd-rom (*0-12-709910-7*, AP Prof) Acad Pr.

***VRML: Bringing Virtual Reality to the Internet.** 2nd ed. John R. Vacca. (Illus.). 500p. 1997. pap. text ed. 44.95 (*0-12-710008-3*, AP Prof) Acad Pr.

VRML: Exploring & Building Virtual Worlds on the Internet. Walter Goralski. LC 96-24170. 1996. pap. text ed. 39.95 incl. cd-rom (*0-13-486960-5*) P-H.

VRML: Flying Through the Web: VRML. New Riders Development Group Staff. (Illus.). 384p. (Orig.). 1996. pap. 35.00 incl. cd-rom (*1-56205-521-6*) New Riders Pub.

***VRML: The Definitive Guide.** Ann Gaug & Dean Nevins. Ed. by Paula Ferguson. 600p. (Orig.). 1997. pap. write for info. (*1-56592-341-3*) OReilly & Assocs.

***VRML & 3D on the Web for Dummies.** 2nd ed. David C. Kay. 1997. pap. 29.99 (*0-7645-0173-9*) IDG Bks.

***VRML Annotated Reference.** Rick Carey. (C). 1997. pap. text ed. 39.95 (*0-201-41974-2*) Addison-Wesley.

VRML, Bringing Virtual Reality to the Internet. John R. Vacca. LC 96-3546. 1996. cd-rom 1.95 (*0-12-709911-5*, AP Prof) Acad Pr.

VRML Browsing & Building Cyberspace: Browsing & Building Cyberspace. Mark Pesce. LC 95-24793. (Illus.). 320p. (Orig.). 1995. 40.00 (*1-56205-498-8*) New Riders Pub.

VRML Explorer with CD-ROM. Tom Wegner. 1996. pap. 39.99 incl. cd-rom (*1-883577-74-8*) Coriolis Grp.

VRML for Dummies. Dummies Press Staff. 1996. pap. 29.99 (*1-56884-611-8*) IDG Bks.

VRML Handbook. Jed Hartman & Scot Wernecke. 1996. 24.95 (*0-614-14427-2*) Addison-Wesley.

VRML Handbook: The Official Guide to Constructing Virtual Worlds. Silicon Graphics Incorporated Staff. 204p. (C). 1996. pap. text ed. 29.95 (*0-201-47944-3*) Addison-Wesley.

VRML Power Publishing, & Online Companion. Ventana Development Staff. LC 96-19513. 1996. pap. text ed. 49.95 incl. cd-rom (*1-56604-450-2*) Ventana Communs.

***VRML Programmer's Library.** Kris Jamsa et al. 1997. pap. 49.95 (*1-884133-51-7*) Jamsa Pr.

VRML 2.0 Sourcebook. 2nd ed. Andrea L. Ames et al. LC 96-42409. 1996. pap. text ed. 49.95 incl. cd-rom (*0-471-16507-7*) Wiley.

VRML 2.0: The Next Step in Cyberspace. Mark Pesce. 400p. 1996. 39.95 (*1-56205-663-8*) Mac Comp Pub.

Vrndavana Dhama Kijaya. Dasa D. Majaraja. 1992. 19.95 (*0-945475-00-4*) Mandala Media.

Vroman Effect. Ed. by C. H. Bamford et al. 208p. 1992. 73.50 (*90-6764-139-1*) Coronet Bks.

Vroom! Turbo-Charged Team Building. Michael Shandler & Michael Egan. LC 95-46216. 176p. 1996. pap. 14.95 (*0-8144-7900-6*) AMACOM.

***Vroom Vroom.** Bird & Falk. (New Trend Fiction A Ser.). (J). 1993. pap. text ed. write for info. (*0-582-80044-7*, Pub. by Longman UK) Longman.

***Vroom! Vroom! Making 'Dozers, 'Copters, Trucks & More.** Judy Press. Ed. by Susan Williamson. LC 96-27204. (Little Hands Book Ser.). (Illus.). 144p. (Orig.). (J). (ps up). 1997. pap. 12.95 (*1-885593-04-X*) Williamson Pub Co.

Vrooman Family in America: Descendants of Hendrick Meese Vrooman, Who Came from Holland to America in 1664. G. V. Wickersham & E. B. Comstock. (Illus.). 341p. 1991. reprint ed. pap. 53.00 (*0-8328-1838-0*); reprint ed. lib. bdg. 63.00 (*0-8328-1837-2*) Higginson Bk Co.

Vroomans Nose: A Study. Vincent J. Schaefer. LC 92-37191. (Illus.). 119p. 1992. pap. 12.50 (*0-935796-35-5*) Purple Mnt Pr.

Vrouw Grobelaar & Her Leading Cases. Perceval Gibbon. LC 73-142263. (Short Story Index Reprint Ser.). 1977. 20.95 (*0-8369-3747-3*) Ayer.

Vrtlozi Smrti, Vol. XIII: Draza Mihailovic I Ravna Gora, 18 vols. Milos Acin-Kosta. 380p. 1988. pap. 20.00 (*0-931931-29-0*) Ravnogorski.

Vrtlozi Smrti, Vol. XIII: Draza Mihailovic I Ravna Gora, 18 vols., XIII. Milos Acin-Kosta. 380p. 1988. write for info. (*0-318-63407-4*, DR359MSA68) Ravnogorski.

VS COBOL Eleven: Highlights & Techniques. James C. Janossy. LC 91-40990. 368p. 1992. pap. text ed. 49.95 (*0-471-55892-3*) Wiley.

VS COBOL Eleven: Highlights & Techniques. James C. Janossy. 368p. 1992. 75.00 (*0-471-57205-5*) Wiley.

VS COBOL II: A Guide for Programmers & Managers. 2nd ed. Anne Prince. LC 89-13671. 271p. 1990. pap. 27.50 (*0-911625-54-2*) M Murach & Assoc.

VS COBOL II: Highlights & Techniques. James C. Janossy. 368p. 1992. 35.00 incl. disk (*0-471-57401-5*) Wiley.

VS COBOL II for COBOL programmer. Robert J. Sandler. LC 89-16520. 257p. 1990. pap. text ed. 49.95 (*0-471-62226-5*) Wiley.

V.S. Naipaul. Bruce King. LC 92-21012. (Modern Novelists Ser.). 1993. text ed. 35.00 (*0-312-08646-6*) St Martin.

VSAM: A Comprehensive Guide. Constantine Kaniklidis. 1990. text ed. 35.95 (*0-442-24641-2*) Van Nos Reinhold.

VSAM: AMS & Application Programming. Doug Lowe. LC 86-60204. 260p. 1986. pap. 27.50 (*0-911625-33-X*) M Murach & Assoc.

VSAM: The Complete Guide to Optimization & Design. Eugene S. Hudders. 248p. 1993. pap. text ed. 39.95 (*0-471-56705-1*, GC3144) Wiley.

VSAM Coding in Cobol & VSAM AMS. 208p. 1986. per. 19.95 (*0-9611810-6-0*) CCD Online Syst.

VSAM for the COBOL Programmer. 2nd ed. Doug Lowe. LC 88-60035. 187p. 1989. pap. 22.50 (*0-911625-45-3*) M Murach & Assoc.

VSAM Performance & System Fine-Tuning Quick Reference Handbook. Treva L. Thompson. LC 82-83606. 150p. 1984. 17.50 (*0-942898-02-8*); 10.25 (*0-685-06189-2*) Halpern & Simon.

VSAM Tuning & Advances Topics. Michael D. Sachais. 1990. text ed. 54.95 (*0-442-31882-0*) Van Nos Reinhold.

VSAT Networks. G. Maral. LC 94-37789. (Series in Communication & Distribution). 282p. 1995. text ed. 53.95 (*0-471-95302-4*) Wiley.

VSATs: Status & Potential. 221p. 1991. 1,950.00 (*0-89336-859-8*, G-134) BCC.

VSATs: Very Small Aperture Terminals. J. Everett. (Telecommunications Ser.: No. 28). xxviii, 532p. 1992. boxed 129.00 (*0-86341-200-9*, TE028) Inst Elect Eng.

VSE - ESA JCL: Utilities, Power, & VSAM. H. Frank Graubart-Cervone. LC 93-23183. 1993. text ed. 45.00 (*0-07-024128-7*) McGraw.

VSE - SP & VSE - ESA: A Guide to Performance Tuning. Eugene S. Hudders. 244p. 1993. 44.95 (*0-471-56659-4*, GC7923) Wiley.

VSE COBOL II Power Programmer's Desk Reference. David S. Kirk. 297p. 1993. pap. text ed. 39.95 (*0-471-57358-2*) Wiley.

VSE ESA Concepts & Facilities. William Merrow. 1994. text ed. 50.00 (*0-07-041777-6*) McGraw.

VSE JCL & Subroutines for Application Programmers. Leo J. Langevin. 1992. 34.95 (*0-89435-401-9*) Wiley.

Vse of the Two Mathematicall Instruments, the Crosse Staffe & the Iacobs Staffe, Newly Reviewed & the Second Time Imprinted, 2 pts. Thomas Hood. LC 75-38202. (English Experience Ser.: No. 468). 40p. 1972. reprint ed. 25.00 (*90-221-0468-0*) Walter J Johnson.

Vseobshii Illiustrirovannyi Putevoditel' po Sviatym Mestam Rossiiskoi Imperii i Sv. Afonu. A. A. Pavlovsky. LC 88-61819. (Illus.). 900p. (RUS.). 1988. reprint ed. 85.00 (*0-911971-35-1*); reprint ed. pap. 55.00 (*0-911971-34-3*) Effect Pub.

Vsevolod Meyerhold. Robert Leach. (Directors in Perspective Ser.). (Illus.). 240p. (C). 1993. pap. text ed. 22.95 (*0-521-31843-2*) Cambridge U Pr.

Vsjenoshchnoje Bdjenije see Tserkovno-Pjevcheskiji Sbornik

***VSP Interpretive Processing: Theory & Practice.** Ronald C. Hinds et al. LC 96-46440. (Open File Publications). 1996. pap. 93.00 (*1-56080-042-9*) Soc Expl Geophys.

Vstrechi s Pasternakom. Nina Muravina. LC 90-4742. 223p. (Orig.). (RUS.). 1990. pap. 15.00 (*1-55779-036-1*) Hermitage.

Vtornik Meri. Predstavlenie v Trekh Chastiakh Dlia Kukol Zhivykh Ili Dereniannykh. Ed. by Mikhail A. Kuzmin. 37p. (RUS.). (C). 1994. reprint ed. pap. text ed. 4.00 (*1-57201-001-0*) Berkeley Slavic.

Vu-Calc & Vu-File (The Organizer) Robert B. Masters. LC 83-22489. 176p. 1984. pap. 19.95 (*0-89303-941-1*) P-H.

Vue De la Terre Promise. Georges Duhamel. (Chronique Des Pasquier Ser.: Vol. III). (FRE.). 1973. pap. 10.95 (*0-7859-1749-7*, 2070364046) Fr & Eur.

Vue de la Terre Promise see Chronique des Pasquier

Vuelo, Level 3. Zenia S. Da Silva. (SPA.). 1971. write for info. (*0-02-270770-0*) Macmillan.

Vuelo de los Colibries. Alma Florada. (Illus.). 32p. (J). (gr. 3-6). pap. text ed. 9.95 (*1-56492-211-1*) Laredo.

Vuelo Hacia el Amanecer. Lorenzo. (SPA.). 1995. pap. write for info. (*0-312-95408-5*) St Martin.

Vuelo 714 para Sidney. Herge. (Illus.). 62p. (SPA.). (J). 19.95 (*0-8288-5004-6*) Fr & Eur.

Vuelta a la Galia. Rene De Goscinny & M. Uderzo. (Illus.). (SPA.). (J). 19.95 (*0-8288-4911-0*) Fr & Eur.

Vues sur Rimbaud. Georges Duhamel. 256p. (FRE.). 1952. pap. 45.00 (*0-7859-5429-5*) Fr & Eur.

Vuillard. Stuart Preston. (Masters of Art Ser.). (Illus.). 128p. 1985. 22.95 (*0-8109-1706-8*) Abrams.

Vuillard. Belinda Thomson. (Illus.). 160p. 1988. 45.00 (*0-89659-883-7*) Abbeville Pr.

***Vuillard.** Belinda Thomson. (Illus.). 160p. (Orig.). Date not set. pap. 24.95 (*0-7148-2955-2*, Pub. by Phaidon Press UK) Chronicle Bks.

Vuillard. Jeanine Warnod. (CAL Art Ser.). 1989. 14.95 (*0-517-57277-X*, Crown) Crown Pub Group.

Vuillard: Interiors. Claude Roger-Marx. (Rhythm & Color Two Ser.). 76p. (FRE.). 1948. pap. write for info. (*0-7859-5250-0*) Fr & Eur.

Vuillard, His Life & Work. Claude Roger-Marx. LC 75-41229. reprint ed. 34.00 (*0-404-14718-6*) AMS Pr.

Vuillard's Graphic Work: A Catalogue Raisonne. Claude Roger-Marx. (Illus.). 192p. 1990. 150.00 (*1-55660-123-9*) A Wofsy Fine Arts.

Vulcan: Avro Vulcan B Mk 2-2k. (Aeroguide Ser.: No. 6). 1984. pap. 6.00 (*0-918805-05-8*) Pac Aero Pr.

Vulcan: The Making of a Prairie Community. Paul Voisey. 368p. 1988. 40.00 (*0-8020-2642-7*); pap. 20.95 (*0-8020-6676-3*) U of Toronto Pr.

Vulcan Academy Murders. Jean Lorrah. (Star Trek Ser.: No. 20). (Orig.). 1991. mass mkt. 4.95 (*0-671-74283-3*) PB.

Vulcan & His Times. Philip A. Morris. (Illus.). 64p. (Orig.). 1995. pap. 9.95 (*0-943994-20-9*) Birmingham Hist Soc.

Vulcan's Forge. Roger Leloup. Tr. by Jean-Jacques Surbeck from FRE. (Adventures of Yoko, Vic & Paul Ser.). (Illus.). 49p. (Orig.). (YA). (gr. 12 up). 1989. pap. 6.95 (*0-87416-065-0*, Comcat Comics) Catalan Communs.

Vulcan's Glory. D. C. Fontana. (Star Trek Ser.: No. 44). (Orig.). 1991. mass mkt. 4.95 (*0-671-74291-4*) PB.

***Vulgar Boatman.** Lorraine Forbes. 150p. 1996. 39.95 (*1-888672-12-9*) J Ciano Pubng.

***Vulgar Boatman, Vol. 1.** Lorraine Forbes. 150p. 1996. pap. 29.95 (*1-888672-13-7*) J Ciano Pubng.

Vulgar Modernism: Writing on the Movies & Other Media. J. Hoberman. (Culture & the Moving Image Ser.). (Illus.). (C). 1991. 54.95 (*0-87722-864-7*); pap. 16.95 (*0-87722-866-3*) Temple U Pr.

Vulgar Streak. Wyndham Lewis. LC 85-6099. (Illus.). 273p. (Orig.). (C). 1985. 25.00 (*0-87685-629-6*); pap. 14.00 (*0-87685-628-8*) Black Sparrow.

Vulgar Streak. deluxe ed. Wyndham Lewis. LC 85-6099. (Illus.). 273p. (Orig.). (C). 1985. 30.00 (*0-87685-630-X*) Black Sparrow.

Vulgaria of J. Stanbridge & the Vulgaria of Robert Whittinton. J. Stanbridge. (EETS, OS Ser.: No. 187). 1974. reprint ed. 45.00 (*0-527-00187-2*) Periodicals Srv.

Vulgaria Uiri Doctissimi Guil. Hormani Caesarisburgensis. William Horman. LC 74-28865. (English Experience Ser.: No. 745). 1975. reprint ed. 55.00 (*90-221-0745-0*) Walter J Johnson.

Vulgarity & Authenticity: Dimensions of Otherness in the World of Jean-Paul Sartre. Stuart Z. Charme. LC 90-23296. 272p. (C). 1993. pap. 16.95 (*0-87023-868-X*); lib. bdg. 35.00 (*0-87023-740-3*) U of Mass Pr.

Vulgarization of Art: The Victorians & Aesthetic Democracy. Linda Dowling. (Victorian Literature & Culture Ser.). 192p. (C). 1996. text ed. 32.50 (*0-8139-1634-8*) U Pr of Va.

Vulgate Version of the Arthurian Romances, 8 Vols. in 7. Ed. by H. Oskar Sommer. LC 78-19691. reprint ed. Set. 1,150.00 (*0-404-17630-5*) AMS Pr.

Vulliamy's the Newborn Child. Peter G. Johnston. LC 93-11163. 1994. pap. 39.95 (*0-443-04889-4*) Churchill.

***Vulnerabilities of the Public Switched Network: Potential Implications for the Air Force.** Phillip M. Feldman & Project Air Force U. S. Staff. LC 97-13309. 1997. write for info. (*0-8330-2512-0*) Rand Corp.

Vulnerabilities to Delinquency. Ed. by Dorothy O. Lewis. 343p. 1981. text ed. 37.95 (*0-88331-211-5*) Luce.

***Vulnerability & Adaptation Assessment: An International Handbook.** Jeffrey Lee & Sandra Guill. Ed. by Ron Benioff. LC 96-26719. (Environmental Science & Technology Library). 564p. (C). 1996. lib. bdg. 208.00 (*0-7923-4140-6*) Kluwer Ac.

***Vulnerability & Adaptation to Climate Change: Interim Results from the U. S. Country Studies Program.** United States Country Studies Program Staff. Ed. by Joel B. Smith. LC 96-9393. (Environmental Science & Technology Library). 404p. (C). 1996. lib. bdg. 156.00 (*0-7923-4141-4*) Kluwer Ac.

Vulnerability & Resilience in Human Development: A Festschrift for Ann & Alan Clarke. Ed. by Barbara Tizard & Ved P. Varma. 200p. 1992. 69.00 (*1-85302-105-9*) Taylor & Francis.

***Vulnerability & Stress in Late-Onset Psychiatric Disorders.** David Gutmann. Date not set. 19.95 (*0-465-09056-7*) Basic.

***Vulnerability Assessment of Federal Facilities.** 140p. 1996. reprint ed. pap. 35.00 (*0-7881-3287-3*) DIANE Pub.

Vulnerability, Coping, & Growth: From Infancy to Adolescence. Lois B. Murphy & Alice E. Moriarty. LC 75-2772. 484p. reprint ed. pap. 138.00 (*0-7837-5303-9*, 2080316) Bks Demand.

Vulnerability of Empire. Charles A. Kupchan. LC 93-24323. (Cornell Studies in Security Affairs). (Illus.). 528p. (C). 1993. 49.95 (*0-8014-2885-8*) Cornell U Pr.

Vulnerability of Empire. Charles A. Kupchan. LC 93-24323. (Cornell Studies in Security Affairs). (Illus.). 544p. (C). 1996. pap. 19.95 (*0-8014-8124-4*) Cornell U Pr.

Vulnerability to Drug Abuse. Ed. by Roy Pickens & Meyer Glantz. 547p. 1991. 49.95 (*1-55798-142-6*) Am Psychol.

Vulnerable. Ed. by John L. Palmer et al. LC 88-17397. (Changing Domestic Priorities Ser.). (Illus.). 458p. (Orig.). (C). 1988. pap. text ed. 28.50 (*0-87766-419-6*) Urban Inst.

Vulnerable Age Phenomenon. Michael Inbar. LC 76-23365. (Social Science Frontiers Ser.). 59p. 1977. pap. 9.95 (*0-87154-397-4*) Russell Sage.

Vulnerable Aged: People, Services, & Policies. Ed. by Zev Harel et al. LC 90-9425. 336p. (C). 1990. 42.95 (*0-8261-6860-4*) Springer Pub.

Vulnerable American Politician. King. 1996. 22.00 (*0-02-874032-7*) Free Pr.

Vulnerable American Politician. Kings. 256p. 1997. 24.00 (*0-684-82730-1*) Free Pr.

Vulnerable Brain & Environmental Risks Vol. 3: Toxins in Air & Water. Ed. by R. L. Isaacson & K. F. Jensen. (Illus.). 320p. 1993. 79.50 (*0-306-44611-1*, Plenum Pr) Plenum.

Vulnerable Brain & Environmental Risks, Vol. 1: Malnutrition & Hazard Assessment. Ed. by Robert L. Isaacson & K. F. Jensen. (Illus.). 305p. 1992. 75.00 (*0-306-44148-9*, Plenum Pr) Plenum.

Vulnerable Brain & Environmental Risks, Vol. 2: Toxins in Food. Ed. by Robert L. Isaacson & K. F. Jensen. (Illus.). 345p. 1992. 79.50 (*0-306-44165-9*, Plenum Pr) Plenum.

Vulnerable but Invincible: A Longitudinal Study of Resilient Children & Youth. Emmy E. Werner & Ruth S. Smith. 228p. (C). 1989. reprint ed. pap. text ed. 14.95 (*0-937431-03-6*) Adams Bannister Cox.

***Vulnerable Child.** Richard Weissbourd. 1997. pap. 13.00 (*0-201-92080-8*) Addison-Wesley.

Vulnerable Child, Vol. 1. Ed. by Theodore B. Cohen et al. (Vulnerable Child Monograph). 300p. 1993. 45.00 (*0-8236-6755-3*) Intl Univs Pr.

Vulnerable Child, Vol. 2. Ed. by M. Hossein Etezady et al. (Vulnerable Child Monograph Ser.). 231p. 1995. 37.50 (*0-8236-6756-1*) Intl Univs Pr.

***Vulnerable Child, Vol. III.** Ed. by Theodore B. Cohen et al. 1997. write for info. (*0-8236-6757-X*, BN06757) Intl Univs Pr.

Vulnerable Child: The Hidden Epidemic of Neglected & Troubled Children Even Within the... Richard Weissbourd. LC 95-36789. 256p. 1996. 22.00 (*0-201-48395-5*) Addison-Wesley.

Vulnerable Children in Schools: A Study of Catch 'em Young, a Project Helping 10 Year Olds Transfer School. Hedy Cleaver. 156p. 1991. pap. text ed. 24.95 (*1-85521-211-0*, Pub. by Dartmth Pub UK) Ashgate Pub Co.

Vulnerable Children, Vulnerable Families: The Social Construction of Child Abuse. Susan Janko. 240p. (C). 1994. text ed. 36.00 (*0-8077-3316-4*); pap. text ed. 17.95 (*0-8077-3315-6*) Tchrs Coll.

Vulnerable Country: Civil Resources in the Defence of Australia. Ed. by J. O. Langtry & D. Ball. 704p. 1986. 62.00 (*0-08-033045-2*, K122,K120,K115, Pergamon Pr) Elsevier.

Vulnerable Fortress: Bureaucratic Organization & Management in the Information Age. James R. Taylor & Elizabeth J. Van Every. LC 93-93393. 283p. 1993. 60.00 (*0-8020-2948-5*); pap. 19.95 (*0-685-67886-5*) U of Toronto Pr.

Vulnerable Observer: Anthropology That Breaks Your Heart. Ruth Behar. 176p. 1996. 22.00 (*0-8070-4630-2*) Beacon Pr.

***Vulnerable Observer: Anthropology That Breaks Your Heart.** Ruth Behar. LC 96-11409. 208p. 1997. reprint ed. pap. 12.00 (*0-8070-4631-0*) Beacon Pr.

Vulnerable Planet. John B. Foster. (Cornerstone Bks.). (Illus.). 144p. (Orig.). (C). 1993. pap. text ed. 13.00 (*0-85345-874-X*) Monthly Rev.

Vulnerable Populations: Evaluation & Treatment of Sexually Abused Children & Adult Survivors, Vol. 1. Suzanne M. Sgroi. LC 87-45325. 336p. 1988. 44.95 (*0-669-16336-8*); pap. 27.95 (*0-669-16338-4*) Free Pr.

Vulnerable Populations, Vol. II: Sexual Abuse Treatment for Children, Adult Survivors, Offenders & Persons with Mental Retardation. Ed. by Suzanne M. Sgroi. 448p. 1989. 44.95 (*0-669-20942-2*); pap. 27.95 (*0-669-20943-0*) Free Pr.

Vulnerable Self: Confronting the Ultimate Questions. Avery D. Weisman. 253p. 1993. 26.95 (*0-306-44501-8*, Plenum Insight) Plenum.

Vulnerable Social Worker: Liability for Serving Children & Families. Douglas J. Besharov. LC 85-28437. 275p. 1985. 23.95 (*0-87101-136-0*) Natl Assn Soc Wkrs.

Vulnerable Text: Essays on Renaissance Literature. Thomas M. Greene. 256p. 1986. text ed. 49.50 (*0-231-06246-X*) Col U Pr.

***Vulnerable Years.** Stewart Richardson. Date not set. write for info. (*0-688-00799-6*) Morrow.

Vulp. Mark Dunster. 27p. (Orig.). 1994. pap. 5.00 (*0-89642-236-4*) Linden Pubs.

Vulpes the Red Fox. Jean Craighead George & John George. (Illus.). 224p. (J). (gr. 5-9). 1996. pap. 4.99 (*0-14-037623-2*) Puffin Bks.

Vultee Aircraft, 1932-1947. Jonathan Thompson. LC 92-83781. (American Aircraft Manufacturer Ser.: Vol. 1). (Illus.). 132p. (Orig.). 1993. pap. 29.95 (*0-913322-02-4*) Jonathan T Pub.

Vultee BT-13 Flight Manual. 56p. pap. 12.95 (*0-911139-21-4*) Flying Bks.

***Vulture.** Wayne Grady. 1997. 22.50 (*0-87156-982-5*) Sierra.

Vulture. Susan Schafer. (Remarkable Animals Ser.). 60p. (J). 1995. pap. 5.95 (*0-382-24725-6*, Dillon Silver Burdett) Silver Burdett Pr.

***Vulture.** Gil Scott-Heron. 237p. 1996. reprint ed. pap. text ed. 12.95 (*0-86241-528-4*, Pub. by Payback Pr UK) AK Pr Dist.

Vulture: A Modern Allegory on the Art of Putting Oneself Down. Sidney B. Simon. 72p. 1991. reprint ed. pap. text ed. 5.95 (*1-880424-06-1*) Values.

Vulture & the Bull: Religious Responses to Death. Antonio R. Gualtieri. 194p. (Orig.). (C). 1984. pap. text ed. 23.00 (*0-8191-3964-5*) U Pr of Amer.

Vulture Fund. Stephen W. Frey. LC 96-10617. 384p. 1996. pap. 23.95 (*0-525-93986-5*, Dutton) NAL-Dutton.

***Vulture Fund.** Stephen W. Frey. 1997. pap. 6.99 (*0-451-18479-3*, Sig) NAL-Dutton.

***Vulture Fund.** large type ed. Stephen W. Frey. LC 96-45015. 1996. 25.95 (*1-56895-390-9*, Compass) Wheeler Pub.

Vulture Warriors Campaign Pack. (Paranoia Ser.). 96p. 10.00 (*0-87431-156-X*, 12019) West End Games.

***Vultures.** Mark J. Rauzon. LC 96-31019. (First Bks.). (J). 1997. lib. bdg. 21.00 (*0-531-20271-2*) Watts.

***Vultures.** Mark J. Rauzon. (First Books). 1997. pap. text ed. 6.95 (*0-531-15853-5*) Watts.

***Vultures.** Roland Smith. LC 96-47074. (Early Bird Nature Bks.). (J). 1997. write for info. (*0-8225-3011-2*) Lerner Group.

Vultures. Lynn M. Stone. LC 92-26721. (J). (gr. 2-5). 1993. lib. bdg. 14.96 (*0-87614-768-6*, Carolrhoda) Lerner Group.

Vultures. Lynn M. Stone. LC 88-30196. (Bird Discovery Library). (Illus.). 24p. (J). (gr. 2-4). 1989. lib. bdg. 11.94 (*0-86592-324-8*); lib. bdg. 8.95 (*0-685-58506-9*) Rourke Corp.

Vultures. Lynn M. Stone. 1995. pap. text ed. 7.95 (*0-87614-950-6*) Lerner Group.

Vultures: Doctors, Lawyers, Hospitals, & Insurance Companies--What's Wrong, & What to Do about It. Farid A. Khavari. LC 90-52811. 272p. 1990. 19.95 (*0-915677-52-0*) Roundtable Pub.

Vultures & Butterflies: Living the Contradictions. Susan Classen. LC 92-16148. 184p. (Orig.). 1992. pap. 8.99 (*0-8361-3607-1*) Herald Pr.

Vultures & the Phoenix. Robert W. Millett. LC 81-65877. (Illus.). 168p. 1983. 32.50 (*0-87982-039-X*) Art Alliance.

Vultures of Africa. Peter Mundy et al. (Illus.). 450p. 1992. text ed. 99.95 (*0-12-510585-1*) Acad Pr.

Vultures of the Void: A History of British Science Fiction Publishing, 1946-1956. Philip Harbottle & Stephen Holland. Ed. by Daryl F. Mallett. LC 87-748. (I. O. Evans Studies in the Philosophy & Criticism of Literature: No. 13). (Illus.). 128p. (C). 1992. pap. 17.00 (*0-89370-415-6*); lib. bdg. 27.00 (*0-89370-315-X*) Borgo Pr.

Vulture's Row: Thirty Years in Naval Aviation. Paul T. Gillcrist. (Illus.). 320p. (C). (gr. 13). 1996. 30.00 (*0-7643-0047-4*) Schiffer.

Vulvar Disease. Allison C. Ledger. 1998. text ed. write for info. (*0-7216-5317-0*) Saunders.

Vulvovaginitis. Ed. by Elsner & Martius. 440p. 1993. 185.00 (*0-8247-9040-5*) Dekker.

Vunamami: Economic Transformation in a Traditional Society. Richard F. Salisbury. LC 70-79062. (Illus.). 401p. reprint ed. pap. 114.30 (*0-685-23960-8*, 2031514) Bks Demand.

Vurt. Jeff Noon. LC 94-25544. 1995. 22.00 (*0-517-59991-0*) Crown Pub Group.

Vurt, Vol. 1. Jeff Noon. 384p. 1996. pap. 13.95 (*0-312-14144-0*) St Martin.

VUV & Soft X-Ray Photoionization. Ed. by Shirley U. Becker. (Physics of Atoms & Molecules Ser.). (Illus.). 651p. (C). 1996. 149.50 (*0-306-45038-0*, Plenum Pr) Plenum.

VW at War - Kubelwagon, Schimmwagen & Special Vehicles. Michael Sawodny. LC 91-60858. (Illus.). 48p. 1991. pap. 7.95 (*0-88740-308-5*) Schiffer.

VW Beetle. Paul Wager. 1994. 10.98 (*0-7858-0022-0*) Bk Sales Inc.

VW Beetle. Jonathan Wood. (Collector's Guide Ser.). (Illus.). 128p. 1983. 27.95 (*0-900549-67-X*, Pub. by Motor Racing UK) Motorbooks Intl.

VW Beetle: An Illustrated History. Reichert & Klersy. (Illus.). 160p. 1987. 29.95 (*0-85429-591-7*, F591, Pub. by G T Foulis Ltd) Haynes Pubns.

VW Beetle: The Complete Story. Robert Davies. (Illus.). 200p. 1996. 35.95 (*1-85223-953-0*, Pub. by Crowood UK) Motorbooks Intl.

VW Beetle & Transporter: Guide to Purchase & DIY Restoration. Lindsay Porter. (Illus.). 270p. 1994. 34.95 (*0-85429-474-0*, Pub. by J H Haynes & Co UK) Motorbooks Intl.

VW Beetle Custom Handbook. 2nd ed. Keith Seume. (Illus.). 160p. 1992. pap. 17.95 (*1-870979-30-3*, Pub. by Bay View Bks UK) Motorbooks Intl.

VW Beetle in Motorsports: The Illustrated History 1940's to 1990's. Peter Noad. (Illus.). 144p. 1993. 14.98 (*1-872004-38-5*, Pub. by Windrow & Green UK) Motorbooks Intl.

***VW Beetle Performance Handbook: A Step-by-Step Guide to Upgrading Engine, Transmission & Suspension.** Keith Seume. 1997. pap. text ed. 19.95 (*0-7603-0469-6*) Motorbooks Intl.

VW Beetle, 1949-1960: A Restorer's Guide to Authenticity. Robert Wilson. (Authenticity Ser.). 112p. (Orig.). 1994. pap. 19.95 (*0-929758-03-X*) Beeman Jorgensen.

VW Beetle 1968-1991. R. M. Clarke. (Gold Portfolio Ser.). (Illus.). 172p. 1993. pap. 24.95 (*1-85520-193-3*, Pub. by Brooklands Bks UK) Motorbooks Intl.

***VW Bus.** Andrea Sparrow & David Sparrow. (Color Family Album Ser.). (Illus.). 96p. 1997. 19.95 (*1-874105-78-2*, Pub. by Veloce Pub UK) Motorbooks Intl.

VW Bus Custom Handbook. Laurence Merideth. (Illus.). 128p. 1994. pap. 15.95 (*1-870979-47-8*, Pub. by Bay View Bks UK) Motorbooks Intl.

VW Front Wheel Drive: 1974-90 RTUG. Chilton Automotives Editorial Staff. (Illus.). 384p. 1990. pap. text ed. 16.95 (*0-8019-8041-0*) Chilton.

VW Front Wheel Drive, 1974-90. Chilton Automotives Editorial Staff. 608p. 1995. pap. 21.95 (*0-8019-8663-X*) Chilton.

VW Golf: The Complete Story. James Ruppert. (Illus.). 200p. 1996. 35.95 (*1-85223-996-4*, Pub. by Crowood UK) Motorbooks Intl.

VW Passat Elec. Trouble 90-91. R. Bentley. 1994. 39.95 (*0-8376-0381-1*) Bentley.

VW Power & Style. Ian Kuah. (Illus.). 192p. 1991. 39.95 (*0-947981-49-7*, Pub. by Motor Racing UK) Motorbooks Intl.

VW Transporter-Bus, Nineteen Forty-Nine - Nineteen Sixty-Seven. Walter Zeichner. (Automotive Ser.). (Illus.). 96p. 1989. 19.95 (*0-88740-196-1*) Schiffer.

***VW Transporter Type 2, Bus, Camper & Van.** Malcolm Bobbitt. (Illus.). 160p. 1997. 29.95 (*1-874105-74-X*, Pub. by Veloce Pub UK) Motorbooks Intl.

VW, 1990-93. Chilton Automotives Editorial Staff. 400p. 1993. pap. 21.95 (*0-8019-8429-7*) Chilton.

Vyacheslav Ivanov: Poet, Critic & Philosopher. Ed. by Robert L. Jackson & Lowry Nelson, Jr. LC 85-51637. (Yale Russian & East European Publications: No. 8). 455p. 1986. 32.00 (*0-936586-08-7*) Yale Russian.

Vybrani Lysty Panteleimona Kulisha. George Y. Shevelov. 360p. (UKR.). (C). 1984. 20.00 (*0-916381-01-3*) Ukrainian Arts Sci.

Vygotskian Approaches to Second Language Research. Ed. by James P. Lantolf & Gabriela Appel. LC 93-49680. (Second Language Learning Ser.). 232p. 1994. pap. 39.50 (*1-56750-025-0*); text ed. 73.25 (*1-56750-024-2*) Ablex Pub.

***Vygotsky & Cognitive Science: Language & the Unification of the Social & Computational Mind.** William Frawley. LC 96-30021. 1997. write for info. (*0-674-94347-3*) HUP.

Vygotsky & Education: Instructional Implications & Applications of Socio-Historical Psychology. Ed. by Luis C. Moll. (Illus.). 432p. (C). 1990. text ed. 69.95 (*0-521-36051-X*) Cambridge U Pr.

Vygotsky & Education: Instructional Implications & Applications of Socio-Historical Psychology. Ed. by Luis C. Moll. (Illus.). 456p. (C). 1992. pap. text ed. 25.95 (*0-521-38579-2*) Cambridge U Pr.

Vygotsky & the Social Formation of Mind. James V. Wertsch. 280p. 1988. reprint ed. pap. 16.95 (*0-674-94351-1*) HUP.

Vygotsky in the Classroom: Mediated Literacy Instruction & Assessment. Ed. by Lisbeth Dixon-Krauss. LC 95-9276. 225p. (Orig.). (C). 1996. pap. text ed. 20.76 (*0-8013-1590-5*) Longman.

Vygotsky Reader. Jean Valsiner. Ed. by Rene Van der Veer. (Illus.). 384p. 1994. 55.95 (*0-631-18896-7*); pap. 29.95 (*0-631-18897-5*) Blackwell Pubs.

Vygotsky's Psychology: A Biography of Ideas. Alex Kozulin. LC 90-39118. (Illus.). 286p. 1991. 37.50 (*0-674-94365-1*, KOZVYG) HUP.

Vygotsky's Sociohistorical Psychology: A Paradigm for Today. C. Ratner. LC 90-25506. (Psycholinguistics Ser.). (Illus.). 370p. 1991. 52.50 (*0-306-43656-6*, Plenum Pr) Plenum.

Vysyas: A Sociological Study. C. Dwarakanath Gupta & S. Bhaskar. (C). 1992. 16.00 (*81-7024-450-1*, Pub. by Ashish II) S Asia.

Vzgliani Na Dom Svoi, Putnik - Look at Your Home, Traveller: Ot Gory Hermon Do Eilata. Ilya Shtemler. LC 92-72485. (Illus.). 232p. (RUS.). 1992. 12.00 (*0-911971-74-2*) Effect Pub.

Vzglid 12 Nichto: Rasskazy. Jurii Mamleev. LC 88-83825. (Illus.). 328p. (RUS.). 1989. 32.00 (*0-911971-42-4*); pap. 25.00 (*0-911971-43-2*) Effect Pub.

***V003 Managing Risk.** 4th ed. CUNA (Rees) Staff. 64p. 1996. 11.74 (*0-7872-2908-3*) Kendall-Hunt.

V2 Conspiracy: Asynchronic & a Diachronic Analysis of Verbal Positions in German Languages. Fred Weerman. (Publications in Language Sciences: No. 31). ix, 263p. 1989. pap. 44.65 (*90-6765-409-4*) Mouton.

***V301 Auditing 1.** 4th ed. CUNA (Rees) Staff. 80p. 1996. 11.74 (*0-7872-2910-5*) Kendall-Hunt.

V400 Investment. CUNA (Ewing) Staff. 96p. 1995. 11.74 (*0-7872-1357-8*) Kendall-Hunt.

V401 Pricing. CUNA Staff. 64p. 1995. 11.74 (*0-7872-1641-0*) Kendall-Hunt.

V403 Marketing. CUNA (Ewing). 64p. 1995. 11.74 (*0-7872-1627-5*) Kendall-Hunt.

V404 Strategic Planning. CUNA(Ewing). 80p. 1995. 11.74 (*0-7872-1662-3*) Kendall-Hunt.

V405 Board - Manager Relations. Ewing & CUNA Staff. 80p. 1995. pap. 11.74 (*0-7872-0467-6*) Kendall-Hunt.

W

w see Her Own Rules

W. A. Mozart. Eric Roseberry. LC 60-3144. (Great Masters Ser.). 1960. pap. 4.00 (*0-913932-20-5*) Boosey & Hawkes.

W. A. Mozart, 4 vols. Otto Jahn. 2626p. (GER.). 1976. reprint ed. Set. lib. bdg. 340.00 (*3-487-06092-2*) G Olms Pubs.

W. A. Mozart: "Die Entfuhrung aus dem Serail" Thomas Bauman. (Cambridge Opera Handbooks Ser.). (Illus.). 160p. 1988. text ed. 47.95 (*0-521-32545-5*); pap. text ed. 19.95 (*0-521-31060-1*) Cambridge U Pr.

W. A. Mozart: "Die Zauberflote" Peter Branscombe. (Cambridge Opera Handbooks Ser.). 288p. (C). 1991. pap. text ed. 17.95 (*0-521-31916-1*) Cambridge U Pr.

W. A. Mozart: "Don Giovanni" Ed. by Julian Rushton. (Cambridge Opera Handbooks Ser.). (Illus.). 176p. 1981. pap. text ed. 16.95 (*0-521-29663-3*) Cambridge U Pr.

W. A. Mozart: "Idomeneo" Ed. by Julian Rushton. LC 92-25833. (Cambridge Opera Handbooks Ser.). (Illus.). 192p. (C). 1993. text ed. 49.95 (*0-521-43144-1*); pap. text ed. 18.95 (*0-521-43741-5*) Cambridge U Pr.

W. A. Mozart: "Le Nozze di Figaro" Ed. by Tim Carter. (Cambridge Opera Handbooks Ser.). (Illus.). 180p. 1988. text ed. 47.95 (*0-521-30267-6*); pap. text ed. 17.95 (*0-521-31606-5*) Cambridge U Pr.

W. A. Mozart: Cosi Fan Tutte. Bruce A. Brown. (Opera Handbooks Ser.). (Illus.). 218p. (C). 1995. text ed. 49.95 (*0-521-43134-4*); pap. text ed. 17.95 (*0-521-43735-0*) Cambridge U Pr.

W. A. Mozart: La Clemenza di Tito. Ed. by Klaus Kropfinger. (Cambridge Opera Handbooks Ser.). (Illus.). 224p. (C). 1991. text ed. 47.95 (*0-521-36142-7*); pap. text ed. 17.95 (*0-521-36949-5*) Cambridge U Pr.

W. A. Mozart: Sa Vie Musicale & Son Oeuvre, 2 vols. T. De Wyzewa & G. De Saint-Foix. LC 80-11625. (Music Reprint Ser.). 2274p. 1980. reprint ed. Set. lib. bdg. 125.00 (*0-306-79561-2*) Da Capo.

W. A. P Martin: Pioneer of Progress in China. Ralph Covell. LC 77-13321. 311p. reprint ed. 88.70 (*0-8357-9133-5*, 2012723) Bks Demand.

***W. A. S. P. - First Blood - Last Cuts.** Ed. by Aaron Stang. 124p. (Orig.). (C). 1994. pap. text ed. 19.95 (*0-7604-0003-2*, P1072GTX) Warner Brothers.

***W. A. S. P. - Headless Children.** Ed. by Aaron Stang. 44p. (Orig.). (C). 1993. pap. text ed. 18.95 (*0-7692-0969-6*, P1039GTX) Warner Brothers.

W. B. Yeats. Augustine Martin. 152p. 9000. pap. 10.95 (*0-86140-325-8*) Dufour.

W

An Asterisk (*) at the beginning of an entry indicates that the title is appearing in BIP for the first time.

W. B. Yeats: A Census of the Manuscripts. Conrad A. Balliet. LC 89-17226. 498p. 1990. text ed. 65.00 (0-8240-6629-4, 772) Garland.

W. B. Yeats: A Century of Criticism. Eitel Timm. LC 89-22373. (ENGL Ser.: Vol. 6). xii, 102p. (C). 1990. 38.00 (0-938100-68-8) Camden Hse.

W. B. Yeats: A Classified Bibliography of Criticism Including Additions to Allan Wade's Bibliography of the Writings of W. B. Yeats & a Section of the Irish Literary & Dramatic Revival. 2nd ed. Ed. by Klaus P. Jochum. 1192p. 1990. text ed. 75.00 (0-252-01762-5) U of Ill Pr.

W. B. Yeats: A Critical Introduction. Stan Smith. 178p. (C). 1990. text ed. 59.00 (0-389-20902-3); pap. text ed. 23.00 (0-389-20903-1) B&N Imports.

W. B. Yeats: A Critical Study. Forrest Reid. LC 72-1317. (Studies in Irish Literature: No. 16). 1972. reprint ed. lib. bdg. 75.00 (0-8383-1434-1) M S G Haskell Hse.

W. B. Yeats: A Literary Life. Alasdair D. Macrae. LC 94-20524. (Literary Lives Ser.). 1994. text ed. 39.95 (0-312-12310-8) St Martin.

W. B. Yeats: Images of a Poet. Donald J. Gordon. LC 79-9441. 151p. 1980. reprint ed. text ed. 49.75 (0-313-22069-7, GOWBY, Greenwood Pr) Greenwood.

***W. B. Yeats: Images of Ireland.** A. Legarsment. 1996. 17.98 (0-7628-0721-0) Bk Sales Inc.

***W. B. Yeats: Romantic Visionary.** Chelsea House Publishing Staff. (Illustrated Poetry Anthology Ser.). (Illus.). 1997. 17.95 (1-86019-291-2) Chelsea Hse.

W. B. Yeats: Selected Poetry. 2nd ed. Ed. by A. Norman Jeffares. 256p. 1990. pap. 13.95 (0-330-31520-X, Pub. by Pan Books UK) Trans-Atl Phila.

W. B. Yeats: The Critical Heritage. Ed. by A. Norman Jeffares. (Critical Heritage Ser.). 1977. 69.50 (0-7100-8480-3, RKP) Routledge.

***W. B. Yeats: The Man & the Milieu.** Keiht Alldritt. 1997. 35.00 (0-517-79989-8, Carol Southern Bks) Crown Pub Group.

W. B. Yeats: The Writing of Sophocles' King Oedipus. David R. Clark & James B. McGuire. LC 86-72889. (Memoirs Ser.: Vol. 175). (Illus.). (C). 1989. 40.00 (0-87169-175-2, M175-CLD) Am Philos.

W. B. Yeats: The Writing of "The Player Queen" Compiled by Curtis B. Bradford. LC 73-18798. 483p. 1977. 35.00 (0-87580-048-3) N Ill U Pr.

***W. B. Yeats a Life Vol. 1: A Life, the Apprentice Mage 1865-1914, Vol. 1.** R. F. Foster. (Illus.). 704p. 1997. 35.00 (0-19-211735-1) OUP.

W. B. Yeats & Georgian Ireland. Donald T. Torchiana. LC 91-2819. (Critical Studies in Irish Literature: Vol. 2). 378p. 1992. pap. 14.95 (0-8132-0753-3) Cath U Pr.

W. B. Yeats & His Circle. Catherine Fahy. (Illus.). 64p. (C). pap. text ed. 12.95 (0-907328-15-6, Pub. by Natl Lib Ireland IE) Syracuse U Pr.

W. B. Yeats & T. Sturge Moore: Their Correspondence, 1901-1937. William Butler Yeats. Ed. by Ursula Bridge. LC 78-6910. 213p. 1978. reprint ed. text ed. 38.50 (0-313-20489-6, YEYM, Greenwood Pr) Greenwood.

W. B. Yeats & the Emergence of the Irish Free State, 1918-1939: Living in the Explosion. Bernard G. Krimm. LC 80-51875. 324p. 1981. 20.00 (0-87875-200-5) Whitston Pub.

W. B. Yeats & the Idea of a Theatre. James W. Flannery. 1989. pap. 28.50 (0-300-04627-8) Yale U Pr.

W. B. Yeats & the Idea of a Theatre: The Early Abbey Theatre in Theory & Practice. James W. Flannery. LC 74-29721. 442p. reprint ed. pap. 126.00 (0-8357-8367-7, 2033723) Bks Demand.

W. B. Yeats & the Ideal of "Unity of Being" Rajeshwari Patel. 200p. 1990. text ed. 27.50 (81-85218-13-7, Pub. by Prestige II) Advent Bks Div.

W. B. Yeats & the Theatre of Desolate Reality: Including Vivien & Time, The Irish National Theatre, & The Poet & the Actress. rev. ed. David R. Clark et al. LC 92-25035. (Critical Studies in Irish Literature: Vol. 3). (Illus.). 280p. (C). 1993. reprint ed. 49.95 (0-8132-0773-8); reprint ed. pap. 19.95 (0-8132-0774-6) Cath U Pr.

W. B. Yeats, Self-Critic: A Study of His Early Verse, & the Later Poetry, 2 vols. in one. Thomas F. Parkinson. LC 75-160480. 484p. reprint ed. pap. 138.00 (0-685-23980-2, 2031544) Bks Demand.

***W. B. Yeats's Poetry & Drama Between Late Romanticism & Modernism: An Analysis of Yeats's Poetry & Drama.** Uta Von Reinersdorff-Paczensky & Tenczin. (European University Studies, Series 14: Vol. 320). 256p. 1996. 51.95 (0-8204-3203-2) P Lang Pubng.

***W. B. Yeats's Poetry & Drama Between Late Romanticism & Modernism: An Analysis of Yeats's Poetry & Drama.** Uta Von Reinersdorff-Paczensky & Tenczin. (European University Studies, Series 14: Vol. 320). 256p. 1996. 51.95 (3-631-30428-5) P Lang Pubng.

***W B3 S Algebra: Modules, Semi-Infinite Cohomology & BV Algebras.** P. Bouwknegt et al. LC 96-29230. (Lectures Notes in Physics Ser.). 204p. 1996. 49.00 (3-540-61528-8) Spr-Verlag.

W. C. Fields. Robert L. Taylor. 1989. pap. 9.95 (0-312-03450-4) St Martin.

W. C. Fields: A Bio-Bibliography. Wes D. Gehring. LC 84-4454. (Popular Culture Bio-Bibliographies Ser.). (Illus.). xv, 233p. 1984. text ed. 52.95 (0-313-23875-8, GWC/, Greenwood Pr) Greenwood.

W. C. Fields: A Life in Film. Ronald Fields. (Illus.). 288p. 1984. pap. 14.95 (0-312-85312-2) St Martin.

W. C. Fields: Renowned Comedian of the Early Motion Picture Industry. Blythe F. Finke. Ed. by D. Steve Rahmas. (Outstanding Personalities Ser.: No. 48). 32p. (Orig.). (YA). (gr. 7-12). 1972. lib. bdg. 7.25 (0-87157-552-3) SamHar Pr.

W. C. Fields - an Annotated Guide: Chronology, Bibliographies, Discography, Filmographies, Press Books, Cigarette Cards, Film Clips & Impersonators. David T. Rocks. LC 92-56688. (Illus.). 143p. 1993. lib. bdg. 32.50 (0-89950-794-8) McFarland & Co.

W. C. Fields in French Light. Rochelle Owens. Ed. by Josh Gosciak & Maurice Kenny. LC 86-16843. 60p. (Orig.). 1986. pap. 4.50 (0-936556-14-5) Contact Two.

W. C. White & Ellen G. White: The Relationship Between the Prophet & Her Son. Jerry A. Moon. (Andrews University Seminary Doctoral Dissertation Ser.: Vol. 19). 497p. 1993. pap. 19.99 (1-883925-01-0) Andrews Univ Pr.

W. C. Wilson: The Fifth General Superintendent. Mallalieu Wilson. 96p. (Orig.). 1995. per., pap. 7.99 (0-8341-1557-3) Beacon Hill.

W. Cameron Forbes & the Hoover Commissions to Haiti, 1930. Robert M. Spector. LC 84-7245. 274p. (Orig.). 1984. pap. text ed. 27.00 (0-8191-3975-0); lib. bdg. 55.50 (0-8191-3974-2) U Pr of Amer.

W. D. & H. O. Wills Roll of Honour & War Service Roll, 1914-1918. Picton Publishing Staff. 46p. (C). 1987. pap. 56.00 (0-948251-28-X, Pub. by Picton UK) St Mut.

W. D. Gann Commodity Trading Course. W. D. Gann. (Illus.). 1954. student ed. 1,295.00 (0-939093-01-4) Lambert Gann Pub.

W. D. Gann Method of Trading. Gerald Marisch. 1990. 50.00 (0-930233-42-5) Windsor.

W. D. Gann Stock Market Course. W. D. Gann. (Illus.). 1953. student ed. 1,295.00 (0-939093-00-6) Lambert Gann Pub.

W. D. Hoard: A Man for His Time. Loren H. Osman. LC 84-62450. (Illus.). 451p. 1985. 14.95 (0-932147-00-3) Hoard & Sons Co.

W. D. Howells: Selected Criticism, 3 vols. William Dean Howells. Ed. by David Nordloh. LC 91-7615. (Selected Edition of W. D. Howells Ser.). 352p. 1993. 39.95 (0-253-32857-8); Set. 100.00 (0-253-32860-8) Ind U Pr.

W. D. Howells: Selected Criticism, 3 vols., Vol. I, 352p. William Dean Howells. Ed. by David Nordloh. LC 91-7615. (Selected Edition of W. D. Howells Ser.). 384p. 1993. 39.95 (0-253-32858-6) Ind U Pr.

W. D. Howells: Selected Criticism, 3 vols., Vol, II, 384p. William Dean Howells. Ed. by David Nordloh. LC 91-7615. (Selected Edition of W. D. Howells Ser.). 288p. 1993. Vol. II, 384p. 39.95 (0-253-32859-4) Ind U Pr.

***W. D. the Wonder Dog.** Cary Boggs. LC 96-44990. (Illus.). (J). 1998. 16.00 (0-689-81376-7, Aladdin Paperbacks) S&S Childrens.

W. D.'s Midnight Carnival. W. D. Snodgrass. LC 88-82743. (Illus.). 48p. 1989. 40.00 (0-936725-05-2) Artra Pub.

W. D.'s Midnight Carnival. W. D. Snodgrass. (Illus.). 48p. 1988. pap. 30.00 (0-936725-04-4) A Wofsy Fine Arts.

W. E. B. Du Bois. Ed. by William M. Tuttle, Jr. (Great Lives Observed Ser.). 192p. 1973. 8.95 (0-13-220905-5, Spectrum IN); pap. 2.45 (0-13-220889-X, Spectrum IN) Macmillan Gen Ref.

W. E. B. Du Bois, Vol. II. David L. Lewis. 1996. 35.00 (0-8050-2534-0) H Holt & Co.

W. E. B. Du Bois: A Bibliography of His Published Writings. 3rd ed. Paul G. Partington. 1985. lib. bdg. 35.00 (0-9602538-3-1) P G Partington.

W. E. B. Du Bois: A Bibliography of His Published Writings, Supplement. Paul G. Partington. 1984. pap. 10.00 (0-685-08855-3) P G Partington.

W. E. B. Du Bois: A Bibliography of Writings about Him. rev. ed. Paul G. Partington & Robert W. McDonnell. 1989. lib. bdg. 30.00 (0-9602538-8-2) P G Partington.

W. E. B. Du Bois: A Reader. Ed. by Andrew G. Paschal. LC 92-30128. 376p. 1993. reprint ed. pap. 12.00 (0-02-002351-0) Macmillan.

W. E. B. Du Bois: Biography of a Race, 1868-1919. David L. Lewis. 1994. pap. 17.95 (0-8050-3568-0) H Holt & Co.

W. E. B. Du Bois: Crusader for Peace. Kathryn Cryan-Hicks. LC 91-70820. (Picture-Book Biography). (Illus.). 48p. (J). (gr. 4-8). 1991. 14.95 (1-878668-05-6); pap. 7.95 (1-878668-09-9) Disc Enter Ltd.

W. E. B. Du Bois: Mini Play. (Black Americans Ser.). (J). (gr. 5 up). 1977. 6.50 (0-89550-362-X) Stevens & Shea.

W. E. B. Du Bois: Negro Leader in a Time of Crisis. Francis L. Broderick. xii, 259p. 1959. 35.00 (0-8047-0558-5) Stanford U Pr.

W. E. B. Du Bois: Negro Leader in a Time of Crisis. fac. ed. Francis L. Broderick. LC 59-7422. (Illus.). 111p. pap. 30.00 (0-7837-7265-3, 2047040) Bks Demand.

W. E. B. Du Bois & Racial Relations. Seamus Cavan. LC 92-33015. (Gateway Civil Rights Ser.). (Illus.). 32p. (J). (gr. 2-4). 1993. pap. 4.95 (1-56294-794-X); lib. bdg. 15.40 (1-56294-288-3) Millbrook Pr.

W. E. B. Du Bois in Memoriam: A Centennial Celebration of His Collegiate Education. Ed. by David Pilgrim. LC 90-50113. (Illus.). 150p. (C). 1990. text ed. 34.95 (0-685-35412-1); pap. text ed. 14.95 (1-55605-150-6) Wyndham Hall.

W. E. B. Du Bois on Sociology & the Black Community. W. E. B. Du Bois. Ed. by Dan S. Green & Edwin D. Driver. LC 78-770. 320p. 1980. reprint ed. pap. 17.95 (0-226-16760-7, 866) U Ch Pr.

W. E. B. Du Bois Speaks, 2 vols. Incl. Vol. 1. W. E. B. Du Bois Speaks: Speeches & Addresses 1890-1919. W. E. B. Du Bois. Ed. & Intro. by Philip S. Foner. LC 78-108719. 289p. 1970. reprint ed. lib. bdg. 50.00 (0-87348-181-X); Vol. 1. W. E. B. Du Bois Speaks: Speeches & Addresses 1890-1919. W. E. B. Du Bois. Ed. & Intro. by Philip S. Foner. LC 78-108719. 289p. 1970. reprint ed. pap. 18.95 (0-87348-125-9); Vol. 2. W. E. B. Du Bois Speaks: Speeches & Addresses 1920-1963. W. E. B. Du Bois. LC 78-108719. 1988. reprint ed. lib. bdg. 55.00 (0-87348-182-8); Vol. 2. W. E. B. Du Bois Speaks: Speeches & Addresses 1920-1963. W. E. B. Du Bois. Ed. by Philip S. Foner. LC 78-108719. 346p. 1970. reprint ed. pap. 19.95 (0-87348-126-7); LC 78-108719. write for info. (0-318-54959-X) Pathfinder NY.

W. E. B. Du Bois Speaks: Speeches & Addresses 1890-1919 see W. E. B. Du Bois Speaks

W. E. B. Du Bois Speaks: Speeches & Addresses 1920-1963 see W. E. B. Du Bois Speaks

W. E. B. Dubois. Patricia C. McKissack & Fredrick McKissack, Jr. LC 90-37823. (Impact Biographies Ser.). (Illus.). 112p. (YA). (gr. 7-12). 1990. lib. bdg. 22.70 (0-531-10939-9) Watts.

W. E. B. Dubois: Civil Rights Leader. (Junior Black Americans of Achievement Ser.). (Illus.). 80p. (J). (gr. 3-6). 1995. lib. bdg. 15.95 (0-7910-2382-6) Chelsea Hse.

W. E. B. DuBois: Scholar & Actitist. James Neyland. (Black American Ser.). (Illus.). 192p. (YA). 1993. mass mkt. 3.95 (0-87067-588-5, Melrose Sq) Holloway.

W. E. B. Dubois: Scholar & Activist. Mark Stafford. Ed. by Nathan I. Huggins. LC 89-9705. (Black Americans of Achievement Ser.). (Illus.). 128p. (YA). (gr. 5 up). 1989. pap. 8.95 (0-7910-0238-1); lib. bdg. 19.95 (1-55546-582-X) Chelsea Hse.

***W. E. B. DuBois & American Political Thought: Fabianism & the Color Line.** Adolph L. Reed, Jr. LC 96-847. 288p. 1997. 35.00 (0-19-505174-2) OUP.

W. E. B. Griffin: Three Complete Novels, Set, Bks. 1-3. W. E. B. Griffin. LC 95-39351. (Badge of Honor Ser.). 1996. 12.98 (0-399-14152-9, Putnam) Putnam Pub Group.

W. E. B. Griffin Three Complete Novels: Battleground, Line of Fire, Close Combat: Omnibus Edition. W. E. B. Griffin. 1995. 11.98 (0-399-14013-1, Putnam) Putnam Pub Group.

W. E. Gladstone I: Autobiographica. Ed. by John Brooke & Mary Sorensen. (Prime Ministers' Papers). 270p. 1971. 10.00 (0-11-440015-6, HM00156, Pub. by Stationery Ofc UK) Bernan Associates.

W. E. Gladstone II: Autobiographical Memoranda, 1832-1845. Ed. by John Brooke & Mary Sorensen. (Prime Ministers' Papers). 309p. 1972. 10.00 (0-11-440033-4, HM00334, Pub. by Stationery Ofc UK) Bernan Associates.

W. E. Gladstone III: Autobiographical Memoranda, 1845-1866. Ed. by John Brooke & Mary Sorensen. (Prime Ministers' Papers). 309p. 1978. 10.00 (0-11-440086-5, HM00865, Pub. by Stationery Ofc UK) Bernan Associates.

***W. E. H. Lecky: Historian & Politician 1838-1903.** Donal McCartney. 272p. 9400. 39.95 (1-874675-22-8) Dufour.

W. E. Henley. Kennedy Williamson. LC 74-30419. (English Literature Ser.: No. 33). 1974. lib. bdg. 53.95 (0-8383-1751-0) M S G Haskell Hse.

W. Elmer Schofield: Proud Painter of Modest Lands. Valerie A. Livingston. (Illus.). 64p. (Orig.). (C). 1988. pap. 15.00 (0-9621345-0-3) Moravian Coll.

W. Eugene Smith: His Photographs & Notes. W. Eugene Smith. (Illus.). 148p. 1993. pap. 27.50 (0-89381-534-9) Aperture.

W. Eugene Smith: Master of the Photographic Essay. limited ed. Comment by William S. Johnson. (Illus.). 224p. 1981. 350.00 (0-89381-072-X) Aperture.

W. Eugene Smith & the Photographic Essay. Glenn G. Willumson. (Illus.). 384p. (C). 1992. text ed. 80.00 (0-521-41464-4) Cambridge U Pr.

***W. F. Cody Buffalo Bill: Collector's Guide with Values.** James W. Wejtowicz. (Illus.). 224p. 1997. 24.95 (1-57432-008-4, 4935) Collector Bks.

***W. H. Auden.** Ed. by John Haffenden. (Critical Heritage Ser.). 556p. (C). 1997. text ed. 45.00 (0-415-15940-7) Routledge.

W. H. Auden. Stan Smith. 1990. 39.00 (0-7463-0731-4, Pub. by Northcote House UK) St Mut.

W. H. Auden. Stan Smith. (Writers & Their Works). 107p. 1997. pap. 22.50 (0-7463-0736-5, Pub. by Northcote House UK) Trans-Atl Phila.

W. H. Auden. Francis Scarfe. LC 72-11646. (Studies in Poetry: No. 38). 1973. reprint ed. lib. bdg. 39.95 (0-8383-1691-3) M S G Haskell Hse.

W. H. Auden: "The Map of All My Youth": Early Works, Friends, & Influences. W. H. Auden. Ed. by Katherine Bucknell & Nicholas Jenkins. (Auden Studies Ser.). 264p. 1990. 65.00 (0-19-812964-5) OUP.

W. H. Auden: A Poet of Ideas. Narsingh Srivastava. 314p. 1989. 35.00 (0-317-52162-4, Pub. by S Chand II) St Mut.

W. H. Auden: Collected Poems. Ed. by Edward Mendelson. 1976. 39.95 (0-394-40895-0) Random.

W. H. Auden: In the Autumn of the Age of Anxiety. Alan Levy. LC 82-84008. (Illus.). 160p. (C). 1983. pap. 16.00 (0-932966-31-4) Permanent Pr.

W. H. Auden: The Critical Heritage. Ed. by John Haffenden. (Critical Heritage Ser.). 500p. 1983. 69.50 (0-7100-9350-0, RKP) Routledge.

W. H. Auden: The Far Interior. Ed. by Alan Bold. LC 85-7358. (Critical Studies). 224p. 1985. 58.50 (0-389-20573-7, N8132) B&N Imports.

W. H. Auden: 1907-1973. Edward Mendelson. (Illus.). 64p. (Orig.). 1976. pap. 11.00 (0-87104-264-9) NY Pub Lib.

W. H. Auden - The Commissar & the Yogi: A Study of His Plays & Longer Poems. M. K. Raju. 200p. 1991. text ed. 30.00 (81-85218-25-0, Pub. by Prestige II) Advent Bks Div.

W. H. Auden, a Bibliography 1924-1969. 2nd ed. B. C. Bloomfield & Edward Mendelson. LC 72-77260. 420p. 1973. text ed. 35.00 (0-8139-0395-5, Bibliographic Pr) U Pr of Va.

W. H. Auden, Poems, 1927-1929: A Photographic & Typographic Facsimile of the Original Notebook in the Berg Collection of English & American Literature. limited ed. W. H. Auden. Ed. by Nicholas Jenkins. (Harcourt Brace Jovanovich Fund Ser.: No. 3). (Illus.). 142p. 1989. Limited Edition. 95.00 (0-87104-415-3) NY Pub Lib.

W. H. Chaney. Jack London. 42p. 1992. 1.95 (0-685-65598-9) Star Rover.

W. H. Davies: A Bibliography. Sylvia Harlow. (Illus.). 256p. 1993. 78.00 (0-938768-43-3) Oak Knoll.

W. H. Hudson: The Man, the Novelist, the Naturalist. Amy D. Ronner. LC 85-48068. (Studies in Modern Literature: No. 16). 1986. 34.50 (0-404-61586-4) AMS Pr.

W. H. Hudson & the Elusive Paradise. David Miller. 240p. 1990. text ed. 45.00 (0-312-03698-1) St Martin.

W. H. Price Guide to American Country Antiques, Bk. 14. 14th ed. Don Raycroft & Carol Raycroft. 264p. pap. 15.95 (0-87069-720-X) Chilton.

***W. H. R. Rivers: Pioneer Anthropologist & Psychiatrist of "The Ghost Road"** Richard Slobodin. (Illus.). 320p. 1997. pap. 22.95 (0-7509-1490-4, Pub. by Sutton Pubng UK) Bks Intl VA.

W. Hawkins Ferry Collection. Jan Van der Marck & W. Hawkins Ferry. (Illus.). 50p. 1987. pap. 12.95 (0-8143-2007-4) Wayne St U Pr.

W-Hollow Cookbook. Glennis S. Liles. Ed. by Chuck D. Charles. LC 95-45901. (Illus.). 310p. 1996. 24.00 (0-945084-56-0) J Stuart Found.

W-Hollow Holidays & Holiday Recipes. Glennis S. Liles. 240p. 1995. write for info. (1-886029-07-5) Spider Hill Pr.

W. Horace Carter's Crappie Secrets. W. Horace Carter. LC 91-70622. (Illus.). 360p. (Orig.). 1991. pap. 12.95 (0-937866-24-5) Atlantic Pub Co.

W. I. N. N. Against Suicide. Robert E. Nelson, Jr. Ed. by Diane Parker. 80p. (Orig.). 1993. pap. 6.95 (1-56875-049-8) R & E Pubs.

W. J. Cash: A Life. Bruce Clayton. LC 90-43462. (Southern Biography Ser.). (Illus.). 256p. 1991. 24.95 (0-8071-1647-5) La State U Pr.

***W. J. Cash: A Life.** Bruce Clayton. (Illus.). 256p. 1997. pap. 13.95 (0-8071-2215-7) La State U Pr.

W. J. Cash & the Minds of the South. Ed. by Paul D. Escott. LC 92-9303. (Illus.). 304p. (C). 1992. text ed. 37.50 (0-8071-1773-0) La State U Pr.

***W. J. Stein: A Biography.** Johannes Tautz. Tr. by John M. Wood & Marguerite A. Wood. (Illus.). 304p. 1990. pap. write for info. (0-904693-23-6, Pub. by Temple Ldge Pub UK) Anthroposophic.

***W. Kelly's Writings on Prophecy.** W. Kelly. Ed. by R. A. Huebner. 422p. 1997. lib. bdg. 35.00 (1-888749-01-6) Pres Truth.

W. L. C. & Joe. Donald H. Werner. (Illus.). 288p. 1989. write for info. (0-318-65179-3) Westminster Schl Bd Trust.

W. L. Garrison & His Times. Oliver A. Johnson. LC 74-89400. (Black Heritage Library Collection). 1977. 32.95 (0-8369-8613-X) Ayer.

W Labiryncie (Labyrinth of Life) An Advanced Polish Course. Wieslaw Oleksy & Oscar E. Swan. (Illus.). xiv, 378p. (Orig.). (C). 1993. pap. text ed. 22.95 (0-89357-242-X) Slavica.

W. Lee O'Daniel & Texas Politics, 1938-1942. Seth S. McKay. LC 83-45450. reprint ed. 58.00 (0-404-20164-4) AMS Pr.

***W. M. Thackeray: The Memoirs of Mr. Charles Yellowplush.** Intro. by Sheila Michell. (Pocket Classics Ser.). 128p. 1997. pap. 10.95 (0-7509-1558-7, Pub. by Sutton Pubng UK) Bks Intl VA.

W. M. Thackeray (1811-1863) L'homme, le penseur, le romancier. Raymond Las Vergnas. LC 70-148810. reprint ed. 49.50 (0-404-08876-7) AMS Pr.

W. Norman Cooper: A View of a Holy Man. Roselyn Witt. LC 81-70657. 96p. 1982. 7.50 (0-87516-492-7); pap. 4.50 (0-87516-471-4) DeVorss.

W. Norman Cooper - a Prophet for Our Time. Filip Field. LC 79-52443. 1979. 7.50 (0-87516-417-X); pap. 4.50 (0-87516-372-6) DeVorss.

W. O. Mitchell: An Annotated Bibliography. Sheila Latham. 364p. (C). 1981. pap. text ed. 9.00 (0-920763-59-6, Pub. by ECW Press CN) Genl Dist Srvs.

W. O. Mitchell & His Works. Dick Harrison. (Canadian Author Studies). 68p. (C). 1991. pap. text ed. 9.95 (1-55022-055-1, Pub. by ECW Press CN) Genl Dist Srvs.

W. O. Philbrook Memorial Symposium Proceedings: Toronto, Ontario, Canada, April 17-20, 1988. Philbrook, W. O., Memorial Symposium Staff. LC 88-81558. 291p. 1988. reprint ed. pap. 83.00 (0-608-00469-3, 2061288) Bks Demand.

W-O-T Position or Self-Actualization for Women. Mae A. Junod. 287p. 1981. 3.95 (0-938968-00-9) Impact Pr MI.

***W. O. W. 2000: How to Turn Employees into Owners, How to Create a Profitable Concept, How to Find the W. O. W. Niche, How to Change.** Barry M. Cohen. Ed. by James D. Scurlock. (Illus.). 205p. (Orig.). 1997. pap. 15.00 (0-9657602-0-0) Savannah Corp.

W. P. A. Historical Records Survey: A Guide to the Unpublished Inventories, Indexes, & Transcripts. Compiled by Loretta L. Hefner. LC 80-51489. 1980. pap. text ed. 5.00 (*0-931828-25-2*) Soc Am Archivists.

W. Page Keeton, No. 36: An Oral History Interview. Compiled by Bill Brands. 79p. 1992. 25.00 (*0-935630-42-2*) U of Tex Tarlton Law Lib.

***W. R. Case & Sons Cookbook & Historical Companion.** Case, W. R. & Sons Staff. (Illus.). 160p. 1996. 19.95 (*0-9653124-0-2*) W R Case & Sons.

W. R. Rodgers. Darcy O'Brien. LC 70-124646. (Irish Writers Ser.). 103p. 1975. pap. 1.95 (*0-8387-7630-2*) Bucknell U Pr.

W. Robertson Smith & the Sociological Study of Religion. Thomas O. Beidelman. LC 74-7568. 106p. reprint ed. pap. 30.30 (*0-685-23841-5*, 2056625) Bks Demand.

W. S. Gilbert: A Classic Victorian & His Theatre. Jane W. Stedman. (Illus.). 416p. 1996. 30.00 (*0-19-816174-3*) OUP.

W. S. McCulloch, 4 vols. Ed. by Rook McCulloch. 1392p. 1989. Set. pap. text ed. 84.00 (*0-685-25893-9*) Intersystems Pubns.

W. S. Merwin: Essays on the Poetry. Ed. by Cary Nelson & Ed Folsom. LC 85-24531. (Illus.). 424p. 1987. text ed. 27.50 (*0-252-01277-1*) U of Ill Pr.

W. S. Merwin the Mythmaker. Mark M. Christhilf. LC 85-20123. (Literary Frontiers Ser.: No. 26). 88p. 1986. pap. 9.95 (*0-8262-0478-3*) U of Mo Pr.

W. S. Van Dyke's Journal: White Shadows in the South Seas, 1927-28, & Other Van Dyke on Van Dyke, Vol. 47. Rudy Behlmer. LC 95-34206. (Filmmakers Ser.: No. 47). 160p. 1996. 34.50 (*0-8108-3028-0*) Scarecrow.

W. Shortz Brain Busters. B & P Publishing Co. Staff. 1992. 11.00 (*0-394-23519-3*) Random.

***W. Simsbury Genealogical History, with Short Sketches & Family Records of the Early Settlers of West Simsbury, Now Canton, Connecticut.** Abiel Brown. 151p. 1997. reprint ed. pap. 19.00 (*0-8328-5696-7*) Higginson Bk Co.

W. Somerset Maugham. Ed. by Anthony Curtis & John Whitehead. 480p. 1987. 69.50 (*0-7100-9640-2*, 96402, RKP) Routledge.

***W. Somerset Maugham.** Ed. by Anthony Curtis & John Whitehead. (Critical Heritage Ser.). 488p. (C). 1997. text ed. 35.00 (*0-415-15925-3*) Routledge.

W Symmetry. P. Bouwknegt. (Advanced Series in Mathematical Physics). 904p. 1995. text ed. 109.00 (*981-02-1762-5*) World Scientific Pub.

W. T. Brown's "Scenes in My Life" Reprinted from the Rochester Post-Express, 1886. Carwood G. Clarke. Ed. by James A. Santucci & Michael Gomes. (Theosophical History Occasional Papers: No. IV). (Illus.). i, 40p. (Orig.). 1995. reprint ed. pap. text ed. 17.00 (*1-883279-04-6*) J Santucci.

W Tungsten: Metal, Chemical Reactions with Nonmetals Nitrogen to Arsenic. 8th ed. Gmelin Institute for Inorganic Chemistry of the Max-Planck-Society Staff. (Gmelin Handbook of Inorganic & Organometallic Chemistry Ser.,: Pt. 5b). (Illus.). xiv, 196p. 1993. 865.00 (*0-387-93676-9*) Spr-Verlag.

W Tungsten: Surface Properties - Electron Emission. 8th ed. Gmelin Institute for Inorganic Chemistry of the Max-Planck-Society Staff. (Gmelin Handbook of Inorganic & Organometallic Chemistry Ser.,: Pt. 4). (Illus.). xv, 277p. 1993. 1,155.00 (*0-387-93677-7*) Spr-Verlag.

W (Viva) rev. ed. e. e. Cummings. Ed. by George J. Firmage. (Transcript Edition Ser.). 1979. 9.95 (*0-87140-636-5*) Liveright.

W. W. Denslow. Douglas G. Green & Michael H. Hearn. LC 77-353964. (Clarke Historical Press Juvenile Ser.: No. 2). (Illus.). 225p. 1976. 9.00 (*0-916699-09-9*) CMU Clarke Hist Lib.

W. W. E. Ross & His Works. Don Precosky. (Canadian Author Studies). 26p. (C). 1987. pap. text ed. 9.95 (*0-920763-20-0*, Pub. by ECW Press CN) Genl Dist Srvs.

***W. W. Jacobs Periodical Bibliography.** John Jascoll. (Illus.). 74p. (Orig.). 1996. pap. 30.00 (*0-9643012-7-X*) Hazelwood Pr.

***W. W. Jacobs' Uncollected Cargoes: The Lost Early Periodical Appearances.** W. W. Jacobs. Ed. by John Jascoll. (Illus.). 182p. (Orig.). 1996. pap. 30.00 (*0-9643012-6-1*) Hazelwood Pr.

***W. W. Loring: Florida's Forgotten General.** James W. Raab. (Illus.). 260p. 1996. 35.95 (*0-89745-210-0*); pap. 21.95 (*0-89745-205-4*) Sunflower U Pr.

W. W. True & Just Recorde of the Information, Examination & Confession of All the Witches, Taken at S. Oses in the Countie of Essex. LC 81-4330. 1981. reprint ed. 50.00 (*0-8201-1363-8*) Schol Facsimiles.

W. Wallace White: Caring for the Environment: My Work with Public Health & Reclamation in Nevada. Ed. by Mary E. Glass. 244p. 1970. lib. bdg. 43.50 (*1-56475-098-1*); fiche write for info. (*1-56475-099-X*) U NV Oral Hist.

W-Waves & a Wave Universe. O. Ed Wagner. LC 91-90809. (Illus.). 86p. (Orig.). (C). 1991. pap. text ed. 10.95 (*0-9628853-0-4*) Wagner Physics.

W-Waves & A Wave Universe. rev. ed. O. Ed Wagner. LC 91-66955. (Illus.). 103p. (C). 1991. pap. text ed. 14.95 (*0-9628853-1-2*) Wagner Physics.

***Wa-a-ay Cool Bible Puzzles.** Nancy I. Sanders. (Sizzling Bible Puzzles Ser.). 80p. (J). (gr. 3-7). 1996. pap. 4.99 (*0-570-04791-9*, 56-1811) Concordia.

Wa & the Wala: Islam & Polity in Northwestern Ghana. Ivor Wilks. (African Studies: No. 63). (Illus.). 272p. (C). 1989. text ed. 80.00 (*0-521-36210-5*) Cambridge U Pr.

W.A. Mozart: An Introduction to His Keyboard Works. Ed. by Willard A. Palmer. (Alfred Masterwork Editions Ser.). 64p. (Orig.). 1974. pap. text ed. 7.95 (*0-88284-254-4*, 664) Alfred Pub.

Wa-Si & Related Peoples of Namibia, Botswana, & Angola. rev. ed. Nicholas M. England. LC 94-35557. (Harvard Dissertations in Folklore & Oral Tradition Ser.). (Illus.). 417p. 1995. text ed. 120.00 (*0-8240-2986-0*) Garland.

Wa-Wan Press, 1901-1911, 5 Vols. Vera B. Lawrence. LC 74-97068. (American Music Ser.). 1970. reprint ed. 245.00 (*0-405-02407-X*) Ayer.

WAAAF in Wartime Australia. Joyce A. Thomson. (Illus.). 434p. 1992. pap. 24.95 (*0-522-84525-8*, Pub. by Melbourne Univ Pr AT) Paul & Co Pubs.

Waarheid of Bedrog? Goran Larsson. (Illus.). 85p. (DUT.). 1996. 5.00 (*1-888235-22-5*) AMI-Jerusalem.

Wabadwipa: The Hidden Treasure of the Holy Dhama. Bhaktivinoda Thakur. Ed. by Alan Dulfon & Ray Richards. Tr. by Banu Dasa from BEN. (Illus.). 185p. (Orig.). 1993. pap. 9.95 (*1-884295-02-9*) Ananta Prnting.

Wabanakis of Maine & the Maritimes: A Resource Book about Penobscot, Passamaquoddy, Maliseet, Micmac & Abenaki Indians. (Illus.). 506p. 1989. pap. text ed. 17.00 (*0-910082-17-0*) Am Fr Serv Comm.

Wabansi: Fiend or Friend? Alice F. Zeman. LC 91-92892. (Illus.). 118p. 1991. text ed. 14.75 (*0-9633266-0-0*) A Zeman.

Wabash. Robert Olen Butler. 15.95 (*0-317-57588-0*) Knopf.

Wabash. Donald J. Heimburger. LC 83-83067. (Illus.). 320p. 1996. 43.95 (*0-911581-02-2*) Heimburger Hse Pub.

Wabash: A Novel. Robert Olen Butler. LC 93-37098. 1994. pap. 11.00 (*0-8050-3138-3*) H Holt & Co.

Wabash County, Illinois. Ed. by Theodore G. Risley. (Illus.). 828p. 1994. reprint ed. lib. bdg. 85.00 (*0-8328-3986-8*) Higginson Bk Co.

Wabash in Color. David R. Sweetland. LC 91-60919. (Illus.). 128p. 1991. 45.00 (*1-878887-04-1*) Morning NJ.

Wabash, or Adventures of an English Gentleman's Family in the Interior of America, 2 Vols. J. Richard Beste. LC 75-121498. (Select Bibliographies Reprint Ser.). 1977. 66.95 (*0-8369-5456-4*) Ayer.

Wabash Standard Plans & Reference. Donald J. Heimburger. LC 92-90260. (Illus.). 128p. 1993. pap. 22.95 (*0-911581-27-8*) Heimburger Hse Pub.

WABC Talkradio 77 AM Financial Expert Bill Bresnan Speaks on Real Estate...In Words of One Syllable. Bill Bresnan. (Illus.). 144p. 1987. 17.50 (*0-13-949629-7*) P-H.

Wabi-Sabi for Artists, Designers, Poets & Philosophers. Leonard Koren. LC 94-2537. 96p. (Orig.). 1994. pap. 14.95 (*1-880656-12-4*) Stone Bridge Pr.

Wabi 2 Opening Windows. Fordin & Nolin. 416p. (C). 1996. pap. text ed. 45.00 (*0-13-461617-0*) P-H.

WAC Days of World War Two: A Personal Story. Dorothy M. Weirick. (Illus.). 88p. (Orig.). 1992. pap. 10.75 (*0-918329-26-4*) Royal Lit.

WAC Looks Back: Recollections & Poems of WWII. Doris Thurston. Ed. by Robert Deckert et al. (Illus.). 190p. (Orig.). 1996. per., pap. 14.95 (*1-886137-04-8*) Norvega Pr.

WAC STATS: The Facts about Women. Ed. by Andrea Blum et al. 64p. 1992. pap. 5.00 (*0-9635162-0-5*) Womens Act Coal.

WAC Stats: The Facts about Women. Ed. by Women's Action Coalition Staff. LC 93-3987. 64p. 1993. pap. 5.00 (*1-56584-122-0*) New Press NY.

Wace & Blegen: Pottery As Evidence for Trade in the Aegean Bronze Age 1939-1989. Ed. by Carol Zerner et al. xi, 428p. 1994. lib. bdg. 194.00 (*90-5063-089-8*, Pub. by Gieben NE) Benjamins North Am.

Wachapreague, Virginia: Then & Now. Kirk Mariner. (Illus.). 55p. 1995. pap. 5.95 (*0-9648393-2-6*) Miona Pubns.

Wachstum. Ed. by H. P. Schwarz. (Paediatrische Fortbildungskurse fuer die Praxis Ser.: Vol. 61). (Illus.). x, 82p. 1987. 39.25 (*3-8055-4594-0*) S Karger.

Wachstum der Deutschen Baumwollindustrie Im19. Jahrhundert. Gunter Kirchhain. Ed. by Stuart Bruchey. LC 77-77177. (Dissertations in European Economic History Ser.). (GER.). 1978. lib. bdg. 39.95 (*0-405-10790-0*) Ayer.

Wackiest Jokes in the World. Michael J. Pellowski. (Illus.). 96p. (J). 1995. pap. 4.95 (*0-8069-0494-1*) Sterling.

Wackiest Nature Riddles on Earth. Mike Artell. (Illus.). 96p. (J). (gr. 2-8). 1993. pap. 4.95 (*0-8069-1251-0*) Sterling.

Wackronyms. Alan Katz & Pete Fornatale. LC 96-1065. 144p. (Orig.). 1996. pap. 8.00 (*0-380-78536-6*) Avon.

Wacky Animals Sticker Pad. Illus. by M.J. Studios Staff. 32p. (J). (gr. k-6). 1993. reprint ed. pap. 2.95 (*1-879424-30-4*) Nickel Pr.

Wacky Animals Tracing Fun. Joan Berger. 32p. (J). (ps-3). 1994. pap. 1.95 (*0-590-48125-8*) Scholastic Inc.

***Wacky Basketball Facts: To Bounce Around.** Sheila Sweeny. Ed. by Jill Safro. (Illus.). 32p. (Orig.). (J). (gr. k-3). Date not set. pap. write for info. (*1-886749-22-1*, Spts Illus Kids) Little.

Wacky Cakes & Water Snakes: Four Seasons of Great Family Activities. Stacie H. Barta. LC 95-11634. 1995. pap. 15.95 (*0-14-023387-3*, Penguin Bks) Viking Penguin.

Wacky Football Facts to Kick Around. Sheila Sweeny. Ed. by Jill Safro. (Illus.). 32p. (Orig.). (J). (gr. k-3). Date not set. pap. write for info. (*1-886749-17-5*, Spts Illus Kids) Little.

Wacky Good Clean Jokes for Kids. Bob Phillips. (J). 1996. mass mkt. 3.99 (*1-56507-458-0*) Harvest Hse.

Wacky Inventions at Home. Bedrock Press Staff. (Flintstones Ser.). (J). (ps). 1994. 4.95 (*1-57036-093-6*, Bedrock Press) Turner Pub GA.

Wacky Inventions at Play. Bedrock Press Staff. (Flintstones Ser.). (J). (ps). 1994. 4.95 (*1-57036-095-2*, Bedrock Press) Turner Pub GA.

Wacky Inventions at Work. Bedrock Press Staff. (Flintstones Ser.). (J). (ps). 1994. 4.95 (*1-57036-094-4*, Bedrock Press) Turner Pub GA.

Wacky Inventions on the Move. Bedrock Press Staff. (Flintstones Ser.). (J). (ps). 1994. 4.95 (*1-57036-096-0*, Bedrock Press) Turner Pub GA.

Wacky Jacks: A Houdini Club Magic Mystery. David A. Adler. LC 93-51259. (First Stepping Stone Bks.). (Illus.). 80p. (Orig.). (J). (gr. 1-4). 1994. pap. 2.99 (*0-679-84696-4*) Random.

Wacky Jacks: A Houdini Club Magic Mystery. David A. Adler. LC 93-51259. (First Stepping Stone Bks.). (Illus.). 80p. (Orig.). (J). (gr. 1-4). 1994. lib. bdg. 11.99 (*0-679-94696-9*) Random.

Wacky Puzzles. (J). (gr. 4-7). 1997. pap. 3.95 (*0-8167-2615-9*) Troll Communs.

Wacky Science: A Cookbook for Elementary Teachers. Phil M. Parratore. 152p. 1995. per. 29.90 (*0-8403-9013-0*) Kendall-Hunt.

***Wacky Supernatural.** Greg Belter. (Orig.). 1997. pap. 11.95 (*0-533-12220-1*) Vantage.

Wacky Vehicle Mix-Ups. Christopher Carrie. (Crayola Color & Activity Ser.). (Illus.). 32p. (J). (gr. k up). 1991. 1.49 (*0-86696-303-0*) Binney & Smith.

Wacky Wednesday. Theodore Le Sieg. LC 74-5520. (Illus.). 48p. (J). (gr. k-4). 1974. 7.99 (*0-394-82912-3*); lib. bdg. 11.99 (*0-394-92912-8*) Beginner.

Wacky Weirdos. (Illus.). 14p. (Orig.). (J). (ps-2). 1994. pap. 3.50 (*1-57102-012-8*, Ideals Child) Hambleton-Hill.

Wacky Wisdom. Maurice Benzinger. LC 96-35262. 1997. 7.99 (*0-517-14939-7*) Random Hse Value.

Wacky Witch: Ghastly Guest. A Ghostwriter. (J). 1996. pap. text ed. 2.95 (*0-307-12936-5*, Golden Books) Western Pub.

Wacky Witch War. Ellen Jackson. (J). 1995. pap. 2.95 (*0-8167-3717-7*) Troll Communs.

Wacky Witch's Cookbook. Chris Angelilli. (J). 1996. pap. text ed. 2.95 (*0-307-12930-6*, Golden Books) Western Pub.

Wacky Word Games School Days. pap. 2.95 (*1-879424-75-4*) Nickel Pr.

Wacky Word Search Puzzles. Elvira Gamiello. (Illus.). (Orig.). (J). (gr. 4-6). 1987. pap. 1.95 (*0-942025-03-2*) Kidsbks.

Wacky Words. World Book Editors. (Mind Benders Ser.). 32p. (J). 1996. pap. text ed. 4.95 (*0-7166-4103-8*) World Bk.

Wacky Words for Travelling Tales: Logo Applications in Language Arts. Ellen Siegel. 120p. 1991. teacher ed. 25.00 (*0-924667-81-8*) Intl Society Tech Educ.

Wacky World of Peafowl, Vol. I. Dennis M. Fett. (Illus.). 52p. 1987. pap. 19.95 (*0-9617789-0-3*) D M Fett.

Wacky World of Peafowl, Vol. II. Dennis M. Fett & Debra J. Buck. (Illus.). 86p. (C). 1990. pap. 23.95 (*0-9617789-1-1*) D M Fett.

***Wackysaurus.** Louis Phillips. (J). 1997. pap. 3.99 (*0-14-038648-3*) Viking Penguin.

Wackysaurus: Dinosaur Jokes. Louis Phillips. LC 93-15134. (Illus.). 64p. (J). (gr. 2-5). 1993. pap. 3.99 (*0-14-034687-2*, Puffin) Puffin Bks.

Waco. San Antonio Cartographers Staff. 1996. 2.95 (*0-671-56301-7*) Macmillan.

Waco - Symbol of Courage & Excellence. Fred Kobernuss. (Illus.). 190p. 1993. pap. text ed. 24.95 (*0-943691-07-9*) Aviation Heritage.

***Waco Massacre.** Max. 50p. (Orig.). 1997. pap. 30.00 (*0-922070-79-2*) M Tecton Pub.

***WACO Memories: An American Classic Aircraft.** Joe Palmer et al. Ed. by Paul Avers. (Illus.). 84p. (Orig.). 1998. mass mkt. write for info. (*1-888282-03-5*) Little Otter.

***Waco People...Making a Difference: Representative Wacoans.** Nancy Barcus. (Illus.). 214p. (Orig.). 1996. pap. 15.95 (*0-9650227-1-4*) Arcway Pubns.

WACO Report, Recommendations, Evaluation, Lessons, 4 vols., Set. 1994. lib. bdg. 995.00 (*0-8490-8427-X*) Gordon Pr.

Waco Sites Tour of Troy, Ohio: Waco Sites in & around Troy. Jim Kessler et al. 1995. pap. 6.00 (*1-888282-00-2*) Little Otter.

Waconia, Paradise of the Northwest: The Lake & Its Island, Vol. 1. Waconia Heritage Association Staff. Ed. by Grace Lahr. LC 85-50907. 240p. lib. bdg. 25.00 (*0-9615181-0-3*) Waconia Heritage.

Waco's Champion: Selections from the Papers of Roger Norman Conger. Ed. by Marion Travis. LC 90-83501. (Illus.). 320p. 1990. 25.95 (*1-879030-00-4*) Historic Waco Fndtn.

Waco's Debt. large type ed. J. T. Edson. 1978. 25.99 (*0-7089-0151-4*) Ulverscroft.

***Wacousta.** John Richardson. 1996. pap. text ed. 8.95 (*0-7710-9877-4*) McCland & Stewart.

Wacousta Syndrome: Explorations in the Canadian Langscape. Gaile McGregor. 488p. 1985. 47.50 (*0-8020-2554-4*); pap. 20.95 (*0-8020-6570-8*) U of Toronto Pr.

***WACs: Women's Army Corps.** Vera Williams. LC 97-21767. (Illus.). 155p. 1997. 39.95 (*0-7603-0139-5*) Motorbooks Intl.

Wacs in Khaki. Mary Steelsmith. LC 96-19150. 55p. (Orig.). 1996. pap. 5.00 (*0-88734-310-4*) Players Pr.

WAC's Story: From Brisbane to Manila. rev. ed. Nancy Dammann. 167p. (Orig.). 1992. pap. 8.95 (*0-9609376-1-7*) Soc Change Pr.

Wad of Poems. Gopal Honnalgere. (Redbird Ser.). 1975. 6.75 (*0-88253-670-2*); pap. text ed. 4.00 (*0-88253-669-9*) Ind-US Inc.

Wade Cup in the Cleveland Museum of Art. D. S. Rice. (Islamic Art Reprint Ser.: No. 2). (Illus.). 64p. (C). 1988. reprint ed. lib. bdg. 15.00 (*0-939214-57-1*) Mazda Pubs.

Wade Genealogy: An Account of the Origin of the Name; Pedigrees of Famous Englishmen of That Name; a Genealogy of the Family in Massachusetts & New Jersey. S. C. Wade. (Illus.). 384p. 1989. reprint ed. pap. 57.50 (*0-8328-1207-2*); reprint ed. lib. bdg. 65.50 (*0-8328-1206-4*) Higginson Bk Co.

Wade Hampton & the Negro: The Road Not Taken. Hampton M. Jarrell. (History - United States Ser.). 209p. 1993. reprint ed. lib. bdg. 79.00 (*0-7812-4820-5*) Rprt Serv.

Wade Hampton Pipes: Arts & Crafts Architect in Portland, Oregon. Ann B. Clarke. LC 86-70205. (Illus.). 104p. 1986. pap. 14.95 (*0-8323-0451-4*) Binford Mort.

Wade in the Water. Contrib. by Myra Schubert. (Hymns We Play & Sing Ser.: Bk. VI). 1985. 7.99 (*0-685-68296-X*, MB-555) Lillenas.

Wade in the Water: The Wisdom of the Spirituals. Arthur C. Jones. LC 93-7491. (Illus.). 200p. (Orig.). 1993. 22.00 (*0-88344-923-4*) Orbis Bks.

Wade Price Guide. Robert Prescott-Walker. 1996. pap. 24.94 (*1-870703-61-8*) Chilton.

***Wade Price Trends Bk. 2: The World of Wade.** Ian Warner & Mike Posgay. (Illus.). 160p. 1996. pap. 24.95 (*1-57080-023-5*, 4104) Antique Pubns.

Waders: Their Breeding Haunts & Watchers. Desmond Nethersole-Thompson & Maimie Nethersole-Thompson. (Illus.). 424p. 1991. text ed. 37.00 (*0-85661-042-9*, 784642, Pub. by Poyser UK) Acad Pr.

Wadham Genealogy, Preceded by a Sketch of the Wadham Family in England. H. Stevens. (Illus.). 664p. 1989. reprint ed. pap. 99.00 (*0-8328-1209-9*); reprint ed. lib. bdg. 107.00 (*0-8328-1208-0*) Higginson Bk Co.

Wadhams Genealogy, Preceded by a Sketch of the Wadham Family in England. H. W. Stevens. (Illus.). 652p. 1990. reprint ed. pap. 97.50 (*0-8328-1555-1*); reprint ed. lib. bdg. 105.50 (*0-8328-1554-3*) Higginson Bk Co.

***Wadi al Qawr, Fashgha Vol. 1: The Excavation of a Prehistoric Burial Structure in Ras Al Khaimah.** C. Phillips. (Illus.). 32p. 1987. pap. 8.00 (*0-614-21842-X*) David Brown.

***Wadi ed-Daliyeh I: The Wadi ed-Daliyeh Seal Impressions.** Mary Leith. (Discoveries in the Judaean Desert Ser.: No. XXIV). (Illus.). 272p. 1997. 115.00 (*0-19-826935-8*) OUP.

Wadi Kubbaniya Skeleton: A Late Paleolithic Burial from Southern Egypt. Fred Wendorf & Romuald Schild. Ed. by Angela E. Close. LC 86-1965. (Illus.). 94p. 1986. pap. 12.95 (*0-87074-216-7*) SMU Press.

***Wadiba Tree: A Photographic Story Book.** Ryan G. Nellis. (Illus.). x, 60p. 1997. 33.50 (*0-9654895-0-7*) Creat Media Wrks.

Wading & Shore Birds: A Photographic Study. Roger S. Everett. LC 88-61476. (Illus.). 96p. 1988. pap. 9.95 (*0-88740-132-5*) Schiffer.

Wading Birds. John P. Mackenzie. (Birds of the World Ser.). 1993. 24.95 (*1-55013-279-2*) U of Toronto Pr.

***Wading Birds.** John P. Mackenzie. (Birds of the World Ser.). (Illus.). 144p. (Orig.). 1997. pap. 19.95 (*1-55013-799-9*, Pub. by Key Porter Bks CN) Firefly Bks Ltd.

Wading Birds. Ed. by Alexander Sprunt et al. LC 77-26723. (Research Reports: No. 7). (Illus.). 1978. pap. 11.50 (*0-930698-00-2*) Natl Audubon.

***Wading into Wetlands.** (Ranger Rick's Naturescope Ser.). (Illus.). 96p. (J). (gr. 1-7). 1997. text ed. 19.95 (*0-7910-4837-3*) Chelsea Hse.

Wading into Wetlands. National Wildlife Federation Staff. (J). (gr. k-8). 1991. pap. 7.95 (*0-945051-44-1*, 75025) Natl Wildlife.

Wading into Wetlands. 2nd ed. National Wildlife Federation Staff. LC 97-10377. (Ranger Rick's NatureScope Ser.). (Illus.). 96p. (J). (gr. k-8). 1997. pap. text ed. 12.95 (*0-07-046507-X*) McGraw.

Wading the Russian River. Richard A. Bunch. Ed. by Edward Mycue. (Took Modern Poetry in English Ser.: No. 41). (Illus.). 28p. (Orig.). 1993. pap. 5.00 (*1-879457-43-1*) Norton Coker Pr.

Wadmalaw Island: Leaving Traditional Roots Behind. Allen Mitchell. 120p. (Orig.). 1996. pap. 12.95 (*1-57502-120-X*) Morris Pubng.

Wads: True Homosexual Experiences from STH Writers, Vol. 6. Ed. by Boyd McDonald. (Illus.). 192p. (Orig.). 1985. pap. 12.00 (*0-917342-11-9*) Leyland Pubns.

Wadsworth Anaerobic Bacteriology Manual. 5th ed. Hanna M. Wexler et al. LC 92-49139. 1993. pap. 39.95 (*0-89863-170-X*) Star Pub CA.

Wadsworth Atheneum Paintings: The Netherlands & German Speaking Countries; Fifteenth Through Nineteenth Centuries. LC 77-82219. (Illus.). 208p. 1978. 25.00 (*0-317-13588-0*); pap. 12.00 (*0-317-13589-9*) Wadsworth Atheneum.

Wadsworth Atheneum Paintings II: Italy & Spain, Fourteenth Through Nineteenth Centuries. Jean K. Cadogan et al. LC 77-82219. (Paintings Ser.). (Illus.). 376p. 1992. pap. 50.00 (*0-918333-09-1*) Hudson Hills.

Wadsworth Jarrell: The Artist As Revolutionary. Robert L. Douglas. LC 96-26465. (Illus.). 128p. (Orig.). 1996. pap. 29.95 (*0-7649-0012-9*) Pomegranate Calif.

Waelrant & Laet: Music Publishers in Antwerp's Golden Age. Robert L. Weaver. LC 94-23767. (Detroit Monographs in Musicology: No. 15). 1995. 55.00 (*0-89990-071-2*) Info Coord.

Wafer Fabrication: Performance & Analysis. Linda F. Atherton & Robert W. Atherton. LC 95-40381. (Kluwer International Series in Engineering & Computer Science: SECS 339). 488p. (C). 1995. lib. bdg. 140.00 (*0-7923-9619-7*) Kluwer Ac.

Wafer-Level Integrated Systems: Implementation Issues. Stuart K. Tewksbury. (C). 1989. lib. bdg. 120.00 (*0-7923-9006-7*) Kluwer Ac.

W

An Asterisk (*) at the beginning of an entry indicates that the title is appearing in BIP for the first time.

***Wafer Paper Quilling.** rev. ed. Christina Wise. (Illus.). 52p. 1996. reprint ed. pap. 8.95 (0-9651584-4-6) Wise Astro.

Wafer Paper Uses. Marsha Winbeckler. (Illus.). 24p. (Orig.). 1990. pap. 10.95 (0-930113-13-6) Winbeckler.

Wafer Scale Integration. Ed. by Earl E. Swartzlander, Jr. (C). 1989. lib. bdg. 143.50 (0-7923-9003-2) Kluwer Ac.

***Wafer Tools: The Disposable Shaper Cutter.** E. W. Haug. (1985 Fall Technical Meeting Ser.: Vol. 8). 1985. pap. text ed. 30.00 (1-55589-101-2) AGMA.

Waffen der Alten Araber. Friedrich W. Schwarzlose. xvi, 392p. 1982. reprint ed. write for info. (3-487-07188-6) G Olms Pubs.

Waffen SS. Herbert Walther. LC 89-63358. (Illus.). 240p. 1989. 24.95 (0-88740-204-6) Schiffer.

Waffen-SS. Martin Windrow. (Men-at-Arms Ser.: No. 34). (Illus.). 48p. pap. 11.95 (0-85045-425-5, 9002, Pub. by Osprey UK) Stackpole.

Waffen SS: Hitler's Elite Guard at War, 1939-1945. George H. Stein. LC 66-11049. (Illus.). 366p. 1984. pap. 15.95 (0-8014-9275-0) Cornell U Pr.

***Waffen-SS Commanders: The Army, Corps & Division Leaders of a Legend Augsberger to Kreutz.** Mark C. Yerger. 352p. 1997. 59.95 (0-7643-0356-2) Schiffer.

Waffen-SS Soldier 1940-45. Bruce Quarrie. (Warrior Ser.: No. 2). (Illus.). 64p. pap. 12.95 (1-85532-288-9, 9601, Pub. by Osprey UK) Stackpole.

Waffen-SS Uniforms in Colour. Andrew Steven & P. Amodio. (Europa Militaria Ser.: Vol. 6). (Illus.). 66p. 1990. pap. 15.95 (1-872004-61-X) Motorbooks Intl.

Waffle Cookbook. Leslie Freiberger. (Illus.). 128p. (Orig.). 1992. pap. 11.00 (1-55788-036-0, HP Books) Berkley Pub.

Waffles. Donna R. German. (Illus.). 160p. (Orig.). 1992. pap. 8.95 (1-55867-041-6, Nitty Gritty Ckbks) Bristol Pub Ent CA.

***Waffles.** Dorie Greenspan. 1998. pap. write for info. (0-688-15804-8) Morrow.

Waffles & Wafers: Traditional Recipes for Today's Kitchen. Mary Barile. (Illus.). 66p. 1987. pap. 6.00 (0-937213-01-2) Heritage NY.

Waffles, Flapjacks, Pancakes, Blintzes, Crepes, & Frybread: From Scandinavia & Around the World. 118p. 1993. spiral bd. 5.95 (0-941016-92-7) Penfield.

Waffles from Morning to Midnight. Dorie Greenspan. LC 92-45914. 1993. pap. 15.00 (0-688-12609-X) Morrow.

Wag Wag Wag. Peter Hansard. LC 93-3536. (Read & Wonder Bks.). (Illus.). 32p. (J). (ps up). 1994. 14.95 (1-56402-301-X) Candlewick Pr.

Wag Wag Wag. Peter Hansard. LC 93-3536. (Read & Wonder Bks.). (Illus.). 32p. (J). (ps-1). 1996. reprint ed. pap. 5.99 (1-56402-980-8) Candlewick Pr.

Wage, 2 vols. 641p. 1973. reprint ed. Set. 100.00 (3-487-04597-4) G Olms Pubs.

Wage & Employment Adjustment in Local Labor Markets. Randall W. Eberts & Joe A. Stone. LC 91-41773. 153p. 1992. text ed. 23.00 (0-88099-115-1); pap. text ed. 13.00 (0-88099-116-X) W E Upjohn.

Wage & Employment Patterns in Labor Contracts: Micro-Foundations & Macroeconomics Implications, Vol. 19. Russell W. Cooper. (Fundamentals of Pure & Applied Economics Ser.: Vol. 19). 80, viiip. 1987. pap. text ed. 29.00 (3-7186-0378-0) Gordon & Breach.

Wage & Hour Law: Compliance & Practice, 3 vols. Les A. Schneider & J. Larry Stine. LC 94-43578. 1995. ring bd. 325.00 (0-615-00570-5) Clark Boardman Callaghan.

Wage & Hour Laws, No. 145. 1995. 115.00 (1-56789-019-9) Busn Laws Inc.

Wage & Hour Manual for California Employers. 2nd ed. Richard J. Simmons. 605p. 1994. per. 69.00 (0-943178-10-X) Castle Pubns.

Wage & Salary. Ad Wittemann. LC 88-29920. 11p. 1988. pap. 25.00 (0-938481-11-8) Camelot Consult.

Wage & Salary Administration. (PPF Survey Ser.: No. 147). 1989. 30.00 (1-55871-100-7) BNA Books.

Wage & Salary Administration. (Personnel Policies Forum Surveys Ser.: No. 131). 56p. 1981. 30.00 (0-87179-981-2) BNA.

Wage & Salary Administration. Lawrence S. Aft. (C). 1985. teacher ed. write for info. (0-8359-8529-6, Reston) P-H.

Wage & Salary Administration in India. Alka Gupta. 286p. (C). 1992. 120.00 (81-7041-626-4, Pub. by Scientific Pubs II) St Mut.

Wage & Salary Administration Workshop, 4 vols., Set. Date not set. per. 69.95 (0-614-08816-X, 410) Busn Legal Reports.

Wage & Salary Audit. A. Schofield & T. Husband. 126p. 1977. text ed. 59.95 (0-566-02008-4, Pub. by Gower UK) Ashgate Pub Co.

Wage Bargain & the Labor Market. Harry M. Douty. LC 79-3720. (Policy Studies in Employment & Welfare: No. 37). 160p. reprint ed. pap. 45.60 (0-317-42310-X, 2025806) Bks Demand.

Wage Behavior in the Postwar Period. William G. Bowen. LC 73-10582. (Princeton University Industrial Relations Ser.). (Illus.). 137p. 1973. reprint ed. text ed. 57.50 (0-8371-7013-3, BOWB, Greenwood Pr) Greenwood.

Wage Carrot & the Pension Stick: Retirement Benefits & Labor Force Participation. Laurence J. Kotlikoff & David A. Wise. LC 89-39488. 155p. 1989. text ed. 22.00 (0-88099-082-1); pap. text ed. 12.00 (0-88099-081-3) W E Upjohn.

Wage Curve. David G. Blanchflower & Andrew J. Oswald. (Illus.). 512p. 1994. 42.50 (0-262-02375-X) MIT Pr.

Wage Determination & Distribution in Japan. Toshiaki Tachibanaki. (Japan Business & Economic Ser.). (Illus.). 292p. (C). 1996. 65.00 (0-19-828865-4) OUP.

Wage Determination & Incomes Policy in Open Economies. Anne R. Braun. LC 86-10414. (Illus.). xix, 380p. 1986. pap. 18.50 (0-939934-75-2) Intl Monetary.

Wage Determination & Incomes Policy in Open Economies. Anne R. Braun. LC 86-10414. 400p. reprint ed. pap. 114.00 (0-317-55518-9, 2029549) Bks Demand.

Wage Determination in Asia & Pacific: The Views of Employers' Organisations-Reports & Documents Submitted to an ILO-DANIDA Regional Seminar (Singapore, October 8-12, 1979) (Labour-Management Relations Ser.: No. 58). ii, 169p. (Orig.). 1983. pap. 18.00 (92-2-102492-X) Intl Labour Office.

Wage Determination under Trade Unions. John T. Dunlop. LC 50-58147. (Reprints of Economic Classics Ser.). xi, 230p. 1966. reprint ed. 35.00 (0-678-00137-5) Kelley.

***Wage Differentials.** Tachibanaki. LC 97-6280. 1997. text ed. 79.95 (0-312-17482-9) St Martin.

Wage Differentials. Carrie Glasser. LC 77-76638. (Columbia University. Studies in the Social Sciences: No. 476). (Illus.). 1969. reprint ed. 20.00 (0-404-51476-6) AMS Pr.

Wage Differentials & Economic Growth. Pasquale M. Sgro. 147p. 1980. 44.00 (0-389-20002-6, N6669) B&N Imports.

Wage Differentials in the European Community: Convergence or Divergence? Willem Molle & Aad Van Mourik. (Illus.). 203p. 1989. text ed. 72.95 (0-566-07098-7, Pub. by Avebury Pub UK) Ashgate Pub Co.

Wage Earners' Budgets: A Study of Standards & Cost of Living in New York City. Louise B. More. LC 73-137178. (Poverty U. S. A. Historical Record Ser.). 1977. reprint ed. 23.95 (0-405-03116-5) Ayer.

Wage-Earning Pittsburgh, Vol. 6. Ed. by Paul U. Kellogg. LC 73-11906. (Metropolitan America Ser.). (Illus.). 726p. 1974. reprint ed. 54.95 (0-405-05398-3) Ayer.

Wage-Earning Women. Annie M. MacLean. LC 74-3962. (Women in America Ser.). (Illus.). 218p. 1974. reprint ed. 24.95 (0-405-06111-0) Ayer.

Wage-Earning Women: Industrial Work & Family Life in the United States, 1900-1930. Leslie W. Tentler. 290p. 1982. reprint ed. pap. 9.95 (0-19-503211-X) OUP.

Wage Employment Programmes in Rural Development. Indira Hirway. 1986. 11.00 (81-204-0072-0, Pub. by Oxford IBH II) S Asia.

Wage Equality among Sexes - a Study of Equal Remuneration Act. Ed. by P. N. Pande. 275p. (C). 1992. 150.00 (81-85009-39-2, Pub. by Print Hse II) St Mut.

Wage Flexibility & Unemployment Dynamics. Thomas Hyclak & Geraint Johnes. LC 92-5782. 116p. 1992. pap. 11.00 (0-88099-120-8) W E Upjohn.

Wage Gap: Women Have Made Slow, Steady Progress in the Labor Market since 1979 but the Wage Gap Has Not Narrowed Significantly. National Committee on Pay Equity. (Briefing Papers: No. 1). 7p. 1989. pap. 4.00 (0-685-29940-6) Inst Womens Policy Rsch.

Wage-Hour Guide. ring bd. write for info. (0-318-57377-6) P-H.

Wage Hunters & Gatherers. Jan Breman. 350p. 1995. text ed. 35.00 (0-19-563556-6) OUP.

Wage Inequalities in East & West. Dominique Redor. (Illus.). 240p. (C). 1993. text ed. 59.95 (0-521-39531-3) Cambridge U Pr.

Wage Inequality: International Comparisons of Its Sources. Francine D. Blau & Lawrence M. Kahn. (AEI Studies on Understanding Inequality). 43p. (Orig.). 1996. pap. 9.95 (0-8447-7074-4, AEI Pr) Am Enterprise.

Wage Inflation & the Two-Tier Labour Market. Ioannis Theodossiou. 307p. 1992. 68.95 (1-85628-268-6, Pub. by Avebury Pub UK) Ashgate Pub Co.

Wage Justice: Comparable Worth & the Paradox of Technocratic Reform. Sara M. Evans & Barbara J. Nelson. LC 88-39871. (Illus.). 240p. 1989. 29.95 (0-226-22259-4) U Ch Pr.

Wage Justice: Comparable Worth & the Paradox of Technocratic Reform. Sara M. Evans & Barbara N. Nelson. LC 88-39871. (Women in Culture & Society Ser.). (Illus.). xiv, 240p. 1991. pap. text ed. 13.00 (0-226-22260-8) U Ch Pr.

Wage-Labor & Capital. Karl Marx. Tr. & Intro. by Friedrich Engels. 59p. pap. 5.00 (0-88286-052-6) C H Kerr.

Wage Labor & Guilds in Medieval Europe. Steven A. Epstein. LC 90-40427. viii, 308p. 1991. pap. 16.95 (0-8078-4498-5) U of NC Pr.

Wage Labor & Guilds in Medieval Europe. Steven A. Epstein. LC 90-40427. viii, 308p. 1991. 45.00 (0-8078-1939-5) U of NC Pr.

Wage Labor & Social Change: The Proletariat in Asia & the Pacific. Ed. by Michael Pinches & Salim Lakha. 283p. (Orig.). 1992. pap. 17.50 (971-10-0453-4, Pub. by New Day Pub PH) Cellar.

Wage-Labour & Capital & Value, Price & Profit. Karl Marx. LC 76-10456. (Illus.). 110p. (C). 1976. pap. text ed. 4.25 (0-7178-0470-4) Intl Pubs Co.

Wage Patterns & Wage Policy in Modern China, 1919-1972. Christopher Howe. LC 72-97875. (Cambridge Studies in Chinese History, Literature & Institutions). 187p. reprint ed. pap. 53.30 (0-317-29416-4, 2024473) Bks Demand.

Wage Payment Systems. (Open Learning for Supervisory Management Ser.). 1986. pap. text ed. 19.50 (0-08-034175-6, Pergamon Pr) Elsevier.

Wage Payment Systems. (Open Learning for Supervisory Management Ser.). 1986. pap. text ed. 19.50 (0-08-070091-8, Pergamon Pr) Elsevier.

Wage Policies of Labor Organizations in a Period of Industrial Depression. Vertrees J. Wyckoff. LC 77-89772. (American Labor, from Conspiracy to Collective Bargaining Ser., No. 1). 119p. 1978. reprint ed. 17.95 (0-405-02159-3) Ayer.

Wage Policy & European Integration. Bernhard Seidel. 304p. 1983. text ed. 74.50 (0-566-00357-0, Pub. by Dartmth Pub UK) Ashgate Pub Co.

Wage Policy During the Transition to a Market Economy: Poland, 1990-91. Ed. by Fabrizio Coricelli & Ana Revenga. LC 92-12835. (Discussion Paper Ser.: Vol. 158). 132p. 1992. 9.95 (0-8213-2114-5, 12114) World Bank.

Wage Policy Issues in Economic Development. Ed. by Anthony D. Smith. LC 69-13690. (International Institute for Labor Studies). 1969. text ed. 39.95 (0-312-85330-0) St Martin.

Wage-Price Controls & Labor Market Distortions. Daniel J. Mitchell & Ross E. Azevedo. (Monograph & Research Ser.: No. 16). 174p. 1976. 6.00 (0-89215-056-4) U Cal LA Indus Rel.

Wage-Price Issue: A Theoretical Analysis. William G. Bowen. LC 72-90471. 447p. 1969. reprint ed. text ed. 75.00 (0-8371-2286-4, BOWP, Greenwood Pr) Greenwood.

Wage, Price, Productivity & Industrial Planning. Basudeb Sahoo. 1985. 32.50 (0-8364-1463-2, Pub. by Ashish II) S Asia.

Wage-Price Standards & Economic Policy. Jack A. Meyer. LC 82-8810. (AEI Studies: No. 358). 88p. reprint ed. pap. 25.10 (0-8357-4543-0, 2037440) Bks Demand.

Wage Rates in Philadelphia, Seventeen Ninety to Eighteen Thirty. Donald R. Adams, Jr. LC 75-2572. (Dissertations in American Economic History Ser.). (Illus.). 1975. reprint ed. 31.95 (0-405-07253-8) Ayer.

Wage Restraint & the Control of Inflation: An International Survey. Ed. by Beth Bilson. LC 86-22575. 208p. 1986. text ed. 39.95 (0-312-00374-9) St Martin.

Wage Rigidity & Umemployment. Ed. by Wilfred Beckerman. LC 86-45446. 231p. reprint ed. pap. 65.90 (0-7837-2192-7, 2042530) Bks Demand.

Wage Slave No More: The Independent Contractor's Legal Guide. Stephen Fishman. LC 96-50113. 320p. 1997. pap. text ed. 29.95 incl. disk (0-87337-359-6) Nolo Pr.

Wage the Energy War at Home. Joseph C. Davis & Claxton Walker. LC 78-51121. (Illus.). 1978. 14.95 (0-87523-191-8) Emerson.

Wage, Trade, & Exchange in Melanesia: A Manus Society in the Modern State. James G. Carrier & Achsah H. Carrier. (Studies in Melanesian Anthropology). 160p. (C). 1989. 42.00 (0-520-06389-9) U CA Pr.

Wage War on Silence: A Book of Poems. Vassar Miller. LC 60-13157. (Wesleyan Poetry Program Ser.: Vol. 8). 69p. 1960. 12.95 (0-8195-2008-X, Wesleyan Univ Pr) U Pr of New Eng.

Waged Work at Home: The Social Organization of Industrial Outwork in Hong Kong. Tai Lok Lui. 207p. 1994. 55.95 (1-85628-644-4, Pub. by Avebury Pub UK) Ashgate Pub Co.

Wagen und Fahrwerke der Griechen und Romer und Anderer Alter Volker, 2 vols. Johann C. Ginzrot. (Documenta Hippologica Ser.). xxxiv, 1104p. 1975. reprint ed. Set. write for info. (3-487-08107-5) G Olms Pubs.

Wager. Sally Cheney. (Historical Ser.). 1996. mass mkt. 4.99 (0-373-28934-0, 1-28934-7) Harlequin Bks.

Wager. Steven Linder. 192p. 1986. 14.95 (0-8027-4061-8) Walker & Co.

Wager. Mark Medoff. 1975. pap. 5.25 (0-8222-1214-5) Dramatists Play.

Wager: Aires' Journal. Machado De Assis. Tr. by Robert L. Scott-Buccleuch from POR. LC 90-80799. 160p. 1990. 30.00 (0-7206-0772-8) Dufour.

Wager & Other Stories. Daniel Corkery. (Illus.). (J). 1950. 8.50 (0-8159-7200-8) Devin.

Wager for Love. Rachelle Edwards. 1980. pap. 1.75 (0-449-50021-7, Coventry) Fawcett.

Wager for Love. large type ed. Rachelle Edwards. (Romance Ser.). 1994. pap. 15.99 (0-7089-7618-2, Linford) Ulverscroft.

Wager of Lucien Goldmann: Tragedy, Dialectics, & a Hidden God. Mitchell Cohen. LC 93-40394. 368p. 1994. text ed. 39.50 (0-691-03420-6) Princeton U Pr.

Wager on Love. Prudence Martin. 1991. mass mkt. 3.50 (0-8217-3548-9, Zebra Kensgtn) Kensgtn Pub Corp.

Wager with the Wind: The Don Sheldon Story. James Greiner. (Illus.). 256p. 1982. pap. 11.95 (0-312-85337-8) St Martin.

Wagered Miss Winslow. Kasey Michaels. 192p. (Orig.). 1992. mass mkt. 3.99 (0-380-76302-8) Avon.

Wagered Woman. Christine Rimmer. 1993. mass mkt. 3.39 (0-373-09794-8, 5-09794-4) Silhouette.

***Wagering on Transcendence: The Search for Meaning in Literature.** Phyllis Carey. LC 97-14762. 1997. write for info. (1-55612-982-3) Sheed & Ward MO.

Wagering the Land: Ritual, Capital, & Environmental Degradation in the Cordillera of Northern Luzon, 1900-1986. Martin W. Lewis. LC 91-12307. (C). 1992. 40.00 (0-520-07272-3) U CA Pr.

Wagering to Win! M. Paul Andersen. 186p. 1995. per., pap. 19.95 (0-614-17744-8) Mutuel Pr.

Wagers of Sin. Robert L. Asprin & Linda Evans. (Time Scout Ser.: No. 2). 1996. mass mkt. 5.99 (0-671-87730-5) Baen Bks.

Wages. Maurice H. Dobb. LC 82-994. (Cambridge Economic Handbooks). (Illus.). xv, 201p. 1982. reprint ed. text ed. 55.00 (0-313-23483-3, DOWA, Greenwood Pr) Greenwood.

Wages: A Workers' Education Manual. 3rd ed. x, 179p. (Orig.). 1992. pap. 15.75 (92-2-102961-1) Intl Labour Office.

Wages - Salary - Paychecks. (C). pap. text ed. 9.95 (0-88671-161-4, 81202) Am Guidance.

Wages Act, 1986. Fraser Davidson. 142p. (C). 1986. 125.00 (1-85185-047-3, Pub. by Blackstone Pr UK) St Mut.

Wages, Amenities, & Cost of Living: Theory & Measurement of Geographical Differentials. Kent Halstead. LC 92-80550. 237p. (Orig.). 1992. pap. 45.00 (1-883298-01-6) Res Assoc WA.

Wages & Earnings in the United States, 1860-1890. Clarence D. Long. LC 75-19725. (National Bureau of Economic Research Ser.). (Illus.). 1975. reprint ed. 18.95 (0-405-07603-7) Ayer.

Wages & Earnings in the United States, 1860-1890. Clarence D. Long. (General Ser.: No. 67). 186p. 1960. reprint ed. 48.90 (0-87014-066-3); reprint ed. mic. film 24.50 (0-685-61323-2) Natl Bur Econ Res.

Wages & Economic Control in Norway, 1945-1957. Mark W. Leiserson. LC 59-5565. (Wertheim Publications in Industrial Relations). 190p. 1959. 12.50 (0-674-94470-4) HUP.

Wages & Employment Policy Nineteen Thirty-Six to Nineteen Eighty-Six. Russell Jones. 230p. 1986. text ed. 49.95 (0-04-331110-5); pap. text ed. 19.95 (0-04-331111-3) Routledge Chapman & Hall.

Wages & Hours. (Labor Relations Reporter Ser.). 1938. ring bd. 611.00 (1-55871-035-3) BNA.

Wages & Hours under the Codes of Fair Competition. Leo Wolman. (NBER Bulletin Ser.: No. 54). 1935. reprint ed. 20.00 (0-685-61169-8) Natl Bur Econ Res.

Wages & Payroll Statistics. Bd. with Methods of Family Living Studies.; Methods of Labour Productivity Statistics. (I.L.O. Studies & Reports New Ser.: Nos. 16-18). 1974. reprint ed. 85.00 (0-8115-3337-9) Periodicals Srv.

Wages & Profits in the Capitalist Economy: The Impact of Monopolistic Power on Macroeconomic Performance in the USA & the UK. Andrew Henley. (New Directions in Modern Economics Ser.). (Illus.). 224p. 1990. text ed. 80.00 (1-85278-090-8) E Elgar.

Wages & Salaries Paid Support Personnel in Public Schools, 1987-88. 74p. 1988. 36.00 (0-318-37603-2) Ed Research.

Wages & the Law. Keith Puttick. (C). 1988. pap. 125.00 (0-317-92374-9, Pub. by Scientific UK) St Mut.

Wages & the Law. Keith Puttick. 190p. (C). 1989. pap. 75.00 (0-7219-1110-2, Pub. by IPM Hse UK) St Mut.

Wages & the Working Day. John Keracher. 1946. pap. 1.25 (0-88286-039-9) C H Kerr.

Wages & Unemployment: A Study in Non-Walrasian Macroeconomics. Pierre Picard. LC 92-19475. (Illus.). 312p. (C). 1993. text ed. 54.95 (0-521-35057-3) Cambridge U Pr.

Wages & Wants of Science-Workers. Richard A. Proctor. 270p. 1970. reprint ed. 38.00 (0-7146-1627-3, Pub. by F Cass Pubs UK) Intl Spec Bk.

***Wages Creek.** Jeffrey Hickey. 1997. pap. text ed. 18.95 (1-55656-194-6) Dercum Audio.

Wages During the Depression. Leo Wolman. (NBER Bulletin Ser.: No. 46). 1993. reprint ed. 20.00 (0-685-61156-6) Natl Bur Econ Res.

Wages for Caring: Compensating Family Care of the Elderly. Ed. by Nathan Linsk et al. LC 91-37512. 296p. 1992. text ed. 59.95 (0-275-93635-X, C3635, Praeger Pubs) Greenwood.

Wages, Hours & Strikes: Labor Panaceas in the Twentieth Century. Ed. by Leon Stein & Philip Taft. LC 79-89743. (American Labor, from Conspiracy to Collective Bargaining Ser., No. 1). 528p. 1971. 44.95 (0-405-02152-6) Ayer.

Wages in Germany, 1871-1945. Gerhard Bry & Charlotte Boschan. (General Ser.: No. 68). 512p. 1960. reprint ed. 133.20 (0-87014-067-1) Ayer.

Wages in Practice & Theory. John W. Rowe. LC 70-76356. x, 277p. 1969. reprint ed. 39.50 (0-678-06502-0) Kelley.

Wages in Practice & Theory: McCormick & International Harvester, 1860-1960. Robert W. Ozanne. LC 68-19572. (Illus.). 195p. reprint ed. pap. 55.60 (0-8357-6778-7, 2035454) Bks Demand.

Wages in the Business Cycle: An Empirical & Methodological Analysis. Jonathan Michie. 194p. 1992. 45.00 (0-86187-686-5) St Martin.

Wages, Labour & Regional Development in Brazil. William D. Savedoff. 158p. 1995. 55.95 (1-85628-964-8, Pub. by Avebury Pub UK) Ashgate Pub Co.

Wages, Manufacturers & Workers in the Nineteenth-Century Factory: The Voortman Cotton Mill in Ghent. Peter Scholliers. (Illus.). 256p. 1996. 45.95 (1-85973-093-0) Berg Pubs.

Wages of Conquest: The Mexican Aristocracy in the Context of Western Aristocracies. Hugo G. Nutini. 550p. 1995. text ed. 69.50 (0-472-10484-5) U of Mich Pr.

Wages of Farm & Factory Laborers. Daniel J. Ahearn, Jr. LC 78-76649. (Columbia University. Studies in the Social Sciences: No. 518). 1969. reprint ed. 37.50 (0-404-51518-5) AMS Pr.

Wages of Globalism: Lyndon Johnson & the Limits of American Power. H. W. Brands. 304p. 1995. 30.00 (0-19-507888-8) OUP.

***Wages of Globalism: Lyndon Johnson & the Limits of American Power.** H. W. Brands. LC 96-52764. 304p. 1997. reprint ed. pap. 18.95 (0-19-511377-2) OUP.

Wages of Goodness. Michael Blumenthal. 64p. (C). 1992. pap. 10.95 (0-8262-0833-9); text ed. 18.95 (0-8262-0832-0) U of Mo Pr.

Wages of Guilt: Memories of War in Germany & Japan. Ian Buruma. 1995. pap. 12.95 (0-452-01156-6, Plume) NAL-Dutton.

***Wages of Independence: Capitalism in the Early American Republic.** Ed. by Paul A. Gilje. LC 97-2173. 176p. (Orig.). (C). 1997. pap. text ed. 14.95 (0-945612-52-4) Madison Hse.

***Wages of Independence: Capitalism in the Early American Republic.** Ed. by Paul A. Gilje. 176p. (C). 1997. text ed. 22.95 (0-945612-53-2) Madison Hse.

W

Wages of Motherhood: Inequality in the Welfare State, 1917-1942. Gwendolyn Mink. 208p. 1995. 35.00 (*0-8014-2234-5*) Cornell U Pr.

Wages of Motherhood: Inequality in the Welfare State, 1917-1942. Gwendolyn Mink. 216p. 1996. pap. 12.95 (*0-8014-9534-2*) Cornell U Pr.

Wages of Peace: Disarmament in a Small Industrialized Country. Nils P. Gleditsch et al. 256p. 1994. 65.00 (*0-8039-7750-6*) Sage.

Wages of Sin. Andrew M. Greeley. 1993. mass mkt. 5.99 (*0-515-11222-4*) Jove Pubns.

Wages of Sin. Gerald Haslam. Ed. by Kirk Robertson. LC 80-65780. (Windriver Ser.). (Illus.). 88p. (Orig.). 1980. pap. 4.00 (*0-916918-11-4*) Duck Down.

Wages of Sin. Sherryl Woods. 272p. (Orig.). 1994. mass mkt. 5.50 (*0-446-60088-1*) Warner Bks.

Wages of Sin. large type ed. Andrew M. Greeley. LC 92-30449. 606p. 1993. reprint ed. lib. bdg. 21.95 (*1-56054-562-3*) Thorndike Pr.

Wages of Sin. large type ed. Andrew M. Greeley. LC 92-30449. 606p. 1993. reprint ed. lib. bdg. 14.95 (*1-56054-893-2*) Thorndike Pr.

Wages of Sin: A Reappraisal of the "Succession Narrative" Gillian Keys. (JSOTS Ser.: No. 221). 174p. 1996. 40.00 (*1-85075-621-X*, Pub. by Sheffield Acad UK) CUP Services.

Wages of Sin: America's Dilemma of Profit Against Humanity. John H. Huer. LC 91-3548. 320p. 1991. text ed. 59.95 (*0-275-93932-4*, C3932, Praeger Pubs) Greenwood.

***Wages of Sin: Censorship & the Fallen Woman Film, 1928-1942.** Lea Jacobs. LC 96-51655. (Illus.). 1997. pap. 15.95 (*0-520-20790-4*) U CA Pr.

Wages of Slavery: From Chattel Slavery to Wage Labour in Africa, the Carribean, & England. Ed. by Michael Twaddle. LC 93-4011. (Studies in Slavery). 234p. 1993. text ed. 39.50 (*0-7146-4517-6*, Pub. by F Cass Pubs UK) Intl Spec Bk.

Wages of Unskilled Labor in Manufacturing Industries in the United States, 1890-1924. Whitney Coombs. LC 76-76686. (Columbia University. Studies in the Social Sciences: No. 283). reprint ed. 32.50 (*0-404-51283-6*) AMS Pr.

***Wages of War: The Official Strategy Guide.** Michael Rymaszewski. 240p. 1996. pap. 19.99 (*0-7615-0983-6*) Prima Pub.

Wages of War, Eighteen Sixteen to Nineteen Sixty-Five. J. David Singer & Melvin Small. 1974. write for info. (*0-89138-068-X*) ICPSR.

Wages of Whiteness: Race & the Making of the American Working Class. David R. Roediger. LC 91-18855. (Haymarket Ser.). 192p. (C). (gr. 13). 1991. text ed. 55.00 (*0-86091-334-1*, A6413, Pub. by Vrso UK); pap. text ed. 18.00 (*0-86091-550-6*, A6417, Pub. by Vrso UK) Norton.

Wages of Writing. Paul W. Kingston & Jonathan R. Cole. LC 85-25543. 224p. 1986. text ed. 37.50 (*0-231-05786-5*) Col U Pr.

Wages Policy: Wages, Non-Wage Labour Costs & Their Relation to Employment under Conditions of Structural Adjustment. v, 60p. (Orig.). 1992. pap. 6.75 (*92-2-108258-X*) Intl Labour Office.

Wages, Prices, Profits & Productivity. Ed. by Charles A. Myers. LC 59-12574. 1959. 4.00 (*0-936904-07-0*) Am Assembly.

Wages, Productivity, & Industrialization in Puerto Rico. Lloyd G. Reynolds & Luz M. Torruellas. LC 65-12407. (Yale University, Economic Growth Center, Publications). 373p. reprint ed. pap. 106.40 (*0-317-29718-X*, 2022034) Bks Demand.

Wages Question: A Treatise on Wages & the Wage Class. Francis A. Walker. LC 68-25540. (Reprints of Economic Classics Ser.). iv, 428p. 1968. reprint ed. 49.50 (*0-678-00387-4*) Kelley.

Wages, Regime Switching, & Cycles. 2nd enl. rev. ed. P. Ferri. (Illus.). xii, 171p. 1992. 100.95 (*0-387-55059-3*) Spr-Verlag.

Waggamans & Their Allied Families. Thomas C. Edwards. 1983. 45.00 (*0-686-89726-9*) T C Edwards NJ.

***Waggin' Training.** Michi Fujimoto. (Puzzle Place Sticker Activity Bks.). (Illus.). 24p. (J). (ps-1). 1997. pap. 3.50 (*0-8431-7933-3*) Price Stern Sloan.

***Wagging Their Tongues: A Canine Compendium.** Ariel Books Staff. LC 96-85943. 374p. (Orig.). 1997. pap. 5.95 (*0-8362-2591-0*, Arie Bks) Andrews & McMeel.

Waggoner: A Village & Its Community. Horace Q. Waggoner, Jr. LC 86-50076. (Illus.). 442p. 1986. 27.00 (*0-9616552-0-8*) Waggoner Cent.

***Waggoner, Charles C. Waggoner, Auglaize Co., Ohio, 1805-1879, & Allied Families of Layton, Bitler, Heidrick, Brakney, Hague, Bayliff.** Charles Moffat & Norma Moffat. (Illus.). 86p. 1996. reprint ed. pap. 18.00 (*0-8328-5312-7*); reprint ed. lib. bdg. 28.00 (*0-8328-5311-9*) Higginson Bk Co.

Waggoner Cruising Guide: Essential Boating to Pacific Northwest. 4th rev. ed. Ed. by Robert Hall. (Illus.). 224p. 1997. pap. 12.95 (*0-935727-12-4*) Weatherly Pr.

Waggoner Vignettes: A Capsule History of a Village & Its Community. Horace Q. Waggoner, Jr. LC 86-90187. (Illus.). 52p. 1986. 10.00 (*0-9616552-1-6*) Waggoner Cent.

***Waggoner's Way.** large type ed. Harry Bowling. (Magna Large Print Ser.). 656p. 1996. 25.99 (*0-7505-0984-8*, Pub. by Magna Print Bks UK) Ulverscroft.

Waging Business Warfare. David J. Rogers. 448p. 1988. mass mkt. 4.95 (*0-8217-2510-6*, Zebra Kensgtn) Kensgtn Pub Corp.

Waging Nuclear Peace: The Technology & Politics of Nuclear Weapons. Robert Ehrlich. LC 84-120. 397p. 1985. text ed. 59.50 (*0-87395-919-1*); pap. text ed. 19.95 (*0-87395-920-5*) State U NY Pr.

Waging Peace. John Lamoreau & Ralph Beebe. 1980. pap. 3.95 (*0-913342-31-9*) Barclay Pr.

Waging Peace. Intro. by Marc Miller. (Southern Exposure Ser.). (Illus.). 120p. (Orig.). 1982. pap. 3.00 (*0-943810-14-0*) Inst Southern Studies.

***Waging Peace: Eisenhower's Strategy for National Security.** Robert Bowie & Richard H. Immerman. 352p. 1997. 49.95 (*0-19-506264-7*) OUP.

Waging Peace: Selections from the Baha'i Writings on Universal Peace. Baha'u'llah & Abdu'l-Baha. 1985. pap. 7.95 (*0-933770-34-0*) Kalimat.

Waging Peace II: Vision & Hope for the 21st Century. Ed. by David Krieger & Frank Kelly. LC 92-50434. 226p. 1992. pap. 12.95 (*1-879360-19-5*) Noble Pr.

Waging Peace in Our Schools. Linda Lantieri & Janet Patti. 288p. 1996. 22.00 (*0-8070-3116-X*) Beacon Pr.

Waging Spiritual Warfare. Mark Buntain. 32p. (Orig.). 1993. pap. 1.95 (*0-88243-455-1*, 02-0455) Gospel Pub.

Waging the Battle Against Drunk Driving: Issues, Countermeasures, & Effectiveness. Gerald D. Robin. LC 91-8235. (Contributions in Criminology & Penology Ser.: No. 32). 160p. 1991. text ed. 49.95 (*0-313-27856-3*, RWB, Greenwood Pr); pap. text ed. 16.95 (*0-275-94040-3*, B4040, Praeger Pubs) Greenwood.

***Waging the War on Drugs in Bolivia.** 48p. (Orig.). (C). 1997. pap. text ed. write for info. (*0-929513-36-3*) WOLA.

Waging War: A Philosophical Introduction. Ian Clark. (Illus.). 160p. 1988. 49.95 (*0-19-827325-8*) OUP.

Waging War: A Philosophical Introduction. Ian Clark. 160p. 1991. reprint ed. pap. 19.95 (*0-19-827759-8*) OUP.

Wagner. (Dent Master Musicians Ser.). (Illus.). (C). pap. write for info. (*0-19-816487-4*) OUP.

Wagner. Howard Gray. (Illustrated Lives of the Great Composers Ser.). (Illus.). 144p. 1996. 14.95 (*0-7119-1687-X*, OP 44817) Omnibus NY.

Wagner. Michael Tanner. LC 96-22020. 256p. 1996. 19.95 (*0-691-01162-1*) Princeton U Pr.

Wagner. rev. ed. Barry Millington. (Illus.). 352p. 1992. pap. text ed. 15.95 (*0-691-02722-6*) Princeton U Pr.

Wagner. Robert L. Jacobs. (Music Book Index Ser.). 242p. 1992. reprint ed. lib. bdg. 79.00 (*0-7812-9482-7*) Rprt Serv.

Wagner: A Bibliography, 2 vols., Vol. 1 (1813-64) Curt V. Westernhagen. LC 77-88680. (Illus.). 1979. 69.95 (*0-521-21930-2*) Cambridge U Pr.

Wagner: A Bibliography, 2 vols., Vol. 2 (1864-83) Curt V. Westernhagen. LC 77-88680. (Illus.). 1979. 69.95 (*0-521-21932-9*) Cambridge U Pr.

Wagner: A Biography, 1813 to 1833. Curt V. Westernhagen. Tr. by Mary Whittall. LC 78-2397. (Illus.). 720p. 1981. pap. 33.95 (*0-521-28254-3*) Cambridge U Pr.

Wagner: Music Book Index. Walter J. Turner. 143p. 1993. reprint ed. lib. bdg. 69.00 (*0-7812-9629-3*) Rprt Serv.

Wagner: Prelude & Transfiguration from Wagner's Tristan & Isolde. Ed. by Robert Bailey. (Critical Scores Ser.). (C). 1985. pap. text ed. 9.95 (*0-393-95405-6*) Norton.

Wagner: Race & Revolution. Paul L. Rose. 288p. (C). 1992. text ed. 30.00 (*0-300-05182-4*) Yale U Pr.

Wagner: Race & Revolution. Paul L. Rose. 1996. pap. text ed. 16.00 (*0-300-06745-3*) Yale U Pr.

***Wagner: Wagner.** Rowland Cotterill. (Illus.). 144p. (Orig.). pap. 14.95 (*0-7119-5501-8*, OP 47817) Omnibus NY.

Wagner & Aeschylus: The "Ring" & The "Oresteia" Michael Ewans. LC 82-12762. 272p. 1983. text ed. 54.95 (*0-521-25073-0*) Cambridge U Pr.

Wagner & Beethoven: Richard Wagner's Reception of Beethoven. Klaus Kropfinger. Tr. by Peter Palmer. (Illus.). 260p. (C). 1991. text ed. 80.00 (*0-521-34201-5*) Cambridge U Pr.

Wagner & His Works, 2 Vols. Henry T. Finck. LC 68-25287. (Studies in Music: No. 42). 1969. reprint ed. lib. bdg. 150.00 (*0-8383-0189-4*) M S G Haskell Hse.

Wagner & His Works: The Story of His Life, 2 Vols. Henry T. Finck. LC 68-30999. (Illus.). 1969. reprint ed. Set. text ed. 75.00 (*0-8371-0419-X*, FIWA) Greenwood.

Wagner & His Works: The Story of His Life, 2 Vols, 1. Henry T. Finck. LC 68-30999. (Illus.). 1969. reprint ed. text ed. 45.00 (*0-8371-3533-8*, FIWB) Greenwood.

Wagner & His Works: The Story of His Life, 2 Vols, Vol. 2. Henry T. Finck. LC 68-30999. (Illus.). 1969. reprint ed. text ed. 45.00 (*0-8371-0812-8*, FIWC) Greenwood.

Wagner & His Works: The Story of His Life, with Critical Comments, 2 vols. Henry T. Finck. 1990. reprint ed. lib. bdg. 140.00 (*0-7812-9097-X*) Rprt Serv.

Wagner & Russia. Rosamund Bartlett. (Studies in Russian Literature). (Illus.). 432p. (C). 1995. text ed. 59.95 (*0-521-44071-8*) Cambridge U Pr.

Wagner & the New Consciousness: Language & Love in the Ring. Sandra Corse. LC 88-46186. (Illus.). 216p. 1990. 36.50 (*0-8386-3378-1*) Fairleigh Dickinson.

***Wagner Androgyne.** Jean-Jacques Nattiez. (Princeton Studies in Opera). 1998. pap. text ed. 18.95 (*0-691-04832-0*) Princeton U Pr.

Wagner Androgyne: A Study in Interpretation. Jean-Jacques Nattiez. Tr. by Stewart Spencer. LC 92-23250. (Illus.). 401p. (C). 1993. text ed. 49.50 (*0-691-09141-2*) Princeton U Pr.

Wagner As Man & Artist. Ernest Newman. 1963. 14.50 (*0-8446-2653-8*) Peter Smith.

Wagner Compendium: A Guide to Wagner's Life & Music. Ed. by Barry Millington. (Illus.). 432p. 1992. 35.00 (*0-02-871359-1*) Schirmer Bks.

Wagner-Enzyclopadie. Carl F. Glasenapp. xxx, 925p. 1977. reprint ed. write for info. (*3-487-06260-7*) G Olms Pubs.

Wagner et la France. Revue Musicale Staff. LC 77-4006. (Music Reprint Ser.: 1977). (Illus.). 1977. reprint ed. lib. bdg. 32.50 (*0-306-70889-2*) Da Capo.

Wagner Handbook. Ed. by Ulrich Muller et al. (Illus.). 711p. 1992. text ed. 45.00 (*0-674-94530-1*) HUP.

Wagner in Performance. Ed. by Barry Millington & Stewart Spencer. (Illus.). 224p. (C). 1992. text ed. 32.50 (*0-300-05718-0*) Yale U Pr.

***Wagner in Rehearsal, 1875-1876: The Diaries of Richard Fricke.** Richard Fricke et al. LC 96-46054. (Franz Liszt Studies). 1996. write for info. (*0-945193-86-6*) Pendragon NY.

Wagner in Thought & Practice. Geoffrey Skelton. 220p. 1992. pap. 14.95 (*0-931340-58-6*, Amadeus Pr) Timber.

Wagner Nights: An American History. Joseph Horowitz. LC 93-42410. (California Studies in 19th Century Music: No. 9). (C). 1994. 30.00 (*0-520-08394-6*) U CA Pr.

***Wagner on Conducting.** Richard Wagner. pap. 4.95 (*0-486-25932-3*) Dover.

Wagner on Music & Drama. Ed. by Albert Goldman & Evert Sprinchorn. Tr. by H. Ashton Ellis. (Quality Paperbacks Ser.). 450p. 1988. reprint ed. pap. 14.95 (*0-306-80319-4*) Da Capo.

Wagner Operas. Ernest Newman. 729p. 1991. pap. text ed. 22.95 (*0-691-02716-1*) Princeton U Pr.

Wagner Report Vol. 1: Report of the Independent Review of Residential Care, 1988: A Positive Choice (Report & Recommendations) NISW Staff. (C). 1988. 59.00 (*0-685-28583-9*, Pub. by Natl Inst Soc Work) St Mut.

Wagner Report Vol. 11: Report of the Independent Review of Residential Care: The Research Reviewed (Background Information) Ed. by NISW Staff. (C). 1988. 75.00 (*0-685-28582-0*, Pub. by Natl Inst Soc Work) St Mut.

Wagner Report, Vol. 1: A Positive Choice. Contrib. by Gillian Wagner. (C). 1988. 85.00 (*0-7855-0068-5*, Pub. by Natl Inst Soc Work) St Mut.

Wagner Report, Vol. 2: The Research Reviewed. Contrib. by Gillian Wagner. (C). 1988. 110.00 (*0-7855-0069-3*, Pub. by Natl Inst Soc Work) St Mut.

***Wagner Ware & Other Companies.** 2nd rev. ed. (Illus.). 125p. 1995. pap. 10.95 (*0-89538-061-7*) L-W Inc.

Wagner Writes from Paris: Stories, Essays, & Articles by the Young Composer. Ed. by Robert L. Jacobs & Geoffrey Skelton. 1973. 19.95 (*0-8464-0960-7*) Beekman Pubs.

Wagnerian Romances. Gertrude Brownell. 414p. 1990. reprint ed. lib. bdg. 89.00 (*0-7812-9096-1*) Rprt Serv.

Wagnerism in European Culture & Politics. Ed. by David C. Large & William Weber. LC 83-45936. 304p. 1984. pap. 18.95 (*0-8014-9283-1*) Cornell U Pr.

Wagner's Das Rheingold. Warren Darcy. (Studies in Musical Genesis & Structure). (Illus.). 288p. 1996. pap. 24.95 (*0-19-816603-6*) OUP.

Wagner's Life & Works, 2 vols. Gustav Kobbe. 1972. 100.00 (*0-8490-1270-8*) Gordon Pr.

Wagner's Musical Prose: Texts & Contexts. Thomas S. Grey. (New Perspectives in Music History & Criticism Ser.: No. 2). 432p. (C). 1995. text ed. 69.95 (*0-521-41738-4*) Cambridge U Pr.

Wagner's Opera. Lawrence Gilman. 1988. reprint ed. lib. bdg. 59.00 (*0-7812-0547-6*) Rprt Serv.

Wagner's Operas. Lawrence Gilman. LC 71-181163. 268p. 1937. reprint ed. 39.00 (*0-403-01565-0*) Scholarly.

Wagner's Ring: Listener's Companion & Concordance. J. K. Holman. (Illus.). 400p. 1996. 34.95 (*1-57467-014-X*, Amadeus Pr) Timber.

Wagner's Ring: Turning the Sky Around. M. Owen Lee. LC 94-29968. 120p. 1994. reprint ed. pap. 10.00 (*0-87910-186-5*) Limelight Edns.

Wagner's 'Ring' & Its Symbols: The Music & the Myth. 3rd ed. Robert Donington. (Illus.). 342p. 1974. pap. 19.95 (*0-571-04818-8*) Faber & Faber.

Wagner's Ring of the Nibelung: A Companion. Stewart Spencer & Barry Millington. LC 93-61096. (Illus.). 384p. 1993. 39.95 (*0-500-01567-8*) Thames Hudson.

Wagon. Tony Johnston. LC 95-53103. 1996. lib. bdg. write for info. (*0-688-13537-4*) Scovill Paterson.

Wagon. Tony Johnston. LC 95-53103. (J). 1996. 16.00 (*0-688-13457-2*, Tambourine Bks) Morrow.

Wagon Box Fight. rev. ed. Jerry Keenan. (Illus.). 45p. 1990. pap. 4.95 (*1-878856-00-6*) Ft P Kearney BT Assn.

Wagon Box Fight. 3rd ed. Jerry Keenan. 48p. 1992. pap. 5.95 (*0-89016-101-1*) Lightning Tree.

Wagon-Lit. Joseph Kessel. 125p. (FRE.). 1988. pap. 10.95 (*0-7859-2557-0*, 2070380351) Fr & Eur.

Wagon-Lit. Joseph Kessel. (Folio Ser.: No. 1952). 125p. (FRE.). 1936. pap. 6.95 (*2-07-038035-1*) Schoenhof.

***Wagon Road.** Jack Turney. 233p. 1996. 14.95 (*0-87012-555-9*) McClain.

Wagon Ruts West. Ronald B. Parsley. 1995. pap. 8.95 (*0-533-11536-1*) Vantage.

***Wagon Tongues & the North Star: Tales of the Cattle Trails.** Eva J. Boyd. 1997. pap. 14.95 (*1-55622-535-0*, Rep of TX Pr) Wordware Pub.

***Wagon Train.** Sydelle Kramer. LC 97-9611. (All Aboard Reading Ser.). (Illus.). (J). 1997. write for info. (*0-448-41335-3*, G&D) Putnam Pub Group.

***Wagon Train.** Sydelle A. Kramer. LC 97-9611. (J). Date not set. pap. 3.95 (*0-448-41334-5*) Putnam Pub Group.

Wagon Train. large type ed. Mark Carrel. (Linford Western Library). 368p. 1995. pap. 15.99 (*0-7089-7700-6*, Linford) Ulverscroft.

Wagon Train: A Family Goes West in 1865. Courtni C. Wright. LC 94-18975. (Illus.). 32p. (J). (ps-4). 1995. lib. bdg. 15.95 (*0-8234-1152-4*) Holiday.

Wagon Train Journal, 1839: Travels in the Great Western Prairies, the Anahuac & Rocky Mountains, & in the Oregon Territory. Thomas J. Farnham. 108p. (Orig.). 1979. reprint ed. pap. text ed. 3.95 (*0-914019-02-3*) NW Interpretive.

Wagon Train Nineteen Fifty-Eight. Joy Cowgill. (Illus.). 78p. 1980. pap. 5.00 (*0-916552-21-7*) Acoma Bks.

Wagon Train 911. Jamie Gilson. LC 95-45372. 160p. (J). (gr. 3 up). 1996. 15.00 (*0-688-14550-7*) Lothrop.

Wagon Trains of '44: A Comparative View of the Individual Caravans in the Emigration of 1844 to Oregon. Thomas A. Rumer. LC 89-62716. (American Trails Ser.: No. XVII). (Illus.). 274p. 1991. 35.50 (*0-87062-197-1*) A H Clark.

Wagon Wars: A Sequel to "The Last Free Range" James A. Ritchie. LC 96-43383. 190p. 1997. 20.95 (*0-8027-4157-6*) Walker & Co.

Wagon Wheel Kitchens: Food on the Oregon Trail. Jacqueline Williams. LC 93-3233. (Illus.). 248p. 1993. 29.95 (*0-7006-0609-2*); pap. 14.95 (*0-7006-0610-6*) U Pr of KS.

Wagon Wheels. Barbara Brenner. (Illus.). (J). (ps-3). 1995. pap. 6.95 incl. audio (*0-694-70001-0*) HarperAudio.

Wagon Wheels. Barbara A. Brenner. LC 92-18780. (I Can Read Bk.). (Illus.). 64p. (J). (gr. k-3). 1978. 14.95 (*0-06-020668-3*); lib. bdg. 14.89 (*0-06-020669-1*) HarpC Child Bks.

Wagon Wheels. Barbara A. Brenner. LC 92-18780. (Trophy I Can Read Bk.). (Illus.). 64p. (J). (gr. k-3). 1984. pap. 4.95 (*0-06-444052-4*, Trophy) HarpC Child Bks.

Wagon Wheels. Duncan Searl. Ed. by J. Friedland & R. Kessler. (Novel-Ties Ser.). 1995. student ed., pap. text ed. 15.95 (*1-56982-255-7*) Lrn Links.

Wagon Wheels: A Contemporary Journey on the Oregon Trail. Candy Moulton & Ben Kern. (Illus.). 256p. (Orig.). 1996. 24.95 (*0-931271-37-1*); pap. 14.95 (*0-931271-36-3*) Hi Plains Pr.

Wagon Wheels & Wild Roses: Heirloom Recipes & Oregon Trail Stories from the McCaw Family, 1847-1995. Naomi S. Kulp. 256p. 1996. 22.95 (*0-9648782-0-8*) Wld Rose Pr.

Wagon Wheels A'Rollin. Daisy B. Ackley. (Illus.). 331p. (Orig.). 1994. pap. 26.00 (*1-55613-899-7*) Heritage Bk.

Wagon Wheels Literature Mini-Unit. Janet Lovelady. (Illus.). 32p. (J). (gr. 3-5). 1990. student ed. 4.95 (*1-56096-010-8*) Mari.

Wagonload of Fish. Judit Z. Bodnar. LC 93-19047. (Illus.). 32p. (J). (gr. k-2). 1996. 15.00 (*0-688-12172-1*); lib. bdg. 14.93 (*0-688-12173-X*) Lothrop.

***Wagons & Rails, Colorado Heritage.** Jane V. Barker. Date not set. pap. text ed. 6.95 (*1-878611-09-7*) Silver Rim Pr.

***Wagons & Wagon-Graves of the Early Iron Age in Central Europe.** C. F. Pare. (Illus.). 1992. 135.00 (*0-947816-35-6*, Pub. by Oxford Univ Comm Arch UK) David Brown.

Wagons West! Roy Gerrard. (J). (gr. k-3). 1996. 15.00 (*0-374-38249-2*) FS&G.

Wagons West. VeraLee Wiggins. (Young Reader's Christian Library). (Illus.). 224p. (J). 1995. pap. text ed. 1.39 (*1-55748-675-1*) Barbour & Co.

Wagons West: Off to Oregon. Catherine E. Chambers. LC 83-18276. (Adventures in Frontier America Ser.). (Illus.). 32p. (J). (gr. 5-9). 1984. pap. text ed. 3.50 (*0-8167-0044-3*) Troll Communs.

Wagons West: Trail Tales - 1848. Robert Shellenberger. LC 91-72903. (Illus.). 96p. (J). 1996. reprint ed. pap. 10.95 (*0-9623048-3-2*) Heritage West.

Wagons West, No. 22: New Mexico. Dana F. Ross. 1988. pap. 4.50 (*0-318-37676-8*) Bantam.

Wagontongue. Elmer Kelton. 160p. 1996. mass mkt. 5.50 (*0-553-27467-8*) Bantam.

Wagontongue. Elmer Kelton. (Texas Tradition Ser.: No. 23). 214p. 1996. reprint ed. 21.95 (*0-87565-165-8*); reprint ed. pap. 14.95 (*0-87565-166-6*) Tex Christian.

Wagram 1809. Ian Castle. (Campaign Ser.). (Illus.). 96p. 1994. pap. 14.95 (*1-85532-366-4*, 9532, Pub. by Osprey UK) Stackpole.

Wah Ming Chang: Artist & Master of Special Effects. Gail B. Riley. LC 95-15390. (Multicultural Junior Biographies Ser.). (Illus.). 112p. (J). (gr. 4-10). 1995. lib. bdg. 18.95 (*0-89490-639-9*) Enslow Pubs.

Wah-To-Yah & the Taos Trail. Lewis H. Garrard. (Western Frontier Library: No. 5). 1972. reprint ed. pap. 12.95 (*0-8061-1016-3*) U of Okla Pr.

Wah Wah Book: Original Crybaby Pedal Book. P. Howorth. 48p. 1994. pap. 9.95 (*0-7935-3234-5*, 00696544) H Leonard.

Wahab & His Animal Friends. Chen Li. (Asian Folk Tales Ser.). (Illus.). 24p. (J). 1995. 9.95 (*983-9808-72-9*, Pub. by Delta Edits MY) Weatherhill.

Waheenee: An Indian Girl's Story. Gilbert L. Wilson. LC 81-2970. (Illus.). xv, 189p. 1981. reprint ed. pap. 8.95 (*0-8032-9703-3*, Bison Books) U of Nebr Pr.

***Wahgancan Memories.** Ruth V. Leih. Ed. & Intro. by Janet Leih. 32p. (Orig.). 1997. pap. text ed. 5.00 (*1-877649-30-9*) Tesseract SD.

Wahhabi Movement in India. Qeyamuddin Ahmad. (C). 1994. reprint ed. 32.50 (*81-7304-042-7*, Pub. by Manohar Bk Srv II) S Asia.

Wahiawa Town. Al Plant. (Hawaii Mini History Ser.). (Illus.). 36p. (Orig.). 1995. pap. 3.95 (*0-913611-04-2*) W E C Plant.

Wahili: The Waterboy. Ava Lawrence. (Illus.). 32p. (J). (gr. 2-5). 1996. 14.95 (*0-9651048-0-X*) Papillon TX.

Wah'Kon-Tah: The Osage & the White Man's Road. John J. Mathews. (Civilization of the American Indian Ser.: Vol. 3). (Illus.). 359p. 1981. pap. 16.95 (*0-8061-1699-4*) U of Okla Pr.

Wahl der Parlamente und anderer Staatsorgane: Ein Handbuch. Incl. Vol. 1, Pt. 1. Europa. Ed. by Dolf Sternberger et al. xl, 831p. 1969. 112.00 (*3-11-001156-5*); Vol. 1, Pt. 2. Europa. Ed. by Dolf Sternberger et al. xvi, 656p. 1969. 84.00 (*3-11-001157-3*); (C). 1969. write for info. (*0-318-51652-7*) De Gruyter.

W

An Asterisk (*) at the beginning of an entry indicates that the title is appearing in BIP for the first time.

***Wahl der Zusammenschlubform von Unternehmen Vol. XXIII: Eine Transaktionsokonomische Entscheidungskonzeption.** Bernhard Leitermann. (Schriften zue Unternehmensplanung Ser.: Bd. 41). (Illus.). 317p. (GER.). 1996. pap. 57.95 (3-631-30834-5) P Lang Pubng.

Wahlverwandtschaften. unabridged ed. Goethe. (World Classic Literature Ser.). (GER.). pap. 5.95 (3-89507-010-6, Pub. by Bookking Intl FR) Distribks Inc.

Wahnsinn: Symptom und Befreiung: Funktion und Narrative Vermittlung extremen Irrationalismus im Werk Doris Lessing. Barbara Dahlhaus-Beilner. (Bochum Studies in English: Vol. 17). iv, 261p. (Orig.). (C). 1984. pap. 30.00 (90-6032-259-2, Pub. by B R Gruener NE) Benjamins North Am.

Wahoo: The Patrols of America's Most Famous WWII Submarine. Richard H. Kane. LC 87-6925. 1996. pap. 15.95 (0-89141-572-6) Presidio Pr.

Wahre Tragodie. Helmut Kuhn. 96p. 1970. write for info. (0-318-70950-3) G Olms Pubs.

Wahrheit als Freiheit: Zur Entwicklung der Wahrheitsfrage in der neueren Philosophie. Josef Simon. (C). 1978. 114.60 (3-11-007414-1) De Gruyter.

Wahrheit der Literatur: Studien zur Literaturtheorie des 18. Jahrhunderts. Karl-Heinz Finken. LC 93-18359. (Studies in Modern German Literature: Vol. 58). 209p. (C). 1994. text ed. 39.95 (0-8204-2187-1) P Lang Pubng.

Wahrheit, Perspektive, Interpretation: Nietzsche und die Philosophische Hermeneutik. Johann N. Hofmann. (Monographien und Texte zur Nietzsche-Forschung Ser.: Bd. 28). xiv, 456p. (GER.). (C). 1994. lib. bdg. 186.15 (3-11-014223-6, 127-94) De Gruyter.

***Wahrheit, Referenz, und Realismus: Eine Sprachphilosophische und Metaphysische Studie.** Richard Schantz. (Perspektiven der Analytischen Philosophie - Perspectives in Analytical Philosophy Ser.: Vol. 12). ix, 429p. (GER.). (C). 1996. lib. bdg. 170.40 (3-11-015252-5) De Gruyter.

Wahrheit Uber Den Lugner: Eine Philosophische-Logische Analyse der Antinomie des Lugners. Elke Brendel. (Grundlagen der Kommunikation & Kognition (Foundations of Communication & Cognition) Ser.). xiv, 230p. (GER.). (C). 1992. lib. bdg. 83.10 (3-11-013684-8) De Gruyter.

Wahrheit und Ideologie: Truth & Ideology. Hans Barth. LC 74-25738. (European Sociology Ser.). 352p. 1975. reprint ed. 28.95 (0-405-06494-2) Ayer.

Wahrheit und Kunst, Geschichtsschreibung und Plagiat Im Klassischen Altertum. Hermann Peter. xii, 490p. 1965. reprint ed. write for info. (0-318-70813-2) G Olms Pubs.

Wahrheit Zwischen Erschlossenheit und Verantwortung: Die Rezeption und Transformation der Wahrheitskonzeption Martin Heideggers in der Theologie Rudolf Bultmanns. Eberhard M. Pausch. (Theologische Bibliothek Toepelmann Ser.: Bd. 64). 380p. (GER.). (C). 1994. lib. bdg. 136.95 (3-11-014230-9) De Gruyter.

Wahrig Brockhaus Dictionary of the German Language in 6 vols: Brockhaus Wahrig Deutsches Woerterbuch in 6 Baenden. Gerhard Wahrig. (GER.). 1984. 1,095.00 (0-8288-1983-1, M15508) Fr & Eur.

***Wahrnehmung-Perception.** Romen Banerjee. 1996. 29.00 incl. audio compact disk (3-931126-10-2, Pub. by Die Gestalten GW) Consort Bk Sales.

***Wahrnehmungsdynamik und Ausdruckswahrnehmung: Das Moderne Westliche Konzept der Wahrnehmungsdynamik und seine Entsprechungen im Ostasiatischen Kulturkreis.** Mo-Young Lee. (Europaische Hochschulschriften, Reihe 6: Bd. 563). ix, 159p. (GER.). 1996. 42.95 (3-631-30572-9) P Lang Pubng.

Wahrscheinlichkeitstheorie. A. A. Borowkow. (Mathematische Reihe Ser.: No. 53). 264p. (GER.). 1980. 47.00 (0-8176-0788-9) Birkhauser.

Waianae Book on Hawaiian Health. Terry Shintani & Claire Hughes. 119p. 1990. pap. text ed. 9.95 (0-9646023-0-X) Waianae Coast CHC.

Waianae Coast & Kuaokala Ridge Trail. Faith M. Roelofs. (Exploring Oahu: Field Site Guides for Teachers Ser.). 24p. 1992. pap. write for info. (1-882163-04-4) Moanalua Grdns Fnd.

Waianae Coast & Kuaokala Trail Field Site Guide for Teachers. Faith M. Roelofs. (Exploring the Islands Ser.). 1992. teacher ed. write for info. (1-882163-40-0) Moanalua Grdns Fnd.

Waianae Diet Book on Hawaiian Foods & Recipes. Rozalyn K. Teixeira & Helen K. O'Connor. 96p. 1995. pap. text ed. 10.00 (0-9646023-2-6) Waianae Coast CHC.

Waianae Diet CookBook. Sheila Beckham & Helen K. O'Conner. 89p. 1993. pap. text ed. 7.25 (0-9646023-1-8) Waianae Coast CHC.

Waiariki. Patricia Grace. pap. 10.00 (0-685-65340-4, Three Continents) Lynne Rienner.

Waif -A Prince. W. T. Andrews. LC 73-37581. (Black Heritage Library Collection). 1977. reprint ed. 27.95 (0-8369-8957-0) Ayer.

Waifs & Strays of Celtic Tradition: Argyllshire Series. Ed. by Archibald Campbell. reprint ed. Set. 198.00 (0-404-53530-5) AMS Pr.

Waight & Williams: Evidence: Commentary & Materials. 4th ed. 931p. 1995. 135.00 (0-455-21287-2, Pub. by Law Bk Co AT) Gaunt.

Waight & Williams: Evidence: Commentary & Materials. 4th ed. Peter Waight & Robert Williams. 950p. 1995. pap. 95.00 (0-455-21288-0, Pub. by Law Bk Co AT) Gaunt.

Waihe'e Trail & Haleki'i Field: Site Guide for Teachers. Faith M. Roelofs. (Exploring the Islands Ser.). 36p. 1993. pap. write for info. (1-882163-16-8) Moanalua Grdns Fnd.

Waihee Trail & Halekii Field Site Guide for Teachers. Faith M. Roelofs. 1993. teacher ed. write for info. (0-614-00211-7) Moanalua Grdns Fnd.

Waikamoi & Halemauu Trail: Field Site Guide for Teachers. Faith M. Roelofs. (Exploring the Islands Ser.). 1993. teacher ed. write for info. (1-882163-17-6) Moanalua Grdns Fnd.

Waikiki. Bruce Bowman. 245p. (Orig.). 1988. pap. text ed. 3.95 (0-9620175-0-7) Makai Pub.

Waikiki Beachboy. Grady Timmons. (Illus.). 176p. 1989. text ed. 29.95 (0-915013-10-X) Editions Ltd.

***Waikiki Yesteryear.** Glen Grant. (Illus.). 96p. 1996. pap. 12.95 (1-56647-107-9) Mutual Pub HI.

***Waikiki Yesteryear.** Glen Grant. (Illus.). 96p. 1996. 16.95 (1-56647-142-7) Mutual Pub HI.

Waikiki 100 B. C. to 1900 A. D. An Untold Story. George S. Kanahele. (Illus.). 185p. (C). 1996. 30.00 (0-8248-1790-7) Queen Emma Fnd.

Waikiki/OahuDahu: The Gathering Place. Allan Seiden. pap. 4.95 (0-89610-232-7) Island Heritage.

Waikiki/OahuDahu: The Gathering Place. Allan Seiden. 64p. 1986. pap. 9.95 (0-89610-248-3) Island Heritage.

Waikna: Adventures on the Mosquito Shore by Samuel A. Bard. Ephraim G. Squier. LC 65-28697. (Latin American Gateway Ser.). 414p. reprint ed. pap. 118.00 (0-7837-5825-1, 2045497) Bks Demand.

Wailing in Heaven, Whistling in Hell: New & Selected Works, 1969-1995. deluxe ed. Gregory Greyhawk. Ed. by Michael Annis. (Illus.). 200p. (Orig.). 1996. pap. 20.00 (1-882863-50-X, Boxer Bks) Howling Dog.

Wailing of the Christ Child: A Book of Christmas Poems & Coloring Book. limited ed. Mattie S. Johnson. (Christmas Poems & Coloring Book Ser.). 152p. 1994. pap. 12.95 (1-886663-03-3) Chatman Pub.

Wailing Siren Mystery. rev. ed. Franklin W. Dixon. (Hardy Boys Ser.: Vol. 30). (Illus.). 180p. (J). (gr. 5-9). 1951. 5.95 (0-448-08930-0, G&D) Putnam Pub Group.

Wailing Souls: How I Remember My Brethrens Living in Tenement. Ricardo A. Scott. (Reggae Book of Light Ser.). (Illus.). 60p. (Orig.). (YA). pap. write for info. (1-883427-29-0) Crnerstone GA.

Wailing Winds of Juneau Abbey. Peggy Darty. (gr. k). 1990. mass mkt. 3.95 (0-8217-3075-4, Zebra Kensgtn) Kensgtn Pub Corp.

Wailua Basin & Heiau Complex. Faith M. Roelofs. (Exploring Kauai: Field Site Guides for Teachers Ser.). 1993. pap. write for info. (1-882163-10-9) Moanalua Grdns Fnd.

Wailua Basin & Heiau Complex Field Site Guide for Teachers. Faith M. Roelofs. (Exploring the Islands Ser.). 1994. teacher ed. write for info. (1-882163-21-4) Moanalua Grdns Fnd.

Waimana - The Spring of Mana: Tuhoe History & the Colonial Encounter. Jeffrey Sissons. 305p. 1991. pap. 39.95 (0-908569-59-9, Pub. by U Otago Pr NZ) Intl Spec Bk.

Waimea Canyon & Kaluapuhi Trail Field Site Guide for Teachers. Faith M. Roelofs. (Exploring the Islands Ser.). 1994. teacher ed. write for info. (1-882163-23-0) Moanalua Grdns Fnd.

Waimea Canyon & the Kaluapuhi Trail. Faith M. Roelofs. (Exploring Kauai: Field Site Guides for Teachers Ser.). 1993. pap. write for info. (1-882163-12-5) Moanalua Grdns Fnd.

Waimea Summer. John D. Holt. (Illus.). 1976. pap. 2.50 (0-914916-13-0); text ed. 5.00 (0-914916-12-2) Ku Paa.

Wainscott Weasel. Tor Seidler. LC 92-54526. (Michael di Capua Bks.). (Illus.). 200p. (J). (gr. 2 up). 1993. 20.00 (0-06-205032-X); lib. bdg. 19.89 (0-06-205033-8) HarpC Child Bks.

Wainscott Weasel. Tor Seidler. LC 92-54526. (Trophy Bk.). (Illus.). 200p. (J). (gr. k up). 1996. pap. 9.95 (0-06-205911-4, Trophy) HarpC Child Bks.

Wainwright: Those Who Came Before Us: Wainwrights, Mayhews, Stuyvesants & Others. J. Mayhew Wainwright. 203p. 1993. reprint ed. pap. 32.00 (0-8328-3154-9); reprint ed. lib. bdg. 42.00 (0-8328-3153-0) Higginson Bk Co.

Wainwright Secret. Margaret Chittenden. (Intrigue Ser.: No. 183). 1992. pap. 2.89 (0-373-22183-5, 1-22183-7) Harlequin Bks.

Waira's First Journey. Eusebio Topooco. LC 92-44158. (J). (gr. 4 up). Date not set. lib. bdg. write for info. (0-688-12055-5) Lothrop.

WAIS-R Tutorial Workbook & WISC-R Tutorial Workbook. Dennis P. Swiercinsky. LC 88-20113. (PRO-ED Workbook Ser.). 1988. Incl. GuideCards for each subtest. 22.00 (0-89079-205-4, 1929); Incl. GuideCards for each subtest. student ed. 22.00 (0-89079-206-2, 1930) PRO-ED.

Waist Deep in Montana's Lakes. John Holt. LC 92-12997. (Illus.). 164p. 1992. 24.95 (0-87108-822-3); pap. 15.95 (0-87108-824-X) Pruett.

Waist-High Culture. Thomas Griffith. LC 72-10978. 275p. 1973. reprint ed. text ed. 35.00 (0-8371-6645-4, GRWC, Greenwood Pr) Greenwood.

***Waist-High in the World.** Nancy Mairs. 1997. 22.95 (0-7838-8099-5) Thorndike Pr.

Waist-High in the World: A Life among the Nondisabled. Nancy Mairs. 224p. 1997. 20.00 (0-8070-7086-6) Beacon Pr.

Waist Management Playbook. Rita Losee. 160p. 1994. per., pap. text ed. 19.97 (0-8403-9917-0) Kendall-Hunt.

Waist Not. Richard Martin & Harold Koda. (Illus.). 16p. 1994. 7.95 (1-870997-12-3) Metro Mus Art.

Wait a Minute, You Can Have It All. Shirley S. Fader. 288p. 1994. mass mkt. 4.99 (0-380-72214-3) Avon.

Wait & See. Robert Munsch & Michael Martchenko. 24p. (J). 1993. pap. 5.95 (1-55037-334-X, Pub. by Annick CN); lib. bdg. 15.95 (1-55037-335-8, Pub. by Annick CN) Firefly Bks Ltd.

Wait & See. Dawn L. Watkins. (Light Line Ser.). (Illus.). 46p. (Orig.). (J). (ps-1). 1991. pap. 5.49 (0-89084-576-X) Bob Jones Univ Pr.

Wait & Win. Horatio Alger, Jr. (Works of Horatio Alger Jr.). 1989. reprint ed. lib. bdg. 79.00 (0-7812-3619-3) Rprt Serv.

Wait & Win: The Story of Jack Drumond's Pluck. Horatio Alger, Jr. (Illus.). 279p. 1979. reprint ed. 30.00 (0-686-35756-6) G K Westgard.

Wait & Wonder. Francine M. O'Connor. (Cycle C Ser.). (Illus.). 16p. (J). (gr. 1-3). 1991. pap. 1.95 (0-89243-419-8) Liguori Pubns.

Wait & Wonder, Cycle C. Francine M. O'Connor. (Cycle C Ser.). (Illus.). 16p. (J). (gr. 1-3). 1991. 9.95 (0-89243-418-X) Liguori Pubns.

Wait & Wonder, Cycle A. Francine M. O'Connor. (Illus.). 16p. 1992. 1.95 (0-89243-447-3) Liguori Pubns.

Wait & Wonder, Cycle A. Francine M. O'Connor. (Illus.). 1992. teacher ed. 9.95 (0-89243-448-1) Liguori Pubns.

Wait & Wonder, Cycle B. Francine M. O'Connor. 16p. 1993. 1.95 (0-89243-663-8) Liguori Pubns.

Wait & Wonder, Cycle B. Francine M. O'Connor. 1993. teacher ed. 9.95 (0-89243-664-6) Liguori Pubns.

***Wait for Me.** Stella Cameron. 416p. (Orig.). 1997. mass mkt. 6.50 (0-446-60430-5) Warner Bks.

Wait for Me! Molly Cross. LC 87-12926. (Sesame Street Start-to-Read Bks.). (Illus.). 40p. (J). (ps-3). 1987. 4.95 (0-394-89135-X) Random Bks Yng Read.

Wait for Me. William J. Fling. LC 94-61161. 249p. 1996. 10.95 (1-55523-726-6) Winston-Derek.

***Wait for Me.** Susan Shreve. Date not set. lib. bdg. write for info. (0-688-11164-5, Tambourine Bks) Morrow.

Wait for Me. Susan Shreve. LC 91-30233. (Illus.). 112p. (J). (gr. 3 up). 1992. 13.00 (0-688-11120-3, Tambourine Bks) Morrow.

Wait for Me. Susan Shreve. Ed. by Amy Cohn. LC 91-30233. (Illus.). 96p. (J). (gr. 4 up). 1994. reprint ed. pap. 4.95 (0-688-13622-2) Morrow.

Wait for Me: A True Life Story. Norma K. Avendano. 394p. 1994. pap. text ed. 18.99 (1-57336-900-4) Interactn Pubs.

Wait for Me: The Americanization of Tamara. Tami McIntyre. 1995. 21.50 (0-533-11329-6) Vantage.

Wait for Me & Other Stories. Seth W. Gilkerson. LC 82-82216. 144p. 1982. pap. write for info. (0-88100-014-0) Natl Writ Pr.

Wait for Me at the Bottom of the Pool: The Writings of Jack Smith. Jack Smith. Ed. by J. Hoberman & E. Leffingwell. (High Risk Ser.). (Illus.). 250p. (Orig.). 1996. pap. 15.99 (1-85242-428-1) Serpents Tail.

Wait for Me, Little Girl! Douglas Radcliff-Umstead. 165p. 1989. 25.00 (0-9624254-0-0) DeSoto Pr Inc.

Wait for Me, Watch for Me, Eula Bee. Patricia Beatty. LC 78-12782. 224p. (J). (gr. 5 up). 1990. reprint ed. pap. 3.95 (0-688-10077-5) Morrow.

Wait for the Dark. Ann Crowleigh. 256p. 1993. mass mkt. 3.99 (0-8217-4298-1, Zebra Kensgtn) Kensgtn Pub Corp.

Wait for the Judge. large type ed. Marshall Grover. (Linford Western Library). 288p. 1995. pap. 15.99 (0-7089-7758-8, Linford) Ulverscroft.

Wait for the Lord: Meditations on the Christian Life. Theodore Plantinga. 137p. (Orig.). 1981. pap. 5.75 (0-932914-12-8) Dordt Coll Pr.

Wait for the Muncie Boys: Indiana's Early Circuses. Fred Graham. (Illus.). 125p. 1995. 18.95 (1-878208-71-3) Guild Pr IN.

Wait for the Sunrise. Cassandra Austin. (Historical Ser.). 1993. mass mkt. 3.99 (0-373-28790-9, 1-28790-3) Harlequin Bks.

Wait for the Wake. large type ed. Margaret A. Carr. (Linford Mystery Library). 256p. 1989. pap. 15.99 (0-7089-6736-1, Linford) Ulverscroft.

***Wait for True Love.** Faithe H. Musser. LC 96-90244. (Orig.). 1996. pap. 8.95 (0-533-11974-X) Vantage.

Wait for What Will Come. Barbara Michaels. 1990. mass mkt. 6.99 (0-425-12005-8, Berkley Trade) Berkley Pub.

Wait-Out in Waco. Richard Smith. LC 93-5154. (Day of Disaster Ser.). (J). 1993. lib. bdg. 12.98 (1-56239-260-3) Abdo & Dghtrs.

Wait Quietly: Devotions for a Busy Parent. Dean Merrill. LC 94-11854. 224p. 1994. pap. 9.99 (0-8423-7917-7) Tyndale.

Wait, Skates! Mildred Johnson. LC 82-22228. (Rookie Readers Ser.). (Illus.). 32p. (J). (ps-2). 1983. pap. 3.50 (0-516-42039-9); lib. bdg. 15.00 (0-516-02039-0) Childrens.

***Wait 'Til Harvest.** 2nd rev. ed. Mary E. Croney. LC 89-63576. (Illus.). 144p. (Orig.). 1996. pap. 10.95 (0-9624209-5-6) Landmark ID.

Wait 'til Next Year. Jennison. 1976. 21.95 (0-8488-1524-6) Amereon Ltd.

Wait Till Helen Comes: A Ghost Story. Mary D. Hahn. LC 86-2648. 192p. (J). (gr. 4-7). 1986. 14.95 (0-89919-453-2, Clarion Bks) HM.

Wait till Helen Comes: Ghost Story. Mary D. Hahn. (J). (gr. 3-7). 1987. pap. 4.50 (0-380-70442-0, Camelot) Avon.

***Wait Till Next Year: Summer Afternoons with My Father & Baseball.** Doris K. Goodwin. 1997. 25.00 (0-684-82489-2, S&S) S&S Trade.

Wait till the Moon Is Full. Margaret Wise Brown. LC 48-9278. (Illus.). 32p. (J). (ps-1). 1948. lib. bdg. 14.89 (0-06-020801-5) HarpC Child Bks.

Wait till the Moon Is Full. Margaret Wise Brown. LC 48-9278. (Illus.). 32p. (J). (ps-1). 1948. 15.00 (0-06-020800-7) HarpC Child Bks.

Wait till the Moon Is Full. Margaret Wise Brown. LC 48-9278. (Trophy Picture Bk.). (Illus.). 32p. (J). (ps-3). 1989. pap. 4.95 (0-06-443222-X, Trophy) HarpC Child Bks.

***Wait Till Your Daddy Comes Home.** Patricia Lakin. (J). Date not set. write for info. (0-688-13965-5, Tambourine Bks); lib. bdg. write for info. (0-688-13966-3) Morrow.

Wait until Dark. Frederick Knott. 1967. pap. 5.25 (0-8222-1216-1) Dramatists Play.

Wait until Dark. large type ed. Katrina Wright. (Linford Romance Library). 1991. pap. 15.99 (0-7089-7046-X) Ulverscroft.

Wait until Dark: Seven Scary Sleepover Stories. Sherry Shahan. 96p. (J). 1996. pap. 3.99 (0-440-41293-5) Dell.

Wait until Spring, Bandini. John Fante. LC 82-24412. 270p. 1995. reprint ed. 25.00 (0-87685-555-9); reprint ed. pap. 14.00 (0-87685-554-0) Black Sparrow.

***Waitangi Nights.** Alice Gaines. 320p. (Orig.). 1996. mass mkt. 4.99 (0-505-52153-9) Dorchester Pub Co.

Waite Family of Malden, Massachusetts. D. P. Corey. (Illus.). 129p. 1993. reprint ed. pap. 19.50 (0-8328-3427-0); reprint ed. lib. bdg. 29.50 (0-8328-3426-2) Higginson Bk Co.

Waite Group's C: Step-by-Step. Mitchell Waite & Stephen W. Prata. (Illus.). 600p. 1989. 29.95 (0-672-22651-0) Sams.

Waite Group's C++ Programming. 2nd ed. John Berry. 408p. 1992. 29.95 (0-672-22771-1) Sams.

Waite Groups C Programming Using Turbo C Plus Plus. 2nd ed. Robert Lafore. 778p. 1993. 34.95 (0-672-30399-X) Sams.

Waite Group's Discovering Ms-Dos. 2nd ed. Kate Oday. 1991. 19.95 (0-672-22772-X, Bobbs) Macmillan.

Waite Group's New C Primer Plus. 2nd ed. Mitchell Waite. 736p. 1993. 29.95 (0-672-30319-1) Sams.

Waite Group's Turbo C Programming for the PC. rev. ed. Robert Lafore. (Illus.). 720p. 1989. 29.95 (0-672-22660-X) Sams.

Waite Group's UNIX Primer Plus. 2nd ed. Waite Group Staff. (Waite Group Ser.). 478p. 1990. 29.95 (0-672-22729-0) Sams.

Waite Group's UNIX System V Primer. 2nd ed. Mitchell Waite et al. (Illus.). 592p. 1992. 29.95 (0-672-30194-6) Sams.

Waiter & Waitress Training Manual. 4th ed. Sondra Dahmer. (Hospitality, Travel & Tourism Ser.). 162p. 1996. text ed. 32.95 (0-442-02110-0) Van Nos Reinhold.

Waiter! There's a Blackfly in My Chowder! More Funny Stories about Life in Maine & Life in General. Stephen R. Bull. (Illus.). 150p. (Orig.). 1996. pap. 9.95 (0-9644753-1-6, W001) Mt Blue Pub.

Waiter! There's a Flower in My Soup. Penny Sandora. (Illus.). 192p. 1989. 9.95 (0-917732-38-3) Barnes-Bks.

Waiter, There's a Fly in My Soup. Charles Keller. (J). (gr. 4-7). 1991. pap. 2.95 (0-671-73982-4, S&S Bks Young Read) S&S Childrens.

Waiter, There's a Tie in My Soup. Gary Wise & Lance Aldrich. (Real Life Adventures Collection). (Illus.). 104p. 1993. pap. 6.95 (0-8362-1714-4) Andrews & McMeel.

Waiter-Waitress Manual. B. Aiken. 1976. text ed. 10.12 (0-07-000742-X) McGraw.

Waiting. Ambler. 1991. 75.00 (0-89296-457-X) Mysterious Pr.

Waiting. Virginia Ferguson & Peter Durkin. LC 92-34336. (Voyages Ser.). (Illus.). (J). 1993. 3.75 (0-383-03663-1) SRA McGraw.

Waiting: A Diary of Loss & Hope in Pregnancy. Ellen J. Reich. LC 91-8720. 132p. 1991. pap. 11.95 (0-918393-88-4); lib. bdg. 32.95 (1-56024-087-3) Haworth Pr.

Waiting: Finding Hope When God Seems Silent. Ben Patterson. LC 89-15342. 170p. 1990. reprint ed. pap. 9.99 (0-8308-1296-2, 1296, Saltshaker Bk) InterVarsity.

Waiting: Waiters' True Tales of Crazed Customers, Murderous Chefs, & Tableside Disasters. Bruce G. Henderson. 272p. (Orig.). 1995. pap. 9.95 (0-452-27151-7, Plume) NAL-Dutton.

Waiting & After. Pierre Boenig. 128p. (Orig.). 1989. pap. 9.95 (0-945819-01-3) Sulzburger & Graham Pub.

Waiting at the Altar. Amy Frazier. 1996. mass mkt. 3.99 (0-373-24036-8, 1-24036-5) Silhouette.

***Waiting at the Gate: Creativity & Hope in the Nursing Home.** David R. Johnson & Susan L. Sandel. 178p. 1987. pap. 19.95 (0-86656-710-0) Haworth Pr.

Waiting at the Gate: Creativity & Hope in the Nursing Home. Susan L. Sandel & David R. Johnson. Ed. by Phyllis Foster. LC 87-8713. (Activities, Adaptation & Aging Ser.: Vol. 9, No. 3). 185p. 1987. 32.95 (0-86656-631-7) Haworth Pr.

Waiting at the Water's Edge. Lucinda Coxon. 116p. 1996. pap. 13.95 (1-85411-149-3) Dufour.

Waiting Country: A South African Witness. Mike Nicol. 211p. 1996. pap. 13.95 (0-575-05915-X, Pub. by V Gollancz UK) Trafalgar.

Waiting, Dating & Mating: A Guide to Woman-Man Relationships in the Middle Years. Jefferson Selth. (Illus.). 263p. 1990. pap. 15.95 (0-9624431-0-7) Dumont Pr.

Waiting Day. Harriet Diller. LC 93-16785. (Illus.). (J). (gr. 3 up). 1994. 14.00 (0-671-86579-X, Green Tiger S&S) S&S Childrens.

***Waiting for a Frog.** large type ed. Glenn Coats. (Illus.). 20p. (Orig.). (J). (gr. k-2). 1997. pap. 4.95 (1-879835-90-8) Kaeden Corp.

Waiting for a Hero: Poems. Penelope Austin. LC 87-26354. 80p. (Orig.). 1988. pap. 12.95 (0-8262-0673-5) U of Mo Pr.

Waiting for a Miracle: An Account of Love. Eleanor Hinton. 100p. (Orig.). 1996. pap. write for info. (1-57502-239-7, P0910) Morris Pubng.

W

Waiting for a Miracle: Schools Are Not the Problem. James P. Comer. 1997. pap. 23.95 (*0-525-94144-4*) NAL-Dutton.

Waiting for a "Pearl Harbor" Japan Debates Defense. Tetsuya Kataoka. (Publication Ser.: No. 232). 95p. (Orig.). 1980. pap. 7.95 (*0-8179-7322-2*) Hoover Inst Pr.

Waiting for a Rainbow: Coming of Age In Vietnam. Paul M. Frazee. LC 95-75011. 352p. 1995. pap. 18.95 (*1-882824-11-3*) Graphic Pubs.

Waiting for Amos. Monica Kulling. LC 92-19550. (Illus.). 32p. (J). (ps-2). 1993. text ed. 13.95 (*0-02-751245-2*, Bradbury S&S) S&S Childrens.

Waiting for an Army to Die: The Tragedy of Agent Orange. Fred A. Wilcox. LC 89-5920. 223p. 1989. pap. 10.95 (*0-932020-68-2*) Seven Locks Pr.

Waiting for Anya. Michael Morpurgo. (J). 1991. pap. 14.99 (*0-670-83735-0*) Viking Child Bks.

***Waiting for Anya.** Michael Morpurgo. 1997. pap. 4.99 (*0-14-038431-6*) Viking Penguin.

Waiting for Aquarius. John Levesque. 200p. 1995. lib. bdg. 39.00 (*0-8095-4813-5*) Borgo Pr.

Waiting for Aquarius. John Levesque. 200p. 1993. pap. 14.95 (*0-88962-537-9*) Mosaic.

Waiting for Babel Prophesies of Sunflower Dreams: Poems. Hugo Walter. LC 91-29354. 80p. (Orig.). 1992. pap. 7.50 (*1-56474-005-6*) Fithian Pr.

Waiting for Baby. Tom Birdseye. LC 90-29076. (Illus.). 32p. (J). (ps-3). 1991. lib. bdg. 14.95 (*0-8234-0892-2*) Holiday.

Waiting for Baby. Frank Endersby. (J). (gr. 4 up). 1981. 3.99 (*0-85953-230-5*) Childs Play.

Waiting for Baby Joe. Pat L. Collins. Ed. by Kathy Tucker. LC 89-21457. (Albert Whitman Concept Bks.). (Illus.). 48p. (J). (ps-2). 1990. lib. bdg. 12.95 (*0-8075-8625-0*) A Whitman.

***Waiting for Captain Ha Ha.** Arupa Chiarini. 24p. (Orig.). (J). 1997. pap. 4.00 (*0-87440-038-4*) Bakers Plays.

Waiting for China: The Anglo-Chinese College at Malacca, 1818-1843 & Early 19th Century Missons. Brian Harrison. 228p. 1979. 33.50 (*962-209-011-7*, Pub. by Hong Kong Univ Pr HK) Coronet Bks.

Waiting for Christmas. Monica Greenfield. LC 95-35945. (Illus.). 32p. (J). (ps-1). 1996. 15.95 (*0-590-52700-2*, Scholastic Hardcover) Scholastic Inc.

Waiting for Christmas. Marcia Leonard. 1988. pap. 2.95 (*0-8167-1490-8*) Troll Communs.

Waiting for Christmas. Bethany Roberts. 32p. 1996. pap. 5.95 (*0-395-79728-4*) HM.

Waiting for Christmas: Stories & Activities for Advent. Carol Greene. LC 87-70474. (Illus.). 32p. (Orig.). (J). (ps-5). 1987. pap. 5.99 (*0-8066-2264-4*, 10-6915, Augsburg) Augsburg Fortress.

Waiting-for-Christmas Stories. Bethany Roberts. LC 93-11480. (Illus.). (J). (ps-3). 1994. 13.95 (*0-395-67324-0*) HM.

***Waiting-for-Christmas Stories.** Bethany Roberts. 1997. pap. text ed. 8.95 (*0-395-85813-5*, Clarion Bks) HM.

Waiting for CORAF: A Critique of Law & Rights. Allan C. Hutchinson. 269p. 1995. 55.00 (*0-8020-0672-8*); pap. 17.95 (*0-8020-7625-4*) U of Toronto Pr.

Waiting for Deborah. Betty A. Neels. (Romance Ser.). 1996. 3.25 (*0-373-03400-8*, 1-03400-8) Harlequin Bks.

Waiting for Deborah. large type unabridged ed. (Harlequin Ser.). 1994. lib. bdg. 18.95 (*0-263-13908-5*, Pub. by Mills & Boon UK) Thorndike Pr.

Waiting for Dizzy. Gene Lees. 272p. 1991. 25.00 (*0-19-505670-1*) OUP.

***Waiting for Fidel.** Hunt. 1998. pap. 13.00 (*0-395-86886-6*) HM.

Waiting for Filippo: The Life of Renaissance Architect Pilippo Brunelleschi. Michael Bender. LC 94-32044. (Illus.). 10p. (J). 1995. 19.95 (*0-8118-0181-0*) Chronicle Bks.

Waiting for Food: Restaurant Placemat Drawings. Robert Crumb. (Illus.). 96p. 1996. 29.95 (*0-87816-465-0*) Kitchen Sink.

Waiting for Garbo: 44 Ghazals. Robert Peterson. LC 87-71660. 52p. (Orig.). 1987. pap. 7.95 (*0-933525-30-3*) Black Dog Pr.

Waiting for God. Paul Ableman. 1995. 18.95 (*0-563-37086-6*, BBC-Parkwest) Parkwest Pubns.

Waiting for God. Simone Weil. LC 92-52647. 256p. 1992. pap. 12.00 (*0-06-090295-7*, CN295, PL) HarpC.

Waiting for God. Simone Weil. 238p. 1991. reprint ed. lib. bdg. 33.00 (*0-8095-9093-X*) Borgo Pr.

Waiting for Godot. Samuel Beckett. LC 54-6803. 128p. 1987. pap. 8.95 (*0-8021-3034-8*, Grove) Grove-Atltic.

Waiting for Godot: The Theatrical Notebooks of Samuel Beckett. Ed. by James Knowlson. LC 93-27313. 288p. 1994. 75.00 (*0-8021-1548-9*, Grove) Grove-Atltic.

Waiting for Godot & Endgame. Ed. by Steven Connor. LC 92-2762. (New Casebooks Ser.). 224p. 1992. text ed. 45.00 (*0-312-07950-8*) St Martin.

Waiting for Godot & Other Plays. Eric J. Siry. (Wallet-Size Classics Ser.: No. 2). (Illus.). 16p. (Orig.). 1993. 2.95 (*1-884304-01-X*) Eric Siry.

Waiting for Godot, Endgame, & Other Plays Notes. Jeffrey Fisher & James L. Roberts. (Cliffs Notes Ser.). 64p. (Orig.). 1980. pap. text ed. 4.50 (*0-8220-1354-1*) Cliffs.

Waiting for Jerusalem: Surviving the Holocaust in Romania. I. C. Butnaru. LC 92-31755. (Contributions to the Study of World History Ser.: No. 37). 280p. 1993. text ed. 57.95 (*0-313-28798-8*, GM8798, Greenwood Pr) Greenwood.

Waiting for Lefty. Clifford Odets. 1989. pap. 3.25 (*0-8222-1215-3*) Dramatists Play.

Waiting for Lefty: And Other Plays. Clifford Odets. LC 93-2795. 418p. 1993. pap. 14.00 (*0-8021-3220-0*, Grove) Grove-Atltic.

Waiting for Leila. Achmat Dangor. (Writers Ser.). 140p. 1995. reprint ed. pap. text ed. 12.95 (*0-86975-471-8*, Pub. by Ravan Pr ZA) Ohio U Pr.

Waiting for Li Ming. Alan Cumyn. 274p. 1993. pap. 14.95 (*0-86492-146-2*, Pub. by Goose Ln Edits CN) Genl Dist Srvs.

Waiting for Lunch. Greta Rasmussen. LC 81-82797. (Illus.). 63p. (Orig.). (J). (gr. 2-6). 1981. pap. 8.95 (*0-936110-02-3*) Tin Man Pr.

Waiting for Matt. Gillian Kaye. (Rainbow Romances Ser.). 160p. 1995. 14.95 (*0-7090-5492-0*, 922, Hale-Parkwest) Parkwest Pubns.

***Waiting for Matt.** large type ed. Gillian Kaye. (Linford Romance Library). 224p. 1996. pap. 15.99 (*0-7089-7925-4*) Ulverscroft.

***Waiting for Nick.** Nora Roberts. (Special Edition Ser.). 1997. mass mkt. 3.99 (*0-373-24088-0*, 1-24088-6) Silhouette.

Waiting for Noah. Shulamith L. Oppenheim. LC 89-35561. (Charlotte Zolotow Bk.). (Illus.). 32p. (J). (ps-2). 1990. 12.95 (*0-06-024633-2*) HarpC Child Bks.

Waiting for Nothing & Other Writings. Tom Kromer. Ed. by Arthur D. Casciato & James L. West, III. LC 85-8610. (Illus.). 312p. 1986. pap. 12.95 (*0-8203-0798-X*) U of Ga Pr.

Waiting for Poppa at the Smithtown Diner. Peter Serchuck. 96p. 1990. 10.95 (*0-252-06104-7*) U of Ill Pr.

Waiting for Prime Time: The Women of Television News. Marlene Sanders & Marcia Rock. LC 88-325. (Illus.). 240p. 1988. text ed. 21.95 (*0-252-01435-9*) U of Ill Pr.

Waiting for Prime Time: The Women of Television News. Marlene Sanders & Marcia Rock. LC 93-32320. (Illus.). 256p. 1994. 13.95 (*0-252-06387-2*) U of Ill Pr.

Waiting for Rain: A Farmer's Story. Dan Butterworth. 240p. 1992. 17.95 (*0-945575-78-5*) Algonquin Bks.

***Waiting for Rain: Agriculture & Ecological Imbalance in Cape Verde.** Mark Langworthy & Timothy J. Finan. LC 96-44538. 230p. 1997. 45.00 (*1-55587-709-5*) Lynne Rienner.

***Waiting for Rain: Life & Development in Mali, West Africa.** Lewis W. Lucke. LC 97-66245. 144p. 1998. pap. 16.95 (*0-8158-0529-2*) Chris Mass.

Waiting for Snow in Lewiston: Poems. Augustine Towey. Ed. by Patricia Schultz. LC 90-34542. (Lewiston Poetry Ser.: Vol. 11). 64p. 1990. lib. bdg. 24.95 (*0-88946-892-3*) E Mellen.

Waiting for Something to Happen. Gregory X. Gorman. 80p. 1984. pap. 4.00 (*0-942582-05-5*) Erie St Pr.

Waiting for Spring. R. P. Jones. LC 78-52925. 1978. pap. 4.00 (*0-931594-00-6*) Circinatum Pr.

Waiting for Sunrise. Himanshu Joshi. (C). 1993. 8.00 (*81-7018-748-6*, Pub. by BR Pub II) S Asia.

Waiting for the Apocalypse: Doomsday Deferred. rev. ed. Daniel Cohen. LC 83-62189. (Illus.). 262p. 1983. pap. 22.95 (*0-87975-223-8*) Prometheus Bks.

Waiting for the Apples. Ed. by Kathleen R. Leo et al. LC 82-62746. (Illus.). 100p. (Orig.). (J). (gr. k up). 1983. pap. 6.50 (*0-9606678-2-2*) Sylvan Pubns.

Waiting for the Banana Peel: We Did It Live, the Early TV Shows of Dick Van Dyke & Fran Adams. Fran Kearton. Ed. by Diane Parker. LC 92-50859. 250p. 1993. 22.95 (*0-88247-977-6*, 977) R & E Pubs.

Waiting for the Barbarians. J. M. Coetzee. 160p. 1982. pap. 11.95 (*0-14-006110-X*, Penguin Bks) Viking Penguin.

***Waiting for the Barbarians.** Lewis Lapham. Date not set. 25.00 (*1-85984-882-6*, Pub. by Verso UK) Routledge Chapman & Hall.

***Waiting for the Big One.** unabridged ed. Kathleen M. Cargill. Ed. by Maura Goessling. (Illus.). x, 188p. (Orig.). 1996. pap. 16.95 (*0-9655503-0-3*) Beekeepers Pr.

Waiting for the Boat. Dennis Pottor. 192p. 1994. 11.99 (*1-56865-114-7*, GuildAmerica) Dblday Direct.

Waiting for the Bus: The Private Cold War of Renato Crotti. Renato Crotti. Tr. by Raymond Rosenthal from ITA. LC 94-5603. 320p. (Orig.). 1994. pap. 14.95 (*0-942963-46-6*) Distinctive Pub.

***Waiting for the Coming: The Liturgical Meaning of Advent, Christmas & Epiphany.** J. Neil Alexander. 95p. 1993. pap. 7.95 (*1-56929-011-3*) Pastoral Pr.

Waiting for the Dark. Ivan Iklima. 256p. 1996. pap. 12.00 (*0-312-14092-4*, Picador USA) St Martin.

Waiting for the Dawn: Mircea Eliade in Perspective. Ed. by David Carrasco & Jane M. Law. (Illus.). 176p. 1991. pap. 17.50 (*0-87081-239-4*) Univ Pr Colo.

Waiting for the Earth to Turn Over: Identity & the Late-Twentieth Century American West. Philip Garrison. LC 96-18591. 176p. 1996. 39.95 (*0-87480-517-1*); pap. 12.95 (*0-87480-518-X*) U of Utah Pr.

Waiting for the End of the World. Madison Smartt Bell. 324p. 1986. pap. 9.95 (*0-14-009330-3*, Penguin Bks) Viking Penguin.

Waiting for the Evening Star. Rosemary Wells. LC 92-30492. (Illus.). 40p. (J). (gr. k-3). 1993. pap. 15.00 (*0-8037-1398-3*); lib. bdg. 14.89 (*0-8037-1399-1*) Dial Bks Young.

***Waiting for the Evening Star.** Rosemary Wells. 1997. pap. 6.99 (*0-14-056283-4*, Puffin) Puffin Bks.

Waiting for the Fireworks: Selected Stories. Norman Sage. LC 95-4366. 130p. (Orig.). 1995. pap. 14.95 (*1-57003-064-2*) U of SC Pr.

Waiting for the Harvest. Elaine A. Nielsen. LC 94-73475. 123p. (Orig.). (YA). (gr. 9-12). 1994. pap. 12.00 (*0-9625040-7-6*, 297-231-X) Legendary Pub.

***Waiting for the Healer.** Sweeney. Date not set. write for info. (*0-312-18206-6*) St Martin.

Waiting for the Lame Horse. Joan Burstyn. LC 87-73262. 65p. 1987. pap. 9.00 (*0-9610346-8-8*) Belle Mead Pr.

Waiting for the Mahatma. R. K. Narayan. LC 81-3075. 256p. (C). 1981. reprint ed. pap. 12.95 (*0-226-56828-8*) U Ch Pr.

Waiting for the Martian Express: Cosmic Visitors, Earth Warriors, Luminous Dreams. Richard Grossinger. 194p. 1989. 20.00 (*1-55643-052-3*); pap. 9.95 (*1-55643-051-5*) North Atlantic.

Waiting for the Messiah: Stories to Inspire Jews with Hope. Mordechai Staiman. LC 96-51939. 296p. 1997. 30.00 (*1-56821-986-5*) Aronson.

Waiting for the Messiah in Somerville, Mass. Naomi Feigelson Chase. 64p. 1993. pap. 10.00 (*1-882329-00-7*) Garden St Pr.

Waiting for the Millennium: The United Nations & the Future of World Order. J. Martin Rochester. LC 92-45145. (Studies in International Relations). 361p. (C). 1993. text ed. 39.95 (*0-87249-882-4*) U of SC Pr.

Waiting for the Moon. Kristin Hannah. (Orig.). 1995. mass mkt. 5.99 (*0-449-14909-9*, GM) Fawcett.

Waiting for the Moon. large type ed. Hannah. 1996. 20.00 (*0-7838-1498-4*, GK Hall) Thorndike Pr.

Waiting for the Moon. large type ed. Kristin Hannah. (Orig.). 1996. 22.95 (*0-7862-0625-X*, Thorndike Lrg Prnt) Thorndike Pr.

Waiting for the Morning Train: An American Boyhood. Bruce Catton. LC 87-10613. (Great Lakes Bks.). (Illus.). 278p. 1987. reprint ed. 29.95 (*0-8143-1884-3*); reprint ed. pap. 15.95 (*0-8143-1885-1*) Wayne St U Pr.

Waiting for the News. Leo Litwak. LC 89-5577. (Great Lakes Bks.). 332p. 1990. reprint ed. text ed. 39.95 (*0-8143-2274-3*); reprint ed. pap. text ed. 19.95 (*0-8143-2275-1*) Wayne St U Pr.

Waiting for the Other Shoe to Drop. Patrick Oliphant. (Illus.). 160p. 1994. pap. 9.95 (*0-8362-1765-9*) Andrews & McMeel.

Waiting for the Parade. John Murrell. 112p. (Orig.). 1993. pap. 10.95 (*0-88922-183-9*) Genl Dist Srvs.

Waiting for the Party: The Life of Frances Hodgson Burnett. Ann Thwaite. LC 88-46101. (Illus.). 288p. 1991. pap. 13.95 (*0-87923-790-2*) Godine.

***Waiting for the Rain.** Sheila Gordon. 224p. (J). 1996. mass mkt. 4.99 (*0-440-22698-8*) BDD Bks Young Read.

Waiting for the Rain. Sheila Gordon. LC 87-7638. 224p. (YA). (gr. 7 up). 1987. 15.95 (*0-531-05726-7*) Orchard Bks Watts.

Waiting for the Rain. Sekou J. Karanja. 56p. 1991. pap. 7.95 (*0-941749-26-6*) Black Tie Pr.

Waiting for the Rain: A Study Guide. Dorothy Kirk. Ed. by J. Friedland & R. Kessler. (Novel-Ties Ser.). (YA). (gr. 6-10). 1996. pap. text ed. 15.95 (*1-56982-655-2*) Lrn Links.

***Waiting for the Savior: Reflections of Hope.** John H. Timmerman. LC 97-12917. 168p. 1997. pap. 9.99 (*0-8308-1354-3*, 1354) InterVarsity.

***Waiting for the Sea to Be Blue.** Phillipa Blake. 234p. 1997. 26.00 (*0-7528-0157-0*, Pub. by Orion Bks UK) Trafalgar.

Waiting for the Second Coming: Studies in Thessalonians. Ray Stedman. LC 89-16936. 160p. 1990. pap. 9.99 (*0-929239-14-8*) Discovery Hse Pubs.

***Waiting for the Snow: The Peace Corps Papers of a Charter Volunteer.** Thomas J. Scanlon. (Illus.). 254p. (Orig.). 1996. pap. 14.95 (*1-889274-03-8*) Posterity Press.

Waiting for the Soothsayer. Guy Beining. 1981. pap. 1.50 (*0-686-47954-8*) Ghost Dance.

Waiting for the Spring Freshet. Paul Corrigan. 1984. pap. 3.00 (*0-942396-33-2*) Blackberry ME.

Waiting for the Storm. Gerald Mangan. 64p. (Orig.). 9000. pap. 15.95 (*1-85224-110-1*, Pub. by Bloodaxe Bks UK) Dufour.

***Waiting for the Sun.** Hoskyns. Date not set. pap. 14.95 (*0-312-17056-4*) St Martin.

Waiting for the Sun: Strange Days, Weird Scenes, & the Sound of Los Angeles. Barney Hoskyns. 384p. 1996. 27.50 (*0-312-14444-X*) St Martin.

Waiting for the Sun to Fill with Courage. Leonard J. Cirino. 52p. 1994. pap. 7.00 (*0-944550-37-1*) Pygmy Forest Pr.

Waiting for the Unicorn: Poems & Lyrics of China's Last Dynasty, 1644-1911. Ed. by Irving Y. Lo & William Schultz. LC 85-42816. (Chinese Literature in Translation Ser.). (Illus.). 456p. (C). 1986. 37.95 (*0-253-36321-7*) Ind U Pr.

Waiting for the Unicorn: Poems & Lyrics of China's Last Dynasty, 1644-1911. Ed. by Irving Y. Lo & William Schultz. LC 85-42816. (Chinese Literature in Translation Ser.). 456p. 1987. pap. 8.95 (*0-253-20403-8*) Ind U Pr.

Waiting for the Unicorn: Poems & Lyrics of China's Last Dynasty, 1644-1911. Ed. by Irving Y. Lo & William Schultz. LC 85-42816. (Chinese Literature in Translation Ser.). (Illus.). 456p. (C). 1990. pap. 8.95 (*0-253-20575-1*, MB-575) Ind U Pr.

Waiting for the Verdict. Rebecca H. Davis. Ed. by D. Dingledine. LC 68-57520. (Masterworks of Literature Ser.). pap. 12.95 (*0-685-71560-4*) NCUP.

Waiting for the Verdict. Rebecca H. Davis. LC 68-57520. (Illus.). 361p. reprint ed. lib. bdg. 49.50 (*0-8398-0354-0*) Irvington.

Waiting for the Weekend. Witold Rybczynski. 288p. 1992. pap. 11.95 (*0-14-012663-5*, Penguin Bks) Viking Penguin.

Waiting for the Westbound. Ruth A. Coates. Ed. by Richard L. Polese & Judyth Hill. LC 92-13955. 64p. (Orig.). 1992. per. 8.00 (*0-943734-26-6*) Ocean Tree Bks.

Waiting for the Wind: Thirty-Six Poets of Japan's Late Medieval Age. Steven Carter. (Translations from the Oriental Classics Ser.). 256p. 1989. text ed. 49.50 (*0-231-06854-9*) Col U Pr.

Waiting for the Wind: Thirty-Six Poets of Japan's Late Medieval Age. Steven D. Carter. 353p. 1994. pap. 17.00 (*0-231-06855-7*) Col U Pr.

Waiting for the Wolf Moon. Evelyn Vaughn. (Shadows Ser.). 1993. mass mkt. 3.50 (*0-373-27008-9*, 5-27008-7) Harlequin Bks.

Waiting for Tomorrow. Claire Stevens. LC 95-78931. 120p. (Orig.). (YA). (gr. 9 up). 1995. pap. 5.95 (*0-9647478-3-9*) Summer Snow.

Waiting for Vern. Jim DeVita. 30p. (Orig.). 1995. pap. 3.50 (*1-57514-105-1*, 1048) Encore Perform Pub.

Waiting for Willa. Dorothy Eden. 1980. pap. 1.95 (*0-449-23187-9*, Crest) Fawcett.

Waiting for Winter to End: An Extraordinary Journey Through Soviet Central Asia. Georgie A. Geyer. (Illus.). 256p. 1994. 23.95 (*0-02-881110-0*) Brasseys Inc.

Waiting for World's End: The Diaries of Wilford Woodruff. Wilford Woodruff. Ed. by Susan Staker. LC 92-11207. xxxviii, 455p. (Orig.). 1993. pap. 19.95 (*0-941214-92-3*) Signature Bks.

***Waiting for Yesterday.** Jenny Lykins. 336p. 1997. mass mkt. 5.99 (*0-515-12129-0*) Jove Pubns.

Waiting for You. Margot Early. (Superromance Ser.). 1996. mass mkt. 3.99 (*0-373-70694-4*, 1-70694-4) Harlequin Bks.

***Waiting for You.** C. G. Stevens. 317p. 1996. 15.00 (*0-9655405-2-9*, Psimate Res) Tiatek.

Waiting Game. Diana Hamilton. 1997. mass mkt. 3.50 (*0-373-11858-9*, 1-11858-7) Silhouette.

***Waiting Game.** Juliet Hastings. (Crime & Passion Ser.). (Orig.). 1997. mass mkt. 5.95 (*0-7535-0109-0*, Pub. by Virgin Pub UK) London Brdge.

Waiting Game. Jayne Ann Krentz. (Men Made in America Ser.). 1995. mass mkt. 3.99 (*0-373-45197-0*, 1-45197-0) Harlequin Bks.

Waiting Game. large type ed. Diana Hamilton. (Harlequin Romance Ser.). 1995. lib. bdg. 18.95 (*0-263-14074-1*, Pub. by Mills & Boon UK) Thorndike Pr.

Waiting Game. Alexander Fullerton. 160p. 1983. reprint ed. pap. 5.00 (*0-583-11758-9*, Pub. by Granada UK) Academy Chi Pubs.

Waiting Game: Photographs of the Oakland A's. John Krich. (Illus.). 136p. 1982. 25.00 (*0-913028-92-4*); pap. 8.95 (*0-913028-93-2*) North Atlantic.

Waiting Games. Bruce Hart & Carole Hart. 320p. (YA). (gr. 7 up). 1981. pap. 3.50 (*0-380-79012-2*, Flare) Avon.

Waiting in Line at the Drugstore & Other Writings of James Thomas Jackson. James T. Jackson. LC 93-32763. 277p. 1993. pap. 12.95 (*0-929398-50-5*) UNTX Pr.

Waiting in Line at the Drugstore & Other Writings of James Thomas Jackson. James T. Jackson. LC 93-32763. 277p. 1993. 19.95 (*0-929398-62-9*) UNTX Pr.

Waiting in Style: A Maternity Wardrobe That Works. Alyson Fendel. LC 85-4035. 196p. 1983. pap. 9.95 (*0-87491-702-6*) Acrpls Bks CO.

Waiting in the Future for the Past to Come. Sebiha Khemir. 282p. 1993. 19.95 (*0-7043-7048-4*, Pub. by Quartet UK) Interlink Pub.

Waiting in the Wings: A Larger Audience for the Arts & How to Develop It. Bradley G. Morison & Julie G. Dalgleish. LC 87-940. (Illus.). 176p. (Orig.). 1987. pap. 14.95 (*0-915400-54-5*, 9453, ACA Bks) Am Council Arts.

Waiting in the Wings: A Larger Audience for the Arts & How to Develop It. rev. ed. Bradley G. Morrison & Julie G. Dalgleish. LC 92-33800. 178p. (Orig.). 1992. pap. 14.95 (*1-879903-03-2*) Am Council Arts.

***Waiting in the Wings: Portrait of a Queer Motherhood.** Cherrie Moraga. 120p. 1997. pap. 10.95 (*1-56341-092-3*); lib. bdg. 22.95 (*1-56341-093-1*) Firebrand Bks.

***Waiting in Vain.** Colin Channer. 1997. pap. write for info. (*0-345-41178-1*) Ballantine.

Waiting Land: A Spell in Nepal. Dervla Murphy. LC 85-5736. 216p. 1987. 22.95 (*0-87951-251-2*) Overlook Pr.

Waiting Land: A Spell in Nepal. Dervla Murphy. 216p. 1989. pap. 13.95 (*0-87951-305-5*) Overlook Pr.

Waiting Land: And Other Poems. Marcia M. Capps. LC 89-35147. 64p. (Orig.). 1989. pap. 7.50 (*0-931832-35-7*) Fithian Pr.

Waiting List. Daisy Al-Amir. Tr. by Barbara M. Parmenter from ARA. (Modern Middle Eastern Literature in Translation Ser.). 100p. (C). 1995. pap. text ed. 8.95 (*0-292-79067-8*, Pub. by Ctr Mid East Stud) U of Tex Pr.

Waiting Missionary. David Fessenden. (Missionary - That's Me! Ser.). (Illus.). 32p. (J). (ps-2). 1995. pap. 4.99 (*0-87509-561-5*) Chr Pubns.

Waiting My Turn. Karen Erickson. Date not set. pap. write for info. (*0-14-050995-X*) NAL-Dutton.

Waiting on America: A Food Server's Guide to Greater Income. Mario Ponce. Ed. by Robert Modesto. (Illus.). 144p. (Orig.). (C). 1989. pap. 7.95 (*0-685-27820-4*) Amer Serv Pubns.

Waiting on God. Andrew Murray. 1992. pap. 5.95 (*0-87508-399-4*) Chr Lit.

Waiting on God. Andrew Murray. 160p. 1981. mass mkt. 4.99 (*0-88368-101-3*) Whitaker Hse.

Waiting on God: Trusting Him in Times of Suffering. J. K. Jones, Jr. LC 95-47062. 142p. (Orig.). (C). 1996. pap. 8.99 (*0-89900-747-3*) College Pr Pub.

***Waiting on Halley's Comet: Short-Story Snapshots of the Human Spirit.** John M. Eades. LC 97-14602. 200p. 1997. pap. 10.95 (*1-55874-514-9*) Health Comm.

Waiting on the Lord. Stephen D. Eyre & Jacalyn Eyre. (Spiritual Encounter Guides Ser.). 96p. (Orig.). 1994. wbk. ed., pap. 4.99 (*0-8308-1180-X*, 1180) InterVarsity.

Waiting on the Outside. Kathy Royer. LC 87-21104. 64p. (Orig.). 1987. pap. 4.50 (*0-8361-3454-0*) Herald Pr.

Waiting on Washington: Central American Workers in the Nation's Capital. Terry A. Repak. (Illus.). 240p. (Orig.). (C). 1995. pap. text ed. 16.95 (*1-56639-302-7*); lib. bdg. 59.95 (*1-56639-301-9*) Temple U Pr.

An Asterisk (*) at the beginning of an entry indicates that the title is appearing in BIP for the first time.

Waiting Place. Barbara R. Garrison. LC 92-74409. (Illus.). 112p. (Orig.). 1993. pap. 5.95 (*0-87946-080-6*, 146) ACTA Pubns.

***Waiting Room.** Lisa Loomer. Date not set. pap. 5.25 (*0-8222-1594-2*) Dramatists Play.

Waiting Room: Poems. Wayne Lanter. LC 95-34703. 1995. pap. 12.95 (*0-7734-2747-3*, Mellen Poetry Pr) E Mellen.

Waiting Room: Writing by Children & Adult Patients in a Hospital Setting. Ed. by Todd Beers. (Illus.). 64p. (Orig.). 1991. pap. 5.95 (*0-9618487-2-3*) Writers & Bks.

Waiting Room Germany. Klaus Pohl. 80p. (Orig.). 1996. pap. 13.95 (*1-85459-274-2*, Pub. by N Hern Bks UK) Theatre Comm.

Waiting Sextet. I. Sulieman. 1995. pap. text ed. 20.00 (*0-7935-4821-7*, 00000502) H Leonard.

Waiting Spirits. Bruce Coville. (Chamber of Horrors Ser.: No. 4). (Orig.). (YA). (gr. 6 up). 1996. mass mkt. 3.99 (*0-671-53640-0*) PB.

Waiting Time. Eugenia Price. LC 96-8250. 384p. 1997. 23.95 (*0-385-47938-7*) Doubleday.

***Waiting Time.** large type ed. Eugenia Price. LC 97-339. 1997. write for info. (*0-7862-1065-6*, Thorndike Lrg Prnt); lib. bdg. 27.95 (*0-7862-1064-8*, Thorndike Lrg Prnt) Thorndike Pr.

Waiting to Clear: Brain Injury: Early Stages of Recovery. Mary M. Castiglione & Cynthia C. Johnson. (Illus.). 88p. (Orig.). 1994. pap. text ed. 9.50 (*0-939838-35-4*) Pritchett & Hull.

***Waiting to Excel.** Quentin Huff. 69p. (Orig.). 1997. pap. 7.50 (*0-614-30228-5*) Baraka Pubng.

Waiting to Exhale. Terry McMillan. 1995. pap. 6.99 (*0-671-53745-8*) PB.

***Waiting to Exhale.** Terry McMillan. 1996. mass mkt. 20.97 (*0-671-85153-5*) PB.

Waiting to Exhale. Terry McMillan. 416p. 1992. pap. 22.95 (*0-670-83980-9*, Viking) Viking Penguin.

Waiting to Exhale. large type ed. Terry McMillan. LC 92-27196. (General Ser.). 600p. 1993. pap. 17.95 (*0-8161-5618-2*, GK Hall) Thorndike Pr.

Waiting to Exhale. Terry McMillan. Ed. by Jane Rosenman. 416p. reprint ed. pap. 12.00 (*0-671-50148-8*, WSP) PB.

Waiting to Forget: A Mother's Search for Her Secret Son. Margaret Moorman. 214p. 1996. 25.00 (*0-393-03967-6*) Norton.

Waiting to Waltz: A Childhood. Cynthia Rylant. LC 84-11030. (Illus.). 48p. (J). (gr. 6-8). 1984. text ed. 14.00 (*0-02-778000-7*, Bradbury S&S) S&S Childrens.

Waiting Tree & Other Poems: Sonnets. G. W. Sherman. (Orig.). 1966. pap. 4.00 (*0-685-00355-8*) Cobra Pr.

Waiting Web. large type ed. Mary Mackie. (Linford Romance Library). 272p. 1992. pap. 15.99 (*0-7089-7287-X*, Trailtree Bookshop) Ulverscroft.

Waiting Wife. Linda M. Lanning. 1997. mass mkt. write for info. (*0-8041-0937-0*) Ivy Books.

Waiting with Alistair. Alistair Sampson. LC 78-58578. (Illus.). 176p. 1978. 9.95 (*0-916838-14-5*) Schiffer.

***Waiting with Hope: Reflections by Young Adults for Everyday of Advent.** Ed. by Ron Bagley. 40p. (Orig.). 1997. pap. 6.95 (*1-890516-00-7*) Ctr Minist Dev.

Waiting Years. Fumiko Enchi. Ed. by Shaw. Tr. by John Bester from JPN. LC 72-15864. (Japan's Women Writers Ser.). 204p. 1980. pap. 9.00 (*0-87011-424-7*) Kodansha.

Waitress. D. Smith. 160p. (YA). (gr. 7-9). 1992. pap. 2.95 (*0-590-45063-8*, Point) Scholastic Inc.

Waitresses Handbook: A Guide to the Legal Rights of Waitresses & Other Restaurant Workers. (Women's Legal Defense Fund Staff Ser.). 80p. 1986. pap. 7.00 (*0-932689-17-5*) Women's Legal Defense.

Waitressing: Inside Tips for Better Tips. rev. ed. Marcia Love-Jackson. (Illus.). 44p. 1994. pap. 4.95 (*0-9614315-0-4*) Love-Jackson.

Waiver Distributed among the Departments Election, Estoppel, Contract, Release. John S. Ewart. 1996. reprint ed. 62.00 (*1-57588-084-9*, 310600) W S Hein.

Waiving the Rules: The Constitution under Thatcherism. Ed. by Cosmo Graham & Tony Prosser. 224p. 1989. 90.00 (*0-335-15580-4*, Open Univ Pr); pap. 32.00 (*0-335-15579-0*, Open Univ Pr) Taylor & Francis.

Wajda on Film: A Master's Notes. Andrzej Wajda. (Illus.). 140p. 1991. reprint ed. pap. text ed. 13.95 (*0-918226-29-5*) Acrobat.

Waka Anthology: The Gem-Glistening Cup, Vol. 1. Tr. by Edwin A. Cranston. xxviii, 988p. Date not set. 99.50 (*0-8047-1922-5*) Stanford U Pr.

Wakabayashi Mineral Collection at the University Museum of the University of Tokyo. Ed. by Ryoichi Sadanaga & Michiaki Bunno. 177p. 1974. 57.50 (*0-86008-115-X*, Pub. by U of Tokyo JA) Col U Pr.

***Wake.** Steve Allen. 107p. 1996. pap. 5.25 (*0-87129-719-1*, M80) Dramatic Pub.

Wake County, North Carolina Marriage Bonds & Certificates, 1781-1867, 3 vols., Set. Francis T. Ingmire. 343p. 1994. pap. 30.00 (*0-8095-8706-8*); lib. bdg. 60.00 (*0-8095-8372-0*) Borgo Pr.

***Wake 'em Up! How to Use Humor & Other Professional Techniques to Create Alarmingly Good Business Presentations.** Thomas Antion. LC 96-86293. (Illus.). 336p. (Orig.). 1997. pap. 24.95 (*0-926395-12-2*) Anchor Maryland.

Wake for Donald. Evelyn Hood. LC 96-19096. 55p. (Orig.). 1996. pap. 5.00 (*0-88734-382-1*) Players Pr.

Wake for the Living. Andrew N. Lytle. LC 92-89829. (Southern Classics Ser.). 308p. 1992. reprint ed. pap. 10.95 (*1-879941-10-4*) J S Sanders.

Wake Forest. Kenneth Garrett. (Illus.). 112p. 1987. 37.50 (*0-916509-17-6*) Harmony Hse Pub.

Wake Forest Football Mystery. Carole M. Longmeyer. (Sportsmystery Ser.). (Illus.). (Orig.). (J). (gr. 3 up). 1994. pap. 19.95 (*0-935326-34-0*) Gallopade Pub Group.

Wake Forest Law Review: 1965-1995, 31 vols., Set. Bound set. 1,412.50 (*0-8377-9183-9*) Rothman.

Wake in Transit. David Hayman. LC 89-45980. 224p. 1990. 37.50 (*0-8014-2441-0*) Cornell U Pr.

Wake in Ybor City. Jose Yglesias. 1981. 31.95 (*0-405-13172-0*) Ayer.

Wake Island Pilot: A World War II Memoir. John F. Kinney & James M. McCaffrey. (World War II Commemorative Ser.). (Illus.). 224p. 1995. 24.95 (*1-57488-035-7*) Brasseys Inc.

Wake Me at Midnight. Barthe DeClements. 160p. (J). (gr. 3-7). 1993. pap. 3.99 (*0-14-036486-2*, Puffin) Puffin Bks.

***Wake Me for the Resurrection.** Robert Kirby. LC 96-43697. (Illus.). 152p. (Orig.). 1996. pap. 9.95 (*1-885628-47-1*) Buckaroo Bks.

Wake Me in Spring. James Preller. (Hello Reader! Ser.). (Illus.). (J). (gr. 2). 1994. pap. 2.95 (*0-590-48189-4*, Cartwheel) Scholastic Inc.

Wake Me in the Spring. James Preller. LC 93-16787. (Hello Reader! Ser.). (Illus.). 32p. (J). (gr. k-2). 1994. pap. 3.50 (*0-590-47500-2*, Cartwheel) Scholastic Inc.

Wake Me up & F* Me.** rev. ed. Dee Snyder. 20p. 1996. pap. 3.00 (*0-9637704-3-8*) Red Dragon VA.

Wake Me up When I'm a Size Five. Cathy Guisewite. (Illus.). 128p. (Orig.). 1985. pap. 8.95 (*0-8362-2069-2*) Andrews & McMeel.

Wake Me When It's Funny: How to Break into Show Business & Stay There. Garry Marshall & Lori Marshall. LC 95-6630. 1995. 22.95 (*1-55850-526-1*) Adams Media.

Wake Me When It's Funny: How to Break into Show Business & Stay There. Garry Marshall & Lori Marshall. (Illus.). 352p. 1997. reprint ed. pap. 14.95 (*1-55704-288-8*) Newmarket.

***Wake Me with a Kiss.** Emily Dalton. (American Romance Ser.: No. 685). 1997. mass mkt. 3.75 (*0-373-16685-0*, 1-16685-9) Harlequin Bks.

Wake Not the Dragon. Jo A. Ferguson. 384p. 1996. mass mkt. 4.99 (*0-06-108413-1*) HarpC.

***Wake of Art: Criticism, Philosophy & the Ends of Taste.** Arthur C. Danto. 150p. 1997. pap. 35.00 (*90-5701-221-9*); pap. 18.95 (*90-5701-301-0*) Dist Art Pubs.

Wake of Deconstruction. Barbara Johnson. (Bucknell Lectures in Literary Theory). (Illus.). 1994. text ed. 44.95 (*0-631-19014-7*); pap. text ed. 17.95 (*0-631-18963-7*) Blackwell Pubs.

Wake of Imagination: Toward a Postmodern Culture. Richard Kearney. LC 88-1311. 467p. (Orig.). 1989. pap. text ed. 21.95 (*0-8166-1714-7*) U of Minn Pr.

Wake of Jamey Foster. Beth Henley. 1983. pap. 5.25 (*0-8222-1217-X*) Dramatists Play.

Wake of the Coasters. rev. ed. John F. Leavitt. LC 75-120265. (American Maritime Library: Vol. 2). (Illus.). xvii, 201p. 1984. pap. 21.95 (*0-913372-34-X*) Mystic Seaport.

Wake of the General Bliss. Edward G. Lueders. LC 88-20687. 196p. reprint ed. pap. 55.90 (*0-7837-5533-3*, 2045306) Bks Demand.

Wake of the Gods: Melville's Mythology. H. Bruce Franklin. xii, 236p. 1963. pap. 19.95 (*0-8047-0137-7*) Stanford U Pr.

***Wake of the Whale.** Larry Bailey. 423p. (Orig.). 1997. mass mkt. 4.99 (*1-55197-736-2*, Pub. by Comnwlth Pub CN) Partners Pubs Grp.

Wake-Pick Poems. Kristjana Gunnars. 96p. (Orig.). 1981. pap. 8.95 (*0-88784-089-2*, Pub. by Hse of Anansi Pr CN) Genl Dist Srvs.

Wake Robin. John Burroughs. (Works of John Burroughs). 1989. reprint ed. lib. bdg. 79.00 (*0-7812-2178-1*) Rprt Serv.

Wake the Dead. Dorothy Simpson. (Inspector Luke Thanet Novel Ser.). 256p. 1992. text ed. 19.00 (*0-684-19507-0*) S&S Trade.

Wake to Darkness. Blythe Stephens. (Intimate Moments Ser.: No. 434). 1992. mass mkt. 3.39 (*0-373-07434-4*, 5-07434-9) Harlequin Bks.

Wake Up. Christine Keys. 88p. 1995. pap. 10.00 (*0-8059-3635-1*) Dorrance.

Wake Up! A Sensory Stimulation Program for Nursing Home Residents. Pamela Sander. (Illus.). 89p. (Orig.). (C). 1987. pap. text ed. 11.00 (*1-877735-14-0*, 121) M&H Pub Co TX.

Wake up America! Vol. 1: The Plucked Eagle. John Walsh. (Illus.). 16p. (Orig.). 1996. pap. 1.00 (*0-933731-09-4*, 2) Children of Mary.

***Wake up America - Regain Your American Heritage: Become Financially Fit Through Debt Elimination.** John Rivera & Carol A. Walker. Ed. by Tamara Pluth. (Illus.). 250p. 1997. 19.95 (*0-9657857-0-X*) Financial Frdm Ent.

Wake Up & Cook: Buddhism in Words & Recipes. Carole Tonkinson. LC 96-22923. 208p. 1997. pap. 14.00 (*1-57322-575-4*, Riverhd Trade) Berkley Pub.

***Wake Up & Goodnight.** Charlotte Zolotow. LC 96-43072. (Illus.). (J). 1997. write for info. (*0-694-01032-4*) HarpC.

Wake Up & Preach. James F. Finley. LC 85-26667. 111p. (Orig.). 1986. pap. 5.95 (*0-8189-0492-5*) Alba.

***Wake up & Prosper.** Catskill Eagle Staff. (Illus.). 225p. 1997. 19.99 (*0-9657156-0-4*) Catskill Eagle.

Wake up & Roar: Satsang with H. W. L. Poonja, Vol. 1. H. W. Poonja. Ed. by Eli Jaxon-Bear. LC 92-80404. 166p. 1992. pap. 12.00 (*0-9632194-1-3*) Satsang Fndtn.

Wake up & Roar: Satsang with H. W. L. Poonja, Vol. 2. H. W. Poonja. LC 92-80404. 172p. (Orig.). 1993. pap. 12.00 (*0-9632194-2-1*) Satsang Fndtn.

Wake up & Shake up Your Company. Richard Koch & Andrew Campbell. (Financial Times Management Ser.). 224p. 1993. 39.50 (*0-273-60201-2*, Pub. by Pitman Pub Ltd UK) Trans-Atl Phila.

Wake Up & Smell the Coffee. Tripp Evans & Andrew Frothingham. 384p. (Orig.). 1995. pap. 8.00 (*0-425-15135-2*, Berkley Trade) Berkley Pub.

Wake Up & Smell the Coffee: Advice, Wisdom & Uncommon Good Sense. Ann Landers. (Illus.). 432p. 1996. 23.00 (*0-679-44539-0*, Villard Bks) Random.

Wake Up & Smell the Coffee: Advice, Wisdom, & Uncommon Good Sense. Ann Landers. 1996. 23.00 (*0-614-95764-8*, Villard Bks) Random.

Wake Up & Smell the Coffee: Advice, Wisdom & Uncommon Good Sense. large type ed. Ann Landers. 1996. pap. 23.00 (*0-7838-1710-X*, GK Hall) Thorndike Pr.

Wake Up & Smell the Coffee: Advice, Wisdom, & Uncommon Good Sense. Ann Landers. LC 96-4206. (Illus.). 1996. pap. 23.00 (*0-679-75887-9*) Random Hse Lrg Prnt.

Wake up & Smell the Coffee: Lake States Edition. Laura C. Zahn. (Illus.). 256p. (Orig.). 1994. pap. 15.95 (*0-939301-94-6*) Down to Erth Pubns.

Wake up & Smell the Coffee: Pacific Northwest Edition. Laura C. Zahn. (Illus.). 176p. (Orig.). 1990. pap. 11.95 (*0-939301-10-5*) Down to Erth Pubns.

Wake up & Smell the Coffee: Southwest Edition. Laura C. Zahn. (Illus.). 224p. (Orig.). 1992. pap. 14.95 (*0-939301-92-X*) Down to Erth Pubns.

Wake up & Smell the Coffee: Upper Midwest Edition. Laura C. Zahn. (Illus.). 224p. (Orig.). 1988. pap. 14.95 (*0-939301-03-2*) Down to Erth Pubns.

Wake up & Smell the Formula: The A to No Zzzzz's of Having a Baby. Shoebox Greetings Staff. (Illus.). 72p. (Orig.). 1990. pap. 5.95 (*0-87529-640-8*) Hallmark.

Wake Up, Baby. Joanne F. Oppenheim. (Bank Street Ready-to-Read Ser.). (J). (ps-3). 1990. pap. 3.50 (*0-685-46039-8*, Litl Rooster); lib. bdg. 9.99 (*0-685-54065-0*, Litl Rooster) BDD Bks Young Read.

Wake up, Baby! Joanne F. Oppenheim. (Illus.). 32p. (J). (ps-3). 1990. pap. 3.99 (*0-553-34914-7*) Bantam.

Wake Up Bear. Lynley Dodd. LC 86-42798. (Gold Star First Readers Ser.). (Illus.). 32p. (J). (gr. 1-2). 1988. lib. bdg. 18.60 (*1-55532-124-0*) Gareth Stevens Inc.

Wake up, Bear...It's Christmas! Stephen Gammell. LC 81-5019. (Illus.). 32p. (J). (ps-3). 1981. lib. bdg. 14.93 (*0-688-00693-0*) Lothrop.

Wake up, Bear...It's Christmas! Stephen Gammell. LC 81-5019. (Illus.). 32p. (J). (ps up). 1990. pap. 4.95 (*0-688-09934-3*, Mulberry) Morrow.

Wake-up Call. Gus Bragg. 368p. (Orig.). 1996. mass mkt. 5.99 (*1-55197-186-0*, Pub. by Comnwlth Pub CN) Partners Pubs Grp.

Wake up Call. J. R. Kares. 128p. (Orig.). 1996. pap. 14.00 (*0-9651573-0-X*, 1023) Pleasant Valley.

Wake up Call: (Final Call) Daniel R. Queen. (Illus.). 128p. pap. write for info. (*1-881328-01-5*) Queens Palace.

Wake up Call Prophecies. unabridged ed. Bob R. Short. (Illus.). 232p. (Orig.). 1996. pap. 14.95 (*0-9651408-0-6*) Wake Up Call.

Wake-up Calls. Gerald G. Jampolsky & Diane V. Cirincione. LC 92-23344. 224p. 1992. 15.00 (*1-56170-055-X*, 147) Hay House.

Wake Up Calls: Classic Cases in Business Ethics. Lisa H. Newton & David Schmidt. 256p. (C). 1996. pap. 26.95 (*0-534-25338-5*) Wadsworth Pub.

Wake-up Calls: You Don't Have to Sleepwalk Through Your Life, Love, Or Career! Eric Allenbaugh. 288p. 1992. 18.95 (*0-9631194-1-9*) Discov Pubns.

Wake-Up Calls: You Don't Have to Sleepwalk Through Your Life, Love, or Career. Eric Allenbaugh. 288p. 1994. pap. 11.00 (*0-671-88707-6*, Fireside) S&S Trade.

Wake up, City! Alvin R. Tresselt. LC 88-32594. (Illus.). 32p. (J). (ps-2). 1990. lib. bdg. 13.88 (*0-688-08653-5*) Lothrop.

Wake up, Darling. Alex Gottlieb. 1956. pap. 5.25 (*0-8222-1219-6*) Dramatists Play.

Wake up Dead Man: Afro-American Worksongs from Texas Prisons. Bruce Jackson. LC 70-169857. (Illus.). 326p. 1972. 30.00 (*0-674-94546-8*) HUP.

Wake up Detroit! The EVs Are Coming. Albert C. Smith, Jr. Ed. by Albert Smith, 3rd. LC 81-68726. (Illus.). 128p. (Orig.). 1982. pap. 4.95 (*0-933086-03-2*) Cromwell-Smith.

Wake up, Dormouse, Santa Claus Is Here. Eleonore Schmid. LC 89-42610. (Illus.). 32p. (J). (gr. k-3). 1989. 14.95 (*1-55858-020-4*) North-South Bks NYC.

Wake up Everybody. Colin King. 1996. bds., mass mkt. 4.99 (*0-7459-3341-6*) Lion USA.

Wake up Everybody. Colin King. 12p. (J). 1996. 4.99 (*0-7459-3491-9*) Lion USA.

Wake up, Farm! Alvin R. Tresselt. LC 90-33646. (Illus.). 32p. (J). (ps up). 1991. 14.95 (*0-688-08654-3*) Lothrop.

Wake up from Your Dream. Perry Mafi. 83p. 1990. pap. text ed. 7.95 (*0-9631372-0-4*) P Mafi Writs.

Wake up, Grizzly! Wolfgang Bittner. Tr. by J. Alison James. LC 95-36758. (Illus.). 32p. (J). (ps-3). Date not set. 15.95 (*1-55858-518-4*); lib. bdg. 15.88 (*1-55858-519-2*) North-South Bks NYC.

Wake up! It's Morning-after in America: And We've Been Screwed! Edward Vibert. (Illus.). 128p. (Orig.). 1996. 7.50 (*0-614-00094-7*) Berkshire Assocs.

Wake up, It's Mothers Day. Patricia R. Giff. (Kops Ser.: No. 16). 80p. (J). (ps-3). 1991. mass mkt. 3.99 (*0-440-40455-X*) Dell.

Wake Up, Little Children: A Rise-&-Shine Rhyme. Jim Aylesworth. (Illus.). 32p. (J). (ps-2). 1996. 16.00 (*0-689-31857-X*, Atheneum Bks Young) S&S Childrens.

Wake up Little Susie: Single Pregnancy & Race Before Roe vs. Wade. Rickie Solinger. 324p. (C). (gr. 13). 1992. text ed. 16.95 (*0-415-90448-X*, A5814, Routledge NY) Routledge.

Wake up, Men! Fred Littauer. LC 93-42446. 1994. pap. 10.99 (*0-8499-3831-7*) Word Pub.

Wake Up, Mommy. Matthew V. Smith. (Illus.). 15p. (J). (gr. 1-3). 1992. pap. 10.95 (*1-56606-009-5*) Bradley Mann.

Wake up, Mr. B.! Penny Dale. LC 91-58763. (Illus.). 32p. (J). (ps up). 1992. 14.95 (*1-56402-104-1*) Candlewick Pr.

Wake Up, Mr. B.! Penny Dale. LC 91-58763. (Illus.). 32p. (J). (ps up). 1994. pap. 4.99 (*1-56402-382-6*) Candlewick Pr.

Wake up Mum: A Mother & Son's True Crisis Story of Overcoming Drug Addiction with Love, Laughter & Miraculous Insights. Carmel Greenwood & Chris Taylor. (Illus.). (Orig.). (YA). 16.95 (*0-9646285-0-3*); pap. 12.95 (*0-9646285-1-1*) Carmel Concepts.

***Wake up! On the Road with a Zen Master.** 29.95 (*0-942795-07-5*) Primary Point Pr.

Wake up, Rhonda: How a Courageous Family Rescued Their "Sleeping Beauty" from Severe Brain-Damage. Jo Knott. LC 89-83589. (Illus.). 242p. (Orig.). 1989. 13.95 (*0-9622992-1-9*); pap. 7.95 (*0-9622992-0-0*) Star Orange Park.

Wake up, Sam! Ski Michaels. LC 85-14115. (Illus.). 48p. (Orig.). (J). (gr. 1-3). 1997. pap. 3.50 (*0-8167-0581-X*) Troll Communs.

Wake up, Santa Claus! Marcus Pfister. LC 96-15964. (Illus.). (J). Date not set. lib. bdg. 15.88 (*1-55858-606-7*) North-South Bks NYC.

Wake up, Santa Claus! Marcus Pfister. LC 96-15964. (Illus.). 32p. (J). (gr. k-3). Date not set. 15.95 (*1-55858-605-9*) North-South Bks NYC.

Wake Up Screaming. Vincent Courtney. 384p. 1992. mass mkt. 4.50 (*1-55817-605-5*, Pinncle Kensgtn) Kensgtn Pub Corp.

***Wake up, Sleeping Beauty: A Pop-Up Book with Sounds.** Jonathan Allen. LC 96-49446. (J). 1997. pap. 16.99 (*0-8037-2212-5*) Dial Bks Young.

Wake up! Sun! David Harrison. LC 85-30053. (Step into Reading Bks.). (Illus.). 32p. (J). (ps-1). 1986. lib. bdg. 7.99 (*0-394-98256-8*) Random Bks Yng Read.

Wake up! Sun! David Harrison. LC 85-30053. (Step into Reading Bks.). (Illus.). 32p. (J). (ps-1). 1986. pap. 3.99 (*0-394-88256-3*) Random Bks Yng Read.

Wake up the Echoes: Notre Dame Football. rev. ed. Ken Rappoport. (College Sports Book Ser.). (Illus.). 464p. 1988. 19.95 (*0-87397-309-7*, Strode Pubs) Circle Bk Service.

Wake up Time see Phonics Is My Way Series

Wake-up to Love. Faith Garner. LC 95-94886. 192p. 1995. 17.95 (*0-8034-9145-X*) Bouregy.

Wake up to Murder. Steve Allen. 256p. 1996. 19.95 (*1-57566-090-3*, Knsington) Kensgtn Pub Corp.

***Wake up to Murder.** Steve Allen. 384p. 1997. mass mkt. 5.99 (*1-57566-236-1*, Knsington) Kensgtn Pub Corp.

Wake up to Murder. large type ed. Day Keene. (Linford Mystery Library). 320p. 1993. pap. 15.99 (*0-7089-7418-X*, Traiitree Bookshop) Ulverscroft.

Wake up to Nightmares: The Nightmare Test. C. C. Graves. 96p. (Orig.). (J). 1997. mass mkt. 3.50 (*0-06-106385-1*, Harp PBks) HarpC.

Wake up to Wealth. Bob Mandel. LC 93-38528. 192p. 1995. pap. 9.95 (*0-89087-709-2*) Celestial Arts.

***Wake up to Your Dreams.** Sandra Collier. (YA). pap. 5.99 (*0-590-24761-1*) Scholastic Inc.

***Wake up to Your Inner Courage & Become Steeped in Divine Contentment: A Book of Contemplations.** LC 97-66735. 88p. (Orig.). 1997. pap. 4.75 (*0-911307-55-9*) SYDA Found.

Wake up, Wake up. Rebecca Wildsmith & Brian Wildsmith. LC 92-18704. (J). 1993. pap. write for info. (*0-15-200686-9*) HarBrace.

Wake up Wilson Street. Thomas. 1995. 3.98 (*0-8317-5245-9*) Smithmark.

Wake up Your Creative Genius. Kurt Hanks & Jay Parry. LC 91-20019. (Quick-Read Ser.). (Illus.). 138p. (C). 1990. reprint ed. pap. 13.95 (*1-56052-111-2*) Crisp Pubns.

***Wake up Your Dreams: A Proven Strategy to Help You, 2 cass.** Walt Kallestad. Date not set. audio 14.99 (*0-310-20742-8*) Zondervan.

Wake up Your Dreams: A Proven Strategy to Help You. Walt Kallestad. 208p. 1996. 17.99 (*0-310-20727-4*) Zondervan.

Wake up Your Seniors. Carole S. Jewkes. 286p. (C). 1994. pap. 50.00 (*1-888143-00-2*) Robbins Mgmt.

Wake up Your Seniors: Obra Edition. 6th ed. Carole S. Jewkes. 350p. (C). 1994. pap. 60.00 (*1-888143-01-0*) Robbins Mgmt.

***Wakefield Hall.** Francesca Stanfill. Date not set. write for info. (*0-688-07597-5*) Morrow.

Wakefield Legacy: The Untold Story. Francine Pascal. (Sweet Valley Ser.: No. 2). 352p. (YA). (gr. 7 up). 1992. mass mkt. 4.50 (*0-553-29794-5*, Starfire BDD) BDD Bks Young Read.

Wakefield Manor, Rappahannock County, Virginia, 1734-1992. Robert T. Dennis. vi, 65p. 1993. pap. 15.00 (*0-8095-8707-6*); lib. bdg. 39.00 (*0-8095-8296-1*) Borgo Pr.

Wakefield Memorial, a History, Genealogy, & Biographical Register of the Name & Family. H. Wakefield. (Illus.). 367p. 1989. reprint ed. pap. 55.00 (*0-8328-1211-0*); reprint ed. lib. bdg. 63.00 (*0-8328-1210-2*) Higginson Bk Co.

Wakefield's Christian Theology, 1. Samuel Wakefield. pap. 14.99 (*0-88019-177-5*) Schmul Pub Co.

Wakefield's Christian Theology, 2. Samuel Wakefield. pap. 14.99 (*0-88019-180-5*) Schmul Pub Co.

Wakefield's Course. large type ed. Mazo De la Roche. (Whiteoak Chronicles Ser.). 1973. 12.00 (*0-85456-684-8*) Ulverscroft.

Wakefields of Sweet Valley. Francine Pascal. (Sweet Valley Ser.: No. 1). 352p. (J). 1991. mass mkt. 4.50 (*0-553-29278-1*) Bantam.

W

Wakefulness. Bruce Renner. LC 78-71828. 78p. (Orig.). 1978. pap. 3.75 (0-934332-10-X) LEpervier Pr.

Wakeman Genealogy, 1630-1899, Being a Historical Account of the Descendants of Samuel Wakeman of Hartford, Connecticut, & of John Wakeman, Treasurer of New Haven Colony. R. Wakeman. (Illus.). 438p. 1989. reprint ed. pap. 65.50 (0-8328-1213-7); reprint ed. lib. bdg. 73.50 (0-8328-1212-9) Higginson Bk Co.

Wakemap Mound & Nearby Sites on the Long Narrows of the Columbia River. 2nd ed. Ed. by Emory Strong. (Illus.). 40p. 1977. pap. 5.95 (0-8323-0137-X) Binford Mort.

WakerUppers: A Spirited Collection of Thinking Activities. Greta Rasmussen & Ted Rasmussen. LC 93-95045. (Illus.). 112p. 1994. pap. 11.95 (0-936110-16-3) Tin Man Pr.

Wakes Week: Memories of Mill Town Holidays. John Hudson. 160p. 1992. pap. 16.00 (0-7509-0094-6, Pub. by Sutton Pubng UK) Bks Intl VA.

Wakeup Call. Robert Culver. 1993. pap. 6.95 (1-883858-22-4) Witness CA.

***Waking.** Lin Coghlan. (Nick Hern Bks.). 1997. pap. text ed. 13.95 (1-85459-392-7, Pub. by N Hern Bks UK) Theatre Comm.

Waking. Tom Sleigh. LC 90-31100. (Phoenix Poets Ser.). 108p. 1990. pap. 10.95 (0-226-76239-4) U Ch Pr.

Waking. Tom Sleigh. LC 90-31100. (Phoenix Poets Ser.). 100p. 1990. lib. bdg. 24.00 (0-226-76238-6) U Ch Pr.

Waking at the Bottom of the Dark. Jan Clausen. LC 78-71983. 1979. pap. 3.00 (0-9602284-0-3) Long Haul.

***Waking Beauty.** Paul Witcover. Date not set. pap. write for info. (0-06-105338-4, HarperPrism); mass mkt. write for info. (0-06-105685-5, HarperPrism) HarpC.

***Waking Beauty.** Paul Witcover. 432p. 1997. 24.00 (0-06-105249-3, HarperPrism) HarpC.

Waking Dream: Photography's First Century, Selections from the Gilman Paper Company Collection. Maria M. Hambourg et al. LC 92-45131. 1993. 60.00 (0-87099-662-2, 0-8109-6427-9) Metro Mus Art.

Waking Dream: Unlocking the Symbolic Language of Our Lives. Ray Grasse. (Illus.). 285p. 1996. 22.95 (0-8356-0726-7, Quest); pap. 16.00 (0-8356-0749-6, Quest) Theos Pub Hse.

Waking, Dream & Deep Sleep. Swami Jyotinmayananda. (Illus.). 1974. pap. 3.99 (0-934664-10-2) Yoga Res Foun.

Waking Dream Therapy: Dream Process as Imagination. Gerald N. Epstein. 237p. 1992. pap. 15.00 (1-883148-03-0) ACMI Pr.

Waking Dreams. 3rd ed. Mary Watkins. LC 83-20435. viii, 174p. 1976. reprint ed. pap. 17.00 (0-88214-324-7) Spring Pubns.

Waking from Doctrinal Amnesia: The Healing of Doctrine in the United Methodist Church. William J. Abraham. 128p. (Orig.). 1995. pap. 9.95 (0-687-01718-1) Abingdon.

***Waking from the Dream.** Sam Fullwood. 1997. pap. 14.95 (0-385-47823-2, Anchor NY) Doubleday.

Waking from the Dream: A Wealth of Practical Information Relating to the Buddhist Path to Enlightenment. Detong Choyin. LC 96-46041. 320p. (Orig.). 1996. pap. 18.95 (0-8048-3084-3) C E Tuttle.

Waking From the Dream: My Life in the Black Middle Class. Sam Fulwood, 3rd. LC 95-40930. 304p. 1996. 23.95 (0-385-47822-4, Anchor NY) Doubleday.

Waking Giants: The Presence of the Past in Modernism. Herbert N. Schneidau. 304p. 1991. 45.00 (0-19-506862-9, 11846) OUP.

Waking Moments. Dawn B. Brimley. (Illus.). 50p. (Orig.). 1989. pap. write for info. (0-318-64718-4) D B Brimley.

Waking October Leaves: Reanimations by a Small-Town Girl. Virginia V. Hlavsa. 88p. 1993. 18.95 (1-56809-000-5); pap. 12.50 (1-56809-001-3) Time Being Bks.

Waking of Angantyr: The Scandinavian Past in European Culture. Jorgen H. Jorgensen. Ed. by Else Roesdahl & Preben M. Sorensen. (Acta Jutlandica Ser.). (Illus.). 232p. (Orig.). (DAN, ENG & SWE.). (C). 1996. pap. text ed. 27.00 (87-7288-435-5, Pub. by Aarhus Univ Pr DK) David Brown.

Waking of the Human Soul & the Forming of Destiny - The Need for Understanding Christ. Rudolf Steiner. Tr. by Olin D. Wannamaker. 25p. (GER.). 1983. reprint ed. pap. 3.95 (0-919924-19-0, Pub. by Steiner Book Centre CN) Anthroposophic.

W

Waking Passenger. Charles Black. Ed. by Maxine Cassin. (Journal Press Bks.: Louisiana Legacy). 80p. 1983. pap. 12.00 (0-938498-03-7) New Orleans Poetry.

***Waking Sleeping Beauty: Feminist Voices in Children's Novels.** Roberta S. Trites. LC 96-54875. 168p. 1997. 24.95 (0-87745-590-2); pap. 12.95 (0-87745-591-0) U of Iowa Pr.

Waking Spell. Carol Dawson. 312p. 1992. 19.95 (0-945575-65-3) Algonquin Bks.

Waking the Dead: Correspondences Between Walter Benjamin's Concept of Remembrance & Ingeborg Bachmann's Ways of Dying. Karen Remmler. (Studies in Austrian Literature, Culture & Thought; Translation Ser.). 174p. 1996. 26.95 (1-57241-028-0) Ariadne CA.

Waking the Moon. Elizabeth Hand. 512p. 1996. mass mkt. 5.99 (0-06-105443-7, HarperPrism) HarpC.

Waking the Moon. Elizabeth Hand. 400p. 1995. 19.00 (0-06-105214-0, HarperPrism) HarpC.

Waking the Pembrokeshire Coast Path. Patrick Stark. (C). 1990. pap. text ed. 50.00 (0-685-50437-9, Pub. by Gomer Pr UK) St Mut.

Waking the Slumbering Spirit. John Sandford et al. (Keys of Knowledge Ser.). 152p. 1993. pap. 10.00 (0-9637741-0-7) Clear Stream.

Waking the Tempests: Ordinary Life in the New Russia. Eleanor Randolph. 448p. 1996. 26.00 (0-684-80912-5) S&S Trade.

***Waking the Tiger - Healing Trauma: The Innate Capacity to Transform Overwhelming.** Peter A. Levine. LC 97-3918. 250p. (Orig.). 1997. pap. 12.95 (1-55643-233-X) North Atlantic.

Waking the World: Classic Tales of Women & the Heroic Feminine. A. B. Chinen. 304p. 1996. 24.95 (0-87477-818-2, Tarcher Putnam) Putnam Pub Group.

***Waking the World: Classic Tales of Women & the Heroic Feminine.** A. B. Chinen. 304p. (Orig.). 1997. reprint ed. 14.95 (0-87477-863-8, Tarcher Putnam) Putnam Pub Group.

Waking Their Neighbors Up: The Nashville Agrarians Rediscovered. Thomas D. Young. LC 81-14736. (Mercer University Lamar Memorial Lectures: No. 24). 96p. 1982. 12.00 (0-8203-0600-2) U of Ga Pr.

Waking to My Name: New & Selected Poems. Robert Pack. LC 79-3651. 272p. 1980. 25.00 (0-8018-2357-9) Johns Hopkins.

Waking to Wonder: Wittgenstein's Existential Investigations. Gordon C. Bearn. LC 96-28483. (SUNY Series in Philosophy). 256p. 1997. text ed. 65.50 (0-7914-3029-4); pap. text ed. 24.95 (0-7914-3030-8) State U NY Pr.

Waking Up: Overcoming the Obstacles to Human Potential. Charles T. Tart. LC 86-11844. 223p. 1987. pap. 20.00 (0-87773-426-7) Shambhala Pubns.

Waking up, Alive: The Descent, the Suicide Attempt, & the Return to Life. Richard A. Heckler. 320p. 1996. pap. 12.00 (0-345-40035-6) Ballantine.

Waking up Down South. Patricia B. Mitchell. 1992. pap. 4.00 (0-925117-65-X) Mitchells.

Waking up, Fighting Back: The Politics of Breast Cancer. Roberta Altman. 432p. 1996. 24.95 (0-316-03532-7); 23.95 (0-614-97048-2) Little.

Waking up from a Dream. Benjamin Deam. (Orig.). 1996. pap. write for info. (1-57553-183-6) Watermrk Pr.

Waking up in America. Ted Rall. 128p. (Orig.). 1992. pap. 6.95 (0-312-08518-4) St Martin.

Waking Up in the Middle of the Movie. Phil Kromka. 74p. (Orig.). 1995. pap. 8.95 (0-9652642-0-3) Ctr Hum Understand.

Waking Up Just in Time. Abraham J. Twerski & Charles M. Schulz. LC 95-3550. 1995. pap. 8.95 (0-312-13207-7) St Martin.

Waking up, Late. Gary Eddy. 1977. pap. 2.00 (0-918366-04-6) Slow Loris.

***Waking up Screaming from the American Dream: A Roving Reporter's Dispatches from the Bumpy Road to Success.** Bob Garfield. 320p. 1997. 23.00 (0-684-83218-6) S&S Trade.

Waking up the Organization to Internal Customer Service: Tools to Measure & Improve Human Resources & Other Internal Services. Andrew S. Bargerstock. 140p. 1996. ring bd. 39.00 (0-9639557-5-6, Jacob-Cameron) A R K Co.

Waking up to Wall Street. Danny J. Fontana. 112p. (Orig.). mass mkt. 5.95 (0-9646455-0-5) D Fontana Enter.

Waking up Together. Paul Williams. (Illus.). 202p. 1989. pap. 8.95 (0-934558-17-5) Entwhistle Bks.

***Waking up Together: Illuminations on the Road to Nowhere.** Paul Ferrini. (Illus.). 214p. (Orig.). 1996. 14.95 (1-879159-17-1) Heartways Pr.

Waking up Well. Linda F. Fleming. Ed. by Mary Abrams. 100p. (Orig.). 1990. pap. write for info. (1-877631-03-5) LF Pub VA.

Waking Upside Down. Philip Heckmsn. LC 95-7746. (Illus.). 40p. (J). (gr. 1-5). 1996. 16.00 (0-689-31930-4, Atheneum Bks Young) S&S Childrens.

Wal-Mart. Sandra S. Vance & Roy V. Scott. (Twayne's Evolution of Modern Business Ser.: No. 11). (Illus.). 256p. 1994. pap. 14.95 (0-8057-9833-1, Twayne) Scribnrs Ref.

Wal-Mart: A History of Sam Walton's Retail Phenomenon. Sandra S. Vance & Roy V. Scott. (Twayne's Evolution of Modern Business Ser.: No. 11). (Illus.). 256p. 1994. 26.95 (0-8057-9832-3, Twayne) Scribnrs Ref.

Walahfrid Strabo's Libellus de Exordiis et Incrementis Quarundam in Observationibus Ecclesiasticis Rerum. Walahfrid Strabo. (Mittellateinische Studien und Texte: Vol. 19). (LAT.). 1995. 142.50 (90-04-09669-8) E J Brill.

WALC One (Workbook of Activities for Language & Cognition) For Lower Levels of Cognition & Aphasia. Kathryn J. Tomlin. 1993. spiral bd. 37.95 (1-55999-397-9) LinguiSystems.

WALC Three (Workbook of Activities for Language & Cognition) Word Finding Organization Reasoning Visual Tasks. Kathryn J. Tomlin. 1993. spiral bd. 37.95 (1-55999-398-7) LinguiSystems.

WALC 2, the Original WALC (Workbook of Activities for Language & Cognition) rev. ed. Kathryn J. Tomlin. (Cognitive Rehabilitation Ser.: Pt. 1). 1986. student ed., spiral bd. 37.95 (1-55999-081-3) LinguiSystems.

Waldeck-Rousseau, Combes, & the Church: The Politics of Anticlericalism, 1899-1905. Malcolm O. Partin. LC 74-76167. 311p. reprint ed. pap. 88.70 (0-317-20441-6, 2023432) Bks Demand.

Waldecki Recollected: Poems by an Iconoclastic Surrealist. Michael Waldecki. Ed. by C. E. Caldwell. (Illus.). 120p. (C). Date not set. 17.95 (0-9646803-1-9) Plant Speak Prods.

***Waldemar Story: History of One of the Most Exclusive Camps for Girls in the South.** Sue V. Willet. LC 97-18750. (Illus.). 200p. 1997. 24.95 (1-57168-190-6, 190-6, Eakin Pr) Sunbelt Media.

Waldemar von Knoeringen: Der Veg vom Revolutionaren Sozialismus zur Sozialen Demokratie. Eine Politische Biographie. Hartmut Mehringer. Ed. by Institut fur Zeitgeschichte - Friedrich-Ebert-Stiftung Staff. (Schriftenreihe der Georg-von-Vollmar-Akademie Ser.). 529p. (GER.). 1989. lib. bdg. 38.00 (3-598-22021-9) K G Saur.

Walden. Henry David Thoreau. 298p. 1992. 17.00 (0-679-41896-2, Everymans Lib) Knopf.

Walden. Henry David Thoreau. LC 90-55348. (Courage Literary Classics Ser.). 208p. 1990. 5.98 (0-89471-879-7) Courage Bks.

Walden. Henry David Thoreau. Ed. by J. Lyndon Shanley. 376p. 1988. pap. text ed. 6.95 (0-691-01464-7) Princeton U Pr.

Walden. Henry David Thoreau. LC 91-50120. (Vintage Books - the Library of America). 320p. 1991. pap. 10.50 (0-679-73574-7, Vin) Random.

***Walden.** Henry David Thoreau. LC 96-50149. 1997. 17.00 (0-8070-1418-4) Beacon Pr.

Walden. Henry David Thoreau. Bd. with On the Duty of Civil Disobedience. 256p. 1962. Set pap. 5.00 (0-02-054720-X, 05472, Collier S&S) S&S Trade.

Walden. Henry David Thoreau. Ed. by Paul Sherman. Bd. with Civil Disobedience. LC 60-16148. LC 60-16148. (YA). (gr. 9 up). 1960. Set pap. 11.56 (0-395-05113-4, RivEd) HM.

***Walden.** Henry David Thoreau. 1997. 15.50 (0-679-43457-7, Modern Lib) Random.

***Walden.** Henry David Thoreau. Ed. & Intro. by Stephen A. Fender. (The World's Classics Ser.). (Illus.). 176p. 1997. pap. 8.95 (0-19-282982-3) OUP.

Walden. large type ed. Henry David Thoreau. 450p. 1995. lib. bdg. 24.00 (0-939495-82-1) North Bks.

Walden. Henry David Thoreau. 367p. 1983. reprint ed. lib. bdg. 21.95 (0-89966-466-0) Buccaneer Bks.

Walden, 2 vols., Set. Henry David Thoreau. Ed. by Franklin B. Sanborn. LC 80-2685. reprint ed. 58.50 (0-404-19080-4) AMS Pr.

Walden: A Case Study in Contemporary Criticism. Henry David Thoreau. Ed. by Michael Meyer. 416p. 1995. pap. text ed. 9.31 (0-312-09218-0) St Martin.

Walden: An Annotated Edition. annot. ed. Henry David Thoreau. Ed. by Walter Harding. LC 94-45347. (Illus.). 349p. 1995. 30.00 (0-395-72042-7) HM.

Walden: Essay on Civil Disobedience. Henry David Thoreau. (Airmont Classics Ser.). (YA). (gr. 10 up). 1965. mass mkt. 1.50 (0-8049-0083-3) Airmont.

Walden: On the Duty of Civil Disobedience. Henry David Thoreau. Ed. by Norman H. Pearson. 304p. (C). 1948. pap. text ed. 22.50 (0-03-009320-1) HB Coll Pubs.

Walden see **Writings of Henry D. Thoreau**

***Walden - A Different Drummer by William Melvin Kelley: Curriculum Unit.** Center for Learning Network Staff. (Novel - Drama Ser.). 120p. 1997. teacher ed. 18.95 (1-56077-508-4) Ctr Learning.

Walden AAA Road Atlas, 1989. Walden AAA World Atlas Staff. 1989. pap. write for info. (0-318-64764-8) Random.

***Walden & Civil Discobedience.** Ed. by Thoreau. (C). 1970. text ed. 2.95 (0-06-502367-6) Addison-Wesley.

Walden & Civil Disobedience. Henry David Thoreau. 1970. mass mkt. 5.50 (0-06-080615-X, Harp PBks) HarpC.

Walden & Civil Disobedience. Henry David Thoreau. 256p. 1942. pap. 4.95 (0-451-52377-6, Sig Classics) NAL-Dutton.

Walden & Civil Disobedience. Henry David Thoreau. (American Library). 440p. 1983. pap. 9.95 (0-14-039044-8, Penguin Classics) Viking Penguin.

Walden & On Duty of Civil Disobedience. Henry David Thoreau. 22.95 (0-8488-0644-1) Amereon Ltd.

Walden & On the Duty of Civil Disobedience. Henry David Thoreau. 255p. pap. 11.00 (0-02-54720X-1) Macmillan.

Walden & Other Writings. Henry David Thoreau. (Classics Ser.). 448p. 1983. mass mkt. 3.95 (0-553-21246-X, Bantam Classics) Bantam.

Walden & Other Writings. Henry David Thoreau. Ed. by Brooks Atkinson. (C). 1981. pap. text ed. write for info. (0-07-554267-6, T35) McGraw.

Walden & Other Writings. Henry David Thoreau. Ed. & Intro. by Brooks Atkinson. LC 50-13711. 1977. 10.95 (0-394-60421-0, Modern Lib) Random.

Walden & Other Writings. Henry David Thoreau. Ed. by William L. Howarth. 743p. (C). 1981. pap. text ed. write for info. (0-318-57303-2) Random.

Walden & Other Writings of Henry David Thoreau. Ed. by Brooks Atkinson. LC 92-50225. 784p. 1992. 19.50 (0-679-60004-3, Modern Lib) Random.

Walden & Resistance to Civil Government. 2nd ed. Henry David Thoreau. Ed. by Owen Thomas & William Rossi. (Critical Editions Ser.). (C). 1992. pap. text ed. 9.95 (0-393-95905-8) Norton.

Walden & Selected Essays. Henry David Thoreau. Ed. by George F. Whicher. (University Classics Ser.). 492p. 1992. reprint ed. spiral bd. 59.50 (0-87532-109-7) Hendricks House.

Walden-Gould, CO. rev. ed. Ed. by Trails Illustrated Staff. 1994. 8.99 (0-925873-35-7) Trails Illustrated.

Walden III: A Catholic America. Patrick A. O'Dougherty. LC 96-79986. 92p. (C). 1991. lib. bdg. 10.99 (0-9626665-1-3) Hellenist Amer Co.

Walden in the Western Reserve. Manny Barenholtz. (Illus.). 68p. 1989. 19.95 (0-9617637-1-X) CL Stock Images.

Walden Interviews. Ed. by David Cox. (C). 1990. 75.00 (1-85283-104-9, Pub. by Boxtree Ltd UK) St Mut.

Walden Notes. Joseph R. McElrath, Jr. 1971. pap. 3.95 (0-8220-1358-4) Cliffs.

Walden: or Life in the Woods. unabridged ed. Henry David Thoreau. (Thrift Editions Ser.). (Illus.). 224p. 1995. pap. text ed. 2.00 (0-486-28495-6) Dover.

Walden: or Life in the Woods: Selections from the American. Henry David Thoreau. LC 91-50878. (Pocket Classics Ser.). 1992. pap. 6.00 (0-87773-685-5, Sham Pckt Edits) Shambhala Pubns.

Walden Pond Caper. James Magorian. LC 83-71263. 148p. 1983. pap. 6.00 (0-930674-11-1) Black Oak.

Walden Ponderings: What's Right, What's Wrong, What Matters. Alan R. Walden. LC 95-78991. 288p. 1995. 22.95 (0-9635159-2-6) Pub Concepts.

Walden Remainder. 1992. 1.79 (1-56686-054-7) Mac Pub USA.

Walden Revisited. George F. Whicher. (University Classics Ser.). 93p. 1973. pap. 12.95 (0-87532-063-5) Hendricks House.

Walden (Thoreau) Milton. (Book Notes Ser.). (C). 1984. pap. 2.50 (0-8120-3447-3) Barron.

Walden Three. Jack Catran. 432p. (Orig.). 1989. pap. 14.95 (0-936162-30-9) Jade Pubns.

Walden Two. B. F. Skinner. (C). 1976. write for info. (0-318-56735-0) Macmillan.

Walden Two. B. F. Skinner. 320p. (C). 1976. pap. 5.95 (0-02-411510-X, Macmillan Coll) P-H.

Walden Two Notes. Cynthia C. McGowan. (gr. 10-12). 1979. pap. 3.95 (0-8220-1361-4) Cliffs.

Walden West. August Derleth. LC 92-50264. (North Coast Bks.). (Illus.). 278p. 1992. reprint ed. pap. 12.95 (0-299-13594-2); reprint ed. lib. bdg. 35.00 (0-299-13590-X) U of Wis Pr.

Walden, with Emerson's Essay on Thoreau. rev. ed. Henry David Thoreau. 320p. 1995. pap. 4.95 (0-460-87635-X, Everyman's Classic Lib) C E Tuttle.

Walden Zero: A Novella. Jorn K. Bramann. LC 87-63331. 140p. (Orig.). 1988. pap. 9.99 (0-945073-07-0) Nightsun MD.

Walden's Post Card Enthusiast Revisited. Ed. by Orville C. Walden. LC 82-70058. (Illus.). 224p. 1982. 7.95 (0-913782-09-2) Deltiologists Am.

Walden's Stove Trade Directory, 1892-93. 52p. 1992. reprint ed. pap. 10.00 (0-9612204-2-2) Autonomy Hse.

Waldgesellschaften der Neiderrheinischen Sandplatten, No. 64. Wolfgang Dinter. (Dissertationes Botanicae Ser.). (Illus.). 112p. 1982. pap. text ed. 40.00 (3-7682-1325-0) Lubrecht & Cramer.

Waldheim. Luc Rosenzweig & Bernard Cohen. Tr. by Josephine Bacon from FRE. (Illus.). 224p. 1987. 17.95 (1-55774-010-0) Hemed Bks.

Waldheim Report: International Commission of Historians. William Templer. 224p. 1994. pap. 40.00 (87-7289-206-4, Pub. by Mus Tusculanum DK) Paul & Co Pubs.

Waldo: A Young Wyoming Cowboy. J. C. Cantle. LC 93-80773. (Illus.). 160p. 1994. pap. 12.95 (0-943972-27-2) Adobe Road.

Waldo: Continuation of the Waldo Genealogy 1900-1943. C. S. Waldo. 295p. 1991. reprint ed. pap. 46.50 (0-8328-1950-6); reprint ed. lib. bdg. 56.50 (0-8328-1949-2) Higginson Bk Co.

Waldo: Pioneer Aviator. Waldo D. Waterman & Jack Carpenter. LC 87-73013. (Illus.). 502p. (Orig.). 1988. pap. 18.95 (0-9600736-0-4) Arsdalen Bosch.

Waldo & Magic, Inc. Robert A. Heinlein. 304p. 1986. mass mkt. 5.99 (0-345-33015-3, Del Rey) Ballantine.

Waldo Chronicles: A Training Log. Gwen Ingram. Ed. & Photos by Anne Montgomery. LC 96-76376. (Illus.). viii, 96p. 1996. pap. 10.95 (0-9652182-1-X) Lst Creek Llamaprnts.

***Waldo. Descendants of Cornelius Waldo, with Related Lines & Ancestry for 1-25 Years, 970-1995 (a Continuation of the 1883 & 1943 Waldo Genealogies)** George S. Waldo. 339p. 1996. reprint ed. pap. 49.00 (0-8328-5300-3); reprint ed. lib. bdg. 59.00 (0-8328-5299-6) Higginson Bk Co.

Waldo Duck. Wendy Kanno. (Funny Farm Ser.). (Illus.). (J). (gr. k-2). 1984. 9.95 (0-89868-157-X); pap. 3.95 (0-89868-158-8) ARO Pub.

Waldo Frank. Paul J. Carter. (Twayne's United States Authors Ser.). 1967. pap. 13.95 (0-8084-0313-3, T125) NCUP.

Waldo Frank, Prophet of Hispanic Regeneration. Michael A. Ogorzaly. LC 92-55007. (C). 1994. 36.50 (0-8387-5233-0) Bucknell U Pr.

Waldo Peirce. Margit Varga. (Illus.). 74p. 1941. 9.95 (0-8288-4001-6) Fr & Eur.

Waldo, Tell Me about Christmas. Hans Wilhelm. (Waldo, Tell Me about Ser.). (Illus.). 40p. (J). (gr. 3 up). 1989. 5.95 (0-8378-1846-X) Gibson.

***Waldo, Tell Me about Christmas.** Hans Wilhelm. (Waldo, Tell Me about... Ser.). (Illus.). (J). mass mkt. 5.95 (0-614-24935-X); mass mkt. 5.95 (0-614-24962-7) Regina Pr.

Waldo, Tell Me about Dying. Hans Wilhelm. (Waldo, Tell Me about Ser.). (Illus.). 1993. 5.95 (0-8378-5134-3) Gibson.

Waldo, Tell Me about God. Hans Wilhelm. (Waldo, Tell Me about Ser.). (Illus.). 40p. (J). (gr. 3 up). 1988. 4.95 (0-8378-1809-5) Gibson.

***Waldo, Tell Me about God.** Hans Wilhelm. (Waldo, Tell Me about... Ser.). (Illus.). (J). mass mkt. 5.95 (0-614-24933-3) Regina Pr.

Waldo, Tell Me about Guardian Angels. Hans Wilhelm. (Waldo, Tell Me about Ser.). (Illus.). 40p. (J). (gr. 3 up). 1988. 5.95 (0-8378-1811-7) Gibson.

***Waldo, Tell Me about Guardian Angels.** Hans Wilhelm. (Waldo, Tell Me about... Ser.). (Illus.). (J). mass mkt. 5.95 (0-614-24958-9) Regina Pr.

Waldo, Tell Me about Jesus. Hans Wilhelm. (Waldo, Tell Me about Ser.). (Illus.). 40p. (J). (gr. 3 up). 1988. 5.95 (0-8378-1812-5) Gibson.

***Waldo, Tell Me about Jesus.** Hans Wilhelm. (Waldo, Tell Me about... Ser.). (Illus.). (J). mass mkt. 5.95 (0-614-24934-1) Regina Pr.

An Asterisk (*) at the beginning of an entry indicates that the title is appearing in BIP for the first time.

Waldo, Tell Me about Me. Hans Wilhelm. (Waldo, Tell Me about Ser.). (Illus.). 40p. (J). (gr. 3 up). 1988. 5.95 (*0-8378-1810-9*) Gibson.

*__Waldo, Tell Me about Me.__ Hans Wilhelm. (Waldo, Tell Me about... Ser.). (Illus.). (J). mass mkt. 5.95 (*0-614-24932-5*) Regina Pr.

*__Waldo, Tell Me Where's Grandpa.__ Hans Wilhelm. (Waldo, Tell Me about Ser.). (Illus.). (J). 5.95 (*0-614-22056-4*) Regina Pr.

Waldo Trench. Henry B. Fuller. (Collected Works of Henry B. Fuller). 1988. reprint ed. lib. bdg. 59.00 (*0-7812-1207-3*) Rprt Serv.

Waldo Wizard. (Loony Balloonies Ser.). (Illus.). 8p. (J). (gr. k-3). 1992. pap. 3.95 (*1-56680-603-8*) Mad Hatter Pub.

Waldo y la Gran Busqueda. Martin Handford. LC 92-54508. (Illus.). 32p. (J). (ps up). 1993. 14.88 (*1-56402-230-7*) Candlewick Pr.

*__Waldoboro Vital Records, 1773 to 1891.__ Compiled by W. Colwell et al. 249p. 1997. reprint ed. pap. 25.00 (*0-8328-5922-2*) Higginson Bk Co.

Waldorf Education & Anthroposophy I: Nine Public Lectures, February 23, 1921-September 16, 1922. Rudolf Steiner. (Foundations of Waldorf Education Ser.: No. 13). 1995. pap. 14.95 (*0-88010-387-6*) Anthroposophic.

Waldorf Education & Anthroposophy II: Public Lectures 1923-1924. Rudolf Steiner. Tr. by Roland Everett from GER. (Foundations of Waldorf Education Ser.: No. 13). 288p. (Orig.). 1996. pap. 16.95 (*0-88010-388-4*) Anthroposophic.

Waldorf Hotel. Roger S. Lucas. (Illus.). 66p. 1997. pap. 9.00 (*1-887287-03-5*) Res Rev Pubns.

Waldorf Parenting Handbook: Useful Information on Child Development & Education from Anthroposophical Sources. 2nd rev. ed. Lois Cusick. 1988. pap. 17.95 (*0-916786-75-7*, Saint George Pubns) R Steiner Col Pubns.

Waldorf Song Book. Ed. by Brien Masters. (J). 1988. pap. 8.50 (*0-86315-059-4*, 20243, Pub. by Floris Bks UK) Gryphon Hse.

Waldorf Teacher's Survival Guide. Eugene M. Schwartz. 1992. pap. write for info. (*0-945803-21-4*) R Steiner Col Pubns.

Waldron's Continuation see Sad Shepherd

Waldstein Woolen Mill: Noble Entrepreneurship in 18th Century Bohemia. Herman Freudenberger. (Kress Library of Business & Economics Publication: No. 18). (Illus.). xi, 68p. 1963. pap. 9.95 (*0-678-09912-X*, Kress Lib Business) Kelley.

Walers: Australian Horses Abroad. A. T. Yarwood. (Miegunyah Press Ser.: No. 1:6). 252p. 1989. 39.95 (*0-522-84385-9*, Pub. by Melbourne Univ Pr AT) Paul & Co Pubs.

Wales. Central Office of Info. (Aspects of Britain Ser.). (Illus.). 88p. 1997. pap. 9.95 (*0-11-701754-X*, HM1754X, Pub. by Statnry Ofc UK) Seven Hills Bk.

Wales. William Condry. (Illus.). 239p. (C). 1993. pap. 30.00 (*0-86383-781-6*, Pub. by Gomer Pr UK) St Mut.

Wales. Kath Davies. LC 90-10192. (World in View Ser.). (Illus.). 96p. (YA). (gr. 6-12). 1990. lib. bdg. 25.68 (*0-8114-2437-5*) Raintree Steck-V.

Wales. Huws Gwilym. (World Bibliographical Ser.). 1991. lib. bdg. 77.50 (*1-85109-118-1*) ABC-CLIO.

*__Wales.__ Richard Keen & Ian Burgum. (Country Ser.). (Illus.). 160p. 1997. 24.95 (*0-297-83569-6*, Weidenfeld) Trafalgar.

Wales. Peter Sager. (Pallas Athene Guides Ser.). (Orig.). 1994. pap. 23.95 (*1-873429-00-2*, Pub. by Pallas Athene UK) Boydell & Brewer.

Wales. Ed. by Peter Sager. Tr. by David H. Wilson. (Illus.). 512p. 1995. pap. 24.95 (*1-873429-52-5*, Pub. by Pallas Athene UK) Boydell & Brewer.

Wales. Dorothy B. Sutherland. LC 86-29954. (Enchantment of the World Ser.). (Illus.). 128p. (J). (gr. 5-9). 1987. lib. bdg. 30.00 (*0-516-02794-8*) Childrens.

*__Wales.__ 2nd ed. (Rough Guide Ser.). 1997. pap. 17.95 (*1-85828-245-4*) Viking Penguin.

Wales: A Good Eating Guide. Roger Thomas. 1992. pap. 22.00 (*1-870948-73-4*, Pub. by Quiller Pr UK) St Mut.

Wales: 1937-1940. Ed. by Bloomfield Rhys. 310p. 1969. Set. 55.00 (*0-7146-2217-6*, Pub. by F Cass Pubs UK) Intl Spec Bk.

*__Wales & Cinema: The First Hundred Years.__ (Illus.). 567p. 1997. pap. 34.95 (*0-7083-1370-1*, Pub. by Univ Wales Pr UK) Paul & Co Pubs.

Wales & Cinema: The First One Hundred Years. Dave Berry. (Illus.). 600p. 1995. text ed. 49.95 (*0-614-08374-5*) Ind U Pr.

Wales & Cinema: The First One Hundred Years. David Berry. (Illus.). 584p. 1995. text ed. 49.95 (*0-85170-256-2*) Ind U Pr.

Wales & Medicine. Ed. by John Cule. 249p. (C). 1975. pap. 20.00 (*0-85088-260-5*, Pub. by Gomer Pr UK) St Mut.

Wales & the Wars of the Roses. H. T. Evans. (Illus.). 192p. 1996. 33.95 (*0-7509-0922-6*, Pub. by Sutton Pubng UK) Bks Intl VA.

*__Wales Bed & Breakfast 1997.__ WTB Staff. (Wales Tourist Board Ser.). 145p. (Orig.). 1997. pap. 6.95 (*1-85013-076-0*, Pub. by Jarrold Pub UK) Seven Hills Bk.

Wales Green Guide. Ed. by Michelin Travel Publications, Staff. 1996. per. 20.00 (*2-06-151001-9*, 1510) Michelin.

*__Wales Hotels, Guest Houses & Farmhouses 1997.__ WTB Staff. (Wales Tourist Board Ser.). 1997. pap. 7.95 (*1-85013-074-4*, Pub. by Jarrold Pub UK) Seven Hills Bk.

Wales in America: Scranton & the Welsh, 1860-1920. William D. Jones. 1996. 34.50 (*0-940866-20-X*) U Scranton Pr.

Wales in Pictures. Ed. by Lerner Publications, Department of Geography Staff. (Visual Geography Ser.). (Illus.). 64p. (YA). (gr. 5 up). 1990. lib. bdg. 19.95 (*0-8225-1877-5*, Lerner Publctns) Lerner Group.

Wales in the Reign of James I. G. Dyfnallt Owen. (Royal Historical Society: Studies in History: No. 53). 1988. 63.00 (*0-86193-210-2*) Boydell & Brewer.

Wales in Vision: The People & Politics of Television. Patrick Hannan. 164p. (C). 1990. 27.00 (*0-86383-549-X*, Pub. by Gomer Pr UK) St Mut.

Wales on the Wireless: A Broadcasting Anthology. Ed. by Patrick Hannan. 200p. (C). 1988. 30.00 (*0-86383-447-7*, Pub. by Gomer Pr UK) St Mut.

*__Wales Self Catering 1997.__ WTB Staff. (Wales Tourist Board Ser.). 145p. 1997. pap. 6.95 (*1-85013-075-2*, Pub. by Jarrold Pub UK) Seven Hills Bk.

Wales Today. Don Dale-Jones & W. Randal Jenkins. 144p. (C). 1976. pap. 45.00 (*0-85088-377-6*, Pub. by Gomer Pr UK) St Mut.

*__Wales/West Country/Midlands Map.__ 1996. 8.95 (*2-06-700403-4*, 403) Michelin.

Walford's Guide to Current British Periodicals in the Humanities & Social Sciences. Ed. by Albert J. Walford. LC 85-22665. 479p. 1985. reprint ed. pap. 136.60 (*0-7837-9276-X*, 2060014) Bks Demand.

*__Walford's Guide to Reference Material: Science & Technology, Vol. 1.__ 7th ed. 800p. 1996. 249.00 (*1-85604-165-4*, Pub. by Library Association UK) Bernan Associates.

Walford's Guide to Reference Material, Vol. 2: Social & Historical Sciences, Philosophy & Religion. Ed. by Alan Day et al. 960p. 1994. 210.00 (*1-85604-044-5*, LAP0445, Pub. by Library Association UK) Bernan Associates.

Walford's Oak. Jill M. Phillips. 386p. 1990. 18.95 (*0-8065-1159-1*, Citadel Pr) Carol Pub Group.

Walg: A Novel of Australia. B. Wongar. LC 83-11610. 213p. 1990. reprint ed. pap. 9.95 (*0-8076-1241-3*) Braziller.

Walid & His Friends: An Umayyad Tragedy. Robert Hamilton. (Oxford Studies in Islamic Art: Vol. VI). (Illus.). 196p. 1988. 65.00 (*0-19-728011-0*) OUP.

Waling Guide to Northern Flinders: Gammon Ranges NP & Arkaroola. Adrian Heard. 88p. (C). 1989. pap. text ed. 50.00 (*0-89771-024-X*, Pub. by Bob Mossel AT) St Mut.

*__Walk.__ Edward T. Lyons. (Orig.). 1997. pap. write for info. (*1-57553-484-3*) Watermrk Pr.

Walk. Robert Walser. Tr. by Christopher Middleton from GER. (Extraordinary Classics Ser.). 208p. 1993. reprint ed. pap. 15.99 (*1-85242-276-9*) Serpents Tail.

Walk: Notes on a Romantic Image. Jeffrey C. Robinson. LC 88-37876. (Illus.). 160p. 1989. 24.95 (*0-8061-2181-5*) U of Okla Pr.

Walk: The Measure of Spiritual Maturity. Gene A. Getz. 240p. 1994. 16.99 (*0-8054-6157-4*, 4261-57) Broadman.

Walk: The Trees Are Marked for You. G. Frederick Dirks. 238p. (Orig.). 1989. pap. 14.00 (*0-9621573-0-9*) G F Dirks.

Walk a Black Wind. Michael Collins. 186p. 1989. pap. 3.95 (*0-88184-500-0*) Carroll & Graf.

Walk a Crooked Mile. Catherine Dain. 208p. (Orig.). 1994. mass mkt. 3.99 (*0-515-11310-7*) Jove Pubns.

*__Walk a Green Path.__ Betsy Lewin. (J). Date not set. lib. bdg. 15.93 (*0-688-13426-2*) Lothrop.

Walk a Green Path. Betsy Lewin. LC 94-14824. (Illus.). 32p. (J). (gr. k up). 1995. 15.00 (*0-688-13425-4*) Lothrop.

Walk a Mile in His Truths: More Comedy Sketches on Walking the Talk. Martha Bolton. (Drama Resource Ser.). 1994. 8.99 (*0-8341-9124-5*, MP-751) Lillenas.

Walk a Mile in My Shoes. 1989. pap. 9.95 (*0-87868-349-6*) Child Welfare.

Walk a Straight Line to Freedom. Robert Nells. 1991. 7.95 (*0-533-08956-5*) Vantage.

*__Walk about Nenagh.__ Nancy Murphy. (Illus.). 139p. (Orig.). 1995. pap. 10.00 (*0-946327-12-2*, Pub. by Relay Pubns IE) Irish Bks Media.

Walk about the Villages: A Dramatic Poem. Peter Handke. Tr. & Afterword by Michael Roloff. (Studies in Austrian Literature, Culture, & Thought). Orig. Title: Uber die Dorfer. 153p. (Orig.). 1996. pap. 14.95 (*1-57241-000-0*) Ariadne CA.

Walk Across America. Peter Jenkins. 336p. (Orig.). 1983. mass mkt. 6.99 (*0-449-20455-3*, Crest) Fawcett.

*__Walk Across Corporate America.__ Paul Wolsfeld. Date not set. write for info. (*0-688-08705-1*) Morrow.

*__Walk Across England.__ Richard Long. LC 97-60275. 192p. (Orig.). 1997. pap. 29.95 (*0-500-27976-4*) Thames Hudson.

Walk Across France. Miles Morland. Orig. Title: Miles Away. 256p. 1994. reprint ed. pap. 10.00 (*0-449-90945-X*) Fawcett.

Walk Aerobics. Les Snowdon & Maggie Humphreys. LC 94-46376. (Illus.). 176p. 1995. 21.95 (*0-87951-590-2*) Overlook Pr.

Walk Aerobics. Les Snowdon & Maggie Humphreys. 173p. 1996. pap. 11.95 (*0-87951-665-8*) Overlook Pr.

*__Walk along Land's End: Pioneering California's Coastal Footpath.__ John McKinney. pap. 10.00 (*0-06-258607-6*) HarpC.

Walk, Amble, Stroll. Dee A. Holisky. 1992. pap. 21.95 (*0-8384-2280-2*) Heinle & Heinle.

Walk, Amble, Stroll L1 & L2. Dee A. Holisky. (College ESL Ser.). 1996. pap. 7.95 (*0-8384-5985-4*) Heinle & Heinle.

Walk Among the Tombstones. large type ed. Lawrence Block. LC 93-16773. 1993. lib. bdg. 22.95 (*0-8161-5759-6*, GK Hall) Thorndike Pr.

Walk among the Tombstones. Lawrence Block. 336p. 1993. reprint ed. mass mkt. 5.99 (*0-380-71375-6*) Avon.

Walk among Tombstones. Lawrence Block. 4.98 (*0-8317-8575-6*) Smithmark.

Walk Around the Block: Using Our Communities in the Present to Learn about the Past & Plan for the Future. Ginny Graves. 115p. 1992. teacher ed. 35.00 (*0-9632033-0-4*) Ctr Under Built.

Walk Around the Downs. Roy Chapman. 64p. 1987. pap. 30.00 (*0-905392-04-0*) St Mut.

Walk Around the World: Healings, Miracles, Power Encounters & Other First Person Accounts from Earth's Frontiers. Compiled by Marilynne E. Foster. LC 95-83955. 164p. 1996. pap. 8.99 (*0-87509-639-5*) Chr Pubns.

Walk Away, Joe. Pamela Toth. (Special Edition Ser.). 1993. mass mkt. 3.50 (*0-373-09850-2*, 5-09850-4) Silhouette.

Walk Awhile in My Shoes, Then We Can Walk Together. J. L. Thomas. 310p. 1995. 18.95 (*0-935243-04-6*) Thomas Ent.

*__Walk Back in Time.__ Tabitha Lewis-Blue. Ed. by C. Hsanni Wade. (Illus.). 84p. (Orig.). 1996. pap. 8.75 (*0-9655369-0-4*) Ts Enterprises.

Walk-Behind Lawn Mower Service Manual. 4th ed. Intertec Publishing Staff. 1991. 24.95 (*0-87288-450-3*, WLMS-4) Intertec Pub.

Walk by Faith. Doris Powell. (Illus.). 274p. (Orig.). 1992. pap. 9.95 (*0-9618256-2-6*) D Powell Pub.

Walk by the Seashore. Caroline Arnold. Ed. by Bonnie Brook. (First Facts: Natural Sciences Ser.). (Illus.). 32p. (J). (ps-1). 1990. lib. bdg. 6.95 (*0-671-68662-3*, Silver Pr NJ) Silver Burdett Pr.

Walk by the Seashore. Caroline Arnold. Ed. by Bonnie Brook. (First Facts: Natural Sciences Ser.). (Illus.). 32p. (J). (ps-1). 1990. pap. 4.95 (*0-382-24648-9*, Silver Pr NJ) Silver Burdett Pr.

Walk Cheerfully: The Middleroad. J. Stanley Banker. LC 94-7299. (Illus.). 1994. 9.95 (*0-944350-33-X*) Friends United.

Walk Cheerfully Friends. Seth B. Hinshaw. (Illus.). 152p. (Orig.). 1978. pap. 5.50 (*0-942727-06-1*) NC Yrly Pubns Bd.

Walk, Don't Die: How to Stay Fit, Trim & Healthy Without Killing Yourself. Fred A. Stutman. LC 85-63360. (Illus.). 256p. (Orig.). 1986. 18.95 (*0-934232-06-7*); pap. 9.95 (*0-934232-05-9*) Med Manor Bks.

Walk Don't Run. Elvira Monroe. LC 79-63351. 1979. pap. 3.95 (*0-933174-04-7*) Wide World-Tetra.

Walk, Don't Run: The Doctor's Book of Walking. Fred A. Stutman. LC 79-84815. 97p. 1979. pap. 6.95 (*0-934232-00-8*) Med Manor Bks.

*__Walk Don't Walk.__ Gordan Williams. Date not set. write for info. (*0-688-05112-X*) Morrow.

Walk Down Main Street. Ruth Moore. 386p. 1988. reprint ed. pap. 10.95 (*0-942396-56-1*) Blackberry ME.

Walk down the Tiger's Tail. Ed. by Jill Breckenridge & Bob Kearney. (Illus.). 164p. (Orig.). 1982. pap. 5.00 (*0-927663-09-0*) COMPAS.

Walk Down to the Sea with Me see Short Story Longs

Walk Gently This Good Earth. Margaret Craven. 1995. reprint ed. lib. bdg. 21.95 (*1-56849-646-X*) Buccaneer Bks.

Walk Historic Halifax: Walking Guide to an Historic Capital. Grant MacLean. (Illus.). 128p. 1996. pap. 12.95 (*1-55109-135-6*, Pub. by Nimbus Publishing Ltd CN) Chelsea Green Pub.

Walk-In: An Inspiring Story of a Spiritual Homecoming. Juelle. LC 95-79681. 220p. 1995. pap. 14.95 (*1-885221-24-X*) BookPartners.

Walk in Balance: Meditations with Lynn Andrews. Lynn V. Andrews. LC 92-56125. (Illus.). 279p. 1994. pap. 14.00 (*0-06-250009-0*) Harper SF.

Walk in Balance: The Path to Healthy, Happy, Harmonious Living. Sun Bear & Sheila Mulligan. 224p. 1989. pap. 11.00 (*0-671-76564-7*) P-H.

Walk in Beauty. Ruth Wind. (Special Edition Ser.). 1994. mass mkt. 3.50 (*0-373-09881-2*, 5-09881-9) Silhouette.

Walk in Dry Places. Mel B. 400p. 1996. pap. text ed. 11.00 (*1-56838-127-1*) Hazelden.

Walk in East Berkshire. Mick Tapp. 64p. 1987. pap. 45.00 (*0-905392-28-0*) St Mut.

Walk in Monet's Garden: A Pop-up Book. Illus. by Francesca Crespi. 9p. 1995. 19.95 (*0-8212-2195-7*) Bulfinch Pr.

Walk in My Shoes: Stories of a Trinidadian-American. Rodney Foster. LC 93-86881. (Illus.). 165p. (Orig.). 1993. pap. text ed. 13.95 (*0-9638604-3-7*) Rememb When.

Walk in My Soul. Lucia St. Clair Robson. 1985. pap. 8.95 (*0-345-30789-5*, Ballantine Trade) Ballantine.

Walk in My Soul. Lucia St. Clair Robson. LC 84-91666. 608p. 1987. mass mkt. 5.99 (*0-345-34701-3*) Ballantine.

Walk in Peace: Legends & Stories of the Michigan Indians. 2nd ed. Simon Otto. Ed. by M. T. Bussey. (Illus.). 50p. (J). (gr. 3-4). 1992. pap. 9.95 (*0-9617707-5-9*) Grnd Rpds Intertribal.

Walk in Spirit: Prayers for the Seasons of Life. Lynn V. Andrews. (Illus.). 120p. 1996. 14.95 (*0-9650958-0-0*) Acacia Pubng.

Walk in the Clouds. Deborah Chiel. 1995. mass mkt. 4.99 (*0-451-18593-5*, Sig) NAL-Dutton.

Walk in the Desert. Caroline Arnold. Ed. by Bonnie Brook. (Illus.). 32p. (J). (ps-1). 1990. lib. bdg. 6.95 (*0-671-68664-X*, Silver Pr NJ) Silver Burdett Pr.

Walk in the Desert. Caroline Arnold. Ed. by Bonnie Brook. (First Facts: Natural Sciences Ser.). (Illus.). 32p. (J). (ps-1). 1990. pap. 4.95 (*0-382-24649-7*, Silver Pr NJ) Silver Burdett Pr.

Walk in the Fire: Scenes from the Life of an American Jew, Vol. 4. John Sanford. LC 89-847. 328p. (Orig.). 1989. 20.00 (*0-87685-758-6*); pap. 12.50 (*0-87685-757-8*) Black Sparrow.

Walk in the Fire: Scenes from the Life of an American Jew, Vol. 4, signed ed. deluxe limited ed. John Sanford. LC 89-847. 328p. (Orig.). 1989. 30.00 (*0-87685-759-4*) Black Sparrow.

Walk in the Garden. Christopher L. Hannah. LC 95-62368. 208p. (Orig.). 1996. pap. 12.00 (*0-9623712-9-7*) Tafford Pub.

Walk in the Garden: Biblical Iconographical & Literary Images of Eden. Morris & Sawyer. (Journal for the Study of the Old Testament Supplement Ser.: No. 136). 327p. (C). 1992. 70.00 (*1-85075-338-5*, Pub. by Sheffield Acad UK) CUP Services.

Walk in the Light. Anna M. Cottrell. Ed. by Nancy Wikingstad. LC 87-15821. (Illus.). 128p. (Orig.). 1987. pap. 9.95 (*0-931892-12-0*) B Dolphin Pub.

Walk in the Light: A Pastoral Response to Child Sexual Abuse. USCC Staff. 16p. (Orig.). 1995. pap. 1.25 (*1-57455-000-4*) US Catholic.

Walk in the Night & Other Stories. Alex LaGuma. 129p. 1967. pap. 10.95 (*0-8101-0139-4*) Northwestern U Pr.

Walk in the Paradise Garden. large type ed. Anne Maybury. 1983. 15.95 (*0-7089-1004-1*) Ulverscroft.

*__Walk in the Park.__ Russell L. Drake. 80p. (Orig.). 1997. pap. 14.00 (*0-9657007-0-4*) Exordium Communs.

Walk in the Park: Acadia's Hiking Guide. rev. ed. Tom St. Germain. Ed. by Jay Saunders. (Illus.). 1993. pap. text ed. 10.95 (*0-9629997-4-1*) Parkman Pubns.

Walk in the Rainforest. Kristin J. Pratt. (Illus.). 32p. (J). (ps-7). 1992. 16.95 (*1-878265-99-7*); pap. 7.95 (*1-878265-53-9*) Dawn CA.

*__Walk in the Rose Garden.__ Kristi Stevens. 208p. 1997. 30.00 (*0-06-039198-7*, ReganBooks) HarpC.

Walk in the Sky: The First Ascent of Hidden Peak. Nicholas Clinch. LC 82-18778. (Illus.). 214p. 1982. 18.00 (*0-89886-042-3*) Mountaineers.

Walk in the Spirit. Gloria Copeland. 90p. 1986. pap. 5.95 (*0-88114-280-8*) K Copeland Pubns.

Walk in the Spring Rain & The Orchard Children. Rachel Maddux. LC 92-4980. 344p. 1992. 31.95 (*0-87049-757-X*) U of Tenn Pr.

Walk in the Sun. Harry Brown. 187p. 1985. pap. 3.95 (*0-88184-117-X*) Carroll & Graf.

Walk in the Sun. Philip S. Callahan. LC 88-71244. (Illus.). 242p. 1988. pap. 11.25 (*0-911311-13-0*) Acres USA.

Walk in the Sun. Harry Brown. 1993. reprint ed. lib. bdg. 16.95 (*1-56849-191-3*) Buccaneer Bks.

Walk in the White Horse Country. Nigel Hammond. 80p. 1987. 30.00 (*0-905392-14-0*) St Mut.

Walk in the Wild: Exploring a Wildlife Refuge. Lorraine Ward. (Illus.). 32p. (J). 1993. pap. 7.95 (*0-88106-478-5*); lib. bdg. 16.88 (*0-88106-480-7*) Charlesbridge Pub.

Walk in the Woods. Caroline Arnold. Ed. by Bonnie Brook. (First Facts: Natural Sciences Ser.). (Illus.). 32p. (J). (ps-1). 1990. lib. bdg. 6.95 (*0-671-68661-5*, Silver Pr NJ) Silver Burdett Pr.

Walk in the Woods. Caroline Arnold. Ed. by Bonnie Brook. (First Facts: Natural Sciences Ser.). (Illus.). 32p. (J). (ps-1). 1990. pap. 4.95 (*0-382-24650-0*, Silver Pr NJ) Silver Burdett Pr.

Walk in the Woods. Lee Blessing. 1988. pap. 5.25 (*0-8222-1220-X*) Dramatists Play.

Walk in the Woods. Lee Blessing. 1988. mass mkt. 6.95 (*0-452-26199-6*, Plume) NAL-Dutton.

Walk in the Woods. Cristin Couture. (J). 1993. 15.00 (*0-374-38227-1*) FS&G.

*__Walk in the Woods: A Great Grandpa Day Book.__ Eric Larsen. (Illus.). 32p. (J). (gr. 1-2). 1997. pap. 4.95 (*1-879432-28-5*) Explorers Guide Pub.

Walk in Winter. Sean Street. 40p. 8900. reprint ed. pap. 11.95 (*1-870612-25-6*, Pub. by Enitha Pr UK) Dufour.

Walk in Wolf Wood. Mary Stewart. 192p. 1987. mass mkt. 5.99 (*0-449-21422-2*) Fawcett.

*__Walk in Woods.__ Mouse Works Staff. 1997. 3.98 (*1-57082-563-7*) Mouse Works.

Walk in Yard. Dodd. 300p. (C). lib. bdg. 34.95 (*0-226-15496-3*) U Ch Pr.

Walk in Your Soul: Love Incantations of the Oklahoma Cherokees. Jack F. Kilpatrick & Anna G. Kilpatrick. LC 65-24931. (Illus.). 176p. 1965. pap. 6.95 (*0-87074-186-1*) SMU Press.

Walk-Ins: Soul Exchange. unabridged ed. Karyn K. Mitchell. (Illus.). 200p. (Orig.). Date not set. pap. 19.95 (*0-9640822-4-1*) Mind Rivers.

Walk into April. Sam Ragan. 1986. 10.00 (*0-932662-62-5*) St Andrews NC.

Walk into Darkness. large type ed. Julie Ellis. 288p. 1995. 25.99 (*0-7089-3363-7*) Ulverscroft.

Walk into Shape. Ed. by Consumer Guide Editors. 1997. pap. 5.99 (*0-451-19068-8*, Sig) NAL-Dutton.

Walk into the Night. Beverly Bird. 480p. 1996. mass mkt. 5.99 (*0-7860-0220-4*, Pinncle Kensgtn) Kensgtn Pub Corp.

Walk It Off: Twenty Minutes a Day to Health & Fitness. Suzanne M. Levine & Ronni Sandroff. (Illus.). 224p. (Orig.). 1990. pap. 11.95 (*0-452-26535-5*, Plume) NAL-Dutton.

*__Walk Like a Giant, Sell Like a Madman.__ Ralph R. Roberts. LC 97-8008. 1997. write for info. (*0-88730-843-0*) HarpC.

*__Walk Like an Athlete.__ Jeff Salvage & Gary Westerfield. (Illus.). 128p. (Orig.). 1996. pap. 14.95 (*0-9655328-0-1*) J Salvage.

An Asterisk (*) at the beginning of an entry indicates that the title is appearing in BIP for the first time.

Walk Log: Diary & Guide for the Exercise Walker. Don Lawrence & Debbi Lawrence. (SportsLog Ser.). (Illus.). 192p. 1995. reprint ed. ring bd. 9.95 (*1-57028-053-3*) Masters Pr IN.

Walk Los Angeles: Adventures on the Urban Edge. John C. McKinney. (Illus.). 310p. (Orig.). 1992. pap. 12.95 (*0-685-49237-0*) Olympus Pr.

Walk My Journey, Walk Your Journey: Stop to Learn & Lead a Lesson in Life & Smell the Rose along the Way. John B. Beer. 120p. 1993. 11.95 (*0-8059-3359-X*) Dorrance.

Walk of a Queen. Annie M. Smithson. 1988. pap. 12.95 (*0-85342-864-6*) Dufour.

Walk On. Mel Williamson & George Ford. (Illus.). 32p. (J). (gr. 3 up). 1972. 11.95 (*0-89388-042-6*) Okpaku Communications.

Walk on in Peace. Dorothy Edgerton. LC 82-73133. 64p. (Orig.). 1982. pap. 2.95 (*0-87029-187-4*, 20278-8) Abbey.

Walk on the Canol Road. S. R. Gage. 152p. 1990. 24.95 (*0-88962-439-9*); pap. 12.95 (*0-88962-438-0*) Mosaic.

Walk on the Great Barrier Reef. Caroline Arnold. (Nature Watch Bks.). (Illus.). 48p. (J). (gr. 2-5). 1988. lib. bdg. 14.96 (*0-87614-285-4*, Carolrhoda) Lerner Group.

Walk on the Waves: Matthew 14:13-32: Jesus Walks on the Water. Mary M. Simon. LC 92-21374. (Hear Me Read Ser.: Level 2). (Illus.). 32p. (Orig.). (J). (gr. 1-3). 1993. pap. 3.99 (*0-570-04735-8*, 56-1692) Concordia.

Walk on the Wild Side. Jeanette Jones. 144p. 1995. 30.00 (*1-56980-054-5*) Barricade Bks.

Walk on the Wild Side. Kathleen Korbel. (Intimate Moments Ser.). 1992. mass mkt. 3.39 (*0-373-07457-3*, 5-07457-0) Silhouette.

***Walk on the Wild Side.** Dennis Rodman. LC 96-52389. 1997. mass mkt. 18.95 (*0-385-31897-9*) Doubleday.

***Walk on the Wild Side.** Dennis Rodman & Michael Silver. 1997. 22.95 (*0-614-28178-4*) Delacorte.

Walk on the Wild Side. Connie Roop & Peter Roop. LC 96-7708. (Illus.). 40p. (J). (gr. 3-6). 1997. lib. bdg. 15.90 (*0-7613-0021-X*) Millbrook Pr.

Walk on the Wild Side. Nelson Algren. LC 78-509. 346p. 1978. reprint ed. text ed. 47.50 (*0-313-20294-X*, ALWW, Greenwood Pr) Greenwood.

Walk on the Wild Side. Nelson Algren. (Classic Reprint Ser.). 368p. 1990. reprint ed. pap. 12.95 (*0-938410-80-6*) Thunders Mouth.

Walk on the Wild Side: Urban American Poetry since 1975. Ed. by Nicholas Christopher. LC 93-29443. 230p. 1994. pap. 12.00 (*0-02-042725-5*) Macmillan.

Walk on Water. Don Thornton. 44p. (Orig.). 1985. pap. 4.00 (*0-933727-00-3*) Cajun Pubs.

Walk on Water, Pete! see Peter Promise: Powerful Principles from the Life of Peter

Walk Quietly Through the Night & Cry Softly. Burniece Avery. LC 77-2891. (Illus.). 1977. 7.00 (*0-913642-08-8*) Balamp Pub.

***Walk, Run, Jog for Wellness Everyone.** 3rd ed. Floyd & Parke. 334p. 1996. pap. text ed. 21.95 (*0-88725-235-4*) Hunter Textbks.

Walk, Run, or Retreat: The Modern School Administrator. Neil V. Sullivan et al. LC 71-135013. 192p. reprint ed. 54.80 (*0-8357-9253-6*, 2017642) Bks Demand.

Walk Safe Through the Jungle. Katharine E. Matchette. LC 74-2085. (Illus.). 140p. (J). (gr. 4-9). 1996. pap. 8.75 (*0-9645045-1-0*) Deka Pr.

Walk Santa Barbara: City Strolls & Country Rambles. John C. McKinney & Cheri Rae. (Illus.). 176p. (Orig.). 1990. pap. 10.95 (*0-934161-06-2*) Olympus Pr.

Walk Slowly: Poems & Drawings. John Campos. LC 86-83186. (Illus.). 80p. (Orig.). 1987. pap. 5.00 (*0-917021-02-9*) Lighthouse Pr.

***Walk Softly, This Is God's Country: Sixty-Six Years on the Wind River Indian Reservation.** Beatrice Crofts & Elinore Markley. (Illus.). 160p. 1997. pap. 9.95 (*0-9658855-1-8*) Mortimore Pub.

Walk! Stroll! Hike! Vol. 1: Selected Oregon Trails, Day Walks of Interest for Those Seeking Pleasant Exercise. Greg Foster & Andrea Foster. (Illus.). 104p. (Orig.). 1995. pap. 9.95 (*0-9651059-0-3*) G & A Foster.

Walk! Stroll! Hike! Vol. 2: Selected Oregon Trails, Day Walks of Interest for Those Seeking Pleasant Exercise. Greg Foster & Andrea Foster. (Illus.). 104p. (Orig.). 1996. pap. 9.95 (*0-9651059-1-1*) G & A Foster.

Walk Tall: A Tale of Love & Loyalty. Jean Hamilton. 162p. (C). 1989. 49.00 (*0-905928-96-2*, Pub. by D Brown & Sons Ltd UK) St Mut.

Walk Tall: Affirmations for People of Color. Carleen Brice. 384p. (Orig.). 1994. pap. 9.95 (*0-941405-51-6*) RPI Pubng.

***Walk Tall: Affirmations for People of Color.** Carleen Brice. 384p. 1997. reprint ed. pap. 12.00 (*0-8070-2811-8*) Beacon Pr.

Walk Tall, You're a Daughter of God. Jamie Glenn. LC 94-3696. viii, 125p. (Orig.). (YA). (gr. 7-12). 1994. pap. 7.95 (*0-87579-868-3*) Deseret Bk.

Walk the Crooked Road with the Crooks. Gyeorgos C. Hatonn. (Phoenix Journals). 213p. 1994. pap. 6.00 (*1-56935-040-X*) Phoenix Source.

***Walk the Dark Streets.** (J). 1997. write for info. (*0-614-29221-2*) FS&G.

Walk the Dog Willie. R. Auletta. 1985. pap. 5.95 (*0-88145-032-4*) Broadway Play.

Walk the Edge of Panic. Karl Goodman. LC 85-51447. 192p. 1985. 12.98 (*0-88290-309-8*, 1962) Horizon Utah.

Walk the Four Seasons: Walking & Cross-Training Logbook. Robert Sweetgall. (Illus.). 112p. (Orig.). (C). 1992. student ed., pap. 7.95 (*0-939041-14-6*) Creative Walking.

***Walk the Rainbow: When You Get Tired of Waiting to Exhale.** Christine Johnson. 145p. 1994. pap. text ed. 12.95 (*0-9642257-4-3*) Sido-Mari Pubns.

Walk the Talk: And Get the Results You Want. Eric Harvey & Alexander Lucia. LC 94-69986. 176p. 1995. 18.95 (*1-885228-25-2*) Performce Pub.

Walk the Walk & Talk the Talk: An Ethnography of a Drug Abuse Treatment Facility. Geoffrey R. Skoll. 250p. (C). 1992. 44.95 (*0-87722-917-1*) Temple U Pr.

Walk the World's Rim. Betty Baker. LC 65-11458. 192p. (J). (gr. 5 up). 1965. lib. bdg. 14.89 (*0-06-020381-1*) HarpC Child Bks.

***Walk This Way.** Aerosmith. LC 97-25598. 1997. 25.00 (*0-380-97594-7*) Avon.

Walk This Way. Andrea Bargsley. LC 94-69058. (Illus.). 28p. (J). (gr. k-3). 1994. 14.95 (*1-885340-08-7*) Coming Age Pr.

Walk This Way. Brenda V. Miller. LC 96-94272. (Illus.). 126p. (Orig.). 1996. pap. 7.95 (*0-9635630-1-7*) Global Promise.

Walk This Way: Spirit-Filled Life. Keith Davy. (Inter Acta Ser.). (Illus.). 6p. (C). 1994. teacher ed., ring bd. 1.25 (*1-885702-03-5*, 741-011t, Inter Acta); student ed., ring bd. 3.25 (*1-885702-02-7*, 741-011s, Inter Acta) WSN Pr.

Walk This Way Please: On Foot on the Monterey Peninsula, Carmel, Carmel Valley & Big Sur. Irene Gaasch. (Illus.). 96p. (Orig.). 1984. pap. 6.95 (*0-685-08464-7*) Hummbird Pr.

Walk Through Biosphere 2: Coloring Book. Sandra Dunn. (Imagine a Biosphere Ser.). (Illus.). 16p. (J). (gr. 3 up). 1993. pap. 4.00 (*1-882428-00-5*) Biosphere Pr.

Walk Through Britain. Roy H. Eardley. (Illus.). 136p. 1994. 19.95 (*0-8059-3484-7*) Dorrance.

Walk-Through Computer Book. Date not set. 35.00 (*0-517-70084-0*) Random Hse Value.

Walk Through Fire. William Cobb. 464p. 1993. mass mkt. 5.50 (*0-380-71832-4*) Avon.

Walk Through Graceland Cemetery: A Chicago Architecture Foundation Walking Tour. 3rd ed. Barbara Lanctot. (Illus.). 68p. 1988. pap. 6.95 (*0-9620562-0-0*) Chi Arch Fndtn.

Walk Through Graceland Cemetery: A Chicago Architecture Foundation Walking Tour. 4th ed. Barbara Lanctot. (Illus.). 68p. 1992. reprint ed. pap. text ed. write for info. (*0-318-69176-0*) Chi Arch Fndtn.

Walk Through Lymington. Ed. by Edward King. (C). 1989. 39.00 (*1-85455-056-X*, Pub. by Ensign Pubns & Print UK) St Mut.

Walk Through Our Kitchen Garden. Judy Walter. 60p. (Orig.). 1985. pap. 6.95 (*0-9614650-1-8*) Herb Farm Pr.

***Walk Through Paradise.** Ed. by Nicole Walstrum. 1996. 69.95 (*0-614-23671-1*) Nat Lib Poetry.

Walk Through the Cloisters. Bonnie Young. 1989. 24.95 (*0-8109-1795-5*) Abrams.

Walk Through the Cloisters. rev. ed. Bonnie Young. (Illus.). 144p. (Orig.). 1989. 19.95 (*0-87099-532-4*, 0-8109-1795-5); pap. 12.95 (*0-87099-533-2*) Metro Mus Art.

Walk Through the English Countryside. Barbara Fleming. (C). 1990. text ed. 35.00 (*0-7223-2546-0*, Pub. by A H S Ltd UK) St Mut.

Walk Through the Heavens: A Guide to Stars & Constellations & Their Legends. Milton D. Heifetz & Wil Tirion. (Illus.). 80p. (C). 1996. pap. text ed. 9.95 (*0-521-46980-5*) Cambridge U Pr.

Walk Through the Human Heart: A Poem. Robley Wilson. (Illus.). 16p. (Orig.). 1996. pap. 3.50 (*1-884235-17-4*) Helicon Nine Eds.

Walk Through the Mind of One Traveling the Inner Way. Willie J. Stratford, Sr. 88p. (Orig.). 1992. pap. 9.95 (*0-9635676-0-8*) Writing MD.

Walk Through the Minnesota Zoo. Jeanne M. Gangelhoff & Bradford Belk. (Illus.). 32p. (J). 9.95 (*0-9635006-1-9*) G J & B Pub.

Walk Through the Rain Forest: Life in the Ituri Forest of Zaire. David Jenike & Mark Jenike. (Cincinnati Zoo Bks.). (Illus.). 64p. (J). (gr. 3-8). 1994. lib. bdg. 22.70 (*0-531-11168-7*) Watts.

Walk Through the Rain Forest: Life in the Ituri Forest of Zaire. David Jenike & Mark Jenike. (Cincinnati Zoo Bks.). (Illus.). 56p. (J). (gr. 4-6). 1994. pap. 9.95 (*0-531-15721-0*) Watts.

Walk Through the Woods of Minnesota. Jeanne M. Gangelhoff & Bradford Belk. (Illus.). 32p. 1992. 9.95 (*0-9635006-0-0*) G J & B Pub.

Walk Through the Yellow Pages. Agha S. Ali. (Illus.). 32p. (Orig.). 1987. Hand-sewn wrappers. 20.00 (*0-933313-06-3*); pap. 4.50 (*0-933313-07-1*) SUN Gemini Pr.

Walk Through Walden Woods. Photos by Deck Higgins. LC 94-1802. (J). 1994. 14.95 (*0-590-48505-9*) Scholastic Inc.

Walk Through Wales. Anthony Bailey. LC 92-52577. 304p. 1993. reprint ed. pap. 12.00 (*0-06-118008-4*, PL) HarpC.

***Walk Thru Life with Poems.** M. Eugene Wright. (Orig.). 1997. pap. write for info. (*1-57553-476-2*) Watermrk Pr.

Walk to Complete Fitness. John Johnson. (Illus.). 185p. (Orig.). (C). 1991. pap. text ed. 13.95 (*0-89641-208-3*) American Pr.

Walk to Somewhere: On the Road During the Great Depression. John A. Palmer. Ed. by Suzanne Stasa. (Illus.). 88p. (Orig.). pap. 9.95 (*1-56550-015-6*) Vis Bks Intl.

Walk to the Great Mystery. Virginia A. Stroud. LC 93-32340. (Illus.). 32p. (J). 1995. pap. 14.99 (*0-8037-1636-2*) Dial Bks Young.

Walk to the Western Isles. Frank Delaney. 1994. 30.00 (*0-246-13745-2*) Granada UK.

***Walk to Walla Walla & the Anvil Chorus.** Frank W. Blick. LC 96-90441. (Orig.). 1996. pap. 8.95 (*0-533-12056-X*) Vantage.

Walk to Win: Easy Four-Day Diet & Fitness Plan. Fred A. Stutman. LC 85-63311. (Illus.). 256p. 1990. 19.95 (*0-934232-08-3*); pap. 10.95 (*0-934232-07-5*) Med Manor Bks.

Walk Together Children: The Story of the Birth & Growth of the Interdenominational Theological Center. Harry V. Richardson. 123p. (C). 1981. pap. 8.95 (*0-614-08305-2*) Jrnl Interdenom.

Walk Together, Talk Together. Katharine T. Kinkead. (Illus.). 1962. 3.95 (*0-393-07384-X*) Norton.

Walk Two Moons. Sharon Creech. LC 93-31277. 280p. (J). (gr. 3-7). 1994. 16.00 (*0-06-023334-6*); lib. bdg. 15.89 (*0-06-023337-0*) HarpC Child Bks.

Walk Two Moons. Sharon Creech. LC 93-31277. (Trophy Bk.). 288p. (J). (gr. 5-9). 1996. pap. 4.50 (*0-06-440517-6*, Trophy) HarpC Child Bks.

Walk Two Moons: A Study Guide. Merrily Hansen. Ed. by J. Friedland & R. Kessler. (Novel-Ties Ser.). (J). (gr. 5-6). 1996. pap. text ed. 15.95 (*1-56982-656-0*) Lrn Links.

Walk up a Mountain. Caroline Arnold. Ed. by Bonnie Brook. (First Facts: Natural Sciences Ser.). (Illus.). 32p. (J). (ps-1). 1990. lib. bdg. 6.95 (*0-671-68663-1*, Silver Pr NJ) Silver Burdett Pr.

Walk up a Mountain. Caroline Arnold. Ed. by Bonnie Brook. (First Facts: Natural Sciences Ser.). (Illus.). 32p. (J). (ps-1). 1990. pap. 4.95 (*0-382-24651-9*, Silver Pr NJ) Silver Burdett Pr.

Walk upon the Earth. Mary Talken. (Illus.). 192p. (Orig.). 1987. pap. 3.95 (*0-9619510-0-1*) M Talken.

Walk upon the Wind. Patricia Wilson. (Presents Ser.). 1993. mass mkt. 2.99 (*0-373-11602-0*, 1-11602-9) Harlequin Bks.

Walk When the Moon Is Full. Frances Hamerstrom. LC 75-33878. (Illus.). 64p. (J). (gr. 3-8). 1975. 15.95 (*0-912278-69-2*); pap. 6.95 (*0-912278-84-6*) Crossing Pr.

Walk, Wiggle, & Wave: Movement Experiences Throughout Your Curriculum. Margery A. Kranyik. Ed. by Martha A. Hayes. (Illus.). 48p. 1991. pap. 6.95 (*1-878727-08-7*) First Teacher.

***Walk with a Wolf.** Janni Howker. LC 97-7769. (Illus.). (J). 1998. write for info. (*0-7636-0319-8*) Candlewick Pr.

Walk with Abraham's Family. 1995. pap. 9.95 (*0-87162-679-9*, D4303) Warner Pr.

Walk with Christ Through the Resurrection. Dawson McAllister. (Illus.). (J). (gr. 5-12). 1981. pap. 8.95 (*0-923417-14-1*) Shepherd Minst.

Walk with Christ to the Cross. Dawson McAllister. (Illus.). (J). (gr. 5-12). 1980. pap. 8.95 (*0-923417-09-5*) Shepherd Minst.

Walk with Christ to the Cross. Dawson McAllister & Tim Kimmel. (J). (gr. 5-12). 1981. teacher ed., pap. 5.95 (*0-923417-20-6*) Shepherd Minst.

Walk with God. (Walk with...Ser.). 389p. 1990. 45.00 (*1-57277-101-1*) Script Rsch.

Walk with God. Gloria Copeland. 116p. 1995. pap. 6.95 (*0-88114-985-3*) K Copeland Pubns.

Walk with God. Joan Hill. 134p. (C). 1989. text ed. 39.00 (*1-872795-87-0*, Pub. by Pentland Pr UK) St Mut.

Walk with God: Obedience, 6 tapes, Set. Gloria Copeland. 30p. 1984. 30.00 incl. audio (*0-88114-705-2*) K Copeland Pubns.

Walk with Herbs Bks. I & II. (Walk with...Ser.). 191p. 1990. pap. 35.00 (*1-57277-124-0*) Script Rsch.

Walk with Jesus. (Walk with...Ser.). 338p. 1991. 45.00 (*1-57277-100-3*) Script Rsch.

***Walk with Jesus.** (Illus.). 8p. (J). (ps-1). 1992. 29.99 (*1-888074-36-1*) Pckts Lrning.

Walk with Jesus. Kathleen D. Buehler. 1992. 9.95 (*0-87162-619-5*, D4300) Warner Pr.

Walk with Jesus. Rosalie Willis. 160p. (Orig.). 1996. pap. 10.00 (*0-9650881-0-3*) Praise Pubng.

Walk with Jesus. abr. ed. 196p. 1975. pap. 15.00 (*1-57277-200-X*) Script Rsch.

Walk with Jesus. 196p. 1995. reprint ed. pap. 25.00 incl. audio (*1-57277-125-9*) Script Rsch.

Walk with Jesus: Appendix VII, Vol. 5-B. (Walk with Jesus Ser.). (Illus.). 370p. 1995. 100.00 (*1-57277-700-1*) Script Rsch.

Walk with Jesus: Resources for Holy Week. Steve Petty. 48p. 1989. pap. 2.95 (*0-687-44005-X*) Abingdon.

Walk with Jesus: Stations of the Cross. Henri J. Nouwen. LC 89-27875. (Illus.). 1990. pap. 11.50 (*0-88344-666-9*) Orbis Bks.

Walk with Jesus Vol. 1. unabridged ed. 535p. 1987. 75.00 (*1-57277-202-6*) Script Rsch.

Walk with Jesus Vol. 2-A, Appendix I. 1196p. 1978. 100.00 (*1-57277-225-5*) Script Rsch.

Walk with Jesus Vol. 2-B, Appendix I. 1196p. 1978. 100.00 (*1-57277-300-6*) Script Rsch.

Walk with Jesus Vol. 2-C, Appendix I. 1190p. 1987. 100.00 (*1-57277-325-1*) Script Rsch.

Walk with Jesus Vol. 3, Appendix II. 1169p. 1987. 100.00 (*1-57277-400-2*) Script Rsch.

Walk with Jesus Vol. 4-A, Appendix III. 1146p. 1987. 100.00 (*1-57277-425-8*) Script Rsch.

Walk with Jesus Vol. 4-B, Appendix III. 1148p. 1986. 100.00 (*1-57277-500-9*) Script Rsch.

Walk with Jesus Vol. 4-C, Appendix III. 771p. 1986. 100.00 (*1-57277-525-4*) Script Rsch.

Walk with Jesus Vol. 4-D, Appendix III. 920p. 1987. 100.00 (*1-57277-600-5*) Script Rsch.

Walk with Jesus Vol. 5-A, Appendices IV, V, VI. (Walk with Jesus Ser.). 577p. 1991. 100.00 (*1-57277-625-0*) Script Rsch.

Walk with Jesus on the Mount of Blessings. George R. Knight. LC 96-9263. 1996. write for info. (*0-8280-1108-7*) Review & Herald.

Walk with Me. (Walk with Jesus Ser.). 440p. 1975. pap. 15.00 (*1-57277-201-8*) Script Rsch.

Walk with Me. Naomi Danis. LC 94-16973. (Story Corner Ser.). (Illus.). 24p. (J). (ps). 1995. 6.95 (*0-590-45855-8*, Cartwheel) Scholastic Inc.

***Walk with Me.** Anthony M. DiPaola. (Orig.). 1997. pap. write for info. (*1-57553-495-9*) Watermrk Pr.

Walk with Me. Timothy F. Melich. LC 89-51347. 61p. 1990. pap. 5.95 (*1-55523-266-3*) Winston-Derek.

Walk with Me: Prayers & Meditations. large type ed. Marilyn R. Riddle. (Illus.). 40p. (Orig.). 1982. pap. 7.00 (*0-9603748-2-5*) Sandpiper OR.

***Walk with Me: To the Light.** Cliff Robinson. 76p. (Orig.). 1997. pap. 6.00 (*1-57502-402-0*, PO1246) Morris Pubng.

Walk with Me in White. Elmer T. Church. LC 86-81184. 154p. (J). 1986. per. 5.98 (*0-318-21723-6*) E T Church.

Walk with Moses & Company. 1995. pap. 9.95 (*0-87162-695-0*) Warner Pr.

Walk with Old Testament Heroes. Kathleen D. Buehler. Ed. by Dan Harman. (Illus.). 100p. (Orig.). (J). (gr. 5-7). 1996. pap. 9.95 (*0-87162-680-2*) Warner Pr.

Walk with Peter & Paul. 1993. pap. 9.95 (*0-87162-518-0*) Warner Pr.

Walk with Praise. Janet Van Rys. (Devotional Ser.). (Illus.). 200p. (Orig.). 1986. pap. 4.95 (*0-9616989-0-X*) Jan Van Pubns.

Walk with Prophecy. 116p. 1990. pap. 35.00 (*1-57277-103-8*) Script Rsch.

Walk with Proverbs. (Walk with...Ser.). 75p. 1992. pap. 15.00 (*1-57277-104-6*) Script Rsch.

Walk with the Dead: Through the Inferno That Is Passion. Earl R. Bostic, Jr. LC 94-73498. (Illus.). 160p. (Orig.). 1995. pap. text ed. 11.95 (*0-9644710-1-9*) B-Bye Pub.

***Walk with the Dinosaurs.** Gordy Slack. (I Wish I Could Ser.). (Illus.). 48p. (J). (gr. 4-7). 1997. pap. 6.95 (*1-57098-117-5*) R Rinehart.

Walk with the Eagles: Hunting North American Big Game. Doug Yajko. LC 90-62139. 256p. 1990. 30.00 (*0-9627247-6-9*) Roaring Co.

Walk with the Lord: Sharing the Cross, Sharing the Glory. Anselm W. Romb. LC 89-49678. 328p. (Orig.). 1990. pap. 8.95 (*0-8198-8240-2*) Pauline Bks.

Walk with the Lord - Advent/Christmas: Sharing the Silence, Sharing the Life. Anselm W. Romb. LC 90-44397. 182p. (Orig.). 1990. pap. 6.95 (*0-8198-8245-3*) Pauline Bks.

Walk with the Serenity Prayer. Minirth-Meier Clinic Staff. (Serenity Meditation Ser.). 1991. pap. 8.99 (*0-8407-3236-8*) Nelson.

Walk with the Sickle Moon. Helen Norris. Ed. by Hillel Black. 176p. 1989. 15.95 (*1-55972-001-8*, Birch Ln Pr) Carol Pub Group.

Walk with the Spirit. (Walk with...Ser.). 286p. 1991. 45.00 (*1-57277-102-X*); 25.00 incl. audio (*1-57277-127-5*) Script Rsch.

Walk with Tom Jefferson. Philip Levine. LC 87-46080. 80p. 1988. 16.95 (*0-394-57038-3*); pap. 13.00 (*0-394-75859-5*) Knopf.

Walk with Wonder. Alice M. Glennon. 80p. (Orig.). 1995. pap. write for info. (*1-57553-030-9*) Watermrk Pr.

Walk Your Way to Better Dancing. L. Hostetler. (Ballroom Dance Ser.). 1986. lib. bdg. 79.95 (*0-8490-3354-3*) Gordon Pr.

Walk Your Way to Better Dancing. L. Hostetler. (Ballroom Dance Ser.). 1985. 79.95 (*0-87700-680-6*) Revisionist Pr.

Walk Yourself Thin. David Rives. 1990. 19.95 (*1-878143-00-X*); pap. 12.95 (*1-878143-01-8*) Moon River.

***Walk Yourself Well: Eliminate Back, Shoulder, Knee, Hip, & Other Structural Pain Forever - Without Surgery or Drugs.** Sherri Brourman & Randy Rodman. (Illus.). 256p. 1998. 22.95 (*0-7868-6293-9*) Hyperion.

Walkabout. Aaron Fletcher. 480p. (Orig.). 1992. mass mkt., pap. text ed. 5.99 (*0-8439-3292-9*) Dorchester Pub Co.

***Walkabout.** James V. Marshall. 1992. pap. 5.75 (*0-435-27247-0*) Heinemann.

Walkabout. James V. Marshall. 158p. 1984. pap. 3.95 (*0-88741-099-5*) Sundance Pub.

Walkabout Year: Twelve Months in Australia. Samuel F. Pickering, Jr. (Illus.). 344p. (Orig.). (C). 1995. pap. 19.95 (*0-8262-1043-0*) U of Mo Pr.

Walkaround Model Railroad Track Plans. Don Mitchell. Ed. by Bob Hayden. (Illus.). 72p. (Orig.). 1989. per. 12.95 (*0-89024-081-7*, 12097) Kalmbach.

Walked to Alaska, Clawed by a Bear: The Stupendous 4000 Mile Trek - a True Story of Robert J. Kennedy. Thomas Hall et al. LC 92-64314. (Illus.). 320p. 1993. 19.95 (*0-945848-03-X*) Prince Wales Pub.

Walker: Ancestors of Francis Walker & Sarah Effie Vinton Kelley. J. S. Elston. (Illus.). 134p. 1992. reprint ed. pap. 22.00 (*0-8328-2755-X*); reprint ed. lib. bdg. 32.00 (*0-8328-2754-1*) Higginson Bk Co.

Walker Art Gallery. Edward Morris. (Illus.). 96p. 1994. 30.00 (*1-85759-036-8*) Scala Books.

Walker Between the Worlds. Diane DesRochers. LC 95-3286. (Psi-Fi Ser.). 448p. 1995. mass mkt. 6.99 (*1-56718-224-0*) Llewellyn Pubns.

Walker Common Sense Log Book. Milo Walker & Terri Walker. (Illus.). 126p. (Orig.). 1990. spiral bd. 15.95 (*0-945265-31-X*) Evergreen Pacific.

Walker County, Texas Census Uniquely Reconstructed & Annotated, 1890. Mary C. Moody. 1992. pap. 34.50 (*0-9615836-8-1*) Blackstone Pub.

***Walker Evans.** 2nd ed. Lloyd Fonvielle. (Masters of Photography Ser.). (Illus.). 96p. Date not set. reprint ed. 12.50 (*0-89381-741-4*) Aperture.

Walker Evans: A Biography. Belinda Rathbone. Ed. by Walker Evans. LC 95-3711. (Illus.). 338p. 1995. 27.50 (*0-395-59072-8*) HM.

***Walker Evans: American Photographs.** Walker Evans. (Illus.). 208p. 40.00 (*0-8109-6155-5*) Abrams.

Walker Evans: American Photographs. Walker Evans. (Illus.). 208p. 1990. pap. 22.50 (*0-8109-6030-3*) Abrams.

Walker Evans: American Photographs. Walker Evans. (Illus.). 208p. 1989. 40.00 (*0-87070-237-8*); pap. 29.95 (*0-87070-238-6*, 0-8109-6030-3) Mus of Modern Art.

Walker Evans: Photographs for the Farm Security Admininistration, 1935-1938. Walker Evans. LC 74-149598. (Photography Ser.). 1975. reprint ed. pap. 18.95 (0-306-80008-X); reprint ed. lib. bdg. 39.50 (0-306-70099-9) Da Capo.

Walker Evans: Photographs from the "Let Us Now Praise Famous Men Project" Compiled by William Stott. (Illus.). 1974. pap. 7.00 (0-87959-016-5) U of Tex H Ransom Ctr.

Walker Evans: Photographs of New York State. Leslie G. Katz. (Illus.). 8p. 1980. 10.00 (0-685-70725-3) Gal Assn NY.

Walker Evans: Subways & Streets. Sarah Greenough. LC 91-34122. (Illus.). 132p. (Orig.). 1991. pap. 35.00 (0-89468-166-4) Natl Gallery Art.

Walker Evans: The Getty Museum Collection. Judith Keller. (Illus.). 416p. 1995. 95.00 (0-89236-317-7, J P Getty Museum) J P Getty Trust.

Walker Evans: The Hungry Eye. Gilles Mora. LC 93-16399. 1993. 65.00 (0-8109-3259-8) Abrams.

Walker Evans America. Michael Brix. 1991. 60.00 (0-8478-1344-4) Rizzoli Intl.

Walker Evans & Jane Ninas in New Orleans, 1935-1936. Jeff L. Rosenheim. LC 90-86149. (Illus.). 24p. 1991. pap. 10.00 (0-917860-31-4) Historic New Orleans.

Walker Evans, Incognito, Vol. 1. limited ed. Photos by Walker Evans. LC 95-78621. (Illus.). 42p. 1995. 75.00 (0-87130-057-5) Eakins.

Walker Expedition to Quebec, 1711, Vol. 32. Ed. by Gerald S. Graham. LC 69-14509. 441p. 1969. reprint ed. text ed. 75.00 (0-8371-5072-8, GRWE, Greenwood Pr) Greenwood.

Walker in Jerusalem. Samuel C. Heilman. 1995. 14.95 (0-8276-0556-0) JPS Phila.

Walker in Shadows. Barbara Michaels. 1992. mass mkt. 6.99 (0-425-13399-0, Berkley Trade) Berkley Pub.

***Walker in the City.** Alfred Kazin. 1997. 6.98 (1-56731-212-8, MJF Bks) Fine Comms.

Walker in the City. Alfred Kazin. LC 53-18408. 176p. 1969. reprint ed. pap. 12.00 (0-15-694176-7, Harvest Bks) HarBrace.

***Walker in the Shadows.** large type ed. Barbara Michaels. LC 96-49283. 312p. 1997. pap. 21.95 (0-7838-8073-1, GK Hall) Thorndike Pr.

Walker-McConnell Scale of Social Competence & School Adjustment, Adolescent Version: Re-Order Forms Set of 20. Hill M. Walker. (Illus.). 1995. pap. 19.95 (1-56593-493-8, 1142) Singular Publishing.

Walker-McConnell Scale of Social Competence & School Adjustment, Adolescent Version: User's Manual, Technical Manual, & Forms. Hill M. Walker. (Illus.). 50p. (Orig.). (C). 1995. pap. 54.95 (1-56593-494-6, 1144) Singular Publishing.

Walker-McConnell Scale of Social Competence & School Adjustment, Elementary Version: Re-Order Forms Set of 20. Hill M. Walker. 1995. pap. 19.95 (1-56593-495-4, 1146) Singular Publishing.

Walker-McConnell Scale of Social Competence & School Adjustment, Elementary Version: User's Manual, Technical Manual, & Forms. Hill M. Walker & Scott R. McConnell. 96p. (Orig.). (C). 1995. pap. 54.95 (1-56593-496-2, 1148) Singular Publishing.

Walker Mysteries. large type ed. Incl. Against the Public Interest. Robert Gaines. 10.00 (0-318-66061-X); Chase. Richard Unekis. 10.00 (0-318-66062-8); Confessions of Arsene Lupkin. Maurice Leblanc. 10.00 (0-318-66063-6); Death at Crane's Court. Eilis Dillion. 10.00 (0-318-66064-4); Devil at Your Elbow. D. M. Devine. 10.00 (0-318-66065-2); Diamonds Bid. Julian Rathbone. 10.00 (0-318-66066-0); Exit Screaming. Herbert Dalmas. 10.00 (0-318-66067-9); Farewell Crown, Goodbye King. Margot Bennet. 10.00 (0-318-66068-7); Hands of Innocence. Jeffrey Ashford. 10.00 (0-318-66069-5); Kill the Toff. John Creasey. 10.00 (0-318-66070-9); Treacherous Road. Simon Harvester. 1966. 10.00 (0-318-66072-5); reprint ed. 10.00 (0-318-66060-1) NAVH.

Walker of Time. Helen H. Vick. LC 92-46740. 212p. (Orig.). (YA). (gr. 6-12). 15.95 (0-943173-84-1, Harbinger CO); pap. 9.95 (0-943173-80-9, Harbinger CO) R Rinehart.

***Walker of Time.** Helen H. Vick. 52p. (Orig.). (YA). (gr. 6-12). Date not set. teacher ed., pap. 9.95 (1-57140-004-4, Harbinger CO) R Rinehart.

Walker on Patents, 11 vols. 3rd ed. Ernest B. Lipscomb, III. LC 84-81078. (IP Ser.). 1984. Set. 950.00 (0-685-65399-4) Clark Boardman Callaghan.

Walker on Patents, 11 vols., Set. annuals 3rd rev. ed. Ernest B. Lipscomb, III. LC 84-81078. (IP Ser.). 1984. 950.00 (0-685-59817-9) Clark Boardman Callaghan.

Walker Pass Lodge. Donna Litherland. 220p. (Orig.). 1996. pap. 11.95 (0-9607888-4-0) Barney Pr. A feminist espionage story laid in the desert of the American Southwest, around our bases of China Lake & Edwards Air Force, in 1988, this is a character study of a too tall young woman who has rebelled against mental abuse. The heroine is concerned with being a person in her own right without being controlled. Women have to find power within themselves. Other characters affect the struggle of Amy de Stahl, her questions of identity, of a balance between femininity & strength. Amy does fall in love with another woman in the beginning, but she matures a great deal during the relationship. When Amy as underdog, starts to fight back, that is the end. Descriptions of the Sierra Nevada abound in this book, including the climbing of Mt. Whitney & again, Mt. Conness in Yosemite. Although the story is fictional, much research into the place names such as Robber's Roost, Walker Lodge, & its connection with the astronauts & pilots together with the weapons systems of the salt desert at China Lake make this good reading for history buffs as well as those interested in a fast paced story. $11.95 paper, Barney Press, 3807 Noel Place, Bakersfield, CA 93306. ***Publisher Provided Annotation.***

Walker Percy: A Comprehensive Descriptive Bibliography. Linda W. Hobson. (Illus.). 115p. 1990. text ed. 35.00 (0-917905-06-7) La State U Pr.

Walker Percy: A Life. Patrick Samway. (Illus.). 544p. 1997. 35.00 (0-374-18735-5) FS&G.

***Walker Percy: Prophetic, Existentialist, Catholic Storyteller.** Robert Lauder. (New Connections Ser.: Vol. 12). 144p. (C). 1996. pap. text ed. 24.95 (0-8204-3333-0) P Lang Pubng.

Walker Percy & the Old Modern Age: Reflections on Language, Argument, & the Telling of Stories. Patricia Lewis Poteat. LC 84-10005. (Southern Literary Studies). 177p. 1985. text ed. 30.00 (0-8071-1187-2) La State U Pr.

Walker Percy & the Postmodern World. Mary K. Sweeny. 1987. 10.35 (0-8294-0541-0) Loyola Pr.

Walker Percy, Nineteen Thirty to Nineteen Eighty-Four: A Bibliography. Stuart Wright. 69p. 1986. text ed. 29.50 (0-313-27709-5) Greenwood.

Walker Percy, the Last Catholic Novelist. Kieran Quinlan. LC 95-44232. (Southern Literary Studies). 256p. (C). 1996. text ed. 35.00 (0-8071-2044-8) La State U Pr.

Walker Percy's Feminine Characters. Ed. by Lewis A. Lawson & Elzbieta Oleksy. 135p. 1995. 18.50 (0-87875-456-3) Whitston Pub.

Walker Washington Guide. 8th rev. ed. John Walker & Katherine Walker. LC 91-20439. (Illus.). 320p. 1991. pap. 8.95 (0-939009-54-4) EPM Pubns.

Walker's Appeal & Garnet's Address: To the Slaves of the United States of America. David Walker & Henry H. Garnet. LC 79-75853. 108p. 1989. reprint ed. pap. 18.95 (0-88143-109-5) Ayer.

Walker's Appeal & Garnet's Address to the Slaves of the United States of America. David Walker & Henry H. Garnet. 104p. 1994. pap. 4.95 (1-55523-540-9) Winston-Derek.

Walker's Appeal & Garnet's Address to the Slaves of the United States of America. David Walker & Henry H. Garnet. LC 78-77508. (American Negro: His History & Literature. Series 2). 1969. reprint ed. 22.95 (0-405-01901-7) Ayer.

Walker's Bats of the World. Ronald M. Nowak. (Illus.). 1995. pap. 19.95 (0-8018-4986-1) Johns Hopkins.

Walker's Building Estimator's Reference Book. 25th ed. Robert S. Siddens. LC 93-72719. (Illus.). 1544p. 1994. pap. 69.95 (0-911592-25-3) F R Walker.

Walker's Building Estimator's Reference Book. 26th rev. ed. Ed. by Scott Siddens. 1998. pap. text ed. write for info. (0-911592-26-1) F R Walker.

Walker's Companion. Elizabeth Ferber et al. Ed. by David R. Wallace. LC 95-4551. (Nature Company Guide Ser.). (Illus.). 288p. (J). (gr. 3 up). 1995. 29.95 (0-7835-4754-4) Time-Life.

Walker's Companion Ireland: Twenty-Three Superb Walks Complete with Route Maps & Colour Photographs. David Herman. (Illus.). 128p. 1995. pap. 12.95 (0-7063-7352-9, Pub. by Ward Lock UK) Sterling.

Walker's Companion to the Wade Roads. Joan Baker & Arthur Baker. 120p. (C). 1987. 70.00 (0-906664-18-7, Pub. by Mercat Pr Bks UK) St Mut.

Walkers Go Hiking. Morrell Gipson et al. LC 90-13797. (Magic Mountain Fables Ser.). (Illus.). 24p. (J). (gr. k-3). 1990. lib. bdg. 14.60 (0-944483-91-7) Garrett Ed Corp.

Walker's Guidebook: Serendipitous Outings Near New York City. 3rd ed. Marina Harrison & Lucy D. Rosenfeld. LC 88-21608. (Illus.). 198p. (Orig.). 1995. pap. 13.95 (0-935576-50-9) Kesend Pub Ltd.

Walker's Guidebook to All San Diego. William Carroll. (Explore San Diego County Ser.). Orig. Title: Beach... Park...Mall Walking in San Diego. (Illus.). 410p. (Orig.). 1996. pap. 16.95 (0-910390-47-9, Coda Pubns) Auto Bk.

Walker's Insulation Techniques & Estimating Handbook. Harry Hardenbrook. (Illus.). 128p. pap. 12.95 (0-685-06830-7) S&S Trade.

Walker's Insulation Techniques & Estimating Handbook. 2nd rev. ed. Harry Hardenbrook. Ed. by Gary D. Cook. (Illus.). 131p. (C). 1983. pap. text ed. 12.95 (0-911592-51-2) F R Walker.

Walker's Journal. Robert Sweetgall & John Dignam. (Illus.). 128p. 1986. pap. 7.95 (0-939041-02-2) Creative Walking.

Walker's Journey Home. Helen H. Vick. LC 94-39796. 192p. (Orig.). (YA). (gr. 7-12). 1995. 14.95 (1-57140-000-1, Harbinger CO); pap. 9.95 (1-57140-001-X, Harbinger CO) R Rinehart.

***Walker's Journey Home.** Helen H. Vick. 48p. (J). pap. 9.95 (1-57140-013-3) R Rinehart.

Walker's Mammals of the World, 2 vols. 5th rev. ed. Ronald M. Nowak. LC 91-27011. (Illus.). 1732p. 1991. Set. 95.00 (0-8018-3970-X) Johns Hopkins.

Walker's Manual for Construction Cost Estimating. Vick S. Crespin et al. Ed. by Frank R. Walker Company. (Illus.). 128p. (C). 1981. pap. 19.95 (0-911592-85-7) F R Walker.

***Walker's Manual of Community Bank Stocks.** 608p. 1997. 100.00 (0-9652088-7-7) Walkers Manual.

***Walker's Manual of Unlisted Stocks.** 2nd ed. 600p. 1997. 85.00 (0-9652088-8-5) Walkers Manual.

Walker's Manual of Western Corporations, 1995, 2 vols. annuals Ed. by E. Walsh. 2600p. 1995. boxed 390.00 (1-879346-23-0) Walkers Research.

Walker's Manual of Western Corporations, 1995, 2 vols., Set, incls. quarterly suppls. annuals Ed. by E. Walsh. 3000p. 1995. boxed 480.00 (1-879346-24-9) Walkers Research.

Walker's Mission. Don Hepler. 192p. 1992. 17.95 (0-8034-8979-X) Bouregy.

Walkers of Hanningfield: Surveyors & Mapmakers Extraordinary. A. C. Edwards & K. C. Newton. 152p. 1986. 125.00 (0-7212-0614-X, Pub. by Regency Press UK) St Mut.

Walkers of the Wind. William Sarabande. (First Americans Ser.: No. IV). 448p. 1990. mass mkt. 5.99 (0-553-28579-3) Bantam.

Walker's Pocket Estimator. 25th ed. Robert S. Siddens. 260p. 1994. pap. text ed. 9.95 (0-911592-44-X) F R Walker.

***Walker's Point.** Marilee Dunker. (Portraits Ser.). 1997. pap. 8.99 (1-55661-997-6) Bethany Hse.

Walker's Quantity Surveying & Basic Construction Estimating. G. Patrick Bourgeois et al. Ed. by Walker, Frank R., Company Staff. (Illus.). 128p. (C). 1981. pap. 19.95 (0-911592-75-X) F R Walker.

Walker's Remodeling Estimators Reference Book. 2nd ed. Robert S. Siddens. (Illus.). 340p. 1987. text ed. 29.95 (0-911592-61-X) F R Walker.

Walker's Rhyming Dictionary of the English Language: In Which the Whole Language Is Arranged According to Its Terminations. enl. rev. ed. J. Walker. 558p. 1983. reprint ed. 19.95 (0-7100-9306-3, RKP) Routledge.

Walker's Yearbook. Margot Doss. 1989. pap. 9.95 (0-917583-15-9, Dont Call Frisco) Lexikos.

Walkin' Maurie Kerrigan. Ed. by Ann Percy & Dosh Emery. LC 89-90794. (Illus.). 36p. (Orig.). 1989. pap. 9.95 (0-9618920-1-3) M Kerrigan.

Walkin' & Talkin' Revisited: (Silver Anniversary Edition) Rudy Topinka. 148p. 1989. pap. 8.95 (0-9624616-0-1) Pine River WI.

Walkin' Occam's Razor. Margareta Waterman. (Illus.). 46p. (Orig.). 1991. pap. 6.00 (1-878888-08-0) Nine Muses.

Walkin' over Medicine: Traditional Health Practices in African-American Life. Loudell F. Snow. LC 92-37482. 311p. (C). 1993. pap. text ed. 22.95 (0-8133-1799-1) Westview.

Walkin' the Park: The Insiders Guide to Hiking at Acadia National Park. Thomas A. St. Germain, Jr. (Illus.). 96p. (Orig.). 1991. spiral bd. 10.95 (0-9629997-0-9) Parkman Pubns.

***Walking.** 1997. write for info. (0-8069-9814-8) Sterling.

Walking. Ruth Rudner. LC 95-1520. (Outdoor Pursuits Ser.). (Illus.). 136p. (Orig.). 1995. pap. 13.95 (0-87322-668-2, PRUD0668) Human Kinetics.

Walking. Henry David Thoreau. LC 92-38877. 60p. (Orig.). 1988. pap. 5.95 (1-55709-100-5) Applewood.

Walking. Henry David Thoreau. LC 93-42719. (Little Book of Wisdom Ser.). 96p. (Orig.). 1994. pap. 8.00 (0-06-251113-0) Harper SF.

Walking. Henry David Thoreau. (Illus.). (Orig.). 1989. write for info. (0-318-65879-8) Heritage Dallas.

Walking. Stephen Vincent. 72p. (Orig.). 1993. pap. 9.00 (1-881523-05-5) Junction CA.

Walking: A Complete Guide to the Complete Exercise. Casey Meyers. 1992. pap. 12.00 (0-679-73777-4, Vin) Random.

Walking a Line. Tom Paulin. 128p. (Orig.). 1995. pap. 9.95 (0-571-17081-1) Faber & Faber.

Walking a Sacred Path: Rediscovering the Labyrinth As a Spiritual Tool. Lauren Artress. 1995. 18.00 (1-57322-007-8, Riverhead Books) Putnam Pub Group.

Walking a Sacred Path: Rediscovering the Labyrinth As a Spiritual Tool. Lauren Artress. 1996. pap. text ed. 11.00 (1-57322-547-9, Riverhd Trade) Berkley Pub.

Walking Across Egypt. Clyde Edgerton. 218p. 1987. 14.95 (0-912697-51-2) Algonquin Bks.

Walking Across Egypt. Clyde Edgerton. 240p. 1988. mass mkt. 5.99 (0-345-34649-1) Ballantine.

***Walking Across Egypt.** Clyde Edgerton. 1997. pap. 11.95 (0-345-41907-3) Ballantine.

Walking after Midnight. M. Jones. 368p. 1995. pap. 13.00 (0-06-092211-7, PL) HarpC.

Walking after Midnight. Maureen McCoy. pap. 5.95 (0-685-18036-0) PB.

Walking after Midnight. Richard Nusser. 432p. 1990. mass mkt. 3.95 (0-380-70939-2) Avon.

Walking after Midnight. Karen Robards. 416p. 1995. mass mkt. 5.99 (0-440-21590-0) Dell.

Walking after Midnight: Gay Men's Life Stories. Hall Carpenter Archives Staff. (Illus.). 224p. 1989. 35.00 (0-415-02956-2, A3634) Routledge.

Walking after Midnight: Gay Men's Life Stories. Hall Carpenter Archives Staff. (Illus.). 224p. (C). 1989. pap. 12.95 (0-415-02957-0, A3638) Routledge.

Walking Alone & Marching Together: A History of the Organized Blind Movement in the United States, 1940-1990. Floyd Matson. (Illus.). 1117p. 1990. text ed. 30.00 (0-9624122-1-X) Natl Fed Blind.

Walking Along the Missouri River. John McKernan. LC 77-8920. (Lost Roads Poetry Ser.: No. 5). (J). 1978. pap. 4.00 (0-918786-09-6) Lost Roads.

Walking among the Unseen. Hannah Hurnard. 207p. 1977. mass mkt. 5.99 (0-8423-7805-7) Tyndale.

Walking Amsterdam. Robin Gauldie. (Illus.). 192p. (Orig.). 1996. pap. 14.95 (0-8442-9200-1, Passport Bks) NTC Pub Grp.

Walking & Eating in Tuscany & Umbria. James Lasdun & Pia Davis. 1997. pap. write for info. (0-14-024476-X) Viking Penguin.

***Walking & Eating in Tuscany & Umbria.** James Lasdun & Pia Davis. 1997. pap. 16.95 (0-14-026460-4) Viking Penguin.

Walking & Leaping. Merlin R. Carothers. 129p. (Orig.). 1974. pap. 6.95 (0-943026-05-9) Carothers.

Walking & Running. Time-Life Books Editors. (Fitness, Health & Nutrition Ser.). (Illus.). 144p. (J). 1989. 17.27 (0-8094-6130-7); lib. bdg. 23.27 (0-8094-6131-5) Time-Life.

Walking & Talking with Jesus: Building Faith Before Tragedy. Marolyn Ford. 190p. (Orig.). 1992. pap. 7.99 (0-9634057-1-3, TX3448-984) Full Court MI.

Walking Around Budapest: Budapest Corvina, 1988. K. Rohonyi & M. Marot. (Illus.). 156p. (C). 1988. pap. 70.00 (0-569-08215-3, Pub. by Collets) St Mut.

Walking Around in South Street: Discoveries in New York's Old Shipping District. Ellen F. Rosebrock. (Illus.). (Orig.). 1974. pap. 3.95 (0-913344-17-6) South St Sea Mus.

Walking As Jesus Walked: Disciple Making Like Jesus. Ed. by Millie H. Griswold. 95p. 1996. student ed., pap. write for info. (1-881909-23-9); teacher ed., pap. write for info. (1-881909-22-0) Advent Christ Gen Conf.

Walking Austria's Alps: Hut to Hut. Jonathan Hurdle. LC 88-1767. (Illus.). 240p. (Orig.). 1988. pap. 10.95 (0-89886-159-4) Mountaineers.

***Walking Back from Woodstock.** Earl S. Braggs. 80p. (Orig.). 1996. pap. 10.00 (0-938078-48-8) Anhinga Pr.

***Walking Back the Cat.** Robert Littell. LC 96-49507. 218p. 1997. 23.95 (0-87951-764-6) Overlook Pr.

Walking Back the Cat. Robert Littell. 1996. write for info. (0-614-09426-7) Random.

***Walking Back the Cat.** Robert Littell. 1997. 21.00 (0-679-43567-0) Random.

Walking Backward in the Wind, 12. Helen M. Fields. LC 94-30503. (Chisholm Trail Ser.). 230p. (Orig.). 1995. pap. 16.95 (0-87565-137-2) Tex Christian.

Walking Beside Jesus in the Holy Land. Isabelle W. Bacon. 100p. (Orig.). 1990. pap. 6.95 (0-915597-53-5) Amana Bks.

***Walking Between Darkness & Hell.** Ethel M. Siwemuke. 127p. (Orig.). 1997. mass mkt. 4.99 (1-55197-662-5, Pub. by Comnwlth Pub CN) Partners Pubs Grp.

Walking Between the Times: Paul's Moral Reasoning. J. Paul Sampley. LC 90-26775. 128p. (Orig.). 1991. pap. 13.00 (0-8006-2479-3, 1-2479, Fortress Pr) Augsburg Fortress.

Walking Black & Tall. rev. ed. Omar Fletcher. 224p. (Orig.). 1984. mass mkt. 2.25 (0-87067-241-X, BH241) Holloway.

Walking Britain's Coast: An Aerial Guide. Richard Sale et al. (Illus.). 190p. 1993. 30.00 (0-04-440481-6, Pub. by HarpC UK) HarpC.

Walking Britain's Skyline: Forty-Five Classic Routes. Tony Greenbank. (Illus.). 224p. 1993. 39.95 (1-85223-287-0, Pub. by Crowood Pr UK) Trafalgar.

Walking California's State Parks: Guide to over 100 Historic Parks, Preserves & Wilderness Areas. John Mckinney. 1994. write for info. (0-318-72331-X) HarpC West.

Walking Cape Ann. Helen Naismith. (Illus.). 254p. (Orig.). 1994. pap. 11.95 (0-938459-08-2) Ten Pound Isl Bk.

Walking Cincinnati: Scenic Hikes Through the Parks & Neighborhoods of Greater Cincinnati & Northern Kentucky. 2nd ed. Darcy Folzenlogen & Robert Folzenlogen. LC 93-61339. (Illus.). 160p. 1993. per., pap. 12.95 (0-9620685-5-1) Willow Pr CO.

Walking City: The Montgomery Bus Boycott, 1955-1956. Pref. by David J. Garrow. LC 89-9869. (Martin Luther King, Jr., & the Civil Rights Movement Ser.: Vol. 7). 662p. 1989. 125.00 (0-926019-03-1) Carlson Pub.

Walking Coat. Pauline Watson. LC 81-7395. (Illus.). 32p. (J). (gr. k-3). 1995. pap. 3.95 (0-689-80420-2, Aladdin Paperbacks) S&S Childrens.

***Walking Colorado Springs.** Judith C. Galas & Cindy West. LC 97-8607. (Illus.). 160p. 1997. pap. 10.95 (1-56044-535-1) Falcon Pr MT.

Walking Common Ground: Nineteenth & Twentieth Century Immigrant Women in America. Kristine Leach. 112p. 1996. 69.95 (1-57292-021-1); pap. text ed. 49.95 (1-57292-020-3) Austin & Winfield.

Walking Cure. Bernar Macfadden. (Illus.). 179p. 1984. reprint ed. pap. text ed. 15.00 (0-87556-391-0) Saifer.

Walking Dead. Fritz Hamilton. 125p. (Orig.). 1991. pap. 6.95 (0-941720-86-1) Slough Pr TX.

Walking Dead. Pat Holliday. 124p. (Orig.). 1982. pap. 3.95 (0-937408-29-8) GMI Pubns Inc.

Walking Dead: A Marine's Story of Vietnam. Craig Roberts & Charles W. Sasser. 1989. mass mkt. 5.99 (0-671-65777-1) PB.

Walking Dead Man. Mary Kittredge. 1993. mass mkt. 3.99 (0-312-95157-4) St Martin.

Walking Death Valley. McKinney. pap. 11.00 (0-06-258515-0, PL) HarpC.

Walking Delegate. Leroy Scott. LC 68-57549. 372p. reprint ed. lib. bdg. 29.50 (0-8398-1853-X) Irvington.

Walking Delegate. Leroy Scott. 372p. 1986. reprint ed. pap. text ed. 7.95 (0-8290-1950-2) Irvington.

Walking Diet: Walk Back to Fitness in 30 Days. Les Snowdon & Maggie Humphreys. LC 92-35036. (Illus.). 192p. 1993. 21.95 (0-87951-492-2) Overlook Pr.

Walking Diet: Walk Your Way to Fitness in 30 Days. Les Snowdon & Maggie Humphreys. (Illus.). 192p. 1995. pap. 11.95 (0-87951-596-1) Overlook Pr.

Walking Distance. Debra Allbery. LC 91-50111. (Poetry Ser.). 64p. (C). 1991. 19.95 (0-8229-3687-9); pap. 10.95 (0-8229-5458-3) U of Pittsburgh Pr.

Walking Doll: Or, the Asters & Disasters of Society. Robert H. Newell. LC 74-171061. reprint ed. 41.50 (0-404-03664-3) AMS Pr.

W

Walking down the Stairs. Galway Kinnell. Ed. by Donald Hall. LC 77-23752. (Poets on Poetry Ser.). 1978. pap. 13.95 (0-472-52530-1) U of Mich Pr.
Walking down the Wild: A Journey Through the Yellowstone Rockies. Gary Ferguson. LC 94-42960. 1995. pap. 12.00 (0-06-258581-9) HarpC.
Walking Drum. Louis L'Amour. 480p. 1985. pap. 5.50 (0-553-28040-6) Bantam.
Walking Dunes. Sandra J. Scofield. LC 91-35580. 247p. 1992. 22.00 (1-877946-12-5) Permanent Pr.
Walking Easy in the Austrian Alps: A Hiking Guide for Active Adults. Chet Lipton & Carolee Lipton. (Walking Easy Ser.). (Illus.). 208p. (Orig.). 1994. pap. 10.95 (0-933469-16-0) Gateway Bks.
Walking Easy in the French Alps: A Hiking Guide for Active Adults. Chet Lipton & Carolee Lipton. (Walking Easy Ser.). (Illus.). 224p. (Orig.). 1995. pap. 11.95 (0-933469-21-7) Gateway Bks.
Walking Easy in the Italian Alps: A Hiking Guide for Active Adults. Chet Lipton & Carolee Lipton. (Walking Easy Ser.). (Illus.). 224p. (Orig.). 1995. pap. 11.95 (0-933469-22-5) Gateway Bks.
Walking Easy in the San Francisco Bay Area: A Hiking Guide for Active Adults. Wendy Logsdon & Roger Rapoport. (Walking Easy Ser.). (Illus.). 184p. (Orig.). 1995. pap. 11.95 (0-933469-20-9) Gateway Bks.
Walking Easy in the Swiss Alps: A Hiking Guide for Active Adults. Chet Lipton & Carolee Lipton. (Illus.). 192p. 1993. pap. 10.95 (0-933469-15-2) Gateway Bks.
Walking Easy in the World's Best Places. Jay B. Teasdel. Ed. by Madeleine A. Teasdel. (Illus.). 279p. (Orig.). 1992. pap. 10.95 (0-9633918-0-1) Gulf Atlantic.
Walking Easy in the World's Best Places. 2nd ed. Jay B. Teasdel. 1995. pap. 12.95 (0-9633918-3-6) Gulf Atlantic.
Walking Europe from Top to Bottom. Susanna Margolis & Ginger Harmon. LC 85-18469. (Adventure Travel Guide Ser.). (Illus.). 320p. (Orig.). 1986. pap. 10.95 (0-87156-752-0) Sierra.
Walking Fire. Valerie Miner. LC 93-35569. (SUNY Series, The Margins of Literature). 254p. 1994. 39.50 (0-7914-2007-8); pap. 19.95 (0-7914-2008-6) State U NY Pr.
Walking Fish. James P. McMahon. Ed. by Jane Weinberger. LC 90-70520. (Illus.). 54p. (Orig.). (J). (ps-3). 1990. pap. 6.95 (0-932433-70-7) Windswept Hse.
Walking for Fitness. 2nd ed. Lon H. Seiger & James Hesson. 256p. (C). 1993. per. write for info. (0-697-12662-5) Brown & Benchmark.
***Walking for Fitness.** 3rd ed. Seiger-Hesson. 1997. pap. text ed. 11.00 (0-697-34535-1) McGraw.
Walking for Freedom: The Montgomery Bus Boycott. Richard Kelso. LC 92-18080. (Stories of America Ser.). (Illus.). 52p. (J). (gr. 2-5). 1992. lib. bdg. 24.26 (0-8114-7218-3) Raintree Steck-V.
Walking for Fun & Fitness. 2nd ed. Jerald D. Hawkins & Sandra M. Hawkins. (Illus.). 144p. 1996. pap. 15.95 (0-89582-321-7) Morton Pub.
Walking for Health. 1991. lib. bdg. 75.00 (0-8490-5140-1) Gordon Pr.
Walking for Health. Lon H. Seiger & James Hesson. 176p. 1990. text ed. write for info. (0-697-11014-1) Brown & Benchmark.
Walking for Health & Fitness. Ann Ward & James M. Rippe. LC 65-10200. (Illus.). 32p. 1988. pap. text ed. 1.20 (0-397-50855-7, Lippnctt) Lppncott-Raven.
Walking for Health Fitness & Sport. Bob Carlson. 320p. (Orig.). 1996. pap. 15.95 (1-55591-236-2) Fulcrum Pub.
Walking for Little Children: Creative Workshops for Teaching Walking & Wellness. Robert Sweetgall & Robert Neeves. (Illus.). 64p. 1988. pap. 5.00 (0-939041-03-0) Creative Walking.
Walking Four Ways in the Wind. John Allman. LC 79-83974. (Contemporary Poets Ser.). 94p. 1979. pap. 9.95 (0-691-01359-4) Princeton U Pr.
Walking Guide to Oregon's Ancient Forest. Wendell Wood. Ed. by Scott Greacen. (Illus.). 250p. (Orig.). 1991. pap. 12.95 (0-9624877-9-1) Oregon Natural Res.
Walking Guide to the Campus: The University of Chicago. University of Chicago Staff. (Illus.). 96p. 1992. pap. text ed. 4.95 (0-226-84178-2) U Ch Pr.
Walking Home from the Ice-House. Vern Rutsala. LC 80-70566. (Poetry Ser.). 1981. 20.95 (0-915604-47-7); pap. 11.95 (0-915604-48-5) Carnegie-Mellon.
Walking Home Through Bear Valley. Greg Darms. 32p. 1995. pap. 6.00 (1-887853-02-2) Radiolarian.
Walking Humbly with God: The Life & Writings of Rabbi Hershel Jonah Matt. Ed. by Daniel C. Matt. LC 92-26969. 1993. 25.00 (0-88125-430-4) Ktav.
Walking in a Landscape of Words. Pamela Hoxsey. LC 96-61927. 1997. pap. write for info. (0-9649247-2-2) Edwin Hse.
Walking in Baltimore: An Intimate Guide to the Old City. Frank R. Shivers. (Illus.). 320p. 1995. pap. 16.95 (0-8018-4868-7); text ed. 35.95 (0-8018-4872-5) Johns Hopkins.
Walking in Beauty: A Collection of the Psychological Insights & Spiritual Wisdom of Dick Olney. Dick Olney & Roslyn Moore. 120p. (Orig.). 1996. pap. 14.95 (0-9646999-0-7) DO Publng.
***Walking in Britain.** David Else. (Illus.). 480p. 1997. pap. 17.95 (0-86442-478-7) Lonely Planet.
***Walking in God's Presence.** Kevin Strong. (Illus.). 110p. 1997. 19.95 (1-885938-07-1) Cathdrl Fndtn Pr.
Walking in God's Truth: Ten Commandments-Lord's Prayer. rev. ed. Allen J. Foss. (Illus.). 276p. (YA). (gr. 6-8). 1989. pap. text ed. 5.95 (0-943167-04-3) Faith & Fellowship Pr.
Walking in Hampshire. 64p. 1987. 30.00 (0-905392-33-7) St Mut.
***Walking in Indian Moccasins: The Native Policies of Tommy Douglas & the CCF.** R. Laurie Brown. (Illus.). 288p. 1997. 65.00 (0-7748-0610-9, Pub. by U BC Pr) U of Wash Pr.
Walking in London (Piano - Vocal) Concrete Blonde. Ed. by Milton Okun. (Illus.). 56p. (Orig.). 1992. pap. text ed. 14.95 (0-89524-750-X) Cherry Lane.
Walking in Love. A. B. Simpson. 1995. pap. text ed. 8.99 (0-87509-601-8) Chr Pubns.
Walking in Missionary Shoes. Lima L. Williams. 1986. pap. 4.99 (0-87162-417-6, D8750) Warner Pr.
Walking in Stone. John Spaulding. LC 88-31768. (Wesleyan New Poets Ser.). 63p. 1989. pap. 11.95 (0-8195-1176-5, Wesleyan Univ Pr); text ed. 25.00 (0-8195-2174-4, Wesleyan Univ Pr) U Pr of New Eng.
Walking in Switzerland: Walking Guide. Clem Lindenmayer. (Illus.). 352p. 1996. pap. 14.95 (0-86442-327-6) Lonely Planet.
Walking in the Air see Snowman Board Books
***Walking in the Anointing.** Stephen Wynacht. 72p. (Orig.). 1997. pap. 3.95 (0-9633111-4-X) S Wynacht Minist.
Walking in the Clouds. large type ed. Judy Lomax. 352p. 1983. 25.99 (0-7089-0960-4) Ulverscroft.
Walking in the Garden. Gillian Nelson. 1994. lib. bdg. 19.00 (0-7278-4619-1) Severn Hse.
Walking in the Kingdom of God: A Lenten Meditation for the Busy Christian. Carl F. Peltz. 80p. (Orig.). 1994. pap. 4.95 (0-8146-2256-9, Liturg Pr Bks) Liturgical Pr.
Walking in the Kingdom of God: An Advent Meditation for the Busy Christian. Carl F. Peltz. 48p. (Orig.). (C). 1993. pap. 3.95 (0-8146-2238-0) Liturgical Pr.
Walking in the Light. Neil T. Anderson. LC 92-41361. 1993. reprint ed. pap. 10.99 (0-8407-4386-6) Nelson.
Walking in the Light: A Bible Study for New Believers. Al Gossan, Jr. (Illus.). 16p. (Orig.). 1992. pap. 2.50 (0-932581-99-4) Word Aflame.
Walking in the Sacred Manner: Holy Women, Healers, & Pipe Carriers - The Medicine Women of the Plains Indians. Mark St. Pierre & Tilda Longsoldier. 1995. pap. 12.00 (0-684-80200-7, Litl Simon S&S) S&S Childrens.
***Walking in the Shade: The Growing Point.** Doris M. Lessing. LC 97-9959. 1997. write for info. (0-06-018295-4) HarpC.
Walking in the Spirit. Sharon Daugherty. 128p. 1991. 4.99 (0-89274-502-9, HH-502) Harrison Hse.
Walking in the Truth: Perseverers & Deserters: The First, Second, & Third Letters of John. Gerard S. Sloyan. Ed. by Andrew Overman & Howard C. Kel. LC 95-24861. (New Testament in Context Ser.). 96p. (Orig.). (C). 1995. pap. 11.00 (1-56338-128-1) TPI PA.
Walking in the Way. John Tallach. 1995. 5.99 (0-906731-28-3, Pub. by Christian Focus UK) Spring Arbor Dist.
Walking in the Ways of the Lord: The Ethical Authority of the Old Testament. Christopher J. Wright. LC 95-49665. 319p. (Orig.). 1996. pap. 19.99 (0-8308-1867-7, 1867) InterVarsity.
Walking in the World. Marjorie Von Harten. 1978. 4.95 (0-900306-46-7, Pub. by Coombe Springs Pr UK) Claymont Comm.
Walking in Tower Grove Park: A Victorian Strolling Park. rev. ed. Robert E. Knittel. LC 83-82822. (Illus.). 105p. 1984. pap. 8.95 (0-933038-03-8) Grass Hooper Pr.
Walking in Tower Grove Park: A Victorian Strolling Park. 2nd rev. ed. Robert E. Knittel. LC 83-82822. (Illus.). 105p. 1984. 12.95 (0-933038-05-4) Grass Hooper Pr.
Walking in Two Worlds: Paper Doll Book for Boys, Bk. 51. (J). (ps-3). write for info. (0-931363-51-9) Celia Totus Enter.
Walking in Two Worlds: Paper Doll Book for Girls, Bk. 50. (J). (ps-3). write for info. (0-931363-50-0) Celia Totus Enter.
Walking in Two Worlds: Women's Spiritual Paths. Ed. by Kay Vander Vort et al. LC 92-29064. 1992. pap. 14.95 (0-87839-071-5) North Star.
Walking in Zen, Sitting in Zen. Rajneesh Osho Staff. Ed. by Rajneesh Foundation Intl. Staff. LC 82-24025. (Responses to Questions Ser.). 444p. (Orig.). 1982. pap. 10.95 (0-88050-668-7) Osho America.
Walking into Darkness: How to Care for the Alzheimer Patient. James J. Joyce. 8p. (Orig.). write for info. (0-9642138-0-X) Joyce Homecare.
Walking into December. Hazel E. Bybee. 110p. 1993. pap. text ed. 10.00 (1-881908-04-6) PanPress.
Walking into the River: A Novel. Lorian Hemingway. LC 92-20043. 1992. 20.00 (0-671-74642-1) S&S Trade.
Walking into the Sun: Stories My Grandfather Told. Jon Schreiber. LC 90-84628. (Illus.). 178p. (Orig.). 1991. pap. 9.95 (0-932581-3-4) CA Health Pubns.
Walking into the Wind. Santoka. LC 87-71413. (Illus.). 152p. 1994. pap. 15.00 (0-932274-41-2) Cadmus Eds.
Walking into the Wind. limited ed. Santoka. LC 87-71413. (Illus.). 152p. 1994. bds. 35.00 (0-932274-42-0) Cadmus Eds.
Walking Ireland's Mountains. David Herman. (Illus.). 144p. (Orig.). 1994. 25.95 (0-86281-471-5, Pub. by Appletree Pr IE); pap. 13.95 (0-86281-459-6, Pub. by Appletree Pr IE) Irish Bks Media.
Walking Is Wild, Weird & Wacky. rev. ed. Nancy R. Thatch. LC 89-13547. (Books for Students by Students). (Illus.). 32p. (J). (ps-2). 1989. lib. bdg. 14.95 (0-933849-29-X) Landmark Edns.
***Walking It Off, Vol. 1.** Peacock. 1997. 24.95 (0-8050-2533-2) H Holt & Co.
***Walking Kung: Breathing for Health.** Sheng K. Yun. LC 97-1467. (Illus.). 224p. (Orig.). 1997. pap. 14.95 (0-87728-895-X) Weiser.
Walking Larder: Patterns of Domestication Pastoralism, & Predation. Juliet C. Brock. (One World Archaeology Ser.: No. 2). (Illus.). 384p. 1988. text ed. 75.00 (0-04-445013-3) Routledge Chapman & Hall.
Walking Larder: Patterns of Domestication, Pastoralism, & Predation. Juliet Clutton-Brock. (One World Archaeology Ser.: No. 2). 384p. (C). 1990. pap. text ed. 29.95 (0-04-445900-9) Routledge Chapman & Hall.
Walking Larder: Patterns of Domestication, Pastoralism, & Predation. Juliet Clutton-Brock. (One World Archaeology Ser.: No. 2). 384p. (C). 1990. text ed. 75.00 (0-685-46017-7) Routledge Chapman & Hall.
Walking Liberty Half Dollars. A. Swiatek. LC 83-71497. 1984. pap. 10.00 (0-685-10799-X); lib. bdg. 18.00 (0-942666-23-2) S J Durst.
Walking Light: Essays & Memoirs. Stephen Dunn. LC 92-31578. 224p. 1993. 20.95 (0-393-03488-7) Norton.
Walking Like a Son of God. Harold Vincent. 96p. (Orig.). 1989. pap. 3.00 (0-9622950-3-5) CTP Lafayette.
Walking London. Andrew Duncan. (Illus.). 184p. 1992. 11.95 (1-56757-009-7) Appleton Comms.
Walking London. Andrew Duncan. 184p. 1995. pap. 12.95 (0-8442-9213-3, Passport Bks) NTC Pub Grp.
Walking London: Thirty Original Walks in & Around the Capital. Andrew Duncan. 128p. (C). 1989. 110.00 (1-85368-073-7, Pub. by New Holland Pubs UK) St Mut.
Walking Man. William Heath. LC 93-80382. 80p. (Orig.). 1994. pap. 8.95 (0-944806-07-4) Icarus Books.
***Walking Meditation: Pakua - The Martial Art of the I Ching.** Paul Crompton. (Illus.). 192p. 1997. pap. 14.95 (1-85230-897-4) Element MA.
Walking Muse: Horace on the Theory of Satire. Kirk Freudenburg. LC 92-8534. 288p. 1992. text ed. 47.50 (0-691-03166-5) Princeton U Pr.
Walking Naboth's Vineyard: New Studies of Swift. Ed. by Christopher Fox & Brenda Tooley. LC 94-15112. (Ward-Phillips Lectures in English Language & Literature Ser.: Vol. 13). (C). 1995. text ed. 38.00 (0-268-01950-9) U of Notre Dame Pr.
***Walking Naked: Survival of a Shattered Soul.** 165p. (Orig.). pap. 12.00 (0-9656867-0-1) Sylvia Hess.
Walking Nightmare. Alicia Scott. (Intimate Moments Ser.). 1994. mass mkt. 3.50 (0-373-07586-3, 1-07586-0) Harlequin Bks.
Walking North. Beverly V. Head. 1995. pap. 9.00 (0-87013-402-7) Mich St U Pr.
Walking North with Keats. Carol K. Walker. (Illus.). 216p. (C). 1992. text ed. 40.00 (0-300-04824-6) Yale U Pr.
Walking Off Weight: A 14-Step, 14-Day Walking-Weight Loss Program That Lasts for Life. R. Sweetgall et al. 96p. 1989. pap. 8.95 (0-939041-10-3) Creative Walking.
Walking off Weight Program. 96p. (YA). 1989. pap. 34.95 incl. vhs (1-57970-019-5, SV7240) Audio-Forum.
Walking on Air. R. S. Jones. LC 95-17166. 224p. 1995. 21.95 (0-395-74545-4) HM.
Walking on Air. R. S. Jones. Date not set. pap. 21.95 (0-670-84885-9) Viking Penguin.
Walking on Air. R. S. Jones. 1999. pap. 10.95 (0-14-017666-7) Viking Penguin.
Walking on Air. Casey Roberts. (Superromance Ser.: No. 493). 1992. mass mkt. 3.39 (0-373-70493-3, 1-70493-1) Harlequin Bks.
Walking on Air. Pierre Delattre. LC 87-80013. 243p. 1987. reprint ed. pap. 8.00 (0-915308-95-9) Graywolf.
Walking on Alligators: A Book of Meditations for Writers. Susan Shaughnessy. LC 92-53904. 224p. 1993. pap. 10.00 (0-06-250758-3) Harper SF.
Walking on Borrowed Land. William A. Owens. LC 87-40266. (Texas Tradition Ser.: No. 9). 320p. 1988. reprint ed. pap. 11.95 (0-87565-028-7) Tex Christian.
Walking on Cork: Poems. Jean Arnold. 96p. (Orig.). 1991. 14.95 (0-944266-10-X); pap. 8.95 (0-944266-11-8) Maecenas Pr.
Walking on Eggshells. Judith Ciminio. 210p. (Orig.). 1997. mass mkt. 4.99 (1-55197-059-7, Pub. by Comnwlth Pub CN) Partners Pubs Grp.
Walking on Eggshells: Practical Counsel for Women in or Leaving a Violent Relationship. Brian K. Ogawa. LC 89-51441. (Illus.). 68p. (Orig.). 1989. pap. 10.00 (0-9621260-1-2) VWAD.
Walking on Eggshells: Practical Counsel for Women in or Leaving a Violent Relationship. Brian K. Ogawa. LC 95-52905. 48p. 1996. reprint ed. pap. 8.95 (1-884244-11-4) Volcano Pr.
Walking on Frogs. John Cassidy. LC 89-84279. 64p. 9000. pap. 11.95 (1-85224-089-X, Pub. by Bloodaxe Bks UK) Dufour.
Walking on Hot Coals. Kamille M. DuSsette. 82p. (Orig.). 1989. pap. write for info. (0-9621430-0-6) K M duSsette.
Walking on Ice: Stories. Susan Hubbard. 128p. 1990. 19.95 (0-8262-0752-9) U of Mo Pr.
Walking on Lotus Flowers. Martine Batchelor. 224p. 1996. pap. 18.00 (0-7225-3231-8) Harper SF.
Walking on the Edge: How Infiltrated Earth First! Barry Clausen & Dana R. Pomeroy. Ed. by William Pickell. LC 94-60636. (Illus.). 320p. (Orig.). 1994. pap. 14.95 (0-936783-12-5) Merril Pr.
***Walking on the Road of Life.** Marjorie L. Burgess. (Orig.). 1997. pap. write for info. (1-57553-493-2) Watermrk Pr.
Walking on Thorns: The Call to Christian Obedience. Allan A. Boesak. LC 84-13782. 75p. (Orig.). reprint ed. pap. 25.00 (0-8357-4355-1, 2037183) Bks Demand.
Walking on Walnuts: My Grandmothers' Recipes for Rugelach, Romance, and Surviving in the Real World. Nancy Ring. (Illus.). 304p. 1996. 21.95 (0-553-09664-8) Bantam.
***Walking on Walnuts: My Grandmothers' Recipes for Rugelach, Romance, & Surviving the Real World.** Nancy Ring. 352p. 1997. mass mkt. 12.95 (0-553-37516-4) Bantam.
Walking on Water. Robert Ball. LC 92-64376. 1992. pap. 12.95 (0-8314-0079-X) Sci & Behavior.
***Walking on Water.** John F. Deane. 78p. 9600. pap. 11.95 (1-873790-53-8) Dufour.
Walking on Water. Mario A. Petaccia. (Illus.). 64p. 1986. 15.00 (0-89304-075-4, CCC195); pap. 7.50 (0-89304-076-2) Cross-Cultrl NY.
Walking on Water: A Comprehensive Guide to Snowshoeing & Related Activities. Carl E. Heilman, II. Ed. by Maureen J. Heilman. 1997. pap. write for info. (0-9613161-1-X) CMCG Pubns.
Walking on Water: Faith & Doubt in the Christian Life. Wayne Brouwer. LC 94-3931. 135p. 1994. 9.75 (1-56212-055-7) CRC Pubns.
Walking on Water: Reflections on Faith & Art. Madeleine L'Engle. 198p. (Orig.). 1995. pap. 10.00 (0-86547-487-7, North Pt Pr) FS&G.
Walking on Water: Reflections on Faith & Art. Madeleine L'Engle. LC 80-21066. (Wheaton Literary Ser.). 198p. (Orig.). 1980. pap. 9.99 (0-87788-919-8) Shaw Pubs.
***Walking on Water: Reflections on Life & Faith from a Writer's Notebook.** Ted Pepple. 112p. (Orig.). 1997. pap. 7.95 (0-9655980-0-4) T Pepple.
Walking on Water: Sermons on the Miracles of Jesus. James O. Gilliom. LC 95-5371. (Protestant Pulpit Exchange Ser.). 96p. (Orig.). 1995. pap. 8.95 (0-687-01138-8) Abingdon.
Walking on Water: Sydney Theatre Company at the Wharf. Compiled by Kim Spanks & Sharon Baird. 126p. (C). 1995. pap. 14.95 (0-86819-428-X) Aubrey Bks.
Walking on Water see Spirituality & Recovery: A Guide to Positive Living
Walking on Water & Other Stories. Ed. & Intro. by Allen Wier. LC 95-31869. 248p. (C). 1996. pap. 29.95 (0-8173-0785-0) U of Ala Pr.
Walking Papers. Jay Cronley. LC 87-43234. 320p. 1988. 16.95 (0-394-56947-4) Random.
Walking Paris. Giles Desmons. 208p. 1995. pap. 12.95 (0-8442-9214-1, Passport Bks) NTC Pub Grp.
Walking People: A Native American Oral History. Paula Underwood. Ed. by Barbara McNeill & Jeanne L. Slobod. LC 93-27754. (Illus.). 839p. 1993. 48.00 (1-879678-07-1); pap. 28.00 (1-879678-10-1) Tribe Two Pr.
***Walking Point: True-Life Experiences of a Founding Member of the Elite Navy SEALs.** James Watson & Kevin Dockery. LC 96-31032. 320p. 1997. 23.00 (0-688-14302-4) Morrow.
***Walking Possession.** Hamilton. 1996. pap. write for info. (0-201-32796-1) Addison-Wesley.
Walking Possession: Essay & Previews 1968-1993. Ian Hamilton. Ed. by James Broll. 320p. 1996. 25.00 (0-201-48397-1) Addison-Wesley.
Walking Proud. M. A. Scally. (J). 1990. 12.95 (0-87498-100-X) Assoc Pubs DC.
Walking Rain. Susan Wade. 370p. 1996. mass mkt. 5.99 (0-553-56865-5, Fanfare) Bantam.
Walking San Diego: Where to Go to Get Away from It All & What to Do When You Get There. Lonnie B. Hewitt & Barbara C. Moore. LC 89-13053. (Illus.). 240p. (Orig.). 1989. pap. 14.95 (0-89886-221-3) Mountaineers.
***Walking San Francisco on the Barbary Coast Trail.** 2nd rev. ed. Daniel Bacon. (Orig.). Date not set. pap. 13.95 (0-9646804-1-6) Quicksilvr CA.
Walking Shadow. Robert B. Parker. 304p. 1995. mass mkt. 6.99 (0-425-14774-6) Berkley Pub.
Walking Shadow. Brian M. Stableford. 224p. 1989. pap. 3.95 (0-88184-502-7) Carroll & Graf.
Walking Shadow. large type ed. Robert B. Parker. LC 94-19124. 1994. 25.95 (1-56895-106-X) Wheeler Pub.
***Walking Shadows.** (Knockout Ser.). Date not set. text ed. write for info. (0-582-25061-7, Pub. by Longman UK) Longman.
Walking Shadows: Shakespeare in the National Film & Television Archive. Ed. by Luke McKernan & Olwen Terris. (Archive Monographs). (Illus.). 280p. 1994. text ed. 45.00 (0-85170-414-X) Ind U Pr.
Walking Shadows: Shakespeare in the National Film & Television Archive. Ed. by Luke McKernan & Olwen Terris. (Archive Monographs). (Illus.). 280p. 1994. pap. 21.95 (0-85170-486-7) Ind U Pr.
Walking Softly. Mary Waller. LC 92-60810. 100p. 1993. 7.95 (1-55523-544-1) Winston-Derek.
Walking Softly in the Wilderness: The Sierra Club Guide to Backpacking. rev. ed. John Hart. LC 83-19592. (Outdoor Activities Guides Ser.). (Illus.). 448p. 1984. pap. 15.00 (0-87156-813-6) Sierra.
***Walking Songs: Poem Meditations.** Velande Taylor. 32p. (Orig.). 1997. pap. 8.00 (0-9649947-3-9) WrdCraft Bks.
***Walking Southeast Alaska: 40 Walks & Easy Hikes for Inside Passage Travelers.** Andromeda Romano-Lax. LC 97-897. (Illus.). 192p. (Orig.). 1997. pap. 13.95 (0-89997-208-X) Wilderness Pr.
Walking Stars. Victor Villasenor. LC 94-7404. 1994. 14.95 (1-55885-118-6) Arte Publico.
Walking Sticks. Catherine Dike. 1989. pap. 25.00 (0-7478-0079-0, Pub. by Shire UK) St Mut.
***Walking Sticks.** Tamara Green. LC 97-7332. (New Creepy Crawly Collection). (Illus.). (J). 1997. lib. bdg. write for info. (0-8368-1917-9) Gareth Stevens Inc.
Walking Sticks. Edward Hart. (Illus.). 96p. 1993. pap. 15.95 (1-85223-756-2, Pub. by Crowood Pr UK) Trafalgar.
Walking Stones. Mollie Hunter. LC 95-37916. (Magic Carpet Book Ser.). 176p. (J). (gr. 3 up). 1996. pap. 5.00 (0-15-200995-7) HarBrace.
Walking Swiftly: Writings & Images on the Occasion of Robert Bly's 65th Birthday. Ed. by Thomas R. Smith. (Illus.). 288p. 1992. 19.95 (0-915408-48-1) Ally Pr.

W

***Walking Switzerland - The Swiss Way: From Vacation Apartments, Hotels, Mountain Inns, & Huts.** 2nd rev. ed. Philip Lieberman & Marcia Lieberman. LC 96-6542. (Illus.). 288p. (Orig.). 1997. pap. 16.95 (*0-89886-511-5*) Mountaineers.

Walking TCU: A Historical Perspective. Joan Swaim. LC 91-38344. 176p. 1992. pap. 10.95 (*0-87565-104-6*) Tex Christian.

Walking the Alpine Parks of France & Northwest Italy. Marcia Leiberman & Philip Leiberman. (Illus.). 240p. 1994. pap. 14.95 (*0-89886-398-8*) Mountaineers.

Walking the Appalachian Trail. Larry Luxenberg. (Illus.). 256p. 1994. pap. 16.95 (*0-8117-3095-6*) Stackpole.

***Walking the Black Cat.** Charles Simic. 1996. 24.00 (*0-614-20810-6*, Harvest Bks); pap. 13.00 (*0-614-20809-2*, Harvest Bks) HarBrace.

Walking the Black Cat: Poems. Charles Simic. LC 96-17064. 1996. 24.00 (*0-15-100219-3*); pap. 13.00 (*0-15-600481-X*) HarBrace.

Walking the Blind Dog: Poems by G. E. Murray. G. E. Murray. 112p. (Orig.). 1992. 10.95 (*0-252-06231-0*) U of Ill Pr.

Walking the Blue Ridge: A Guide to the Trails of the Blue Ridge Parkway. rev. ed. Leonard M. Adkins. LC 92-17117. xiv, 521p. (Orig.). 1992. pap. 13.95 (*0-8078-4401-2*) U of NC Pr.

Walking the Bridge of Your Nose. Michael Rosen. LC 95-3007. (Illus.). 64p. (J). (gr. 1-5). 1995. 14.95 (*1-85697-596-7*, Kingfisher LKC) LKC.

Walking the California Coast: One Hundred Adventures along the West Coast. John McKinney. LC 93-14604. (Walking the West Ser.). (Illus.). 272p. 1994. pap. 14.00 (*0-06-258513-4*) Harper SF.

Walking the Cat, by Tommy "Tip" Paine: Gordon Liddy Is My Muse, II. John Calvin Batchelor. LC 95-14537. 1995. pap. 12.00 (*0-8050-3789-6*, Owl) H Holt & Co.

Walking the Central California Coast: A Day Hiker's Guide. John McKinney. LC 95-51516. 256p. 1996. pap. 14.00 (*0-06-258636-X*) Harper SF.

Walking the Central Scottish Way. Earl B. Wilkie. (Illus.). 240p. 1996. pap. 22.95 (*1-85158-747-0*, Pub. by Mnstream UK) Trafalgar.

Walking the Dead. Lori Anderson. (Illus.). 24p. (Orig.). (C). 1991. pap. 4.95 (*0-9623693-2-2*) Heaven Bone Pr.

Walking the Dead. Keith Curran. 1992. pap. 5.25 (*0-8222-1218-8*) Dramatists Play.

Walking the Dead Diamond River. Edward Hoagland. 340p. 1993. pap. 15.95 (*1-55821-216-7*) Lyons & Burford.

Walking the Denver-Boulder Region. Darcy Folzenlogen & Robert Folzenlogen. LC 91-68587. (Illus.). 214p. (Orig.). 1992. pap. 14.95 (*0-9620685-3-5*) Willow Pr CO.

Walking the Dog. Bernard Mac Laverty. 200p. 1996. pap. 11.00 (*0-393-31453-7*, Norton Paperbks) Norton.

Walking the Dog: And Other Stories. Bernard MacLaverty. LC 94-36707. 208p. 1995. 20.00 (*0-393-03758-4*) Norton.

Walking the Dog & Other Stories. Marian Eldridge. LC 83-12884. 220p. 1985. pap. 14.95 (*0-7022-1785-9*) Intl Spec Bk.

Walking the East Mojave: A Visitor's Guide to Mojave National Park. John McKinney & Cheri Rae. LC 93-26564. (Illus.). 224p. 1994. pap. 12.00 (*0-06-258512-6*) Harper SF.

Walking the Edge. Alice Mead. 190p. (J). (gr. 4-7). 1995. lib. bdg. 14.95 (*0-8075-8649-8*) A Whitman.

Walking the Empowerment Tightrope: Balancing Management Authority & Employee Influence. Robert P. Crosby. LC 92-60828. 208p. 1992. pap. 19.95 (*0-925652-15-6*) Orgn Design & Dev.

Walking the GR Five: Larche to Nice: A Guide to 550 Kilometers of Footpaths of the Southern Alps & Haute Provence, Including the Tour de l'Ubeye. French Ramblers Association Staff. (Footpaths of Europe Ser.). (Illus.). 225p. (Orig.). 1991. pap. 19.95 (*1-85365-223-7*, Pub. by McCarta UK) Seven Hills Bk.

Walking the GR Five: Vosges to Jura: A Guide to 550 Kilometers of Footpaths Through an Area of Scenic Grandeur, Abundant Forests & Superb Architecture. French Ramblers Association Staff. (Footpaths of Europe Ser.). (Illus.). 225p. (Orig.). 1991. pap. 19.95 (*1-85365-232-6*, Pub. by McCarta UK) Seven Hills Bk.

Walking the GR5: Modane to Larche: A Guide to 750 Kilometers of This Famous Alpine Footpath Including the Tour de l'Oisans & the Tour du Haut-Dauphine. French Ramblers Association Staff. Ed. by Folly Marland. Tr. by Helen PcPhail from FRE. (Footpaths of Europe Ser.). (Illus.). 200p. (Orig.). 1990. pap. 19.95 (*1-85365-189-3*, Pub. by McCarta UK) Seven Hills Bk.

Walking the High-Tech High Wire: The Technical Entrepreneur's Guide to Running a Successful Enterprise. David Adamson. LC 93-24208. 1993. text ed. 24.95 (*0-07-000468-4*) McGraw.

***Walking the Hudson Batt to Bear: From the Battery to Bear Mountain.** Cy A. Adler. (Illus.). 164p. (Orig.). 1997. pap. 12.95 (*0-914018-04-3*, 7269) Green Eagle Pr.

***Walking the Labyrinth.** Goldstein. Date not set. pap. 9.99 (*0-312-85968-6*) St Martin.

Walking the Labyrinth. Lisa Goldstein. 1996. write for info. (*0-614-09396-1*) Tor Bks.

***Walking the Labyrinth.** Lisa Goldstein. 1997. mass mkt. 5.99 (*0-8125-4469-2*) Tor Bks.

Walking the Labyrinth. Lisa Goldstein. 256p. 1996. 21.95 (*0-312-86175-3*) St Martin.

Walking the Line: Scenes from an Army Childhood. Kevin T. Brophy. (Illus.). 189p. 1995. 29.95 (*1-85158-638-5*, Pub. by Mnstream UK) Trafalgar.

Walking the Log: Memories of a Southern Childhood. Bessie Nickens. LC 94-10803. (Illus.). 32p. (J). (gr. 2 up). 1994. 14.95 (*0-8478-1794-6*) Rizzoli Intl.

Walking the Maine Coast: Thirty-Two Walking Tours from Kittery to the Canadian Border. 2nd ed. John Gibson. LC 90-84960. (Illus.). 146p. 1991. pap. 10.95 (*0-89272-282-7*) Down East.

Walking the Marches. Sam Burnside. 83p. 9000. pap. 10.95 (*0-948339-42-X*, Pub. by Salmon Pubng IE) Dufour.

Walking the New England Coast: Forty-Four Scenic Walks, Strolls, & Day Hikes. John Gibson. LC 91-77672. (Illus.). 208p. 1992. pap. 13.95 (*0-89272-309-2*) Down East.

Walking the Path. Jude LaClaire. (Life Weaving Ser.: Vol. 3). (Illus.). 64p. 1995. spiral bd. write for info. (*0-9629385-3-X*) Heartlnd Personal.

Walking the Path with Sai Baba. Howard Murphet. LC 93-12651. Orig. Title: Invitation to Glory. (Illus.). 208p. (Orig.). 1993. pap. 12.95 (*0-87728-781-3*) Weiser.

Walking the Pembrokeshire Coast Path. Patrick Stark. 84p. (C). 1990. pap. 30.00 (*0-86383-686-0*, Pub. by Gomer Pr UK) St Mut.

Walking the Plank: A True Adventure among Pirates. Stephen Kiesling. LC 94-7436. 256p. (Orig.). 1994. pap. 12.95 (*0-9638461-5-9*) Nordic Knight.

Walking the Point: Male Initiation & the Vietnam Experience. Daryl S. Paulson. LC 94-8249. 96p. (Orig.). 1995. pap. 8.95 (*0-942963-49-0*) Distinctive Pub.

Walking the Rez Road. Jim Northup. LC 92-4418. 176p. 1993. 15.95 (*0-89658-181-0*) Voyageur Pr.

Walking the Rez Road. Jim Northup. LC 92-4418. 176p. 1995. pap. text ed. 12.00 (*0-89658-321-X*) Voyageur Pr.

Walking the Rim. Susan H. Lindquist. LC 91-76966. (Illus.). 144p. (YA). (gr. 7 up). 1992. 14.95 (*1-56397-098-8*) Boyds Mills Pr.

Walking the Road of Faith: Lessons Presented to the Judson C. Ward, Jr. Class of Glenn Memorial United Methodist Church. Judson C. Ward, Jr. Ed. by Beth D. Bassett. LC 94-33908. (Emory Archives & Libraries Ser.: No. 2). 258p. 1994. pap. 24.95 (*0-7885-0024-4*, 700202) Scholars Pr GA.

Walking the Road to Freedom: A Story about Sojourner Truth. Jeri Ferris. (Creative Minds Ser.). (Illus.). 64p. (J). (gr. 3-6). 1988. lib. bdg. 14.21 (*0-87614-318-4*, Carolrhoda) Lerner Group.

Walking the Road to Freedom: A Story about Sojourner Truth. Jeri Ferris. (Creative Minds Biographies Ser.). (Illus.). 64p. (J). (gr. 3-6). 1989. reprint ed. pap. 5.95 (*0-87614-505-5*, Lerner Publctns) Lerner Group.

Walking the Tightrope: A Feminist Reading of Therese Huber's Short Prose Narratives. Vibha B. Gokhale. (GERM Ser.). x, 136p. (C). 1996. 55.95 (*1-57113-016-0*) Camden Hse.

Walking the Trail: One Man's Journey Along the Cherokee Trail of Tears. Jerry Ellis. 272p. 1991. pap. 10.95 (*0-385-30826-4*, Delta) Dell.

Walking the Trail: One Man's Journey along the Cherokee Trail of Tears. large type ed. Jerry Ellis. LC 92-43588. (Americana Ser.). 353p. 1993. reprint ed. lib. bdg. 13.95 (*1-56054-885-1*) Thorndike Pr.

Walking the Trail: One Man's Journey along the Cherokee Trail of Tears. large type ed. Jerry Ellis. LC 92-43588. (Americana Ser.). 353p. 1993. reprint ed. lib. bdg. 20.95 (*1-56054-642-5*) Thorndike Pr.

***Walking the Twilight.** Northland Publishing Staff. 1997. pap. text ed. 14.95 (*0-87358-695-6*) Northland AZ.

Walking the Twilight: Women Writers of the Southwest. Ed. by Kathryn Wilder. LC 94-28280. 240p. (Orig.). 1994. pap. 14.95 (*0-87358-585-2*) Northland AZ.

Walking the Twilight Vol. II: Women Writers of the Southwest. Ed. by Kathryn Wilder. LC 94-28280. 256p. (Orig.). 1996. pap. 14.95 (*0-87358-648-4*) Northland AZ.

Walking the Ulster Way: A Journal & Guide. rev. ed. Alan Warner. (Illus.). 200p. 1992. pap. 11.95 (*0-86281-227-5*, Pub. by Appletree Pr IE) Irish Bks Media.

Walking the Victorian Streets: Women, Representation, & the City. Deborah E. Nord. (Illus.). 280p. 1995. 39.95 (*0-8014-3196-4*); pap. 16.95 (*0-8014-8291-7*) Cornell U Pr.

Walking the Walk: Realizing Your Personal Relationship with God. Willa M. Thompson. 60p. 1991. pap. 6.95 (*0-9631152-0-0*) W M Thompson.

Walking the Winds: A Hiking & Fishing Guide to Wyoming's Wind River Range. Rebecca Woods. 224p. 1994. pap. text ed. 12.95 (*0-9642423-0-3*) Whte Willow.

Walking the World Wide Web: Your Personal Guide to the Best of the Web. 2nd ed. Shannon R. Turlington. 792p. 1996. pap. 39.95 incl. cd-rom (*1-56604-298-4*) Ventana Communs.

Walking the Yukon: A Solo Journey Through the Land of Beyond. Chris Townsend. 1993. pap. text ed. 13.95 (*0-07-065249-X*) McGraw.

Walking the Yukon: A Solo Trek Through the Land of Beyond. Chris Townsend. LC 93-9479. 1993. 13.95 (*0-87742-380-6*, Ragged Mntn) Intl Marine.

Walking Through Brittany: A Guide to 1100 Kilometers of Footpaths Through the Countryside & Villages of Brittany. French Ramblers Association Staff. Tr. by Jane Chalk et al. from FRE. (Footpaths of Europe Ser.). (Illus.). 198p. (Orig.). 1990. pap. 19.95 (*1-85365-160-5*, Pub. by McCarta UK) Seven Hills Bk.

Walking Through Clear Water in a Pool Painted Black. Cookie Mueller. 150p. 1990. pap. 6.00 (*0-936756-61-6*) Autonomedia.

***Walking Through Deep Snow.** Mary A. Wehler. Ed. by Larry Smith. 104p. pap. 12.95 (*0-911051-91-0*) Plain View.

Walking Through France. Robin Neillands. 1995. pap. text ed. 10.95 (*1-85253-312-9*, Pub. by Quiller Pr UK) St Mut.

Walking Through History: The Seaports of Black Rock & Southport. Charles Brilvitch. (Illus.). 1977. pap. 3.50 (*0-614-05155-X*) Fairfield Hist.

Walking Through Stress: Meditation in Motion. Richard L. Harding. (Illus.). 201p. (Orig.). 1989. pap. 11.95 (*0-945946-09-0*) Cassandra Pr.

Walking Through the Fire: Finding the Purpose of Pain in the Christian Life. James R. Lucas. 224p. 1996. pap. 12.99 (*0-8054-6194-9*, 4261-94) Broadman.

***Walking Through the Jungle.** Illus. by Debbie Harter. LC 96-46706. 32p. (J). (ps-k). 1997. 14.95 (*0-531-30035-8*) Orchard Bks Watts.

Walking Through the Jungle. Julie Lacome. LC 92-53018. (Illus.). 32p. (J). (ps). 1993. 13.95 (*1-56402-137-8*) Candlewick Pr.

Walking Through the Jungle. Julie Lacome. LC 92-53018. (Illus.). (J). (ps up). 1995. pap. 4.99 (*1-56402-526-8*) Candlewick Pr.

Walking Through the Woods. Mary F. Van De Vyver. 80p. 1994. pap. text ed. 5.00 (*1-883520-05-3*) Jeremiah Pr.

Walking Through Walls: A Presentation of Tibetan Meditation. Geshe G. Lodro. Ed. by Jeffrey Hopkins et al. LC 92-16321. 400p. 1992. 35.00 (*1-55939-008-5*); pap. 19.95 (*1-55939-004-2*) Snow Lion Pubns.

Walking Through Walls: Practical Esoteric Psychology. Will Parfitt. 1993. pap. 14.95 (*1-85230-115-5*) Element MA.

Walking to Cootehill: New & Selected Poems, 1958-1992. John Engels. LC 92-31706. 174p. (C). 1993. pap. 14.95 (*0-87451-611-0*); text ed. 30.00 (*0-87451-610-2*) U Pr of New Eng.

Walking to Fitness. Seth Bauer. (Illus.). 128p. (Orig.). 1991. pap. 8.95 (*0-9630398-0-6*) Walking.

Walking to La Milpa: Living in Guatemala with Armies, Demons, Abrazos & Death. Marcos M. Villatoro. LC 95-45126. 180p. (Orig.). 1996. 19.95 (*1-55921-164-4*) Moyer Bell.

***Walking to Mercury.** Starhawk. LC 96-30290. 544p. 1997. 23.95 (*0-553-10233-8*) Bantam.

Walking To New Orleans see Rhythm & Blues in New Orleans

Walking to Santiago. Neil Curry. 66p. 9300. pap. 17.95 (*1-870612-13-2*, Pub. by Enitha Pr UK) Dufour.

Walking to School. Libby Gleeson. LC 92-31945. (Voyages Ser.). (Illus.). (J). 1993. 2.50 (*0-383-03602-X*) SRA McGraw.

Walking to School. Ethel Turner. (Illus.). 24p. (Orig.). (J). (gr. k-2). 1995. pap. 7.95 (*0-85091-654-2*, Pub. by Lothian Pub AT) Seven Hills Bk.

Walking to the Edge: Essays of Resistance. Margaret Randall. 220p. (Orig.). 1991. 25.00 (*0-89608-398-5*); pap. 12.00 (*0-89608-397-7*) South End Pr.

Walking to Waldheim. Mayo Simon. 1995. 5.25 (*0-87129-471-0*, W22) Dramatic Pub.

Walking to, Walking with, Walking Through: Sermons for Lent, Holy Week, & Easter - Gospel. Glenn E. Ludwig. LC 93-51081. (Orig.). 1994. pap. 9.50 (*0-7880-0005-5*) CSS OH.

Walking to Where the River Ends. Wang Fang-Yu et al. (Illus.). 96p. 1980. pap. 22.50 (*0-208-01882-4*, Archon Bks) Shoe String.

Walking to Work: Tramps in America, 1790-1935. Ed. by Eric H. Monkkonen. LC 83-21807. 259p. reprint ed. pap. 73.90 (*0-7837-1844-6*, 2042044) Bks Demand.

Walking Together: Outreach & Evangelization for Youth. Robert P. Stamschror. (Illus.). (Orig.). 1995. pap. 15.95 (*0-88489-293-X*) St Marys.

Walking Together in Faith: A Workbook for Sponsors of Christian Initiation. Thomas H. Morris. 224p. 1992. pap. 12.95 (*0-8091-3289-3*) Paulist Pr.

Walking Together to God. Ann Gallagher et al. (Grade School Chastity - Project Genesis Ser.). (Illus.). 72p. (Orig.). (J). (gr. 4). 1996. teacher ed., pap. text ed. write for info. (*1-885845-12-X*); student ed., pap. text ed. write for info. (*1-885845-13-8*) Leaflet Missal.

Walking Tour in Southern France: Ezra Pound among the Troubadours. Ezra Pound. LC 92-19890. (Illus.). 160p. 1992. 22.95 (*0-8112-1223-8*) New Directions.

Walking Tour of Dublin Churches. Illus. by Liam C. Martin. 64p. 1989. pap. 22.00 (*1-85390-945-9*, Pub. by Veritas IE) St Mut.

Walking Tour of Historic Roscoe Village. Geri Nichols. (Illus.). 34p. (Orig.). 1989. pap. 3.50 (*1-880443-03-1*) Roscoe Village.

Walking Tour of Historic Roscoe Village. rev. ed. write for info. (*0-318-70038-7*) Roscoe Village.

Walking Tour of the University at Buffalo: And Other Area Architectural Treasures. Frances Rupley. LC 93-12107. (Illus.). 119p. (Orig.). (C). 1993. pap. 14.95 (*0-87975-813-9*) Prometheus Bks.

Walking Tour of the University of Georgia. F. N. Boney. LC 88-25997. (Illus.). 112p. (Orig.). 1989. pap. 8.95 (*0-8203-1081-6*) U of Ga Pr.

Walking Tours of Downtown Rochester: Images of History. Cynthia Howk et al. (Illus.). 50p. (Orig.). 1992. pap. 4.95 (*0-9641706-2-0*) Rorval Pubns.

Walking Tours of Old Washington & Alexandria. Paul Hogarth. LC 85-12907. (Illus.). 144p. (Orig.). 1985. pap. 12.50 (*0-914440-85-3*) EPM Pubns.

***Walking Towards Pentecost.** Anne N. Rupp. 157p. 1996. pap. 14.95 (*1-877871-95-8*, 2686) Ed Ministries.

***Walking Towards Walden.** John H. Mitchell. LC 96-51483. 1997. pap. 13.00 (*0-201-15487-0*) Addison-Wesley.

Walking Towards Walden: A Pilgrimage in Search of Place. John H. Mitchell. LC 95-20789. 320p. 1995. 23.00 (*0-201-40672-1*) Addison-Wesley.

***Walking Trails of Eastern & Central Wisconsin.** Bob Crawford. LC 97-6432. 1997. write for info. (*0-299-15570-6*) U of Wis Pr.

***Walking Trails of Eastern & Central Wisconsin.** Bob Crawford. LC 97-6432. (North Coast Bks.). (Illus.). 200p. 1997. pap. 16.95 (*0-299-15574-9*) U of Wis Pr.

Walking Trails of Southern Wisconsin. Robert F. Crawford. LC 93-39165. 1994. 35.00 (*0-299-13840-2*); pap. 16.95 (*0-299-13844-5*) U of Wis Pr.

Walking Trees: Portraits of Teachers & Children in the Culture of Schools. 2nd ed. Ralph Fletcher. LC 90-36357. (Illus.). 238p. 1995. pap. 14.95 (*0-435-08121-7*, 08121) Heinemann.

Walking Trees & Other Scary Stories. Roberta Brown. 139p. (J). (gr. 4 up). 1991. pap. 7.95 (*0-87483-143-1*) August Hse.

Walking up a Rainbow. Theodore Taylor. 256p. (YA). 1996. mass mkt. 4.50 (*0-380-72592-4*, Flare) Avon.

Walking up a Rainbow: Being the True Version of the Long & Hazardous Journey of Susan D. Carlisle, Mrs. Myrtle Dessery, Drover Bert Pettit & Cowboy Clay Carmer & Others. Theodore Taylor. LC 94-16548. 276p. (YA). (gr. 7 up). 1994. 15.00 (*0-15-294512-1*) HarBrace.

***Walking Victims.** Adele Mayer. 134p. 1997. pap. 15.95 (*1-55691-126-2*, 262) Learning Pubns.

Walking Wellness Student Workbook. Robert Sweetgall. Ed. by Robert Neeves. (Illus.). 80p. (J). (gr. 4-8). 1986. student ed. 5.00 (*0-939041-00-6*); teacher ed. 12.95 (*0-939041-01-4*) Creative Walking.

Walking Wellness Teacher's Guide. Robert Sweetgall. Ed. by Robert Neeves. (Illus.). 144p. 1988. 13.00 (*0-939041-05-7*) Creative Walking.

Walking West. Noelle Sickles. 320p. 1995. 22.95 (*0-312-13208-5*) St Martin.

Walking Wisdom for Women: Plusing Your Walk for Fitness, Career & Romance. Elaine P. Ward. LC 95-69495. (Illus.). 126p. (Orig.). 1996. pap. 12.95 (*1-884647-02-2*) N A R F.

***Walking with a Himalayan Master: An American's Odyssey.** Justin O'Brien. (Illus.). 300p. (Orig.). 1997. 22.00 (*0-936663-19-7*) Yes Intl.

***Walking with Angels.** 1996. 8.95 (*0-8378-4999-3*) Gibson.

Walking with Beauty: The Art & Life of Gerard Curtis Delano. Richard G. Bowman. (Illus.). 174p. 1990. 67.50 (*0-9625410-0-1*) R G Bowman.

Walking with Christ. rev. ed. Navigators Staff. (Design for Discipleship Ser.: Bk. 3). (Illus.). 48p. 1980. pap. 4.00 (*0-89109-038-X*) NavPress.

Walking with Contemplation: A Walker's Guide. Ed. by P. K. Colleran. (Illus.). 230p. (Orig.). 1983. pap. 4.95 (*0-9609102-0-4*) CAFH Found Inc.

Walking with Faith. Walter J. Woods. (Orig.). 1997. pap. write for info. (*0-8146-5824-5*) Liturgical Pr.

Walking with God. D. Martyn Lloyd-Jones. LC 92-21507. (Studies in First John). 144p. (C). 1993. pap. 9.99 (*0-89107-735-9*) Crossway Bks.

Walking with God. Harold Penninger. LC 96-60487. 128p. 1996. per. 7.95 (*1-57258-114-X*) Teach Servs.

Walking with God: Daily Bread. (Illus.). (J). (gr. k-4). 1972. pap. text ed. 6.99 (*1-55976-300-0*) CEF Press.

Walking with God: Leaders Guide I. 500p. 1992. teacher ed., pap. 22.99 (*0-310-59203-8*) Zondervan.

Walking with God: Leaders Guide II. 500p. 1992. teacher ed., pap. 22.99 (*0-310-59213-5*) Zondervan.

Walking with God: Reflections on Life's Meaning. Adolfo Quezada. LC 90-60305. 96p. (Orig.). 1990. pap. 3.50 (*0-89243-320-5*) Liguori Pubns.

Walking with God: The Young Person's Prayer Diary. 1996. pap. 12.99 (*0-927545-79-9*) YWAM Pub.

Walking with God Through Genesis. Ellen Blackwell. (Walking with God Ser.). 384p. (Orig.). 1995. pap. 15.99 (*1-56043-839-8*) Destiny Image.

Walking with God Through the Twelve Steps: What I Learned about Honesty, Healing, Reconciliation & Wholeness. Frances Jay & Joyce Turk. 112p. (Orig.). 1996. pap. 8.95 (*0-87946-134-9*) ACTA Pubns.

Walking with Him: A Biblical Guide Through Thirty Days of Spiritual Exercises. Josef Neuner. 290p. (C). 1985. 2.50 (*0-8294-0533-X*) Loyola Pr.

Walking with Jesus. Mary C. Meyer. LC 92-10912. 80p. (Orig.). 1992. pap. 10.99 (*0-8361-3574-1*) Herald Pr.

Walking with Jesus: Luke. Linda R. McGinn. (Women in the Word Ser.). 96p. (Orig.). (YA). (gr. 10). 1995. pap. 3.99 (*0-8010-5009-X*) Baker Bks.

Walking with Jesus Leader's Guide: Luke. Linda R. McGinn. (Women in the Word Ser.). 64p. (Orig.). 1995. teacher ed., pap. 7.99 (*0-8010-5247-5*) Baker Bks.

***Walking with Lions.** Clive J. Buchanan & Michale J. Bandley. (Illus.). (Orig.). 1996. pap. 14.95 (*1-890261-00-9*) Missions Pub.

***Walking with Mama.** Barbara W. Stynes. Ed. by Glenn J. Hovemann. (Illus.). 24p. (J). (ps-2). 1997. 14.95 (*1-883220-56-4*); pap. 6.95 (*1-883220-57-2*) Dawn CA.

***Walking with Muir Across Yosemite.** Thomas R. Vale & Geraldine R. Vale. LC 97-20321. (Illus.). 160p. 1998. 32.95 (*0-299-15690-7*) U of Wis Pr.

***Walking with Muir Across Yosemite.** Thomas R. Vale & Geraldine R. Vale. LC 97-20321. (Illus.). 160p. 1998. pap. 14.95 (*0-299-15694-X*) U of Wis Pr.

Walking with My Lord. Stefanie Sakuma. (Inspirational Ser.). 25p. 1990. pap. text ed. 6.95 (*1-878385-02-X*, Audiobridge); pap. text ed. 14.95 incl. audio (*1-878385-04-6*, Audiobridge); audio 9.95 (*1-878385-03-8*, Audiobridge) Media Bridge.

Walking with My Lord. large type ed. write for info. (*0-318-68659-7*, 7270) LBW.

***Walking with Presidents: Louis Martin & the Rise of Black Political Power.** Alex Poinsett. LC 97-1997. 288p. 1997. 21.95 (*1-56833-093-6*) Madison Bks UPA.

Walking With Saints: Through the Best & Worst Times of Our Lives. Calvin Miller. LC 94-32745. 1995. pap. 16.99 (*0-7852-8006-5*) Nelson.

Walking with Spring. Earl Shaffer. (Illus.). 160p. 1996. reprint ed. pap. 8.95 (*0-917953-84-3*) Appalachian Trail.

W

An Asterisk (*) at the beginning of an entry indicates that the title is appearing in BIP for the first time.

Walking with the Angels: The Valiant Papers & the Philippian Fragment. Calvin Miller. LC 94-7402. (Illus.). 222p. (gr. 10). 1994. reprint ed. pap. 15.99 (*0-8010-6308-6*) Baker Bks.

Walking with the Giants - Chinese Edition. Warren W. Wiersbe. Tr. by Wesley K. Shao. 262p. (CHI.). 1991. 12.00 (*1-56582-010-X*) Christ Renew Min.

Walking with the Great Apes: Jane Goodall, Dian Fossey, Birute Galdikas. Sy Montgomery. 1992. pap. 15.00 (*0-395-61156-3*) HM.

Walking with the Lord. John-Roger. 1991. 12.50 (*0-914829-30-0*) Mandeville LA.

Walking with the Night: The Afro-Cuban World of Santeria. Raul Canizares. (Illus.). 160p. 1992. pap. 12.95 (*0-89281-366-0*) Inner Tradit.

Walking with the Pilgrim Pope: Pope John Paul II Speaks Through Words & Pictures. Ed. by Charles Mangan. LC 94-69789. 52p. 1995. pap. 5.95 (*1-882972-43-0*) Queenship Pub.

Walking with the River. Bob Boldman. 32p. 1980. pap. 3.50 (*0-913719-14-5*) High-Coo Pr.

***Walking with the Savior.** Max Lucado. 1996. 13.99 (*0-8423-7930-4*) Tyndale.

Walking with the Shepherd. Isabel Anders. LC 93-47218. 1994. 7.99 (*0-8407-9402-9*) Nelson.

Walking with the Walkers. Edward R. Walker, III. (Illus.). 128p. 1981. pap. 9.95 (*0-932807-08-9*) Overmountain Pr.

Walking with the Wise: God's Plan for Parents & Teens. Benny Phillips & Sheree Phillips. Ed. by Greg Somerville. 176p. (Orig.). (YA). (gr. 7-12). 1994. pap. 8.00 (*1-881039-04-8*) People of Destiny.

Walking with Wildflowers: A Field Guide to the St. Louis Area. Karen S. Haller. LC 93-48414. (Illus.). 272p. (C). 1994. pap. 22.50 (*0-8262-0950-5*) U of Mo Pr.

Walking Wolf. Nancy A. Collins. 1995. 25.00 (*0-929480-42-2*) Mark Ziesing.

Walking Words. Eduardo Galeano. Tr. by Mark Fried. (Illus.). 328p. 1995. 23.00 (*0-393-03782-7*) Norton.

Walking Words: With Woodcuts by Jose Francisco Borges. Eduardo Galeano. 328p. 1997. pap. 15.00 (*0-393-31514-2*) Norton.

Walking Worthy. Ed Robinson. 32p. 1989. pap. 3.25 (*0-8341-1273-6*) Beacon Hill.

Walking Wounded. Beverly Barbo. LC 87-72944. (Illus.). 248p. (Orig.). 1987. 13.95 (*0-944996-00-0*); pap. 9.95 (*0-944996-01-9*) Carlsons.

Walking Wounded. Robert Devereaux. 382p. 1996. mass mkt. 5.50 (*0-440-21794-6*) Dell.

Walking Wounded: A Look at Faith Theology. Jeremy Reynolds. LC 94-72827. 224p. 1995. pap. 10.99 (*0-614-06757-X*) Huntington Hse.

Walking Wounded: Men's Lives During & since the Vietnam War. Steve Trimm. Ed. by Edward Tick. (Frontiers in Psychotherapy Ser.). 192p. (C). 1993. pap. 39.50 (*0-89391-807-5*); text ed. 73.25 (*0-89391-806-7*) Ablex Pub.

***Walking 14th Street Home: Poems 1990-1992.** Gia Hansbury. 24p. 1992. 5.00 (*1-890044-00-8*) Riverstone PA.

***Walkingsticks.** Patrick Merrick. LC 96-46957. (Nature Bks.). 32p. (J). (gr. 1-5). 1997. lib. bdg. 22.79 (*1-56766-383-4*) Childs World.

Walkingsticks. Ulrich Stoeber. (Illus.). 244p. 1996. pap. 29.95 (*0-7643-0154-3*) Schiffer.

***Walkman.** (Young Dragon Readers 3 Ser.). (J). 1995. pap. text ed. write for info. (*962-359-536-0*) Addison-Wesley.

***Walks Alone.** Brian Burks. LC 97-14738. (J). 1998. write for info. (*0-15-201612-0*) HarBrace.

Walks Among the Poor of Belfast. W. M. O'Hanlon. 1971. reprint ed. 22.00 (*0-8464-0961-5*) Beekman Pubs.

Walks & Hikes in the Foothills & Lowlands Around Puget Sound. Harvey Manning & Penny Manning. (Illus.). 288p. 1995. pap. 14.95 (*0-89886-431-3*) Mountaineers.

Walks & Hikes on the Beaches Around Puget Sound. Harvey Manning & Penny Manning. (Illus.). 288p. 1995. pap. 14.95 (*0-89886-411-9*) Mountaineers.

Walks & Rambles in & Around St. Louis. Robert Rubright. (Walks & Rambles Ser.). (Illus.). 264p. (Orig.). 1995. pap. 14.00 (*0-88150-344-4*, Backcountry) Countryman.

Walks & Rambles in Dutchess & Putnam Counties: A Guide to Ecology & History in Eastern Hudson Valley Parks. Peggy Turco. LC 89-28231. (Walks & Rambles Ser.). 224p. 1990. pap. 14.00 (*0-88150-169-7*, Backcountry) Countryman.

Walks & Rambles in Ohio's Western Reserve: Discovering Nature & History in the Northeastern Corner. Jay Abercrombie. (Walks & Rambles Ser.). (Illus.). 208p. (Orig.). 1996. pap. 15.00 (*0-88150-285-5*, Backcountry) Countryman.

Walks & Rambles in Rhode Island: A Guide to the Natural & Historic Wonders of the Ocean State. 2nd ed. Ken Weber. LC 85-26843. (Walks & Rambles Ser.). (Illus.). 192p. 1993. pap. 13.00 (*0-88150-261-8*, Backcountry) Countryman.

Walks & Rambles in Southwestern Ohio: From the Stillwater to the Ohio River. Ralph Ramey. (Walks & Rambles Ser.). (Illus.). 192p. (Orig.). 1994. pap. 12.00 (*0-88150-250-2*, Backcountry) Countryman.

Walks & Rambles in the Western Hudson Valley: Landscape, Ecology, & Folklore in Orange & Ulster Counties. Peggy Turco. LC 95-50968. (Walks & Rambles Ser.). 224p. 1996. pap. 15.00 (*0-88150-376-2*, Backcountry) Countryman.

Walks & Rambles in Westchester & Fairfield Counties: A Nature Lover's Guide to 36 Parks & Sanctuaries. 2nd rev. ed. Katherine S. Anderson & Peggy Turco. (Walks & Rambles Ser.). 176p. 1993. pap. 12.00 (*0-88150-277-4*, Backcountry) Countryman.

Walks & Rambles on Cape Cod & the Islands: A Naturalist's Hiking Guide. Ned Friary & Glenda Bendure. (Walks & Rambles Ser.). (Illus.). 184p. (Orig.). 1992. pap. 12.00 (*0-88150-223-5*, Backcountry) Countryman.

Walks & Rambles on Long Island. Alice M. Geffen & Carole Berglie. LC 95-52150. (Walks & Rambles Ser.). 176p. 1996. pap. 14.00 (*0-88150-339-8*, Backcountry) Countryman.

Walks & Rambles on the Delmarva Penisula: A Guide for Hikers & Naturalists. Jay Abercrombie. LC 85-15813. (Walks & Rambles Ser.). (Illus.). 208p. (Orig.). 1985. pap. 13.00 (*0-942440-27-7*, Backcountry) Countryman.

Walks & Tours in Britain: AA Weekend Walks in Britain. Automobile Association Staff. 320p. 1997. pap. 25.00 (*0-393-31501-0*) Norton.

***Walks Around Cork.** Vincent Godsil. 142p. 1996. pap. 16.95 (*1-898256-19-5*) Dufour.

Walks Around London: Celebration of the Capital. Ian Norrie & Dorothy Bohm. (Illus.). 160p. 1986. pap. 14.95 (*0-233-97853-4*, Pub. by A Deutsch UK) Trafalgar.

***Walks in Beauty.** Hazel Krantz. (J). 1997. write for info. (*0-87358-667-0*, Rising Moon Bks) Northland AZ.

***Walks in Beauty.** Hazel Krantz. LC 96-40477. 200p. (YA). (gr. 6 up). 1997. pap. 6.95 (*0-87358-671-9*) Northland AZ.

Walks in Corsica. Footpaths Staff. 1990. pap. 19.95 (*1-85365-199-0*, Pub. by McCarta UK) Seven Hills Bk.

Walks in Hemingway's Paris: A Guide to Paris for the Literary Traveler. Noel R. Fitch. 1990. 16.95 (*0-312-05177-8*) St Martin.

Walks in Hemingway's Paris: A Guide to Paris for the Literary Traveler. Noel R. Fitch. (Illus.). 208p. 1992. pap. 9.95 (*0-312-07113-2*) St Martin.

Walks in Nature's Empire: Exploring the Nature Conservancy's Preserves in New York State. Scott E. Anderson. (Illus.). 224p. (Orig.). 1995. pap. 15.00 (*0-88150-313-4*) Countryman.

***Walks in Rome.** F. T. Prince. Date not set. pap. 34.00 (*0-85646-196-2*, Pub. by Anvil Press UK); pap. 14.95 (*0-85646-197-0*, Pub. by Anvil Press UK) Dufour.

Walks in Shakespeare Country. Joe Taylor & Chas Cook. (Illus.). 226p. (C). 1988. 40.00 (*0-946328-23-4*, Pub. by Thornhill Pr UK) St Mut.

Walks in South Lancashire & on Its Borders. Samuel Bamford. LC 72-80019. xvi, 288p. 1972. reprint ed. lib. bdg. 45.00 (*0-678-08023-2*) Kelley.

Walks in Stardust. Lynn A. McKee. 352p. (Orig.). 1994. mass mkt. 5.50 (*0-7865-0021-2*) Diamond.

Walks in the Cairngorms. E. L. Cross. 86p. 1989. pap. 50.00 (*0-946487-09-X*, Pub. by Luath Pr UK) St Mut.

Walks in the Cevennes: A Guide to 400 Kilometers of Footpaths Through Mountains Including the Tour Du Mont Lozere & Gardors Valleys, & Tour Du Mont Aigoual. French Ramblers Association Staff. (Footpaths of Europe Ser.). (Illus.). 225p. (Orig.). 1991. pap. 19.95 (*1-85365-233-4*, Pub. by McCarta UK) Seven Hills Bk.

Walks in the Sun. Dan Coldsmith. 256p. 1993. mass mkt. 4.99 (*0-553-56364-5*) Bantam.

Walks in the Trossachs & Rob Roy Country. Rennie McOwan. 184p. (C). 1991. pap. text ed. 39.00 (*86-15-30563-3*, Pub. by St Andrew UK) St Mut.

Walks in the Trossachs & Rob Roy Country. Rennie McOwan. 192p. (C). 1992. pap. 35.00 (*0-685-66160-1*, Pub. by St Andrew UK) St Mut.

Walks in the Trossachs & Rob Roy Country. Rennie McOwan. 192p. 1993. pap. 35.00 (*0-7152-0563-3*, Pub. by St Andrew UK) St Mut.

Walks in the World: Representation & Experience in Modern American Poetry. Roger Gilbert. 303p. 1991. text ed. 42.50 (*0-691-06858-5*) Princeton U Pr.

Walks in Welcoming Places: Outings in the Northeast for Strollers of All Ages & the Disabled. Marina Harrison & Lucy D. Rosenfeld. LC 95-8792. (Illus.). 164p. (Orig.). 1996. pap. 14.95 (*0-935576-49-5*) Kesend Pub Ltd.

Walks of Dreams. large type ed. Joan Garrison. (Linford Romance Library). 256p. 1994. pap. 15.99 (*0-7089-7508-9*, Linford) Ulverscroft.

Walks on the Lizard. Bob Acton. (C). 1989. pap. text ed. 24.95 (*0-85025-308-X*, Pub. by Tor Mark Pr UK) St Mut.

Walks on Water. Ed. by Deborah Levy. 160p. (C). 1992. pap. 19.95 (*0-413-67120-8*, A0655, Pub. by Methuen UK) Heinemann.

Walks the Fire: A Novel. Stephanie G. Whitson. LC 94-29787. (Prairie Winds Ser.: Bk. 1). 1995. pap. 9.99 (*0-7852-7981-4*) Nelson.

Walks Through Amsterdam. Bert W. Lief & L. M. Keely. 1991. pap. 3.00 (*0-912693-60-6*, 1054) VLE Ltd.

Walks Through Barcelona. Bert W. Lief & L. M. Keely. 1992. pap. 3.00 (*0-912693-62-2*, 1050) VLE Ltd.

Walks Through Brussels. Bert W. Lief & L. M. Keely. 1991. pap. 3.00 (*0-912693-61-4*, 1053) VLE Ltd.

Walks Through Dublin. Bert W. Lief & L. M. Keely. 1994. pap. 3.00 (*0-912693-71-1*, 1055) VLE Ltd.

Walks Through London. Bert W. Lief. 1995. pap. 3.00 (*0-912693-63-0*, 1043) VLE Ltd.

Walks Through Madrid. Bert W. Lief & L. M. Keely. 1992. pap. 3.00 (*0-912693-64-9*, 1044) VLE Ltd.

Walks Through Munich. Bert W. Lief. 1995. pap. 3.00 (*0-912693-65-7*, 1046) VLE Ltd.

Walks Through Paris. Bert W. Lief & L. M. Keely. 1995. pap. 3.00 (*0-912693-66-5*, 1045) VLE Ltd.

Walks Through Rome. Bert W. Lief & L. M. Keely. 1996. pap. 3.00 (*0-912693-67-3*, 1047) VLE Ltd.

Walks Through Seville. Bert W. Lief & L. M. Keely. 1992. pap. 3.00 (*0-912693-68-1*, 1051) VLE Ltd.

Walks Through Stuttgart. Bert W. Lief & L. M. Keely. 1988. pap. 3.00 (*0-912693-57-6*, 1048) VLE Ltd.

Walks Through Vienna. Bert W. Lief & L. M. Keely. 1992. pap. 3.00 (*0-912693-69-X*, 1052) VLE Ltd.

Walks Through Zurich. Bert W. Lief & L. M. Keely. 1992. pap. 3.00 (*0-912693-70-3*, 1049) VLE Ltd.

Walks Two Worlds. Robert B. Fox. LC 83-513. (Illus.). 62p. (Orig.). (J). (gr. 4-6). 1983. pap. 6.95 (*0-86534-015-3*) Sunstone Pr.

Walks, Walls & Fences. James E. Russell. Ed. by Marilyn M. Auer. LC 81-65752. (Illus.). 144p. (Orig.). 1981. pap. 9.95 (*0-932944-36-1*) Creative Homeowner.

Walks, Walls & Patios. Jim Barrett. LC 94-69655. 176p. 1997. pap. 14.95 (*1-880029-47-2*) Creative Homeowner.

Walks With Nature in Rocky Mountain National Park see **Short Hikes in Rocky Mountain National Park**

Walkshaping: Indoors or Out, Six Weeks to a Better Body. Gary Yanker. 1996. pap. 12.95 (*0-688-14621-X*, Quill) Morrow.

Walkshaping: Six Weeks to a Better Body. Gary Yanker. LC 93-14514. (Illus.). 192p. 1994. 20.00 (*0-345-38380-X*, Ballantine Trade) Ballantine.

Walkure: Complete Vocal & Orchestral Score. Richard Wagner. LC 77-84850. (Music Scores Ser.). 1978. reprint ed. pap. 24.95 (*0-486-23566-1*) Dover.

Walkure: Libretto. Richard Wagner. 64p. (ENG & GER.). 1986. pap. 4.95 (*0-7935-5382-2*, 50340320) H Leonard.

Walkway Surfaces: Measurement of Slip Resistance - STP 649. Ed. by C. Anderson & J. Senne. 117p. 1982. pap. 15.00 (*0-8031-0596-7*, 04-649000-47) ASTM.

***Walkway to the Future: Implementing the NCTM Standards at the K-4 Level.** Jean Morrow & Ruth H. Miles. (Illus.). Date not set. text ed. write for info. (*0-614-19586-1*, G196) Janson Pubns.

Wall. Eve Bunting. (Illus.). 32p. (J). (ps-3). 1990. 14.95 (*0-395-51588-2*, Clarion Bks) HM.

Wall. Eve Bunting. (J). (ps-3). 1992. pap. 5.95 (*0-395-62977-2*, Clarion Bks) HM.

Wall. William R. Gardiner. (Illus.). 96p. (Orig.). (C). 1987. pap. 7.95 (*0-9619400-0-X*) Gardiner Pub.

Wall. Lonnie B. Hewitt & Penny Bernal. LC 94-33732. (Spotlight Ser.). 1994. 4.00 (*0-07-028587-X*) McGraw.

***Wall. Evangeline Ivers. LC 97-60652. (Illus.). 144p. 1997. pap. 7.95 (*0-9650821-1-3*) Lazarus Trust. THE WALL is a haunting novel of estrangement & reconciliation set in rural Vermont in the mid-19th century. Two fast friends plan their futures together until they become divided over the affections of a beautiful young woman who returns to the small town of Old Bell Falls. The grudge between them takes the form of a stone wall that divides the property they once shared. This grudge is the legacy passed down to young James William Howe & his cousins, & it becomes the motivation for what happens when they encounter Gamallel Stethington Mead one Christmas Eve, alone, on the frozen edges of Abnak Pond... The stone wall itself becomes a subtle symbol of the walls that divide us--jealousy, pride, anger--& how these walls obstruct us from seeing others as human beings like ourselves. And in the end, the story is a tale of what it takes to bring these barriers down.**

Publisher Provided Annotation.

Wall. Ardath Mayhar. LC 86-31453. (Illus.). 136p. (Orig.). 1987. pap. 6.95 (*0-917053-06-0*) Space And.

Wall. Peter Meyer. 1996. 12.99 (*0-517-15022-0*) Random.

Wall. Gale T. Richardson. 9p. (Orig.). 1989. pap. write for info. (*0-9614337-1-X*) Poetry Unltd.

Wall. Mary R. Rinehart. 352p. 1989. mass mkt. 3.99 (*0-8217-4017-2*, Zebra Kensgtn) Kensgtn Pub Corp.

Wall. Peter Vansittart. LC 90-80799. 208p. 9000. 32.00 (*0-7206-0784-1*, Pub. by P Owen Ltd UK) Dufour.

Wall. Marlen Haushofer. 224p. 1991. reprint ed. pap. 9.95 (*0-939416-54-9*) Cleis Pr.

Wall. John R. Hersey. LC 87-45944. 644p. 1988. reprint ed. pap. 14.00 (*0-394-75696-7*, Vin) Random.

Wall: A Day in the Life of the Vietnam Veterans Memorial. Life Magazine Editors. LC 93-14677. (Illus.). 96p. (Orig.). 1993. pap. 15.95 (*0-312-09478-7*, Thomas Dunne Bks) St Martin.

Wall: A Pilgrimage. Jan Stuckey. 15p. (Orig.). 1989. pap. 4.00 (*0-88680-321-7*) I E Clark.

Wall: Intimacy. 3rd ed. Jean-Paul Sartre. Tr. by Lloyd Alexander from FRE. LC 73-88731. 1969. pap. 9.95 (*0-8112-0190-2*, NDP272) New Directions.

Wall & Floor Systems: Design & Performance of Light Frame Structures. 263p. 1983. 26.00 (*0-8403-2949-0*, 7317) Forest Prod.

Wall & the Garden: Selected Massachusetts Election Sermons, 1670-1775. Ed. by A. W. Plumstead. LC 68-19742. 398p. reprint ed. pap. 113.50 (*0-318-39689-0*, 2033284) Bks Demand.

***Wall & Water Gardens.** Gertrude Jekyll. Date not set. write for info. (*0-8434-6217-5*, Pub. by McGrath NH) Ayer.

Wall Around Eden. Joan Slonczewski. 288p. 1990. mass mkt. 3.95 (*0-380-71177-X*) Avon.

Wall Came Tumbling Down. Jerry Bornstein. 1990. 12.99 (*0-517-03306-2*) Random Hse Value.

Wall Came Tumbling Down. Margaret C. Cockrell. 55p. (Orig.). 1994. pap. write for info. (*0-9642017-0-4*) Armeria Pr.

Wall Chart: IMO Dangerous Goods Labels, Placards & Mark. International Maritime Organization Staff. 1992. text ed. 110.00 (*0-89771-872-0*, Pub. by Intl Maritime Org UK) St Mut.

Wall Chart: IMO Dangerous Goods, Labels, Placards & Mark (1994 Edition) International Maritime Organization Staff. 1994. pap. 30.00 (*0-7855-0497-4*, Pub. by Intl Maritime Org UK) St Mut.

Wall Construction & Finishing. Elizabeth Williams & Robert Williams. 1989. pap. 14.95 (*0-07-155298-7*) McGraw.

Wall Construction & Finishing. Elizabeth Williams & Robert Williams. (Illus.). 192p. 1989. 23.95 (*0-8306-9087-5*, 3087); pap. 14.95 (*0-8306-9387-4*, 3087) McGraw-Hill Prof.

Wall Dressing: Wall Furnishings. Judy Smith. (Interior Focus Ser.). (Illus.). 96p. 1997. 12.95 (*1-85967-224-8*, Lorenz Bks) Anness Pub.

Wall-Eyed Caesar's Ghost & Other Sketches. Jane Cotton. LC 77-106281. (Short Story Index Reprint Ser.). 1977. 18.95 (*0-8369-3315-X*) Ayer.

***Wall Finishes Etc.** Cowles Creative Publishing Staff. LC 96-37445. (Creative Touches Ser.). (Illus.). 64p. (Orig.). 1997. pap. 9.95 (*0-86573-882-3*) Cowles Creative.

Wall Framing. Charley G. Chadwick et al. Ed. by Lois G. Harrington. (Basic Carpentry Skills Ser.). (Illus.). 16p. (Orig.). (YA). (gr. 10-12). 1989. 3.00 (*0-89606-332-1*, 701TK); pap. text ed. 8.00 (*0-89606-266-X*, 701) Am Assn Voc Materials.

Wall Games. large type ed. Michael Dobbs. 1991. 25.99 (*0-7089-2551-0*) Ulverscroft.

Wall in My Backyard: East German Women in Transition. Ed. by Dinah Dodds & Pam Allen-Thompson. LC 94-18664. (Illus.). 192p. (C). 1994. pap. 14.95 (*0-87023-933-3*) U of Mass Pr.

Wall in My Backyard: East German Women in Transition. Ed. by Dinah Dodds & Pam Allen-Thompson. LC 94-18664. (Illus.). 192p. (C). 1995. 30.00 (*0-87023-932-5*) U of Mass Pr.

Wall in Wales. Nicolas McDowall. 1963. 70.00 (*0-907664-27-X*, Pub. by Old Stiles UK) St Mut.

Wall of Blood, Bk. 1. Fred L. Brown. LC 92-70364. (Illus.). 384p. (Orig.). (C). 1992. pap. 14.95 (*0-942551-00-1*) Combat Ready.

Wall of Brass. Robert Daley. 1994. write for info. (*0-318-72700-5*) Little.

Wall of Brass. Robert Daley. 384p. 1995. mass mkt. 6.50 (*0-446-36566-1*, Warner Vision) Warner Bks.

Wall of Brass: A Novel. Robert Daley. 1994. 22.95 (*0-316-17206-5*) Little.

Wall of Controversy. Francis G. Lee. LC 85-19697. 132p. 1986. pap. 10.50 (*0-89874-828-3*) Krieger.

Wall of Darkness. Ferando Alfonsi. 64p. 1980. pap. 7.50 (*0-89304-599-3*); pap. 7.50 (*0-89304-598-5*) Cross-Cultrl NY.

Wall of Eyes. Margaret Millar. 224p. 1986. pap. 4.95 (*0-930330-42-0*) Intl Polygonics.

Wall of Fire. Gilbert Morris. LC 94-43872. (Appomattox Saga Ser.: Vol. 7). 352p. 1995. 10.99 (*0-8423-8126-0*) Tyndale.

Wall of Flame. Gar Wilson. (Super Phoenix Force Ser.: No. 4). 1991. mass mkt. 4.50 (*0-373-62204-X*) Harlequin Bks.

Wall of Flames: The Minnesota Forest Fire of 1894. Lawrence H. Larsen. LC 84-61133. 187p. 1984. 9.85 (*0-911042-29-6*) NDSU Inst Reg.

Wall of Fog: Struggle with Blindness. Thomas A. Gonzales. (Orig.). 1994. audio 14.95 (*0-9647289-1-5*) Blind Pr.

Wall of Fog: Struggle with Blindness. Thomas A. Gonzales. 164p. (Orig.). 1994. 14.95 (*0-9647289-0-7*) Blind Pr.

Wall of Glass. Walter Satterthwait. 1989. mass mkt. 3.50 (*0-373-26032-6*) Harlequin Bks.

Wall of Glass. Walter Satterthwait. 1993. mass mkt. 3.99 (*0-373-83265-6*, 1-83265-8) Harlequin Bks.

Wall of Light: Nikola Tesla & the Venusian Space Ship, the X-12. Arthur H. Matthews. 140p. 1973. reprint ed. spiral bd. 13.50 (*0-7873-0588-X*) Hlth Research.

Wall of Love. large type ed. Florence Stuart. 1990. pap. 15.99 (*0-7089-6887-2*) Ulverscroft.

Wall of Mirrors: Nationalism & Perceptions of the Border at Niagara Falls. Patrick McGreevy. (Borderlands Monographs: No. 5). 1-18p. (C). 1991. pap. text ed. 5.00 (*0-9625055-4-4*) Canadian-Amer Ctr.

Wall of Names: The Story of the Vietnam Veterans Memorial A Step 4 Book - Grades 2-4. Judy Donnelly. LC 90-30275. (Step into Reading Bks.). (Illus.). 48p. (Orig.). (J). (gr. 2-4). 1991. pap. 3.99 (*0-679-80169-3*); lib. bdg. 9.99 (*0-679-90169-8*) Random Bks Yng Read.

Wall of Paradise: Essays on Milton's Poetics. John M. Steadman. LC 85-9671. 156p. 1985. text ed. 27.50 (*0-8071-1230-5*) La State U Pr.

***Wall of Separation? Debating the Public Role of Religion.** Mary C. Segers. 200p. 1997. 48.50 (*0-8476-8387-7*) Rowman.

***Wall of Separation? Debating the Public Role of Religion.** Mary C. Segers. 200p. 1997. pap. 14.95 (*0-8476-8388-5*) Rowman.

***Wall of Sky Wall of Eye.** Lethem. Date not set. pap. 13.95 (*0-312-86353-5*) St Martin.

Wall of the Earth. Giorgio Caproni. 1992. pap. 10.00 (*0-920717-53-5*) Guernica Editions.

***Wall of the Sky, the Wall of the Eye.** Jonathan Lethem. 1997. pap. write for info. (*0-614-27321-8*) Tor Bks.

Wall of the Sky, the Wall of the Eye: Stories. Jonathan Lethem. LC 95-32093. 304p. 1996. 23.00 (*0-15-100180-4*) HarBrace.

Wall of Water. Sherry Kramer. 1989. pap. 5.95 (*0-88145-080-4*) Broadway Play.

Wall Painting in Bulgaria: 9th to 19th Centuries. L. Prashkov. (C). 1981. 95.00 (*0-685-34406-1*) Collets.

Wall Paintings from Central India. R. A. Agarwala. (Illus.). (C). 1987. 74.95 (*0-317-66132-9*) Asia Bk Corp.

Wall Paintings from Central India. R. A. Agarwala. (C). 1987. 78.50 (*0-8364-2203-1*, Pub. by Sundeep II) S Asia.

Wall Paintings from the Oecus of the Villa of Publius Fannius Synistor in Boscoreale. Frank G. Muller. (Iconological Studies in Roman Art: Vol. 2). (Illus.). x, 156p. 1994. lib. bdg. 57.00 (*90-5063-256-4*, Pub. by Gieben NE) Benjamins North Am.

Wall Paintings of Punjab & Haryana. Kanwarjit S. Kang. (Illus.). 193p. 1985. 105.00 (*0-318-36348-8*) Asia Bk Corp.

Wall Paintings of the Western Himalayas. Mira Seth. 1976. 55.00 (*0-940500-96-5*, Pub. by Pubns Div II) Asia Bk Corp.

Wall Paintings of Thera. Christos Doumas. Ed. by Diana Zafiropoulou. Tr. by Alex Doumas from GRE. (Illus.). 188p. (C). 1993. boxed 60.00 (*960-220-274-2*, Pub. by Thera Fnd UK) DAP Assocs.

Wall Pockets of the Past. Fredda Perkins. 1995. pap. text ed. 17.95 (*0-89145-682-1*, 4572) Collector Bks.

Wall Quilts. Marsha R. McCloskey. 1990. pap. 5.95 (*0-486-26370-3*) Dover.

Wall Reliefs of Joe Goode. Helene Winer. (Illus.). 8p. 1971. 1.00 (*0-915478-22-6*) Montgomery Gallery.

Wall Scenes from the Tomb of Amenhotep (Huy) Governor of Bahria Oasis. Charles C. Van Siclen, III. (Illus.). xi, 43p. 1981. pap. text ed. 12.50 (*0-933175-00-0*) Van Siclen Bks.

Wall Shadows: A Study in American Prisons. Frank Tannenbaum. LC 70-156033. reprint ed. 32.50 (*0-404-09183-0*) AMS Pr.

Wall Street. John Calvin Batchelor. Date not set. 25.00 (*0-8050-5072-8*) H Holt & Co.

Wall Street. Doug Henwood. LC 97-13488. 240p. 1995. 25.00 (*0-86091-495-X*, B0539, Pub. by Vrso UK) Norton.

*__Wall Street.__ Doug Henwood. 1997. 25.00 (*0-614-28236-5*, Pub. by Verso UK) Routledge Chapman & Hall.

Wall Street. Walter Werner & Steven Smith. 1991. text ed. 37.50 (*0-231-07302-X*) Col U Pr.

Wall Street. William C. Moore. LC 66-19018. 1969. reprint ed. pap. 12.00 (*0-87034-041-7*) Fraser Pub Co.

*__Wall Street: A History.__ Charles Geisst. (Illus.). 480p. 1997. 30.00 (*0-19-511512-0*) OUP.

Wall Street: Asset or Liability? Compiled by James G. Hodgson. LC 75-2641. (Wall Street & the Security Market Ser.). 1975. reprint ed. 26.95 (*0-405-06966-9*) Ayer.

Wall Street: Changing Fortunes. Maxine Friedman. (Illus.). 58p. (Orig.). 1990. pap. 9.24 (*0-9616415-8-4*) Fraunces Tavern.

Wall Street: The Other Las Vegas. Nicolas Darvas. 192p. 1986. reprint ed. pap. 7.95 (*0-8184-0398-5*) Carol Pub Group.

Wall Street: The Story of a Street. Frederick T. Hill. 1977. lib. bdg. 69.95 (*0-8490-2804-3*) Gordon Pr.

Wall Street - How It Works. Jeffrey B. Little & Lucien Rhodes. 1977. pap. 2.95 (*0-8306-3002-3*, 30002, Liberty Hse) TAB Bks.

Wall Street & FDR. Antony C. Sutton. 1993. reprint ed. lib. bdg. 16.95 (*0-89968-325-8*, Lghtyr Pr) Buccaneer Bks.

*__Wall Street & Poker-Same Game.__ 112p. (Orig.). 1996. pap. 9.95 (*1-884570-61-5*) Research Triangle.

Wall Street & Regulation. Samuel L. Hayes, III. 1987. text ed. 29.95 (*0-07-103238-X*) McGraw.

Wall Street & the Bolshevik Revolution. Antony C. Sutton. 1993. reprint ed. lib. bdg. 16.95 (*0-89968-324-X*, Lghtyr Pr) Buccaneer Bks.

Wall Street & the Rise of Bolshevism & National Socialism, 2 vols. 1991. lib. bdg. 99.95 (*0-8490-5041-3*) Gordon Pr.

Wall Street & the Security Markets, 58 vols, Vol. 30. Ed. by Vincent P. Carosso. 1975. reprint ed. Vols. 30-58. 770.00 (*0-405-19007-7*) Ayer.

Wall Street & the Security Markets, 58 vols, Vols. 1-29. Ed. by Vincent P. Carosso. 1975. reprint ed. 2,103.00 (*0-405-12493-7*) Ayer.

Wall Street & Wildflowers: Choices about Life in Corporate America. Michael J. Vander Mark. 224p. 1996. 22.95 (*0-9650390-0-5*); pap. 17.95 (*0-9650390-1-3*) Spirit At Wrk.

Wall Street & World Revolution, 2 vols., Set. 1991. lib. bdg. 169.00 (*0-8490-4452-9*) Gordon Pr.

Wall Street Blues. Jerome Tuccille. 224p. 1988. 15.95 (*0-8184-0455-8*) Carol Pub Group.

Wall Street Christmas. Photos by Robert Gambee. (Illus.). 1990. 49.95 (*0-393-02835-6*) Norton.

*__Wall Street City.__ David L. Brown & Kassandra Bentley. LC 97-12706. 304p. 1997. pap. 27.95 (*0-471-17878-0*) Wiley.

Wall Street Enjuicia al Socialismo (Socialism on Trial) 2nd ed. James P. Cannon. 188p. (SPA.). 1981. pap. 16.95 (*0-87348-617-X*) Pathfinder NY.

Wall Street Gurus: How You Can Profit From Investment Newsletters. Peter Brimelow. 238p. 1988. 19.95 (*0-9620125-1-3*) Minerva Bks.

Wall Street in History. Martha J. Lamb. LC 92-71285. (Illus.). 95p. (Orig.). 1992. reprint ed. pap. 15.00 (*0-87034-104-9*) Fraser Pub Co.

Wall Street in Your Pocket. Joseph Marks. Ed. by Diana Marks. 170p. (Orig.). 1995. pap. write for info. (*1-885591-77-2*) Morris Pubng.

*__Wall Street Joke Book.__ LC 96-40527. 1997. pap. 7.95 (*0-312-15684-7*) St Martin.

Wall Street Journal. Murray & Birnbaum. 1987. write for info. (*0-318-61167-8*) Random.

*__Wall Street Journal Almanac.__ Ed. by Wall St. Journal Staff. 1997. pap. 10.95 (*0-345-40521-8*) Ballantine.

Wall Street Journal Applications in Finance 1993. 2nd ed. Paul Bolster. 32p. (C). 1992. text ed. 6.95 (*0-256-11900-7*) Irwin.

Wall Street Journal Applications in Finance, 1994 Edition. 3rd ed. Paul Bolster. 32p. (C). 1993. per. 6.95 (*0-256-13843-5*) Irwin.

*__Wall Street Journal Book of International Investing: Everything You Need to Know about Investing in Foreign Markets.__ John A. Prestbo & Douglas R. Sease. LC 96-35266. (Illus.). 288p. 1997. 24.95 (*0-7868-6092-8*) Hyperion.

Wall Street Journal Book of Personal Technology. Walter S. Mossberg. 288p. 1995. pap. 15.00 (*0-8129-2602-1*, Times Bks) Random.

*__Wall Street Journal Guide to Anderstanding Money & Markets.__ Rich Wurman. (C). 1994. text ed. 9.95 (*0-673-97176-7*) Addison-Wesley.

Wall Street Journal Guide to Planning Your Financial Future: The Easy-to-Read Guide to Lifetime Planning for Retirement. Kenneth M. Morris & Alan M. Siegel. 1995. pap. 14.95 (*0-684-80202-3*, Fireside) S&S Trade.

Wall Street Journal Guide to Understanding Money & Investing. Kenneth M. Morris & Alan M. Siegel. 176p. 1994. pap. 14.95 (*0-671-89451-X*, Fireside) S&S Trade.

Wall Street Journal Guide to Understanding Money & Markets. Alan M. Siegel et al. (Financial Reference Guidebook Ser.). (Illus.). 120p. 1989. pap. 12.95 (*0-13-945148-X*, Access NY) HarpC.

Wall Street Journal, Guide to Understanding Money & Markets. Rich Wurman. 1990. pap. text ed. 13.95 (*0-06-772516-3*) HarpC.

Wall Street Journal Guide to Understanding Personal Finance. Morris. LC 96-30011. 1997. pap. 18.95 incl. disk (*0-684-83362-X*) S&S Trade.

*__Wall Street Journal Guide to Understanding Personal Finance.__ Morris. 1997. pap. 18.95 incl. disk (*0-684-84697-7*) S&S Trade.

Wall Street Journal Guide to Understanding Personal Finance. Kenneth M. Morris & Aland M. Siegel. 176p. 1993. pap. 14.95 (*0-671-87964-2*, Fireside) S&S Trade.

Wall Street Journal Guide to Understanding Personal Finance. Kenneth M. Morris. LC 96-30011. 1997. pap. 14.95 (*0-684-83361-1*) S&S Trade.

Wall Street Journal Guide to Understanding Taxes: An Easy-to-Understand, Easy-to-Use Primer that Takes the Mystery Out of Income Taxes. Kenneth M. Morris & Alan M. Siegel. 128p. 1995. pap. 14.95 (*0-671-50235-2*, Fireside) S&S Trade.

Wall Street Journal Lifetime Guide to Money: Everything You Need to Know about Managing Your Finances--For Every Stage of Life. Wall Street Journal Personal-Finance Team Staff. Ed. by C. Frederic Wiegold. LC 95-45519. 624p. 1997. 29.95 (*0-7868-6132-0*) Hyperion.

Wall Street Journal on Accounting. Lee Berton & Jonathan B. Schiff. 350p. 1989. text ed. 45.00 (*1-55623-225-X*) Irwin Prof Pubng.

Wall Street Journal on Marketing. Ronald Alsop & Bill Abrams. 304p. (C). 1986. pap. text ed. 20.50 (*0-256-05679-X*) Irwin.

Wall Street Journal Stylebook. 3rd ed. Paul R. Martin. LC 92-73699. 200p. 1992. 18.00 (*1-881944-00-X*) Dow Jones & Co.

Wall Street Journal Stylebook. 4th ed. Paul R. Martin. 1995. 18.00 (*1-881944-03-4*, Wall St Jrnl) Dow Jones & Co.

Wall Street Journal Views America Tomorrow. Ed. by Donald Moffitt. LC 76-52501. 190p. reprint ed. pap. 54.20 (*0-317-27197-0*, 2023931) Bks Demand.

Wall Street Journal's Understanding Money & Investing. Morris & Siegel. 1994. pap. text ed. 17.20 (*0-13-169210-0*) P-H.

Wall Street Made Simple. Merle E. Dowd. 240p. 1992. pap. 12.95 (*0-385-41786-1*) Doubleday.

*__Wall Street Money Machine.__ Wade B. Cook. 1997. pap. text ed. 24.95 (*0-910019-73-8*) Lghthse Pub Gp.

Wall Street Money Machine: New & Incredible Strategies for Cash Flow & Wealth. Wade B. Cook. 220p. 1996. text ed. 24.95 (*0-910019-70-3*) Lghthse Pub Gp.

Wall Street Office Systems. Olinzock & Santos. (KM - Office Procedures Ser.). 1990. text ed. 13.95 (*0-538-11324-3*) S-W Pub.

Wall Street Office Systems, Integrated. Olinzock & Santos. (KM - Office Procedures Ser.). 1990. wbk. ed., pap. 7.95 (*0-538-11336-7*); wbk. ed., pap. 7.95 (*0-538-11337-5*) S-W Pub.

Wall Street Office Systems, Integrated. Olinzock & Santos. (KM - Office Procedures Ser.). 1990. wbk. ed., pap. 7.95 (*0-538-11338-3*) S-W Pub.

Wall Street Office Systems, Integrated. Olinzock & Santos. (KM - Office Procedures Ser.). 1990. wbk. ed., pap. 7.95 (*0-538-11339-1*) S-W Pub.

Wall Street People Vol. 1: True Stories of Today's Masters & Moguls, 1. Charles D. Ellis & James R. Vertin. LC 96-15864. 448p. 1996. text ed. 39.95 (*0-471-12397-8*) Wiley.

Wall Street People Vol. 2: True Stories of Yesterday's Barons of Finance, Vol. 2. Charles D. Ellis & James R. Vertin. (Investment Ser.). 352p. 1997. 39.95 (*0-471-12396-X*) Wiley.

Wall Street Picks for 1997: An Insider's Guide to the Year's Best Stocks & Mutual Funds. Kirk Kazanjian. LC 96-46562. 276p. (Orig.). 1996. pap. 19.95 (*0-7931-2348-8*, 5680-3302) Dearborn Finan.

Wall Street Point of View. Henry Clews. LC 68-28620. (Illus.). 290p. 1968. reprint ed. text ed. 59.75 (*0-8371-0048-8*, CLWS, Greenwood Pr) Greenwood.

Wall Street Speculation: Its Tricks & Tragedies. Franklin C. Keyes. 1969. reprint ed. pap. 11.00 (*0-87034-053-0*) Fraser Pub Co.

Wall Street Stories. Edwin Lefevre. LC 75-150478. (Short Story Index Reprint Ser.). 1977. reprint ed. 19.95 (*0-8369-3819-4*) Ayer.

Wall Street Talk: How to Understand Your Broker. Barbara Quint. (Illus.). 1983. 11.95 (*0-8027-0754-8*); pap. 5.95 (*0-8027-7232-3*) Walker & Co.

Wall Street Thesaurus. Paul Sarnoff. 1963. 19.95 (*0-8392-1127-9*) Astor-Honor.

Wall Street Ventures & Adventures Through Forty Years. Richard D. Wyckoff. 400p. 1986. reprint ed. 19.95 (*0-934380-13-9*, 174) Traders Pr.

Wall Street Ventures & Adventures Through 40 Years. Richard D. Wyckoff. LC 85-70938. 313p. 1985. reprint ed. pap. 21.00 (*0-87034-078-6*) Fraser Pub Co.

Wall Street Waltz: Financial Markets at a Glance. Kenneth L. Fisher. 250p. 1987. 31.95 (*0-931133-04-1*, Busn Class) Pac Pub Grp.

Wall Street Wit & Wisdom: A Collection of Savvy Investment Tips, Clever Quotes & Humorous... Robert H. Thomas. 1996. pap. text ed. 7.95 (*0-9649201-0-7*) Marbo Ent.

*__Wall Street Words: An Essential A to Z Guide for Today's Investor.__ David L. Scott. LC 97-10608. 1997. pap. write for info. (*0-395-88607-4*) HM.

*__Wall Street Words: An Essential A to Z Guide for Today's Investor.__ David L. Scott. LC 97-10608. 1997. pap. 12.00 (*0-395-85392-3*) HM.

Wall Street Words: Every Investor's Guide to Financial Terms - Words & Wisdom from the Experts. David L. Scott. 416p. 1989. pap. 8.95 (*0-395-46777-2*) HM.

Wall Street Words: From Annuities to Zero Coupon Bonds. rev. ed. Richard J. Maturi. 150p. 1995. per. 16.95 (*1-55738-865-2*) Irwin Prof Pubng.

Wall Street Words: The Basics & Beyond. Richard J. Maturi. (Investor's Quick Reference Ser.). 150p. 1991. per. 14.95 (*1-55738-195-X*) Irwin Prof Pubng.

*__Wall Street's Picks for 1998: An Insider's Guide to the Year's Best Stocks & Mutual Funds.__ Kirk Kazanjian. 276p. (Orig.). 1997. pap. 19.95 (*0-7931-2733-5*, 5680-3303) Dearborn Finan.

Wall Street's Reference Guide. Gregory Erickson. 1985. pap. 17.95 (*0-8359-8534-2*, Reston); text ed. 26.67 (*0-8359-8535-0*, Reston) P-H.

*__Wall That Did Not Fall: The Story of Rahab's Faith.__ Marilyn Lashbrook. (Me Too Bks.). (Illus.). 30p. (J). 1996. 7.95 (*0-87973-865-0*) Our Sunday Visitor.

Wall That Did Not Fall: The Story of Rahab's Faith. Marilyn Lashbrook. LC 87-63420. (Me Too! Bks.). (Illus.). 32p. (J). (ps). 1988. 5.95 (*0-86606-433-8*, 864) Treasure Pub.

Wall That Did Not Fall (Rahab) see Muro Que No Se Cayo (Rahab)

Wall to Wall. Douglas Woolf. LC 84-21374. 196p. 1984. reprint ed. 20.00 (*0-916583-06-6*); reprint ed. pap. 7.95 (*0-916583-07-4*) Dalkey Arch.

Wall to Wall: From Beijing to Berlin by Rail. Mary Morris. 272p. 1992. pap. 10.95 (*0-14-019939-X*, Penguin Bks) Viking Penguin.

Wall-to-Wall America: A Cultural History of Post Office Murals in the Great Depression. Karal A. Marling. LC 82-2622. (Illus.). 364p. 1982. pap. text ed. 15.95 (*0-8166-1117-3*) U of Minn Pr.

Wall-to-Wall History. R. Hodges. 1990. pap. 18.95 (*0-7156-2342-7*, Pub. by Duckworth UK) Focus Pub-R Pullins.

Wall to Wall Speaks. David Mus. (Contemporary Poets Ser.). 112p. 1988. pap. 10.95 (*0-691-01444-2*); text ed. 23.95 (*0-691-06728-7*) Princeton U Pr.

*__Wall-to-Wall Thanksgiving.__ large type ed. Ed. & Intro. by Kenneth Jernigan. (Kernel Book Ser.: Vol. 13). (Illus.). 96p. (Orig.). 1997. pap. 3.00 (*1-885218-11-7*) Natl Fed Blind.

Wall Water & Woodland Gardens. Gertrude Jekyll. 1994. 29.50 (*1-85149-197-X*) Antique Collect.

Wall Water Gardens. rev. ed. Gertrude Jekyll. LC 82-16419. (Jekyll Garden Bks.). (Illus.). 337p. 1983. reprint ed. 26.95 (*0-88143-002-1*) Ayer.

Wall Water Gardens. rev. ed. Gertrude Jekyll. LC 82-16419. (Jekyll Garden Bks.). (Illus.). 337p. 1984. reprint ed. pap. 11.95 (*0-88143-059-5*) Ayer.

Walla Walla: A Nice Place to Raise a Family, 1920 -1954. Robert A. Bennett. 200p. 1987. 24.95 (*0-936546-13-1*); pap. 16.95 (*0-936546-12-3*) Pioneer Pr Bks.

Walla Walla: A Town Built to Be a City, 1900-1919. Robert A. Bennett. 232p. 1982. 21.95 (*0-936546-06-9*); pap. 14.95 (*0-936546-07-7*) Pioneer Pr Bks.

Walla Walla: Portrait of a Western Town, 1804-1898. Robert A. Bennett. 180p. 1980. 21.95 (*0-936546-01-8*); pap. 14.95 (*0-936546-00-X*) Pioneer Pr Bks.

Wallabadah Manuscript. deluxe limited ed. R. Millis. 256p. 89.95 (*0-86840-304-0*, Pub. by New South Wales Univ Pr AT) Intl Spec Bk.

Wallaby Track. Aaron Fletcher. (Outback Saga Ser.). 480p. (Orig.). 1994. mass mkt., pap. text ed. 5.99 (*0-8439-3615-0*) Dorchester Pub Co.

Wallace. Marshall Frady. 1996. pap. 15.00 (*0-679-77128-X*); pap. 15.00 (*0-614-12566-9*) Random.

Wallace. Sydney Goodsir-Smith. 128p. (Orig.). 1996. pap. 10.95 (*0-7145-4075-7*) Riverrun NY.

*__Wallace: A Biography.__ Peter Reese. 1997. pap. text ed. 14.95 (*0-86241-607-8*) Canon USA.

*__Wallace: A Biography.__ Peter Reese. (Canongate Classic Ser.). (Illus.). 256p. 1996. pap. 14.95 (*0-86241-608-6*, Pub. by Canongate Bks UK) Interlink Pub.

Wallace: Genealogical Data Pertaining to Descendants of Peter Wallace & Elizabeth Woods, His Wife. G. S. Wallace. (Illus.). 275p. 1992. reprint ed. pap. 43.00 (*0-8328-2757-6*); reprint ed. lib. bdg. 53.00 (*0-8328-2756-8*) Higginson Bk Co.

Wallace A. Rainey & Jessie I. Ringer: Their Ancestors, Descendants & Allied Families. Ralph E. Rainey. LC 85-90199. (Illus.). 402p. 1985. 35.00 (*0-9615061-0-5*) Rainey R.

*__Wallace & Gromit: A Close Shave.__ Nick Park. (J). 1996. pap. 7.99 (*0-385-32321-2*, DD Bks Yng Read) BDD Bks Young Read.

*__Wallace & Gromit: The Wrong Trousers.__ Nick Park. (J). 1996. pap. 7.99 (*0-385-32320-4*, DD Bks Yng Read) BDD Bks Young Read.

*__Wallace & Gromit Postcard Book.__ (J). 1996. pap. 6.99 (*0-385-32322-0*, DD Bks Yng Read) BDD Bks Young Read.

Wallace & Natural Selection. H. Lewis McKinney. LC 72-75203. (Studies in the History of Science & Medicine: No. 8). (Illus.). 116p. reprint ed. 33.10 (*0-8357-9597-7*, 2013373) Bks Demand.

Wallace Berman: Support the Revolution. Wallace Berman. 1993. 39.95 (*90-800968-3-0*) Dist Art Pubs.

Wallace Berman Vol. 1: Retrospective. Contrib. by Wallace Berman. LC 78-70599. (Illus.). 118p. (Orig.). 1978. pap. 22.50 (*0-911291-03-2*) Fellows Cont Art.

Wallace-Bruce & Closely Related Families, History & Genealogy. James Wallace. (Illus.). 389p. 1993. reprint ed. pap. 59.50 (*0-8328-3091-7*); reprint ed. lib. bdg. 69.50 (*0-8328-3090-9*) Higginson Bk Co.

Wallace Collection. John Ingamells. (Illus.). 132p. 1990. 30.00 (*1-870248-43-0*) Scala Books.

Wallace Collection Catalogue of Ceramics I: Pottery, Maiolica, Faience, Stoneware. A. V. Norman. (Illus.). 450p. 1976. pap. 19.95 (*0-900785-06-3*, Pub. by Wallace Collect UK) Antique Collect.

Wallace Collection Catalogue of European Arms & Armour, 2 vols., Set. J. G. Mann. (Illus.). pap. 50.00 (*0-614-11688-0*, Pub. by Wallace Collect UK) Antique Collect.

Wallace Collection Catalogue of European Arms & Armour, Vol. I. J. G. Mann. (Illus.). 714p. pap. write for info. (*0-900785-05-5*, Pub. by Wallace Collect UK) Antique Collect.

Wallace Collection Catalogue of European Arms & Armour, Vol. II. J. G. Mann. (Illus.). 304p. pap. write for info. (*0-900785-20-9*, Pub. by Wallace Collect UK) Antique Collect.

Wallace Collection Catalogue of Furniture, 3 vols., Set. Peter Hughes. (Illus.). 1700p. 1996. 495.00 (*0-900785-56-X*, Pub. by Wallace Collect UK) Antique Collect.

Wallace Collection Catalogue of Miniatures. Graham Reynolds. (Illus.). 366p. 1980. pap. 19.95 (*0-900785-21-7*, Pub. by Wallace Collect UK) Antique Collect.

Wallace Collection Catalogue of Pictures I: British, German, Italian, Spanish. John Ingamells. (Illus.). 464p. 1985. pap. 45.00 (*0-900785-16-0*, Pub. by Wallace Collect UK) Antique Collect.

Wallace Collection Catalogue of Pictures II: French Nineteenth Century. John Ingamells. (Illus.). 326p. 1986. pap. 45.00 (*0-900785-19-5*, Pub. by Wallace Collect UK) Antique Collect.

Wallace Collection Catalogue of Pictures III: French Before 1815. John Ingamells. (Illus.). 410p. 1989. pap. 45.00 (*0-900785-36-5*, Pub. by Wallace Collect UK) Antique Collect.

Wallace Collection Catalogue of Pictures IV: Dutch & Flemish. John Ingamells. (Illus.). 493p. 1992. pap. 45.00 (*0-900785-38-1*, Pub. by Wallace Collect UK) Antique Collect.

Wallace Collection Catalogue of Sculpture, 2 vols., Set. J. G. Mann. (Illus.). 258p. 1931. pap. 19.95 (*0-900785-02-0*, Pub. by Wallace Collect UK) Antique Collect.

Wallace Collection Catalogue of Sevres Porcelain. Rosalind Savill. 1988. 395.00 (*0-900785-27-6*, Pub. by Wallace Collect UK); pap. 245.00 (*0-900785-31-4*, Pub. by Wallace Collect UK) Antique Collect.

Wallace Harrison - A Painter: A Collection of His Work. Wallace Harrison. LC 86-210786. (Illus.). 96p. (C). 1983. text ed. 40.00 (*0-933951-25-6*) Locust Hill Pr.

Wallace Herndon Smith: Paintings. Lee Hall. (Illus.). 176p. 1987. 19.95 (*0-295-96460-X*) U of Wash Pr.

Wallace Herndon Smith: Rediscovered. Charles E. Buckley. 64p. 1992. pap. 17.95 (*0-9632870-1-X*) D A Hanks.

*__Wallace Homestead Price Guide to American Country Antiques.__ Don Raycraft & Carol Raycraft. (Illus.). 256p. (Orig.). 1997. pap. 16.95 (*0-87069-721-8*, WHACA) Krause Pubns.

Wallace-Homestead Price Guide to American Country Antiques. 13th ed. Don Raycraft & Carol Raycraft. (Illus.). 272p. 1993. pap. 15.95 (*0-87069-586-X*, Wallace-Hmestead) Chilton.

Wallace-Homestead Price Guide to Coca-Cola Collectibles. Deborah G. Hill. LC 82-62060. (Illus.). 192p. 1991. pap. 15.95 (*0-87069-591-6*) Chilton.

Wallace Homestead Price Guide to Plastic Collectibles: Updated Prices. 216p. 1992. pap. 17.95 (*0-87069-652-1*) Chilton.

Wallace Milroy's Malt Whisky Alamanac: A Taster's Guide. Wallace Milroy. (Illus.). 144p. 1991. 10.95 (*0-312-06542-6*) St Martin.

Wallace Neff, Eighteen Ninety-Five to Nineteen Eighty-Two: The Romance of Regional Architecture. Alson Clark et al. (Illus.). 144p. 1989. pap. 24.95 (*0-87328-128-4*) Huntington Lib.

Wallace Nutting: Supreme Edition, General Catalog. Wallace Nutting. LC 77-608284. 160p. 1978. pap. 10.95 (*0-916838-09-9*) Schiffer.

Wallace Nutting Expansible Catalog. Wallace Nutting. Ed. by Michael Ivankovich. LC 87-70415. (Illus.). 175p. (Orig.). 1987. reprint ed. pap. 12.95 (*0-9615843-3-5*) Diamond Pr PA.

Wallace Nutting's Biography. Wallace Nutting. 1976. 24.95 (*0-8488-0599-2*) Amereon Ltd.

Wallace P. Roudebush: Spirit of the Institution. Christopher A. Maraschiello. 100p. (Orig.). 1993. pap. text ed. write for info. (*0-918761-04-2*) Miami U Pubns.

*__Wallace Stegner.__ Jackson Benson. 1997. pap. 15.95 (*0-14-024796-3*) Viking Penguin.

W

Wallace Stegner. Merrill Lewis & Lorene Lewis. LC 72-619569. (Western Writers Ser.: No. 4). (Illus.). 48p. (Orig.). (C). 1972. pap. 4.95 (*0-88430-003-X*) Boise St U W Writ Ser.

Wallace Stegner: A Descriptive Bibliography. Ed. by James R. Hepworth. LC 89-82163. (American Authors Ser.). 280p. 1991. 50.00 (*0-917652-80-0*) Confluence Pr.

Wallace Stegner: His Life & Work. Jackson J. Benson. 480p. 1996. pap. 32.95 (*0-670-86222-3*) Viking Penguin.

Wallace Stegner: Man & Writer. Ed. by Charles E. Rankin. LC 96-4422. 272p. (C). 1996. 45.00 (*0-8263-1741-3*) U of NM Pr.

Wallace Stegner: Man & Writer. Charles E. Rankin. 272p. 1996. pap. text ed. 19.95 (*0-8263-1756-1*) U of NM Pr.

***Wallace Stegner & the Continental Vision: Critical Essays & Commentary.** Curt Meine. LC 97-14838. 240p. 1997. text ed. 24.95 (*1-55963-537-1*) Island Pr.

Wallace Steven Revisited. Janet McCann. (Twayne's United States Authors Ser.). 1995. 22.95 (*0-8057-7644-3*, Twayne) Scribnrs Ref.

***Wallace Stevens.** Ed. by Cranes Doyle. (Critical Heritage Ser.). 520p. (C). 1997. text ed. 45.00 (*0-415-15943-1*) Routledge.

Wallace Stevens. Frank Kermode. (Writers & Critics Ser.). 134p. 1979. 24.50 (*0-912378-07-7*) Chips Bksearch.

Wallace Stevens. Helen H. Vendler. 96p. 1986. pap. 9.50 (*0-674-94575-1*) HUP.

Wallace Stevens: A Celebration. Ed. by Frank Doggett & Robert Buttel. LC 79-18877. 384p. 1980. reprint ed. pap. 109.50 (*0-7837-8583-6*, 2049398) Bks Demand.

Wallace Stevens: A Descriptive Bibliography. J. M. Edelstein. LC 72-91106. (Series in Bibliography). (Illus.). 456p. 1973. 100.00 (*0-8229-3268-7*) U of Pittsburgh Pr.

Wallace Stevens: A Poet's Growth. George S. Lensing. LC 86-7280. xii, 313p. 1986. pap. text ed. 16.95 (*0-8071-1671-8*) La State U Pr.

***Wallace Stevens: A Spiritual Poet in a Secular Age.** Charles M. Murphy. LC 96-51500. 144p. (Orig.). 1997. pap. 9.95 (*0-8091-3708-9*) Paulist Pr.

Wallace Stevens: A World of Transforming Shapes. Alan Perlis. LC 74-19631. 160p. 1975. 27.50 (*0-8387-1651-2*) Bucknell U Pr.

Wallace Stevens: An Anatomy of Figuration. Eugene P. Nassar. LC 64-24495. 229p. reprint ed. pap. 65.30 (*0-317-28693-5*, 2055280) Bks Demand.

Wallace Stevens: An Annotated Secondary Bibliography. John N. Serio. LC 93-1005. (Series in Bibliography). 456p. (C). 1994. text ed. 100.00 (*0-8229-3836-7*) U of Pittsburgh Pr.

Wallace Stevens: An Approach to His Poetry & Thought. Robert Pack. LC 68-24044. 203p. 1967. reprint ed. 45.00 (*0-87752-082-8*) Gordian.

***Wallace Stevens: Collected Poetry & Prose.** Wallace Stevens. Ed. by Frank Kermode & Joan Richardson. 1997. 35.00 (*0-614-29418-5*) Library of America.

***Wallace Stevens: Imagination & Faith.** Ed. by A. K. Morris. 1909. text ed. write for info. (*0-691-00249-5*) Princeton U Pr.

Wallace Stevens: Imagination & Faith. Adalaide K. Morris. LC 73-2495. (Princeton Essays in Literature Ser.). 218p. 1974. reprint ed. pap. 62.20 (*0-7837-9288-3*, 2060027) Bks Demand.

Wallace Stevens: Musing the Obscure. Ronald Sukenick. 234p. (C). 1991. reprint ed. pap. 9.95 (*0-9626530-1-2*) In Pr CO.

Wallace Stevens: The Critical Heritage. Charles Doyle. (Critical Heritage Ser.). 500p. 1985. 69.50 (*0-7100-9647-X*, RKP) Routledge.

Wallace Stevens: The Intensest Rendezvous. Barbara M. Fisher. LC 89-16608. 185p. 1990. text ed. 30.00 (*0-8139-1248-2*) U Pr of Va.

Wallace Stevens: The Plain Sense of Things. James Longenbach. 352p. 1991. pap. 22.00 (*0-19-507022-4*) OUP.

Wallace Stevens: The Poems of Our Climate. Harold Bloom. 416p. 1980. pap. 17.95 (*0-8014-9185-1*) Cornell U Pr.

Wallace Stevens: The Poetics of Modernism. Albert Gelpi. (Cambridge Studies in American Literature & Culture: No. 13). (Illus.). 176p. (C). 1990. pap. text ed. 18.95 (*0-521-38699-3*) Cambridge U Pr.

Wallace Stevens: Whole Harmonium. Richard A. Blessing. LC 71-105612. 1970. 34.50 (*0-8156-2145-0*) Syracuse U Pr.

Wallace Stevens: Words Chosen Out of Desire. Helen H. Vendler. LC 83-23588. (Hodges Lectures). 96p. (C). 1984. 12.00 (*0-87049-427-9*) U of Tenn Pr.

Wallace Stevens: Words Chosen Out of Desire. Helen H. Vendler. LC 83-23588. (Hodges Lectures). 95p. 1984. reprint ed. pap. 27.10 (*0-608-01436-2*, 2062198) Bks Demand.

***Wallace Stevens, a Spiritual Poet in a Secular Age.** Charles M. Murphy. 1997. pap. 12.95 (*0-614-27481-8*) Paulist Pr.

Wallace Stevens & Company: The Harmonium Years, 1913-1923. Glen G. MacLeod. LC 83-3624. (Studies in Modern Literature: No. 3). 133p. reprint ed. pap. 38.00 (*0-8357-1405-5*, 2070504) Bks Demand.

Wallace Stevens & Literary Canons. John T. Newcomb. LC 91-31930. 1992. 37.50 (*0-87805-525-8*) U Pr of Miss.

Wallace Stevens & Modern Art: From the Armory Show to Abstract Expressionism. Glen G. MacLeod. LC 92-25358. (C). 1993. text ed. 37.50 (*0-300-05360-6*) Yale U Pr.

Wallace Stevens & Poetic Theory: Conceiving the Supreme Fiction. Bobby J. Leggett. LC 86-16125. 236p. 1987. reprint ed. pap. 67.30 (*0-608-00292-5*, 2059320) Bks Demand.

Wallace Stevens & the Actual World. Alan Filreis. (Illus.). 391p. 1991. text ed. 47.50 (*0-691-06864-X*) Princeton U Pr.

Wallace Stevens & the Feminine. Melita C. Schaum. LC 92-23098. (Illus.). 232p. 1993. text ed. 34.95 (*0-8173-0666-8*) U of Ala Pr.

Wallace Stevens & the Idealist Tradition. Margaret Peterson. LC 83-4996. (Studies in Modern Literature: No. 24). 199p. reprint ed. pap. 56.80 (*0-8357-1452-7*, 2070517) Bks Demand.

Wallace Stevens & the Pennsylvania Keystone: The Influence of Origins on His Life & Poetry. Thomas F. Lombardi. LC 95-19124. (Illus.). 296p. 1996. 43.50 (*0-945636-79-2*) Susquehanna U Pr.

Wallace Stevens & the Question of Belief: Metaphysician in the Dark. David R. Jarraway. LC 92-28610. (Horizons in Theory & American Culture Ser.). xiii, 376p. 1993. text ed. 45.00 (*0-8071-1759-5*) La State U Pr.

Wallace Stevens Case: Law & the Practice of Poetry. Thomas C. Grey. 155p. (C). 1991. 29.00 (*0-674-94577-8*) HUP.

Wallace Stevens, Harmonium, & the Whole of Harmonium. Kia Penso. LC 91-22649. 128p. (C). 1991. lib. bdg. 28.50 (*0-208-02305-4*, Archon Bks) Shoe String.

Wallace Stevens' Supreme Fiction: A New Romanticism. Joseph Carroll. LC 87-4070. 328p. 1987. text ed. 45.00 (*0-8071-1367-0*) La State U Pr.

Wallace Stevens, the Making of the Poem. Frank A. Doggett. LC 79-22772. 176p. reprint ed. pap. 50.20 (*0-8357-8368-5*, 2034123) Bks Demand.

Wallawa Country: 1867-1877. Grace Bartlett. 110p. 1984. 16.95 (*0-87770-330-2*) Ye Galleon.

Walled Garden in Moylough. Joan McBreen. 80p. pap. 10.95 (*1-885266-07-3*) Story Line.

Walled Garden of Truth: The Hadiqa of Hakim Sanai. Hakim Sanai. 1974. 16.00 (*0-900860-35-9*, Pub. by Octagon Pr UK) ISHK.

Walled Gardens: Scenes from an Anglo-Irish Childhood. Annabel Goff. (Illus.). 255p. 1994. pap. 27.50 (*0-907871-42-9*, Pub. by Constable Pubs UK) Trans-Atl Phila.

Walled in Light: St. Colette. Mother Mary Francis. 247p. 1985. pap. 9.50 (*0-8199-0889-4*, Frncscn Herld) Franciscan Pr.

Walled Towns. Ralph A. Cram. 1973. 59.95 (*0-8490-1271-6*) Gordon Pr.

Walled Towns. Ralph A. Cram. LC 19-18459. 107p. (J). 1987. reprint ed. pap. 8.00 (*0-942153-15-4*) Entropy Conserv.

Walled Towns in Ireland. John Bradley. (Irish Treasures Ser.). (Illus.). 48p. (Orig.). (YA). 1995. pap. 8.95 (*0-946172-46-3*, Pub. by Town Hse IE) R Rinehart.

Walled Towns of Ireland, Vol. 1. Avril Thomas. (Illus.). 224p. 1992. 47.50 (*0-7165-2474-0*, Pub. by Irish Acad Pr IE) Intl Spec Bk.

Walled Towns of Ireland, Vol. 2. Avril Thomas. (Illus.). 1992. 47.50 (*0-7165-2475-9*, Pub. by Irish Acad Pr IE) Intl Spec Bk.

Walled-Up Wife: A Casebook. Ed. by Alan Dundes. LC 96-1225. (Illus.). 222p. 1996. 50.00 (*0-299-15070-4*); pap. 16.95 (*0-299-15074-7*) U of Wis Pr.

Wallenberg: Lost Hero. Danny Smith. 192p. 1987. pap. 10.95 (*0-87243-155-X*) Templegate.

Wallenberg's Diary. Charles H. Martin. 224p. 1995. pap. 4.99 (*1-896329-15-2*, Pub. by Comnwlth Pub CN) Partners Pubs Grp.

Wallenstein & Mary Stuart. J. Friedrich Von Schiller. (German Library: Vol. 16). 400p. 1990. 29.50 (*0-8264-0335-2*); pap. text ed. 16.95 (*0-8264-0336-0*) Continuum.

***Waller.** 3rd ed. Waller. LC 97-16576. 1997. pap. text ed. 34.67 (*0-13-744368-4*) P-H.

Waller Scrapbook: Hero or Butcher of Samar? Ed. by Calvert W. Tazewell. LC 90-80405. (Tazewell & Allied Families Scrapbooks Ser.: Vol. 7). 88p. (Orig.). 1990. pap. 11.00 (*1-878515-07-1*) W S Dawson.

Wallet of Kai Lung. Ernest Bramah. 337p. 1977. lib. bdg. 15.95 (*0-89966-269-2*) Buccaneer Bks.

Wallet of Time, 2 Vols. William Winter. LC 79-83400. (Illus.). 1972. 86.95 (*0-405-09095-1*) Ayer.

Wallet of Time, 2 Vols. William Winter. LC 76-84347. (Essay Index Reprint Ser.). 1977. 71.95 (*0-8369-1113-X*) Ayer.

Wallet of Time, 2 Vols., Vol. 1. William Winter. LC 79-83400. (Illus.). 1972. 43.95 (*0-405-09096-X*) Ayer.

Wallet of Time, 2 Vols., Vol. 2. William Winter. LC 79-83400. (Illus.). 1972. 43.95 (*0-405-09097-8*) Ayer.

Wallet of Time: Containing Personal, Biographical, & Critical Reminiscence of the American Theater, 2 vols., Set. (American Biography Ser.). 1991. reprint ed. lib. bdg. 148.00 (*0-7812-8422-8*) Rprt Serv.

Walleye. Dick Sternberg. LC 85-72015. (Hunting & Fishing Library). (Illus.). 160p. 1986. 19.95 (*0-86573-013-X*) Cowles Creative.

Walleye Fishing Today. Tom Zenanko. (Illus.). 212p. (Orig.). 1982. pap. 9.95 (*0-9610296-0-9*) Zenanko Outdoors.

Walleye Tactics, Tips & Tales. Mark Strand. LC 90-60123. (Complete Angler's Library). 314p. 1990. write for info. (*0-914697-28-5*) N Amer Outdoor Grp.

Walleye Trouble Shooting. Mike McClelland. (Illus.). 224p. (Orig.). 1996. 14.95 (*0-9622571-8-4*); pap. 17.95 (*0-9622571-9-2*); lib. bdg. 14.95 (*0-9622571-7-6*) Fishing Enterprises.

Walleye Warriors: An Effective Alliance Against Racism & for the Earth. Rick Whaley & Walter Bresette. 288p. 1994. lib. bdg. 39.95 (*0-86571-256-5*) New Soc Pubs.

Walleye Warriors: An Effective Alliance Against Racism & for the Earth. Rick Whaley & Walter Bresette. 288p. 1994. pap. 17.95 (*0-86571-257-3*) New Soc Pubs.

Walleye Wisdom. Al Lindner. 1994. pap. text ed. 11.95 (*0-929384-49-0*) In-Fisherman.

Walleye Wisdom: An In-Fisherman Handbook of Strategies. Al Lindner et al. (Illus.). 388p. (Orig.). 1983. pap. 11.95 (*0-9605254-1-6*) In-Fisherman.

Wallflower. William Bayer. 1992. mass mkt. 5.99 (*0-515-10843-X*) Jove Pubns.

Wallflower. Linda F. Lee. 272p. (Orig.). 1995. mass mkt. 4.99 (*0-515-11683-1*) Jove Pubns.

***Wallflowers: Bringing down the House.** Jennette DeLisa. 72p. (Orig.). 1997. pap. text ed. 21.95 (*1-57623-934-9*, 0019B) Warner Brothers.

Wallied Gardens: Scenes from an Anglo-Irish Childhood. Goff A. Davis. 1989. 19.95 (*0-394-56837-0*) Knopf.

Wallin: The Michigan Wallins: a History, from Stratford-on-Avon, 1791, to Wallinwood-on-the-Grand, 1933. Van A. Wallin. (Illus.). 129p. 1993. reprint ed. pap. 22.00 (*0-8328-3158-1*); reprint ed. lib. bdg. 32.00 (*0-8328-3157-3*) Higginson Bk Co.

Wallingford Riegger: Two Essays in Musical Biography. Stephen Spackman. LC 82-82102. (I.S.A.M. Monographs: No. 17). (Illus.). 60p. (Orig.). 1982. pap. 10.00 (*0-914678-18-3*) Inst Am Music.

Wallington. Raleigh Trevelyan. (Illus.). 96p. 1995. pap. 9.95 (*0-7078-0230-X*, Pub. by Natl Trust UK) Trafalgar.

Wallington's World: A Puritan Artisan in Seventeenth-Century London. Paul S. Seaver. LC 84-40447. 272p. 1985. 42.50 (*0-8047-1267-0*); pap. 12.95 (*0-8047-1432-0*) Stanford U Pr.

Wallis: Secret Lives of the Duchess of Windsor: The Scandalous Truth about the Century's Most Infamous Woman. Charles Higham. (Illus.). 591p. (Orig.). 1989. pap. 19.95 (*0-330-30724-X*, Pub. by Pan Books UK) Trans-Atl Phila.

Wallis & Edward - Letters 1931-1937: The Intimate Correspondence of the Duke & Duchess of Windsor. Ed. by Michael Bloch. 368p. 1988. mass mkt. 4.95 (*0-380-70362-9*) Avon.

Wallop & Whizz & the Bottle of Fizz. Philip Hawthorne. (Rhyming Stories Ser.). (Illus.). 24p. (J). (gr. 1 up). 1996. pap. 4.95 (*0-7460-1700-6*, Usborne); lib. bdg. 12.95 (*0-88110-851-0*, Usborne) EDC.

Walloping Window-Blind. Charles E. Carryl. LC 92-40338. (Illus.). (J). (gr. k-5). 1994. 16.00 (*0-688-12517-4*); lib. bdg. 15.93 (*0-688-12518-2*) Lothrop.

Wallowing in Trivia Grits. Samantha Touchtome, pseud. (Adult Poetry Ser.). (Illus.). 96p. (Orig.). 1987. pap. 6.95 (*0-915199-09-2*) Pen-Dec.

Wallpaper. Clare Taylor. 1989. pap. 25.00 (*0-7478-0140-1*, Pub. by Shire UK) St Mut.

Wallpaper & the Artist: From Durer to Warhol. Marilyn O. Hapgood. LC 92-14717. (Illus.). 272p. 1992. 85.00 (*0-89659-933-7*) Abbeville Pr.

Wallpaper from Space. Daniel Pinkwater. LC 95-36393. (Illus.). (J). (gr. 1-4). 1996. 15.00 (*0-689-80764-3*, Atheneum Bks Young) S&S Childrens.

Wallpaper in America: From the Seventeenth Century to World War I. Catherine Lynn. (Illus.). 1980. 45.00 (*0-393-01448-7*) Norton.

***Wallpapering.** Steven Cory. Ed. by David W. Toht. (Easy Step Ser.). (Illus.). 64p. (Orig.). 1997. pap. 6.95 (*0-89721-345-9*, 05985) Ortho Info.

Wallpapering. Outlet Book Co. Staff. 1994. 3.99 (*0-517-08781-2*) Random Hse Value.

Wallraf-Richartz Museum, Cologne. Intro. by Rainer Budde. (Illus.). 128p. 1991. 30.00 (*1-870248-76-7*) Scala Books.

Walls. Henry Pluckrose. LC 94-45584. (New Look Ser.). (Illus.). 24p. (J). (gr. k-3). 1996. lib. bdg. 15.00 (*0-516-08239-6*) Childrens.

Walls. rev. ed. James J. Callahan. 176p. 1996. pap. 10.00 (*0-9636270-1-5*) Callahan Assocs.

Walls: Essays, 1985-1990. Kenneth A. McClane. LC 90-22624. (African American Life Ser.). 122p. 1991. 12.95 (*0-8143-2134-8*) Wayne St U Pr.

Walls: Physical & Psychological. Robert E. Reuman. LC 66-24444. (Orig.). 1966. pap. 3.00 (*0-87574-147-9*) Pendle Hill.

Walls: Resisting the Third Reich - One Woman's Story. Hiltgunt Zassenhaus. LC 92-40910. 256p. 1993. reprint ed. pap. 10.00 (*0-8070-6345-2*) Beacon Pr.

Walls: Siteworks for the Gym. Roger Hull. (Illus.). 1981. pap. 1.00 (*0-914435-04-3*) Marylhurst Art.

Walls & Bars. 3rd ed. Eugene V. Debs. 286p. (C). 1983. reprint ed. lib. bdg. 24.95 (*0-88286-010-0*) C H Kerr.

Walls & Bars. Eugene V. Debs. LC 74-172574. (Criminology, Law Enforcement, & Social Problems Ser.: No. 161). 1973. reprint ed. 15.00 (*0-87585-161-4*) Patterson Smith.

Walls & Ceilings. (Home Repair & Improvement Ser.). (Illus.). 136p. 1980. 14.60 (*0-8094-3450-4*); lib. bdg. 20.60 (*0-8094-3451-2*) Time-Life.

Walls & Ceilings. Time-Life Books Editors. LC 95-49608. (Home Repair & Improvement Ser.). (Illus.). 128p. 1996. 14.95 (*0-7835-3900-2*) Time-Life.

Walls & Mirrors: Mexican Americans, Mexican Immigrants, & the Politics of Ethnicity. David G. Gutierrez. LC 94-1892. 1995. 40.00 (*0-520-08322-9*) U CA Pr.

Walls & Mirrors: Mexican Americans, Mexican Immigrants, & the Politics of Ethnicity. David G. Gutierrez. LC 94-1892. 321p. 1995. pap. 15.00 (*0-520-20219-8*) U CA Pr.

Walls & Mirrors: Western Representations of Really Existing German Socialism in the German Democratic Republic. Duncan Smith. 222p. (Orig.). (C). 1988. pap. text ed. 21.00 (*0-8191-6710-X*); lib. bdg. 42.00 (*0-8191-6709-6*) U Pr of Amer.

Walls & Molding: How to Care for Old & Historic Wood & Plaster. Natalie Shivers. LC 89-78511. (Respectful Rehabilitation Ser.). (Illus.). 200p. (Orig.). 1995. pap. text ed. 16.95 (*0-471-14432-0*) Wiley.

Walls & Screens. Diana Saville. (Illus.). 64p. 1994. 7.98 (*1-55859-660-7*) Abbeville Pr.

***Walls & Woodwork.** Mike Lawrence & Fred Milson. (Home Decorator Ser.). 96p. 1997. pap. 15.95 (*1-85368-738-3*, Pub. by New Holland Pubs UK) Sterling.

Walls Are Crumbling. John M. Oesterreicher. (Illus.). 10.00 (*0-8159-7201-6*) Devin.

Walls Around Us: The Thinking Person's Guide to How a House Works. David Owen. LC 92-50070. 1992. pap. 13.00 (*0-679-74144-5*, Vin) Random.

Walls Belong to Kids: Literature. Anthony Flores & Jerry Dodge. 80p. (J). (gr. 2-5). 8.99 (*0-86653-956-5*, FE0956) Fearon Teach Aids.

Walls Belong to Kids: Math. Anthony Flores & Jerry Dodge. 80p. (J). (gr. 2-5). 1996. 9.99 (*0-86653-909-3*, FE3862) Fearon Teach Aids.

Walls Belong to Kids: Science. Anthony Flores & Jerry Dodge. 80p. (J). (gr. 2-5). 8.99 (*0-86653-955-7*, FE0955) Fearon Teach Aids.

Walls Belong to Kids: Social Studies. Anthony Flores & Jerry Dodge. 80p. (J). (gr. 2-5). 8.99 (*0-86653-954-9*, FE0954) Fearon Teach Aids.

Walls Belong to Kids Set, 4 bks., Set. Anthony Flores & Jerry Dodge. (J). (gr. 2-5). 34.99 (*1-56417-690-8*, FE7690) Fearon Teach Aids.

Walls Built on Sand: Migration, Exclusion, & Society in Kuwait. Anh Nga Longva. LC 96-49172. (C). 1997. text ed. 59.00 (*0-8133-2758-X*) Westview.

Walls Came Tumbling Down. Robert A. Wilson. LC 96-68643. 192p. (Orig.). 1996. pap. 14.95 (*1-56184-091-2*) New Falcon Pubns.

Walls Came Tumbling Down. Mary W. Ovington. LC 69-18543. (American Negro: His History & Literature. Series 2). 1969. reprint ed. 29.95 (*0-405-01884-3*) Ayer.

Walls Came Tumbling Down: The Collapse of Communism in Eastern Europe. Gale Stokes. LC 92-44862. 336p. (C). 1993. reprint ed. pap. text ed. 18.95 (*0-19-506645-6*) OUP.

Walls, Ceilings & Woodwork. Time-Life Books Editors. (Fix-It-Yourself Ser.). (Illus.). 144p. 1987. 17.27 (*0-8094-6212-5*); lib. bdg. 23.27 (*0-8094-6213-3*) Time-Life.

Walls Collide As You Expand, Dwarf Maple. James Chapman. LC 92-75669. 92p. (Orig.). (C). 1993. pap. 6.00 (*1-879193-01-9*) Fugue State.

Walls Come True: An Opera for Spoken Voices (The Structure of Destruction, Pt. II) Douglas Messerli. (Littoral Bks.). 96p. (Orig.). 1994. pap. 12.95 (*1-55713-180-5*) Sun & Moon CA.

Walls, Floors & Ceilings. Judson Mead. Ed. by Roundtable Press Editors. LC 84-17052. (Illus.). 160p. (Orig.). 1984. pap. 9.95 (*0-932944-72-8*) Creative Homeowner.

Walls of Air. Barbara Hambly. 297p. (Orig.). 1983. mass mkt. 4.95 (*0-345-29670-2*, Del Rey) Ballantine.

***Walls of Air.** Barbara Hambly. (The Darwath Trilogy Ser.). 1997. mass mkt. 5.99 (*0-345-91170-9*, Del Rey) Ballantine.

Walls of Blue Coquina. Sam Harrison. 1990. 19.95 (*0-15-194195-5*) HarBrace.

***Walls of Carthage.** Harry Clifton. 46p. 7700. pap. 10.95 (*0-902996-50-9*) Dufour.

Walls of Circumstance: Studies in Nineteenth-Century Music. Eric F. Jensen. LC 92-25210. (Illus.). 170p. 1992. 25.00 (*0-8108-2588-0*) Scarecrow.

Walls of Constantinople. B. Granville Baker. LC 72-178513. (Medieval Studies). reprint ed. 37.50 (*0-404-56509-3*) AMS Pr.

Walls of Fear. Ed. by Kathryn D. Cramer. 400p. 1991. mass mkt. 4.99 (*0-380-70789-6*) Avon.

***Walls of Jericho.** Rudolph Fisher. (X Press Black Classics Ser.). 168p. 1996. pap. 9.95 (*1-874509-28-X*, Pub. by X Pr UK) LPC InBook.

***Walls of Jericho.** Jon Land. LC 96-27427. 1997. 23.95 (*0-312-86267-9*) Forge NYC.

***Walls of Jericho.** Mann. 1997. pap. 15.00 (*0-15-600501-8*) HarBrace.

Walls of Jericho. Rudolph Fisher. LC 69-18590. (American Negro: His History & Literature. Series 2). 1978. reprint ed. 32.95 (*0-405-01862-2*) Ayer.

Walls of Jericho. Rudolph Fisher. LC 94-2140. 300p. (C). 1994. reprint ed. pap. 15.95 (*0-472-06565-3*); reprint ed. text ed. 34.50 (*0-472-09565-X*) U of Mich Pr.

Walls of Jericho: Lyndon Johnson, Hubert Humphrey, Richard Russell, & the Struggle for Civil Rights. Robert Mann. LC 95-30058. 609p. 1996. 32.00 (*0-15-100065-4*) HarBrace.

***Walls of Jericho: Lyndon Johnson, Hubert Humphrey, Richard Russell, & the Struggle for Civil Rights.** Robert Mann. 1997. pap. 15.00 (*0-614-27376-5*, Harvest Bks) HarBrace.

Walls of My Heart. Bruce Thompson & Barbara Thompson. LC 88-92665. (Illus.). 258p. 1989. pap. 8.95 (*0-935779-13-2*) Crown Min.

Walls of Plato's Cave: The Science & Philosophy of Consciousness, Brain & Perception. John R. Smythies. (Philosophy Ser.). 251p. 1994. 63.95 (*1-85628-882-X*, Pub. by Avebury Pub UK) Ashgate Pub Co.

***Walls of Terror.** Frank Simon. LC 97-16923. 368p. (Orig.). 1997. pap. 12.99 (*0-89107-952-1*) Crossway Bks.

Walls of Thebes. Poems. David R. Slavitt. LC 85-23845. 51p. 1986. pap. 6.95 (*0-8071-1307-7*) La State U Pr.

Walls of This House Have Tongues. Stefan Hyner. 1986. pap. 3.00 (*0-942396-34-0*) Blackberry ME.

Walls Rise Up: A Novel. George S. Perry. LC 93-37785. (Texas Tradition Ser.: No. 21). 154p. 1994. 19.95 (*0-87565-126-7*) Tex Christian.

***Walls, Walks & Patios.** Creative Homeowner Press Staff. 1997. pap. text ed. 14.95 (*1-880029-97-9*) Creative Homeowner.

W

An Asterisk (*) at the beginning of an entry indicates that the title is appearing in BIP for the first time.

Wally Armstrong Golf Log. Wally Armstrongs Golf Log. (Illus.). 144p. 1994. pap. 13.95 (*1-885198-00-0*) Sports Log Pubs.

Wally Hunt's Vermont. Ed. by James Hayford. 56p. (Orig.). 1983. pap. 4.00 (*0-9610860-0-9*) Orleans.

Wally Koala & Friends. Toni Mazzola & Mimi Guten. Ed. by Keri Cohen. LC 93-94001. (Wally Koala Ser.). (Illus.). 24p. (J). (ps-3). 1993. 9.95 incl. audio (*1-883747-00-7*) WK Prods.

Wally Koala & the Little Green Peach. Toni Mazzola & Mimi Guten. Ed. by Keri Cohen. LC 93-94002. (Wally Koala Ser.). (Illus.). 22p. (J). (ps-3). 1993. 9.95 (*1-883747-01-5*) WK Prods.

Wally Laughs-Easy. large type ed. Dane Coolidge. LC 93-44661. 1994. lib. bdg. 15.95 (*0-7862-0160-6*) Thorndike Pr.

Wally Lewis: The Last Emperor. Adrian McGregor. 1993. pap. 18.95 (*0-7022-2493-6*, Pub. by Univ Queensland Pr AT) Intl Spec Bk.

Wally Moore's Wedding & Banquet Reference. Wallace Moore. 154p. 1991. spiral bd. write for info. (*0-9631447-0-7*) T C & I.

Wally, the Scholarly Walrus. Lee Hill. (J). 1990. 6.95 (*0-533-08401-6*) Vantage.

Wally the Whale Who Loved Balloons. Yuichi Watanabe. Tr. by Diane T. Ooka from JPN. (Illus.). 32p. (J). (ps-4). 1982. 11.95 (*0-89346-150-4*) Heian Intl.

Wally the Wordworm. Clifton Fadiman. LC 83-9181. (Illus.). (J). (gr. 3 up). 1984. 12.95 (*0-88045-038-X*); audio 21.90 (*0-88045-101-7*); audio 8.95 (*0-88045-098-3*) Stemmer Hse.

Wally Whale & Friends. Pam Adams. (J). (gr. 4 up). 1981. pap. 7.99 (*0-85953-268-2*) Childs Play.

***Wally Whale Tubby Book.** 8p. (J). 1987. pap. write for info. (*1-55513-654-0*, Chariot Bks) Chariot Victor.

Wally Wooluf & Other Stories: A Young Person's Guide to Humor. Tom Mooney. pap. 3.00 (*0-317-28510-6*) Mooney.

Wally's Stories: Conversations in the Kindergarten. Vivian G. Paley. LC 80-21882. 223p. 1987. pap. text ed. 10.95 (*0-674-94593-X*) HUP.

***Walnut Canyon National Monument.** Scott Thybony. LC 96-70560. 16p. 1996. pap. 3.95 (*1-877856-72-X*) SW Pks Mnmts.

Walnut Canyon National Monument: Deutsch. Scott Thybony. Ed. by T. J. Priehs. Tr. by Southwest Translators Staff. LC 91-61568. 16p. (GER.). 1991. pap. 3.95 (*1-877856-00-2*) SW Pks Mnmts.

Walnut Creek Learns the Alphabet: From Settlement to Suburbia - a History of Walnut Creek Through the Great Depression. 2nd ed. Jeane Elder. LC 74-84514. (Illus.). 144p. 1974. pap. 6.95 (*0-914974-01-7*) Holmgangers.

Walnut Grove. Jane G. Rushing. xiv, 255p. 1992. reprint ed. pap. 12.00 (*0-89672-278-3*) Tex Tech Univ Pr.

Walnut Grove: The Photograph Album. Shirley M. Kelley. (Illus.). 230p. 1993. pap. write for info. (*0-935648-43-7*) Halldin Pub.

Walnut Grove - The Good Old Days. Shirley M. Kelley. (Illus.). 124p. 1991. pap. write for info. (*0-935648-35-6*) Halldin Pub.

Walnut King: And Other Stories. John Mort. 184p. (Orig.). 1990. pap. 8.00 (*0-9617499-2-X*) Woods Colt Pr.

Walnut Pickles & Watermelon Cake: A Century of Michigan Cooking. Larry B. Massie & Priscilla Massie. LC 89-16448. (Great Lakes Bks.). (Illus.). 354p. 1990. 29.95 (*0-8143-1939-4*) Wayne St U Pr.

Walnut Sapling on Masih's Grave & Other Stories by Iranian Women. Ed. by John Green & Farzin Yazdanfar. 208p. (C). 1993. pap. 13.95 (*0-435-08626-X*, 08626) Heinemann.

Walnut Street Prison Workshop. John L. Cotter et al. (Illus.). 1988. pap. 7.50 (*0-916530-12-4*) Athenaeum Phila.

***Walnut Tree Waits for Its Bees.** James C. Hopkins. (Premier Ser.: Vol. 5). (Illus.). 25p. 1997. 5.00 (*0-9654421-7-9*) Mica Press.

Walnut Trees. John F. Prevost. LC 96-309. (Trees Ser.). (J). 1996. lib. bdg. 13.98 (*1-56239-618-8*) Abdo & Dghtrs.

Walnut Trees of Altenburg. Andre Malraux. Tr. by A. W. Fielding from FRE. LC 88-37363. 224p. 1989. lib. bdg. 35.00 (*0-86527-392-8*) Fertig.

Walnut Trees of Altenburg. Andre Malraux. Tr. by A. W. Fielding. LC 88-37363. 226p. 1992. pap. 13.95 (*0-226-50289-9*) U Ch Pr.

Walpole. John M. Morley. LC 76-110858. 251p. 1971. reprint ed. text ed. 59.75 (*0-8371-4527-9*, MOHW, Greenwood Pr) Greenwood.

Walpole & the Patriots: Politics, Poetry, & Myth, 1725-1742. Christine Gerrard. (Illus.). 350p. 1995. 59.00 (*0-19-812982-3*) OUP.

Walpole & the Robinocracy. Paul Langford. LC 85-6609. (English Satirical Print Ser.). 252p. 1986. lib. bdg. 100.00 (*0-85964-175-9*) Chadwyck-Healey.

Walpole & the Wits: The Relation of Politics to Literature. Bertrand A. Goldgar. LC 76-6809. 266p. reprint ed. pap. 75.90 (*0-7837-6883-4*, 2046713) Bks Demand.

Walpole As It Was & As It Is: Containing the Complete Civil History of the Town from 1749 to 1879, Also...a History of the 150 Families that Settled in the Town Previous to 1820... George Aldrich. (Illus.). 404p. 1995. reprint ed. lib. bdg. 42.50 (*0-8328-4646-5*) Higginson Bk Co.

Walpurgis Night. Joan Cofrancesco. Ed. by Kathleen Iddings. LC 93-84138. 80p. (Orig.). 1993. per. 10.00 (*0-931289-13-0*) San Diego Poet Pr.

Walrasian Microeconomics: An Introduction to the Economic Theory of Market Behavior. Donald W. Katzner. LC 86-26622. (Illus.). 500p. (C). 1988. text ed. 42.36 (*0-201-10461-X*) Addison-Wesley.

Walrasian Vision of the Microeconomy: An Elementary Exposition of the Structure of Modern General Equilibrium Theory. Donald W. Katzner. LC 89-35171. 164p. 1989. text ed. 47.50 (*0-472-09409-2*); pap. text ed. 18.95 (*0-472-06409-6*) U of Mich Pr.

Walras's Market Models. Donald A. Walker. (Illus.). 400p. (C). 1996. text ed. 59.95 (*0-521-56268-6*) Cambridge U Pr.

Walrus: On Location. Kathy Darling. LC 90-33376. (Illus.). 40p. (J). (gr. 2 up). 1991. 14.95 (*0-688-09032-X*) Lothrop.

Walrus' Adventure in Alphabet Town. Janet Riehecky. LC 92-1330. (Read Around Alphabet Town Ser.). (Illus.). 32p. (J). (ps-2). 1992. lib. bdg. 17.50 (*0-516-05423-6*) Childrens.

Walrus & the Carpenter. Lewis Carroll. LC 85-7591. (Illus.). 32p. (J). (gr. 2-4). 1990. reprint ed. pap. 4.95 (*0-8050-1482-9*, Owlet BYR) H Holt & Co.

Walrus & the Warwolf. Hugh Cook. LC 88-70886. (Chronicles of an Age of Darkness Ser.: No. 4). (Illus.). 486p. 9300. 30.00 (*0-86140-294-4*, Pub. by Colin Smythe Ltd UK) Dufour.

Walrus & the Warwolf. Hugh Cook. 1992. 30.00 (*0-8023-1287-X*) Dufour.

***Walrus on Location.** Kathy Darling. (Illus.). 40p. (J). 3.98 (*0-8317-2833-7*) Smithmark.

Walrus Was Paul: The Great Beatle Death Clues of 1969. R. Gary Patterson. (Illus.). 162p. (Orig.). 1994. pap. 19.95 (*0-9641163-0-8*) Excursion Prods.

Walrus Was Paul: The Great Beatle Death Clues of 1969. R. Gary Patterson. 176p. (Orig.). 1996. reprint ed. pap. 16.95 (*0-9646452-1-1*) Dowling Pr.

Walruses. Emilie U. Lepthien. LC 96-13921. (True Bks.). 48p. (J). 1996. lib. bdg. 19.00 (*0-516-20162-X*) Childrens.

***Walruses.** Emilie U. Lepthien. (True Bks.). 48p. (J). 1997. pap. 6.95 (*0-516-26117-7*) Childrens.

Walruses. Sarah Palmer. (Sea Mammal Discovery Library). (Illus.). 24p. (J). (gr. k-5). 1989. lib. bdg. 11.94 (*0-86592-358-2*); lib. bdg. 8.95 (*0-685-58621-9*) Rourke Corp.

Walruses. Charles Rotter. LC 92-8410. (Nature Bks.). (J). (gr. 2-6). 1992. lib. bdg. 22.79 (*0-89565-841-0*) Childs World.

Walsh. rev. ed. Sharon Pollock. (NFS Canada Ser.). 1993. pap. 11.95 (*0-88922-215-0*) Genl Dist Srvs.

***Walsh & Hoyt's Clinical Neuro-Ophthalmology.** 5th ed. Neil R. Miller et al. LC 96-50372. 1997. write for info. (*0-683-30230-2*); write for info. (*0-683-30231-0*); write for info. (*0-683-30232-9*); write for info. (*0-683-30233-7*); write for info. (*0-683-30234-5*) Williams & Wilkins.

Walsh & Hoyt's Clinical Neuro-Ophthalmology, Vol. 1. 4th ed. Neil R, Miller. (Illus.). 382p. 1982. lib. bdg. 115.00 (*0-683-06020-1*) Williams & Wilkins.

Walsh & Hoyt's Clinical Neuro-Ophthalmology: Infections & Inflammation of the Central Nervous System & Non-organic (Functional) Neuro-Opthalmologic Disease, Vol. 5, Pts. 1 & 2. 4th ed. Neil R. Miller. (Illus.). 2693p. 1994. 225.00 (*0-683-06024-4*) Williams & Wilkins.

Walsh & Hoyt's Clinical Neuro-Ophthalmology, Vol. 4: Vascular Disease. 4th ed. Neil R. Miller. (Illus.). 947p. 1991. 170.00 (*0-683-06023-6*) Williams & Wilkins.

Walsh & Hoyt's Clinical Neuro-Opthalmology, Vol. 2. 4th ed. Neil R. Miller. (Illus.). 750p. 1984. 135.00 (*0-683-06021-X*) Williams & Wilkins.

Walsh & Hoyt's Clinical Neuro-Opthalmology, Vol. 3. 4th ed. Ed. by Neil R. Miller. 734p. 1987. 140.00 (*0-683-06022-8*) Williams & Wilkins.

Walsh Heritage-Walsh Co. Historical Society, 4 vols., Set. 50.00 (*0-686-30746-1*) Assoc Print.

Walsh Heritage-Walsh Co. Historical Society, 4 vols., Vols. 1 & 2. 20.00 (*0-686-30747-X*) Assoc Print.

Walsh Heritage-Walsh Co. Historical Society, 4 vols., Vols. 3 & 4. 30.00 (*0-686-30748-8*) Assoc Print.

Walsh Series: An Introduction to Dyadic Harmonic Analysis Co-publication with Academiai Kiado, Budapest, Hungary. F. Schipp et al. 528p. 1990. 216.00 (*0-7503-0068-X*) IOP Pub.

Walsh Series & Transforms: Theory & Applications. B. Golubov et al. (C). 1991. lib. bdg. 210.00 (*0-7923-1100-0*) Kluwer Ac.

***Walshingham Prayer Book: A Meditative Companion & Guide.** Elizabeth Obbard. (Illus.). 128p. 1997. pap. 11.95 (*1-85311-170-8*, Pub. by Canterbury Press Norwich UK) Morehouse Pub.

Walston Citation at Glance. Date not set. pap. text ed. write for info. (*0-314-05897-4*) West Pub.

Walt: Backstage Adventures with Walt Disney. Charles Shows. (Illus.). 212p. 1980. 10.95 (*0-934846-01-4*) Wind Song.

Walt Bellamy: The Saturnine Center. Ronald L. Thomas. 1985. pap. 8.95 (*0-933085-00-1*) Antaeus Pr.

Walt Disney: A Bio-Bibliography. Kathy M. Jackson. LC 92-19842. (Popular Culture Bio-Bibliographies Ser.). 364p. 1993. text ed. 55.00 (*0-313-25898-8*, JWD, Greenwood Pr) Greenwood.

Walt Disney: A Biography. Barbara Ford. (Illus.). 160p. (J). (gr. 4-7). 1989. 15.95 (*0-8027-6864-4*); lib. bdg. 16.85 (*0-8027-6865-2*) Walker & Co.

Walt Disney: An American Original. Bob Thomas. (Illus.). 384p. 1994. 19.95 (*0-7868-6129-0*); pap. 14.95 (*0-7868-6027-8*) Hyperion.

Walt Disney: Creator of Mickey Mouse. Michael D. Cole. LC 95-31202. (People to Know Ser.). (Illus.). 112p. (YA). (gr. 6 up). 1996. lib. bdg. 18.95 (*0-89490-694-1*) Enslow Pubs.

Walt Disney: His Life in Pictures. Russell Schroeder. LC 96-17248. (Illus.). 1996. lib. bdg. 14.89 (*0-7868-5043-4*) Disney Pr.

Walt Disney: His Life in Pictures. Ed. by Russell Schroeder. LC 96-17248. (Illus.). 64p. 1996. 14.95 (*0-7868-3116-2*) Disney Pr.

Walt Disney: Hollywood's Dark Prince. Marc Eliot. LC 92-38788. 1993. 21.95 (*1-55972-174-X*, Birch Ln Pr) Carol Pub Group.

***Walt Disney: Young Movie Maker.** Marie Hammontree. (Childhood of Famous Americans Ser.). (Illus.). (J). (gr. 3-7). 1997. pap. 4.99 (*0-614-29081-3*, Aladdin Paperbacks) S&S Childrens.

Walt Disney Bambi. (J). pap. 1.99 (*0-307-07100-6*) Western Pub.

Walt Disney Choose Your Own Adventure. (J). (ps-1). 1985. write for info. (*0-318-59135-9*) Bantam.

Walt Disney Easy Piano Solos, Bk. 1. 1993. 4.95 (*0-7935-2212-9*, 00292025) H Leonard.

Walt Disney Easy Piano Solos, Bk. 2. 1993. 4.95 (*0-7935-2213-7*, 00292026) H Leonard.

Walt Disney Fairy Tale Treasury: Blue. Disney Studios Staff. (Penguin-Disney Ser.). (J). 1991. 9.98 (*0-8317-9291-4*) Viking Child Bks.

Walt Disney Fairy Tale Treasury: Red. Disney Studios Staff. (Penguin-Disney Ser.). (J). 1991. 9.98 (*0-8317-9292-2*) Viking Child Bks.

Walt Disney Imagineering: A Behind the Dreams Look at Making the Magic Real. Imagineers Staff. (Illus.). 200p. 1996. 50.00 (*0-7868-6246-7*) Hyperion.

Walt Disney-One Hundred One Dalmatas: Un Libro para Contar. Fran Manushkin. Tr. by Daniel M. Santacruz from ENG. LC 93-70677. (Libros Buena Vista Ser.). (Illus.). 32p. (SPA.). (J). 1994. pap. 5.95 (*1-56282-568-2*) Disney Pr.

Walt Disney-One Hundred One Dalmatas: Un Libro para Contar. Fran Manushkin. Tr. by Daniel m. Santacruz from ENG. LC 93-70677. (Libros Buena Vista Ser.). (Illus.). 32p. (SPA.). (J). 1994. lib. bdg. 13.89 (*1-56282-697-2*) Disney Pr.

Walt Disney Pictures Presents the Little Mermaid: Ariel above the Sea. Stephanie Colmenson. (Golden Easy Readers Ser.). (Illus.). (J). (gr. k-2). 1991. 4.25 (*0-307-11697-2*, Golden Pr) Western Pub.

Walt Disney World - 1991: The Official Guide. Stephen Birnbaum. 240p. (Orig.). 1991. pap. 10.95 (*0-380-71216-4*) Avon.

Walt Disney World & Epcot Center. Valerie Childs. (J). 1990. 7.99 (*0-517-48085-9*) Random Hse Value.

Walt Disney World & Orlando Pocket Guide. Berlitz Staff. (Pocket Guides Ser.). (Illus.). 144p. 1994. pap. 7.95 (*2-8315-0702-2*) Berlitz.

Walt Disney World, Epcot & Universal Studios, Florida, 1995. Corey Sandler. (EconoGuide Ser.). (Illus.). 288p. 1994. pap. 9.95 (*0-8092-3508-0*) Contemp Bks.

Walt Disney World for Couples. Rick Perlmutter & Gail Perlmutter. 1996. pap. 14.95 (*0-7615-0321-8*) Prima Pub.

***Walt Disney World for Couples.** 2nd rev. ed. Rick Perlmutter & Gayle Perlmutter. LC 97-5569. 368p. 1997. per. 15.00 (*0-7615-0940-2*) Prima Pub.

Walt Disney World Unfolds. (Illus.). 1996. pap. 5.95 (*0-7868-8151-8*) Hyperion.

***Walt Disney World, Universal Studios & Orlando '98.** Fodors Travel Staff. 1997. pap. 14.00 (*0-679-03544-3*) Fodors Travel.

Walt Disney World, Universal Studios Florida, EPCOT, & Other Major Central Florida Attractions. Corey Sandler. (Contemporary's Econoguide '97 Ser.). (Illus.). 368p. 1996. pap. 12.95 (*0-8092-3318-5*) Contemp Bks.

***Walt Disney World with Kids.** Kim Wiley. 1997. pap. 13.00 (*0-7615-0808-2*) Prima Pub.

Walt Disney World with Kids, 1993 Edition: Including Epcot Center, Disney-MGM Studios, Universal Studios, & Typhoon Lagoon. Kim W. Wiley. 336p. 1992. pap. 9.99 (*1-55958-276-6*) Prima Pub.

Walt Disney World with Kids, 1994 Edition: The Unofficial Guide. Kim W. Wiley. LC 93-34368. 1993. pap. 9.99 (*1-55958-416-5*) Prima Pub.

Walt Disney World with Kids, 1995. Kim W. Wiley. 1994. pap. 9.99 (*1-55958-557-9*) Prima Pub.

Walt Disney World with Kids 1996. Kim Wiley. 336p. 1995. pap. text ed. 9.95 (*0-7615-0133-9*) Prima Pub.

Walt Disney World with Kids, 1997 Edition. Kim W. Wiley. 352p. 1996. per. 13.00 (*0-7615-0407-9*) Prima Pub.

Walt Disney World, 1989. Stephen Birnbaum. 1989. pap. write for info. (*0-318-64763-X*) HM.

Walt Disney World, 1990: The Official Guide. Steve Burnbaum. 1989. pap. 10.95 (*0-380-71004-8*) Avon.

Walt Disney's Alice in Wonderland. Illus. by Franc Maten. (J). (ps-2). 1991. write for info. (*0-307-12341-3*, Golden Pr) Western Pub.

Walt Disney's Alice in Wonderland: Book of Colors. Rita Balducci. (Board Bks.). (Illus.). 12p. (J). (ps). 1993. bds. 1.95 (*0-307-06079-9*, 6079, Golden Pr) Western Pub.

Walt Disney's Alice's Tea Party. Lyn Calder. LC 91-73810. (Illus.). 48p. (J). (gr. k-4). 1992. 12.95 (*1-56282-145-8*); lib. bdg. 12.89 (*1-56282-199-7*) Disney Pr.

Walt Disney's Alice's Tea Party. Lyn Calder. LC 91-73810. (Illus.). 48p. (J). (gr. k-4). 1994. pap. 5.95 (*1-56282-648-4*) Disney Pr.

Walt Disney's Bambi. Illus. by Isidre Mones. (Little Nugget Bks.). 28p. (J). (ps). 1992. bds. 3.50 (*0-307-12535-1*, 12535, Golden Books) Western Pub.

***Walt Disney's Bambi.** Stacey Stevens. (Illus.). (J). (ps-k). 1997. pap. 4.95 (*0-614-28694-8*) Disney Pr.

***Walt Disney's Bambi.** limited ed. Disney Studio Staff. (Sketchbook Ser.). (Illus.). 104p. 1997. 100.00 (*1-55709-342-3*) Applewood.

***Walt Disney's Bambi: The Sketchbook Series.** (Sketchbook Ser.). (Illus.). 88p. 1997. 29.95 (*0-7868-6302-1*) Hyperion.

Walt Disney's Bambi: The Sketchbook Series. Illus. by David Pacheco & Jesse Clay. LC 92-54876. (Illustrated Classics). 96p. (J). 1993. 14.95 (*1-56282-442-2*) Disney Pr.

Walt Disney's Bambi: The Sketchbook Series. Adapted by Joanne Ryder. LC 92-54875. (Junior Novel Ser.). (Illus.). 64p. (J). (gr. 2-6). 1993. pap. 3.50 (*1-56282-444-9*) Disney Pr.

Walt Disney's Bambi: Thumper's Book of Opposites. Rita Balducci. (Golden Board Bks.). (Illus.). 12p. (J). (ps). 1993. bds. 1.95 (*0-307-06124-8*, 6124, Golden Books) Western Pub.

Walt Disney's Bambi & the Butterfly. Little Golden Books Staff. (First Little Golden Bks). (Illus.). 24p. (J). (ps). 1983. bds. 1.09 (*0-307-10152-5*, Golden Books) Western Pub.

Walt Disney's Bambi Bambi Count to Five. Diane Muldron. (Golden Board Bks.). (Illus.). 12p. (J). (ps). 1991. bds. 1.95 (*0-307-06114-0*, Golden Books) Western Pub.

Walt Disney's Bambi's Forest: A Year in the Life of the Forest. Joanne Ryder. LC 93-72551. (Illus.). 32p. (J). (gr. k-3). 1994. 11.95 (*1-56282-643-3*); lib. bdg. 11.89 (*1-56282-698-0*) Disney Pr.

Walt Disney's Bambi's Fragrant Forest. LC 74-33127. (Golden Scratch & Sniff Bks.). (Illus.). 32p. (J). (ps-2). 1988. write for info. (*0-307-13530-6*) Western Pub.

Walt Disney's Beauty & the Beast: A Gift of Love. (Golden Book and Necklace Ser.). (Illus.). 32p. (J). (ps-2). 1995. bds. 8.95 (*0-307-16152-8*, Golden Pr) Western Pub.

Walt Disney's Cinderella. Disney, Walt, Productions Staff. LC 74-22325. (Disney's Wonderful World of Reading Ser.: No. 16). (Illus.). 48p. (J). (ps-3). 1974. 6.95 (*0-394-82552-7*) Random Bks Yng Read.

Walt Disney's Cinderella. Illus. by Isidre Mones. (Little Nugget Bks.). 28p. (J). (ps). 1992. bds. write for info. (*0-307-12530-0*, 12530, Golden Pr) Western Pub.

Walt Disney's Cinderella: The Three Wishes. (Golden Book and Necklace Ser.). (Illus.). 32p. (J). (ps-2). 1995. bds. 8.95 (*0-307-16153-6*, Golden Pr) Western Pub.

Walt Disney's Dumbo. Illus. by Ron Dias. LC 88-80740. (Big Golden Bks.). 24p. (J). (ps-1). 1988. write for info. (*0-307-11994-7*) Western Pub.

Walt Disney's Dumbo. Illus. by Phil Ortiz & Diana Wakeman. (Little Nugget Bks.). 28p. (J). (ps). 1992. bds. 3.50 (*0-307-12533-5*, 12533, Golden Books) Western Pub.

Walt Disney's Dumbo the Circus Baby. Diane Muldrow. (Golden Sturdy Shape Bks.). (Illus.). 14p. (J). (ps). 1993. bds. 3.95 (*0-307-12397-9*, Golden Books) Western Pub.

Walt Disney's Fantasia. John Culhane. (Illus.). 224p. 1987. pap. 19.98 (*0-8109-8078-9*, Abradale Pr) Abrams.

Walt Disney's Favorites: Twelve Favorite Little Golden Books - Classics Ser. (Illus.). 288p. (J). (ps). 1992. Set. boxed write for info. (*0-307-15491-2*, 15491, Golden Pr) Western Pub.

Walt Disney's I Am Winnie the Pooh. Betty Birney. (Golden Sturdy Bks.). (Illus.). 24p. (J). (ps). 1994. bds. 3.95 (*0-307-12456-8*, Golden Books) Western Pub.

Walt Disney's Lady & the Tramp. Rita Balducci. (J). (ps). 1994. 3.95 (*0-307-12549-1*, Golden Pr) Western Pub.

Walt Disney's Lady & the Tramp. Illus. by Franc Mateu. LC 93-71378. (Illustrated Classics). 96p. (J). 1994. 14.95 (*1-56282-613-1*); lib. bdg. 14.89 (*1-56282-615-8*) Disney Pr.

Walt Disney's Lady & the Tramp. Adapted by Todd Strasser. LC 93-71379. (Junior Novelization Ser.). (Illus.). 64p. (J). (gr. 2-6). 1994. pap. 3.50 (*1-56282-614-X*) Disney Pr.

***Walt Disney's Little Mermaid.** Walt Disney Studios Staff. (Sketchbook Ser.). (Illus.). 1997. write for info. (*1-55709-344-X*) Applewood.

Walt Disney's Mickey & the Beanstalk. Illus. by Phil Wilson. LC 92-53445. (Animated Film Picture Bks.). 48p. (J). 1993. 12.95 (*1-56282-385-X*) Disney Pr.

Walt Disney's Mickey's Christmas Carol. (Illus.). 24p. (J). (ps-3). 1990. 3.50 (*0-307-12179-8*, Golden Books) Western Pub.

Walt Disney's Mickey's Christmas Carol. Golden Books Publishing. (J). 1996. 2.50 (*0-307-98789-2*, Golden Books) Western Pub.

Walt Disney's Minnie Mouse & the Friendship Lockets. (Golden Book & Necklace Ser.). (Illus.). 32p. (J). (ps-2). 1995. bds. 8.95 (*0-307-16150-1*, Golden Pr) Western Pub.

Walt Disney's One Hundred One Dalmatians. Illus. by Gil DiCicco. LC 90-85424. (Illustrated Classics). 96p. (J). 1991. 14.95 (*1-56282-010-9*) Disney Pr.

Walt Disney's One Hundred One Dalmatians. Illus. by Gil Dicicco. LC 90-85425. (Junior Novelization Ser.). 72p. (J). (gr. 2-6). 1991. pap. 3.50 (*1-56282-013-3*) Disney Pr.

Walt Disney's One Hundred One Dalmatians. Illus. by Isidre Mones. (Little Nugget Bks.). 28p. (J). (ps-3). 1994. write for info. (*0-307-12546-7*, Golden Books) Western Pub.

Walt Disney's One Hundred One Dalmatians: A Counting Book. Fran Manushkin. LC 90-85426. (Illus.). 32p. (J). (ps-k). 1991. 9.95 (*1-56282-012-5*); lib. bdg. 9.89 (*1-56282-032-X*) Disney Pr.

Walt Disney's One Hundred One Dalmatians: A Counting Book. Fran Manushkin. LC 92-53493. (Illus.). 32p. (J). (ps-k). 1993. pap. 4.95 (*1-56282-324-8*) Disney Pr.

Walt Disney's Peter Pan. (Vocal Selections Ser.). (Illus.). 32p. (J). (gr. 4-12). 1985. pap. 7.95 (*0-88188-414-6*, HL 00360819) H Leonard.

Walt Disney's Pinocchio. Illus. by Gil DiCicco. LC 91-73814. (Illustrated Classics). 96p. (J). 1992. 14.95 (*1-56282-136-9*) Disney Pr.

Walt Disney's Pinocchio. Disney. 1984. 3.50 (*0-307-10580-6*) Western Pub.

Walt Disney's Pinocchio. Adapted by Gina Ingoglia. LC 91-73974. (Junior Novel Ser.). (Illus.). 64p. (J). (gr. 2-6). 1992. pap. 3.50 (*1-56282-033-8*) Disney Pr.

Walt Disney's Pinocchio. Illus. by Fred Marvin. (Little Nugget Bks.). 28p. (J). (ps). 1992. bds. 3.50 (*0-307-12532-7*, 12532, Golden Books) Western Pub.

Walt Disney's Pinocchio Fun with Shapes & Sizes. Marc Gave. (Golden Sturdy Shape Bks.). (Illus.). 14p. (J). (ps). 1992. bds. 3.95 (*0-307-12332-4*, 12332, Golden Books) Western Pub.

Walt Disney's Play with Bambi. (Golden Touch & Feel Bks.). (Illus.). (J). (ps). 1991. 6.50 (*0-307-12002-3*, Golden Books) Western Pub.

***Walt Disney's Railroad Story: The Small-Scale Fascination That Led to a Full-Scale Kingdom.** Michael Broggie. (Illus.). 400p. 1997. 59.95 (*1-56342-006-6*, B926) Pentrex Pub.

***Walt Disney's Read & Grow Library, 19 vols.** Disney Enterprises, Inc. Staff. Incl. Vol. 1. Mickey's Alphabet Soup. (Illus.). 44p. (J). (gr. 1-6). 1997. 3.49 (*1-885222-76-9*); Vol. 2. Count on Donald. (Illus.). 44p. (J). (gr. 1-6). 1997. 3.49 (*1-885222-77-7*); Vol. 3. Colors, Colors Everywhere!. (Illus.). 44p. (J). (gr. 1-6). 1997. 3.49 (*1-885222-78-5*); Vol. 4. Missing Shapes Mix-Up. (Illus.). 44p. (J). (gr. 1-6). 1997. 3.49 (*1-885222-79-3*); Vol. 5. Amazing Muffin Search. (Illus.). 44p. (J). (gr. 1-6). 1997. 3.49 (*1-885222-80-7*); Vol. 6. Mickey's World of Words. (Illus.). 44p. (J). (gr. 1-6). 1997. 3.49 (*1-885222-81-5*); Vol. 7. Telling Time with Goofy. (Illus.). 44p. (J). (gr. 1-6). 1997. 3.49 (*1-885222-82-3*); Vol. 8. Follow Your Nose, Donald. (Illus.). 44p. (J). (gr. 1-6). 1997. 3.49 (*1-885222-83-1*); Vol. 9. Goofy Shapes Up. (Illus.). 44p. (J). (gr. 1-6). 1997. 3.49 (*1-885222-84-X*); Vol. 10. Look Before You Leap!. (Illus.). 44p. (J). (gr. 1-6). 1997. 3.49 (*1-885222-85-8*); Vol. 11. Minnie's Small Wonders. (Illus.). 44p. (J). (gr. 1-6). 1997. 3.49 (*1-885222-86-6*); Vol. 12. Daisy's Nature Hunt. (Illus.). 44p. (J). (gr. 1-6). 1997. 3.49 (*1-885222-87-4*); Vol. 13. Mickey's Weather Machine. (Illus.). 44p. (J). (gr. 1-6). 1997. 3.49 (*1-885222-88-2*); Vol. 14. Donald Duck Directs. (Illus.). 44p. (J). (gr. 1-6). 1997. 3.49 (*1-885222-89-0*); Vol. 15. Minnie's Surprise Trip. (Illus.). 44p. (J). (gr. 1-6). 1997. 3.49 (*1-885222-90-4*); Vol. 16. All in a Day's Work. (Illus.). 44p. (J). (gr. 1-6). 1997. 3.49 (*1-885222-91-2*); Vol. 17. Uncle Scrooge Comes Home. (Illus.). 44p. (J). (gr. 1-6). 1997. 3.49 (*1-885222-92-0*); Vol. 18. Laugh-Along Mystery. (Illus.). 44p. (J). (gr. 1-6). 1997. 3.49 (*1-885222-93-9*); Vol. 19. Parents' Guide. (Illus.). 44p. (J). (gr. 1-6). 1997. 3.49 (*1-885222-94-7*); 1997. 66.60 (*1-885222-75-0*) Advance Pubs.

Walt Disneys Sketch Book of Snow White: Walt Disney's Sketchbook of Snow White & the Seven Dwarfs. Walt Disney. LC 93-16898. (Illus.). 110p. 1993. reprint ed. 29.95 (*1-55709-207-9*) Applewood.

Walt Disney's Sleeping Beauty. Betty Birney. (J). (ps). 1993. 3.95 (*0-307-12528-9*, Golden Pr) Western Pub.

Walt Disney's Sleeping Beauty. Illus. by Ric Gonzalez & Dennis Durrell. LC 92-56158. (Illustrated Classics). 96p. (J). 1993. 14.95 (*1-56282-366-3*); lib. bdg. 14.89 (*1-56282-367-1*) Disney Pr.

Walt Disney's Sleeping Beauty. Adapted by A. L. Singer. LC 92-56157. (Junior Novelization Ser.). (Illus.). 80p. (J). (gr. 2-6). 1993. pap. 3.50 (*1-56282-368-X*) Disney Pr.

***Walt Disney's Sleeping Beauty.** Walt Disney Studios Staff. (Sketchbook Ser.). (Illus.). 1997. write for info. (*1-55709-343-1*) Applewood.

Walt Disney's Snow White & the Seven Dwarfs. Walt Disney. 1986. 10.45 (*0-307-60305-9*) Western Pub.

Walt Disney's Snow White & the Seven Dwarfs. Disney, Walt, Productions Staff. (Disney's Wonderful World of Reading Ser.: No. 8). (Illus.). (J). (ps-3). 1973. 6.95 (*0-394-82625-6*) Random Bks Yng Read.

Walt Disney's Snow White & the Seven Dwarfs. Illus. by Fred Marvin. LC 92-53430. (Illustrated Classics). 96p. (J). 1993. 14.95 (*1-56282-362-0*) Disney Pr.

Walt Disney's Snow White & the Seven Dwarfs. Illus. by Fred Marvin & Fernando Guell. LC 92-53430. (Illustrated Classics). 96p. (J). 1993. lib. bdg. 14.89 (*1-56282-363-9*) Disney Pr.

Walt Disney's Snow White & the Seven Dwarfs. Illus. by Isidre Mones. (Little Nugget Bks.). 28p. (J). (ps). 1992. bds. write for info. (*0-307-12531-9*, 12531, Golden Pr) Western Pub.

Walt Disney's Snow White & the Seven Dwarfs. Adapted by Jim Razzi. LC 92-53431. (Junior Novel Ser.). (Illus.). 64p. (J). (gr. 2-6). 1993. pap. 3.50 (*1-56282-364-7*) Disney Pr.

Walt Disney's Snow White & the Seven Dwarfs Counting Book. Lewis Patrick. (Little Nugget Bks.). (Illus.). 28p. (J). (ps). 1993. bds. 3.50 (*0-307-12529-7*, Golden Books) Western Pub.

Walt Disney's Story Land. (J). (ps-3). 1991. write for info. (*0-318-68555-8*, Golden Pr) Western Pub.

Walt Disney's the Grasshopper & the Ants. Margaret Wise Brown. LC 93-70938. (Illus.). 32p. (J). 1993. 12.95 (*1-56282-534-8*); lib. bdg. 12.89 (*1-56282-535-6*) Disney Pr.

Walt Disney's the Jungle Book. Denise L. Patrick. (J). (ps). 1994. 3.95 (*0-307-12548-3*, Golden Pr) Western Pub.

Walt Disney's the Jungle Book. Adapted by Jim Razzi. LC 91-58975. (Junior Novel Ser.). (Illus.). 64p. (J). (gr. 2-6). 1992. pap. 3.50 (*1-56282-243-8*) Disney Pr.

Walt Disney's the Jungle Book. Illus. by Chris Schnabel. LC 91-71352. (Illustrated Classics). (J). 1992. 14.95 (*1-56282-057-5*) Disney Pr.

Walt Disney's the Little Mermaid. (Big Golden Bks.). (J). (ps-3). 1991. write for info. (*0-307-12345-6*, Golden Pr) Western Pub.

Walt Disney's the Little Mermaid: Ariel's New Treasure. (Golden Book and Necklace Ser.). (Illus.). 32p. (J). (ps-2). 1995. bds. 8.95 (*0-307-16151-X*, Golden Pr) Western Pub.

Walt Disney's the Mickey Mouse Book. (Golden Super Shape Bks.). (Illus.). 24p. (J). (ps). 1965. pap. write for info. (*0-307-10077-4*) Western Pub.

Walt Disney's the Old Mill. Margaret Wise Brown. LC 93-74249. (Illus.). 32p. (J). (ps-3). 1994. 12.95 (*1-56282-644-1*); lib. bdg. 12.89 (*1-56282-645-X*) Disney Pr.

Walt Disney's Three Little Pigs. Illus. by Gil DiCicco. LC 92-53443. 32p. (J). 1993. 12.95 (*1-56282-381-7*) Disney Pr.

Walt Disney's Treasury of Children's Classics. Ed. by Darlene Geis. LC 95-12135. (Illus.). 320p. (J). 1995. reprint ed. 29.95 (*0-7868-3086-7*) Disney Pr.

Walt Disney's Treasury of Silly Symphonies see Treasury of Cartoon Classics: Walt Disney's Silly Symphonies

Walt Disney's Uncle Remus Stories. Joel C. Harris. Ed. by Marion Palmer. (Deluxe Golden Bks.). (Illus.). (J). (gr. 3-5). 1964. write for info. (*0-307-15551-X*) Western Pub.

Walt Disney's Winnie the Pooh: Pooh Can ... Can You? Carol North. (Golden Board Bks.). (Illus.). 12p. (J). (ps). 1993. bds. 1.95 (*0-307-06081-0*, 6081, Golden Books) Western Pub.

Walt Disney's Winnie-the-Pooh All Year Long. Illus. by Bill Williams. (Golden Sturdy Shape Bks.). 14p. (J). (ps). 1981. bds. 3.95 (*0-307-12260-3*, Golden Books) Western Pub.

Walt Disney's Winnie-the-Pooh & the Pebble Hunt. (J). 1982. 1.19 (*0-307-10121-5*, Golden Pr) Western Pub.

Walt Disney's Winnie-the-Pooh & the Pebble Hunt. Little Golden Books Staff. (J). 1.19 (*0-307-68121-1*, Golden Pr) Western Pub.

Walt Disney's Winnie the Pooh Has Ears. Golden Staff. (Shaped Little Nugget Bks.). (Illus.). 14p. (J). (ps). 1995. bds. 2.95 (*0-307-12726-5*, Golden Books) Western Pub.

Walt Disney's Winnie the Pooh Scratch & Sniff Book. (Golden Scratch & Sniff Bks.). (Illus.). 32p. (J). (ps-2). 1989. write for info. (*0-307-13528-4*) Western Pub.

Walt Disney's 101 Dalmatians: Snow Puppies. Barbara Bazaldua. (J). 1996. 2.50 (*0-307-98786-8*, Golden Books) Western Pub.

Walt Disney's 101 Dalmations. P. Z. Mann. (J). 1996. pap. text ed. 2.95 (*0-307-12842-3*, Golden Books) Western Pub.

Walt in Wonderland: The Silent Films of Walt Disney. Russell Merritt & J. B. Kaufman. 176p. (C). 1994. 39.95 (*0-8018-4907-1*) Johns Hopkins.

Walt Kelly Collector's Guide: A Bibliography & Price Guide. Steve A. Thompson. LC 88-4361. (Illus.). (C). 1988. pap. 15.95 (*0-945185-01-4*) Spring Hollow Bks.

Walt Kuhn, Painter: His Life & Work. Philip R. Adams. LC 78-3502. (Illus.). 308p. 1978. 83.50 (*0-8142-0258-6*) Ohio St U Pr.

Walt Whitman. Richard M. Bucke. 1972. 59.95 (*0-8490-1272-4*) Gordon Pr.

***Walt Whitman.** Ed. by Milton Hindus. (Critical Heritage Ser.). 304p. (C). 1997. text ed. 15.00 (*0-415-15945-8*) Routledge.

***Walt Whitman.** Ed. by Jonathan Levin. LC 97-433. (Poetry for Young People Ser.). (Illus.). 48p. (J). 1997. 14.95 (*0-8069-9530-0*) Sterling.

Walt Whitman. Nancy Loewen. LC 93-15081. 1994. lib. bdg. 17.95 (*0-88682-608-X*) Creative Ed.

Walt Whitman. Nancy Loewen. (Illus.). 48p. (YA). (gr. 5 up). 1995. 16.95 (*0-15-200919-1*) HarBrace.

Walt Whitman. Catherine Reef. LC 94-7405. (Illus.). 148p. (J). (gr. 10 up). 1995. 16.95 (*0-395-68705-5*, Clarion Bks) HM.

Walt Whitman. rev. ed. Gay W. Allen. LC 68-30926. (Illus.). 252p. reprint ed. pap. 71.90 (*0-7837-3614-2*, 2043480) Bks Demand.

Walt Whitman. John Bailey. LC 74-131615. 1970. reprint ed. 49.00 (*0-403-00502-7*) Scholarly.

Walt Whitman. John Baily. 1988. reprint ed. lib. bdg. 59.00 (*0-7812-0051-2*) Rprt Serv.

Walt Whitman. William Clarke. LC 77-130249. (Studies in Whitman: No. 28). 1970. reprint ed. lib. bdg. 49.95 (*0-8383-1139-3*) M S G Haskell Hse.

Walt Whitman. John A. Symonds. LC 67-29559. 1972. reprint ed. 19.95 (*0-405-09020-X*, Pub. by Blom Pubns UK) Ayer.

Walt Whitman: A Descriptive Bibliography. Joel Myerson. LC 92-25927. (Series in Bibliography). (Illus.). 1128p. (C). 1993. text ed. 250.00 (*0-8229-3739-5*) U of Pittsburgh Pr.

***Walt Whitman: A Gay Life.** Gary Schmidgall. LC 97-14311. 1997. pap. 29.95 (*0-525-94373-0*) NAL-Dutton.

Walt Whitman: A Supplementary Bibliography, 1961-1967. James T. Tanner. LC 67-65586. (Serif Series: Bibliographies & Checklists: No. 5). 65p. reprint ed. pap. 25.00 (*0-7837-0578-6*, 2040922) Bks Demand.

Walt Whitman: Critical Assessments, 4 vols., Set. Ed. by Graham Clarke. (Critical Assessments of Writers in English Ser.). 2112p. (C). (gr. 13). 1994. text ed. 545.00 (*1-873403-16-X*, C0580) Routledge.

Walt Whitman: Here & Now. Ed. by Joan P. Kreig. LC 85-922. viii, 248p. 1985. text ed. 49.95 (*0-313-24895-8*, KWW/, Greenwood Pr) Greenwood.

Walt Whitman: His Life & Work. Bliss Perry. (BCL1-PS American Literature Ser.). 318p. 1992. reprint ed. lib. bdg. 89.00 (*0-7812-6899-0*) Rprt Serv.

Walt Whitman: In Life or Death Forever. Francis O. Mattson. (Illus.). 45p. 1992. pap. 10.00 (*0-87104-431-5*) NY Pub Lib.

Walt Whitman: La Naissance Du Poete. Jean Catel. (BCL1-PS American Literature Ser.). 483p. 1992. reprint ed. lib. bdg. 99.00 (*0-7812-6920-2*) Rprt Serv.

Walt Whitman: La Naissance Du Poete. Jean Catel. 1971. reprint ed. 39.00 (*0-403-00900-6*) Scholarly.

Walt Whitman: Notebooks & Unpublished Prose Manuscripts, 6 vols., Set. Walt Whitman. Ed. by Edward F. Grier et al. (Collected Writings of Walt Whitman: Vols. 17-22). 2353p. (C). 1984. text ed. 432.00 (*0-8147-2989-4*) NYU Pr.

Walt Whitman: Selected Poems. Walt Whitman. (Bloomsbury Poetry Classics Ser.). 1993. 9.95 (*0-312-09754-9*) St Martin.

Walt Whitman: The Centennial Essays. Ed. by Ed Folsom. LC 93-40838. (Illus.). 286p. 1994. pap. 17.95 (*0-87745-462-0*) U of Iowa Pr.

Walt Whitman: The Contemporary Reviews. Ed. by Kenneth M. Price. (American Critical Archives Ser.: No. 9). 500p. (C). 1996. text ed. 95.00 (*0-521-45387-9*) Cambridge U Pr.

Walt Whitman: The Man & His Work. Leon Bazalgette. Tr. by Ellen Fitzgerald. LC 72-128770. 1971. reprint ed. lib. bdg. 60.50 (*0-8154-0352-6*) Cooper Sq.

Walt Whitman: The Man & the Poet. James Thomson. LC 71-163457. (Studies in Whitman: No. 28). 1971. reprint ed. lib. bdg. 59.95 (*0-8383-1319-1*) M S G Haskell Hse.

***Walt Whitman: The Measure of His Song.** Jim Perlman. 1997. pap. text ed. 20.00 (*0-930100-78-6*) Holy Cow.

Walt Whitman: The Measure of His Song. Louis Simpson et al. Ed. by Ed Folsom et al. LC 80-85268. (Illus.). 454p. (Orig.). (C). 1981. pap. 10.00 (*0-930100-08-5*) Holy Cow.

Walt Whitman: The Measure of His Song. Louis Simpson et al. Ed. by Ed Folsom et al. LC 80-85268. (Illus.). 454p. (Orig.). (C). 1981. 20.00 (*0-930100-09-3*) Holy Cow.

Walt Whitman: The Poem As Private History. Graham Clarke. 176p. 1991. text ed. 35.00 (*0-312-03744-9*) St Martin.

Walt Whitman: The Prophet of the New Era. W. Hayes. LC 73-17310. (Studies in Whitman: No. 28). 1973. reprint ed. lib. bdg. 75.00 (*0-8383-1715-4*) M S G Haskell Hse.

Walt Whitman: Yesterday & Today. Henry E. Legler. LC 76-2434. (Studies in Whitman: No. 28). 1976. lib. bdg. 32.95 (*0-8383-2118-6*) M S G Haskell Hse.

Walt Whitman, a Study. John A. Symonds. LC 68-54301. reprint ed. 27.50 (*0-404-06327-6*) AMS Pr.

Walt Whitman & Emily Dickinson: Poetry of the Central Consciousness. Agnieszka Salska. LC 84-17286. 256p. 1985. pap. text ed. 20.95 (*0-8122-1203-7*) U of Pa Pr.

Walt Whitman & His Poetry. Henry B. Binns. LC 75-120971. (Poetry & Life Ser.). reprint ed. 16.00 (*0-404-52502-4*) AMS Pr.

Walt Whitman & Rabindranath Tagore: A Study in Comparison. C. N. Sastry. (New World Literature Ser.: No. 46). (C). 1992. 12.00 (*81-7018-698-6*, Pub. by BR Pub II) S Asia.

***Walt Whitman & Sir William Osler: A Poet & His Physician.** Philip W. Leon. (Illus.). 212p. 1995. 42.00 (*0-614-30480-6*, Pub. by E C W Pr CN) Aubrey Bks.

Walt Whitman & Sir William Osler: A Poet & His Physician. Philip W. Leon. (Illus.). 212p. 1995. pap. 29.95 (*1-55022-252-X*, Pub. by E C W Pr CN) Aubrey Bks.

Walt Whitman & Sir William Osler: A Poet & His Physician. Philip W. Leon. 1995. 32.00 (*1-55022-251-1*, Pub. by ECW Pr CN) LPC InBook.

Walt Whitman & the American Reader. Ezra Greenspan. (Cambridge Studies in American Literature & Culture: No. 46). (Illus.). 250p. (C). 1990. text ed. 59.95 (*0-521-38469-9*) Cambridge U Pr.

Walt Whitman & the Body Beautiful. Harold Aspiz. LC 79-28280. 304p. 1980. 29.95 (*0-252-00799-9*) U of Ill Pr.

Walt Whitman & the Citizen's Eye. James Dougherty. LC 92-14096. (Illus.). 344p. (C). 1993. text ed. 42.50 (*0-8071-1772-2*) La State U Pr.

Walt Whitman & the Critics: A Checklist of Criticism, 1900-1978. Jeanetta Boswell. LC 80-20528. (Author Bibliographies Ser.: No. 51). 270p. 1980. 25.00 (*0-8108-1355-6*) Scarecrow.

Walt Whitman & the French Impressionists: A Study of Analogies. Jessica Haigney. LC 90-5796. (Studies in American Literature: Vol. 10). 132p. 1990. lib. bdg. 69.95 (*0-88946-114-7*) E Mellen.

Walt Whitman & the Germans. Richard H. Riethmueller. 1972. 59.95 (*0-8490-1273-2*) Gordon Pr.

Walt Whitman & the Visual Arts. Ed. by Geoffrey M. Sill & Roberta K. Tarbell. LC 91-9551. (Illus.). 220p. (C). 1991. text ed. 45.00 (*0-8135-1730-3*) Rutgers U Pr.

Walt Whitman & the World. Ed. by Gay W. Allen & Ed Folsom. LC 95-479. 480p. 1995. text ed. 49.95 (*0-87745-497-3*) U of Iowa Pr.

Walt Whitman & the World. Ed. by Gay W. Allen & Ed Folsom. LC 95-479. 480p. 1995. pap. 22.95 (*0-87745-498-1*) U of Iowa Pr.

***Walt Whitman & 19th-Century Women Reformers.** Sherry Ceniza. LC 97-24621. 1998. write for info. (*0-8173-0893-8*) U of Ala Pr.

Walt Whitman Archive Vol. 1: A Facsimile of the Poet's Manuscripts: Whitman Manuscripts at the Library of Congress, Pts. 1 & 2. Walt Whitman & Joel Myerson. LC 93-13841. (Illus.). 760p. 1993. text ed. 195.00 (*0-8153-1110-9*) Garland.

Walt Whitman Archive Vol. 2: A Facsimile of the Poet's Manuscripts: Whitman Manuscripts at Duke University & the Humanities Research Center of the University of Texas. Ed. by Joel Myerson. LC 93-13839. (Illus.). 742p. 1993. text ed. 195.00 (*0-8153-1111-7*) Garland.

Walt Whitman Archive Vol. 3: A Facsimile of the Poet's Manuscripts: Whitman Manuscripts at the University of Virginia, Pts. 1 & 2. Walt Whitman. Ed. by Joel Myerson. LC 93-150056. (Illus.). 680p. 1993. text ed. 160.00 (*0-8153-1209-1*) Garland.

Walt Whitman As Critic of Literature. Maurice O. Johnson. LC 71-122991. (Studies in Whitman: No. 28). 1970. reprint ed. lib. bdg. 39.95 (*0-8383-1124-5*) M S G Haskell Hse.

Walt Whitman Bathing: Poems. David Wagoner. 88p. 1996. 11.95 (*0-252-06570-0*) U of Ill Pr.

Walt Whitman Handbook. Gay W. Allen. (University Classics Ser.). 560p. reprint ed. spiral bd. 59.50 (*0-87532-050-3*) Hendricks House.

Walt Whitman, His Life & Work. Bliss Perry. LC 79-86165. reprint ed. 35.00 (*0-404-04995-8*) AMS Pr.

Walt Whitman in England. Harold W. Blodgett. 1972. 59.95 (*0-8490-1274-0*) Gordon Pr.

Walt Whitman in Hell. T. R. Hummer. LC 96-2083. (Southern Messenger Poets Ser.). 80p. (C). 1996. pap. 10.95 (*0-8071-2061-8*) La State U Pr.

Walt Whitman in Mickle Street. Elizabeth L. Keller. LC 76-160160. (Studies in Whitman: No. 28). 1971. reprint ed. lib. bdg. 59.95 (*0-8383-1296-9*) M S G Haskell Hse.

Walt Whitman of Mickel Street: A Centennial Collection. Ed. by Geoffrey M. Sill. LC 93-35741. (Illus.). 336p. (C). 1994. pap. text ed. 18.95 (*0-87049-842-8*); lib. bdg. 36.00 (*0-87049-835-5*) U of Tenn Pr.

Walt Whitman Reader. Walt Whitman. LC 92-54931. (Literary Classics Ser.). 320p. 1993. 5.98 (*1-56138-268-X*) Courage Bks.

Walt Whitman's America. David S. Reynolds. 1996. pap. 19.00 (*0-679-76709-6*, Vin) Random.

Walt Whitman's America: A Cultural Biography. David S. Reynolds. LC 94-12841. (Illus.). 671p. 1995. 35.00 (*0-394-58023-0*) Knopf.

Walt Whitman's Backward Glances. Walt Whitman. LC 68-57347. (Essay Index Reprint Ser.). 1977. 15.95 (*0-8369-0991-7*) Ayer.

Walt Whitman's Civil War. Walter Lowenfels. (Quality Paperbacks Ser.). (Illus.). 368p. 1989. pap. 14.95 (*0-306-80355-0*) Da Capo.

Walt Whitman's Estimate of Shakespeare. Clifton J. Furness. (Studies in Whitman: No. 28). 1970. reprint ed. pap. 39.95 (*0-8383-0032-4*) M S G Haskell Hse.

Walt Whitman's Journalism: A Bibliography. William White. LC 68-58207. 81p. reprint ed. pap. 25.00 (*0-317-10412-8*, 2000972) Bks Demand.

Walt Whitman's Language Experiment. James P. Warren. LC 89-37353. 224p. 1990. lib. bdg. 30.00 (*0-271-00688-9*) Pa St U Pr.

Walt Whitman's Mrs. G. 1991. 42.50 (*0-8386-3381-1*) Fairleigh Dickinson.

Walt Whitman's Mrs. G: A Biography of Anne Gilchrist. Marion W. Alcaro. LC 89-46136. (Illus.). 288p. 1991. 42.50 (*0-685-48674-5*) Fairleigh Dickinson.

Walt Whitman's Native Representations. Ed Folsom. (Cambridge Studies in American Literature & Culture: No. 78). (Illus.). 208p. (C). 1994. text ed. 59.95 (*0-521-45357-7*) Cambridge U Pr.

***Walt Whitman's Native Representative.** Walt Whitman. 1997. 17.95 (*0-521-58572-4*) Cambridge U Pr.

Walt Whitman's New York. Ed. by Henry M. Christman. LC 74-39704. (Select Bibliographies Reprint Ser.). 1977. reprint ed. 18.95 (*0-8369-9933-9*) Ayer.

Walt Whitman's New York, from Manhattan to Montauk. 2nd ed. Ed. by Henry M. Christman. (Illus.). 208p. (C). 1989. pap. 9.95 (*0-941533-77-8*) New Amsterdam Bks.

Walt Whitman's Poetry: A Study & a Selection. E. Holmes. LC 72-6289. (Studies in Whitman: No. 28). 132p. 1972. reprint ed. lib. bdg. 75.00 (*0-8383-1628-X*) M S G Haskell Hse.

Walt Whitman's "Song of Myself" A Mosaic of Interpretations. Edwin H. Miller. LC 88-38069. 209p. 1989. pap. 19.95 (*0-87745-345-4*) U of Iowa Pr.

Walt Whitman's Workshop: A Collection of Unpublished Manuscripts. Walt Whitman. (BCL1-PS American Literature Ser.). 265p. 1992. reprint ed. lib. bdg. 79.00 (*0-7812-6919-9*) Rprt Serv.

Walter. David Cook. LC 84-5116. 206p. 1985. 15.95 (*0-87951-972-X*) Overlook Pr.

Walter. David Cook. 216p. 1988. Tusk. pap. 8.95 (*0-87951-205-9*) Overlook Pr.

Walter: An Airman's Life. Marcia A. Brenneman. (Illus.). 278p. (Orig.). 1989. pap. 21.95 (*0-9625652-0-2*) M Brenneman.

Walter Abish to William S. Burroughs see Library of Literary Criticism

Walter & His Adventure. Pam Whitehurst. LC 95-62381. (Illus.). 44p. (J). (ps-3). 1996. 7.95 (*1-55523-790-8*) Winston-Derek.

Walter & Miller's Textbook of Radiotherapy: Radiation Physics, Therapy, & Oncology. 5th ed. C. K. Bomford et al. LC 92-48182. 624p. 1993. pap. text ed. 75.00 (*0-443-02873-7*) Churchill.

***Walter & the Tugboat.** (Ready Readers Stage I Ser.). (Illus.). 32p. (J). (gr. k-2). 1995. pap. write for info. (*1-56144-744-7*, Honey Bear Bks) Modern Pub NYC.

Walter Anderson Birthday Book. Walter Anderson. Ed. & Intro. by Patti C. Black. (Illus.). 125p. 1986. text ed. 15.00 (*0-938896-47-4*) Mississippi Archives.

Walter Anderson for Children: An Activity Book from the Mississippi State Historical Museum. Ed. by Ann M. Morrison & Patti C. Black. (Illus.). 64p. (Orig.). (J). (ps-8). 1984. pap. 12.95 (*0-938896-39-3*) Mississippi Archives.

Walter Anderson's Illustrations of Epic & Voyage. Ed. by Redding S. Sugg, Jr. LC 80-12239. (Illus.). 149p. 1980. 19.95 (*0-8093-0973-4*) S Ill U Pr.

Walter B. Cannon: The Life & Times of a Young Scientist. Saul Benison et al. LC 86-25951. (Illus.). 528p. 1987. 39.95 (*0-674-94580-8*) Belknap Pr.

Walter Bagehot. William Irvine. 300p. (C). 1970. reprint ed. lib. bdg. 36.00 (*0-208-00900-0*, Archon Bks) Shoe String.

Walter Benjamin. Norbert Bolz & Willem Van Reijen. Tr. by Laimdota Mazzarins. LC 95-9006. 128p. (C). 1996. text ed. 39.95 (*0-391-03941-5*) Humanities.

Walter Benjamin. Norbert Bolz & Willem Van Reijen. Tr. by Laimdota Mazzarins. LC 95-9006. 128p. (C). 1996. pap. 12.50 (*0-391-03942-3*) Humanities.

Walter Benjamin. Ed. by Joan Nordquist. (Social Theory: A Bibliographic Ser.: No. 15). 60p. (Orig.). (C). 1989. pap. 15.00 (*0-937855-28-6*) Ref Rsch Serv.

Walter Benjamin: A Biography. Momme Brodersen. LC 96-48951. (Illus.). 316p. 1995. 35.00 (*1-85984-967-9*, Pub. by Vrso UK) Norton.

Walter Benjamin: An Intellectual Biography. Bernd Witte. Tr. by James Rolleston from GER. LC 91-7666. (Kritik: German Literary Theory & Cultural Studies). 226p. 1991. text ed. 29.95 (*0-8143-2017-1*) Wayne St U Pr.

***Walter Benjamin: An Intellectual Biography.** 2nd ed. Bernd Witte. Tr. by James Rolleston. (Illus.). 226p. 1997. reprint ed. pap. text ed. 16.95 (*0-8143-2018-X*) Wayne St U Pr.

Walter Benjamin: Or Towards a Revolutionary Criticism. Terry Eagleton. 200p. (Orig.). (C). 1985. pap. text ed. 19.00 (*0-86091-733-9*, A1024, Pub. by Vrso UK) Norton.

Walter Benjamin: Selected Writings: 1913-1926, Vol. 1. Ed. by Marcus Bullock & Michael W. Jennings. (Illus.). 512p. 1996. 35.00 (*0-674-94585-9*) Belknap Pr.

***Walter Benjamin: The Colour of Experience.** Howard Caygill. LC 97-16700. 208p. (C). 1997. pap. write for info. (*0-415-08959-X*) Routledge.

***Walter Benjamin: The Colour of Experience.** Howard Caygill. LC 97-16700. 208p. (C). 1998. text ed. write for info. (*0-415-08958-1*) Routledge.

Walter Benjamin: Theoretical Questions. Ed. by David S. Ferris. LC 95-30006. 1996. 39.50 (*0-8047-2569-1*); pap. 14.95 (*0-8047-2570-5*) Stanford U Pr.

***Walter Benjamin Vol. 1: Selected Writings, 1913-1926.** Ed. by Marcus Bullock. 1996. 35.00 (*0-614-20693-6*) HUP.

Walter Benjamin, an Aesthetic of Redemption. Richard Wolin. LC 93-30241. (Weimar & Now Ser.: Vol. 7). 1994. 14.00 (*0-520-08400-4*) U CA Pr.

Walter Benjamin & the Antinomies of Tradition. John McCole. LC 92-21431. 352p. 1993. 47.50 (*0-8014-2465-8*); pap. 18.95 (*0-8014-9711-6*) Cornell U Pr.

Walter Benjamin & the Bible. Brian Britt. 200p. 1996. 29.50 (*0-8264-0879-6*) Continuum.

Walter Benjamin & the Demands of History. Michael P. Steinberg. (Illus.). 272p. 1996. 42.50 (*0-8014-3135-2*); pap. 16.95 (*0-8014-8257-7*) Cornell U Pr.

Walter Benjamin for Children: An Essay on His Radio Years. Jeffrey Mehlman. LC 92-28496. 126p. (C). 1993. 19.95 (*0-226-51865-5*) U Ch Pr.

Walter Benjamin on Experience & History: Profane Illumination. Jasiel Cesar. LC 92-3641. 240p. 1992. lib. bdg. 89.95 (*0-7734-9812-5*) E Mellen.

***Walter Benjamin's Other History: Of Stones, Animals, Human Beings & Angels.** Beatrice Hanssen. 1998. 35.00 (*0-520-20841-2*) U CA Pr.

Walter Benjamin's Passages. Pierre Missac. Tr. by Shierry W. Nicholsen. (Studies in Contemporary German Social Thought). (Illus.). 256p. 1995. 25.00 (*0-262-13305-9*) MIT Pr.

Walter Benjamin's Passages. Pierre Missac. (Studies in Contemporary German Social Thought). (Illus.). 256p. 1996. pap. 12.50 (*0-262-63175-X*) MIT Pr.

Walter Benjamin's Philosophy: Destruction & Experience. Andrew Benjamin & Peter Osborne. LC 93-16566. (Warwick Studies in European Philosophy). 224p. (C). (gr. 13). 1993. pap. 19.95 (*0-415-08369-9*, B2229, Routledge NY); text ed. 69.95 (*0-415-08368-0*, B2225, Routledge NY) Routledge.

Walter Bower's Scotichronicon, Bks. III & IV. Ed. by John McQueen & Winifred McQueen. (Scotichronicon Ser.). 400p. 1989. Books III & IV. text ed. 70.00 (*0-08-036410-1*, Pub. by Aberdeen U Pr) Macmillan.

Walter Bower's Scotichronicon, Vol. 5, Bks. IX & X. Ed. by Simon Taylor. 400p. 1990. text ed. 70.00 (*0-08-037985-0*, Pub. by Aberdeen U Pr) Macmillan.

Walter Boyd: A Merchant Banker in the Age of Napoleon. S. R. Cope. 197p. 1987. text ed. 49.95 (*0-312-01247-0*) St Martin.

Walter Breen's Complete Encyclopedia of U. S. & Colonial Coins. Walter Breen. LC 79-6855. (Illus.). 768p. 1987. 100.00 (*0-385-14207-2*) Doubleday.

Walter Breen's Encyclopedia of United States & Colonial Proof Coins, 1722-1977. rev. ed. Walter Breen. (Illus.). 340p. 1989. pap. 29.95 (*0-943161-21-5*) Bowers & Merena.

Walter Burleigh, De Puritate Artis Logicae Tractatus Longior. Ed. by Philotheus Boehner. xvi, 264p. 1955. pap. 11.00 (*1-57659-057-7*) Franciscan Inst.

Walter Burleigh De Puritate Artis Logicae Tractus Langios. Philotheus Boehner. Incl. Tractatus Brevior. 1955. lib. bdg. (*0-318-51913-5*); (Text Ser.). 1955. 6.00 (*0-686-17965-X*) Franciscan Inst.

Walter Burley Griffin in America. Mati Maldre & Paul Kruty. LC 95-11632. (Illus.). 192p. 1996. 49.95 (*0-252-02193-2*) U of Ill Pr.

Walter Camp, the Father of American Football. Harford Powel, Jr. LC 70-126246. (Select Bibliographies Reprint Ser.). (Illus.). 1977. 20.95 (*0-8369-5473-4*) Ayer.

Walter Clinton Jackson Essays in the Social Sciences. University of North Carolina Woman's College Faculty Staff. Ed. by Vera Largeut. LC 79-167431. (Essay Index Reprint Ser.). 1977. reprint ed. 21.95 (*0-8369-2725-7*) Ayer.

Walter Cronkite. Walter Cronkite. Date not set. 19.95 (*0-312-00454-0*) St Martin.

Walter D. Edmonds, Storyteller. Lionel D. Wyld. LC 82-10443. (New York State Bks.). (Illus.). 168p. 1982. text ed. 32.50 (*0-8156-0180-8*) Syracuse U Pr.

Walter Darby Bannard. Jane H. Cone. LC 73-87987. (Illus.). 1973. pap. 2.98 (*0-912298-34-0*) Baltimore Mus.

Walter De La Mare: A Biography & Critical Study. Rodolphe L. Megroz. 1988. reprint ed. lib. bdg. 69.00 (*0-7812-0050-4*) Rprt Serv.

Walter De la Mare: A Biography & Critical Study. Rodolphe L. Megroz. LC 72-145175. 305p. 1972. reprint ed. 39.00 (*0-403-01103-5*) Scholarly.

Walter De La Mare: A Critical Study. Forrest Reid. LC 73-131813. 1970. reprint ed. 39.00 (*0-403-00700-3*) Scholarly.

Walter De la Mare: An Exploration. J. Atkins. LC 75-22359. (Studies in Poetry: No. 38). 1975. lib. bdg. 49.95 (*0-8383-2105-4*) M S G Haskell Hse.

Walter De La Mare, a Study of His Poetry. Henry C. Duffin. (Select Bibliographies Reprint Ser.). 1977. 23.95 (*0-8369-5043-7*) Ayer.

Walter De La Mare, a Study of His Poetry. Henry C. Duffin. LC 71-95424. (Studies in Poetry: No. 38). 1970. reprint ed. lib. bdg. 58.95 (*0-8383-0972-0*) M S G Haskell Hse.

***Walter Dean Myers.** Diane Patrick-Wexler. (J). (gr. 4-8). Date not set. pap. 5.95 (*0-8114-9796-8*) Raintree Steck-V.

Walter Dean Myers. Diane Patrick-Wexler. (Contemporary Biographies Ser.). (J). (gr. 4-8). 1996. lib. bdg. 24.26 (*0-8172-3979-0*) Raintree Steck-V.

***Walter Dean Myers.** large type ed. Diane Patrick-Wexler. (Contemporary African Americans Ser.). 54p. (J). (gr. 4-8). 22.83 (*0-615-10999-3*, L-86309-00 APHB) Am Printing Hse.

***Walter Dean Myers.** large type ed. Diane Patrick-Wexler. 54p. (J). (gr. 4-8). 1996. pap. 13.50 (*0-614-20569-7*, L-86309-00 APHB) Am Printing Hse.

Walter Dragun's Town: Crafts & Trade in the Middle Ages. Sheila Sancha. LC 88-34066. (Illus.). 64p. (J). (gr. 4 up). 1989. lib. bdg. 15.89 (*0-690-04806-8*, Crowell Jr Bks) HarpC Child Bks.

Walter Dusenbery: Classical Echoes. Daniel E. Stetson & Tim Threlfall. Ed. by Kevin Boatright. LC 85-73204. (Illus.). 20p. (Orig.). 1985. pap. text ed. 5.00 (*0-932660-10-X*) U of NI Dept Art.

***Walter Emerson Baum 1884-1956 Pennsylvania Artist: Founder of Baum School of Art & Allentown Art Museum.** Martha Hutson-Saxton. (Illus.). 240p. 1997. 60.00 (*0-9658157-0-6*) Hutson Assoc.

Walter F. Isaacs: An Artist in America, 1886-1964. Spencer Moseley & Gervais Reed. LC 74-28489. (Index of Art in the Pacific Northwest Ser.: No. 8). (Illus.). 124p. 1982. 20.00 (*0-295-95950-9*) U of Wash Pr.

Walter Francis Dillingham, 1875-1963: Hawaiian Entrepreneur & Statesman. H. Brett Melendy. LC 96-3699. (Studies in American History: Vol. 10). (Illus.). 356p. 1996. 99.95 (*0-7734-8793-X*) E Mellen.

Walter Frye & the Contenance Angloise. Sylvia W. Kenney. (Music Reprint Ser.). 1980. reprint ed. 35.00 (*0-306-76011-8*) Da Capo.

Walter George Smith. Thomas A. Bryson. LC 77-9967. 239p. reprint ed. pap. 68.20 (*0-685-17833-1*, 2029500) Bks Demand.

Walter Goodwin Davis: A Scholar's Unique Contribution to New England Genealogy. Danny D. Smith. LC 85-61390. (Special Publications of Maine Genealogical Society: No. 1). 80p. 1985. pap. text ed. 11.00 (*0-9615551-0-6*) ME Geneal Soc.

Walter Gropius. Sigfried Giedion. (Illus.). 256p. 1992. reprint ed. pap. 17.95 (*0-486-27118-8*) Dover.

Walter Gropius Archive, Vol. II: (1930-1936) Winfried Nerdinger. LC 90-3058. 500p. 1990. reprint ed. text ed. 175.00 (*0-8240-3341-8*) Garland.

Walter Gropius Archive, Vol. III: (1936-1957) Winfried Nerdinger. LC 90-3058. (Illus.). 500p. 1990. reprint ed. text ed. 200.00 (*0-8240-3342-6*) Garland.

Walter Gropius Archive, 1945-1969, Vol. 4: The Work of the Architects Collaborative. Ed. by John C. Harkness. LC 90-3058. (Illus.). 520p. 1991. text ed. 200.00 (*0-8240-3343-4*) Garland.

Walter Gropius, 1911-1930: Collection of the Busch-Reisinger Museum. Ed. by Winifred Nerdinger. LC 90-3058. (Walter Gropius Archive Ser.: Vol. I of 4). (Illus.). 500p. 1990. reprint ed. text ed. 175.00 (*0-8240-3340-X*) Garland.

Walter, Hamilton & Israel's Principles of Pathology for Dental Students. 5th ed. J. B. Walter & Margaret C. Grundy. (Dental Ser.). (Illus.). 496p. (Orig.). 1992. pap. text ed. 72.00 (*0-443-04124-5*) Churchill.

Walter Hammond: Test Match Career. Spellmount Ltd. Publishers Staff. (C). 1986. 75.00 (*1-871876-10-9*, Pub. by Spellmount UK) St Mut.

Walter Hard's Vermont People. Walter Hard. 96p. 1981. pap. 5.95 (*0-911570-18-7*) Vermont Bks.

Walter Hasenclever's Humanitarianism: Themes of Protest in His Work. Alfred Hoelzel. LC 83-48134. (American University Studies: Germanic Languages & Literature: Ser. I, Vol. 11). 272p. (C). 1983. pap. text ed. 28.40 (*0-8204-0014-9*) P Lang Pubng.

Walter Hilton: The Scale of Perfection. annot. ed. Tr. by John P. Clark & Rosemary Dorward. (Classics of Western Spirituality Ser.). 1990. 24.95 (*0-8091-0440-7*); pap. 17.95 (*0-8091-3194-3*) Paulist Pr.

Walter Hines Page: The Southerner as American, 1855-1918. John M. Cooper, Jr. LC 77-4390. (Illus.). 490p. reprint ed. pap. 139.70 (*0-8357-3884-1*, 2036616) Bks Demand.

***Walter Hood.** Spacemaker Press Staff. Date not set. pap. 19.95 (*0-688-15362-3*) Morrow.

***Walter Hood: Urban Diaries.** Walter Hood. (Land Marks Ser.). 1997. pap. text ed. 24.95 (*1-888931-03-5*) Watson-Guptill.

Walter Hottle Bottle. Bronwen Scarffe. LC 92-34271. (Voyages Ser.). (Illus.). (J). 1993. 14.00 (*0-383-03664-X*) SRA McGraw.

Walter Johnson. Jack Kavanagh. (Baseball Legends Ser.). (Illus.). 64p. (J). (gr. 3 up). 1992. lib. bdg. 15.95 (*0-7910-1179-8*) Chelsea Hse.

Walter Johnson: A Life. Jack Kavanagh. LC 94-42221. (Illus.). 318p. 1995. 24.95 (*0-912083-81-6*) Diamond Communications.

Walter Johnson: A Life. rev. ed. Jack Kavanagh. LC 94-42221. 300p. 1996. pap. 14.95 (*0-912083-94-8*) Diamond Communications.

Walter Johnson: Baseball's Big Train. Henry W. Thomas. (Illus.). 1995. 24.95 (*0-9645439-0-7*) Phenom Pr.

Walter Knott - Keeper of the Flame. Helen Kooiman. LC 73-83770. (Illus.). 224p. 1973. 7.95 (*0-916434-07-9*) Plycon Pr.

Walter Launt Palmer. Maybelle Mann. LC 84-50506. (Illus.). 192p. 1989. 35.00 (*0-88740-001-9*) Schiffer.

Walter Legge: A Discography. Compiled by Alan Sanders. LC 84-8991. (Discographies Ser.: No. 11). xx, 452p. 1984. text ed. 69.50 (*0-313-24441-3*, SDW/, Greenwood Pr) Greenwood.

Walter Lippmann: Cosmopolitanism in the Century of Total War. D. Steven Blum. LC 84-7041. 208p. 1984. 37.50 (*0-8014-1676-0*) Cornell U Pr.

Walter Lippmann: Odyssey of a Liberal. Barry D. Riccio. LC 92-37471. 376p. (C). 1993. text ed. 39.95 (*1-56000-096-1*) Transaction Pubs.

Walter Lippmann - Odyssey of a Liberal. Barry D. Riccio. 260p. (Orig.). (C). 1995. pap. text ed. 24.95 (*1-56000-859-8*) Transaction Pubs.

Walter Lippmann, a Study in Personal Journalism. David E. Weingast. LC 75-97383. 155p. 1970. reprint ed. text ed. 39.75 (*0-8371-2970-2*, WEWL, Greenwood Pr) Greenwood.

***Walter Lippmann & His Times.** Ed. by Marquis W. Childs & James Reston. 246p. Date not set. 18.95 (*0-8369-0106-1*) Ayer.

Walter Lippmann & the American Century. Ronald Steel. LC 81-40077. (Illus.). 704p. 1981. pap. 26.00 (*0-394-74731-3*, Vin) Random.

Walter Long, Ireland, & the Union, 1905-1920. John Kendle. 264p. 1992. 55.00 (*0-7735-0908-9*, Pub. by McGill CN) U of Toronto Pr.

Walter M. Miller, Jr. A Bio-Bibliography. William H. Roberson & Robert L. Battenfeld. LC 92-7335. (Bio-Bibliographies in American Literature Ser.: No. 3). 192p. 1992. text ed. 42.95 (*0-313-27651-X*, RWA, Greenwood Pr) Greenwood.

Walter Muir Whitehill, Director & Librarian, Boston Athenaeum, 1946-1973: A Bibliography & Verses by Friends Presented on His Retirement. Compiled by Marez E. D'Orbessan. (Illus.). 36p. (Orig.). 1974. pap. 1.50 (*0-934552-30-4*) Boston Athenaeum.

Walter Northway. Ed. by Yvonne Yarber & Curt Madison. Tr. by Della Northway et al. (Illus.). x, 53p. (Orig.). 1996. reprint ed. pap. 12.00 (*1-55500-030-4*) Alaska Native.

Walter O. Evans Collection of African American Art. Walter O. Evans. (Illus.). 96p. 1991. 50.00 (*0-9630764-1-8*); pap. 35.00 (*0-9630764-2-6*) W O Evans Collect.

Walter Pater. Laurel Brake. 1990. 40.00 (*0-7463-0711-X*, Pub. by Northcote UK) St Mut.

Walter Pater. Laurel Brake. (Writers & Their Work Ser.). 95p. 1996. pap. text ed. 15.00 (*0-7463-0716-0*, Pub. by Nrthcote House UK) U Pr of Miss.

Walter Pater. F. Greenslet. LC 73-21634. (English Literature Ser.: No. 33). 1974. lib. bdg. 75.00 (*0-8383-1798-7*) M S G Haskell Hse.

Walter Pater. Gerald C. Monsman. LC 76-58511. (Twayne's English Authors Ser.). 213p. (C). 1977. lib. bdg. 17.95 (*0-8057-6676-6*) Irvington.

Walter Pater. Arthur C. Benson. (BCL1-PR English Literature Ser.). 226p. 1992. reprint ed. lib. bdg. 79.00 (*0-7812-7612-8*) Rprt Serv.

Walter Pater: An Annotated Bibliography of Writings about Him. Ed. by Franklin E. Court. LC 78-56125. (Annotated Secondary Bibliography Series on English Literature in Transition, 1880-1920). 411p. 1980. 48.00 (*0-87580-072-6*) N Ill U Pr.

Walter Pater: An Imaginative Sense of Fact. Ed. by Philip Dodd. 104p. 1981. 32.50 (*0-7146-3183-3*, Pub. by F Cass Pubs UK) Intl Spec Bk.

Walter Pater: Lover of Strange Souls. Denis Donoghue. LC 94-12843. 364p. 1995. 28.00 (*0-679-43753-3*) Knopf.

Walter Pater: The Critic As Artist of Ideas. William E. Buckler. 350p. (C). 1976. text ed. 40.00 (*0-8147-1092-1*) NYU Pr.

Walter Pater: The Critic As Artist of Ideas. William E. Buckler. 350p. (C). 1993. pap. text ed. 14.00 (*0-8147-1213-4*) NYU Pr.

Walter Pater: The Critical Heritage. Ed. by R. M. Seiler. (Critical Heritage Ser.). 1979. 65.00 (*0-7100-0380-3*, RKP) Routledge.

Walter Pater: Three Major Texts, (The Renaissance, Appreciations & Imaginary Portraits) Ed. by William E. Buckler. LC 85-29738. 576p. (C). 1986. text ed. 48.00 (*0-8147-1088-3*); pap. text ed. 16.00 (*0-8147-1089-1*) NYU Pr.

Walter Pater see Victorian Thinkers

Walter Pater & the French Tradition. John J. Conlon. LC 81-65458. 180p. 1982. 29.50 (*0-8387-5016-8*) Bucknell U Pr.

Walter Pater's Art of Autobiography. Gerald C. Monsman. LC 80-11941. 184p. reprint ed. pap. 52.50 (*0-8357-3753-5*, 2036479) Bks Demand.

Walter Pater's Renaissance. Paul Barolsky. LC 85-43561. 228p. 1987. 28.50 (*0-271-00436-3*) Pa St U Pr.

Walter Payton. Philip Koslow. LC 94-1352. (Football Legends Ser.). (Illus.). 64p. (J). (gr. 3 up). 1994. lib. bdg. 15.95 (*0-7910-2455-5*) Chelsea Hse.

Walter Pichler: Drawings, Sculpture, Buildings. LC 93-22423. (Illus.). 216p. 1993. 60.00 (*0-910413-97-5*) Princeton Arch.

Walter Prescott Webb: In Stephens County. Mike Kingston. (Illus.). 128p. 1985. 9.95 (*0-89015-503-8*) Sunbelt Media.

Walter P38 Auto Pistol Caliber 9mm Parabellum. 1986. lib. bdg. 79.95 (*0-8490-3483-3*) Gordon Pr.

Walter Rauscenbusch: Selected Writings. Ed. by Winthrop S. Hudson. (Sources of American Spirituality Ser.). 252p. (C). 1985. text ed. 14.95 (*0-8091-0356-7*) Paulist Pr.

Walter Reed: A Biography. William B. Bean. LC 81-16123. 208p. reprint ed. pap. 59.30 (*0-685-44473-2*, 2033005) Bks Demand.

***Walter Reed Doctor in Uniform.** L. N. Wood. lib. bdg. 22.95 (*0-8488-2085-1*) Amereon Ltd.

Walter Reuther: Modern Leader of the United Automobile Workers Union. Gerald Kurland. Ed. by D. Steve Rahmas. LC 72-89213. (Outstanding Personalities Ser.: No. 52). 32p. 1972. lib. bdg. 7.25 (*0-87157-545-0*) SamHar Pr.

***Walter Reuther: The Most Dangerous Man in Detroit.** Nelson Lichtenstein. LC 96-33058. 1997. 19.95 (*0-252-06626-X*) U of Ill Pr.

Walter Reuther & the Rise of the Autoworkers. John Barnard. (Library of American Biography). 256p. pap. 15.95 (*1-886746-33-8*, 93483) Talman.

Walter Rodney. Eusi Kwayana. 52p. (Orig.). 1991. pap. text ed. 7.95 (*0-911565-14-0*) Calaloux Pubns.

Walter Rodney, Revolutionary & Scholar: A Tribute. Ed. by Edward A. Alpers & Pierre-Michel Fontaine. 200p. (Orig.). 1982. pap. 10.00 (*0-918456-08-8*, Crossroads) African Studies Assn.

Walter Rodney Speaks: The Making of an African Intellectual. Frwd. by Robert Hill et al. LC 87-72611. 175p. 1990. 29.95 (*0-86543-071-3*); pap. 9.95 (*0-86543-072-1*) Africa World.

Walter Rosenblum. Walter Rosenblum. (Illus.). 224p. 1991. 49.95 (*0-89381-472-5*) Aperture.

Walter S. Landor. Ernest Dillworth. (Twayne's English Authors Ser.). 198p. 1968. pap. text ed. 4.95 (*0-8290-1951-0*); lib. bdg. 17.95 (*0-8057-1312-3*) Irvington.

Walter Savage Landor: A Biography, 8 bks., Set. John Forster. LC 79-115241. 1971. reprint ed. 59.00 (*0-403-00407-1*) Scholarly.

Walter Savage Landor, a Biography. John Forster. (BCL1-PR English Literature Ser.). 693p. 1992. reprint ed. lib. bdg. 109.00 (*0-7812-7588-1*) Rprt Serv.

Walter Scott. Robin Mayhead. LC 72-88622. (British Authors-Introductory Critical Studies). 142p. reprint ed. pap. 40.50 (*0-685-15593-5*, 2026348) Bks Demand.

Walter Scott: "Waverley" Richard Humphrey. LC 92-42217. (Landmarks of World Literature Ser.). (Illus.). 153p. (C). 1993. text ed. 34.95 (*0-521-37291-7*); pap. text ed. 12.95 (*0-521-37888-5*) Cambridge U Pr.

Walter Scott: American Frontier Evangelist. William A. Gerrard, III. 252p. (C). 1992. pap. 9.99 (*0-89900-405-9*) College Pr Pub.

Walter Scott: The Making of the Novelist. Jane Millgate. 223p. 1984. pap. 14.95 (*0-8020-6692-5*) U of Toronto Pr.

Walter Scott: The Making of the Novelist. Jane Millgate. LC 84-243112. 237p. reprint ed. pap. 67.60 (*0-8357-4144-3*, 2036917) Bks Demand.

Walter Scott see Early English Novelist: Critical Heritage

Walter Scott & Scotland. Ed. by Paul H. Scott. (C). 1994. pap. 39.95 (*0-85411-056-9*, Pub. by Saltire Soc) St Mut.

Walter Scott Driskill: Without Cutting Corners. Glen Evans. Ed. by Ceila D. Robbins. (Illus.). 224p. 1992. write for info. (*0-944641-04-0*) Greenwich Pub Group.

***Walter Scott Publishing Company: A Bibliography.** John Turner. LC 97-731. (Bibliography Ser.). (Illus.). 416p. 1997. 100.00 (*0-8229-3965-7*) U of Pittsburgh Pr.

Walter Sherwoods Probation. Horatio Alger, Jr. (Works of Horatio Alger Jr.). 1989. reprint ed. lib. bdg. 79.00 (*0-7812-3620-7*) Rprt Serv.

Walter Sickert: Drawings. Anna G. Robins. LC 96-14107. (Illus.). 1996. text ed. 59.95 (*1-85928-310-1*, Pub. by Scolar Pr UK) Ashgate Pub Co.

Walter Sickert As Printmaker. Aimee Troyen. LC 78-68824. (Illus.). 90p. 1979. pap. 6.00 (*0-685-59701-6*) Yale Ctr Brit Art.

Walter Sickert, 1860-1942 Paintings. Ed. by Wendy Baron & Richard Shone. LC 92-31004. (Illus.). 384p. (C). 1993. 65.00 (*0-300-05373-8*) Yale U Pr.

Walter Syndrome. Richard Neely. 224p. 1993. pap. 3.95 (*0-88184-917-0*) Carroll & Graf.

Walter the Baker. Eric Carle. LC 93-20124. (J). (gr. 1-8). 1993. 15.95 (*0-88708-331-5*, Picture Book Studio) S&S Childrens.

Walter the Baker. Eric Carle. LC 94-32364. (J). (ps-3). 1995. 16.00 (*0-689-80078-9*, S&S Bks Young Read) S&S Childrens.

Walter the Warlock. Deborah Hautzig. (Illus.). 80p. (J). 1996. pap. 3.99 (*0-679-87341-4*) Random.

Walter the Warlock. Deborah Hautzig. (Illus.). (J). 1996. lib. bdg. 11.99 (*0-679-97341-9*) Random.

Walter the Wolf. Marjroie W. Sharmat. LC 74-26659. (Illus.). 32p. (J). (ps-3). 1989. pap. 5.95 (*0-8234-0778-0*) Holiday.

Walter Van Tilburg Clark. L. L. Lee. LC 73-8337. (Western Writers Ser.: No. 8). 50p. 1973. pap. 4.95 (*0-88430-007-2*) Boise St U W Writ Ser.

W

Walter Van Tilburg Clark: Critiques. Ed. by Charlton G. Laird. LC 83-6789. (Illus.). 312p. 1983. 24.95 (0-87417-077-X) U of Nev Pr.

Walter Wanger, Hollywood Independent. Matthew Bernstein. 1994. 35.00 (0-520-08127-7) U CA Pr.

Walter Wangerin, Jr. - Shaping Our Lives with Words of Power, Vol. 1. Dianne R. Portfleet. LC 96-94304. 192p. (Orig.). (C). 1996. pap. 12.00 (0-9652129-0-4) Greenleaf-Witcop.

Walter Warthog. large type ed. Betty Leslie-Melville. 1993. 13.50 (0-614-09859-9, L-34123-00) Am Printing Hse.

Walter Washington. Ed. by J. Rupert Picott. (YA). 1990. 5.95 (0-87498-094-1) Assoc Pubs DC.

Walter West's Probation: The Birth of Massac County, a Novel of the Regulator-Flathead War. George W. May. (Illus.). 322p. 1993. 12.00 (0-9605566-8-0) G W May.

Walter White & the Power of Organized Protest. Robert E. Jakoubek. (Gateway Civil Rights Ser.). (Illus.). 32p. (J). (gr. 2-4). 1994. pap. 4.95 (1-56294-697-8); lib. bdg. 15.40 (1-56294-378-2) Millbrook Pr.

Walter Winchell. Michael Herr. LC 90-50494. 176p. 1991. pap. 9.00 (0-679-73393-0, Vin) Random.

Walter Worm's Good Turn. Barbara Beak. LC 91-33548. (J). 1992. 3.99 (0-85953-785-4) Childs Play.

Walter's Boy. Steve Hopkins. Ed. by Marv Balousek. (Illus.). 207p. 1993. pap. 12.95 (1-878569-16-3) Badger Bks Inc.

Walter's Tail. Ernst. 1997. 5.99 (0-689-80963-8) S&S Childrens.

Walter's Tail. Lisa C. Ernst. LC 91-19948. (Illus.). 40p. (J). (ps-2). 1992. lib. bdg. 14.95 (0-02-733564-X, Bradbury S&S) S&S Childrens.

Waltham Book Human-Companion Animal Interaction. Ed. by I. Robinson. LC 95-21317. (Waltham Centre for Pet Nutrition Ser.: No. 4). 1995. text ed. 65.00 (0-08-042284-5, Pergamon Pr); pap. text ed. 37.50 (0-08-042285-3, Pergamon Pr) Elsevier.

Waltham Book of Clinical Nutrition. Ed. by Josephien Wills & Kenny Simpson. LC 93-27493. 1994. text ed. 60.00 (0-08-040839-7, Ed Skills Dallas) Elsevier.

Waltham Book of Companion Animal Nutrition. Ed. by I. H. Burger. (Waltham Centre for Pet Nutrition Ser.: Vol. 2). 150p. 1993. text ed. 65.00 (0-08-040843-5, Pergamon Pr); pap. text ed. 37.50 (0-08-040844-3, Pergamon Pr) Elsevier.

Waltham Book of Dog & Cat Behaviour. Ed. by C. G. Thorne. 250p. 1992. text ed. 55.00 (0-08-040821-4, Pergamon Pr); pap. text ed. 30.00 (0-08-040822-2, Pergamon Pr) Elsevier.

Waltham Book of Dog & Cat Nutrition. 2nd ed. Ed. by A. T. Edney. 130p. 1988. text ed. 46.00 (0-08-035730-X, Pergamon Pr); pap. text ed. 18.50 (0-08-035729-6, Pergamon Pr) Elsevier.

Waltham Chronicle. Ed. by Leslie Watkiss & Marjorie Chibnall. Tr. by Marjorie Chibnall. (Medieval Texts Ser.). (Illus.). 792p. 1994. 48.00 (0-19-822164-9) OUP.

Waltham Pocket Watch Identification & Price Guide. Roy Ehrhardt. (Illus.). 1976. reprint ed. spiral bd. 25.00 (0-913902-17-9) Heart Am Pr.

***Waltharius.** Karl Strecker. 162p. (GER.). 1988. 49.80 (3-615-00033-1, Pub. by Weidmann GW) Lubrecht & Cramer.

Waltharius. Gernot Wieland. (Latin Commentaries Ser.). 109p. (Orig.). (C). 1986. pap. text ed. 6.00 (0-929524-53-5) Bryn Mawr Commentaries.

Walther & Houston's Orthodontic Notes. 5th rev. ed. Ed. by Malcolm J. Jones & Richard G. Oliver. 240p. 1995. pap. text ed. 35.00 (0-7236-1005-3) Buttrwrth-Heinemann.

Walther Rathenau: His Life & Work. Harry K. Kessler. LC 68-9663. 1970. reprint ed. 9.00 (0-86527-203-4) Fertig.

Walther Rathenau, His Life & Work. Harry K. Kessler. LC 70-181937. reprint ed. 20.00 (0-404-03665-1) AMS Pr.

***Walther von Chatillon: Die Lieder.** Karl Stecker. xx, 64p. (GER.). 1964. write for info. (3-296-21210-8, Pub. by Weidmann GW) Lubrecht & Cramer.

Walther von Chatillon: Verskonkordanz zur Alexandreis des Walther von Chatillon. Walther Von Chatillon. Ed. by Jutta Grub & Heinz E. Stiene. (Alpha-Omega, Reihe B Ser.: Bd. III). viii, 968p. (GER.). 1985. write for info. (3-487-07677-2) G Olms Pubs.

Walther von der Vogelweide: A Complete Reference Work Headword & Rhymeword Concordances to His Poetry. Clifton Hall & Samuel Coleman. 512p. 1995. 125.00 (0-87081-359-5) Univ Pr Colo.

***Walthers Big Trains Catalog.** (Illus.). 450p. 1997. pap. 19.98 (0-941952-52-5) W K Walthers.

Walther's Pastorale: American Lutheran Pastoral Theology. Carl F. Walther. LC 94-74311. (Illus.). 304p. (C). 1995. pap. 7.95 (0-9644799-0-7) Luth News.

Walthers 1995 HO Catalog: A Walthers Catalog & Reference Manual. (Illus.). 896p. 1994. pap. 16.98 (0-941952-40-1, 913-638) W K Walthers.

Walthers 1996 HO Catalog. (Illus.). 928p. 1995. pap. 18.98 (0-941952-44-4) W K Walthers.

Walthers 1996 N&Z Catalog: Walthers Catalog & Reference Manual. (Illus.). 464p. 1995. pap. 15.98 (0-941952-45-2, 913-636) W K Walthers.

***Walthers 1997 HO Catalog.** (Illus.). 250p. 1996. pap. 19.98 (0-941952-47-9) W K Walthers.

***Walthers 1997 N&Z Catalog.** (Illus.). 449p. Date not set. pap. 16.98 (0-941952-48-7) W K Walthers.

***Walthers 1998 HO Catalog.** (Illus.). 928p. 1997. pap. 19.98 (0-941952-50-9) W K Walthers.

***Walthers 1998 NZ Catalog.** (Illus.). 449p. 1997. pap. 16.98 (0-941952-51-7) W K Walthers.

Walton Backwaters. Wilson Ltd. Staff & Imray L. Norie. (C). 1981. 60.00 (0-685-40427-7, Pub. by Imray Laurie Norie & Wilson UK) St Mut.

Walton Experience. Travis Walton. 1994. lib. bdg. 25.95 (1-56849-440-8) Buccaneer Bks.

***Walton Fallacies Arising From.** 1996. lib. bdg. 130.00 (0-7923-4100-7) Kluwer Ac.

Walton Ford & Julie Jones. Meyer R. Rubinstein & Barry Schwabsky. Ed. by Jan Riley. (Illus.). 48p. (C). 1993. pap. 25.00 (0-917562-63-1) Contemp Arts.

Walton's Little Black D Whst. 5.50 (0-7866-1606-7, 95199IWW) Mel Bay.

***Waltz.** Paul Bottomer. (Dance Crazy Ser.). (Illus.). 64p. 1997. 12.95 (1-85967-396-1, Lorenz Bks) Anness Pub.

Waltz. Kevin McIlvoy. LC 80-26883. (Illus.). 105p. 1981. pap. 7.00 (0-89924-032-1) Lynx Hse.

Waltz (American) Earl Atkinson. (Ballroom Dance Ser.). 1983. lib. bdg. 250.00 (0-87700-479-X) Revisionist Pr.

Waltz from Masquerade: Piano 4 Hands. Khachaturian. 20p. 1986. pap. 5.95 (0-7935-3780-0, 50335730) H Leonard.

Waltz in Marathon. Charles Dickinson. 272p. 1993. reprint ed. pap. 10.00 (0-380-71949-5) Avon.

Waltz into Darkness. William Irish. 1976. 24.95 (0-8488-0538-0) Amereon Ltd.

Waltz into Darkness. Cornell Woolrich. 320p. 1995. pap. 6.95 (0-14-023973-1, Penguin Bks) Viking Penguin.

Waltz Kings of Old Vienna. Ada B. Teetgen. LC 78-107833. (Select Bibliographies Reprint Ser.). 1977. 24.95 (0-8369-5198-0) Ayer.

Waltz Made Easy. (Ballroom Dance Ser.). 1985. lib. bdg. 78.00 (0-87700-673-3) Revisionist Pr.

Waltz of Hearts. large type ed. Barbara Cartland. 239p. 1993. 25.99 (0-7505-0362-9) Ulverscroft.

***Waltz of the Scarecrows.** Constance McGeorge. LC 97-1347. (Illus.). (J). 1998. write for info. (0-8118-1727-X) Chronicle Bks.

Waltz Time, No. 85. 96p. 1987. per. 7.95 (0-7935-2456-3, 00243859) H Leonard.

Waltz (Viennese) Earl Atkinson. 1983. lib. bdg. 250.00 (0-87700-486-2) Revisionist Pr.

Waltz with the Devil. Paul Fouliard. LC 93-77787. 273p. (Orig.). 1993. pap. 12.95 (1-878044-06-0) Mayhaven Pub.

Waltzer. Henry J. Ambers. LC 76-114002. 320p. 1970. 19.95 (0-9600874-4-3) Edelweiss Pr.

Waltzes: For Folk Instruments & Country Dancing. Ryan J. Thomson. (Illus.). 80p. (Orig.). 1995. pap. 12.95 (0-931877-25-3) Captain Fiddle Pubns.

Waltzes & Scherzos, Vols. IX, XII, V. Frederic Chopin. (Music Scores Ser.). (Illus.). 208p. 1983. reprint ed. pap. 9.95 (0-486-24316-8) Dover.

***Waltzing in Ragtime.** Eileen Charbonneau. 1997. mass mkt. 6.99 (0-8125-4468-4) Forge NYC.

Waltzing in Ragtime. Eileen Charbonneau. LC 96-3148. 480p. 1996. 26.95 (0-312-86180-X) St Martin.

Waltzing Matilda. Alice Notley. 7.00 (0-317-17176-3); pap. 3.50 (0-317-17177-1) Kulchur Foun.

Waltzing Matilda. A. B. Paterson. (Illus.). 32p. (J). (ps-1). 1991. 7.95 (0-207-17098-3) HarperColl Wrld.

Waltzing with a Moose: Following the Wizard's Path to Corporate Creativity. Courtney Price. 70p. pap. 8.95 (0-944303-08-0) Entre Ed Fndtn.

***Waltzing with Mannequins.** John Orozco. 156p. (Orig.). 1998. mass mkt. 4.99 (1-55237-429-7, Pub. by Comnwlth Pub CN) Partners Pubs Grp.

Waltzing Words. Margaret B. Waters. 85p. (Orig.). 1989. pap. 7.50 (0-9624949-4-1) M B Waters.

Walzer Nr. 1-30. Joseph Lanner. (Samtliche Weke fur Klavier Ser.: Vol. 1). (Illus.). 1973. reprint ed. pap. 65.00 (0-8450-1011-5) Broude.

Walzer Nr. 31-51. Joseph Lanner. (Samtliche Werke fur Klavier Ser.: Vol. 2). 1973. reprint ed. pap. 65.00 (0-8450-1012-3) Broude.

Walzer Nr. 52-70. Joseph Lanner. (Samtliche Werke fur Klavier Ser.: Vol. 3). (Illus.). 1973. reprint ed. pap. 65.00 (0-8450-1013-1) Broude.

Walzer Nr. 71-93. Joseph Lanner. (Samtliche Werke fur Klavier Ser.: Vol. 4). 1973. reprint ed. pap. 65.00 (0-8450-1014-X) Broude.

Walzer Nr. 94-106: Anhang. Joseph Lanner. (Samtliche Werke fur Klavier Ser.: Vol. 5). (Illus.). 1973. reprint ed. pap. 65.00 (0-8450-1015-8) Broude.

Walzer 1-38 see Werke Fur Pianoforte

Walzer 123-150 see Werke Fur Pianoforte

Walzer 39-68 see Werke Fur Pianoforte

Walzer 69-96 see Werke Fur Pianoforte

Walzer 97-122 see Werke Fur Pianoforte

Wampanoag. Katherine M. Doherty & Craig A. Doherty. (First Bks.). (Illus.). 64p. (J). (gr. 4-6). 1995. lib. bdg. 21.00 (0-531-20208-9) Watts.

***Wampanoag.** Alice Flanagan. LC 97-15090. (True Book Ser.). 1997. write for info. (0-516-20629-X) Childrens.

Wampanoag. Katherine Doherty. (First Bks.). (Illus.). 64p. (J). (gr. 4-6). 1996. reprint ed. pap. 6.95 (0-531-15765-2) Watts.

Wampanoag see Indians of North America

***Wampanoag Indians.** Bill Lund. LC 97-6397. (Native Peoples Ser.). (J). 1998. write for info. (1-56065-564-X) Capstone Pr.

Wampanoag Traveler: Being, in Letters, the Life & Times of Loranzo Newcomb, American & Natural Historian. Brendan Galvin. LC 88-31447. xi, 64p. 1989. pap. 6.95 (0-8071-1542-8); text ed. 13.95 (0-8071-1541-X) La State U Pr.

Wampeters, Foma & Granfalloons. Kurt Vonnegut, Jr. 320p. 1992. mass mkt. 6.50 (0-440-18533-5) Dell.

***Wamphyri.** (Necroscope Ser.). 18.00 (0-87431-479-8, 25007) West End Games.

Wampum & Old Gold. Hervey Allen. LC 70-144716. (Yale Series of Younger Poets: No. 9). reprint ed. 18.00 (0-404-53809-6) AMS Pr.

Wampum & Shell Articles Used by the New York Indians. William M. Beauchamp. LC 76-43663. (New York State Museum Bulletin Ser.: No. 41, Vol. 8). reprint ed. 49.50 (0-404-15496-4) AMS Pr.

Wampum Belts & Peace Trees: George Morgan, Native Americans & Revolutionary Diplomacy. Gregory Schaaf. LC 90-3973. (Illus.). 272p. 1990. 12.99 (1-55591-064-5) Fulcrum Pub.

Wampum, War & Trade Goods West of the Hudson. Gilbert W. Hagerty. LC 85-957. (Illus.). 312p. 1987. 40.00 (0-932334-15-6, NY74035) Hrt of the Lakes.

Wan Hu Is in the Stars. Jennifer Armstrong. LC 94-14815. (Illus.). 32p. (J). (gr. k up). 1995. 15.00 (0-688-12457-7, Tambourine Bks); lib. bdg. 14.93 (0-688-12458-5, Tambourine Bks) Morrow.

Wan Qingli: The Scholar Artist in Modern China. Novelene G. Ross et al. (Illus.). 12p. 1988. pap. 3.00 (0-939324-34-2) Wichita Art Mus.

***wan You Do This Old Badger?** Bunting. (J). Date not set. write for info. (0-15-201654-6, HB Juv Bks) HarBrace.

Wanano Indians of the Brazilian Amazon: A Sense of Space. Janet Chernela. (Illus.). 207p. (Orig.). 1996. pap. 16.95 (0-292-71186-7) U of Tex Pr.

Wanano Indians of the Brazilian Amazon: A Sense of Space. Janet M. Chernela. LC 92-4734. (Illus.). 207p. 1993. text ed. 32.50 (0-292-78522-4) U of Tex Pr.

Wanasema: Conversations with African Writers. Ed. by Don Burness. LC 82-91981. (Monographs in International Studies, Africa: No. 46). 108p. 1985. pap. text ed. 11.00 (0-89680-129-2, Ohio U Ctr Intl) Ohio U Pr.

Wanawake Watatu Wa Kiswahili: Hadithi za Maisha Kutoka Mombasa, Kenya. Ed. by Margaret Strobel & Sarah M. Mirza. Tr. by Sarah M. Mirza. LC 90-84389. (Illus.). 104p. 1991. pap. 10.95 (0-253-28855-X) Ind U Pr.

Wanawake Watatu Wa Kiswahili: Hadithi za Maisha Kutoka Mombasa, Kenya. Ed. by Margaret Strobel & Sarah M. Mirza. Tr. by Sarah M. Mirza. LC 90-84389. (Illus.). 104p. 1991. 19.95 (0-253-36336-5) Ind U Pr.

Wanda. 1992. mass mkt. 4.95 (1-56333-002-4) Masquerade.

Wanda Gag. Karen N. Hoyle. (Twayne's United States Authors Ser.). 139p. 1994. 22.95 (0-8057-3968-8, Twayne) Scribnrs Ref.

Wanda Gag: A Catalogue Raisonne of the Prints. Audur H. Winnan. LC 92-20937. (Illus.). 352p. 1993. 75.00 (1-56098-221-7) Smithsonian.

Wanda Gag: Author & Illustrator of Childrens Books. Nancy E. Duin. Ed. by D. Steve Rahmas. (Outstanding Personalities Ser.: No. 57). 32p. 1972. lib. bdg. 7.25 (0-87157-546-9) SamHar Pr.

Wanda Hickey's Night of Golden Memories & Other Disasters. Jean Shepherd. LC 72-161317. (Illus.). 352p. 1976. pap. 10.95 (0-385-11632-2, Dolp) Doubleday.

Wanda Rings. Wanda Todd. Ed. & Illus. by Janet Leih. 32p. (Orig.). 1994. pap. 7.00 (1-877649-21-X) Tesseract SD.

Wanda the Worrywart. Mary Towne. Ed. by Ruth Ashby. 144p. 1993. reprint ed. pap. 2.99 (0-671-70899-6, Minstrel Bks) PB.

Wanda Water, the Traveling Reporter. Lynne Hudgins. (Nature's Natives Ser.). 24p. (J). (gr. 3-6). 1996. text ed. 3.50 (1-889203-01-7) L Hudgins.

***Wanda Water, the Traveling Reporter.** Lynne Hudgins. (Illus.). 32p. (J). (gr. 3-6). 1996. text ed. 5.50 (1-889203-08-4) L Hudgins.

Wanda's Roses. Pat Brisson. LC 93-72916. (Illus.). 32p. (J). (ps-3). 1994. 14.95 (1-56397-136-4) Boyds Mills Pr.

Wandel der Staatsverfassungen. Heinrich Ryffel. LC 72-7904. (Greek History Ser.). (GER.). 1973. reprint ed. 25.95 (0-405-04800-9) Ayer.

Wanderer. Henri Alain-Fournier. 1981. pap. 3.95 (0-452-00754-2, Mer) NAL-Dutton.

Wanderer. Ed. by A. J. Bliss & T. P. Dunning. (Old English Ser.). 1969. pap. text ed. 5.95 (0-89197-572-1) Irvington.

Wanderer. Frances Burney. (World's Classics Ser.). 1008p. 1991. pap. 12.95 (0-19-282133-4) OUP.

Wanderer. Mark Dunster. 11p. (Orig.). 1992. pap. 4.00 (0-89642-209-7) Linden Pubs.

Wanderer. Kahlil Gibran. (Kahlil Gibran Pocket Library). 1995. 12.00 (0-679-43923-4) Knopf.

Wanderer. Ed. by Leslie. 116p. 1985. pap. text ed. 13.95 (0-85989-261-1, Pub. by Univ Exeter Pr UK) Northwestern U Pr.

Wanderer. Donald E. McQuinn. 800p. 1994. mass mkt. 6.99 (0-345-39018-0, Del Rey) Ballantine.

Wanderer. Sterling Hayden. 1995. reprint ed. lib. bdg. 32.95 (1-56849-677-X) Buccaneer Bks.

Wanderer. Fritz Leiber. (Orig.). 1993. reprint ed. lib. bdg. 18.95 (0-89968-349-5, Lghtyr Pr) Buccaneer Bks.

Wanderer: A Colloquial Poems. William E. Channing, II. (Works of William Ellery Channing II). 1990. reprint ed. lib. bdg. 79.00 (0-7812-2265-6) Rprt Serv.

Wanderer in the Spirit Lands. Franchezzo. 1993. pap. text ed. 14.00 (1-883389-50-X) Asn Int Mastery.

Wanderer in the Spirit Lands. Tr. by Franchezzo & A. Farnese. 286p. 1965. reprint ed. spiral bd. 12.50 (0-7873-0333-X) Hlth Research.

Wanderer King. Theodore Deppe. 80p. (Orig.). 1996. pap. 9.95 (1-882295-08-0) Alicejamesbooks.

Wanderer of St. Paul - The First Decade, 1867-1877: A Mirror of the German-Catholic Immigrant Experience in Minnesota, 9. John S. Kulas. LC 94-24566. (New German-American Studies: Vol. 9). 304p. (C). 1996. text ed. 53.95 (0-8204-2677-6) P Lang Pubng.

Wanderer of the Wasteland. Zane Grey. 432p. 1990. mass mkt. 3.99 (0-06-100092-2, Harp PBks) HarpC.

Wanderer Springs. Robert Flynn. LC 86-30014. 340p. 1987. 19.95 (0-87565-071-6) Tex Christian.

Wanderers. Richard Price. 256p. 1993. pap. 9.00 (0-380-77474-7) Avon.

Wanderers. W. W. Worster. 24.95 (0-8488-0686-7) Amereon Ltd.

Wanderers: Selected Poems & Translations. Antony Oldknow. 80p. 1994. 8.00 (1-881604-19-5) Scopcraeft.

Wanderer's Chronicles. Matt Forbeck. 1996. 20.00 (0-7869-0367-8) TSR Inc.

Wanderer's First Summer. Janice Erbach. 176p. (Orig.). (YA). (gr. 8-12). 1994. pap. 7.95 (0-919591-94-9, Pub. by Polestar Bk Pubs CN) Orca Bk Pubs.

Wanderer's Guide to New Mexico: Sally into the Southwest Quadrant. K. Hilleson. (Wanderer's Guide Ser.: Vol. 1). (Illus.). 80p. (Orig.). 1985. pap. 6.95 (0-9615195-0-9) Nakii Ent.

Wanderers in Space: Exploration & Discovery in the Solar System. Kenneth R. Lang. 334p. 1991. pap. text ed. 29.95 (0-521-42252-3) Cambridge U Pr.

Wanderground. Sally M. Gearhart. 196p. 1984. reprint ed. pap. 8.95 (0-932870-55-4) Alyson Pubns.

Wanderin Girl. Glenyse Ward. 160p. (C). 1991. 39.00 (0-7316-1623-5, Pub. by Pascoe Pub AT) St Mut.

Wandering: How to Cope with This Alarming Behavioral Problem. Marianne Caldwell. 1996. 10.95 (0-943873-23-1) Elder Bks.

Wandering & Feasting: A Washington Cookbook. Mary H. Caditz. LC 96-13943. (Illus.). 264p. (Orig.). (C). 1996. pap. 22.95 (0-87422-138-2) Wash St U Pr.

Wandering & Home: Beckett's Metaphysical Narrative. Eyal Amiran. 240p. (C). 1993. 35.00 (0-271-00860-1) Pa St U Pr.

Wandering & Return in "Finnegans Wake" An Integrative Approach to Joyce's Fictions. Kimberly J. Devlin. 224p. 1991. text ed. 37.50 (0-691-06886-0) Princeton U Pr.

***Wandering & Return in Finnegan's Wake: An Integrative Approach to Joyce's Fictions.** Kimberly J. Devlin. LC 90-47136. reprint ed. pap. 62.20 (0-608-04586-1, 2065356) Bks Demand.

Wandering Aramean: Collected Aramaic Essays. Joseph A. Fitzmyer. LC 77-21379. (Society of Biblical Literature. Monograph Ser.: No. 25). 310p. reprint ed. pap. 88.40 (0-7837-5455-8, 2045220) Bks Demand.

Wandering Arm. Sharan Newman. 352p. 1995. 23.95 (0-312-85829-9) Forge NYC.

***Wandering Arm.** Sharan Newman. 1996. mass mkt. 5.99 (0-8125-5089-7) Forge NYC.

Wandering Border. Jaan Kaplinski. Tr. by Riina Tamm et al. from EST. LC 87-71141. 96p. (Orig.). 1987. 15.00 (1-55659-009-1); pap. 9.00 (1-55659-010-5) Copper Canyon.

Wandering City. Robert Kendall. (CSU Poetry Ser.: No. XXXIII). 74p. (Orig.). 1992. 12.00 (0-914946-86-2); pap. 8.00 (0-914946-87-0) Cleveland St Univ Poetry Ctr.

Wandering Continents & Spreading Sea Floors on an Expanding Earth. Lester C. King. LC 83-1345. (Illus.). 244p. reprint ed. pap. 69.60 (0-8357-3090-5, 2039347) Bks Demand.

Wandering Fire. Guy G. Kay. (Fionavar Tapestry Ser.: No. 2). 400p. 1992. pap. 5.99 (0-451-45156-2, ROC) NAL-Dutton.

Wandering Ghost: The Odyssey of Lafcadio Hearn. Jonathan Cott. (Illus.). 464p. 1992. reprint ed. pap. 14.95 (4-7700-1659-X) Kodansha.

Wandering Ghosts. Francis M. Crawford. (Works of Francis Marion Crawford Ser.). 1990. reprint ed. lib. bdg. 79.00 (0-7812-2561-2) Rprt Serv.

Wandering Girl. Glenyse Ward. 144p. 1992. mass mkt. 3.99 (0-449-70414-9) Fawcett.

Wandering Gun. large type ed. Sam Gort. 192p. 1994. pap. 17.99 (1-85389-423-0, Dales) Ulverscroft.

Wandering in Arabia, Vol. 1. Ed. by Charles M. Doughty. (C). 1988. 150.00 (1-85077-190-1, Pub. by Darf Pubs Ltd UK) St Mut.

Wandering in Arabia, Vol. 2. Charles M. Doughty. (C). 1988. 135.00 (1-85077-191-X, Pub. by Darf Pubs Ltd UK) St Mut.

Wandering in the Fields: for Professor Kazuhik Nishijima on the Occasion of His Sixtieth Birthday. Ed. by K. Kawarabayashi & A. Ukawa. 524p. (C). 1987. text ed. 144.00 (9971-5-0363-8) World Scientific Pub.

Wandering in the Wilderness. Cora E. Cypser. 1995. pap. 7.95 (0-9625774-1-3) Kim Pathways.

Wandering Irish in Europe: Their Influence from the Dark Ages to Modern Times. Matthew J. Culligan & Peter Cherici. (Illus.). 350p. 1996. 22.95 (0-9651244-0-1) Derrynane Pr.

Wandering Island. Karl Kirchwey. 68p. (Orig.). 1990. pap. 9.95 (0-691-01481-7); text ed. 21.95 (0-691-06847-X) Princeton U Pr.

Wandering Jew. Ed. by M. E. Burton. LC 83-51130. 80p. 1984. 12.95 (0-938310-02-X) Volunteer Pubns.

Wandering Jew. Michelene Wandor & Mike Alfreds. (Methuen New Theatrescripts Ser.). 72p. (C). 1988. pap. 9.95 (0-413-17920-6, A0309) Heinemann.

Wandering Jew. Percy Bysshe Shelley. Ed. by Bertram Dobell. LC 74-30292. (Shelley Society, Second Ser.: No. 12). 1887. reprint ed. 34.50 (0-404-11510-1) AMS Pr.

Wandering Jew: Essays in the Interpretation of a Christian Legend. Ed. by Galit Hasan-Rokem & Alan Dundes. LC 84-48248. (Illus.). 288p. 1986. 35.00 (0-253-36340-3) Ind U Pr.

Wandering Jew & the Pound of Flesh. Moncure D. Conway. (Works of Moncure Daniel Conway Ser.). 1990. reprint ed. lib. bdg. 79.00 (0-7812-2335-0) Rprt Serv.

Wandering Knights: China Legacies, Lived & Recalled. Robert W. Barnett. LC 89-29563. 156p. (gr. 13). 1990. text ed. 51.95 (0-87332-513-3, East Gate Bk) M E Sharpe.

Wandering Lands & Animals: The Story of Continental Drift & Animal Populations. Edwin H. Colbert. 352p. 1985. reprint ed. pap. 9.95 (0-486-24918-2) Dover.

Wandering Marin Trails: A Hiking Guide to Trails of Central Marin. rev. ed. Tacy Dunham. (Marin Trail Guide Ser.). (Illus.). 56p. 1989. reprint ed. pap. 6.95 (0-685-44725-1) Cttnwd Pr.

W

An Asterisk (*) at the beginning of an entry indicates that the title is appearing in BIP for the first time.

Wandering Minstrels. large type ed. Mary Delorme. 1990. 25.99 (*0-7089-2296-1*) Ulverscroft.
Wandering Natural Products Chemist. Koji Nakanishi. Ed. by Jeffrey I. Seeman. LC 90-45062. (Profiles, Pathways, & Dreams Ser.). (Illus.). 200p. 1991. 34.95 (*0-8412-1775-0*) Am Chemical.
Wandering of Humanity. Jacques Camatte. 1975. pap. 1.25 (*0-934868-06-9*) Black & Red.
Wandering of Peoples. A. C. Haddon. (Illus.). 1984. 36.00 (*0-941694-21-6*) Cliveden Pr.
Wandering on the Outside. 2nd ed. Karren L. Alenier. LC 74-30470. (Illus.). 1979. per. 8.00 (*0-915380-00-5*) Word Works.
Wandering on the Way: Early Taoist Tales & Parables of Chuang Tzu. Victor H. Mair. 384p. 1997. pap. 17.95 (*0-553-37476-1*) Bantam.
***Wandering Peoples: Colonialism, Ethnic Spaces, & Ecological Frontiers in Northwestern Mexico, 1700-1850.** Cynthia R. Radding. LC 96-35147. (Latin America Otherwise Ser.). (Illus.). 368p. 1997. pap. text ed. 19.95 (*0-8223-1899-7*); lib. bdg. 59.95 (*0-8223-1907-1*) Duke.
Wandering Regiment: The Diary of Capt. Ralph Ely. Ed. by George M. Blackburn. (Illus.). 73p. (Orig.). 1965. pap. 5.00 (*0-915056-18-6*, Central MI Univ Pr) Hardscrabble Bks.
Wandering Scholars. Helen Waddell. 332p. 1990. 47.50 (*0-472-09412-2*); pap. 18.95 (*0-472-06412-6*) U of Mich Pr.
Wandering Stars: Russian Emigre Theatre, 1905-1940. Ed. by Laurence Senelick. LC 92-20191. (Studies in Theatre History & Culture). (Illus.). 263p. 1992. 39.95 (*0-87745-389-6*) U of Iowa Pr.
Wandering Through Paradox: China's Academe & Other Curious Places. LC 95-83878. 242p. 1996. 14.95 (*0-9650983-0-3*) Four Winds Press.
Wandering Through the Wild Nature Mazes. Strong & Sal Guastella. (J). 1992. pap. 2.50 (*0-590-45016-6*) Scholastic Inc.
Wandering Through Winter. Edwin W. Teale. 1990. pap. 12.95 (*0-312-04458-5*) St Martin.
Wandering Trails. Esther L. Vogt. LC 93-74957. (Heart for the Prairie Ser.: Bk. 3). 260p. 1994. pap. 8.99 (*0-88965-103-5*, Pub. by Horizon Books CN) Chr Pubns.
Wandering Under Summer: A Cycle of Poems. Miyoko Tanahashi. (Illus.). 1974. pap. 2.00 (*0-936072-00-8*) Soc New Lang Study.
Wandering Uterus: Politics & the Reproductive Rights of Women. Cheryl Meyer. LC 96-35694. 208p. (C). 1997. 42.50 (*0-8147-5563-1*); pap. 16.95 (*0-8147-5562-3*) NYU Pr.
Wandering Words. Edwin Arnold. LC 75-39660. (Essay Index Reprint Ser.). (Illus.). 1977. reprint ed. 30.95 (*0-8369-2739-7*) Ayer.
Wanderings. pap. 6.95 (*0-7935-2990-5*, 00290446) H Leonard.
Wanderings. Robert Herrick. (Collected Works of Robert Herrick). 1988. reprint ed. lib. bdg. 79.00 (*0-7812-1280-4*) Rprt Serv.
Wanderings: Chaim Potok's History of the Jews. Chaim Potok. 576p. 1987. mass mkt. 6.99 (*0-449-21582-2*) Fawcett.
***Wanderings: Exploring Moral Landscapes Past & Present.** Tony L. Moyers. LC 96-3428. 276p. 1996. pap. text ed. 34.00 (*0-7618-0486-2*) U Pr of Amer.
Wanderings see Collected Works of Robert Herrick
Wanderings among the Falashas in Abyssinia. 2nd rev. ed. Henry A. Stern. (Illus.). 1322p. 1968. reprint ed. 45.00 (*0-7146-1878-0*, Pub. by F Cass Pubs UK) Intl Spec Bk.
Wanderings in North Africa. James Hamilton. 360p. 1990. 122.00 (*1-85077-024-7*, Pub. by Darf Pubs Ltd UK) St Mut.
Wanderings in the Southwest, 1855. J. D. Stillman. LC 88-71687. (Western Frontiersman Ser.: No. XXIII). (Illus.). 194p. 1990. 37.50 (*0-87062-192-0*) A H Clark.
Wanderings in West Africa. Richard F. Burton. Orig. Title: Wanderings in West Africa from Liverpool to Fernando Po. (Illus.). 624p. reprint ed. pap. 12.95 (*0-486-26890-X*) Dover.
Wanderings in West Africa from Liverpool to Fernando Po see Wanderings in West Africa
Wanderings of a Spiritualist. Arthur Conan Doyle. (Visions Ser.). (Illus.). 300p. 1996. pap. 14.95 (*0-914171-73-9*) Ronin Pub.
Wanderings of an Artist among the Indians of North America. unabridged ed. Paul Kane. (Illus.). 384p. 1996. reprint ed. pap. text ed. 9.95 (*0-486-29031-X*) Dover.
Wanderings of Odysseus: The Story of the Odyssey. Rosemary Sutcliff. LC 95-15518. (Illus.). 120p. (J). (gr. 5-8). 1996. 22.50 (*0-385-32205-4*) Delacorte.
Wanderings of Peoples. Alfred C. Haddon. LC 76-44730. (Illus.). reprint ed. 45.00 (*0-404-15931-1*) AMS Pr.
Wanderjahr: The Education of a Surgeon. Edward D. Churchill. Ed. by J. Gordon Scannell. (Illus.). xi, 213p. 1991. 18.95 (*0-88135-067-2*) F A Countway.
Wanderjahre of a Revolutionist: And Other Essays on American Music. Arthur Farwell. Ed. by Thomas Stoner. (Symposium on Developmental Psychopathology Ser.). (Illus.). 280p. (C). 1996. 49.50 (*1-878822-48-9*) Univ Rochester Pr.
Wanderlust. Danielle Steel. 384p. 1986. 17.95 (*0-385-29463-8*) Delacorte.
Wanderlust. Danielle Steel. 512p. 1987. mass mkt. 6.50 (*0-440-19361-3*, Dell Trade Pbks) Dell.
Wanderlust: Homoerotic Tales of Travel. Ed. by David Laurents. (Orig.). 1996. mass mkt. 5.95 (*1-56333-395-3*, Badboy) Masquerade.
Wanderlust: Northeastern U. S. A. & Eastern Canada 93. David Ehrich. 300p. (Orig.). 1993. 10.95 (*0-942986-11-3*) LongRiver Bks.
Wanderlust: Work by Eight Contemporary Photographers from the Hallmark Photographic Collection. Keith F. Davis. (Illus.). 92p. (Orig.). 1987. pap. 14.95 (*0-87529-621-1*) Hallmark.
Wandjuk Marika: Life Story. Told to Jenny Isaacs. 176p. 1995. 34.95 (*0-7022-2564-9*, Pub. by Univ Queensland Pr AT) Intl Spec Bk.
Wandloser Raum see Room Without Walls: Selected Poems
Wandlungen der Modernen Gesellschaft: Transformations of Modern Society. Karl Renner. LC 74-25776. (European Sociology Ser.). 227p. 1975. reprint ed. 24.95 (*0-405-06530-2*) Ayer.
***Wandlungen des Doppelgangers: Shakespeare - E. T. A. Hoffmann - Pirandello - Von der Kwillingskomodie (The Comedy of Errors) zur Identitatsgefahurdung (Prinzessin Brambilla; Il fu Mattia Pascal)** Sandro M. Moraldo. 236p. (GER.). 1996. 51.95 (*3-631-49313-4*) P Lang Pubng.
Wandor's Journey. Roland Green. 1976. pap. 1.95 (*0-380-00328-7*) Avon.
Wang An-Kuo's Jade Rewards & Millet Dream. Jonathan Pease. (American Oriental Ser.: Vol. 77). iv, 106p. 1994. 18.00 (*0-940490-77-3*) Am Orient Soc.
***Wang Fan: Selected Paintings.** Fan Wang. Ed. by Haibo Luo. Tr. by Gang Jin from CHI. (Contemporary Chinese Artists Ser.). (Illus.). 218p. 1996. 39.95 (*0-9644818-6-3*) Waymont Intl.
Wang Kuo-wei: An Intellectual Biography. Joey Bonner. (East Asian Monographs: No. 101). (Illus.). 336p. 1986. 39.95 (*0-674-94594-8*) HUP.
Wang Kuo-wei's Jen-chien Tz'u-hua: A Study in Chinese Literary Criticism. Wang Kuo-wei. Tr. by Adele A. Rickett from CHI. 150p. 1977. 27.50 (*962-209-003-6*, Pub. by Hong Kong Univ Pr HK) Coronet Bks.
Wang Shiwei & "Wild Lilies" Rectification & Purges in the Chinese Communist Party, 1942-1944. Dai Qing. Ed. by David E. Apter & Timothy Cheek. Tr. by Nancy Liu & Lawrence R. Sullivan from CHI. LC 93-34022. 224p. (C). (gr. 13). 1994. pap. text ed. 28.95 (*1-56324-256-7*, East Gate Bk) M E Sharpe.
Wang Shou-Jen As a Statesman. Yu-Chuan Chang. LC 75-32330. (Studies in Chinese History & Civilization). 517p. 1975. reprint ed. text ed. 65.00 (*0-313-26958-0*, U6958, Greenwood Pr) Greenwood.
Wang WP & WP Plus: The Useable Portable Guide. Jon Haber & Herbert R. Haber. 32p. (Orig.). 1989. pap. 4.95 (*0-945765-13-4*) Useable Portable Pubns.
Wang Yang-Ming & Karl Barth: A Confucian-Christian Dialogue. Heup Y. Kim. 248p. (C). 1996. lib. bdg. 37.00 (*0-7618-0226-6*) U Pr of Amer.
Waning Authority of Christ in the Churches. Aiden W. Tozer. (Heritage Ser.). pap. 1.49 (*0-87509-611-5*) Chr Pubns.
Waning of Humaneness. Konrad Lorenz. 1987. 17.95 (*0-316-53291-6*) Little.
Waning of Old Corruption: The Politics of Economical Reform in Britain, 1779-1846. Philip Harling. (Illus.). 320p. (C). 1996. 72.00 (*0-19-820576-7*) OUP.
Waning of the Communist State: Economic Origins of the Political Decline in China & Hungary. Ed. by Andrew G. Walder. LC 94-26931. (Studies on China: Vol. 21). 1995. 40.00 (*0-520-08851-4*) U CA Pr.
Waning of the Renaissance 1640-1740: Studies in the Thought & Poetry of Henry More, John Norris & Isaac Watts. J. Hoyles. (International Archives of the History of Ideas Ser.: No. 39). 281p. 1971. lib. bdg. 82.50 (*90-247-5077-6*, Pub. by M Nijhoff NE) Kluwer Ac.
Waning of the West. Stan Steiner. 1990. pap. 9.95 (*0-312-05534-X*) St Martin.
***Wank: The Tapes.** Lars Eighner. (Orig.). 1997. mass mkt. 6.95 (*1-56333-588-3*, Badboy) Masquerade.
Wankel Rotary Engine: Introduction & Guide. Harris E. Dark. LC 73-16676. 159p. reprint ed. pap. 45.40 (*0-685-16399-7*, 2056224) Bks Demand.
Wanley Manuscripts: A Critical Commentary. James Wrightson. LC 89-7928. (British Music Theses Ser.). 900108p. 1990. text ed. 20.00 (*0-8240-2337-4*) Garland.
Wann Schreibt Man Gross, Wann Scheibt Man Klein. (Duden-Taschenbucher Ser.: No. 6). 251p. 1981. 12.25 (*3-411-01916-6*, Pub. by Bibliogr Inst Brockhaus GW) Langenscheidt.
***Wanna-be: "You Have Thirty Minutes..."** T. Wolfe Tone. 96p. 1996. mass mkt. 2.95 (*1-887900-15-2*) Peanut Books.
***Wanna Be a Cowboy.** Cactus C. Buethe. (Illus.). 80p. (Orig.). 1995. pap. 10.00 (*0-944551-10-6*, SunDance Press) Rainbow Tree Pubns.
Wanna Bet? Vicki Cobb & Kathy Darling. 160p. 1994. pap. 3.99 (*0-380-71722-0*, Camelot) Avon.
Wanna Bet! Science Challenges Bound to Fool You. Vicki Cobb & Kathy Darling. LC 92-8962. (J). 1993. 13.00 (*0-688-11213-7*) Lothrop.
***Wanna Go to Sally's?** Carlee Swann. LC 77-17769. (Illus.). 93p. 1977. per. 5.00 (*0-614-24783-7*) Tesseract SD.
***Wanna Play!** Playwrights Canada Press Staff. 1997. pap. text ed. 14.95 (*0-88754-495-9*, Pub. by Playwrights CN Pr CN) Theatre Comm.
Wanna Trade? Carol Reinsma. LC 95-17545. (J). 1995. 7.50 (*1-56212-111-1*) CRC Pubns.
Wannabe. Daniel J. Monti. Orig. Title: America's Suburban Gangs. 240p. (Orig.). 1994. 56.95 (*1-55786-614-7*); pap. 19.95 (*1-55786-615-5*) Blackwell Pubs.
Wannabe. Shelley Stoehr. 192p. (YA). 1997. 15.95 (*0-385-32223-2*, Delacorte Pr Bks) BDD Bks Young Read.
***Wannabe.** Weinberger. LC 97-16873. Date not set. pap. 11.95 (*0-312-15708-8*) St Martin.
Wannabe: A Would-Be Player's Misadventures in Hollywood. Everett Weinberger. 224p. 1995. 17.95 (*1-55972-268-1*, Birch Ln Pr) Carol Pub Group.
***Wannabe Guide to Classical Music.** Jack Mingo. (Illus.). 100p. (Orig.). 1997. pap. 9.95 (*1-57143-055-5*) RDR Bks.
Wannabe Guide to Golf. Jack Mingo. (Illus.). 100p. 1997. pap. 9.95 (*1-57143-040-7*) RDR Bks.
***Wannabe Guide to Marketing.** Jim Meade. (Illus.). 100p. (Orig.). 1997. pap. 9.95 (*1-57143-056-3*) RDR Bks.
Wannabe Guide to Wine. Jack Mingo. LC 95-72162. (Illus.). 100p. 1995. pap. 9.95 (*1-57143-039-3*) RDR Bks.
***Wannabes.** Mark Mazza. 577p. (Orig.). 1997. mass mkt. 5.99 (*1-55197-632-3*, Pub. by Comnwlth Pub CN) Partners Pubs Grp.
***Wannier-Stark Effects in Semiconductor Superlattices: Selected Papers.** 500p. 1997. lib. bdg. 61.00 (*981-02-2741-8*) World Scientific Pub.
Want a Job? Get Some Experience. Want Experience? Get a Job. Don Berliner. LC 78-18304. 192p. reprint ed. pap. 54.80 (*0-317-26944-5*, 2023589) Bks Demand.
Want Ad Killer. Andy Stack, pseud. 242p. 1983. pap. 5.50 (*0-451-16688-4*, Sig) NAL-Dutton.
Want Ads: I Want to Be a Woman. Reita Hamilton. LC 77-72146. (Illus.). 1977. pap. 3.50 (*0-914598-40-6*) Pr MacDonald & Reinecke.
Want Bone. Robert Pinsky. 1991. pap. 12.00 (*0-88001-251-X*) Ecco Pr.
Want You Soonest: Memoirs of a War Reporter. Frank Goldsworthy. 240p. 1996. 22.00 (*0-8059-3885-0*) Dorrance.
***Wanted!** Caroline B. Cooney. (YA). (gr. 6 up). 1997. mass mkt. 4.50 (*0-590-98849-2*) Scholastic Inc.
Wanted. Yaacov Eliav. Tr. by Mordecai Schreiber. LC 84-50676. 272p. 1984. 22.95 (*0-88400-107-5*) Shengold.
Wanted! Arthur W. Knight. 20p. (Orig.). 1988. pap. 4.00 (*0-916155-08-0*) Trout Creek.
Wanted. Patricia Potter. 448p. 1994. pap. 5.50 (*0-553-56600-8*) Bantam.
Wanted! Joann Ross. 1996. mass mkt. 3.50 (*0-373-25709-0*, 1-25709-6) Harlequin Bks.
Wanted. Eva Toth. Ed. by Richard Seehuus. Tr. by Laura Schiff & Peter Jay from HUN. 16p. (Orig.). 1992. pap. 4.00 (*1-881489-01-9*) Poetry Miscellany.
Wanted. large type ed. Patricia Potter. LC 95-5403. (Large Print Bks.). 1995. pap. 21.95 (*1-56895-125-6*) Wheeler Pub.
Wanted. Richard D. Coss. LC 88-38703. (Illus.). 112p. (Orig.). 1989. reprint ed. pap. 5.95 (*0-88289-707-1*) Pelican.
Wanted: A Chaperone. Paul L. Ford. (Notable American Authors Ser.). 1992. reprint ed. lib. bdg. 90.00 (*0-7812-2878-6*) Rprt Serv.
Wanted: A Dad to Brag About. Charlotte Maclay. (American Romance Ser.). 1996. mass mkt. 3.75 (*0-373-16643-5*, 1-16643-8) Harlequin Bks.
Wanted: A Match-Maker. Paul L. Ford. (Notable American Authors Ser.). 1992. reprint ed. lib. bdg. 90.00 (*0-7812-2877-8*) Rprt Serv.
***Wanted: Best Friend.** A. M. Monson. (Illus.). (J). (ps-3). 1997. 14.99 (*0-614-28689-1*) Dial Bks Young.
Wanted: Christmas Mommy. Judy Christenberry. 1995. mass mkt. 3.50 (*0-373-16612-5*, 1-16612-3) Harlequin Bks.
Wanted: First Child: A Birth-Mother's Story. Rebecca Harsin. LC 90-13887. 144p. (Orig.). 1991. pap. 9.95 (*0-931832-69-1*) Fithian Pr.
Wanted: Missionary to Mexico. Harry Emrich. (Illus.). 285p. (Orig.). 1992. pap. 8.95 (*0-9632190-0-6*) Longwood.
Wanted: Mom & Me. Kayla Daniels. 1997. mass mkt. 3.99 (*0-373-07760-2*, 1-07760-1) Silhouette.
***Wanted: One Son.** Laurie Paige. 1997. mass mkt. 3.25 (*0-373-19246-0*, 1-19246-7) Silhouette.
Wanted: Perfect Parents. John Himmelman. LC 93-22201. (Illus.). 32p. (J). (ps-3). 1993. pap. 13.95 (*0-8167-3028-8*) BrdgeWater.
Wanted: Perfect Parents. John Himmelman. LC 93-22201. (Illus.). 32p. (J). (ps-3). 1996. pap. 4.95 (*0-8167-3029-6*) BrdgeWater.
Wanted: Perfect Partner. Debbie Macomber. (Yours Truly Ser.). 1995. mass mkt. 3.50 (*0-373-52001-8*, 1-52001-4) Silhouette.
Wanted: Pot Bellied Pigs. Colene Copeland. LC 93-78897. (Illus.). 158p. (J). (gr. 1-7). 1993. 9.95 (*0-939810-15-8*); pap. 4.95 (*0-939810-16-6*) Jordan Valley.
Wanted: Rowing Coach. Brad A. Lewis. 213p. (Orig.). 1995. pap. 11.95 (*1-888478-02-0*) Shark Pr.
Wanted: The Search for Nazis in America. Howard Blum. 1978. pap. 1.95 (*0-449-23409-6*, Crest) Fawcett.
Wanted: UFO. Beatrice Gormley. 128p. (J). 1992. pap. 2.99 (*0-380-71313-6*, Camelot) Avon.
Wanted: Wife. Stella Bagwell. (Romance Ser.). 1996. mass mkt. 3.25 (*0-373-19140-5*, 1-19140-2) Silhouette.
Wanted: Wife. Kate Hoffmann. (Temptation Ser.). 1994. mass mkt. 2.99 (*0-373-25575-6*, 1-25575-1) Harlequin Bks.
Wanted--A Wife. large type ed. Mary Williams. (Linford Romance Library). 240p. 1992. pap. 15.99 (*0-7089-7208-X*, Trailtree Bookshop) Ulverscroft.
***Wanted: A Few Bold Riders.** Darice Bailer. (Smithsonian Odyssey Ser.). (Illus.). (J). (gr. 1-4). 1997. audio 7.95 (*1-56899-469-9*) Soundprints.
***Wanted: A Few Bold Riders.** Darice Bailer. (Smithsonian Odyssey Ser.). (Illus.). 32p. (J). (gr. 1-4). 1997. 19.95 incl. audio (*1-56899-472-9*) Soundprints.
***Wanted: A Few Bold Riders, Incl. toy.** Darice Bailer. (Smithsonian Odyssey Ser.). (Illus.). 32p. (J). (gr. 1-4). 1997. 29.95 (*1-56899-466-4*) Soundprints.
***Wanted: A Few Bold Riders, Incl. toy.** Darice Bailer. (Smithsonian Odyssey Ser.). (Illus.). 32p. (J). (gr. 1-4). 1997. pap. 17.95 (*1-56899-467-2*) Soundprints.
***Wanted: A Few Bold Riders, Incl. toy.** Darice Bailer. (Smithsonian Odyssey Ser.). (Illus.). 32p. (J). (gr. 1-4). 1997. pap. write for info. incl. audio (*1-56899-468-0*) Soundprints.
***Wanted: A Few Bold Riders, Incl. toy.** Darice Bailer. (Smithsonian Odyssey Ser.). (Illus.). (J). (gr. 1-4). 1997. audio write for info. (*1-56899-470-2*) Soundprints.
***Wanted: A Few Bold Riders, Incl. toy.** Darice Bailer. (Smithsonian Odyssey Ser.). (Illus.). 32p. (J). (gr. 1-4). 1997. write for info. incl. audio (*1-56899-471-0*) Soundprints.
***Wanted Across Time.** Eugenia Riley. 1997. mass mkt. 5.99 (*0-380-78909-4*) Avon.
Wanted Alive. Erin Maure. 111p. (Orig.). 1983. pap. 8.95 (*0-88784-097-3*, Pub. by Hse of Anansi Pr CN) Genl Dist Srvs.
Wanted & Unwanted Childbearing in the United States, 1973-88: PHS 91-1250. No. 189. write for info. (*0-318-69620-7*) Natl Ctr Health Stats.
Wanted: Best Friend. A. M. Monson. (J). 1997. pap. 14.99 (*0-8037-1483-1*); pap. 14.89 (*0-8037-1485-8*) Dial Bks Young.
***Wanted by Cracken.** (Star Wars Supplements Ser.). 15.00 (*0-87431-189-6*, 40062) West End Games.
Wanted by Satan but Chosen by God. Betty Jordan. LC 93-95005. 75p. (Orig.). 1996. pap. 7.95 (*0-533-10914-0*) Vantage.
Wanted Dead or Alive. Clay Dawson. (Long Rider Ser.: No. 27). 1993. mass mkt. 3.99 (*1-55773-961-7*) Diamond.
Wanted Dead or Alive. Historical Briefs, Inc. Staff. Ed. by Thomas Antonucci & Michael Antonucci. 200p. 1994. pap. 19.95 (*0-89677-055-9*) Hist Briefs.
Wanted Dead or Alive: The American West in Popular Culture. Ed. by Richard Aquila. LC 95-32476. (Illus.). 296p. 1996. 29.95 (*0-252-02224-6*) U of Ill Pr.
Wanted Dead or Alive: The American West in Popular Culture. Ed. by Richard Aquila. LC 95-32476. 1996. pap. write for info. (*0-252-06527-1*) U of Ill Pr.
Wanted Dead Or Alive: The True Story of Harriet Tubman. Ann McGovern. 64p. (J). (gr. 2-4). 1991. 3.95 (*0-590-44212-0*) Scholastic Inc.
Wanted! Dumb or Alive. Daniel Butler & Alan Ray. LC 96-32030. (America's Dumbest Criminals Ser.: No. 2). 240p. (Orig.). 1996. pap. 7.95 (*1-55853-421-0*) Rutledge Hill Pr.
Wanted for Murder: Thriller Edition. Francine Pascal. (Sweet Valley University Ser.). 288p. (YA). (gr. 8-12). 1995. mass mkt. 4.50 (*0-553-56688-1*) Bantam.
***Wanted: Husband, Will Train.** Marie Ferrarella. 1997. mass mkt. 3.99 (*0-373-24132-1*, 1-24132-2) Silhouette.
Wanted Man: (American Heroes) Kathleen Creighton. (Intimate Moments Ser.). 1994. mass mkt. 3.50 (*0-373-07547-2*, 5-07547-8) Silhouette.
Wanted Man: In Search of Bob Dylan. Ed. by John Bauldie. (Citadel Underground Ser.). (Illus.). 224p. (Orig.). 1991. pap. 9.95 (*0-8065-1266-0*, Citadel Pr) Carol Pub Group.
Wanted Man see Henry Cecil Reprint Series
Wanted: Mother. Annette Broadrick et al. 1996. mass mkt. 4.99 (*0-373-48318-X*, 1-48318-9) Harlequin Bks.
Wanted to Ask. Ken Gaub. 1990. pap. 27.95 (*0-926775-56-1*) Sensible Des.
Wanted to Buy. 5th ed. Sharon Huxford & Bob Huxford. 304p. 1995. pap. 9.95 (*0-89145-651-1*, 3978) Collector Bks.
***Wanted to Buy: A Listing of Serious Buyers Paying Cash for Everything Collectible!** 6th ed. Ed. by Bob Huxford & Sharon Huxford. 288p. 1996. pap. 9.95 (*0-89145-791-7*, 4879) Collector Bks.
Wanted: Wife & Mother. large type ed. Barbara McMahon. (Romance Ser.). 1995. mass mkt. 2.99 (*0-373-03369-9*, 1-03369-5) Harlequin Bks.
Wanted: Wife & Mother. large type ed. Barbara McMahon. (Harlequin Romance Ser.). 1995. 20.95 (*0-263-14322-8*, Pub. by Mills & Boon UK) Thorndike Pr.
Wanted...Mud Blossom. Betsy C. Byars. (Illus.). 160p. (J). (gr. 4-8). 1991. 14.95 (*0-385-30428-5*) Delacorte.
Wanted...Mud Blossom. Betsy C. Byars. 160p. (J). (gr. 4-7). 1993. pap. 4.50 (*0-440-40761-3*) Dell.
Wanting a Country for This Weather. Robin E. Van Loben Sels. LC 93-20914. 64p. 1993. pap. 12.95 (*0-7734-2783-X*, Mellen Poetry Pr) E Mellen.
***Wanting & Choosing: Essays on Subjectivity in Political Economy.** David P. Levine. LC 97-23783. 1998. write for info. (*0-415-16661-6*) Routledge.
Wanting Another Child: How to Cope with Secondary Infertility. Harriet F. Simons. 190p. 23.00 (*0-02-928938-6*, Free Press) Free Pr.
Wanting Only to Be Heard. Jack Driscoll. LC 92-5109. 208p. (Orig.). 1992. 22.50 (*0-87023-808-6*) U of Mass Pr.
Wanting Only to Be Heard. Jack Driscoll. LC 95-5109. 208p. (Orig.). 1995. pap. 14.95 (*0-87023-979-1*) U of Mass Pr.
Wanting Seed. Anthony Burgess. 288p. 1996. reprint ed. pap. 13.00 (*0-393-31508-8*) Norton.
Wanting to Know the End. Judy Goldman. Ed. by Rodger Moody. 28p. 1993. pap. text ed. 5.00 (*1-878851-04-7*) Silverfish Rev Pr.
Wantok. W. P. Botha. (African Writers Ser.). 182p. 1995. pap. 10.95 (*0-435-90969-X*, 90969) Heinemann.
Wanton. Rosemary Rogers. 336p. 1985. mass mkt. 6.50 (*0-380-86165-8*) Avon.
Wanton Angel. Elizabeth Chadwick. 448p. 1992. mass mkt., pap. text ed. 4.50 (*0-8439-3275-9*) Dorchester Pub Co.
Wanton Angel. Linda L. Miller. Ed. by Linda Marrow. 352p. 1991. mass mkt. 5.99 (*0-671-73772-4*) PB.

W

Wanton Eyes & Chaste Desires: Female Sexuality in The Faerie Queene. Sheila T. Cavanagh. LC 93-40515. 1994. 27.95 (0-253-31367-8); pap. 15.95 (0-253-20889-0) Ind U Pr.

Wanton Fires. large type ed. Meriol Trevor. 356p. 1981. 25.99 (0-7089-0722-9) Ulverscroft.

Wanton Women. 512p. 1994. pap. 5.95 (0-7867-0111-0) Carroll & Graf.

Wantons. 210p. 1986. pap. 4.50 (0-88184-262-1) Carroll & Graf.

***Want's Federal-State Court Directory, 1998.** 23th rev. ed. (Your Nation's Courts Ser.: No. 23). 240p. (Orig.). 1997. pap. 35.00 (0-942008-82-0) Want Pub.

Waorani. Robarchek. (C). 1997. pap. text ed. write for info. (0-15-503797-8) HB Coll Pubs.

Waorani: People of the Ecuadoran Rain Forest. Alexandra Siy. LC 92-36985. (Global Villages Ser.). (Illus.). 80p. (YA). (gr. 5 up). 1993. lib. bdg. 14.95 (0-87518-550-9, Dillon Silver Burdett) Silver Burdett Pr.

Wapack Trail Guide: Hikes, History, & Nature. John Flanders. (Illus.). 98p. 1991. pap. 9.95 (0-9636062-0-4) Frnds Wapack.

Wapiti-Hoo: A Bedtime Adventure. John F. Smith. (Illus.). (J). (ps-k). 1995. 15.95 (1-884375-01-4) Chinky-Po Tree.

Wapiti Wilderness: The Life of Olaus & Margaret Murie in Jackson Hole, Wyoming. Margaret Murie & Olaus Murie. (Illus.). 302p. 1985. pap. 17.50 (0-87081-155-X) Univ Pr Colo.

Wappen-Bilder-Lexikon: German, French & English. Ottfried Neubecker. 418p. (ENG, FRE & GER.). 1974. 49.95 (0-7859-8519-0, 3870450223) Fr & Eur.

Wappen des Boemischen Adels. Graf Meraviglia-Crivelli. 316p. (CZE & GER.). 1990. reprint ed. 152.00 (0-317-03842-7) Szwede Slavic.

Wappen des Maehrischen Adels. H. Kadich & C. Blazek. 331p. (CZE & GER.). 1990. reprint ed. 185.00 (0-317-03843-5) Szwede Slavic.

Wappo: A Report. Yolande S. Beard. 1979. pap. 8.50 (0-939046-26-1) Malki Mus Pr.

Wappo: A Report. Yolande S. Beard. 88p. (C). 1993. reprint ed. lib. bdg. 27.00 (0-8095-6204-9) Borgo Pr.

Wappo Texts - First Series. fac. ed. Paul A. Radin. (University of California Publications in American Archaeology & Ethnology: Vol. 19: 1). 152p. (C). 1924. reprint ed. pap. text ed. 13.70 (1-55567-235-3) Coyote Press.

Wapshot Chronicle. John Cheever. LC 91-58072. 1992. pap. 13.00 (0-679-73899-1, Publishers Media) Random.

Wapshot Scandal. John Cheever. LC 91-58073. 1992. pap. 14.00 (0-679-73900-9, Vin) Random.

Wapurgisnacht. Gustav Meyrick. Tr. by Michael Mitchell. (Studies in Austrian Literature, Culture, & Thought. Translation Ser.). 1993. pap. 12.50 (0-929497-71-6) Ariadne CA.

WAQFS in India: A Study of Administration & Statutory Control. M. A. Qureshi. 1990. 78.50 (81-212-0282-5, Pub. by Gian Publng Hse II) S Asia.

WAQFS in India: A Study of Administrative & Legislative Control. M. A. Qureshi. (C). 1990. 280.00 (0-89771-239-0) St Mut.

WAQFS in India: A Study of Administrative & Statutory Control. Ed. by M. A. Qureshi. (C). 1990. 275.00 (0-89771-141-6) St Mut.

War. Deborah Chiel. 224p. (Orig.). 1994. mass mkt. 4.99 (0-515-11447-2) Jove Pubns.

***War.** Dennis Foon. (J). 1997. pap. text ed. 10.95 (0-921368-53-4, Pub. by Bain & Cox CN) Genl Dist Srvs.

War. Ed. by Lawrence Freedman. LC 93-21348. (Oxford Readers Ser.). 400p. 1994. pap. 17.95 (0-19-289254-1) OUP.

War. Simon Hawke. (Birthright Ser.). 1996. 21.99 (0-7869-0495-X) TSR Inc.

***War.** Simon Hawke. (Birthright Ser.). 1997. pap. 5.99 (0-7869-0720-7) TSR Inc.

War. John Keegan. 1998. pap. 29.95 (0-670-85299-6) Viking Penguin.

War. Klaus Rifbjerg. Tr. by Steven T. Murray & Tiina Nunnally from DAN. LC 95-5738. (International Poetry Ser.: No. 3). 80p. 1995. pap. 10.00 (0-940242-66-4) Fjord Pr.

War. Klaus Rifbjerg. Tr. by Tiina Nunnally & Steven T. Murray from DAN. LC 95-5738. (International Poetry Ser.: No. 3). 80p. 1995. 20.00 (0-940242-67-2) Fjord Pr.

War, No. 4. Doug Murray. 48p. 1989. 3.50 (0-87135-551-5) Marvel Entmnt.

War: A Call to the Inner Land. Eberhard Arnold. 135p. (Orig.). 1985. pap. 1.00 (0-8091-2851-9) Plough.

War: A Classic Collection of 56 Great War Stories of Our Time. Jon E. Lewis. 1995. 12.98 (0-88365-909-3) Galahad Bks.

***War: A Matter of Principles.** Evans. LC 96-39674. 1997. text ed. 65.00 (0-312-17318-0) St Martin.

War: A Medical, Psychological & Scientific Subject Analysis with Research Index & Bibliography. John C. Bartone. LC 83-71661. 160p. 1984. 44.50 (0-941864-91-X); pap. 39.50 (0-941864-90-1) ABBE Pubs Assn.

War: A Memoir. Marguerite Duras. Tr. by Barbara Bray from FRE. 192p. (Orig.). 1994. pap. 10.00 (1-56584-221-9) New Press NY.

War: A Primer for Christians. Joseph Allen. 1991. pap. 3.95 (0-687-44012-2) Abingdon.

***War: An Epic Poem in 24 Books.** John Gurney. (Illus.). 474p. 1996. pap. 29.95 (3-7052-0978-7, Pub. by Univ of Salzburg AT) Intl Spec Bk.

War: Controlling Escalation. Richard Smoke. 419p. 1978. 36.50 (0-674-94595-6) HUP.

War: Ends & Means. Paul Seabury. 1990. pap. 18.00 (0-465-09068-0) Basic.

War: Four Christian Views. Herman A. Hoyt et al. Ed. by Robert G. Clouse. 216p. (Orig.). 1981. pap. 10.99 (0-88469-097-0) BMH Bks.

War: Four Christian Views. rev. ed. Ed. by Robert G. Clouse. LC 91-71185. 210p. 1991. pap. 10.99 (0-8308-1309-8, 1309) InterVarsity.

War: Stonewall Jackson's Campaigns & Battles. James B. Wood. 70p. 1988. pap. 15.00 (0-87556-357-0) Saifer.

War: The Global Battlefield. Linda MacRae-Campbell & Micki McKisson. (Our Only Earth Ser.). 104p. (J). (gr. 4-12). 1990. 19.95 (0-913705-51-9) Zephyr Pr AZ.

War: Toward a Solution. Tom Mooney. pap. 2.00 (0-317-28513-0) Mooney.

War - A Trilogy. Calvert G. Ross et al. 174p. 1993. pap. 6.95 (1-56794-052-8, C-2330) Star Bible.

War, a Cruel Necessity. Hinde. 1995. text ed. 59.50 (1-85043-824-2, Pub. by I B Tauris UK) St Martin.

War, a Legacy of Madness: Man's Wretched Little Test of Testosterone. Ann Gasser. 44p. (Orig.). 1991. pap. 3.50 (1-884257-03-8) AGEE Keyboard.

War Above the Clouds: Siachen Glacier. Martin A. Sugarman. 144p. 45.95 (1-883071-04-6); pap. text ed. 34.95 (1-883071-03-8) Sugarman Prods.

War According to Anna. Kamilla C. Chadwick. 132p. (Orig.). 1986. pap. 8.95 (0-940249-00-6) Seven Stones Pr.

War after War. Ed. by Nancy J. Peters et al. (City Lights Review Ser.: No. 5). (Illus.). 256p. (Orig.). 1992. pap. 11.95 (0-87286-260-7) City Lights.

War Aftermath Depose. Tyrone Dancy. (Orig.). 1995. pap. write for info. (1-56167-279-3) Watermrk Pr.

War Against Authority: From the Crisis of Legitimacy to a New Social Contract. Nicholas N. Kittrie. LC 94-47530. 352p. 1995. 29.95 (0-8018-5050-9) Johns Hopkins.

***War Against Children: How the Drugs, Programs, & Theories of the Psychiatric Establishment Are Threatening America's Children with a Medical "Care" for Violence.** Peter R. Breggin & Ginger R. Breggin. 280p. 1994. write for info. (0-614-24091-3) Lake Hse Bks.

War Against Children: The Government's Intrusion into Schools, Families & Communities in Search of a Medical "Cure" for Violence. Peter R. Breggin & Ginger R. Breggin. 272p. 1994. 21.95 (0-312-11065-0) St Martin.

***War Against Children of Color: Psychiatry Targets Inner City Youth.** Peter Breggin. LC 97-13741. 1997. 29.95 (1-56751-127-9) Common Courage.

***War Against Children of Color: Psychiatry Targets Inner City Youth.** Peter Breggin & Ginger R. Breggin. LC 97-13741. 1997. pap. 18.95 (1-56751-126-0) Common Courage.

War Against Gender Bias. Indira Kulshrestha. 1992. 18.95 (81-207-1248-X, Pub. by Sterling Pubs II) Apt Bks.

War Against Germany: Europe & Adjacent Areas. Center of Military History Staff. (Brassey's WWII Commemorative Series & Association of the U. S. Army Book Ser.). 464p. 1997. pap. write for info. (1-57488-101-9) Brasseys Inc.

War Against Germany: Europe & Adjacent Areas. U. S. Army, Center of Military History Staff. LC 93-34602. (Brassey's WWII Commemorative Series & Association of the U. S. Army Book Ser.). (Illus.). 448p. 1994. 30.00 (0-02-881093-7) Brasseys Inc.

War Against Germany & Italy see War in the Mediterranean: A WWII Pictorial History

War Against Germany & Italy & Adjacent Mediterranean Areas, 2 vols., Set. 1995. lib. bdg. 600.00 (0-8490-6670-0) Gordon Pr.

War Against Germany, Europe & Adjacent Areas: A Pictorial Record, 2 vols., Set. 1995. lib. bdg. 600.00 (0-8490-6671-9) Gordon Pr.

War Against Gravity. Kristine Rosemary. 192p. 1993. pap. 10.95 (0-930773-24-1); lib. bdg. 20.95 (0-930773-20-9) Black Heron Pr.

War Against Hepatitis B: A History of the International Task Force on Hepatitis B Immunization. William A. Muraskin. LC 94-43276. (Illus.). 248p. 1995. 29.95 (0-8122-3267-4) U of Pa Pr.

War Against Hitler: Military Strategy in the West. Albert A. Nofi. 274p. 1995. pap. text ed. 15.95 (0-938289-49-7) Combined Pub.

War Against Iraq: Handbook for the Anti-Imperialists. Arthur Henson. 147p. (Orig.). 1992. pap. text ed. 3.95 (0-9631692-3-8) Unity Struggle.

War Against Japan. Sidney C. Moody & Associated Press Photographers. LC 94-18411. 192p. 1994. 19.95 (0-89141-495-9) Presidio Pr.

War Against Japan: A Pictorial Record, 2 vols., Set. 1995. lib. bdg. 600.00 (0-8490-6672-7) Gordon Pr.

War Against Japan: Pictorial Record. Center of Military History Staff. (World War II Commemorative, Association of the U. S. Army Book Ser.). (Illus.). 512p. 1997. pap. 24.95 (1-57488-102-7) Brasseys Inc.

War Against Japan: Pictorial Record. U. S. Army, Center of Military History Staff. (Association of the U. S. Army Book Series & World War II Commemorative Ser.). (Illus.). 496p. 1994. 30.00 (0-02-881101-1) Brasseys Inc.

War Against Nuclear Power. Eric N. Skousen. (Illus.). 211p. (Orig.). 1981. pap. 7.95 (0-88080-002-X) Natl Ctr Constitutional.

War Against Paris, 1871. Robert Tombs. LC 80-42024. (Illus.). 272p. 1981. 59.95 (0-521-23551-0); pap. text ed. 24.95 (0-521-28784-7) Cambridge U Pr.

War Against Population: The Economics & Ideology of Population Control. Jacqueline Kasun. LC 87-83505. 225p. (Orig.). 1988. pap. 16.95 (0-89870-191-0) Ignatius Pr.

War Against Proslavery Religion: Abolitionism & the Northern Churches, 1830-1865. John R. McKivigan. LC 83-45933. 328p. 1984. 39.95 (0-8014-1589-6) Cornell U Pr.

War Against Silence after Trauma: Unmasking & Managing the Stress of Change. Emily Dee. LC 92-75053. x, 246p. (Orig.). 1993. 16.95 (0-9626818-2-2); pap. 9.95 (0-9626818-3-0) Loess Hills Pr.

***War Against the Family: A Parent Speaks Out.** William D. Gairdner. 1997. pap. text ed. 15.95 (0-7737-5648-5, Pub. by Stoddart Pubng CN) Genl Dist Srvs.

***War Against the Greens.** David Helvarg. 512p. 1997. pap. 16.00 (0-87156-907-8) Sierra.

War Against the Greens: The Wise-Use Movement, the New Right & Anti-Environmental Violence. David Helvarg. LC 94-1493. 512p. 1994. 25.00 (0-87156-459-9) Sierra.

War Against the Idols: The Reformation of Worship from Erasmus to Calvin. Carlos M. Eire. 320p. 1986. text ed. 69.95 (0-521-30685-X) Cambridge U Pr.

War Against the Idols: The Reformation of Worship from Erasmus to Calvin. Carlos M. Eire. 320p. 1989. pap. text ed. 21.95 (0-521-37984-9) Cambridge U Pr.

War against the Intellect: Episodes in the Decline of Discourse. Peter Shaw. LC 88-32115. 201p. 1989. pap. 14.95 (0-87745-240-7) U of Iowa Pr.

War Against the Jews: 1933-1945. Lucy S. Dawidowicz. 640p. 1986. pap. 15.95 (0-553-34532-X) Bantam.

War Against the Jews & the Betrayal of the Jewish People. 1996. lib. bdg. 251.95 (0-8490-6048-6) Gordon Pr.

War Against the Mafia. Don Pendleton. 1988. pap. 3.50 (1-55817-024-3) Kensgtn Pub Corp.

***War Against the Panthers: A Study of Repression.** Huey P. Newton. 176p. 22.00 (0-86316-246-0) Writers & Readers.

War Against the Panthers: A Study of Repression in America. Huey P. Newton. 1995. 24.95 (0-933121-98-9) Black Classic.

War Against the Poor: Low Intensity Conflict & Christian Faith. Jack Nelson-Pallmeyer. LC 88-38165. 125p. 1989. pap. 11.50 (0-88344-589-1, 589-1) Orbis Bks.

War Against the Poor: The Underclass & Anti-Poverty Policy. Herbert J. Gans. 208p. 1996. pap. 14.00 (0-465-01991-9) Basic.

War Against the Seals: A History of the North American Seal Fishery. Briton C. Busch. (Illus.). 432p. 1987. pap. 24.95 (0-7735-0610-1, Pub. by McGill CN) U of Toronto Pr.

War Against the Wolf: America's Campaign to Exterminate the Wolf. Ed. by Rick McIntyre. LC 94-28038. (Illus.). 496p. 1995. 24.95 (0-89658-264-7) Voyageur Pr.

War Against War: The Horrors of War. 1991. lib. bdg. 69.95 (0-8490-4708-0) Gordon Pr.

War Against Women. Marilyn French. 224p. 1993. pap. 12.00 (0-345-38248-X, Ballantine Trade) Ballantine.

War, Aggression & Self Defence. Yoram Dinstein. 324p. (C). 1988. text ed. 190.00 (0-949009-15-6, Pub. by Grotius Pubns UK) St Mut.

War, Aggression, & Self-Defence. 2nd ed. Yoram Dinstein. LC 93-50563. 356p. (C). 1994. text ed. 95.00 (0-521-46526-5) Cambridge U Pr.

War All the Time: Poems 1981-1984. Charles Bukowski. LC 84-20390. 280p. 1996. reprint ed. 25.00 (0-87685-638-5); reprint ed. pap. 14.00 (0-87685-637-7) Black Sparrow.

***War along the Bayous: Louisiana's 1864 Red River Campaign.** William R. Brooksher. (Illus.). 272p. 1998. 25.95 (1-57488-139-6) Brasseys Inc.

War along the Niagara: Essays on the War of 1812 & Its Legacy. Intro. by R. Arthur Bowler. (Illus.). 120p. (Orig.). (C). 1991. pap. 7.95 (0-941967-11-5) Old Fort Niagara Assn.

War, an Essay. Jonathan Dymond. 1973. 59.95 (0-8490-1275-9) Gordon Pr.

War & Aftermath in Vietnam. T. Louise Brown. 288p. (C). (gr. 13). 1991. text ed. 79.95 (0-415-01403-4, A5595) Routledge.

War & American Thought: From the Revolution to the Monroe Doctrine. Reginald C. Stuart. LC 81-19358. 262p. reprint ed. pap. 74.70 (0-7837-0314-7, 2040636) Bks Demand.

War & American Women: Heroism, Deeds & Controversy. William B. Breuer. LC 96-9013. 256p. 1997. text ed. 24.95 (0-275-95717-9, Praeger Pubs) Greenwood.

War & an Irish Town. 2nd rev. ed. Eamonn McCann. LC 93-36051. 176p. (C). 54.00 (0-7453-0830-9, Pub. by Pluto Pr UK); pap. 15.95 (0-7453-0725-6, Pub. by Pluto Pr UK) LPC InBook.

War & Anti-War: Making Sense of Today's Global Chaos. Alvin Toffler & Heidi Toffler. 1995. pap. write for info. (0-446-67083-9); mass mkt. 6.99 (0-446-60259-0) Warner Bks.

War & Anti-War in the Twenty-First Century. Alvin Toffler. 1993. 22.95 (0-316-85024-1) Little.

War & Architecture - Rat i Arhitektura. Lebbeus Woods. LC 93-37703. (Pamphlet Architecture Ser.: Vol. 15). (Illus.). 40p. (Orig.). (CRO & ENG.). 1993. pap. 10.95 (1-56898-011-6) Princeton Arch.

War & Border Societies. Ed. by Anthony Goodman & Anthony Tuck. LC 91-40569. 224p. (C). (gr. 13). 1992. text ed. 69.95 (0-415-08021-5, A9950) Routledge.

War & Breed. David S. Jordan. 1990. lib. bdg. 79.95 (0-8490-4055-8) Gordon Pr.

War & Change in Twentieth Century Europe. Arthur Marwick et al. (War, Peace & Social Change Series: Europe, 1900-1955). 144p. 1990. 90.00 (0-335-09313-2, Open Univ Pr); pap. 29.00 (0-335-09312-4, Open Univ Pr) Taylor & Francis.

War & Change in World Politics. Robert G. Gilpin. LC 81-2885. (Illus.). 288p. 1983. pap. text ed. 20.95 (0-521-27376-5) Cambridge U Pr.

War & Children. Anna Freud & Dorothy T. Burlingham. Ed. by Philip R. Lehrman. LC 73-7699. 191p. 1973. reprint ed. text ed. 41.50 (0-8371-6942-9, FRWC, Greenwood Pr) Greenwood.

War & Chivalry: The Conduct & Perception of War in England & Normandy, 1066-1217. Matthew Strickland. (Illus.). 448p. (C). 1996. text ed. 69.95 (0-521-44392-X) Cambridge U Pr.

War & Christianity. Elliott Coues. 1973. 250.00 (0-8490-1276-7) Gordon Pr.

War & Cinema: The Logics of Perception. Paul Virilio. Tr. by Patrick Camiller. 200p. (C). 1988. pap. text ed. 19.00 (0-86091-928-5, Pub. by Vrso UK) Norton.

War & Conflict: Selected Images from the National Archives, 1765-1970. Jonathan Heller. LC 89-39644. (Illus.). 366p. 1990. 25.00 (0-911333-77-0, 100014) National Archives & Recs.

***War & Conflict Quotations: A Worldwide Dictionary of Pronouncements from Military Leaders, Politicians, Philosophers, Writers & Others.** Michael C. Thomsett & Jean F. Thomsett. LC 97-47324. 296p. 1997. lib. bdg. 45.00 (0-7864-0314-4) McFarland & Co.

War & Conscience in the Nuclear Age. Sydney D. Bailey. LC 87-18755. 200p. 1988. text ed. 39.95 (0-312-01345-0) St Martin.

War & Democracy. Peter T. Manicas. 384p. 1989. text ed. 56.95 (0-631-15836-7) Blackwell Pubs.

***War & Development: The Study of Post-Conflict Integration in Southern Africa.** Rosemary Preston. text ed. 65.95 (0-471-96941-9) Wiley.

War & Diplomacy: The Making of a Grand Alliance. Oleg A. Rzheshevsky. (History of Russia Ser.: Vol. 2). 350p. 1996. text ed. 63.00 (3-7186-5790-2, Harwood Acad Pubs) Gordon & Breach.

War & Drought in Sudan: Essays on Population Displacement. Eltigani E. Eltigani. LC 94-34182. (Illus.). 128p. (C). 1995. lib. bdg. 29.95 (0-8130-1336-4) U Press Fla.

War & Economy in the Third Reich. R. J. Overy. (Illus.). 410p. 1995. pap. 24.95 (0-19-820599-6) OUP.

War & Education. Porter E. Sargent. 1975. lib. bdg. 300.00 (0-87700-244-4) Revisionist Pr.

War & Ethnicity: Global Connections & Local Violence. Ed. by David Turton. LC 96-48994. (Illus.). 296p. 1997. 71.00 (1-878822-82-9) Univ Rochester Pr.

War & Existence: A Philosophical Inquiry. Michael Gelven. LC 92-41697. 288p. (C). 1994. 40.00 (0-271-01052-5); pap. 16.95 (0-271-01054-1) Pa St U Pr.

War & Famine in Africa: Oxfam Research Discussion Papers. Mark Duffield. (Oxfam Research Discussion Papers). 36p. (C). Date not set. 15.95 (0-85598-161-X, Pub. by Oxfam UK) Humanities.

War & Four Other Plays. Jean-Claude Van Itallie. 1967. pap. 5.25 (0-8222-1202-1) Dramatists Play.

War & Government in Britain, 1598-1650. Ed. by Mark C. Fissel. LC 90-21943. (War, Armed Forces & Society Ser.). 320p. 1991. text ed. 59.95 (0-7190-2887-6, Pub. by Manchester Univ Pr UK) St Martin.

War & Government in Early Modern France: Picardy, 1470-1560. David Potter. LC 92-11887. (Illus.). 384p. (C). 1993. text ed. 69.95 (0-521-43189-1) Cambridge U Pr.

War & Healing: Stanhope Bayne-Jones & the Maturing of American Medicine. Albert E. Cowdrey. Ed. by William J. Cooper, Jr. LC 91-32513. (Southern Biography Ser.). (Illus.). 264p. (C). 1992. text ed. 42.50 (0-8071-1717-X) La State U Pr.

War & Hunger: Rethinking International Responses to Complex Emergencies. Ed. by Joanna Macrae et al. LC 94-41463. (C). 1995. pap. 25.00 (1-85649-292-3, Pub. by Zed Bks Ltd UK) Humanities.

War & Hunger: Rethinking International Responses to Complex Emergencies. Ed. by Joanna Macrea & Anthony Zwi. LC 94-41463. 256p. (C). 1995. text ed. 59.95 (1-85649-291-5, Pub. by Zed Bks Ltd UK) Humanities.

War & Identity in France. Ed. by Colin W. Nettelbeck. 176p. (C). 1994. pap. text ed. 22.95 (0-423-51700-7) Routledge Chapman & Hall.

***War & Identity in France.** Ed. by Colin W. Nettlebeck. (Twentieth Century French Texts Ser.). 176p. 1994. pap. text ed. 22.95 (0-415-11949-9) Routledge.

War & Ideology. Eric Carlton. 216p. (C). 1990. pap. text ed. 66.50 (0-389-20945-7) B&N Imports.

War & Imperialism in Republican Rome, 327-70 B. C. William V. Harris. 312p. 1985. pap. 35.00 (0-19-814866-6) OUP.

War & Insurance. Norman Hill et al. (Economic & Social History of the World War Ser.). (GER.). 1927. 100.00 (0-317-27648-4) Elliots Bks.

War & Insurance. Josiah Royce. LC 75-3336. reprint ed. 34.50 (0-404-59339-9) AMS Pr.

War & International Ethics: Tradition & Today. W. L. LaCroix. 316p. (Orig.). (C). 1988. pap. text ed. 26.00 (0-8191-6708-8); lib. bdg. 51.00 (0-8191-6707-X) U Pr of Amer.

War & Intervention in Lebanon: The Israeli-Syrian Deterrence Dialogue. Yair Evron. LC 87-2851. 350p. 1987. text ed. 41.50 (0-8018-3569-0) Johns Hopkins.

War & Its Consequences: Lessons from the Persian Gulf Conflict. Ed. by John O'Loughlin et al. LC 93-34027. (C). 1994. 14.50 (0-06-502260-2) Addson-Wesley Educ.

War & Its Discontents: Pacifism & Quietism in the Abrahamic Traditions. Ed. by J. Patout Burns. LC 95-42086. 240p. 1996. 55.00 (0-87840-603-4) Georgetown U Pr.

War & Law since 1945. Geoffrey Best. 580p. 1994. 49.95 (0-19-821991-1) OUP.

***War & Law since 1945.** Geoffrey Best. 456p. 1997. reprint ed. pap. 24.95 (0-19-820699-2) OUP.

W

An Asterisk (*) at the beginning of an entry indicates that the title is appearing in BIP for the first time.

War & Lechery. William Sylvester. LC 95-78184. 101p. (Orig.). 1995. pap. 12.00 (*0-912592-39-7*) Ashland Poetry.

***War & Memory in the 20th Century.** Berg. 1997. 45.50 (*1-85973-194-5*, Pub. by Berg Pubs UK); pap. 19.50 (*1-85973-199-6*, Pub. by Berg Pubs UK) NYU Pr.

War & Military Reform in the Roman Republic: 578-589 B.C. John M. Carter. 95p. (Orig.). 1980. pap. 24.95 (*0-89126-096-X*) MA-AH Pub.

War & Morality. Ed. by Richard A. Wasserstrom. 136p. (C). 1970. pap. 21.95 (*0-534-00681-7*) Wadsworth Pub.

War & Order: Reflections on Vietnam & History. George Liska. LC 68-9697. (Washington Center of Foreign Policy Research. Studies in International Affairs: No. 11). 127p. reprint ed. pap. 36.20 (*0-317-19922-6*, 2023126) Bks Demand.

War & Other Essays. William G. Sumner. Ed. by Albert G. Keller. LC 76-93379. (Essay Index Reprint Ser.). 1977. 29.95 (*0-8369-1530-5*) Ayer.

War & Other Essays. William G. Sumner. Ed. & Intro. by Albert G. Keller. LC 78-108124. 1970. reprint ed. 32.50 (*0-404-06304-7*) AMS Pr.

***War & Peace.** Adapted by Helen Edmundson. 160p. (Orig.). 1996. pap. 16.95 (*1-85459-306-4*, Pub. by N Hern Bks UK) Theatre Comm.

War & Peace. Toni Goffe. LC 91-18197. (J). (gr. 4 up). 1991. 7.99 (*0-85953-366-2*); pap. 3.99 (*0-85953-356-5*) Childs Play.

War & Peace. Silbajori. 1995. pap. 13.95 (*0-8057-4459-2*) Macmillan.

War & Peace. Silbajori. 1995. 23.95 (*0-8057-9449-2*, Twayne) Scribnrs Ref.

War & Peace, 3 vols. Leo Tolstoy. Tr. by Louise Maude & Aylmer Maude from RUS. LC 92-52894. (Everyman's Library of Children's Classics). 1993. Boxed. 40.00 (*0-679-40573-9*) Knopf.

War & Peace. Leo Tolstoy. Tr. by Ann Dunnigan. 1968. pap. 8.95 (*0-451-52326-1*, Sig Classics) NAL-Dutton.

War & Peace. Leo Tolstoy. 1989. pap. 5.95 (*0-451-52116-1*) NAL-Dutton.

War & Peace. Leo Tolstoy. Ed. by Henry Gifford. Tr. by Louise Maude & Aylmer Maude. (World's Classics Ser.). (Illus.). 1392p. 1991. pap. 10.95 (*0-19-282780-4*, 312) OUP.

War & Peace. Leo Tolstoy. Tr. by Constance Garnett. 1408p. 1994. 23.00 (*0-679-60084-1*) Random.

War & Peace. Leo Tolstoy. Tr. by Rosemary Edmonds. 1, 454p. 1982. pap. 12.95 (*0-14-044417-3*, Penguin Classics) Viking Penguin.

War & Peace. Leo Tolstoy. (C). 1966. pap. text ed. 16.95 (*0-393-09672-6*) Norton.

***War & Peace.** Michael Twinn. (J). 1996. lib. bdg. 11.95 (*0-85953-854-0*) Childs Play.

War & Peace, 5 vols., 1. large type ed. Leo Tolstoy. 1976. 25.99 (*0-85456-625-2*) Ulverscroft.

War & Peace, 5 vols., 2. large type ed. Leo Tolstoy. 1976. 25.99 (*0-85456-626-0*) Ulverscroft.

War & Peace, 5 vols., 3. large type ed. Leo Tolstoy. 1976. 25.99 (*0-85456-627-9*) Ulverscroft.

War & Peace, 5 vols., 4. large type ed. Leo Tolstoy. 1976. 25.99 (*0-85456-628-7*) Ulverscroft.

War & Peace, 5 vols., 5. large type ed. Leo Tolstoy. 1976. 25.99 (*0-85456-629-5*) Ulverscroft.

War & Peace, 5 vols., Set. large type ed. Leo Tolstoy. 1976. 55.00 (*0-85456-624-4*) Ulverscroft.

War & Peace, Vol. I. Leo Tolstoy. 1989. reprint ed. lib. bdg. 49.95 (*0-89966-646-9*) Buccaneer Bks.

War & Peace, Vol. II. Leo Tolstoy. 1989. reprint ed. lib. bdg. 49.95 (*0-89966-647-7*) Buccaneer Bks.

***War & Peace: Between Israel & Its Neighbors.** Raji Dabit. viii, 208p. 1997. pap. write for info. (*0-9657058-0-3*) R P Caudill.

War & Peace: Observations on our Times. Howard Fast. LC 92-26859. 304p. (gr. 13). 1992. 45.00 (*1-56324-207-9*) M E Sharpe.

War & Peace: Perspectives in the Nuclear Age. Ed. by Ulrich Goebel & Otto Nelson. LC 88-50215. (Studies in Comparative Literature). vi, 149p. 1988. 22.95 (*0-89672-158-2*); pap. 12.95 (*0-89672-168-X*) Tex Tech Univ Pr.

War & Peace: The Evils of the First, & a Plan for Preserving the Last. William Jay. LC 70-137547. (Peace Movement in America Ser.). xiv, 69p. 1972. reprint ed. lib. bdg. 21.95 (*0-89198-075-X*) Ozer.

War & Peace: The Maude Translation, Backgrounds & Soruces, Essays in Criticism. 2nd ed. Leo Tolstoy. Ed. by George Gibian. LC 94-29261. (Critical Editions Ser.). (C). 1995. pap. text ed. 16.95 (*0-393-96647-X*) Norton.

War & Peace: The Views from Moscow & Beijing. Banning N. Garrett & Bonnie S. Glaser. LC 84-80320. (Policy Papers in International Affairs: No. 20). 160p. 1984. pap. text ed. 7.95 (*0-87725-520-2*) U of Cal IAS.

War & Peace: Toynbee, Hawtrey, Wright. Lynchburg College Faculty Staff. 366p. (Orig.). (C). 1993. pap. text ed. 24.95 (*0-8191-9285-6*) U Pr of Amer.

War & Peace: Toynbee, Hawtrey, Wright. Lynchburg College Faculty Staff. (Lynchburg College Symposium Readings Ser.: Vol. II). 366p. (Orig.). (C). 1993. lib. bdg. 45.00 (*0-8191-9324-0*) U Pr of Amer.

War & Peace Cycles: Poverty Amid Plenty. 1991. lib. bdg. 79.95 (*0-8490-4468-5*) Gordon Pr.

War & Peace from Genesis to Revelation. Vernard Eller. LC 80-26280. (Christian Peace Shelf Ser.). 232p. 1981. pap. 11.99 (*0-8361-1947-9*) Herald Pr.

War & Peace in Europe, 1815-1970. E. L. Woodward. 292p. 1963. 37.50 (*0-7146-1530-7*, Pub. by F Cass Pubs UK) Intl Spec Bk.

War & Peace in Ireland: Britain & the IRA in the New World Order. Mark Ryan. LC 94-8049. (C). 59.95 (*0-7453-0923-2*, Pub. by Pluto Pr UK); pap. 15.95 (*0-7453-0924-0*, Pub. by Pluto Pr UK) LPC InBook.

War & Peace in Israeli Politics: Labor Party Positions on National Security. Efraim Inbar. LC 90-43019. 180p. 1991. lib. bdg. 36.50 (*1-55587-236-0*) Lynne Rienner.

War & Peace in Literature. Lucy Dougall. 128p. 1981. 5.00 (*0-318-16880-4*) World Without War.

War & Peace in the Baltic: 1560-1790. Stewart P. Oakley. LC 92-6571. (War in Context Ser.). 240p. (C). (gr. 13). 1993. text ed. 62.95 (*0-415-02472-2*, A7943) Routledge.

***War & Peace in the Global Village.** Marshall McLuhan & Quentin Fiore. 1997. pap. text ed. 9.95 (*1-888869-07-0*) HardWired.

War & Peace in the Law of Islam. Majid Khadduri. LC 77-2418. reprint ed. 24.50 (*0-404-10925-X*) AMS Pr.

War & Peace in the Middle East: A Critique of American Policy. Avi Shlaim. 160p. 1995. pap. 9.95 (*0-14-024564-2*, Penguin Bks) Viking Penguin.

War & Peace in the Nuclear Age. (Dantes Subject Standardized Tests Ser.: DANTES-63). pap. 23.95 (*0-8373-6663-1*) Nat Learn.

War & Peace in the 1940s, Vol. 2: The History. Harold Gauer. (Illus.). 280p. (Orig.). 1991. pap. 19.95 (*1-877831-03-4*) Prec Process.

War & Peace in Vietnam. Richard West. Date not set. 24.95 (*0-7493-2450-3*) Heinemann.

War & Peace in Western Australia: The Social & Political Impact of the Great War 1914-1926. Bobbie Oliver. 314p. 1995. pap. 24.95 (*1-875560-57-2*, Pub. by Univ of West Aust Pr AT) Intl Spec Bk.

War & Peace Literature for Children & Young Adults: A Resource Guide to Significant Issues. Virginia A. Walter. LC 92-29729. 184p. 1993. pap. 29.95 (*0-89774-725-9*) Oryx Pr.

War & Peace News. Glasgow Media Group Staff. LC 85-11594. 354p. 1985. 85.00 (*0-335-15071-3*, Open Univ Pr); pap. 32.00 (*0-335-10598-X*, Open Univ Pr) Taylor & Francis.

War & Peace Notes. Marianne Sturman. 1967. pap. 4.50 (*0-8220-1366-5*) Cliffs.

War & Peace since 1945. John F. Bradley. 204p. 1989. text ed. 46.50 (*0-88033-964-0*) East Eur Monographs.

War & Peace Through Women's Eyes: A Selective Bibliography of Twentieth-Century American Women's Fiction. Susanne Carter. LC 91-33399. (Bibliographies & Indexes in Women's Studies: No. 14). 336p. 1992. text ed. 59.95 (*0-313-27771-0*, CWE, Greenwood Pr) Greenwood.

War & Peace with China: Experiences in the Foreign Service of the U.S. Marshall Green et al. (Illus.). 224p. 1994. per., pap. 15.00 (*1-885965-00-1*) Dacor Pr.
WHAT WILL CHINA DO TO HONG KONG & TAIWAN? For answers, this book looks deeply into the events that formed the present Chinese leadership: the drastic break with Mao's commitment to Stalin & his ignorance of economic factors, & the resulting internal chaos. Instead of opinion or self-serving reminiscence, read this solid, comprehensive, yet lively account of experiences by three U.S. Foreign Service Officers who led the professional China staff of successive presidents & Secretaries of State, & who dealt themselves with Chinese leaders in the radical turnabout of U.S. & Chinese policy. WAR & PEACE WITH CHINA deals authentically, from first-hand experiences, with: strategic & economic forces at work; the Taiwan issue: not what it seems; Hong Kong more important for impact on China than the converse; priorities in China's foreign & domestic policies. "Fascinating..of great value...important contribution to history."--William Bundy, ex-Editor of FOREIGN AFFAIRS & Assistant Secretary of State for East Asia. "Highly effective & authoritative view by insiders of our relations with China, filled with lively human interest."--Arthur Hummel, retired Ambassador to China & current consultant. Published by Diplomatic & Consular Officers Retired (DACOR PRESS). To order, send $15 to: DACOR Press, 4858 Cordell Ave., Bethesda, MD 20814-3011. MasterCard or Visa. Credit card orders (give number & expiration date) may also be faxed to 301-654-5508. ***Publisher Provided Annotation.***

War & Peas. Jill Churchill. 224p. 1996. 20.00 (*0-380-97323-5*) Avon.

***War & Peas.** Jill Churchill. LC 96-54878. (Americana Ser.). 275p. 1997. 24.95 (*0-7862-1049-4*) Thorndike Pr.

***War & Photography: Cultural History.** Caroline Brothers. 304p. (C). 1997. 55.00 (*0-415-13099-9*) Routledge.

War & Politics. Bernard Brodie. 514p. (C). 1974. pap. write for info. (*0-685-28575-8*) Macmillan.

War & Politics. Bernard Brodie. 514p. (C). 1974. pap. text ed. 50.00 (*0-02-315020-3*, Macmillan Coll) P-H.

War & Politics in Cambodia: A Communications Analysis. LC 73-81737. 186p. reprint ed. pap. 53.10 (*0-317-26848-1*, 2023450) Bks Demand.

War & Politics in China. John T. Pratt. LC 78-146869. (Select Bibliographies Reprint Ser.). 1977. reprint ed. 24.95 (*0-8369-5636-2*) Ayer.

War & Politics in Ireland, 1649-1730. J. G. Simms. 335p. 1986. text ed. 55.00 (*0-907628-72-9*) Hambledon Press.

War & Politics in Twentieth Century Europe: Essays in Military & Diplomatic History, 1. R. H. Haigh et al. 1982. pap. 41.95 (*0-89126-105-2*) MA-AH Pub.

War & Politics in Twentieth Century Europe: Essays in Military & Diplomatic History, 2. R. H. Haigh et al. 1982. 48.00 (*0-89126-106-0*) MA-AH Pub.

War & Politics in Twentieth Century Europe: Essays in Military & Diplomatic History, 3. R. H. Haigh et al. 1982. 27.95 (*0-89126-114-1*) MA-AH Pub.

War & Politics in Twentieth Century Europe: Essays in Military & Diplomatic History, 4. R. H. Haigh et al. 1982. 37.95 (*0-89126-115-X*) MA-AH Pub.

War & Politics in Twentieth Century Europe: Essays in Military & Diplomatic History, 5. R. H. Haigh et al. 1982. 45.95 (*0-89126-116-8*) MA-AH Pub.

War & Politics in Twentieth Century Europe: Essays in Military & Diplomatic History, 6. R. H. Haigh et al. 1982. 27.95 (*0-89126-117-6*) MA-AH Pub.

War & Popular Culture: Resistance in Modern China, 1937-1945. Chang-tai Hung. LC 93-4738. 1994. 37.00 (*0-520-08236-2*) U CA Pr.

War & Presidential Power: A Chronicle of Congressional Surrender. Thomas F. Eagleton. 1974. 8.95 (*0-87140-581-4*) Liveright.

War & Progress: Britain, 1914-1945. LC 96-16228. (Economic & Social History of Britain Ser.). (C). 1997. pap. text ed. 27.50 (*0-582-04586-X*, Pub. by Longman UK) Longman.

War & Progress: Britain, 1914-1945. Peter Dewey. LC 96-16228. (Economic & Social History of Britain Ser.). (C). 1997. text ed. 59.50 (*0-582-04587-8*, Pub. by Longman UK) Longman.

***War & Public Health.** Ed. by Barry S. Levy & Victor W. Sidel. (Illus.). 368p. 1996. 55.00 (*0-19-510814-0*) OUP.

War & Race: The Black Officer in the American Military, 1915 to 1941. Gerald W. Patton. LC 80-24629. (Contributions in Afro-American & African Studies: No. 62). (Illus.). 232p. 1981. text ed. 55.00 (*0-313-22176-6*, PWR/, Greenwood Pr) Greenwood.

War & Reason: Domestic & International Imperatives. Bruce Bueno de Mesquita & David Lalman. 336p. (C). 1992. pap. 18.00 (*0-300-05922-1*); text ed. 45.00 (*0-300-05202-2*) Yale U Pr.

***War & Reflection.** Walter W. Benjamin. Ed. by Douglas Benson. LC 96-70760. (Illus.). 256p. (Orig.). 1996. pap. 12.95 (*0-9640439-1-2*) Red Oak MN.

War & Reform: British Politics During the Second World War. Ed. by Kevin Jefferys. LC 93-30885. 1994. text ed. 49.95 (*0-7190-3970-3*, Pub. by Manchester Univ Pr UK); text ed. 19.95 (*0-7190-3971-1*, Pub. by Manchester Univ Pr UK) St Martin.

War & Refugees. Richard Lawless & Liala Manahan. (Illus.). 280p. 1992. 47.50 (*0-86187-900-7*) St Martin.

War & Remembrance. Herman Wouk. LC 78-16490. 1978. 29.95 (*0-316-95501-9*) Little.

War & Remembrance. Herman Wouk. 1392p. 1992. mass mkt. 6.99 (*0-316-95515-9*) Little.

War & Responsibility. John H. Ely. 254p. 1993. pap. text ed. 16.95 (*0-691-02552-5*) Princeton U Pr.

War & Responsibility: Constitutional Lessons of Vietnam & Its Aftermath. John H. Ely. LC 92-45769. 256p. 1993. text ed. 35.00 (*0-691-08643-5*) Princeton U Pr.

War & Revolution: Excerpts from the Letters & Diaries of the Countess Olga Poutiatine. Olga Poutiatine. Ed. & Tr. by George A. Lensen. LC 74-164854. (Illus.). 111p. 1971. 12.50 (*0-910512-12-4*) Diplomatic IN.

War & Revolution: Lenin & the Myth of Revolutionary Defeatism. Hal Draper. Ed. by E. Haberkern. LC 95-42979. (Revolutionary Studies Ser.). 256p. (C). 1996. text ed. 49.95 (*0-391-03930-X*) Humanities.

War & Secession: Pakistan, India, & the Creation of Bangladesh. Leo E. Rose. (Illus.). 350p. 1991. reprint ed. pap. 15.00 (*0-520-07665-6*) U CA Pr.

War & Society: The United States, 1941-1945. Richard Polenberg. LC 80-10734. (Critical Periods of History Ser.). 298p. 1980. reprint ed. text ed. 55.00 (*0-313-22348-3*, POWS, Greenwood Pr) Greenwood.

War & Society in Africa. Ed. by Bethwell A. Ogot. 276p. 1972. pap. 22.50 (*0-7146-4009-3*, Pub. by F Cass Pubs UK) Intl Spec Bk.

War & Society in Ancient Mesoamerica. Ross Hassig. 347p. (C). 1992. 50.00 (*0-520-07734-2*) U CA Pr.

War & Society in Britain 1899-1945. Rex Pope. (C). 1900. pap. text ed. 13.50 (*0-582-03531-7*) Addison-Wesley.

War & Society in Colonial Connecticut. Harold E. Selesky. 256p. (C). 1990. 30.00 (*0-300-04552-2*) Yale U Pr.

***War & Society in Early Modern Europe 1495-1715.** Frank Tallett. (War in Context Ser.). 320p. (C). 1997. pap. 19.95 (*0-415-16073-1*) Routledge.

War & Society in East Central Europe, Vol. IV. Ed. by Bela K. Kiraley. 1984. 40.00 (*0-317-18770-8*) East Eur Monographs.

War & Society in East Central Europe: East European Society in the First World War. Ed. by Bela K. Kiraly & Nandor F. Dreiszinger. 623p. 1986. 83.00 (*0-88033-089-9*) East Eur Monographs.

War & Society in East Central Europe During the Eighteenth & Nineteenth Centuries: Special Topics & Generalizations, Vol. 1. Ed. by Bela K. Kiraly & Gunther E. Rothenberg. (Studies on Society in Change: No. 10). 1979. 22.50 (*0-930888-04-9*) Brooklyn Coll Pr.

War & Society in East Central Europe During the 18th & 19th Centuries, Vol. I. Ed. by Bela K. Kiraly & Gunther E. Rothenberg. (Special Topics & Generalizations on the 18th & 19th Centuries Ser.). 478p. (C). 1986. reprint ed. lib. bdg. 64.00 (*0-8191-5560-8*, Atlantic Rsch & Pubns Inc) U Pr of Amer.

War & Society in Europe, Eighteen Seventy to Nineteen Seventy. Brian Bond. LC 83-40281. 256p. 1984. text ed. 29.95 (*0-312-85547-8*) St Martin.

War & Society in Europe of the Old Regime, 1618-1789. M. S. Anderson. LC 88-4466. 240p. 1988. text ed. 39.95 (*0-312-01879-7*) St Martin.

War & Society in Europe, 1618-1648. Josef V. Polisensky. LC 77-71423. (Illus.). 1978. 64.95 (*0-521-21659-1*) Cambridge U Pr.

War & Society in Europe, 1870-1970. Brian Bond. 256p. 1986. pap. 16.95 (*0-19-520502-2*) OUP.

War & Society in Habsburg Spain. I. A. Thompson. (Collected Studies: Vol. CS376). 368p. 1992. 98.95 (*0-86078-328-6*, Pub. by Variorum UK) Ashgate Pub Co.

War & Society in Renaissance Europe, 1450-1620. J. R. Hale. LC 85-23106. 282p. 1986. reprint ed. pap. text ed. 14.95 (*0-8018-3196-2*) Johns Hopkins.

***War & Society in the Ancient World: War & Society in the Greek World, & War & Society in the Roman World.** Ed. by John Rich & Graham Shipley. 608p. (C). 1993. text ed. 85.00 (*0-415-06645-X*) Routledge.

War & Society in the Eastern Mediterranean, 7th-15th Centuries. Ed. by Yaacov Lev. LC 96-16295. (Medieval Mediterranean Ser.: Vol. 9). (Illus.). 448p. 1997. text ed. 162.75 (*90-04-10032-6*, NLG252) E J Brill.

War & Society in the Greek World. Ed. by John Rich & Graham Shipley. LC 92-29074. (Leicester-Nottingham Studies in Ancient Society: Vol. 4). 288p. (C). (gr. 13). 1993. text ed. 59.95 (*0-415-06643-3*, Routledge NY) Routledge.

War & Society in the Greek World. John Rich & Graham Shipley. (Leicester-Nottingham Studies in Ancient Society). (Illus.). 264p. (C). 1995. pap. 17.95 (*0-415-12166-3*, C0202) Routledge.

War & Society in the Roman World. Ed. by John Rich & Graham Shipley. LC 92-36698. (Leicester-Nottingham Studies in Ancient Society: Vol. 5). 320p. (C). (gr. 13). 1993. text ed. 59.95 (*0-415-06644-1*) Routledge.

War & Society in the Roman World. John Rich & Graham Shipley. (Leicester-Nottingham Studies in Ancient Society). 320p. (C). 1995. pap. 18.95 (*0-415-12167-1*, C0218) Routledge.

War & Society in the Seventeenth Century. George N. Clark. LC 85-12551. viii, 157p. 1985. reprint ed. text ed. 43.75 (*0-313-24948-2*, CWSO, Greenwood Pr) Greenwood.

War & Society in Twentieth-Century France. Ed. by Michael Scriven & Peter Wagstaff. LC 91-16316. 320p. 1992. 38.95 (*0-85496-292-1*) Berg Pubs.

War & State Making: The Shaping of the Global Powers. Karen A. Rasler & William R. Thompson. (Studies in International Conflict: Vol. 2). 272p. (C). (gr. 13). 1989. text ed. 62.95 (*0-04-445097-4*) Routledge Chapman & Hall.

War & Television. Bruce Cumings. 320p. (C). (gr. 13). 1994. pap. text ed. 19.00 (*0-86091-682-0*, Pub. by Vrso UK) Norton.

War & Terrorism in International Affairs. Gerardo J. Schamis. Tr. by Danielle Salti from SPA. LC 79-91346. 100p. (Orig.). 1980. pap. 21.95 (*0-87855-808-X*) Transaction Pubs.

War & the Breed. D. S. Jordan. (Illus.). 1988. 30.00 (*0-941694-33-X*) Cliveden Pr.

***War & the British.** Noakes. Date not set. text ed. write for info. (*1-86064-306-X*, Pub. by I B Tauris UK) St Martin.

War & the Christian Conscience: How Shall Modern War Be Conducted Justly? Paul Ramsey. LC 61-10666. xxiv, 331p. 1961. reprint ed. pap. text ed. 16.95 (*0-8223-0361-2*) Duke.

War & the Christian Conscience: How Shall Modern War be Conducted Justly? Paul Ramsey. LC 61-10666. 353p. reprint ed. pap. 100.70 (*0-317-26099-5*, 2023766) Bks Demand.

War & the City. Gregory J. Ashworth. (Illus.). 240p. (C). (gr. 13). 1991. text ed. 49.95 (*0-415-05347-1*, A6146) Routledge.

War & the Environment. Elizabeth Sirimarco. LC 93-1194. (Environment Alert! Ser.). (J). 1993. lib. bdg. 18.60 (*0-8368-1014-7*) Gareth Stevens Inc.

War & the Gospel. Jean Lasserre. Tr. by O. Coburn. 248p. 1962. 10.00 (*0-227-67635-1*) Attic Pr.

War & the Gospel. Jean Lasserre. LC 62-52667. 246p. reprint ed. pap. 70.20 (*0-7837-5106-0*, 2044805) Bks Demand.

***War & the Illiberal Conscience.** Christopher Coker. 4p. 1997. text ed. 35.00 (*0-8133-3369-5*) Westview.

War & the Liberal Conscience. Michael Howard. (C). 1978. 30.00 (*0-8135-0866-5*) Rutgers U Pr.

War & the Liberal Conscience. Michael Howard. 160p. 1987. pap. text ed. 15.00 (*0-8135-1197-6*) Rutgers U Pr.

War & the Media: Propaganda & Persuasion in the Gulf War. Philip M. Taylor. 288p. 1992. text ed. 19.95 (*0-7190-3754-9*, Pub. by Manchester Univ Pr UK) St Martin.

***War & the Pity of War.** Philip. 1997. write for info. (*0-395-84982-9*) Ticknor & Fields.

War & the Poet. Ed. by Richard Eberhart & Selden Rodman. LC 73-19574. 240p. 1974. reprint ed. text ed. 48.50 (*0-8371-7287-X*, EBWP, Greenwood Pr) Greenwood.

***War & the Red Cross.** Berry. LC 96-48926. 1997. text ed. 35.00 (*0-312-16517-X*) St Martin.

War & the Rise of the State: The Military Foundations of Modern Politics. Bruce Porter. 350p. 1994. 27.95 (*0-02-925095-1*, Free Press) Free Pr.

***War & the Royal Houses of Europe in the Twentieth Century.** Anthony Devere-Summers. (Illus.). 176p. 1997. 24.95 (*1-85409-310-X*, Pub. by Arms & Armour UK) Sterling.

War & the Russian Government. Paul P. Gronsky & Nicholas J. Astrov. 45.00 (*0-86527-207-7*) Fertig.

War & the Soviet Union. Herbert S. Dinerstein. LC 75-45031. 268p. 1976. reprint ed. text ed. 59.75 (*0-8371-8658-7*, DIWS, Greenwood Pr) Greenwood.

War & Trade in Northern Seas: Anglo-Scandinavian Economic Relations in the Mid-Eighteenth Century. Heinz S. Kent. LC 72-75304. (Cambridge Studies in Economic History). 256p. reprint ed. pap. 73.00 (*0-317-28402-9*, 2022457) Bks Demand.

War & Wartime Changes: The Transformation of Arkansas, 1940-1945. C. Calvin Smith. LC 85-16474. 176p. 1986. 20.00 (*0-938626-56-6*) U of Ark Pr.

War & Welfare: Social Engineering in America, 1890-1925. John F. McClymer. LC 79-54060. (Contributions in American History Ser.: No. 84). xvi, 248p. 1980. text ed. 55.00 (*0-313-21129-9*, MWW/, Greenwood Pr) Greenwood.

War & Western Civilization, 1832-1932. John F. Fuller. LC 72-102238. (Select Bibliographies Reprint Ser.). 1977. 26.95 (*0-8369-5123-9*) Ayer.

War & Woman. J. T. Elias. 578p. 24.95 (*1-878648-01-2*) Flying Eightball Prodns.

War & Women's Employment: The Experience of the U. K. & the U. S. A. 1946. Bd. with Wartime Labour Conditions & Reconstruction Planning in India. (I.L.O. Studies & Reports New Ser.: Nos. 1 & 2). 1974. reprint ed. 60.00 (*0-8115-3328-X*) Periodicals Srv.

***War & Words: The Northern Ireland Media Reader.** Ed. by Bill Rolston & David Miller. 300p. (Orig.). 1996. pap. 25.95 (*1-900960-00-1*, Pub. by Beyond the Pale IE) Irish Bks Media.

War As a Political Weapon in the Nuclear Age. Nirmal Jindal. 1987. 42.00 (*81-7076-011-9*, Pub. by Intellectual II) S Asia.

War As a Social Institution: The Historian's Perspective. American Historical Association Staff. Ed. by Jessie D. Clarkson & Thomas C. Cochran. LC 73-38408. reprint ed. 22.50 (*0-404-01575-1*) AMS Pr.

***War As an Instrument of Policy: Past, Present, & Future.** David W. Nowlin & Ronald J. Stupak. LC 97-25301. 1997. write for info. (*0-7618-0843-4*); pap. write for info. (*0-7618-0844-2*) U Pr of Amer.

War As I Knew It. George S. Patton. (War Ser.). 416p. 1983. mass mkt. 6.99 (*0-553-25991-1*) Bantam.

War As I Knew It: General George S. Patton, Jr. George S. Patton. (Illus.). 448p. 1995. pap. 16.95 (*0-395-73529-7*) HM.

War at Bent's Fort: 1832-1869. John Legg. 1994. mass mkt. 4.99 (*0-312-95053-5*) St Martin.

***War at Every Man's Door: The Struggle for East Tennessee, 1860-1869.** Noel C. Fisher. LC 97-9886. (Civil War America Ser.). 288p. (C). (gr. 13). 1997. 34. 95 (*0-8078-2367-8*) U of NC Pr.

War at Home: Covert Action Against U. S. Activists & What We Can Do about It. Brian Glick. LC 88-30840. (Illus.). 72p. (Orig.). 1989. pap. 5.00 (*0-89608-349-7*) South End Pr.

War at Nugget Creek. large type ed. Wayne C. Lee. (Sagebrush Large Print Westerns Ser.). 179p. 1995. lib. bdg. 17.95 (*1-57490-004-8*) T T Beeler.

War at Sea: A Naval History of World War II. Nathan Miller. 576p. 1995. 32.50 (*0-684-80380-1*) S&S Trade.

***War at Sea: A Naval History of World War II.** Nathan Miller. (Illus.). 608p. 1997. reprint ed. pap. 17.95 (*0-19-511038-2*) OUP.

War at Sea: The Imperial War Museum Book. Julian Thompson. (Illus.). 288p. 1996. 24.95 (*0-7603-0263-4*) Motorbooks Intl.

***War at Sea & the Air.** (World War One Ser.). Date not set. pap. text ed. write for info. (*0-582-22098-X*, Pub. by Longman UK) Longman.

War at Sea 1939-1945. Jurgen Rohwer. (Illus.). 250p. 1996. 45.00 (*1-55750-915-8*) Naval Inst Pr.

War at Sea, 1939-1945, Vol. III, Pt. 2. Stephen W. Roskill. (Illus.). 632p. 1994. reprint ed. 49.95 (*0-89839-210-1*) Battery Pr.

War at Sea, 1939-45. Edward Smithies & Colin J. Bruce. (Illus.). 206p. 1992. 39.50 (*0-09-471590-4*, Pub. by Constable Pubs UK) Trans-Atl Phila.

War at Sixteen: Autobiography, Vol. 2. Julian Green. Tr. by Euan Cameron from FRE. LC 93-656. 224p. (YA). 1993. 24.95 (*0-7145-2969-9*) M Boyars Pubs.

War at Troy: What Homer Didn't Tell. Smyrnaeus Quintus. Tr. & Intro. by Frederick M. Combellack. LC 67-24612. 288p. reprint ed. pap. 82.10 (*0-7837-1988-4*, 2042262) Bks Demand.

War Babies. Frederick Busch. LC 89-35209. 128p. 1989. 15.95 (*0-8112-1103-7*) New Directions.

***War Baby.** Penny McDaniel-Hayko. LC 96-94604. v, 124p. (Orig.). 1996. pap. 9.95 (*0-9653811-3-7*) Hasor-Plenny.

War Baby Express. Roseann Lloyd. 108p. (Orig.). 1996. pap. 10.95 (*0-930100-68-9*) Holy Cow.

War, Battering, & Other Sports: The Gulf Between American Men & Women. James McBride. LC 94-39404. (Religion/Society - Society/Religion Ser.). (Illus.). 240p. (C). 1995. pap. 49.95 (*0-391-03882-6*); text ed. 17.50 (*0-391-03881-8*) Humanities.

***War Before Civilization.** Lawrence H. Keeley. (Illus.). 272p. 1997. reprint ed. pap. 13.95 (*0-19-511912-6*) OUP.

War Before Civilization: The Myth of the Peaceful Savage. Lawrence H. Keeley. (Illus.). 272p. 1996. 25.00 (*0-19-509112-4*) OUP.

War Behind the Barbed Wire: The Daily Bulletin of Oflag 64. J. Frank Diggs. (Illus.). 192p. 1994. 24.95 (*0-918339-27-8*) Vandamere.

War Behind the Lines. Wallace B. Black & Jean F. Blashfield. LC 91-40866. (World War II 50th Anniversary Ser.). (Illus.). 48p. (J). (gr. 5-6). 1992. lib. bdg. 12.95 (*0-89686-564-9*, Crstwood Hse) Silver Burdett Pr.

War Behind the War, 1914-1918: A History of the Political & Civilian Fronts. Frank P. Chambers. LC 72-4267. (World Affairs Ser.: National & International Viewpoints). (Illus.). 638p. 1972. reprint ed. 39.95 (*0-405-04564-6*) Ayer.

War Beneath the Sea: Submarine Conflict During World War II. Peter Padfield. LC 95-46299. 1996. text ed. 30. 00 (*0-471-14624-2*) Wiley.

War Between Brothers. deluxe ed. Time-Life Books Editors. Ed. by Sarah Brash. LC 96-20773. (American Story Ser.). 192p. 1996. write for info. (*0-7835-6257-8*) Time-Life.

War Between Brothers see American Story

War Between Peru & Chile 1879-1882. Clements R. Markham. 1976. lib. bdg. 59.95 (*0-8490-2805-1*) Gordon Pr.

War Between the Classes. Gloria D. Miklowitz. 176p. (J). (gr. 6 up). 1986. pap. 4.50 (*0-440-99406-3*, LLL BDD) BDD Bks Young Read.

War Between the Classes: A Study Guide. Barbara Reeves. Ed. by Joyce Friedland & Rikki Kessler. (Novel-Ties Ser.). (J). (gr. 7-10). 1991. pap. text ed. 15.95 (*0-88122-586-X*) Lrn Links.

War Between the Generals. David Irving. (Illus.). 480p. 1981. 17.95 (*0-685-04740-7*) St Martin.

War Between the Pitiful Teachers & the Splendid Kids. Stanley Kiesel. 208p. (YA). (gr. 7 up). 1982. mass mkt. 3.50 (*0-380-57802-6*, Flare) Avon.

War Between the Tates. Alison Lurie. 1991. pap. 8.95 (*0-380-71135-4*) Avon.

War Between the Tates. Alison Lurie. LC 73-3991. 1974. 16.95 (*0-394-46201-7*) Random.

War Between the Twins. Francine Pascal. (Sweet Valley Twins Ser.: No. 37). 144p. (J). (gr. 4-7). 1990. pap. 3.50 (*0-553-15779-5*) Bantam.

War Between the Union & the Confederacy. William C. Oates. (Illus.). 808p. 1995. 50.00 (*0-89029-017-2*) Morningside Bkshop.

War Between the United States & Mexico. limited ed. George W. Kendall. (Illus.). 100p. 1994. boxed 295.00 (*0-87611-147-9*) Tex St Hist Assn.

War Between the United States & Mexico Illustrated. George W. Kendall. LC 94-11461. (Illus.). 1994. 75.00 (*0-87611-138-X*) Tex St Hist Assn.

War Between the Vowels & the Consonants. Priscilla Turner. LC 95-37587. (Illus.). 32p. (J). (ps-3). 1996. 15. 00 (*0-374-38236-0*) FS&G.

War Beyond the Stars. Joel French & Jane French. LC 79-90267. (Illus.). 128p. 1979. pap. 4.95 (*0-89221-067-2*) New Leaf.

War Bird: The Life & Times of Elliott White Springs. Burke Davis. LC 87-5934. (Illus.). x, 293p. (C). 1987. 27.50 (*0-8078-1752-X*) U of NC Pr.

War Birds: Diary of an Unknown Aviator. John M. Grider. Ed. by Elliott W. Springs. LC 87-33538. (Military History Ser.: No. 6). (Illus.). 227p. 1988. reprint ed. 19. 95 (*0-89096-327-4*) Tex A&M Univ Pr.

War Bonds. Gregory Klink. LC 89-84018. 56p. (Orig.). 1995. pap. 9.95 (*0-9622668-0-9*) Home Place.

War Books. Jean N. Cru. 210p. 1988. pap. 12.50 (*0-916304-22-1*) SDSU Press.

War Breaker. Jim DeFelice. 400p. 1996. reprint ed. mass mkt. 6.99 (*0-8439-4043-3*, Leisure Bks) Dorchester Pub Co.

War Bride. large type ed. Heinz G. Konsalik. 432p. 1983. 25.99 (*0-7089-0906-X*) Ulverscroft.

War by Other Means: Economic Espionage in America. John Fialka. LC 96-16699. 288p. 1997. 25.00 (*0-393-04014-3*) Norton.

War by Other Means: National Liberation & Revolution. Carlyle A. Thayer. 282p. 1989. 34.95 (*0-04-820045-X*) Routledge Chapman & Hall.

War by Other Means: National Liberation & Revolution in Viet-Nam, 1954-60. Carlyle A. Thayer. 256p. 1991. pap. text ed. 24.95 (*0-04-370187-6*, Pub. by Allen Unwin AT) Paul & Co Pubs.

War by Stealth: Australians & the Allied Intelligency Bureau 1942-45. Alan Powell. 480p. 1996. 59.95 (*0-522-84691-2*, Pub. by Melbourne Univ Pr AT) Paul & Co Pubs.

War Called Peace: Khrushchev's Communism. Harry A. Overstreet & Bonaro W. Overstreet. 1961. 4.95 (*0-393-05286-9*) Norton.

War Canoe. Jamie S. Bryson. LC 89-17580. 198p. (Orig.). (J). 1990. pap. 9.95 (*0-88240-368-0*) Alaska Northwest.

War Ceremony & Peace Ceremony of the Osage Indians. Francis La Flesche. (Bureau of American Ethnology Bulletins Ser.). 280p. 1995. lib. bdg. 89.00 (*0-7812-4101-4*) Rprt Serv.

War, Chaos, & History. Roger A. Beaumont. LC 94-19595. 323p. 1994. text ed. 57.50 (*0-275-94949-4*, Praeger Pubs) Greenwood.

War Chest: An Adam Horne Adventure. Porter Hill. 224p. 1989. 17.95 (*0-8027-1049-2*) Walker & Co.

War Chief. Edgar Rice Burroughs. 17.95 (*0-8488-1258-1*) Amereon Ltd.

War Chief. Edgar Rice Burroughs. 1976. reprint ed. lib. bdg. 16.95 (*0-89966-044-4*) Buccaneer Bks.

War Chiefs: Geronimo. Bill Dugan. 320p. (Orig.). 1997. mass mkt. 5.50 (*0-06-100298-4*, Harp PBks) HarpC.

War Child. Stephen Gray. 1994. per. 14.95 (*1-897959-01-X*) LPC InBook.

War Child. Dieter Steiner & Diane Marcou. LC 95-17841. (Illus.). 376p. (Orig.). 1995. pap. 11.95 (*0-9633083-4-3*) Quixote Pubns.

War Child's Children: A Story of the Third Arkansas Cavalry. Calvin L. Collier. (Illus.). 139p. 1965. 19.95 (*0-685-06989-3*) J W Bell.

War Clouds on the Horn of Africa: The Widening Storm. rev. ed. Tom J. Farer. LC 78-75279. 1979. pap. 5.00 (*0-87003-013-2*) Carnegie Endow.

War Clouds on the Horn of Africa: The Widening Storm. 2nd rev. ed. Tom J. Farer. LC 78-75279. 1979. text ed. 10.00 (*0-87003-014-0*) Carnegie Endow.

War Comes Again: Civil War - World War II: Comparative Vistas. Ed. by Gabor Boritt. LC 94-36511. (Gettysburg Lectures). 288p. 1995. 25.00 (*0-19-508845-X*) OUP.

War Comes to Alaska: The Dutch Harbor Attack, June 3-4, 1942. Norman E. Rourke. LC 96-53353. (Illus.). 144p. (Orig.). 1997. pap. 12.95 (*1-57249-028-4*, Burd St Pr) White Mane Pub.

War Comes to Long An: Revolutionary Conflict in a Vietnamese Province. Jeffrey Race. LC 79-145793. 1972. pap. 15.00 (*0-520-02361-7*) U CA Pr.

War Comes to the Middle Kingdom. L. Krieger et al. (Illus.). 192p. (Orig.). 1991. pap. 10.95 (*0-945092-24-5*) EZ Nature.

War Comes to Willy Freeman. James L. Collier & Christopher Collier. 192p. (J). (gr. k-6). 1987. mass mkt. 3.99 (*0-440-49504-0*, YB BDD) BDD Bks Young Read.

War Comes to Willy Freeman. Duncan Searl. Ed. by J. Friedland & R. Kessler. (Novel-Ties Ser.). 1995. student ed., pap. text ed. 15.95 (*1-56982-300-6*) Lrn Links.

War Comics. Lisa Bloomfield. (Illus.). 32p. (Orig.). 1989. pap. 3.00 (*0-917061-28-4*) Top Stories.

War Commentaries of Caesar. Julius Caesar. 1976. 25.95 (*0-8488-0344-2*) Amereon Ltd.

War, Cooperation, & Conflict: The European Possessions in the Caribbean, 1939-1945. Fitzroy A. Baptiste. LC 87-8643. (Contributions in Comparative Colonial Studies: No. 23). 365p. 1988. text ed. 59.95 (*0-313-25472-9*, BWC/, Greenwood Pr) Greenwood.

War Correspondent. Michael Moynihan. 256p. 1994. 42.50 (*0-85052-413-X*, Pub. by L Cooper Bks UK) Trans-Atl Phila.

War Correspondents American Civil War. Ian F. Beckett. (War Correspondents Ser.). (Illus.). 256p. 1993. 35.99 (*0-7509-0044-X*, Pub. by Sutton Pubng UK) Bks Intl VA.

War Costs & Their Financing: A Study of the Financing of the War & the After-War Problems of Debt & Taxation. Ernest L. Bogart & Russell C. Leffingwell. LC 74-75232. (United States in World War I Ser.). xxiv, 510p. 1974. reprint ed. lib. bdg. 52.95 (*0-89198-095-4*) Ozer.

War Craft: Orcs & Humans Official Secrets & Solutions. Ed Dille. 1995. pap. text ed. 9.95 (*0-7615-0143-6*) Prima Pub.

War Cries. David W. Ross. 384p. (Orig.). 1995. mass mkt. 5.99 (*0-380-78024-0*) Avon.

War Cries: A Collection of Plays. Diane Glancy. 1996. pap. 16.95 (*0-930100-54-9*) Holy Cow.

War Cries on Horseback. Stephen Longstreet. reprint ed. lib. bdg. 26.95 (*0-89190-143-4*, Rivercity Pr) Amereon Ltd.

War, Crime & the Covenant. Geza Roheim. Ed. by V. C. Branham. LC 46-5116. (Journal of Clinical Psychopathology. Monograph Ser.: No. 1). 166p. reprint ed. pap. 47.40 (*0-317-08250-7*, 2010705) Bks Demand.

***War Crimes.** William W. Horne. 1997. 29.95 (*1-57500-009-1*) TV Bks.

War Crimes: A Report on United States War Crimes Against Iraq. Ramsey Clark et al. LC DS79.736.W37. (Illus.). 300p. (Orig.). 1992. pap. text ed. 12.95 (*0-944624-15-4*) Maisonneuve Pr.

War Crimes & Laws of War. 2nd ed. Donald A. Wells. (Social Philosophy Research Institute Bks.: No. 1). 194p. (C). 1990. pap. text ed. 26.00 (*0-8191-7932-9*); lib. bdg. 44.50 (*0-8191-7931-0*) U Pr of Amer.

War Crimes in Bosnia-Hercegovina, Vol. I. Ed. by Human Rights Watch Staff. 368p. (Orig.). 1992. pap. 20.00 (*1-56432-083-9*) Hum Rts Watch.

War Crimes in Bosnia-Hercegovina, Vol. II. Ed. by Human Rights Watch Staff. 440p. (Orig.). 1993. pap. 20.00 (*1-56432-097-9*) Hum Rts Watch.

War Crimes in International Law. Ed. by Yoram Dinstein & Mala Tabory. LC 96-8151. 1996. text ed. 177.00 (*90-411-0237-X*, Pub. by M Nijhoff NE) Kluwer Ac.

War Crimes in the Balkans: Medicine under Siege in the Former Yugoslavia 1991-1995. Physicians for Human Rights Staff. 100p. 1996. pap. text ed. 10.00 (*1-879707-20-9*) Phy Human Rights.

War Crimes in Vietnam. Bertrand R. Russell. LC 67-23969. 178p. reprint ed. pap. 50.80 (*0-317-08492-5*, 2001708) Bks Demand.

War Crimes, War Criminals, & War Crimes Trials: An Annotated Bibliography & Source Book. Ed. by Karen Winnovich. LC 86-9985. (Bibliographies & Indexes in World History Ser.: No. 4). 568p. 1986. text ed. 75.00 (*0-313-24412-X*, TUW/) Greenwood.

War Criminal: The Life & Death of Hirota Koki. Saburo Shiroyama. Tr. by John Bester from JPN. LC 76-9361. 1980. pap. 6.95 (*0-87011-368-2*) Kodansha.

War Criminals in Canada. James E. McKenzie. (Illus.). 225p. (Orig.). 1995. pap. 18.95 (*1-55059-109-6*, Pub. by Detselig CN) Temeron Bks.

War Culture: Social Change & Changing Experience in World War II. Ed. by Kirkham & Thoms. (C). 1996. pap. 19.50 (*0-85315-824-X*, Pub. by Lawrence & Wishart UK) NYU Pr.

War, Culture & Economy in Java: 1677-1726. Merle Ricklefs. 224p. 1993. pap. text ed. 24.95 (*1-86373-380-9*, Pub. by Allen Unwin AT) Paul & Co Pubs.

War, Culture, & Society in Renaissance Venice: Essays in Honour of John Hale. Ed. by David S. Chambers et al. LC 93-27448. 276p. 1993. boxed 65.00 (*1-85285-090-6*) Hambledon Press.

War, Culture, & the Media: Representations of the Military in 20th Century Britain. Ed. by Ian Stewart & Susan L. Carruthers. 208p. 1996. 39.50 (*0-8386-3702-7*) Fairleigh Dickinson.

War Cycles - Peace Cycles: The Necessity for War in Modern Finance. Richard K. Hoskins. 250p. 1995. pap. 10.00 (*1-881867-26-9*) Virginia Pub.

***War Dance.** Tim Sebastian. 320p. 1997. pap. 8.95 (*0-7528-0170-8*, Pub. by Orion Bks UK) Trafalgar.

***War Dance.** Tim Sebastian. 320p. 1997. 26.00 (*1-85797-621-5*, Pub. by Orion Bks UK) Trafalgar.

War Dance. Eric G. Howe. LC 70-153642. (Studies in Philosophy: No. 40). 1971. reprint ed. lib. bdg. 75.00 (*0-8383-1243-8*) M S G Haskell Hse.

War Dance: Plains Indian Musical Performance. William K. Powers. LC 90-32421. (Illus.). 199p. 1990. 29.95 (*0-8165-1170-5*) U of Ariz Pr.

War Dance: Plains Indian Musical Performance. William K. Powers. LC 90-32421. (Illus.). 199p. 1993. reprint ed. pap. 12.95 (*0-8165-1365-1*) U of Ariz Pr.

***War Declared...the Five-Pronged Attack Against Cancer: Complete 5-Part Cancer Fighting Program with the 100% All Natural Nutritional Supplement Green Tea-Plus.** S. J. Farley. (Illus.). 104p. (Orig.). 1996. pap. text ed. 29.95 (*1-889623-02-4*) Alternat Med Pub.

War Department, 1861. A. Howard Meneely. LC 72-127434. (Columbia University. Studies in the Social Sciences: No. 300). 1970. reprint ed. 27.50 (*0-404-51300-X*) AMS Pr.

War, Depression, Prohibition & Racism: The Response of the Sunday School to an Era of Crisis, 1933-1941. Kent L. Johnson. 280p. (C). 1991. lib. bdg. 46.50 (*0-8191-8357-1*) U Pr of Amer.

War Despatches: Indo-Pak Conflict 1965. Harbakhsh Singh. (C). 1991. 32.00 (*81-7062-117-8*, Pub. by Lancer Intl II) S Asia.

War Despatches of Kenneth Slessor Official Australian Correspondent, 1940-1944. Kenneth Slessor. LC 87-10457. (Illus.). 493p. 1988. text ed. 49.95 (*0-7022-2076-0*, Pub. by Univ Queensland Pr AT) Intl Spec Bk.

***War Diaries: Politics & War in the Mediterranean, January 1943 - May 1945.** Harold Macmillan. (Illus.). 804p. 1984. 67.50 (*0-333-37198-4*, Pub. by Macmlln UK) Trans-Atl Phila.

War Diaries: The 1861 Kanawha Valley Campaigns. David L. Phillips. (Illus.). 479p. (C). 1990. 40.00 (*0-9628218-0-2*) Gauley Mount Pr.

War Diaries of Kenneth Slessor: Official Australian Correspondent 1940-1944. Ed. by Clement Semmler. 1986. 49.95 (*0-7022-1879-0*, Pub. by Univ Queensland Pr AT) Intl Spec Bk.

War Diaries of Neville Duke: DSO, OBE, DFC (Two Bars), AFC Czech Military Cross 1941-1944. Ed. by Norman Franks. (Illus.). 240p. 1995. 29.95 (*1-898697-16-7*, Pub. by Grub St Pubns UK) Seven Hills Bk.

War Diaries of U-764: Fact or Fiction? Heinz F. Guske. (Illus.). 192p. (C). 1992. pap. text ed. 9.95 (*0-939631-43-1*) Thomas Publications.

War Diaries of Vladimir Dedijer: From April 8, 1941 to November 7, 1944, 3 vols., 1. Vladimir Dedijer. (Illus.). 550p. 1989. 65.00 (*0-472-10091-2*) U of Mich Pr.

War Diaries of Vladimir Dedijer: From April 8, 1941 to November 7, 1944, 3 vols., 2. Vladimir Dedijer. (Illus.). 550p. 1989. 65.00 (*0-472-10109-9*) U of Mich Pr.

War Diaries of Vladimir Dedijer: From April 8, 1941 to November 7, 1944, 3 vols., 3. Vladimir Dedijer. (Illus.). 550p. 1989. 65.00 (*0-472-10110-2*) U of Mich Pr.

War Diaries of Vladimir Dedijer: From April 8, 1941 to November 7, 1944, 3 vols., Set. Vladimir Dedijer. (Illus.). 550p. 1989. 175.00 (*0-472-10123-4*) U of Mich Pr.

War Diary & Letters of Stephen Minot Weld, 1861-1865. Stephen M. Weld, Jr. (American Biography Ser.). 433p. 1991. reprint ed. lib. bdg. 89.00 (*0-7812-8409-0*) Rprt Serv.

War Diary of a Combat Artist: Captain Harry Everett Townsend. Ed. by Alfred E. Cornebise. (Illus.). 344p. 1991. 39.95 (*0-87081-231-9*) Univ Pr Colo.

War Diary of Hauptmann Helmut Lipfert: JG 52 on the Russian Front 1943-1945. Helmut Lipfert & Werner Girbig. Tr. by David Johnston. LC 92-61775. (Illus.). 224p. 1993. 29.95 (*0-88740-446-4*) Schiffer.

War Diary of the Chief of the General Staff, Janos Voros: From April 17 to October 15, 1944. Hungarian Historical Research Society Staff. LC 77-95242. Orig. Title: Vitez Voros Janos M. kir Vezerezredes Vezerkari Fonok Naploja. 297p. 1979. pap. 14.95 (*0-935484-03-5*) Universe Pub Co.

War Diary of the Emperor Frederick III, 1870-1871. Frederick III. Tr. by A. R. Allinson from GER. viii, 356p. 1988. reprint ed. lib. bdg. 40.00 (*0-86527-376-6*) Fertig.

War Diary of the Emperor Frederick the Third, 1870-1871. Ed. by A. R. Allinson. LC 77-114529. (Illus.). 355p. 1971. reprint ed. text ed. 45.00 (*0-8371-4824-3*, FRWD, Greenwood Pr) Greenwood.

War Diary, 1938-1945. 1995. (*0-7858-0280-0*) Bk Sales Inc.

War, Diplomacy, & Development: The United States & Mexico 1938-1954. Stephen R. Niblo. Ed. by William H. Beezley & Judith Ewell. (Latin American Silhouettes Ser.). (Illus.). 320p. 1995. 50.00 (*0-8420-2550-2*) Scholarly Res Inc.

***War Dog: A Novel.** Martin Booth. LC 96-52570. (J). 1997. 15.00 (*0-689-81380-5*, Aladdin Paperbacks) S&S Childrens.

***War Dog Heroes.** Jeanette Sanderson. (J). 1997. mass mkt. 3.50 (*0-590-50954-3*) Scholastic Inc.

War Dogs: Canines in Combat. Michael Lemish. (Illus.). 304p. 1996. 22.95 (*1-57488-017-9*) Brasseys Inc.

War Drums. John Vornholt. Ed. by Dave Stern. (Star Trek: The Next Generation Ser.: No. 23). 288p. (Orig.). 1992. mass mkt. 4.99 (*0-671-79236-9*) PB.

An Asterisk (*) at the beginning of an entry indicates that the title is appearing in BIP for the first time.

War Drums & Wagon Wheels: The Story of Russell, Majors, & Waddell. Mary Lee Settle. LC 65-18414. 278p. reprint ed. pap. 79.30 (*0-7837-4666-0*, 2044393) Bks Demand.

War Drums at Eden Prairie. Gladys T. Nelson. (Illus.). (J). (gr. 5-9). 1977. 5.95 (*0-87839-023-5*) North Star.

War Eagle: A Life of General Eugene A. Carr. James T. King. LC 63-14694. (Illus.). 350p. reprint ed. pap. 99.80 (*0-8357-4581-3*, 2037509) Bks Demand.

War Eagle: The Story of Auburn Football. rev. ed. Clyde Bolton. (College Sports Bks.). (Illus.). 358p. 1987. pap. 11.95 (*0-87397-302-X*, Strode Pubs) Circle Bk Service.

War Eagle Wholegrain & Honey Cookbook. Zoe Caywood. 1991. write for info. (*0-9616521-1-X*) War Eagle Cks.

War Eagle Wholegrain Cookbook II. Zoe Caywood. 1994. write for info. (*0-614-06219-5*) War Eagle Cks.

War Eagles. Frank Burleson. (Apache Wars Saga). 352p. (Orig.). 1995. mass mkt., pap. 4.50 (*0-451-18090-9*) NAL-Dutton.

War Eagles. James S. Childers. Ed. by James A. Gray. 369p. reprint ed. 24.00 (*0-941624-71-4*) Eagle Publ.

War, Economy & Society: 1939-1945. Alan S. Milward. LC 76-40823. (History of the World Economy in the Twentieth Century Ser.: Vol. 5). 1977. pap. 15.00 (*0-520-03942-4*) U CA Pr.

War Eighteen Twelve. George May. (Illus.). 43p. (Orig.). 1962. pap. 3.00 (*0-911872-28-0*) Mackinac St Hist Pks.

War Ethics in Islam. Hassan Hathout. 60p. 1991. pap. text ed. 3.00 (*1-881504-01-8*) Minaret Pubns.

War Everyone Lost - & Won: America's Intervention in Viet Nam's Twin Struggles. rev. ed. Timothy J. Lomperis. LC 92-36594. 203p. 1992. 20.95 (*0-87187-825-9*) Congr Quarterly.

War, Famine & Our Food Supply. Robert B. Marston. LC 75-26308. (World Food Supply Ser.). (Illus.). 1976. reprint ed. 23.95 (*0-405-07787-4*) Ayer.

War Fever. J. G. Ballard. 1991. 18.95 (*0-374-28645-0*) FS&G.

War Finance, 2 vols. Ed. by Larry Neal. (International Library of Macroeconomic & Financial History: Vol. 12). 1880p. 1994. 550.00 (*1-85278-663-9*) E Elgar.

War Finance, Reconstruction, Hyperinflation, & Stabilization in Hungary, 1938-48. Pierre L. Siklos. LC 90-48958. 304p. 1991. text ed. 55.00 (*0-312-05708-3*) St Martin.

War Flying in France. George A. Vaughn, Jr. (Illus.). 160p. (Orig.). 1980. pap. 33.95 (*0-89126-082-X*) MA-AH Pub.

War for America Vol. 1: The Fight for Independence, 1775-1783. Jeremy Black. 1994. text ed. 19.95 (*0-312-12346-9*) St Martin.

War for America, 1775-1783. Piers Mackesy. LC 92-37789. xxx, 569p. (C). 1993. pap. 21.50 (*0-8032-8192-7*, Bison Books) U of Nebr Pr.

***War for America's Natural Resources.** William R. Nester. LC 96-35139. 1997. text ed. 59.95 (*0-312-16589-7*); text ed. 18.95 (*0-312-16591-9*) St Martin.

War for Brooklyn's Independence. Jack Delman. 286p. (Orig.). 1996. mass mkt. 4.99 (*1-55197-079-1*, Pub. by Comnwlth Pub CN) Partners Pubs Grp.

***War for Heart & Soul of a Highland Maya Town.** Robert S. Carlsen. LC 96-35613. (Illus.). 224p. 1997. 35.00 (*0-292-71193-X*); pap. 14.95 (*0-292-71194-8*) U of Tex Pr.

War for Independence: A Military History. Howard H. Peckham. LC 58-5685. (Chicago History of American Civilization Ser.). 235p. 1958. pap. text ed. 15.95 (*0-226-65316-1*) U Ch Pr.

War for Independence: The Story of the American Revolution. Albert Marrin. LC 87-13711. (Illus.). 288p. (YA). (gr. 5 up). 1988. lib. bdg. 19.00 (*0-689-31390-X*, Atheneum Bks Young) S&S Childrens.

War for Lebanon: 1970-1985. rev. ed. Itamar Rabinovich. LC 83-45935. 243p. (C). 1984. 39.95 (*0-8014-1870-4*); pap. 14.95 (*0-8014-9313-7*) Cornell U Pr.

War for Love. Bill Lonecke. 280p. (Orig.). 1997. pap. 10.95 (*1-57532-002-9*) Press-Tige Pub.

War for Oil? Energy Issues & the Gulf War of 1991. John Roberts. 20p. 1991. pap. 10.00 (*0-918714-28-1*) Intl Res Ctr Energy.

War for South Viet Nam: Nineteen Fifty-Four to Nineteen Seventy-Five. Anthony J. Joes. LC 88-25184. 192p. 1989. text ed. 55.00 (*0-275-93162-5*, C3162, Praeger Pubs) Greenwood.

War for South Viet Nam: Nineteen Fifty-Four to Nineteen Seventy-Five. Anthony J. Joes. LC 88-25184. 192p. 1990. pap. text ed. 14.95 (*0-275-93892-1*, B3892, Praeger Pubs) Greenwood.

***War for the Ark.** Rick Gauger. 1998. mass mkt. write for info. (*0-345-34932-6*, Del Rey) Ballantine.

War for the German Mind: Re-Educating Hitler's Soldiers. Arthur L. Smith, Jr. LC 95-20955. 224p. 1996. 39.95 (*1-57181-892-8*) Berghahn Bks.

War for the Oaks. Emma Bull. 320p. 1996. mass mkt. 5.99 (*0-614-96135-1*) Ace Bks.

War for the Plains. (American Indians Ser.). (Illus.). 176-184p. 1994. 19.95 (*0-8094-9445-0*); lib. bdg. write for info. (*0-8094-9446-9*) Time-Life.

War for What. Francis W. Springer. 224p. (Orig.). 1990. pap. 5.95 (*0-931709-02-4*) B Coats.

***War from My Window: A Child's View of the Second World War.** Ann Stalcup. (Illus.). 100p. (J). (gr. 4-8). 1998. lib. bdg. write for info. (*0-208-02482-4*, Linnet Bks) Shoe String.

***War from My Window: A Child's View of the Second World War.** Ann Stalcup. (Illus.). 100p. (J). (gr. 4-8). 1998. pap. text ed. write for info. (*0-208-02491-3*, Linnet Bks) Shoe String.

War from the Top: German & British Military Decision Making During World War II. Alan F. Wilt. LC 89-45566. (Illus.). 400p. 1990. 14.95 (*0-253-36455-8*) Ind U Pr.

War from Within. Sophie Goetzel-Leviathan. Ed. by Rebecca Fromer. LC 86-62879. 89p. 1987. pap. 7.95 (*0-943376-29-7*) Magnes Mus.

***War from Within: German Women in the First World War.** Ute Daniel. Ed. by Jay Winter. Tr. by Margaret Ries from GER. (Legacy of the Great War Ser.). 256p. 1997. 49.95 (*0-85496-892-X*); pap. 19.95 (*1-85973-147-3*) Berg Pubs.

War Gallery of the Winter Palace: Voennaia Galereia Zimnego Dvortsa. V. M. Glinka & A. V. Pomarnatsii. 240p. 1981. 66.00 (*0-317-57480-9*) St Mut.

War Game. Michael Foreman. (Illus.). 72p. (J). (gr. 3-7). 1994. 16.95 (*1-55970-242-7*) Arcade Pub Inc.

War Game. large type ed. Anthony Price. (Adventure Suspense Ser.). 512p. 1988. 25.99 (*0-7089-1870-0*) Ulverscroft.

War Game: A Critique of Military Problem Solving. Garry D. Brewer & Martin Shubik. (Illus.). 404p. (C). 1979. 39.95 (*0-674-94600-6*) HUP.

War God. Patrick F. Rogers. 1990. mass mkt. 4.50 (*1-55817-436-2*, Pinncle Kensgtn) Kensgtn Pub Corp.

War Gods. Brady Computer Books Staff. 1996. 9.99 (*1-56686-541-7*) Brady Pub.

War Gods Official Arcade. PCS Staff. 128p. 1996. per., pap. 9.99 (*0-7615-0767-1*) Prima Pub.

***War Gods Official Game Secrets.** 128p. 1997. per. 12.99 (*0-7615-1080-X*) Prima Pub.

War Government, Federal & State, 1861-65. William B. Weeden. LC 75-87685. (Law, Politics & History Ser.). 1972. reprint ed. lib. bdg. 49.50 (*0-306-71707-7*) Da Capo.

War Hangover. Gregory W. Bitz. LC 87-71864. (Illus.). 272p. (Orig.). 1988. pap. 11.95 (*0-944357-67-9*) Angel Wing Pr.

War Heaven. Mack Maloney. 432p. 1991. mass mkt. 4.95 (*0-8217-3414-8*, Zebra Kensgtn) Kensgtn Pub Corp.

War Heroes: Stories of Congressional Medal of Honor Recipients. Kent DeLong. LC 92-39283. 224p. 1993. text ed. 21.95 (*0-275-94309-7*, C4309, Praeger Pubs) Greenwood.

War Hero's Wife. Martha L. Thomas. 192p. 1988. 17.95 (*0-8027-1042-5*) Walker & Co.

War History of American Railroads. Walker D. Hines. LC 74-75240. (United States in World War I Ser.). xviii, 327p. 1974. reprint ed. lib. bdg. 37.95 (*0-89198-104-7*) Ozer.

War, Holocaust & Stalinism: A Documented History of the Jewish Anti-Fascist Committee in the USSR. Shimon Redlich. (History of Russia Ser: Vol. 1). 500p. 1995. text ed. 74.00 (*3-7186-5739-2*, Harwood Acad Pubs) Gordon & Breach.

War Hound & the World's Pain: A Fable. Michael Moorcock. LC 81-9030. 239p. 1981. 25.00 (*0-671-43708-9*) Ultramarine Pub.

War in Afghanistan. Mark Urban. LC 87-14375. 240p. 1988. text ed. 49.95 (*0-312-01205-5*) St Martin.

War in Algeria: Background for Crisis. Tanya S. Matthews. LC 62-10305. 165p. reprint ed. pap. 47.10 (*0-7837-0457-7*, 2040780) Bks Demand.

War in America to Seventeen Seventy-Five: Before Yankee Doodle. John M. Dederer. (American Social Experience Ser.: No. 16). 328p. (C). 1990. text ed. 40.00 (*0-8147-1828-0*) NYU Pr.

War in American Culture: Society & Consciousness During World War II. Lewis Erenberg & Susan E. Hirsch. 360p. 1996. pap. text ed. 17.95 (*0-226-21512-1*) U Ch Pr.

War in American Culture: Society & Consciousness During World War II. Ed. by Lewis A. Erenberg & Susan E. Hirsch. 360p. 1996. lib. bdg. 50.00 (*0-226-21511-3*) U Ch Pr.

War in an Empty House. Don Domanski. 70p. (Orig.). 1982. pap. 6.95 (*0-88784-094-9*, Pub. by Hse of Anansi Pr CN) Genl Dist Srvs.

War in Ancient India. Dikshitar Ramachandra. (C). 1987. reprint ed. 26.00 (*81-208-0382-5*, Pub. by Motilal Banarsidass II) S Asia.

War in Aquarius: Memoir of an American Infantryman in Action along the Cambodian Border During the Vietnam War. Dennis Kitchin. LC 93-43782. 216p. 1994. pap. 22.95 (*0-89950-949-5*) McFarland & Co.

War in Cambodia 1970-75. K. Conboy & K. Bowra. (Men-at-Arms Ser.: No. 209). (Illus.). 48p. pap. 11.95 (*0-85045-851-X*, 9142, Pub. by Osprey UK) Stackpole.

War in Central Asia: Four Hundred Years in the History of a Muslim Shrine, 1480-1889. R. D. McChesney. 347p. 1991. text ed. 67.50 (*0-691-05584-X*) Princeton U Pr.

War in China: America's Role in the Far East. Varian Fry. LC 76-111741. (American Imperialism: Viewpoints of United States Foreign Policy, 1898-1941 Ser.). 1970. reprint ed. 13.95 (*0-405-02021-X*) Ayer.

War in Cuba, Being a Full Account of Her Great Struggle for Freedoms. Gonzalo De Quesada. LC 79-111731. (American Imperialism: Viewpoints of United States Foreign Policy, 1898-1941 Ser.). 1970. reprint ed. 41.95 (*0-405-02047-3*) Ayer.

War in Europe: Battles in the Balkans, Vol. 4. Edwin P. Hoyt. 175p. (Orig.). 1992. mass mkt. 4.99 (*0-380-76483-0*) Avon.

War in Europe: From the Kasserine Pass to Berlin, 1941-1945. John P. Langellier. LC 95-15139. (GI: The Illustrated History of the American Soldier, His Uniform, & His Equipment Ser.: Vol. 1). (Illus.). 80p. 1995. pap. 12.95 (*1-85367-220-3*, Pub. by Greenhill Bks UK) Stackpole.

War in Europe: North African Struggle, Vol. 5. Edwin P. Hoyt. 160p. (Orig.). 1993. mass mkt. 4.99 (*0-380-76673-6*) Avon.

War in Europe: Nuclear & Conventional Perspectives. Hylke Tromp. 366p. 1989. text ed. 57.95 (*0-566-07022-7*, Pub. by Dartmth Pub UK) Ashgate Pub Co.

War in Europe, Vol. 1: Blitzkrieg. Edwin P. Hoyt. 256p. (Orig.). 1991. mass mkt. 4.99 (*0-380-76155-6*) Avon.

War in Europe, Vol. 2: The Fall of France. Edwin P. Hoyt. 224p. (Orig.). 1991. mass mkt. 4.99 (*0-380-76156-4*) Avon.

War in Europe, Vol. 3: The Battle of Britain. Edwin P. Hoyt. 1992. mass mkt. 4.50 (*0-380-76482-2*) Avon.

War in European History. Michael C. Howard. 176p. 1976. pap. text ed. 15.95 (*0-19-289095-6*) OUP.

***War in Former Yugoslavia.** Nathaniel Harris. LC 97-3249. (New Perspectives Ser.). (J). 1998. write for info. (*0-8172-5014-X*) Raintree Steck-V.

***War in France & Flanders.** L. F. Ellis. (Official History Ser.: Vol. 12). (Illus.). 564p. 1996. reprint ed. 54.95 (*0-89839-253-5*) Battery Pr.

War in Georgia. Jerrie Oughton. LC 96-22029. (J). 1997. 14.95 (*0-395-81568-1*) HM.

War in Goethe's Writings: Representation & Assessment. Edward T. Larkin. LC 92-10192. 268p. 1992. lib. bdg. 69.95 (*0-7734-9540-1*) E Mellen.

***War in Heaven.** Kent Nussey. 192p. 1997. pap. 18.99 (*1-895837-42-1*, Pub. by Insomniac Pr CN) Login Pubs Consort.

War in Heaven! The Case for a Solar System War. C. L. Turnage. (Illus.). 208p. 1996. spiral bd., pap. 20.00 (*0-9645885-2-8*, FD33) Flying Disk Pubns.

War in Heaven see Novels

War in High Himalaya: The Indian Army in Crisis, 1962. D. K. Palit. (C). 1991. 30.00 (*81-7062-138-0*, Pub. by Lancer International II) S Asia.

War in Indo-China, 1945-1954. Jaques Dalloz. 288p. (C). 1990. lib. bdg. 68.00 (*0-389-20897-3*) B&N Imports.

War in Italy, 1943-1945: A Brutal Story. Richard Lamb. LC 95-41048. (Illus.). 363p. 1996. reprint ed. pap. 14.95 (*0-306-80688-6*) Da Capo.

War in Kansas. G. Douglas Brewerton. LC 74-164381. (Black Heritage Library Collection). reprint ed. 31.95 (*0-8369-8840-X*) Ayer.

War in Kentucky: From Shiloh to Perryville. James L. McDonough. LC 94-4508. (Illus.). 408p. (C). 1994. 34.00 (*0-87049-847-9*) U of Tenn Pr.

War in Kentucky: From Shiloh to Perryville. James L. McDonough. (Illus.). 408p. 1996. pap. 16.95 (*0-87049-935-1*) U of Tenn Pr.

War in Korea. R. C. Thomas. 110p. (C). 1987. pap. 22.00 (*81-7002-006-9*, Pub. by Himalayan Bks II) St Mut.

War in Laos: 1954-1975. Kenneth Conboy. (Vietnam Studies Group). (Illus.). 64p. pap. 10.95 (*0-89747-315-9*) Squad Sig Pubns.

War in Laos 1960-75. Kenneth Conboy. (Men-at-Arms Ser.: No. 217). (Illus.). 48p. pap. 11.95 (*0-85045-938-9*, 9150, Pub. by Osprey UK) Stackpole.

War in Melville's Imagination. Joyce S. Adler. (Gotham Library). 208p. (C). 1981. text ed. 36.00 (*0-8147-0574-X*) NYU Pr.

***War in Mexico.** Anton Adams. (Illus.). 208p. 1997. 39.95 (*1-883476-08-9*) Emperors Pr.

War in Modern Societies see Warfare in the Modern World: A Short but Critical Analysis

War in Nicaragua. William Walker. LC 84-22224. 448p. 1985. reprint ed. pap. 15.95 (*0-8165-0882-8*) U of Ariz Pr.

***War in Nicaragua: The Effects of Low-Intensity Conflict on an Underdeveloped Country.** 56p. 1993. pap. 6.00 (*0-614-29345-6*) Intl Phys PONW.

War in North Africa, 1940-1943: A Selected Bibliography. Colin F. Baxter. LC 95-39434. (Bibliographies of Battles & Leaders Ser.: No. 16). 144p. 1996. text ed. 49.95 (*0-313-29120-9*, Greenwood Pr) Greenwood.

War in Slow Motion: The Economic & Social Impact of Militarism. Zelle W. Andrews. 1985. 6.95 (*0-377-00155-4*) Friendship Pr.

War in South Africa. Prussia Kriegministerium Staff. Tr. by Hubert Du Cane. LC 69-19361. 374p. 1970. reprint ed. text ed. 59.75 (*0-8371-5089-2*, PRW&, Greenwood Pr) Greenwood.

War in South Vietnam: The Years of the Offensive, 1965-1968. John Schlight. LC 88-14030. (Illus.). 419p. 1988. text ed. 31.00 (*0-16-002247-9*, S/N 008-070-00612-0) USGPO.

War in South Vietnam: The Years of the Offensive, 1965-1968. Richard Woolf. 1988. 31.00 (*0-912799-51-X*) Off Air Force.

War in Southwest Virginia 1861-65. 7th ed. Gary C. Walker. (Illus.). 215p. (C). 1985. reprint ed. Numbered & autographed. 27.95 (*0-9617896-9-7*) A & W Enterprises.

War in Tethyr. Victor Milan. (The Nobles Ser.). 320p. (Orig.). 1995. pap. 5.99 (*0-7869-0184-5*) TSR Inc.

War in the Age of Intelligent Machines. Manuel DeLanda. LC 89-27027. (Illus.). 272p. 1991. pap. 16.95 (*0-942299-75-2*) Zone Bks.

***War in the Air: True Accounts of the 20th Century's Most Dramamtic Air Battles by the Men Who Fought Them.** Stephen Coonts. 1997. pap. 14.00 (*0-671-88191-4*) PB.

War in the Air: True Accounts of the 20th Century's Most Dramatic Air Battles - by the Men Who Fought Them. Ed. & Compiled by Stephen Coonts. LC 96-33736. 1996. 24.00 (*0-671-88190-6*) PB.

***War in the Air: True Accounts of the 20th Century's Most Dramatic Air Battles - By the Men Who Fought Them.** Stephen Coonts. LC 96-49227. 1997. 24.95 (*0-7862-0974-7*) G K Hall.

***War in the Air: True Accounts of the 20th Century's Most Dramatic Air Battles - By The Men Who Fought Them.** large type ed. Stephen Coonts. LC 96-49227. 578p. 1997. 26.95 (*0-7862-0973-9*, Thorndike Lrg Prnt) Thorndike Pr.

War in the Boats: My WWII Submarine Battles. William J. Ruhe. (Brassey's WWII Commemorative Ser.). 360p. 1994. 24.95 (*0-02-881084-8*) Brasseys Inc.

War in the Boats: My WWII Submarine Battles. William J. Ruhe. (Illus.). 303p. 1996. pap. 17.95 (*1-57488-028-4*) Brasseys Inc.

War in the Culture. Bork. 1994. 24.95 (*0-02-903763-8*) S&S Trade.

War in the Desert: An R. A. F. Frontier Campaign. John B. Glubb. LC 80-1929. reprint ed. 38.00 (*0-404-18964-4*) AMS Pr.

War in the Desert: The Eighth Army at El Alamein. James Lucas. (Illus.). 288p. 1983. 16.95 (*0-8253-0153-X*) Beaufort Bks NY.

War in the Far East. Fiona Reynolds. 80p. (Orig.). (C). 1995. pap. text ed. 6.50 (*0-435-31882-9*) Heinemann.

War in the Gulf. Barbara Bardes. Date not set. pap. text ed. write for info. (*0-314-92938-X*) West Pub.

***War in the Gulf, 1990-91: The Iraq-Kuwait Conflict & Its Implications: Views from the Other Side.** Majid Khadduri & Edmund Ghareeb. 320p. 1997. text ed. 35.00 (*0-19-508384-9*) OUP.

War in the Hebrew Bible: A Study in the Ethics of Violence. Susan Niditch. 192p. 1995. pap. 13.95 (*0-19-509840-4*) OUP.

War in the Himalaya. D. K. Palit. 1992. text ed. 55.00 (*0-312-06147-1*) St Martin.

War in the Information Age: New Challenges for U. S. Security Policy. Ed. by Robert L. Pfaltzgraff & Richard H. Shultz. LC 96-22516. (Institute for Foreign Policy Analysis Special Report Ser.). 400p. 1997. 39.95 (*1-57488-118-3*) Brasseys Inc.

War in the Islands: Undercover Operations in the Aegean 1942-4. Adrian Seligman. (Illus.). 224p. 1996. 30.95 (*0-7509-1180-8*, Pub. by Sutton Pubng UK) Bks Intl VA.

***War in the Land of Egypt.** Muhammad Y. Quayd et al. LC 97-21922. 1997. pap. write for info. (*1-56656-227-9*) Interlink Pub.

***War in the Mediterranean: A WWII Pictorial History.** Center of Military History Staff. LC 97-23500. Orig. Title: The War Against Germany & Italy. (Illus.). 465p. 1997. 29.95 (*1-57488-130-2*) Brasseys Inc.

War in the Mediterranean, 1803 to 1810. Piers Mackesy. LC 81-6457. (Illus.). xviii, 430p. 1981. reprint ed. text ed. 75.00 (*0-313-22913-9*, MAWM, Greenwood Pr) Greenwood.

War in the Middle Ages. Philippe Contamine. Tr. by Michael Jones. 420p. 1992. reprint ed. pap. 25.95 (*0-631-14469-2*) Blackwell Pubs.

War in the Modern Great Power System, 1495-1975. Jack S. Levy. LC 83-10249. 232p. 1983. 25.00 (*0-8131-1497-7*) U Pr of Ky.

War in the Modern World. Theodore Ropp. LC 60-5274. 416p. reprint ed. pap. 118.60 (*0-317-08033-4*, 2010250) Bks Demand.

War in the Modern World. Theodore Ropp. LC 81-6448. xv, 400p. 1981. reprint ed. text ed. 89.50 (*0-313-22844-2*, ROWM, Greenwood Pr) Greenwood.

***War in the Narrow Seas: Coastal Forces Operations in World War II.** David Jefferson. (Illus.). 176p. 1996. 37.95 (*1-85260-499-9*, Pub. by J H Haynes & Co UK) Motorbooks Intl.

***War in the Pacific.** Jerome T. Hagen. Ed. by Helen Chapin. LC 96-77738. (Illus.). xii, 248p. (Orig.). (C). 1996. pap. 15.70 (*0-9653927-0-8*) Hawaii Pac Univ.

War in the Pacific. Bernard C. Nalty. 1991. 29.98 (*0-8317-6788-X*) Smithmark.

War in the Pacific. Clark G. Reynolds. 1990. 15.99 (*0-517-69321-6*) Random Hse Value.

War in the Pacific: A Study of Navies, Peoples, & Battle Problems. Sutherland Denlinger & Charles B. Gary. LC 77-111752. (American Imperialism: Viewpoints of United States Foreign Policy, 1898-1941 Ser.). 1977. reprint ed. 23.95 (*0-405-02011-2*) Ayer.

***War in the Pacific: From Pearl Harbor to Okinawa, 1941-1945.** Jonathan Gawne. LC 96-32216. (GU: The Illustrated History of the American Soldier). (Illus.). 80p. 1996. pap. 12.95 (*1-85367-253-X*, Pub. by Greenhill Bks UK) Stackpole.

***War in the Pacific: From Pearl Harbor to Tokyo Bay.** Harry A. Gailey. LC 94-32493. 560p. 1997. pap. 18.95 (*0-89141-616-1*) Presidio Pr.

War in the Pacific: Iwo Jima, No. 9. Ed. by Edwin P. Hoyt. 224p. (Orig.). 1992. mass mkt. 4.99 (*0-380-76582-9*) Avon.

War in the Pacific: MacArthur's Return, Vol. 8. Edwin P. Hoyt. 224p. (Orig.). 1992. mass mkt. 4.99 (*0-380-76165-3*) Avon.

War in the Pacific Vol. 2: Stirrings. Edwin P. Hoyt. 192p. (Orig.). 1990. mass mkt. 3.95 (*0-380-75793-1*) Avon.

***War in the Pacific Encyclopedia.** James F. Dunnigan & Alber A. Nofi. LC 97-15634. 1998. write for info. (*0-8160-3438-9*) Facts on File.

***War in the Pacific Encyclopedia.** James F. Dunnigan & Albert A. Nofi. LC 97-15634. 1998. write for info. (*0-8160-3437-0*); write for info. (*0-8160-3439-7*) Facts on File.

War in the Pacific, No. 5: Aleutians. Edwin P. Hoyt. 192p. (Orig.). 1992. mass mkt. 4.99 (*0-380-76316-8*) Avon.

War in the Pacific, Vol. 3: South Pacific. Edwin P. Hoyt. 232p. (Orig.). 1991. mass mkt. 4.50 (*0-380-76158-0*) Avon.

War in the Painted Buttes. Peter Field. 176p. 1988. mass mkt. 2.75 (*0-380-70423-4*) Avon.

War in the Persian Gulf. 1990. lib. bdg. 79.95 (*0-87700-908-2*) Revisionist Pr.

W

An Asterisk (*) at the beginning of an entry indicates that the title is appearing in BIP for the first time.

War in the Persian Gulf. Fred Bratman. (Headliners Ser.). (Illus.). 64p. (YA). (gr. 7 up). 1991. pap. 6.95 (*1-878841-61-0*) Millbrook Pr.

War in the Pews. Frank Martin. 180p. (Orig.). 1995. pap. 9.99 (*0-8308-1640-2*, 1640) InterVarsity.

War in the Poetry of George Seferis. Carmen Capri-Karka. LC 85-62597. 232p. 1986. 25.00 (*0-918618-28-2*); pap. 11.00 (*0-918618-27-4*) Pella Pub.

War in the Third Dimension: Essays in Contemporary Air Power. Ed. by R. A. Mason. 228p. 1986. 23.00 (*0-08-031188-1*, Pub. by Brasseys UK) Brasseys Inc.

War in the Tribal Zone: Expanding States & Indigenous Warfare. R. Brian Ferguson & Neal L. Whitehead. LC 91-39599. (Advanced Seminar Ser.). 303p. (Orig.). 1992. 35.00 (*0-933452-79-9*); pap. 15.95 (*0-933452-80-2*) Schol Am Res.

War in the Twentieth Century. Willard Waller. 1973. 250.00 (*0-87700-201-0*) Revisionist Pr.

War in the Twentieth Century: Sources in Theological Ethics. Ed. by Richard B. Miller. LC 92-2318. (Library of Theological Ethics). 320p. (Orig.). 1993. pap. 25.00 (*0-664-25323-7*) Westminster John Knox.

War in the West: Pea Ridge & Prairie Grove. William L. Shea. LC 96-24827. (Civil War Campaigns & Commanders Ser.). (Illus.). 126p. (Orig.). 1996. pap. 12.95 (*1-886661-14-6*, 61146) Ryan Place Pub.

War in the Woods: Estonia's Struggle for Survival, 1944-56. Mart Laar. Tr. by Tiina Ets from EST. (Illus.). 272p. 1992. 38.00 (*0-929590-08-2*); pap. 18.95 (*0-929590-09-0*) Compass Pr.

War in the Woods: The Day the United States Began July 9, 1755. Edward L. Tottle. LC 91-73245. (American Freedom Ser.). (Illus.). 544p. 1991. pap. 20.00 (*0-937117-06-4*) Educ Materials.

War in the Woods: The Day the United States Began July 9, 1755. Edward L. Tottle. (American Freedom Ser.). (Illus.). (YA). (gr. 10 up). 1992. text ed. 29.00 (*0-937117-05-6*) Educ Materials.

War in the World-System. Ed. by Robert K. Shaeffer. LC 88-35757. (Contributions in Economics & Economic History Ser.: No. 93). 144p. 1989. text ed. 45.00 (*0-313-25429-X*, SLV/, Greenwood Pr) Greenwood.

War in Val d'Orcia: An Italian War Diary, 1943-1944. Iris Origo. LC 82-49344. 256p. 1984. pap. 13.95 (*0-87923-476-8*) Godine.

***War in Vietnam.** David K. Wright. LC 88-14981. Date not set. write for info. (*0-516-02288-1*) Childrens.

***War in Vietnam.** David K. Wright. LC 88-11104. Date not set. pap. write for info. (*0-516-02289-X*) Childrens.

War in Vietnam: The Influence of Concepts on Policy. Michael Nacht. (CISA Working Papers: No. 26). 28p. (Orig.). 1980. pap. 15.00 (*0-86682-025-6*) Ctr Intl Relations.

War in Yugoslavia: The Breakup of a Nation. Edward R. Ricciuti. LC 92-32126. (Headliners Ser.). (Illus.). 64p. (J). (gr. 5-8). 1993. pap. 6.95 (*1-56294-750-8*); lib. bdg. 17.40 (*1-56294-375-8*) Millbrook Pr.

War in Yugoslavia: The Return of Nationalism. Tim Walker & Close Up Foundation Staff. LC 93-28942. 30p. (YA). (gr. 7-12). 1993. pap. 6.95 (*0-932765-50-5*, 1381-94) Close Up Fnd.

War in 2020. Ralph Peters. Ed. by Paul McCarthy. 624p. (Orig.). 1992. reprint ed. pap. 6.50 (*0-671-75172-7*, Pocket Star Bks) PB.

War Inconsistent with the Religion of Jesus Christ. David L. Dodge. LC 75-137540. (Peace Movement in America Ser.). xxiv, 168p. 1972. reprint ed. lib. bdg. 24.95 (*0-89198-067-9*) Ozer.

War Industries Board: Business-Government Relations during World War 1. Robert D. Cuff. LC 72-4002. 320p. 1973. 40.00 (*0-8018-1360-3*) Johns Hopkins.

War, Industry & Society: The Midlands 1939-45. David Thoms. 224p. 1989. 62.00 (*0-415-02272-X*, A3568) Routledge.

War Injuries of the Upper Extremity. Ed. by J. Engel & I. Kessler. (Progress in Surgery Ser.: Vol. 16). (Illus.). 1979. pap. 78.50 (*3-8055-2900-7*) S Karger.

War Inside My Heart. Paul Rodriguez. 1995. pap. 8.95 (*0-533-11541-8*) Vantage.

War Is a Dinosaur, & Other Songs of Hope, Love & Weltschmerz. Teddy Milne. LC 86-64053. 96p. (J). 1987. pap. 9.95 (*0-938875-04-3*) Pittenbrauch Pr.

War Is a Racket. Smedley Butler. 1973. 250.00 (*0-87700-153-7*) Revisionist Pr.

War Is Good for Babies & Other Young Children. Deborah Dwork. 300p. 1987. 45.00 (*0-422-60660-X*, 1200, Pub. by Tavistock UK) Routledge Chapman & Hall.

War Is Kind. Stephen Crane. (Works of Stephen Crane Ser.). 1990. reprint ed. lib. bdg. 79.00 (*0-7812-2434-9*) Rprt Serv.

War is the Enemy. A. J. Muste. (C). 1942. pap. 3.00 (*0-87574-015-4*) Pendle Hill.

War Is the Health of the State. Randolph Bourne. 1991. lib. bdg. 75.00 (*0-8490-4141-4*) Gordon Pr.

War, Its Causes & Correlates. Ed. by Martin A. Nettleship et al. (World Anthropology Ser.). (Illus.). xviii, 814p. 1975. 82.35 (*90-279-7659-7*) Mouton.

War, Jews, & the New Europe: The Diplomacy of Lucien Wolf, 1914-1919. Mark Levene. (Littman Library of Jewish Civilization). (Illus.). 346p. 1992. 45.00 (*0-19-710072-4*) Bnai Brith Bk.

War Journal of an Innocent Soldier. John T. Bassett. 160p. 1991. mass mkt. 4.50 (*0-380-71130-3*) Avon.

War Journal of an Innocent Soldier. John T. Bassett. LC 89-14973. 128p. (C). 1989. lib. bdg. 22.50 (*0-208-02260-0*, Archon Bks) Shoe String.

War Journal of Louis N. Beaudry, Fifth New York Cavalry: The Diary of a Union Chaplain, Commencing February 16, 1863. Louis N. Beaudry. Ed. by Richard E. Beaudry. LC 96-24267. 246p. 1996. lib. bdg. 31.50 (*0-7864-0260-1*) McFarland & Co.

War Journey. Wade Hawsey. Ed. by Bette G. Wahlfeldt. (Illus.). 30p. (Orig.). 1986. pap. 4.95 (*0-961628-0-6*) BW Enterprises.

***War Junkie.** Joe Sacco. 136p. 1995. pap. 14.95 (*1-56097-170-3*) Fantagraph Bks.

War, Justice & Public Order: England & France in the Late Middle Ages. Richard W. Kaeuper. 464p. 1988. 95.00 (*0-19-822873-2*) OUP.

War Kids 1941-1945: WWII Through the Eyes of Children. Lloyd Hornbostel. LC 95-41236. (Illus.). 128p. (Orig.). 1995. pap. 10.95 (*1-880090-27-9*) Galde Pr.

War Law, Set. S. Coleman Charlton et al. (Rolemaster Ser.). (Illus.). 160p. (Orig.). (C). 1991. boxed 30.00 (*1-55806-099-5*, 1110) Iron Crown Ent Inc.

War Ledger. A. F. Organski & Jacek Kugler. LC 79-23366. (Illus.). 304p. 1981. pap. text ed. 14.50 (*0-226-63280-6*) U Ch Pr.

War Letters: A Tour in the 'Nam' Cheryl Sweet. 175p. 1995. pap. 15.00 (*1-888292-01-6*) Pygmalion Press.

War Letters to a Wife. Rowland Feilding. 384p. 1988. 90.00 (*0-947893-16-4*, Pub. by Gliddon Bks UK) St Mut.

War, Literature & the Arts in 16th Century Europe. Ed. by J. R. Mulryne & Margaret Shewring. LC 88-36592. (Illus.). 208p. 1989. text ed. 45.00 (*0-312-03107-6*) St Martin.

War Lords. Alan J. Taylor. (Illus.). 1979. pap. 11.95 (*0-14-004638-0*, Penguin Bks) Viking Penguin.

War Lords of Washington. Bruce Catton. LC 70-90481. 313p. 1969. reprint ed. text ed. 35.00 (*0-8371-2149-3*, CAWL, Greenwood Pr) Greenwood.

***War Love Your Enemies: Medjugorje 12 Years Later.** Rene Laurentin. LC 94-65099. 145p. (Orig.). 1994. pap. 7.95 (*1-882972-26-0*, 3023) Queenship Pub.

War Lover: A Study of Plato's Republic. Leon H. Craig. 504p. (C). 1994. 78.00 (*0-8020-0586-1*) U of Toronto Pr.

***War Lover: A Study of Plato's Republic.** Leon H. Craig. LC 96-187300. 1997. pap. text ed. 34.75 (*0-8020-7942-3*) U of Toronto Pr.

War-Lyrics & Other Poems. Henry H. Brownell. LC 72-4953. (Romantic Tradition in American Literature Ser.). 256p. 1972. 21.95 (*0-405-04625-1*) Ayer.

War Machine. Dave Gibbons. Ed. by Richard Burton. (Illus.). 80p. (YA). 1993. text ed. 14.95 (*1-56862-018-7*) Tundra MA.

War Machine. Patrick F. Rogers. (Omega Ser.). 1993. mass mkt. 3.50 (*0-373-63207-X*, 1-63207-4) Harlequin Bks.

War Machine: The Case Against the Arms Race. James A. Joyce. 14.95 (*0-7043-2254-4*, Pub. by Quartet UK) Charles River Bks.

War Machine: The Rationalization of Slaughter in the Modern Age. Daniel Pick. (Illus.). 288p. (C). 1993. text ed. 35.00 (*0-300-05417-3*) Yale U Pr.

War Machine: The Rationalization of Slaughter in the Modern Age. Daniel Pick. 1996. pap. text ed. 18.00 (*0-300-06719-4*) Yale U Pr.

War-Making Powers of the President: Constitutional & International Law Aspects. Ann Van Wynen Thomas & A. J. Thomas, Jr. LC 82-10541. 192p. 1982. 15.00 (*0-87074-185-3*) SMU Press.

War Man. Chuck Dixon & Juan Zanotto. 64p. 1992. 9.95 (*0-87135-856-5*) Marvel Entmnt.

War Managers: American Generals Reflect on Vietnam. Douglas Kinnard. (Quality Paperbacks Ser.). (Illus.). 225p. 1991. reprint ed. pap. 12.95 (*0-306-80449-2*) Da Capo.

War Memoirs of David Lloyd George, 6 vols., Set. David Lloyd George. LC 75-41179. reprint ed. 450.00 (*0-404-15040-3*) AMS Pr.

War Memoirs of Robert Lansing, Secretary of State. Robert Lansing. LC 78-110853. 383p. 1971. reprint ed. text ed. 65.00 (*0-8371-4520-1*, LAWM, Greenwood Pr) Greenwood.

War Memorials: From Antiquity to the Present. Alan Borg. (Illus.). 153p. 1991. 57.50 (*0-85052-363-X*, Pub. by L Cooper Bks UK) Trans-Atl Phila.

War Memorials As Political Landscape: The American Experience & Beyond. James M. Mayo. LC 87-22328. 219p. 1988. text ed. 59.95 (*0-275-92812-8*, C2812, Praeger Pubs) Greenwood.

War Memories of the Alcala Veterans. Ed. by Alberto T. Marquez. (Illus.). 158p. (Orig.). 1992. pap. 13.75 (*971-10-0461-5*, Pub. by New Day Pub PH) Cellar.

War Minstrels. Karen Haber. 304p. 1995. mass mkt. 4.99 (*0-88677-669-4*) DAW Bks.

War Moon. Tom Cooper. 384p. 1987. mass mkt. 3.50 (*0-373-97031-5*) Harlequin Bks.

War, Morality, & the Military Profession. 2nd rev. ed. Ed. by Malham H. Wakin. 521p. (C). 1986. pap. text ed. 30.50 (*0-8133-0360-5*) Westview.

War Mountain. Jerry Ahern. (Survivalist Ser.: No. 25). 320p. 1993. mass mkt. 3.50 (*0-8217-4100-4*, Zebra Kensgtn) Kensgtn Pub Corp.

War Movies. CineBooks Staff. LC 89-60760. (CineBooks Home Library Ser.: No. 6). 256p. (Orig.). 1997. pap. 9.95 (*0-933997-25-6*) CineBks.

War Music: A Version of Books 1-4 & 16-19 of Homer's "Iliad" Christopher Logue. LC 96-48168. 256p. 1996. pap. 14.00 (*0-374-52494-7*, Noonday) FS&G.

War Music: An Account of Books 16 to 19 of Homer's Iliad. Christopher Logue. 256p. 1988. pap. 14.00 (*0-374-52089-5*) FS&G.

War, Nationalism & Peasants: Java under the Japanese Occupation, 1942-1945. Shigeru Sato. LC 94-31953. 300p. (C). (gr. 13). 1994. text ed. 69.95 (*1-56324-544-2*, East Gate Bk); pap. text ed. 27.95 (*1-56324-545-0*) M E Sharpe.

War Neuroses. Roy R. Grinker, Sr. & John P. Spiegel. Ed. by Richard H. Kohn. LC 78-22381. (American Military Experience Ser.). 1980. reprint ed. lib. bdg. 15.95 (*0-405-11858-9*) Ayer.

War Never Ends. Robie Wiesner. 144p. (Orig.). 1991. pap. 8.95 (*0-9630483-0-9*) Hudson Annex.

War News: A Young Reporter in Indochina. Robert S. Anson. 317p. 1989. 19.95 (*0-685-28399-2*) S&S Trade.

War Nobody Won: The Modoc War from the Army's Point of View. Edward E. Hathaway. (Illus.). 134p. (C). 1995. pap. text ed. 11.95 (*0-929408-15-2*) Amer Eagle Pubns Inc.

War North of Rome: June 1944-May 1945. Thomas R. Brooks. LC 96-17257. (Illus.). 408p. 1996. 27.50 (*1-885119-26-7*) Sarpedon.

War Notes: From the Letters of Sgt. Raymond McNabney. Raymond McNabney. Ed. by E. Andra Whitworth. LC 94-71567. (Illus.). 224p. (Orig.). 1994. pap. 12.95 (*0-9640706-0-X*) Cock-a-Hoop.

War Nurses. Shaaron Cosner. (American History Series for Young People). (YA). (gr. 7 up). 1988. 16.95 (*0-8027-6826-1*); 17.85 (*0-8027-6828-8*) Walker & Co.

War of a Jewish Partisan: A Youth Imperiled by His Russian Comrades & Nazi Conquerors. Yechiel Granatstein. (ArtScroll History Ser.). (Illus.). 256p. 1986. 17.99 (*0-89906-476-0*) Mesorah Pubns.

War of American Independence. R. E. Evans. (Cambridge Introduction to World History Topic Bks.). (Illus.). 48p. (YA). (gr. 7 up). 1976. pap. 9.95 (*0-521-20903-X*) Cambridge U Pr.

War of American Independence: Military Attitudes, Policies & Practice, 1763-1789. Don Higginbotham. LC 83-2374. 521p. 1983. reprint ed. pap. text ed. 18.95 (*0-930350-44-8*) NE U Pr.

War of American Independence, 1775-1783. Stephen Conway. 256p. 1995. text ed. 49.95 (*0-340-62520-1*, Pub. by E Arnld UK); text ed. 17.95 (*0-340-57626-X*, Pub. by E Arnld UK) St Martin.

War of Another Kind: A Southern Community in the Great Rebellion. Wayne K. Durrill. 304p. 1994. pap. 16.95 (*0-19-508923-5*) OUP.

War of Conquest: How It Was Waged Here in Mexico: the Aztecs' Own Story. Bernardino De Sahagun. Tr. by Arthur J. Anderson & Charles F. Dibble. LC 78-60241. (Illus.). 112p. reprint ed. pap. 32.00 (*0-8357-4373-X*, 2037202) Bks Demand.

***War of Darkness Game.** Mayfair Games Staff. 1986. pap. 7.00 (*0-912771-66-6*) Mayfair Games.

War of Desire & Technology at the Close of the Mechanical Age. Allucquere R. Stone. LC 95-17286. 210p. 1995. 25.00 (*0-262-19362-0*) MIT Pr.

War of Desire & Technology at the Close of the Mechanical Age. Allucquere R. Stone. (Illus.). 224p. 1996. pap. 10.00 (*0-262-69189-2*) MIT Pr.

War of 1812. Kathlyn Gay & Martin Gay. (Voices from the Past Ser.). (Illus.). 64p. (J). (gr. 5-8). 1996. lib. bdg. 15.98 (*0-8050-2846-3*) TFC Bks NY.

War of Eighteen Twelve. Miriam Greenblatt. Ed. by John Bowman. (America at War Ser.). (Illus.). 128p. (J). (gr. 4-11). 1994. 17.95 (*0-8160-2879-6*) Facts on File.

War of Eighteen Twelve. Francis F. Beirne. (History - United States Ser.). 410p. 1993. reprint ed. lib. bdg. 99.00 (*0-7812-4825-6*) Rprt Serv.

War of Eighteen Twelve, 22. Harry L. Coles. LC 65-17283. (Chicago History of American Civilization Ser.). (Illus.). 312p. 1966. pap. text ed. 16.95 (*0-226-11350-7*) U Ch Pr.

War of Eighteen Twelve: A Forgotten Conflict. Donald R. Hickey. (Illus.). 480p. 1990. pap. text ed. 16.95 (*0-252-06059-8*) U of Ill Pr.

War of Eighteen Twelve: Past Justifications & Present Interpretations. Ed. by George R. Taylor. LC 80-12565. (Problems in American Civilization). xii, 114p. 1980. reprint ed. text ed. 35.00 (*0-313-22356-4*, TATW, Greenwood Pr) Greenwood.

***War of 1812 Eyewitness Accounts: An Annotated Bibliography.** Compiled by John C. Fredriksen. LC 96-43982. (Bibliographies & Indexes in Military Studies: Vol. 8). 336p. 1997. text ed. 79.50 (*0-313-30291-X*, Greenwood Pr) Greenwood.

War of Eighteen Twelve Genealogy. 88p. 1994. pap. 12.00 (*0-913857-07-6*) Genealog Sources.

War of Eighteen Twelve Soldier at New Orleans. (Soldier Ser.). 48p. (J). (gr. 5-6). 1991. lib. bdg. 17.80 (*1-56065-001-X*) Capstone Pr.

War of Eyes & Other Stories. Wanda Coleman. LC 88-14714. 246p. (Orig.). 1988. 20.00 (*0-87685-737-3*); pap. 14.00 (*0-87685-735-7*) Black Sparrow.

***War of Gods.** Anderson. LC 97-19383. 1997. 22.95 (*0-312-86315-2*) St Martin.

War of Gods: Religion & Politics in Latin America. Michael Lowy. 192p. (C). 1996. text ed. 60.00 (*1-85984-907-5*, Pub. by Vrso UK); pap. text ed. 18.00 (*1-85984-002-7*, Pub. by Vrso UK) Norton.

***War of Great Proportions.** Richard Overy. Date not set. write for info. (*0-688-10842-3*) Morrow.

War of Ideas in Spain: Philosophy, Politics & Education. Jose Castilejo. 1976. lib. bdg. 59.95 (*0-8490-2806-X*) Gordon Pr.

War of Independence. John Fiske. (Notable American Authors Ser.). 1992. reprint ed. lib. bdg. 75.00 (*0-7812-2850-6*) Rprt Serv.

War of Independence: American Phase. Claude H. Van Tyne. (BCL1 - U. S. History Ser.). 518p. 1991. reprint ed. lib. bdg. 99.00 (*0-7812-6108-2*) Rprt Serv.

War of Information: The Conflict Between Public & Private U. S. Foreign Policy on El Salvador, 1979-1992. Michael R. Little. (Illus.). 210p. (C). 1993. lib. bdg. 42.00 (*0-8191-9311-9*) U Pr of Amer.

War of Invention: Science in the Great War 1914-18. Guy Hartcup. 208p. 1988. 50.00 (*0-08-033591-8*, Pub. by Brasseys UK) Brasseys Inc.

War of Jenkins' Ear. Michael Morpurgo. LC 94-7602. 192p. (J). (gr. 3-7). 1995. 16.95 (*0-399-22735-0*, Philomel Bks) Putnam Pub Group.

***War of Jenkin's Ear.** Michael Morpurgo. 176p. (Orig.). (YA). (gr. 7 up). 1997. pap. 5.95 (*0-698-11550-3*, Paperstar) Putnam Pub Group.

War of Love: (Presents Plus) Carole Mortimer. (Presents Ser.). 1995. pap. 3.25 (*0-373-11727-2*, 1-11727-4) Harlequin Bks.

War of No War: Yodhya of Ayodhya. Kunhunni Gupta. (C). 1992. text ed. 16.00 (*81-7001-087-X*, Pub. by Chanakya II) S Asia.

War of Numbers: An Intelligence Memoir. Sam Adams. 256p. 1994. 22.00 (*1-883642-23-X*) Steerforth Pr.

War of Numbers: An Intelligence Memoir. Sam Adams. 256p. 1995. pap. 13.00 (*1-883642-46-9*) Steerforth Pr.

War of Quito. Pedro De Cieza de Leon. Ed. by Clements R. Markham. (Hakluyt Society Second Ser.: Vol. 31). 224p. 1996. 45.00 (*0-85115-969-9*, Pub. by Hakluyt Soc UK) Boydell & Brewer.

***War of Saint Sardos.** P. Chaplais. (Camden Third Ser.). 35.00 (*0-86193-087-8*) David Brown.

War of Shadows: The Struggle for Utopia in the Peruvian Amazon. Michael F. Brown & Eduardo Fernandez. LC 90-26076. (Illus.). 275p. 1991. 30.00 (*0-520-07435-1*) U CA Pr.

War of Shadows: The Struggle for Utopia in the Peruvian Amazon. Michael F. Brown. (C). 1993. pap. 14.00 (*0-520-07448-3*) U CA Pr.

War of Space Notes. E. Sevin. (Keyboard Theory Ser.). 1990. 1.95 (*0-685-32007-3*, G046) Hansen Ed Mus.

War of the Austrian Succession. M. S. Anderson. LC 94-15591. (Modern Wars in Perspective Ser.). 264p. (C). 1995. pap. text ed. 23.50 (*0-582-05950-X*, 76986, Pub. by Longman UK) Longman.

War of the Austrian Succession. Reed Browning. (Illus.). 464p. 1994. 60.00 (*0-7509-0578-6*, Pub. by Sutton Pubng UK) Bks Intl VA.

War of the Austrian Succession. Reed Browning. LC 93-12439. 445p. 1993. text ed. 45.00 (*0-312-09483-3*) St Martin.

War of the Austrian Succession. Reed Browning. 480p. 1995. pap. 18.00 (*0-312-12561-5*) St Martin.

***War of the Black Heavens: The Battles of Western Broadcasting in the Cold War.** Michael Nelson. LC 97-13789. (Illus.). 336p. 1997. 29.95 (*0-8156-0479-3*) Syracuse U Pr.

War of the Christs & Emilia's Case. Josep M. Sola-Sole. LC 92-20665. (Catalan Studies: Translations & Criticism: Vol. 5). 256p. 1993. 49.95 (*0-8204-2006-9*) P Lang Pubng.

War of the Classes. Jack London. (Illus.). 278p. 1982. pap. 6.95 (*0-932458-11-4*) Star Rover.

War of the Cottontails: Memoirs of a WWII Bomber Pilot. William R. Cubbins. LC 88-26227. (Illus.). 300p. 1989. 19.95 (*0-912697-96-2*) Algonquin Bks.

War of the Dinosaurs. Charles Hinton. LC 95-94344. (Illus.). 112p. (Orig.). (J). 1995. pap. text ed. 14.95 (*0-9639934-4-5*) C Hinton.

War of the Dispossessed: Honduras & El Salvador, 1969. Thomas P. Anderson. LC 80-24080. (Illus.). xiv, 203p. 1981. text ed. 25.00 (*0-8032-1009-4*) U of Nebr Pr.

War of the Doomed: Jewish Armed Resistance in Poland, 1942-1944. Shmuel Krakowski. LC 83-18537. 340p. (C). 1984. 44.50 (*0-8419-0851-6*) Holmes & Meier.

War of the Dots. Robert B. Irwin. 56p. 1970. pap. 12.95 (*0-89128-069-3*) Am Foun Blind.

War of the End of Democracy: Mario Vargas Llosa vs. Alberto Fujimori. Jeff Daeschner. 360p. 1993. pap. 25.00 (*1-886617-10-4*) Peru Rept.

War of the End of the World. Mario Vargas Llosa. Tr. by Helen R. Lane. 1985. pap. 11.95 (*0-380-69987-7*) Avon.

War of the End of the World. Mario Vargas Llosa. Tr. by Helen Lane from SPA. 624p. 1984. 18.95 (*0-374-28651-5*) FS&G.

War of the End of the World. Mario Vargas Llosa. 1997. pap. 14.95 (*0-14-026260-1*, Penguin Bks) Viking Penguin.

War of the End of the World. limited ed. Mario Vargas Llosa. Tr. by Helen Lane from SPA. 624p. 1984. 75.00 (*0-374-28652-3*) FS&G.

War of the Fatties & Other Stories from Aztec History. Salvador Novo. Tr. by Michael Alderson from SPA. 256p. (C). 1993. pap. 14.95 (*0-292-75554-6*); text ed. 37.50 (*0-292-79059-7*) U of Tex Pr.

War of the Fists: Popular Culture & Public Violence in Late Renaissance Venice. Robert C. Davis. 240p. 1994. 45.00 (*0-19-508403-9*); pap. 19.95 (*0-19-508404-7*) OUP.

War of the Flea: A Study of Guerrilla Warfare. Robert Taber. (Theory & Practice Ser.). 1970. pap. 1.95 (*0-8065-0225-8*, Citadel Pr) Carol Pub Group.

War of the Gaedhil with Gaill, or the Invasion of Ireland by the Danes & Other Norsemen: Irish Text with Translation. Ed. by James Todd. (Rolls Ser.: No. 48). 1974. reprint ed. 70.00 (*0-8115-1107-3*) Periodicals Srv.

War of the Generations: The Revolt of Eleven Seventy-Three to Seventy-Four. Thomas M. Jones. LC 80-18411. (Monograph Publishing; Sponsor Ser.). 242p. reprint ed. pap. 69.00 (*0-317-28156-9*, 2022592) Bks Demand.

War of the Godfathers. William R. Roemer. 1991. mass mkt. 5.99 (*0-8041-0831-5*) Ivy Books.

War of the Jewels: The Later Silmarillion, Part 2. J. R. Tolkien. Ed. by Christopher Tolkein. (History of Middle-Earth Ser.: Vol. XI). 496p. 1994. 27.95 (*0-395-71041-3*) HM.

War of the Mines: Cambodia, Landmines & the Impoverishment of a Nation. Paul Davies. (Illus.). 172p. (C). pap. 24.95 (*0-7453-0860-0*, Pub. by Pluto Pr UK) LPC InBook.

War of the Mines: Cambodia, Landmines & the Impoverishment of a Nation. Paul Davies & Nic Dunlop. LC 94-2724. 172p. (C). 79.95 (*0-7453-0859-7*, Pub. by Pluto Pr UK) LPC InBook.

An Asterisk (*) at the beginning of an entry indicates that the title is appearing in BIP for the first time.

War of the Mountain Man. William W. Johnstone. 288p. 1995. mass mkt. 4.50 (*0-8217-5083-6*, Zebra Kensgtn) Kensgtn Pub Corp.

*__War of the Mountain Man.__ William W. Johnstone. 1996. mass mkt. 4.99 (*0-8217-5610-9*) Kensgtn Pub Corp.

War of the Nations: A Pictorial Portfolio of World War I. 1976. 42.95 (*0-405-09858-8*, 19527) Ayer.

War of the Raven. Andrew Kaplan. 416p. 1991. mass mkt. 4.99 (*0-380-71472-8*) Avon.

War of the Rebellion. Chauncey F. Grosvenor. 166p. (Orig.). 1994. pap. text ed. 17.50 (*0-7884-0049-5*) Heritage Bk.

War of the Regulation & the Battle of Alamance, May 16, 1771. William S. Powell. (Illus.). 32p. 1976. reprint ed. pap. 3.00 (*0-86526-102-4*) NC Archives.

War of the Ring: The History of the Lord of the Rings, Pt. 3. J. R. R. Tolkien. 544p. 1990. 29.95 (*0-395-56008-X*) HM.

War of the Rising Sun & Tumbling Bear: A Military History of the Russo-Japanese War (1904-1905) Richard M. Connaughton. 320p. 1989. 49.95 (*0-415-00906-5*) Routledge.

War of the Roses: Through the Lives of Five Men & Women of the Fifteenth Century. Desmond Seward. (Illus.). 416p. 1996. pap. 14.95 (*0-14-023402-0*, Penguin Bks) Viking Penguin.

War of the Saints. Jorge Amado. LC 93-5310. 368p. 1995. pap. 13.95 (*0-553-37440-0*) Bantam.

War of the Sexes - Battle Plan A - Initial Encounters. John W. Walkington. LC 96-92106. 176p. 1996. 19.95 (*1-888922-03-6*, JW-1110); pap. 14.95 (*1-888922-04-4*, JW-1101) Natl Inst Masculine.

War of the Spanish Succession, 1702-1713: A Selected Bibliography. Compiled by W. Clavin Dickinson & Eloise R. Hitchcock. LC 95-41984. (Bibliographies of Battles & Leaders Ser.: No. 15). 160p. 1996. text ed. 65.00 (*0-313-28302-8*, Greenwood Pr) Greenwood.

War of the Spirits. Sandra Cerda. (Orig.). 1996. pap. 5.00 (*0-9643649-1-3*) N Life Minist.

War of the Springing Tigers. Gerard H. Corr. 200p. 1979. 12.95 (*0-318-36623-1*) Asia Bk Corp.

War of the Theatres. Josiah H. Penniman. LC 73-126649. reprint ed. 32.50 (*0-404-04992-3*) AMS Pr.

War of the Twins, Vol. 2. Margaret Weis & Tracy Hickman. (Dragon Lance Legends Ser.: Vol. III). 1995. pap. 5.99 (*0-7869-0263-9*) TSR Inc.

War of the Wenuses. C. L. Graves & Edward V. Lucas. LC 74-15979. (Science Fiction Ser.). (Illus.). 140p. 1975. reprint ed. 18.95 (*0-405-06293-1*) Ayer.

War of the Wizards. Stephen Wyllie. LC 93-14494. (Illus.). (J). 1994. pap. 18.95 (*0-8037-1690-7*) Dial Bks Young.

War of the Words: The Gulf War Quote by Quote. Wes Janz & Vickie Abrahamson. (Illus.). (Orig.). 1991. pap. 12.95 (*0-9630330-1-8*) Bobbleheads Pr.

War of the Words: Twenty-Five Years of Super Bowl Head-Butts & High-Fives. Wes Janz & Vickie Abrahamson. LC 91-77226. (Illus.). 140p. (Orig.). 1991. pap. 12.95 (*0-9630330-2-6*) Bobbleheads Pr.

War of the Worlds. 1993. pap. 5.25 (*0-19-585466-7*) OUP.

*__War of the Worlds.__ Peter Glassman. (J). Date not set. write for info. (*0-688-13137-9*, Morrow Junior) Morrow.

War of the Worlds. H. G. Wells. (Airmont Classics Ser.). (J). (gr. 8 up). 1964. mass mkt. 2.50 (*0-8049-0045-0*, CL-45) Airmont.

War of the Worlds. H. G. Wells. (J). (gr. 4-7). 1997. pap. 2.95 (*0-89375-347-5*) Troll Communs.

War of the Worlds. H. G. Wells. 176p. 1988. mass mkt. 3.50 (*0-553-21338-5*) Bantam.

War of the Worlds. H. G. Wells. Ed. by Arthur C. Clarke. 208p. 1993. pap. 3.95 (*0-460-87303-2*, Everyman's Classic Lib) C E Tuttle.

War of the Worlds. H. G. Wells. 224p. (YA). 1986. mass mkt. 5.95 (*0-451-52276-1*, Sig Classics) NAL-Dutton.

War of the Worlds. H. G. Wells. 226p. (YA). 1993. pap. 2.50 (*0-8125-0515-8*) Tor Bks.

War of the Worlds. H. G. Wells. Ed. by Brian W. Aldiss & David Y. Hughes. (World's Classics Ser.). (Illus.). 208p. 1995. pap. 6.95 (*0-19-282826-6*) OUP.

*__War of the Worlds.__ H. G. Wells. (Illustrated Classics Collection 2). 64p. 1994. pap. 4.95 (*0-7854-0676-X*, 40424) Am Guidance.

War of the Worlds. large type ed. H. G. Wells. LC 94-43663. 236p. 1995. 20.95 (*0-7838-1224-8*, GK Hall) Thorndike Pr.

*__War of the Worlds.__ unabridged ed. H. G. Wells. 175p. 1997. reprint ed. pap. 14.95 (*1-57002-050-7*) Univ Publng Hse.

War of the Worlds. H. G. Wells. 1981. reprint ed. lib. bdg. 17.95 (*0-89966-376-1*) Buccaneer Bks.

*__War of the Worlds.__ H. G. Wells. LC 96-43700. (Thrift Editions Ser.). 160p. 1997. reprint ed. pap. text ed. 1.50 (*0-486-29506-0*) Dover.

War of the Worlds: Cyberspace & the High-Tech Assault on Reality. Mark Slouka. 208p. 1996. pap. 12.00 (*0-465-00487-3*) Basic.

*__War of the Worlds: Global Dispatches.__ Kevin J. Anderson. 1997. mass mkt. 6.50 (*0-553-57598-8*, Spectra) Bantam.

War of the Worlds: Global Dispatches: Anthology. Ed. by Kevin J. Anderson. LC 95-45125. 320p. 1996. 22.95 (*0-553-10353-9*) Bantam.

War of the Worlds: Student Activity Book. Marcia Sohl & Gerald Dackerman. (Now Age Illustrated Ser.). (Illus.). (J). (gr. 4-10). 1976. student ed. 1.25 (*0-88301-198-0*) Pendulum Pr.

War of the Worlds, Vol. 1, Bk. 1: The Invasion Begins. Scott Finley & Brooks Hagan. (Illus.). 93p. 1990. pap. 9.95 (*0-944735-33-9*) Malibu Comics Ent.

*__War of Three Waters.__ Douglas Niles. (Watershed Trilogy Ser.: Bk. 3). (Orig.). 1997. pap. 14.00 (*0-614-27309-9*) Ace Bks.

War of Titans: Blake's Critique of Milton & the Politics of Religion. Jackie DiSalvo. LC 82-11136. 403p. 1983. reprint ed. pap. 114.90 (*0-608-00903-2*, 2061697) Bks Demand.

War of Tomorrow: Arctic Strike, A Visual Novel of Michael A. Parker. Michael A. Parker. (Illustrated History of Near Future Warfare Ser.: No. 2). (Illus.). 224p. (Orig.). 1991. mass mkt. 6.95 (*0-380-75844-X*) Avon.

War of Visions: Conflicts of Identities in the Sudan. Francis M. Deng. 577p. (C). 1995. 52.95 (*0-8157-1794-6*); pap. 24.95 (*0-8157-1793-8*) Brookings.

*__War of Witches: A Journey into the Underworld of the Contemporary Aztecs.__ Timothy J. Knab. (C). 1997. pap. text ed. 16.00 (*0-8133-3387-3*) Westview.

War of Witches: Journey into the World of the Contemporary Aztecs. Timothy J. Knab. LC 94-41813. 224p. 1995. pap. write for info. (*0-06-251280-3*) Harper SF.

War of Witches: Journey into the World of the Contemporary Aztecs. Timothy J. Knab. LC 94-41813. 224p. 1995. 22.00 (*0-06-251264-1*) Harper SF.

War of Witches: Journey into the World of the Contemporary Aztecs. Timothy J. Knab. LC 94-41813. 1995. pap. 12.00 (*0-06-251265-X*) Harper SF.

War of Wits: The Anatomy of Espionage & Intelligence. Ladislas Farago. LC 75-31362. (Illus.). 379p. 1976. reprint ed. text ed. 35.00 (*0-8371-8518-1*, FAWW, Greenwood Pr) Greenwood.

War of Words: Chicano Protest in the 1960's & 1970's. John C. Hammerback et al. LC 85-5598. (Contributions in Ethnic Studies: No. 12). x, 187p. 1985. text ed. 49.95 (*0-313-24825-7*, JWW/, Greenwood Pr) Greenwood.

War of 1812. LC 65-89168. (Massachusetts Historical Society Picture Books Ser.). 16p. 1962. pap. 4.00 (*0-934909-18-0*) Mass Hist Soc.

War of 1812. John K. Mahon. (Quality Paperbacks Ser.). (Illus.). xii, 476p. 1991. reprint ed. pap. 15.95 (*0-306-80429-8*) Da Capo.

War of 1812: A Short History. Donald R. Hickey. LC 94-17031. 152p. 1995. pap. text ed. 8.95 (*0-252-06430-5*) U of Ill Pr.

War of 1812: Second Fight for Independence. Alden R. Carter. LC 92-11438. (First Bks.). (Illus.). 64p. (J). (gr. 5-8). 1992. lib. bdg. 21.00 (*0-531-20080-9*) Watts.

War of 1812: Second Fight for Independence. Alden R. Carter. (First Bks.). (Illus.). 64p. (J). (gr. 5-8). 1993. pap. 6.95 (*0-531-15659-1*) Watts.

War of 1898 & U. S. Interventions, 1898-1934: An Encyclopedia. Ed. by Benjamin R. Beede. LC 93-49579. (Military History of the U. S. Ser.: Vol. 2). 784p. 1994. text ed. 95.00 (*0-8240-5624-8*, H933) Garland.

War Office at War. Sam Fay. 1976. reprint ed. 15.00 (*0-85409-883-6*) Charles River Bks.

War on a Distant Moon. Tod Foley. Ed. by Leo LaDell. (Space Master Ser.). (Illus.). 32p. (Orig.). (YA). (gr. 12). 1988. pap. 6.00 (*1-55806-020-0*, 9104) Iron Crown Ent Inc.

War on Christ in America: The Christian Fortress America under Siege Christophobes of the Media & of the Supreme Court in Action - Demonic Maladies of the Western Culture, Freud, Marx, Skinner & Other Ugly Pagans. Ratibor-Ray M. Jurjevich. 538p. 1985. pap. 22.95 (*0-930711-01-7*) Ichthys Bks.

*__War on Crime: Gangsters, G-Men, & the Politics of Mass Culture.__ Claire B. Potter. (Illus.). 272p. 1998. 50.00 (*0-8135-2486-5*) Rutgers U Pr.

*__War on Crime: Gangsters, G-Men, & the Politics of Mass Culture.__ Claire B. Potter. (Illus.). 272p. 1998. pap. 20.00 (*0-8135-2487-3*) Rutgers U Pr.

War on Debt: Breaking the Power of Debt. John Avanzini. (Financial Freedom Ser.). 190p. 1990. pap. 7.95 (*1-878605-00-3*) HIS Pub Co.

War on Drugs. Neville Steele, II. LC 92-91382. 64p. 1994. pap. 8.95 (*1-56002-294-9*, Univ Edtns) Aegina Pr.

War on Drugs: Examining Cause & Effect Relationships. Neal Bernards. LC 91-22021. (Opposing Viewpoints Juniors Ser.). (Illus.). 36p. (J). (gr. 4-7). 1991. lib. bdg. 12.96 (*0-89908-612-8*) Greenhaven.

War on Drugs: Federal Assistance to State & Local Drug Enforcement. (Illus.). 50p. (Orig.). (C). 1993. pap. text ed. 20.00 (*0-7881-0009-2*) DIANE Pub.

War on Drugs II: The Continuing Epic of Heroin, Cocaine, & Public Policy. 2nd ed. James A. Inciardi. LC 91-24736. 315p. (C). 1992. pap. text ed. 24.95 (*1-55934-016-9*, 1016) Mayfield Pub.

War on Drugs, War on People. Steve Otto. LC 95-46098. x, 203p. (Orig.). 1995. pap. 15.00 (*0-86663-249-2*) Ide Hse.

War on Drugs (1989) 90p. 1989. pap. text ed. 10.00 (*1-56986-064-5*) Federal Bar.

War on Labor & the Left: Understanding America's Unique Conservatism. Patricia C. Sexton. 325p. (C). 1992. pap. text ed. 24.00 (*0-8133-1063-6*) Westview.

War on Light: The Destruction of the Image of God in Man Through Modern Art. Margaret E. Stucki. 1975. 25.00 (*0-686-23419-7*) Birds' Meadow Pub.

War on Poverty Revisited: The Community Services Block Grant Program in the Reagan Years. Michael Givel. 264p. (C). 1990. lib. bdg. 46.00 (*0-8191-7872-1*) U Pr of Amer.

War on Powder River. Helena H. Smith. LC 65-28734. (Illus.). xiv, 328p. 1967. pap. 14.95 (*0-8032-5188-2*, Bison Books) U of Nebr Pr.

War on the Bank of the United States. Thomas F. Gordon. LC 68-18219. (Reprints of Economic Classics Ser.). 155p. 1968. reprint ed. 35.00 (*0-678-00380-7*) Kelley.

War on the Frontier. (Civil War Ser.). (Illus.). 176p. 1986. lib. bdg. 25.93 (*0-8094-4781-9*) Time-Life.

War on the Great Lakes: Essays Commemorating the 175th Anniversary of the Battle of Lake Erie. Ed. by William J. Welsh & David C. Skaggs. LC 90-5345. 160p. 1991. 29.00 (*0-87338-424-5*); pap. 17.50 (*0-87338-425-3*) Kent St U Pr.

War on the Homefront: State Intervention in Queensland, 1938-1948. Kay Saunders. 190p. (Orig.). 1993. pap. text ed. 19.95 (*0-7022-2377-8*, Pub. by Univ Queensland Pr AT) Intl Spec Bk.

War on the Land: Ecology & Politics in Central America. William J. Weinberg. LC 91-13782. 192p. (C). 1991. pap. 15.00 (*0-86232-947-7*, Pub. by Zed Bks Ltd UK); text ed. 49.95 (*0-86232-946-9*, Pub. by Zed Bks Ltd UK) Humanities.

War on the Mississippi. (Civil War Ser.). (Illus.). 176p. 1985. 18.95 (*0-8094-4744-4*); lib. bdg. 25.93 (*0-8094-4745-2*) Time-Life.

War on the Poor: A Defense Manual. Nancy Folbre. 128p. (Orig.). Date not set. pap. 11.95 (*1-56584-262-6*) New Press NY.

*__War on the Potomac.__ Elly Sutton. Ed. by Helena Bowman. LC 96-79123. (Illus.). 288p. (Orig.). 1996. pap. 9.95 (*0-932820-01-8*) M P Pubs.

War on the Saints. Jessie Penn-Lewis. (Orig.). 1993. pap. 7.95 (*0-87508-963-1*) Chr Lit.

*__War on the Saints.__ Jessie Penn-Lewis. 324p. (Orig.). 1996. mass mkt. 4.99 (*0-88368-455-1*) Whitaker Hse.

War on the Saints. Jessie Penn-Lewis & Evan Roberts. 325p. 1994. reprint ed. 12.50 (*0-913926-04-3*) T E Lowe.

War on the Short Waves see **Propaganda by Short Wave**

War on the Webfoot Saloon & Other Tales of Feminine Adventures. Malcolm Clark, Jr. & Kenneth W. Porter. (Illus.). 54p. 1969. pap. 2.95 (*0-87595-023-X*) Oregon Hist.

War on the West: Government Tyranny on America's Great Frontier. William P. Pendley. 314p. 1995. 21.95 (*0-89526-482-X*) Regnery Pub.

War on Two Fronts: Shiloh to Gettysburg. rev. ed. John Cannan. (Eyewitness History of the Civil War Ser.). 413p. 1994. pap. 16.95 (*0-938289-42-X*, 7307) Combined Pub.

War on War. Lowell Jaeger. 90p. 1988. pap. 10.95 (*0-87421-138-7*) Utah St U Pr.

War on War: Lenin, the Zimmerwald Left, & the Origins of Communist Internationalism. R. Craig Nation. LC 89-35744. 304p. 1989. text ed. 52.95 (*0-8223-0944-0*) Duke.

War on Waste: Can America Win Its Battle with Garbage? Louis Blumberg & Robert Gottlieb. LC 89-11169. (Illus.). 303p. (Orig.). 1989. 34.95 (*0-933280-92-0*); pap. 19.95 (*0-933280-91-2*) Island Pr.

*__War on Waste II.__ Roger V. Dickerson. 120p. 46.00 (*0-614-25583-X*, 00GM52102) Print Indus Am.

War on Waste II. Roger V. Dickeson. Ed. by Norman W. Scharpf. 125p. 1991. 38.40 (*0-933505-18-3*) Graph Comm Assn.

*__War or Peace?__ Burg. (C). Date not set. pap. write for info. (*0-8147-1271-1*) NYU Pr.

War or Peace? Nationalism, Democracy, & American Foreign Policy in Post-Communist Europe. Steven L. Burg. 280p. (C). 1996. 35.00 (*0-8147-1270-3*) NYU Pr.

War or Peace in the Twentieth Century. Eleanor Roosevelt Institute Staff. Ed. by Sue R. Roff. (Illus.). 270p. (YA). (gr. 8-12). 1984. ring bd. 69.95 (*0-89908-502-4*) Greenhaven.

War Out of Niagara: Walter Butler & the Tory Rangers. Howard Swiggett. 309p. 1993. reprint ed. lib. bdg. 89.00 (*0-7812-5200-8*) Rprt Serv.

War Outside Ireland. Michael Joyce. LC 82-80497. 192p. (Orig.). 1982. pap. 8.50 (*0-943608-01-5*) Tinkers Dam Pr.

War Over Walloomscoick: Land Use & Settlement Pattern on the Bennington Battlefield-1777. Philip L. Lord, Jr. (Bulletin Ser.: No. 473). (Illus.). 190p. (Orig.). (C). 1989. pap. text ed. 15.00 (*1-55557-186-7*) NYS Museum.

War Paint. (Executioner Ser.). 1994. mass mkt. 3.50 (*0-373-61188-9*, 1-61188-8) Harlequin Bks.

War Paint: Blackfoot & Sarcee Painted Buffalo Robes in the Royal Ontario Museum. Arni Brownstone. (Illus.). 96p. 1993. pap. 24.95 (*0-88854-408-1*, Pub. by Royal Ont Mus CN) U of Toronto Pr.

War Papers & Personal Reminiscences, 1861-1865, Vol. I: Missouri. (Military Order of the Loyal Legion of the United States Ser.: Vol. 14). 451p. 1992. reprint ed. 40.00 (*1-56837-169-1*) Broadfoot.

War Papers of Vermont: And Miscellaneous States Papers & Addresses. (Military Order of the Loyal Legion of the United States Ser.: 57). (Illus.). 438p. 1994. 40.00 (*1-56837-270-1*) Broadfoot.

War Papers Read Before the Indiana Commandery. (Military Order of the Loyal Legion of the United States Ser.: Vol. 24). (Illus.). 521p. 1992. reprint ed. 40.00 (*1-56837-179-9*) Broadfoot.

War Papers, Vol. I: Maine. (Military Order of the Loyal Legion of the United States Ser.: Vol. 16). (Illus.). 343p. 1992. reprint ed. 40.00 (*1-56837-171-3*) Broadfoot.

War Papers, Vol. II: Maine. (Military Order of the Loyal Legion of the United States Ser.: Vol. 17). (Illus.). 341p. 1992. reprint ed. 40.00 (*1-56837-172-1*) Broadfoot.

War Papers, Vol. III: Maine. (Military Order of the Loyal Legion of the United States Ser.: Vol. 18). (Illus.). 350p. 1992. reprint ed. 40.00 (*1-56837-173-X*) Broadfoot.

War Papers, Vol. IV: Maine. (Military Order of the Loyal Legion of the United States Ser.: Vol. 19). (Illus.). 339p. 1992. reprint ed. 40.00 (*1-56837-174-8*) Broadfoot.

War Papers, Vol. 1: Commandery of the State. (Military Order of the Loyal Legion of the United States Ser.: Vol. 56). 453p. 1994. reprint ed. 40.00 (*1-56837-238-8*) Broadfoot.

War Papers, Vol. 1: Commandery of the State of Massachusetts. (Military Order of the Loyal Legion of the United States Ser.: Vol. 52). 327p. 1994. reprint ed. 40.00 (*1-56837-244-2*) Broadfoot.

War Papers, Vol. 1: Commandery of the State of Michigan. (Military Order of the Loyal Legion of the United States Ser.: Vol. 50). (Illus.). 555p. 1993. reprint ed. 40.00 (*1-56837-242-6*) Broadfoot.

War Papers, Vol. 1: District of Columbia. (Military Order of the Loyal Legion of the United States Ser.: Vol. 42). 494p. 1994. reprint ed. 40.00 (*1-56837-272-8*) Broadfoot.

War Papers, Vol. 2: Commandery of the State of Michigan. (Military Order of the Loyal Legion of the United States Ser.: Vol. 51). 325p. 1993. reprint ed. 40.00 (*1-56837-243-4*) Broadfoot.

War Papers, Vol. 2: Commandery of the State of Wisconsin. (Military Order of the Loyal Legion of the United States Ser.: Vol. 47). 443p. 1993. reprint ed. 40.00 (*1-56837-239-6*) Broadfoot.

War Papers, Vol. 2: District of Columbia. (Military Order of the Loyal Legion of the United States Ser.: Vol. 43). (Illus.). 488p. 1994. reprint ed. 40.00 (*1-56837-273-6*) Broadfoot.

War Papers, Vol. 3: Commandery of the District of Columbia, Papers 49-70. (Military Order of the Loyal Legion of the United States Ser.: Vol. 44). (Illus.). 482p. 1993. reprint ed. 40.00 (*1-56837-274-4*) Broadfoot.

War Papers, Vol. 3: Commandery of the State of Wisconsin. (Military Order of the Loyal Legion of the United States Ser.: Vol. 48). (Illus.). 545p. 1993. reprint ed. 40.00 (*1-56837-240-X*) Broadfoot.

War Papers, Vol. 4: Commandery of the District of Columbia, Papers 71-98. (Military Order of the Loyal Legion of the United States Ser.: Vol. 45). (Illus.). 510p. 1993. reprint ed. 40.00 (*1-56837-225-6*) Broadfoot.

War Papers, Vol. 4: Commandery of the State of Wisconsin. (Military Order of the Loyal Legion of the United States Ser.: Vol. 49). (Illus.). 479p. 1993. reprint ed. 40.00 (*1-56837-241-8*) Broadfoot.

*__War Party.__ John S. Daniels. LC 96-44968. (Nightingale Ser.). 1997. pap. 18.95 (*0-7838-2004-6*) G K Hall.

War Party. Louis L'Amour. 160p. 1982. mass mkt. 3.99 (*0-553-25393-X*) Bantam.

War Party. Louis L'Amour. 1996. audio 9.99 (*0-553-47434-0*) Bantam.

*__War Party.__ large type ed. Louis L'Amour. LC 96-36269. 1998. 20.00 (*0-7838-1952-8*) G K Hall.

War Party. Max Brand. LC 81-38502. 224p. 1982. reprint ed. 16.00 (*0-8376-0460-5*) Bentley.

War Path. John B. Jones. (Notable American Authors Ser.). 1992. reprint ed. lib. bdg. 90.00 (*0-7812-3521-9*) Rprt Serv.

War-Path & Bivouac: or The Conquest of the Sioux. John F. Finerty. LC 94-8099. (Western Frontier Library: Vol. 18). (Illus.). 358p. 1994. pap. 12.95 (*0-8061-1413-4*) U of Okla Pr.

War Patrol of the PCE(R)852. Alfred Samuels. 1989. lib. bdg. write for info. (*0-9622415-0-4*) Pubs Syndication.

War Patrols of the USS Flasher. William R. McCants. Ed. by Ginny Turner. 480p. 1994. 27.00 (*1-57087-054-3*) Prof Pr NC.

War, Peace & All That Jazz. Joy Hakim. LC 93-28768. (History of US Ser.: Vol. 9). (Illus.). 160p. (J). 1995. pap. 10.95 (*0-19-507762-8*); lib. bdg. 14.95 (*0-19-507761-X*) OUP.

War, Peace & All That Jazz. Joy Hakim. LC 93-28768. (History of US Ser.: Vol. 9). 192p. (J). (gr. 3-10). 1995. 15.95 (*0-19-509514-6*) OUP.

War, Peace, & International Politics. 6th ed. David W. Ziegler. LC 92-42865. (C). 1993. 27.50 (*0-673-52287-3*) Addson-Wesley Educ.

War, Peace & International Politics. 7th ed. David W. Ziegler. LC 96-6373. (C). 1997. text ed. 38.50 (*0-673-52501-5*) Addson-Wesley Educ.

War, Peace, & Love. Martin L. Sommers. 280p. (Orig.). 1996. pap. 16.95 (*0-9651872-0-9*) Gondola Pubng.

War, Peace & Politics: The U. S. & New World Order. Carl Kaysen. (CISA Working Papers, New: No. 7). 1994. pap. 15.00 (*0-86682-098-1*) Ctr Intl Relations.

War, Peace & Revolution: International Socialism at the Crossroads, 1914-1918. David Kirby. LC 86-11895. 340p. 1986. text ed. 39.95 (*0-312-85587-7*) St Martin.

War, Peace, & Social Change: A Reader. Ed. by Clive Emsley et al. 368p. 1990. 90.00 (*0-335-09291-8*, Open Univ Pr); pap. 24.00 (*0-335-09290-X*, Open Univ Pr) Taylor & Francis.

War, Peace, & Structural Violence: Peace Activism & the African-American Historic Experience. Juliet E. Walker. Ed. by Victoria Cuffel. (Lecture Ser.: No. 14). 91p. (Orig.). 1992. pap. 4.00 (*1-881157-14-8*) In Ctr Global.

War, Peace, & the Bible. Joseph C. Swaim. LC 81-16889. 143p. reprint ed. pap. 40.80 (*0-8357-8551-3*, 2034897) Bks Demand.

War, Peace & the Presidency. Henry Paolucci. LC 68-8774. 20.00 (*0-685-06495-6*) Bagehot Council.

War Pictures from the South. Bela Estvan. LC 74-179516. (Select Bibliographies Reprint Ser.). 1977. reprint ed. 35.95 (*0-8369-6645-7*) Ayer.

War Pilot of Orange. Bob Vanderstok. LC 87-62612. 242p. (Orig.). 1987. pap. 10.95 (*0-933126-89-1*) Pictorial Hist.

War Plan Orange: The U. S. Strategy to Defeat Japan, 1897-1945. Edward S. Miller. LC 91-14361. (Illus.). 509p. 1991. 34.95 (*0-87021-759-3*) Naval Inst Pr.

War Plans of the Great Powers, 1880-1914. Ed. by Paul M. Kennedy. (Illus.). 280p. 1985. pap. text ed. 22.95 (*0-04-940082-7*) Routledge Chapman & Hall.

War Play Dilemma: Balancing Needs & Values in the Early Childhood Classroom. Nancy Carlsson-Paige & Diane Levin. (Early Childhood Education Ser.). 120p. (C). 1987. pap. text ed. 13.95 (*0-8077-2875-6*) Tchrs Coll.

War Plays. Edward Bond. (Methuen New Theatrescripts Ser.). 51p. (Orig.). (C). 1988. pap. 6.95 (*0-413-57240-4*, A0310, Pub. by Methuen UK) Heinemann.

War Plays. Edward Bond. (Methuen Modern Plays Ser.). 363p. (Orig.). (C). 1991. pap. 19.95 (*0-413-64600-9*, A0558, Pub. by Methuen UK) Heinemann.

War Poems: A War Poem Folio. Roberta Mendel. (Death Song Ser.). 21p. (Orig.). 1996. pap. 9.00 (*0-936424-10-9*, 012) Pin Prick.

War Poems of Siegfried Sassoon. Siegfried Sassoon. Ed. by Rupert Hart-Davis. LC 82-24202. 160p. 1983. pap. 13. 958.95 (*0-571-13015-1*) Faber & Faber.

War Poetry of the South. Ed. by William G. Simms. LC 72-4974. (Romantic Tradition in American Literature Ser.). 494p. 1978. reprint ed. 40.95 (*0-405-04644-8*) Ayer.

War Poets. (Poets Ser.). 146p. 1993. 5.95 (*0-7117-0398-1*, Pub. by Jarrold Pub UK) Seven Hills Bk.

War Poets. Robert Giddings. 1990. pap. 9.99 (*0-517-05436-1*) Random Hse Value.

War, Politics, & Culture in Fourteenth-Century England. James Sherborne. LC 93-49640. 224p. 1994. boxed 55. 00 (*1-85285-086-8*) Hambledon Press.

War, Politics & Finance under Edward the First. Michael Prestwich. (Modern Revivals in History Ser.). 318p. 1992. 59.95 (*0-7512-0000-X*, Pub. by Gregg Revivals UK) Ashgate Pub Co.

War, Politics & Power. Karl Von Clausewitz. Tr. by Edward M. Collins. LC 63-1381. 304p. 1962. pap. 9.95 (*0-89526-999-6*) Regnery Pub.

***War, Politics, & Power.** Karl Von Clausewitz. (Gateway Ser.). 304p. 1997. pap. 12.95 (*0-89526-401-3*, Gateway Editions) Regnery Pub.

War Pony. Donald E. Worcester. LC 83-40486. (Chaparral Bks.). (Illus.). 96p. (J). (gr. 4 up). 1984. reprint ed. 10.95 (*0-912646-85-3*) Tex Christian.

War Potential of Nations. Klaus E. Knorr. LC 78-13603. (Illus.). 310p. 1978. reprint ed. text ed. 65.00 (*0-313-21049-7*, KNWA, Greenwood Pr) Greenwood.

War Powers: The President, the Congress, & the Question of War. Donald L. Westerfield. LC 95-43774. 264p. 1996. text ed. 59.95 (*0-275-94701-7*, Praeger Pubs) Greenwood.

War Powers Resolution: Its Implementation in Theory & Practice. Robert F. Turner. LC 82-24192. (Philadelphia Policy Papers). (Orig.). 1983. pap. 4.95 (*0-910191-06-9*) For Policy Res.

War Powers Resolution & U. S. Policy in Lebanon, 1982-1984. Vincent A. Auger. (Pew Case Studies in International Affairs). 50p. (C). 1993. pap. text ed. 3.50 (*1-56927-358-8*) Geo U Inst Dplmcy.

War Prayer. Mark Twain. 5p. (Orig.). 1994. pap. 2.00 (*1-57514-266-X*, 3056) Encore Perform Pub.

War Prayer. Mark Twain. LC 68-29574. (Illus.). 96p. (Orig.). 1984. pap. 8.00 (*0-06-091113-1*, CN 1113, PL) HarpC.

War Prayer. Mark Twain. 96p. (Orig.). 1991. reprint ed. lib. bdg. 27.00 (*0-8095-9061-1*) Borgo Pr.

War Prizes. Phil Butler. (Illus.). 320p. 1994. 49.95 (*0-904597-86-5*) Specialty Pr.

War, Progress, & the End of History: Three Conversations, Including a Short Story of the Antichrist. Vladimir Solovyov. Tr. by Alexander Bakshy & Thomas Beyer, Jr. from RUS. 192p. (Orig.). 1990. pap. 14.95 (*0-940262-35-5*) Lindisfarne Bks.

War Propaganda & the U. S. Harold Lavine & James Wechsler. 1972. 59.95 (*0-8490-1277-5*) Gordon Pr.

War Propaganda & the United States. Harold Lavine & James A. Wechsler. LC 72-4668. (International Propaganda & Communications Ser.). (Illus.). 389p. 1972. reprint ed. 21.95 (*0-405-04753-3*) Ayer.

War, Prosperity & Depression: The U. S. Economy, 1917-1945. Peter Fearon. LC 87-21571. x, 294p. 1987. pap. 17.95 (*0-7006-0349-2*) U Pr of KS.

War, Prosperity & Depression see U. S. History - Two

War Psalms of the Prince of Peace. Jim E. Adams. 1991. pap. 6.99 (*0-87552-093-6*, Pub. by Evangelical Pr) Presby & Reformed.

War Puzzle. John A. Vasquez. LC 92-25775. (Studies in International Relations: No. 27). (Illus.). 368p. (C). 1993. text ed. 59.95 (*0-521-36673-9*); pap. text ed. 19.95 (*0-521-36674-7*) Cambridge U Pr.

War Remembered. Clark Dougan et al. 1986. 16.30 (*0-201-11275-2*) Addison-Wesley.

War Reminiscences. Aristides Montiero. 1976. 22.95 (*0-8488-1104-6*) Amereon Ltd.

War Requiem: The Film. Derek Jarman. (Illus.). 64p. 1990. pap. 11.95 (*0-571-14115-3*) Faber & Faber.

War Resistance in Historical Perspective. Larry Gara. LC 74-123299. (C). 1970. pap. 3.00 (*0-87574-171-1*) Pendle Hill.

War, Revolution & Japan. Ed. by Ian Neary. 128p. (C). 1993. pap. text ed. 15.00 (*1-873410-08-5*, Pub. by Curzon Press UK) UH Pr.

War, Revolution & Peace: Essays in Honor of Charles B. Burdick. Ed. by Joachim Remak. (Illus.). 298p. (C). 1987. lib. bdg. 50.00 (*0-8191-6342-2*) U Pr of Amer.

War, Revolution, & Peace in Russia: The Passages of Frank Golder, 1914-1927. Ed. by Terence Emmons & Bertrand M. Patenaude. (Publication Ser.: No. 411). (Illus.). 360p. (Orig.). (C). 1992. text ed. 38.95 (*0-8179-9191-3*); pap. text ed. 24.95 (*0-8179-9192-1*) Hoover Inst Pr.

War, Revolution, & Society in Romania: The Road to Independence. Ilie Ceausescu. (East European Monographs: No. 135). 298p. 1983. text ed. 60.00 (*0-88033-023-6*) East Eur Monographs.

War, Revolution, & the Bureaucratic State: Politics & Army Administration in France, 1791-1799. Howard G. Brown. (Oxford Historical Monographs). 330p. 1995. 55. 00 (*0-19-820542-2*) OUP.

War, Revolution & the Ku Klux Klan: A Study of Intolerance in a Border City. Shawn Lay. LC 85-90937. 224p. 1985. 20.00 (*0-87404-094-9*) Tex Western.

***War Scare: Nuclear Countdown after the Soviet Fall.** Peter Pry. LC 97-3854. 1997. 22.95 (*1-57036-357-9*) Turner Pub GA.

War Scare on the Rio Grande: Robert Runyon's Photographs of the Border Conflict, 1913-1916. Frank N. Samponaro. (Illus.). 1991. 29.95 (*0-87611-099-5*) Tex St Hist Assn.

War Scare on the Rio Grande: Robert Runyon's Photographs of the Border Conflict, 1913-1916. limited ed. Frank N. Samponaro. (Illus.). 1991. boxed 125.00 (*0-87611-100-2*) Tex St Hist Assn.

War Scenes I Shall Never Forget. Carita Spencer. (American Biography Ser.). 72p. 1991. reprint ed. lib. bdg. 59.00 (*0-7812-8358-2*) Rprt Serv.

War Secrets in the Ether. rev. ed. Wilhelm F. Flicke. 245p. 1994. pap. 26.80 (*0-89412-233-9*) Aegean Park Pr.

War Sketches & Incidents Vol. II: Iowa. (Military Order of the Loyal Legion of the United States Ser.: Vol. 56). 508p. 1994. 40.00 (*1-56837-248-5*) Broadfoot.

War Sketches & Indicents as Related by Companions of the Iowa Commandery Vol. 1: Iowa. (Military Order of the Loyal Legion of the United States Ser.: 55). 400p. 1994. write for info. (*1-56837-247-7*) Broadfoot.

War Slang: American Fighting Words & Phrases from the Civil War to the Gulf War. Paul Dickson. Ed. by Paul McCarthy. 416p. (Orig.). 1995. pap. 18.00 (*0-671-75024-0*) PB.

War Stars: The Superweapon & the American Imagination. H. Bruce Franklin. (Illus.). 288p. 1990. reprint ed. pap. 10.95 (*0-19-506692-8*) OUP.

War, State & Society in Wurttemberg, 1677-1793. Peter H. Wilson. (Cambridge Studies in Early Modern History). 320p. (C). 1995. 69.95 (*0-521-47302-0*) Cambridge U Pr.

War Still Raging. Charles Matherson & C. Stephen Byrum. (Illus.). 376p. 1991. 19.95 (*1-879908-01-8*) Milton Pub.

War, "Stonewall" Jackson, His Campaigns & Battles, & the Regiment As I Saw Them. James H. Wood. 200p. 1984. reprint ed. 27.95 (*0-913419-03-6*) Amereon Ltd.

War Stories. Date not set. write for info. (*0-312-93135-2*) St Martin.

War Stories: A Collection of One Hundred Fifty Little Known Human Interest Stories of the Campaign & Battle of Gettysburg. Gregory A. Coco. (Illus.). 72p. (C). 1992. pap. text ed. 5.95 (*0-939631-55-5*) Thomas Publications.

***War Stories: Accounts of People Victimized by Invasions of Privacy.** Robert E. Smith. v, 99p. (Orig.). 1997. pap. text ed. 17.50 (*0-930072-12-X*) Privacy Journal.

War Stories: An Oral History of Life Behind Bars. Susann Walens. LC 96-21322. (Criminology & Crime Control Policy Ser.). 200p. 1997. text ed. 49.95 (*0-275-95575-3*, Praeger Pubs) Greenwood.

War Stories: Civil War in West Virginia. Ed. by David L. Phillips. (Illus.). 490p. (C). 1991. 30.00 (*0-9628218-1-0*) Gauley Mount Pr.

War Stories: Poems. H. R. Coursen. Ed. by Lewis Turco. LC 84-72827. (Illus.). 48p. 1984. 4.00 (*0-910380-05-8*) Cider Mill.

War Stories: Poems about Long Ago & Now. Howard Nemerov. LC 87-5097. (Illus.). x, 70p. 1989. pap. 9.95 (*0-226-57243-9*) U Ch Pr.

War Stories: The Culture of Foreign Correspondents. Mark Pedelty. LC 94-23388. 256p. (C). (gr. 13). 1995. pap. 16. 95 (*0-415-91124-9*, B4913, Routledge NY); text ed. 62. 95 (*0-415-91123-0*, B4909, Routledge NY) Routledge.

War Stories: Veterans Remember WWII. University of Nevada Oral History Program Staff. Ed. by R. T. King. (Illus.). 200p. (Orig.). 1995. pap. 19.95 (*1-56475-369-7*) U NV Oral Hist.

War Stories & Poems. Rudyard Kipling. (World's Classics Ser.). 352p. 1990. pap. 7.95 (*0-19-282656-5*) OUP.

***War Stories from the Field.** rev. ed. Joseph Hession et al. (Illus.). 286p. 1997. pap. 24.95 (*0-942627-39-3*) Woodford Pubng.

War Stories of the Green Berets: The Viet Nam Experience. Hans Halberstadt. (Illus.). 222p. 1994. 19. 95 (*0-87938-955-9*) Motorbooks Intl.

War Story. Patricia Brown. LC 93-80596. 140p. (Orig.). 1994. pap. 8.00 (*0-9625313-5-9*) Mntn Pr MA.

War Story. Jim Morris. 308p. 1994. text ed. 29.95 (*0-87364-147-7*) Paladin Pr.

War, Strategy & Intelligence. Michael I. Handel. 1989. 49. 50 (*0-7146-3311-9*, Pub. by F Cass Pubs UK); pap. 24.50 (*0-7146-4066-2*, Pub. by F Cass Pubs UK) Intl Spec Bk.

War, Strategy, & International Politics: Essays in Honour of Sir Michael Howard. Ed. by Lawrence Freedman et al. 336p. 1992. 75.00 (*0-19-822292-0*) OUP.

War Surgery: Field Manual. Hans Husum. LC 96-1310. (Illus.). 1996. write for info. (*983-9747-14-2*, Pub. by Zed Bks Ltd UK); pap. write for info. (*983-9747-12-6*, Pub. by Zed Bks Ltd UK) Humanities.

War Surgery: Field Manual. Hans Husum et al. (Illus.). 762p. (C). 1996. pap. 110.00 (*1-85649-390-3*, Pub. by Zed Bks Ltd UK); text ed. 225.00 (*1-85649-389-X*, Pub. by Zed Bks Ltd UK) Humanities.

***War Syndromes of the Persian Gulf Battles: Index of New Information with References.** John C. Bartone. 165p. 1997. 47.50 (*0-7883-1528-5*) ABBE Pubs Assn.

***War Syndromes of the Persian Gulf Battles: Index of New Information with References.** John C. Bartone. 165p. 1997. pap. 44.50 (*0-7883-1529-3*) ABBE Pubs Assn.

War System of the Commonwealth of Nations. Charles Sumner. LC 70-137552. (Peace Movement in America Ser.). 71p. 1972. reprint ed. lib. bdg. 19.95 (*0-89198-082-2*) Ozer.

War Talks in Kansas. (Military Order of the Loyal Legion of the United States Ser.: Vol. 15). (Illus.). 391p. 1992. reprint ed. 40.00 (*1-56837-170-5*) Broadfoot.

War Tax Resistance: A Guide to Withholding Your Support from the Military. rev. ed. Ed Hedemann & War Resisters League Staff. (Illus.). 144p. 1992. pap. 12.00 (*0-86571-245-X*) War Res League.

War, Taxation & Rebellion in Early Tudor England: Henry VIII, Wolsey & the Amicable Grant of 1525. G. W. Bernard. LC 86-13065. 208p. 1986. text ed. 39.95 (*0-312-85611-3*) St Martin.

War Taxes. Elaine J. Crauderueff. LC 89-61822. (Orig.). 1989. pap. 3.00 (*0-87574-286-6*) Pendle Hill.

War, Terrible War. Joy Hakim. (History of US Ser.: Vol. 6). (Illus.). 160p. (J). (gr. 3-10). 1994. pap. 10.95 (*0-19-507756-3*); lib. bdg. 14.95 (*0-19-507755-5*) OUP.

War, Terrible War. Joy Hakim. (History of US Ser.: Vol. 6). (Illus.). 160p. (J). (gr. 3-10). 1994. 15.95 (*0-19-509511-1*) OUP.

War That Never Was. Michael A. Palmer. (Illus.). 368p. 1994. 19.95 (*0-918339-28-6*) Vandamere.

War That Wasn't. Turner Publishing Company Staff. LC 93-61018. 104p. 1993. 48.00 (*1-56311-117-9*) Turner Pub KY.

War the Women Lived: Female Voices from the Confederate South. Ed. & Intro. by Walter Sullivan. LC 95-36150. 352p. (C). 1996. 24.95 (*1-879941-30-9*) J S Sanders.

War Through Children's Eyes: The Soviet Occupation of Poland & the Deportations, 1939-1941. Ed. by Irena Grudzinska-Gross & Jan. T. Gross. LC 80-83832. (Publication Series: Archival Documentaries: No. 247). 260p. 1981. reprint ed. pap. 7.95 (*0-8179-7472-5*) Hoover Inst Pr.

War-Time Journal of a Georgia Girl. Eliza F. Andrews. Ed. by Spencer B. King, Jr. LC 75-39489. 416p. 1981. reprint ed. pap. 14.95 (*0-87797-214-1*) Cherokee.

***War-Time Journal of Georgia Girl, 1864-1865.** Eliza F. Andrews. LC 97-24622. (Illus.). 440p. 1997. pap. 16.95 (*0-8032-5931-X*, Bison Books) U of Nebr Pr.

War-Time Strikes & Their Adjustment. Alexander M. Bing. LC 79-156405. (American Labor Ser., No. 2). 1977. reprint ed. 25.95 (*0-405-02915-2*) Ayer.

War to End All Wars: The American Military Experience in World War I. Edward M. Coffman. LC 86-15918. 412p. (C). 1986. reprint ed. pap. 16.95 (*0-299-10964-X*) U of Wis Pr.

***War to Petrify the Heart: The Civil War Letters of a Dutchess County, N. Y. Volunteer.** Richard T. Van Wyck. Ed. by Virginia Kaminsky. LC 97-3120. (Illus.). 384p. (Orig.). 1997. pap. 24.95 (*1-883789-11-7*) Blk Dome Pr.

***War to Petrify the Heart: The Civil War Letters of a Dutchess County, N. Y. Volunteer.** Richard T. Van Wyck. Ed. by Virginia Kaminsky. LC 97-3120. (Illus.). 384p. 1997. 35.95 (*1-883789-12-5*) Blk Dome Pr.

War to Win: Company B 813th Tank Destroyers. Harry D. Dunnagan. Ed. by Vicki H. Warner. (Illus.). 214p. 1992. 17.95 (*0-9631959-1-3*) Royall Dutton Bks.

War Today: East vs. West: Battlefield Europe. write for info. (*0-318-59603-2*) S&S Trade.

War Today: East vs. West: The Machinery of Destruction. write for info. (*0-318-59604-0*) S&S Trade.

War Today: East vs. West: The Nuclear Duel. write for info. (*0-318-59606-7*) S&S Trade.

War Today: East vs. West: The Strategy of Combat. write for info. (*0-318-59710-1*) S&S Trade.

***War-Torn Kingdom.** Dave Morris & Jamie Thompson. (Quest Role-Playing Bks.). (Illus.). 112p. (YA). (gr. 4 up). 1997. pap. 9.95 (*0-8431-7926-0*) Price Stern Sloan.

War-Torn Valley. Joyce Miller. 256p. 1990. 8.10 (*0-317-02913-4*) Rod & Staff.

War Toys. Jesse Ramage. LC 81-84846. 1982. 8.95 (*0-87212-160-7*) Libra.

War Trails of the Blue Ridge. Shepherd M. Dugger. (Illus.). 1974. 6.00 (*0-686-15219-0*) Puddingstone.

War Trap. Bruce Bueno de Mesquita. LC 80-24631. (Illus.). 238p. (C). 1981. 50.00 (*0-300-02558-0*) Yale U Pr.

War Trap. Bruce Bueno de Mesquita. LC 80-24631. (Illus.). 238p. (C). 1983. pap. 15.00 (*0-300-03091-6*, Y-469) Yale U Pr.

War Variations: Bilingual Edition. Amelia Roselli. Tr. by Lucia Re & Paul Vangelisti. (Classics Ser.: No. 81). 160p. (Orig.). 1996. pap. 11.95 (*1-55713-208-9*) Sun & Moon CA.

War, Violence, & Children in Uganda. Ed. by Cole P. Dodge & Magne Raundalen. 159p. 1987. pap. 21.00 (*82-00-18408-0*) Scandnvan Univ Pr.

***War, Violence, & the Modern Condition.** Ed. by Bernd Hueppauf. LC 96-48552. (European Cultures: Vol. 10). (Illus.). vii, 145p. (C). 1997. text ed. 131.45 (*3-11-014702-5*) De Gruyter.

War! War! War! rev. ed. Cincinnatus. 291p. 1984. reprint ed. pap. 6.00 (*0-89562-100-2*) Sons Lib.

***War Wind 2.** Michael Knight. 1997. pap. 19.99 (*0-7615-1151-2*) Prima Pub.

War, Wings & a Western Youth, 1925-1945. Ted C. Hinckley. LC 95-71348. (Illus.). 225p. 1996. 19.95 (*1-57197-009-6*) Pentland Press.

War with Catiline, War with Jugurtha, Etc. Sallust. (Loeb Classical Library: No. 116). 562p. 18.95 (*0-674-99128-1*) HUP.

War with Empty Hands: Self Defense Against Aggression. 1991. lib. bdg. 79.95 (*0-8490-4745-5*) Gordon Pr.

War with Empty Hands: Self-Defense Against Aggression. 2nd ed. Lenox Cramer. (Illus.). 209p. (Orig.). 1991. pap. 16.95 (*0-939427-41-9*, 05017) Alpha Pubns OH.

War with Empty Hands, Supplement 1: Advanced Training. Lenox Cramer. LC 91-73340. (Shadow Warrior Ser.). (Illus.). 96p. (Orig.). 1991. pap. 10.00 (*0-939427-42-7*, 05055) Alpha Pubns OH.

War with Empty Hands, Supplement 2: Field Craft. Lenox Cramer. LC 91-73340. (Shadow Warrior Ser.). (Illus.). 82p. 1991. pap. 14.00 (*0-939427-43-5*, 05056) Alpha Pubns OH.

War with Germany. Leonard P. Ayres. Ed. by Richard H. Kohn. LC 78-22374. (American Military Experience Ser.). (Illus.). 1980. reprint ed. lib. bdg. 15.95 (*0-405-11852-X*) Ayer.

War with Grandpa. Robert K. Smith. (Illus.). 128p. (J). (gr. 5-9). 1984. mass mkt. 3.99 (*0-440-49276-9*, YB BDD) BDD Bks Young Read.

War with Grandpa: A Study Guide. Toni Albert. Ed. by Joyce Friedland & Rikki Kessler. (Novel-Ties Ser.). (J). (gr. 3-6). 1991. pap. text ed. 15.95 (*0-88122-578-9*) Lrn Links.

War with Hannibal. Titus Livy. Tr. by Aubrey De Selincourt. (Classics Ser.). (Orig.). 1965. pap. 12.95 (*0-14-044145-X*, Penguin Classics) Viking Penguin.

War with Mexico. William J. Jacobs. LC 92-46115. (Spotlight on American History Ser.). (Illus.). 64p. (J). (gr. 4-6). 1993. pap. 5.95 (*1-56294-776-1*); lib. bdg. 16. 40 (*1-56294-366-9*) Millbrook Pr.

War with Mexico Reviewed. Abiel A. Livermore. Ed. by Carlos E. Cortes. LC 76-1287. (Chicano Heritage Ser.). 1977. reprint ed. 26.95 (*0-405-09511-2*) Ayer.

War with Military & Civil Aspects: Subject Analysis with Bibliography. John C. Bartone. LC 87-47631. 160p. 1987. 44.50 (*0-88164-542-7*); pap. 39.50 (*0-88164-543-5*) ABBE Pubs Assn.

War with Mutant Spider Ants. Edward Packard. (Choose Your Own Adventure Ser.: No. 152). 128p. (YA). 1994. pap. 3.50 (*0-553-56399-8*) Bantam.

War with Spain. Henry C. Lodge. LC 70-111702. (American Imperialism: Viewpoints of United States Foreign Policy, 1898-1941 Ser.). 1970. reprint ed. 24.95 (*0-405-02035-X*) Ayer.

War with Spain in 1898. David F. Trask. LC 96-21710. xiv, 654p. 1996. pap. 29.95 (*0-8032-9429-8*, Bison Books) U of Nebr Pr.

War with the Newts. Karel Capek. Tr. by Ewald Osers from CZE. LC 89-25373. 240p. 1990. pap. 11.95 (*0-945774-10-9*, PG5038.C3V33) Catbird Pr.

War with the Newts. Karel Capek. 348p. 1985. pap. 12.95 (*0-8101-0663-9*) Northwestern U Pr.

***War with the Newts.** Karel Capek. Tr. by M. Weatherall & R. Weatherall from CZE. 384p. 1996. pap. 14.95 (*0-8101-1468-2*) Northwestern U Pr.

War with the Newts. Karel Capek. Tr. by M. Weatherall & R. Weatherall from CZE. LC 75-41049. (BCL Ser. II). reprint ed. 27.50 (*0-404-14649-X*) AMS Pr.

***War with Two Voices.** Laurence Deonna. (Illus.). 240p. 1989. 24.00 (*1-57889-006-3*); pap. 12.00 (*1-57889-005-5*) Passeggiata.

War with Words: Stucture & Transcendence. Harley C. Shands. LC 77-144009. (Approaches to Semiotics Ser.: No. 12). 1971. text ed. 30.00 (*90-279-1603-9*) Mouton.

War Within: America's Battle over Vietnam. Tom Wells. LC 93-28460. 1994. 30.00 (*0-520-08367-9*) U CA Pr.

War Within: America's Battle Over Vietnam. Tom Wells. 720p. 1996. pap. 19.95 (*0-8050-4491-4*, Owl) H Holt & Co.

***War Within: Experiencing Victory in the Battle for Sexual Purity.** Robert Daniels. LC 96-45359. 224p. 1997. pap. 11.99 (*0-89107-933-5*) Crossway Bks.

War Within: From Victorian to Modernist Thought in the South, 1919-1945. Daniel J. Singal. LC 81-16358. (Fred W. Morrison Series in Southern Studies). (Illus.). xvi, 455p. (C). 1982. text ed. 39.95 (*0-8078-1505-5*); pap. text ed. 19.95 (*0-8078-4087-4*) U of NC Pr.

War Within: Haunted by Confederate Ghosts, the South Still Struggles with Its Misremembered Past. Ed. by Robert Hinton. (Southern Exposure Ser.). (Illus.). 64p. (Orig.). 1990. pap. 5.00 (*0-943810-44-2*) Inst Southern Studies.

War Within & Without. Anne M. Lindbergh. 1995. pap. 14. 95 (*0-15-694703-X*) HarBrace.

***War Without Bloodshed.** Clift. 1997. pap. 14.00 (*0-684-83346-8*) S&S Trade.

War Without Bloodshed: The Art of Politics. Eleanor Clift & Tom Brazaitis. (Illus.). 400p. 1996. 25.00 (*0-684-80084-5*) S&S Trade.

War Without Mercy: Race & Power in the Pacific War. John Dower. LC 85-43462. 416p. 1987. 22.00 (*0-394-50030-X*) Pantheon.

War Without Mercy: Race & Power in the Pacific War. John Dower. LC 85-43462. 416p. 1987. pap. 15.00 (*0-394-75172-8*) Pantheon.

War Without Winners: Afghanistan's Uncertain Transition after the Cold War. Rasul B. Rais. (Illus.). 301p. 1994. 32.00 (*0-19-577535-X*) OUP.

***War Woman.** Conley. LC 97-18593. 1997. 25.95 (*0-312-17058-0*) St Martin.

War, Women & Poetry, 1914-1945: British & German Writers & Activists. Joan M. Byles. LC 94-48454. 200p. 1995. 34.50 (*0-87413-563-X*) U Delaware Pr.

War World III: Sauron Dominion. Created by Jerry Pournelle. 368p. 1991. mass mkt. 4.95 (*0-671-72072-4*) Baen Bks.

War Wounds of Limbs: Surgical Management. Robin M. Coupland. LC 93-7780. (Illus.). 101p. 1993. 70.00 (*0-7506-1491-9*) Buttrwrth-Heinemann.

War Year. Joe W. Haldeman. (Vietnam Ser.). 128p. 1984. mass mkt. 2.95 (*0-380-67975-2*) Avon.

War Years: A Global History of the Second World War. Lloyd E. Lee. LC 88-37938. 496p. (C). 1989. pap. 22.95 (*0-04-445265-9*) Routledge Chapman & Hall.

War Years: A Global History of the Second World War. Lloyd E. Lee. 496p. 1989. 55.00 (*0-04-445266-7*) Routledge Chapman & Hall.

***War Years & the People of Antelope County, Nebraska.** Compiled by Betty Reinke. 168p. 1995. 35.00 (*0-88107-249-4*) Curtis Media.

***War Years & the Veterans of Cheyenne-Kiowa County, Colorado.** Compiled by Betty Sterns & Betty Jacobs. 102p. 1995. 35.00 (*0-88107-257-5*) Curtis Media.

W

War Years with Jeb Stuart. William W. Blackford. LC 93-8969. (Illus.). 322p. 1993. pap. 14.95 (*0-8071-1880-X*) La State U Pr.

War Years with Jeb Stuart. William W. Blackford. (History - United States Ser.). 322p. 1993. reprint ed. lib. bdg. 89.00 (*0-7812-4819-1*) Rprt Serv.

***War, 1939-1945: A Documentary History.** Ed. by Desmond Flower & James Reeves. LC 96-44131. (Illus.). 1142p. 1997. reprint ed. pap. 24.95 (*0-306-80763-7*) Da Capo.

***Warane der Welt, Welt der Warane.** rev. ed. Daniel Bennett. (Illus.). 400p. (ENG & GER.). 1997. pap. 87.50 (*3-930612-05-4*, Pub. by Edition Chimaira GW) Bibliomania.

Waray-English Dictionary. George Tramp. LC 95-83712. 1996. 69.00 (*1-881265-35-8*) Dunwoody Pr.

Warbasse History: A Study in the Sociology of Heredity in Two Parts. James P. Warbasse. (Illus.). 226p. 1991. reprint ed. pap. 34.00 (*0-8328-1952-2*); reprint ed. lib. bdg. 44.00 (*0-8328-1951-4*) Higginson Bk Co.

Warbirds. Richard Herman, Jr. 432p. 1990. mass mkt. 4.95 (*0-380-70838-8*) Avon.

Warbirds: Airpower. Outlet Book Co. Staff. 1990. 19.99 (*0-517-01218-9*) Random Hse Value.

Warbirds of the Sea: A History of Aircraft Carriers & Carrier-Based Aircraft. Walter A. Musciano. LC 93-87478. (Illus.). 592p. 1994. 49.95 (*0-88740-583-5*) Schiffer.

Warbirds of the Sea: Part One, 1911-1945. Walter A. Musciano. (Illus.). 304p. 1992. 29.95 (*0-8306-4235-8*, 4281, TAB-Aero) TAB Bks.

Warbirds of World War II, No. 1. Ed. by Ray Merriam. (World War II Historical Society Monograph Ser.). 50p. 1995. pap. 5.00 (*1-57638-002-5*) Merriam Pr.

Warbirds of World War II, No. 2. Ed. by Ray Merriam. (World War II Historical Society Monograph Ser.). 52p. 1995. pap. 5.00 (*1-57638-003-3*) Merriam Pr.

Warbirds of World War II, No. 3. Ed. by Ray Merriam. (World War II Historical Society Monograph Ser.). 50p. 1995. pap. 5.00 (*1-57638-004-1*) Merriam Pr.

Warbirds of World War II, No. 4. Ed. by Ray Merriam. (World War II Historical Society Monograph Ser.). 50p. 1995. pap. 5.00 (*1-57638-005-X*) Merriam Pr.

Warbirds Worldwide, No. 25. Paul Coogan. (Illus.). 58p. 1993. pap. 10.95 (*1-870601-32-7*) Motorbooks Intl.

Warbirds Worldwide, No. 27. Paul Coggan. 58p. 1994. pap. 10.95 (*1-870601-36-X*, Pub. by Warbirds Worldwide UK) Motorbooks Intl.

Warbirds Worldwide, No. 30. Paul Coggan. (Illus.). 60p. 1994. pap. 10.95 (*1-870601-39-4*, Pub. by Warbirds Worldwide UK) Motorbooks Intl.

Warbirds Worldwide, No. 31. Paul Coggan. (Illus.). 50p. 1995. pap. 10.95 (*1-870601-41-6*, Pub. by Warbirds Worldwide UK) Motorbooks Intl.

***Warbirds Worldwide, No. 37.** (Illus.). 50p. 1996. pap. 10.95 (*1-870601-50-5*, Pub. by Warbirds Worldwide UK) Motorbooks Intl.

***Warbirds Worldwide, No. 38.** (Illus.). 50p. 1996. pap. 10.95 (*1-870601-52-1*, Pub. by Warbirds Worldwide UK) Motorbooks Intl.

***Warbirds Worldwide, No. 39.** (Illus.). 50p. 1997. pap. 10.95 (*1-870601-53-X*, Pub. by Warbirds Worldwide UK) Motorbooks Intl.

Warbirds Worldwide, Vol. 34. Ed. by Warbirds Worldwide Editors. (Illus.). 50p. 1995. pap. 10.95 (*1-870601-47-5*, Pub. by Warbirds Worldwide UK) Motorbooks Intl.

Warbirds Worldwide, Vol. 35. Ed. by Warbirds Worldwide Editors. (Illus.). 50p. 1996. pap. 10.95 (*1-870601-48-3*, Pub. by Warbirds Worldwide UK) Motorbooks Intl.

Warbirds Worldwide, Vol. 36. Ed. by Warbirds Worldwide Editors. (Illus.). 50p. 1996. pap. 10.95 (*1-870601-49-1*, Pub. by Warbirds Worldwide UK) Motorbooks Intl.

Warbirds Worldwide No. 32. Paul Coggan. (Illus.). 50p. 1995. pap. 10.95 (*1-870601-43-2*, Pub. by Warbirds Worldwide UK) Motorbooks Intl.

Warbirds Worldwide No. 33. Paul Coggan. (Illus.). 50p. 1995. pap. 10.95 (*1-870601-44-0*, Pub. by Warbirds Worldwide UK) Motorbooks Intl.

Warbirds Worldwide Directory: An International Survey of the World's Warbird Population. 3rd ed. Chapman et al. (Illus.). 700p. 1996. pap. 44.95 (*1-870601-46-7*, Pub. by Warbirds Worldwide UK) Motorbooks Intl.

Warble Fly Control in Europe: A Symposium in the EC Programme of Coordination of Research on Animal Pathology, Brussels, 16-17 September 1982. Ed. by Chantal Boulard & H. Thornberry. 168p. (C). 1984. text ed. 70.00 (*90-6191-529-5*, Pub. by A A Balkema NE) Ashgate Pub Co.

***Warblers of Europe & Asia.** Jeff Baker. 360p. 1997. text ed. 49.50 (*0-691-01169-9*) Princeton U Pr.

Warblers of the Americas: An Indentification Guide. Jon Curson et al. LC 94-7470. 1994. 40.00 (*0-395-70998-9*) HM.

Warbonnets. CCTP Staff. (Illus.). 17p. 1995. pap. 5.00 (*0-9624883-6-4*) Reddick Enterp.

***Warbreeds.** Prima Publishing Staff. 1997. pap. 19.99 (*0-7615-1200-4*) Prima Pub.

Warburgs: The Twentieth Century Odyssey of a Remarkable Jewish Family. Ron Chernow. 1994. pap. 16.00 (*0-679-74359-6*, Vin) Random.

Warchild. Andrew Cartmel. (Dr. Who New Adventures Ser.). 288p. (Orig.). 1996. mass mkt. 5.95 (*0-426-20464-6*, Pub. by Virgin Pub UK) London Brdge.

Warchild. Ed. by John Ordover. (Star Trek: Deep Space Nine Ser.: No. 7). 288p. (Orig.). 1994. mass mkt. 5.50 (*0-671-88116-7*) PB.

Warchild, Vol. 1. Rob Liefeld. Ed. by Matt Hawkins. (Illus.). 104p. 1996. reprint ed. pap. 12.95 (*1-888610-03-4*) Mximum Pr.

Warcraft & the Fragility of Virtue: An Essay in Aristotelian Ethics. Grady S. Davis. LC 91-20166. 216p. (Orig.). (C). 1992. pap. 19.95 (*0-89301-154-1*) U of Idaho Pr.

***Warcraft II: Dark Saga Official Strategy Guide.** 96p. 1997. per. 12.99 (*0-7615-1184-9*) Prima Pub.

WarCraft II: Tides of Darkness: The Official Strategy Guide. Ed Dille. 1996. pap. 19.95 (*0-7615-0188-6*) Prima Pub.

WarCraft II Vol. II: Beyond the Dark Portal: Official Secrets & Solutions. Mark Walker. 144p. 1996. per., pap. 14.99 (*0-7615-0787-6*) Prima Pub.

***Ward.** Leigh Greenwood. (Cowboys Ser.). 400p. (Orig.). 1997. mass mkt. 5.99 (*0-8439-4299-1*, Leisure Bks) Dorchester Pub Co.

Ward Attending: The Forty Day Month. Lucy M. Osborn & Neal A. Whitman. 194p. 1991. text ed. 30.00 (*0-940193-09-4*) Univ UT Sch Med.

Ward Brothers' Decoys: A Collector's Guide. Ronald J. Gard & Brian J. McGrath. LC 89-60836. (Illus.). 136p. 1989. text ed. 60.00 (*0-9620155-1-2*) T B Reel.

Ward Clerk Skills. Beverly J. Rambo. LC 77-1819. (Nursing & Allied Health Ser.). 1978. text ed. 25.95 (*0-07-051176-4*) McGraw.

Ward Eight. Joseph Dinneen. LC 76-6335. (Irish Americans Ser.). 1976. reprint ed. 29.95 (*0-405-09331-4*) Ayer.

Ward Family & Their 'Helps' Domestic Work, Workers, & Relationships on a New England Farm, 1787-1866. Holly V. Izard. (Illus.). 29p. (Orig.). 1993. pap. 9.00 (*0-944026-46-X*) Am Antiquarian.

***Ward 5B.** Rebecca Ranson. Date not set. pap. write for info. (*0-670-81138-6*) Viking Penguin.

***Ward Lock Encyclopedia of Gardening.** Anita Pereire. 1997. pap. text ed. 29.95 (*0-7063-7639-0*, Pub. by Ward Lock UK) Sterling.

Ward Lock Encyclopedia of Practical Gardening: The Definitive Single-Volume Guide to Garden Plants & Gardening Techniques. Anita Pereire. (Illus.). 702p. 1995. 35.00 (*0-7063-7409-6*, Pub. by Ward Lock UK) Sterling.

Ward Management & Teaching. Jean Barrett. 423p. (C). 1989. 75.00 (*81-7002-032-8*, Pub. by Himalayan Bks II) St Mut.

Ward Management & Teaching. 3rd ed. Ellen L. Perry. (Illus.). 304p. 1988. 26.00 (*0-685-32962-3*, Bailliere-Tindall) Saunders.

Ward Ritchie: The Lagune Verde Imprenta Years, 1975-1990. Bernard N. Jazzar & Wendy M. Mayfield. Ed. by Constance W. Glenn et al. 32p. (Orig.). 1991. pap. write for info. (*0-936270-31-4*) CA St U LB Art.

***Ward Rounds for Medical Students: Clinical Medicine.** G. Sandler. (Illus.). 288p. (Orig.). (C). (gr. 13 up). 1989. pap. text ed. 38.00 (*0-412-30960-2*) Chapman & Hall.

Ward Sister at Catherine's. Mary B. Williams. (Rainbow Romances Ser.). 160p. 1993. 14.95 (*0-7090-4934-X*, Hale-Parkwest) Parkwest Pubns.

Ward Sister at Catherine's. large type ed. Mary-Beth Williams. (Romance Ser.). 256p. 1995. pap. 15.99 (*0-7089-7677-8*, Linford) Ulverscroft.

Ward Six & Other Stories. Anton P. Chekhov. 1976. 19.95 (*0-8488-1267-0*) Amereon Ltd.

Ward Six & Other Stories. Anton P. Chekhov. Tr. by Ronald Hingley. (World's Classics Ser.). 272p. 1988. pap. 5.95 (*0-19-282174-1*) OUP.

Ward Six & Other Stories. Anton P. Chekhov. 384p. 1986. reprint ed. lib. bdg. 18.95 (*0-89966-523-3*) Buccaneer Bks.

Ward Street. Melvin Mincey. (Illus.). 281p. (Orig.). 1994. pap. text ed. 8.95 (*0-9637969-0-9*) Mincey Pub Hse.

Ward Street see Worm That Never Dies

Ward Valley: An Examination of Seven Issues in Earth Sciences & Ecology. 1995. pap. text ed. 39.00 (*0-309-05288-2*) Natl Acad Sci.

Warday. Whitley Strieber & James W. Kunetka. 528p. 1988. mass mkt. 5.95 (*0-446-35727-8*) Warner Bks.

Wardell Buffalo Trap Forty Eight SU 301: Communal Procurement in the Upper Green River Basin, Wyoming. George C. Frison. LC 73-623151. (Anthropological Papers: No. 48). 117p. reprint ed. pap. 33.40 (*0-7837-0552-2*, 2040886) Bks Demand.

Warden. Jack Rudman. (Career Examination Ser.: C-894). 1994. pap. 49.95 (*0-8373-0894-1*) Nat Learn.

Warden. Glen Trevor. 21.95 (*0-8488-1208-5*) Amereon Ltd.

Warden. Anthony Trollope. 240p. 1991. 15.00 (*0-679-40551-8*, Everymans Lib) Knopf.

Warden. Anthony Trollope. Ed. by Barbara Dennis. 352p. 1994. pap. 4.50 (*0-460-87416-0*, Everyman's Classic Lib) C E Tuttle.

Warden. Anthony Trollope. 216p. 1983. pap. 2.50 (*0-451-51815-2*, Sig Classics) NAL-Dutton.

Warden. Anthony Trollope. (World's Classics Ser.). (Illus.). 316p. 1980. pap. 5.95 (*0-19-281506-7*) OUP.

Warden. Anthony Trollope. Ed. & Intro. by Robin Gilmour. (English Library). 240p. 1984. pap. 8.95 (*0-14-043214-0*, Penguin Classics) Viking Penguin.

Warden. large type ed. Anthony Trollope. 220p. 1991. 21.95 (*1-85089-433-7*, Pub. by ISIS UK) Transaction Pubs.

Warden see Barsetshire Novels

***Warden of the Queen's March.** Nigel Tranter. 356p. 1997. pap. 10.95 (*0-340-54597-6*, Pub. by H & S UK) Trafalgar.

Warden Wore Pink. Tekla D. Miller. LC 96-83321. 240p. (Orig.). 1996. pap. 11.95 (*1-879418-24-X*) Biddle Pub.

Warden (1855) Anthony Trollope. 272p. 1993. 5.95 (*0-14-043803-3*, Penguin Classics) Viking Penguin.

Warding of Witch World. Andre Norton. (Secrets of the Witch World Ser.: Vol. 3). 528p. 1996. 22.95 (*0-446-51991-X*) Warner Bks.

Warding of Witch World. Andre Norton. (Secrets of the Witch World Ser.: Vol. 3). 608p. 1998. mass mkt. 6.50 (*0-446-60369-4*, Aspect) Warner Bks.

Wardrobe Cluster: Wardrobe Cluster Concept, No. 3. Judith A. Rasband. (Wardrobe Strategies Ser.: 3). 1996. 85.00 (*0-8273-6164-5*) Delmar.

Wardrobe Evaluation, No. 5. Judith A. Rasband. (Wardrobe Strategies Ser.: 5). 1996. 85.00 (*0-8273-6166-1*) Delmar.

Wardrobe for a Little Girl 1900-1910. Susan B. Sirkis. (Wish Booklets Ser.: Vol. 10). 44p. 1972. pap. 5.95 (*0-913786-10-1*) Wish Bklets.

Wardrobe from the King. Berit Kjos. (Women's Inductive Bible Study Ser.). 96p. 1988. pap. text ed. 6.50 (*0-89693-419-5*, 6-1419, Victor Bks) Chariot Victor.

Wardrobe Strategies for Women. Judith A. Rasband. LC 94-8251. (Illus.). 394p. (Orig.). 1996. pap. text ed. 38.00 (*0-8273-6159-9*) Delmar.

Wardrobe Strategies for Women. Judith A. Rasband. (Fashion Merchandising Ser.). 1996. teacher ed., pap. 12.00 (*0-8273-6160-2*) Delmar.

Wards: An Introduction to Clinical Clerkships. Paul L. Fine. LC 94-11844. 216p. 1994. pap. text ed. 24.95 (*0-316-28322-3*) Lppncott-Raven.

***Ward's Anaesthetic Equipment.** 4th ed. Andrew Davey & John T. Moyle. (Illus.). 399p. 1997. write for info. (*0-7020-2169-5*, Pub. by W B Saunders UK) Saunders.

Ward's Anaesthetic Equipment 3. 3rd ed. Davey. 1992. text ed. 97.00 (*0-7020-1435-4*) HarBrace.

Ward's Automotive Yearbook. Ed. by Harry A. Stark. 1980. 60.00 (*0-686-18833-0*) Wards Comm.

Ward's Automotive Yearbook. Ed. by Harry A. Stark. LC 40-33639. 1982. 75.00 (*0-686-35855-4*) Wards Comm.

Ward's Automotive Yearbook 1982. Ed. by Harry A. Stark. 1982. 75.00 (*0-614-10577-3*, 40-33639) Wards Comm.

Ward's Automotive Yearbook 1983. 45th ed. Ed. by Harry A. Stark. LC 40-33639. (Illus.). 400p. 1983. 85.00 (*0-910589-00-3*) Wards Comm.

Ward's Automotive Yearbook 1984. Ed. by Harry A. Stark. 1984. 95.00 (*0-614-10578-1*) Wards Comm.

Ward's Automotive Yearbook 1985. Ed. by Harry A. Stark. 1985. 110.00 (*0-614-10579-X*) Wards Comm.

Ward's Automotive Yearbook 1986. Ed. by Harry A. Stark. 1986. 125.00 (*0-614-10580-3*) Wards Comm.

Ward's Automotive Yearbook 1987. Ed. by Harry A. Stark. 1987. 140.00 (*0-614-10581-1*) Wards Comm.

Ward's Automotive Yearbook 1988. Ed. by Harry A. Stark. 1988. 150.00 (*0-614-10582-X*) Wards Comm.

Ward's Automotive Yearbook 1989. Ed. by Harry A. Stark. 1989. 160.00 (*0-614-10583-8*) Wards Comm.

Ward's Automotive Yearbook 1990. Ed. by James W. Bush & Harry A. Stark. 1990. 175.00 (*0-614-10584-6*) Wards Comm.

Ward's Automotive Yearbook 1991. Ed. by James W. Bush. 1991. 190.00 (*0-614-10585-4*) Wards Comm.

Ward's Automotive Yearbook 1992. James W. Bush. 1992. 205.00 (*0-614-10586-2*) Wards Comm.

Ward's Automotive Yearbook 1993. Ed. by Deebe Ferris. 1993. 220.00 (*0-910589-10-0*) Wards Comm.

Ward's Automotive Yearbook 1994. Ed. by Deebe Ferris. 1994. 250.00 (*0-910589-11-9*) Wards Comm.

Ward's Automotive Yearbook 1995. Deebe Ferris. 1995. 275.00 (*0-910589-12-7*) Wards Comm.

Ward's Business Directory of U. S. Private & Public Companies, 4 Vols. 90th ed. 1990. Set. 995.00 (*0-8103-4857-8*) Gale.

Ward's Business Directory of U. S. Private & Public Companies, Vols. 1-3. 90th ed. 1990. 885.00 (*0-8103-6832-3*) Gale.

Ward's Business Directory of U. S. Private & Public Companies, Vol. 4: Ranked by Sales Within Industry. 90th ed. 1990. 625.00 (*0-8103-4864-0*) Gale.

Ward's Business Directory Supplement 96. Edgar. 1996. suppl. ed. write for info. (*0-7876-0793-2*) Gale.

Ward's Business Directory, Vol. 1: U. S. Largest Private Companies Plus Selected Public Companies 1989. 89th ed. Meglio. 1300p. 1989. 395.00 (*0-8103-4805-5*) Gale.

Ward's Business Directory, Vol. 2: U. S. Private Companies up to 11 Million in Sales 1989. 89th ed. Meglio. 1300p. 1989. 395.00 (*0-8103-4806-3*) Gale.

Ward's Business Directory, Vol. 3: U. S. Private Companies-Private & Public Companies, 1989. 89th ed. Meglio. 1000p. 1989. 595.00 (*0-8103-4807-1*) Gale.

Ward's Business Directory, 1989, 3 Vols. 89th ed. Meglio. 3600p. 1989. Set. 845.00 (*0-8103-4804-7*) Gale.

Ward's Business Directory, 1989, 2 vols., Vols. 1 & 2. 89th ed. Meglio. 2600p. 1989. 745.00 (*0-8103-4819-5*) Gale.

***Ward's Business Directory 1989, Vols. 1 & 3.** 1989. 745.00 (*0-8103-4821-7*, 00007448, Gale Res Intl) Gale.

Ward's Business Directory 1989, 2 vols., Vols. 2 & 3. 89th ed. Meglio. 2300p. 1989. 745.00 (*0-8103-4822-5*) Gale.

Ward's Business Directory 1991, 4 Vols. 91th ed. Meglio. 1991. 1,050.00 (*0-8103-7463-3*) Gale.

Ward's Business Directory 1991, 3 vols. 91th ed. Julie E. Towell. 1991. 930.00 (*0-8103-7813-2*) Gale.

Ward's Business Directory 1991, Vol. 4. 91th ed. Julie E. Towell. 1991. 655.00 (*0-8103-7817-5*) Gale.

Ward's Business Directory 1992, 3 vols. 92th ed. Julie E. Towell. 1991. 995.00 (*0-8103-7814-0*); 1,150.00 (*0-8103-7559-1*) Gale.

Ward's Business Directory 1992, Vol. 4. 92th ed. Julie E. Towell. 1991. 675.00 (*0-8103-7818-3*) Gale.

Ward's Business Directory 1993, 4 vols. 93th ed. Julie E. Towell. 1992. 1,045.00 (*0-8103-7815-9*); 1,210.00 (*0-8103-7566-4*) Gale.

Ward's Business Directory 1993, Vol. 5. 93th ed. Julie E. Towell. 1992. 710.00 (*0-8103-7819-1*) Gale.

Ward's Business Directory 1994, 5 Vols. 94th ed. Julie E. Towell. 1993. 1,400.00 (*0-8103-8083-8*); 1,250.00 (*0-8103-8084-6*) Gale.

Ward's Business Directory 1994, Vol. 4. 94th ed. Julie E. Towell. 1993. 795.00 (*0-8103-8088-9*) Gale.

***Ward's Business Directory 1995, 5 vols.** 95th ed. 1994. 1,500.00 (*0-7876-0509-3*, 00152903, Gale Res Intl); 1,300.00 (*0-8103-8829-4*, 00005580, Gale Res Intl) Gale.

Ward's Business Directory 1995, 6 vols., Set. 95th ed. Ed. by Susan E. Edgar. 10561p. 1994. 1,650.00 (*0-8103-8828-6*, 030804) Gale.

Ward's Business Directory 1995, Vol. 4. Julie E. Towell. 1994. write for info. (*0-8103-8853-7*, 030811) Gale.

***Ward's Business Directory 1995, Vol. 5.** 95th ed. 1994. 825.00 (*0-8103-8833-2*, 00009448, Gale Res Intl) Gale.

Ward's Business Directory 1995 Vol. 6, Pts. 1 & 2: State Rankings by Sales Within 4 Digit SIC. 95th ed. Ed. by Susan E. Edgar. 2853p. 1994. 825.00 (*0-7876-0382-1*, 189382) Gale.

Ward's Business Directory 1996, 4 vols. & supplement, Set. 96th ed. S. Edgar. (Ward's Business Directory Ser.). 7600p. 1995. 1,635.00 (*0-8103-5651-1*, 101659) Gale.

Ward's Business Directory 1996, 6 vols., Vol. 1. Edgar. 1995. write for info. (*0-8103-5646-5*) Gale.

Ward's Business Directory 1996, 5 vol. set, Vol. 1-5. 96th ed. 1995. 1,845.00 (*0-7876-0765-7*) Gale.

Ward's Business Directory 1996, 6 vols., Vol. 2. Edgar. 1995. write for info. (*0-8103-5647-3*) Gale.

Ward's Business Directory 1996, 6 vols., Vol. 3. Edgar. 1995. write for info. (*0-8103-5648-1*) Gale.

Ward's Business Directory 1996, 6 vols., Vol. 4. Edgar. 1995. write for info. (*0-8103-5649-X*) Gale.

Ward's Business Directory 1996, Vol. 5. 96th ed. Ed. by S. Edgar. (Ward's Business Directory Ser.). 1375p. 1995. 850.00 (*0-8103-5650-3*, 101658) Gale.

Ward's Business Directory 1996, 2 pts., Vol. 6. 96th ed. Ed. by S. Edgar. 2850p. 1995. 825.00 (*0-7876-0760-6*, 109933) Gale.

Ward's Business Directory 1996, Vol. 6, Pt. 1. Edgar. 1995. write for info. (*0-7876-0366-X*) Gale.

Ward's Business Directory 1996, Vol. 6, Pt. 2. 96th ed. Edgar. 1995. write for info. (*0-7876-0758-4*) Gale.

Ward's Business Directory 1996 Vol. 11: Of U. S. Private & Public Companies, 6 vols., Set. 96th ed. Ed. by Susan E. Edgar. (Ward's Business Directory Ser.: Vols. 1-6). 557p. 1995. 1,995.00 (*0-8103-5645-7*, 109956) Gale.

Ward's Business Directory 1997, Vol. 4. 97th ed. Edgar. 1996. 1,700.00 (*0-8103-6161-2*) Gale.

Ward's Business Directory 1997, Vol. 5. 97th ed. Edgar. 1996. 885.00 (*0-8103-6166-3*) Gale.

***Ward's Business Directory 1997, 2 pts., Vol. 6.** Edgar. 1996. 855.00 (*0-7876-0761-4*) Gale.

Ward's Business Directory 1997, Vol. 7. 97th ed. Edgar. 1996. suppl. ed. 2,075.00 (*0-8103-6160-4*) Gale.

***Ward's Business Directory 1997 & Supplement, 5 vols.** 1996. 1,920.00 (*0-7876-1492-0*, 00156772, Gale Res Intl) Gale.

***Ward's Business Directory 1998, Vol. 5.** 98th ed. 1997. 885.00 (*0-7876-1005-4*, 00156051, Gale Res Intl) Gale.

***Ward's Business Directory 1998, Vol. 6, 2 Pts.** 1997. 855.00 (*0-7876-1006-2*, 00156052, Gale Res Intl) Gale.

***Ward's Business Directory 1998 & Supplement, 5 vols.** 1997. 1,920.00 (*0-7876-1493-9*, 00156773, Gale Res Intl) Gale.

***Ward's Business Directory 1998 & Supplement, 7 vols.** 98th ed. 1997. 2,075.00 (*0-7876-1000-3*, 00156046, Gale Res Intl) Gale.

Ward's History of Coffee County. Warren P. Ward. LC 78-13236. 1978. reprint ed. 25.00 (*0-87152-290-X*) Reprint.

***Ward's Insurance Results, Life-Health, 1997.** Ward Financial Group Staff. 575p. 1997. 525.00 (*0-9642358-6-2*) Ward Financial.

***Ward's Insurance Results, Property-Casualty, 1997.** Ward Financial Group Staff. 1997. 525.00 (*0-9642358-7-0*) Ward Financial.

Ward's Natural Sign Language Thesaurus of Useful Signs N' Synonyms. Jill Ward. Ed. by John Joyce. LC 77-93547. (Illus.). 1978. 29.95 (*0-917002-18-0*, 446) Joyce Media.

Wards of Liberty. Myra Kelly. LC 74-140332. (Short Story Index Reprint Ser.). (Illus.). 1977. 20.95 (*0-8369-3724-4*) Ayer.

Ward's Private Company Profiles. Ed. by Jennifer A. Mast. 750p. 1993. 139.00 (*0-8103-9140-6*, 101789) Gale.

***Ward's Private Company Profiles.** 3rd ed. 1998. 145.00 (*0-8103-9312-3*, 00002819, Gale Res Intl) Gale.

***Ward's Private Company Profiles.** 4th ed. Date not set. 145.00 (*0-8103-9313-1*, 00002868, Gale Res Intl) Gale.

Ward's Private Company Profiles, Vol. 2. 2nd ed. Ed. by Jennifer A. Mast. 699p. 1994. 139.00 (*0-8103-9311-5*) Gale.

Wards Sales Prospector 1992, Vol. 2. 92th ed. Ed. by Kenneth Estell. 1200p. 1992. 175.00 (*0-8103-8890-1*, 022280) Gale.

Wards Sales Prospector 1992, Vol. 3. 92th ed. Ed. by Kenneth Estell. 1200p. 1992. 175.00 (*0-8103-8891-X*, 022305) Gale.

Wards Sales Prospector 1992, Vol. 1: A Directory of Leads by State & by Industry. 92th ed. Ed. by Kenneth Estell. 1200p. 1992. 175.00 (*0-8103-8889-8*, 022255) Gale.

Wards Sales Prospector 1992, Vol. 4: A Directory of Leads by State & by Industry. 92th ed. Ed. by Kenneth Estell. 1200p. 1992. 175.00 (*0-8103-8892-8*, 022330) Gale.

Wards Sales Prospector 1992, Vol. 5: A Directory of Leads by State & by Industry. 92th ed. Ed. by Kenneth Estell. 1200p. 1992. 175.00 (*0-8103-8893-6*, 022355) Gale.

Ward's Who's Who Among U. S. Motor Vechicle Manufacturers. Ed. by David C. Smith. 1977. 29.75 (*0-686-18832-2*) Wards Comm.

Ward's Worldwide Automotive Decade of Data - Production, 1994: Passenger Car & Commercial Vehicle Production, 1984-1993. Max Pemberton. (Worldwide Automotive Decade of Data, 1994 Ser.). (Illus.). (Orig.). (C). 1994. pap. 450.00 (*0-910589-98-4*) Wards Comm.

Ward's Worldwide Automotive Decade of Data - Sales, 1994: Passenger Car & Commercial Vehicle Sales, 1984-1993. Max Pemberton. (Worldwide Automotive Decade of Data, 1994 Ser.). (Illus.). (Orig.). (C). 1994. pap. 450.00 (*0-910589-99-2*) Wards Comm.

Ward's Worldwide Automotive Decade of Data, 1994. Max Pemberton. (Illus.). (Orig.). (C). 1994. pap. 750.00 (*0-910589-97-6*) Wards Comm.

Ward's 1994 Worldwide Vehicle Parc. Max Pemberton. (Illus.). (Orig.). (C). pap. 950.00 (*0-910589-50-X*) Wards Comm.

Ward's 1995 Worldwide Automotive Decade of Data - Sales: Passenger Car & Commercial Vehicle Sales - 1985-1994. annuals (Ward's 1995 Worldwide Automotive Decade of Data Ser.). (Orig.). (C). 1995. pap. 475.00 (*0-910589-96-8*) Wards Comm.

Ward's 1995 Worldwide Automotive Decade of Data - Sales & Production: Passenger Car & Commercial Vehicles - 1985-1994, 2 vols., Set. (Ward's 1995 Worldwide Automotive Decade of Data Ser.). (Orig.). (C). 1995. pap. write for info. (*0-910589-94-1*) Wards Comm.

Ward's 1995 Worldwide Automotive Decade of Data - Production: Passenger Car & Commercial Vehicle Production - 1985-1994. annuals (Ward's 1995 Worldwide Automotive Decade of Data Ser.). (Orig.). (C). 1995. pap. 475.00 (*0-910589-95-X*) Wards Comm.

***Ward's 1996 Worldwide Automotive Decade of Data: Passenger Car & Commercial Vehicle Production 1986-1995.** (Orig.). 1996. pap. 495.00 (*0-910589-92-5*) Wards Comm.

***Ward's 1996 Worldwide Automotive Decade of Data: Passenger Car & Commercial Vehicle Production 1986-1995, Set, production & sales vols.** (Orig.). 1996. pap. 800.00 (*0-910589-91-7*) Wards Comm.

***Ward's 1996 Worldwide Automotive Decade of Data: Passenger Car & Commercial Vehicle Sales 1986-1995.** (Orig.). 1996. pap. 495.00 (*0-910589-93-3*) Wards Comm.

Wardship: The Law & Practice. Nasreen Pearce. 126p. 1986. 104.00 (*0-906840-97-X*, Pub. by Fourmat Pub UK) St Mut.

Ware Genealogy: Robert Ware of Dedham, Massachusetts, 1642-1699, & His Lineal Descendants. E. Ware. (Illus.). 335p. 1989. reprint ed. pap. 50.00 (*0-8328-1225-0*); reprint ed. lib. bdg. 58.00 (*0-8328-1224-2*) Higginson Bk Co.

Ware, MA. Ware Historical Society Staff. (Images of America Ser.). 1996. pap. 16.99 (*0-7524-0453-9*, Arcdia) Chalford.

Warehouse Accounting & Control: Guidelines for Distribution & Financial Management. Ernst & Whinney. 268p. 1984. pap. 40.00 (*0-86641-106-2*, 84158) Inst Mgmt Account.

Warehouse Accounting & Control: Guidelines for Distribution & Financial Managers. Ernst & Whinney Staff & Cleveland Consulting Associates Staff. 1985. 50.00 (*0-318-03941-9*); 25.00 (*0-318-03942-7*) Coun Logistics Mgt.

Warehouse & Distribution Automation Handbook. Nicholas D. Adams. 640p. 1996. text ed. 79.95 (*0-07-000400-5*) McGraw.

Warehouse Distribution & Operations Handbook. David E. Mulcahy. 544p. 1993. text ed. 89.50 (*0-07-044002-6*) McGraw.

Warehouse Examiner. Jack Rudman. (Career Examination Ser.: C-895). 1994. pap. 27.95 (*0-8373-0895-X*) Nat Learn.

Warehouse Lighting. (Design Guides Ser.). (Illus.). 26p. 1992. pap. 18.00 (*0-87995-101-X*, DG-2-92) Illum Eng.

Warehouse Management Handbook. 2nd ed. James A. Tompkins. (Illus.). 992p. 1997. text ed. 89.95 (*0-07-065295-3*) McGraw.

Warehouse Operations. Stephen L. Frey. 295p. 1983. 39.95 (*0-930206-14-2*) Weber Systems.

Warehouse Priest. Paul Marx. (Illus.). 364p. 1994. 8.00 (*1-55922-031-7*); pap. 5.00 (*1-55922-032-5*) Human Life Intl.

Warehouse Receiving & Transfer Reports GCA Standard 126-1992: Supplement to Specification EMBARC: Electronic Manifesting & Bar Coding of Paper Stock Shipments. Alan Kotok. 18p. (Orig.). 1992. pap. 42.00 (*0-933505-24-8*) Graph Comm Assn.

Warehouse Sanitation Manual. 144p. 1979. pap. 12.50 (*0-318-12793-8*) Am Inst Baking.

Warehouse Supervisor. Jack Rudman. (Career Examination Ser.: C-926). 1994. pap. 29.95 (*0-8373-0926-3*) Nat Learn.

Warehouseman. Jack Rudman. (Career Examination Ser.: C-890). 1994. pap. 23.95 (*0-8373-0890-9*) Nat Learn.

Warehousing Profitably A Manager's Guide. Kenneth B. Ackerman. (Illus.). text ed. 69.75 (*0-9631776-1-3*) K B Ackerman.

Warehousing Violence. Mark S. Fleisher. (Frontiers of Anthropology Ser.: Vol. 3). 320p. (C). 1989. text ed. 52.00 (*0-8039-3122-0*); pap. text ed. 25.00 (*0-8039-3123-9*) Sage.

***Warendorf Belgian Company Law.** (Letr Ser.). 1996. lib. bdg. 146.00 (*90-411-0284-1*) Kluwer Ac.

Warfare. Robert Harrison. LC 73-82852. (Basic Concepts in Anthropology Ser.). 65p. (C). reprint ed. pap. 25.00 (*0-8357-9056-8*, 2015880) Bks Demand.

Warfare: A Chronological History. Robin Cross. 1991. 29.98 (*1-55521-722-2*) Bk Sales Inc.

Warfare: A Study of Military Methods from the Earliest Times. Oliver L. Spaulding et al. LC 72-4301. (World Affairs Ser.: National & International Viewpoints). 616p. 1977. reprint ed. 37.95 (*0-405-04592-1*) Ayer.

Warfare: The Relation of War to Society. Ludwig Renn. Tr. by Edward Fitzgerald. LC 79-160989. (Select Bibliographies Reprint Ser.). 1977. reprint ed. 23.95 (*0-8369-5857-8*) Ayer.

Warfare Accomplished. Edith Pargeter. 362p. 1991. pap. 13.95 (*0-7472-3399-3*, Pub. by Headline UK) Trafalgar.

Warfare along the Mississippi. Ed. by Norman E. Clarke, Sr. (Illus.). 153p. 1961. 7.50 (*0-915056-19-4*, Clarke Hist Collect Central MI Univ) Hardscrabble Bks.

Warfare & Armed Conflicts: A Statistical Reference to Casualty & Other Figures, 1618-1991, 2 vols., Set. Michael D. Clodfelter. LC 91-52632. 1466p. (C). 1992. lib. bdg. 155.00 (*0-89950-544-9*) McFarland & Co.

Warfare & Diplomacy in Pre-Colonial West Africa. 2nd ed. Robert S. Smith. LC 89-16510. 176p. (C). 1989. text ed. 39.75 (*0-299-12330-8*); pap. text ed. 14.95 (*0-299-12334-0*) U of Wis Pr.

Warfare & Diplomacy in Precolonial Nigeria: Essays in Honor of Robert Smith. Ed. by Toyin Falola. LC 92-13651. (Illus.). (Orig.). 1992. pap. 25.00 (*0-942615-14-X*) U Wis African Stud.

***Warfare & Empires: Contact & Conflict Between European & Non-European Military & Maritime Forces & Cultures.** Ed. by Douglas M. Peers. (Expanding World Ser.: Vol. 24). 350p. 1997. text ed. 98.95 (*0-86078-528-9*, Pub. by Variorum UK) Ashgate Pub Co.

Warfare & the Third Reich: The Rise & Fall of Hitler's Armed Forces. Christopher Chant. 1996. 14.98 (*0-8317-7289-1*) Smithmark.

Warfare & Welfare: Integrating Security Policy into Socio-Economic Policy. Jan Tinbergen & Dietrich Fischer. LC 87-9625. 203p. 1987. text ed. 39.95 (*0-312-00957-7*) St Martin.

***Warfare at Sea.** LC 97-20297. (Illus.). 96p. 1997. 13.98 (*0-7603-0405-X*) Motorbooks Intl.

Warfare, Culture, & Environment. R. Brian Ferguson. LC 83-21452. (Studies in Anthropology). 1984. text ed. 80.00 (*0-12-253780-7*) Acad Pr.

Warfare Evangelism. J. Kip Givens. 1994. pap. 9.95 (*0-9641158-1-6*) Redemp Fellowship.

Warfare for Wealth: Early Indian Perspective. Ranabir Chakravarti. 1986. 34.00 (*0-8364-1570-1*, KL Mukhopadhyay) S Asia.

Warfare, Ideology & Indoctrinability: Evolutionary Perspectives. Ed. by Irenaus Eibl-Eibesfeldt & Frank K. Salter. LC 97-3888. (Illus.). 450p. 1997. 49.95 (*1-57181-923-1*) Berghahn Bks.

Warfare in a Fragile World: Military Impact on the Human Environment. Ed. by Taylor & Francis, Ltd. Staff. 250p. 1980. 45.00 (*0-85066-187-0*) Taylor & Francis.

Warfare in Ancient Greece: A Sourcebook. Michael M. Sage. 320p. (C). 1996. pap. 19.95 (*0-415-14355-1*); text ed. 65.00 (*0-415-14354-3*) Routledge.

Warfare in Antiquity: History of the Arbor War, Vol. I. Hans Delbruck. Tr. by Walter J. Renfroe, Jr. LC 89-24980. (Illus.). 604p. 1990. pap. 24.00 (*0-8032-9199-X*, Bison Books) U of Nebr Pr.

Warfare in Feudal Europe, 730-1200. John Beeler. LC 74-148018. (Illus.). 288p. 1973. pap. 13.95 (*0-8014-9120-7*) Cornell U Pr.

Warfare in Roman Europe, A.D. 350-425. Hugh Elton. LC 95-17531. (Oxford Classical Monographs). (Illus.). 336p. (C). 1996. 72.00 (*0-19-815007-5*, Clarendon Pr) OUP.

***Warfare in Roman Europe AD, 350-425.** Hugh Elton. (Oxford Classical Monographs). 336p. 1997. pap. 22.00 (*0-19-815241-8*) OUP.

Warfare in the Ancient World. Ed. by John Hackett. (Illus.). 256p. 1990. 35.00 (*0-8160-2459-6*) Facts on File.

Warfare in the Book of Mormon. Ed. by William J. Hamblin & Stephen D. Ricks. LC 90-80965. (Illus.). x, 534p. 1990. 19.95 (*0-87579-300-2*) Deseret Bk.

Warfare in the Classical World: An Illustrated Encyclopedia of Weapons, Warriors & Warfare in the Ancient Civilizations of Greece & Rome. John Warry. LC 95-18643. (Illus.). 224p. 1995. pap. 19.95 (*0-8061-2794-5*) U of Okla Pr.

Warfare in the Far North: Finland, Russia & Germany. 1994. lib. bdg. 250.00 (*0-8490-6446-5*) Gordon Pr.

Warfare in the Latin East, 1192-1291. Christopher Marshall. 320p. (C). 1992. text ed. 64.95 (*0-521-39428-7*) Cambridge U Pr.

Warfare in the Latin East, 1192-1291. Christopher Marshall. (Studies in Medieval Life & Thought: No. 17). (Illus.). 308p. (C). 1994. pap. text ed. 22.95 (*0-521-47742-5*) Cambridge U Pr.

Warfare in the Modern World: A Short but Critical Analysis. unabridged ed. Julien Freund. Ed. & Tr. by Simona Draghici from FRE. LC 96-39242. Orig. Title: War in Modern Societies. 102p. 1996. pap. text ed. 5.95 (*0-943045-07-X*) Plutarch Pr DC.

Warfare in the Sokoto Caliphate: Historical & Sociological Perspectives. Joseph P. Smaldone. LC 75-27795. (African Studies Ser.: No. 19). 240p. reprint ed. pap. 68.40 (*0-685-20570-3*, 2030620) Bks Demand.

Warfare in the Twentieth Century: Theory & Practice. Ed. by Colin J. McInnes & Gary D. Sheffield. LC 88-5615. 256p. (C). 1988. pap. 19.95 (*0-04-355035-5*) Routledge Chapman & Hall.

Warfare in the Twentieth Century: Theory & Practice. Ed. by Colin J. McInnes & Gary D. Sheffield. 256p. 1988. text ed. 55.00 (*0-04-355034-7*) Routledge Chapman & Hall.

***Warfare in the Western World Vol. 1: Military Operations from 1600 to 1871.** Robert Doughty et al. 532p. (C). 1996. text ed. 49.16 (*0-669-20939-2*) HM College Div.

***Warfare in the Western World Vol. 2: Military Operations since 1871.** Robert Doughty et al. 564p. (C). 1996. text ed. 49.16 (*0-669-20940-6*) HM College Div.

Warfare of a Nation. Friedrich Meinecke. 1977. 59.95 (*0-8490-2807-8*) Gordon Pr.

Warfare of the Spirit: Developing Spiritual Maturity. Aiden W. Tozer. LC 93-72164. 177p. (Orig.). 1993. pap. 8.99 (*0-87509-545-3*) Chr Pubns.

Warfare under the Anglo-Norman Kings, 1066-1135. Stephen Morillo. LC 94-18931. (Illus.). 219p. (C). 1994. 53.00 (*0-85115-555-3*, Boydell Pr) Boydell & Brewer.

***Warfare under the Anglo-Norman Kings, 1066-1135.** Stephen Morillo. (Illus.). 218p. 1997. pap. 9.00 (*0-85115-689-4*) Boydell & Brewer.

Warfare Weapons. K. Neill Foster. 1995. pap. 8.99 (*0-88965-116-7*, Pub. by Horizon Books CN) Chr Pubns.

Warfare with Satan. Jessie Penn-Lewis. 111p. Date not set. pap. text ed. 4.95 (*0-87508-731-0*) Chr Lit.

Warfield Bride. Bronwyn Williams. 384p. (Orig.). 1994. mass mkt. 4.99 (*0-451-40455-6*, Topaz) NAL-Dutton.

Warfighters: A History of the USAF Weapons School & the 57th Wing. Rick Linares & Chuck Lloyd. (Illus.). 264p. (C). (gr. 13). 1996. 50.00 (*0-7643-0044-X*) Schiffer.

***Warfighters 2: The Story of the U. S. Marine Corps Aviation Weapons & Tactics Squadron One (MAWTS-1)** Rick Llinares & Chuck Lloyd. 352p. 1997. 59.95 (*0-7643-0329-5*) Schiffer.

Warfighting: Maneuver Warfare in the U. S. Marine Corps. Ed. by H. T. Hayden. 208p. 1995. 29.95 (*1-85367-198-3*, Pub. by Greenhill Bks UK) Stackpole.

Warfighting: The U. S. Marine Corps Books on Strategy. 112p. 1995. pap. 10.00 (*0-385-47834-8*) Doubleday.

Wargs! Philip W. Helms & David L. Dettman. 26p. (Orig.). 1993. pap. 7.50 (*1-881799-06-9*) Am Tolkien Soc.

***Warhammer: Game Fantasy.** Games Workshop Staff. 1992. 54.99 (*0-425-13931-X*) Berkley Pub.

Warhead. 1994. mass mkt. 4.99 (*0-373-61897-2*, 1-61897-4) Harlequin Bks.

***Warhead.** Jeffrey Layton. 448p. (Orig.). 1997. mass mkt. 5.99 (*0-380-79154-4*) Avon.

***Warhogs: A History of War Profits in America.** Stuart D. Brandes. LC 96-53139. (Illus.). 432p. 1997. 34.95 (*0-8131-2020-9*) U Pr of Ky.

Warhol. David Bourdon. (Illus.). 1989. 49.50 (*0-8109-1761-0*) Abrams.

Warhol. David Bourdon. (Illus.). 432p. 1995. pap. 24.95 (*0-8109-2634-2*) Abrams.

***Warhol.** Klaus Honnef. 1994. pap. text ed. 9.99 (*3-8228-0565-3*) Taschen Amer.

Warhol: Conversations about the Artist. Patrick S. Smith. Ed. by Stephen C. Foster. LC 87-28565. (Studies in the Fine Arts: The Avant-Garde: No. 59). 392p. reprint ed. pap. 111.80 (*0-8357-1836-0*, 2070771) Bks Demand.

Warhol: Ten Lizes. Franette Guerin-Fermigier & Richard Nicolas. (Art Play Book Ser.). 32p. 1991. 19.95 (*0-8109-3952-5*) Abrams.

***Warhol: The Biography.** Victor Bockris. (Illus.). 570p. 1997. reprint ed. pap. 17.95 (*0-306-80795-5*) Da Capo.

Warhol Shadows. Afterword by Walter Hopps. LC 87-42780. (Illus.). 65p. (C). 1987. pap. 12.50 (*0-939594-07-2*) Menil Collect.

Warhola Untitled, No. 5. James Warhola. (J). Date not set. 15.00 (*0-671-89553-2*, S&S Bks Young Read) S&S Childrens.

Warhola Untitled #4. James Warhola. (J). 1997. 15.00 (*0-689-80559-4*) S&S Childrens.

Warhorse. John Cunningham. 1992. mass mkt. 3.99 (*0-8125-1360-6*) Tor Bks.

Warhosts of Vastmark. Janny Wurts. 1996. mass mkt. 5.99 (*0-614-15546-0*, HarperPrism) HarpC.

Wari: The Pacaas Novos Language of Western Brazil. Daniel L. Everett & Barbara Kern. LC 95-43985. (Descriptive Grammar Ser.). 280p. (C). 1997. text ed. 120.00 (*0-415-00999-5*) Routledge.

Wari Imperialism in Middle Horizon Peru. Katharina J. Schreiber. LC 91-44776. (Anthropological Papers: No. 87). xvii, 332p. (Orig.). 1992. pap. 18.00 (*0-915703-26-2*) U Mich Mus Anthro.

Warkeep 2030. Michael Kasner. 1992. mass mkt. 4.99 (*0-373-62014-4*, 1-62014-5) Harlequin Bks.

Warkis of the Famous & Worthie Knicht, Schir David Lyndesay. Newly Correctit & Augmentit. David Lindsay. LC 75-171797. (English Experience Ser.: No. 352). 362p. 1971. reprint ed. 44.00 (*90-221-0352-8*) Walter J Johnson.

Warlock. Andrew Cartmel. (Dr. Who New Adventures Ser.). (Illus.). 1995. mass mkt. 5.95 (*0-426-20433-6*, Pub. by Virgin Pub UK) London Brdge.

Warlock. Ray Garton. 1989. pap. 3.50 (*0-380-75712-5*) Avon.

Warlock. Oakley Hall. (Western Literature Ser.). 488p. 1996. pap. 17.00 (*0-87417-268-3*) U of Nev Pr.

Warlock. Jim Harrison. 272p. 1982. pap. 12.95 (*0-385-29134-5*, Delta) Dell.

Warlock. Ernest J. Martin. LC 82-61712. (Illus.). 296p. (Orig.). 1983. pap. 5.95 (*0-910759-00-6*) Mars Pubns.

Warlock: Black Spiral. Brandon Blackmoor & Susan Blackmoor. 250p. (YA). (gr. 10 up). pap. 25.00 (*0-9641722-4-0*) Black Gate.

Warlock & Son. Christopher Stasheff. 1991. mass mkt. 5.99 (*0-441-87314-6*) Ace Bks.

Warlock Enraged. Christopher Stasheff. 256p. 1986. reprint ed. mass mkt. 5.50 (*0-441-87334-0*) Ace Bks.

Warlock Heretical. Christopher Stasheff. 224p. 1987. mass mkt. 4.99 (*0-441-87286-7*) Ace Bks.

Warlock in Spite of Himself. Christopher Stasheff. 1986. mass mkt. 5.50 (*0-441-87337-5*) Ace Bks.

Warlock Insane. Christopher Stasheff. 256p. 1989. mass mkt. 4.99 (*0-441-87364-2*) Ace Bks.

Warlock Is Missing. Christopher Stasheff. (Warlock Ser.: Vol. 7). 208p. 1986. reprint ed. pap. text ed. 4.99 (*0-441-84826-5*) Ace Bks.

Warlock Rock. Christopher Stashoff. 288p. 1990. mass mkt. 5.99 (*0-441-87313-8*) Ace Bks.

Warlock Unlocked. Christopher Stasheff. 288p. 1986. mass mkt. 4.99 (*0-441-87332-4*) Ace Bks.

Warlock Wandering. Christopher Stasheff. 304p. 1987. mass mkt. 4.99 (*0-441-87362-6*) Ace Bks.

Warlock's Companion. Christopher Stasheff. 240p. 1988. mass mkt. 4.99 (*0-441-87341-3*) Ace Bks.

Warlord. Elizabeth Elliott. 400p. 1995. mass mkt. 5.50 (*0-553-56910-4*, Fanfare) Bantam.

Warlord. Jason Frost. 1983. mass mkt. 3.50 (*0-8217-1189-X*, Zebra Kensgtn) Kensgtn Pub Corp.

Warlord: Tojo Against the World. Edwin P. Hoyt. (Illus.). 276p. 1993. 24.95 (*0-8128-4017-8*, Scrbrough Hse) Madison Bks UPA.

Warlord, No. 3: Badland. Jason Frost. 1984. mass mkt. 2.50 (*0-8217-1437-6*, Zebra Kensgtn) Kensgtn Pub Corp.

Warlord of Mars. Edgar Rice Burroughs. 158p. 1985. mass mkt. 4.99 (*0-345-32453-6*, Del Rey) Ballantine.

Warlord of Mars. Edgar Rice Burroughs. 1976. reprint ed. lib. bdg. 21.95 (*0-89966-045-2*) Buccaneer Bks.

Warlord Politics in China, 1916-1928. Hsi-sheng Ch'i. LC 75-7482. xiv, 282p. 1976. 42.50 (*0-8047-0894-0*) Stanford U Pr.

Warlords: A Verse Drama. Nicholas Hagger. 1995. pap. 24.95 (*1-85230-648-3*) Element MA.

WarLords: Ancient-Celtic-Medieval. Tim Newark. (Illus.). 432p. 1996. 34.95 (*1-85409-349-5*, Pub. by Arms & Armour UK) Sterling.

Warlords & Holymen: Scotland, Eighty to One Thousand, A.D. Alfred P. Smyth. 279p. 1989. pap. 20.00 (*0-7486-0100-7*, Pub. by Edinburgh U Pr UK) Col U Pr.

Warlords, Artists, & Commoners: Japan in the Sixteenth Century. Ed. by George Elison & Bardwell L. Smith. LC 80-24128. (Illus.). 378p. 1987. pap. text ed. 17.00 (*0-8248-1109-7*) UH Pr.

Warlords II Deluxe: The Official Strategy Guide. Ed Dille. 1995. pap. text ed. 19.95 (*0-7615-0254-8*) Prima Pub.

***Warlords III.** Rick Barba. 1997. pap. 19.99 (*0-7615-1199-7*) Prima Pub.

Warlords of Nin. Stephen R. Lawhead. (Dragon King Trilogy Ser.: Bk. 2). 416p. 1992. mass mkt. 5.99 (*0-380-71630-5*, AvoNova) Avon.

Warlords of Nin, Bk. 2. Stephen R. Lawhead. (Dragon King Trilogy Ser.: Vol. 2). 368p. 1996. pap. 13.00 (*0-310-20503-4*) Zondervan.

Warlords of the Ancient Americas: Central America. Peter G. Tsouras. (Illus.). 240p. 1996. 29.95 (*1-85409-237-5*, Pub. by Arms & Armour UK) Sterling.

Warlords of the Desert. Jessica M. Ney. (Middle Earth Ser.). (Illus.). 40p. (Orig.). (YA). (gr. 12). 1989. pap. 7.00 (*1-55806-058-8*, 8012) Iron Crown Ent Inc.

Warlove, the Hipocrite II. Thomas K. Siemer. 276p. 1986. pap. 9.95 (*0-940157-02-0*) Abbeyhills O C.

Warlpiri Morpho-Syntax: A Lexicalist Approach. Jane Simpson. (Studies in Natural Language & Linguistic Theory). (C). 1991. lib. bdg. 149.50 (*0-7923-1292-9*) Kluwer Ac.

Warm Air Heating for Climate Control. 3rd ed. Cooper & Lee. LC 92-41644. 1993. text ed. 65.00 (*0-13-102369-1*) P-H.

Warm Air Heating for Climate Control. 3rd ed. William B. Cooper et al. LC 92-41644. 564p. (C). 1993. text ed. 76.00 (*0-13-606104-4*) P-H.

Warm & Caring Thoughts from a Sensitive Politician. Bob Dole. 112p. 1995. 6.95 (*0-8216-1005-8*) Carol Pub Group.

Warm & Wearable: Crochet & Knit. Workbasket Magazine Staff. 1994. pap. 9.95 (*0-86675-307-9*) KC Pub.

Warm & Welcome Place. June Strong. LC 93-17787. 1993. pap. 9.99 (*0-8280-0730-6*) Review & Herald.

***Warm & Wondrous Wintertime.** Becky Daniel. (Illus.). 192p. (Orig.). 1996. pap. text ed. 12.95 (*1-56490-023-1*) G Grimm Assocs.

"Warm & Zealous Spirit" John J. Zubly & the American Revolution, a Selection of His Writings. Ed. by Randall M. Miller. LC 81-22367. xii, 211p. 1982. text ed. 14.95 (*0-86554-028-4*, MUP-H029) Mercer Univ Pr.

Warm As Wool. Scott R. Sanders. LC 91-34987. (Illus.). 32p. (J). (gr. k-5). 1992. lib. bdg. 16.00 (*0-02-778139-9*, Bradbury S&S) S&S Childrens.

***Warm at Home.** Roni Schotter. (Illus.). 28p. (J). 3.98 (*0-7651-0032-0*) Smithmark.

Warm-Blooded Animals. Maurice Burton. (World of Science Ser.). (Illus.). 64p. (YA). (gr. 4-7). 1985. 15.95 (*0-8160-1059-5*) Facts on File.

Warm-Climate Gardening: Tips - Techniques - Plans - Projects for Humid or Dry Conditions. Barbara Pleasant. Ed. by Gwen Steege. LC 92-54255. (Illus.). 208p. 1993. pap. 12.95 (*0-88266-818-8*, Garden Way Pub) Storey Comm Inc.

Warm December. Vega Studios Staff. LC 91-9146. 112p. 1992. pap. text ed. 9.95 (*1-880729-01-6*) Vega Pr.

Warm Desert Environment. Andrew Goudie & John Wilkinson. LC 76-9731. (Cambridge Topics in Geography Ser.). 96p. reprint ed. pap. 27.40 (*0-317-26407-9*, 2024463) Bks Demand.

Warm Heart Surgery. Ed. by Tomas A. Salerno. 240p. 1995. 125.00 (*0-340-61023-9*, Pub. by Ed Arnold UK) OUP.

Warm Hearts & Cold Noses: A Common Sense Guide to Understanding the Family Dog. Ernie Smith. LC 87-10173. (Illus.). 96p. (Orig.). 1987. pap. 10.95 (*0-86534-109-5*) Sunstone Pr.

Warm Liguid Life: Memories, Dreams, & Inspirations. Marianne Weidlein. 1993. pap. 14.95 (*0-9629636-2-3*) Aimari Pr.

Warm Memories. Frank Nance. 106p. (Orig.). 1985. pap. text ed. 5.00 (*0-9615739-1-0*) F Nance.

Warm, Moist, Salty God: Women Journeying Towards Wisdom. Edwina Gateley. LC 93-11919. 128p. (Orig.). 1993. pap. 7.95 (*0-940147-26-2*) Source Bks CA.

Warm Place. Nancy Farmer. LC 94-21984. 160p. (J). (gr. 4-6). 1995. 15.95 (*0-531-06888-9*); lib. bdg. 16.99 (*0-531-08738-7*) Orchard Bks Watts.

Warm Place. Nancy Farmer. 160p. (J). (gr. 4-6). 1996. pap. 3.99 (*0-14-037956-8*) Viking Penguin.

An Asterisk (*) at the beginning of an entry indicates that the title is appearing in BIP for the first time.

W

Warm Rooms & Cold. Lars Gustafsson. Tr. by Yvonne L. Sandstroem from SWE. (Orig.). 1975. pap. 6.95 (*0-914278-05-3*) Copper Beech.

Warm Snuggles & Cold Ouchies: A Parable for Children Over & Under 21. Jim Ballard. LC 75-25393. (Mandala Series in Education). 1975. pap. 4.50 (*0-916250-05-9*) Irvington.

Warm Springs. Kerry S. Keys. 54p. 1995. pap. 7.00 (*0-930502-39-6*) Pine Pr.

Warm Storm. Rochelle L. Holt. Ed. by Patricia Schultz. LC 91-7879. (Mellen Poetry Ser.: Vol. 14). 72p. 1991. pap. 12.95 (*0-7734-9790-0*) E Mellen.

Warm Trend. Cory Brown. LC 88-64018. 54p. (Orig.). 1989. 15.95 (*0-930501-18-7*) Livingston U Pr.

Warm Trend. Cory Brown. LC 88-64018. 54p. (Orig.). 1989. pap. 7.95 (*0-930501-19-5*) Swallows Tale Pr.

Warm under the Cat: Haiku & Senryu Poems. Caroline G. Banks. 40p. (Orig.). 1995. pap. 5.00 (*0-9645254-0-2*) Wllngtn Pr.

Warm-Up Exercises, Bk. I. Rita Kisner & Brooke Knowles. 100p. (J). (gr. 5-12). 1984. spiral bd. 19.00 (*0-9610370-8-3*) Thinking Pubns.

Warm-up Exercises, Bk. II. Rita Kisner & Brooke Knowles. 100p. 1985. spiral bd. 19.00 (*0-9610370-9-1*) Thinking Pubns.

Warm-up Exercises: Calisthenics for the Brain, Bk. III. Rita Kisner & B. Knowles. 107p. (J). (gr. 5-12). pap. 19.00 (*0-930599-77-2*) Thinking Pubns.

Warm up for Little League Baseball. rev. ed. Morris A. Shirts. Ed. by Patricia MacDonald. (Illus.). (J). (gr. 3-6). 1990. pap. 2.99 (*0-671-70119-3*, Archway) PB.

Warm-Ups for Brass Instruments. Mitchell. 1990. 8.95 (*0-685-32177-0*, M372) Hansen Ed Mus.

Warm Ups for Meeting Leaders. Susan Bianchi & Jan Butler. Ed. by Jean Parcher & Cathy Lewis. LC 84-61535. (Illus.). 138p. (Orig.). 1984. 29.95 (*0-930733-00-2*) Quality Groups Pub.

Warm Weather Activities: A Coloring Book with Games & Projects That Kids Can Do Again & Again. Jennifer W. McIntosh. Ed. by Kathleen Gavin & Marshall Gavin. (Kids on the Go Ser.). (Illus.). 56p. (Orig.). (J). (ps-8). 1994. pap. 3.95 (*1-885437-04-8*) B dazzle.

Warm Weather & Bad Whiskey: The 1886 Laredo Election Riot. Jerry D. Thompson. LC 91-65783. 218p. 1991. 25.00 (*0-87404-212-7*) Tex Western.

Warm Welcomes. Joan Zeigler. (Illus.). 28p. (Orig.). 1986. pap. 5.95 (*0-933491-12-3*) Hot off Pr.

Warm Winter Love. large type ed. Constance Walker. 181p. 1993. reprint ed. lib. bdg. 13.95 (*1-56054-601-8*) Thorndike Pr.

Warman's American Pottery & Porcelain. Susan Bagdade & Al Bagdade. LC 94-3191. (Encyclopedia of Antiques & Collectibles Ser.). 320p. 1994. 19.95 (*0-87069-693-9*, Wallace-Hmestead) Chilton.

Warman's Americana & Collectibles. 6th ed. Ed. by Harry L. Rinker, Jr. (Illus.). 608p. 1993. pap. 15.95 (*0-87069-684-X*) Chilton.

Warman's Americana & Collectibles. 7th ed. Harry L. Rinker. 608p. 1995. pap. 16.95 (*0-87069-742-0*) Chilton.

***Warman's Americana & Collectibles.** 8th ed. Ed. by Ellen Schroy. (Illus.). 400p. 1997. pap. 17.95 (*0-614-30888-7*, WAMC8) Krause Pubns.

***Warman's Americana & Collectibles.** 8th ed. Ellen Schroy. 1997. pap. text ed. 17.95 (*0-87069-752-8*) Chilton.

Warman's Antique American Games, 1840-1940. rev. ed. Lee Dennis. LC 85-50969. (Illus.). 232p. 1991. pap. 17.95 (*0-87069-630-0*) Chilton.

Warman's Antiques & Collectibles Price Guide. 30th ed. Ed. by Harry L. Rinker. 1996. pap. 15.95 (*0-87069-746-3*) Chilton.

***Warman's Antiques & Collectibles Price Guide.** 31th ed. Ed. by Ellen T. Schroy. 1997. pap. 16.95 (*0-87069-750-1*) Chilton.

Warman's Antiques & Collectibles Price Guide 1995. 29th ed. Harry L. Rinker. 864p. 1995. pap. 18.95 (*0-87069-734-X*) Chilton.

Warman's Coins & Currency. Allen G. Berman. 368p. 1994. pap. 19.95 (*0-87069-710-2*) Chilton.

Warman's Coins & Currency. 2nd ed. Allen G. Berman & Alex G. Malloy. 1996. pap. text ed. 19.95 (*0-87069-747-1*, Wallace-Hmestead) Chilton.

Warman's Country Antiques & Collectibles. 2nd ed. Dana G. Morykan & Harry L. Rinker. LC 93-45256. (Encyclopedia of Antiques & Collectibles Ser.). 384p. 1994. 18.95 (*0-87069-699-8*, Wallace-Hmestead) Chilton.

Warman's Country Antiques & Collectibles. 3rd ed. Dana G. Morykan & Harry L. Rinker. 1996. pap. 14.95 (*0-87069-743-9*) Chilton.

***Warman's Depression Glass: A Value & Identification Guide.** Ed. by Ellen Schroy. (Illus.). 224p. (Orig.). 1997. pap. 24.95 (*0-87069-754-4*, WDC01) Krause Pubns.

Warman's English & Continental Pottery & Porcelain. 2nd ed. Susan Bagdade & Al Bagdade. LC 91-50430. 416p. 1991. pap. 19.95 (*0-87069-577-0*) Chilton.

Warman's Furniture. LC 92-50191. (Illus.). 336p. 1993. pap. 14.95 (*0-87069-626-2*) Chilton.

Warman's Glass. 2nd ed. Ellen T. Schroy. 352p. 1995. pap. 19.95 (*0-87069-738-2*) Chilton.

Warman's Jewelry. Christie Romero. 304p. 1995. pap. 18.95 (*0-87069-696-3*) Chilton.

Warman's Paper. Norman Martinus & Harry L. Reinker. (Illus.). 432p. 1994. pap. 18.95 (*0-87069-672-6*) Chilton.

Warman's Pattern Glass. Ed. by Ellen T. Schroy. LC 92-56761. 192p. 1993. pap. 15.95 (*0-87069-673-4*, Wallace-Hmestead) Chilton.

Warmblood Guidebook. Charlene Strickland. LC 92-35016. (Illus.). 256p. 1992. 34.95 (*0-939481-28-6*) Half Halt Pr.

Warmed by Love. Leonard Nimoy. LC 83-71747. 150p. 1983. text ed. 16.95 (*0-88396-200-4*) Blue Mtn Pr CO.

Warmed Heart: A 30-day Journey in the Company of John Wesley. Mark A. Harmon. 80p. 1995. per., pap. 6.99 (*0-8341-1555-7*) Beacon Hill.

Warmeleitung see Heat Conduction

***Warming Fires: Stories for All Seasons.** Jeff Kunkel. 192p. (Orig.). 1997. pap. 13.95 (*1-883953-20-0*, Face to Face) Midwest Trad.

***Warming Fires: Stories for All Seasons.** Jeff Kunkel. LC 97-16081. 192p. 1997. 18.95 (*1-883953-21-9*, Face to Face) Midwest Trad.

Warming of Bornoir's Bed. Sara G. Long. LC 90-70447. (Illus.). 464p. (Orig.). 1992. pap. 12.00 (*1-56002-104-7*) Aegina Pr.

Warming Tract: A Guide to Good Writing from Sports Stories. Michael Paul. LC 86-90402. 54p. (Orig.). (YA). (gr. 7-12). pap. 5.00 (*0-9616367-0-X*) Michael Paul.

Warming Up for the GED. 2nd ed. Ed. by Chuck Herring. 103p. 1980. write for info. (*0-937128-00-7*) GED Inst.

Warmth & the Light: Illuminating Approaches to the Weekly Portion. Aron Soloveitchik. 19.95 (*0-685-63108-7*) Feldheim.

***Warmth & Wonder of Christmas: Devotions to Put a Glow in the Heart of a Family.** Robert Strand. LC 96-69690. 100p. 1996. boxed 10.95 (*0-89221-336-1*) New Leaf.

Warmth Course. Rudolf Steiner. Ed. by G. A. Balaster & A. Dollfus. Tr. by George Adams from GER. 197p. (Orig.). 1988. pap. 20.00 (*0-936132-33-7*) Merc Pr NY.

Warmth of Life. Carol A. Vercz. 1993. 3.75 (*0-910119-15-5*) SOCO Pubns.

Warmups & Workouts: Exercises for Learning(r) Jane Folk. (Illus.). 1995. 22.95 (*0-937857-60-2*, 1486) Speech Bin.

Warmups for Meeting Leaders. Sue Bianchi et al. LC 84-61535. (Illus.). 138p. 1990. ring bd. 49.95 (*0-88390-249-4*, Pfffr & Co) Jossey-Bass.

Warmwater Streams Symposium. Ed. by Louis A. Krumholz. LC 81-65542. 422p. 1981. pap. 15.00 (*0-913235-21-0*) Am Fisheries Soc.

WARN Act: A Manager's Compliance Guide to Workforce Reductions. Joseph A. Brislin. LC 90-2133. 1990. 195.00 (*1-55871-171-6*, BSP 173) BNA Plus.

WARN Act & State Plant-Closing Handbook. Ed. by James F. Fitzpatrick. LC 93-10327. 1993. 45.00 (*0-87179-796-8*) BNA Books.

Warn Your Children. William Tell. LC 95-91022. (Orig.). 1996. pap. 8.95 (*0-533-11824-7*) Vantage.

Warned Off. large type ed. Richard Pitman. (Ulverscroft). 512p. 1994. 25.99 (*0-7089-3048-4*) Ulverscroft.

Warneford V. C. The First Naval Airmen to Be Awarded the VC. Ed. by Mary Gibson. 128p. (C). 1990. pap. 35.00 (*0-902633-91-0*, Pub. by Picton UK) St Mut.

Warner & Laura. Giles Tippette. (Illus.). (J). 1995. mass mkt. 4.99 (*0-671-87160-9*) PB.

Warner Bros. Presents Children's Favorite Songs. Ed. by Carol Cuellar. 180p. (Orig.). (YA). 1995. pap. text ed. 18.95 (*0-89724-619-5*, MF9521) Warner Brothers.

Warner Bros. Presents Christmas Favorites. Ed. by Carol Cuellar. 200p. (Orig.). 1995. pap. text ed. 16.95 (*0-89724-885-6*, AF9547) Warner Brothers.

Warner Bros. Presents Mellow Rock Classics. Ed. by Carol Cuellar. 392p. (Orig.). (YA). 1995. pap. text ed. 18.95 (*0-89724-606-3*, MF9509) Warner Brothers.

Warner Bros. Presents Television Favorites. Ed. by Carol Cuellar. (Warner Bros. Presents Ser.). 252p. (YA). 1995. pap. text ed. 18.95 (*0-89724-944-5*, MF9561) Warner Brothers.

Warner Bros. Presents Wedding Favorites. Ed. by Carol Cuellar. 320p. (Orig.). (YA). 1995. pap. text ed. 18.95 (*0-89724-712-4*, MF9534) Warner Brothers.

***Warner Brothers Animation Art.** Beck & Friedwald. 1997. 75.00 (*0-88363-107-5*) H L Levin.

Warner Brothers Cartoons. Will Friedwald & Jerry Beck. LC 80-27839. 287p. 1981. 27.50 (*0-8108-1396-3*) Scarecrow.

Warner Brothers Present 70s & 80s. Warner. 1995. pap. 18.95 (*0-89724-519-9*, MF9502) Warner Brothers.

Warner Brothers Presents Rock n Roll. Warner. 1995. pap. 18.95 (*0-89724-699-3*, MF9531) Warner Brothers.

Warning: Anthology of Poetry from Prisoners of Oklahoma. Ed. by Mary McAnally. 1980. pap. 5.00 (*0-931350-03-4*) Moonlight Pubns.

Warning! Cute Kid Stories Ahead! St. Paul Pioneer Press Staff. Ed. by Dan Kelly. 176p. 1995. pap. 8.95 (*0-8362-0585-5*) Andrews & McMeel.

Warning: Dying May Be Hazardous to Your Wealth. 2nd ed. Adriane Berg. LC 94-44542. 224p. 1995. pap. 16.99 (*1-56414-161-6*) Career Pr Inc.

Warning: Inadequate Low-Income Subsidy Design Can Cause Problems for Health Care Reform. David A. Super et al. 108p. (Orig.). 1994. pap. 12.00 (*1-57291-000-3*) Ctr on Budget.

Warning: The Coming Great Crash in the Stock Market. Joseph Granville. 402p. 1985. 18.95 (*0-88191-034-1*) Freundlich.

Warning & Response to the Mount St. Helen's Eruption. Thomas F. Saarinen & James L. Sell. LC 84-46. (SUNY Series in Environmental Public Policy). 240p. 1985. text ed. 64.50 (*0-87395-915-9*); pap. text ed. 21.95 (*0-87395-916-7*) State U NY Pr.

Warning! Dating May Be Hazardous to Your Health! Claudette McShane. LC 88-60718. 192p. (Orig.). 1988. pap. 9.95 (*0-941300-08-0*) Mother Courage.

Warning Design: A Research Prospective. Judy Edworthy & Austin Adams. 256p. 1996. 89.95 (*0-7484-0090-7*); pap. 44.95 (*0-7484-0467-8*) Taylor & Francis.

Warning for Fair Women. LC 70-133757. (Tudor Facsimile Texts. Old English Plays Ser.: No. 84). reprint ed. 49.50 (*0-404-53384-1*) AMS Pr.

Warning for Fair Women: A Critical Edition. Charles D. Cannon. LC 73-81080. (Studies in English Literature: No. 86). 241p. 1975. text ed. 58.50 (*90-279-3134-8*) Mouton.

Warning from the West Indies. William M. Macmillan. LC 73-160982. (Select Bibliographies Reprint Ser.). 1977. reprint ed. 25.95 (*0-8369-5850-0*) Ayer.

Warning in the 1260, 1290, 1335 - Dan. 12. M. G. Berry. LC 90-70564. 197p. (Orig.). 1990. per. 14.95 (*0-945383-20-7*, 945-5805) Teach Servs.

Warning of Kashmir. G. S. Raghvan. (C). 1993. reprint ed. 14.00 (*81-7041-824-0*, Pub. by Anmol II) S Asia.

Warning Out in New England. Josiah H. Benton. LC 70-137370. (Select Bibliographies Reprint Ser.). 1977. 16.95 (*0-8369-5571-4*) Ayer.

Warning Out in New England, 1656-1817. Josiah H. Benton. 131p. 1995. reprint ed. pap. 17.50 (*0-8328-4492-6*); reprint ed. pap. 17.50 (*0-8328-4610-4*); reprint ed. lib. bdg. 27.50 (*0-8328-4491-8*); reprint ed. lib. bdg. 27.50 (*0-8328-4609-0*) Higginson Bk Co.

Warning! Revelation - English. Larry Wilson. LC 88-51477. 208p. 1994. per. 5.00 (*1-57258-006-2*) Teach Servs.

***Warning Shot.** Egleton. 1997. 22.95 (*0-312-15685-5*) St Martin.

***Warning Signals: Basic Criteria for Tracking at-Risk Infants & Toddlers.** James Blackman. 10p. Date not set. pap. 3.50 (*0-943657-08-3*, 67) Zero To Three.

Warning! The New Mass. Gommar A. De Pauw. (Illus.). 100p. 1989. reprint ed. write for info. (*0-318-65212-9*) CTM Pubns.

Warning This Is Not a Book. Pete Babones. (New Shoes Ser.). 83p. (Orig.). 1995. pap. 7.00 (*0-9641196-3-3*) Champion Bks.

Warning to Conquerors. Donagh MacDonagh. LC 68-26023. 69p. 6800. 15.95 (*0-8023-1167-9*) Dufour.

Warning: Writer at Work: The Best Collectibles of Larry L. King. Larry L. King. LC 84-24013. (Illus.). 290p. 1985. 17.95 (*0-87565-004-X*); pap. 10.95 (*0-87565-016-3*) Tex Christian.

Warnings. Margaret Buffie. 256p. (YA). (gr. 7-9). 1994. pap. 3.25 (*0-590-43666-X*) Scholastic Inc.

Warnings: An Anthology on the Nuclear Peril. Ed. by John Witte. LC 84-14761. (Illus.). 210p. 1984. pap. 8.00 (*0-918402-08-5*) NW Review Bks.

Warnings from the Far South: Democracy vs. Dictatorship in Uruguay, Argentina & Chile. William C. Davis. LC 95-7017. 256p. 1995. text ed. 59.95 (*0-275-95021-2*, Praeger Pubs) Greenwood.

Warnings of God. Billy J. Daugherty. 32p. (Orig.). 1993. pap. 0.50 (*1-56267-073-5*) Victory Ctr OK.

Warnings to the Churches. J. C. Ryle. 176p. 1992. pap. 4.99 (*0-85151-043-4*) Banner of Truth.

Warnings, Vol. 1: Fundamentals, Design & Evaluation Methodologies. Mark R. Lehto & James M. Miller. LC 86-22866. (Illus.). 287p. 1986. 55.00 (*0-940537-00-1*) Fuller Tech.

Warnock's Eighteen Percent: Children with Special Needs in the Primary School. Caroline Gipps et al. 200p. 1987. 55.00 (*1-85000-139-1*, Falmer Pr); pap. 28.00 (*1-85000-140-5*, Falmer Pr) Taylor & Francis.

***Warp.** Grossman. LC 97-21423. 1997. 10.95 (*0-312-17059-9*) St Martin.

Warp: A Weaving Reference. Blair Tate. (Illus.). 133p. (Orig.). 1992. pap. 14.95 (*0-937274-33-X*) Lark Books.

Warp & Peace. Jonathan Brannen. 18p. (Orig.). 1989. pap. 3.00 (*0-926935-17-8*) Runaway Spoon.

Warp & Weft: A Textile Terminology. Dorothy K. Burnham. 1994. 35.00 (*0-88854-256-9*, Pub. by Royal Ont Mus CN) U of Toronto Pr.

***Warp & Weft: In Search of the I Ching.** G. W. Dickinson. (Orig.). 1997. pap. 23.95 (*1-86163-006-9*, Pub. by Capall Bann Pubng UK) Holmes Pub.

Warp Angel. Stuart Hopen. 288p. 1995. 21.95 (*0-312-85903-1*) Tor Bks.

***Warp Angel.** Stuart Hopen. 1996. mass mkt. 5.99 (*0-8125-3653-3*) Tor Bks.

Warp Book. Barrie Sosinsky. 1995. pap. 24.95 (*0-7615-0034-0*) Prima Pub.

***Warp Knit Fabric Construction: From Stitch Formation to Stitch Construction.** C. Wilkens. 1995. pap. 54.00 (*0-614-20906-4*, Pub. by Textile Inst UK) St Mut.

Warp of Ulster's Past: Interdisciplinary Perspectives on the Irish Linen Industry. Marilyn Cohen. LC 96-28130. 1996. text ed. 49.95 (*0-312-12907-6*) St Martin.

Warp Painting: A Manual for Weavers. Dominie Nash. (Illus.). 32p. (Orig.). 1990. pap. 7.95 (*0-9623468-2-9*) Stellar Pub Hse.

WARP Server: Installation & Administration Guide. John Whatley. (Illus.). 352p. 1996. pap. text ed., pap. 39.95 incl. cd-rom (*0-07-913071-2*) McGraw.

Warp Weighted Loom. Marta Hoffmann. 1980. reprint ed. pap. 16.95 (*82-00-08094-3*) Robin & Russ.

Warp World 3030. T. M. West. (J). 1995. pap. text ed. 4.95 (*0-8114-9321-0*) Raintree Steck-V.

Warp Zone Shakespeare! Active Learning Lessons for the Gifted. Betty Eidenier. (J). (gr. 6-12). 1990. 12.00 (*0-910609-23-3*) Gifted Educ Pr.

Warpath. Tony Daniel. 320p. 1994. mass mkt. 4.99 (*0-8125-1966-3*) Tor Bks.

Warpath. Jake McMasters. (White Apache Ser.: No. 2). 176p. (Orig.). 1994. mass mkt., pap. text ed. 3.99 (*0-8439-3575-8*) Dorchester Pub Co.

Warpath. large type ed. Elliot Long. 224p. 1996. pap. 17.99 (*1-85389-598-9*, Dales) Ulverscroft.

***Warpath: A Story of the 345th Bombardment Group (M) "The Air Apaches" in World War II.** fac. ed. (Illus.). 304p. 1997. reprint ed. 49.95 (*0-7643-0218-3*) Schiffer.

Warpath: The True Story of the Fighting Sioux Told in a Biography of Chief White Bull. Stanley Vestal. LC 84-3557. (Illus.). xxxviii, 291p. 1984. reprint ed. pap. 11.00 (*0-8032-9601-0*, Bison Books) U of Nebr Pr.

Warpath Across the Pacific: The Illustrated History of the 345th Bombardment Group During WWII. 4th rev. ed. Lawrence J. Hickey. LC 89-84113. (Eagles over the Pacific Ser.: Vol. I). (Illus.). 448p. 1996. 75.00 (*0-913511-02-1*) Intl Res & Pub.

***Warpath to Alaska.** Blake Smith. 272p. (Orig.). 1997. pap. 16.95 (*0-88839-401-2*) Hancock House.

Warpaths: Invasions of North America, 1513-1765. Ian K. Steele. (Illus.). 288p. (C). 1994. reprint ed. 25.00 (*0-19-508222-2*) OUP.

Warpaths: Invasions of North America, 1513-1765. Ian K. Steele. (Illus.). 288p. (C). 1995. reprint ed. pap. text ed. 16.95 (*0-19-508223-0*) OUP.

Warped Disks & Inclined Rings Around Galaxies. Ed. by F. Briggs et al. 350p. (C). 1991. text ed. 69.95 (*0-521-40184-4*) Cambridge U Pr.

Warped Star Trek Deep Space Nine. K. W. Jeter. 1996. mass mkt. 5.99 (*0-671-56781-0*, PB Trade Paper) PB.

Warping All by Yourself. Cay Garrett. LC 74-9515. (Illus.). 192p. 1974. pap. 7.50 (*0-934026-39-4*) Interweave.

***Warping & Morphing of Graphical Objects: Book & CD.** Jonas Gomes et al. 400p. 1998. pap. 65.95 (*1-55860-464-2*) Morgan Kaufmann.

Warping Back to Front. Louise E. Fredrickson & Linda Stevens-Sloan. (Illus.). (Orig.). (C). 1989. pap. text ed. 10.00 (*0-9623054-0-5*) L&L Pubns FL.

Warping Calculations. Ed. by Wira Staff. 1984. 65.00 (*0-317-43588-4*) St Mut.

Warping Equipment: Its Choice & Design, with Descriptions of Certain Machines. Ed. by Wira Staff. 1988. 30.00 (*0-317-43591-4*) St Mut.

Warping to the Internet. N. Salomon. 1995. 29.95 incl. cd-rom (*1-55755-284-3*) Abacus MI.

***Warping Your Loom & Tying on New Warps.** 2nd rev. ed. Peggy Osterkamp. (Peggy Osterkamp's New Guide to Weaving Ser.: No. 2). (Illus.). 188p. (Orig.). 1997. pap. 29.95 (*0-9637793-2-X*) Lease Sticks.

Warplanes of the Luftwaffe. World Airpower Journal Staff. 256p. 1995. 34.95 (*1-880588-10-2*) AIRtime Pub.

Warps. Hironori Yasuda. (Super Special Background Patterns (SPATS) Ser.: No. 12). (Illus.). 208p. 1993. pap. 29.95 (*4-87708-103-8*, Pub. by KDC Co Ltd JA) Bks Nippan.

Warrant: Cherry Pie. 80p. 1991. otabind 19.95 (*0-7935-0761-8*, 00694781) H Leonard.

Warrant: Dirty Rotten Filthy Stinking Rich. 112p. 1991. otabind 19.95 (*0-7935-0879-7*, 00694787) H Leonard.

Warrant: Dirty Rotten Filthy Stinking Rich - Cherry Pie. 112p. 1991. otabind 16.95 (*0-7935-0411-2*, 00694763) H Leonard.

Warrant: The Current Debate. Alvin Plantinga. LC 92-13183. 256p. 1993. pap. 23.00 (*0-19-507862-4*) OUP.

Warrant & Proper Function. Alvin Plantinga. LC 92-408. 272p. 1993. pap. 19.95 (*0-685-56686-2*) OUP.

Warrant & Proper Function. Alvin Plantinga. LC 92-408. 272p. 1993. 55.00 (*0-19-507863-2*) OUP.

***Warrant & Transfer Officer.** Jack Rudman. (Career Examination Ser.: Vol. C-3817). 1997. pap. 27.95 (*0-8373-3817-4*) Nat Learn.

***Warrant for Genocide: The Key Elements of Turko-Armenian Conflict.** Vahakn N. Dadrian. Date not set. text ed. write for info. (*1-886434-03-4*) Blue Crane Bks.

***Warrant for Genocide: The Myth.** 1996. 19.95 (*1-897959-25-7*, Pub. by Serif UK) LPC InBook.

Warrant in Contemporary Epistemology: Essays in Honor of Planting's Epistemology. Ed. by Jonathan L. Kvanvig. 320p. (C). 1996. lib. bdg. 62.50 (*0-8476-8158-0*) Rowman.

Warrant in Contemporary Epistemology: Essays in Honor of Planting's Epistemology. Ed. by Jonathan L. Kvanvig. 400p. (C). 1996. pap. text ed. 26.95 (*0-8476-8159-9*) Rowman.

Warranties: Planning Analysis & Implementation. James R. Brennan. LC 94-4631. 1994. text ed. 49.00 (*0-07-007567-0*) McGraw.

Warranties in Cross-Border Acquisitions. Ed. by M. Rubino-Sammartano. LC 93-23307. (International Bar Association Ser.). 480p. (C). 1993. lib. bdg. 185.50 (*1-85333-946-6*, Pub. by Graham & Trotman UK) Kluwer Ac.

Warranting Assent: Case Studies in Argument Evaluation. Ed. by Edward Schiappa. LC 94-13642. (SUNY Series in Speech Communication). 330p. (C). 1995. text ed. 59.50 (*0-7914-2363-8*); pap. text ed. 19.95 (*0-7914-2364-6*) State U NY Pr.

Warrantless Search Law Deskbook. Paul R. Joseph. LC 91-12047. (Criminal Law Ser.). 1991. ring bd. 125.00 (*0-87632-812-5*) Clark Boardman Callaghan.

Warrants & Convertible Debt As Financing Vehicles in the Private Placement Market. Thomas R. Piper & Jaspar H. Arnold, III. (Explorations in Economic Research Four Ser.: No. 2). 26p. 1977. reprint ed. 35.00 (*0-685-61411-5*) Natl Bur Econ Res.

Warrants, Options & Convertibles. Quinten Price & Capel, James, & Company Staff. 180p. 1990. 115.00 (*0-946559-75-9*, Pub. by IFR Pub UK) Am Educ Systs.

Warranty Cost Analysis. Ed. by Blischke & Murthy. 752p. 1993. 225.00 (*0-8247-8911-3*) Dekker.

***Warranty Law in Tort & Contract Actions, Vol. 1.** Fred O. Harris & Alphonse M. Squillante. 1989. text ed. 130.00 (*0-471-62332-6*) Wiley.

***Warranty Law in Tort & Contract Actions, Vol. 2.** Fred O. Harris & Alphonse M. Squillante. 1989. text ed. 130.00 (*0-471-62333-4*) Wiley.

W

Warranty Service for Builders & Remodelers. Carol Smith. Ed. by Sharon Costello. (Customer Service Ser.). (Illus.). 191p. (Orig.). 1991. pap. 22.00 (*0-86718-367-5*) Home Builder.

Warren-Adams Letters, Being Chiefly a Correspondence among John Adams, Samuel Adams, & James Warren, 2 Vols. Massachusetts Historical Society Staff. LC 79-158225. reprint ed. Set. 125.00 (*0-404-06854-5*) AMS Pr.

Warren Akin Candler: The Conservative As Idealist. Mark K. Bauman. LC 80-22230. 290p. 1981. 25.00 (*0-8108-1368-8*) Scarecrow.

Warren-Ballard Debate. Thomas B. Warren & L. S. Ballard. 1979. pap. 10.00 (*0-934916-39-X*) Natl Christian Pr.

Warren-Barnhart Debate on Ethics. Thomas B. Warren & Joe Barnhart. 1981. pap. 14.00 (*0-934916-47-0*) Natl Christian Pr.

Warren Beatty & Desert Eyes: A Life & a Story. David Thomson. LC 87-45934. 480p. 1988. reprint ed. pap. 9.95 (*0-394-75756-4*, Vin) Random.

Warren Brandt: A Retrospective. Gerrit Henry. Ed. by Ruth K. Beesch. (Illus.). 32p. (C). 1992. pap. text ed. 15.00 (*0-9627541-3-7*) UNC Greensboro.

Warren Buffett: The Good Guy of Wall Street. Andrew Kilpatrick. (Illus.). 304p. 1995. pap. 14.95 (*1-55611-432-X*) D I Fine.

***Warren Buffett Speaks: Wit & Wisdom from the World's Greatest Investor.** Janet C. Lowe. LC 96-38904. 1997. text ed. 16.95 (*0-471-16996-X*) Wiley.

Warren Buffett Way: Investment Strategies of the World's Greatest Investor. Robert G. Hagstrom. 288p. 1994. text ed. 24.95 (*0-471-04460-1*) Wiley.

Warren Buffett Way: Investment Strategies of the World's Greatest Investor. Robert G. Hagstrom. LC 94-20586. 274p. 1995. pap. text ed. 14.95 (*0-471-13298-5*) Wiley.

***Warren Buffett Way: Investment Strategies of the World's Greatest Investor.** Robert G. Hagstrom. 1997. pap. text ed. 6.99 (*0-471-17750-4*) Wiley.

Warren Cole, MD, & the Ascent of Scientific Surgery. Dennis Connaughton. (Illus.). 272p. 1991. 24.95 (*0-9628799-0-8*) W & C Cole Found.

Warren Cole, M.D., & the Ascent of Scientific Surgery. Dennis Connaughton. 272p. 1991. text ed. 24.95 (*0-252-01884-2*) U of Ill Pr.

Warren Commission Report. 1992. pap. 12.95 (*0-312-08257-6*) St Martin.

***Warren County, Kentucky, Deed Books, 1821-1825.** (Orig.). 1997. pap. 20.00 (*1-57445-028-X*) TLC Genealogy.

Warren County, Mississippi, Probate Index. Mary L. Ragland & Jane J. Williams. 242p. (Orig.). 1993. pap. text ed. 21.00 (*0-685-70624-9*) Heritage Bk.

Warren County North Carolina Census 1790. Courtney York & Gerlene York. (Orig.). 1972. pap. 12.00 (*0-916660-09-5*) Hse of York.

Warren County North Carolina Census 1810. Courtney York & Gerlene York. (Orig.). 1970. pap. 12.00 (*0-916660-14-1*) Hse of York.

Warren County, North Carolina Marriage Bonds & Certificates, 1780-1867. Francis T. Ingmire. 162p. 1994. pap. 18.00 (*0-8095-8708-4*); lib. bdg. 45.00 (*0-8095-8373-9*) Borgo Pr.

Warren County Running: An In-Depth Race History. Jim Roberts, Jr. (Illus.). 144p. (Orig.). 1995. pap. 13.00 (*0-9645729-2-3*, 500) J W Roberts.

Warren County Story (Tennessee) Ed. by Eugene M. Wiseman. LC 95-60351. (Illus.). 576p. 1995. lib. bdg. 50.00 (*1-881851-08-7*) Genealogy Pub.

Warren County Virginia Marriages, Eighteen Thirty-Six to Eighteen Fifty. John Vogt & T. William Kethley, Jr. (Virginia Historic Marriage Register Ser.). (Illus.). vii, 48p. (Orig.). 1983. pap. 5.00 (*0-935931-20-1*) Borgo Pr.

Warren County Virginia Marriages, Eighteen Thirty-Six to Eighteen Fifty. John Vogt & T. William Kethley, Jr. (Virginia Historic Marriage Register Ser.). vii, 48p. (C). 1983. reprint ed. lib. bdg. 25.00 (*0-8095-8234-1*) Borgo Pr.

Warren County, Virginia Mortality Schedules, 1850, 1860, 1870. Louise Henry. 59p. 1994. pap. 10.00 (*0-8095-8709-2*); lib. bdg. 29.00 (*0-8095-8143-4*) Borgo Pr.

Warren Court: A Retrospective. Bernard Schwartz. 416p. 1996. 45.00 (*0-19-510439-0*) OUP.

Warren Court: Constitutional Decision As an Instrument of Reform. Archibald S. Cox. LC 68-21971. 144p. 1968. 12.95 (*0-674-94740-1*) HUP.

Warren Court: In Historical & Political Perspective. Mark V. Tushnet. 1996. pap. text ed. 14.50 (*0-8139-1665-8*) U Pr of Va.

Warren Court & Its Critics. Clifford M. Lytle. LC 66-28788. 149p. reprint ed. pap. 42.50 (*0-317-28216-6*, 2022756) Bks Demand.

Warren Court & the Constitution: A Critical View of Judicial Activism. John D. Carter. LC 73-7828. 176p. 1972. 19.95 (*0-911116-98-2*) Pelican.

Warren Court in Historical & Political Perspective. Mark V. Tushnet. LC 93-12626. (Constitutionalism & Democracy Ser.). 256p. (C). 1993. text ed. 35.00 (*0-8139-1459-0*) U Pr of Va.

Warren Family: One Thousand Years of History. 1982. 75.00 (*0-946095-00-0*, Pub. by Gresham Bks); pap. 50.00 (*0-946095-01-9*, Pub. by Gresham Bks) St Mut.

Warren Family of Trigg County, Kentucky. Martha J. Stone. (Illus.). 411p. 1990. 49.95 (*0-9617084-5-X*) Martha J Stone.

Warren-Flew Debate on the Existence of God. Ed. by Thomas B. Warren & A. G. N. Flew. 1977. pap. 10.00 (*0-934916-40-3*); audio 30.00 (*0-685-03498-4*); vhs 75.00 (*0-685-03499-2*) Natl Christian Pr.

Warren G. Harding. Linda R. Wade. LC 88-38057. (Encyclopedia of Presidents Ser.). (Illus.). 100p. (J). (gr. 3 up). 1989. lib. bdg. 22.00 (*0-516-01368-8*) Childrens.

Warren G. Harding: A Bibliography. Compiled by Richard G. Frederick. LC 92-8211. (Bibliographies of the Presidents of the United States Ser.: No. 28). 416p. 1992. text ed. 65.00 (*0-313-28186-6*, AP28, Greenwood Pr) Greenwood.

Warren G. Harding: Twenty-Ninth President of the United States. Anne Canadeo. Ed. by Richard G. Young. LC 89-39952. (Presidents of the United States Ser.). (Illus.). 128p. (J). (gr. 5-9). 1990. lib. bdg. 17.26 (*0-944483-64-X*) Garrett Ed Corp.

Warren G Harding Papers: An Inventory to the Microfilm Edition. Andrea D. Lentz. 283p. 1970. 4.00 (*0-318-03212-0*) Ohio Hist Soc.

***Warren G. Magnuson & the Shaping of Twentieth-Century America.** Shelby Scates. LC 97-24392. (Illus.). 392p. 1997. 27.50 (*0-295-97631-4*) U of Wash Pr.

Warren Hastings. Alfred C. Lyall. LC 73-140364. (Select Bibliographies Reprint Ser.). 1977. reprint ed. 20.95 (*0-8369-5607-9*) Ayer.

Warren Hastings: Volume Six of Rulers of India. L. J. Trotter. Ed. by William W. Hunter. LC 70-39407. (Select Bibliographies Reprint Ser.). 1977. reprint ed. 19.95 (*0-8369-9922-3*) Ayer.

Warren, Jackson & Allied Families: Being the Ancestry of Jesse Warren & Betsey Jackson. B. W. Davis. (Illus.). 207p. 1992. reprint ed. pap. 32.50 (*0-8328-2759-2*); reprint ed. lib. bdg. 42.50 (*0-8328-2758-4*) Higginson Bk Co.

Warren Mackenzie: American Potter. David Lewis. (Illus.). 192p. 1991. 65.00 (*4-7700-1528-3*) Kodansha.

Warren MacKenzie, Potter: A Retrospective. David Lewis. Ed. by Susan Brown. LC 89-51231. (Illus.). 128p. (Orig.). 1989. pap. text ed. 30.00 (*0-938713-05-1*) Univ MN Art Mus.

Warren-Matson Debate on the Existence of God. Thomas B. Warren & Wallace I. Matson. LC 78-64546. 1981. 15.00 (*0-934916-45-4*); pap. 11.00 (*0-934916-41-1*) Natl Christian Pr.

***Warren Miller, on Film in Print.** 2nd ed. Warren Miller. (Illus.). 271p. 1995. 24.95 (*0-9636144-1-X*) W Miller Prods.

Warren Miller's Learn to Ski & Snowboard Better. Miller. 1996. pap. 13.00 (*0-684-80012-8*) S&S Trade.

Warren Miller's Ski Fever! Warren Miller. (Illus.). 168p. 1995. pap. 20.00 (*0-06-258662-9*, Harp PBks) Harper SF.

Warren Miller's Ski Fever! Tehabi Books, Inc. Staff. Ed. by Richard L. Needham. (Illus.). 168p. (Orig.). 1995. 40.00 (*1-887656-00-6*) Tehabi Bks.

Warren Neidich: Historical In(ter) vention. Ron Platt et al. LC 91-14972. (Illus.). 16p. 1991. pap. 5.00 (*0-938437-38-0*) MIT List Visual Arts.

Warren Nelson: Gaming from the Old Days to Computers. Ed. by Mary E. Glass. 187p. 1978. lib. bdg. 37.50 (*1-56475-177-5*); fiche write for info. (*1-56475-178-3*) U NV Oral Hist.

Warren on Homicide Permanent Edition, 5 vols., Set. Oscar L. Warren. Date not set. suppl. ed. 147.50 (*0-89941-612-8*, 500570) W S Hein.

Warren R. Austin at the U. N., 1946-1953. George T. Mazuzan. LC 76-52990. 245p. reprint ed. pap. 69.90 (*0-7837-0504-2*, 2040828) Bks Demand.

Warren, RI. Macaulay & Chaney. (Images of America Ser.). 1997. pap. 16.99 (*0-7524-0447-4*, Arcdia) Chalford.

Warren Rohrer. Contrib. by Howard Hussey. (Illus.). 32p. 1989. pap. 15.00 (*0-9623799-8-0*) Locks Gallery.

Warren Rohrer. Contrib. by Steven Z. Levine. (Illus.). 6p. 1991. pap. 2.00 (*1-879173-06-9*) Locks Gallery.

Warren Rohrer: New Painting. David Carrier. LC 93-79953. (Illus.). 36p. (Orig.). 1993. pap. text ed. 15.00 (*1-879173-16-6*) Locks Gallery.

Warren Spahn. Peter Bjarkman. (Baseball Legends Ser.). (Illus.). 64p. (J). (gr. 3 up). 1994. lib. bdg. 15.95 (*0-7910-1191-7*) Chelsea Hse.

Warren the Worm Stories. Jack F. Welsh. (Illus.). (Orig.). (J). (gr. 1-4). 1996. pap. 6.95 (*0-533-11771-2*) Vantage.

***Warren the Worm Stories, Vol. II.** Jack F. Welch. (Illus.). (J). (ps-3). 1997. pap. 6.95 (*0-533-12226-0*) Vantage.

Warren Township, NJ. Alan A. Siegel. (Images of America Ser.). (Illus.). 128p. 1996. pap. 16.99 (*0-7524-0439-3*, Arcdia) Chalford.

Warren Wagontrain Raid. Benjamin Capps. LC 89-42897. (Southwest Life & Letters Ser.). (Illus.). 328p. 1989. reprint ed. pap. 12.95 (*0-87074-295-7*) SMU Press.

Warrenpoint. Denis Donoghue. (Illus.). 1990. 19.45 (*0-394-53966-4*) Knopf.

Warrenpoint. Denis Donoghue. (Irish Studies). 196p. (C). 1994. reprint ed. pap. 16.95 (*0-8156-0303-7*) Syracuse U Pr.

Warren's Abstract Machine: A Tutorial Reconstruction. Hassan Ait-Kaci. (Logic Programming - Research Reports & Notes). 125p. 1991. 30.00 (*0-262-01123-9*) MIT Pr.

Warrens & Related Families of North Carolina & Virginia. Holland D. Warren. 442p. 1990. 48.50 (*0-912081-13-9*) Delmar Co.

Warren's Forms of Agreements, 4 vols. Oscar L. Warren & Gloria C. Markuson. 1954. Updates. ring bd. write for info. (*0-8205-1770-4*) Bender.

Warren's Forms of Agreements: Business Forms. Anelia C. Greenhill. (Desk Edition Ser.). 1975. Updates. ring bd. write for info. (*0-8205-1771-2*) Bender.

Warren's Heaton on Surrogates' Court Practice, 22 vols., Set. 6th ed. Oscar L. Warren & Gloria C. Markuson. 1940. ring bd. write for info. (*0-8205-1780-1*) Bender.

Warren's Movie Poster Price & Guide. Jon R. Warren. (Illus.). 450p. 1992. 29.95 (*0-9634319-0-0*) Am Collect Exch.

Warren's Negligence in the New York Courts, 23 vols. 3rd ed. Oscar L. Warren. LC 67-9319. 1966. Updates. ring bd. write for info. (*0-8205-1790-9*) Bender.

Warren's Operation. G. P. Marzoli & S. Versontini. (Illus.). 90p. 1981. 69.00 (*0-387-10785-1*) Spr-Verlag.

Warren's Weed New York Real Property, 14 vols., Set. Oscar L. Warren & Gloria C. Markuson. 1950. ring bd. write for info. (*0-8205-1800-X*) Bender.

Warrick County. Peyton Autry. (Illus.). 144p. 1986. 21.95 (*0-9617663-1-X*); pap. 14.95 (*0-9617663-0-1*) McDowell Pubns.

Warriner: The Colonial & European Ancestry of Julia Adelaide Warriner. Richard L. Dickson. (Illus.). 123p. 1991. reprint ed. pap. 19.50 (*0-8328-2057-1*); reprint ed. lib. bdg. 29.50 (*0-8328-2063-6*) Higginson Bk Co.

Warring According to Prophecy. Terry Crist. 64p. 1992. pap. 4.99 (*0-88368-225-7*) Whitaker Hse.

Warring According to Prophecy. Terry M. Crist, Jr. Ed. by Jimmy Peacock. (Illus.). 63p. (Orig.). (C). 1990. pap. 4.95 (*0-9623768-2-5*) T Crist Ministries.

Warrington Colescott. Margaret Andera et al. LC 96-77357. (Illus.). 32p. (Orig.). 1996. pap. 10.95 (*0-944110-48-7*) Milwauk Art Mus.

Warrington Colescott: Forty Years of Printmaking: A Retrospective, 1948-1988. Richard Cox & Carlton Overland. (Illus.). (Orig.). (C). 1988. pap. 19.95 (*0-932900-19-4*) Elvejhem Mus.

Warrior. Don Bendell. 352p. (Orig.). 1995. pap. 4.50 (*0-451-18241-3*, Sig) NAL-Dutton.

Warrior. Nicole Jordan. 416p. (Orig.). 1995. mass mkt. 4.99 (*0-380-77831-9*) Avon.

Warrior. Elizabeth Lowell. 1995. mass mkt. 4.99 (*1-55166-032-6*, 1-66032-3, Mira Bks) Harlequin Bks.

Warrior. Donald E. McQuinn. (Military Science Fiction Promotion Ser.). 672p. 1991. mass mkt. 5.99 (*0-345-37348-0*, Del Rey) Ballantine.

Warrior: One Man's Environmental Crusade. Pete Wilkinson & Julia Schofield. LC 95-82204. (Illus.). 142p. 1996. 29.95 (*0-7188-2910-7*, Lutterworth-Parkwest) Parkwest Pubns.

Warrior: The First Modern Battleship. Walter D. Brownlee. (Cambridge Introduction to World History Topic Bks.). (Illus.). 48p. (YA). (gr. 7 up). 1985. pap. text ed. 10.95 (*0-521-27579-2*) Cambridge U Pr.

Warrior - The First & Last. Maritime Books Staff. (C). 1986. text ed. 75.00 (*0-907771-34-3*, Pub. by Maritime Bks UK) St Mut.

Warrior & the Priest: Woodrow Wilson & Theodore Roosevelt. John M. Cooper, Jr. (Illus.). 456p. 1985. pap. text ed. 16.95 (*0-674-94751-7*) Belknap Pr.

Warrior & the Wise Man. David Wisniewski. LC 88-21678. (Illus.). 32p. (J). (gr. k-3). 1989. 16.00 (*0-688-07889-3*); lib. bdg. 15.93 (*0-688-07890-7*) Lothrop.

Warrior at Rest: A Collection of Poetry by Jane Chambers. Jane Chambers. LC 84-4377. 72p. 1984. 6.95 (*0-935672-12-5*) T n T Class.

Warrior Blends with Life: A Modern Tao. Michael LaTorra. LC 93-12491. 1993. pap. 12.95 (*1-55643-160-0*) North Atlantic.

Warrior Born. Jake McMasters. (White Apache Ser.: No. 3). 176p. (Orig.). 1994. mass mkt., pap. text ed. 3.99 (*0-8439-3613-4*) Dorchester Pub Co.

***Warrior Born & Quick Killer, 2 vols. in 1.** Jake McMasters. (White Apache Ser.). 352p. 1997. reprint ed. mass mkt. 4.99 (*0-8439-4231-2*) Dorchester Pub Co.

Warrior Breed. Joseph E. Johnson. 254p. 1996. write for info. (*1-885807-02-3*) Johnson Pubng.

Warrior Bride. Tamara Leigh. 384p. 1994. mass mkt. 5.50 (*0-553-56533-8*) Bantam.

Warrior Chiefs of Southern Africa. Ian J. Knight. (Illus.). 192p. 1995. 24.95 (*1-85314-106-2*) Sterling.

Warrior Code of India's Sacred Song. rev. ed. Mary C. Smith. LC 92-998. (Folklore & Oral Tradition Ser.). 174p. 1992. text ed. 20.00 (*0-8240-2898-8*) Garland.

Warrior Cults: A History of Magical, Mystical & Murderous. Paul Elliott. (Illus.). 208p. 1996. 24.95 (*0-7137-2531-1*, Pub. by Blandford Pr UK) Sterling.

Warrior Diplomats: Guardians of the National Security & a Modernization of Turkey. Metin Tamkoc. LC 73-93301. 414p. reprint ed. pap. 118.00 (*0-317-27776-6*, 2025228) Bks Demand.

Warrior Dreams. James W. Gibson. 357p. 1994. pap. 12.00 (*0-8090-1578-1*) Hill & Wang.

Warrior Dreams. Kathleen Harrington. 416p. (Orig.). 1992. mass mkt. 4.50 (*0-380-76581-0*) Avon.

Warrior Dreams: The Martial Arts & the American Imagination. John J. Donohue. LC 93-9019. 160p. 1994. text ed. 49.95 (*0-89789-346-8*, Bergin & Garvey) Greenwood.

Warrior Enchantresses. Ed. by Kathleen M. Massie-Ferch & Martin H. Greenberg. 352p. 1996. mass mkt. 5.50 (*0-88677-690-2*) DAW Bks.

Warrior for Freedom: Admiral Robert B. Carney. Betty C. Taussig. (Illus.). 296p. 1995. pap. 27.95 (*0-89745-189-9*) Sunflower U Pr.

Warrior for Gringostroika. Guillermo Gomez-Pena. LC 93-14529. (Illus.). 176p. (Orig.). 1993. pap. 14.00 (*1-55597-199-7*) Graywolf.

Warrior Fury. Judd Cole. (Cheyenne Ser.: No. 18). 176p. (Orig.). 1996. mass mkt. 3.99 (*0-8439-4048-4*, Leisure Bks) Dorchester Pub Co.

***Warrior Generals.** Thomas Buell. 1998. pap. write for info. (*0-609-80173-2*, Crown) Crown Pub Group.

***Warrior Generals: Combat Leadership in the Civil War.** Thomas B. Buell. LC 96-32959. 1997. 35.00 (*0-517-59571-0*) Crown Pub Group.

Warrior Gentlemen: "Gurkhas" in the Western Imagination. Lionel Caplan. LC 94-37858. 192p. 1995. 32.00 (*1-57181-852-9*) Berghahn Bks.

Warrior Ghost Plays from Japanese Noh Theater: Parallel Translations with Running Commentary. Chifumi Shimazaki. (Cornell East Asia Ser.: No. 60). (Illus.). 240p. (Orig.). (C). 1993. pap. 12.00 (*0-939657-60-0*) Cornell East Asia Pgm.

Warrior Goddess: Athena. Doris Gates. (Greek Myths Ser.). (Illus.). (J). (gr. 3-7). 1982. pap. 4.99 (*0-14-031530-6*, Puffin) Puffin Bks.

Warrior Government in Early Medieval Japan: A Study of the Kamakura Bakufu, Shugo & Jiteo. Jeffrey P. Mass. LC 74-75875. (Yale Historical Publications: Miscellany: No. 103). 269p. reprint ed. pap. 76.70 (*0-8357-8369-3*, 2033815) Bks Demand.

***Warrior Heart.** Bonander. 1997. mass mkt. 5.99 (*0-671-52981-1*, Pocket Books) PB.

Warrior Herdsmen. Elizabeth M. Thomas. (Illus.). 1981. pap. 10.95 (*0-393-00040-0*) Norton.

Warrior Heritage: A Psychological Perspective of Cambodian Trauma. Seanglim Bit. 250p. 1991. 19.95 (*0-9628625-0-9*) Seanglim Bit.

Warrior in Two Camps: Ely S. Parker, Union General & Seneca Chief. William H. Armstrong. (Iroquois Bks.). (Illus.). 256p. 1990. pap. text ed. 15.95 (*0-8156-2495-6*) Syracuse U Pr.

Warrior in White see Saint John Masias: Marvelous Dominican Gatekeeper of Lima, Peru

***Warrior Lawyer: Powerful Strategies for Winning Legal Battles.** LC 96-54272. 1997. write for info. (*1-57105-050-7*) Bridge St Bks.

Warrior Legacy. Jerry L. Aiello. 350p. 1995. pap. text ed. 29.95 (*1-883702-10-0*) Aiello Grp.

Warrior Lives. Joel Rosenberg. (Guardians of the Flame Ser.: No. 5). 272p. 1990. pap. 4.99 (*0-451-45001-9*, ROC) NAL-Dutton.

Warrior Maiden: A Hopi Legend. Ellen Schecter. (Bank Street Ready-to-Read Ser.). 48p. (J). (ps-3). 1992. pap. 3.99 (*0-553-37022-7*) Bantam.

***Warrior Maiden: A Hopi Legend.** Ellen Schecter. LC 96-33280. (Bank Street Ready-to-Read Bks.). (Illus.). 48p. (J). (gr. 2-4). 1997. lib. bdg. 17.27 (*0-8368-1696-X*) Gareth Stevens Inc.

Warrior Marks. Alice Walker. 1993. 24.95 (*0-15-100061-1*) HarBrace.

Warrior Marks: Female Genital Mutilation & the Sexual Binding of Women. Alice Walker & Pratibha Parmar. 1995. pap. 15.00 (*0-15-600214-0*) HarBrace.

Warrior MCV 1988-94. Christopher F. Foss. (New Vanguard Ser.). (Illus.). 48p. 1994. pap. 12.95 (*1-85532-379-6*, 9343, Pub. by Osprey UK) Stackpole.

Warrior Merchants: Textiles, Trade, & Territory in South India. Mattison Mines. (Illus.). 192p. 1985. 64.95 (*0-521-26714-5*) Cambridge U Pr.

Warrior Moon. Marilyn Jordan. 400p. (Orig.). 1996. mass mkt. 5.50 (*0-505-52083-4*) Dorchester Pub Co.

Warrior Moon. Sara Orwig. 384p. 1995. mass mkt. 4.99 (*0-8217-5041-6*, Zebra Kensgtn) Kensgtn Pub Corp.

Warrior of Mars. John R. Fearn. (Drew Ser.: No. 2). 1995. pap. 15.00 (*0-936071-48-6*) Gryphon Pubns.

Warrior of the Heart. Dan A. Barker. (Vietnam Generation Ser.). 278p. (Orig.). (C). 1992. pap. 15.00 (*0-9628524-7-3*) Burning Cities Pr.

Warrior of the Mist: A Title Suggested by Luculluss Virgil McWhorter: A Biography of Qualchan, Chief Owhi's Son. Terry G. Boyden. LC 95-34789. 372p. 1996. pap. 14.95 (*0-87770-557-7*) Ye Galleon.

Warrior of the Mist: A Title Suggested by Luculluss Virgil McWhorter: a Biography of Qualchan, Chief Owhi's Son. Terry G. Boyden. LC 96-8156. 1996. 24.95 (*0-87770-586-0*) Ye Galleon.

Warrior of the Mist: A Title Suggested by Luculluss Virgil McWhorter: A Biography of Qualchan, Chief Owhi's Son. Abel De Petit-Thouars. Tr. by Charles N. Rudkin. 1995. 15.95 (*0-87770-554-2*) Ye Galleon.

***Warrior of the Skies.** John A. Giegling. (Illus.). 135p. (J). 1970. per. 3.95 (*0-614-24786-1*) Tesseract SD.

Warrior of Zen: The Diamond-Hard Wisdom Mind of Suzuki Shosan. Ed. & Tr. by Arthur Braverman. (Illus.). 128p. 1994. pap. 10.00 (*1-56836-031-2*) Kodansha.

Warrior Outlaws. Mark K. Roberts. 256p. 1993. mass mkt. 3.50 (*0-8217-4374-0*, Zebra Kensgtn) Kensgtn Pub Corp.

Warrior Queens. Antonia Fraser. 1989. 22.95 (*0-394-54939-2*) Knopf.

Warrior Queens. Antonia Fraser. 1994. pap. 14.00 (*0-394-25932-7*) Random.

Warrior Queens. Antonia Fraser. LC 89-40487. 1990. pap. 14.00 (*0-679-72816-3*, Vin) Random.

Warrior Queens. Antonia Fraser. 1996. 14.98 (*0-8317-5614-4*) Smithmark.

***Warrior Returns.** Allan Cole. 1997. mass mkt. 6.99 (*0-345-41312-1*, Del Rey) Ballantine.

Warrior Returns: An Epic Fantasy of the Anteros. Allan Cole. 352p. (J). 1996. 23.00 (*0-345-39459-3*, Del Rey) Ballantine.

Warrior Rule in Japan. Ed. by Marius Jansen. 270p. (C). 1995. text ed. 59.95 (*0-521-48239-9*) Cambridge U Pr.

Warrior Rule in Japan. Ed. by Marius Jansen. 270p. (C). 1995. pap. text ed. 18.95 (*0-521-48404-9*) Cambridge U Pr.

Warrior Saint. Paul S. Rees. 1987. pap. 7.99 (*0-88019-213-5*) Schmul Pub Co.

Warrior Scarlet. Rosemary Sutcliff. LC 94-39547. 240p. (YA). (gr. 5 up). 1994. pap. 5.95 (*0-374-48244-6*, Sunburst Bks) FS&G.

Warrior Scarlet. Rosemary Sutcliff. 1995. 18.50 (*0-8446-6838-9*) Peter Smith.

Warrior Secrets: A Handbook of the Martial Arts. Keith D. Yates. (Illus.). 200p. 1985. pap. 20.00 (*0-87364-306-2*) Paladin Pr.

W

Warrior Song of King Gesar. Douglas J. Penick. LC 96-20173. (Illus.). 176p. 1996. 16.95 (*0-86171-113-0*) Wisdom MA.

Warrior Songs for the White Cavalry. 4th ed. Intro. by Frank W. Sandford. 464p. 1972. 10.00 (*0-910840-14-8*) Kingdom.

***Warrior to Dreadnought: Warship Development 1860-1905.** David K. Brown. (Illus.). 208p. 1997. 59.95 (*1-86176-022-1*) Naval Inst Pr.

Warrior Training Manual: International Procedure, Protocol & Techniques for the Traditional Martial Artist. Jerry L. Aiello. 250p. 1993. pap. text ed. 24.95 (*1-883702-05-4*) Aiello Grp.

Warrior Who Killed Custer: The Personal Narrative of Chief Joseph White Bull. Dakota Chief White Bull. Ed. by James H. Howard. LC 68-25321. 106p. reprint ed. pap. 30.30 (*0-317-27116-4*, 2024691) Bks Demand.

***Warrior Who Would Rule Russia: A Profile of Aleksandr Lebed.** Benjamin S. Lambeth. LC 96-41162. (Illus.). 153p. 1996. pap. 15.00 (*0-8330-2447-7*, MR-805-AF) Rand Corp.

Warrior Wisdom. Ed. by Daniel Moore. LC 93-83457. (Illus.). 192p. 1993. 11.95 (*1-56138-312-0*) Running Pr.

Warrior Witch of Hel. Asa Drake. 240p. 1985. pap. 2.95 (*0-445-20039-1*) Warner Bks.

***Warrior Within.** Robert Moore & Douglas Gillette. 302p. 4.98 (*0-8317-4346-8*) Smithmark.

Warrior Within: A Guide to Applying Your Warrior Spirit. Jerry L. Aiello. (Warrior Ser.). 114p. 1992. pap. text ed. 12.00 (*1-883702-01-1*) Aiello Grp.

Warrior Within: A Guide to Inner Power. Shale Paul. LC 83-72057. (Illus.). 160p. (Orig.). 1984. 12.95 (*0-913787-01-9*); pap. 9.95 (*0-913787-02-7*) Delta G Pr.

Warrior Within: Accessing the Knight in the Male Psyche. Robert Moore & Douglas Gillette. 328p. 1993. pap. 11.00 (*0-380-72069-8*) Avon.

Warrior Within: The Philosophies of Bruce Lee for Better Understanding the World Around You & Achieving a Rewarding Life. John Little. (Illus.). 160p. 1996. pap. 14.95 (*0-8092-3194-8*) Contemp Bks.

Warrior Woman: A Journal of My Life As an Artist. 2nd ed. Tina Le Marque. LC 91-73200. (Illus.). 160p. 1991. pap. 18.95 (*0-9630131-0-6*) Artists & Writers.

Warrior Women: The Anonymous Tractatus de Mulieribus. Deborah L. Gera. LC 96-9610. (Mnemosyne, Bibliotheca Classica Batava Ser.). 205p. 1996. 74.25 (*90-04-10665-0*) E J Brill.

Warrior Women & Popular Balladry, 1650-1850. Dianne Dugaw. (Cambridge Studies in Eighteenth-Century English Literature & Thought: No. 4). (Illus.). 256p. (C). 1989. text ed. 59.95 (*0-521-37254-2*) Cambridge U Pr.

Warrior Women & Popular Balladry, 1650-1850. Dianne Dugaw. LC 95-34137. xvi, 250p. 1995. pap. text ed. 14.95 (*0-226-16916-2*) U Ch Pr.

Warriors. Garneau & Gaboriau. 1994. per. 12.95 (*0-88922-282-7*) Genl Dist Srvs.

Warriors. Tom Sirotnak & Ken Walker. LC 95-11875. 192p. 1995. pap. 9.99 (*0-8054-6262-7*, 4262-62) Broadman.

Warriors. limited rev. ed. Richard L. Stack. Ed. by American Historical Foundation Staff. (Illus.). 95p. (Orig.). 1986. reprint ed. 24.00 (*0-933489-05-6*) Amer Hist Found.

Warriors. rev. ed. Richard L. Stack. Ed. by American Historical Foundation Staff. (Illus.). 95p. (Orig.). 1986. reprint ed. pap. 9.95 (*0-933489-04-8*) Amer Hist Found.

***Warriors, Vol. 7.** Jim Walker. (Wells Fargo Trail Ser.). Date not set. pap. text ed. 8.99 (*1-55661-702-X*) Bethany Hse.

Warriors: Navajo Code Talkers. Kenji Kawano. LC 90-53285. (Illus.). 128p. (Orig.). 1990. pap. 19.95 (*0-87358-513-5*) Northland AZ.

Warriors: Reflections on Men in Battle. Glenn J. Gray. 1967. pap. text ed. 18.25 (*0-06-131294-0*) HarpC.

Warriors: The United States Marines. Ed. by Ross A. Howell, Jr. LC 88-80089. (Illus.). 200p. 1988. 24.95 (*0-943231-08-6*) Howell Pr VA.

Warriors: Warfare & the Native Americans. Norman B. Hunt. (Illus.). 256p. 1995. 24.99 (*0-517-14033-0*) Random Hse Value.

Warriors: Words: A Consideration of Language & Leadership. Keith S. Felton. LC 94-37392. (Praeger Series in Political Communication). 224p. 1995. text ed. 55.00 (*0-275-94992-3*, Praeger Pubs) Greenwood.

Warriors Against Israel. Donald Neff. 600p. (Orig.). 1988. 19.95 (*0-915597-59-4*) Amana Bks.

Warriors & Adventurers. David M. Brownstone & Irene M. Franck. (Work Throughout History Ser.). (Illus.). 192p. 1988. 17.95 (*0-8160-1452-3*) Facts on File.

***Warriors & Adventurers.** Irene M. Franck & David M. Brownstone. LC 87-19947. (Work Throughout History Ser.). 192p. 1988. reprint ed. pap. 54.80 (*0-608-02830-4*, 2063897) Bks Demand.

Warriors & Chiefs. Charles L. Convis. (True Tales of the Old West Ser.: Vol. 1). (Illus.). ii, 62p. (Orig.). 1996. pap. 7.95 (*0-9651954-1-4*) Athena Inst.

Warriors & Churchmen in the High Middle Ages: Essays Presented to Karl Leyser. Ed. by Timothy Reuter. LC 92-22268. 304p. 1992. boxed 55.00 (*1-85285-063-9*) Hambledon Press.

Warriors & Guardians: Native Highland Trees. Hugh Fife. (Natural Heritage Ser.). (Illus.). 192p. (C). 1994. pap. write for info. (*1-874640-65-3*, Pub. by Argyll Pubng UK) St Mut.

Warriors & Lovers: True Homosexual Military Stories, Vol. 2. Ed. by Winston Leyland. 160p. (Orig.). 1992. pap. 14.95 (*0-943595-37-1*) Leyland Pubns.

Warriors & Maidens. Carolyn Osborn. LC 90-49280. 188p. 1991. 19.95 (*0-87565-084-8*) Tex Christian.

Warriors & Priests. John Terra. 1996. 20.00 (*0-7869-0368-6*) TSR Inc.

Warriors & Seafarers. Anne Millard. (Picture History Ser.). (Illus.). (J). (gr. 4-9). 1977. pap. 6.95 (*0-86020-140-6*, Usborne); lib. bdg. 14.95 (*0-88110-108-7*, Usborne) EDC.

Warriors & Wildmen: Men, Masculinity, & Gender. Stephen Wicks. LC 96-3623. 176p. 1996. text ed. 45.00 (*0-89789-454-5*, Bergin & Garvey) Greenwood.

***Warriors & Witches: Myths of Southern Europe.** Stewart Ross. LC 97-19217. (Best Tales Ever Told Ser.). (Illus.). 44p. (YA). (gr. 5 up). 1997. lib. bdg. 17.90 (*0-7613-0705-2*, Copper Beech Bks) Millbrook Pr.

Warrior's Apprentice. Lois M. Bujold. 320p. 1991. reprint ed. mass mkt. 5.99 (*0-671-72066-X*) Baen Bks.

***Warriors Arise: Becoming a True Disciple of Christ.** Jerry Williams. LC 97-65079. 160p. (Orig.). 1997. pap. 14.95 (*0-9656407-0-1*) Harvest Pub.

Warriors at Suez. Donald Neff. 479p. 1987. pap. 9.95 (*0-915597-58-6*) Amana Bks.

Warriors at Work: How Guinea Was Really Set Free. Mustafah Dhada. (Illus.). 352p. 1993. 34.95 (*0-87081-287-4*) Univ Pr Colo.

Warriors Book of Poetry & Prose & the Word. Edna B. Stigger. 72p. (Orig.). 1996. pap. 9.99 (*1-889208-03-5*) Glad Tidngs Pub.

***Warrior's Bride.** Lisa Samson. LC 97-2664. (Abbey Ser.: No. 3). 400p. (Orig.). 1997. pap. 9.99 (*1-56507-636-2*) Harvest Hse.

Warrior's Camera: The Cinema of Akira Kurosawa. Stephen Prince. (Illus.). 370p. 1991. pap. text ed. 18.95 (*0-691-00859-0*) Princeton U Pr.

Warrior's Challenge: David Zeisberger. Dave Jackson & Meta Jackson. LC 96-25292. (Trailblazer Ser.: Vol. 20). (J). (gr. 3-8). 1996. pap. 5.99 (*1-55661-473-X*) Bethany Hse.

Warriors, Conjurers & Priests: Defining African-Centered Literary Criticism. Joyce A. Joyce. 300p. (C). 1993. 29.95 (*0-685-70135-2*); pap. 16.95 (*0-88378-099-2*) Third World.

Warrior's Deception (March Madness) Diana Hall. (Historical Ser.). 1996. mass mkt. 4.50 (*0-373-28909-X*, 1-28909-9) Harlequin Bks.

Warrior's Destiny. Betty Brooks. 1995. pap. 4.99 (*0-8217-4999-4*) NAL-Dutton.

Warriors Don't Cry. abr. ed. Melba P. Beals. Ed. by Anne Greenberg. 240p. (YA). (gr. 7 up). 1995. mass mkt. 3.99 (*0-671-89900-7*, Archway) PB.

Warriors Don't Cry: A Searing Memoir of the Battle to Integrate Little Rock's Central High. Melba P. Beals. Ed. by Julie Rubenstein. 336p. (Orig.). 1995. pap. 12.00 (*0-671-86639-7*, WSP) PB.

Warrior's Dream. Seth Williams. (Orig.). 1996. pap. write for info. (*1-57553-126-7*) Watermrk Pr.

Warrior's Edge. John B. Alexander et al. 240p. 1992. mass mkt. 4.99 (*0-380-71674-7*) Avon.

Warriors for Jerusalem. Donald Neff. 430p. pap. 9.95 (*0-915597-57-8*) Amana Bks.

Warriors for the Working Day. Brian J. Dooley. (Illus.). 109p. (Orig.). 1991. pap. 12.50 (*1-55613-468-1*) Heritage Bk.

Warriors for the Working Day. Roland J. Green. 384p. (Orig.). 1994. pap. 5.50 (*0-451-45349-2*, ROC) NAL-Dutton.

Warrior's Gift. Mack Faith. LC 85-24693. (Associated Writing Programs Novel Award Ser.). 250p. 1986. 24.95 (*0-87745-143-5*) U of Iowa Pr.

Warrior's Gift: A Novel. Mack Faith. LC 85-24693. 250p. reprint ed. pap. 71.30 (*0-7837-1622-2*, 2041915) Bks Demand.

Warriors, Gods & Spirits from Central & South American Mythology. Douglas Gifford. LC 93-1013. (World Mythology Ser.). (Illus.). 128p. (J). (gr. 6 up). 1993. pap. 14.95 (*0-87226-915-9*) P Bedrick Bks.

Warriors, Gods & Spirits from Central & South American Mythology. Douglas Gifford. LC 93-1013. (World Mythology Ser.). (Illus.). 128p. (YA). (gr. 6 up). 1993. lib. bdg. 24.95 (*0-87226-914-0*) P Bedrick Bks.

***Warrior's Honor.** Ignatieff. 1997. 24.95 (*0-8050-5518-5*) H Holt & Co.

***Warrior's Honor.** Ignatieff. 1998. pap. 15.00 (*0-8050-5519-3*) H Holt & Co.

Warriors in Peacetime: The Military & Democracy in Latin America, New Directions for U.S. Policy. Ed. by Gabriel Marcella. LC 94-1380. 190p. (C). 1994. 37.50 (*0-7146-4585-0*, Pub. by F Cass Pubs UK); pap. 19.50 (*0-7146-4115-4*) Intl Spec Bk.

Warriors in Undress. Francis J. Hudleston. LC 73-93346. (Essay Index Reprint Ser.). 1977. 21.95 (*0-8369-1298-5*) Ayer.

Warriors into Traders: The Power of the Market in Early Greece. David W. Tandy. LC 96-23278. (Classics & Contemporary Thought Ser.). 1997. 45.00 (*0-520-20269-4*) U CA Pr.

Warrior's Journey Home: Healing Men, Healing the Planet. Jed Diamond. LC 93-86801. 268p. (Orig.). 1994. 15.95 (*1-879237-61-X*); pap. 13.95 (*1-879237-60-1*) New Harbinger.

***Warrior's Lady.** Madeline Baker. 448p. 1997. mass mkt. 5.99 (*0-8439-4305-X*, Leisure Bks) Dorchester Pub Co.

Warriors, Merchants, & Slaves: The State & the Economy in the Middle Niger Valley, 1700-1914. Richard L. Roberts. LC 86-23138. 305p. 1987. 45.00 (*0-8047-1378-2*) Stanford U Pr.

Warriors of Blood & Dreams. Ed. by Roger Zelazny. 432p. (Orig.). 1995. mass mkt. 5.99 (*0-380-77422-4*, AvoNova) Avon.

***Warriors of Disinformation: American Propaganda, Soviet Lies, & the Winning of the Cold War - An Insider's Account.** Alvin A. Snyder. 1997. pap. 13.95 (*1-55970-389-X*) Arcade Pub Inc.

Warriors of God. William Christie. 1995. mass mkt. 4.99 (*0-312-95393-3*) St Martin.

Warriors of God: Jihad (Holy War) & the Fundamentalists of Islam. Antoine J. Abraham & George Haddad. LC 89-40174. 85p. 1990. text ed. 34.95 (*1-55605-123-9*); pap. text ed. 14.95 (*1-55605-122-0*) Wyndham Hall.

Warriors of Isis. Jean Stewart. (Orig.). 1995. pap. 10.99 (*1-883061-03-2*) Rising NY.

Warriors of Japan, As Portrayed in the War Tales. Paul Varley. LC 93-43651. (Illus.). 292p. (C). 1994. text ed. 43.00 (*0-8248-1575-0*); pap. text ed. 16.95 (*0-8248-1601-3*) UH Pr.

Warriors of Medieval Times. John Matthews & Bob Stewart. (Illus.). 192p. 1993. pap. 14.95 (*1-85314-115-1*, Pub. by Firebird Bks UK) Sterling.

Warriors of the Apocalypse: Rage. Ethan Skemp. (Werewolf Ser.). (Illus.). 128p. (Orig.). 1996. pap. 15.00 (*1-56504-318-9*, 3403) White Wolf.

Warriors of the Heart. Danaan Parry. LC 90-70815. (Illus.). 224p. (Orig.). 1991. pap. 9.95 (*0-913319-09-0*) Erthstewards.

***Warriors of the Heart: A Handbook for Conflict Resolution.** Danaan Parry. (Illus.). 190p. 1997. reprint ed. pap. 11.95 (*0-9653808-2-3*) Erthstewards.

***Warriors of the Morning Calm.** B. C. Stevens. 167p. (Orig.). 1998. mass mkt. 4.99 (*1-55237-415-7*, Pub. by Comnwlth Pub CN) Partners Pubs Grp.

***Warriors of the Plains.** Thomas E. Mails. Ed. by Anthony Meisel. LC 97-12696. (Library of Native Peoples). (Illus.). 96p. (Orig.). (YA). 1997. pap. 10.00 (*1-57178-045-9*) Coun Oak Bks.

Warriors of the Rainbow: Strange & Prophetic Dreams of the Indian Peoples. William Willoya & Vinson Brown. (Illus.). 94p. (J). 1962. pap. 7.95 (*0-911010-24-6*) Naturegraph.

***Warriors of the Rising Sun: A History of the Japanese Military.** Robert B. Edgerton. LC 96-47472. (Illus.). 384p. 1997. 29.95 (*0-393-04085-2*) Norton.

***Warriors of the Steppe: A Military History of Central Asia, 500 B. C. to 1700 A. D.** Erik Hildinger. LC 97-25574. (Illus.). 272p. 1997. 24.95 (*1-885119-43-7*) Sarpedon.

Warriors of the Storm. Jack L. Chalker. (Rings of the Master Ser.: Bk. III). 352p. (Orig.). 1987. mass mkt. 4.95 (*0-345-32562-1*, Del Rey) Ballantine.

Warriors of the Way, 2 vols. in 1. Harry Harrison & John Holm. (Illus.). 800p. 1995. 14.98 (*1-56865-146-5*, GuildAmerica) Dblday Direct.

Warriors of Tibet: The Story of Aten & the Khampa's Fight for the Freedom of Their Country. Jamyang Norbu. (Tibet Book - Yellow Ser.). 152p. 1986. pap. 12.95 (*0-86171-050-9*) Wisdom MA.

Warriors of Truth: Adult Survivors Healing from Childhood Sexual Abuse. Kim McGregor. 280p. 1994. pap. 29.95 (*0-908569-84-X*, Pub. by U Otago Pr NZ) Intl Spec Bk.

***Warriors of Virtue: The Novel.** Robert Tine. 256p. 1997. mass mkt. 5.99 (*1-57297-243-2*) Blvd Books.

Warriors of Whiskey City. Robin Gibson. LC 96-96411. 192p. 1996. 17.95 (*0-8034-9215-4*, Avalon Bks) Bouregy.

Warrior's Path. Louis L'Amour. 240p. (Orig.). 1984. mass mkt. 3.99 (*0-553-27690-5*) Bantam.

***Warrior's Prize.** Georgina Gentry. 416p. 1997. mass mkt. 5.99 (*0-8217-5565-X*, Zebra Kensgtn) Kensgtn Pub Corp.

Warrior's Prize. Patricia Williams. 304p. (Orig.). 1994. mass mkt. 4.99 (*0-7865-0040-9*) Diamond.

Warrior's Quest. Margaret Moore. (Historical Ser.). 1993. mass mkt. 3.99 (*0-373-28775-5*, 1-28775-4) Harlequin Bks.

***Warrior's Song.** Janis R. Hudson. 352p. 1997. mass mkt. 4.99 (*0-8217-5603-6*, Zebra Kensgtn) Kensgtn Pub Corp.

Warrior's Song. Judith Pella. LC 95-45622. (Lone Star Legacy Ser.: Vol. 3). 384p. (Orig.). 1996. pap. 10.99 (*1-55661-655-4*) Bethany Hse.

Warrior's Tale. Allan Cole & Chris Bunch. (The Wizards of Fantasy Promotion). 1995. mass mkt. 5.99 (*0-345-38734-1*, Del Rey) Ballantine.

Warriors, the United States Marines. Karl C. Lippard. LC 83-90360. (Illus.). 239p. 1983. 34.95 (*0-9611880-0-6*); lthr. 250.00 (*0-9611880-1-4*) Vietnam Mar.

Warriors to Managers: The French Military Establishment since 1945. Michel L. Martin. LC 79-28114. 446p. reprint ed. pap. 127.20 (*0-7837-2456-X*, 2042609) Bks Demand.

***Warriors, Warthogs, & Wisdom: An African Childhood.** Lyall Watson & Keith R. West. LC 96-34537. (J). 1997. 16.95 (*0-7534-5066-6*, Kingfisher LKC) LKC.

Warrior's Way. Margaret Moore. 1994. mass mkt. 3.99 (*0-373-28824-7*, 1-28824-0) Harlequin Bks.

Warrior's Way. Robert S. De Ropp. 366p. 1992. reprint ed. pap. 18.95 (*0-89556-079-8*) Gateways Bks & Tapes.

Warrior's Way: Israel's Most Decorated Tank Commander Relives His Greatest Battles. Avigdor Kahalani. 320p. (Orig.). 1993. pap. 5.99 (*1-56171-239-6*, S P I Bks) Sure Seller.

Warrior's Way: The Challenging Life Games. Robert S. DeRopp. 1984. 18.75 (*0-8446-6174-0*) Peter Smith.

Warriors Who Ride the Wind. William F. Band. (American Heroes Ser.). (Illus.). 267p. 1993. 19.95 (*0-916693-20-1*) Castle Bks.

***Warrior's Wisdom: The Combat Guide to Corporate Life.** Arthur I. Clark. LC 96-46200. 128p. 1997. pap. 12.00 (*0-399-51938-6*, Perigee Bks) Berkley Pub.

***Warriors Within.** Alan Perelson. 1998. write for info. (*0-201-44215-9*) Addison-Wesley.

Warrior's Woman. Johanna Lindsey. 432p. (Orig.). 1990. mass mkt. 6.99 (*0-380-75301-4*) Avon.

Warrior's Woman. large type ed. Johanna Lindsey. 496p. (Orig.). 1997. 26.95 (*0-7838-1837-8*, GK Hall) Thorndike Pr.

Wars & Peace Treaties 1816-Present. Erik Goldstein. 320p. (C). (gr. 13). 1992. text ed. 59.95 (*0-415-07822-9*, A7449) Routledge.

Wars & Population. B. Urlanis. 320p. 1971. 27.00 (*0-8464-1149-0*) Beekman Pubs.

***Wars & Revolutions.** write for info. (*0-7131-6158-2*, Pub. by E Arnold UK) Routledge Chapman & Hall.

Wars & Revolutions: Britain, 1760-1815. Ian R. Christie. (New History of England Ser.). (Illus.). 368p. 1982. 37.50 (*0-674-94760-6*) HUP.

Wars & Revolutions: Britain, 1760-1815. Ian R. Christie. (New History of England Ser.). 368p. 1985. pap. 15.95 (*0-674-94761-4*) HUP.

***Wars & Warriors.** David H. Caldwell. (Discovering Historic Scotland Ser.). (Illus.). 96p. 1998. pap. 14.95 (*0-11-495786-X*, Pub. by Statnry Ofc UK) Seven Hills Bk.

***Wars End.** (Torg Ser.). 18.00 (*0-87431-358-9*, 20590) West End Games.

***War's End: A Memoir.** Charles W. Sweeney et al. LC 96-48526. 1997. write for info. (*0-380-97349-9*) Avon.

Wars I Have Seen. Esther S. Blanc. LC 93-60727. (Illus.). 126p. (Orig.). 1996. pap. 12.95 (*0-912078-80-4*) Volcano Pr.

Wars in the Caucasus, 1990-1995. Edgar O'Ballance. LC 96-42273. 255p. 1997. 45.00 (*0-8147-6192-5*) NYU Pr.

***Wars in the Midst of Peace: The International Politics of Ethnic Conflict.** Ed. by David Carment & Patrick James. LC 96-51262. (Policy & Institutional Studies). 320p. 1997. 45.00 (*0-8229-3975-4*); pap. 19.95 (*0-8229-5626-8*) U of Pittsburgh Pr.

Wars in the Third World since 1945. 2nd ed. Guy Arnold. 672p. 1995. 95.00 (*0-304-33086-8*) Cassell.

Wars, Internal Conflicts, & Political Order: A Jewish Democracy in the Middle East. Gad Barzilai. LC 92-37349. (SUNY Series in Israeli Studies). 311p. 1996. text ed. 71.50 (*0-7914-2943-1*); pap. text ed. 23.95 (*0-7914-2944-X*) State U NY Pr.

Wars Lost Battles Won: Lost Wars, No. 349. Adam Reviczky. 384p. 1993. text ed. 56.50 (*0-88033-246-8*) Col U Pr.

Wars of Alexander. Ed. by Hoyt N. Duggan & Thorlac Turville-Petre. (SS 10 Ser.: No. 10). 468p. 1989. 75.00 (*0-19-722410-5*) OUP.

Wars of Alexander. Ed. by Walter W. Skeat. (EETS, ES Ser.: No. 47). 1974. reprint ed. 70.00 (*0-527-00256-9*) Periodicals Srv.

Wars of America: Christian Views. Ed. by Ronald A. Wells. LC 91-3290. (C). 1991. 24.95 (*0-86554-334-8*, MUP/H263); pap. 14.95 (*0-86554-394-1*, MUP/P092) Mercer Univ Pr.

Wars of America: From 1600 to 1900, Vol. 1. Robert Leckie. LC 92-54863. (Illus.). 640p. 1993. pap. 17.00 (*0-06-092409-8*, PL) HarpC.

Wars of Cyrus. LC 74-133758. (Tudor Facsimile Texts. Old English Plays Ser.: No. 73). reprint ed. 49.50 (*0-404-53373-6*) AMS Pr.

Wars of Eduard Shevardnadze. Carolyn M. Ekedahl & Melvin A. Goodman. LC 96-1961. 1997. 29.95 (*0-271-01604-3*) Pa St U Pr.

Wars of Frederick II. David W. Felder. 56p. 1995. pap. text ed. 8.95 (*0-910959-76-5*, B&G 26B) Wellington Pr.

Wars of Frederick the Great. Dennis E. Showalter. LC 95-13124. (Modern Wars in Perspective Ser.). 352p. (C). 1995. pap. text ed. 23.50 (*0-582-06259-4*, Pub. by Longman UK) Longman.

Wars of French Decolonization. Anthony Clayton. LC 93-29506. (Modern Wars in Perspective Ser.). (C). 1994. text ed. 62.50 (*0-582-09802-5*) Longman.

Wars of French Decolonization. Anthony Clayton. LC 93-29506. (Modern Wars in Perspective Ser.). (C). 1995. pap. text ed. 25.50 (*0-582-09801-7*) Longman.

***Wars of German Unification.** Showalter. Date not set. text ed. write for info. (*0-340-58017-8*) St Martin.

Wars of Gods & Men. Zecharia Sitchin. 384p. 1985. mass mkt. 6.99 (*0-380-89585-4*) Avon.

Wars of Gods & Men: The Third Book of The Earth Chronicles. Zecharia Sitchin. (Earth Chronicles Ser.). (Illus.). 384p. 1992. reprint ed. 21.95 (*0-939680-90-4*) Bear & Co.

Wars of Independence. Richard Sanchez. LC 94-33364. (Hispanic Heritage Ser.: 4). 1994. lib. bdg. 15.98 (*1-56239-334-0*) Abdo & Dghtrs.

Wars of Japan. Ronald L. Tarnstrom. LC 91-66182. (Fifty Centuries of Warfare Ser.). (Illus.). 280p. 1992. 28.95 (*0-922037-10-8*) Trogen Bks.

***Wars of Light & Shadow No. 3.** Janny Wurts. 1975. mass mkt. write for info. (*0-06-105466-6*, HarperPrism) HarpC.

***Wars of Light & Shadow No. 4.** Janny Wurts. mass mkt. write for info. (*0-06-105467-4*, HarperPrism) HarpC.

***Wars of Light & Shadow No. 4.** Janny Wurts. 1975. write for info. (*0-06-105220-5*) HarpC.

Wars of Light & Shadow Vol. 2: Warhosts & Vastmark: Ships of Merior. Janny Wurts. 512p. 1996. mass mkt. 5.99 (*0-06-105667-7*) HarpC.

Wars of Love. Mark Schorer. LC 82-61041. 176p. 1982. reprint ed. 22.00 (*0-933256-34-5*) Second Chance.

Wars of Love. Mark Schorer. LC 82-61041. 176p. 1984. reprint ed. pap. 16.00 (*0-933256-35-3*) Second Chance.

Wars of Napoleon. Charles J. Esdaile. LC 94-44377. (Modern Wars in Perspective Ser.). (J). (gr. 2 up). 1995. pap. text ed. 23.50 (*0-582-05955-0*, Pub. by Longman UK) Longman.

Wars of Napoleon. Charles J. Esdaile. LC 94-44377. (Modern Wars in Perspective Ser.). (J). (gr. 2 up). 1996. text ed. 48.95 (*0-582-05954-2*, Pub. by Longman UK) Longman.

Wars of Napoleon. Ed. by Thomas Griess. LC 85-18602. (West Point Military History Ser.). (Illus.). 210p. 1985. 25.00 (*0-89529-308-0*) Avery Pub.

W

Wars of Napoleon. Ed. by Thomas E. Griess. LC 85-18602. (West Point Military History Ser.). (Illus.). 206p. pap. 19.95 (0-89529-271-8) Avery Pub.

Wars of Our Ancestors: A Novel by Miguel Delibes. Miguel Delibes. Tr. by Agnes Moncy from SPA. LC 91-32399. 312p. 1992. 40.00 (0-8203-1418-8) U of Ga Pr.

Wars of Peggy Hull: The Life & Times of the First Accredited Woman Foreign Correspondent. Wilda M. Smith & Eleanor A. Bogart. LC 89-51841. (Illus.). 300p. 1991. 30.00 (0-87404-215-1) Tex Western.

Wars of Succession: How Businesses Survive Generations. Roger Fritz. 300p. 1997. pap. 17.95 (1-56343-137-8) Merritt Pub.

Wars of the Americas. David F. Marley. 448p. 1996. lib. bdg. 75.00 (0-87436-837-5) ABC-CLIO.

Wars of the Iroquois. George T. Hunt. 209p. 1993. reprint ed. lib. bdg. 79.00 (0-7812-5158-3) Rprt Serv.

Wars of the Iroquois: A Study in Intertribal Relations. George T. Hunt. LC 40-3755. 224p. reprint ed. pap. 63.90 (0-8357-4750-6, 2037672) Bks Demand.

Wars of the Lord, Vol. 2. Levi B. Gershom, pseud. Tr. by Seymour Feldman from HEB. 288p. 1987. 34.95 (0-8276-0275-8) JPS Phila.

Wars of the Lord: Immortality of the Soul, Vol. I. Levi B. Gershom. Tr. by Seymour Feldman from HEB. 256p. (C). 1984. 34.95 (0-8276-0220-0) JPS Phila.

Wars of the Rajas: Being the History of Anantapuram: Written in Telugu: in or about the Years 1750-1810. Tr. by Charles P. Brown. (C). 1988. reprint ed. 17.50 (81-206-0365-6, Pub. by Asian Educ Servs II) S Asia.

Wars of the Roses. William W. Lace. LC 95-14367. (World History Ser.). (Illus.). 112p. (J). (gr. 5-12). 1996. lib. bdg. 17.96 (1-56006-419-6) Lucent Bks.

Wars of the Roses. J. R. Lander. (Illus.). 256p. (C). 1992. pap. text ed. 20.00 (0-7509-0018-0, Pub. by Sutton Pubng UK) Bks Intl VA.

Wars of the Roses. Ed. by A. J. Pollard. LC 95-9735. 1995. text ed. 49.95 (0-312-12697-2); text ed. 19.95 (0-312-12699-9) St Martin.

Wars of the Roses. David Tipton. 64p. (C). 1988. pap. 35.00 (0-947612-07-6, Pub. by Rivelin Grapheme Pr) St Mut.

Wars of the Roses. Alison Weir. (Illus.). 480p. 1996. pap. 12.95 (0-345-40433-5) Ballantine.

Wars of the Roses. Terence Wise. (Men-at-Arms Ser.: No. 145). (Illus.). 48p. pap. 11.95 (0-85045-520-0, 9077, Pub. by Osprey UK) Stackpole.

Wars of the Roses. Jon Nichol. (Resource Units Middle Ages, 1066-1485 Ser.). (Illus.). 24p. 1974. reprint ed. teacher ed., pap. 13.25 (0-582-39390-6) Longman.

Wars of the Roses: A Concise History. Charles L. Ross. LC 85-52289. (Illus.). 190p. 1986. pap. 15.95 (0-500-27407-X) Thames Hudson.

Wars of the Roses: Lancastrians & Yorkists. Davis R. Cook. (Seminar Studies in History). (Illus.). (C). Date not set. pap. text ed. 13.50 (0-582-35384-X) Longman.

Wars of the Roses: Military Activity & English Society, 1452-1497. Anthony Goodman. (Illus.). 300p. 1981. 35.00 (0-7100-0728-0, RKP) Routledge.

Wars of the Roses: Military Activity & English Society, 1452-97. Anthony Goodman. 289p. (C). (gr. 13). 1990. pap. 17.95 (0-415-05264-5, A5221) Routledge.

Wars of the Roses: Peace & Conflict in Fifteenth-Century England. John Gillingham. LC 81-83851. (Illus.). 308p. 1981. reprint ed. pap. 87.80 (0-7837-9868-7, 2060594) Bks Demand.

***Wars of the Roses: Politics & the Constitution in England, c. 1437-1509.** Christine Carpenter. (Medieval Textbooks Ser.). 400p. (C). 1997. text ed. 59.95 (0-521-26800-1) Cambridge U Pr.

***Wars of the Roses: Politics & the Constitution in England, c. 1437-1509.** Christine Carpenter. (Medieval Textbooks Ser.). 400p. (C). 1997. pap. text ed. 19.95 (0-521-31874-2) Cambridge U Pr.

Wars of the Roses: Through the Lives of Five Men & Women of the Fifteenth Century. Desmond Seward. (Illus.). 416p. 1995. pap. 26.95 (0-670-84258-3, Viking) Viking Penguin.

Wars of the Roses in Fiction: An Annotated Bibliography, 1440-1994. Compiled by Roxane C. Murph. LC 95-12746. (Bibliographies & Indexes in World History Ser.: Vol. 41). 224p. 1995. text ed. 69.50 (0-313-29709-6, Greenwood Pr) Greenwood.

Wars of the Third Kind: Conflict in Underdeveloped Countries. Edward E. Rice. 186p. 1988. pap. 14.00 (0-520-07195-6) U CA Pr.

Wars of Watergate: The Last Crisis of Richard Nixon. Stanley I. Kutler. (Illus.). 750p. 1992. pap. 15.95 (0-393-30827-8) Norton.

War's Other Voices: Women Writers in the Lebanese Civil War. Miriam Cooke. (Cambridge Middle East Library: No. 14). 218p. 1988. text ed. 59.95 (0-521-34192-2) Cambridge U Pr.

War's Other Voices: Women Writers on the Lebanese Civil War. Miriam Cooke. 228p. (C). 1996. pap. 15.95 (0-8156-0377-0, COWOP) Syracuse U Pr.

Wars, Revolutions, Dictatorships. Ed. by Stanislav Andreski. 240p. 1992. text ed. 45.00 (0-7146-3452-2, Pub. by F Cass Pubs UK) Intl Spec Bk.

Wars That Changed the World: Group 2, 6 vols. LC 87-36748. (Illus.). 192p. (J). (gr. 3-9). 1988. Set. lib. bdg. 68.12 (0-86307-929-6) Marshall Cavendish.

Wars That Changed the World Series: Group 1, 4 vols. (Illus.). 128p. (J). (gr. 3-9). 1991. Set. lib. bdg. 45.41 (1-85435-258-X) Marshall Cavendish.

Wars We Took to Vietnam: Cultural Conflict & Storytelling. Milton J. Bates. LC 95-46772. 325p. (C). 1996. 50.00 (0-520-20432-8); pap. 18.95 (0-520-20433-6) U CA Pr.

Wars Within. William F. Smith. 375p. 1994. 19.95 (0-9643493-0-2) TopWood Pubng.

Wars Without Splendor: The U. S. Military & Low-Level Conflict. Ernest Evans. LC 86-22756. (Contributions in Military Studies: No. 58). 174p. 1987. text ed. 45.00 (0-313-25126-6, EWS/, Greenwood Pr) Greenwood.

Warsaw. Joanna Regulska & Adam Kowalewski. (World Cities Ser.). 224p. 1994. text ed. 49.95 (0-470-22014-7) Halsted Pr.

Warsaw. Joanna Regulska & Adam Kowalewski. (World Cities Ser.). 224p. 1995. text ed. 65.00 (0-471-94969-8) Wiley.

Warsaw: A Novel of Resistance. Albert Litewka. 512p. 1989. 21.95 (0-685-31318-2) IMA NYC.

Warsaw: The Cabaret Years. Ron Nowicki. LC 92-16660. (Illus.). 288p. 1992. 30.00 (1-56279-030-7) Mercury Hse Inc.

***Warsaw: Warsaw.** LC 97-15211. (Eyewitness Travel Guides Ser.). 288p. 1997. 22.95 (0-7894-1614-X) DK Pub Inc.

Warsaw Aflame. Leszek Szymanski et al. Tr. by Stanislaw. (Illus.). 192p. 1973. 10.95 (0-914310-00-3) Polamerica Pr.

Warsaw Before the First World War: Poles, & Jews in the Third City of the Russian Empire. Stephen D. Corrsin. 183p. 1989. text ed. 52.50 (0-88033-171-2) East Eur Monographs.

Warsaw Between the World Wars: Profile of the Capital City in a Developing Land, 1918-1939. Edward D. Wynot, Jr. (East European Monographs: No. 129). 375p. 1983. text ed. 68.50 (0-88033-018-X) East Eur Monographs.

Warsaw Convention. Elmar Giemulla & Ronald Schmid. LC 92-31472. 1992. 169.00 (90-6544-918-3) Kluwer Law Tax Pubs.

Warsaw Convention Annotated: A Legal Handbook. Lawrence B. Goldhirsch. (C). 1988. lib. bdg. 194.50 (90-247-3619-6) Kluwer Ac.

Warsaw Diary of Adam Czerniakow. Raul Hilberg et al. LC 78-9272. (Illus.). 448p. 1982. pap. 12.95 (0-8128-6110-8, Scrbrough Hse) Madison Bks UPA.

Warsaw Document: A Quiller Adventure. Adam Hall. 320p. 1993. mass mkt. 4.50 (0-06-100529-0, Harp PBks) HarpC.

Warsaw Economy in Transition. David Dowall et al. 224p. 1996. 59.95 (1-85972-339-X, Pub. by Avebury Pub UK) Ashgate Pub Co.

Warsaw Ghetto: A Christian's Testimony. Wladyslaw Bartoszewski. LC 87-42842. (Illus.). 160p. (C). 1988. 14.95 (0-8070-5602-2) Beacon Pr.

Warsaw Ghetto: The Twenty-Fifth Anniversary of the Uprising. (Illus.). 1989. 27.00 (0-317-03849-4) Szwede Slavic.

Warsaw Ghetto Diary. Michael Zylberberg. 7.95 (0-87677-104-5) Hartmore.

Warsaw Ghetto in Photographs. Illus. by Ulrich Keller. LC 83-20540. (Photography Ser.). 160p. 1984. pap. 9.95 (0-486-24665-5) Dover.

Warsaw Ghetto Uprising. Elaine Landau. LC 92-15851. (Illus.). 144p. (YA). (gr. 6 up). 1992. lib. bdg. 14.95 (0-02-751392-0, Mac Bks Young Read) S&S Childrens.

Warsaw Pact: Alliance in Transition? Ed. by David Holloway & Jane M. Sharp. LC 84-7093. (Cornell Studies in Security Affairs). 290p. 1984. reprint ed. pap. 82.70 (0-608-01689-6, 2062345) Bks Demand.

Warsaw Pact: Political Purpose & Military Means. Ed. by Robert W. Clawson & Lawrence S. Kaplan. LC 81-86387. 297p. (C). 1982. pap. text ed. 13.95 (0-8420-2199-X); lib. bdg. 40.00 (0-8420-2198-1) Scholarly Res Inc.

Warsaw Pact Air Forces. Hans-Heiri Stapfer. (Specials Ser.). (Illus.). 80p. 1991. pap. 11.95 (0-89747-266-7, 6054) Squad Sig Pubns.

Warsaw Pact & the Balkans: Moscow's Southern Flank. Ed. by Jonathan Eyal. LC 89-30604. (Illus.). 240p. 1989. text ed. 55.00 (0-312-03151-3) St Martin.

Warsaw Pact Ground Forces. Gordon L. Rottman. (Elite Ser.: No. 10). (Illus.). 64p. pap. 12.95 (0-85045-730-0, 9409, Pub. by Osprey Pubng Ltd UK) Stackpole.

Warsaw Requiem. Bodie Thoene. (Zion Covenant Ser.: Vol. 6). Orig. Title: Bk. 6. 512p. (Orig.). 1991. pap. 11.99 (1-55661-188-9) Bethany Hse.

Warsaw Sparks. Gary Gildner. LC 89-20381. (Singular Lives: The Iowa Series in North American Autobiography). (Illus.). 255p. 1990. 27.95 (0-87745-270-9); pap. 14.95 (0-87745-276-8) U of Iowa Pr.

***Warsaw to Wrigley: A Foreign Correspondent's Tale of Coming Home from Communism to the Cubs.** Joseph A. Reaves. LC 97-9839. (Illus.). 240p. 1997. 24.95 (1-888698-07-1) Diamond Communications.

Warsaw Treaty Organization: A Political & Organizational Analysis. Neil Fodor. LC 90-8108. 230p. 1990. text ed. 49.95 (0-312-04622-7) St Martin.

Warsaw Visitor & Tales from the Vienna Streets. William Saroyan. 160p. (C). 1990. 23.95 (0-8093-1695-1); pap. 13.95 (0-8093-1696-X) S Ill U Pr.

***Warscape, with Lovers.** Marilyn Krysl. (Poetry Ser.: Vol. LII). 92p. (Orig.). 1997. 17.50 (1-880834-29-4); pap. 10.00 (1-880834-28-6) Cleveland St Univ Poetry Ctr.

Warship, Vol. I. Ed. by Anthony Preston. LC 78-55455. (Illus.). 256p. 1978. 41.95 (0-87021-975-8) Naval Inst Pr.

Warship, Vol. II. (Illus.). 287p. 1980. 41.95 (0-87021-976-6) Naval Inst Pr.

Warship, Vol. III. Ed. by John Roberts. LC 78-55455. (Illus.). 288p. 1981. 41.95 (0-87021-977-4) Naval Inst Pr.

Warship, Vol. IV. Ed. by John Roberts. LC 78-55455. (Illus.). 286p. 1981. 41.95 (0-87021-979-0) Naval Inst Pr.

Warship, Vol. V. John Roberts. LC 78-55455. (Illus.). 288p. 1982. 41.95 (0-87021-980-4) Naval Inst Pr.

Warship, Vol. VII. Ed. by John Roberts. LC 78-55455. (Illus.). 288p. 1984. 41.95 (0-87021-982-0) Naval Inst Pr.

Warship, Vol. VIII. (Illus.). 288p. 1985. 41.95 (0-87021-983-9) Naval Inst Pr.

Warship, Vol. IX. Ed. by Andrew D. Lambert. LC 78-55455. (Illus.). 288p. 1986. 41.95 (0-87021-984-7) Naval Inst Pr.

Warship, Vol. X. Ed. by Andrew D. Lambert. LC 78-55455. (Illus.). 288p. 1987. 41.95 (0-87021-985-5) Naval Inst Pr.

Warship Losses of World War Two. David Brown. (Illus.). 256p. (Orig.). 1995. pap. 19.95 (1-55750-914-X) Naval Inst Pr.

***Warship Pictorial No. 1: USS Indianapolis CA-35.** Ed. by Steve Wiper. (Illus.). 56p. 1999. pap. 12.95 (0-9654829-0-1) Classic Warships.

Warship, 1989. (Illus.). 256p. 1989. 41.95 (0-87021-999-5) Naval Inst Pr.

Warship, 1990. Ed. by Robert Gardiner. LC 90-62895. (Illus.). 256p. 1991. 41.95 (1-55750-903-4) Naval Inst Pr.

Warship 1991. Ed. by Robert Gardiner. (Illus.). 256p. 1991. 41.95 (1-55750-907-7) Naval Inst Pr.

Warship 1994. (Illus.). 256p. 1994. 41.95 (0-85177-630-2) Naval Inst Pr.

Warship 1995. Ed. by John Roberts. (Illus.). 256p. 1995. 41.95 (0-85177-654-X) Naval Inst Pr.

***Warship 1996.** Ed. by David McLean & Tony Preston. (Illus.). 256p. 1997. 42.95 (0-85177-685-X) Naval Inst Pr.

***Warship 1997.** Ed. by David McLean & Antony Preston. (Illus.). 224p. 1997. 41.95 (0-85177-722-8) Naval Inst Pr.

Warships & Their Story. R. A. Fletcher. 1977. lib. bdg. 69.95 (0-8490-2808-6) Gordon Pr.

Warship's Data, No. 3: U. S. S. Iowa. Robert F. Sumrall. LC 86-61291. (Illus.). 54p. 1987. pap. text ed. 8.95 (0-933126-77-8) Pictorial Hist.

Warships of the Civil War Navies. Paul H. Silverstone. (Illus.). 288p. 1989. 45.95 (0-87021-783-6) Naval Inst Pr.

Warships of the Imperial Japanese Navy, 1869-1945. Hansgeorg Jentschura et al. Tr. by David Brown & Anthony Preston. LC 75-43861. (Illus.). 284p. 1976. 36.95 (0-87021-893-X) Naval Inst Pr.

***Warships of the U. S. S. R. & Russia, 1945-1995.** A. S. Pavlov. Ed. by Norman Friedman. Tr. by Gregory Tokar. LC 96-30077. (Illus.). 304p. 1997. 59.95 (1-55750-671-X) Naval Inst Pr.

Warships of the World. Gino Galuppiny. (Illus.). 320p. 1989. 29.99 (0-517-68252-4) Random Hse Value.

Warships of the World: An Illustrated Encyclopedia. Gino Galluppini. (Illus.). 320p. 1986. 69.95 (0-8129-1129-6, Times Bks) Random.

Warstrider. William H. Keith, Jr. 352p. (Orig.). 1993. mass mkt. 4.99 (0-380-76879-8, AvoNova) Avon.

Warstrider: Jackers. William H. Keith, Jr. 384p. (Orig.). 1994. mass mkt. 4.99 (0-380-77591-3, AvoNova) Avon.

Warstrider: Netlink. William H. Keith, Jr. (Warstrider Ser.: No. 5). 352p. (Orig.). 1995. mass mkt. 4.99 (0-380-77968-4, AvoNova) Avon.

Warstrider: Rebellion. William H. Keith, Jr. 352p. (Orig.). 1993. mass mkt. 4.99 (0-380-76880-1, AvoNova) Avon.

Warstrider: Symbionts. William H. Keith, Jr. (Warstrider Ser.: Vol. 4). 336p. (Orig.). 1995. mass mkt. 4.99 (0-380-77592-1, AvoNova) Avon.

Warstrider No. 6: Battlemind. William H. Keith, Jr. (Warstrider Ser.: No. 6). 304p. (Orig.). 1996. mass mkt. 5.99 (0-380-77969-2, AvoNova) Avon.

***Warthog, Vol. 1.** George. (Illus.). (J). 1998. 14.95 (0-7868-3166-9) Disney Pr.

Warthog: Flying the A-10 in the Gulf War. William L. Smallwood. LC 92-23201. (Illus.). 267p. 1993. 24.95 (0-02-881021-X) Brasseys Inc.

Warthog: Flying the A-10 in the Gulf War. William L. Smallwood. (Illus.). 267p. 1995. pap. 14.95 (0-02-881123-2) Brasseys Inc.

***Warthogs.** Edwards. 1998. 14.95 (0-7868-0399-1); 14.89 (0-7868-2351-8) Hyperion.

Warthogs. Don Rothaus. LC 95-12143. (Nature Bks.). (Illus.). 32p. (J). (gr. 2-6). 1995. lib. bdg. 22.79 (1-56766-185-8) Childs World.

***Warthogs of Wartonia in Justice for All.** Stephen Van Rathje & James C. Baley. LC 94-90349. (Illus.). 64p. (J). (gr. 3-6). 1996. 17.95 (1-56002-475-5, Univ Edtns) Aegina Pr.

Wartide. John Barnes. (Time Raider Ser.: No. 604). 1992. mass mkt. 3.50 (0-373-63604-0, 1-63604-2) Harlequin Bks.

Wartime. Milovan Djilas. LC 80-16174. 496p. 1980. pap. 7.95 (0-15-694712-9, Harvest Bks) HarBrace.

Wartime: Understanding & Behavior in the Second World War. Paul Fussell, Jr. (Illus.). 350p. 1989. 30.00 (0-19-503797-9) OUP.

Wartime: Understanding & Behavior in the Second World War. Paul Fussell, Jr. (Illus.). 352p. 1990. reprint ed. pap. 13.95 (0-19-506577-8) OUP.

Wartime Agriculture in Australia & New Zealand, 1939-50. John G. Crawford et al. (Illus.). xiii, 354p. 1954. 47.50 (0-8047-0455-4) Stanford U Pr.

Wartime America: The World War II Home Front. John W. Jeffries. LC 96-18600. 224p. 1996. 24.95 (1-56663-118-1) I R Dee.

Wartime America: The World War II Home Front. John W. Jeffries. LC 96-18600. (American Ways Ser.). 224p. 1997. pap. 9.95 (1-56663-119-X) I R Dee.

Wartime America Plans for a New Hungary: Developments from the U. S. Department of State, 1942-44. Ed. by Ignac Romsics. (Atlantic Studies on Society & Change: No. 77). 316p. (C). 1993. text ed. 47.50 (0-88033-251-4) Col U Pr.

Wartime & Aftermath: English Literature & Its Background, 1939-60. Bernard Bergonzi. LC 92-26593. 240p. 1993. pap. 15.95 (0-19-289222-3) OUP.

Wartime Children, Nineteen Thirty-Nine to Nineteen Forty-Five. Eleanor Allen. (Junior Reference Ser.). (Illus.). 64p. (J). (gr. 6 up). 1983. 14.95 (0-7136-1503-6) Dufour.

Wartime Correspondence: Between President Roosevelt & Pope Pius 12th. Ed. & Intro. by Myron Taylor. (FDR & the Era of the New Deal Ser.). 1975. reprint ed. lib. bdg. 22.50 (0-306-70709-8) Da Capo.

Wartime Correspondence Between President Roosevelt & Pope Pius XII. Franklin Roosevelt. (American Autobiography Ser.). 127p. 1995. reprint ed. lib. bdg. 69.00 (0-7812-8629-8) Rprt Serv.

Wartime Diaries of Lionel Robbins & James Meade, 1943-5. Ed. by Susan Howson & D. E. Moggridge. LC 90-48160. 300p. 1991. text ed. 69.95 (0-312-05741-5) St Martin.

Wartime Exile, the Exclusion of the Japanese Americans from the West Coast see U. S. War Relocation Authority

Wartime Farm & Food Policy. Iowa State College, Economics & Sociology Department Staff. LC 75-26304. (World Food Supply Ser.). (Illus.). 1976. reprint ed. 45.95 (0-405-07783-1) Ayer.

Wartime Handling of Evacuee Property see U. S. War Relocation Authority

Wartime Journalism, 1939-1943. Paul De Man. Ed. by Werner Hamacher et al. LC 88-17234. x, 399p. 1988. pap. text ed. 20.00 (0-8032-6576-X, Bison Books) U of Nebr Pr.

Wartime Labour Conditions & Reconstruction Planning in India see War & Women's Employment: The Experience of the U. K. & the U. S. A. 1946

Wartime Letters. Emil H. Gabelmann. 1996. text ed. 20.00 (1-884680-05-4) Gabelmann Pr.

***Wartime Lies.** Louis Begley. 1997. pap. 12.00 (0-449-00117-2) Fawcett.

Wartime Lies. Louis Begley. 192p. 1992. mass mkt. 5.99 (0-8041-0990-7) Ivy Books.

Wartime Log. Art Beltrone & Lee Beltrone. (Illus.). 208p. 1995. 34.95 (0-943231-90-6) Howell Pr VA.

Wartime Missions of Harry L. Hopkins. Matthew B. Wills. LC 95-72729. (Illus.). 112p. 1996. 17.95 (1-57197-012-6) Pentland Pr.

Wartime Papers of Robert E. Lee. Ed. by Clifford Dowdey & Louis H. Manarin. (Quality Paperbacks Ser.). (Illus.). xiv, 994p. 1987. reprint ed. pap. 19.95 (0-306-80282-1) Da Capo.

***Wartime Passenger Ship Disasters.** David Williams. (Illus.). 92p. 1997. 42.95 (1-85260-565-0) Haynes Pubns.

***Wartime Poland, 1939-1945: A Select Annotated Bibliography of Books in English.** Walter Okonski. LC 96-33027. (Bibliographies & Indexes in World History Ser.). 128p. 1997. text ed. 65.00 (0-313-30004-6) Greenwood.

Wartime Production Controls. David Novick et al. LC 76-5795. (FDR & the Era of the New Deal Ser.). 1976. reprint ed. lib. bdg. 49.50 (0-306-70818-3) Da Capo.

Wartime "Prosperity" & the Future. Wesley C. Mitchell. (Occasional Papers: No. 9). 48p. 1943. reprint ed. 20.00 (0-87014-324-7); reprint ed. mic. film 20.00 (0-685-61241-4) Natl Bur Econ Res.

Wartime Relations of the Federal Government & the Public Schools, 1917-1918. Lewis P. Todd. LC 76-165743. (American Education, Ser, No. 2). 1975. reprint ed. 23.95 (0-405-03614-0) Ayer.

Wartime Scrapbook: From Blitz to Victory 1939-1945. Robert Opie. (Illus.). 64p. 1995. 17.95 (1-872727-08-5) Pincushion Pr.

Wartime Shipyard: A Study in Social Disunity. Katherine Archibald. LC 76-7621. (FDR & the Era of the New Deal Ser.). 1976. reprint ed. 27.50 (0-306-70802-7) Da Capo.

Wartime Shipyard: Study in Social Disunity. Katherine Archibald. Ed. by Leon Stein. LC 77-70478. (Illus.). 1977. reprint ed. lib. bdg. 25.95 (0-405-10152-X) Ayer.

Wartime Strikes. Martin Glaberman. (Illus.). (Orig.). 1980. pap. 12.00 (0-935590-11-0) Bewick Edns.

Wartime System of Labor Service in Hungary. Ed. by Randolph L. Braham. 154p. 1995. 24.00 (0-88033-317-0) East Eur Monographs.

Wartime Technological Developments, 2 Vols. United States Bureau of Labor Statistics Staff & U. S. Congress, Senate Committee on Military Affairs, Subcommittee on War Mobilization. LC 78-22407. (American Military Experience Ser.). 1980. reprint ed. lib. bdg. 46.95 (0-405-11882-1) Ayer.

Wartime Washington: The Civil War Letters of Elizabeth Blair Lee. Ed. by Virginia J. Laas. (Illus.). 588p. 1991. text ed. 39.95 (0-252-01802-8) U of Ill Pr.

Wartime Washington: The Secret OSS Journal of James Grafton Rogers. Ed. by Thomas F. Troy. LC 86-28184. (Foreign Intelligence Book Ser.). 400p. 1986. text ed. 47.95 (0-313-27075-9, U7075, Greenwood Pr) Greenwood.

Wartime Women: Sex Roles, Family Relations, & the Status of Women During World War II. Karen L. Anderson. LC 80-1703. (Contributions in Women's Studies: No. 20). 198p. 1981. text ed. 45.00 (0-313-20884-0, AWW/, Greenwood Pr) Greenwood.

Wartime Writings Nineteen Thirty-Nine to Nineteen Forty-Four. Antoine de Saint-Exupery. LC 85-30566. 1986. 12.95 (0-15-194680-9) HarBrace.

An Asterisk (*) at the beginning of an entry indicates that the title is appearing in BIP for the first time.

Wartime Writings, 1939-1944. Antoine de Saint-Exupery. Tr. by Norah Purcell. 250p. 1990. pap. 8.95 (*0-15-694740-4*, Harvest Bks) HarBrace.

Wartime Writings 1939-1944. Antoine de Saint-Exupery. Tr. by Norah Purcell. 1990. 8.95 (*0-685-47700-2*) HarBrace.

***Warton's History of English Poetry, 4 vols.** Ed. by David Fairer. (Cultural Formations Ser.). 2010p. (C). (gr. 13). 1997. text ed. write for info. (*0-415-14871-5*) Routledge.

Warts. Susan Shreve. (J). (gr. 2). 1996. 15.00 (*0-688-14378-4*, Tambourine Bks) Morrow.

***Warts & All.** Drew Friedman & Josh A. Freidman. 88p. pap. 9.95 (*1-56097-143-6*) Fantagraph Bks.

Wartville Wizard. Don Madden. LC 92-22246. (Illus.). 32p. (J). (gr. k-3). 1993. reprint ed. pap. 5.99 (*0-689-71667-2*, Aladdin Paperbacks) S&S Childrens.

Warum Geburten Doch Gerecht Sind see Why Was I Born?: Bridging Birth & Justice

Warum Gibt Es in Den Vereinigten Staaten Keinen Sozialismus see Why Is There No Socialism in the United States

Warum Ich Sagen Kann Ich Bin Gott: Ich Bin Gott. Herbert L. Beierle. 1995. pap. 2.00 (*0-940480-15-8*) UNI Press.

***Warware Stepanowa: Ein Leben fur den Konstruktivismus.** Alexander N. Lawrentiew. Tr. by Ala Smeljanskaja et al. from RUS. (Illus.). 192p. (GER.). (C). 1988. 126.00 (*3-8170-2016-3*, Pub. by Knstvrlag Weingrtn GW) Intl Bk Import.

Warwick County: Virginia Publick Claims. Janice L. Abercrombie & Richard Slatten. (Virginia Publick Claims Ser.). ix, 13p. 1992. pap. 5.00 (*0-8095-8710-6*) Borgo Pr.

Warwick County: Virginia Publick Claims. Janice L. Abercrombie & Richard Slatten. (Virginia Publick Claims Ser.). ix, 13p. (C). 1992. reprint ed. lib. bdg. 25.00 (*0-8095-8366-6*) Borgo Pr.

Warwick Heiress. large type ed. Margaret Abbey. LC 94-33760. (Nightingale Ser.). 1995. pap. 16.95 (*0-8161-7497-0*, GK Hall) Thorndike Pr.

Warwick Mountain Series. Photos by Philip Perkis. LC 78-61647. (Illus.). 1978. 24.00 (*0-932526-01-2*) Nexus Pr.

Warwick, RI. Don D'Amato. (Images of America Ser.). 128p. 1996. pap. 16.99 (*0-7524-0265-X*, Arcdia) Chalford.

Warwick the Kingmaker. Paul M. Kendall. (Illus.). 416p. 1987. reprint ed. pap. 9.95 (*0-393-30380-2*) Norton.

Warwick the Kingmaker. Charles W. Oman. LC 79-137383. (Select Bibliographies Reprint Ser.). 1977. reprint ed. 18.95 (*0-8369-5584-6*) Ayer.

Warwick Valley Cooking. Ed. by Joan Masson et al. (Illus.). 160p. 1989. 7.50 (*0-9623003-0-6*) Friends A Wisner.

Warwick Woodlands. Henry W. Herbert. (Notable American Authors Ser.). 1992. reprint ed. lib. bdg. 90.00 (*0-7812-3093-4*) Rprt Serv.

Warwick's Three Hundred Fifty Year Heritage: A Pictorial History. Donald A. D'Amato. LC 92-21790. 1992. write for info. (*0-89865-845-4*) Donning Co.

Warwickshire Christmas. David Green. (Illus.). 160p. 1991. pap. 15.00 (*0-86299-766-6*, Pub. by Sutton Pubng UK) Bks Intl VA.

Warwickshire Grazier & London Skinner, 1532-1555: The Account Book of Peter Temple & Thomas Heritage. N. W. Alcock. (Records of Social & Economic History Ser.: Vol. IV). (Illus.). 1981. 22.98 (*0-19-726008-X*) David Brown.

Warwickshire Hundred Rolls of 1279-80: Stoneleigh & Kineton Hundreds. Ed. by Trevor John. (Records of Social & Economic History, New Series British Academy: No. XIX). (Illus.). 300p. 1993. 110.00 (*0-19-726122-1*) OUP.

***Warwickshire Railways.** Mike Hitches & Jim Roberts. (Photographic History of Railways Ser.). (Illus.). 128p. 1997. pap. 19.95 (*0-7509-1366-5*, Pub. by Sutton Pubng UK) Bks Intl VA.

Warwickshire Word-Book Comprising Obsolescent & Dialect Words, Colloquialisms, Etc. G. T. Northall. (English Dialect Society Publications: No. 79). 1974. reprint ed. pap. 35.00 (*0-8115-0497-2*) Periodicals Srv.

***WarWind.** Michael Knight. 240p. 1996. per. 16.99 (*0-7615-1009-5*) Prima Pub.

Wary Fugitives: Four Poets & the South. Louis D. Rubin. LC 77-25479. (Walter Lynwood Fleming Lectures in Southern History Ser.). 400p. 1978. reprint ed. pap. 114.00 (*0-7837-9867-9*, 2060593) Bks Demand.

***Wary Heart.** large type ed. Lynn Granger. (Dales Large Print Ser.). 224p. 1996. pap. 17.99 (*1-85389-642-X*, Dales) Ulverscroft.

Wary Warriors: Future Directions in Japanese Security Policies. N. D. Levin et al. 146p. 1993. pap. 15.00 (*0-8330-1406-4*, MR-101) Rand Corp.

Warzones. Chris Giannou. text ed. write for info. (*0-7167-2945-8*) W H Freeman.

Was. Geoff Ryman. 384p. 1993. pap. 11.95 (*0-14-017872-4*, Penguin Bks) Viking Penguin.

Was a War Correspondent in the Battle of the Sexes. 1991. pap. 13.95 (*0-87949-320-8*) Ashley Bks.

Was Baseball Really Invented in Maine? A Warm & Wonderful Look at the History of Professional Baseball in Maine & at Every Mainer Who's Ever Played in the Majors. Will Anderson. LC 91-90687. (Illus.). 188p. (Orig.). 1992. pap. 17.95 (*0-9601056-5-4*) Anderson & Sons.

Was Bhagwan Shree Rajneesh Poisioned by Ronald Regans America? Sue Appleton. 1989. 4.95 (*3-89338-041-8*) Osho America.

***Was Blind But Now I See.** Flagg. 1997. 30.00 (*0-8147-2643-7*) NYU Pr.

Was C. G. Jung a Mystic? And Other Essays. Aniell Jaffe. 214p. 1995. pap. 12.95 (*3-85630-508-4*, Pub. by Daimon Pubs SZ) Continuum.

Was Calvin a Theonomist? Gary North. 20p. (Orig.). 1990. pap. 1.00 (*0-930464-36-2*) Inst Christian.

Was Christ God? Spiros Zodhiates. 336p. 1966. pap. 7.99 (*0-89957-504-8*) AMG Pubs.

Was Christopher Columbus a Jew? Walter F. McEntire. 1976. lib. bdg. 59.95 (*0-8490-1278-3*) Gordon Pr.

Was George Washington Really the Father of Our Country? A Clinical Geneticist Looks at World History. Robert Marion. LC 93-26588. (Illus.). 206p. 1993. 22.95 (*0-201-62255-6*) Addison-Wesley.

Was He Anyone? N. F. Simpson. 69p. 1973. pap. 5.00 (*0-87129-157-6*, W10) Dramatic Pub.

Was Huck Black? Mark Twain & African-American Voices. Shelley F. Fishkin. LC 92-31228. 288p. 1993. 30.00 (*0-19-508214-1*) OUP.

Was Huck Black? Mark Twain & African-American Voices. Shelley F. Fishkin. (Illus.). 288p. 1994. reprint ed. pap. 12.95 (*0-19-508914-6*) OUP.

Was It a Classical Triangle? Mark Mitnik. (Illus.). 192p. (Orig.). (RUS.). 1988. pap. 12.00 (*0-9622027-0-3*) M Mitnik.

Was It Heaven or Hell: The Triumphs & Torments of Mark Twain. Billie Valentine-Fonorow. LC 94-90812. 199p. 1995. pap. 16.95 (*0-9644557-0-6*) Fonorow & Assocs.

Was It Murder? James Hilton. LC 78-74115. 1979. reprint ed. pap. 5.95 (*0-486-23774-5*) Dover.

Was It Not I? And Other Questions God Asks. W. E. McCumber. 196p. 1994. pap. 10.99 (*0-8341-1485-2*) Beacon Hill.

***Was It Something I Said?** Valerie Block. LC 97-16735. 1998. write for info. (*1-56947-109-6*) Soho Press.

Was It Something I Said? Lorene Machado. LC 96-18623. 128p. 1996. pap. 9.95 (*1-57544-000-8*) Genl Pub Grp.

Was It Something I Said? Jean Thesman. 160p. 1988. mass mkt. 2.75 (*0-380-75462-2*, Flare) Avon.

Was It Worth It? A Collection of International Cartoons about Columbus & His Trip to America. Michael A. Ricci & Joseph G. Szabo. 112p. 1992. pap. 12.95 (*0-9631600-0-1*) WittyWrld ICM.

Was Jesus a Republican or a Democrat. Tony Campolo. LC 95-31479. 192p. 1995. 17.99 (*0-8499-1009-9*) Word Pub.

Was Jesus Christ a Negro? The African Origin of the Myths & Legends of the Garden of Eden. John G. Jackson. LC 87-80245. 50p. 1987. pap. 5.95 (*0-938818-11-2*) ECA Assoc.

Was Jesus Crucified? A. Deedat. pap. 3.00 (*0-933511-85-X*) Kazi Pubns.

Was Jesus Crucified. Ahmed Deedat. Ed. by Al I. Obaba. 49p. (Orig.). (YA). 1991. pap. text ed. 2.00 (*0-916157-72-5*) African Islam Miss Pubns.

Was Jesus Influenced by Buddhism? Dwight Goddard. 249p. 1971. reprint ed. spiral bd. 12.00 (*0-7873-0350-X*) Hlth Research.

Was Jesus Influenced by Buddhism? A Comparative Study of the Lives & Thoughts of Jesus & Gautama. D. Goddard. 1991. lib. bdg. 69.95 (*0-8490-4310-7*) Gordon Pr.

Was Jesus Influenced by Buddhism? A Comparative Study of the Lives & Thoughts of Gautama & Jesus. Dwight Goddard. 250p. 1996. pap. 19.95 (*1-56459-883-7*) Kessinger Pub.

Was Jesus of Nazareth God or Man, Christ or Spirit Medium? E. W. Sprague. 180p. 1993. reprint ed. spiral bd. 8.50 (*0-7873-0813-7*) Hlth Research.

Was Jesus of Nazareth the Messiah? Alphonso de Espina & the "Fortalitium Fidei" Stephen J. McMichael. LC 93-39350. (South Florida Studies in the History of Judaism). 703p. 1994. 134.95 (*1-55540-930-X*, 240096) Scholars Pr GA.

***Was Jesus Really Like Us?** T. A. Davis. 189p. (Orig.). Date not set. pap. 7.95 (*0-614-30878-X*) Hartland Pubns.

Was Jonestown a CIA Experiment: A Review of the Evidence. Michael Meiers. LC 88-30698. (Studies in American Religion: Vol. 35). (Illus.). 575p. 1988. 119.95 (*0-88946-013-2*) E Mellen.

***Was Lady Godiva Involved in a Coverup? & Other Logic Puzzles.** Roger Hufford. LC 88-12584. 1989. pap. 7.95 (*0-13-944778-4*) P-H.

Was Pythagoras Chinese? An Examination of Right Triangle Theory in Ancient China. Frank Swetz & T. I. Kao. LC 76-41806. (Penn State Studies: No. 39). (Illus.). 1977. pap. 10.00 (*0-271-01238-2*) Pa St U Pr.

Was Roosevelt Pushed into War? Harry E. Barnes. 1971. 200.00 (*0-87700-285-1*) Revisionist Pr.

Was Sie Schon Immer Ueber Angst Wissen Wollten! Angst, Angsterkrankungen, Behandlungsmoeglichkeiten. 2nd ed. H. U. Wittchen et al. (Illus.). vi, 72p. 1994. pap. 17.50 (*3-8055-6005-2*) S Karger.

Was Sind Erignisse? Eine Studie Zur Analytischen Ontologie. Ralf Stoecker. (Quellen und Studien zur Philosophie Ser.: No. 29). xiv, 253p. (GER.). (C). 1992. lib. bdg. 103.10 (*3-11-012909-4*) De Gruyter.

Was That a Tax Lawyer Who Just Flew Over? From Outside the Offices of Fairweather, Winters & Sommers. Arnold B. Kanter. (Illus.). 224p. (Orig.). 1996. pap. 13.95 (*0-945774-31-1*) Catbird Pr.

Was the AIDS Epidemic Unnecessary: How the Bureaucracy Has Spread the Disease. 1992. lib. bdg. 79.95 (*0-8490-5358-7*) Gordon Pr.

Was the Buddha a Bhikkhu? A Rejoinder to a Reply to Forty-Three Years Ago. Sangharakshita. 58p. (Orig.). 1996. pap. 6.99 (*0-904766-71-3*) Windhorse Pubns.

Was the Industrial Revolution Necessary? Ed. by Graeme D. Snooks. LC 93-45688. 176p. (C). (gr. 13). 1994. text ed. 59.95 (*0-415-10868-3*, B3917, Routledge NY) Routledge.

Was the Industrial Revolution Necessary? Ed. by Graeme D. Snooks. LC 93-45688. 176p. (C). 1994. pap. 19.95 (*0-415-10869-1*, B3921) Routledge.

Was the Red Flag Flying There? Marxist Politics & the Arab-Israeli Conflict in Egypt & Israel, 1948-1965. Joel Beinin. LC 89-49036. 328p. 1990. 45.00 (*0-520-07035-6*); pap. 14.00 (*0-520-07036-4*) U CA Pr.

Was the Vietnam War Legal? rev. ed. Steven Cohen & Millard Clements. Ed. by Jerold M. Starr. (Lessons of the Vietnam War Ser.). (Illus.). 32p. (C). 1991. pap. text ed. 5.00 (*0-945919-03-4*) Ctr Social Studies.

Was There a Pepsi Generation Before Pepsi Discovered It? Stanley C. Hollander & Richard Germain. LC 92-13905. (Illus.). 176p. 1993. 29.95 (*0-8442-3456-7*, NTC Busn Bks) NTC Pub Grp.

Was There an Alternative? Trotskyism: a Look Through the Years. Vadim Z. Rogovin. (Orig.). 1997. pap. 21.95 (*0-929087-71-2*) Labor Pubns Inc.

Was This Heaven? A Self-Portrait of Iowa on Early Postcards. Lyell D. Henry, Jr. LC 95-17620. (Bur Oak Original Ser.). (Illus.). 268p. 1995. 29.95 (*0-87745-520-1*) U of Iowa Pr.

Was Wales Industrialised? Essays in Modern Welsh History. John Williams. 272p. 1995. 40.00 (*1-85902-139-5*, Pub. by Gomer Pr UK) St Mut.

Was War Necessary? National Security & U. S. Entry into War. Melvin Small. LC 80-13536. (Sage Library of Social Research: No. 105). 311p. reprint ed. pap. 88.70 (*0-8357-8511-4*, 2034804) Bks Demand.

***Wasatch & Beyond: Mountain Bike Trail Guide.** LC 96-76166. 84p. (Orig.). 1996. pap. 8.95 (*0-9652355-0-5*, 9601) Hgh Desert UT.

Wasatch Front - Strawberry Valley, UT. rev. ed. Ed. by Trails Illustrated Staff. (Illus.). 1994. 8.99 (*0-925873-90-X*) Trails Illustrated.

Wasatch Quartzite. John W. Gottman. (Illus.). 1979. pap. 3.00 (*0-915272-23-7*) Wasatch Pubs.

***Wasatch Range.** Stuart Ruckman & Bret Ruckman. (Classic Rock Climbs Ser.: Vol. 11). (Illus.). (Orig.). 1997. pap. 10.95 (*1-57540-036-7*) Chockstone Pr.

Wasatch Rock Climbs. Les Ellison & Brian Smoot. LC 84-713333. (Illus.). 302p. 1984. pap. 14.50 (*0-930410-20-3*) Amer Alpine Club.

***Wasatch Ski Atlas: A Photographic Collection.** Angus M. Thuermer et al. (Illus.). 28p. (Orig.). 1996. pap. 13.95 (*0-9655673-1-1*) Proj X Pubns.

Wasatch Tours: An Introduction. 2nd ed. Alexis Kelner & David Hanscom. (Illus.). 256p. 1993. pap. 14.95 (*1-884744-02-8*) Wasatch Tours.

Wasatch Tours Vol. 2: The Northern Wasatch. David Hanscom & Alexis Kelner. (Illus.). 256p. (Orig.). (YA). 1995. pap. 17.95 (*1-884744-03-6*) Wasatch Tours.

Wasatch Winter Trails. John Veranth. (Illus.). 128p. 1991. pap. 7.00 (*0-915272-36-9*) Wasatch Pubs.

WASCO: An Epic Novel of Early San Francisco & the Untamed Oregon Frontier. Martel Scroggin. LC 87-71308. 264p. 1987. pap. 8.95 (*0-8323-0457-3*) Binford Mort.

Wash. Philip K. Gotanda. 1991. pap. 5.25 (*0-8222-1222-6*) Dramatists Play.

Wash. Philip K. Gotanda. LC 92-13221. 64p. (C). 1992. pap. 9.95 (*0-435-08613-8*, 08613) Heinemann.

Wash & Be Healed: The Water-Cur Movement & Women's Health. Susan Cayleff. (Health, Society, & Policy Ser.). 257p. 1991. pap. 18.95 (*0-87722-859-0*) Temple U Pr.

Wash & Brush up. Eleanor Allen. (Junior Reference Ser.). (Illus.). 64p. (J). (gr. 7 up). 1984. 14.95 (*0-7136-1639-3*) Dufour.

Wash Day. Ron Bacon. LC 92-34270. (Voyages Ser.). (Illus.). (J). 1993. 2.50 (*0-383-03665-8*) SRA McGraw.

Wash Day. Frank Endersby. (J). (gr. 4 up). 1981. 3.99 (*0-85953-273-9*) Childs Play.

Wash Me on Home Mama. Peter Najarian. 86p. (Orig.). 1978. pap. 5.95 (*0-917658-10-8*) BPW & P.

***Wash Your Hair with Whipped Cream: And Hundreds More Offbeat Uses for Even More Brand-Name Products.** Joey Green. LC 97-12161. (Illus.). 176p. 1997. pap. 8.95 (*0-7868-8276-X*) Hyperion.

Washakie: An Account of Indian Resistance of the Covered Wagon & Union Pacific Railroad Invasions of Their Territory. Grace R. Hebard. LC 76-43733. reprint ed. 52.50 (*0-404-15575-8*) AMS Pr.

Washakie, Chief of the Shoshones. Grace R. Hebard. LC 95-33119. (Illus.). xxv, 325p. 1995. pap. 12.00 (*0-8032-7278-2*, Bison Books) U of Nebr Pr.

Washburn: Over 100 Years of Fine Stringed Instruments. John Teagle. (Illus.). pap. 29.95 (*0-8256-1435-X*, AM 92230) Omnibus NY.

Washburn: Over 100 Years of Fine Stringed Instruments. John Teagle. (Illus.). 39.95 (*0-8256-1436-8*, AM 92231) Omnibus NY.

Washburn: The Richard Washburn Family Genealogy; a Family History of 200 Years, with Some Connected Families. Ada C. Haight. Ed. by Frank C. Lewis. (Illus.). 1271p. 1992. reprint ed. pap. 139.50 (*0-8328-2417-8*); reprint ed. lib. bdg. 149.50 (*0-8328-2416-X*) Higginson Bk Co.

Washburn, a Town History: Settlers of Salmon Brook, Maine. Ray H. Carter. (Illus.). 192p. 1987. 25.00 (*0-933858-18-3*); pap. 17.50 (*0-933858-10-8*) Kennebec River.

Washburn Reader. Ed. by Robert Stein. (Illus.). 238p. 1984. pap. 6.95 (*0-939391-02-3*) B Woodley Pr.

Washburne's Tables. Randel Washburne. 16p. (Orig.). pap. 5.95 (*0-935727-01-9*) Weatherly Pr.

Washday on Noah's Ark: A Story of Noah's Ark. Illus. & As told by Glen Rounds. LC 91-4507. 32p. (J). (ps-3). 1985. lib. bdg. 15.95 (*0-8234-0555-9*) Holiday.

Washday on Noah's Ark: A Story of Noah's Ark. Illus. & As told by Glen Rounds. LC 91-4507. 32p. (J). (ps-3). 1991. pap. 5.95 (*0-8234-0880-9*) Holiday.

Washed by a Wave of Wind: Science Fiction from the Corridor. Ed. by M. Shayne Bell. LC 93-13567. xxii, 378p. (Orig.). 1993. pap. 18.95 (*1-56085-038-8*) Signature Bks.

Washed Out Bridges & Other Disasters. Garry B. Trudeau. (Illus.). 1994. pap. 7.95 (*0-8362-1747-0*) Andrews & McMeel.

Washi Crafts: Working with Japanese Paper. Andrea Heinrichsohn. (Illus.). 96p. (Orig.). 1996. pap. 16.00 (*0-87040-961-1*) Kodansha.

Washing Away of Wrongs: Forensic Medicine in Thirteenth-Century China. Sung Tz'u. Tr. by Brian E. McKnight & Joseph Needham from CHI. LC 81-6195. (Science, Medicine, & Technology in East Asia Ser.: No. 1). (Illus.). 181p. (Orig.). 1981. pap. text ed. 25.00 (*0-89264-800-7*) Ctr Chinese Studies.

Washing Silk: The Life & Selected Poetry of Wei Chung, (834?-910) Robin D. Yates. LC 87-29642. (Harvard-Yenching Institute Monograph: No. 26). 280p. 1988. 30.00 (*0-674-94775-4*) Coun East Asian Stud.

Washing the Cow's Skull: Texas Poetry in Translation. Ed. by Dave Oliphant & Luis A. Ramos-Garcia. 400p. (ENG & SPA.). (C). 1981. pap. 15.00 (*0-933384-05-X*) Prickly Pear.

Washing the Elephant: An Authorized Biography of Bettie Esther Parham. Joseph Osborne & Bettie E. Parham. (Illus.). 192p. 1994. text ed. 19.95 (*0-8059-3479-0*) Dorrance.

Washing "the Great Unwashed" Public Baths in Urban America, 1840-1920. Marilyn T. Williams. 190p. 1991. 47.50 (*0-8142-0537-2*) Ohio St U Pr.

Washing the Stones: Selected Poems 1975-1995. Maude Meehan. LC 95-29997. 240p. (Orig.). 1996. pap. 13.00 (*0-918949-85-8*) Papier-Mache Press.

Washing the Willow Tree Loon. Jacqueline B. Martin. LC 94-11787. (J). (ps-4). 1995. 16.00 (*0-689-80415-6*, Atheneum S&S) S&S Trade.

Washington. LC 96-23438. (One Nation Ser.). 1996. write for info. (*1-56065-441-4*) Capstone Pr.

***Washington.** (Celebrate the States Ser.). (Illus.). 144p. (J). (ps up). 1998. lib. bdg. 22.95 (*0-7614-0422-8*, Benchmark NY) Marshall Cavendish.

Washington. Bradlee. 192p. 1996. pap. 25.00 (*0-7893-0054-0*) St Martin.

***Washington.** Capstone Press Geography Department Staff. (One Nation Ser.). (Illus.). 48p. (J). (gr. 3-7). 1996. 18.40 (*0-516-20268-5*) Childrens.

Washington. Compass American Guide Staff. (Compass American Guides Ser.). 1995. pap. 17.95 (*1-878867-58-X*, Compass Amrcn) Fodors Travel.

Washington. Nancy M. Davies. (American Traveler Ser.). 1990. 7.98 (*0-8317-8838-0*) Smithmark.

Washington. Dennis B. Fradin & Judith B. Fradin. LC 94-14549. (From Sea to Shining Sea Ser.). (Illus.). 64p. (J). (gr. 3-5). 1994. lib. bdg. 24.00 (*0-516-03847-8*) Childrens.

***Washington.** Dennis B. Fradin. (From Sea to Shining Sea Ser.). 64p. (J). 1997. pap. 5.95 (*0-516-26129-0*) Childrens.

Washington. Douglas S. Freeman. 1995. pap. 23.00 (*0-684-82637-2*, Touchstone Bks) S&S Trade.

Washington. Jaffe. 1992. 22.95 (*0-13-933979-5*) P-H.

Washington. Photos by John Marshall. LC 88-80536. (Illus.). 160p. 1988. 39.95 (*0-932575-64-1*) Gr Arts Ctr Pub.

Washington. Sandy E. Powell. LC 92-13366. (Hello U. S. A. Ser.). (J). (gr. 3-6). 1993. lib. bdg. 18.95 (*0-8225-2726-X*, Lerner Publctns) Lerner Group.

Washington. R. C. Stein. LC 91-13509. (America the Beautiful Ser.). 144p. (J). (gr. 4 up). 1991. lib. bdg. 28.30 (*0-516-00493-X*) Childrens.

Washington. Kathleen Thompson. LC 95-25733. (Portrait of America Library). 48p. (YA). (gr. 3 up). 1996. lib. bdg. 22.83 (*0-8114-7393-7*) Raintree Steck-V.

Washington. Kathleen Thompson. LC 95-25733. (Portrait of America Library). 48p. (YA). (gr. 3 up). 1996. pap. text ed. 5.95 (*0-8114-7474-7*) Raintree Steck-V.

Washington: A Centennial Atlas. James W. Scott. 1990. 42.00 (*1-882008-03-0*) WWU CPNS.

Washington: A Centennial History. Robert E. Ficken & Charles P. LeWarne. (Illus.). 232p. 1988. 19.95 (*0-295-96693-9*) U of Wash Pr.

Washington: A Guide to the Evergreen State. Federal Writers' Project. 688p. 1941. reprint ed. 79.00 (*0-403-02196-0*) Somerset Pub.

Washington: A Guide to the Evergreen State. Federal Writers' Project Staff & Writers Program-WPA Staff. (American Guide Ser.). 1989. reprint ed. lib. bdg. 79.00 (*0-7812-1046-1*, 1046) Rprt Serv.

Washington: A History of the Evergreen State. Mary W. Avery. LC 61-8211. (Illus.). 374p. 1965. 25.00 (*0-295-95126-5*) U of Wash Pr.

Washington! Adventure for Kids. 2nd ed. Marti Weston & Florri Decell. LC 90-70168. 64p. (J). (gr. 1-9). 1990. pap. 6.95 (*0-918339-13-8*) Vandamere.

Washington: City & Capital. Federal Writers' Project. 528p. 1942. reprint ed. 95.00 (*0-403-02237-1*) Somerset Pub.

***Washington: City on a Hill.** Bob Levey & Nan Siemer. LC 97-12602. (Urban Tapestry Ser.). (Illus.). 1997. 44.95 (*1-881096-41-6*) Towery Pub.

Washington: Hello U. S. A. Sandy E. Powell. (J). 1996. pap. text ed. 5.95 (*0-8225-9738-1*) Lerner Group.

Washington: Off the Beaten Path: A Guide to Unique Places. 2nd ed. Todd Litman & Suzanne Kort. LC 96-11928. (Off the Beaten Path Ser.). (Illus.). 160p. 1995. pap. 10.95 (*1-56440-898-1*) Globe Pequot.

***Washington: Pride & Glory of America.** Isabella Brega. (Travel America Ser.). 1997. 15.98 (*0-7651-9401-5*) Smithmark.

W

Washington: Readings in the History of the Evergreen State. Ed. by Burton J. Williams. 1977. pap. 25.00 (*0-87291-090-3*) Coronado Pr.

Washington: Seasons of the Capital. Philip Kopper. LC 92-38747. (Illus.). 112p. 1993. 19.95 (*1-880216-08-6*, Elliott Clark) Black Belt Comm.

Washington: The Indispensable Man. James T. Flexner. 1994. pap. 16.95 (*0-316-28616-8*) Little.

Washington: The Indispensable Man. James T. Flexner. 1979. pap. 3.95 (*0-451-62213-8*, ME2213, Ment) NAL-Dutton.

Washington: The State & It's Educational System. Harold L. Hodgkinson. 10p. 1990. 7.00 (*0-937846-62-7*) Inst Educ Lead.

Washington: Writings. George Washington. Ed. by John Rhodehamel. LC 96-9665. 1149p. 1997. 40.00 (*1-883011-23-X*) Library of America.

Washington see Atlas of Historical County Boundaries

Washington, Adams, & Jefferson. Michael Weber. LC 95-43544. (Complete History of Our Presidents Ser.: Vol. 1). (J). 1996. write for info. (*0-86593-406-1*) Rourke Corp.

Washington, Adams, & Jefferson: The Building of a New Nation. Stephen Meyeroff. (Student's Guide Through American History Ser.). (Illus.). (YA). (gr. 8-12). 1998. write for info. (*0-9646602-2-9*) Oak Tree Pubs.

Washington Administrative Law Practice Manual. Administrative Law Section of the Washington State Bar Association Staff. 470p. 1993. suppl. ed. 32.00 (*0-685-74273-3*) MICHIE.

Washington Administrative Law Practice Manual. Ed. by WA State Bar Association, Administrative Law Section Staff. 470p. 1994. spiral bd. 95.00 (*0-409-20038-7*) MICHIE.

***Washington Allston, Secret Societies & the Alchemy of Anglo-American Painting.** David Bjelajac. (Cambridge Studies in American Visual Culture). (Illus.). 272p. (C). 1997. text ed. 65.00 (*0-521-43153-0*) Cambridge U Pr.

***Washington Almanac of International Trade & Business, 1998, Vol. IV. 4th rev. ed. Ed. by William A. Scouton & Gary P. Osifchin. (Illus.). 800p. 1998. pap. 225.00 (*1-886222-10-X*) Almanac Pub.**

Now in its fourth edition, this Almanac is the only comprehensive reference available covering thousands of contacts in Washington, D.C. & beyond who deal with issues concerning global trade & foreign policy. It is an indispensable road map for anyone with an interest in the international arena, guiding them to the policymakers & offices with responsibility for a range of issues from export promotion, to diplomatic relations, to military procurement, to the global environment. In all, over 10,000 contacts throughout all levels of the U.S. Government, at the foreign embassies, within state governments, & in the private sector, are listed. Included are profiles of more than 600 ambassadors, congressional staffers, & executive branch appointees as well as descriptions of hundreds of government programs & offices. Also included are descriptions & contact information for over 500 private trade associations, think tanks, & nonprofit institutions with international involvement. "For those who want a one-stop approach for coverage of the international community in Washington, this new Almanac will be welcome."--American Reference Books Annual. "Recommended to all libraries."--CHOICE. "This Almanac is irrefutable testament to Greater Washington's prominence in the global arena."--Louise Tucker, Director, International Business Center, The Greater Washington Board of Trade. Order from: Almanac Publishing, P. O. Box 3785, Washington, D.C. 20007. 202-206-2297, 888-8-ALMANAC, FAX 202-223-3504.

Publisher Provided Annotation.

***Washington Almanac of International Trade Business 1996/97.** 3rd ed. Ed. by William Scouton & Gary P. Osifehin. (Illus.). 800p. (C). 1996. pap. 225.00 (*1-886222-05-3*) Almanac Pub.

Washington & His Colleagues: A Chronicle of the Rise & Fall of Federalism. Henry J. Ford. (BCL1 - U. S. History Ser.). 235p. 1992. reprint ed. lib. bdg. 79.00 (*0-7812-6137-6*) Rprt Serv.

Washington & His Comrades in Arms: A Chronicle of the War of Independence. George M. Wrong. (BCL1 - U. S. History Ser.). 295p. 1991. reprint ed. lib. bdg. 79.00 (*0-7812-6109-0*) Rprt Serv.

Washington & His Generals: Or, Legends of the American Revolution, George Lippard. LC 70-164570. (American Fiction Reprint Ser.). Orig. Title: The Legends of the American Revolution, 1776. 1977. reprint ed. 35.95 (*0-8369-7047-0*) Ayer.

Washington & Lee. William Strode. (Illus.). 112p. 1986. 35.00 (*0-916509-06-0*) Harmony Hse Pub.

Washington & Lee Law Review: 1939-1995/96, 53 vols., Set. Bound set. 2,160.00 (*0-8377-9184-7*) Rothman.

Washington & Old Dominion Railroad. 4th ed. Ames W. Williams. 206p. 1989. reprint ed. pap. 16.75 (*0-926984-00-4*) Arlington Historical.

Washington & Oregon, A Map History of the Oregon Country. Martha B. Parker. 1988. 25.00 (*0-685-19905-3*) Ye Galleon.

Washington & Oregon in Color. Ray Atkeson. (Illus.). 24p. 1954. pap. 1.00 (*0-8323-0077-2*) Binford Mort.

Washington & Other State Greats (Biographies!) Carole Marsh. (Carole Marsh Washington Bks.). (Illus.). (J). 1994. pap. 19.95 (*0-7933-2225-1*); lib. bdg. 29.95 (*0-7933-2224-3*); disk 29.95 (*0-7933-2226-X*) Gallopade Pub Group.

Washington & the American Revolution: A Guide to the Campaigns in Pennsylvania & New Jersey. Anita D. Blackaby. LC 86-70173. 112p. (Orig.). 1986. pap. 8.50 (*0-9616323-0-5*) CARS.

Washington & the Poet. Ed. by Francis C. Rosenberger. LC 77-81771. 87p. reprint ed. pap. 25.00 (*0-317-55499-9*, 2029601) Bks Demand.

Washington & the Revolutionists: A Characterization of Recovery Policies & of the People Who Are Giving Them Effect. Roger W. Babson. LC 76-111812. (Essay Index Reprint Ser.). 1977. reprint ed. 23.95 (*0-8369-1642-5*) Ayer.

Washington & the Theatre. Paul L. Ford. LC 67-13345. (Illus.). 1972. reprint ed. 13.95 (*0-405-08527-3*) Ayer.

Washington & the Virginia Backcountry. Warren R. Hofstra. LC 96-16602. (Illus.). 256p. 1997. 34.95 (*0-945612-50-8*) Madison Hse.

Washington & Two Marches: 1963 & 1983. Samuel F. Yette & Frederick W. Yette. (Illus.). (YA). 1984. 25.00 (*0-911253-02-5*); pap. 16.95 (*0-911253-03-3*) Cottage Bks.

Washington & Two Marches: 1963 & 1983. deluxe limited ed. Samuel F. Yette & Frederick W. Yette. (Illus.). (YA). 1984. 50.00 (*0-317-11590-1*) Cottage Bks.

Washington & Washington Writing, Vol. M12. Ed. by David McAleavey. 1986. 7.00 (*1-888028-10-6*) GWU Ctr WAS.

Washington Appellate Practice Deskbook, 2 vols., Set. 1993. 180.00 (*0-88129-242-7*) Wash Bar CLE.

Washington Apple Country. Rick Steigmeyer. 1995. 39.95 (*1-55868-240-6*) Gr Arts Ctr Pub.

Washington Area, Health & Fitness Guide. Ellen A. Heard. (Illus.). 144p. (Orig.). 1993. pap. 9.95 (*0-9634883-0-9*, Haras Salohcin Pr) E A Heard.

Washington Area Library Directory. Ed. by David Shumaker. 180p. 1992. 90.00 (*0-9635577-1-8*); pap. 75.00 (*0-9635577-0-X*) Data-Matic Systs.

Washington Area Restaurant Menu Book. 3rd ed. Carol P. Stowell. (Illus.). 144p. 1989. pap. 7.95 (*0-918339-11-1*) Vandamere.

Washington Art: A Guide to Galleries, Art Consultants & Museums. Carolyn Blakeslee et al. (Illus.). 1988. pap. 13.95 (*0-945388-00-4*) Art Calendar.

Washington at Work. 2nd ed. Cohen. 1994. pap. text ed. 24.00 (*0-02-323200-5*, Macmillan Coll) P-H.

Washington Atlas & Gazetteer. 3rd ed. DeLorme Mapping Company Staff. (Atlas & Gazetteer Ser.). (Illus.). 128p. (Orig.). 1996. pap. 16.95 (*0-89933-245-5*, 5353) DeLorme Map.

Washington Automotive Directory. Ed. by T. L. Spelman. 1985. 24.95 (*1-55527-033-6*) Auto Contact Inc.

Washington Babylon. Alexander Cockburn & Ken Silverstein. (Illus.). 224p. 1996. pap. 17.00 (*1-85984-092-2*, Pub. by Vrso UK) Norton.

Washington Babylon. Alexander Cockburn & Ken Silverstein. (Illus.). 224p. (C). (gr. 13 up). 1996. text ed. 60.00 (*0-86091-427-5*, Pub. by Vrso UK) Norton.

Washington Babylon. Thomas. 1995. 25.00 (*0-684-19634-4*) PB.

***Washington Backcountry Almanac 1997: National Parks - National Forests - Wilderness Areas.** annuals rev. ed. Mountaineers Staff. Ed. by Ken Lans. (Illus.). 112p. 1997. pap. 5.95 (*0-89886-508-5*) Mountaineers.

Washington-Baltimore Mountain Bike Book: Out of the Gridlock - into the Woods. Scott Adams. (Illus.). 208p. (Orig.). 1994. pap. 12.95 (*1-882997-03-4*) Beachway Pr.

Washington-Baltimore Sports Quiz: Senators, Orioles, Redskins, Colts, Bullets, Capitals. Brenda Alesii & Daniel Locche. LC 92-38083. 1993. 9.95 (*0-8065-1424-8*) Carol Pub Group.

Washington Baltimore Telephone Want Ads. Beth Campbell. 156p. 1989. pap. 6.95 (*0-918339-12-X*) Vandamere.

Washington Bandits, Bushwackers, Outlaws, Crooks, Devils, Ghosts, Desperadoes & Other Assorted & Sundry Characters! Carole Marsh. (Carole Marsh Washington Bks.). (Illus.). (J). 1994. pap. 19.95 (*0-7933-1177-2*); lib. bdg. 29.95 (*0-7933-1178-0*); disk 29.95 (*0-7933-1179-9*) Gallopade Pub Group.

Washington Bible Class. Mary A. Dodge. (Notable American Authors Ser.). 1992. reprint ed. lib. bdg. 90.00 (*0-7812-2662-7*) Rprt Serv.

Washington Biographical Dictionary: People of All Times & All Places Who Have Been Important to the History & Life of the State. LC 93-32623. 1995. 79.00 (*0-403-09935-8*) Somerset Pub.

Washington Black Book: The Directory to the Washington Press Corps. Ed. by Marina Newmyer. LC 88-5181. 500p. (Orig.). 1988. pap. 103.50 (*0-8191-6878-5*) Madison Bks UPA.

Washington Book of Facts & Fancies, Caprices & Curiosities: The Insider's Guide to the Passions, Possessions & Pleasures of the Power Elite in the Nation's Capital. James J. Sheeran. LC 93-92634. (Illus.). 416p. 1993. 18.95 (*0-9622977-4-7*) Palm Beach Soc.

Washington Bookstore Book: A Surprising Guide to Our State's Bookstores & Their Specialties for Students, Teachers, Writers & Publishers. Carole Marsh. (Washington Bks.). (Illus.). 1994. pap. 19.95 (*0-7933-2997-3*); lib. bdg. 29.95 (*0-7933-2996-5*); disk 29.95 (*0-7933-2998-1*) Gallopade Pub Group.

Washington Building Contracts & Construction Law. David Trachtenberg. 400p. 1994. spiral bd. 95.00 (*1-56257-222-9*) MICHIE.

Washington Bullets. Richard Rambeck. (NBA Today Ser.). 32p. (YA). (gr. 5 up). 1993. lib. bdg. 14.95 (*0-88682-523-7*) Creative Ed.

Washington Business Directory, 1997. rev. ed. 3280p. 1996. boxed 445.00 (*1-56105-794-0*) Am Busn Direct.

***Washington Business Directory 1997.** rev. ed. American Business Directories Staff. 3280p. 1996. boxed 445.00 (*1-56105-877-7*) Am Busn Direct.

***Washington Business Directory 1998.** rev. ed. American Business Directories Staff. 3408p. 1997. boxed 445.00 (*1-56105-964-1*) Am Busn Direct.

Washington By-Line. Bess Furman. (American Autobiography Ser.). 348p. 1995. reprint ed. lib. bdg. 89.00 (*0-7812-8525-9*) Rprt Serv.

Washington by Night: Vintage Photographs from the 30's. Volkmar K. Wentzel. 304p. 1992. 39.95 (*1-56373-019-7*) Fulcrum Pub.

Washington Capitols. David Smale. LC 94-4304. (NHL Today Ser.). 32p. (J). 1995. lib. bdg. 15.95 (*0-88682-691-8*) Creative Ed.

Washington Cascades. (Northwest Mythic Landscape Ser.). (Illus.). 28p. 1992. text ed. 5.95 (*0-912365-66-8*) Sasquatch Bks.

Washington Census Index 1850 Mortality Schedule. (Illus.). lib. bdg. 30.00 (*0-89593-794-8*) Accelerated Index.

Washington Census Index 1860 Mortality Schedule. (Illus.). lib. bdg. 30.00 (*0-89593-525-2*) Accelerated Index.

Washington Census Index 1870 Mortality Schedule. (Illus.). lib. bdg. 30.00 (*0-89593-526-0*) Accelerated Index.

Washington Census Index 1880 Mortality Schedule. (Illus.). 1980. lib. bdg. 32.00 (*0-89593-527-9*) Accelerated Index.

Washington Census Index 1890 Union Veterans. Ronald V. Jackson. (Illus.). 1985. lib. bdg. 55.00 (*0-89593-799-9*) Accelerated Index.

Washington City Is Burning. Harriette G. Robinet. LC 95-33382. (J). (gr. 3-7). 1996. 16.00 (*0-689-80773-2*, Atheneum S&S) S&S Trade.

Washington Civil Practice Deskbook. Eleanor C. Hoague & Butterworth Staff. 700p. 1993. spiral bd. 110.00 (*0-88063-814-1*) MICHIE.

Washington Civil Procedure Deskbook: 1992 Edition, Set, Vols. I-III. 1992. 295.00 (*0-88129-237-0*) Wash Bar CLE.

Washington Civil Procedure Deskbook: 1992 Edition, Vol. III. write for info. (*0-88129-236-2*) Wash Bar CLE.

Washington Classic Christmas Trivia: Stories, Recipes, Activities, Legends, Lore & More! Carole Marsh. (Washington Bks.). (Illus.). (J). 1994. pap. 19.95 (*0-7933-1180-2*); lib. bdg. 29.95 (*0-7933-1181-0*); disk 29.95 (*0-7933-1182-9*) Gallopade Pub Group.

Washington Close-ups. Edward G. Lowry. LC 70-142656. (Essay Index Reprint Ser.). 1977. 23.95 (*0-8369-2057-0*) Ayer.

Washington Co., TN: Death Record Abstracts 1908-1916. Eddie M. Nikazy. 316p. (Orig.). 1994. pap. text ed. 23.00 (*0-7884-0100-9*) Heritage Bk.

Washington Coastales. Carole Marsh. (Carole Marsh Washington Bks.). (Illus.). (J). 1994. pap. 19.95 (*0-7933-2219-7*); lib. bdg. 29.95 (*0-7933-2218-9*); disk 29.95 (*0-7933-2220-0*) Gallopade Pub Group.

Washington Coastales! Carole Marsh. (Washington Bks.). (J). 1994. lib. bdg. 29.95 (*0-7933-7312-3*) Gallopade Pub Group.

Washington Comes of Age: The State in the National Experience. Ed. by David H. Stratton. LC 92-33109. (Pettyjohn Lectures). 171p. (Orig.). 1993. 25.00 (*0-87422-093-9*); pap. 17.95 (*0-87422-091-2*) Wash St U Pr.

Washington Commercial Law Deskbook & 1985 Supplement, 4 vols. 1982. Set. ring bd. 375.00 (*0-88129-069-6*) Wash Bar CLE.

Washington Community: Eighteen Hundred to Eighteeen Twenty-Eight. James S. Young. LC 66-14080. 307p. 1986. pap. text ed. 19.50 (*0-231-08381-5*) Col U Pr.

Washington Community Property Deskbook. 2nd ed. 1989. ring bd. 95.00 (*0-88129-220-6*) Wash Bar CLE.

Washington Compromise: How Government Betrays the National Interest. Joseph Churba. (Illus.). 342p. (C). Date not set. lib. bdg. 26.00 (*0-7618-0087-5*) U Pr of Amer.

Washington Conference: Naval Rivalrly, East Asian Stability & the Road to Pearl Harbor. Ed. by Erik Goldstein & John Maurer. 300p. 1994. 35.00 (*0-7146-4559-1*, Pub. by F Cass Pubs UK); pap. 19.50 (*0-7146-4136-7*, Pub. by F Cass Pubs UK) Intl Spec Bk.

Washington Conference, 1956 see Research Opportunities in Renaissance Drama: The Reports of the Modern Language Association Conferences

Washington Connection & Third World Facism, Vol. I. Noam Chomsky & Edward S. Herman. LC 79-64085. (Political Economy of Human Rights Ser.: Vol. I). 441p. 1979. 40.00 (*0-89608-091-9*); pap. 16.00 (*0-89608-090-0*) South End Pr.

Washington Cookbook. Janet Walker. (Illus.). 128p. (Orig.). 1994. pap. 5.95 (*0-914846-97-3*) Golden West Pub.

Washington Cookbook. Ed. by Washington Opera Women's Committee. LC 82-225247. (Illus.). 200p. 1982. pap. 10.00 (*0-9610542-0-4*) Wash Opera.

Washington Corporate Forms, 2 vols. David D. Hoff & Morris Kremen. 970p. 1994. Set. spiral bd. 160.00 (*0-8342-0146-1*); suppl. ed., ring bd. 79.00 (*0-685-74635-6*) MICHIE.

Washington Correspondents. Leo C. Rosten. LC 73-19175. (Politics & People Ser.). 456p. 1974. reprint ed. 30.95 (*0-405-05896-9*) Ayer.

***Washington County: Its History to the Close of the Nineteenth Century. With Biographical Sketches.** Ed. by William L. Stone & A. Dallas Wait. (Illus.). 888p. 1997. reprint ed. lib. bdg. 89.50 (*0-8328-6269-X*) Higginson Bk Co.

Washington County: Politics & Community in Antebellum America. Paul Bourke & Donald DeBats. LC 94-34055. (Reconfiguring American Political History). (Illus.). 312p. 1995. text ed. 45.00 (*0-8018-4950-0*) Johns Hopkins.

Washington County, Alabama, the History Of, Vol. II. Washington County Historical Society Staff. Ed. by Barbara Waddell. (Illus.). 436p. 1989. 50.00 (*0-89308-632-0*, AL 17) Southern Hist Pr.

Washington County, Arkansas, Sheriff's Census for 1865. Nancy Maxwell. 67p. (Orig.). 1994. pap. text ed. 16.50 (*1-55613-885-7*) Heritage Bk.

Washington County, Colorado. Otis Public Library Staff. (Illus.). 323p. 1989. 45.00 (*0-88107-140-4*) Curtis Media.

Washington County Frontier Rangers. Paul W. Myers. 1988. pap. text ed. 7.00 (*0-933227-85-X*) Closson Pr.

Washington County, History of Leitersburg District, Washington County, Including Its Original Land Tenure: First Settlement: Material Development; Biographical Sketches, Etc. Herbert C. Bell. 331p. 1995. lib. bdg. 39.00 (*0-8328-4693-7*) Higginson Bk Co.

Washington County, Illinois. Turner Publishing Company Staff. LC 90-71724. 350p. 1990. 48.00 (*0-614-07275-1*) Turner Pub KY.

Washington County, Kentucky. Washington County Genealogical Society Staff. (Illus.). 350p. 1991. 65.00 (*1-56311-014-8*) Turner Pub KY.

Washington County, Kentucky Taxpayers, 1792-1799. T. L.C. Genealogy Staff. 78p. (Orig.). 1992. spiral bd., pap. 10.00 (*1-886633-11-8*) TLC Genealogy.

Washington County, Maryland, Genealogical Research Guide. George E. Russell. (Illus.). 48p. 1993. pap. 11.00 (*0-914385-14-3*) Catoctin Pr.

Washington County Men & Women of Nebraska: A Book of Portraits, Washington County Edition, Containing an Historical Review of Washington County, Compiled from Public & Private Records. Ed. by Daniel M. Carr. (Illus.). 198p. 1995. reprint ed. lib. bdg. 29.50 (*0-8328-5054-3*) Higginson Bk Co.

Washington County, Ohio: Marriages 1804-1823. Fay Maxwell. 26p. 1974. 6.00 (*1-885463-29-4*) Ohio Genealogy.

Washington County, PA WB Index 1781-1900. Ed. by Bob Closson & Mary Closson. 74p. per. 9.50 (*0-933227-22-1*) Closson Pr.

Washington County, Pennsylvania Marriages, 1780-1857. Compiled by James B. Whisker. 16p. 1988. pap. 5.00 (*0-933227-79-5*) Closson Pr.

Washington County, Tennessee, Marriages, 1780-1870. Goldene F. Burgner. (Illus.). 224p. 1985. 27.50 (*0-89308-564-2*, TN 89) Southern Hist Pr.

Washington County, Tennessee, Wills: 1777-1872. Goldene F. Burgher. (Illus.). 144p. 1983. pap. 25.00 (*0-89308-285-6*) Southern Hist Pr.

Washington County, Virginia Records, Vol. 34. Beverly Fleet. (Virginia Colonial Abstracts Ser.). 83p. 1949. 15.00 (*0-89308-392-5*, VA 76) Southern Hist Pr.

Washington Court Rules Annotated, with Forms, 3 Binders. LC 70-2815. 297.00 (*0-317-00420-4*) Lawyers Cooperative.

Washington Court Rules Annotated, with Forms, 3 Binders. LC 70-2815. 1993. Suppl. 1993. suppl. ed. 67.50 (*0-317-03169-4*) Lawyers Cooperative.

Washington Crafts: Then & Now. Gloria E. Crouse. Ed. by Penelope Loucas. (Illus.). 34p. (Orig.). 1989. pap. 2.00 (*0-924335-08-4*) Tacoma Art Mus.

Washington Crime Perspective 1996. Ed. by Kathleen O. Morgan et al. 24p. 1996. pap. 19.00 (*1-56692-546-0*) Morgan Quitno Corp.

***Washington Crime Perspective 1997.** Ed. by Kathleen O. Morgan & Scott E. Morgan. 24p. 1997. pap. 19.00 (*1-56692-796-X*) Morgan Quitno Corp.

Washington Criminal Practice in Courts of Limited Jurisdiction, 2 vols., Set. Linda S. Portnoy & Eileen P. Farley. LC 92-42802. 1150p. 1994. spiral bd. 175.00 (*1-56257-834-0*) MICHIE.

Washington "Crinkum-Crankum" A Funny Word Book about Our State. Carole Marsh. (Washington Bks.). (Illus.). (J). (gr. 3-12). 1994. 29.95 (*0-7933-4949-4*); pap. 19.95 (*0-7933-4950-8*); disk 29.95 (*0-7933-4951-6*) Gallopade Pub Group.

Washington Cycle. Les Whitten. LC 78-59772. (Illus.). 44p. (Orig.). 1979. pap. 6.00 (*0-912292-50-4*) Smith.

Washington, D. C. (Album Ser.: No. 5). 1976. pap. 7.95 (*0-87130-055-9*) Eakins.

***Washington D. C.** (Rough Guide Ser.). 1997. pap. 14.95 (*1-85828-246-2*) Viking Penguin.

***Washington, D. C.** Dan Elish. LC 97-15042. (Celebrate the States Ser.: Group 4). (Illus.). 94p. (YA). (gr. 4 up). 1998. lib. bdg. 23.95 (*0-7614-0423-6*, Benchmark NY) Marshall Cavendish.

Washington, D. C. Dennis B. Fradin. LC 91-32919. (From Sea to Shining Sea Ser.). (Illus.). 64p. (J). (gr. 3-5). 1992. pap. 5.95 (*0-516-43851-4*); lib. bdg. 24.00 (*0-516-03851-6*) Childrens.

***Washington, D. C.** Arthur Frommer. (Frommer's Portable Guide Ser.). 1997. pap. 8.95 (*0-02-861551-4*) Macmillan.

Washington, D. C. Bill Harris. 1996. 24.99 (*0-517-63114-8*) Random Hse Value.

W

Washington, D. C. Carol Highsmith. 1997. 14.99 (*0-517-18460-5*) Random Hse Value.

***Washington, D. C.** Carol M. Highsmith & Ted Landphair. LC 97-11303. (Pictorial Souvenir Ser.). 1997. write for info. (*0-517-20142-9*) Crown Pub Group.

Washington, D. C. Joyce Johnston. LC 92-44848. (Hello U. S. A. Ser.). (J). (gr. 3-6). 1993. lib. bdg. 18.95 (*0-8225-2751-0*, Lerner Publctns) Lerner Group.

Washington D. C. Robert Llewellyn. 176p. 1994. 14.98 (*0-8317-9472-0*) Smithmark.

Washington, D. C. Nancy Loewen. (Great Cities of the U. S. A. Ser.). (Illus.). (YA). (gr. 5 up). 1989. lib. bdg. 15.94 (*0-86592-544-5*); lib. bdg. 11.95 (*0-685-58590-5*) Rourke Corp.

Washington, D. C. National Park Service Staff. LC 87-600287. (Handbook Ser.: No. 102). (Illus.). 176p. (Orig.). 1988. pap. 5.00 (*0-912627-36-0*) Natl Park Serv.

Washington, D. C. Catherine Reef. LC 89-12025. (Downtown America Ser.). (Illus.). 60p. (J). (gr. 3 up). 1990. lib. bdg. 13.95 (*0-87518-411-1*) Silver Burdett Pr.

***Washington, D. C.** St. Martin's Press Staff. (Let's Go Ser.). 1997. pap. 14.99 (*0-312-16904-3*) St Martin.

***Washington, D. C.** St. Martin's Press Staff. (Marcellino's Restaurant Report Ser.). 1997. pap. 9.99 (*0-312-16923-X*) St Martin.

Washington, D. C. Kathleen Thompson. (Portrait of America Library). 48p. (J). (gr. 4 up). 1996. lib. bdg. 22.83 (*0-8114-7394-5*) Raintree Steck-V.

Washington, D. C. Kathleen Thompson. (Portrait of America Library). 48p. (J). (gr. 4 up). 1996. pap. text ed. 5.95 (*0-8114-7475-5*) Raintree Steck-V.

Washington, D. C. Gore Vidal. 384p. 1986. mass mkt. 5.99 (*0-345-34236-4*) Ballantine.

***Washington, D. C.** rev. ed. Insights Guides Staff. (Insight Guides Ser.). 1996. pap. 21.95 (*0-395-81933-4*) HM.

Washington, D. C. rev. ed. Deborah Kent. LC 90-35386. (America the Beautiful Ser.). (Illus.). 144p. (J). (gr. 4 up). 1992. lib. bdg. 28.30 (*0-516-00497-2*) Childrens.

***Washington, D. C.** A. L. Carlisle. (Illus.). Date not set. reprint ed. pap. 6.95 (*1-879295-20-2*) L B Prince.

***Washington, D. C., Set 8.** (Questivities Ser.). 1995. 9.95 (*1-880505-69-X*, CLC0181) Pieces of Lrning.

Washington, D. C. A Photographic Journey. (Illus.). 1991. 15.99 (*0-517-05306-3*) Random Hse Value.

Washington, D. C. A Picture Memory. 1990. 8.99 (*0-517-01748-2*) Random Hse Value.

Washington, D. C. A Smithsonian Book of the Nation's Capitol. LC 92-17647. (Illus.). 240p. 1992. 39.95 (*0-89599-032-6*) Smithsonian Bks.

Washington, D. C. A Traveler's Guide to the District of Columbia & Nearby Attractions. LC 87-600287. (Illus.). 176p. 1989. Incl. index. pap. 6.50 (*0-16-003553-8*, 024-005-01034-3) USGPO.

***Washington, D. C. A Traveler's Guide to the District of Columbia & Nearby Attractions.** 1997. lib. bdg. 251.75 (*0-8490-8168-8*) Gordon Pr.

Washington, D. C. A Walk Thru. Alma Schulmerich. LC 78-57022. (Illus.). 72p. 1978. pap. 3.95 (*0-8323-0305-4*) Binford Mort.

Washington, D. C. Downtown America. Catherine Reef. (J). (gr. 4-7). 1996. pap. text ed. 7.95 (*0-382-24803-1*) Silver Burdett Pr.

Washington, D. C. Nation's Capital Picture Book. rev. ed. (Illus.). 32p. 1994. pap. 3.95 (*1-879295-11-3*) L B Prince.

Washington, D. C.: A Prospice: A Community Study of Political Socialization. Michael J. Murray. LC 78-61328. 300p. text ed. 26.50 (*0-9614642-1-6*) Media Arts.

Washington, D. C. Access. rev. ed. Richard S. Wurman. (Access Travel Guides Ser.). (Illus.). 168p. 1989. pap. 12.95 (*0-318-40047-2*, Access NY) HarpC.

Washington, D. C. & Other State Greats (Biographies) Carole Marsh. (Washington, D.C. Bks.). (Illus.). (YA). (gr. 3-12). 1994. pap. 19.95 (*0-7933-1481-X*); lib. bdg. 29.95 (*0-7933-1480-1*); disk 29.95 (*0-7933-1482-8*) Gallopade Pub Group.

Washington D. C. & the Potomac Region. Bonnie Jacob. (American Enterprise Ser.). (Illus.). 208p. 1992. 32.95 (*0-89781-430-4*) Am Historical Pr.

Washington D. C. Area Business Directory, 1997. rev. ed. 1328p. 1996. boxed 395.00 (*1-56105-791-6*) Am Busn Direct.

***Washington, D. C. Area Business Directory 1997.** rev. ed. American Business Directories Staff. 1328p. 1996. boxed 395.00 (*1-56105-874-2*) Am Busn Direct.

Washington, D. C. Bandits, Bushwackers, Outlaws, Crooks, Devils, Ghosts, Desperadoes & Other Assorted & Sundry Characters! Carole Marsh. (Carole Marsh Washington, D.C. Bks.). (Illus.). (YA). (gr. 3-12). 1994. pap. 19.95 (*0-7933-0261-7*); lib. bdg. 29.95 (*0-7933-0262-5*); disk 29.95 (*0-7933-0263-3*) Gallopade Pub Group.

Washington, D. C. Bookstore Book: A Surprising Guide to Our State's Bookstores & Their Specialties for Students, Teachers, Writers & Publishers. Carole Marsh. (Washington, D.C. Bks.). (Illus.). 1994. pap. 19.95 (*0-7933-2880-2*); lib. bdg. 29.95 (*0-7933-2879-9*); disk 29.95 (*0-7933-2881-0*) Gallopade Pub Group.

Washington, D. C. Classic Christmas Trivia: Stories, Recipes, Activities, Legends, Lore & More! Carole Marsh. (Carole Marsh Washington, D.C. Bks.). (Illus.). (YA). (gr. 3-12). 1994. pap. 19.95 (*0-7933-0264-1*); lib. bdg. 29.95 (*0-7933-0265-X*); disk 29.95 (*0-7933-0266-8*) Gallopade Pub Group.

Washington, D. C. Coastales. Carole Marsh. (Carole Marsh Washington, D.C. Bks.). (Illus.). (YA). (gr. 3-12). 1994. pap. 19.95 (*0-7933-1475-5*); lib. bdg. 29.95 (*0-7933-1474-7*); disk 29.95 (*0-7933-1476-3*) Gallopade Pub Group.

Washington, D. C. Coastales! Carole Marsh. (Washington, D.C. Bks.). (J). 1994. lib. bdg. 29.95 (*0-7933-7273-9*) Gallopade Pub Group.

Washington D. C. "Crinkum-Crankum" A Funny Word Book about Our State. Carole Marsh. (Washington, D.C. Bks.). (Illus.). (J). (gr. 3-12). 1994. 29.95 (*0-7933-4952-4*); pap. 19.95 (*0-7933-4953-2*); disk 29.95 (*0-7933-4954-0*) Gallopade Pub Group.

Washington, D. C. Dingbats! Bk. 1: A Fun Book of Games, Stories, Activities & More about Our State That's All in Code! for You to Decipher. Carole Marsh. (Washington, D.C. Bks.). (Illus.). (J). (gr. 3-12). 1994. pap. 29.95 (*0-7933-3798-4*); lib. bdg. 29.95 (*0-7933-3797-6*); disk 29.95 (*0-7933-3799-2*) Gallopade Pub Group.

Washington D. C. en Espanol. Annick Sanjurjo & Albert J. Casciero. 224p. 1992. pap. 11.95 (*0-9633827-0-5*) So Cross Pr.

Washington, D. C. Ethnic Restaurant Guide: Your Passport to Great Ethnic Dining. Jonathan Stein. (Passport Press Travel Guides Ser.). 128p. (Orig.). 1993. pap. 9.95 (*1-883323-01-0*) Open Rd Pub.

Washington, D. C. Festival Fun for Kids! Includes Reproducible Activities for Kids! Carole Marsh. (Washington, D.C. Bks.). (Illus.). (J). (gr. 3-12). 1994. pap. 19.95 (*0-7933-3951-0*); lib. bdg. 29.95 (*0-7933-3950-2*); disk 29.95 (*0-7933-3952-9*) Gallopade Pub Group.

Washington, D. C. Green Guide. Michelin Staff. 1991. pap. 18.95 (*0-7859-9171-9*) Fr & Eur.

Washington, D. C. Green Guide English Edition. Michelin Staff. pap. 17.95 (*0-7859-7182-3*, 206701577X) Fr & Eur.

Washington, D. C. Guidebook for Kids. rev. ed. Carol Bluestone & Susan Irwin. LC 87-50322. (Illus.). 64p. (J). (gr. 3-9). 1995. pap. 7.95 (*0-9601022-4-8*) Noodle Pr.

Washington D. C. Hot Air Balloon Mystery. Carole Marsh. (Washington, D.C. Bks.). (Illus.). (J). (gr. 2-9). 1994. 29.95 (*0-7933-2390-8*); pap. 19.95 (*0-7933-2391-6*); disk 29.95 (*0-7933-2392-4*) Gallopade Pub Group.

Washington, D. C. Jeopardy! Answers & Questions about Our State! Carole Marsh. (Washington, D.C. Bks.). (Illus.). (J). (gr. 3-12). 1994. pap. 19.95 (*0-7933-4104-3*); lib. bdg. 29.95 (*0-7933-4103-5*); disk 29.95 (*0-7933-4105-1*) Gallopade Pub Group.

***Washington D. C. Jobbank.** Date not set. pap. 16.95 (*1-55850-781-7*) Adams Media.

Washington D. C. Jobbank, 1996. Adams Publishing Staff. 1995. pap. text ed. 15.95 (*1-55850-571-7*) Adams Media.

Washington, D. C. Jobbank, 1997. Adams Publishing Staff. 1996. pap. text ed. 15.95 (*1-55850-669-1*) Adams Media.

Washington, D. C. "Jography" A Fun Run Thru Our State! Carole Marsh. (Washington, D.C. Bks.). (Illus.). (YA). (gr. 3-12). 1994. pap. 19.95 (*1-55609-561-9*); lib. bdg. 29.95 (*1-55609-562-7*); disk 29.95 (*0-7933-1460-7*) Gallopade Pub Group.

Washington, D. C. Kid's Cookbook: Recipes, How-to, History, Lore & More! Carole Marsh. (Carole Marsh Washington, D.C. Bks.). (Illus.). (YA). (gr. 3-12). 1994. pap. 19.95 (*0-7933-0273-0*); lib. bdg. 29.95 (*0-7933-0274-9*); disk 29.95 (*0-7933-0275-7*) Gallopade Pub Group.

Washington, D. C. Library Book: A Surprising Guide to the Unusual Special Collections in Libraries Across Our State for Students, Teachers, Writers & Publishers. Carole Marsh. (Washington, D.C. Bks.). (Illus.). 1994. pap. 19.95 (*0-7933-3030-0*); lib. bdg. 29.95 (*0-7933-3029-7*); disk 29.95 (*0-7933-3031-9*) Gallopade Pub Group.

Washington, D. C. Media Book: A Surprising Guide to the Amazing Print, Broadcast & Online Media of Our State for Students, Teachers, Writers & Publishers - Includes Reproducible Mailing Labels Plus Activities for Young People! Carole Marsh. (Washington, D.C. Bks.). (Illus.). 1994. pap. 19.95 (*0-7933-3186-2*); lib. bdg. 29.95 (*0-7933-3185-4*); disk 29.95 (*0-7933-3187-0*) Gallopade Pub Group.

Washington, D. C. Monuments in Architectural & Historical Review. Jack Meyer. (Illus.). 21p. (Orig.). 1993. pap. 4.00 (*0-9631727-1-9*) CSU Pubns.

Washington, D. C. Museums: A Ross Guide. Betty Ross. (Illus.). 325p. (Orig.). 1992. pap. 14.95 (*0-9616144-3-9*) Americana Pr.

Washington D. C. Museums: Museums, Historic Houses, Art Galleries & Other Special Places. 3rd ed. Betty Ross. LC 91-39333. (Illus.). 328p. 1992. pap. 14.95 (*0-939009-85-4*) EPM Pubns.

Washington D. C. Mystery Van Takes Off! Book 1: Handicapped Washington D. C. Kids Sneak Off on a Big Adventure. Carole Marsh. (Washington, D.C. Bks.). (Illus.). (J). (gr. 3-12). 1994. 29.95 (*0-7933-5105-7*); pap. 19.95 (*0-7933-5106-5*); disk 29.95 (*0-7933-5107-3*) Gallopade Pub Group.

Washington, D. C. One Hundred Years Ago. Compiled by Skip Whitson. (Historical Ser.). (Illus.). (Orig.). 1976. pap. 6.50 (*0-89540-023-5*, SB-023) Sun Pub.

***Washington D. C. Picture Book: Nation's Capital.** rev. ed. Michael Prince. (Illus.). 32p. 1997. pap. 3.95 (*1-879295-19-9*) L B Prince.

Washington, D. C. Plenary Publication, 1990. Ed. by Andrew V. Frankel & Charles B. Heck. (Trialogue Ser.: No. T42). (Illus.). 76p. (Orig.). 1991. pap. text ed. 6.00 (*0-930503-64-3*) Trilateral Comm.

Washington, D. C. Quiz Bowl Crash Course! Carole Marsh. (Carole Marsh Washington, D.C. Bks.). (Illus.). (YA). (gr. 3-12). 1994. pap. 19.95 (*0-7933-1472-0*); lib. bdg. 29.95 (*0-7933-1471-2*); disk 29.95 (*0-7933-1473-9*) Gallopade Pub Group.

Washington, D. C. Rollercoasters! Carole Marsh. (Washington, D.C. Bks.). (Illus.). (YA). (gr. 3-12). 1994. pap. 19.95 (*0-7933-5249-5*); lib. bdg. 29.95 (*0-7933-5248-7*); disk 29.95 (*0-7933-5250-9*) Gallopade Pub Group.

Washington, D. C. School Trivia: An Amazing & Fascinating Look at Our State's Teachers, Schools & Students! Carole Marsh. (Washington, D.C. Bks.). (Illus.). (YA). (gr. 3-12). 1994. pap. 19.95 (*0-7933-0270-6*); lib. bdg. 29.95 (*0-7933-0271-4*); disk 29.95 (*0-7933-0272-2*) Gallopade Pub Group.

***Washington, D. C. Sightseeing Map.** 1994. 3.95 (*2-06-700049-7*, 49) Michelin.

Washington, D. C. Sightseers' Guide. annuals Anthony S. Pitch. LC 86-70380. (Illus.). 128p. (Orig.). 1996. pap. 5.95 (*0-931719-04-6*) Mino Pubns.

Washington, D. C. Silly Basketball Sportsmysteries, Vol. 1. Carole Marsh. (Washington, D.C. Bks.). (Illus.). (YA). (gr. 3-12). 1994. pap. 19.95 (*0-7933-0267-6*); lib. bdg. 29.95 (*0-7933-0268-4*); disk 29.95 (*0-7933-0269-2*) Gallopade Pub Group.

Washington, D. C. Silly Basketball Sportsmysteries, Vol. 2. Carole Marsh. (Washington, D.C. Bks.). (Illus.). (YA). (gr. 3-12). 1994. pap. 19.95 (*0-7933-1484-4*); lib. bdg. 29.95 (*0-7933-1483-6*); disk 29.95 (*0-7933-1485-2*) Gallopade Pub Group.

Washington, D. C. Silly Football Sportsmysteries, Vol. 1. Carole Marsh. (Washington, D.C. Bks.). (Illus.). (YA). (gr. 3-12). 1994. pap. 19.95 (*0-7933-1463-1*); lib. bdg. 29.95 (*0-7933-1462-3*); disk 29.95 (*0-7933-1464-X*) Gallopade Pub Group.

Washington, D. C. Silly Trivia! Carole Marsh. (Washington, D.C. Bks.). (Illus.). (YA). (gr. 3-12). 1994. pap. 19.95 (*1-55609-559-7*); lib. bdg. 29.95 (*1-55609-560-0*); disk 29.95 (*0-7933-1459-3*) Gallopade Pub Group.

Washington, D. C., Then & Now: 69 Sites Photographed in the Past & Present. Charles S. Kelly. (Americana Ser.). 160p. (Orig.). 1984. pap. 9.95 (*0-486-24586-1*) Dover.

Washington D. C. Timeline: A Chronology of Washington D. C. History, Mystery, Trivia, Legend, Lore & More. Carole Marsh. (Washington, D.C. Bks.). (Illus.). (J). (gr. 3-12). 1994. pap. 19.95 (*0-7933-5900-7*); lib. bdg. 29.95 (*0-7933-5899-X*); disk 29.95 (*0-7933-5901-5*) Gallopade Pub Group.

Washington, D. C., Williamsburg, Busch Gardens, Richmond, & Other Area Attractions. Corey Sandler. (Contemporary's Econoguide '97 Ser.). (Illus.). 288p. 1996. pap. 14.95 (*0-8092-3315-0*) Contemp Bks.

Washington, D. C., 1997. Fodor's Travel Staff. (Illus.). 1996. pap. 14.00 (*0-679-03322-X*) Fodors Travel.

Washington, D. C.'s (Most Devastating!) Disasters & (Most Calamitous!) Catastrophies! Carole Marsh. (Washington, D.C. Bks.). (Illus.). (YA). (gr. 3-12). 1994. pap. 19.95 (*0-7933-0258-7*); lib. bdg. 29.95 (*0-7933-0259-5*); disk 29.95 (*0-7933-0260-9*) Gallopade Pub Group.

Washington D. C.'s Unsolved Mysteries (& Their "Solutions") Includes Scientific Information & Other Activities for Students. Carole Marsh. (Washington, D.C. Bks.). (Illus.). (J). (gr. 3-12). 1994. pap. 19.95 (*0-7933-5747-0*); lib. bdg. 29.95 (*0-7933-5746-2*); disk 29.95 (*0-7933-5748-9*) Gallopade Pub Group.

Washington, D.C. (Pocket Guides Ser.). 1993. pap. 7.95 (*2-8315-2320-6*) Berlitz.

Washington, DC. Michael D. Brown. Ed. by Julia Schieken. (Illus.). 20p. 1995. pap. 7.95 (*1-887498-01-X*) Winterberry Pub.

Washington, D.C. Joyce Johnston. 1995. pap. text ed. 5.95 (*0-8225-9704-7*) Lerner Group.

Washington DC. Santi Visalli. 192p. 1996. 40.00 (*0-7893-0075-3*) Universe.

Washington D.C. A City & Capital. Federal Writers' Project Staff & Writers Program-WPA Staff. (American Guide Ser.). 1989. reprint ed. lib. bdg. 89.00 (*0-7812-1061-5*, 1061) Rprt Serv.

Washington D.C. Ninety-One Pictures - Nation's Capital. rev. ed. (Illus.). 32p. 1992. pap. 3.95 (*1-879295-09-1*) L B Prince.

***Washington, D.C. The Nations Capital Viewbook.** (Illus.). 24p. 1995. write for info. (*0-9656315-0-8*) Coffman Pubns.

***Washington, DC & the Capital Region.** Kap Stann et al. (Illus.). 624p. 1997. pap. 19.95 (*0-86442-437-X*) Lonely Planet.

***Washington, DC Area Business Directory 1998.** rev. ed. American Business Directories Staff. 1360p. 1997. boxed 395.00 (*1-56105-961-7*) Am Busn Direct.

Washington, D.C. at Its Best. Robert S. Kane. LC 90-63158. (World at Its Best Travel Ser.). 222p. 1995. pap. 12.95 (*0-8442-9584-1*, Passport Bks) NTC Pub Grp.

Washington D.C. Facts & Factivities. Carole Marsh. (Carole Marsh State Bks.). (Illus.). 1996. 29.95 (*0-614-11559-0*, C Marsh); teacher ed., pap. 19.95 (*0-7933-7863-X*) Gallopade Pub Group.

***Washington, DC Green Guide.** Michelin Staff. (Illus.). 1997. pap. 18.00 (*2-06-157703-2*, 1577) Michelin.

Washington DC Green Guide. 2nd ed. Ed. by Michelin Travel Publications, Staff. (Orig.). 1994. per. 18.00 (*2-06-157702-4*, 1577) Michelin.

Washington, D.C. Indian Dictionary for Kids! Carole Marsh. (Carole Marsh State Bks.). (J). (gr. 2-9). 1996. 29.95 (*0-7933-7668-8*, C Marsh); pap. 19.95 (*0-7933-7669-6*, C Marsh) Gallopade Pub Group.

Washington, D.C. Silly Football Sportsmysteries, Vol. 2. Carole Marsh. (Carole Marsh Washington, D.C. Bks.). (Illus.). (YA). (gr. 3-12). 1994. pap. 19.95 (*0-7933-1466-6*); lib. bdg. 29.95 (*0-7933-1465-8*); disk 29.95 (*0-7933-1467-4*) Gallopade Pub Group.

Washington D.C. Souvenir Book: English Text - Texte Francais - Deutscher Text - Texto Espanol. rev. ed. Illus. by Wener Bertech. 96p. (ENG, FRE, GER & SPA.). 1992. pap. 9.75 (*1-879295-08-3*) L B Prince.

Washington DC Vegetarian Resourcebook 1996: Delights of the Garden's Exhaustive Guide to Vegetarian & Health-Related Resources for Washington, DC, Maryland & Virginia. Ed. by Matthew G. Tollin. (Nineteen Ninety-Six Vegetarian Resourcebook Ser.). (Illus.). 184p. (Orig.). 1995. pap. 12.95 (*0-9641284-1-1*) Four Winds DC.

***Washington, D.C. 5-Language Book.** (Illus.). 24p. 1996. write for info. (*0-9656315-1-6*) Coffman Pubns.

***Washington, DC '98.** Fodors Travel Staff. 1997. pap. 14.50 (*0-679-03545-1*) Fodors Travel.

Washington Deco: Art Deco Design in the Nation's Capital. Hans Wirz & Richard Striner. LC 84-600183. (Illus.). 128p. 1984. 32.50 (*0-87474-970-0*, STWD) Smithsonian.

Washington Despatches, 1941 to 1945: Weekly Political Reports from the British Embassy. Ed. by H. G. Nicholas. LC 80-6208. xviii, 718p. (C). 1985. pap. text ed. 24.00 (*0-226-58005-9*) U Ch Pr.

Washington Dingbats! Bk. 1: A Fun Book of Games, Stories, Activities & More about Our State That's All in Code! for You to Decipher. Carole Marsh. (Washington Bks.). (Illus.). (J). (gr. 3-12). 1994. pap. 19.95 (*0-7933-3915-4*); lib. bdg. 29.95 (*0-7933-3914-6*); disk 29.95 (*0-7933-3916-2*) Gallopade Pub Group.

Washington Discovery Guide: A Remarkably Useful Travel Companion for Motorists, RVers & Other Explorers. Ed. by Don Martin & Betty Martin. (Discovery Guide Ser.). (Illus.). 352p. (Orig.). 1994. pap. 13.95 (*0-942053-16-8*) Pine Cone Pr CA.

Washington Driver's Handbook: A Guide to Capital Cruising. Ira Gershkoff & Richard Trachtman. 1984. 47.60 (*0-201-11019-9*) Addison-Wesley.

Washington Earthquake Handbook: An Easy-to-Understand Information & Survival Guide. Vern Cope. LC 93-91101. (Illus.). 152p. (Orig.). 1994. pap. 11.95 (*0-9635564-4-4*) V Cope.

***Washington Entrepreneur's Guide.** 2nd ed. Univerity Press Staff. 1997. pap. text ed. 19.95 (*0-9624819-5-5*) University MT.

***Washington Environmental Law Handbook.** 3rd ed. Preston, Gates & Ellis Staff. (State Environment Law Ser.). 450p. (Orig.). 1997. pap. text ed. 95.00 (*0-86587-556-1*) Gov Insts.

Washington Environmental Regulations & Liability. Jeff Belfiglio. 450p. 1994. ring bd. 90.00 (*1-56257-193-1*) MICHIE.

Washington Facts & Factivities. Carole Marsh. (Carole Marsh State Bks.). (Illus.). 1996. 29.95 (*0-614-11560-4*, C Marsh); teacher ed., pap. 19.95 (*0-7933-7941-5*, C Marsh) Gallopade Pub Group.

Washington Family Law Deskbook & 1991 Supplement, 2 vols. 1989. Set. ring bd. 195.00 (*0-88129-225-7*) Wash Bar CLE.

Washington Family Law Deskbook & 1991 Supplement. 1991. Supplement 1991. suppl. ed. 50.00 (*0-88129-231-1*) Wash Bar CLE.

Washington Federal Census Index, 1850. Ronald V. Jackson. (Illus.). lib. bdg. 48.00 (*0-89593-793-X*) Accelerated Index.

Washington Federal Census Index, 1860. Ronald V. Jackson. (Illus.). lib. bdg. 48.00 (*0-89593-796-4*) Accelerated Index.

Washington Federal Census Index, 1870. Ronald V. Jackson. (Illus.). 1977. lib. bdg. 58.00 (*0-89593-797-2*) Accelerated Index.

Washington Federal Census Index, 1880. Ronald V. Jackson. (Illus.). 1980. lib. bdg. 80.00 (*0-89593-798-0*) Accelerated Index.

Washington Festival Fun for Kids! Includes Reproducible Activities for Kids! Carole Marsh. (Washington Bks.). (Illus.). (J). (gr. 3-12). 1994. pap. 19.95 (*0-7933-4068-3*); lib. bdg. 29.95 (*0-7933-4067-5*); disk 29.95 (*0-7933-4069-1*) Gallopade Pub Group.

Washington Fishing: The Complete Guide to More Than 1, 600 Fishing Spots on Streams, Rivers, Lakes & the Coast. Terry Rudnick. (Complete Guide Ser.). (Illus.). 608p. (Orig.). 1996. pap. 19.95 (*0-935701-95-8*) Foghorn Pr.

Washington for the Curious: A Guide. Clarence Stilwill et al. LC 94-72411. 450p. 1996. pap. 21.95 (*0-9639134-1-7*) Peak Media.

***Washington for Women.** Jacci Duncan. 1996. pap. text ed. 16.95 (*1-56833-088-X*) Madison Bks UPA.

Washington Foundation Directory: How to Get Your Slice of the Pie. 3rd ed. Mardell Moore & Charna Klein. 500p. Date not set. pap. 44.92 (*0-614-14931-2*) Consult Serv NW.

Washington Foundation Directory, 1994: How to Get Your Slice of the Pie. 2nd ed. Mardell Moore & Charna Klein. 456p. 1994. pap. 39.83 (*0-9617216-2-6*) Consult Serv NW.

Washington Frugal Mania: A Money Saving Guide to the National Capital Area. Sarah Crim & Gwen Moulton. 181p. 1996. pap. 12.95 (*0-9653092-0-7*) Capital Frugalist.

Washington Geography. Randy L. Womack. (Illus.). 80p. (YA). (gr. 4 up). 1996. student ed. 8.95 (*1-56500-036-6*) Gldn Educ.

Washington Gladden Collection: An Inventory to the Microfilm Edition. Gary J. Arnold. 235p. 1972. 3.00 (*0-318-03209-0*) Ohio Hist Soc.

Washington Goes to War. David Brinkley. 304p. 1989. mass mkt. 5.99 (*0-345-35979-8*) Ballantine.

Washington Goes to War. David Brinkley. (Illus.). 352p. 1996. pap. 12.00 (*0-345-40730-X*) Ballantine.

W

*__Washington Government! The Cornerstone of Everday Life in Our State!__ Carole Marsh. (Carole Marsh Washington Bks.). (Illus.). (J). (gr. 3-12). 1996. pap. 19.95 (*0-7933-6323-3*); lib. bdg. 29.95 (*0-7933-6322-5*); disk 29.95 (*0-7933-6324-1*) Gallopade Pub Group.

Washington Governments Performance Standards, 1990. Ed. by Greg Michels. (Governments Performance Standards Ser.). (Illus.). 150p. 1990. text ed. 125.00 (*1-55507-505-3*) Municipal Analysis.

Washington Grangers Celebrate a Century: History, Fraternal Organization (100th Anniversary), Agriculture. Gus Norwood. LC 88-50556. (Illus.). (Orig.). 1988. 7.95 (*0-929612-01-9*); pap. 4.95 (*0-929612-02-7*) WA State Grange.

Washington Guardianship Law: Administration & Litigation. 2nd ed. Gerald B. Treacy, Jr. LC 92-13694. 500p. 1993. suppl. ed. 30.00 (*0-685-74432-9*) MICHIE.

Washington Guardianship Law: Administration & Litigation. 2nd ed. Gerald B. Treacy, Jr. LC 92-13694. 500p. 1994. spiral bd. 95.00 (*1-56257-663-1*) MICHIE.

Washington Guide to Self-Publishing: Producing, Marketing & Selling Your Book in the National Capital Area. Lisa Saunders & Jack Schadegg. (Illus.). 90p. (Orig.). 1996. pap. 12.95 (*0-9649403-1-0*) L Saunders.

Washington Handbook. 2nd ed. Dianne J. Lyons. LC 90-36336. (Illus.). 400p. (YA). (gr. 9-12). 1990. pap. 12.95 (*0-918373-58-1*) Moon Trvl Hdbks.

Washington Handbook: Includes Seattle, Mt. Rainier, & Olympic National Park. 5th rev. ed. Don Pitcher. (Moon Travel Hnadbooks Ser.). (Illus.). 630p. 1997. pap. 19.95 (*1-56691-045-5*) Moon Trvl Hdbks.

Washington Health Care Perspective 1996. Ed. by Kathleen O. Morgan et al. 24p. 1996. pap. 19.00 (*1-56692-646-7*) Morgan Quitno Corp.

*__Washington Health Care Perspective 1997.__ Ed. by Kathleen O. Morgan & Scott E. Morgan. 24p. 1997. pap. 19.00 (*1-56692-746-3*) Morgan Quitno Corp.

Washington Heights-Inwood Neighborhood: Assessment of Health Care Needs. North Manhattan Health Action Group Report Staff & CCS Center for Health & Human Services Staff. 129p. (Orig.). 1984. pap. text ed. 12.00 (*0-88156-054-5*) Comm Serv Soc NY.

Washington Heights-Inwood Neighborhoods: Assessment of Health Care Needs-Appendices. North Manhattan Health Action Group & CSS & Center for Health & Human Services. 175p. (Orig.). 1984. pap. text ed. 15.00 (*0-88156-055-3*) Comm Serv Soc NY.

Washington High Bench: A Biographical History of the State Supreme Court, 1889-1991. Charles H. Sheldon. LC 91-42576. (Illus.). 396p. 1992. 35.00 (*0-87422-080-7*); pap. 25.00 (*0-87422-076-9*) Wash St U Pr.

Washington Historical Atlas: Who Did What Where & When. Laura Bergheim. LC 90-50502. (Illus.). 348p. (Orig.). (C). 1992. pap. 15.95 (*0-933149-42-5*) Woodbine House.

*__Washington History! Surprising Secrets about Our State's Founding Mothers, Fathers & Kids!__ Carole Marsh. (Carole Marsh Washington Bks.). (Illus.). (J). (gr. 3-12). 1996. pap. 19.95 (*0-7933-6170-2*); lib. bdg. 29.95 (*0-7933-6169-9*); disk 29.95 (*0-7933-6171-0*) Gallopade Pub Group.

Washington Hostess Cookbook. 1990. 19.99 (*0-517-65875-5*) Random Hse Value.

Washington Hot Air Balloon Mystery. Carole Marsh. (Carole Marsh Washington Bks.). (Illus.). (J). (gr. 2-9). 1994. 29.95 (*0-7933-2741-5*); pap. 19.95 (*0-7933-2742-3*); disk 29.95 (*0-7933-2743-1*) Gallopade Pub Group.

Washington in Focus: A Photo History of the Nation's Capital. Philip Bigler. LC 88-23096. (Illus.). 144p. (Orig.). 1988. pap. 8.95 (*0-918339-07-3*) Vandamere.

Washington in Perspective 1996. Ed. by Kathleen O. Morgan et al. 26p. 1996. pap. 19.00 (*1-56692-596-7*) Morgan Quitno Corp.

*__Washington in Perspective 1997.__ Ed. by Kathleen O. Morgan & Scott E. Morgan. 26p. 1997. pap. 19.00 (*1-56692-696-3*) Morgan Quitno Corp.

Washington, Inc. Blueprint for America: A Corporate Approach to Balancing the Federal Budget. Rick Friedman. LC 93-90486. 224p. 1993. pap. 14.50 (*0-9637145-1-1*) Blueprint Pub.

Washington Indian Dictionary for Kids! Carole Marsh. (Carole Marsh State Bks.). (J). (gr. 2-9). 1996. 29.95 (*0-7933-7785-4*, C Marsh); pap. 19.95 (*0-7933-7786-2*, C Marsh) Gallopade Pub Group.

Washington Information Directory, 1994-1995. LC 72-646321. 1148p. 1994. 99.95 (*0-87187-798-8*) Congr Quarterly.

Washington Information Directory, 1995-1996. Congressional Quarterly, Inc. Staff. LC 72-646321. 1143p. 1995. 99.95 (*0-87187-847-X*) Congr Quarterly.

Washington Information Directory, 1995-1996. Congressional Quarterly, Inc. Staff. 1995. 132.00 (*5-550-94047-7*) Congr Quarterly.

Washington Information Directory 1996-1997. LC 72-646321. 1100p. 1996. 105.00 (*0-87187-896-8*) Congr Quarterly.

*__Washington Inscription on All Stones Still Standing in Cemeteries in the Town of Washington, Connecticut.__ Helen S. Boyd. 105p. 1997. reprint ed. pap. 15.00 (*0-8328-5691-6*) Higginson Bk Co.

Washington Iron Works of Franklin County, Virginia, 1773 - 1850. John S. Salmon. (Illus.). ix, 88p. 1986. 17.50 (*0-88490-137-8*) Library of VA.

Washington Irving. Harriot Curtis. (Works of Harriot Curtis Ser.). 1990. reprint ed. lib. bdg. 90.00 (*0-7812-2470-5*) Rprt Serv.

Washington Irving. Henry A. Pochmann. 1988. reprint ed. lib. bdg. 75.00 (*0-7812-0193-4*) Rprt Serv.

Washington Irving: An American Study, 1802-1832. William L. Hedges. LC 80-23564. (Goucher College Ser.). xiv, 274p. 1980. reprint ed. text ed. 52.50 (*0-313-21159-0*, HEWI, Greenwood Pr) Greenwood.

*__Washington Irving: Great American Short Stories I.__ Illus. by Tracy Hall. LC 94-75012. (Classic Short Stories Ser.). 80p. 1994. pap. 5.95 (*0-7854-0575-5*, 40001) Am Guidance.

Washington Irving: Representative Selections. Washington Irving. Ed. by Henry A. Pochmann. 1971. 59.00 (*0-403-01039-X*) Scholarly.

Washington Irving: The Critical Reaction. Ed. by James W. Tuttleton. LC 89-45870. (Studies in the Nineteenth Century: No. 10). 1993. 39.50 (*0-404-61490-6*) AMS Pr.

Washington Irving: The Western Works. Richard Cracroft. LC 74-1973. (Western Writers Ser.: No. 14). 48p. 1974. pap. 4.95 (*0-88430-013-7*) Boise St U W Writ Ser.

Washington Irving & the House of Murray: Geoffrey Crayon Charms the British, 1817-1856. Washington Irving. Ed. by Ben H. McClary. LC 73-77843. 287p. reprint ed. pap. 81.80 (*0-317-29308-7*, 2022219) Bks Demand.

Washington Irving Diary, Spain 1828-1829. Washington Irving. (BCL1-PS American Literature Ser.). 142p. 1992. reprint ed. lib. bdg. 69.00 (*0-7812-6758-7*) Rprt Serv.

Washington Irving to Henry Wadsworth Longfellow see Bibliography of American Literature

Washington Irving's Life of Mohammed. Washington Irving. Ed. by Charles Getchell. (Illus.). 288p. (Orig.). 1989. reprint ed. pap. 11.95 (*0-938864-12-2*) Ipswich Pr.

Washington Irving's Pilgrim of Love: From the Tales of the Alhambra. 2nd ed. Ed. by Frank Calderon. (Illus.). 64p. (J). (gr. 4 up). 1990. text ed. 19.95 (*0-939193-20-5*) Edit Concepts.

Washington Irving's Rip Van Winkle. Lara R. Bergen & Washington Irving. (All Aboard Reading Ser.). (J). Date not set. pap. 3.95 (*0-448-41136-9*, G&D) Putnam Pub Group.

*__Washington Irving's Rip Van Winkle.__ Illus. by Donald Cook. LC 96-24335. (All Aboard Reading Ser.). 48p. (J). (gr. 1-3). 1997. lib. bdg. 13.99 (*0-448-41733-2*, G&D) Putnam Pub Group.

Washington Irving's Rip Van Winkle. Illus. & Adapted by Thomas Locker. 40p. (J). 1994. pap. 5.99 (*0-14-055284-7*, Puff Pied Piper) Puffin Bks.

Washington Irving's Sunnyside. Kathleen E. Johnson. (Illus.). 64p. (Orig.). 1995. pap. 8.95 (*0-912882-81-6*) Sleepy Hollow.

Washington Is Leaking. Art Buchwald. 1978. pap. 2.95 (*0-449-23294-8*, Crest) Fawcett.

*__Washington Island: A Part of the History of Washington Township.__ 3rd rev. ed. Conan B. Eaton. Orig. Title: Washington Island 1836-1876. (Illus.). 1997. pap. write for info. (*0-9640210-9-9*) Jackson Harbor.

Washington Island Guidebook. William H. Olson & Charles J. Olson. 52p. 1994. pap. 4.98 (*0-9640210-0-5*) Jackson Harbor.

Washington Island Guidebook. William H. Olson & Charles J. Olson. (Illus.). 56p. 1995. 14.99 (*0-9640210-6-4*) Jackson Harbor.

Washington Island 1836-1876 see Washington Island: A Part of the History of Washington Township

Washington Itself: An Informal Guide to the Capital of the United States. 2nd ed. E. J. Applewhite. (Illus.). 368p. 1993. reprint ed. pap. 14.95 (*1-56833-008-1*) Madison Bks UPA.

Washington Jeopardy! Answers & Questions about Our State! Carole Marsh. (Washington Bks.). (Illus.). (J). (gr. 3-12). 1994. pap. 19.95 (*0-7933-4221-X*); lib. bdg. 29.95 (*0-7933-4220-1*); disk 29.95 (*0-7933-4222-8*) Gallopade Pub Group.

Washington Job Source. 4th ed. Benjamin S. Psillas & Mary McMahon. 480p. 1997. 15.95 (*0-9635651-7-6*) Metcom.

Washington Job Source: Everything You Need to Land the Internship, Entry-Level or Middle Management Job of Your Choice. 3rd ed. Benjamin S. Psillas. 436p. 1995. pap. 15.95 (*0-9635651-2-5*) Metcom.

Washington Jobs: How to Find & Get the Job You Want in the Washington Area. Beth Campbell. 180p. 1992. pap. 9.95 (*0-918339-21-9*) Vandamere.

Washington "Jography" A Fun Run Thru Our State! Carole Marsh. (Carole Marsh Washington Bks.). (Illus.). (J). 1994. pap. 19.95 (*0-7933-2202-2*); lib. bdg. 29.95 (*0-7933-2201-4*); disk 29.95 (*0-7933-2203-0*) Gallopade Pub Group.

Washington Kid's Cookbook: Recipes, How-to, History, Lore & More! Carole Marsh. (Carole Marsh Washington Bks.). (Illus.). (J). 1994. pap. 19.95 (*0-7933-1189-6*); lib. bdg. 29.95 (*0-7933-1190-X*); disk 29.95 (*0-7933-1191-8*) Gallopade Pub Group.

Washington Land Surveying Law: Questions & Answers. John E. Keen. 27p. (C). 1995. pap. text ed. 20.00 (*1-56569-043-5*) Land Survey.

Washington Land Use & Environmental Law & Practice. Richard L. Settle. 378p. 1983. boxed 65.00 (*0-409-20359-9*) MICHIE.

Washington Landmarks: A Collection of Architecture & Historical Details. Charles J. Ziga & Annie L. Roberts. 64p. 1993. 9.95 (*0-9636673-1-9*) DoveTail Bks.

Washington Law Review: 1925-1996, 71 vols., Set. Bound set. 3,372.50 (*0-8377-9185-5*) Rothman.

Washington Lawyer: A Series of Lectures Delivered under the Auspices of the Julius Rosenthal Foundation at Northwestern University School of Law in April, 1952. Charles A. Horsky. LC 81-646. viii, 179p. 1981. reprint ed. text ed. 49.75 (*0-313-22736-5*, HOWL) Greenwood.

Washington Library Book: A Surprising Guide to the Unusual Special Collections in Libraries Across Our State for Students, Teachers, Writers & Publishers - Includes Reproducible Mailing Labels Plus Activities for Young People! Carole Marsh. (Washington Bks.). (Illus.). 1994. pap. 19.95 (*0-7933-3147-1*); lib. bdg. 29.95 (*0-7933-3146-3*); disk 29.95 (*0-7933-3148-X*) Gallopade Pub Group.

Washington, Library of Congress, MS M21.M185 Case. Ed. by Alexander Silbiger. (Seventeenth-Century Keyboard Music Ser.). 225p. 1987. text ed. 25.00 (*0-8240-8020-3*) Garland.

Washington Life Insurance Trust Deskbook. 1992. suppl. ed. 75.00 (*0-88129-233-8*) Wash Bar CLE.

Washington Life Insurance Trust Deskbook. 1993. suppl. ed. 20.00 (*0-88129-244-3*) Wash Bar CLE.

Washington Llorens, Celoso Guardian del Jardin de Academo. Ed. by Angel Calderon-Cruz. LC 90-84793. (Illus.). 156p. (Orig.). (C). 1990. pap. text ed. 8.00 (*0-9622522-6-3*) Editorial Academica.

Washington Lobby. 5th ed. LC 86-29030. 250p. 1987. pap. 21.95 (*0-87187-408-3*) Congr Quarterly.

Washington Lobbyists. Lester W. Milbrath. LC 76-5789. (Illus.). 431p. 1976. reprint ed. text ed. 105.00 (*0-8371-8802-4*, MIWL, Greenwood Pr) Greenwood.

Washington Lobbyists Survey, 1956-1957. Lester W. Milbrath. 1972. write for info. (*0-89138-054-X*) ICPSR.

Washington, Louisiana: Fabulous Inland Port; Historic Gateway to the Southwest. Sue Eakin. LC 88-83294. (Illus.). 170p. 1988. lib. bdg. 24.95 (*0-944419-03-8*) Everett Cos Pub.

*__Washington Manual.__ rev. ed. 592p. spiral bd. 32.95 (*0-614-19717-1*, OP930895WE) AMA.

Washington Manual of Medical Therapeutics. 28th ed. Little Brown Staff. 640p. 1995. spiral bd. 34.95 (*0-316-92433-4*) Lppncott-Raven.

*__Washington Manual of Surgery.__ Washington University Department of Medicine & Gerard M. Doherty. LC 96-33002. 600p. 1996. spiral bd. 34.95 (*0-316-92446-6*) Lppncott-Raven.

*__Washington Manufacturers Register, 1997.__ 14th ed. 696p. 1996. pap. 99.00 (*1-57541-026-5*) Database Pub Co.

Washington Matthews: Studies of Navajo Culture, 1880-1894. Katherine S. Halpern. LC 97-13901. 304p. 1996. 70.00 (*0-8263-1631-X*) U of NM Pr.

Washington Medal. Howard P. Arnold. 1976. 3.00 (*0-89073-040-7*) Boston Public Lib.

Washington Media Book: A Surprising Guide to the Amazing Print, Broadcast & Online Media of Our State for Students, Teachers, Writers & Publishers - Includes Reproducible Mailing Labels Plus Activities for Young People! Carole Marsh. (Washington Bks.). (Illus.). 1994. pap. 19.95 (*0-7933-3303-2*); lib. bdg. 29.95 (*0-7933-3302-4*); disk 29.95 (*0-7933-3304-0*) Gallopade Pub Group.

*__Washington Money Go-Round, Vol. 1.__ Jack Anderson. 288p. (C). 1997. 28.95 (*0-9637899-3-7*) Elliott & James Pubs.

Washington Monument. Craig A. Doherty & Katherine M. Doherty. Ed. by Bruce Glassman. LC 94-24477. (Building America Ser.). (Illus.). 48p. (J). (gr. 3-7). 1995. lib. bdg. 15.95 (*1-56711-110-6*) Blackbirch.

Washington Motor Vehicle Accident Deskbook & 1995 Supplement. LC 87-51491. 1988. ring bd. 155.00 (*0-88129-218-4*) Wash Bar CLE.

Washington Motor Vehicle Accident Insurance Deskbook & 1995 Supplement. 1989. 105.00 (*0-88129-222-2*) Wash Bar CLE.

Washington Motor Vehicle Accident Insurance 1995 Supplement. 1995. 25.00 (*0-88129-248-6*) Wash Bar CLE.

Washington Motor Vehicle Accident Litigation Deskbook & 1995 Supplement. LC 90-70740. 1990. ring bd. 155.00 (*0-88129-229-X*) Wash Bar CLE.

Washington Motor Vehicle Accident Litigation 1995 Supplement. 1995. 35.00 (*0-88129-246-X*) Wash Bar CLE.

Washington Motor Vehicle Accident 1995 Supplement. 1995. 35.00 (*0-88129-247-8*) Wash Bar CLE.

Washington Mountain Ranges. Robert U. Steelquist. (Washington Geographic Ser.: No. 1). (Illus.). 104p. (Orig.). 1986. pap. 9.95 (*0-938314-25-4*) Am Wrld Geog.

Washington Municipal Expenditures, 1941-1957: An Economic Analysis. Albert A. Montgomery. LC 63-63374. (Illus.). 179p. reprint ed. pap. 51.10 (*0-8357-8370-7*, 2034104) Bks Demand.

Washington Municipal Financing. Roy J. Koegen. LC 92-74088. 1992. 110.00 (*0-317-05378-7*) Lawyers Cooperative.

Washington Mystery Van Takes Off! Book 1: Handicapped Washington Kids Sneak Off on a Big Adventure. Carole Marsh. (Washington Bks.). (Illus.). (J). (gr. 3-12). 1994. 29.95 (*0-7933-5102-2*); pap. 19.95 (*0-7933-5103-0*); disk 29.95 (*0-7933-5104-9*) Gallopade Pub Group.

Washington National Cathedral: This Bible in Stone. Robert E. Kendig. LC 95-24820. (Illus.). 176p. (Orig.). 1995. pap. 29.95 (*0-939009-91-9*) EPM Pubns.

*__Washington Notary Law Primer.__ 2nd ed. National Notary Association Editors. LC 86-60899. 120p. 1993. pap. 12.95 (*0-933134-28-2*) Natl Notary.

Washington Objections at Trial. Robert H. Aronson et al. 200p. 1992. pap. 39.50 (*0-88063-825-7*) MICHIE.

Washington on Foot: Twenty-Three Walking Tours of Washington, D. C., & Old Town Alexandria. 4th rev. ed. Ed. by John J. Protopappas & Alvin R. McNeal. LC 83-12880. (Illus.). 224p. 1992. pap. 6.95 (*1-56098-176-8*) Smithsonian.

Washington on My Mind. Falcon Press Staff. LC 96-85303. 120p. 1996. 29.95 (*1-56044-495-9*) Falcon Pr MT.

Washington on View: The Nation's Capital since 1790. John W. Reps. LC 90-46782. (Illus.). xi, 297p. (C). 1991. 60.00 (*0-8078-1948-4*) U of NC Pr.

*__Washington, Oregon & Alaska Limited Liability Company Forms & Practice Manual.__ Charles H. Purcell. LC 96-37712. 674p. 1997. ring bd. 149.95 (*1-57400-026-8*) Data Trace Pubng.

Washington Outdoor Activity Guide. Archie Satterfield. (Outdoor Activity Guide Ser.). (Illus.). 120p. (Orig.). 1994. pap. 9.95 (*1-56626-049-3*) Country Rds.

Washington, PA WWII. Historical Briefs, Inc. Staff. Ed. by Thomas Antonucci & Michael Antonucci. 176p. 1994. pap. 14.95 (*0-614-03688-7*) Hist Briefs.

Washington Parks Guide. Chris Boyce. Ed. by Barbara McCaig. 100p. (Orig.). 1988. pap. text ed. 5.95 (*0-317-67996-1*) Affordable Adven.

Washington Partnership Law & Practice Handbook 1984 & 1992 Supplement. 1984. 145.00 (*0-88129-239-7*) Wash Bar CLE.

Washington Partnership Law & Practice Handbook 1992 Supplement. 1992. suppl. ed. 50.00 (*0-88129-238-9*) Wash Bar CLE.

Washington Past & Present: A Guide to the Nation's Capital. rev. ed. Donald R. Kennon & Richard Striner. (Illus.). 144p. (YA). (gr. 7-12). 1993. reprint ed. pap. 5.00 (*0-685-64855-9*) US Capitol Hist.

Washington-Peking-Taipei: A Decade after Normalization. Roy A. Werner et al. LC 89-61644. (Proceedings of the Annual Asia-Pacific Regional Study Ser.). 1989. 5.00 (*0-935082-13-1*) Southern Ctr Intl Stud.

Washington Politics: Published under the Auspices of the Citizenship Clearing House. Daniel M. Ogden, Jr. & Hugh A. Bone. LC 80-25647. (Illus.). vi, 77p. 1981. reprint ed. text ed. 35.00 (*0-313-22803-5*, OGWP, Greenwood Pr) Greenwood.

Washington Post Deskbook on Style. Ed. by Robert A. Webb. 1978. write for info. (*0-07-068397-2*) McGraw.

Washington Post Deskbook on Style. 2nd ed. Compiled by Thomas W. Lippman. 1989. pap. text ed. 9.95 (*0-07-068414-6*) McGraw.

*__Washington Post Dining Guide.__ Phyllis C. Richman. Ed. by Noel Epstein. (Illus.). iii, 248p. (Orig.). 1996. pap. 11.95 (*0-9625971-3-9*) Washington Post.

Washington Post Sunday Crossword Puzzle. Stanley Newman. 1997. pap. 9.00 (*0-8129-2649-8*, Times Bks) Random.

Washington Post Sunday Crossword Puzzles, Vol. 1. Ed. by William Lutwiniak & William R. Mackaye. 64p. 1991. pap. 8.50 (*0-8129-1933-5*, Times Bks) Random.

Washington Post Sunday Crossword Puzzles, Vol. 2. Ed. by William Lutwiniak & William R. Mackaye. 64p. 1991. pap. 8.50 (*0-8129-1934-3*, Times Bks) Random.

Washington Post Sunday Crossword Puzzles, Vol. 3. William Lutwiniak. 1992. pap. 8.00 (*0-8129-2109-7*, Times Bks) Random.

Washington Post Sunday Crossword Puzzles, Vol. 4. William R. Mackaye. 1994. pap. 8.50 (*0-8129-2396-0*, Times Bks) Random.

Washington Post Sunday Crossword Puzzles, Vol. 5. Ed. by William R. MacKaye. 64p. 1996. pap. 8.50 (*0-8129-2648-X*, Times Bks) Random.

Washington Postcard Catalog. James L. Lowe. LC 74-30734. (Illus.). 128p. 1986. pap. 5.95 (*0-913782-06-8*) Deltiologists Am.

Washington Property & Casualty Course. James J. Smith. 1991. 50.00 (*1-56461-030-6*, 26970) Rough Notes.

Washington Public Shore Guide: Marine Waters. James W. Scott & Melly A. Reuling. LC 85-40976. (Illus.). 342p. 1986. 35.00 (*0-295-96334-4*) U of Wash Pr.

Washington Quarters, No. 2. 1988. 2.20 (*0-307-09031-0*) Western Pub.

Washington Quarters Nineteen Sixty-Five to Date. 2.25 (*0-307-09040-X*, Golden Pr) Western Pub.

Washington Quarters, No. 1: 1932-1945. 1988. 1.90 (*0-307-09018-3*) Western Pub.

Washington Quiz Bowl Crash Course! Carole Marsh. (Carole Marsh Washington Bks.). (Illus.). (J). 1994. pap. 19.95 (*0-7933-2216-2*); lib. bdg. 29.95 (*0-7933-2215-4*); disk 29.95 (*0-7933-2217-0*) Gallopade Pub Group.

*__Washington Real Estate Fundamentals.__ 9th rev. ed. Kathryn J. Haupt & David L. Rockwell. (Illus.). 553p. (Orig.). 1997. pap. text ed. 36.25 (*1-887051-04-X*) Rockwell WA.

*__Washington Real Estate Fundamentals Workbook.__ 3rd rev. ed. Kathryn J. Haupt & David L. Rockwell. Ed. by Megan Dorsey. (Illus.). 304p. (Orig.). 1997. pap. text ed. 27.45 (*1-887051-05-8*) Rockwell WA.

Washington Real Estate Law. 3rd rev. ed. Alan N. Tonnon. (Illus.). 536p. (Orig.). 1995. pap. text ed. 32.95 (*0-915799-98-7*) Rockwell WA.

Washington Redskins. Bob Italia. LC 95-43589. (Inside the NFL Ser.). (J). 1996. lib. bdg. 15.98 (*1-56239-465-7*) Abdo & Dghtrs.

*__Washington Redskins.__ Thom Loverro. LC 96-41452. 1996. 39.95 (*0-87833-136-0*); 75.00 (*0-87833-137-9*) Taylor Pub.

Washington Redskins. Richard Rambeck. (NFL Today Ser.). (J). (gr. 4 up). 1991. lib. bdg. 14.95 (*0-88682-386-2*) Creative Ed.

Washington Redskins. 2nd rev. ed. Steve Potts. (NFL Today Ser.). (Illus.). 32p. (J). (gr. 4-8). 1996. lib. bdg. 14.95 (*0-88682-803-1*) Creative Ed.

Washington Redskins Trivia Book. Leonard Shapiro. (Illus.). 112p. (Orig.). 1992. pap. 8.99 (*0-312-08519-2*) St Martin.

Washington Reflections: Littlebook. Photos by Charles Gurche. (Illus.). 64p. 1996. 14.95 (*1-56579-138-X*) Westcliffe Pubs.

Washington Reporters. Stephen Hess. LC 80-70077. 174p. 1981. 32.95 (*0-8157-3594-4*); pap. 12.95 (*0-8157-3593-6*) Brookings.

W

An Asterisk (*) at the beginning of an entry indicates that the title is appearing in BIP for the first time.

***Washington Representatives 1997.** 21th ed. Ed. by J. Valerie Steele et al. 1255p. 1997. pap. 85.00 (*1-880873-24-9*) Columbia Bks.

Washington Revealed: The Only Guide to Washington, D. C. That Allows You to Focus on Your Individual Interest. Maxine H. Atwater. LC 91-28555. 240p. 1992. pap. text ed. 14.95 (*0-471-54673-9*) Wiley.

***Washington Rock.** 2nd ed. Jeff Smoot. (Illus.). 1997. pap. write for info. (*1-57540-089-8*) Chockstone Pr.

Washington Rollercoasters! Carole Marsh. (Washington Bks.). (Illus.). (YA). (gr. 3-12). 1994. pap. 19.95 (*0-7933-5366-1*); lib. bdg. 29.95 (*0-7933-5365-3*); disk 29.95 (*0-7933-5367-X*) Gallopade Pub Group.

Washington Rules of Court Annotated, 1994. 1400p. (Orig.). 1994. pap. 50.00 (*0-614-10384-3*) MICHIE.

Washington Rules of Court Annotated, 1994 Edition. Michie Butterworth Editorial Staff. 50.00 (*1-55834-178-1*) MICHIE.

Washington San Juan Islands: Littlebook. Photos by Charles Gurche. (Illus.). 64p. 1996. 14.95 (*1-56579-139-8*) Westcliffe Pubs.

Washington School Trivia: An Amazing & Fascinating Look at Our State's Teachers, Schools & Students! Carole Marsh. (Carole Marsh Washington Bks.). (Illus.). (J). 1994. pap. 19.95 (*0-7933-1186-1*); disk 29.95 (*0-7933-1188-8*) Gallopade Pub Group.

Washington School Trivia: An Amazing & Fascinating Look at Our State's Teachers, Schools & Students! Carole Marsh. (Carole Marsh Washington Bks.). (Illus.). (J). 1997. lib. bdg. 29.95 (*0-7933-1187-X*) Gallopade Pub Group.

Washington Seen: A Photographic History, 1875-1965. Fredric M. Miller & Howard Gillette, Jr. LC 95-2948. (Illus.). 288p. 1995. 35.95 (*0-8018-4979-9*) Johns Hopkins.

Washington Sentinels. Mokhless Al-Hariri. 224p. 1992. 43.00 (*0-9624483-3-8*) GDG Pubns.

Washington Sentinels. limited ed. Mokhless Al-Hariri. 224p. 1992. Washington, D.C. Bicentennial Limited Edition. 75.50 (*0-9624483-2-X*) GDG Pubns.

Washington Silly Basketball Sportsmysteries, Vol. 1. Carole Marsh. (Carole Marsh Washington Bks.). (Illus.). (J). 1994. pap. 19.95 (*0-7933-1183-7*); lib. bdg. 29.95 (*0-7933-1184-5*); disk 29.95 (*0-7933-1185-3*) Gallopade Pub Group.

Washington Silly Basketball Sportsmysteries, Vol. 2. Carole Marsh. (Carole Marsh Washington Bks.). (Illus.). (J). 1994. pap. 19.95 (*0-7933-2228-6*); lib. bdg. 29.95 (*0-7933-2227-8*); disk 29.95 (*0-7933-2229-4*) Gallopade Pub Group.

Washington Silly Football Sportsmysteries, Vol. 1. Carole Marsh. (Carole Marsh Washington Bks.). (Illus.). (J). 1994. pap. 19.95 (*0-7933-2207-3*); lib. bdg. 29.95 (*0-7933-2206-5*); disk 29.95 (*0-7933-2208-1*) Gallopade Pub Group.

Washington Silly Football Sportsmysteries, Vol. 2. Carole Marsh. (Carole Marsh Washington Bks.). (Illus.). (J). 1994. pap. 19.95 (*0-7933-2210-3*); disk 29.95 (*0-7933-2211-1*) Gallopade Pub Group.

Washington Silly Trivia! Carole Marsh. (Carole Marsh Washington Bks.). (Illus.). (J). 1994. pap. 19.95 (*0-7933-2199-9*); lib. bdg. 29.95 (*0-7933-2198-0*); disk 29.95 (*0-7933-2200-6*) Gallopade Pub Group.

Washington Society in the Early Republic: Writings of Margaret Bayard Smith. Margaret B. Smith. Ed. by Fredrika J. Teute & Joyce Appleby. 300p. (C). (gr. 13). 1998. text ed. 47.95 (*1-56324-811-5*); pap. text ed. 15.95 (*1-56324-812-3*) M E Sharpe.

Washington, Somoza, & the Sandinistas: State & Regime in U. S. Policy Toward Nicaragua, 1969-1981. Morris H. Morley. LC 93-34540. 352p. (C). 1994. text ed. 80.00 (*0-521-45081-0*) Cambridge U Pr.

Washington Songs & Lore. Ed. by Chrystle L. Snider et al. (Illus.). 200p. (J). (gr. 1-12). 1988. pap. 15.95 (*0-9616441-3-3*) Melior Dist.

Washington Songs & Lore. abr. ed. Ed. by Chrystle L. Snider et al. (Illus.). 72p. (J). (gr. 1-12). 1988. Abridged ed., 72 pg. spiral bd. 8.95 (*0-9616441-4-1*) Melior Dist.

Washington Square. Henry James. (Classics Ser.). (YA). (gr. 10 up). 1970. mass mkt. 1.50 (*0-8049-0210-0*, CL-210) Airmont.

Washington Square. Henry James. Date not set. lib. bdg. 20.95 (*0-8488-0544-5*) Amereon Ltd.

Washington Square. Henry James. 1964. pap. 4.95 (*0-451-52499-3*, Sig Classics) NAL-Dutton.

Washington Square. Henry James. Ed. by Mark Le Fanu. (World's Classics Ser.). 224p. (C). 1983. pap. 4.95 (*0-19-281611-X*) OUP.

***Washington Square.** Henry James. LC 97-25219. 1998. 14.50 (*0-679-60276-3*, Modern Lib) Random.

Washington Square. Henry James. LC 95-39366. 1996. 22.00 (*0-684-81911-2*) S&S Trade.

Washington Square. Henry James. Ed. & Intro. by Brian Lee. (English Library). 224p. 1984. pap. 7.95 (*0-14-043226-4*, Penguin Classics) Viking Penguin.

Washington Square. large type ed. Henry James. 330p. 1995. lib. bdg. 24.00 (*0-939495-81-3*) North Bks.

Washington Square. Henry James. 192p. 1986. reprint ed. lib. bdg. 17.95 (*0-89966-532-2*) Buccaneer Bks.

Washington Square Ensemble. Madison Smartt Bell. 352p. 1984. pap. 11.95 (*0-14-007025-7*, Penguin Bks) Viking Penguin.

Washington Square Moves. Matthew Witten. 1994. pap. 5.25 (*0-8222-1409-1*) Dramatists Play.

Washington Star Garden Book: The Encyclopedia of Gardening for the Chesapeake & Potomac Region. rev. ed. Deborah Fialka. (Illus.). 250p. 1994. pap. 15.95 (*0-915168-50-2*) Wash Bk Trad.

Washington State. rev. ed. Charles P. LeWarne. LC 85-20977. (Illus.). 438p. 1993. text ed. 50.00 (*0-295-97301-3*) U of Wash Pr.

Washington State: A Photographic Journey. Bill Harris. (Illus.). 1991. 15.99 (*0-517-06028-0*) Random Hse Value.

Washington State: Materials for Lesson-Planners, Grades 5-12. Bob Graef. 66p. 1993. teacher ed. 34.50 (*0-9641783-0-3*) Grassrts WA.

Washington State: National Parks, Historic Sites, Recreation Areas, & Natural Landmarks. Ruth Kirk. LC 74-6020. (Illus.). 64p. 1974. pap. 4.95 (*0-295-95323-3*) U of Wash Pr.

Washington State Advanced Technology 1993 Directory. Glenn R. Avery. (Illus.). 324p. 1993. pap. 34.00 (*0-9634596-0-0*) Commerce Pub.

Washington State Advanced Technology 1994 Directory. Glenn R. Avery. (Illus.). 296p. (Orig.). 1994. pap. text ed. 34.00 (*0-9634596-1-9*) Commerce Pub.

Washington State Advanced Technology 1995 Directory. Glenn R. Avery. (Illus.). 296p. (Orig.). 1995. pap. 34.00 (*0-9634596-2-7*) Commerce Pub.

Washington State Advanced Technology 1996 Directory. Ed. by Glenn R. Avery. 232p. (Orig.). 1996. pap. 34.00 (*0-9634596-3-5*) Commerce Pub.

Washington State Almanac, 1995: An Economic & Demographic Overview of Counties & Cities. Ed. by James Fox. (Illus.). 124p. 1995. pap. 18.95 (*0-9640012-4-1*) Public Sector.

Washington State Anti-Sex Discrimination Legislation. (Illus.). 125p. (Orig.). (C). 1993. pap. text ed. 35.00 (*1-56806-912-X*) DIANE Pub.

Washington State Atlas & Databook. 4th ed. Ed. by Richard Yates & Charity Yates. (Illus.). 1995. pap. 12.95 (*0-9640012-5-X*) Public Sector.

Washington State Environmental Policy Act, 1987-1993: A Legal & Policy Analysis. Richard L. Settle. 450p. 1991. ring bd. 85.00 (*0-409-20360-2*) MICHIE.

Washington State Environmental Policy Act, 1987-1993: A Legal & Policy Analysis. Richard L. Settle. 450p. 1994. suppl. ed., ring bd. 47.50 (*0-86678-047-5*) MICHIE.

***Washington State Fishing Guide.** S. Jones. 1995. pap. 14.95 (*0-939936-04-6*) Jones Pub.

Washington State Fishing Guide. 6th rev. ed. Stan Jones. (Illus.). 334p. (Orig.). 1984. pap. 8.95 (*0-939936-02-X*) Jones Pub.

Washington State International Trade Directory. Howard S. Hirshman. 394p. 1983. 58.00 (*0-318-00151-9*) Robinson Pub.

Washington State Men of Valor: Medal of Honor Action, Biography & Citation of 81 Recipients of Our Nation's Highest Award. 2nd rev. ed. Donald K. Ross. LC 94-68497. (Illus.). 259p. 1994. 22.00 (*0-9620552-1-2*) Rokalu Pr.

Washington State on the Air. Burt Harrison. (Illus.). 97p. 1993. pap. 12.95 (*0-614-14815-4*) Wash St U Pr.

Washington State Parks: A Complete Recreation Guide. Marge Mueller & Ted Mueller. LC 92-39612. (Illus.). 288p. (Orig.). 1993. pap. 16.95 (*0-89886-324-4*) Mountaineers.

Washington State Place Names. rev. ed. James W. Phillips. LC 73-159435. (Illus.). 186p. 1971. pap. 9.95 (*0-295-95498-1*) U of Wash Pr.

Washington State Place Names: From Alki to Yelm. Doug Brokenshire. LC 93-18926. 336p. (Orig.). 1993. pap. 14.95 (*0-87004-356-0*) Caxton.

***Washington State Retirement & Relocation Guide.** Dick Gilbert. (Illus.). 350p. (Orig.). 1997. pap. write for info. (*1-56559-111-9*) HGI Mrktng.

Washington State Trout Fishing: A Guide to Lakes. Daniel B. Homel. (Illus.). 112p. 1995. pap. 9.95 (*1-879522-03-9*) Forrest Pk.

Washington State Yearbook, 1996: A Guide to Government in the Evergreen State. Ed. by Richard Yates & Charity Yates. (Illus.). 294p. 1996. pap. 20.95 (*0-9640012-6-8*) Public Sector.

Washington States Most Influential. Phil Harrison et al. 256p. (Orig.). 1993. per. 29.95 (*0-9636726-0-6*) Harrison & Assocs.

Washington Station. Yuri B. Shvets. 1995. 23.00 (*0-671-88397-6*) S&S Trade.

Washington Statutory Time Limitations: Washington State. 2nd ed. Butterworth Staff. 650p. 1994. ring bd. 85.00 (*0-250-40722-1*) MICHIE.

Washington Story: Behind the Scenes in the Federal Government - An Official under Civil Service Describes His Experiences. A. C. Rosander. LC 85-227965. xiii, 546p. 1985. 7.95 (*0-9615168-0-1*) Natl Directions.

Washington Substantive Criminal Law Notebook. 1992. 75.00 (*0-88129-232-X*) Wash Bar CLE.

Washington Survival. Betty L. Hall & Ken Holmes. 160p. (Orig.). (gr. 10-12). 1981. pap. text ed. 5.84 (*0-936159-05-7*) Westwood Pr.

Washington Tax Decisions: Index. Butterworth Staff. 100p. 1992. ring bd. 50.00 (*1-56257-738-7*) MICHIE.

Washington Tax Decisions Excise Tax Bulletin. Ed. by Butterworth Staff. 840p. 1993. ring bd. 160.00 (*0-614-05996-8*) MICHIE.

Washington Tax Decisions, 1987-1993, 10 vols. Ed. by Butterworths Staff & Washington State Dept. of Revenue Staff. 70.00 (*0-614-05996-8*) MICHIE.

Washington Tax Decisions, 1987-1993, 10 vols. WA State Department of Revenue Staff & Butterworth Staff. 500p. 1993. ring bd. 650.00 (*0-409-20007-7*) MICHIE.

Washington Taxes: A Taxpayer's Manual for Practice Before the Department of Revenue. Martin Silver. 380p. 1992. ring bd. 95.00 (*1-56257-702-6*) MICHIE.

Washington Taxes: A Taxpayer's Manual for Practice Before the Department of Revenue. Martin Silver. 350p. 1994. suppl. ed., ring bd. 48.50 (*0-685-74456-6*) MICHIE.

Washington Territorial Census Index, 1857-61. Ronald V. Jackson. (Illus.). 1982. lib. bdg. 40.00 (*0-89593-795-6*) Accelerated Index.

Washington Through a Purple Veil: Memoirs of a Southern Woman. Lindy Boggs. 1994. 24.95 (*0-15-193106-2*) HarBrace.

Washington Through a Purple Veil: Memoirs of a Southern Woman. large type ed. Lindy Boggs. (Niagara Large Print Ser.). 501p. 1995. 27.99 (*0-7089-5816-8*) Ulverscroft.

Washington Timeline: A Chronology of Washington History, Mystery, Trivia, Legend, Lore & More. Carole Marsh. (Washington Bks.). (Illus.). (J). (gr. 3-12). 1994. pap. 19.95 (*0-7933-6017-X*); lib. bdg. 29.95 (*0-7933-6016-1*); disk 29.95 (*0-7933-6018-8*) Gallopade Pub Group.

Washington Trial Handbook. Dale M. Foreman. LC 88-71138. 1988. 110.00 (*0-317-02931-2*) Lawyers Cooperative.

Washington Trial Handbook. Dale M. Foreman. LC 88-71138. 1994. Suppl. 1994. suppl. ed. 42.50 (*0-317-03964-4*) Lawyers Cooperative.

Washington Trivia. Patricia C. Hedtke & John Z. Hedtke. LC 91-34089. 192p. (Orig.). 1991. pap. 5.95 (*1-55853-137-8*) Rutledge Hill Pr.

Washington University in St. Louis: A History. Ralph E. Morrow. LC 96-6388. 757p. 1996. 69.95 (*1-883982-10-3*) MO Hist Soc.

Washington University Papyri I, Nos. 1-61: Non-Literary Texts. Ed. by Verne B. Schuman. LC 79-14199. (American Studies in Papyrology: No. 17). 113p. reprint ed. pap. 32.30 (*0-7837-5493-0*, 2045258) Bks Demand.

Washington Used & Rare, Notes on a Weekend in Washington's Antiquarian Bookshops. Henry Turlington. viii, 39p. (Orig.). 1979. pap. 4.95 (*0-938768-01-8*) Oak Knoll.

Washington, Vol. 2: Capital City, 1879-1950. Constance M. Green. LC 62-7402. 600p. pap. 171.00 (*0-7837-0103-9*, 2040381) Bks Demand.

Washington Walkabout. Steve Breakstone. Ed. by Jerry Marsh & Rory Hurt. (Illus.). 256p. (Orig.). (YA). 1992. pap. 13.95 (*0-9632724-4-6*) Balance Pubns.

***Washington Waste Minimisation Workshop: Vol. I: Five Waste Streams to Reduce; Vol. II: Which Policies, Which Tools?, 2 vols.** OECD Staff. 560p. (Orig.). 1996. pap. 108.00 (*92-64-15295-4*, 97-96-10-1) OECD.

Washington Way. Jeffrey B. Morris. (Great Presidential Decisions Ser.). (Illus.). 128p. (J). (gr. 5 up). 1994. lib. bdg. 22.95 (*0-8225-2928-9*, Lerner Publctns) Lerner Group.

Washington, Westminster & Whitehall. Walter Williams. (Illus.). 268p. 1988. text ed. 59.95 (*0-521-35185-5*) Cambridge U Pr.

Washington Whitewater: The Thirty-Four Best Whitewater Rivers. rev. ed. Douglass North. LC 91-39562. (Illus.). 304p. 1992. pap. 18.95 (*0-89886-327-9*) Mountaineers.

Washington Wildflowers: Littlebook. Photos by Charles Gurche. (Illus.). 64p. 1996. 14.95 (*1-56579-137-1*) Westcliffe Pubs.

Washington Wildlife. Loralie Cecotti. (Color-A-Story Ser.). (Illus.). 24p. (Orig.). (J). (gr. k-5). 1984. pap. text ed. 2.75 (*0-318-04105-7*) Coffee Break.

***Washington Wildlife Viewing Guide.** Jim Butler. (Watchable Wildlife Ser.). 112p. Date not set. pap. 7.95 (*0-919433-78-2*) Lone Pine.

Washington Wildlife Viewing Guide. Joe La Tourrette. LC 92-53272. (Illus.). 96p. (Orig.). 1992. pap. 5.95 (*1-56044-150-X*) Falcon Pr MT.

Washington Wives. 1993. 4.99 (*1-56171-194-2*) Sure Seller.

***Washington Wizards.** Paul Joseph. LC 96-39614. (Inside the NBA Ser.). (J). 1997. write for info. (*1-56239-778-8*) Abdo & Dghtrs.

***Washington Wizards.** Richard Rambeck. LC 96-52960. (NBA Today Ser.). (J). 1997. lib. bdg. 15.95 (*0-88682-892-9*) Creative Ed.

Washington Workbook for Child Advocates-104th Congress. 200p. 1995. pap. 12.95 (*0-87868-625-8*) Child Welfare.

Washington, 1939 see General Assembly Proceedings

***Washington 97: A Comprehensive Directory of the Key Institutions & Leaders of the National Capital Area.** 14th ed. Ed. by R. Willson Hardy et al. 1235p. 1997. pap. 85.00 (*1-880873-25-7*) Columbia Bks.

Washingtoniana: Photographs; Collections in the Prints & Photographs Division of the Library of Congress. Kathleen K. Collins. LC 87-600421. (Illus.). 310p. 1989. 25.00 (*0-8444-0588-4*, 030-000-00210-5) Lib Congress.

Washington's Audacious State Capital & Its Builders. Norman J. Johnston. (Illus.). 192p. 1987. 30.00 (*0-295-96467-7*) U of Wash Pr.

Washington's Best Lake Fly Fishing. Nathan Caproni. 180p. 1995. pap. 21.95 (*1-57188-027-5*) F Amato Pubns.

Washington's Birthday. Dennis B. Fradin. LC 89-7664. (Best Holiday Bks.). (Illus.). 48p. (J). (gr. 1-4). 1990. lib. bdg. 17.95 (*0-89490-235-0*) Enslow Pubs.

Washington's Birthday: For Chamber Orchestra. Charles E. Ives. 44p. 1992. pap. 15.00 (*0-7935-0431-7*) H Leonard.

Washington's Chinaware. 1982. 40.00 (*0-8109-1779-3*) Abrams.

Washington's Coast. Robert U. Steelquist. (Washington Geographic Ser.: No. 2). (Illus.). 96p. (Orig.). 1987. pap. 14.95 (*0-938314-28-9*) Am Wrld Geog.

***Washington's Dirigible.** John Barnes. 240p. 1997. mass mkt. 5.99 (*0-06-105660-X*, HarperPrism) HarpC.

Washington's Farewell Address. Ed. by Victor H. Paltsits. LC 74-137706. (New York Public Library Publications in Reprint). (Illus.). 1971. reprint ed. 31.95 (*0-405-01742-1*) Ayer.

Washington's Historical Markers. W. M. Scofield. (Illus.). 80p. 1967. pap. 1.95 (*0-911518-15-0*) Touchstone Oregon.

Washington's Inaugural Address of 1789. LC 86-5166. (Milestone Documents in the National Archives Ser.). (Illus.). 18p. 1986. pap. 3.50 (*0-911333-39-8*, 200101) National Archives & Recs.

Washington's Irish Policy 1916-1986: Independence, Partition, Neutrality. Sean Cronin. 200p. (Orig.). (C). 1987. pap. 18.95 (*0-937702-08-0*) Irish Bks Media.

Washington's Last Cantonment: High Time for a Peace. Janet Dempsey. LC 86-10691. (Illus.). 250p. 1990. 24.95 (*0-912526-39-4*) Lib Res.

Washington's (Most Devastating!) Disasters & (Most Calamitous!) Catastrophies! Carole Marsh. (Carole Marsh Washington Bks.). (Illus.). (J). 1994. pap. 19.95 (*0-7933-1174-8*); lib. bdg. 29.95 (*0-7933-1175-6*); disk 29.95 (*0-7933-1176-4*) Gallopade Pub Group.

***Washington's New Poor Law: Welfare Reform & the Jobs Illusion.** Sheila D. Collins & Gertrude S. Goldberg. 160p. 1997. 27.50 (*0-614-30134-3*) Apex Pr.

***Washington's New Poor Law: Welfare Reform & the Jobs Illusion.** Sheila D. Collins & Gertrude S. Goldberg. 160p. (Orig.). 1997. pap. 14.50 (*0-945257-83-X*) Apex Pr.

***Washington's New Poor Law: Welfare Reform & the Jobs Illusion.** Sheila D. Collins & Gertrude S. Goldberg. 160p. 1997. 27.50 (*0-945257-84-8*) Apex Pr.

Washington's Partisan War, 1775-1783. Mark V. Kwasny. LC 96-14559. 448p. (C). 1996. 35.00 (*0-87338-546-2*) Kent St U Pr.

Washington's Rail Trails: A Guide for Walkers, Bicyclists, Equestrians. Fred Wert. LC 91-33507. (Illus.). 160p. (Orig.). 1992. pap. 10.95 (*0-89886-299-X*) Mountaineers.

Washington's Road see Historic Highways of America...with Maps & Illustrations

Washington's Secret War Against Afghanistan. Phillip Bonosky. LC 84-19139. 264p. (Orig.). reprint ed. pap. 75.30 (*0-7837-0585-9*, 2040929) Bks Demand.

Washington's Taiwan Dilemma: From Abandonment to Salvation. David M. Finkelstein. 392p. (C). 1994. lib. bdg. 56.00 (*0-913969-64-8*) Univ Pub Assocs.

Washington's Unsolved Mysteries (& Their "Solutions") Includes Scientific Information & Other Activities for Students. Carole Marsh. (Washington Bks.). (Illus.). (J). (gr. 3-12). 1994. pap. 19.95 (*0-7933-5864-7*); lib. bdg. 29.95 (*0-7933-5863-9*); disk 29.95 (*0-7933-5865-5*) Gallopade Pub Group.

Washington's War on Nicaragua. Holly Sklar. LC 88-10160. 480p. 1988. pap. 15.00 (*0-89608-295-4*); lib. bdg. 35.00 (*0-89608-296-2*) South End Pr.

Washington's Wild Rivers: The Unfinished Work. Tim McNulty. LC 89-13562. (Illus.). 144p. 1990. 14.98 (*0-89886-170-5*) Mountaineers.

Washington's "Wild Scotsman" The Early Aeronautical Adventures of L. Guy Mecklem, 1896-1910. Eklund. (Occasional Papers: No. 2). 1986. pap. 2.95 (*0-318-23322-3*) WWU CPNS.

Washlanders. Ed. by Phil Gray. 196p. (C). 1990. 47.85 (*0-86138-071-1*, Pub. by T Dalton UK) St Mut.

Washo Indians. Samuel A. Barrett. LC 76-43651. (Bulletin of the Public Museum of the City of Milwaukee Ser.: Vol. 2, No. 1). reprint ed. 29.50 (*0-404-15485-9*) AMS Pr.

Washo Indians of California & Nevada. Ed. by Warren Azevedo. (Utah Anthropological Papers: No. 67). reprint ed. 22.50 (*0-404-60667-9*) AMS Pr.

Washo Language of East Central California & Nevada. fac. ed. A. L. Kroeber. (University of California Publications in American Archaeology & Ethnology: Vol. 4: 5). 66p. (C). 1907. reprint ed. pap. text ed. 5.90 (*1-55567-167-5*) Coyote Press.

Washo-Northern Paiute Peyotism: A Study in Acculturation. fac. ed. Omer C. Stewart. Ed. by A. L. Kroeber et al. (University of California Publications in American Archaeology & Ethnology: No. 40:3). 85p. (C). 1944. reprint ed. pap. 7.75 (*1-55567-314-7*) Coyote Press.

Washo Religion. fac. ed. James F. Downs. Ed. by J. H. Rowe et al. (University of California Publications: No. 16:9). 26p. (C). 1961. reprint ed. pap. 2.75 (*1-55567-150-0*) Coyote Press.

Washo Shamans & Peyotists: Religious Conflict in an American Indian Tribe. Edgar E. Siskin. LC 83-14573. (Illus.). 264p. reprint ed. pap. 75.30 (*0-8357-4377-2*, 2037208) Bks Demand.

Washo Texts. fac. ed. Grace Sangberg. (University of California Publications in American Archaeology & Ethnology: Vol. 22: 3). 56p. (C). 1927. reprint ed. pap. text ed. 5.30 (*1-55567-257-4*) Coyote Press.

Washout. Carrick. (J). Date not set. mass mkt. 4.95 (*0-395-50960-2*) HM.

Washout! The Aviation Cadet Story. Charles A. Watry. LC 83-72383. (Illus.). 192p. (Orig.). 1983. pap. 10.95 (*0-914379-00-3*) CalAero.

Wasichu. Barry Brierley. 345p. 1993. 21.95 (*0-9637792-0-6*); pap. write for info. (*0-9637792-1-4*) Lagare.

***Wasichu.** Barry Brierley. (Illus.). (Orig.). 1996. pap. 15.00 (*1-889657-02-6*) Bear Bks AZ.

Wasichu. limited ed. Barry Brierley. 345p. 1993. 75.00 (*0-9637792-9-X*) Lagare.

Wasi'chu: The Continuing Indian Wars. Bruce Johansen & Roberto Maestas. LC 79-10153. 266p. reprint ed. pap. 75.90 (*0-7837-3925-7*, 2043773) Bks Demand.

***Wasichu's Return.** Barry Brierley. 336p. Date not set. 23.95 (*1-889657-19-0*) Bear Bks AZ.

***Wasichu's Return.** Barry Brierley. (Illus.). 336p. 1996. pap. 14.00 (*1-889657-20-4*) Bear Bks AZ.

Wasita in a Lebanese Context: Social Exchange among Villagers & Outsiders. Frederick C. Huxley. (Anthropological Papers: No. 64). (Illus.). (Orig.). 1978. pap. 3.00 (*0-932206-62-X*) U Mich Mus Anthro.

Wasn't That a Time! Firsthand Accounts of the Folk Music Revival. Ed. by Ronald D. Cohen. LC 94-24902. (American Folk Music & Musicians Ser.: No. 1). (Illus.). 258p. 1995. 32.50 (*0-8108-2955-X*) Scarecrow.

W

An Asterisk (*) at the beginning of an entry indicates that the title is appearing in BIP for the first time.

Wasn't That Very Clever of Me. Pamela J. Tarchinski. LC 89-83922. (Illus.). 64p. 1989. 22.95 (*0-9623049-0-5*) Hold Tight Too Pr.

Wasp. David Hawcock. (Bouncing Bugs Ser.). (Illus.). (J). (ps-3). 1996. 6.99 (*0-614-15722-6*) Random.

Wasp. large type ed. Ursula Curtiss. (Linford Mystery Library). 329p. 1989. pap. 15.99 (*0-7089-6642-X*, Linford) Ulverscroft.

***Wasp: A Play in One Act.** Steve Martin. (Illus.). 65p. 1996. 65.00 (*0-9657858-0-7*) V Dailey.

***Wasp Cookbook.** Alexandra Wentworth. 128p. 1997. 12.95 (*0-446-91210-7*) Warner Bks.

Wasp Farm. Howard E. Evans. LC 77-90903. (Illus.). 208p. (C). 1985. pap. 14.95 (*0-8014-9315-3*) Cornell U Pr.

Wasp Genus Gastrosericus Spinola, 1839: Hymenoptera: Sphecidae. Wojciech J. Pulawski. LC 95-71265. (Memoirs of the California Academy of Sciences Ser.: No. 18). (Illus.). 1995. 40.00 (*0-940228-36-X*) Calif Acad Sci.

Wasp Is Not a Bee. Marilyn Singer. (Illus.). 32p. (J). 1995. 15.95 (*0-8050-2820-X*, Bks Young Read) H Holt & Co.

Wasp Without a Sting: The Memoirs of a Person of No Particular Importance. James H. Grew. (Illus.). 204p. (Orig.). 1995. pap. 11.95 (*0-9645988-0-9*) E S Grew.

Wasps. Sylvia A. Johnson. LC 83-23847. (Lerner Natural Science Bks.). (Illus.). 48p. (J). (gr. 4 up). 1984. lib. bdg. 21.50 (*0-8225-1460-5*, Lerner Publctns) Lerner Group.

Wasps: An Account of the Biology & Natural History of Social & Solitary Wasps. J. Philip Spradbery. LC 73-7872. (Biology Ser.). (Illus.). 424p. 1973. 50.00 (*0-295-95287-3*) U of Wash Pr.

Wasps: The Comedies of Aristophanes. Alan H. Sommerstein. (Classical Texts Ser.: Vol. 4). 1983. 49.95 (*0-85668-212-8*, Pub. by Aris & Phillips UK); pap. 24.95 (*0-85668-213-6*, Pub. by Aris & Phillips UK) David Brown.

Wasps see Frogs & Other Plays

Wasps at Home. Bianca Lavies. LC 90-27338. (Illus.). 32p. (J). (gr. 2-5). 1991. pap. 13.95 (*0-525-44704-0*) Dutton Child Bks.

Wasps of the Genus Trypoxylon Subgenus Trypargilum in North America (Hymenoptera: Sphecidae) Rollin E. Coville. LC 81-16395. (University of California Publications in Entomology: No. 97). 155p. 1981. pap. 44.20 (*0-7837-7476-1*, 2049198) Bks Demand.

Wassala Valley Shootout. large type ed. Elliot Long. (Linford Western Library). 224p. 1993. pap. 15.99 (*0-7089-7444-9*, Linford) Ulverscroft.

Wasser und Elektrolythaushalt: Physiologie und Pathophysiologie. H. Reissigl et al. (Handbuch der Infusionstherapie und Klinischen Ernaehrung Ser.: Band 1). viii, 160p. 1984. 63.25 (*3-8055-3745-X*) S Karger.

Wasserbau: Englisch - Deutsch Deutsch - Englisch. Reinhard Pohl. 1991. 49.95 (*0-685-40786-1*) Fr & Eur.

Wasserbau: Englisch-Deutsch-Englisch. Reinhard Pohl. (DUT & ENG.). 49.95 (*0-8288-7936-2*, F58909) Fr & Eur.

Wassilly Kandinsky. Ed. by Andreas Huneke. 100p. 1995. text ed. 15.00 (*3-364-00332-7*) Gordon & Breach.

Wassily Kandinsky & Gabriele Munter. Annegret Hoberg et al. (Pegasus Library). (Illus.). 160p. 1995. 25.00 (*3-7913-1374-6*, Pub. by Prestel GW) te Neues.

Wastage of Primary Education. K. Venkatsubramaniam. 86p. 1978. 5.50 (*0-318-36833-1*) Asia Bk Corp.

Waste. Kay Davis & Wendy Oldsfield. LC 91-23414. (Starting Science Ser.). (Illus.). 32p. (J). (gr. 2-5). 1991. pap. 4.95 (*0-8114-1531-7*); lib. bdg. 19.97 (*0-8114-3000-6*) Raintree Steck-V.

Waste. Robert Herrick. Ed. by Carlos E. Cortes. LC 76-1280. (Chicano Heritage Ser.). 1977. reprint ed. lib. bdg. 36.95 (*0-405-09507-4*) Ayer.

Waste. Robert Herrick. (Collected Works of Robert Herrick). 1988. reprint ed. lib. bdg. 79.00 (*0-7812-1279-0*) Rprt Serv.

Waste. Wesley Marx. LC 79-137805. (Man & His Environment Ser.). 189p. reprint ed. pap. 53.90 (*0-317-11223-6*, 2013235) Bks Demand.

Waste: Choices for Communities. Andy Knaus. (Community Action Guide Ser.). 22p. (Orig.). 1988. pap. text ed. 4.00 (*0-937345-05-9*) CONCERN.

Waste see Collected Works of Robert Herrick

Waste Age & Recycling Times' Recycling Handbook. Compiled by John T. Aquino. LC 95-14479. 304p. 1995. 55.00 (*1-56670-068-X*, L1068) Lewis Pubs.

Waste Analysis. Environmental Protection Agency Staff. 198p. 1994. pap. text ed. 69.00 (*0-86587-414-X*) Gov Insts.

***Waste Analysis at Facilities That Generate, Treat, Store, & Dispose of Hazardous Wastes: A Guidance Manual.** (Illus.). 193p. (C). 1996. reprint ed. pap. 30.00 (*0-7881-3173-7*) DIANE Pub.

Waste Analysis at Facilities that Generate, Treat, Store & Dispose of Hazardous Wastes: A Manual. 1995. lib. bdg. 299.99 (*0-8490-8379-6*) Gordon Pr.

Waste & Recycling. Janine Amos. LC 92-16339. (What About...? Ser.). (Illus.). 32p. (J). (gr. 2-3). 1992. lib. bdg. 21.40 (*0-8114-3406-0*) Raintree Steck-V.

***Waste & Recycling.** Janine Amos. (What About...? Ser.). 1996. pap. 4.95 (*0-8114-4914-9*) Raintree Steck-V.

Waste & Recycling. Barbara James. LC 89-26274. (Conserving Our World Ser.). (Illus.). 48p. (J). (gr. 4-9). 1990. pap. 5.95 (*0-8114-3457-5*); lib. bdg. 24.26 (*0-8114-2386-7*) Raintree Steck-V.

Waste & Spoilage in the Printing Industry: Sheetfed Edition. 36p. 1987. 65.00 (*0-318-21973-5*, XP111) NAPL.

Waste & Spoilage in the Printing Industry: Web Press Edition. 32p. 1987. 65.00 (*0-318-21974-3*, XP114) NAPL.

Waste & Want. Susan Strasser. 1996. write for info. (*0-8050-4830-8*) H Holt & Co.

Waste Audit Study: Drug Manufacturing & Processing Industry. (Illus.). 195p. (Orig.). (C). 1994. pap. text ed. 40.00 (*0-7881-0429-2*) DIANE Pub.

Waste Audit Study: Fiberglass-Reinforced & Composite Plastic Products. (Illus.). 175p. (Orig.). (C). 1994. pap. text ed. 40.00 (*0-7881-0428-4*) DIANE Pub.

Waste Away: A Curriculum on Solid Waste. Vermont Institute of Natural Science Staff. Ed. by Bonnie Ross. (Illus.). 120p. (Orig.). 1990. pap. 18.95 (*0-9617627-2-1*) VT Inst Nat Sci.

Waste Chasers: A Pocket Companion to Quality & Productivity. Conway Quality Inc. Staff. (Illus.). 105p. (Orig.). 1992. pap. write for info. (*0-9631464-1-6*) Conway Qual.

Waste Compactors. Richard K. Miller & Marcia E. Rupnow. LC 90-83890. (Survey on Technology & Markets Ser.: No. 186). 50p. 1991. pap. text ed. 200.00 (*1-55865-210-8*) Future Tech Surveys.

Waste Containment Facilities: Guidance for Construction, Quality Assurance, & Quality Control of Liner & Cover Systems. David E. Daniel & Robert M. Koerner. LC 95-31293. 1995. 48.00 (*0-7844-0111-X*) Am Soc Civil Eng.

Waste Containment Facilities: Guidance for Construction, Quality Assurance & Quality Control of Liner & Cover Systems. David E. Daniel & Robert M. Koerner. 376p. 1995. 48.00 (*0-7844-0003-2*) Am Soc Civil Eng.

Waste Containment Systems: Construction, Regulation & Performance. Ed. by Rudolph Bonaparte. LC 90-49336. 272p. 1990. pap. text ed. 29.00 (*0-87262-787-X*) Am Soc Civil Eng.

Waste Containment Systems, Waste Stabilization & Landfills: Design & Evaluation. Hari D. Sharma & Sangeeta P. Lewis. 588p. 1994. text ed. 79.95 (*0-471-57536-4*) Wiley.

Waste Crisis. Jenny E. Tesar. (Our Fragile Planet Ser.). (Illus.). 128p. (YA). (gr. 9-12). 1991. 18.95 (*0-8160-2491-X*) Facts on File.

Waste Disposal & Evaporites: Contributions to Long-Term Safety. Albert G. Herrmann & Bernhard Knipping. LC 92-42109. (Lecture Notes in Earth Sciences Ser.: Vol. 45). 1993. write for info. (*3-540-56232-X*); 69.95 (*0-387-56232-X*) Spr-Verlag.

Waste Disposal by Landfill: Proceedings of the Symposium GREEN '93, Geotechnics Related to the Environment, Bolton, UK, 6-10 September 1993. Ed. by R. W. Sarsby. (Illus.). 700p. 1995. 110.00 (*90-5410-356-6*) Balkema RSA.

Waste Disposal in Academic Institutions. James A. Kaufman. (Illus.). 208p. 1990. 89.95 (*0-87371-256-0*, L256) Lewis Pubs.

Waste Disposal in Rocks. R. Pusch. LC 93-48194. (Developments in Geotechnical Engineering Ser.: Vol. 76). 510p. 1994. 205.00 (*0-444-89449-7*) Elsevier.

Waste Energy Utilization Technology. Yen-Hsiung Kiang. LC 80-24125. (Energy, Power, & Environment Ser.: No. 10). 265p. reprint ed. pap. 75.60 (*0-7837-3895-1*, 2043743) Bks Demand.

Waste Generating Processes in Research & Educational Institutions: Guide to Pollution Prevention. (Illus.). 51p. (Orig.). (C). 1994. pap. text ed. 25.00 (*1-56806-085-8*) DIANE Pub.

Waste Generator's Compliance Manual. Ethan S. Naftalin. 452p. (Orig.). 1995. pap. text ed. 89.00 (*0-86587-507-3*) Gov Insts.

Waste Geotechnics. R. N. Yong. (Developments in Geotechnical Engineering Ser.). Date not set. text ed. write for info. (*0-444-89847-6*) Elsevier.

Waste Heat Boiler Deskbook. V. Ganapathy. (Illus.). 1991. 69.00 (*0-88173-122-6*, 0267) Fairmont Pr.

***Waste Incineration & Human Health.** 315p. 1997. 44.95 (*0-309-06371-X*) Natl Acad Pr.

Waste Incineration & the Environment. Ed. by R. E. Hester & R. M. Harrison. 158p. 1994. 52.00 (*0-85404-205-9*, R4205) CRC Pr.

Waste Isolation Pilot Plant: A Potential Solution for the Disposal of Transuranic Waste. National Research Council, Waste Isolation Pilot Plant Committee. 175p. (Orig.). (C). 1996. pap. text ed. 40.00 (*0-309-05491-5*) Natl Acad Pr.

Waste Land. Ed. by Tony Davies & Nigel Wood. LC 93-20998. (Theory in Practice Ser.). 1994. 19.95 (*0-335-15716-5*, Open Univ Pr) Taylor & Francis.

***Waste Land.** T. S. Eliot. 1997. pap. 4.00 (*0-15-600534-4*) HarBrace.

Waste Land. Grover C. Smith. (Unwin Critical Library). 200p. 1983. pap. 13.95 (*0-04-800020-5*); text ed. 34.95 (*0-04-800015-9*) Routledge Chapman & Hall.

Waste Land: Facsimile & Transcript. annot. ed. T. S. Eliot. Ed. by Valerie Eliot. LC 73-12627. 184p. 1974. reprint ed. pap. 19.00 (*0-15-694870-2*, Harvest Bks) HarBrace.

***Waste Land: Meditations on a Ravaged Landscape.** David T. Hanson et al. (Illus.). 160p. 1997. 40.00 (*0-89381-726-0*) Aperture.

Waste Land: Some Commentaries. Eric Mesterton. LC 75-22205. (Studies in T. S. Eliot: No. 11). 1975. lib. bdg. 75.00 (*0-8383-2085-6*) M S G Haskell Hse.

Waste Land & Other Poems. T. S. Eliot. LC 56-58835. 88p. (Orig.). 1955. pap. 7.00 (*0-15-694877-X*, Harvest Bks) HarBrace.

Waste Land & Other Poems. T. S. Eliot. LC 56-58835. 96p. (Orig.). 1992. reprint ed. lib. bdg. 16.95 (*0-89966-898-4*) Buccaneer Bks.

Waste Land As Grail Romance: Eliot's Use of the Medieval Grail Legends. Everett A. Gillis. (Graduate Studies: No. 6). 26p. 1974. pap. 2.00 (*0-89672-013-6*) Tex Tech Univ Pr.

Waste Lands. Stephen King. (Dark Tower Ser.: Vol. III). 592p. 1993. pap. 6.99 (*0-451-17331-7*, Sig) NAL-Dutton.

Waste Lands. Stephen King. 1992. 34.95 (*0-453-00770-8*, NAL Bks) NAL-Dutton.

Waste Lands. Stephen King. (Dark Tower Ser.: Vol. III). (Illus.). 432p. 1992. reprint ed. pap. 17.95 (*0-452-26740-4*, Plume) NAL-Dutton.

Waste Lands Development & Their Utilisation. K. A. Shandrnarayan. 496p. (C). 1992. 185.00 (*81-85046-80-8*, Pub. by Scientific UK) St Mut.

Waste Lands Diagnosis & Treatment. Hridai R. Yadav. 1987. 34.00 (*0-8364-2262-7*, Pub. by Concept II) S Asia.

Waste Location: Spatial Aspects of Waste Management, Hazards & Disposal. Ed. by Michael Clark et al. (Natural Environment: Problems & Management Ser.). (Illus.). 272p. (C). 1991. text ed. 110.00 (*0-415-04824-9*, A6464) Routledge.

Waste Management. (Illus.). 107p. 1968. 10.00 (*0-318-16390-X*, 107) Regional Plan Assn.

***Waste Management.** Bernd Bilitewski et al. LC 96-35760. 650p. 1996. 69.00 (*3-540-59210-5*) Spr-Verlag.

Waste Management. Ed. by Jeremy Woolfe. viii, 277p. 1981. lib. bdg. 100.50 (*90-277-1338-3*) Kluwer Ac.

Waste Management: An American Corporate Success Story. Timothy Jacobson. LC 92-28617. (Illus.). 340p. 1992. 21.95 (*0-89526-511-7*) Regnery Pub.

Waste Management: From Risk to Remediation. Mohammad Jamshidi et al. 1994. text ed. 48.00 (*0-13-123134-0*) P-H.

***Waste Management: The Duty of Care - A Code of Practice.** 65p. 1996. pap. 15.00 (*0-11-753210-X*, HM3210X, Pub. by Stationery Ofc UK) Bernan Associates.

Waste Management: Towards a Sustainable Society. Om P. Kharbanda & E. A. Stallworthy. LC 89-18496. 240p. 1990. text ed. 55.00 (*0-86569-000-6*, T000, Auburn Hse) Greenwood.

Waste Management & Resource Recovery. Robert B. Wenger et al. 544p. 1995. 69.95 (*0-87371-572-1*, L572) Lewis Pubs.

Waste Management & Resources Recovery Information Database. Randall L. Voight. (C). 1986. 1,250.00 (*0-930318-07-2*); 125.00 (*0-930318-18-8*) Intl Res Eval.

Waste Management & Soil Pollution Technology in Europe. 135p. 1993. 1,500.00 (*0-89336-966-7*, E-066) BCC.

***Waste Management & Utilization in Food Production & Processing.** Task Force of Scientists Staff. LC 92-10235. (Illus.). 125p. (Orig.). 1995. pap. 22.00 (*1-887383-02-6*) CAST.

***Waste Management Concepts.** Neal K. Ostler & John T. Nielsen. LC 97-22365. (Prentice Hall's Environmental Technology Ser.). 1998. write for info. (*0-02-389545-4*) P-H.

Waste Management for Health Care Facilities. rev. ed. Linda D. Lee. (Management & Compliance Ser.: Vol. 1). (Illus.). 300p. 1992. ring bd. 110.00 (*0-87258-585-9*, 055401) Am Hospital.

***Waste Management in Petrochemical Complexes.** S. A. Almeida et al. (Water Science & Technology Ser.: Vol. 20). 296p. 1989. 61.00 (*0-08-037366-6*, Pergamon Pr) Elsevier.

Waste Management in the Chemical & Petrochemical Industries. Fontes & Lima. (Water Science & Technology Ser.: No. 29-8). 292p. 1994. pap. 152.00 (*0-08-042541-0*, Pergamon Pr) Elsevier.

***Waste Management in the Coastal Areas of the ASEAN Region: Roles of Governments, Banking Institutions, Donor Agencies, Private Sector & Communities.** Ed. by T. E. Chua & L. R. Garces. (ICLARM Conference Proceedings Ser.: No. 33). 218p. 1992. per. write for info. (*971-8709-10-X*, Pub. by ICLARM PH) Intl Spec Bk.

Waste Management in the States. Leslie Cole. LC 82-147343. 30p. reprint ed. pap. 25.00 (*0-317-10672-4*, 2020427) Bks Demand.

Waste Management Law: A Practical Handbook. 2nd ed. John Garbutt. 274p. 1995. pap. text ed. 35.00 (*0-471-95227-3*) Wiley.

Waste Management Problems in Agro-Industries: Proceedings of an IAWPRC Symposium Held in Istanbul, Turkey, 25-27 September 1989. Ed. by M. Henze et al. (Water Science & Technology Ser.: WST 22). 296p. 1990. pap. 120.50 (*0-08-040778-1*, Pergamon Pr) Elsevier.

Waste Management Problems in Agro-Industries 1992. Ed. by M. Henze et al. (Water Science & Technology Ser.). 284p. 1993. pap. 114.25 (*0-08-042349-3*, Pergamon Pr) Elsevier.

***Waste Management Solutions for Health Care Facilities.** Ed. by Randall Abate. 500p. 1997. ring bd. 245.00 (*0-929321-37-5*) WEKA Pub.

Waste Materials in Construction. J. J. Goumans et al. (Studies in Environmental Science: Vol. 48). 672p. 1991. 318.75 (*0-444-89089-0*) Elsevier.

Waste Materials Used in Concrete Manufacturing. Ed. by Satish Chandra. LC 96-12577. 1996. 86.00 (*0-8155-1393-3*) Noyes.

Waste Minimisation: A Chemist's Approach. Ed. by K. Martin & T. W. Bastock. 155p. 1994. 79.00 (*0-85186-585-2*, R6585) CRC Pr.

Waste Minimization & Cost Reduction for the Process Industries. Paul N. Cheremisinoff. (Illus.). 331p. 1995. 64.00 (*0-8155-1388-7*) Noyes.

Waste Minimization & Pollution Prevention. Richard K. Miller & Marcia E. Rupnow. (Survey on Technology & Markets Ser.: No. 224). 50p. 1993. pap. text ed. 200.00 (*1-55865-254-X*) Future Tech Surveys.

Waste Minimization & Recycling. Ed. by Nicholas P. Cheremisinoff. LC 92-12009. (Encyclopedia of Environmental Control Technology Ser.: Vol. 5). 1992. 155.00 (*0-87201-258-1*) Gulf Pub.

Waste Minimization As a Strategic Weapon. David F. Ciambrone. 272p. 1995. 65.00 (*1-56670-135-X*, L1135) Lewis Pubs.

Waste Minimization Manual. Ed. by Government Institutes, Inc. Staff. 181p. 1987. pap. 69.00 (*0-86587-731-9*) Gov Insts.

Waste Minimization Through Process Design. Ed. by Alan P. Rossiter. LC 94-49707. 1995. text ed. 55.00 (*0-07-053957-X*) McGraw.

***Waste Minimizaton in the Oil Field.** (Illus.). 115p. 1996. reprint ed. pap. 30.00 (*0-7881-3194-X*) DIANE Pub.

Waste Not Want Not. Robert Allen. 1991. 16.95 (*1-85383-095-X*, Pub. by Erthscan Pubns UK) Island Pr.

Waste Not, Want Not: Food Preservation in Britain From Early Times to the Present Day. Ed. by Anne Wilson. (Illus.). 166p. 1992. 38.50 (*0-7486-0119-8*, Pub. by Edinburgh U Pr UK) Col U Pr.

Waste of the West: Public Lands Ranching. Lynn Jacobs. (Illus.). 602p. (Orig.). 1991. pap. 28.00 (*0-9629386-0-2*) L Jacobs.

Waste of Timelessness: And Other Early Stories. Anais Nin. LC 74-28648. viii, 110p. 1994. reprint ed. pap. 9.95 (*0-8040-0981-3*) Swallow.

Waste Oil: Reclaiming Technology, Utilization & Disposal. Mueller Associates, Inc. Staff. LC 88-38438. (Pollution Technology Review Ser.: No. 166). (Illus.). 193p. 1989. 39.00 (*0-8155-1193-0*) Noyes.

Waste Oil Recycling & Resource Recovery. Richard K. Miller & Marcia E. Rupnow. LC 90-83880. (Survey on Technology & Markets Ser.: No. 176). 50p. 1991. pap. text ed. 200.00 (*1-55865-200-0*) Future Tech Surveys.

Waste Recycling for Sustainable Development Vol. 1: The Case of Obsolete Oil & Gas Production Structures in Asia & the Pacific Waters: An Overview. 86p. 1994. 20.00 (*92-1-119642-6*) UN.

Waste Recycling for Sustainable Development Vol. 2: The Case of Obsolete Oil & Gas Production Structures in Asia & the Pacific Waters: Country Perspective. 93p. 1995. 17.00 (*92-1-127047-2*) UN.

***Waste Reduction.** E2: Environment & Education Staff. Ed. by Cathy Anderson et al. (Environmental ACTION Ser.). (Illus.). 100p. (Orig.). (YA). (gr. 6-12). 1997. teacher ed., pap. text ed. 13.95 (*0-201-49536-8*, SE:30676) Seymour Pubns.

***Waste Reduction.** E2: Environment & Education Staff. Ed. by Cathy Anderson et al. (Environmental ACTION Ser.). (Illus.). 170p. (Orig.). (YA). (gr. 6-12). 1997. pap. text ed. 5.95 (*0-201-49537-6*, TE: 30625) Seymour Pubns.

Waste Reduction: Policy & Practice. Piper et al. 1990. pap. 39.95 (*1-55840-272-1*) Exec Ent Pubns.

Waste Reduction: Policy & Practice. Waste Management, Inc. Staff & Piper & Marbury Staff. 111p. 1994. pap. text ed. 49.95 (*0-471-11263-1*) Wiley.

***Waste Reduction for Pollution Prevention.** Paul N. Cheremisinoff & Louise M. Ferrante. LC 92-6801. 1992. write for info. (*0-7506-0601-0*) Buttrwrth-Heinemann.

Waste Reduction in English & Spanish. 52p. 1989. 15.00 (*0-318-32903-4*) F Drazan.

Waste Reduction Priorities in Manufacturing: A DOE/CWRT Workshop. Jack Eisenhauer & Shawna McQueen. LC 94-35651. 1994. 25.00 (*0-8169-0656-4*) Am Inst Chem Eng.

Waste Shredders. Richard K. Miller & Marcia E. Rupnow. LC 90-83889. (Survey on Technology & Markets Ser.: No. 185). 50p. 1991. pap. text ed. 200.00 (*1-55865-209-4*) Future Tech Surveys.

***Waste Stabilisation Ponds & the Reuse of Pond Effluents.** H. W. Pearson & F. B. Green. (Water Science & Technology Ser.: Vol. 31). 432p. 1995. 115.00 (*0-08-042666-2*, Pergamon Pr) Elsevier.

Waste Stabilization Ponds. E. F. Gloyna. (Monograph Ser.: No. 60). 175p. 1971. pap. text ed. 20.00 (*92-4-140060-9*, 1140060) World Health.

Waste Stabilization Ponds: Proceedings of an IAWPRC Specialized Conference Held in Lisbon, Portugal, 29 June - 2 July 1987. D. Duncan Mara & Marecos Do Monte. (Water Science & Technology Ser.: 19). (Illus.). 417p. 1988. pap. 54.00 (*0-08-035598-6*, Pergamon Pr) Elsevier.

***Waste Stabilization Ponds - Technology & Applications: Selected Proceedings of the 3rd IAWQ International Symposium on Waste Stabilization Ponds, Technology & Applications.** Ed. by D. D. Mara et al. (Water Science & Technology 33 Ser.). 262p. 1996. pap. text ed. 128.00 (*0-08-042900-9*, Pergamon Pr) Elsevier.

Waste Testing & Quality Assurance, Vol. 2. Ed. by David Friedman. (Special Technical Publication (STP) Ser.: STP 1062). (Illus.). 474p. 1990. text ed. 58.00 (*0-8031-1293-9*, 04-010620-56) ASTM.

Waste Testing & Quality Assurance, Vol. 3. Ed. by David Friedman. 411p. 1992. 61.00 (*0-8031-1294-7*, 04-010750-56) ASTM.

Waste Testing & Quality Assurance, STP 999. Ed. by David Friedman. LC 88-19458. (Special Technical Publication (STP) Ser.). (Illus.). 184p. 1988. text ed. 29.00 (*0-8031-1175-4*, 04-999000-56) ASTM.

Waste-to-Energy. Richard K. Miller & Marcia E. Rupnow. (Survey on Technology & Markets Ser.: No. 213). 50p. 1994. pap. text ed. 200.00 (*1-55865-244-2*) Future Tech Surveys.

Waste to Energy: Impact, Directions & Trends, No. E-053. Business Communications Co., Inc. Staff. 155p. 1990. 1,950.00 (*0-89336-785-0*) BCC.

Waste-to-Energy Commercial Facilities Profiles: Technical, Operational & Economic Perspectives. Dick Richards et al. LC 89-70986. (Pollution Technology Review Ser.: No. 177). (Illus.). 423p. 1990. 58.00 (*0-8155-1226-0*) Noyes.

W

An Asterisk (*) at the beginning of an entry indicates that the title is appearing in BIP for the first time.

Waste-to-Energy in the United States: A Social & Economic Assessment. T. Randall Curlee et al. LC 93-26467. 280p. 1994. text ed. 69.50 (0-89930-844-9, Quorum Bks) Greenwood.

Waste Treatment & Disposal. Ed. by R. E. Hester & R. M. Harrison. (Issues in Environmental Science & Technology Ser.: Issue 3). 158p. 1995. 29.95 (0-85404-210-5, R4210) CRC Pr.

Waste Treatment & Utilization 3: Proceedings of IWTUS-3, the Third International Waste Treatment & Utilization Symposium, Frauenfeld, Switzerland, August 27-31, 1984. Ed. by J. D. Bryers et al. (Illus.). 328p. 1985. 153.00 (0-08-032605-6, Pub. by PPL UK) Franklin.

Waste Treatment in Agriculture. Peter N. Hobson & A. M. Robertson. (Illus.). x, 257p. 1977. 66.75 (0-85334-736-0, Pub. by Elsevier Applied Sci UK) Elsevier.

***Waste Treatment Plants.** Ed. by C. A. Sastry et al. 1995. text ed. 45.00 (0-471-14301-4) Wiley.

Waste Treatment Systems. Center for Occupational Research & Development Staff. (EUTEC Power Plant Operator Curriculum Ser.). (Illus.). 36p. (C). 1985. pap. text ed. write for info. (1-55502-224-3) CORD Commns.

Waste Treatment Technology Reviews. Donald Saxman. 277p. 1995. 1,500.00 (0-614-10888-8, DNT94) BCC.

Waste Water & Effluent Technology Handbook. Dare. 1997. text ed. write for info. (1-85617-283-X) Elsevier.

***Waste Water Management for Coastal Cities: The Ocean Disposal Option.** 2nd ed. Charles G. Gunnerson & Jonathan A. French. LC 96-27517. (Environmental Engineering Ser.). 345p. 1996. 133.00 (3-540-59216-4) Spr-Verlag.

Waste Water Technology. (Illus.). 1190p. 1989. 126.00 (0-387-17450-8) Spr-Verlag.

Wasted. Linda Wolfe. Ed. by Julie Rubenstein. 384p. 1990. reprint ed. mass mkt. 5.99 (0-671-70900-3) PB.

Wasted: A Teenagers's Drug Odyssey. Craig Fraser & Deidre Sullivan. 1989. 18.95 (0-318-42497-5) NAL-Dutton.

***Wasted: Eating Disorders & the Culture of Control.** Marya Hornbacher. LC 97-21375. 304p. 1997. 23.00 (0-06-018739-5) HarpC.

***Wasted: Tales of a Gen X Drunk.** Mark G. Judge. 1997. pap. 21.95 (0-614-27646-2) Hazelden.

***Wasted: Tales of a GenX Drunk.** Mark G. Judge. LC 97-9225. 250p. 1997. text ed. 21.95 (1-56838-142-5) Hazelden.

***Wasted: The Plight of America's Unwanted Children.** Patrick T. Murphy. LC 97-8978. 192p. 1997. 22.50 (1-56663-163-7) I R Dee.

Wasted Americans: Cost of Our Welfare Dilemma. Edgar May. LC 80-19500. (Illus.). xi, 227p. 1980. reprint ed. text ed. 59.75 (0-313-22674-1, MAWAM, Greenwood Pr) Greenwood.

Wasted Away: The Worldwide Party Guide. Scott Stavrou. LC 95-74950. 176p. (Orig.). 1996. pap. 12.95 (1-884818-10-2) Pride-Frost.

Wasted Land. Gerald W. Johnson. LC 78-130556. (Select Bibliographies Reprint Ser.). 1977. reprint ed. 17.95 (0-8369-5529-3) Ayer.

Wasted Lives: A Study of Children in Mental Hospitals & Their Families. Lillian C. Kovar. LC 78-23248. 1979. text ed. 29.95 (0-89876-051-8) Gardner Pr.

Wasted on the Young. Ralph Schoenstein. LC 73-11795. 112p. 1974. 4.95 (0-672-51839-2, Bobbs) Macmillan.

***Wasted Space, Vol. 1.** Elizabeth Manz. 1996. mass mkt. 5.99 (0-312-95981-8) St Martin.

Wasted Valor: The Confederate Dead at Gettysburg. Gregory A. Coco. (Illus.). 192p. (C). 1995. reprint ed. pap. text ed. 11.95 (0-939631-83-0) Thomas Publications.

***Wasted Years.** Harvey. 1998. pap. 6.95 (0-8050-5499-5) H Holt & Co.

Wasted Years. John Harvey. 352p. 1994. mass mkt. 4.99 (0-380-72182-1) Avon.

Wasted Years. large type ed. Mary A. Larkin. 569p. 1994. 25.99 (0-7505-0598-2) Ulverscroft.

Wasteland. T. S. Eliot. 1997. pap. 9.95 (0-14-086398-2) Viking Penguin.

Wasteland. Jo Sinclair. (Gems of American Jewish Literature Ser.). 348p. 1987. pap. 12.95 (0-8276-0280-4) JPS Phila.

Wasteland: A Novel. Peter McCabe. LC 93-2238. 258p. 1994. 20.00 (0-684-19681-6) S&S Trade.

***Wasteland of Strangers.** Bill Pronzini. LC 96-50927. 256p. 1997. 21.95 (0-8027-3301-8) Walker & Co.

Wastelands & Afforestation. Irshad Khan. 176p. (C). 1987. 12.75 (81-204-0212-X, Pub. by Oxford IBH II) S Asia.

Wastelands Development & Their Utilization. K. A. Shnakarnarayana. (C). 1988. text ed. 200.00 (0-7855-0107-X, Pub. by Scientific Pubs II); text ed. 225.00 (0-685-63522-8, Pub. by Scientific Pubs II) St Mut.

Wastelands of Fire: Selected Poems of Ku Sang. Ku Sang. Tr. by Anthony Teague. LC 89-82407. 144p. 9000. pap. 16.95 (0-948259-82-5, Pub. by Forest Bks UK) Dufour.

Wastepaper Theater Anthology. Edwin Honig et al. (Pourboire Ser.). 1979. pap. 5.00 (0-930900-56-1) Burning Deck.

Wastes in Marine Environments. Compiled by Office of Technology Assessment Staff. LC 66-65012. 320p. 1987. 78.95 (0-89116-793-5) Hemisp Pub.

Wastes Management International: Yearbook of Products & Services 1994. Ed. by Jeremy Gambrill. 185p. 1994. text ed. 165.00 (0-471-93328-7) Wiley.

Wastewater Biology: The Microlife. Water Pollution Control Federation Staff. LC 90-35373. (Illus.). (Orig.). 1990. pap. 40.00 (0-943244-49-8) Water Environ.

Wastewater Biology - The Life Processes: A Special Publication. Michael H. Gerardi & Water Environment Federation Staff. Ed. by Technical Practice Committee, Operations & Maintenance Subcommittee Staff. LC 94-37376. 1994. 45.00 (1-881369-93-5) Water Environ.

***Wastewater Biosolids to Compost.** Frank R. Spellman. LC 96-60894. 256p. 1996. pap. text ed. 59.95 (1-56676-461-0) Technomic.

Wastewater Collection & Transportation, Vol. 1. N. I. Likhachev et al. (Design Handbook of Wastewater Systems). 150p. 1986. 100.00 (0-89864-021-0) Allerton Pr.

Wastewater Collection & Transportation see Design Handbook of Wastewater Systems

Wastewater Collection Systems Management. Ed. by Stephen B. Tilson. LC 92-31596. (Manual of Practice Ser.: No. 7). 1992. pap. 42.00 (1-881369-01-3) Water Environ.

Wastewater Conference Proceedings: First Conference, 1974. Incl. Wastewater Conference Proceedings: Second Conference, 1975. 214p. 30.00 (0-250-40209-2); Wastewater Conference Proceedings: Third Conference, 1976. 213p. 30.00 (0-250-40156-8); Wastewater Conference Proceedings: Fourth Conference, 1977. 232p. 30.00 (0-250-40210-6); Wastewater Conference Proceedings: Fifth Conference, 1978. 295p. 30.00 (0-250-40277-7); Wastewater Conference Proceedings: Sixth Conference, 1979. 514p. 30.00 (0-250-40345-5); 163p. 30.00 (0-250-40208-4) Natl Sanit Foun.

Wastewater Conference Proceedings: Fifth Conference, 1978 see Wastewater Conference Proceedings: First Conference, 1974

Wastewater Conference Proceedings: Fourth Conference, 1977 see Wastewater Conference Proceedings: First Conference, 1974

Wastewater Conference Proceedings: Second Conference, 1975 see Wastewater Conference Proceedings: First Conference, 1974

Wastewater Conference Proceedings: Sixth Conference, 1979 see Wastewater Conference Proceedings: First Conference, 1974

Wastewater Conference Proceedings: Third Conference, 1976 see Wastewater Conference Proceedings: First Conference, 1974

Wastewater Disinfection. Water Pollution Control Federation Staff. (Manual of Practice Ser.: No. MFD10). 165p. 1986. pap. 40.00 (0-943244-64-1) Water Environ.

***Wastewater Disinfection.** Water Pollution Control Federation Staff & Water Environment Federation Staff. LC 96-24225. (Manual of Practice Ser.). 1996. write for info. (1-57278-036-3) Water Environ.

Wastewater Disinfection: A State-of-the Art Report. Water Pollution Control Federation Staff. (Manual of Practice Ser.: No. P0005). 78p. 1984. pap. 29.50 (0-943244-54-4) Water Environ.

Wastewater Engineering. Bill T. Ray. (Civil Engineering Ser.). 1998. pap. 76.95 (0-534-95100-7) PWS Pubs.

Wastewater Engineering: Collection & Pumping of Wastewater. Metcalf & Eddy, Inc. Staff & George Tchobanoglous. (Water Resources & Engineering Ser.). (Illus.). 448p. (C). 1981. text ed. write for info. (0-07-041680-X) McGraw.

Wastewater Engineering: Treatment, Disposal & Reuse. 3rd ed. Metcalf & Eddy, Inc. Staff & George Tchobanoglous. Ed. by Franklin L. Burton. (Water Resources & Environmental Engineering Ser.). 1991. text ed. write for info. (0-07-041690-7) McGraw.

Wastewater Management: A Guide to Information Sources. Ed. by George Tchobanoglous et al. LC 74-11570. (Man & the Environment Information Guide Ser.: Vol. 2). 216p. 1976. 68.00 (0-8103-1338-3) Gale.

***Wastewater Management in Coastal Areas.** J. Bontoux & J. Bebin. (Water Science & Technology Ser.: Vol. 25). 304p. 1993. 147.00 (0-08-042191-1, Pergamon Pr) Elsevier.

Wastewater Management Problems in Agro-Industries 1995: Selected Proceedings of the Third IAWQ International Symposium on Waste Management Problems in Agro-Industries, held in Mexico City, 4-6 October 1995. Ed. by B. Jimenez et al. 190p. 1995. pap. text ed. write for info. (0-08-042888-6, Pergamon Pr) Elsevier.

Wastewater Microbiology. Gabriel Bitton. (Ecological & Applied Microbiology Ser.). 488p. 1994. text ed. 132.95 (0-471-30985-0, Wiley-Interscience); pap. text ed. 69.95 (0-471-30986-9) Wiley.

Wastewater Organisms: A Color Atlas. Berk. (Illus.). 48p. 1993. 89.95 (0-87371-623-X, L623) Lewis Pubs.

Wastewater Permitting & Finance: New Issues in Water Quality Protection. Larry Morandi. (State Legislative Reports: Vol. 17, No. 8). 8p. 1992. pap. text ed. 5.00 (1-55516-280-0, 7302-1708) Natl Conf State Legis.

***Wastewater Reclamation & Reuse.** R. Mujeriego & T. Asano. (Water Science & Technology Ser.: Vol. 24). 378p. 1991. 143.00 (0-08-041837-6, Pergamon Pr) Elsevier.

***Wastewater Reclamation & Reuse 1995: Selected Proceedings of the IAWQ 2nd International Symposium on Wastewater Reclamation & Reuse, Held in Iraklio, Crete, Greece, 17-20 October 1995.** Ed. by T. Angelakis et al. 492p. 1996. pap. 255.00 (0-08-042903-3, Pergamon Pr) Elsevier.

Wastewater Renovation & Reuse: Proceedings of the International Conference on the Renovation & Reuse of Wastewater Through Aquatic & Terrestrial Systems. Ed. by Frank M. D'Itri. LC 76-54588. (Pollution Engineering & Technology Ser.: Vol. 3). 736p. reprint ed. pap. 180.00 (0-317-08391-0, 2055036) Bks Demand.

Wastewater Reuse for Golf Course Irrigation: Proceedings of the Golf Course Wastewater Symposium, 1993. United States Golf Association Staff. 304p. 1994. 59.95 (1-56670-090-6, L1090) Lewis Pubs.

Wastewater Sampling for Process & Quality Control. Water Environment Federation Staff. LC 96-24226. 1996. write for info. (1-57278-037-1) Water Environ.

Wastewater Sampling for Process & Quality Control, 1980: Manual of Practice, Operation & Maintenance-I. Water Pollution Control Federation Staff. 103p. 1980. pap. 15.00 (0-943244-21-8, M0M1) Water Environ.

Wastewater Sludge Dewatering. Ed. by J. A. Hansen et al. (Water Science & Technology Ser.: Vol. 28). 308p. 1993. pap. 163.75 (0-08-042348-5, Pergamon Pr) Elsevier.

***Wastewater Stabilization Ponds Principles of Planning & Practice.** (WHO/EMRO Technical Publication Ser.: No. 10). 1987. pap. text ed. 25.00 (92-9021-001-X) World Health.

Wastewater Technician. Jack Rudman. (Career Examination Ser.: C-3412). 1994. pap. 27.95 (0-8373-3412-8) Nat Learn.

Wastewater Treatment. 1995. 89.00 (3-540-58816-7) Spr-Verlag.

Wastewater Treatment. R. E. Bartlett. (Illus.). xii, 326p. 1971. 61.00 (0-685-43725-6, Pub. by Elsevier Applied Sci UK) Elsevier.

Wastewater Treatment. Donald W. Sundstrom & Herbert E. Klei. LC 78-13058. (Illus.). 1979. 56.00 (0-13-945832-8) P-H.

***Wastewater Treatment.** 3rd ed. Barnes. 1987. pap. text ed. write for info. (0-582-29726-5, Pub. by Longman UK) Longman.

Wastewater Treatment: Biological & Chemical Processes. Mogens Henze. LC 95-10558. (Environmental Engineering Ser.). 375p. 1995. 89.00 (0-387-58816-7) Spr-Verlag.

***Wastewater Treatment: Biological & Chemical Processes.** 2nd ed. M. Henze. LC 97-14897. (Environmental Engineering Ser.). 1997. write for info. (3-540-62702-2) Spr-Verlag.

Wastewater Treatment: Troubleshooting & Problem Solving. Glenn M. Tillman. 150p. (C). 1996. text ed. 44.95 (1-57504-000-X) Ann Arbor Chelsea.

Wastewater Treatment, an Environmental Primer. Illus. by Jonathan Skaines. LC 93-91544. 72p. (C). 1993. pap. 12.95 (0-929244-00-1) Lone Oak Pub Co.

Wastewater Treatment & Disposal: Engineering & Ecology in Pollution Control. S. J. Arceivala. LC 81-1521. (Pollution Engineering & Technology Ser.: Vol. 15). (Illus.). 904p. reprint ed. pap. 180.00 (0-685-24140-8, 2033012) Bks Demand.

Wastewater Treatment & Use in Agriculture. F.A.O. Staff & M. B. Pescod. 1994. pap. 150.00 (81-7233-094-4, Pub. by Scientific Pubs II) St Mut.

Wastewater Treatment by Immobilized Cells. Tyagi & Vembu. 296p. 1990. 193.00 (0-8493-5176-6, TD475) CRC Pr.

Wastewater Treatment by Ion Exchange. B. A. Bolto & L. Pawlowski. 250p. 1987. 69.95 (0-419-13320-8, 2968, E & FN Spon) Routledge Chapman & Hall.

Wastewater Treatment Plant Design. Water Pollution Control Federation Staff. (Manual of Practice Ser.: No. M0008). (Illus.). 550p. pap. 23.00 (0-943244-08-0, M0008) Water Environ.

Wastewater Treatment Plant Maintenance Supervisor. Jack Rudman. (Career Examination Ser.: C-3064). 1994. pap. 34.95 (0-8373-3064-5) Nat Learn.

Wastewater Treatment Plants: Planning, Design & Operation. Syed R. Qasim. 704p. (C). 1985. text ed. 58.75 (0-03-062449-5) SCP.

Wastewater Treatment Plants: Planning, Design, & Operation. Syed R. Qasim. LC 93-61610. 746p. 1994. text ed. 89.95 (1-56676-134-4) Technomic.

Wastewater Treatment Technology. Ed. by Paul N. Cheremisinoff. (Encyclopedia of Environmental Control Technology Ser.: Vol. 3). 684p. 1989. 155.00 (0-87201-247-6) Gulf Pub.

Wastewater Treatment Using Genetically Engineered Microorganisms. Masanori Fujita & Michihiko Ike. LC 94-60490. 185p. 1994. pap. 59.95 (1-56676-139-5) Technomic.

Wastewater Treatment with Microbial Films. Shigehisa Iwai & Takane Kitao. (Illus.). 183p. 1994. pap. 59.95 (1-56676-112-3) Technomic.

Wasting America's Future: The Children's Defense Fund Report on the Costs of Child Poverty. Children's Defense Fund Staff. 192p. 1994. 35.00 (0-8070-4106-8); pap. 18.00 (0-8070-4107-6) Beacon Pr.

Wasting Assets: Natural Resources in the National Income Accounts. Robert C. Repetto et al. 120p. (Orig.). 1989. pap. text ed. 10.00 (0-915825-31-7) World Resources Inst.

Wasting Away: The Undermining of Canada's Health Care System. Pat Armstrong & Hugh Armstrong. 256p. 1996. pap. 24.95 (0-19-541070-X) OUP.

Wasting My Life. James Miranda. Ed. by R. Crowder. LC 93-72729. (Illus.). 132p. (C). 1993. 21.95 (0-935763-02-3); pap. 9.95 (0-935763-03-1) Chester Hse Pubs.

Wasting the Rain: Rivers, People, & Planning in Africa. W. M. Adams. LC 92-22825. 240p. (C). 1993. pap. text ed. 17.95 (0-8166-2270-1) U of Minn Pr.

Wasting Time in School: An Experiential Account of Chaplaincy in Secondary Schools. Mary McKeon. 128p. 1993. 25.00 (0-85439-461-3, Pub. by St Paul Pubns UK) St Mut.

Wastrel. Margaret Moore. 1996. pap. 4.99 (0-373-28944-8, 1-28944-6) Harlequin Bks.

Wat Haripunjaya: A Study of the Royal Temple of the Buddha's Relic, Lamphun, Thailand. Donald K. Swearer. LC 75-33802. (American Academy of Religion. Studies in Religion: No. 10). 106p. reprint ed. pap. 30.30 (0-7837-5482-5, 2045247) Bks Demand.

Wat Tyler: A Dramatic Poem. Robert Southey. LC 90-118875. 100p. 1989. reprint ed. 35.00 (1-85477-025-X, Pub. by Woodstock Bks UK) Cassell.

Watashi No Nihon Tuttle Activity Books for Young Learners of Japanese Book I: My Homestay Family. Kumi Kato et al. (Key Centre for Asian Languages & Studies Language). (Illus.). 64p. (Orig.). (ENG & JPN.). (YA). 1995. pap. 9.95 (0-8048-2010-4) C E Tuttle.

Watashi No Nihon Tuttle Activity Books for Young Learners of Japanese Book II: My Day at School. Kumi Kato et al. (Key Centre for Asian Languages & Studies Language). (Illus.). 64p. (Orig.). (ENG & JPN.). (YA). 1995. pap. 9.95 (0-8048-2012-0) C E Tuttle.

Watashi No Nihon Tuttle Activity Books for Young Learners of Japanese Book III: My Day in Tokyo. Kumi Kato et al. (Key Centre for Asian Languages & Studies Language). (Illus.). 64p. (Orig.). (ENG & JPN.). (YA). 1995. pap. 9.95 (0-8048-2011-2) C E Tuttle.

Watauga Drawdown. Don Johnson. 66p. 1990. 12.95 (0-932807-56-9); pap. 8.95 (0-932807-54-2) Overmountain Pr.

Wataugans. Max Dixon. (Illus.). 80p. 1989. reprint ed. pap. 6.95 (0-932807-47-X) Overmountain Pr.

Watbanaland. Doug Wright. 1995. pap. 5.25 (0-8222-1480-6) Dramatists Play.

***Watch: House of the Sun.** Wayne Jones. 128p. 1998. pap. write for info. (0-425-16157-9, Berkley Trade) Berkley Pub.

Watch: Stories. Rick Bass. 1994. pap. 9.95 (0-393-31135-X) Norton.

Watch a Miracle Begin. Shoddy Chase. Ed. by Delores Crittenden. 1992. write for info. (0-9628168-0-9) Keys Freedom.

Watch & Be Ready: Nineteen Ninety Two Millions Disappear. D. A. Miller. 1992. pap. 4.95 (1-878993-34-8) Jeremiah Films.

Watch & Be Ready: Preparing for the Second Coming of the Lord. Compiled by Robert L. Millet. LC 94-27762. iv, 230p. 1994. 14.95 (0-87579-911-6) Deseret Bk.

Watch & Chronometer Jeweling. N. B. Sherwood. (Illus.). 120p. 1988. pap. 11.95 (0-930163-14-1) Arlington Bk.

Watch & Clock Encyclopedia. Antique Collector's Club Staff. 1994. 39.00 (0-7198-0170-2) Antique Collect.

Watch & Clock Encyclopedia. Donald DeCarle. (Illus.). 1959. 35.00 (0-685-22155-5) Wehman.

Watch & Clock Information, Please. Orville R. Hagans. 1981. 30.00 (0-918845-03-3) Am Watchmakers.

Watch & Clock Making. David Glasgow. (Illus.). 1977. reprint ed. 25.00 (0-7158-1215-7) Charles River Bks.

Watch & Clockmaker's Handbook, Dictionary & Guide. F. J. Britten. 1996. 29.50 (1-85149-192-9) Antique Collect.

Watch & Clockmakers' Handbook, Dictionary & Guide. F. J. Britten. (Illus.). 500p. 1976. reprint ed. 29.50 (0-902028-46-4) Antique Collect.

Watch and Pray: Meditations in Dramatic Form for the Season of Lent. Neil E. Orts. LC 95-25340. (Orig.). 1996. pap. 6.95 (0-7880-0390-9) CSS OH.

Watch & Ward see Works of Henry James Jr.: Collected Works

***Watch Below.** James White. LC 96-27411. 1996. pap. 15.00 (1-882968-08-5) Old Earth Bks.

Watch Escapement. Henry B. Fried. (Illus.). 191p. 1974. pap. 17.95 (0-930163-68-0) Arlington Bk.

Watch Fire. Christopher Merrill. 190p. (Orig.). 1994. pap. 14.00 (1-877727-43-1) White Pine.

Watch Fires: A Civil War Story. Cecelia D. Johnson. 1993. pap. 9.95 (0-943135-50-8) Gallagher Jordan.

Watch for a Tall White Sail. Margaret E. Bell. 190p. 1992. reprint ed. lib. bdg. 16.95 (0-89966-912-3) Buccaneer Bks.

Watch for Evil. Caroline H. Keith. 390p. (Orig.). 1990. pap. 12.95 (0-9627467-0-3) Bacalou Pub.

Watch for Me on the Mountain. Forrest Carter. 320p. 1990. pap. 11.95 (0-385-30082-4, Delta) Dell.

Watch for Me on the Mountain. large type ed. Forrest Carter. 1982. 15.95 (0-7089-0771-7) Ulverscroft.

***Watch for Opportunities: A Challenge for Creativity in the Child.** Barbara D. Heavilin. (Illus.). 32p. (J). (gr. k up). 1995. pap. text ed. 8.29 (0-9648730-2-8) Shoe Hse.

Watch for Trams. Colin Jones. (Illus.). 1994. 29.95 (0-86417-544-2, Pub. by Kangaroo Pr AT) Seven Hills Bk.

Watch Harry Grow! Demi. LC 84-60109. (Follow-Me Bks.). (Illus.). 26p. (J). (ps-1). 1984. bds. 3.50 (0-394-86857-9) Random Bks Yng Read.

***Watch Hill Hurricane September 21, 1938.** Helen J. Lee et al. (Illus.). 24p. 1996. 10.00 (0-614-30504-7) Book & Tackle.

***Watch Hour.** Camille Yarbrough. Date not set. 14.95 (0-399-22614-1) Putnam Pub Group.

***Watch in the Night.** A. Wilson. Date not set. pap. 12.00 (0-393-31725-0) Norton.

Watch in the Night: Being the Conclusion of the Lampitt Chronicles. A. N. Wilson. LC 96-28636. 256p. 1996. 23.00 (0-393-04042-9) Norton.

Watch It Grow! Julian Rowe & Molly Perham. LC 94-12258. (First Science Ser.). (Illus.). 32p. (J). (gr. 1-4). 1994. pap. 4.95 (0-516-48141-X); lib. bdg. 19.90 (0-516-08141-1) Childrens.

Watch It Made in the U. S. A Visitor's Guide to the Companies That Make Your Favorite Products. Bruce Brumberg & Karen Axelrod. (Illus.). 328p. (Orig.). 1995. pap. 16.95 (1-56261-157-7) John Muir.

***Watch It Made in the U. S. A. A Visitor's Guide to the Companies That Make Your Favorite Products.** 2nd rev. ed. Bruce Brumberg & Karen Axelrod. LC 97-11093. 368p. 1997. pap. 17.95 (1-56261-337-5) John Muir.

Watch-Keeping Certificate. Brown, Son & Ferguson Ltd. Staff. (C). 1987. 45.00 (0-685-45086-4, Pub. by Brwn Son Ferg) St Mut.

Watch Me. A. J. Holt. 1995. pap. 24.95 (0-7871-0521-X, Dove Bks) Dove Audio.

Watch Me. A. J. Holt. LC 95-31732. 1995. 22.95 (0-312-13614-5) St Martin.

***Watch Me.** A. J. Holt. 1996. mass mkt. 6.99 (0-312-95997-4) St Martin.

***Watch Me Dance.** Pinkney. 1997. pap. write for info. (0-15-200631-1) HarBrace.

***Watch Me Dance.** Andrea Pinkney. (Illus.). (J). 1997. bds. write for info. (0-614-29233-6, Red Wagon Bks) HarBrace.

***Watch Me Go! The Art & Skills of Communication (A Beginning Program, Reading & Comprehensive Language Arts)** Patricia Thurman. (Illus.). 260p. 1996. wbk. ed., pap. text ed. 29.00 (0-9654764-0-5) Creat Acad.

***Watch Me Learn.** (Fisher-Price Preschool Workbook Series II). (Illus.). 72p. (J). (ps). 1997. pap. write for info. (1-56144-922-9, Honey Bear Bks) Modern Pub NYC.

Watch Me Sing, Vol. 1. Janeen Brady. (Illus.). 31p. (J). (ps-2). 1977. audio 8.95 (0-944803-10-5) Brite Music.

Watch Me Sing, Vol. 2. Janeen Brady. (Illus.). 30p. (J). (ps-2). 1986. audio 8.95 (0-944803-12-1) Brite Music.

Watch Me Sing: Songbook, Vol. 1. Janeen Brady. (Illus.). 31p. (J). (ps-2). 1977. pap. text ed. 6.95 (0-944803-09-1) Brite Music.

Watch Me Sing: Songbook, Vol. 2. Janeen Brady. (Illus.). 30p. (J). (ps-2). 1986. pap. text ed. 6.95 (0-944803-11-3) Brite Music.

Watch My Back: A Bouncer's Story. Geoff Thompson. 176p. 1995. pap. 24.95 (0-87364-838-2) Paladin Pr.

Watch of the Future: The Story of the Hamilton Electric Watch. 2nd rev. ed. Rene Rondeau. (Illus.). 168p. (Orig.). 1992. 29.95 (0-9622219-1-0) R Rondeau.

Watch Officer's Guide. 13th ed. Rev. by James Stavridis. LC 91-32947. (Illus.). 352p. 1992. 18.95 (1-55750-904-2) Naval Inst Pr.

Watch on the Rhine. Lillian Hellman. 1944. pap. 5.25 (0-8222-1223-4) Dramatists Play.

Watch on the Right: Conservative Intellectuals in the Reagan Era. J. David Hoeveler, Jr. LC 90-13021. (History of American Thought & Culture Ser.). 348p. 1991. 8.95 (0-299-12810-5) U of Wis Pr.

Watch Out! Richard Hefter. LC 83-2190. (Stickybear Bks.). (Illus.). 32p. (J). (ps-1). 1983. 5.95 (0-911787-03-8) Optimum Res Inc.

***Watch Out! Big Bro's Coming!** Jez Alborough. (Illus.). (J). (ps-3). 1997. 16.99 (0-614-28640-9) Candlewick Pr.

Watch Out! Big Bro's Coming! Jez Alborough. LC 96-30318. (Illus.). 32p. (J). (ps-3). 1997. 16.99 (0-7636-0130-6) Candlewick Pr.

Watch Out for Big Bad Brad. (J). (gr. 2 up). 1991. pap. 1.97 (1-56297-115-8) Lee Pubns KY.

Watch Out for Chicken Feet in Your Soup. Tomie DePaola. (Illus.). 32p. (J). (gr. k-4). 1985. pap. 5.95 (0-671-66745-9, S&S Bks Young Read) S&S Childrens.

Watch Out for Clever Women! Cuidado Con las Mujeres Astutas. Joe Hayes. LC 93-73417. 80p. (Orig.). (J). (gr. 3-7). 1994. 17.95 (0-938317-21-0); pap. 10.95 (0-938317-20-2) Cinco Puntos.

Watch Out for My Nest. Nancy Northrop. (Illus.). 44p. (Orig.). (J). (gr. 1-5). 1994. pap. 5.95 (0-9627894-3-7) LNR Pubns.

Watch Out for Room 13. Laban C. Hill. (Choose Your Own Nightmare Ser.: No. 11). 112p. (J). 1996. pap. 3.50 (0-553-48330-7) BDD Bks Young Read.

***Watch Out for Room 13.** Laban C. Hill. LC 96-36058. (Choose Your Own Nightmare Ser.: No. 11). (Illus.). 96p. (J). (gr. 4 up). 1997. lib. bdg. 15.93 (0-8368-1723-0) Gareth Stevens Inc.

Watch Out for Sharks! Caroline Arnold. (J). (gr. 3-6). 1994. pap. 6.95 (0-395-69941-X, Clarion Bks) HM.

Watch Out for the Chicken Feet in Your Soup. Tomie De Paola. LC 74-8201. (Illus.). 32p. (J). (gr. k-4). 1974. 12.95 (0-685-35587-X, S&S Bks Young Read); pap. 5.95 (0-685-35588-8, S&S Bks Young Read) S&S Childrens.

Watch Out for the Golly Whompers. Dorothy D. Corrigan. LC 88-50754. (Illus.). 35p. (J). (gr. k-3). 1988. 6.95 (1-55523-149-7) Winston-Derek.

Watch Out for the Little Guys. Steve Bloom. 1989. pap. 3.95 (0-312-91742-2) St Martin.

Watch Out! I'm Peeking in Your Window! Shirley Lueth. 140p. (Orig.). 1986. pap. 7.95 (0-937911-00-3) Lueth Hse Pub.

Watch Out! Man-Eating Snake. Patricia R. Giff. (New Kids at the Polk Street School Ser.: No. 1). 80p. (Orig.). (J). (gr. k-6). 1988. pap. 3.50 (0-440-40085-6, YB BDD) BDD Bks Young Read.

Watch Out! Man-Eating Snake. Patricia R. Giff. (Orig.). (J). (gr. 1-4). 1990. 18.00 (0-8446-6378-6) Peter Smith.

Watch Out, Pollyanna! Ruth I. Dowell. (Illus.). 40p. (J). (gr. 2-6). 1986. pap. 4.00 (0-945842-02-3) Pollyanna Prodns.

Watch Out, Ronald Morgan. Patricia R. Giff. (Picture Puffins Ser.). (Illus.). 32p. (J). (gr. k-4). 1986. pap. 4.99 (0-14-050638-1, Puffin) Puffin Bks.

Watch Out! We're Talking: Speaking Out about Incest & Abuse. Intro. by Janice Mirikitani et al. 206p. (Orig.). 1993. pap. 12.95 (0-9622574-2-7) Glide Word.

Watch Out! Word Bird. Jane B. Moncure. (Word Bird Library). (Illus.). 32p. (J). (ps-2). 1982. lib. bdg. 21.36 (0-89565-219-6) Childs World.

Watch Out World...Here Comes Barbell Brock, Vol. 1: America's Funniest Strongman. Ronald Martin. (Illus.). 64p. (Orig.). 1988. pap. 3.00 (0-685-22540-2) Christian H & D Pubs.

Watch over Mortality: The Philosophical Story of Julian Marias. Harold Raley. LC 96-3773. (SUNY Series in Latin American & Iberian Thought & Culture). 320p. (C). 1996. text ed. 65.50 (0-7914-3153-3); pap. text ed. 21.95 (0-7914-3154-1) State U NY Pr.

Watch Repairer's Manual. 4th rev. ed. Henry B. Fried. (Illus.). 35.00 (0-918845-11-4) Am Watchmakers.

Watch Repairing As a Hobby. D. W. Fletcher. LC 84-24634. (Illus.). 12p. 1995. reprint ed. pap. 5.00 (0-930163-24-9) US Bks.

Watch Repairing, Cleaning & Adjusting. F. J. Garrard. (Illus.). 214p. 1988. pap. 16.95 (0-930163-17-6) Arlington Bk.

Watch That Made the Dollar Famous. rev. ed. Townsend & Ralph Whitmer. 45p. 1994. 25.00 (0-913902-39-X) Heart Am Pr.

Watch the Birdie. Norman Krasna. 1969. pap. 5.25 (0-8222-1224-2) Dramatists Play.

Watch the Bubbles Rise. I. J. Donnelly & B. A. Christian. LC 90-55254. 104p. (Orig.). 1991. pap. 7.00 (1-56002-063-6) Aegina Pr.

***Watch the Day Move.** Lomonaco. (J). Date not set. 14.95 (0-399-22162-X) Putnam Pub Group.

Watch the Flame. Eleni Fourtouni. (Greek Women Poets Ser.). 78p. (Orig.). 1983. pap. 11.95 (0-915017-04-0) Thelpini Pr.

Watch the Lamb. Terry Bell. 156p. 1989. pap. 5.99 (0-89225-344-4) Gospel Advocate.

Watch the Skies! A Chronicle of the Flying Saucer Myth. Curtis Peebles. 432p. (Orig.). 1995. mass mkt. 6.99 (0-425-15117-4) Berkley Pub.

Watch the Skies! A Chronicle of the Flying Saucer Myth. Curtis Peebles. LC 93-26819. 368p. (Orig.). 1994. 24.95 (1-56098-343-4) Smithsonian.

Watch the Stars Come Out. Riki Levinson. LC 84-28672. (Illus.). 32p. (J). (ps-3). 1985. pap. 15.00 (0-525-44205-7) Dutton Child Bks.

Watch the Stars Come Out. Riki Levinson. (Illus.). 32p. (J). 1995. pap. 5.99 (0-14-055506-4) Puffin Bks.

Watch Them Grow. Linda Martin. LC 93-25426. (Illus.). 48p. (J). (ps-1). 1994. 14.95 (1-56458-458-5) DK Pub Inc.

***Watch Us Play.** Miela Ford. LC 97-6948. 24p. (J). (ps up). 1998. 15.00 (0-688-15606-1); lib. bdg. 14.93 (0-688-15607-X) Greenwillow.

Watch What I Can Do! see Hewitt Early Readers: Level II

Watch What I Do: Programming by Demonstration. Ed. by Ellen Cypher. LC 93-18319. 672p. 1993. 52.50 (0-262-03213-9) MIT Pr.

Watch Where the Wolf Is Going. Antonio Skarmeta. 192p. (Orig.). 1991. 18.95 (0-930523-83-0); pap. 10.95 (0-930523-84-9) Readers Intl.

***Watch Where You Go!** Sally Nol. (FRE.). (J). pap. 5.99 (0-590-24231-8) Scholastic Inc.

Watch Where You Go. Sally Noll. LC 92-25333. (J). 1993. reprint ed. pap. 3.99 (0-14-054884-X) Puffin Bks.

Watch William Walk. Ann Jonas. LC 96-7467. (Illus.). 24p. (J). (ps up). 1997. 15.00 (0-688-14172-2); lib. bdg. 14.93 (0-688-14175-7) Greenwillow.

Watch with Me. Wendell Berry. 224p. 1995. pap. 11.00 (0-679-75854-2) Pantheon.

Watch-Word!!! Argus J. Tresidder. 110p. 1981. reprint ed. 2.50 (0-940328-00-3) Marine Corps.

Watch World Events Relating to the Bible in 1989. Charles R. Taylor. (Today in Bible Prophecy Ser.). Orig. Title: Watch, 1989. (Illus.). 120p. (Orig.). 1989. pap. 3.95 (0-937682-10-1) Today Bible.

Watch Your Child's Weight. Jennifer J. Ashcroft & R. Glynn Owens. 160p. 1987. pap. 10.95 (0-19-261645-5) OUP.

Watch Your Cleavage, Check Your Zipper! Guy Lebow. 1994. pap. 5.99 (1-56171-284-1, S P I Bks) Sure Seller.

Watch Your Dreams. Ann R. Colton. LC 96-83735. 124p. 1960. pap. 15.95 (0-917189-18-3) A R Colton Fnd.

Watch Your Language: Bk. 1. Ed. by Brian Schenk et al. 192p. 1988. pap. text ed. 6.30 (0-8428-9700-3); Exercise wkbk. student ed., pap. text ed. 4.00 (0-8428-9706-2); Student ans. bk. student ed., pap. text ed. 1.40 (0-8428-9707-0) Cambridge Bk.

Watch Your Language: Bk. 1. Ed. by Brian Schenk et al. 192p. 1988. Student ans. bk. student ed., pap. text ed. 1.40 (0-8428-9701-1) Cambridge Bk.

Watch Your Language: Bk. 2. Ed. by Brian Schenk et al. 192p. 1988. pap. text ed. 6.30 (0-8428-9702-X); Exercise wkbk. student ed., pap. text ed. 4.00 (0-8428-9708-9); Student ans. bk. student ed., pap. text ed. 1.40 (0-8428-9703-8) Cambridge Bk.

Watch Your Language! Mother Tongue & Her Wayward Children. Robert Gorrell. LC 93-33528. 232p. 1994. 21.95 (0-87417-235-7) U of Nev Pr.

Watch Your Life & Doctrine Closely. Darvin H. Raddatz. 94p. (Orig.). 1990. pap. 5.99 (0-8100-0348-1, 070757) Northwest Pub.

Watch Your Step: The Amazing World Beneath Your Feet. Stephen Tchudi. (J). Date not set. 15.95 (0-689-80580-2) S&S Childrens.

Watch Your Step: The Amazing World Beneath Your Feet. Stephen Tchudi. (J). 1995. 15.95 (0-684-19713-8, Atheneum Bks Young) S&S Childrens.

Watch Your Step, Mr. Rabbit! Richard Scarry. LC 90-34336. (Pictureback Ser.). (Illus.). 24p. (Orig.). (J). (ps-2). 1991. pap. 3.25 (0-679-81072-2) Random Bks Yng Read.

***Watch Your Step, Mr. Rabbit.** Richard Scarry. (J). 1997. lib. bdg. 11.99 (0-679-98650-2) Random Bks Yng Read.

***Watch Your Step, Mr. Rabbit.** Richard Scarry. (J). 1997. pap. 3.99 (0-679-88650-8) Random.

Watch, 1989 see Watch World Events Relating to the Bible in 1989

Watchable Birds of the Rocky Mountains. Mary T. Gray. Ed. by Kathleen Ort. (Illus.). 163p. (Orig.). 1992. pap. 14.00 (0-87842-281-1) Mountain Pr.

Watchable Birds of the Southwest. Mary T. Gray. LC 95-34354. 187p. 1995. pap. 14.00 (0-87842-322-2) Mountain Pr.

Watchboy, What of the Night? Turner Cassity. 1991. pap. 15.00 (0-936576-15-4) Symposium Pr.

Watchdog & the Coyotes. Bill Wallace. 105p. (J). (gr. 3-6). Date not set. pap. 3.50 (0-671-89075-1, PB Trade Paper) PB.

Watchdog & the Coyotes. Bill Wallace. 105p. (J). (gr. 3-6). 1995. 14.00 (0-671-53620-6, PB Hardcover) PB.

Watchdog Concept: The Press & the Courts in Nineteenth-Century America. Timothy W. Gleason. LC 89-15265. 160p. 1990. reprint ed. pap. 45.60 (0-608-00111-2, 2060876) Bks Demand.

Watchdog of Loyalty: The Minnesota Commission of Public Safety During World War I. Carl H. Chrislock. LC 91-11228. (Illus.). xvi, 387p. 1991. 39.95 (0-87351-263-4); pap. 19.95 (0-87351-264-2) Minn Hist.

Watchdogs of Terror. Peter Deriabin. LC 84-11873. (Foreign Intelligence Book Ser.). 469p. 1984. text ed. 65.00 (0-313-27040-6, U7040, Greenwood Pr) Greenwood.

Watchdogs of Wall Street. Hillel Black. LC 75-2621. (Wall Street & the Security Market Ser.). 1975. reprint ed. 23.95 (0-405-06948-0) Ayer.

Watched. Dee Holmes. (Intimate Moments Ser.). 1994. mass mkt. 3.50 (0-373-07591-X, 1-07591-0) Harlequin Bks.

***Watcher.** James Howe. (Illus.). (YA). (gr. 7 up). 1997. 15.00 (0-614-29092-9, Atheneum Bks Young) S&S Childrens.

Watcher. James Howe. 172p. (J). 1997. 15.00 (0-689-80186-6, Atheneum Bks Young) S&S Childrens.

Watcher. Lael J. Littke. 208p. (YA). (gr. 7-9). 1994. pap. 3.50 (0-590-47088-4) Scholastic Inc.

Watcher. Brenda Silsbe. (Illus.). 24p. (J). (ps-2). 1995. pap. 4.95 (1-55037-384-6, Pub. by Annick CN) Firefly Bks Ltd.

Watcher. Brenda Silsbe. (Illus.). 24p. (J). (ps-2). 1995. lib. bdg. 15.95 (1-55037-385-4, Pub. by Annick CN) Firefly Bks Ltd.

***Watcher: Werewolf.** Charles Grant. 288p. 1997. mass mkt. 5.50 (0-06-105672-3, HarperPrism) HarpC.

Watcher & Other Stories. Italo Calvino. Tr. by William Weaver & Archibald Colquhoun from ITA. LC 75-9829. 181p. 1975. pap. 9.00 (0-15-694952-0, Harvest Bks) HarBrace.

Watcher & Other Weird Stories. Joseph S. Le Fanu. Ed. by Devendra P. Varma. LC 76-5279. (Collected Works). (Illus.). 1977. reprint ed. 26.95 (0-405-09241-5) Ayer.

Watcher at the Nest. M. M. Nice. (Illus.). 1990. 11.75 (0-8446-2656-2) Peter Smith.

Watcher by the Threshold. John Buchan. 1988. reprint ed. lib. bdg. 59.00 (0-7812-0013-X) Rprt Serv.

Watcher by the Threshold. John Buchan. 1971. reprint ed. 39.00 (0-403-00880-8) Scholarly.

Watcher from Another World. J. Wilson. 1995. 5.99 (1-871676-72-X, Pub. by Christian Focus UK) Spring Arbor Dist.

Watcher from the Shore. Ayako Sono. Tr. by Edward Putzar. 376p. 1990. 19.95 (0-87011-938-9) Kodansha.

Watcher in the Dark. Beverly Hastings. 160p. (YA). 1986. pap. 3.99 (0-425-10131-2, Berkley-Pacer) Berkley Pub.

Watcher in the Woods. Patricia Sibley. (Illus.). 128p. text ed. 25.95 (0-905483-82-0, Pub. by Whittet Bks UK) Diamond Farm Bk.

Watcher of Waipuna & Other Stories. Gary Pak. LC 92-426. (Bamboo Ridge Ser.: Nos. 55-56). 179p. 1992. pap. 8.00 (0-910043-28-0) Bamboo Ridge Pr.

Watcher on the Cast-Iron Balcony. Hal Porter. (Orig.). 1993. pap. 16.95 (0-7022-2558-4, Pub. by Univ Queensland Pr AT) Intl Spec Bk.

Watcher on the Shore. large type ed. Isobel Lambot. 336p. 1988. 25.99 (0-7089-1914-6) Ulverscroft.

***Watcher on the Wharf.** Bird & Falk. (New Trend Fiction C Ser.). (J). 1993. pap. text ed. write for info. (0-582-80041-2, Pub. by Longman UK) Longman.

Watchers. Raymond E. Fowler. 416p. 1991. pap. 5.99 (0-553-28733-8) Bantam.

Watchers. Dean R. Koontz. 496p. 1988. mass mkt. 7.50 (0-425-10746-9) Berkley Pub.

Watchers. large type ed. Dean R. Koontz. 744p. 1991. reprint ed. lib. bdg. 20.95 (1-56054-221-7) Thorndike Pr.

Watchers: A Mystery at Alton Towers. Helen Cresswell. LC 93-41683. 160p. (J). (gr. 3-7). 1994. text ed. 15.95 (0-02-725371-6, Mac Bks Young Read) S&S Childrens.

***Watchers & Seekers: Creative Writing by Black Women in Britain.** Ed. by Rhonda Cobham & Merle Collins. pap. 13.95 (0-7043-4024-0, Pub. by Womens Press UK) Trafalgar.

Watchers at the Strait Gate: Mystical Tales. Russell Kirk. LC 84-267. (Illus.). 256p. 1984. 14.95 (0-87054-098-X) Arkham.

Watchers at the Well, 3 vols. in 1. Jack L. Chalker. 800p. 1994. 14.98 (1-56865-123-6, GuildAmerica) Dblday Direct.

Watchers by the Pool. Margaret Reinhold. (Illus.). 192p. 1993. 18.95 (0-7867-0009-2) Carroll & Graf.

Watchers II Vol. 1: Exploring UFO's & the Near Death Experience. Raymond E. Fowler. Ed. by Amy O. Demmon. (Illus.). 57p. 1996. pap. 18.95 (0-962524-30-5) Blue Wtr Pubng.

Watcher's Mask. Laurie J. Marks. 288p. (Orig.). 1992. mass mkt. 4.99 (0-88677-510-8) DAW Bks.

Watchers, Moles, & Assassins. Steve Thompson. 286p. (Orig.). 1996. mass mkt. 4.99 (1-55197-188-7, Pub. by Comnwlth Pub CN) Partners Pubs Grp.

Watchers of the Sky. Alfred Noyes. 1988. reprint ed. lib. bdg. 59.00 (0-7812-0390-2) Rprt Serv.

Watchers of the Sky. Alfred Noyes. LC 72-131790. 1971. reprint ed. 29.00 (0-403-00677-5) Scholarly.

***Watchers Out of Time.** H. P. Lovecraft & August Derleth. 4.95 (0-7867-0769-0) Carroll & Graf.

Watchers Out of Time. H. P. Lovecraft & August Derleth. 272p. 1991. pap. 4.95 (0-88184-769-0) Carroll & Graf.

Watcher's Three. Linda Gregorino & Melva Libb. (Illus.). 64p. 3.95 (0-936369-46-9) Son Rise Pubns.

Watches, Their History Decoration & Mechanism. G. H. Baillie. (Illus.). 379p. 1979. 75.00 (0-7198-0140-0, Pub. by NAG Press UK) Antique Collect.

Watchfriends & Rack Screams: Works from the Final Period, 1945-48. Antonin Artaud. Ed. by Clayton Eshleman & Bernard Bador. Tr. by Bernard Bador. 352p. 1995. pap. 15.95 (1-878972-18-9) Exact Change.

Watchful Eye: American Justice in the Age of the Television Trial. Paul Thaler. LC 93-4257. 264p. 1994. text ed. 59.95 (0-275-94215-5, Praeger Pubs) Greenwood.

Watchful Eye: American Justice in the Age of the Television Trial. Paul Thaler. LC 93-4257. 264p. 1994. pap. text ed. 18.95 (0-275-95133-2, Praeger Pubs) Greenwood.

Watchful Heart: Daily Reading with Ruth Burrows. Ed. by Elizabeth R. Obbard. 1992. pap. 6.95 (0-87193-283-0) Dimension Bks.

Watching. Todd Moore. 36p. (Orig.). 1985. pap. 4.00 (0-935390-10-3) Wormwood Bks & Mag.

***Watching.** John Ryan. 1997. 22.00 (0-8038-9398-1) Hastings.

Watching & Wondering: Observing & Recording Child Development. Judith G. Isaksen. LC 86-60469. 231p. (C). 1986. pap. 24.95 (0-87484-755-9, 755) Mayfield Pub.

Watching Birds in Ireland. Clive Hutchinson. (Illus.). 144p. (Orig.). 1995. pap. 9.95 (0-946172-08-0, Pub. by Town Hse IE) R Rinehart.

Watching Bradley Grow: A Story about Premature Birth. Elizabeth Murphy-Melas. (Illus.). (J). (gr. k-4). 1995. pap. 8.95 (1-56352-282-9) Longstreet Pr Inc.

Watching Channel One: The Convergence of Students, Technology, & Private Business. Ed. by Ann De Vaney. LC 93-28980. (SUNY Series, Education & Culture). 244p. 1994. text ed. 64.50 (0-7914-1947-9); pap. text ed. 21.95 (0-7914-1948-7) State U NY Pr.

Watching Children Read & Write: Observational Records for Children with Special Needs. Max Kemp. (Illus.). 263p. (Orig.). 1990. pap. text ed. 36.00 (0-435-08514-X, 08514) Heinemann.

Watching Dallas. Ien Ang. 1986. pap. 8.95 (0-416-41640-3) Routledge Chapman & Hall.

Watching Dallas: Soap Opera & the Melodramatic Imagination. Ien Ang. 224p. (C). 1985. pap. 9.50 (0-415-04598-3, 9781) Routledge Chapman & Hall.

Watching Dan Quayle: Problems in Participant Observation. Richard F. Fenno, Jr. 1990. pap. 1.00 (1-55614-132-7) U of SD Gov Res Bur.

Watching Desert Wildlife. Caroline Arnold. LC 93-48076. (Nature Watch Bks.). (Illus.). (J). (gr. 2-5). 1994. lib. bdg. 14.21 (0-87614-841-0, Carolrhoda) Lerner Group.

Watching English Change: An Introduction to the Study of Linguistic Change in the Twentieth Century. Laurie Bauer. LC 93-38602. (Learning about Language Ser.). 1994. write for info. (0-582-21089-5) Longman.

Watching for Willa. Helen R. Myers. (Shadows Ser.). 1995. mass mkt. 3.50 (0-373-27049-6, 1-27049-5) Silhouette.

Watching Foxes. Jim Arnosky. LC 84-20157. (Illus.). 24p. (J). (ps-3). 1985. 12.95 (0-688-04259-7); lib. bdg. 12.88 (0-688-04260-0) Lothrop.

Watching from the Sky. Ed. by Martha Ann Blackman. (Illus.). 32p. (Orig.). 1989. pap. 6.00 (0-914485-12-1) Trill Pr.

Watching How or Why. Larry Eigner. 1977. 5.00 (0-685-88994-7); bds., boxed 10.00 (0-685-88993-9) Elizabeth Pr.

Watching Kansas Wildlife: A Guide to 101 Sites. Bob Gress & George A. Potts. LC 92-41094. (Illus.). xiii, 104p. (Orig.). 1993. pap. 9.95 (0-7006-0594-0) U Pr of KS.

Watching, Listening & Loving. Bonnie Seefeldt. 77p. 1985. pap. 10.00 (1-884112-04-8) See More Bks.

Watching Media Learning. David Buckingham. 224p. 1990. 75.00 (1-85000-652-0, Falmer Pr); pap. 33.00 (1-85000-653-9, Falmer Pr) Taylor & Francis.

***Watching My Language.** William Safire. 1997. write for info. (0-679-44905-1) Random.

Watching My Language. William Safire. LC 95-3800. 1997. 27.50 (0-679-42387-7) Random.

***Watching Nature.** Monica Russo. Date not set. write for info. (0-8069-9515-7) Sterling.

***Watching Nature: A Mid-Atlantic Natural History.** Mark S. Garland. LC 97-846. (Illus.). 256p. (Orig.). 1997. pap. 15.95 (1-56098-742-1) Smithsonian.

***Watching Our Crops.** Clifton Taulbert. 1998. pap. 8.95 (0-14-024434-4) Viking Penguin.

***Watching Our Crops Come In.** Clifton M. Taulbert. 1997. pap. 15.95 (0-670-85952-4, Viking) Viking Penguin.

***Watching Our Feathered Friends.** Dean T. Spaulding. LC 96-25128. (Birder's Bookshelf Ser.). (J). 1997. write for info. (0-8225-3177-1) Lerner Group.

Watching Over Israel from Elijah. Mendelssohn. 8p. 1986. pap. 1.25 (0-7935-5479-9, 50293760) H Leonard.

Watching Police, Watching Communities. Michael McConville & Dan Shepherd. LC 91-29553. 288p. (C). 1992. text ed. 110.00 (0-415-07364-2, Routledge NY) Routledge.

Watching Politicians: Essays on Participant Observation. Richard F. Fenno, Jr. LC 89-26974. 133p. (Orig.). 1990. pap. 11.95 (0-87772-323-0) UCB IGS.

W

Watching Race: Television & the Struggle for "Blackness" Herman Gray. LC 94-31783. 224p. 1995. 22.95 (*0-8166-2250-7*) U of Minn Pr.

Watching Race: Television & the Struggle for "Blackness" Herman Gray. LC 94-31783. 216p. (C). 1997. pap. text ed. 16.95 (*0-8166-2251-5*) U of Minn Pr.

Watching Shakespeare on Television. Herbert R. Coursen. LC 92-55123. 1993. 34.50 (*0-8386-3521-0*) Fairleigh Dickinson.

Watching Television. Ed. by Todd Gitlin. LC 86-42640. 256p. 1987. pap. 13.00 (*0-394-74651-1*) Pantheon.

***Watching the Contortionists.** Laura L. Washburn. 1997. pap. 5.00 (*1-889806-14-5*) Devils Millhopper.

Watching the Detectives: Essays on Crime Fiction. Ed. by Ian A. Bell & Graham Daldry. LC 89-24158. 249p. 1990. text ed. 39.95 (*0-312-04068-7*) St Martin.

Watching the Fire-Eater. Robert Minhinnick. 139p. 1993. pap. 15.95 (*1-85411-075-6*, Pub. by Seren Bks UK) Dufour.

Watching the Fire Eater. Robert Minhinnick. 139p. 1993. pap. 15.95 (*0-685-67834-2*, Pub. by Seren Bks UK) Dufour.

***Watching the Morning Grow.** Pearse Hutchinson. 48p. 7200. pap. 11.95 (*0-904011-00-3*) Dufour.

***Watching the River Flow: Observations on Bob Dylan's Art-in-Progress, 1966-1995.** Paul Williams. 256p. 1997. 39.95 (*0-934558-18-3*) Entwhistle Bks.

Watching the Rose. Geras. 1997. pap. write for info. (*0-15-201517-5*) HarBrace.

Watching the Watchers: Corporate Governance for the 21st Century. Robert Monks & Nell Minnow. 320p. 1996. text ed. 24.95 (*1-55786-866-2*) Blackwell Pubs.

Watching the World. Raymond Clapper. (FDR & the Era of the New Deal Ser.). 1975. reprint ed. 45.00 (*0-306-70730-6*) Da Capo.

Watching the World's Weather. William J. Burroughs. (Illus.). 250p. (C). 1991. text ed. 28.95 (*0-521-34342-9*) Cambridge U Pr.

Watching Their Figures - a Guide to Citizen's Charter Indicators. 80p. 1994. pap. 25.00 (*0-11-886123-9*, HM61239, Pub. by Stationery Ofc UK) Bernan Associates.

Watching TV with the Red Chinese. Luke Whisnant. 320p. 1994. pap. 10.99 (*0-446-67007-3*) Warner Bks.

Watching TV with the Red Chinese: A Novel. Luke Whisnant. LC 92-10034. 320p. 1992. 17.95 (*0-945575-83-1*) Algonquin Bks.

Watching Vanessa. unabridged ed. Patricia M. Tiffin. LC 97-3560. 320p. 1997. 22.00 (*1-880909-54-5*) Baskerville.

***Watching Wanda: The Migration of a Gray Whale.** Stacey Ytuarte & Frederick Spurgeon. (Illus.). 53p. (J). (gr. 3-5). 1996. 14.95 (*0-9653150-0-2*) Seascript Pubns.

***Watching Water Birds.** Jim Arnosky. LC 97-7594. (J). 1997. write for info. (*0-7922-7073-8*) Natl Geog.

***Watching Water Birds.** Jim Aronsky. (Illus.). (J). 1997. write for info. (*0-614-29272-7*) Natl Geog.

Watching Whales. Jason Cooper. LC 96-19192. (Read All About Whales Ser.). (J). 1996. write for info. (*0-86593-451-7*) Rourke Corp.

Watching Wildlife: A Companion to the Watchable Wildlife Series. Mark D. Duda. LC 95-26073. (Watchable Wildlife Ser.). (Illus.). 117p. 1995. pap. 9.95 (*1-56044-315-4*) Falcon Pr MT.

Watching Wildlife: The National Wildlife Federation Guide to Observing Animals in the Wild. Joe La Tourrette. LC 96-44345. (Illus.). 160p. 1997. pap. 12.95 (*0-8050-4685-2*, Owl) H Holt & Co.

Watching Wisteria: Poems by Duane Locke. Duane Locke. LC 95-60912. 80p. 1995. 19.95 (*0-9632547-4-X*); pap. 9.95 (*0-9632547-5-8*) Vida Pub.

Watchmaker's Daughter. J. Watson. 5.99 (*1-85792-116-X*, Pub. by Christian Focus UK) Spring Arbor Dist.

Watchmaker's Lathe. Ward Goodrich. (Illus.). 264p. 1987. pap. 16.95 (*0-930163-34-6*) Arlington Bk.

***Watchman.** Jonathan Littman. 1997. 24.95 (*0-316-52857-9*) Little.

Watchman. Jack Rudman. (Career Examination Ser.: C-891). 1994. pap. 23.95 (*0-8373-0891-7*) Nat Learn.

Watchman see Collected Works of Samuel T. Coleridge

***"Watchman? How Far Gone Is the Night?" "The End Is Coming on the Four Corners of the Land"** John M. Stephenson. (Illus.). 262p. (Orig.). 1995. pap. 12.95 (*0-9636077-1-5*) Living-Faith.

Watchman in Babylon: A Study Guide to Ezekiel. John Job. 112p. (Orig.). 1982. pap. 6.95 (*0-85364-339-3*) Attic Pr.

Watchman Nee: A Seer Of The Divine Revelation In The Present Age. Witness Lee. 348p. boxed 17.25 (*0-87083-625-0*, 20001901) Living Stream Ministry.

Watchman Nee's Testimony. Watchman Nee. 57p. per. 2.25 (*0-87083-051-1*, 20006001) Living Stream Ministry.

***Watchman on the Walls: Praying Character into Your Child.** rev. ed. Gary Harrell et al. text ed. 12.95 (*1-57229-026-9*) FamilyLife.

Watchman Warning: The Endtimes Are Unfolding. John M. Stephenson. (Illus.). 470p. 1994. pap. 24.95 (*0-9636077-0-7*) Living-Faith.

***Watchman 1796.** Samuel T. Coleridge. 324p. 1998. 75.00 (*1-85477-198-1*, Pub. by Woodstock Bks UK) Cassell.

Watchman's Stone. large type ed. Rona Randall. 464p. 1995. 25.99 (*0-7089-3280-0*) Ulverscroft.

Watchmen. Ben Bova. 432p. 1994. mass mkt. 5.99 (*0-671-87598-1*) Baen Bks.

Watchmen. Alan Moore. Ed. by Barry Marx. 416p. 1989. pap. 19.95 (*0-930289-23-4*) DC Comics.

Watchmen. Alan Moore & Dave Gibbons. 384p. 1987. pap. 14.95 (*0-446-38689-8*) Warner Bks.

***Watchmen: Draw Your Way Through the Bible.** Dan Peters. (Picturethis! Ser.: No. 5). (Illus.). 70p. 1997. ring bd. write for info. (*1-890598-15-1*) PictureThis.

Watchmen of the House. S. R. Holman. LC 96-92295. 180p. (Orig.). 1996. pap. 12.95 (*1-889298-59-X*, 3000) Wordspace.

Watchmen on the Walls: Pastors Equipping Christians for Their Civil Duties. Bruce Anderson et al. 70p. 1995. pap. 5.95 (*1-887456-02-3*) Providence Found.

Watchmen Who Wouldn't Quit. Pam Campbell & Stan Campbell. (BibleLog Ser.). 180p. (Orig.). 1992. pap. 8.99 (*0-89693-874-3*, 6-1874, Victor Bks) Chariot Victor.

Watchstanding Guide for the Merchant Marine. Robert J. Meurn. LC 89-71208. (Illus.). 256p. 1990. text ed. 27.50 (*0-87033-409-3*) Cornell Maritime.

Watchtower Files. Duane Magnani & Arthur Barrett. LC 84-28318. 304p. (Orig.). 1985. pap. 10.99 (*0-87123-816-0*) Bethany Hse.

Watcom C/C++ Unleashed. 900p. Date not set. 49.99 (*0-672-30893-2*) Sams.

Water. Frank Asch. LC 93-47967. (Gulliver Green Book Ser.). (Illus.). 32p. (J). (ps-2). 1995. 14.00 (*0-15-200189-1*, Gulliver Bks) HarBrace.

Water. Ashokamitran. (Asian Writers Ser.). 96p. 1994. pap. 9.95 (*0-435-95085-1*, 95085) Heinemann.

Water. Paul Caro. 132p. 1993. pap. text ed. 11.95 (*0-07-009990-1*) McGraw.

Water. Andrew Charman. LC 93-20880. (What About...? Ser.). (J). 1994. lib. bdg. 19.97 (*0-8114-5508-4*) Raintree Steck-V.

Water. Chris Ellis. (Illus.). 48p. (J). (gr. 7-9). 1992. 13.95 (*0-563-34756-2*, BBC-Parkwest); pap. 7.95 (*0-563-34616-7*, BBC-Parkwest) Parkwest Pubns.

Water. Franks. 1989. 19.00 (*0-85186-473-2*) CRC Pr.

***Water.** Kay. 832p. 1997. text ed. write for info. (*0-419-21840-8*, E & FN Spon) Routledge Chapman & Hall.

Water. Jenny Markert. (Images Ser.). (J). (gr. 5 up). 1992. lib. bdg. 16.95 (*0-88682-431-1*) Creative Ed.

Water. Diane McClymont. Ed. by Richard Young. LC 91-20536. (First Technology Library). (Illus.). 32p. (J). (gr. 3-5). 1991. lib. bdg. 15.93 (*1-56074-006-X*) Garrett Ed Corp.

Water. Sally Morgan & Adrian Morgan. LC 93-31721. (Designs in Science Ser.). (Illus.). 48p. (YA). (gr. 5-9). 1994. 14.95 (*0-8160-2982-2*) Facts on File.

***Water.** Steve Parker. (Library of Science Projects). (Illus.). 44p. (YA). (gr. 4 up). 1996. lib. bdg. 15.95 (*0-86307-627-0*) Marshall Cavendish.

Water. J. M. Parramon et al. (Four Elements Ser.). 32p. (J). (ps). 1985. pap. 6.95 (*0-8120-3599-2*) Barron.

Water. Molly Perham & Julian Rowe. LC 94-39691. (MapWorlds Ser.). (Illus.). 32p. (J). (gr. 5-8). 1996. lib. bdg. 18.60 (*0-531-14361-9*) Watts.

Water. Philip Sauvain. LC 91-19145. (Way It Works Ser.). (Illus.). 48p. (J). (gr. 4-8). 1992. lib. bdg. 13.95 (*0-02-781078-X*, Mac Bks Young Read) S&S Childrens.

Water. Bonita Searle-Barnes. LC 50-88. (Wonder of God's World Ser.). (Illus.). 32p. (J). (gr. k-3). 1993. 6.99 (*0-7459-2693-2*) Lion USA.

Water. Andrienne Soutter-Perrot. (My First Nature Bks.). (J). (gr. 5 up). 1992. lib. bdg. 10.95 (*0-88682-549-0*) Creative Ed.

Water. Sue Thomas. 240p. 1994. 21.95 (*0-87951-532-5*) Overlook Pr.

Water. Sue Thomas. 240p. 1995. pap. 11.95 (*0-87951-600-3*) Overlook Pr.

Water. Pierre-Marie Valat. Tr. by Peter Christiansen. (First Discovery Book Ser.). (Illus.). 24p. (J). 1996. 11.95 (*0-590-62369-9*, Cartwheel) Scholastic Inc.

Water. Brenda Walpole. Ed. by Rebecca Stefoff. LC 90-40381. (Threads Ser.). (Illus.). 32p. (J). (gr. 3-5). 1990. lib. bdg. 15.93 (*0-944483-72-0*) Garrett Ed Corp.

Water. Cyril S. Fox. LC 75-138233. (Illus.). 148p. 1972. reprint ed. text ed. 52.50 (*0-8371-5590-8*, FOWA, Greenwood Pr) Greenwood.

Water: A Comprehensive Treatise, 6 vols. Ed. by Felix Franks. Incl. Vol. 1. Physics & Physical Chemistry of Water. 596p. 1972. 125.00 (*0-306-37181-2*); Vol. 2. Water in Crystalline Hydrates. 682p. 1973. 125.00 (*0-306-37182-0*); Vol. 7. Water & Aqueous Solutions at Subzero Temperatures. 400p. 1982. 125.00 (*0-306-40710-8*); (Illus.). write for info. (*0-318-55338-4*, Plenum Pr) Plenum.

***Water: A Natural History.** Alice Outwater. 224p. 1997. pap. 18.00 (*0-465-03780-1*) Basic.

Water: A Resource in Crisis. Eileen Lucas. LC 91-36137. (Saving Planet Earth Ser.). (Illus.). 128p. (J). (gr. 4-8). 1991. lib. bdg. 29.30 (*0-516-05509-7*) Childrens.

Water: A Thematic Unit. David Jefferies. (Thematic Units Ser.). (Illus.). 80p. (Orig.). (J). (gr. 3-5). 1993. student ed., pap. 9.95 (*1-55734-231-8*) Tchr Create Mat.

Water: Almost Enough for Everyone. Stephanie Ocko. (Illus.). 140p. (YA). (gr. 7 up). 1995. 16.00 (*0-689-31797-2*, Atheneum Bks Young) S&S Childrens.

***Water: An Amazing Pop-Up, Pull-Tab, Lift-the-Flap Guide.** Francois Michel. (Illus.). 10p. (J). 4.98 (*0-8317-2834-5*) Smithmark.

Water: Canadian Needs & Resources. 3rd ed. J. S. Cram. LC 74-171154. (Environment Ser.). 220p. reprint ed. pap. 62.70 (*0-317-28411-8*, 2022290) Bks Demand.

Water: Healer or Poison? Jan De Vries. (By Appointment Only Ser.). 123p. 1988. pap. 11.95 (*1-85158-341-6*, Pub. by Mnstream UK) Trafalgar.

Water: Its Global Nature. Michael Allaby. (Elements Ser.). (Illus.). 208p. 1992. 35.00 (*0-8160-2526-6*) Facts on File.

Water: Nature's Precious Resource. National Rivers Authority Staff. 96p. 1994. pap. 45.00 (*0-11-886523-4*, HM65234, Pub. by Stationery Ofc UK) Bernan Associates.

Water: Opposing Viewpoints. Ed. by Carol Wekesser. LC 93-12374. 192p. (YA). 1994. pap. 12.96 (*1-56510-063-8*); lib. bdg. 20.96 (*1-56510-064-6*) Greenhaven.

Water: Rethinking Management in an Age of Scarcity. Sandra Postel. LC 84-52522. (Worldwatch Papers). 1984. pap. 4.00 (*0-916468-62-3*) Worldwatch Inst.

***Water: Sheba's Story.** Alice R. Hayes. LC 97-2929. (Illus.). 32p. 1997. 26.95 (*1-880404-17-6*) Bkwrights.

***Water: Sheba's Story.** Alice R. Hayes. (Illus.). 32p. 1997. pap. 17.95 (*1-880404-19-2*) Bkwrights.

Water: Simple Experiments for Young Scientists. Larry White. LC 94-10818. (Gateway Science Ser.). (Illus.). 48p. (J). (gr. 2-4). 1995. lib. bdg. 14.90 (*1-56294-472-X*) Millbrook Pr.

Water: Simple Experiments for Young Scientists. Larry White. (Gateway Science Ser.). (Illus.). 48p. (J). (gr. 2-4). 1996. pap. 6.95 (*0-7613-0090-2*) Millbrook Pr.

Water: The Book of John. (New International Version Ser.). 80p. (CHI & ENG.). 1983. pap. (*1-880349-50-7*) Pocket Testament.

Water: The Elements. Ken Robbins. (Elements Ser.). (Illus.). 48p. (J). 1994. 16.95 (*0-8050-2257-0*, Bks Young Read) H Holt & Co.

Water: The International Crisis. Robin Clarke. LC 92-36487. (Illus.). 193p. (Orig.). (C). 1993. 30.00 (*0-262-03208-2*); pap. 15.95 (*0-262-53116-X*) MIT Pr.

Water: The Nature, Uses, & Future of Our Most Precious & Abused Resource. Fred Powledge. 384p. 1983. pap. 7.95 (*0-374-51798-3*) FS&G.

Water- What It Is, What It Does. Judith S. Seixas. LC 86-14926. (Greenwillow Read-Alone Bks.). (Illus.). 56p. (J). (gr. 1-4). 1987. 16.00 (*0-688-06607-0*); lib. bdg. 15.93 (*0-688-06608-9*) Greenwillow.

Water, a Gift of Nature: The Story Behind the Scenery. Sandra Robinson et al. LC 93-77028. (Illus.). 48p. (Orig.). 1993. pap. 7.95 (*0-88714-077-7*) KC Pubns.

***Water, a Story of Hope.** (Illus.). 24p. 1995. pap. 5.00 (*0-614-30378-8*, S4A) Terrene Inst.

Water Activity: Theory & Applications to Food. Beuchat & Louis B. Rockland. (IFT Basic Symposium Ser.: Vol. 2). 424p. 1987. 125.00 (*0-8247-7759-X*) Dekker.

Water Aerobics. A. Lynn Berle. 128p. (C). 1996. pap. text ed. 20.94 (*0-7872-2166-X*) Kendall-Hunt.

***Water Affordability Programs.** Margot F. Saunders et al. LC 97-22150. 1998. write for info. (*0-89867-912-5*) AWWA Research.

Water Allocation & Water Markets: An Analysis of Gains-from-Trade in Chile. Robert R. Hearne & K. William Easter. LC 95-50699. (Technical Paper Ser.: No. 315). 96p. 1996. 7.95 (*0-8213-3528-6*, 13528) World Bank.

Water Allocation, Rights, & Pricing: Examples from Japan & the United States. John R. Teerink & Masahiro Nakashima. LC 92-47122. (Discussion Paper Ser.: No. 198). 75p. 1993. 6.95 (*0-8213-2332-6*, 12332) World Bank.

Water Analysis. Ed. by W. Fresenius et al. (Illus.). 850p. (C). 1996. 125.00 (*0-387-17723-X*) Spr-Verlag.

***Water Analysis: A Practical Guide.** 1996. text ed. 125.00 (*3-540-17723-X*) Spr-Verlag.

Water Analysis: A Practical Treatise on the Examination of Potable Water. J. Alfred Wanklyn & Ernest T. Chapman. Ed. by Barbara G. Rosenkrantz. LC 76-40651. (Public Health in America Ser.). (Illus.). 1977. reprint ed. lib. bdg. 19.95 (*0-405-09834-0*) Ayer.

Water Analysis: Some Revised Methods for Limnologists. F. J. Mackereth et al. 1978. 39.00 (*0-900386-31-2*) St Mut.

Water & Aqueous Solutions. Ed. by G. W. Neilson & J. E. Enderby. (Illus.). 362p. 1986. 100.00 (*0-85274-576-1*) IOP Pub.

Water & Aqueous Solutions at Subzero Temperatures. see Water: A Comprehensive Treatise

Water & Architecture: Architecture, History, & Myth. Photos by Jane Lidz. LC 93-27389. 1994. 60.00 (*0-8109-3975-4*) Abrams.

Water & Biological Macromolecules. Ed. by Eric Westhof. 1993. 131.00 (*0-8493-7570-3*, QP535) CRC Pr.

Water & Clay. Saud Al-Harkan. 136p. 1994. 39.95 (*0-9642938-1-1*) Ravenala Pubns.

Water & Dreams: An Essay on the Imagination of Matter. Gaston Bachelard. Tr. by Edith R. Farrell from FRE. LC 83-23641. (Bachelard Translation Ser.). 213p. 1994. pap. 18.00 (*0-911005-25-0*) Dallas Inst Pubns.

Water & Electrolytes in Pediatrics. 2nd ed. Laurence Finberg et al. LC 92-24338. (Illus.). 288p. 1993. text ed. 57.50 (*0-7216-3468-0*) Saunders.

Water & Energy: Technical & Policy Issues. Ed. by F. Kilpatrick & D. Matchett. LC 82-71351. 668p. 1982. pap. 57.00 (*0-87262-308-4*) Am Soc Civil Eng.

Water & Energy Development in an Arid Environment: The Colorado River Basin. Gaylord V. Skogerboe. 1982. pap. 63.00 (*0-08-028752-2*, Pergamon Pr) Elsevier.

Water & Energy, 2001: Proceedings of the International Conference, New Delhi, India, Oct. 9-12, 1995. (Illus.). 1000p. 1996. 130.00 (*90-5410-718-9*, Pub. by A A Balkema NE) Ashgate Pub Co.

***Water & Environmental Management: Design & Construction of Works.** M. D. Haigh & C. P. James. LC 91-33043. (Ellis Horwood Series in Environmental Management, Science & Technology). 1991. write for info. (*0-13-952672-2*, Pub. by E Horwood UK) P-H.

***Water & Floating.** David Evans & Claudette Williams. (Let's Explore Science Ser.). (Illus.). (J). 12.95 (*0-590-74593-X*) Scholastic Inc.

Water & Floating. Alan Ward. LC 92-6260. (Project Science Ser.). (Illus.). 32p. (J). (gr. k-4). 1992. lib. bdg. 20.00 (*0-531-14230-2*) Watts.

Water & Grass: Study in the Pastoral Economy of Southern Europe. Else H. Carrier. LC 77-87717. reprint ed. 49.50 (*0-404-16579-6*) AMS Pr.

***Water & Industrial Tanks.** Richard K. Miller & Christy H. Gunter. (Market Research Survey Ser.: No. 318). 50p. 1996. 200.00 (*1-55865-341-4*) Future Tech Surveys.

Water & Ions in Biological Systems. Ed. by V. Vasilescu. (Congress Reports: No. 2). 500p. 1988. 106.50 (*0-8176-1941-0*) Birkhauser.

Water & Ions in Biomolecular Systems. V. Vasilescu. 1990. 79.50 (*0-8176-2359-0*) Birkhauser.

Water & Land Management in Arid Ecology: Policy & Socio-Scientific Perspectives on Soil-Crop-Water Synergy. P. C. Mathur. 1991. 34.00 (*81-7033-126-9*, Pub. by Rawat II) S Asia.

Water & Life: Comparative Analysis of Water Relationships at the Organismic, Cellular & Molecular Level. George N. Somero. (Illus.). 404p. 1992. 181.95 (*0-387-54112-8*) Spr-Verlag.

Water & Life: Poetry in English & Italian. Adolph Caso. 1976. pap. 9.95 (*0-8283-1682-1*) Branden Pub Co.

Water & Light: A Diver's Journey to a Coral Reef. Stephen Harrigan. LC 93-25658. 288p. 1994. reprint ed. pap. 12.00 (*0-87156-453-X*) Sierra.

Water & Light: Looking Through Lenses. Michinori Murata. LC 92-19969. (Illus.). (J). (gr. 1-3). 1993. lib. bdg. 18.95 (*0-8225-2904-1*, Lerner Publctns) Lerner Group.

Water & Metropolitan Man. 94p. 1969. pap. 9.00 (*0-87262-011-5*) Am Soc Civil Eng.

Water & Other Liquids. Robert C. Mebane & Thomas R. Rybolt. (Everyday Material Science Experiments Ser.). (Illus.). 64p. (J). (gr. 5-8). 1995. lib. bdg. 15.98 (*0-8050-2840-4*) TFC Bks NY.

Water & Peace: Water Resources & the Arab-Israeli Peace Process. Elisha Kally & Gideon Fishelson. LC 92-23454. 152p. 1993. text ed. 47.95 (*0-275-94365-8*, C4365, Praeger Pubs) Greenwood.

Water & Peace in the Middle East: Proceedings of the First Israeli-Palestinian International Academic Conference on Water, Zurich, Switzerland, December 1992. Ed. by John Isaac & H. Shuval. 550p. 1994. 253.25 (*0-444-81464-7*) Elsevier.

Water & Poverty in the Southwest. Franklin L. Brown. Ed. by Helen M. Ingram. LC 87-19217. 237p. 1987. reprint ed. pap. 67.60 (*0-608-02349-3*, 2062990) Bks Demand.

Water & Power: And Other Stories. Greg Boyd. LC 90-83543. 128p. (Orig.). 1991. pap. 7.95 (*1-878580-33-7*) Asylum Arts.

Water & Power: The Conflict over Los Angeles' Water Supply in the Owens Valley. William L. Kahrl. (Illus.). 584p. 1982. pap. 16.00 (*0-520-05068-1*) U CA Pr.

Water & Power: The Politics of a Scarce Resource in the Jordan River Basin. Miriam R. Lowi. LC 92-38277. (Middle East Library: No. 31). (Illus.). 276p. (C). 1993. text ed. 59.95 (*0-521-43164-6*) Cambridge U Pr.

Water & Power: The Politics of a Scarce Resource in the Jordan River Basin. Miriam R. Lowi. (Middle East Library: No. 31). (Illus.). 320p. (C). 1995. pap. text ed. 20.95 (*0-521-55836-0*) Cambridge U Pr.

Water & Revenue Losses: Unaccounted-for Water. 198p. 1990. pap. 32.00 (*0-89867-417-4*, 90531) Am Water Wks Assn.

Water & Royal Fireworks Music. George F. Handel. 1986. pap. 6.95 (*0-486-25070-9*) Dover.

Water & Salt Regimes of Soils: Modelling & Management. Ed. by E. A. Sokolenko. Tr. by R. K. Mishra from RUS. 254p. (C). 1984. text ed. 70.00 (*90-6191-425-6*, Pub. by A A Balkema NE) Ashgate Pub Co.

***Water & Sanitation in Islam: The Right Path to Health, Health Education Through Religion, 2.** 1996. pap. text ed. 10.00 (*92-9021-169-5*) World Health.

Water & Sediment Reconnaissance of the Hanford Shoreline. Norm Buske & Linda Josephson. LC 88-84103. (Illus.). 62p. 1989. pap. 5.00 (*0-932975-03-8*) N Buske.

Water & Shadows. Brown Miller. 1969. pap. 6.00 (*0-912136-15-4*) Twowindows Pr.

Water & Sky: Reflections of a Northern Year. Alan S. Kesselheim. LC 89-7937. (Illus.). 328p. 1989. 8.99 (*1-55591-046-7*) Fulcrum Pub.

Water & Society: The Social & Ecological Effects of Water Exploitation in Developing Countries, Part 1. C. G. Widstrand et al. 1982. pap. 29.00 (*0-08-028751-4*, Pergamon Pr) Elsevier.

Water & Steam. J. Straub. 1980. pap. 26.00 (*0-08-025429-2*, Pergamon Pr) Elsevier.

Water & Steam. J. Straub. 1980. 75.00 (*0-08-025430-6*, Pergamon Pr) Elsevier.

Water & Storm Polemics Against Baalism in the Deuteronomic History. Fred E. Woods. LC 93-2973. (American University Studies: American Literature: Ser. VII, Vol. 150). 172p. (C). 1994. text ed. 37.95 (*0-8204-2111-1*) P Lang Pubng.

Water & the Arid Lands of the Western United States. Ed. by Mohamed T. El-Ashry & Diana C. Gibbons. (Illus.). 475p. 1988. text ed. 85.00 (*0-521-35040-9*) Cambridge U Pr.

Water & the City: The Next Century. Ed. by Howard Rosen & Ann D. Keating. (Illus.). 300p. (C). 1990. 25.00 (*1-882102-01-0*) Pub Works Hist Soc.

Water & the Cycle of Life. Joseph Cocannouer. 14.95 (*0-8159-7202-4*) Devin.

Water & the Environment. Ed. by J. C. Currie & A. T. Pepper. LC 92-30401. (Ellis Horwood Series in Environmental Management, Science & Technology). 380p. 1993. 72.00 (*0-13-950692-6*, Pub. by Tavistock-E Horwood UK) Routledge Chapman & Hall.

Water & the Environment. J. Rose. (Environmental Topics Ser.). 458p. 1991. text ed. 146.00 (*2-88124-747-4*) Gordon & Breach.

***Water & the Future of the Southwest.** Ed. by Zachary A. Smith. LC 89-33728. (University of New Mexico Public Policy Ser.). (Illus.). 288p. 1989. reprint ed. pap. 82.10 (*0-608-04150-5*, 2064883) Bks Demand.

W

Water & the Land: A History of Irrigation in America. Robert M. Morgan. Ed. by Bruce M. Shank. (Illus.). 200p. 1993. 36.95 (*0-935030-02-6*); 12.00 (*0-317-36872-9*) Irrigation.

Water & the Leaf: Oriental Poems for Meditation. Angela Lobo-Cobb. (Illus.). pap. write for info. (*0-318-57646-5*) Bloomsberry Pr.

***Water & the New States of Central Asia.** Philip P. Micklin. 60p. 1997. pap. 12.95 (*1-86203-000-6*, Pub. by Royal Inst Intl Affairs UK) Brookings.

Water & Waste Control for the Plating Shop. Joseph B. Kushner & Arthur S. Kushner. 242p. (C). 1993. text ed. 35.00 (*1-56990-052-3*) Hanser-Gardner.

Water & Waste Control for the Plating Shop. 3rd rev. ed. J. Kushner & Arthur S. Kushner. 284p. (C). 1994. pap. text ed. write for info. (*1-56990-138-4*) Hanser-Gardner.

Water & Wastewater Engineering, 2 vols., Vol 1, Water Supply & Wastewater Removal. Gordon M. Fair & Daniel A. Okun. LC 66-16139. reprint ed. pap. 128.00 (*0-317-11201-5*, 2055401) Bks Demand.

Water & Wastewater Engineering, 2 vols., Vol 2, Water Purification & Wastewater Treatment. Gordon M. Fair & Daniel A. Okun. LC 66-16139. reprint ed. Vol. 2, Water Purification & Wastewater Treatment & Disposal. pap. 160.00 (*0-317-11202-3*) Bks Demand.

Water & Wastewater Engineering Hydraulics. T. J. Casey. (Illus.). 240p. 1992. pap. 45.00 (*0-19-856359-0*) OUP.

Water & Wastewater Examination Manual. V. Dean Adams. (Illus.). 265p. 1990. 59.95 (*0-87371-199-8*, L199) Lewis Pubs.

Water & Wastewater Laboratory Techniques. Roy-Keith Smith. LC 95-10980. 1995. write for info. (*1-57278-014-2*) Water Environ.

Water & Wastewater Microbiology: Proceedings of the IAWPRC Conference Held in Newport Beach, California, U. S. A., February 8-11, 1988. Ed. by D. Jenkins & B. H. Olson. (Water Science & Technology Ser.). (Illus.). 562p. 1989. pap. 108.00 (*0-08-037367-4*, Pergamon Pr) Elsevier.

Water & Wastewater Project Financing. Curley. 256p. 1993. 59.95 (*0-87371-486-5*, L486) Lewis Pubs.

Water & Wastewater Systems Analysis: Developments in Water Science. Ed. by D. Stephenson. 232p. 1988. 113.25 (*0-444-42945-X*) Elsevier.

Water & Wastewater Technology. 3rd ed. Mark J. Hammer, Jr. LC 95-30584. 519p. 1995. text ed. 77.00 (*0-13-205626-7*) P-H.

Water & Wastewater Treatment Chemicals: U. S. Products, Applications, Markets. 239p. 1993. pap. 129.95 (*1-56676-088-7*, 760887) Technomic.

Water & Water Policy in World Food Supplies: Proceedings of the Conference May 26-30, 1985. Ed. by Wayne R. Jordan. LC 86-23065. (Illus.). 472p. 1987. 69.50 (*0-89096-278-2*) Tex A&M Univ Pr.

Water & Water Pollution Handbook, Vol. 1. Ciaccio. 480p. 1971. 210.00 (*0-8247-1104-1*) Dekker.

Water & Water Pollution Handbook, Vol. 2. Ed. by Leonard L. Ciaccio. LC 78-134780. (Illus.). 362p. reprint ed. pap. 103.20 (*0-7837-7134-7*, 2052528) Bks Demand.

Water & Water Pollution Handbook, Vol. 3. Ciaccio. 528p. 1972. 210.00 (*0-8247-1117-3*) Dekker.

Water & Water Pollution Handbook, Vol. 4. Ciaccio. 648p. 1973. 210.00 (*0-8247-1118-1*) Dekker.

Water & Weather, No. 1. Charles F. Cochrane. (How to Draw & Paint Ser.). (Illus.). 32p. (Orig.). 1989. pap. 6.95 (*0-929261-67-4*, HT155) W Foster Pub.

Water & Windfall. Marilyn A. Francis. (Illus.). 48p. 1982. 20.00 (*0-88014-039-9*) Mosaic Pr OH.

Water & Womanhood: Religious Meanings of Rivers in Maharashtra. Anne Feldhaus. LC 94-36158. (Illus.). 288p. (C). 1995. 51.00 (*0-19-509122-1*); pap. text ed. 20.95 (*0-19-509283-X*) OUP.

Water Animals. Mark Carwardine. Ed. by Richard G. Young. LC 89-7879. (Looking at How Animals Live Ser.). (Illus.). 45p. (J). (gr. 3-5). 1989. lib. bdg. 14.60 (*0-944483-31-3*) Garrett Ed Corp.

Water As a Productive Environment. C. F. Hickling. LC 75-4394. 200p. (C). 1975. text ed. 29.95 (*0-312-85680-6*) St Martin.

Water at the Surface of the Earth: Student Edition. David H. Miller. LC 82-13769. (International Geophysics Ser.). (C). 1982. pap. text ed. 74.00 (*0-12-496752-3*) Acad Pr.

Water Atlas of Virginia: Basic Facts about Virginia's Water Resources. Frits Van Der Leeden. LC 93-60888. 105p. 1994. lib. bdg. 49.95 (*0-9638711-0-2*) Tennyson Pr.

Water Audits & Leak Detection, No. M36. 96p. 1990. pap. 40.00 (*0-89867-485-9*, 30036) Am Water Wks Assn.

***Water Babies.** Photos by Tom Arma. (Illus.). 14p. (J). (ps). 1997. bds. 5.95 (*0-448-41567-4*, G&D) Putnam Pub Group.

Water Babies. Margie Franklin. 1991. 12.95 (*1-878096-07-9*) Best E TX Pubs.

Water Babies. Charles Kingsley. (Classics Ser.). 192p. (J). (gr. 5 up). 1986. pap. 2.99 (*0-14-035035-7*, Puffin) Puffin Bks.

Water Babies. Charles Kingsley. (Children's Classics Ser.). (Illus.). 256p. (J). (gr. k-6). 1986. 10.99 (*0-517-61817-6*) Random Hse Value.

Water-Babies. Charles Kingsley. Ed. by Brian Alderson. LC 94-11775. (The World's Classics Ser.). 272p. 1995. pap. 7.95 (*0-19-282238-1*) OUP.

Water Babies. Charles Kingsley. (J). 1995. pap. 3.99 (*0-14-036736-5*, Viking) Viking Penguin.

***Water-Babies.** Charles Kingsley. 1997. 22.00 (*0-688-14831-X*, Morrow Junior) Morrow.

Water-Babies. Charles Kingsley. (Illus.). 256p. (YA). 1987. reprint ed. lib. bdg. 22.95 (*0-89966-579-9*) Buccaneer Bks.

Water Baby: The Story of Alvin. Victoria A. Kaharl. (Illus.). 400p. 1990. 25.00 (*0-19-506191-8*) OUP.

Water Baby (Family Man) Roz D. Fox. (Superromance Ser.). 1996. mass mkt. 3.99 (*0-373-70686-3*, 1-70686-0) Harlequin Bks.

Water Balance in Schizophrenia. Ed. by David B. Schnur & Darrell G. Kirch. (Progress in Psychiatry Ser.: No. 48). 302p. 1996. text ed. 38.50 (*0-88048-485-3*, 8485) Am Psychiatric.

Water Baptism. Guy BonGiovanni. 24p. (Orig.). (C). 1983. pap. 1.00 (*0-912981-05-9*) Hse BonGiovanni.

Water Baptism. Perry A. Gaspard. 1983. pap. 2.00 (*0-931867-01-0*) Abundant Life Pubns.

Water Baptism: Its History, Importance, & Cessation. Vernon A. Schutz. 48p. 1988. 2.95 (*0-89814-043-9*) Grace Publns.

Water Baptism: Weapon or Ritual. Wayne C. Gwilliam. 40p. (Orig.). 1993. pap. 3.75 (*0-9631477-6-5*) Reach Out NY.

***Water Baptism, Who Needs It?** T. D. Jakes, Sr. (Orig.). 1997. pap. write for info. (*1-890521-05-1*) Jakes Ent.

Water-Based Inks: A Screenprinting Manual for Studio & Classroom. 2nd ed. Lois M. Johnson & Hester Stinnett. Ed. by Marie Naples. LC 87-82964. (Illus.). 40p. (C). 1990. reprint ed. lab manual ed. 16.00 (*0-9627916-1-X*) Univ of Arts Pr.

Water-Based Paint Formulations, Vol. 3. Ernest W. Flick. LC 75-2939. 502p. 1994. 72.00 (*0-8155-1345-3*) Noyes.

Water Basin Supervisor. Jack Rudman. (Career Examination Ser.: C-3492). 1994. Cloth bdg. avail. pap. 29.95 (*0-8373-3492-6*) Nat Learn.

Water Beetles & Other Things (Half a Century's Work) F. Balfour-Browne. 226p. 1962. 50.00 (*0-317-07182-3*) St Mut.

Water Bioengineering Techniques. H. M. Schiechtl & R. Stern. LC 96-38475. 256p. 1996. text ed. 69.95 (*0-632-04066-1*) Blackwell Sci.

Water Birds. Marj Dunmire. (Illus.). 48p. (J). (gr. 2-8). 1990. pap. 4.95 (*0-942559-06-1*) Pegasus Graphics.

Water Birds of California. Howard L. Cogswell. (California Natural History Guides Ser.: No. 40). 1977. pap. 11.00 (*0-520-02699-3*) U CA Pr.

Water Birds of North America, 2 Vols. Spencer F. Baird et al. (Natural Sciences in America Ser.). (Illus.). 1974. 81.95 (*0-405-05716-4*) Ayer.

Water Birth: A Midwife's Perspective. Susanna Napierala. LC 93-49703. (Illus.). 256p. 1994. pap. text ed. 16.95 (*0-89789-285-2*, Bergin & Garvey) Greenwood.

Water-Bombs. Steven Herrick. (YA). 1995. pap. 12.95 (*0-7022-2807-9*, Pub. by Univ Queensland Pr AT) Intl Spec Bk.

Water Book. D. A. Rain. (Illus.). 1993. 29.95 (*0-8283-1956-1*) Branden Pub Co.

Water-Borne Coatings: The Environmentally-Friendly Alternative. Klaus Doren et al. 1994. write for info. (*1-56990-139-2*, Pub. by C Hanser GW) Hanser-Gardner.

Water Borne Disease. Paul Hunter. LC 97-17109. Date not set. text ed. write for info. (*0-471-96646-0*) Wiley.

Water Bottles. Waterborn. 1996. pap. write for info. (*0-345-40535-8*) Ballantine.

Water Boundaries. George Cole. (Riparian Boundaries Ser.: No. 1). (Illus.). 1997. 55.00 (*0-910845-13-1*, 645) Wiley.

***Water Boundaries.** George M. Cole. LC 96-44730. text ed. 54.95 (*0-471-17929-9*) Wiley.

Water Boy. Gary Reiswig. 304p. 1993. 20.00 (*0-671-79506-6*) S&S Trade.

Water Brought Us: The Story of the Gullah-Speaking People. Muriel M. Branch. LC 94-49593. (J). 1995. pap. 16.99 (*0-525-65185-3*, Cobblehill Bks) Dutton Child Bks.

***Water Buffalo Days: Growing up in Vietnam.** Quang Nhuong Huynh. LC 96-35058. (Illus.). 128p. (J). (gr. 2-5). 1997. 13.95 (*0-06-024957-9*); lib. bdg. 13.89 (*0-06-024958-7*) HarpC Child Bks.

Water Bug Story. Dorothy Britt. (Illus.). 10p. (Orig.). (J). 1992. pap. 4.95 (*1-881809-32-3*) Gabriel TX.

Water Bugs & Dragonflies: Explaining Death to Children. Doris Stickney. (Looking up Ser.). (Illus.). 24p. (J). 1982. pap. 1.95 (*0-8298-0609-1*) Pilgrim OH.

***Water Bugs & Dragonflies: Explaining Death to Young Children.** Doris Stickney. LC 97-13957. (Illus.). 32p. 1997. 9.95 (*0-8298-1180-X*) Pilgrim OH.

Water-Bug's Mittens. limited ed. James Dickey. 1980. 40.00 (*0-89723-021-3*) Bruccoli.

Water Can Be Fun! How to Create a Successful Science Fair. 80p. 1991. pap. 32.00 (*0-89867-539-1*, 20254) Am Water Wks Assn.

Water Can Undermine Your Health. 1992. lib. bdg. 79.95 (*0-8490-8816-X*) Gordon Pr.

Water Can Undermine Your Health. rev. ed. N. W. Walker. (Illus.). 120p. 1996. pap. 5.95 (*0-89019-037-2*) Norwalk Pr.

***Water Cannibals.** P. B. Shaw. (Lieutenant Abe Rainfinch Mystery Ser.). 224p. 1997. 20.95 (*0-8027-3293-3*) Walker & Co.

Water Carriers in Hades: A Study of Catharsis Through Toil in Classical Antiquity. Eva Keuls. (Illus.). 179p. 1974. pap. text ed. 54.00 (*0-317-54499-3*, Pub. by AM Hakkert NE) Coronet Bks.

Water Carriers in Hades: A Study of Catharsis Through Toil in Classical Antiquity. Eva Keuls. 179p. 1974. pap. 64.00 (*90-256-0699-7*, Pub. by A M Hakkert NE) Benjamins North Am.

Water Channels. Alan S. Verkman. LC 93-34244. (Molecular Biology Intelligence Unit Ser.). 128p. 1993. 89.95 (*1-57059-017-6*) R G Landes.

Water Chemicals Codex. National Research Council Staff. 73p. (C). 1982. pap. text ed. 12.95 (*0-309-03338-1*) Natl Acad Pr.

Water Chemistry. Vernon L. Snoeyink & David Jenkins. LC 79-21331. (SPE Monographs). 463p. 1980. Net. text ed. 61.00 (*0-471-05196-9*); Net. pap. text ed. 29.50 (*0-471-06272-3*) Wiley.

Water Chemistry Manual for Water & Spentwater Personnel. Gaines B. Jackson. LC 92-13869. 704p. (gr. 13). 1992. text ed. 84.95 (*0-442-01060-5*) Chapman & Hall.

Water Chemistry of Nuclear Reactor Systems 3: Proceedings of an International Conference Organized by the British Nuclear Energy Society, 2 vols. 541p. 1983. Set. 168.00 (*0-7277-0202-5*, Pub. by T Telford UK) Am Soc Civil Eng.

Water Chlorination: Chemistry, Environmental Impact & Health Effects, Vol. 6. Ed. by Robert L. Jolley et al. (Illus.). 1048p. 1990. 129.95 (*0-87371-167-X*, L167) Lewis Pubs.

Water Chlorination Principles & Practices, No. M20. 96p. 1973. pap. 30.00 (*0-89867-078-0*, 30020) Am Water Wks Assn.

Water Colour on Porcelain: A Guide to the Use of Water Soluble Colourants. Arne Ase. (Illus.). 260p. 1989. 56.50 (*82-00-06524-3*) Scandnvan Univ Pr.

Water-Colourist. Sebastian Barry. 56p. 8300. pap. 10.95 (*0-85105-412-9*, Pub. by Colin Smythe Ltd UK) Dufour.

Water Conduits in the Kathmandu Valley, Set. Raimund Becker-Ritterspach. (Illus.). 119p. (C). 1995. 147.50 (*81-215-0690-5*, Pub. by M Manoharial II) Coronet Bks.

***Water Conservation.** Evett. (Environmental Engineering Ser.). 1998. text ed. 69.95 (*0-442-02530-0*) Van Nos Reinhold.

Water Conservation. William O. Maddaus. 100p. 1987. pap. 36.00 (*0-89867-387-9*, 20238) Am Water Wks Assn.

Water Conservation: Needs & Implementing Strategies. 277p. 1979. pap. 22.00 (*0-87262-198-7*) Am Soc Civil Eng.

Water Conservation & Pollution, Vol. 9. Soemarto et al. (Water Science & Technology Ser.: Vol. 31). 204p. 1995. pap. 115.00 (*0-08-042663-8*, Pergamon Pr) Elsevier.

Water, Conservation & Reclamation: Building Sustainable Communities, an Environmental Guide for Local Government. Center for the Study of Law & Politics Staff. 135p. 1990. 40.00 (*1-880386-01-1*) Ctr Study Law.

Water Conservation in Buildings. 1990. 36.00 (*0-86022-263-2*, Pub. by Build Servs Info Assn UK) St Mut.

Water Conservation Manager's Guide to Residential Retrofit. (Illus.). 52p. 1993. pap. 33.00 (*0-89867-664-9*, 20250) Am Water Wks Assn.

Water-Conserving Gardens & Landscapes. John M. O'Keefe. Ed. by Constance Oxley. LC 91-51124. (Down-to-Earth Bk.). (Illus.). 160p. 1992. pap. 12.95 (*0-88266-786-6*, Garden Way Pub) Storey Comm Inc.

Water Contamination & Health Integration of Exposure Assessment, Toxicology, & Risk Assessment. Rhoda Wang. LC 93-48586. (Environmental Science & Pollution Ser.: Vol. 9). 544p. 1994. 195.00 (*0-8247-8922-9*) Dekker.

Water Coolant Technology of Power Reactors. Paul Cohen. LC 79-57306. (Monographs). 250p. 1980. reprint ed. 32.00 (*0-89448-020-0*, 300016) Am Nuclear Soc.

Water-Cooling Towers. National Fire Protection Association Staff. 1992. 20.25 (*0-317-63332-5*, 214-92) Natl Fire Prot.

***Water Crisis: Ending the Policy Drought.** Terry L. Anderson. LC 97-14369. 1997. 19.95 (*1-882577-43-4*); pap. text ed. 10.95 (*1-882577-44-2*) Cato Inst.

Water Crisis: The Next Middle East Crisis? George E. Gruen. (Special Reports). (Illus.). 91p. (Orig.). 1991. pap. 10.00 (*0-943058-14-7*) S Wiesenthal Ctr.

***Water, Culture & Power: Local Struggles in a Global Context.** John M. Donahue. 430p. 1997. text ed. 50.00 (*1-55963-521-5*); pap. text ed. 30.00 (*1-55963-522-3*) Island Pr.

Water Cycle - Atmosphere (First) 1992. 20.00 (*1-56638-148-7*) Math Sci Nucleus.

Water Cycle - Literature Books (K-Sixth) 1992. 112.30 (*1-56638-204-1*) Math Sci Nucleus.

Water Cycle - Oceans (Fifth) 1992. 25.00 (*1-56638-152-5*) Math Sci Nucleus.

Water Cycle - The Earth's Gift. J. R. Blueford et al. (J). (gr. k-6). 1992. 19.95 (*1-56638-146-0*) Math Sci Nucleus.

Water Cycle - Water (Fourth) 1992. 25.00 (*1-56638-150-9*) Math Sci Nucleus.

Water Cycle - Water (Second) 1992. 45.00 (*1-56638-149-5*) Math Sci Nucleus.

Water Cycle - Water (Sixth) 1992. 25.00 (*1-56638-219-X*) Math Sci Nucleus.

Water Cycle - Weather (Fourth) 1992. 25.00 (*1-56638-151-7*) Math Sci Nucleus.

Water Cycle - Weather (K) 1992. 20.00 (*1-56638-147-9*) Math Sci Nucleus.

Water Cycle - Weather (Sixth) 1992. 25.00 (*1-56638-153-3*) Math Sci Nucleus.

Water Dance. Thomas Locker. LC 95-47861. (J). 1997. write for info. (*0-15-201284-2*) HarBrace.

***Water Dance.** Thomas Locker. (J). (ps-5). 1997. 16.00 (*0-614-28814-2*) HarBrace.

Water Dancer. Jenifer Levin. LC 93-44118. 1994. pap. 10.95 (*0-452-27257-2*, Plume) NAL-Dutton.

Water Dancing. Pearl P. Duncan. LC 90-85712. 124p. (Orig.). 1991. pap. 9.50 (*1-56002-026-1*) Aegina Pr.

Water Deficits: Plant Responses from Cell to Community. Ed. by J. A. Smith & H. Griffiths. (Environmental Plant Biology Ser.). (Illus.). 345p. 1993. 147.50 (*1-872748-06-6*, Pub. by Bios Scientific UK) Coronet Bks.

Water Demand for Steam Electric Generation: An Economic Projection Model. Paul H. Cootner & George O. Lof. LC 65-27669. 156p. reprint ed. pap. 44.50 (*0-7837-3137-X*, 2020959) Bks Demand.

***Water Demand Forecasting.** Gardiner & Herrington. (Illus.). 148p. 1986. text ed. 49.50 (*0-86094-214-7*) Chapman & Hall.

Water Detectives: The Adventures of Mitch & Molly. Karen O'Connor. LC 92-24649. (God's Green Earth Ser.). (Illus.). 80p. (Orig.). (J). (gr. 1-4). 1993. pap. 4.99 (*0-570-04727-7*, 56-1686) Concordia.

Water Development & Management, 4 vols. Ed. by United Nations Staff. Incl. Part 1. . 1978. 172.00 (*0-08-023402-X*); Part 2. . 1978. 243.00 (*0-08-023404-6*); Part 3. . 1978. 338.00 (*0-08-023406-2*); Part 4. . 1978. 478.00 (*0-08-023408-9*); 1978. 1,230.00 (*0-08-021987-X*, Pub. by Pergamon Repr UK) Franklin.

Water Development & the Environment. James. 400p. 1992. 89.95 (*0-87371-522-5*, L522) Lewis Pubs.

***Water Disinfection & Natural Organic Matter: Characterization & Control.** Ed. by Roger A. Minear & Gary L. Amy. LC 96-36454. (Acs Symposium Ser.: Vol. 649). (Illus.). 400p. 1996. 109.95 (*0-8412-3464-7*) Am Chemical.

Water Distribution in Ancient Rome: The Evidence of Frontinus. Harry B. Evans. (Illus.). 220p. (C). 1993. text ed. 44.50 (*0-472-10464-0*) U of Mich Pr.

***Water Distribution in Ancient Rome: The Evidence of Frontinus.** Harry B. Evans. (C). 1997. reprint ed. pap. 27.95 (*0-472-08446-1*) U of Mich Pr.

Water Distribution Operator Training Handbook. 232p. 1986. pap. 27.00 (*0-89867-013-6*, 20103) Am Water Wks Assn.

Water Distribution System Operation & Maintenance. 3rd ed. Kenneth D. Kerri. (Illus.). 514p. (C). 1994. pap. text ed. 20.00 (*1-884701-16-7*) CA St U Ofc Water.

Water Distribution Systems: A Troubleshooting Manual. James W. Male & Thomas M. Walski. (Illus.). 128p. 1990. 84.95 (*0-87371-232-3*, L232) Lewis Pubs.

Water Distribution Systems: Simulation & Sizing. Thomas M. Walski et al. (Illus.). 352p. 1990. 87.95 (*0-87371-233-1*, L233) Lewis Pubs.

Water District Clerk. Jack Rudman. (Career Examination Ser.: C-3378). 1994. pap. 23.95 (*0-8373-3378-4*) Nat Learn.

Water District Superintendent. Jack Rudman. (Career Examination Ser.: C-3342). 1994. pap. 39.95 (*0-8373-3342-3*) Nat Learn.

Water District Supervisor. Jack Rudman. (Career Examination Ser.: C-2625). 1994. pap. 34.95 (*0-8373-2625-7*) Nat Learn.

Water Dog. Wolter. 1964. pap. 24.95 (*0-525-24734-3*) NAL-Dutton.

Water Dog. Richard A. Wolters. 1964. 14.95 (*0-525-24430-1*, Dutton) NAL-Dutton.

***Water down under '94, Vol. 1.** Contrib. by Claus Schonfeldt et al. (National Conference Proceedings 94 Ser.: Vol. 10). (Illus.). 650p. 1994. pap. 106.00 (*0-85825-607-X*, Pub. by Inst Engrs Aust-EA Bks AT) Accents Pubns.

Water Dragons, Sailfin Lizards, & Basilisks. John Coborn. (Illus.). 64p. 1996. pap. 9.95 (*0-7938-0281-4*, RE118) TFH Pubns.

***Water Dreams & Other Poems by Debra Wilk.** Debra Wilk. 124p. (Orig.). 1996. pap. 9.00 (*1-879025-10-8*) Christopher-Burghardt.

Water, Earth, & Fire: Land Use & Environmental Planning in the New Jersey Pine Barrens. Jonathan Berger & John W. Sinton. LC 84-47963. (Illus.). 248p. (C). 1985. text ed. 38.00 (*0-8018-2398-6*) Johns Hopkins.

Water, Ecology, Pollution, & Management. B. Sambasiva. (C). 1991. 59.00 (*0-8364-2655-X*, Pub. by Chugh Pubns II) S Asia.

Water Efficiency: A Resource for Utility Managers, Community Planners, & Other Decisionmakers. Rocky Mountain Institute Water Program Staff. 114p. (Orig.). 1991. pap. text ed. 15.00 (*1-881071-02-2*, W91-27) Rocky Mtn Inst.

Water Efficient Landscape Guidelines. (Illus.). 184p. 1993. pap. 51.00 (*0-89867-679-7*, 20305) Am Water Wks Assn.

Water Encyclopedia. 2nd ed. Ed. by Frits Van Der Leeden et al. (Geraghty & Miller Ground Water Ser.). (Illus.). 824p. 1990. 151.95 (*0-87371-120-3*, L120) Lewis Pubs.

Water Energy. Graham Rickard. (Alternative Energy Ser.). (Illus.). 32p. (J). (gr. 4-6). 1991. lib. bdg. 18.60 (*0-8368-0710-3*) Gareth Stevens Inc.

Water Engineering & Landscape: Water Control & Landscape Transformation in the Modern Period. Ed. by D. Cosgrove & G. Petts. (Illus.). 192p. 1992. 51.95 (*1-85293-069-1*, Pub. by Pinter Pubs Ltd UK) CRC Pr.

***Water Environmental Markets: Asia.** 143p. 1996. 185.00 (*0-614-29516-5*) R K Miller Assocs.

***Water Environmental Markets: Asia.** Karen P. Griffith. 143p. 1997. 185.00 (*1-881503-71-2*) R K Miller Assocs.

***Water Environmental Markets: Canada.** 108p. 1996. 135.00 (*0-614-29515-7*) R K Miller Assocs.

***Water Environmental Markets: Canada.** Karen P. Griffith. 108p. 1997. 135.00 (*1-881503-69-0*) R K Miller Assocs.

***Water Environmental Markets: Latin America.** 160p. 1996. 185.00 (*0-614-29517-3*) R K Miller Assocs.

***Water Environmental Markets: Latin America.** Karen P. Griffith. 182p. 1997. 185.00 (*1-881503-73-9*) R K Miller Assocs.

***Water Environmental Markets: State-by-State.** Richard K. Miller et al. 340p. 1997. 185.00 (*0-614-29518-1*) R K Miller Assocs.

***Water Environmental Markets: State-by-State.** Richard K. Miller et al. 220p. 1997. 185.00 (*1-881503-78-X*) R K Miller Assocs.

Water Exercise for Therapy & Fitness. Martha White. LC 94-44193. (Illus.). 128p. (Orig.). 1995. pap. 14.95 (*0-87322-726-3*, PWHI0726) Human Kinetics.

Water Exercises for All Ages. Jaye D. Slater. (Illus.). 44p. (Orig.). 1981. 5.00 (*0-9607454-0-8*) Slater Pub.

An Asterisk (*) at the beginning of an entry indicates that the title is appearing in BIP for the first time.

Water Features for Small Gardens. Francesca Greenoak. (Illus.). 96p. 1996. 22.95 (*1-57076-053-5*, Trafalgar Sq Pub) Trafalgar.

Water Finds Its Own Level. Paul M. Eko. Ed. by Paula Scalist. 105p. (YA). 1990. pap. 8.95 (*0-685-28132-9*) Backwards & Backwards.

Water Fitness after Forty. Ruth Sova. LC 95-8270. (Illus.). 176p. (Orig.). 1995. pap. 15.95 (*0-87322-604-6*, PSOV0604) Human Kinetics.

Water Fitness During Your Pregnancy. Jane Katz. LC 94-17659. 248p. 1994. pap. 17.95 (*0-87322-495-7*, PKAT0495) Human Kinetics.

Water Flow & Solute Transport in Soils: Developments & Applications. Ed. by Gedeon Dagan & David A. Russo. LC 92-47096. (Advanced Series in Agricultural Sciences: Vol. 20). 1993. 145.00 (*0-387-56216-8*) Spr-Verlag.

Water Flow in Soils. Miyazaki. (Books in Soils, Plants & the Environment: Vol. 28). 312p. 1993. 160.00 (*0-8247-8982-2*) Dekker.

*__Water Flowers.__ Edward Gorey. 64p. Date not set. 11.95 (*0-8253-0412-1*) P Weed Bks.

Water Flowers. Edward Gorey. LC 82-73193. (Illus.). 64p. 1986. reprint ed. 11.95 (*0-926637-13-4*) P Weed Bks.

Water Flowing Home. Sherman Alexie. (Orig.). 1995. pap. 20.00 (*0-931659-25-6*) Limberlost Pr.

Water Flowing Home. limited ed. Sherman Alexie. (Orig.). 1995. 125.00 (*0-931659-26-4*) Limberlost Pr.

Water Fluoridation Principles & Practices, Vol. M4. (Illus.). 80p. 1995. pap. 40.00 (*0-89867-794-7*, 30004) Am Water Wks Assn.

Water Flying Concepts. 2nd ed. Dale DeRemer. LC 89-91576. (Illus.). 288p. (C). 1989. 35.00 (*0-89100-385-1*, EA-385) D De Remer.

Water Flying Concepts. 2nd ed. Dale DeRemer. LC 89-91576. (Illus.). 270p. (C). 1991. pap. text ed. 14.95 (*0-89100-374-6*, EA-374) IAP.

*__Water Flying Concepts: An Advanced Text on Wilderness Water Flying.__ 2nd ed. Dale Deremer. LC 89-91576. (Illus.). 288p. 1997. pap. 19.95 (*0-9622159-1-0*) D De Remer.

Water for Agriculture: Facing the Limits. Sandra Postel. (Orig.). (C). 1989. pap. 5.00 (*0-916468-94-1*) Worldwatch Inst.

*__Water for Agriculture & Wildlife & the Environment - Win Win Opportunities: Proceedings of the 1996 USCID Wetlands Seminar.__ Ed. by Jerry Schaack & Susan S. Anderson. 332p. 1997. pap. 36.00 (*1-887903-02-X*) US Comm Irrigation.

Water for Human Consumption, Vol. 1. (Water Resources Ser.: Vol. 2). (Illus.). 626p. 1983. pap. 100.00 (*0-907567-60-6*, Tycooly Pub); text ed. 230.00 (*0-907567-61-4*, Tycooly Pub) Weidner & Sons.

Water for Human Consumption, Vol. 2. (Water Resources Ser.: Vol. 3). (Illus.). 167p. 1983. pap. 55.00 (*0-907567-55-X*, Tycooly Pub); text ed. 85.00 (*0-907567-54-1*, Tycooly Pub) Weidner & Sons.

Water for Larsa: An Old Babylonian Archive Dealing with Irrigation. Stanley D. Walters. LC 76-99845. (Yale Near Eastern Researches Ser.: Vol. 4). 236p. reprint ed. pap. 67.30 (*0-317-10222-2*, 2022050) Bks Demand.

Water for New York: A Study in State Administration of Water Resources. Roscoe C. Martin. LC 60-9946. 1960. 34.95 (*0-8156-2028-4*) Syracuse U Pr.

Water for New York City: A 300 Year History. rev. ed. Edward H. Hall. (Illus.). 145p. 1993. reprint ed. pap. 12.50 (*0-910746-12-5*) Hope Farm.

*__Water for One, Water for Everyone: A Counting Book of African Animals.__ Stephen R. Swinburne. LC 97-14429. (J). 1998. lib. bdg. write for info. (*0-7613-0269-7*) Millbrook Pr.

Water for Resource Development: Proceedings of a Specialty Conference Sponsored by Hydraulics Division. Ed. by David L. Schreiber. 912p. 1984. 80.00 (*0-87262-409-9*) Am Soc Civil Eng.

Water for Subsurface Injection - STP 735. Ed. by Johnson et al. 150p. 1981. 14.00 (*0-8031-0800-1*, 04-735000-16) ASTM.

Water for Sustainable Development in the 21st Century, Oxford University Press, Oxford, 1993. Glenn E. Stout. (Water Resource Management Ser.). 273p. 1993. 40.00 (*0-19-563302-4*) Intl Water Resc.

Water for the Angels: Mini-Play. (California History Ser.). (J). (gr. 5 up). 1978. 6.50 (*0-89550-332-8*) Stevens & Shea.

Water for the Cities: A History of the Urban Water Supply Problem in the United States. Nelson M. Blake. LC 56-13576. (Maxwell School Ser.: No. 3). 357p. reprint ed. pap. 101.80 (*0-685-20512-6*, 2029971) Bks Demand.

Water for the Future: Water Resources Developments in Perspective. Ed. by W. O. Wunderlich & J. Egbert Prins. 445p. (C). 1987. text ed. 130.00 (*90-6191-695-X*, Pub. by A A Balkema NE) Ashgate Pub Co.

Water for the Thousand Millions, Vol. 4. Ed. by Arnold Pacey. LC 77-23127. 1977. pap. 8.00 (*0-08-021805-9*, Pergamon Pr) Elsevier.

Water for Western Agriculture. Kenneth D. Frederick & James C. Hanson. LC 82-47985. 241p. 1982. 17.95 (*0-8018-2832-5*) Resources Future.

Water for World Development: Proceedings of the Sixth IWRA World Congress on Water Resources, 4 vols. Ed. by Kaz Adamowski et al. 2814p. (Orig.). 1988. pap. 50.00 (*0-923227-02-4*) Intl Water Resc.

Water-Formed Scale Deposits. Jack C. Cowan & Donald J. Weintritt. LC 75-5089. (Illus.). 606p. reprint ed. pap. 172.80 (*0-8357-8371-5*, 2034173) Bks Demand.

Water Forum, Nineteen Eighty-Six: World Water Issues in Evolution, 2 vols. Ed. by Mohammad Karamouz et al. (Conference Proceedings Ser.). 2227p. 1986. Set. 195.00 (*0-87262-545-1*) Am Soc Civil Eng.

Water Forum '81, 2 vols., Set. LC 81-67746. 1404p. 1981. pap. 100.00 (*0-87262-275-4*) Am Soc Civil Eng.

Water from the Moon. Rory Barnes & James Birrell. 184p. 1989. pap. 7.95 (*0-14-011739-3*, Penguin Bks) Viking Penguin.

Water from the Moon. Thomas R. Crowe. LC 93-92605. (Night Sun Trilogy Ser.: Bk. 3). 80p. 1993. pap. 9.95 (*1-883197-03-1*) New Native Pr.

Water from the Moon. Jane B. Zalben. LC 86-46439. 160p. (YA). (gr. 8 up). 1987. 15.00 (*0-374-38238-7*) FS&G.

Water from the Moon. large type ed. Lesley Denny. 592p. 1988. 25.99 (*0-7089-1863-8*) Ulverscroft.

Water from the Moon & Other Love Stories. Lawrence Kinsman. 256p. (Orig.). 1995. pap. 12.95 (*0-9648817-0-5*) Abelard Pr.

Water from the Rock: Black Resistance in a Revolutionary Age. Sylvia R. Frey. 388p. 1991. text ed. 49.50 (*0-691-04784-7*); pap. text ed. 17.95 (*0-691-00626-1*) Princeton U Pr.

Water from the Rock: Finding Grace in Times of Grief. Lyn M. Fraser. LC 94-25003. 88p. 1994. pap. 6.95 (*0-8091-3504-3*) Paulist Pr.

Water from the Well. Myra McLarey. 256p. 1996. pap. 11.00 (*0-684-83097-3*) S&S Trade.

Water Fun & Fitness. Terri Elder. LC 95-2204. (Illus.). 152p. (Orig.). 1995. pap. 14.95 (*0-87322-501-5*, BELD0501) Human Kinetics.

Water Garden. Anthony Paul. 167p. 1986. pap. 18.00 (*0-14-046756-4*, Penguin Bks) Viking Penguin.

Water Garden. Anthony Paul & Yvonne Rees. 168p. 1996. 19.95 (*2-01-402515-0*, Penguin Bks) Viking Penguin.

Water Garden. Anthony Paul & Yvonne Rees. (Illus.). 168p. 1986. pap. 19.95 (*0-14-025150-2*, Penguin Bks) Viking Penguin.

*__Water Garden: A Practical Guide to Planning & Planting.__ Peter Robinson. (Illus.). 128p. 1997. pap. 16.95 (*0-8069-0846-7*) Sterling.

Water Garden Plants: The Complete Guide. David Case. (Illus.). 160p. 1994. pap. 22.95 (*1-85223-812-7*, Pub. by Crowood Pr UK) Trafalgar.

Water Gardener. Anthony Archer-Wills. LC 92-44565. (Illus.). 192p. 1993. 45.00 (*0-8120-6332-5*) Barron.

*__Water Gardening.__ Peter Robinson. 1997. 34.95 (*0-614-27228-9*) DK Pub Inc.

Water Gardening. Ed. by Wilfred V. Schmidlin. (Plants & Gardens Ser.). (Illus.). 1990. per., pap. 7.95 (*0-945352-14-X*) Bklyn Botanic.

Water Gardening. Joseph Tomocek & Leslie Garisto. (American Garden Guides Ser.). 224p. 1996. pap. 25.00 (*0-679-75860-7*) Pantheon.

Water Gardening: Water Lilies & Lotuses. Perry D. Slocum et al. (Illus.). 434p. 1996. 59.95 (*0-88192-335-4*) Timber.

Water Gardening Basics. William C. Uber. LC 88-160279. (Illus.). 174p. (Orig.). (C). 1988. pap. 21.95 (*0-944933-01-7*) Dragonflyer Pr.

Water Gardening Basics. William C. Uber. LC 88-160279. (Illus.). 174p. (Orig.). (C). 1995. 31.95 (*0-944933-00-9*) Dragonflyer Pr.

*__Water Gardening for Everyone.__ Phillip Swindell. 1996. 12.95 (*0-903001-72-1*, Pub. by Burall Floraprint UK) J Markham & Assocs.

Water Gardening in Containers: Small Ponds Indoors & Out. Helen Nash & C. Greg Speichert. LC 96-11986. (Illus.). 128p. 1996. 24.95 (*0-8069-8197-0*) Sterling.

*__Water Gardens.__ (Taylor's Weekend Gardening Guide Ser.). 1997. pap. 12.95 (*0-614-27237-8*) HM.

Water Gardens. Carol Spier. 72p. 1996. pap. text ed. 12.95 (*1-56799-272-2*, Friedman-Fairfax) M Friedman Pub Grp Inc.

Water Gardens. Peter Stadelman. 144p. 1992. pap. 14.95 (*0-8120-4928-4*) Barron.

*__Water Gardens.__ Sunset Editors. 1997. 19.99 (*0-376-03848-9*, Sunset) Sunset Bks Inc.

Water Gardens. Philip Swindells. (Planning & Planting Ser.). (Illus.). 96p. 1996. 12.95 (*0-7063-7491-6*, Pub. by Ward Lock UK) Sterling.

Water Gardens: A Firefly Gardener's Guide. David Archibald. Ed. by Mary Patton. (Illus.). 96p. 1996. pap. text ed. 10.95 (*1-895565-96-0*, Pub. by Camden Hse CN) Firefly Bks Ltd.

*__Water Gardens: A Guide to Creating, Caring for & Enjoying Aquatic Landscaping.__ Terri Dunn. 1997. 16.98 (*0-7651-9479-1*) Smithmark.

Water Gardens: A Harrowsmith Gardener's Guide. Ed. by David Archibald & Mary Patton. (Illus.). 96p. (Orig.). 1990. pap. 10.95 (*0-920656-96-X*, Pub. by Camden Hse CN) Firefly Bks Ltd.

Water Gardens: How to Design, Install, Plant & Maintain a Home Water Garden. Jacqueline Heriteau & Charles Thomas. (Illus.). 240p. 1996. pap. 18.95 (*0-395-70935-0*) HM.

*__Water Gardens: Simple Projects, Contemporary Designs.__ Hazel White. LC 97-6981. 1998. pap. 16.95 (*0-8118-1406-8*) Chronicle Bks.

Water Gardens: Step by Step to Success. Brian Leverett. (Crowood Gardening Guides Ser.). (Illus.). 128p. 1996. pap. 17.95 (*1-85223-977-8*, Pub. by Crowood Pr UK) Trafalgar.

Water Gardens for Plants & Fish. Charles B. Thomas. (Illus.). 189p. (YA). (gr. 7 up). 1988. lib. bdg. 24.95 (*0-86622-942-6*, TS-102) TFH Pubns.

Water Ghost. Christina Russell. LC 94-74534. (Illus.). 192p. (J). (gr. 3-7). 1995. 14.95 (*1-56397-413-4*) Boyds Mills Pr.

Water Ghost & Others. John K. Bangs. 1972. reprint ed. pap. text ed. 12.95 (*0-8290-0677-X*); reprint ed. lib. bdg. 29.50 (*0-8422-8005-7*) Irvington.

Water Girl. Joyce C. Thomas. 1986. mass mkt. 3.50 (*0-380-89532-3*, Flare) Avon.

Water Ground Stone: The Ground of Japanese Poetry. Thomas Fitzsimmons. (Reflections Ser.: No. 4). (Illus.). 160p. (C). 1994. 25.00 (*0-942668-39-1*); pap. text ed. 16.95 (*0-942668-40-5*) Katydid Bks.

Water Habitat Convention: Stories & Word Mapping Activity Workbook. Story Time Stories That Rhyme Staff. (Illus.). 50p. (Orig.). (J). (gr. 4-7). 1992. ring bd. 25.95 (*1-56820-018-8*) Story Time.

*__Water Hammer.__ write for info. (*0-340-64597-0*, Pub. by E Arnold UK) Routledge Chapman & Hall.

Water Hammer: Practical Solutions. D. B. Sharp. (Illus.). 192p. 1996. text ed. 95.00 (*0-470-23599-3*) Wiley.

Water Hammer in Hydraulics & Wave Surges in Electricity. Louis J. Bergeron. 337p. reprint ed. pap. 96.10 (*0-317-10793-3*, 2011588) Bks Demand.

Water Hammer in Pipe-Line Systems. Josef Zaruba. LC 92-15017. (Developments in Water Science Ser.: Vol. 43). 362p. 1993. 246.50 (*0-444-98722-3*) Elsevier.

Water Hazard. Scott Borg. 416p. 1996. mass mkt. 5.99 (*0-440-21214-6*) Dell.

Water, Health, & Society: Selected Papers. Abel Wolman. Ed. by Gilbert F. White. LC 69-16005. 412p. reprint ed. pap. 117.50 (*0-317-11256-2*, 2055237) Bks Demand.

Water Heater Workbook: A Hands-on Guide to Water Heaters. Larry Weingarten & Suzanne Weingarten. LC 92-80345. (Illus.). 154p. (Orig.). 1992. spiral bd. 12.00 (*0-9630344-0-5*) Elemental.

Water House. Antonio Olinto. 416p. 1985. pap. 9.95 (*0-88184-229-X*) Carroll & Graf.

Water, Human Values & the Eighties. Ed. by M. L. De Wayne. 100p. 1981. pap. 16.75 (*0-08-028098-6*, Pergamon Pr) Elsevier.

Water Hyacinth: Proceedings of the International Conference on Water Hyacinth. UN Environment Programme. 1026p. 1984. 60.00 (*0-685-17134-5*, G.V.E. 84.0.1) UN.

Water Hydraulics Control Technology. Erik Trostmann. 192p. 1995. 29.75 (*0-8247-9680-2*) Dekker.

Water (I) see 1997 Annual Book of ASTM Standards: Water & Environmental Technology, Section 11

Water, Ice, & Stone. Bill Green. 22.95 (*0-06-016631-2*, HarpT) HarpC.

Water, Ice, & Stone: Science & Memory on the Antarctic Lakes. Bill Green. 1995. 23.00 (*0-517-58759-9*, Harmony) Crown Pub Group.

Water (II) see 1997 Annual Book of ASTM Standards: Water & Environmental Technology, Section 11

Water in Biology, Chemistry & Physics: Experimental Overviews & Computational Methodologies. G. W. Robinson et al. (Series in Contemporary Chemical Physics: Vol. 8). 500p. 1996. text ed. 84.00 (*981-02-2451-6*, CPcBPYg-B2923) World Scientific Pub.

Water in California. Norris Hundley, Jr. Ed. by John A. Schutz. (Golden State Ser.). 1997. 10.00 (*0-685-58339-2*) MTL.

Water in Crisis: A Guide to the World's Freshwater Resources. Ed. by Peter H. Gleick. LC 92-30061. 504p. 1993. 58.00 (*0-19-507627-3*); pap. 31.95 (*0-19-507628-1*) OUP.

Water in Crystalline Hydrates see Water: A Comprehensive Treatise

Water in Environmental Planning. Thomas Dunne & Luna B. Leopold. LC 78-8013. (Illus.). 818p. (C). 1995. text ed. write for info. (*0-7167-0079-4*) W H Freeman.

Water in Exterior Building Walls: Problems & Solutions. Ed. by Thomas A. Schwartz. LC 91-44783. (ASTM Special Technical Publication Ser.: Vol. 1107). 242p. 1991. reprint ed. pap. 69.00 (*0-608-00555-X*, 2061438) Bks Demand.

Water in Foods. Fito et al. 1994. 305.00 (*1-85861-037-0*, Pergamon Pr) Elsevier.

*__Water in Nebraska: Use, Politics, Policies.__ James Aucoin. LC 83-12512. (Illus.). 183p. 1984. reprint ed. pap. 52.20 (*0-608-02667-0*, 2063320) Bks Demand.

*__Water in New Mexico: A History of Its Management & Use.__ Ira G. Clark. LC 86-30819. (Illus.). 857p. 1987. reprint ed. pap. 180.00 (*0-608-04151-3*, 2064884) Bks Demand.

Water in Plants Bibliography Vol. 9: 1983. Ed. by J. Solarova & Jane Pospisilova. 1984. pap. text ed. 143.50 (*90-6193-520-2*) Kluwer Ac.

Water in Polymers. Ed. by Stanley P. Rowland. LC 80-13860. (ACS Symposium Ser.: No. 127). 1980. 65.95 (*0-8412-0559-0*) Am Chemical.

*__Water in Polymers.__ Ed. by Stanley P. Rowland. LC 80-13860. (ACS Symposium Ser.: Vol. 127). 606p. 1980. reprint ed. pap. 172.80 (*0-608-03064-3*, 2063517) Bks Demand.

Water in the Arab World: Perspectives & Prognoses. Ed. by Peter Rogers & Peter Lydon. LC 94-37287. 1994. write for info. (*0-674-94789-4*) HUP.

Water in the Arab World: Perspectives & Prognoses. Ed. by Peter Rogers & Peter Lydon. (Illus.). 389p. 1995. pap. text ed. 25.00 (*0-674-94780-0*, ROGWAT) HUP.

Water in the Garden: A Complete Guide to the Design & Installation of Ponds, Fountains, Streams, & Waterfalls. James Allison. (Illus.). 160p. 1991. 32.50 (*0-8212-1839-5*) Bulfinch Pr.

Water in the Global Environment. Marvin Waterstone. (Pathways in Geography Ser.: No. 3). (Illus.). 57p. (Orig.). pap. text ed. 5.00 (*0-9627379-5-X*) NCFGE.

Water in the Hispanic Southwest: A Social & Legal History, 1550-1850. Michael C. Meyer. LC 83-24276. 209p. 1996. pap. 16.95 (*0-8165-1595-6*) U of Ariz Pr.

Water in the Middle East: Legal, Political & Commercial Implications. Ed. by J. A. Allan & Chibli Mallat. 320p. 1995. text ed. 75.00 (*1-85043-645-2*, Pub. by I B Tauris UK) St Martin.

Water in the Pearl. Carol Cox. 1982. pap. 6.50 (*0-914610-28-7*) Hanging Loose.

Water in the West. Ed. by J. B. Smallwood, Jr. (Illus.). 86p. 1983. pap. text ed. 15.00 (*0-89745-024-8*) Sunflower U Pr.

Water in the Wilderness. T. D. Jakes. 1995. pap. 5.95 (*1-56229-432-6*) Pneuma Life Pub.

Water in the Wilderness: A Biblical Motif & Its Mythological Background. William H. Propp. LC 87-16314. (Harvard Semitic Monographs). 152p. 1987. 16.95 (*1-55540-157-0*, 04-00-40) Scholars Pr GA.

Water in the 21st Century: Conservation, Demand, & Supply. Ed. & Pref. by Lloyd H. Austin. (Technical Publications: No. 95-1). (Illus.). 736p. (Orig.). 1995. pap. 66.00 (*1-882132-32-7*) Am Water Resources.

Water in Wood. Christen Skaar. LC 70-39754. (Syracuse Wood Science Ser.: No. 4). 232p. reprint ed. pap. 66.20 (*0-317-08521-2*, 2051340) Bks Demand.

Water Insects. Sylvia A. Johnson. (Natural Science Ser.). (Illus.). 48p. (J). (gr. 4 up). 1989. lib. bdg. 21.50 (*0-8225-1489-3*, Lerner Publctns) Lerner Group.

Water (Intermediate) Robyn F. Spizman & Marianne D. Garber. (Illus.). 48p. (J). (gr. 4-7). 1992. student ed. 6.99 (*0-86653-676-0*, 1410) Good Apple.

Water into Wine: A Study of Ritual Idiom in the Middle East. Ethel S. Drower. LC 77-87663. reprint ed. 23.50 (*0-404-16401-3*) AMS Pr.

*__Water into Wine: A Wine Lover's Cruise Through the Vineyards of France.__ Hilary Wright. (Illus.). 176p. 1997. 35.00 (*1-85626-217-0*, C Kyle) Trafalgar.

Water into Wine: An Investigation of the Concept of Miracle. Robert A. Larmer. 160p. 1988. 44.95 (*0-7735-0615-2*, Pub. by McGill CN) U of Toronto Pr.

*__Water into Wine? An Investigation of the Concept of Miracle.__ Robert A. Larner. 1996. pap. text ed. 16.95 (*0-7735-1527-5*, Pub. by McGill CN) U of Toronto Pr.

Water into Wine & the Beheading of John the Baptist: Early Jewish-Christian Interpretation of Esther 1 in John 2: 1-11 & Mark 6: 17-29. Roger Aus. LC 88-11521. (Brown Judaic Studies). 96p. 1988. 27.95 (*1-55540-245-3*, 14-01-50) Scholars Pr GA.

Water into Wine. Stories. Helen Norris. LC 87-34289. (Illinois Short Fiction Ser.). 160p. 1988. 14.95 (*0-252-01540-1*) U of Ill Pr.

Water Is Wide. Pat Conroy. 320p. 1987. reprint ed. mass mkt. 6.50 (*0-553-26893-7*) Bantam.

Water Is Wide. Pat Conroy. (Illus.). 288p. 1990. reprint ed. 25.00 (*0-937036-03-X*) Old NY Bk Shop.

Water Island Study: Economic Development Options. B. Potter et al. 170p. 1980. 20.00 (*0-318-14620-7*) Isl Resources.

Water Island Study: Summary Report & Fiscal Analysis. Ben Posner. 64p. 1980. 10.00 (*0-318-14621-5*) Isl Resources.

Water Jet Symposium: Proceedings. Ed. by Fun-Den Wang et al. LC 81-21616. (Illus.). 248p. 1982. pap. text ed. 16.00 (*0-918062-48-9*) Colo Sch Mines.

Water King: Anthony Chabot: His Life & Times. Sherwood D. Burgess. (Illus.). 200p. (Orig.). 1992. pap. 14.95 (*0-932857-04-3*) Ag Access.

Water King's Laughter. Esther M. Friesner. 288p. 1989. mass mkt. 3.95 (*0-380-75410-X*) Avon.

Water Knowledge Transfer. Ed. by Neil S. Grigg. LC 78-63016. 1978. 40.00 (*0-918334-25-X*) WRP.

Water, Land, & Law in the West: The Limits of Public Policy, 1850-1920. Donald J. Pisani. LC 96-14093. (Development of Western Resources Ser.). 248p. 1996. 29.95 (*0-7006-0795-1*) U Pr of KS.

Water Law. 2nd ed. William Goldfarb. 304p. (C). 1988. 79.00 (*0-87371-111-4*, L111) Lewis Pubs.

Water Law: A Growing Dimension of Poverty Law, A Water-Law Resource & Litigation Manual for Low-Income Advocates. Margot J. Steadman & Alice G. Hector. (Illus.). 538p. (Orig.). 1982. pap. 33.50 (*0-941077-14-4*, 33,680) NCLS Inc.

Water Law: Adaptable to Courses Utilizing Trelease & Gould's Casebook on Water Law. Casenotes Publishing Co., Inc. Staff. Ed. by Norman S. Goldenberg & Peter Tenen. (Legal Briefs Ser.). 1986. pap. write for info. (*0-87457-143-X*, 1580) Casenotes Pub.

Water Law, Cases & Materials. 4th ed. Frank J. Trelease & George Gould. LC 86-4105. (American Casebook Ser.). 816p. (C). 1986. text ed. 52.00 (*0-314-98400-3*) West Pub.

Water Law in a Nutshell. 2nd ed. David H. Getches. (Nutshell Ser.). 459p. 1991. reprint ed. pap. 18.50 (*0-314-73779-0*) West Pub.

*__Water Law in a Nutshell.__ 3rd ed. David H. Getches. LC 96-51716. (Nutshell Ser.). 435p. (C). 1996. pap. text ed. write for info. (*0-314-21157-8*) West Pub.

Water Law in Historical Perspective. Ludwik A. Teclaff. LC 85-21899. xi, 617p. 1985. lib. bdg. 75.00 (*0-89941-460-5*, 305530) W S Hein.

Water-Level Controls on Halite Sedimentation: Permian Cyclic Evaporites of the Palo Duro Basin. S. D. Hovorka. (Report of Investigations Ser.: No. RI 214). (Illus.). 51p. 1994. pap. 7.00 (*0-614-01863-3*) Bur Econ Geology.

Water Level Route. 2nd ed. Charles M. Knoll. 1984. pap. 9.95 (*0-9605296-2-4*) Natl Rail Rochester.

Water Life. Cecilia Fitzsimons. LC 95-18859. (Nature's Hidden Worlds Ser.). (Illus.). (J). 1996. lib. bdg. 24.26 (*0-8172-3971-5*) Raintree Steck-V.

Water Life. Cecilia Fitzsimons. (J). 1996. pap. text ed. 5.95 (*0-8172-4185-X*) Raintree Steck-V.

Water, Life. Augustus Graham. 101p. 1993. pap. write for info. (*0-9636740-0-5*) Eldorado Pr.

Water Lillies: An Anthology of Spanish Women Writers from the Fifteenth Through the Nineteenth Century. Ed. by Amy Kaminsky. 592p. 1995. text ed. 54.95 (*0-8166-1944-1*); pap. text ed. 21.95 (*0-8166-1946-8*) U of Minn Pr.

Water Lily Princess. Barbara A. Zahrt. 1995. pap. 7.95 (*0-533-11320-2*) Vantage.

Water Link: A History of Puget Sound As a Resource. Daniel J. Chasan. (Puget Sound Bks.). (Illus.). 192p. 1981. pap. 9.95 (*0-295-95782-4*) U of Wash Pr.

W

Water Magic. (Illus.). (J). (ps-2). 1991. pap. 5.10 (*0-8136-5696-6*); lib. bdg. 7.95 (*0-8136-5196-4*) Modern Curr.

Water Magic: Healing Bath Recipes for the Body, Spirit & Soul. Mary Muryn. LC 95-21969. 1995. pap. 11.00 (*0-684-80142-6*, Fireside) S&S Trade.

Water Magic Water Activities for Students & Teachers. 48p. (J). (gr. k-3). 1991. pap. 6.00 (*0-89867-573-1*, 70060) Am Water Wks Assn.

Water Main Evaluation for Rehabilitation - Replacement. 197p. 1987. pap. 47.00 (*0-915295-10-5*, 90509) Am Water Wks Assn.

Water Maintainance Foreman. Jack Rudman. (Career Examination Ser.: C-2925). 1994. pap. 29.95 (*0-8373-2925-6*) Nat Learn.

Water Maintainance Man. Jack Rudman. (Career Examination Ser.: C-2657). 1994. pap. 27.95 (*0-8373-2657-5*) Nat Learn.

Water Management: Proceedings of the USCID 1987 Regional Meetings. Ed. by Susan S. Anderson et al. 592p. (Orig.). 1988. pap. 40.00 (*0-9618257-1-5*) US Comm Irrigation.

Water Management & Agricultural Development: A Case Study of the Cuyo Region of Argentina. Kenneth D. Frederick. LC 74-24402. (Resources for the Future Research Paper). (Illus.). 208p. 1975. 16.50 (*0-8018-1701-3*) Johns Hopkins.

***Water Management & Environmental Protection in Asia & the Pacific.** Ed. by Ichiro Kato et al. LC 84-164800. 212p. 1983. reprint ed. pap. 60.50 (*0-608-03651-X*, 2064477) Bks Demand.

Water Management for Irrigation & Drainage: Proceedings of the ASCE Irrigation & Drainage Division Specialty Conference on July 20-22, (1977: Reno, Nevada), 1. LC 78-101244. (Illus.). reprint ed. pap. 111.50 (*0-317-10797-6*, 2019557) Bks Demand.

Water Management for Irrigation & Drainage: Proceedings of the ASCE Irrigation & Drainage Division Specialty Conference on July 20-22, (1977: Reno, Nevada), 2. LC 78-101244. (Illus.). reprint ed. pap. 48.00 (*0-317-10798-4*, X1977) Bks Demand.

Water Management in Ancient Greek Cities. Dora P. Crouch. 336p. 1993. 70.00 (*0-19-507280-4*) OUP.

Water Management in Desert Environments: A Comparative Analysis. Bruce R. Roberts. LC 93-12681. (Lecture Notes in Earth Sciences Ser.: Vol. 48). 1993. Acid-free paper. 103.95 (*0-387-56562-0*) Spr-Verlag.

Water Management in Reservoirs. L. Votruba & V. Broza. (Developments in Water Science Ser.: No. 33). 450p. 1989. 214.50 (*0-444-98933-1*) Elsevier.

Water Management in the Yellow River Basin of China. Charles Greer. LC 78-15303. 192p. reprint ed. pap. 54.80 (*0-8357-7741-3*, 2036098) Bks Demand.

Water Management in the '90s: A Time for Innovation, Proceedings of the 20th Anniversary Conference, Seattle, Washington, May 1-5, 1993. Ed. by Katherine Hon. LC 93-3571. 912p. 1993. 64.00 (*0-87262-912-0*) Am Soc Civil Eng.

Water Management in Urban Areas. Ed. by Mark L. Loethen. (Technical Publications: No. 95-4). (Illus.). 354p. (Orig.). 1995. pap. 40.00 (*1-882132-35-1*) Am Water Resources.

Water Management in Urban Areas: Proceedings, November 5-10, 1995, Houston, TX. American Water Resources Association, Conference (31st, 1995, Houston, TX) Staff. Ed. by Mark L. Loethen. LC 95-80552. (American Water Resources Association Technical Publication Ser.: Vol. TPS-95-4). 363p. 1995. reprint ed. pap. 103.50 (*0-608-02439-2*, 2063082) Bks Demand.

Water Management Innovations in England. Lyle E. Craine. LC 70-75182. 135p. reprint ed. pap. 38.50 (*0-7837-3136-1*, 2052109) Bks Demand.

Water Management Institutions along the Texas-Mexico Border. Contrib. by David Eaton. (Policy Research Project Report: No. 56). 74p. 1983. pap. 7.50 (*0-89940-658-0*) LBJ Sch Pub Aff.

Water Management Models: A Guide to Software. Ralph A. Wurbs. LC 94-23463. (C). 1995. text ed. 61.00 (*0-13-161621-8*) P-H.

Water Management of River Systems: 27 Annual Conference & Resource Development of the Lower Mississippi River, Symposium Proceedings, New Orleans, LA, September 8-13, 1991. American Water Resources Association Staff. Ed. by Dhamo Dhamotharan. LC 91-75128. (American Water Resources Association Technical Publication Ser.: Vol. TPS-91-3). 504p. 1991. reprint ed. pap. 143.70 (*0-7837-9223-9*, 2049974) Bks Demand.

Water Management of the Amazon Basin: Proceedings from an International Seminar in Manaus, Brazil, August 1990. Ed. by UNESCO Staff et al. 288p. 1991. 20.00 (*92-9089-017-7*) Intl Water Resc.

Water Management Organizations in the People's Republic of China. James E. Nickum. LC 80-5458. (China Book Project Ser.). (Illus.). 285p. reprint ed. pap. 81.30 (*0-685-23742-7*, 2032783) Bks Demand.

Water Management Program Coordinator. Jack Rudman. (Career Examination Ser.: C-3208). 1994. pap. 39.95 (*0-8373-3208-7*) Nat Learn.

***Water Mangement Guidelines for the Greenhouse Industry: A Guide for Protecting Our Natural Water Resources.** rev. ed. Ed. by Don C. Wilkerson. 44p. 1996. pap. 20.00 (*0-7881-3311-X*) DIANE Pub.

***Water Marketing: The Next Generation.** Ed. by Terry L. Anderson & Peter J. Hill. LC 96-31065. (Political Economy Forum Ser.: No. 37). 216p. 1996. 57.50 (*0-8476-8397-4*); pap. 22.95 (*0-8476-8398-2*) Rowman.

Water Matters Vol. 2: Water Resources Teacher's Guide. Jane N. Crowder & Joe Cain. (Illus.). 32p. (J). (gr. 3-8). 1994. teacher ed., pap. text ed. 14.00 (*0-87355-127-3*, PB116X2) Natl Sci Tchrs.

Water Meadows. large type ed. Emma Blair. 752p. 1994. 27.99 (*0-7089-8777-X*) Ulverscroft.

Water Measurement Manual. USDI Staff. (C). 1985. text ed. 75.00 (*81-85046-19-0*, Pub. by Scientific Pubs II) St Mut.

Water Measurement Manual: A Manual Pertaining Primarily to Measurement of Water for Irrigation Projects. 327p. 1987. 100.00 (*0-685-18863-9*, Pub. by Scientific UK) St Mut.

Water Meter Reader. Jack Rudman. (Career Examination Ser.: C-2224). 1994. pap. 23.95 (*0-8373-2224-3*) Nat Learn.

Water Meterman. Jack Rudman. (Career Examination Ser.: C-2225). 1994. pap. 23.95 (*0-8373-2225-1*) Nat Learn.

Water Meters, No. M6: Selection, Installation, Testing & Maintenance. 106p. 1988. pap. 45.00 (*0-89867-357-7*, 30006) Am Water Wks Assn.

***Water Method Man.** Irving. 1989. mass mkt. 4.95 (*0-671-69180-5*, Pocket Books) PB.

***Water-Method Man.** John Irving. 1997. pap. 11.00 (*0-345-41800-X*) Ballantine.

Water Method Man. John Irving. 384p. 1990. mass mkt. 5.99 (*0-345-36742-1*) Ballantine.

Water-Mill Inns of France: A Gastronomic Guide to Romantic Country Inns. Marv Luther & Nona Luther. LC 95-71951. 232p. 1996. pap. 16.95 (*0-9649085-4-9*) Corinthian CA.

***Water Mill, NY Celebrating Community 1644-1994.** Marlene E. Haresign & Marsha Kranes. Date not set. pap. 20.95 (*0-8488-1772-9*); lib. bdg. 31.95 (*0-8488-1771-0*) Amereon Ltd.

Water Mills of the Missouri Ozarks. George G. Suggs, Jr. LC 89-25082. (Illus.). 224p. 1990. 37.95 (*0-8061-2259-5*) U of Okla Pr.

Water Mills of the Missouri Ozarks. George G. Suggs. LC 89-25082. 1993. pap. 17.95 (*0-8061-2432-6*) U of Okla Pr.

Water Mirror Reflecting Heaven. Tripitaka Master Hua. Tr. by Buddhist Text Translation Society from CHI. (Illus.). 82p. (Orig.). 1982. pap. 4.00 (*0-88139-501-3*) Buddhist Text.

Water Mite Genera & Subgenera. David Cook. (Memoir Ser.: No. 21). (Illus.). 860p. 1974. 75.00 (*1-56665-019-4*) Assoc Pubs FL.

Water Mites from Australia. David Cook. (Memoir Ser.: No. 40). (Illus.). 568p. 1986. 55.00 (*1-56665-038-0*) Assoc Pubs FL.

Water Mites from Chile. David Cook. (Memoir Ser.: No. 42). (Illus.). 356p. 1988. 45.00 (*1-56665-040-2*) Assoc Pubs FL.

Water Mites from India. David R. Cook. (Memoir Ser.: No. 9). (Illus.). 411p. 1967. 45.00 (*1-56665-007-0*) Assoc Pubs FL.

Water Mites of Liberia. David R. Cook. (Memoir Ser.: No. 6). (Illus.). 418p. 1966. 45.00 (*1-56665-004-6*) Assoc Pubs FL.

Water Moccasins. Kate G. Harper. 1993. pap. 10.95 (*0-9639528-1-1*) Valentine CA.

Water Music. T. Coraghessan Boyle. (Contemporary American Fiction Ser.). 448p. 1983. pap. 12.99 (*0-14-006550-4*, Penguin Bks) Viking Penguin.

Water Music. Robert Haight. 28p. (Orig.). 1993. pap. text ed. 5.00 (*1-56439-031-4*) Ridgeway.

Water Music: Poems for Children. Jane Yolen. LC 94-79163. (Illus.). 40p. (J). (gr. 3-7). 1995. 16.95 (*1-56397-336-7*, Wordsong) Boyds Mills Pr.

***Water My Soul: Only God Can Show Us How to Nurture the Life Within.** Luci Shaw. LC 97-14231. (Spiritual Directions Ser.). 1998. write for info. (*0-310-20202-7*) Zondervan.

Water Nepal Vol. 4, No. 1: Himalayan Ganga. P. Knowles. 1994. pap. 75.00 (*0-7855-0422-2*, Pub. by Ratna Pustak Bhandar) St Mut.

Water of Kane. O. A. Bushnell. LC 80-5463. 472p. 1980. 12.95 (*0-8248-0714-6*) UH Pr.

Water of Kane: And Other Legends of the Hawaiian Islands. rev. ed. Mary K. Pukui & Caroline Curtis. (Illus.). 221p. (YA). (gr. 7-12). 1994. pap. 9.95 (*0-87336-020-6*) Kamehameha Schools.

Water of Life. Armstrong. 111p. 1971. pap. 11.95 (*0-85032-052-6*, Pub. by C W Daniel UK) Natl Bk Netwk.

***Water of Life.** Amatullah Armstrong. 78p. 1996. pap. 24.00 (*0-614-21377-0*, 1420) Kazi Pubns.

Water of Life. John W. Armstrong. 136p. (C). 1971. pap. 19.95 (*0-8464-1060-5*) Beekman Pubs.

Water of Life. John Bunyan. pap. 1.59 (*0-87377-984-3*) GAM Pubns.

Water of Life. Glenn Clark. 1979. pap. 5.95 (*0-910924-86-4*) Macalester.

Water of Life. Illus. by Trina S. Hyman. LC 84-19226. 40p. (J). (gr. k-3). 1986. lib. bdg. 15.95 (*0-8234-0552-4*) Holiday.

Water of Life. Illus. by Trina S. Hyman. LC 84-19226. 40p. (J). (gr. k-3). 1991. pap. 5.95 (*0-8234-0907-4*) Holiday.

Water of Life: A Jungian Journey Through Hawaiian Myth. Rita Knipe. LC 89-5040. (Illus.). 1989. text ed. 24.00 (*0-8248-1242-5*) UH Pr.

Water of Life: A Tale of the Grateful Dead. 2nd ed. Alan Trist. (Illus.). 48p. (J). (gr. 4-6). 1989. pap. 12.00 (*0-938493-23-X*) Hulogosi Inc.

Water of Light: A Miscellany in Honor of Brewster Ghiselin. Ed. by Henry Taylor. LC 73-93299. 287p. reprint ed. pap. 81.80 (*0-7837-5536-8*, 2045309) Bks Demand.

***Water of Marah.** David Miller. (Sun & Moon Classics Ser.: Vol. 118). 1997. pap. 11.95 (*1-55713-360-3*) Sun & Moon CA.

***Water of the Wondrous Isles: 1913 Edition.** Ed. by Peter Faulkner. (William Morris Library). 408p. 1996. reprint ed. pap. write for info. (*1-85506-256-9*) Bks Intl VA.

Water on Mars. Michael H. Carr. (Illus.). 256p. 1996. 70.00 (*0-19-509938-9*) OUP.

Water on the Brain. Denys Gamblin. 96p. 1979. 7.00 (*0-7277-0070-7*, Pub. by T Telford UK) Am Soc Civil Eng.

Water on the Plateau, Vol. 53, No. 3. 32p. 1981. pap. 4.95 (*0-89734-077-9*) Mus Northern Ariz.

Water over the Dam at Mountain View in the Adirondacks. Floy S. Hyde. LC 73-126350. 1984. 18.00 (*0-317-56106-5*) F S Hyde.

***Water over the Falls: 101 of the Most Memorable Events at Niagara Falls.** Paul Gromosiak. (Illus.). 90p. 1996. pap. 5.95 (*1-879201-16-X*) Meyer Enter.

Water Over the Road see NEA Series

Water, Peace & the Middle East: Negotiating Resources in the Jordan Basin. Ed. by J. A. Allan. 208p. 1996. text ed. 59.50 (*1-86064-055-9*, Pub. by I B Tauris UK) St Martin.

Water People: A Deep Dive into the Forgotten Ocean of Male Spirit. Rich Zubaty. LC 96-67221. 128p. 1996. pap. 5.95 (*1-882342-21-6*) Panther IL.

***Water Pipe/Sewer Maintenance Services.** Richard K. Miller et al. (Market Research Survey Ser.: No. 275). 50p. 1996. 200.00 (*1-55865-304-X*) Future Tech Surveys.

Water Planet. Ralph Fletcher. 48p. (Orig.). (J). (ps-3). 1991. pap. 5.95 (*0-9628238-5-6*) Arrowhead Bks.

Water Plant Operator. Jack Rudman. (Career Examination Ser.: C-897). 1994. pap. 27.95 (*0-8373-0897-6*) Nat Learn.

Water Plant Operator Trainee. Jack Rudman. (Career Examination Ser.: C-886). 1994. pap. 23.95 (*0-8373-0886-0*) Nat Learn.

Water Plant Supervisor. Jack Rudman. (Career Examination Ser.: C-2445). 1994. pap. 34.95 (*0-8373-2445-9*) Nat Learn.

***Water Plants: At-a-Glance Guide to Varieties, Cultivation & Care.** Andrew Mikolajski. Ed. by Peter McHoy. (The New Plant Library). (Illus.). 64p. 1997. 9.95 (*1-85967-390-2*, Lorenz Bks) Anness Pub.

***Water Play.** Photos by Margaret Miller. (Illus.). (J). (ps-k). 1997. 4.99 (*0-614-29107-0*, Litl Simon S&S) S&S Childrens.

***Water Policy: Allocation & Management in Practice.** Ed. by Howsam. (Illus.). 400p. 1996. text ed. 64.50 (*0-419-21650-2*, E & FN Spon) Routledge Chapman & Hall.

Water Policy & Management: Solving the Problems, Proceedings of a Conference. Ed. by Darrell G. Fontane & Harry N. Tuvel. 920p. 1994. 81.00 (*0-685-75152-X*, 40020-2) Am Soc Civil Eng.

Water Policy & Water Markets: Selected Papers & Proceedings from the World Bank's Ninth Annual Irrigation & Drainage Seminar Held in Annapolis, Maryland, December 8-10, 1992. Ed. by Guy J. Le Moigne et al. LC 94-18954. (Technical Papers Ser.: Vol. 249). 1994. 8.95 (*0-8213-2861-1*) World Bank.

Water Policy Initiatives: Positions of the National Water Policy Committee of the ASCE on the President's June 1978 Statements. 280p. 1979. pap. 20.00 (*0-87262-193-6*) Am Soc Civil Eng.

***Water Politics: Continuity & Change.** Helen M. Ingram. LC 89-70524. (Illus.). 166p. 1990. reprint ed. pap. 47.40 (*0-608-04152-1*, 2064885) Bks Demand.

Water Pollution. Kathlyn Gay. LC 90-376. (Impact Bks.). (Illus.). 112p. (YA). (gr. 7-12). 1990. lib. bdg. 22.70 (*0-531-10949-6*) Watts.

Water Pollution. Ed. by O. Hutzinger. (Handbook of Environmental Chemistry Ser.: Vol. 5, Pt. A). (Illus.). 288p. 1991. 128.00 (*0-387-51599-2*) Spr-Verlag.

Water Pollution. Darlene R. Stille. LC 89-25344. (New True Bks.). (Illus.). 48p. (J). (gr. k-4). 1990. pap. 5.50 (*0-516-41190-X*); lib. bdg. 19.00 (*0-516-01190-1*) Childrens.

Water Pollution. A. K. Tripathi & S. N. Pandey. (C). 1990. 48.00 (*81-7024-267-3*, Pub. by Ashish II) S Asia.

Water Pollution: A Guide to Information Sources. Ed. by Allen W. Knight & Mary Ann Simmons. LC 73-17537. (Man & the Environment Information Guide Ser.: Vol. 9). 288p. 1980. 68.00 (*0-8103-1346-4*) Gale.

Water Pollution: Causes & Effects in Australia & New Zealand. 3rd ed. D. W. Connell. 1993. pap. 29.95 (*0-7022-2337-9*, Pub. by Univ Queensland Pr AT) Intl Spec Bk.

***Water Pollution: Differences among the States in Issuing Permits Limiting the Discharge of Pollutants.** (Illus.). 34p. (Orig.). (C). 1996. pap. 20.00 (*0-7881-3015-3*) DIANE Pub.

Water Pollution: Disposal & Reuse, Vol. 1. James E. Zajic. LC 70-163919. 405p. reprint ed. pap. 115.50 (*0-685-16365-2*, 2027129) Bks Demand.

Water Pollution: Disposal & Reuse, Vol. 2. James E. Zajic. LC 70-163919. 269p. reprint ed. pap. 76.70 (*0-7837-0019-9*, 2027129) Bks Demand.

Water Pollution: Economic Aspects & Research Needs. Allen V. Kneese. (Resources for the Future Ser.). 120p. 1962. pap. 6.95 (*0-8018-0343-8*) Johns Hopkins.

Water Pollution: Economic Aspects & Research Needs. Allen V. Kneese. LC 62-12587. 119p. reprint ed. pap. 34.00 (*0-685-23700-1*, 2032156) Bks Demand.

Water Pollution: Information on the Use of Alternative Wastewater Treatment Systems. (Illus.). 51p. (Orig.). (C). 1994. pap. text ed. 20.00 (*0-7881-1508-1*) DIANE Pub.

Water Pollution: Law & Liability. Ed. by Patricia Thomas. (International Bar Association Ser.). 384p. (C). 1993. lib. bdg. 160.00 (*1-85333-874-5*, Pub. by Graham & Trotman UK) Kluwer Ac.

Water Pollution: Poor Quality Assurance & Limited Pollutant Coverage Undermine EPA's Control of Toxic Substances. (Illus.). 87p. (Orig.). (C). 1995. pap. text ed. 30.00 (*0-7881-1750-5*) DIANE Pub.

Water Pollution see Environmental Law

Water Pollution & Fish Physiology. Alan G. Heath. LC 86-24348. 272p. 1987. 146.00 (*0-8493-4649-5*, SH174, CRC Reprint) Franklin.

Water Pollution & Fish Physiology. 2nd ed. Alan G. Heath. 384p. 1995. 89.95 (*0-87371-632-9*, L632) Lewis Pubs.

Water Pollution & Hazardous Wastes, 1989. Jackson B. Battle & Mark Squillace. (Environmental Law Casebook Ser.: Vol. 2A). 299p. 1989. suppl. ed., pap. 35.00 (*0-87084-085-1*) Anderson Pub Co.

Water Pollution & Toxicology. Ed. by S. K. Shukla. (C). 1992. 34.00 (*81-7169-204-4*, Commonwealth) S Asia.

Water Pollution & Water Quality in Massachusetts' Coastal Zone: A Municipal Officials Primer. Madeleine Hall-Arber. 7.00 (*1-56172-005-4*) MIT Sea Grant.

Water Pollution Assessment: Automatic Sampling & Measurement - STP 582. 126p. 1975. pap. 6.50 (*0-8031-0597-5*, 04-582000-16) ASTM.

***Water Pollution Biology.** 2nd ed. P. D. Abel. 256p. 1997. 84.95 (*0-7484-0661-1*, Pub. by Tay Francis Ltd UK); pap. 34.95 (*0-7484-0619-0*, Pub. by Tay Francis Ltd UK) Taylor & Francis.

Water Pollution Biology. 2nd ed. P. D. Abel. 1996. pap. text ed. 50.00 (*0-13-057530-5*) P-H.

Water Pollution Biology: A Laboratory-Field Handbook. Robert A. Coler & John P. Rockwood. LC 89-50810. 117p. 1989. pap. 39.95 (*0-87762-655-3*) Technomic.

Water Pollution Control. BNA's Environment & Safety Services Staff. (Policy & Practice Ser.). 1979. ring bd. 612.00 (*0-87179-913-8*) BNA.

Water Pollution Control Equipment & Services. Ed. by Peter Allen. 228p. 1989. pap. 1,795.00 (*0-941285-51-0*) FIND-SVP.

Water Pollution Control Handbook. Dennison. (Industrial Health & Safety Ser.). 1995. text ed. 59.95 (*0-442-02037-6*) Van Nos Reinhold.

***Water Pollution Control in Asia.** K. Yamamoto et al. (Advances in Water Pollution Control Ser.: Vol. 6). 732p. 1989. 175.00 (*0-08-036884-0*, Pergamon Pr) Elsevier.

Water Pollution Control in Developing Countries: Proceedings of the WHO Expert Committee, Geneva, 1972. WHO Staff. (Technical Report Ser.: No. 404). 1968. pap. text ed. 5.00 (*92-4-120404-4*, 1100404) World Health.

Water Pollution Control in the Danube Basin. Ed. by M. Miloradov. (Water Science & Technology Ser.: No. 22). (Illus.). 303p. 1990. pap. 120.50 (*0-08-040765-X*, Pergamon Pr) Elsevier.

Water Pollution II: Modelling, Measuring, & Prediction. Ed. by L. C. Wrobel & C. A. Brebbia. LC 93-71022. (Water Pollution Ser.). 760p. 1993. 242.00 (*1-56252-168-3*, 2459) Computational Mech MA.

Water Pollution III: Modelling, Measuring & Prediction. Ed. by L. C. Wrobel et al. LC 95-67474. (Water Pollution Ser.: Vol. 3). 536p. 1995. text ed. 199.00 (*1-56252-234-5*, 3102) Computational Mech MA.

Water Pollution in Europe. 116p. 1993. 1,500.00 (*0-89336-960-8*, E-065) BCC.

Water Pollution Incidents in England & Wales 1993. HMSO Staff. (Water Quality Ser.: No. 21). 68p. 1994. pap. 11.00 (*0-11-886512-9*, HM65129, Pub. by Stationery Ofc UK) Bernan Associates.

Water Pollution IV: Modelling, Measuring & Prediction. (Water Pollution Ser.: Vol. 4). 400p. 1997. 180.00 (*1-85312-470-2*, 4702) Computational Mech MA.

Water Pollution Microbiology, Vol. 1. Ed. by Ralph Mitchell. LC 73-168641. 428p. reprint ed. pap. 122.00 (*0-317-26263-7*, 2055711) Bks Demand.

Water Pollution Research & Control: Proceedings of the Eleventh Biennial Conference of the International Association on Water Pollution Research, Capetown, March 29-April 2, 1982, Vol. 14, No. 11. Ed. by S. H. Jenkins. (Illus.). 1500p. 1983. 215.00 (*0-08-029689-0*, Pergamon Pr) Elsevier.

Water Pollution Research & Control, Amsterdam 1984: Proceedings of the 12th Biennial Conference of the International Association on Water Pollution Research & Control Held in Amsterdam, The Netherlands, 17-20 September 1984. Ed. by L. Lijklema et al. 1985. 330.00 (*0-08-033657-4*, Pub. by PPL UK) Elsevier.

Water Pollution Research & Control, Brighton: Fourteenth Biennial Conference Proceedings of the International Association on Water Pollution Research & Control Held in Brighton, U.K., 18-21 July, 1988. IAPRC Programme Committee. Ed. by L. Lijklema. (Water Science & Technology Ser.: No. 21). (Illus.). 2004p. 1990. Set. 527.25 (*0-08-040152-X*, 1908; 2400, Pergamon Pr) Elsevier.

Water Pollution Research & Control, Kyoto: Proceedings of the Fifteenth Biennial Conference of the International Association on Water Pollution Research & Control, Held in Kyoto, Japan, 29 July-3 August 1990, 4 vols. Ed. by P. Grau & IAPRC Programme Committee Staff. (Water Science & Technology Ser.: No. 23). (Illus.). 2238p. 1991. Set. 470.00 (*0-08-040774-9*, Pergamon Pr) Elsevier.

An Asterisk (*) at the beginning of an entry indicates that the title is appearing in BIP for the first time.

Water Pollution Research & Development: Proceedings of the IAWPR International Conference on Water Pollution Research, 10th, Toronto, June, 1980. IAWPR International Conference Staff. Ed. by S. H. Jenkins. (Water Science & Technology Ser.). (Illus.). 1388p. 1981. 235.00 (*0-08-026025-X*, Pergamon Pr) Elsevier.

Water Pollution: Supplement see Environmental Law

Water Polo. 2nd ed. Charles F. Cicciarella. 132p. 1994. pap. text ed. 11.95 (*0-89641-066-8*) American Pr.

Water Potential Relations in Soil Microbiology. Ed. by J. F. Parr et al. 151p. 1981. pap. 6.25 (*0-89118-767-7*) Soil Sci Soc Am.

Water Power: How It Works. Robert A. Howard. (Illus.). 28p. 1979. pap. 1.50 (*0-614-16879-1*) Hagley Museum.

Water Power Development, Vol. 1. E. Mosonyi. 1074p. (C). 1987. 350.00 (*0-569-09084-9*, Pub. by Collets) St Mut.

Water Power Development, Vol. 2. E. Mosonyi. 748p. (C). 1965. 350.00 (*0-685-36847-5*, Pub. by Collets) St Mut.

Water Power Development Vol. 1: Low Head Power Plants, Vol. 1. E. Mosonyi. 1074p. (C). 1987. 300.00 (*963-05-4271-4*, Pub. by Akad Kiado HU) St Mut.

Water Power Development Vol. 11: High Head Power Plants. E. Mosonyi. 1091p. (C). 1991. 435.00 (*963-05-5885-8*, Pub. by Akad Kiado HU) St Mut.

Water Precious Water. (J). (gr. 2-6). 1988. 16.95 (*1-881431-22-3*, 1301) AIMS Educ Fnd.

Water Preparation in Thermal Power Stations Using Municipal Waste Waters. K. M. Abdullayev et al. 300p. 1992. text ed. 205.00 (*0-13-929977-7*) P-H.

Water (Prevention & Control of Pollution) Act, 1974. 2nd ed. Vijay Malik. (C). 1991. 95.00 (*0-685-39522-7*) St Mut.

Water (Primary) Ava D. Drutman. (Illus.). 48p. (J). (gr. 1-3). 1992. student ed. 6.99 (*0-86653-604-3*, 1407) Good Apple.

Water Problems of Urbanizing Areas. Compiled by William Whipple, Jr. 358p. 1979. pap. 22.00 (*0-87262-145-6*) Am Soc Civil Eng.

Water Production Functions for Irrigated Agriculture. Roger W. Hexem & Earl O. Heady. LC 77-17200. (Illus.). 231p. 1978. reprint ed. pap. 65.90 (*0-608-00029-9*, 2060795) Bks Demand.

Water Production Using Nuclear Energy. Ed. by Roy G. Post & Robert L. Seale. LC 66-24303. (Illus.). 392p. reprint ed. pap. 111.80 (*0-317-10713-5*, 2055358) Bks Demand.

Water Program Specialist. Jack Rudman. (Career Examination Ser.: C-3488). 1994. pap. 34.95 (*0-8373-3488-8*) Nat Learn.

Water Proof Chart to Long Island Sound, No. 1. Embassy Guides Staff. 1993. pap. 19.95 (*0-930527-23-2*) Embassy Marine.

Water Pumping Devices: A Handbook for Users & Choosers. 2nd ed. Peter Frankel. 312p. (Orig.). 1996. pap. 34.50 (*1-85339-346-0*, Pub. by Intermed Tech UK) Women Ink.

Water Pup. Peter Parnall. LC 92-40850. (Illus.). 144p. (J). (gr. 3 up). 1993. 13.95 (*0-02-770151-4*, Mac Bks Young Read) S&S Childrens.

Water Purification Market. Ed. by Peter Allen. 300p. 1987. pap. 1,250.00 (*0-941285-09-X*) FIND-SVP.

Water Quality. 2nd ed. 1995. write for info. (*0-89867-804-8*) Am Water Wks Assn.

Water Quality: Management & Pollution Control Problems. S. H. Jenkins. 1973. 169.00 (*0-08-017006-4*, Pergamon Pr) Elsevier.

Water Quality: Management of a Natural Resource. James A. Perry & Elizabeth Vanderklein. LC 96-857. (Illus.). 450p. (Orig.). 1996. pap. text ed. 69.95 (*0-86542-469-1*) Blackwell Sci.

Water Quality: Urban Runoff Solutions. Laurel Berman et al. (Special Reports: No. 61). 32p. (Orig.). 1991. pap. text ed. 35.00 (*0-917084-18-7*) Am Public Works.

Water Quality & Availability: A Reference Handbook. E. Willard Miller & Ruby M. Miller. LC 92-33057. (Contemporary World Issues Ser.). 430p. 1992. lib. bdg. 39.50 (*0-87436-647-X*) ABC-CLIO.

Water Quality & Diffuse Pollution. Vladimir Novotny. 1994. text ed. 93.95 (*0-442-00559-8*) Van Nos Reinhold.

Water Quality & Its Control. Miko Hino. (Hydraulic Structures Design Manual Ser.: Vol. 5). (Illus.). 262p. 1994. text ed. 110.00 (*90-5410-123-7*, Pub. by A A Balkema NE) Ashgate Pub Co.

Water Quality & Management for Recreation & Tourism: Proceedings of IAWPRC Conference, Brisbane, Australia, 10-15 July 1988. Ed. by B. Rigden & L. Henry. (Water Science & Technology Ser.: No. 21). (Illus.). 318p. 1989. pap. 107.50 (*0-08-037383-6*, Pergamon Pr) Elsevier.

Water Quality & the Early Life History of Fishes. Ed. by L. A. Fuiman. LC 93-73537. (Symposium Ser.: No. 14). 172p. 1993. pap. 27.50 (*0-913235-86-5*) Am Fisheries Soc.

Water Quality & Treatment. Ed. by R. Urbistondo & L. R. Bays. 76p. 1985. 24.00 (*0-08-031432-5*, Pergamon Pr) Elsevier.

Water Quality & Treatment. 4th ed. 960p. 1990. text ed. 110.00 (*0-07-001540-6*, 10053) McGraw.

Water-Quality Assessment of the Kentucky River Basin, Kentucky: Analysis of Available Surface Water Quality Data Through 1986. James L. Smoot et al. Vol. B, Vol. 2351-B. write for info. (*0-318-72289-5*) US Geol Survey.

Water-Quality Assessment of the Lower Kansas River Basin, Kansas & Nebraska: Surface-Water-Quality Analysis of Available Data Through 1986. Ed. by P. R. Jordan & J. K. Stamer. Vol. B. 1995. write for info. (*0-318-72600-9*) US Geol Survey.

Water Quality Assessments: A Guide to the Use of Biota, Sediments & Water in Environmental Monitoring. Ed. by Deborah Chapman. (Illus.). 586p. 1992. 85.00 (*0-412-44840-8*, A7504) Chapman & Hall.

Water Quality Control Specialist. Jack Rudman. (Career Examination Ser.: C-3337). 1994. pap. 34.95 (*0-8373-3337-7*) Nat Learn.

Water Quality Controls at Shiplocks: Prevention of Salt & Fresh Water Exchange. J. Kerstma et al. (Illus.). 130p. (C). 1994. text ed. 55.00 (*90-5410-142-3*, Pub. by A A Balkema NE) Ashgate Pub Co.

Water Quality Criteria. American Society for Testing & Materials Staff. LC 67-14533. (American Society for Testing & Materials Special Technical Publication Ser.: 416). 127p. reprint ed. pap. 36.20 (*0-317-10923-5*, 2000707) Bks Demand.

Water Quality Data: Analysis & Interpretation. Arthur W. Hounslow. 416p. 1995. 79.95 (*0-87371-676-0*, L676) Lewis Pubs.

Water Quality Deterioration in a Suburbanizing Basin: Brandywine Creek, Pennsylvania. Thomas R. Hammer. (Discussion Paper Ser.: No. 78). 1974. pap. 10.00 (*1-55869-133-2*) Regional Sci Res Inst.

***Water Quality for Agriculture.** rev. ed. 186p. 1994. 25.00 (*92-5-102263-1*, F2825, Pub. by FAO IT) Bernan Associates.

Water Quality for Dialysis: Current Concepts in Hemodialyzer Reprocessing. 2nd ed. AAMI Staff. (Illus.). 59p. (Orig.). 1993. pap. 90.00 (*1-57020-003-3*, WQD-209) Assn Adv Med Instrn.

***Water Quality for Fish Culture.** Poxton. (Chapman & Hall Aquaculture Ser.). (Illus.). 352p. (C). (gr. 13 up). 1997. text ed. 69.95 (*0-412-44860-2*, Chap & Hall NY) Chapman & Hall.

Water Quality for Freshwater Fish: Further Advisory Criteria. Ed. by Gwyneth Howells. LC 93-40991. (Environmental Topics Ser.: Vol. 6). 290p. 1994. text ed. 95.00 (*2-88124-922-1*) Gordon & Breach.

Water-Quality Hydrology see Proceedings of the International Conference on Hydrology & Water Resources, New Delhi, India, December 1993

Water Quality Impact Analysis. Ed. by S. K. Shukla. (C). 1992. 32.00 (*81-7169-212-5*, Commonwealth) S Asia.

Water-Quality Impacts of Unsewered Housing. William T. Howard & Thomas R. Hammer. (Discussion Paper Ser.: No. 66). 1973. pap. 10.00 (*1-55869-134-0*) Regional Sci Res Inst.

Water Quality in Catchment Ecosystems. Ed. by Anthony M. Gower. LC 79-42907. (Institution of Environmental Sciences Ser.). 347p. reprint ed. pap. 98.90 (*0-685-20750-1*, 2030391) Bks Demand.

Water Quality in Latin America: Balancing the Microbial & Chemical Risks in Drinking Water Disinfection. Ed. by G. Craun. 211p. 1996. pap. 52.50 (*0-944398-48-0*) ILSI.

Water Quality in Latin America: Balancing the Microbial & Chemical Risks in Drinking Water Disinfection. Ed. by G. Craun. 211p. (SPA.). 1996. pap. 52.50 (*0-944398-49-9*) ILSI.

Water Quality in North American River Systems. Ed. by C. Dale Becker & Duane A. Neitzel. LC 92-4935. 328p. 1992. per. 44.95 (*0-935470-50-6*) Battelle.

Water Quality Indicators Guide: Surface Waters. 1992. lib. bdg. 79.95 (*0-8490-8758-9*) Gordon Pr.

Water Quality Indicators Guide: Surface Waters. Charles R. Terrell & Patricia B. Perfetti. (Illus.). 129p. (Orig.). (C). 1993. pap. text ed. 35.00 (*1-56806-182-X*) DIANE Pub.

Water Quality Indicator's Guide: Surface Waters. Terrene Institute (TTI) Staff. 144p. 1996. per., pap. text ed. 26.95 (*0-7872-1787-5*) Kendall-Hunt.

Water Quality Indicators Guide: Surface Waters. 2nd ed. Charles R. Terrell & Patricia B. Perfetti. (Illus.). 208p. (Orig.). 1996. pap. 26.95 (*0-614-14301-2*) Terrene Inst.

Water Quality Instrumentation. Richard K. Miller & Marcia E. Rupnow. LC 90-83896. (Survey on Technology & Markets Ser.: No. 192). 50p. 1991. pap. text ed. 200.00 (*1-55865-216-7*) Future Tech Surveys.

***Water Quality Instrumentation.** Richard K. Miller et al. (Market Research Survey Ser.: No. 277). 50p. 1996. 200.00 (*1-55865-305-8*) Future Tech Surveys.

Water Quality International 1994 Part 1: Combined Sewer Overflows & Urban Storm Drainage. Ballay. (Water Science & Technology Ser.). 212p. 1995. pap. 90.75 (*0-08-042547-X*, Pergamon Pr) Elsevier.

***Water Quality International '92 Washington, D. C., 1992.** M. Suzuki & IAWPRC Programme Committee. (Water Science & Technology Ser.: Vol. 26). 2757p. 1993. 1,202.50 (*0-08-042044-3*, Pergamon Pr) Elsevier.

Water Quality International 94 Pt. 2: Watermatex 94 - Systems Analysis & Computing in Water Quality Management. Ed. by D. Ballay et al. (Water Science & Technology Ser.: Vol. 30). 234p. 1994. pap. 100.75 (*0-08-042548-8*, Pergamon Pr) Elsevier.

Water Quality International 94 Pt. 4: Design & Operation of Wastewater. Ballay et al. (Water Science & Technology Ser.). (Illus.). 290p. 1995. pap. 138.50 (*0-08-042549-6*, Pergamon Pr) Elsevier.

Water Quality International 94 Pt. 5: Water Quality Management in Central Eastern Europe. Ballay et al. (Water Science & Technology Ser.). 280p. 1995. pap. 138.50 (*0-08-042553-4*, Pergamon Pr) Elsevier.

Water Quality International 94 Pt. 6: Nutrient Removal. Ed. by D. Ballay et al. (Water Science & Technology Ser.: Vol. 30). 378p. 1995. pap. 160.50 (*0-08-042554-2*, Pergamon Pr) Elsevier.

***Water Quality International '94 Pt. 7: Groundwater Contamination, Environmental Restoration & Diffuse Source Pollution.** Ed. by D. Ballay et al. (Water Science & Technology Ser.: Vol. 30). 184p. 1995. pap. 69.25 (*0-08-042617-4*) Elsevier.

***Water Quality International '94 Pt. 8: Anaerobic Digestion; Sludge Management; Appropriate Technologies.** D. Ballay et al. (Water Science & Technology Ser.: Vol. 30). 314p. 1995. 138.50 (*0-08-042629-8*, Pergamon Pr) Elsevier.

***Water Quality International '94 Pt. 9: Special Applications & Emerging Technologies; Specific Pollutants & Treatment Technologies; Water Reuse - Industrial & Municipal Applications.** D. Ballay & IAWQ Programme Committee. (Water Science & Technology Ser.: Vol. 30). 260p. 1995. 115.00 (*0-08-042630-1*, Pergamon Pr) Elsevier.

Water Quality International 94 Pt. 10: Water Quality Monitoring. Ballay et al. (Water Science & Technology Ser.). 304p. 1995. pap. 138.50 (*0-08-042638-7*, Pergamon Pr) Elsevier.

Water Quality International 94 Pt. 11: Petrochemical Waste Management. 2nd ed. Ballay et al. (Water Science & Technology Ser.). 274p. 1995. pap. 115.00 (*0-08-042632-8*, Pergamon Pr) Elsevier.

Water Quality International 94 - WST 30-3 Pt. 3: Chemical & Petrochemical Waste Management. Ballay et al. (Water Science & Technology Ser.). 286p. 1995. pap. 115.00 (*0-08-042550-X*, Pergamon Pr) Elsevier.

***Water Quality International '96: River Basin Management; Management & Institutional Affairs; Environmental Engineering Education.** Ed. by D. Ballay et al. 214p. 1997. pap. 128.00 (*0-08-043092-9*, Pergamon Pr) Elsevier.

***Water Quality International '96: Wet Weather Pollution Control; Sewage Design, Operation & Maintenance; Instrumentation, Control & Automation; Large Wastewater Treatment Plants; Sludge Management; Cross Media Pollution & Volatile Organic Emissions.** Ed. by D. Ballay et al. (Water Science & Technology Ser.). 594p. 1996. pap. text ed. 255.00 (*0-08-043086-4*, Pergamon Pr) Elsevier.

***Water Quality International '96 Pt. 1: Nutrient Removal.** Ed. by D. Ballay et al. 504p. 1996. pap. 255.00 (*0-08-043081-3*, Pergamon Pr) Elsevier.

***Water Quality International '96 Pt. 3: Modelling of Activated Sludge Processes; Microorganisms in Activated Sludge & Biofilm Processes; Anaerobic Biological Treatment; Biofouling.** Ed. by D. Ballay et al. 544p. 1996. pap. 255.00 (*0-08-043085-6*, Pergamon Pr) Elsevier.

***Water Quality International '96 Pt. 4: Environmental Contaminants; Health-Related Water Microbiology; Coastal Pollution & Eutrophication; Environmental Restoration, Groundwater Contamination & Management; Solid Waste Disposal.** Ed. by D. Ballay et al. 474p. 1996. pap. 255.00 (*0-08-043087-2*, Pergamon Pr) Elsevier.

***Water Quality International '96 Pt. 5: Innovative Treatment Technologies; Membrane Technology.** Ed. by D. Ballay et al. 270p. 1996. pap. 128.00 (*0-08-043088-0*, Pergamon Pr) Elsevier.

***Water Quality International '96 Pt. 6: Chemical, Petrochemical & Hazardous Waste Management.** Ed. by D. Ballay et al. 196p. 1997. pap. 128.00 (*0-08-043089-9*, Pergamon Pr) Elsevier.

***Water Quality International '96 Pt. 7: Agro-Industries Technologies & Waste Stabilization Ponds; Wastewater Reclamation & Reuse.** Ed. by D. Ballay et al. 270p. 1997. pap. 128.00 (*0-08-043091-0*, Pergamon Pr) Elsevier.

Water Quality Issues at Fossil Fuel Plants: Proceedings of a Symposium Sponsored by the Energy Division. Ed. by William G. Dinchak & Michael J. Mathis. 90p. 1985. 14.00 (*0-87262-490-0*) Am Soc Civil Eng.

Water Quality Issues of the California-Baja California Border Region. Ed. by Clifton G. Metzner, Jr. (Border Issue Ser.). 84p. 1989. 10.00 (*0-925613-02-9*) SDSU Inst Reg Studies.

Water Quality Management. Peter A. Krenkel & Vladimir Novotny. LC 80-516. 1980. text ed. 151.00 (*0-12-426150-7*) Acad Pr.

Water Quality Management: An Introduction. George Tchobanoglous & Edward D. Schroeder. (Illus.). 1985. teacher ed. write for info. (*0-201-05434-5*) Addison-Wesley.

Water Quality Management: An Introduction. George Tchobanoglous & Edward D. Schroeder. (Illus.). (C). 1985. text ed. 70.95 (*0-201-05433-7*) Addison-Wesley.

Water Quality Management - Nonpoint Source Pollution Digest. 321p. pap. 70.00 (*1-881369-30-7*) Water Environ.

Water Quality: Management & Pollution Control Problems see Progress in Water Technology

Water Quality Management for Pond Fish Culture. C. E. Boyd. (Developments in Aquaculture & Fisheries Science Ser.: Vol. 9). 318p. 1982. 166.25 (*0-444-42054-1*) Elsevier.

Water Quality Management for the Metals & Minerals Industries, a Short Course (In Conjunction with the 104th AIME Annual Meeting, New York, 1975) Metallurgical Society of AIME Staff. 147p. reprint ed. pap. 41.90 (*0-317-10692-9*, 2004307) Bks Demand.

***Water Quality Management Plan North Sea: Framework for Analysis.** Rob Koudstaal. (Coastal Waters Ser.: No. 1). 141p. 1987. 70.00 (*90-6191-748-4*, Pub. by A A Balkema NE) Ashgate Pub Co.

***Water Quality Measurement: The Modern Analytical Techniques.** Harry B. Mark, Jr. Ed. by James S. Mattson. LC 81-5408. (Pollution Engineering & Technology Ser.: Vol. 18). reprint ed. pap. 141.10 (*0-608-04612-4*, 2065381) Bks Demand.

Water Quality Modeling. LC 95-75944. (Illus.). 539p. (Orig.). 1995. pap. 44.00 (*0-929355-64-4*, P0595) Am Soc Ag Eng.

Water Quality Modeling Vol. 2: Biochem - Geochem Cycles - Rivers. McCutcheon. 1995. 195.00 (*0-8493-6972-X*) CRC Pr.

Water Quality Modeling, Vol. 1: River Transport & Surface Exchange. Steve C. McCutcheon. (Illus.). 553p. 1990. 241.95 (*0-8493-6971-1*, TD370) CRC Pr.

Water Quality Modeling, Vol. 3: Applications to Estuaries. Lung & French. 208p. 1993. 159.95 (*0-8493-6973-8*, TD370) CRC Pr.

Water Quality Modeling, Vol. 4: Decision Support Techniques. Henderson-Sell. (Illus.). 462p. 1991. 228.95 (*0-8493-6974-6*, TD370) CRC Pr.

Water Quality Modelling. Ed. by Roger A. Falconer. 128p. 1992. 63.95 (*1-85742-034-9*, Pub. by Avebury Technical UK) Ashgate Pub Co.

Water Quality Monitoring in the Asian & Pacific Region. (Water Resources Ser.: No. 67). 345p. 1991. 37.00 (*92-1-119568-3*) UN.

Water Quality Parameters: A Symposium. Symposium on Water Quality Parameters - Selection, Measurement, & Monitoring Staff. LC 74-28980. (ASTM Special Technical Publication Ser.: No. 573). (Illus.). 590p. reprint ed. pap. 168.20 (*0-7837-4416-1*, 2044160) Bks Demand.

Water Quality, Planning & Management. Ed. by D. Ouazar et al. (Computer Methods & Water Resources Ser.: Vol. 6). 310p. 1988. 116.95 (*0-387-18858-4*) Spr-Verlag.

Water Quality, Protection & Remediation: Building Sustainable Communities, an Environmental Guide for Local Government. 326p. 1991. 40.00 (*1-880386-08-9*) Ctr Study Law.

Water Quality Standards for Wetlands: National Guidance. (Illus.). 60p. (Orig.). (C). 1994. pap. text ed. 20.00 (*0-7881-0639-2*) DIANE Pub.

Water Quality Standards Handbook. Environmental Protection Agency Staff. 482p. 1995. pap. text ed. 95.00 (*0-86587-468-9*) Gov Insts.

Water Quality Student Workbook, Vol. 4. (Principles & Practices of Water Supply Operations Ser.). 96p. 1995. pap. 18.00 (*0-89867-813-7*, 1968) Am Water Wks Assn.

Water Quantity - Quality Management & Conflict Resolution: Institutions, Processes & Economic Analyses. Ed. by Ariel Dinar & Edna T. Loehman. LC 94-13729. 552p. 1995. text ed. 75.00 (*0-275-94782-3*, Praeger Pubs) Greenwood.

Water Rates, No. M1. 4th ed. 92p. 1990. pap. 40.00 (*0-89867-574-X*, 30001) Am Water Wks Assn.

***Water Rates & Related Charges, No. M26.** 2nd ed. 110p. 1996. pap. 60.00 (*0-89867-817-X*, 30026) Am Water Wks Assn.

Water Re-Use & the Cities. Roger E. Kasperson & Jeanne X. Kasperson. 238p. (C). 1986. 305.00 (*0-685-54223-8*, Pub. by Scientific UK) St Mut.

Water Re-Use & the Cities. Ed. by Roger E. Kasperson & Jeanne X. Kasperson. (C). 1987. text ed. 305.00 (*0-685-22076-1*, Pub. by Scientific UK) St Mut.

Water Re-Use & the Cities. Ed. by Roger E. Kasperson & Jeanne X. Kasperson. LC 75-44888. 252p. reprint ed. pap. 71.90 (*0-7837-0378-3*, 2040698) Bks Demand.

Water Reactor Fuel Extended Burnup Study. IAEA Staff. (Technical Reports: No. 343). 60p. 1992. pap. 30.00 (*92-0-103992-1*, STI/DOC/343, Pub. by IAEA AU) Bernan Associates.

Water Relations of Plants. Ed. by Paul J. Kramer. 428p. 1983. text ed. 69.00 (*0-12-425040-8*) Acad Pr.

Water Relations of Plants & Soils. Paul J. Kramer & John S. Boyer. (Illus.). 495p. 1995. boxed 69.95 (*0-12-425060-2*) Acad Pr.

Water Relations of Terrestrial Arthropods. Neil F. Hadley. (Illus.). 356p. 1994. text ed. 79.95 (*0-12-312990-7*) Acad Pr.

Water Relationships in Foods: Advances in the 1980s & Trends for the 1990s. Ed. by H. Levine & L. Slade. (Advances in Experimental Medicine & Biology Ser.: Vol. 302). (Illus.). 850p. 1991. 175.00 (*0-306-43936-0*, Plenum Pr) Plenum.

Water Rescue. 7th ed. Kidd-Czajkowski & First Due Rescue Company Staff. 70p. (C). (gr. 13). 1994. teacher ed., pap. 37.00 (*0-8151-5088-1*) Mosby Yr Bk.

Water Rescue: Basic Skills for Emergency Responders. David Smith & Sara J. Smith. LC 93-30283. 368p. (C). (gr. 13). 1993. pap. text ed. 25.95 (*0-8016-6343-1*) Mosby Yr Bk.

Water Research. Ed. by Allen V. Kneese & Stephen C. Smith. 526p. 1967. 30.00 (*0-8018-0344-6*) Resources Future.

Water Research -- Contaminants in Drinking Water: Index of New Information & Research Reference Book. Susan H. Silena. 150p. 1996. 47.50 (*0-7883-1126-3*); pap. 44.50 (*0-7883-1127-1*) ABBE Pubs Assn.

Water Research -- Strange Substances (Mutagens, Teratogens, Asbestos, Fibers & Other Substances) in Drinking Water: Index of New Information & Research Reference Book. Susan H. Silena. 150p. 1996. 47.50 (*0-7883-1128-X*); pap. 44.50 (*0-7883-1129-8*) ABBE Pubs Assn.

Water Research--Drinking Water & Its Contents of Potential Cancer-Causing Substances: Index of New Information & Research Reference Book. Susan H. Silena. 150p. 1996. 47.50 (*0-7883-1130-1*); pap. 44.50 (*0-7883-1131-X*) ABBE Pubs Assn.

Water-Resisting Basements, Report 139. Construction Industry Research & Information Association Staff. 189p. 1995. 115.00 (*0-7277-2042-2*) Am Soc Civil Eng.

Water Resouces Administration in the United States: Policy, Practice, & Emerging Issues: Selected Papers from the American Water Resources Association National Forum on Water Management Policy, June 28-July 1, 1992, Washington, DC. National Forum on Water Management Policy Staff. Ed. by Martin Reuss. LC 93-7668. (Illus.). 326p. 1993. reprint ed. pap. 93.00 (*0-7837-9226-3*, 2049977) Bks Demand.

Water Resource Challenges in the Ganges-Brahmaputra River Basin: Hydropower, Deforestation, Legal Institutions. David Eaton & Mahesh C. Chaturvedi. (Policy Research Project Report: No. 101). 72p. 1993. pap. 10.50 (*0-89940-709-9*) LBJ Sch Pub Aff.

W

Water Resource Development & Management in the Edwards Aquifer Region. Contrib. by Emmette S. Redford. (Policy Research Project Report: No. 1). 63p. 1972. pap. 3.00 (*0-89940-600-9*) LBJ Sch Pub Aff.

Water Resource Investment & the Public Interest: An Analysis of Federal Expenditures in Ten Southern States. Robert H. Haveman. LC 65-18545. 213p. reprint ed. pap. 60.80 (*0-8357-3257-6*, 2039478) Bks Demand.

Water Resource Management. 4th ed. A. Dan Tarlock et al. (University Casebook Ser.). 930p. 1993. text ed. 45.95 (*1-56662-068-6*) Foundation Pr.

Water Resource Management: An Annotated Bibliography. British Computer Society Staff. Ed. by R. A. Newell. LC 81-40231. (Use of Computers for National Development Ser.). 79p. reprint ed. pap. 25.00 (*0-685-44432-5*, 2032668) Bks Demand.

Water Resource Management: Principles, Cases & Regulations. Neil S. Grigg. (Illus.). 544p. 1996. text ed. 69.95 (*0-07-024782-X*) McGraw.

Water Resource Management in Northern Mexico. Ronald G. Cummings. LC 72-3612. 80p. reprint ed. pap. 25.00 (*0-317-26458-3*, 2023794) Bks Demand.

Water Resource Planning & Development. Margaret S. Peterson. (Illus.). 240p. 1984. text ed. 61.00 (*0-13-945908-1*) P-H.

Water Resources. Ed. by Asit K. Biswas. LC 96-38133. (Illus.). 1000p. 1997. text ed. 65.00 (*0-07-005483-5*) McGraw.

Water Resources: A Changing Strategy? Conference Proceedings. 220p. 1980. 62.00 (*0-7277-0097-9*, Pub. by T Telford UK) Am Soc Civil Eng.

Water Resources: Distribution, Use & Management. John R. Mather. (Environmental Science & Technology Ser.: No. 1-121). 439p. 1983. text ed. 74.95 (*0-471-89401-X*) Wiley.

Water Resources: Planning & Management. Otto J. Helweg. 378p. (C). 1992. reprint ed. lib. bdg. 61.50 (*0-89464-610-9*) Krieger.

Water Resources: Present & Future Uses. Frederick H. Newell. LC 72-2859. (Use & Abuse of America's Natural Resources Ser.). (Illus.). 350p. 1972. reprint ed. 23.95 (*0-405-04523-9*) Ayer.

Water Resources Administration in the United States: Policy, Practice, & Emerging Issues. Ed. by Martin Reuss. LC 93-7668. 300p. (C). 1993. 40.00 (*0-87013-333-0*) Mich St U Pr.

Water Resources Administration in the United States Policy, Practice, & Emerging Issues. Ed. by Martin Reuss. LC 93-7668. (Technical Publications: No. 92-3). (Illus.). 314p. 1993. 40.00 (*1-882132-19-X*, CIP) Am Water Resources.

***Water Resources & Agricultural Development in the Tropics.** C. J. Barrow. 1987. pap. 24.95 (*0-582-30137-8*, Pub. by Longman UK) Longman.

Water Resources & Conflict in the Middle East. Nurit Kliot. LC 93-32288. 368p. (C). (gr. 13). 1993. text ed. 160.00 (*0-415-09752-5*, Routledge NY) Routledge.

Water Resources & Environmental Hazards: Emphasis on Hydrologic & Cultural Insight in the Pacific Rim. Ed. by Raymond Herrmann. (Technical Publications: No. 95-2). 300p. 1995. pap. 50.00 (*1-882132-33-5*) Am Water Resources.

Water Resources & Land-Use Planning: A Systems Approach. P. LaConte & Y. Y. Haimes. 1982. lib. bdg. 158.50 (*90-247-2726-X*) Kluwer Ac.

Water Resources & Public Policy. Ed. by Dean E. Mann et al. 304p. (Orig.). 1985. pap. 15.00 (*0-918592-79-8*) Pol Studies.

Water Resources & the Law. Summer Institute on International & Comparative Law Staff. (Michigan Legal Publications). xi, 614p. 1986. reprint ed. lib. bdg. 50.00 (*0-89941-496-6*, 304230) W S Hein.

Water Resources & the National Welfare. Walter U. Garstka. LC 77-74260. 1978. 45.00 (*0-918334-19-5*) WRP.

Water Resources & Water Management. M. K. Jermar. (Developments in Water Science Ser.: No. 28). 386p. 1987. 176.75 (*0-444-42717-1*) Elsevier.

Water Resources Atlas of Florida. Ed. by Edward A. Fernald & Donald J. Patton. (Illus.). 291p. 1984. 29.50 (*0-9606708-1-5*) Florida State U Inst.

Water Resources Development in Asia & the Pacific: Dam Safety Evaluation & Monitoring, Water Tariffs & Rain-Water Harvesting. (Water Resources Ser.: No. 63). 136p. 15.50 (*92-1-119466-0*) UN.

Water Resources Development in Asia & the Pacific: Some Issues & Concerns. (Water Resources Ser.: No. 62). 202p. 1988. pap. 21.00 (*92-1-119443-1*, 87.II.F.15) UN.

Water Resources Development in Developing Countries. D. Stephenson & Margaret S. Peterson. (Developments in Water Science Ser.: No. 41). 290p. 1991. 148.25 (*0-444-88956-6*) Elsevier.

Water Resources Development of the Mighty Himalayan Rivers: Indus, Ganga-Yamuna, Brahamaputra Rivers. S. N. Bastola. 1994. pap. 75.00 (*0-7855-0423-0*, Pub. by Ratna Pustak Bhandar) St Mut.

***Water Resources Education, Training, & Practice: Opportunities for the Next Century.** Ed. by John J. Warwick. (Technical Publication Ser.: Vol. 97-1). 500p. 1997. pap. write for info. (*1-882132-40-8*) Am Water Resources.

Water Resources Engineering. 4th ed. Ray K. Linsley. 1992. text ed. write for info. (*0-07-038010-4*) McGraw.

Water Resources Engineering. 4th ed. Ray K. Linsley. 1993. Solutions manual. lab manual ed., student ed., pap. text ed. write for info. (*0-07-038012-0*) McGraw.

Water Resources Engineering: Proceedings of the First International Conference, 2. Ed. by William H. Espey, Jr. & Phil G. Combs. LC 95-34193. 1948p. 1995. 170.00 (*0-7844-0108-X*) Am Soc Civil Eng.

Water Resources Engineering Risk Assessment. Ed. by J. Ganoulis. (NATO ASI Series G: Ecological Sciences: Vol. 29). xii, 539p. 1992. 199.00 (*0-387-54602-2*) Spr-Verlag.

***Water Resources Environmental Markets.** 245p. 1996. 185.00 (*0-614-29514-9*) R K Miller Assocs.

***Water Resources Environmental Markets.** Richard K. Miller et al. 245p. 1997. 185.00 (*1-881503-65-8*) R K Miller Assocs.

Water Resources for Agricultural Production in the U. S. LC 85-71168. 39p. 1985. pap. 19.50 (*0-916150-72-0*, Z0985) Am Soc Ag Eng.

Water Resources for Lodging Operations. Ed. by David M. Stipanuk & Stephani Robson. 1995. pap. write for info. (*0-86612-127-7*) Educ Inst Am Hotel.

Water Resources for Our Cities. Duane Baumann & Daniel Dworkin. Ed. by Salvatore J. Natoli. LC 78-59100. (Resource Papers for College Geography). (Illus.). 1978. pap. text ed. 15.00 (*0-89291-130-1*) Assn Am Geographers.

Water Resources, Geography & Law. Olen P. Matthews. LC 84-70006. 1984. pap. 15.00 (*0-89291-174-3*) Assn Am Geographers.

Water Resources Geography & Law. Glen P. Matthews. 1987. reprint ed. 60.00 (*81-85046-45-X*, Pub. by Scientific UK) St Mut.

Water Resources Handbook. Larry W. Mays. 1996. text ed. 125.00 (*0-07-041150-6*) McGraw.

Water Resources in Pennsylvania: Availability, Quality & Management. Ed. by Shyamal K. Majumdar et al. LC 89-63978. (Illus.). xiii, 580p. (C). 1990. text ed. 45.00 (*0-945809-02-6*) Penn Science.

Water Resources in the Arid Realm. Clive Agnew & Ewan W. Anderson. LC 91-38302. (Physical Environment Ser.). (Illus.). 320p. (C). 1992. pap. 35.00 (*0-415-07969-1*, A7332); text ed. 85.00 (*0-415-04346-8*, A7259) Routledge.

Water Resources Infrastructure: Need, Economics & Financing - Proceedings of the Symposium. Ed. by John F. Scott & Reza M. Khanbilvardi. LC 90-450. 225p. 1990. pap. text ed. 29.00 (*0-87262-755-1*) Am Soc Civil Eng.

Water Resources Institutions: Principles & Practices. Harald D. Frederiksen. LC 92-21129. (Technical Paper Ser.: No. 191). 50p. 1992. 6.95 (*0-8213-2295-8*, 12295) World Bank.

Water Resources Legislation & Administration in Selected Caribbean Countries. (Natural Resources Water Ser.: No.16). 171p. 1986. pap. 16.50 (*92-1-123105-1*, E.86.II. H.2) UN.

Water Resources Management. 160p. (SPA.). 1994. 6.95 (*0-8213-2638-4*, 12638) World Bank.

Water Resources Management. 160p. (ARA.). 1994. 6.95 (*0-8213-2639-2*, 12639) World Bank.

Water Resources Management. LC 93-31793. (Policy Study Ser.). 160p. 1994. 6.95 (*0-8213-2636-8*, 12636) World Bank.

Water Resources Management: In Search of an Environmental Ethic. David L. Feldman. LC 90-43987. 296p. 1991. text ed. 40.00 (*0-8018-4075-9*) Johns Hopkins.

Water Resources Management: In Search of an Environmental Ethic. David L. Feldman. LC 90-43987. 296p. 1995. pap. text ed. 16.95 (*0-8018-5125-4*) Johns Hopkins.

Water Resources Management: Modern Decision Techniques: Selected Papers from the International Symposium on the Application of Systems Analysis to Water Resources Management, Perugia, 1986. Ed. by Marcello Benedini et al. (IAHR Proceedings Ser.: No. 4). (Illus.). 155p. (C). 1992. text ed. 99.00 (*90-6191-148-6*, Pub. by A A Balkema NE) Ashgate Pub Co.

Water Resources Management in Asia Vol. I: Main Report. Harold D. Frederiksen et al. LC 93-26158. (Technical Paper Ser.: No. 212). 184p. 1993. 10.95 (*0-8213-2527-2*, 12527) World Bank.

Water Resources Management in Industrial Areas. Ed. by Leo R. Beard & W. H. Maxwell. (Water Resources Ser.: Vol. 1). 463p. 1982. 75.00 (*0-907567-30-4*, Tycooly Pub); pap. 55.00 (*0-907567-31-2*, Tycooly Pub) Weidner & Sons.

Water Resources Management in the Face of Climatic/ Hydrologic Uncertainties. Ed. by Zdzislaw Kaczmarek et al. LC 95-48402. (Water Science & Technology Library: Vol. 18). 408p. (C). 1996. lib. bdg. 169.00 (*0-7923-3927-4*) Kluwer Ac.

Water Resources Management under Drought or Water Shortage Conditions: Proceedings: EWRA 95 Symposium (1995: Nicosia, Cyprus) Ed. by Nicos X. Tsiourtis. (Illus.). 311p. (C). 1995. 90.00 (*90-5410-534-8*, Pub. by A A Balkema NE) Ashgate Pub Co.

Water Resources of a Western New York Region: A Case Study of Water Resources & Use in the Genesee Valley & Western Lake Ontario Basin. Erich F. Bordne. LC 60-9945. (Illus.). 149p. (Orig.). 1960. pap. 35.00 (*0-89366-007-8*) Ultramarine Pub.

Water Resources of Boulder County, Colorado. D. C. Hall et al. (Bulletin Ser.: No. 42). (Illus.). 97p. (Orig.). 1980. pap. 4.00 (*1-884216-04-8*) Colo Geol Survey.

Water Resources of Latin America & the Caribbean: Planning, Hazards & Pollution. 260p. 1990. 17.50 (*92-1-121158-1*) UN.

Water Resources Planning. Andrew A. Dzurik. 256p. (C). 1990. lib. bdg. 44.95 (*0-8476-7391-X*, R7391) Rowman.

Water Resources Planning. 2nd rev. ed. Andrew A. Dzurik. LC 96-23295. 372p. (C). 1996. lib. bdg. 44.95 (*0-8476-8081-9*) Rowman.

Water Resources Planning & Management: Proceedings of the Water Resources Sessions at Water Forum '92. Mohammad Karamouz. LC 92-23812. 928p. 1992. 75.00 (*0-87262-876-0*) Am Soc Civil Eng.

Water Resources Planning & Management: Proceedings of the 16th Annual Conference: Sacramento, CA, May 21-25, 1989. Water Resources Planning & Management Conference Staff. Ed. by Steven C. Harris. (Illus.). 842p. reprint ed. pap. 180.00 (*0-8357-4213-X*, 2036995) Bks Demand.

Water Resources Planning & Management see Proceedings of the International Conference on Hydrology & Water Resources, New Delhi, India, December 1993

Water Resources Planning & Management & Urban Water Resources. Ed. by Jerry L. Anderson. LC 91-12629. 1058p. 1991. pap. text ed. 90.00 (*0-87262-805-1*) Am Soc Civil Eng.

Water Resources Planning in New England. Stuart G. Koch. LC 79-66453. 198p. reprint ed. pap. 56.50 (*0-7837-0379-1*, 2040699) Bks Demand.

Water Resources Planning to Meet Long-Term Demand: Guidelines for Developing Countries. (Natural Resources-Water Ser.: No. 21). 117p. 1989. 13.50 (*92-1-104301-8*, E. 88. II.A.17) UN.

Water Resources Policy & the Nineteen Seventy-Seven South Dakota Legislature. Lawrence L. Downey. 1977. 1.00 (*1-55614-015-0*) U of SD Gov Res Bur.

Water Resources Policy for Asia: Proceeding of the Regional Symposium on Water Resources Policy in Agro-Socio-Economic Development, Dhaka, Bangladesh, 4-8 August 1985. Ed. by Mohammed Ali et al. 640p. (C). 1987. text ed. 130.00 (*90-6191-684-4*, Pub. by A A Balkema NE) Ashgate Pub Co.

Water Resources Problems Related to Mining. Ed. by Richard F. Hadley & David T. Snow. LC 75-13433. (American Water Resources Association Proceedings Ser.: No. 18). 242p. reprint ed. pap. 69.00 (*0-685-15204-9*, 2056156) Bks Demand.

Water Resources Protection Technology. J. Toby Tourbier & Richard Westmacott. LC 80-54911. (Illus.). 178p. (C). 1981. pap. 36.95 (*0-87420-595-6*, W08) Urban Land.

Water Resources Related to Mining & Energy - Preparing for the Future: Proceedings of the Symposium. Symposium on Water Resources Related to Mining & Energy - Preparing for the Future Staff. Ed. by Richard F. Dworsky. LC 87-72488. (American Water Resources Association Technical Publication Ser.: No. TPS-87-4). (Illus.). 564p. reprint ed. pap. 160.80 (*0-8357-3168-5*, 2039431) Bks Demand.

Water Resources Research: Problems & Potentials for Agriculture & Rural Communities. Ed. by Ted L. Napier et al. LC 83-4821. 247p. 1983. 7.00 (*0-935734-10-4*) Soil & Water Conserv.

Water Reuse. Water Pollution Control Federation Staff. (Manual of Practice, Systems Management Ser.: No. 3). (Illus.). 118p. (Orig.). 1983. pap. text ed. 23.00 (*0-943244-45-5*, MSM3) Water Environ.

Water Reuse Digest. 128p. 1992. pap. 55.00 (*1-881369-18-8*) Water Environ.

Water Rights: Scarce Resource Allocation, Bureaucracy, & the Environment. Ed. by Terry L. Anderson. LC 83-3855. (Illus.). 348p. 1983. pap. 14.95 (*0-936488-51-4*) PRIPP.

Water Rights & Energy Development in the Yellowstone River. Constance M. Boris & John V. Krutilla. LC 79-3741. (Resources for the Future Ser.). 1980. text ed. 25.00 (*0-8018-2368-4*) Johns Hopkins.

Water Rights & Energy Development in the Yellowstone River Basin: An Integrated Analysis. Constance M. Boris & John V. Krutilla. LC 79-3741. (Illus.). 294p. reprint ed. pap. 83.80 (*0-685-23693-5*, 2032144) Bks Demand.

Water Rights & Irrigation Practices in Lahj: A Study of the Application of Customary & Shri'ah Law in South-West Arabia. A. M. Maktari. LC 76-145606. (Oriental Publications: No. 21). (Illus.). 212p. 1972. text ed. 64.95 (*0-521-07930-6*) Cambridge U Pr.

Water Rights in the Fifty States & Territories. Kenneth Wright. 132p. 1990. pap. 39.00 (*0-89867-466-2*, 20247) Am Water Wks Assn.

Water Rights in the Western States, Enlarged to June 1, 1911, 2 Vols., Set. 3rd rev. ed. Samuel C. Wiel. Ed. by Stuart Bruchey. LC 78-53571. (Development of Public Land Law in the U. S. Ser.). 1979. reprint ed. lib. bdg. 119.95 (*0-405-11391-9*) Ayer.

Water Rites. Guy N. Smith. 256p. 1997. mass mkt. 4.99 (*0-8217-5553-6*, Zebra Kensgtn) Kensgtn Pub Corp.

***Water, Rivers & Creeks.** Luna B. Leopold. LC 97-9507. 1997. 30.00 (*0-935702-98-9*) Univ Sci Bks.

Water, Rock & Sand: Poems. Peter S. Levi. LC 63-2158. 6200. 15.95 (*0-8023-1071-0*) Dufour.

Water-Rock Interaction: Proceedings of the 7th International Symposium (WRI-7), Park City, Utah, U. S. A. 13-18 July 1992, 2 vols. Ed. by Yousif K. Kharaka & Ann S. Maest. (Illus.). 1730p. (C). 1992. Set. 190.00 (*90-5410-075-3*, Pub. by A A Balkema NE) Ashgate Pub Co.

Water-Rock Interaction: Proceedings of the 8th International Symposium (WRI-8), Vladiwostok, Russia, 15-19 August 1995. Ed. by Y. K. Khakara & Oleg Chudaev. (Illus.). 1500p. (C). 1995. text ed. 165.00 (*90-5410-549-6*, Pub. by A A Balkema NE) Ashgate Pub Co.

Water-Rock Interaction (WRI-Six) Proceedings of the International Symposium, Malvern, UK, 3 - 8 August 1989. Ed. by Douglas L. Miles. (Illus.). 838p. (C). 1989. text ed. 130.00 (*90-6191-970-3*, Pub. by A A Balkema NE) Ashgate Pub Co.

Water Row Review, No. 3. Ed. by Jeffrey H. Weinberg. 50p. 1988. pap. 10.00 (*0-934953-19-8*) Water Row Pr.

Water Row Review One. Ed. by Jeffrey H. Weinberg. (Illus.). 60p. (Orig.). (C). pap. 10.00 (*0-934953-16-3*) Water Row Pr.

Water Runs to What Is Wet. Heather S. Steliga. (Burning Deck Poetry Ser.). 56p. 1980. 15.00 (*0-930900-97-9*); pap. 4.00 (*0-930900-98-7*) Burning Deck.

Water Safety. American Red Cross Staff. 176p. (gr. 13). 1995. teacher ed. 3.50 (*0-8151-0810-9*) Mosby Yr Bk.

Water Safety. Cynthia F. Klingel. LC 86-72673. (Safety First Ser.). (J). (ps up). 1986. lib. bdg. 12.95 (*0-87191-740-8*) Creative Ed.

Water Safety. Nancy Loewen. LC 95-44769. (Safety Sense Ser.). (Illus.). 24p. (J). (gr. k-3). 1996. lib. bdg. 19.93 (*1-56766-261-7*) Childs World.

Water Safety Instructor's Candidate Kit. rev. ed. American Red Cross Staff. (gr. 13). 1995. 46.00 (*0-8151-0598-3*) Mosby Yr Bk.

Water Safety Instructor's Manual. American Red Cross Staff. 1977. 10.00 (*0-8016-7549-9*) Mosby Yr Bk.

Water Safety Instructor's Manual. American Red Cross Staff. 336p. (gr. 13). 1995. teacher ed., pap. text ed. 12.40 (*0-8151-0596-7*) Mosby Yr Bk.

Water Safety with Teddy Ruxpin. Michelle Baron. (Teddy Ruxpin Safe 'n' Sound Ser.). (Illus.). 34p. (J). (ps). 1988. 9.95 incl. audio (*0-934323-74-7*) Alchemy Comms.

Water Sampler. (Career Examination Ser.: C-3655). pap. 29.95 (*0-8373-3655-4*) Nat Learn.

Water Sampling for Pollution Regulation. Keith D. Harsham. 152p. 1995. text ed. 74.00 (*2-88449-039-6*) Gordon & Breach.

Water Sampling for Pollution Regulation. Keith D. Harsham. (Environmental Topics Ser.). 152p. 1995. pap. text ed. 28.00 (*2-88449-040-X*) Gordon & Breach.

***Water, Sanitary & Waste Services for Buildings.** 4th ed. A. F. Wise. (C). 1995. pap. text ed. 50.95 (*0-582-23085-3*, Pub. by Longman UK) Longman.

Water Saving Techniques for Plant Growth. Ed. by H. J. Verplancke et al. LC 92-17201. 252p. (C). 1992. lib. bdg. 133.00 (*0-7923-1851-X*) Kluwer Ac.

Water Scarcity: Impacts on Western Agriculture. Ed. by Ernest A. Engelbert & Ann F. Scheuring. LC 84-48702. (Illus.). 550p. (C). 1985. pap. 18.00 (*0-520-05313-3*) U CA Pr.

Water Scarcity in Developing Countries: Reconciling Development & Environmental Protection. Ed. by David Seckler & Deborah D. Moore. 80p. (Orig.). (C). 1993. pap. text ed. 9.95 (*0-933595-80-8*) Winrock Intl.

Water Science. Deborah Seed. (Illus.). (J). (gr. 2-7). 1992. pap. 9.95 (*0-201-57778-X*) Addison-Wesley.

Water Science & Technology, Vol. 14, Nos. 1-2. 1982. pap. 88.00 (*0-08-029095-7*, Pergamon Pr) Elsevier.

Water Science & Technology Series. Water Science & Technology Staff. Date not set. pap. write for info. (*0-08-044393-1*, Pergamon Pr) Elsevier.

Water Science & Technology Series. Water Science & Technology Staff. Date not set. write for info. (*0-08-044398-2*, Pergamon Pr) Elsevier.

Water Science & Technology, Vol. 24, No. 7 see Advanced Wastewater Treatment & Reclamation

Water Science, Water Fun: Great Things to Do with H2O. Noel Fiarotta & Phyllis Fiarotta. LC 96-25719. (Illus.). 80p. (J). 1996. 17.95 (*0-8069-4248-7*) Sterling.

Water Sediments & Ecology of the Mangrove Lagoon & Benner Bay, St. Thomas. Maynard Nichols. (Illus.). 159p. 1977. 20.00 (*0-318-14622-3*) Isl Resources.

***Water Seekers.** 3rd rev. ed. Remi Nadeau. (Illus.). 286p. 1997. pap. 14.95 (*0-9627104-5-8*) Crest Pubs.

Water Sensitivity: Binder Validation. Abdulla-Al-Joaid et al. 104p. (Orig.). (C). 1994. pap. text ed. 10.00 (*0-309-05810-4*, SHRP-A-402) SHRP.

Water Sensitivity of Asphalt-Aggregate Mixes: Test Selection. Ronald L. Terrel & Saleh Al-Swailmi. (SHRP Ser.: A-403). (Illus.). 183p. (Orig.). (C). 1994. pap. text ed. 15.00 (*0-309-05820-1*) Natl Res Coun.

Water Service Agencies: Interim California Statewide Alpha Listing. 80p. (Orig.). (C). 1993. pap. text ed. 30.00 (*0-7881-0022-X*) DIANE Pub.

Water Service Foreman. Jack Rudman. (Career Examination Ser.: C-2918). 1994. pap. 29.95 (*0-8373-2918-3*) Nat Learn.

Water Shall Flow from the Rock. Arie S. Issar. (Illus.). 224p. 1989. 43.95 (*0-387-51621-2*) Spr-Verlag.

Water Shell. Gretchen Schields. LC 94-15606. (Illus.). 40p. (J). (gr. 1-5). 1995. 16.00 (*0-15-200404-1*, Gulliver Bks) HarBrace.

Water Shortage: Lessons in Conservation from the Great California Drought, 1976-77. A. Berk et al. 220p. 1984. reprint ed. lib. bdg. 47.50 (*0-8191-4092-9*) U Pr of Amer.

***Water Skiing.** Ben Favret & Dave Benzel. LC 96-40091. (Illus.). 248p. (Orig.). 1997. pap. 19.95 (*0-88011-522-X*, PFAV0522) Human Kinetics.

Water Skiing. John West. (Skills of the Game Ser.). (Illus.). 112p. 1991. pap. 19.95 (*1-85223-563-2*, Pub. by Crowood Pr UK) Trafalgar.

Water Sky. Jean Craighead George. LC 86-45496. (Illus.). 224p. (YA). (gr. 6 up). 1987. lib. bdg. 13.89 (*0-06-022199-2*) HarpC Child Bks.

Water Sky. Jean Craighead George. LC 86-45496. (Trophy Bk.). (Illus.). 224p. (YA). (gr. 5 up). 1989. pap. 3.95 (*0-06-440202-9*, Trophy) HarpC Child Bks.

***Water Slashing on a Rock.** Rawlins. 1998. 27.00 (*0-8050-5240-2*) H Holt & Co.

Water Snakes of North America. W. P. Mara. (Illus.). 64p. 1995. pap. 9.95 (*0-7938-0288-1*, RE137) TFH Pubns.

Water Snake's Year. Doris Gove. LC 90-673. (Illus.). 40p. (J). (gr. 2-6). 1991. lib. bdg. 13.95 (*0-689-31597-X*, Atheneum Bks Young) S&S Childrens.

W

An Asterisk (*) at the beginning of an entry indicates that the title is appearing in BIP for the first time.

Water Solubility of Phosphate Fertilizers: Agronomic Aspects - A Literature Review. Orvis P. Engelstad & Deborah T. Hellums. LC 92-30387. (Paper Ser.: No. P-17). (Illus.). 20p. (Orig.). 1993. pap. text ed. 4.00 (*0-88090-098-9*) Intl Fertilizer.

***Water-Soluble Poly-N-Vinylamides: Synthesis & Physico-Chemical Properties.** Yurii E. Kirsh. LC 97-17696. 1998. write for info. (*0-471-97630-X*) Wiley.

Water Soluble Polymers. Business Communications Co., Inc. Staff. 212p. 1991. 2,250.00 (*0-89336-761-3*, C-012N) BCC.

Water Soluble Polymers: Beauty with Performance. Ed. by J. E. Glass. LC 86-3534. (Advances in Chemistry Ser.: No. 213). (Illus.). xii, 444p. 1986. 89.95 (*0-8412-0931-6*) Am Chemical.

Water-Soluble Polymers: Synthesis, Solution Properties, & Applications. Ed. by Shalaby W. Shalaby et al. LC 91-751. (Symposium Ser.: No. 467). (Illus.). 536p. 1991. 109.95 (*0-8412-2101-4*) Am Chemical.

Water-Soluble Polymers for Petroleum Recovery. G. Allan Stahl. LC 88-12531. (Illus.). 366p. 1988. 105.00 (*0-306-42915-2*, Plenum Pr) Plenum.

Water Soluble Synthetic Polymers: Properties & Behavior, 2 Vols., Vol. I. P. Molyneux. 240p. 1983. 191.00 (*0-8493-6135-4*, QD382) CRC Pr.

Water Soluble Synthetic Polymers: Properties & Behavior, 2 Vols., Vol. II. P. Molyneux. 280p. 1984. 194.95 (*0-8493-6136-2*, QD382) CRC Pr.

***Water-Soluble Vitamin Assays in Human Nutrition.** Ball. (Illus.). 432p. 1994. text ed. 172.95 (*0-412-58370-4*, Chap & Hall NY) Chapman & Hall.

Water Song. Michael S. Weaver. Ed. by Charles H. Rowell. (Callaloo Poetry Ser.). (Illus.). 80p. (C). 1985. pap. text ed. 8.95 (*0-912759-05-4*) U Pr of Va.

Water Source Heat Pump Handbook. R. Dexheimer. 180p. 1985. 18.75 (*1-56034-059-2*) Natl Grnd Water.

Water Sources Student Workbook, Vol. 1. (Principles & Practices of Water Supply Operations Ser.). 62p. 1995. pap. 17.00 (*0-89867-810-2*, 1965) Am Water Wks Assn.

***Water Spaces of the World Vol. 1: A Pictorial Review.** (Illus.). 224p. 45.00 (*1-875498-36-2*) AIA Press.

***Water Splashing on a Rock.** Rawlins. 1999. 12.95 (*0-8050-5239-9*) H Holt & Co.

***Water Sports: An Outdoor Activity Handbook.** Hugh McManners. (An Outdoor Adventure Handbk.). (Illus.). 48p. (J). 1997. pap. 10.95 (*0-7894-1479-1*) DK Pub Inc.

Water Spray Fixed Systems for Fire Protection. National Fire Protection Association Staff. 43p. 1990. 20.25 (*0-317-63052-0*, 15-90) Natl Fire Prot.

Water Squeeze. Mary O'Neill. LC 89-77456. (SOS Planet Earth Ser.). (Illus.). 32p. (J). (gr. 3-6). 1989. lib. bdg. 13.50 (*0-8167-2080-0*) Troll Communs.

Water Squeeze. Mary O'Neill. LC 89-77456. (SOS Planet Earth Ser.). (Illus.). 32p. (J). (gr. 3-6). 1997. pap. 5.95 (*0-8167-2081-9*) Troll Communs.

Water, Stones, & Fossil Bones. Ed. by Karen K. Lind. (CESI Sourcebook Ser.: Vol. VI). (Illus.). 140p. 1991. pap. text ed. 18.50 (*0-87355-101-X*) Natl Sci Tchrs.

Water Stress on Plants. G. M. Simpson. LC 81-7376. (Illus.). 336p. 1981. text ed. 59.95 (*0-275-90719-8*, C0719, Praeger Pubs) Greenwood.

Water Subsidies: Impact of Higher Irrigation Rates on Central Valley Project Farmers. (Illus.). 92p. (Orig.). (C). 1995. pap. text ed. 25.00 (*0-7881-1851-X*) DIANE Pub.

Water Superintendent. Jack Rudman. (Career Examination Ser.: C-1534). 1994. pap. 39.95 (*0-8373-1534-4*) Nat Learn.

Water Supplies & Economic Growth in an Arid Environment: An Arizona Case Study. Maurice M. Kelso et al. LC 72-92106. 349p. reprint ed. pap. 99.50 (*0-685-15954-X*, 2056211) Bks Demand.

Water Supplies & the Treatment & Disposal of Effluents. A. H. Little. 71p. 1975. 60.00 (*0-686-63808-5*) St Mut.

Water Supplies & the Treatment & Disposal of Effluents. A. H. Little. 71p. (C). 1975. pap. text ed. 75.00 (*0-900739-21-5*, Pub. by Textile Inst UK) St Mut.

Water Supplies for Fire Protection. 4th ed. IFSTA Committee. Ed. by Gene P. Carlson & Michael A. Wieder. LC 87-83192. (Illus.). 268p. 1988. pap. text ed. 25.00 (*0-87939-073-5*) IFSTA.

Water Supplies for Rural Communities. Colin Ball & Mog Ball. 64p. (Orig.). 1991. pap. 11.50 (*0-614-09485-2*, Pub. by Intermed Tech UK) Women Ink.

Water Supplies for Suburban & Rural Fire Fighting. National Fire Protection Association Staff. 63p. 1993. 22.25 (*0-317-63539-5*, 1231-89) Natl Fire Prot.

***Water Supply.** 4th ed. A. C. Twort et al. text ed. 59.95 (*0-470-23709-0*) Wiley.

Water Supply. 4th ed. A. C. Twort et al. 511p. 1995. pap. 62.95 (*0-340-57587-5*, Pub. by E Arnold UK) Routledge Chapman & Hall.

Water Supply: Energy an Environment Technology Sourcebook. Unifem Staff. (Energy & Environment Technology Source Book Ser.). 80p. (Orig.). 1996. pap. 15.50 (*1-85339-344-4*, Pub. by Intermed Tech UK) Women Ink.

Water Supply: Second Altantic Workshop: Prooceedings of the Specialised Workshop of the ISWA Held in Nice, France, 3-7 March 1984. Ed. by R. Urbistondo & L. R. Bays. 176p. 1985. pap. 73.00 (*0-08-034131-4*, Pub. by PPL UK) Elsevier.

Water Supply: The Decade-Half Way: Part of the Proceedings of the Regional Conference of the IWSA Held in Conjunction with the 3rd Congress of the UADE in Libreville, Gabon, 10-15 June, 1985. Ed. by G. Dassonville. 372p. 1986. pap. 66.00 (*0-08-034142-X*, Pub. by PPL UK) Elsevier.

Water Supply & Pollution Control. 5th ed. Warren Viessman, Jr. & Mark J. Hammer. LC 92-17473. (C). 1993. text ed. 84.68 (*0-06-500058-7*) Addson-Wesley Educ.

***Water Supply & Sanitation for Rural Areas.** F. El-Gohary et al. (Water Science & Technology Ser.: Vol. 27). 188p. 1993. 114.25 (*0-08-042337-X*, Pergamon Pr) Elsevier.

Water Supply & Sewerage. 6th ed. Terrence McGhee. (Water Resources & Environmental Engineering Ser.). 665p. 1991. text ed. 55.00 (*0-07-060938-1*) McGraw.

Water Supply & Treatment. Ed. by Jack G. Walters. 87p. 1989. pap. 27.00 (*0-89852-456-3*, 0101R156) TAPPI.

Water Supply & Treatment. 2nd ed. Ed. by Jack G. Walters. LC 89-152903. (Illus.). 93p. reprint ed. pap. 24.20 (*0-8357-6345-5*, 2035618) Bks Demand.

Water Supply & Treatment: State-of-the-Art. Technical Association of the Pulp & Paper Industry Staff. LC 79-120640. 94p. reprint ed. pap. 26.80 (*0-317-29320-6*, 2022337) Bks Demand.

Water Supply & Water Reuse: 1991 & Beyond, Hyatt Islandia, San Diego, CA, June 2-6, 1991. Symposium on Water Supply & Water Reuse Staff. Ed. by Harold E. Bailey et al. LC 91-71247. (American Water Resources Association Technical Publication Ser.: Vol. TPS-91-2). (Illus.). 488p. 1991. reprint ed. pap. 139.10 (*0-7837-9222-0*, 2049973) Bks Demand.

Water Supply Development & Concentrate Disposal for Membr. Thomas M. Missimer. 272p. 1994. 75.95 (*0-87371-954-9*, L954) Lewis Pubs.

Water Supply Planning. David W. Prasifka. LC 93-28392. 282p. 1994. 42.50 (*0-89464-838-1*) Krieger.

Water Supply, Sanitation, & Environmental Sustainability: The Financing Challenge. Ismail Serageldin. LC 94-34389. 1994. 6.95 (*0-8213-3022-5*) World Bank.

Water Supply System Rehabilitation. Thomas M. Walski. 336p. 1987. 31.00 (*0-87262-618-0*) Am Soc Civil Eng.

***Water Supply Systems: New Technologies.** C. Maksimovic et al. LC 96-32374. (NATO ASI Ser.: Environment: Vol. 15). 615p. 1996. 219.50 (*3-540-61533-4*) Spr-Verlag.

Water Systems Construction Inspector. (Career Examination Ser.: C-3413). 1994. pap. 39.95 (*0-8373-3413-6*) Nat Learn.

Water Systems Seventy-Nine: Proceedings of the ASCE Water Resources Planning & Management Division Specialty Conference, University of Houston, Hilton Hotel Center, February 25-28, 1979. American Society of Civil Engineers Staff. LC 79-105513. 237p. reprint ed. pap. 67.60 (*0-317-10837-9*, 2019548) Bks Demand.

Water Tables. James Seay. LC 73-15014. (Wesleyan Poetry Program Ser.: Vol. 72). 71p. 1974. pap. 11.95 (*0-8195-1072-6*, Wesleyan Univ Pr) U Pr of New Eng.

Water Tanks for Private Fire Protection. National Fire Protection Association Staff. 63p. 1993. 20.75 (*0-317-63060-1*, 22-93) Natl Fire Prot.

***Water Technology & Development.** Hvidt. Date not set. text ed. write for info. (*1-86064-216-0*, Pub. by I B Tauris UK) St Martin.

Water Technology Industry Reviews. Hilton & Sara Kochummen. 270p. 1995. 1,500.00 (*0-614-10924-8*, DWA94) BCC.

Water Temple. Hans-Eberhad Hess. 1994. 45.00 (*1-85490-387-X*) Academy Ed UK.

Water Tender. Jack Rudman. (Career Examination Ser.: C-1649). 1994. reprint ed. pap. 27.95 (*0-8373-1649-9*) Nat Learn.

Water, the Source of Life: Glaciers, Springs Oceans, Tide Pools, Lakes, Swamps, & Oases. Scholastic Staff. (Voyages of Discovery Ser.). 48p. (J). (gr. 3 up). 1996. pap. 19.95 (*0-590-47650-5*, Scholastic Voy Discov) Scholastic Inc.

Water Today & Tomorrow: Proceedings of a Specialty Conference Sponsored by the Irrigation & Drainage Division. Ed. by John A. Replogle & Kenneth G. Renard. 740p. 1984. 61.00 (*0-87262-408-0*) Am Soc Civil Eng.

Water Towers. Bernd Bechr & Hilla Becher. (Illus.). 223p. 1988. 65.00 (*0-262-02277-X*) MIT Pr.

Water Trails of Washington. rev. ed. Werner Furrer. (Illus.). (Orig.). 1979. pap. 5.95 (*0-913140-31-7*) Signpost Bk Pub.

Water Transfer from Soil to the Atmosphere As Related to Climate & Soil Properties. Charles Wendt. LC 73-136103. 101p. 1970. 19.00 (*0-403-04546-0*) Scholarly.

Water Transfers: Economic Efficiency & Alternative Institutions. Loyal M. Hartman & Don Seastone. LC 70-108382. 144p. reprint ed. pap. 41.10 (*0-317-28863-6*, 2020963) Bks Demand.

Water Transfers: More Efficient Water Use Possible, If Problems Are Addressed. (Illus.). 132p. (Orig.). (C). 1995. pap. text ed. 30.00 (*0-7881-1729-7*) DIANE Pub.

Water Transmission & Distribution, Vol. 3. 2nd ed. LC 95-48298. (Principles & Practices of Water Supply Operations Ser.). Orig. Title: Introduction to Water Distribution. 550p. 1996. 89.00 (*0-89867-821-8*, 1957) Am Water Wks Assn.

Water Transmission & Distribution Instructor Guide, Vol. 3. (Principles & Practices of Water Supply Operations Ser.). (Illus.). 1996. spiral bd. 99.00 (*0-89867-807-2*, 1962) Am Water Wks Assn.

Water Transmission & Distribution Student Workbook. (Principles & Practices of Water Supply Operations Ser.). 1996. pap. 18.00 (*0-89867-812-9*, 1967) Am Water Wks Assn.

Water Transport in Biological Membranes, Vol. I. Gheorghe Benga. 304p. 1988. 135.00 (*0-8493-6082-X*, QH509, CRC Reprint) Franklin.

Water Transport in Biological Membranes, Vol. II. Gheorghe Benga. 304p. 1988. 170.00 (*0-8493-6083-8*, QH509, CRC Reprint) Franklin.

Water Treatment. (Principles of Steam Generation Ser.: Module 2). (Illus.). 80p. 1982. spiral bd. 25.50 (*0-87683-252-4*) GP Courseware.

Water Treatment. (Illus.). 410p. 1984. 295.00 (*0-87683-369-5*); ring bd. 149.50 (*0-87683-368-7*) GP Courseware.

Water Treatment. 1993. 150.00 (*0-86022-319-1*, Pub. by Build Servs Info Assn UK) St Mut.

Water Treatment. Center for Occupational Research & Development Staff. (EUTEC Environmental & Chemical Analysis Curriculum Ser.). (Illus.). 224p. (C). 1985. pap. text ed. write for info. (*1-55502-206-5*) CORD Commns.

Water Treatment: Industrial, Commercial & Municipal. 3rd ed. D. C. Brandvold. (Illus.). 164p. (C). 1994. pap. text ed. 15.00 (*0-9610178-1-3*) DCB Enter.

Water Treatment: Industrial-Commercial-Municipal. 2nd ed. D. C. Brandvold. (Illus.). 1982. pap. 5.00 (*0-9610178-0-5*) DCB Enter.

Water Treatment: Refining Petrochemicals & Gas Processing Techniques. Francois Berne & Jean Cordonnier. (Illus.). 266p. (C). 1994. 340.00 (*2-7108-0673-8*, Pub. by Edits Technip FR) St Mut.

Water Treatment Basics: From Pretreatment to Wastewater Seminar, 1986: The Peabody, Memphis, TN, October 15-17. Technical Association of the Pulp & Paper Industry Staff. (TAPPI Notes Ser.). (Illus.). 85p. pap. 25.00 (*0-317-58158-9*, 2029694) Bks Demand.

***Water Treatment Chemicals.** Richard K. Miller et al. (Market Research Survey Ser.: No. 278). 50p. 1996. 200.00 (*1-55865-302-3*) Future Tech Surveys.

Water Treatment Chemicals: An Industrial Guide. Ed. by Ernest W. Flick. LC 91-30708. 510p. 1992. 76.00 (*0-8155-1291-0*) Noyes.

Water Treatment Chemicals & Equipment: Outlook for the 1990s. 193p. 1996. 1,995.00 (*0-945235-52-6*) Lead Edge Reports.

Water Treatment Essentials for Boiler Plant Operation. Robert G. Nunn. LC 96-47395. (Illus.). 224p. 1996. text ed. 49.00 (*0-07-048219-5*) McGraw.

***Water Treatment Glossary: English/French-French/English.** Degremont. 336p. (ENG & FRE.). 1995. 175.00 (*0-7859-9273-1*) Fr & Eur.

Water Treatment Instructor's Guide, Vol. 2. 2nd ed. (Principles & Practices of Water Supply Operations Ser.). 153p. 1995. spiral bd., pap. 69.00 (*0-89867-811-0*, 1961) Am Water Wks Assn.

Water Treatment Membrane Processes: A Joint Project by Three of the Worlds Largest Agencies. American Water Works Association Research Foundation et al. LC 96-17666. 1996. text ed. 79.00 (*0-07-001559-7*) McGraw.

Water Treatment Plant Design for Practicing Engineers. Ed. by Robert L. Sanks. LC 77-76914. 1978. 105.00 (*0-7506-9183-2*) Buttrwrth-Heinemann.

Water Treatment Plant Operation, Vol. I. 3rd ed. Kenneth D. Kerri. (Illus.). 689p. (C). 1994. pap. text ed. 30.00 (*1-884701-12-4*) CA St U Ofc Water.

Water Treatment Plant Operation, Vol. II. 2nd ed. Kenneth D. Kerri. (Illus.). 689p. (C). 1993. pap. text ed. 30.00 (*1-884701-13-2*) CA St U Ofc Water.

Water Treatment Plant Operation, Vols. I & II. Kenneth D. Kerri. (Illus.). 1356p. 1993. pap. text ed. 60.00 (*1-884701-14-0*) CA St U Ofc Water.

Water Treatment Plant Waste Management. 480p. 1987. pap. 52.00 (*0-89867-404-2*, 90527) Am Water Wks Assn.

Water Treatment Principles & Design. James M. Montgomery. LC 85-5344. 696p. 1985. text ed. 99.95 (*0-471-04384-2*, Wiley-Interscience) Wiley.

Water Treatment Processes: Simple Options. Saravanamuthu Vigneswaran & C. Visvanathan. Ed. by Wai-Fah Chen. (New Directions in Civil Engineering Ser.). 224p. 1995. 69.95 (*0-8493-8283-1*, 8283) CRC Pr.

Water Treatment Specification Manual. Frank Rosa. LC 92-45808. 1993. 29.95 (*0-912524-80-4*) Busn News.

Water Treatment Troubleshooting & Problem Solving. Glenn M. Tillman. 150p. (C). 1996. text ed. 44.95 (*1-57504-001-8*) Ann Arbor Chelsea.

***Water under a Film of Ice.** Patricia C. Peters. LC 96-42368. 64p. 1997. pap. 12.95 (*0-7734-2685-X*, Mellen Poetry Pr) E Mellen.

Water under Fish. Leslie L. Fields. (Dog River Review Poetry Ser.). 56p. (Orig.). 1994. pap. 4.95 (*0-916155-28-5*) Trout Creek.

***Water under the Bridge.** large type ed. Susan Sallis. (Magna Large Print Ser.). 624p. 1996. 25.99 (*0-7505-0980-5*, Pub. by Magna Print Bks UK) Ulverscroft.

Water Up, Water Down: The Hydrologic Cycle. Sally M. Walker. (Earth Watch Bks.). 48p. (J). (gr. 1-4). 1992. lib. bdg. 14.96 (*0-87614-695-7*, Carolrhoda) Lerner Group.

***Water Upside down '94, Vol. 2, Pts. A & B.** Contrib. by Claus Schonfeldt et al. (National Conference Proceedings 94 Ser.: Vol. 14). (Illus.). 762p. 1994. pap. 115.50 (*0-85825-620-7*, Pub. by Inst Engrs Aust-EA Bks AT) Accents Pubns.

***Water Upside down '94, Vol. 3.** Contrib. by Claus Schonfeldt et al. (National Conference Proceedings 94 Ser.: Vol. 15). (Illus.). 503p. 1994. pap. 91.50 (*0-85825-621-5*, Pub. by Inst Engrs Aust-EA Bks AT) Accents Pubns.

Water Usage in Wet Processing & Problems Associated with Treatment & Re-use of Effluents. Ed. by Wira Staff. 1988. 35.00 (*0-317-43603-1*) St Mut.

Water Use by Naturally Occurring Vegetation: Including an Annotated Bibliography. Eldon L. Johns. 252p. 1989. ring bd. 24.00 (*0-87262-732-2*) Am Soc Civil Eng.

Water Use Inspector. Jack Rudman. (Career Examination Ser.: C-898). 1994. pap. 23.95 (*0-8373-0898-4*) Nat Learn.

Water Use Statistics in the Long-Term Planning of Water Resources Development. (Water Resources Ser.: No. 64). 114p. 15.50 (*92-1-119545-4*, E.89.II.F.12) UN.

Water Utility Accounting. 3rd ed. 334p. 1995. 78.00 (*0-89867-237-6*, 10007) Am Water Wks Assn.

Water Utility Capital Financing, No. M29. 68p. 1988. pap. 40.00 (*0-89867-426-3*, 30029) Am Water Wks Assn.

Water Utility Experience with Plastic Service Pipe. (Illus.). 64p. 1992. pap. 30.00 (*0-89867-616-9*, 90593) Am Water Wks Assn.

Water Utility Management Practices, No. M5. 168p. 1989. pap. 45.00 (*0-89867-063-2*, 30005) Am Water Wks Assn.

Water Utilization in the Yarmuck-Jordan, 1192-1992. J. W. Eaton & David J. Eaton. (Working Paper Ser.: No. 71). 16p. 1993. pap. 5.50 (*0-89940-554-1*) LBJ Sch Pub Aff.

***Water Vapor Measurement: Methods & Instrumentation.** Pieter R. Wiederhold. LC 97-1910. 384p. 1997. 135.00 (*0-8247-9319-6*) Dekker.

Water Vapor Transmission Through Building Materials & Systems: Mechanisms & Measurement. Ed. by M. Bomberg & Heinz R. Trechsel. LC 89-34778. (Special Technical Publication Ser.: No. STP 1039). (Illus.). 180p. 1989. text ed. 24.00 (*0-8031-1254-8*) ASTM.

Water Virology: Water Science & Technology, Vol. 15, No. 5. Ed. by W. O. Grabow. (Illus.). 166p. 1983. pap. 44.00 (*0-08-030440-0*, Pergamon Pr) Elsevier.

Water Virology 1984: Proceedings of an IAWPRC Seminar Held in Amsterdam & Bilthoven, The Netherlands, 19-21 September 1984. Ed. by W. O. Grabow. 1985. pap. 48.00 (*0-08-033659-0*, Pub. by PPL UK) Elsevier.

Water Voices. Toby Speed. LC 95-10588. (Illus.). (J). 1997. 15.95 (*0-399-22631-1*, Putnam) Putnam Pub Group.

Water Walker. Nancy Willard. 1989. 18.95 (*0-394-57208-4*); pap. 9.95 (*0-679-72171-1*) Knopf.

Water Wars: The Fight to Control & Conserve Nature's Most Precious Resource. Olga Cossi. LC 92-43968. (Earthcare Bks.). (Illus.). 128p. (J). (gr. 6-7). 1993. lib. bdg. 13.95 (*0-02-724595-0*, New Dscvry Bks) Silver Burdett Pr.

Water, Wastewater & Sludge Filtration. Ed. by Saravanamuthu Vigneswaran & Roger B. Aim. 304p. 1989. 228.95 (*0-8493-6983-5*, TD441) CRC Pr.

Water Watch Book 'n Rain Gauge. Patrick S. Kelly. 1991. pap. 15.95 (*0-939251-61-2*) Accord CO.

Water, Water Everywhere. Joanne Barkan. Ed. by Bonnie Brook. (First Facts Ser.). (Illus.). 32p. (J). (ps-1). 1990. lib. bdg. 6.95 (*0-671-68653-4*, Silver Pr NJ) Silver Burdett Pr.

Water, Water Everywhere. Mark J. Rauzon & Cynthia O. Bix. LC 92-34521. (Illus.). 32p. (J). (gr. 1-4). 1994. 14.95 (*0-87156-598-6*) Sierra Club Childrens.

Water, Water Everywhere. Mark J. Rauzon & Cynthia O. Bix. (Illus.). 32p. (J). (gr. 1-4). 1995. pap. 5.95 (*0-87156-383-5*) Sierra Club Childrens.

***Water Water Everywhere.** Thomas-Cochran. (What a Wonderful World 1 Ser.). 1991. pap. text ed. write for info. (*0-582-90958-9*, Pub. by Longman UK) Longman.

Water, Water Everywhere: A Book about the Water Cycle. Melvin Berger & Gilda Berger. LC 95-16024. (Discovery Readers Ser.). (Illus.). 48p. (J). (gr. k-4). 1995. per., pap. 4.50 (*1-57102-042-X*, Ideals Child); lib. bdg. 12.00 (*1-57102-056-X*, Ideals Child) Hambleton-Hill.

Water, Water, Everywhere, So Many Drops to Drink. Phyllis Reisdorf. (Illus.). 52p. (Orig.). 1988. pap. 4.95 (*0-317-93900-9*) P Reisdorf.

***Water! Water! Water!** Thomas-Cochran. (What a Wonderful World Intro Ser.). 1993. pap. text ed. write for info. (*0-582-91091-9*, Pub. by Longman UK) Longman.

Water, Water...Everywhere. Vic Lockman. 36p. 1992. 4.00 (*0-936175-17-6*) V Lockman.

Water Wave Kinematics. Ed. by A. Torum & O. T. Gudmestad. (C). 1990. lib. bdg. 308.50 (*0-7923-0638-4*) Kluwer Ac.

Water Wave Mechanics for Engineers & Scientists. R. G. Dean & R. A. Dalrymple. (Advanced Series in Ocean Engineering: Vol. 2). 368p. 1991. text ed. 67.00 (*981-02-0420-5*); pap. text ed. 32.00 (*981-02-0421-3*) World Scientific Pub.

***Water Wave Propagation over Uneven Bottoms.** LC 96-29860. 988p. 1997. 96.00 (*981-02-3993-9*) World Scientific Pub.

***Water Wave Propagation over Uneven Bottoms.** LC 96-29860. 988p. 1997. 96.00 (*981-02-3994-7*) World Scientific Pub.

***Water Wave Propagation over Uneven Bottoms.** LC 96-29860. 988p. 1997. 60.00 (*981-02-3995-5*) World Scientific Pub.

***Water Wave Propagation over Uneven Bottoms.** LC 96-29860. 988p. 1997. 60.00 (*981-02-3996-3*) World Scientific Pub.

Water Wave Propagation Over Uneven Bottoms. M. W. Dingemans. LC 96-29860. 700p. 1997. text ed. 99.00 (*981-02-0426-4*); pap. text ed. 53.00 (*981-02-0427-2*) World Scientific Pub.

Water Waves: Relating Modern Theory to Advanced Engineering Practice, 3. M. Rahman. (Institute of Mathematics & Its Applications Monograph). (Illus.). 220p. 1995. 85.00 (*0-19-853478-7*) OUP.

Water Waves: The Mathematical Theory with Applications. J. J. Stoker. LC 91-41111. (Classics Library: No. 1826). 600p. 1992. pap. text ed. 59.95 (*0-471-57034-6*) Wiley.

Water Waves Generated by Underwater Explosion. Bernard Le Mehaute & Shen Wang. LC 94-45506. (Advanced Series in Ocean Engineering). 400p. 1996. text ed. 74.00 (*981-02-2083-9*) World Scientific Pub.

Water Waves Generated by Underwater Explosion. Bernard Le Mehaute & Shen Wang. LC 94-45506. (Advanced Series in Ocean Engineering). 400p. 1996. pap. text ed. 43.00 (*981-02-2132-0*) World Scientific Pub.

Water Ways. Laurence W. Thomas. LC 93-15927. 64p. 1993. pap. 12.95 (*0-7734-2761-9*, Mellen Poetry Pr) E Mellen.

Water Well & Aquifer Test Analysis (Plus Computer Program) Phil Hall. 428p. 1996. boxed 82.00 (*0-918334-93-4*, WWAT) WRP.

Water-Well Design & Construction. R. L. Harlan et al. (Developments in Geotechnical Engineering Ser.: No. 60). 206p. 1989. 140.75 (*0-444-87480-1*) Elsevier.

Water Well Drillers Beginning Training Manual. 2nd ed. 84p. 1974. 10.00 (*1-56034-049-5*, T044) Natl Grnd Water.

Water Well Technology. O. P. Handa. (Illus.). 316p. (C). 1989. text ed. 46.00 (*90-6191-969-X*, Pub. by A A Balkema NE) Ashgate Pub Co.

Water Well Technology. O. P. Handa. (C). 1988. 22.00 (*81-204-0338-X*, Pub. by Oxford IBH II) S Asia.

Water Wells - Monitoring, Maintenance, Rehabilitation: Proceedings of the International Groundwater Engineering Conference. Ed. by P. Howsam. 440p. 1991. 86.95 (*0-442-31375-6*) Chapman & Hall.

Water Wheel. Betsy Ford. Ed. by Edward Mycue. (Took Modern Poetry in English Ser.: No. 3). (Illus.). 28p. (Orig.). 1992. pap. 5.00 (*0-9625855-4-8*) Norton Coker Pr.

Water, Wind & Fire: Understanding the New Birth & the Baptism of the Holy Spirit. Mac Hammond. 34p. (Orig.). 1993. pap. 1.00 (*1-57399-004-3*) Mac Hammond.

***Water, Wind & Fire: Understanding the New Birth & the Baptism of the Holy Spirit.** Mac Hammond. (Orig.). 1996. pap. 1.00 (*1-57399-025-6*) Mac Hammond.

Water-Wise Vegetables. Steve O. Solomon. (Cascadia Gardening Ser.). (Illus.). 96p. (Orig.). 1993. pap. 8.95 (*0-912365-75-7*) Sasquatch Bks.

Water-Witch. James Fenimore Cooper. (BCL Ser.). reprint ed. 37.50 (*0-404-00629-9*) AMS Pr.

Water Witch. James Fenimore Cooper. (Works of James Fenimore Cooper Ser.). 1990. reprint ed. lib. bdg. 79.00 (*0-7812-2379-2*) Rprt Serv.

Water-Witch: Or, the Skimmer of the Seas. James Fenimore Cooper. LC 04-15437. 1896. 13.00 (*0-403-00244-3*) Scholarly.

***Water Witches.** Bohjalian. 1997. pap. 13.00 (*0-684-82612-7*, Scribners PB Fict) S&S Trade.

Water Witches. Chris Bohjalian. LC 94-9816. (Hardscrabble Bks.). 351p. 1995. 24.95 (*0-87451-687-0*) U Pr of New Eng.

Water Witching. Kathleene West. LC 84-71254. 64p. 1984. pap. 7.00 (*0-914742-82-5*) Copper Canyon.

Water Witching in the Garden: Poems. Donna Biffar. LC 95-39508. 64p. 1995. pap. 12.95 (*0-7734-2670-1*, Mellen Poetry Pr) E Mellen.

Water Witching U. S. A. 2nd ed. Evon Z. Vogt & Ray Hyman. LC 79-240. xii, 272p. 1979. pap. text ed. 13.50 (*0-226-86297-6*, P814) U Ch Pr.

***Water Wizard: Water's Mysteries Revealed.** Viktor Schauberger. 228p. (Orig.). 1997. pap. 14.95 (*1-85860-048-0*, Pub. by Gateway Books UK) ACCESS Pubs Network.

Water Wonders. Dale McCreedy & Julia Andrews. (National Science Partnership for Girl Scouts & Science Museums Ser.). (Illus.). 72p. (Orig.). 1995. pap. 8.00 (*0-9625622-6-2*) Franklin PA.

Water Wonders. Meredith Corporation, Better Homes & Gardens Staff. (Max the Dragon Project Book Ser.). (Illus.). 32p. (J). (ps-12). 1991. lib. bdg. 11.95 (*1-878363-60-3*) Forest Hse.

Water Won't Quench the Fire Cycle B: Sermons for the Sundays after Pentecost (First Third), Gospel Texts. William G. Carter. LC 96-4985. 99p. (Orig.). 1996. pap. 8.50 (*0-7880-0797-1*) CSS OH.

***Water Workout.** Ken Poulsen & Gail Poulsen. (Illus.). 31p. 1996. spiral bd. 20.00 (*0-9654087-0-1*) LFI Pubns.

Water Workouts. 2nd ed. Knopf et al. 150p. 1992. pap. text ed. 14.95 (*0-88725-173-0*) Hunter Textbks.

***Water Workouts: A Guide to Fitness, Training, & Performance Enhancement in the Water.** Steve Tarpinian & Brian J. Awbrey. LC 97-2427. (Illus.). 160p. (Orig.). 1997. pap. 14.95 (*1-55821-396-1*) Lyons & Burford.

Water Works: A Survey of Great Lakes - St. Lawrence River Waterfront Development. Daniel K. Ray. Ed. by Paul Botts. (Illus.). 72p. (Orig.). (C). 1991. 16.95 (*0-921578-06-7*) Harbor Hse MI.

***Water Worlds: Experience 4-H Natural Resources.** 2nd ed. Janet E. Hawkes et al. (Illus.). 62p. (Orig.). (J). (gr. 4-7). 1990. reprint ed. pap. 6.00 (*1-57753-036-5*, 147L518) Corn Coop Ext.

Waterbearer. Austin Repath. 200p. (Orig.). 1994. pap. 12.95 (*0-9697399-0-7*) Reed Pr.

Waterbird & Mammal Censuses at Siuslaw Estuary, Lane County, Oregon. Range D. Bayer & Roy W. Lowe. LC 87-83287. (Studies in Oregon Ornithology: No. 4). (Illus.). x, 101p. 1988. pap. 10.00 (*0-939819-03-1*) Gahmken Pr.

Waterbirds of the Northeast. Winston Williams. 120p. 1989. pap. 15.95 (*0-911977-09-0*) World FL.

***Waterbirth Handbook: The Gentle Art of Waterbirthing.** Roger Lichy. 216p. (Orig.). 1993. pap. 14.95 (*0-946551-70-7*, Pub. by Gateway Books UK) ACCESS Pubs Network.

***Waterborn.** J. Gregory Keyes. 1997. mass mkt. 5.99 (*0-345-39670-7*, Del Rey) Ballantine.

Waterborn: Children of the Changeling. J. Gregory Keyes. 448p. (YA). 1996. 22.00 (*0-345-40393-2*, Del Rey) Ballantine.

Waterborne Coatings & Additives, No. 165. Ed. by David R. Karsa & W. D. Davies. 257p. 1995. 99.00 (*0-85404-740-9*) CRC Pr.

Waterborne Commerce of British Columbia & Washington, 1850-1870. Hitchman. (Occasional Papers: No. 7). 1986. pap. 4.00 (*0-318-23326-6*) WWU CPNS.

Waterborne Diseases in the United States. Ed. by Gunther F. Craun. 336p. 1986. 173.00 (*0-8493-5937-6*, RA642, CRC Reprint) Franklin.

Waterbound. Jane Stemp. LC 95-50534. 240p. (YA). (gr. 7 up). 1996. pap. 15.99 (*0-8037-1994-9*) Dial Bks Young.

Waterboy. John Chesire. 140p. (Orig.). 1996. pap. 3.95 (*1-57502-179-X*, PO803) Morris Pubng.

Waterboys. Eric Gabriel. LC 88-7849. 234p. 1989. 18.95 (*0-916515-54-0*) Mercury Hse Inc.

Waterbury Clock Company 1867. 1976. pap. 7.95 (*0-915706-09-1*) Am Reprints.

Waterbury Clocks: History, Identification, & Price Guide. Tran D. Ly. (Illus.). 304p. 1989. 39.50 (*0-930163-40-0*); pap. 29.50 (*0-685-60153-6*) Arlington Bk.

Waterbury Clocks: Price Guide Up-Date, 1996. Tran D. Ly. (Illus.). 12p. 1996. pap. 5.00 (*0-930163-69-9*) Arlington Bk.

Waterbury Clocks: The Complete Illustrated Catalog of 1983. 2nd ed. Waterbury Clock Co. Staff. (Illus.). 128p. 1983. reprint ed. pap. 7.95 (*0-486-24460-1*) Dover.

Waterbury, CT. Fred Chesson. (Images of America Ser.). 128p. 1996. pap. 16.99 (*0-7524-0421-0*, Arcdia) Chalford.

Waterbury, CT. Historical Briefs, Inc. Staff. Ed. by Thomas Antonucci & Michael Antonucci. 176p. 1991. pap. 12.95 (*0-89677-024-9*) Hist Briefs.

Watercolor. Michael Clarke. LC 92-54547. (Eyewitness Art Ser.). (Illus.). 64p. 1993. 16.95 (*1-56458-174-8*) DK Pub Inc.

Watercolor. Duane R. Light. (Artist's Library). (Illus.). 64p. (Orig.). 1989. pap. 7.95 (*0-929261-02-X*, AL02) W Foster Pub.

Watercolor. Polly Raynes. (Workstations Ser.). (Illus.). 48p. (YA). (gr. 9 up). 1993. 21.95 (*0-8431-3663-4*) Price Stern Sloan.

Watercolor. Isidro Sanchez. (I Draw, I Paint Ser.). (Illus.). 48p. (J). 1991. pap. 7.95 (*0-8120-4717-6*) Barron.

Watercolor: A Painting Study Guide. Pat Regan. (Illus.). 68p. pap. 12.95 (*0-9615826-0-X*) P Regan.

***Watercolor: A Personal View.** John Yardley. (Illus.). 128p. 1997. 29.95 (*0-7153-0333-3*, Pub. by D & C Pub UK) Sterling.

Watercolor: A Step-By-Step Guide to Watercolor Techniques. Angela Gair. 96p. 1996. pap. 14.95 (*1-85238-540-5*, Pub. by New Holland Pubs UK) Sterling.

Watercolor: Barron's Art Handbook. Barron Staff. 1996. 9.95 (*0-8120-6617-0*) Barron.

Watercolor: Drybrush Technique. Gene Franks. (Artist's Library). (Illus.). 64p. (Orig.). 1989. pap. 7.95 (*0-929261-12-7*, AL12) W Foster Pub.

Watercolor: Free & Easy. Eric Wiegardt. LC 95-35787. (Illus.). 128p. 1996. 27.99 (*0-89134-613-9*, North Lght Bks) F & W Pubns Inc.

Watercolor: Go with the Flow. Guy Lipscomb. LC 92-34438. (Illus.). 144p. 1993. 29.95 (*0-8230-3189-6*, Watsn-Guptill) Watsn-Guptill.

Watercolor: Let the Medium Do It. Valfred Thelin & Patricia Burlin. (Illus.). 144p. 1988. 29.95 (*0-8230-5667-8*, Watsn-Guptill) Watsn-Guptill.

Watercolor: You Can Do It! Tony Couch. (Illus.). 176p. 1996. pap. 24.99 (*0-89134-697-X*, North Lght Bks) F & W Pubns Inc.

***Watercolor - The Garden Scene T. V. Book.** Susan S. Brown. 94p. 1995. pap. 11.95 (*1-56770-339-9*) S Scheewe Pubns.

Watercolor & Acrylic Painting Materials & Their Uses. William F. Powell. (Artist's Library). (Illus.). 64p. (Orig.). 1990. pap. 7.95 (*1-56010-060-5*, AL18) W Foster Pub.

Watercolor & Collage Workshop. Gerald Brommer. (Illus.). 144p. 1986. 27.50 (*0-8230-5652-X*, Watsn-Guptill) Watsn-Guptill.

***Watercolor & Collage Workshop: Make Better Paintings Through Mastery of Collage Techniques.** Gerald Brommer. 1997. pap. text ed. 19.95 (*0-8230-5643-0*) Watsn-Guptill.

Watercolor & How. Graham Scholes. (Illus.). 144p. 1989. 27.50 (*0-8230-5656-2*, Watsn-Guptill) Watsn-Guptill.

Watercolor Bold & Free. Lawrence C. Goldsmith. (Illus.). 160p. 1980. 29.95 (*0-8230-5654-6*, Watsn-Guptill) Watsn-Guptill.

Watercolor Book: Materials & Techniques for Today's Artist. David Dewey. (Illus.). 176p. 1995. 35.00 (*0-8230-5641-4*) Watsn-Guptill.

Watercolor Bright & Beautiful. Richard C. Karwoski. (Illus.). 144p. 1988. 29.95 (*0-8230-5653-8*, Watsn-Guptill) Watsn-Guptill.

***Watercolor Charms, Vol. 7.** (Illus.). 1996. pap. write for info. (*1-56770-376-3*) S Scheewe Pubns.

Watercolor Class: An Innovative Course in Transparent Watercolor. Michael Crespo. (Illus.). 256p. 1994. pap. 24.95 (*0-8230-5659-7*, Watson-Guptill Bks) Watsn-Guptill.

Watercolor Color. Ray Smith. LC 92-38771. (DK Art School Ser.). (Illus.). 72p. 1993. 16.95 (*1-56458-276-0*) DK Pub Inc.

Watercolor Fast & Loose. Ron Ranson. (Illus.). 128p. 1996. pap. 19.95 (*0-7153-0369-4*, Pub. by D & C Pub UK) Sterling.

Watercolor Fix-It Book. Tony Van Hasselt & Judi Wagner. (Illus.). 144p. (Orig.). 1995. pap. 22.99 (*0-89134-680-5*, North Lght Bks) F & W Pubns Inc.

Watercolor for the Artistically Undiscovered. Thacher Hurd & John Cassidy. 72p. 1992. 19.95 (*1-878257-44-7*) Klutz Pr.

***Watercolor for the Serious Beginner: Basic Lessons in Becoming a Good Painter.** Mary Whyte. LC 97-18887. 1997. pap. text ed. 19.95 (*0-8230-5660-0*) Watsn-Guptill.

Watercolor from the Heart. Barbara Nechis. (Illus.). 144p. (Orig.). 1993. 29.95 (*0-8230-1624-2*, Watsn-Guptill) Watsn-Guptill.

Watercolor Fun & Easy. Beverly Kaiser. 100p. 1991. pap. text ed. 7.50 (*1-56770-243-0*) S Scheewe Pubns.

***Watercolor Garden Treasures.** Susan S. Brown. 1996. pap. 11.95 (*1-56770-361-5*) S Scheewe Pubns.

Watercolor Handbook: Learning from the Masters. Ettore Maiotti. (Illus.). 160p. 1986. 15.00 (*0-517-56306-1*, C P Pubs) Crown Pub Group.

Watercolor Impressions. Pat M> Magaret & Donna I. Slusser. 1995. pap. 26.95 (*1-56477-116-4*, B233) That Patchwork.

***Watercolor Journey.** Ellie Cook. (Illus.). (Orig.). 1997. pap. 9.50 (*1-56770-381-X*) S Scheewe Pubns.

Watercolor Landscape. Ray Smith. LC 92-38770. (DK Art School Ser.). (Illus.). 72p. 1993. 16.95 (*1-56458-275-2*) DK Pub Inc.

***Watercolor Landscapes T. V. Book.** Susan S. Brown. 1996. pap. 11.95 (*1-56770-360-7*) S Scheewe Pubns.

Watercolor Made Easy: Techniques for Simplifying the Painting Process. Janet Walsh. LC 94-12267. (Illus.). 144p. 1994. 29.95 (*0-8230-5657-0*) Watsn-Guptill.

***Watercolor Made Easy 3.** Kathy George. 68p. 1994. pap. 9.50 (*1-56770-301-1*) S Scheewe Pubns.

Watercolor Memories. Ellie Cook. 100p. 1992. pap. text ed. 9.50 (*1-56770-246-5*) S Scheewe Pubns.

***Watercolor Memories of the Hills.** John Kollock. (Illus.). 80p. 1996. 40.00 (*0-9613242-2-8*) Saturday Shop.

Watercolor Naturals. Betty Denton. (Illus.). 28p. (Orig.). (C). 1993. pap. 7.95 (*0-9628339-2-4*) Giftways-B Denton.

Watercolor Painter's Handbook. Patricia Monahan & Jenny Rodwell. (Illus.). 256p. 1996. 29.95 (*0-289-80136-2*, Pub. by Studio Vista Bks UK) Sterling.

Watercolor Painter's Pocket Palette. Ed. by Moira Clinch. (Illus.). 64p. 1991. 17.99 (*0-89134-401-2*, 30341, North Lght Bks) F & W Pubns Inc.

Watercolor Painter's Solution Book. Angela Gair. (Illus.). 144p. 1991. pap. 19.99 (*0-89134-397-0*, 30307, North Lght Bks) F & W Pubns Inc.

Watercolor Painting. Wendon Blake. (Artist's Painting Library). (Illus.). 80p. 1979. pap. 12.95 (*0-8230-5673-2*, Watsn-Guptill) Watsn-Guptill.

Watercolor Painting. Hubert Gautier. (Printed Sources of Western Art Ser.). 154p. (FRE.). 1981. reprint ed. boxed 30.00 (*0-915346-63-X*) A Wofsy Fine Arts.

Watercolor Painting Kit. Duane R. Light. (Illus.). 32p. (YA). (gr. 7 up). 1995. pap. 14.95 (*1-56010-191-1*) W Foster Pub.

Watercolor Painting on the Trail: A Hiking Artist's Handbook. Judith Campbell. LC 93-11461. (Illus.). 160p. (Orig.). 1993. pap. 18.95 (*1-878239-29-5*) AMC Books.

Watercolor Painting Techniques. Ed. by David Lewis. (Illus.). 144p. 1983. pap. 16.95 (*0-8230-5669-4*, Watsn-Guptill) Watsn-Guptill.

Watercolor Paper Handbook: A Selection Guide for Artists. Werner Mertz. (Illus.). 112p. 1991. 18.95 (*0-8230-5678-3*, Watsn-Guptill) Watsn-Guptill.

***Watercolor, Pen & Ink.** Jane Wunder. 62p. 1996. pap. 9.50 (*1-56770-357-7*) S Scheewe Pubns.

Watercolor Portraiture: A Practical Guide. Phoebe Flory et al. 192p. 1985. reprint ed. pap. 5.95 (*0-486-24972-7*) Dover.

Watercolor Quilts. Pat S. Magaret & Donna I. Slusser. Ed. by Barbara Weiland. LC 93-8551. (Illus.). 118p. (Orig.). 1993. pap. 24.95 (*1-56477-031-1*, B161) That Patchwork.

Watercolor Red Yellow Blue: Intermediate Techniques of Bringing Color to Life with a Primary Palette. John Koser. (Illus.). 144p. 1990. 29.95 (*0-8230-5679-1*, Watsn-Guptill) Watsn-Guptill.

Watercolor Rendering. Hayashi Studio Staff. (Illus.). 152p. 1995. pap. 29.95 (*4-7661-0643-1*, Pub. by Graphic Sha JA) Bks Nippan.

Watercolor Right from the Start. Hilary Page. LC 92-17440. (Illus.). 144p. 1992. 29.95 (*0-8230-5688-0*, Watsn-Guptill) Watsn-Guptill.

Watercolor Secrets for Painting Light. rev. ed. Betty L. Schlemm. Ed. by Herbert Rogoff. (Illus.). 128p. 1996. 27.99 (*0-929552-11-3*) Art Instr Assocs.

Watercolor Sketches of Thomas Moran: Yellowstone & Grand Teton National Park. Illus. by Thomas Moran. 8p. 1991. pap. 9.95 (*0-931895-21-9*) Grand Teton NHA.

***Watercolor Step by Step.** Susan S. Brown. 102p. 1994. pap. 11.95 (*1-56770-294-5*) S Scheewe Pubns.

Watercolor Still Life. Elizabeth J. Lloyd. LC 93-47008. (DK Art School Ser.). (Illus.). 72p. 1994. 16.95 (*1-56458-490-9*) DK Pub Inc.

Watercolor Strategy. Michael G. Booth. 150p. 1996. pap. text ed. 25.00 (*1-888236-00-0*) Art Wise.

Watercolor Tricks & Techniques. Cathy Johnson. (Illus.). 160p. 1992. pap. 22.99 (*0-89134-447-0*, 30440, North Lght Bks) F & W Pubns Inc.

***Watercolor Troubleshooter.** Don Harrison. LC 97-15291. 1998. write for info. (*0-7641-0323-7*) Barron.

Watercolor U. S. A. National Invitational Exhibition, 1976. Allen S. Weller. (Watercolor U. S. A. Ser.). (Illus.). (Orig.). 1976. pap. text ed. 5.00 (*0-934306-00-1*) Springfield.

Watercolor U. S. A. 1986: The Monumental Image. William C. Landwehr. LC 86-61583. (Illus.). 80p. (Orig.). 1986. pap. text ed. 15.00 (*0-934306-06-0*) Springfield.

Watercolor U. S. A. 1996. Jerry A. Berger & Deborah J. Schlier. (Illus.). 24p. (Orig.). 1996. pap. 5.00 (*0-934306-12-5*) Springfield.

***Watercolor U. S. A. 1997.** Deborah J. Schlier et al. (Illus.). 24p. (Orig.). 1997. pap. 3.00 (*0-934306-16-8*) Springfield.

Watercolor with Mixed Media. Duane R. Light. (Artist's Library). (Illus.). 64p. (Orig.). 1989. pap. 7.95 (*1-56010-032-X*, AL16) W Foster Pub.

Watercolor Workbook. Bud Biggs & Lois Marshall. (Illus.). 160p. 1987. pap. 22.99 (*0-89134-203-6*, 8841, North Lght Bks) F & W Pubns Inc.

Watercolor Workshop, No. 1. Rose Edin. (How to Draw & Paint Ser.). (Illus.). 32p. (Orig.). 1989. pap. 6.95 (*0-929261-23-2*, HT213) W Foster Pub.

Watercolor Workshop, No. 2. Rose Edin. (How to Draw & Paint Ser.). (Illus.). 32p. (Orig.). 1992. pap. 6.95 (*1-56010-077-X*, HT236) W Foster Pub.

***Watercolor World of Cheng-Khee Chee.** Cheng-Khee Chee. Ed. & Tr. by Sylvia Tan. (Illus.). viii, 200p. (CHI & ENG.). 1997. 65.00 (*0-9655807-0-9*) Chee Studio.

Watercolorist's Complete Guide to Color. Tom Hill. (Illus.). 144p. 1992. 27.99 (*0-89134-430-6*, North Lght Bks) F & W Pubns Inc.

***Watercolorist's Garden.** Jill Bays. 128p. 1997. pap. 19.95 (*0-7153-0620-0*, Pub. by D & C Pub UK) Sterling.

***Watercolorist's Guide to Mixing Colors.** Jenny Rodwell. (Illus.). 128p. 1997. 27.99 (*0-89134-797-6*, North Lght Bks) F & W Pubns Inc.

Watercolor...Let's Think about It! 4th ed. Judi Betts. (Illus.). 114p. 1984. pap. 17.00 (*0-9616679-0-7*) Aquarelle Pr.

***Watercolors.** M. Angels Comella. LC 96-33017. (Painting & Drawing Ser.). (J). 1997. pap. 5.95 (*0-382-39847-5*, Silver Pr NJ); lib. bdg. 15.95 (*0-382-39852-1*, Silver Pr NJ) Silver Burdett Pr.

Watercolors. Walter Foster. (How to Draw & Paint Ser.). (Illus.). 32p. (Orig.). 1989. pap. 6.95 (*0-929261-56-9*, HT5) W Foster Pub.

***Watercolors.** Smithmark Staff. (Art School Ser.). 1996. 7.98 (*0-7651-9728-6*) Smithmark.

Watercolors: A Concise History. Graham Reynolds. (World of Art Ser.). (Illus.). 1986. pap. 14.95 (*0-500-20109-9*) Thames Hudson.

Watercolors - Landscape. Brian Bagnall et al. (Artist's Workshop Ser.). (Illus.). 64p. 1994. pap. 9.95 (*1-56010-180-6*, AW03) W Foster Pub.

***Watercolors Anyone Can Paint, Vol. 25.** Susan S. Brown. 94p. 1995. pap. 11.95 (*1-56770-325-9*) S Scheewe Pubns.

Watercolors by John Piper. David F. Jenkins. (Illus.). 48p. (Orig.). 1992. pap. 15.95 (*1-85444-025-X*, 025-X, Pub. by Ashmolean Mus UK) A Schwartz & Co.

Watercolors by Kandinsky at the Guggenheim Museum. Susan B. Hirschfield. 1994. 45.00 (*0-8109-6873-8*) Abrams.

Watercolors by Kandinsky at the Guggenheim Museum: A Selection from the Solomon R. Guggenheim Museum & the Hilla von Rebay Foundation. Guggenheim Museum Staff. Ed. by Anthony Calnek. (Illus.). 185p. (Orig.). 1991. 42.00 (*0-89207-069-2*); pap. write for info. (*0-89207-070-6*) S R Guggenheim.

***Watercolors by Martha Odum: January 25-March 16, 1997.** Martha Odum & Jennifer Deprima. LC 96-52377. 1997. write for info. (*0-915977-32-X*) Georgia Museum of Art.

Watercolors by Paul Signac. Charles Cachin. Ed. by Lauri Thompson. Tr. by Isabel Balzer from FRE. (Illus.). 42p. 1990. pap. text ed. 15.00 (*0-942779-06-1*) Greenberg Voin Doren.

Watercolors for the Birds of America. John J. Audubon. Ed. by Annette Blaugrund & Theodore E. Stebbins, Jr. LC 93-3219. (Illus.). 1993. 75.00 (*0-679-42059-2*, Villard Bks) Random.

Watercolors for the Birds of America. John J. Audubon. Ed. by Annette Blaugrund & Theodore E. Stebbins, Jr. LC 93-3219. (Illus.). 1994. pap. write for info. (*0-679-74837-7*) Random.

Watercolors from the Abstract Expressionist Era. Jeffrey Wechsler. (Illus.). 28p. 1990. 9.00 (*0-915171-15-5*) Katonah Gal.

Watercolors Made Easy. 1996. 12.99 (*0-517-14296-1*) Random Hse Value.

Watercolors of Carolyn Brady: Including a Catalogue Raisonne 1972-1990. Irene McManus. LC 91-71548. (Illus.). 192p. 1991. 50.00 (*1-55595-048-5*) Hudson Hills.

Watercolors of Dixie. Ben E. Looney. 1974. 20.00 (*0-87511-075-4*) Claitors.

Watercolors of Italy. Mignonette Y. Cheng et al. 39.50 (*0-472-10738-0*) U of Mich Pr.

Watercolors of Paul Jacoulet. Richard Miles. (Illus.). 84p. 1989. 60.00 (*1-877921-02-5*); pap. 27.50 (*1-877921-01-7*) Pacific Asia.

Watercolors of the Rio Grande. Michael Frary. LC 84-40128. (Illus.). 134p. 1984. 29.95 (*0-89096-207-3*) Tex A&M Univ Pr.

Watercolors Step-by-Step. Kolan Peterson. (How to Draw & Paint Ser.). (Illus.). 32p. (Orig.). 1989. pap. 6.95 (*0-929261-47-X*, HT205) W Foster Pub.

Watercolour Flowers. David Easton. (Illus.). 128p. 1994. pap. 22.95 (*0-7134-7604-4*, Pub. by Batsford UK) Trafalgar.

***Watercolour Landscapes Made Easy.** Richard Taylor. (Illus.). 128p. 1997. 29.95 (*0-7134-7955-8*, Pub. by Batsford UK) Trafalgar.

Watercolour Painting Art Workshop. Paul Taggart. (Illus.). 128p. 1993. 29.95 (*0-09-177016-5*, Pub. by Ebury Pr UK) Trafalgar.

An Asterisk (*) at the beginning of an entry indicates that the title is appearing in BIP for the first time.

*Watercolour Painting with Aubrey Phillips. Aubrey Phillips. (Illus.). 128p. 1997. 35.00 (0-7134-7080-1, Pub. by Batsford UK) Trafalgar.

Watercolour Painting with Karen Simmons see Painting the Colors of Nature: A Watercolorist's Guide

Watercolours & Drawings: Akvareli i Risunki v Gosudarstvennom Russkom Muzee. V. A. Pushkarev. (Illus.). 1982. 125.00 (0-317-57493-0) St Mut.

Watercolours & Drawings of Russian & Soviet Artists in the Pushkin Fine Arts Museum. A. Alexandrova. (Illus.). (ENG & RUS.). 1982. 65.00 (0-317-57489-2) St Mut.

Watercolours & Drawings of the Eighteenth & First Half of the Nineteenth Century in the Tretyakov Gallery. M. A. Nemirovskaias. (Illus.). 162p. (ENG & RUS.). 1982. 173.00 (0-317-57485-X) St Mut.

Watercolours from the Turner Bequest, 1819-1845. (Tate Gallery Publications). (Illus.). 1968. 12.50 (0-405-00224-6) Ayer.

Watercomp '93: Computing for the Water Industry Today & Tomorrow. Ed. by Roger G. Hadgraft. (National Conference Publication Ser.: No. 93/2). (Illus.). 442p. (Orig.). 1993. pap. 84.00 (0-317-05536-4, Pub. by Inst Engrs Aust-EA Bks AT) Accents Pubns.

Watercraft on Stamps. Katherine A. Kirk. (Illus.). 172p. 1991. pap. 17.00 (0-935991-11-5) Am Topical Assn.

Watercraft Patrol & Survival Tactics. Donald M. Turner et al. 292p. 1990. pap. 35.95 (0-398-06467-9) C C Thomas.

Watercraft Patrol & Survival Tactics. Donald M. Turner & Tony Lesce. (Illus.). 292p. (C). 1990. text ed. 52.95 (0-398-05712-5) C C Thomas.

*Waterdance. Graphis Staff. 1995. 39.95 (0-688-14789-5) Morrow.

*Waterdance. Graphis Staff. 1997. pap. 24.95 (0-688-15205-8) Morrow.

Waterdance. Ed. by B. Martin Pedersen. (Illus.). 192p. 1996. pap. 24.95 (1-888001-20-8) Graphis US.

Waterdeep. Richard Awlinson. LC 88-51725. (Forgotten Realms Avatar Trilogy Ser.: Bk. 3). 352p. 1989. pap. 5.99 (0-88038-759-9) TSR Inc.

Waterdrum Science: Science Through American Indian Arts & Culture. Carolyn A. Petty. Ed. by Benjamin Duranske. LC 94-78267. (Illus.). 290p. (J). (gr. 4-8). 1994. lib. bdg. 28.50 (0-9642898-0-6) Larchmere Ltd.

*Watered-Down Electricity: Using Water to Explain Electricity. John A. Fife. LC 95-90925. (Illus.). 64p. (Orig.). 1996. pap. 8.95 (1-56002-636-7, Univ Edtns) Aegina Pr.

Watered Garden. J. Boyd Nicholson. (Illus.). 96p. 1994. 21.95 (1-882701-03-8) Uplook Min.

Waterfall. Margaret Drabble. 1989. pap. 8.95 (0-317-02811-1) NAL-Dutton.

*Waterfall. Robin J. Gunn. 1998. pap. 8.99 (1-57673-221-5) Multnomah Pubs.

Waterfall Lover's Guide to the Pacific Northwest: Where to Find More Than 500 Scenic Waterfalls in WA, OR & ID. 2nd ed. Gregory Plumb. LC 89-12959. (Illus.). 192p. 1989. pap. 12.95 (0-89886-191-8) Mountaineers.

Waterfall Walks & Drives in Georgia, Alabama & Tennessee. Mark Morrison. (Illus.). 176p. (Orig.). 1996. pap. 9.95 (0-9636070-2-2) H F Pub GA.

Waterfall Walks & Drives in Northeast Georgia & the Western Carolinas. Mark Morrison. 76p. 1992. pap. 7.95 (0-9636070-0-6) H F Pub GA.

Waterfall Walks & Drives in the Western Carolinas. Mark Morrison. (Illus.). 128p. (Orig.). 1994. pap. 8.95 (0-9636070-1-4) H F Pub GA.

Waterfalls: Nature's Thundering Splendor. Jenny Wood. (Wonderworks of Nature Ser.). (Illus.). 32p. (J). (gr. 3-4). 1991. lib. bdg. 19.93 (0-8368-0633-6) Gareth Stevens Inc.

Waterfalls & Cascades of the Great Smoky Mountains. rev. ed. Hal Hubbs et al. 80p. 1993. pap. 7.95 (0-9630682-4-5) Panther TN.

Waterfalls & Gorges of the Finger Lakes. Derek Doeffinger. LC 96-8826. (Illus.). 128p. (Orig.). 1996. pap. 29.95 (0-935526-24-2) McBooks Pr.

Waterfalls of Colorado. Marc Conly. LC 92-42496. (Illus.). 52p. 1993. pap. 18.95 (0-87108-823-1) Pruett.

Waterfalls of Grand Teton National Park: A National Park Waterfall Guide. Charles Maynard. (Illus.). 70p. (Orig.). 1996. pap. text ed. 5.95 (1-887205-07-1) Panther TN.

Waterfalls of Scotland: Worth Gaun a Mile Tae See. Louis Stott. (Illus.). 264p. 1987. text ed. 25.00 (0-08-032424-X, Pub. by Aberdeen U Pr) Macmillan.

Waterfalls of Slunj. Heimito Von Doderer. Tr. by Ernst Kaiser & Eithne Wilkins from GER. LC 87-83303. 406p. 1987. reprint ed. pap. 15.00 (0-941419-11-8, Eridanos Library) Marsilio Pubs.

*Waterfalls of Slunj, Vol. 159. Doderer Von Heimito. (Sun & Moon Classics Ser.). 1997. pap. text ed. 14.95 (1-55713-320-4) Sun & Moon CA.

Waterfalls of Tennessee: A Guide to over 200 Falls in the Volunteer State. Gregory Plumb. (Illus.). 256p. (Orig.). 1996. pap. 17.95 (1-57072-057-6) Overmountain Pr.

Waterfalls of the Blue Ridge: A Guide to the Blue Ridge Parkway & Great Smoky Mountains. rev. ed. Nicole Blouin et al. (Illus.). 172p. 1997. pap. 14.95 (0-89732-128-6) Menasha Ridge.

Waterfalls of the Southern Appalachians. 2nd ed. Brian A. Boyd. (Illus.). 112p. 1993. pap. 7.95 (0-9625737-3-6) Ferncreek Pub.

Waterfalls of the Southern Appalachians: A Viewer's Guide to 40 Waterfalls of Northern Georgia, Western North Carolina, & Western South Carolina. Brian A. Boyd. Ed. by K. Boyd. (Illus.). 68p. (Orig.). 1990. pap. 6.95 (0-9625737-1-X) Ferncreek Pub.

Waterfalls of the White Mountains: 30 Trips to 100 Waterfalls. Bruce Bolnick & Doreen Bolnick. LC 89-18636. (Illus.). 336p. (Orig.). 1990. pap. 15.00 (0-88150-160-3, Backcountry) Countryman.

Waterfalls of Yellowstone National Park: A National Park Waterfall Guide. Charles Maynard. 120p. 1996. pap. text ed. 11.95 (1-887205-06-3) Panther TN.

Waterfields Guide to Computer Software: (Word Processing, Spreadsheet, Database Operating System, & More) Ed. by Arthur L. Delcher. (Waterfields Computer Guide Ser.). (Illus.). 150p. (Orig.). 1995. pap. 12.95 (1-886271-05-4) Waterflds Pr.

Waterfield's Guide to Computer Terms. Ed. by A. L. Delcher. (Computer Guide Ser.). 160p. 1995. pap. 12.95 (1-886271-00-3) Waterflds Pr.

Waterflood Calculations for Hand-Held Computers. fac. ed. Forrest A. Garb. LC 81-20274. (Illus.). 104p. pap. 29.70 (0-7837-7409-5, 2047203) Bks Demand.

Waterflooding. G. Paul Wilhite. 326p. 1986. 57.50 (1-55563-005-7, 31804) Soc Petrol Engineers.

Waterford Water Cure: A Numismatic Inquiry. Q. David Bowers. (Illus.). 224p. 1992. text ed. 49.95 (0-943161-45-2) Bowers & Merena.

Waterfowl. Dave Beaty. LC 92-32319. (Nature Bks.). 32p. (J). (gr. 2-6). 1993. lib. bdg. 22.79 (1-56766-006-1) Childs World.

Waterfowl. John P. Mackenzie. (Illus.). 144p. 1988. 24.95 (1-55971-018-7) NorthWord.

Waterfowl. 2nd ed. 1987. write for info. (0-318-62427-3) Rolfs Gall.

Waterfowl, Vol. 2. Rolf A. Pederson. (Orig.). 1983. pap. 9.95 (0-910579-01-6) Rolfs Gall.

Waterfowl: An Identification Guide to the Ducks, Geese & Swans of the World. Steven Madge. (Illus.). 288p. 1992. pap. 29.95 (0-395-46726-8) HM.

*Waterfowl: Care, Breeding & Conservation. Simon Tarsnane. 280p. (Orig.). 1996. pap. 24.95 (0-88839-391-1) Hancock House.

Waterfowl & Wetlands: Toward Bioeconomic Analysis. Judd Hammack & Gardner M. Brown, Jr. LC 74-6815. (Resources for the Future Research Paper). (Illus.). 108p. 1974. 10.00 (0-8018-1625-4) Johns Hopkins.

Waterfowl & Wetlands: Toward Bioeconomic Analysis. Judd Hammack & Gardner M. Brown. LC 74-6815. 110p. reprint ed. pap. 31.40 (0-685-23699-4, 2032151) Bks Demand.

Waterfowl Art of Maynard Reece. Maynard Reece. (Illus.). 160p. 1985. 49.50 (0-8109-1797-1) Abrams.

Waterfowl Carving, Blue Ribbon Techniques. William Veasey & Cary S. Hull. LC 82-50616. (Illus.). 272p. 1982. 35.00 (0-916838-67-6) Schiffer.

Waterfowl Carving with J. D. Sprankle: The Fully Illustrated Reference to Carving & Painting 25 Decorative Ducks. Roger Schroeder & James D. Sprankle. LC 85-9748. (Illus.). 256p. 1985. 29.95 (0-8117-3094-8) Stackpole.

Waterfowl Decoys of Michigan & the Lake St. Clair Region. Ed. by Clune Walsh, Jr. & Lowell G. Jackson. (Illus.). 114p. 1983. 65.00 (0-8103-4243-X); 250.00 (0-8103-4244-8) Gale.

Waterfowl Down & Feathers. (Latin American Products Included in the U. S. General System of Preferences Ser.). 1978. pap. text ed. 3.00 (0-8270-3380-X) OAS.

Waterfowl Ecology. Myrfyn Owen & Jeffrey M. Black. (Tertiary Level Biology Ser.). (Illus.). 200p. 1990. text ed. 69.95 (0-412-02191-9, A3617, Chap & Hall NY) Chapman & Hall.

Waterfowl Ecology. Myrfyn Owen & Jeffrey M. Black. (Tertiary Level Biology Ser.). (Illus.). 200p. (gr. 13). 1990. pap. text ed. 46.50 (0-412-02201-X, A3621, Chap & Hall NY) Chapman & Hall.

Waterfowl Ecology & Management. Guy A. Baldassarre & Eric Bolen. 609p. 1994. text ed. 84.95 (0-471-59770-8) Wiley.

Waterfowl Ecology & Management: Selected Readings. Compiled by John T. Ratti et al. LC 82-70782. (Illus.). xvi, 1328p. (Orig.). (C). 1982. pap. 29.00 (0-933564-09-0) Wildlife Soc.

Waterfowl Heritage: North Carolina Decoys & Gunning Lore. William N. Conoley, Jr. (Illus.). 336p. 1983. 39.95 (0-9610358-1-1) Webfoot Inc.

Waterfowl Identification: The LeMaster Method. Richard LeMaster. LC 96-20744. (Illus.). 76p. 1996. spiral bd., pap. 7.95 (0-8117-2982-6) Stackpole.

Waterfowl Illustrated. Tricia Veasey. LC 83-61648. (Illus.). 296p. 1983. 45.00 (0-916838-89-7) Schiffer.

Waterfowl of North America. LC 87-5638. 1992. 70.00 (0-9618270-0-9) GSJ Press.

Waterfowl Painting: Blue Ribbon Techniques. William Veasey. LC 83-61645. (Illus.). 224p. 1983. 45.00 (0-916838-90-0) Schiffer.

Waterfowl Studies: Dabbling & Whistling Ducks. Bruce Burk. LC 84-51284. (Waterfowl Studies: Vol. I). (Illus.). 240p. 1984. 35.00 (0-88740-025-6) Schiffer.

Waterfowl Studies: Diving Ducks. Bruce Burk. LC 84-51283. (Waterfowl Studies: Vol. II). (Illus.). 280p. 1984. 39.95 (0-88740-026-4) Schiffer.

Waterfowl Studies: Geese & Swans. Bruce Burk. LC 84-51260. (Waterfowl Studies: Vol. III). (Illus.). 200p. 1984. 29.95 (0-88740-027-2) Schiffer.

*Waterfowling Horizons: Hunting Ducks & Geese in the 21st Century. Christopher Smith & Jason Smith. 1997. 49.95 (1-885106-50-5) Wild Adven Pr.

*Waterfowling Horizons: Shooting Ducks & Geese in the Twenty-First Century. limited ed. Christopher Smith & Jason Smith. (Illus.). 320p. 1997. lthr. 125.00 (1-885106-51-3) Wild Adven Pr.

Waterfront. Budd Schulberg. LC 79-11704. 1979. reprint ed. lib. bdg. 20.00 (0-8376-0434-6) Bentley.

Waterfront Directory of Lucas & Wood Counties, Ohio. Eugene P. Van Voorhis. (Illus.). 54p. (Orig.). 1989. pap. 5.00 (0-9603006-6-X) Waterfront OH.

Waterfront Directory of Ottawa County, Ohio. Eugene P. Van Voorhis. 1985. pap. 5.00 (0-9603006-5-1) Waterfront OH.

Waterfront Journals. David Wojnarowicz. LC 95-45735. 144p. 1996. 20.00 (0-8021-1585-3, Grove) Grove-Atltic.

*Waterfront Journals. David Wojnarowicz. 384p. 1997. pap. 12.00 (0-8021-3504-8, Grove) Grove-Atltic.

Waterfront Living: A Report on Permanent & Seasonal Residents in Northern Michigan. Robert W. Marans et al. LC 76-620083. 301p. 1976. pap. 12.00 (0-87944-218-2) Inst Soc Res.

Waterfront Living: A Report on Permanent & Seasonal Residents in Northern Michigan. Robert W. Marans et al. LC 76-620083. (Illus.). 301p. reprint ed. pap. 85.80 (0-7837-5252-0, 2044989) Bks Demand.

Waterfront Peacemaker. Dennis J. Comey. LC 82-60025. 202p. 1983. pap. 5.95 (0-916101-03-7) St Joseph.

Waterfront Planning & Development. Ed. by A. Ruth Fitzgerald. LC 86-25929. 108p. 1986. pap. 17.00 (0-87262-576-1) Am Soc Civil Eng.

Waterfront Revitalization. Eric J. Fournier. LC 95-1911. (CPL Bibliographies Ser.: No. 310). 46p. 1994. pap. 10.00 (0-86602-310-0, Sage Prdcls Pr) Sage.

Waterfront Revitalization for Smaller Communities. Intro. by Robert F. Goodwin. 207p. (Orig.). 1988. pap. 12.00 (0-934539-04-9) Wash Sea Grant.

Waterfront Supercargo. Tom Murray. (Little Bks.). 59p. (Orig.). 1980. pap. 2.25 (0-917300-10-6) Singlejack Bks.

Waterfront Workers of New Orleans: Race, Class, & Politics, 1863-1923. Eric Arnesen. LC 93-33057. (Illus.). 384p. 1994. reprint ed. pap. text ed. 15.95 (0-252-06377-5) U of Ill Pr.

Watergate. National Archives Trust Fund Board Staff. 48p. 1992. 5.95 (0-8403-7401-1) Kendall-Hunt.

Watergate. Scott Westerfeld. (Turning Points in American History Ser.). (Illus.). 64p. (YA). (gr. 5 up). 1991. pap. 7.95 (0-382-24120-7) Silver Burdett Pr.

Watergate: An Annotated Bibliography of Sources in English, 1972-1982. Myron J. Smith, Jr. LC 83-4408. 344p. 1983. 29.50 (0-8108-1623-7) Scarecrow.

Watergate: The Corruption of American Politics & the Fall of Richard Nixon. Fred Emery. LC 95-12511. 1995. pap. 15.00 (0-684-81323-8, Fireside) S&S Trade.

Watergate: The Fall of Richard M. Nixon. Ed. by Stanley I. Kutler. 256p. (Orig.). (C). 1996. pap. text ed. 16.50 (1-881089-30-4) Brandywine Press.

Watergate & Afterward: The Legacy of Richard M. Nixon. Ed. by Leon Friedman & William F. Levantrosser. LC 90-20677. (Contributions in Political Science Ser.: No. 274). 392p. 1992. text ed. 59.95 (0-313-27781-8, FWG/, Greenwood Pr) Greenwood.

Watergate & the Constitution. Philip B. Kurland. LC 77-18338. 272p. 1978. lib. bdg. 15.00 (0-226-46393-1) U Ch Pr.

Watergate & the White House, Vol. 1, June 1972-July 1973. Ed. by Edward W. Knappman. LC 73-83049. reprint ed. pap. 62.00 (0-317-26133-9, 2025164) Bks Demand.

Watergate & the White House, Vol. 2, July-Dec 1973. Ed. by Edward W. Knappman. LC 73-83049. reprint ed. pap. 72.50 (0-317-26134-7) Bks Demand.

Watergate & the White House, Vol. 3, Jan-Sept 1974. Ed. by Edward W. Knappman. LC 73-83049. reprint ed. pap. 104.50 (0-317-26135-5) Bks Demand.

Watergate Games: Strategies, Choices, Outcomes. Douglas Muzzio. LC 81-16964. 176p. (C). 1982. text ed. 24.00 (0-8147-5384-1) NYU Pr.

Watergate Investigation Index: House Judiciary Committee Hearings & Report on Impeachment. Compiled by Hedda Garza. LC 85-2040. 261p. 1985. 125.00 (0-8420-2186-8) Scholarly Res Inc.

Watergate Investigation Index: Senate Select Committee Hearings & Reports on Presidential Campaign Activities. Compiled by Hedda Garza. LC 82-7353. 326p. 1982. lib. bdg. 125.00 (0-8420-2175-2) Scholarly Res Inc.

Watergate Reforms: Ten Years Later. 48p. 1984. 2.00 (0-914389-15-7) Common Cause.

*Watergate Scandal in American History. David Fremon. (In American History Ser.). (Illus.). (YA). (gr. 5 up). 1997. lib. bdg. 18.95 (0-89490-883-9) Enslow Pubs.

Watergate Victory: Mardian's Appeal. Arnold Rochvarg. LC 95-5695. 280p. (C). 1995. lib. bdg. 36.00 (0-8191-9916-8) U Pr of Amer.

Watergrate: How to Train Taxed Prisoners. Harold C. Billings, Jr. LC 84-90959. 276p. 1985. pap. 14.95 (0-9613642-0-3) H C Billings.

Waterhammer Analysis. John Parmakian. 1955. pap. 6.95 (0-486-61061-6) Dover.

Waterhole: How to Dig Your Own Well. Bob Mellin. LC 91-72454. (Illus.). 75p. (Orig.). 1992. pap. 8.95 (0-935902-21-X) Balboa Pub.

Waterhouse: The Families of Jacob Waterhouse, 1605-1676. Jerry E. Waterous. (Illus.). 228p. 1993. reprint ed. pap. 34.00 (0-8328-3086-0); reprint ed. lib. bdg. 44.00 (0-8328-3085-2) Higginson Bk Co.

Waterhouse-Frost. Raymond F. Frost. LC 95-70927. (Illus.). 211p. 1996. 34.95 (1-57197-001-0) Pentland Pr.

Waterhyacinth: Biology, Ecology & Management. Brij Gopal. (Aquatic Plant Studies: No. 1). 484p. 1987. 228.25 (0-444-42706-6) Elsevier.

Watering Hole: A User's Guide to Montana Bars. Joan Melcher. (Illus.). 128p. (Orig.). 1980. pap. text ed. 3.95 (0-938314-00-9) Am Wrld Geog.

Watering Holes of Scotland. Kensington West Productions Ltd. Staff. 1996. pap. 26.95 (1-871349-91-5, Pub. by Kensington West UK) BookWorld Dist.

*Watering Holes of Scotland. Kensington West Productions, Ltd. Staff. (Illus.). 224p. pap. 26.95 (1-871349-56-7, Pub. by Kensington West UK) BookWorld Dist.

Watering Systems for Lawn & Garden: A Do-It-Yourself Guide. R. Dodge Woodson. Ed. by Deborah Balmuth. LC 95-30587. (Illus.). 144p. (Orig.). 1996. pap. 16.95 (0-88266-906-0, 906-0, Storey Pub) Storey Comm Inc.

Watering the Roots in a Democracy: A Manual on How to Combine Literature & Writing in the Public Library. Judy Hogan. (Illus.). 270p. (Orig.). 1989. pap. 10.00 (0-932112-28-5) Carolina Wren.

Watering the Valley: Development along the High Plains Arkansas River, 1870-1950. James E. Sherow. LC 90-12695. (Development of Western Resources Ser.). (Illus.). xiv, 226p. 1990. 29.95 (0-7006-0440-5) U Pr of KS.

Watering Trough, Homestead Humor. Alice Schumacher & Dorothy Bohn. LC 88-92741. 1989. 12.95 (0-9621822-0-6) Schumacher-Bohn.

Waterjet Cutting. Fairmont Press Staff & Miller. 1991. text ed. 63.00 (0-13-947573-7) P-H.

Waterjet Cutting. Richard K. Miller. LC 88-45797. 165p. 1990. text ed. 62.95 (0-88173-068-8) Fairmont Pr.

Waterjet Cutting: A Survey on Technology & Markets, No. 5. Richard K. Miller & Terri C. Walker. LC 88-80483. 36p. 1988. pap. text ed. 200.00 (1-55865-004-0) Future Tech Surveys.

*Waterjetting Technology. Summers. (Illus.). 904p. 1995. text ed. 159.95 (0-419-19660-9, E & FN Spon) Routledge Chapman & Hall.

Waterland. Graham Swift. 1992. write for info. (0-679-74033-3) McKay.

Waterland. Graham Swift. 1992. pap. 12.00 (0-679-73979-3, Vin) Random.

Waterland: A Gathering from Holland. John S. Wade. 1977. pap. 4.00 (0-914974-12-2) Holmgangers.

Waterlilies-a Monograph of the Genus Nymphaea. fac. ed. Henry S. Conard. (Illus.). 336p. 1991. 395.00 (0-948697-17-2, Pub. by Lark Pubns UK) St Mut.

Waterlily. Ella C. Deloria. LC 87-21462. xii, 246p. 1988. pap. 10.95 (0-8032-6579-4, Bison Books) U of Nebr Pr.

*Waterlily. Anne Geddes. 1997. 19.95 (0-8362-3649-1) Andrews & McMeel.

Waterline. Arno Minkkinen. (Illus.). 112p. 1994. 40.00 (0-89381-591-8) Aperture.

Waterline. Arno Minkkinen. (Illus.). 112p. 1994. pap. 29.95 (0-89381-648-5) Aperture.

Waterlines. Ann W. Walka. (Illus.). 64p. 1993. per. 9.95 (0-614-04179-1) Red Lake Bks.

Waterlines: Journeys on a Desert River. Ann W. Walka. (Illus.). 64p. (Orig.). 1993. pap. 9.95 (1-884546-00-5) Red Lake Bks.

Waterloo. Philip Sauvain. LC 92-29564. (Great Battles & Sieges Ser.). (Illus.). 32p. (YA). (gr. 6 up). 1993. lib. bdg. 13.95 (0-02-781096-8, Mac Bks Young Read) S&S Childrens.

Waterloo. large type ed. Frederick E. Smith. (General Ser.). 384p. 1993. 25.99 (0-7089-2831-5) Ulverscroft.

Waterloo. Charles Grant. (Wargaming in History Ser.). (Illus.). 112p. (Orig.). (C). 1990. reprint ed. lib. bdg. 27.00 (0-8095-7581-7) Borgo Pr.

*Waterloo: A Near Run Thing. David Howarth. (Great Battles Ser.). 1997. pap. 21.95 (1-900624-02-8, Pub. by Windrush Pr UK) Interlink Pub.

Waterloo: New Perspectives. David Hamilton-Williams. LC 94-10058. 416p. 1994. text ed. 27.95 (0-471-05225-6) Wiley.

Waterloo: New Perspectives - The Great Battle Reappraised. David Hamilton-Williams. 384p. 1996. pap. text ed. 19.95 (0-471-14571-8) Wiley.

Waterloo at Dawning. George Dallas. LC 97-13625. 1997. 30.00 (0-8050-3184-7) H Holt & Co.

*Waterloo at Dawning, Vol. 1. Dallas. 1997. pap. 15.95 (0-8050-3185-5) St Martin.

Waterloo Campaign: June 1815. Albert A. Nofi. (Illus.). 352p. 1993. 24.95 (0-938289-29-2, 7324) Combined Pub.

Waterloo Creek. Roger Milliss. 1995. pap. 51.95 (0-86840-326-1, Pub. by New South Wales Univ Pr AT) Intl Spec Bk.

Waterloo Diamonds. Richard Panek. 304p. 1995. 22.95 (0-312-13209-3) St Martin.

Waterloo Directory of Irish Newspapers & Periodicals 1800-1900. Ed. by John S. North. 838p. (C). 1986. lib. bdg. 300.00 (0-921075-00-6) N Waterloo Acad Pr.

Waterloo Directory of Scottish Newspapers & Periodicals, 1800-1900, 2 vols. Ed. by John S. North. (Illus.). 2199p. (C). 1989. Set. lib. bdg. 640.00 (0-921075-05-7) N Waterloo Acad Pr.

Waterloo Directory of Victorian Periodicals. Ed. by Michael Wolff et al. 1203p. 1981. 529.00 (0-08-026079-9, Pub. by Pergamon Repr UK) Franklin.

Waterloo Express. Paulette Jiles. 83p. (Orig.). 1973. pap. 6.95 (0-88784-028-0, Pub. by Hse of Anansi Pr CN) Genl Dist Srvs.

*Waterloo Lectures. Charles C. Chesney. LC 97-19005. (Napoleonic Library). 1997. write for info. (1-85367-288-2) Stackpole.

Waterloo Letters. Ed. by H. T. Siborne. 464p. 1993. 40.00 (1-85367-156-8, 5449) Stackpole.

Waterloo Mennonites: A Community in Paradox. J. Winfield Fretz. (Illus.). 272p. (C). 1989. pap. 19.95 (0-88920-984-7); text ed. 29.95 (0-88920-985-5) Wilfrid Laurier.

Waterloo, No. 11: Sharpe's Final Adventure. Bernard Cornwell. 384p. 1991. pap. 10.95 (0-14-008473-8, Penguin Bks) Viking Penguin.

Waterloo Promenade & Its Environs. R. Smith & D. Shaw. (C). 1984. text ed. 50.00 (0-685-22168-7, Pub. by Univ Nottingham UK) St Mut.

Waterloo 1815. Geoffrey Wootten. (Campaign Ser.: No. 15). (Illus.). 96p. pap. 14.95 (1-85532-210-2, 9514, Pub. by Osprey UK) Stackpole.

Waterman: Descendants of Richard Waterman of Providence, RI, with Records of Many Other Family Groups of the Waterman Name. Donald L. Jacobus & Edgar F. Waterman. 808p. 1991. reprint ed. pap. 109.00 (0-8328-1956-5); reprint ed. lib. bdg. 119.00 (0-8328-1955-7) Higginson Bk Co.

Waterman: Descendants of Robert Waterman of Marshfield, MA Through Seven Generations. Donald L. Jacobus. (Illus.). 818p. 1991. reprint ed. pap. 109.00 (0-8328-1954-9); reprint ed. lib. bdg. 119.00 (0-8328-1953-0) Higginson Bk Co.

Waterman of the Chesapeake Bay. 2nd ed. John H. Whitehead, III. LC 87-13405. (Illus.). 168p. 1987. 29.95 (0-87033-374-7, Tidewtr Pubs) Cornell Maritime.

Waterman, Vol. 2: Descendants of Robert Waterman of Marshfield, MA, from Seventh Generation. Jacobus & Edgar F. Waterman. (Illus.). 784p. 1991. reprint ed. pap. 109.00 (0-8328-1766-X); reprint ed. lib. bdg. 119.00 (0-8328-1765-1) Higginson Bk Co.

Waterman's Boy. Susan Sharpe. LC 89-39332. 96p. (J). (gr. 3-6). 1990. lib. bdg. 16.00 (0-02-782351-2, Bradbury S&S) S&S Childrens.

Waterman's Child. Barbara Mitchell. LC 94-40734. (Illus.). 32p. (J). (gr. k up). 1997. lib. bdg. 15.93 (0-688-10862-8) Lothrop.

Waterman's Child. Daniel S. Souci. LC 94-40734. (Illus.). 32p. (J). (gr. k up). 1997. 16.00 (0-688-10861-X) Lothrop.

Waterman's Children. John Bensko. LC 93-32434. 104p. 1994. pap. 9.95 (0-87023-902-3); lib. bdg. 20.00 (0-87023-901-5) U of Mass Pr.

Watermark. Joseph Brodsky. 96p. 1992. 15.00 (0-374-14812-0) FS&G.

Watermark. Joseph Brodsky. 135p. 1993. pap. 11.00 (0-374-52382-7) FS&G.

Watermark. Laura Chester. 1978. pap. 10.00 (0-935724-81-8) Figures.

Watermark. Susan Friedland. LC 87-42545. 24p. 1987. pap. 3.00 (0-87376-053-0) Red Dust.

Watermark. Dixie Partridge. LC 91-16235. (Eileen W. Barnes Award Ser.). (Illus.). 80p. (Orig.). 1991. pap. 7.00 (0-938158-11-2) Saturday Pr.

Watermark. deluxe ed. Laura Chester. 1978. 15.00 (0-935724-56-7) Figures.

Watermark Guide to Fishing in Kansas. George Stanley. 150p. 1991. pap. 20.00 (0-922820-14-7) Watermrk Pr.

Watermatex 'Ninety-One: Proceedings of the Second International Conference on Systems Analysis in Water Quality Management, Held in Durham, New Hampshire, USA, 3-6 June 1991. Ed. by M. B. Beck et al. (Water Science & Technology Ser.: No. 24). (Illus.). 366p. 1991. pap. 157.00 (0-08-041161-4, Pergamon Pr) Elsevier.

Watermedia Techniques for Releasing the Creative Spirit. Marilyn H. Phillis. LC 92-13481. (Illus.). 144p. 1992. 29.95 (0-8230-5698-8, Watsn-Guptill) Watsn-Guptill.

Watermelon. Marian Keyes. 612p. 1995. pap. 11.95 (1-85371-508-5, Pub. by Poolbeg Pr IE) Dufour.

***Watermelon & Rustic Edges, Vol. 2.** Lorrine Thurlow. 58p. 1996. pap. 9.50 (1-56770-353-4) S Scheewe Pubns.

Watermelon Day. Kathi Appelt. LC 95-38200. (Illus.). 32p. (J). (ps-2). 1996. 14.95 (0-8050-2304-6) H Holt & Co.

Watermelon Dress: Portrait of a Woman. Paulette C. White. LC 83-82773. (Illus.). 61p. (YA). (gr. 7-12). 1984. pap. 6.00 (0-916418-53-7) Lotus.

Watermelon in a Cucumber Patch. G. I. Shaw. LC 93-81154. 96p. (Orig.). (YA). (gr. 8-11). 1994. pap. 5.00 (0-9639450-0-9, Joy Bks) Joy Ent.

Watermelon Kid. Novel. Bill Terry. LC 84-5730. 166p. 1984. 16.95 (0-8071-1177-5) La State U Pr.

Watermelon Magic: Seeds of Wisdom, Slices of Life. Wally Amos & Stuart Glauberman. LC 96-16177. 144p. 1996. 14.95 (1-885223-47-1) Beyond Words Pub.

Watermelon Man. Katie Donovan et al. 64p. 9400. pap. 12.95 (1-85224-215-9, Pub. by Bloodaxe Bks UK) Dufour.

Watermelon Man. Waldman. (J). 1996. 14.95 (0-689-31738-7, Atheneum Bks Young) S&S Childrens.

Watermelon Rinds & Cherry Pits. Murray Jackson. LC 90-83555. 1990. 7.00 (0-940713-04-7) Broadside Pr.

Watermelon Treat. Terry Latterman. Ed. by Mary E. Hawkins. LC 85-63266. (Illus.). 48p. (J). (gr. 1-4). 1987. 8.95 (0-934739-03-X); pap. 5.95 (0-934739-04-8) Pussywillow Pub.

Watermelon Uses: Uses for the Watermelon. rev. ed. Recycling Consortium Staff. 1992. ring bd. 19.95 (0-317-04799-X) Prosperity & Profits.

***Watermelon Wedges & Rustic Edges, Vol. I.** Lorrine Thurlow. 62p. 1996. pap. 9.50 (1-56770-342-9) S Scheewe Pubns.

***Watermelon Wedges & Rustic Edges, Vol. 3.** Lorrine Thurlow. 48p. 1996. pap. 9.50 (1-56770-362-3) S Scheewe Pubns.

Watermelons, Walnuts & the Wisdom of Allah: And Other Tales of the Hoca. Barbara K. Walker. (Illus.). 72p. (J). 1991. reprint ed. 17.50 (0-89672-254-6) Tex Tech Univ Pr.

Watermen. James A. Michener. (Illus.). 1979. 12.95 (0-394-50660-X) Random.

Watermen. Randall S. Peffer. LC 79-9896. (Maryland Paperback Bookshelf Ser.). 208p. 1985. reprint ed. pap. 12.95 (0-8018-2737-X) Johns Hopkins.

Waterplants & Wetland Processes. J. Pokorny et al. (Advances in Limnology Ser.: Heft 27). (Illus.). 265p. 1988. pap. text ed. 78.00 (3-510-47025-7) Lubrecht & Cramer.

Waterpower Ninety-One: A New View of Hydro Resources, 3 vols., Set. Ed. by David D. Darling. LC 89-647159. 2275p. 1991. pap. 150.00 (0-87262-814-0) Am Soc Civil Eng.

Waterpower '85, 3 vols. Ed. by Michael J. Roluti. (Conference Proceedings Ser.). 2280p. 1986. Set. 140.00 (0-87262-536-2) Am Soc Civil Eng.

Waterpower '87, 3 vols., Set. Ed. by Brian W. Clowes. 2622p. 1988. 150.00 (0-87262-630-X, 630-8) Am Soc Civil Eng.

Waterpower '89, 3 vols. Ed. by Anthony J. Eberhardt. 1934p. 1989. pap. text ed. 150.00 (0-87262-723-3) Am Soc Civil Eng.

Waterpower '95: Proceedings; International Conference on Hydropower (1995: San Francisco, Calif.), 3 Vols., Set. Ed. by John J. Cassidy. LC 95-24175. 5868p. 1995. pap. 190.00 (0-7844-0099-7) Am Soc Civil Eng.

Waterpowered Mills in Cass County. Stan Hamper. (Illus.). 170p. 1993. pap. 15.95 (1-883228-01-8) Invictus MI.

Waterproof Chart from Block Island to Nantucket Sound. Embassy Guides Staff. 1992. pap. 14.95 (0-930527-24-0) Embassy Marine.

Waterproof Chart to Massachusetts & Cape Cod. Embassy Guides Staff. 1992. pap. 14.95 (0-930527-25-9) Embassy Marine.

Waterproof Guide to Corals & Fishes. Idaz Greenberg. (Illus.). 64p. 1977. Soft plastic pages, rust-proof bdg. pap. 13.95 (0-913008-07-9) Seahawk Pr.

Waterproofing & Dampproofing Concrete. 44p. 1983. pap. 11.95 (0-924659-18-1, 4470) Aberdeen Group.

Waterproofing the Building Envelope. Michael T. Kubal. LC 92-102795. 1992. text ed. 50.00 (0-07-035859-1) McGraw.

Waters. Edith N. Chase. (Illus.). 24p. (J). (ps-1). 1995. 14.95 (1-895565-77-4) Firefly Bks Ltd.

Waters - Places - a Time. Larry Eigner. Ed. by Robert Grenier. LC 82-24359. 166p. (Orig.). (C). 1983. pap. 10.00 (0-87685-497-8) Black Sparrow.

Waters & Water Rights, 1991 Edition: 1991 Edition, 7 vols. Ed. by Robert E. Beck. 1991. Set. 695.00 (0-87473-753-2) MICHIE.

Water's Dictionary of Florida Law. Robert C. Waters. 740p. 1991. boxed 75.00 (0-409-27219-1) MICHIE.

Water's Edge: Domestic Politics & the Making of American Foreign Policy. Paula Stern. LC 78-55331. (Contributions in Political Science Ser.: No. 15). xix, 265p. 1979. text ed. 59.95 (0-313-20520-5, SWE/, Greenwood Pr) Greenwood.

Water's Edge: Women Who Push the Limits in Rowing, Kayaking & Canoeing. Linda Lewis. LC 92-4361. (Illus.). 288p. (Orig.). 1992. pap. 14.95 (1-878067-18-4) Seal Pr WA.

Water's Edge & Beyond: Defining the Limits to Domestic Influence on United States Middle East Policy. Mitchell G. Bard. 176p. (C). 1990. 44.95 (0-88738-346-7) Transaction Pubs.

Water's for Fighting: The Edwards Aquifer Dilemma. (Working Paper Ser.). 34p. 1994. pap. 5.50 (0-89940-557-6) LBJ Sch Pub Aff.

Water's Journey. Eleanor Schmid. LC 89-42872. (Illus.). 32p. (J). (gr. k-3). Date not set. 14.95 (1-55858-013-1) North-South Bks NYC.

Waters of America: 19th-Century American Paintings of Rivers, Streams, Lakes, & Waterfalls. (Illus.). x, 106p. 1984. pap. 10.00 (0-917860-18-7) Historic New Orleans.

Waters of Becoming. Tom Keene. 1989. pap. 10.00 (0-941179-23-0) Latitudes Pr.

Waters of Darkness: Scenes from the Life of an American Jew, Vol. 2. John Sanford. LC 85-13514. 294p. (Orig.). 1986. 20.00 (0-87685-672-5); pap. 12.50 (0-87685-671-7) Black Sparrow.

Waters of Egypt. Anthony Bryson. (C). 1990. 150.00 (1-898162-45-X, Pub. by IMMEL Pubng UK); pap. 125.00 (0-685-74644-5, Pub. by IMMEL Pubng UK) St Mut.

Waters of Fire. Sister Vandana. (Wellspring Bks.). 192p. 1987. pap. 9.95 (0-317-65964-2) Amity Hse Inc.

Waters of Forgetting. Barry Seiler. LC 93-43410. (Akron Series in Poetry). 62p. 1994. 19.95 (0-9622628-7-0); pap. 10.95 (0-9622628-8-9) U Akron Pr.

Waters of Hope: Himalaya-Ganga Development & Cooperation for a Billion People. Ed. by B. G. Verghese. (C). 1990. 54.00 (81-204-0519-6, Pub. by Oxford IBH II) S Asia.

***Waters of Life.** Finn Bevan. LC 97-11697. (Landscapes of Legend Ser.). (Illus.). (J). 1997. write for info. (0-516-20350-9) Childrens.

Waters of Mormon. Robert H. Moss. LC 86-81775. 176p. 1986. 12.98 (0-88290-285-7) Horizon Utah.

Waters of Oblivion: The British Invasion of the Rio de la Plata, 1806-07. Ian Fletcher. 176p. (C). 1991. 95.00 (0-946771-69-3, Pub. by Spellmount UK) St Mut.

Waters of Reflection: Meditations for Every Day. Sandra Drescher-Lehman. LC 93-1433. 180p. (Orig.). 1993. pap. 8.95 (1-56148-084-3) Good Bks PA.

Waters of Siloe. Thomas Merton. LC 79-10372. 377p. 1979. pap. 12.00 (0-15-694954-7, Harvest Bks) HarBrace.

Waters of the Canadian Arctic. Donat Pharand. LC 86-26395. (Studies in Polar Research). (Illus.). 300p. 1988. text ed. 85.00 (0-521-32503-X) Cambridge U Pr.

Waters of the Lonely Way: A Chronicle of Weston, Vermont from 1761-1978. Ernestine D. Pannes. LC 82-13314. (Illus.). 352p. 1982. 22.00 (0-914016-89-X) Phoenix Pub.

Waters of the Nile: An Annotated Bibliography. Robert O. Collins. 343p. 1991. lib. bdg. 100.00 (0-905450-84-1, Pub. by H Zell Pubs UK) Bowker-Saur.

Waters of the Nile: Hydropolitics & the Jonglei Canal 1900-1988. Robert O. Collins. LC 94-39649. 468p. (C). 1996. reprint ed. pap. text ed. 24.95 (1-55876-099-7) Wiener Pubs Inc.

Waters of the West. Kenneth Pringle. 1976. lib. bdg. 59.95 (0-8490-2809-4) Gordon Pr.

Waters of the World, Use & Conservation: International Aquatic Conference, Quebec, Canada, November 14-17, 1972. International Aquatic Conference (1972: Quebec) Staff. Ed. by Harold T. Friermood. LC 75-330579. (Illus.). 192p. reprint ed. pap. 54.80 (0-8357-3832-9, 2036557) Bks Demand.

Waters of Thirst. Adam Mars-Jones. 1995. pap. 11.00 (0-679-75960-3) Random.

Waters of Time. large type ed. Doris Howe. 304p. 1989. 25.99 (0-7089-2038-1) Ulverscroft.

***Waters of Ulan.** Kenneth Ziegler. 300p. (Orig.). 1997. pap. 18.95 (1-881636-14-3) Windsor Hse Pub Grp.

***Waters of Ulan.** Kenneth Ziegler. LC 96-61819. 266p. 1997. pap. 11.95 (1-881636-23-2) Windsor Hse Pub Grp.

Waters of Zion: The Law, Policy, & Politics of Water in Utah. Ed. by Daniel C. McCool. 256p. (Orig.). 1995. pap. text ed. 24.95 (0-87480-473-6) U of Utah Pr.

Waters Re-Born. Neeli Cherkovski. 1975. pap. 2.50 (0-88031-017-0) Invisible-Red Hill.

Waters under the Bridge: Twentieth Century Tollcross, Fountainbridge & the West Port. Drew Easton. (Illus.). 196p. 1990. pap. 14.00 (0-08-040906-7, Pub. by Aberdeen U Pr) Macmillan.

Water's Way: Life along the Chesapeake. Tom Horton. LC 91-36706. 132p. 1992. 24.95 (1-880216-01-9, Elliott Clark) Black Belt Comm.

Waterscaping: Plants & Ideas for Natural & Created Water Gardens. Judy Glattstein. LC 93-33378. (Illus.). 192p. 1994. 27.95 (0-88266-608-8, Garden Way Pub); pap. 18.95 (0-88266-606-1, Garden Way Pub) Storey Comm Inc.

Watershed. Percival Everett. LC 95-80896. 202p. 1996. 22.95 (1-55597-237-3) Graywolf.

Watershed. G. P. Gallivan. (Irish Play Ser.). 1981. pap. 3.95 (0-912262-75-3) Proscenium.

Watershed: A Successful Voyage into Integrative Learning. Mark Springer. 208p. (C). 1994. pap. text ed. 24.00 (1-56090-088-1) Natl Middle Schl.

Watershed Approach to Urban Runoff: Handbook for Decisionmakers. Ed. by Rachel Reeder. (Illus.). 115p. (Orig.). 1996. pap. 16.95 (1-880686-05-8) Terrene Inst.

***Watershed Collection.** Joan Finnigan. 80p. 1988. 26.95 (0-919627-66-8, Pub. by Quarry Pr CN) LPC InBook.

***Watershed Collection.** Joan Finnigan. 80p. 1988. pap. 16.95 (0-919627-68-4, Pub. by Quarry Pr CN) LPC InBook.

Watershed Development in Asia: Strategies & Technologies. Ed. by John B. Doolette & William B. Magrath. (Technical Paper Ser.: No. 127). 236p. 1990. 13.95 (0-8213-1606-0, 11606) World Bank.

Watershed Hydrology, Second Edition. Peter E. Black. 430p. (C). 1996. text ed. 49.95 (1-57504-027-1) Ann Arbor Chelsea.

***Watershed in Rwanda: The Evolution of President Clinton's Humanitarian Intervention Policy.** John A. Ausink. (Pew Case Studies in International Affairs). 50p. (C). 1997. text ed. 3.50 (1-56927-374-X) Geo U Inst Dplmcy.

Watershed Maintainer. Jack Rudman. (Career Examination Ser.: C-284). 1994. pap. 23.95 (0-8373-0284-6) Nat Learn.

Watershed Management: Balancing Sustainability & Environmental Change. Ed. by Robert J. Naiman. (Illus.). 542p. 1992. 79.00 (0-387-97790-2) Spr-Verlag.

Watershed Management: Balancing Sustainability & Environmental Change. Ed. by Robert J. Naiman. (Illus.). 560p. 1995. 42.95 (0-387-94232-7) Spr-Verlag.

Watershed Management: Planning for the 21st Century: Proceedings of the Symposium Organized by the Watershed Management Committee of the Water Resources Engineering Division, American Society of Civil Engineers, in Conjunction with the ASCE's First International Conference on Resources Engineering in San Antonio, Texas, in Cooperation with American Society of Agricultural Engineers...(et al): San Antonio, Texas, Augus. Ed. by Tim J. Ward. 456p. 1995. 45.00 (0-7844-0102-0) Am Soc Civil Eng.

Watershed Management: Proceedings, Utah State University, Logan, Utah, August 11-13, 1975. 789p. reprint ed. pap. 180.00 (0-317-10825-5, 2019536) Bks Demand.

Watershed Management in India. J. V. Murty. 1995. write for info. (81-224-0566-5, Pub. by Wiley Estrn II) Franklin.

Watershed Management in the Eighties: Proceedings of a Symposium Sponsored by the Irrigation & Drainage Division. Ed. by E. Bruce Jones & Timothy J. Ward. 319p. 1985. 34.00 (0-87262-449-8) Am Soc Civil Eng.

Watershed Management 1980, 2 vols., Set. LC 80-69952. 1122p. 1980. pap. 75.00 (0-87262-250-9) Am Soc Civil Eng.

Watershed of Empire: Essays on New Deal Foreign Policy. Ed. by Leonard P. Liggio & James J. Martin. LC 76-4291. 1976. pap. 3.95 (0-87926-020-3) R Myles.

Watershed of Juvenile Justice. 7.00 (0-318-20318-9) Natl Coun Crime.

Watershed Planning: A Selected Research Bibliography, No. 1014. Frank L. Kudrna. 1976. 5.50 (0-686-20391-7, Sage Prdcls Pr) Sage.

Watershed Planning & Analysis in Action. Ed. by Robert E. Riggins et al. 596p. 1990. pap. text ed. 50.00 (0-87262-767-5) Am Soc Civil Eng.

Watershed Rehabilitation. B. VanHaveren. 1988. text ed. write for info. (0-442-28848-4) Van Nos Reinhold.

Watershed Research Traditions in Human Communication Theory. Ed. by Donald P. Cushman & Branislav Kovacic. LC 94-37655. (SUNY Series, Human Communication Processes). 312p. (C). 1995. text ed. 64.50 (0-7914-2597-5) State U NY Pr.

Watershed Research Traditions in Human Communication Theory. Ed. by Donald P. Cushman & Branislav Kovacic. LC 94-37655. (SUNY Series, Human Communication Processes). 312p. (C). 1995. pap. text ed. 21.95 (0-7914-2598-3) State U NY Pr.

***Watershed Restoration Management: Physical, Chemical, & Biological Considerations.** Ed. by Jeffrey J. McDonnell et al. (Technical Publications: No. 96-1). (Illus.). 514p. (Orig.). pap. 45.00 (1-882132-37-8) Am Water Resources.

Watershed Restoration Management: Physical, Chemical, & Biological Considerations: New York City Water Supply Studies. Ed. by Jeffrey J. McDonnell et al. (Technical Publications: No. 96-2). (Illus.). 174p. (Orig.). 1996. pap. 25.00 (1-882132-38-6, TPS96-1) Am Water Resources.

***Watershed Restoration Management: Physical, Chemical, & Biological Considerations: American Water Resources Association, Symposium Proceedings.** American Water Resources Association Staff. Ed. by Jeffrey J. McDonnell et al. LC 96-85383. (American Water Resources Association Technical Publication Ser.: No. TPS-96-1). (Illus.). 534p. 1996. reprint ed. pap. 152.20 (0-608-04277-3, 2065030) Bks Demand.

***Watershed Trilogy Book: Darkenheight, Vol. 2.** Douglas Niles. (Watershed Trilogy Ser.). 480p. 1997. mass mkt. 6.99 (0-441-00456-3) Ace Bks.

Watersheds. Betty Gray. 64p. (Orig.). 1987. pap. 1.95 (1-85239-003-4, Greenwood Pr) Greenwood.

Watersheds: Classic Cases in Environmental Ethics. Lisa H. Newton & Catherine K. Dillingham. 249p. 1994. pap. 16.50 (0-534-21180-1) Wadsworth Pub.

Watersheds: Mastering Life's Unpredictable Crises. Robert H. Lauer & Jeanette C. Lauer. 272p. 1988. 16.95 (0-316-51629-5) Little.

***Watersheds in Higher Education.** Ed. by James J. Van Patten. LC 97-18638. (Studies in Education: Vol. 32). 200p. 1997. text ed. 79.95 (0-7734-8605-4) E Mellen.

Watersheds '94 Respect, Rethink, Restore Proceedings of the Fifth Biennial Watershed Management Conference. Ed. by Hannah Kerner & Jeff Woledos, 3rd. write for info. (1-887192-02-6) U Cal CWWR.

Watership Down. Richard Adams. 1976. mass mkt. 6.99 (0-380-00293-0) Avon.

Watership Down. Richard Adams. LC 73-6044. 429p. (YA). 1974. 40.00 (0-02-700030-3) Macmillan.

***Watership Down.** Richard Adams. 1997. 27.50 (0-684-83605-X, Scrbnr) Scribnrs Ref.

***Watership Down.** large type ed. Richard Adams. 642p. 1997. 24.95 (0-7838-8081-2, GK Hall) Thorndike Pr.

Watership Down. 20th anniversary ed. Richard Adams. 480p. 1976. pap. 12.00 (0-380-00428-3) Avon.

Watership Down. Richard Adams. 1994. reprint ed. lib. bdg. 37.95 (1-56849-250-2) Buccaneer Bks.

***Watership Down by Richard Adams: Curriculum Unit.** Center for Learning Network Staff. (Novel Ser.). 88p. Date not set. teacher ed. 18.95 (1-56077-352-9) Ctr Learning.

Waterside: A Pictorial Past. Clare Murley & Fred Murley. (C). 1989. 50.00 (1-85455-068-3, Pub. by Ensign Pubns & Print UK) St Mut.

Waterside Escapes in the Northeast: Great Getaways by Lake, River & Sea. 3rd rev. ed. Betsy Wittemann & Nancy Woodworth. LC 87-50272. (Illus.). 442p. 1996. reprint ed. 15.95 (0-934260-79-6) Wood Pond.

Waterside Reflections. Van Egan. (Illus.). 188p. 1996. pap. 14.95 (1-57188-048-8) F Amato Pubns.

***Waterskiing.** (Illus.). 48p. (YA). (gr. 6-12). 1996. pap. 2.40 (0-8395-3348-9, 33348) BSA.

Waterskiing: A Waterskiers Guide. Jack Travers. 96p. (C). 1990. text ed. 59.00 (0-906754-51-8, Pub. by Fernhurst Bks UK) St Mut.

***Waterskiing: Getting Off the Ground!** Gary B. Solomon. (Illus.). 144p. (Orig.). 1997. pap. 14.95 (1-883085-13-6, 90320) Aquatics Unltd.

Waterskiing & Kneeboarding. Cheryl Walker. (Action Sports Ser.). (Illus.). 48p. (J). (gr. 3-6). 1992. lib. bdg. 17.80 (1-56065-056-7) Capstone Pr.

***Waterskiing & Kneeboarding.** Cheryl Walker. (Action Sports Ser.). (Illus.). 48p. (J). (gr. 3-4). 1992. 18.40 (0-516-35056-0) Childrens.

***Watersleep.** Axler. (Deathlands Ser.: No. 39). 1997. mass mkt. 5.50 (0-373-62539-1, 1-62539-1, Wrldwide Lib) Harlequin Bks.

Watersmeet. Nancy Garden. LC 83-11512. 202p. (J). (gr. 5 up). 1983. 13.95 (0-374-38244-1) FS&G.

Watersmeet. large type ed. Philip Boast. 1993. 39.95 (0-7066-1023-7, Pub. by Remploy Pr CN) St Mut.

Watersplash. Patricia Wentworth. 1987. pap. 3.50 (0-446-34448-6) Warner Bks.

Watersplash. large type ed. Patricia Wentworth. 1976. 12.00 (0-85456-489-6) Ulverscroft.

Watersplash. Patricia Wentworth. 1976. reprint ed. lib. bdg. 22.95 (0-88411-741-3, 741) Amereon Ltd.

Watersplash. Patricia Wentworth. 1994. reprint ed. lib. bdg. 32.95 (1-56849-359-2) Buccaneer Bks.

Watersports Guide to Cancun: Includes Isla Mujeres, Playa del Carmen, Akumal & Tulum. Stuart Cummings & Susanne Cummings. LC 93-15534. 1993. 11.95 (1-55992-073-4, Pisces Bks) Gulf Pub.

Watersteps Round Europe: From Greece to England by Barge. Bill Cooper & Laurel Cooper. LC 96-8267. (Illus.). 176p. 1996. pap. 17.95 (1-57409-016-X) Sheridan.

Watersteps Through France: To the Camargue by Canal. Bill Cooper & Laurel Cooper. (Illus.). 192p. 1996. pap. 17.95 (1-57409-017-8) Sheridan.

Waterton - Glacier International Peace Park. David Petersen. LC 92-9208. (New True Bks.). (Illus.). 48p. (J). (gr. k-4). 1992. lib. bdg. 19.00 (0-516-01946-5) Childrens.

An Asterisk (*) at the beginning of an entry indicates that the title is appearing in BIP for the first time.

Waterton-Glacier International Peace Park. David Petersen. LC 92-9208. (New True Bks.). (Illus.). 48p. (J). (gr. k-4). 1993. pap. 5.50 (*0-516-41946-3*) Childrens.

Watertower. Gary Crew. (Illus.). 32p. (J). 1995. 12.95 (*1-86374-200-X*, Pub. by ERA Pubns AT) ACCESS Pubs Network.

***Watertower.** Gary Crew. LC 97-23095. 1997. write for info. (*1-56656-233-3*, Crocodile Bks) Interlink Pub.

Watertrips: A Guide to East Coast Cruise Ships, Ferryboats, & Island Excursions. Theodore W. Scull. 1987. pap. text ed. 10.95 (*0-07-156798-4*) McGraw.

Waterville, ME. Frank Sleeper. 1995. pap. 16.99 (*0-7524-0213-7*, Arcdia) Chalford.

Watervliet Shaker Cemetery, Albany, N. Y. Elizabeth D. Shaver. 1986. pap. 2.50 (*0-317-56377-7*) Shaker Her Soc.

Watervliet Shaker Meeting House. Elizabeth D. Shaver. 6p. 1986. pap. 2.50 (*0-317-56375-0*) Shaker Her Soc.

Waterway. Berard Haile. LC 79-66605. (American Tribal Religions Ser.: Vol. 5). (Illus.). vi, 153p. 1979. pap. text ed. 12.95 (*0-89734-030-2*, Mus Northern Ariz) U of Nebr Pr.

Waterway Guide: Great Lakes, 1994. Ed. by Judith Powers. (Illus.). 1993. pap. 33.95 (*0-915962-77-2*) Intertec GA.

***Waterway Guide: Mid-Atlantic Edition, 1997.** Ed. by Judith Powers. (Illus.). 1997. pap. 33.95 (*0-915962-90-X*) Intertec IL.

***Waterway Guide: Northern Edition, 1997.** Ed. by Judith Powers. (Illus.). 1997. pap. 33.95 (*0-915962-91-8*) Intertec IL.

***Waterway Guide: Southern Edition, 1997.** (Illus.). 1997. pap. 33.95 (*0-915962-89-6*) Intertec IL.

Waterway Industrial Sites: A Chicago Case Study. David M. Solzman. LC 66-29231. (University of Chicago, Department of Geography, Research Paper Ser.: No. 107). 151p. reprint ed. pap. 43.10 (*0-8357-3718-7*, 2036440) Bks Demand.

Waterway User Taxes: The Public Value of Navigation Programs, the Rationale for Cost Recovery...Major Arguments, Pro & Con. Ed. by Harry N. Cook. 48p. (Orig.). 1994. pap. 7.50 (*0-934292-12-4*) Natl Waterways.

Waterways: Poetry in the Mainstream Cumulative Index 1979-1986. Richard A. Spiegel. (Illus.). 45p. (C). 1987. pap. 10.00 (*0-934830-40-1*) Ten Penny.

Waterways: Poetry in the Mainstream, 1987. Richard A. Spiegel. (Illus.). 16p. 1988. pap. 5.00 (*0-934830-41-X*) Ten Penny.

Waterways see Historic Highways of America...with Maps & Illustrations

Waterways Management Supervisor. Jack Rudman. (Career Examination Ser.: C-3414). 1994. pap. 34.95 (*0-8373-3414-4*) Nat Learn.

Waterways of Europe. (Insight Guides Ser.). 1993. pap. 23.95 (*0-395-66294-X*) HM.

Waterweed in the Wash-houses: A Novel. Jeanne Hyvrard. Tr. by Elsa Copeland. 128p. 1996. pap. 16.50 (*0-7486-0822-2*, Pub. by Edinburgh U Pr UK) Col U Pr.

***Waterwise Swimming & Water Safety.** rev. ed. Mary B. Sultenfuss. (Illus.). 90p. 1995. pap. 6.00 (*1-890064-08-4*) Waterwise.

***Waterwise Water Safety Coloring Book.** Mary B. Sultenfuss. (Illus.). 20p. (Orig.). (J). (ps-2). 1995. pap. 1.50 (*1-890064-11-4*) Waterwise.

Waterworks. E. L. Doctorow. 400p. 1995. mass mkt. 6.99 (*0-451-18563-3*, Sig) NAL-Dutton.

Waterworks. E. L. Doctorow. LC 96-29871. 1997. pap. 11.95 (*0-452-27549-0*, Plume) NAL-Dutton.

Waterworks. Jeanne C. James & Randy F. Granovetter. (Illus.). 64p. 1987. pap. text ed. 8.95 (*0-88076-084-2*, 15046) Kaplan Pr.

Waterworks. Paul Violi. (Illus.). 24p. 1972. pap. 2.00 (*0-915124-06-8*, Toothpaste) Coffee Hse.

Waterworks. deluxe ed. E. L. Doctorow. 1994. 100.00 (*0-679-43196-9*) Random.

Waterworks-Accounting. 18th ed. Philip E. Fess & Carl S. Warren. (Ab-Accounting Principles Ser.). 1996. pap. 21.95 (*0-538-83946-5*) S-W Pub.

Waterworks in the Athenian Agora. Mabel L. Lang. LC 69-22670. (Excavations of the Athenian Agora Picture Bks.: No. 11). (Illus.). 32p. 1968. pap. 3.00 (*0-87661-611-2*) Am Sch Athens.

Waterworld. Max A. Collins. (Orig.). 1995. mass mkt. 5.99 (*1-57297-001-4*); mass mkt. 3.99 (*1-57297-002-2*) Blvd Books.

***Watery Grave.** Bruce Alexander. 320p. 1997. mass mkt. 5.99 (*0-425-16036-X*, Prime Crime) Berkley Pub.

Watery Grave: A Sir John Fielding Mystery. Bruce Alexander. 272p. 1996. 22.95 (*0-399-14155-3*, Putnam) Putnam Pub Group.

WATFIV. James D. Moore. 1975. pap. write for info. (*0-87909-876-7*, Reston) P-H.

Watkins: A Beginning Genealogy. Jayne E. Bickford. (Illus.). 704p. 1994. reprint ed. pap. text ed. 72.50 (*1-55613-903-9*) Heritage Bk.

Watkins Bender-Gestalt Scoring System. Ernest O. Watkins. LC 76-13899. 1976. 18.00 (*0-685-44981-5*) Acad Therapy.

Watkins Bender-Gestalt Scoring System. Ernest O. Watkins. LC 76-13899. 1976. lab manual ed. 18.00 (*0-87879-142-6*); student ed. 50.00 (*0-685-44980-7*); 15.00 (*0-685-31201-1*) Acad Therapy.

Watkins Reynolds Matthews: A Biography. Lawrence Clayton. LC 93-45374. 1994. 16.95 (*0-89015-950-5*) Sunbelt Media.

Watling Operator's Companion. Ed. by Dan R. Post. LC 79-53627. (Slot Machines of Yesteryear Ser.). (Illus.). 1979. 21.95 (*0-911160-74-4*) Post Group.

Watoto! An African Activity Book. Michelle D. Wright. Ed. by Iva D. Wright & Rose D. Chaney. Tr. by John M. Mwangi. (Illus.). 32p. (Orig.). (J). (gr. 3-7). 1996. pap. 7.95 (*0-9652316-0-7*, Alexdras Treas) Griot Publns.

Watsa...Unbelief. Michael P. Gallagher. LC 95-17431. (W. A.T.S. About...Ser.). 96p. (Orig.). (C). 1995. pap. 6.95 (*0-8091-3596-5*) Paulist Pr.

Watson: History & Genealogy of the Watson Family, Descendants of Matthew Watson Who Came to America in 1718. J. D. Bemis & A. A. Bemis. 163p. 1994. reprint ed. pap. 27.00 (*0-8328-4064-5*); reprint ed. lib. bdg. 37.00 (*0-8328-4063-7*) Higginson Bk Co.

Watson & Crick: Decoding the Secrets of DNA. Victoria Sherrow. LC 94-43493. (Partners II Ser.). 112p. (J). (gr. 5 up). 1995. lib. bdg. 16.95 (*1-56711-133-5*) Blackbirch.

Watson Genealogy, "Of Sceptred Race" A. Watson. (Illus.). 389p. 1989. reprint ed. pap. 58.50 (*0-8328-1231-5*); reprint ed. lib. bdg. 66.50 (*0-8328-1230-7*) Higginson Bk Co.

Watson-Guptill Sketchbook: Black. Watson-Guptill Staff. 1996. 6.95 (*0-8230-0518-6*); 9.95 (*0-8230-0519-4*) Watsn-Guptill.

Watson-Guptill Sketchbook: Hunter Green. Watson-Guptill Publications Staff. 224p. 1993. bds. 6.95 (*0-8230-0510-0*); bds. 9.95 (*0-8230-0511-9*) Watsn-Guptill.

Watson-Guptill Sketchbook: Navy Blue. Watson-Guptill Publications Staff. 224p. 1993. bds. 9.95 (*0-8230-0515-1*) Watsn-Guptill.

Watson-Guptill Sketchbook: Navy Blue. Watson-Guptill Publications, Staff. 1993. bds. 6.95 (*0-8230-0514-3*) Watsn-Guptill.

Watson-Guptill Sketchbooks: Carmine Red. Watson-Guptill Publications Staff. 224p. 1993. bds. 6.95 (*0-8230-0512-7*); bds. 9.95 (*0-8230-0513-5*) Watsn-Guptill.

Watsons. Jane Austen. LC 72-9808. 318p. 1973. reprint ed. text ed. 59.75 (*0-8371-6598-9*, AUTW, Greenwood Pr) Greenwood.

Watsons. Jane Austen. Ed. by R. W. Chapman. LC 85-7352. (Jane Austen Library: vol. 4). 164p. (C). 1985. reprint ed. text ed. 25.00 (*0-485-10503-9*, Pub. by Athlone Pr UK) Humanities.

Watson's Apology. Beryl Bainbridge. 224p. 1988. pap. text ed. write for info. (*0-07-003255-6*) McGraw.

Watson's Classic Book on the Play of the Hand at Bridge. Louis H. Watson. Ed. by Sam Fry, Jr. LC 75-5240. 1971. pap. 12.00 (*0-06-463209-1*, EH 209) HarpC.

***Watsons Clinical Nursing.** 5th ed. Walsh. 1997. pap. text ed. write for info. (*0-7020-2025-7*, Bailliere-Tindall) Saunders.

Watsons Go to Birmingham - 1963. Christopher P. Curtis. LC 95-7091. 192p. (J). (gr. 5 up). 1995. 14.95 (*0-385-32175-9*, Delacorte Pr Bks) BDD Bks Young Read.

***Watsons Go to Birmingham - 1963.** Christopher P. Curtis. 224p. (J). (gr. 4-8). 1997. pap. 4.99 (*0-440-41412-1*) BDD Bks Young Read.

Watsonville: Memories That Linger, Vol. 1. Betty Lewis. LC 76-41500. 220p. 1986. 13.95 (*0-9617681-0-X*) Otter B Bks.

Watsonville: Memories That Linger, Vol. 2. Betty Lewis. LC 76-41500. (Illus.). 154p. 1980. 13.95 (*0-934136-08-4*) Otter B Bks.

Watsu: Freeing the Body in Water. Harold Dull. 52p. 1993. pap. 12.95 (*0-944202-04-7*) Harbin Springs.

Watsuji Tetsuro's Rinrigaku: Ethics in Japan. Watsuji Tetsuro. Tr. by Yamamoto Seisaku & Robert E. Carter. LC 96-27890. (SUNY Series in Modern Japanese Philosophy). 381p. 1996. text ed. 65.50 (*0-7914-3093-6*); pap. text ed. 21.95 (*0-7914-3094-4*) State U NY Pr.

Watt. Samuel Beckett. 29.95 (*0-685-37202-2*, F86120) Fr & Eur.

Watt. Samuel Beckett. LC 58-9097. 262p. 1970. pap. 11.95 (*0-8021-5140-X*, Grove) Grove-Atltic.

Watt Matthews of Lambshead: A Photographic Study of a Man & His Ranch. Laura C. Wilson. (Illus.). 139p. 1990. 39.95 (*0-87611-090-1*) Tex St Hist Assn.

Watt Pottery. Dennis M. Thompson & W. Bryce Watt. LC 94-65634. (Illus.). 240p. 1994. 39.95 (*0-88740-614-9*) Schiffer.

Watt Pottery Identification & Value Guide. Sue Morris. 160p. 1996. 19.95 (*0-89145-527-2*) Collector Bks.

Watta-Dwellers: A Sociological Study of Selected Urban Low-Income Communities in Sri Lanka. Kalinga T. Silva & Karunatissa Athukorala. 242p. (C). 1991. lib. bdg. 47.50 (*0-8191-8106-4*) U Pr of Amer.

Watteau. Donald Posner. LC 83-45154. (Illus.). 288p. 1983. 95.00 (*0-8014-1571-3*) Cornell U Pr.

Watteau, Antoines: Paintings & Drawings from Soviet Museums. Yuri A. Zolotov. 116p. (C). 1985. 150.00 (*0-685-34411-8*, Pub. by Collets) St Mut.

Watteau Drawings: Forty-Four Plates. Antoine Watteau. 43p. (Orig.). 1985. pap. 3.95 (*0-486-24958-1*) Dover.

Watteau in Venice. Philippe Sollers. 288p. 1994. text ed. 22.00 (*0-684-19451-1*) S&S Trade.

Watteau's Painted Conversations: Art, Literatura, & Talk in Seventeenth- & Eighteenth-Century France. Mary Vidal. LC 92-9695. (Illus.). 248p. (C). 1992. text ed. 57.00 (*0-300-05480-7*) Yale U Pr.

Watteau's Shepherds: The Detective Novel in Britain 1914-1940. Leroy L. Panek. LC 79-83887. 232p. 14.95 (*0-87972-131-6*); pap. 7.95 (*0-87972-132-4*) Bowling Green Univ Popular Press.

***Wattle.** Maria Hitchcock. 208p. (Orig.). 24.95 (*0-644-12678-7*, Pub. by Aust Gov Pub AT) Aubrey Bks.

***Wattle Hurdles & Leather Gaiters.** John Randall. (Illus.). 202p. 1995. pap. 13.95 (*0-85236-306-0*, Pub. by Farming Pr UK) Diamond Farm Bk.

Wattles: Autobiography of Gurdon Wallace Wattles, with Genealogy. G. W. Wattles. (Illus.). 268p. 1994. reprint ed. pap. 42.00 (*0-8328-4246-X*); reprint ed. lib. bdg. 52.00 (*0-8328-4245-1*) Higginson Bk Co.

Wattles - Autobiography of Gurdon Wallace Wattles, with Genealogy. G. W. Wattles. (Illus.). 268p. 1994. reprint ed. pap. 42.00 (*0-8328-4552-3*); reprint ed. lib. bdg. 52.00 (*0-8328-4551-5*) Higginson Bk Co.

Watts Hospital of Durham, North Carolina, 1895-1976: Keeping the Doors Open. P. Preston Reynolds. LC 91-77158. (Illus.). 133p. (Orig.). 1992. 24.95 (*0-9631387-1-5*); pap. 15.95 (*0-9631387-0-7*) Fund Adv Sci.

***Watts Riots.** Liza N. Burby. LC 96-54585. (World History Ser.). (Illus.). (J). (gr. 4-12). 1997. lib. bdg. 17.96 (*1-56006-300-9*) Lucent Bks.

Watts Teen Health Dictionary. Charlotte Isler & Alwyn T. Cohall. (Projects for Young Scientists Ser.). (Illus.). 128p. (YA). (gr. 9-12). 1995. lib. bdg. 22.00 (*0-531-11233-0*) Watts.

Watts Teen Health Dictionary. Charlotte Isler & Alwyn T. Cohall. LC 95-22166. (Illus.). 192p. (YA). (gr. 7-12). 1996. lib. bdg. 26.60 (*0-531-11236-5*) Watts.

Watts Teen Health Dictionary. Charlotte Isler. 1996. pap. 16.00 (*0-531-15792-X*) Watts.

***Watts Towers of Los Angeles.** Goldstone. (Conservation & Cultural Heritage Ser.). 1997. 24.95 (*0-89236-491-2*) J P Getty Trust.

Watts Towers of Los Angeles. Leon Whiteson. (Illus.). 95p. 29.95 (*0-88962-394-5*); pap. 14.95 (*0-88962-393-7*) Mosaic.

***Watunna: An Orinoco Creation Cycle.** 2nd ed. Marc De Civrieux. Ed. & Tr. by David M. Guss from SPA. LC 97-20813. (Illus.). 232p. 1997. reprint ed. pap. 12.95 (*0-292-71589-7*) U of Tex Pr.

Watusi Titanic. Connie Deanovich. 80p. (Orig.). 1996. pap. 12.00 (*0-943221-24-2*) Timken Pubs.

Wau-Bun: The "Early Day" in the Northwest. Juliette M. Kinzie. (Prairie State Bks.). (Illus.). 288p. 1992. 14.95 (*0-252-06232-9*); text ed. 25.95 (*0-252-01934-2*) U of Ill Pr.

Wau-Mato. Dorothy Carey. LC 91-67098. 280p. 1992. 11.95 (*1-55523-485-2*) Winston-Derek.

Waucoma Twilight: Generations of the Farm. Dona Schwartz. LC 91-37956. (Series in Ethnographic Inquiry). (Illus.). 176p. (Orig.). 1992. pap. text ed. 24.95 (*1-56098-181-4*) Smithsonian.

***Waud's Employment Law 97.** 11th ed. Christopher Waud & Andrew Barns. (Human Resource Management Ser.). 1997. pap. 29.95 (*0-7494-1827-3*) Kogan Page Ltd.

Waukegan Schools: A History in Sketches, 1840's-1990's. Lorraine D. Newby. Ed. by Lynn Schornick. LC 89-52037. (Illus.). 48p. (Orig.). 1989. pap. 10.00 (*0-9625103-0-0*) Waukegan Pk Dist.

Waupaca County: Seven A. M. Jerry McGinley. 46p. 1986. 20.00 (*0-9616222-0-2*); pap. 5.50 (*0-9616222-1-0*) Indian Crossing Bks.

Wausau in Nineteen Hundred. rev. ed. George A. Martin. Ed. by John Janke & Jane J. Johnson. (Illus.). 140p. 1987. 19.95 (*0-9617780-1-6*) Birch Lake Pr.

Wave. John M. Bennett. 10p. (Orig.). 1993. pap. 2.00 (*0-935350-40-3*) Luna Bisonte.

Wave. Margaret Hodges. (Illus.). (J). (gr. k-3). 1964. 3.50 (*0-395-06817-7*) HM.

Wave. Morton Rhue. 143p. (YA). (gr. 7 up). 1981. mass mkt. 4.50 (*0-440-99371-7*, LLL BDD) BDD Bks Young Read.

Wave. Evelyn Scott. LC 95-47385. (Voices of the South Ser.). 632p. (C). 1996. reprint ed. pap. 14.95 (*0-8071-2068-5*) La State U Pr.

WAVE: Procedures Manual. rev. ed. WAVE, Inc. Staff. 143p. 1991. reprint ed. teacher ed. 100.00 (*1-881176-08-8*) WAVE.

WAVE: Student Workbook, Level 1. rev. ed. WAVE, Inc. Staff. 102p. 1991. reprint ed. student ed. 12.00 (*1-881176-00-2*) WAVE.

WAVE: Student Workbook, Level 2. rev. ed. WAVE, Inc. Staff. 100p. 1991. reprint ed. student ed. 12.00 (*1-881176-01-0*) WAVE.

WAVE: Student Workbook, Level 3. rev. ed. WAVE, Inc. Staff. 115p. 1991. reprint ed. student ed. 12.00 (*1-881176-02-9*) WAVE.

WAVE: Student Workbook, Level 4. rev. ed. WAVE, Inc. Staff. 54p. 1991. reprint ed. student ed. 12.00 (*1-881176-03-7*) WAVE.

WAVE: Teacher Guidebook, Level 1. rev. ed. WAVE, Inc. Staff. 329p. 1991. reprint ed. teacher ed. 100.00 (*1-881176-04-5*) WAVE.

WAVE: Teacher Guidebook, Level 2. rev. ed. WAVE, Inc. Staff. 344p. 1991. reprint ed. teacher ed. 100.00 (*1-881176-05-3*) WAVE.

WAVE: Teacher Guidebook, Level 3. rev. ed. WAVE, Inc. Staff. 313p. 1991. reprint ed. teacher ed. 100.00 (*1-881176-06-1*) WAVE.

WAVE: Teacher Guidebook, Level 4. rev. ed. WAVE, Inc. Staff. 155p. 1991. reprint ed. teacher ed. 100.00 (*1-881176-07-X*) WAVE.

Wave - Study Guide. Gloria Levine & Kathleen M. Fischer. Ed. by Joyce Friedland & Rikki Kessler. (Novel-Ties Ser.). (YA). (gr. 6-10). 1993. pap. text ed. 15.95 (*0-88122-132-5*) Lrn Links.

Wave Action. Irene Lumgair. (How to Draw & Paint Ser.). (Illus.). 32p. (Orig.). 1995. pap. 6.95 (*1-56010-143-1*, HT244) W Foster Pub.

Wave & Stability in Fluids. D. Y. Hsieh & S. P. Ho. LC 94-30388. 400p. 1994. text ed. 55.00 (*981-02-1870-2*) World Scientific Pub.

Wave & Wind Directionality: Applications to the Design of Structures, International Conference, Paris, 29-30 September-1st-October 1981. Editions Technip Staff. (Illus.). 600p. (C). 1982. pap. 720.00 (*2-7108-0426-3*, Pub. by Edits Technip FR) St Mut.

Wave Breaking: A Numerical Study. Ed. by M. C. Lemos et al. (Lecture Notes in Engineering Ser.: Vol. 71). (Illus.). viii, 196p. 1992. 68.95 (*0-387-54942-0*) Spr-Verlag.

***Wave Collapse.** (Nonlinear Dynamics Ser.). 300p. 1997. text ed. 40.00 (*981-02-3086-9*) World Scientific Pub.

Wave Collapse in Nonlinear Media: Academy of Sciences Research in the Former Soviet Union. Vadim F. Shvets. (Foreign Technology Assessment Ser.). xii, 135p. (Orig.). 1994. pap. 55.00 (*1-881874-13-3*) Global Cnslts.

Wave Dancer is Missing: My Pretty Mermaid. M. J. Carr. 32p. (J). (ps-3). 1993. pap. 2.50 (*0-590-46604-6*) Scholastic Inc.

Wave Directional Spectra. I. K. Tsanis & C. Valeo. (Environmental Hydraulics Ser.: No. 3). 370p. 1996. 137.00 (*1-56252-305-8*, 3811) Computational Mech MA.

Wave Dynamics & Radio Probing of the Ocean Surface. Ed. by O. M. Phillips & Klaus Hasselmann. 687p. 1986. 135.00 (*0-306-41992-0*, Plenum Pr) Plenum.

Wave Flow of Liquid Films. S. V. Alekseenko et al. 313p. 1994. 135.00 (*1-56700-021-5*) Begell Hse.

Wave Forces on Inclined & Vertical Wall Structures: Task Committee on Forces on Inclined & Vertical Wall Structures of the Committee on Waves & Wave Forces of the Waterway, Port, Coastal & Ocean Engineering Division. ASCE, Waterway, Port, Coastal & Ocean Division, Committee on Waves & Wave Forces, Task Committee on Forces on Inclined & Vertical Wall Structures Staff. LC 95-8330. 408p. 1995. 36.00 (*0-7844-0080-6*) Am Soc Civil Eng.

Wave Functions: An Explanatory Hypothesis. James S. Hughes. (Illus.). 70p. 1976. 50.00 (*0-915386-02-X*) Arctinurus Co.

Wave Goodbye. Rob Reid. LC 95-21733. (Illus.). 24p. (J). (ps-1). 1996. 14.95 (*1-880000-30-X*) Lee & Low Bks.

Wave He Caught. Rick Noguchi. (Orig.). 1995. pap. 6.00 (*0-9628094-7-0*) Pearl Edit.

Wave Heating & Current Drive in Plasmas. Ed. by V. L. Granatstein & P. L. Colestock. LC 85-12634. 510p. 1985. text ed. 261.00 (*2-88124-057-7*) Gordon & Breach.

Wave Hello to Thomas! A Thomas the Tank Engine Lift-&-Peek-a-Board Book. Illus. by Owain Bell. LC 92-80747. (Lift-&-Peek-a-Board Bks.). 14p. (J). (ps). 1993. 4.99 (*0-679-83877-5*) Random Bks Yng Read.

Wave in Her Pocket. Lynn Joseph. 1996. pap. 5.95 (*0-395-81309-3*) HM.

Wave in Her Pocket: Stories from Trinidad. Lynn Joseph. Ed. by Dinah Stevenson. (Illus.). 64p. (J). (gr. 3-7). 1991. 14.95 (*0-395-54432-7*, Clarion Bks) HM.

Wave Instabilities in Space Plasmas. Ed. by Peter J. Palmadesco & K. Papadopoulos. (Astrophysics & Space Science Library: No. 74). 1979. lib. bdg. 104.50 (*90-277-1028-7*) Kluwer Ac.

***Wave Interaction with Permeable Coastal Structures.** M. R. Van Gent. (Illus.). vii, 177p. (Orig.). 1995. pap. 59.50 (*90-407-1182-8*, Pub. by Delft U Pr NE) Coronet Bks.

Wave Interactions & Fluid Flows. Alex D. Craik. (Cambridge Monographs on Mechanics & Applied Mathematics). (Illus.). 336p. 1988. pap. text ed. 34.95 (*0-521-36829-4*) Cambridge U Pr.

Wave Interactions As a Seismo-Acoustic Source. Alick C. Kibblewhite & Cheng Y. Wu. (Lecture Notes in Earth Sciences Ser.: Vol. 59). 1996. pap. 99.00 (*0-387-60721-8*); text ed. 99.00 (*3-540-60721-8*) Spr-Verlag.

Wave Kinematics & Environmental Forces. Ed. by Society for Underwater Technology Staff. (Advances in Underwater Technology, Ocean Science, & Offshore Engineering Ser.). 356p. (C). 1993. lib. bdg. 144.00 (*0-7923-2184-7*) Kluwer Ac.

Wave Me No Flags: Challenging the Twenty-First Century. Luc Meyer. 1995. pap. 11.95 (*0-533-11078-5*) Vantage.

Wave Mechanics. G. Ludwig. 1968. 106.00 (*0-08-012302-3*, Pub. by Pergamon Repr UK) Franklin.

Wave Mechanics & Its Applications. P. Gombas & D. Kisdi. LC 73-5789. 250p. 1973. text ed. 116.00 (*0-08-016979-1*, Pub. by Pergamon Repr UK) Franklin.

Wave Mechanics Applied to Semiconductor Heterostructures. Gerald Bastard. LC 90-47219. (Monographs of Physics). 357p. 1991. pap. text ed. 74.95 (*0-470-21708-1*) Halsted Pr.

Wave Motion: Theory, Modelling, & Computation. Ed. by A. Chorin & A. J. Majda. (Mathematical Sciences Research Institute Publications: Vol. 7). (Illus.). 350p. 1987. 59.95 (*0-387-96594-7*) Spr-Verlag.

Wave Motion & Vibration Theory: Proceedings of the Symposium in Applied Mathematics, Carnegie Institute of Technology, 1952, Vol. 5. Ed. by A. E. Heins. LC 50-1183. 169p. 1954. 35.00 (*0-8218-1305-6*, PSAPM/5) Am Math.

Wave Motion in Elastic Solids. Karl F. Graff. 1991. pap. 15.95 (*0-486-66745-6*) Dover.

Wave of Mouth Stories. Jane Reichhold. 184p. (Orig.). 1993. pap. 9.00 (*0-944676-09-X*) AHA Bks.

Wave of the Future: The United Nations & Naval Peacekeeping. Robert S. Staley, II. LC 92-21076. (International Peace Academy Occasional Paper Ser.). 64p. 1992. pap. text ed. 6.95 (*1-55587-379-0*) Lynne Rienner.

Wave of the Sea-Wolf. David Wisniewski. LC 93-18265. (J). 1994. 16.95 (*0-395-66478-0*, Hills Med) HM.

Wave Optics. J. Petykiewicz. (C). 1992. lib. bdg. 251.00 (*0-7923-0683-X*) Kluwer Ac.

Wave Packets & Their Bifurcations in Geophysical Fluid Dynamics. H. Yang. Ed. by F. John et al. (Applied Mathematical Sciences Ser.: Vol. 85). (Illus.). 184p. 1990. 58.95 (0-387-97257-9) Spr-Verlag.

Wave-Particle Duality. Ed. by Franco Selleri. (Illus.). 330p. 1992. 95.00 (0-306-44163-2, Plenum Pr) Plenum.

***Wave Phenomena.** 1988. pap. 10.95 (0-486-65818-X) Dover.

Wave Phenomena. Ed. by Lui Lam & H. C. Morris. (Illus.). xii, 275p. 1988. 87.95 (0-387-96921-7) Spr-Verlag.

Wave Physics: Oscillations Solitions & Chaos. Stephen Nettel. 1992. 39.00 (0-387-55715-6) Spr-Verlag.

Wave Physics: Oscillations, Solitons, Chaos. Stephen Nettel. 272p. 1995. 39.00 (3-540-58504-4) Spr-Verlag.

Wave Physics: Oscillations, Solitons, Chaos. 2nd enl. ed. Stephen Nettel. 1994. write for info. (0-387-58504-4) Spr-Verlag.

Wave Physics: Up to Solitons & Chaos. Stephen Nettel. (Illus.). 260p. (C). 1992. text ed. 33.00 (0-387-53295-1) Spr-Verlag.

Wave Pipelining: Theory & CMOS Implementation. C. Thomas Gray. LC 93-27386. (Kluwer International Series in Engineering & Computer Science). 224p. (C). 1993. lib. bdg. 101.00 (0-7923-9398-8) Kluwer Ac.

Wave Propagation: An Invariant Imbedding Approach. Richard E. Bellman & R. Vasudevan. 1986. lib. bdg. 146.00 (90-277-1766-4) Kluwer Ac.

Wave Propagation & Emerging Technologies: 1994 International Mechanical Engineering Congress & Exposition, Chicago, Illinois - November 6-11, 1994. Ed. by V. K. Kinra et al. (AMD Ser.: Vol. 188). 224p. 1994. 80.00 (0-7918-1434-3, G00929) ASME.

Wave Propagation & Inversion. Ed. by W. E. Fitzgibbon & M. F. Wheeler. LC 92-16401. (Miscellaneous Bks.: No. 35). vii, 134p. 1992. pap. 32.00 (0-89871-300-5) Soc Indus-Appl Math.

***Wave Propagation & Scattering in Random Media.** Akira Ishimaru. LC 96-31357. (IEEE/OUP Series on Electromagnetic Wave Theory). 608p. 1996. 89.95 (0-7803-3409-4, PC5677) Inst Electrical.

***Wave Propagation & Scattering in Random Media.** Akira Ishimaru. (IEEE/OUP Series on Electromagnetic Wave Theory). (Illus.). 600p. 1997. 125.00 (0-19-859226-4) OUP.

Wave Propagation & Turbulent Media. Roy N. Adams & Eugene D. Denman. LC 66-30179. (Modern Analytic & Computational Methods in Science & Mathematics Ser.). 134p. reprint ed. pap. 38.20 (0-317-08452-6, 2007766) Bks Demand.

***Wave Propagation in Elastic Solids.** J. D. Achenbach. (North-Holland Series in Applied Mathematics & Mechanics: Vol. 16). 426p. 1984. reprint ed. pap. 99.00 (0-7204-0325-1) Elsevier.

Wave Propagation in Electromagnetic Media. J. L. Davis. (Illus.). xi, 294p. 1989. 87.00 (0-387-97066-5) Spr-Verlag.

Wave Propagation in Gas-Liquid Media. Ed. by V. E. Nakoryakov et al. LC 93-15417. 240p. 1993. 138.00 (0-8493-9906-8, QC153) CRC Pr.

Wave Propagation in Layered Anisotropic Media: With Applications to Composites. Adnan H. Nayfeh. LC 95-36456. (Applied Mathematics & Mechanics Ser.: Vol. 39). 346p. 1995. 158.75 (0-444-89018-1) Elsevier.

Wave Propagation in Petroleum Engineering. Wilson C. Chin. LC 93-48179. 400p. 1994. 85.00 (0-88415-169-7) Gulf Pub.

***Wave Propagation in Petroleum Engineering: Modern Applications to Drillstring Vibrations, Measurement-While-Drilling, Swab-Surge, & Geophysics.** Wilson C. Chin. LC 93-48179. (Illus.). 408p. pap. 116.30 (0-608-05081-4, 2065635) Bks Demand.

Wave Propagation in Random Media (Scintillation) Ed. by V. I. Tatarskii et al. 500p. 1993. 30.00 (0-8194-1962-1, PM09) SPIE.

Wave Propagation in Solids. Ed. by Julius Miklowitz. LC 72-101230. 189p. reprint ed. pap. 53.90 (0-317-08536-0, 2010125) Bks Demand.

Wave Propagation in Solids & Fluids. J. L. Davis. (Illus.). 400p. 1988. 118.95 (0-387-96739-7) Spr-Verlag.

Wave Propagation in Structures. James F. Doyle. (Illus.). x, 258p. 1989. 69.95 (0-387-97078-9) Spr-Verlag.

***Wave Propagation in Structures: Spectral Analysis Using Fast Fourier Transforms.** 2nd ed. James F. Doyle. LC 97-1015. (Mechanical Engineering Ser.). 1997. write for info. (0-387-94940-2) Spr-Verlag.

Wave Propagation in the Ionosphere. Karl Rawer. LC 92-24066. (Developments in Electromagnetic Theory & Application Ser.: No. 5). 424p. (C). 1993. lib. bdg. 218.50 (0-7923-0775-5) Kluwer Ac.

Wave Propagation, Scattering Theory. Ed. by M. S. Birman. LC 93-31285. (Translations Ser.: Series 2, Vol. 157). 280p. 1993. 105.00 (0-8218-7507-8, TRANS2/157) Am Math.

Wave Resistance: The Low Speed-Limit. T. Francis Ogilvie. (University of Michigan, Dept. of Naval Architecture & Marine Engineering, Report Ser.). 34p. reprint ed. pap. 25.00 (0-317-28265-4, 2022627) Bks Demand.

***Wave Riding the Safe Way: A Self Study Course for Personal Watercraft.** Mosby. 64p. (gr. 13). 1997. pap. text ed. 9.95 (0-8151-2507-0) Mosby Yr Bk.

Wave-Rings in the Water: My Years with the Women of Postwar Japan. Carmen Johnson. LC 96-11798. (Illus.). 200p. (Orig.). 1996. pap. 12.00 (0-9647124-1-5) C River Pr.

Wave-Run. Tod Thilleman. 1995. pap. 7.95 (1-881471-10-1) S Duyvil.

Wave Scattering from Rough Surfaces. Alexander G. Voronovich. LC 93-47583. (Wave Phenomena Ser.: No. 17). 1994. 99.95 (0-387-57439-5) Spr-Verlag.

Wave Scattering from Statistically Rough Surfaces. F. G. Bass & Marjorie Fuchs. LC 77-23113. 1979. 241.00 (0-08-019896-1, Pub. by Pergamon Repr UK) Franklin.

Wave Separation. F. Gangleaud & Jean-Luc Mari. 1994. 175.00 (2-7708-0653-X, Pub. by Edits Technip FR) St Mut.

Wave Separation. Franois Glangeaud & Jean-Luc Mari. (Illus.). 86p. (C). 1994. pap. text ed. 35.00 (2-7108-0659-2) Technip.

Wave That Will Beach Us Both. Charles Rafferty. Ed. by Shirley Warren. 28p. 1994. pap. 5.00 (1-877801-26-7) Still Waters.

Wave the Flag for Hudson High. John R. Behee & Tom Saylor. LC 77-89960. (Illus.). 1977. pap. 9.95 (0-914464-02-7) J & J Bks.

Wave Theory & Applications. D. R. Bland. (Oxford Applied Mathematics & Computing Science Ser.). (Illus.). 328p. 1988. 70.00 (0-19-859654-5); pap. 29.95 (0-19-859669-3) OUP.

Wave Theory of Difference & Similarity. Ed. by S. W. Link. (Scientific Psychology Ser.). 384p. (C). 1992. text ed. 79.95 (0-8058-0926-0) L Erlbaum Assocs.

Wave Theory of Light & Spectra. Ed. by I. Bernard Cohen. LC 80-2102. (Development of Science Ser.). (Illus.). 1981. lib. bdg. 38.95 (0-405-13867-9) Ayer.

***Wave Three.** Richard Poe. 1997. pap. 18.95 (0-7615-0673-X) Prima Pub.

Wave Three: The New Era in Network Marketing. Richard Poe. LC 94-9089. 1994. pap. 14.95 (1-55958-501-3) Prima Pub.

Wave Three to Building Your Downline: Your Guide to Building a Successful Network Marketing Empire. Richard Poe. 256p. 1996. pap. 14.95 (0-7615-0439-7) Prima Pub.

***Wave Three Way to Building Your Downline.** Richard Poe. 1997. pap. 18.95 (0-7615-0757-4) Prima Pub.

Wave Turbulence under Parametric Excitation. Ed. by V. S. L'Vov & B. Fuchssteiner. LC 94-25113. (Nonlinear Dynamics Ser.). 352p. 1994. 108.95 (0-387-51991-2) Spr-Verlag.

Wave Watch. 2nd ed. Lesley Choyce. 120p. (J). (gr. 6-9). 1994. reprint ed. 16.95 (0-88780-081-5, Pub. by Formac Pubng CN); reprint ed. pap. 6.95 (0-88780-300-8, Pub. by Formac Pubng CN) Formac Dist Ltd.

Wave Watcher. Jan Gregory. (Illus.). 176p. 1992. 19.95 (0-9633503-0-7) PCS Presents.

Wavecrest. large type ed. Bill Knox. 560p. 1987. 25.99 (0-7089-1658-9) Ulverscroft.

***Wavefields & Reciprocity: Proceedings of a Symposium in Honour of A. T. de Hoop.** Ed. by P. M. Van den Berg et al. (Illus.). 151p. 1996. text ed. 57.50 (90-407-1402-9, Pub. by Delft U Pr NE) Coronet Bks.

Waveforms: A Modern Guide to Nonsinusoidal Waves & Nonlinear Processes. Homer B. Tilton. LC 85-12427. 245p. 1986. 33.95 (0-13-946096-9, Busn) P-H.

Waveguide Components for Antenna Feed Systems: Theory & CAD. Jaroslaw Uher et al. LC 93-12331. (Antenna Ser.). 498p. 1993. text ed. 69.00 (0-89006-582-9) Artech Hse.

Waveguide Handbook. Ed. by James R. Wait et al. (Electromagnetic Waves Ser.). 446p. 1986. boxed 95.00 (0-86341-058-8, EW021) Inst Elect Eng.

Waveguide Optoelectronics. Ed. by John H. Marsh & Richard M. De La Rue. LC 92-33757. (NATO Advanced Study Institutes Series E, Applied Sciences: Vol. 226). 1992. lib. bdg. 204.50 (0-7923-2033-6) Kluwer Ac.

***Waveguides & Waveguide Materials.** (Report Ser.: No. GB-190). 278p. 1996. 3,000.00 (1-56965-236-8) BCC.

Wavelength. Mary J. Mullen. 240p. 1995. pap. 5.95 (0-9645523-0-2) Custom Media Design.

Wavelength Division Multiplexing. Jean Laude. 224p. 1993. 49.00 (0-13-489865-6) P-H.

Wavelengths of X-Ray Emission Lines & Absorption Edges. Ed. by Y. Cauchois et al. LC 78-40419. 1978. pap. text ed. 80.00 (0-685-04017-8, Pub. by Pergamon Repr UK) Franklin.

***Wavelet Analysis with Applications to Image Processing.** L. Prasad & S. S. Iyengar. LC 97-11042. 1997. write for info. (0-8493-3169-2) CRC Pr.

Wavelet Applications in Chemical Engineering. Ed. by Rudolphe L. Motard & Babu Joseph. LC 94-13695. (International Series in Engineering & Computer Science, VLSI, Computer Architecture, & Digital Screen Processing: Vol. 272). 344p. (C). 1994. lib. bdg. 122.50 (0-7923-9461-5) Kluwer Ac.

***Wavelet Applications IV.** Ed. by Harold H. Szu. 69p. 1997. pap. 107.00 (0-8194-2493-5) SPIE.

Wavelet Basics. Y. T. Chan. 144p. (C). 1994. lib. bdg. 81.50 (0-7923-9536-0) Kluwer Ac.

Wavelet Methods for Pointwise Regularity & Local Oscillations of Functions. Stephane Jaffard & Yves Meyer. LC 96-21892. (Memoirs of the American Mathematical Society Ser.: Vol. 123/587). 1996. 36.00 (0-8218-0475-8, MEMO/123/587) Am Math.

Wavelet Packet Laboratory for Windows. Digital Diagnostics Corp. Staff & Yale University Staff. 1994. student ed., spiral bd., pap. 350.00 incl. 3.5 hd (1-56881-036-9) AK Peters.

***Wavelet Theory & Harmonic Analysis in Applied Sciences.** Carlos E. D'Attellis & Elena M. Fernandez-Berdaguer. LC 97-184. 1997. write for info. (3-7643-3953-5) Birkhauser.

***Wavelet Theory & Harmonic Analysis in Applied Sciences.** Ed. by Carlos E. D'Attellis & Elana M. Fernandez-Berdaguer. LC 97-184. (Applied & Numerical Harmonic Analysis Ser.). 400p. 1997. 65.00 (0-8176-3953-5) Spr-Verlag.

Wavelet Theory & Its Applications. Randy K. Young. LC 92-23362. (International Series in Engineering & Computer Science, VLSI, Computer Architecture, & Digital Screen Processing: SECS 189). 240p. (C). 1992. lib. bdg. 91.50 (0-7923-9271-X) Kluwer Ac.

Wavelets. Charles K. Chui. (Approximations & Decomposition Ser.). 1992. text ed. 98.00 (981-02-1127-9) World Scientific Pub.

Wavelets. Charles K. Chui. (Series on Approximations & Decomposition). 1993. text ed. 58.00 (981-02-1222-4) World Scientific Pub.

Wavelets. Ed. by J. M. Combes et al. (Illus.). ix, 315p. 1989. pap. 88.10 (0-387-51159-8) Spr-Verlag.

Wavelets. Yves Meyer. (Studies in Advanced Mathematics: No. 37). 220p. (C). 1993. text ed. 69.95 (0-521-42000-8) Cambridge U Pr.

***Wavelets: A Mathematical Tool for Signal Processing.** Charles K. Chui. LC 96-51635. (SIAM Monographs on Mathematical Modeling & Computation: Vol. MMC1). (Illus.). 216p. (Orig.). 1997. pap. text ed. 36.50 (0-89871-384-6, MM01) Soc Indus-Appl Math.

Wavelets: A Selected Collection of Published Papers. I. Daubechies. (Series in Approximations & Decomposition). 500p. 1997. text ed. 78.00 (981-02-2409-5) World Scientific Pub.

Wavelets: A Tutorial in Theory & Applications. Ed. by Charles K. Chui. (Wavelet Analysis & Its Applications Ser.: Vol. 2). (Illus.). 723p. 1992. text ed. 74.00 (0-12-174590-2) Acad Pr.

Wavelets: Algorithms & Applications. Yves Meyer. LC 93-15100. (Miscellaneous Bks.: No. 38). xi, 133p. 1993. pap. 20.75 (0-89871-309-9) Soc Indus-Appl Math.

Wavelets: An Analysis Tool. Matthius Holschneider. (Oxford Mathematical Monographs). (Illus.). 416p. 1995. 85.00 (0-19-853481-7) OUP.

Wavelets: An Elementary Treatment of Theory & Application. Tom H. Koornwinder. (Approximations & Decomposition Ser.). 240p. 1993. text ed. 67.00 (981-02-1388-3) World Scientific Pub.

Wavelets: An Elementary Treatment of Theory & Applications. Ed. by Tom H. Koornwinder. (Series in Approximations & Decomposition: Vol. 1). 240p. 1993. write for info. (981-02-2486-9) World Scientific Pub.

Wavelets: Theory, Algorithms, & Applications. Ed. by Charles K. Chui et al. (Wavelet Analysis & Its Applications Ser.: Vol. 5). (Illus.). 627p. 1994. text ed. 59.95 (0-12-174575-9) Acad Pr.

Wavelets: Theory & Applications. Jameson. Ed. by M. Y. Hussaini & Erlebacher. (ICASE-LaRC Short Course Series in Science & Engineering). (Illus.). 512p. 1996. 65.00 (0-19-509423-9) OUP.

Wavelets Vol. 2: Calderon-Zygmund Operators & Multilinear Operators. Yves Meyer & Ronald Coifman. (Studies in Advanced Mathematics: Vol. 48). (Illus.). 400p. (C). 1997. text ed. 59.95 (0-521-42001-6) Cambridge U Pr.

Wavelets & Applications: Proceedings of the International Conference Marseille, France, May 1989. Ed. by Yves Meyer et al. (Recherches en Mathematiques Appliquees - Research Notes in Applied Mathematics Ser.: Vol. 20). (Illus.). xii, 450p. 1992. 96.95 (0-387-54516-6) Spr-Verlag.

Wavelets & Filter Banks. Gilbert Strang & Truong Nguyen. LC 96-28791. (Illus.). 672p. (C). 1996. text ed. 62.50 (0-9614088-7-1) Wellesley-Cambridge Pr.

***Wavelets & Multiscale Signal Processing.** Cohen & Ryan. (Applied Mathematics & Mathematical Computation Ser.). (Illus.). 248p. 1995. text ed. 64.50 (0-412-57590-6, Chap & Hall NY) Chapman & Hall.

Wavelets & Operators. Yves Meyer. (Cambridge Studies in Advanced Mathematics: No. 37). 240p. (C). 1995. pap. 27.95 (0-521-45869-2) Cambridge U Pr.

Wavelets & Other Orthogonal Systems with Applications. Gilbert G. Walter. 272p. 1994. 59.95 (0-8493-7878-8, 7878) CRC Pr.

***Wavelets & Renormalization.** (Approximations & Decompositions Ser.). 350p. 1997. 33.00 (981-02-2624-1) World Scientific Pub.

Wavelets & Singular Integrals on Curves & Surfaces. G. David. 107p. 1992. 35.95 (0-387-53902-6) Spr-Verlag.

Wavelets & Statistics. N. Wermuth & K. Krickeberg. (Lecture Notes in Statistics Ser.: Vol. 103). 424p. 1996. 49.95 (0-387-94564-4) Spr-Verlag.

Wavelets & Subband Coding. Martin Vetterli & Jelena Kovacevic. LC 95-5967. (C). 1995. text ed. 71.00 (0-13-097080-8) P-H.

Wavelets & Their Applications. Ruskai et al. (C). 1992. 67.50 (0-86720-225-4) Jones & Bartlett.

Wavelets for Computer Graphics: Theory & Applications. Eric Stollnitz et al. 250p. (Orig.). 1996. pap. 49.95 (1-55860-375-1) Morgan Kaufmann.

Wavelets, Fractals, & Fourier Transforms. Ed. by M. Farge et al. LC 93-3195. (Institute of Mathematics & Its Applications Conference Series, New Ser.: New Series 34). 424p. 1993. 110.00 (0-19-853647-X, Old Oregon Bk Store) OUP.

Wavelets, Images & Surface Fitting. P. J. Laurent. Ed. by A. LeMehaute & Larry L. Schumaker. LC 94-11330. 544p. 1994. text ed. 82.00 (1-56881-040-7) AK Peters.

Wavelets in Geophysics. Ed. by Efi Foufoula-Georgiou & Praveen Kumar. (Wavelet Analysis & Its Applications Ser.: Vol. 4). (Illus.). 373p. 1994. text ed. 63.00 (0-12-262850-0) Acad Pr.

Wavelets in Image Communication. M. Barlaud. (Advances in Image Communication Ser.: Vol. 5). 270p. 1994. 168.75 (0-444-89281-8) Elsevier.

Wavelets in Medicine & Biology. Ed. by Akram Aldroubi & Michael Unser. LC 95-46327. 608p. 1996. 74.95 (0-8493-9483-X) CRC Pr.

Wavelets, Mathematics & Applications. Ed. by Michael W. Frazier & John J. Benedetto. 592p. 1993. 74.95 (0-8493-8271-8, QA403) CRC Pr.

***Wavelets, Multilevel Methods & Elliptic PDEs.** Ed. by Mark Ainsworth. (Numerical Mathematics & Scientific Computation Ser.). (Illus.). 304p. 1997. 65.00 (0-19-850190-0) OUP.

***Wavelets Theory & Applications.** Louis et al. text ed. 79.95 (0-471-96481-6) Wiley.

Wavell in the Middle East, 1939-1941: A Study in Generalship. Harold E. Raugh, Jr. (Illus.). 348p. 1993. 54.00 (0-08-040983-0, Pub. by Brasseys UK) Brasseys Inc.

***Wavenumber Calibration Tables from Heterodynes Frequency Measurements.** Arthur G. Maki & Joseph S. Wells. (Illus.). 654p. (C). 1997. reprint ed. pap. text ed. 65.00 (0-7881-3784-0) DIANE Pub.

Wavering Friendship: Russia & Austria 1876-1878. George H. Rupp. LC 76-8455. (Perspectives in European History Ser.: No. 11). xiv, 599p. 1976. reprint ed. lib. bdg. 57.50 (0-87991-617-6) Porcupine Pr.

Waverley. Walter Scott. Ed. by Andrew Hook. (English Library). 608p. 1981. pap. 9.95 (0-14-043071-7, Penguin Classics) Viking Penguin.

Waverley. Walter Scott. Ed. & Intro. by Claire Lamont. (World's Classics Ser.). 480p. 1986. pap. 6.95 (0-19-281722-1) OUP.

Waverley Dictionary. May Rogers. 1972. 75.00 (0-8490-1279-1) Gordon Pr.

Waverly Honor: A Workbook of Embroidery Design. Martha A. Hart & Hester Neblett. Ed. by Mary Digges & Dick Digges. (Illus.). 240p. 1989. 29.95 (0-929339-02-9) Embroidery Research Pr Inc.

Wavertree: An Ocean Wanderer. George Spiers. (Illus.). 134p. 1969. 4.50 (0-913344-01-X) South St Sea Mus.

Waves. Bei Dao. Tr. by Bonnie S. McDougall & Susette T. Cooke from CHI. LC 89-13346. 224p. 1990. 22.95 (0-8112-1133-9); pap. 10.95 (0-8112-1134-7, NDP693) New Directions.

Waves. Barbara Beveridge. LC 92-31948. (Voyages Ser.). (Illus.). (J). 1993. 3.75 (0-383-03603-8) SRA McGraw.

Waves. Shin-Jae Kang. Tr. by Tina Sallee from KOR. 160p. 1988. pap. 19.95 (0-7103-0281-9) Routledge Chapman & Hall.

Waves. Donald Verger. LC 95-70055. 64p. 1995. pap. 6.95 (1-887716-00-9) Designs Disc.

Waves. Virginia Woolf. LC 77-92142. 297p. 1901. pap. 11.00 (0-15-694960-1, Harvest Bks) HarBrace.

Waves: An Anthology of Gay Literature. Ethan Mordden. LC 93-40349. 1994. pap. 12.00 (0-679-74477-0, Vin) Random.

Waves: The Invisible Universe. Gloria Skurzynski. (Illus.). 48p. (J). 1996. 16.95 (0-7922-3520-7) Natl Geog.

Waves: Two Short Novels. Masuji Ibuse. Ed. by Shaw & Tsuizaki. Tr. by Anthony Liman & David Aylward. 176p. 1993. pap. 8.00 (4-7700-1745-6) Kodansha.

Waves see Berkeley Physics Course

Waves & Distributions. T. Jonsson & J. Yngvason. 196p. 1995. text ed. 48.00 (981-02-0974-6) World Scientific Pub.

Waves & Fields in Inhomogeneous Media. Weng Cho Chew. LC 94-32641. (Electromagnetic Waves Ser.). 632p. 1994. 79.95 (0-7803-1116-7) Inst Electrical.

Waves & Fields in Inhomogeneous Media. Weng Cho Chew. (IEEE/OUP Series on Electromagnetic Wave Theory). (Illus.). 632p. (C). 1996. 125.00 (0-19-859224-8) OUP.

Waves & Instabilities in Plasmas. Ed. by F. Cap. (CISM International Centre for Mechanical Sciences Ser.: Vol. 349). 282p. 1995. 81.95 (3-211-82636-X) Spr-Verlag.

Waves & Instabilities in Plasmas. Ed. by L. Chen. 188p. (C). 1987. text ed. 70.00 (9971-5-0389-1); pap. text ed. 37.00 (9971-5-0390-5) World Scientific Pub.

Waves & Licence. Stephen T. Booker. (Illus.). 65p. (Orig.). 1983. pap. 4.00 (0-912678-55-0, Greenfld Rev Pr) Greenfld Rev Lit.

Waves & Nonlinear Processes in Hydrodynamics. Ed. by John Grue et al. (Fluid Mechanics & Its Applications Ser.: Vol. 34). 1996. lib. bdg. 198.00 (0-7923-4031-0) Kluwer Ac.

Waves & Optics Simulations: The Consortium for Upper-Level Physics Software. Wolfgang Christian et al. LC 95-24813. 257p. 1995. pap. text ed. write for info. (0-471-54887-1) Wiley.

***Waves & Oscillations.** F. Kneubuehl. 1997. 69.00 (3-540-62001-X) Spr-Verlag.

Waves & Particles in Light & Matter. Ed. by A. Van der Merwe & A. Garuccio. (Illus.). 624p. (C). 1994. 135.00 (0-306-44732-0, Plenum Pr) Plenum.

Waves & Patterns in Chemical & Biological Media. Ed. by Harry L. Swinney & Valintine Krinsky. (Illus.). 260p. 1991. pap. 27.50 (0-262-69150-7, Bradford Bks) MIT Pr.

Waves & Plagues: The Art of Masami Teraoka. Howard A. Link. (Illus.). 96p. 1989. 29.95 (0-87701-602-X); pap. 16.95 (0-87701-590-2) Chronicle Bks.

Waves & Stability in Continuous Media. Ed. by S. Rionero. 444p. (C). 1991. text ed. 118.00 (981-02-0554-6) World Scientific Pub.

Waves & Tides. Patricia Armentrout. LC 96-2882. (Earthly Oddities Ser.). 1996. write for info. (1-57103-157-X) Rourke Pr.

Waves & Tides. Open University Team Staff. (Open University Oceanography Ser.). 1989. pap. text ed. 11.75 (0-08-036933-2, Pergamon Pr) Elsevier.

Waves & Turbulence in Stably Stratified Flows. Ed. by S. D. Mobbs & J. C. King. LC 92-32076. (Institute of Mathematics & Its Applications Conference Series, New Ser.: New Series 40). (Illus.). 480p. (C). 1993. 120.00 (0-19-853661-5, Clarendon Pr) OUP.

W

An Asterisk (*) at the beginning of an entry indicates that the title is appearing in BIP for the first time.

Waves Called Solitons: Concepts & Experiments. M. Remoissenet. LC 93-36462. 1994. 49.00 (*0-387-57000-4*) Spr-Verlag.
Waves Called Solitons: Concepts & Experiments. 2nd ed. M. Remoissenet. (Illus.). 255p. 1996. pap. 49.95 (*3-540-60502-9*) Spr-Verlag.
Waves, Formations & Values in the World System, Vol. 2: World Society Studies. Ed. by Volker Bornschier & Peter Lengyel. 311p. (C). 1992. 49.95 (*1-56000-056-2*) Transaction Pubs.
Waves in Astrophysics. Ed. by J. H. Hunter, Jr. & R. E. Wilson. LC 95-48345. (Annals of the New York Academy of Sciences Ser.: Vol. 773). 1996. write for info. (*0-89766-957-6*); pap. 80.00 (*0-89766-958-4*) NY Acad Sci.
Waves in Dark Matter. O. Ed Wagner. LC 95-90745. (Illus.). 200p. (Orig.). (C). 1995. pap. text ed. 19.95 (*0-9628853-2-0*) Wagner Physics.
Waves in Fluids. James Lighthill. LC 77-8174. (Illus.). 504p. 1979. pap. text ed. 47.95 (*0-521-29233-6*) Cambridge U Pr.
Waves in Focal Regions: Propagation, Diffraction & Focusing of Light, Sound & Water Waves. J. J. Stamnes. (Optics & Optoelectronics Ser.). (Illus.). 618p. 1986. 254.00 (*0-85274-468-4*) IOP Pub.
Waves in the Bathtub. Eugenie Fernandes. (Illus.). 32p. (J). (gr. k-4). 1996. 12.95 (*1-55209-010-8*) Firefly Bks Ltd.
***Waves in the Bathtub.** Eugenie Fernandes. 1997. pap. text ed. 5.95 (*1-55209-147-3*) Firefly Bks Ltd.
Waves of Change: Business Evolution Through Information Technology. James L. McKenney. 1995. text ed. 29.95 (*0-07-103600-8*) McGraw.
Waves of Change: Business Revolution Through Information Technology. James L. McKenney et al. LC 94-3471. 256p. 29.95 (*0-87584-564-9*) Harvard Busn.
Waves of Democracy: Social Movements & Political Change. John Markoff. 1996. pap. 18.95 (*0-8039-9019-7*) Pine Forge.
Waves of Fortune: The Past, Present & Future of the UK Continental Shelves in the Oil & Gas Industries. David Upton. LC 96-11983. 1996. write for info. (*0-471-96341-0*) Wiley.
***Waves of Power: Dynamics of Global Technology Leadership, 1964-2010.** David C. Moschella. LC 96-49652. 1997. 29.95 (*0-8144-0379-4*) AMACOM.
***Waves of Spirit: Practical Ways to Face Today's Life Challenges.** Eileen Caddy. Ed. by Judi Buttner. (Guidebooks for Growth Together). 128p. (Orig.). 1996. pap. 10.95 (*1-899171-75-4*, Pub. by Findhorn Pr UK) Words Distrib.
***Waves of Time: Long-Term Change & International Relations.** K. R. Dark. LC 97-10239. 224p. 1997. 70.00 (*1-85567-402-5*, Pub. by Pntr Pubs UK) Bks Intl VA.
Waves Stability in Continuous Media: Proceedings of the 7th International Conference. S. Rionero & T. Ruggeri. 448p. 1994. text ed. 112.00 (*981-02-1878-8*) World Scientific Pub.
Waves That Heal. Mark Clement. 63p. 1963. reprint ed. spiral bd. 7.00 (*0-7873-1164-2*) Hlth Research.
Waves That Heal: The New Science of Radiobiology. (Alternative Energy & Medicine Ser.). 1991. lib. bdg. 69.95 (*0-8490-4311-5*) Gordon Pr.
Waves, Tides & Shallow-Water Processes. Ed. by Open University Team Staff. (Open University Oceanography Ser.). 188p. 1989. pap. text ed. 34.95 (*0-08-036371-7*, Prgamon Press) Buttrwrth-Heinemann.
***Wavetech's Russian/English Oil & Gas Translator: Abbreviations, Parameters, Units.** Wavetech Geophysical, Inc. Staff. 109p. (ENG & RUS.). 1996. 99.95 (*0-87814-653-9*) PennWell Bks.
Wavewalker. Stella Duffy. (Mask Noir Ser.). 196p. (Orig.). 1996. pap. 13.99 (*1-85242-508-3*) Serpents Tail.
Waving. Peter Sis. LC 86-25762. (Illus.). 24p. (J). (ps-1). 1988. 12.95 (*0-688-07159-7*); lib. bdg. 12.88 (*0-688-07160-0*) Greenwillow.
Waving at Trains. John Dickson. 96p. (Orig.). 1986. 9.95 (*0-939395-06-1*); pap. 5.95 (*0-939395-07-X*) Thorntree Pr.
Waving from Shore. Lisel Mueller. LC 89-12144. 64p. 1989. pap. 7.95 (*0-8071-1576-2*); text ed. 14.95 (*0-8071-1575-4*) La State U Pr.
***Waving the Flag: Constructing a National Cinema in Britain.** Andrew Higson. (Illus.). 336p. 1997. pap. 26.00 (*0-19-874229-0*) OUP.
Wax & Casting: A Notebook of Process & Technique. Roger Armstrong. (Illus.). 160p. 1988. pap. 19.95 (*0-89863-038-X*) Star Pub CA.
Wax Binder & Slurry Test Handbook. 144p. pap. 60.00 (*0-87433-105-6*, IV8801) Am Foundrymen.
Wax Crayon. Albert Rovira. (I Draw, I Paint Ser.). (Illus.). 48p. (J). 1991. pap. 7.95 (*0-8120-4718-4*) Barron.
***Wax Crayons.** M. Angels Comella. LC 96-32334. (Painting & Drawing Ser.). (J). 1997. pap. 5.95 (*0-382-39848-3*, Silver Pr NJ); lib. bdg. 15.95 (*0-382-39851-3*, Silver Pr NJ) Silver Burdett Pr.
Wax Museum. Devra N. Speregen. LC 95-18328. (Eek! Stories to Make You Shriek Ser.). (Illus.). 48p. (J). (gr. 1-3). 1996. pap. 3.95 (*0-448-41273-X*, G&D) Putnam Pub Group.
***Wax Tablets of the Mind: Cognitive Studies of Memory & Literacy in Classical Antiquity.** Jocelyn P. Small. LC 96-37725. 464p. (C). 1997. text ed. write for info. (*0-415-14983-5*) Routledge.
Wax-up for Functional Occlusion. Lang et al. (Illus.). 28p. 1989. ring bd. 24.00 (*0-86715-217-6*) Quint Pub Co.
Waxes: Chemistry, Molecular Biology & Functions. Ed. by Richard J. Hamilton. (Oily Press Lipid Library: Vol. 6). (Illus.). 360p. (C). 1995. 76.00 (*0-9514171-5-0*, Pub. by Oily Pr UK) Matreya.
Waxing & Care of Skis & Snowboards. M. Michael Brady & Leif Torgersen. LC 96-19830. 1996. 7.95 (*0-89997-199-7*) Wilderness Pr.
Waxing Made Easy: A Step-by-Step Guide. Renee Poignard. LC 93-25343. 108p. 1993. pap. 13.95 (*1-56253-171-9*) Milady Pub.
Waxing Nostalgic: A Gil Thorp Collection. Jack Berrill. 256p. 1993. pap. 19.95 (*0-930099-09-5*) Take Five Pubs.
Waxworks Spies. large type ed. Howard C. Davis. (Mystery Library). 352p. 1995. pap. 15.99 (*0-7089-7649-2*, Linford) Ulverscroft.
Way. C. Allan Boyles. LC 90-83636. 323p. 1990. 20.00 (*0-9627283-0-6*) Theophysics.
Way. Elise N. Morgan. (Meditation Ser.). 1972. 6.95 (*0-87516-332-7*) DeVorss.
Way. Leslie Scalapino. LC 87-82589. 148p. 1988. pap. 12.00 (*0-86547-320-X*) O Bks.
Way: A Text Book for the Student of Rosicrucian Philosophy. Freeman B. Dowd. 152p. 1972. reprint ed. spiral bd. 8.50 (*0-7873-0294-5*) Hlth Research.
Way: A Text Book for the Student of the Rosicrucian Philosophy (1917) Freeman B. Dowd. 152p. 1996. pap. 17.95 (*1-56459-661-3*) Kessinger Pub.
Way: A Walk with Paul, the Apostle. Richard J. Aschwanden. 156p. (Orig.). 1990. pap. 5.00 (*0-913071-09-9*) Rama Pub Co.
***Way: An Ecological World-View.** Edward Goldsmith. LC 97-20009. 1998. write for info. (*0-8203-1976-7*) U of Ga Pr.
Way: Catholic Edition. rev. ed. LC 72-84415. 1116p. 1973. pap. 16.95 (*0-87973-831-6*) Our Sunday Visitor.
Way: Living in Love. Elena S. Whiteside. LC 72-89132. 1988. 9.95 (*0-8159-7226-1*) Devin.
Way: Mini Book. Josemaria Escriva. 411p. 1985. pap. 6.95 (*0-933932-54-5*) Scepter Pubs.
Way: The Discovery of the Grail of Immortality. Rhuddlwm Gawr. LC 85-73759. (Illus.). (Orig.). (J). 1987. 18.95 (*0-931760-50-X*, CP 10128); pap. 15.95 (*0-931760-28-3*) Camelot GA.
Way: When There's No Where Else to Turn. Cheryl Mayfield & Dennis McGee. 96p. 1996. 11.95 (*1-887750-25-8*) Rutledge Bks.
Way a Bear Is. David Dale. 46p. (Orig.). 1993. pap. 8.95 (*0-9622429-4-2*) Big Mtn.
Way a Live Thing Moves. Virginia B. Young. 52p. (Orig.). 1989. pap. 8.95 (*0-317-93453-8*) Croton Review.
Way Ahead: A Visionary Perspective for the New Millenium. Eddie Shapiro. 1992. pap. 13.95 (*1-85230-317-4*) Element MA.
Way Alone: Your Path to Excellence in the Martial Arts. Loren W. Christensen. (Illus.). 128p. 1987. pap. 10.00 (*0-87364-421-2*) Paladin Pr.
Way & Its Power: A Study of the Tao Te Ching & Its Place in Chinese Thought. Intro. by Arthur Waley. LC 58-5092. 262p. 1958. pap. 10.95 (*0-8021-5085-3*, Grove) Grove-Atltic.
Way & the Mountain. Marco Pallis. 226p. 9100. pap. 22.00 (*0-7206-0841-4*) Dufour.
Way & the Power: Secrets of Japanese Strategy. Fredrick J. Lovret. (Illus.). 328p. 1987. pap. 16.95 (*0-87364-409-3*) Paladin Pr.
Way & the Wilderness. Kenneth Robinson. 248p. 1994. text ed. 30.00 (*1-85821-083-6*) World Scientific Pub.
Way Back. Clifford Bias. LC 84-52289. (Illus.). 160p. (Orig.). 1985. pap. 8.95 (*0-87728-607-8*) Weiser.
Way Back. Enrico Palandri. (Masks Ser.). 1994. pap. 14.99 (*1-85242-246-7*) Serpents Tail.
Way Back: George Moore's "The Untilled Field" & "The Lake" Ed. by Robert Welch. LC 82-11449. (Appraisal Ser.). 140p. (C). 1982. text ed. 42.00 (*0-389-20318-1*, BNB 07156) B&N Imports.
Way Back: The Autobiography of Jesse Galvan, Jr. Jesse Galvan, Jr. LC 92-85259. (Illus.). iv, 124p. 1993. 22.00 (*0-934955-25-5*) Watercress Pr.
Way Back: The Stories of Gay & Lesbian Alcoholics. 1982. 3.95 (*0-686-32944-9*) Whitman Walker.
Way Back Home. Peggy O'Mara. 1993. pap. 10.95 (*0-914257-09-9*) Mothering Magazine.
Way Back in Papua. John H. Holmes. LC 75-35122. reprint ed. 32.50 (*0-404-14138-2*) AMS Pr.
Way Back in the Ozarks. Howard J. Hefley. 280p. 1992. pap. 5.95 (*0-929292-26-X*) Hannibal Bks.
Way Back in the Ozarks: The Tale of Danny Boy, Bk. 2. Howard J. Hefley. 260p. 1993. pap. 5.95 (*0-929292-38-3*) Hannibal Bks.
Way Back Now: Collected Poems. Reuben Halpern. (Illus.). 74p. 1996. per., pap. 10.00 (*1-882260-10-4*) Carrier Pigeon.
Way Back to Wisdom. Margaret Therese of Jesus. (Illus.). 147p. (Orig.). 1988. pap. 10.38 (*0-9625008-0-1*) Wisdoms Pub Hse.
Way Back When. James C. Hefley. 250p. 1992. pap. 5.95 (*0-929292-08-1*) Hannibal Bks.
Way Back When. D. F. Kelly. 1993. 18.95 (*0-533-10297-9*) Vantage.
Way Back Yonder. Abigail T. Leland. Ed. by Priscilla L. Perkins. (Illus.). 64p. (Orig.). 1993. pap. 10.00 (*1-881459-11-X*) Eagle Pr SC.
Way Baseball Works. Dan Gutman. 1996. 30.00 (*0-684-81606-7*) S&S Trade.
Way Below E. Patrick J. Murphy. 230p. (Orig.). 1994. pap. 14.00 (*1-877727-42-3*) White Pine.
Way Beneath. Angus Wells. (Kingdoms Ser.: No. 3). 384p. 1991. mass mkt. 5.99 (*0-553-28823-7*, Spectra) Bantam.
Way Beyond. William L. Mikulas. LC 87-40131. (Illus.). 150p. (Orig.). 1987. pap. 7.95 (*0-8356-0625-2*, Quest) Theos Pub Hse.
Way Beyond "Art" rev. ed. Alexander Dorner. LC 59-3452. 156p. reprint ed. pap. 44.50 (*0-317-10179-X*, 2050282) Bks Demand.
Way Beyond the I. Q. Guide to Improving Intelligence & Creativity. J. P. Guilford. LC 77-80536. 1977. pap. 13.95 (*0-930222-01-6*) Creat Educ Found.
Way Beyond Therapy. Charles M. Schulz. LC 96-15796. (Peanuts at Work & Play Bks.). (Illus.). 144p. 1996. 10.95 (*0-00-225193-0*) Collins SF.
Way Broadly: Managing Time, Money, Uncertainty & Folly in Fixed Price Software Supply. Darius A. Irani. Ed. by Alison W. Snowden. vi, 130p. (Orig.). 1996. pap. 10.00 (*0-9650794-0-6*) BTGG.
***Way Computer Graphics Works.** Olin Lathrop. LC 96-42688. 256p. 1997. pap. text ed. 32.95 (*0-471-13040-0*) Wiley.
Way Computers & MS-DOS Work. Simon Collin. LC 94-3490. (WYSIWYG Ser.). 128p. 1994. 19.95 (*1-55615-697-9*) Microsoft.
Way Cool Bible: Topical Selection Teac. Tracy Balzer & Cary Balzer. 55p. 1993. pap. 4.95 (*0-917851-61-7*) Bristol Hse.
Way Cool Bible: Topical Selections. Dan Wright. 52p. 1993. pap. 4.95 (*0-917851-60-9*) Bristol Hse.
Way Cool Web Sites. Jerry Yang. 1996. pap. 24.99 (*0-7645-7002-1*) IDG Bks.
Way Demon Angels Trick, Trap, & Trample. Jack W. Hayford. 54p. (Orig.). 1995. pap. text ed. 2.95 (*0-916847-17-9*) Living Way.
Way Down. John Burt. (Contemporary Poets Ser.). 80p. 1988. pap. 10.95 (*0-691-01443-4*); text ed. 21.95 (*0-691-06727-9*) Princeton U Pr.
Way down Deep: Strange Ocean Creatures. Patricia Demuth. (All Aboard Reading Ser.: Level 2). (Illus.). 48p. (J). (gr. 1-3). 1995. pap. 3.95 (*0-448-40851-1*, G&D) Putnam Pub Group.
Way Down East, or Portraitures of Yankee Life. Seba Smith. 1972. reprint ed. lib. bdg. 29.00 (*0-8290-1659-7*) Irvington.
Way Down on the High Lonely: A Neal Carey Mystery. Don Winslow. 288p. 1993. 19.95 (*0-312-09934-7*, Thomas Dunne Bks) St Martin.
Way Down South. Rozanne L. Williams. (Emergent Reader Bks.). 16p. 1994. 2.49 (*0-916119-62-9*) Creat Teach Pr.
Way Down South. Rozanne L. Williams. (Emergent Reader Big Bks.). (Illus.). 46p. (Orig.). (J). (gr. k-2). 1995. pap. 11.98 (*1-57471-074-5*) Creat Teach Pr.
Way down Yonder in Plaquemines. Janice P. Buras. LC 96-7767. (Illus.). 256p. 1996. pap. 14.95 (*1-56554-229-0*) Pelican.
Way down Yonder in the Indian Nation: Writings from America's Heartland. Michael Wallis. (Illus.). 240p. 1993. 18.95 (*0-312-09410-8*) St Martin.
***Way Down Yonder Indian Nation.** Wallis. 1997. pap. 11.95 (*0-312-15242-6*) St Martin.
Way Down Yonder on Troublesome Creek & The Wolfpen Rusties see Rusties, Riddles, & Gee-Haw Whimmy-Diddles
Way English Works: How to Understand It & Use It. Kenneth Oliver. 288p. (Orig.). 1994. pap. 19.95 (*1-56883-036-X*) Colonial Pr AL.
Way for the Pilgrim: A Book of Meditations. J. Barrie Shepherd. 160p. (C). 1991. pap. text ed. 39.00 (*86-15-30654-0*, Pub. by St Andrew UK) St Mut.
Way for the Pilgrim: A Book of Meditations. J. Barrie Shepherd. 160p. (C). 1992. pap. 39.00 (*0-685-60698-8*, Pub. by St Andrew UK) St Mut.
Way for the Pilgrim: A Book of Meditations. J. Barrie Shepherd. 160p. 1993. pap. 22.00 (*0-7152-0654-0*, Pub. by St Andrew UK) St Mut.
Way for the Weekend: New York. Eleanor Berman. LC 92-53471. 1994. pap. 15.00 (*0-517-88166-7*) Crown Pub Group.
Way, Furrow, Forge. 991p. 1994. pap. 16.95 (*0-933932-69-3*) Scepter Pubs.
Way God Fights. Lois Barrett. LC 87-11936. (Peace & Justice Ser.: Vol. 1). 96p. (Orig.). 1987. pap. 6.99 (*0-8361-3447-8*) Herald Pr.
***Way Home.** Angela Benson. 304p. 1997. mass mkt. 4.99 (*0-7860-0373-1*, Pinncle Kensgtn) Kensgtn Pub Corp.
***Way Home.** Megan Chance. 1997. mass mkt. 5.99 (*0-06-108491-3*, Harp PBks) HarpC.
Way Home. Marlene Goodman. 128p. (Orig.). 1990. pap. 7.95 (*0-945127-01-4*) Upword Pr.
Way Home. Lesley Koplow. 1999. pap. 9.00 (*0-452-27046-4*, Plume) NAL-Dutton.
***Way Home.** Dorothy Lewis. 140p. (Orig.). 1996. pap. 10.95 (*1-899171-60-6*, Pub. by Findhorn Pr UK) Words Distrib.
Way Home. Judith B. Richardson. (J). (gr. k). 13.95 (*0-685-41406-X*) Macmillan.
Way Home. Leigh Sauerwein. LC 93-10097. (J). 1994. 15.00 (*0-374-38247-6*) FS&G.
Way Home. Dorothy H. Wells. 96p. (C). 1990. 39.00 (*0-85439-413-3*, Pub. by St Paul Pubns UK) St Mut.
Way Home: A Child Therapist Looks at the Inner Lives of City Children. Lesley Koplow. 240p. 1994. 4.99 (*0-451-62862-4*, Ment) NAL-Dutton.
Way Home: Beyond Feminism, Back to Reality. Mary Pride. LC 84-73078. 240p. 1985. pap. 12.99 (*0-89107-345-0*) Crossway Bks.
Way Home: Photographs from the Heart of Texas. June Van Cleef. LC 91-43305. (Charles & Elizabeth Prothro Texas Photography Ser.: No. 4). (Illus.). 160p. 1992. 24.50 (*0-89096-444-0*) Tex A&M Univ Pr.
***Way Home Is Longer.** Christopher Renino. LC 96-40464. 1997. 23.95 (*0-312-15686-3*) St Martin.
Way I Feel. Debra W. Alexander. 16p. (YA). (gr. 6-12). 1993. 3.95 (*1-56688-064-5*) Bur For At-Risk.
***Way I Feel.** Miguel Chavarria. (Orig.). 1996. pap. write for info. (*1-57553-322-7*) Watermrk Pr.
Way I Feel. . . Sometimes. Beatrice S. De Regniers. LC 87-18245. (Illus.). 48p. (J). (gr. 1-4). 1988. 14.95 (*0-89919-647-0*, Clarion Bks) HM.
Way I Feel Text & Prints. (Illus.). 18p. 1992. pap. text ed. 52.50 (*0-935493-78-6*) Modern Learn Pr.
Way I Feel...Sometimes. Beatrice Schenk de Regniers. (Illus.). (J). (gr. 1-4). 1988. 13.95 (*0-318-35052-1*, Clarion Bks) HM.
Way I Remember It. Antonino Mazza. (Essential Poets Ser.: No. 56). 64p. 1994. pap. 10.00 (*0-920717-74-8*) Guernica Editions.
***Way I Remember It.** Walter Rudin. LC 96-27190. (History of Mathematics Ser.: Vol. 12). 1996. 29.00 (*0-8218-0633-5*, HMATH/12) Am Math.
Way I Remember It: Growing up in Moore Co. NC & in World War II. Glenn A. Flinchum. Ed. by MaryBelle Campbell. (Illus.). 96p. (Orig.). 1991. per., pap. 9.00 (*1-879009-04-8*) S P-Persephone Pr.
Way I Saw It. Dwight L. Barton. (Illus.). 152p. (Orig.). Date not set. pap. 9.00 (*0-944996-12-4*) Carlsons.
Way I See It. Patti Davis. 304p. (Orig.). 1993. mass mkt. 5.99 (*0-515-11089-2*) Jove Pubns.
Way I See It: We Refused to Be What They Wanted Us to Be. Ricardo A. Scott. (Reggae Book of Light Ser.). (Illus.). 65p. (Orig.). pap. write for info. (*1-883427-31-2*) Crnerstone GA.
Way I Started. Gary W. Hawk. 44p. 1979. pap. text ed. 6.00 (*1-56770-120-5*) S Scheewe Pubns.
Way I Want to Remember: Poems. Colette L. Huxford. LC 96-11663. 64p. 1996. pap. 12.95 (*0-7734-2692-2*, Mellen Poetry Pr) E Mellen.
***Way in the Wilderness.** Sally Demaray. 1997. pap. text ed. 89.95 (*1-888445-03-3*) Sonstar Pubns.
Way in the Wilderness. Elizabeth Wagler. 240p. (J). 1995. 7.85 (*0-614-17641-7*, 2462) Rod & Staff.
Way in the Wilderness: Essays in Messianic Jewish Thought. 2nd ed. Ed. by M. G. Einspruch. 101p. 1989. pap. 4.95 (*1-880226-08-1*) M J Pubs.
Way in the World. V. S. Naipaul. 1995. pap. 14.00 (*0-679-76166-7*) Random.
***Way in the World.** V. S. Naipaul. Date not set. 23.50 (*0-8446-6909-1*) Peter Smith.
Way in the World: A Sequence. V. S. Naipaul. 1994. 23.00 (*0-394-56478-2*) Knopf.
Way into Town. Roy Bentley. (Orig.). 1984. pap. 2.00 (*0-936563-03-6*) Signpost.
***Way Is Within: A Spiritual Journey.** Ron Rahtbum. 272p. 1997. pap. 13.00 (*0-425-15460-2*, Berkley Trade) Berkley Pub.
Way Is Within: A Spiritual Journey. Ron Rathbun. LC 94-68656. (Illus.). 271p. (Orig.). 1995. pap. 14.95 (*0-9643519-4-3*) Quiescence CA.
Way It Happens to You. Harold Bond. LC 79-50730. 1979. 6.95 (*0-933706-08-1*); pap. 3.95 (*0-933706-09-X*) Ararat Pr.
Way It Is: One Water, One Aie, One Mother Earth. Corbin Harney. LC 94-35990. (Illus.). 232p. (Orig.). 1995. pap. 16.00 (*0-931892-80-5*) B Dolphin Pub.
Way It Is (un-RUSH-ed) Ed Marshall & Lincoln Beta Club Staff. Ed. by Jillian Kyle. (Illus.). 120p. (Orig.). 1993. pap. 8.95 (*0-938041-15-0*) Arc Pr AR.
Way It Really Was. (C). 1988. 35.00 (*0-86236-101-X*, Pub. by Granary UK) St Mut.
Way It Spozed to Be. James Herndon. Ed. by Susannah Sheffer. (Innovators in Education Ser.). (Orig.). 1995. pap. 13.95 (*0-86709-407-9*, 0407) Boynton Cook Pubs.
***Way It Was.** (Illus.). 32p. 1996. pap. 4.95 (*0-913515-02-7*, Elliott Clark) Black Belt Comm.
Way It Was. D. June Cox. (Illus.). 124p. (Orig.). 1989. pap. 23.20 (*0-685-44898-3*) D J Cox.
Way It Was. June D. Cox. (Orig.). 1989. write for info. (*0-9624954-0-9*) R B Clarkson.
Way It Was. Herb Plambeck. 300p. (Orig.). 1993. pap. 12.95 (*0-9635812-2-8*) Sigler Print.
Way It Was: Biography. E. Krohn. 1993. 16.99 (*0-89906-564-3*); 13.99 (*0-89906-565-1*) Mesorah Pubns.
Way It Was: Eighteen Fifty to Nineteen Thirty Photographs of Montgomery & Her Central Alabama Neighbors. Beth T. Muskat & Mary A. Neeley. LC 85-50334. (Illus.). 185p. 1985. 20.00 (*0-9614653-0-1*) Landmarks Found.
Way It Was: Pearl Harbor - The Original Photographs. Donald M. Goldstein et al. (World War II Commemorative Ser.). (Illus.). 192p. 1995. pap. 17.95 (*0-02-881120-8*) Brasseys Inc.
Way It Was: Sex, Surgery, Treasure, & Travel, 1907-1987. George Crile, Jr. LC 92-2971. (Illus.). 432p. 1992. 35.00 (*0-87338-465-2*) Kent St U Pr.
Way It Was & Other Writings. Jesus Colon. Ed. by Edna Acosta-Belen & Virginia A. Korrol. LC 92-42443. 180p. (Orig.). 1993. pap. 12.00 (*1-55885-057-0*) Arte Publico.
Way It Was in Charleston. Laura W. Waring. Ed. by Thomas R. Waring, Jr. (How We Lived Ser.: No. 2). (Illus.). 1988. pap. 9.95 (*0-8159-7220-2*) Devin.
Way It Was in North Rockland. Norman Baker. 1973. pap. 3.90 (*0-911183-10-8*) Rockland County Hist.
Way It Was in the South: The Black Experience in Georgia. Donald L. Grant. 608p. 1993. 27.50 (*1-55972-153-7*, Birch Ln Pr) Carol Pub Group.
Way it Was in the U.S.A. A Pictoral Panorama of America, 1850-1890. Clarence P. Horning. (Illus.). 521p. 1995. 25.00 (*0-89659-001-1*) Abbeville Pr.
Way It Was Maple Heights, Ohio. John Straka. LC 87-83641. (Illus.). 128p. 1988. 9.95 (*0-9619942-0-7*) Jonelen Pr.
Way It Was...& Is: The Story of the Ewing Family & Their Historic Farmhouse. Vernon Ewing. (Illus.). 24p. (Orig.). 1996. pap. 8.00 (*0-9617799-8-5*) Book Lode.
Way It Wasn't: Great Science Fiction Stories of Alternate History. Compiled by Martin H. Greenberg. 405p. 1996. pap. 14.95 (*0-8065-1769-7*, Citadel Pr) Carol Pub Group.

W

An Asterisk (*) at the beginning of an entry indicates that the title is appearing in BIP for the first time.

Way, Learning, & Politics: Essays on the Confucian Intellectual. Tu Wei-ming. LC 93-18447. (SUNY Series in Chinese Philosophy & Culture). 202p. (C). 1993. text ed. 59.50 (*0-7914-1775-1*); pap. text ed. 19.95 (*0-7914-1776-X*) State U NY Pr.

Way Life Works. Mahlon B. Hoagland. 1995. 7.00 (*0-8129-2667-6*) Random.

Way Life Works. Mahlon B. Hoagland & Bert Dodson. LC 94-48780. 1995. 35.00 (*0-8129-2020-1*, Times Bks) Random.

***Way Life Works.** Mahlon B. Hoagland & B. Dodson. 1997. pap. 22.00 (*0-8129-2888-1*, Times Bks) Random.

Way-Marked Trails of Ireland. rev. ed. Michael Fewer. (Illus.). 224p. 1996. pap. 19.95 (*0-7171-2386-3*, Pub. by Gill & MacMill IE) Irish Bks Media.

Way Men Act. Elinor Upman. Ed. by Jane Rosenman. 320p. 1993. reprint ed. pap. 12.00 (*0-671-74841-6*, WSP) PB.

Way Men Think: Intellect, Intimacy, & the Erotic Imagination. Liam Hudson & Bernadine Jacot. (Illus.). 232p. (C). 1992. text ed. 32.50 (*0-300-04997-8*) Yale U Pr.

Way Men Think: Intellect, Intimacy, & the Erotic Imagination. Liam Hudson & Bernadine Jacot. (Illus.). 232p. (C). 1993. pap. 15.00 (*0-300-05753-9*) Yale U Pr.

Way Microsoft Excel for Windows 95 Works: The Ultimate How-to Guide for Beginners - in Full Color! Brynly Clarke. (WYSIWYG Ser.). 128p. 1995. pap. 19.95 (*1-55615-821-1*) Microsoft.

Way Microsoft Excel 5 for Windows Works. Brynly Clarke. (WYSIWYG Ser.). 128p. 1994. pap. 18.95 (*1-55615-570-0*) Microsoft.

Way Microsoft Word for Windows 95 Works: The Ultimate How-to Guide for Beginners - in Full Color! Peter Gloster. (WYSIWYG Ser.). 128p. 1995. pap. 19.95 (*1-55615-820-3*) Microsoft.

Way More Free Stuff from the Internet. Patrick Vincent. 1995. pap. text ed. 19.99 (*1-883577-50-0*) Coriolis Grp.

Way Mothers Are: Thirtieth Anniversary Edition. rev. ed. Miriam Schlein. Ed. by Kathy Tucker. LC 92-21516. (Illus.). 32p. (J). (ps). 1993. lib. bdg. 14.95 (*0-8075-8691-9*) A Whitman.

Way Must Be Tried: Memoirs of a University Man. Murray Ross. 288p. 1992. 29.95 (*0-7737-2571-7*) Genl Dist Srvs.

Way Nature Works. (Illus.). 360p. 1992. 35.00 (*0-02-508110-1*) Macmillan.

Way of a Boy: A Memoir of Java. Ernest Hillen. 216p. 1995. pap. 9.95 (*0-14-017975-5*, Pelican Bks) Viking Penguin.

Way of a Dog. Albert P. Terhune. (J). 1992. reprint ed. lib. bdg. 24.95 (*0-89966-986-7*) Buccaneer Bks.

Way of a Fighter. Claire L. Chennault. 1991. 35.00 (*0-685-41106-0*) Beachcomber Bks.

Way of a Fighter: Memoirs. Claire L. Chennault. (History - United States Ser.). 375p. 1993. reprint ed. lib. bdg. 89.00 (*0-7812-4813-2*) Rprt Serv.

Way of a Man: Wild River Trilogy. Laurie Paige. (Special Edition Ser.). 1993. mass mkt. 3.50 (*0-373-09849-9*, 5-09849-6) Silhouette.

Way of a Physician: The Biologos, Biopsychosocial Way, Survival & the Parasympathetic Towards an Ethic & a Way of Life. Stacey B. Day. LC 81-80988. (Monograph on Health Communications & Biopsychosocial Health). Orig. Title: Le Medicine Reprend Lui-Meme. 80p. 1982. write for info. (*0-934314-04-7*, SBD/BIO/81SKI) Intl Found Biosocial Dev.

Way of a Pilgrim: And the Pilgrim Continues His Way. Helen Bacovcin. 208p. 1978. pap. 8.95 (*0-385-46814-8*) Doubleday.

Way of a Pilgrim: And the Pilgrim Continues His Way. Reginald M. French. LC 90-55773. 1991. pap. 12.00 (*0-06-063017-5*) Harper SF.

Way of a Pilgrim: The Pilgrim Continues His Way. Tr. by R. M. French. LC 89-11105. (Illus.). 213p. (SPA.). 1990. pap. 9.95 (*0-932727-30-1*); lib. bdg. 16.95 (*0-932727-26-3*) Hope Pub Hse.

Way of a Pilgrim & the Pilgrim Continues His Way. 242p. 1994. pap. 8.95 (*1-880364-12-3*) New Sarov.

Way of a Transgressor. Negley Farson. 447p. 1984. pap. 9.95 (*0-88184-089-0*) Carroll & Graf.

Way of a Warrior: A Journey into Secret Worlds of Martial Arts. 3rd ed. John F. Gilbey. LC 83-2130. (Illus.). 215p. 1992. pap. 12.95 (*1-55643-126-0*) North Atlantic.

Way of Abhyasa: Meditation in Practice. J. P. Vaswani. LC 95-8746. (Illus.). 112p. (Orig.). 1995. pap. 9.95 (*0-89243-826-6*, Triumph Books) Liguori Pubns.

***Way of Abu Madyan.** Vincent Cornell. 1996. write for info. (*0-614-21378-9*, 1292) Kazi Pubns.

Way of Abu Madyan. Abu Madyan. Ed. & Tr. by Vincent Cornell. (Golden Palm Ser.). (ARA.). (C). 1995. 39.95 (*0-946621-34-9*, Pub. by Islamic Texts UK) Intl Spec Bk.

Way of Abu Madyan. Abu Madyan. Ed. & Tr. by Vincent J. Cornell. (Golden Palm Ser.). (ARA.). (C). 1996. pap. text ed. 35.00 (*0-946621-35-7*, Pub. by Islamic Texts UK) Intl Spec Bk.

Way of Acting: The Theatre Writings of Tadashi Suzuki. Tr. by J. Thomas Rimer. LC 86-5894. (Illus.). 188p. 1985. pap. 9.95 (*0-930452-56-9*) Theatre Comm.

***Way of Agape.** Chuck Missler & Nancy Missler. (King's High Way Ser.). 109p. Date not set. pap. 5.95 (*1-880532-89-1*) Koinonia Hse.

Way of Agape. Chuck Missler & Nancy Missler. Ed. by Tracy McDonald et al. (Illus.). (Orig.). 1996. reprint ed. pap. text ed. 12.95 (*1-880532-56-5*) Koinonia Hse.

Way of Agape: Personal Application Workbook. Chuck Missler & Nancy Missler. (Orig.). 1994. pap. text ed. 5.95 (*1-880532-57-3*) Koinonia Hse.

Way of Agape Leadership Manual. Nancy Missler. Ed. by Tracy McDonald. 1996. 19.95 (*1-880532-46-8*) Koinonia Hse.

Way of All Flesh. Samuel Butler. (Airmont Classics Ser.). (J). (gr. 11 up). 1965. mass mkt. 2.50 (*0-8049-0090-6*, CL-90) Airmont.

Way of All Flesh. Samuel Butler. 24.95 (*0-88411-788-X*) Amereon Ltd.

Way of All Flesh. Samuel Butler. 1960. mass mkt. 4.95 (*0-452-00882-4*, Mer) NAL-Dutton.

Way of All Flesh. Samuel Butler. LC 92-52916. 400p. 1992. 17.00 (*0-679-41718-4*, Everymans Lib) Knopf.

Way of All Flesh. Samuel Butler. 416p. 1993. pap. 7.95 (*0-460-87240-0*, Everyman's Classic Lib) C E Tuttle.

Way of All Flesh. Samuel Butler. LC 92-39870. (World's Classics Ser.). 520p. 1993. pap. 8.95 (*0-19-282980-7*) OUP.

Way of All Flesh. Samuel Butler. Ed. by Richard Hogart & James Cochrane. (English Library). 446p. 1966. pap. 10.95 (*0-14-043012-1*, Penguin Classics) Viking Penguin.

Way of All Flesh. J. D. Stanley. LC 93-94979. 160p. (Orig.). 1995. pap. 10.00 (*1-56002-399-6*, Univ Edtns) Aegina Pr.

Way of All Flesh. Samuel Butler. 345p. 1983. reprint ed. lib. bdg. 17.95 (*0-89966-310-9*) Buccaneer Bks.

Way of All the Earth: Experiments in Truth & Religion. John S. Dunne. LC 78-1575. 1978. reprint ed. pap. 15.00 (*0-268-01928-2*); reprint ed. text ed. 29.00 (*0-268-01927-4*) U of Notre Dame Pr.

Way of an Eagle. Robert Darden & P. J. Richardson. LC 95-33301. 272p. 1996. 19.99 (*0-7852-7701-3*) Nelson.

Way of an Eagle in the Air: The Paintings of Shlomo Katz at the United States Air Force Academy Cadet Chapel. Shlomo Katz. (Illus.). 112p. (Orig.). 1991. 125.00 (*0-9624181-1-0*) Stuart Allen.

Way of an Indian. Frederic Remington. LC 76-50438. 1976. 25.00 (*0-89436-000-0*) Memento.

Way of an Investigator: A Scientist's Experiences in Medical Research. Walter B. Cannon. 1984. pap. 5.95 (*0-393-30125-7*) Norton.

Way of an Investigator: A Scientist's Experiences in Medical Research. Walter B. Cannon. LC 65-20089. 239p. reprint ed. pap. 68.20 (*0-685-15934-5*, 2026393) Bks Demand.

Way of Anthroposophy: Answers to Modern Questions. Stewart Easton. 102p. (Orig.). 1986. pap. 10.95 (*0-85440-464-3*, Steinerbks) Anthroposophic.

***Way of Art.** 10.95 (*1-56176-154-0*) Mystic Fire.

Way of Art: Inner Vision-Outer Expression. Kelly Fearing et al. (Illus.). 80p. (J). (gr. 7-8). 1986. Tchr's manual, 80 pages. teacher ed. 6.00 (*0-87443-068-2*) Benson.

Way of Art: Inner Vision-Outer Expression, Vol. I. Kelly Fearing et al. (Illus.). 160p. (J). (gr. 7-8). 1986. pap. 17.79 (*0-87443-066-6*) Benson.

Way of Art: Inner Vision-Outer Expression, Vol. II. Kelly Fearing et al. (Illus.). 160p. (J). (gr. 7-8). 1986. text ed. 17.79 (*0-87443-067-4*) Benson.

Way of Aten & the Ancient Egyptian Proverbs. Ed. & Intro. by Tyrone J. Greer. 79p. (Orig.). 1994. pap. 5.95 (*0-9630951-2-9*) Karnak Co.

Way of Attainment. Sydney T. Klein. 220p. 1981. pap. 17.00 (*0-89540-106-1*, SB-106) Sun Pub.

Way of Being. Carl R. Rogers. 416p. 1995. pap. 11.95 (*0-395-75530-1*) HM.

Way of Biblical Justice. Jose Gallardo. LC 82-83386. (Mennonite Faith Ser.: No. 11). 80p. (Orig.). 1983. pap. 1.99 (*0-8361-3321-8*) Herald Pr.

Way of Cartouche: An Oracle of Ancient Egyptian Magic. Murry Hope. (Illus.). 25p. 1985. 27.95 (*0-312-85823-X*); 239.40 (*0-312-85824-8*) St Martin.

Way of Christ. Pope John Paul, II. Ed. & Compiled by Tony Castle. LC 95-30100. 64p. (Orig.). 1995. pap. 4.95 (*0-8245-2007-6*) Crossroad NY.

Way of Christian Living. John H. Timmerman. LC 87-12455. 157p. (Orig.). reprint ed. pap. 44.80 (*0-8357-4368-3*, 2037197) Bks Demand.

Way of Christian Service. Zacharias T. Fomum. 1990. 13.95 (*0-533-08451-2*) Vantage.

Way of Chuang Tzu. Thomas Merton. LC 65-27556. (Illus.). 1969. reprint ed. pap. 7.95 (*0-8112-0103-1*, NDP276) New Directions.

Way of Chuang Tzu. Thomas Merton. LC 91-50903. (Pocket Classics Ser.). 194p. 1992. reprint ed. pap. 6.00 (*0-87773-676-6*) Shambhala Pubns.

Way of Chuang Tzu: A Personal & Spiritual Interpretation of the Classic Philosopher of Taoism. Thomas Merton. 160p. 1994. pap. 21.00 (*0-86012-239-5*, Pub. by Srch Pr UK) St Mut.

Way of Contentment. Ekiken Kaibara. Bd. with Greater Learning for Women. LC 79-65352. (Studies in Japanese History & Civilization). 239p. 1979. reprint ed. Set text ed. 59.95 (*0-313-27033-3*, U7033) Greenwood.

Way of Council. Jack Zimmerman & Virginia Coyle. LC 96-21974. 322p. (Orig.). 1996. pap. 16.95 (*1-883647-05-3*, Bramble Bks) Bramble Co.

***Way of Death: Merchant Capitalism & the Angolan Slave Trade, 1730-1830.** Joseph C. Miller. LC 87-40368. (Illus.). 800p. (Orig.). 1997. pap. 24.95 (*0-299-11564-X*) U of Wis Pr.

Way of Delphi: Reusing Objects Components Properties & Events. Gary Entsminger. 464p. 1996. pap. 39.95 incl. disk (*0-13-455271-7*) P-H.

Way of Desert Spirituality: The Rule of Life of the Hermits of Bethlehem of the Heart of Jesus. Eugene L. Romano. LC 92-37733. 124p. 1993. pap. 6.95 (*0-8189-0661-8*) Alba.

Way of Discipleship to Christ. Stephen Isaac. LC 76-57021. 61p. 1976. pap. 7.00 (*0-910378-12-6*) Christward.

Way of Divine Love. Josefa Menendez. LC 79-112493. 504p. 1993. reprint ed. pap. 18.50 (*0-89555-030-X*); reprint ed. pap. 8.50 (*0-89555-276-0*) TAN Bks Pubs.

Way of Divine Union: Being a Doctrine of Experience in the Life of Sanctity, Considered on the Faith of Its Testimonies & Interpreted after a New Manner. A. E. Waite. 360p. 1993. reprint ed. pap. 27.00 (*1-56459-389-4*) Kessinger Pub.

Way of Doctoring. Ainslie Meares. 180p. (Orig.). 1994. pap. 12.95 (*0-85572-150-2*, Pub. by Hill Content Pubng AT) Seven Hills Bk.

Way of Duty: A Woman & Her Family in Revolutionary America. Richard Buel, Jr. & Joy D. Buel. 336p. 1995. pap. 12.00 (*0-393-31210-0*, Norton Paperbks) Norton.

Way of Eating for Pleasure & Health. Michael Blate & Gail C. Watson. (G-Jo Institute Fabulous Foods Ser.). 130p. (Orig.). 1983. pap. 8.95 (*0-916878-15-5*) Falkyn Inc.

Way of Energy: A Gaia Original. Lam Kam Chuen. (Illus.). 192p. (Orig.). 1991. pap. 15.95 (*0-671-73645-0*, Fireside) S&S Trade.

Way of Escape. Neil T. Anderson. 1994. pap. 9.99 (*1-56507-170-0*) Harvest Hse.

Way of Ethical Humanism. Gerald A. Larue. 96p. 1989. pap. 10.95 (*0-913111-22-8*) Centerline.

Way of Everyday Life. Hakuyu T. Maezumi & John D. Loori. LC 78-8309. (Illus.). 1978. pap. 9.95 (*0-916820-06-8*) Center Pubns.

Way of Faith: Words of Admonition & Encouragement for the Journey Based on the Letter to the Hebrews. Ed. by James M. Pitts. 176p. (Orig.). 1985. pap. 8.95 (*0-913029-10-6*) Stevens Bk Pr.

Way of Faithfulness: Contemplation & Formation in the Church. Padraic O'Hare. LC 93-22668. 192p. 1993. pap. 13.50 (*1-56338-066-8*) TPI PA.

Way of Faithfulness: Study Guide to Christians in Japan. Patricia J. Patterson. (Orig.). 1991. pap. 5.95 (*0-377-00220-8*) Friendship Pr.

Way of Flame: A Guide to the Forgotten Mystical Tradition of Jewish Meditation. Avram Davis. LC 95-46074. 1996. pap. 10.00 (*0-06-061753-5*) Harper SF.

***Way of God: Derech Hashem.** Moshe C. Luzzatto & Aryeh Kaplan. LC 96-30224. (Torah Classics Library). 1996. 17.95 (*0-87306-769-X*) Feldheim.

Way of God's Will. Sun M. Moon. 418p. (Orig.). reprint ed. pap. 6.95 (*0-910621-31-4*) HSA Pubns.

***Way of Happening.** Chappell. Date not set. write for info. (*0-312-18033-0*) St Martin.

Way of Heaven. Manly P. Hall. pap. 10.95 (*0-89314-833-4*) Philos Res.

Way of Heaven: An Introduction to the Confucian Religious Life. R. L. Taylor. (Iconography of Religions Ser.: Vol. XII-3). (Illus.). xi, 37p. 1986. pap. 51.50 (*90-04-07423-6*) E J Brill.

Way of Herbs. rev. ed. Michael Tierra. Ed. by Eric Tobias. 414p. (Orig.). 1990. pap. 6.99 (*0-671-72403-7*) PB.

Way of His Own. T. A. Dyer. (YA). 1990. pap. 5.95 (*0-395-54969-8*) HM.

Way of Holines. Phoebe Palmer. 1988. pap. 9.99 (*0-88019-233-X*) Schmul Pub Co.

Way of Holiness. K. Prior. 7.99 (*1-85792-109-7*, Pub. by Christian Focus UK) Spring Arbor Dist.

Way of Holiness. Samuel L. Brengle. 1966. reprint ed. 4.95 (*0-86544-008-5*) Salv Army Suppl South.

Way of Hope: Michio Kushi's Anti-AIDS Program. Tom Monte. 1990. pap. 12.95 (*0-446-39174-3*) Warner Bks.

Way of Ignatius Loyola: Contemporary Approaches to the Spiritual Exercises. Intro. by Philip Sheldrake. LC 91-73016. (Studies on Jesuit Topics Series IV: No. 13). xiii, 270p. 1991. 29.95 (*0-912422-67-X*); pap. 19.95 (*0-912422-65-3*) Inst Jesuit.

Way of Illumination, Vol. 1: The Sufi Message. Hazrat I. Khan. (C). 1988. 17.00 (*81-208-0497-X*, Pub. by Motilal Banarsidass II); pap. 8.75 (*0-685-37679-6*, Pub. by Motilal Banarsidass II) S Asia.

Way of Initiation: How to Attain Knowledge of the Higher Worlds. Rudolf Steiner. 63p. 1960. reprint ed. spiral bd. 8.50 (*0-7873-0830-7*) Hlth Research.

Way of Inspiration: Teachings of Native American Elder Joseph Rael. Joseph Rael. (Illus.). 64p. 1996. 12.95 (*1-57178-034-3*) Coun Oak Bks.

Way of Integral Life. Hua-Ching Ni. LC 88-63991. 408p. (Orig.). 1989. 20.00 (*0-937064-21-1*); pap. 14.00 (*0-937064-20-3*) SevenStar Comm.

Way of Java. Entsminger. LC 96-51649. 1997. pap. 34.95 (*0-13-491978-5*) P-H.

Way of Jesus Christ: Christology in Messianic Dimensions. Jurgen Moltmann. Tr. by Margaret Kohl from GER. LC 93-29961. (Works of Jurgen Moltmann). 416p. 1993. pap. 20.00 (*0-8006-2826-8*, 1-2826, Fortress Pr) Augsburg Fortress.

Way of Karate. George E. Mattson. 200p. 1992. pap. 18.95 (*0-8048-1852-5*) C E Tuttle.

Way of Karate. George E. Mattson. 21.95 (*0-685-22157-1*) Wehman.

Way of Karma. Charles Breaux. LC 92-45543. 196p. (Orig.). 1993. pap. 14.95 (*0-87728-773-2*) Weiser.

Way of Language: An Introduction. Fred West. 250p. (Orig.). (C). 1975. pap. text ed. 18.75 (*0-15-595130-0*) HB Coll Pubs.

Way of Lao Tzu. Wing-Tsit Chan. 296p. (C). 1963. pap. text ed. 15.20 (*0-02-320700-0*, Macmillan Coll) P-H.

Way of Liberation: Essays & Lectures on the Transformation of the Self. Alan Watts. Ed. by Mark Watts & Rebecca Shropshire. LC 82-21917. 120p. 1983. reprint ed. pap. 12.95 (*0-8348-0181-7*) Weatherhill.

Way of Life. Charles Davis. Ed. by Nancy K. Newman. 132p. (Orig.). 1989. pap. 5.00 (*0-685-26555-2*) CMC Pr FL.

Way of Life. Eliza. (Orig.). 1992. pap. 12.95 (*1-881333-00-0*) White Mount Pubns.

Way of Life. Charles Hodge. 1978. pap. 7.50 (*0-85151-273-9*) Banner of Truth.

Way of Life. H. Glyn Joner & Barbara Collins. (Illus.). 192p. 1987. 32.95 (*0-85236-166-1*, Pub. by Farming Pr UK) Diamond Farm Bk.

Way of Life. Jim Kinter. Ed. by Joseph E. Walker. LC 74-29188. (Lancaster County During the American Revolution Ser.). (Illus.). 64p. 1975. pap. 5.00 (*0-915010-04-6*) Sutter House.

Way of Life. Lao Tzu. 1955. pap. 4.99 (*0-451-62674-5*, Ment) NAL-Dutton.

Way of Life. William Osler. 1937. text ed. 11.95 (*0-06-141860-9*) Lppncott-Raven.

***Way of Life.** Richard A. Snow, Jr. 158p. (Orig.). 1997. mass mkt. 4.99 (*1-55197-599-8*, Pub. by Comnwlth Pub CN) Partners Pubs Grp.

Way of Life. D. E. Pohren. (Illus.). 194p. (Orig.). 1988. reprint ed. 19.95 (*0-933224-02-8*, Pub. by Soc Sp Studies SP); reprint ed. pap. 16.50 (*0-933224-03-6*, Pub. by Soc Sp Studies SP) Bold Strummer Ltd.

Way of Life. Hendrik Roehrman. LC 70-144677. Orig. Title: Marlow & Shakespeare. reprint ed. 21.50 (*0-404-05386-6*) AMS Pr.

Way of Life: A Human-Spiritual Growth Series for Lay Groups. Kathleen O'Sullivan. 126p. 1989. pap. 22.00 (*0-86217-203-9*, Pub. by Veritas IE) St Mut.

Way of Life: An Address Delivered to Yale Students Sunday Evening, April 20, 1913. William Osler. (Illus.). 54p. 1969. 18.95 (*0-398-01433-7*) C C Thomas.

Way of Life: King, Householder, Renouncer: Essays in Honour of Louis Dumont. Ed. by Triloki N. Madan. (C). 1988. reprint ed. 31.00 (*81-208-0527-5*, Pub. by Motilal Banarsidass II) S Asia.

Way of Life: Macrobiotics & the Spirit of Christianity. John Ineson. LC 85-80539. 274p. 1986. 15.95 (*0-87040-635-3*) Japan Pubns USA.

Way of Life: Tao Te Ching. Lao Tzu. Tr. by R. B. Blakney. 1955. pap. 3.95 (*0-451-62563-3*, Ment) NAL-Dutton.

Way of Life Abundant. Luis F. Zapata & Christopher J. Hibbard. (Illus.). 160p. (Orig.). 1995. pap. 15.95 (*0-9623614-7-X*) Disciples Pr.

Way of Life & Death: Three Centuries of Prussian-German Militarism, An Anthropological Approach. Emilio Willems. LC 85-22488. 256p. (Orig.). 1986. pap. text ed. 19.95 (*0-8265-1214-3*) Vanderbilt U Pr.

Way of Life Be a Saint! Union with the Blessed Trinity As Reflected in the Holy Family. Luke Zimmer. LC 94-67387. 37p. 1996. pap. 1.95 (*1-882972-37-6*) Queenship Pub.

Way of Life Be a Saint! Union with the Blessed Trinity As Reflected in the Holy Family. Luke Zimmer. Tr. by Gracie Ruiz from ENG. 52p. (SPA.). 1996. pap. 1.95 (*1-882972-42-2*) Queenship Pub.

Way of Living. Lucy Laurie. 109p. (C). 1990. text ed. 40.00 (*0-85439-348-X*, Pub. by St Paul Pubns UK) St Mut.

Way of Looking at Things: Selected Papers. Stephen P. Schlein. 816p. 1995. pap. 17.95 (*0-393-31314-X*, Norton Paperbks) Norton.

Way of Looking at Things: Selected Papers of Erik H. Erikson 1930-1980. Ed. by Stephen P. Schlein. 1987. 29.95 (*0-393-02267-6*) Norton.

Way of Love. Joan W. Anglund. 1993. 9.95 (*0-679-73112-1*) Random.

Way of Love. Pope John Paul, II. Ed. & Compiled by Tony Castle. LC 95-30101. 64p. 1995. pap. 4.95 (*0-8245-2006-8*) Crossroad NY.

Way of Love: Bhagavata Doctrine of Bhaki. Subhash Anand. 248p. (C). 1996. 29.00 (*81-215-0665-4*, Pub. by Munshiram Manoharial II) S Asia.

Way of Love see Best Gift Is Love: Meditations

Way of Man: According to the Teaching of Hasidism. Martin Buber. 44p. 1995. pap. 5.95 (*0-8065-0024-7*, Citadel Pr) Carol Pub Group.

Way of Man, 1959. Martin Buber. 3.00 (*0-87574-106-1*) Pendle Hill.

***Way of Mary.** Harvey. 24.00 (*0-06-063589-4*); pap. 13.00 (*0-06-063590-8*) HarpC.

***Way of Mary: Praying & Living Her Words.** Alphonsus Liguori. LC 96-78940. 192p. (Orig.). 1997. pap. 4.95 (*0-7648-0033-7*) Liguori Pubns.

Way of Merlyn: The Male Path in Wicca. Ly Warren-Clarke & Kathryn Matthews. 160p. (Orig.). 1991. pap. 10.95 (*1-85327-041-5*, Pub. by Prism Pr UK) Assoc Pubs Grp.

Way of Microwave Cooking - Como Trabajo el Microonda. Claudette Harshberger. Tr. by Alfredo Borunda. 120p. (Orig.). (ENG & SPA.). 1981. pap. 7.50 (*0-9606100-0-6*) Pan Prods.

Way of Mysticism. Joseph James. 256p. 1981. pap. 20.00 (*0-89540-086-3*, SB-086) Sun Pub.

Way of Mysticism: An Anthology. Joseph James. 1977. lib. bdg. 59.95 (*0-8490-2810-8*) Gordon Pr.

Way of Myth: Talking with Joseph Campbell. Joseph Campbell. LC 94-6186. (Pocket Classics Ser.). 240p. 1994. reprint ed. pap. 6.00 (*1-57062-042-3*, Sham Pocket Class) Shambhala Pubns.

Way of No Thinking: The Prophocies of Japan's Kunihiro Yamate. Robert Engler & Yuriko Hayashi. 318p. (Orig.). 1995. pap. 15.95 (*1-57178-008-4*) Coun Oak Bks.

Way of No Way. Jerry Beasley. (Illus.). 160p. pap. 19.95 (*0-87364-668-1*) Paladin Pr.

***Way of Our People.** Arnold Griese. LC 96-85988. (Illus.). 72p. (J). 1997. pap. text ed. 7.95 (*1-56397-648-X*) Boyds Mills Pr.

Way of Passion: A Celebration of Rumi. Andrew Harvey. LC 93-48302. 319p. (Orig.). (C). 1994. 20.00 (*1-883319-20-X*) Frog Ltd CA.

Way of Peace. James Allen. 113p. 1992. pap. 10.00 (*0-89540-229-7*, SB-229) Sun Pub.

Way of Peace. John C. Wenger. LC 77-86349. (Mennonite Faith Ser.: Vol. 4). 72p. 1977. pap. text ed. 2.99 (*0-8361-1835-9*) Herald Pr.

An Asterisk (*) at the beginning of an entry indicates that the title is appearing in BIP for the first time.

Way of Peace & Blessedness. 4th ed. Swami Paramananda. 105p. 1961. 6.95 (*0-911564-06-3*) Vedanta Ctr.

Way of Perfection. St. Teresa of Avila. 288p. 1991. pap. 9.95 (*0-385-06539-6*, D176, Image Bks) Doubleday.

Way of Poetry. Ed. by John Drinkwater. LC 73-116399. (Granger Index Reprint Ser.). 1977. 18.95 (*0-8369-6140-4*) Ayer.

Way of Positive Humanism. Gerald A. Larue. 96p. 1989. pap. 10.95 (*0-913111-25-2*) Centerline.

Way of Power. Red Hawk. LC 96-75395. 96p. (Orig.). 1996. pap. 10.00 (*0-934252-64-5*) Hohm Pr.

Way of Prayer. Pope John Paul, II. Ed. & Compiled by Tony Castle. LC 95-30096. 64p. (Orig.). 1995. pap. 4.95 (*0-8245-2008-4*) Crossroad NY.

Way of Real Wealth: Creating a Future That Is Financially Secure, Emotionally Satisfying, Spiritually Fulfilling. Mark Waldman. LC 93-1207. 224p. 1994. pap. 12.00 (*0-89486-902-7*, 5050A) Hazelden.

***Way of Seeing.** Mabel Drew. 118p. 1993. pap. 12.95 (*1-55082-096-6*, Pub. by Quarry Pr CN) LPC InBook.

Way of Seeing. Philip Rusten. (Illus.). 96p. 1978. 23.00 (*0-686-29711-3*) Way of Seeing.

Way of Seeing. rev. ed. Helen Levitt. LC 81-82838. (Illus.). 100p. 1989. reprint ed. pap. text ed. 24.95 (*0-8223-1005-8*) Duke.

Way of Seeing. 3rd rev. ed. Helen Levitt. LC 81-82838. (Illus.). 100p. 1989. reprint ed. text ed. 41.95 (*0-8223-1004-X*) Duke.

Way of Spiritual Direction. Francis K. Nemeck & Marie T. Coombs. LC 84-81254. 220p. 1985. pap. 10.95 (*0-8146-5447-9*) Liturgical Pr.

Way of Splendor: Jewish Mysticism & Modern Psychology. Edward Hoffman. LC 89-6720. 264p. 1992. reprint ed. pap. 22.50 (*0-87668-269-7*) Aronson.

Way of St. Francis: The Challenge of Franciscan Spirituality for Everyone. Murray Bodo. 160p. 1995. pap. 8.95 (*0-86716-244-9*) St Anthony Mess Pr.

Way of St. James, 3 vols. Georgianna G. King. LC 78-63469. reprint ed. Set. 140.00 (*0-404-17160-5*) AMS Pr.

Way of Strategy. William A. Levinson. 246p. 1995. 30.00 (*0-87389-228-3*, H0778) ASQC Qual Pr.

Way of Suffering: A Geography of Crisis. Jerome Miller. LC 88-4703. 215p. 1988. 10.95 (*0-87840-465-1*) Georgetown U Pr.

***Way of Sufi Chivalry.** Ibn Al-Husayn & Al-Sulami. 122p. 1996. pap. 10.95 (*0-614-21379-7*, 1293); pap. 10.95 (*0-614-21563-3*, 1293) Kazi Pubns.

Way of Sufi Chivalry: Futuwwah. Ibn Al-Husayn Al-Sulami. 192p. 1991. reprint ed. pap. 10.95 (*0-89281-317-2*) Inner Tradit.

Way of Tamarisk. large type ed. Vicky Maxwell. 318p. 1980. 25.99 (*0-7089-0593-5*) Ulverscroft.

Way of Tantra: Ananda Marga Yoga Philosophy. (Illus.). 92p. (Orig.). 1989. pap. 6.00 (*0-88476-026-X*) Ananda Marga.

Way of the Ab: A Way of Living. Anita M. Klinger & Lori Harding. (Illus.). 175p. (Orig.). 1992. pap. text ed. 9.95 (*0-9635147-0-9*) Marshall Graph.

***Way of the Algonquin: Timeless Wisdom from Contemporary Native Americans.** Evan T. Pritchard. LC 97-7492. 114p. (Orig.). 1997. pap. 12.95 (*1-57178-042-4*) Coun Oak Bks.

Way of the Ascetics: The Ancient Tradition of Discipline & Inner Growth. Tito Colliander. Tr. by Katharine Ferre from SWE. LC 61-7341. 110p. 1982. 8.00 (*0-06-061526-5*, Y004) St John Kronstadt.

Way of the Ascetics: The Ancient Tradition of Discipline & Inner Growth. Ed. by Tito Colliandor. Tr. by Katharine Ferre from SWE. LC 85-83900. 110p. 1985. pap. 7.95 (*0-88141-049-7*) St Vladimirs.

Way of the Black Messiah: The Hermeneutical Challenge of Black Theology As a Theology of Liberation. Theo Witvliet. 352p. 1987. 39.95 (*0-940989-09-3*); 22.95 (*0-940989-04-2*) Meyer Stone Bks.

Way of the Bodhisattva: A Translation of the Bodhicharyavatara. Shantideva. Tr. by Padmakara Translation Group Staff from SAN. LC 96-25650. (Dragon Editions Ser.). 240p. (Orig.). 1997. pap. 14.00 (*1-57062-253-1*) Shambhala Pubns.

***Way of the Boundary Crosser: An Introduction to Jewish Flexidoxy.** Gershon Winkler. LC 97-25800. 1998. write for info. (*0-7657-9986-3*) Aronson.

Way of the Brush: Painting Techniques of China & Japan. Fritz Van Briessen. LC 62-14119. (Illus.). 330p. 1962. reprint ed. 49.95 (*0-8048-0625-X*) C E Tuttle.

Way of the Buddha. Cottie A. Burland. (Way Ser.). 64p. (J). (gr. 3-7). 1988. pap. 10.95 (*0-7175-0590-1*) Dufour.

Way of the Bull. Leo F. Buscaglia. LC 73-83777. 176p. 1973. 9.95 (*0-913590-08-8*) SLACK Inc.

Way of the Bull. Leo F. Buscaglia. 192p. 1986. mass mkt. 5.99 (*0-449-21130-4*) Fawcett.

Way of the Carpenter: Tools & Japanese Architecture. William H. Coaldrake. (Illus.). 220p. 1990. 35.00 (*0-8348-0231-7*) Weatherhill.

Way of the Child. David Patterson. LC 86-83410. 280p. (Orig.). pap. 11.95 (*0-89896-168-8*) Larksdale.

Way of the Churches of Christ in New England. John Cotton. (Works of John Cotton Ser.). 1990. reprint ed. lib. bdg. 90.00 (*0-7812-2317-2*) Rprt Serv.

Way of the Circle. James Vollbracht. LC 92-45871. (Illus.). 48p. (J). (gr. 4-8). 1993. pap. 6.95 (*0-915166-76-3*) Impact Pubs CA.

Way of the Congregational Churches Clearde. John Cotton. (Works of John Cotton Ser.). 1990. reprint ed. lib. bdg. 79.00 (*0-7812-2319-9*) Rprt Serv.

Way of the Cross. 33p. (Orig.). 1957. pap. 0.95 (*0-8146-0664-4*) Liturgical Pr.

***Way of the Cross.** (Saint Joseph Picture Bks.). (Illus.). 1992. pap. 1.25 (*0-89942-497-X*, 497-00) Catholic Bk Pub.

Way of the Cross. Slavko Barbaric. 62p. 1991. pap. 4.95 (*0-940535-29-7*, UP129) Franciscan U Pr.

***Way of the Cross.** Inos Biffi. LC 96-45055. (Illus.). 48p. (YA). (gr. 5 up). 1997. 12.00 (*0-8028-5135-5*, Eerdmans Bks) Eerdmans.

***Way of the Cross.** Anna M. Canopi & Richard De Menocal. 63p. pap. 2.95 (*0-8198-8270-4*) Pauline Bks.

Way of the Cross. K. Cavanagh. (J). Date not set. pap. text ed. 1.25 (*0-88271-211-X*) Regina Pr.

Way of the Cross. Plinio C. De Oliveira. Ed. by Edward Parrot. Tr. by TFP Publications Dept. Staff from POR. (Illus.). 64p. (Orig.). 1990. pap. 3.95 (*1-877905-16-X*) Am Soc Defense TFP.

Way of the Cross. Roy Hession. 1991. pap. 4.50 (*0-87508-238-6*) Chr Lit.

***Way of the Cross.** Alphonsus Liguori. 1987. pap. 0.60 (*0-89942-014-1*, 14/05) Catholic Bk Pub.

Way of the Cross. Mary C. Morrison. LC 85-60516. 32p. (Orig.). 1985. pap. 3.00 (*0-87574-260-2*) Pendle Hill.

Way of the Cross. Louis M. Savary. (J). (ps-3). Date not set. pap. text ed. 1.95 (*0-88271-160-1*) Regina Pr.

Way of the Cross. Hans U. Von Balthasar. 64p. (C). 1990. 29.00 (*0-85439-320-X*, Pub. by St Paul Pubns UK) St Mut.

***Way of the Cross.** Hans U. Von Balthasar. 63p. pap. 4.95 (*0-8198-8241-0*) Pauline Bks.

Way of the Cross: A Reflection on Economic Justice for All. Carmen B. Mele. 21p. (Orig.). 1992. pap. 0.95 (*0-8146-2034-5*) Liturgical Pr.

Way of the Cross: According to the Method of St. Alphonsus Liguori. Alphonsus Ligouri. 1995. reprint ed. pap. 1.00 (*0-89555-313-9*) TAN Bks Pubs.

Way of the Cross: According to the Method of St. Francis of Assisi. M. A. Schumacher. 36p. 1995. pap. 1.00 (*0-89555-314-7*) TAN Bks Pubs.

Way of the Cross: Christian Individuation & Psychological Temperament. Richard Grant. (Illus.). 52p. 1989. pap. 9.95 (*1-878287-25-7*) Type & Temperament.

Way of the Cross: Following Jesus in the Gospel of Mark. Joel B. Green. LC 91-71794. 112p. 1991. pap. 5.95 (*0-88177-103-1*, DR103) Discipleship Res.

Way of the Cross: Spanish-Language Edition. Clemens Schmidt. 32p. (Orig.). (SPA.). 1996. pap. 0.95 (*0-8146-2399-9*) Liturgical Pr.

Way of the Cross: The Passion of Christ in the Americas. Ed. by Virgil Elizondo. Tr. by John Drury from ITA. LC 92-19802. (Illus.). 100p. (Orig.). 1992. pap. 11.50 (*0-88344-819-X*) Orbis Bks.

Way of the Cross: The Pilgrimage at Jerusalem. Ade Bethune. (Illus.). 32p. (Orig.). 1986. pap. 1.00 (*0-934134-94-4*) Sheed & Ward MO.

Way of the Cross: Way of Justice. Leonardo Boff. Tr. by John Drury from POR. LC 79-23776. 144p. (Orig.). 1980. pap. 13.50 (*0-88344-701-0*) Orbis Bks.

Way of the Cross for Caregivers to the Sick. Ronald Tokarz. 21p. (Orig.). 1993. pap. 1.95 (*0-8146-2234-8*) Liturgical Pr.

Way of the Cross for Children. H. J. Richards. 24p. (J). 1989. pap. 2.95 (*0-8146-1805-7*) Liturgical Pr.

Way of the Cross for Congregational Use. Jeremy Harrington. 32p. 1994. pap. text ed. 1.25 (*0-86716-220-1*) St Anthony Mess Pr.

Way of the Cross for Parents. Susan Jones. 32p. 1996. pap. text ed. 1.95 (*0-89622-667-0*) Twenty-Third.

Way of the Cross for the Bereaved. Terence P. Curley. LC 95-48356. (Illus.). 64p. (Orig.). 1996. pap. 3.95 (*0-8189-0752-5*) Alba.

Way of the Cross for Those Who Are HIV Positive & Those Living with AIDS. Ronald Tokarz. 21p. (Orig.). 1993. pap. 1.95 (*0-8146-2233-X*) Liturgical Pr.

Way of the Cross in Santa Maria. Rene Laurentin. LC 93-83641. 86p. 1993. pap. 5.95 (*1-882972-03-1*) Queenship Pub.

***Way of the Cross in Scripture & Meditation.** John A. Hammes. (Illus.). 136p. pap. 1.95 (*0-8198-8205-4*) Pauline Bks.

Way of the Cross Leads Home: A Domestication of American Methodism. A. Gregory Schneider. LC 92-23087. (Religion in North America Ser.). 292p. 1993. 31.50 (*0-253-35094-8*) Ind U Pr.

Way of the Dead Indians: Guajiro Myths & Symbols. Michel Perrin. Tr. by Michael Fineberg from FRE. (Sourcebooks in Anthropology: No. 13). (Illus.). 229p. 1987. pap. 14.95 (*0-292-79039-2*); text ed. 30.00 (*0-292-79032-5*) U of Tex Pr.

Way of the Doll: The Art & Craft of Personal Transformation. Cassandra Light. LC 94-48177. (Illus.). 96p. 1996. pap. 18.95 (*0-8118-0698-7*) Chronicle Bks.

***Way of the Dragon.** Hiroi Oji. (Samurai Crusader Ser.). 1997. pap. text ed. 15.95 (*1-56931-164-1*, Viz Comics) Viz Commns Inc.

Way of the Dream: Conversations on Jungian Dream Interpretation with Marie-Louise Franz. Fraser Boa. LC 94-6184. 192p. 1994. pap. 12.00 (*1-57062-036-9*) Shambhala Pubns.

***Way of the Eagle.** Ned Conquest. LC 94-72041. 319p. 1994. 19.95 (*0-9627485-2-8*) Apollonian Pr.

Way of the Eagle. Jerry Fankhauser. 133p. (Orig.). 1987. pap. 10.00 (*0-911197-10-9*) J Fankhauser.

Way of the Eagle. Jerry Fankhauser. 133p. (Orig.). 1987. pap. 10.00 (*0-9617006-4-5*) J Fankhauser.

Way of the Eagle. 7th ed. Charles J. Biddle. (Great War Ser.: No. 7). (Illus.). 297p. 1990. reprint ed. 34.95 (*0-89839-152-0*) Battery Pr.

Way of the Earth. Teri McLuhan. 560p. 1994. 30.00 (*0-671-75939-6*) S&S Trade.

Way of the Earth: Encounters with Nature in Ancient & Contemporary Thought. T. C. MuLuhan. 1995. pap. 17. 50 (*0-684-80157-4*, Touchstone Bks) S&S Trade.

Way of the Earth: Native America & the Environment. John Bierhorst. LC 93-28971. (Illus.). 336p. (YA). (gr. 7 up). 1994. 15.00 (*0-688-11560-8*, Morrow Junior) Morrow.

Way of the English Mystics: An Anthology & Guide for Pilgrims. Gordon L. Miller. 192p. (Orig.). 1996. pap. 19.95 (*0-8192-1675-5*) Morehouse Pub.

Way of the Essenes: Christ's Hidden Life Remembered. Anne Meurois-Givaudan & Daniel Meurois-Givaudan. 383p. 1993. reprint ed. pap. 16.95 (*0-89281-322-9*, Destiny Bks) Inner Tradit.

Way of the Essentialist: Contra Sartres Existentialism. John E. Boyle. (Primers for the Age of Inner Space Ser.: No. 5). 166p. 1993. pap. 15.00 (*0-917888-08-1*) Wheat Forders.

Way of the Essentialist: Contra Sartres Existentialism. John E. Boyle. (Primers for the Age of Inner Space Ser.: No. 5). 166p. 1993. 20.00 (*0-917888-01-4*) Wheat Forders.

Way of the Explorer: An Apollo Astronaut's Journey Through the Material & Mystical Worlds. Edgar Mitchell & Dwight Williams. 224p. (Orig.). 1996. 24.95 (*0-399-14161-8*, Putnam) Putnam Pub Group.

Way of the Ferret: Finding Educational Resources on the Internet. Judi B. Harris. (Illus.). 209p. 1994. pap. text ed. 24.95 (*1-56484-085-9*) Intl Society Tech Educ.

Way of the Flame: A Guide to the Forgotten Mystical Tradition of Jewish Meditation. Avram Davis. LC 95-46074. 160p. 1996. 17.00 (*0-06-061752-7*) Harper SF.

Way of the Fox: American Strategy in the War for America, 1775-1783. Dave R. Palmer. LC 74-5992. (Contributions to Military History Ser.: No. 8). 229p. 1975. text ed. 37.50 (*0-8371-7531-3*, PAF/, Greenwood Pr) Greenwood.

Way of the Fussbudget Is Not Easy. Charles M. Schulz. LC 85-82547. 192p. 1986. pap. 5.95 (*0-03-005619-5*, Owl) H Holt & Co.

Way of the Fussbudget Is Not Easy. Charles M. Schulz. (Peanuts Classics Ser.). 128p. 1993. pap. 7.95 (*0-8050-2697-5*) H Holt & Co.

Way of the Goddess: A Journey of Self Awareness. Shantara M. Khalsa. (Illus.). 212p. (Orig.). 1994. pap. 11.95 (*0-9598048-3-8*, WOTG) Bks Light Pub.

Way of the Greeks. Frank R. Earp. LC 75-136393. reprint ed. 37.50 (*0-404-02234-0*) AMS Pr.

Way of the Grizzly. Dorothy H. Patent. LC 86-17562. (Illus.). 64p. (J). (gr. 4 up). 1991. pap. 5.95 (*0-395-58112-5*, Clarion Bks) HM.

Way of the Guerrilla: Achieving Success & Balance As an Entrepreneur in the 21st Century. Jay C. Levinson. 288p. 1997. 19.95 (*0-395-77018-1*) HM.

Way of the Heart. Henri J. Nouwen. (Epiphany Bks.). 1985. mass mkt. 5.99 (*0-345-32959-7*) Ballantine.

***Way of the Heart.** large type ed. Rebecca Marsh. (Linford Romance Library). 256p. 1997. pap. 16.99 (*0-7089-5039-6*) Ulverscroft.

Way of the Heart: Desert Spirituality & Contemporary Ministry. Henri J. Nouwen. 1991. pap. 9.00 (*0-06-066330-8*) Harper SF.

Way of the Heart: The Rajneesh Movement. Judith Thompson & Paul Heelas. LC 87-29792. (New Religious Movements Ser.: No. 3). 142p. 1988. reprint ed. lib. bdg. 29.00 (*0-8095-7038-6*) Borgo Pr.

Way of the Heavenly Sword: The Japanese Army in the 1920's. Leonard A. Humphreys. LC 94-15612. xi ,p. 1995. 39.50 (*0-8047-2375-3*) Stanford U Pr.

Way of the Hindu. Swami Yogeshananda. (Way Ser.). 64p. (J). (gr. 3-7). 1980. pap. 10.95 (*0-7175-0626-6*) Dufour.

Way of the Hummingbird: In Legend, History & Today's Gardens. Virginia C. Holmgren. LC 89-659. 160p. (Orig.). (C). 1988. reprint ed. lib. bdg. 27.00 (*0-8095-4026-6*) Borgo Pr.

Way of the Jewish Mystics. Compiled by Perle Besserman. LC 93-36510. (Pocket Classics Ser.). 272p. 1994. pap. 7.00 (*0-87773-983-8*, Sham Pocket Class) Shambhala Pubns.

Way of the Jews. Louis Jacobs. (Way Ser.). 64p. (J). (gr. 3-7). 1987. pap. 10.95 (*0-7175-0875-7*) Dufour.

Way of the Journal: A Journal Therapy Workbook for Healing. Kathleen Adams. LC 93-84727. ix, 79p. (Orig.). 1993. pap. 15.95 (*0-9629164-2-0*) Sidran Pr.

Way of the Kabbalah. Z'ev Ben Shimon Halevi. LC 91-9411. 224p. 1991. pap. 14.00 (*0-87728-305-2*) Weiser.

Way of the King: Sermons for Pentecost, First Lesson, Cycle B. Charles J. Curley. LC 93-2756. 1993. pap. 5.95 (*1-55673-613-4*, 9338) CSS OH.

Way of the Leader. Donald G. Krause. LC 96-22371. 192p. 1997. pap. 12.00 (*0-399-52267-0*, Perigee Bks) Berkley Pub.

Way of the Levites. Blanche Beeston. 186p. 1989. pap. text ed. 7.95 (*0-9616488-6-4*) Alef Bet Comns.

Way of the Lord: A New Testament Pilgrimage. Brother John of Taize. 200p. (Orig.). 1990. pap. 13.95 (*0-912405-69-4*) Pastoral Pr.

Way of the Lord: A New Testament Pilgrimage. John Taize. 232p. 1989. pap. 24.00 (*1-85390-170-9*, Pub. by Veritas IE) St Mut.

Way of the Lord: Christological Exegesis of the Old Testament in the Gospel of Mark. Joel Marcus. 256p. 1992. text ed. 25.00 (*0-664-21949-7*) Westminster John Knox.

Way of the Magus: Rune-Lore & Secret Wisdom of the Northern Tradition. Michael Howard. (Illus.). (Orig.). 1996. pap. 21.95 (*1-898307-82-2*, Pub. by Capall Bann Pubng UK) Holmes Pub.

Way of the Masks. Claude Levi-Strauss. Tr. by Sylvia Modelski from FRE. LC 82-2723. (Illus.). 276p. 1988. pap. 18.95 (*0-295-96636-X*) U of Wash Pr.

Way of the Mother: The Lost Journey of the Feminine. Carol W. LaChance. 160p. 1991. pap. 12.95 (*1-85230-267-4*) Element MA.

Way of the Muslim. Muhammad Iqbal. (Way Ser.). 64p. (J). (gr. 3-7). 1983. pap. 10.95 (*0-7175-0632-0*) Dufour.

Way of the Mystic. Betty Bethards & Catalfo. 1995. pap. 12.95 (*1-85230-690-4*) Element MA.

***Way of the Mystic.** Joan Borysenko. 200p. 1997. write for info. (*1-56170-392-3*, 898) Hay House.

Way of the Mystics. H. C. Graef. 1977. lib. bdg. 59.95 (*0-8490-2811-6*) Gordon Pr.

Way of the Orisa. Philip J. Neimark. LC 92-53903. 208p. 1993. pap. 13.00 (*0-06-250557-2*) Harper SF.

Way of the Owl: Succeeding with Integrity in a Conflicted World. Frank Rivers. LC 95-20645. 160p. pap. 11.00 (*0-06-251397-4*) Harper SF.

Way of the Painter. Dale Marsh. 64p. (C). 1990. 100.00 (*0-86439-071-8*, Pub. by Boolarong Pubns AT) St Mut.

Way of the Peaceful Warrior: A Book That Changes Lives. LC 83-83240. 1988. audio 10.95 (*0-915811-10-3*) H J Kramer Inc.

Way of the Peaceful Warrior: A Book That Changes Lives. rev. ed. Dan Millman. LC 83-83240. 216p. (C). 1984. reprint ed. pap. 11.95 (*0-915811-00-6*) H J Kramer Inc.

***Way of the Pilgrim.** Tr. by R. M. French. 128p. 1995. pap. 5.95 (*0-687-86513-1*) Abingdon.

Way of the Pipa: Structure & Imagery in Chinese Lute Music. John E. Myers. LC 91-33965. (World Music Ser.). (Illus.). 152p. 1992. lib. bdg. 35.00 (*0-87338-455-5*) Kent St U Pr.

Way of the Rainbow Warrioress: A Handbook of Practical Wisdom. Janice Tucker. (Illus.). (Orig.). 1989. pap. 6.95 (*0-9622061-0-5*) El Rancho Pr.

Way of the Ronin: Riding the Waves of Change at Work. Beverly A. Potter. (Illus.). 252p. 1989. reprint ed. pap. 9.95 (*0-914171-26-7*) Ronin Pub.

***Way of the Sages: How to Understand & Practice Ancient Mystical Philosophy.** unabridged ed. Abhaya A. Muata. (Illus.). 160p. (Orig.). 1997. pap. 14.99 (*1-884564-23-2*) Cruzian Mystic.

Way of the Saints: The Collected Short Writings of Kirpal Singh. 2nd ed. Kirpal Singh. Ed. by Russell Perkins. LC 76-21987. 402p. 1989. 10.00 (*0-89142-026-6*) Sant Bani Ash.

Way of the Samurai. Eiji Yoshikawa. Tr. by Charles S. Terry from JPN. (Musashi Bks.: No. I). 1990. mass mkt. 4.50 (*0-671-73483-0*) PB.

***Way of the Samurai Musashi, Bk. 1.** Yoshikawa. 1989. mass mkt. 3.95 (*0-671-66421-2*) PB.

Way of the Scarlet Pimpernel. Baroness E. Orczy. 24.95 (*0-8488-1442-8*) Amereon Ltd.

Way of the Scarlet Pimpernel. Emmuska Orczy. 318p. 1983. reprint ed. lib. bdg. 27.95 (*0-89966-461-X*) Buccaneer Bks.

Way of the Scout. Tom Brown, Jr. 288p. (Orig.). 1995. pap. 12.00 (*0-425-14779-7*, Berkley Trade) Berkley Pub.

***Way of the Scout.** Tom Brown, Jr. 288p. 1997. mass mkt. 6.99 (*0-425-15910-8*) Berkley Pub.

Way of the Sea. Norman Duncan. LC 76-121537. (Short Story Index Reprint Ser.). 1977. 23.95 (*0-8369-3493-8*) Ayer.

Way of the Sea see Corridors of Time: New Haven & London, 1927-1956

Way of the Seeded Earth, 2 vols. Joseph Campbell. 1989. 50.00 (*0-685-74089-7*, PL) HarpC.

Way of the Shaman. Michael Harner. LC 89-46444. (Illus.). 208p. 1990. reprint ed. pap. 12.00 (*0-06-250373-1*) Harper SF.

Way of the Sikh. W. H. McLeod. (Way Ser.). 64p. (J). (gr. 4-8). 1986. pap. 10.95 (*0-7175-0731-9*) Dufour.

Way of the Skeptical Nutrition. Weiner. 1981. 12.95 (*0-02-625620-7*) Macmillan.

Way of the Soul. 2nd ed. Maria Illo. 36p. 1994. pap. 5.00 (*0-9613159-1-1*) Emerald Forest.

***Way of the Spirit.** Time-Life Books Editors. LC 96-48059. (Illus.). 228p. 1997. write for info. (*0-7835-4908-3*) Time-Life.

Way of the Stars. Ghislaine Vautier. (Illus.). 32p. (J). 1989. pap. text ed. 9.95 (*0-521-37913-X*) Cambridge U Pr.

Way of the Sufi. Idries Shah. 283p. 1983. 25.00 (*0-900860-80-4*, Pub. by Octagon Pr UK) ISHK.

Way of the Sufi. Idries Shah. 320p. 1991. reprint ed. pap. 12.95 (*0-14-019252-2*, Arkana) Viking Penguin.

Way of the Sun. White Eagle Staff. 112p. 1982. 9.95 (*0-85487-055-5*, Pub. by White Eagle UK) DeVorss.

***Way of the Sun Dragon: Chinese Martial Art of Tai-Yang Lung Tao.** Kenneth A. Smith. LC 92-31468. (Illus.). 136p. pap. 38.80 (*0-608-04961-1*, 2065540) Bks Demand.

***Way of the Superior Man: A Man's Guide to Mastering the Challenge of Women, Work, & Sexual Desire.** David Deida. LC 96-72534. 256p. 1997. 23.95 (*1-889762-10-5*) Plexus.

Way of the Sword: Musashi, Bk. III. Eiji Yoshikawa. 1989. mass mkt. 4.99 (*0-671-67721-7*) PB.

Way of the Topi. Thomas Anderson. (Orig.). (J). (gr. 6-9). 1996. pap. write for info. (*0-88092-125-0*) Royal Fireworks.

***Way of the Traitor: A Samurai Mystery.** Laura J. Rowland. LC 96-41706. 1997. 24.00 (*0-679-44900-0*, Vin) Random.

Way of the Trout: Anglers, Wild Fish & Running Water. M. R. Montgomery. 288p. 1993. reprint ed. pap. 11.00 (*0-380-71884-7*) Avon.

***Way of the Warrior.** James. LC 97-20324. 1997. 21.95 (*0-312-17061-0*) St Martin.

Way of the Warrior. Time-Life Books Editors. LC 92-22261. (American Indians Ser.). 1993. write for info. (*0-8094-9416-7*); lib. bdg. write for info. (*0-8094-9417-5*) Time-Life.

Way of the Warrior: The Paradox of the Martial Arts. Howard Reid & Michael Croucher. (Illus.). 240p. 1991. 35.00 (*0-87951-433-7*) Overlook Pr.

W

An Asterisk (*) at the beginning of an entry indicates that the title is appearing in BIP for the first time.

Way of the Warrior: The Paradox of the Martial Arts. Howard Reid & Michael Croucher. (Illus.). 240p. 1995. pap. 23.95 (0-87951-606-2) Overlook Pr.

Way of the Warrior: The Violent Side. Loren Christiansen. 128p. 1991. 15.00 (0-87364-627-4) Paladin Pr.

Way of the Warrior: Walking the Sacred Path. David Scott. 269p. (Orig.). 1995. pap. 12.95 (0-9636435-7-6) M A P.

***Way of the Warrior-Trader: The Financial Risk-Taker's Guide to Samurai Courage, Confidence, & Discipline.** LC 96-40909. 240p. 1997. 24.95 (0-7863-1163-0) Irwin Prof Pubng.

Way of the Wasp: How It Made America, & How It Can Save It, So to Speak. Richard Brookhiser. 261p. 1990. text ed. 24.95 (0-02-904721-8, Free Press) Free Pr.

Way of the Whitetail: Magic & Mystery. Dennis L. Olson. (Illus.). 160p. 1994. 35.00 (1-55971-427-1) NorthWord.

Way of the Wicked. Catherine Lanigan. 448p. (Orig.). 1993. mass mkt. 4.99 (0-380-76947-6) Avon.

Way of the Willow. Linda Shaw. (Men Made in America Ser.). 1994. mass mkt. 3.59 (0-373-45160-1, 1-45160-8) Silhouette.

Way of the Willow Branch. Emery Bernhard. LC 95-9977. (Illus.). 32p. (J). (ps-3). 1996. 15.00 (0-15-200844-6) HarBrace.

***Way of the Winner.** Mac Hammond. 1996. pap. 1.00 (1-57399-030-2) Mac Hammond.

Way of the Winner: Running the Race to Victory. Mac Hammond. 27p. 1993. pap. 1.00 (1-57399-005-1) Mac Hammond.

Way of the Wizard. Deepak Chopra. 176p. 1996. 15.95 (0-517-70434-X, Harmony) Crown Pub Group.

Way of the Wolf. Martin Bell. (Epiphany Bks.). 144p. 1983. mass mkt. 5.99 (0-345-30522-1) Ballantine.

Way of the Wolf. Rebecca Daniels. (Montana Mavericks Ser.). 1995. pap. 3.99 (0-373-50171-4, 1-50171-7) Harlequin Bks.

Way of the Wolf. L. David Mech. LC 91-14415. (Illus.). 120p. 1991. 29.95 (0-89658-163-2) Voyageur Pr.

Way of the Wolf. L. David Mech. LC 91-14415. (Illus.). 120p. 1995. pap. text ed. 19.95 (0-89658-179-9) Voyageur Pr.

Way of the Woman Writer. Janet L. Roseman. LC 94-22764. 156p. (Orig.). 1994. lib. bdg. 29.95 (1-56024-905-6) Haworth Pr.

Way of the Woman Writer. Janet L. Roseman. LC 94-22764. (Illus.). 120p. (Orig.). 1994. pap. 12.95 (1-56023-860-7) Haworth Pr.

Way of the World. Nicholas Bouvier. Tr. by Robyn Marsack. 220p. (FRE.). 1992. pap. 14.95 (0-910395-87-X) Marlboro Pr.

Way of the World. Nicolas Bouvier. Tr. by Robyn Marsack from FRE. LC 92-60851. 220p. 1992. 29.95 (0-910395-86-1) Marlboro Pr.

Way of the World. William Congreve. Ed. by Henry T. Perry. (Crofts Classics Ser.). 128p. 1951. pap. write for info. (0-88295-024-X) Harlan Davidson.

Way of the World. William Congreve. LC 59-1770. 128p. 1996. pap. 6.95 (1-85459-198-3, Pub. by N Hern Bks UK) Theatre Comm.

Way of the World. William Congreve. 80p. 1993. reprint ed. pap. text ed. 1.00 (0-486-27787-9) Dover.

Way of the World. William Congreve. Ed. by Kathleen M. Lynch. LC 65-10543. xxii, 136p. 1965. reprint ed. pap. text ed. 8.95 (0-8032-5354-0, Bison Books) U of Nebr Pr.

Way of the World: Level 10. Evertts. 1986. 32.00 (0-03-002354-8) HB Schl Dept.

Way of the World: The Bildungsroman in European Culture. Franco Moretti. 288p. 1987. 60.00 (0-86091-159-4, A1199, Pub. by Verso UK) Routledge Chapman & Hall.

Way of the World: The Bildungsroman in European Culture. Franco Moretti. 288p. (C). 1987. pap. text ed. 20.00 (0-86091-891-2, A1128, Pub. by Vrso UK) Norton.

***Way of the World Level 10.** Evertts. 1986. wbk. ed., pap. text ed. 13.50 (0-03-002358-0) HR&W Schl Div.

Way of the World see Restoration Plays

Way of the World see Six Restoration Plays

Way of the World 1983: Level 10. Evertts. 1983. wbk. ed., pap. 14.75 (0-03-069268-7) HB Schl Dept.

Way of Theology in Karl Barth: Essays & Comments. Ed. by H. Martin Rumscheidt. LC 86-15069. (Princeton Theological Monographs: No. 8). 1986. pap. 12.00 (0-915138-61-1) Pickwick.

Way of Things. Kathleen Iddings. 60p. (Orig.). 1984. pap. 4.95 (0-942424-06-9) W Anglia Pubns.

Way of Things: A Philosophy of Knowledge, Nature & Value. William P. Montague. LC 75-3283. reprint ed. 49.50 (0-404-59271-6) AMS Pr.

Way of Thinking: A Primer on the Art of Being a Doctor. Eugene A. Stead, Jr. Ed. by Barton F. Haynes. LC 95-68700. (Illus.). 180p. 1995. pap. 24.95 (0-89089-753-0) Carolina Acad Pr.

Way of Torah: An Introduction to Judaism. 5th ed. Jacob Neusner. LC 92-12408. 212p. (C). 1993. pap. 26.95 (0-534-16938-4) Wadsworth Pub.

***Way of Torah: An Introduction to Judaism.** 6th ed. Jacob Neusner. LC 96-39049. (The Religious Life in History Ser.). (C). 1997. pap. text ed. 26.95 (0-534-51568-1) Wadsworth Pub.

Way of Tradition, Vol. 1. Sun M. Moon. 326p. reprint ed. pap. 6.95 (0-910621-22-5) HSA Pubns.

Way of Tradition, Vol. 2. Sun M. Moon. 295p. reprint ed. pap. 6.95 (0-910621-23-3) HSA Pubns.

Way of Tradition III. Sun M. Moon. 541p. reprint ed. pap. 6.95 (0-910621-24-1) HSA Pubns.

Way of Tradition IV. Sun M. Moon. 462p. 1980. pap. 8.00 (0-910621-35-7) HSA Pubns.

Way of Transformation. Karlfried G. Durckheim. (Unwin Paperbacks Ser.). 112p. 1988. pap. 10.95 (0-04-291014-5) Routledge Chapman & Hall.

Way of Transformation. Karlfried G. Durckheim. 1990. pap. 10.95 (0-04-292020-5) Routledge Chapman & Hall.

Way of Transformation: Daily Life As Spiritual Exercise. Karlfried G. Durckheim. 1988. pap. 10.95 (0-685-44222-5) Routledge Chapman & Hall.

Way of Universal Teaching. Michael Schwartz & Phyllis Schwartz. 144p. 1994. pap. 13.00 (1-886722-00-5) Maps Pub.

Way of Vaisnava Sages: A Medieval Story of South Indian Sadhus. N. S. Narasimha & Ramananda Babaji. LC 86-28251. (Sanskrit Notes of Visnu-vijay Swami Ser.). 422p. (Orig.). 1987. lib. bdg. 59.50 (0-8191-6060-1) U Pr of Amer.

Way of Vincent de Paul: A Contemporary Spirituality in the Service of the Poor. 3rd ed. Robert C. Maloney. 176p. 1992. pap. 9.95 (1-56548-001-5) New City.

***Way of Water & Sprouts of Virtue.** Sarah Allan. LC 96-36341. (SUNY Series in Chinese Philosophy & Culture). (Illus.). 195p. (C). 1997. pap. text ed. 17.95 (0-7914-3386-2) State U NY Pr.

***Way of Water & Sprouts of Virtue.** Sarah Allan. LC 96-36341. (SUNY Series in Chinese Philosophy & Culture). (Illus.). 195p. (C). 1997. text ed. 53.50 (0-7914-3385-4) State U NY Pr.

Way of Wind. Paul J. Lederer. (Indian Heritage Ser.: No. 5). 1989. pap. 3.50 (0-451-14038-9) NAL-Dutton.

Way of Wisdom: An Investigation of the Meanings of the Letters of the Hebrew Alphabet Considered as a Remnant of Chaldean Wisdom. Florence Farr. 1994. pap. 4.95 (1-55818-290-X, Sure Fire) Holmes Pub.

Way of Woman: Awakening the Perennial Feminine. Helen M. Luke. LC 95-15929. 256p. 1995. 22.50 (0-385-47850-X) Doubleday.

Way of Woman: Awakening the Perennial Feminine. Helen M. Luke. 224p. 1996. pap. 10.95 (0-385-48574-3) Doubleday.

Way of Women & Other Essays. Helen Luke. 144p. 1995. 17.95 (0-930407-32-6) Parabola Bks.

Way of Work & a Way of Life: Coal Mining in Thurber, Texas, 1888-1926. Marilyn D. Rhinehart. LC 91-35907. (Southwestern Studies: No. 9). (Illus.). 192p. 1992. 39.50 (0-89096-499-8) Tex A&M Univ Pr.

Way of Working: The Spiritual Dimension of Craft. 5th ed. Ed. by D. M. Dooling & Pamela L. Travers. 128p. 1986. reprint ed. pap. text ed. 8.95 (0-930407-01-6) Parabola Bks.

Way of World. 2nd ed. William Congreve. (New Mermaid Ser.). (C). Date not set. pap. text ed. 6.95 (0-393-90074-6) Norton.

Way of Z: Formal Methods Demystified. Jonathan Jacky. 320p. (C). 1996. text ed. 74.95 (0-521-55041-6) Cambridge U Pr.

Way of Z: Practical Programming with Formal Methods. Jonathan Jacky. 320p. (C). 1996. pap. text ed. 29.95 (0-521-55976-6) Cambridge U Pr.

Way of Zen. Alan Watts. 1989. pap. 10.00 (0-679-72301-3, Vin) Random.

Way Off Broadway: A Complete Guide to Producing Musicals with School & Community Groups. Lynn M. Soeby. LC 91-52744. (Illus.). 167p. 1991. pap. 24.95 (0-89950-629-1) McFarland & Co.

Way off the Church Wall. Rob Portlock. LC 89-11230. (Illus.). 108p. (Orig.). 1989. pap. 6.99 (0-8308-1281-4, 1281) InterVarsity.

Way Out. 1971. pap. 6.95 (0-87516-302-5) DeVorss.

Way Out. James H. Carlisle. LC 93-94243. 168p. (Orig.). 1994. pap. 8.00 (1-56002-410-0, Univ Edtns) Aegina Pr.

Way Out. Jeanne Guyon. (Orig.). 1993. pap. 9.95 (0-940232-20-0) Seedsowers.

Way Out: A Story of the Cumberland Today. Emerson Hough. 1976. lib. bdg. 14.75 (0-89968-048-8, Lghtyr Pr) Buccaneer Bks.

Way Out: Anarchist, Mutualist & Individualist Essays. Laurance Labadie. (Men & Movements in the History & Philosophy of Anarchism Ser.). 1980. lib. bdg. 250.00 (0-686-60065-7) Revisionist Pr.

Way Out: Libertarian & Mutualist Essays on Free Banking, Free Land & Individualism. Vardis Fisher et al. 1979. lib. bdg. 250.00 (0-87700-267-3) Revisionist Pr.

Way Out Book. John-Roger. 1980. pap. 5.00 (0-914829-23-8) Mandeville LA.

Way Out Here: Modern Life in Ice-Age Alaska. Richard Leo. 208p. (Orig.). 1996. pap. 14.95 (1-57061-061-4) Sasquatch Bks.

Way Out in Idaho: A Centennial Collection of Stories & Songs. Intro. by Rosalie Sorrels. LC 90-83710. (Illus.). 240p. 1991. pap. 25.00 (0-917652-83-5) Confluence Pr.

Way Out in Space. Illus. by Nate Evans. (Sticker Stories Ser.). 16p. (Orig.). (J). (ps). 1996. pap. 4.95 (0-448-41308-6, G&D) Putnam Pub Group.

Way Out of Agnosticism: Or the Philosophy of Free Religion. Francis E. Abbot. LC 75-3014. (Philosophy in America Ser.). reprint ed. 34.50 (0-404-59008-X) AMS Pr.

Way out of Educational Confusion. John Dewey. LC 72-104267. 41p. 1971. reprint ed. text ed. 45.00 (0-8371-3918-X, DEEC, Greenwood Pr) Greenwood.

***Way Out of No Way.** Jacqueline Woodson. (YA). (gr. 7 up). 1997. mass mkt. 4.50 (0-449-70460-2, Juniper) Fawcett.

Way Out of No Way: The Spiritual Memoirs of Andrew Young. Andrew J. Young. 192p. 1995. pap. 14.99 (0-7852-7508-8) Nelson.

Way Out of No Way: Writing about Growing up Black in America. Ed. by Jacqueline Woodson. 160p. (YA). (gr. 7 up). 1996. 15.95 (0-8050-4570-8, B Martin BYR) H Holt & Co.

Way Out of the Dead End: A Plea for Peace. Huschmand Sabet. Tr. by Patricia Crampton from GER. 1986. 13.50 (0-85398-245-7); pap. 7.95 (0-85398-240-6) G Ronald Pub.

Way Out of the Trap: An Innovative & Unique Ten-Step Program for Spiritual Growth. Nathan Rutstein. Ed. by Beth Hinshaw. LC 92-63009. 176p. (Orig.). 1995. pap. 11.95 (0-9633001-2-1) Whitcomb MA.

Way Out of Vietnam. Patricia. 166p. (Orig.). 1980. pap. 3.00 (0-935146-21-0) Morningland.

Way Out on the Mountain. William R. Filler. LC 90-60091. 1990. 18.95 (0-87212-237-9) Libra.

Way Out West. Jane Stern. LC 92-56223. 416p. 1994. pap. 18.00 (0-06-092560-4, HarpT) HarpC.

***Way Out West: Story of the Pony Express.** Darice Bailer. LC 97-7206. (Smithsonian Odyssey Ser.). (Illus.). 32p. (J). (gr. 1-4). 1997. 14.95 (1-56899-464-8); pap. 5.95 (1-56899-465-6) Soundprints.

***Way Out West Lives.** Jillian Lund. 1997. pap. 4.99 (0-14-056232-X) Viking Penguin.

Way Out West Lives a Coyote Named Frank. Jillian Lund. LC 91-46011. (Illus.). 32p. (J). (ps-2). 1993. pap. 14.99 (0-525-44982-5) Dutton Child Bks.

Way Past Cool. Jess Mowry. 288p. 1992. 17.00 (0-374-28669-8) FS&G.

Way Past Cool. Jess Mowry. LC 92-54377. 320p. 1993. pap. 12.00 (0-06-097545-8, PL) HarpC.

Way Past Dead. Steven Womack. (Orig.). 1995. mass mkt. 5.99 (0-345-39043-1) Ballantine.

Way Prepared: Arabic & Islamic Studies in Honor of Bayly Winder. Ed. by Farhad Kazemi & Robert D. McChesney. (Illus.). 352p. (C). 1988. text ed. 40.00 (0-8147-4591-1) NYU Pr.

Way Schools Work: A Sociological Analysis of Education. Kathleen P. Bennett & Margaret D. LeCompte. Orig. Title: How Schools Work. 320p. (C). 1995. pap. text ed. 23.95 (0-685-73079-4) Longman.

Way Schools Work: A Sociological Analysis of Education. 2nd ed. Kathleen B. DeMarrais & Margaret D. LeCompte. LC 94-21574. 384p. (C). 1995. pap. text ed. 39.95 (0-8013-1245-0) Longman.

Way Science Works: An Illustrated Exploration of Technology in Action. Frwd. by John Durant. 288p. 1995. 35.00 (0-02-860822-4) Macmillan Info.

Way She Looks Tonight. Marian Fowler. LC 96-3117. 336p. 1996. 24.95 (0-312-14757-0) St Martin.

Way Some People Live. John Cheever. 1994. lib. bdg. 24.95 (1-56849-389-4) Buccaneer Bks.

Way South. large type ed. Robert J. Conley. LC 94-16395. 254p. 1994. lib. bdg. 17.95 (0-7862-0242-4) Thorndike Pr.

Way Station. Lesley Einer. 58p. (Orig.). 1993. pap. 5.00 (0-9620822-4-4) Sage Shadow Pr.

Way Station. Clifford D. Simak. 240p. 1986. mass mkt. 5.99 (0-345-33246-6, Avery Pub) Ballantine.

Way Station. Clifford D. Simak. 1993. reprint ed. lib. bdg. 18.95 (0-89968-367-3, Lghtyr Pr) Buccaneer Bks.

Way Station. Clifford D. Simak. LC 79-20182. 1980. reprint ed. lib. bdg. 18.00 (0-8376-0440-0) Bentley.

Way Stations. Henry Gould. 36p. (Orig.). 1990. pap. 4.00 (0-945926-17-0) Paradigm RI.

Way Stations to Heaven. 224p. 1996. 15.95 (0-02-860576-4) Macmillan.

Way That I Followed: A Naturalist's Journey Around Ireland. Frank Mitchell. (Illus.). 288p. 1995. 35.00 (0-946172-21-8, TCH220X, Pub. by Town Hse IE); pap. 21.95 (0-946172-20-X, Pub. by Town Hse IE) R Rinehart.

***Way That Water Enters Stone: Stories.** John Dufresne. 1997. pap. 10.95 (0-452-27731-0, Plume-Truman Talley Bks) NAL-Dutton.

Way the Angel Spreads Her Wings. Barry Callaghan. LC 90-24641. 296p. 1991. 22.50 (0-86538-073-2) Ontario Rev NJ.

Way the Earth Works. Peter J. Wyllie. 296p. (C). 1976. Net. pap. text ed. 34.50 (0-471-96896-X) Wiley.

Way the Modern World Works: World Hegemony to World Impasse. Peter J. Taylor. 1996. text ed. 60.00 (0-471-96586-3) Wiley.

Way, the Truth & the Light. Hua-Ching Ni. LC 92-50543. 232p. 1993. 22.95 (0-937064-67-X) SevenStar Comm.

Way, the Truth, & the Light. Hua-Ching Ni. LC 92-50543. 232p. (Orig.). 1994. pap. 14.95 (0-937064-56-4) SevenStar Comm.

***Way, the Truth, the Light: Secrets of My Culture.** John Ravenscroft. 115p. (Orig.). 1997. mass mkt. 4.99 (1-55237-153-0, Pub. by Comnwlth Pub CN) Partners Pubs Grp.

Way, the Walk, the Warfare of the Believer. Frederick K. Price. 403p. (Orig.). 1994. pap. 10.99 (1-883798-06-X) Faith One.

***Way the Wind Blew.** Ron Jacobs. (C). 1997. text ed. 60.00 (1-85984-861-3, Pub. by Verso UK) Routledge Chapman & Hall.

***Way the Wind Blew: A History of the Weather Underground.** Ron Jacobs. 1997. pap. 18.00 (1-85984-167-8, Pub. by Verso UK) Routledge Chapman & Hall.

Way the Words Are Taken. Robin Fulton. (C). 1994. pap. 39.95 (0-86334-064-4, Pub. by Saltire Soc) St Mut.

Way the World Is. John C. Polkinghorne. LC 84-1527. 140p. reprint ed. pap. 39.90 (0-685-15952-3, 2027549) Bks Demand.

Way the World Is: Cultural Processes & Social Relations among the Mombasa Swahili. Marc J. Swartz. (Illus.). 450p. 1991. 45.00 (0-520-07137-9) U CA Pr.

Way the World Works. 3rd ed. Jude Wanniski. 1989. 24.95 (0-938081-04-7); pap. 12.95 (0-938081-05-5) Polyconomics.

Way the World Works: The Journey from Chaos to Peace. Myra Estelle. 70p. (Orig.). 1996. pap. 12.00 (0-9651771-0-6) Myco Pr.

Way They Learn. Cynthia U. Tobias. LC 94-14104. 1994. 14.99 (1-56179-253-5) Focus Family.

Way They Learn. Cynthia U. Tobias. 1995. pap. 10.99 (1-56179-414-7) Focus Family.

Way They Saw Us: The South Dakota State Historical Society Collection of Images from the Nineteenth-Century Illustrated Press. John E. Miller & Mark J. Halvorson. Ed. by Nancy T. Koupal. LC 89-50608. (Illus.). 64p. (Orig.). 1989. pap. 6.95 (0-9622621-0-2) SD State Hist Soc.

Way They Should Go: Correcting Children Correctly. 2nd ed. Laura L. Tolles. Ed. by Carolyn Goyne. (Illus.). 84p. (Orig.). reprint ed. pap. text ed. 4.50 (0-9634371-0-0) L L Tolles.

Way They Should Go: Correcting Children Corrrectly. 2nd ed. Laura L. Tolles & Carolyn Goyne. (Illus.). 84p. 1995. pap. text ed. 4.50 (1-55673-016-0) L L Tolles.

***Way They Wore, Doll Costumes & Accessories 1925-1980.** Florence Therialt. (Illus.). 120p. 1996. pap. 33.00 (0-614-23816-1, N4787) Hobby Hse.

Way Things Are. Phillip Corwin. 96p. (Orig.). (C). 1985. pap. 5.95 (0-933515-06-5) Exile Pr.

Way Things Are. Allen Wheelis. Ed. by Jeff Putnam. 181p. 1994. 18.00 (1-880909-14-6) Baskerville.

Way Things Are: A Living Approach to Buddhism for Today's World. Ole Nydahl & Lama O. Nydahl. LC 96-35059. (Illus.). 96p. (Orig.). 1996. pap. 10.00 (0-931892-38-4) B Dolphin Pub.

***Way Things Are: Basic Readings in Metaphysics.** William R. Carter et al. LC 97-10598. 1997. write for info. (0-07-010198-1) McGraw.

***Way Things Are: The Basic Precepts of Reality & Common Sense.** Charles Hoppins. Ed. by Sarah Roberts. LC 97-60599. 186p. (Orig.). 1997. pap. 15.95 (1-882567-26-9) Wstrn Res Inst.

Way Things Are: The Stories of Rachel Maddux. Rachel Maddux. LC 91-40099. 296p. 1992. 28.95 (0-87049-751-0) U of Tenn Pr.

Way Things Are: Thoughts on the Mystery & Meaning of Life. Peter W. Jedlicka. LC 95-41482. 144p. 1996. 12.95 (0-944957-81-1) Rivercross Pub.

Way Things Are or Could Be. Myrtle Stedman. LC 96-19959. 1996. pap. write for info. (0-86534-255-5) Sunstone Pr.

Way Things Aren't: Rush Limbaugh's Reign of Error. 1995. pap. 41.70 (1-56584-299-5) New Press NY.

Way Things Aren't: Rush Limbaugh's Reign of Error. Fairness & Accuracy in Reporting Staff. LC 94-46494. 128p. 1995. 6.95 (1-56584-260-X) New Press NY.

Way Things Ought to Be. large type ed. Rush H. Limbaugh, III. LC 92-38202. (General Ser.). 1993. lib. bdg. 23.95 (0-8161-5731-6, GK Hall) Thorndike Pr.

Way Things Ought to Be. Rush Limbaugh. Ed. by Judith Regan. 352p. 1993. reprint ed. pap. 6.99 (0-671-75150-6, Pocket Star Bks) PB.

Way Things Oughta' Be Told. Burt Grossman & Bill Kushner. Ed. by Susan Smith. (Illus.). 320p. 1996. 24.50 (1-885758-06-5) Quality Sports.

Way Things Really Are. Roger B. Hooper. 80p. (Orig.). 1992. pap. 5.95 (0-929956-09-5) Hooper Group.

***Way Things Work, 2 Vols.** 1996. 39.95 incl. cd-rom (0-7894-1599-2) DK Pub Inc.

Way Things Work. David Macaulay. (Illus.). 400p. (J). (ps up). 1988. 29.95 (0-395-42857-2) HM.

Way Through the Mountains. Steve Frazee. 352p. 1996. reprint ed. mass mkt., pap. text ed. 4.99 (0-8439-3945-1) Dorchester Pub Co.

Way Through the Sea. Robert Elmer. (Young Underground Ser.: Vol. 1). 176p. (J). (gr. 3-8). 1994. pap. 5.99 (1-55661-374-1) Bethany Hse.

Way Through the Wilderness: The Natchez Trace & the Civilization of the Southern Frontier. William C. Davis. LC 94-42289. 400p. 1995. 30.00 (0-06-016921-4) HarpC.

Way Through the Wilderness: The Natchez Trace & the Civilization of the Southern Frontier. William C. Davis. (Illus.). 416p. 1996. pap. 16.95 (0-8071-2132-0) La State U Pr.

Way Through the Woods. Colin Dexter. 1994. mass mkt. 5.99 (0-8041-1142-1) Ivy Books.

Way Through the Woods. large type ed. Colin Dexter. LC 93-13448. 1993. lib. bdg. 21.95 (1-56054-764-2) Thorndike Pr.

Way Through the Woods. large type ed. Colin Dexter. LC 93-13448. 1994. lib. bdg. 14.95 (1-56054-765-0) Thorndike Pr.

Way to a Man's Heart. Candy Coleman. (Illus.). 32p. (Orig.). 1979. pap. text ed. 3.00 (0-943768-02-0) C Coleman.

Way to a New Life. John C. Wenger. LC 77-86326. (Mennonite Faith Ser.: Vol. 3). 72p. 1977. reprint ed. pap. 25.00 (0-608-01745-0, 2062403) Bks Demand.

Way to an "A" How to Help Your Child Succeed in School. Jan Barrick. LC 93-26787. 150p. 1994. pap. 12.95 (1-56825-009-6); pap. 29.95 incl. vhs (1-56825-010-X) Rainbow Books.

***Way to Awaken: Exercises to Enliven Body, Self & Soul.** Robert Masters. LC 96-54724. (Illus.). 288p. 1997. pap. 12.95 (0-8356-0754-2, Quest) Theos Pub Hse.

Way to Be Free. J. G. Bennett. 196p. 1980. pap. 12.50 (0-87728-491-1) Weiser.

***Way to Bethlehem.** Inos Biffi. LC 97-21274. (Illus.). (J). 1997. write for info. (0-8028-5159-2) Eerdmans.

Way to Bliss in Three Books, 1658, 3 bks. Elias Ashmole. 221p. 1993. Set. pap. 24.95 (1-56459-347-9) Kessinger Pub.

Way to Captain Yankee's. Anne Rockwell. LC 92-44644. (Illus.). 32p. (J). (ps-2). 1994. lib. bdg. 13.95 (0-02-777271-3, Mac Bks Young Read) S&S Childrens.

Way to Christ. Pope John Paul, II. LC 83-48426. 1994. pap. 12.00 (0-06-064216-5) Harper SF.

W

An Asterisk (*) at the beginning of an entry indicates that the title is appearing in BIP for the first time.

Way to Christ: Of True Repentance; of True Resignation; of Regeneration; of the Supersensual Life. Jacob Boehme. 159p. 1992. pap. 12.95 (*1-56459-218-9*) Kessinger Pub.

Way to Cook. Julia Child. LC 89-45832. (Illus.). 544p. 1989. 65.00 (*0-394-53264-3*) Knopf.

Way to Cook. Julia Child. (Illus.). 1993. pap. 35.00 (*0-679-74765-6*) Knopf.

Way to Danish. 3rd ed. E. Norlev. 306p. 1983. pap. 58.00 (*87-16-00998-3*) IBD Ltd.

Way to Durable Peace. M. N. Roy. (C). 1986. 6.50 (*0-8364-2198-1*, Pub. by Minerva II) S Asia.

Way to Eternal Life. Gordon Lindsay. (Literature Crusade Ser.). 1965. pap. 0.95 (*0-614-06170-9*) Christ for the Nations.

Way to Eternal Life (El Camino A la Vida Eterna) Gordon Lindsay. (SPA.). 1965. pap. 0.95 (*0-89985-374-9*) Christ for the Nations.

Way to Freedom: Core Teachings of Tibetan Buddhism. Dalai Lama. Ed. by Don Lopez. LC 94-31891. 144p. 1994. 16.00 (*0-06-061722-5*) Harper SF.

***Way to Garden: A Hands-on Primer for Every Season.** Margaret Roach. LC 97-13997. 1998. write for info. (*0-517-70733-0*, C P Pubs) Crown Pub Group.

Way to Get Dead. large type ed. William Newton. (Linford Mystery Library). 1991. pap. 15.99 (*0-7089-7071-0*) Ulverscroft.

Way to Get What You Want. W. M. Davis. 1941. pap. 3.50 (*0-88027-022-5*) Firm Foun Pub.

Way to Glory: Major General Sir Henry Havelock - the Christian Soldier. John Pollock. (History Makers Ser.). 304p. 1996. reprint ed. pap. 11.99 (*1-85792-245-X*, Pub. by Christian Focus UK) Spring Arbor Dist.

Way to Go: Academic Travel Pack. Gloria M. Prather & Alfred G. Prather. Ed. by Arden C. Prather & Ellen Smith. (Illus.). 48p. (J). (gr. k-2). 1987. student ed. write for info. (*0-9619655-0-9*) Academic Parks Co.

Way to Go! Crating Artwork for Travel. Stephen A. Horne. (Illus.). 53p. 1985. 10.00 (*0-934483-05-1*) Gal Assn NY.

Way to Go, Coach! A Scientifically Validated Approach to Coaching Effectiveness. Ronald E. Smith & Frank L. Smoll. 140p. (Orig.). 1996. pap. 15.95 (*1-886346-01-1*) Warde Pubs.

Way to God. Dwight L. Moody. 160p. 1984. mass mkt. 4.99 (*0-88368-131-5*) Whitaker Hse.

Way to God. Dwight L. Moody. (Moody Classics Ser.). 1996. mass mkt., pap. 4.99 (*0-8024-5447-X*) Moody.

Way to God: A Biography of George More. Mary More. (C). 1990. text ed. 45.00 (*0-947988-45-9*, Pub. by Wild Goose Pubns UK) St Mut.

Way to God see Camino Hacia Dios

Way to God as Taught by Sri Ramakrishna. Swami Lokeswarananda. 475p. pap. 20.00 (*0-87481-693-9*) Vedanta Ctr.

Way to God As Taught by Sri Ramakrishna. Swami Lokeswarananda. 457p. (Orig.). 1993. pap. 20.00 (*0-87481-572-X*, Pub. by Ramakrishna Math II) Vedanta Pr.

Way to Godhood. R. Swinburne Clymer. 192p. 1970. reprint ed. spiral bd. 10.50 (*0-7873-0181-7*) Hlth Research.

Way to Godhood (1914) R. Swinburne Clymer. 189p. 1996. pap. 17.95 (*1-56459-667-2*) Kessinger Pub.

Way to Greece. Harold Melcher & Joan Melcher. LC 84-18400. (Illus.). 113p. (Orig.). 1984. pap. 8.95 (*0-87233-077-X*) Bauhan.

Way to Ground Zero: The Atomic Bomb in American Science Fiction. Martha A. Bartter. LC 88-15461. (Contributions to the Study of Science Fiction & Fantasy Ser.: No. 33). 290p. 1988. text ed. 55.00 (*0-313-25892-9*, BBT/, Greenwood Pr) Greenwood.

Way to Grow: Dynamic Church Growth Through Small Groups. Ronald J. Lavin. 208p. (Orig.). 1996. pap. 15.00 (*0-7880-0733-5*) CSS OH.

Way to Happiness. Alfred A. Montapert. LC 77-13678. 1978. pap. 10.00 (*0-9603174-3-0*) Bks of Value.

Way to Happiness. Alfred A. Montapert. (Eternal Quest of Mankind Ser.). 1978. pap. 10.00 (*0-13-946228-7*) Borden.

Way to Happiness. Iverna M. Tompkins. 176p. 1983. pap. text ed. 2.50 (*0-9611260-0-0*) I Tompkins.

Way to Happiness. deluxe ed. L. Ron Hubbard. 1984. 37.50 (*0-88404-411-4*) Bridge Pubns Inc.

***Way to Happiness: A Common Sense Guide to Better Living.** L. Ron Hubbard. Date not set. pap. 12.95 (*1-57318-040-8*) Bridge Pubns Inc.

Way to Happiness: An Inspiring Guide to Peace, Hope & Contentment. Fulton J. Sheen. LC 97-19481. 1997. reprint ed. mass mkt. 5.95 (*0-8189-0775-4*) Alba.

***Way to Happiness: With White Eagle As Guide in Meditation.** Ylana Hayward. (Illus.). 128p. (Orig.). 1995. pap. write for info. (*0-85487-094-6*, Pub. by White Eagle UK) DeVorss.

Way to Health. Robert R. Leichtman & Carl Japikse. 128p. 1995. pap. 9.95 (*0-89804-805-2*, Enthea Pr) Ariel GA.

Way to Health & Fitness. (Illus.). 1996. write for info. (*1-886614-14-8*) Intl Masters Pub.

Way to Heavens Doore: An Introduction to Liturgical Process & Musical Style. Steven Plank. LC 94-34082. (Studies in Liturgical Musicology: No. 2). 183p. 1994. 27.50 (*0-8108-2953-3*) Scarecrow.

Way to Heron Mountain. Ed Zahniser. LC 86-61605. (Illus.). 38p. 1986. pap. 5.95 (*0-935939-01-6*) Night Tree Pr.

Way to Independence: Memories of a Hidatsa Indian Family, 1840-1920. Carolyn Gilman et al. LC 87-11152. (Illus.). xii, 371p. (Orig.). 1987. 24.95 (*0-87351-218-9*) Minn Hist.

Way to Inner Freedom. Erik Blumenthal. 144p. (Orig.). 1994. pap. 7.50 (*1-85168-011-X*) Onewrld Pubns.

Way to Inner Peace. rev. ed. Fulton J. Sheen. LC 94-41422. 224p. 1995. pap. 5.95 (*0-8189-0713-4*) Alba.

Way to Invest: A Five-Step Blueprint for Investing in Mutual Funds with As Little As $50 Per Month. Ginita Wall. 224p. (Orig.). 1995. pap. 10.95 (*0-8050-3493-5*, Owl) H Holt & Co.

Way to Leadership see 7 Classic Strategies in Selling

Way to Liberation: Moksha Dharma of Mahabharata, 2 vols. Swami Jyotir Maya Nanda. (Illus.). 1976. Ea. pap. 9.95 (*0-934664-11-0*) Yoga Res Foun.

Way to Life & How to Live It. Charles F. Gilmore. (Illus.). 112p. (Orig.). 1993. pap. 5.95 (*0-9627630-3-9*) Light & Living.

Way to Life & Immortality. R. Swinburne Clymer. 244p. 1948. 7.95 (*0-932785-48-4*) Philos Pub.

Way to Life & Immortality. R. Swinburne Clymer. 208p. 1976. reprint ed. spiral bd. 8.25 (*0-7873-0182-5*) Hlth Research.

Way to Life & Immortality: A Textbook That Shall Lead Man from Weakness, Disease, & Death, to Freedom from These Things (1914) R. Swinburne Clymer. 208p. 1996. pap. 18.95 (*1-56459-726-1*) Kessinger Pub.

Way to Locate Acu-Points. Ed. by Yang Jiasan. Tr. by Meng Xiankun & Li Xuewu from CHI. (Illus.). 72p. (Orig.). 1982. pap. 14.95 (*0-8351-1028-1*) China Bks.

Way to Love: The Last Meditations of Anthony de Mello. Anthony De Mello. 160p. 1992. 16.00 (*0-385-24938-1*) Doubleday.

Way to Love: The Last Meditations of Anthony de Mello. Anthony De Mello. LC 94-23993. Orig. Title: Call to Love. 208p. 1995. pap. 6.00 (*0-385-24939-X*) Doubleday.

***Way to Make Perfect Mountains: Native American Legends of Sacred Mountains.** Illus. by Leonard Chana. LC 96-40531. Orig. Title: A God on Every Mountain Top. 64p. 1997. pap. 9.95 (*0-938317-26-1*) Cinco Puntos.

***Way to Mans Heart, Vol. 1.** Dorsey. 1997. mass mkt. write for info. (*0-312-96333-5*) St Martin.

Way to Modern Man: An Introduction to Human Evolution. Fred T. Adams. LC 68-28011. (Anthropology & Education Ser.). 296p. reprint ed. pap. 84.40 (*0-317-41948-X*, 2025986) Bks Demand.

Way to Nirvana: Six Lectures on Ancient Buddhism As a Discipline of Salvation. Louis D. La Vallee Poussin. LC 77-27154. (Hibbert Lectures: 1916). reprint ed. 39.50 (*0-404-60417-X*) AMS Pr.

Way to Oneness. 4th ed. Disciples of Morningland. 1979. pap. 3.95 (*0-935146-00-8*) Morningland.

Way to Peace. 196p. 1988. pap. 2.95 (*0-87481-579-7*, Pub. by Ramakrishna Math II) Vedanta Pr.

Way to Peace: Liberation Through the Bible. L. John Topel. LC 78-9148. 207p. (Orig.). reprint ed. pap. 59.00 (*0-7837-5527-9*, 2045297) Bks Demand.

Way to Play, Bk. 1. Robert Pace. 32p. 1988. pap. 4.50 (*0-7935-3704-5*, 00371214) H Leonard.

Way To Practice The Lord's Present Move. Witness Lee. 156p. per. 6.00 (*0-87083-233-6*, 12025001) Living Stream Ministry.

Way To Practice the Lord's Present Recovery. Witness Lee. 50p. 2.00 (*0-87083-433-9*, 12026001) Living Stream Ministry.

***Way to Rainy Mountain.** N. Scott Momaday. LC 96-28570. 88p. 1996. 24.95 (*0-8165-1701-0*) U of Ariz Pr.

Way to Rainy Mountain. N. Scott Momaday. LC 69-19154. (Illus.). 90p. 1976. reprint ed. pap. 8.95 (*0-8263-0436-2*) U of NM Pr.

Way to Save: Ten-Step Blueprint Lifetime Security. Ginita Wall. 224p. 1994. pap. 8.95 (*0-8050-2705-X*) H Holt & Co.

Way to Sketch: With Special Reference to Water Color. Vernon Blake. (Illus.). 144p. 1981. reprint ed. pap. 4.95 (*0-486-24119-X*) Dover.

Way to Spiritual Mastery. Robert Wall Crary. LC 91-60438. 208p. (Orig.). 1991. pap. 10.95 (*0-914711-02-4*) Rishis Inst.

Way to Start a Day. Byrd Baylor. LC 78-113. (Illus.). 32p. (J). (ps-3). 1978. lib. bdg. 14.95 (*0-684-15651-2*, C Scribner Sons Young) S&S Childrens.

Way to Start a Day. Byrd Baylor. LC 85-28802. (Illus.). 32p. (J). (gr. 1-4). 1986. reprint ed. pap. 4.95 (*0-689-71054-2*, Aladdin Paperbacks) S&S Childrens.

Way to Survive the AIDS Epidemic: Based on the Metaphysical Teachings of the Ancient Masters. Thomas A. Berg. LC 84-108491. 84p. 1984. pap. 4.95 (*0-9613110-0-2*) Palm Pubns.

Way to the Cats. Yehoshua Kenaz. Tr. by Dalya Bilu from HEB. 325p. 1994. 20.00 (*1-883642-20-5*) Steerforth Pr.

Way to the Cats. Yehoshua Kenaz. Tr. by Dalya Bily from HEB. 325p. 1995. pap. 14.00 (*1-883642-48-5*) Steerforth Pr.

Way to the Crib. Friedrich Hoffmann & Reinhard Herrmann. (Illus.). 100p. 1989. 30.00 (*0-85439-299-8*, Pub. by St Paul Pubns UK) St Mut.

Way to the Heart of Christmas. 3rd ed. Brian Linard. 105p. 1994. pap. 6.95 (*1-56548-025-2*) New City.

Way to the Inner Mysteries: The Way to the Inner Mysteries. White Eagle Staff. (Spiritual Unfoldment Ser.: Vol. 3). 114p. 1987. 11.95 (*0-85487-075-X*, Pub. by White Eagle UK) DeVorss.

Way to the Kingdom. 2nd ed. 345p. 1972. reprint ed. pap. 11.95 (*0-87516-164-2*) DeVorss.

Way to the Labyrinth: Memories of East & West. Alain Danielou. Tr. by Marie-Claire Cournand from FRE. LC 86-28660. 352p. 1987. 23.95 (*0-8112-1014-6*); pap. 13.95 (*0-8112-1015-4*, NDP634) New Directions.

Way to the Light. Tobler. Date not set. write for info. (*0-312-03001-0*) St Martin.

Way to the Light: Pilgrimage of a Reiki Master. Yasmin Verschure. LC 96-8714. (Illus.). 256p. (Orig.). 1996. pap. 16.95 (*0-87728-877-1*) Weiser.

Way to the Mysteries. L. Gordon Plummer. 126p. 1992. pap. 10.00 (*0-913004-73-1*) Point Loma Pub.

***Way to the Pond.** Ann Racuya-Robbins. (Sesquin Americas Ser.). (Illus.). 250p. (Orig.). 1998. pap. 14.95 (*1-884434-08-8*) Images For Media.

***Way to the Quran.** Khurram Murad. 145p. 1996. pap. 8.95 (*0-614-21077-1*, 1294) Kazi Pubns.

Way to the Spirit. Adnan Sarhan. 70p. 1989. pap. 5.00 (*1-884328-07-5*) Sufi Fnd Amer.

***Way to the Towers of Silence.** Jack Royce. LC 97-60212. (Illus.). 1997. pap. 7.95 (*1-884953-03-4*, WTOS-0004) Eaton St Pr.

Way to the Uncle Sam Hotel. William D. Brown. (Orig.). 1966. pap. 2.75 (*0-940556-00-6*) Coyote.

Way to the West: Essays on the Central Plains. Elliott West. LC 95-4351. (Calvin P. Horn Lectures in Western History & Culture). (Illus.). 320p. 1995. 49.95 (*0-8263-1652-2*); pap. 19.95 (*0-8263-1653-0*) U of NM Pr.

Way to the Western Sea: Lewis & Clark Across the Continent. David Lavender. 464p. 1990. pap. 14.00 (*0-385-41155-3*, Anchor NY) Doubleday.

Way to Tin Pan Alley: American Popular Song 1866-1910. Nicholas E. Tawa. 296p. 1990. 35.00 (*0-02-872541-7*) Schirmer Bks.

Way to True Worship: A Popular Story of Hinduism. Anoop Chandola. 152p. (Orig.). (C). 1990. pap. text ed. 21.00 (*0-8191-8048-3*); lib. bdg. 44.00 (*0-8191-8047-5*) U Pr of Amer.

Way to Wealth. Benjamin Franklin. 30p. 1988. 8.95 (*0-918222-88-5*) Applewood.

***Way to Wealth.** Benjamin Franklin. Date not set. lib. bdg. 12.95 (*0-8488-1827-X*) Amereon Ltd.

Way to Wealth, Wherein Is Plainly Taught a Remedy for Sedicion. Richard Crowley. LC 74-28843. (English Experience Ser.: No. 724). 1975. reprint ed. 10.00 (*90-221-0724-8*) Walter J Johnson.

Way to Wear'Em: One Hundred & Fifty Years of Punch on Fashion. Christina Walkley. (Illus.). 190p. 1985. 36.00 (*0-317-61362-6*, Pub. by P Owen Ltd UK) Dufour.

Way to Wear'em: One Hundred Fifty Years of Punch on Fashion. Christina Walkley. (Illus.). 192p. 8500. 39.00 (*0-7206-0627-6*, Pub. by P Owen Ltd UK) Dufour.

***Way to Win: Success Manuals & Manhood in Gilded Age America.** LC 96-51450. 272p. (C). (gr. 13). 1997. pap. 17.95 (*0-8078-4658-9*) U of NC Pr.

Way to Wisdom: An Introduction to Philosophy. Karl Jaspers. Tr. by Ralph Manheim. (C). 1960. pap. 12.00 (*0-300-00134-7*, Y27) Yale U Pr.

Way to Write for Children. Joan Aiken. 112p. 1982. pap. 7.95 (*0-312-85840-X*) St Martin.

Way to Wyoming. Dan Parkinson. 432p. 1988. mass mkt. 3.95 (*0-8217-2411-8*, Zebra Kensgtn) Kensgtn Pub Corp.

Way to Xanadu. Caroline Alexander. 1994. 23.00 (*0-679-41900-4*) Knopf.

***Way Toward Health: A Seth Book.** Jane Roberts. 336p. (Orig.). 1997. pap. 17.95 (*1-878424-30-0*) Amber-Allen Pub.

Way Towards the Blessed Life see Characteristics of the Present Age

Way, Truth & Life: Living with Jesus Our Personal Savior. Henry Libersat. LC 88-34206. 110p. (Orig.). 1989. pap. 7.95 (*0-8198-8237-2*) Pauline Bks.

Way up from Down. Priscilla Slagle. 1992. mass mkt. 5.99 (*0-312-92914-5*) St Martin.

Way up North in Dixie: A Black Family's Claim to the Confederate Anthem. Howard L. Sacks & Judith R. Sacks. LC 92-39328. (Illus.). 272p. 1996. pap. 15.95 (*1-56098-259-4*) Smithsonian.

Way Was Through Woods: The Story of Tomo-Chi-Chi. 2nd ed. Sara H. Banks. LC 93-85477. 92p. (J). (gr. 5 up). 1993. pap. 7.95 (*1-879373-59-9*) R Rinehart.

Way We Are. Margaret Visser. 320p. 1996. 23.95 (*0-571-19885-6*) Faber & Faber.

***Way We Are: The Astonishing Anthropology of Everyday Life.** Margaret Visser. LC 96-50313. 288p. 1997. pap. 14.00 (*1-56836-186-6*, Kodansha Globe) Kodansha.

Way We Ate: Pacific Northwest Cooking, 1843-1900. Jacqueline Williams. LC 96-21942. (Illus.). 240p. (Orig.). 1996. 29.95 (*0-87422-137-4*); pap. 18.95 (*0-87422-136-6*) Wash St U Pr.

Way We Build Now. Andrew Orton. (Illus.). 530p. 1988. pap. 80.95 (*0-7476-0011-2*) Chapman & Hall.

***Way We Build Now: Form, Scale & Technique.** Andrew Orton. (Illus.). 544p. (Orig.). 1991. pap. text ed. 98.95 (*0-419-15780-8*, E & FN Spon) Routledge Chapman & Hall.

Way We Die Now. Charles Willeford. 1996. mass mkt. 4.99 (*0-440-21885-3*) Dell.

Way We Drove: Toronto's Love Affair with the Automobile. Bill Sherk. 1994. pap. text ed. 19.95 (*1-55046-065-X*, Pub. by Boston Mills Pr CN) Genl Dist Srvs.

Way We Eat. Richard Sax. 1996. text ed. 32.95 (*0-442-01800-2*) Van Nos Reinhold.

Way We Flew: America's Romance with Air Travel: From Biplanes to the Dawn of the Jet Age 1920s-1960s. Michael O'Leary. (Illus.). 132p. 1998. 29.95 (*0-89658-333-3*) Voyageur Pr.

Way We Grow. Anne W. Garland. 1993. pap. 8.95 (*0-425-14061-X*) Berkley Pub.

Way We Know in Dreams: Stories. Gordon Weaver. LC 93-38323. 240p. (C). 1994. 26.95 (*0-8262-0931-9*) U of Mo Pr.

Way We Know in Dreams: Stories. Gordon Weaver. 240p. (C). 1994. pap. 16.95 (*0-8262-1008-2*) U of Mo Pr.

Way We Live. Kathleen Jamie. LC 87-73050. 64p. (Orig.). 1988. pap. 12.95 (*1-85224-034-2*, Pub. by Bloodaxe Bks UK) Dufour.

Way We Live, 3 Bks., Bk. 1. Neena Kaushal & Satya Uberoi. 335p. 1983. pap. text ed. 12.50 (*0-86131-364-X*, Pub. by Orient Longman Ltd II) Apt Bks.

Way We Live, 3 Bks., Bk. 2. Neena Kaushal & Satya Uberoi. 335p. 1983. pap. text ed. 3.95 (*0-86131-365-8*, Pub. by Orient Longman Ltd II) Apt Bks.

Way We Live: Practical Economics for Everyday Living. John M. Shaw. Ed. by Tate Baird. (Illus.). 145p. (Orig.). 1992. teacher ed., pap. 6.19 (*0-614-02538-9*) Univ Class.

Way We Live: Practical Economics for Everyday Living. John M. Shaw. Ed. by Tate Baird. LC 92-61667. (Illus.). 145p. (Orig.). 1992. boxed 14.95 (*0-914127-05-5*) Univ Class.

Way We Live: Stories by Utah Women. Ed. by Ellen Fagg. LC 94-38215. xii, 211p. (Orig.). 1994. pap. 14.95 (*1-56085-062-0*) Signature Bks.

Way We Live see English for Today

Way We Live Now. Susan Sontag. Ed. by Howard Hodgkin. (Illus.). 64p. 1991. pap. 35.00 (*0-374-52305-3*, Noonday) FS&G.

Way We Live Now. Anthony Trollope. Ed. by Robert Tracy. LC 74-132935. (Library of Literature). 1974. pap. 13.95 (*0-672-61016-7*, LL32, Bobbs) Macmillan.

Way We Live Now. Anthony Trollope. Ed. by John Sutherland. (World's Classics Ser.). 494p. 1982. pap. 10.95 (*0-19-281576-8*) OUP.

Way We Live Now. Anthony Trollope. 496p. 1994. 8.95 (*0-14-043836-X*, Penguin Classics) Viking Penguin.

Way We Live Now. Anthony Trollope. 816p. 1995. pap. 10.95 (*0-14-043392-9*, Penguin Classics) Viking Penguin.

Way We Live Now. Anthony Trollope. 832p. 1996. 21.00 (*0-679-60183-X*, Modern Lib) Random.

Way We Live Now. large type ed. Berard Levin. (Illus.). 200p. 1991. 22.95 (*1-85290-019-9*, Pub. by ISIS UK) Transaction Pubs.

Way We Live Now. Anthony Trollope. (Illus.). 416p. 1982. reprint ed. pap. 8.95 (*0-486-24360-5*) Dover.

Way We Live Now: American Married Life. Harris. 1995. 22.50 (*0-671-65763-1*) S&S Trade.

Way We Live Now: American Plays & the AIDS Crisis. William M. Hoffman et al. Ed. by M. Elizabeth Osborn. LC 90-10829. 304p. 1990. 24.95 (*1-55936-005-4*); pap. 14.95 (*1-55936-006-2*) Theatre Comm.

Way We Live Now: Dilemmas in Contemporary Culture. Richard Hoggart. 400p. 1996. 35.00 (*0-7011-6501-4*, Pub. by Chatto & Windus UK) Trafalgar.

Way We Lived: California Indian Stories, Songs & Reminiscences. rev. ed. Ed. by Malcolm Margolin. (Illus.). 260p. (C). 1993. lib. bdg. 39.00 (*0-8095-4983-2*) Borgo Pr.

Way We Lived: California Indian Stories, Songs & Reminiscences. rev. ed. Ed. by Malcolm Margolin. (Illus.). 248p. 1993. pap. 14.95 (*0-930588-55-X*) Heyday Bks.

Way We Lived: Durham, 1900-1920. James G. Leyburn. Ed. by Lon K. Savage. 220p. 1987. 16.95 (*0-9617256-1-3*) Northcross Hse.

***Way We Lived: Essays & Documents in American Social History, Vol. 1.** 3rd ed. Ed. by Frederick M. Binder & David M. Reimers. 322p. (C). 1996. pap. text ed. 27.56 (*0-669-39714-8*) HM College Div.

***Way We Lived: Essays & Documents in American Social History, Vol. 2.** 3rd ed. Ed. by Frederick M. Binder & David M. Reimers. 323p. (C). 1996. pap. text ed. 27.56 (*0-669-39715-6*) HM College Div.

Way We Lived: Essays & Sources in American Social History, 2 vols., Vol. II. Frederick M. Binder & David M. Reimers. LC 87-81182. 328p. (C). 1988. pap. text ed. 28.36 (*0-669-09031-X*) HM College Div.

Way We Never Were: American Families & the Nostalgia Trap. Stephanie Coontz. LC 91-59009. 400p. 1993. reprint ed. pap. 16.00 (*0-465-09097-4*) Basic.

Way We Pray. Leonel L. Mitchell. 80p. (Orig.). 1984. pap. 1.95 (*0-88028-039-5*, 759) Forward Movement.

***Way We Really Are: Ending the War over America's Changing Families.** Stephanie Coontz. LC 96-45068. 224p. 1997. 22.00 (*0-465-07787-0*) Basic.

Way We Really Live. Sam B. Warner. 1978. 8.00 (*0-89073-053-9*) Boston Public Lib.

Way We See It: Photography from the Children of Charlotte's Inner City. Frye Gaillard & Rachel Gaillard. Ed. by Jerry Bledsoe. (Illus.). 80p. (Orig.). 1995. pap. 11.95 (*1-878086-46-4*) Down Home NC.

Way We Were. Ken Bell. (Illus.). 256p. 1988. 45.00 (*0-8020-3990-1*) U of Toronto Pr.

***Way We Were.** large type ed. Marie Joseph. (Charnwood Large Print Ser.). 384p. 1997. 29.50 (*0-7089-8933-0*, Charnwood) Ulverscroft.

***Way We Were: A Pictorial History of Clark County, Arkansas.** Compiled by Joe May. (Illus.). 134p. 1996. 35.00 (*0-88107-260-5*) Curtis Media.

***Way We Were Before Our Destruction: Lives of Jewish Students from Vilna, Who Perished During the Holocaust.** Yulian I. Rafes. Ed. by Paul Glasser. LC 97-60290. (Illus.). 220p. (Orig.). 1997. pap. write for info. (*1-885563-06-X*) VIA Press MD.

Way We Were Fifty Years Ago: East of Modesto to Empire & Beyond. Franklin Beard. 300p. 1985. text ed. 37.50 (*0-945037-02-3*) Southern Mines Pr.

Way We Were in Marion County. Ray Cunningham. LC 95-92146. 77p. (Orig.). 1995. pap. 5.95 (*0-9631251-3-3*) R Cunningham.

Way We Were, the Way We Can Be: A Vision for the Middle School. 3rd rev. ed. Ann Ross & Karen D. Olsen. Ed. by Kristen Little. (Illus.). 292p. (Orig.). 1995. pap. 24.95 (*1-878631-24-1*) S Kovalik.

Way We Wore: Styles of the 1930s & '40s. Marsha Hunt. (Illus.). 460p. (C). 1994. 49.95 (*1-882747-00-3*) Fallbrook Pub.

Way We Work: A Practical Approach for Dealing with People on the Job. Cynthia U. Tobias. 1995. 19.99 (*1-56179-407-4*); audio 16.99 (*1-56179-408-2*) Focus Family.

W

Way We Write Now: Short Stories from the AIDS Crisis. Ed. by Sharon O. Warner. LC 94-45456. 272p. 1995. pap. 12.95 (*0-8065-1638-0*, Citadel Pr) Carol Pub Group.

Way West. A. B. Guthrie, Jr. LC 92-37982. 352p. 1993. pap. 13.00 (*0-395-65662-1*) HM.

Way West. A. B. Guthrie, Jr. 350p. 1992. reprint ed. lib. bdg. 32.95 (*0-89968-305-3*, Lghtyr Pr) Buccaneer Bks.

Way West - Stories, Essays & Verse Accounts: 1963-1993. Edward Dorn. LC 93-24338. 281p. (Orig.). 1993. pap. 14.00 (*0-87685-905-8*) Black Sparrow.

Way West: Traveling the Oregon Trail, a Play see Perspectives on History Series: Part II

Way with Pain. Mary Batchelor. (Pocketbooks Ser.). (Illus.). 48p. (Orig.). 1990. pap. 2.99 (*0-7459-1600-7*) Lion USA.

Way with Widows. Harold Adams. LC 94-1245. 142p. 1994. 18.95 (*0-8027-3190-2*) Walker & Co.

Way with Widows. large type ed. Harold Adams. LC 94-31222. (Nightingale Ser.). 219p. 1995. pap. 17.95 (*0-7838-1144-6*, GK Hall) Thorndike Pr.

Way with Words. Arthur H. Bell. 1991. 31.95 (*0-87280-121-7*, 3323, Asher-Gallant) Caddylak Systs.

***Way with Words.** Garlick & Taylor. 1995. pap. text ed. write for info. (*0-582-80363-2*, Pub. by Longman UK) Longman.

Way with Words: On Creative Writing. Edna Gilbert. 95p. 1968. pap. 3.25 (*0-85225-533-0*) Ed Solutions.

Way with Words: The Language of English Renaissance Literature. Gert Ronberg. 192p. 1992. pap. 14.95 (*0-340-49307-0*, A6109, Pub. by E Arnold UK) Routledge Chapman & Hall.

Way with Words: The Story of Literacy Volunteers of America. Ruth J. Colvin. 52p. 1987. pap. text ed. 4.00 (*0-930713-38-9*) Lit Vol Am.

Way with Words, Level 1: Vocabulary Development Activities for Learners of English. Stuart Redman & Robert Ellis. Ed. by Mike McCarthy. (Illus.). 112p. (C). 1990. teacher ed., pap. text ed. 14.95 (*0-521-35918-X*) Cambridge U Pr.

Way with Words, Level 1: Vocabulary Development Activities for Learners of English. Stuart Redman & Robert Ellis. Ed. by Mike McCarthy. (Illus.). 106p. (C). 1990. student ed., pap. text ed. 11.95 (*0-521-35917-1*); digital audio 17.95 (*0-521-35026-3*) Cambridge U Pr.

Way Without Words: "A Guide for Spiritually Emerging Adults" Marsha Sinetar. LC 91-43891. 188p. 1992. pap. 9.95 (*0-8091-3303-2*) Paulist Pr.

Way You Believe. Lauren King. LC 91-73705. 82p. 1991. pap. 9.95 (*0-913342-70-X*) Barclay Pr.

***Way You Look Tonight, Vol. 1.** Thompson. 1997. mass mkt. write for info. (*0-312-96331-9*) St Martin.

***Way You Wear Your Hat.** Bill Zehme. 1997. 23.00 (*0-06-018289-X*) HarpC.

Wayfarer. Natsume Soseki. Tr. & Intro. by Beongcheon Yu. LC 66-26974. 326p. reprint ed. pap. 93.00 (*0-7837-3625-8*, 2043491) Bks Demand.

***Wayfarer: New Fiction by Korean Women.** Ed. by Bruce Fulton & J. Chan Fulton. Tr. by J. Chan Fulton from KOR. LC 96-39431. 200p. (Orig.). 1997. pap. 14.95 (*1-879679-09-4*) Women Translation.

Wayfarer in a World in Upheaval. Bernard L. Ginsburg. Ed. by Nathan Kravetz. LC 93-12024. (Studies in Judaica & the Holocaust: No. 12). 128p. 1993. pap. 17.00 (*0-8095-1400-1*); lib. bdg. 27.00 (*0-8095-0400-6*) Borgo Pr.

Wayfarer in the Land. Watchman Nee. 176p. 1975. reprint ed. mass mkt. 4.99 (*0-8423-7823-5*) Tyndale.

Wayfarer Poems. T. A. Gibson. 68p. (Orig.). 1994. pap. 7.95 (*0-9643896-7-3*) T A Gibson.

***Wayfarer Poems.** T. A. Gibson. 100p. (Orig.). 1997. mass mkt. 5.99 (*1-55197-739-7*, Pub. by Comnwlth Pub CN) Partners Pubs Grp.

Wayfarers. Knut Hamsun. Tr. by James McFarlane from NOR. (Sun & Moon Classics Ser.: No. 88). 468p. 1995. pap. 13.95 (*1-55713-211-9*) Sun & Moon CA.

Wayfarers: Meher Baba with the God-Intoxicated. William Donkin. (Illus.). 450p. 1988. reprint ed. 30.00 (*0-913078-65-4*) Sheriar Pr.

Wayfarers in Arcady. Charles Vince. LC 71-90688. (Essay Index Reprint Ser.). 1977. 19.95 (*0-8369-1236-5*) Ayer.

Wayfarer's Words, 3 vols. C. Rhys Davids. LC 78-72414. reprint ed. Set. 125.00 (*0-404-17600-3*) AMS Pr.

W

Wayfaring Princes: A Tale of Questing & Adventure. Edith Lawrence. (Illus.). 136p. (Orig.). (J). (gr. 4-7). 1987. pap. 8.00 (*0-936132-86-8*) Merc Pr NY.

Wayfaring Sin-Eater & Other Tales of Appalachia. James G. Jones. 128p. 1992. reprint ed. pap. 8.00 (*0-87012-464-1*) McClain.

Wayfaring Stranger. Burl Ives. (American Autobiography Ser.). 253p. 1995. reprint ed. lib. bdg. 79.00 (*0-7812-8564-X*) Rprt Serv.

Wayfaring with Birds. Ina Griffin. LC 86-19799. (Illus.). 288p. (Orig.). 1987. pap. 9.95 (*0-936784-23-7*) J Daniel.

Wayfinder's Story. Fred Saberhagen. (Lost Swords Ser.: Bk. 7). 256p. 1993. mass mkt. 4.99 (*0-8125-0575-1*) Tor Bks.

***Wayfinding.** Lynn Wilcox. 201p. 1996. pap. text ed. 13.00 (*0-910735-87-5*) MTO Printing & Pubn Ctr.

Wayfinding: People, Signs & Architecture. Paul Arthur. 1992. text ed. 58.00 (*0-07-551016-2*) McGraw.

Waylander. David Gemmell. 1995. mass mkt. 5.99 (*0-345-37907-1*, Del Rey) Ballantine.

Wayless Way Pt. 1. rev. ed. Willard Gellis. (Orpheophrenia Ser.). 68p. Date not set. reprint ed. pap. write for info. (*0-917455-13-4*) Big Foot NY.

Waylon: A Biography. R. Serge Denisoff. LC 82-24786. 389p. reprint ed. 110.90 (*0-685-16002-5*, 2027556) Bks Demand.

Waylon: An Autobiography. Waylon Jennings & Lenny Kaye. LC 96-2587. (Illus.). 432p. 1996. 23.00 (*0-446-51865-4*) Warner Bks.

***Waylon: An Autobiography.** Waylon Jennings & Lenny Kaye. 464p. 1998. mass mkt. 6.99 (*0-446-60512-3*) Warner Bks.

Waylon Jennings Discography. Compiled by John L. Smith. LC 95-14502. (Discographies Ser.: No. 61). 400p. 1995. text ed. 75.00 (*0-313-29745-2*, Greenwood Pr) Greenwood.

Waymarks: An Artist's Attempt at a Natural Religion. Geoffrey E. Makins. (C). 1988. 51.00 (*1-85072-026-6*, Pub. by W Sessions UK) St Mut.

Waymarks: The Notre Dame Inaugural Lectures in Anthropology. Ed. by Kenneth Moore. LC 86-40339. 160p. 1988. text ed. 22.00 (*0-268-01939-8*); pap. text ed. 11.50 (*0-268-01941-X*) U of Notre Dame Pr.

Wayne Anderson's Horrorble Book. Wayne Anderson. (Illus.). 24p. (J). 1996. 14.95 (*0-7894-1119-9*) DK Pub Inc.

Wayne Community College. Rosalyn Lomax. 112p. (C). 1995. per., pap. 15.69 (*0-7872-1553-8*) Kendall-Hunt.

***Wayne County Marriages & Deaths Copied from the Wayne Sentinel (1823-60) Published in Palmyra, & the Newark Weekly Courier (1869-73)** Compiled by Harriett M. Wiles. (Illus.). 127p. 1997. reprint ed. pap. 16.00 (*0-8328-6271-1*) Higginson Bk Co.

Wayne County Mediation Program in the Eastern District of Michigan. Federal Judicial Center Staff & Kathy L. Shuart. (Illus.). v, 60p. 1984. write for info. (*0-318-60744-1*) Bates Info Serv.

Wayne County, Missouri. Rose F. Cramer. (Illus.). 734p. 1972. 11.00 (*0-911208-22-4*) Ramfre.

Wayne County, TN: History & Families. Turner Publishing Company Staff. LC 95-60269. 600p. 1995. 48.00 (*1-56311-193-4*) Turner Pub KY.

Wayne Estes: A Hero's Legacy. Eleanor Olson. (Illus.). (YA). (gr. 7-12). 1991. pap. text ed. 6.00 (*0-9628317-0-0*) E Olson.

***Wayne Evans on AS/400 Security.** Ed. by Martin Pluth. 300p. 1997. pap. text ed. write for info. (*1-883884-36-5*) Midrange Comput.

Wayne Gretsky. Richard Rambeck. LC 95-5624. (Sports Superstars Ser.). (Illus.). 24p. (J). (gr. 2-6). 1995. lib. bdg. 21.36 (*1-56766-203-X*) Childs World.

Wayne Gretzky. James Beckett. (Beckett Great Sports Heroes Ser.). (Illus.). 128p. 1996. 15.00 (*0-676-60032-8*, House of Collect) Ballantine.

Wayne Gretzky. Aleksandrs Rozens. LC 93-18132. (J). 1993. 15.93 (*0-86592-119-9*); 11.95 (*0-685-66586-0*) Rourke Enter.

***Wayne Gretzky.** Josh Wilker. (Ice Hockey Legends Ser.). 1997. 14.95 (*0-7910-4554-4*) Chelsea Hse.

Wayne Gretzky: A Biography. Gerry Redmond. (Illus.). 112p. (Orig.). 1993. pap. 9.95 (*1-55022-190-6*, Pub. by ECW Pr CN) LPC InBook.

Wayne Gretzky: Hockey Great. Thomas R. Raber. (Sports Achievers Ser.). (Illus.). 64p. (J). (gr. 4-9). 1991. lib. bdg. 13.50 (*0-8225-0539-8*, Lerner Publctns) Lerner Group.

Wayne Gretzky: Hockey Great. Thomas R. Raber. (YA). 1992. pap. 4.95 (*0-8225-9601-6*, Lerner Publctns) Lerner Group.

Wayne Gretzky: Profil d'un Joueur de Hockey. Craig T. Wolff. (Illus.). 64p. (FRE.). (J). (ps-5). 1984. pap. 2.25 (*0-380-85753-7*, Camelot) Avon.

***Wayne Gretzky, Star Center.** Frank Fortunato. LC 97-20163. (Sports Reports Ser.). (J). 1998. write for info. (*0-89490-930-4*) Enslow Pubs.

Wayne Morse: A Bio-Bibliography. Lee Wilkins. LC 85-10028. (Bio-Bibliographies in Law & Political Science Ser.: No. 1). xiv, 115p. 1985. text ed. 42.95 (*0-313-24268-2*, WIM/, Greenwood Pr) Greenwood.

***Wayne Morse: A Political Biography.** Mason Drukman. LC 97-3380. 1997. write for info. (*0-87595-263-1*) Oregon Hist.

***Wayne Rainey: The Two Lives of a World Champion.** Michael Scott. 1997. 34.95 (*1-85960-401-3*, Pub. by J H Haynes & Co UK) Motorbooks Intl.

***Wayne State University.** Ed. by A. Dayle Wallace. 269p. Date not set. 20.95 (*0-8369-2727-3*) Ayer.

Wayne Thiebaud. Karen Tsujimoto. LC 85-40351. (Illus.). 208p. (Orig.). 1985. pap. 27.50 (*0-295-96269-0*) San Fran MOMA.

Wayne Thiebaud, Paintings & Works on Paper. Douglas McClellan. (Illus.). 8p. (Orig.). 1976. pap. 5.00 (*0-939982-00-5*) Sesnon Art Gall.

Wayne Wheeler, Dry Boss. Justin Steuart. LC 75-100207. (Illus.). 304p. 1971. reprint ed. text ed. 59.75 (*0-8371-4033-1*, STWW, Greenwood Pr) Greenwood.

***Waynesboro: History of Settlements in the County Formerly Called Cumberland...in Its Beginnings Through Its Growth.** Benjamin M. Nead. (Illus.). 427p. 1997. reprint ed. lib. bdg. 45.00 (*0-8328-6460-9*) Higginson Bk Co.

Waynesboro, PA. Historical Briefs, Inc. Staff. Ed. by Thomas Antonucci & Michael Antonucci. 176p. 1993. pap. 14.95 (*0-89677-032-X*) Hist Briefs.

Ways & Crossways. Paul Claudel. Tr. by Fr. J. O'Conner. LC 67-28732. (Essay Index Reprint Ser.). 1977. 23.95 (*0-8369-0313-7*) Ayer.

***Ways & Means.** Mayfair Games Staff. 1996. 25.00 (*1-56905-021-X*) Mayfair Games.

Ways & Means see Henry Cecil Reprint Series

Ways & Means of Payment: A Full Analysis of the Credit System, with Its Various Modes of Adjustment. Stephen Colwell. LC 65-23212. (Reprints of Economic Classics Ser.). xii, 644p. 1965. reprint ed. 57.50 (*0-678-00110-3*) Kelley.

Ways & Power of Love. C. Kay Allen. LC 92-71904. 1993. pap. 8.95 (*1-55503-406-3*, 01111213) Covenant Comms.

Ways Children Learn Music: An Introduction & Practical Guide to Music Learning Theory. Eric Bluestine. LC 95-32684. 168p. (Orig.). 1995. pap. 12.95 (*0-941050-71-8*, G4355) GIA Pubns.

***Ways In: Poems from Hollywood.** Mark Dunster. 19p. (Orig.). 1997. pap. 5.00 (*0-89642-364-6*) Linden Pubs.

Ways in Approaches to Reading & Writing about Literature. Gilbert H. Muller & John A. Williams. LC 93-1666. 1993. pap. text ed. write for info. (*0-07-044203-7*) McGraw.

Ways in Mystery: Explorations in Mystical Awareness & Life. Luther Askeland. LC 96-46096. 216p. (Orig.). 1997. pap. 17.00 (*1-883991-16-1*) Whte Cloud Pr.

Ways into the Logic of Alexander of Aphrodisias. Kevin L. Flannery. 228p. 1994. 81.75 (*90-04-09998-0*) E J Brill.

Ways into Work. J. Murray-Robertson. Ed. by R. Waller. (C). 1986. 35.00 (*0-09-165541-2*, Pub. by S Thornes Pubs UK) St Mut.

Ways into Work. Ed. by J. Murray-Robertson. (C). 1989. 30.00 (*0-09-165531-5*, Pub. by S Thornes Pubs UK) St Mut.

Ways of Art: Literature, Music, Painting in France: A Critical Work, II. Robert G. Cohn. (Stanford French & Italian Studies: Vol. 40). 384p. 1986. pap. 46.50 (*0-915838-52-4*) Anma Libri.

Ways of Assessing Children & Curriculum: Stories of Early Childhood Practice, Vol. 37. Ed. by Celia Genishi. LC 92-13805. (Early Childhood Education Ser.). 232p. (C). 1992. text ed. 17.95 (*0-8077-3186-2*); pap. text ed. 17.95 (*0-8077-3185-4*) Tchrs Coll.

Ways of Being. Herbert W. Schneider. LC 72-9832. 116p. 1974. reprint ed. text ed. 45.00 (*0-8371-6149-5*, SCWB, Greenwood Pr) Greenwood.

Ways of Being Religious: Readings for a New Approach to Religion. Frederick J. Streng et al. (Illus.). 608p. 1973. text ed. 48.75 (*0-13-946277-5*) P-H.

***Ways of Co-Existing: Urban, Suburban, & Global Communities.** Frederick Baker. 256p. (C). 1997. per. 37.95 (*0-7872-3887-2*) Kendall-Hunt.

Ways of Communicating: The Darwin College Lectures, 1989. Ed. by David H. Mellor. (Illus.). 208p. (C). 1991. text ed. 39.95 (*0-521-37074-4*) Cambridge U Pr.

Ways of Confucianism: Investigations in Chinese Philosophy. David S. Nivison. Ed. by Bryan Van Norden. LC 96-39050. 354p. (Orig.). 1996. 46.95 (*0-8126-9339-6*); pap. 19.95 (*0-8126-9340-X*) Open Court.

Ways of Dying. Zakes Mda. (Southern African Writing Ser.). 192p. 1995. pap. 10.95 (*0-19-571106-8*) OUP.

Ways of Enlightenment: Buddhist Studies at the Nyingma Institute. LC 93-1546. 371p. 1993. pap. 25.00 (*0-89800-254-0*) Dharma Pub.

Ways of Enspiriting: Transformative Practices for the Twenty-First Century. Warren Ziegler. (Orig.). 1995. pap. 14.95 (*0-9643701-0-7*) FIA Intl.

Ways of Escape: Modern Transformation in Leisure & Travel. Chris Rojek. LC 93-33328. (Postmodern Social Futures Ser.). 250p. (C). 1994. lib. bdg. 47.50 (*0-8476-7898-9*) Rowman.

Ways of Escape & a Sort of Life. Graham Greene. (Uniform Editions Ser.). 320p. 1994. 20.00 (*0-670-75262-2*) Viking Penguin.

***Ways of Falling.** Peter Sirr. 86p. 1991. pap. 12.95 (*1-85235-073-3*) Dufour.

Ways of Film Studies: Film Theory & the Interpretation of Film. Gaston Roberge. (C). 1992. 26.00 (*81-202-0348-8*, Pub. by Ajanta II) S Asia.

Ways of God. St. Thomas Aquinas Staff. LC 95-36706. 90p. (Orig.). 1995. pap. 4.95 (*0-918477-30-1*) Sophia Inst Pr.

Ways of Imperfection. Simon Tugwell. 252p. 1985. pap. 12.95 (*0-87243-164-9*) Templegate.

Ways of Indian Magic. Teresa VanEtten. LC 85-2722. (Illus.). 96p. (Orig.). 1985. pap. 8.95 (*0-86534-061-7*) Sunstone Pr.

Ways of Indian Wisdom. Teresa VanEtten. LC 86-5924. 117p. (Orig.). 1987. pap. 10.95 (*0-86534-090-0*) Sunstone Pr.

***Ways of Knowing.** Nancy Ware. 240p. (C). 1996. pap. text ed. 40.89 (*0-7872-2886-9*) Kendall-Hunt.

Ways of Knowing. 2nd ed. Tim Summerlin et al. 400p. (C). 1996. per., pap. text ed. 34.12 (*0-8403-9464-0*) Kendall-Hunt.

Ways of Knowing: Essays on Marge Piercy. Ed. by Sue Walker & Eugenie Hamner. LC 90-60602. 182p. (Orig.). (C). 1991. pap. text ed. 12.95 (*0-685-50964-8*) Negative Capability Pr.

Ways of Knowing: Literature & the Intellectual Life of Children. Ed. by Kay E. Vandergrift. 432p. 1996. 39.50 (*0-8108-3087-6*) Scarecrow.

Ways of Knowing & Caring for Older Adults. Ed. by Mary Burke & Susan Sherman. LC 93-38938. 1993. 29.95 (*0-88737-593-6*) Natl League Nurse.

Ways of Knowledge & Experience. Louis A. Reid. 287p. 1961. 69.50 (*0-614-00166-8*) Elliots Bks.

Ways of Life. N. Middleton. (C). 1981. teacher ed. 280.00 incl. audio (*0-86158-627-1*, Pub. by S Thornes Pubs UK) St Mut.

Ways of Life. Van Binh Nguyen. 1995. pap. 10.95 (*0-533-11333-4*) Vantage.

***Ways of Living: Cultural Consciousness & the Environment.** Richard Jacobs. 284p. (C). 1996. pap. text ed. 37.74 (*0-7872-2848-6*) Kendall-Hunt.

Ways of Living: Self-Care Strategies for Special Needs. Ed. by Charles Christiansen. 600p. (C). 1994. text ed. 65.00 (*1-56900-008-5*) Am Occup Therapy.

Ways of Lying: Dissimulation, Persecution, & Conformity in Early Modern Europe. Perez Zagorin. 337p. 1990. 42.50 (*0-674-94834-3*) HUP.

***Ways of Meaning: An Introduction to a Philosophy of Language.** 2nd ed. Mark Platts. LC 96-45206. (Illus.). 276p. 1997. pap. 25.00 (*0-262-66107-1*) MIT Pr.

***Ways of Meaning: An Introduction to a Philosophy of Language.** 2nd ed. Mark D. Platts. 1997. write for info. (*0-262-16166-4*) MIT Pr.

Ways of Medieval Life & Thought. Frederick M. Powicke. LC 64-13394. (Illus.). 1949. 28.00 (*0-8196-0137-3*) Biblo.

Ways of Mental Prayer. Domitry V. Lehodey. LC 82-50584. 408p. 1994. reprint ed. pap. 14.00 (*0-89555-178-0*) TAN Bks Pubs.

Ways of My Grandmothers. Beverly Hungry-Wolf. LC 79-91645. 224p. 1981. pap. 10.00 (*0-688-00471-7*, Quill) Morrow.

Ways of Nature. John Burroughs. LC 77-157963. (Essay Index Reprint Ser.). 1977. reprint ed. 21.95 (*0-8369-2217-4*) Ayer.

Ways of Nature. John Burroughs. (Works of John Burroughs). 1989. reprint ed. lib. bdg. 79.00 (*0-7812-2192-7*) Rprt Serv.

Ways of Paradox & Other Essays. enl. rev. ed. Willard V. Quine. LC 75-19554. 364p. 1976. pap. 14.95 (*0-674-94837-8*) HUP.

Ways of Philosophy. Milton K. Munitz. (C). 1979. text ed. write for info. (*0-02-384850-2*, Macmillan Coll) P-H.

Ways of Philosophy: Searching for a Worthwhile Life. A. L. Herman. (Studies in the Humanities). 347p. 1990. 35.95 (*1-55540-515-0*, 00 01 17); pap. 19.95 (*1-55540-516-9*, 00 01 17) Scholars Pr GA.

Ways of Rain: And Other Poems by Hugo Lindo. Hugo Lindo. Ed. by Yvette E. Miller. Tr. by Elizabeth G. Miller. LC 86-18577. (Discoveries Ser.). 160p. (ENG & SPA.). 1986. pap. 14.95 (*0-935480-24-2*) Lat Am Lit Rev Pr.

Ways of Reading. 4th ed. David Bartholomae. 1996. teacher ed., pap. text ed. 10.00 (*0-312-11707-8*) St Martin.

***Ways of Reading.** 5th ed. Bartholomae. Date not set. pap. text ed. write for info. (*0-312-17893-X*); teacher ed., pap. text ed. write for info. (*0-312-17894-8*) St Martin.

Ways of Reading: Advanced Reading Skills for Students of English Literature. Martin Montgomery et al. LC 91-39237. 256p. (C). (gr. 13). 1992. pap. 24.95 (*0-415-05320-X*, A7142) Routledge.

Ways of Reading: An Anthology for Writers. 4th ed. David Bartholomae & Anthony Petrosky. 1996. pap. text ed. 22.50 (*0-312-11564-4*) St Martin.

Ways of Reading Booklet. 3rd ed. David Bartholomae. 1996. suppl. ed., pap. text ed. 5.50 (*0-312-14955-7*) St Martin.

Ways of Reason: Guide to Talmudic Reasoning & Logic. Moshe C. Luzzatto. 1992. 23.95 (*0-87306-495-X*) Feldheim.

Ways of Religion: An Introduction to the Major Traditions. 2nd ed. Ed. by Roger Eastman. LC 92-19530. 504p. 1993. 27.95 (*0-19-507596-X*) OUP.

***Ways of Scope Taking.** Szabolcsi. 1997. pap. text ed. 49.00 (*0-7923-4451-0*) Kluwer Ac.

***Ways of Scope Taking.** Anna Szabolcsi. 1997. lib. bdg. 170.00 (*0-7923-4446-4*) Kluwer Ac.

Ways of Seeing. John Berger. 1990. 22.25 (*0-8446-6175-9*) Peter Smith.

Ways of Seeing. John Berger. 1977. mass mkt. 5.95 (*0-14-021631-6*, Penguin Bks) Viking Penguin.

Ways of Seeing. John Berger. 1990. pap. 11.95 (*0-14-013515-4*) Viking Penguin.

Ways of Studying Children: An Observation Manual for Early Childhood Teachers. 2nd ed. Millie C. Almy & Celia Genishi. LC 79-13881. 1979. pap. text ed. 17.95 (*0-8077-2551-X*) Tchrs Coll.

Ways of Sunlight. Sam Selvon. (Caribbean Writers Ser.). 1989. pap. 8.95 (*0-685-32994-1*, TG7163) Longman.

Ways of the Bird: A Naturalist's Guide to Bird Behavior. Sarita Van Vleck. 144p. 1993. pap. 12.95 (*1-55821-223-X*) Lyons & Burford.

Ways of the Christian Mystics. Thomas Merton. LC 94-8330. (Pocket Classics Ser.). 200p. 1994. pap. 6.00 (*1-57062-030-X*, Sham Pocket Class) Shambhala Pubns.

Ways of the Hand: The Organization of Improvised Conduct. David Sudnow. (Illus.). 192p. 1978. 25.00 (*0-674-94833-5*) HUP.

Ways of the Hand: The Organization of Improvised Conduct. David Sudnow. LC 92-34315. (Illus.). 170p. (C). 1993. pap. 15.95 (*0-262-69161-2*) MIT Pr.

Ways of the Hour. James Fenimore Cooper. (Pocket Classics Ser.). 336p. 1996. pap. 10.95 (*0-7509-1158-1*, Pub. by Sutton Pubng UK) Bks Intl VA.

Ways of the Hour. James Fenimore Cooper. (Works of James Fenimore Cooper Ser.). 1990. reprint ed. lib. bdg. 79.00 (*0-7812-2397-0*) Rprt Serv.

Ways of the Lonely Ones. Manly P. Hall. pap. 9.95 (*0-89314-368-5*) Philos Res.

Ways of the Righteous. LC 94-40780. (ENG & HEB.). 1994. 24.95 (*0-87306-697-9*) Feldheim.

Ways of the Sages & the Way of the World: The Minor Tractates of the Babylonian Talmud. Marcus Van Loopik. (Texte und Studien zum Antiken Judentum: No. 26). 389p. 1991. 114.50 (*3-16-145644-0*, Pub. by J C B Mohr GW) Coronet Bks.

Ways of the Sea. Charles G. Davis. (Illus.). 185p. (YA). 1994. pap. 13.95 (*0-941567-51-6*) South St Sea Mus.

Ways of the Service. Frederick Palmer. LC 70-100290. (Short Story Index Reprint Ser.). 1977. 21.95 (*0-8369-3326-5*) Ayer.

Ways of the Sierra Madre: Crafts of the Sierra Madre. Eugene H. Boudreau. LC 74-22999. (Illus.). 96p. 1974. 6.00 (*0-686-10332-7*) Redbud Press.

Ways of the South Sea Savage. Robert W. Williamson. LC 75-35169. (Illus.). reprint ed. 57.50 (*0-404-14183-8*) AMS Pr.

Ways of the Strega - Italian Witchcraft: Its Legends, Lore, & Spells. Raven Grimassi. LC 95-38486. (Llewellyn's World Religion & Magic Ser.). (Illus.). 320p. 1995. pap. 20.00 (*1-56718-253-4*) Llewellyn Pubns.

Ways of the White Folks. Langston Hughes. LC 90-50180. (Vintage Classics Ser.). 256p. 1990. pap. 11.00 (*0-679-72817-1*, Vin) Random.

An Asterisk (*) at the beginning of an entry indicates that the title is appearing in BIP for the first time.

Ways of the Wild: A Practical Guide to the Outdoors. Kevin Callan. 250p. 1993. pap. 16.95 (1-55111-024-5) Broadview Pr.

Ways of the World: A History of the World's Roads & of the Vehicles That Used Them. Maxwell G. Lay. LC 91-23148. (Illus.). 500p. (C). 1992. text ed. 50.00 (0-8135-1758-3) Rutgers U Pr.

Ways of the World: Comedy & Society. Robert B. Heilman. LC 77-15186. 400p. 1978. 25.00 (0-295-95587-2) U of Wash Pr.

Ways of Thinking. James Davies. LC 91-18025. (American University Studies: Philosophy: Ser. V, Vol. 131). 258p. 1991. 44.95 (0-8204-1692-4) P Lang Pubng.

Ways of Thinking: The Limits of Rational Thought & Artificial Intelligence. L. Mero. 260p. (C). 1990. text ed. 61.00 (981-02-0266-0); pap. text ed. 30.00 (981-02-0267-9) World Scientific Pub.

Ways of Thinking of Eastern Peoples, 10 vols. Hajime Nakamura. (Documentary Reference Collections). 1988. Set. 395.00 (0-318-35983-9, CMJ/, Greenwood Pr) Greenwood.

Ways of Thinking of Eastern Peoples, 10 vols., Vol. 1. Hajime Nakamura. LC 88-21947. (Documentary Reference Collections). 657p. 1988. text ed. 69.50 (0-313-26556-9, CMJ01, Greenwood Pr) Greenwood.

***Ways of Thinking of Eastern Peoples: India-China-Tibet-Japan.** Hajime Nakamura. LC 96-41818. 1997. write for info. (0-7103-0571-0, Pub. by Kegan Paul Intl UK) Col U Pr.

Ways of Thinking of Eastern Peoples: India, China, Tibet, Japan. rev. ed. Hajime Nakamura. Ed. by Philip P. Wiener. 732p. (C). 1981. pap. text ed. 20.00 (0-8248-0078-8) UH Pr.

Ways of Thinking of Eastern Peoples: India-Tibet-China-Japan. Hajime Nakamura. 1991. 27.00 (81-208-0764-2, Pub. by Motilal Banarsidass II) S Asia.

Ways of Training: Recipes for Teacher Training. T. Woodward. (Pilgrims Longman Resource Bks.). 184p. 1993. pap. text ed. 21.32 (0-582-06493-7, 79847) Longman.

Ways of Trout. Leonard M. Wright, Jr. LC 84-27086. (Illus.). 160p. 1985. pap. 12.95 (1-55821-092-X) Lyons & Burford.

***Ways of War: The Era of World War II in Children's & Young Adult Fiction: An Annotated Bibliography.** M. Paul Holsinger. 503p. 1995. 57.50 (0-8108-2925-8) Scarecrow.

Ways of War & Peace. Michael Doyle. Date not set. write for info. (0-393-03931-5) Norton.

Ways of War & Peace: Realism, Liberalism, & Socialism. Michael W. Doyle. LC 96-15090. 416p. 1997. 30.00 (0-393-03826-2) Norton.

Ways of War & Peace: Realism, Liberalism, & Socialism. Michael W. Doyle. LC 96-15090. (C). 1997. pap. text ed. 29.95 (0-393-96947-9) Norton.

Ways of Wills: Trust & Estate Planning for Government Employees. 3rd ed. G. Jerry Shaw et al. 242p. 1994. pap. text ed. 14.95 (0-936295-42-2) FPMI Comns.

Ways of Wisdom: Great Thoughts from Great Thinkers. Bill Miller. 64p. 1992. pap. 4.95 (0-9630439-4-3) Bayrock.

Ways of Wisdom: Readings on the Good Life. Ed. by Steve Smith. (Illus.). 312p. (Orig.). (C). 1983. pap. text ed. 25.00 (0-8191-3388-4) U Pr of Amer.

Ways of Work: Nyingma in the West. LC 87-22990. (Nyingma in America Ser.). 439p. 1987. pap. 14.95 (0-89800-135-8) Dharma Pub.

Ways of Work: Nyingma in the West. LC 87-22990. (Nyingma in America Ser.). 350p. 1987. 26.00 (0-614-95899-7) Dharma Pub.

Ways of Worldmaking. Nelson Goodman. LC 78-56364. (Illus.). 160p. (C). 1978. 29.95 (0-915144-52-2); pap. 8.95 (0-915144-51-4) Hackett Pub.

Ways of Yoga. Gurani Anjali. 110p. (Orig.). 1993. pap. 10.95 (0-933989-01-6, Baker & Taylor) Vajra Print & Pub.

Ways Out: The Book of Changes for Peace. Ed. by Gene Knudsen-Hoffman. LC 87-35219. 192p. 1988. pap. 9.95 (0-936784-51-2) J Daniel.

Ways Out of the Arms Race. Ed. by T. Kibble. 392p. (C). 1989. text ed. 70.00 (9971-5-0863-X) World Scientific Pub.

Way's Packet Directory, 1848-1994: Passenger Steamboats of the Mississippi River System since the Advent of Photography in Mid-Continent America. rev. ed. Frederick Way, Jr. LC 83-8210. (Illus.). 638p. 1994. pap. text ed. 34.95 (0-8214-1106-3) Ohio U Pr.

Way's Steam Towboat Directory. Compiled by Frederick Way, Jr. LC 90-39814. (Illus.). 320p. 1990. 34.95 (0-8214-0969-7) Ohio U Pr.

Ways That Are Wary. Lemuel De Bra. LC 79-101796. (Short Story Index Reprint Ser.). 1977. 20.95 (0-8369-3184-X) Ayer.

Ways to Better Breathing. Carola H. Speads. Orig. Title: Breathing the ABC's. (Illus.). 128p. (Orig.). 1992. pap. 9.95 (0-89281-397-0) Inner Tradit.

Ways to Better Breathing. Carola H. Speads. LC 85-90511. Orig. Title: Breathing the ABC's. (Illus.). 144p. (Orig.). 1986. reprint ed. pap. 8.95 (0-9615659-1-8) F Morrow.

Ways to Bring Back Prosperity & Prosper in Today's Economy Despite Recession. 1992. lib. bdg. 88.95 (0-8490-8766-X) Gordon Pr.

***Ways to Grow: 101 Virtue-Building Devotions.** Eldon Weisheit. LC 96-41015. 1997. 12.99 (0-570-04887-7, 12-3304) Concordia.

Ways to Improve United States Foreign Educational Aid see Education & Foreign Aid

Ways to Love Iris & Other People. Judith Kinter. (Illus.). (Orig.). 1996. pap. 9.95 (0-9651945-0-7) Mocamus Tree.

Ways to Make A's. Karl Davidson. (Illus.). 127p. (Orig.). 1992. pap. 8.95 (0-9630884-3-2) Team Effort.

Ways to Pray with Children: Prayers, Activities, & Services. Barbara A. Bretherton. LC 95-78538. 80p. (Orig.). (J). 1996. pap. 9.95 (0-89622-670-0) Twenty-Third.

Ways to Say I Love You to Those You Love the Most. Stephen Arterburn. 1994. 6.98 (0-88365-858-5) Galahad Bks.

Ways to Self-Realization. Sadhu. 1975. pap. 7.00 (0-87980-248-0) Wilshire.

***Ways to Successful Strategies in Drug Research & Development.** H. Harold Sellacek et al. (Illus.). xiii, 266p. 1996. 90.00 (3-527-29415-5, VCH) Wiley.

Ways to Teach Biology: The Whys & Hows of Changing to a Process Approach. Sharon L. Hanks. (American University Studies: Language: Ser. XIV, Vol. 23). 200p. (C). 1989. text ed. 31.95 (0-8204-0957-X) P Lang Pubng.

Ways to the Center: An Introduction to World Religions. 4th ed. Denise L. Carmody & John T. Carmody. 489p. (C). 1993. pap. 43.95 (0-534-19182-7) Wadsworth Pub.

Ways to World Meaning, Vol. 64: Annual ACPA Proceedings, 1990. Ed. by Dominic Balestra & Lawrence P. Schrenk. 1991. pap. 20.00 (0-918090-24-5) Am Cath Philo.

Ways to Writing: Purpose, Task, Process. 3rd ed. Linda C. Stanley et al. (Illus.). 656p. (C). 1991. pap. text ed. 39.00 (0-02-415651-5, Macmillan Coll) P-H.

Ways Toward Wellness. Paul Terry et al. 96p. 1990. student ed. write for info. (1-884153-04-6) Prk Nicollet.

***Ways We Live: Exploring Community.** Susan Berlin. (Illus.). 176p. (Orig.). 1997. pap. 16.95 (0-86571-363-4) New Soc Pubs.

***Ways We Live: Exploring Community.** Susan Berlin. (Illus.). 176p. 1997. lib. bdg. 39.95 (0-86571-362-6) New Soc Pubs.

***Ways We Touch.** Miller Williams. 1997. 15.95 (0-252-02362-5) U of Ill Pr.

***Ways We Touch: Poems.** Miller Williams. LC 96-51233. 1997. pap. write for info. (0-252-06646-4) U of Ill Pr.

Ways We Want Our Class to Be: Class Meetings That Build Commitment to Kindness & Learning. Developmental Studies Center Staff. 120p. (Orig.). 1996. pap. 14.95 (1-885603-80-0) Develop Studies.

***Ways We Want Our Class to Be Collegial Study Guide.** Developmental Studies Center Staff. (Building Schoolwide Community Ser.). (Illus.). 56p. 1997. pap. 9.95 (1-57621-140-1) Develop Studies.

***Ways We Worship.** W. McElrath. LC 96-39694. 1997. 14.95 (0-8120-6625-1) Barron.

Ways Which Be in Christ. Alice I. Cravens. 1990. pap. 4.25 (0-89137-449-3) Quality Pubns.

Ways with Words: Language, Life & Work in Communities & Classrooms. Shirley B. Heath. LC 82-22062. 448p. 1983. text ed. 70.00 (0-521-25334-9); pap. text ed. 26.95 (0-521-27319-6) Cambridge U Pr.

Ways with Wreaths. Esther Hands. (Illus.). 28p. (Orig.). 1986. pap. 5.95 (0-933491-14-X) Hot off Pr.

Ways You Can Help. Margie Cook. (Orig.). 1995. pap. write for info. (0-446-60227-2) Warner Bks.

Ways You Can Help. Margie Cook. (Orig.). 1995. pap. write for info. (0-446-67149-5) Warner Bks.

Ways You Can Help: Creative, Practical Suggestions for Family & Friends of Patients & Caregivers. Margaret Cooke & Elizabeth Putnam. LC 95-3524. 160p. (Orig.). 1996. pap. 9.99 (0-446-67125-8) Warner Bks.

***Wayside: Its History, the Authors, in Photographs & Prose.** Jan Sciacca & Robert Derry. (Illus.). 40p. (Orig.). 1997. pap. 3.75 (1-888213-06-X) Eastern Acorn.

Wayside Courtships. Hamlin Garland. LC 70-103509. (Short Story Index Reprint Ser.). 1977. 20.95 (0-8369-3251-X) Ayer.

Wayside Courtships. Hamlin Garland. (Collected Works of Hamlin Garland). 1988. reprint ed. lib. bdg. 79.00 (0-7812-1224-3) Rprt Serv.

Wayside Courtships see Collected Works of Hamlin Garland

Wayside Mechanic: An Analysis of Skill Acquisition in Ghana. Stephen D. McLaughlin. 329p. (Orig.). 1980. pap. 6.00 (0-932288-58-8) Ctr Intl Ed U of MA.

Wayside Motor Inn. A. R. Gurney. 1978. pap. 5.25 (0-8222-1225-0) Dramatists Play.

Wayside Plants of the Islands: A Guide to the Lowland Flora of the Pacific Islands. W. Arthur Whistler. (Illus.). 202p. (C). 1995. text ed. 27.00 (0-9645426-1-7); pap. text ed. 19.95 (0-9645426-0-9) Isle Botanica.

Wayside Poems of the Early Eighteenth Century: An Anthology. Edmund C. Blunden & Bernard Mellor. LC 64-54686. 174p. reprint ed. pap. 49.60 (0-317-28807-5, 2020773) Bks Demand.

Wayside Poems of the Seventeenth Century. Edmund Blunden & Bernard Mellor. 152p. (C). 1963. text ed. 30.00 (0-85656-048-0, Pub. by Hong Kong U Pr HK) St Mut.

Wayside Revelations. Roy W. Henry. LC 94-61730. (Illus.). xii, 141p. (Orig.). 1994. pap. 14.95 (0-945530-12-9) Wordsworth KS.

***Wayside School, 3 vols.** Louis Sachar. 1996. boxed, pap. text ed. 13.50 (0-380-79171-4) Avon.

Wayside School Gets a Little Stranger. Louis Sachar. (J). (gr. 3-7). 1996. pap. 4.50 (0-380-72381-6, Camelot) Avon.

Wayside School Gets a Little Stranger. Louis Sachar. LC 94-25448. (Illus.). 176p. (J). (gr. 3 up). 1995. 16.00 (0-688-13694-X, Morrow Junior) Morrow.

Wayside School Is Falling Down. Louis Sachan. LC 88-674. (Illus.). 192p. (J). (gr. 3-7). 1989. 16.00 (0-688-07868-0) Lothrop.

Wayside School Is Falling Down. Louis Sachar. 192p. (J). 1990. pap. 4.50 (0-380-75484-3, Camelot) Avon.

Wayside Simples & Grateful Herbs. Vincent Abraitys. LC 76-19236. (Illus.). 1980. pap. 8.95 (0-914366-08-4) Columbia Pub.

Wayside Sketches. Sarah A. Cooke. pap. 6.99 (0-88019-196-1) Schmul Pub Co.

Wayside Sonnets 1750-1850. Edmund Blunden & Bernard Mellor. 182p. (C). 1971. text ed. 25.00 (0-85656-001-4, Pub. by Hong Kong U Pr HK) St Mut.

Wayside Sonnets, 1750-1850: An Anthology Gathered by Edmund Blunden & Bernard Mellor. Edmund Blunden. LC 73-170371. 181p. 1971. reprint ed. pap. 51.60 (0-608-02389-2, 2063030) Bks Demand.

***Wayside Tales.** Vincent Starrett. (Vincent Starrett Memorial Library: Vol. 12). 289p. 1997. 25.00 (1-896648-05-3) Battered Silicon.

Wayside Tavern. large type ed. Norah Lofts. 1982. 15.95 (0-7089-0838-1) Ulverscroft.

Wayside Wildflowers of the Pacific Northwest. Dee Strickler. LC 92-76062. (Wildflower Ser.). (Illus.). 272p. (Orig.). 1993. pap. 19.95 (1-56044-185-2) Falcon Pr MT.

Waysiders: Stories of Connacht. Seumas O'Kelly. LC 73-150480. (Short Story Index Reprint Ser.). 1977. reprint ed. 19.95 (0-8369-3821-6) Ayer.

Wayward. (Orig.). 1992. mass mkt. 4.95 (1-56333-004-0) Masquerade.

Wayward. Ned Gander. 14.95 (0-9610750-0-7) N Gander Pub.

Wayward & the Seeking: A Collection of Writings by Jean Toomer. Ed. by Darwin T. Turner. LC 74-11026. 1980. pap. 12.95 (0-88258-028-0) Howard U Pr.

Wayward Angel. Patricia Rice. 1997. pap. 5.99 (0-451-40724-5) NAL-Dutton.

Wayward Angel. Sue Rich. 1995. mass mkt. 5.99 (0-671-89807-8) PB.

***Wayward Angels.** Zannah. (Heart Prints of Angels Collection Ser.: Vol. 3). 76p. (Orig.). 1997. pap. 6.95 (1-890613-05-3) West Coast Media.

Wayward Bride. large type ed. Daphne Clair. 1994. 26.95 (0-685-73035-2, Pub. by Magna Print Bks UK) Ulverscroft.

Wayward Bride. large type ed. Daphne Clair. (Magna Large Print Ser.). 1994. 25.99 (0-7505-0660-1, Pub. by Magna Print Bks UK) Ulverscroft.

Wayward Bus. John Steinbeck. (Fiction Ser.). 320p. 1979. mass mkt. 7.95 (0-14-005001-9, Penguin Bks) Viking Penguin.

Wayward Bus. John Steinbeck. (Twentieth Century Classics Ser.). 304p. 1995. pap. 10.95 (0-14-018752-9, Penguin Classics) Viking Penguin.

Wayward Capitalists. Susan P. Shapiro. LC 83-2337. 229p. 1987. pap. 14.00 (0-300-03933-6, Y-633) Yale U Pr.

Wayward Girls & Wicked Women: An Anthology of Subversive Stories. Ed. by Angela Carter. 352p. 1989. pap. 12.00 (0-14-010371-6, Penguin Bks) Viking Penguin.

Wayward Head & Heart. Claude P. Crebillon. Tr. by Barbara Bray. LC 78-16439. 221p. 1978. reprint ed. text ed. 55.00 (0-313-20578-7, CRWH, Greenwood Pr) Greenwood.

***Wayward Knights.** TSR Inc. Staff. 1997. pap. 5.99 (0-7869-0696-0) TSR Inc.

***Wayward Lady.** Nan Ryan. mass mkt. write for info. (0-06-108516-2) HarpC.

Wayward Liberal: A Political Biography of Donald Richberg. Thomas E. Vadney. LC 75-132832. 235p. reprint ed. pap. 67.00 (0-317-42032-1, 2025965) Bks Demand.

***Wayward Monks & the Religious Revolution of the Eleventh Century.** Phyllis G. Jestice. LC 96-49111. (Studies in Intellectual History: No. 76). (Illus.). 320p. 1997. 106.25 (90-04-10722-3, NLG 170) E J Brill.

Wayward Muse: A Historical Survey of Painting in Buffalo. Susan Krane. (Illus.). 208p. 1987. pap. 22.95 (0-914782-63-0) Buffalo Fine-Albrght-Knox.

Wayward Nuns in Medieval Literature. Graciela Daichman. (Illus.). 240p. (Orig.). 1986. pap. text ed. 15.95 (0-8156-2379-8) Syracuse U Pr.

Wayward Preacher in the Literature of African American Women. James R. Saunders. LC 94-41242. 175p. 1995. lib. bdg. 27.50 (0-7864-0060-9) McFarland & Co.

Wayward Professor. Joel J. Gold. (Illus.). viii, 192p. 1989. 14.95 (0-7006-0404-9) U Pr of KS.

Wayward Puritans: A Study in the Sociology of Deviance. Kai T. Erikson. LC 66-16140. (Deviance & Criminology Ser.). 228p. (C). 1986. pap. text ed. 29.00 (0-02-332200-4, Macmillan Coll) P-H.

***Wayward Reflections on the History of Philosophy.** James A. Diefenbeck. 322p. 1996. lib. bdg. 42.00 (0-7618-0466-8) U Pr of Amer.

Wayward Reporter: The Life of A. J. Liebling. Raymond Sokolov. LC 84-45026. 368p. 1984. pap. 10.95 (0-916870-63-4) Creat Arts Bk.

Wayward Seeds of Grass. large type ed. Padder Nash. (Linford Mystery Library). 1991. pap. 15.99 (0-7089-7131-8) Ulverscroft.

Wayward Servants: The Two Worlds of the African Pygmies. Colin M. Turnbull. LC 75-5002. (Illus.). 390p. 1976. reprint ed. text ed. 37.00 (0-8371-7927-0, TUWS, Greenwood Pr) Greenwood.

Wayward Technology. Ernst Braun. LC 83-22586. (Contributions in Sociology Ser.: No. 48). xi, 224p. 1984. text ed. 37.50 (0-313-24398-0, BWT/, Greenwood Pr) Greenwood.

Wayward Welfare State. Roger Freeman. (Publication Ser.: No. 249). (Illus.). 511p. 1981. pap. 5.40 (0-8179-7492-X) Hoover Inst Pr.

Wayward Wife. George S. Lewis. LC 86-62543. 25p. (Orig.). 1986. text ed. 10.95 (0-937771-03-1); pap. text ed. 8.95 (0-937771-04-X); lib. bdg. 10.95 (0-937771-11-2) Spencers Intl.

Wayward Wife. Sally Wentworth. (Presents Ser.). 1993. mass mkt. 2.99 (0-373-11605-5, 1-11605-2) Harlequin Bks.

***Wayward Wind.** James Galway. 1983. pap. 12.95 (0-89898-689-3, P0466FLX) Warner Brothers.

Wayward Wind. Dorothy Garlock. 384p. (Orig.). 1986. mass mkt. 5.99 (0-445-20214-9) Warner Bks.

Wayword Dictionary: JBR Yant's Definitions from Hell. John Bryant. 125p. (Orig.). 1995. pap. 10.95 (1-886739-22-6) Socratic Pr.

Wayzgoose: A South African Satire. Roy Campbell. LC 72-131660. 1971. reprint ed. 29.00 (0-403-00547-7) Scholarly.

***W.B. Yeats.** Ed. by A. Norman Jeffares. (Critical Heritage Ser.). 500p. (C). 1997. text ed. 45.00 (0-415-15939-3) Routledge.

W.B. Yeats, Dramatist of Vision. A. S. Knowland. (Irish Literary Studies: Vol. # 17). 256p. 8300. 54.95 (0-86140-117-4, Pub. by Colin Smythe Ltd UK) Dufour.

WCCN Wireless Handbook: RF Terminals & LANs. Tom Polizzi. (WCCN Wireless Handbook Ser.). (Illus.). 96p. 1993. pap. text ed. 27.95 (0-9638649-0-4) WCCN Pubng.

WCCN Wireless Handbook: RF Terminals & LANs. 2nd ed. Tom Polizzi. (Wireless Handbook Ser.). 1995. write for info. (0-9638649-3-9) WCCN Pubng.

***WCCN Wireless Handbook - RF Systems Integrators & Selected Software.** 2nd ed. Bernadette C. Polizzi. 208p. 1997. write for info. (0-9638649-4-7) WCCN Pubng.

***WCCN Wireless Handbook - RF Terminals & LANs.** 3rd ed. Tom Polizzi. 182p. 1997. write for info. (0-9638649-5-5) WCCN Pubng.

WCCN Wireless Handbook-Leading RF Systems Integrators & Selected Applications. Ed. by Bernadette C. Polizzi. (Illus.). 192p. 1995. write for info. (0-9638649-2-0) WCCN Pubng.

WCCN Wireless Handbook on Event-Time Data Processing. Tom Polizzi. (Wireless Handbook Ser.). (Illus.). 100p. 1994. write for info. (0-9638649-1-2) WCCN Pubng.

WCFL, Chicago's Voice of Labor, 1926-78. Nathan Godfried. LC 96-10132. 1997. text ed. 49.95 (0-252-02287-4); pap. text ed. 19.95 (0-252-06592-1) U of Ill Pr.

WCRP: A History of the World Conference on Religion & Peace. Homer A. Jack. (Illus.). 596p. (Orig.). 1993. pap. 25.00 (0-935934-09-X) World Confer Rel & Peace.

WCW & Others. Ed. by Dave Oliphant & Thomas Zigal. (Illus.). 128p. 1984. pap. 16.95 (0-87959-103-X) U of Tex H Ransom Ctr.

***WCW vs. the World: Official Secrets & Solutions.** 40p. 1997. per. 3.99 (0-7615-1223-3) Prima Pub.

***WD-40 Book.** Jim & Tim - The Duct Tape Guys Staff. 128p. 1997. pap. 7.00 (1-887317-15-5) Bad Dog Pr.

We. Charles A. Lindbergh. 1976. 25.95 (0-8488-1412-6) Amereon Ltd.

We. Margaret Randall. 1978. pap. 1.50 (0-918266-10-6) Smyrna.

We. Eugene Zamiatin. Tr. by Gregory Zilboorg. (C). 1959. mass mkt. 5.95 (0-525-47039-5, Dutton) NAL-Dutton.

We. Eugene Zamiatin. 1991. pap. 10.00 (0-14-016710-2, Penguin Bks) Viking Penguin.

We. Yevgeny Zamyatin. Tr. by Mirra Ginsburg. 256p. 1983. mass mkt. 5.99 (0-380-63313-2) Avon.

We. Yevgeny Zamyatin. Tr. & Intro. by Clarence Brown. 240p. 1993. pap. 11.95 (0-14-018585-2, Penguin Classics) Viking Penguin.

We. unabridged ed. Yevgeny Zamyatin. (World Classic Literature Ser.). (RUS.). pap. 6.95 (2-87714-267-1, Pub. by Bookking Intl FR) Distribks Inc.

We. Charles A. Lindbergh. (Illus.). 318p. 1991. reprint ed. lib. bdg. 35.95 (0-89966-832-1) Buccaneer Bks.

We: Understanding the Psychology of Romantic Love. Robert A. Johnson. LC 83-47725. 224p. 1985. pap. 14.00 (0-06-250436-3) Harper SF.

We Add Value. Associated Equipment Distributors Staff. 1986. 145.00 incl. vhs (0-318-19182-2) Assn Equip Distrs.

We Address You! How a Home or Office Address Affects the Environment. Maryanna Korwitts & Jim Gash. 1994. pap. 5.95 (1-887270-03-5) Weve Got Your Number.

We Adopted You, Benjamin Koo. Linda W. Girard. Ed. by Abby Levine. LC 88-23653. (Illus.). 32p. (J). (gr. 2-6). 1989. pap. 5.95 (0-8075-8695-1); lib. bdg. 14.95 (0-8075-8694-3) A Whitman.

We Ain't Going Back No More, No How, Vol. 2. Mike F. Holodnak. LC 77-71882. 1977. pap. 7.95 (0-9601084-2-4) Jacek.

***We Ain't What We Was: Civil Rights in the New South.** Frederick M. Wirt. LC 96-32710. (Illus.). 280p. 1997. pap. text ed. 16.95 (0-8223-1893-8); lib. bdg. 49.95 (0-8223-1901-2) Duke.

We All Fall Down. Robert Cormier. 208p. (J). 1993. mass mkt. 4.99 (0-440-21556-0) Dell.

We All Fall Down. Rennie McQuilkin. LC 87-60219. (Illus.). 76p. (Orig.). (C). 1986. 15.95 (0-930501-14-4); pap. 8.95 (0-930501-15-2) Livingston U Pr.

We All Fall Down. large type ed. Robert Cormier. LC 93-13717. 1993. pap. 16.95 (1-56054-774-X) Thorndike Pr.

We All Fall Down: A Chronicle of an Impeachment Foretold. William Keisling. LC 96-16274. (Illus.). 336p. 1996. 24.00 (1-882611-08-X) Yardbird Bks.

We All Fought for Freedom: Women in Poland's Solidarity Movement. Kristi S. Long. (Studies in Ethnographic Imagination). 192p. (C). 1996. text ed. 54.00 (0-8133-2968-X) Westview.

We All Go Together: Creative Activities for Children to Use with Multicultural Folksongs. Doug Lipman. LC 93-34071. (Illus.). 232p. 1993. pap. 26.50 incl. audio (0-89774-764-X) Oryx Pr.

We All Got History. Nick Salvatore. 1997. pap. 14.00 (0-679-77635-4) Random.

We All Got History: The Memory Books of Amos Webber. Nick Salvatore. (Illus.). 448p. 1996. 25.00 (0-8129-2681-1, Times Bks) Random.

We All Have a Share: A Catholic Vision of Prosperity Through Productivity. Richard C. Haas. LC 94-73613. 190p. (Orig.). 1995. pap. 14.95 (0-87946-103-9) ACTA Pubns.

We All Lead Different Lives. (Shorewood Art Programs for Education Ser.). 8p. 1974. teacher ed. 107.00 (0-88185-013-6); 143.00 (0-685-07213-4) Shorewood Fine Art.

We All Live on Earth: A Sketchbook. Delores Solberg. LC 81-20733. 87p. reprint ed. pap. 25.00 (0-317-55558-8, 2029625) Bks Demand.

We All Live Together Plus. (Songs for Kids Ser.). (Illus.). 160p. (Orig.). (J). 1993. pap. 19.95 (0-7935-2378-8, 00815003) H Leonard.

We All Lost the Cold War. Richard N. Lebow & Janice G. Stein. (Studies in International History & Politics). 552p. 1993. text ed. 55.00 (0-691-03308-0) Princeton U Pr.

We All Lost the Cold War. Richard N. Lebow. 566p. (C). 1993. pap. text ed. 19.95 (0-691-01941-X) Princeton U Pr.

***We All Shine on: The Stories Behind Every John Lennon Song.** Paul Du Noyer. 1997. pap. text ed. 19.00 (0-06-273491-1, Harper Ref) HarpC.

We All Wore Blue. Muriel G. Pushman. Ed. by Winifred Denny. (Illus.). 208p. (Orig.). 1989. 22.95 (0-940495-13-9) Pickering Pr.

We All Wore Blue: Funny, Romantic & Moving - a Young Girl's Adventures in the Wartime WAAF. Muriel G. Pushman. 175p. 1995. pap. 10.95 (0-86051-940-6, Robson-Parkwest) Parkwest Pubns.

We, Also, Were There. Archie Hall. (C). 1989. 45.00 (0-86303-269-9) St Mut.

We Always Lie to Strangers. Vance Randolph. LC 74-12852. (Illus.). 309p. 1974. reprint ed. text ed. 35.00 (0-8371-7765-0, RAAL, Greenwood Pr) Greenwood.

We & Our Relationship to the Three Worlds Around Us. Taco Bay. LC 79-27423. 28p. (Orig.). 1996. pap. 2.95 (0-935690-00-X) Schaumburg Pubns.

We Animals: Poems of Our World. Nadya Aisenberg. LC 88-35043. 1989. pap. 10.95 (0-87156-685-0) Sierra.

We Are. Ilene L. Dunn. 10p. 1995. write for info. (1-887975-01-2) Romance & Miracles.

We Are. Ed. by Lisa Kanemoto. 88p. (Orig.). pap. 14.95 (0-9613699-0-6) Outreach Press.

We Are a Little Land: Cultural Assumptions in Danish Everyday Life. Judith E. Hansen. Ed. by Francesco Cordasco. LC 80-861. (American Ethnic Groups Ser.). 1981. lib. bdg. 23.95 (0-405-13424-X) Ayer.

We Are a People! Initiatives in Hispanic-American Theology. Ed. by Roberto S. Goizueta. LC 92-23666. 144p. (Orig.). 1992. pap. 17.00 (0-8006-2577-3, 1-2577, Fortress Pr) Augsburg Fortress.

We Are a People in This World: The Lakota Sioux & the Massacre at Wounded Knee. Conger Beasley, Jr. LC 94-48101. 172p. 1995. 20.00 (1-55728-387-7); pap. 14.00 (1-55728-386-9) U of Ark Pr.

***We Are a Rainbow.** Nancy Tabor. LC 97-14305. 1997. pap. write for info. (0-88106-417-3) Charlesbridge Pub.

We Are a Thunderstorm. Amity Gaige. Ed. by Nancy R. Thatch. LC 90-5922. (Books for Students by Students). (Illus.). 26p. (J). 1990. lib. bdg. 14.95 (0-933849-27-3) Landmark Edns.

We Are Acadians: Nous Sommes Acadiens. Myron Tassin. LC 76-25036. (Illus.). 96p. 1976. 8.95 (0-88289-117-0) Pelican.

We Are Accountable. Leonard Edelestein. (C). 1945. pap. 3.00 (0-87574-024-3) Pendle Hill.

We Are All Close: Conversations with Israel Writers. Haim Chertok. LC 89-80058. 265p. 1989. pap. 19.95 (0-8232-1223-8) Fordham.

We Are All Continental Afrikans. Afrikadzata Deku. LC 91-72659. (Afrikan-Centric Pan-Afrikan Poetry Ser.). 44p. 1994. pap. 10.00 (1-56454-001-4) Cont Afrikan.

We Are All Different & That's Okay! Sheila Holden. LC 94-96449. (Illus.). 26p. (Orig.). (J). (ps-6). 1994. pap. text ed. 5.95 (1-886401-00-4) S Holden Bks.

We Are All Leaders: The Alternative Unionism of the Early 1930s. Ed. by Staughton Lynd. 1995. write for info. (0-614-96404-0) U of Ill Pr.

"We Are All Leaders" The Alternative Unionism of the Early 1930s. Ed. by Staughton Lynd. (Working Class in American History Ser.). 336p. 1996. text ed. 44.95 (0-252-02243-2); pap. text ed. 17.95 (0-252-06547-6) U of Ill Pr.

We Are All Living with AIDS: How You Can Set Policies & Guidelines for the Workplace. Earl C. Pike. 416p. 1993. pap. 14.95 (0-925190-68-3) Fairview Press.

***We Are All Multiculturalists Now.** Nathan Glazer. LC 96-39900. 179p. 1997. 19.95 (0-674-94851-3) HUP.

We are All POWs. Chuck Noell & Gary Wood. LC 75-13032. 96p. reprint ed. pap. 27.40 (0-685-16035-1, 2026839) Bks Demand.

***We Are All Related: A Celebration of Our Cultural Heritage.** Illus. by Cunningham, G. T., Elementary School Students. 64p. (Orig.). (J). (gr. 4-7). 1997. pap. 15.95 (0-9680479-0-4, Pub. by Polestar Bk Pubs CN) Orca Bk Pubs.

***We Are All Schismatics.** Elias Zoghby. Tr. by Philip Khairallah from FRE. LC 96-39393. 192p. (Orig.). 1996. pap. 9.95 (1-56125-019-8) Educ Services.

We Are All Self-Employed: The New Social Contract for Working in a Changed World. Cliff Hakim. LC 94-21708. 246p. 1994. 24.95 (1-881052-47-8) Berrett-Koehler.

We Are All Self-Employed: The New Social Contract for Working in a Changed World. Cliff Hakim. LC 94-21708. 246p. 1995. pap. 14.95 (1-881052-79-6) Berrett-Koehler.

We Are All the Black Boy. Michael Warr. 52p. (Orig.). (C). 1991. pap. 6.95 (0-9624287-1-X) Tia Chucha Pr.

We Are All the Target: A Handbook of Terrorism Avoidance & Hostage Survival. Douglas S. Derrer. LC 92-4415. 112p. 1992. pap. 15.95 (1-55750-150-5) Naval Inst Pr.

We Are All Together Now: Fredrick Douglass, William Lloyd Garrison, & the Prophetic Tradition. 9,501th ed. William B. Rogers. LC 94-24749. (Studies in African American History & Culture). 182p. 1995. text ed. 44.00 (0-8153-1868-5) Garland.

We Are All Water Babies. Jessica Johnson & Michel Odent. LC 95-6376. (Illus.). 128p. 1995. pap. 24.95 (0-89087-758-0) Celestial Arts.

We Are America. Anna Joy. (Illus.). 580p. (Orig.). (C). 1994. pap. text ed. write for info. (0-15-501480-3) HB Coll Pubs.

We Are America. 2nd ed. Joy & Jacobus. (C). 1994. teacher ed., pap. text ed. 33.75 (0-15-502364-0) HB Coll Pubs.

We Are America. 3rd ed. Joy. (C). 1997. teacher ed., text ed. 28.00 (0-15-505239-X); text ed. 25.25 (0-15-505240-3) HarBrace.

We Are America: A Cross-Cultural Reader & Guide. Anna Joy. 600p. (C). 1992. teacher ed. write for info. (0-318-69137-X); pap. text ed. 21.50 (0-15-595146-7) HB Coll Pubs.

***We Are an Easter People: Leader's Guide.** 10.35 (0-687-61292-6) Abingdon.

We Are an Easter People: The Triumph of God's Love in Our Lives. John Carr & Adrienne Carr. 64p. (Orig.). 1990. Leader's guide, 64 pgs. teacher ed., pap. 6.95 (0-8358-0602-2); Participant's guide, 48p. student ed., pap. 4.95 (0-8358-0603-0) Upper Room Bks.

We Are an Easter People-Participant's Notebook: The Triumph of God's Love in Our Lives. John Carr. 1990. pap. 4.95 (0-687-61293-4) Abingdon.

We Are, Are We? Bill Brown. (Orig.). 1992. pap. 12.00 (0-940556-06-5) Coyote.

We Are Authors, Too! Ed. by Brigitta Geltrich. (Illus.). 44p. (Orig.). (YA). 1985. pap. text ed. 4.75 (0-936945-07-9) Creat with Wds.

We Are Best Friends. Aliki. LC 81-6549. (Illus.). 32p. (J). (gr. k-3). 1982. 16.00 (0-688-00822-4); lib. bdg. 15.93 (0-688-00823-2) Greenwillow.

We Are Best Friends. Aliki. LC 81-6549. (Illus.). 32p. (J). (ps up). 1987. reprint ed. pap. 4.95 (0-688-07037-X, Mulberry) Morrow.

We Are But Women: Women In Ireland's History. Roger Sawyer. LC 93-508. 256p. (C). (gr. 13). 1993. text ed. 49.95 (0-415-05866-X) Routledge.

We Are Children Just the Same: Vedem, the Secret Magazine of the Boys of Theresienstadt. Ed. by Paul Wilson. LC 94-12698. 1995. 29.95 (0-8276-0534-X) JPS Phila.

We Are Dressing Up. Jane Walker. (Magic Window Puzzle Bks.). (Illus.). 8p. (J). (gr. k-2). 1996. 3.99 (0-88705-958-9, Wshng Well Bks) Joshua Morris.

We Are Everywhere: A Historical Sourcebook in Gay & Lesbian Politics. Ed. by Mark Blasius & Shane Phelan. 600p. (C). (gr. 13). 1997. text ed. 75.00 (0-415-90858-2, B2934) Routledge.

We Are Everywhere: A Historical Sourcebook in Gay & Lesbian Politics. Ed. by Mark Blasius & Shane Phelan. 600p. (C). (gr. 13). 1997. pap. 24.95 (0-415-90859-0, B2938) Routledge.

We Are Experiencing Parental Difficulties...Please Stand By. Rick Kirkman & Jerry Scott. (Baby Blues Scrapbook Ser.: No. 5). (Illus.). 128p. 1995. pap. 8.95 (0-8362-1781-0) Andrews & McMeel.

***We Are Family.** JoAnne Nelson. LC 93-12176. (Primarily Health Ser.). (Illus.). (J). (ps-2). 1995. 6.00 (0-7802-3257-7) Wright Group.

***We Are Family: Queer Parents Tell Their Stories.** Turan Ali & Catherine Treasure. 1996. 60.00 (0-614-22137-4) Cassell.

***We Are Family: Queer Parents Tell Their Stories.** Turan Ali & Catherine Treasure. 1996. pap. 17.95 (0-614-22138-2) Cassell.

We Are Family: The Ultimate Destiny of Creation. Kenna Farris. write for info. (0-318-60371-3) Port Love Intl.

We Are Fishing. Jane Walker. LC 95-62457. (Magic Window Puzzle Stories Ser.). (Illus.). 13p. (Orig.). (J). (gr. k-2). 1996. 3.99 (0-88705-948-1, Wshng Well Bks) Joshua Morris.

We Are Forever Voyageurs of Space. Ronald J. McMillan. LC 92-59947. 550p. 1993. pap. 18.95 (1-55523-572-7) Winston-Derek.

We Are Forgiven. Domenic Vadala. (Orig.). 1993. pap. 9.95 (0-9635920-0-9) Sun Books.

We Are Friends. Eve Feldman. (Real Readers Ser.: Level Blue). (Illus.). 32p. (J). (gr. 1-4). 1989. lib. bdg. 21.40 (0-8172-3517-5) Raintree Steck-V.

We Are Friends. Eve Feldman. (Real Reading Ser.: Level Blue). (Illus.). 32p. (J). (gr. 1-4). 1989. pap. 3.95 (0-8114-6716-3) Raintree Steck-V.

***We Are Gathered Here.** Micah Perks. 1997. pap. 13.95 (0-312-15294-9) St Martin.

We Are Gathered Here: A Novel. Micah Perks. LC 95-33693. 336p. 1995. 22.95 (0-312-14065-7, Wyatt Bk) St Martin.

We Are Gifts from God. Ann Gallagher et al. (Grade School Chastity - Project Genesis Ser.). (Illus.). 48p. (Orig.). (J). (gr. k-k). 1996. teacher ed., pap. text ed. write for info. (1-885845-04-9); student ed., pap. text ed. write for info. (1-885845-05-7) Leaflet Missal.

We Are Here: Politics of Aboriginal Land Tenure. Ed. by Edwin N. Wilmsen. 222p. 1989. pap. 14.00 (0-520-07206-5) U CA Pr.

We Are Here: Songs of the Holocaust in Yiddish & Singable English Translation. Eleanor G. Mlotek & Malke Gottlieb. 104p. 1983. 10.00 (0-686-40805-5) Workmen's Circle.

We Are Hindus. Vithal P. Kanitkar. 168p. (C). 1988. pap. text ed. 45.00 (0-7152-0620-6) St Mut.

We Are Hindus. Vithal P. Kanitkar. 168p. (C). 1989. pap. 30.00 (0-685-60671-6, Pub. by St Andrew UK) St Mut.

We Are Holding the President Hostage. Warren Adler. 304p. 1988. pap. 4.50 (0-373-97072-2) Harlequin Bks.

We Are Home: Spirituality of the Environment. Shannon Jung. LC 92-37876. 176p. 1993. pap. 12.95 (0-8091-3364-4) Paulist Pr.

***We Are in for It! The First Battle of Kernstown.** Gary Ecelbarger. LC 97-22162. (Illus.). 328p. 1997. 29.95 (1-57249-053-5, Burd St Pr) White Mane Pub.

We Are Leaving Here Forever!, Vol. 4. Ilya Nabakov. (Illus.). 326p. 1993. pap. 95.00 (0-8109-2541-9) Abrams.

We Are Like Dreamers. Walter Beyerlin. Tr. by Dinah Livingstone from GER. 76p. 1982. 19.95 (0-567-09315-8, Pub. by T & T Clark UK) Bks Intl VA.

We Are Loved. (RUS.). 1995. pap. 2.99 (1-85792-081-3, Pub. by Christian Focus UK) Spring Arbor Dist.

We Are Loved. C. Mackenzie. (J). 1995. 2.99 (1-871676-53-3, Pub. by Christian Focus UK) Spring Arbor Dist.

We Are Men: Memoirs of W. W. II & the Korean War. Wilbert L. Walker. LC 72-81006. 129p. 1972. 9.00 (0-935428-01-1) Heritage Pr.

We Are Mesquakie, We Are One. Hadley Irwin. 128p. (Orig.). (J). (gr. 3-6). 1996. reprint ed. pap. 9.95 (1-55861-148-7) Feminist Pr.

We Are Metis: The Ethnography of a Halfbreed Community in Northern Alberta. Paul Driben. LC 83-45353. (Immigrant Communities & Ethnic Minorities in the U. S. & Canada Ser.: No. 2). (Illus.). 1985. 37.50 (0-404-19406-0) AMS Pr.

We Are Monsters. Mary Packard. LC 96-1466. (My First Hello Reader! Ser.). (Illus.). 32p. (J). (ps-k). 1996. 3.99 (0-590-68995-9, Cartwheel) Scholastic Inc.

We Are Moving. Jane Walker. LC 95-62456. (Magic Window Puzzle Stories Ser.). (Illus.). 13p. (Orig.). (J). (gr. k-2). 1996. 3.99 (0-88705-947-3, Wshng Well Bks) Joshua Morris.

We Are Moving: A Let's Make a Book about It Book. Rachel Biale. (Illus.). 48p. (J). (ps-3). 1996. pap. 7.95 (1-883672-32-5) Tricycle Pr.

***We Are Muslim, Al-Hamdu Lillah.** unabridged ed. Kathy Fannoun. Ed. by Fadel Abdallah & Mahlaqa Patel. LC 94-77887. (Islamic Akhlaq Ser.). (Illus.). 16p. (J). (ps-k). 1994. mass mkt. 5.00 (1-56316-319-5) Iqra Intl Ed Fdtn.

We Are Muslim Children. Saida Chaudhry. (J). (gr. 4). 1993. pap. 4.00 (0-89259-126-9) Am Trust Pubns.

We Are No Longer "a Couple" Gary Browe. LC 92-81968. (Illus.). 128p. (Orig.). 1992. pap. 9.95 (0-8187-0162-5) Harlo Press.

We Are Not Afraid: History of the Northern Ireland Civil Rights Movement, 1968-1978. Ed. by Thomas R. Eckenrode. 79p. 1996. pap. text ed. 7.50 (0-9648601-1-2) Stella Matutina.

We Are Not Alone: A Baby Blues Book. Rick Kirkman & Jerry Scott. (Little Gift Bks.). (Illus.). 1996. 4.95 (0-8362-1325-4) Andrews & McMeel.

We Are Not Alone: Learning to Live with Chronic Illness. Sefra K. Pitzele. LC 86-40200. 336p. 1986. pap. 10.95 (0-89480-139-2, 1139) Workman Pub.

We Are Not Alone: Learning to Live with Chronic Illness. Howard I. Shapiro. LC 84-16378. (Illus.). 320p. 1985. pap. 14.95 (0-918351-01-4) Thompson Co Inc.

We Are Not Alone: Studies in the Covenant of God. Rodney J. Buchanan. 95p. 1994. pap. 7.95 (0-917851-98-6) Bristol Hse.

We Are Not Alone: The Continuing Search for Extraterrestrial Intelligence. rev. ed. Walter Sullivan. LC 93-46130. (Illus.). 368p. 1994. pap. 13.95 (0-452-27224-6, Plume) NAL-Dutton.

"We Are Not Beggars" - a Private Sector: Economic Revitalization Plan for the Black Inner City. 2nd ed. James McRae. 57p. (Orig.). 1996. pap. text ed. 10.00 (0-9651347-1-7) J McRae.

We Are Not Forgotten. Joel Martin & Patricia Romanowski. 1992. mass mkt. 6.99 (0-425-13288-9) Berkley Pub.

***We Are Not Gathered Here Alone: A Novel of the Creek Nation. Donovan Hamilton. LC 96-95510. 296p. (Orig.). 1997. pap. 14.95 (0-9656141-0-7) D Hamilton.**

Set in the Creek Nation in the early 1900s before Oklahoma Statehood, this novel chronicles the challenges faced by one branch of the famous & wealthy Perryman Family with its prosperous cattle empire. The oldest son, Moses, has married a young Caucasian miss much to the dislike of one of his full-blood siblings. While many characters are featured, the events of this panorama center around his wife, Lula Dunbar Perryman, who bears him three daughters. Although the erosion of Creek traditions is obvious to all, it is more noticeable to the Indians, themselves, especially in their dialogue with the U.S. Government. Based on exhausting research & with actual incidents & historically fictionalized people, the story ends on a positive note despite physical & emotional conflicts. A large number of characters are called by their real names, including Lula who was the author's grandmother. Sweeping historical & cultural themes; quite an accomplishment. ***Publisher Provided Annotation.***

We Are Not in This Together. William Kittredge. LC 83-82866. (Short Fiction Ser.). 128p. (C). 1984. pap. 10.00 (0-915308-44-4) Graywolf.

We Are One. Sara A. Bender & Robert A. Bender. (Illus.). 97p. (Orig.). 1986. pap. 6.95 (0-9624630-0-0) SA & RA Bender.

***We Are One.** Valerie F. Harris & Eula V. Jones. 29p. (J). (gr. k-6). Date not set. pap. write for info. (1-889654-02-7) Enricharamics.

We Are One: A Challenge to Traditional Christianity. Ellwood W. Norquist. 176p. 1995. pap. 14.95 (0-9646995-2-4) CC Publng.

We Are One Another. Arthur Guirdham. 238p. pap. 26.95 (0-8464-4311-2) Beekman Pubs.

We Are One Another. Arthur Guirdham. (Guirdham Trilogy Ser.). 191p. 1991. pap. 17.95 (0-85207-248-1, Pub. by C W Daniel UK) Natl Bk Netwk.

***We Are Our Own.** Ray McCreary. 155p. (Orig.). 1997. mass mkt. 4.99 (1-55197-754-0, Pub. by Comnwlth Pub CN) Partners Pubs Grp.

We Are Overcome: Thoughts on Being Black in America. Bonnie Allen. 1995. 16.00 (0-517-59759-4, Crown) Crown Pub Group.

We Are Shopping. Jane Walker. (Magic Window Puzzle Bks.). (Illus.). 8p. (J). (gr. k-2). 1996. 3.99 (0-88705-957-0, Wshng Well Bks) Joshua Morris.

We Are Sisters. Dee Brestin. LC 96-21413. 192p. 1996. pap. 8.99 (1-56476-604-7, Victor Bks) Chariot Victor.

We Are Staying: The Alyawarre Struggle for Land at Lake Nash. Pamela Lyon. 240p. (C). 1990. 60.00 (0-7316-7458-8, Pub. by Pascoe Pub AT) St Mut.

We Are Still Here! The Algonquian Peoples of Long Island Today. John A. Strong. LC 96-86274. (Illus.). 96p. (Orig.). 1996. pap. 12.00 (1-55787-147-7, Empire State Bks) Hrt of the Lakes.

We Are Still Married. Garrison Keillor. 352p. 1990. pap. 12.95 (0-14-013156-6) Viking Penguin.

We Are Still Married. large type ed. Garrison Keillor. (General Ser.). 427p. 1990. pap. 13.95 (0-8161-4870-8, GK Hall); lib. bdg. 21.95 (0-8161-4868-6, GK Hall) Thorndike Pr.

We Are Stories We Tell: The Best Short Stories by American Women since 1945. Ed. by Wendy Martin. 272p. 1990. pap. 15.00 (0-679-72881-3) Pantheon.

We Are Ten. Fannie Hurst. LC 72-178442. (Short Story Index Reprint Ser.). 1977. reprint ed. 36.95 (0-8369-4043-1) Ayer.

***We Are the Angels: Healing Your Past, Present, & Future with the Lords of Karma.** Diane Stein. (Illus.). 128p. (Orig.). 1997. pap. 14.95 (0-89594-878-8) Crossing Pr.

We Are the Beloved: A Special Gift for Family & Friends. Ken Blanchard. LC 94-33605. 80p. 1994. 9.99 (0-310-48820-6) Zondervan.

***We Are the Children of the Forest.** Louise Phillips. Ed. by Jane Weinberger. (Illus.). 48p. (J). (ps-4). 1997. 15.95 (1-883650-42-9) Windswept Hse.

We Are the Church: 52 Second Lesson Text Children's Object Lessons. Wesley T. Runk. LC 94-8316. 1994. 9.50 (0-7880-0100-0) CSS OH.

We Are the Church Together: Cultural Diversity in Congregational Life. Charles R. Foster & Theodore Brelsford. LC 96-12885. 192p. (Orig.). 1996. pap. 17.00 (1-56338-169-9) TPI PA.

We Are the Circle: Accompaniment Book. Julie Howard. 64p. (Orig.). 1993. spiral bd. 9.95 (0-8146-2232-1) Liturgical Pr.

We Are the Circle: Celebrating the Feminine in Song & Ritual. Julie Howard. LC 93-594. 88p. 1993. pap. 6.95 (0-8146-2231-3) Liturgical Pr.

We Are the Fire: A Selection of Poems. Toby Olson. LC 84-4772. 128p. 1984. 14.95 (0-8112-0913-X); pap. 7.50 (0-8112-0914-8, NDP580) New Directions.

We Are the Landlords Now: A Report on Community-Based Housing Management. Doug Turetsky. 94p. 1993. 9.00 (0-88156-153-3) Comm Serv Soc NY.

***We Are the Light of God: A Little Book about Enlightenment.** Linda Bernat. LC 97-12701. (Illus.). 32p. (Orig.). 1997. pap. 4.95 (1-889059-07-2) Regent Pr.

We Are the Masters of Our Fate. Stephen Tarver. 140p. 1984. 8.00 (0-9614237-1-4) Powder River.

***We Are the Miracle: Seeking Blessings, Asking Guidance, Finding Help.** Susan Maguire. LC 96-38334. 208p. (Orig.). 1997. pap. 14.95 (0-915556-30-8) Great Ocean.

We Are the Music Masters. Jesse E. Brannen. LC 93-94370. 360p. (Orig.). 1995. pap. 14.95 (1-56002-429-1, Univ Edtns) Aegina Pr.

We Are the Original People. Marieke Clarke. (C). 1991. 28.00 (81-202-0243-0, Pub. by Ajanta II) S Asia.

We Are the People Our Parents Warned Us Against. Nicholas Von Hoffman. (Illus.). 288p. 1989. reprint ed. pap. text ed. 6.95 (0-929587-06-5, Elephant Paperbacks) I R Dee.

We Are the Pharisees. Kathleen Kern. LC 94-28471. 160p. (Orig.). 1995. pap. 9.99 (0-8361-3671-3) Herald Pr.

We Are the Shakers. A. F. Joy. Orig. Title: The Queen of the Shakers. (Illus.). 130p. (Orig.). 1985. pap. 5.00 (0-934703-00-0) Saturscent Pubns.

We Are the Shakers. abr. rev. ed. A. F. Joy. Orig. Title: The Queen of the Shakers. (Illus.). 130p. (Orig.). 1985. pap. 5.50 (0-318-18279-3) A F Joy.

We Are the Way We Are. Sondra Anice Barnes. LC 86-72759. (Illus.). 85p. (Orig.). 1986. pap. 6.00 (0-9602534-1-6) Brason-Sargar.

W

An Asterisk (*) at the beginning of an entry indicates that the title is appearing in BIP for the first time.

We Are the World We Walk Through. Margaret Laird. 297p. 1993. pap. 12.95 (0-9638172-0-5) M Laird Fnd.

We Are the Young Magicians. Ruth Forman. LC 92-37807. (Barnard New Women Poets Ser.). 96p. 1993. pap. 12.00 (0-8070-6821-7) Beacon Pr.

We Are Three. Jelaluddin Rumi. Tr. by Coleman Barks. 132p. 1987. pap. 7.50 (0-9618916-0-2) Maypop.

We Are Tomorrow's Past. large type ed. Betty King. 304p. 1994. 25.99 (0-7089-3095-6) Ulverscroft.

We are Twins: But Who Am I? Betty J. Case. LC 91-65981. 203p. 1991. 18.95 (0-9629948-0-4) Tibbutt Pub.

***We Are Waiting on You.** 1995. pap. 1.20 (0-8341-9329-9) Lillenas.

We Are Witnesses: Five Diaries of Teenagers Who Died in the Holocaust. Jacob Boas. (YA). (gr. 5 up). 1996. pap. 3.99 (0-590-84475-X) Scholastic Inc.

We Are Witnesses: The Diaries of Five Teenagers Who Died in the Holocaust. Ed. by Jacob Boas. LC 94-43889. (J). (gr. 7 up). 1995. 15.95 (0-8050-3702-0, Bks Young Read) H Holt & Co.

We Are Writers, Too!, Vol. I. Ed. by Brigitta Geltrich. (Annual Anthology by Young Writers & Poets Ser.). (Illus.). 44p. (Orig.). (YA). 1988. pap. text ed. 7.50 (0-936945-16-8) Creat with Wds.

We Are Writers, Too!, Vol. II: The Year Round--Seasons. Ed. & Illus. by Brigitta Geltrich. (Annual Anthology by Young Writers & Poets Ser.). 64p. (Orig.). (YA). 1989. pap. text ed. 7.50 (0-936945-17-6) Creat with Wds.

We Are Writers, Too!, Vol. III: Time. Ed. by Brigitta Geltrich. (Annual Anthology by Young Writers & Poets Ser.). (Illus.). 88p. (Orig.). (YA). 1990. pap. text ed. 8.00 (0-936945-18-4) Creat with Wds.

We Are Writers, Too!, Vol. IV: Caring. Ed. by Brigitta Geltrich. (Annual Anthology by Young Writers & Poets Ser.). (Illus.). 83p. (Orig.). (YA). 1991. pap. text ed. 9.00 (0-936945-19-2) Creat with Wds.

We Are Writers, Too!, Vol. V: America. Ed. & Illus. by Brigitta Geltrich. (Annual Anthology by Young Writers & Poets Ser.). 100p. (Orig.). (YA). 1992. pap. text ed. write for info. (0-936945-21-4) Creat with Wds.

We Are Writers, Too!, Vol. VI. Ed. & Intro. by Brigitta Geltrich. (Annual Anthology by Young Writers & Poets Ser.). (Illus.). 108p. (Orig.). (YA). 1993. pap. text ed. 11.00 (0-936945-23-0) Creat with Wds.

We Are Writers, Too! Vol. VII. Ed. & Intro. by Brigitta Geltrich. (Annual Anthology by Young Writers & Poets Ser.). 108p. (Orig.). (YA). 1994. pap. text ed. write for info. (0-614-03698-4) Creat with Wds.

We Are Your Servants: Augustine's Homilies on Ministry. Ed. by John E. Rotelle. Tr. by Audrey Fellowes from LAT. LC 86-71645. 156p. 1986. pap. 4.50 (0-941491-10-2) Augustinian Pr.

***We Are Your Sisters: Black Women in the 19th Century.** Ed. by Dorothy Sterling. (Illus.). 560p. 1997. reprint ed. pap. 15.95 (0-393-31629-7) Norton.

We Are Your Sons: The Legacy of Ethel & Julius Rosenberg. 2nd ed. Robert Meeropol & Michael Meeropol. LC 85-30892. (Illus.). 508p. 1986. text ed. 34.95 (0-252-01263-1) U of Ill Pr.

We Ask for Baptism: A New Sourcebook for Parents & Godparents. William J. Belford. 50p. 1992. pap. 2.50 (0-8146-6065-7, Pueblo Bks) Liturgical Pr.

We Ask for British Justice: Workers & Racial Difference in Late Imperial Britain. Laura Tabili. LC 94-7305. (Wilder House Series in Politics, History, & Culture). (Illus.). 272p. 1994. 36.50 (0-8014-2904-8) Cornell U Pr.

We Ask Forgiveness: A Young Child's Book for Reconciliation. rev. ed. Corinne Hart & Ellen Shannon. (Illus.). 32p. (J). (ps-2). 1991. pap. 1.90 (1-55944-005-8) Franciscan Comns.

We Ask Only a Fair Trial: A History of the Black Community of Evansville, Indiana. Darrel E. Bigham. LC 86-45892. (Midwestern History & Culture Ser.; Blacks in the Diaspora Ser.). (Illus.). 302p. 1987. 39.95 (0-253-36326-8) Ind U Pr.

We Aspired: The Last Innocent Americans. Pete Sinclair. LC 93-3859. (Illus.). 192p. (Orig.). 1993. pap. 12.00 (0-87421-166-2) Utah St U Pr.

We Band of Brothers: The Sullivans & World War II. Jack R. Satterfield. 261p. (Orig.). 1995. pap. 15.00 (0-931209-58-7) Mid-Prairie Bks.

We Barons. Marian B. Goldner. 1993. 60.00 (0-9614989-5-1) Banmar Inc.

We Be Here When the Morning Comes. Bryan Woolley. LC 75-18285. 168p. reprint ed. pap. 47.90 (0-317-26724-8, 2024362) Bks Demand.

We Become a Picnic: (Selected Poems 1971-1983) Larry Jones. 60p. 1994. pap. 5.00 (1-886206-12-0) Venom Pr.

We Beheld His Glory. Nicolai S. Arsen'ev. Tr. by Mary A. Ewer. LC 76-113545. reprint ed. 37.50 (0-404-00407-5) AMS Pr.

We Beheld His Glory: Rosedale Bible Institute - The First Forty Years: 1952-1992. Elmer S. Yoder & Jewel Showlater. 280p. 1992. pap. 9.49 (0-9633310-0-0) Rosedale Bks.

We Believe. (Christ Our Life Ser.). (Illus.). 1992. pap. text ed. 9.00 (0-8294-0365-5) Loyola Pr.

We Believe. (Christ Our Life Ser.). (Illus.). 1992. teacher ed. 10.60 (0-8294-0668-9) Loyola Pr.

We Believe. David M. Thomas & Mary J. Calnan. (Catechism of the Catholic Church Ser.: Vol. 1). 146p. (Orig.). 1994. pap. 8.95 (0-88347-295-3, 7295) Res Christian Liv.

We Believe... A Guide to a Better Understanding of the Bible As a Source Book for the Humanities. 1987. 0.75 (0-89942-247-0, 247/05) Catholic Bk Pub.

We Believe: A Study of the Book of Confessions for Church Officers. rev. ed. Harry W. Eberts, Jr. LC 93-39392. 128p. (Orig.). 1994. pap. 9.00 (0-664-25374-1) Westminster John Knox.

We Believe... A Survey of the Catholic Faith. rev. ed. Oscar Lukefahr. LC 90-60495. 224p. (Orig.). 1995. pap. 7.95 (0-89243-536-4) Liguori Pubns.

We Believe: Doctrines & Principles of the Church of Jesus Christ of Latter Day Saints. Rulon T. Burton. 1400p. (Orig.). 1994. lib. bdg. 39.95 (0-9640696-0-1) Tabernacle Bks.

We Believe: Doctrines & Principles of the Church of Jesus Christ of Latter Day Saints. Rulon T. Burton. 1200p. (Orig.). 1995. pap. 24.95 (0-9640696-2-8) Tabernacle Bks.

***We Believe: Growing Spiritually Through the Catechism of the Catholic Church, Vol. 1.** Henry Libersat. LC 96-50958. (Catholic Confession of Faith Ser.). 80p. 1997. pap. 5.95 (0-8198-8288-7) Pauline Bks.

We Believe: Junior High Basic Belief Studies. Ed. by Sara L. Anderson & Charles Cooper. (Illus.). Date not set. teacher ed., pap. 7.95 (1-885224-05-2); student ed., pap. 5.95 (1-885224-06-0) Bristol Hse.

We Believe: The Articles of Faith. Margaret Yorgason & Annette Ward. 1994. pap. 5.95 (0-88494-916-8) Bookcraft Inc.

***We Believe - Discovery.** rev. ed. Ed. by Sara L. Anderson & Charles Cooper. 64p. (YA). 1988. student ed., pap. 5.95 (1-885224-09-5) Bristol Hse.

We Believe in God. Ed. by John V. Taylor. 184p. 1987. pap. 7.95 (0-8192-1407-8) Morehouse Pub.

We Believe, Therefore We Speak. David Valleskey. 310p. (Orig.). 1995. 23.99 (0-8100-0540-9, 15N0563); pap. 12.99 (0-8100-0539-5, 15N0562) Northwest Pub.

We Believe...Workbook: A Survey of the Catholic Faith. rev. ed. Oscar Lukefahr. 64p. (Orig.). 1995. student ed. 2.95 (0-89243-539-9) Liguori Pubns.

We Belong Dead: Frankenstein in the Cinema. Ed. by Gary J. Svehla & Susan Svehla. (Illus.). 320p. (Orig.). 1997. pap. 20.00 (1-887664-09-2) Midnght Marquee Pr.

We Belong Together: The Churches in Solidarity with Women. Ed. by Sarah Cunningham. (Orig.). 1992. pap. 7.95 (0-377-00242-9) Friendship Pr.

We Bombed in Burbank: A Joyride to Primetime. Vance Muse. 279p. 1994. 22.00 (0-201-62223-8) Addison-Wesley.

***We Breathe the Sky.** David R. Good. 62p. 1996. pap. text ed. 12.00 (0-9646851-0-8) Scrubjay Pr.

We Bring Her Flowers. Sharon A. Dunn. LC 90-3626. 96p. (Orig.). 1990. pap. 8.95 (0-931832-62-4) Fithian Pr.

We Build Poeple: Making Disciples for the 21st Century. Michael H. Clarensau et al. 144p. (Orig.). 1996. pap. 3.95 (0-88243-698-8, 02-0698) Gospel Pub.

We Built Jerusalem: Tales of Pioneering Days. Arye Lipshitz. Tr. by Misha Louvish. LC 84-45016. 176p. 1985. 14.95 (0-8453-4787-X, Cornwall Bks) Assoc Univ Prs.

***We Call It Prescott.** Jack August. 1996. pap. text ed. 12.95 (0-916179-57-5) Ariz Hwy.

"We Called Each Other Comrade" Charles H. Kerr & Company, Radical Publishers. Allen Ruff. LC 96-1008. 1997. text ed. 49.95 (0-252-02277-7) U of Ill Pr.

"We Called Each Other Comrade" Charles H. Kerr & Company, Radical Publishers. Allen Ruff. LC 96-1008. 1997. pap. text ed. 19.95 (0-252-06582-4) U of Ill Pr.

We Called Him Casper. James E. Vincent. Ed. by Frank Cannon. (Psychic Phenomena Series: A History). (Illus.). (Orig.). 1987. 6.00 (0-317-00997-4) RAPCOM Enter.

***We Called It Culture: The Story of Chautaugua.** Victoria Case. 272p. 1970. 18.95 (0-8369-8051-4) Ayer.

We Called It Macaroni: An American Heritage of Southern Italian Cooking. Nancy V. Barr. (Illus.). 1990. 25.00 (0-394-55798-0) Knopf.

We Called It Macaroni: An American Heritage of Southern Italian Cooking. Nancy V. Barr. (Illus.). 368p. 1996. pap. 18.00 (0-679-76577-8) Random.

We Called It Music. Eddie Condon & Thomas Sugrue. (Roots of Jazz Ser.). (Illus.). 341p. 1987. reprint ed. lib. bdg. 35.00 (0-306-76267-6) Da Capo.

We Called It Music: A Generation of Jazz. Eddie Condon & Thomas Sugrue. (Illus.). 375p. 1992. reprint ed. pap. 13.95 (0-306-80466-2) Da Capo.

We Came All the Way from Cuba So You Could Dress Like This? Stories. Achy Obejas. LC 94-18194. 160p. (Orig.). 1994. pap. 10.95 (0-939416-93-X) Cleis Pr.

We Came Back to Jesus. Bob Lord & Penny Lord. (Illus.). 205p. (Orig.). 1988. 12.95 (0-926143-04-2); pap. 8.95 (0-926143-05-0) Journeys Faith.

We Came from Vietnam. Muriel Stanek. Ed. by Ann Fay. LC 84-29927. (Illus.). 48p. (J). (gr. 1-6). 1985. lib. bdg. 11.95 (0-8075-8699-4) A Whitman.

We Came to Australia. Thomas Jenkins. LC 78-448322. (Illus.). 280p. reprint ed. pap. 79.80 (0-317-11339-9, 2019383) Bks Demand.

***"We Came to Fight" The History of the 5th New York Veteran Volunteer Infantry, Duryees Zouaves (1863-1865)** unabridged ed. Patrick A. Schroeder. (Illus.). 500p. 1997. 40.00 (1-889246-07-7) P A Schroeder.

We Came to Love. Michael Hathaway. LC 94-44066. 1994. write for info. (1-886557-00-4) Obelus Bks.

We Came to Play: Writings on Basketball. Ed. by Q. R. Hand & John Ross. LC 95-45632. 1996. pap. 16.95 (1-55643-162-7) North Atlantic.

We Came to Town. Ed. by Caroline Kerfoot. (Illus.). 74p. 1986. pap. 12.95 (0-86975-251-0, Pub. by Ravan Pr ZA) Ohio U Pr.

We Can!, 2 vols. Robin R. Star. (J). (gr. 4 up). 1980. Set. lib. bdg. 4.95 (0-685-00153-9) Alexander Graham.

We Can!, 2 vols., Vol. 1, 88p. Robin R. Star. (J). (gr. 4 up). 1980. Vol. 1 88 pgs. write for info. (0-88200-135-3, C2670) Alexander Graham.

We Can!, 2 vols., Vol. 2, 98p. Robin R. Star. (J). (gr. 4 up). 1980. Vol. 2 98 pgs. write for info. (0-88200-136-1, C2786) Alexander Graham.

We Can All Be Doctors of Commonsense. Elizabeth Bowden. 156p. (C). 1990. 60.00 (0-9589059-3-2, Pub. by Pascoe Pub AT) St Mut.

We Can All Get Along: Fifty Steps You Can Take to Help End Racism. Clyde W. Ford. LC 93-1930. 208p. 1994. pap. 9.95 (0-440-50570-4) Dell.

We Can All Get Along IF. 126p. (Orig.). 1994. pap. text ed. 6.95 (0-9641423-0-9) Tales Pr.

We Can Build see Homeplay: Joyful Learning for Children & Adults, Series I

We Can Build You. Philip K. Dick. 1994. pap. 11.00 (0-679-75296-X) Random.

We Can Change America...& Here's How! Darylann Whitemarsh. 1991. pap. 9.95 (0-929292-05-7) Hannibal Bks.

We Can Change the World. Mark Kram. (Illus.). 56p. (Orig.). 1991. pap. 5.95 (0-317-04659-4) Mark Kram.

We Can Change the World: The Real Meaning of Everyday Life. David G. Stratman. LC 90-92305. 320p. (Orig.). 1991. 19.95 (0-9628566-1-4); pap. 9.95 (0-9628566-0-6) New Dem Bks.

We Can Do It! Laura Dwight. (Illus.). 32p. (J). (ps-4). 1992. 7.95 (1-56288-301-1) Checkerboard.

We Can Eat the Plants. Rozanne L. Williams. (Emergent Reader Big Bks.). (Illus.). 8p. (Orig.). (J). (gr. k-2). 1995. pap. 7.98 (1-57471-012-5) Creat Teach Pr.

We Can Eat the Plants, Level I. Rozanne L. Williams. (Emergent Reader Science Ser.). 8p. 1994. 1.59 (0-916119-26-2, 3502) Creat Teach Pr.

***We Can Get Along: A Child's Book of Choices.** Lauren M. Payne & Claudia Rohling. Ed. by Pamela Espeland. LC 96-29528. (Illus.). 36p. (Orig.). (J). 1997. pap. 9.95 (1-57542-013-9) Free Spirit Pub.

We Can Implement Cost-Effective Information Systems NOW: Proceedings. 126p. 12.00 (0-318-14034-9) EDUCOM.

We Can Make Graphs. Rozanne L. Williams. (Emergent Reader Bks.). (Illus.). 8p. (Orig.). (J). (gr. k-2). 1995. pap. 1.59 (1-57471-000-1) Creat Teach Pr.

We Can Make Graphs. Rozanne L. Williams. (Emergent Reader Big Bks.). (Illus.). 8p. (Orig.). (J). (gr. k-2). 1996. pap. 7.98 (1-57471-104-0) Creat Teach Pr.

***We Can Make It: Stories of Disabled Women in Developing Countries.** Susan Epstein. 50p. 1997. pap. 13.50 (92-2-110327-7) Intl Labour Office.

We Can Make It...Together: A Daring Vision of the Future for Black Americans. Jordan. LC 84-234729. 1984. 6.00 (0-685-09709-9) Jordan Enter.

We Can Play. Julia B. McFann. (Illus.). 13p. (Orig.). (J). (gr. 1). 1993. pap. text ed. write for info. (1-882225-15-5) Tott Pubns.

***We Can Prevent Wars! A Guidebook for World Peace.** rev. ed. Crandall R. Kline, Jr. 180p. (Orig.). 1997. pap. 6.50 (0-9640656-1-4) C R Kline.

We Can Print Anything. Arlene Spencer. Ed. by Mary Caroland. LC 90-71227. 235p. 1991. pap. 8.95 (1-55523-380-5) Winston-Derek.

We Can Read. Beth A. Wise & Amy Levin. (Learn Today for Tomorrow Ser.). (Illus.). 32p. (J). (gr. k-1). 1997. student ed., pap. 2.25 (1-878624-63-6) McClanahan Bk.

***We Can Read.** Beth A. Wise. (J). (gr. k-1). 1997. wbk. ed., pap. text ed. 2.25 (1-56293-969-6) McClanahan Bk.

We Can Read: Story Pack-54 Little Stories. Priscilla L. McQueen. (J). 1973. pap. 18.66 (0-685-47089-X) McQueen.

***We Can Reclaim Our Errant Youth.** A. I. Schepps. LC 95-91047. (Orig.). 1997. pap. 9.95 (0-533-11833-6) Vantage.

We Can Save Ourselves...How to Live Better on Fewer Energy Dollars, Vol. 4. 68p. 1978. 2.50 (0-317-34114-6, 017811) Edison Electric.

***We Can Share at School.** Rozanne L. Williams. (Social Studies Learn to Read Ser.). (Illus.). 8p. (Orig.). (J). (ps-2). 1996. pap. 1.59 (1-57471-125-3, 3906) Creat Teach Pr.

***We Can Share at School.** Rozanne L. Williams. (Social Studies Big Bks.). (Illus.). 8p. (Orig.). (J). (ps-2). 1997. pap. 7.98 (1-57471-171-7, 3963) Creat Teach Pr.

We Can Share It. 2nd ed. Sarah Tatler. (Let Me Read Ser.). (Illus.). (J). (ps-2). 1995. bds. 2.95 (0-673-36274-4, GoodYrBooks) Addson-Wesley Educ.

We Can Sing: Beginner Sequence. Ellis Richardson. (Read Aloud Ser.: Bk. A). (Illus.). 24p. (Orig.). 1988. pap. text ed. 4.00 (1-56775-005-2, BGSA3) ISM Teach Systs.

We Can Speak for Ourselves: Self-Advocacy by Mentally Handicapped People. Paul Williams & Bonnie Shoultz. 245p. (C). 1988. reprint ed. pap. text ed. 10.00 (0-253-36365-9) Brookline Bks.

We Can Try to Fly Away: Beginner Sequence. Ellis Richardson. (Read Aloud Ser.: Bk. C). 20p. (Orig.). 1988. pap. text ed. 4.00 (1-56775-007-9, BGSC5) ISM Teach Systs.

We Can Use Computers, Bk. C. (J). Date not set. pap. 3.95 (0-590-49544-5) Scholastic Inc.

We Can Use Computers, Bk. C. Date not set. teacher ed., pap. 5.95 (0-590-49550-X) Scholastic Inc.

We Can Use Computers, Bk. D. (J). Date not set. pap. 3.95 (0-590-49545-3) Scholastic Inc.

We Can Use Computers, Bk. D. Date not set. teacher ed., pap. 5.95 (0-590-49551-8) Scholastic Inc.

We Can Use Computers, Bk. A. (J). Date not set. pap. 3.95 (0-590-49542-9) Scholastic Inc.

We Can Use Computers, Bk. A. Date not set. teacher ed., pap. 5.95 (0-590-49548-8) Scholastic Inc.

We Can Use Computers, Bk. B. (J). Date not set. pap. 3.95 (0-590-49543-7) Scholastic Inc.

We Can Use Computers, Bk. B. Date not set. teacher ed., pap. 5.95 (0-590-49549-6) Scholastic Inc.

We Can Use Computers, Bk. E. (J). Date not set. pap. 3.95 (0-590-49546-1) Scholastic Inc.

We Can Use Computers, Bk. E. Date not set. teacher ed., pap. 5.95 (0-590-49552-6) Scholastic Inc.

We Can Use Computers, Bk. F. (J). Date not set. pap. 3.95 (0-590-49547-X) Scholastic Inc.

We Can Use Computers, Bk. F. Date not set. teacher ed., pap. 5.95 (0-590-49553-4) Scholastic Inc.

We Can Work It Out: How to Solve Conflicts, Save Your Marriage & Strenjthen Your Love for Each Other. Clifford Notarius. Ed. by Howard Markman. LC 94-14009. 336p. (Orig.). 1994. pap. 12.95 (0-399-52137-2, Berkley Trade) Berkley Pub.

We Cannot but Tell: A Practical Guide to Heart to Heart Evangelism. Ross Tooley. 177p. 1993. pap. 7.99 (0-927545-42-X) YWAM Pub.

We Cannot Escape History: Lincoln & the Last Best Hope of Earth. Ed. by James M. McPherson. LC 95-2279. 184p. 1995. 27.95 (0-252-02190-8) U of Ill Pr.

We Cannot Find Words. Tad Dunne. 1985. pap. 6.95 (0-87193-262-8) Dimension Bks.

***We Can't Eat Prestige: The Women Who Organized Harvard.** John Hoerr. LC 97-1722. (Labor & Social Change Ser.). 256p. (C). 1997. 29.95 (1-56639-535-6) Temple U Pr.

We Can't Forget. Doris Eggleston. (Illus.). 400p. (Orig.). 1995. pap. 18.00 (1-886094-20-9) Chicago Spectrum.

We Care: A Preschool Curriculum for Children Ages 2-5. Bertie W. Kingore & Glenda M Higbee. (Illus.). 464p. (Orig.). 1988. pap. 29.95 (0-673-18574-5, GoodYrBooks) Addson-Wesley Educ.

We Care for Summer. Bertie W. Kingore & Brenda Higbee. (Illus.). 224p. (Orig.). (J). (ps). 1992. pap. 13.95 (0-673-36017-2, GoodYrBooks) Addson-Wesley Educ.

We Celebrate. David M. Thomas & Mary J. Calnan. (Catechism of the Catholic Church Ser.: Vol. 2). 126p. (Orig.). 1994. pap. 8.95 (0-88347-296-1, 7296) Res Christian Liv.

We Celebrate: Prayer Services for Special Occasions. LC 90-82094. 152p. (Orig.). 1990. spiral bd. 9.95 (0-87793-432-0) Ave Maria.

***We Celebrate Advent: A Prayer Service for Children.** Cynthia L. Trainque. 8p. (J). (gr. 1-5). pap. 1.50 (0-8198-8274-7) Pauline Bks.

We Celebrate Christmas. Bobbie Kalman. (Holidays & Festivals Ser.). (Illus.). 56p. (J). (gr. 3-4). 1985. 21.28 (0-86505-040-6); pap. 8.95 (0-86505-050-3) Crabtree Pub Co.

We Celebrate Easter. Bobbie Kalman. (Holidays & Festivals Ser.). (Illus.). 56p. (J). (gr. 3-4). 1985. 21.28 (0-86505-042-2); pap. 8.95 (0-86505-052-X) Crabtree Pub Co.

We Celebrate Family Days. Bobbie Kalman. (Holidays & Festivals Ser.). (Illus.). 56p. (J). (gr. 3-4). 1986. 21.28 (0-86505-048-1); pap. 8.95 (0-86505-058-9) Crabtree Pub Co.

We Celebrate Halloween. Bobbie Kalman. (Holidays & Festivals Ser.). (Illus.). 56p. (J). (gr. 3-4). 1985. 21.28 (0-86505-039-2); pap. 8.95 (0-86505-049-X) Crabtree Pub Co.

We Celebrate Hanukkah. Bobbie Kalman. (Holidays & Festivals Ser.). (Illus.). 56p. (J). (gr. 3-4). 1986. 21.28 (0-86505-045-7); pap. 8.95 (0-86505-055-4) Crabtree Pub Co.

We Celebrate Harvest. Bobbie Kalman. (Holidays & Festivals Ser.). (Illus.). 56p. (J). (gr. 3-4). 1986. 21.28 (0-86505-044-9); pap. 8.95 (0-86505-054-6) Crabtree Pub Co.

We Celebrate New Year. Bobbie Kalman. (Holidays & Festivals Ser.). (Illus.). 56p. (J). (gr. 3-4). 1985. 21.28 (0-86505-041-4); pap. 8.95 (0-86505-051-1) Crabtree Pub Co.

We Celebrate Our Marriage. John Van Bemmel & Dolores Van Bemmel. (Greeting Book Line Ser.). 32p. (Orig.). 1986. pap. 1.95 (0-89622-304-3) Twenty-Third.

We Celebrate Spring. Bobbie Kalman. (Holidays & Festivals Ser.). (Illus.). 56p. (J). (gr. 3-4). 1985. 21.28 (0-86505-043-0); pap. 8.95 (0-86505-053-8) Crabtree Pub Co.

***We Celebrate the Mystery: Growing Spiritually Through the Catechism of the Catholic Church, Vol. 2.** Henry Libersat. LC 96-50959. (Catholic Confession of Faith Ser.). 97p. (Orig.). 1997. pap. 5.95 (0-8198-8289-5) Pauline Bks.

We Celebrate Valentine's Day. Bobbie Kalman. (Holidays & Festivals Ser.). (Illus.). 56p. (J). (gr. 3-4). 1986. 21.28 (0-86505-047-3); pap. 8.95 (0-86505-057-0) Crabtree Pub Co.

We Celebrate Winter. Bobbie Kalman. (Holidays & Festivals Ser.). (Illus.). 56p. (J). (gr. 3-4). 1986. 21.28 (0-86505-046-5); pap. 8.95 (0-86505-056-2) Crabtree Pub Co.

***We Changed the World: African Americans 1945-1970.** Vincent Harding. (YA). (gr. 12 up). 1997. 21.00 (0-614-25380-2) OUP.

We Changed the World: African Americans 1945-1970 see Young Oxford History of African Americans

We Charge Genocide: The Historic Petition to the United Nations for Relief from a Crime of the United States Government Against the Negro People. Civil Rights Congress Staff. Ed. by William L. Patterson. LC 76-140208. 256p. reprint ed. pap. 73.00 (0-317-28065-1, 2025547) Bks Demand.

We, Chile: Personal Testimonies of the Chilean Arpilleristas. Ed. by Emma Sepulveda. Tr. by Bridget Morgan from SPA. LC 95-83885. (Illus.). 192p. (Orig.). (C). 1996. pap. 15.95 (1-885214-08-1) Azul Edits.

We Chose Cape Cod. Scott Corbett. LC 52-13127. 1970. reprint ed. pap. 9.95 (0-85699-007-8) Chatham Pr.

We Chose Cape Cod. Scott Corbett. 320p. 1984. reprint ed. pap. 8.95 (0-940160-27-7) Parnassus Imprints.

We Christians & Jews. Paul J. Kirsch. LC 74-26332. 160p. reprint ed. pap. 45.60 (0-685-16032-7, 2026838) Bks Demand.

We Claim the Title. Burton F. Anderson. LC 94-61241. (Illus.). 418p. 1994. reprint ed. pap. 14.95 (0-9643110-0-3) Tracy Pubng.
We Claimed This Land: Portland's Pioneer Land Settlers. Eugene E. Snyder. LC 89-60948. (Illus.). 288p. 1989. 24.95 (0-8323-0471-9); pap. 14.95 (0-8323-0468-9) Binford Mort.
We Come As Eagles. Harold Klemp. (Mahanta Transcripts Ser.: Bk. 9). 164p. 1994. pap. 14.00 (1-57043-010-1) ECKANKAR.
***We Come to Object: The Peasants of Morelos & the National State.** Arturo Warman. LC 80-8092. (Johns Hopkins Studies in Atlantic History & Culture). 328p. 1980. reprint ed. pap. 93.50 (0-608-03664-1, 2064490) Bks Demand.
We Confess: The Sacraments. Herman Sasse. Tr. by Norman Nagel. (We Confess Ser.: Vol. II). 160p. 1985. pap. 14.99 (0-570-03982-7, 12-2899) Concordia.
We Could Have Finished Last Without You. Bill Borst. 48p. (Orig.). 1986. pap. 3.95 (0-9612260-3-X) Krank Pr.
We Could've Finished Last Without You: An Irreverent Look at the Atlanta Braves. Bob Hope. LC 90-63895. 192p. 1991. 16.95 (0-929264-84-3) Longstreet Pr Inc.
We Cried Together. Apurba Maitra. 1983. 11.00 (0-8364-0952-3, Pub. by Mukhopadhyaya II) S Asia.
We Cry for Our Land: Farm Workers in South Africa. Wendy Davies. (Illus.). 64p. (C). 1990. pap. 8.95 (0-85598-143-1, Pub. by Oxfam UK) Humanities.
We Dance Because We Can: People of the Powwow. Photos by Don Contreras. (Illus.). 1996. 29.95 (1-56352-287-X) Longstreet Pr Inc.
We Danced All Night: My Life Behind the Scenes with Alan Jay Lerner. Doris Shapiro. LC 93-19654. 1993. pap. 12.00 (0-942637-98-4) Barricade Bks.
We Dare to Dream: Doing Theology As Asian Women. Ed. by Virginia Fabella & Sun Si Lee Park. LC 90-102425. 166p. 1990. reprint ed. pap. 47.40 (0-7837-9846-6, 2060575) Bks Demand.
***We Delivered.** Lyle E. Dupra. (Illus.). 170p. 1997. pap. 23.95 (0-89745-212-7) Sunflower U Pr.
We Did It, Tara! Katy Hall. Ed. by Lisa Clancy. (Peabody Rebus Reading Program Ser.: No. 4). 144p. (Orig.). (J). (gr. 3-6). 1995. pap. 3.50 (0-671-89787-X, Minstrel Bks) PB.
We Did It Their Way. unabridged ed. William F. Bane. Ed. by Mary K. Matson & Oka Negley. (Illus.). 230p. 1996. 19.62 (0-9652452-0-9) Bane-Clene.
We Didn't Ask Utopia: A Quaker Family in Soviet Russia. Harry Timbres & Rebecca Timbres. LC 76-115590. (Russia Observed Ser., No. 1). 1970. reprint ed. 19.95 (0-405-03067-3) Ayer.
We Didn't Mean to. Sharon Addy. LC 80-24976. (Life & Living from a Child's Point of View Ser.). (Illus.). 32p. (J). (gr. k-6). 1981. lib. bdg. 21.40 (0-8172-1370-8) Raintree Steck-V.
We Didn't Mean to Go to Sea. Arthur Ransome. 344p. 1994. pap. 12.95 (0-87923-991-3) Godine.
***We Didn't Pass Through the Golden Door: The Filipino American Experience.** Reuben S. Seguritan. 240p. (Orig.). 1997. pap. 17.00 (0-9655951-0-2) R S Seguritan.
We Die Alone. David Howarth. LC 96-83530. (Adventure Library: Vol. 7). (Illus.). 224p. 1996. reprint ed. lib. bdg. 25.00 (1-885283-06-7) Advent Library.
We Discovered Alien Bases on the Moon. Fred Steckling. LC 81-90609. (Illus.). 192p. 1981. pap. 14.95 (0-942176-00-6) GAF Intl.
We Dissent. Ed. by Hoke Norris. LC 73-6210. 211p. 1973. reprint ed. text ed. 55.00 (0-8371-6889-9, NOWD, Greenwood Pr) Greenwood.
We Do Have a Choice: Please Choose Jesus. Harry O. Nawroth. 110p. pap. 4.95 (1-883537-52-5) Nawroth Pub.
We Do It for Jesus - Mother Teresa & Her Missionaries. Edward L. Joly. 182p. 1977. 8.95 (0-318-37371-8) Asia Bk Corp.
We Do Not Die. Hilton Hotema. 50p. 1962. reprint ed. spiral bd. 5.00 (0-7873-0439-5) Hlth Research.
We Don't Even Want to March Straight: Why Queers Should Oppose the Military. Peter Tachell. Date not set. pap. 4.95 (0-304-33373-5, Pub. by Cassell Pubng UK) LPC InBook.
We Don't Kill Snakes Where We Come From: Two Years in a Greek Village. John Levy. LC 92-81744. 128p. 1994. pap. 8.00 (1-882168-02-X) Querencia Bks.
We Don't Make the Weather! Don Wigington. LC 92-70187. (Illus.). 138p. (Orig.). 1992. pap. 7.95 (0-9628296-6-8) Bounds Pub.
We Don't Speak Great Things - We Live Them. Mark Felix & Justin Martyr. Tr. by Robert E. Wallis & Marcus Dods from GRE. 160p. (Orig.). 1990. pap. 7.95 (0-924722-01-0) Scroll Pub.
We Drink from Our Own Wells: The Spiritual Journey of a People. Gustavo Gutierrez. Tr. by Mattew J. O'Connell from SPA. LC 83-22008. Orig. Title: Beber en Supropio Pozo: En el Itinerario Espiritual de un Pueblo. 208p. (Orig.). 1984. pap. 16.00 (0-88344-707-X) Orbis Bks.
We Each Have a Dream. (Shorewood Art Programs for Education Ser.). 12p. 1974. teacher ed. 107.00 (0-88185-050-0); 143.00 (0-685-07224-X) Shorewood Fine Art.
We Eat Dinner in the Bathtub. Angela S. Medearis. (Hello Reader! Ser.: Level 1). (Illus.). (J). 1996. write for info. (0-590-73886-0) Scholastic Inc.
We Eat the Mines & the Mines Eat Us: Dependency & Exploitation in Bolivian Tin Mines. June Nash. (Illus.). 384p. 1993. pap. 19.00 (0-231-08051-4); text ed. 49.50 (0-231-08050-6) Col U Pr.
We Endeavor. Charles H. Spurgeon. 1975. mass mkt. 5.00 (1-56186-315-7) Pilgrim Pubns.
We Fall & Rise, 1889-1914: Russian-Language Newspapers in New York City. Robert A. Karlowich. LC 91-28068. (Illus.). 356p. 1991. 39.50 (0-8108-2474-4) Scarecrow.
We Fed Them Cactus. 2nd ed. Fabiola Cabeza de Baca. LC 93-11951. (Paso por Aqui Ser.). (Illus.). 218p. 1994. pap. 15.95 (0-8263-1503-8) U of NM Pr.
We Fight for Freedom: Massachusetts, African Americans, & the Civil War. (Picture Bks.). 32p. 1993. pap. 7.95 (0-934909-66-0) Mass Hist Soc.
We Fight for Oil. Ludwell Denny. 1979. lib. bdg. 59.95 (0-8490-3014-5) Gordon Pr.
***We Find the Jury Guilty.** D. R. Ayres. (Railway Fiction Ser.: Vol. 4). (Illus.). 324p. (Orig.). 1997. pap. 8.95 (0-943857-10-4) D R Ayres.
We Fished All Night. Willard Motley. LC 73-18875. reprint ed. 39.50 (0-404-11370-2) AMS Pr.
We Flew over the Bridge: The Memoirs of Faith Ringgold. Faith Ringgold. LC 95-12988. (Illus.). 304p. 1995. 29.95 (0-8212-2071-3) Bulfinch Pr.
***We Follow Jesus.** (Image of God Ser.). (J). (gr. 4). 1996. pap. text ed. 10.95 (0-614-24899-X) Ignatius Pr.
We-Force in Management: How to Build & Sustain Cooperation. Lawrence G. Hrebiniak. 154p. 19.95 (0-02-915345-X, Free Press) Free Pr.
We Fought Together for Freedom. Ed. by Indian Council for Historical Research Staff, Delhi. 280p. 1995. 24.00 (0-19-563286-9) OUP.
***We Gain More Than We Give: Teaming in Middle Schools.** Thomas S. Dickinson & Thomas O. Erb. LC 96-47731. 1997. pap. write for info. (1-56090-103-9) Natl Middle Schl.
We Gather in Christ: Our Identity As Assembly. Worship Office of the Archdiocese of Cincinnati Staff. LC 96-39188. 80p. (Orig.). 1996. pap. 9.00 (1-56854-149-X, WGIC) Liturgy Tr Pubns.
We Gather Together: Food & Festival in American Life. Ed. by Theodore C. Humphrey & Lin T. Humphrey. LC 91-29267. 301p. 1991. reprint ed. pap. 85.80 (0-608-02076-1, 2062729) Bks Demand.
We Gather Together: The Story of Thanksgiving. Ralph Linton & Adelin Linton. (Illus.). 100p. 1990. reprint ed. lib. bdg. 34.00 (1-55888-883-7) Omnigraphics Inc.
We Give Thanks. Doris Willis. (Bible Board Book Ser.). 1991. pap. 3.95 (0-687-03128-1) Abingdon.
***We Give Thanks.** Linda R. Wisdom. 1998. mass mkt. 4.50 (0-373-81041-5, 1-81041-5) Harlequin Bks.
We Give Thanks: Preparation for Early Communion. Iris V. Cully. (Illus.). (Orig.). 1976. student ed., wbk. ed., pap. text ed. 3.95 (0-8192-4070-2); teacher ed., pap. text ed. 5.50 (0-8192-4069-9); teacher ed., pap. text ed. 3.25 (0-8192-4071-0) Morehouse Pub.
***We Give You Thanks: Three Services of Thanksgiving.** Gail G. Martin. 50p. 1996. pap. 9.50 (1-57438-002-8, 2692) Ed Ministries.
We Go to Mass. George Brundage. (Illus.). 16p. (J). 1994. bds. 2.50 (0-89942-841-X, 841/22) Catholic Bk Pub.
***We Go to Mass: Coloring.** K. Cavanagh. Date not set. pap. text ed. 0.99 (0-88271-175-X) Regina Pr.
***We Got Here Together.** Stafford. 1987. pap. write for info. (0-15-201597-3) HarBrace.
We Got Here Together. Kim R. Stafford. LC 93-9814. (Illus.). 40p. (J). (ps-3). 1994. 14.00 (0-15-294891-0) HarBrace.
We Got My Brother at the Zoo. John Hassett & Ann Hassett. LC 92-1681. (J). 1993. 14.95 (0-395-62429-0) HM.
We Gotta Get Outta This Place: Politics & Popular Culture in Contemporary America. Lawrence Grossberg. 352p. (C). (gr. 13). 1992. pap. 16.95 (0-415-90330-0, A4619, Routledge NY) Routledge.
We Grow in God's Love. Ann Gallagher et al. (Grade School Chastity - Project Genesis Ser.). (Illus.). 48p. (Orig.). (J). (gr. 1). 1996. teacher ed., pap. text ed. write for info. (1-885845-06-5); student ed., pap. text ed. write for info. (1-885845-07-3) Leaflet Missal.
We Grow up Fast Nowadays: Conversations with a New Generation. Jeffrey Artenstein. 204p. 1991. 19.95 (0-929923-46-4) Lowell Hse.
We Grow up Fast Nowadays: Conversations with a New Generation. Jeffrey Artenstein. 192p. 1993. pap. 12.95 (1-56565-020-4) Lowell Hse.
We Grow up Fast Nowadays: Conversations with America's Youth. Jeffrey Artenstein. 1991. 19.95 (0-929923-69-3) Lowell Hse.
We Had a Picnic This Sunday Past. Jacqueline Woodson. LC 96-16312. (Illus.). (J). 1999. write for info. (0-7868-0242-1); lib. bdg. write for info. (0-7868-2192-2) Hyprn Child.
We Had Everything but Money. Ed. by Deb Mulvey. LC 92-60979. 164p. 1992. 14.95 (0-89821-099-2, 11572) Reiman Pubns.
We Had Joy, We Had Fun: The "Lost" Recording Artists of the Seventies. Barry Scott. LC 93-46448. (Illus.). 250p. (Orig.). 1994. pap. 14.95 (0-571-19835-X) Faber & Faber.
***We Happy Wasps: Virginia in the Days of Jim Crow & Harry Byrd.** Parke Rouse, Jr. (Illus.). 244p. (Orig.). 1996. pap. 17.95 (0-87517-091-9) Dietz.
We Hatch Our Embryo: Selected Poems by Wilson Reid Ogg. Wilson R. Ogg. (Illus.). 70p. (Orig.). 1988. pap. 5.00 (0-929707-02-8) Pinebrook CA.
We Hate Everything but Boys. Linda Lewis. (J). (gr. 5 up). pap. 2.99 (0-671-72225-5, Archway) PB.
We Hate Rain! James Stevenson. LC 87-21204. (Illus.). 32p. (J). (gr. k-3). 1988. 12.95 (0-688-07786-2); lib. bdg. 12.88 (0-688-07787-0) Greenwillow.
We Have a Baby. Cathryn Falwell. LC 92-40268. (J). 1993. 15.00 (0-395-62038-4, Clarion Bks) HM.
We Have a Dream: African-American Visions of Freedom. Compiled by Diana Wells. LC 93-20000. (Illus.). 288p. 1993. 21.95 (0-88184-941-3); pap. 11.95 (0-88184-957-X) Carroll & Graf.
We Have a Duty: The Supreme Court & the Watergate Tapes Litigation. Howard Ball. LC 90-3135. (Contributions in Legal Studies: No. 60). 184p. 1990. text ed. 49.95 (0-313-26565-8, BWB, Greenwood Pr) Greenwood.
***We Have a Great High Priest: A Brief Study of the Book of Hebrews.** 225p. (Orig.). 1997. pap. text ed. 22.50 (0-9654519-7-6) Bedrock Pub.
We Have a Lift-Off: History of Shuttle Missions Photographs of Shuttle Launches. Ed Case. (Illus.). 1992. pap. 14.95 (0-9633033-0-9) Ed Case.
We Have a Little Sister: Marguerite: The Midwest Years. John Sanford. LC 95-33054. (Illus.). 300p. 1995. 25.00 (0-88496-399-3) Capra Pr.
We Have a New Baby. Christine H. Tangvald. LC 87-35457. (Please Help Me God Ser.). 24p. (J). (ps-2). 1988. 8.99 (1-55513-503-X, Chariot Bks) Chariot Victor.
We Have a Problem: A Parent's Sourcebook. Jane Marks. LC 92-7391. 449p. 1992. text ed. 23.95 (0-88048-504-3, 8504) Am Psychiatric.
***We Have a Side.** Vincent Johnson. 16p. (Orig.). 1996. pap. 9.95 (1-885206-41-0, Iliad Pr) Cader Pubng.
We Have all Gone Away. Curtis Harnack. LC 87-34498. (Iowa Heritage Collection). (Illus.). 188p. 1988. reprint ed. pap. 9.95 (0-8138-1903-2) Iowa St U Pr.
We Have Already Cried Many Tears: The Stories of Three Portuguese Migrant Women. Caroline B. Brettel. (Illus.). 170p. 1983. 18.95 (0-87073-232-5); pap. 13.95 (0-87073-233-1) Schenkman Bks Inc.
We Have Already Cried Many Tears: The Stories of Three Portuguese Migrant Women. Caroline B. Brettell. (Illus.). 151p. (C). 1995. reprint ed. pap. text ed. 10.50 (0-88133-878-8) Waveland Pr.
We Have Always Lived in the Castle. Shirley Jackson. 224p. 1984. pap. 9.95 (0-14-007107-5, Penguin Bks) Viking Penguin.
We Have Always Lived in the Castle. Shirley Jackson. 1994. reprint ed. lib. bdg. 21.95 (0-89968-532-3) Buccaneer Bks.
We Have Always Lived in the Castle: Acting Edition. adapted ed. Shirley Jackson. 1967. pap. 5.25 (0-8222-1226-9) Dramatists Play.
We Have Always Lived in the Castle: Acting Edition. Shirley Jackson. reprint ed. lib. bdg. 22.95 (0-89190-623-1, Am Repr) Amereon Ltd.
We Have Arrived in Amritsar: And Other Stories. Bhisham Sahni. 1990. text ed. 7.95 (0-86131-998-2, Pub. by Orient Longman Ltd II) Apt Bks.
We Have Been Believers: An African-American Systematic Theology. James H. Evans, Jr. LC 92-15333. 192p. (Orig.). 1992. pap. 15.00 (0-8006-2672-9, 1-2672, Fortress Pr) Augsburg Fortress.
We Have Conquered the Pain: The Discovery of Anesthesia. Dennis B. Fradin. LC 95-35538. (Illus.). 160p. (J). (gr. 7-10). 1996. 16.00 (0-689-50587-6, McElderry) S&S Childrens.
We Have Done with Pleading: The Women's 1913 Anti-Pass Campaign. Julia Wells. (History Workshop Topic Ser.: No. 3). (Illus.). (Orig.). (C). 1992. pap. text ed. 9.95 (0-86975-415-7) Ohio U Pr.
We Have Eaten the Forest: The Story of a Montagnard Village in the Central Highlands of Vietnam. Georges Condominas. Ed. by Philip Turner. Tr. by Adrienne Foulke. (Illus.). 464p. 1994. pap. 16.00 (1-56836-023-1) Kodansha.
We Have Enough Clothes. Bill Keane. Date not set. pap. write for info. (0-449-14817-3) Fawcett.
We Have Fun. (Key Words Readers Ser.: A Series, No. 641-2a). (Illus.). (J). (ps-5). 3.50 (0-7214-0002-7, Ladybrd) Penguin.
We Have Fun. (Series S705: No. 2). (Illus.). (J). (ps-5). Ser. S705, No. 2. student ed. 1.95 (0-7214-3063-5, Ladybrd) Penguin.
***We Have Fun.** Ladybird Staff. (J). 1997. pap. 3.50 (0-7214-5762-2) Dutton Child Bks.
***We Have Gone to the Beach.** Cynthia Huntington. 80p. (Orig.). 1996. pap. 9.95 (1-882295-11-0) Alicejamesbooks.
***We Have Heard with Our Ears, O God: Sources of the Communal Laments in the Psalms.** Walter C. Bouzard. LC 97-7383. (Dissertation Series - Society of Biblical Literature). 1997. write for info. (0-7885-0354-5) Scholars Pr GA.
We Have Just Begun to Not Fight. Heather Frazer. 1996. pap. 28.95 (0-8057-9134-5, Twayne) Scribnrs Ref.
We Have Just Begun to Not Fight: An Oral History of Conscientious Objectors in Civilian Public Service During WWII. Heather T. Frazer & John O'Sullivan. LC 95-20068. (Twayne's Oral History Ser.: Vol. 18). 1996. pap. write for info. (0-8057-9225-2, Twayne) Scribnrs Ref.
We Have Kept the Faith: New & Selected Poems. Francis Stuart. 47p. 1982. pap. 7.95 (0-906897-34-3) Dufour.
***We Have Kept the Faith: Poems 1918-1992.** Francis Stuart. 80p. 9200. pap. 10.95 (1-85186-101-7) Dufour.
We Have Lived & Loved Before. Susan J. Cassidy, pseud. et al. LC 91-77037. (Illus.). 64p. (Orig.). 1992. pap. 7.95 (1-879559-05-6) Galaxy WV.
***We Have Lost Our Fathers, & Other Poems.** Nicholas Rinaldi. LC 80-22908. (Contemporary Poetry Ser.). (Illus.). 88p. reprint ed. pap. 25.10 (0-608-04485-7, 2065230) Bks Demand.
We Have Marched Together: The Working Children's Crusade. Stephen Currie. LC 95-47686. (J). Date not set. lib. bdg. write for info. (0-8225-1733-7, Lerner Publctns) Lerner Group.
***We Have Met Before: The Siddha Yoga Meditation Tour with Gurumayi Chidulisananda.** LC 96-70976. (Illus.). 160p. 1996. pap. 34.95 (0-911307-50-8) SYDA Found.
We Have Never Been Modern. Bruno Latour. Tr. by Catherine Porter from FRE. LC 93-15226. 168p. 1993. pap. 14.95 (0-674-94839-4) HUP.
We Have Never Been Modern. Bruno Latour. Tr. by Catherine Porter from FRE. LC 93-15226. 167p. 1993. 32.50 (0-674-94838-6) HUP.
We Have No Leaders: African Americans in the Post-Civil Rights Era. Robert C. Smith & Ronald W. Walters. LC 95-52681. (SUNY Series in Afro-American Studies). 352p. (C). 1996. text ed. 46.50 (0-7914-3135-5) State U NY Pr.
We Have No Leaders: African Americans in the Post-Civil Rights Era. Robert C. Smith & Ronald W. Waters. LC 95-52681. (SUNY Series in Afro-American Studies). 352p. (C). 1996. pap. 16.95 (0-7914-3136-3) State U NY Pr.
We Have Reason to Believe: Some Aspects of Jewish Theology Examined in the Light of Modern Thought. 4th rev. ed. Louis Jacobs. LC 95-11920. 168p. 1995. 22.50 (0-85303-310-2, Pub. by Vallentine Mitchell UK); pap. 12.50 (0-85303-314-5, Pub. by Vallentine Mitchell UK) Intl Spec Bk.
We Have Stories to Tell. Ed. by Richard Krawiec. (Illus.). 71p. (Orig.). 1994. pap. 8.00 (0-9640528-1-4, Voices Commun Pr) Jacar Pr Lit.
We Have the Right to Exist: A Translation of Aboriginal Thought: The First Book Ever Published from an Ahnishinahbaeotjibway Perspective. Wub-e-ke-niew. (Illus.). 420p. (Orig.). 1995. pap. 16.00 (0-9628181-4-3) Black Thistle Pr.
We Have This Hope. Jonathan Gallagher. LC 92-42961. 1993. pap. 0.97 (0-8163-1142-0) Pacific Pr Pub Assn.
***We Have This Ministry: The Essence of Being a Pastor.** Samuel D. Proctor & Gardner C. Taylor. LC 96-34975. 160p. (Orig.). 1996. pap. 14.00 (0-8170-1248-6) Judson.
***We Have to Escape.** Judith Makranczy. (YA). (gr. 7 up). 1997. pap. 7.99 (0-88092-373-3) Royal Fireworks.
We Have Tomorrow. Louis B. Reynolds. Ed. by Raymond H. Woolsey. 480p. 1984. 29.99 (0-8280-0232-0) Review & Herald.
We Have Watched You... 30p. 1994. pap. 3.99 (1-881542-03-3) Blue Star Prodns.
We Heard the Angels of Madness: How One Family Dealt with Manic Depression. Diane Berger. 1992. pap. 10.00 (0-688-11615-9, Quill) Morrow.
We Heard the Bird Sing: Interacting with Anthony de Mello, S.J. Compiled by Aurel Brys & Joseph Pulickal. LC 95-24093. 122p. (C). 1995. pap. 12.95 (0-8294-0866-5) Loyola Pr.
We Hide, You Seek. Jose Aruego. LC 78-13638. (Illus.). 32p. (J). (gr. k-3). 1979. 16.00 (0-688-80201-X); lib. bdg. 15.93 (0-688-84201-1) Greenwillow.
We Hide, You Seek. Jose Aruego. LC 78-13638. (Illus.). 32p. (J). (ps up). 1988. pap. 4.95 (0-688-07815-X, Mulberry) Morrow.
***We Hold the Rock: The Indian Occupation of Alcatraz Island, 1969-1971.** Troy Johnson. (Illus.). 64p. 1997. pap. 9.95 (1-883869-28-5) Gldn Gate Natl Parks Assoc.
We Hold These Truths: A Reverent Review of the U. S. Constitution. Lawrence P. McDonald. 1992. pap. 11.95 (0-9632809-1-0) L McDonald Mem.
We Hold These Truths: Catholic Reflections on the American Proposition. John C. Murray & Walter Burghardt. LC 60-12876. 350p. 1985. reprint ed. 19.50 (0-934134-83-9); reprint ed. pap. 15.95 (0-934134-50-2) Sheed & Ward MO.
We Hold These Truths, & More: Further Catholic Reflections on the American Proposition: Essays on the Political Philosophy of Father John Courtney Murray, S. J. Ed. by Donald J. D'Elia & Stephen M. Krason. LC 92-40082. 263p. 1993. pap. 15.00 (0-940535-48-3, UP148) Franciscan U Pr.
***We Hold This Treasure: The Story of Gillette Children's Hospital.** Steven E. Koop. Ed. by Priscilla Farnham. (Illus.). 184p. 1997. 49.00 (1-890434-03-5) Afton Hist Soc.
We Home School. Debbie Strayer. (Illus.). 30p. 1991. pap. 7.00 (1-880892-16-2) Com Sense FL.
***We Imagine, We Draw Animals.** Parramon Editorial Team Staff. LC 97-12302. (We Imagine, We Draw Ser.). (J). 1997. 12.95 (0-7641-5044-8) Barron.
***We Imagine, We Draw Landscapes.** Parramon Editorial Team Staff. LC 97-17667. (We Imagine, We Draw Ser.). 1997. 12.95 (0-7641-5041-3) Barron.
***We Imagine, We Draw Objects.** Parramon Editorial Team Staff. LC 97-21413. 1997. 12.95 (0-7641-5042-1) Barron.
We Imperialists: Notes on Ernest Seilliere's "Philosophy of Imperialism" Cargill Sprietsma. LC 70-176005. reprint ed. 22.50 (0-404-06198-2) AMS Pr.
***We Interrupt This Broadcast.** K. K. Beck. 1997. 20.00 (0-89296-642-4) Mysterious Pr.
We Interrupt This Program... A Citizen's Guide to Using the Media for Social Change. Robbie Gordon. LC 79-624735. (Illus.). (Orig.). (C). 1978. pap. 10.00 (0-934210-03-9) Devlp Commy.
We Irish: On Irish Literature & Society. Denis Donoghue. 284p. (C). 1988. pap. 12.00 (0-520-06425-9) U CA Pr.
We Jazz June. Sharon L. Goodman. 10p. 1989. pap. text ed. 1.00 (0-935369-16-3) In Tradition Pub.
We Joined the Navy (Winton) Maritime Books Staff. (C). 1986. text ed. 60.00 (0-907771-38-6, Pub. by Maritime Bks UK) St Mut.
We Just Got On with It. Bette Anderson. 176p. 1990. 54.00 (0-948251-58-1, Pub. by Picton UK) St Mut.
We Just Toughed It Out: Women Heads of Households on the Llano Estacado. Georgellen Burnett. (Southwestern Studies: No. 90). 65p. 1990. pap. 10.00 (0-87404-176-7) Tex Western.
We Keep a Light. large type ed. E. M. Richardson. 1990. 25.99 (0-7089-2227-9) Ulverscroft.

W

An Asterisk (*) at the beginning of an entry indicates that the title is appearing in BIP for the first time.

We Keep a Pig in the Parlor. Suzanne Bloom. (Illus.). 32p. (J). (ps-1). 1988. 13.95 (*0-517-56829-2*, Clarkson Potter) Crown Bks Yng Read.

We Keep a Store. Anne Shelby. LC 89-35105. (Illus.). 32p. (J). (ps-2). 1990. lib. bdg. 16.99 (*0-531-08456-6*) Orchard Bks Watts.

We Keep America on Top of the World: Television Journalism & the Public Sphere. Daniel C. Hallin. LC 93-21867. (Communication & Society Ser.). 208p. (C). 1993. pap. write for info. (*0-415-09143-8*, Routledge NY) Routledge.

We Kids. Darwin Gross. 189p. 1991. 6.95 (*0-931689-19-8*) D Gross.

We Killed Mangy-Dog & Other Mozambique Stories. Luis B. Honwana. (African Writers Ser.). 117p. (C). 1969. pap. 8.95 (*0-435-90060-9*, 90060) Heinemann.

We Kiss Monsters. Charlotte Agell. LC 95-30923. (J). 1996. write for info. (*0-15-200949-3*) HarBrace.

We Knew Jesus. Marian Hostetler. LC 93-5563. 160p. (Orig.). (J). (gr. 4-8). 1994. pap. 5.99 (*0-8361-3653-5*) Herald Pr.

We Knew Paul. Marian Hostetler. LC 92-10562. 128p. (Orig.). (J). (gr. 4-8). 1992. pap. 5.99 (*0-8361-3589-X*) Herald Pr.

We Knew Paul: Conversations with Friends & Students of Paul Rosenfels. Intro. by Dean Hannotte. LC 90-35815. (Orig.). 1991. pap. 9.95 (*0-932961-09-6*) Ninth St Ctr.

***We Knew You Wouldn't Remember, So We Wrote It Down: A Collection of Memories & Recipes from the Murry Girls.** Margie M. Morgan & Robbie M. Alford. 1997. ring bd. 14.95 (*0-9658678-0-3*) Eagles Trning.

***We Know We're Not Alone: The Voices of Women Living with HIV/AIDS in the Metropolitan DC Area.** unabridged ed. Edna A. Viruell-Fuentes & Leslie R. Wolfe. (Illus.). 64p. (Orig.). 1997. pap. write for info. (*1-877966-36-3*) Ctr Women Policy.

We Know What to Do: A Political Maverick Talk to America. Lamar Alexander. LC 95-21711. 224p. 1995. 23.00 (*0-688-14288-5*) Morrow.

We Know Where You Live. Jean Taylor. LC 94-37238. 240p. (Orig.). 1995. pap. 9.95 (*1-878067-62-1*) Seal Pr WA.

We Laughed, We Cried: Life with Fibromyalgia. Ed. by Kit Gardiser & Kathleen Kerry. (Illus.). 126p. (Orig.). 1995. pap. 12.00 (*0-9630002-1-7*) KMK Assocs.

We Learn All about Community Helpers. Sharon MacDonald. (J). (ps-1). 1988. pap. 7.99 (*0-8224-4599-9*) Fearon Teach Aids.

We Learn All about Dinosaurs. Sharon MacDonald. (J). (ps-1). 1988. pap. 7.99 (*0-8224-4595-6*) Fearon Teach Aids.

We Learn All about Endangered Species. Sharon MacDonald. 1992. pap. 9.99 (*0-86653-944-1*) Fearon Teach Aids.

We Learn All about Fall. Sharon MacDonald. (J). (ps-1). 1988. pap. 7.95 (*0-8224-4596-4*) Fearon Teach Aids.

We Learn All about Farms. Sharon MacDonald. (J). (ps-1). 1988. pap. 7.99 (*0-8224-4594-8*) Fearon Teach Aids.

We Learn All about Machines. Sharon Macdonald. 1991. 7.99 (*0-8224-4590-5*) Fearon Teach Aids.

We Learn All about Protecting Our Environment. Sharon MacDonald. 1992. pap. 9.99 (*0-86653-942-5*) Fearon Teach Aids.

We Learn All about Series, 9 bks., Set. Sharon MacDonald. (J). (ps-1). 55.99 (*1-56417-740-8*, FE0020) Fearon Teach Aids.

We Learn All about Spring. Sharon Macdonald. 1991. 7.99 (*0-8224-4591-3*) Fearon Teach Aids.

We Learn all about the Circus. Sharon MacDonald. (J). (ps-1). 1988. pap. 7.99 (*0-8224-4598-0*) Fearon Teach Aids.

We Learn All about the Earth's Habitats. Sharon MacDonald. 1992. pap. 9.99 (*0-86653-943-3*) Fearon Teach Aids.

We Learn All about the Environment Series, 3 bks., Set. Sharon MacDonald. (J). (ps-1). 25.99 (*1-56417-756-4*, FE7564) Fearon Teach Aids.

We Learn All about Transportation. Sharon Macdonald. 1991. 7.99 (*0-8224-4592-1*) Fearon Teach Aids.

We Learn All about Winter. Sharon MacDonald. (J). (ps-1). 1988. pap. 7.99 (*0-8224-4597-2*) Fearon Teach Aids.

We Learn at Play see Story Books for We Can Read

We Learn English Through Action. Bertha E. Segal. 106p. (J). (gr. 3-12). 1994. 13.99 (*0-938395-11-4*) B Segal.

We Led the Way, 1980 see Darby's Rangers: We Led the Way

We Left Jehovah's Witnesses: A Non-Prophet Organization. Edmond C. Gruss. 1974. pap. 7.99 (*0-87552-307-2*, Pub. by Evangelical Pr) Presby & Reformed.

We Liberals. Nelson A. Crawford. LC 68-22908. (Essay Index Reprint Ser.). 1977. 18.95 (*0-8369-0349-8*) Ayer.

We Light the Candles: Devotions Related to Family Use of the Advent Wreath. Catharine Brandt. 40p. (J). pap. 4.99 (*0-8066-1544-3*, 10-15443, Augsburg) Augsburg Fortress.

We Like Ike: The Eisenhower Presidency & 1950s America. Ed. by Dennis Medina. LC 90-70503. (Illus.). 114p. (Orig.). 1990. pap. 5.00 (*0-939324-42-3*) Wichita Art Mus.

***We Like It Where? Sovereign State of Winneconne.** Compiled by Polly Zimmerman. LC 97-25232. (Illus.). 168p. 1997. 24.95 (*0-938627-35-X*) New Past Pr.

We Like Kids! A Multicultural Storybook, Pre-Grade 3. Jeff Brown. (Illus.). 88p. (Orig.). 1994. pap. 13.95 incl. audio (*0-673-36167-5*, GoodYrBooks) Addson-Wesley Educ.

We Like Kids! Letters & Numbers Songbook. Jeff Brown. (Illus.). 88p. (J). (ps-3). 1994. pap. 13.95 (*0-673-36126-8*, GoodYrBooks) Addson-Wesley Educ.

We Like Kids! Songs for the Earth. Jeff Brown et al. (Illus.). 80p. (Orig.). (J). (ps-3). 1992. pap. 13.95 (*0-673-36052-0*, GoodYrBooks) Addson-Wesley Educ.

We Like Kids! Songbook. Jeff Brown et al. (Illus.). 88p. (Orig.). (J). (ps-3). 1992. pap. 13.95 (*0-673-36038-5*, GoodYrBooks) Addson-Wesley Educ.

We Like to Do Things. Golden Books Staff. (First Little Golden Bks.). (Illus.). 24p. (J). 1995. 1.09 (*0-307-30273-3*, Golden Pr) Western Pub.

We Like to Graph see Math Set

We Like to Help. (Key Words Readers Ser.: B Series, No. 641-6b). (Illus.). (J). (ps-5). 3.50 (*0-7214-0542-8*, Ladybrd) Penguin.

We Like to Help. (Series S705: No. 6). (Illus.). (J). (ps-5). Ser. S705, No. 6. student ed. 1.95 (*0-317-04015-4*, Ladybrd) Penguin.

We Like to Nurse. Chia Martin. LC 94-77052. (Illus.). 36p. (Orig.). (J). 1994. pap. 9.95 (*0-934252-45-9*) Hohm Pr.

***We Live Eternal.** Darnell L. Sherman. LC 95-83386. 238p. (Orig.). 1996. pap. 14.95 (*0-7880-0657-6*) CSS OH.

We Live Forever. Lehman Strauss. LC 86-2738. 122p. 1947. pap. 7.99 (*0-87213-830-5*) Loizeaux.

We Live in Bodies. Ellen Watson. 80p. (Orig.). 1997. pap. 9.95 (*1-882295-12-9*) Alicejamesbooks.

***We Live in Germany, Too!** 40p. 1994. 3.15 (*0-8341-1488-7*) Nazarene.

***We Live the Good Life: Growing Spiritually Through the Catechism of the Catholic Church, Vol. 3.** Henry Libersat. LC 96-50957. (Catholic Confession of Faith Ser.). 120p. 1997. pap. 5.95 (*0-8198-8290-9*) Pauline Bks.

We Live to Paint Again. Lester Polakov. 216p. 1993. pap. 25.00 (*0-9639720-0-6*) Logbooks Pr.

We Lived in a Little Cabin in the Yard. Ed. by Belinda Hurmence. LC 94-28622. (Illus.). 103p. (Orig.). 1994. pap. 7.95 (*0-89587-118-1*) Blair.

We Lived There Too: In Their Own Words & Pictures - Pioneer Jews & the Westward Movement of America 1630-1930. Kenneth Libo & Irving Howe. (Illus.). 4p. 1985. pap. 14.95 (*0-312-85867-1*) St Martin.

We Lived with Dignity: The Jewish Proleteriat of Amsterdam, 1900-1940. Selma Leydesdorff. Tr. by Frank Heny from DUT. (Illus.). 288p. 1994. reprint ed. text ed. 39.95 (*0-8143-2338-3*) Wayne St U Pr.

We Love. David M. Thomas & Mary J. Calnan. (Catechism of the Catholic Church Ser.: Vol. 3). 126p. (Orig.). 1994. pap. 8.95 (*0-88347-297-X*, 7297) Res Christian Liv.

We Love Fruit! Fay Robinson. LC 92-13312. (Rookie Read-about Science Ser.). (Illus.). 32p. (J). (ps-2). 1992. lib. bdg. 17.30 (*0-516-06006-6*) Childrens.

We Love Fruit! Fay Robinson. LC 92-13312. (Rookie Read-about Science Ser.). (Illus.). 32p. (J). (ps-2). 1993. pap. 3.95 (*0-516-46006-4*) Childrens.

We Love Fruit Big Book! Fay Robinson. LC 92-13312. (Rookie Read-about Science Ser.). (Illus.). 32p. (J). (ps-2). 1992. pap. 32.40 (*0-516-49633-6*) Childrens.

***We Love Jesus Coloring Fun: My Bible Pals.** Standard Publishing Staff. (J). 1997. pap. text ed. 1.49 (*0-7847-0601-8*) Standard Pub.

We Love Music of the Fifties & Sixties. rev. ed. (We Love Ser.). 128p. 1985. pap. 14.95 (*0-89724-045-6*, VF1987) Warner Brothers.

We Love only Older Boys. Linda Lewis. 176p. (Orig.). (YA). (gr. 7 up). 1990. pap. 2.95 (*0-671-69558-4*, Archway) PB.

We Love Our New Home. Eugene Beuth. LC 93-77946. (Illus.). 34p. (Orig.). (J). (ps). 1993. pap. 12.95 (*0-9636417-2-7*) Make-Hawk Pub.

We Love the Dirt. Tony Johnston. LC 96-10588. (Hello Reader! Ser.). (Illus.). 1997. 3.50 (*0-590-92953-4*) Scholastic Inc.

***We Love Them.** 2nd ed. Martin Waddell. LC 96-49845. (Illus.). (J). 1997. write for info. (*0-7636-0339-2*) Candlewick Pr.

We Love Them Regardless. Lawrence Hallum. LC 90-80687. 172p. (Orig.). 1990. pap. 6.99 (*0-89900-356-7*) College Pr Pub.

We Love to Cook (If It's Easy) Jessica B. Fay & Merle J. Oliver. LC 75-2850. (Illus.). 123p. 1975. pap. 3.95 (*0-88435-003-7*) Chateau Pub.

We Love You - Adoption Book. Maxine Teplitz. 1991. pap. write for info. (*1-882479-02-5*) I Love You Bks.

We Love You Grant Gould: Book of Poems. Bruce Gould & Christine Gould. 96p. 1991. pap. 9.95 (*0-685-50888-9*) B Gould Pubns.

We Love You Tiffany Anne: Book of Poems. Bruce Gould & Christine Gould. 99p. 1985. pap. 9.95 (*0-918706-00-9*) B Gould Pubns.

We Made a Garden. Margery Fish. LC 83-16489. (Illus.). 120p. (Orig.). 1984. pap. 9.95 (*0-571-13141-7*) Faber & Faber.

We Made a Garden. Margery Fish. Ed. by Graham S. Thomas. (RHS Classic Garden Writers Ser.). (Illus.). 184p. (Orig.). 1995. 19.95 (*0-88192-341-9*) Timber.

We Made It Through the Winter. Walter O'Meara. (Illus.). xi, 128p. 1987. pap. 7.95 (*0-87351-212-X*) Minn Hist.

We Made Our Own Fun! Reiman Publications Staff. Ed. by Bettina Miller. LC 95-72529. 164p. Date not set. 16.95 (*0-89821-155-7*) Reiman Pubns.

We Make the Road by Walking: Conversations on Education & Social Change. Myles Horton & Paulo Freire. Ed. by Brenda Bell et al. (Illus.). 272p. 1990. pap. 17.95 (*0-87722-775-6*) Temple U Pr.

We March As One. 48p. 1987. reprint ed. 6.00 (*0-8266-0380-7*, Merkos LInyonei Chinuch) Kehot Pubn Soc.

We May Ride Away: Beginner Sequence. Ellis Richardson. (Read Aloud Ser.: Bk. B). 20p. (Orig.). 1988. pap. text ed. 4.00 (*1-56775-006-0*, BGSB4) ISM Teach Systs.

***We Mean Business.** Norman. 1993. student ed., pap. text ed. write for info. (*0-582-09905-6*, Pub. by Longman UK) Longman.

***We Mean Business.** rev. ed. Norman. 1993. wbk. ed., pap. text ed. write for info. (*0-582-22582-5*, Pub. by Longman UK) Longman.

We Mean Business: Building Communication Competence in Business & Professions. William I. Gorden & Randi J. Nevins. LC 92-18520. (C). 1993. text ed. 35.50 (*0-06-500048-X*) Addson-Wesley Educ.

***We Mean to Be Counted: White Women & Politics in Antebellum Virginia.** Elizabeth Varon. LC 97-21587. (Gender & American Culture Ser.). 1998. write for info. (*0-8078-2390-2*); pap. write for info. (*0-8078-4696-1*) U of NC Pr.

We Miss You: An Outreach Program for Inactive Catholics, Reproducible. Gary Petri et al. 96p. 1995. pap. 49.95 (*1-55612-613-1*, LL1613) Sheed & Ward MO.

We Montanans. Norma Tirrell. (Illus.). 160p. 1988. pap. 9.95 (*0-938314-51-3*) Am Wrld Geog.

We Moon '96: Gaia Rhythms for Wnyn. 1996. pap. 13.95 (*0-9510661-7-X*) Mother Tongue Ink.

We Murderers: A Play in Three Acts. Einar I. Haugen & Guomundur Kamban. LC 70-98124. (Nordic Translation Ser.). 99p. 1970. reprint ed. pap. 28.30 (*0-608-01879-1*, 2062531) Bks Demand.

We Must Love One Another or Die: Larry Kramer - His Life & Legacy. Larry Mass. (Sexual Politics Ser.). 320p. 1996. write for info. (*0-304-33545-2*) Cassell.

We Must Obey God. Samuel E. Waldron. (Orig.). 1991. write for info. (*0-9622508-9-9*) Simpson NJ.

We Must Re-Civilize America. Donald Tivens. Ed. by Randy Tivens. 160p. (Orig.). 1996. pap. text ed. 14.95 (*0-9640631-3-1*) Landmark Pub Inc.

We Must Take Charge! Our Schools & Our Future. Chester E. Finn, Jr. 365p. 1993. pap. 14.95 (*0-02-910276-6*, Free Press) Free Pr.

We Need a Hero! Heldentenors from Wagner's Time to the Present, A Critical History. Carla M. Verdino-Sullwold. LC 88-27685. (Illus.). 466p. 1989. pap. 34.95 (*0-9620958-1-8*) Weiala Pr.

***We Need a Moose.** Lynne Fairbridge. (Illus.). 32p. (J). 1996. 11.99 (*1-56476-565-2*, Victor Bks) Chariot Victor.

***We Need Each Other.** Thomas-Cochran. (What a Wonderful World 2 Ser.). 1992. pap. text ed. write for info. (*0-582-90966-X*, Pub. by Longman UK) Longman.

We Need Men: The Union Draft in the Civil War. James W. Geary. LC 90-21636. (Illus.). 300p. 1991. lib. bdg. 32.00 (*0-87580-157-9*) N Ill U Pr.

We Need Not Walk Alone: After the Death of a Child. 2nd ed. Ed. by Mary Cleckley et al. (Illus.). 234p. (Orig.). 1991. pap. 14.95 (*1-878615-00-9*) Compassionate Friend.

We Need One Another. D. H. Lawrence. LC 74-1421. (Studies in D. H. Lawrence: No. 20). 1974. lib. bdg. 75.00 (*0-8383-2031-7*) M S G Haskell Hse.

We Need to Talk: Opening Doors of Communication with Your Mate. Robert Barnes & Rosemary J. Barnes. 224p. 1996. pap. 12.99 (*0-310-20805-X*) Zondervan.

We Never Left the Garden. Pamela Galadrial. 232p. 1996. pap. text ed. 12.95 (*0-9647585-1-2*) Mt Tallac Pr.

We Never Make Mistakes: Two Short Novels. Aleksandr I. Solzhenitsyn. 144p. 1996. pap. 11.00 (*0-393-31474-X*, Norton Paperbks) Norton.

We Never Said Goodbye: The Tragedy of Alzheimer's Disease. Isobelle Gidley & Richard Shears. 191p. 1985. 14.95 (*0-86861-551-X*) Routledge Chapman & Hall.

We Never Went to the Moon: America's Thirty Billion Dollar Swindle! Bill Kaysing & Randy Reid. 87p. 1976. reprint ed. spiral bd. 11.00 (*0-7873-0487-5*) Hlth Research.

***We Never Wore Shoes: Growing up on Ft. Myers Beach.** Jean F. Matthew. (Illus.). 593p. (YA). 1994. 29.95 (*0-9644574-6-6*) Shoeless Pub.

***We Now Know: Rethinking Cold War History.** John L. Gaddis. 420p. 1997. text ed. 30.00 (*0-19-878070-2*) OUP.

We of the Third Sex: Literary Representations of Homosexuality in Wilhelmine Germany. James W. Jones. LC 90-41219. (German Life & Civilization Ser.: Vol. 7). 348p. (C). 1990. text ed. 64.95 (*0-8204-1209-0*) P Lang Pubng.

We Offer Ourselves As Evidence: Toward Workers' Control of Occupational Health. Bennett M. Judkins. LC 85-24775. (Contributions in Labor Studies: No. 61). 272p. 1986. text ed. 55.00 (*0-313-24898-2*, JWO/, Greenwood Pr) Greenwood.

We Open on Venus. Christopher Stasheff. (Orig.). 1994. mass mkt. 5.99 (*0-345-36891-6*, Del Rey) Ballantine.

We Oughta Be In Pictures. Julia Willis. 208p. (Orig.). 1993. pap. 9.95 (*0-9624751-8-1*) Alamo Sq Pr.

We Overcame: History of the Civil Rites of the Disabled. Richard Bryant. 350p. (C). 1993. pap. text ed. 17.95 (*0-9631345-2-3*) Regal Direct.

We Own It: Starting & Managing Co-ops, Collectives & Employee-Owned Ventures. Peter J. Honigsberg et al. 165p. 1982. 14.50 (*0-318-17055-8*) NASCO.

We Own It: Starting & Managing Cooperatives & Employee-Owned Businesses. rev. ed. Peter J. Honigsberg et al. 147p. 1991. pap. 14.00 (*0-917510-08-9*) Bell Springs Pub.

***We Paid Our Dues: Women Trade Union Leaders of the Caribbean.** A. Lynn Bolles. LC 95-50954. (C). 1996. pap. 21.95 (*0-88258-085-X*) Howard U Pr.

***We Passed This Way: A Coast to Coast Bicycle Trip with Historical Reflections.** Dick Swinnerton. Ed. by Alisa B. Oliver. 224p. (Orig.). 1997. pap. 16.95 (*0-9641606-5-X*) Easy Break.

We People Here: Nahuatl Accounts of the Conquest of Mexico. Ed. & Tr. by James Lockhart. (Repertorium Columbianum Ser.: No. 1). 304p. 1994. 45.00 (*0-520-07875-6*) U CA Pr.

We Planned It That Way. Frank Knox. LC 77-37889. (Select Bibliographies Reprint Ser.). 1977. reprint ed. 16.95 (*0-8369-6726-7*) Ayer.

We Play on a Rainy Day. Angela S. Medearis. (Hello Reader! Ser.). (Illus.). 32p. (J). 1996. pap. 3.50 (*0-590-26265-3*, Cartwheel) Scholastic Inc.

We Played the Game: Sixty-Five Players Remember Baseball's Greatest Era, 1947-1964. Ed. by Danny Peary. LC 93-26497. 672p. 1994. 35.00 (*0-7868-6008-1*) Hyperion.

We Played the Game: Sixty-Five Players Remember Baseball's Greatest Era, 1947-1964. Ed. by Danny Peary. (Illus.). 672p. 1995. pap. 19.95 (*0-7868-8091-0*) Hyperion.

We Plow God's Fields: The Life of James G.K. McClure. John C. Ager. (Illus.). 477p. 1991. 22.00 (*0-913239-63-1*); pap. 17.00 (*0-913239-68-2*) Appalach Consortium.

We Pointed Them North: Recollections of a Cowpuncher. E. C. Abbott. LC 55-9632. 1955. pap. 12.95 (*0-8061-1366-9*) U of Okla Pr.

We Praise You, O Lord! Patricia Fritz. 1985. pap. 3.95 (*0-8091-2518-8*) Paulist Pr.

We Pray. David M. Thomas et al. LC 74-84712. (Catechism of the Catholic Church Ser.: Vol. 4). (Illus.). 77p. 1994. reprint ed. pap. 8.95 (*0-88347-298-8*, 7298) Res Christian Liv.

***We Pray: Growing Spiritually Through the Catechism of the Catholic Church, Vol. 4.** Henry Libersat. LC 96-37932. (Catholic Confession of Faith Ser.). 56p. (Orig.). 1997. pap. 5.95 (*0-8198-8291-7*) Pauline Bks.

We Pray at Mass. Illus. by Ferelith E. Williams. 32p. (J). 1989. pap. 3.95 (*0-8146-1798-0*) Liturgical Pr.

We Preach Christ Crucified: Cowley's Lent Book for 1995. Kenneth Leech. 105p. 1995. pap. 9.95 (*1-56101-105-3*) Cowley Pubns.

We Proclaim. Ed. by Blair G. Meeks. (Liturgy Ser.). 96p. (Orig.). 1993. pap. 10.95 (*0-918208-62-9*) Liturgical Conf.

We Protest: The Public Order Debate. Peter Thornton. 1988. 30.00 (*0-946088-21-7*, Pub. by NCCL UK) St Mut.

We Pulled Together & Won! Personal Memories of the World War II Years. Ed. by Deb Mulvey. LC 93-84612. (Illus.). 164p. 1993. 14.95 (*0-89821-112-3*, 12300) Reiman Pubns.

We Read More Stories. (J). teacher ed. 4.72 (*0-917186-12-5*) McQueen.

We Read More Stories, Set. (J). pap. 10.62 (*0-917186-11-7*) McQueen.

We Refuse to Starve in Silence. Croucher. (C). 1987. pap. 19.95 (*0-85315-681-6*, Pub. by Lawrence & Wishart UK) NYU Pr.

We Rejoice in the Light: Candlelighting Ceremonies for Advent. Sandra J. Dixon. 64p. 1988. pap. 5.99 (*0-8272-4223-9*) Chalice Pr.

We Remember: Twenty-Four Members of Kibbutz Megido Testify. Denise Nevo. Ed. by Mira Berger. 336p. 1994. 22.95 (*0-88400-176-8*) Shengold.

We Remember Bataan & Corregidor: The Story of the American & Filipino Defenders of Bataan & Corregidor & Their Captivity. Mariano Villarin. (Illus.). 335p. 1990. 21.95 (*0-9626127-0-7*) M Villarin.

We Remember Cuba. John H. Parker. Ed. by Giles S. Gianelloni. (Illus.). 233p. (Orig.). 1993. pap. 21.95 (*0-9635705-0-1*) Gldn Quill FL.

We Remember D-Day. Frank Shaw. 277p. 1995. 26.95 (*1-85695-027-1*, Pub. by ISIS UK) Transaction Pubs.

We Remember D-Day, Vol. 2. large type ed. Frank Shaw & Joan Shaw. 256p. 1996. 21.95 (*1-85695-029-8*, Pub. by ISIS UK) Transaction Pubs.

We Remember Jesus: Lent, Easter, & Early Church. Carolyn Willmore. (Good Steward's Craft Bks.). 64p. 1995. pap. 8.95 (*0-687-00784-4*) Abingdon.

We Remember the Battle of Britain. large type ed. Frank Shaw & Joan Shaw. (Illus.). 240p. 1994. 24.95 (*1-85695-101-4*, Pub. by ISIS UK) Transaction Pubs.

We Remember the Holocaust. David A. Adler. 160p. (J). (gr. 4-7). 1995. pap. 10.95 (*0-8050-3715-2*, Bks Young Read) H Holt & Co.

We Remember the Home Guard. Frank Shaw & Joan Shaw. 332p. 1995. 24.95 (*1-85089-585-6*, Pub. by ISIS UK) Transaction Pubs.

We Ride for Circle 6: Larry & Stretch. large type ed. Marshall Grover. (Linford Western Library). 272p. 1996. pap. 15.99 (*0-7089-7877-0*, Linford) Ulverscroft.

We Rode the Wind: Recollections of Native American Life. Ed. & Contrib. by Jane B. Katz. LC 94-34946. (Illus.). 128p. (YA). (gr. 6 up). 1995. lib. bdg. 21.50 (*0-8225-3154-2*, Runestone Pr) Lerner Group.

We Sagebrush Folks. Annie P. Greenwood. LC 87-38312. (Illus.). 496p. 1988. reprint ed. pap. 19.95 (*0-89301-122-3*) U of Idaho Pr.

We Saw Brother Francis. Francis De Beer. 145p. 1983. 9.00 (*0-8199-0803-7*, Frncscn Herld) Franciscan Pr.

We Saw Him Act: A Symposium on the Art of Sir Henry Irving. Ed. by Harry A. Saintsbury & Cecil Palmer. LC 78-113453. (Illus.). 1972. 24.95 (*0-405-08909-0*) Ayer.

We Saw Lincoln Shot: One Hundred Eyewitness Accounts. Timothy S. Good. 256p. 1995. pap. 17.95 (*0-87805-779-X*); text ed. 42.50 (*0-87805-778-1*) U Pr of Miss.

We Say No: Chronicles 1963-1991. Eduardo Galeano. Tr. by Mark Fried. 296p. 1992. pap. 11.95 (*0-393-30898-7*) Norton.

We Say Thanks: A Young Child's Book for Eucharist. rev. ed. Corinne Hart. (Illus.). 32p. (J). (ps-2). 1991. pap. 1.90 (*1-55944-004-X*) Franciscan Comns.

We Say We Love Each Other. Minnie B. Pratt. LC 92-24947. 112p. (Orig.). 1992. pap. 8.95 (*1-56341-023-0*); lib. bdg. 18.95 (*1-56341-024-9*) Firebrand Bks.

An Asterisk (*) at the beginning of an entry indicates that the title is appearing in BIP for the first time.

We Scholars: Changing the Culture of the University. David Damrosch. LC 94-32442. (Illus.). 237p. 1995. text ed. 32.50 (*0-674-94842-4*, DAMWES); pap. text ed. 15.95 (*0-674-94843-2*, DAMWEX) HUP.

We See All. Bruce Bailey. 281p. 1983. 35.00 (*0-317-69293-3*) B M Bailey.

We Shake in a Quake. Hannah G. Givon. LC 96-2227. (Illus.). 32p. (J). (ps-3). 1996. 12.95 (*1-883672-25-2*) Tricycle Pr.

***We Shall All Be Changed: Social Problems & Theological Renewal.** James Evans. 1997. pap. 12.00 (*0-8006-3084-X*, Fortress Pr) Augsburg Fortress.

We Shall Be Heard: An Index to Speeches by American Women, 1978-1985. Beverley Manning. LC 88-6644. 626p. 1988. 62.50 (*0-8108-2122-2*) Scarecrow.

***We Shall Fall As the Leaves.** Howard E. Greager. LC 89-90613. 193p. 1996. 21.95 (*0-614-30010-X*) H E Greager.

We Shall Judge Angels. Harold J. Chadwick. LC 94-70064. 348p. (Orig.). 1994. pap. 8.95 (*0-88270-706-X*) Bridge-Logos.

We Shall Live Again: The 1870 & 1890 Ghost Dance Movements As Demographic Revitalization. Russell Thornton. (ASA Rose Monograph Ser.). (Illus.). 112p. 1986. text ed. 44.95 (*0-521-32894-2*) Cambridge U Pr.

We Shall Not Be Moved: The Women's Factory Strike of 1909. Joan Dash. LC 95-19404. (Illus.). 166p. (J). (gr. 3-7). 1996. 15.95 (*0-590-48409-5*) Scholastic Inc.

We Shall Not Overcome: Populism & Southern Blue-Collar Workers. fac. ed. Robert E. Botsch. LC 80-11567. 253p. 1980. reprint ed. pap. 72.20 (*0-7837-8054-0*, 2047807) Bks Demand.

We Shall Overcome: Heroes of the Civil Rights Movement. Fred Powledge. LC 92-25184. (Illus.). 224p. (YA). (gr. 7 up). 1993. lib. bdg. 17.00 (*0-684-19362-0*, C Scribner Sons Young) S&S Childrens.

We Shall Overcome: Martin Luther King, Jr. & the Black Freedom Struggle. Ed. by Peter J. Albert & Ronald Hoffman. (Illus.). 304p. 1993. reprint ed. pap. 14.95 (*0-306-80511-1*) Da Capo.

***We Shall Overcome: The Role of the Black Church in Shaping Black Political Leaders.** Linda F. Williams. 450p. pap. write for info. (*0-465-09828-2*) Basic.

***We Shall Overcome: The Role of the Black Church in Shaping Black Political Leadership.** Linda F. Williams. 448p. Date not set. 25.00 (*0-465-09819-3*) Basic.

We Shall Return! MacArthur's Commanders & the Defeat of Japan, 1942-1945. Ed. by William M. Leary. LC 88-2731. 320p. 1988. 32.00 (*0-8131-1654-6*) U Pr of Ky.

We Shall Rise Again. Reg Groves. (C). 1996. pap. 13.50 (*1-899438-16-5*, Pub. by Porcupine Bks UK) Humanities.

***We Shall See Jesus.** 1994. pap. 1.20 (*0-8341-9221-7*) Lillenas.

We Share the Road, Poems. Lawrence H. Janssen. LC 89-81992. 112p. (Orig.). 1989. pap. 6.95 (*0-917575-06-7*) Cedars WI.

***We Shook the Family Tree.** Hildegarde Dolson. 71p. 1947. pap. 5.00 (*0-87129-765-5*, W13) Dramatic Pub.

***We Shoot Every Third Salesperson...the Second One Just Left.** Ary Group, Inc. Staff. 128p. 1997. per. 18.95 (*0-7872-4167-9*) Kendall-Hunt.

***We Should Be So Lucky.** Kathy Levine. 1997. 24.00 (*0-671-00848-X*, PB Hardcover) PB.

We Should Be Thankful. James Swartzentruber. (God Is Good Ser.). (J). 1976. 2.50 (*0-686-18188-3*) Rod & Staff.

We Should Have Killed the King. J. G. Eccarius. 194p. (Orig.). 1990. pap. 5.00 (*0-9622937-1-7*) III Pub.

We Signed Away Our Lives: How One Family Gave Everything for the Gospel. Kari T. Malcolm. LC 90-38692. 184p. (Orig.). 1990. pap. 8.99 (*0-8308-1718-2*, 1718) InterVarsity.

We Simply Had to Laugh. Ed. by Dorothy M. Obe. 85p. (C). 1989. text ed. 39.00 (*1-872795-23-4*, Pub. by Pentland Pr UK) St Mut.

We Sing Our Struggle: A Tribute to Us All. Ed. by Mary McAully. (Illus.). 82p. (Orig.). 1982. pap. 7.50 (*0-943594-03-0*) Cardinal Pr.

We Sing the City. Mary B. Lundgren. LC 93-34860. (Illus.). (J). 1997. 14.95 (*0-395-68188-X*, Clarion Bks) HM.

***We So Seldom Look on Love.** Barbara Gowdy. 1997. pap. text ed. 13.00 (*1-883642-00-0*) Steerforth Pr.

W

We Speak for Ourselves. Jack Babuscio. 224p. 1988. pap. 13.95 (*0-687-86470-4*) Abingdon.

We Speak for Ourselves: Experiences in Homosexual Counselling. Jack Babuscio. LC 77-78623. 160p. reprint ed. pap. 45.60 (*0-685-16028-9*, 2026837) Bks Demand.

We Speak for Ourselves: Population & Development: Voices from Latin America & the Caribbean. Patricia Ardila et al. (Illus.). 44p. 1994. pap. 5.95 (*1-879358-04-2*) Panos Inst.

We Speak for Ourselves: Social Justice, Race, & Environment. Robert Bullard et al. Ed. by Dana Alston et al. (Illus.). 50p. (Orig.). 1990. pap. write for info. (*1-879358-01-8*) Panos Inst.

We Speak for Peace: An Anthology. Ed. by Ruth H. Jacobs. 330p. (Orig.). 1993. pap. 14.00 (*1-879198-08-8*) Knwldg Ideas & Trnds.

***We Speak Silent.** Hannah Weiner. (Roof Bks.). 79p. (Orig.). 1996. pap. 9.95 (*0-937804-68-1*, Roof Bks) Segue NYC.

We Specialize in the Wholly Impossible: A Reader in Black Women's History. Ed. by Darlene C. Hine et al. LC 94-41968. (Black Women in United States History Ser.: Vol. 17). 618p. (YA). 1994. pap. 19.95 (*0-926019-81-3*) Carlson Pub.

We Specialize in the Wholly Impossible: A Reader in Black Women's History. Ed. by Darlene C. Hine et al. LC 94-41968. (Black Women in United States History Ser.: Vol. 17). 618p. (YA). 1995. 75.00 (*0-926019-80-5*) Carlson Pub.

We Spend Our Years As a Tale That Is Told: Oral Historical Narrative in a South African Chiefdom. Isabel Hofmeyr. LC 93-33815. 328p. 1994. 10.00 (*0-435-08099-7*, 08099); pap. 22.95 (*0-435-08951-X*, 08951) Heinemann.

We Stand Our Ground: Three Women, Their Vision, Their Poems. Kimiko Hahn et al. (Illus.). 6p. 19.95 (*0-945368-01-1*); pap. 9.95 (*0-945368-00-3*) IKON.

We Stand Together: Reconciling Men of Different Color. Rodney L. Cooper. 1995. pap. 10.99 (*0-8024-9181-2*) Moody.

We Survived: A Mother's Story of Japanese Captivity. Nell Van De Graaff. 250p. (Orig.). 1989. pap. text ed. 14.95 (*0-7022-2187-2*, Pub. by Univ Queensland Pr AT) Intl Spec Bk.

We Survived the Holocaust. Elaine Landau. LC 91-16982. (International Affairs Ser.). (Illus.). 144p. (YA). (gr. 9-12). 1991. lib. bdg. 22.70 (*0-531-11115-6*) Watts.

We Survived Yesterday. John Reseck. 1994. pap. 12.95 (*1-882180-18-6*) Griffin CA.

We Swam the Grand Canyon: The True Story of a Cheap Vacation That Got a Little Out of Hand. Bill Beer. 171p. 1995. pap. 12.00 (*0-9634055-9-4*) Fifteen Minute Pr.

We Teach Them All: Teachers Writing about Diversity. Ed. by June Kuzmeskus. 160p. (Orig.). 1996. pap. text ed. 14.00 (*1-57110-032-6*) Stenhse Pubs.

We Teach with Technology: New Visions for Education. Greg P. Kearsley et al. LC 91-44315. 176p. 1992. pap. text ed. 17.95 (*0-938661-37-X*) Franklin Beedle.

We Tell It to Our Children - The Story of Passover: A Haggadah for Seders with Young Children. MaryAnn B. Wark. LC 87-63604. (Illus.). 150p. (Orig.). (J). (ps-6). 1988. Leader's Edition with Puppets. teacher ed., spiral bd. 12.95 (*0-9619880-9-6*) Mensch Makers Pr.
Children's active participatory Haggadah makes the Passover story into an engaging drama of the Exodus story. A complete guide, including multi-national recipes, for putting on the traditional Seder meal for Passover. Text is a musical puppet show with Judaically-meaningful lyrics set to simple American folk tunes. Everyone participates in singing throughout the service. This Leader's edition has 9 cut out puppets who are the "guests" from the past, who in a "you-are-there" style tell the story of the Exodus. Parts for non-readers & early readers. Guest edition - no puppets with full text also available. Endorsed by rabbis, religious educators (Jewish & Christian), children's book store owners, preschool teachers, parents & grandparents nationwide. For home or model seders. Authentically Jewish; easy for non-Jews. Developmentally appropriate for children. Downright fun for adults. Other unique features include the Passover food symbols, like matzoh, explained at the appropriate time in the story; special sections to personalize & teach about world Jewry. Difficult concepts like slavery are taught through action, songs, & pictures. Lyrics respond to children's thinking while tackling complicated issues surrounding freedom. Plentiful, detailed drawings emphasize immediacy of ideas & illustrate every idea & ceremonial symbol. ***Publisher Provided Annotation.***

We Tell It to Our Children - The Story of Passover: A Haggadah for Seders with Young Children: Guest Edition - No Puppets. 2nd ed. Mary A. Wark. LC 88-92282. (Illus.). 126p. (Orig.). (J). (ps-6). 1988. spiral bd. 6.95 (*0-9619880-8-8*) Mensch Makers Pr.

We Thank God. Marion Josef. (Illus.). 28p. (Orig.). (J). (gr. k-4). 1993. pap. 0.95 (*0-8198-8267-4*) Pauline Bks.

We That Were Young. Irene Rathbone. LC 88-31029. 528p. 1989. 35.00 (*1-55861-001-4*); pap. 10.95 (*1-55861-002-2*) Feminist Pr.

We, the Alien: An Introduction to Cultural Anthropology. Paul Bohannan. (Illus.). 344p. (Orig.). (C). 1992. pap. text ed. 28.95 (*0-88133-637-8*) Waveland Pr.

We, the American Women: A Documentary History. rev. ed. Beth M. Kava & Jeanne Bodin. 362p. 1987. 29.95 (*0-574-01058-0*); student ed. 3.95 (*0-574-01057-2*); pap. text ed. 18.95 (*0-574-01055-6*) SRA.

We, the Arcturian's. Betty Rice et al. LC 90-82682. (Illus.). 336p. (Orig.). 1990. pap. 14.95 (*0-9627417-0-1*) Athena NM.

We the Black Jews: Witness to the "White Jewish Race" Myth. Yosef Ben-Jochannan. LC 92-81884. 424p. reprint ed. pap. 24.95 (*0-933121-40-7*) Black Classic.

We, the Bride. Francis Clare. LC 90-63012. 160p. (Orig.). 1990. pap. 7.95 (*0-89221-187-3*) New Leaf.

We, the Church: Eight Small Group Studies. David Misenheimer. 1993. pap. 12.95 (*0-933173-61-X*) Chging Church Forum.

We the Condemned. large type ed. Norman A. Lazenby. (Linford Mystery Library). 272p. 1992. pap. 15.99 (*0-7089-7229-2*, Trailtree Bookshop) Ulverscroft.

We the Creators: From Shame to Honor. Shelby Boone. LC 89-91709. (Illus.). 386p. (Orig.). 1989. pap. 17.95 (*0-9622054-0-0*) Breakthrgh MN.

We the Dangerous: Selected Poems. Janice Mirikitani. 176p. 1995. pap. 12.95 (*0-89087-767-X*) Celestial Arts.

We, the Divided Self. John G. Watkins & Rhonda J. Johnson. 140p. 1982. text ed. 18.95 (*0-8290-1011-4*); One hr. audio cassette (for prof. use only). audio 12.00 (*0-8290-1412-8*) Irvington.

***We the Earth.** Katherine Scholes. 1996. 17.95 (*0-85572-258-4*, Pub. by Hill Content Pubng AT) Seven Hills Bk.

We the Enemy. large type ed. Peter Essex. 576p. 1988. 27.99 (*0-7089-8451-7*, Charnwood) Ulverscroft.

We, the Generation in the Wilderness. Ricardo Feirstein. Tr. by J. Kates & Stephen Sadow from SPA. (Ford-Brown Latin American Ser.: Vol. 2). 72p. (Orig.). 1989. pap. 7.00 (*0-918644-17-8*) Ford-Brown.

We, the Human Beings: Twenty-Seven Contemporary Native American Artists. 2nd ed. College of Wooster Art Museum Staff et al. Ed. by Kathleen M. Zurko. LC 93-72134. (Illus.). 52p. (C). 1993. 20.00 (*0-9604658-6-3*) Coll Wooster.

We, the Humans: Is There Meaning in Our Life? Boris M. Segal. 400p. (Orig.). 1995. pap. 12.95 (*0-9644617-0-6*) Wise Owl NY.

***We the Jury: The Impact of Jurors on Our Basic Freedoms.** Godfrey D. Lehman. LC 97-11435. 1997. 26.95 (*1-57392-144-0*) Prometheus Bks.

We, the Jury: The Jury System & the Ideal of Democracy. Jeffrey Abramson. 320p. 1995. pap. 14.00 (*0-465-09116-4*) Basic.

We the Living. Ayn Rand. 1960. pap. 6.99 (*0-451-15860-1*, Sig) NAL-Dutton.

We the Living. Ayn Rand. 1998. pap. 16.95 (*0-14-086311-7*) Viking Penguin.

We the Living: Sixtieth Anniversary Edition. anniversary ed. Ayn Rand. 448p. 1996. mass mkt., pap. 6.99 (*0-451-18784-9*, Sig) NAL-Dutton.

We the Living: 60th Anniversary Edition. anniversary ed. Ayn Rand. 433p. 1995. pap. 25.95 (*0-525-94054-5*, Dutton) NAL-Dutton.

***We the Media.** Don Hazen. Date not set. pap. 16.95 (*1-56584-380-0*) New Press NY.

We, the Nation: The Lost Decades. Nani A. Palkhivala. (C). 1994. 9.50 (*81-85944-90-3*, Pub. by UBS Pubs Dist II) S Asia.

We, the Navigators: The Ancient Art of Landfinding in the Pacific. 2nd ed. David Lewis. Ed. by Derek Oulton. LC 93-44019. (Illus.). 384p. (C). 1994. pap. 24.95 (*0-8248-1582-3*) UH Pr.

We, the Other People: Alternative Declarations of Independence by Labor Groups, Farmers, Woman's Rights Advocates, Socialists, & Blacks, 1829-1975. Ed. by Philip S. Foner. LC 76-10736. 211p. reprint ed. pap. 60.20 (*0-7837-5735-2*, 2045396) Bks Demand.

We the People. Budziszews. 1989. wbk. ed., pap. text ed. 13.25 (*0-03-023557-X*) HR&W Schl Div.

We the People. Budziszews. 1989. teacher ed., wbk. ed., pap. text ed. 16.75 (*0-03-023558-8*) HR&W Schl Div.

***We the People.** Budzuszews. 1989. text ed. 70.50 (*0-03-022888-3*) HR&W Schl Div.

***We the People.** Benjamin Ginsberg. (C). Date not set. student ed., text ed. write for info. (*0-393-97177-5*) Norton.

We the People. Margaret Weir. (C). Date not set. teacher ed., pap. text ed. write for info. (*0-393-97029-9*) Norton.

We the People. Margaret Weis. LC 96-39782. (C). 1997. text ed. 56.95 (*0-393-97027-2*) Norton.

We the People. Margaret Weis. (C). Date not set. student ed., pap. text ed. write for info. (*0-393-97028-0*) Norton.

We, the People. Leo Huberman. (Illus.). 384p. 1970. reprint ed. pap. 12.00 (*0-85345-134-6*) Monthly Rev.

***We The People, Chapter 17.** Benjamin Ginsberg. (C). Date not set. pap. text ed. write for info. (*0-393-10173-8*) Norton.

***We the People, Chapter 18.** Benjamin Ginsberg. (C). Date not set. pap. text ed. write for info. (*0-393-10174-6*) Norton.

***We the People, Chapter 19.** Benjamin Ginsberg. (C). Date not set. pap. text ed. write for info. (*0-393-10175-4*) Norton.

***We the People: A Concise Introduction to American Politics.** 2nd ed. Thomas E. Patterson. LC 97-11441. 1997. write for info. (*0-07-049400-2*) McGraw.

We the People: A Story of Internment in America. Mary Tsukamoto & Elizabeth Pinkerton. LC 87-205205. (Illus.). 324p. 1988. 30.00 (*0-944665-41-1*); pap. 15.00 (*0-944665-42-X*) Laguna Pubs.

We, the People: American Character & Social Change. Ed. by Gordon J. DiRenzo. LC 76-51926. (Contributions in Sociology Ser.: No. 24). (Illus.). 339p. 1977. text ed. 69.50 (*0-8371-9481-4*, DWP/, Greenwood Pr) Greenwood.

We the People: An Atlas of America's Ethnic Diversity. James P. Allen & Eugene J. Turner. LC 87-28194. xii, 315p. 1987. 175.00 (*0-02-901420-4*, Free Press) Free Pr.

***We the People: An Introduction to American Politics.** Benjamin Ginsberg et al. LC 96-39657. (C). 1997. pap. text ed. 39.95 (*0-393-97136-8*) Norton.

We, the People: Australian Republican Government. Ed. by George Winterton. 224p. 1994. pap. 19.95 (*1-86373-640-9*, Pub. by Allen Unwin AT) Paul & Co Pubs.

We the People: Bits, Bytes & Highlights of the U. S. Constitution & Bill of Rights from Honey Bees Tye & Sy. D. M. Wolf. LC 88-117385. (Illus.). 32p. (Orig.). (J). (gr. 4-5). 1987. pap. 4.95 (*0-9617057-1-X*) Storyviews Pub.

We the People: Community Forums on the Constitution. 1986. pap. 10.00 (*0-685-43850-3*, 468-0011) Amer Bar Assn.

We, the People: Formative Documents of America's Democracy. Adolph Caso. (Illus.). 336p. (C). 1995. 22.95 (*0-8283-2006-3*) Branden Pub Co.

We the People: Foundations, Vol. 1. Bruce A. Ackerman. 369p. (C). 1991. text ed. 24.95 (*0-674-94840-8*) Belknap Pr.

We the People: Foundations, Vol. 1. Bruce A. Ackerman. 384p. (C). 1993. pap. text ed. 10.95 (*0-674-94841-6*) HUP.

We, the People? Satiric Prints of the 1930s. Richard N. Masteller. LC 89-50444. (Illus.). 75p. (Orig.). (C). 1989. pap. 7.00 (*1-880269-05-8*) D H Sheehan.

We the People: Testbook. Budziszews. 1989. pap. text ed. 13.75 (*0-03-023559-6*) HR&W Schl Div.

We the People: The Constitution of the United States of America. Peter Spier. (Illus.). 48p. (J). (ps). 1991. pap. 7.95 (*0-385-41903-1*) Doubleday.

We the People: The Economic Origins of the Constitution. Forrest McDonald. 455p. (C). 1992. pap. text ed. 24.95 (*1-56000-574-2*) Transaction Pubs.

We the People: The History of America from Colonization to Lincoln's Inauguration. rev. ed. 235p. (YA). (gr. 9-12). 1994. pap. text ed. 149.95 incl. audio (*1-887942-07-6*) Gateway Educ Prods.

***We the People: The Story of America.** Ed. by Randall. (C). 1998. student ed., text ed. write for info. (*0-673-99216-0*) Addison-Wesley.

***We the People: The Story of America, Vol. 1.** Ed. by Randall. (C). 1998. text ed. write for info. (*0-673-99217-9*) Addison-Wesley.

***We the People: The Story of the America, Vol. 2.** Ed. by Randall. (C). 1998. text ed. write for info. (*0-673-99218-7*) Addison-Wesley.

We, the People: The Story of the United States Capitol. (Illus.). 144p. 1985. pap. 6.95 (*0-614-13951-1*) Natl Geog.

We the People: The Story of the United States Capitol. 14th ed. Lonnelle Aikman. Ed. by National Geographic Society Staff. LC 91-65042. (Illus.). 144p. 1991. reprint ed. pap. 5.00 (*0-916200-10-8*); reprint ed. text ed. 10.00 (*0-916200-09-4*) US Capitol Hist.

***We the People: To Save America.** Velna Reniak. 58p. 1997. pap. 7.00 (*0-8059-4066-9*) Dorrance.

We the People: Voices & Images of the New Nation. Alfred F. Young et al. (Critical Perspectives on the Past Ser.). (Illus.). 380p. (C). 1993. 59.95 (*0-87722-937-6*); pap. 24.95 (*0-87722-938-4*) Temple U Pr.

We the People & Others: Duality & America's Treatment of Its Racial Minorities. Benjamin B. Ringer. 1178p. 1985. pap. text ed. 28.50 (*0-422-60160-8*, 9677, Pub. by Tavistock UK) Routledge Chapman & Hall.

We the People & Others: Duality & America's Treatment of the Racial Minorities. Benjamin B. Ringer. 1165p. 1983. 75.00 (*0-422-78180-0*, NO. 3734, Pub. by Tavistock UK) Routledge Chapman & Hall.

We, the People! Bay Area Activism in the 1960s: Three Case Studies. Richard DeLuca. LC 93-16623. (Great Issues of the Day Ser.: No. 7). (Illus.). 144p. 1994. pap. 19.00 (*0-89370-254-4*); lib. bdg. 29.00 (*0-89370-154-8*) Borgo Pr.

We the People Have Credit Rights Too. Pearl B. Polto & Rick Bell. 110p. (Orig.). 1993. pap. 5.95 (*0-9636397-0-6*) P B Polto.

We the People of the United States. Lynne Glasner & Marilyn Thypin. (Government Ser.: Bk. 2). (Illus.). 96p. (Orig.). (YA). (gr. 7-12). 1993. pap. text ed. 6.00 (*0-941342-20-4*, 1042) Entry Pub.

We, the People of the World... Special Programs in Citizenship Education: Comparative Legal Systems. Told to Spice V Teachers Staff. LC 91-72238. 250p. 1991. lab manual ed. 15.00 (*1-879953-04-8*) CRD Law-Related.

We the People 89. Budziszews. 1989. 51.75 (*0-03-022887-5*) HB Schl Dept.

We, the Puerto Rican People: A Story of Oppression & Resistance. Juan A. Silen. Tr. by Cedric Belfrage. LC 70-158926. (Illus.). 132p. reprint ed. pap. 37.70 (*0-7837-3926-5*, 2043774) Bks Demand.

We the Sheeple: The Fleecing of the American Criminal Justice System. Peter G. Schmidt. 450p. (Orig.). 1995. pap. 22.95 (*0-9647827-0-7*) Lawmann Pubs.

We, the Tikopia: A Sociological Study of Kinship in Primitive Polynesia. abr. ed. Raymond Firth. LC 83-42540. (Illus.). xxviii, 497p. 1963. reprint ed. 59.50 (*0-8047-1201-8*); reprint ed. pap. 19.95 (*0-8047-1202-6*) Stanford U Pr.

We the Undersigned. Alexander Gelman. Tr. by A. De Vreeze & Michael Mackenzie from RUS. 1992. pap. 5.00 (*0-87129-170-3*, W65) Dramatic Pub.

We the Unreconciled. Sujatha Modayil. (Redbird Ser.). 52p. 1975. 10.00 (*0-88253-672-9*); pap. text ed. 4.80 (*0-88253-671-0*) Ind-US Inc.

We the Women: Career Firsts of Nineteenth-Century America. Madeleine B. Stern. LC 93-45996. xvii, 415p. 1994. pap. 12.95 (*0-8032-9223-6*, Bison Books) U of Nebr Pr.

We the Women of Hawaii Cookbook. Ed. by Jean Keys & Adele Davis. 397p. (Orig.). 1987. reprint ed. pap. 9.95 (*0-916630-47-1*) Pr Pacifica.

We Think the World Is Round. Ray Gilbert. (Illus.). 24p. (Orig.). (J). (ps-7). 1992. pap. 6.95 incl. audio (*0-943351-56-1*, XE 2001) Astor Bks.

We Think the World of You. Joe R. Ackerley. 1961. 11.95 (*0-685-06622-3*) Astor-Honor.

We Thought at Least the Roof Would Fall. Leslie Mellichamp. LC 87-2231. (Illus.). 140p. (Orig.). 1987. pap. 5.95 (*0-936015-07-1*) Pocahontas Pr.

We Thought We Could Whip Them in Two Weeks. William O. Trafton. 110p. (Orig.). (C). 1990. pap. 10.00 (*971-10-0397-X*, Pub. by New Day Pub PH) Cellar.

We Three Cats, 3 vols. Ed. by Malachi McCormick. 84p. 1991. Set. boxed 20.00 (*0-943984-43-2*) Stone St Pr.

We Three Cats, 3 vols., 1. Ed. by Malachi McCormick. 84p. 1991. write for info. (*0-943984-44-0*) Stone St Pr.

An Asterisk (*) at the beginning of an entry indicates that the title is appearing in BIP for the first time.

We Three Cats, 3 vols., 2. Ed. by Malachi McCormick. 84p. 1991. write for info. (0-943984-45-9) Stone St Pr.

We Three Cats, 3 vols., 3. Ed. by Malachi McCormick. 84p. 1991. write for info. (0-943984-46-7) Stone St Pr.

***We Three Kings.** Illus. by Laura Rader. (Little Angels Ser.). 4p. (J). (ps up). 1997. bds. 2.99 (1-57584-159-2) Rdrs Dgst Yng Fam.

***We Three Kings.** Illus. by Laura Rader. (Little Angels Ser.). 6p. (J). (ps). 1997. bds. 2.99 (0-7847-0634-4, 24-03744) Standard Pub.

We Three Were All Alone. Barney Wagner. (Illus.). 152p. 1996. 15.00 (0-8059-3973-3) Dorrance.

We Too Are Drifting. Gale Wilhelm. 128p. 1985. pap. 6.95 (0-930044-61-4) Naiad Pr.

We Too Are Drifting. Gale Wilhelm. LC 75-12359. (Homosexuality Ser.). 1975. reprint ed. 13.95 (0-405-07380-1) Ayer.

We Too Are the People. Louise V. Armstrong. LC 78-137155. (Poverty U. S. A. Historical Record Ser.). 1971. reprint ed. 38.95 (0-405-03093-2) Ayer.

***We Too Sing America.** Chitra B. Divakaruni. LC 97-17611. 1997. pap. text ed. write for info. (0-07-017084-3) McGraw.

We Took the Train. Ed. by H. Roger Grant. (Illus.). 212p. 1990. 29.50 (0-87580-156-0) N Ill U Pr.

We Took to the Woods. Louise D. Rich. 250p. 1992. reprint ed. lib. bdg. 18.95 (0-89966-913-1) Buccaneer Bks.

We Took to the Woods. Louise D. Rich. (Illus.). 1975. reprint ed. pap. 10.95 (0-89272-016-6) Down East.

We Touched, You & I: A Collection of Poems. Gerald H. Adams. LC 95-90298. 50p. (Orig.). 1996. pap. 7.95 (0-533-11527-2) Vantage.

We Travel an Appointed Way. Aiden W. Tozer. LC 88-70130. 145p. (Orig.). 1988. pap. 8.99 (0-87509-407-4) Chr Pubns.

We Tried: Government Service in India & Nepal. Nancy Dammann. LC 95-71920. (Illus.). 196p. 1995. pap. 9.95 (0-9609376-3-3) Soc Change Pr.

***We Trust in the Name of the Lord Our God.** 1996. pap. 1.20 (0-8341-9614-X) Lillenas.

We Two Know the Script; We have Become Good Friends: Linguistic & Social Aspects of The Women's Script Literacy in Southern Hunan, China. William W. Chiang. (Illus.). 336p. (Orig.). (C). Date not set. pap. text ed. 38.50 (0-7618-0014-X); lib. bdg. 59.50 (0-7618-0013-1) U Pr of Amer.

***We Use Our Senses.** large type ed. Kathy Kelley. (Cuddlebook Ser.). (Illus.). 7p. (Orig.). (J). (ps). 1997. pap. text ed. 5.95 (1-57332-078-1) HighReach Lrning.

We Vermonters: Perspectives on the Past - A Bibliography. Ed. & Pref. by Kristin Peterson-Ishaq. (Illus.). 177p. (Orig.). 1995. pap. 14.00 (0-944277-29-2) U VT Ctr Rsch VT.

We Walk the Way of the New World. Don L. Lee. LC 70-121885. (YA). (gr. 12 up). 1970. 6.00 (0-910296-26-X) Broadside Pr.

We Walked to Moscow. Jerry Lehmann. Ed. by Arthur Harvey. 100p. (Orig.). 1966. pap. 7.50 (0-934676-07-0) Greenlf Bks.

We Wanna Boogie: An Illustrated History of the American Rockabilly Movement. 2nd ed. Randy McNutt. (Illus.). 288p. 1989. pap. 24.95 (0-940152-05-3) Hamilton Hobby.

***We Want Jobs: A History of Affirmative Action.** Robert J. Weiss. LC 96-30018. (Studies in African American History & Culture). 312p. 1997. text ed. 59.00 (0-8153-2750-1) Garland.

We Want Jobs! A Story of the Great Depression. Robert J. Norrell. LC 92-18082. (Stories of America Ser.). (Illus.). 40p. (J). (gr. 2-5). 1992. lib. bdg. 25.68 (0-8114-7229-9) Raintree Steck-V.

***We Want to Live, 2 vols., Set.** Aaionus Vonderplanitz. 310p. 1997. 29.95 (1-889356-77-8, 41747) Carnelian Bay.

We Want to Win! Steve De Masco & Alex Simmons. LC 91-40935. (Cool Karate School Ser.). (Illus.). 64p. (J). (gr. 1-4). 1993. text ed. 9.95 (0-8167-3100-4) Troll Communs.

We Want to Win! Steve De Masco & Alex Simmons. LC 91-40935. (Cool Karate School Ser.). (Illus.). 64p. (J). (gr. 1-4). 1997. teacher ed., pap. 2.50 (0-8167-3101-2) Troll Communs.

***We Wear the Mask: African Americans Write American Literature, 1760-1870.** LC 96-53974. 1997. write for info. (0-231-08094-8) Col U Pr.

***We Wear the Mask: African Americans Write American Literature, 1760-1870.** LC 96-53974. 1997. pap. write for info. (0-231-08095-6) Col U Pr.

We Were Baptized Too: Claiming God's Grace for Lesbians & Gays. Marilyn B. Alexander & James Preston. LC 95-46241. 176p. (Orig.). 1996. pap. 17.00 (0-664-25628-7) Westminster John Knox.

***We Were Each Other's Prisoners: An Oral History of World War II American & German Prisoners of War.** Lewis H. Carlson. LC 96-39116. (Illus.). 272p. 1997. 25.00 (0-465-09120-2) Basic.

***We Were Here.** Vance Muse. 1997. write for info. (0-679-44204-9) Pantheon.

We Were Making History: Women in the Telangana People's Struggle. Stree S. Sangathana et al. LC 88-29785. 224p. (C). 1989. pap. 17.50 (0-86232-679-6, Pub. by Zed Bks Ltd UK); text ed. 55.00 (0-86232-678-8, Pub. by Zed Bks Ltd UK) Humanities.

We Were Next to Nothing: An American POW's Account of Japanese Prison Camps & Deliverance in World War II. Carl S. Nordin. LC 96-39692. 264p. 1997. lib. bdg. 28.95 (0-7864-0274-1) McFarland & Co.

We Were Not Summer Soldiers: The Indian War Diary of Plympton J. Kelly, 1855-1856. Anno. & Intro. by W. N. Bischoff. LC 76-11999. (Illus.). 190p. 1976. 8.95 (0-917048-00-8) Wash St Hist Soc.

***We Were So Beloved: Autobiography of a German Jewish Community.** Gloria Kirchheimer & Manfred Kirsheimer. LC 97-4824. (Illus.). 440p. 1997. 34.95 (0-8229-3997-5) U of Pittsburgh Pr.

We Were Soldiers Once...& Young: Ia Drang, the Battle That Changed the War in Vietnam. Harold G. Moore & Joseph Galloway. LC 93-15836. (Illus.). 448p. 1993. reprint ed. pap. 14.00 (0-06-097576-8, PL) HarpC.

We Were the Mulvaneys. Joyce Carol Oates. LC 96-17267. 432p. 1996. pap. 24.95 (0-525-94223-8) NAL-Dutton.

***We Were the Mulvaneys.** Joyce Carol Oates. 1997. pap. 15.95 (0-452-27720-5, Plume) NAL-Dutton.

We Were the Ninth: A History of the Ninth Regiment, Ohio Volunteer Infantry, April 17, 1861 to June 7, 1864. Constantin Grebner. LC 87-3884. 348p. reprint ed. pap. 99.20 (0-7837-1983-3, 2042257) Bks Demand.

We Were the People: Voices from East Germany's Revolutionary Autumn of 1989. Dirk Philipsen. LC 92-12762. 432p. 1992. text ed. 54.95 (0-8223-1282-4); pap. text ed. 19.95 (0-8223-1294-8) Duke.

We Were There: A Way of the Cross. Sarah A. O'Malley. (Illus.). 40p. (Orig.). 1996. pap. 1.95 (0-8146-2355-7, Liturg Pr Bks) Liturgical Pr.

We Were There: Women in the New Testament. Luch Fuchs. LC 93-24987. 1994. pap. 7.95 (0-8189-0648-0) Alba.

We Were Tired of Living in a House. Liesel M. Skorpen. LC 96-4903. (Illus.). (J). 1996. 15.95 (0-399-23016-5, Putnam) Putnam Pub Group.

We Who Live in the Castle: An Allegorical Novel. Frances E. Crary. LC 91-75127. 310p. (Orig.). 1991. pap. 6.95 (0-9629950-4-5) Ashbrook Pub.

We Who Were Raised Poor: Ending the Oppression of Classism. Gwen Brown. 1994. pap. 2.00 (0-913937-90-8) Rational Isl.

We Will Celebrate a Church Wedding. George R. Szews. 88p. 1983. pap. 3.50 (0-8146-1288-1) Liturgical Pr.

We Will Glorify: Personal Worship Journal. Chapel of the Air Ministries Staff. (1994 4-Week Worship Celebration Ser.). (Illus.). 64p. (Orig.). 1994. student ed., pap. text ed. 4.99 (1-879050-45-5) Chapel of Air.

***We Will Know What War Is.** Stephen Cresswell. 106p. 1993. pap. 8.00 (0-87012-503-6) McClain.

We Will Meet Again in Heaven: One Family's Remarkable Struggle with Death & Life. Christel Zachert & Isabell Zachert. Tr. by Stephen Trobisch from GER. LC 95-11807. 1995. pap. 12.99 (0-8066-2752-2, Augsburg) Augsburg Fortress.

We Will Never Forget. Jim Ross & Paul Myers. LC 96-18285. 271p. 1996. pap. 15.95 (1-57168-081-0, Eakin Pr) Sunbelt Media.

***We Will Not Be Strangers: Korean War Letters Between a M. A. S. H. Surgeon & His Wife.** Dorothy G. Horwitz & Mel Horwitz. LC 96-35654. 1997. 24.95 (0-252-02204-1) U of Ill Pr.

We Will Not Hang Our Harps on the Willows: Global Sisterhood & God's Song. Barbel Von Wartenberg-Potter. LC 87-34712. (Illus.). 144p. 1988. 10.95 (0-940989-34-4) Meyer Stone Bks.

We Will Remember. Elizabeth Darrell. 464p. 1996. 26.95 (0-312-14066-5) St Martin.

We Will Rise in Our Might: Workingwomen's Voices from Nineteenth-Century New England. Mary H. Blewett. LC 91-55077. (Documents in American Social History Ser.). (Illus.). 224p. 1991. 39.95 (0-8014-2246-9); pap. 14.95 (0-8014-9537-7) Cornell U Pr.

We Will Smash This Prison: Indian Women in Struggle. Gail Omvedt. 189p. 1979. 19.95 (0-318-37315-7) Asia Bk Corp.

We Will Stand by You: Serving in the Pawnee, 1942-1945. Theodore C. Mason. LC 95-24848. (Bluejacket Bks.). (Illus.). 284p. 1996. pap. 14.95 (1-55750-581-0) Naval Inst Pr.

We Will Wait: Wives of French Prisoners of War, 1940-45. Sarah Fishman. (Illus.). 320p. (C). 1992. text ed. 42.50 (0-300-04774-6) Yale U Pr.

We Win: A Complete Physical Education Program for the Entire Family Without Competition. Alexander Marini. 1995. pap. text ed. 19.95 (1-56857-017-1) Noble Pub Assocs.

We Wish to See Jesus. Eduardo Pironio. 214p. 1982. pap. 10.50 (0-8189-0392-9) Alba.

We Wish to See Jesus. Ed. by Eduardo Pironio. (C). 1988. 39.00 (0-85439-198-3, Pub. by St Paul Pubns UK) St Mut.

We Wish You a Merry Christmas. Illus. by Tracey C. Pearson. LC 82-22224. 32p. (J). (ps up). 1983. pap. 3.95 (0-8037-0310-4) Dial Bks Young.

We Wish You a Merry Christmas. J. Vreeman. (Illus.). 16p. (Orig.). (J). 1985. pap. 3.95 (0-918789-02-8) FreeMan Prods.

We Wish You a Merry Christmas - Victorian Caroling Kit. John Grossman et al. Ed. by Sally Kovalchick. LC 94-19221. (Illus.). 96p. (Orig.). 1994. pap. 24.95 (1-56305-307-1, 3307) Workman Pub.

We Wish You a Merry Murder. Valerie Wolzien. (Holiday Mysteries Ser.). (Orig.). 1991. mass mkt. 4.99 (0-449-14723-1, GM) Fawcett.

***We Wish You a Scary Christmas, No. 16.** M. T. Coffin. (Spinetinglers Ser.: No. 16). 144p. (Orig.). (J). 1996. pap. 3.50 (0-380-78996-5, Camelot) Avon.

We Women. Edith Sodergran. 1977. 2.50 (0-685-89006-6) Oyez.

We Won't Go Back: Making the Case for Affirmative Action. Charles R. Lawrence & Mari J. Matsuda. LC 96-46158. 288p. 1997. 25.00 (0-395-79125-1) HM.

We Won't Murder: Being the Story of Men Who Followed Their Conscientious Scruples & Helped Give Life to Democracy. Paul C. French. LC 79-137541. (Peace Movement in America Ser.). 189p. 1972. reprint ed. lib. bdg. 22.95 (0-89198-068-7) Ozer.

We Wore Jump Boots & Baggy Pants. John Ospital. (Illus.). 118p. (Orig.). 1977. pap. 8.75 (0-89839-047-8) Battery Pr.

We Worship. (Christ Our Life Ser.). 1992. teacher ed. 10.60 (0-8294-0679-4); pap. text ed. 9.00 (0-8294-0677-8) Loyola Pr.

We Worship As We Live: A Devotional Journey Through the Years. Carl H. Lee. 96p. 1996. pap. 21.95 (0-9630111-1-1) Concordia Coll.

We Would Lie on the Air. Anna M. Coleman. (Illus.). 32p. (Orig.). 1987. pap. 10.00 (0-944290-00-0) Light Speed.

We Would Not Kill. Hobart Mitchell. LC 83-81893. 300p. (Orig.). 1983. pap. 13.95 (0-913408-63-8) Friends United.

We Would See Jesus. Roy Hession. 1992. pap. 4.95 (0-87508-237-8) Chr Lit.

***We Write to Read: A Practical Approach to Integration of Vertical Print Letter Patterns.** 5th rev. ed. Charles H. Trafford & Rand H. Nelson. (Illus.). 40p. (J). 1996. pap. text ed. 1.95 (1-890666-01-7, 011696) Peterson Direct.

***We Write to Read: Advanced Cursive.** 5th rev. ed. Charles H. Trafford & Rand H. Nelson. (Illus.). 40p. (J). (gr. 5-8). 1996. pap. text ed. 1.95 (1-890666-05-X, 051696) Peterson Direct.

***We Write to Read: Teacher Handbook for Advanced Cursive Writing.** 5th rev. ed. Charles H. Trafford & Rand H. Nelson. (Illus.). 32p. 1996. teacher ed., pap. 3.40 (1-890666-11-4, 482096) Peterson Direct.

***We Write to Read: Teacher Handbook for Book Three, Transition to Cursive.** 5th rev. ed. Charles H. Trafford & Rand H. Nelson. (Illus.). 40p. 1996. teacher ed., pap. 3.40 (1-890666-10-6, 032096) Peterson Direct.

***We Write to Read: Teacher Handbook for Book Two, Cursive Readiness.** 5th rev. ed. Charles H. Trafford. (Illus.). 48p. 1996. teacher ed., pap. 3.40 (1-890666-09-2, 022096) Peterson Direct.

***We Write to Read: Teacher Handbook for Early Childhood & Kindergarten.** 5th rev. ed. Rand H. Nelson & Charles H. Trafford. (Illus.). 28p. 1997. teacher ed., pap. 3.40 (1-890666-07-6, 112007) Peterson Direct.

***We Write to Read: Teacher Handbook for Grade One.** 5th rev. ed. Charles H. Trafford & Rand H. Nelson. (Illus.). 48p. 1996. teacher ed., pap. 3.40 (1-890666-08-4) Peterson Direct.

***We Write to Read: The Left-Handed Writer.** Charles H. Trafford. (Illus.). 10p. 1987. reprint ed. teacher ed., per. 2.05 (1-890666-13-0) Peterson Direct.

***We Write to Read Bk. 2: A Practical Approach to the Introduction of Cursive Writing Patterns.** 5th rev. ed. Charles H. Trafford & Rand H. Nelson. (Illus.). 40p. (J). (gr. 2). 1996. pap. text ed. 1.95 (1-890666-02-5, 021696) Peterson Direct.

***We Write to Read Bk. 3: A Practical Transition to Applied Cursive Writing.** 5th rev. ed. Charles H. Trafford & Rand H. Nelson. (Illus.). 40p. (J). (gr. 3). 1996. pap. text ed. 1.95 (1-890666-03-3, 031696) Peterson Direct.

***We Write to Read Bk. 4: Learning to Work with Adult Tools.** 5th rev. ed. Charles H. Trafford & Rand H. Nelson. (Illus.). 40p. (J). (gr. 4). 1996. pap. text ed. 1.95 (1-890666-04-1, 041696) Peterson Direct.

We Write What We Can Read. student ed. 9.13 (0-917186-02-8) McQueen.

WEA Education Year Book 1918. H. D. Hughes & G. F. Brown. (C). 1981. 110.00 (0-902031-57-0, Pub. by Univ Nottingham UK) St Mut.

WEA Education Year Book, 1918. H. D. Hughes & G. Brown. 538p. (C). 1982. reprint ed. text ed. 65.00 (0-685-22161-X, Pub. by Univ Nottingham UK) St Mut.

Weak & Electromagnetic Interactions in Nuclei. Ed. by H. V. Klapdor. (Illus.). 1090p. 1987. 119.95 (0-387-17255-6) Spr-Verlag.

Weak & Electromagnetic Interactions in Nuclei: Proceedings of 3rd International Symposium. T. S. Vylov. 944p. 1993. text ed. 178.00 (981-02-1211-9) World Scientific Pub.

***Weak & Electromagnetic Interactions in Nuclei (WEIN '95)** 772p. 1995. 87.00 (981-02-2507-5) World Scientific Pub.

Weak & Young Measure Valued Solutions to Evolution. Jindrich Necas. 288p. 1996. 55.00 (0-412-57750-X) Chapman & Hall.

Weak Chaos & Quasi-Regular Patterns. George M. Zaslavsky et al. (Nonlinear Science Ser.: No. 1). (Illus.). 253p. (C). 1992. pap. text ed. 34.95 (0-521-43828-4) Cambridge U Pr.

Weak Chaos & Quasiregular Patterns. George M. Zaslavsky et al. (Nonlinear Science Ser.: No. 1). (Illus.). 272p. (C). 1991. text ed. 95.00 (0-521-37317-4) Cambridge U Pr.

Weak Convergence & Empirical Processes: With Applications to Statistics. Aad Van Der Vaart & Jon A. Wellner. LC 95-49099. (Springer Series in Statistics). 496p. 1996. 49.95 (0-387-94640-3) Spr-Verlag.

***Weak Convergence Approach to the Theory of Large Deviations.** Paul Dupuis & Richard S. Ellis. LC 96-27513. (Wiley Series in Probability & Mathematical Statistics). 488p. 1997. text ed. 79.95 (0-471-07672-4) Wiley.

Weak Convergence Methods & Singularly Perturbed Stochastic Control & Filtering Problems. Harold J. Kushner. (Systems & Control: Foundations & Applications Ser.: Vol. 3). 256p. 1990. 57.50 (0-8176-3437-1) Birkhauser.

Weak Convergence Methods for Nonlinear Partial Differential Equations. Evans. LC 89-27844. (CBMS Regional Conference Series in Mathematics: No. 74). 80p. 1990. 15.00 (0-8218-0724-2, CBMS/74) Am Math.

Weak Convergence of Measures: Applications in Probability. P. Billingsley. (CBMS-NSF Regional Conference Ser.: No. 5). v, 31p. 1972. pap. text ed. 12.00 (0-89871-176-2) Soc Indus-Appl Math.

Weak Foundations: The Economy of El Salvador in the Nineteenth Century, 1821-1898. Hector Lindo-Fuentes. (Illus.). 275p. 1990. 40.00 (0-520-06927-7) U CA Pr.

Weak in the World of the Strong: The Developing Countries in the International System. Robert L. Rothstein. LC 77-7889. 399p. reprint ed. pap. 113.80 (0-8357-7071-0, 2033594) Bks Demand.

Weak in the World of the Strong: The Third World in the International System. Robert L. Rothstein. LC 77-7889. (Institute of War & Peace Studies). 1977. text ed. 58.00 (0-231-04338-4) Col U Pr.

Weak Interaction in Nuclear, Particle & Astrophysics. K. Grotz & H. V. Klapdor. LC 90-37411. (Illus.). 480p. 1990. 191.00 (0-85274-312-2); pap. 65.00 (0-85274-313-0) IOP Pub.

Weak Interaction Physics: Nineteen Seventy-Seven Proceedings. Conference on the Present Status of Weak Interaction Physics, Indiana Univ., Bloomington, May 16-17, 1977. Ed. by D. B. Lichtenberg. LC 77-83344. (AIP Conference Proceedings Ser.: Vol. 37). (Illus.). 1977. lib. bdg. 13.00 (0-88318-136-3) Am Inst Physics.

Weak Interactions: Proceedings of the International Summer School for Theoretical Physics, 2nd, University of Karlsruhe, 1969. International Summer School for Theoretical Physics Staff. Ed. by G. Hoehler. (Tracts in Modern Physics Ser.: Vol. 52). (Illus.). v, 214p. 1970. 28.95 (0-387-05015-9) Spr-Verlag.

Weak Interactions & CP Violation: Beijing Workshop. Tao Huang & Dan-Di Wu. 360p. 1990. text ed. 113.00 (981-02-0105-2) World Scientific Pub.

Weak Interactions & Neutrinos: Proceedings of the 12th Symposium on Theoretical Physics. J. E. Kim & S. K. Kim. 364p. 1994. text ed. 99.00 (981-02-1843-5) World Scientific Pub.

Weak Interactions & Neutrinos: Proceedings of the 8th International Workshop, Javea, Spain, Sept. 5-11. 1982. Ed. by A. Morales. 820p. 1983. 125.00 (9971-950-89-8) World Scientific Pub.

Weak Interactions as Probes of Unification: Virginia Polytechnic Institute 1980. Ed. by G. B. Collins et al. (AIP Conference Proceedings Ser.: No. 72). 689p. 1981. lib. bdg. 39.50 (0-88318-171-1) Am Inst Physics.

Weak Interactions in Nuclei. Barry Holstein. (Physics Ser.). (Illus.). 360p. (C). 1989. text ed. 57.50 (0-691-08523-4) Princeton U Pr.

***Weak Neutral Currents: The Discovery of the Electroweak Force, Vol. 95.** David B. Cline. (Frontiers in Physics Ser.). 1998. 64.95 (0-201-93347-0) Addison-Wesley.

Weak Rock: Soft, Fractured & Weathered Rock: Proceedings of the International Symposium, Tokyo, 21-24 September 1981, 3 vols. Ed. by K. Akai et al. 1549p. 1981. Set. text ed. 490.00 (90-6191-209-1, Pub. by A A Balkema NE) Ashgate Pub Co.

Weak Rock Tunneling: A Simplified Analytical Simulation, a PC-Based Model & Design Charts for Engineering Practice. F. O. Francis. (Illus.). 256p. (C). 1994. 70.00 (90-5410-145-8, Pub. by A A Balkema NE) Ashgate Pub Co.

Weak States in the International System. 2nd ed. Michael I. Handel. 1990. text ed. 39.50 (0-7146-3385-2, Pub. by F Cass Pubs UK); pap. text ed. 22.50 (0-7146-4073-5, Pub. by F Cass Pubs UK) Intl Spec Bk.

Weak Strongman: Samson. Marilyn Lashbrook. LC 90-60456. (Me Too! Readers Ser.). (Illus.). 32p. (J). (gr. k-3). 1990. 5.95 (0-86606-442-7, 873) Treasure Pub.

***"Weak" Subject: Modernity, Eros, & Women's Dramatic Writing.** Serena Anderlini-D'Onofrio. LC 97-13826. 1997. write for info. (0-8386-3730-2) Fairleigh Dickinson.

Weak Superconductivity. Ed. by S. Benacka & M. Kedro. 290p. (C). 1990. text ed. 139.00 (0-941743-78-0) Nova Sci Pubs.

Weak Superconductivity: Proceedings of the 2nd Soviet-Italian Symposium, Naples, Italy, 5-7 May 1987. Antonio Barone. Ed. by A. I. Larkin. (Progress in High Temperature Superconductivity: Vol. IV). 420p. (C). 1988. text ed. 121.00 (9971-5-0504-5) World Scientific Pub.

Weak Superconductivity: Proceedings of the 6th International Symposium. Ed. by S. Benacka et al. 280p. (C). 1991. text ed. 81.00 (981-02-0795-6) World Scientific Pub.

Weak Thing in Moni Land. Gracie Cutts. (Junior Jaffray Collection: Bk. 2). 29p. (J). (ps-2). 1991. pap. 3.99 (0-87509-451-1) Chr Pubns.

Weak Thing in Moni Land: The Story of Bill & Gracie Cutts. William A. Cutts. LC 90-80454. (Jaffray Collection of Missionary Portraits). (Illus.). 168p. (Orig.). (YA). 1990. pap. 8.99 (0-87509-429-5) Chr Pubns.

Weak Thought & Its Strength. Dario Antiseri. (Avebury Series on Philosophy). 144p. 1996. 51.95 (1-85972-257-1, Pub. by Avebury Pub UK) Ashgate Pub Co.

Weak Type Estimates for Cesaro Sums of Jacobi Polynomial Series. Sagun Chanillo & Benjamin Muckenhoupt. LC 92-38214. (Memoirs of the American Mathematical Society Ser.: No. 487). 90p. 1993. pap. 29.00 (0-8218-2548-8, MEMO/102/487) Am Math.

Weaker Section in India: Undiscovered Past, Uncertain Present & Unpredictable Future Index to Writings in Indian Scholarly Journals & 10 National Newspapers Classified under 1500 Descriptors 1886-1900. Ed. by S. P. Agarwal. (Concepts in Communication Informatics & Librarianship Ser.). (C). 1992. 50.00 (81-7022-416-0, Pub. by Concept II) S Asia.

W

Weaker Sections in Indian Villages, 2 vols., Set. Ajit K. Danda. (C). 1993. 64.00 (*81-210-0303-2*, Pub. by Inter-India Pubns) S Asia.

Weaker Vessel. Antonia Fraser. 1994. pap. 18.00 (*0-394-25931-9*) Random.

Weaker Vessel: Woman's Lot in Seventeenth Century England. Antonia Fraser. (Illus.). 550p. 1985. pap. 18.00 (*0-394-73251-0*, Vin) Random.

Weakest Goeth to the Wall. LC 78-133759. (Tudor Facsimile Texts. Old English Plays Ser.: No. 91). reprint ed. 49.50 (*0-404-53391-4*) AMS Pr.

***Weakly Connected Neural Networks.** Frank C. Hoppensteadt. LC 97-14324. 1997. 59.95 (*0-387-94948-8*) Spr-Verlag.

Weakly Differential Functions. William P. Ziemer. (Graduate Texts in Mathematics Ser.: Vol. 120). (Illus.). 370p. 1989. 53.95 (*0-387-97017-7*) Spr-Verlag.

Weakly Nonlinear Dirichlet Problems on Long or Thin Domains. Edward N. Dancer. LC 93-2236. (Memoirs of the American Mathematical Society Ser.: No. 501). 66p. 1993. pap. 26.00 (*0-8218-2563-1*, MEMO/105/501) Am Math.

Weakly Semialgebraic Spaces. M. Knebusch. (Lecture Notes in Mathematics Ser.: Vol. 1367). xx, 376p. 1989. 54.95 (*0-387-50815-5*) Spr-Verlag.

Weakness. Bernard O'Donoghue. 80p. 1992. pap. 13.95 (*0-7011-3859-9*, Pub. by Chatto & Windus UK) Trafalgar.

Weakness Is a Crime: The Life of Bernarr Macfadden. Robert Ernst. (Illus.). 376p. 1990. pap. 17.95 (*0-8156-0252-9*); text ed. 39.95 (*0-8156-2512-X*) Syracuse U Pr.

Weakness of the Will. Justin Gosling. 256p. (C). (gr. 13). 1990. text ed. 49.95 (*0-415-03435-3*, A4680) Routledge.

Weakness of the Will in Medieval Thought: From Augustine to Buridan. Risto Saarinen. LC 94-15058. (Studien und Texte zur Geistesgeschichte des Mittelalters Ser.: Bd. 44). 1994. 99.00 (*90-04-09994-8*) E J Brill.

Wealdwife's Tale. Paul Hazel. 304p. 1994. mass mkt. 4.99 (*0-380-71880-4*, AvoNova) Avon.

Wealdwife's Tale. Paul Hazel. LC 92-25069. 1993. 20.00 (*0-688-12188-8*) Morrow.

Wealth: An Owner's Manual: a Sensible, Steady, Sure Course to Becoming & Staying Rich. Michael Stolper & Everett Mattlin. LC 91-42316. (Illus.). 272p. 1993. pap. 12.00 (*0-88730-645-4*) Harper Busn.

Wealth: How to Get It, How to Keep It. Lynn R. Niedermeier & Herb D. Vest. 160p. 1995. pap. 14.95 (*0-8144-7891-3*) AMACOM.

***Wealth: How to Get It How to Keep It.** Herb D. Vest. 156p. 3.98 (*0-7651-0106-8*) Smithmark.

***Wealth Accumulation Planning (For 329)** 3rd rev. ed. R. Robert Rackley. (ChFC Ser.). 1996. 160.00 (*1-57195-082-6*) Insurance Achiev.

Wealth Against Commonwealth. Ed. by Henry D. Lloyd. LC 76-7. 184p. 1976. reprint ed. text ed. 45.00 (*0-8371-8726-5*, LLWA, Greenwood Pr) Greenwood.

***Wealth & Beneficence in the Pastoral Epistles: A Bourgeois Form of Early Christianity?** Reggie M. Kidd. 231p. 1990. 24.95 (*1-55540-445-6*, 062122); pap. 14.95 (*1-55540-446-4*) Scholars Pr GA.

Wealth & Culture. Eduard C. Lindeman. 155p. 1987. 44.95 (*0-88738-170-7*) Transaction Pubs.

Wealth & Economic Status: A Perspective on Racial Inequity. William P. O'Hare. 38p. 1983. pap. 12.25 (*0-941410-35-8*) Jt Ctr Pol Studies.

Wealth & Freedom: An Introduction to Political Economy. David P. Levine. (Illus.). 192p. (C). 1995. pap. text ed. 17.95 (*0-521-44791-7*) Cambridge U Pr.

Wealth & Freedom: An Introduction to Political Economy. David P. Levine. (Illus.). 203p. (C). 1995. text ed. 54.95 (*0-521-44314-8*) Cambridge U Pr.

Wealth & Health. LC 72-133760. (Tudor Facsimile Texts. Old English Plays Ser.: No. 26). reprint ed. 49.50 (*0-404-53326-4*) AMS Pr.

Wealth & Hierarchy in the Intermediate Area. Ed. by Frederick W. Lange. LC 90-43419. (Illus.). 476p. 1992. 36.00 (*0-88402-191-2*) Dumbarton Oaks.

Wealth & Higher Consciousness. John-Roger. 160p. 1988. 12.00 (*0-914829-51-3*) Mandeville LA.

Wealth & Honour: Portsmouth During the Golden Age of Privateering, 1775-1815, No. 12. Edward C. Winslow, III. (Illus.). 320p. 1988. 30.00 (*0-915819-11-2*) Portsmouth Marine Soc.

Wealth & Personal Incomes. A. B. Atkinson et al. LC 77-30556. 1978. 74.00 (*0-08-022450-4*, Pub. by Pergamon Repr UK) Franklin.

Wealth & Poverty. 2nd ed. George Gilder. LC 93-9717. 320p. 1993. pap. 19.95 (*1-55815-240-7*) ICS Pr.

Wealth & Poverty: An Economic History of the Twentieth Century. Ed. by Sidney Pollard. (Illus.). 256p. 1990. 40.00 (*0-19-520821-8*) OUP.

Wealth & Poverty in the Instruction of Amenemope & the Hebrew Proverbs: A Comparative Case Study in the Social Location & Function of Ancient Near Eastern Wisdom Literature. Harold C. Washington. LC 94-40162. (Dissertation Ser.: Vol. 142). 252p. 1994. 29.95 (*0-7885-0072-4*, 062142) Scholars Pr GA.

Wealth & Poverty in the Instruction of Amenemope & the Hebrew Proverbs: A Comparative Case Study with the Social Location & Function of Ancient Near Eastern Wisdom Literature. Harold C. Washington. LC 94-40162. (Dissertation Ser.: Vol.142). 252p. 1994. pap. 19.95 (*0-7885-0073-2*, 06 21 42) Scholars Pr GA.

Wealth & Poverty in the Teachings of the Church Fathers. James Thornton. 168p. (Orig.). (C). 1993. pap. 8.95 (*0-9634692-1-5*) St John Chrysostom.

Wealth & Poverty of Nations. David Landes. Date not set. 30.00 (*0-393-04017-8*) Norton.

Wealth & Power in America: An Analysis of Social Class & Income Distribution. Gabriel Kolko. LC 81-6856. xvi, 178p. 1981. reprint ed. text ed. 49.75 (*0-313-23182-6*, KOWP, Greenwood Pr) Greenwood.

Wealth & Power in American Zion. Anson Shupe. LC 92-16594. 324p. 1992. reprint ed. lib. bdg. 99.95 (*0-7734-9549-5*) E Mellen.

Wealth & Progress. George Gunton. LC 71-130549. (Select Bibliographies Reprint Ser.). 1977. 23.95 (*0-8369-5522-6*) Ayer.

Wealth & Rebellion: Elsie Clews Parsons, Anthropologist & Folklorist. Rosemary L. Zumwalt & Roger D. Abrahams. (Illus.). 400p. (C). 1992. text ed. 47.50 (*0-252-01909-1*) U of Ill Pr.

Wealth & Taxable Capacity. Josiah C. Stamp. LC 79-150200. (Select Bibliographies Reprint Ser.). 1977. reprint ed. 20.95 (*0-8369-5713-X*) Ayer.

Wealth & the Demand for Art in Italy, 1300-1600. Richard A. Goldthwaite. LC 92-38328. 304p. (C). 1993. 35.00 (*0-8018-4612-9*) Johns Hopkins.

Wealth & the Demand for Art in Italy, 1300-1600. Richard A. Goldthwaite. 304p. 1995. reprint ed. pap. 15.95 (*0-8018-5235-8*) Johns Hopkins.

Wealth & the Power of Wealth in Classical Athens. rev. ed. John K. Davies. Ed. by W. R. Connor. LC 80-2647. (Monographs in Classical Studies). 1981. lib. bdg. 26.95 (*0-88143-019-6*) Ayer.

Wealth & the Wealthy in the Modern World. W. D. Rubenstein. LC 80-14632. 1980. text ed. 32.50 (*0-312-85936-8*) St Martin.

Wealth & Want. Stanley Lebergott. LC 75-4460. 229p. reprint ed. pap. 65.30 (*0-7837-6773-0*, 2046603) Bks Demand.

Wealth & Welfare. Jeremias Gotthelf. Tr. by J. Firth from GER. vi, 507p. 1976. reprint ed. 45.00 (*0-86527-325-1*) Fertig.

Wealth Angles. Ed. by Laura Bernstein. 238p. 1991. 29.00 (*0-945332-28-9*) Agora Inc MD.

Wealth As Peril & Obligation: The New Testament on Possessions. Sondra E. Wheeler. LC 95-9161. 1995. pap. 15.00 (*0-8028-0733-X*) Eerdmans.

Wealth Building for Middle Income Americans. Michael A. Beitler. LC 95-94391. 141p. (Orig.). 1995. pap. 19.95 (*0-9646434-3-X*) Contntl Pub SC.

Wealth Building Lessons of Booker T. Washington. T. M. Pryor. LC 95-67017. (Illus.). 150p. 1995. 15.95 (*1-878647-21-0*) Duncan & Duncan.

Wealth Building Strategies: How to Become a Better Consumer of Financial Products & Get Ahead in Today's Financially Complex World. Eric Gelb. 32p. (Orig.). 1997. pap. 7.95 (*0-9631289-8-1*) Career Advan.

Wealth Creation & Wealth Sharing: A Colloquium on Corporate Governance & Investment in Human Capital. Ed. by Margaret M. Blair. 100p. 1996. pap. 12.95 (*0-8157-0949-8*) Brookings.

Wealth Creation As a "Sin" Jonathan R. Macey. (Independent Policy Reports). 32p. (Orig.). 1996. pap. 5.95 (*0-945999-44-5*) Independent Inst.

Wealth Creation in China. Rupert A. Hodder. LC 92-43312. 152p. 1993. text ed. 49.95 (*0-470-22004-X*, Belhaven) Halsted Pr.

Wealth Creation in Eastern Europe: Financial Management Issues & Strategies. Ed. by Fred R. Kaen. LC 91-47937. (Journal of Multinational Financial Management). 112p. 1992. lib. bdg. 39.95 (*1-56024-305-8*) Haworth Pr.

***Wealth Enhancement & Preservation. 2nd ed. Ed. by Robert A. Esperti & Renno L. Peterson. 526p. 1996. reprint ed. 29.95 (*0-922943-08-7*, NNI-221BK) Esperti Petrsn.**
In a clear & precise, question-&-answer format, WEALTH offers a myriad of highly sophisticated estate & financial planning strategies to enhance & preserve wealth. It is the product of an extensive national research & writing project that involved the collaboration of over sixty of America's leading financial advisors. Their expertise & longstanding record of planning successes bring an especially direct practicality to the subject of planning. WEALTH brings to the forefront the critically important questions being asked by people all over the United States & the answers that these expert financial advisors provide so individuals can create meaningful estate, financial, investment, insurance & retirement plans; & charitable giving programs. The collection of specialized knowledge in WEALTH ENHANCEMENT & PRESERVATION was brought together for the first time in a single text by the Esperti Peterson Institute, & Robert A. Esperti & Renno L. Peterson, authors of LOVING TRUST (Viking) & PROTECT YOUR ESTATE (McGraw-Hill) among other widely acclaimed books on tax & estate planning. Books are available by writing or calling Esperti Peterson Institute, 410 17th Street, Suite 1260, Denver, CO 80202; Tel: (800) 638-8681; FAX: (303) 446-6060. ***Publisher Provided Annotation.***

Wealth for All: Economics, 2 Bks., Book 2. rev. ed. R. E. McMaster, Jr. 280p. 1982. 14.95 (*0-9605316-2-9*) Reaper Pub.

Wealth from Diversity: Innovation, Structural Change & Finance for Regional Development in Europe. J. S. Metcalfe. Ed. by Xavier Vence-Deza. LC 96-8870. (Economics of Science, Technology & Innovation Ser.). 408p. (C). 1996. lib. bdg. 140.00 (*0-7923-4115-5*) Kluwer Ac.

Wealth Holders of America, 1988. 830p. (Orig.). 1988. pap. 395.00 (*0-929094-00-X*) Biodata Inc.

Wealth in a Decade. Brett Machtig. LC 96-9322. 256p. 1996. text ed. 24.95 (*0-7863-1072-3*) Irwin Prof Pubng.

Wealth in Western Thought: The Case for & Against Riches. Paul G. Schervish. LC 93-23469. 272p. 1994. text ed. 59.95 (*0-275-94677-0*, Praeger Pubs) Greenwood.

Wealth, Kinship & Culture: The 17th-Century Newdigates of Arbury & Their World. Vivienne Larminie. (Royal Historical Society Studies in History: No. 72). (Illus.). 259p. (C). 1995. 71.00 (*0-86193-231-5*, Royal Historical Soc) Boydell & Brewer.

Wealth Management: The Financial Advisor's Guide to Investing & Managing Your Client's Assets. Harold R. Evensky. 472p. 1996. text ed. 50.00 (*0-7863-0478-2*) Irwin Prof Pubng.

***Wealth Management Index: The Financial Advisor's System for Assessing & Managing Your Client's Plans & Goals.** Ross Levin. LC 96-3466. 168p. 1996. text ed. 50.00 (*0-7863-1020-0*) Irwin Prof Pubng.

Wealth Now Answers Manual. Richard Staff. (Illus.). 223p. (Orig.). 1993. pap. 29.00 (*0-9640217-9-X*) Results Now.

Wealth of a Nation in the National Museums of Scotland. Ed. by Jenni Calder. (Illus.). 208p. 1995. pap. 29.95 (*0-86267-265-1*, 2651, Pub. by Natl Mus Scotland UK) A Schwartz & Co.

Wealth of a Spiritual Woman. Linda G. Beatty. LC 94-60969. 111p. (Orig.). 1994. pap. 10.95 (*1-55523-721-5*) Winston-Derek.

***Wealth of Cities: How America Wrecked Its Cities & How They Can Grow Rich Again.** John O. Norquist. 1998. write for info. (*0-201-44213-2*) Addison-Wesley.

Wealth of Communities: Stories of Success in Local Environmental Management. Charlie Pye-Smith et al. LC 94-75606. (Library of Management for Development). (Illus.). x, 213p. (Orig.). 1994. pap. 18.95 (*1-56549-038-X*) Kumarian Pr.

***Wealth of Devotion.** Chandrahasa Das. LC 97-65783. 128p. (Orig.). 1997. pap. 7.95 (*0-9657306-2-X*) Omegaman Prod.

Wealth of England from Fourteen Ninety-Six to Seventeen Sixty. George N. Clark. LC 85-27270. (Home University of Modern Knowledge Ser.). 207p. 1986. reprint ed. text ed. 59.75 (*0-313-25045-6*, CLWE, Greenwood Pr) Greenwood.

***Wealth of Experience: A Guide to Activities for Older People.** 2nd ed. Meredith Budge. 300p. 1994. pap. 45.00 (*0-8036-0104-2*) Davis Co.

Wealth of Happiness & Many Bitter Trials: The Journals of Sir Alfred Edward Pease a Restless Man. Joseph G. Pease. 384p. 1990. 85.00 (*1-85072-107-6*, Pub. by W Sessions UK) St Mut.

Wealth of India: Raw Materials, Vol. 1:A. Scientific Publishers Staff. 513p. (C). 1988. 94.00 (*0-317-92332-3*, Pub. by Scientific UK) St Mut.

Wealth of Japan. Edmund O'Connor. Ed. by Malcolm Yapp et al. (World History Program Ser.). (Illus.). 32p. (YA). (gr. 6-11). 1980. reprint ed. pap. text ed. 4.72 (*0-89908-212-2*) Greenhaven.

Wealth of Love. large type ed. Kay Winchester. 320p. 1992. 25.99 (*0-7089-2581-2*) Ulverscroft.

Wealth of Nations. Adam Smith. 23.95 (*0-8488-1170-4*) Amereon Ltd.

Wealth of Nations. Adam Smith. Ed. & Intro. by Andrew Skinner. (English Library). 544p. 1982. pap. 9.95 (*0-14-043208-6*, Penguin Classics) Viking Penguin.

Wealth of Nations. Adam Smith. 656p. 1991. 20.00 (*0-679-40564-X*, Everymans Lib) Knopf.

Wealth of Nations. Adam Smith. (Modern Library College Editions). 512p. (C). 1985. pap. text ed. write for info. (*0-07-554596-9*) McGraw.

Wealth of Nations. Adam Smith. (Great Minds Ser.). 590p. 1991. pap. 9.95 (*0-87975-705-1*) Prometheus Bks.

Wealth of Nations. Adam Smith. Ed. & Intro. by Edwin Cannan. LC 37-3720. 1977. 16.95 (*0-394-60409-1*, Modern Lib) Random.

Wealth of Nations. Adam Smith. 1104p. 1994. 22.00 (*0-679-42473-3*, Modern Lib) Random.

Wealth of Nations. abr. ed. Adam Smith. LC 93-24370. (Hackett Classics Ser.). 352p. (C). 1993. pap. 8.95 (*0-87220-204-6*); lib. bdg. 27.95 (*0-87220-205-4*) Hackett Pub.

Wealth of Nations: An Inquiry into the Nature & Causes, 2 vols. in one. Adam Smith. Ed. by Edwin Cannan. LC 76-21934. 1146p. 1977. pap. 19.95 (*0-226-76374-9*, P707) U Ch Pr.

Wealth of Nations & the Environment. Mikhail Bernstam. 71p. (C). 1991. text ed. 70.00 (*0-255-36240-4*, Pub. by Inst Economic Affairs UK) St Mut.

Wealth of Nations in Crisis. Ronald C. Nairn. LC 79-90284. 289p. 1979. 12.95 (*0-934018-00-6*, Houston Metropolitan Mag) ARC Comms.

***Wealth of Nations in the Twentieth Century: The Policies & Institutional Determinants of Economic Development.** Ed. by Ramon H. Myers. LC 96-35432. (Publication Ser.). 1996. 34.95 (*0-8179-9451-3*); pap. 24.95 (*0-8179-9452-1*) Hoover Inst Pr.

Wealth of Nature: Environmental History & the Ecological Imagination. Donald Worster. LC 92-15360. 272p. 1993. 30.00 (*0-19-507624-9*) OUP.

Wealth of Nature: Environmental History & the Ecological Imagination. Donald Worster. 272p. 1994. reprint ed. pap. 13.95 (*0-19-509264-3*) OUP.

Wealth of Oceans: Environment & Development on Our Ocean Planet. Michael L. Weber & Judith A. Gradwohl. LC 94-35997. (Illus.). 256p. 1995. 25.00 (*0-393-03764-9*) Norton.

Wealth of Poor Nations. C. Suriyakumaran. LC 83-17672. 336p. 1984. text ed. 35.00 (*0-312-85942-2*) St Martin.

Wealth of Races: The Present Value of Benefits from Past Injustices. Ed. by Richard F. America. LC 89-25728. (Contributions in Afro-American & African Studies: No. 132). 232p. 1990. text ed. 55.00 (*0-313-25753-1*, ARR/, Greenwood Pr) Greenwood.

***Wealth of States: A Comparative Sociology of International Economic & Political Change.** John M. Hobson. (Cambridge Studies in International Relations: No. 52). 300p. (C). 1997. 59.95 (*0-521-58149-4*); pap. 19.95 (*0-521-58862-6*) Cambridge U Pr.

Wealth of States: Policies for a Dynamic Economy. Rober Vaughan et al. LC 85-29082. 154p. 1985. 16.95 (*0-934842-23-X*) CSPA.

Wealth of the Gentry, Fifteen Forty to Sixteen Sixty: East Anglican Studies. Alan Simpson. LC 61-13873. 234p. reprint ed. pap. 66.70 (*0-317-28119-4*, 2024105) Bks Demand.

Wealth of the Solomons: A History of a Pacific Archipelago, 1800-1978. Judith A. Bennett. LC 86-16080. (Pacific Islands Monographs: No. 3). (Illus.). 544p. 1986. text ed. 38.00 (*0-8248-1078-3*) UH Pr.

Wealth of the Windsors. Andrew Morton. (Illus.). 192p. 1994. reprint ed. pap. 10.95 (*1-55970-261-3*) Arcade Pub Inc.

Wealth of the World: The Proven Wealth Transfer System. John F. Avanzini. 162p. (Orig.). 1989. pap. 7.99 (*0-89274-580-0*, HH580) Harrison Hse.

Wealth of Thought: Franz Boaz on Native American Art. Franz Boaz. Ed. by Aldona Jonaitis. (Illus.). 352p. 1994. pap. 24.95 (*0-295-97384-6*); text ed. 50.00 (*0-295-97325-0*) U of Wash Pr.

Wealth of Wisdom: A Treasury of Basic Values. 366p. 1995. spiral bd. 7.00 (*1-882835-30-1*) STA-Kris.

Wealth on Minimal Wage: Living Well on Less. James W. Steamer. LC 96-36015. 208p. (Orig.). 1996. pap. 16.95 (*0-7931-2240-6*, 5680-3501) Dearborn Finan.

Wealth Power. Eric Savage. 288p. 1993. pap. 39.95 (*0-911752-68-4*) Neo-Tech Pub.

Wealth Power: How to Work With Your Financial Advisors to Maximize, Protect & Control Your Assets. James F. Vigue. (Your Assets Ser.). 213p. (Orig.). 1991. pap. 12.95 (*0-9629858-0-5*) Cnslts Pr.

Wealth Preservation & Protection for Closely-Held Business Owners (& Others) Jonathan G. Blattmach. LC 93-8803. (Libey Business Library). 640p. 1993. 190.00 (*1-882222-03-2*) Libey Pub.

Wealth Ranking Annual 1995. Mark W. Scott. 1996. 95.00 (*1-56995-062-8*) Taft Group.

Wealth Ranking Annual 1997. Mark W. Scott. 95.00 (*1-56995-064-4*) Taft Group.

Wealth Rankings Annual, 1994. 1995. 99.00 (*1-56995-061-X*, 600517) Taft Group.

Wealth Rankings Annual 1996. Mark W. Scott. 1997. 95.00 (*1-56995-063-6*) Taft Group.

***Wealth Starts at Home: And 15 Other Financial Secrets That Could Make You a Fortune.** David Darcangelo. LC 96-40001. 216p. 1997. 22.95 (*0-7863-1128-2*) Irwin Prof Pubng.

Wealth, Virtual Wealth & Debt: An Expose of Our Iniquitous Banking System. Frederick Soddy. 1992. lib. bdg. 79.95 (*0-8490-5280-7*) Gordon Pr.

Wealth Watchers: H. D. Vest's Wealth-Building Program for Life. Herb D. Vest & Lynn R. Niedermeier. 240p. 1995. text ed. 24.95 (*0-7863-0467-7*) Irwin Prof Pubng.

Wealth Weapon: U. S. Foreign Policy & Multinational Corporations. Ben J. Wattenberg & Richard J. Whalen. LC 79-66448. 127p. 1980. 34.95 (*0-87855-340-1*); pap. 21.95 (*0-87855-820-9*) Transaction Pubs.

Wealth Well-Given: The Enterprise & Benevolence of Lord Nuffield. Ed. by F. John Minns. (Illus.). 336p. 1994. 28.00 (*0-7509-0656-1*, Pub. by Sutton Pubng UK) Bks Intl VA.

Wealth Within. Ainslie Meares. 170p. (Orig.). 1994. pap. 13.95 (*0-85572-086-7*, Pub. by Hill Content Pubng AT) Seven Hills Bk.

Wealth Within Reach: Kwik Kopy Story. Bud Hadfield. 268p. 1992. 23.00 (*0-9645102-0-0*) Cyprss Pub.

Wealth Within Reach: Winning Strategies for Success from the Unconventional Wisdom of Bud Hadfield. rev. ed. Bud Hadfield. 270p. 1995. text ed. 23.95 (*0-9645102-1-9*) Cyprss Pub.

Wealth Without Guilt. Roland J. Hill. Ed. by Kenneth McFarland. 80p. 1995. 12.00 (*0-9639357-1-2*) Helping Hands.

Wealth Without Work: Keys to More Thru Management. Clifton M. Whitley. write for info. (*0-935497-02-1*) Fountainhead.

Wealthbuilder by Money Magazine: Taking Control of Your Financial Destiny. Donald R. Woodwell & Doris Woodwell. 240p. 1991. pap. 26.00 (*1-55623-441-4*) Irwin Prof Pubng.

Wealth's Thesaurus. Sue Hu. LC 92-80922. (Illus.). 64p. (Orig.). (CHI & ENG.). (C). 1993. 900.00 (*1-881797-00-7*); pap. 180.00 (*0-9623736-7-2*); pap. text ed. 12.00 (*1-881797-01-5*) WE Enterprises.

Wealthy & Wise: How You & America Can Get the Most of Your Giving. Claude Rosenberg. 1994. 24.95 (*0-316-75741-1*) Little.

Wealthy Barber: Everyone's Common-Sense Guide to Becoming Financially Independent. 2nd rev. ed. David Chilton. 208p. 1995. pap. text ed. 12.95 (*0-7615-0166-5*) Prima Pub.

Wealthy Barber: The Common-Sense Guide to Becoming Financially Independent. David Chilton. 208p. 1991. 19.95 (*1-55958-096-8*) Prima Pub.

W

An Asterisk (*) at the beginning of an entry indicates that the title is appearing in BIP for the first time.

Wealthy Citizens of New York. Moses Y. Beach. LC 73-1992. (Big Business; Economic Power in a Free Society Ser.). 1980. reprint ed. 17.95 (*0-405-05117-4*) Ayer.

Wealthy 100: From Benjamin Franklin to Bill Gates; a Ranking of the Richest Americans, Past & Present. Michael M. Klepper & Robert E. Gunther. (Illus.). 24.95 (*1-55972-341-6*, Birch Ln Pr) Carol Pub Group.

***Wealthy Tortoise: How to Get Rich Without Risk - Slowly. Jan Richmond. LC 96-69503. (Illus.). 120p. (Orig.). 1997. pap. 12.95 (*0-9653237-7-3*, 1456) Suntrak.**

"You could get rich by playing the lottery, but chances are you won't. But you may well be rich if you follow THE WEALTHY TORTOISE by Jan Richmond. This book tells you how, with a collection of personal stories & easy-to-read methods. Anyone can do it."--RICHARD A. VOKE, FORMER MAJORITY LEADER, MASSACHUSETTS HOUSE OF REPRESENTATIVES. "THE WEALTHY TORTOISE is written in a witty & engaging style. Jan Richmond shares personal experiences, enlightening the reader with sound investment strategies, & proving the absolute necessity of methodical long range financial planning. Richmond successfully argues the point that one can attain financial goals & independence WITHOUT TAKING UNDUE RISKS. Her approach is disciplined & proactive. This book should be used as a textbook for Investing 101."--LIESELOTTE JOSLYN, VICE PRESIDENT, CHITTENDEN BANK. "THE WEALTHY TORTOISE is for everyone. Richmond presents a solid strategy for financial success based on the slow, steady progress of the tortoise in its fabled race against the upstart hare. Many real-life examples explain financial terms. Richmond identifies three essential ingredients of her financial plan - a reasonable goal, a specific & verifiable method & a way to track progress so minor deviations can be instantly corrected."--HIROKO TATBE, CFP, SENIOR VICE PRESIDENT & TREASURER, DAL-ICHI KANGYO BANK OF CALIFORNIA. To order: Suntrak, Inc., R.R.#1 Box 1890, Berwal Road, Arlington, VT 05250. Telephone: 802-375-6588.

Publisher Provided Annotation.

Wealthy Women. Lynda Logan-Frank et al. 1985. 14.95 (*0-910019-35-5*) Lghthse Pub Gp.

Weaning: And Other Stories. Nell Brasher. 192p. 1993. 19.95 (*1-881548-01-5*) Crane Hill AL.

Weaning: Why, What, & When? Ed. by Angel Ballabriga & Jean Rey. (Nestle Nutrition Workshop Ser.: Vol. 10). 240p. 1987. 45.50 (*0-685-38974-X*, 1699) Lppncott-Raven.

Weaning & Human Development. Gordon R. Forrer. LC 72-79731. 1969. 12.95 (*0-87212-020-1*) Libra.

***Weaning of America: The Case Against Dairy Products.** LC 97-70573. (Illus.). 115p. (Orig.). Date not set. pap. 10.95 (*0-9630275-1-4*) Innerpeace.

Weaning of Baby Roy. Dan Lenihan. 48p. (Orig.). 1989. pap. 4.00 (*0-935390-14-6*) Wormwood Bks & Mag.

Weaning Ways: A Mothers' Collection of Nursing & Weaning Experiences. Siena Klein-Owen. LC 89-91701. 100p. 1989. pap. 11.00 (*0-9624133-0-5*) Shared Experiences.

Weapon Masters of Okinawa: An Informal History of the Ryukyu Kobudo (Ancient Weapon Ways) Sid Campbell. (Audio Cassette Book). 25p. 1988. audio 29.95 (*0-682-87110-9*) Gong Prods.

***Weapon of Prayer.** E. M. Bounds. 190p. 1996. mass mkt. 4.99 (*0-88368-457-8*) Whitaker Hse.

Weapon of Prayer. deluxe ed. Basilea M. Schlink. 1974. 0.95 (*3-87209-658-3*) Evang Sisterhood Mary.

Weapon of Prayer. rev. ed. E. M. Bounds. (E. M. Bounds Classics on Prayer Ser.). 120p. (gr. 10). 1991. pap. 6.99 (*0-8010-1004-7*) Baker Bks.

Weapon of Theory: A Post-Cold-War Primer on Marxism. Markar Melkonian. 170p. 1994. pap. 12.00 (*0-9641569-0-3*) Sardarabad.

Weapon on the Wall. Murray Dyer. 1979. 28.95 (*0-405-10599-1*) Ayer.

***Weapon Shops of Isher.** A. E. Van Vogt. Date not set. lib. bdg. 18.95 (*0-8488-0851-7*) Amereon Ltd.

Weapon Shops of Isher. A. E. Van Vogt. 1993. reprint ed. lib. bdg. 18.95 (*0-89968-381-9*, Lghtyr Pr) Buccaneer Bks.

Weapon Systems of the U. S. Army: An Overview of Major Systems - Close Combat, Air Defense, Fire Support, Combat Support, Combat Service, Control Command, Communications, Soldier Support & Strategic Defense. (Military Science Ser.). 1991. lib. bdg. 250.00 (*0-8490-5462-1*) Gordon Pr.

***Weapon Systems, U. S. Army, 1996.** 272p. 1996. pap. text ed. 55.00 (*1-57979-155-7*) BPI Info Servs.

***Weapon Systems, U. S. Army, 1997.** (Illus.). 272p. 1997. 55.00 (*1-57979-210-3*, 2117) BPI Info Servs.

***Weapon Systems, U. S. Army, 1997.** (Illus.). 262p. (Orig.). 1997. pap. 55.00 (*0-7881-3995-9*) DIANE Pub.

Weaponeer: An Encyclopedia of Improvised Home Weapons. 1991. lib. bdg. 250.00 (*0-8490-4747-1*) Gordon Pr.

Weaponless Control: For Law Enforcement & Security Personnel. Jeff Cope & Kenneth Goddard. (Illus.). 302p. 1979. pap. 35.95 (*0-398-06076-2*) C C Thomas.

Weaponless Control: For Law Enforcement & Security Personnel. fac. ed. Jeff Cope & Kenneth Goddard. (Illus.). 302p. 1979. 51.95 (*0-398-03902-X*) C C Thomas.

Weaponless Warriors. Richard Kim. Ed. by John Scurra. LC 74-21218. (History & Philosophy Ser.). (Illus.). 1974. pap. text ed. 12.95 (*0-89750-041-5*, 313) Ohara Pubns.

Weaponry in Space: The Dilemma of Security. Ed. by Y. Velikhov et al. 174p. 1987. 22.95 (*0-08-034752-5*, Pergamon Pr) Elsevier.

Weapons: An International Encyclopedia from 5000 B.C. to 2000 A.D. Diagram Group Staff. (Illus.). 336p. (Orig.). 1991. 29.95 (*0-312-03951-4*); pap. 18.95 (*0-312-03950-6*) St Martin.

Weapons Acquisition: A Rare Opportunity for Lasting Change. (Illus.). 84p. (Orig.). (C). 1993. pap. text ed. 25.00 (*1-56806-311-3*) DIANE Pub.

Weapons Acquisition: Low-Rate Initial Production Used to Buy Weapon Systems Prematurely. (Illus.). 44p. (Orig.). (C). 1995. pap. text ed. 30.00 (*0-7881-1763-7*) DIANE Pub.

Weapons Acquisition: Precision Guided Munitions Inventory, Production & Development. 55p. (Orig.). (C). 1995. pap. text ed. 25.00 (*0-7881-2490-0*) DIANE Pub.

***Weapons Acquisition: Warranty Law Should Be Repealed.** (Illus.). 44p. (Orig.). (C). 1996. pap. 20.00 (*0-7881-3395-0*) DIANE Pub.

Weapons Against Chaos. Mary Ewald. 1986. 14.95 (*0-8159-7225-3*) Devin.

Weapons & Armor: A Pictorial Archive of Woodcuts & Engravings. Ed. by Harold H. Hart. (Illus.). 192p. reprint ed. pap. 8.95 (*0-486-24242-0*) Dover.

Weapons & Equipment for Counter-Terrorism. 1992. lib. bdg. 88.95 (*0-8490-5378-1*) Gordon Pr.

Weapons & Equipment of the German Cavalry in World War II. Klaus C. Richter. Tr. by David Johnston from GER. (Illus.). 48p. 1995. pap. 8.95 (*0-88740-816-8*) Schiffer.

Weapons & Equipment of the German Fallschirmtruppe 1941-1945. Alex Buchner & David Johnston. (Illus.). 48p. (YA). 1996. pap. 10.00 (*0-88740-964-4*) Schiffer.

Weapons & Equipment of the German Mountain Troops in WW II. Roland Kaltenegger et al. Tr. by Edward Force from GER. (Illus.). 48p. (Orig.). 1995. pap. 8.95 (*0-88740-756-0*) Schiffer.

***Weapons & Equipment of the Napoleonic Wars.** Philip J. Haythornthwaite. (Illus.). 192p. 1997. 27.95 (*1-85409-393-2*, Pub. by Arms & Armour UK) Sterling.

***Weapons & Equipment of the SAS.** Peter Darman. LC 97-2556. 1997. write for info. (*1-85367-294-7*) Stackpole.

Weapons & Fighting Arts of Indonesia. Donn F. Draeger. 256p. 1992. pap. 21.95 (*0-8048-1716-2*) C E Tuttle.

Weapons & Warfare: From the Stone Age to the Space Age. Milton Meltzer. LC 95-48464. (Illus.). 96p. (J). (gr. 3-7). 1996. 16.95 (*0-06-024875-0*); lib. bdg. 16.89 (*0-06-024876-9*) HarpC Child Bks.

Weapons & Warfare in Anglo-Saxon England. Ed. by Sonia C. Hawkes. (Illus.). 216p. 1989. 45.00 (*0-947816-21-6*, Pub. by Oxford Univ Comm Arch UK) David Brown.

***Weapons & Warfare in Renaissance Europe: Gunpowder, Technology, & Tactics.** Bert S. Hall. LC 96-43295. (Studies in the History of Technology). (Illus.). 296p. 1997. 29.95 (*0-8018-5531-4*) Johns Hopkins.

Weapons Animals Wear. Lynn M. Stone. LC 96-24223. (Animal Weapons Ser.). 1996. write for info. (*1-57103-163-4*) Rourke Pr.

***Weapons, Culture & Self-Interest: Soviet Defense Managers in the New Russia.** Kimberly M. Zisk. LC 97-26199. 1998. write for info. (*0-231-11078-2*); pap. write for info. (*0-231-11079-0*) Col U Pr.

Weapons Don't Make War: Policy, Strategy, & Military Technology. Colin S. Gray. LC 92-10090. (Modern War Studies). xii, 236p. 1993. 29.95 (*0-7006-0559-2*) U Pr of KS.

Weapons Effects Against Fortifications (1900-1980) Ed. by Bruce A. Hanesalo. 1996. vinyl bd. 15.00 (*1-886848-20-3*) Mil-Info.

Weapons for the World Update: The U. S. Corporate Role in International Arms Transfer. Steven D. Lydenberg. 72p. 1977. 5.00 (*0-318-35442-X*) CEP.

Weapons for Victory: The Hiroshima Decision Fifty Years Later. Robert J. Maddox. 200p. (C). 1995. 19.95 (*0-8262-1037-6*) U of Mo Pr.

Weapons in Ancient China. Yang Hong. 181p. 1992. text ed. 89.65 (*1-880132-03-6*) Sci Pr NY.

Weapons Law. J. B. Hill. (Waterlow Practitioner's Library). 96p. (Orig.). 1989. pap. 21.95 (*0-08-033104-1*, Waterlow) Macmillan.

***Weapons Legacy of the Cold War: Problems & Opportunities.** Ed. by Dietrich Schroeer & Alessandro Pascolini. LC 97-19614. (ISODARCO Ser.). 250p. 1997. text ed. 63.95 (*1-85521-945-X*, Pub. by Ashgate UK) Ashgate Pub Co.

Weapons of Chess: An Omnibus of Chess Strategy. Bruce Pandolfini. 272p. 1989. pap. 11.00 (*0-671-65972-3*, Fireside) S&S Trade.

***Weapons of Mass Destruction: An Update Reducing the Threat from the Former Soviet Union.** 78p. 1995. pap. text ed. 30.00 (*1-57979-133-6*) BPI Info Servs.

Weapons of Mass Destruction: Costs Versus Benefits. Ed. by Kathleen C. Bailey. (C). 1994. 16.00 (*81-7304-099-0*, Pub. by Manohar II) S Asia.

***Weapons of Mass Destruction: New Perspectives on Counterproliferation.** (Illus.). 248p. 1995. pap. text ed. 45.00 (*1-57979-167-0*) BPI Info Servs.

Weapons of Mass Destruction: New Perspectives on Counterproliferation. Ed. by William H. Lewis & Stuart E. Johnson. (Illus.). 247p. (Orig.). (C). 1995. pap. text ed. 45.00 (*0-7881-2127-8*) DIANE Pub.

Weapons of Mass Destruction: Nonlethality, Information Warfare, & Airpower in the Age of Chaos. Chris Morris et al. (Illus.). 47p. (Orig.). (C). 1995. pap. text ed. 30.00 (*0-7881-1670-3*) DIANE Pub.

Weapons of Mass Destruction: Reducing the Threat from the Former Soviet Union. (Illus.). 62p. (Orig.). (C). 1994. pap. text ed. 30.00 (*0-7881-1506-5*) DIANE Pub.

Weapons of Mass Destruction: Reducing the Threat from the Former Soviet Union: An Update. 77p. (Orig.). (C). 1995. pap. text ed. 20.00 (*0-7881-2487-0*) DIANE Pub.

***Weapons of Mass Destruction: Status of the Cooperative Threat Reduction Program.** (Illus.). 35p. (Orig.). (C). 1996. pap. 25.00 (*0-7881-3580-5*) DIANE Pub.

Weapons of Mass Destruction: The Cases of Iran, Syria & Libya. Kenneth R. Timmerman. (Simon Wiesenthal Center Special Reports). (Illus.). 133p. (Orig.). 1992. pap. 10.00 (*0-614-03226-1*) S Wiesenthal Ctr.

***Weapons of Mass Destruction & Terrorism.** James Campbell. (Illus.). 600p. (Orig.). 1967. pap. text ed. 29.95 (*0-9628700-3-X*) Inter Pact Pr.

Weapons of Our Warfare: Help for Troubled Minds. (Illus.). 144p. 1987. pap. 3.95 (*0-936369-06-X*) Son-Rise Pubns.

Weapons of Righteousness. Alden Reed. 80p. (Orig.). 1993. pap. 5.99 (*1-56043-751-0*) Destiny Image.

Weapons of the American Civil War. Ian V. Hogg. 1995. 15.98 (*0-7858-0430-7*) Bk Sales Inc.

Weapons of the Elite Forces. David Miller & Gerard Ridefort. (New Illustrated Guide Ser.). (Illus.). 160p. 1992. 5.98 (*0-8317-5057-X*) Smithmark.

***Weapons of the Spirit: Living a Holy Life in Unholy Times.** Ed. by David Scott & Mike Aquilina. 275p. 1997. 24.95 (*0-615-11007-X*) Our Sunday Visitor.

Weapons of the Weak. James C. Scott. LC 85-51779. 414p. 1987. pap. 19.00 (*0-300-03641-8*, Y-665) Yale U Pr.

Weapons of Tomorrow. Brian Beckett. 160p. 1983. 17.95 (*0-306-41383-3*, Plenum Pr) Plenum.

Weapons of War. Bob Italia. LC 91-73074. (War in the Gulf Ser.). (J). (gr. 4 up). 1991. lib. bdg. 13.99 (*1-56239-027-9*) Abdo & Dghtrs.

Weapons of Women Writers Vol. 16: Bertha Von Suttner's Die Waffen Nieder! As Political Literature in the Tradition of Harriet Beecher Stowe's Uncle Tom's Cabin. Regina Braker. LC 94-3633. (Austrian Culture Ser.: 16). 155p. (C). 1995. text ed. 46.95 (*0-8204-2626-1*) P Lang Pubng.

Weapons of World War II, No. 1. Ed. by Ray Merriam. (World War II Historical Society Monograph Ser.). 50p. 1995. pap. 5.00 (*1-57638-001-7*) Merriam Pr.

Weapons Proliferation & World Order: After the Cold War. Brad Roberts. 416p. 1996. 115.00 (*90-411-0205-1*) Kluwer Law Tax Pubs.

Weapons Proliferation in the 1990s. Ed. by Brad Roberts. (Washington Quarterly Reader Ser.). (Illus.). 473p. 1995. pap. 18.00 (*0-262-68086-6*) MIT Pr.

Weapons Systems, U. S. Army, 1995. (Illus.). 236p. (Orig.). 1996. pap. 55.00 (*0-7881-2672-5*) DIANE Pub.

***Weapons under Fire.** Lauren Holland. LC 97-21805. (Social-Psychology Reference Ser.). 335p. 1997. 50.00 (*0-8153-2067-1*); pap. 20.95 (*0-8153-2068-X*) Garland.

Weapons Without a Cause. Farrell. 1996. text ed. 59.95 (*0-312-16103-4*) St Martin.

Weapons Women Use: A Guide to the Man Going Through Divorce. James A. Cular. 36p. (Orig.). 1995. 6.95 (*0-9647707-0-9*) QQs Inc.

Weaponsmakers: Personal & Professional Crisis During the Vietnam War. Jeffrey Schevitz. LC 78-21046. 224p. 1979. pap. text ed. 16.95 (*0-87073-933-6*) Transaction Pubs.

Wear a Green Kirtle. large type ed. Philippa Wiat. 352p. 1994. 25.99 (*0-7089-3088-3*) Ulverscroft.

Wear & Erosion - Metal Corrosion see 1997 Annual Book of ASTM Standards: Metals Test Methods & Analytical Procedures, Section 3

Wear & Fracture Prevention: Proceedings of a Conference Held May 21-22, 1980, Peoria, Illinois. American Society for Metals Staff. LC 81-67226. (Materials-Metalworking Technology Ser.). 319p. reprint ed. pap. 91.00 (*0-317-26752-3*, 2024351) Bks Demand.

Wear & Friction of Elastomers. Ed. by Robert Denton & M. K. Keshavan. LC 92-17236. (Special Technical Publication Ser.: No. 1145). (Illus.). 135p. 1992. text ed. 40.00 (*0-8031-1467-2*, 04-011450-27) ASTM.

***Wear & Scare, Vol. 26.** M. T. Coffin. (Spinetinglers Ser.). 1997. pap. text ed. 3.99 (*0-380-78928-0*) Avon.

Wear & Tear: or Hints for the Overworked. 5th ed. Silas W. Mitchell. LC 73-2407. (Mental Illness & Social Policy; the American Experience Ser.). 1973. reprint ed. 16.95 (*0-405-05217-0*) Ayer.

***Wear Behavior of Plastics on Plastics.** M. P. Wolverton & J. E. Theberge. (Technical Papers). 1982. pap. text ed. 30.00 (*1-55589-116-0*) AGMA.

Wear Control Handbook. Ed. by M. Peterson & W. Winer. 1500p. 95.00 (*0-317-33640-1*, G00169) ASME.

Wear Corrosion Interactions in Liquid Media. Ed. by A. A. Sagues & E. I. Meletis. (Illus.). 200p. 1991. 10.00 (*0-87339-174-8*, 1748) Minerals Metals.

***Wear-Corrosion Interactions in Liquid Media: Proceedings of a Symposium Sponsored by the Corrosion & Environmental Effects Committee, Held at the Fall Meeting of the Minerals, Metals, & Materials Society in Indianapolis, IN, October 1-5, 1989.** Ed. by Alberto A. Sagues & Efstathios I. Meletis. LC 91-61220. (Illus.). 211p. pap. 60.20 (*0-608-04899-2*, 2065591) Bks Demand.

Wear in Plastics Processing: How to Understand, Protect & Avoid. Gunter Mennig. 436p. (C). 1995. text ed. write for info. (*1-56990-137-6*) Hanser-Gardner.

***Wear Me.** 1996. 55.00 (*0-688-14524-8*) Morrow.

Wear Me - Fashion Graphics Interaction: A View from London. Booth Clibborn Editions Staff. 1996. 49.95 (*0-8230-6527-8*) Watsn-Guptill.

Wear of Agricultural Machine Parts. Ed. by M. Severnev. Tr. by S. Kaila from RUS. 271p. (C). 1985. text ed. 130.00 (*90-6191-454-X*, Pub. by A A Balkema NE) Ashgate Pub Co.

Wear of Materials: Proceedings, 9th International Conference, San Francisco, USA, April 1993. Ed. by Kenneth C. Ludema et al. xxiv, 1170p. 1993. 390.75 (*0-444-81471-X*) Elsevier.

Wear of Materials, 1977: Presented at the I. International Conference on Wear of Materials Staff. Ed. by W. A. Glaeser et al. LC 77-72209. (Illus.). 593p. reprint ed. pap. 169.10 (*0-8357-2867-6*, 2039103) Bks Demand.

Wear of Materials, 1979: Presented at the International Conference on Wear of Materials, Dearborn, Michigan, April 16-18, 1979. International Conference on Wear of Materials Staff. Ed. by K. C. Ludema et al. LC 77-72209. (Illus.). 703p. reprint ed. pap. 180.00 (*0-8357-2903-6*, 2039139) Bks Demand.

Wear of Materials, 1981: Presented at the International Conference on Wear of Materials, San Francisco, CA, March 30-April 1, 1981. International Conference on Wear of Materials Staff. Ed. by S. K. Rhee et al. LC 77-72209. (Illus.). 820p. reprint ed. pap. 180.00 (*0-8357-2878-1*, 2039115) Bks Demand.

Wear of Rock Cutting Tools: Laboratory Experiments on the Abrasivity of Rock. H. J. Deketh. (Illus.). 202p. (C). 1995. 70.00 (*90-5410-620-4*, Pub. by A A Balkema NE) Ashgate Pub Co.

***Wear of Total Hip Protheses.** Oonishi. (Illus.). 288p. 1997. text ed. write for info. (*0-412-64330-8*, Chap & Hall NY) Chapman & Hall.

***Wear on Gear Teeth.** E. Buckingham. (Technical Papers). 1926. pap. text ed. 30.00 (*1-55589-239-6*) AGMA.

Wear Particles - From the Cradle to the Grave: Proceedings of the 18th Leeds-Lyon Symposium on Tribology Held at the Institut National des Sciences Appliquees, Lyon, France, 3rd-6th September 1991. Ed. by Duncan Dowson. LC 92-17688. (Tribology Ser.: Vol. 21). 550p. 1992. 282.25 (*0-444-89336-9*) Elsevier.

Wear-Resistant Ceramic Parts. 261p. 1992. 2,750.00 (*0-89336-902-0*, GB-152) BCC.

***Wear Studies of Fine Pitch Gear Materials.** R. J. Benson. (Technical Papers). 1957. pap. text ed. 30.00 (*1-55589-348-1*) AGMA.

Wear Testing of Advanced Materials. Ed. by Ramesh Divakar & Peter J. Blau. LC 92-2357. (Special Technical Publication Ser.: No. 1167). (Illus.). 180p. 1992. text ed. 45.00 (*0-8031-1476-1*, 04-011670-27) ASTM.

Wear Tests for Plastics: Selection & Use- STP 701. Ed. by Raymond G. Bayer. 106p. 1981. pap. 18.00 (*0-8031-0599-1*, 04-701000-19) ASTM.

***Wearable & Decorative Stencilling: Patterns, Projects & Possibilities.** Joanne Malone. LC 96-38700. 1997. 27.95 (*0-8069-9446-0*) Sterling.

Wearable Art. Kathy Lamancusa. (Creative Home Design Ser.). 128p. 1992. 19.95 (*0-8306-4027-4*, 3900); pap. 10.95 (*0-8306-4026-6*, 3900) McGraw-Hill Prof.

Wearable Art for Kids. (Illus.). 64p. 1994. spiral bd. 5.98 (*0-7853-0285-9*, 3616800) Pubns Intl Ltd.

Wearable Art for Kids. (Art-Crafts-Cooking-Drawing Books for Children Ser.). (Illus.). 64p. (J). (gr. 2-6). 1995. lib. bdg. 16.95 (*1-56674-101-7*, HTS Bks) Forest Hse.

Wearable Parables: Proverbs for Program People. rev. ed. Hal Ackerman. 1994. pap. 2.00 (*0-89230-247-X*) Do It Now.

Wearable Quilts: Sewing Timeless Fashions Using Traditional Patterns. Roselyn Gadia-Smitley. LC 92-41341. (Illus.). 224p. 1993. pap. 14.95 (*0-8069-8800-2*) Sterling.

Wearing of Costume: The Changing Techniques of Wearing Clothes & How to Move in Them, from Roman Britain to the Second World War. Ruth M. Green. LC 95-25662. (Illus.). 171p. (Orig.). 1996. pap. 17.95 (*0-89676-141-X*, Costume & Fashion Pr) QSMG Ltd.

Wearing of the Gray. John E. Cook. 601p. 1987. reprint ed. 30.00 (*0-942211-69-3*) Olde Soldier Bks.

***Wearing of the Gray: Being Personal Portraits, Scenes & Adventures of the War.** John E. Cooke. (Illus.). 624p. 1997. pap. 19.95 (*0-8071-2216-5*) La State U Pr.

***Wearing Purple.** Lydia Alexander et al. 1998. 19.95 (*0-517-70834-5*, Harmony) Crown Pub Group.

Wearing the Edged Weapons of the Third Reich: A Pictorial Study, Vol. 2. Thomas M. Johnson. Ed. by Johnson Reference Books Staff. Tr. by Mark Ready & Bonnie Jones. LC 77-82820. (Illus.). 71p. (Orig.). 1992. pap. 25.00 (*0-944432-02-6*) Johnson Ref Bks.

Wearing the Morning Star: Native American Songs & Poems. Ed. & Intro. by Brian Swann. 208p. 1996. 23.00 (*0-679-44827-6*) Random.

Weary & the Wary: U. S. & Japanese Security Policies in Transition. Robert E. Osgood. LC 71-186510. (Washington Center of Foreign Policy Research. Studies in International Affairs: No. 16). 106p. reprint ed. pap. 30.30 (*0-317-19919-6*, 2023132) Bks Demand.

***Weary Feet Rested Souls.** Townsend Davis. LC 97-6749. 1997. 27.50 (*0-393-04592-7*) Norton.

Weary Sons of Freud. Catherine Clement. Tr. by Nicole Ball. 115p. 1987. 44.95 (*0-86091-177-2*, A0635, Pub. by Verso UK) Routledge Chapman & Hall.

Weary Sons of Freud. Catherine Clement. Tr. by Nicole Ball. 115p. (C). 1987. pap. text ed. 17.00 (*0-86091-888-2*, A0639, Pub. by Vrso UK) Norton.

Weary Titan: Britain & the Experience of Relative Decline, 1895-1905. Aaron L. Friedberg. (Illus.). 376p. (C). 1988. pap. text ed. 17.95 (0-691-00844-2) Princeton U Pr.

***Weary Warriors: Lessons from Christian Workers Who Burned Out.** Carrie S. Coffman. (Illus.). 248p. (Orig.). 1997. pap. 12.95 (0-9633283-2-8) Apples of Gold.

Weasel. Cynthia DeFelice. 128p. (J). (gr. 5). 1991. pap. 4.50 (0-380-71358-6, Camelot) Avon.

Weasel. Cynthia DeFelice. LC 89-37794. 128p. (YA). (gr. 5 up). 1990. 15.00 (0-02-726457-2, Mac Bks Young Read) S&S Childrens.

Weasel. Fred Marsocci. Ed. by J. Friedland & R. Kessler. (Novel-Ties Ser.). 1993. student ed., pap. text ed. 15.95 (0-88122-901-6) Lrn Links.

Weasel. large type ed. Cynthia DeFelice. 1991. pap. 34.00 (0-614-09879-3, L-04422-00) Am Printing Hse.

Weasel in the Turkey Pen. Marie Harris. LC 92-18015. 1993. 18.00 (0-914610-80-5); pap. 10.00 (0-914610-76-7) Hanging Loose.

Weasels. Lynn M. Stone. LC 94-46894. (Wild Animals of the Woods Ser.). (J). (gr. 2-6). 1995. write for info. (1-57103-097-2) Rourke Pr.

Weasels & Wisemen. Kane. Date not set. text ed. write for info. (0-312-16086-0) St Martin.

Weather. 64p. (YA). (gr. 6-12). 1963. pap. 2.40 (0-8395-3274-1, 33274) BSA.

Weather. LC 95-147. (DK Pockets Ser.). (Illus.). 160p. (YA). (gr. 7 up). 1995. pap. 5.95 (0-7894-0218-1, 5-70631) DK Pub Inc.

Weather. (Discover Ser.). (Illus.). 48p. (J). 1993. 9.98 (1-56173-425-X) Pubns Intl Ltd.

***Weather.** LC 97-3324. (Reader's Digest Explores Ser.). 1997. write for info. (0-89577-975-7) RD Assn.

Weather. (My First Learning Ser.). (Illus.). 24p. (J). (gr. k-2). 1995. text ed. write for info. (1-56144-740-4) Modern Pub NYC.

Weather. Date not set. pap. 4.99 (0-7214-5604-9, Ladybrd) Penguin.

***Weather.** (Discovery Box Ser.). 32p. (J). (gr. 1-5). 1997. 11.95 (0-590-92674-8) Scholastic Inc.

Weather. Book Division Staff & Tom Kierein. LC 94-25394. (National Geographic Action Bk.). (J). 1995. 16.00 (0-7922-2782-4) Natl Geog.

Weather. Martyn Bramwell. (Earth Science Library). (Illus.). 32p. (J). (gr. 5-8). 1994. lib. bdg. 18.60 (0-531-14306-6) Watts.

Weather. William J. Burroughs & Sally Morgan. Ed. by Richard Whitaker. LC 95-20621. (Nature Company Guides Ser.). (Illus.). 288p. (J). (gr. 4-7). 1996. 29.95 (0-8094-9374-8) Time-Life.

Weather. Ed Catherall. LC 90-10025. (Exploring Science Ser.). (Illus.). 48p. (J). (gr. 4-8). 1990. lib. bdg. 24.26 (0-8114-2596-7) Raintree Steck-V.

Weather. Brian Cosgrove. LC 90-4887. (Eyewitness Bks.: No. 28). (Illus.). 64p. (J). (gr. 5 up). 1991. 19.00 (0-679-80784-5) Knopf Bks Yng Read.

Weather. Brian Cosgrove. LC 90-4887. (Eyewitness Bks.: No. 28). (Illus.). 64p. (J). (gr. 5 up). 1991. lib. bdg. 20.99 (0-679-90784-X) Knopf Bks Yng Read.

Weather. Kay Davis & Wendy Oldsfield. LC 91-30066. (Starting Science Ser.). (Illus.). 32p. (J). (gr. 2-5). 1991. pap. 4.95 (0-8114-1535-X) Raintree Steck-V.

Weather. Pascale De Bourgoing. (Illus.). 24p. (J). 1991. 11.95 (0-590-45234-7, Cartwheel) Scholastic Inc.

Weather. Robert DeWeese & Jo E. Moore. (Illus.). 48p. (J). (gr. 3-6). 1994. pap. text ed. 5.95 (1-55799-279-7, EMC 284) Evan-Moor Corp.

***Weather.** Ann Flagg. (J). 1997. pap. 9.95 (0-590-13111-7) Scholastic Inc.

Weather. Anita Ganeri. LC 92-26987. (Nature Detective Ser.). 32p. (J). 1993. 18.60 (0-531-14250-7) Watts.

Weather. Melissa Getzoff. LC 94-26982. (First-Start Science Ser.). (Illus.). 32p. (J). (ps-2). 1996. pap. 2.95 (0-8167-3608-1) Troll Communs.

Weather. J. F. Griffiths. 162p. 1990. text ed. 362.00 (2-88124-765-2) Gordon & Breach.

Weather. Photos by Melanie Hall. LC 92-14913. (Charlotte Zolotow Bk.). (Illus.). 64p. (J). (gr. k-3). 1994. 14.95 (0-06-021463-5); lib. bdg. 14.89 (0-06-021462-7) HarpC Child Bks.

***Weather.** Andrew Haslam & Barbara Taylor. LC 96-53572. (Make-It-Work! Ser.). (J). 1997. pap. write for info. (0-7166-5113-0) World Bk.

Weather. Paul Humphrey. LC 96-18103. (Step-by-Step Geography Ser.). (J). 1997. lib. bdg. 17.00 (0-516-20238-3) Childrens.

Weather. Robin Kerrod. LC 93-49706. (Let's Investigate Science Ser.). (Illus.). (J). 1994. lib. bdg. 17.95 (1-85435-630-5) Marshall Cavendish.

Weather. Robin Kerrod. (Learn about Ser.). (Illus.). 64p. (J). (gr. 3-7). 1997. 7.95 (1-85967-189-6, Lorenz Bks) Anness Pub.

Weather. David Lambert. LC 89-20304. (Our Planet Ser.). (Illus.). 32p. (J). (gr. 4-6). 1990. pap. 4.95 (0-8167-1980-2); lib. bdg. 12.95 (0-8167-1979-9) Troll Communs.

***Weather.** Marsden. (Oliver & Boyd Georaphy Ser.). (J). 1992. pap. text ed. write for info. (0-05-005025-7) Addison-Wesley.

Weather. Fred Martin. LC 95-38353. (J). 1996. lib. bdg. write for info. (1-57572-022-1) Rigby Interact Libr.

Weather. National Science Resources Center Staff. (Science & Technology for Children Ser.). (Illus.). 188p. (Orig.). (J). (gr. 1). 1995. teacher ed., pap. text ed. write for info. (0-89278-713-9) Carolina Biological.

Weather. National Science Resources Center Staff. (Science & Technology for Children Ser.). (Illus.). 16p. (Orig.). (J). (gr. 1). 1995. wbk. ed., pap. text ed. write for info. (0-89278-714-7) Carolina Biological.

Weather. Henry Pluckrose. LC 93-45660. (Walkabout Ser.). 32p. (J). 1994. lib. bdg. 17.60 (0-516-08123-3) Childrens.

Weather. Henry Pluckrose. (Walkabout Ser.). (J). (ps-2). 1994. pap. 4.95 (0-516-40123-8) Childrens.

Weather. Tony Potter. (Illus.). 48p. (J). (gr. 7-9). 1992. 13.95 (0-563-21428-7, BBC-Parkwest); pap. 7.95 (0-563-21427-9, BBC-Parkwest) Parkwest Pubns.

Weather. Tony Ross. LC 94-36612. (Little Princess Board Bks.). (Illus.). 14p. (J). (ps). 1995. pap. 6.00 (0-15-200320-7, Red Wagon Bks) HarBrace.

Weather. Seymour Simon. LC 92-31069. (Illus.). 40p. (J). (gr. k up). 1993. 15.00 (0-688-10546-7, Morrow Junior); lib. bdg. 14.93 (0-688-10547-5, Morrow Junior) Morrow.

Weather. Harris Winitz. (All about Language Ser.). (Illus.). 50p. (YA). (gr. 7 up). 1986. pap. text ed. 19.00 incl. audio (0-939990-47-4) Intl Linguistics.

Weather. rev. ed. Herbert S. Zim et al. (Golden Guide Ser.). (Illus.). 160p. 1987. reprint ed. pap. 5.50 (0-307-24051-7, Golden Pr) Western Pub.

Weather. 2nd ed. Louis J. Battan. (Illus.). 160p. (C). 1985. text ed. write for info. (0-13-947698-9) P-H.

***Weather.** 2nd rev. ed. Christine Dillon. (My First Report Ser.). (Illus.). 32p. (J). (gr. 1-3). 1997. 5.95 (1-57896-004-5, 1765) Hewitt Res Fnd.

***Weather, Set 4.** (Questivities Ser.). 1995. 9.95 (1-880505-65-7, CLC0177) Pieces of Lrning.

Weather: A Thematic Unit. Diane Williams. (Thematic Units Ser.). (Illus.). 80p. (J). (gr. 1-3). 1991. student ed. 9.95 (1-55734-273-3) Tchr Create Mat.

Weather: A User's Guide to the Atmosphere. Ti Sanders. (Illus.). 280p. 1985. pap. 14.95 (0-89651-907-4) Hardwood Pr.

Weather: An Integrated Unit. Kathy Rogers. (Primary Thematic Units Ser.). (Illus.). 96p. (Orig.). 1993. pap. 12.95 (0-944459-77-3) ECS Lrn Systs.

Weather: Complete Unit. National Science Resources Center Staff. (Science & Technology for Children Ser.). (Illus.). (Orig.). (J). (gr. 1). 1995. write for info. (0-89278-721-X) Carolina Biological.

Weather: Drama of the Heavens. Rene Chabout. Tr. by I. Mark Paris. (Discoveries Ser.). (Illus.). 160p. 1996. pap. text ed. 12.95 (0-8109-2878-7) Abrams.

Weather: Hands on Elementary School Science. Linda Poore. 48p. 1994. teacher ed. 35.00 (1-883410-11-8) L Poore.

Weather: How to Watch & Understand the Weather & Its Changes. John Farndon. LC 91-58210. (Eyewitness Explorers Ser.). (Illus.). 64p. 1992. lib. bdg. 10.99 (1-56458-020-2) DK Pub Inc.

Weather: How to Watch & Understand the Weather & Its Changes. John Farndon. LC 91-58210. (Eyewitness Explorers Ser.). (Illus.). 64p. (J). (gr. 3 up). 1992. 9.95 (1-56458-019-9) DK Pub Inc.

Weather: Spanish Theme Pack & ESL Theme Link Set, Set. (Que Maravilla! Ser.). (Illus.). (Orig.). 1993. pap. 215.00 (1-56334-376-2) Hampton-Brown.

Weather: Teacher's Theme Guide. (Wonders! Ser.). (Illus.). (Orig.). 1992. pap. 29.95 (1-56334-162-X) Hampton-Brown.

Weather: The Nature Company Journals. Time-Life Books Editors. 1996. 14.95 (0-8094-9380-2) Time-Life.

Weather: Understanding the Forces of Nature. Louise Quayle. (Illus.). 128p. 1990. 14.99 (0-517-67663-X) Random Hse Value.

Weather Almanac. 5th ed. Ed. by James A. Ruffner & Frank E. Bair. 811p. 1986. 120.00 (0-8103-1497-5) Gale.

Weather Almanac. 6th ed. Ed. by James A. Ruffner & Frank E. Bair. 800p. 1991. 125.00 (0-8103-2843-7) Gale.

Weather Almanac. 7th ed. 1995. 130.00 (0-8103-6980-X) Gale.

Weather Almanac. 8th ed. Ed. by Richard A. Wood. 750p. 1997. 130.00 (0-8103-5522-1) Gale.

Weather America: The Latest Detailed Climatological Data for over 4,000 Places - with Rankings. Ed. by Alfred N. Garwood. LC 96-9003. (Illus.). 1412p. 1996. 99.95 (1-884925-60-X) Toucan Valley.

***Weather Analysis.** Date not set. write for info. (0-614-30275-7) Weather Wkbk.

Weather Analysis. Dusan Djuric. 304p. 1994. text ed. 74.00 (0-13-501149-3) P-H.

Weather & Agriculture. J. Taylor. LC 67-13993. 1967. 104.00 (0-08-012213-2, Pub. by Pergamon Repr UK) Franklin.

Weather & Bird Behavior. 2nd ed. Norman Elkins. (Illus.). 240p. 1990. text ed. 37.00 (0-85661-051-8, 784651, Pub. by Poyser UK) Acad Pr.

Weather & Climate. Paul E. Lydolph. LC 84-18080. (Illus.). 230p. (C). 1985. 45.00 (0-86598-120-5, R3924) Rowman.

Weather & Climate. John Mason. (Our World Ser.). (Illus.). 48p. (J). (gr. 5-8). 1991. lib. bdg. 12.95 (0-382-24225-4) Silver Burdett Pr.

Weather & Climate. Reginald C. Sutcliffe. (Advancement of Science Ser.). (Illus.). (C). 1967. text ed. 5.95 (0-393-06329-1) Norton.

Weather & Climate. Time-Life Books Editors. (Understanding Science & Nature Ser.). 176p. (J). 1992. 17.95 (0-8094-9683-6) Time-Life.

Weather & Climate. F. Watt. (Science & Experiments Ser.). (Illus.). 48p. (J). (gr. 4-11). 1992. pap. 7.95 (0-7460-0683-7, Usborne); lib. bdg. 15.95 (0-88110-511-2, Usborne) EDC.

Weather & Climate: Geography Facts & Experiments. Barbara Taylor. LC 92-28420. (Young Discoverers Ser.). 32p. (J). (gr. 1-4). 1993. pap. 6.95 (1-85697-940-7, Kingfisher LKC) LKC.

Weather & Climate: Geography Facts & Experiments. Barbara Taylor. Ed. by Kingfisher Books Staff. LC 92-28420. (Young Discoverers Ser.). 32p. (J). (gr. 1-4). 1993. lib. bdg. 13.90 (1-85697-626-2, Kingfisher LKC) LKC.

Weather & Climate: Text-Exercises-Weather Maps. John J. Hidore. LC 84-61956. 238p. 1984. pap. 15.95 (0-941226-05-0) Park Pr Co.

***Weather & Climate in Africa.** Buckle. 1996. pap. text ed. write for info. (0-582-09333-3, Pub. by Longman UK) Longman.

***Weather & Climate Modification.** 1980. 60.00 (0-8103-1017-1, 00008422, Gale Res Intl) Gale.

Weather & Climate of Australia & New Zealand. Andrew Sturman & Nigel Tapper. (Illus.). 480p. 1996. 125.00 (0-19-553923-0); pap. 75.00 (0-19-553393-3) OUP.

Weather & Climate of the Antarctic. W. Schwerdtfeger. (Developments in Atmospheric Science Ser.: Vol. 15). 1984. 117.50 (0-444-42293-5, I-092-84) Elsevier.

Weather & Climate of the Great Lakes Region. Val Eichenlaub. LC 78-51526. (Illus.). 1979. text ed. 25.50 (0-268-01929-0); pap. text ed. 14.00 (0-268-01930-4) U of Notre Dame Pr.

Weather & Climate Responses to Solar Variations. Ed. by Billy M. McCormac. LC 82-73247. 636p. reprint ed. pap. 180.00 (0-685-16387-3, 2027297) Bks Demand.

Weather & Climate San Salvador Island, Bahamas. Ronald V. Shaklee. (Illus.). 67p. (Orig.). (C). 1996. pap. text ed. 8.00 (0-935909-57-5) Bahamian.

Weather & Cosmos. Dennis Klocek. 1991. pap. 11.95 (0-945803-05-2) R Steiner Col Pubns.

Weather & Forecasting. Storm Dunlop. (Field Guide Ser.). 160p. 1987. pap. 10.95 (0-02-013700-1) Macmillan.

Weather & Its Causes. Frank Schaffer Publications, Inc. Staff. (Science Notes Ser.). (Illus.). 8p. 1996. 2.49 (0-86734-889-5, FS-62026) Schaffer Pubns.

Weather & People. Morgan & Moran. 150p. (C). 1996. pap. text ed. 36.40 (0-02-383811-6, Macmillan Coll) P-H.

Weather & Seasons. Sterling Staff. (BipQuiz Ser.). (J). (gr. 4-7). 1995. pap. 2.95 (0-8069-0937-4) Sterling.

Weather & the Bible: 100 Questions & Answers. Donald B. DeYoung. LC 92-6248. 162p. (YA). (gr. 10). 1992. pap. 8.99 (0-8010-3013-7) Baker Bks.

Weather & the Epidemiology of the African Armyworm (Spodoptera Exempta) M. R. Tucker. 70p. 1993. pap. 49.00 (0-85954-346-3, Pub. by Nat Res Inst UK) St Mut.

Weather & Us. Ann Merk & Jim Merk. LC 94-13322. (Weather Report Ser.). (Illus.). (J). (gr. 3 up). 1994. write for info. (0-86593-387-1) Rourke Corp.

Weather & War. T. A. FitzPatrick. 146p. (C). 1989. text ed. 65.00 (1-872795-39-0, Pub. by Pentland Pr UK) St Mut.

Weather & Water. B. W. Atkinson et al. LC 85-6594. (Reviews of U. K. Statistical Sources Ser.: Vol. 7). (Illus.). 240p. 1985. 114.25 (0-08-031844-4, Pergamon Pr) Elsevier.

Weather & Weather Maps. Ed. by Gosta H. Liljequist. (Contributions to Current Research in Geophysics Ser.: 10). 265p. (C). 1982. text ed. 71.95 (0-8176-1192-4) Birkhauser.

Weather & Yield. J. Petr. (Developments in Crop Science Ser.: Vol. 20). 288p. 1991. 203.25 (0-444-98803-3) Elsevier.

Weather at Sea. 2nd ed. David D. Houghton. 80p. (Orig.). (C). 1990. text ed. 65.00 (0-906754-64-X, Pub. by Fernhurst Bks UK) St Mut.

Weather Atlas. 2nd ed. 1905. 98.00 (0-8103-5505-1) Gale.

Weather Atlas of the United States. U. S. Environmental Data Service Staff. LC 74-11931. 272p. 1975. 98.00 (0-8103-1048-1) Gale.

Weather Book. Janet Kauffman. 71p. (Orig.). 1981. 9.95 (0-89672-090-X); pap. 4.95 (0-89672-089-6) Tex Tech Univ Pr.

***Weather Book.** Charles Meyer. Date not set. write for info. (0-688-03774-7) Morrow.

***Weather Book.** Michael Oard. 72p. 1996. 15.95 (0-89051-211-6, WEABOO) Master Bks.

Weather Central. Ted Kooser. (Poetry Ser.). 100p. (Orig.). (C). 1994. 19.95 (0-8229-3796-4); pap. 10.95 (0-8229-5527-X) U of Pittsburgh Pr.

Weather, Climate & Human Affairs. Hubert H. Lamb. 416p. 1988. text ed. 99.00 (0-415-00674-0) Routledge.

Weather Companion: An Album of Meteorological History, Science, Legend, & Folklore. Gary Lockhart. LC 88-6884. (Illus.). 230p. 1988. pap. text ed. 16.95 (0-471-62079-3) Wiley.

Weather Company. Bernie Fass & Rosemary Caggiano. 48p. (J). (gr. k-8). 1978. pap. 14.95 (0-86704-004-1) Clarus Music.

Weather Concepts & Terminology. Joe R. Eagleman. (Illus.). 128p. (C). 1989. wbk. ed., pap. text ed. 13.95 (1-877696-00-5) Trimedia Pub.

Weather Conspiracy: The Coming of the New Ice Age. Impact Team Staff. 1977. pap. 1.95 (0-345-27209-9) Ballantine.

Weather Cycles: Real or Imaginary? William J. Burroughs. (Illus.). 250p. (C). 1992. text ed. 59.95 (0-521-38178-9) Cambridge U Pr.

Weather Cycles: Real or Imaginary? William J. Burroughs. (Illus.). 215p. (C). 1995. pap. text ed. 20.95 (0-521-47869-3) Cambridge U Pr.

Weather Dance see Homeplay: Joyful Learning for Children & Adults, Series I

Weather Dude: A Musical Guide to the Atmosphere. Nick Walker. (Illus.). 46p. (Orig.). (J). (gr. 1-5). 1994. 14.95 incl. audio (0-9643389-0-4) Small Gate Media.

Weather, Electricity, Environmental Investigations. Sandra Markle. (Enrichment & Gifted Ser.). 112p. (J). (gr. 4-6). 1982. 10.95 (0-88160-082-2, LW 902) Learning Wks.

Weather Everywhere. Denise Casey. LC 92-23239. (Illus.). 40p. (J). 1995. lib. bdg. 15.00 (0-02-717777-7, Mac Bks Young Read) S&S Childrens.

Weather Experiments. Vera Webster. LC 81-17062. (New True Bks.). (Illus.). 48p. (J). (gr. k-4). 1982. pap. 5.50 (0-516-41662-6); lib. bdg. 19.00 (0-516-01662-8) Childrens.

Weather Eye. Lesley Howarth. LC 94-48918. 224p. (YA). (gr. 8-10). 1995. 16.95 (1-56402-616-7) Candlewick Pr.

Weather Eye. Brendan McWilliams. (Illus.). 160p. (Orig.). 1994. pap. 11.95 (1-874675-38-4, Pub. by Lilliput Pr Ltd IE) Irish Bks Media.

***Weather Eye.** Lesley Howarth. LC 94-48918. 224p. (YA). (gr. 8-10). 1997. reprint ed. pap. 4.99 (0-7636-0243-4) Candlewick Pr.

Weather Eyes in the Sky: America's Meteorological Satellites. Joseph G. Vaeth. LC 65-12760. 134p. reprint ed. pap. 38.20 (0-317-09224-3, 2012372) Bks Demand.

Weather Factor. (Illus.). 275p. 1989. reprint ed. pap. 20.00 (0-933876-98-X) Am Meteorological.

Weather Facts. A. Ganeri. (Facts & Lists Ser.). (Illus.). 48p. (J). (gr. 3-7). 1987. pap. 5.95 (0-86020-975-X); lib. bdg. 13.95 (0-88110-241-5) EDC.

***Weather Flying.** 4th ed. Robert N. Buck. 1997. 29.95 (0-07-008761-X); text ed. 29.95 (0-07-008716-4) McGraw.

Weather for Aircrews. 1996. lib. bdg. 253.75 (0-8490-6024-9) Gordon Pr.

***Weather for Hillwalkers & Climbers.** Malcolm Thomas. (Illus.). 96p. pap. 17.95 (0-7509-1080-1, Pub. by Sutton Pubng UK) Bks Intl VA.

Weather for Poetry: Essays, Reviews & Notes on Poetry, 1977-1981. Donald Hall. LC 82-8544. (Poets on Poetry Ser.). 304p. 1982. pap. 13.95 (0-472-06340-5) U of Mich Pr.

Weather for the IFR Pilot. IFR & IFR Refresher Editors. (Instrument Pilots Library). 192p. 1993. 23.95 (1-879620-17-0) Belvoir Pubns.

Weather for the Mariner. 3rd ed. William J. Kotsch. LC 83-13084. 315p. 1983. 26.95 (0-87021-756-9) Naval Inst Pr.

Weather for the New Pilot. Tom Morrison. LC 91-19260. (Illus.). 186p. 1991. 16.95 (0-8138-1773-0) Iowa St U Pr.

***Weather Forcasting: Radar Availability Requirement Not Being Met.** (Illus.). 48p. (C). 1996. pap. 25.00 (0-7881-3436-1) DIANE Pub.

Weather Forecast For Utopia & Vicinity: Poems Nineteen Sixty-Seven to Nineteen Eighty-Two. Charles Simic. LC 83-527. 56p. (Orig.). 1983. pap. 4.95 (0-930794-83-4) Station Hill Pr.

Weather Forecast For Utopia & Vicinity: Poems Nineteen Sixty-Seven to Nineteen Eighty-Two. deluxe limited ed. Charles Simic. LC 83-527. 56p. (Orig.). 1983. 30.00 (0-88268-030-7) Station Hill Pr.

Weather Forecasting. Gail Gibbons. LC 86-7602. (Illus.). 32p. (J). (gr. k-3). 1987. 14.00 (0-02-737250-2, Four Winds Pr) S&S Childrens.

Weather Forecasting. Gail Gibbons. LC 92-22264. (Illus.). 32p. (J). (ps-3). 1993. reprint ed. pap. 5.99 (0-689-71683-4, Mac Bks Young Read) S&S Childrens.

Weather Forecasting: A Young Meteorologist's Guide. Dan Ramsey. (Illus.). 144p. (YA). 1990. 19.95 (0-8306-8338-0, 3338); pap. 10.95 (0-8306-3338-3) McGraw-Hill Prof.

Weather Forecasting: Rules, Techniques & Procedures. George Elliott. 154p. (C). 1988. pap. text ed. 15.95 (0-89641-171-0) American Pr.

Weather Forecasting: Unmet Needs & Unknown Costs Warrant Reassessment of Observing System Plans. (Illus.). 49p. (Orig.). (C). 1995. pap. text ed. 25.00 (0-7881-1800-5) DIANE Pub.

Weather Forecasting for Agriculture & Industry: A Symposium. Ed. by James A. Taylor. LC 72-6550. (Illus.). 250p. 1973. 30.00 (0-8386-1260-1) Fairleigh Dickinson.

Weather Forecasts. Wilson Ltd. Staff & Imray L. Norie. (C). 1989. 50.00 (0-685-40421-8, Pub. by Imray Laurie Norie & Wilson UK) St Mut.

Weather from Above: America's Meteorological Satellites. Janice Hill. 96p. 1991. pap. 11.95 (0-87474-467-9) Smithsonian.

Weather Graph Explorations: Intermediate. Debby Head & Libby Pollett. (Collecting & Analyzing Data Ser.: Collection I). 12p. 1994. teacher ed., pap. 9.95 (1-885775-03-2) BBY Pubns.

Weather Graph Explorations: Primary. Debby Head & Libby Pollett. (Collecting & Analyzing Data Ser.: Collection I). 11p. 1994. teacher ed., pap. 9.95 (1-885775-02-4) BBY Pubns.

Weather Handbook. Alan Watts. (Illus.). 187p. 1994. 19.95 (0-924486-76-7) Sheridan.

Weather Handbook. rev. ed. Ed. by H. McKinley Conway & Linda L. Liston. LC 90-82037. (Illus.). 548p. 1990. 39.95 (0-910436-29-0) Conway Data.

Weather, Health & Biomedicine: Subject Analysis Index with Research Bibliography. American Health Research Institute Staff. LC 85-47846. 150p. 1987. 37.50 (0-88164-354-8); pap. 34.50 (0-88164-355-6) ABBE Pubs Assn.

***Weather in Africa.** M. Gellhorn. 1989. pap. text ed. 14.95 (0-907871-01-1, Pub. by Eland UK) London Brdge.

Weather In Africa: Three Novellas. Martha Gellhorn. (Eland Travel Fiction Ser.). 296p. 1993. reprint ed. pap. 14.95 (0-87052-759-2) Hippocrene Bks.

Weather in the Garden. Jane Taylor. 384p. 1996. 34.95 (0-89831-050-4) Sagapr.

Weather in the Lab: Simulate Nature's Phenomena. Thomas R. Baker. 1993. pap. text ed. 11.95 (0-07-005088-0) McGraw.

Weather in the Lab: Simulate Nature's Phenomena. Thomas R. Baker. LC 92-34050. 1993. write for info. (0-8306-4309-5); pap. 11.95 (0-8306-4307-9) McGraw-Hill Prof.

Weather in U. S. Agriculture. 1991. lib. bdg. 250.00 (0-8490-4940-7) Gordon Pr.

Weather in U. S. Agriculture. 1991. lib. bdg. 250.00 (0-8490-4489-8) Gordon Pr.

W

Weather in United States Agriculture: Monthly Temperature & Precipitation by State & Farm Production Region, 1950-1988. 1990. lib. bdg. 250.00 (0-8490-4030-2) Gordon Pr.

Weather Is Front Page News. Ti Sanders. (Illus.). 224p. 1984. 21.95 (0-89651-902-3); pap. 14.95 (0-89651-903-1) Hardwood Pr.

Weather Kids: Natural Disasters. MaryKate Jordan. Ed. by Joy Johnson. (Illus.). 34p. (J). (gr. k-5). 1993. pap. 5.25 (1-56123-065-0) Centering Corp.

Weather Lore. Richard Inwards. 1976. lib. bdg. 59.95 (0-8490-2812-4) Gordon Pr.

Weather Lore. Richard Inwards. (Illus.). 1977. reprint ed. 8.95 (0-85409-577-2) Charles River Bks.

Weather Magic in Inner Asia. Adam Molnar. (Uralic & Altaic Ser.: Vol. 158). 174p. 1995. 22.00 (0-933070-33-0) Ind U Res Inst.

Weather-Magic in Inner Asia. Adam Molnar. (Indiana University Uralic & Altaic Ser.: Vol. 158). 174p. 1995. 22.00 (0-614-14918-5) Res Inst Inner Asian Studies.

Weather Map Folio. Constantine N. Zois. (Meteorology/ Oceanography Workbooks). 1989. lab manual ed. 40.00 (1-888950-03-X) Xenon Hse.

Weather Map Study. rev. ed. Fred W. Decker. (C). 1981. pap. 1.25 (0-931778-02-6) Weather Wkbk.

*Weather Maps: How to Read & Interpret All the Basic Weather Charts. 2nd unabridged ed. Peter R. Chaston. (Illus.). 230p. (Orig.). 1997. per., pap. 29.00 (0-9645172-4-8) Chaston Scient.

Weather Matrix & Human Behavior. Michael A. Persinger. LC 80-18422. 346p. 1980. text ed. 65.00 (0-275-90536-5, C0536, Praeger Pubs) Greenwood.

Weather of Old Seasons. Maria M. Gillan. Ed. by Stanley H. Barkan. Tr. by Nina Scammacca & Nat Scammacca. (Review Women Writers Chapbook Ser.: No. 8). 48p. (ENG & ITA.). 1989. 15.00 (0-89304-435-0, CCC167); pap. 5.00 (0-89304-436-9) Cross-Cultrl NY.

Weather of Old Seasons: Mini Book. Maria M. Gillan. Ed. by Stanley H. Barkan. Tr. by Nina Scammacca & Nat Scammacca. (Review Women Writers Chapbook Ser.: No. 8). 48p. (ENG & ITA.). 1989. 15.00 (0-89304-437-7); pap. 5.00 (0-89304-438-5) Cross-Cultrl NY.

Weather of Southern California. Harry P. Bailey. (California Natural History Guides Ser.: No. 17). (Illus.). (Orig.). 1966. pap. 7.00 (0-520-00062-5) U CA Pr.

Weather of the Eye. Thomas E. Kennedy. 1996. per. write for info. (1-884754-23-6) Potpourri Pubns.

Weather of the Heart. Madeleine L'Engle. LC 78-62202. (Wheaton Literary Ser.). 96p. 1978. pap. 9.99 (0-87788-931-7) Shaw Pubs.

Weather of the Heart: Glimpses of God in Sunlight & Storm. Gigi G. Tchividjian. 280p. (YA). (gr. 10). 1993. reprint ed. 16.99 (0-8010-8907-7, Ravens Ridge) Baker Bks.

Weather of the House. Suzanne Clark. (Chapbook Ser.: No. 4). 36p. 1994. pap. 6.00 (1-885912-01-3) Sows Ear Pr.

Weather of the San Francisco Bay Region. Harold Gilliam. (California Natural History Guides Ser.: No. 6). (Illus.). (Orig.). 1962. pap. 9.00 (0-520-00469-8) U CA Pr.

Weather of U. S. Cities. 3rd ed. Ed. by James A. Ruffner & Frank E. Bair. 1200p. 1987. 190.00 (0-8103-2102-5) Gale.

*Weather of United States Cities. 2nd ed. 1985. 165.00 (0-8103-1640-4, 00008376, Gale Res Intl) Gale.

Weather of United States Cities. 5th ed. 1996. 210.00 (0-8103-5525-6) Gale.

Weather Pack. (Illus.). (J). (gr. 3-6). 1992. pap. 7.95 (1-56680-502-3) Mad Hatter Pub.

Weather Patterns & Phenomena: A Pilot's Guide. Thomas P. Turner. LC 94-14289. (Illus.). 223p. 1994. pap. text ed. 16.95 (0-07-065602-9) McGraw-Hill Prof.

Weather Patterns of East Anglia. Alfred Glenn. 256p. 1990. 51.00 (0-86138-044-4, Pub. by T Dalton UK) St Mut.

Weather Pioneers: The Signal Corps Station at Pikes Peak. Phyllis Smith. LC 92-39291. (Illus.). 135p. 1993. pap. 12.95 (0-8040-0970-8); text ed. 24.95 (0-8040-0969-4) Swallow.

Weather Pop-Up Book. Francis Wilson. (Illus.). (J). (gr. 5 up). 1987. pap. 15.00 (0-671-63699-5, S&S Bks Young Read) S&S Childrens.

Weather Predicting: The Hermetic System of Astrological Weather Analysis. C. C. Zain. (Brotherhood of Light Home Study Ser.: Course 15). 1976. pap. 10.95 (0-87887-361-9) Church of Light.

Weather Prophet: A Caribbean Journey. Lucretia Stewart. 256p. 1996. 29.95 (0-7011-3735-5, Pub. by Chatto & Windus UK) Trafalgar.

Weather Proverbs. H. H. Dunwoody et al. 1977. lib. bdg. 69.95 (0-8490-2813-2) Gordon Pr.

Weather Proverbs. rev. ed. George D. Freier. LC 92-12307. (Illus.). 224p. (Orig.). 1992. pap. 12.95 (1-55561-045-5) Fisher Bks.

Weather Radar & Flood Forecasting. C. Kirby & V. K. Collinge. 296p. 1987. text ed. 285.00 (0-471-91296-4) Wiley.

Weather Radar Networking: COST 73 Project: Final Report. Ed. by D. H. Newsome. LC 92-26375. 272p. (C). 1992. lib. bdg. 117.50 (0-7923-1939-7) Kluwer Ac.

Weather Radar Networking: Seminar on COST Project 73. Ed. by C. G. Collier & M. Chapuis. (C). 1990. lib. bdg. 206.00 (0-7923-0672-4) Kluwer Ac.

Weather Radio: A Complete Guide to Receiving NOPP, Volmet, Weather Fax, Weather Satellites & Other Weather Information Sources. Anthony R. Curtis. 126p. 1992. 14.95 (0-936653-32-9) Tiare Pubns.

Weather Report. Mike Graf. (J). (gr. 3-6). 1989. pap. 14.99 (0-8224-7511-1) Fearon Teach Aids.

Weather Report. Jane Yolen. LC 92-81075. (Illus.). 64p. (J). 1993. 16.95 (1-56397-101-1, Wordsong) Boyds Mills Pr.

Weather Reports. Quincy Troupe. LC 91-72805. 176p. 1991. pap. 12.00 (0-86316-108-1) Writers & Readers.

Weather Reports: New & Selected Poems. Quincy Troupe. LC 91-72805. 160p. 1991. 22.00 (0-86316-003-4) Writers & Readers.

*Weather-Resistant Polyolefin-Covered Wire & Cable. 30.00 (0-614-18711-7, S-70-547-1992) Insulated Cable.

Weather Revolution: Innovations & Imminent Breakthroughs in Accurate Forecasting. Jack Fishman & R. Kalish. (Illus.). 292p. (C). 1994. text ed. 27.95 (0-306-44764-9, Plenum Pr) Plenum.

Weather Rocks & Landforms. C. Curtis. (Down to Earth Ser.). (C). 1983. 50.00 (0-09-149141-X, Pub. by S Thornes Pubs UK) St Mut.

Weather Satellite Handbook. 1994. pap. 20.00 (0-87259-448-3) Am Radio.

Weather Satellites: Systems, Data, & Environmental Applications. Ed. by Krishna P. Rao. (Illus.). 518p. 1990. 95.00 (0-933876-87-4) Am Meteorological.

Weather Satellites, Stereoscopy & Sounding: Proceedings of the Topical Meeting of the COSPAR Interdisciplinary Scientific Commission A (Meetings A3 & A4) of the COSPAR 24th Plenary Meeting held in Ottawa, Canada, 16 May-2 June, 1982, Vol. 2/6. Ed. by H. Yates & A. F. Hasler. (Illus.). 190p. 1983. pap. 50.00 (0-08-030428-1, Pergamon Pr) Elsevier.

Weather Signs. Ann Merk & Jim Merk. LC 94-13323. (Weather Report Ser.). (J). (gr. 3 up). 1994. write for info. (0-86593-388-X) Rourke Corp.

Weather Sky. Bruce McMillan. (Illus.). 40p. (J). (gr. 5 up). 1996. 16.95 (0-374-38261-1) FS&G.

Weather Sky. Bruce McMillan. 40p. (J). 1996. pap. 6.95 (0-374-48266-7, Sunburst Bks) FS&G.

*Weather Sourcebook: Your One-Stop Resource for Everything You Need to Know to Feed Your Weather Habit. 2nd rev. ed. Ronald L. Wagner & Bill Adler, Jr. LC 97-4475. (Illus.). 224p. 1997. pap. 19.95 (0-7627-0080-7) Globe Pequot.

Weather Spotters Guide. F. Wilson & F. Mansfield. (Spotter's Guides Ser.). (Illus.). 64p. (J). (gr. 4 up). 1995. pap. 4.95 (0-86020-270-4, Usborne) EDC.

Weather Station: Guide to Science Anytime 1995. annuals 95th ed. (J). 1995. pap. text ed. 9.00 (0-15-306058-1) HarBrace.

Weather Support for Army Tactical Operations. 1995. lib. bdg. 255.95 (0-8490-6555-0) Gordon Pr.

Weather Systems. Leslie F. Musk et al. (Cambridge Topics in Geography Ser.). (Illus.). 160p. 1988. pap. text ed. 22.95 (0-521-27874-0) Cambridge U Pr.

Weather That Kills: A Poetry Collection. Patricia S. Jones. LC 94-45775. 96p. (Orig.). 1995. pap. 11.95 (1-56689-029-2) Coffee Hse.

Weather the Cuckoo Likes: The Sourcebook of the Cut-Ups Project. Robin D. Laws. (Over the Edge Ser.). 96p. 1994. pap. 12.95 (1-887801-12-X, Atlas Games) Trident MN.

Weather the Storm. Jean Ferris. (YA). 1996. mass mkt. 3.99 (0-380-78200-6) Avon.

Weather Theme Pack: Level 2. (Wonders! Ser.). (Illus.). (Orig.). 1992. teacher ed., pap. 159.00 (1-56334-222-7) Hampton-Brown.

Weather Tomorrow: Why Can't They Get It Right? Bob Lynott. LC 86-83330. 190p. (Orig.). 1987. pap. 15.00 (0-9618077-0-9) Gadfly Pr.

Weather Tracker's CD-ROM Discovery Kit. Gregory C. Aaron. (Illus.). 64p. (J). 1995. pap. 29.95 incl. cd-rom (1-56138-641-3) Running Pr.

Weather Tracker's Kit. Gregory Aaron. (Discovery Kit Ser.). (Illus.). 64p. (Orig.). (J). (gr. 3 up). 1991. 17.95 (0-89471-998-X) Running Pr.

*Weather Watch. Adam Ford. (J). Date not set. pap. write for info. (0-688-00550-0) Lothrop.

Weather Watch. Dale McCreedy & Elizabeth McAndrew. (National Science Partnership for Girl Scouts & Science Museums Ser.). (Illus.). 63p. (Orig.). 1995. pap. 8.00 (0-9625622-7-0) Franklin PA.

Weather Watch. Doris Roetger. (J). (gr. k-3). 1991. pap. 8.99 (0-86653-969-7) Fearon Teach Aids.

Weather Watch! Julian Rowe & Molly Perham. LC 94-16944. (First Science Ser.). (Illus.). 32p. (J). (gr. 1-4). 1994. pap. 4.95 (0-516-48142-8) Childrens.

Weather Watch: Big Book. Ina Cumpiano. (Wonders! Ser.). (Illus.). 24p. (Orig.). (J). (gr. 1-3). 1992. pap. text ed. 29.95 (1-56334-065-8) Hampton-Brown.

Weather Watch: Forecasting the Weather. Jonathan D. Kahl. LC 95-9725. (How's the Weather? Ser.). 72p. (J). (gr. 5-8). 1996. lib. bdg. 19.95 (0-8225-2529-1, Lerner Publctns) Lerner Group.

Weather Watch: Small Book. Ina Cumpiano. (Wonders! Ser.). (Illus.). 24p. (Orig.). (J). (gr. 1-3). 1992. pap. text ed. 6.00 (1-56334-071-2) Hampton-Brown.

Weather Watch Science Anytime Guide. HB Staff. 1995. pap. 8.00 (0-15-306063-8) HB Schl Dept.

Weather Whys. Mike Artell. 96p. (Orig.). (J). (gr. k up). 1995. pap. 12.95 (0-673-36173-X, GoodYrBooks) Addson-Wesley Educ.

*Weather Wisdom. Wolfgang Mieder & Mildred Kingsbury. 478p. (C). 1996. text ed. 49.95 (0-8204-3326-8) P Lang Pubng.

*Weather Wise: Creative Activities about the Environment. Robynne Eagan & Tracey A. Schofield. Ed. by Judy Mitchell. (Illus.). 160p. (Orig.). 1997. teacher ed., pap. 14.95 (1-57310-072-2) Teachng & Lrning Co.

Weather-Wise Boater. Mal Sillars & Don Hill. (Illus.). 64p. (Orig.). 1987. pap. 5.95 (0-9616885-3-X) M Sillars.

Weather Wit. Norman Dvoskin. 80p. 1994. pap. 6.95 (0-9645637-0-3) Belrock Printing.

Weather Wizard's Cloud Book. Louis D. Rubin, Sr. & Jim Duncan. (Illus.). 87p. 1984. pap. 8.95 (0-912697-10-5) Algonquin Bks.

Weather Wizard's 5-Year Weather Diary. Ed. by Robert A. Rubin. (Illus.). 400p. 1991. 13.95 (0-945575-85-8, 71585) Algonquin Bks.

Weather Words & What They Mean. Gail Gibbons. LC 89-39515. (Illus.). 32p. (J). (ps-3). 1990. lib. bdg. 15.95 (0-8234-0805-1) Holiday.

Weather Words & What They Mean. Gail Gibbons. LC 89-39515. (Illus.). 32p. (J). (ps-3). 1992. pap. 6.95 (0-8234-0952-X) Holiday.

Weather Words of Polynesia. William Churchill. LC 08-11468. (AAA Memoirs: No. 7). 1907. 25.00 (0-527-00506-1) Periodicals Srv.

Weather Workbook. Melvin Kazeck & J. Bridwell. 1971. pap. 6.80 (0-87563-045-6) Stipes.

Weather Workbook. rev. ed. Fred W. Decker. (C). 1981. pap. 8.00 (0-931778-03-4) Weather Wkbk.

*Weather Workbook, 1997 Revision. Date not set. write for info. (0-614-30274-9) Weather Wkbk.

Weatherby: The Man, the Gun, the Legend. Grits Gresham & Tom Gresham. (Illus.). 304p. 1992. 24.95 (0-944438-02-4) Cane River AK.

Weatherby Genealogy, 1682-1936. George W. Weatherby, Jr. 110p. 1994. reprint ed. pap. 19.50 (0-8328-4395-4); reprint ed. lib. bdg. 29.50 (0-8328-4394-6) Higginson Bk Co.

Weathered Wood & Rust. Mel Steele. 100p. 1993. 150.00 (0-9638631-0-X) Chainsaw Pubng.

Weathering. Pearl Karrer. 40p. (Orig.). 1993. pap. 8.00 (0-9624178-0-7) Slapering Hol.

Weathering: Poems & Translations. Alastair Reid. LC 87-30048. 144p. 1988. pap. 14.95 (0-8203-0990-7) U of Ga Pr.

Weathering & Degradation of Plastics. Ed. by S. H. Pinner. 144p. 1966. text ed. 141.00 (0-677-11830-9) Gordon & Breach.

Weathering of Polymers. A. Davis & D. Sims. (Illus.). 300p. 1983. 93.75 (0-85334-226-1, I-266-83, Pub. by Elsevier Applied Sci UK) Elsevier.

*Weathering, Soils & Paleosols. I. P. Martini & W. Chesworth. (Developments in Earth Surface Processes Ser.: Vol. 2). 618p. 1992. 197.75 (0-444-89198-6) Elsevier.

Weathering Stock Market Storms: Learning about Risk Control Timing. James D. Nisbet. (Illus.). 208p. (C). 29.95 (0-9640139-0-8) Capital Bks.

Weathering the Midlife Storm. Bobb Biehl. LC 96-23081. 224p. 1996. 17.99 (1-56476-583-0, Victor Bks) Chariot Victor.

Weathering the Peace: The Ohio National Guard in the Interwar Years 1919-1940. Ed. by Robert L. Daugherty. (Illus.). 320p. (Orig.). (C). 1992. lib. bdg. 39.75 (1-882090-03-9) Wright State Univ Pr.

Weathering the Storm. Dan Clark. 1990. pap. 7.95 (0-945167-19-9) British Amer Pub.

Weathering the Storm. Wally Seccombe. 352p. (C). 1996. pap. text ed. 20.00 (1-85984-064-7, Pub. by Vrso UK) Norton.

Weathering the Storm: Tornadoes, Television, & Turmoil. Gary A. England. LC 95-44997. (Illus.). 264p. 1996. 24.95 (0-8061-2823-2) U of Okla Pr.

*Weathering the Storm: Tornadoes, Television, & Turmoil. Gary A. England. LC 95-44997. (Illus.). 264p. 1997. pap. 16.95 (0-8061-2942-5) U of Okla Pr.

Weathering the Storm: Working-Class Families from the Industrial Revolution to the Fertility Decline. Wally Seccombe. LC 93-36720. 288p. (C). 1993. text ed. 65.00 (0-86091-333-3, B0540, Pub. by Vrso UK) Norton.

Weathering the Wilderness: The Sierra Club Guide to Practical Meteorology. William E. Reifsnyder. LC 79-20859. (Outdoor Activities Guides Ser.). (Illus.). 288p. 1982. pap. 12.00 (0-87156-266-9) Sierra.

Weathering Well with Colorant & Additives: Regional Technical Conference, October 11-13, 1993, Stouffer Orlando Resort, Orlando, FL. Society of Plastics Engineers Staff. (Illus.). 326p. 1993. reprint ed. pap. 93.00 (0-7837-9702-8, 2060433) Bks Demand.

*Weathering Winter: A Gardener's Daybook. Carl H. Klaus. LC 97-5720. (Bur Oak Original Ser.). 202p. 1997. 19.95 (0-87745-594-5) U of Iowa Pr.

*Weatherlight Revealed: A Review of the Weatherlight Edition of Magic:The Gathering. Eric Tam. 1997. pap. text ed. 14.95 (1-55622-577-6) Wordware Pub.

Weatherly Waypoint Guide, Vol. 1. Robert Hale. (Illus.). 80p. (Orig.). 1993. pap. 14.95 (0-935727-09-4) Weatherly Pr.

Weatherly Waypoint Guide, Vol. II. Robert Hale. (Illus.). 80p. (Orig.). 1994. pap. 14.95 (0-935727-10-8) Weatherly Pr.

Weatherman. Steve Thayer. 1996. mass mkt. 6.50 (0-451-18438-6, Sig) NAL-Dutton.

Weatherman. Steve Thayer. 1995. pap. 22.95 (0-670-77309-3) Viking Penguin.

Weatherman. Doug Wallace. 186p. (Orig.). 1991. pap. write for info. (0-932281-08-7) Quill Pubns GA.

Weathermen Let Them Fly: Story of the Eighth Air Force 18th Weather Squadron. Ewing F. Brown. Ed. by James W. Hill. (Illus.). 110p. (Orig.). 1994. pap. 13.95 (0-9640988-0-6) Eighth Air Force.

Weatherproofing. (Home Repair & Improvement Ser.). (Illus.). 136p. 1977. 14.60 (0-8094-2370-7); lib. bdg. 20.60 (0-8094-2371-5) Time-Life.

Weathersfield: Century One. John L. Hurd. LC 75-22317. (Illus.). 256p. 1975. 15.00 (0-914016-18-0) Phoenix Pub.

Weathersfield: Century Two. John L. Hurd. LC 75-22317. (Illus.). 1978. 15.00 (0-914016-55-5) Phoenix Pub.

Weathertop, the Tower of the Wind. Ruth Sochard. Ed. by Peter C. Fenlon, Jr. 32p. (Orig.). (YA). (gr. 10-12). 1987. pap. 6.00 (0-915795-89-2, 8201) Iron Crown Ent Inc.

Weathervane Secrets. Mabel Reaveley. LC 83-25854. (Illus.). (Orig.). 1984. pap. 6.95 (0-87233-075-3) Bauhan.

Weathervanes. Patricia Mockridge & Philip Mockridge. 1989. pap. 25.00 (0-7478-0191-6, Pub. by Shire UK) St Mut.

Weatherwatch. Valerie Wyatt. 1990. pap. 9.95 (0-201-15404-8) Addison-Wesley.

Weatherwatcher's Diary. Carol Thiessen. 1987. pap. text ed. 9.95 (0-660-10351-6) U of Toronto Pr.

Weatherwise: Learning about the Weather. Jonathan Kahl. (How's the Weather? Ser.). (Illus.). 64p. (J). (gr. 4 up). 1992. lib. bdg. 19.95 (0-8225-2525-9, Lerner Publctns) Lerner Group.

*Weatherwise Forecasting. Thorn Bacon. Date not set. write for info. (0-688-04320-8) Hearst Bks.

*Weatherworks Discovery Kit. Andrew Deacon. 32p. (YA). (gr. 3 up). 1997. 16.95 (0-7624-0149-4) Running Pr.

Weave a Dream Activity Book, Unit 7. (Networks Ser.). 1991. 3.90 (0-88106-756-3, N234) Charlesbridge Pub.

Weave a Dream Activity Book (EV), Unit 7. (Networks Ser.). 1991. 3.90 (0-88106-755-5) Charlesbridge Pub.

Weave a Dream Anthology, Unit 7. (Networks Ser.). 1991. 7.45 (0-88106-753-9, N231) Charlesbridge Pub.

*Weave a Garment of Brightness: A Gathering of Prayers from Around the World. Wayne L. Jones. 144p. 1997. pap. 10.00 (0-425-15774-1, Berkley Trade) Berkley Pub.

Weave a Loving Webb. large type ed. Stella Whitelaw. 1990. pap. 15.99 (0-7089-6889-9, Traitree Bookshop) Ulverscroft.

Weave It! Quilt It! Wear It! Mary A. Caplinger. Ed. by Barbara Weiland. LC 95-48409. (Illus.). 88p. (Orig.). 1996. pap. 24.95 (1-56477-142-3, B259) That Patchwork.

Weave Me a Dream. Mary McGuinness. 1996. pap. 1.78 (0-8217-5558-7) Kensgtn Pub Corp.

Weave of Women. E. M. Broner. LC 84-48548. 314p. 1985. reprint ed. pap. 10.95 (0-253-20354-6, MB 354) Ind U Pr.

*Weave of Words. Robert D. San Souci. LC 97-5046. (Illus.). (J). 1997. write for info. (0-531-30053-6); lib. bdg. write for info. (0-531-33053-2) Orchard Bks Watts.

*Weave Room. Michael Chitwood. LC 97-8422. (Phoenix Poets Ser.). 1996. pap. 10.95 (0-226-10398-6); lib. bdg. 21.00 (0-226-10397-8) U Ch Pr.

Weaver & Koehler's Programmed Mathematics of Drugs & Solutions. 5th ed. Virginia Arcangelo. (Illus.). 160p. 1992. pap. text ed. 17.95 (0-397-54918-0) Lppncott-Raven.

Weaver Fever. Jackie Robinson. 14p. 1991. pap. text ed. 6.50 (1-885156-01-4) Animas Quilts.

Weaver-God, He Weaves: Melville & the Poetics of the Novel. Christopher Sten. LC 95-37382. 480p. 1996. 39.00 (0-87338-537-3) Kent St U Pr.

Weaver, History & Genealogy of a Branch of the Weaver Family. Lucius E. Weaver. 743p. 1993. reprint ed. pap. 105.00 (0-8328-3565-X); reprint ed. lib. bdg. 115.00 (0-8328-3564-1) Higginson Bk Co.

Weaver Named Kabir: Selected Verses, with a Detailed Historical & Biographical Introduction. Charlotte Vaudeville. 384p. 1993. 26.00 (0-19-563078-5) OUP.

Weaver of Worlds: A Woman's Journey in Tapestry. David Jongeward. (Illus.). 160p. (Orig.). 1991. pap. 12.95 (0-89281-270-2) Inner Tradit.

*Weavers. Leonard E. Fisher. LC 96-36135. (Colonial Craftsmen Ser.). (J). 1997. lib. bdg. write for info. (0-7614-0509-7, Benchmark NY) Marshall Cavendish.

Weaver's & PWC Index: 1981-1995. Compiled by Lee Anderst. 45p. (Orig.). 1996. pap. 9.95 (0-9646391-1-4) XRX Inc.

Weaver's Book of Eight-Shaft Patterns: From the Friends of Handwoven. Ed. by Carol Strickler. LC 91-28618. (Illus.). 240p. 1991. 36.95 (0-934026-67-X) Interweave.

Weaver's Book of Fabric Design. Janet Phillips. (Illus.). 148p. 1983. pap. 11.95 (0-312-85980-5) St Martin.

Weaver's Book of Scottish Tartans. Harriet Tidball. LC 76-23997. (Guild Monographs: No. 5). (Illus.). 46p. 1962. pap. 9.95 (0-916658-05-8) Shuttle Craft.

Weaver's Choice: Patterns in American Coverlets. Janice T. Wass. (Handbook of Collections: No. 6). (Illus.). 76p. (Orig.). (C). 1988. pap. 15.95 (0-89792-118-6) Ill St Museum.

Weaver's Draft Book & Clothiers Assistant. Compiled by John Hargrove. (AAS Facsimiles Ser.: No. 2). 1979. pap. 10.00 (0-912296-17-8, U Pr of Va) Am Antiquarian.

Weavers Draft Book & Clothiers Assistant. John Hargrove. 28p. 1979. pap. 10.00 (0-614-10095-X) Oak Knoll.

Weaver's Garden. Rita Buchanan. LC 86-83425. (Illus.). 230p. 1987. 16.95 (0-934026-28-9) Interweave.

Weaver's Horse. Jill Creighton & Robert Creighton. (J). (gr. 2-4). 1991. 15.95 (1-55037-181-9, Pub. by Annick CN); pap. 5.95 (1-55037-178-9, Pub. by Annick CN) Firefly Bks Ltd.

Weaver's Knot: The Contradictions of Class Struggle & Family Solidarity in Western France, 1750-1914. Tessie P. Liu. (Illus.). 296p. 1994. 45.00 (0-8014-2738-X); pap. 17.95 (0-8014-8019-1) Cornell U Pr.

Weavers, Merchants, & Kings: The Inscribed Rugs of Armenia. Lucy Der Manuelian & Murray L. Eiland. LC 84-48115. (Illus.). 216p. (Orig.). 1984. 40.00 (0-295-96548-7) U of Wash Pr.

Weavers of Death. Mohamed Abdel-Al. 158p. 1996. pap. 12.95 (1-85756-285-2, Pub. by Janus Pubng UK) Paul & Co Pubs.

Weavers of Dreams. 2nd ed. David J. Thompson. (Illus.). 152p. (Orig.). (C). 1994. pap. write for info. (88-85641-05-9, B6) U CA Ctr Cooperatives.

W

Weavers of Revolution: The Yarur Workers & Chile's Road to Socialism. Peter Winn. (Illus.). 354p. (C). 1989. pap. text ed. 18.95 (0-19-504558-0) OUP.

Weavers of the Song: The Oral Poetry of Arab Women in Israel & the West Bank. Mishael Caspi & Julia A. Blessing. 146p. (Orig.). 1991. pap. 14.00 (0-89410-651-1, Three Contnts); text ed. 28.00 (0-89410-650-3, Three Contnts) Lynne Rienner.

Weavers of Tradition & Beauty: Basketmakers of the Great Basin. Mary L. Fulkerson & Kathleen Curtis. LC 95-8555. (Illus.). 128p. 1995. pap. 19.95 (0-87417-260-8) U of Nev Pr.

Weavers of Wisdom. Anne Bancroft. 192p. 1990. pap. 10.00 (0-14-019193-3, Penguin Bks) Viking Penguin.

Weaver's Study Course: Sourcebook for Ideas & Techniques. Else Regensteiner. LC 87-61437. (Illus.). 176p. 1987. pap. 19.95 (0-88740-112-0) Schiffer.

Weaver's Tale. Kate Sedley. 256p. 1994. 20.95 (0-312-10474-X) St Martin.

Weaver's Tale. Kate Sedley. 224p. 1995. mass mkt. 4.50 (0-06-104336-2, Harp PBks) HarpC.

Weaver's Workbook. Hilary Chetwynd. (Color Craft Workbooks Ser.). (Illus.). 96p. 1988. pap. 16.95 (0-312-02120-8) St Martin.

Weaverville: Trinity County, California. Patricia J. Hicks & Frank E. Hicks, Jr. LC 90-81526. (Illus.). 70p. (Orig.). 1990. pap. 7.25 (0-9626392-1-4) I Collect Facts.

Weaverville, a Jewel of a Town. Patricia J. Hicks. LC 93-91494. (Illus.). 72p. (Orig.). 1993. teacher ed., pap. 7.25 (0-9626392-4-9) I Collect Facts.

Weaves of the Incas. Ulla Nass. (Illus.). 108p. 1980. pap. 16.95 (0-9606468-1-7) Nass.

Weaveworld. Clive Barker. 1996. pap. 6.99 (0-671-31152-2) S&S Trade.

Weaveworld. Clive Barker. 1989. mass mkt. 6.99 (0-671-70418-4) PB.

Weaveworld, No. 1. Saltzgaber et al. 64p. 1991. 4.95 (0-87135-850-6) Marvel Entmnt.

Weaveworld, No. 2. Saltzgaber et al. 64p. 1991. 4.95 (0-87135-851-4) Marvel Entmnt.

Weaveworld, No. 3. Saltzgaber et al. 64p. 1992. 4.95 (0-87135-852-2) Marvel Entmnt.

***Weaving.** (Discovery Box Ser.). 32p. (J). (gr. 1-5). 1997. 11.95 (0-590-89665-2) Scholastic Inc.

Weaving. Lori V. Schue. (ArtWorks for Kids Ser.: Vol. 3). (Illus.). 48p. (J). (gr. 1-6). 1995. teacher ed., pap. text ed. 9.95 (1-55799-364-5, EMC 293) Evan-Moor Corp.

Weaving: A Handbook of Fiber Arts. 2nd ed. Shirley E. Held. LC 77-24219. (Illus.). 288p. (C). 1978. 21.95 (0-03-042821-1); pap. text ed. 39.25 (0-03-022691-0) HB Coll Pubs.

Weaving: A Handbook of the Fibers. 3rd ed. Held. (C). 1996. pap. text ed. write for info. (0-15-501512-5) HarBrace.

Weaving: A Manual of Techniques. Rosemary Bridgman. (Illus.). 224p. 1992. 45.00 (1-85223-444-X, Pub. by Crowood Pr UK) Trafalgar.

Weaving: An Analysis of the Constitution of Objects. J. K. Swindler. 188p. 1991. text ed. 48.00 (0-8476-7667-6) Rowman.

***Weaving: Conversion of Yarn to Fabric.** 2nd ed. P. R. Lord & M. H. Mohamed. (Merrow Technical Library: Vol. 12). 1982. pap. 35.00 (0-904095-38-X, Pub. by Textile Inst UK) St Mut.

***Weaving: Technology & Operations.** A. Omerod & W. S. Sondhelm. 1995. 90.00 (1-870812-76-X, Pub. by Textile Inst UK) St Mut.

Weaving: The Fabric of a Woman's Life. Elinor M. Greenberg. LC 91-72466. 224p. (Orig.). (C). 1991. pap. 12.95 (0-9629764-0-7) EMG & Assocs.

Weaving: The Irish Inheritance. E. F. Sutton. 64p. 1980. 9.95 (0-8159-7227-X) Devin.

Weaving a California Tradition: A Native American Basketmaker. Linda Yamane. (J). 1996. pap. text ed. 6.95 (0-8225-9730-6) Lerner Group.

Weaving a California Tradition: Native American Basketmaking. Linda Yamane. LC 96-13388. (Illus.). (J). 1996. 19.95 (0-8225-2660-3, Lerner Publctns) Lerner Group.

Weaving a Canadian Allegory: Anonymous Writing, Personal Reading. Loretta Czernis. 134p. (C). 1994. text ed. 29.95 (0-88920-232-X) Wilfrid Laurier.

***Weaving a Family.** Peggy Weber. ix, 115p. (Orig.). 1996. pap. 9.50 (0-9655594-0-8) P Weber.

***Weaving a Future Together: Women & Participatory Development.** Kamala Peiris. 96p. (Orig.). 1997. pap. 14.95 (90-6224-972-8, Pub. by Uitgeverij Arkel NE) LPC InBook.

Weaving a Legacy: The Don & Jean Stuck Coverlet Collection. Clarita S. Anderson. LC 94-47602. 1995. 42.95 (0-918881-33-1) Columbus Mus Art.

Weaving a Legacy: The Don & Jean Stuck Coverlet Collection. Clarita S. Anderson. LC 94-47602. (Illus.). 234p. 1995. 49.50 (0-8109-3984-3) Abrams.

Weaving a Life: The Story of Mary Meigs Atwater. Mary J. Reiter. Ed. by Veronica Patterson. 208p. (Orig.). 1992. pap. 14.95 (0-934026-77-7) Interweave.

Weaving a Navajo Blanket. Gladys A. Reichard. LC 73-86437. (Illus.). 256p. 1974. reprint ed. 4.95 (0-486-22992-0) Dover.

Weaving a Tapestry: Loneliness, Spiritual Well-Being, & Communal Support. Carol A. Wintermyer. LC 93-16058. 110p. (C). 1993. lib. bdg. 24.00 (0-8191-9179-5) U Pr of Amer.

Weaving a Tapestry of Resistance: The Places, Power & Poetry of a Sustainable Society. Sharon E. Sutton. LC 95-44320. (Critical Studies in Education & Culture). 256p. 1996. pap. text ed. 19.95 (0-89789-278-X, Bergin & Garvey) Greenwood.

Weaving a Tapestry of Resistance: The Places, Power & Poetry of a Sustainable Society. Sharon E. Sutton. LC 95-44320. (Critical Studies in Education & Culture). 264p. 1996. text ed. 59.95 (0-89789-277-1, Bergin & Garvey) Greenwood.

Weaving a Traditional Coverlet. Helen Jarvis. LC 88-83440. (Illus.). 96p. (Orig.). 1989. pap. 12.95 (0-934026-43-2) Interweave.

Weaving a Web of Magic: A Potpourri of Rituals, Chants, Dances, Webs, Cords, Runes, Talismans, & Magical Information. Rhiannon Ryall. (Illus.). (Orig.). 1996. pap. 19.95 (1-898307-92-X, Pub. by Capall Bann Pubng UK) Holmes Pub.

Weaving a World: Textiles & the Navajo Way of Seeing. Paul Zolbrod & Roseann Willink. (Illus.). 144p. 1996. pap. 29.95 (0-89013-307-7) Museum NM Pr.

Weaving & Colcha from the Hispanic Southwest: Authentic Designs. Ed. by William Wroth. LC 85-71306. (Illus.). 112p. (Orig.). 1985. pap. 12.95 (0-941270-27-0) Ancient City Pr.

***Weaving & Designing Woven Fabrics.** Peggy Osterkamp. (Peggy Osterkamp's New Guide to Weaving Ser.: No. 3). (Illus.). 200p. (Orig.). pap. write for info. (0-9637793-3-8) Lease Sticks.

Weaving Areas: Design & Analysis. (National Cooperative Highway Research Program Report Ser.: No. 159). 119p. 1975. 6.40 (0-309-02336-X) Transport Res Bd.

Weaving As an Art Form. Theo Moorman. LC 86-61202. (Illus.). 104p. 1986. pap. 12.95 (0-88740-068-X) Schiffer.

Weaving Book: Patterns & Ideas. Helen Bress. (Illus.). 548p. 1990. reprint ed. 49.95 (0-9620543-0-5) Flower Valley Pr.

***Weaving Contemporary Rag Rugs: New Designs & Traditional Techniques.** Heather Allen. LC 97-19740. 1997. write for info. (1-887374-39-6) Lark Books.

***Weaving Country Baskets.** Gillooly. LC 96-39296. (Storey Publishing Bulletin Ser.). 1996. pap. write for info. (0-88266-588-X, Storey Pub) Storey Comm Inc.

Weaving Identities: Construction of Dress & Self in a Highland Guatemala Town. Carol Hendrickson. LC 95-7296. (Orig.). 1995. pap. 15.95 (0-292-73120-5); pap. 15.95 (0-292-73100-0); text ed. 35.00 (0-292-73099-3) U of Tex Pr.

Weaving in the Women: Transforming the High School English Curriculum. Liz Whaley & Liz Dodge. LC 93-17827. 300p. 1993. pap. text ed. 26.00 (0-86709-327-7, 0327) Boynton Cook Pubs.

Weaving Inkle Bands. Harriet Tidball. LC 76-24016. (Guild Monographs: No. 27). (Illus.). 40p. 1969. pap. 9.95 (0-916658-27-9) Shuttle Craft.

Weaving Is Fun. A. V. White. LC 74-27568. (Illus.). 96p. 1975. reprint ed. pap. 3.95 (0-486-22724-3) Dover.

Weaving It Together. Broukal. (College ESL Ser.: Bk. 4). 1996. pap. 21.95 (0-8384-6594-3) Heinle & Heinle.

Weaving It Together. Broukal. (College ESL Ser.: Bk. 4). 1996. student ed., pap. 7.95 (0-8384-6595-1) Heinle & Heinle.

Weaving It Together - 1. Broukal. (College ESL Ser.). 1994. pap. 20.95 (0-8384-4221-8) Heinle & Heinle.

Weaving It Together - 3. Broukal. (College ESL Ser.). Date not set. pap. 17.95 (0-614-10348-7) Heinle & Heinle.

Weaving It Together - 3. Broukal. (College ESL Ser.). 1994. pap. 20.95 (0-8384-4222-6) Heinle & Heinle.

Weaving It Together Two. Broukal. 1993. pap. 20.95 (0-8384-3977-2) Heinle & Heinle.

Weaving It Together Two. Broukal. 1993. teacher ed., pap. 9.95 (0-8384-4201-3) Heinle & Heinle.

Weaving It Together 1. Broukal. (College ESL Ser.). 1994. suppl. ed., pap. 6.95 (0-8384-5414-3) Heinle & Heinle.

Weaving Mountain Memories: Recollections of the Allenspark Area. Lorna Knowlton. Ed. by Sybil Barnes. (Illus.). 288p. (Orig.). 1989. pap. 8.95 (0-9626381-0-2) Estes Pk Area Hist Mus.

Weaving New Visions: Art Therapy in Collaboration with Allied Professions. Ed. by Irene R. David & Mary Buckley. 178p. (Orig.). pap. 20.00 (1-882147-50-2) Am Art Therapy.

***Weaving New Worlds: Southeastern Cherokee Women & Their Basketry.** Sarah H. Hill. LC 96-47882. (Illus.). 448p. (C). 1997. 45.00 (0-8078-2345-7); pap. 22.50 (0-8078-4650-3) U of NC Pr.

Weaving of a Dream. Marilee Heyer. (Illus.). 32p. (J). (ps-3). 1989. pap. 5.99 (0-14-050528-8, Puffin) Puffin Bks.

Weaving of Glory. George H. Morrison. 192p. 1994. pap. 9.99 (0-8254-3291-X) Kregel.

Weaving of Hearts. Cynthia E. Cowen. 1991. pap. 5.95 (1-55673-392-5, 9210) CSS OH.

Weaving of the Southwest. Marian Rodee. LC 86-63764. (Illus.). 248p. 1987. 39.95 (0-88740-095-7); pap. 24.95 (0-88740-091-4) Schiffer.

Weaving of Wonder: Fables to Summon Inner Wisdom. Charlotte R. Brown & Karolyne S. Rogers. LC 95-7722. 128p. 1995. pap. 12.95 (1-880913-14-3) Innisfree Pr.

***Weaving Ourselves into the Land: Charles Godfrey Leland, "Indians," & the Study of Native American Religions.** Thomas C. Parkhill. LC 96-41611. (Native American Religions Ser.). (Illus.). 256p. (C). 1997. pap. text ed. 18.95 (0-7914-3454-0) State U NY Pr.

***Weaving Ourselves into the Land: Charles Godfrey Leland, "Indians," & the Study of Native American Religions.** Thomas C. Parkhill. LC 96-41611. (SUNY Series in Native American Religions). (Illus.). 256p. (C). 1997. text ed. 59.50 (0-7914-3453-2) State U NY Pr.

Weaving Overshot: Redesigning the Tradition. Donna L. Sullivan. (Illus.). 160p. 1996. pap. 19.95 (1-883010-23-3) Interweave.

***Weaving Partnerships & Communities: Visions, Voices, Ventures: Proceedings of the 34th Annual Meeting - Eastern Academy of Management.** Ed. by Bonita Betters-Reed & Madeline Crocitto. 300p. 1997. write for info. (0-916958-15-9) Eastrn Acad Mgmt.

Weaving Rag Rugs: A Women's Craft in Western Maryland. Geraldine N. Johnson. LC 84-17398. 196p. 1985. 30.00 (0-87049-451-1) U of Tenn Pr.

***Weaving Rag Rugs: A Women's Craft in Western Maryland.** Geraldine N. Johnson. LC 84-17398. (Illus.). 204p. 1985. reprint ed. pap. 58.20 (0-608-02608-5, 2063266) Bks Demand.

Weaving Roses of Rhode Island. Isadora Safner. LC 85-82321. (Illus.). 160p. 1986. 15.00 (0-934026-19-X) Interweave.

Weaving, Spinning & Dyeing: A Beginner's Manual. V. Howar. 1976. 11.95 (0-13-947812-4, Spectrum IN) Macmillan Gen Ref.

Weaving, Spinning & Dyeing Book. 2nd ed. Rachel Brown. (Illus.). 1983. pap. 40.00 (0-394-71595-0) Knopf.

Weaving Technology in India. Puneet Kishore. 1990. text ed. 15.95 (0-7069-4938-2, Pub. by Vikas II) S Asia.

***Weaving Textile Reuse into Waste Reduction.** Brenda Platt. LC 97-3520. 1997. write for info. (0-917582-93-4) Inst Local Self Re.

Weaving That Sings: Variations on the Theo Moorman Technique. Joyce Harter & Nadine Sanders. (Illus.). 128p. 1995. pap. 29.95 (0-9644315-0-5) Loomis Studio.

Weaving the Net: Conditional Engagement with China. Ed. by James Shinn. LC 96-2302. 284p. 1996. 19.95 (0-87609-190-7) Coun Foreign.

Weaving the Sermon: Preaching in a Feminist Perspective. Christine M. Smith. LC 88-27942. 192p. 1989. pap. 16.00 (0-664-25031-9) Westminster John Knox.

Weaving the Sheets. Judith Root. 1988. pap. 11.95 (0-88748-070-5) Carnegie-Mellon.

Weaving the Threads of Life: The Khita Gyn-Eco-Logical Healing Cult among the Yaka. Rene Devisch. LC 93-355. (Illus.). 352p. (ENG & FRE.). 1993. pap. text ed. 19.95 (0-226-14362-7) U Ch Pr.

Weaving the Threads of Life: The Khita Gyn-Eco-Logical Healing Cult among the Yaka. Rene Devisch. LC 93-355. (Illus.). 344p. (ENG & FRE.). 1993. lib. bdg. 53.95 (0-226-14361-9) U Ch Pr.

Weaving the Visions: New Patterns in Feminist Spirituality. Ed. by Judith Plaskow & Carol P. Christ. 352p. 1989. pap. 16.00 (0-06-061383-1) Harper SF.

Weaving Wildly. rev. ed. Mary Lou Stahl. (Illus.). 48p. 1994. pap. 5.00 (1-886075-05-0) Grass Rt Ent.

Weaving Wildly: Mats & Baskets the Choctaw Way. Mary Lou Stahl. (Illus.). 80p. (Orig.). 1997. pap. 15.95 (1-880319-04-7) Biotech.

Weaving with Coconut Palm. George B. Stevenson. (Illus.). 1970. pap. 2.50 (0-916224-40-6) Banyan Bks.

Weaving with Reeds & Fibers. Osma G. Tod & Oscar H. Benson. (Illus.). 224p. 1975. reprint ed. pap. 5.95 (0-486-23143-7) Dover.

Weaving with Wheat: A Manual for Beginning Wheat Weavers, No. I. Clara Poore. (Illus.). 16p. 1982. pap. 4.00 (0-9613993-1-7) Wheat N Flower.

Weaving Woman: Musings & Meditations on the Feminine Mythos. Barbara Black Koltuv. LC 90-6736. (Illus.). 143p. (Orig.). 1990. pap. 9.95 (0-89254-019-2) Nicolas-Hays.

Weaving Your Way from Arithmetic to Mathematics with Manipulatives. Mary Laycook & Peggy McLean. Ed. & Illus. by Margaret Smart. 133p. (J). (gr. k-8). 1993. pap. text ed. 18.95 (1-882293-00-2, A-1680) Activity Resources.

Weavings from Nahuala: A Mayan Tradition. Richard D. Mandel. Ed. by Salvatore G. Cilella. Tr. by Patricia B. McRae. (Illus.). 28p. (SPA.). (C). 1992. write for info. (0-9627858-1-4) Columbia Mus Art.

Weavings Reader. LC 92-61443. 254p. 1993. 19.95 (0-8358-0680-4) Upper Room Bks.

***Weavings Reader.** John Mogabgab. 29.75 (0-687-61302-7) Abingdon.

Web. Jerry Ahern. (Survivalist Ser.: No. 5). 1983. mass mkt. 2.50 (0-8217-1145-8, Zebra Kensgtn) Kensgtn Pub Corp.

Web. Jonathan Kellerman. 432p. 1996. mass mkt. 6.99 (0-553-57227-X) Bantam.

Web. L. Orde. 1988. pap. 2.95 (0-8217-2672-2) NAL-Dutton.

***Web.** Helen M. Osterman. Ed. by Carolyn S. Zagury. LC 96-61492. 184p. (Orig.). 1997. pap. 12.95 (1-880254-41-7) Vista.

***Web.** Robert Perine. 248p. (Orig.). 1997. mass mkt. 4.99 (1-55197-620-X, Pub. by Comnwlth Pub CN) Partners Pubs Grp.

***Web.** Jan Pienkowski. (Creepy Creatures Ser.). (J). 1997. 5.95 (0-8362-5160-1) Andrews & McMeel.

Web. large type ed. Jonathan Kellerman. LC 96-10191. (Alex Delaware Ser.). 1996. 26.95 (1-56895-311-9, Compass) Wheeler Pub.

Web. Emerson Hough. LC 73-90178. (Mass Violence in America Ser.). 1969. reprint ed. 41.95 (0-405-01319-1) Ayer.

Web: Stories by Argentine Women. Ed. by Ernest H. Lewald. LC 81-51646. 135p. 1983. 26.00 (0-89410-085-8, Three Contnts) Lynne Rienner.

***Web Access Framework: C++ Objects for Internet Programming.** Chris E. Richardson. 1996. pap. 39.95 (0-13-494394-5) P-H.

***Web Advertising: Market Analysis & Forecast.** Elizabeth Estroff et al. Ed. by Karen Burka. (Illus.). 170p. 1996. 995.00 (0-88709-119-9) Simba Info Inc.

Web Advertising & Marketing. Thomas Kuegler. 1996. pap. text ed. 34.95 (0-7615-0383-8) Prima Pub.

Web after Hours. Bill Mann. 1995. pap. 21.95 (0-7615-0377-3) Prima Pub.

Web after Work for Dummies. Jill Ellsworth. 1996. pap. 19.99 (1-56884-649-5) IDG Bks.

***Web after Work for Dummies.** 2nd ed. Jill Ellsworth. 1997. pap. 19.99 (0-7645-0116-X) IDG Bks.

***Web & New Media Pricing Guide.** Michelle Szabo & J. P. Frenza. 320p. 1996. pap. 40.00 (1-56830-336-X) Hayden.

***Web Animation Bible.** Kris Jamsa & Jamsa Press Staff. (Orig.). 1997. pap. 54.95 (1-884133-60-6) Jamsa Pr.

***Web Animation for Dummies.** Dummies Technology Press Staff. 1997. pap. 24.99 (0-7645-0195-X) IDG Bks.

***Web Animation with Macromedia Flash 2.** Ken Milburn. 1997. pap. text ed. 34.99 (1-56604-732-3) Ventana Communs.

Web Architect Handbook. Charles Stross. (C). 1996. pap. text ed. 30.95 (0-201-87735-X) Addison-Wesley.

***Web Architecture.** Rosenfeld & Morville. Ed. by Linda Mui. (Orig.). 1997. pap. write for info. (1-56592-282-4) OReilly & Assocs.

***Web Audio Studio.** (Orig.). pap. write for info. (1-56592-353-7) OReilly & Assocs.

***Web Authoring Desk Reference.** Bob Benedict et al. 800p. 1997. 55.00 (1-56830-352-1) Hayden.

***Web-Based Instruction.** Ed. by Badrul H. Khan. LC 96-52250. (Illus.). 480p. 1997. 89.95 (0-87778-296-2); pap. text ed. 59.95 (0-87778-297-0) Educ Tech Pubns.

***Web-Based Training Cookbook.** Brandon Hall. LC 97-14629. 432p. 1997. pap. 39.99 incl. cd-rom (0-471-18021-1) Wiley.

Web Bound. 2nd ed. Art Mac Cammon. 180p. 1996. pap. 14.95 (0-9650520-0-1) N A International.

***Web Broadcasting Development for Dummies.** 1997. pap. 29.99 (0-7645-0309-X) IDG Bks.

Web Browsing with America On-Line. Barrie Sosinsky. 1995. pap. text ed. 22.95 (0-7615-0298-X) Prima Pub.

Web Browsing with Microsoft Network. Jeff Bankston. 1995. pap. text ed. 22.95 (0-7615-0288-2) Prima Pub.

Web Browsing with Netcom Cruiser 2.0. Pat McGregor. 1995. pap. text ed. 24.95 (0-7615-0240-8) Prima Pub.

Web Browsing with Netscape Navigator 1.1. Steve Davis. 1995. pap. text ed. 24.95 (0-7615-0239-4) Prima Pub.

Web Browsing with Prodigy: Exploring New Worlds of Graphics, Text, & Sound on the World Wide Web. John P. Withers. 1995. pap. text ed. 22.95 (0-7615-0214-9) Prima Pub.

Web Bundle Macintosh: Publish It on the Web, Webmaster, New & Improved Stupid Mac Tricks. Barbara Pfaffenberger. 1996. pap. text ed. 44.95 (0-12-799046-1, AP Prof) Acad Pr.

Web Bundle Windows: Publish It on the Web, Webmaster Windows, New & Improved Stupid Windows... Barbara Pfaffenberger. 1996. pap. text ed. 44.95 (0-12-799045-3, AP Prof) Acad Pr.

***Web Casting Bible.** Noel Moore. 1997. pap. 49.99 (0-7645-8045-0) IDG Bks.

***Web Catalog Cookbook.** Cliff Allen & Deborah Kania. LC 97-9529. 512p. 1997. pap. 44.99 incl. cd-rom (0-471-18331-8) Wiley.

***Web Client Programming with Perl.** Clinton Wong. Ed. by Linda Mui. (Illus.). 250p. 1997. pap. 29.95 (1-56592-214-X) OReilly & Assocs.

***Web Commerce Engineering.** Daniel Minoli. LC 97-19682. (Illus.). 288p. 1997. pap. text ed. 44.95 (0-07-042978-2) McGraw.

***Web Commerce Unleashed.** Edmund T. Smith. 950p. Date not set. 49.99 (1-57521-250-1, SamsNet Bks) Mac Comp Pub.

Web Concept & Design. Crystal Waters. 288p. 1996. pap. text ed. 39.99 (1-56205-648-4) New Riders Pub.

***Web Concept & Design.** 2nd ed. Crystal Waters. 1997. 45.00 (1-56205-783-9) New Riders Pub.

***Web Database Construction Kit with Cold Fusion 2.0.** Ben Forta. 850p. 1996. pap. text ed. 59.99 incl. cd-rom (0-7897-0970-8) Que.

***Web Database Interactive Course.** Gunnit Khurana. LC 97-19465. 1997. 59.99 (1-57169-097-2) Sams.

Web Database Primer Plus. Piroz Mohseni. (Illus.). 700p. (Orig.). 1996. pap. 49.99 (1-57169-070-0, Waite Grp Pr) Sams.

***Web Database Publishing for Dummies.** Dummies Technology Press. 1997. pap. 24.99 (0-7645-0149-6) IDG Bks.

***Web Database Publishing with Filemaker Pro X.** Don Crabb. 1997. pap. text ed. 39.95 (1-55851-514-3) MIS Press.

Web Derivatives. Hewitt Kenyon & Anthony P. Morse. LC 73-2858. (Memoirs Ser.: No. 1/132). 177p. 1973. pap. 18.00 (0-8218-1832-5, MEMO/1/132) Am Math.

***Web Design: Studio Secrets.** Craig Kanarick & Thomas Muller. 256p. 1997. pap. 44.99 incl. cd-rom (0-7645-4025-4) IDG Bks.

***Web Design & Desktop Publishing for Dummies.** 2nd ed. Roger C. Parker. 1997. pap. 19.99 (0-7645-0139-9) IDG Bks.

Web Design Finesse. David G. Weinman. 1996. pap. write for info. (0-679-76964-1) Random.

***Web Design Resources Directory.** Eileen Mullin. 1997. pap. 39.99 (0-614-28475-9, Lycos Pr) Que.

***Web Design Resources Directory: Tools & Techniques for Creating Your Home Page.** Eileen Mullin. 400p. 1997. 29.99 (0-7897-1060-9) Mac Comp Pub.

***Web Design Studio Secrets.** Craig Kanarick & Thomas Muller. 256p. 1997. pap. write for info. (0-614-26289-5) IDG Bks.

***Web Design Template Sourcebook.** Lisa Schmeiser. 250p. 1997. 35.00 (1-56205-754-5) New Riders Pub.

***Web Designer's Guide to Castanet.** Hayden Books Staff. 1997. 39.99 (1-56830-387-4) Hayden.

***Web Designer's Guide to Cookies.** Hayden Development Group Staff. 400p. 1997. 45.00 (1-56830-358-0) Mac Comp Pub.

W

An Asterisk (*) at the beginning of an entry indicates that the title is appearing in BIP for the first time.

***Web Designer's Guide to Dynamic HTML.** Jason Wolf & Timothy Webster. 600p. 1997. pap. text ed. 39.99 incl. cd-rom (*1-56830-418-8*) Hayden.

***Web Designer's Guide to FrontPage 97.** Justin Higgins & David Cohn. 1997. pap. 39.99 (*0-614-28470-8*, Hayden Sftwre) MCP SW Interactive.

***Web Designer's Guide to Frontpage 98.** 2nd ed. Craig Vitter. 1997. 45.00 (*1-56830-432-3*) Hayden.

***Web Designer's Guide to Netcasts & Chats.** Hayden Developement Group Staff. 450p. 1997. 45.00 (*1-56830-359-9*) Mac Comp Pub.

***Web Designer's Guide to Photoshop.** Hayden Development Team Staff. 500p. 1997. 45.00 (*1-56830-415-3*) Hayden.

***Web Designer's Guide to PNG, GIF, JPEG.** Timothy Webster. 288p. 1997. 49.99 (*1-56830-363-7*) Hayden.

***Web Designer's Guide to Typography.** Leary. 350p. 1997. 39.99 (*1-56830-337-8*) Mac Comp Pub.

***Web Designer's Guide to Typography.** Michael Leary & Galapagos Design Group Staff. 1997. pap. 39.99 (*0-614-28471-6*, Hayden Sftwre) MCP SW Interactive.

***Web Developers Guide to Java Beans.** Jalal Feghhi. 1997. pap. text ed. 39.99 incl. cd-rom (*1-57610-121-5*) Coriolis Grp.

Web Developers Guide to Javascript. Peter Aitken. 1996. pap. text ed. 39.99 incl. cd-rom (*1-883577-97-7*) Coriolis Grp.

***Web Developers Guide to Multicasting.** Nels Johnson. 1997. pap. text ed. 39.99 incl. cd-rom (*1-57610-117-7*) Coriolis Grp.

Web Developers Guide to Multimedia & Video. Nels Johnson. 1996. pap. text ed. 39.99 incl. cd-rom (*1-883577-96-9*) Coriolis Grp.

Web Developers Guide to Sound & Music. Anthony Helmstetter. 1996. pap. text ed. 39.99 incl. cd-rom (*1-883577-95-0*) Coriolis Grp.

***Web Developer's Guide to Visual J++ & ActiveX.** Trevor Harmon. 39.99 (*1-57610-062-6*) Coriolis Grp.

***Web Developer's SECRETS.** Harold Davis. 512p. (Orig.). 1997. pap. write for info. (*0-614-26301-8*) IDG Bks.

***Web Developer's Secrets.** Harold Davis. 1997. pap. 44.99 (*0-7645-8015-9*) IDG Bks.

Web Dictionary. William H. Holt & Rockie J. Morgan. 1996. 12.95 (*0-945264-16-X*) Resolution Busn Pr.

W.E.B. Du Bois: His Contributions to Pan-Africanism. Kwadwo O. Pobi-Asamani. LC 93-4385. (Black Political Studies: No. 4). 136p. 1994. 29.00 (*0-89370-351-6*); pap. 19.00 (*0-89370-451-2*) Borgo Pr.

Web Empowerment Book. F. Jas. Ed. by R. Abraham et al. 208p. 1995. 27.95 (*0-387-94431-1*) Spr-Verlag.

Web-Enabled Enterprise. Robert Coen & Mark C. Hoogenboom. LC 97-19219. (Illus.). 400p. 1997. text ed. 54.95 (*0-07-011774-8*) McGraw.

***Web-Enabling MS Access 97.** Stephen Forte. 1997. 49.99 (*1-56205-773-1*) New Riders Pub.

***Web Enabling MS Access 97.** Stephen Forte. 1997. 45.00 (*0-7897-1382-9*) Que.

Web Explorer Pocket Companion. Jeff Duntemann et al. 1995. pap. 12.99 (*1-883577-54-3*) Coriolis Grp.

***Web F/X.** Kevin Hampton. 1996. pap. 39.99 (*0-7645-4010-6*) IDG Bks.

***Web Gateway Tools: Connecting IBM & Lotus Applications to the Web.** Ed. by Josephine Cheng & Susan Malaika. LC 96-29922. 1997. pap. text ed. 34.95 (*0-471-17555-2*) Wiley.

***Web Graphics: Studio Secrets.** Craig Kanarick & Thomas Muller. 245p. 1997. pap. 44.99 incl. cd-rom (*0-7645-4024-6*) IDG Bks.

***Web Graphics Bible.** Ron Wodaski. 848p. 1997. pap. write for info. (*0-614-26307-7*) IDG Bks.

***Web Graphics Bible.** Ron Wodaski. 1997. pap. 49.99 (*0-7645-3055-0*) IDG Bks.

***Web Graphics for Dummies.** Dummies Technology Press Staff. 1997. pap. 24.99 (*0-7645-0211-5*) IDG Bks.

***Web Graphics Interactive Course.** Greg Holden. LC 97-16867. 656p. 1997. 49.99 (*1-57169-108-1*, Waite Grp Pr) Sams.

Web Graphics Sourcebook. Ed Tittel et al. LC 96-25882. 752p. 1996. pap. text ed. 44.95 incl. cd-rom (*0-471-15692-2*) Wiley.

***Web Graphics Studio Secrets.** Craig Kanarick & Thomas Muller. 256p. (Orig.). 1997. pap. write for info. (*0-614-26330-1*) IDG Bks.

***Web Graphics Toolkit.** Doctor Ozone. 1997. 39.99 (*1-56205-775-8*) New Riders Pub.

***Web Graphics Tools & Techniques.** Peter Kentie. 320p. (C). 1997. pap. text ed. 39.95 (*0-201-68813-1*) Peachpit Pr.

***Web Graphics Visual Quick Reference.** Bray Jones. 192p. 1997. 19.99 (*0-7897-1137-0*) Mac Comp Pub.

Web Guide. Robert L. Richardson. LC 95-69986. 306p. 1995. 24.99 (*0-7821-1726-0*) Sybex.

Web Handling - 1992. Ed. by J. K. Good. (AMD Ser.: Vol. 149). 144p. 1992. 45.00 (*0-7918-1104-2*, G00748) ASME.

Web Head. Mary J. Mara. 272p. 1995. pap. 24.95 (*1-56609-176-4*) Peachpit Pr.

Web in the Sea: Jung, Sophia, & the Geometry of the Soul. Alice O. Howell. LC 92-56482. 284p. (Orig.). 1993. pap. 14.00 (*0-8356-0688-0*, Quest) Theos Pub Hse.

Web Is the Message: Ten Key Principles of Effective Web Publishing. Bryan Pfaffenberger & Dave Wall. (Illus.). 350p. 1996. pap. 19.95 (*1-56604-370-0*) Ventana Communs.

***Web Journal, Vol. 2, Issue 2.** Ed. by Donna Woouteiler. 1997. pap. write for info. (*0-614-30644-2*) OReilly & Assocs.

***Web Journal, Vol. 2, Issue 3.** Ed. by Donna Woouteiler. 1997. pap. write for info. (*1-56592-329-4*) OReilly & Assocs.

***Web Journal, Vol. 2, Issue 4.** (Orig.). pap. write for info. (*1-56592-349-9*) OReilly & Assocs.

***Web Journal - Summer 1997.** (Orig.). pap. write for info. (*1-56592-348-0*) OReilly & Assocs.

Web Journal of Current Legal Issues: 1995 Yearbook. Ed. by Michael Allen. 365p. 1995. pap. 74.00 (*1-85431-515-3*, Pub. by Blackstone Pr UK) Gaunt.

***Web Management with Microsoft Visual SourceSafe.** Chris Densehikoff. 300p. 1997. 39.99 (*0-7897-1233-4*) Que.

***Web Manual of Style.** Robin Zeff. 1997. 39.99 (*0-7897-1456-6*) Que.

***Web Marketing Cookbook.** Janice M. King et al. LC 96-47738. 384p. 1997. pap. 39.95 incl. cd-rom (*0-471-17911-6*) Wiley.

Web Master: An Introduction to Electronic Publishing on the Global Internet. Dennis Woo. 1995. pap. 19.95 (*0-387-94433-8*) Spr-Verlag.

***Web Mastering for Dummies.** Brenda Kienan. 1997. pap. 19.99 (*0-7645-0171-2*) IDG Bks.

Web Master's Guide: Windows NT Version. Mary Bennion & Geoff Galitz. 1996. pap. 26.95 (*0-13-459397-9*) P-H.

Web Master's Guide - Windows 95. Mary Bennion & Geoff Galitz. 1996. pap. 26.95 (*0-13-459413-4*) P-H.

Web Master's Guide to Cool Web Pages. John Fisher. 432p. 1996. per. 40.00 (*0-7615-0726-4*) Prima Pub.

***Web Motion Encyclopedia.** Jerry Kindall. LC 97-20303. 1997. write for info. (*1-57169-107-3*, Waite Grp Pr) Sams.

***Web Multimedia Development.** David Miller. 600p. 1996. 44.99 (*1-56205-683-2*) Mac Comp Pub.

Web Multimedia for Dummies. Greg Harvey. 1996. pap. text ed. 29.99 incl. cd-rom (*0-7645-0025-2*) IDG Bks.

Web Multimedia Publishing: Create Interactive Internet Programs with the Macintosh. Lauren Steinhauer. 400p. 1996. pap. text ed. 39.95 incl. cd-rom (*0-471-16503-4*) Wiley.

***Web Navigation Design.** (Orig.). pap. write for info. (*1-56592-351-0*) OReilly & Assocs.

***Web Navigator.** Paul Gilster. LC 97-3517. 1997. pap. text ed. 24.95 (*0-471-16495-X*) Wiley.

***Web Objects: Designing, Building, & Deploying Object-Oriented Applications for the Web.** Ron Ben-Natan. (Illus.). 450p. 1997. pap. text ed. 39.95 (*0-07-006281-1*); pap. text ed. 39.95 (*0-07-006366-4*) McGraw.

Web of Adaptation: Bird Studies in the American Topics. David W. Snow. LC 75-24891. (Illus.). 160p. 1976. write for info. (*0-8129-0603-9*, Times Bks) Random.

Web of Adaptation: Bird Studies in the American Tropics. David W. Snow. LC 85-7890. (Comstock Ser.). 192p. (C). 1985. pap. 13.95 (*0-8014-9316-1*) Cornell U Pr.

Web of Angels. John M. Ford. 320p. (Orig.). 1992. mass mkt. 4.99 (*0-8125-0959-5*) Tor Bks.

Web of Being: The Novels of Robert Penn Warren. Barnett Guttenberg. LC 74-26892. 187p. reprint ed. pap. 53.30 (*0-8357-3255-X*, 2039476) Bks Demand.

Web of Belief. 2nd ed. J. S. Ullian & Willard V. Quine. 1978. text ed. write for info. (*0-07-553609-9*) McGraw.

Web of Censorship. Zamir Niazi. 250p. 1995. text ed. 26.00 (*0-19-577543-0*) OUP.

Web of Darkness. Sean Sellers. 1990. pap. 6.95 (*0-932081-26-6*) Victory Hse.

Web of Darkness. large type ed. Helen Brooks. (Harlequin Romance Ser.). 1995. lib. bdg. 18.95 (*0-263-14072-5*, Pub. by Mills & Boon UK) Thorndike Pr.

Web of Deceit. Gary C. King. 320p. 1994. mass mkt. 5.99 (*0-7860-0069-4*, Pinncle Kensgtn) Kensgtn Pub Corp.

Web of Deceit. Catherine Lanigan. 400p. 1987. mass mkt. 4.50 (*0-380-75311-1*) Avon.

***Web of Deceit.** Brenda Sue & Hope Dale. 360p. (Orig.). 1998. mass mkt. 8.99 (*1-889501-65-4*, Appaloosa) Sovereign.

Web of Deception. Jane Peart. LC 95-49284. (Edgecliffe Manor Mystery Ser.: No. 2). 208p. (Orig.). (gr. 10). 1996. pap. 10.99 (*0-8007-5598-7*) Revell.

Web of Disinformation: Churchill's Yugoslav Blunder. David Martin. 464p. 1990. 29.95 (*0-15-180704-3*) HarBrace.

Web of Dreams. V. C. Andrews. Ed. by Linda Marrow. 432p. 1990. pap. 6.99 (*0-671-72949-7*) PB.

Web of Dreams. large type ed. V. C. Andrews. (General Ser.). 581p. 1991. pap. 17.95 (*0-8161-5039-7*, GK Hall); lib. bdg. 20.95 (*0-8161-5038-9*, GK Hall) Thorndike Pr.

Web of Easter Island. Donald Wandrei. 1994. reprint ed. lib. bdg. 29.95 (*1-56849-356-8*) Buccaneer Bks.

Web of Fear. 1994. pap. 5.95 (*0-426-11084-6*, Dr Who) Carol Pub Group.

Web of Gold. Elaine Aitken. (Rainbow Romances Ser.: No. 899). 160p. 1994. 14.95 (*0-7090-4971-4*, Hale-Parkwest) Parkwest Pubns.

Web of Good Manners: Grown-up Manners for Young People. Phyllis Hillings. LC 92-85125. (Illus.). 96p. (J). (gr. 3 up). 1993. 14.95 (*0-9634642-1-3*) Manhattan Pr.

Web of Hate: Inside Canada's Far Right Network. Warren Kinsella. 1996. pap. 13.00 (*0-00-638051-4*) Harper SF.

***Web of Heroes.** Keith Bailey. (Illus.). 224p. 1996. pap. 25.95 (*1-57872-005-2*, 0005BG) Web Games.

Web of Horror. Franklin W. Dixon. Ed. by Ann Greenberg. (Hardy Boys Casefiles Ser.: No. 53). 160p. (Orig.). (J). (gr. 6 up). 1991. mass mkt. 3.99 (*0-671-73089-4*, Archway) PB.

***Web of Horrors.** Keith Bailey & Gino Dykstra. (Illus.). 224p. 1996. pap. 25.95 (*1-57872-004-4*, 0004BG) Web Games.

Web of Inclusion: Building an Organization for Everyone. Sally Helgesen. LC 94-23322. 1995. 24.95 (*0-385-42365-9*) Doubleday.

Web of Inclusion: Building an Organization for Everyone. Sally Helgesen. 320p. 1995. 24.95 (*0-385-42364-0*) Doubleday.

Web of Inclusion: Faculty Helping Faculty. Ed. by Patricia Bayles & Jodi Parks-Doyle. 1995. pap. 29.95 (*0-614-06211-X*) Natl League Nurse.

Web of Indian Life, an Indian Study on Love & Death, Studies from an Eastern Home, Lectures & Articles see Complete Works of Sister Nivedita

***Web of Interactions: Humans & the Land Through Time.** Emily W. Russell. LC 96-37098. 1997. write for info. (*0-300-06830-1*) Yale U Pr.

Web of Leadership Vol. 3: The Presidency in Higher Education. William G. Tierney. LC 88-13180. (Contemporary Ethnographic Studies: Vol. 3). 241p. 1988. 73.25 (*0-89232-959-9*) Jai Pr.

Web of Life. Melvin Berger. Ed. by Natalie Lunis. (Ranger Rick Science Spectacular Ser.). 16p. (J). (gr. 2-4). 1994. pap. 14.95 (*1-56784-206-2*) Newbridge Comms.

***Web of Life.** Ed. by M. Biswas et al. (Perspectives in Science & Engineering Ser.: Vol. 1). 224p. 1997. text ed. 58.00 (*3-7186-5927-1*, Harwood Acad Pubs) Gordon & Breach.

Web of Life. John Davidson. 408p. (Orig.). pap. 29.95 (*0-8464-4312-0*) Beekman Pubs.

Web of Life. John Davidson. 191p. 1988. pap. 19.95 (*0-85207-199-X*, Pub. by C W Daniel UK) Natl Bk Netwk.

Web of Life. Robert Herrick. 321p. 1980. reprint ed. lib. bdg. 15.95 (*0-89968-189-1*, Lghtyr Pr) Buccaneer Bks.

Web of Life. Robert Herrick. LC 75-104482. 356p. reprint ed. lib. bdg. 14.75 (*0-8398-0780-5*) Irvington.

Web of Life. Robert Herrick. (Collected Works of Robert Herrick). 1988. reprint ed. lib. bdg. 79.00 (*0-7812-1264-2*) Rprt Serv.

Web of Life: A New Scientific Understanding of Living Systems. Fritjof Capra. LC 96-12576. (Illus.). 304p. 1996. 23.95 (*0-385-47675-2*, Anchor NY) Doubleday.

***Web of Life: A New Understanding of Living Systems.** Fritjof Capra. 358p. 1997. pap. 14.00 (*0-385-47676-0*, Anchor NY) Doubleday.

Web of Life: Student Book. Melvin Berger. Ed. by Natalie Lunis. (Ranger Rick Science Spectacular Ser.). (Illus.). 16p. (Orig.). (J). (gr. 2-4). 1996. pap. write for info. (*1-56784-231-3*) Newbridge Comms.

***Web of Life: Theme Pack.** Melvin Berger. Ed. by Natalie Lunis. (Ranger Rick Science Spectacular Ser.). (Illus.). (Orig.). (J). (gr. 2-4). 1996. pap. write for info. (*1-56784-276-3*) Newbridge Comms.

Web of Life: Weaving the Values That Sustain Us. Richard Louv. (Illus.). 250p. 1996. 14.95 (*1-57324-036-2*) Conari Press.

Web of Life see Collected Works of Robert Herrick

***Web of Light: Rites for Witches in the New Age.** Morwyn. 256p. 1996. 19.95 (*0-924608-17-X*) Schiffer.

Web of Literacy. Sara. 1996. pap. text ed. 20.00 (*0-312-14979-4*) St Martin.

Web of Loving Lies. Barbara Leigh. (Historical Ser.). 1993. mass mkt. 3.99 (*0-373-28777-1*, 1-28777-0) Harlequin Bks.

Web of Meaning: Essays on Writing, Teaching, Learning, & Thinking. Janet Emig. Ed. by Dixie Goswami & Maureen Butler. LC 83-2667. 178p. (Orig.). (C). 1983. pap. text ed. 21.50 (*0-86709-047-2*, 0047) Boynton Cook Pubs.

***Web of Memories.** large type ed. Clare Lavenham. (Magna Large Print Ser.). 248p. 1997. 27.50 (*0-7505-1060-9*) Ulverscroft.

Web of Metaphor: Studies in the Imagery of Montaigne's Essays. Carol Clark. LC 77-93404. (French Forum Monographs: No. 7). 191p. (Orig.). 1978. pap. 10.95 (*0-917058-06-2*) French Forum.

Web of Murder. Jonathan Troy. 1964. pap. 5.25 (*0-8222-1227-7*) Dramatists Play.

***Web of Poverty: Psychosocial Perspectives.** Anne-Marie Ambert. LC 97-14968. 1997. write for info. (*0-7890-0231-0*); pap. write for info. (*0-7890-0232-9*) Haworth Pr.

Web of Progress: Private Values & Public Styles in Boston & Charleston, 1828-1843. William H. Pease & Jane H. Pease. LC 91-4003. 352p. 1991. pap. 20.00 (*0-8203-1390-4*) U of Ga Pr.

Web of Relationship: Women in the Short Fiction of Mary Wilkins Freeman. Mary R. Reichardt. LC 91-32352. 208p. 1992. 32.50 (*0-87805-555-X*) U Pr of Miss.

Web of Smoke. Erin Grady. 288p. (Orig.). 1994. mass mkt. 5.50 (*0-380-77720-7*) Avon.

Web of Southern Social Relations: Women, Family, & Education. Ed. by Walter J. Fraser, Jr. et al. LC 85-1054. 280p. 1987. pap. 18.00 (*0-8203-0942-7*) U of Ga Pr.

***Web of Stars.** Keith Bailey. Ed. by Gino Dykstra & Fritzen Ravenswood. (Illus.). 208p. (Orig.). 1995. pap. 25.95 (*1-57872-002-8*, 0002BG) Web Games.

***Web of Stories.** Ford. 1997. pap. text ed. 39.33 (*0-13-455651-8*) P-H.

Web of the Romulans. M. S. Murdock. (Star Trek Ser.: No. 10). 1989. mass mkt. 5.50 (*0-671-70093-6*) PB.

Web of the Universe. E. L. Gardner. 115p. 1993. reprint ed. spiral bd. 8.50 (*0-7873-0343-7*) Hlth Research.

Web of the Universe: Jung, the "New Physics" & Human Spirituality. John Hitchcock. (Jung & Spirituality Ser.). 1991. pap. 14.95 (*0-8091-3267-2*) Paulist Pr.

Web of Their Lives: Macbeth & Human Greatness. Arthur T. Levinson. 120p. 1984. pap. 7.95 (*0-9613268-0-8*) Byrnam Pr.

Web of Treason. large type ed. Olive Fish. (Dales Romance Ser.). 319p. 1993. pap. 17.99 (*1-85389-396-X*) Ulverscroft.

Web of Victory: Grant at Vicksburg. Earl S. Miers. LC 84-9717. (Illus.). 320p. 1984. pap. 14.95 (*0-8071-1199-6*) La State U Pr.

Web of Violence: From Interpersonal to Global. Jennifer E. Turpin. 224p. 1996. text ed. 39.95 (*0-252-02261-0*); pap. text ed. 15.95 (*0-252-06561-1*) U of Ill Pr.

***Web of Water: Life in Redwood Creek.** Maya Khosla. LC 96-78728. (Illus.). 72p. (Orig.). 1997. pap. 10.95 (*1-883869-27-7*) Gldn Gate Natl Parks Assoc.

***Web of Words Bk. 1: Selected Poetry & Prose from ShowEMall! Writers' Block.** Gail Janssen et al. (Illus.). 100p. 1997. pap. 15.00 (*0-9657917-0-X*) Show Em.

Web Offset Press Operating. 4th ed. GATF Staff. (Illus.). 352p. 1996. text ed. 60.00 (*0-88362-181-9*) Graphic Arts Tech Found.

Web Offset Printers, Heatset see 1996 PIA Ratios

Web Page Creative Techniques. Hayden Development Group Staff. 528p. 1996. pap. text ed. 50.00 (*1-56830-307-6*) Hayden.

Web Page Design: A Different Multimedia. Mary Morris. 352p. 1996. pap. 24.95 (*0-13-239880-X*) P-H.

Web Page Design Cookbook: All the Ingredients You Need to Creat 5-Star Web Pages. William K. Horton et al. LC 95-41350. 624p. 1995. pap. text ed., pap. 34.95 incl. cd-rom (*0-471-13039-7*) Wiley.

***Web Page Essentials.** Paul Zimmerman. 1996. 22.99 (*1-57576-368-0*) Sams.

Web Page Recipe Book. Barrie Sosinsky. 284p. 1996. pap. 29.95 incl. cd-rom (*0-13-460296-X*) P-H.

Web Page Wizardry. Dick Oliver. 448p. 1996. pap. text ed. 39.99 incl. cd-rom (*1-57521-092-4*, SamsNet Bks) Sams.

***Web Page Workbook: Academic Edition.** LC 97-7625. 1997. 19.95 (*1-887902-21-X*) Franklin Beedle.

Web Power with Visual Basic Script & Activex. Ken Spencer. 1996. pap. 34.99 (*0-7645-8010-8*) IDG Bks.

Web Programming. Steve Weakley & Kris Jamsa. 600p. 1996. pap. 49.95 incl. cd-rom (*1-884133-27-4*) Jamsa Pr.

***Web Programming Desktop Reference 6-in-1.** Mike Afergan et al. 1104p. 1996. 49.99 (*0-7897-1028-5*) Mac Comp Pub.

***Web Programming Handbook: HTML, CGI & Java.** Gary Cornell & Marty Hall. 600p. 1997. pap. 44.95 (*0-13-625666-X*) P-H.

***Web Programming Languages Sourcebook.** Gordon McComb. LC 97-3988. 1997. pap. text ed. 49.95 incl. cd-rom (*0-471-17576-5*) Wiley.

Web Programming Secrets with HTML, CGI, & PERL5. Ed Tittel. 1996. pap. 44.99 (*1-56884-848-X*) IDG Bks.

***Web Programming Unleashed.** Bob Breedlove. 950p. 1996. 49.99 (*1-57521-117-3*) Mac Comp Pub.

Web Programming with Java. Sams Development Group Staff. 512p. 1996. pap. text ed. 39.99 incl. cd-rom (*1-57521-113-0*, SamsNet Bks) Sams.

***Web Programming With Microsoft Tools 6 in 1.** Que Development Group, Staff. 1000p. 1997. 59.99 (*0-7897-1215-6*) Que.

Web Programming with Visual BASIC. Craig Eddy & Brad Haasch. 400p. 1996. 39.99 (*1-57521-106-8*) Mac Comp Pub.

***Web Programming with Visual BASIC.** 2nd ed. Craig Eddy & Brad Haasch. 500p. 1996. 39.99 (*1-57521-248-X*, SamsNet Bks) Mac Comp Pub.

Web Programming with Visual Basic Script. Daniel Mezick. 500p. Date not set. pap. text ed. 39.99 incl. cd-rom (*1-57521-116-5*, SamsNet Bks) Sams.

Web Programming with Visual J++ Sams Development Group Staff. 600p. 1997. pap. text ed. 39.99 incl. cd-rom (*1-57521-174-2*, SamsNet Bks) Sams.

***Web Psychos, Stalkers, & Pranksters: How to Protect Yourself in Cyberspace.** Michael Banks. 1997. pap. 24.99 (*0-614-28446-5*); pap. text ed. 24.99 (*1-57610-137-1*) Coriolis Grp.

Web Publisher's Construction Kit with VRML/Live 3D: Creating 3D Web Worlds. David Fox & Phillip Shaddock. LC 96-7214. 720p. (Orig.). 1996. pap. 39.99 incl. cd-rom (*1-57169-068-9*, Waite Grp Pr) Sams.

Web Publisher's Constuction Kit with HTML 3.2: Publishing Your Own HTML Pages on the Internet. David Fox & Troy Downing. (Web Publisher's Construction Kits Ser.). (Illus.). 936p. (Orig.). 1996. 44.99 (*1-57169-040-9*) Mac Comp Pub.

Web Publishers Design Guide for Macintosh. Mary Fahey. 1995. pap. 34.99 incl. cd-rom (*1-883577-63-2*) Coriolis Grp.

***Web Publishers Design Guide for Windows.** 2nd ed. Mary Jo Fahey. 1997. pap. text ed. 39.99 (*1-57610-109-6*) Coriolis Grp.

Web Publishers Design Guide for Windows 95. Mary Fahey. 1995. pap. 34.99 incl. cd-rom (*1-883577-61-6*) Coriolis Grp.

***Web Publishers Guide to Fusion.** Dan Shafer. 1997. pap. text ed. 34.99 incl. cd-rom (*1-57610-124-X*) Coriolis Grp.

***Web Publisher's Illustrated Quick Reference.** Ralph Grabowski. LC 96-25481. (Illus.). 272p. 1996. pap. 34.95 (*0-387-94831-7*) Spr-Verlag.

Web Publishers 3D & Animation Design Guide for Macintosh. Mary J. Fahey. 1996. pap. text ed. 34.99 incl. cd-rom (*1-883577-94-2*) Coriolis Grp.

Web Publishers 3D & Animation Design Guide for Windows. Mary J. Fahey. 1996. pap. text ed. 34.99 incl. cd-rom (*1-883577-93-4*) Coriolis Grp.

***Web Publishing.** Daniel Speers. (C). 1998. pap. text ed. write for info. (*0-201-30420-1*) Addison-Wesley.

***Web Publishing: Strategies for Making Money Online.** 292p. 1995. 1,250.00 (*0-614-25703-4*) Simba Info.

***Web Publishing: Strategies for Making Money Online.** 2nd ed. 1997. write for info. (*0-614-25704-2*) Simba Info.

***Web Publishing & Programming Resource Kit.** 3300p. 1997. 149.99 (*1-57521-239-0*, SamsNet Bks) Sams.

***Web Publishing Design Guide for Macintosh.** 2nd ed. Mary J. Fahey. 1997. pap. text ed. 39.99 (*1-57610-108-6*) Coriolis Grp.

W

***Web Publishing for Teachers.** Bard Williams. 1997. pap. text ed. 24.99 (0-7645-0172-0) IDG Bks.

Web Publishing Unleashed. William Stanek. 1996. 49.99 incl. cd-rom (0-614-14455-8) Macmillan.

***Web Publishing Unleashed: Professional Reference Edition.** William Stanek. 1200p. 1996. 69.99 incl. cd-rom (1-57521-198-X, SamsNet Bks) Sams.

***Web Publishing with Activex Controls.** Doug Lloyd. LC 96-38077. 1997. pap. 39.99 incl. cd-rom (1-56604-647-5) Ventana Communs.

Web Publishing with Adobe Acrobat & PDF w/CD-ROM. Bruce Page & Diana Holm. LC 96-18035. 352p. 1996. pap. 39.95 (0-471-14948-9) Wiley.

Web Publishing with Adobe Pagemill. Daniel Gray. LC 96-19509. 450p. 1996. pap. text ed. 34.99 incl. cd-rom (1-56604-458-8) Ventana Communs.

***Web Publishing with Corel WordPerfect Suite 8: The Official Guide.** Jeff Hadfield. 1997. pap. 34.99 (0-07-882348-X) Osborne-McGraw.

***Web Publishing with FrontPage 97.** 2nd ed. Martin S. Matthews. 1997. pap. text ed. 29.99 (0-07-882312-9) Osborne-McGraw.

***Web Publishing with Macromedia Backstage.** R. Shammms Mortier. LC 96-35966. 500p. 1997. 49.99 (1-56604-598-3) Ventana Communs.

***Web Publishing with Microsoft Frontpage 3.** 11th ed. Barrie Sosinsky. (VCG Ventana Press Ser.). 1997. pap. text ed. 34.99 incl. cd-rom (1-56604-742-0) Ventana Communs.

Web Publishing with Microsoft FrontPage 97. Charles Brannon. LC 96-37901. 500p. 1996. pap. text ed. 34.99 incl. cd-rom (1-56604-478-2) Ventana Communs.

Web Publishing with Netscape for Busy People, No. 6. Christian Crumlish & Malcolm Humes. (Busy People Bks.). 304p. 1996. pap. text ed. 22.95 (0-07-882144-4) Osborne-McGraw.

***Web Publishing with QuarkImmedia.** Roger Sperberg. 450p. 1996. 39.99 (1-56604-525-8) Ventana Communs.

***Web Scripting Secret Weapons.** Scott Walter. 416p. 1996. pap. text ed. 39.99 incl. cd-rom (0-7897-0947-3) Que.

***Web Scripting Unleashed.** Sams Development Group Staff. 800p. Date not set. 49.99 (1-57521-182-3) Mac Comp Pub.

Web Search Strategies. Bryan Pfaffenberger. (Illus.). 416p. 1995. pap. 29.95 incl. disk (1-55828-470-2) MIS Press.

***Web Security & Commerce.** Simson Garfinkel. 500p. 1997. pap. text ed. 32.95 (1-56592-269-7) OReilly & Assocs.

***Web Security Sourcebook.** Aviel D. Rubin et al. 352p. 1997. pap. 29.99 (0-471-18148-X) Wiley.

Web Server Construction Kit: Macintosh Edition. Stewart Buskirk. 400p. 1996. pap. text ed. 45.00 incl. cd-rom (1-56830-271-1) Hayden.

***Web Server Construction Kit for Windows 95 & NT 4.** David Wolfe. 1997. 49.99 (0-7897-1320-9) Que.

Web Server Handbook. Peter L. Palmer. 1996. pap. 34.95 (0-13-239930-X) P-H.

Web Server Handbook: The Complete Guide to Setting Up the Web Server. Cynthia Chin-Lee & Comet. 700p. 1997. pap. text ed. 39.95 (0-07-882215-7) McGraw.

***Web Server Technologies, Professional Reference.** Phil Beetley. 1997. pap. text ed. 50.00 (1-56205-772-3) New Riders Pub.

Web Server Technology: The Advanced Guide for World Web Information Providers. Nancy Yeager. LC 96-16330. 1996. pap. text ed. 34.95 (1-55860-376-X) Morgan Kaufmann.

***Web Server Toolkit for Windows 95 & NT 4.** David Wolfe & Rolf Crozier. 550p. 1997. pap. 39.99 incl. cd-rom (0-471-18332-6) Wiley.

***Web Sights & Sounds Bible.** Philip Shaddock. 1997. pap. text ed. 49.99 incl. cd-rom (0-7645-3080-1) IDG Bks.

***Web Sights & Sounds Bible.** Phillip Shaddock. 900p. (Orig.). 1997. pap. write for info. (0-614-26321-2) IDG Bks.

Web Site Administrators Survival Guide. Erin Zhu. 784p. 1996. pap. text ed. 49.99 incl. cd-rom (1-57521-018-5, SamsNet Bks) Sams.

***Web Site Construction.** Andy Hanson. 1997. pap. 32.95 (0-614-28453-8) Franklin Beedle.

***Web Site Construction: From the Ground Up.** Andy Hanson. 1997. pap. text ed. 32.95 (1-887902-22-8) Franklin Beedle.

Web Site Construction Kit for Windows NT. 500p. 1996. 49.99 (1-57521-047-9, SamsNet Bks) Sams.

Web Site Construction Kit for Windows 95. Christopher Brown & Zimmerman. 560p. 1996. 49.99 (1-57521-072-X, SamsNet Bks) Sams.

Web Site Development Kit with Microsoft Resources. James Townsend. 784p. 1996. pap. text ed. 49.99 incl. cd-rom (1-57521-095-9, SamsNet Bks) Sams.

***Web Site Management Excellence.** Linda Brigman. 300p. 1996. 29.99 (0-7897-0911-2) Mac Comp Pub.

Web Site Programming with Java. D. Harms. (Illus.). 336p. 1996. pap. 39.95 incl. cd-rom (0-07-912986-2) McGraw.

***Web Site Programming with Java 1.1.** David Harms et al. (Illus.). 604p. 1997. pap. text ed., pap. 39.95 incl. cd-rom (0-07-913178-6) McGraw.

Web Site Review Index: An Index to Reviews, Rankings, Ratings, & Other Descriptive Commentary on World Wide Web Sites. Ed. by Dennis LaBeau. 1998. pap. 85.00 (0-7808-0096-6) Omnigraphics Inc.

Web Site Source Book: A Guide to Major U. S. Businesses, Organizations, & Other Information Resources on the World Web. Ed. by Darren L. Smith. 400p. 1996. pap. 65.00 (0-7808-0095-8) Omnigraphics Inc.

***Web Site Source Book, 1997 Edition: A Guide to Major U. S. Businesses, Organizations, Agencies, Institutions, & Other Information Resources on the World Wide Web.** 2nd ed. Ed. by Darren L. Smith. Date not set. pap. 65.00 (0-7808-0169-5) Omnigraphics Inc.

***Web Site Source Book 1998: A Guide to Major U. S. Businesses, Organizations, Agencies, Institutions, & Other Information Resources on the World Web.** 3rd ed. 1000p. 1997. pap. 85.00 (0-7808-0283-7, B2001-1998) Omnigraphics Inc.

Web Site Stats: Tracking Hits & Analyzing Web Traffic. Rick Stout. 350p. 1996. pap. text ed. 29.95 (0-07-882236-X) Osborne-McGraw.

Web Site Wizardry. Marianne Krcma. 1996. pap. text ed. 34.99 incl. cd-rom (1-883577-87-X) Coriolis Grp.

***Web Sites for Health Professionals.** Mark Kittleson. 60p. 1997. pap. 11.95 (0-7637-0511-X) Jones & Bartlett.

***Web Storefront Construction Kit.** Raymond Novello. 450p. 1997. 39.99 (0-7897-1265-2) Que.

***Web Style Sheets.** Bryan McCormick. LC 97-20221. 400p. 1997. 39.99 (1-56205-740-5) Mac Comp Pub.

***Web-Teaching: A Guide to Designing Interactive Teaching for the World Wide Web.** David W. Brooks. LC 97-1861. (Innovations in Science Education & Technology Ser.). (Illus.). 236p. (C). 1997. pap. 25.00 (0-306-45552-8, Plenum Pr) Plenum.

Web That Has No Weaver. Ted J. Kaptchuk. 432p. 1984. pap. text ed. 18.95 (0-8092-2933-1) Contemp Bks.

***Web Tips: For Beginners & Professionals.** Dave Reed. (Illus.). 40p. (Orig.). 1997. write for info. (0-9637448-3-6) Comments Friends.

Web to Catch a Spider. large type ed. Cyril A. Joyce. (Linford Mystery Library). 304p. 1992. pap. 15.99 (0-7089-7238-1) Ulverscroft.

***Web Video Toolkit.** Martin A. Nemzow. (Illus.). 416p. 1997. pap. text ed. 29.95 (0-07-046404-9) McGraw.

***Web Wealth: How to Turn the World Wide Web into a Cash Hose for You & Your Business...Whatever You're Selling.** Jeffrey Lant. 248p. 1997. pap. 24.95 (0-940374-37-4) JLA Pubns.

***Web Weavers & Other Spiders.** Bobbie Kalman. (Crabapple Ser.). 32p. (J). 1996. pap. 5.95 (0-86505-732-X) Crabtree Pub Co.

***Web Weavers & Other Spiders.** Bobbie Kalman. LC 96-42408. (Crabapple Ser.). 32p. (J). 1996. lib. bdg. 18.08 (0-86505-632-3) Crabtree Pub Co.

Web Weaving: Designing & Managing an Effective Web Site. Eric Tilton et al. 512p. (C). 1996. pap. text ed. 24.95 (0-201-48959-7) Addison-Wesley.

***Web Without a Weaver: How the Internet Is Shaping Our Future.** Victor Grey. LC 97-91877. 248p. (Orig.). 1997. pap. 14.95 (0-9658516-0-5) Open Heart.

Web Works: A Norton Pocket Guide. Martin Irvine. 150p. 1996. pap. 15.00 (0-393-31520-7) Norton.

***Web Yellow Pages Simplified.** Ruth Maran. 1996. pap. 29.99 (0-7645-6005-0) IDG Bks.

Webb for All Seasons: Poems by Charles Harper Webb. 76p. 1992. 23.95 (0-930090-57-8); pap. 8.95 (0-930090-59-4) Applezaba.

Webb for All Seasons: Poems by Charles Harper Webb. deluxe ed. 76p. 1992. 30.00 (0-930090-58-6) Applezaba.

Webb on Watercolor. Frank Webb. (Illus.). 160p. 1994. pap. 22.95 (0-89134-478-0, North Lght Bks) F & W Pubns Inc.

Webb Report Binders, Years 1985 thru 1987 Vols. I-IV: The Webb Report Newsletters. Susan L. Webb. 114p. 1985. ring bd. 59.95 (1-878269-22-4) Pacific Resource.

Webber Quartet, 4 Vols. deluxe ed. Helen Webber. (J). (gr. k-6). Set. boxed 35.00 (0-8392-3070-2) Astor-Honor.

Webbing. Drummond Hadley. LC 67-20765. (Writing Ser.: No. 15). 38p. (Orig.). 1967. pap. 2.00 (0-87704-006-0) Four Seasons Foun.

Webbing Way: Integrating the Curriculum Through Writing. Susan Hughes. (Illus.). 198p. (Orig.). 1994. teacher ed., pap. 19.00 (1-895411-63-7) Peguis Pubs Ltd.

Webbing with Literature: Creating Story Maps with Children's Books. 2nd ed. Karen D. Bromley. 1995. pap. text ed. 30.00 (0-205-16975-9) Allyn.

Webbs & Their Work. Ed. by Margaret I. Cole. LC 84-22459. (Illus.). xvi, 304p. 1985. reprint ed. text ed. 59.75 (0-313-24677-7, COWW, Greenwood Pr) Greenwood.

Webb's Guide to the Official Records of the Colony of Natal. 3rd rev. ed. Compiled by Jennifer Verbeek et al. 412p. 1984. 49.95 (0-86980-363-8, Pub. by Univ Natal Pr SA) Intl Spec Bk.

Webb's Guide to the Official Records of the Colony of Natal. 3rd rev. ed. Compiled by Jennifer Verbeek et al. 1984. pap. 19.95 (0-86980-387-5, Pub. by Univ Natal Pr SA) Intl Spec Bk.

***Webcaster Macintosh.** Bob Levitus & Jeff Evans. (Illus.). 500p. 1997. pap. text ed. 39.95 (0-12-445606-5, AP Prof) Acad Pr.

***Webcaster Windows.** Bob Levitus & Jeff Evans. (Illus.). 500p. 1997. pap. text ed., pap. 39.95 incl. cd-rom (0-12-445604-9, AP Prof) Acad Pr.

***Webcasting: Broadcast Marketing over the Net.** Jessica Keyes. LC 97-8025. (Illus.). 320p. 1997. pap. text ed. 24.95 (0-07-034581-3) McGraw.

***Webcasting Handbook.** Kitty Wells & Frank Schwartz. 1997. 39.99 (0-7897-1305-5) Macmillan.

WEB/CGI Scripting with PERL: A Programmer's Guide to the Common Gateway Interface & Other WEB Resources. Lincoln D. Stein. (C). 1998. pap. text ed. write for info. (0-201-63489-9) Addison-Wesley.

Webcraft: Dynamic Content Using HTML. Eyzaguirre. 1995. pap. text ed. 29.95 (1-56276-322-9, Ziff-Davis Pr) Que.

Webelos Den Activities. (Illus.). 96p. 1988. pap. 3.15 (0-8395-3853-7, 33853) BSA.

Webelos Scout Book. rev. ed. Boy Scouts of America Staff. (Illus.). 416p. (J). (gr. 4-6). 1987. pap. 4.95 (0-8395-3235-0, 33235) BSA.

Weber. Anthony Friese-Greene. (Illustrated Lives of the Great Composers Ser.). (Illus.). 144p. 1996. 14.95 (0-7119-2081-8, OP 45665) Omnibus NY.

Weber. 2nd ed. William Saunders. LC 69-11670. (Music Reprint Ser.). 1970. reprint ed. lib. bdg. 42.50 (0-306-71200-8) Da Capo.

Weber! The American Adventure of Captain Charles M. Weber. James M. Shebl. LC 92-61559. (Illus.). 192p. (Orig.). 1993. 35.00 (0-9621586-0-7) Sn Joaquin Cty Hist Soc.

Weber! The American Adventure of Captain Charles M. Weber. Wayne M. Shebl. LC 92-61559. (Illus.). 192p. (Orig.). 1993. pap. 19.95 (0-9621586-1-5) Sn Joaquin Cty Hist Soc.

Weber & Dellorto Carburetor Expert. Des Hammill. (Illus.). 96p. 1996. pap. text ed. 17.95 (1-874105-67-7, Pub. by Veloce Pub UK) Motorbooks Intl.

Weber & Islam: A Critical Study. Bryan S. Turner. 1978. reprint ed. pap. 15.95 (0-7100-8942-2, RKP) Routledge.

Weber & Rickert: Concept Formation in the Social Sciences. Guy Oakes. (Studies in Contemporary German Social Thought). 200p. 1988. 24.00 (0-262-15034-4) MIT Pr.

Weber & Rickert: Concept Formation in the Social Sciences. Guy Oakes. (Studies in Contemporary German Social Thought). 200p. 1990. reprint ed. pap. 9.95 (0-262-65037-1) MIT Pr.

Weber & the Marxist World. Johannes Weiss. Tr. by Elizabeth King-Utz & Michael J. King. (International Library of Sociology). 320p. 1986. text ed. 60.00 (0-7100-9981-9, 99819, RKP) Routledge.

Weber, Irrationality, & Social Order. Alan Sica. 350p. 1988. 45.00 (0-520-06149-7) U CA Pr.

Weber, Irrationality & Social Order. Alan Sica. 321p. 1988. pap. 14.00 (0-520-07200-6) U CA Pr.

Weber-Marx Dialogue. Ed. by Robert J. Antonio & Ronald M. Glassman. LC 85-3148. xxii, 336p. 1985. 35.00 (0-7006-0265-8); pap. 14.95 (0-7006-0312-3) U Pr of KS.

Weber River: A Study of Grass Roots Democracy in Water Development. Richard W. Sadler & Richard C. Roberts. (Illus.). 300p. 1993. 26.95 (0-87421-164-6) Utah St U Pr.

WEBER! The American Adventure of Captain Charles M. Weber. James M. Shebl. (Illus.). 150p. 1988. write for info. (0-318-62769-8) Sn Joaquin Cty Hist Soc.

Weber, the Ideal Type & Contemporary Social Theory. Susan J. Hekman. LC 82-40381. 223p. 1983. reprint ed. pap. 63.60 (0-608-00894-X, 2061688) Bks Demand.

Weberian & Marxian Analysis of Law: Development & Functions of Law in a Capitalist Mode of Production. Dragan Milovanovic. 240p. 1989. text ed. 52.95 (0-566-07000-6, Pub. by Dartmth Pub UK) Ashgate Pub Co.

Weberian Sociological Theory. Randall Collins. (Illus.). 320p. 1986. pap. text ed. 19.95 (0-521-31426-7) Cambridge U Pr.

Weberian Theory of Human Society: Structure & Evolution. Walter L. Wallace. LC 93-37868. (Arnold & Caroline Rose Monograph Series of the American Sociological Association). 335p. (C). 1994. text ed. 59.00 (0-8135-2069-X) Rutgers U Pr.

Webern & the Lyric Impulse: Songs & Fragments on Poems of George Trakl. Anne C. Schreffler. (Studies in Musical Genesis & Structure). (Illus.). 272p. 1995. text ed. 59.00 (0-19-816224-3) OUP.

Webern Studies. Ed. by Kathryn Bailey. (Illus.). 300p. (C). 1996. text ed. 64.95 (0-521-47526-0) Cambridge U Pr.

Weber's Electrodynamics, 66. A. Torres Assis. LC 94-32309. (Fundamental Theories of Physics Ser.). 288p. (C). 1994. lib. bdg. 137.50 (0-7923-3137-0) Kluwer Ac.

Weber's Protestant Ethic: Origins, Evidence, Contexts. Ed. by Hartmut Lehmann & Guenther Roth. (Publications of the German Historical Institute, Washington, D.C.). 300p. (C). 1993. text ed. 59.95 (0-521-44062-9) Cambridge U Pr.

Weber's Protestant Ethic: Origins, Evidence, Contexts. Ed. by Hartmut Lehmann & Guenther Roth. (Publications of the German Historical Institute, Washington, D.C.). 416p. (C). 1995. pap. text ed. 19.95 (0-521-55829-8) Cambridge U Pr.

Webfoot Reader. 2nd ed. University of Oregon Staff. 282p. 1991. pap. 22.00 (0-536-58625-X) Ginn Pr.

Webfoot Volunteer: The Diary of William M. Hilleary, 1864-1866. fac. ed. William M. Hilleary. Ed. by Herbert B. Nelson & Preston E. Onstad. LC 65-65228. (Oregon State Monographs, Studies in History: No. 5). 260p. 1965. reprint ed. pap. 74.10 (0-608-01022-7, 2061880) Bks Demand.

Webheads' Guide to Netscape. B. Heslop & Angell David. 1996. pap. 30.00 (0-679-76892-0) Random.

Webley Story. William C. Dowell. (Illus.). 337p. 1987. 59.95 (0-939683-04-0) Armory Pubns.

***Webmaster.** Dennis Woo & Ray Cole. 1996. 24.95 (0-614-20324-4) Spr-Verlag.

***Webmaster Engineer Certification Handbook.** Net Guru Technologies, Inc. Staff. 1997. pap. text ed. 74.95 incl. cd-rom (0-07-913287-1) McGraw.

Webmaster Expert Solutions. Que Development Group Staff. 1224p. 1996. pap. text ed. 59.99 incl. cd-rom (0-7897-0801-9) Que.

***Webmaster in a Nutshell: A Desktop Quick Reference.** Stephen Spainhour & Valerie Quercia. (Illus.). 394p. (Orig.). 1996. pap. 19.95 (1-56592-229-8) OReilly & Assocs.

***Webmaster Macintosh.** 2nd ed. Bob Levitus & Jeff Evans. (Illus.). 525p. 1997. pap. 34.95 (0-12-445602-2, AP Prof) Acad Pr.

***Webmaster Resource Library.** Dean Rositano & Robert Rositano. 1996. 150.00 (0-7897-0872-8) Mac Comp Pub.

Webmaster Strategies. Michael Sullivan-Trainor. 1996. pap. 29.99 (1-56884-820-X) IDG Bks.

***Webmaster Windows.** 2nd ed. Bob Levitus & Jeff Evans. (Illus.). 490p. 1997. pap. 34.95 incl. cd-rom (0-12-445600-6, AP Prof) Acad Pr.

Webmastering Live Wire Pro. Lipshultz. 1996. pap. text ed. 39.99 incl. audio compact disk (0-7821-1933-6) Sybex.

Webmastering RealAudio Server 2. Jae Yang. 1996. pap. text ed. 39.99 incl. cd-rom (0-7821-1932-8) Sybex.

Webmaster's Guide to HTML: For Advanced Web Developers. N. Muller. 1996. pap. text ed., pap. 34.95 incl. disk (0-07-912273-6) McGraw.

Webmaster's Guide to Internet Connectivity. Eit. 560p. 1996. pap. 35.00 (1-56205-574-7) New Riders Pub.

***Webmaster's Guide to Lotus Domino.** James D. Cimino. (Illus.). 400p. (Orig.). 1997. pap. 39.95 (1-886801-11-8) Chrles River Media.

Webmaster's Guide to Plug Ins. Que Development Group Staff. 528p. 1996. pap. text ed. 49.99 incl. cd-rom (0-7897-0845-0) Que.

Webmaster's Guide to VB Script. Jim Keogh. (Illus.). 254p. 1996. pap. 29.95 (0-12-703875-2) Acad Pr.

Webmaster's Handbook: Perl Power for Your WWW Server. Christian Neuss & Johan Vromans. (Illus.). 200p. 1996. pap. 29.95 incl. cd-rom (1-85032-253-8) ITCP.

***Webmasters Mojo.** Dan Brown. 1997. pap. 49.99 incl. cd-rom (1-56604-638-6) Ventana Communs.

Webmaster's Professional Reference. New Riders Development Group Staff. (Illus.). 1248p. (Orig.). 1996. pap. text ed. 55.00 (1-56205-473-2) New Riders Pub.

***Webmaster's Toolkit.** Michael Erwin. 1997. pap. text ed., pap. 39.99 incl. cd-rom (0-07-882334-X) Osborne-McGraw.

***WebNet 96: World Conference of the Web Society Proceedings.** Ed. by Hermann Maurer. 602p. (Orig.). 1996. pap. write for info. (1-880094-24-X) Assn Advan Comput Educ.

***Webonomics: The Nine Essential Principles for Growing Your Business on the World Wide Web.** Evan I. Schwartz. LC 96-47780. 256p. 1997. 25.00 (0-553-06172-0) Broadway BDD.

Webs & Arrows. Russell N. Barton. (YA). 1995. 19.95 (0-9650434-0-1, 0010); pap. write for info. (0-9650434-1-X, 0010) Ridgewood MN.

Webs & Scales: Physical & Ecological Processes in Marine Fish Recruitment. Michael M. Mullin. LC 93-10188. (Washington Sea Grant Ser.). 144p. 1993. 25.00 (0-295-97244-0); pap. 15.00 (0-295-97245-9) U of Wash Pr.

***Webs Basic Gaming System.** 2nd ed. Keith Bailey. Ed. & Illus. by Fritzen Ravenswood. 86p. (Orig.). 1996. pap. 14.95 (1-57872-001-X, 0001BG) Web Games.

Webs of Influence. John Soper & Mimi Soper. 48p. 1995. pap. 5.99 (0-87509-589-5) Chr Pubns.

***Webs of Life - Group 1, 4 vols.** P. Fleisher. (Illus.). 40p. (J). (gr. 2-4). 1997. lib. bdg. write for info. (0-7614-0435-X, Benchmark NY) Marshall Cavendish.

WebServer Construction Kit for Mac. Stewart Buzkirk. 1996. 45.00 incl. cd-rom (0-614-14448-5) Macmillan.

***Website Graphics: The Best of Global Site Design.** Willem Velthoven & Jorinde Seijdel. LC 97-60326. (Illus.). 192p. 1997. 55.00 (0-500-01788-3) Thames Hudson.

***Website Management & Internet Advertising Trends.** (Illus.). (Orig.). per. write for info. (1-56318-052-9) Assn Natl Advertisers.

***Website Pro, Version 2.0.** 1997. pap. write for info. (1-56592-327-8) OReilly & Assocs.

Website Sound. New Riders Development Group Staff. LC 96-46749. 448p. 1996. pap. text ed. 44.99 incl. cd-rom (1-56205-626-3) New Riders Pub.

Website 1.1. O'Reilly & Associates, Inc. Staff. (Illus.). 500p. (Orig.). 1996. 249.00 incl. disk (1-56592-173-9) OReilly & Assocs.

Webster. Mark Dunster. (John Brown, First Prolog Ser.). 1977. pap. 4.00 (0-89642-009-4) Linden Pubs.

Webster: The Critical Heritage. Don Moore. (Critical Heritage Ser.). 172p. 1981. 69.50 (0-7100-0773-6, RKP) Routledge.

Webster & Hayne's Speeches in the United States Senate. Daniel Webster & Robert Y. Hayne. LC 71-37318. (Black Heritage Library Collection). 1977. reprint ed. 15.95 (0-8369-8955-4) Ayer.

Webster Comprehensive Dictionary: International Edition, 2 vols. 1514p. 1992. Set. write for info. (0-89434-136-7) Ferguson.

Webster Contemporary Dictionary, Illustrated Edition **see New International Webster's Pocket Dictionary**

Webster County Moccasin Tracks & Other Imprints. William C. Dodrill. (Illus.). 298p. 1995. reprint ed. lib. bdg. 37.50 (0-8328-5137-X) Higginson Bk Co.

Webster Dictionary. 448p. pap. 5.95 (0-317-68268-7) Book Essentials.

Webster Illustrated Contemporary Dictionary. (Illus.). 1122p. 1992. write for info. (0-89434-134-0) Ferguson.

Webster Illustrated Contemporary Dictionary: New Standard Edition. 1930p. 1992. write for info. (0-89434-140-5) Ferguson.

Webster Illustrated Dictionary Encyclopedia. 1989. 12.99 (0-517-68835-2) Random Hse Value.

Webster, Massachusetts Vital Records to 1850. Jay M. Holbrook. LC 78-60365. 336p. 1980. lib. bdg. 35.00 (0-931248-08-6) Holbrook Res.

Webster New World Compact Dictionary of American English: Based upon Webster's New World Dictionary. 1981. 6.00 (0-671-41802-5) S&S Trade.

Webster, Noah-Dissertation on the Supposed Change in the Temperature of Winter: Wright, Elizur-Dissertation on the Production of Vapor, Etc. Noah Webster et al. (Connecticut Academy of Arts & Sciences Ser., Trans.: Vol. 1, Pt. 1). 1810. 350.00 (0-685-22872-X) Elliots Bks.

***Webster Parish, Louisiana Cemetaries.** John C. Head & Wanda V. Head. 195p. 1996. pap. text ed. 20.00 (1-57088-043-3) J&W Ent.

W

***Webster Parish, Louisiana Marriage Records 1871-1901.** John C. Head & Wanda V. Head. 70p. 1987. pap. text ed. 15.00 (*1-57088-013-1*) J&W Ent.

Webster v. Reproductive Health Services: Briefs & Related Documents. Ed. by Maria E. Protti. LC 90-83331. 818p. 1990. lib. bdg. 195.00 incl. fiche (*0-89941-741-8*, 306660) W S Hein.

Webster's American Dictionary. LC 96-26807. 1997. 9.95 (*0-679-45213-3*, Vin) Random.

Webster's American Dictionary. Webster. Date not set. pap. write for info. (*0-451-18026-7*, Sig) NAL-Dutton.

***Webster's American Family Dictionary.** 1997. write for info. (*0-679-45801-8*, Random Ref) Random.

Webster's American Military Biographies. Ed. by Robert McHenry. 1990. 23.00 (*0-8446-6143-0*) Peter Smith.

Webster's American Military Biographies. Ed. by Robert McHenry. LC 84-8004. 548p. 1984. reprint ed. pap. 13.95 (*0-486-24758-9*) Dover.

Webster's Atlas of the World. Random House Value Publishing Staff. 1994. 9.99 (*0-517-12071-2*) Random Hse Value.

Webster's Basic English Dictionary. Merriam-Webster Editorial Staff. LC 83-13709. 608p. 1995. 14.95 (*0-87779-150-3*) Merriam-Webster Inc.

Websters Classic Dictionary. Date not set. pap. text ed. 5.95 (*1-56987-359-3*) Landoll.

Webster's College Dictionary. 2nd ed. Random House Staff. LC 97-903. 1997. 23.95 (*0-679-45570-1*, Random Ref) Random.

Webster's College Encyclopedia. LC 93-387. 1993. 35.00 (*0-671-85016-4*, Webstrs New) Macmillan Gen Ref.

***Webster's College Thesaurus.** Random House, Incorporated Staff. 1998. pap. 12.95 (*0-375-70065-X*, Random Ref) Random.

Webster's Compact Dictionary. Ed. by Merriam-Webster Editorial Staff. LC 87-21956. 432p. 1995. 6.50 (*0-87779-488-X*) Merriam-Webster Inc.

Webster's Compact Dictionary of Quotations. LC 92-2455. 432p. 1995. 6.50 (*0-87779-284-4*) Merriam-Webster Inc.

Webster's Compact Dictionary of Synonyms. Merriam-Webster Editorial Staff. LC 86-33138. 384p. 1995. 6.50 (*0-87779-186-4*) Merriam-Webster Inc.

Webster's Compact Rhyming Dictionary. Merriam-Webster Editorial Staff. LC 86-33165. 400p. 1995. 6.50 (*0-87779-185-6*) Merriam-Webster Inc.

Webster's Compact Writers Guide. Merriam-Webster Editorial Staff. LC 86-28650. 336p. 1995. 6.50 (*0-87779-187-2*) Merriam-Webster Inc.

Webster's Computer Dictionary: (Vest Pocket) 256p. 1994. write for info. (*1-881275-21-3*) Pamco Pub.

***Webster's Concise Biographical Dictionary.** LC 96-49634. 1997. write for info. (*0-7651-9434-1*) Smithmark.

***Webster's Concise Reference Library.** Merriam-Webster Editorial Staff. 1996. 9.98 (*0-7651-9746-4*) Smithmark.

Webster's Crossword Puzzle Dictionary. 256p. 1994. pap. write for info. (*1-884907-09-1*) Paradise Miami.

Websters Crossword Puzzle Dictionary. Date not set. pap. text ed. 4.95 (*1-56987-354-2*) Landoll.

Webster's Desk Dictionary. Webster Staff. 1996. 6.99 (*0-517-18198-3*) Random Hse Value.

Webster's Desk Dictionary of the English Language. (Illus.). 1088p. 1990. 9.99 (*0-517-03371-2*) Random Hse Value.

Webster's Desk Thesaurus. Webster Staff. 1996. 6.99 (*0-517-18085-5*) Random Hse Value.

Websters Dictionary. Date not set. pap. text ed. 4.95 (*1-56987-350-X*) Landoll.

***Webster's Dictionary.** Date not set. pap. 1.25 (*0-517-18640-3*) Random Hse Value.

Webster's Dictionary. Random House. (Orig.). 1996. mass mkt. 5.99 (*0-345-40095-X*) Ballantine.

Webster's Dictionary. Watermill Press Staff. (J). (gr. 4-7). 1992. pap. 4.95 (*0-8167-2917-4*) Troll Communs.

Webster's Dictionary. V. Nichols. Ed. by L. Kauffman. (Illus.). 448p. 1993. reprint ed. pap. 2.99 (*1-879424-00-2*); reprint ed. pap. 1.99 (*1-879424-12-6*) Nickel Pr.

Webster's Dictionary & Thesaurus. rev. ed. V. Nichols. Ed. by L. Kaufmann. (C). 1991. reprint ed. pap. 7.95 (*1-879424-14-2*) Nickel Pr.

Webster's Dictionary of American Authors. Merriam-Webster Editorial Staff. LC 95-48311. 1996. 14.98 (*0-8317-7158-5*) Smithmark.

***Webster's Dictionary of American Women.** Merriam-Webster Editorial Staff. 1996. 12.98 (*0-7651-9793-6*) Smithmark.

Webster's Dictionary of English Usage see Merriam-Webster's Dictionary of English Usage

Webster's Dictionary of Quotations. LC 95-10997. 1995. write for info. (*0-8317-1541-3*) Smithmark.

Webster's Dictionary of Synonyms & Antonyms. 1996. write for info. (*0-8317-6102-4*) Smithmark.

Webster's Dictionary of Word Origins. LC 95-9075. 1995. write for info. (*0-8317-1542-1*) Smithmark.

Webster's Encyclopedia of Dictionaries. 39.95 (*0-685-70713-X*) Wehman.

Webster's Encyclopedia Unabridged Dictionary. 1996. 16.00 (*0-517-15026-3*) Random Hse Value.

Webster's Encyclopedic Unabridged Dictionary. Random House Value Publishing Staff. 1996. 9.50 (*0-517-15141-3*) Random Hse Value.

Webster's Encyclopedic Unabridged Dictionary of the English Language. (Illus.). 2120p. 1989. 12.50 (*0-517-68781-X*) Random Hse Value.

Webster's English-French - Francais-Anglais Dictionary. Watermill Press Staff. 224p. (J). (gr. 4-7). 1992. pap. 2.95 (*0-8167-2919-0*) Troll Communs.

Webster's English-French Rack Size. V. Nichols. 288p. (Orig.). (ENG & FRE.). 1993. pap. 1.99 (*1-879424-57-6*) Nickel Pr.

Webster's English-Portuguese Dictionary: Webster's Diccionario Ingles-Portugues. Antoio Houaiss. 928p. (ENG & POR.). 1982. 75.00 (*0-8288-0492-3*, M14135) Fr & Eur.

Webster's English-Spanish'- Espanol-Ingles Dictionary. Watermill Press Staff. 224p. (J). (gr. 4-7). 1992. pap. 4.95 (*0-8167-2918-2*) Troll Communs.

Webster's English Spanish Dictionary. V. Nichols. 336p. (Orig.). (ENG & SPA.). 1992. pap. 1.99 (*1-879424-11-8*) Nickel Pr.

Webster's English Spanish Rack Dictionary. V. Nichols. 288p. (Orig.). (ENG & SPA.). 1993. pap. 1.99 (*1-879424-58-4*) Nickel Pr.

Webster's English Spanish Vest Pocket. V. Nichols. 192p. (Orig.). (ENG & SPA.). 1992. pap. 1.95 (*1-879424-24-X*) Nickel Pr.

Webster's FactFinder Handbook: (Vest Pocket) 256p. 1994. write for info. (*1-881275-22-1*) Pamco Pub.

Webster's Family Dictionary. LC 97-14176. 1997. 4.50 (*0-517-18361-7*) Random Hse Value.

Websters' First New Intergalactic Wickedary of the English Language: Conjured by Mary Daly in Cahoots with Jane Caputi. Mary Daly & Jane Caputi. LC 93-25752. 336p. 1994. pap. 17.00 (*0-06-251037-1*) Harper SF.

Webster's French-English, English-French Dictionary. 256p. 1991. pap. 2.49 (*0-517-67045-3*) Random Hse Value.

Webster's French-English English-French Dictionary. Ed. by R. F. Patterson. 256p. (Orig.). 1993. pap. 5.95 (*0-938261-15-0*) PSI & Assocs.

Websters French/English Dictionary. (ENG & FRE.). Date not set. pap. text ed. 4.95 (*1-56987-358-5*) Landoll.

Webster's Giant Print Dictionary. V. Nichols. Ed. by L. Kauffman. (Illus.). 288p. 1993. pap. 2.99 (*1-879424-53-3*) Nickel Pr.

Webster's Gold. Georgia A. Johnson. LC 89-92739. 65p. (Orig.). 1990. pap. 12.95 (*0-9626450-1-X*) G A Johnson Pub.

Webster's Grammar Guide: (Vest Pocket) 256p. 1994. write for info. (*1-881275-19-1*) Pamco Pub.

Webster's Guide to Abbreviations. Ed. by Merriam-Webster Editorial Staff. LC 83-15286. 400p. 1995. 6.50 (*0-87779-072-8*) Merriam-Webster Inc.

Websters Home Medical Dictionary. Date not set. pap. text ed. 5.95 (*1-56987-356-9*) Landoll.

Websters Household Home Repair Dictionary. Date not set. pap. text ed. 4.95 (*1-56987-355-0*) Landoll.

Webster's II: New College Dictionary. LC 95-5833. (Illus.). 1536p. 1995. 22.00 (*0-395-70869-9*) HM.

***Webster's II: New Riverside Notebook Dictionary.** 64p. 1987. pap. 2.95 (*0-395-39571-2*) HM.

***Webster's II Children's Dictionary.** LC 96-21176. (J). 1997. pap. 13.00 (*0-395-84825-3*) HM.

Webster's II New Riverside Children's Dictionary. LC 96-21176. (Illus.). 800p. (J). 1985. pap. 12.95 (*0-395-37884-2*) HM.

***Webster's II New Riverside Desk Dictionary.** Daniel Webster. 1995. 9.00 (*0-395-74450-4*) HM.

Webster's II New Riverside Student's Notebook Dictionary. 64p. pap. 2.50 (*0-317-64611-7*) HM.

Webster's II New Riverside University Dictionary. Ed. by Marion Severynse. 1984. write for info. (*0-318-61166-X*) HM.

Webster's Instant Word Guide. Merriam-Webster Editorial Staff. LC 79-20748. 384p. 1995. 6.50 (*0-87779-273-9*) Merriam-Webster Inc.

Webster's Intermediate Dictionary, 13 vols. large type ed. 3876p. reprint ed. Set. 581.40 (*0-317-01961-9*, J-27370-00) Am Printing Hse.

Webster's International Dictionary, 2 vols. 1990. 89.50 (*0-911156-72-0*) Bern Porter.

***Webster's Large Print Dictionary.** Random House Staff. 1998. write for info. (*0-375-40114-8*, Random Ref) Random.

***Webster's Large Print Dictionary.** Ed. by Random House Staff. 1998. pap. write for info. (*0-375-70106-0*, Random Ref) Random.

Websters Large Print Dictionary. large type ed. Date not set. pap. text ed. 4.95 (*1-56987-357-7*) Landoll.

Websters' Leap. Eileen Dunlop. LC 95-2075. (Illus.). 176p. (J). (gr. 4 up). 1995. 15.95 (*0-8234-1193-1*) Holiday.

Webster's Legal Secretaries Handbook. Merriam-Webster Editorial Staff. (Illus.). 672p. 1995. 14.95 (*0-87779-034-5*) Merriam-Webster Inc.

Webster's Legal Speller. Merriam-Webster Editorial Staff. LC 76-9633. 368p. 1995. 6.50 (*0-87779-038-8*) Merriam-Webster Inc.

Webster's Marketing Bibliography: Company & Industry Studies, 2 vols., Bk. 1. Frederick A. Webster. (Series XIII-1 & 2). 460p. (C). 1986. lib. bdg. 67.00 (*1-55575-694-8*) Websters Biblio.

Webster's Marketing Bibliography: Company & Industry Studies, 2 vols., Bk. 2. Frederick A. Webster. (Series XIII-1 & 2). 442p. (C). 1986. lib. bdg. 65.00 (*1-55575-696-4*) Websters Biblio.

Webster's Marketing Bibliography: Foundations of Marketing Thought. Frederick A. Webster. (Series I-1). 282p. (C). 1986. lib. bdg. 48.00 (*1-55575-602-6*) Websters Biblio.

Webster's Marketing Bibliography: Management of the Channel of Distribution. Frederick A. Webster. (Series VI-2). 484p. (C). 1986. lib. bdg. 70.00 (*1-55575-670-0*) Websters Biblio.

Webster's Marketing Bibliography: Management of the Product Variable, 2 vols., Bk. 1. Frederick A. Webster. (Series V-1 & 2). 353p. (C). 1986. lib. bdg. 54.50 (*1-55575-660-3*) Websters Biblio.

Webster's Marketing Bibliography: Management of the Product Variable, 2 vols., Bk. 2. Frederick A. Webster. (Series V-1 & 2). 242p. (C). 1986. lib. bdg. 41.00 (*1-55575-662-X*) Websters Biblio.

Webster's Marketing Bibliography: Marketing Management & the External Environment Interface. Frederick A. Webster. (Series II-3). 446p. (C). 1986. lib. bdg. 65.50 (*1-55575-622-0*) Websters Biblio.

Webster's Marketing Bibliography: Marketing Management Control: Tools & Techniques. Frederick A. Webster. (Series II-4). 213p. (C). 1986. lib. bdg. 37.50 (*1-55575-626-3*) Websters Biblio.

Webster's Marketing Bibliography: Marketing Management Decision Theory. Frederick A. Webster. (Series I-2). 345p. (C). 1986. lib. bdg. 53.50 (*1-55575-604-2*) Websters Biblio.

Webster's Marketing Bibliography: Marketing Research Applications: Product, Physical Distribution & Price. Frederick A. Webster. (Series IV-3). 265p. (C). 1986. lib. bdg. 44.00 (*1-55575-654-9*) Websters Biblio.

Webster's Marketing Bibliography: Marketing Research: Tools & Techniques. Frederick A. Webster. (Series IV-2). 376p. (C). 1986. lib. bdg. 57.00 (*1-55575-652-2*) Websters Biblio.

Webster's Marketing Bibliography: Marketing Services, General Product Issues, Books on Products as a Controllable Marketing Variable. Frederick A. Webster. (Series V-4). 287p. (C). 1986. lib. bdg. 46.50 (*1-55575-666-2*) Websters Biblio.

Webster's Marketing Bibliography: Miscellaneous Marketing Management Issues. Frederick A. Webster. (Series II-6). 328p. (C). 1986. lib. bdg. 51.25 (*1-55575-630-1*) Websters Biblio.

Webster's Marketing Bibliography: Miscellaneous Marketing Research Issues. Frederick A. Webster. (Series IV-5). 295p. (C). 1986. lib. bdg. 47.00 (*1-55575-658-1*) Websters Biblio.

Webster's Marketing Bibliography: Personal Selling, Sales Promotion, Public Relations. Frederick A. Webster. (Series VII-4). 234p. (C). 1986. lib. bdg. 40.00 (*1-55575-682-4*) Websters Biblio.

Webster's Marketing Bibliography: Product, Physical Distribution, Promotion & Price Theory. Frederick A. Webster. (Series I-6). 240p. (C). 1986. lib. bdg. 40.50 (*1-55575-612-3*) Websters Biblio.

Webster's Marketing Bibliography: The Consumer-Buyer Decision - Making Process, 2 vols., Bk. III-1. Frederick A. Webster. (Series III-1 & 2). 243p. (C). 1986. lib. bdg. 41.50 (*1-55575-632-8*) Websters Biblio.

Webster's Marketing Bibliography: The Consumer-Buyer Decision - Making Process, 2 vols., Bk. III-2. Frederick A. Webster. (Series III-1 & 2). 271p. (C). 1986. lib. bdg. 47.50 (*1-55575-634-4*) Websters Biblio.

Webster's Marketing Bibliography: The Geography of Markets & Marketing. Frederick A. Webster. (Series VI-1). 555p. (C). 1986. lib. bdg. 79.00 (*1-55575-668-9*) Websters Biblio.

Webster's Marketing Bibliography: The Marketing Management Commitment. Frederick A. Webster. (Series II-1). 152p. (C). 1986. lib. bdg. 30.25 (*1-55575-616-6*) Websters Biblio.

Webster's Marketing Bibliography: The Wholesale Sector. Frederick A. Webster. (Series VI-3). 332p. (C). 1986. lib. bdg. 52.00 (*1-55575-672-7*) Websters Biblio.

Webster's Marketing Bibliography: Theory of Marketing Communications, Spatial Marketing Models: Health Care Marketing Management Models & Studies, & Miscellaneous Theoretical Marketing Constructs. Frederick A. Webster. (Series I-7). 451p. (C). 1986. lib. bdg. 66.00 (*1-55575-614-X*) Websters Biblio.

***Webster's Medical Spell Check.** Random House Staff. 1998. write for info. (*0-375-40152-0*, Random Ref) Random.

Webster's Medical Speller. 2nd ed. Ed. by Merriam-Webster Editorial Staff. LC 87-26947. 400p. 1995. 6.50 (*0-87779-137-6*) Merriam-Webster Inc.

***Webster's Middle School Dictionary.** (J). (gr. 6-8). write for info. (*0-03-096483-0*) Merriam-Webster Inc.

***Webster's Middle School Dictionary, 4 vols.** large type ed. 1064p. (J). (gr. 6-8). 266.00 (*0-614-20563-8*, L-36935-00 APHB) Am Printing Hse.

Webster's New American Crossword Dictionary. LC 95-2047. (Illus.). 752p. 1995. 7.98 (*0-8317-9164-0*) Smithmark.

Webster's New American Dictionary. (Illus.). 704p. 1995. 9.98 (*0-8317-9165-9*) Smithmark.

Webster's New Business Writers Guide. Merriam-Webster Editorial Staff. LC 95-46614. 1996. write for info. (*0-8317-7159-3*) Smithmark.

Webster's New Compact Dictionary. LC 84-4798. 1979. 3.99 (*0-8407-4081-6*) Nelson.

***Webster's New Complete Medical Dictionary.** Merriam-Webster Staff. 1997. 7.98 (*0-7651-9435-X*) Smithmark.

Webster's New Complete Thesaurus. Merriam-Webster Editorial Staff. LC 95-16737. 1995. write for info. (*0-8317-1543-X*) Smithmark.

Webster's New Dictionary & Roget's Thesaurus. Ed. by William Morris. LC 86-5133. 1008p. 1984. pap. 2.99 (*0-8407-4924-4*) Nelson.

Webster's New Encyclopedic Dictionary. Webster Staff. 1993. 19.95 (*0-9637056-0-1*) Blck Dog & Leventhal.

Webster's New Encyclopedic Dictionary. rev. ed. Ed. by B. D. & L. Staff. LC 95-13165. 1696p. 24.98 (*1-884822-20-7*); pap. 15.98 (*1-884822-25-8*) Blck Dog & Leventhal.

Webster's New Geographical Dictionary. Merriam-Webster Editorial Staff. (Illus.). 1408p. 1995. 24.95 (*0-87779-446-4*) Merriam-Webster Inc.

***Webster's New Home & Office Desk Reference.** Merriam-Webster Editorial Staff. LC 96-50140. 1997. 14.98 (*0-7651-9718-9*) Smithmark.

***Webster's New Lexicon Dictionary, 2 vols.** 1990. 89.50 (*0-911156-52-6*) Bern Porter.

Webster's New Word Dictionary. Jane S. Whitfield. 1990. mass mkt. 6.50 (*0-671-72692-7*) PB.

Webster's New World - Kenkyusha Japanese-English Character Reading Dictionary. Jack Halpern. (Illus.). 2200p. (ENG & JPN.). 1990. 60.00 (*0-685-31177-5*, Webstrs New) Macmillan Gen Ref.

***Webster's New World Children's Dictionary.** Victoria Neufeldt & Fernando De Mello Vianna. LC 97-7211. (J). 1997. 16.95 (*0-02-861888-2*) Macmillan.

Webster's New World Children's Dictionary. Webster's New World Dictionaries Editors. (Illus.). 912p. (J). 1991. 16.00 (*0-13-945726-7*, Webstrs New) Macmillan Gen Ref.

Webster's New World College Dictionary. 3rd ed. 1600p. 1989. 79.95 (*0-13-949298-4*, Webstrs New) Macmillan Gen Ref.

***Webster's New World College Dictionary.** 3rd ed. Victoria Neufeldt & David B. Guralnik. LC 96-44362. 1997. 23.95 (*0-02-861673-1*); 27.95 (*0-02-861674-X*); 21.95 (*0-02-861675-8*) Macmillan.

Webster's New World College Dictionary. 3rd expanded rev. ed. Webster's New World College Dictionary Staff. (Illus.). 1600p. 1995. boxed 40.00 (*0-02-860587-X*, Webstrs New) Macmillan Gen Ref.

Webster's New World College Dictionary. 3rd expanded rev. ed. Webster's New World College Dictionary Staff. (Illus.). 1600p. 1995. boxed, lib. bdg. 45.00 (*0-02-860588-8*, Webstrs New) Macmillan Gen Ref.

Webster's New World College Third & Revised Thesaurus, 2 vols., Set. 1988. boxed 35.95 (*0-671-92701-9*) P-H Gen Ref & Trav.

***Webster's New World Compact Japanese Dictionary.** 2nd ed. 528p. (JPN.). 1997. pap. 6.50 (*0-02-861726-6*, Webstrs New) Macmillan Gen Ref.

Webster's New World Compact Japanese Dictionary Japanese-English, English-Japanese. 1985. pap. 8.95 (*0-671-55159-0*) S&S Trade.

Webster's New World Crossword Puzzle Dictionary. 3rd ed. Jane S. Whitfield. 1996. 12.95 (*0-02-861212-4*) Macmillan.

Webster's New World Crossword Puzzle Dictionary. 3rd ed. Compiled by Jane S. Whitfield. LC 96-2077. 1996. 16.95 (*0-02-861213-2*) Macmillan.

Websters New World Dictionary. 1995. pap. 4.99 (*0-671-51982-4*) PB.

Webster's New World Dictionary. Prentice. 1995. pap. 11.00 (*0-671-8944X-4*) PB.

Webster's New World Dictionary. Ed. by Scott Shannon. 704p. 1995. pap. 11.00 (*0-671-89448-X*, PB Trade Paper) PB.

Webster's New World Dictionary. 3rd deluxe expanded rev. ed. Webster's New College Dictionary Staff. (Illus.). 1600p. 1995. 80.00 (*0-02-860586-1*, Webstrs New) Macmillan Gen Ref.

Webster's New World Dictionary. 3rd ed. (C). 1988. 17.95 (*0-685-21887-2*) S&S Trade.

Webster's New World Dictionary. 3rd ed. Webster's New World Editors. 1994. 15.00 (*0-671-79765-4*) S&S Trade.

Webster's New World Dictionary: College Edition. 3rd ed. LC 93-2961. 1600p. 1988. Leatherkraft thumb-indexed. 22.00 (*0-13-949314-X*, Webstrs New) Macmillan Gen Ref.

Webster's New World Dictionary: College Edition. 3rd expanded rev. ed. Webster's New College Dictionary Staff. (Illus.). 1600p. 1995. 24.95 (*0-02-860334-6*, Webstrs New) Macmillan Gen Ref.

Webster's New World Dictionary: College Edition-Indexed. 3rd expanded rev. ed. Webster's New World Dictionary Staff. (Illus.). 1600p. 1995. 22.95 (*0-02-860333-8*, Webstrs New) Macmillan Gen Ref.

Webster's New World Dictionary: College Edition-Plain. 3rd expanded rev. ed. Webster's New World College Dictionary Staff. (Illus.). 1600p. 1995. 19.95 (*0-02-860332-X*, Webstrs New) Macmillan Gen Ref.

Webster's New World Dictionary: School Edition. 21.99 (*0-8136-1995-5*, J619955) Good Apple.

Webster's New World Dictionary: 4th College Edition. 4th ed. Newfeldt. 1997. 18.00 (*0-671-84886-0*) Macmillan.

Webster's New World Dictionary & Thesaurus. Webster's New World Dictionary Staff. LC 95-17738. 1995. 19.95 (*0-02-860574-8*, Webstrs New) Macmillan Gen Ref.

Webster's New World Dictionary & Thesaurus. Websters New World Staff. 768p. 1996. pap. text ed. 12.95 (*0-02-861318-X*, Webstrs New) Macmillan Gen Ref.

Webster's New World Dictionary & Thesaurus: Leather-Kraft Boxed Set. 1984. Set. 35.00 (*0-671-93463-5*) S&S Trade.

Webster's New World Dictionary for Young Adults. (Illus.). 1056p. (YA). (gr. 6-10). 1992. 18.00 (*0-13-945734-8*, Webstrs New) Macmillan Gen Ref.

Webster's New World Dictionary for Young Adults see Webster's New World Student's Dictionary

***Webster's New World Dictionary for Young Readers & Writers.** 926p. (J). 1996. 23.35 (*0-382-21325-4*) Silver Burdett Pr.

Webster's New World Dictionary of Acronyms & Abbreviations. Auriel Douglas & Michael Strumpf. 352p. 1988. pap. 7.95 (*0-13-947136-7*, Webstrs New) Macmillan Gen Ref.

Webster's New World Dictionary Of Computer Terms. 5th ed. Donald D. Spencer. 1994. pap. 9.95 (*0-671-89993-7*) P-H.

Webster's New World Dictionary of Mathematics. William Karush. (Illus.). 336p. 1989. pap. 12.00 (*0-13-192667-5*) P-H.

***Webster's New World Dictionary of Media & Comminications.** 2nd ed. Richard Weiner. 1996. 39.95 (*0-02-861474-7*) Macmillan.

Webster's New World Dictionary of Media & Communications. rev. ed. Richard Weiner. 676p. 1996. 39.95 (*0-02-860611-6*) Macmillan.

***Webster's New World Dictionary of Quotable Definitions.** E. Brussell. 680p. 39.95 (*0-13-949272-0*) P-H.

W

Webster's New World Dictionary of the American Language. rev. ed. Ed. by David B. Guralnik. 704p. 1984. pap. 9.95 (*0-446-38240-X*) Warner Bks.

Webster's New World Dictionary of the American Language: Second College Edition, 24 vols. large type ed. Ed. by David B. Guralnik. 7352p. (YA). (gr. 10 up). Set. 1,300.34 (*0-317-01962-7*, 4-27260-00) Am Printing Hse.

Webster's New World Dictionary of the American Language: 100,000 Entry Edition. pap. 9.95 (*0-452-00619-8*, F619, Mer) NAL-Dutton.

***Webster's New World Dictionary of the Culinary Arts.** Steven Labensky et al. LC 96-47579. 1997. 26.40 (*0-13-182726-X*) P-H.

***Webster's New World Easy Crossword Key.** James Capps. 1997. 10.95 (*0-02-861837-8*) Macmillan.

Webster's New World Encyclopedia. Ed. by Stephen P. Elliot & Martha Goldstein. (Illus.). 1248p. 1992. 75.00 (*0-13-947482-X*, Webstrs New) Macmillan Gen Ref.

Webster's New World Encyclopedia Pocket Edition. 9th rev. ed. Ed. by Stephen P. Elliot & Martha Goldstein. LC 93-388. (Illus.). 928p. 1993. pap. 14.00 (*0-671-85035-0*, Webstrs New) Macmillan Gen Ref.

Webster's New World French Dictionary. 960p. 1992. pap. 12.00 (*0-13-953613-2*, Webstrs New) Macmillan Gen Ref.

Webster's New World French Dictionary. Robert A. Collins. 536p. (ENG & FRE.). 1981. 19.95 (*0-8288-1211-X*, S60720) Fr & Eur.

Webster's New World French Dictionary, Pocket Edition. Websters New World Staff. 1996. pap. text ed. 4.95 (*0-02-861412-7*, Webstrs New) Macmillan Gen Ref.

Webster's New World German Dictionary. LC 92-16695. 1056p. 1992. pap. 12.00 (*0-13-953621-3*, Webstrs New) Macmillan Gen Ref.

Webster's New World German Dictionary, Pocket Edition. Websters New World Staff. 1996. pap. text ed. 4.95 (*0-02-861410-0*, Webstrs New) Macmillan Gen Ref.

Webster's New World Guide to Punctuation. Michael Strumpf & Auriel Douglas. (Webster's New World). 1988. pap. 5.95 (*0-13-947896-5*) S&S Trade.

Webster's New World Hebrew Dictionary. 1994. pap. 18.00 (*0-671-88991-5*, Webstrs New) Macmillan Gen Ref.

Webster's New World Italian Dictionary. 1024p. 1992. pap. 12.95 (*0-13-953639-6*, Webstrs New) Macmillan Gen Ref.

Webster's New World Italian Dictionary, Pocket Edition. Websters New World Staff. 1996. pap. text ed. 4.95 (*0-02-861413-5*, Webstrs New) Macmillan Gen Ref.

Webster's New World Italian-English Dictionary. write for info. (*0-318-59605-9*) S&S Trade.

***Webster's New World Japanese Dictionary.** 2nd ed. 528p. 1997. pap. 6.95 (*0-02-861725-8*, Webstrs New) Macmillan Gen Ref.

Webster's New World Japanese Dictionary, Pocket Edition. Websters New World Staff. 1996. pap. text ed. 11.95 (*0-02-861411-9*, Webstrs New) Macmillan Gen Ref.

***Webster's New World Large Print Dictionary.** large type ed. 35.00 (*0-7838-1905-6*, GK Hall) Thorndike Pr.

Webster's New World Large-Print Dictionary. large type ed. Webster's New World Dictionary Staff. 1040p. 1992. 40.00 (*0-671-86862-4*, Webstrs New) Macmillan Gen Ref.

***Webster's New World Misspeller's Dictionary.** 2nd ed. Michael Agnes. LC 96-51674. 1997. 4.95 (*0-02-861720-7*) Macmillan.

Webster's New World Office Professional's Handbook. 5th ed. Plain English Inc. Staff. 704p. 1996. 15.95 (*0-02-860619-1*, Webstrs New) Macmillan Gen Ref.

Webster's New World Pocket Dictionary. 2nd ed. Webster's New World Dictionary of American English Staff. LC 92-39176. 1993. pap. 4.00 (*0-671-86613-3*, Webstrs New) Macmillan Gen Ref.

***Webster's New World Pocket Dictionary.** 3rd ed. Websters New World Staff. 1997. pap. text ed. 4.95 (*0-02-861887-4*) Macmillan.

***Webster's New World Pocket Thesaurus.** Websters New World Staff. 1997. pap. text ed. 4.95 (*0-02-861886-6*) P-H Gen Ref & Trav.

Webster's New World Power Reading. Rozakis. 1995. pap. 12.95 (*0-671-51897-6*) S&S Trade.

Webster's New World Power Vocabulary. 2nd ed. Elizabeth Morse-Cluley & Richard Read. LC 93-47434. (Orig.). 1994. 10.00 (*0-671-88821-8*) P-H Gen Ref & Trav.

Webster's New World Spanish Dictionary. 1040p. 1992. pap. 12.00 (*0-13-953647-7*, Webstrs New) Macmillan Gen Ref.

Webster's New World Spanish Dictionary, Pocket Edition. Websters New World Staff. 1996. pap. text ed. 4.95 (*0-02-861414-3*, Webstrs New) Macmillan Gen Ref.

Webster's New World Spanish-English Dictionary: Collins Concise Edition. write for info. (*0-318-59602-4*) S&S Trade.

Webster's New World Speller - Divider. 2nd ed. 384p. 1992. pap. 8.00 (*0-13-953654-X*, Webstrs New) Macmillan Gen Ref.

Webster's New World Speller - Divider: Based upon Webster's New World Dictionary of the American Language, College Edition. 3rd ed. Compiled by Shirley M. Miller. 1992. write for info. (*0-318-69384-4*, Webstrs New) Macmillan Gen Ref.

Webster's New World Stedman's Concise Medical Dictionary. Simon & Schuster Staff. 848p. 1991. text ed. write for info. (*0-89303-951-9*) P-H.

Webster's New World Stedman's Concise Medical Dictionary. Webster's New World Editors. 1993. 24.00 (*0-671-86863-2*) S&S Trade.

Webster's New World Student Writing Handbook. 2nd ed. Sharon Sorenson. 608p. 1992. pap. 16.00 (*0-13-951955-6*, Webstrs New) Macmillan Gen Ref.

***Webster's New World Student Writing Handbook.** 3rd ed. Sharon Sorenson. 608p. 1997. pap. 16.95 (*0-02-861705-3*, Webstrs New) Macmillan Gen Ref.

Webster's New World Student's Dictionary. Ed. by Jonathan L. Goldman & Andrew N. Sparks. LC 96-4585. Orig. Title: Webster's New World Dictionary for Young Adults. (Illus.). 1056p. (J). 1996. write for info. (*0-02-861319-8*) Macmillan.

Websters New World Thesaurus. 1995. pap. 4.99 (*0-671-51983-2*) PB.

Webster's New World Thesaurus. 1998. 16.00 (*0-02-860335-4*) Macmillan.

Webster's New World Thesaurus. 1996. 12.95 (*0-02-860336-2*) Macmillan.

Webster's New World Thesaurus. Charlton A. Laird. 1995. pap. 10.95 (*0-671-84871-2*) S&S Trade.

Webster's New World Thesaurus. Pocket & Charlton A. Laird. 1995. pap. text ed. 16.00 (*0-205-19987-9*) P-H.

Webster's New World Thesaurus. rev. ed. Laird Charlton. 1988. 16.00 (*0-13-947151-0*, Webstrs New) Macmillan Gen Ref.

Webster's New World Thesaurus. rev. ed. Charlton G. Laird. 854p. 1985. 16.00 (*0-671-60437-6*, Webstrs New) Macmillan Gen Ref.

Webster's New World Thesaurus. 3rd deluxe ed. Webster's New World Dictionaries Editors. LC 96-2072. (Illus.). 1995. 16.00 (*0-02-860337-0*) Macmillan.

Webster's New World Thesaurus. 3rd ed. Webster New World Editors. 1996. 16.00 (*0-671-89899-X*) Macmillan.

Webster's New World Thesaurus. 3rd ed. Webster's New World Dictionaries Editors. LC 96-2072. (Illus.). 1996. 18.95 (*0-02-861320-1*) Macmillan.

Webster's New World Thesaurus. 3rd ed. Webster's New World Dictionaries Editors. LC 96-2072. (Illus.). 1996. pap. write for info. (*0-614-12738-6*) Macmillan.

Webster's New World Thesaurus. Charlton Laird. Ed. by Scott Shannon. 512p. 1995. reprint ed. pap. 11.00 (*0-671-89450-1*, PB Trade Paper) PB.

Webster's New World Vest Pocket Dictionary. 2nd ed. Webster's New World Staff. 1994. pap. 3.00 (*0-671-88993-1*, Webstrs New) Macmillan Gen Ref.

Webster's New Young America Dictionary. (Illus.). 720p. (J). (gr. 2-6). 1995. 9.98 (*0-8317-9166-7*) Smithmark.

Webster's Official Crossword Puzzle Dictionary. Merriam-Webster Editorial Staff. LC 81-38341. 768p. 1995. 17.95 (*0-87779-021-3*) Merriam-Webster Inc.

Webster's Pocket Dictionary II. rev. ed. Houghton Mifflin Reference Staff. 1991. pap. 3.95 (*0-395-60173-8*) HM.

***Webster's Pocket French Dictionary.** Random House Staff. 1998. pap. write for info. (*0-375-70156-7*, Random Ref) Random.

***Webster's Pocket German Dictionary.** Ed. by Random House Staff. 1998. pap. write for info. (*0-375-70160-5*, Random Ref) Random.

***Webster's Pocket Italian Dictionary.** Ed. by Random House Staff. 1998. pap. write for info. (*0-375-70159-1*, Random Ref) Random.

***Webster's Pocket Japanese Dictionary.** Ed. by Random House Staff. 1998. pap. write for info. (*0-375-70163-X*, Random Ref) Random.

***Webster's Pocket Spanish Dictionary.** Ed. by Random House Staff. 1998. pap. write for info. (*0-375-70157-5*, Random Ref) Random.

Webster's Pocket Spanish-English Dictionary. 192p. (ENG & SPA.). 1994. pap. write for info. (*1-884907-12-1*) Paradise Miami.

***Webster's Pocket Thesaurus.** Ed. by Random House Staff. 1998. pap. write for info. (*0-375-70158-3*, Random Ref) Random.

Websters Promotional Dictionary. Date not set. pap. text ed. 3.95 (*1-56987-351-8*) Landoll.

Webster's Quick Note. 32p. 1994. pap. write for info. (*1-884907-13-X*) Paradise Miami.

Webster's Quotations: (Vest Pocket) 256p. 1994. write for info. (*1-881275-20-5*) Pamco Pub.

***Webster's Real Estate Law in North Carolina, 2 vols.** 4th ed. Patrick K. Hetrick & James B. McLaughlin, Jr. 1994. 150.00 (*1-55834-200-1*, 62793-11) MICHIE.

***Webster's Real Estate Law in North Carolina.** 4th ed. Patrick K. Hetrick & James B. McLaughlin, Jr. 1995. suppl. ed. 40.00 (*0-614-25255-5*, 62792-11) MICHIE.

Webster's Real Estate Law in North Carolina with 1991 Cumulative Supplement. 3rd ed. Patrick K. Hetrick & James B. McLaughlin, Jr. 835p. 1988. 85.00 (*0-87473-413-4*) MICHIE.

Webster's Real Estate Law in North Carolina with 1991 Cumulative Supplement. 3rd ed. Patrick K. Hetrick & James B. McLaughlin. 835p. 1991. suppl. ed. 35.00 (*0-87473-863-6*) MICHIE.

Webster's Scholastic Dictionary. (J). (gr. 9 up). mass mkt. 2.95 (*0-8049-2001-X*, D1) Airmont.

Webster's Spanish-English English-Spanish Dictionary. Ed. by R. F. Patterson. 192p. (Orig.). (ENG & SPA.). 1993. pap. 2.95 (*0-938261-02-9*) PSI & Assocs.

Websters Spanish/English Dictionary. (ENG & SPA.). Date not set. pap. text ed. 3.95 (*1-56987-360-7*) Landoll.

Websters Speller. Date not set. pap. text ed. 3.95 (*1-56987-353-4*) Landoll.

Webster's Speller. V. Nichols & L. Kauffman. 288p. pap. 1.99 (*1-879424-02-9*) Nickel Pr.

Webster's Ten Volume Family Encyclopedia. 2800p. 1991. pap. 19.95 (*1-880459-00-0*) Arrow Trad.

Websters Thesaurus. Date not set. pap. text ed. 3.95 (*1-56987-352-6*) Landoll.

Webster's Thesaurus. V. Nichols. Ed. by L. Kauffman. 288p. 1993. reprint ed. pap. 1.99 (*1-879424-01-0*) Nickel Pr.

Webster's Third New International Dictionary. rev. unabridged ed. LC 93-10630. 2783p. 1961. 99.95 (*0-87779-201-1*); 109.95 (*0-87779-206-2*) Merriam-Webster Inc.

Webster's Third on Nonstandard Usage; Social Aspects of Bilingualism in San Antonio, Texas; Names in Gardening; Needed Research in American English (1943); Needed Research in American English (1963) Jean Malmstrom et al. (Publications of the American Dialect Society). 69p. 1964. pap. text ed. 7.05 (*0-8173-0641-2*) U of Ala Pr.

Webster's Three Piece Box Set. V. Nichols & L. Kauffman. 1024p. (Orig.). 1991. pap. 9.95 (*1-879424-03-7*) Nickel Pr.

Webster's Twenty-First Century Chronology - World History. LC 93-7025. 1993. pap. 7.99 (*0-8407-6879-6*) Nelson.

Webster's 21st Century Large-Print Dictionary. large type ed. Princeton Language Institute Staff. 608p. 1996. pap. 19.95 (*0-385-31643-7*, Delta) Dell.

Websters Two In One Dictionary & Thesaurus. Date not set. pap. text ed. 6.95 (*1-56987-361-5*) Landoll.

Webster's Two in One Dictionary & Thesaurus. V. Nichols. Ed. by L. Kauffman. (Illus.). 352p. pap. 1.99 (*1-879424-42-8*) Nickel Pr.

***Webster's Unabridged Dictionary.** Random House Value Publishing Staff. 1997. 9.50 (*0-517-18367-6*) Random Hse Value.

Webster's Vest Pocket Dictionary. V. Nichols & L. Kauffman. 192p. 1992. reprint ed. pap. 1.95 (*1-879424-33-9*) Nickel Pr.

Webster's Vest Pocket Dictonary. 1995. pap. 2.15 (*0-395-74448-2*) HM.

Webster's Vest Pocket Thesaurus. V. Nichols & L. Kauffman. 192p. 1993. reprint ed. pap. 1.95 (*1-879424-34-7*) Nickel Pr.

***WEBTV for Dummies.** Brad Hill. 1997. pap. 19.99 (*0-7645-0150-X*) IDG Bks.

Webvisions: An Inside Look at Successful Business Strategies on the Net. Eugene Marlowee. LC 96-41531. 273p. 1997. text ed. 29.95 (*0-442-02453-5*) Van Nos Reinhold.

***Webwise: The Cyberia Guide to Smart Web Publishing.** Cyberia Staff. 1996. pap. text ed. 39.95 incl. cd-rom (*0-07-709312-7*) McGraw.

Webworks. Martin Irvine. (C). Date not set. pap. text ed. 12.95 (*0-393-97109-0*) Norton.

***WECAFC: Report of the Workshop on the Use of Length-Frequency Data for the Assessment of Fishery Resources of the Caribbean Islands, Trois-Ilets, Martinique, 1991.** 49p. 1992. 12.00 (*92-5-103294-7*, Pub. by FAO IT) Bernan Associates.

***WECAFC: Report of the 1st Session of the Working Party on Fishery Economics & Planning, Saint George's, Grenada, 1989.** 68p. (ENG & SPA.). 1989. 12.00 (*92-5-002885-7*, Pub. by FAO IT) Bernan Associates.

***WECAFC: Report of the 2nd Workshop on the Biological & Economical Modelling of the Shrimp Resources on the Guyana-Brazil Shelf.** 95p. 1989. 12.00 (*92-5-102843-5*, Pub. by FAO IT) Bernan Associates.

***WECAFC: Report of the 6th Session of the Working Party on Assessment of Marine Fishery Resources, Saint George's, Grenada, 1989.** 133p. (ENG & SPA.). 1990. 17.00 (*92-5-002954-3*, Pub. by FAO IT) Bernan Associates.

***WECAFC - Report of Session of Committee for Development & Management of Fisheries, Lesser Antilles.** (Fisheries Reports: No. 539). 106p. 1996. pap. 10.00 (*92-5-003836-4*, F38364, Pub. by FAO IT) Bernan Associates.

Wechsel der Modalitatsbestimmungen. Urbanus Bomm. 197p. 1975. reprint ed. 40.00 (*3-487-05716-6*) G Olms Pubs.

Wechselspiel. Dreke & Lind. 160p. 1986. 35.00 (*3-468-49994-9*) Langenscheidt.

Wechselspiel: A Tu Per Tu. Michael Dreke & Wolfgang Lind. 112p. (ITA.). 1996. wbk. ed. 35.00 (*3-468-49997-3*) Langenscheidt.

Wechselspiel: Espanol en Pareja (Paired Activities) Dreke et al. 136p. 1991. 35.00 (*3-468-49998-1*) Langenscheidt.

Wechselspiel: Espanol en Pareja (Paired Activities) Michael Dreke & Wolfgang Lind. 136p. (SPA.). 1996. wbk. ed. 33.50 (*3-468-44998-4*) Langenscheidt.

Wechselspiel: Face to Face. Michael Dreke & Wolfgang Lind. 160p. 1996. wbk. ed. 35.00 (*3-468-49999-X*) Langenscheidt.

Wechsler Scales: Index of Modern Information. Andrew S. Zunotto. LC 88-47637. 150p. 1988. 44.50 (*0-88164-822-1*); pap. 39.50 (*0-88164-823-X*) ABBE Pubs Assn.

Wechsler's Measurement & Appraisal of Adult Intelligence. 5th ed. Joseph D. Matarazzo & David Wechsler. (Illus.). 572p. 1972. 38.95 (*0-19-502296-3*) OUP.

Wed Again. Elda Minger. (American Romance Ser.). 1993. mass mkt. 3.50 (*0-373-16510-2*, 1-16510-9) Harlequin Bks.

We'd Have a Great Relationship If It Weren't for You: Regaining Love & Intimacy Through Mutuality. Bruce Derman & Michael Hauge. 335p. (Orig.). 1994. pap. 12.95 (*1-55874-316-2*, 3162) Health Comm.

***We'd Like You to Know about the Church of the Nazarene.** 32p. 1977. 1.50 (*0-8341-0453-9*) Nazarene.

Wed Offset Printers, Non-Heatset see 1996 PIA Ratios

***Wed to a Stranger?** Jule McBride. (Hidden Identity Ser.). 1997. mass mkt. 3.75 (*0-373-22418-4*, 1-22418-7) Harlequin Bks.

Wedded Bliss: A Victorian Bride's Handbook. Molly D. Blayney. (Illus.). 128p. 1991. 9.95 (*1-55859-332-2*) Abbeville Pr.

Wedded Life. 1979. 3.35 (*0-686-30767-4*) Rod & Staff.

Wedded to the Cause: Ukrainian-Canadian Women & Ethnic Identity. Frances Swyripa. LC 92-95029. 328p. 1993. 50.00 (*0-8020-5008-5*); pap. 20.95 (*0-8020-6939-8*) U of Toronto Pr.

Weddell Sea Ecology: Results of EPOS European "Polarstern" Study. Ed. by Gotthif Hempel. LC 92-34144. 280p. 1993. 98.00 (*3-540-55605-2*) Spr-Verlag.

Weddell Sea Tectonics & Gondwana Break-Up. Ed. by B. C. Storey et al. (Geological Society Special Publications Classics Ser.: No. 108). (Illus.). vi, 280p. 1996. 93.00 (*1-897799-59-4*, 347, Pub. by Geol Soc Pub Hse UK) AAPG.

Weddell Seal, Consummate Diver. Gerald L. Kooyman. LC 80-18794. 145p. reprint ed. pap. 41.40 (*0-318-34815-2*, 2031678) Bks Demand.

Wedding. 1993. pap. 4.95 (*1-55037-281-5*, Pub. by Annick CN); lib. bdg. 14.95 (*1-55037-280-7*, Pub. by Annick CN) Firefly Bks Ltd.

***Wedding.** Marion C. Beavers. LC 96-61785. 208p. (Orig.). 1997. pap. 10.99 (*1-883893-83-6*) WinePress Pub.

Wedding. Elias Canetti. Tr. by Gitta Honegger. 1986. pap. 8.95 (*1-55554-008-2*) PAJ Pubns.

Wedding. Anton P. Chekhov. Ed. by William-Alan Landes. Tr. by Sergius Ponomarov. 55p. (Orig.). 1996. pap. 5.00 (*0-88734-358-9*) Players Pr.

Wedding. Emma Darcy. (Presents Ser.: No. 463). 1992. pap. 2.89 (*0-373-11463-X*, 1-11463-6) Harlequin Bks.

Wedding. Julie Garwood. 480p. 1996. 23.00 (*0-671-87099-8*) PB.

***Wedding.** Julie Garwood. 1997. mass mkt. 6.99 (*0-671-87100-5*) PB.

***Wedding.** Anne Geddes. 1997. 24.95 (*0-8362-3700-5*) Andrews & McMeel.

Wedding. Hannigan. (J). pap. 4.95 (*0-7136-4112-6*, 93346, Pub. by A&C Black UK) Talman.

Wedding. Edith Layton. 1995. mass mkt. 5.50 (*0-671-88300-3*) PB.

Wedding. Francine Pascal. 224p. (YA). 1993. mass mkt. 3.99 (*0-553-29855-0*) Bantam.

Wedding. Danielle Steel. LC 94-44391. 1997. 25.95 (*0-385-31437-X*) Delacorte.

***Wedding.** Danielle Steel. 1997. 29.95 (*0-385-31794-8*) Doubleday.

Wedding. Dorothy West. LC 94-27285. 256p. 1995. 20.00 (*0-385-47143-2*) Doubleday.

Wedding. Dorothy West. 256p. 1996. 9.95 (*0-385-47144-0*, Anchor NY) Doubleday.

Wedding. Stanislaw Wyspianski. Ed. by Gerald T. Kapolka. 200p. 1990. 22.50 (*0-88233-556-1*) Ardis Pubs.

Wedding. large type ed. Emma Darcy. LC 95-53793. 210p. 1996. 22.95 (*0-7838-1241-8*, GK Hall) Thorndike Pr.

***Wedding.** large type ed. Julie Garwood. LC 96-27671. (Basic Ser.). 608p. 1996. 26.95 (*0-7862-0883-X*, Thorndike Lrg Prnt); write for info. (*0-7862-0884-8*) Thorndike Pr.

Wedding. large type ed. Dorothy West. LC 95-5411. 314p. 1995. lib. bdg. 22.95 (*0-7862-0431-1*) Thorndike Pr.

Wedding. limited ed. Dorothy West. 1995. 200.00 (*0-385-47915-8*) Doubleday.

Wedding: (Hindu) (Illus.). pap. write for info. (*0-938924-16-8*) Sri Shirdi Sai.

Wedding: A Novel. Grace Lumpkin. LC 75-28481. (Lost American Fiction Ser.). 325p. 1976. reprint ed. 14.95 (*0-8093-0767-7*) S Ill U Pr.

Wedding: New Pictures from the Continuing "Living Room" Series. Irvine Welsh. (Illus.). 80p. 1996. 40.00 (*0-89381-607-8*) Aperture.

Wedding Advisor. Jeanette Senkowski. 224p. (Orig.). 1995. pap. 16.95 (*1-887177-05-1*) Bridal Buying Bur.

Wedding after the Manner of Friends. rev. ed. Seth B. Hinshaw. 14p. (Orig.). 1984. pap. 1.50 (*0-942727-10-X*) NC Yrly Pubns Bd.

Wedding Album. Nancy Cogan & Roni Akmon. (Wedding Album Ser.). 84p. 1994. 35.95 (*1-884807-00-3*) Blushing Rose.

Wedding Album. Smallwood. 48p. 1996. 30.00 (*0-00-225125-6*, HarpT) HarpC.

Wedding Album: Floral Cover Version. Nancy C. Akmon & Roni Akmon. (Wedding Album Ser.). (Illus.). 84p. 1995. 35.95 (*1-884807-12-7*) Blushing Rose.

Wedding Album Kit: Preserving the Precious. Jeanne English. 58p. 1990. 14.95 (*0-614-00294-X*) Restorat Source.

Wedding & Sacred Music for All Organs, EFS69. (Illus.). 160p. 1948. pap. 12.95 (*0-8256-2069-4*, AM40288) Music Sales.

Wedding Anniversary Idea Book. Rayburn W. Ray & Rose A. Ray. 96p. (Orig.). 1985. pap. 7.95 (*0-939298-43-0*, 430) J M Prods.

Wedding Assignment: Assignment: Romance. Cathryn Clare. (Intimate Moments Ser.). 1996. mass mkt. 3.99 (*0-373-07702-5*, 1-07702-3) Silhouette.

Wedding at Touisset. Richard W. Nason. LC 75-538. (Illus.). 56p. 1975. pap. 6.00 (*0-912292-37-7*) Smith.

Wedding Bargain. Emily French. (Historical Ser.). 1996. mass mkt. 4.99 (*0-373-28936-7*, 1-28936-2) Harlequin Bks.

Wedding Bells. Lydia Browne. 336p. (Orig.). 1994. mass mkt. 4.99 (*1-55773-971-4*) Diamond.

Wedding Bells. Mike Gellerman. 183p. (Orig.). 1987. pap. 3.50 (*0-9617913-0-6*) Orienta Pub.

Wedding Bells. Patricia Rice. 352p. 1996. pap. 5.99 (*0-451-18785-7*, Sig) NAL-Dutton.

Wedding Bells Ahead. Arleta Richardson. LC 87-461. (Grandma's Attic Ser.). 156p. (J). (gr. 3-7). 1995. pap. 4.99 (*1-55513-668-0*, Chariot Bks) Chariot Victor.

Wedding Bells & Diaper Pins. Natalie Patrick. (Romance Ser.). 1995. mass mkt. 2.99 (*0-373-19095-6*, 1-19095-8) Silhouette.

Wedding Bells for Beatrice. Betty A. Neels. (Romance Ser.). 1995. mass mkt. 2.99 (*0-373-03371-0*, 1-03371-1) Harlequin Bks.

Wedding Bells for Beatrice. large type ed. Betty A. Neels. 1995. lib. bdg. 18.95 (*0-263-13939-5*) Thorndike Pr.

W

An Asterisk (*) at the beginning of an entry indicates that the title is appearing in BIP for the first time.

Wedding Book. Ariel Books Staff. (Illus.). 80p. 1992. 4.95 (0-8362-3011-6, Arie Bks) Andrews & McMeel.

Wedding Book. Ed. by John Brimhall. 32p. (YA). 1995. pap. text ed. 6.95 (0-89724-849-X, BMP507) Warner Brothers.

Wedding Bouquet: Low Voice-Piano 17 Celebrated Wedding Songs. 72p. 1987. pap. 12.95 (0-7935-4815-2, 50329290) H Leonard.

Wedding Cake Book. Dede Wilson. LC 97-9514. 1997. 35. 00 (0-02-861234-5) P-H Gen Ref & Trav.

***Wedding Cakes: A Wilton Album.** (Illus.). 80p. (Orig.). 1989. pap. 7.99 (0-912696-43-5) Wilton.

Wedding Cakes: Exciting Designs with Full Step-by-Step Instructions. Sylvia Coward. (Illus.). 80p. 1995. pap. 14. 95 (1-85368-293-4, Pub. by New Holland Pubs UK) Sterling.

Wedding Cakes & Cultural History. Simon R. Charsley. LC 91-24278. 350p. (Orig.). (C). 1992. pap. 16.95 (0-415-02649-0, A6791) Routledge.

Wedding Cakes & Cultural History. Simon R. Charsley. LC 91-24278. 350p. (Orig.). (C). (gr. 13). 1992. text ed. 52. 95 (0-415-02648-2, A6787) Routledge.

Wedding Ceremonies: Planning Your Special Day. Jo Packham. LC 92-44207. (Illus.). 112p. 1993. pap. 5.95 (0-8069-8834-7, Chapelle) Sterling.

Wedding Ceremonies, Dating & Love Customs of Cultures Worldwide, Including Royalty. Carolyn Mordecai. (Illus.). 280p. 1997. write for info. (0-9613823-2-5) Nittany Pr.

Wedding Classics: High Voice. 1992. pap. 16.95 incl. audio (0-7935-0929-7, 00747015) H Leonard.

Wedding Collection: Twenty-Six Basic Wedding Ceremonies for Pastors. Morris Chapman. 1991. 14.99 (0-8054-2004-5, 4220-04) Broadman.

Wedding Contract. Kelly Jamison. 1996. mass mkt. 3.99 (0-373-24014-7, 1-24014-2) Silhouette.

Wedding Date. Christie Ridgway. (Yours Truly Ser.). 1996. mass mkt. 3.50 (0-373-52012-3, 1-52012-1) Silhouette.

Wedding Day. Mark Dunster. 53p. (Orig.). 1986. pap. 5.00 (0-89642-139-2) Linden Pubs.

Wedding Day. Ed. by Edwin Su et al. (Magazine Collection - Marriage Ser.). 242p. 1992. pap. 7.50 (1-882324-01-3) Ambssdrs Christ.

Wedding Day: And Other Stories, Vol. 1. Kay Boyle. LC 72-4420. (Short Story Index Reprint Ser.). 1977. reprint ed. 18.95 (0-8369-4171-3) Ayer.

Wedding Day & Other Korean Plays. Yong Jin O et al. Ed. by UNESCO, Korean National Commission Staff. Tr. by G. Slettland et al. from KOR. (Korean Novels, Plays & Poetry Ser.: No. 2). xiii, 211p. 1983. 20.00 (0-89209-013-8) Pace Intl Res.

Wedding Day in Literature & Art. C. F. Carter. 1972. 59.95 (0-8490-1280-5) Gordon Pr.

Wedding Day in Literature & Art: A Collection of the Best Descriptions of Wedding from the Works of the World's Leading Novelists & Poets. rev. ed. Charles F. Carter. LC 89-71340. (Illus.). xii, 294p. 1990. reprint ed. lib. bdg. 38.00 (1-55888-923-X) Omnigraphics Inc.

***Wedding Day Mystery.** Carolyn Keene. (J). 1997. pap. 3.99 (0-671-00050-0, Minstrel Bks) PB.

***Wedding Days.** Susan Gordon. Date not set. write for info. (0-688-14860-3) Morrow.

***Wedding Deception.** Carolyn Greene. 1997. mass mkt. 3.50 (0-373-44019-7, 1-44019-7) Harlequin Bks.

Wedding Diary. Nancy Cogan & Roni Akmon. (Wedding Album Ser.). 120p. 1994. 8.95 (1-884807-01-1) Blushing Rose.

Wedding Directory for Greater Spartanburg & Greer, 1990-1991. Sandra Sheldon & Martin Sheldon. (Illus.). 64p. (Orig.). 1990. pap. text ed. 2.50 (0-9623130-1-7) Info Servs SC.

***Wedding Directory, 1997: A Guide to Reception Sites & Wedding Related Services in Massachusetts.** Christine M. Young. 148p. 1996. pap. 8.95 (0-9620049-7-9) C D Young Pubns.

Wedding Dress. Maria McBride-Mellinger. LC 93-17435. 1993. 40.00 (0-679-41884-9) Random.

Wedding Dress. Marian Wells. LC 82-14623. 272p. 1982. pap. 7.99 (0-87123-610-9) Bethany Hse.

Wedding Dress. Marian Wells. 256p. 1994. mass mkt. 5.99 (1-55661-522-1) Bethany Hse.

***Wedding Dress.** Carrie Young. 1996. pap. 9.95 (0-385-31899-5, Delta) Dell.

Wedding Dress: Stories from the Dakota Plains. Carrie Young. LC 92-6522. (Bur Oak Original Ser.). 135p. 1992. 16.95 (0-87745-386-1) U of Iowa Pr.

Wedding Dress: Stories from the Dakota Plains. large type ed. Carrie Young. LC 94-14520. 198p. 1994. lib. bdg. 20. 95 (0-7862-0252-1) Thorndike Pr.

Wedding Dress Disaster. Eric D. Stoffle. LC 96-18587. (Shoebox Kids Ser.). (J). 1997. 5.99 (0-8163-1355-5) Pacific Pr Pub Assn.

Wedding Dress Style. Catherine Woram. 1993. 12.98 (1-55521-968-3) Bk Sales Inc.

Wedding Effect. large type ed. Sophie Weston. 288p. 1995. 21.50 (0-263-14266-3, Pub. by M & B UK) Ulverscroft.

***Wedding Escapade.** Kate Denton. 1997. mass mkt. 3.25 (0-373-15698-7, 1-15698-3); mass mkt. 3.25 (0-373-03452-0, 1-03452-9) Harlequin Bks.

***Wedding Essentials.** Cristina Neale. 95p. (Orig.). 1996. pap. 17.95 (0-9654572-0-6) Wedding Essent.

***Wedding Fake Book: C Edition, More Than 150 Traditional & Popular Songs for Piano - Vocal - Guitar.** Ed. by Carol Cuellar. 164p. (Orig.). (YA). 1991. pap. text ed. 12.95 (0-7692-0140-7, F3101FBX) Warner Brothers.

Wedding Fashion Paper Dolls in Full Color. Tom Tierney. (Illus.). (J). (gr. k-3). 1993. pap. 4.50 (0-486-27635-X) Dover.

Wedding Fashions, 1860-1912: Three Hundred Eighty Designs from "La Mode Illustree" Ed. by JoAnne Olian. (Illus.). 96p. 1994. reprint ed. pap. text ed. 10.95 (0-486-27882-4) Dover.

Wedding Fashions 1860-1980. Avril Lansdell. 1989. pap. 25.00 (0-85263-839-6, Pub. by Shire UK) St Mut.

Wedding Feast. Richard Edelman. (Illus.). 1970. pap. 1.50 (0-685-04680-X) Oyez.

***Wedding Fever.** Susan Crosby. (Desire Ser.). 1997. mass mkt. 3.50 (0-373-76061-2, 1-76061-0) Silhouette.

***Wedding Fever.** large type ed. Lee Wilkinson. (Mills & Boon Large Print Ser.). 288p. 1997. 22.50 (0-263-14926-9) Ulverscroft.

Wedding Floral Guest Book. Nancy Akmon. (Wedding Album Ser.). (Illus.). 84p. 1996. 13.95 (1-884807-18-6) Blushing Rose.

Wedding Flowers. Fiona Barnett. 1991. 24.95 (0-671-72834-2) S&S Trade.

Wedding Flowers. Pauline Mann. (Illus.). 64p. 1985. 19.95 (0-7134-4636-6, Pub. by Batsford UK) Trafalgar.

Wedding for Emily. large type ed. Elizabeth August. LC 93-21000. 1993. pap. 13.95 (0-7862-0057-X) Thorndike Pr.

Wedding for Emily Smytheshire. Elizabeth August. (Romance Ser.). 1993. pap. 2.75 (0-373-08953-8, 5-08953-7) Silhouette.

Wedding Gamble. Muriel Jensen. (American Romance Ser.). 1994. mass mkt. 3.50 (0-373-16549-8, 1-16549-7) Harlequin Bks.

Wedding Gamble. Cait Logan. 378p. 1996. mass mkt. 5.99 (0-440-22241-9) Dell.

***Wedding Gift.** Moshe Goldberger. 95p. 1996. 7.95 (1-56871-095-X) Targum Pr.

Wedding Gift: And Other Angling Stories. John T. Foote. 144p. 1992. 18.95 (1-55821-163-2) Lyons & Burford.

Wedding Gift Goof. Carolyn Keene. (Nancy Drew Notebooks Ser.: No. 13). (Illus.). (J). (gr. 4-7). 1996. pap. 3.50 (0-671-53552-8) PB.

Wedding Guest. large type ed. Anna Gilbert. LC 94-1082. 1994. lib. bdg. 19.95 (0-7862-0192-4) Thorndike Pr.

Wedding Guest & Gift Organizer. Don M. Horner & Dee A. Withrow. (Illus.). 76p. (Orig.). 1989. pap. write for info. (0-9623236-9-1) DMH Pub Co Inc.

Wedding Guest Book. Nancy Cogan & Roni Akmon. (Wedding Album Ser.). 84p. 1994. 13.95 (1-884807-04-6) Blushing Rose.

Wedding Guest Book. Helen Exley. (Record Bks.). (Illus.). 80p. 1995. 12.00 (1-85015-608-5) Exley Giftbooks.

***Wedding Guest Book.** Wedding Collection Staff. Date not set. 5.99 (0-517-17689-0) Random Hse Value.

Wedding Hints & Reminders. Sharon Dlugosch. LC 89-9741. 156p. (Orig.). 1989. pap. 8.95 (0-918420-09-1) Brighton Pubns.

Wedding in Ancient Athens. John H. Oakley & Rebecca H. Sinos. LC 93-17881. (Studies in Classics). (Illus.). 144p. (C). 1993. text ed. 40.00 (0-299-13720-1) U of Wis Pr.

Wedding in Hell: Poems. Charles Simic. LC 94-11941. 1994. write for info. (0-15-100123-5); pap. write for info. (0-15-600129-2) HarBrace.

Wedding Invitation. Marisa Carroll. 1994. mass mkt. 3.50 (0-373-70598-0, 1-70598-7) Harlequin Bks.

Wedding Is a Family Affair. deluxe ed. Brenda Hunter & Kristen Blair. (Illus.). 128p. 1995. 14.99 (0-88070-836-0, Multnomah Bks) Multnomah Pubs.

Wedding Jokes. Bill Stott. Ed. by Helen Exley & Samantha Armstrong. (Joke Bks.). (Illus.). 60p. 1992. 6.99 (1-85015-320-5) Exley Giftbooks.

Wedding Kiss. Robin Wells. (Romance Ser.). 1996. mass mkt. 3.25 (0-373-19185-5, 1-19185-7) Silhouette.

Wedding Knot. Pamela Toth. (Special Edition Ser.). 1994. mass mkt. 3.50 (0-373-09905-3, 1-09905-0) Harlequin Bks.

Wedding Memories. Beverly Clark. 64p. 1990. 16.95 (0-934081-05-0) Wlshre Pubns.

Wedding Memories. Jane Kozlouski & Mark Jacobsen. Ed. by Judi Jacobsen. (Wedding Ser.). (Illus.). 96p. 1990. 22. 95 (0-9623800-2-4) Madison Pk Grtings.

Wedding Memories. Lucy Rigg. (Illus.). 64p. 21.00 (0-614-01771-8) Gibson.

Wedding Memory Keepbook. Linda C. Franklin. (Illus.). 60p. 1985. 20.00 (0-934504-50-4) Michel Pub Co.

Wedding Music: An Index to Collections. William D. Goodfellow. LC 92-13745. 205p. 1992. 25.00 (0-8108-2575-9) Scarecrow.

Wedding Music Essentials. Pamela Foard & Gail Nelson. LC 92-64383. 91p. 1992. pap. 19.95 incl. audio (0-9633888-0-0, PNWM01) Preludes Nouveaux.

Wedding Music Essentials. rev. ed. Gail Nelson & Pamela Foard. LC 93-85452. 90p. 1993. pap. 19.95 incl. audio (0-9633888-1-9, PNWM02) Preludes Nouveaux.

***Wedding Music for Flute & Guitar.** Mychal Gendron. (Editiones Classicae Ser.). 1993. pap. 17.95 incl. audio (0-7866-1107-3, 94737P) Mel Bay.

Wedding Music Guide. Jane Salemson. 26p. 1993. pap. 18. 95 incl. audio (0-9636516-9-2) JDJ Pubns.

Wedding Night. Ira Alterman & Herbert I. Kavet. 1994. pap. 5.95 (0-88032-444-9) Ivory Tower Pub.

Wedding Night. Gary Devon. 1995. 21.00 (0-684-80183-3) S&S Trade.

***Wedding Night.** Gary Devon. 1997. mass mkt. 5.99 (0-380-72812-5) Avon.

Wedding Nightmares. Told to Bride's Magazine Editors. LC 92-53565. (Illus.). 128p. (Orig.). 1993. pap. 8.95 (0-452-26768-4, Plume) NAL-Dutton.

Wedding Notebook for the Bride. Linda C. Franklin. (Old Fashioned Keepbook Ser.). (Illus.). 128p. 1980. 12.00 (0-934504-02-4) Michel Pub Co.

Wedding Notebook for the Bride. Linda Franklin. (Keepbooks Ser.). (Illus.). 96p. 1990. reprint ed. 16.00 (0-685-30140-0) Country Diary.

Wedding Occasions: One Hundred & One New Party Themes for Wedding Showers, Rehearsal Dinners, Engagement Parties & More! Cynthia L. Sowden. LC 90-1488. 158p. (Orig.). 1990. pap. 9.95 (0-918420-10-5) Brighton Pubns.

Wedding of a Poet. Ibrahim Sinasi. Tr. by Edward Allworth. (Illus.). 1981. pap. 4.95 (0-918680-15-8) Bagehot Council.

Wedding of G. Washington Bear. Rachel N. Pittman. (Illus.). 42p. (Orig.). (J). (ps-5). 1986. pap. 6.95 (0-9615382-1-X) Pittman Pub.

Wedding of Her Dreams. Karen T. Whittenburg. (American Romance Ser.). 1994. mass mkt. 3.50 (0-373-16528-5, 1-16528-1) Harlequin Bks.

Wedding of the Birds. Jack L. Welch & Grace R. Yost. LC 95-61660. (Illus.). 16p. (Orig.). (J). 1996. pap. 6.95 (0-9641433-1-3) Welch & Welch.

Wedding of the Dead: Ritual, Poetics, & Popular Culture in Transylvania. Gail Kligman. LC 87-25638. (Studies on the History of Society & Culture: No. 4). 1988. pap. 17. 00 (0-520-06964-1) U CA Pr.

Wedding of the Siamese Twins. Burton Cohen. 1989. pap. 5.25 (0-8222-1228-5) Dramatists Play.

Wedding of the Waters. Craig J. Carrozzi. LC 88-60526. (Illus.). 396p. (Orig.). (YA). 1988. pap. 14.95 (0-9620286-0-6) Suthrn Trails Pub.

Wedding of Your Own. Padraig McCarthy. 108p. 1989. pap. 22.00 (0-86217-107-5, Pub. by Veritas IE) St Mut.

Wedding of Zein. Tayeb Salih. Tr. by Denys Johnson-Davies from ARA. 120p. (Orig.). 1978. reprint ed. 15.00 (0-89410-200-1, Three Contnts); reprint ed. pap. 10.00 (0-89410-201-X, Three Contnts) Lynne Rienner.

Wedding of Zein & Other Sudanese Stories. Tayeb Salih. (African Writers Ser.). 120p. (C). 1991. pap. 8.95 (0-435-90047-1, 90047) Heinemann.

Wedding Organizer: The Bar - Bat Mitzvah Organizer. Margaret M. Mitchell. 50p. 1990. student ed. 14.00 (0-9641090-0-X) Wedding Organizer.

Wedding Organizer or How to Plan a Smooth Trip Down the Aisle. rev. ed. Marguerite B. Herring. LC 82-81574. 157p. 1982. reprint ed. pap. 10.95 (0-931948-36-3) Peachtree Pubs.

***Wedding Origami.** Florence Temko & V'ann Cornelius. (My Favorite Origami Ser.). (Illus.). 14p. (Orig.). (YA). (gr. 5 up). 1996. pap. 5.95 (0-89346-838-X) Heian Intl.

Wedding Pages. rev. ed. Monica M. Foster. Ed. by Kenneth L. Nanfito. (Illus.). 176p. 1994. reprint ed. student ed. 9.95 (0-929879-00-7) Wedding Info Network.

Wedding Pages. 7th rev. ed. Monica M. Foster. Ed. by Nancy Stillmnnks. (Illus.). 176p. 1994. pap. 19.95 (0-929879-01-5) Wedding Info Network.

***Wedding Pages.** 7th rev. ed. Monica McFarland. (Illus.). 176p. 1996. pap. text ed. 19.95 (0-929879-02-3) Wedding Info Network.

Wedding Party Responsibility Cards: Christian Edition. Alex Lluch & Elizabeth Lluch. 48p. 1994. pap. 6.95 (0-9639654-9-2) Wedding Solns.

***Wedding Photographers' Book of Contracts, Policies, Procedures.** Steve Herzog. (Professional Photography Ser.). (Illus.). 76p. (Orig.). 1995. pap. text ed. 24.95 (0-9633158-3-8) Incite Pubns.

Wedding Photographer's Handbook. Robert Hurth & Sheila Hurth. (Illus.). 172p. 1996. pap. 24.95 (0-936262-44-3) Amherst Media.

Wedding Photography. Rotovision S. A. Staff. (Pro-Photo Ser.). (Illus.). 160p. 1995. pap. 29.95 (0-8230-6469-7, Amphoto) Watsn-Guptill.

Wedding Photography: Building a Profitable Pricing Strategy. 2nd ed. Steve Herzog. (Professional Photography Ser.). (Illus.). 222p. 1992. pap. text ed. 39. 95 (0-9633158-0-3) Incite Pubns.

Wedding Photography: Down the Aisle Backwards. Steve Sint. (Illus.). 175p. (Orig.). (C). Date not set. pap. 29.95 (1-883403-36-7, H 705, Silver Pixel Pr) Saunders Photo.

Wedding Photography & Video: The Bride & Groom's Guide. Chuck DeLaney. LC 93-71918. 160p. (Orig.). 1994. pap. 10.95 (1-880559-10-2) Allworth Pr.

Wedding Pianist. 1993. 8.99 (0-8341-9240-3, MB-650) Lillenas.

***Wedding Pictures: A Novel.** Kathy Osborn & Jacqueline Carey. LC 96-33988. 1997. 22.95 (0-8118-1109-3) Chronicle Bks.

Wedding Planner. 125p. 1992. write for info. (1-882157-00-1); pap. write for info. (1-882157-02-8) Hodges & Irvine.

Wedding Planner. Diana Ajjan. 160p. (Orig.). 1994. pap. 3.99 (0-425-14104-7) Berkley Pub.

***Wedding Planner.** Diana Ajjan. 1994. pap. 3.99 (0-425-14106-3) Berkley Pub.

Wedding Planner. Genevieve Morgan. 130p. 1996. 24.95 (0-8118-0994-3) Chronicle Bks.

Wedding Planner. Martha Stewart. (Illus.). 256p. 1988. Slipcased, hidden spiral bdg. boxed, spiral bd. 37.50 (0-517-56566-8, C P Pubs) Crown Pub Group.

***Wedding Planner.** Martha Stewart. Date not set. 9.99 (0-517-19273-X) Random Hse Value.

Wedding Planner: Your Step-by-Step Guide to Planning Your Wedding from Engagement to Honeymoon. Valerie Hathaway et al. (Illus.). 32p. (Orig.). 1993. pap. 8.00 (0-9618935-3-2) Linholm.

Wedding Planner & Record Book: Wedding Planning Made Simple & Memorable. 80p. 1996. 17.95 (0-7894-0446-X) DK Pub Inc.

Wedding Planner for Brides: Questions You Need to Ask When Planning the Perfect Wedding. JoAnn K. Leonard. 190p. 1994. reprint ed. pap. 24.95 (0-9629412-5-5) Garnet Rose.

***Wedding Planner Tames Rancher!** Pamela Ingrahm. (Desire Ser.: No. 1086). 1997. mass mkt. 3.50 (0-373-76086-8, 1-76086-7) Silhouette.

Wedding Planners Inc. Wedding Guide. Wedding Planners Inc. Staff. (Illus.). 62p. (Orig.). 1988. pap. 7.95 (0-9619779-1-4) Wedding Planners.

Wedding Plans: 50 Unique Themes for the Wedding of Your Dreams. Sharon Dlugosch. LC 96-12326. 1996. 10.95 (0-918420-28-8) Brighton Pubns.

Wedding Procession of the Rag Doll & the Broom Handle & Who Was in It. Carl Sandburg. LC 67-10211. (Voyager Picture Bks.). (Illus.). 32p. (J). (ps-3). 1978. pap. 4.00 (0-15-695487-7, Voyager Bks) HarBrace.

***Wedding Quilt.** Nazworth. 1997. mass mkt. 4.50 (0-373-87012-4) Harlequin Bks.

Wedding Raffle. Geralyn Dawson. 1996. mass mkt. 5.99 (0-671-00126-4) PB.

***Wedding Ransom.** Dawson. 1998. mass mkt. 5.99 (0-671-00127-2) PB.

Wedding Readings: Centuries of Writing & Rituals on Love & Marriage. Intro. by Eleanor Munro. 262p. 1996. pap. 12.95 (0-14-008879-2, Viking) Viking Penguin.

Wedding Receptions: Arranging a Joyous Celebration. Jo Packham. LC 93-25930. (Wedding Ser.). 112p. 1993. pap. 5.95 (0-8069-8833-9, Chapelle) Sterling.

Wedding Report: A Prototypical Approach to the Study of Traditional Text Types. Hans-Jurg Suter. LC 93-10695. (Pragmatics & Beyond Ser.: No. 27). xii, 314p. 1993. 74. 00 (1-55619-295-9) Benjamins North Am.

Wedding Resource Directory: An Annual Directory of Wedding Services in the Denver-Boulder Area. 3rd ed. M. Susan Portz. (Illus.). 110p. 1989. pap. 8.95 (0-9617718-2-8) Bascom Pr.

Wedding Resource Directory: An Annual Directory of Wedding Services in the Denver-Boulder Area. 4th ed. M. Susan Portz. (Illus.). 104p. 1990. write for info. (0-318-66813-0); pap. 8.95 (0-9617718-3-6) Bascom Pr.

***Wedding Rings & Baby Things.** Teresa Southwick. (Romance Ser.). 1997. 3.25 (0-373-19209-6, 1-19209-5) Silhouette.

Wedding Secrets. Melissa Lowell. (Silver Blades Super Ser.: Vol. 2). 144p. (J). 1997. pap. 3.99 (0-553-48523-7) Bantam.

Wedding Sentiments. Ariel Books Staff. (Illus.). 16p. 1994. 4.95 (0-8362-3057-4, Arie Bks) Andrews & McMeel.

Wedding Shower Book. 2nd ed. Janet Anastasio. LC 94-3728. 1995. pap. 7.95 (1-55850-407-9) Adams Media.

***Wedding Showers for Couples: Over 100 Theme Showers.** Pamela Thomas. LC 96-94875. (Illus.). 120p. (Orig.). 1997. pap. 11.95 (0-9615882-4-1) Bridal Guide.

Wedding Song. Naguib Mahfouz. 176p. 1989. pap. 9.95 (0-385-26464-X, Anchor NY) Doubleday.

Wedding Song. large type ed. Rebecca Lang. 288p. 1996. 21.50 (0-263-14633-2, Pub. by M & B UK) Ulverscroft.

Wedding Song: (Weddings, Inc.) Vicki L. Thompson. (Temptation Ser.). 1994. mass mkt. 2.99 (0-373-25602-7, 1-25602-3) Harlequin Bks.

Wedding Song of Wisdom. G. R. Mead. 107p. 1992. pap. 12.95 (1-56459-155-7) Kessinger Pub.

***Wedding Song of Wisdom.** G. R. Mead. Date not set. reprint ed. pap. 6.95 (1-55818-383-3, Alexandrian) Holmes Pub.

***Wedding Songs for the Solo Guitarist: A Collection of Love Songs.** rev. ed. 48p. (Orig.). (YA). 1995. pap. text ed. 17.95 incl. audio compact disk (0-89724-585-7, F3055GTXCD) Warner Brothers.

Wedding Sourcebook. Madeline Barillo. LC 95-43582. (Illus.). 336p. 1996. 30.00 (1-56565-448-X) Lowell Hse.

***Wedding Sourcebook.** Madeline Barillo. 1997. pap. text ed. 16.00 (1-56565-650-4) Lowell Hse.

***Wedding Sourcebook Planner.** Madeline Barillo. Date not set. pap. 15.00 (1-56565-649-0) Contemp Bks.

Wedding Speeches. Lee Jarvis. 128p. (Orig.). 1993. pap. 9.95 (0-572-01781-2, Pub. by W Foulsham UK) Trans-Atl Phila.

Wedding Speeches & Toasts. 2nd ed. Barbara Jeffery. 96p. (Orig.). 1995. pap. 6.95 (0-572-00779-5, Pub. by Foulsham UK) Assoc Pubs Grp.

Wedding Styles for the Unique Bride. Rita Williamson. (Illus.). (Orig.). 1994. pap. 27.50 (0-572-01745-6, Pub. by W Foulsham UK) Trans-Atl Phila.

Wedding Time. Heidi Larson. (Way We Live Ser.). (Illus.). 25p. (J). (gr. 2-4). 1991. 15.95 (0-237-60146-X, Pub. by Evans Bros Ltd UK) Trafalgar.

Wedding to Remember. Emma Darcy. 1994. mass mkt. 2.99 (0-373-11659-4, 1-11659-9) Harlequin Bks.

***Wedding to Remember.** Emma Darcy. (And the Winner Is...Ser.). 1997. mass mkt. 3.99 (0-373-48346-5, 1-48346-0) Harlequin Bks.

***Wedding to Remember.** large type ed. Emma Darcy. (Magna Large Print Ser.). 263p. 1997. 27.50 (0-7505-1096-X) Ulverscroft.

Wedding Toasts & Speeches: Finding the Perfect Words. Jo Packham. LC 92-41319. (Illus.). 96p. 1993. pap. 5.95 (0-8069-8832-0, Chapelle) Sterling.

Wedding Tour: January to June Eighteen Seventy-Three & Visit to the Vienna Exhibition. Emily Birchall. Ed. by David Verey. LC 85-18463. (Illus.). 166p. 1985. text ed. 29.95 (0-312-85998-8) St Martin.

Wedding Treasures. Customs Creations Staff. (Illus.). 28p. (Orig.). 1986. pap. 5.95 (0-933491-15-8) Hot off Pr.

Wedding Troika. Jovan V. Vukcevich. 1980. pap. 4.95 (0-910286-80-9) Boxwood.

Wedding Venture. Nikki Benjamin. (Intimate Moments Ser.). 1995. mass mkt. 3.75 (0-373-07645-2, 1-07645-4) Silhouette.

Wedding Videographer's Handbook. Stanley J. Modrzyk. 82p. (Orig.). 1986. pap. 4.50 (0-939751-00-3) Seeing Is Believing Video.

Wedding Vows. (Little Gift Bks.). (Illus.). 80p. 1996. 4.95 (0-8362-1057-3) Andrews & McMeel.

W

Wedding Vows: How to Express Your Love in Your Own Words. Peg Kehret. Ed. by Arthur L. Zapel. LC 89-32089. 112p. (Orig.). 1989. pap. 10.95 (*0-916260-59-3*, B151) Meriwether Pub.

Wedding Warnings: What Every Bride & Groom Must Know but Were Never Told until Now! Thomas Riccardo. Ed. by Brenda Becka. 120p. (Orig.). pap. text ed. write for info. (*0-9633972-0-6*) Club Wed Pubns.

***Wedding Wise Workbook.** Suzanne Kresse. 128p. 1998. pap. write for info. (*0-425-15615-X*, Berkley Trade) Berkley Pub.

***Wedding Wish.** Susan Florence. (New Loving Thoughts Ser.). 40p. 1996. 6.95 (*0-8378-8072-6*) Gibson.

Wedding Wonders: Tales & Traditions, Customs & Curiosities. Kimberly B. Allen. Ed. by Patrick Caton. LC 96-76132. 168p. 1996. 5.95 (*1-56245-264-9*) Great Quotations.

Wedding Workbook: Everything You Need for Planning Your Wedding. Marlene S. Holloway. 66p. (Orig.). 1994. 24.95 (*0-9644351-0-1*) Marlenes Wedding Coll.

***Weddings.** Beverly Clark. 1996. 60.00 (*0-934081-14-X*) Wlshre Pubns.

***Weddings.** Cowie Colin. LC 97-14916. 1998. 65.00 (*0-316-24661-1*) Little.

Weddings. Ann Morris. LC 94-48040. (Illus.). 32p. (J). (gr. k-2). 1995. 15.00 (*0-688-13272-3*); lib. bdg. 14.93 (*0-688-13273-1*) Lothrop.

Weddings. Martha Stewart & Elizabeth B. Hawes. (Illus.). 384p. 1987. 70.00 (*0-517-55675-8*, C P Pubs) Crown Pub Group.

Weddings: The 'How-To' Manual for Non-Denominational Ministers & Chaplains: And What Should Be Discussed with Couples Planning Their Wedding. Rev. by John E. Forbes-Cunningham. (Illus.). 160p. (Orig.). 1993. student ed., pap. 19.95 (*0-9637049-1-5*) Anglican Pubns.

Weddings by Design: A Guide to Non-Traditional Ceremonies. Richard Leviton. LC 92-53058. 208p. 1994. pap. 14.00 (*0-06-251007-X*) Harper SF.

Weddings, Christenings & Anniversaries in Lace. Ed. by Bridget M. Cook. (Illus.). 48p. 1996. pap. 19.95 (*0-7134-7789-X*, Pub. by Batsford UK) Trafalgar.

***Weddings, Dating, & Love Customs of Cultures Worldwide, Including Royalty.** Carolyn Mordecai. LC 96-68875. (Illus.). 280p. 1997. 28.00 (*0-614-29356-1*) Nittany Pr.

Weddings for Complicated Families: The New Etiquette. Margorie Engel. 1993. pap. 14.95 (*0-9635257-0-0*) Mt Ivy Pr.

***Weddings for Dummies.** Marcy Blum. 1997. pap. 19.99 (*0-7645-5055-1*) IDG Bks.

Weddings for Grownups. Carroll Stoner. LC 92-21868. 224p. 1993. pap. 12.95 (*0-8118-0229-9*) Chronicle Bks.

Weddings for Grownups: Everything You Need to Know to Plan Your Wedding Your Way. rev. ed. Carroll Stoner. LC 96-41633. 224p. 1997. pap. 17.95 (*0-8118-1421-1*) Chronicle Bks.

***Weddings from the Heart.** Daphne R. Kingma. 1997. 7.98 (*1-56731-177-6*, MJF Bks) Fine Comms.

Weddings from the Heart: Contemporary & Traditional Ceremonies for an Unforgettable Wedding. expanded rev. ed. Daphne R. Kingma. 180p. 1995. lib. bdg. 35.00 (*0-8095-5889-0*) Borgo Pr.

Weddings from the Heart: Contemporary & Traditional Ceremonies for an Unforgettable Wedding. expanded rev. ed. Daphne R. Kingma. (Illus.). 200p. 1995. pap. 12.95 (*0-943233-94-1*) Conari Press.

Weddings, Funerals, Liturgy of the Hours. Ed. by Virgil C. Funk. (Pastoral Music in Practice Ser.: No. 3). (Orig.). 1990. pap. 9.95 (*0-912405-75-9*) Pastoral Pr.

Weddings in Style: A Northern California Guide to Extraordinary Wedding & Party Sites. Denise Beatty & Dana Beatty. (Illus.). 300p. (Orig.). 1990. pap. 19.95 (*0-9625196-3-4*) D & D Beatty.

Weddings in the Wine Country: Beautiful Locations for Your Romantic Northern California Wedding. Debbie Doumitt. 200p. (Orig.). 1995. pap. 16.95 (*0-9643567-2-4*) Bird Rock Pr.

Weddings in Tripolitania. Abdelkafi. 126p. 1987. 100.00 (*0-317-62541-1*, Pub. by Darf Pubs Ltd UK) St Mut.

Weddings in Tripolitania. A. Abdelkafi. 126p. (C). 1989. 35.00 (*1-85077-945-7*, Pub. by Darf Pubs Ltd UK) St Mut.

Wedding's Over: What Now? Eddie Lewis. 1989. 9.95 (*0-89137-574-0*); pap. 6.75 (*0-685-35356-7*) Quality Pubns.

Weddings Southern Style. Beverly R. Church & Lisa R. Harrison. (Illus.). 256p. 1993. 50.00 (*1-55859-290-3*) Abbeville Pr.

Weddings with More Love Than Money. Abby Ruoff. 200p. 1995. pap. 14.95 (*0-88179-117-2*) Hartley & Marks.

Weddiquette: Answers to All Your Wedding Ettiquette Questions. Yetta F. Gruen. LC 94-34803. 1995. pap. 10.95 (*0-14-024139-6*, Penguin Bks) Viking Penguin.

Wedekind: Plays One. Frank Wedekind. 209p. (C). 1993. pap. 15.95 (*0-413-67540-8*, A0675, Pub. by Methuen UK) Heinemann.

Wedemeyer on War & Peace. Ed. by Keith E. Eiler. (Publication Ser.: No. 367). 272p. 1987. pap. 18.95 (*0-8179-8672-3*); text ed. 25.95 (*0-8179-8671-5*) Hoover Inst Pr.

Wedemeyer Reports! Albert C. Wedemeyer. pap. 19.95 (*0-8159-7216-4*) Devin.

***Wedge.** Patricia Armentrout. LC 97-15158. (Simple Machines Ser.). 1997. write for info. (*1-57103-181-2*) Rourke Pr.

Wedge: History & Genealogy. James D. Beissel, Sr. Ed. by Janice M. Stoltzfus. LC 90-80964. (Illus.). 462p. 1991. text ed. 60.00 (*0-9623159-0-7*) Crystal Educn.

Wedge: History & Genealogy. James D. Beissel, Sr. Ed. by Janice N. Stoltzfus. LC 90-80964. (Illus.). 462p. 1991. text ed. 60.00 (*0-685-54348-X*) Crystal Educn.

Wedge: The Extraordinary Communications of an Earthbound Spirit. Margaret Moon & Maurine. (Illus.). 136p. 1975. pap. 3.95 (*0-87542-497-X*) Llewellyn Pubns.

Wedge-Game Pocket Campanion. Jim McLean & John Andrisani. LC 95-23231. (Illus.). 128p. 1995. 10.00 (*0-06-270141-X*, Harper Ref) HarpC.

Wedge Goes to Arizona. J. T. Edson. 288p. 1996. mass mkt. 4.99 (*0-440-22218-4*) Dell.

Wedge of Gold. W. A. Scott. 1974. pap. 4.99 (*0-87377-080-3*) GAM Pubns.

Wedge of Words. 2nd ed. Frederic Will. LC 61-15828. (Tower Poetry Ser.: No. 1). (Illus.). 1963. reprint ed. 10.00 (*0-87959-055-6*) U of Tex H Ransom Ctr.

Wedge's Gamble. Michael A. Stackpole. (Star Wars X-Wing Ser.: No. 2). 384p. (YA). 1996. mass mkt. 5.99 (*0-553-56802-7*) Bantam.

Wedgewood: Their Music, Their Journey. Wedgwood Trio & Marilyn Thomsen. LC 96-6353. 1996. pap. 10.99 (*0-8163-1343-1*) Pacific Pr Pub Assn.

Wedgwood, 2 vols. R. Reilly. LC 89-21609. 1989. Set. 850.00 (*0-935859-85-3*, Stockton Pr) Groves Dictionaries.

Wedgwood. Geoffrey Wills. 1989. 14.98 (*1-55521-389-8*) Bk Sales Inc.

Wedgwood. deluxe ed. Gene Garrison. (Illus.). 48p. 1982. 28.00 (*0-88014-061-5*) Mosaic Pr OH.

Wedgwood. John M. Graham, II & Hensleigh C. Wedgwood. LC 71-128384. (Brooklyn Museum Publications in Reprint). (Illus.). 122p. 1974. reprint ed. 15.95 (*0-405-00878-3*) Ayer.

Wedgwood: Its Competitors & Imitators, 1800-1830. 1977. 40.00 (*0-89344-021-3*) Ars Ceramica.

Wedgwood: The New Illustrated Dictionary. Robin Reilly. (Illus.). 1994. 89.50 (*1-85149-209-7*) Antique Collect.

Wedgwood & Bentley Pottery from the Kadison Collection. LC 83-16635. (Illus.). 71p. 1983. pap. 9.00 (*0-87328-081-4*) Huntington Lib.

Wedgwood & His Imitators. 2nd rev. ed. Hannah H. Moore. LC 76-2888. (Illus.). 1978. 29.95 (*0-89344-005-1*) Ars Ceramica.

Wedgwood Ceramics 1846-1959. Maureen Batkin. (Illus.). 1982. 95.00 (*0-903685-11-6*, Pub. by R Dennis UK) Antique Collect.

Wedgwood Circle: 1730-1897; Four Generations of Wedgwoods & Their Friends. Hensleigh C. Wedgewood. LC 80-65213. (Illus.). 408p. 1980. 22.50 (*0-89860-038-3*) Eastview.

Wedgwood Handbook. Eliza Meteyard. 1972. 250.00 (*0-8490-1281-3*) Gordon Pr.

Wedgwood in the Collection of the R. W. Norton Art Gallery. (Illus.). 101p. 1980. pap. 10.00 (*0-913060-18-6*) Norton Art.

Wedgwood International Seminar: An Index to the Published Proceedings, 1956-1992. Alton C. Powell. LC 94-66653. 56p. 1994. pap. text ed. 17.00 (*0-9641682-0-0*) A C Powell.

Wedgwood Jasper. Robin Reilly. LC 94-60284. (Illus.). 408p. 1994. 60.00 (*0-500-01624-0*) Thames Hudson.

Wedgwood Ware. Robert Copeland. (Illus.). 1995. pap. 25.00 (*0-7478-0296-3*, Pub. by Shire UK) St Mut.

Wedlock... The Common Sense Marriage. Sherman N. Miller & Gwynelle W. Miller. 224p. (Orig.). 1994. pap. 12.95 (*0-9640915-6-9*) S N M Pubng.

Wedlock: Two Novellas. Mark Spencer. 157p. 1990. pap. 7.50 (*0-922820-02-3*) Watermrk Pr.

Wedlock's the Devil: Eighteen Fourteen to Eighteen Fifteen see Byron's Letters & Journals

Wednesday Game. Martin Yoseloff. LC 87-47860. 240p. 1988. 15.95 (*0-8453-4808-6*, Cornwall Bks) Assoc Univ Prs.

***Wednesday Girl.** Julie Nisargand. 192p. (Orig.). 1997. pap. 10.00 (*0-9654757-1-9*) Anima Bks CA.

Wednesday Is Spaghetti & Macaroni & Fettucine & Pasta Salads & More: And Macaroni & Fettucine & Pasta Salads & More. Time-Life Books Editors. LC 95-10416. (Everyday Cookbooks Ser.). 128p. 1995. 14.95 (*0-8094-9188-5*) Time-Life.

Wednesday Nights. Camarin Grae. 384p. 1994. pap. 10.95 (*1-56280-060-4*) Naiad Pr.

Wednesday Surprise. Eve Bunting. (Illus.). 32p. (J). (ps-3). 1900. pap. 5.95 (*0-395-54776-8*, Clarion Bks) HM.

Wednesday Surprise. Eve Bunting. 32p. (J). (gr. k-3). 1989. 15.00 (*0-89919-721-3*, Clarion Bks) HM.

Wednesday Surprise. Houghton Mifflin Company Staff. (Literature Experience 1991 Ser.). (J). (gr. 3). 1990. pap. 8.48 (*0-395-55151-X*) HM.

Wednesday the Rabbi Got Wet. Harry Kemelman. (Rabbi Ser.). 1987. mass mkt. 5.99 (*0-449-21328-5*) Fawcett.

Wednesday Workout: Practical Techniques for Rehearsing the Church Choir Series & Series Editor. Richard Devinney. LC 93-8285. 96p. (Orig.). 1993. pap. 9.95 (*0-687-44312-1*) Abingdon.

Wednesdays at the Pier: Visitors & Regulars at the San Monica Pier. Tom Zimmerman. 1991. pap. 11.95 (*1-56171-048-2*) Sure Seller.

Wednesday's Child. Peter Robinson. 320p. 1995. mass mkt. 5.99 (*0-425-14834-3*, Prime Crime) Berkley Pub.

Wednesday's Child. Deborah N. Shlian. 1986. 3.95 (*0-317-52123-3*) PB.

Wednesday's Child: An Inspector Banks Mystery. Peter Robinson. 352p. 1994. 20.00 (*0-684-19644-1*) S&S Trade.

Wednesday's Child: An Inspector Banks Mystery. large type ed. Peter Robinson. LC 94-19361. 1994. pap. 18.95 (*0-7862-0276-9*) Thorndike Pr.

Wednesday's Child Is Full of Woe: Helping Children Is Full of Grief. Kathie J. Johnson et al. (Illus.). 192p. 1991. pap. 11.95 (*1-879695-00-6*) Hill Hse Pubs.

***Wednesday's Children.** Robin Hyde. 224p. 1996. 24.95 (*0-908569-72-6*, Pub. by U Otago Pr NZ) Intl Spec Bk.

Wednesday's Children: A Study of Child Neglect & Abuse. Leontine Young. LC 78-12941. 195p. 1979. reprint ed. text ed. 59.75 (*0-313-20637-6*, YOWC, Greenwood Pr) Greenwood.

Wee Bit of Texas. Rita Kerr. (Illus.). 80p. (J). (gr. 1-4). 1991. 11.95 (*0-89015-809-6*) Sunbelt Media.

Wee Book. Kita Antonia. (Illus.). 32p. (Orig.). (J). (gr. k-3). 1995. pap. 12.00 (*1-887116-11-7*) Saxon West Pubns.

Wee Color Wee Sing America. Susan H. Nipp & Pamela C. Beall. (Illus.). 48p. (J). (ps-2). 1989. pap. 1.95 (*0-8431-2277-3*) Price Stern Sloan.

Wee Color Wee Sing Australia. Susan H. Nipp & Pamela C. Beall. (Wee Color, Wee Sing Coloring Activity Packages Ser.). 48p. (J). (ps-2). 1989. pap. 1.95 (*0-8431-4725-3*) Price Stern Sloan.

Wee Cookbook. 4th ed. Irish Children's Fund Families & Friends Staff. (Illus.). 300p. pap. 7.95 (*0-9614331-2-4*) Irish Childs Fund.

Wee Folks A B C's of the Bible. Elisabeth R. Scovil. LC 95-20326. (Wee Books for Wee Folks). (Illus.). 64p. (J). (ps-2). 1996. reprint ed. 6.95 (*1-55709-413-6*) Applewood.

Wee Folks Inching On: A Phonetic Approach to Beginning Reading. Charlotte M. Hill. Ed. by Theodore Fields. LC 90-832256. (Wee Folks Readers Ser.: Vol. 2). (Illus.). 89p. (J). (gr. k-3). 1991. pap. text ed. 7.95 (*0-9620182-4-4*) Charill Pubs.

Wee Folks Learn to Read: A Phonetic Approach to Beginning Reading. Charlotte M. Hill. Ed. by Elaine Young et al. LC 90-83256. (Wee Folks Readers Ser.: Vol. 1). (Illus.). 77p. (Orig.). (J). (gr. k-3). 1991. reprint ed. pap. text ed. 7.95 (*0-9620182-3-6*) Charill Pubs.

Wee Folks Moving Up: A Phonetic Approach to Beginning Reading. Charlotte M. Hill. LC 91-70303. (Wee Folks Readers Ser.: Vol. 3). (Illus.). (Orig.). (J). (gr. k-3). 1991. pap. text ed. 7.95 (*0-9620182-5-2*) Charill Pubs.

Wee Folks on Top: Adventures in Reading. Charlotte M. Hill & Fred D. Hill. Ed. by Cleona Shortridge. LC 92-90056. (Wee Folks Readers Ser.: Vol. 5). (Illus.). 66p. (Orig.). (J). (gr. 3-5). 1992. pap. 8.95 (*0-9620182-7-9*) Charill Pubs.

Wee Folks Reading Series: A Phonetic Approach to Beginning Reading, 5 vols. Charlotte M. Hill. Ed. by Cleona Shortridge. LC 90-832256. (Illus.). 70p. (Orig.). (J). (gr. k-5). 1992. Set. pap. write for info. (*0-9620182-9-5*) Charill Pubs.

Wee Folks Soaring High: A Phonetic Approach to Beginning Reading. Charlotte M. Hill. Ed. by Cleona Shortridge. LC 91-73581. (Wee Folks Readers Ser.: Vol. 4). (Illus.). 101p. (Orig.). (J). (gr. k-3). 1992. pap. text ed. 7.95 (*0-9620182-6-0*) Charill Pubs.

***Wee Frannie Frog & the Noisy Croaking: A Teeny Tiny Bedtime Story, Vol. 3.** Virginia M. Whitcanack. LC 96-61456. (Illus.). 16p. (Orig.). (J). (ps-4). 1996. pap. 4.45 (*1-889484-02-4*) TBS Publng.

Wee G. Harriet Ziefert. LC 96-4203. (Illus.). (J). 1997. write for info. (*0-614-97949-8*, Atheneum Bks Young) S&S Childrens.

Wee G. Harriet Ziefert. (J). 1997. 15.00 (*0-689-81064-4*) S&S Childrens.

Wee Green Witch. Mary Leister. LC 78-12380. (Illus.). 44p. (J). (ps up). 1978. 12.95 (*0-916144-30-5*) Stemmer Hse.

Wee Little Flea Circus. Dan Witkowski. (J). 1995. 14.99 (*0-679-87698-7*) Random.

Wee Little Woman. Byron Barton. LC 94-18683. (Illus.). 32p. (J). (ps-1). 1995. 13.95 (*0-06-023387-7*); lib. bdg. 14.89 (*0-06-023388-5*) HarpC Child Bks.

Wee Mouse Who Was Afraid of the Dark. Margo Lundell. (All Aboard Bks.). (Illus.). 32p. (J). (ps-3). 1991. pap. 2.95 (*0-448-40060-X*, G&D) Putnam Pub Group.

Wee Mouse's Peekaboo House. Illus. by Jean Hirashima. LC 89-64279. (Peek-a-Boo Board Bks.). 14p. (J). (ps). 1991. 3.99 (*0-679-80786-1*) Random Bks Yng Read.

Wee Pals: Musical. Ole Kittleson & Morrie Turner. 54p. 1984. pap. 5.00 (*0-87129-109-6*, W02) Dramatic Pub.

Wee Peter Puffin. Jane S. Weinberger. LC 84-51988. (Illus.). 40p. (J). (ps-8). 1984. reprint ed. pap. 9.95 (*0-932433-03-0*) Windswept Hse.

Wee Science. Laura Candler. (Illus.). 200p. 1994. pap. text ed. 22.00 (*1-879097-25-7*) Kagan Cooperative.

Wee Scot Book: Scottish Poems & Stories. Ed. by Linda Greenberg. LC 93-28728. (Illus.). (J). 1994. 19.95 (*1-56554-018-2*); audio 9.95 (*1-56554-019-0*) Pelican.

***Wee Sing: More Bible Songs.** Pamela C. Beall & Susan H. Nipp. (Illus.). 64p. (J). (ps-3). 1997. 12.95 incl. audio compact disk (*0-8431-7881-7*, Wee Sing) Price Stern Sloan.

***Wee Sing: Silly Songs.** Pamela C. Beall & Susan H. Nipp. (Illus.). 64p. (J). (ps-3). 1997. 12.95 incl. audio compact disk (*0-8431-7878-7*, Wee Sing) Price Stern Sloan.

***Wee Sing: Sing-Alongs.** Pamela C. Beall & Susan H. Nipp. (Illus.). 64p. (J). (ps-3). 1997. 12.95 incl. audio compact disk (*0-8431-7880-9*, Wee Sing) Price Stern Sloan.

***Wee Sing: Sing & Play.** Pamela C. Beall & Susan H. Nipp. 64p. (J). (ps-3). 1997. 12.95 incl. audio compact disk (*0-8431-7879-5*, Wee Sing) Price Stern Sloan.

Wee Sing see Wee Sing Children's Songs & Fingerplays

Wee Sing America. Pamela C. Beall & Susan H. Nipp. (Wee Sing Ser.). (Illus.). 64p. (J). (ps-2). 1987. 9.95 incl. audio (*0-8431-3799-1*); pap. 2.95 (*0-8431-3805-X*) Price Stern Sloan.

Wee Sing & Play. Pamela C. Beall & Susan H. Nipp. (Wee Sing Ser.). (Illus.). 64p. (Orig.). (J). (ps-2). 1983. pap. 2.95 (*0-8431-3812-2*); pap. 9.95 incl. audio (*0-8431-3796-7*) Price Stern Sloan.

Wee Sing Around the Campfire see Wee Sing Sing-Alongs

Wee Sing Around the World. Pamela C. Beall & Susan H. Nipp. (Wee Sing Ser.). (Illus.). 65p. (J). (ps-6). 1994. 9.95 incl. audio (*0-8431-3729-0*); pap. 2.95 (*0-8431-3740-1*) Price Stern Sloan.

Wee Sing Bible Songs. (Wee Sing Ser.). (J). 1992. pap. 2.95 (*0-8423-8069-8*) Tyndale.

Wee Sing Bible Songs. Pamela C. Beall & Susan H. Nipp. (Wee Sing Ser.). (Illus.). 64p. (J). (ps-2). 1986. pap. 2.95 (*0-8431-3806-8*); pap. 9.95 incl. audio (*0-8431-3795-9*) Price Stern Sloan.

***Wee Sing Bible Songs.** Pamela C. Beall & Susan H. Nipp. (Wee Sing Ser.). (Illus.). 64p. (J). (ps-3). 1996. pap. 12.95 incl. audio compact disk (*0-8431-7938-4*) Price Stern Sloan.

***Wee Sing Children's Songs & Fingerplay.** Pamela C. Beall & Susan H. Nipp. (Wee Sing Ser.). (Illus.). 64p. (J). (ps-3). 1996. pap. 12.95 incl. audio compact disk (*0-8431-7940-6*) Price Stern Sloan.

Wee Sing Children's Songs & Fingerplays. Pamela C. Beall & Susan H. Nipp. (Wee Sing Ser.). Orig. Title: Wee Sing. (Illus.). 64p. (J). (ps-2). 1982. 9.95 incl. audio (*0-8431-3793-2*); pap. 2.95 incl. audio (*0-8431-3807-6*) Price Stern Sloan.

Wee Sing Dinosaurs. Pamela C. Beall et al. (Wee Sing Ser.). (Illus.). 64p. (J). (ps-2). 1991. pap. 2.95 (*0-8431-3809-2*); pap. 9.95 incl. audio (*0-8431-3801-7*) Price Stern Sloan.

Wee Sing for Baby. Pamela C. Beall. (J). (ps). 1996. pap. text ed. 2.95 (*0-8431-7942-2*) Price Stern Sloan.

***Wee Sing for Baby.** Pamela C. Beall & Susan H. Nipp. (Illus.). 64p. (J). (ps). 1996. pap. 9.95 incl. audio (*0-8431-7990-2*, Wee Sing) Price Stern Sloan.

***Wee Sing for Baby.** Pamela C. Beall & Susan H. Nipp. (Wee Sing Ser.). (Illus.). 64p. (J). (ps-3). 1996. pap. 12.95 incl. audio compact disk (*0-8431-7949-X*, Wee Sing) Price Stern Sloan.

Wee Sing for Christmas. Pamela C. Beall & Susan H. Nipp. (Wee Sing Ser.). (Illus.). 64p. (Orig.). (J). (ps-2). 1984. pap. 2.95 (*0-8431-3808-4*); pap. 9.95 incl. audio (*0-8431-3800-9*) Price Stern Sloan.

Wee Sing Fun 'n' Folk. Pamela C. Beall & Susan H. Nipp. (Wee Sing Ser.). (Illus.). 64p. (Orig.). (J). (ps-2). pap. 2.95 (*0-8431-3810-6*); pap. 9.95 incl. audio (*0-8431-3802-5*) Price Stern Sloan.

Wee Sing More Bible Song. Pamela C. Beall. (Wee Sing Ser.). (Illus.). 64p. (J). (ps-3). 1995. 2.95 incl. audio (*0-8431-3892-0*) Price Stern Sloan.

Wee Sing More Bible Song. Susan H. Nipp. (Wee Sing Ser.). (Illus.). 1995. pap. 9.95 incl. audio (*0-8431-3891-2*) Price Stern Sloan.

Wee Sing More Bible Songs. (Wee Sing Ser.). (J). 1995. pap. 2.95 (*0-8423-8085-X*) Tyndale.

Wee Sing Nursery Rhymes & Lullabies. Pamela C. Beall & Susan H. Nipp. (Wee Sing Ser.). (Illus.). 64p. (Orig.). (J). (ps-2). 1985. pap. 2.95 (*0-8431-3811-4*); pap. 9.95 incl. audio (*0-8431-3794-0*) Price Stern Sloan.

***Wee Sing Nursery Rhymes & Lullabies.** Pamela C. Beall & Susan H. Nipp. (Wee Sing Ser.). (Illus.). 64p. (Orig.). (J). (ps-3). 1996. pap. 12.95 incl. audio compact disk (*0-8431-7939-2*) Price Stern Sloan.

Wee Sing Sing-Alongs. Pamela C. Beall & Susan H. Nipp. (Wee Sing Ser.). Orig. Title: Wee Sing Around the Campfire. (Illus.). 64p. (J). (ps-2). 1983. pap. 2.95 (*0-8431-3814-9*); pap. 9.95 incl. audio (*0-8431-3804-1*) Price Stern Sloan.

Wee Sir Gibbie of the Highlands. George MacDonald. Ed. by Michael R. Phillips. (George MacDonald Classics for Young Readers Ser.). 242p. (J). (gr. 2-7). 1990. 10.99 (*1-55661-139-0*) Bethany Hse.

Wee Taste O'Scotland. Mary McGregor, pseud. & Michael Peyton. (Illus.). 100p. (Orig.). 1995. wbk. ed., spiral bd. 12.95 (*1-885527-07-1*) Feather Fables.

***Wee Willie Winkie.** Lucy Cousins. (J). 1997. pap. 5.99 (*0-525-45751-8*) NAL-Dutton.

Wee Willie Winkie. Rudyard Kipling. 432p. 1988. mass mkt. 5.95 (*0-14-043303-1*, Penguin Classics) Viking Penguin.

Wee Willie Winkie. Rudyard Kipling. Ed. & Intro. by Hugh Haughton. 432p. (J). 1989. pap. 9.95 (*0-14-018380-9*, Penguin Classics) Viking Penguin.

***Wee Willie Winkie.** Ed. by Iona A. Opie. (Illus.). 16p. (J). 1997. 7.99 (*0-7636-0356-2*) Candlewick Pr.

Wee Willie Winkie & other Stories. Rudyard Kipling. 1976. 19.95 (*0-8488-1071-6*) Amereon Ltd.

Wee Willie Winkle. Dianne O. Burke. (Rhyme-along Book). (Illus.). 12p. (J). (ps). 1994. bds. 3.95 (*1-56565-096-4*) Lowell Hse Juvenile.

Weed among the Roses. Eva Vogiel. LC 93-12143. 1993. 14.95 (*0-87306-635-9*); pap. 11.95 (*0-87306-637-5*) Feldheim.

***Weed & Crop Resistance to Herbicides.** 1997. lib. bdg. 280.00 (*0-7923-4581-9*) Kluwer Ac.

***Weed Control.** Warren Somerville. (Illus.). 144p. 1997. pap. write for info. (*0-7506-8933-1*, 31071) Buttrwrth-Heinemann.

Weed Control Economics. Kenneth M. Menz. (Applied Botany & Crop Science Ser.). 177p. 1987. text ed. 79.00 (*0-12-068278-8*) Acad Pr.

Weed Control for the Home Gardener. Aldous. Ed. by John Patrick. (Lothian Australian Garden Ser.). (Illus.). 64p. (Orig.). 1995. pap. 10.95 (*0-85091-462-0*, Pub. by Lothian Pub AT) Seven Hills Bk.

Weed Control Handbook, Vol. 1: Principles. 8th ed. Ed. by Raymond J. Hance & K. R. Holly. (Illus.). 576p. (C). 1989. text ed. 125.00 (*0-632-02459-3*) Blackwell Sci.

Weed Control in Limited-Tillage Systems. Ed. & Intro. by A. F. Wiese. 298p. 1985. text ed. 22.50 (*0-318-32864-X*) Weed Sci Soc.

Weed Control in Vegetable Production: Proceedings of the EC Experts' Group Meeting, Stuttgart, 28-31 October 1986. Ed. by R. Cavalloro & A. El Titi. 316p. (C). 1988. text ed. 75.00 (*90-6191-845-6*, Pub. by A A Balkema NE) Ashgate Pub Co.

Weed Control Methods for Public Health Applications. Edward O. Gangstad. 320p. 1980. 129.00 (*0-8493-5326-2*, SB614, CRC Reprint) Franklin.

An Asterisk (*) at the beginning of an entry indicates that the title is appearing in BIP for the first time.

Weed Control Methods for Recreation Facility Management. Edward O. Gangstad. 312p. 1982. 119.00 (*0-8493-5330-0*, SB614, CRC Reprint) Franklin.

Weed Control Methods for Rights of Way Management. Ed. by Edward O. Gangstad. 1982. 156.00 (*0-8493-5329-7*, SB614, CRC Reprint) Franklin.

Weed Control Methods for River Basin Management. Ed. by Edward O. Gangstad. 232p. 1978. 95.00 (*0-8493-5328-9*, SB614, CRC Reprint) Franklin.

Weed Control on Vine & Soft Fruits: Proceedings. Ed. by R. Cavalloro & D. W. Robinson. 176p. 1987. text ed. 70.00 (*90-6191-691-7*, Pub. by A A Balkema NE) Ashgate Pub Co.

Weed Ecology: Implications for Management. 2nd ed. Steven R. Radosevich et al. LC 96-19470. 1996. text ed. 89.95 (*0-471-11606-8*) Wiley.

Weed Ecology: Implications for Vegetation Management. Steven R. Radosevich & Jodie S. Holt. 265p. 1984. text ed. 84.95 (*0-471-87674-7*) Wiley.

Weed Flora of Egypt. Loutfy Boulos & M. Nabil El-Hadidi. (Illus.). 370p. 1995. 40.00 (*977-424-323-4*, Pub. by Am Univ Cairo Pr UA) Col U Pr.

Weed Flora of Egypt: A Practical Guide. Loutfy Boulos & M. Nabil El-Hadidi. 1985. pap. 20.00 (*977-424-038-3*, Pub. by Am Univ Cairo Pr UA) Col U Pr.

Weed Flora of Kashmir Valley. M. K. Kaul. 422p. (C). 1886. 275.00 (*81-85046-28-X*, Pub. by Scientific UK) St Mut.

Weed Is a Flower: The Life of George Washington Carver. Aliki. (Illus.). 32p. (J). (ps-3). 1988. pap. 14.00 (*0-671-66118-3*, S&S Bks Young Read); pap. 5.95 (*0-671-66490-5*, S&S Bks Young Read) S&S Childrens.

Weed Is a Seed. Ferida Wolff. LC 94-45505. (Illus.). 32p. (J). (ps-2). 1996. 14.95 (*0-395-72291-8*) Ticknor & Flds Bks Yng Read.

Weed Management for Developing Countries. R. Labrada et al. (Plant Production & Protection Papers: Vol. 12). 402p. 1994. 50.00 (*92-5-103427-3*, F34273, Pub. by FAO IT) Bernan Associates.

Weed Management in Agroecosystems Ecological Approaches: Ecological Approaches, 2 vols., Vol. I. Ed. by Miguel A. Altieri & Matthew Z. Liebman. LC 87-25619. 192p. 1988. 204.00 (*0-8493-6816-2*, SB611, CRC Reprint) Franklin.

*__Weed Management in Rice.__ Food & Agriculture Organization Staff. (Plant Produciton & Protections Papers: No. 139). 272p. 1997. pap. 44.00 (*92-5-103912-7*, F39127, Pub. by FAO IT) Bernan Associates.

Weed Physiology, Vol. I: Reproduction & Ecophysiology. Ed. by Stephen O. Duke. 176p. 1985. 153.00 (*0-8493-6313-6*, SB611) CRC Pr.

*__Weed Proceedings of the Second National Conference of South Africa.__ 352p. 1977. pap. 70.00 (*0-86961-095-3*, Pub. by A A Balkema NE) Ashgate Pub Co.

Weed Science: Principles. 2nd ed. Wood P. Anderson. (Illus.). 655p. (C). 1983. text ed. 67.00 (*0-314-69632-6*) West Pub.

Weed Science: Principles & Applications. 3rd ed. W. Powell Anderson. LC 95-30901. 410p. (C). 1996. text ed. 69.25 (*0-314-04627-5*) West Pub.

Weed Science: Principles & Practices. 3rd ed. Floyd M. Ashton & Thomas J. Monaco. LC 90-24784. 480p. 1991. text ed. 84.95 (*0-471-60084-9*) Wiley.

Weed Science in the Tropics. I. Okezie Akobundu. LC 87-8128. 538p. reprint ed. pap. 153.40 (*0-8357-7540-2*, 2036263) Bks Demand.

Weed Seeds of the Great Plains: A Handbook for Identification. Linda W. Davis. LC 93-15615. (Illus.). 208p. 1993. 25.00 (*0-7006-0651-3*) U Pr of KS.

Weed Time: Essays from the Edge of a Country Yard. John Lane. 70p. (Orig.). 1996. pap. 8.00 (*0-9638731-3-X*) Holocene Pr.

Weedee Peepo: A Collection of Essays - Una Coleccion de ensayos. 2nd ed. Jose A. Burciaga. Ed. by Patricia De La Fuente. (Illus.). 207p. (Orig.). 1992. reprint ed. pap. text ed. 10.95 (*0-938738-06-2*) U TX Pan Am Pr.

Weeder in the Garden of the Lord: Anthony Comstock's Life & Career. Anna L. Bates. 226p. (C). Date not set. lib. bdg. 39.50 (*0-7618-0076-X*) U Pr of Amer.

Weeder's Digest: The Best of Green Prints. Pat Stone. 208p. (Orig.). 1996. pap. 15.95 (*1-55591-257-5*) Fulcrum Pub.

Weeding & Maintenance of Reference Collections. Ed. by Sydney J. Pierce. LC 90-30910. (Reference Librarian Ser.: No. 29). 183p. 1990. text ed. 49.95 (*1-56024-001-6*) Haworth Pr.

Weeding & Maintenance of Reference Collections. Ed. by Sydney J. Pierce. LC 90-30910. (Reference Librarian Ser.: No. 29). (Illus.). 183p. (C). 1995. reprint ed. pap. text ed. 19.95 (*1-56024-976-5*) Haworth Pr.

Weeding & Sowing: Preface to a Science of Mathematical Education. Hans Freudenthal. ix, 314p. 1977. lib. bdg. 123.50 (*90-277-0789-8*) Kluwer Ac.

Weeding & Sowing: Preface to a Science of Mathematical Education. Hans Freudenthal. ix, 314p. 1980. pap. text ed. 55.00 (*90-277-1072-4*) Kluwer Ac.

Weeding Library Collections: Library Weeding Methods. 3rd ed. Stanley J. Slote. xxii, 284p. 1989. lib. bdg. 42.00 (*0-87287-633-0*) Libs Unl.

*__Weeding Library Collections: Library Weeding Methods.__ 4th ed. Stanley J. Slote. LC 96-54865. 1997. pap. write for info. (*1-56308-565-8*) Libs Unl.

*__Weeding Library Collections: Library Weeding Methods.__ 4th rev. ed. Stanley J. Slote. LC 96-54865. (Illus.). 290p. 1997. lib. bdg. 55.00 (*1-56308-511-9*) Libs Unl.

Weeding of Collections in Sci-Tech Libraries. Ed. by Ellis Mount. LC 85-27010. (Science & Technology Libraries: Vol. 6, No. 3). 164p. 1986. text ed. 29.95 (*0-86656-552-3*) Haworth Pr.

Weeding Out the Target Population: The Law of Accountability in a Manpower Program. James Latimore. LC 84-8952. (Contributions in Sociology Ser.: No. 54). (Illus.). x, 176p. 1985. text ed. 49.95 (*0-313-24495-2*, LWT/, Greenwood Pr) Greenwood.

*__Weeding Out the Tears: A Mother's Story of Love, Loss, & Renewal.__ Jeanne White & Susan Dworkin. LC 96-47132. 248p. 1997. 22.00 (*0-380-97328-6*) Avon.

Weeding the Cosmos: Selected Haiku. John Brandi. 132p. (Orig.). 1994. pap. 10.00 (*0-9631909-1-1*) La Alameda Pr.

Weeding the Duchess. Sarah Maclay. 1979. pap. 5.00 (*0-686-71066-5*) Black Stone.

Weeds. Edith S. Kelley. LC 72-75333. (Lost American Fiction Ser.). 349p. 1972. 14.95 (*0-8093-0587-9*) S Ill U Pr.

Weeds. Alexander C. Martin. (Golden Guide Ser.). (Illus.). 160p. (YA). (gr. 7 up). 1973. pap. 5.50 (*0-307-24353-2*, Golden Pr) Western Pub.

Weeds. 2nd ed. Walter C. Muenscher. LC 79-48017. (Comstock Bk.). (Illus.). 560p. 1987. pap. 22.50 (*0-8014-9417-6*) Cornell U Pr.

Weeds. Edith S. Kelley. LC 81-22061. 368p. 1996. reprint ed. pap. 15.95 (*1-55861-154-1*) Feminist Pr.

Weeds: Guardians of the Soil. Joseph Cocannouer. (Illus.). pap. 15.95 (*0-8159-7205-9*) Devin.

Weeds among the Wheat: Discernment: Where Prayer & Action Meet. Thomas H. Green. LC 84-70663. 208p. (Orig.). 1984. pap. 5.95 (*0-87793-318-9*) Ave Maria.

Weeds & Poisonous Plants of Wyoming & Utah. Ed. by Thomas D. Whitson. (Illus.). 284p. (Orig.). 1987. pap. 13.50 (*0-941570-06-1*) U of Wyoming.

Weeds & What They Tell. E. E. Pfeiffer. 96p. pap. 4.50 (*0-938250-04-3*) Bio-Dynamic Farm.

Weeds, Control Without Poisons. Charles Walters. LC 90-84508. 320p. 1990. pap. 20.00 (*0-911311-25-4*) Acres USA.

Weeds in Winter. Lauren Brown. (Illus.). 1986. reprint ed. pap. 10.95 (*0-393-30348-9*) Norton.

Weeds 'n Walleyes. 64p. 1990. 6.95 (*0-685-48130-1*) Fishing Hot.

Weeds 'n Walleyes. Greg Bohn. LC 92-74158. (Secrets of a Northwoods Walleye Guide Ser.: Vol. 3). 1989. write for info. (*0-939314-51-7*) Fishing Hot.

Weeds of Cotton: Characterization & Control. Ed. by John R. Abernathy. LC 92-6771. (Cotton Foundation Reference Bks.: No. 2). 1992. lib. bdg. 45.00 (*0-939809-02-8*) Cotton Found.

Weeds of Kentucky & Adjacent States: A Field Guide. Patricia D. Haragan. LC 90-24566. (Illus.). 304p. 1991. text ed. 29.00 (*0-8131-1743-7*) U Pr of Ky.

Weeds of Lebanon. Winnie Edgecombe. (Illus.). 1970. pap. 20.00 (*0-8156-6001-4*, Am U Beirut) Syracuse U Pr.

*__Weeds of the Northeast.__ Richard H. Uva et al. LC 96-36434. (Comstock Bks.). (Illus.). 416p. 1996. 60.00 (*0-8014-3391-6*, Comstock Pub); pap. 29.95 (*0-8014-8334-4*, Comstock Pub) Cornell U Pr.

*__Weeds of the West.__ Whitson. (Illus.). 630p. 1996. pap. 25.95 (*0-941570-13-4*) U of Wyoming.

Weeds of the Woods: Small Trees & Shrubs of the Eastern Forest. Glen Blouin. 125p. 1992. per. 11.95 (*0-86492-127-6*, Pub. by Goose Ln Edits CN) Genl Dist Srvs.

Weeds? or Wildflowers! Dori J. Somers. LC 87-72456. (Illus.). 110p. (Orig.). 1987. pap. 6.50 (*0-318-23571-4*) Choice Fullerton.

Weeds Used in Medicine. Alice Hinkel. (Alternative Medicine Ser.). 1991. lib. bdg. 69.00 (*0-8490-4277-1*) Gordon Pr.

Weeds Used in Medicine. Alice Henkel. 45p. 1970. reprint ed. spiral bd. 5.00 (*0-7873-0406-9*) Hlth Research.

*__Weegee.__ 2nd ed. Allene Talmey. (Masters of Photography Ser.). (Illus.). 96p. Date not set. reprint ed. 12.50 (*0-89381-749-X*) Aperture.

Weegee's People. Arthur F. Weegee, pseud. (Quality Paperbacks Ser.). (Illus.). 242p. 1985. reprint ed. pap. 13.95 (*0-306-80242-2*) Da Capo.

*__Weegee's World.__ Weegee et al. LC 97-11990. 1997. 75.00 (*0-8212-2375-5*) Little.

Week. Crag Hill. 55p. (Orig.). 1992. pap. 7.00 (*0-926935-59-3*) Runaway Spoon.

Week. Francis H. Colson. LC 73-7697. 126p. 1974. reprint ed. text ed. 38.50 (*0-8371-6940-2*, CTHW, Greenwood Pr) Greenwood.

Week at the Fair: A Country Celebration. Patricia H. Easton. LC 94-48120. (Illus.). 48p. (J). (gr. 2-4). 1995. lib. bdg. 15.90 (*1-56294-527-0*) Millbrook Pr.

Week at the Fair: A Country Celebration. Patricia H. Easton. (Illus.). 48p. (J). (gr. 2-4). 1995. 14.95 (*1-56294-932-2*) Millbrook Pr.

Week by Week: Plans for Observing & Recording Young Children. Barbara A. Nilsen. (Early Childhood Education Ser.). 416p. 1997. 39.95 (*0-8273-7646-4*) Delmar.

Week by Week to a Strong Heart. Marvin Moser & Brenda L. Becker. 336p. 1994. mass mkt. 5.50 (*0-380-72089-2*) Avon.

Week-End a Zuydcoote. Robert Merle. 256p. (FRE.). 1976. pap. 10.95 (*0-7859-4057-X*, 2070367716) Fr & Eur.

Week-End Book of Humor. Ed. by P. G. Wodehouse & Scott Meredith. LC 71-134162. (Essay Index Reprint Ser.). 1977. 19.95 (*0-8369-2094-5*) Ayer.

Week-End Menus. Julee Rosso. 1997. pap. 10.00 (*0-517-88525-5*, Crown) Crown Pub Group.

Week-End Menus. Julee Rosso. 1998. 16.00 (*0-517-70286-X*) Random Hse Value.

Week-End Wodehouse. P. G. Wodehouse. (Pimlico Ser.). (Illus.). 430p. 1993. reprint ed. pap. 15.95 (*0-7126-5034-2*, Pub. by Pimlico) Trafalgar.

Week in Daily Prayer. Barry Trick. 71p. (Orig.). 1992. pap. text ed. 3.95 (*0-8146-2015-9*) Liturgical Pr.

Week in Europe. Dylan Iorwerth. 140p. 1996. pap. 18.95 (*0-7083-1326-4*, Pub. by Univ Wales Pr UK) Paul & Co Pubs.

Week in the Life of an Airline Pilot. William Jaspersohn. (J). (gr. 4-7). 1991. 14.95 (*0-316-45822-8*) Little.

Week in the Life of the Church. Laurie S. Monsees. 1992. 5.00 (*0-8309-0606-1*) Herald Hse.

Week in the Woods. Heather S. Thomas. Ed. by Raymond H. Woolsey. 64p. (J). (gr. 2-4). 1988. pap. 4.99 (*0-8280-0435-8*) Review & Herald.

Week in Turenevo & Other Stories. Leo Tolstoy. LC 75-15693. 187p. 1975. reprint ed. text ed. 35.00 (*0-8371-8224-7*, TOWT, Greenwood Pr) Greenwood.

Week Like Any Other: Novellas & Stories. Natalya Baranskaya. Tr. by Pieta Monks. LC 89-34486. 231p. 1989. pap. 10.95 (*0-931188-80-6*) Seal Pr WA.

Week of Raccoons. Gloria Whelan. LC 87-16800. (Illus.). 40p. (J). (ps-1). 1988. lib. bdg. 12.99 (*0-394-98396-3*) Knopf Bks Yng Read.

Week of Salvation: History & Traditions of Holy Week. James Monti. LC 93-83256. 400p. (Orig.). 1993. 19.95 (*0-87973-532-5*, 532) Our Sunday Visitor.

Week of the Whales & Other Stories. Leoncio P. Deriada. 132p. (Orig.). 1994. pap. 9.75 (*971-10-0483-6*, Pub. by New Day Pub PH) Cellar.

Week on the Concord & Merimack Rivers. Henry David Thoreau. 504p. 1987. reprint ed. pap. 9.95 (*0-940160-36-6*) Parnassus Imprints.

Week on the Concord & Merrimac Rivers. Henry David Thoreau. (BCL1 - United States Local History Ser.). 355p. 1991. reprint ed. lib. bdg. 89.00 (*0-7812-6269-0*) Rprt Serv.

Week on the Concord & Merrimack Rivers. Henry David Thoreau. 1998. pap. 9.95 (*0-14-043442-9*) Viking Penguin.

Week on the Concord & Merrimack Rivers. Henry David Thoreau. (American Biography Ser.). 610p. 1991. reprint ed. lib. bdg. 89.00 (*0-7812-8389-2*) Rprt Serv.

*__Week on the Concord & Merrimack Rivers.__ Ed. by Elizabeth H. Witherell et al. LC 78-51201. (Writings of Henry D. Thoreau). 611p. 1980. reprint ed. pap. 174.20 (*0-608-02516-X*, 2063160) Bks Demand.

Week on the Concord & Merrimack Rivers see Writings of Henry D. Thoreau

Week Past Forever. Cynthia D. Devore. LC 93-7722. (Children of Courage Ser.). (J). 1993. lib. bdg. 14.98 (*1-56239-246-8*) Abdo & Dghtrs.

Week That Changed the World. Ernest C. Wilson. LC 68-15193. 1968. 9.95 (*0-87159-170-7*) Unity Bks.

Week the World Heard Gallaudet. Jack R. Gannon. LC 88-38682. (Illus.). 176p. 1989. 29.95 (*0-930323-54-8*); pap. 19.95 (*0-930323-50-5*) Gallaudet Univ Pr.

Week 'Til the Wedding. Beth Henderson. 1996. mass mkt. 3.50 (*0-373-52031-X*, 1-52031-1) Silhouette.

Week, Walden, The Maine Woods, Cape Cod. Robert F. Sayre. LC 85-5175. 1114p. 1989. 30.00 (*0-940450-27-5*) Library of America.

*__Week with Elephants: Proceedings of the International Seminar on the Conservation of the Asian Elephants.__ Ed. by J. C. Daniel & Hemant Datye. (Illus.). 544p. 1997. 17.95 (*0-19-563850-6*) OUP.

Weekday Gourmet: Healthful, Delicious Meals in 30 Minutes or Less. Linda Ferrari. 192p. 1996. per. 14.95 (*0-7615-0404-4*) Prima Pub.

Weekday Liturgies for Children: Creative Ways to Celebrate Year-Round. Kathleen Glavich. LC 96-60316. 248p. 1996. pap. 29.95 (*0-89622-694-8*) Twenty-Third.

Weekday Prayer Book. United Synagogue Staff & Morris Silverman. 9.65 (*0-87677-070-7*) Prayer Bk.

Weekday Prayer Book. enl. ed. United Synagogue Staff & Morris Silverman. 39.00 (*0-87677-071-5*) Prayer Bk.

Weekday Prayerbook. 6.25 (*0-686-96031-9*) USCJE.

Weekday Readings: A Daily Eucharistic Lectionary for the Weekdays Following the First Sunday After Epiphany & the Feast of Pentecost, a Lectionary Authorized for Study & Evaluation. Ed. by Joseph P. Russell. 53p. 1995. pap. 10.95 (*0-89869-249-0*) Church Pub Inc.

Weekdays Are Quick Meals: From Speedy Stir-Fries to Soups to Skillet Dishes & More. Time-Life Books Editors. LC 96-7946. (Everyday Cookbooks Ser.). 128p. 1996. pap. 9.95 (*0-7835-4834-6*) Time-Life.

Weekend. Peter Cameron. LC 93-37428. 1994. 17.00 (*0-374-28739-2*) FS&G.

Weekend. Peter Cameron. LC 94-43823. 1995. pap. 9.95 (*0-452-27411-7*) NAL-Dutton.

Weekend. Mark Dunster. LC 74-438797. (Rin Ser.: Pt. 6). 1974. 4.00 (*0-89642-038-8*) Linden Pubs.

Weekend. Christopher Pike. (Orig.). (J). 1986. pap. 2.75 (*0-590-42968-X*) Scholastic Inc.

Weekend. Christopher Pike. 240p. (Orig.). (YA). (gr. 7-9). 1986. pap. 3.50 (*0-590-44256-2*) Scholastic Inc.

Weekend. Gore Vidal. 1968. pap. 5.25 (*0-8222-1230-7*) Dramatists Play.

Weekend! A Menu Cookbook for Relaxed Entertaining. Edith Stovel & Pamela Wakefield. Ed. by Deborah Balmuth. LC 94-7937. (Illus.). 224p. 1994. pap. 12.95 (*0-88266-847-1*, Storey Pub) Storey Comm Inc.

*__Weekend Adventures in Northern California.__ 6th ed. Carole T. Meyers. LC 96-47236. (Illus.). 416p. (Orig.). 1997. pap. 17.95 (*0-917120-15-9*) Carousel Pr.

Weekend Adventures Outside Tokyo: Travel with a Historical Twist. Tae Moriyama. (Illus.). 358p. (Orig.). 1990. pap. 19.95 (*4-07-975049-8*, Pub. by Shufunomoto Co Ltd JA) C E Tuttle.

Weekend Breaks & Day Trips. Euromonitor Staff. 76p. 1987. 705.00 (*0-86338-219-3*, Pub. by Euromonitor Pubns UK) Gale.

Weekend Galley. Charlene McCaull. (Illus.). 56p. 1984. pap. 6.95 (*0-916669-01-7*) Alcyone Pubns.

Weekend Garden Guide: Work-Saving Ways to a Beautiful Backyard. Susan A. Roth. 1996. pap. 15.95 (*0-87596-695-0*) Rodale Pr Inc.

*__Weekend Gardener.__ Keely Shaye-Smith. 224p. 1998. 30.00 (*0-06-270153-3*, HarperStyle) HarpC.

Weekend Getaways in Louisiana. Mary Fonseca. (Illus.). 480p. 1996. pap. 14.95 (*1-56554-096-4*) Pelican.

Weekend Girls. large type ed. Jonathan Burke. (Linford Mystery Library). 320p. 1987. pap. 15.99 (*0-7089-6456-7*, Linford) Ulverscroft.

Weekend Gold Miner. rev. ed. A. H. Ryan. Ed. by Robin Shepherd. 1991. 5.50 (*0-935182-46-2*) Gem Guides Bk.

*__Weekend Golfer.__ William J. Mace. LC 96-69829. 80p. (Orig.). 1997. pap. 11.95 (*1-57197-038-X*) Pentland Pr.

Weekend Healer. Bryden MacDonald. 1996. pap. text ed. 10.95 (*0-88922-360-2*) Genl Dist Srvs.

Weekend in September. John E. Weems. LC 79-7415. (Illus.). 192p. 1993. reprint ed. pap. 13.95 (*0-89096-390-8*) Tex A&M Univ Pr.

Weekend in the City. Lee Lorenz. (Illus.). 32p. (J). (gr. k-3). 1991. 15.95 (*0-945912-15-3*) Pippin Pr.

Weekend Journeys. Philadelphia Inquirer Staff. (Illus.). 336p. 1988. pap. 9.95 (*0-912608-59-5*) Mid Atlantic.

Weekend Journeys: 62 Getaways Within a Day's Drive of Philidelphia. Philadelphia Inquirer Staff. (Illus.). 304p. 1995. pap. 9.95 (*0-8362-7037-1*) Andrews & McMeel.

Weekend Kitchen: Menus & Recipes for Relaxed Entertaining, Family Fun & a Head Start On. Joanne L. Hayes. 1992. pap. 11.00 (*0-517-58328-3*, Harmony) Crown Pub Group.

Weekend Mechanic's Automotive Body Repair Guide. Robert Grossblatt & Billy Boynton. 1991. text ed. 23.95 (*0-07-157514-6*) McGraw.

Weekend Mechanic's Automotive Body Repair Guide. Robert Grossblatt & Billy Boynton. (Illus.). 224p. 1990. pap. 13.95 (*0-8306-3497-5*) McGraw-Hill Prof.

Weekend Mechanic's Automotive Body Repair Guide. Robert Grossblatt & Billy Boynton. (Illus.). 224p. 1990. 24.95 (*0-8306-7497-7*, 3497) TAB Bks.

Weekend Mechanic's Guide to Engine Rebuilding. Paul Dempsey. (Weekend Mechanic Ser.). (Illus.). 256p. (Orig.). 1989. pap. 12.95 (*0-8306-3180-1*) McGraw-Hill Prof.

Weekend Mechanic's Guide to Peak Performance & Handling. Bill Farlow. 1989. 19.95 (*0-07-156447-0*) McGraw.

Weekend Navigator. Bruce Fraser. 1981. 18.15 (*0-8286-0090-2*) J De Graff.

Weekend Novelist. Robert J. Ray. LC 93-15108. 288p. 1994. pap. 11.95 (*0-440-50594-1*) Dell.

*__Weekend Projects Plus: Complete Step-by-Step Instructions for 40 Woodworking Projects You Can Build in a Weekend.__ Nick Engler. (Illus.). 320p. 1998. 29.95 (*0-87596-785-X*) Rodale Pr Inc.

Weekend Quilt. Leslie Linsley. 1992. pap. 14.95 (*0-312-07116-7*) St Martin.

Weekend Quilt. Leslie Linsley. (Illus.). 160p. 1992. pap. 14.95 (*0-685-50332-1*) St Martin.

*__Weekend Quilter.__ Rosemary Wilkinson. LC 97-18504. 1997. write for info. (*0-89577-995-1*) RD Assn.

Weekend Refinishers. Bruce E. Johnson. 1989. pap. 12.00 (*0-345-35866-X*) Ballantine.

*__Weekend Sentences, No. 85.__ Jack Martin. 20p. (Orig.). 1997. pap. 6.95 (*0-614-24054-9*) Pudding Hse Pubns.

Weekend Tennis: How to Have Fun & Win at the Same Time. Bill Talbert. 1976. pap. 3.00 (*0-87980-277-4*) Wilshire.

*__Weekend Territory.__ Pearce. (Clipper Fiction Ser.). (J). 1993. pap. text ed. write for info. (*0-582-80053-6*, Pub. by Longman UK) Longman.

Weekend to Remember. Miranda Lee. 1996. pap. 3.50 (*0-373-11855-4*, 1-11855-3) Harlequin Bks.

Weekend to Remember. large type ed. Miranda Lee. 1996. lib. bdg. 19.95 (*0-263-14592-1*, Pub. by Mills & Boon UK) Thorndike Pr.

Weekend Visit. 176p. 1990. mass mkt. 4.95 (*0-929654-64-1*, 31) Blue Moon Bks.

*__Weekend Warriors.__ Paul L. Cooper. (Illus.). 250p. 1996. pap. 23.95 (*0-89745-202-X*) Sunflower U Pr.

Weekend Warriors: Alcohol in a Micronesian Culture. Mac Marshall. Ed. by Robert B. Edgerton & L. L. Langness. LC 78-64597. 170p. (C). 1979. pap. 14.95 (*0-87484-455-X*, 455) Mayfield Pub.

Weekend Was Murder! Joan L. Nixon. 208p. (YA). 1994. mass mkt. 3.99 (*0-440-21901-9*) Dell.

Weekend Was Murder! large type ed. Joan L. Nixon. 225p. 1993. reprint ed. lib. bdg. 15.95 (*1-56054-598-4*) Thorndike Pr.

Weekend Was Murder: Homicide As Entertainment. Susan Casey. 240p. (Orig.). 1987. pap. 5.95 (*0-15-695300-5*, Harvest Bks) HarBrace.

Weekend Wife: (Sister Switch) Carolyn Zane. (Romance Ser.). 1995. mass mkt. 2.99 (*0-373-19082-4*, 1-19082-6) Silhouette.

Weekend with Degas. Rosabianca Skira-Venturi. LC 91-38364. (Weekend with...Ser.). (Illus.). 64p. (J). (gr. 1-6). 1992. 19.95 (*0-8478-1439-4*) Rizzoli Intl.

Weekend with Diego Rivera. Barbara Braun. LC 93-38905. 64p. (J). 1994. 19.95 (*0-8478-1749-0*) Rizzoli Intl.

Weekend with Leonardo Da Vinci. Rosabianca Skira-Venturi. (Illus.). 64p. (J). (gr. 4-7). 1993. 19.95 (*0-8478-1440-8*) Rizzoli Intl.

Weekend with Matisse. Florian Rodari. Tr. by Joan Knight from FRE. LC 93-41671. 64p. (J). 1994. 19.95 (*0-8478-1792-X*) Rizzoli Intl.

Weekend with Picasso. Florian Rodari. LC 91-12427. (Illus.). 64p. 1996. 9.95 (*0-8478-1920-5*) Rizzoli Intl.

Weekend with Rembrandt. Pascal Bonafoux. LC 91-40507. (Weekend with...Ser.). (Illus.). 64p. (J). (gr. 1-6). 1992. 19.95 (*0-8478-1441-6*) Rizzoli Intl.

W

Weekend with Renoir. Rosabianca S. Venturi. LC 91-12426. (Illus.). 64p. 1996. 9.95 (*0-8478-1921-3*) Rizzoli Intl.

Weekend with Rousseau. Gilles Plazy. LC 93-12187. (Illus.). 64p. (J). 1993. 19.95 (*0-8478-1717-2*) Rizzoli Intl.

***Weekend with the Great War: Proceedings of the Fourth Annual Great War Interconference Seminar, Lisle, Illinois, 16-18 September 1995.** Steven Weingartner et al. LC 96-37490. Date not set. pap. write for info. (*1-57249-068-3*) White Mane Pub.

***Weekend with the Great War: Proceedings of the Fourth Annual Great War Interconference Seminar 16-18 September 1994.** Cantigny First Foundation Staff. Ed. by Steven Weingartner. (Illus.). 320p. Date not set. pap. 24.95 (*0-614-24050-6*, WM Kids) White Mane Pub.

***Weekend with the One You Love: A Do-It-Yourself Marriage Retreat.** Art Hunt. 160p. 1997. pap. 8.99 (*1-57673-096-4*, Multnomah Bks) Multnomah Pubs.

Weekend with Van Gogh. Rosabianca Skira-Venturi. Tr. by Ann K. Beneduce. LC 94-16262. (Illus.). 64p. (J). (gr. 3-7). 1994. 19.95 (*0-8478-1836-5*) Rizzoli Intl.

Weekend with Velazquez. Tr. by Ann K. Beneduce. LC 92-33350. (Illus.). 64p. (J). 1993. 19.95 (*0-8478-1647-8*) Rizzoli Intl.

Weekend with Wendell. Kevin Henkes. LC 85-24822. (Illus.). 32p. (J). (ps-3). 1986. 16.00 (*0-688-06325-X*); lib. bdg. 15.93 (*0-688-06326-8*) Greenwillow.

Weekend with Wendell. Kevin Henkes. LC 85-24822. (Illus.). 32p. (J). (ps up). 1995. reprint ed. pap. 4.95 (*0-688-14024-6*, Mulberry) Morrow.

Weekend with Winslow Homer. Ann K. Beneduce. LC 93-12189. (Illus.). 64p. (J). 1993. 19.95 (*0-8478-1622-2*) Rizzoli Intl.

Weekend with Winslow Homer. Ann K. Beneduce. 64p. 1996. 9.95 (*0-8478-1919-1*) Rizzoli Intl.

Weekend Woodworker. John A. Nelson. LC 89-70250. (Illus.). 304p. 1990. pap. 14.95 (*0-87857-904-4*, 14-997-1) Rodale Pr Inc.

Weekend Woodworker: Projects for the Home Craftsman: Cabinets & Chests, Tables & Chairs, Kitchen Projects, Accents, Outdoor Projects, Toys. Illus. by Sally Onopa. LC 92-32816. 1993. pap. 14.95 (*0-87596-575-X*) Rodale Pr Inc.

Weekend Woodworker: Quick & Easy Country Projects. Selected by Rodale Books Editors. (Illus.). 256p. (Orig.). 1994. pap. 14.95 (*0-87596-621-7*) St Martin.

Weekend Woodworker, Quick-&-Easy Projects: Furniture & Accents, Plywood Projects, Toys, Kitchen Projects, Shelving & Storage. Selected by Rodale Books Editors. LC 91-33573. (Illus.). 256p. (Orig.). 1992. 22.95 (*0-87596-128-2*, 14-047-2); pap. 12.95 (*0-87857-997-4*, 14-047-1) Rodale Pr Inc.

Weekenders' Club. Ralph Arnote. 1996. mass mkt. write for info. (*0-8125-3880-3*) Forge NYC.

Weekender's Gardening Manual: Easy-Care Gardens in Two Hours (or Less!) a Week. Patricia A. Taylor. LC 85-21856. (Illus.). 144p. 1989. pap. 15.95 (*0-8050-1024-6*, Owl) H Holt & Co.

Weekender's Guide: Points of Interest & Walks Along the Paved Roads of Anza-Borrego Desert State Park. Paul R. Johnson. Ed. by Rose Houk et al. (Illus.). 32p. (Orig.). 1987. pap. 5.95 (*0-910805-05-9*) Anza-Borrego.

Weekender's Guide to the Four Seasons. 8th ed. Robert Shosteck. Ed. by Susan C. Dore. LC 88-17999. 504p. 1988. reprint ed. pap. 15.95 (*0-88289-701-2*) Pelican.

***Weekending in New England.** rev. ed. Betsy Wittemann & Nancy Woodworth. (Illus.). 448p. 1997. pap. text ed. 16.95 (*0-934260-81-8*) Wood Pond.

Weekends: Great Ideas for Memorable Adventures. Sidney Simon & Hanoch McCarty. 180p. (Orig.). 1994. pap. 10.00 (*1-55874-300-6*, 3006) Health Comm.

Weekends Are Entertaining: From Cocktail Parties & Brunches to Dinner for Two or Twenty. Time-Life Books Editors. LC 96-12345. (Everyday Cookbooks Ser.). 128p. 1996. pap. 9.95 (*0-7835-4833-8*) Time-Life.

Weekends Away! Camping & Cooking in Texas State Parks. rev. ed. Sheryl Smith-Rodgers. 160p. 1996. pap. 15.95 (*1-57168-093-4*) Sunbelt Media.

Weekends for Two: The Mid-Atlantic Area. 2nd ed. June H. Marquis. 108p. 1989. pap. 7.95 (*0-89709-177-9*) Liberty Pub.

Weekends for Two in New England: 50 Romantic Getaways. Bill Gleeson. (Illus.). 120p. 1996. pap. 14.95 (*0-8118-0857-2*) Chronicle Bks.

Weekends for Two in Southern California: 50 Romantic Getaways. Bill Gleeson. LC 92-13495. 128p. 1992. pap. 14.95 (*0-8118-0149-7*) Chronicle Bks.

***Weekends for Two in Southern California: 50 Romantic Getaways.** Bill Gleeson. 1998. pap. text ed. 16.95 (*0-8118-1574-9*) Chronicle Bks.

Weekends for Two in the Pacific Northwest: Fifty Romantic Getaways. Bill Gleeson. LC 93-2224. 132p. 1994. pap. 14.95 (*0-8118-0378-3*) Chronicle Bks.

Weekends for Two in the Southwest: 50 Romantic Getaways. Bill Gleeson. LC 95-49867. (Illus.). 120p. 1997. pap. 16.95 (*0-8118-0884-X*) Chronicle Bks.

***Weekends in New York.** 5th ed. Fodors Travel Staff. 1997. pap. 14.50 (*0-679-03546-X*) Fodors Travel.

Weekends Like Other People. David Blomquist. 1983. pap. 5.25 (*0-8222-1229-3*) Dramatists Play.

***Weekends with Impressionists.** Westervelt. Date not set. 18.95 (*0-7893-0111-3*) Universe.

Weekly Feeder. Cori Kirkpatrick. 71p. 1995. spiral bd. 19.95 (*1-883697-43-3*) Hara Pub.

Weekly Guide for Daily Bible Readings, the Sundays after Pentecost, Year One see Daily Lectionary - Years One & Two

Weekly Law Reports Reprint. boxed 10,300.00 (*0-406-08800-4*, U.K.) MICHIE.

Weekly Menu Planner & Shopping List. Victor M. Spadaccini. (Illus.). 53p. (Orig.). 1989. pap. 6.95 (*0-911493-05-0*) Blue Sky.

Weekly Menu Planning List: Mom's Meal Planners. rev. ed. KayLee Parker. 52p. 1995. pap. 3.95 (*1-883924-05-7*, 240) Your Moms Organizers.

Weekly Midrash: Tzenah U'R'enah, 2 vols., Set. Tr. by Miriam S. Zakon from YID. (ArtScroll Judaica Classics Ser.). 1993. 34.99 (*0-89906-925-8*) Mesorah Pubns.

Weekly Prayer & Study Journal. Gary C. Wharton. 1996. spiral bd. 3.99 (*1-56570-031-7*) Meridian MI.

Weekly Prayer Services for Parish Meetings, Cycle C. Ed. by Marliss Rogers. LC 94-60153. 120p. (Orig.). 1994. pap. 12.95 (*0-89622-599-2*) Twenty-Third.

Weekly Prayer Services for Parish Meetings, Year A. Ed. by Marliss Rogers. LC 94-60153. 118p. (Orig.). 1995. pap. 12.95 (*0-89622-646-8*) Twenty-Third.

Weekly Prayer Services for Parish Meetings, Year B: Lectionary Based on Year B. Marliss Rogers. LC 94-60153. 120p. (Orig.). 1996. pap. 12.95 (*0-89622-693-X*) Twenty-Third.

Weekly Prayer Services for Teenagers, Years A & B: Lectionary Based for the School Year. Valerie Schneider. LC 97-60532. 104p. (Orig.). (YA). 1996. pap. 12.95 (*0-89622-692-1*) Twenty-Third.

Weekly Reports on All Legislation. Ed. by Butterworth Staff. ring bd. 1,500.00 (*0-614-05997-6*) MICHIE.

Weekly Reports on Banking. Ed. by Butterworth Staff. ring bd. 1,620.00 (*0-614-05998-4*) MICHIE.

Weekly Reports on Commerce & Consumer Affairs. Ed. by Butterworth Staff. ring bd. 1,500.00 (*0-614-05999-2*) MICHIE.

Weekly Reports on Insurance. Ed. by Butterworth Staff. ring bd. 1,620.00 (*0-614-06000-1*) MICHIE.

Weekly Reports on Labor-Management. Ed. by Butterworth Staff. ring bd. 1,620.00 (*0-614-06001-X*) MICHIE.

Weekly Reports on Taxes. Ed. by Butterworth Staff. ring bd. 1,800.00 (*0-614-06002-8*) MICHIE.

Weeks after Pentecost, Year Two see Daily Lectionary - Years One & Two

Weeks Hall: The Master of the Shadows. Morris Raphael. LC 81-90439. (Illus.). 207p. (J). (gr. 5-12). 1981. 14.95 (*0-9608866-1-3*) M Raphael.

Weeks Hall Tapes. Morris Raphael. LC 83-91286. 90p. (Orig.). 1983. pap. 7.95 (*0-9608866-2-1*) M Raphael.

Weenie-Toons! Women Cartoonists Mock Cocks. Ed. by Roz Warren. 40p. 1992. pap. 5.00 (*0-9632526-0-7*) Laugh Lines.

***Weep No More My Lady.** Mary Higgins Clark. 1997. pap. 11.95 (*0-385-31921-5*) Doubleday.

Weep No More, My Lady. Mary Higgins Clark. 384p. 1993. reprint ed. mass mkt. 6.99 (*0-440-20098-9*) Dell.

Weep No More My Lady. Mary Higgins Clark. 1993. reprint ed. lib. bdg. 27.95 (*0-89968-446-7*, Lghtyr Pr) Buccaneer Bks.

Weep Not Child. Ngugi Wa Thiong'o. (African Writers Ser.). 136p. (C). 1964. pap. 9.95 (*0-435-90830-8*, 90830) Heinemann.

Weep Not for Me. Gary Cohen. 179p. 1995. pap. 6.99 (*0-89957-099-2*) AMG Pubs.

Weep Not for Me. Moultrie Guerry. 51p. 1984. pap. 2.95 (*0-89536-974-5*) Univ South Pr.

Weep Not for Me: Meditations on the Cross & the Resurrection. John V. Taylor. (Risk Book Ser.). 56p. 1986. pap. 3.50 (*2-8254-0850-6*) Wrld Coun Churches.

Weep Not for Me: Meditations on the Cross & the Resurrection. John V. Taylor. LC 86-71639. (Risk Book Ser.: No. 27). 56p. reprint ed. pap. 25.00 (*0-7837-5999-1*, 2045809) Bks Demand.

***Weep Not for Me: Women, Ballads & Infanticide in Early Modern Scotland.** Deborah A. Symonds. LC 97-13086. (Illus.). 288p. 1997. 55.00 (*0-271-01616-7*); pap. 18.95 (*0-271-01617-5*) Pa St U Pr.

Weep Not for Me, Dear Mother. Elizabeth W. Roberson. LC 95-26298. (Illus.). 168p. (Orig.). 1996. reprint ed. pap. 19.95 (*1-56554-186-3*) Pelican.

Weep Some More, My Lady. Sigmund G. Spaeth. LC 80-11295. (Music Reprint Ser.). (Illus.). xv, 268p. 1980. reprint ed. lib. bdg. 35.00 (*0-306-76003-7*) Da Capo.

Weeping Angel. Stef A. Holm. (Illus.). (J). 1995. mass mkt. 5.99 (*0-671-51045-2*) PB.

Weeping Angel Prediction. Michael X. Barton. 30p. 1985. reprint ed. spiral bd. 7.00 (*0-7873-1279-7*) Hlth Research.

Weeping Crab. Iefke Goldberger. 36p. (Orig.). 1984. pap. 4.95 (*0-913370-16-9*, Sol Press) Wisconsin Bks.

Weeping in the Playtime of Others: The Plight of Incarcerated Children. Kenneth Wooden. 1976. pap. text ed. 6.95 (*0-07-071643-9*) McGraw.

***Weeping May Endure for a Night.** Phillip Cohen. (Illus.). 111p. (Orig.). 1996. pap. 6.00 (*0-9656046-0-8*) Lghthse Pub TN.

Weeping Moon. G. Clifton Wisler. 320p. (Orig.). 1995. mass mkt. 5.50 (*0-515-11678-5*) Jove Pubns.

Weeping Season. Gauri Pant. (Redbird Ser.). 36p. 1975. 4.80 (*0-88253-717-2*); pap. 4.00 (*0-88253-847-0*) Ind-US Inc.

Weeping Violins: The Gypsy Tragedy in Europe. Betty Alt & Silvia Folts. (C). 1996. pap. 20.00 (*0-943549-39-6*); text ed. 45.00 (*0-943549-31-0*) TJU Pr.

Weeping Willow. Ruth White. 256p. (YA). (gr. 7 up). 1992. 16.00 (*0-374-38255-7*) FS&G.

Weeping Willow. Ruth White. (YA). (gr. 7 up). 1994. pap. 3.95 (*0-374-48280-2*) FS&G.

Weeping Willow Trees. John F. Prevost. LC 96-6061. (Trees Ser.). (Illus.). (J). 1996. lib. bdg. 13.98 (*1-56239-619-6*) Abdo & Dghtrs.

Weeping Woman: La Llorona & Other Stories. Alma Luz Villanueva. LC 93-29735. 168p. 1994. 15.00 (*0-927534-38-X*) Biling Rev-Pr.

WEESKA Accounting & Finance. Jae K. Shim. (What Every Engineer Should Know Ser.: Vol. 32). 264p. 1994. 49.75 (*0-8247-9271-8*) Dekker.

WEESKA Computer Modeling & Simulation. Ingels. (What Every Engineer Should Know Ser.: Vol. 15). 176p. 1985. 59.75 (*0-8247-7444-2*) Dekker.

WEESKA Corrosion. Albert Schweitzer. (What Every Engineer Should Know Ser.: Vol. 21). 144p. 1987. 59.75 (*0-8247-7755-7*) Dekker.

WEESKA Developing Plastics Products. Bruce C. Wendle. (What Every Engineer Should Know Ser.: Vol. 29). 200p. 1991. 59.75 (*0-8247-8485-5*) Dekker.

WEESKA Electronic Communications Systems. McKay. (What Every Engineer Should Know Ser.: Vol. 25). 264p. 1988. 55.00 (*0-8247-8008-6*) Dekker.

WEESKA Engineering Information Resources. Schenk & Webster. (What Every Engineer Should Know Ser.: Vol. 13). 232p. 1984. 59.75 (*0-8247-7244-X*) Dekker.

WEESKA Engineering Work Stations. Harlow. (What Every Engineer Should Know Ser.: Vol. 16). 168p. 1986. 59.75 (*0-8247-7509-0*) Dekker.

WEESKA Finite Element Analysis. 2nd rev. ed. Ed. by John R. Brauer. LC 93-12659. (What Every Engineer Should Know Ser.: Vol. 31). 346p. 1993. 59.75 (*0-8247-8954-7*) Dekker.

WEESKA Lasers. Winburn. (What Every Engineer Should Know Ser.: Vol. 22). 224p. 1987. 59.75 (*0-8247-7748-4*) Dekker.

WEESKA Manufacturing Cost Estimating. Malstrom. (What Every Engineer Should Know Ser.: Vol. 6). 200p. 1981. 55.00 (*0-8247-1511-X*) Dekker.

WEESKA Microcomputer Software. Keith Wehmeyer. (What Every Engineer Should Know Ser.: Vol. 14). (Illus.). 184p. 1984. 59.75 (*0-8247-7275-X*) Dekker.

WEESKA Microcomputer Systems Design & Debugging. Bill Wray & Bill Crawford. (What Every Engineer Should Know Ser.: Vol. 12). (Illus.). 200p. 1984. 55.00 (*0-8247-7160-5*) Dekker.

WEESKA Microcomputers Hardware - Software Design: A Step-by-Step Example. 2nd ed. Ed. by William S. Bennett. (What Every Engineer Should Know Ser.: Vol. 27). 272p. 1990. 55.00 (*0-8247-8193-7*) Dekker.

WEESKA Product Liability. James F. Thorpe & Middendorf. (What Every Engineer Should Know Ser.: Vol. 2). 118p. 1979. 55.00 (*0-8247-6876-0*) Dekker.

WEESKA Quality Control. Thomas Pyzdek. (What Every Engineer Should Know Ser.: Vol. 26). 274p. 1988. 59.75 (*0-8247-7966-5*) Dekker.

WEESKA Reliability & Risk Analysis. Mohammed Modarres. LC 92-32998. (What Every Engineer Should Know Ser.: Vol. 30). 360p. 1992. 59.75 (*0-8247-8958-X*) Dekker.

WEESKA Robots. Maurice Zeldman. (What Every Engineer Should Know Ser.: Vol. 11). (Illus.). 224p. 1984. 59.75 (*0-8247-7123-0*) Dekker.

WEESKA Technology Transfer & Innovation. Mogavero & Shane. (What Every Engineer Should Know Ser.: Vol. 8). 168p. 1982. 59.75 (*0-8247-1863-1*) Dekker.

WEESKA Threaded Fasteners: Materials & Design. Blake. (What Every Engineer Should Know Ser.: Vol. 18). 216p. 1986. 59.75 (*0-8247-7554-6*) Dekker.

Weet. John Wilson. 148p. 1996. pap. text ed. 7.95 (*0-929141-40-7*, Pub. by Napoleon Pubng CN) ACCESS Pubs Network.

Weetman Pearson, First Viscount Cowdray, 1856-1927. John A. Spender. Ed. by Mira Wilkins. LC 76-40616. (European Business Ser.). (Illus.). 1977. reprint ed. lib. bdg. 31.95 (*0-405-09801-4*) Ayer.

Weetzie Bat. Francesca L. Block. LC 88-6214. (Charlotte Zolotow Bk.). 96p. (YA). (gr. 7 up). 1989. 12.95 (*0-06-020534-2*); lib. bdg. 14.89 (*0-06-020536-9*) HarpC Child Bks.

Weetzie Bat. Francesca L. Block. LC 88-6214. (Charlotte Zolotow Bk.). 96p. (YA). (gr. 7 up). 1991. pap. 3.95 (*0-06-447068-7*, Trophy) HarpC Child Bks.

Weeuns Journey of Two Cousins. Beatrice Tallarico & S. Callis Stone. (Illus.). 39p. (J). (gr. 2-8). 1984. 12.95 (*0-936191-13-9*) Tallstone Pub.

Weevils in the Wheat: Interviews with Virginia Ex-Slaves. Ed. by Charles L. Perdue, Jr. et al. LC 79-65433. (Midland Bks.: No. 237). (Illus.). 405p. (C). 1992. reprint ed. pap. text ed. 18.50 (*0-8139-1370-5*) U Pr of Va.

Weezer, Weezer. 19.95 (*0-7935-4581-1*, 00690071) H Leonard.

WEF Conference, 1992: Set of Symposia & Abstracts. 1992. Set. pap. 800.00 (*1-881369-15-3*) Water Environ.

***WEFA Industrial Monitor 1997.** WEFA Inc. Staff. 275p. 1997. 59.95 (*0-471-19946-X*) Wiley.

Weft-Faced Pattern Weaves: Tabby to Taquete. Nancy A. Hoskins. LC 91-66162. (Illus.). 352p. 1992. pap. 40.00 (*0-295-97199-1*) U of Wash Pr.

Weft Twining. Virginia I. Harvey & Harriet Tidball. LC 76-24017. (Guild Monographs: No. 28). (Illus.). 39p. 1969. pap. 7.95 (*0-916658-28-7*) Shuttle Craft.

***Weg (-ung) Im Denken Ferdinand Ebners: Ein Reise-Berich von Einer Zwischen-Station und Vom Sich An-Bahnenden Ein-/Durch-Horen, -Blicken.** Franz Scharl. (Europaische Hochschulschriften Ser.: Reihe 20, Bd. 525). 639p. (GER.). 1997. 95.95 (*3-631-30578-8*) P Lang Pubng.

***Weg des Films, 2 vols.** Friedrich Von Zglinicki. (Weitere Monographien Zur Filmgeschichte Ser.). xxxi, 678p. (GER.). 1979. write for info. (*3-487-08166-0*) G Olms Pubs.

Weg ins Freie. Roman. Arthur Schnitzler. 384p. (GER.). 1990. pap. 18.00 (*3-596-29405-3*, Pub. by Fischer Taschbch Verlag GW) Intl Bk Import.

Weg von der Dudennorm: Arno Schmidts Weg von den "Sturenburg-Geschichten" xur "Inselstrasse" Jens Simon. xii, 225p. (GER.). (C). 1991. lib. bdg. 75.40 (*3-11-012828-4*) De Gruyter.

Weg Zum Lesen. 3rd ed. Van H. Vail. 361p. (GER.). (C). 1986. pap. text ed. 21.50 (*0-15-517351-0*); audio 83.00 (*0-15-517352-9*) HB Coll Pubs.

WEGA - Large Wind Turbines. E. Hau et al. (Illus.). x, 143p. 1993. 86.95 (*0-387-56592-2*) Spr-Verlag.

***WEGA II Large Wind Turbines Intermediate Design Report, EUR 16902.** European Commission Staff. 164p. 1996. pap. 30.00 (*92-827-8903-9*, CG-NA-16902-ENC, Pub. by Europ Com UK) Bernan Associates.

Wege der Weisheit: Die Legren Amenemopes und Proverbein 22, 17-24, 22. Diethard Roemheld. (Beiheft zur Zeitschrift fuer die Alttestamentliche Wissenschaft Ser.: No. 184). x, 233p. (GER.). (C). 1989. lib. bdg. 69.25 (*3-11-011958-7*) De Gruyter.

***Wegman Video Movie Guide 1997.** Martin & Porter. 1996. mass mkt. 7.99 (*0-345-41988-X*) Ballantine.

Wegner's Bibliography on Deer & Deer Hunting: A Comprehensive Annotated Compilation of Books in English Pertaining to Deer & Their Hunting, 1413-1991. Robert Wegner. LC 92-60899. 333p. 1992. 45.00 (*0-9633094-0-4*) St Huberts Pr.

Wegner's Bibliography on Deer & Deer Hunting: A Comprehensive Annotated Compilation of Books in English Pertaining to Deer & Their Hunting, 1413-1991. deluxe ed. Robert Wegner. LC 92-60899. 333p. 1992. lthr. 150.00 (*0-9633094-1-2*) St Huberts Pr.

Wegweiser Durch die Grammatik von Heinrich Bauer: Verzeichnisse und Erlauterungen. J. Meder. (GER.). (C). 1991. lib. bdg. 220.00 (*3-11-012577-3*) De Gruyter.

Wegweiser Durch die Literatur der Urkundensammlungen, 2 vols. Hermann Oesterley. vi, 997p. 1969. reprint ed. Set. write for info. (*0-318-71849-9*) G Olms Pubs.

Wehrmacht: Diceless Science-Fiction Wargaming. T. Bradley Back & Timothy J. Gallion. (Illus.). 120p. (Orig.). 1996. pap. 24.95 (*0-9653173-0-7*) Tyrant Games.

***Wehrmacht: The Illustrated History of the German Army in WWII.** John Pinot. LC 97-14736. (Illus.). 176p. 1997. 24.95 (*0-7603-0387-8*) Motorbooks Intl.

Wehrmacht & German Rearmament. Anthony J. Nicholls. LC 81-178952. 165p. reprint ed. pap. 47.10 (*0-8357-8372-3*, 2034016) Bks Demand.

Wehrmacht Auxiliary Forces. N. Thomas & C. Jurado. (Men-at-Arms Ser.: No. 254). (Illus.). 48p. pap. 11.95 (*1-85532-257-9*, 9225, Pub. by Osprey UK) Stackpole.

***Wehrmacht Weapons Testing Ground at Kummersdorf.** Wolfgang Fleischer. 200p. 1997. 29.95 (*0-7643-0273-6*) Schiffer.

Wei Wei & Other Friends. Louis Simpson. (Illus.). 24p. (J). 1990. pap. 25.00 (*0-930126-30-0*) Typographeum.

Wei Yuan & China's Rediscovery of the Maritime World. Jane K. Leonard. (East Asian Monographs: No. 111). (Illus.). 300p. 1984. 30.00 (*0-674-94855-6*) HUP.

Wei Yuan & China's Rediscovery of the Maritime World. Jane K. Leonard. (Harvard East Asian Monographs: No. 111). (Illus.). 300p. 1983. 20.00 (*0-317-01568-0*) Harvard E Asian.

***Weib Offnen, um das Schwarz Hervorkommen zu Lassen: Zur Schrift in der Dramatik Victoria Benedictssons und Cecilie Loveids.** Corinna Vonhoegen. Ed. by Heiko Uecker. (Texte und Untersuchungen zur Germanistik und Skandinavistik Ser.: Bd. 37). 235p. (GER.). 1996. 44.95 (*3-631-30494-3*) P Lang Pubng.

***Weibliche und die Unmoglichkeit Seiner Integration: Eine Studie der "Gothic Fiction" nach C. G. Jung.** Elvira Weibmann-Orzlowski. (Europaische Hochschulschriften, Reihe 14: Bd. 323). 266p. 1997. 51.95 (*3-631-30950-3*) P Lang Pubng.

Weibull Analysis. Bryan Dodson. LC 94-26849. 256p. 1994. pap. 50.00 incl. disk (*0-87389-295-X*, H0851) ASQC Qual Pr.

Weida. Charline T. Rotha. 204p. 1993. pap. 11.95 (*0-685-69189-6*) Prof Pr NC.

Weider System of Bodybuilding. Joe Weider. Ed. by Bill Reynolds. (Illus.). 240p. (Orig.). 1983. pap. 14.95 (*0-8092-5559-6*) Contemp Bks.

Weidmannsche Buchhandlung in Berlin, 1680-1930. Ernst Vollert. x, 164p. 1983. write for info. (*3-615-00003-X*) G Olms Pubs.

Weiga of Temagami. Cy Warman. LC 76-140346. (Short Story Index Reprint Ser.). 1977. 19.95 (*0-8369-3738-4*) Ayer.

***Weigh Down Diet: The Inspirational Way to Lose Weight, Stay Slim & Find a New You.** Gwen Shamblim. (Illus.). 288p. 1997. 21.00 (*0-385-48762-2*) Doubleday.

Weigh-In. Winthrop Smith. (Illus.). 170p. (Orig.). 1996. pap. 12.95 (*1-879194-20-1*) GLB Pubs.

***Weigh It Up.** Andy Cooke. (Bear's Playschool Kits Ser.). (J). 1997. pap. 8.95 (*0-8120-8488-8*) Barron.

***Weigh Less, Live Longer: Dr. Lou Aronne's "Getting Healthy" Plan.** Louis J. Aronne & Fred Graver. 320p. 1997. pap. text ed. 5.99 (*0-471-17695-8*) Wiley.

Weigh Less, Live Longer: Dr. Lou Aronne's "Getting Healthy" Plan for Permanent Weight Control. Louis J. Aronne. (Illus.). 320p. 1995. text ed. 22.95 (*0-471-58112-7*) Wiley.

Weigh of Life. Beverly Slay. (Illus.). 1993. pap. 14.95 (*0-9639799-0-6*) Weigh of Life.

Weigh Out: A Medically Supervised Weight Loss Program Used for Twenty Years by a Group of California Physicians. 2nd ed. Sandra Stoddard & Wendy Keown. 200p. (Orig.). 1993. pap. 14.95 (*0-9637877-0-5*) Phys Weight.

Weigh to Win at Weight Loss. Lynn Hill. (Weigh to Win Ser.). 180p. (Orig.). 1992. pap. 10.99 (*0-89693-059-9*, 6-1059, Victor Bks) Chariot Victor.

Weigh to Win Daily Journal. Lynn Hill. (Weigh to Win Ser.). 132p. (Orig.). 1992. pap. 6.99 (*0-89693-060-2*, 6-1060, Victor Bks) Chariot Victor.

Weigh to Win Daily Journal. Lynn Hill. (Weigh to Win Ser.). (Orig.). 1994. 19.99 (*1-56476-446-X*, 6-3446, Victor Bks) Chariot Victor.

Weighed & Found Wanting: Putting the Toronto Blessing in Context. Bill Randles. (Illus.). 249p. (Orig.). 1995. pap. 10.00 (*0-9646626-1-2*) B Randles.

Weighed & Found Wanting: The American Catholic Bishops & Their Pastoral Letter on War & Peace. 2nd ed. Gommar A. De Pauw. (Illus.). 180p. 1989. write for info. (*0-318-65211-0*) CTM Pubns.

Weighed & Wanting. George MacDonald. (George MacDonald Original Works: Series VII). 625p. 1996. 20.00 (*1-881084-43-4*) Johannesen.

Weighed in the Balance. Anne Perry. 384p. 1996. 23.00 (*0-449-91078-4*) Fawcett.

***Weighed in the Balance.** Anne Perry. 1997. mass mkt. 6.99 (*0-8041-1562-1*) Ivy Books.

***Weighed in the Balance.** large type ed. Anne Perry. LC 96-37675. 588p. 1997. 26.95 (*0-7862-0978-X*, Thorndike Lrg Prnt) Thorndike Pr.

Weigher. Jack Rudman. (Career Examination Ser.: C-2674). 1994. pap. 23.95 (*0-8373-2674-5*) Nat Learn.

Weighing. Ron Marson. (Task Cards Ser.: No. 5). (Illus.). 56p. (YA). (gr. 7-12). 1990. teacher ed. 9.50 (*0-941008-75-4*) Tops Learning.

***Weighing an Elephant.** Illus. by He Youzhi. 91p. (J). 1981. pap. 6.95 (*0-8351-2548-3*) China Bks.

Weighing & Measuring. Terry Jennings. (Making Science Work Ser.). (Illus.). 1996. lib. bdg. 21.40 (*0-8172-3963-4*) Raintree Steck-V.

Weighing Delight & Dole: A Study of Comedy, Tragedy & Anxiety. Peter B. Waldeck. (American University Studies: Comparative Literature: Ser. III, Vol. 26). 275p. (C). 1989. text ed. 36.60 (*0-8204-0846-8*) P Lang Pubng.

Weighing Goods: Equality, Uncertainty & Time. John Broome. Ed. by Alan Hamun & Philip Pettit. (Economics & Philosophy Ser.). 255p. 1995. pap. 23.95 (*0-631-19972-1*) Blackwell Pubs.

Weighing Imponderables & Other Quantitative Science Around 1800. John L. Heilbron. LC 91-62713. (Berkeley Papers in History of Science: No. 13). 337p. (Orig.). 1993. pap. text ed. 20.00 (*0-918102-17-0*) U Cal Hist Sci Tech.

Weighing the Options: Criteria for Evaluating Weight-Management Programs. Institute of Medicine, Committee to Develop Criteria for Evaluating the Outcome of Approaches to Prevent & Treat Obesity Staff. Ed. by Paul R. Thomas. LC 94-44625. (Illus.). 296p. (Orig.). (C). 1995. pap. 24.95 (*0-309-05131-2*) Natl Acad Pr.

Weighing the Variables: A Guide to Ag Credit Management. David Kohl. Ed. by Kathy Topping. 160p. (C). student ed. 60.00 (*0-89982-336-X*) Am Bankers.

Weight. Henry Pluckrose. (Math Counts Ser.). 32p. (J). 1995. lib. bdg. 17.80 (*0-516-05460-0*) Childrens.

Weight. Henry Pluckrose. (Math Counts Ser.). (J). 1995. pap. 4.95 (*0-516-45460-9*) Childrens.

Weight: A Teenage Concern. Elaine Landau. 160p. (YA). (gr. 7 up). 1991. pap. 15.00 (*0-525-67335-0*, Lodestar Bks) Dutton Child Bks.

***Weight & Win Get Started Set.** 1994. write for info. (*1-56476-289-0*, Victor Bks) Chariot Victor.

***Weight & Win Management System.** 1992. write for info. (*1-56476-039-1*, Victor Bks) Chariot Victor.

Weight Be Gone. Jay F. Vincent. 12p. 1995. pap. text ed. 5.95 (*0-9647859-0-0*) V-Enter.

Weight Control. Charles Citrenbaum. Date not set. student ed., pap. 10.95 incl. reel tape (*0-393-70016-X*) Norton.

***Weight Control.** Stephen Terrass. 1995. pap. 8.00 (*0-7225-3149-4*) Thorsons SF.

Weight Control: A Guide for Counselors & Therapists. Ed. by Aaron M. Atlschul. LC 87-11725. 305p. 1987. text ed. 65.00 (*0-275-92697-4*, C2697, Praeger Pubs) Greenwood.

Weight Control: A Nutritional Approach. Louise Tenney. (Todays Health Ser.: No. 6). pap. 3.95 (*0-913923-33-8*) Woodland UT.

Weight Control: The Behavioural Strategies. Michael D. LeBow. LC 79-41728. (Illus.). 358p. reprint ed. pap. 102.10 (*0-685-20593-2*, 2030527) Bks Demand.

***Weight Control: The Current Perspective.** Ed. by Cottrell. (Illus.). 128p. 1995. text ed. 64.50 (*0-412-73600-4*, Chap & Hall NY) Chapman & Hall.

Weight Control & Reduction Business, No. GA-069. Business Communications Co., Inc., Staff. 110p. 1990. 1,950.00 (*0-89336-464-9*) BCC.

Weight Control, Stress & Amino Acid Therapy. 1996. lib. bdg. 251.95 (*0-8490-5895-3*) Gordon Pr.

Weight Control Ways. Joan Bissen et al. 56p. 1990. student ed. write for info. (*1-884153-01-1*) Prk Nicollet.

Weight-Distance Taxes & Other Highway User Taxes. (Legislative Finance Papers: No. 71). 1989. 10.00 (*1-55516-071-9*, 5101-71) Natl Conf State Legis.

Weight Functions & Stress Intensity Factor Solutions. Xue-Ren Wu & A. J. Carlsson. (Illus.). 528p. 1991. 142.00 (*0-08-041702-7*, Pergamon Pr) Elsevier.

Weight Lifting. Jeff Savage. (Working Out Ser.). (Illus.). (YA). (gr. 5 up). 1995. pap. 7.95 (*0-382-24949-6*, Crstwood Hse) Silver Burdett Pr.

Weight Lifting & Conditioning Exercises. 2nd ed. Maurice Johnson. (Illus.). 110p. 1992. pap. 14.95 (*0-945483-21-X*) E Bowers Pub.

Weight Lifting & Progressive Resistance Exercise. Jim Murray. 95p. reprint ed. pap. 27.10 (*0-317-28592-0*, 2055167) Bks Demand.

***Weight Loss: The Psychological Approach.** Gert Bursey. LC 97-66630. (Illus.). 110p. (Orig.). 1997. pap. 9.50 (*0-9657078-0-6*) Reliable Wght Consult.

***Weight Loss & Cellulite Control: A Fighting Chance for Weight Loss.** rev. ed. Linda R. Page. (Healthy Healing Library Ser.: Vol. 12). (Illus.). 32p. 1996. pap. 3.50 (*1-884334-37-7*) Hlthy Healing.

Weight Loss & Fitness Facts: Diet - Exercise - Disease Prevention. Cindy Bracken. (Illus.). 36p. (Orig.). 1993. pap. 10.00 (*0-9638588-1-5*) Weight Loss.

Weight Loss & Fitness Facts: Diet-Exercise-Disease Prevention. Cindy Bracken. (Illus.). 36p. 1994. pap. 55.00 incl. vhs (*0-9638588-0-7*) Weight Loss.

Weight Loss for African-Americans: A Cultural Lifestyle Change. Charles W. Johnson. 152p. 1994. pap. 11.95 (*0-9624889-4-1*) Seymour-Smith.

Weight Loss for the Middle-Aged Athlete. Bruce C. Vandre. (How to Succeed in Fitness Ser.). 192p. (Orig.). 1987. pap. 10.95 (*0-942223-00-4*) VanPress.

Weight Loss for the Mind. Stuart Wilde. 112p. pap. 3.95 (*1-56170-162-9*, 186) Hay House.

Weight Loss Made Easy: Hundreds of Tips for a Weight Loss Life-Style. Cecelia Phillips. LC 88-91234. 150p. (Orig.). 1993. write for info. (*0-9618870-3-6*); pap. 14.95 (*0-9618870-2-8*) L C Ellsworth.

Weight Loss Through Persistence: Making Science Work for You. Daniel S. Kirschenbaum. LC 93-86803. 281p. (Orig.). 1994. pap. 13.95 (*1-879237-64-4*) New Harbinger.

Weight Loss to Super Wellness. Ted L. Edwards, Jr. & Barbara Lau. (Illus.). 176p. (Orig.). 1982. pap. text ed. 12.95 (*0-938934-07-4*) Hills Med.

Weight Loss to Super Wellness. 2nd ed. Ted L. Edwards, Jr. LC 87-31863. (Illus.). 176p. (Orig.). 1988. pap. 14.95 (*0-87322-924-X*, PEDW0348) Human Kinetics.

***Weight Loss Workbook: The Essential Companion for Any Weight Loss Program.** June Rodriguez. 144p. 1998. spiral bd. 14.00 (*1-56836-201-3*) Kodansha.

Weight Machines. Michael T. Cannell & Judith Zimmer. Ed. by Susan Wallach. LC 84-40602. (AT Home Gym Ser.). 64p. 1985. pap. 2.95 (*0-394-72974-9*, Villard Bks) Random.

Weight Maintenance Survival Guide. Kelly D. Brownell & Judith Rodin. 165p. (Orig.). 1990. pap. 17.95 (*1-878513-01-X*) Am Hlth Pub.

Weight Management & Eating Disorders: HP 625. Rita Jones. 226p. (C). 1993. student ed., spiral bd. write for info. (*0-933915-48-9*) CA College Health Sci.

***Weight Management for Type II Diabetes: An Action Plan.** Jackie Labat & Annette Maggi. 176p. (Orig.). 1997. pap. 12.95 (*1-56561-114-4*) Chronimed.

Weight Management the Fitness Way. Dorothy E. Dusek. 304p. (Orig.). 1989. pap. 35.00 (*0-86720-416-8*) Jones & Bartlett.

Weight No Longer. William G. Johnson & Peter Stalonas. LC 80-21663. 188p. 1981. 16.95 (*0-88289-261-4*) Pelican.

Weight No More: A Weight-Loss Program That Can Work. Eric A. Mein. (Natural Remedies for Common Ailments & Conditions Ser.). 76p. (Orig.). 1990. pap. 4.95 (*0-87604-260-4*, 351) ARE Pr.

Weight of Evidence. large type ed. Roger Ormerod. (Linford Mystery Large Print Ser.). 1994. pap. 15.99 (*0-7089-7634-4*) Ulverscroft.

Weight of Glory. C. S. Lewis. 144p. 1996. pap. 9.00 (*0-684-82384-5*, Touchstone Bks) S&S Trade.

Weight of Glory: A Vision & Practice for Christian Faith: The Future of Liberal Theology. Ed. by D. W. Hardy & P. H. Sedgwick. 312p. 1991. 29.95 (*0-567-09579-7*, Pub. by T & T Clark UK) Bks Intl VA.

Weight of Glory: A Vision & Practice for Christian Faith: The Future of Liberal Theology. Ed. by D. W. Hardy & P. H. Sedgwick. 312p. 1994. pap. text ed. 24.95 (*0-567-29269-X*, Pub. by T & T Clark UK) Bks Intl VA.

Weight of Light. Betty P. Nelson. 320p. 1993. pap. 12.95 (*0-312-09936-3*) St Martin.

Weight of Love. John Herman. 336p. 1995. 23.95 (*0-385-47815-1*, N A Talese) Doubleday.

Weight of Numbers. Judith Baumel. LC 87-21180. (Wesleyan Poetry Ser.). 72p. 1988. pap. 11.95 (*0-8195-1145-5*, Wesleyan Univ Pr); text ed. 25.00 (*0-8195-2144-2*, Wesleyan Univ Pr) U Pr of New Eng.

Weight of the Body. Michal Reed. (Artists' Bks.). (Illus.). 32p. (Orig.). 1995. pap. 12.00 (*0-89822-110-2*) Visual Studies.

Weight of the Heart. David Citino. (QRL Poetry Bks.: Vol. XXXV). 1996. 20.00 (*0-614-15861-3*) Quarterly Rev.

Weight of the World. Peter Handke. Tr. by Ralph Manheim from GER. 288p. 1984. 16.95 (*0-374-28745-7*) FS&G.

Weight of the Yen. R. Taggart Murphy. 320p. 1996. 25.00 (*0-393-03832-7*) Norton.

***Weight of the Yen: How Denials Imperils America's Future & Ruins an Alliance.** R. Taggart Murphy. 352p. 1997. pap. 13.95 (*0-393-31657-2*) Norton.

***Weight of Water.** Shreve. 1998. pap. 13.95 (*0-316-78037-5*) Little.

Weight of Water. Anita Shreve. LC 96-21326. 1997. 22.95 (*0-316-78997-6*) Little.

***Weight of Water.** large type ed. Anita Shreve. LC 97-5421. (Basic Ser.). 401p. 1997. 25.95 (*0-7862-1095-8*, Thorndike Lrg Prnt) Thorndike Pr.

Weight of Winter. Cathie Pelletier. LC 92-39708. 432p. reprint ed. pap. 12.00 (*0-671-79387-X*, WSP) PB.

Weight, Sex, & Marriage: A Delicate Balance. Richard B. Stuart & Jacobson. 1994. lib. bdg. 14.95 (*0-89862-060-0*, 2060) Guilford Pr.

***Weight Theory for Integral Transforms on Spaces of Homogenous Type.** LC 96-31180. (Pitman Monographs & Surveys in Pure & Applied Mathematics). 1997. write for info. (*0-582-30295-1*) Longman.

***Weight Training.** Brown & Benchmark Staff. LC 97-11006. (Elements of Learning Ser.). 120p. (C). 1997. per. write for info. (*0-697-29463-3*) Brown & Benchmark.

***Weight Training.** Lombardi. Date not set. pap. text ed. 15.50 (*0-697-10737-X*) McGraw.

Weight Training. 3rd ed. Jim Hesson. (Illus.). 160p. 1995. pap. text ed. 15.95 (*0-89582-293-8*) Morton Pub.

Weight Training. 5th ed. Philip J. Rasch. 128p. (C). 1989. per. write for info. (*0-697-10417-6*) Brown & Benchmark.

Weight Training: A Practical Approach to "Total" Fitness. Richard Trestrail. 112p. (C). 1994. per., pap. text ed. 11.02 (*0-8403-9735-6*) Kendall-Hunt.

Weight Training: A Step-by-Step Guide to the Development of a Safe & Sound Program. Anthony Glass. 144p. (C). 1994. per. 15.91 (*0-8403-9450-0*) Kendall-Hunt.

Weight Training: Steps to Success. Thomas R. Baechle & Barney R. Groves. LC 91-25316. 208p. 1992. pap. 14.95 (*0-88011-451-7*, PBAE0451) Human Kinetics.

Weight Training, A Scientific Approach. Michael H. Stone & Harold S. O'Bryant. (Illus.). 364p. (C). 1986. pap. 17.95 (*0-8087-6942-1*) Burgess MN Intl.

Weight Training & Fitness for Health & Performance. Seidler. 144p. (C). 1990. spiral bd. 18.84 (*0-8403-6312-5*) Kendall-Hunt.

Weight Training & Lifting. John Lear. pap. 19.95 (*0-7136-5674-3*, 91804, Pub. by A&C Black UK) Talman.

Weight Training & Total Fitness...in a Nutshell. Terry Moss. LC 94-77894. (Nutshell Ser.). 53p. 1994. pap. 4.95 (*1-885962-52-5*) Lincoln Lrning.

Weight Training Calorie Register. rev. ed. Jim Bennett. 96p. 1991. pap. 7.95 (*1-879031-02-7*) JBBA Pub.

***Weight Training Everyone.** 4th ed. Signorile et al. 218p. 1993. pap. text ed. 15.95 (*0-88725-196-X*) Hunter Textbks.

Weight Training for Beginners, Vol. 1. Bill Reynolds. (Illus.). 96p. 1982. pap. 8.95 (*0-8092-5728-9*) Contemp Bks.

***Weight Training for Dummies.** Liz W. Neporent. 1997. pap. 19.99 (*0-7645-5036-5*) IDG Bks.

Weight Training for Gifted Athletes. William J. Maitland. LC 89-90833. (Illus.). 147p. (Orig.). (YA). (gr. 8 up). 1990. pap. 17.95 (*0-936759-01-1*) Maitland Enter.

***Weight Training for Life.** 4th ed. James Hesson. (Illus.). 160p. (C). 1997. pap. text ed. 15.95 (*0-89582-393-4*) Morton Pub.

Weight Training for Strength & Fitness. L. J. Silvester. 256p. 1992. pap. 15.00 (*0-86720-139-8*) Jones & Bartlett.

Weight Training for Women. Thomas D. Fahey & Gayle Hutchinson. LC 91-18357. 189p. (C). 1992. pap. 14.95 (*1-55934-048-7*) Mayfield Pub.

Weight Training Instruction: Steps to Success. Thomas R. Baechle & Barney R. Groves. LC 93-38005. (Steps to Success Activity Ser.). (Illus.). 208p. 1994. pap. text ed. 19.95 (*0-87322-618-6*, PBAE0618) Human Kinetics.

***Weight Training Logbook.** 50p. 1997. pap. 8.95 (*0-9645470-1-5*) LOC CO.

***Weight Training Made Easy: Transform Your Body in Four Simple Steps.** Joyce L. Vedral. (Illus.). 304p. 1997. pap. 14.99 (*0-446-67109-6*); pap. text ed. 89.94 (*0-446-16481-X*) Warner Bks.

Weight Training Record. 2nd ed. Jim Bennett. 208p. 1995. spiral bd., pap. 10.95 (*1-879031-07-8*) JBBA Pub.

Weight Training Workbook. 2nd ed. JIm Bennett. (Weight Training Ser.). (Illus.). 256p. 1995. spiral bd., pap. 12.95 (*1-879031-06-X*) JBBA Pub.

Weight Training Workbook for Women. Jim Bennett. (Illus.). 256p. (Orig.). 1996. spiral bd., pap. 12.95 (*1-879031-08-6*) JBBA Pub.

Weight Traning. Christopher M. Norris. pap. 20.95 (*0-7136-3771-4*, 92982, Pub. by A&C Black UK) Talman.

***Weight Watchers Complete Cookbook & Program.** Weight Watchers Staff. 1998. 16.95 (*0-02-862077-1*) Macmillan.

Weight Watcher's Complete Cookbook & Program Basics. Weight Watchers International, Inc. Staff. LC 94-15686. 1994. 29.95 (*0-671-88184-1*) Macmillan.

Weight Watcher's Complete Exercise Book. Weight Watchers International, Inc. Staff. 144p. 1994. 14.00 (*0-02-860081-9*) Macmillan.

Weight Watchers Cut the Fat! Cookbook. Weight Watchers International, Inc. Staff. LC 95-38385. 224p. 1995. 23.00 (*0-02-860390-7*) Macmillan.

***Weight Watchers Fast & Fabulous Cookbook.** Weight Watchers International, Inc. Staff. 1996. 12.98 (*0-7651-9794-4*) Smithmark.

Weight Watchers Fast & Fabulous Recipes. Weight Watchers International, Inc. Staff. (Weight Watchers Ser.). 1996. write for info. (*0-525-94266-1*) NAL-Dutton.

***Weight Watchers Fast Food Companion.** (Illus.). 170p. (Orig.). 1996. pap. 1.99 (*0-9658090-7-2*) Inventory Mngmnt.

Weight Watchers Fat Sorter. Augustus Y. Napier. 1995. pap. 3.00 (*0-671-50126-7*) S&S Trade.

Weight Watchers Favorite Homestyle Recipes. LC 93-37107. 1994. pap. 14.95 (*0-452-27050-2*) NAL-Dutton.

Weight Watchers Favorite Homestyle Recipes. large type ed. Weight Watchers International, Inc. Staff. LC 93-17804. (Illus.). 1994. Alk. paper. 25.95 (*0-8161-5825-8*, GK Hall) Thorndike Pr.

Weight Watchers Favorite Recipes. Weight Watchers International, Inc. Staff. 1988. pap. 11.95 (*0-452-26465-0*, Plume) NAL-Dutton.

Weight Watchers Favorite Recipes. Weight Watchers International, Inc. Staff. 1996. write for info. (*0-525-94267-X*) NAL-Dutton.

***Weight Watchers Favorite Recipes.** Weight Watchers International, Inc. Staff. 1996. 12.98 (*0-7651-9795-2*) Smithmark.

***Weight Watchers Food Companion.** (Illus.). 150p. (Orig.). 1995. pap. 1.99 (*0-9658090-6-4*) Inventory Mngmnt.

Weight Watchers Health & Fitness. Weight Watchers International, Inc. Staff. 1994. pap. 10.00 (*0-671-89262-2*) S&S Trade.

Weight Watcher's Healthy Life-Style Cookbook. Weight Watchers International, Inc. Staff. (Illus.). 416p. 1991. 19.95 (*0-525-24935-4*, Dutton) NAL-Dutton.

Weight Watcher's Healthy Life-Style Cookbook. Weight Watchers International, Inc. Staff. 1996. write for info. (*0-525-94264-5*) NAL-Dutton.

Weight Watchers Healthy Life-Style Cookbook. large type ed. Weight Watchers International, Inc. Staff. LC 93-37107. 500p. 1992. pap. 15.95 (*0-8161-5249-7*, GK Hall) Thorndike Pr.

Weight Watchers Healthy Life-Style Cookbook. Weight Watchers International, Inc. Staff. (Illus.). 368p. 1992. reprint ed. pap. 12.95 (*0-452-26755-2*, Plume) NAL-Dutton.

***Weight Watchers Healthy Style Cookbook.** Weight Watchers International, Inc. Staff. 1996. 12.98 (*0-7651-9796-0*) Smithmark.

***Weight Watchers Managing Stress.** 1997. pap. 9.00 (*0-614-19375-3*) Macmillan.

***Weight Watchers Meals in Minutes.** Weight Watchers International, Inc. Staff. 1996. 12.98 (*0-7651-9797-9*) Smithmark.

Weight Watchers Meals in Minutes Cookbook. Weight Watchers International, Inc. Staff. (Illus.). 416p. 1991. pap. 11.95 (*0-452-26570-3*, Plume) NAL-Dutton.

Weight Watchers Meals in Minutes Cookbook. Weight Watchers International, Inc. Staff. 1996. write for info. (*0-525-94265-3*) NAL-Dutton.

Weight Watchers Meditational, No. 2. Weight Watchers International, Inc. Staff. 1995. pap. 10.00 (*0-671-88984-2*) S&S Trade.

Weight Watchers New 365-Day Menu Cookbook. LC 96-11094. 192p. 1996. 29.95 (*0-02-861295-7*) Macmillan.

Weight Watchers Quick & Easy Menu Cookbook: Over 250 Seasonal Recipes & Menus Based on The Quick Success Program. (Illus.). 1989. pap. 10.95 (*0-452-26248-8*, Plume) NAL-Dutton.

Weight Watchers Quick & Easy Menus. Weight Watchers International, Inc. Staff. 1989. pap. 11.95 (*0-452-26475-8*, Plume) NAL-Dutton.

Weight Watcher's Quick Meals. 1995. 27.50 (*0-02-860351-6*) Macmillan.

***Weight Watchers Quick Meals.** Weight Watchers Staff. 1997. 14.95 (*0-02-862078-X*) Macmillan.

Weight Watchers Quick Start Plus Program Cookbook. Jean T. Nidetch. 1986. pap. 12.00 (*0-452-26477-4*, Plume) NAL-Dutton.

Weight Watchers Quick Start Program Cookbook: Including the Full Exchange Plan. Jean T. Nidetch. (Illus.). 416p. 1984. 18.50 (*0-453-01010-5*) NAL-Dutton.

Weight Watchers Quick Success Program Cookbook. Jean T. Nidetch. (Illus.). 448p. 1990. pap. 10.95 (*0-452-26428-6*, Plume) NAL-Dutton.

***Weight Watchers Simply the Best 250 Prize-Winning Family Recipes.** Weight Watchers International Staff. LC 97-4287. 1997. 21.95 (*0-02-861940-4*) Macmillan.

Weight Watcher's Slim Way to Grilling. Weight Watchers International, Inc. Staff. 1996. 17.00 (*0-02-861461-5*) Macmillan.

Weight Watcher's Slim Ways: Chicken. Weight Watchers International, Inc. Staff. 192p. 1995. 16.00 (*0-02-860364-8*) Macmillan.

***Weight Watchers Slim Ways: Italian.** Weight Watchers International, Inc. Staff. LC 96-46918. 1997. write for info. (*0-02-861498-4*) Macmillan.

Weight Watchers Slim Ways Grilling. Weight Watchers International, Inc. Staff. LC 95-49104. 192p. 1996. 17.00 (*0-02-861007-5*) Macmillan.

Weight Watchers Slim Ways Hearty Meals. LC 96-11095. 1996. 12.00 (*0-614-13027-1*) Macmillan.

Weight Watchers Slim Ways Mexican. 1996. 17.00 (*0-02-860384-2*) Macmillan.

Weight Watcher's Slim Ways with Chicken. 1995. 15.00 (*0-671-51718-X*) Macmillan.

Weight Watcher's Stress Meditational. Weight Watchers International, Inc. Staff. LC 96-54718. 1997. 9.95 (*0-02-861000-8*) Macmillan.

Weight Watcher's Success Every Day. 1994. pap. 10.00 (*0-671-88983-4*) Macmillan.

Weight Watchers Success Every Day: Everyday Inspiration for Weight Loss & Maintenance. Weight Watchers International, Inc. Staff. 384p. 1995. 9.95 (*0-02-860392-3*) Macmillan.

Weight Watchers Three Hundred & Sixty-Five Day Menu Cookbook. Weight Watchers International, Inc. Staff. 1986. pap. 9.95 (*0-452-25958-4*, Plume) NAL-Dutton.

***Weight Watchers Versatile Vegetarian: 150 Easy Recipes for Every Day.** Weight Watchers International Staff. LC 97-4285. 1997. 19.95 (*0-02-861852-1*) Macmillan.

Weight Watchers 1001 Ways to Win at Losing. LC 96-26603. 1997. pap. 5.95 (*0-02-861497-6*) Macmillan.

Weight Watchers 101 More Secrets of Success. Weight Watchers International, Inc. Staff. LC 96-24780. 1997. write for info. (*0-02-861499-2*) Macmillan.

Weight Watchers 101 Secrets for Success: Weight Loss Tips from Weight Watchers Leaders. 112p. 1995. 5.95 (*0-02-860986-7*) Macmillan.

Weight Watchers 1997 Planner for Success: Organize Your Life & Your Healthier Lifestyle. Weight Watchers International, Inc. Staff. 160p. 1996. 15.00 (*0-02-861020-2*) Macmillan.

Weight Watchers 365 Day Cookbook. Weight Watchers International, Inc. Staff. 432p. 1996. 29.95 (*0-02-861015-6*) Mac Pub USA.

Weighted Approximation with Varying Weights. Vilmos Totik. LC 93-49416. (Lecture Notes in Mathematics Ser.: Vol. 1569). vi, 115p. 1994. 29.95 (*0-387-57705-X*) Spr-Verlag.

W

Weighted Approximations in Probability & Statistics. Miklos Csorgo & L. Horvath. LC 92-27167. 442p. 1993. text ed. 119.00 (0-471-93635-9) Wiley.

Weighted Bootstrap. Philippe Barbe & Patrice Bartail. LC 95-5885. (Lecture Notes in Statistics Ser.: Vol. 98). 1995. 43.95 (0-387-94478-8) Spr-Verlag.

Weighted Empiricals & Linear Models. Hira L. Koul. LC 92-54658. (IMS Lecture Notes - Monograph Ser.: Vol. 21). x, 264p. 1992. pap. 30.00 (0-940600-28-5) Inst Math.

Weighted Energy Methods in Fluid Dynamics & Elasticity. Giovanni P. Galdi & S. Rionero. LC 85-12662. (Lecture Notes in Mathematics Ser.: Vol. 1134). vii, 126p. 1985. 29.95 (0-387-15645-3) Spr-Verlag.

Weighted Hardy Spaces. J. O. Stromberg & A. Torchinsky. (Lecture Notes in Mathematics Ser.: Vol. 1381). v, 193p. 1989. 32.95 (0-387-51402-3) Spr-Verlag.

Weighted Norm Inequalities in Orlicz & Lorentz Spaces. V. Kokilashvili & M. Krbec. 200p. (C). 1991. text ed. 43.00 (981-02-0612-7) World Scientific Pub.

Weighted Polynomial Approximation. H. N. Mhaskar. (Series on Decompositions & Approximation). 300p. 1997. text ed. 74.00 (981-02-1312-3) World Scientific Pub.

***Weightier Matters: For the Believer & the Nonbeliever Alike.** Park E. Garnes, Sr. LC 96-90751. (Orig.). 1997. pap. 10.95 (0-533-12161-2) Vantage.

Weightier Matters of the Law: Essays on Law & Religion. Ed. by John Witte, Jr. & Frank S. Alexander. LC 87-28845. (Studies in Religion). 450p. 1988. 41.95 (1-55540-179-1, 01-00-51) Scholars Pr GA.

Weighting Game: The Truth about Weight Control. Lawrence E. Lamb. 196p. 1988. 15.95 (0-8184-0487-6) Carol Pub Group.

Weighting Game: The Truth about Weight Control. Lawrence E. Lamb. 1991. pap. 10.95 (0-8184-0551-1) Carol Pub Group.

Weightless Workout. Jerry Robinson. (Illus.). 158p. (Orig.). 1990. pap. 19.95 (0-944831-26-5) Health Life.

Weightlifting. LC 96-24725. (Extreme Sports Ser.). 1996. write for info. (1-56065-431-7) Capstone Pr.

***Weightlifting.** Bill Lund. (Extreme Sports Ser.). (Illus.). 48p. (J). (gr. 3-7). 1996. 18.40 (0-516-20258-8) Childrens.

Weightlifting: A Guide for Parents & Coaches. Cooper Publishing Group Staff. (USOC Sports Education Ser.). (Illus.). 128p. 1997. pap. 18.00 (1-884125-59-X) Cooper Pubng.

Weightlifting & Bodybuilding: Total Fitness for Men & Women. Donald D. Macchia. 200p. 1987. pap. 24.95 (0-8304-1183-6) Nelson-Hall.

Weights & Measures. Robin Kerrod. LC 90-25570. (Secrets of Science Ser.: Group 2). (Illus.). 32p. (J). (gr. 3-8). 1991. lib. bdg. 10.95 (1-85435-269-5) Marshall Cavendish.

Weightshaping - Body Sculpting & Human Performance: An Instruction Manual. Don McDaniel. (Illus.). 130p. (Orig.). 1994. pap. text ed. 14.95 (0-9624378-0-8) Life Fitness.

Weighty Word Book. Paul M. Levitt et al. LC PZ7.L5824 W4. (Illus.). 99p. (Orig.). (J). (gr. 4-9). 1990. reprint ed. 17.95 (0-9627979-0-1) Manuscripts.

Weiher in der Franch-Comte: Eine Florist-Isch-Oekologische und Vegetationskundliche Untersuchung, 1 & 2. Otto Schaefer-Guignier. (Dissertationes Botanicae Ser.: No. 213). (Illus.). 403p. (GER.). 1994. pap. 129.00 (3-443-64125-3) Lubrecht & Cramer.

Weiher in der Franch-Comte: Eine Floristisch-Oekologische und Vegetationskundliche Untersuchung, 2 vols. Otto Schaefer-Guignier. (Dissertationes Botanicae Ser.: Vol. 213). (Illus.). 403p. (GER.). 1994. pap. 129.00 (3-443-04125-6) Lubrecht & Cramer.

Weil Representation I: Intertwining Distributions & Discrete Spectrum. Stephen Rallis & Gerard Schiffmann. LC 80-12191. (Memoirs of the American Mathematical Society Ser.: No. 25/231). 203p. 1980. pap. 17.00 (0-8218-2231-4, MEMO/25/231) Am Math.

***Weilka Encyklopedia Powszwchna PWN, 13 vols.** Contrib. by Bogdan Suchodolski. (POL.). 1970. 1,000.00 (0-614-25049-8) Szwede Slavic.

Weil's Code of Massachusetts Regulations, Set, Vols. 1-25. rev. ed. Date not set. 2,566.00 (0-916812-97-9) Weil Pub.

Weil's Code of Massachusetts Regulations, Vol. 1. rev. ed. Date not set. 192.00 (0-916812-72-3) Weil Pub.

Weil's Code of Massachusetts Regulations, Vol. 2. rev. ed. Date not set. 192.00 (0-916812-73-1) Weil Pub.

Weil's Code of Massachusetts Regulations, Vol. 3. rev. ed. Date not set. 192.00 (0-916812-74-X) Weil Pub.

Weil's Code of Massachusetts Regulations, Vol. 4. rev. ed. Date not set. 192.00 (0-916812-75-8) Weil Pub.

Weil's Code of Massachusetts Regulations, Vol. 5. rev. ed. Date not set. 192.00 (0-916812-76-6) Weil Pub.

Weil's Code of Massachusetts Regulations, Vol. 6. rev. ed. Date not set. 192.00 (0-916812-77-4) Weil Pub.

Weil's Code of Massachusetts Regulations, Vol. 7. rev. ed. Date not set. 192.00 (0-916812-78-2) Weil Pub.

Weil's Code of Massachusetts Regulations, Vol. 8. rev. ed. Date not set. 192.00 (0-916812-79-0) Weil Pub.

Weil's Code of Massachusetts Regulations, Vol. 9. rev. ed. Date not set. 192.00 (0-916812-80-4) Weil Pub.

Weil's Code of Massachusetts Regulations, Vol. 10. rev. ed. Date not set. 192.00 (0-916812-81-2) Weil Pub.

Weil's Code of Massachusetts Regulations, Vol. 11. rev. ed. Date not set. 192.00 (0-916812-82-0) Weil Pub.

Weil's Code of Massachusetts Regulations, Vol. 12. rev. ed. Date not set. 192.00 (0-916812-83-9) Weil Pub.

Weil's Code of Massachusetts Regulations, Vol. 13. rev. ed. Date not set. 192.00 (0-916812-84-7) Weil Pub.

Weil's Code of Massachusetts Regulations, Vol. 14. rev. ed. Date not set. 192.00 (0-916812-85-5) Weil Pub.

Weil's Code of Massachusetts Regulations, Vol. 15. rev. ed. Date not set. 192.00 (0-916812-86-3) Weil Pub.

Weil's Code of Massachusetts Regulations, Vol. 16. rev. ed. Date not set. 192.00 (0-916812-87-1) Weil Pub.

Weil's Code of Massachusetts Regulations, Vol. 17. Date not set. 192.00 (0-916812-88-X) Weil Pub.

Weil's Code of Massachusetts Regulations, Vol. 18. rev. ed. Date not set. 192.00 (0-916812-89-8) Weil Pub.

Weil's Code of Massachusetts Regulations, Vol. 19. rev. ed. Date not set. 192.00 (0-916812-90-1) Weil Pub.

Weil's Code of Massachusetts Regulations, Vol. 20. rev. ed. Date not set. pap. 192.00 (0-916812-91-X) Weil Pub.

Weil's Code of Massachusetts Regulations, Vol. 21. rev. ed. Date not set. 192.00 (0-916812-92-8) Weil Pub.

Weil's Code of Massachusetts Regulations, Vol. 22. rev. ed. Date not set. 192.00 (0-916812-93-6) Weil Pub.

Weil's Code of Massachusetts Regulations, Vol. 23. rev. ed. Date not set. 192.00 (0-916812-94-4) Weil Pub.

Weil's Code of Massachusetts Regulations, Vol. 24. rev. ed. Date not set. 192.00 (0-916812-95-2) Weil Pub.

Weil's Code of Massachusetts Regulations, Vol. 25. rev. ed. Date not set. 192.00 (0-916812-96-0) Weil Pub.

Weil's Code of Wyoming Rules. 1995. write for info. (0-614-03799-9) Weil Pub.

Weil's Code of Wyoming Rules, 11 vols., Set. rev. ed. Weil Publishing Co. Inc. Staff. 10000p. (C). 1995. 1,095.00 (0-916812-71-5) Weil Pub.

Weil's Code of Wyoming Rules, Vol. 1. rev. ed. Weil Publishing Co., Inc. Staff. Ed. by Nancy Provencal. 1000p. (C). 1995. 190.00 (0-916812-56-1) Weil Pub.

Weil's Code of Wyoming Rules, Vol. 2. rev. ed. Weil Publishing Co., Inc. Staff. Ed. by Nancy Provencal. 1000p. (C). 1995. 190.00 (0-916812-57-X) Weil Pub.

Weil's Code of Wyoming Rules, Vol. 3. rev. ed. Weil Publishing Co., Inc. Staff. Ed. by Nancy Provencal. 1000p. (C). 1995. 190.00 (0-916812-58-8) Weil Pub.

Weil's Code of Wyoming Rules, Vol. 4. rev. ed. Weil Publishing Co., Inc. Staff. Ed. by Nancy Provencal. 1000p. (C). 1995. 190.00 (0-916812-59-6) Weil Pub.

Weil's Code of Wyoming Rules, Vol. 5. rev. ed. Weil Publishing Co., Inc. Staff. Ed. by Nancy Provencal. 1000p. (C). 1995. 190.00 (0-916812-60-X) Weil Pub.

Weil's Code of Wyoming Rules, Vol. 6. rev. ed. Weil Publishing Co., Inc. Staff. Ed. by Nancy Provencal. 1000p. (C). 1995. 190.00 (0-916812-61-8) Weil Pub.

Weil's Code of Wyoming Rules, Vol. 7. rev. ed. Weil Publishing Co., Inc. Staff. Ed. by Nancy Provencal. 1000p. (C). 1995. 190.00 (0-916812-62-6) Weil Pub.

Weil's Code of Wyoming Rules, Vol. 8. rev. ed. Weil Publishing Co. Inc. Staff. 1,000p. (Orig.). (C). 1995. 190.00 (0-916812-63-4) Weil Pub.

Weil's Code of Wyoming Rules, Vol. 9. rev. ed. Weil Publishing Co., Inc. Staff. Ed. by Nancy Provencal. 1000p. (C). 1995. 190.00 (0-916812-64-2) Weil Pub.

Weil's Code of Wyoming Rules, Vol. 10. rev. ed. Weil Publishing Co. Inc. Staff. 1000p. (Orig.). (C). 1995. 190.00 (0-916812-65-0) Weil Pub.

Weil's Code of Wyoming Rules Index, Index. rev. ed. Weil Publishing Co. Inc. Staff. 200p. (Orig.). (C). 1995. 125.00 (0-916812-70-7) Weil Pub.

Weil's Index to Code of Massachusetts Regulations. rev. ed. Weil Publishing Co. Inc. Staff. 100p. (C). 1995. 159.00 (0-916812-55-3) Weil Pub.

Weil's Representation & the Spectrum of the Metaplectic Group. S. S. Gelbart. (Lecture Notes in Mathematics Ser.: Vol. 530). 1976. 24.95 (0-387-07799-5) Spr-Verlag.

Weil's Wyoming Government Register. 1995. pap. write for info. (0-614-03800-6) Weil Pub.

Weimar: Why Did German Democracy Fail? Ed. by Ian Kershaw. LC 89-70130. (Debates in Modern History Ser.). 234p. 1990. text ed. 35.00 (0-312-04470-4) St Martin.

Weimar & the Rise of Hitler. 3rd ed. Anthony J. Nicholls. LC 90-48823. (Making of the Twentieth Century Ser.). (C). 1991. pap. text ed. 19.00 (0-312-05713-X) St Martin.

Weimar & the Vatican, 1919-1933. Stewart A. Stehlin. LC 83-42544. (Illus.). 512p. 1983. pap. text ed. 26.95 (0-691-10195-7) Princeton U Pr.

Weimar Chronicle: Prelude to Hitler. Alex De Jonge. 1979. pap. 8.95 (0-452-00868-9, Mer) NAL-Dutton.

Weimar Correspondence: Letters of Friedrich & Sophie Tieck to Amalie Voigt 1804-1837. Ed. & Tr. by James Trainer. (GERM Ser.). xxvi, 196p. (C). 1995. 59.95 (1-57113-029-2) Camden Hse.

Weimar Culture: The Outsider As Insider. Peter Gay. LC 81-2046. (Illus.). xv, 205p. 1981. reprint ed. text ed. 59.75 (0-313-22972-4, GAWC, Greenwood Pr) Greenwood.

Weimar Etudes. Henry Pachter. Ed. by Stephen E. Bronner. LC 82-1122. (Illus.). 360p. 1982. text ed. 45.00 (0-231-05360-6) Col U Pr.

Weimar Germany. Bookbinder. 1997. text ed. 59.95 (0-7190-4286-0); text ed. 16.95 (0-7190-4287-9) St Martin.

Weimar Germany: Germany 1918-33. Ed. by Josh Brooman. (Twentieth Century History Ser.). (Illus.). 32p. (Orig.). 1985. pap. text ed. 10.92 (0-582-22372-5, 70925) Longman.

Weimar Intellectuals & the Threat of Modernity. Dagmar Barnouw. LC 87-45246. 352p. 1988. 35.00 (0-253-36427-2) Ind U Pr.

Weimar Prussia, Nineteen Eighteen to Nineteen Twenty-Five: The Unlikely Rock of Democracy. Dietrich Orlow. LC 85-1187. (Illus.). 375p. 1991. 49.95 (0-8229-3519-8) U of Pittsburgh Pr.

Weimar Prussia, 1925-33: The Illusion of Strength. Dietrich Orlow. LC 91-8117. 480p. 1991. 49.95 (0-8229-3684-4) U of Pittsburgh Pr.

Weimar Republic. Eberhard Kolb. (Illus.). 250p. (C). 1988. pap. 19.95 (0-415-09077-6, Routledge NY) Routledge.

Weimar Republic. Detlev J. Peukert. Tr. by Richard Deveson from GER. 352p. 1992. 28.00 (0-8090-9674-9) Hill & Wang.

Weimar Republic. Detlev J. Peukert. 216p. 1993. pap. 13.00 (0-8090-1556-0) Hill & Wang.

Weimar Republic. 2nd ed. John Hiden. (Seminar Studies in History). 128p. (C). 1996. pap. text ed. 12.50 (0-582-28706-5, Pub. by Longman UK) Longman.

Weimar Republic: Germany, 1918-1933. Helmut Heiber. Tr. by W. E. Yuill from GER. LC 93-1115. (Illus.). 288p. 1993. 58.95 (0-631-18698-0) Blackwell Pubs.

Weimar Republic: Germany, 1918-1933. Helmut Heiber. Tr. by William E. Yuill from GER. LC 93-1115. (Illus.). 288p. 1993. pap. 21.95 (0-631-18699-9) Blackwell Pubs.

Weimar Republic, Overture to the Third Reich. Godfrey Scheele. LC 75-25268. 360p. 1975. reprint ed. text ed. 35.00 (0-8371-8388-X, SCWR, Greenwood Pr) Greenwood.

Weimar Republic Sourcebook. Ed. by Anton Kaes et al. LC 93-42108. (Weimar & Now Ser.: No. 3). (C). 1994. 55.00 (0-520-06774-6) U CA Pr.

Weimar Republic Sourcebook. Ed. by Anton Kaes et al. LC 93-42108. 1995. pap. 24.95 (0-520-06775-4) U CA Pr.

Weimaraner Champions, 1952-1987. Camino E. E. & Bk. Co. Staff. (Illus.). 158p. 1988. pap. 36.95 (0-940808-81-1) Camino E E & Bk.

Weimaraner Champions, 1988-1994. Camino E. E. & Bk. Co. Staff & Jan Linzy. (Illus.). 105p. 1996. pap. 32.95 (1-55893-043-4) Camino E E & Bk.

Weimaraner Today. Vicky Bambridge. (Illus.). 160p. 1993. 24.95 (0-948955-17-1, Pub. by Ringpr Bks UK) Seven Hills Bk.

Weimaraners. Anna K. Nicholas. (Illus.). 192p. 1995. 9.95 (0-7938-1476-6) TFH Pubns.

***Weimaraners.** Anna K. Nicholas. (Illus.). 192p. 1995. 9.95 (0-7938-1100-7, KW-096) TFH Pubns.

Weimer: Biographical Sketches & Family Records of the Gabriel Weimer & David Weimer Families. L. C. Potts. (Illus.). 270p. 1992. reprint ed. pap. 42.50 (0-8328-2334-1); reprint ed. lib. bdg. 52.50 (0-8328-2333-3) Higginson Bk Co.

Weinstein, Korn & Miller CPLR Manual. 2nd ed. Oscar G. Chase. 1980. Updates. ring bd. write for info. (0-8205-1802-6) Bender.

Weinstein's Evidence: United States Rules, 7 vols., Set. Jack B. Weinstein & Margaret A. Berger. 1975. ring bd. write for info. (0-8205-1803-4) Bender.

Weinstein's Evidence Manual. Weinstein & Berger. (C). 1987. ring bd. write for info. (0-8205-0541-2) Bender.

Weinstock among the Dying. Michael Blumenthal. LC 93-14214. 386p. 1993. 22.95 (0-944072-34-8) Zoland Bks.

Weir. Ruth Moore. 1986. pap. 10.95 (0-942396-48-0) Blackberry ME.

Weir Mitchell, His Life & Letters. Anna R. Burr. 1993. reprint ed. lib. bdg. 89.00 (0-7812-5440-X) Rprt Serv.

Weir of Hermiston. Robert Louis Stevenson. Ed. by Catherine Kerrigan. 224p. 1996. 35.00 (0-7486-0473-1, Pub. by Edinburgh U Pr UK) Col U Pr.

***Weir of Hermiston.** Robert Louis Stevenson. 1997. pap. 9.95 (0-14-043560-3) Viking Penguin.

Weir of Hermiston: An Unfinished Romance. Robert Louis Stevenson. LC 78-150563. (Short Story Index Reprint Ser.). 1977. reprint ed. 18.95 (0-8369-3861-5) Ayer.

Weir of Hermiston & Other Stories. Robert Louis Stevenson. Ed. & Intro. by Paul Binding. (English Library). 320p. 1980. pap. 10.95 (0-14-043138-1, Penguin Classics) Viking Penguin.

Weird? Etienne Delessert. LC 93-27455. (Yok-Yok Ser.). (Illus.). 32p. (J). (gr. 1-8). 1994. 10.95 (0-88682-645-4, 97933-098) Creative Ed.

Weird! The Complete Book of Halloween Words. Peter R. Limburg. 176p. (J). 1991. pap. 3.50 (0-380-71172-9, Camelot) Avon.

Weird! The Complete Book of Halloween Words. Peter R. Limburg. LC 88-38678. (Illus.). 128p. (J). (gr. 4-10). 1989. lib. bdg. 13.95 (0-02-759050-X, Bradbury S&S) S&S Childrens.

Weird & Spooky Tales. (Illus.). 192p. (J). (gr. 3-8). 1997. pap. 13.95 (0-87460-391-9) Lion Bks.

Weird & the Beautiful. Richard Headstrom. LC 81-67780. (Illus.). 240p. 1984. 14.95 (0-8453-4727-6, Cornwall Bks) Assoc Univ Prs.

Weird & Tragic Shores: The Story of Charles Francis Hall, Explorer. Chauncey C. Loomis. LC 90-21280. (Illus.). xii, 403p. 1991. reprint ed. pap. 12.95 (0-8032-7937-X, Bison Books) U of Nebr Pr.

Weird & Wacky Science Series, 6 vols., Set. (Illus.). (J). (gr. 4-10). 1996. lib. bdg. 107.70 (0-89490-662-3) Enslow Pubs.

Weird & Wacky Word Search Puzzles. Elvira Gamiello. (Illus.). (Orig.). (J). (gr. 4-6). 1988. pap. 1.95 (0-942025-42-3) Kidsbks.

***Weird & Wonderful.** (Funfax Eyewitness Library). 1997. pap. 1.95 (0-7894-1842-8) DK Pub Inc.

Weird & Wonderful. Owl Magazine Editors. (Illus.). 96p. (J). (gr. 3 up). 1992. pap. 4.95 (0-919872-81-6, Pub. by Greey dePencier CN) Firefly Bks Ltd.

Weird & Wonderful Ants. Lynn Poole & Gray Poole. (Illus.). (J). (gr. 5 up). 1961. 8.95 (0-8392-3041-9) Astor-Honor.

Weird & Wonderful Wildlife. John May et al. LC 82-25245. (Illus.). 224p. 1983. pap. 19.95 (0-87701-295-4) Chronicle Bks.

Weird Animals. Bobbie Kalman & Tammy Everts. (Crabapple Ser.). (Illus.). 32p. (J). (ps-3). 1994. lib. bdg. 18.08 (0-86505-617-X) Crabtree Pub Co.

Weird Animals. Bobbie Kalman & Tammy Everts. (Crabapple Ser.). (Illus.). 32p. (Orig.). (J). (ps-3). 1994. pap. 5.95 (0-86505-717-6) Crabtree Pub Co.

Weird Business. Ed. by Joe R. Lansdale & Richard Klaw. (Illus.). 420p. 1995. 29.95 (1-885418-02-7) MOJO Pr.

***Weird but True.** Janet Goldenberg. (Trophy Book Ser.). (Illus.). 96p. (J). (gr. 3-7). 1997. pap. 4.95 (0-06-446190-4, Trophy) HarpC Child Bks.

Weird Cars. Ed. by John Gunnell. LC 93-77540. (Illus.). 304p. (Orig.). 1993. pap. 16.95 (0-87341-253-2, CT01) Krause Pubns.

Weird Colonial Boy. Paul Voermans. 224p. 1994. pap. 9.95 (0-575-05715-7, Pub. by V Gollancz UK) Trafalgar.

***Weird Creatures of the Wild.** Theresa Greenaway. LC 97-3337. (Illus.). 24p. (J). 1997. 9.95 (0-7894-1510-0) DK Pub Inc.

Weird Facts to Blow Your Mind. Judith F. Clark. LC 93-12251. (Facts to Blow Your Mind Ser.). (Illus.). 48p. (Orig.). (J). (gr. 1-6). 1993. pap. 4.95 (0-8431-3579-4) Price Stern Sloan.

Weird Football Game. Kincaid Summer School Students. (Wee Write Bks.: No. 9). (Illus.). 25p. (J). (ps-4). 1995. pap. 8.95 (1-884987-31-1) WeWrite.

***Weird History 101: My Dinner with Attila the Hun, I Started World War I, Watching Custer's Last Stand.** John R. Stephens. LC 97-7531. 1997. pap. text ed. 12.95 (1-55850-715-9) Adams Media.

Weird Is the Night. Fred Rogerson. 50p. 1973. pap. 3.00 (0-87129-114-2, W14) Dramatic Pub.

Weird on the Outside. Shelley Stoehr. 224p. (YA). (gr. 9 up). 1996. mass mkt. 3.99 (0-440-22010-6, LLL BDD) BDD Bks Young Read.

Weird Parents. Audrey Wood. Ed. by Phyllis J. Fogelman. LC 88-25742. (Illus.). 32p. (J). (ps-3). 1990. pap. 14.99 (0-8037-0648-0); lib. bdg. 11.89 (0-8037-0649-9) Dial Bks Young.

Weird Parents. Audrey Wood. (Illus.). 32p. (J). (ps-3). 1995. pap. 4.99 (0-14-054924-2, Puff Pied Piper) Puffin Bks.

Weird People: We Are Stranger Than We Think. Jocelyn Little. LC 95-51256. 128p. 1996. pap. 7.95 (0-8069-3850-1) Sterling.

Weird Pet Poems. Evans & Rogers. LC 96-30302. (J). 1997. 16.00 (0-689-80734-1) S&S Childrens.

***Weird Places.** Bill Bridges. (Illus.). 80p. 1997. pap. 12.00 (1-888906-05-7) Holistic Design.

Weird Rooms. Mal Sharpe & Sandra Sharpe. LC 96-22401. (Illus.). 96p. 1996. 25.00 (0-7649-0010-2) Pomegranate Calif.

***Weird Science.** (Wild Side Ser.). (Illus.). (J). (gr. 1-7). 12.66 (0-614-20171-3) Contemp Bks.

Weird Tale: Arthur Machen - Lord Dunsany - Algernon Blackwood - M. R. James - Ambrose Bierce - H. P. Lovecraft. S. T. Joshi. LC 89-37753. 304p. (C). 1990. pap. 12.95 (0-292-79057-0); text ed. 27.50 (0-292-79050-3) U of Tex Pr.

Weird Tales, 2 Vols. Ernst T. Hoffman. Tr. by J. T. Bealby from GER. LC 74-125218. (Short Story Index Reprint Ser.). 1977. 35.95 (0-8369-3586-1) Ayer.

Weird Tales. Jonas L. Lie. 128p. 1996. pap. 12.95 (1-57216-021-7) Penfield.

Weird Tales: Thirty-Two Unearthed Terrors. Stefan R. Dziemianowicz. LC 87-34125. 1988. 7.99 (0-517-66123-3, Crown) Crown Pub Group.

Weird Tales from Northern Seas, from the Danish of Jonas Lie. Jonas L. Lie. LC 79-81272. (Short Story Index Reprint Ser.). (Illus.). 1977. 17.95 (0-8369-3024-X) Ayer.

Weird Tales from Shakespeare. Ed. by Katharine Kerr & Martin H. Greenberg. 320p. (Orig.). 1994. mass mkt. 4.99 (0-88677-605-8) DAW Bks.

Weird Tales of the Supernatural. Kurt Singer. 25.95 (0-8488-0631-X) Amereon Ltd.

Weird Walkers. Anthony D. Fredericks. LC 95-35666. (World of Discovery Ser.). (Illus.). 48p. (J). (gr. 3-9). 1996. 9.95 (1-55971-541-3) NorthWord.

Weird Wambo. (Junior African Writers Ser.). (Illus.). 128p. (J). (gr. 3-4). 1995. pap. 3.89 (0-7910-3019-9) Chelsea Hse.

Weird Water & Fuzzy Logic: More Notes of a Fringe Watcher. Martin Gardner. 284p. 1996. 25.95 (1-57392-096-7) Prometheus Bks.

***Weird Weather.** Simons. 1997. 22.95 (0-316-79179-2) Little.

***Weird Weddings: True Stories about Nonsense in Nuptials.** Dale J. Pritchard. 109p. (Orig.). 1997. wbk. ed., pap. 19.95 (0-9649856-9-1) Christina Pub.

Weird, Weird West, No. 16. Marty Engle & Barnes. (Strange Matter Ser.). 140p. (J). (gr. 4 up). 1996. pap. 3.99 (1-56714-055-6) Montage Bks.

***Weird Wide Web.** Erfert Fenton & David Pogue. 1997. pap. 12.99 (0-614-28458-9) IDG Bks.

Weird Wolf. Margery Cuyler. LC 89-1541. (Illus.). 80p. (J). (gr. 2-4). 1991. pap. 4.95 (0-8050-1643-0, Owl) H Holt & Co.

Weird Words. Irwin M. Berent & Rod L. Evans. 256p. (Orig.). 1995. pap. text ed. 5.99 (0-425-14404-6) Berkley Pub.

Weird Worlds. 2nd ed. Date not set. pap. 1.50 (0-590-05781-2) Scholastic Inc.

Weird Worlds, No. 5. (J). pap. 1.50 (0-590-30038-5) Scholastic Inc.

***Weird Zone: Revenge of the Tiki Men!, Vol. 8.** Tony Abbott. (Weird Zone Ser.). (J). 1997. pap. text ed. 3.50 (0-590-67440-4) Scholastic Inc.

***Weird Zone #5.** Tony Abbott. (Wierd Zone Ser.: No. 5). (J). 1997. mass mkt. 2.99 (0-590-67437-4) Scholastic Inc.

Weird Zone #4. Tony Abbott. (Weird Zone Ser.: No. 4). (J). (gr. 2-5). 1996. pap. 2.99 (0-590-67436-6) Scholastic Inc.

***Weird Zone #6.** Tony Abbott. (J). 1997. mass mkt. 3.50 (0-590-67438-2) Scholastic Inc.

Weirdo. Theodore Taylor. 240p. (YA). 1993. mass mkt. 4.50 (0-380-72017-5, Flare) Avon.

An Asterisk (*) at the beginning of an entry indicates that the title is appearing in BIP for the first time.

Weirdo. Theodore Taylor. 304p. (YA). (gr. 7 up). 1991. 16.00 (*0-15-294952-6*, HB Juv Bks) HarBrace.

Weirdo Art of R. Crumb: His Early Period, 1981-1985. Robert Crumb. 1995. pap. 19.95 (*0-86719-339-5*) Last Gasp.

Weirdos from Another Planet! A Calvin & Hobbes Collection. Bill Watterson. (Illus.). 128p. (Orig.). 1990. pap. 9.95 (*0-8362-1862-0*) Andrews & McMeel.

Weirdos of the Universe, Unite! Pamela F. Service. 160p. (YA). 1993. mass mkt. 4.50 (*0-449-70429-7*) Fawcett.

***Weirdstone of Brisingamen.** Garner. 1998. pap. write for info. (*0-15-201766-6*) HarBrace.

***Weirdsville U. S. A. The Obsessive Universe of David Lynch.** Paul A. Woods. (Illus.). 192p. 1997. pap. 19.95 (*0-85965-255-6*, Pub. by Plexus UK) Publishers Group.

Weirs & Flumes for Low Measurement. fac. ed. Peter Ackers et al. LC 78-317. (Illus.). 371p. 1978. pap. 105.80 (*0-7837-7669-1*, 2047422) Bks Demand.

Weirs Beach, NH. Warren Huse. (Images of America Ser.). 128p. 1996. pap. 16.99 (*0-7524-0429-6*, Arcdia) Chalford.

Weir's Handbook of Experimental Immunology. 5th ed. Lenore Herzenberg et al. (Illus.). 2752p. 1996. text ed. 595.00 (*0-86542-421-7*) Blackwell Sci.

Weir's Handbook of Experimental Immunology. 5th ed. Lenore Herzenberg et al. (Illus.). 1996. cd-rom 295.00 (*0-86542-566-3*) Blackwell Sci.

***Weir's Handbook of Experimental Immunology.** 5th ed. Donald M. Weir. LC 96-35330. 1996. write for info. (*0-86542-569-8*); write for info. (*0-86542-570-1*) Blackwell Sci.

***Weir's Handbook of Experimental Immunology.** 5th ed. Donald M. Weir. 1996. write for info. (*0-86542-572-8*) Blackwell Sci.

Weir's Way. Tom Weir. 240p. (C). 1989. 50.00 (*0-903065-34-7*, Pub. by G Wright Pub Ltd) St Mut.

Weiser Family. H. M. Richards. (Illus.). 115p. 1992. reprint ed. pap. 18.50 (*0-8328-2761-4*); reprint ed. lib. bdg. 28.50 (*0-8328-2760-6*) Higginson Bk Co.

***Weiser Indians: Shoshoni Peacemakers.** Hank Corless. (Illus.). 170p. (Orig.). 1996. reprint ed. pap. 14.95 (*0-87004-376-5*, 037650) Caxton.

Weisheit in Israel see Wisdom in Israel

Weisheit und Pradestination: Weisheitliche Urordnung und Pradestination in den Textfunden von Qumran. Armin Lange. (Studies on the Texts of the Desert of Judah: No. 18). (Illus.). xii, 345p. (GER.). 1995. 115.50 (*90-04-10432-1*) E J Brill.

Weiss Labor Law in Germany. 1995. lib. bdg. 73.50 (*90-411-0016-4*) Kluwer Ac.

***Weiss Ratings' HMO & Health Insurance Directory Vol. 8: A Guide to Health Insurers with Their Safety Ratings Including Blue Cross/Blue Shield Plans.** Ed. by Ted Brownstein. 230p. 1997. reprint ed. pap. 176.00 (*1-889499-13-7*) Weiss Ratings.

***Weiss Ratings' Insurance Safety Directory Vol. 23: A Guide to Life, Health & Annuity Insurers with Their Safety Ratings.** Ed. by Ted Brownstein. 350p. (Orig.). 1996. reprint ed. pap. 438.00 (*1-889499-04-8*) Weiss Ratings.

***Weiss Ratings' Property & Casualty Insurance Safety Directory Vol. 13: A Guide to Auto, Home, & Business Insurers with Their Safety Ratings.** Ed. by Ted Brownstein. 350p. 1997. reprint ed. pap. 176.00 (*1-889499-16-1*) Weiss Ratings.

Weisse Rose und Ihre Flugblatter. Hinrich Siefken. 192p. 1994. text ed. 17.95 (*0-7190-4177-5*, Pub. by Manchester Univ Pr UK) St Martin.

Weissenbaum's Eye. George Stetten. LC 88-90397. 212p. (Orig.). 1989. pap. 4.95 (*0-923056-00-9*) Zwitter Pr.

Weissenberger's Federal Evidence. Glen Weissenberger. 1992. suppl. ed. 28.50 (*0-87084-924-7*) Anderson Pub Co.

Weissenberger's Federal Evidence. 2nd ed. Glen Weissenberger. LC 94-45181. 948p. 1995. pap. text ed. 75.00 (*0-87084-920-4*) Anderson Pub Co.

Weissenhof 1927 & the Modern Movement in Architecture. Richard Pommer & Christian F. Otto. LC 90-33628. (Illus.). 432p. 1991. 78.00 (*0-226-67515-7*) U Ch Pr.

Weissmann Travel Planner for Western & Eastern Europe, 1994-1995. Ed. by Arnie Weissmann. (Illus.). 350p. 1994. lib. bdg. 49.95 (*0-945305-13-3*) Hoovers TX.

Weissmann Travel Reports: North America Profiles 1997. rev. ed. Arnie Weissmann. (Illus.). 1000p. 1997. ring bd. 329.00 (*0-945305-07-9*) Weissmann Travel.

Weissmann Travel Reports' International Profiles. rev. ed. Arnie Weissmann. Orig. Title: Fuller-Weissmann Report. (Illus.). 1300p. 1997. ring bd. 329.00 (*0-945305-04-4*) Weissmann Travel.

Weissmann Travel Reports' Travel Geography & Destinations. rev. ed. Arnie Weissmann. Orig. Title: Fuller Weissmann Report - Travel Geography & Destinations. (C). 1996. pap. text ed. 24.95 (*0-945305-05-2*) Weissmann Travel.

Weissmann Travel Reports' Travel Geography & Destinations - Instructor's Manual. rev. ed. Arnie Weissmann. Orig. Title: Fuller Weissmann Report - Student Edition Instructor's Manual. (C). 1996. pap. text ed. write for info. (*0-945305-06-0*) Weissmann Travel.

Weissmuller to Spitz. Buck Dawson. 236p. 1991. 32.95 (*1-880236-02-8*) Hoffman FL.

Weitchie: Spirit of the Redwoods. David Coe. 220p. (Orig.). 1990. pap. 9.95 (*0-936609-20-6*) QED Ft Bragg.

Weite Land: Dramen 1910-1912. Arthur Schnitzler. 304p. (GER.). 1995. pap. 18.00 (*3-596-11508-6*, Pub. by Fischer Taschbch Verlag GW) Intl Bk Import.

Weiter! Grammatik. Isabelle S. Un-Gorrell. 398p. 1993. pap. text ed. 27.50 (*0-471-57658-1*) Wiley.

***Weiter! Grammatik & Weiter! Lesen, Reden, und Schreiben Set.** Isabelle Salaun. (GER.). 1995. pap. text ed. write for info. (*0-471-15512-8*) Wiley.

Weiter! Lesen, Reden & Schreiben. Isabelle Salaun-Gorrell. 326p. 1994. 27.50 (*0-471-57659-X*) Wiley.

***Weitz Saga.** Howard J. Brumley, Sr. 21.00 (*0-614-23859-5*) Am Hist Soc Ger.

***Weizman Institute of Science.** Weizman Institute of Science Staff. Date not set. write for info. (*0-688-12115-2*) Hearst Bks.

Welborn Beeson on the Oregon Trail in 1853 see Oregon & Applegate Trail Diary of Welborn Beeson in 1853: The Unabridged Diary with Introduction & Contemporary Comments by Bert Webber

Welch Clock Company Catalogue, 1900. (Illus.). 64p. pap. 5.95 (*0-930163-70-2*) Arlington Bk.

Welch Clocks. Tran D. Ly. (Illus.). 304p. 1992. 39.50 (*0-930163-38-9*); pap. 32.95 (*0-685-60154-4*) Arlington Bk.

Welch Clocks: Price Guide Up-Date, 1992. Tran D. Ly. 8p. 1992. pap. 5.00 (*0-930163-64-8*) Arlington Bk.

Welch's Grape Juice. William Chazanof. 1979. pap. 13.95 (*0-8156-2211-2*) Syracuse U Pr.

Welcome! A Biblical & Practical Guide to Receiving New Members. Ervin R. Stutzman. LC 90-38164. 176p. (Orig.). 1990. pap. 9.99 (*0-8361-3530-X*) Herald Pr.

Welcome: A Foreigner's Guide to Successful Living in the Southern United States. Irva R. Hayward. 1994. pap. 13.95 (*0-9624032-7-X*) Best Times Inc.

Welcome! A Guide for the Paris Musician. Michael Gilligan. 1980. pap. 1.95 (*0-915866-10-2*) Am Cath Pr.

Welcome: Christian Parenting. Judith Tate-O'Brien. 68p. (Orig.). 1980. teacher ed. 3.00 (*0-936098-36-8*); pap. 4.00 (*0-936098-37-6*) Intl Marriage.

Welcome! Tools & Techniques for New Member Ministry. Andrew D. Weeks. LC 92-72458. (Orig.). 1992. pap. 15.95 (*1-56699-057-2*, AL136) Alban Inst.

***Welcome All Wonders - A Composer's Journey.** J. A. Redford. 1997. 17.99 incl. cd-rom (*0-614-28273-X*) Baker Bks.

Welcome Baby. Lucy Rigg. (Illus.). 1992. 18.50 (*0-8378-4154-2*) Gibson.

Welcome Baby: A Guide to the First Six Weeks. George E. Verrilli & Anne M. Mueser. LC 81-16696. (Illus.). 96p. 1981. pap. 6.95 (*0-312-86121-4*) St Martin.

Welcome Back, Michael. Bob Sakamoto. 1995. pap. 9.99 (*0-451-82307-9*) NAL-Dutton.

Welcome Back, Snow White. Walt Disney Productions Staff. (Walt Disney's Fun-to-Read Library Ser.: Vol. 11). (Illus.). 44p. (J). (gr. 1-6). 1986. reprint ed. 3.49 (*1-885222-23-8*) Advance Pubs.

Welcome Back, Stacey. Ann M. Martin. (Baby-Sitters Club Ser.: No. 28). 192p. (J). (gr. 4-6). 1989. pap. 3.50 (*0-590-42501-3*, Apple Paperbacks) Scholastic Inc.

Welcome Back, Stacey! large type ed. Ann M. Martin. (Baby-Sitters Club Ser.: Vol. 28). 176p. (J). 1994. lib. bdg. 15.93 (*0-8368-1249-2*) Gareth Stevens Inc.

***Welcome Back Stacy, Vol. 28.** M. Martin Ann. (J). 1949. pap. text ed. 3.99 (*0-590-67396-3*) Scholastic Inc.

Welcome Back, Sun. Michael Emberley. LC 92-9786. (J). (gr. 4 up). 1993. 14.95 (*0-316-23647-0*) Little.

Welcome Back to Brooklyn. Brian Merlis. 172p. 19.95 (*1-878741-14-4*) Israelowitz Pub.

Welcome Back to Jesus. Lyle Pointer. (Christian Living Ser.). 40p. (Orig.). 1987. pap. 3.25 (*0-8341-1190-X*) Beacon Hill.

Welcome Back to Nursing. Wendy Green. LC 92-49296. 144p. 1993. pap. 19.95 (*0-632-03556-0*) Blackwell Sci.

Welcome Back to Pokeweed Public School. John Bianchi. (Illus.). 24p. (Orig.). (J). (gr. 1-5). 1996. 15.95 (*0-921285-45-0*, Pub. by Bungalo Bks CN); pap. 4.95 (*0-921285-44-2*, Pub. by Bungalo Bks CN) Firefly Bks Ltd.

Welcome Back to School Book. Dianne McCune et al. (Illus.). 112p. (J). (gr. k-4). 1987. pap. 12.99 (*0-86653-383-4*, GA1001) Good Apple.

Welcome, Blessed Morning! G. Franklin Gray & Charles A. Woods. Ed. by Michael L. Sherer. (Orig.). 1987. pap. 3.65 (*0-89536-849-8*, 7808) CSS OH.

Welcome Brothers: Poems of a Changing Man's Consciousness. David Steinberg. (Illus.). 1976. pap. 3.00 (*0-914906-04-6*) Red Alder.

Welcome for Annie. Helen Craig. LC 92-43770. (Illus.). 32p. (J). (ps up). 1994. pap. 4.99 (*1-56402-144-0*) Candlewick Pr.

Welcome for Every Child: Care, Education & Family Support for Infants & Toddlers in Europe. Sheila B. Kamerman & Alfred J. Kahn. Ed. by Emily Fenichel. 72p. (Orig.). 1994. pap. 10.00 (*0-943657-31-8*) Zero To Three.

Welcome for Every Child: How France Protects Maternal & Child Health - A New Frame of Reference for the United States. Gail Richardson. 62p. (Orig.). 1994. pap. text ed. 10.00 (*1-57285-011-6*) Nat Ctr Educ.

***Welcome, Holy Spirit.** rev. ed. Benny Hinn. 300p. 1997. pap. 12.99 (*0-7852-7169-4*) Nelson.

Welcome, Holy Spirit: How You Can Experience the Dynamic Work of the Holy Spirit in Your Life. Benny Hinn. 144p. 1995. 16.99 (*0-7852-7982-2*) Nelson.

***Welcome Home.** Emilie Barnes. LC 96-53617. (Illus.). 125p. (Orig.). 1997. 19.99 (*1-56507-586-2*) Harvest Hse.

Welcome Home! James Bitney & Yvette Nelson. (Illus.). 48p. 1987. pap. 5.60 (*0-89505-508-2*, T1810) Tabor Pub.

Welcome Home! Joe J. Christensen. 1995. pap. 5.95 (*0-88494-981-8*) Bookcraft Inc.

Welcome Home. B. North. 1995. 5.99 (*1-871676-03-7*, Pub. by Christian Focus UK) Spring Arbor Dist.

Welcome Home! Sylvia White. LC 94-38290. (World of Difference Ser.). (Illus.). 32p. (J). (gr. 2-5). 1995. lib. bdg. 19.50 (*0-516-08193-4*) Childrens.

Welcome Home! Sylvia White. (World of Difference Ser.). (J). 1995. pap. 6.95 (*0-516-48193-2*) Childrens.

Welcome Home. Alice D. Miller. 1994. reprint ed. lib. bdg. 21.95 (*1-56849-524-2*) Buccaneer Bks.

Welcome Home: A Time for Uniting. Rota Eileen. Ed. by Linda K. Caputi & Eckroate Norma. LC 87-63572. 294p. pap. 12.00 (*0-9619931-0-3*) Sand Cstle Pub.

Welcome Home: Following Your Soul's Journey Home. Sandra Ingerman. LC 93-4429. 208p. 1994. pap. 14.00 (*0-06-250267-0*) Harper SF.

Welcome Home: Scripture, Prayers, & Blessings for the Household. Ed. by Samuel Torvend. LC 94-45263. 1995. pap. 10.99 (*0-8066-2806-5*) Augsburg Fortress.

Welcome Home: Scripture, Prayers & Blessings for the Household: Year of Mark. Augsburg Fortress Staff. LC 96-21208. 1996. 10.99 (*0-8066-2840-5*) Augsburg Fortress.

***Welcome Home: The Enterprise Foundation & Homeownership.** Photos by Janis Rettaliata et al. (Illus.). 20p. 1997. pap. 3.00 (*0-942901-06-1*) Enterprise Foundation.

Welcome Home, Daddy! Kristin Morgan. (Romance Ser.). 1996. mass mkt. 3.25 (*0-373-19150-2*, 1-19150-1) Silhouette.

Welcome Home for the Holidays. Vickie L. Hutchins & JoAnn Martin. (Illus.). 220p. pap. 14.95 (*0-9632978-1-3*) Gooseberry Patch.

Welcome Home, Jellybean. Marlene F. Shyer. (J). (gr. 5-10). 1996. 17.75 (*0-8446-6884-2*) Peter Smith.

Welcome Home, Jellybean. Marlene F. Shyer. LC 87-19483. 160p. (J). (gr. 3-7). 1988. reprint ed. pap. 3.95 (*0-689-71213-8*, Aladdin Paperbacks) S&S Childrens.

Welcome Home Jellybean: A Study Guide. Joyce Friedland & Rikki Kessler. (Novel-Ties Ser.). 1983. teacher ed., wbk. ed., pap. text ed. 15.95 (*0-88122-016-7*) Lrn Links.

Welcome Home, Raspberry & The Lucky Ones. Tony Marchant. (Methuen Theatrescripts Ser.). 77p. (C). 1988. pap. 7.95 (*0-413-53820-6*, A0313) Heinemann.

Welcome Home to Deering, New Hampshire. Evangeline K. Poling. LC 78-808. (Illus.). 1978. 12.00 (*0-914016-48-2*) Phoenix Pub.

Welcome Home to Lenexa. Intro. by Judy Rix. (Illus.). 96p. 1993. write for info. (*0-9638542-0-8*) Geo Graphics.

***Welcome Home to Lenexa Traditions.** Judy Rix. (Illus.). 100p. (Orig.). 1997. pap. write for info. (*0-9638542-3-2*) Geo Graphics.

Welcome in the Spring: Morris & Sword Dances for Children. Paul Kerlee. 66p. 1994. pap. 17.00 (*0-937203-63-7*); pap. 24.95 incl. audio (*0-937203-64-5*) World Music Pr.

Welcome Inn, Vol. 3. Ed Okonowicz. (Spirits Between the Bays Ser.). (Illus.). 96p. (Orig.). 1995. pap. 8.95 (*0-9643244-4-X*) Myst & Lace.

Welcome, Jesus! Joan D. Ritchings. 20p. 1988. pap. 5.00 (*0-9608078-1-0*) Gray Moose.

***Welcome Jesus!** Carol Wehrheim. (Word & Picture Bks.: Set 3). (Illus.). 12p. (J). (gr. k). 1997. bds. 4.95 (*0-8298-1227-X*) Pilgrim OH.

Welcome, Little Baby. Aliki. LC 86-7648. (Illus.). 24p. (J). (ps up). 1987. 16.00 (*0-688-06810-3*) Greenwillow.

Welcome Little Baby: Miniature Edition. Aliki. (Illus.). 24p. (J). (ps up). 1993. reprint ed. pap. 4.95 (*0-688-12665-0*, Tupelo Bks) Morrow.

***Welcome, Mei Su.** (Four Little Friends Ser.). (Illus.). 24p. (J). (gr. 1-4). 1995. write for info. (*1-56144-731-5*, Honey Bear Bks) Modern Pub NYC.

Welcome of Tears: The Tapirape Indians of Central Brazil. Charles Wagley. (Illus.). 328p. (C). 1983. reprint ed. pap. text ed. 12.95 (*0-88133-030-2*) Waveland Pr.

Welcome, Silence: My Triumph over Schizophrenia. Carol S. North. 240p. 1989. reprint ed. mass mkt. 4.99 (*0-380-70627-X*) Avon.

Welcome Speeches & More. Carol Cupples. 64p. (Orig.). 1993. pap. 5.95 (*0-687-27192-4*) Abingdon.

Welcome Speeches & Responses. Compiled by H. Herschell Hobbs. 136p. (gr. 10). 1987. pap. 6.99 (*0-8010-4307-7*) Baker Bks.

Welcome Speeches & Responses for All Occasions. (Orig.). 1992. pap. 5.95 (*0-687-44307-5*) Abingdon.

Welcome, Stranger: Welcome Friend. JoAnn Cairns. LC 87-82531. 144p. 1988. pap. 3.95 (*0-88243-626-0*, 02-0626) Gospel Pub.

Welcome Sweet Babe: A Book of Christenings. Ed. & Intro. by Christina Walkley. LC 87-71418. (Illus.). 167p. 8800. 32.00 (*0-7206-0685-3*, Pub. by P Owen Ltd UK) Dufour.

Welcome Table: African-American Heritage Cooking. Jessica Harris. 1995. 24.00 (*0-671-79360-8*) S&S Trade.

Welcome Table: Planning Masses with Children. Elizabeth M. Jeep et al. (Illus.). 89p. 1982. pap. 5.95 (*0-930467-38-8*, WTBL) Liturgy Tr Pubns.

Welcome Table African American Heritage Cooking. Jessica B. Harris. 1996. pap. 12.00 (*0-684-81837-X*) S&S Trade.

Welcome the Child: A Child Advocacy Guide for Churches. Kathleen Guy & Shannon Daley. 1994. pap. 9.95 (*0-377-00266-6*) Friendship Pr.

Welcome the Traveler Home: Jim Garland's Story of the Kentucky Mountains. Jim Garland. Ed. by Julia S. Ardery. LC 80-50564. 275p. reprint ed. pap. 78.40 (*0-7837-5809-X*, 2045476) Bks Demand.

Welcome the Word. Joan Brown. 304p. 1993. pap. 29.95 (*0-225-66525-5*, Pub. by Geoffrey Chapman UK) Morehouse Pub.

Welcome to. . . CD Rom. Tom Benford. 1995. pap. 19.95 (*1-55828-265-3*) MIS Press.

Welcome to. . . Networks: A Guide to LAN'S. Levy. 1993. pap. 19.95 (*1-55828-259-9*) MIS Press.

Welcome to a New World: An Invitation from the Gospel of St. John. Ernest W. Saunders. Ed. by Constance Hunting. 126p. (C). 1995. pap. 12.95 (*0-913006-57-2*) Puckerbrush.

Welcome to America: Memories of a Bintel Brief. Barbara Lesser. LC 96-37911. 128p. 1996. pap. 7.95 (*1-55783-259-5*) Applause Theatre Bk Pubs.

Welcome to America: What a Wonderful Country! Aziem Peera. (Illus.). 78p. (Orig.). 1996. pap. 6.95 (*0-9652988-0-9*) Asante Intl.

Welcome to America, Mr. Sherlock Holmes: Victorian America Meets Arthur Conan Doyle. Christopher Redmond. 236p. (Orig.). 1993. pap. 20.00 (*0-88924-184-8*, Pub. by Simon & Pierre Pub CN) Empire Pub Srvs.

Welcome to Bayou Town! Cherie D. Schadler. LC 96-15572. (Illus.). 32p. (J). (gr. k-5). 1996. 14.95 (*1-56554-161-8*) Pelican.

***Welcome to Bear Country.** (Berenstain Bears Ser.). Date not set. 5.95 (*1-57719-060-2*) GT Pubng Corp.

Welcome to Calculus & Mathematica. William Davis. (C). 1994. pap. text ed. 10.95 (*0-201-58463-8*) Addison-Wesley.

***Welcome to Camp Nightmare.** R. L. Stine. LC 97-13832. (Goosebumps Ser.). (J). 1997. lib. bdg. write for info. (*0-8368-1981-0*) Gareth Stevens Inc.

Welcome to Camp Nightmare. R. L. Stine. (Goosebumps Ser.). 160p. (J). (gr. 4-6). 1993. pap. 3.99 (*0-590-46619-4*) Scholastic Inc.

Welcome to Camp Nightmare. R. L. Stine. (Goosebumps TV Ser.: No. 3). (J). (gr. 4-7). 1996. pap. 3.99 (*0-590-74588-3*) Scholastic Inc.

Welcome to Carnie. Wil Denson. (Illus.). (Orig.). (YA). (gr. 7-12). 1989. pap. 4.00 (*0-88680-315-2*) I E Clark.

Welcome to Chillsville Elementary: Ghoul School, No. 1. Jane King. (J). (gr. 2-4). 1996. mass mkt. 3.50 (*0-671-51023-1*) PB.

Welcome to Club Mom: The Adventure Begins. Leslie L. Spirson. LC 94-21021. (Illus.). 1994. pap. 8.00 (*0-88166-221-6*, 067151153X) Meadowbrook.

Welcome to Club Mom: The Adventure Begins: Humor and Truth in Pregnancy and the First Year of Motherhood. Leslie L. Spirson. 203p. 1994. pap. 8.00 (*0-671-51153-X*) S&S Trade.

Welcome to Club Scud: A Doonesbury Book. Garry B. Trudeau. (Illus.). 96p. (Orig.). 1991. pap. 7.95 (*0-8362-1882-5*) Andrews & McMeel.

Welcome to Concepts in Graphic Design. David A. Holzgang & Lesley Strothers. 1993. pap. 19.95 (*1-55828-306-4*) MIS Press.

***Welcome to Dead House.** R. L. Stine. LC 97-19367. (Goosebumps Ser.). (J). 1997. write for info. (*0-8368-1973-X*) Gareth Stevens Inc.

Welcome to Dead House. R. L. Stine. (Goosebumps Ser.: No. 1). 160p. (J). (gr. 4-6). 1992. pap. 3.99 (*0-590-45365-3*, Apple Paperbacks) Scholastic Inc.

Welcome to Dilworth: The Largest Railroad Village in Western Minnesota. Ed. by Wayne Gudmundson. (Prairie Documents Photographic Book Ser.). (Illus.). 112p. 1991. pap. 10.00 (*0-9629472-0-2*) MSU Mass Commns.

Welcome to Dinsmore, the World's Greatest Store. William Boniface. (Illus.). 48p. (J). 1995. 14.95 (*0-8362-0743-2*) Andrews & McMeel.

Welcome to Divnograd: An Illustrated Workbook for Students of Russian. 2nd ed. Ed. by Samuel D. Cioran & Gennadi A. Kalinin. (Illus.). 180p. (Orig.). (ENG & RUS.). (C). 1994. reprint ed. pap. text ed. 22.95 (*0-87501-103-9*) Ardis Pubs.

Welcome to DOS: Mastering the Basics. Paul L. Browning. 112p. (Orig.). (C). 1991. pap. text ed. 12.95 (*0-929915-05-4*) Headline Bks.

Welcome to Earth, Mom: Tales of a Single Mother. Adair Lara. 192p. 1992. pap. 9.95 (*0-8118-0090-3*) Chronicle Bks.

Welcome to English, Nos. 1-3. John Chapman. (gr. 3-6). 1978. teacher ed. 7.50 (*0-88345-355-X*) Prentice ESL.

Welcome to English: Let's Begin. John Chapman. (Welcome to English Ser.). (Illus.). 48p. (J). (gr. 1 up). 1980. teacher ed. 4.50 (*0-88345-423-8*, 18493); pap. 3.25 (*0-88345-422-X*, 18480) Prentice ESL.

Welcome to English: Let's Begin, Bk. 4. Lismore. 1980. pap. 11.20 (*0-13-949694-7*) Prentice ESL.

Welcome to English: Let's Begin, Nos. 4-5. John Chapman. (Welcome to English Ser.). (Illus.). 48p. (J). (gr. 1 up). 1980. teacher ed. 7.50 (*0-88345-368-1*, 18499) Prentice ESL.

Welcome to Exit Four: Enter at Own Risk. Rosemary Parrillo. LC 93-72527. 224p. (Orig.). 1994. pap. 12.00 (*0-9635720-1-6*) August Pr.

***Welcome to Flanders Fields.** Daniel G. Dancocks. 1996. mass mkt. 2.99 (*0-7710-2546-7*) McCland & Stewart.

Welcome to Four Way: The Town That Time Forgot. Kent R. Brown. 1993. pap. 5.00 (*0-87129-303-X*, W75) Dramatic Pub.

Welcome to Georgia, Kids! A Collection of Stories & Art by Georgia's Children. Ed. by Kay Borden. (Illus.). 48p. (Orig.). (J). (gr. 1-6). 1996. pap. 15.95 (*0-9637477-4-6*) Franklin-Sarrett Pubs.

Welcome to Good Cooking. Janice Parrino. LC 87-90514. (Illus.). (Orig.). pap. write for info. (*0-9618347-0-6*) N A & J Parrino.

Welcome to Grand Teton: An Explosion of Life & Color. Jackie Gilmore. Ed. by NPS Staff. Tr. by Wordmill Staff. 24p. (JPN.). (J). 1991. Japanese. write for info. (*0-931895-16-2*); German. pap. 4.95 (*0-931895-15-4*); Spanish. pap. 4.95 (*0-931895-18-9*); French. pap. 4.95 (*0-931895-17-0*) Grand Teton NHA.

Welcome to Grand Teton National Park: An Explosion of Life & Color. Jackie Gilmore. Ed. by NPS Staff. (Illus.). 24p. (J). 1991. pap. 4.95 (*0-931895-19-7*) Grand Teton NHA.

***Welcome to Great Britain & the U. S. A.** Laird. 1993. pap. text ed. write for info. (*0-582-08955-7*, Pub. by Longman UK) Longman.

Welcome to Happy, Texas, The Town Without a Frown. Mary V. Wilhelm. 224p. (Orig.). 1995. pap. 13.95 (*0-9645029-0-9*) Twn Without Frwn.

W

An Asterisk (*) at the beginning of an entry indicates that the title is appearing in BIP for the first time.

Welcome to Hard Times. E. L. Doctorow. 1994. lib. bdg. 24.95 (*1-56849-393-2*) Buccaneer Bks.

Welcome to Hard Times. E. L. Doctorow. 1988. mass mkt. 5.99 (*0-449-21602-0*, Crest) Fawcett.

Welcome to Hard Times. E. L. Doctorow. 224p. 1975. pap. 9.95 (*0-394-73107-7*) Random.

Welcome to Hard Times. E. L. Doctorow. LC 96-681. 1996. pap. 10.95 (*0-452-27571-7*, Plume) NAL-Dutton.

Welcome to Hard Times: The Fiscal Consequences of German Unity. Ullrich Heilemann & Wolfgang H. Reinicke. 115p. (C). 1995. pap. 16.95 (*0-8157-3543-X*) Brookings.

Welcome to Heights High: The Crippling Politics of Restructuring America's Public Schools. Diana Tittle. (Urban Life & Urban Landscape Ser.). 304p. (C). 1996. 39.50 (*0-8142-0682-4*); pap. 18.95 (*0-8142-0683-2*) Ohio St U Pr.

Welcome to Heights High: The Deadly Politics of Restructuring America's Public Schools. Diana Tittle. 1995. 23.95 (*1-879360-34-9*) Noble Pr.

***Welcome to Hell: Letters & Writings from Death Row.** Ed. by Jan Arriens. LC 96-9868. (Illus.). 280p. 1997. text ed. 42.50 (*1-55553-289-6*); pap. text ed. 15.95 (*1-55553-290-X*) NE U Pr.

Welcome to High School. Diane Eble et al. 144p. 1991. pap. 9.99 (*0-310-71151-7*) Zondervan.

***Welcome to Horror Hospital.** (Choose Your Own Nightmare Ser.: No. 16). (J). 1997. pap. 3.50 (*0-553-48457-5*) BDD Bks Young Read.

Welcome to Hospitality: An Introduction. Kye-Sung Chon et al. LC 93-49743. 1994. Template disk only. disk write for info. (*0-538-71125-6*) S-W Pub.

Welcome to Hospitality: An Introduction. Kye-Sung Chon et al. LC 93-49743. 1995. 43.00 (*0-538-71246-5*) S-W Pub.

Welcome to Internet: From Mystery to Mastery. Corey Sandler. 1993. pap. 19.95 (*1-55828-308-0*) MIS Press.

Welcome to... Internet: From Mystery to Mastery. 2nd ed. Tom Badgett & Corey Sandler. 400p. 1995. pap. 19.95 (*1-55828-424-9*) MIS Press.

Welcome to Israel: A Bridges for Peace Study Tour. Shirley Ruble. (Illus.). 110p. (Orig.). 1993. pap. 10.00 (*1-878703-01-3*) Legal Pubns.

Welcome to Junior High. L. E. Blair. (Girl Talk Ser.: Bk. 1). 128p. (J). (gr. 2 up). 1990. pap. write for info. (*0-307-22001-X*) Western Pub.

Welcome to Lickskillet: And Other Crazy Places in the Deep South. Kathy Kemp & Keith Boyer. 192p. 1996. 21.95 (*1-881548-22-8*) Crane Hill AL.

***Welcome to Lumpy Gravy.** John Long. 1997. pap. 55.60 (*0-7611-0858-0*); pap. text ed. 6.95 (*0-7611-0735-5*) Workman Pub.

Welcome to Me, Myself & I... A Collection of Poetry. Jorge L. Arteta. 88p. 1995. pap. 7.95 (*1-881539-06-7*) Tabby Hse Bks.

Welcome to Memory Management. Phillip R. Robinson. LC 94-17282. 1994. pap. 19.95 (*1-55828-343-9*) MIS Press.

Welcome to Multimedia. Linda Tway. 1995. pap. 29.95 (*1-55828-242-4*) MIS Press.

Welcome to My Contri! Geoffrey Fox. 164p. 1992. reprint ed. pap. 9.00 (*0-931642-27-2*) Lintel.

***Welcome to My Country.** Lauren Slater. LC 96-29849. 208p. 1997. pap. 12.95 (*0-385-48739-8*, Anchor NY) Doubleday.

Welcome to My Country. Lauren Slater. 199p. 1996. 22.00 (*0-679-44785-7*) Random.

***Welcome to My Country.** Lauren Slater. Date not set. write for info. (*0-679-44783-0*) Random.

Welcome to My Dreams: A Collection of Poems. Mary A. Sorrell. 50p. 1985. pap. 5.95 (*0-89697-269-0*) Intl Univ Pr.

Welcome to My Studio. Helen Van Wyk. (Illus.). 128p. 1994. 27.99 (*0-89134-582-5*, North Lght Bks) F & W Pubns Inc.

Welcome to My Studio: Adventures in Oil Painting. Helen Van Wyk. Ed. by Herbert Rogoff. (Illus.). 128p. (Orig.). 1989. pap. 19.95 (*0-929552-05-9*) Art Instr Assocs.

Welcome to My Studio: Adventures in Oil Painting. rev. ed. Helen Van Wyk. Ed. by Herbert Rogoff. (Illus.). 128p. (Orig.). 1994. 24.95 (*0-929552-08-3*) Art Instr Assocs.

Welcome to My World. Sylvia L. Camp. 1985. pap. 5.50 (*0-89137-435-3*) Quality Pubns.

***Welcome to My World No. 1.** Elizabeth Winfrey. (Party of Five: Claudia Ser.). (Orig.). (J). (gr. 3-6). 1997. mass mkt. 3.99 (*0-671-00676-2*, Minstrel Bks) PB.

Welcome to Nashville. Eddie Cope. (Illus.). 52p. (Orig.). 1993. 15.00 (*0-88680-389-6*) I E Clark.

Welcome to New Baby. Ed. by Helen Exley. (To Give & to Keep Ser.). (Illus.). 28p. 1994. 6.99 (*1-85015-436-8*) Exley Giftbooks.

***Welcome to New York.** Michael E. Brown. (Illus.). 7.95 (*0-935039-30-9*) Stwise Maps.

Welcome to New York: How to Settle & Survive. 3rd ed. Roberta Seret. 368p. 1989. pap. 11.95 (*0-9612432-1-X*) Am Welcome Serv.

Welcome to New York: How to Settle & Survive in New York. Roberta Seret. LC 83-72988. (Illus.). 306p. (Orig.). 1984. pap. text ed. 9.95 (*0-9612432-0-1*) Am Welcome Serv.

Welcome to New York: How to Settle & Survive in New York. 4th ed. 275p. 1992. pap. 13.95 (*0-9612432-2-8*) Am Welcome Serv.

Welcome to New York City. (Illus.). 28p. (Orig.). (J). (ps up). 1996. pap. 3.99 (*0-9652726-0-5*) Totally Graphic.

***Welcome to Our Church: A Guide for Ushers & Greeters.** Annette Schroeder. 1997. pap. 3.00 (*0-570-03560-0*) Concordia.

Welcome to Our City: A Play in Ten Scenes. fac. ed. Thomas Wolfe. Ed. & Intro. by Richard S. Kennedy. LC 82-20838. (Southern Literary Studies). 140p. 1983. reprint ed. pap. 39.90 (*0-7837-7752-3*, 2047508) Bks Demand.

Welcome to Our Company: Your Office Manual. Yolanda Nave. LC 88-40251. 96p. 1988. pap. 6.95 (*0-89480-608-4*, 1608) Workman Pub.

Welcome to Our Hospital. L. S. Howard. 60p. 1995. pap. 9.95 (*1-879895-23-4*) Lushelho Hse.

Welcome to Our Wesleyan Church. Joseph Liddick & Robin George. (Illus.). 37p. Date not set. ring bd. 4.95 (*0-89827-052-9*, GMH57) Wesleyan Pub Hse.

***Welcome to Paradise.** large type ed. John Atkinson. (Illus.). 58p. (Orig.). (J). (gr. k-5). 1995. pap. 5.99 (*0-929155-06-8*) Windward Bks.

***Welcome to Paris.** Illus. by Keith Batchellar & American Artists Staff. (Anastasia Ser.). 10p. (J). (ps-3). 1997. 6.98 (*0-694-01086-3*, Festival) HarpC Child Bks.

Welcome to PC Sound, Music & MIDI. Tom Benford. 1995. pap. 29.95 (*1-55828-316-1*) MIS Press.

Welcome to Personal Computers. Kris Jamsa. Ed. by Cary Weinberger. 250p. (Orig.). 1992. pap. 19.95 (*1-55828-188-6*) MIS Press.

Welcome to... Personal Computers: From Mystery to Mastery. 3rd ed. Kris Jamsa. 400p. 1995. pap. 19.95 (*1-55828-421-4*) MIS Press.

Welcome to Personal Finance on Your Computer: A Guide to Saving, Spending, Taxing & Investing with Your Computer. Phillip R. Robinson. 1994. pap. 19.95 (*1-55828-372-2*) MIS Press.

Welcome to Programming. Al Stephens. 1993. pap. 24.95 incl. disk (*1-55828-309-9*) MIS Press.

Welcome to Querecho Flats. Curt Brummett. LC 95-17104. (Illus.). 112p. 1995. pap. 9.95 (*0-87905-697-5*) Gibbs Smith Pub.

Welcome to Reality: The Nightmares of Philip K. Dick. Ed. by Uwe Anton. Tr. by Jim Young. 208p. 1991. reprint ed. 55.00 (*0-9623824-4-2*); reprint ed. pap. 12.95 (*0-9623824-5-0*) Broken Mirrors Pr.

Welcome to Sharmunding. Janet Blakeley. 64p. (Orig.). 1991. pap. 12.00 (*0-910973-08-3*) Arrowhead AZ.

Welcome to Success in E. S. L. Apple Pie (Personalized Instruction in English) Cecilia D. Kabisch. (Illus.). (J). (gr. k-6). 1982. teacher ed. write for info. (*0-911149-07-4*); Set. 85.00 (*0-911149-08-2*); text ed. write for info. (*0-911149-00-7*) Apple Pie Pub Co.

Welcome to Success in E. S. L. Apple Pie (Personalized Instruction in English), No. 1. Cecilia D. Kabisch. (Illus.). (J). (gr. k-6). 1982. student ed. write for info. (*0-911149-01-5*) Apple Pie Pub Co.

Welcome to Success in E. S. L. Apple Pie (Personalized Instruction in English), No. 2. Cecilia D. Kabisch. (Illus.). (J). (gr. k-6). 1982. write for info. (*0-911149-02-3*) Apple Pie Pub Co.

Welcome to Success in E. S. L. Apple Pie (Personalized Instruction in English), No. 3. Cecilia D. Kabisch. (Illus.). (J). (gr. k-6). 1982. write for info. (*0-911149-03-1*) Apple Pie Pub Co.

Welcome to Success in E. S. L. Apple Pie (Personalized Instruction in English), No. 4. Cecilia D. Kabisch. (Illus.). (J). (gr. k-6). 1982. write for info. (*0-911149-04-X*) Apple Pie Pub Co.

Welcome to Sunday. Vincent Ryan. 96p. 1989. pap. 22.00 (*0-86218-000-7*, Pub. by Veritas IE) St Mut.

Welcome to Sylvan Pines: An Adventure for Over the Edge. Stephan M. Sechi. (Over the Edge Ser.). 32p. 1993. pap. 8.00 (*1-887801-09-X*, Atlas Games) Trident MN.

Welcome to Teaching... & Our Schools. Robert L. DeBruyn. LC 84-60402. 60p. (Orig.). 1985. pap. 4.95 (*0-914607-05-7*) Master Tchr.

Welcome to the Ark. Stephanie S. Tolan. (YA). (gr. 5 up). 1996. 15.00 (*0-688-13724-5*, Morrow Junior) Morrow.

Welcome to the Arrow-Catcher Fair. Lewis Nordan. (Vintage Contemporaries Ser.). 1989. pap. 6.95 (*0-679-72164-9*, Vin) Random.

Welcome to the Arrow-Catcher Fair: Stories. Lewis Nordan. LC 83-7888. 127p. 1983. pap. 9.95 (*0-8071-1134-1*) La State U Pr.

Welcome to the Barbecue. rev. ed. Ron Kolm. LC 81-90000. (Illus.). 50p. 1990. pap. 5.00 (*0-9605626-5-6*) Low-Tech.

***Welcome to the Big Comfy Couch.** (Big Comfy Couch Ser.). 12p. (J). (ps). 1997. 5.95 (*0-448-41641-7*, G&D) Putnam Pub Group.

Welcome to the Big Ten: The 1993 Penn State Football Season. Kip Richeal. LC 94-67276. (Illus.). 250p. 1994. 19.95 (*1-57167-000-9*) Sagamore Pub.

Welcome to the Board: Your Guide to Effective Participation. Fisher Howe. (Non Profit Sector Ser.). 137p. text ed. 19.95 (*0-7879-0089-3*) Jossey-Bass.

Welcome to the BSC, Abby. Ann M. Martin. (Baby-Sitters Club Ser.: No. 90). 192p. (gr. 4-6). 1995. pap. text ed. 3.99 (*0-590-22874-9*) Scholastic Inc.

***Welcome to the Church of the Nazarene: An Introduction to Membership.** 96p. 1988. pap. 5.99 (*0-8341-1256-6*) Nazarene.

***Welcome to the Church of the Nazarene: An Introduction to Membership.** Richard Parrott. 56p. 1988. pap. 2.99 (*0-8341-1255-8*) Nazarene.

Welcome to the Club. Richard D. Simonds, Jr. 102p. (Orig.). 1989. pap. 4.95 (*0-9623193-0-9*) Boz Pub.

***Welcome to the Dollhouse.** Todd Solondz. LC 96-25011. (Orig.). 1996. pap. write for info. (*0-571-19900-3*); pap. 12.95 (*0-571-19050-2*) Faber & Faber.

***Welcome to the End of the World: Prophecy, Rage, & the New Age.** Teresa Kennedy. LC 96-53032. (Illus.). 240p. 1997. 19.95 (*0-87131-817-2*) M Evans.

Welcome to the Family. Date not set. teacher ed., pap. 1.00 (*0-87162-507-5*, D08941) Warner Pr.

Welcome to the Family. James Bitney & Yvette Nelson. 112p. (J). (gr. 4-6). 1988. student ed., pap. text ed. 9.50 (*0-89505-658-5*, T18X1) Tabor Pub.

Welcome to the Family. Kenneth Copeland. 26p. 1979. pap. 1.00 (*0-938458-06-X*) K Copeland Pubns.

***Welcome to the Family: An Introduction to Evangelical Christianity.** Timothy R. Phillips & Dennis L. Okholm. 344p. (C). 1996. pap. 15.99 (*0-8010-9035-0*, Bridgept Bks) Baker Bks.

Welcome to the Family: Teacher's Edition. James Bitney & Yvette Nelson. 176p. 1988. pap. text ed. 24.95 (*0-89505-659-3*, T18X2) Tabor Pub.

Welcome to the Family: The Complete Resource for Integrating New Members into the Life of Your Congregation. 64p. 1996. ring bd. 49.95 (*0-9651998-0-0*) Grt Commission.

Welcome to the Family: Understanding Your New Relationship to God & Others. EvanTell Resources Staff & Larry Moyer. 80p. 1996. pap. 5.99 (*0-8254-3176-X*) Kregel.

Welcome to the Federal Government. Shaw et al. 50p. 1993. pap. text ed. 6.95 (*0-936295-38-4*) FPMI Comns.

Welcome to the Green House. Jane Yolen. (Illus.). 32p. (J). (ps-3). 1993. lib. bdg. 15.95 (*0-399-22335-5*, Putnam) Putnam Pub Group.

***Welcome to the Greenhouse.** Jane Yolen. (Illus.). 32p. (Orig.). (J). (ps-3). 1997. pap. 5.95 (*0-698-11445-0*, Paperstar) Putnam Pub Group.

Welcome to the Home of Your Heart. Dorothy M. Brinkman. LC 90-61688. 290p. 1990. pap. 11.95 (*0-941300-17-X*) Mother Courage.

Welcome to the Hospital. Mary Becker et al. (Illus.). 28p. (J). 1994. pap. write for info. incl. audio (*0-934323-79-8*) Alchemy Comms.

***Welcome to the Icehouse.** Jane Yolen. LC 97-9609. (Illus.). (J). 1998. write for info. (*0-399-23011-4*) Putnam Pub Group.

Welcome to the Jungle. Geoffrey T. Holtz. LC 95-7938. 1995. pap. 14.95 (*0-312-13210-7*) St Martin.

Welcome to the Jungle: New Positions in Black Cultural Studies. Kobena Mercer. LC 93-48150. 288p. (gr. 13). 1994. pap. 17.95 (*0-415-90635-0*) Routledge.

Welcome to the Jungle: New Positions in Black Cultural Studies. Kobena Mercer. LC 93-48150. 288p. (C). (gr. 13). 1994. text ed. 59.95 (*0-415-90634-2*) Routledge.

Welcome to the Magic Theatre. 2nd ed. Dick McLeester. LC 76-29541. (Illus.). (Orig.). 1977. pap. 3.75 (*0-686-23238-0*) Health Journal.

Welcome to the Middle East, Bk. I. Ed. by Gretchen Winkleman. (Active Learning in Social Science Ser.). (Illus.). 129p. (Orig.). 1994. student ed., pap. 19.50 (*1-884397-00-X*) Fresno Pacific.

Welcome to the Middle East, Bk. II. Ed. by Gretchen Winkleman. (Active Learning in Social Science Ser.). 130p. (J). (gr. 5-9). 1995. lab manual ed., pap. 19.50 (*1-884397-02-6*) Fresno Pacific.

Welcome to the Monkey House. Kurt Vonnegut, Jr. 320p. 1970. mass mkt. 6.50 (*0-440-19478-4*) Dell.

Welcome to the Monkey House. Kurt Vonnegut, Jr. 1970. 5.25 (*0-87129-575-X*, W15) Dramatic Pub.

***Welcome to the Moon: Twelve Lunar Expeditions for Small Telescopes.** Robert B. Kelsey. LC 97-12303. (Illus.). 80p. (Orig.). 1997. pap. 9.95 (*0-87961-245-2*) Naturegraph.

Welcome to the Moon & Other Plays. John P. Shanley. 1985. pap. 5.25 (*0-8222-1231-5*) Dramatists Play.

Welcome to the Mustard Seed Cafe: Ten Interactive Scripts Presenting the Parables. Dean Kephart. 1992. 35.00 (*0-685-68684-1*); 5.00 (*0-685-74655-0*) Lillenas.

Welcome to the Mustard Seed Cafe: Ten Interactive Scripts Presenting the Parables. Dean Kephart. 1992. 8.99 (*0-685-68683-3*, MP-676) Lillenas.

Welcome to the New Tax-Free Economy: Taxes As We Know Them Are No Longer Necessary. Frank Alexander. 17p. (Orig.). 1992. pap. 3.00 (*0-915256-33-9*, Kokono) Front Row.

***Welcome to the North Pole: Santa's Village in Applique.** Becky Goldsmith & Linda Jenkins. Ed. by Janet White. LC 97-9753. (Illus.). 48p. (Orig.). 1997. pap. 10.95 (*1-56477-194-6*, B308) That Patchwork.

Welcome to the Oasis & Other Stories. Virgil Suarez. LC 91-31374. 124p. (Orig.). 1992. pap. 9.50 (*1-55885-043-0*) Arte Publico.

Welcome to the Pleasuredome: Inside Las Vegas. David Spanier. LC 93-20330. (Gambling Studies Ser.). (Illus.). 288p. 1993. reprint ed. pap. 17.95 (*0-87417-213-6*) U of Nev Pr.

Welcome to the Professional World. Gary Martin. Ed. by David B. Reyner & Carole Massey-Reyner. LC 96-76112. (Illus.). 100p. (Orig.). 1996. pap. 24.95 (*0-9650514-6-3*) Lrning Tree CA.

Welcome to the Ranks of the Enchanted. Michael David. LC 91-65535. 160p. 1992. pap. 6.95 (*1-55523-438-0*) Winston-Derek.

Welcome to the Real Corporate World: Surviving & Succeeding in a Large Corporation. Dan England, pseud. LC 93-80942. (Illus.). 140p. (Orig.). 1994. pap. 12.95 (*0-9633671-1-0*) Greenfield Ctr.

***Welcome to the Real Working World: What Every Employee Must Know to Succeed.** Frank G. Doerger. LC 97-4950. 160p. 1997. pap. 9.95 (*1-57544-052-0*) Genl Pub Grp.

Welcome to the Real World. Lisa Birnbach. 1987. write for info. (*0-318-61412-X*, Villard Bks) Random.

***Welcome to the Real World: You've Got an Education, Now Get a Life!** Stacy Kravetz. LC 96-43602. 304p. (Orig.). (C). 1997. pap. 13.00 (*0-393-31611-4*) Norton.

Welcome to the Revolution: Managing Paradox in the Information Age. Tom Cannon. (Illus.). 320p. 1997. 25.00 (*0-273-62049-5*) Pitman Publng.

Welcome to the Revolution: The Literary Legacy of Mack Reynolds. Curtis C. Smith. LC 95-5022. (Milford Ser.: Popular Writers of Today: Vol. 64). 136p. 1995. pap. 19.00 (*1-55742-236-2*); lib. bdg. 29.00 (*1-55742-235-4*) Borgo Pr.

Welcome to the Sea of Sand. Jane Yolen. LC 94-28103. (J). (ps-3). 1996. 15.95 (*0-399-22765-2*, Putnam) Putnam Pub Group.

***Welcome to the Stock Show.** Jean M. Greenlaw. 1997. pap. 15.99 (*0-525-67525-6*) NAL-Dutton.

Welcome to the Table! James Bitney & Yvette Nelson. (Illus.). 64p. (Orig.). 1987. pap. text ed. 5.60 (*0-89505-509-0*, T1820) Tabor Pub.

***Welcome to the Terror-Go-Round, Vol. 12.** A. G. Cascone. (Deadtime Stories Ser.). (J). 1997. pap. 3.50 (*0-8167-4293-6*) Troll Communs.

Welcome to the Theatre. Sandra N. Boyce. (Illus.). 400p. 1987. pap. 22.95 (*0-8304-1083-X*) Nelson-Hall.

Welcome to the Underground & Other Stories. Sonia Games. 100p. (Orig.). (J). (gr. 3-8). 1996. per. 5.99 (*0-9650736-0-2*) Super Bks & Tapes.

***Welcome to the United States Airforce.** Charles M. Wachob. 70p. 1997. pap. 9.95 (*1-884778-17-8*) Old Mountain.

Welcome to the Way: Parish Manual. James Bitney & Yvette Nelson. 48p. (Orig.). 1989. pap. text ed. 6.95 (*0-89505-583-X*, T1850) Tabor Pub.

Welcome to the Way, Jr. High Catechist's Guide. James Bitney & Yvette Nelson. (Illus.). 160p. (Orig.). 1989. teacher ed., pap. text ed. 26.20 (*0-89505-581-3*, T2514) Tabor Pub.

Welcome to the Way, Jr. High Student Edition. James Bitney & Yvette Nelson. (Illus.). 80p. (Orig.). (J). (gr. 6-8). 1989. pap. text ed. 8.50 (*0-89505-585-6*, T2512) Tabor Pub.

Welcome to the Way, Sr. High Catechist's Guide. James Bitney & Yvette Nelson. (Illus.). 160p. 1989. teacher ed., pap. text ed. 26.20 (*0-89505-584-8*, T2518) Tabor Pub.

Welcome to the Way, Sr. High Student Edition. James Bitney & Yvette Nelson. (Illus.). 80p. (YA). (gr. 9-12). 1989. pap. text ed. 8.50 (*0-89505-580-5*, T2513) Tabor Pub.

***Welcome to the White House: A Children's Guide to Where the President Lives.** Betty Debnam. (Illus.). 96p. (Orig.). (J). 1997. pap. 6.95 (*0-8362-2153-2*) Andrews & McMeel.

Welcome to the Wicked Wax Museum. R. L. Stine. (Give Yourself Goosebumps Ser.: No. 12). (J). (gr. 2-5). 1996. pap. 3.99 (*0-590-84772-4*) Scholastic Inc.

***Welcome to the Williamsburg Inn.** Hugh Desamper & Colonial Williamsburg Foundation Staff. LC 97-10002. 1997. write for info. (*0-87935-169-1*) Colonial Williamsburg.

Welcome to the Wonderful World of Horses! What a Beginner Needs to Know. Linda Liestman. 56p. (YA). (gr. 5 up). 1994. pap. text ed. 6.00 (*1-887811-09-5*) N Amer Horsemens.

***Welcome to the Word Worksheets.** Joan Brown. Date not set. pap. 25.95 (*0-225-66650-2*, Pub. by Geoffrey Chapman UK) Morehouse Pub.

Welcome to the World. Illus. by Flavia. 32p. 1993. 6.95 (*0-8362-4704-3*) Andrews & McMeel.

Welcome to the World: A Celebration of Birth & Babies from Many Cultures. Compiled by Nikki Siegen-Smith. LC 96-1747. (Illus.). 48p. 1996. 17.95 (*0-531-36006-7*) Orchard Bks Watts.

Welcome to the World - A Jewish Baby's Record Book. Women's League for Conservative Judaism Staff. (Illus.). 40p. 1985. 15.00 (*0-936293-00-4*) WLCJ.

***Welcome to the World of Bears.** Diane Swanson. 1997. pap. 5.95 (*1-55110-519-5*, Pub. by Whitecap Bks CN) Gr Arts Ctr Pub.

Welcome to the World of Computers. Connie Acton & Woody Greene. (Illus.). 256p. (YA). 1995. pap. text ed. 18.95 (*1-887281-01-0*) Labyrinth CA.

Welcome to the World of Computers: Version 4.0 for Windows 95. Connie Acton & Woody Greene. (Illus.). 239p. (YA). 1996. pap. text ed. 18.95 (*1-887281-09-6*) Labyrinth CA.

***Welcome to the World of Independent Contractors & Other Contindent Contractors & Other Contingent Workers.** 396p. 1996. pap. 29.00 (*0-614-26847-8*, 15195BLS03) Commerce.

***Welcome to the World of Otters.** Diane Swanson. 1997. pap. 5.95 (*1-55110-520-9*, Pub. by Whitecap Bks CN) Gr Arts Ctr Pub.

***Welcome to the World of Owls.** Diane Swanson. 1997. pap. text ed. 5.95 (*1-55110-614-0*, Pub. by Whitecap Bks CN) Gr Arts Ctr Pub.

Welcome to the World of Whales. Diane Swanson. (Illus.). 32p. (J). (ps-2). 1996. pap. 5.95 (*1-55110-490-3*) Gr Arts Ctr Pub.

***Welcome to the World of Wild Cats.** Diane Swanson. 1997. pap. text ed. 5.95 (*1-55110-615-9*, Pub. by Whitecap Bks CN) Gr Arts Ctr Pub.

Welcome to the World of Wolves. Diane Swanson. (Illus.). 32p. (J). (ps-2). 1996. pap. 5.95 (*1-55110-491-1*) Gr Arts Ctr Pub.

Welcome to the Zone. David Chelsea. Ed. by Phil Amara. (Illus.). 96p. 1994. pap. 9.95 (*0-87816-312-3*) Kitchen Sink.

Welcome to This World: A Love Letter to Little Ones. Debby Boone. (Illus.). (Orig.). (J). 1995. 14.99 (*1-56507-302-9*) Harvest Hse.

Welcome to This World Baby Book. Debby Boone & Gabriel Ferrer. (Illus.). 25-30p. 1996. 22.99 (*1-56507-413-0*) Harvest Hse.

Welcome to Vietnam, Macho Man: Reflections of a Khe Sanh Vet. 2nd ed. Ernest Spencer. Ed. by Toni Murray. 192p. 1988. 15.95 (*0-9618529-0-9*) Corps Press.

An Asterisk (*) at the beginning of an entry indicates that the title is appearing in BIP for the first time.

Welcome to Wall Street. Global Investments Staff. LC 93-90425. 1994. pap. 14.95 (*0-9637196-3-7*) Global Investmts.
Welcome to Washington. rev. ed. Eugenia M. Horstman. (Illus.). 36p. (Orig.). 1987. pap. 6.95 (*0-936478-11-X*) Interpretive Pubns.
Welcome to Washington. rev. ed. Eugenia M. Horstman. (Illus.). 36p. (Orig.). (JPN.). 1988. reprint ed. pap. 6.95 (*0-936478-12-8*) Interpretive Pubns.
Welcome to Welsh. pap. 9.50 (*0-89979-031-3*) British Am Bks.
Welcome to Welsh. Heini Gruffudd. (WEL.). 1993. pap. 9.95 (*0-86243-069-0*) Intl Spec Bk.
Welcome to Your Baby Boy. Ed. by Helen Exley. (So-Much-More-Than-a-Card Ser.). (Illus.). 28p. (Orig.). 1995. pap. 2.99 (*1-85015-659-X*) Exley Giftbooks.
Welcome to Your Baby Girl. Ed. by Helen Exley. (So-Much-More-Than-a-Card Ser.). (Illus.). 28p. (Orig.). 1995. pap. 2.99 (*1-85015-676-X*) Exley Giftbooks.
***Welcome To Your Face Lift.** Helen Bransford. 1997. 22.95 (*0-385-48549-2*) Doubleday.
Welcome to Your First Small Group. Judy Hamlin. 64p. (Orig.). 1993. pap. 3.50 (*1-56476-100-2*, 6-3100, Victor Bks) Chariot Victor.
***Welcome to Your Future! A Manual for Millionaires (& Those Thinking of Becoming One)** Richard S. Greenburg. (Wealth Steps Ser.). (Illus.). 375p. (Orig.). 1996. pap. write for info. (*1-890202-01-0*, Ascend Busn) Ascend Intl.
Welcome to Your Midlife Crisis. Paul Valle. Ed. by Cliff Carle. 1996. pap. text ed. 5.95 (*1-57644-000-1*) CCC Pubns.
Welcome Tomorrow. Ed. by Arnold Reisman & Ellen Reisman. LC 82-91107. (Illus.). 1982. pap. 6.95 (*0-686-39632-4*); 4.17 (*0-912269-00-6*) North Coast Pubs.
Welcomes & Ceremonies for the Year's Program. 32p. 1994. reprint ed. pap. 3.00 (*0-88053-332-3*, S-086) Macoy Pub.
Welcoming a Visitation of the Holy Spirit. Wesley Campbell. 1995. pap. 10.99 (*0-88419-410-8*) Creation House.
Welcoming Babies. Margy Burns Knight. LC 94-6854. (Illus.). 19p. (J). (gr. k up). 1994. 14.95 (*0-88448-123-9*) Tilbury Hse.
***Welcoming Change: Discovering Hope in Life's Transitions.** James E. Miller. LC 97-21457. (The Willowgreen Ser.). 1997. pap. 14.99 (*0-8066-3338-7*, Augsburg) Augsburg Fortress.
Welcoming Children: Experimental Children's Sermons. Brant D. Baker. 1995. pap. 8.99 (*0-8066-2835-9*) Augsburg Fortress.
Welcoming Congregation: Resources for Affirming Gay, Lesbian & Bisexual Persons. Ed. by Scott W. Alexander. 164p. 1993. pap. 25.00 (*1-55896-190-9*) Unitarian Univ.
Welcoming Hearth. Elizabeth R. Skoglund. 194p. 1993. pap. 8.99 (*0-8423-7919-3*) Tyndale.
Welcoming Heaven: Prayers & Reflections for the Dying & Those Who Love Them. Josephine M. Ford. LC 90-70558. 148p. (Orig.). 1990. 19.95 (*0-89622-442-2*) Twenty-Third.
Welcoming Land. large type ed. Una Rothwell. 336p. 1987. 25.99 (*0-7089-1661-9*) Ulverscroft.
***Welcoming Life: An M. F. K. Fisher Scrapbook.** Dominique Gioia. LC 96-54641. 1997. 35.00 (*1-887178-32-5*) Counterpt DC.
Welcoming New Christians: A Guide for the Christian Initiation of Adults. Jane H. Peifer & John Stahl-Wert. LC 94-74576. 142p. 1995. pap. 24.95 (*0-87303-298-5*) Faith & Life.
Welcoming Students Who Are Deaf-Blind into Typical Classrooms: Facilitating School Participation, Learning, & Friendship. Norris G. Haring & Romer. 480p. 1995. pap. 37.00 (*1-55766-144-8*) P H Brookes.
Welcoming the Japanese Visitor: Insights, Tips, Tactics. Kazuo Nishiyama. LC 95-46072. (Illus.). 224p. (C). 1996. pap. 19.95 (*0-8248-1759-1*, Kolowalu Bk) UH Pr.
Welcoming the New Catholic. 3rd rev. ed. Ronald J. Lewinski. LC 93-50845. (Font & Table Ser.). 98p. 1994. pap. 5.95 (*1-56854-013-2*, WNEW-3) Liturgy Tr Pubns.
***Welcoming the Presence of the Holy Spirit.** Larry Keefauver. 1997. pap. 5.99 (*0-88419-470-1*) Creation House.
Welcoming the Stranger: A Public Theology of Worship & Evangelism. Patrick R. Keifert. 184p. (Orig.). 1992. pap. 14.00 (*0-8006-2492-0*, 1-2492, Fortress Pr) Augsburg Fortress.
Welcoming the Undesirables: Brazil & the Jewish Question. Jeffrey Lesser. LC 93-21199. 1994. 42.00 (*0-520-08412-8*); pap. 18.00 (*0-520-08413-6*) U CA Pr.
Welcoming the World: A History of Salt Lake County. Linda Sillitoe. (Illus.). 250p. 1996. write for info. (*0-9651857-0-2*) Salt Lke Cty.
Welcoming Your Second Baby. 2nd ed. Vicki Lansky. 112p. 1990. pap. 6.95 (*0-916773-12-4*) Book Peddlers.
Weld Decay in Austenitic Stainless Steels. T. G. Goach & D. C. Willingham. 18p. 1975. pap. 53.00 (*0-85300-095-6*, Pub. by Woodhead Pubng UK) Am Educ Systs.
Weld Failures. Ed. by J. D. Harrison. (Illus.). 560p. (Orig.). (C). 1989. pap. 245.00 (*0-85300-234-7*, Pub. by Woodhead Pubng UK) Am Educ Systs.
***Weld Integrity & Performance.** Steve Lampman & ASM International Staff. LC 97-10740. 400p. 1997. 145.00 (*0-87170-600-8*, 6593) ASM.
Weld Pool Oscillation for Penetration Sensing & Control. Ton Aendenroomer. (Illus.). 151p. (Orig.). 1996. pap. 82.50 (*90-407-1229-8*, Pub. by Delft U Pr NE) Coronet Bks.
Weld Residual Stresses & Plastic Deformation: Presented at the 1989 ASME Pressure Vessels & Piping Conference, JSME Co-Sponsorship, Honolulu, Hawaii, July 23-27, 1989. ASME Pressure Vessels & Piping Conference Staff. Ed. by Edmund F. Rybicki et al. LC 89-45821. (PVP Ser.: Vol. 173). 79p. 1989. reprint ed. pap. 25.00 (*0-608-00286-0*, 2059314) Bks Demand.
Weld Symbols on Drawings. (Illus.). 38p. 1982. pap. 49.95 (*0-85300-157-X*, Pub. by Woodhead Pubng UK) Am Educ Systs.
Weldability of Steels. 4th ed. R. D. Stout. 1987. 50.00 (*0-318-22288-4*) Welding Res Coun.
Welded see Six Short Plays of Eugene O'Neill
Welded Interior Beam-to-Column Connections. 40p. 1959. 10.00 (*1-56424-025-8*, T105) Am Inst Steel Construct.
Welded Stainless Steel Pipe from Malaysia: An International Trade Investigation. Olympia D. Hand. (Illus.). 82p. (Orig.). (C). 1995. pap. text ed. 30.00 (*0-7881-2386-6*) DIANE Pub.
Welded Structures '90: International Conference, November 1990. (Illus.). 272p. 1991. pap. 245.00 (*1-85573-030-8*, Pub. by Woodhead Pubng UK) Am Educ Systs.
Welded Wire Fabric for Shear Reinforcement. (PCI Journal Reprints Ser.). 6p. 1985. pap. 10.00 (*0-318-19750-2*, JR222) P-PCI.
Welder. Jack Rudman. (Career Examination Ser.: C-892). 1994. pap. 23.95 (*0-8373-0892-5*) Nat Learn.
Welder Trade Practicals. Central Instruc Media Inst. Staff. 1995. write for info. (*81-224-0737-4*, Pub. by Wiley Estrn II) Franklin.
Welder's Bible. 2nd ed. Don Geary. 1992. text ed. 29.95 (*0-07-023546-5*); pap. text ed. 21.95 (*0-07-023547-3*) McGraw.
Welder's Bible. 2nd ed. Don Geary. (Illus.). 480p. 1992. 29.95 (*0-8306-3826-1*, 4116); pap. 21.95 (*0-8306-3825-3*, 4116) McGraw-Hill Prof.
***Welder's Handbook.** Richard Finch. LC 96-44794. 196p. 1997. pap. 16.95 (*1-55788-264-9*, HP Books) Berkley Pub.
Welding. Jerry Galyen & Sear. 1989. text ed. 42.00 (*0-13-950098-7*) P-H.
Welding. Jack Rudman. (Occupational Competency Examination Ser.: OCE-33). 1994. pap. 27.95 (*0-8373-5733-0*) Nat Learn.
Welding. D. Smith. 1984. text ed. 43.95 (*0-07-000757-8*) McGraw.
Welding. 7th rev. ed. Ed. by Deere & Company Staff. (Fundamentals of Service Ser.). (Illus.). 160p. 1991. pap. text ed. 14.95 (*0-86691-220-7*, FOS5207NC) Deere & Co.
***Welding.** 7th rev. ed. Ed. by Deere & Company Staff. (Fundamentals of Service Ser.). 147p. 1991. 147.95 incl. sl. (*0-614-24210-X*, FOS5207S) Deere & Co.
***Welding, Level 1.** 1996. student ed., ring bd. 80.00 (*0-13-264938-1*, Prentice Hall) P-H.
Welding, Level 1. National Center for Construction Education & Research Staff. (Wheels of Learning Ser.). 1996. teacher ed., ring bd. 50.00 (*0-13-265661-2*) P-H.
Welding, Level 2. National Center for Construction Education & Research Staff. (Wheels of Learning Ser.). 1996. teacher ed., ring bd. 80.00 (*0-13-265679-5*) P-H.
Welding: Level 1. Ed. by National Center for Construction Staff. 1996. pap. text ed. 50.00 (*0-13-462847-0*) P-H.
Welding: Level 1. Ed. by National Center for Construction Staff. 1996. teacher ed., pap. text ed. 50.00 (*0-13-462854-3*) P-H.
Welding: Level 2. Ed. by National Center for Construction Staff. 1996. pap. text ed. 80.00 (*0-13-462862-4*) P-H.
Welding: Level 2. Ed. by National Center for Construction Staff. 1996. teacher ed., pap. text ed. 80.00 (*0-13-462870-5*) P-H.
Welding: Level 3. Ed. by National Center for Construction Staff. 1996. pap. text ed. 80.00 (*0-13-462888-8*) P-H.
Welding: Level 3. Ed. by National Center for Construction Staff. 1996. teacher ed., pap. text ed. 80.00 (*0-13-462896-9*) P-H.
Welding: Principles & Applications. Larry Jeffus & Harold Johnson. LC 83-71046. (C). 1984. text ed. 39.95 (*0-8273-1806-5*) Delmar.
***Welding: Principles & Applications.** Larry F. Jeffus. LC 97-13165. 1997. write for info. (*0-8273-8240-5*) Delmar.
Welding: Principles & Applications. 2nd ed. Larry Jeffus. (Welding Ser.). 1984. teacher ed. 13.95 (*0-8273-1807-3*) Delmar.
Welding: Principles & Applications. 2nd ed. Larry Jeffus & Harold Johnson. (C). 1988. pap. 36.95 (*0-8273-2982-2*) Delmar.
Welding: Principles & Applications. 3rd ed. Larry Jeffus. LC 92-26657. 764p. 1993. text ed. 41.95 (*0-8273-5048-1*) Delmar.
Welding: Principles & Applications Instructor's Guide. 3rd ed. Larry Jeffus. 234p. 1993. teacher ed. 20.95 (*0-8273-5050-3*) Delmar.
Welding: Series. Gellerman. 1997. pap. 12.95 (*0-8273-7630-8*); pap. 18.95 (*0-8273-7632-4*) Delmar.
Welding: Techniques & Rural Practice. Peter Cryer & Jim Heather. 1996. pap. 44.95 (*0-7506-8921-8*) Buttrwrth-Heinemann.
Welding: Theory & Practice. Ed. by D. L. Olson et al. (Materials Processing Theory & Practice Ser.: No. 8). 390p. 1990. 216.75 (*0-444-87427-5*, North Holland) Elsevier.
Welding: Trainee Guide, Level 2. National Center for Construction Education & Research Staff. (Wheels of Learning Ser.). 1996. student ed., pap. text ed. 80.00 (*0-13-266024-5*) P-H.
Welding & Brazing of Carbon Steels, 2 bks., Bk. 1: Arc Welding. Ed. by Charles A. Davis. LC 76-44372. (Metalworking & Manufacturing Processes Ser.). (Illus.). reprint ed. Bk. 1-Arc Welding. pap. 43.00 (*0-317-09871-3*, 2019480) Bks Demand.
Welding & Brazing of Carbon Steels, 2 bks., Bk. 2, High-Deposition-Rate & Special-Application. Ed. by Charles A. Davis. LC 76-44372. (Metalworking & Manufacturing Processes Ser.). (Illus.). reprint ed. Bk. 2-High-Deposition-Rate & Special-Application Welding. pap. 34.80 (*0-317-09872-1*) Bks Demand.
Welding & Brazing of Carbon Steels, Bk. 3: Resistance Welding. American Society for Metals Staff. Ed. by Charles A. Davis. LC 76-44372. reprint ed. Book 3: Resistance Welding. pap. 37.80 (*0-317-26234-3*, 2052147) Bks Demand.
Welding & Brazing of Carbon Steels, Bk. 4: Gas Welding & Brazing. American Society for Metals Staff. Ed. by Charles A. Davis. LC 76-44372. reprint ed. Book 4: Gas Welding & Brazing. pap. 43.00 (*0-317-26235-1*) Bks Demand.
Welding & Brazing Techniques for Nuclear Reactor Components. Gerald M. Slaughter. LC 64-16362. (Monograph Series on Metallurgy in Nuclear Technology). 204p. reprint ed. pap. 58.20 (*0-317-08660-X*, 2050847) Bks Demand.
Welding & Cutting. J. A. Oates. (Illus.). pap. 6.00 (*0-85344-094-8*) Apple Blossom.
Welding & Cutting: A Guide to Fusion Welding & Associated Cutting Processes. Peter T. Houldcroft & Robert John. (Illus.). 240p. 1989. 36.95 (*0-8311-1184-4*) Indus Pr.
Welding & Other Joining Processes. R. A. Lindberg & N. R. Braton. 1985. pap. text ed. 30.00 (*0-9606344-6-0*) Blitz Pub Co.
***Welding & Surfacing Reviews: Brazing of Steel Structures, Vol. 4, Pt. 1.** V. D. Tabelev. (Welding & Surfacing Reviews Ser.). 1995. pap. text ed. 116.00 (*3-7186-5757-0*) Gordon & Breach.
Welding & Surfacing Reviews: Electron Beam Welding: Achievements & Problems (a Review) B. E. Paton & O. K. Nazarenko. (Soviet Technology Reviews Ser.: Vol. 1, Pt. 1). ii, 54p. 1989. pap. text ed. 52.00 (*3-7186-4946-2*) Gordon & Breach.
Welding & Surfacing Reviews: Explosion Welding Criteria, Vol. 3. B. E. Paton. (Welding & Surfacing Reviews Ser: Vol. 3, Pt. 4). 127p. 1994. pap. text ed. 214.00 (*3-7186-5725-2*, Harwood Acad Pubs) Gordon & Breach.
Welding & Surfacing Reviews: Laser-Arc Discharge, Vol. 3. B. E. Paton. (Welding & Surfacing Reviews Ser: Vol. 3, Pt. 3). 148p. 1994. pap. text ed. 249.00 (*3-7186-5726-0*, Harwood Acad Pubs) Gordon & Breach.
Welding & Surfacing Reviews: Metallurgy of Welding & Welding Materials. I. K. Pokhodnaya & V. V. Podgaetsky. Ed. by B. E. Paton. (Soviet Technology Reviews Ser.: Vol. 1, Pt. 2). 86p. 1989. pap. text ed. 56.00 (*3-7186-4947-0*) Gordon & Breach.
Welding & Surfacing Reviews: Special Electrometallurgy (a Review) B. I. Medovar et al. Ed. by B. E. Paton. (Soviet Technology Reviews Ser.: Vol. 1, Pt. 5). 68p. 1989. pap. text ed. 62.00 (*3-7186-4976-4*) Gordon & Breach.
Welding & Surfacing Reviews: Surfacing in the U. S. S. R. P. V. Gladkii et al. Ed. by B. E. Paton. (Soviet Technology Reviews Ser.: Vol. 1, Pt. 4). iv, 66p. 1989. pap. text ed. 61.00 (*3-7186-4957-8*) Gordon & Breach.
Welding & Surfacing Reviews: The Flash Butt Welding of Pipes & Rails. S. I. Kuchuk-Yatsenko & V. T. Cherednichok. Ed. by B. E. Paton. (Soviet Technology Reviews Ser.: Vol. 1, Pt. 3). iv, 78p. 1989. pap. text ed. 74.00 (*3-7186-4948-9*) Gordon & Breach.
***Welding & Surfacing Reviews: Welding of Composite Materials, Vol. 4, Pt. 2.** V. R. Ryabeo. (Welding & Surfacing Reviews Ser.). 1995. pap. text ed. 70.00 (*3-7186-5758-9*) Gordon & Breach.
Welding & Surfacing Reviews Vol. 1, Pg. 6: Nitrogen & Hydrogen in Molten Metals & Alloys. G. M. Grigorenko. (Soviet Technology Reviews Ser.: Sec. C). 1990. 44.00 (*3-7186-5016-9*, Harwood Acad Pubs) Gordon & Breach.
Welding & Surfacing Reviews Vol. 3, Pt. 2: Fatigue Strength of Welded Structures, Vol. 3. B. E. Paton. (Welding & Surfacing Reviews Ser). 100p. 1994. pap. text ed. 168.00 (*3-7186-5724-4*, Harwood Acad Pubs) Gordon & Breach.
Welding & Weld Automation in Shipbuilding. Ed. by R. Denale. (Illus.). 257p. 1996. 90.00 (*0-87339-322-8*) Minerals Metals.
Welding Blueprints & Symbols. Craig Stinchcomb. LC 94-46981. 261p. 1995. pap. text ed. 30.60 (*0-13-436296-9*) P-H.
Welding Careers. Mark Rowh. (Opportunities in...Ser.). 160p. 1992. pap. 10.95 (*0-8442-8599-4*, VGM Career Bks) NTC Pub Grp.
Welding Careers. Mark Rowh. (Opportunities in...Ser.). 160p. 1994. 13.95 (*0-8442-8598-6*, VGM Career Bks) NTC Pub Grp.
Welding Cast Irons. Ed. by C. L. Cottrell. (Illus.). 28p. 1986. pap. 55.00 (*0-85300-176-6*, Pub. by Woodhead Pubng UK) Am Educ Systs.
Welding Certification Questionnaire. Henry L. Jackson. 150p. (C). 1992. pap. text ed. 42.50 (*1-881870-00-6*) BJ Pubns.
Welding Coated Steels. 40p. 1978. pap. 55.00 (*0-85300-115-4*, Pub. by Woodhead Pubng UK) Am Educ Systs.
Welding Codes, Standards & Specifications. Jeffrey D. Mouser. (Illus.). 608p. 1997. text ed. 69.95 (*0-07-043550-2*) McGraw.
Welding Craft Practice, 2 Vols. 2nd ed. Ed. by N. Parkin & C. R. Flood. Incl. Vol. 1. Oxy-Acetylene Gas Welding & Related Studies. LC 79-40237. 1979. 78.00 (*0-08-024220-0*); Vol. 2. Electric Arc Welding & Related Studies. LC 79-40237. 1980. text ed. 80.00 (*0-08-024260-X*); Vol. 2. Electric Arc Welding & Related Studies. LC 79-40237. 1980. pap. text ed. 19.00 (*0-08-024259-6*); LC 79-40237. (International Series on Monographs on Materials Science & Technology). 1979. Set pap. write for info. (*0-318-55240-X*, Pub. by Pergamon Repr UK) Franklin.
Welding Creep-Resisting Steels. 38p. 1976. pap. 55.00 (*0-85300-102-2*, Pub. by Woodhead Pubng UK) Am Educ Systs.
Welding Dissimilar Metals: Specially Commissioned Papers. (Illus.). 72p. 1986. pap. 79.95 (*0-85300-158-8*, Pub. by Woodhead Pubng UK) Am Educ Systs.
Welding Encyclopedia. 18th ed. Ed. by Ted B. Jefferson & D. T. Jefferson. (Monticello Bks.). 1988. 27.50 (*0-318-35129-3*) Jefferson Pubns.
Welding Engineer. Jack Rudman. (Career Examination Ser.: C-1533). 1994. pap. 27.95 (*0-8373-1533-6*) Nat Learn.
Welding Fume Control: A Demonstration Project (WFDP) 65p. 1982. 32.00 (*0-686-43388-2*) Am Welding.
Welding Fumes. V. G. Voitkevich. 176p. 1994. pap. 135.00 (*1-85573-185-1*, Pub. by Woodhead Pubng UK) Am Educ Systs.
Welding Fundamentals. Mike Gellerman. LC 94-35393. 1995. text ed. 41.95 (*0-8273-5937-3*) Delmar.
Welding Fundamentals: Workbook. Gellerman. 288p. 1995. student ed. 16.95 (*0-8273-6740-6*) Delmar.
Welding Guidelines with Aircraft Supplement. William Kielhorn. LC 93-5514. (IAP Training Ser.). (Illus.). 187p. 1978. pap. text ed. 12.45 (*0-89100-076-3*, EA-WB-1) IAP.
Welding Handbook, Vol. 1 (WHB-1.8) Welding Technology. 8th enl. ed. 638p. 1987. 118.00 (*0-87171-281-4*) Am Welding.
Welding Handbook, Vol. 2 (WHB-2.8) Welding Processes. 8th enl. ed. (Illus.). 955p. 1991. 118.00 (*0-87171-354-3*) Am Welding.
Welding Handbook, Vol. 5 (WHB-5) Engineering, Costs, Quality & Safety. 7th ed. 460p. 1984. 36.50 (*0-87171-239-3*) Am Welding.
Welding Health & Safety Resource Manual. American Industrial Hygiene Association. 40p. 1984. 22.00 (*0-932627-17-X*) Am Indus Hygiene.
Welding Inspection, Course 28. (Illus.). 410p. (C). 1979. ring bd. 95.00 (*0-87683-104-8*) GP Courseware.
Welding Inspection, Course 28. Center for Occupational Research & Development Staff. (Nuclear Technology Ser.). (Illus.). 440p. (C). 1984. pap. text ed. 35.00 (*1-55502-117-4*) CORD Commns.
Welding Inspection (WI) 222p. 1980. 39.00 (*0-87171-177-X*) Am Welding.
Welding Lab Manual. Douglas C. Snyder. 94p. (C). 1994. spiral bd. 17.79 (*0-8403-9467-5*) Kendall-Hunt.
***Welding Management: Techniques for Welding Leadership.** John Menhart & Donald Lynn. Ed. by Amy J. Nickel. (Illus.). 128p. (Orig.). 1997. pap. 45.00 (*1-881113-10-8*) Croydon Grp.
Welding Mechanisation & Automation in World Shipbuilding: Production Methods & Trends Based on Yard Capacity. R. Boekholt. 350p. 1995. pap. 585.00 (*1-85573-219-X*, Pub. by Woodhead Pubng UK) Am Educ Systs.
Welding Metallurgy. Sindo Dou. LC 87-2218. 411p. 1987. text ed. 112.00 (*0-471-84090-4*) Wiley.
Welding Metallurgy Vol. 1: Fundamentals. 4th ed. G. E. Linnert. (Illus.). 940p. 1995. 99.00 (*0-87171-457-4*, wM1) Am Welding.
Welding Metallurgy of Non-Ferrous Metals & Cast Iron. Welding Institute Staff. 78p. 1995. pap. 49.95 (*1-85573-174-6*, Pub. by Woodhead Pubng UK) Am Educ Systs.
Welding Metallurgy of Stainless & Heat-Resisting Steels. Rene Castro & J. J. De Cadenet. LC 74-76582. 200p. reprint ed. pap. 57.00 (*0-317-26032-4*, 2024434) Bks Demand.
Welding Metallurgy of Stainless Steels. Welding Institute Staff. 72p. 1995. pap. 49.95 (*1-85573-173-8*, Pub. by Woodhead Pubng UK) Am Educ Systs.
Welding Metallurgy of Steels. Welding Institute Staff. 82p. 1995. pap. 49.95 (*1-85573-172-X*, Pub. by Woodhead Pubng UK) Am Educ Systs.
Welding Metallurgy of Structural Steels: Proceedings of an International Symposium on Welding Metallurgy of Structural Steels Sponsored by the TMS Ferrous Metallurgy Committee & the Heat Treatment Committee & Co-Sponsored by the Edison Welding Institute, Held at the Annual Meeting of the Metallurgy Society Inc. in Denver, Colorado, February 22-26, 1987. international Symposium on Welding Metallurgy of Structural Steels Staff. Ed. by Jay Y. Koo. LC 87-42882. (Illus.). 647p. reprint ed. pap. 180.00 (*0-7837-4079-4*, 2052476) Bks Demand.
Welding of High Alloy Castings see Steel Casting Handbook Supplements
Welding of HSLA Structural Steels: Proceedings of an International Conference. American Society for Metals Staff. Ed. by A. B. Rothwell & J. Malcolm Gray. LC 78-18220. (Materials Metalworking Technology Ser.). 805p. reprint ed. pap. 180.00 (*0-317-27699-9*, 2019490) Bks Demand.
Welding of Line Pipe Steels. 1977. 20.00 (*0-318-18633-0*) Welding Res Coun.
Welding of Open Web Steel Joists. (Technical Digest Ser.: No. 8). 1983. 12.50 (*0-318-01793-8*) Steel Joist Inst.
Welding of Sand Cast Incramet 800. British Welding Research Association Staff. 75p. 1965. 11.25 (*0-317-34556-7*, 57) Intl Copper.

W

An Asterisk (*) at the beginning of an entry indicates that the title is appearing in BIP for the first time.

Welding of Tubular Structures. International Institute of Welding Staff. (Illus.). 574p. 1984. 80.00 (*0-08-031647-6*, Pub. by Pergamon Repr UK); pap. 33.75 (*0-08-031155-5*, Pub. by Pergamon Repr UK) Franklin.

Welding of Tubular Structures (WTS) 500p. 1984. 50.00 (*0-317-17734-6*) Am Welding.

Welding Practices & Procedures. Richard Carr & Robert O'Con. (Illus.). 416p. 1983. pap. text ed. write for info. (*0-13-948059-5*) P-H.

Welding Principles & Applications: Study Guide - Lab Manual. 3rd ed. Larry Jeffus & Dewayne Roy. 330p. 1993. 19.95 (*0-8273-6016-9*) Delmar.

Welding Principles & Practices, No. 2. Raymond Sacks. 1986. pap. 31.95 (*0-02-666140-3*) Macmillan.

Welding Print Reading. John R. Walker. (Illus.). 238p. 1996. 25.28 (*1-56637-267-4*) Goodheart.

Welding Process Technology. Peter T. Houldcroft. LC 76-47408. (Illus.). 270p. 1977. text ed. 64.95 (*0-521-21530-7*) Cambridge U Pr.

Welding Processes. 3rd ed. Edward E. Roden et al. 400p. (C). 1985. teacher ed. 14.95 (*0-8273-2136-8*) Delmar.

Welding Processes. 3rd ed. Edward M. Roden et al. 400p. (C). 1984. text ed. 37.95 (*0-8273-2133-3*) Delmar.

Welding Processes & Power Sources. 3rd ed. Edwards R. Pierre. (Student Study Guide Ser.). (Illus.). 416p. (C). 1984. text ed. write for info. (*0-8087-3369-9*); student ed. write for info. (*0-8087-3370-2*) Burgess MN Intl.

Welding Processes & Practices. Leonard Koellhoffer et al. 482p. 1988. text ed. 39.50 (*0-471-81671-X*); Wkbk. student ed. 18.50 (*0-471-81668-X*) P-H.

Welding Projects: A Design Approach. J. A. Pender & J. Masson. 1976. text ed. 35.95 (*0-07-077330-0*) McGraw.

Welding Safety. Gary Hutchinson. LC 81-730682. 1982. student ed. 5.00 (*0-8064-0247-4*, 515); audio, vhs 149.00 (*0-8064-0248-2*) Bergwall.

Welding Series. 1997. pap. 18.95 (*0-8273-7629-4*) Delmar.

Welding Series. Rowe. 1997. 12.95 (*0-8273-7615-4*) Delmar.

Welding Series: Gas Tung Metal Arc Welding. Rowe. 1997. 26.95 (*0-8273-7616-2*) Delmar.

***Welding Skills.** 2nd ed. R. T. Miller. 456p. 1997. 32.96 (*0-8269-3007-7*) Am Technical.

Welding Skills & Practices. Joseph W. Giachino et al. LC 77-123471. 432p. reprint ed. pap. 123.20 (*0-317-10910-3*, 2012979) Bks Demand.

Welding Skills & Techniques. Robert P. Schmidt. (C). 1982. teacher ed. write for info. (*0-8359-8612-8*, Reston) P-H.

Welding Steels Without Hydrogen Cracking. 2nd ed. N. Bailey et al. (Illus.). 160p. 1993. 128.00 (*0-614-02558-3*, 6324U) ASM Intl.

Welding Structural Steels. Earl Kent. 1977. pap. text ed. 10.00 (*0-918782-01-5*) E Kent.

Welding Technology. Gower A. Kennedy. LC 72-92622. 1974. 26.50 (*0-672-97505-X*, Bobbs) Macmillan.

Welding Technology. Gower A. Kennedy. 1985. 37.32 (*0-02-682220-2*) Macmillan.

Welding Technology. 2nd ed. Joseph W. Giachino et al. (Illus.). 489p. 1973. pap. 22.96 (*0-8269-3063-8*) Am Technical.

Welding Technology. 2nd ed. Gower A. Kennedy. 598p. 1982. teacher ed. write for info. (*0-672-97136-4*); text ed. write for info. (*0-672-97778-8*); lab manual ed. write for info. (*0-672-97990-X*) Macmillan.

Welding Technology: Paton Institute. 234p. 1994. pap. 285.00 (*1-85573-153-3*, Pub. by Woodhead Pubng UK) Am Educ Systs.

Welding Technology Fundamentals. William A. Bowditch & Kevin E. Bowditch. LC 96-3968. (Illus.). 368p. 1997. 35.96 (*1-56637-314-X*) Goodheart.

Welding Technology in Japan, Pt. I Processes & II Management Systems. 1982. 25.00 (*0-318-18640-3*) Welding Res Coun.

Welding Technology Today: Principles & Practices. Craig Stinchcomb. 496p. 1988. text ed. 75.00 (*0-13-924416-6*) P-H.

Welding Technology Workbook. Gower A. Kennedy. 1982. pap. 14.64 (*0-02-682230-X*) Macmillan.

Welding Theory & Application. 1991. lib. bdg. 79.69 (*0-8490-4112-0*) Gordon Pr.

Welding Theory & Application. 1995. lib. bdg. 263.95 (*0-8490-6570-4*) Gordon Pr.

Welding under Extreme Conditions. Ed. by International Institute of Welding Staff. (Proceedings of the International Conferences on Basement Tectonics Ser.). (Illus.). 308p. 1989. 142.00 (*0-08-037863-3*, Pergamon Pr) Elsevier.

Welding's Engineering Data Sheets. 9th ed. (Monticello Bks.). 188p. 1978. pap. 12.00 (*0-686-12001-9*) Jefferson Pubns.

Weldon Kees: A Critical Introduction. Ed. & Intro. by Jim Elledge. LC 85-14170. 263p. 1985. 25.00 (*0-8108-1830-2*) Scarecrow.

Weldon Kees & the Midcentury Generation: Letters, 1935-1955. Weldon Kees. Ed. by Robert E. Knoll. LC 86-1288. (Illus.). viii, 253p. 1986. text ed. 25.00 (*0-8032-2709-4*) U of Nebr Pr.

Weldon Rising & Disappeared. Phyllis Nagy. 1996. pap. 15.95 (*0-413-70150-6*, Pub. by Methuen UK) Heinemann.

Weldtech Series in Welding: Oxyacetylene Welding, Cutting, & Brazing. Chrysler Learning, Inc. (Illus.). 80p. 1983. pap. text ed. 17.00 (*0-13-948091-9*) P-H.

Welfare. Norman Barry. (Concepts in Social Thought Ser.). 160p. (C). 1990. pap. text ed. 13.95 (*0-8166-1883-6*) U of Minn Pr.

***Welfare.** Norman P. Barry. 160p. 1990. pap. 9.99 (*0-335-15595-2*, Open Univ Pr) Taylor & Francis.

Welfare. Ed. by Charles Cozic & Paul A. Winters. LC 96-31261. (Opposing Viewpoints Ser.). (Illus.). (J). (gr. 5-12). 1997. pap. 12.96 (*1-56510-519-2*) Greenhaven.

Welfare. Ed. by Paul Winters & Charles Cozic. LC 96-31261. (Opposing Viewpoints Ser.). (Illus.). (J). (gr. 5-12). 1997. lib. bdg. 20.96 (*1-56510-520-6*) Greenhaven.

Welfare: A Novocain. Lateef Muhammad. Ed. by Sabir K. Muhammad. 75p. (Orig.). (C). 1991. lib. bdg. 5.00 (*0-9627663-1-3*) Designer Comns.

Welfare: The Political Economy of Welfare Reform in the United States. Martin Anderson. (Publication Ser.: No. 181). 1978. 6.78 (*0-8179-6811-3*) Hoover Inst Pr.

Welfare: The Social Issues in Philosophical Perspective. Nicholas Rescher. LC 70-158184. 198p. reprint ed. pap. 56.50 (*0-317-26659-4*, 2025444) Bks Demand.

***Welfare Vol. 1: Aggregate Consumer Behavior.** Dale W. Jorgenson. (Illus.). 464p. 1997. 45.00 (*0-262-10062-2*) MIT Pr.

***Welfare Vol. 2: Measuring Social Welfare.** Dale W. Jorgenson. LC 96-44875. (Illus.). 448p. 1997. 45.00 (*0-262-10063-0*) MIT Pr.

Welfare Activities of Federal, State, & Local Governments in California, 1850-1934. Frances Cahn & Valeska Bary. LC 75-17212. (Social Problems & Social Policy Ser.). 1976. reprint ed. 36.95 (*0-405-07484-0*) Ayer.

Welfare & Citizenship: Beyond the Crisis of the Welfare State? Ian Culpitt. (Theory, Culture & Society Ser.). 224p. (C). 1992. 65.00 (*0-8039-8617-3*); pap. 24.95 (*0-8039-8618-1*) Sage.

Welfare & Competition. Tibor Scitovsky. (Modern Revivals in Economics Ser.). 490p. (C). 1993. text ed. 85.95 (*0-7512-0253-3*, Pub. by Gregg Revivals UK) Ashgate Pub Co.

Welfare & Efficiency: Their Interactions in Western Europe & Implications for International Economic Relations. Theodor Geiger & Frances M. Geiger. LC 78-63434. 160p. 1978. 7.00 (*0-89068-045-0*) Natl Planning.

***Welfare & Enlightenment: An Enquiry into the Rational Foundations of the Welfare State.** Hans Lindahl. 334p. (Orig.). 1995. pap. 72.50 (*90-6186-671-5*, Pub. by Leuven Univ BE) Coronet Bks.

Welfare & Freedom American Style II: The Role of the Federal Government, 1941-1980. Richard K. Caputo. LC 93-43063. (Federal Responses to People in Need Ser.: Vol. 2). 694p. (C). 1994. lib. bdg. 64.50 (*0-8191-9398-4*) U Pr of Amer.

Welfare & Housing Law. (Human Rights for All Ser.: Bk. 5). 99p. 1992. student ed. write for info. (*0-7021-2477-X*, Pub. by Juta SA); teacher ed. write for info. (*0-7021-2478-8*, Pub. by Juta SA) Gaunt.

Welfare & Housing of Laboratory Primates. UFAW Staff. (C). 1988. 160.00 (*0-900767-48-0*) St Mut.

Welfare & Husbandry of Calves. Ed. by J. P. Signoret. 1982. lib. bdg. 100.50 (*90-247-2680-8*) Kluwer Ac.

Welfare & Ideology. Victor George. 256p. 1995. pap. text ed. 29.95 (*0-13-320649-1*) P-H.

Welfare & Inequality: National & International Perspectives on the Australian Welfare State. Peter Saunders. LC 93-34166. (Illus.). 328p. (C). 1994. pap. write for info. (*0-521-45594-4*) Cambridge U Pr.

Welfare & Inequality: National & International Perspectives on the Australian Welfare State. Peter Saunders. LC 93-34166. (Illus.). 328p. (C). 1994. text ed. 64.95 (*0-521-45456-5*) Cambridge U Pr.

Welfare & Pension Plans Disclosure Act of 1958: Legislative History. U. S. Solicitor of the Department of Labor Staff. LC 63-26. xxxvi, 568p. 1978. reprint ed. lib. bdg. 52.50 (*0-930342-97-6*, 200680) W S Hein.

Welfare & Policy: Agendas & Issues. Ed. by Neil Lunt & Douglas Coyle. 224p. 1996. 75.00 (*0-7484-0401-5*); pap. 25.95 (*0-7484-0402-3*) Taylor & Francis.

Welfare & Poverty in Conakry: Assessment & Determinants. Carlo Del Ninno. (Working Papers: No. 66). 60p. (C). 1994. pap. 7.00 (*1-56401-166-6*) Cornell Food.

Welfare & the Ageing Experience: A Multidisciplinary Analysis. Ed. by Bill Bytheway & Julia Johnson. 221p. 1990. text ed. 59.95 (*1-85628-102-7*, Pub. by Avebury Pub UK) Ashgate Pub Co.

Welfare & the Poor in the Nineteenth Century City: Philadelphia, 1800-1854. Priscilla F. Clement. LC 83-49357. (Illus.). 224p. 1985. 32.50 (*0-8386-3216-5*) Fairleigh Dickinson.

Welfare & the Well-Being of Children, Vol. 59. Janet Currie. (Fundamentals of Pure & Applied Economics Ser.). 176p. 1995. pap. text ed. 22.00 (*3-7186-5624-8*, Harwood Acad Pubs) Gordon & Breach.

***Welfare & Values: Challenging the Culture of the Unconcern.** Peter Askonas & Stephen F. Frowen. LC 96-46620. 1997. text ed. 69.95 (*0-312-17256-7*) St Martin.

Welfare & Work Incentives. Ed. by A. B. Atkinson & Gunnar V. Morgensen. (Illus.). 3344p. 1994. 65.00 (*0-19-828860-3*) OUP.

Welfare & Worker Participation: Eight Case Studies. Patrick Kerans et al. LC 87-11878. 260p. 1988. text ed. 59.95 (*0-312-00908-9*) St Martin.

***Welfare As We Knew It: A Political History of the American Welfare State.** Charles Noble. LC 97-23704. 240p. 1997. pap. 17.95 (*0-19-511337-3*) OUP.

***Welfare As We Knew It: A Political History of the American Welfare State.** Charles Noble. LC 97-23704. 240p. 1997. 39.95 (*0-19-511336-5*) OUP.

***Welfare As We Know It: A Family-Level Analysis of AFDC Receipt.** Thomas R. Barton & Vijayan K. Pillai. LC 97-1987. (Studies in Health & Human Services: Vol. 27). 180p. 1997. text ed. 79.95 (*0-7734-8670-4*) E Mellen.

Welfare Aspects of Industrial Markets. Ed. by Alexis P. Jacquemin & H. W. DeJong. (Nijenrode Studies in Economics: No. 2). 1977. lib. bdg. 81.50 (*90-207-0625-X*) Kluwer Ac.

***Welfare Aspects of Transgenic Animals: Proceedings, EC-Workshop of October 30, 1995.** L. F. Van Zutphen et al. LC 97-7996. 1997. write for info. (*3-540-61839-2*) Spr-Verlag.

***Welfare Benefits: Potential to Recover Hundreds of Millions More in Overpayments.** Ed. by Suzanne C. Sterling et al. (Illus.). 54p. (C). 1997. reprint ed. pap. 30.00 (*0-7881-4102-3*) DIANE Pub.

Welfare Benefits Guide, 1990-91. Paul Routh & Ronald Kladder. 1993. pap. 128.00 (*0-685-31929-6*) Clark Boardman Callaghan.

Welfare Bind. Naomi Gottlieb. LC 73-17259. 206p. 1974. text ed. 45.00 (*0-231-03762-7*) Col U Pr.

Welfare Bureaucracies: Their Design & Changes in Response to Social Problems. David Billis. 252p. 1985. 34.95 (*0-435-82059-1*, Pub. by Avebury Pub UK) Ashgate Pub Co.

***Welfare Capitalism in Taiwan.** Ku. LC 96-46499. 1997. text ed. 69.95 (*0-312-17416-0*) St Martin.

Welfare Connection. Suzanne Taylor-Moore. 64p. 1982. pap. 4.95 (*0-938758-14-4*) MTM Pub Co.

Welfare Consequences of Selling Public Enterprise: An Empirical Analysis. Ahmed Galal et al. LC 94-22971. 1994. 6.95 (*0-8213-2976-6*) World Bank.

Welfare Consequences of Selling Public Enterprise: Case Studies from Chile, Malaysia, Mexico & the U. K. Ahmed Galal et al. LC 93-45504. 750p. 1994. 49.95 (*0-19-520995-8*) OUP.

Welfare Debate of Nineteen Seventy-Eight. Gordon L. Weil. LC 78-19555. 134p. 1978. 8.00 (*0-915312-08-5*) Inst Socioecon.

Welfare, Democracy & the New Deal. William R. Brock. 300p. 1988. text ed. 69.95 (*0-521-33379-2*) Cambridge U Pr.

Welfare Dependence & Welfare Policy: A Statistical Study. Vicky N. Albert. LC 88-15495. (Studies in Social Welfare Policies & Programs: No. 8). 211p. 1988. text ed. 55.00 (*0-313-26175-X*, AWD/, Greenwood Pr) Greenwood.

Welfare Economic Theory. John O'Connell. LC 82-1760. 206p. (C). 1982. text ed. 35.00 (*0-86569-087-1*, Auburn Hse); pap. text ed. 15.00 (*0-86569-074-X*, Auburn Hse) Greenwood.

Welfare Economics & Externalities in an Open Ended Universe: A Modern Austrian Perspective. Roy E. Cordato. LC 92-19778. 160p. 1992. lib. bdg. 77.50 (*0-7923-9246-9*, Pub. by Klwr Acad Pubs NE) Kluwer Ac.

Welfare Economics & India. Ed. by Bhaskar Dutta. (India Readings: Themes in Economics Ser.). (Illus.). 264p. 1994. 29.95 (*0-19-563103-X*) OUP.

Welfare Economics & Social Choice Theory. Allan M. Feldman. 240p. (C). 1980. lib. bdg. 52.50 (*0-89838-033-2*) Kluwer Ac.

Welfare Economics & the Theory of Economic Policy. Pieter Hennipman. Ed. by Donald Walker et al. LC 94-40773. 328p. 1995. 80.00 (*1-85898-242-1*) E Elgar.

Welfare Economics of Alternative Renewable Resource Strategies: Forested Wetlands & Agricultural Production. Robert N. Stavins. LC 90-3324. (Environment: Problems & Solutions Ser.: Vol. 7). 240p. 1990. text ed. 20.00 (*0-8240-0440-X*) Garland.

Welfare Economics of International Trade, Vol. 54. Murray C. Kemp & Henry Y. Wan. LC 93-16716. 46p. 1993. pap. text ed. 18.00 (*3-7186-5382-6*) Gordon & Breach.

Welfare Economics of the Liberal Society: A Study in Markets, Voting, & Predation. Daniel Usher. 500p. (C). 1992. text ed. 67.50 (*0-472-10396-2*) U of Mich Pr.

Welfare Economics of the Second Best. Ed. by Dieter Bos & C. Seidl. (Journal of Economics: Suppl. 5). (Illus.). viii, 280p. 1986. 94.95 (*0-387-81942-8*) Spr-Verlag.

Welfare Effects of Value-Added Harmonization in Europe: A Computable General Equilibrium Analysis. Hans Fehr. LC 95-1438. 1995. 89.00 (*3-540-58826-4*) Spr-Verlag.

Welfare for Weapons Dealers: The Hidden Costs of the Arms Trade. William D. Hartung. Ed. by Peter J. Schmuhl. (Papers). 68p. 1996. pap. 10.00 (*0-911646-64-7*) World Policy.

***Welfare Guidelines for the Re-Introduction of Captive Bred Mammals to the Wild.** International Academy of Animal Welfare Sciences Staff. 1992. pap. 30.00 (*0-900767-80-4*, Pub. by Univs Fed Animal Welfare UK) St Mut.

Welfare, Happiness & Ethics. L. W. Sumner. LC 96-8172. 256p. 1996. 35.00 (*0-19-824440-1*) OUP.

Welfare Housing Consultant. Jack Rudman. (Career Examination Ser.: C-3331). 1994. pap. 34.95 (*0-8373-3331-8*) Nat Learn.

Welfare, Ideology & Need: Developing Perspectives on the Welfare State. Martin Hewitt. 256p. (C). 1992. text ed. 59.50 (*0-389-20983-X*) B&N Imports.

Welfare Implications of Female Headship in Jamaican Households. Frederic Louat et al. LC 93-21834. (Living Standards Measurement Study Working Paper Ser.: No. 96). 92p. 1993. 7.95 (*0-8213-2384-9*, 12384) World Bank.

***Welfare in America.** Vaughn D. Bornet. (Illus.). 319p. 1997. 15.00 (*0-9632366-4-4*) Bornet Bks.

***Welfare in America: Christian Perspectives on a Policy in Crisis.** Ed. by James W. Skillen & Stanley W. Carlson-Thies. LC 95-42240. 603p. 1995. pap. 24.00 (*0-8028-4127-9*) Eerdmans.

***Welfare in America: How Social Science Fails the Poor.** William M. Epstein. LC 97-14661. 256p. 1997. 45.00 (*0-299-15590-0*); pap. 19.95 (*0-299-15594-3*) U of Wis Pr.

***Welfare in America: Robin Hood in Reverse.** Ed. by Shenhar Venakhi. LC 97-750. (Illus.). 247p. (C). 1997. lib. bdg. 59.00 (*1-56072-408-0*) Nova Sci Pubs.

***Welfare in Newly-Industrialized Society: The Construction of the Welfare State in Hong Kong.** Raymond Chan. 336p. 1996. text ed. 67.95 (*1-85972-464-7*, Pub. by Avebury Pub UK) Ashgate Pub Co.

Welfare in Rural Areas: The North Carolina-Iowa Income Maintenance Experiment. Ed. by John L. Palmer & Joseph A. Pechman. LC 77-91826. (Studies in Social Economics). 273p. 1978. 34.95 (*0-8157-6896-6*); pap. 14.95 (*0-8157-6895-8*) Brookings.

Welfare Is Not for Women: Toward a Model of Advocacy to Meet the Needs of Women in Poverty. Diana M. Pearce. 17p. 1989. pap. 5.00 (*0-685-29943-0*) Inst Womens Policy Rsch.

Welfare Justice: Restoring Social Equity. Neil Gilbert. LC 94-38146. 1995. 30.00 (*0-300-06202-8*) Yale U Pr.

***Welfare Justice: Restoring Social Equity.** Neil Gilbert. 208p. 1997. pap. 14.00 (*0-300-07060-8*) Yale U Pr.

Welfare, Justice, & Freedom. Scott Gordon. LC 80-14571. 256p. 1980. text ed. 49.50 (*0-231-04976-5*) Col U Pr.

Welfare, Justice, & Freedom. Scott Gordon. LC 80-14571. 256p. 1983. pap. text ed. 17.50 (*0-231-04977-3*) Col U Pr.

Welfare Law. Ed. by Peter Robson. (International Library of Essays in Law & Legal Theory). 550p. (C). 1992. 150.00 (*0-8147-7426-1*) NYU Pr.

Welfare, Law & Citizenship. Hartley Dean. 224p. 1995. pap. 29.00 (*0-13-355264-0*) P-H Gen Ref & Trav.

Welfare Magnets: A New Case for a National Standard. Paul E. Peterson & Mark C. Rom. 178p. 1990. 32.95 (*0-8157-7022-7*); pap. 12.95 (*0-8157-7021-9*) Brookings.

Welfare Management System Coordinator. Jack Rudman. (Career Examination Ser.: C-3024). 1994. pap. 39.95 (*0-8373-3024-6*) Nat Learn.

Welfare Measurement, Sustainability & Green National Accounting: A Growth Theoretical Approach. Thomas Aronsson et al. LC 96-23170. (New Horizons in Environmental Economics Ser.). 192p. 1997. 80.00 (*1-85898-485-8*) E Elgar.

Welfare Medical Care: An Experiment. Charles H. Goodrich et al. LC 77-85075. (Illus.). 361p. 1970. 34.50 (*0-674-94895-5*) HUP.

Welfare Mother. Susan Sheehan. 144p. 1977. pap. 3.95 (*0-451-62682-6*, Ment) NAL-Dutton.

Welfare Mothers Movement: A Decade of Change for Poor Women? Susan H. Hertz. LC 81-40358. (Illus.). 200p. (Orig.). 1981. pap. text ed. 22.50 (*0-8191-1781-1*) U Pr of Amer.

***Welfare Myths: Fact or Fiction? Exploring the Truth about Welfare.** Adele M. Blong et al. (Illus.). 48p. 1996. pap. 8.00 (*0-9653488-0-6*) Ctr Soc Welfare.

Welfare of Children. Duncan Lindsey. (Illus.). 288p. 1994. 32.00 (*0-19-508518-3*) OUP.

Welfare of Pet Marmosets. Captive Care Working Party, Primate Society of Great Britain Staff & UFAW Staff. (C). 1996. pap. 23.00 (*0-900767-42-1*, Pub. by Univs Fed Animal Welfare UK) St Mut.

***Welfare of Pet Parrots.** Dilys J. Roe. 1991. pap. 22.00 (*0-900767-75-8*, Pub. by Univs Fed Animal Welfare UK) St Mut.

Welfare of the Elderly: An Economic Analysis & Policy Prescription. W. Kip Viscusi. LC 78-31223. (Wiley Series in Urban Research). 263p. reprint ed. pap. 75.00 (*0-317-09193-X*, 2055533) Bks Demand.

Welfare or Welfare State? Contradictions & Dilemmas in Social Policy. David Marsland. LC 95-33088. 1996. text ed. 49.95 (*0-312-12920-3*); text ed. 18.95 (*0-312-12921-1*) St Martin.

Welfare Paradox: Income Maintenance & Personal Social Services in Norway & Britain. Ivar Lodemel. 270p. 1996. write for info. (*82-00-21242-4*) Scandnvan Univ Pr.

Welfare Plan Guide: Practical Solutions to Administration & Management. Consul Alexander. 384p. (C). 1996. text ed. 50.00 (*0-7863-0534-7*) Irwin Prof Pubng.

Welfare, Planning, & Employment: Selected Essays in Economic Theory. Abram Bergson. 288p. 1982. 39.50 (*0-262-02175-7*) MIT Pr.

Welfare Policy & Politics in Japan: Beyond the Developmental State. Stephen J. Anderson. 1994. 46.95 (*1-56924-953-9*) Marlowe & Co.

***Welfare Policy in American Politics.** Anne M. Cammisa. (Dilemmas in American Politics Ser.). (C). 1997. text ed. 45.00 (*0-8133-2995-7*); pap. text ed. 15.95 (*0-8133-2996-5*) Westview.

Welfare Politics in Mexico. Peter M. Ward. (London Research Series in Geography: No. 9). (Illus.). 192p. 1986. text ed. 37.85 (*0-04-361058-7*) Routledge Chapman & Hall.

Welfare Programs: Ineffective Federal Oversight Permits Costly Automated System Problems. 52p. (Orig.). (C). 1993. pap. text ed. 25.00 (*1-56806-899-9*) DIANE Pub.

Welfare Realities: From Rhetoric to Reform. Mary J. Bane & David T. Ellwood. LC 93-45029. 238p. 1994. 32.00 (*0-674-94912-9*) HUP.

Welfare Realities: From Rhetoric to Reform. Mary Jo Bane & David T. Ellwood. 240p. 1996. pap. 16.95 (*0-674-94913-7*) HUP.

***Welfare Reform.** Gary Bryner. (C). Date not set. pap. text ed. write for info. (*0-393-97135-X*) Norton.

Welfare Reform. Ed. by Charles Cozic. LC 96-33567. (At Issue Ser.). (J). (gr. 5-12). 1996. pap. 8.96 (*1-56510-545-1*) Greenhaven.

Welfare Reform. Ed. by Charles Cozic. LC 96-33567. (At Issue Ser.). (J). (gr. 5-12). 1996. lib. bdg. 14.96 (*1-56510-546-X*) Greenhaven.

Welfare Reform. Mary E. Hombs. LC 96-47515. (Contemporary World Issues Ser.). 288p. 1996. lib. bdg. 39.50 (*0-87436-844-8*) ABC-CLIO.

Welfare Reform, No. 28. Ed. by Hodis Rhodes. Incl. Vol. II. Income Maintenance Policy: An Analysis of Historical & Legislative Precedents. 145p. 1978. 2.00 (*0-89940-622-X*); Vol. III. Analyses of Contemporary Welfare Reform Issues. 98p. 1978. 3.00 (*0-89940-623-8*); Vol. IV. Family Independence Project: An Alternative Welfare Reform Approach. 130p. 1978. 2.00 (*0-89940-624-6*); (Policy Research Project Report Ser.). 1978. write for info. (*0-89940-503-7*) LBJ Sch Pub Aff.

Welfare Reform: A Response to Unemployed Two-Parent Families. Patrick M. Cunningham. LC 92-32112. (Children of Poverty Ser.). 184p. 1993. text ed. 53.00 (*0-8153-1114-1*) Garland.

***Welfare Reform: Conference Report Text, 1996.** 700p. pap. 29.00 (*0-614-26830-3*, 21496BLS01) Commerce.

Welfare Reform: Consensus or Conflict? Ed. by James S. Denton & Daniel P. Moynihan. (Illus.). 136p. (Orig.). (C). 1988. pap. text ed. 15.00 (*0-8191-6903-X*, Natl Forum Found); lib. bdg. 37.00 (*0-8191-6902-1*, Natl Forum Found) U Pr of Amer.

***Welfare Reform: Helping the Least Fortunate Become Less Dependent.** Richard L. Koon. LC 96-49747. (Children of Poverty Ser.). (Illus.). 231p. 1997. text ed. 51.00 (*0-8153-2799-4*) Garland.

Welfare Reform: State & Federal Roles. Wilbur J. Cohen & W. Joseph Heffernan. (Policy Research Project Report: No. 59). 163p. 1984. pap. 9.95 (*0-89940-661-0*) LBJ Sch Pub Aff.

Welfare Reform: The Politics of Wealth & Poverty. Ed. by Gary E. McCuen. (Ideas in Conflict Ser.). (Illus.). 184p. (YA). (gr. 7-12). 1996. lib. bdg. 12.95 (*0-86596-136-0*) G E M.

***Welfare Reform & Teen Parents.** Bronwyn Mayden & Thomas Brooks. 17p. 1996. pap. 6.95 (*0-87868-657-6*) Child Welfare.

Welfare Reform & the Carter Public Service Employment Program: A Critique. David I. Meiselman. LC 77-95219. 1978. pap. 2.50 (*0-916770-05-2*) Law & Econ U Miami.

Welfare Reform in California. Eugene Smolensky et al. LC 92-43736. 53p. (C). 1992. pap. 3.95 (*0-87772-337-0*) UCB IGS.

Welfare Reformed: A Compassionate Approach. Ed. by David W. Hall. 256p. (Orig.). 1994. pap. 10.99 (*0-87552-301-3*, Pub. by Evangelical Pr) Presby & Reformed.

Welfare Representative. Jack Rudman. (Career Examination Ser.: C-899). 1994. pap. 23.95 (*0-8373-0899-2*) Nat Learn.

Welfare Resources Supervisor. Jack Rudman. (Career Examination Ser.: C-3332). 1994. pap. 29.95 (*0-8373-3332-6*) Nat Learn.

Welfare Society & the Helping Professions. Schenk. pap. 22.95 (*0-87411-086-6*) Copley Pub.

Welfare State: Concept & Development. 2nd ed. David C. Marsh. LC 79-41439. (Aspects of Modern Sociology: the Social Structure of Modern Britain Ser.). 120p. reprint ed. pap. 34.20 (*0-685-20295-X*, 2030329) Bks Demand.

Welfare State: No Mercy for the Middle Class. John McKay. LC 95-76043. 289p. 1995. 22.00 (*0-9645693-0-2*) Liberty Books.

Welfare State: Privatisation, Deregulation, Commercialisation of the Private Sector: Alternative Strategies for the 1990's. Dexter Whitfield. 545p. (C). 77.50 (*0-7453-0608-X*, Pub. by Pluto Pr UK); pap. 27.50 (*0-7453-0080-4*, Pub. by Pluto Pr UK) LPC InBook.

Welfare State: The Selected Essays of Assar Lindbeck, Vol. II. Assar Lindbeck. (Economists of the Twentieth Century Ser.). 328p. 1993. 85.00 (*1-85278-721-X*) E Elgar.

Welfare State America: Safety Net or Social Contract? Michael Kronenwetter. LC 92-35880. (Impact Bks.). 128p. (YA). (gr. 7-12). 1993. lib. bdg. 22.70 (*0-531-13010-X*) Watts.

Welfare State & Beyond: Success & Problems in Scandinavia. Gunnar Heckscher. LC 83-21883. (Nordic Ser.: No. 11). 283p. reprint ed. pap. 80.70 (*0-7837-2948-0*, 2057506) Bks Demand.

Welfare State & Canadian Federalism. rev. ed. Keith G. Banting. 280p. 1987. pap. 22.95 (*0-7735-0631-4*, Pub. by McGill CN) U of Toronto Pr.

Welfare State & Equality: Structural & Ideological Roots of Public Expenditures. Harold L. Wilensky. 1975. pap. 11.00 (*0-520-02908-9*) U CA Pr.

Welfare State & Its Aftermath. S. N. Eisenstadt & Ora Ahimeir. (Illus.). 336p. 1985. 64.50 (*0-389-20529-X*, 08091) B&N Imports.

Welfare State & Woman Power: Essays in State Feminism. Helga M. Hernes. 176p. 1987. 37.50 (*82-00-18495-1*) Scandnvan Univ Pr.

Welfare State As Employer. Ed. by Jon E. Kolberg. LC 90-33125. (Comparative Public Policy Analysis Ser.). 224p. (gr. 13). 1991. text ed. 59.95 (*0-87332-648-2*) M E Sharpe.

Welfare State Crisis & the Transformation of Social Service Work. Michael Fabricant & Steve Burghardt. LC 91-21549. 272p. (gr. 13). 1992. text ed. 59.95 (*0-87332-642-3*); pap. text ed. 25.95 (*0-87332-643-1*) M E Sharpe.

Welfare State in Britain: A Political History Since 1945. Michael Hill. 200p. 1993. 80.00 (*1-85278-436-9*) E Elgar.

Welfare State in Britain: A Political History since 1945. Michael Hill. LC 92-42191. 200p. 1993. pap. 25.00 (*1-85278-437-7*) E Elgar.

Welfare State in Capitalist Society: Policies of Retrenchment & Maintenance in Europe, North America, & Australia. Ramesh Mishra. 208p. 1990. text ed. 60.00 (*0-8020-5895-7*); pap. text ed. 19.95 (*0-8020-6829-4*) U of Toronto Pr.

Welfare State in New Zealand. John B. Condliffe. LC 73-19123. (Illus.). 396p. 1975. reprint ed. text ed. 38.50 (*0-8371-7298-5*, CONZ, Greenwood Pr) Greenwood.

***Welfare State in Transition: Reforming the Swedish Model.** Richard B. Freeman et al. LC 96-50195. 1996. 74.00 (*0-226-26178-6*) U Ch Pr.

Welfare State in Transition: The Theory & Practice of Welfare Pluralism. Norman Johnson. LC 87-20585. 256p. (C). 1987. pap. text ed. 17.95 (*0-87023-618-0*); lib. bdg. 30.00 (*0-87023-617-2*) U of Mass Pr.

Welfare State of Britain & India. N. C. Basuraychaudhuri. (C). 1989. 29.00 (*81-85195-20-X*) S Asia.

Welfare State to Welfare Society: Restructuring New Zealand's Social Services. Angela Barretta-Herman. LC 93-32456. (Children of Poverty Ser.). 376p. 1993. text ed. 68.00 (*0-8153-1545-7*) Garland.

Welfare States & Working Mothers: The Scandinavian Experience. Arnlaug Leira. (Illus.). 192p. (C). 1992. 44.95 (*0-521-41720-1*) Cambridge U Pr.

Welfare States in Hard Times: Problems, Policy & Politics in Denmark & Sweden. rev. ed. Eric Einhorn & John Logue. LC 84-672797. (Illus.). 72p. (C). 1982. pap. 3.95 (*0-933522-12-6*) Kent Popular.

Welfare States in Transition: National Adaptations in Global Economics. Ed. by Gosta Esping-Andersen. 272p. 1996. 79.95 (*0-7619-5047-8*); pap. 26.95 (*0-7619-5048-6*) Sage.

Welfare System: Help or Hindrance to the Poor? Marianne LeVert. LC 94-21815. (Issue & Debate Ser.). (Illus.). 112p. (YA). (gr. 7 up). 1995. lib. bdg. 17.90 (*1-56294-455-X*) Millbrook Pr.

Welfare System Reform: Coordinating Federal, State, & Local Public Assistance Programs. Ed. by Edward T. Jennings, Jr. & Neal S. Zank. LC 92-21361. (Studies in Social Welfare Policies & Programs: No. 16). 264p. 1993. text ed. 57.95 (*0-313-28485-7*, ZHD, Greenwood Pr) Greenwood.

Welfare the Elusive Consensus: Where We Are, How We Got There, & What's Ahead. Lester M. Salamon. LC 78-12163. (Praeger Special Studies). 257p. 1978. text ed. 55.00 (*0-275-90315-X*, C0315, Praeger Pubs) Greenwood.

Welfare Theory & Social Policy: Reform or Revolution? Phil Lee & Colin Raban. 224p. (C). 1988. text ed. 45.00 (*0-8039-8130-9*); pap. text ed. 22.00 (*0-8039-8131-7*) Sage.

***Welfare to Work: Child Care Assistance Limited; Welfare Reform May Expand Needs.** (Illus.). 32p. (Orig.). (C). 1996. pap. 20.00 (*0-7881-3025-0*) DIANE Pub.

Welfare to Work: Current AFDC Program Not Sufficiently Focused on Employment. (Illus.). 41p. (Orig.). (C). 1995. pap. text ed. 25.00 (*0-7881-1766-1*) DIANE Pub.

Welfare to Work: Implementation & Evaluation of Transitional Benefits Need HHS Action. (Illus.). 52p. (Orig.). (C). 1993. pap. text ed. 25.00 (*1-56806-495-0*) DIANE Pub.

Welfare to Work: Measuring Outcomes for Jobs Participants. (Illus.). 43p. (Orig.). (C). 1995. pap. text ed. 25.00 (*0-7881-1815-3*) DIANE Pub.

Welfare to Work: Most A. F. D. C. Training Programs Not Emphasizing Job Placement. (Illus.). 96p. (Orig.). (C). 1995. pap. text ed. 20.00 (*0-7881-2077-8*) DIANE Pub.

***Welfare to Work: State Programs Have Tested Some of the Proposed Reforms.** Stephanie L. Shipman & Daniel G. Rodriguez. (Illus.). 32p. (C). 1997. reprint ed. pap. text ed. 30.00 (*0-7881-4101-5*) DIANE Pub.

Welfare Trends in the Scandinavian Countries. Hannu Uusitalo. LC 91-26045. 432p. (gr. 13). 1993. text ed. 69.95 (*0-87332-844-2*) M E Sharpe.

***Welfare Waivers Implementation: States Work to Change Welfare Culture, Community Involvement, & Service Delivery.** (Illus.). 56p. (Orig.). (C). 1996. pap. 25.00 (*0-7881-3458-2*) DIANE Pub.

Welfare Work in Mill Villages: The Story of Extra-Mill Activities in North Carolina. Harriet L. Herring. LC 74-137170. (Poverty U. S. A. Historical Record Ser.). 1971. reprint ed. 24.95 (*0-405-03108-4*) Ayer.

Welfare Work in Mill Villages: The Story of Extra-Mill Activities in North Carolina. Harriet L. Herring. LC 68-55773. (Criminology, Law Enforcement, & Social Problems Ser.: No. 20). 1968. reprint ed. 24.00 (*0-87585-020-0*) Patterson Smith.

Welfarism in Contract Law. Ed. by Roger Brownsword et al. 360p. 1994. 59.95 (*1-85521-246-3*, Pub. by Dartmth Pub UK) Ashgate Pub Co.

***Well.** Mildred Taylor. (J). 1998. pap. 3.99 (*0-14-038642-4*) Viking Penguin.

Well: David's Story. Mildred D. Taylor. LC 94-25360. (J). (gr. 1-8). 1995. pap. 14.89 (*0-8037-1803-9*) Dial Bks Young.

Well: David's Story. Mildred D. Taylor. LC 94-25360. (J). (gr. 3-7). 1995. pap. 14.99 (*0-8037-1802-0*) Dial Bks Young.

Well - Connected Macintosh. Tony Bove & Cheryl Rhodes. 1987. pap. 11.95 (*0-15-695666-7*, Harvest Bks) HarBrace.

Well Acquainted with Books: The Founding Framers of 1787: With James Madison's List of Books for Congress. Robert A. Rutland. LC 87-2805. 95p. 1987. 6.95 (*0-8444-0561-2*) Lib Congress.

***Well Adjusted Cat: Feline Chiropractic Methods You Can Do.** Daniel Kamen. (Illus.). 166p. 1997. pap. 13.95 (*1-57129-044-3*) Brookline Bks.

***Well Adjusted Dog: Canine Chiropractic Methods You Can Do.** Daniel Kamen & Brookline Books Staff. (Illus.). 166p. (Orig.). 1997. pap. 16.95 (*1-57129-030-3*) Brookline Bks.

Well Advised: A Practical Guide to Everyday Health Decisions. Park Nicollet. 1996. 12.95 (*1-56066-626-9*) Great Performance.

Well Advised: A Practical Guide to Everyday Health Decisions. Park Nicollet. 1996. 12.95 (*1-56066-627-7*) Great Performance.

We'll All Go Home in the Spring: Personal Accounts & Adventures As Told by the Pioneers of the West. Ed. by Robert A. Bennett. LC 83-63182. 382p. 1984. pap. 10.95 (*0-936546-08-5*) Pioneer Pr Bks.

We'll All Wear Silk Hats: The Erie & Chiricahua Cattle Companies & the Rise of Corporate Ranching in the Sulphur Spring Valley of Arizona, 1883-1909. Lynn R. Bailey. (Great West & Indian Ser.: 61). (Illus.). 1994. 26.95 (*0-87026-088-X*) Westernlore.

Well, Almost Everything You Always Wanted to Know about Iodo-Shimshu: But Were Afraid to Ask. 96p. 1987. reprint ed. pap. 3.95 (*0-912624-09-4*) Nembutsu Pr.

Well, Almost...But Not Quite. Henry P. Hosey, 2nd. 30p. (J). Date not set. text ed. write for info. (*0-9648216-1-3*) Brown Basket Pubns.

"We'll Always Have Paris" The Definitive Guide to Great Lines from the Movies. Robert A. Nowlan & Gwendolyn W. Nowlan. LC 95-25203. 704p. 1995. pap. 21.00 (*0-06-272506-8*, PL) HarpC.

Well & Good: Case Studies in Bio-Medical Ethics. 2nd rev. ed. John E. Thomas & Wilfrid J. Waluchow. 240p. 1990. pap. text ed. 16.95 (*0-921149-64-6*) Broadview Pr.

Well & the Cathedral. 5th ed. Ira Progoff. LC 76-20823. (Entrance Meditation Ser.). 166p. 1983. pap. 9.95 (*0-87941-005-1*) Dialogue Hse.

Well & the Tree: World & Time in Early Germanic Culture. Paul C. Bauschatz. LC 81-14766. (Illus.). 280p. 1982. reprint ed. pap. 59.30 (*0-7837-9206-9*, 2049956) Bks Demand.

Well & Truly. Evelyn W. Mayerson. 400p. 1991. pap. 5.50 (*0-451-16988-3*, Sig) NAL-Dutton.

***Well at the World's End.** Neil Gunn. 294p. 1997. pap. 12.95 (*0-86241-645-0*, Pub. by Canongate Bks UK) Interlink Pub.

Well at the World's End. William Morris. (Pocket Classics Ser.). 592p. 1996. pap. 13.95 (*0-7509-1207-3*, Pub. by Sutton Pubng UK) Bks Intl VA.

Well Baby Book: A Comprehensive Manual of Baby Care, from Conception to Age Four. enl. rev. ed. Mike Samuels & Nancy H. Samuels. (Illus.). 402p. 1991. pap. 18.00 (*0-671-73412-1*) Summit Bks.

***Well Balanced Meal: The Very Best of Four Food Groups of the Apocalypse.** David J. Kellett. (Illus.). 80p. (Orig.). (C). 1996. pap. 8.95 (*0-9655060-0-2*) Small Fish.

Well-Being: Its Meaning, Measurement & Moral Importance. James Griffin. 424p. 1989. reprint ed. pap. 28.00 (*0-19-824843-1*) OUP.

Well-Being Journal: Drawing on Your Inner Power to Heal Yourself. Lucia Capacchione. 192p. (Orig.). (C). 1989. lib. bdg. 45.00 (*0-8095-6141-7*) Borgo Pr.

Well-Being Journal: Drawing on Your Inner Power to Heal Yourself. Lucia Capacchione. 168p. (Orig.). 1989. pap. 12.95 (*0-87877-141-7*, 641) Newcastle Pub.

Well-Being of Animals in Zoo & Aquarium Sponsored Research. Ed. by J. Bielitzki et al. 1996. 50.00 (*0-614-06552-6*) Scientists Ctr.

Well-Being of Children & Youth in Pennsylvania: Demographic Trends. Pennsylvania State Data Center Staff. 14p. (Orig.). 1993. pap. 10.00 (*0-939667-26-6*) Penn State Data Ctr.

Well-Being of Organizations. Ed. by C. West Churchman. (Systems Inquiry Ser.). 380p. 1987. pap. text ed. 15.95 (*0-914105-39-6*) Intersystems Pubns.

Well-Beloved. Thomas Hardy. (World's Classics Ser.). (Illus.). 366p. 1987. pap. 6.95 (*0-19-281721-3*) OUP.

Well, Bless Your Heart: High Fiber, Low Fat, Low Cholesterol Recipes, 2 vols., Set. Patricia B. Mitchell. Incl. Vol. 1 Breakfasts & Lunches. (Illus.). 37p. 1989. pap. 4.00 (*0-925117-13-7*); Vol. 2 Dinners & Desserts. 38p. 1992. pap. 4.00 (*0-925117-56-0*); 1992. Set pap. 8.00 (*0-925117-64-1*) Mitchells.

Well-Bred Muse. Keith Garebian. (Illus.). 178p. 1995. lib. bdg. 39.00 (*0-8095-4920-4*) Borgo Pr.

Well-Bred Muse: Selected Theatre Writings 1978-1988. Keith Garebian. (Illus.). 178p. pap. 14.95 (*0-88962-460-7*) Mosaic.

We'll Bring the World His Truth: Missionary Adventures from Around the World. Dean Hughes & Tom Hughes. LC 94-8988. (Illus.). vi, 115p. (YA). (gr. 4-12). 1995. 12.95 (*1-57345-090-1*) Deseret Bk.

***We'll Build a Museum!** unabridged ed. Marvin Beloff. Ed. by Jim Smith & Jackie Smith. 1994. pap. 25.00 (*0-9656290-0-7*) Marvs Mike.

Well-Built Elephant & Other Roadside Attractions: A Tribute to American Eccentricity. J. J. Andrews. LC 83-11107. (Illus.). 146p. 1983. pap. 16.95 (*0-685-07029-8*) St Martin.

Well-Built House. rev. ed. Jim Locke. 320p. 1992. pap. 12.95 (*0-395-62951-9*, R Todd) HM.

***Well Built Mycenae Fasc. 21: Mycenaean Pictorial Pottery.** Joost Crouwel. Ed. by E. French & K. Wardle. (Illus.). 1991. pap. 15.00 (*0-946897-18-2*, Pub. by Oxbow Bks UK) David Brown.

***Well Built Mycenae Fasc. 27: Ground Stone.** D. Evely & Curtis Runnels. Ed. by E. French & K. Wardle. (Illus.). 44p. 1992. pap. 15.00 (*0-946897-35-2*, Pub. by Oxbow Bks UK) David Brown.

***Well Built Mycenae Fasc. 36: The Hellenistic Dye-Works.** L. C. Bowkett. (Illus.). 55p. 1995. 22.00 (*0-946897-84-0*, Pub. by Oxbow Bks UK) David Brown.

Well Cast Lines. John Merwin. 1995. pap. 10.00 (*0-684-81151-0*, Fireside) S&S Trade.

Well Cat Book: The Classic Comprehensive Handbook of Cat Care. Terri McGinnis. LC 95-25789. (Illus.). 336p. 1996. pap. 15.00 (*0-679-77000-3*) Random.

Well Cat Book: The Classic Comprehensive Handbook of Cat Care. rev. ed. Terri McGinnis. LC 92-56834. 292p. 1993. 23.00 (*0-394-58769-3*) Random.

Well Cementing. Cinda Cyrus. Ed. by Jeanette R. Paxson. (Oil & Gas Production Ser.). (Illus.). 82p. (Orig.). (C). 1983. pap. text ed. 15.00 (*0-88698-112-3*, 3.30610) PETEX.

Well Cementing. Ed. by E. B. Nelson. (Developments in Petroleum Science Ser.: No. 28). 496p. 1990. 226.75 (*0-444-88751-2*) Elsevier.

Well-Clad Windowsills: Houseplants for Four Exposures. Tovah Martin. LC 93-39565. 1994. 27.50 (*0-671-85015-6*, Hortcultre Bks) Macmillan Gen Ref.

Well Cleanout & Repair Methods. Frwd. by W. E. Boyd. (Well Servicing & Workover Ser.: Lesson 8). (Illus.). 32p. (Orig.). 1971. pap. text ed. 12.00 (*0-88698-064-X*, 3.70810) PETEX.

Well Completion Methods. (Well Servicing & Workover Ser.: Lesson 4). (Illus.). 49p. (Orig.). 1971. pap. text ed. 12.00 (*0-88698-060-7*, 3.70410) PETEX.

Well Completions. rev. ed. (SPE Reprint Ser.). 344p. 1970. 10.20 (*0-317-32941-3*, 30505) Soc Petrol Engineers.

Well Connected Architecture. Ian Ritchie. (Academy Educational Ser.). (Illus.). 144p. (Orig.). 1994. pap. 30.00 (*1-85490-292-X*) Academy Ed UK.

Well Connected Architecture. Ian Ritchie. (Academy Educational Ser.). (Illus.). 144p. 1994. 45.00 (*1-85490-294-6*) Academy Ed UK.

Well Connected Office. Mark E. Laubach. 250p. 1993. pap. 35.00 (*0-13-950965-8*) P-H.

Well Construction Engineering. William C. Lyons et al. 250p. 1993. boxed 64.00 (*0-13-953423-7*) P-H.

Well Control for Completion & Workover. Well Control School Staff. (Illus.). 416p. 1992. boxed 40.00 (*0-88698-155-7*, 2.80210) PETEX.

Well Design: Drilling & Production. Benjamin C. Craft et al. 1962. text ed. 72.00 (*0-13-950022-7*) P-H.

Well-Designed Interface: Crafting the Best UI for Your Window-Based Applications. Tandy Trower. (Code Ser.). 250p. Date not set. pap. 24.95 (*1-57231-332-3*) Microsoft.

Well Dog Book: The Classic, Comprehensive Handbook of Dog Care. Terri McGinnis. LC 91-52680. (Illus.). 272p. 1992. 23.00 (*0-394-58768-5*) Random.

Well Dog Book: The Classic, Comprehensive Handbook of Dog Care. Terri McGinnis. (Illus.). 288p. 1996. pap. 15.00 (*0-679-77001-1*) Random.

Well-Done Roasts: Witty Insults, Quips, & Wisecracks Perfect for Every Imaginable Occasion. Andrew Frothingham & William R. Evans, III. 176p. 1992. 13.95 (*0-312-08334-3*, Thomas Dunne Bks) St Martin.

Well Dressed Potato. Christie Katona & Thomas Katona. (Illus.). 160p. (Orig.). 1993. pap. 8.95 (*1-55867-092-0*, Nitty Gritty Ckbks) Bristol Pub Ent CA.

Well Drilling Manual. 72p. 8.75 (*1-56034-051-7*, T047) Natl Grnd Water.

Well Drilling Manual. Scientific Publishers Staff. (Illus.). (C). 1986. 125.00 (*81-85046-25-5*, Pub. by Scientific UK) St Mut.

Well Drilling Operations. 249p. 1965. 8.75 (*1-56034-052-5*, T048) Natl Grnd Water.

Well Drilling Operations. 1995. lib. bdg. 260.95 (*0-8490-6613-1*) Gordon Pr.

Well-Enchanting Skill: Music, Poetry, & Drama in the Culture of the Renaissance (Essays in Honour of F. W. Sternfeld) Ed. by John Caldwell et al. (Illus.). 288p. 1990. 80.00 (*0-19-316124-9*) OUP.

Well-Executed Failure: The Sullivan Campaign Against the Iroquois, July-September 1779. Joseph R. Fischer. LC 96-25192. (Illus.). 230p. 1997. 29.95 (*1-57003-137-1*) U of SC Pr.

Well-Fed Baby. O. Robin Sweet & Thomas A. Bloom. LC 94-1551. 1994. pap. 12.00 (*0-02-045370-1*) Macmillan.

Well-Fed Backpacker. June Fleming. 1986. pap. 10.00 (*0-394-73804-7*, Vin) Random.

Well-Filled Microwave Cookbook. Victoria Wise & Susanna Hoffman. LC 95-32830. 448p. 1996. pap. 14.95 (*1-56305-177-X*, 3177) Workman Pub.

Well-Filled Tortilla Cookbook. Victoria Wise & Susanna Hoffman. LC 89-40730. 256p. 1990. pap. 9.95 (*0-89480-364-6*, 1364) Workman Pub.

We'll Find the Way: History of Hondo Army Air Field. Robert D. Thompson. (Illus.). 205p. (C). 1992. 22.95 (*0-89015-871-1*) Sunbelt Media.

Well-Functioning Families for Adoptive & Foster Children: A Handbook for Child Welfare Workers. Joyce S. Cohen & Anne Westhues. 176p. 1990. pap. 18.95 (*0-8020-6754-9*) U of Toronto Pr.

Well Governed Son. Charles DeGravelles. Ed. by Maxine Cassin. LC 87-62144. (Journal Press Bks.: Louisiana Legacy). (Illus.). 80p. (Orig.). 1987. pap. text ed. 12.00 (*0-938498-07-X*) New Orleans Poetry.

We'll Have Fun. O'Hara. 1996. 1.99 (*0-679-77100-X*, Modern Lib) Random.

Well-Heeled Murders. Cherry Hartman. 224p. 1996. pap. 10.95 (*1-883523-10-9*) Spinsters Ink.

Well, I Never! Heather Eyles. (Illus.). 32p. (J). (ps-3). 1990. 11.95 (*0-87951-383-7*) Overlook Pr.

Well, I Never! Susan Pearson. LC 89-48016. (Illus.). 40p. (J). (ps-1). 1990. pap. 15.00 (*0-671-69199-6*, S&S Bks Young Read) S&S Childrens.

Well in Dialogue Games: A Discourse Analysis of the Interjection "Well" in Idealized Conversation. Lauri Carlson. LC 85-4029. (Pragmatics & Beyond Ser.: Vol. V-5). ix, 104p. (Orig.). 1985. pap. 38.00 (*0-915027-27-5*) Benjamins North Am.

Well-Intentioned Dragons: Ministering to Problem People in the Church. Marshall Shelley. 160p. 1994. pap. 8.99 (*1-55661-515-9*) Bethany Hse.

W

An Asterisk (*) at the beginning of an entry indicates that the title is appearing in BIP for the first time.

Well It's Not My Fault! About the San Andreas Fault & Other Things. John Lenihan. LC 87-28103. (Illus.). 223p. (gr. 12 up). 1988. pap. 7.95 (*0-944838-00-6*) Med Physics Pub.

Well, I've Never Met a Native: Stories of the Coastal People of Alabama. Joy C. Buskens. LC 86-90380. (Illus.). 330p. 1986. 19.95 (*0-9616351-1-8*); pap. 14.95 (*0-9616351-0-X*) J C Buskens.

*__Well-Known Formulas & Modified Applications.__ Ed. by Ping Chen & Lin Chinian. LC 96-78114. (Advanced Traditional Chinese Medicine Ser.: Vol. 5). 250p. (YA). (gr. 12 up). Date not set. 83.00 (*90-5199-302-1*, 302-1) IOS Press.

Well-Known Movie Themes Piano Solo. 9.95 (*0-7935-4806-3*, 00294021) H Leonard.

Well Known Piano Solos. Charles W. Wilkinson. 1976. lib. bdg. 29.00 (*0-403-03767-0*) Scholarly.

Well Known Piano Solos. Charles Wilkinson. 1988. reprint ed. lib. bdg. 59.00 (*0-317-90878-2*) Rprt Serv.

Well Known Violincello Solos. E. Vander Straeton. 1976. lib. bdg. 49.00 (*0-403-03804-9*) Scholarly.

Well Known Violincello Solos. Edmund S. Van der Straeten. 1988. reprint ed. lib. bdg. 59.00 (*0-7812-0461-5*) Rprt Serv.

Well-Known Violoncello Solos. Edmund S. Van der Straeten. 161p. 1991. reprint ed. 69.00 (*0-7812-9303-0*) Rprt Serv.

*__Well Log Formation Evaluation.__ Richard H. Merkel. (AAPG Continuing Education Course Note Ser.: Vol. 14). 92p. 1979. reprint ed. pap. 26.30 (*0-608-02773-1*, 2063839) Bks Demand.

Well Logging: Fundamentals of Methods. Yury I. Gorbachev. LC 94-30635. 324p. 1995. text ed. 150.00 (*0-471-95368-7*) Wiley.

Well Logging for Earth Scientists. D. V. Ellis. 450p. 1987. 100.00 (*0-444-01180-3*) P-H.

Well Logging for the Nontechnical Person. David E. Johnson & Kathryne E. Pile. 228p. 1988. 69.95 (*0-87814-329-7*) PennWell Bks.

Well Logging in Hydrogeology. Dominique Chapellier. (Illus.). (C). 1992. text ed. 75.00 (*90-5410-207-1*, Pub. by A A Balkema NE) Ashgate Pub Co.

Well Logging Methods: Well Servicing & Workover, Lesson 3. 2nd ed. Ed. by Ron Baker. (Illus.). 54p. (Orig.). 1992. pap. text ed. 15.00 (*0-88698-151-4*, 3-70320) PETEX.

Well Logging, No. I: Rock Properties. J. R. Jorden et al. 175p. 1985. 55.00 (*0-89520-323-5*, 30409) Soc Petrol Engineers.

Well Logging, No. 2: Electric & Acoustic Logging. J. R. Jorden et al. 192p. 1986. 61.00 (*1-55563-002-2*, 30410) Soc Petrol Engineers.

Well-Loved Tales from Shakespeare. Bernard Miles. LC 85-63829. (Illus.). 128p. (J). (gr. 2 up). 1986. 12.95 (*0-528-82758-8*) Checkerboard.

Well Made in America: Lessons from Harley-Davidson on Being the Best. Peter C. Reid. 1991. pap. text ed. 14.95 (*0-07-051801-7*) McGraw.

Well-Managed Classroom: Promoting Student Success Through Social Skill Instruction. Theresa Connolly et al. 160p. 1995. pap. text ed. 24.95 (*0-938510-61-4*, 48-005) Boys Town Pr.

Well-Managed Health Care Organization. 3rd ed. John R. Griffith. LC 95-18402. 779p. 1995. 58.00 (*1-56793-034-4*, 0966) Health Admin Pr.

Well-Mannered Assassin. Aline, Countess of Romanones Staff. 368p. (Orig.). 1995. pap. text ed. 5.99 (*0-515-11533-9*) Jove Pubns.

Well-Mannered Assassin. large type ed. Aline. LC 94-20267. 584p. 1994. lib. bdg. 24.95 (*0-8161-7447-4*, GK Hall) Thorndike Pr.

Well-Mannered Balloon. Nancy Willard. Ed. by Diane D'Andrade. LC 76-29158. (Illus.). 32p. (J). (ps-3). 1991. pap. 4.00 (*0-15-294986-0*, HB Juv Bks) HarBrace.

*__Well-Mannered War.__ Gareth Roberts. 256p. (Orig.). 1997. mass mkt. 5.95 (*0-426-20506-5*, Pub. by Virgin Pub UK) London Brdge.

We'll Meet Again. Forman. Date not set. 15.95 (*0-689-80536-5*) S&S Childrens.

We'll Meet Again. Forman. (J). 1995. 15.95 (*0-684-19737-5*, Atheneum Bks Young) S&S Childrens.

We'll Meet Again. large type ed. Philippa Carr. LC 93-8425. 1993. lib. bdg. 22.95 (*1-56054-795-2*) Thorndike Pr.

*__We'll Never Forget You, Roberto Clemente.__ Trudie Engel. (J). 1997. pap. text ed. 3.99 (*0-590-68881-2*) Scholastic Inc.

Well, No One's Ever Complained Before... Judith Stewart. 96p. 1910. pap. 9.95 (*1-85230-082-5*) Element MA.

Well Now: A Manager's Guide to Worksite Health Promotion. James M. Eddy & Harold S. Kahler, Jr. 64p. 1992. pap. 10.00 (*0-9628334-1-X*) WELCOA.

*__Well of Creativity.__ Jean Houston et al. Ed. by Michael Toms. LC 97-11927. 250p. (Orig.). 1997. pap. 12.95 (*1-56170-375-3*, 894) Hay House.

Well of Days. Gleb Struve. 351p. 1976. reprint ed. 45.00 (*0-86527-326-X*) Fertig.

Well of Loneliness. Radclyffe Hall. 440p. 1996. pap. 10.95 (*0-385-41609-1*, Anchor NY) Doubleday.

Well of Loneliness. Radclyffe Hall. 1992. reprint ed. lib. bdg. 31.95 (*0-89966-948-4*) Buccaneer Bks.

Well of Remembrance: Rediscovering the Earth Wisdom Myths of Northern Europe. Ralph Metzner. 375p. 1994. pap. 16.00 (*1-57062-028-8*) Shambhala Pubns.

Well of Remembrance: Rediscovering the Earth Wisdom Myths of Northern Europe. Ralph Metzner. 1995. 24.75 (*0-8446-6826-5*) Peter Smith.

Well of Saint Clare. Anatole France. Tr. by Alfred Allinson. LC 70-121549. (Short Story Index Reprint Ser.). 1977. 21.95 (*0-8369-3505-5*) Ayer.

Well of Shiuan, Bk. 2. C. J. Cherryh. 256p. (Orig.). 1978. pap. 4.50 (*0-88677-322-9*) DAW Bks.

Well of the Saints. John Millington Synge. LC 82-4367. (Irish Dramatic Texts Ser.). 90p. 1982. reprint ed. pap. 25.70 (*0-7837-9123-2*, 2049924) Bks Demand.

Well of the Saints see Complete Plays of John M. Synge

Well of the Unicorn. Pratt Fletcher. 1981. mass mkt. 5.99 (*0-345-29729-6*) Ballantine.

Well of Understanding. Johonet H. Carpenter. LC 82-61176. (Illus.). 136p. 1982. 15.95 (*0-9609378-0-3*) Sophia Pr.

*__Well Ordered Life: Five Novellas.__ Lawrence Kinsman. LC 97-72926. 256p. 1997. 23.00 (*0-9648817-1-3*) Abelard Pr.

Well-Painted Passion. large type ed. Cynthia Harrod-Eagles. (Dales Large Print Ser.). 254p. 1995. pap. 17.99 (*1-85389-448-6*, Dales) Ulverscroft.

Well Performance. Michael Golan & Curtis H. Whitson. LC 85-10869. (Illus.). 1987. text ed. 65.00 (*0-934634-75-0*, TN870.G63) Intl Human Res.

Well-Placed Weed: The Bountiful Gardens of Ryan Gainey. Ryan Gainey. LC 93-10416. 176p. 1993. 29.95 (*0-87833-837-3*) Taylor Pub.

*__Well-Planned Garden: A Practical Guide to Planning & Planting.__ Rupert Golby. 1997. pap. text ed. 16.95 (*0-8069-4267-3*) Sterling.

Well-Planned Garden & Planting: A Practical Guide to Planning & Planting. Rupert Golby. LC 95-32220. (Wayside Gardens Collection). 128p. 1996. 19.95 (*0-8069-4266-5*) Sterling.

*__Well Pleasured Lady.__ Christina Dodd. 384p. (Orig.). 1997. mass mkt. 5.99 (*0-380-79089-0*) Avon.

Well-Posed Optimization Problems. Asen Dontchev & Tullio Zolezzi. LC 93-15612. (Lecture Notes in Mathematics Ser.: Vol. 1543). 1993. 79.95 (*0-387-56737-2*) Spr-Verlag.

Well-Posedness of Parabolic Difference Operations. A. Ashyralyev & P. E. Sobolevskii. Tr. by A. Iacob. LC 94-4711. (Operator Theory, Advances & Applications Ser.). 1994. 163.00 (*0-8176-5024-5*) Birkhauser.

Well-Prepared Pianist. Contrib. by N. Jane Tan's. Date not set. 5.95 (*0-614-12707-6*) Willis Music Co.

Well Preserved. Malvina Kinard. (Illus.). 160p. (Orig.). 1994. pap. 10.95 (*0-87983-573-7*) Keats.

*__Well-Protected Domains.__ Deringil. Date not set. text ed. write for info. (*1-86064-307-8*, Pub. by I B Tauris UK) St Martin.

We'll Race You, Henry: A Story about Henry Ford. Barbara Mitchell. (Creative Minds Ser.). (Illus.). 64p. (J). (gr. 3-6). 1986. lib. bdg. 14.21 (*0-87614-291-9*, Carolrhoda) Lerner Group.

We'll Race You, Henry: A Story about Henry Ford. Barbara Mitchell. (Creative Minds Bks.). (Illus.). (J). (gr. 3-6). 1987. reprint ed. pap. 5.95 (*0-87614-471-7*, First Ave Edns) Lerner Group.

Well Regulated Militia: The Battle over Gun Control. William Weir. LC 96-16147. xvi, 309p. 1997. lib. bdg. 35.00 (*0-208-02423-9*, Archon Bks) Shoe String.

We'll Ride Elephants Through Brooklyn. Susan L. Roth. (J). (ps up). 1989. 13.95 (*0-374-38258-1*) FS&G.

*__Well Rounded: Eight Simple Steps for Changing Your Life. ..Not Your Size.__ Catherine Lippincott. 240p. 1997. 22.00 (*0-671-54508-6*) PB.

Well Said: Advanced English Pronunciation. Linda Grant. LC 92-40903. 1993. pap. 26.95 (*0-8384-3963-2*) Heinle & Heinle.

Well Said: Advanced English Pronunciation. Linda Grant. LC 92-40903. 1993. teacher ed., pap. 9.95 (*0-8384-4132-7*); student ed. 58.95 incl. audio (*0-8384-4131-9*) Heinle & Heinle.

Well Said: Advanced English Pronunciation. Linda Grant. LC 92-40903. 1993. audio 29.95 (*0-8384-4250-1*); cd-rom 28.95 (*0-8384-5094-6*); audio compact disk 29.95 (*0-8384-4249-8*) Heinle & Heinle.

Well-Schooled in Murder. Elizabeth George. 448p. 1991. 6.50 (*0-553-28734-6*) Bantam.

Well Seasoned. 448p. 1982. spiral bd. 14.95 (*0-939114-42-9*) Starr-Toof.

Well-Seasoned Appetite. Molly O'Neill. LC 94-43961. 464p. 1995. pap. 25.95 (*0-670-85574-X*, Viking) Viking Penguin.

Well Seasoned Appetite. Molly O'Neill. 1997. pap. 15.95 (*0-14-023782-8*) Viking Penguin.

Well-Seasoned Wok. Martin Yan. LC 92-10614. (Illus.). 192p. (Orig.). 1993. pap. 15.95 (*0-9627345-5-1*) Harlow & Ratner.

Well Service & Workover Profitability. 2nd ed. Ed. by Mildred Gerding. (Well Servicing & Workover Ser.: Lesson 12). (Illus.). 32p. 1980. pap. text ed. 12.00 (*0-88698-068-2*, 3.71220) PETEX.

Well Servicing & Repair. (Well Servicing & Workover Ser.: Lesson 7). (Illus.). 61p. (Orig.). 1971. pap. text ed. 12.00 (*0-88698-063-1*, 3.70710) PETEX.

Well-Set Table. Ryan Gainey & Frances Schultz. (Illus.). 168p. 1996. 30.00 (*0-87833-945-0*) Taylor Pub.

*__Well Spoken.__ Ramsey. Date not set. pap. text ed. write for info. (*0-582-02090-5*, Pub. by Longman UK) Longman.

Well Spoken: Oral Communication Skills for Business. Kenneth R. Mayer. 246p. (C). 1989. pap. text ed. 19.00 (*0-15-595154-8*) Dryden Pr.

Well-Spring of Morality. J. D. Thomas. LC 87-70804. 120p. 1987. 12.95 (*0-89112-028-9*); pap. 7.95 (*0-89112-029-7*) Abilene Christ U.

We'll Stand by the Union: Robert Gould Shaw & the Black 54th Massachusetts Regiment. Peter Burchard. Ed. by John A. Scott. LC 92-37132. (Makers of America Ser.). (Illus.). 144p. (J). (gr. 6-9). 1993. 17.95 (*0-8160-2609-2*) Facts on File.

Well Stimulation Treatments. Frwd. by W. E. Boyd. (Well Servicing & Workover Ser.: Lesson 11). (Illus.). 44p. (Orig.). 1971. pap. text ed. 12.00 (*0-88698-067-4*, 3.71110) PETEX.

Well-Tempered Accompanist: Music Book Index. Coenraad V. Bos. 162p. 1993. reprint ed. lib. bdg. 69.00 (*0-7812-9658-7*) Rprt Serv.

Well-Tempered Announcer: A Pronunciation Guide to Classical Music. Robert A. Fradkin. LC 95-360. 256p. 1996. pap. 24.95 (*0-253-21064-X*) Ind U Pr.

Well Tempered Clavier: A Handbook for Keyboard Teachers & Performers. Laurette Goldber. LC 95-78709. (Illus.). 120p. (Orig.). 1995. pap. 28.00 (*0-9648179-0-X*) MusicSources CHIP.

Well-Tempered Clavier: Books I & II Complete. Johann Sebastian Bach. (Music Ser.). 208p. (Orig.). 1984. pap. 8.95 (*0-486-24532-2*) Dover.

Well-Tempered Critic. Northrop Frye. LC 63-9716. 160p. reprint ed. pap. 45.60 (*0-7837-1504-8*, 2057286) Bks Demand.

Well Tempered Digital Design. R. B. Seidensticker. LC 85-1376. (C). 1986. pap. text ed. 46.25 (*0-201-06747-1*) Addison-Wesley.

*__Well-Tempered Garden.__ Christopher Lloyd. (Horticulture Garden Classics Ser.). 1997. pap. 16.95 (*1-55821-593-X*, 1593X) Lyons & Burford.

Well-Tempered Keyboard Teacher. Marienne Uszler et al. 446p. (C). 1990. 38.00 (*0-02-871780-5*) Schirmer Bks.

*__Well Tempered Keyboard Teacher.__ 2nd ed. Uszler & Gordon. 1998. 27.00 (*0-02-864788-2*) S&S Trade.

Well-Tempered Object: Musical Applications of Object Oriented Software Technology. Ed. by Stephen T. Pope. (Illus.). 200p. 1991. 31.50 (*0-262-16126-5*) MIT Pr.

Well-Tempered Self: Formations of the Cultural Subject. Toby Miller. LC 93-13102. (C). 1994. text ed. 45.00 (*0-8018-4603-X*); pap. text ed. 15.95 (*0-8018-4604-8*) Johns Hopkins.

Well-Tempered Violin. Michael McLean. 52p. 1992. pap. text ed. 8.95 (*0-87487-434-3*) Summy-Birchard.

Well Test Analysis for Fractured Reservoir Evaluation. Ed. by G. Da Prat. (Developments in Petroleum Science Ser.: No. 27). 240p. 1990. 145.00 (*0-444-88691-5*) Elsevier.

Well Testing. John Lee. 150p. 1982. 40.00 (*0-89520-317-0*) Soc Petrol Engineers.

Well Testing in Heterogeneous Formations. Tatian D. Streltsova. LC 87-21669. (Exxon Monographs). 413p. 1988. text ed. 165.00 (*0-471-63169-8*) Wiley.

*__Well Timed Enchantment.__ Vandevelde. LC 97-17352. 1998. pap. write for info. (*0-15-201765-8*) HarBrace.

We'll to the Woods No More. Edouard Dujardin. Tr. by Stuart Gilbert from FRE. LC 89-13019. (Illus.). 176p. 1990. pap. 9.95 (*0-8112-1113-4*, NDP682) New Directions.

Well-Trained Computer: Designing Systematic Instructional Materials for the Classroom Microcomputer. Mynga K. Futrell & Paul Geisert. LC 84-1629. (Illus.). 290p. 1984. 39.95 (*0-87778-190-7*) Educ Tech Pubns.

*__Well Trained Dog.__ Contrib. by Herbert Axelrod. (Cats & Dogs). (Illus.). (YA). (gr. 3 up). 1998. lib. bdg. 19.95 (*0-7910-4812-8*) Chelsea Hse.

Well Trained Llama: A Trainers Guide. rev. ed. Betty Barkman & Paul Barkman. LC 88-93027. (Illus.). 95p. (Orig.). (YA). (gr. 9 up). 1989. pap. text ed. 25.00 (*0-945860-01-3*) Birch Bark Pr.

Well-Trained Tongue: Formation in the Ministry of Reader. Aelred R. Rosser. LC 96-8689. 120p. 1996. 9.00 (*1-56854-124-4*) Liturgy Tr Pubns.

Well-Tun'd Word: Musical Interpretations of English Poetry, 1597-1651. Elise B. Jorgens. LC 81-13090. 318p. reprint ed. pap. 90.70 (*0-7837-2942-1*, 2057512) Bks Demand.

Well-Tuned Harp. Geraldine C. Little. LC 87-28838. (Illus.). 72p. (Orig.). 1988. pap. 7.00 (*0-938158-09-0*) Saturday Pr.

We'll Understand It Better by & By: Pioneering African American Gospel Composers. Ed. by Bernice J. Reagon. LC 91-37954. (Illus.). 432p. 1992. pap. text ed. 24.95 (*1-56098-167-9*) Smithsonian.

*__Well Versed Anthology.__ Ed. by Lily Gebhart. 112p. (Orig.). 1996. pap. 6.95 (*0-9645010-2-3*, Well Versed Pub) Prem Raja Baba.

Well-Versed Cat: Poems of Celebration. LC 93-83459. (Miniature Editions Ser.). (Illus.). 128p. 1993. 4.95 (*1-56138-311-2*) Running Pr.

Well Versed in Business: Straight Talk Can You Relate? Greg LaConte. (Illus.). 128p. 1994. pap. 10.00 (*0-9642872-0-X*) LaConte & Assocs.

Well Watered Garden. Harriet Crosby. 1995. pap. 14.99 (*0-7852-8318-8*) Nelson.

Well Watered Garden Gift Pack. Howard Crosby. 1995. pap. text ed. 16.98 (*0-7852-6969-X*) Nelson.

*__Well Wealth Reality.__ Keith Waldrop & Rosmarie Waldrop. LC 97-17843. 80p. 1997. pap. 14.00 (*0-942996-30-5*) Post Apollo Pr.

Well Wished. Billingsley. LC 96-24511. (J). 1997. 16.00 (*0-689-81210-8*) S&S Childrens.

Well-Wishers. Edward Eager. (Illus.). 240p. (J). (gr. 3-7). 1990. pap. 5.00 (*0-15-294994-1*, Odyssey) HarBrace.

Well-Woman. Margery Morgan. 128p. (Orig.). 1993. pap. 9.95 (*0-563-36307-X*, BBC-Parkwest) Parkwest Pubns.

Well-Woman Cookbook. Patricia Panahi. (Illus.). 175p. (Orig.). 1996. pap. 14.95 (*1-56072-343-2*) Nova Sci Pubs.

*__Well Women: Healing the Female Body Through Traditional Chinese Medicine.__ Marie E. Cargill. 1998. pap. text ed. write for info. (*0-89789-543-6*, Bergin & Garvey) Greenwood.

Well Worn Path. Jay H. Cravens. LC 93-94302. 512p. (Orig.). 1995. pap. 14.95 (*1-56002-418-6*, Univ Edtns) Aegina Pr.

Well Worth the Wait. Gloria Copeland. 15p. 1995. pap. 1.00 (*0-88114-980-2*) K Copeland Pubns.

Well Written Paper. 2nd ed. Rosemary Camilleri. 28p. (C). 1995. pap. text ed. 5.00 (*0-9649117-9-5*) R Camilleri.

Well Wrought Urn: Studies in the Structure of Poetry. Cleanth Brooks. LC 47-3143. 300p. (Orig.). (YA). (gr. 7 up). 1956. pap. 12.00 (*0-15-695705-1*, Harvest Bks) HarBrace.

*__Wellbeing of the Elderly: Approaches to Multidimensional Assessment.__ G. Fillenbaum. (WHO Offset Publications: No. 84). 99p. 1984. 11.00 (*92-4-170084-X*) World Health.

Wellborn Science: Eugenics in Germany, France, Brazil & Russia. Ed. by Mark B. Adams. (Monographs in the History & Philosophy of Biology). 256p. 1990. 60.00 (*0-19-505361-3*) OUP.

Wellensittiche-Mein Hobby see Budgerigars

Weller-Strawser Scales of Adaptive Behavior for the Learning Disabled Manual (WSSAB) Carol Weller & Sherri Strawser. (Orig.). 1981. student ed., pap. 36.00 (*0-685-41954-1*, 258-9-AN); student ed. 36.00 (*0-685-00088-5*, 258-9-BN); student ed. 15.00 (*0-87879-258-9*, 258-9); 18.00 (*0-685-00090-7*, 259-7N); 18.00 (*0-685-00091-5*, 260-ON); 15.00 (*0-685-00092-3*, 258-9-S) Acad Therapy.

Welles Anthology: A Critical Edition. Ed. by Sharon L. Jansen & Kathleen H. Jordan. (Medieval & Renaissance Texts & Studies: Vol. 75). 336p. 1991. 28.00 (*0-86698-085-7*, MR75) MRTS.

Wellesley. Photos by Dan Dry. (First Edition Ser.). (Illus.). 112p. 1988. 39.00 (*0-916509-42-7*) Harmony Hse Pub.

Wellesley Affair: Richard Marquess Wellesley & the Conduct of Anglo-Spanish Diplomacy, 1809-1812. John K. Severn. LC 80-25416. (Illus.). 303p. reprint ed. pap. 86.40 (*0-7837-4907-4*, 2044572) Bks Demand.

Wellesley Aron: Rebel with a Cause, a Memoir. Helen Silman-Cheong. 1992. text ed. 27.00 (*0-85303-245-9*, Pub. by Vallentine Mitchell UK) Intl Spec Bk.

Wellesley College Studies in Psychology see Voluntary Isolation of Control in a Natural Muscle Group

Wellesley Index to Victorian Periodicals, 1824-1900, Vol. IV. Ed. by Jean H. Slingerland. 826p. 1987. 175.00 (*0-8020-5721-7*) U of Toronto Pr.

Wellesley Index to Victorian Periodicals 1824-1900: Epitome & Index, Vol. V. Ed. by Walter E. Houghton et al. xiv, 923p. 1989. 195.00 (*0-8020-2688-5*) U of Toronto Pr.

Wellesley Island Farms. Roger S. Lucas. (Illus.). 60p. 1998. pap. 9.00 (*1-887287-04-3*) Res Rev Pubns.

Wellesley Series, 4 vols., Set. Cain. 1600p. (C). 1996. boxed, text ed. 625.00 (*0-415-13325-4*) Routledge.

Wellesley Series Pt. 1: Language & Linguistics, 4 vols., Set. Roy Harris. 1600p. (C). (gr. 13). 1995. boxed, text ed. 615.00 (*0-415-12206-6*, C0440) Routledge.

Wellfire. (Executioner Ser.). 1994. mass mkt. 3.50 (*0-373-61189-7*, 1-61189-6) Harlequin Bks.

Wellfleet Whale & Companion Poems. deluxe limited ed. Stanley Kunitz. LC 83-61493. 1983. 20.00 (*0-935296-37-9*) Sheep Meadow.

Wellhead Protection: A Guide for Small Communities. Tom Belk. (Illus.). 144p. (Orig.). (C). 1994. pap. text ed. 40.00 (*0-7881-1470-0*) DIANE Pub.

Wellin Magic. (Wellinworld Tapes & Books for Children: 2-9). 36p. (J). (ps-4). 1985. 8.95 (*0-88684-180-1*); audio write for info. (*0-318-59512-5*) Listen USA.

Wellington. William O. Morris. LC 73-14459. (Heroes of the Nations Ser.). reprint ed. 30.00 (*0-404-58277-X*) AMS Pr.

Wellington: Pillar of State. E. Longford. 574p. 1975. 10.00 (*0-586-04155-9*, Pub. by Granada UK) Academy Chi Pubs.

Wellington: The Geodetic Giant. Martin Bowman. LC 89-69823. (Illus.). 176p. 1990. text ed. 32.00 (*0-87474-263-3*) Smithsonian.

Wellington: The Years of the Sword. Elizabeth Longford. 1996. 14.98 (*0-8317-5646-2*) Smithmark.

Wellington after Waterloo. Neville Thompson. 304p. 1986. 45.00 (*0-7102-0747-6*, 07476, RKP) Routledge.

Wellington Commander: The Iron Duke's Generalship. Paddy Griffith et al. LC 85-31141. 224p. 1986. 45.00 (*0-907319-08-4*) Faber & Faber.

Wellington in the Peninsula, 1808-1814. Jac Weller. LC 92-26683. 396p. 1992. 37.50 (*1-85367-127-4*) Stackpole.

Wellington Sears Handbook of Industrial Textiles. Ed. by Sabit Adanur. LC 95-61229. 850p. 1995. text ed. 169.95 (*1-56676-340-1*) Technomic.

Wellington's Army: Recreated in Colour Photographs. Neil Leonard. (Europa Militaria Ser.: No. 15). (Illus.). 96p. 1994. pap. 19.95 (*1-872004-79-2*, Pub. by Windrow & Green UK) Motorbooks Intl.

Wellington's Army, 1809-1814. Charles W. Oman. 440p. 1986. 40.00 (*0-947898-41-7*) Stackpole.

Wellington's Generals. Michael Barthorp. (Men-at-Arms Ser.: No. 84). (Illus.). 48p. pap. 11.95 (*0-85045-299-6*, 9212, Pub. by Osprey UK) Stackpole.

Wellington's Guards. Ian Fletcher. (Elite Ser.). (Illus.). 64p. 1994. pap. 12.95 (*1-85532-392-3*, 9467, Pub. by Osprey UK) Stackpole.

Wellington's Heavy Cavalry. Bryan Fosten. (Men-at-Arms Ser.: No. 130). (Illus.). 48p. pap. 11.95 (*0-85045-474-3*, 9062, Pub. by Osprey UK) Stackpole.

Wellington's Highlanders. Stuart Reid. (Men-at-Arms Ser.: No. 253). (Illus.). 48p. pap. 11.95 (*1-85532-256-0*, 9224, Pub. by Osprey UK) Stackpole.

Wellington's Infantry. Bryan Fosten. (Men-at-Arms Ser.: No. 114). (Illus.). 48p. pap. 11.95 (*0-85045-395-X*, 9047, Pub. by Osprey UK) Stackpole.

Wellington's Infantry, Vol. 2. Bryan Fosten. (Men-at-Arms Ser.: No. 119). (Illus.). 48p. pap. 11.95 (*0-85045-419-0*, 9052, Pub. by Osprey UK) Stackpole.

Wellington's Light Cavalry. Bryan Fosten. (Men-at-Arms Ser.: No. 126). (Illus.). 48p. pap. 11.95 (*0-85045-449-2*, 9058, Pub. by Osprey UK) Stackpole.

W

Wellington's Men: Some Soldier Autobiographies. Ed. by W. H. Fitchett. 1977. reprint ed. 27.00 (0-7158-1151-7) Charles River Bks.
Wellington's Military Machine. Philip J. Haythornthwaite. 192p. (C). 1991. 95.00 (0-946771-88-X, Pub. by Spellmount UK) St Mut.
Wellington's Military Machine. Philip J. Haythornthwaite. (Illus.). 192p. 1994. 29.95 (1-885119-11-9) Sarpedon.
Wellington's Regiments: The Men & Their Battles 1808-1815, Vol. 2: The Household Regiments. Text by Ian Fletcher. (Illus.). 224p. (C). 1995. 45.00 (1-873376-06-5, Pub. by Spellmnt Pubs UK) Howell Pr VA.
Wellington's Specialist Troops. Philip J. Haythornthwaite. (Men-at-Arms Ser.: No. 204). (Illus.). 48p. pap. 11.95 (0-85045-862-5, 9137, Pub. by Osprey UK) Stackpole.
Wellington's Surgeon General, Sir James McGrigor. Richard L. Blanco. LC 74-75477. 257p. reprint ed. pap. 73.30 (0-317-28968-3, 2023759) Bks Demand.
Wellington's War: His Peninsular Dispatches. Julian Rathbone. (Illus.). 352p. 1995. pap. 14.95 (0-7181-3841-4, Penguin Bks) Viking Penguin.
***Wellingtons, Watts & Windsor Knots: How the Names Became the Words.** Andrew Sholl. LC 97-20940. (Artful Wordsmith Ser.). 1997. write for info. (0-8442-0416-1) NTC Pub Grp.
Wellness. Jan G. Bishop & Steven G. Aldana. 350p. (C). 1997. pap. text ed. write for info. (0-89787-635-0) Gorsuch Scarisbrick.
Wellness. Greenberg & Dintiman. 400p. 1996. pap. 30.00 (0-205-26078-0) Allyn.
Wellness. Brian Lowdon et al. 1995. pap. 56.00 (0-949823-49-X, Pub. by Deakin Univ AT) St Mut.
Wellness: A Lifetime Commitment. Floyd et al. 408p. 1993. pap. text ed. 28.95 (0-88725-154-4) Hunter Textbks.
Wellness: A Way of Life. University of Delaware Staff. 204p. (C). 1994. spiral bd. 20.94 (0-8403-6964-6) Kendall-Hunt.
Wellness: AIDS, STD & Other Communicable Diseases. James Jackson. 184p. (C). 1991. per. 13.50 (0-87967-868-2) Dushkin Pub.
Wellness: Alcohol Use & Abuse. Richard G. Schlaadt. 160p. (C). 1991. per. 13.50 (0-87967-867-4) Dushkin Pub.
Wellness: An Arthritis Reality. 2nd ed. Beth Ziebell. 176p. 1992. per., pap. text ed. 19.95 (0-8403-7212-4) Kendall-Hunt.
Wellness: Choices for Health & Fitness. Rebecca Donatelle et al. LC 94-15968. 1994. write for info. (0-8053-3037-2) Benjamin-Cummings.
Wellness: Choices for Health & Fitness. Rebecca Donatelle. (C). 1995. pap. text ed. 29.25 (0-8053-0370-7) Benjamin-Cummings.
Wellness: Choices for Health & Fitness. Donatelleetalo. (Health Sciences Ser.). 1995. pap. 33.95 (0-534-33951-4) Brooks-Cole.
***Wellness: Choices for Health & Fitness.** 2nd ed. Donatelle. (Health Sciences Ser.). 1998. pap. 30.95 (0-534-34836-X) Brooks-Cole.
Wellness: Drugs, Society & Behavior. Richard G. Schlaadt. 160p. (C). 1991. per. 13.50 (0-87967-869-0) Dushkin Pub.
Wellness: Environment & Health. Robert Kime. 160p. (C). 1991. per. 13.50 (0-87967-870-4) Dushkin Pub.
Wellness: Exercise & Physical Fitness. Gary Klug & Janice Lettunich. 176p. (C). 1991. per. 13.50 (0-87967-871-2) Dushkin Pub.
Wellness: Healthful Aging. James A. Porterfield & Richard St. Pierre. 160p. (C). 1991. per. 13.50 (0-87967-866-6) Dushkin Pub.
Wellness: Just a State of Mind? Eldon Taylor. Ed. by Suzanne Brady. (Illus.). 128p. 1993. pap. 5.95 (1-55978-034-7) R K Bks.
Wellness: Major Chronic Diseases. Paula Ciesielski. 176p. (C). 1991. per. 13.50 (0-87967-873-9) Dushkin Pub.
Wellness: Nutrition & Health. Judith S. Hurley. 192p. 1992. 13.50 (0-87967-875-5) Dushkin Pub.
Wellness: Pregnancy, Childbirth & Parenting. Robert Kime. 160p. (C). 1991. per. 13.50 (0-87967-876-3) Dushkin Pub.
Wellness: Safety & Accident Prevention. David Lawson. 128p. (C). 1991. per. 13.50 (0-87967-864-X) Dushkin Pub.
Wellness: Small Changes You Can Use to Make a Big Difference. John Travis & Regina S. Ryan. (Illus.). 80p. (Orig.). 1991. pap. 6.95 (0-89815-402-2) Ten Speed Pr.
Wellness: Stress Management. Randall Cottrell. 160p. (C). 1991. per. 13.50 (0-87967-872-0) Dushkin Pub.
Wellness: The Informed Health Consumer. Robert Kime. 160p. (C). 1991. per. 13.50 (0-87967-865-8) Dushkin Pub.
Wellness: The Inside Story. Julia Swarner. (Lifeline Ser.). 95p. 1991. pap. 2.97 (0-8163-0935-3) Pacific Pr Pub Assn.
Wellness: The Wellness Life-Style. Richard G. Schlaadt. 160p. (C). 1991. 13.50 (0-87967-879-8) Dushkin Pub.
Wellness: Tobacco & Health. Richard G. Schlaadt. 160p. (C). 1991. per. 13.50 (0-87967-877-1) Dushkin Pub.
Wellness: Weight Control. Randall Cottrell. 176p. (C). 1991. per. 13.50 (0-87967-878-X) Dushkin Pub.
Wellness - Guidelines for a Healthy Lifestyle. Brent O. Hafen & Werner W. Hoeger. (Illus.). 352p. (C). 1994. pap. text ed. 26.95 (0-89582-230-X) Morton Pub.
Wellness Activities for Youth. Sandy Queen. 154p. 1992. spiral bd. 19.95 (0-938586-70-X) Whole Person.
Wellness Activities for Youth, Vol. 1. Sandy Queen. 160p. 1994. 19.95 (1-57025-026-X) Whole Person.
Wellness Activities for Youth, Vol. 2. Sandy Queen. 160p. 1994. 19.95 (0-938586-98-X) Whole Person.
***Wellness Against All Odds.** Sherry A. Rogers. LC 94-65045. 384p. 1994. reprint ed. pap. 17.95 (0-9618821-5-8) Prestige NY.
***Wellness & Chiropractic.** Edmund J. Burke & Brent Gravelle. (Illus.). 304p. 1997. pap. 29.95 (0-614-24660-1) Mouvement Pubns.
***Wellness & Chiropractic.** Edmund J. Burke & Brent Gravelle. (Illus.). 304p. (Orig.). 1997. pap. text ed. 29.95 (0-614-26225-9) Mouvement Pubns.
Wellness & Lifestyle Renewal: A Manual for Personal Change. Mark S. Rosenfeld. (Orig.). 1993. pap. text ed. 28.00 (0-910317-92-5) Am Occup Therapy.
***Wellness & the Liberal Arts.** Cheryl McClary & Keith Ray. 140p. (C). 1996. per., pap. text ed. 21.99 (0-7872-2679-3) Kendall-Hunt.
Wellness & the Liberal Arts. Keith Ray & Cheryl McClary. 92p. (C). 1994. per. 11.49 (0-8403-9212-5) Kendall-Hunt.
Wellness & the Liberal Arts: Preliminary Edition. Cheryl McClary & Keith Ray. 92p. (C). 1994. spiral bd. 11.49 (0-8403-9362-8) Kendall-Hunt.
Wellness at Work: Building Resilience to Job Stress. Valerie O'Hara. LC 95-69482. 238p. (Orig.). 1995. pap. 17.95 (1-57224-030-X) New Harbinger.
Wellness Book: The Comprehensive Guide to Maintaining Health & Treating Stress-Related Illness. Mind-Body Medical Institute Staff et al. (Illus.). 352p. 1991. 21.95 (1-55972-092-1, Birch Ln Pr) Carol Pub Group.
Wellness Book: The Comprehensive Guide to Maintaining Health & Treating Stress-Related Illness. New England Deaconess Hospital & Harvard Medical School Mind-Body Medical Institute Associates Staff et al. LC 92-39899. (Illus.). 512p. 1993. pap. 15.00 (0-671-79750-6) S&S Trade.
Wellness Book of I.B.S. How to Achieve Relief from Irritable Bowel Syndrome & Live a Symptom-Free Life. Deralee Scanlon & Barbara C. Becnel. 192p. 1991. pap. 10.95 (0-312-85226-6) St Martin.
Wellness Community Guide to Fighting for Recovery from Cancer. expanded rev. ed. Harold H. Benjamin. LC 95-11417. Orig. Title: From Victim to Victor. 256p. 1995. pap. 12.95 (0-87477-794-1, Tarcher Putnam) Putnam Pub Group.
Wellness Daybook: The Personal Health Management Book. Emilia D. Pisani. 175p. 1993. pap. text ed. 15.95 (0-9637571-0-5) Design Data.
Wellness Encyclopedia of Food & Nutrition: How to Buy, Store, & Prepare Every Fresh Food. Univ. of California at Berkeley Wellness Letter Editors & Sheldon Margen. LC 92-13017. (Illus.). 512p. 1992. 29.95 (0-929661-03-6, Random) Rebus.
Wellness-Fitness Products: Light-Healthy Foods & Soft Drinks, Dietary Supplements, Home Exercise Equipment, No. GA-083. 1994. 2,550.00 (1-56965-102-7) BCC.
Wellness for Helping Professionals: Creating Compassionate Cultures. John W. Travis & Meryn G. Callander. (Illus.). 416p. 1990. pap. 34.95 (0-9625882-1-0) Wellness Assocs.
Wellness Guide to Lifelong Fitness. University of California at Berkeley Wellness Letter Staff & Timothy P. White. (Illus.). 480p. 1993. 29.95 (0-929661-08-7) Rebus.
***Wellness Guidelines for a Healthy Lifestyle.** 2nd ed. Brent Q. Hafen & Werner W. Hoeger. (Illus.). 352p. (C). 1997. pap. text ed. 26.95 (0-89582-397-7) Morton Pub.
Wellness in the Workplace: How to Plan, Implement & Evaluate a Wellness Program. Merlene T. Sherman. LC 89-81245. (Fifty-Minute Ser.). 93p. (Orig.). 1990. pap. 10.95 (1-56052-020-5) Crisp Pubns.
Wellness Index. 24p. 1990. pap. 3.95 (0-89815-054-X) Ten Speed Pr.
Wellness Inventory. 3rd ed. John W. Travis. (Illus.). 12p. 1988. pap. 1.95 (0-9625882-0-2) Wellness Assocs.
Wellness Lowfat Cookbook: Hundreds of Delicious Recipes & a Revolutionary New Eating Plan that can Help Prevent Heart Disease. Ed. by Wellness Cooking School Staff. (Illus.). 256p. 1994. 24.95 (0-929661-11-7) Rebus.
Wellness Medicine. Robert A. Anderson. LC 87-70316. (Illus.). 520p. 1987. lib. bdg. 34.95 (0-942767-00-4) Amer Health Pr.
Wellness Medicine. 2nd ed. Robert A. Anderson. 494p. 1990. reprint ed. pap. 17.95 (0-87983-533-8) Keats.
Wellness Nursing: Concepts, Theory, Research & Practice. Carolyn C. Clark. 368p. (C). 1986. pap. 36.95 (0-8261-5150-7) Springer Pub.
Wellness Nursing Diagnosis for Health Promotion. Karen M. Stolte. 336p. 1995. spiral bd. 18.95 (0-397-55082-0) Lppncott-Raven.
***Wellness Nutrition Counter: The Essential Guide to Complete Nutritional Information on over 6,000 Foods & Products.** Sheldon Margen. LC 97-17959. 1997. write for info. (0-929661-38-9) Rebus.
Wellness Practitioner: Concepts, Research, & Strategies. 2nd expanded rev. ed. Carolyn C. Clark. LC 95-47784. (Illus.). 368p. 1996. 46.95 (0-8261-5151-5) Springer Pub.
Wellness Programs for Taft-Hartley Funds. Bernard Handel & Mitchell Langbert. Ed. by Mary Brennan. LC 92-73536. 165p. (Orig.). 1992. pap. 25.00 (0-89154-455-0) Intl Found Employ.
Wellness Resources: An Annotated Guide to Essential Books, Periodicals, A-V Materials & Teaching Tools for Trainers, Consultants, Counselors, Educators, & Health Professionals. Rev. & Selected by Jim Polidora. LC 94-42228. 1995. 34.95 (1-57025-065-0) Whole Person.
Wellness Rx: Dr. Taub's 7-Day Program for Radiant Health & Energy. Edward A. Taub. LC 94-7752. 1994. pap. text ed. 10.95 (0-13-082463-1) P-H.
Wellness Rx: Dr. Taub's 7-Day Program for Radiant Health & Energy. Edward A. Taub. LC 94-7752. 1994. write for info. (0-13-082471-2) P-H.
Wellness Tree. Judith Cox. LC 95-76782. (Illus.). 32p. (J). (gr. k-4). 1995. 19.95 (1-878044-29-X) Mayhaven Pub.
Wellness Tree: Dynamic Six-Step Program for Rejuvenating Health the Creating Optimal Wellness. 2nd ed. Justin O'Brien. LC 93-10357. (Illus.). 250p. (Orig.). (C). 1993. pap. 16.00 (0-936663-08-1) Yes Intl.
Wellness Tree Activity Book. Judith Cox. (Illus.). 32p. (Orig.). (J). (gr. k-4). 1995. pap. 2.95 (1-878044-35-4) Mayhaven Pub.
Wellness vs. Neurotic Styles: Holistic or Monomanic Use of the Four Functions. Terence Duniho. 1991. pap. text ed. 5.95 (1-878287-31-1, BDAB) Type & Temperament.
Wellness Way of Life. Gwen Robbins et al. 416p. (C). 1990. per. write for info. (0-697-06331-3) Brown & Benchmark.
Wellness Way of Life. 2nd ed. Gwen Robbins et al. 496p. (C). 1993. per. write for info. (0-697-12659-5) Brown & Benchmark.
Wellness Way of Life. 3rd ed. Gwen Robbins et al. 448p. (C). 1996. per. write for info. (0-697-25915-3) Brown & Benchmark.
***Wellness Way of Life.** 4th ed. Robbins. 1998. pap. text ed. 15.50 (0-697-29578-8) McGraw.
Wellness Way to Weight Loss. Elizabeth M. Gallup. LC 90-41746. (Illus.). 320p. 1990. 21.95 (0-306-43568-3, Plenum Pr) Plenum.
Wellness Workbook. 2nd ed. John W. Travis & Regina S. Ryan. LC 86-6052. 256p. 1986. pap. 16.95 (0-89815-179-1) Ten Speed Pr.
***Wells: Poems from Hollywood.** Mark Dunster. 21p. 1997. pap. 5.00 (0-89642-360-3) Linden Pubs.
Wells & Septic Systems. 2nd ed. Mac Alth et al. 1991. 25.95 (0-07-157780-7); pap. text ed. 18.95 (0-07-157779-3) McGraw.
Wells & Septic Systems. 2nd ed. Max Alth. 272p. 1991. 25.95 (0-8306-2137-7); pap. 18.95 (0-8306-2136-9) McGraw-Hill Prof.
***Wells Brothers, the Young Cattle Kings.** Andy Adams. LC 96-52808. (Illus.). xvii, 370p. 1997. pap. 12.95 (0-8032-5929-8, Bison Books) U of Nebr Pr.
Wells Construction. Richard E. Brush. (C). 1988. text ed. 250.00 (0-685-44233-0, Pub. by Scientific UK) St Mut.
Wells Fargo & Co. in Idaho Territory. W. Turrentine Jackson. (Illus.). iv, 120p. (Orig.). 1984. pap. 5.95 (0-931406-05-6) Idaho State Soc.
Wells Fargo Decoys: Larry & Stretch. large type ed. Marshall Grover. (Linford Western Library). 272p. 1996. pap. 15.99 (0-7089-7820-7, Linford) Ulverscroft.
Wells, Fargo Detective: A Biography of James B. Hume. Richard Dillon. LC 86-11304. (Vintage West Ser.). (Illus.). 334p. 1986. reprint ed. pap. 14.95 (0-87417-113-X) U of Nev Pr.
Wells Fargo in Arizona Territory. Lillian G. Theobald. LC 78-67555. 1978. pap. 10.00 (0-910152-10-1) AZ Hist Foun.
Wells, ME. H. Shelley. (Images of America Ser.). 128p. 1996. pap. 16.99 (0-7524-0261-7, Arcdia) Chalford.
Wells of Abundance. E. V. Ingraham. 1938. pap. 6.95 (0-87516-028-X) DeVorss.
Wells of Discontent. Charles G. Daughters. Ed. by Stuart Bruchey & Vincent P. Carosso. LC 78-18959. (Small Business Enterprise in America Ser.). (Illus.). 1979. reprint ed. lib. bdg. 30.95 (0-405-11463-X) Ayer.
Wells of Glory. Mary McReynolds. LC 95-48801. (Legacy of the Land Ser.: Bk. 1). 320p. 1996. pap. 9.99 (0-89107-889-4) Crossway Bks.
Wells of Hell. Graham Masterton. 320p. 1990. pap. 3.95 (0-8125-2211-7) Tor Bks.
Wells of Memphis. James Pritchett. Ed. by Margaret Owens et al. 256p. (Orig.). 1996. pap. 12.00 (0-9643232-1-4) Pandamonium.
Wells of Phyre: An Arbiter Tale. L. Warren Douglas. 1996. mass mkt. 5.50 (0-451-45470-7, ROC) NAL-Dutton.
Wells of Power: The Oil Fields of South-Western Asia. Olaf Caroe. (Middle East in the 20th Century Ser.). 1976. reprint ed. lib. bdg. 29.50 (0-306-70825-6) Da Capo.
Wells of Salvation. Edmund E. Wells. (Orig.). pap. 2.00 (0-686-30400-4) WOS.
Wells of Salvation: Meditations of Isaiah. Charles Ellis & Norma Ellis. 224p. (Orig.). 1986. pap. 8.99 (0-85151-457-X) Banner of Truth.
Wells of the Spirit. Bill Adams. 56p. 1993. pap. 9.95 (0-85819-849-5, Pub. by JBCE AT) Morehouse Pub.
***Wells' Supportive Therapies in Health Care.** Ed. by Richard Wells & Verena Tschudin. (Illus.). 299p. 1994. pap. write for info. (0-7020-1591-1, Pub. by W B Saunders UK) Saunders.
Wellsite Geological Techniques for Petroleum Exploration: Methods & Systems of Formation Evaluation. M. Ghosh et al. (Illus.). 515p. (C). 1988. text ed. 120.00 (90-6191-905-3, Pub. by A A Balkema NE) Ashgate Pub Co.
Wellspring. D. Phillip Caron. Ed. by Curtis R. McGuirt. (Illus.). 28p. (Orig.). 1994. pap. 4.00 (1-885799-01-2) October Release.
Wellspring: A Story from the Deep Country. Barbara Dean. LC 79-2606. (Illus.). 208p. 1979. pap. 9.95 (0-933280-01-7) Island Pr.
***Wellspring: A Weekly Devotional for Single Parents.** Lynda Hunter. LC 96-47495. 1997. 12.99 (1-56179-532-1) Focus Family.
Wellspring: Poems. Sharon Olds. LC 95-15835. 112p. 1996. 21.00 (0-679-44592-7) Knopf.
Wellspring: Poems. Sharon Olds. LC 95-15835. 112p. 1996. pap. 13.00 (0-679-76560-3) Knopf.
***Wellspring of Light.** Jacob Boehme. Tr. by Evelyn Sire. (Orig.). 1997. pap. 8.95 (1-55818-390-6) Holmes Pub.
Wellspring of Worship. Jean Corbon. 208p. 1988. pap. 12.95 (0-8091-2968-X) Paulist Pr.
Wellsprings: A Book of Spiritual Exercises. Anthony DeMello. LC 86-4478. 240p. 1986. pap. 11.00 (0-385-19617-2, Image Bks) Doubleday.
Wellsprings of a Nation: America Before 1801. Rodger D. Parker. LC 77-72082. (Illus.). 1977. pap. 10.00 (0-912296-13-5) Am Antiquarian.
Wellsprings of Achievement: Cultural & Economic Dynamics in Early Modern England & Japan. Ed. by Penelope Gouk. 288p. 1995. 77.50 (0-86078-465-7, Pub. by Variorum UK) Ashgate Pub Co.
Wellsprings of Imagination: The Homes of Children's Authors. Mark West. 154p. 1992. 24.95 (1-55570-097-7) Neal-Schuman.
Wellsprings of Knowledge: Building & Sustaining the Sources of Innovation. Dorothy Leonard-Barton. LC 95-14582. 352p. 1995. 29.95 (0-87584-612-2) Harvard Busn.
Wellsprings of Knowledge: Building & Sustaining the Sources of Innovation. Dorothy Leonard-Barton. 1995. text ed. 29.95 (0-07-103640-7) McGraw.
Wellsprings of Life: Understanding Proverbs. Donald P. Orthner. (Illus.). xii, 228p. (Orig.). (YA). (gr. 9 up). 1989. pap. 7.95 (0-317-93833-9) Adon Bks.
Wellsprings of Literary Creation: An Analysis of Male & Female "Artist Stories" from the German Romantics to the Present. Ursula R. Mahlendorf. LC 84-72198. (GERM Ser.: Vol. 18). (Illus.). 292p. 1985. 35.00 (0-938100-34-3) Camden Hse.
Wellsprings of Music. Curt Sachs. Ed. by Jaap Kunst. LC 77-23410. 1977. reprint ed. pap. 12.95 (0-306-80073-X) Da Capo.
Wellsprings of the American Spirit. Ed. by F. Ernest Johnson. (Religion & Civilization Series of the Institute for Religious & Social Studies). 241p. 1964. reprint ed. lib. bdg. 60.50 (0-8154-0121-3) Cooper Sq.
Wellsprings of Torah. Alexander Z. Friedman. Tr. by Gertrude Hirschler from YID. 584p. 1980. reprint ed. boxed 22.50 (0-910818-20-7) Judaica Pr.
Wellsprings of Wisdom: A Study of Abu Yaqub al-Sijmistani's "Kitab Al-Yanabi" Paul E. Walker. LC 94-13755. (Illus.). 256p. (C). 1994. text ed. 30.00 (0-87480-421-3) U of Utah Pr.
WELS & Other Lutherans. Edward C. Fredrich, III et al. LC 94-74993. 104p. (Orig.). 1995. pap. 7.99 (0-8100-0543-3, 15N2002) Northwest Pub.
Welsch: Entwicklung Multimedia. 1996. 67.00 (3-540-60317-4) Spr-Verlag.
Welsh. Alice Thomas Ellis. 152p. 1991. 21.95 (1-85089-536-8, Pub. by ISIS UK) Transaction Pubs.
Welsh Academy English-Welsh Dictionary. Ed. by Bruce Griffiths & Dafydd G. Jones. 1710p. (ENG & WEL.). 1996. 85.00 (0-7083-1186-5, Pub. by Univ Wales Pr UK) Paul & Co Pubs.
Welsh Ambassadors: Powys Lives & Letters. Louis Marlow. LC 73-157126. 273p. 1971. text ed. 29.95 (0-912568-04-6) Colgate U Pr.
Welsh & Their Country: Selected Readings in the Social Sciences. Open University Team Staff et al. 365p. (C). 1986. pap. 30.00 (0-86383-245-8, Pub. by Gomer Pr UK) St Mut.
Welsh Castles of Edward I. Arnold Taylor. 129p. 1986. boxed 12.00 (0-907628-71-0) Hambledon Press.
Welsh Celtic Myth in Modern Fantasy: Contributions to the Study of Science Fiction & Fantasy, No. 35. C. W. Sullivan, III. LC 88-24714. 197p. 1989. text ed. 49.95 (0-313-24998-9, SUL, Greenwood Pr) Greenwood.
Welsh Champions. Wynne Davies. 63p. 1990. pap. 21.00 (0-85131-396-5, Pub. by J A Allen & Co UK) St Mut.
Welsh Chapels. Anthony Jones. (Illus.). 160p. 1996. pap. 15.95 (0-7509-1162-X, Pub. by Sutton Pubng UK) Bks Intl VA.
Welsh Childhood. Alice T. Ellis. (Illus.). 186p. 1997. 34.95 (1-55921-198-9) Moyer Bell.
Welsh Church: From Conquest to Reformation. Glanmor Williams. LC 91-14353. 632p. 1993. 36.00 (1-55728-224-2) U of Ark Pr.
Welsh Classics, Vol. 1: Dafydd ap Gwilym: Poems, Vol. 1. Ed. by Lynn Hughes & Rachel Bromwich. 1207p. (C). 1982. text ed. 95.00 (0-85088-815-8, Pub. by Gomer Pr UK) St Mut.
Welsh Cob Champions. Wynne Davies. 1990. pap. 21.00 (0-85131-410-4, Pub. by J A Allen & Co UK) St Mut.
Welsh Connection. Ed. by William Tydeman. 211p. (C). 1986. pap. 20.00 (0-86383-395-0, Pub. by Gomer Pr UK) St Mut.
Welsh Country Diary. William Condry. 176p. 1993. pap. 23.00 (0-86383-872-3, Pub. by Gomer Pr UK) St Mut.
Welsh Courting Customs. Catrin Stevens. 198p. 1993. 30.00 (0-86383-658-5, Pub. by Gomer Pr UK) St Mut.
Welsh Dictionary. Edwin Lewis. (Teach Yourself Ser.). 302p. 1994. pap. 14.95 (0-8442-3842-2, Teach Yourslf) NTC Pub Grp.
Welsh-English - English-Welsh Dictionary. H. Meurig Evans & W. O. Thomas. (ENG & WEL.). 49.50 (0-87557-091-7) Saphrograph.
Welsh-English, English-Welsh Dictionary. 612p. 1993. pap. 24.95 (0-7818-0136-2) Hippocrene Bks.
Welsh Fairy Book. W. Jenkyn Thomas. (Illus.). 310p. reprint ed. pap. 16.95 (0-7083-1257-8, Pub. by Univ Wales Pr UK) Paul & Co Pubs.
Welsh Family Coats of Arms. Robert J. Lewis. (Illus.). 96p. (Orig.). 1995. pap. text ed. 22.00 (0-7884-0156-4) Heritage Bk.
Welsh Family History: A Guide to Research. Ed. by John Rowlands. (Illus.). 316p. 1994. pap. 19.95 (0-614-03826-X, 5030) Genealog Pub.
Welsh Fare. Ed. by S. Minwel Tibbott. 88p. (C). 1989. 65.00 (0-85485-040-6, Pub. by D Brown & Sons Ltd UK) St Mut.
Welsh Fever: Welsh Activities in the United States & Canada Today. David Greenslade. (Illus.). 344p. 1986. text ed. 16.95 (0-905928-56-3) B Hirsch.
Welsh Folk Customs. Trefor M. Owen. 197p. 1987. pap. 20.00 (0-85088-347-4, Pub. by Gomer Pr UK) St Mut.

W

Welsh Folk Customs. Trefor M. Owne. 197p. (C). 1987. text ed. 40.00 (*0-685-50525-1*, Pub. by Gomer Pr UK) St Mut.

Welsh Folk-Lore: A Collection of Folk-Tales & Legends of North Wales. Elias Owen. 1977. reprint ed. 29.00 (*0-7158-1179-7*) Charles River Bks.

Welsh for Customs. Trefor M. Owen. 197p. (C). 1987. pap. 50.00 (*0-685-60036-X*, Pub. by Gomer Pr UK) St Mut.

Welsh Heirs. Glynn Jones. 158p. (C). 1977. text ed. 35.00 (*0-85088-495-0*, Pub. by Gomer Pr UK) St Mut.

Welsh Hymns & Their Tunes. Alan Luff. LC 90-81524. 255p. (Orig.). (C). 1990. 14.95 (*0-916642-42-9*, 63) Hope Pub.

Welsh in Wisconsin. Phillips G. Davies. LC 82-10283. (Illus.). 39p. 1982. pap. 3.00 (*0-87020-214-6*) State Hist Soc Wis.

Welsh Is Fun! Heini Gruffudd & Elwyn Ioan. (WEL.). 1971. pap. 8.50 (*0-9500178-4-1*, Pub. by Y Llfa UK) Intl Spec Bk.

Welsh Is Fun. Heini Gruffudd & Elwyn Ioan. 1987. pap. 7.50 (*0-89979-060-7*) British Am Bks.

Welsh Is Fun-Tastic! Heini Gruffudd & Elwyn Ioan. (WEL.). 1975. pap. 8.50 (*0-9500178-7-6*, Pub. by Y Llfa UK) Intl Spec Bk.

Welsh Knight: Paradoxicality in Chretien's Erec et Enide. Rupert T. Pickens. LC 76-47499. (French Forum Monographs: No. 6). 163p. (Orig.). 1977. pap. 10.95 (*0-917058-05-4*) French Forum.

***Welsh Language & Welsh Dissertations.** Alun E. Davies. 384p. 1997. 60.00 (*0-7083-1210-1*, Pub. by Univ Wales Pr UK) Paul & Co Pubs.

***Welsh Learner's Dictionary.** Henri Gruffurd. 320p. 1996. pap. 14.95 (*0-86243-363-0*, Pub. by Y Llfa UK) Intl Spec Bk.

***Welsh Learner's Phrase Book.** Leonard Hayles. (Illus.). 200p. 1996. pap. 20.00 (*0-86243-364-9*, Pub. by Y Lolfa UK) St Mut.

Welsh Legends & Folklore. D. Parry-Jones. 1972. 59.95 (*0-8490-1282-1*) Gordon Pr.

Welsh Lineage of John Lewis (1592-1657), Emigrant to Gloucester, Virginia. rev. ed. Grace M. Moses. 68p. 1995. reprint ed. pap. 10.00 (*0-685-62585-0*, 9263) Clearfield Co.

Welsh Literature & the Classical Tradition. Ceri Davies. 220p. 1996. 39.95 (*0-7083-1321-3*, Pub. by Univ Wales Pr UK) Paul & Co Pubs.

Welsh Metrics. J. Glyn Davies. LC 78-72625. (Celtic Language & Literature Ser.: Goidelic & Brythonic). reprint ed. 27.50 (*0-404-17547-3*) AMS Pr.

Welsh Mormon Writings from 1844 to 1862: A Historical Bibliography. Ronald D. Dennis. (Specialized Monograph Ser.: Vol. 4). 1988. 11.95 (*0-88494-656-8*) Bookcraft Inc.

Welsh Mountain Pony. Wynne Davies. 134p. 1990. 52.00 (*0-85131-571-2*, Pub. by J A Allen & Co UK) St Mut.

Welsh Names for Children. Heini Gruffudd. (WEL.). reprint ed. pap. 8.50 (*0-904864-99-5*, Pub. by Y Llfa UK) Intl Spec Bk.

Welsh Nation Builders. Gwynfor Evans. 357p. (C). 1988. 35.00 (*0-86383-417-5*, Pub. by Gomer Pr UK); pap. 21.00 (*0-86383-401-9*, Pub. by Gomer Pr UK) St Mut.

Welsh Nationalism in the Twentieth Century: The Ethnic Option & the Modern State. Charlotte A. Davies. LC 88-28832. 153p. 1989. text ed. 55.00 (*0-275-93116-1*, C3116, Praeger Pubs) Greenwood.

Welsh People. John Rhys & David B. Jones. LC 68-25263. (British History Ser.: No. 30). 1969. reprint ed. lib. bdg. 75.00 (*0-8383-0233-5*) M S G Haskell Hse.

Welsh Personal Names. Heini Gruffudd. pap. 12.50 (*0-89979-032-1*) British Am Bks.

Welsh Pilgrim's Manual. Ed. by Brendan O'Malley. 147p. (C). 1989. pap. 20.00 (*0-86383-583-X*, Pub. by Gomer Pr UK) St Mut.

Welsh Poems & Ballads. George H. Borrow. LC 78-72620. (Celtic Language & Literature Ser.: Goidelic & Brythonic). reprint ed. 37.50 (*0-404-17537-6*) AMS Pr.

Welsh Pony Champions. Ed. by Wynne Davies. 80p. 1990. pap. 30.00 (*0-85131-458-9*, Pub. by J A Allen & Co UK) St Mut.

Welsh Proverbs. H. H. Vaughan. 1973. 59.95 (*0-8490-1283-X*) Gordon Pr.

Welsh Revival: Its Origin & Development. Thomas Phillips. 147p. 1995. pap. 8.50 (*0-85151-685-8*) Banner of Truth.

Welsh Sail. Susan C. Jones. 103p. (C). 1976. pap. 20.00 (*0-85088-306-7*, Pub. by Gomer Pr UK) St Mut.

Welsh Saints: A Study in Patterned Lives. Elissa Henken. 220p. (C). 1991. 79.00 (*0-85991-317-1*) Boydell & Brewer.

Welsh Sheep & Their Wool. John Williams-Davies. 74p. (C). 1981. pap. 20.00 (*0-85088-964-2*, Pub. by Gomer Pr UK) St Mut.

Welsh, Spoken, No. One: Catchphrase, 2 texts, Set. Basil Davies & Cennard Davies. 258p. 1980. pap. 135.00 incl. audio (*0-88432-209-2*, AFWE10) Audio-Forum.

Welsh, Spoken, No. Two: Catchphrase. 183p. 1984. pap. 45.00 incl. audio (*0-88432-399-4*, AFWE20) Audio-Forum.

***Welsh Springer Spaniel: AKC Rank #117.** Linda Brennan. (Rare Breed Ser.). (Illus.). 96p. 1997. 19.95 (*0-7938-0762-X*, RS-112) TFH Pubns.

Welsh Springer Spaniel Champions, 1952-1989. Camino E. E. & Bk. Co. Staff. (Illus.). 125p. 1990. pap. 36.95 (*1-55893-013-2*) Camino E E & Bk.

Welsh Stick Chairs: A Workshop Guide to the Windsor Chair. John Brown. LC 93-28897. (Illus.). 93p. 1993. reprint ed. pap. 14.95 (*0-941936-28-7*) Linden Pub Fresno.

***Welsh Surnames & Given Names & Their Meanings.** Annie Lloyd. 144p. (Orig.). 1996. 15.00 (*0-9644567-3-7*) A Lloyd.

Welsh Syntax: A Government-Binding Approach. Louisa Sadler. 224p. 1987. lib. bdg. 49.95 (*0-7099-4483-7*, Pub. by Croom Helm UK) Routledge Chapman & Hall.

Welsh Terrier. Bardi McLennan. (Illus.). 192p. 1993. 14.95 (*0-86622-585-4*, KW213) TFH Pubns.

Welsh Terrier. Bardi Mclennan. Ed. by Luana Luther. (Pure-Breds Ser.). (Illus.). 280p. Date not set. 28.50 (*0-944875-38-6*) Doral Pub.

Welsh Verse: Translations. 3rd rev. ed. Ed. by Tony Conran et al. 355p. 1993. pap. 17.95 (*1-85411-081-0*, Pub. by Seren Bks UK) Dufour.

Welsh Wars of Edward First: Medieval Military History. John Morris. LC 68-25253. (British History Ser.: No. 30). 1969. reprint ed. lib. bdg. 75.00 (*0-8383-0221-1*) M S G Haskell Hse.

Welsh Wars of Edward I. John E. Morris. LC 96-7110. (Medieval Military Library). (Illus.). 352p. 1995. 22.95 (*0-938289-67-5*); pap. 14.95 (*0-938289-68-3*) Combined Pub.

Welsh Wars of Edward the First. J. E. Morris. 352p. 1996. 70.00 (*0-7509-1168-9*, Pub. by Sutton Pubng UK) Bks Intl VA.

Welsh Women: An Annotated Bibliography of Women in Wales & Women of Welsh Descent in America. Constance W. Holt. 707p. 1993. 69.50 (*0-8108-2610-0*) Scarecrow.

Welshman's Way. Margaret Moore. 1995. mass mkt. 4.50 (*0-373-28895-6*, 1-28895-0) Harlequin Bks.

Welshness Performed: Welsh Concepts of Person & Society. Carol Trosset. LC 93-13100. (Anthropology of Form & Meaning Ser.). 183p. 1993. 36.00 (*0-8165-1378-3*) U of Ariz Pr.

Welt der einfachen Formen: Studien zur Motiv- Wort- und Quellenkunde. Kurt Ranke. (C). 1978. 176.95 (*3-11-007420-6*) De Gruyter.

Welt der Galgenlieder Christian Morgensterns und der viktorianische Nonsense. Ernst Kretschmer. 338p. 1983. 103.10 (*3-11-009506-8*) De Gruyter.

Welt der Roemer: Studien Zu Ihrer Literatur, Geschichte und Religion. Carl J. Classen & Hans Bernsdorff. Ed. by Meinolf Vielberg. (Untersuchungen zur Antiken Literatur und Geschichte Ser.: Vol. 41). viii, 281p. (GER.). (C). 1993. lib. bdg. 129.25 (*3-11-013840-9*) De Gruyter.

Welt des Menschen-Die Welt der Philosophie: Festschrift fur Jan Patocka. W. Biemel. (Phaenomenologica Ser.: No. 72). 337p. 1976. lib. bdg. 175.00 (*90-247-1899-6*, Pub. by M Nijhoff NE) Kluwer Ac.

Welt Des Puppenspiels: The World of Puppetry. John Blundall et al. Ed. by Unima Commission for Publication Staff. Tr. by Christa Schuenke & Frank Reiter. (Illus.). 246p. 1989. 57.50 (*3-362-00244-7*, Pub. by Henschelverlag Kunst und Gesellschaft) Am Ctr UNIMA.

Welt, Geschichte, Mythos, Politik. Gerd Brand. (C). 1978. 76.95 (*3-11-007505-9*) De Gruyter.

Welt im Widerspruch: Gedanken zu Einer Phanomenologie als Ethischer Fundamentalphilosophie. Stephan Strasser. (Phaenomenologica Ser.: Vol. 124). 224p. 1991. lib. bdg. 121.50 (*0-7923-1404-2*, Pub. by Klwr Acad Pubs NE) Kluwer Ac.

***Welt Lohn - Das Herzmaere - Heinrich Von Kempten.** Edward Schroeder. (Konrad von Wurzburg Ser.: Teil 1). xxviii, 78p. (GER.). 1970. write for info. (*3-296-20401-6*, Pub. by Weidmann GW) Lubrecht & Cramer.

Weltalter, Goldene Zeit und Sinnverwandte Vorstellungen. Bodo Gatz. viii, 238p. (GER.). 1967. write for info. (*3-318-70621-0*) G Olms Pubs.

***Weltbild der Vergilischen "Georgika" in Seinem Verhaltnis Zu "De Rerum Natura" des Lukrez.** Sabine Schäfer. (Studien Zur Klassischen Philologie Ser.: Bd. 102). 166p. (GER.). 1996. 42.95 (*3-631-30849-3*) P Lang Pubng.

Weltbuch fur Familiennamen. Numa Research Department Staff. 95p. 1994. 53.00 (*1-885808-03-8*); pap. text ed. 46.00 (*1-885808-04-6*) Numa Corp.

Weltenwuerfe: Ludwig Binswangers Phaenomenologische Psychologie. Max Herzog. (Phaenomenologisch-Psychologische Forschungen Ser.: No. 17). xxxii, 315p. (GER.). (C). 1994. lib. bdg. 129.25 (*3-11-014213-9*) De Gruyter.

Weltgeschichte des Tanzes. Curt Sachs. xi, 325p. (GER.). 1992. reprint ed. write for info. (*3-487-06086-8*) G Olms Pubs.

Weltgeschichtliche Betrachtungen. Jacob Burchhardt. Ed. by J. P. Mayer. LC 78-67340. (European Political Thought Ser.). (GER.). 1979. reprint ed. lib. bdg. 37.95 (*0-405-11683-7*) Ayer.

***Weltlichkeit des Glaubens in der Alten Kirche: Festschrift Fuer Ulrich Wickert Zum Siebzigsten Geburtstag.** Ed. by Dietmar Wyrwa. (Beihefte zur Zeitschrift fuer Neutestamentliche Wissenschaft Ser.: Vol. 85). x, 480p. (GER.). (C). 1997. lib. bdg. 183.70 (*3-11-015441-2*) De Gruyter.

Weltraumrecht: Law of Outer Space. Stephan Von Welck & Renate Platzoder. 825p. (ENG & GER.). 1987. 251.00 (*3-7890-1228-9*, Pub. by Nomos Verlags GW) Intl Bk Import.

Welts: Female Domination in an American Marriage. Gloria Wallace & Dave Wallace. 128p. (Orig.). 1995. pap. 12.95 (*0-9640963-9-0*) Artemis Creat.

Weltstadt in Krisen: Berlin, 1949-1958. Diethelm Prowe. (Veroeffentlichungen der Historischen Kommission zu Berlin, Band 67, Beitraege zu Inflation und Wiederaufbau in Deutschland und Europa 1914-1924: Vol. 42). x, 359p. (C). 1973. 112.35 (*3-11-003876-5*) De Gruyter.

***Weltverantwortung des Christen: Zum Gedenken an Ernst Michel (1889-1964) Dokumentationen.** Arnulf Grob et al. (Illus.). ix, 276p. (GER.). 1996. 54.95 (*3-631-50033-5*) P Lang Pubng.

Welty. 1,977th ed. Patti C. Black. LC 77-82045. (Old Capitol Museum Ser.). (Illus.). 28p. (Orig.). 1977. pap. 6.95 (*0-87805-337-9*) U Pr of Miss.

Welty: A Life in Literature. Ed. by Albert J. Devlin. LC 87-14267. (Illus.). 290p. 1987. 37.50 (*0-87805-315-8*) U Pr of Miss.

Welty Collection: A Guide to the Eudora Welty Manuscripts & Documents at the Mississippi Department of Archives & History. Suzanne Marrs. LC 88-17537. (Illus.). 244p. 1988. text ed. 35.00 (*0-87805-366-2*) U Pr of Miss.

Welty's Book of Procedures for Meetings, Boards, Committees & Officers. Joel D. Welty. 276p. 1982. 9.95 (*0-89803-086-2*) NASCO.

Welzenbach's Climbs. Eric Roberts. LC 81-80502. (Illus.). 272p. 1981. 14.95 (*0-89886-018-0*) Mountaineers.

Weminuche Wilderness, CO. rev. ed. Ed. by Trails Illustrated Staff. 1994. 8.99 (*0-925873-57-8*) Trails Illustrated.

***We'Moon Unbound '98: GAIA Rhythms for Womyn.** (Illus.). 224p. (Orig.). 1997. 14.85 (*1-890931-00-4*) Mother Tongue Ink.

We'Moon '97: Gaia Rhythms for Womyn. (Illus.). 224p. (Orig.). 1996. pap. 13.95 (*0-9510661-8-8*) Mother Tongue Ink.

***We'Moon '98: GAIA Rhythms for Womyn.** (Illus.). 224p. (Orig.). 1997. pap. 14.85 (*0-9510661-9-6*) Mother Tongue Ink.

Wempires. Daniel Pinkwater. LC 90-46925. (Illus.). 32p. (J). (gr. k-3). 1991. lib. bdg. 13.95 (*0-02-774411-6*, Mac Bks Young Read) S&S Childrens.

Wemyss Chronology of the American Stage from 1752-1852. Francis C. Wemyss. LC 67-31455. 191p. 1972. reprint ed. 23.95 (*0-405-09058-7*, Pub. by Blom Pubns UK) Ayer.

Wen Bon: A Naval Air Intelligence Officer Behind Japanese Lines in China in WWII. Byron R. Winborn. LC 94-17451. (War & the Southwest Ser.: No. 2). (Illus.). 253p. 1994. 29.95 (*0-929398-77-7*) UNTX Pr.

***Wen-Jen Hua: Chinese Literati Painting from the Collection of Mr. & Mrs. Mitchell Hutchinson.** Tseng Y. Ecke. Ed. by Howard A. Link. (Illus.). 130p. (Orig.). (C). 1988. pap. 17.50 (*0-937426-09-1*) Honolu Arts.

Wen, the Botany, & the Mexican Hat: The Adventures of the First Women Through Grand Canyon on the Nevills Expedition. William Cook. 151p. 1987. reprint ed. lib. bdg. 29.00 (*0-8095-6118-2*) Borgo Pr.

Wen-Tzu: Understanding the Mysteries. Lao Tzu. Tr. by Thomas Cleary from CHI. LC 92-53700. (Dragon Editions Ser.). Orig. Title: Further Teachings of Lao-tzu. 168p. (Orig.). 1992. pap. 14.00 (*0-87773-862-9*, Sham Dragon Edits) Shambhala Pubns.

***Wen Xuan, or Selections of Refined Literature: Rhapsodies on Natural Phenomena, Birds & Animals, Aspirations & Feelings, Vol. 3.** Xiao Tong. Tr. by David R. Knechtges. 458p. 1996. text ed. 75.00 (*0-691-02126-0*) Princeton U Pr.

Wenatchie Bend. large type ed. Giff Cheshire. LC 96-8317. (Sagebrush Large Print Westerns Ser.). 272p. 1996. lib. bdg. 17.95 (*1-57490-018-8*) T T Beeler.

Wenceslas Square. Larry Shue. 1989. pap. 5.25 (*0-8222-1232-3*) Dramatists Play.

Wenceslaus Hollar: A Bohemian Artist in England. Richard T. Godfrey. (Illus.). 224p. 1994. 45.00 (*0-300-06166-8*) Yale U Pr.

Wenceslaus Hollar: Delineator of His Time. Katherine S. Van Eerde. (Special Publications Ser.). 1978. 30.00 (*0-8139-0297-5*) Folger Bks.

Wenceslaus Hollar: Delineator of His Time. Katherine S. Van Eerde. (Illus.). 121p. 1990. 40.00 (*0-918016-51-7*) Folger Bks.

Wenceslaus Hollar 1607-1677. Frwd. by Naomi R. Kline. 1979. write for info. (*0-9601342-2-0*) PSC Art Gall.

Wenceslaus Holler & His Views of London & Windsor in the Seventeenth Century: And His Views of London & Windsor in the Seventeenth Century. Arthur M. Hind. LC 68-56500. (Illus.). 106p. 1972. reprint ed. lib. bdg. 20.95 (*0-405-08622-9*, Pub. by Blom Pubns UK) Ayer.

Wench Is Dead. Colin Dexter. 192p. 1991. mass mkt. 5.99 (*0-553-29120-3*) Bantam.

Wench Is Dead. large type ed. Colin Dexter. 1991. 25.99 (*0-7089-2512-X*) Ulverscroft.

Wendal, His Cat, & the Progress of Man: An Illustrated Novel. V. Campudoni. LC 93-81135. (Illus.). 108p. 1994. 12.00 (*1-56352-128-8*) Longstreet Pr Inc.

Wende Des Lebens: Untersuchungen Zu Einem Situations-Motiv Der Bibel. Armin Schmitt. (Beihefte zur Zeitschrift fuer die Alttestamentliche Wissenschaft Ser.: No. 237). x, 323p. (GER.). (C). 1996. lib. bdg. 124.95 (*3-11-014757-2*) De Gruyter.

Wende '89 Von der DDR Zu Den Funf Neuen Landern. Ed. by P. Hutchinson & A. G. Jones. (Bristol German Texts Ser.). 96p. (GER.). 1992. pap. 14.95 (*1-85399-304-2*, Pub. by Brstl Class Pr UK) Focus Pub-R Pullins.

Wendell. Eric J. Nones. (J). (ps up). 1989. 13.95 (*0-374-38266-2*) FS&G.

Wendell Berry. Andrew J. Angyal. LC 95-2290. (United States Authors Ser.: Vol. TUSAS 654). 1995. 23.95 (*0-8057-4628-5*, Twayne) Scribnrs Ref.

Wendell Berry. Ed. by Paul Merchant. LC 91-73134. (American Authors Ser.). 250p. (Orig.). 1991. 25.00 (*0-917652-89-4*); pap. 15.00 (*0-917652-88-6*) Confluence Pr.

Wendell Brazeau: A Search for Form. Spencer Moseley & Millard B. Rogers. LC 76-49167. (Index of Art in the Pacific Northwest Ser.: No. 12). (Illus.). 96p. 1977. 16.50 (*0-295-95555-4*); pap. 8.95 (*0-295-95546-5*) U of Wash Pr.

Wendell Castle: Environmental Works. Peter T. Joseph & Matthew Kangas. (Illus.). 30p. (Orig.). 1993. pap. text ed. 15.00 (*1-881658-07-4*) P J Gallery.

Wendell Franklin. Wendell Franklin. LC 94-74712. (Oral History Ser.). 162p. 1995. pap. 12.95 (*1-882766-01-6*) Dirs Guild Am.

Wendell Phillips. James J. Green. LC 44-5915. 39p. reprint ed. pap. 25.00 (*0-317-28069-4*, 2025545) Bks Demand.

Wendell Phillips: Liberty's Hero. James B. Stewart. LC 85-23793. (Illus.). xiii, 356p. 1986. text ed. 45.00 (*0-8071-1257-7*) La State U Pr.

Wendell Phillips: Orator & Agitator. Lorenzo Sears. LC 67-13340. 1972. reprint ed. 34.95 (*0-405-08942-2*, Pub. by Blom Pubns UK) Ayer.

Wendell Willkie: Fighter for Freedom. Ellsworth Barnard. LC 66-19668. 628p. 1971. 45.00 (*0-87023-088-3*) U of Mass Pr.

Wendell Willkie: Hoosier Internationalist. Ed. by James H. Madison. LC 91-12758. (Illus.). 214p. 1992. text ed. 8.95 (*0-253-33619-8*) Ind U Pr.

Wendigen see Frank Lloyd Wright: The Complete 1925 "Wendingen" Series

Wendigo Border. Catherine Montrose. 288p. (Orig.). 1995. mass mkt. 4.99 (*0-8125-2432-2*) Tor Bks.

Wendle, What Have You Done? Peggy P. Anderson. LC 93-11291. (J). 1994. 13.95 (*0-395-64346-5*) HM.

Wendover, Acme, & Virginia Point. Stephen M. Reeves. LC 80-54382. 158p. 1981. 29.95 (*0-938794-01-9*) Red River Pub Co.

Wendy. Richard Hart. LC 78-72870. 1979. pap. 3.95 (*0-9602100-0-8*) St Wrks Cooperative.

Wendy & Emery Reves Collection. Robert V. Rozelle et al. (Illus.). 224p. 1985. 35.00 (*0-9609622-8-X*); pap. 24.95 (*0-9609622-9-8*) U of Tex Pr.

Wendy & the Whine. Carol Greene. (Illus.). 32p. (J). (gr. 1-4). 1987. pap. 5.99 (*0-570-04157-0*, 56-1615) Concordia.

Wendy Edwards: Paintings & Drawings. Ronald J. Onorato. (Illus.). 16p. (Orig.). 1989. pap. 5.00 (*0-933519-18-4*) D W Bell Gallery.

Wendy Maruyama. Peter T. Joseph & Emma Cobb. (Illus.). (Orig.). 1992. pap. text ed. 15.00 (*1-881658-02-3*) P J Gallery.

Wendy on the Warpath. Nancy K. Robinson. LC 93-32739. (J). (gr. 3 up). 1994. 13.95 (*0-590-45571-0*) Scholastic Inc.

Wendy Perrin's Secrets Every Smart Traveler Should Know. Wendy Perrin. LC 96-48213. 1997. pap. 15.00 (*0-679-03351-3*) Fodors Travel.

Wendy Wahl: Textural Compositions. Intro. by Emma Cobb. (Illus.). 6p. (Orig.). pap. text ed. 10.00 (*0-614-02571-0*) P J Gallery.

Wendy's Adventure in Never Land. Walt Disney Productions Staff. (Walt Disney's Fun-to-Read Library Ser.: Vol. 9). (Illus.). 44p. (J). (gr. 1-6). 1986. reprint ed. 3.49 (*1-885222-21-1*) Advance Pubs.

Wendy's Gift. Vel Priebe. (Kinderbook Ser.). (Illus.). 24p. (Orig.). (J). (ps-2). 1988. pap. 1.50 (*0-919797-67-9*) Kindred Prods.

Wendy's Wish. T. J. Bradstreet. (Darkest Wish Ser.: No. 3). 160p. (Orig.). (J). 1996. pap. 3.99 (*0-380-77819-X*, Camelot) Avon.

Wenham Tea House Cookbook. Wenham Village Improvement Society Staff. LC 92-25281. 1992. spiral bd. 15.95 (*0-87197-344-8*) Favorite Recipes.

Wenner Gren International Series. Wenner Gren International Series Staff. Date not set. write for info. (*0-08-044446-6*, Pergamon Pr) Elsevier.

Went Missing. 9th ed. Frederick Stonehouse. LC 84-70847. (Illus.). 1984. pap. 11.95 (*0-932212-37-9*) Avery Color.

Went the Day Well? BFI Film Classics. Penelope Houston. (Illus.). 64p. 1992. pap. 9.95 (*0-85170-318-6*, Pub. by British Film Inst UK) Ind U Pr.

Wentworth Genealogy in England & America, Vol. 1. J. Wentworth. (Illus.). 711p. 1989. reprint ed. pap. 106.50 (*0-8328-1239-0*); reprint ed. lib. bdg. 104.50 (*0-8328-1238-2*) Higginson Bk Co.

Wentworth Genealogy in England & America, Vol. 2. J. Wentworth. (Illus.). 803p. 1989. reprint ed. pap. 120.50 (*0-8328-1241-2*); reprint ed. lib. bdg. 128.50 (*0-8328-1240-4*) Higginson Bk Co.

Wentworth Genealogy in England & America, Vol. 3. J. Wentworth. (Illus.). 727p. 1989. reprint ed. pap. 109.00 (*0-8328-1243-9*); reprint ed. lib. bdg. 117.00 (*0-8328-1242-0*) Higginson Bk Co.

Wentworth Papers 1597-1628. J. P. Cooper. (Camden Fourth Ser.: No. 12). 347p. 27.00 (*0-901050-20-2*) David Brown.

Wenzel's Menu Maker. 2nd ed. George Wenzel, Jr. Ed. by CBL Staff. LC 79-13732. 1196p. 1979. text ed. 166.95 (*0-8436-2135-4*) Van Nos Reinhold.

Wenzel's Menu Maker. 3rd ed. Lewis Reed. 1997. text ed. 166.95 (*0-442-01283-7*) Van Nos Reinhold.

Wept of Wish-Ton-Wish, 2 vols. in one. James Fenimore Cooper. (BCL Ser. I). reprint ed. 42.50 (*0-404-01715-0*) AMS Pr.

Wept of Wish-Ton-Wish, 2 vols. in 1. James Fenimore Cooper. LC 74-107169. 1971. reprint ed. 39.00 (*0-403-00432-2*) Scholarly.

Wept of Wishton Wish. James Fenimore Cooper. (Works of James Fenimore Cooper Ser.). 1990. reprint ed. lib. bdg. 79.00 (*0-7812-2378-4*) Rprt Serv.

***WEPZA International Directory of Export Processing Zones & Free Trade Zones.** 3rd ed. 1997. pap. 95.00 (*0-945951-17-5*) Flagstaff Inst.

***Wepza International Directory of Export Processing Zones & Free Zones.** 2nd ed. Flagstaff Institute Staff. 310p. 1996. text ed. 65.00 (*0-945951-14-0*) Flagstaff Inst.

An Asterisk (*) at the beginning of an entry indicates that the title is appearing in BIP for the first time.

Wer Ist Schuld? Eckhard Frick. (Philosophische Texte und Studien: Vol. 33). 220p. (GER.). 1993. write for info. (3-487-09685-4) G Olms Pubs.

***Wer Studiert Heute Theologie? Studienbeweggrunde und Studienberlaufe Bei Theologiestudierenden Eine Langzeitstudie.** Theodor W. Kohler & Bernard Schwaiger. (Theologie & Empirie Ser.: Vol. 26). 221p. 1996. pap. 35.00 (90-390-0541-9, Pub. by KOK Pharos NE) Eisenbrauns.

Wer War Wer in der DDR: Ein Biographisches Handbuch. Ed. by Bernd-Rainer Barth et al. 864p. (GER.). 1995. pap. 26.25 (3-596-12767-X, Pub. by Fischer Taschbch Verlag GW) Intl Bk Import.

Wer Zuletzt Lacht. Peter Fabrizius. Ed. by Clair H. Bell. LC 52-7510. (Illus.). (GER.). 1963. pap. text ed. 9.95 (0-89197-468-7) Irvington.

***Werbefilm.** Ingrid Westbrock. (Studien Zur Filmgeschichte Ser.: Vol. 1). 126p. (GER.). 1983. write for info. (3-487-07453-2) G Olms Pubs.

Werbel Approved Course for Rental Vehicle Companies & Their Franchisees. Harold Luckstone, Jr. & Richard W. Holliday. 64p. 1991. pap. text ed. 7.95 (1-884803-14-8) Werbel Pub.

Werbel Life Insurance Primer. Raymond A. D'Amico. 256p. (C). 1996. pap. 19.95 (1-884803-03-2) Werbel Pub.

Werbel Multiple Choice Practice Questions for New York Addendum Property & Casualty Insurance. rev. ed. Marilyn J. Needleman. 112p. (C). 1996. pap. text ed. 11.95 (1-884803-01-6) Werbel Pub.

Werbel's New York Addendum: Property & Casualty Insurance. rev. ed. Sandra G. Blundetto. 138p. (C). 1996. pap. text ed. 10.75 (1-884803-00-8) Werbel Pub.

Werberecht der Rechtsanwalte. Gerhard Ring. 269p. (GER.). 1990. pap. 44.00 (3-7890-1907-0, Pub. by Nomos Verlags GW) Intl Bk Import.

Werberwoerterbuch-Advertising Dictionary-Dictionaire de la Publicite. Ed. by Wolfgang J. Koschnick. xi, 299p. (ENG, FRE & GER.). (C). 1994. lib. bdg. 52.00 (3-11-014341-0, 7-94) De Gruyter.

***Werbewirksam Handeln in Einer Fremden Kultur: Eine Untersuchung Interkultureller Unterschiede Zwischen dem Deutschen und dem Chinesischen Werbenden Sprechen aus Ubersetzungswissenschaftlicher Sicht.** Jianbin Wang. (GER.). 1996. 44.95 (3-631-30413-7) P Lang Pubng.

Werden und Wesen Des 107 Psalms. Walter Beyerlin. (Beiheft 153 zur Zeitschrift fuer die Alttestamentliche Wissenschaft Ser.). (C). 1979. 77.70 (3-11-007755-8) De Gruyter.

We're a Family, Aren't We? Nancy Cushman. 1979. 8.50 (0-686-24268-8) T Weatherby.

We're All Animals Coloring Book. People for the Ethical Treatment of Animals Staff. (Illus.). 16p. (Orig.). (J). (gr. k-5). pap. text ed. 3.35 (0-9622101-0-2) Peta Pubns.

We're All Artists: Watercolor for Everyone. Teresa Ascone. (Illus.). 148p. (Orig.). (C). 1994. 36.95 (1-883724-01-5); otabind, pap. 19.95 (1-883724-00-7) Alaskan Portfolio.

We're All Doing Time. Bo Lozoff. LC 84-62787. (Illus.). 336p. (Orig.). (C). 1985. pap. 10.00 (0-9614444-0-1) Human Kind Found.

We're All in This Alone. Ludlow Porch. LC 94-77591. 160p. 1994. 16.95 (1-56352-171-7) Longstreet Pr Inc.

We're All in This Together: Families Facing Breast Cancer. Irene Virag. (Illus.). 96p. 1995. pap. 14.95 (0-8362-7050-9) Andrews & McMeel.

We're All Kin: A Cultural Study of a Mountain Neighborhood. F. Carlene Bryant. LC 81-473. 160p. 1981. 22.00 (0-87049-312-4) U of Tenn Pr.

We're All Mad, You Know. Gary McGuire. Ed. & Intro. by Craig Roberts. (Illus.). 219p. (Orig.). 1996. pap. 11.95 (0-9652385-0-4) M Lee Pr.

We're All Special. Arlene Maguire. (Illus.). 164p. (J). (ps up). 1995. 12.00 (0-9641330-3-2) Portunus Pubng.

We're Back: A Dinosaur's Story. Hudson Talbott. 32p. (J). (ps-2). 1988. lib. bdg. 15.00 (0-517-56599-4) Crown Bks Yng Read.

We're Back! A Dinosaur's Story. Hudson Talbott. LC 87-5355. (Illus.). 32p. (J). (ps-2). 1993. pap. 4.99 (0-517-58985-0) Crown Bks Yng Read.

We're Counting on You, Grover! Michaela Muntean. (Sesame Street Growing-up Bks.). (Illus.). (J). (ps). 1991. write for info. (0-307-12050-3, Golden Pr) Western Pub.

We're Czechs. Robert L. Skrabanek. LC 87-18002. (Centennial Series of the Association of Former Students: No. 25). (Illus.). 256p. (C). 1995. pap. 14.95 (0-89096-413-0) Tex A&M Univ Pr.

We're Different, We're the Same. Bobbi J. Kates. LC 91-38545. (Sesame Street Picturebacks Ser.). (Illus.). 32p. (Orig.). (J). (ps-3). 1992. pap. 3.25 (0-679-83227-0) Random Bks Yng Read.

We're Doing Cinderella. Sheila L. Rinear. 24p. (Orig.). (YA). (gr. 6-11). 1993. pap. 3.00 (1-57514-127-2) Encore Perform Pub.

We're Driving Our Kids Crazy: The Shift to Non-Guilt Parenting. Arlie J. Payne. Ed. by Diane Parker. LC 90-50893. (Illus.). 150p. (Orig.). 1991. pap. 7.95 (0-88247-864-8) R & E Pubs.

We're Fighting a War. Be There! large type ed. Pete Peterson et al. (Illus.). 160p. (Orig.). 1996. pap. 9.95 (1-889103-01-2) Lead Mine Pr.

We're Finally Alone: Now What Do We Do? Greg Johnson. LC 95-40115. 1996. pap. 10.99 (0-8423-7848-0) Tyndale.

We're Friends Because... Joan Hutson. (Illus.). 32p. (J). (gr. 5-9). 1995. 5.95 (0-8198-8244-5) Pauline Bks.

We're from Duffield. 3rd ed. Stanley C. Perkins. (Illus.). 147p. 1982. 10.00 (0-9614640-1-1); pap. 7.50 (0-9614640-2-X) Broadblade Pr.

We're Going on a Bear Hunt. Michael Rosen. LC 88-13338. (Illus.). 40p. (J). (ps-4). 1989. lib. bdg. 16.00 (0-689-50476-4, McElderry) S&S Childrens.

We're Going on a Bear Hunt. Michael Rosen. LC 92-8836. (Illus.). 40p. (J). (ps-1). 1992. 5.95 (0-689-71653-2, Aladdin Paperbacks) S&S Childrens.

***We're Going on a Bear Hunt.** Michael Rosen. (Illus.). (J). 1997. write for info. (0-614-29303-0, Litl Simon S&S) S&S Childrens.

***We're Going to Meeting for Worship.** Abby A. Hadley. (Illus.). 32p. (J). (ps-3). 1972. reprint ed. pap. 5.00 (1-888305-02-9) Friends Genl Conf.

We're Going to the Doctor. Harry Bornstein. (Signed English Ser.). (Illus.). 28p. (J). (ps-3). 1974. pap. 5.50 (0-913580-26-0, Pub. by K Green Pubns) Gallaudet Univ Pr.

We're Growing Together. Candice F. Ransom. LC 92-7424. (Illus.). 32p. (J). (ps-2). 1993. lib. bdg. 14.95 (0-02-775666-1, Bradbury S&S) S&S Childrens.

***We're Growing Together.** Candice F. Ransom. (Illus.). 32p. (J). 3.98 (0-7651-0033-9) Smithmark.

***We're Having a Kitten.** Swanson. LC 97-24682. 1997. 16.95 (0-312-17062-9) St Martin.

We're Having a Party. Lucy Rigg. (Tiny Touch Bks.). (Illus.). 1994. 7.50 (0-8378-7624-9) Gibson.

***We're Having a Puppy.** Swanson. LC 97-22123. 1997. 16.95 (0-312-17063-7) St Martin.

We're Heaven Bound! Portrait of a Black Sacred Drama. Gregory D. Coleman. LC 94-15273. (Illus.). 200p. 1994. 24.95 (0-8203-1684-9) U of Ga Pr.

We're Here: Conversations with Lesbian Women. Angela Stewart-Park & Jules Cassidy. 3.95 (0-7043-3117-9, Pub. by Quartet UK) Charles River Bks.

***We're in Business.** Norman. Date not set. wbk. ed., pap. text ed. write for info. (0-582-74871-2, Pub. by Longman UK); student ed., pap. text ed. write for info. (0-582-74872-0, Pub. by Longman UK) Longman.

We're in the Money: Depression America & Its Films. Andrew Bergman. LC 74-159533. (Illus.). (C). 1971. text ed. 28.00 (0-8147-0964-8) NYU Pr.

We're in the Money: Depression America & Its Films. Andrew Bergman. (Illus.). 224p. 1992. reprint ed. pap. text ed. 9.95 (0-929587-85-5, Elephant Paperbacks) I R Dee.

We're in This Thing Together. Perry Tanksley. 1974. 4.50 (0-8007-0664-1) Allgood Bks.

We're in This Together, Lord: Bible Devotions for Girls. Evelyn A. Wade. LC 92-30987. (Young Reader's Ser.). 112p. (J). (gr. 3-7). 1992. pap. 5.99 (0-8066-2649-6, 9-2649) Augsburg Fortress.

Were in This Together, Patti! Katy Hall. (Peabody Rebus Reading Program Ser.). (Orig.). (J). (gr. 3-6). 1995. pap. 3.50 (0-671-52051-2, Minstrel Bks) PB.

We're in This War Too: World War II Letters from American Women in Uniform. Ed. by Judy B. Litoff & David C. Smith. LC 93-36523. (Illus.). 288p. 1994. 25.00 (0-19-507504-8) OUP.

***We're Just Good Friends: Women & Men in Nonromantic Relationships.** Kathy Werking. LC 97-2904. (Personal Relationships Ser.). 193p. 1997. lib. bdg. 26.95 (1-57230-187-2, 0187) Guilford Pr.

We're Living with Tragedy Baby. Esther K. Heggie. (Orig.). 1987. pap. text ed. 2.00 (0-938885-03-0) Shu Pub.

We're Making Breakfast for Mother. Shirley Neitzel. LC 96-10417. (Illus.). 32p. (J). (ps up). 1997. 15.00 (0-688-14575-2); lib. bdg. 14.93 (0-688-14576-0) Greenwillow.

We're No Angels. David Mamet. LC 59-25204. 144p. 1990. pap. 7.95 (0-8021-3202-2, Grove) Grove-Atltic.

We're Not Bananas! The Concept of People in the Principle of Self-Determination & Its Implications for the United Nations. Harris O. Schoenberg. Ed. by Walter Hoffmann. (Monograph in CURE Ser.: No. 11). 68p. 1993. pap. text ed. 5.00 (1-881520-01-3) Ctr U N Reform Educ.

***We're Not in Kansas Anymore, Sis.** Loretta Jackson & Vickie Britton. 364p. (Orig.). 1997. pap. write for info. (1-57502-483-7, P01443) Morris Pubng.

We're Number One: State--Ole Miss Jokes. rev. ed. Sally Walton & Faye Wilkinson. (Illus.). 72p. 1980. reprint ed. pap. 4.95 (0-937552-04-6) Quail Ridge.

We're Number One: Where America Stands & Falls in the New World Order. Andrew Shapiro. 1992. pap. 10.00 (0-679-73893-2, Vin) Random.

We're off to Thunder Mountain. Margaret Y. Phinney. LC 95-8418. (J). 1995. write for info. (1-57255-032-5) Mondo Pubng.

We're off to Thunder Mountain. Margaret Y. Phinney. LC 95-8418. 16p. (J). (ps-3). 1995. pap. 3.95 (1-57255-031-7) Mondo Pubng.

We're on a Mission from God: The Generation X Guide to John Paul II & the Real Meaning of Life. Mary B. Bonacci. LC 95-78279. 216p. (Orig.). 1996. pap. 11.95 (0-89870-567-3) Ignatius Pr.

***Were Our Mouths Filled with Song: Studies in Liberal Jewish Liturgy.** LC 96-51937. (Monographs of the Hebrew Union College). 1997. 49.95 (0-87820-419-9) Hebrew Union Coll Pr.

"We're People First" The Social & Emotional Lives of Individuals with Mental Retardation. Elaine E. Castles. LC 95-34409. 224p. 1996. text ed. 35.00 (0-275-95243-6, Praeger Pubs) Greenwood.

We're Poor Little Lambs: The Last Misson of Crew 22 & "Picadilly Lilly," 100th Bombardment Group, October 8, 1943. Paul M. Andrews. Ed. by Charles P. McDowell. LC 95-60246. (Illus.). 96p. (Orig.). 1995. pap. 12.95 (0-915779-04-8) Foxfall Pr.

We're Ready for You, Mr. Grodin: Behind the Scenes at Talk Shows, Movies, & Elsewhere. Charles Grodin. 1994. text ed. 20.00 (0-02-545795-0, L Drew Bks) S&S Trade.

We're Right & You're Not. James Carville. 1995. write for info. (0-614-15014-0) Random.

We're Right, They're Wrong: A Progressive Program. James Carville. 144p. 1996. pap. 10.00 (0-679-76978-1) Random.

We're Roasting Harry Tuesday Night: How to Plan, Write & Conduct the Business-Social Roast. Ed McManus & Bill Nicholas. 221p. 1984. 18.95 (0-13-950163-0, Busn) P-H.

We're Rooted Here & They Can't Pull Us Up: Essays in African Canadian Women's History. Dionne Brand et al. Ed. by Peggy Bristow. (Illus.). 192p. (C). 1994. 45.00 (0-8020-5943-0); pap. 17.95 (0-8020-6881-2) U of Toronto Pr.

We're Running Late! Teachable Moments for Working Mothers. Kass Dotterweich. LC 96-4571. (Teachable Moment Bks.). (Illus.). 128p. (Orig.). 1996. pap. 8.95 (0-89243-924-6) Liguori Pubns.

We're So Big & Powerful That Nothing Bad Can Happen to Us. Ian I. Mitroff. 1990. 19.95 (1-55972-051-4, Birch Ln Pr) Carol Pub Group.

We're So Lucky! A Book about Our Bubbies & Zaidies. Ruth Finkelstein. (Illus.). 26p. (J). (ps-5). 1996. 12.95 (0-9628157-3-X) R Finkelstein.

Were the Hawaiian Islands Visited by the Spaniards Before Their Discovery by Captain Cook in 1778? Erik W. Dahlgren. LC 75-35187. (Illus.). reprint ed. 67.50 (0-404-14216-8) AMS Pr.

We're the Noisy Dinosaurs!, Set. John Watson. LC 91-58764. (Illus.). 32p. (J). (ps up). 1992. 14.95 (1-56402-089-4) Candlewick Pr.

Were They Pushed or Did They Jump? An Analysis of Educational Decisions in North-West Italy. Diego Gambetta. (Studies in Rationality & Social Change). 270p. 1987. text ed. 80.00 (0-521-32490-4) Cambridge U Pr.

Were They Pushed or Did They Jump? Individual Decision Mechanisms in Education. Diego Gambetta. LC 96-10243. 234p. (C). 1996. reprint ed. pap. text ed. 24.95 (0-8133-3154-4) Westview.

Were They Really the Good Old Days? Eunice Kanne. (Illus.). 160p. (Orig.). 1994. pap. 10.00 (0-938627-25-2) New Past Pr.

We're Very Good Friends, My Brother & I. P. K. Hallinan. (Illus.). 24p. (J). (ps-3). 1990. pap. 4.95 (0-8249-8469-2, Ideals Child) Hambleton-Hill.

We're Very Good Friends, My Father & I. P. K. Hallinan. (Illus.). 24p. (J). (ps-3). 1990. per., pap. 4.95 (0-8249-8520-6, Ideals Child) Hambleton-Hill.

We're Very Good Friends, My Grandma & I. P. K. Hallinan. (Illus.). 24p. (J). (ps-3). 1989. per., pap. 4.95 (0-8249-8548-6, Ideals Child) Hambleton-Hill.

We're Very Good Friends, My Grandpa & I. P. K. Hallinan. (Illus.). 24p. (J). (ps-3). 1989. per., pap. 4.95 (0-8249-8549-4, Ideals Child) Hambleton-Hill.

We're Very Good Friends, My Mother & I. P. K. Hallinan. (Illus.). 24p. (J). (ps-3). 1990. per., pap. 4.95 (0-8249-8519-2, Ideals Child) Hambleton-Hill.

We're Very Good Friends, My Sister & I. P. K. Hallinan. (Illus.). 24p. (J). (ps-3). 1990. pap. 4.95 (0-8249-8470-6, Ideals Child) Hambleton-Hill.

Were We Our Brothers' Keepers? The Public Response of Jews to the Holocaust, 1938-1944. Haskel Lookstein. (Illus.). 288p. 1985. 18.95 (0-87677-148-7) Hartmore.

***Were We the Enemy? A Saga of Hiroshima Survivors in America.** Rinjiro Sodei. (Transitions: Asia & Asian America Ser.). 1997. 49.95 (0-8133-2960-4) Westview.

Were-Wolf. Douglas A. Menville. LC 75-46280. (Supernatural & Occult Fiction Ser.). (Illus.). 1976. reprint ed. lib. bdg. 17.95 (0-405-08138-3) Ayer.

Were-Wolves & Will-O-the-Wisps: French Tales of Mackinac Retold. Dirk Gringhuis. (Illus.). 106p. (Orig.). 1974. pap. 6.00 (0-911872-14-0) Mackinac St Hist Pks.

We're Worth It! Women & Collective Action in the Insurance Workplace. Cynthia B. Costello. 168p. 1992. text ed. 23.50 (0-252-01803-6) U of Ill Pr.

Were You Always a Criminal? Freddie Greenfield. (Illus.). 88p. (Orig.). 1989. pap. 7.95 (0-915480-18-2) Fag Rag.

Were You Born under a Lucky Star. A. Alpheus. 217p. 1969. reprint ed. spiral bd. 7.00 (0-7873-0031-4) Hlth Research.

Were You There? Godforsakenness in Slave Religion. David E. Goatley. LC 95-47052. (Bishop Henry McNeal Turner-Sojourner Truth Ser.: Vol. 11). 125p. (Orig.). 1996. pap. 14.50 (1-57075-063-7) Orbis Bks.

Were You There When They Crucified My Lord? A Negro Spiritual in Illustrations. Allan R. Crite. LC 70-84107. (Illus.). 94p. reprint ed. 26.95 (0-8434-0048-X) Ayer.

Were Your Ancestors in the Newspaper. Arlene H. Eakle. 62p. 1974. pap. 18.00 (0-940764-12-1) Genealog Inst.

Wereing. Rodman Philbrick. (Werewolf Chronicles Ser.: No. 3). (J). (gr. 4-7). 1996. pap. text ed. 3.99 (0-590-69241-0) Scholastic Inc.

Werewolf. William Gleason. 22p. 1972. pap. 3.00 (0-87129-095-2, W16) Dramatic Pub.

Werewolf. Jim Pipe. (In the Footsteps of... Ser.). (Illus.). 40p. (J). (gr. 4-6). 1996. pap. 6.95 (0-7613-0465-7, Copper Beech Bks); lib. bdg. 16.40 (0-7613-0450-9, Copper Beech Bks) Millbrook Pr.

Werewolf. Montague Summers. 308p. 1973. pap. 3.95 (0-8065-0392-0, Citadel Pr) Carol Pub Group.

Werewolf. Montague Summers. 1997. 9.99 (0-517-18093-6) Random Hse Value.

***Werewolf.** Charles Whiting. 1996. pap. text ed. 16.95 (0-85052-513-6, Pub. by L Cooper Bks UK) Trans-Atl Phila.

Werewolf: A True Story of Demonic Possession. Ed Warren. 1992. mass mkt. 4.50 (0-312-92864-5) St Martin.

Werewolf: Hell-Storm. James A. Moore. (World of Darkness Ser.). 304p. 1996. mass mkt. 5.50 (0-06-105675-8, HarperPrism) HarpC.

Werewolf: The Apocalypse. 2nd ed. (Werewolf Ser.). 1994. 28.00 (1-56504-112-7, 3600) White Wolf.

***Werewolf: The Wild West.** Various. 1997. 28.00 (1-56504-340-5) White Wolf.

Werewolf & Vampire in Romania. Harry A. Senn. (East European Monographs: No. 99). 148p. 1982. text ed. 41.00 (0-914710-93-1) East Eur Monographs.

***Werewolf Chronicles, Vol. 2.** Steve Crow et al. (Werewolf Ser.). (Illus.). 1997. pap. 15.00 (1-56504-322-7, 3207) White Wolf.

***Werewolf Chronicles: For Werewolf, the Apocalypse, Vol. 1.** White Wolf Staff. 1997. pap. 15.00 (1-56504-321-9) White Wolf.

Werewolf Complex: America's Fascination with Violence. Denis Duclos. Ed. by Bruce Kapferer & John Gledhill. (Global Issues Ser.). 256p. 1996. 38.95 (1-85973-146-5); pap. 16.95 (1-85973-151-1) Berg Pubs.

***Werewolf Followed Me Home.** Stanley. LC 97-3579. (Scaredy Cats Ser.: No. 7). (J). 1997. mass mkt. 3.99 (0-689-81614-6) S&S Childrens.

Werewolf Moon. Sharon Green. (Intrigue Ser.). 1993. pap. 2.89 (0-373-22224-6, 1-22224-9) Harlequin Bks.

Werewolf, Nineteen Forty-Four to Nineteen Forty-Five. 1980. 9.95 (3-87943-700-9) Beachcomber Bks.

Werewolf of Fever Swamp. R. L. Stine. (Goosebumps Ser.: Nov. 14). 160p. (J). (gr. 4-6). 1993. pap. 3.99 (0-590-49449-X) Scholastic Inc.

Werewolf of Paris. Guy Endore. 256p. 1992. pap. 10.95 (0-8065-1287-3, Citadel Pr) Carol Pub Group.

Werewolf of Paris. Guy Endore. 1993. reprint ed. lib. bdg. 18.95 (0-89968-425-4, Lghtyr Pr) Buccaneer Bks.

Werewolf Players Guide. (Werewolf Ser.). 1994. 18.00 (1-56504-057-0, 3202) White Wolf.

Werewolf Principle. Clifford D. Simak. 192p. 1994. 3.95 (0-7867-0100-5) Carroll & Graf.

Werewolf Screen. James A. Moore. 1996. 10.00 (1-56504-113-5, 3601) White Wolf.

Werewolf Sequence (a Poem in 100 Sequences) Martin J. Rosenblum. 150p. (Orig.). 1974. pap. 50.00 (0-87924-029-6) Membrane Pr.

Werewolf Storytellers Handbook. White Wolf Staff. 128p. 1994. per., pap. 18.00 (1-56504-131-3, 3205) White Wolf.

Werewolf Tonight. Don Whittington. 144p. (Orig.). (J). (gr. 3-7). 1995. pap. 3.50 (0-380-77513-1, Camelot) Avon.

Werewolf vs. Comanche: The Official Strategy Guide. Tom Basham. 1995. pap. text ed. 19.95 (0-7615-0053-7) Prima Pub.

Werewolf Wars. Randall Goldman. 159p. (Orig.). 1996. mass mkt. 4.99 (1-55197-265-4, Pub. by Comnwlth Pub CN) Partners Pubs Grp.

Werewolves. Jerry Ahern. 1990. mass mkt. 4.50 (1-55817-335-8, Pinncle Kensgtn) Kensgtn Pub Corp.

Werewolves. Daniel Cohen. 128p. (YA). (gr. 5-12). 1996. pap. 14.99 (0-525-65207-8, Cobblehill Bks) Dutton Child Bks.

Werewolves. Martin H. Greenberg. 320p. (Orig.). 1995. mass mkt. 5.50 (0-88677-654-6) DAW Bks.

Werewolves & Stories about Them. Eric Kudalis. (Monsters & Their Stories Ser.). 48p. (J). (gr. 3-10). 1994. lib. bdg. 17.80 (1-56065-215-2) Capstone Pr.

***Werewolves & Stories about Them.** Eric Kudalis. (Classic Monster Stories Ser.). (Illus.). 48p. (J). (gr. 3-7). 1994. 18.40 (0-516-35215-6) Childrens.

Werewolves Don't Go to Summer Camp. Debbie Dadey & Marcia Jones. 128p. (J). (gr. 2-5). 1991. pap. 2.99 (0-590-44061-6) Scholastic Inc.

***Werewolves Don't Go to Summer Camp.** Debbie Dadey & Marcia T. Jones. (FRE.). (J). pap. 5.99 (0-590-73940-9) Scholastic Inc.

Werewolves for Lunch. Erica Farber & J. R. Sansevere. LC 95-6798. (Creepy Critters Ser.). (Illus.). 80p. (J). (gr. 1-5). 1996. pap. 3.99 (0-679-87359-7, Bullseye Bks) Random Bks Yng Read.

Werewolves, Ghost & Vampire Jokes You Can Sink Your Teeth Into. Dianne Woo. 128p. (Orig.). (J). 1994. mass mkt. 3.99 (0-8125-2049-1) Tor Bks.

Werewolves of London. Brian M. Stableford. 462p. 1994. 4.95 (0-7867-0180-3) Carroll & Graf.

***Wergin on Skat & Sheepshead.** Joseph P. Wergin. 312p. 1975. pap. 4.50 (0-614-28575-5) Wergin Distrib.

Werhrmacht War Crimes Bureau, 1939-1945. Alfred M. De Zayas. LC 88-31596. (Illus.). xx, 364p. 1989. pap. 16.95 (0-8032-9908-7, Bison Books) U of Nebr Pr.

Werkbund. Lucius Burckhardt. 118p. 1987. 90.00 (0-85072-108-3) St Mut.

Werkbund: Design Theory & Mass Culture Before the First World War. Frederic J. Schwartz. LC 96-14708. 1996. write for info. (0-300-06849-2) Yale U Pr.

***Werkbund: Design Theory & Mass Culture before the First World War.** Frederic J. Schwartz. (Illus.). 288p. 1996. 50.00 (0-300-06898-0) Yale U Pr.

Werke, 2 Vols. in 1. P. G. Lejeune-Dirichlet. Ed. by Leopold Kronecker. LC 68-54716. 1969. reprint ed. 75.00 (0-8284-0225-6) Chelsea Pub.

Werke, 43 vols., Set. Karl Marx & Frederick Engels. write for info. (3-320-01316-5) Adlers Foreign Bks.

Werke, 3 vols., Set. Adelbert Von Chamisso. LC 75-41053. (BCL Ser.: No. II). 1976. reprint ed. 72.50 (0-404-14850-6) AMS Pr.

Werke, 14 vols. in 12, Set. Carl F. Gauss. (Illus.). 7776p. (GER & LAT.). 1981. reprint ed. lib. bdg. 1,595.00 (3-487-04632-6) G Olms Pubs.

Werke, 5 vols., Set. Leopold Kronecker. LC 66-20394. 1969. reprint ed. 175.00 (0-8284-0224-8) Chelsea Pub.

Werke, 5 vols., Set. Paracelsus. (GER.). reprint ed. 369.60 (3-7965-0471-X) Adlers Foreign Bks.

W

Werke, Vol. 2. Johannes von Paltz. (Illus.). 504p. 1983. 176.95 (*3-11-004955-4*) De Gruyter.

***Werke: Samtliche Romane und Novellenbucher, 19 vols.** Ed. by Wolfgang Mohrig. (Literatur der Romantik Ser.: Vol. 1). (GER.). 1994. reprint ed. write for info. (*3-487-09158-5*) G Olms Pubs.

***Werke Band 10: Der Begriff der Religion Im System der Philosophie.** Thomas Becker. 216p. (GER.). 1996. reprint ed. write for info. (*3-487-06400-6*) G Olms Pubs.

Werke Fur Pianoforte, 7 vols., Set. Johann Strauss, Sr. Incl. Vol.1. Walzer 1-38. (Illus.). 176p. 1976. pap. 75.00 (*0-89371-001-6*); Vol. 2. Walzer 39-68. (Illus.). 184p. 1976. pap. 75.00 (*0-89371-002-4*); Vol. 3. Walzer 69-96. (Illus.). 184p. 1976. pap. 75.00 (*0-89371-003-2*); Vol. 4. Walzer 97-122. (Illus.). 168p. 1976. pap. 75.00 (*0-89371-004-0*); Vol. 5. Walzer 123-150. (Illus.). 176p. 1976. pap. 75.00 (*0-89371-005-9*); Vol. 6. Polkas/Galoppe/Marsche. (Illus.). 144p. 1976. pap. 75.00 (*0-89371-006-7*); Vol. 7. Quadrillen. (Illus.). 160p. 1976. pap. 75.00 (*0-89371-007-5*); Illus.). (GER.). 1976. reprint ed. Set pap. 375.00 (*0-89371-000-8*) Broude Intl Edns.

Werke Jacob Grimms, Bd. 17-18: Deutsche Rechtsaltertumer, 2 vols., Set. Jacob Grimms. 971p. (GER.). 1992. reprint ed. write for info. (*3-487-09596-3*) G Olms Pubs.

Werke Jacob Grimms, Bd. 29: Uber den Altdeutschen Meistergesang. Jacob Grimms. 196p. (GER.). 1993. reprint ed. write for info. (*3-487-09682-X*) G Olms Pubs.

Werke und Briefe. Historisch-kritische Ausgabe (Hamburger Klopstock-Ausgabe) Incl. Section Briefe I. Briefe 1738-1750. Ed. by Friedrich G. Klopstock et al. 1978. 172.00 (*3-11-007257-2*); Section Briefe II. Briefe 1751-1752. Ed. by Friedrich G. Klopstock et al. 1985. 252.00 (*3-11-010552-7*); Section Briefe VII. Briefe 1776-1782 (1) Text. Ed. by Friedrich G. Klopstock et al. 1982. 118.75 (*3-11-008128-8*); Section Briefe VII. Briefe 1776-1782 (2) Apparat-Kommentar (Nr. 1-131). Ed. by Friedrich G. Klopstock et al. 1982. 199.00 (*3-11-008932-7*); Section Briefe VII. Briefe 1776-1782 (3) Apparat-Kommentar (Nr. 132-244) Anhang. Ed. by Friedrich G. Klopstock et al. 1982. 199.00 (*3-11-008933-5*); Section Werke II. Epigramme. Text und Apparat. Ed. by Friedrich G. Klopstock et al. 1982. 199.00 (*3-11-008735-9*); Section Werke IV, Bd. 4. Messias. Band 4 Apparat. 1984. 265.50 (*3-11-008898-3*); Section Addenda, Bd. 2. Klopstock, Arbeitstagebuch. 1977. 165.50 (*3-11-005713-1*); Section Addenda, Bd. 3. Zeitgenossischen Drucke von Klopstocks Werken. Band 1 Bibliographie. 1981. 213.85 (*3-11-008119-9*); Section Addenda, Bd. 3. Zeitgenossischen Drucke von Klopstocks Werken. Band 2 Bibliographie. 1981. 213.85 (*3-11-008570-4*); (GER.). write for info. (*0-318-61114-7*); write for info. (*0-318-61118-X*) De Gruyter.

Werke Wilhelm Grimms, Bd. 31-35: Kleinere Schriften. Wilhelm Grimms. (GER.). 1992. reprint ed. write for info. (*3-487-09617-X*) G Olms Pubs.

Werken voor Clavecimbel. Joseph-Hector Fiocco. 1971. pap. 20.00 (*0-8450-0103-5*) Broude.

Werken voor Clavecimbel. Jean-Baptiste Loeillet. 1973. pap. 20.00 (*0-8450-0106-X*) Broude.

Werkstatt des Pheidias In Olympia: Zweiter Teil: Werkstattfunde. Wolfgang Schiering. Ed. by German Archeological Institute Staff. (Olympische Forschungen Ser.: Vol. XVIII). xiv, 172p. (GER.). (C). 1991. lib. bdg. 152.35 (*3-11-012468-8*) De Gruyter.

Werkstoffe. 3rd ed. 1995. 30.00 (*0-387-58186-3*) Spr-Verlag.

Werkzeug. (Meyers Klien Kinderbibliothek). 24p. (GER.). (J). 1994. 13.25 (*3-411-08711-0*) Langenscheidt.

Werner: A Tragedy. George Gordon Byron. 232p. 1970. pap. 54.95 (*3-7705-0360-0*) Adlers Foreign Bks.

Werner & Ingbar's the Thyroid: A Fundamental & Clinical Text. 7th ed. Ed. by Lewis E. Braverman & Robert D. Utiger. LC 95-39527. 1124p. 1996. text ed. 190.00 (*0-397-51406-9*) Lppncott-Raven.

Werner Drewes: A Catalogue Raisonne of His Prints. (Illus.). 458p. 1984. 165.00 (*3-921561-31-0*, Pub. by Edition Cantz GW) Dist Art Pubs.

Werner Heisenberg: A Bibliography of His Writings. Compiled by David Cassidy & Martha Baker. LC 82-60498. (Berkeley Papers in History of Science: No. 9). 153p. (Orig.). 1984. pap. 10.00 (*0-918102-10-3*) U Cal Hist Sci Tech.

Werner Jaeger Reconsidered: Proceedings of the Second Oldfather Conference. Ed. by William M. Calder, III. LC 92-15977. (Illinois Studies in the History of Classical Scholarship: Vol. 3). 342p. 1992. pap. 44.95 (*1-55540-729-3*, 330003) Scholars Pr GA.

***Werner Koerbs: Vom Sinn der Leibesubungen Zur Zeit der Italienischen Renaissance.** Wolfgang Decker. iv, 161p. (GER.). 1988. 49.80 (*3-615-00037-4*, Pub. by Weidmann GW) Lubrecht & Cramer.

Werner Krauss. W. Goetz. 1976. lib. bdg. 59.95 (*0-8490-2814-0*) Gordon Pr.

Werner Von Braun: Space Visionary & Rocket Engineer. Ray Spangenburg & Diane K. Moser. LC 94-22520. (Makers of Modern Science Ser.). (Illus.). 144p. (J). (gr. 5-12). 1995. 17.95 (*0-8160-2924-5*) Facts on File.

Werner Von Siemens: Inventor & International Entrepreneur. Wilfried Feldenkirchen. LC 94-29670. (Historical Perspectives on Business Enterprise Ser.). (Illus.). 216p. 1994. pap. text ed. 12.50 (*0-8142-0659-X*) Ohio St U Pr.

Werner's Manual for Prison Law Libraries. 2nd ed. Arturo A. Flores. (American Association of Law Libraries Publications Ser.: No. 36). xiv, 174p. 1990. 22.50 (*0-8377-0136-8*) Rothman.

***Wernher der Schweizer.** Deutschen Akademie der Wissenschaften Staff & Max Papke. (Deutsche Texte des Mittelalters Ser.: Band XXVII). xviii, 287p. (GER.). 1967. write for info. (*3-296-17227-0*, Pub. by Weidmann GW) Lubrecht & Cramer.

Wernher Von Braun: Crusader for Space, a Biographical Memoir. rev. ed. Ernst Stuhlinger & Frederick I. Ordway, 3rd. 392p. 1995. 49.50 (*0-89464-969-8*) Krieger.

Wernher Von Braun: Crusader for Space, Combined Edition. 2nd ed. Ernst Stuhlinger & Frederick I. Ordway, 3rd. LC 93-10678. (Illus.). 540p. 1996. pap. 55.00 (*0-89464-980-9*) Krieger.

***Wernher von Braun: Space Pioneer.** John C. Goodrum. LC 78-94442. (Heroes of Space Ser.). (Illus.). 166p. 1969. 10.95 (*0-87397-201-5*, Strode Pubs) Circle Bk Service.

Wernher Von Braun - Crusader for Space: An Illustrated Memoir. Ernst Stuhlinger & Frederick I. Ordway, III. LC 93-10678. (Illus.). 174p. 1994. 29.50 (*0-89464-824-1*) Krieger.

Wernicke-Korsakoff Syndrome & Related Neurologic Disorders Due to Alcoholism & Malnutrition. 2nd ed. Maurice Victor et al. LC 88-30965. (Contemporary Neurology Ser.: No. 30). (Illus.). 231p. (C). 1989. 55.00 (*0-8036-8921-7*) Davis Co.

Wertheimer's Seminars Revisited: Problem Solving & Thinking, 3 vols., Vol. 1. Abraham S. Luchins & Edith H. Luchins. (Illus.). 439p. reprint ed. pap. 114.20 (*0-8357-4204-0*, 2036983) Bks Demand.

Wertheimer's Seminars Revisited: Problem Solving & Thinking, 3 vols., Vol. 2. Abraham S. Luchins & Edith H. Luchins. (Illus.). 430p. reprint ed. pap. 122.60 (*0-8357-4205-9*) Bks Demand.

Wertheimer's Seminars Revisited: Problem Solving & Thinking, 3 vols., Vol. 3. Abraham S. Luchins & Edith H. Luchins. (Illus.). 445p. reprint ed. pap. 126.90 (*0-8357-4206-7*) Bks Demand.

Werther's Goethe: The Game of Literary Creativity. Deirdre Vincent. 304p. 1992. 50.00 (*0-8020-5018-2*) U of Toronto Pr.

Wertmuller: Artist & Immigrant Farmer. Franklin D. Scott. 1963. 1.00 (*0-318-03685-1*) Swedish-Am.

Wes Craven's New Nightmare: The Real Story. David Bergantino. 224p. 1994. mass mkt. 4.99 (*0-8125-5166-4*) Tor Bks.

Wes Jordan - Profile of a Rodmaker: Cross - South Bend - Orvis. Dick Spurr & Gloria Jordan. 192p. 1993. 29.95 (*1-882418-01-8*); pap. 21.95 (*1-882418-02-6*) Centenn Pubns.

Wes Montgomery. Adrian Ingram. 126p. 1993. pap. 19.95 (*0-9506224-9-4*, 00183830, Pub. by Ashley Mark Pub UK) H Leonard.

Wes Montgomery, Artist: Transcriptions for Guitar. 96p. 1988. per. 14.95 (*0-7935-3140-3*, 00675536) H Leonard.

***Wesakejack & the Bears.** Bill Ballantyne. (Illus.). 32p. (J). 1997. pap. 6.95 (*0-921368-72-0*, Pub. by Bain & Cox CN) Genl Dist Srvs.

Wesakejack & the Bears. Bill Ballantyne. (Illus.). 1995. 12.95 (*0-921368-46-1*) LPC InBook.

Wesakejack & the Bears. Bill Ballantyne. (Illus.). 1995. text ed. 18.95 incl. reel tape (*0-921368-48-8*) LPC InBook.

***Wesakejack & the Bears.** Bill Ballantyne. (Illus.). 32p. 1997. pap. 12.95 incl. audio (*0-921368-74-7*, Pub. by Bain & Cox CN) Genl Dist Srvs.

Wesakejack & the Flood. Ballantyne. 1995. 18.95 incl. audio (*0-921368-47-X*, Pub. by Blizzard Pub CN) Genl Dist Srvs.

Wesakejack & the Flood. Bill Ballantyne. 1995. 12.95 (*0-921368-45-3*, Pub. by Blizzard Pub CN) Genl Dist Srvs.

***Wesakejack & the Flood.** Bill Ballantyne. (Illus.). 32p. (J). 1997. pap. 6.95 (*0-921368-71-2*, Pub. by Bain & Cox CN) Genl Dist Srvs.

***Wesakejack & the Flood.** Bill Ballantyne. (Illus.). 32p. 1997. pap. 12.95 incl. audio (*0-921368-73-9*, Pub. by Bain & Cox CN) Genl Dist Srvs.

Wescon '95. IEEE (Region Six) Staff. Ed. by IEEE (Institute of Electrical & Electronics Engineers, Inc.) Staff. LC 95-76248. 794p. 1995. pap. text ed. 134.00 (*0-7803-2636-9*, 95CH35791); lib. bdg. 134.00 (*0-7803-2637-7*, 95CB35791); fiche 134.00 (*0-7803-2638-5*, 95CM35791) Inst Electrical.

Wescon '96. IEEE Staff. LC 96-75711. 750p. 1996. write for info. (*0-7803-3276-8*, 96CH35927); pap. write for info. (*0-7803-3274-1*, 96CH35927); lib. bdg. write for info. (*0-7803-3275-X*, 96CH35927) Inst Electrical.

***Wesen und Lehre des Sports.** Carl Diem. x, 271p. (GER.). 1969. write for info. (*3-296-80200-2*, Pub. by Weidmann GW) Lubrecht & Cramer.

Wesen und Sinn Des Spiels: The Essence & Meaning of Games. Jacobus J. Buytendijk. LC 75-35064. (Studies in Play & Games). (Illus.). (GER.). 1976. reprint ed. 19.95 (*0-405-07915-X*) Ayer.

Wesen und Wandlungen Des Humanismus. Horst Rudiger. 323p. 1966. write for info. (*0-318-71278-4*) G Olms Pubs.

***Wesendonk Lieder & Other Songs.** Richard Wagner. pap. 7.95 (*0-486-27070-X*) Dover.

Wesentliche Vereinigung. Manfred Gerland. (Theologische Texte und Studien: Bd. 2). xii, 186p. (GER.). 1992. write for info. (*3-487-09664-1*) G Olms Pubs.

Wesker on File. Compiled by Simon Trussler & Glenda Leeming. (Methuen Writer-Files Ser.). 96p. (C). 1988. pap. 7.95 (*0-413-53660-2*, A0314) Heinemann.

Wesker the Playwright. Glenda Leeming. 224p. (C). 1988. pap. 11.95 (*0-413-49240-0*, A0315, Pub. by Methuen UK) Heinemann.

***Wesley & Sanctification.** Harald Lindstrom. (Orig.). 1996. reprint ed. pap. 15.00 (*0-916035-72-7*) Evangel Indiana.

Wesley & the People Called Methodist. Richard P. Heitzenrater. 256p. (Orig.). 1995. 34.95 (*0-687-01682-7*); pap. 19.95 (*0-687-44311-3*) Abingdon.

***Wesley & the Quadrilateral: Renewing the Conversation.** W. Stephen Gunter. LC 97-19088. 1997. write for info. (*0-687-06055-9*) Abingdon.

Wesley & Wendell: At Home. Shep Ireland. (Illus.). 40p. (J). (gr. 1). 1991. lib. bdg. 4.75 (*0-8378-0330-6*) Gibson.

Wesley & Wendell: Happy Birthday. Shep Ireland. (Illus.). 40p. (J). (gr. 1). 1991. lib. bdg. 4.75 (*0-8378-0333-0*) Gibson.

Wesley & Wendell: In the Garden. Shep Ireland. (Illus.). 40p. (J). (gr. 1). 1991. lib. bdg. 4.75 (*0-8378-0331-4*) Gibson.

Wesley & Wendell: Vacation. Shep Ireland. (Illus.). 40p. (J). (gr. 1). 1991. lib. bdg. 4.75 (*0-8378-0332-2*) Gibson.

***Wesley Bourne: A Retrospective on the Foundations of McGill Anesthesia.** Joan Bevan & Maria Pacelli. (Fontanus Monographs). (Illus.). 140p. 1997. 45.00 (*0-7735-1455-4*, Pub. by McGill CN) U of Toronto Pr.

Wesley Century. T. Crichton Mitchell. (Great Holiness Classics Ser.: Vol. 2). 508p. 1984. 29.99 (*0-8341-0910-7*) Beacon Hill.

Wesley Clair Mitchell: The Economic Scientist. Ed. by Arthur F. Burns. (General Ser.: No. 53). 401p. 1952. reprint ed. 104.30 (*0-87014-052-3*) Natl Bur Econ Res.

Wesley Family Book of Days. Ed. by Susan I. Pellowe. LC 94-68425. (Illus.). 172p. (Orig.). 1994. pap. 12.00 (*0-9623507-1-0*) Renard Prodns.

Wesley Hymns. Compiled by Ken Bible. 1982. 5.99 (*0-685-69276-0*, MB-510) Lillenas.

Wesley-Langshaw Correspondence: Charles Wesley, His Sons, and the Lancaster Organists. Ed. by Arthur W. Wainwright. LC 93-25483. 108p. 1993. 29.95 (*1-55540-848-6*, 700501); pap. 11.95 (*1-55540-849-4*) Scholars Pr GA.

***Wesley Memorials, Memorials of the Wesley Family, Including biographical & Historical Sketches of All the Members of the Family for 250 Years, with a Genealogical Table (England & America)** George J. Stevenson. 562p. 1996. reprint ed. pap. 87.00 (*0-8328-5264-3*) Higginson Bk Co.

***Wesley Memorials, Memorials of the Wesley Family, Including Biographical Sketches of All the Members of the Family for 250 Years, with a Genealogical Table (England & America)** George J. Stevenson. 562p. 1996. reprint ed. lib. bdg. 97.00 (*0-8328-5263-5*) Higginson Bk Co.

Wesley Mitchell (1874-1948), John Commons (1862-1945), Clarence Ayers (1891-1972) Ed. by Mark Blaug. (Pioneers in Economics Ser.: Vol. 33). 288p. 1992. 100.00 (*1-85278-496-2*) E Elgar.

Wesley on Perfection. J. A. Wood. pap. 12.99 (*0-88019-120-1*) Schmul Pub Co.

Wesley Quotations: Excerpts from the Writings of John Wesley & Other Family Members. Compiled by Betty M. Jarboe. LC 90-43028. (Illus.). 253p. 1990. 29.50 (*0-8108-2357-8*) Scarecrow.

Wesley Workbook: A Brief Biography Plus a Study Guide to the Standard Sermons. Ed. by Victor P. Reasoner & Robert L. Brush. 95p. 1996. spiral bd. 8.95 (*0-9629383-5-1*) Fundmntl Wesleyan.

Wesleyan Doctrine Made Plain: Programmed Instruction Text Plus Supplement. John Connor. (Illus.). 336p. (Orig.). Date not set. pap. 8.95 (*0-89827-048-0*, BK077) Wesleyan Pub Hse.

Wesleyan-Holiness Theology. J. Kenneth Grider. 592p. 1994. 49.99 (*0-8341-1512-3*) Beacon Hill.

Wesleyan Themes. G. W. Wilson. 1986. pap. 8.99 (*0-88019-204-6*) Schmul Pub Co.

***Wesleyan Theology.** Langford. 44.50 (*0-8010-2046-8*); pap. 25.25 (*0-8010-2026-3*) Baker Bks.

Wesleyan Theology: A Sourcebook. Thomas A. Langford. LC 84-7170. 320p. (C). 1984. pap. 14.95 (*0-939464-41-1*, Labyrinth); lib. bdg. 30.00 (*0-939464-40-3*, Labyrinth) Baker Bks.

Wesleyan Tradition: Four Decades of American Poetry. Ed. by Michael Collier. LC 93-17846. (Wesleyan Poetry Ser.). 316p. (C). 1993. pap. 14.95 (*0-8195-1229-X*, Wesleyan Univ Pr) U Pr of New Eng.

Wesleyan Tradition: Four Decades of American Poetry. Ed. by Michael Collier. LC 93-17846. 316p. 1993. text ed. 35.00 (*0-8195-2210-4*, Wesleyan Univ Pr) U Pr of New Eng.

Wesleyan Transformations. Earl D. Brewer & Mance C. Jackson, Jr. 87p. (C). 1988. pap. 6.95 (*1-884805-00-0*) Jrnl Interdenom.

Wesleyan University, 1831-1910: Collegiate Enterprise in New England. David B. Potts. (Illus.). 368p. (C). 1992. text ed. 35.00 (*0-300-05160-3*) Yale U Pr.

Wesley's Christology: An Interpretation. John Deschner. LC 85-2274. 244p. 1985. reprint ed. pap. 12.95 (*0-87074-200-0*) SMU Press.

Wesley's Veterans, 7 vols., 2. John Telford. 1979. pap. 5.99 (*0-88019-134-1*) Schmul Pub Co.

Wesley's Veterans, 7 vols., 3. John Telford. 1979. pap. 5.99 (*0-88019-135-X*) Schmul Pub Co.

Wesley's Veterans, 7 vols., 4. John Telford. 1979. pap. 5.99 (*0-88019-136-8*) Schmul Pub Co.

Wesley's Veterans, 7 vols., 5. John Telford. 1979. pap. 5.99 (*0-88019-137-6*) Schmul Pub Co.

Wesley's Veterans, 7 vols., 6. John Telford. 1979. pap. 5.99 (*0-88019-138-4*) Schmul Pub Co.

Wesley's Veterans, 7 vols., 7. John Telford. 1979. pap. 5.99 (*0-88019-139-2*) Schmul Pub Co.

Wesley's Veterans, 7 vols., Set. John Telford. 1979. pap. 39.99 (*0-88019-140-6*) Schmul Pub Co.

Wesley's 52 Standard Sermons. John Wesley. 543p. 1996. 29.99 (*0-88019-231-3*) Schmul Pub Co.

Wesner Conjectures. R. Wesner. LC 82-21421. 128p. 1985. pap. 4.95 (*0-88437-070-4*) Psych Dimensions.

***Wesoomi Gardening Journal: A Better Way to Plan & Record Your Gardening Adventure.** William E. Steinman. (Illus.). 176p. (Orig.). 1996. pap. 9.95 (*0-9653732-0-7*) Wesoomi Pub.

***Wessex.** Rob Talbot & Robin Whiteman. (Country Ser.). (Illus.). 160p. 1997. pap. 17.95 (*1-85799-930-4*, Pub. by Phoenix Hse UK) Trafalgar.

Wessex. Robin Whiteman. (Country Ser.). (Illus.). 160p. 1994. 24.95 (*0-297-83260-3*, Weidenfeld) Trafalgar.

Wessex from A. D. One Thousand. J. H. Bettey. (Regional History of England Ser.). 352p. 1986. text ed. 42.95 (*0-582-49207-6*) Longman.

Wessex Images. John Chandler. (Illus.). 192p. 1991. 30.00 (*0-86299-739-9*, Pub. by Sutton Pubng UK) Bks Intl VA.

Wessex in Early Middle Ages. write for info. (*0-8386-3621-7*) Fairleigh Dickinson.

Wessex in the Early Middle Ages. Barbara Yorke. LC 95-14446. (Studies in the Early History of Britain). 392p. 1995. 95.00 (*0-7185-1314-2*, Pub. by Leicester Univ Pr); pap. 19.95 (*0-7185-1856-X*, Pub. by Leicester Univ Pr) Bks Intl VA.

Wessex Poems. Thomas Hardy. LC 93-41356. (Decadents, Symbolists, Anti-Decadents Ser.). 1994. 55.00 (*1-85477-145-0*, Pub. by Woodstock Bks UK) Cassell.

***Wessex Tales.** Hardy. (Longman Literature Ser.). 1995. pap. text ed. write for info. (*0-582-25405-1*, Pub. by Longman UK) Longman.

Wessex Tales. Thomas Hardy. 1976. 22.95 (*0-8188-0518-8*) Amereon Ltd.

Wessex Tales. Thomas Hardy. (World's Classics Ser.). 288p. 1991. pap. 5.95 (*0-19-282720-0*, 6498) OUP.

Wessex to A. D. 1000. Barry Cunliffe. (C). 1993. pap. text ed. 39.95 (*0-582-49280-7*) Addison-Wesley.

Wessex Way. Alan Proctor. (C). 1988. pap. 40.00 (*0-904110-83-4*, Pub. by Thornhill Pr UK) St Mut.

West. William C. Davis & Joseph G. Rosa. 176p. 1994. 19.98 (*0-8317-9367-8*) Smithmark.

West. Jill C. Wheeler. LC 94-12498. (This Land Is Your Land Ser.). (Illus.). 32p. (J). 1994. lib. bdg. 15.98 (*1-56239-298-0*) Abdo & Dghtrs.

West. Photos by Eliot Porter. (Illus.). 1996. reprint ed. 17.98 (*1-56731-147-4*, MJF Bks) Fine Comms.

West: A Treasury of Art & Literature. T. W. Watkins & Joan P. Watkins. (Illus.). 384p. 1994. 75.00 (*0-88363-794-4*) H L Levin.

West: An Illustrated History. Contrib. by Geoffrey C. Ward et al. (Illus.). 528p. 1996. 60.00 (*0-316-92236-6*) Little.

***West: An Illustrated History.** Geoffrey C. Ward. Date not set. write for info. (*0-614-20965-X*) Little.

West: An Illustrated History for Children. Dayton Duncan. LC 95-26722. (Illus.). (J). (gr. 3-7). 1996. 19.95 (*0-316-19628-2*); pap. 10.95 (*0-316-19632-0*) Little.

West: Stories from Ireland. Eddie Stack. 120p. (Orig.). 1989. pap. 8.50 (*0-943873-11-8*) Elder Bks.

***West: The History of a Region in Confederation.** rev. ed. John Conway. bds. 29.95 (*1-55028-408-8*, Pub. by J Lorimer CN) Formac Dist Ltd.

***West: The History of a Region in Confederation.** rev. ed. John Conway. pap. 19.95 (*1-55028-409-6*, Pub. by J Lorimer CN) Formac Dist Ltd.

West: The Way It Really Was! Nevada. Norm Nielson. Ed. by Phyllis B. Turner. 218p. (Orig.). 1994. pap. 12.95 (*0-9625020-3-0*) Tales Nevada.

West Africa: An Introduction to Its History. Michael Crowder. (Illus.). (C). 1977. pap. text ed. 26.50 (*0-582-60003-0*, 74468) Longman.

West Africa: Ghana, Stencils. Mira Bartok & Christine Ronan. (Ancient & Living Cultures Ser.). (Illus.). 32p. (Orig.). (J). (gr. 3 up). 1992. pap. 9.95 (*0-673-36053-9*, GoodYrBooks) Addson-Wesley Educ.

West Africa: Nigeria: Stencils. Mira Bartok & Christine Ronan. (Ancient & Living Cultures Ser.). (Illus.). 32p. (Orig.). (J). 1993. pap. 9.95 (*0-673-36137-3*, GoodYrBooks) Addson-Wesley Educ.

West Africa: Travel Survival Kit. 3rd ed. Alex Newton & David Else. (Illus.). 928p. 1995. pap. 21.95 (*0-86442-294-6*) Lonely Planet.

West Africa Atlas. Oilfield Publications Limited Staff. (C). 1993. 1,250.00 (*1-870945-12-3*, Pub. by Oilfield Pubns UK) St Mut.

West Africa Fertilizer Study: Chad, Vol. VI. R. B. Diamond et al. (Technical Bulletin Ser.: No. T-8). (Illus.). 55p. (Orig.). 1977. pap. 4.00 (*0-88090-007-5*) Intl Fertilizer.

West Africa Fertilizer Study: Mauritania, Vol. VII. R. B. Diamond et al. (Technical Bulletin Ser.: No. T-9). (Illus.). 39p. (Orig.). 1978. pap. 4.00 (*0-88090-008-3*) Intl Fertilizer.

West Africa Fertilizer Study: Niger, Vol. V. R. B. Diamond et al. (Technical Bulletin Ser.: No. T-7). (Illus.). 47p. (Orig.). 1978. pap. 4.00 (*0-88090-006-7*) Intl Fertilizer.

West Africa Fertilizer Study: Regional Overview, Vol. I. R. B. Diamond et al. (Technical Bulletin Ser.: No. T-3). 79p. (Orig.). 1977. pap. 4.00 (*0-88090-039-3*) Intl Fertilizer.

West Africa Fertilizer Study: Senegal, Vol. II. R. B. Diamond et al. (Technical Bulletin Ser.: No. T-4). (Illus.). 64p. (Orig.). 1977. pap. 4.00 (*0-88090-003-2*) Intl Fertilizer.

West Africa Fertilizer Study: Upper Volta, Vol. IV. R. B. Diamond et al. (Technical Bulletin Ser.: No. T-6). (Illus.). 60p. (Orig.). 1977. pap. 4.00 (*0-88090-005-9*) Intl Fertilizer.

West Africa Partitioned: The Elephants & the Grass, Vol. 2. John D. Hargreaves. LC 74-10451. 240p. 1985. text ed. 35.00 (*0-299-09990-3*) U of Wis Pr.

West African Christianity: The Religious Impact. Lamin Sanneh. 304p. (Orig.). 1983. pap. 20.00 (*0-88344-703-7*) Orbis Bks.

W

West African Church History, No. 2: Christian Missions & Theological Training, 1842-1970. John K. Agbeti. LC 86-149803. xv, 262p. 1991. pap. 61.00 (*90-04-09100-9*) E J Brill.

West African Countries & Peoples, British & Native. James A. Horton. (B. E. Ser.: No. 11). 1868. 45.00 (*0-8115-2962-2*) Periodicals Srv.

West African Culture Dynamics: Archaeological & Historical Perspectives. Ed. by B. K. Swartz, Jr. (World Anthropology Ser.). (Illus.). xiv, 630p. 1980. text ed. 92.35 (*90-279-7920-0*) Mouton.

West African Economic & Social History. Ed. by David Henige & T. C. McCaskie. LC 91-143798. (Illus.). 227p. (Orig.). 1990. pap. 26.00 (*0-942615-07-7*) U Wis African Stud.

West African Folk-Tales. W. H. Barker. (B. E. Ser.: No. 41). (Illus.). 1917. 25.00 (*0-8115-2992-4*) Periodicals Srv.

West African Folktales. 160p. 1994. pap. 14.95 (*0-8442-5812-1*, Passport Bks) NTC Pub Grp.

West African Folktales. Tr. & Compiled by Jack Berry. 229p. (Orig.). 1991. 29.95 (*0-8101-0979-4*); pap. 14.95 (*0-8101-0993-X*) Northwestern U Pr.

West African Governments & Volunteer Development Organizations: Priorities for Partnership. Willard R. Johnson & Vivian R. Johnson. LC 89-39288. (Illus.). 132p. (C). 1990. pap. text ed. 19.00 (*0-8191-7747-4*); lib. bdg. 39.00 (*0-8191-7746-6*) U Pr of Amer.

***West African Herbaria of Isert & Thonning.** F. N. Hepper. 227p. 1976. 18.00 incl. fiche (*0-9504876-0-0*, Pub. by Royal Botnic Grdns UK) Balogh.

West African Kingdoms in the Nineteenth Century. Ed. by Daryll Forde & P. M. Kaberry. LC 67-82613. (Illus.). 303p. reprint ed. pap. 86.40 (*0-8357-3218-5*, 2057090) Bks Demand.

West African Leadership. Magnus J. Sampson. 160p. 1969. 37.50 (*0-7146-1766-0*, Pub. by F Cass Pubs UK) Intl Spec Bk.

West African Marine Fisheries: Alternatives for Management. James A. Crutchfield & Rowena Lawson. LC 73-10843. (Program of International Studies of Fishery Arrangements. Papers: Paper No. 3). 78p. reprint ed. pap. 25.00 (*0-317-28865-2*, 2020960) Bks Demand.

West African Monetary Union: An Analytical Review. Rattan J. Bhatia. (Occasional Paper Ser.: No. 35). 59p. 1985. pap. 7.50 (*1-55775-083-1*) Intl Monetary.

West African Orogens & Circum-Atlantic Correlatives: IGCP-Project 233. Ed. by R. D. Dallmeyer & P. P. Lecorche. (Illus.). ix, 405p. 1991. 199.95 (*0-387-52412-6*) Spr-Verlag.

West African Passage: A Journey Through Nigeria, Chad & the Cameroons. Margery Perham. 245p. 8300. 40.00 (*0-7206-0609-8*, Pub. by P Owen Ltd UK) Dufour.

West African Poetry: A Critical History. Robert G. Fraser. (Illus.). 352p. 1986. text ed. 75.00 (*0-521-30993-X*); pap. text ed. 29.95 (*0-521-31223-X*) Cambridge U Pr.

West African Pop Roots. John Collins. 350p. (C). 1992. pap. 19.95 (*0-87722-916-3*) Temple U Pr.

West African Pop Roots. John Collins. 350p. (C). 1992. 59.95 (*0-87722-793-4*) Temple U Pr.

***West African Popular Theatre.** Karin Barber et al. LC 96-42321. (Drama & Performance Studies). 1997. pap. write for info. (*0-253-21077-1*) Ind U Pr.

***West African Popular Theatre.** Karin Barber et al. LC 96-42321. (Drama & Performance Studies). 1997. write for info. (*0-253-33204-4*) Ind U Pr.

West African Psychology. Edward G. Parrinder. LC 74-15076. reprint ed. 37.50 (*0-404-12125-X*) AMS Pr.

***West African Rhythms for the Drum Set.** Royal Hartigan. Ed. by Dan Thress. (Illus.). 112p. (Orig.). 1995. pap. text ed. 24.95 (*0-89724-732-9*, MMBK0057CD) Warner Brothers.

West African Sahel: Human Agency & Environmental Change. Jeffrey A. Gritzner. (Research Papers: No. 226). (Illus.). (Orig.). 1988. pap. 12.00 (*0-89065-130-2*) U Ch Pr.

West African Secret Societies: Their Organizations, Officials & Teaching. Frederick W. Butt-Thompson. 1969. reprint ed. 20.00 (*0-87266-003-6*) Argosy.

West African Secret Societies, Their Organizations, Officials & Teaching. Frederick W. Butt-Thompson. LC 70-109320. (Illus.). 320p. 1970. reprint ed. text ed. 52.50 (*0-8371-3585-0*, BWA&, Greenwood Pr) Greenwood.

West African Studies. 3rd ed. Mary Kingsley. (Illus.). 507p. 1964. 55.00 (*0-7146-1822-5*, Pub. by F Cass Pubs UK) Intl Spec Bk.

West African Sufi: The Religious Heritage & Spiritual Quest of Cerno Bokar Saalif Taal. Louis Brenner. LC 83-4803. 215p. (C). 1984. 35.00 (*0-520-05008-8*) U CA Pr.

***West African Sufi: The Religious Heritage & Spiritual Search of Cerno Bokar Saalif Taal.** Louis Brenner. 214p. 1996. 49.95 (*0-614-21380-0*, 1296) Kazi Pubns.

West African Trade: A Study of Competition, Oligopoly & Monopoly in a Changing Economy. Peter T. Bauer. LC 67-19585. (Reprints of Economic Classics Ser.). xix, 450p. 1967. reprint ed. 49.50 (*0-678-06510-1*) Kelley.

West African Traders in Ghana in the Nineteenth & Twentieth Centuries. Kwame Arhin. LC 79-40716. (Legon History Ser.). 160p. reprint ed. pap. 45.60 (*0-8357-3586-9*, 2034471) Bks Demand.

West African Trickster Tales. As told by Martin Bennett. (Myths & Legends Ser.). (Illus.). 128p. (YA). 1994. pap. 12.95 (*0-19-274172-1*) OUP.

West African Urbanization: A Study of Voluntary Associations in Social Change. Kenneth L. Little. LC 65-14349. 187p. reprint ed. pap. 53.30 (*0-317-20625-7*, 2024579) Bks Demand.

West African Wager: Houphouet Versus Nkrumah. Jon Woronoff. LC 72-5155. 371p. 1972. 24.00 (*0-8108-0523-5*) Scarecrow.

West Against the Wind. Liza K. Murrow. LC 87-45337. 240p. (YA). (gr. 7 up). 1987. 15.95 (*0-8234-0668-7*) Holiday.

West & Eastern Europe: Economic Statecraft & Political Change. Thomas A. Baylis. LC 93-14139. 256p. 1993. text ed. 57.95 (*0-275-94676-2*, C4676, Praeger Pubs); pap. text ed. 20.95 (*0-275-94734-3*, Praeger Pubs) Greenwood.

West & Reconstruction. Eugene H. Berwanger. LC 80-26357. (Illus.). 304p. 1981. text ed. 29.95 (*0-252-00868-5*) U of Ill Pr.

West & the Rest of Us: White Predators, Black Slavers & the African Elite. Chinweizu. 544p. 1978. pap. 9.95 (*0-88357-016-5*); text ed. 21.95 (*0-88357-015-7*) NOK Pubs.

West & the Soviet Union: Politics & Policy. Ed. by Gregory Flynn. LC 89-27906. 270p. 1990. 39.95 (*0-8357-7956-4*); text ed. 15.95 (*0-312-04098-9*) St Martin.

West & the Soviet Union: Politics & Policy. Gregory Flynn. 1990. text ed. 39.95 (*0-312-04097-0*) St Martin.

West & the Third World: Essays in Honour of J. D. B. Miller. Ed. by Robert O'Neill & R. J. Vincent. LC 89-70079. 256p. 1990. text ed. 55.00 (*0-312-04096-2*) St Martin.

West & the World: A History of Civilization, Vol. 1. 2nd ed. Kevin Reilly. 384p. (C). 1989. pap. text ed. 45.95 (*0-06-045346-X*) Addson-Wesley Educ.

West & the World: A History of Civilization, Vol. 2. 2nd ed. Kevin Reilly. 432p. (C). 1989. pap. text ed. 39.00 (*0-06-045347-8*) Addson-Wesley Educ.

***West & the World: A History of Civilization from the Ancient World to 1700.** Kevin Reilly. LC 96-37674. 1997. write for info. (*1-55876-152-7*) M Wiener.

West & the World since Nineteen Hundred Forty Five. 4th ed. Blackburn. 1995. pap. text ed. 12.00 (*0-312-11193-2*) St Martin.

***West & Wood's Introduction to Foodservice.** 8th ed. Ed. by June Payne-Palacio & Monica Theis. LC 96-27613. 1996. 61.00 (*0-13-495425-4*, Merrill Coll) P-H.

West Aroostook County, ME. J. Greaves. (Images of America Ser.). 1995. pap. 16.99 (*0-7524-0237-4*, Arcdia) Chalford.

West As America: Reinterpreting Images of the Frontier. Ed. by William H. Truettner. LC 90-41379. (Illus.). 408p. (C). 1991. 65.00 (*1-56098-023-0*) Smithsonian.

West As Romantic Horizon. William H. Goetzmann & Joseph C. Porter. LC 81-12424. (Joslyn Art Museum Ser.). (Illus.). 128p. 1981. pap. 20.00 (*0-936364-05-X*) U of Nebr Pr.

West at Its Best: Selections from the Tombstone Epitaph. (Illus.). 200p. (Orig.). 1998. pap. write for info. (*1-877704-27-X*) Pioneer Pr.

West Baltimore Neighborhoods: Sketches of Their History, 1840-1960. Roderick N. Ryon. LC 93-60361. (Orig.). 1993. pap. write for info. (*0-9636930-0-X*) R N Ryon.

West Bank & Gaza: Toward the Making of a Palestinian State. Emile A. Nakhleh. LC 79-536. (AEI Studies: No. 232). (Illus.). 73p. reprint ed. pap. 25.00 (*0-8357-4544-9*, 2037442) Bks Demand.

West Bank & the Rule of Law: A Study. Raja Shehadeh. LC 81-139864. 130p. 1980. reprint ed. pap. 37.10 (*0-608-00496-0*, 2061315) Bks Demand.

West Bank-Gaza Strip. Rebecca Stefoff. (Let's Visit Places & Peoples of the World Ser.). (Illus.). 104p. (J). (gr. 5 up). 1988. lib. bdg. 19.95 (*1-55546-782-2*) Chelsea Hse.

West Bank Palestinian Family. Ibrahim W. Ata. 250p. 1987. text ed. 55.00 (*0-7103-0186-3*) Routledge Chapman & Hall.

West Belfast: A Novel. Danny Morrison. LC 95-71037. 255p. 1995. pap. 12.95 (*1-57098-043-8*) R Rinehart.

West Bengal & the Federalizing Process in India. Marcus F. Franda. LC 68-10391. 269p. 1968. reprint ed. pap. 76.70 (*0-7837-9339-1*, 2060080) Bks Demand.

West Bengal Economy: Past, Present & Future. Kalipada Basu. (C). 1989. 34.00 (*0-8364-2480-8*, Pub. by Firma KLM II) S Asia.

West Berlin: History of the Nineteen Seventy-One Agreement. V. Vysotsky. (Illus.). 355p. 1975. 22.00 (*0-8464-0964-X*) Beekman Pubs.

West Beyond the West: A History of British Columbia. rev. ed. Jean Barman. (Illus.). 520p. 1996. pap. 21.95 (*0-8020-7185-6*) U of Toronto Pr.

West Branch of the Penobscot & the Kennebec Gorge Flip Map. Ron Rathnow. LC 87-34978. (Great American Rivers Flip Map Ser.). (Illus.). 57p. 1989. pap. 5.95 (*0-89732-081-6*) Menasha Ridge.

West Branch Trolleys: Street Railways of Lycoming & Clinton Counties, Pennsylvania. Paul J. Schieck & Harold E. Cox. (Illus.). (Orig.). 1978. pap. 11.00 (*0-911940-29-4*) Cox.

West Business Law. Carper. Date not set. teacher ed., text ed. 58.95 (*0-314-01952-9*) West Pub.

West by Covered Wagon: A Journey on the Oregon Trail. Dorothy H. Patent. LC 94-48233. (Illus.). 32p. (J). (gr. 3-7). 1995. 15.95 (*0-8027-8377-5*); lib. bdg. 16.85 (*0-8027-8378-3*) Walker & Co.

West by Southwest: Letters of Joseph Pratt Allyn, a Traveller on the Santa Fe Trail, 1863. David K. Strate. LC 83-83152. (Illus.). 194p. (Orig.). 1984. pap. 7.95 (*1-882404-00-9*) KS Herit Ctr.

West by Steamboat. Tim McNeese. LC 91-22822. (Americans on the Move Ser.). (Illus.). 48p. (J). (gr. 5). 1993. lib. bdg. 11.95 (*0-89686-728-5*, Crstwood Hse) Silver Burdett Pr.

West, Central & East Africa see Encyclopedia of World Geography

West Central Wisconsin: A History, Set, Vols. 1 & 2. John G. Gregory. (Illus.). 994p. 1994. reprint ed. lib. bdg. 99.50 (*0-8328-3869-1*) Higginson Bk Co.

West Central Wisconsin: A History, Vol. 4. John Gregory. (Illus.). 730p. 1994. reprint ed. lib. bdg. 74.50 (*0-8328-3871-3*) Higginson Bk Co.

West Central Wisconsin, Vol. 3: A History. John G. Gregory. (Illus.). 737p. 1994. reprint ed. lib. bdg. 74.50 (*0-8328-3870-5*) Higginson Bk Co.

West Civilization: Testbank, 3 Vols. Marvin Perry. (C). 1996. teacher ed., pap. 11.96 (*0-395-81114-7*) HM.

West Coast Birds, Vol 1. large type ed. Chris C. Fisher. (Illus.). 128p. (Orig.). 1996. pap. 11.95 (*1-55105-049-8*, 1-55105) Lone Pine.

West Coast Chinese Boy. Sing Lim. LC 79-67110. (Illus.). 64p. (J). (gr. 5 up). 1991. pap. 7.95 (*0-88776-270-0*) Tundra Bks.

West Coast Duchamp. Intro. by Bonnie Clearwater. LC 91-70132. (Illus.). 128p. (Orig.). 1991. 55.00 (*0-9628514-0-X*) Grassfield Pr.

West Coast Fossils: A Guide to the Ancient Life of Vancouver Island. Rolf Ludvigsen. 1994. pap. text ed. 12.95 (*1-55110-149-1*, Pub. by Whitecap Bks CN) Gr Arts Ctr Pub.

West Coast Impressions: The Dynamic British Columbia Landscape. Kathryn Graham. (Illus.). 80p. 1995. pap. 14.95 (*1-895714-68-0*, Pub. by Raincoast Bks CN) Orca Bk Pubs.

West Coast Jazz: Modern Jazz in California, 1945-1960. Ted Gioia. 432p. 1992. 25.00 (*0-19-506310-4*) OUP.

West Coast Journeys, 1865-1879: The Travelogue of a Remarkable Woman. Caroline C. Leighton. LC 95-12198. 192p. 1995. pap. 14.95 (*1-57061-012-6*) Sasquatch Bks.

West Coast Kitchen Garden: Growing Culinary Herbs & Vegetables. Andrew Yeoman. 1995. pap. text ed. 12.95 (*1-55110-279-X*, Pub. by Whitecap Bks CN) Gr Arts Ctr Pub.

***West Coast of North & South America, Including Hawaii, Including the Alaskan Supplement.** Noaa. (Tide Tables, 1998 Ser.). 1997. pap. text ed. 13.95 (*0-07-047117-7*) McGraw.

West Coast of Puerto Rico. Wilson Ltd. Staff & Imray L. Norie. (C). 1983. 53.00 (*0-685-40411-0*, Pub. by Imray Laurie Norie & Wilson UK) St Mut.

West Coast of Scotland: Crinan to Mallaig & Barra. Imray, Laurie, Norie & Wilson Ltd. Staff. (Illus.). (C). 1989. text ed. 60.00 (*0-685-40202-9*, Pub. by Imray Laurie Norie & Wilson UK) St Mut.

West Coast of Scotland: Mallaig to Rudha Reidh & Sound of Harris. Imray, Laurie, Norie & Wilson Ltd. Staff. (Illus.). (C). 1988. text ed. 75.00 (*0-685-40201-0*, Pub. by Imray Laurie Norie & Wilson UK) St Mut.

West Coast River Angling. Eric Carlisle. (Illus.). 192p. 1990. 12.95 (*0-88839-212-5*) Hancock House.

West Coast Seafood Recipes. Blaine Freer. (Illus.). 1995. spiral bd. 14.95 (*1-57188-046-1*) F Amato Pubns.

West Coast Shipping. Michael K. Stammers. 1989. pap. 25.00 (*0-85263-642-3*, Pub. by Shire UK) St Mut.

West Coast Town & Country B & B's U. S. A. - Canada: Directory of Homes & Inns. 8th ed. (Illus.). 150p. 1991. pap. 7.50 (*0-945796-03-X*) NW Bed Breakfast.

West Coast Town & Country B & B's U. S. A. - Canada: Directory of Homes & Inns. 9th ed. 112p. 1992. pap. 7.95 (*0-945796-04-8*) NW Bed Breakfast.

West Coast Town B & B's U. S. A. & Canada: Directory of Homes & Inns. 6th ed. Ed. by NW Bed & Breakfast Reservation Service Staff. (Illus.). 150p. (C). 1989. per. 9.50 (*0-945796-01-3*) NW Bed Breakfast.

West Coast Trail & Nitinat Lakes: A Trail Guide. 7th rev. ed. Sierra Club of Western Canada Staff. (Illus.). 96p. 1994. pap. 10.95 (*0-89886-399-6*) Mountaineers.

West Coast Whale Watching: The Complete Guide to Observing Marine Mammals. Richard C. Kreitman & Mary J. Schramm. 1995. pap. 15.00 (*0-06-258619-X*) HarpC.

West Coast Workboats: An Illustrated Guide to Work Vessels from Bristol Bay to San Diego. Archie Satterfield. (Illus.). 128p. (Orig.). 1993. pap. 11.95 (*0-912365-51-X*) Sasquatch Bks.

West Collection. West Publishing Company Editorial Staff. (Illus.). 224p. 1986. pap. text ed. 60.00 (*0-314-95791-X*) West Pub.

West Collection. limited ed. West Publishing Company Editorial Staff. (Illus.). 224p. 1986. 75.00 (*0-317-45599-0*) West Pub.

West Country. Rob Talbot & Robin Whiteman. (Country Ser.). (Illus.). 160p. 1994. 24.95 (*0-297-83158-5*) Trafalgar.

***West Country.** Robin Whiteman & Rob Talbot. (Country Ser.). (Illus.). 160p. 1997. pap. 17.95 (*0-297-83568-8*, Weidenfeld) Trafalgar.

West Country Wicca. Rhiannon Ryall. 1994. pap. 19.95 (*1-898307-02-4*, Pub. by Capall Bann Pubng UK) Holmes Pub.

West Country Wicca. Rhiannon Ryall. (Illus.). 104p. 1990. pap. 8.95 (*0-919345-98-0*) Phoenix WA.

West Countrymen in Prince Edward's Isle: A Fragment of the Great Migration. Basil Greenhill & Ann Giffard. LC 67-113574. 248p. reprint ed. pap. 70.70 (*0-685-15341-X*, 2026521) Bks Demand.

West Covina: Fulfilling the Promise. Barbara Pronin. 1989. 29.95 (*0-89781-291-3*) Am Historical Pr.

West Downs: A Portrait of an English Preparatory School. Mark Hichens. 206p. (C). 1989. text ed. 69.00 (*1-872795-76-5*, Pub. by Pentland Pr UK) St Mut.

West Eighty-Five: Art & the Law. West Publishing Company Editorial Staff. LC 85-50908. (Illus.). 120p. 1985. pap. text ed. write for info. (*0-314-93133-3*) West Pub.

West End. Laura Van Wormer. 1990. mass mkt. 5.95 (*0-312-92262-0*) St Martin.

West End Adventures, 3 bks., Set. Gary Grady & Suzanne Goldberg. (Sherlock Holmes, Consulting Detective Ser.). (Illus.). (Orig.). 1995. boxed, pap. 25.00 (*1-883240-70-0*) Chessex.

West End Horror. large type ed. Nicholas Meyer. 1978. 25.99 (*0-7089-0098-4*) Ulverscroft.

West End Horror: From the Memoris of John H. Watson. Nicholas Meyer. 1994. pap. 8.95 (*0-393-31153-8*) Norton.

West End Shuffle. Natalie J. Prior. (YA). 1996. pap. 12.95 (*0-7022-2882-6*, Pub. by Univ Queensland Pr AT) Intl Spec Bk.

West End Women: Women on the London Stage, 1918-1962. Maggie B. Gale. LC 96-18241. (Gender in Performance Ser.). 272p. (C). 1996. text ed. 65.00 (*0-415-08495-4*) Routledge.

West End Women: Women on the London Stage, 1918-1962. Maggie B. Gale. LC 96-18241. (Gender in Performance Ser.). 272p. (C). 1996. pap. 18.95 (*0-415-08496-2*) Routledge.

West European Allies, the Third World, & U. S. Foreign Policy: Post-Cold War Challenge. Richard J. Payne. LC 91-2563. (Contributions in Political Science Ser.: No. 282). 256p. 1991. pap. text ed. 17.95 (*0-275-93626-0*, B3626, Praeger Pubs) Greenwood.

West European Allies, The Third World, & U. S. Foreign Policy: Post-Cold War Challenges. Richard J. Payne. LC 91-11334. (Contributions in Political Science Ser.: No. 282). 256p. 1991. text ed. 59.95 (*0-313-27460-6*, PWN/, Greenwood Pr) Greenwood.

West European Arms Control Policy. Ed. by Robbin F. Laird. LC 89-16819. (Duke Press Policy Studies). 210p. 1989. text ed. 46.95 (*0-8223-0955-6*) Duke.

West European Communism & American Foreign Policy. Michael A. Ledeen. 310p. 1987. 39.95 (*0-88738-140-5*) Transaction Pubs.

West European Communist Parties after the Revolutions of 1989. Ed. by Martin J. Bull & Paul Heywood. LC 94-14211. 1994. text ed. 65.00 (*0-312-12268-3*) St Martin.

West European Economic Handbook, Vol. 3. 2nd ed. 1995. write for info. (*0-8103-9807-9*, 073078, Pub. by Euromonitor Pubns UK) Gale.

West European Industrial Enzyme Markets: New Applications Emerge Out of Changing Technology. Market Intelligence Staff. 248p. (Orig.). 1993. 3,800.00 (*1-56753-897-5*) Frost & Sullivan.

West European Market for Fluorochemicals. Market Intelligence Staff. 443p. 1993. 4,450.00 (*1-56753-554-2*) Frost & Sullivan.

West European Pacifism & the Strategy for Peace. Ed. by Peter Van den Dungen. LC 84-11585. 208p. 1985. text ed. 39.95 (*0-312-86284-9*) St Martin.

West European Party System. Ed. by Peter Mair. (Oxford Readings in Politics & Government Ser.). 376p. 1990. 65.00 (*0-19-827584-6*); pap. text ed. 18.95 (*0-19-827583-8*) OUP.

West European Population Change. Allan M. Findlay & Paul White. 304p. 1987. 59.95 (*0-7099-3667-2*, Pub. by Croom Helm UK) Routledge Chapman & Hall.

West European Prime Ministers. Ed. by G. W. Jones. 1991. text ed. 35.00 (*0-7146-3425-5*, Pub. by F Cass Pubs UK) Intl Spec Bk.

West European Pulp & Paper Chemical Markets. Market Intelligence Staff. 322p. 1994. 3,800.00 (*1-56753-598-4*) Frost & Sullivan.

West European Terrorism & Counter-Terrorism: The Evolving Dynamic. Peter Chalk. 256p. 1997. text ed. 59.95 (*0-312-12971-8*) St Martin.

West Explored: The Gerald Peters Collection of Western American Art. Julie Schimmel. LC 88-82174. (Illus.). 93p. 1988. 35.00 (*0-935037-25-X*); pap. 25.00 (*0-935037-22-5*) G Peters Gallery.

West Family Data Base, Vol I. Howard E. West, Jr. 444p. 1994. reprint ed. pap. text ed. 53.00 (*1-55613-961-6*) Heritage Bk.

West Federal Tax Binder. William Hoffman. Date not set. pap. text ed. write for info. (*0-314-00857-8*) West Pub.

West Federal Taxation: Comprehensive Volume, 1997 Edition. Eugene Willis et al. 1200p. 1996. text ed. write for info. (*0-314-08818-0*) West Pub.

West Federal Taxation Corporation Practice Set. (C). 1995. write for info. (*0-615-00551-9*) West Pub.

West Federal Taxation Individual Practice Set. (C). 1995. write for info. (*0-615-00552-7*) West Pub.

West Florida Controversy, 1798-1813: A Study in American Diplomacy. Isaac J. Cox. (BCL1 - United States Local History Ser.). 699p. 1991. reprint ed. lib. bdg. 109.00 (*0-7812-6301-8*) Rprt Serv.

West Forty Second Street. Kornblum. Date not set. pap. 9.95 (*0-14-014547-8*) Viking Penguin.

West from Fort Bridger: The Pioneering of the Immigrant Trails across Utah, 1846-1850. rev. ed. Ed. by J. Roderic Korns et al. LC 94-16876. (Illus.). 350p. 1995. reprint ed. pap. 15.00 (*0-87421-189-1*) Utah St U Pr.

West from Fort Pierre: The World of Scotty Philip. James M. Robinson. (Great West & Indian Ser.: Vol. 43). (Illus.). 1974. 19.95 (*0-87026-032-4*) Westernlore.

West from Home: Letters of Laura Ingalls Wilder, San Francisco 1915. Laura Ingalls Wilder. Ed. by Roger L. MacBride. LC 73-14342. 176p. (YA). (gr. 7 up). 1974. lib. bdg. 15.89 (*0-06-024111-X*) HarpC Child Bks.

West from Home: Letters of Laura Ingalls Wilder, San Francisco 1915. Laura Ingalls Wilder. Ed. by Roger L. MacBride. LC 73-14342. (Trophy Bk.). (Illus.). 144p. (YA). (gr. 7 up). 1976. pap. 3.95 (*0-06-440081-6*, Trophy) HarpC Child Bks.

W

West from Home: Letters of Laura Ingalls Wilder, San Francisco 1915. Laura Ingalls Wilder. Ed. by Roger L. MacBride. LC 73-14342. 144p. (YA). (gr. 7 up). 1974. 14.00 (*0-06-024110-1*) Zondervan.

West from Omaha: A Railroader's Odyssey. Jack A. Pfeifer. Ed. by Pacific Fast Mail Staff. 207p. 1990. 59.50 (*0-915713-20-9*) Pac Fast Mail.

West from Singapore. Louis L'Amour. 176p. 1987. mass mkt. 3.99 (*0-553-26353-6*) Bantam.

West from the Columbia: Views at the River Mouth. Robert Adams. (Illus.). 84p. 1995. 50.00 (*0-89381-642-6*) Aperture.

West from the Fathers to the Reformation see Cambridge History of the Bible

West Futuna Aniwa: An Introduction to a Polynesian Outlier Language. Janet W. Dougherty. LC 82-7005. (Publications in Linguistics: Vol. 102). 732p. (C). 1984. pap. 45.00 (*0-520-09657-6*) U CA Pr.

West German Cinema since 1945: A Reference Handbook. Richard C. Helt & Marie Helt. LC 87-16429. (Illus.). 758p. 1987. 52.50 (*0-8108-2053-6*) Scarecrow.

West German Cinema, 1985-1990: A Reference Handbook. Richard C. Helt & Marie E. Helt. 275p. 1992. 35.00 (*0-8108-2647-X*) Scarecrow.

West German Economy Nineteen Forty-Five to Nineteen Fifty-Five. Alan Kramer. LC 90-784. (German Studies). 309p. 1991. 19.95 (*0-85496-241-7*) Berg Pubs.

West German Filmmakers on Film: Visions & Voices. Ed. by Eric Rentschler. LC 87-14856. (Modern German Voices Ser.). 300p. 1988. 49.00 (*0-8419-0984-9*); pap. 22.50 (*0-8419-0985-7*) Holmes & Meier.

West German Foreign Policy: The Domestic Setting. Gebhard Schweigler. (Washington Papers: No. 106). 136p. 1984. pap. 9.95 (*0-275-91635-9*, B1635, Praeger Pubs) Greenwood.

***West German Lay Judges: Recruitment & Representativeness.** John P. Richert. LC 82-20251. (Illus.). 233p. reprint ed. pap. 66.50 (*0-608-04504-7*, 2065249) Bks Demand.

West German Model: Perspectives on a Stable State. Ed. by William E. Paterson & Gordon Smith. (Illus.). 184p. 1981. 35.00 (*0-7146-3180-9*, Pub. by F Cass Pubs UK); pap. 12.50 (*0-7146-4034-4*, Pub. by F Cass Pubs UK) Intl Spec Bk.

West German Peace Movement & the National Question. Kim R. Holmes. LC 84-3745. (Foreign Policy Reports). 73p. 1984. 11.95 (*0-89549-058-7*) Inst Foreign Policy Anal.

West German Political Parties: CDU, CSU, FDP, SPD, the Greens. Peter Radunski et al. Ed. by Robert G. Livingston & Peter G. Kielmannsegg. LC 86-73191. (German Issues Ser.: No. 4). 102p. 1986. pap. 7.50 (*0-941441-00-8*) Am Inst Contemp Ger Studies.

West German Politics. Lewis J. Edinger. LC 85-11703. (Illus.). 350p. 1985. text ed. 52.50 (*0-231-06090-4*); pap. text ed. 17.00 (*0-231-06091-2*) Col U Pr.

West German Politics in the Mid-Eighties: Crisis & Continuity. Ed. by H. G. Wallach & George K. Romoser. LC 84-18071. 288p. 1985. text ed. 79.50 (*0-275-90178-5*, C0178, Praeger Pubs) Greenwood.

West Germanic Inflection, Derivation & Compounding. Joseph B. Voyles. LC 72-94456. (Janua Linguarum, Ser. Practica: No. 145). 204p. (Orig.). 1974. pap. text ed. 60.80 (*90-279-2711-1*) Mouton.

West Germany. Donald S. Detwiler & Ilse E. Detwiler. (World Bibliographical Ser.: No. 72). 300p. 1988. lib. bdg. 70.00 (*1-85109-017-7*) ABC-CLIO.

West Germany: A Geography of Its People. Trevor Wild. LC 79-55698. (Illus.). 255p. 1980. text ed. 42.00 (*0-06-497658-0*, N6741) B&N Imports.

***West Germany: Geography of People.** M. Wild. Date not set. pap. text ed. write for info. (*0-582-30078-9*, Pub. by Longman UK) Longman.

West Germany: Internal Structures & External Relations: Foreign Policy of the Federal Republic of Germany. Frank R. Pfetsch. LC 87-29129. 288p. 1988. text ed. 59.95 (*0-275-92868-3*, C2868, Praeger Pubs) Greenwood.

West Germany: On the Road to Reunification. Sean Dolan. (Let's Visit Places & Peoples of the World Ser.). (Illus.). 128p. (J). (gr. 5 up). 1991. lib. bdg. 19.95 (*0-7910-1367-7*) Chelsea Hse.

West Germany: Politics & Society. David Childs & Jeffrey Johnson. 1981. text ed. 39.95 (*0-312-86300-4*) St Martin.

West Germany: Politics of Non-Planning. Hans J. Arndt. LC 66-17524. (National Planning Ser.: No. 8). 186p. reprint ed. pap. 53.10 (*0-317-28999-3*, 2020394) Bks Demand.

West Germany & the European Community: Changing Interests & Competing Policy Objectives. Werner J. Feld. LC 81-8599. 160p. 1981. text ed. 45.00 (*0-275-90621-3*, C0621, Praeger Pubs) Greenwood.

West Germany Today. Ed. by Karl Koch. 220p. (C). 1989. pap. text ed. 11.95 (*0-415-01685-1*, A3717) Routledge.

***West Germany under Construction: Politics, Society, & Culture in the Adenauer Era.** Ed. by Robert G. Mueller. LC 96-38008. (Social History, Popular Culture, & Politics In Germany Ser.). (C). 1997. pap. 24.95 (*0-472-06648-X*) U of Mich Pr.

***West Germany under Construction: Politics, Society, & Culture in the Adenauer Era.** Ed. by Robert G. Mueller. LC 96-38008. (Social History, Popular Culture, & Politics in Germany Ser.). (C). 1997. text ed. 54.50 (*0-472-09648-6*) U of Mich Pr.

West Germany's Foreign Policy: The Impact of the Social Democrats & the Greens. Diane Rosolowsky. LC 87-12017. (Contributions in Political Science Ser.: No. 192). 168p. 1987. text ed. 45.00 (*0-313-25672-1*, RWG/, Greenwood Pr) Greenwood.

West Germany's Internal Security Policy: State & Terrorism in the 1970s & 1980s. Peter J. Katzenstein. (Western Societies Papers). 80p. (Orig.). 1991. pap. 11.95 (*0-8014-9652-7*) Cornell U Pr.

West Germany's Trade with the East: Hypotheses & Perspectives. Frank D. Weiss. 120p. 1983. lib. bdg. 44.50 (*3-16-344677-9*, Pub. by J C B Mohr GW) Coronet Bks.

West Governments Performance Standards, 1990. Ed. by Greg Michels. (Governments Performance Standards Ser.). (Illus.). 150p. 1990. text ed. 125.00 (*1-55507-510-X*) Municipal Analysis.

West Greenlandic. Michael Fortescue. LC 84-19862. (Descriptive Grammars Ser.). 384p. 1984. 72.50 (*0-7099-1069-X*, Pub. by Croom Helm UK) Routledge Chapman & Hall.

West Ham United. Charles P. Korr. 1986. pap. 16.95 (*0-7156-2126-2*, Pub. by Duckworth UK) Focus Pub-R Pullins.

West Ham United: The Making of a Football Club. Charles P. Korr. (Sport & Society Ser.). (Illus.). 272p. 1987. text ed. 27.95 (*0-252-01405-7*) U of Ill Pr.

West Haven, Classroom Culture & Society in a Rural Elementary. Norris B. Johnson. LC 84-17371. (Illus.). 320p. 1985. reprint ed. pap. 91.20 (*0-7837-9035-X*, 2049786) Bks Demand.

***West Hawaii Street Guide, Vol. 1.** 2nd rev. ed. Stephen C. Graves. (Illus.). 52p. (Orig.). 1996. pap. 9.95 (*0-9653374-0-5*) Rec Copy Serv.

West Hemisphere Trade Integration: A Canadian-Latin American Dialogue. Lipsey. LC 96-9135. 308p. 1996. text ed. 49.95 (*0-312-16189-1*) St Martin.

West Highland Cattle! The Grand Olde Breed. John M. Anderson. (Illus.). 96p. 1985. 14.00 (*0-9615813-0-1*) J Mac Anderson.

West Highland Steam. Picton Publishing Staff. (C). 1987. 32.00 (*0-317-90389-6*, Pub. by Picton UK) St Mut.

West Highland Steamers. Ed. by G. E. Langmuir. (C). 1987. 175.00 (*0-85174-505-9*, Pub. by Brwn Son Ferg) St Mut.

West Highland Tales from the Dewar Manuscripts, Bk. 1: The Appin Murder. Stuart Titles Ltd. Staff. 65p. (C). 1988. 30.00 (*0-948474-01-7*, Pub. by Stuart Titles Ltd UK) St Mut.

West Highland Tales from the Dewar Manuscripts, Bk. 11: Charles Stuart of Ardsheil. Stuart Titles Ltd. Staff. (C). 1988. 30.00 (*0-948474-03-3*, Pub. by Stuart Titles Ltd UK) St Mut.

West Highland White Terrier: An Owner's Guide to a Happy, Healthy Pet. Seymour Weiss. LC 96-20461. 1996. pap. 12.95 (*0-87605-494-7*) Howell Bk.

West Highland White Terriers. Ingrid Bolle-Kleinbub. (Pet Owner's Manuals Ser.). 96p. (Orig.). 1994. pap. 6.95 (*0-8120-1950-4*) Barron.

West Highland White Terriers. Roger White. (Owner's Companion Ser.). (Illus.). 224p. 1993. 39.95 (*1-85223-667-1*, Pub. by Crowood Pr UK) Trafalgar.

West Highland White Terriers, AKC Rank No. 36. Martin Weil. (Illus.). 224p. 1996. pap. 9.95 (*0-7938-2385-4*, KW113S) TFH Pubns.

West Highland White Terriers Champions, 1952-1990. Camino E. E. & Bk. Co. Staff. (Illus.). 200p. 1993. pap. 36.95 (*1-55893-017-5*) Camino E E & Bk.

West Images of Psychology. Date not set. write for info. (*0-314-05533-9*) West Pub.

West in Global Context. Kirsch & Albert Schweitzer. 480p. (C). 1996. pap. text ed. 31.33 (*0-13-485210-9*) P-H.

West in Russia & China: Religious & Secular Thought in Modern Times, 2 vols. Donald W. Treadgold. Incl. Vol. 1. Russia, 1472-1917. LC 72-78886. pap. 91.00 (*0-685-42734-X*); Vol. 2. China, 1582-1949. LC 72-78886. pap. 68.50 (*0-685-09014-0*); LC 72-78886. reprint ed. Set pap. write for info. (*0-318-58061-6*, 2022474) Bks Demand.

West in Sketch & Verse. 2nd ed. Dan Hoover. (Illus.). 40p. (Orig.). 1993. pap. 7.99 (*0-941875-18-0*) Wolverine Distrib.

West India Pickles. William P. Talboys. 1977. text ed. 21.95 (*0-8369-9255-5*, 9108) Ayer.

West Indian-American Experience. Warren J. Halliburton. LC 93-19233. (Coming to America Ser.). (Illus.). 64p. (J). (gr. 4-6). lib. bdg. 16.90 (*1-56294-340-5*) Millbrook Pr.

West Indian Americans. Alexandra Bandon. LC 93-27201. (Footsteps to America Ser.). (Illus.). 112p. (YA). (gr. 6 up). 1994. lib. bdg. 13.95 (*0-02-768148-3*, New Dscvry Bks) Silver Burdett Pr.

West Indian & Calypso. Compiled by Jerry Silverman. (Traditional Black Music Ser.). (Illus.). 80p. (YA). (gr. 5 up). 1995. lib. bdg. 18.95 (*0-7910-1840-7*) Chelsea Hse.

West Indian Community of Greater Hartford: Connecticut. rev. ed. Lynroy A. Grant & Frank A. Stone. 52p. 1985. 5.00 (*0-317-65372-5*) I N Thut World Educ Ctr.

West Indian Family Structure. Michael G. Smith. LC 84-45531. (American Ethnological Society Monographs: No. 36). 1988. reprint ed. 35.00 (*0-404-62935-0*) AMS Pr.

West Indian Fish Tale (& Other Stories) A. L. Anduze. 56p. 1993. pap. 8.95 (*0-932831-09-5*) Eastern Caribbean Inst.

West Indian Folk-Tales. Philip Sherlock. 1990. 20.25 (*0-8446-6658-0*) Peter Smith.

West Indian Folk Tales. Philip M. Sherlock. (Illus.). 151p. (YA). (gr. 3 up). 1988. pap. 12.95 (*0-19-274127-6*) OUP.

West Indian Green Monkeys: Problems in Historical Biogeography. W. W. Denham. (Contributions to Primatology Ser.: Vol. 24). (Illus.). viii, 80p. 1987. 38.50 (*3-8055-4518-5*) S Karger.

West Indian Reports, 42 vols., Set. boxed 5,360.00 (*0-406-87800-5*, U.K.) MICHIE.

West Indian Slavery: Selected Pamphlets. LC 75-100310. 1971. reprint ed. text ed. 65.00 (*0-8371-2954-0*, WEI&, Negro U Pr) Greenwood.

West Indian Women at War. Bousquet. (C). 1991. pap. 19.95 (*0-85315-743-X*, Pub. by Lawrence & Wishart UK) NYU Pr.

West Indian Workers & the United Fruit Company in Costa Rica, 1870-1940. Aviva Chomsky. LC 95-21958. (Illus.). 312p. (C). 1996. text ed. 35.00 (*0-8071-1979-2*) La State U Pr.

West Indians & Their Language. P. Roberts. 224p. 1988. text ed. 61.95 (*0-521-35136-7*); pap. text ed. 21.95 (*0-521-35955-4*) Cambridge U Pr.

West Indies. Helen Arnold. LC 96-3497. (Postcards From Ser.). (Illus.). (J). 1997. lib. bdg. 21.40 (*0-8172-4021-7*) Raintree Steck-V.

West Indies. Don Brothers. (Let's Visit Places & Peoples of the World Ser.). (Illus.). 128p. (J). (gr. 5 up). 1989. lib. bdg. 19.95 (*1-55546-793-8*) Chelsea Hse.

West Indies. C. Washington Eves. 1976. lib. bdg. 59.95 (*0-8490-2815-9*) Gordon Pr.

West Indies. David Flint. LC 92-43914. (On the Map Ser.). (Illus.). 32p. (J). (gr. 3-4). 1993. lib. bdg. 22.83 (*0-8114-2942-3*) Raintree Steck-V.

West Indies. Ron Ramdin. LC 91-7490. (World in View Ser.). (Illus.). 96p. (YA). (gr. 6-12). 1991. lib. bdg. 25.68 (*0-8114-2442-1*) Raintree Steck-V.

West Indies. William Russell. LC 93-49339. (J). 1994. write for info. (*1-55916-035-7*) Rourke Bk Co.

West Indies: Patterns of Development, Culture & Environmental Change since 1492. David Watts. (Studies in Historical Geography: No. 8). (Illus.). 600p. (C). 1990. pap. text ed. 36.95 (*0-521-38651-9*) Cambridge U Pr.

West Indies see Coins of the British Commonwealth of Nations to the End of the Reign of George VI

West Indies Before & since Emancipation Compromising the Windward & Leeward Islands' Military Command. John Davy. 1971. reprint ed. 49.50 (*0-7146-1935-3*, Pub. by F Cass Pubs UK) Intl Spec Bk.

West Indies Cookbook: Classic Recipes from the Spicy Caribbean. Connie Krochmal & Arnold Krochmal. (Border Bks.). 128p. (Orig.). 1993. pap. 9.95 (*0-9623865-3-7*) Out West Pub.

West Indies Federation. David Lowenthal. LC 76-21682. (American Geographical Society; Research Ser.: No. 23). (Illus.). 142p. 1976. reprint ed. text ed. 49.75 (*0-8371-9005-3*, LOWI, Greenwood Pr) Greenwood.

West Indies in Eighteen Thirty-Seven. Joseph Sturge & Thomas Harvey. 475p. 1968. reprint ed. 47.50 (*0-7146-1900-0*, Pub. by F Cass Pubs UK) Intl Spec Bk.

West Internal Revenue Code of 1986 & Treasury Regulations: Annotated & Selected. James E. Smith. 1600p. 1995. pap. text ed. 28.75 (*0-314-04172-9*) West Pub.

West Internal Revenue Code of 1986 & Treasury Regulations: Annotated & Selected Readings, 1996 Edition. James E. Smith. 1820p. (C). 1996. pap. text ed. 31.75 (*0-314-06354-4*) West Pub.

West Irish Folk-Tales & Romances. Compiled by William Larminie. LC 72-4191. (Select Bibliographies Reprint Ser.). 1977. reprint ed. 19.95 (*0-8369-6888-3*) Ayer.

West Is Left on the Map. Anselm Hollo. (Illus.). 32p. (Orig.). 1993. pap. 4.95 (*1-880743-02-7*) Dead Metaphor.

West Is West: Rudyard Kipling in San Francisco. limited ed. Lois Rather. (Illus.). 1976. 35.00 (*0-686-20624-X*) Rather Pr.

West, Japan, & Cape Route Imports: The Oil & Non-Fuel Mineral Trades. Charles Perry. LC 82-80947. (Special Report Ser.). 88p. 1982. 11.95 (*0-89549-042-0*) Inst Foreign Policy Anal.

West Landscaping. Sunset Books Staff. 416p. 1997. pap. 29.95 (*0-376-03905-1*, Sunset) Sunset Bks Inc.

***West Legal Desk Reference.** Hussey & William P. Statsky. (LQ - Paralegal Ser.). (C). 1990. pap. 45.00 (*0-314-79997-4*) West Pub.

West Legal Thesaurus. William P. Statsky. Date not set. text ed. 45.25 (*0-314-53872-0*) West Pub.

West Less Traveled: The Best & Lesser Known Parks, Monuments & Natural Areas. Jan Bannan. 288p. (Orig.). 1996. pap. 16.95 (*1-55591-261-3*) Fulcrum Pub.

***West Long Branch, NJ.** H. Pike. (Images of America Ser.). pap. 16.99 (*0-7524-0472-5*, Arcdia) Chalford.

West Lothian: An Illustrated Architectural Guide. Richard Jaques & Charles McKean. (Illus.). 96p. (C). 1994. pap. text ed. 35.00 (*1-873190-25-5*, Pub. by Rutland Pr UK) St Mut.

West Main School, a History Book: The Story of a School in Ravenna, Ohio, U. S. A. Lois F. Lewis. (Illus.). (Orig.). (J). (gr. 5). 1988. pap. text ed. 2.00 (*0-9620136-0-9*) L F Lewis.

West Malaysia & Singapore. Wendy Moore. (Passport's Regional Guides of Malaysia Ser.). (Illus.). 288p. 1994. pap. 17.95 (*0-8442-9891-3*, Passport Bks) NTC Pub Grp.

West Malaysia & Singapore. Wendy Moore. 288p. 1993. pap. 19.95 (*0-945971-64-8*) Periplus.

West Malaysia & Singapore: A Selected Bibliography. Karl J. Pelzer. LC 72-87853. (Bibliographies Ser.). 400p. 1971. 25.00 (*0-87536-235-4*) HRAFP.

West Marin Diary. John Grissim. (Orig.). 1991. pap. 10.00 (*0-912449-35-7*) Floating Island.

West Meets East: The Travels of Alexander. Suzanne S. Art. (Illus.). 199p. (Orig.). (J). (gr. 4-8). 1996. pap. text ed. 14.67 (*1-877653-43-8*, 81) Wayside Pub.

West Memphis Mojo. Martin Jones. 69p. (Orig.). 1987. pap. 5.95 (*0-88145-049-9*) Broadway Play.

West Mexico, from Sea to Sierra: A Traveler's Handbook to the Baja California Peninsula & Mexico's West Coast. Charles A. Kulander. (Illus.). 352p. (Orig.). 1992. pap. 16.95 (*0-9629043-3-3*) La Paz Pub.

West Midlands in the Early Middle Ages. Ed. by Margaret Gelling. 240p. 1992. text ed. 75.00 (*0-7185-1170-0*); pap. text ed. write for info. (*0-7185-1395-9*) St Martin.

West Molokai Field Site Guide for Teachers. Faith M. Roelofs. (Exploring the Islands Ser.). 1994. teacher ed. write for info. (*1-882163-28-1*) Moanalua Grdns Fnd.

West Mound Surface Clearance see Abu Salabikh Excavations

West Nashville: Its People & Environs. Sarah F. Kelley. (Illus.). 443p. 1987. 39.95 (*0-9615960-0-7*) S F Kelley Pub.

West of Barbwire. large type ed. Lee Floren. (Linford Western Library). 272p. 1994. pap. 15.99 (*0-7089-7576-3*, Linford) Ulverscroft.

West of Bohemia. large type ed. Jessica Steele. (Harlequin Ser.). 1994. lib. bdg. 19.95 (*0-263-13771-6*) Thorndike Pr.

***West of Cheyenne.** Lee Hoffman. LC 96-52577. (Sagebrush Large Print Westerns Ser.). 1997. lib. bdg. 17.95 (*1-57490-111-7*, Beeler LP Bks) T T Beeler.

West of Chicago. Dave Etter. 81p. (Orig.). 1982. 4.50 (*0-685-08289-X*) Spoon Riv Poetry.

West of Cimarron. G. Clifton Wisler. 1985. pap. 2.50 (*0-8217-1681-6*) Kensgtn Pub Corp.

West of Darkness. John Barton. 128p. 1987. 9.95 (*0-920806-90-2*, Pub. by Penumbra Pr CN) U of Toronto Pr.

***West of Dodge.** Louis L'Amour. 252p. 1997. mass mkt. 4.99 (*0-553-57697-6*) Bantam.

West of Dodge. large type ed. Louis L'Amour. LC 96-20872. (Western Ser.). 380p. 1996. 21.95 (*0-7862-0803-1*, Thorndike Lrg Prnt) Thorndike Pr.

West of Dodge: Frontier Stories. Louis L'Amour. LC 95-4508. 192p. 1996. 19.95 (*0-553-10143-9*) Bantam.

West of Eden: A History of Art & Literature of Yosemite. David Robertson. (Illus.). 174p. 1984. 15.95 (*0-939666-40-5*); pap. 9.95 (*0-939666-41-3*) Yosemite Assn.

West of Eden: The End of Innocence at Apple Computer. Frank Rose. LC 88-40302. 288p. 1990. 19.95 (*0-685-23144-5*); pap. 8.95 (*0-685-23145-3*) Viking Penguin.

West of Eden: Writers in Hollywood, 1928-1940. Richard Fine. LC 93-2036. (Studies in the History of Film & Television). (Illus.). 216p. 1993. reprint ed. pap. text ed. 14.95 (*1-56098-263-2*) Smithsonian.

West of Everything: The Inner Life of the Westerns. Jane P. Tompkins. (Illus.). 208p. 1992. 25.00 (*0-19-507305-3*) OUP.

West of Everything: The Inner Life of the Westerns. Jane P. Tompkins. 272p. 1993. pap. 13.95 (*0-19-508268-0*) OUP.

West of Hell's Fringe: Crime, Criminals, & the Federal Peace Officer in Oklahoma Territory, 1889-1907. Glenn Shirley. LC 77-9112. (Illus.). 512p. 1990. pap. 17.95 (*0-8061-2264-1*) U of Okla Pr.

West of Ireland: Including Connemara. Trish Fitzpatrick & Tony Whilde. (Direct from Ireland Ser.). 276p. 1995. pap. text ed. 14.95 (*0-8442-9712-7*, Passport Bks) NTC Pub Grp.

West of Key West. Ed. by John Cole. LC 95-52458. 224p. 1996. 50.00 (*0-8117-1881-6*) Stackpole.

West of Littleton: A Short History of the Rural Communities of Slate Ledge, Partridge Lake, Pattenville, & West Littleton, New Hampshire. Wilbur W. Willey. (Illus.). 66p. (Orig.). 1992. pap. 10.95 (*0-9645740-1-2*) Wldwood W.

West of Mass. Jim McCrary. Ed. by John Moritz & Curtis Dillon. (Illus.). 76p. (Orig.). 1992. pap. 8.00 (*1-881175-01-4*) Tansy Pr.

West of Orange see Dead at the Box Office

West of Owen Wister: Selected Short Stories. Owen Wister. LC 74-175805. 265p. 1972. reprint ed. pap. 75.60 (*0-7837-8904-1*, 2049615) Bks Demand.

West of Quarantine. large type ed. Todhunter Ballard. LC 96-18186. 1996. pap. 20.00 (*0-7838-1849-1*, GK Hall) Thorndike Pr.

West of Rimrock - Draw or Drag, 2 vols. in 1. Wayne D. Overholser. 384p. 1994. mass mkt., pap. text ed. 4.99 (*0-8439-3635-5*) Dorchester Pub Co.

West of Rome. John Fante. LC 86-12995. 192p. 1995. reprint ed. 20.00 (*0-87685-678-4*); reprint ed. pap. 13.00 (*0-87685-677-6*) Black Sparrow.

West of Sheba. Aisha Mohammed. LC 91-66858. 527p. 1991. pap. 11.95 (*1-55523-477-1*) Winston-Derek.

West of the Divide: Voices from a Ranch & Reservation. Jim Carrier. LC 91-58482. 192p. 1992. 8.99 (*1-55591-093-9*) Fulcrum Pub.

West of the Great Divide: Norwegian Migration to the Pacific Coast, 1847-1893. Kenneth O. Bjork. LC 58-4511. (Publications of the Norwegian-American Historical Association). 678p. reprint ed. pap. 180.00 (*0-317-27953-X*, 2056021) Bks Demand.

West of the Imagination. William H. Goetzmann & William N. Goetzmann. (Illus.). 1989. pap. 17.95 (*0-393-30565-1*) Norton.

West of the Mad Coyote: Poems. Larry K. Jacobson. LC 84-1094. 90p. (Orig.). 1984. pap. 9.95 (*0-916447-02-2*) Edit Review.

***West of the Moon.** Booth. (J). (gr. 2). 1989. pap. text ed. 34.75 (*0-03-926811-X*); student ed., pap. text ed. 12.50 (*0-03-926812-8*) HR&W Schl Div.

West of the Moon. James A. Whistler. (Illus.). 103p. 1995. pap. 16.95 (*0-7206-0918-6*, Pub. by P Owen Ltd UK) Dufour.

West of the Neosho. George B. Yandell. 368p. 1996. mass mkt. 5.99 (*1-896329-93-4*, Pub. by Comnwlth Pub CN) Partners Pubs Grp.

West of the Pecos. Zane Grey. 336p. 1992. mass mkt. 3.99 (*0-06-100467-7*, Harp PBks) HarpC.

An Asterisk (*) at the beginning of an entry indicates that the title is appearing in BIP for the first time.

West of the Pecos. Tim Kelly. 1971. pap. 5.00 (*0-87129-370-6*, W17) Dramatic Pub.
West of the Pecos. large type ed. Zane Grey. LC 96-19310. (Sagebrush Large Print Westerns Ser.). 320p. 1996. lib. bdg. 18.95 (*1-57490-019-6*) T T Beeler.
West of the Rockies: From Campfire to Candlelight. Ed. by Patti Milius. (Illus.). 360p. 1994. 17.95 (*0-9641314-0-4*) JSLOGJ.
West of the Scioto. Robert E. Lowe. LC 90-92260. (Illus.). 210p. (Orig.). 1993. pap. text ed. write for info. (*1-878455-05-2*) Markas Pub.
West of the Thirties: Discoveries among the Navajo & Hopi. Edward T. Hall. LC 94-36043. 224p. 1995. pap. 11.95 (*0-385-42422-1*, Anchor NY) Doubleday.
West of the West: Imagining California: An Anthology. Ed. by Leonard Michaels et al. 1995. 13.00 (*0-520-20164-7*) U CA Pr.
West of Venus. Judy Troy. LC 96-49498. 1997. 23.00 (*0-679-45153-6*) Random.
West of Warsaw. Frank Serafino. LC 82-73450. 248p. 1983. 13.95 (*0-910977-00-3*) Avenue Pub.
West of West. Brian Lalor. (Illus.). 160p. (Orig.). 1990. pap. 19.95 (*0-86322-109-2*, Pub. by Brandon Bk Pubs IE) Irish Bks Media.
West of Wichita: Settling the High Plains of Kansas, 1865-1890. Craig Miner. LC 85-26013. (Illus.). viii, 304p. 1986. pap. 12.95 (*0-7006-0364-6*) U Pr of KS.
West of Wild Bill Hickok. Joseph G. Rosa. LC 81-21945. (Illus.). 202p. 1994. pap. 14.95 (*0-8061-2680-9*) U of Okla Pr.
West of Yesterday. limited ed. Paul Monette. 1994. 100.00 (*0-312-11406-0*) St Martin.
West of Yesterday, East of Summer: New & Selected Poems, 1973-1993. Paul Monette. LC 94-16119. 1994. 17.95 (*0-312-11379-X*) St Martin.
West of Yesterday, East of Summer: New & Selected Poems (1973-1993) Paul Monette. 1995. pap. 9.95 (*0-312-13616-1*) St Martin.
West Pacific Rim: An Introduction. Rupert A. Hodder. LC 92-27957. 153p. 1992. text ed. 59.95 (*0-470-21963-7*); pap. text ed. 27.95 (*0-470-21964-5*) Halsted Pr.
West Pacific Rim: An Introduction. Rupert A. Hodder. LC 92-27957. 153p. 1993. pap. text ed. 45.00 (*0-471-94648-6*) Wiley.
West Palm Beach: Centennial Reflections. H. J. Roberts. LC 94-68705. (Illus.). 300p. 1994. 25.95 (*1-884243-02-9*) Sunshine Sentinel.
West Parker Remembers When. Elizabeth B. Kelley. (Illus.). 67p. (Orig.). (C). 1988. pap. 12.50 (*0-945677-03-0*) Riverby Bks.
West Pathway: New Poems. Steve Ellis. 63p. 9400. pap. 12.95 (*1-85224-235-3*, Pub. by Bloodaxe Bks UK) Dufour.
West Point. Libby Hughes. LC 92-20641. (Places in American History Ser.). (Illus.). 72p. (J). (gr. 4 up). 1993. lib. bdg. 14.95 (*0-87518-529-0*, Dillon Silver Burdett) Silver Burdett Pr.
***West Point.** Libby Hughes. (Places in American History Ser.). (Illus.). 72p. (J). (gr. 4). 1997. pap. 7.95 (*0-382-24777-9*, Dillon Silver Burdett) Silver Burdett Pr.
West Point. David Pahl. 1987. 7.98 (*0-671-08917-X*) S&S Trade.
West Point: An Artist's Sketchbook. Robert A. Getz & Edward Moses. (Illus.). 60p. 1994. pap. 19.95 (*1-884824-06-4*) Tryon Pubng.
West Point Atlas of American Wars Vol. 1: 1689-1900. Vincent J. Esposito. 336p. 1995. 75.00 (*0-8050-3391-2*) H Holt & Co.
West Point Way of Leadership. Larry Donnithorne. 192p. 1994. 22.50 (*0-385-41703-9*) Doubleday.
West Point Wooing & Other Stories. Clara L. Burnham. LC 79-94709. (Short Story Index Reprint Ser.). 1977. 20.95 (*0-8369-3088-6*) Ayer.
West Pointers & Early Washington. John A. Hemphill. Ed. by Robert C. Cumbow. 235p. (YA). (gr. 4-9). 1992. 29.95 (*0-9635925-0-5*) W Pt Soc Puget.
***West Pole.** Diane Glancy. LC 96-36471. 216p. 1997. pap. text ed. 17.95 (*0-8166-2894-7*) U of Minn Pr.
West Pole. limited ed. Diane H. Glancy. (Winter Book Ser.: Vol. 7). (Illus.). 22p. 1994. 180.00 (*1-879832-07-0*); lib. bdg. 80.00 (*1-879832-08-9*) MN Ctr Book Arts.
West Portals of Chartres Cathedral, I: The Iconology of the Creation. Jan Van der Meulen & Nancy W. Price. LC 80-5586. (C). 1981. pap. text ed. 24.00 (*0-8191-1403-0*); lib. bdg. 56.00 (*0-8191-1402-2*) U Pr of Amer.
West River Voting Patterns. Alan L. Clem. 1965. 5.00 (*1-55614-016-9*) U of SD Gov Res Bur.
West Rock to the Barndoor Hills: The Traprock Ridges of Connecticut. Cara Lee. (Illus.). 60p. 1985. pap. 5.00 (*0-942081-00-5*) CT DEP CGNHS.
West Roxbury, MA. Anthony Sammarco. (Images of America Ser.). 1997. pap. 16.99 (*0-7524-0452-0*, Arcdia) Chalford.
***West! Sail West, Man! Around the World in Twenty Feet.** Hein Zenker. LC 97-90189. (Illus.). 312p. 1997. pap. 18.95 (*0-9658773-0-2*) Windjammer.
West Side: Narrow Gauge in the Sierra. Mallory H. Ferrell. Ed. by Pacific Fast Mail Staff. (Illus.). 320p. 1992. 59.50 (*0-915713-02-0*) Pac Fast Mail.
West Side Stories. Ed. by George Bailey. LC 91-77074. (Chicago Voices Ser.). 181p. 1994. reprint ed. pap. 9.95 (*0-929968-39-5*) Another Chicago Pr.
West Side Stories: A Multicultural Anthology of Contemporary Short Stories. Intro. by George Bailey. (Orig.). 1992. pap. 9.95 (*0-9627425-1-1*) City Stoop Pr.
West Side Story. (Vocal Score Ser.). 208p. 1986. pap. 40.00 (*0-7935-2010-X*, 50338100) H Leonard.
West Side Story. Leonard Bernstein et al. 1958. 13.95 (*0-394-40788-1*) Random.
West Side Story. Irving Shulman. (Orig.). 1990. mass mkt. 5.50 (*0-671-72566-1*) PB.
West Side Story: A Novelization. Irving Shulman. 17.95 (*0-8488-0847-9*) Amereon Ltd.
West Side Story: Choral Selection. Leonard Bernstein. 32p. 1986. pap. 2.50 (*0-7935-5497-7*, 50307850) H Leonard.
West Side Story: Easy Piano Selections. Leonard Bernstein. 20p. 1986. pap. 4.95 (*0-7935-2009-6*, 50329750) H Leonard.
West Side Story: Orchestra Set/Full Score/Parts. Leonard Bernstein. 1986. pap. text ed. 75.00 (*0-7935-4873-X*, 50343100) H Leonard.
West Side Story: Piano. Leonard Bernstein. 12p. 1986. pap. 5.95 (*0-7935-5006-8*, 50288290) H Leonard.
West Side Studies, 2 Vols., Set. Incl. Vol. 1. Boyhood & Lawlessness & the Neglected Girl. Ruth S. True. LC 73-11932. 1974. (*0-318-50912-1*); Vol. 2. Middle West Side by Ortho G. Cartwright & Mothers Who Must Earn by Katharine Anthony. Richard C. Wade. LC 73-11932. 1974. (*0-318-50913-X*); LC 73-11932. (Metropolitan America Ser.). (Illus.). 778p. 1974. reprint ed. 54.95 (*0-405-05434-3*) Ayer.
West Side Waltz. Ernest Thompson. 1982. pap. 5.25 (*0-8222-1233-1*) Dramatists Play.
West Sociology Astound Wind. Date not set. 45.00 (*0-314-06212-2*) West Pub.
West Sussex Probate Inventories, Fifteen Twenty-One to Eighteen Thirty-Four. Timothy J. McCann. 1981. 110.00 (*0-86260-005-7*) St Mut.
West Sussex Village Book. Tony Wales. 224p. 1987. 30.00 (*0-905392-34-5*) St Mut.
West System Products Technical Manual: United Kingdom Version. Ted Hugger. (Illus.). 32p. 1989. write for info. (*0-318-65786-4*) Gougeon Brothers.
West Texas Adventure. Bill Lewis. 180p. 1993. pap. 9.95 (*1-57087-007-1*) Prof Pr NC.
West Texas & the Big Bend. Eric O'Keefe. (Texas Monthly Guidebooks Ser.). 1995. 16.95 (*0-87719-250-2*) Gulf Pub.
***West Texas Weddings: The West Texans.** Ginger Chambers. 1997. mass mkt. 3.99 (*0-373-70730-4*, 1-70730-6) Harlequin Bks.
West That Never Was. Tony Thomas. 1989. pap. 14.95 (*0-8065-1121-4*, Citadel Pr) Carol Pub Group.
West That Was. John E. Eggen. LC 91-65653. (Illus.). 184p. 1991. 29.95 (*0-88740-330-1*) Schiffer.
West That Was: Featuring the Writings of Michael P. Jones & the Artwork of Will Lehnen. Michael P. Jones. (Illus.). 8p. (Orig.). 1984. pap. text ed. write for info. (*0-89904-087-X*) Crumb Elbow Pub.
West to Cambodia. Samuel L. Marshall. (Vietnam War Ser.: No. 6). (Illus.). 253p. 1984. reprint ed. 27.95 (*0-89839-078-8*) Battery Pr.
West to East: A Teenager's Journey to China. Gao Qian. 1996. pap. 12.95 (*0-614-12546-4*) China Bks.
***West to East: A Young Girl's Journey to China.** Qian Gao. (Illus.). 192p. (YA). 1996. pap. 12.95 (*0-8351-2549-1*) China Bks.
West to East: Tales of the Twenties & Thirties. Teo Savory. 200p. 1989. 22.50 (*0-87775-208-7*) Unicorn Pr.
West to Eden. Gloria Goldreich. 1989. mass mkt. 4.95 (*0-380-70601-6*) Avon.
West to Eden: Texans in Hollywood. Donald Clarke. Ed. by Edwin M. Eakin. (Illus.). 240p. 1988. 15.95 (*0-89015-617-4*) Sunbelt Media.
***West to Opportunity: The Diary of Teresa Angelino Viscardi.** Jim Murphy. LC 97-23064. (Dear America Ser.). (J). 1998. write for info. (*0-590-73888-7*) Scholastic Inc.
West to the Pacific: The Story of the Lewis & Clark Expedition. Ronald K. Fisher. Ed. by Merle Wells. LC 88-72198. (Illus.). 152p. (Orig.). 1989. pap. 9.95 (*0-941734-01-3*) Alpha Om ID.
***West Transformed.** Hollister. (C). Date not set. pap. text ed. write for info. (*0-15-508117-9*); teacher ed., pap. text ed. 26.75 (*0-15-508118-7*); pap. text ed. 26.75 (*0-15-508119-5*) HB Coll Pubs.
***West Transformed.** 2nd ed. Hollister. (C). Date not set. student ed., pap. text ed. write for info. (*0-15-508124-1*); pap. text ed. write for info. (*0-15-508125-X*) HB Coll Pubs.
***West Transformed, Vol. C.** Hollister. (C). Date not set. pap. text ed. write for info. (*0-15-508128-4*) HB Coll Pubs.
***West Transformed, Vol. A.** Hollister. (C). Date not set. pap. text ed. write for info. (*0-15-508126-8*) HB Coll Pubs.
***West Transformed, Vol. B.** Hollister. (C). Date not set. pap. text ed. write for info. (*0-15-508127-6*) HB Coll Pubs.
West Victoria Separation Movement. K. K. Donaghue. 1984. pap. 21.00 (*0-949759-40-6*, Pub. by Deakin Univ AT) St Mut.
***West Virginia.** (Illus.). 1997. write for info. (*0-89933-246-3*, 5403) DeLorme Map.
West Virginia. Domenica DiPiazza. LC 93-46906. (Hello U. S. A. Ser.). (Illus.). 72p. (J). (gr. 3-6). 1995. lib. bdg. 18.95 (*0-8225-2745-6*, Lerner Publctns) Lerner Group.
West Virginia. Dennis B. Fradin & Judith B. Fradin. LC 94-17016. (From Sea to Shining Sea Ser.). (Illus.). 64p. (J). (gr. 3-5). 1994. lib. bdg. 24.00 (*0-516-03848-6*) Childrens.
West Virginia. Arnout Hyde, Jr. LC 80-82049. (Illus.). 128p. 1980. 25.00 (*0-685-00000-1*); 125.00 (*0-9604590-1-4*) A Hyde.
West Virginia. R. Conrad Stein. LC 90-33848. (America the Beautiful Ser.). (Illus.). 144p. (J). (gr. 4 up). 1990. lib. bdg. 28.50 (*0-516-00494-8*) Childrens.
West Virginia. Kathleen Thompson. LC 87-26483. (Portrait of America Library). 48p. (J). (gr. 3 up). 1996. lib. bdg. 22.83 (*0-8114-7395-3*) Raintree Steck-V.
West Virginia. Kathleen Thompson. LC 87-26483. (Portrait of America Library). 48p. (J). (gr. 3 up). 1996. pap. text ed. 5.95 (*0-8114-7476-3*) Raintree Steck-V.
West Virginia: A Guide to the Mountain State. Federal Writers' Project. LC 72-84516. (American Guidebook Ser.). 1980. reprint ed. lib. bdg. 79.00 (*0-686-34458-8*) Somerset Pub.
West Virginia: A Guide to the Mountain State. Federal Writers' Project Staff & Writers Program-WPA Staff. (American Guide Ser.). 1989. reprint ed. lib. bdg. 79.00 (*0-7812-1047-X*, 1047) Rprt Serv.
West Virginia: A Guide to Unique Places. Stephen Soltis. LC 94-43643. (Off the Beaten Path Ser.). (Illus.). 160p. (Orig.). 1995. pap. 10.95 (*1-56440-634-2*) Globe Pequot.
West Virginia: A History. John A. Williams. (States & the Nation Ser.). (Illus.). 1984. pap. 12.95 (*0-393-30182-6*) Norton.
West Virginia: A History. 2nd ed. Otis K. Rice & Stephen W. Brown. LC 93-17819. (Illus.). 376p. 1994. Alk. paper. 32.00 (*0-8131-1854-9*) U Pr of Ky.
West Virginia: Documents in the History of a Rural Industrial State. 2nd ed. Ronald Lewis & John Hennen. 444p. (C). 1996. per. 40.89 (*0-7872-2540-1*) Kendall-Hunt.
West Virginia: Mountain Majesty. James E. Casto. Ed. by Ken Sullivan. (Illus.). 256p. 1996. 49.95 (*0-9651580-0-4*) Publns Mgmt Assoc.
West Virginia: Our Land - Our People. William T. Doherty. Ed. by Marshall Buckalew. (Illus.). 320p. (J). (gr. 8). 1990. 25.00 (*0-914498-07-X*); teacher ed., ring bd. 25.00 (*0-914498-10-X*) WV Hist Ed Found.
West Virginia: Our State. Tony L. Williams. Ed. by Marshall Buckalew. (Illus.). 288p. (J). (gr. 4). 1990. 20.00 (*0-914498-09-6*); teacher ed., ring bd. 25.00 (*0-685-25544-1*) WV Hist Ed Found.
West Virginia: The State & Its People. 4th ed. Otis K. Rice. 1979. reprint ed. 10.00 (*0-87012-129-4*) McClain.
West Virginia: 1870 Census Index. Ed. by Bradley W. Steuart. 1096p. 1990. lib. bdg. 175.00 (*1-877677-07-8*) Precision Indexing.
West Virginia - Collected Works of Federal Writers Project. Federal Writers' Project Staff. 1991. reprint ed. lib. bdg. 98.00 (*0-7812-5808-1*) Rprt Serv.
West Virginia Air Power: A Pictorial History of the 130th & 167th Tactical Airlift Groups. Jack H. Smith. (Illus.). 80p. (Orig.). 1992. pap. 9.95 (*0-929521-53-6*) Pictorial Hist.
West Virginia & Other State Greats (Biographies) Carole Marsh. (Carole Marsh West Virginia Bks.). (Illus.). (J). 1994. pap. 19.95 (*0-7933-2257-X*); lib. bdg. 29.95 (*0-7933-2256-1*); disk 29.95 (*0-7933-2258-8*) Gallopade Pub Group.
West Virginia & the Captains of Industry. John A. Williams. LC 75-35409. 1976. 17.95 (*0-87012-237-1*) West Va U Pr.
West Virginia Bandits, Bushwackers, Outlaws, Crooks, Devils, Ghosts, Desperadoes & Other Assorted & Sundry Characters! Carole Marsh. (Carole Marsh West Virginia Bks.). (Illus.). (J). 1994. pap. 19.95 (*0-7933-1201-9*); lib. bdg. 29.95 (*0-7933-1202-7*); disk 29.95 (*0-7933-1203-5*) Gallopade Pub Group.
West Virginia Baptist History: The Convention Years, 1865-1965. Truett Rogers. 1994. 21.95 (*0-929915-12-7*) Headline Bks.
West Virginia Biographical Supplement: Biographies of Confederates Living Outside the South. Robert White. Ed. by Clement A. Evans. (Confederate Military History Extended Edition Ser.: Vol. III). (Illus.). 595p. 1987. reprint ed. 50.00 (*1-56837-022-9*) Broadfoot.
West Virginia Birds: Distribution & Ecology. George A. Hall. (Special Publications: No. 7). (Illus.). 188p. (Orig.). 1983. 11.95 (*0-935868-05-4*) Carnegie Mus.
West Virginia Book of Lists. Gerald Tomlinson & Richard C. Weigen. LC 94-76304. (Illus.). 192p. (Orig.). 1994. pap. 11.95 (*0-917125-03-7*) Home Run Pr.
West Virginia Bookstore Book: A Surprising Guide to Our State's Bookstores & Their Specialties for Students, Teachers, Writers & Publishers. Carole Marsh. (West Virginia Bks.). (Illus.). 1994. pap. 19.95 (*0-7933-3000-9*); lib. bdg. 29.95 (*0-7933-2999-X*); disk 29.95 (*0-7933-3001-7*) Gallopade Pub Group.
West Virginia Breeding Bird Atlas. Albert R. Buckelew & George A. Hall. (Pitt Series in Nature & Natural History). (Illus.). 232p. (C). 1994. 27.50 (*0-8229-3850-2*) U of Pittsburgh Pr.
West Virginia Business Directory, 1997. rev. ed. 672p. 1996. boxed 295.00 (*1-56105-795-9*) Am Busn Direct.
***West Virginia Business Directory 1997.** rev. ed. American Business Directories Staff. 672p. 1996. boxed 295.00 (*1-56105-878-5*) Am Busn Direct.
***West Virginia Business Directory 1998.** rev. ed. American Business Directories Staff. 704p. 1997. boxed 295.00 (*1-56105-965-X*) Am Busn Direct.
West Virginia Census Index 1850 Mortality. Ronald V. Jackson. (Illus.). lib. bdg. 35.00 (*0-89593-531-7*) Accelerated Index.
West Virginia Census Index 1860 Mortality. Ronald V. Jackson. (Illus.). lib. bdg. 35.00 (*0-89593-532-5*) Accelerated Index.
West Virginia Census Index 1870 Mortality. Ronald V. Jackson. (Illus.). 1981. lib. bdg. 39.00 (*0-89593-533-3*) Accelerated Index.
West Virginia Census Index 1880 Mortality. Ronald V. Jackson. (Illus.). 1980. lib. bdg. 49.00 (*0-89593-534-1*) Accelerated Index.
West Virginia Central & Pittsburgh Railway Company. Sam Griffin. 1992. reprint ed. pap. 8.00 (*0-87012-418-8*) McClain.
West Virginia Classic Christmas Trivia: Stories, Recipies, Activities, Legends, Lore & More! Carole Marsh. (Carole Marsh West Virginia Bks.). (Illus.). (J). 1994. pap. 19.95 (*0-7933-1204-3*); lib. bdg. 29.95 (*0-7933-1205-1*); disk 29.95 (*0-7933-1206-X*) Gallopade Pub Group.
West Virginia Coastales. Carole Marsh. (Carole Marsh West Virginia Bks.). (Illus.). (J). 1994. pap. 19.95 (*0-7933-2251-0*); disk 29.95 (*0-7933-2252-9*) Gallopade Pub Group.
West Virginia Coastales. Carole Marsh. (Carole Marsh West Virginia Bks.). (Illus.). (J). 1997. lib. bdg. 29.95 (*0-7933-2250-2*) Gallopade Pub Group.
West Virginia Coastales! Carole Marsh. (West Virginia Bks.). (J). 1994. lib. bdg. 29.95 (*0-7933-7313-1*) Gallopade Pub Group.
West Virginia Code Annotated, 25 vols. write for info. (*0-87215-138-7*) MICHIE.
West Virginia Code Annotated. write for info. (*0-614-06003-6*) MICHIE.
West Virginia County Maps. rev. ed. Ed. by C. J. Puetz. (Illus.). 144p. (Orig.). 1995. pap. 14.85 (*0-916514-16-1*) Cnty Maps.
West Virginia Court Rules Annotated. Michie Company Editorial Staff. 1309p. 1992. 45.00 (*0-87473-879-2*) MICHIE.
West Virginia Court Rules, 1994 Edition. Michie Butterworth Editorial Staff. pap. 55.00 (*1-55834-050-5*) MICHIE.
West Virginia Crime Perspective 1996. Ed. by Kathleen O. Morgan et al. 24p. 1996. pap. 19.00 (*1-56692-547-9*) Morgan Quitno Corp.
***West Virginia Crime Perspective 1997.** Ed. by Kathleen O. Morgan & Scott E. Morgan. 24p. 1997. pap. 19.00 (*1-56692-797-8*) Morgan Quitno Corp.
West Virginia Criminal & Traffic Law Manual, 1993 Edition. 30.00 (*0-614-06004-4*) MICHIE.
West Virginia "Crinkum-Crankum" A Funny Word Book about Our State. Carole Marsh. (West Virginia Bks.). (Illus.). (J). (gr. 3-12). 1994. 29.95 (*0-7933-4955-9*); pap. 19.95 (*0-7933-4956-7*); disk 29.95 (*0-7933-4957-5*) Gallopade Pub Group.
West Virginia Dingbats! Bk. 1: A Fun Book of Games, Stories, Activities & More about Our State That's All in Code! for You to Decipher. Carole Marsh. (West Virginia Bks.). (Illus.). (J). (gr. 3-12). 1994. pap. 19.95 (*0-7933-3918-9*); lib. bdg. 29.95 (*0-7933-3917-0*); disk 29.95 (*0-7933-3919-7*) Gallopade Pub Group.
West Virginia Environmental Law Handbook. Jackson & Kelly Staff. (State Environmental Law Ser.). 400p. 1990. pap. text ed. 89.00 (*0-86587-227-9*) Gov Insts.
West Virginia Estate Settlements: An Index to Wills, Inventories, Appraisements, Land Grants & Surveys to 1850. Ross B. Johnston. LC 76-53168. 176p. 1988. reprint ed. 15.00 (*0-317-31647-8*) Genealog Pub.
West Virginia Facts & Factivities. Carole Marsh. (Carole Marsh State Bks.). (Illus.). 1996. 29.95 (*0-614-11562-0*, C Marsh); teacher ed., pap. 19.95 (*0-7933-7943-1*, C Marsh) Gallopade Pub Group.
West Virginia Federal Census Index, 1860. (Illus.). 1988. lib. bdg. 140.00 (*0-89593-528-7*) Accelerated Index.
West Virginia Federal Census Index, 1870 (with Addendum) Ronald V. Jackson. (Illus.). 1988. lib. bdg. 350.00 (*0-89593-529-5*) Accelerated Index.
West Virginia Festival Fun for Kids! Includes Reproducible Activities for Kids! Carole Marsh. (West Virginia Bks.). (Illus.). (J). (gr. 3-12). 1994. pap. 19.95 (*0-7933-4071-3*); lib. bdg. 29.95 (*0-7933-4070-5*); disk 29.95 (*0-7933-4072-1*) Gallopade Pub Group.
West Virginia Folk Music. John A. Cuthbert. 185p. 1982. 12.00 (*0-937058-12-2*) West Va U Pr.
West Virginia Geology, Archeology, & Pedology: A Bibliography & Index. William H. Gillespie & John A. Clendening. 241p. 1964. 15.00 (*0-937058-42-4*) West Va U Pr.
West Virginia Government. William E. Coffey et al. Ed. by Marshall Buckalew & Eugenia G. Thoenen. (Illus.). 112p. (Orig.). (J). (gr. 8). 1984. pap. 10.00 (*0-914498-05-3*) WV Hist Ed Found.
***West Virginia Government! The Cornerstone of Everyday Life in Our State!** Carole Marsh. (Carole Marsh West Virginia Bks.). (J). (gr. 3-12). 1996. pap. 19.95 (*0-7933-6326-8*); lib. bdg. 29.95 (*0-7933-6325-X*); disk 29.95 (*0-7933-6327-6*) Gallopade Pub Group.
West Virginia Governments Performance Standards, 1990. Ed. by Greg Michels. (Governments Performance Standards Ser.). (Illus.). 150p. 1990. text ed. 125.00 (*1-55507-506-1*) Municipal Analysis.
West Virginia Health - Administrative Code Annotated. Ed. by C. Page Hamrick, III. 550p. 1985. ring bd. 295.00 (*0-937683-03-5*) WV Busn Pub.
West Virginia Health Care Perspective 1996. Ed. by Kathleen O. Morgan et al. 24p. 1996. pap. 19.00 (*1-56692-647-5*) Morgan Quitno Corp.
***West Virginia Health Care Perspective 1997.** Ed. by Kathleen O. Morgan & Scott E. Morgan. 24p. 1997. pap. 19.00 (*1-56692-747-1*) Morgan Quitno Corp.
***West Virginia Hiking Trails: Hiking the Mountain State.** 2nd rev. ed. Allen De Hart. Orig. Title: Hiking the Mountain State. (Illus.). 416p. 1997. pap. 16.95 (*1-878239-56-2*) AMC Books.
West Virginia Hillbilly. John G. Rexroad. 1992. pap. 9.95 (*0-87012-494-3*) McClain.
West Virginia Historical Almanac. Sam Clagg. 1975. pap. 8.00 (*0-87012-231-2*) McClain.
West Virginia History. William T. Doherty & Phil Conley. (Illus.). 494p. (J). (gr. 8). 1974. 10.25 (*0-914498-00-2*) WV Hist Ed Found.

W

***West Virginia History! Surprising Secrets about Our State's Founding Mothers, Fathers & Kids!** Carole Marsh. (Carole Marsh West Virginia Bks.). (Illus.). (J). (gr. 3-12). 1996. pap. 19.95 (*0-7933-6173-7*); lib. bdg. 29.95 (*0-7933-6172-9*); disk 29.95 (*0-7933-6174-5*) Gallopade Pub Group.

West Virginia Hot Air Balloon Mystery. Carole Marsh. (Carole Marsh West Virginia Bks.). (Illus.). (J). (gr. 2-9). 1994. 29.95 (*0-7933-2750-4*); pap. 19.95 (*0-7933-2751-2*); disk 29.95 (*0-7933-2752-0*) Gallopade Pub Group.

West Virginia in Perspective 1996. Ed. by Kathleen O. Morgan et al. 26p. 1996. pap. 19.00 (*1-56692-597-5*) Morgan Quitno Corp.

***West Virginia in Perspective 1997.** Ed. by Kathleen O. Morgan & Scott E. Morgan. 26p. 1997. pap. 19.00 (*1-56692-697-1*) Morgan Quitno Corp.

West Virginia in the 1990s: Opportunities for Economic Progress. Robert J. Dilger & Tom S. Witt. (Illus.). 347p. (C). 1993. pap. 16.00 (*0-937058-31-9*) West Va U Pr.

West Virginia Indian Dictionary for Kids! Carole Marsh. (Carole Marsh State Bks.). (J). (gr. 2-9). 1996. 29.95 (*0-7933-7788-9*, C Marsh); pap. 19.95 (*0-7933-7789-7*, C Marsh) Gallopade Pub Group.

West Virginia Input-Output Study 1975: Modeling a Regional Economy. Anthony L. Loviscek et al. 37p. 1979. pap. 10.00 (*0-930284-01-1*) West Va U Pr.

West Virginia Italian Heritage Festival Cookbook. Martina Neely. (Illus.). 112p. (Orig.). 1980. pap. 5.00 (*0-686-37047-3*) Back Fork Bks.

West Virginia Jeopardy! Answers & Questions about Our State! Carole Marsh. (West Virginia Bks.). (Illus.). (J). (gr. 3-12). 1994. pap. 19.95 (*0-7933-4224-4*); lib. bdg. 29.95 (*0-7933-4223-6*); disk 29.95 (*0-7933-4225-2*) Gallopade Pub Group.

West Virginia "Jography" A Fun Run Thru Our State! Carole Marsh. (Carole Marsh West Virginia Bks.). (Illus.). (J). 1994. pap. 19.95 (*0-7933-2234-0*); lib. bdg. 29.95 (*0-7933-2233-2*); disk 29.95 (*0-7933-2235-9*) Gallopade Pub Group.

West Virginia Journal of Psychological Reach & Practice: The Journal of the West Virginia Psychological Association. Ed. by Kevin Larkin. (C). 1992. pap. text ed. write for info. (*0-9634170-4-5*) WVa Psychol Assn.

West Virginia Journal of Psychological Research & Practice: The Journal of the West Virginia Psychological Association. Ed. by Kevin Larkin. 1992. write for info. (*0-9634170-0-2*) WVa Psychol Assn.

West Virginia Kid's Cookbook: Recipes, How-to, History, Lore & More! Carole Marsh. (Carole Marsh West Virginia Bks.). (Illus.). (J). 1994. pap. 19.95 (*0-7933-1213-2*); lib. bdg. 29.95 (*0-7933-1214-0*); disk 29.95 (*0-7933-1215-9*) Gallopade Pub Group.

West Virginia Library Book: A Surprising Guide to the Unusual Special Collections in Libraries Across Our State for Students, Teachers, Writers & Publishers. Carole Marsh. (West Virginia Bks.). (Illus.). 1994. pap. 19.95 (*0-7933-3150-1*); lib. bdg. 29.95 (*0-7933-3149-8*); disk 29.95 (*0-7933-3151-X*) Gallopade Pub Group.

***West Virginia Logging Railroads.** William Warden. (Illus.). 108p. 1996. 29.95 (*1-883089-03-4*) TLC VA.

West Virginia Media Book: A Surprising Guide to the Amazing Print, Broadcast & Online Media of Our State for Students, Teachers, Writers & Publishers - Includes Reproducible Mailing Labels Plus Activities for Young People! Carole Marsh. (West Virginia Bks.). (Illus.). 1994. pap. 19.95 (*0-7933-3306-7*); lib. bdg. 29.95 (*0-7933-3305-9*); disk 29.95 (*0-7933-3307-5*) Gallopade Pub Group.

West Virginia Mine Wars: An Anthology. Ed. by David A. Corbin. LC 90-64144. 165p. (Orig.). 1991. pap. 9.95 (*0-9627486-0-9*) Applchin Eds.

West Virginia Mystery Van Takes Off! Book 1: Handicapped West Virginia Kids Sneak Off on a Big Adventure. Carole Marsh. (West Virginia Bks.). (Illus.). (J). (gr. 3-12). 1994. 29.95 (*0-7933-5108-1*); pap. 19.95 (*0-7933-5109-X*); disk 29.95 (*0-7933-5110-3*) Gallopade Pub Group.

West Virginia "No-Fault" Divorce Formbook. Ed. by James F. Humphreys & C. Page Hamrick, III. (West Virginia Legal Formbooks Ser.). 60p. (Orig.). 1985. pap. 24.95 (*0-937683-04-3*) WV Busn Pub.

West Virginia One-Day Trip Book: More Than 150 Jaunts in the Magic Mountain State. Suzanne Lord & Jon Metzger. LC 93-16659. (Illus.). 304p. (Orig.). 1993. pap. 12.95 (*0-939009-70-6*) EPM Pubns.

West Virginia Place Names: Origins & History. Quinith Janssen & William Fernbach. LC 84-80786. (Illus.). 87p. (Orig.). 1984. pap. 5.95 (*0-918441-00-5*) J & F Ents.

West Virginia Politics & Government. Richard A. Brisbin, Jr. et al. LC 96-14437. (Politics & Governments of the American States Ser.). xx, 218p. 1996. text ed. 40.00 (*0-8032-1271-2*); pap. text ed. 17.00 (*0-8032-6128-4*, Bison Books) U of Nebr Pr.

West Virginia Practice Handbook, 2 vols., Set. 3rd ed. West Virginia State Bar, Young Lawyers Section Staff. 1988. ring bd. 160.00 (*0-87473-370-7*) MICHIE.

West Virginia Quiz Bowl Crash Course! Carole Marsh. (Carole Marsh West Virginia Bks.). (Illus.). (J). 1994. pap. 19.95 (*0-7933-2248-0*); lib. bdg. 29.95 (*0-7933-2247-2*); disk 29.95 (*0-7933-2249-9*) Gallopade Pub Group.

West Virginia Rollercoasters! Carole Marsh. (West Virginia Bks.). (Illus.). (YA). (gr. 3-12). 1994. pap. 19.95 (*0-7933-5369-6*); lib. bdg. 29.95 (*0-7933-5368-8*); disk 29.95 (*0-7933-5370-X*) Gallopade Pub Group.

West Virginia School Trivia: An Amazing & Fascinating Look at Our State's Teachers, Schools & Students! Carole Marsh. (Carole Marsh West Virginia Bks.). (Illus.). (J). 1994. pap. 19.95 (*0-7933-1210-8*); lib. bdg. 29.95 (*0-7933-1211-6*); disk 29.95 (*0-7933-1212-4*) Gallopade Pub Group.

West Virginia Silly Basketball Sportsmysteries, Vol. 1. Carole Marsh. (Carole Marsh West Virginia Bks.). (Illus.). (J). 1994. pap. 19.95 (*0-7933-1207-8*); lib. bdg. 29.95 (*0-7933-1208-6*); disk 29.95 (*0-7933-1209-4*) Gallopade Pub Group.

West Virginia Silly Basketball Sportsmysteries, Vol. 2. Carole Marsh. (Carole Marsh West Virginia Bks.). (Illus.). (J). 1994. pap. 19.95 (*0-7933-2260-X*); lib. bdg. 29.95 (*0-7933-2259-6*); disk 29.95 (*0-7933-2261-8*) Gallopade Pub Group.

West Virginia Silly Football Sportsmysteries, Vol. 1. Carole Marsh. (Carole Marsh West Virginia Bks.). (Illus.). (J). 1994. pap. 19.95 (*0-7933-2239-1*); lib. bdg. 29.95 (*0-7933-2238-3*); disk 29.95 (*0-7933-2240-5*) Gallopade Pub Group.

West Virginia Silly Football Sportsmysteries, Vol. 2. Carole Marsh. (Carole Marsh West Virginia Bks.). (Illus.). (J). 1994. pap. 19.95 (*0-7933-2242-1*); lib. bdg. 29.95 (*0-7933-2241-3*) Gallopade Pub Group.

West Virginia Silly Trivia! Carole Marsh. (Carole Marsh West Virginia Bks.). (Illus.). (J). 1994. pap. 19.95 (*0-7933-2231-6*); lib. bdg. 29.95 (*0-7933-2230-8*); disk 29.95 (*0-7933-2232-4*) Gallopade Pub Group.

West Virginia State Constitution: A Reference Guide. Robert M. Bastress. LC 95-10220. (Reference Guides to the State Constitutions of the United States: No. 22). 336p. 1995. text ed. 95.00 (*0-313-27409-6*, Greenwood Pr) Greenwood.

West Virginia Studies, Our Heritage. William T. Doherty. Ed. by Marshall Buckalew. (Illus.). 306p. (gr. 8). 1984. 20.00 (*0-914498-04-5*); teacher ed. 10.00 (*0-914498-06-1*) WV Hist Ed Found.

West Virginia Survival. Betty L. Hall & Helen Jones. 160p. (Orig.). (gr. 10-12). pap. text ed. 5.84 (*0-03-051201-8*) Westwood Pr.

West Virginia Taxation - Administrative Code Annotated, 2 vols., Set. Ed. by C. Page Hamrick, III. 1930p. 1984. ring bd. 195.00 (*0-937683-00-0*) WV Busn Pub.

West Virginia Taxation - Administrative Code Annotated, 2 vols., Vol. I, 1094p. Ed. by C. Page Hamrick, III. 1930p. 1984. write for info. (*0-937683-01-9*) WV Busn Pub.

West Virginia Taxation - Administrative Code Annotated, 2 vols., Vol. II, 836p. Ed. by C. Page Hamrick, III. 1930p. 1984. write for info. (*0-937683-02-7*) WV Busn Pub.

West Virginia Taxation - Administrative Decisions Annotated, 2 vols., Set. Ed. by C. Page Hamrick, III. 1073p. 1990. 250.00 (*0-937683-05-1*) WV Busn Pub.

West Virginia Taxation - Administrative Decisions Annotated, 2 vols., Vol. I, 517p. Ed. by C. Page Hamrick, III. 1073p. 1990. Vol. I, 517p. write for info. (*0-937683-06-X*) WV Busn Pub.

West Virginia Taxation - Administrative Decisions Annotated, 2 vols., Vol. II, 556p. Ed. by C. Page Hamrick, III. 1073p. 1990. write for info. (*0-937683-07-8*) WV Busn Pub.

West Virginia Tech: A History. 2nd ed. Ronald R. Alexander. LC 92-61982. (Illus.). 188p. 1992. text ed. 14.95 (*0-929521-66-8*) Pictorial Hist.

West Virginia Timeline: A Chronology of West Virginia History, Mystery, Trivia, Legend, Lore & More. Carole Marsh. (West Virginia Bks.). (Illus.). (J). (gr. 3-12). 1994. pap. 19.95 (*0-7933-6020-X*); lib. bdg. 29.95 (*0-7933-6019-6*); disk 29.95 (*0-7933-6021-8*) Gallopade Pub Group.

West Virginia UFO's: Close Encounters in the Mountain State. Bob Teets. 1994. pap. 14.95 (*0-929915-13-5*) Headline Bks.

West Virginia University. William T. Doherty. LC 82-62028. 384p. 1982. 25.00 (*0-937058-16-5*) West Va U Pr.

West Virginia University. Jack Mellott. (Illus.). 112p. 1987. 37.50 (*0-916509-13-3*) Harmony Hse Pub.

West Virginia Veterans Census Index, 1890. Ronald V. Jackson. (Illus.). lib. bdg. 55.00 (*0-89593-530-9*) Accelerated Index.

West Virginian. Sharon Brondos. (Superromance Ser.). 1995. pap. 3.75 (*0-373-70630-8*, 1-70630-8) Harlequin Bks.

West Virginian. Sharon Brondos. (Superromance Ser.). 1995. mass mkt. 3.75 (*0-373-70657-X*, 1-70657-1) Harlequin Bks.

***West Virginians in the American Revolution.** Ross B. Johnston. 320p. 1995. pap. 20.00 (*0-614-23555-3*, 3055) Clearfield Co.

West Virginia's (Most Devastating!) Disasters & (Most Calamitous!) Catastrophies! Carole Marsh. (Carole Marsh West Virginia Bks.). (Illus.). (J). 1994. pap. 19.95 (*0-7933-1198-5*); lib. bdg. 29.95 (*0-7933-1199-3*); disk 29.95 (*0-7933-1200-0*) Gallopade Pub Group.

West Virginia's Unsolved Mysteries (& Their "Solutions") Includes Scientific Information & Other Activities for Students. Carole Marsh. (West Virginia Bks.). (Illus.). (J). (gr. 3-12). 1994. pap. 19.95 (*0-7933-5867-1*); lib. bdg. 29.95 (*0-7933-5866-3*); disk 29.95 (*0-7933-5868-X*) Gallopade Pub Group.

West vs. Islam. S. Abul Ala Maududi. 317p. (C). 1991. text ed. 19.95 (*1-56744-413-X*) Kazi Pubns.

West, West, West. Elizabeth Cunningham. LC 91-71392. (Illus.). 132p. 1991. pap. 25.00 (*0-9629111-0-0*, Bison Books) U of Nebr Pr.

West Wind. Mary Oliver. 1996. pap. write for info. (*0-15-600213-2*) HarBrace.

***West Wind.** Mary Oliver. 1997. 21.00 (*0-395-85082-7*) HM.

West Wind. Mary Oliver. 1996. write for info. (*0-15-100159-6*) HarBrace.

West Wind. Linda Winstead. 368p. (Orig.). 1995. mass mkt., pap. text ed. 4.99 (*0-8439-3796-3*) Dorchester Pub Co.

***West Wind Review.** Ed. & Intro. by Gillian Gillette. (Illus.). 224p. (Orig.). Date not set. pap. 10.00 (*0-9630694-6-2*) So Oregon.

West Wind Review. Intro. by Sue E. Rosenberg. 216p. (C). 1994. write for info. (*0-9630694-3-8*) So Oregon.

West Wind Review: Reality. Intro. by Clifford Cowley. 192p. (C). 1992. write for info. (*0-9630694-1-1*) So Oregon.

West Wind Review Vol. 15: Sites, Vol. 15. 15th ed. Ed. by Mitzi Miles-Kubota. (Illus.). 224p. (YA). (gr. 10 up). 1996. pap. 10.00 (*0-9630694-5-4*) So Oregon.

West Winds Four: An Anthology. California Writers' Club Staff. LC 89-11401. 232p. (Orig.). 1990. pap. 9.95 (*0-89407-097-5*) Strawberry Hill.

***West Witch.** large type ed. Lance Howard. (Linford Western Library). 272p. 1997. pap. 16.99 (*0-7089-7989-0*, Linford) Ulverscroft.

West with Columbus. (J). 1991. pap. write for info. (*0-590-28401-0*) Scholastic Inc.

West with the Night. Mcdougal. Date not set. text ed. 15.96 (*0-395-77502-7*) HM.

West 47th. Gerald A. Browne. 390p. 1996. 23.95 (*0-446-51662-7*) Warner Bks.

West 47th. Gerald A. Browne. 416p. 1997. pap. 6.99 (*0-446-60413-5*, Warner Vision) Warner Bks.

***Westborough Bessboro: History of Westport, Essex County.** Caroline H. Royce. (Illus.). 616p. 1997. reprint ed. lib. bdg. 64.00 (*0-8328-6279-7*) Higginson Bk Co.

Westbound Pioneer: Overland Emigration to Oregon. Cecil K. Byrd. (Illus.). 1989. pap. 5.00 (*1-879598-06-X*) IN Univ Lilly Library.

Westbrook Maine Cemeteries: Plus Surrounding Towns of Cumberland, Falmouth, Gorham, Portland & Windham. (Illus.). viii, 447p. (Orig.). 1996. pap. 35.00 (*0-7884-0401-6*, K175) Heritage Bk.

Westbrook, ME. Westbrook Historical Society Staff. (Images of America Ser.). 1996. pap. 16.99 (*0-7524-0446-6*, Arcdia) Chalford.

***Westchester County: New York's Golden Apple.** Paul Votano et al. LC 96-37122. 1996. write for info. (*1-885352-43-3*) Community Comm.

***Westchester County: New York's Golden Apple.** Paul Votano et al. LC 96-37122. 1997. 45.00 (*1-885352-42-5*) Community Comm.

***Westchester County During the American Revolution.** Henry B. Dawson. (Illus.). 281p. 1997. reprint ed. lib. bdg. 35.00 (*0-8328-6277-0*) Higginson Bk Co.

***Westchester County During the Revolution, 1775-1783.** Otto Hufeland. (Illus.). 471p. 1997. reprint ed. lib. bdg. 4.50 (*0-8328-6282-7*) Higginson Bk Co.

***Westchester County Treasures Hunt Tour: Treason in the American Revolution.** (Illus.). 93p. 1980. pap. 8.95 (*0-614-26443-X*) Purple Mnt Pr.

***Westchester Health & Human Services Directory.** 2nd rev. ed. Orig. Title: Health & Human Services Directory for Westchester. 1997. pap. 59.95 (*0-9655840-0-3*) Family Info & Referral.

Westchester Historian: Index to Volumes 1-65, 1925-1989. Elizabeth G. Fuller. 88p. (Orig.). 1990. pap. 25.00 (*0-915585-02-2*) West Cnty Hist Soc.

Westchester Public Records Guide. Fred D. Knapp. 50p. 1992. pap. text ed. 4.95 (*0-9629879-4-8*) REYN.

***Westchester School-to-Work Initiative: Prospects & Challenges.** Steve Farkas & Will Friedman. 21p. (Orig.). 1995. pap. 10.00 (*1-889483-12-5*) Public Agenda.

***Westchester Weather Book.** Jerome S. Thaler. (Illus.). 136p. 1977. pap. 10.00 (*0-614-26445-6*) Purple Mnt Pr.

***Westcott's Plant Disease Handbook.** 5th ed. R. Horst. (Illus.). 976p. (C). (gr. 13 up). 1993. text ed. 92.50 (*0-412-06721-8*) Chapman & Hall.

Westcott's Plant Disease Handbook. 5th ed. R. K. Horst. 1990. text ed. 69.95 (*0-442-31853-7*) Chapman & Hall.

***Westeners Through Chinese Eyes.** Ed. by Wang Jianguang. 230p. 1995. 6.95 (*7-119-01216-9*, Pub. by Foreign Lang CH) China Bks.

***Westerbork Observatory, Continuing Adventure In Radio Astronomy.** Ernst Raimond & Ren E. Genee. (Astrophysics & Space Science Library). 1996. lib. bdg. 95.00 (*0-7923-4150-3*) Kluwer Ac.

Westering. Dan Parkinson. 352p. 1989. mass mkt. 3.95 (*0-8217-2559-9*, Zebra Kensgtn) Kensgtn Pub Corp.

Westering. 2nd ed. Thomas H. Ferril. Ed. by Orvis Burmaster. LC 86-71597. (Ahsahta Press Modern & Contemporary Poets of the West Ser.). 85p. 1986. reprint ed. pap. 6.95 (*0-916272-32-X*) Ahsahta Pr.

***Westering: An Epic Story of Hope, Bravery & Shameful Treachery.** Ann Sutcliff. 486p. 1997. pap. 18.95 (*1-85756-286-0*, Pub. by Janus Pubng UK) Paul & Co Pubs.

Westering: Jamie. Vera Saban. Ed. by Kitty Crane. (This Is America: The Westering Ser.: Vol. 3). (Illus.). 600p. (Orig.). 1996. pap. 15.95 (*0-914565-46-X*, Timbertrails) Capstan Pubns.

Westering: Joanna. Vera Saban. LC 94-13759. (This Is America Ser.). (J). 1994. 15.95 (*0-914565-43-5*) Capstan Pubns.

Westering: Rebecca. Vera Saban. Ed. by Kitty Crane. (This Is America, the Westering Ser.: Vol. 2). 650p. (Orig.). 1995. pap. 15.95 (*0-914565-45-1*, Timbertrails) Capstan Pubns.

Westering Experience in American Literature: Bicentennial Essays. Ed. by Merrill Lewis & L. L. Lee. LC 77-80814. 1977. pap. 4.95 (*0-930216-01-6*) West Wash Univ.

Westering Man: The Life of Joseph Walker. Bil Gilbert. LC 84-22055. 352p. 1985. pap. 17.95 (*0-8061-1934-9*) U of Okla Pr.

Westering Women & the Frontier Experience, 1800-1915. Sandra L. Myres. LC 82-6956. (Histories of the American Frontier Ser.). (Illus.). 385p. 1982. pap. 16.95 (*0-8263-0626-8*) U of NM Pr.

Westerly: Finding an Integrative Focus for a Nursing Home Activity Program. Barbara De la Cuesta. (Illus.). 157p. (Orig.). (C). 1993. pap. text ed. 9.50 (*1-877735-45-0*, 256) M&H Pub Co TX.

***Westerly Looks to Asia.** Ed. by Bruce Bennett et al. pap. 25.00 (*1-86342-169-6*, Pub. by Univ of West Aust Pr AT) Intl Spec Bk.

Westerly, RI. K. Fink. (Images of America Ser.). 1995. pap. 16.99 (*0-7524-0252-8*, Arcdia) Chalford.

Westerly Trend. Godfrey Sykes. LC 84-8906. (Illus.). 332p. 1985. reprint ed. 38.50 (*0-8165-0888-7*) U of Ariz Pr.

Western Abenaki Dictionary Vol. 1: Abenaki-English, Vol. 1. Gordon M. Day. (Mercury Ser.: No. 128). 612p. 1994. pap. 34.95 (*0-660-14024-1*, Pub. by Can Mus Civil CN) U of Wash Pr.

Western Abenaki Dictionary Vol. 2: English-Abenaki. Gordon M. Day. (Mercury Ser.: No. 129). 612p. 1995. pap. 34.95 (*0-660-14030-6*, Pub. by Can Mus Civil CN) U of Wash Pr.

Western Abenakis of Vermont, 1600-1800: War, Migration & the Survival of an Indian People. Colin G. Calloway. LC 89-40736. (Civilization of the American Indian Ser.: No. 197). (Illus.). 352p. 1990. 32.95 (*0-8061-2274-9*) U of Okla Pr.

Western Abenakis of Vermont, 1600-1800: War, Migration & the Survival of an Indian People. Colin G. Calloway. LC 89-40736. (Civilization of the American Indian Ser.: Vol. 197). (Illus.). 376p. 1994. pap. 14.95 (*0-8061-2568-3*) U of Okla Pr.

Western Acropolis of Learning: The University of California in 1897. Roy Lowe. LC 96-33926. (Chapters in the History of the University of California Ser.: Vol. 5). (Illus.). 47p. 1996. pap. 10.00 (*0-87772-368-0*) UCB IGS.

Western Africa to 1860 A.D. A Provisional Historical Schem Based on Climate Periods. George E. Brooks. (African Studies Working Papers). 231p. 1985. pap. text ed. 15.00 (*0-941934-67-5*) Indiana Africa.

Western African Slavery & Atlantic Commerce: The Senegal River Valley, 1700-1860. James F. Searing. LC 92-27508. (African Studies: Vol. 78). 250p. (C). 1993. text ed. 59.95 (*0-521-44083-1*) Cambridge U Pr.

Western Allegan County, Michigan. Kit Lane. (Illus.). 541p. 1988. 62.50 (*0-88107-122-6*) Curtis Media.

Western Allegan County Pioneer Days. Henry H. Hutchins. LC 95-68819. (Illus.). 96p. (Orig.). 1995. pap. 7.50 (*1-877703-07-9*) Pavilion Pr.

Western Alliance after INF: Redefining U. S. Policy Toward Europe & the Soviet Union. Michael R. Lucas. LC 89-38359. 266p. 1989. lib. bdg. 35.00 (*1-55587-159-3*) Lynne Rienner.

Western Allies & the Politics of Food: Agrarian Management in Postwar Germany. John E. Farquharson. LC 85-3977. 279p. 1987. 19.95 (*0-907582-24-9*) Berg Pubs.

Western Alphabet. Geoffrey O'Gara. LC 83-51556. (Illus.). 64p. (Orig.). 1983. pap. 3.95 (*0-915333-00-7*) Trotevale.

Western American Alpines. Ira N. Gabrielson. LC 71-174546. (Illus.). 1972. reprint ed. 10.00 (*0-685-61146-9*) Theophrastus.

Western American Indian: Case Studies in Tribal History. Ed. by Richard N. Ellis. LC 70-181597. xiv, 203p. 1972. pap. text ed. 4.95 (*0-8032-5754-6*, Bison Books) U of Nebr Pr.

Western American Indian: Case Studies in Tribal History. Ed. by Richard N. Ellis. LC 70-181597. 217p. 1972. reprint ed. pap. 61.90 (*0-608-00490-1*, 2061309) Bks Demand.

Western American Literary Criticism. Martin Bucco. LC 84-70250. (Western Writers Ser.: No. 62). 57p. (Orig.). 1984. pap. 4.95 (*0-88430-036-6*) Boise St U W Writ Ser.

Western American Novelists Vol. 1: Walter Van Tilburg Clark, Dan Cushmann, H. L. Davis, Vardis Fisher, A. B. Guthrie, Jr., William Humphrey, & Dorothy M. Johnson, Vol. 1. Martin Kich. LC 95-36470. (Reference Library of the Humanities: Vol. 1347). 896p. 1995. text ed. 135.00 (*0-8240-7389-4*, H1347) Garland.

***Western American Writers 1965-1990.** Martin Kich. (Literature Reference Ser.). 1997. text ed. 65.00 (*0-8240-5899-2*) Garland.

Western Americana: Frontier History of the Trans-Mississippi West; a Guide to the Microfilm Collection, 2 vols. Intro. by Archibald Hanna. 610p. 1980. Set. 215.00 (*0-89235-030-X*) Primary Srce Media.

Western Americana Catalogue Prices, 1995 Vol. 9: 19,000 Price Entries on Non-Texas Western Americana Offered for Sale in 1995. Shelly Morrison. 242p. (Orig.). 1996. pap. 38.50 (*0-926158-26-0*) W M Morrison.

Western Americana in the California State Library. Ed. by Gary E. Strong & Gary F. Kurutz. 44p. 1985. pap. 6.95 (*0-929722-07-8*) CA State Library Fndtn.

Western & Arctic Canadian Biostratigraphy: The Proceedings of the P. S. Warren Biostratigraphy Symposium Organized by the Geological Association of Canada & the Edmonton Geological Society, Held at the University of Alberta, Edmonton, Alberta, May 19, 1976. Ed. by C. R. Stelck & B. D. Chatterton. LC 80-480812. (Geological Association of Canada. Special Paper Ser.: No. 18). (Illus.). 616p. reprint ed. pap. 175.60 (*0-685-44472-4*, 2033004) Bks Demand.

An Asterisk (*) at the beginning of an entry indicates that the title is appearing in BIP for the first time.

Western & Eastern Rambles: Travel Sketches of Nova Scotia. Joseph Howe. Ed. by M. G. Parks. LC 72-97424. (Illus.). 216p. reprint ed. pap. 61.60 (*0-8357-8373-1*, 2034049) Bks Demand.

Western & Frontier Film & Television Credits: 1903-1995, 2 vols., Set. Harris M. Lentz, III. LC 95-43360. 1796p. 1996. lib. bdg. 175.00 (*0-7864-0158-3*) McFarland & Co.

Western & Frontier Film & Television Credits: 1903-1995, Vol. 1. Harris M. Lentz, III. 1996. lib. bdg. write for info. (*0-7864-0217-2*) McFarland & Co.

Western & Frontier Film & Television Credits: 1903-1995, Vol. 2. Harris M. Lentz, III. 1996. lib. bdg. write for info. (*0-7864-0218-0*) McFarland & Co.

Western & Northern Europe see Balance of Births & Deaths

Western & Provincial Byzantine Coins in the British Museum: Vandals, Ostrogoths, Lombards & the Empire of Thessalonica, Nicaea & Trebizond. Warwick Wroth. (Illus.). xcvi, 344p. 1997. 65.00 (*0-89005-519-X*) Ares.

Western & Soviet Historiography: Recent Views. Ed. by Henry Kozicki. 240p. 1993. text ed. 49.95 (*0-312-05214-6*) St Martin.

Western & Wildlife: Selections from the Samuel B & Marion Lawrence Collection. Intro. by Francis Martin, Jr. (Illus.). 45p. (Orig.). 1987. pap. 10.00 (*0-9615828-1-2*) Cornell Fine Arts.

Western Apache Heritage: People of the Mountain Corridor. Richard J. Perry. (Illus.). 314p. (C). 1991. text ed. 37.50 (*0-292-76524-X*) U of Tex Pr.

Western Apache Language & Culture: Essays in Linguistic Anthropology. Keith H. Basso. LC 89-20242. 192p. 1990. 36.95 (*0-8165-1094-6*) U of Ariz Pr.

Western Apache Language & Culture: Essays in Linguistic Anthropology. Keith H. Basso. LC 89-20242. (Illus.). 195p. 1992. reprint ed. pap. text ed. 13.95 (*0-8165-1323-6*) U of Ariz Pr.

Western Apache Material Culture: The Goodwin & Guenther Collections. Ed. by Alan Ferg. LC 86-30806. (Illus.). 176p. 1987. pap. 25.95 (*0-8165-1028-8*) U of Ariz Pr.

Western Apache Raiding & Warfare. Grenville Goodwin. Ed. by Keith H. Basso. LC 73-142255. (Illus.). 330p. 1994. reprint ed. pap. 18.95 (*0-8165-0297-8*) U of Ariz Pr.

***Western Apache Witchcraft.** Keith H. Basso & Morris E. Opler. (Anthropological Papers: No. 15). 80p. 1969. write for info. (*0-8165-1730-4*) U of Ariz Pr.

Western Apache Witchcraft. Keith H. Basso. LC 69-16329. (University of Arizona, Anthropological Papers: No. 15). 81p. reprint ed. pap. 25.00 (*0-317-28645-5*, 2055359) Bks Demand.

Western Approach to Karma & Reincarnation. Rudolf Steiner. Ed. & Intro. by R. M. Querido. LC 95-43107. (Vista Ser.). 256p. (Orig.). 1996. pap. 16.95 (*0-88010-399-X*) Anthroposophic.

Western Approach to Zen. Christmas Humphreys. LC 72-76428. 212p. 1981. reprint ed. pap. 8.95 (*0-8356-0550-7*, Quest) Theos Pub Hse.

Western Approaches to the British Isles. Imray, Laurie, Norie & Wilson Ltd. Staff. (Illus.). (C). 1989. text ed. 60.00 (*0-685-40198-7*, Pub. by Imray Laurie Norie & Wilson UK) St Mut.

Western Approaches to the Soviet Union. Gregory F. Treverton et al. Ed. by Michael Mandelbaum. LC 88-39780. 125p. 1988. reprint ed. pap. 35.70 (*0-608-02003-6*, 2062659) Bks Demand.

Western Arizona Ghost Towns. Stanley W. Paher. (Illus.). 64p. 1991. 7.95 (*0-913814-89-X*) Nevada Pubns.

Western Arkansas Death Record Index, 1914-1923: Crawford, Franklin, Johnson, Logan, Montgomery, Polk, Pope, Scott, Sebastian, & Yell Counties. Ed. by Desmond W. Allen. 61p. (Orig.). 1996. pap. 15.00 (*1-56546-082-0*) Arkansas Res.

Western Arkansas Death Record Index, 1934-1940: Crawford, Franklin, Johnson, Logan, Montgomery, Polk, Pope, Scott, Sebastian, & Yell Counties. Ed. by Desmond W. Allen. 50p. (Orig.). 1996. pap. 15.00 (*1-56546-090-1*) Arkansas Res.

***Western Art Book.** Don Hagerty. (Illus.). 208p. 1997. 55.00 (*0-87358-600-X*) Northland AZ.

***Western Art Book.** limited ed. Don Hagerty. (Illus.). 208p. 1997. 250.00 (*0-87358-691-3*) Northland AZ.

Western Art Masterpieces. T. H. Watkins & Joan P. Watkins. (Illus.). 120p. 1996. 35.00 (*0-88363-596-8*) S&S Trade.

Western Artists - African Art. Jack Flam. LC 94-75230. (Illus.). 102p. 1994. pap. 25.00 (*0-945802-15-3*) Museum African.

Western Asceticism. Ed. by Owen Chadwick. LC 58-8713. (Library of Christian Classics). 364p. 1979. pap. 25.00 (*0-664-24161-1*, Westminster) Westminster John Knox.

Western Asia: An Annotated Historical Bibliography. Don Y. Lee. LC 84-70884. 213p. (C). 1984. 43.50 (*0-939758-07-5*) Eastern Pr.

Western Asiatic Antiquities. Edgar Peltenburg. 1992. text ed. 90.00 (*0-7486-0224-0*, Pub. by Edinburgh U Pr UK) Col U Pr.

Western Astrology & Chinese Medicine. Jonathan C. Willmott. 192p. 1985. reprint ed. pap. 9.95 (*0-89281-109-9*) Inner Tradit.

Western Attitudes Toward Death: From the Middle Ages to the Present. Philippe Aries. Tr. by Patricia M. Ranum from FRE. LC 73-19340. (Symposia in Comparative History Ser.). (Illus.). 122p. 1974. pap. 11.95 (*0-8018-1762-5*) Johns Hopkins.

***Western Australia.** 2nd ed. Jeff Williams. (Illus.). 310p. 1998. pap. 14.95 (*0-86442-544-9*) Lonely Planet.

Western Australia: Travel Survival Kit. Jeff Williams. (Illus.). 320p. 1995. pap. 13.95 (*0-86442-268-7*) Lonely Planet.

***Western Australia Between the Wars 1919-1939.** Ed. by Jenny Gregory. (Studies in Western Australian History: Vol. XI). pap. 19.95 (*0-86422-097-9*, Pub. by Univ of West Aust Pr AT) Intl Spec Bk.

Western Australian Introduction to Law. 3rd ed. M. V. Brown & J. A. Hacket. 1989. Australia. 36.00 (*0-409-30129-9*, AT) MICHIE.

Western Australian Law Reports. Council of Law Reporting of Western Australia Staff. Set. 726.00 (*0-409-34108-8*) MICHIE.

Western Australian Plant Names & Their Meanings: A Glossary. F. A. Sharr. 304p. 1996. pap. 16.95 (*1-875560-43-2*, Pub. by Univ of West Aust Pr AT) Intl Spec Bk.

Western Bahr Al-Ghazal under British Rule, 1898-1956. Ahmad A. Sikainga. LC 90-41421. (Monographs in International Studies, Africa: No. 57). 195p. (Orig.). (C). 1991. pap. text ed. 15.00 (*0-89680-161-6*) Ohio U Pr.

Western Bird Song. 2nd ed. Peterson. Date not set. write for info. (*0-395-35541-9*) HM.

***Western Bird Songs, Vol. 2.** Roger T. Peterson. (Peterson Field Guide Ser.). 1992. 35.00 (*0-395-51746-X*) HM.

Western Birds. (American Nature Guide Ser.). 1992. 9.98 (*0-8317-6966-1*) Smithmark.

Western Birds, Vol. 3. LC 87-3425. (Audubon Handbks.). (Illus.). 340p. 1988. text ed. 17.95 (*0-07-019977-9*) McGraw.

Western Books on China Published up to 1850. John Lust. (Illus.). 352p. 1987. 67.50 (*1-870076-02-8*, Pub. by Bamboo Pub UK) Antique Collect.

Western Boxing & World Wrestling: Story & Practice. John F. Gilbey. 149p. (Orig.). 1986. pap. 9.95 (*1-55643-178-3*) North Atlantic.

Western Broadcasting over the Iron Curtain. Ed. by K. R. Short. LC 86-6730. 288p. 1986. text ed. 35.00 (*0-312-86343-8*) St Martin.

Western Canada. Ed. by Ian MacPherson. (Illus.). 80p. 1985. pap. text ed. 15.00 (*0-89745-064-7*) Sunflower U Pr.

Western Canada: Ulysses Travel Guide. 1996. pap. text ed. 16.95 (*2-89464-007-2*) Ulysses Travel.

***Western Canada Bed & Breakfast Guide: Over 400 B&Bs in British Columbia & Alberta.** Sarah Bell. LC 96-69680. (Illus.). 311p. (Orig.). 1997. pap. 14.95 (*0-919574-05-X*) Gordon Soules Bk.

***Western Canada Travel Smart Trip Planner.** Lyn Hancock. (Travel Smart Trip Planner Ser.). 272p. 1998. pap. 15.95 (*1-56261-320-0*) John Muir.

Western Canon: The Books & School of the Ages. Harold Bloom. LC 93-43542. 1994. 29.95 (*0-15-195747-9*) HarBrace.

Western Canon: The Books & School of the Ages. Harold Bloom. 608p. 1994. 29.95 (*0-15-100133-2*) HarBrace.

Western Canon: The Books & School of the Ages. Harold Bloom. LC 95-1680. 560p. 1995. pap. 15.00 (*1-57322-514-2*, Riverhd Trade) Berkley Pub.

Western Captive: Or, the Times of Tecumseh. Elizabeth O. Smith. LC 78-72172. reprint ed. 37.50 (*0-404-17534-1*) AMS Pr.

Western Carpetbagger: The Extraordinary Memoirs of Senator Thomas Fitch. Thomas Fitch. Ed. & Intro. by Eric N. Moody. (Illus.). 286p. 1991. reprint ed. pap. 5.25 (*0-930830-15-6*) Great Basin.

Western Cattle Industry. O. J. Fargo. (Western History Ser.). (Illus.). 57p. (Orig.). (YA). (gr. 5 up). 1990. pap. 1.50 (*0-924702-21-4*) Grn Valley Area.

***Western Central Atlantic Fishery Commission Report of the 8th Session.** (Fisheries Reports: Vol. 543). 50p. 1996. pap. 10.00 (*92-5-103889-9*, F38895, Pub. by FAO IT) Bernan Associates.

***Western Central Atlantic Fishery Commission Report of the 8th Session.** (Fisheries Reports: No. 543). 50p. 1996. pap. 10.00 (*0-614-30311-7*, F38895, Pub. by FAO IT) Bernan Associates.

Western Characters: Or, Types of Border Life in the Western States. John L. McConnel. LC 75-110. (Mid-American Frontier Ser.). (Illus.). 1975. reprint ed. 33.95 (*0-405-06877-8*) Ayer.

Western Chou Civilization. Cho-Yun Hsu & Katheryn M. Linduff. LC 87-6178. (C). 1988. text ed. 50.00 (*0-300-03772-4*) Yale U Pr.

Western Christian Thought in the Middle Ages. Sydney H. Mellone. 1977. lib. bdg. 250.00 (*0-8490-2816-7*) Gordon Pr.

Western Church from the Tenth to the Early Twelfth Century. Gerd Tellenbach. Tr. by Timothy Reuter. LC 92-13778. (Cambridge Medieval Textbooks Ser.). 464p. (ENG & GER.). (C). 1993. text ed. 80.00 (*0-521-43105-0*); pap. text ed. 24.95 (*0-521-43711-3*) Cambridge U Pr.

Western Church in the Later Middle Ages. Francis Oakley. LC 79-7621. 346p. (C). 1985. 45.00 (*0-8014-1208-0*); pap. 15.95 (*0-8014-9347-1*) Cornell U Pr.

Western Circuit Assize Orders 1629-1648: A Calendar. J. S. Cockburn. (Camden Fourth Ser.: No. 17). 366p. 27.00 (*0-901050-29-6*) David Brown.

Western Civilization. (C). 1994. suppl. ed., teacher ed., pap. 9.96 (*0-395-68839-6*) HM.

Western Civilization. Blackburn. 1990. teacher ed., pap. text ed. 5.00 (*0-312-04790-8*) St Martin.

Western Civilization. Nobel. (C). 1993. pap. 45.16 (*0-395-55122-6*) HM.

Western Civilization. Thomas F. Noble. (C). Date not set. suppl. ed., teacher ed., pap. write for info. (*0-395-69143-5*); suppl. ed., teacher ed., text ed. write for info. (*0-395-69141-9*) HM.

Western Civilization. Thomas F. Noble. (C). 1994. student ed., pap. 18.36 (*0-395-55128-5*) HM.

Western Civilization. Thomas F. Noble. (C). 1994. student ed., pap. 18.36 (*0-395-55127-7*) HM.

Western Civilization. Thomas F. Noble. (C). 1994. teacher ed., pap. 7.96 (*0-395-68838-8*) HM.

Western Civilization, 5 Vols. Marvin Perry. (C). 1995. teacher ed., pap. 11.96 (*0-395-75048-2*) HM.

Western Civilization, 5 Vols. Marvin Perry. (C). 1995. student ed., pap. 16.76 (*0-395-75046-6*) HM.

Western Civilization, 2 Vols. Marvin Perry. (C). 1992. student ed., pap. 15.96 (*0-395-63882-8*) HM.

Western Civilization, 2 Vols. Marvin Perry. (C). 1992. teacher ed., pap. 4.76 (*0-395-63788-0*) HM.

Western Civilization, 2 Vols. Marvin Perry. (C). 1992. student ed., pap. 31.16 (*0-395-63787-2*) HM.

Western Civilization, 5 Vols. Marvin Perry. (C). 1995. suppl. ed., teacher ed., pap. 11.96 (*0-395-75049-0*) HM.

Western Civilization. Jack Rudman. (College Level Examination Ser.: CLEP-29). 1994. pap. 23.95 (*0-8373-5329-7*) Nat Learn.

Western Civilization. Jack Rudman. (Regents College Proficiency Examination Ser.: Vol. CPEP-16). 1994. pap. 23.95 (*0-8373-5416-1*) Nat Learn.

Western Civilization. 2nd ed. Jackson J. Spielvogel. Ed. by Baxter. LC 93-27127. 1100p. (C). 1994. text ed. 62.50 (*0-314-02794-7*) West Pub.

Western Civilization. 3rd ed. Jackson J. Spielvogel. 1080p. 1997. text ed. write for info. (*0-314-09674-4*) West Pub.

***Western Civilization.** 3rd ed. Jackson J. Spielvogel. LC 96-30605. 500p. 1997. pap. write for info. (*0-314-20523-3*); pap. write for info. (*0-314-20524-1*); pap. write for info. (*0-314-20525-X*); pap. write for info. (*0-314-20526-8*); pap. write for info. (*0-314-20527-6*); pap. write for info. (*0-314-20533-0*) West Pub.

Western Civilization, 1. 12th ed. Edward Burns. (C). Date not set. student ed., pap. text ed. 18.95 (*0-393-96209-1*) Norton.

Western Civilization, Vol. 1. Jackson J. Spielvogel. Ed. by Baxter. 613p. (C). 1991. pap. text ed. 38.25 (*0-314-82893-1*) West Pub.

***Western Civilization, Vol. 2.** King. Date not set. pap. text ed. write for info. (*0-312-11109-6*) St Martin.

Western Civilization, 5 Vols., Vol. 2. Marvin Perry. (C). 1995. student ed., pap. 16.76 (*0-395-75047-4*) HM.

Western Civilization, Vol. 2. Birdsall S. Viault. 1990. pap. text ed. 10.95 (*0-07-015396-5*) McGraw.

Western Civilization, Vol. 2. 12th ed. Edward Burns. (C). Date not set. student ed., pap. text ed. 18.95 (*0-393-96210-5*) Norton.

Western Civilization: A Brief History. 2nd ed. Robin W. Winks. 495p. (C). 1988. pap. text ed. 28.75 (*0-939693-05-4*) Collegiate Pr.

***Western Civilization: A Brief History, 3 Vols.** 3rd ed. Marvin Perry. (C). 1996. student ed., pap. text ed. 15.96 (*0-395-81113-9*) HM.

***Western Civilization: A Brief History: To 1789, 3 Vols.** 3rd ed. Marvin Perry. 340p. (C). 1997. pap. text ed. 30.76 (*0-395-81111-2*) HM.

Western Civilization: A Brief Introduction. F. Roy Willis. 656p. (C). 1987. pap. text ed. 40.60 (*0-02-428110-7*, Macmillan Coll) P-H.

Western Civilization: A Critical Guide to Documentary Films. Neil M. Heyman. LC 95-35676. 264p. 1995. text ed. 59.95 (*0-313-28438-5*, Greenwood Pr) Greenwood.

Western Civilization: Ideas, Politics, & Society. 3rd ed. Marvin Perry et al. 1989. lab manual ed., student ed. write for info. (*0-318-63330-2*) HM.

***Western Civilization: Ideas, Politics, & Society: From the 1400s, 5 Vols.** Marvin Perry et al. 604p. (C). 1995. pap. text ed. 44.76 (*0-395-74460-1*) HM.

Western Civilization: Ideas, Politics & Society: From the 1400s, 4 Vols. 4th ed. Marvin Perry et al. (C). 1991. pap. 53.56 (*0-395-59333-6*) HM.

Western Civilization: Images & Interpretations. 3rd ed. Dennis Sherman. 1991. pap. text ed. write for info. (*0-07-056784-0*) McGraw.

Western Civilization: Since 1300. Jackson J. Spielvogel. Ed. by Baxter. LC 93-27127. 1100p. (C). 1994. pap. text ed. 50.25 (*0-314-02795-5*) West Pub.

Western Civilization: Since 1550. Jackson J. Spielvogel. Ed. by Baxter. LC 93-27127. 1100p. (C). 1994. pap. text ed. 44.25 (*0-314-02797-1*) West Pub.

Western Civilization: Sources, Images, & Intrepretations. 4th ed. Ed. by Dennis Sherman. LC 94-16726. 1994. pap. text ed. 18.13 (*0-07-056948-7*) McGraw.

Western Civilization: Sources, Images, & Intrepretations, Vol. 2. 4th ed. Ed. by Dennis Sherman. LC 94-16726. 1994. pap. text ed. 18.13 (*0-07-056949-5*) McGraw.

Western Civilization: Sources, Images, & Intrepretations, Vol. 3. 4th ed. Ed. by Dennis Sherman. LC 94-16726. 1994. pap. text ed. 18.75 (*0-07-056950-9*) McGraw.

Western Civilization: To 1500. Jackson J. Spielvogel. Ed. by Baxter. LC 93-27127. 1100p. (C). 1994. pap. text ed. 41.00 (*0-314-02798-X*) West Pub.

Western Civilization: To 1715. Jackson J. Spielvogel. Ed. by Baxter. LC 93-27127. 1100p. (C). 1994. pap. text ed. 44.25 (*0-314-02796-3*) West Pub.

Western Civilization: 1300-1815. Jackson J. Spielvogel. Ed. by Baxter. LC 93-27127. 1100p. (C). 1994. pap. text ed. 41.00 (*0-314-02799-8*) West Pub.

***Western Civilization Vol. 1: Ancient History Syllabus.** Michael G. Gaunt. 26p. (YA). (gr. 9-12). 1996. pap. text ed. 4.95 (*0-913717-05-3*, 2316) Hewitt Res Fnd.

***Western Civilization Vol. 1: The Earliest Civilizations Through the Reformation, Vol. 1.** 9th ed. William Hughes. (Annual Ser.). (Illus.). 256p. (C). 1997. pap. text ed. 11.75 (*0-697-36313-9*) Dushkin Pub.

Western Civilization Vol. I: To 1700: Sources, Images & Interpretations. 4th ed. Dennis Sherman. 1994. pap. text ed. write for info. (*0-07-057059-0*) McGraw.

Western Civilization Vol. 2. Nobel. (C). 1993. pap. 45.16 (*0-395-55123-4*) HM.

Western Civilization Vol. 2, 2 Vols. Marvin Perry. (C). 1992. pap. 31.16 (*0-395-63881-X*) HM.

***Western Civilization Vol. 2: Medieval History Syllabus.** Michael G. Gaunt. 25p. (YA). (gr. 9-12). 1996. pap. text ed. 4.95 (*0-913717-06-1*, 2315) Hewitt Res Fnd.

***Western Civilization Vol. A: The Continuing Experiment: To 1500.** Thomas F. Noble et al. 544p. (C). 1994. pap. text ed. 40.36 (*0-395-55124-2*) HM.

***Western Civilization Vol. B: The Continuing Experiment: 1300 to 1815.** Thomas F. Noble et al. 382p. (C). 1994. pap. text ed. 40.36 (*0-395-55125-0*) HM.

***Western Civilization Vol. C: The Continuing Experiment: 1815 to Present.** Thomas F. Noble et al. 446p. (C). 1994. pap. text ed. 40.36 (*0-395-55126-9*) HM.

***Western Civilization Vol. I: Ideas, Politics, & Society: To 1789, 5 Vols.** 5th ed. Marvin Perry et al. 457p. (C). 1995. pap. text ed. 43.56 (*0-395-74458-X*) HM.

***Western Civilization Vol. II: A Brief History: From the 1400s, 3 Vols.** 3rd ed. Marvin Perry. 460p. (C). 1997. pap. text ed. 30.76 (*0-395-81112-0*) HM.

***Western Civilization Vol. II: Ideas, Politics, & Society: From the 1600s, 5 Vols.** 5th ed. Marvin Perry et al. 524p. (C). 1995. pap. text ed. 43.56 (*0-395-74459-8*) HM.

Western Civilization: A Concise History: From Early Societies to the Present. Glenn Blackburn. 640p. (Orig.). (C). 1990. teacher ed. write for info. (*0-318-68117-X*) St Martin.

Western Civilization: A Concise History, Vol. I: From Early Societies to the Reformation. Glenn Blackburn. 267p. (Orig.). (C). 1990. teacher ed. write for info. (*0-318-68115-3*); pap. text ed. 19.50 (*0-312-01861-4*) St Martin.

Western Civilization: A Concise History, Vol. II: From the Birth of Modern Science to the Present. Glenn Blackburn. 554p. (Orig.). (C). 1990. teacher ed. write for info. (*0-318-68116-1*); pap. text ed. 19.50 (*0-312-01862-2*) St Martin.

Western Civilization at the University of Chicago: An Introduction for Teachers. Eric Cochrane. 48p. 1988. pap. write for info. (*0-226-06955-9*) U Ch Pr.

Western Civilization Complete. Thomas F. Noble. (C). 1994. text ed. 63.16 (*0-395-55121-8*) HM.

Western Civilization Condemned by Itself, 2 vols. Maryam Jameelah. Set. pap. 45.00 (*0-933511-86-8*) Kazi Pubns.

Western Civilization in Biological Perspective: Patterns in Biohistory. Stephen Boyden. (Illus.). 384p. 1990. reprint ed. pap. 35.00 (*0-19-857742-7*) OUP.

Western Civilization in the Near East. Hans Kohn. Tr. by E. W. Dickes. LC 37-23489. reprint ed. 20.00 (*0-404-03739-9*) AMS Pr.

Western Civilization, Islam & Muslims. A. H. Nadvi. 18.50 (*0-933511-87-6*) Kazi Pubns.

***Western Civilization Mapping Workbook, Vol. 1.** 2nd ed. Wilson. (C). 1998. pap. text ed. write for info. (*0-321-01878-8*) Addison-Wesley.

***Western Civilization Mapping Workbook, Vol. 2.** 2nd ed. Wilson. (C). 1998. pap. text ed. write for info. (*0-321-01877-X*) Addison-Wesley.

Western Civilization Through Muslim Eyes. Sayyed M. Musavi. Tr. by F. J. Goulding from PER. 146p. 1977. 14.95 (*0-941722-20-1*); pap. 7.95 (*0-941722-06-6*) Book Dist Ctr.

Western Civilization to 1500. 2nd ed. Walther Kirchner. LC 90-56010. (College Outline Ser.). (Illus.). 320p. (Orig.). 1991. pap. 14.00 (*0-06-467101-1*, Harper Ref) HarpC.

Western Civilization, 1789-1919. John S. Jackson. (C). 1988. pap. 20.75 (*0-911337-01-6*) Intell Pr CA.

Western Civilizations, Their History & Their Culture. 12th ed. LC 92-41530. (C). 1993. text ed. 59.95 (*0-393-96206-7*) Norton.

Western Civilizations, Their History & Their Culture, 1. LC 92-41530. (C). 1993. pap. text ed. 44.95 (*0-393-96207-5*) Norton.

Western Civilizations, Their History & Their Culture, 2. LC 92-41530. (C). 1993. pap. text ed. 44.95 (*0-393-96208-3*) Norton.

Western Clearings. Caroline Kirkland. 1972. reprint ed. lib. bdg. 29.00 (*0-8422-8088-X*) Irvington.

Western Clearings. Caroline Kirkland. (C). 1986. reprint ed. pap. text ed. 7.95 (*0-8290-1948-0*) Irvington.

Western Coinages of Nero. David W. MacDowall. LC 74-82869. (Numismatic Notes & Monographs: No. 161). (Illus.). 281p. (Orig.). 1979. pap. 40.00 (*0-89722-176-1*) Am Numismatic.

Western Community & the Gorbachev Challenge. Ed. by Armand Clesse & Thomas C. Schelling. 408p. 1989. 63.00 (*3-7890-1789-2*, Pub. by Nomos Verlags GW) Intl Bk Import.

***Western Companies Interested in Doing Business in Russia.** 2nd ed. Russian Information & Business Center, Inc. Staff. (Russian Business Library). 400p. 1997. pap. 99.00 (*1-57751-313-4*) Russ Info & Busn Ctr.

Western Companies Interested in Doing Business in Russia, 96. 2nd rev. ed. (Russian Business Library). (Illus.). 300p. 1996. pap. 99.00 (*1-57751-003-8*) Russ Info & Busn Ctr.

Western Conceptions of the Individual. Brian Morris. 528p. (C). 1992. pap. text ed. 19.95 (*0-85496-801-6*) Berg Pubs.

Western Containment Policies Towards Yugoslavia, 1948-1953. D. B. Heuser. 256p. 1989. 49.95 (*0-415-01303-8*) Routledge.

Western Contribution to Buddhism. William Peiris. 372p. 1974. lib. bdg. 79.95 (*0-87968-550-6*) Krishna Pr.

Western Cover. (Dudley the Dragon Flip 'N' Fun Pad Ser.). (Illus.). 64p. (J). (gr. k-2). 1995. pap. write for info. (*1-56144-662-9*, Honey Bear Bks) Modern Pub NYC.

Western Crisis Over Southern Africa. Colin Legum. LC 79-9723. (Current Affairs Ser.). (Illus.). (C). 1979. pap. 17.95 (*0-8419-0496-0*, Africana) Holmes & Meier.

W

Western Dada Orbit Vol. 7: United States, Italy, Spain, Holland & Belgium. Milman. 1996. 85.00 (*0-8161-7386-9*, GK Hall) Thorndike Pr.

*__Western Decorative Arts: Medieval, Renaissance, & Historicizing Styles Including Metalwork, Enamels, & Ceramics, Vol. I.__ Rudolf Distelberger et al. (Illus.). 334p. 1996. 160.00 (*0-89468-162-1*) Natl Gallery Art.

Western Diseases: Their Dietary Prevention & Reversibility. Ed. by Norman J. Temple & Denis P. Burkitt. LC 94-14051. 453p. 1994. 49.50 (*0-89603-264-7*) Humana.

Western Diseases: Their Emergence & Prevention. Ed. by H. C. Trowell & D. P. Burkitt. LC 80-28917. (Illus.). 474p. (C). 1981. 52.95 (*0-674-95020-8*) HUP.

Western Doctrines on East-West Trade: Theory, History & Policy. Peter Van Ham. LC 91-9241. 300p. 1992. text ed. 45.00 (*0-312-06033-5*) St Martin.

Western Dominance & Political Islam: Challenge & Response. Khalid B. Sayeed. LC 94-4119. 197p. (C). 1994. pap. text ed. 19.95 (*0-7914-2266-6*) State U NY Pr.

Western Dominance & Political Islam: Challenge & Response. Khalid B. Sayeed. LC 94-4119. 197p. (C). 1994. text ed. 59.50 (*0-7914-2265-8*) State U NY Pr.

Western Echoes. Earl F. Moore. LC 23-939860. (Illus.). 198p. (J). (gr. 4-12). 1980. 12.95 (*0-939860-00-7*) Tremaine Graph & Pub.

Western Economists & Eastern Societies: Agents of Change in South Asia, 1950-1970. George Rosen. LC 84-4370. (Studies in Development). 296p. 1985. text ed. 43.00 (*0-8018-3187-3*) Johns Hopkins.

Western Edge. Huppes. 1900. pap. text ed. 0.01 (*90-247-3496-7*, Pub. by M Nijhoff NE) Kluwer Ac.

Western Edge. Huppes. 1987. lib. bdg. 52.50 (*90-247-3495-9*, Pub. by M Nijhoff NE) Kluwer Ac.

Western Edition. Ed. by Michael B. Balmforth. (C). 1989. 105.00 (*0-685-40417-X*, Pub. by Imray Laurie Norie & Wilson UK) St Mut.

Western Electric. Don Zancanella. (John Simmons Short Fiction Award Ser.). 130p. 1996. 19.95 (*0-87745-567-8*) U of Iowa Pr.

Western Electric Researches. George C. Homans. (Reprint Series in Social Sciences). (C). 1993. reprint ed. pap. text ed. 2.30 (*0-8290-3390-4*, S-123) Irvington.

Western Energy Policy. Douglas Evans. LC 78-23315. 1979. text ed. 18.95 (*0-312-86392-6*) St Martin.

Western English Channel Passage Chart. Imray, Laurie, Norie & Wilson Ltd. Staff. (Illus.). (C). 1989. text ed. 60.00 (*0-685-40195-2*, Pub. by Imray Laurie Norie & Wilson UK) St Mut.

Western Enterprise in Far Eastern Economic Development, China & Japan. George C. Allen & Audrey G. Donnithorne. LC 54-1323. 291p. reprint ed. pap. 83.00 (*0-317-28695-1*, 2055254) Bks Demand.

Western Enterprise in Late Ch'ing China: A Selective Survey of Jardine, Matheson & Company's Operations, 1842-1895. Edward LeFevour. LC 73-386. (East Asian Monographs: No. 26). 222p. 1968. pap. 11.00 (*0-674-95010-0*) HUP.

*__Western Ethics: An Historical Introduction.__ Robert L. Arrington. 448p. (C). 1998. text ed. 64.95 (*0-631-19415-0*) Blackwell Pubs.

*__Western Ethics: An Historical Introduction.__ Robert L. Arrington. 448p. (C). 1998. pap. text ed. 25.95 (*0-631-19416-9*) Blackwell Pubs.

Western Europe. 200p. 1987. 80.00 (*0-86338-142-1*, Pub. by Euromonitor Pubns UK) Gale.

*__Western Europe.__ Bealt. 1986. pap. text ed. write for info. (*0-273-25267-4*) Addison-Wesley.

Western Europe. John Dornberg. LC 95-43046. (International Government & Politics Ser.). (Illus.). 296p. 1996. pap. 34.95 (*0-89774-943-X*) Oryx Pr.

Western Europe. Leslie Gardiner. (Illus.). 64p. 1985. pap. 4.95 (*0-933521-16-2*) AGT Pub.

Western Europe. fac. rev. ed. Ed. by Richard J. Mayne. LC 85-29242. (Handbooks to the Modern World Ser.). 717p. 1986. pap. 180.00 (*0-7837-8613-1*, 2059168) Bks Demand.

Western Europe. rev. ed. Frank Hill. (TravelCard Pac Ser.). 1992. Incl. 7 language cards, 1 phrasecard. 4.00 (*0-88699-015-7*) Travel Sci.

Western Europe. 3rd ed. Steve Fallon et al. (Illus.). 1328p. 1997. pap. 24.95 (*0-86442-438-8*) Lonely Planet.

Western Europe: A Political Dictionary. Ernest L. Rossi. (Dictionary Ser.). 300p. 1996. 60.00 (*0-87436-754-9*) ABC-CLIO.

Western Europe: A Survey of Holdings at the Hoover Institution on War, Revolution & Peace. Agnes F. Peterson. LC 72-142950. (Library Survey Ser.: No. 1). 60p. 1970. pap. 1.20 (*0-8179-5012-5*) Hoover Inst Pr.

*__Western Europe: Challenge & Change.__ David A. Pinder. 290p. 1995. pap. text ed. 40.00 (*0-471-94747-4*, GE11) Wiley.

Western Europe: Challenge & Change. Ed. by David A. Pinder. 290p. 1991. reprint ed. pap. text ed. 30.00 (*0-89862-489-4*) Guilford Pr.

Western Europe: Economic & Social Studies: Ireland. Barry Brunt. 256p. (C). 1988. pap. 35.00 (*1-85396-019-5*) St Mut.

Western Europe: Economic & Social Studies: Spain. John Naylon. 192p. (C). 1988. pap. 60.00 (*0-317-93198-9*) St Mut.

*__Western Europe: Geographical Perspectives.__ 3rd ed. Hugh Clout. 1996. pap. 37.95 (*0-582-09283-3*, Pub. by Longman UK) Longman.

*__Western Europe: Language Survival Kit.__ 2nd ed. Ed. by Sally Steward. (Illus.). 520p. 1997. pap. 6.95 (*0-86442-516-3*) Lonely Planet.

Western Europe: Technology & the Future. Stanley Woods. (Atlantic Papers: No. 63). 128p. 1987. pap. 17.95 (*0-7099-5220-1*, Pub. by Croom Helm UK) Routledge Chapman & Hall.

Western Europe & Germany: The Beginnings of European Integration, 1945-1960. Ed. by Clemens A. Wurm et al. LC 94-49205. (German Historical Perspectives Ser.: No. 9). 288p. 1995. 45.95 (*1-85973-052-3*) Berg Pubs.

Western Europe & Germany: The Beginnings of European Integration, 1945-1960. Ed. by Clemens A. Wurm et al. (German Historical Perspectives Ser.). 288p. 1996. pap. 19.95 (*1-85973-182-1*) Berg Pubs.

Western Europe & the Crisis in U. S.-Soviet Relations. Ed. by Richard H. Ullman & Mario Zucconi. LC 86-30625. 144p. 1987. text ed. 55.00 (*0-275-92584-6*, C2584, Praeger Pubs) Greenwood.

Western Europe & the United States: The Uncertain Alliance. Michael Smith. (Studies on Contemporary Europe: No. 6). 1984. pap. text ed. 16.95 (*0-04-327072-7*) Routledge Chapman & Hall.

Western Europe in Color. Alice F. Mutton. (Illus.). 279p. 1972. pap. 12.00 (*0-7137-0555-8*) Transatl Arts.

Western Europe in the Middle Ages: A Short History. 3rd ed. Joseph R. Strayer. (Illus.). 207p. (C). 1991. reprint ed. pap. text ed. 14.95 (*0-88133-624-6*) Waveland Pr.

Western Europe in the Middle Ages: 300-1475. 5th ed. Brian Tierney & Sidney Painter. 1992. text ed. write for info. (*0-07-064613-9*) McGraw.

Western Europe in World Affairs: Continuity, Change, & Challenge. Guy De Carmoy. LC 85-28147. 208p. 1986. text ed. 45.00 (*0-275-92057-7*, C2057, Praeger Pubs) Greenwood.

Western Europe since 1945: A Bibliography. Joan F. Higbee. LC 95-48831. (Scarecrow Area Bibliographies Ser.: Vol. 9). 200p. 1996. text ed. 29.00 (*0-8108-3112-0*) Scarecrow.

Western Europe since 1945: A Political History. 4th ed. Derek W. Urwin. (Illus.). 451p. (C). 1989. pap. text ed. 31.95 (*0-582-49511-3*, 78191) Longman.

*__Western Europe Travellers Survival Kit.__ (Travellers Survival Kit Guides Ser.). 352p. (Orig.). 1997. pap. 16.95 (*1-85458-114-7*, Pub. by Vac Wrk Pubns UK) Seven Hills Bk.

Western Europe 1996. 15th ed. Wayne C. Thompson. 519p. 1996. pap. 19.50 (*1-887985-02-6*) Stryker-Post.

Western European Adjustment to Structural Economic Problems. Marie J. Drouin et al. Ed. by Catherine Albrecht et al. (Illus.). 282p. (Orig.). (C). 1987. pap. text ed. 24.00 (*0-8191-6528-X*, Hudson Instit IN); lib. bdg. 49.50 (*0-8191-6527-1*, Pub. by Hudson Inst) U Pr of Amer.

Western European Censuses, Nineteen Sixty, Vol. 7. Judith Blake & Jerry J. Donovan. LC 76-4558. (Population Monograph: No. 8). 421p. 1976. reprint ed. text ed. 48.50 (*0-8371-8831-8*, BLWE, Greenwood Pr) Greenwood.

Western European Communists & the Collapse of Communism. Ed. by David S. Bell. LC 92-12214. 1993. 38.95 (*0-85496-806-7*) Berg Pubs.

Western European Costume & Its Relation to the Theatre. Iris Brooke. Incl. Vol. 2. 17th Through 19th Centuries. LC 63-18334. 1963. pap. 10.95 (*0-87830-514-9*, Thtre Arts Bks); LC 63-18334. (Illus.). (Orig.). Set pap. write for info. (*0-318-55926-9*, Thtre Arts Bks) Routledge.

Western European Costume Thirteenth to Seventeenth Century. Iris Brooke & William-Alan Landes. LC 93-36612. (Illus.). 192p. 1993. pap. 15.00 (*0-88734-635-9*) Players Pr.

Western European Economic Organizations: Comprehensive Reference Guide. 92th ed. 1992. 145.00 (*0-582-06845-2*, Pub. by Longman Grp UK) Gale.

*__Western European Government & Politics.__ Michael Curtis & Jean Blondel. LC 96-33112. (C). 1997. text ed. 35.95 (*0-673-98257-2*) Longman.

Western European Integration: Implications for U. S. Policy & Strategy. Michael J. Collins. LC 91-26376. 160p. 1992. text ed. 45.00 (*0-275-94170-1*, C4170, Praeger Pubs) Greenwood.

Western European Labor & the American Corporation. Ed. by Alfred Kamin. LC 72-83775. 574p. reprint ed. pap. 163.60 (*0-317-29811-9*, 2016699) Bks Demand.

Western European Market for Chiral Reagents & Instrumentation Markets. Market Intelligence Staff. 196p. 1993. 4,200.00 (*1-56753-578-X*) Frost & Sullivan.

Western European Military Space Policy. Alastair McLean. 200p. 1992. 59.95 (*1-85521-115-7*, Pub. by Dartmth Pub UK) Ashgate Pub Co.

Western European Nuclear Forces: A British, a French & an American View. Nicholas K. Witney et al. xi, 96p. 1995. pap. text ed. 15.00 (*0-8330-1663-6*, MR-587-AF) Rand Corp.

Western European Painting in the Hermitage: 19th to 20th Centuries. Albert G. Kostenevich. 376p. (C). 1987. text ed. 325.00 (*0-569-08990-5*, Pub. by Collets) St Mut.

Western European Painting of the Renaissance. Frank J. Mather. LC 65-28209. (Illus.). reprint ed. lib. bdg. 72.00 (*0-8154-0148-5*) Cooper Sq.

Western European Party Systems: Continuity & Change. Ed. by Hans Daalder & Peter Mair. 466p. 1983. pap. 16.95 (*0-8039-9702-7*) Sage.

Western European Penal Systems: A Critical Anatomy. Ed. by Vincenzo et al. 256p. 1995. 69.95 (*0-8039-7720-4*); pap. 25.95 (*0-8039-7721-2*) Sage.

Western European Political Parties: A Comprehensive Guide. Longman Staff. 550p. 1989. 180.00 (*0-582-00113-7*) Longman.

Western European Sculpture from Soviet Museums: 15th & 16th Centuries. M. Liebmann. (Illus.). 264p. (C). 1988. text ed. 300.00 (*0-685-40254-1*, Pub. by Collets) St Mut.

Western European Sculpture from Soviet Museums, 15th-16th Centuries. M. Liebmann. 264p. (C). 1988. 275.00 (*0-685-34410-X*, Pub. by Collets) St Mut.

Western European Studies: Current Research Trends & Library Resources. Eva M. Sartori. 120p. 1990. pap. 32.95 (*0-8389-7461-9*) Assn Coll & Res Libs.

Western European Synthetic Adhesive Markets. Market Intelligence Staff. 342p. 1994. 3,800.00 (*1-56753-975-0*) Frost & Sullivan.

Western European Thermoplastic Elastomer Markets. Market Intelligence Staff. 191p. 1993. 4,300.00 (*1-56753-517-8*) Frost & Sullivan.

Western European Union & NATO: Building a European Defence Identity Within the Context of Atlantic Solidarity, No. 2. Alfred Cahen. (Atlantic Commentaries Ser.). 150p. 1989. pap. 16.50 (*0-08-037340-2*, Pub. by Brasseys UK) Brasseys Inc.

*__Western European Union & the European Security Debate.__ G. Wyn Rees. (C). 1997. text ed. 55.00 (*0-8133-8961-5*) Westview.

Western European Water-Soluble Polymer Markets. Market Intelligence Staff. 237p. 1994. 3,800.00 (*1-56753-942-4*) Frost & Sullivan.

*__Western Europe's Best-Loved Driving Tours.__ 3rd ed. Arthur Frommer. (Frommer's Driving Tours Ser.). 1997. 19.95 (*0-02-861567-0*) Macmillan.

Western Europe's Global Reach: Regional Cooperation & Worldwide Aspirations. Ed. by Werner J. Feld. (Policy Studies). 1980. 78.00 (*0-08-025130-7*, Pergamon Pr) Elsevier.

Western Expansion & Indigenous People: The Heritage of Las Casas. Ed. by Elias Sevilla-Casas. (World Anthropology Ser.). xiv, 308p. 1977. 40.00 (*90-279-7510-8*) Mouton.

Western Expansionism in the Persian Gulf. V. Mikhin. (C). 1988. 17.50 (*0-8364-2448-4*, Pub. by Allied II) S Asia.

Western Experience, 5 vols. 5th ed. Incl. Vol. 3. Since 1600. , 2 vols. 5th ed. Mortimer Chambers et al. 1991. pap. text ed. (*0-07-010618-5*); Vol. 4. To 1500. , 3 vols. 5th ed. Mortimer Chambers et al. 1991. pap. text ed. (*0-07-010619-3*); Vol. 5. 1300-1815. , 3 vols. 5th ed. Mortimer Chambers & Raymond Crew. 1991. pap. text ed. 33.50 (*0-07-010620-7*); LC 94-17442. 1991. Set text ed. write for info. (*0-07-010616-9*) McGraw.

Western Experience. 6th ed. Mortimer Chambers et al. LC 94-17442. 1995. text ed. 48.75 (*0-07-011066-2*) McGraw.

Western Experience Vol. 1: To the Eighteenth Century, Vol. 2. 6th ed. Mortimer Chambers et al. 1995. pap. text ed. write for info. (*0-07-011068-9*) McGraw.

Western Experience Vol. 2: Since the Sixteenth Century, Vol. 3. 6th ed. Mortimer Chambers et al. 1995. pap. text ed. write for info. (*0-07-011069-7*) McGraw.

Western Experience Vol. 7: From the Renaissance to the Modern Era, Vol. 7. 6th ed. Mortimer Chambers et al. 1994. pap. text ed. write for info. (*0-07-011188-X*) McGraw.

Western Experience Vol. A: Antiquity & the Middle Ages, Vol. 4. 6th ed. Mortimer Chambers et al. 1995. pap. text ed. write for info. (*0-07-011070-0*) McGraw.

Western Experience Vol. B: The Early Modern Era, Vol. 5. 6th ed. Mortimer Chambers et al. 1995. pap. text ed. write for info. (*0-07-011071-9*) McGraw.

Western Experience Vol. C: The Modern Era, Vol. 6. 6th ed. Mortimer Chambers et al. 1995. pap. text ed. write for info. (*0-07-011072-7*) McGraw.

Western Experiment: New England Transcendentalists in the Ohio Valley. Elizabeth R. McKinsey. LC 72-83467. (Essays in History & Literature Ser.). 78p. 1978. pap. 6.50 (*0-674-95040-2*) HUP.

Western Explorations. Charlene Beeler. (Simulation Ser.). 51p. 1991. pap. 19.95 (*1-882664-03-5*) Prufrock Pr.

Western Fairfield County. CCS Inc. Staff. (Street Directions Without a Map Ser.). 100p. 1992. pap. 14.95 (*1-881638-01-4*) CCS Inc.

Western Fertilizer Handbook. 8th ed. California Fertilizer Association Staff. (Illus.). 316p. 1994. pap. text ed. 19.95 (*0-8134-2972-2*, 2490) Interstate.

Western Fertilizer Handbook: Horticulture Edition. California Fertilizer Association Staff. (Illus.). 279p. (Orig.). (C). 1990. teacher ed. 6.95 (*0-8134-2922-6*); pap. text ed. 19.95 (*0-8134-2858-0*) Interstate.

Western Fiction in the Library of Congress Classification Scheme. Michael Burgess & Beverly A. Ryan. LC 87-6309. (Borgo Cataloging Guides Ser.: No. 3). 48p. 1988. pap. 13.00 (*0-89370-922-0*); lib. bdg. 23.00 (*0-89370-822-4*) Borgo Pr.

Western Films: A Brief History. Ed. by Richard W. Etulain. (Illus.). 96p. 1983. pap. text ed. 15.00 (*0-89745-048-5*) Sunflower U Pr.

Western Films: A Complete Guide. Brian Garfield. (Quality Paperbacks Ser.). (Illus.). 400p. 1988. reprint ed. pap. 16.95 (*0-306-80333-X*) Da Capo.

Western Films of John Ford. J. A. Place. (Illus.). 226p. 1974. text ed. 12.00 (*0-8065-0445-5*, Citadel Pr) Carol Pub Group.

Western Films of John Ford. J. A. Place. 1977. pap. 9.95 (*0-8065-0594-X*, Citadel Pr) Carol Pub Group.

Western Fly Fishing Guide. Dave Hughes. (Illus.). 84p. (Orig.). 1987. pap. 5.95 (*0-936608-50-1*) F Amato Pubns.

*__Western Fly-Fishing Strategies.__ Craig Mathews. (Illus.). 256p. 1998. 25.00 (*1-55821-641-3*) Lyons & Burford.

Western Foreign Policy Toward Eastern Europe: Lessons to Be Learned. Tom Lantos. (Nimitz Memorial Lectures: No. 11). 48p. (Orig.). 1995. pap. text ed. 5.95 (*0-87725-610-1*) U of Cal IAS.

Western Forest Industry: An Economic Outlook. John A. Guthrie & George R. Armstrong. LC 61-9914. 352p. reprint ed. pap. 100.40 (*0-317-28864-4*, 2020962) Bks Demand.

Western Forests. Stephen Whitney. Ed. by Charles Elliott. LC 84-48670. (Audubon Society Nature Guides Ser.). (Illus.). 671p. 1985. pap. 19.95 (*0-394-73127-1*) Knopf.

*__Western Front.__ Rosemary Rees. LC 97-4476. (Heinemann History Depth Studies). (Illus.). (J). 1997. write for info. (*1-57572-217-8*) Rigby Interact Libr.

Western Front Companion 1914-1918: A-Z Source to the Battles, Weapons, People, Places and Air Combat. John Laffin. (Illus.). 218p. 1995. 29.95 (*0-7509-0061-X*, Pub. by Sutton Pubng UK) Bks Intl VA.

Western Front Illustrated. John Laffin. (Illus.). 224p. 1991. 34.00 (*0-86299-789-5*, Pub. by Sutton Pubng UK) Bks Intl VA.

*__Western Front Illustrated: 1914-1918.__ John Laffin. (Illus.). 192p. 1997. pap. 22.95 (*0-7509-1438-6*, Pub. by Sutton Pubng UK) Bks Intl VA.

*__Western Front Tank Leader.__ 25.00 (*0-87431-061-X*, 10160) West End Games.

*__Western Front 1915: VCs of the First World War.__ Peter F. Batchelor & Christopher Matson. (Illus.). 224p. 1996. 17.99 (*0-7509-1106-9*, Pub. by Sutton Pubng UK) Bks Intl VA.

*__Western Front 1915-1918, Epilogue 1919-1929, Vol. 8.__ Marquess of Anglesey Staff. (A History of the British Cavalry Ser.). 1997. 75.00 (*0-85052-467-9*, Pub. by L Cooper Bks UK) Trans-Atl Phila.

Western Frontiers of Imperial Rome. Steven K. Drummond & Lynn H. Nelson. LC 93-3650. 288p. (C). 1993. pap. text ed. 24.95 (*1-56324-151-X*) M E Sharpe.

Western Frontiers of Imperial Rome. Steven K. Drummond & Lynn H. Nelson. LC 93-3650. 288p. (C). (gr. 13). 1993. text ed. 67.95 (*1-56324-150-1*) M E Sharpe.

Western Fur Trade. O. J. Fargo. (Western History Ser.). (Illus.). 53p. (Orig.). (YA). (gr. 5 up). 1990. pap. 1.50 (*0-924702-20-6*) Grn Valley Area.

Western Furniture: 1350 to the Present Day. Christopher Wilk. (Illus.). 232p. 1996. 60.00 (*0-7892-0252-2*, Cross Riv Pr) Abbeville Pr.

*__Western Garden Annual 1997.__ Sunset Staff. 1997. pap. text ed. 21.95 (*0-376-03861-6*, Sunset) Sunset Bks Inc.

Western Garden Annual. Sunset Editors. 304p. 1994. 24.99 (*0-376-03855-1*) Sunset Bks Inc.

Western Gardening. Sunset Staff. 1988. 32.00 (*0-376-03895-0*) Sunset Bks Inc.

Western Gazetteer: Or Emigrant's Directory. Samuel R. Brown. LC 79-146380. (First American Frontier Ser.). (Illus.). 1977. reprint ed. 35.95 (*0-405-02831-8*) Ayer.

*__Western Ghats Ecosystem.__ D. N. Tewari. 294p. 1995. pap. 238.00 (*81-7089-224-4*, Pub. by Intl Bk Distr II) St Mut.

Western Ghosts. Ed. by Frank D. McSherry, Jr et al. LC 90-8072. (American Ghost Ser.). 224p. (Orig.). (J). 1990. pap. 9.95 (*1-55853-069-X*) Rutledge Hill Pr.

Western Glass Auctions: Auction Catalog, 3 vols., 1. Dale Mooney. (Illus.). 1991. 16.00 (*1-883192-00-5*) Wstrn Glass.

Western Glass Auctions: Auction Catalog, 3 vols., 2. Dale Mooney. (Illus.). 1992. 18.00 (*1-883192-01-3*) Wstrn Glass.

Western Glass Auctions: Auction Catalog, 3 vols., 3. Dale Mooney. (Illus.). 1992. 20.00 (*1-883192-02-1*) Wstrn Glass.

Western Grazing Grounds & Forest Ranges. William C. Barnes. Ed. by Stuart Bruchey. LC 78-56685. (Management of Public Lands in the U. S. Ser.). (Illus.). 1979. reprint ed. lib. bdg. 29.95 (*0-405-11317-X*) Ayer.

Western Great Lakes Lighthouses: Michigan & Superior. Photos by Bruce Roberts. LC 95-53718. (Lighthouse Ser.). 1996. pap. 19.95 (*1-56440-954-6*) Globe Pequot.

Western Greeks. T. J. Dunbabin. 504p. 1991. pap. 40.00 (*0-89005-300-6*) Ares.

Western Guide to Feng Shui: Creating Balance, Harmony, & Prosperity in Your Environment. Terah K. Collins. LC 95-47274. (Illus.). 224p. (Orig.). 1996. pap. 12.95 (*1-56170-324-9*, 194) Hay House.

Western Gulf of Alaska: A Socio-Economic Study. David T. Kresge et al. LC 74-620053. (Illus.). 200p. 1974. pap. write for info. (*0-88353-014-7*) U Alaska Inst Res.

Western Guns at Dawn: The California Legend of Joaquin Murietta. (Illus.). 105p. (Orig.). 1989. pap. text ed. 5.00 (*0-317-93847-9*) J Robin.

*__Western Gunslingers in Fact & on Film: Hollywood's Famous Lawmen & Outlaws.__ Buck Rainey. 272p. 1997. pap. 35.00 (*0-7864-0396-9*) McFarland & Co.

*__Western Hall of Fame Anthology.__ Martin H. Greenberg & Dale C. Walker. 288p. 1997. mass mkt. 5.99 (*0-425-15906-X*) Berkley Pub.

Western Harvest: Gatherings of an Editor. Frances Ring. LC 90-13882. (Illus.). 192p. (Orig.). 1991. pap. 9.95 (*0-936784-87-3*) J Daniel.

Western Hemisphere: Guarding the United States & Its Outposts. 1996. lib. bdg. 606.95 (*0-8490-6924-6*) Gordon Pr.

Western Hemisphere Economic Integration. Gary C. Hufbauer & Jeffrey J. Schott. LC 94-3985. 279p. 1994. pap. 25.00 (*0-88132-159-1*) Inst Intl Eco.

Western Hemisphere Economic Integration: Economic & Political Determinants of U. S. Policy. Ed. by Jeffrey J. Schott & Gary G. Hufbauer. 74p. 1994. write for info. (*0-940602-84-9*) IADB.

Western Hemisphere Economic Integration: Implications for GATT & Relations with Third Countries. Ed. by Jeffrey J. Schott & Gary G. Hufbauer. 34p. 1994. write for info. (*0-940602-83-0*) IADB.

Western Hemisphere Economic Integration: Starting Point, Long-Term Goals, Readiness Indicators, Paths to Integration. Ed. by Jeffrey J. Schott & Gary G. Hufbauer. 121p. 1994. write for info. (*0-940602-81-4*) IADB.

Western Hemisphere Economic Integration: Subregional Building Blocks. Ed. by Jeffrey J. Schott & Gary G. Hufbauer. 108p. 1994. write for info. (*0-940602-82-2*) IADB.

W

An Asterisk (*) at the beginning of an entry indicates that the title is appearing in BIP for the first time.

Western Hemisphere Immigration & United States Foreign Policy. Ed. by Christopher Mitchell. 384p. 1992. pap. 16.95 (0-271-00791-5); text ed. 45.00 (0-271-00789-3) Pa St U Pr.

***Western Heritage.** Donald Kagan. (C). 1997. pap. text ed. 30.00 (0-13-955493-9) P-H.

***Western Heritage.** 6th ed. Kagan & Steven Ozment. LC 97-23706. (C). 1997. text ed. 61.33 (0-13-617383-7); pap. text ed. 46.67 (0-13-617432-9); pap. text ed. 39.33 (0-13-617440-X); pap. text ed. 39.33 (0-13-617457-4); pap. text ed. 39.33 (0-13-617655-0) P-H.

***Western Heritage, 1.** 6th ed. Kagan & Steven Ozment. (C). 1997. pap. text ed. 46.67 (0-13-617424-8) P-H.

Western Heritage, Vol. 1. abr. ed. Kagan & Steven Ozment. 1995. pap. text ed. 30.67 (0-13-439266-3) P-H.

Western Heritage, Vol. I. 4th rev. ed. Donald Kagan & Steven Ozment. (Illus.). 616p. (C). 1990. pap. text ed. 51.00 (0-02-361911-2, Macmillan Coll) P-H.

Western Heritage, Vol. 1. 5th ed. Brescia. 1994. student ed., pap. text ed. 20.40 (0-02-314090-9, Macmillan Coll) P-H.

Western Heritage, Vol. 1. 5th ed. Donald Kagan. (Illus.). 616p. (C). 1994. pap. text ed. 49.33 (0-02-363275-5, Macmillan Coll) P-H.

Western Heritage, Vol. 2. abr. ed. Kagan & Steven Ozment. 1995. pap. text ed. 30.60 (0-13-439258-2) P-H.

Western Heritage, Vol. 2. 4th rev. ed. Donald Kagan & Steven Ozment. (Illus.). 296p. (C). 1991. student ed., pap. write for info. (0-02-314082-8, Macmillan Coll) P-H.

Western Heritage, Vol. 2. 5th ed. Kagan. 1994. student ed., pap. text ed. 20.40 (0-02-314091-7, Macmillan Coll) P-H.

Western Heritage, Vol. II. 5th ed. Donald Kagan. (Illus.). 616p. (C). 1994. pap. text ed. 51.00 (0-02-363276-3, Macmillan Coll) P-H.

Western Heritage, Vol. A. 5th ed. Donald Kagan. (Illus.). 616p. (C). 1994. pap. text ed. 46.00 (0-02-363277-1, Macmillan Coll) P-H.

Western Heritage, Vol. B. 5th ed. Donald Kagan. (Illus.). 616p. (C). 1994. pap. text ed. 46.00 (0-02-363278-X, Macmillan Coll) P-H.

Western Heritage: Combined Edition. Kagan & Osment. 1995. pap. text ed. 48.00 (0-02-361872-8, Macmillan Coll) P-H.

Western Heritage: Combined Edition. 5th ed. Donald Kagan. (Illus.). 1216p. (C). 1994. teacher ed. write for info. (0-318-72459-6) Macmillan.

Western Heritage: Combined Edition. 5th ed. Donald Kagan. (Illus.). 1264p. (C). 1994. text ed. 68.00 (0-02-363262-3, Macmillan Coll) P-H.

Western Heritage: Man's Encounter with Himself & the World, a Journey for Meaning. Ed. by Francis R. Gendreau & Angelo Caranfa. LC 84-17268. 418p. (Orig.). 1985. pap. text ed. 32.00 (0-8191-4252-2) U Pr of Amer.

Western Heritage: Since Thirteen Hundred. 5th ed. Donald Kagan. (Illus.). 566p. (C). 1994. text ed. 57.00 (0-02-363280-1, Macmillan Coll) P-H.

Western Heritage Pt. I: A Study of the Colonial Architecture of Perth, Western Australia. Ray Oldham & John Oldham. LC 79-670392. 15.00 (0-85564-134-7, Pub. by Univ of West Aust Pr AT) Intl Spec Bk.

***Western Heritage Pt. II: George Temple-Poole: Architect of the Golden Years 1885-1897.** Ray Oldham & John Oldham. lthr. 35.00 (0-85564-173-8) Intl Spec Bk.

***Western Heritage 1300-Present.** 6th ed. Kagan & Steven Ozment. (C). 1997. text ed. 50.67 (0-13-617374-8) P-H.

Western Hero. Matt Forbeck. Ed. by Monte Cook. (Hero System Ser.). (Illus.). 208p. (Orig.). (C). 1991. pap. 20.00 (1-55806-118-5) Iron Crown Ent Inc.

Western Hero in Film & Television: Mass Media Mythology. Rita Parks. LC 81-21826. (Studies in Cinema: No. 10). 198p. reprint ed. pap. 56.50 (0-8357-1287-7, 2070675) Bks Demand.

***Western Hero in History & Legend.** Kent L. Steckmesser. LC 97-14426. (Illus.). 296p. 1997. pap. 15.95 (0-8061-2966-2) U of Okla Pr.

Western Himalayas & Tibet. Thomas Thomson. 1979. 80.00 (0-7855-0325-0, Pub. by Ratna Pustak Bhandar) St Mut.

Western Himalayas & Tibet. Ed. by Thomas Thomson. (Illus.). (C). 1979. 150.00 (0-89771-098-3, Pub. by Ratna Pustak Bhandar) St Mut.

Western Histories of Linguistic Thought: An Annotated Chronological Bibliography, 1822-1976. E. Konrad Koerner. (Studies in the History of Linguistics: No. 11). x, 113p. 1978. 35.00 (90-272-0952-9) Benjamins North Am.

***Western History.** Richard White. Ed. by Eric Foner. (New American History Ser.). 30p. (Orig.). 1997. pap. 5.00 (0-87229-081-6) Am Hist Assn.

Western History from 1500. Walther Kirchner. LC 90-56011. (HarperCollins College Outline Ser.). 352p. (Orig.). 1991. pap. 14.00 (0-06-467102-X, Harper Ref) HarpC.

Western History Overview. O. J. Fargo. (Western History Ser.). (Illus.). 78p. (Orig.). (YA). (gr. 5 up). 1990. pap. 1.50 (0-924702-22-2) Grn Valley Area.

***Western Home: A Literary History of Norwegian America.** text ed. 44.95 (0-252-02327-7) U of Ill Pr.

***Western Home: A Literary History of Norwegian America.** Orm Overland. Ed. by Odd S. Lovoll. (Authors Ser.: Vol. 8). (Illus.). 442p. 1996. 44.95 (0-87732-085-3) Norwegian-Am Hist Assn.

Western Home Plans: Over Two Hundred Fifteen Home Plans. (Illus.). 208p. 1992. pap. 9.95 (0-918894-94-8) Home Planners.

Western Horse: Advice & Training. Dave Jones. LC 73-7422. (Illus.). 184p. 1991. pap. 12.95 (0-8061-2334-6) U of Okla Pr.

Western Horse Behavior & Training. Robert W. Miller. 336p. 1975. pap. 16.95 (0-385-08181-2, Dolp) Doubleday.

Western Horse Tales. Ed. by Don Worcester. LC 93-24240. 28p. (Orig.). 1993. pap. 12.95 (1-55622-316-1, Rep of TX Pr) Wordware Pub.

Western Horseman Collection of Mignery Cartoons. Herb Mignery. Ed. by Cornhusker Press Staff. LC 90-86357. 1991. pap. 24.95 (0-933909-06-3) Cornhusker Pr.

Western Horsemanship. Richard Shrake. Ed. & Intro. by Pat Close. (Illus.). 144p. (Orig.). 1987. pap. 12.95 (0-911647-09-0) Western Horseman.

Western Hostility to Islam & Prophecies of Turkish Doom. Kenneth M. Setton. LC 91-76984. (Memoirs Ser.: Vol. 201). 120p. (C). 1992. 10.00 (0-87169-201-5, M201-SEK) Am Philos.

Western Humanities. 2nd ed. Roy T. Matthews & F. Dewitt Platt. 1994. sl., vhs write for info. (0-614-02479-X) Mayfield Pub.

***Western Humanities.** 2nd ed. Roy T. Matthews & F. DeWitt Platt. (Illus.). 648p. 1996. text ed. 52.95 (1-55934-763-5, 1763) Mayfield Pub.

***Western Humanities.** 3rd ed. Roy T. Matthews & F. Dewitt Platt. LC 96-53229. 1997. write for info. (1-55934-433-4) Mayfield Pub.

Western Humanities, Complete Volume. 2nd ed. Roy T. Matthews & F. Dewitt Platt. 1994. vdisk write for info. (0-614-03281-4) Mayfield Pub.

Western Humanities, Complete Volume. 2nd ed. Roy T. Matthews & F. Dewitt Platt. LC 94-16373. 648p. (C). 1994. pap. text ed. 47.95 (1-55934-412-1, 1412) Mayfield Pub.

Western Humanities, Complete Volume: Test Bank. 2nd ed. Roy T. Matthews & F. Dewitt Platt. 1994. disk write for info. (0-614-03280-6) Mayfield Pub.

Western Humanities, Vol. II. 2nd ed. Roy T. Matthews & F. DeWitt Platt. LC 94-25909. 376p. (C). 1994. pap. text ed. 40.95 (1-55934-421-0, 1421) Mayfield Pub.

Western Humanities: Beginnings Through the Renaissance, Vol. I. Roy T. Matthews & F. Dewitt Platt. LC 94-25909. (Illus.). 360p. (C). 1994. pap. text ed. 40.95 (1-55934-418-0, 1418) Mayfield Pub.

Western Humanities, Instructor's Manual, Complete Volume. 2nd ed. Roy T. Matthews & F. Dewitt Platt. 1994. teacher ed., pap. text ed. write for info. (1-55934-413-X) Mayfield Pub.

Western Hunting Guide. Mike Lapinski. (Illus.). 172p. 1989. 17.95 (0-912299-43-6); pap. 12.95 (0-912299-44-4) Stoneydale Pr Pub.

Western Illinois University 13th Annual Spring Transportation-Physical Distribution Seminar Proceedings: Just in Time: New Dimensions in Logistics. Ed. by David J. Bloomberg. 100p. 1986. pap. 10.50 (0-931497-03-5) WIU CBER.

***Western Illuminated Manuscripts.** Tamara Voronova. (Temporis Ser.). 1996. 55.00 (1-85995-235-6) Parkstone Pr.

Western Images. Becky Anthony. 100p. 1988. pap. text ed. 6.50 (1-56770-186-8) S Scheewe Pubns.

Western Images, Western Landscapes: Travels along U. S. 89. Thomas R. Vale & Geraldine R. Vale. LC 89-5063. (Illus.). 189p. 1990. 33.50 (0-8165-1117-9) U of Ariz Pr.

Western Impact on World Music Change, Adaption, & Survival. Bruno Nettl. 232p. 1985. write for info. (0-317-46649-6) Macmillan.

Western Imperialism Menaces Muslims. Maryam Jameelah. 40p. (Orig.). 1985. pap. 3.00 (1-56744-414-8) Kazi Pubns.

Western Impressions of Nature & Landscape in Southeast Asia. Victor R. Savage. 478p. (Orig.). 1985. pap. 47.50 (9971-69-081-0, Pub. by Sgapore Univ SI) Coronet Bks.

Western India: Bombay, Maharashtra, Karnataka - A Travel Guide. Philip Ward. (Travel Bks.: Vol. 19). (Illus.). 288p. (Orig.). 1991. pap. 21.95 (0-900891-32-7) Oleander Pr.

Western Indian Basketry. Joan M. Jones. (Illus.). 56p. 1988. pap. 7.95 (0-88839-122-6) Hancock House.

Western Influence in Iqbal. T. C. Rastogi. (C). 1987. 34.00 (81-7024-080-8, Pub. by Ashish II) S Asia.

***Western Influences in the Third World.** Ed. by Harold Isaacs. (Journal of Third World Studies: Vol. IV, No. 2). (Orig.). pap. 11.25 (0-614-30658-2) Assn Third Wld.

***Western Influences in the Third World.** Ed. by Harold Isaacs. (Journal of Third World Studies: Vol. IV, No. 2). 234p. 1987. pap. 7.00 (0-931971-06-3) Assn Third Wld.

Western Influences on Political Parties to Eighteen Twenty-Five. H. C. Hockett. LC 75-87650. (American Scene Ser.). 1970. reprint ed. lib. bdg. 24.50 (0-306-71777-8) Da Capo.

Western Inner Workings. William G. Gray. LC 82-62846. (Sangreal Sodality Ser.: Vol. 1). 196p. 1983. pap. 8.95 (0-87728-560-8) Weiser.

Western Intellectual Tradition: From Leonardo to Hegel. Jacob Bronowski & Bruce Mazlish. 1962. pap. text ed. 15.00 (0-06-133001-9, TB 3001, Torch) HarpC.

Western Intellectual Tradition: From Leonardo to Hegel. Jacob Bronowski & Bruce Mazlish. LC 70-167315. (Essay Index Reprint Ser.). 1977. reprint ed. 40.95 (0-8369-2448-7) Ayer.

Western Interactions with Japan: Expansions, the Armed Forces & Readjustment, 1859-1956. Ed. by Peter Lowe & Herman Moeshart. 118p. (C). 1990. pap. text ed. 18.00 (0-904404-84-6, Pub. by Curzon Press UK) UH Pr.

Western Invasions of the Pacific & Its Continents: A Study of Moving Frontiers & Changing Landscapes, 1513-1958. Archibald G. Price. LC 80-14037. (Illus.). xi, 236p. 1980. reprint ed. text ed. 38.50 (0-313-22433-1, PRWE, Greenwood Pr) Greenwood.

Western Island or the Great Basket. Robin Flower. (Oxford Paperbacks Ser.). (Illus.). 148p. 1978. reprint ed. pap. 9.95 (0-19-281234-3) OUP.

Western Islands Handbook. David Perrott. 160p. 1995. pap. 39.95 (0-9511003-4-3, Pub. by Kittiwake Pr UK) St Mut.

Western Isles of Scotland. Francis Thompson. (Illus.). 192p. (C). 1988. 19.95 (0-941533-37-9) New Amsterdam Bks.

Western Jerusalem: University of California Studies on Tasso. Ed. by Luisa Del Giudice. LC 84-20560. (Italian Literary Studies). 150p. (Orig.). (C). 1985. pap. 12.95 (0-915570-22-X) Oolp Pr.

Western Jewish History Center: Guide to Archival & Oral History Collections. Ruth K. Rafael. LC 86-50102. (Illus.). 1987. pap. 24.95 (0-943376-35-1) Magnes Mus.

***Western Jewry & the Zionist Project, 1914-1933.** Michael Berkowitz. (Illus.). 320p. (C). 1996. text ed. 59.95 (0-521-47087-0) Cambridge U Pr.

Western Journal: A Daily Log of the Great Parks Trip, June 20-July 2, 1938. Thomas Wolfe. LC 51-5285. (Pitt Paperback Ser.: No. 29). 87p. 1967. pap. 25.00 (0-7837-8538-0, 2049353) Bks Demand.

Western Journal of Isaac Mayer Wise, 1877. Ed. by William K. Kramer. 1974. pap. 5.00 (0-943376-05-X) Magnes Mus.

***Western Journeys: Discovering the Secrets of the Land.** Daniel Wood & Beverley Sinclair. 192p. (Orig.). 1997. pap. 22.95 (1-55192-069-7, Pub. by Raincoast Bks CN) Orca Bk Pubs.

Western Junior League Cookbook. Ed. by Ann Seranne. (Illus.). 1979. 12.95 (0-679-51454-6) McKay.

Western Karnataka: Its Agrarian Relations A.D. 1500-1800. K. G. Madhava. (C). 1991. 29.50 (81-7013-073-5, Pub. by Navarang II) S Asia.

Western Kentucky University. Lowell H. Harrison. LC 86-32456. (Illus.). 384p. 1987. 24.95 (0-8131-1620-1) U Pr of Ky.

Western King: The Rune Blade Trilogy. Ann Marston. 400p. 1996. mass mkt. 5.50 (0-06-105628-6, HarperPrism) HarpC.

Western Kuksu Cult. fac. ed. E. M. Loeb. (University of California Publications in American Archaeology & Ethnology: Vol. 33: 1). 143p. (C). 1932. reprint ed. pap. text ed. 13.10 (1-55567-288-4) Coyote Press.

Western Lacustrine Bantu (Nyoro, Toro, Nyankore, Kiga, Haya, & Zinza, with Sections on the Amba & Konjo) Brian K. Taylor. LC 62-51775. (Ethnographic Survey of Africa: East Central Africa Ser.: Pt. 13). 167p. reprint ed. pap. 47.60 (0-8357-6973-9, 2039033) Bks Demand.

Western Lands. William S. Burroughs. 272p. 1988. pap. 12.95 (0-14-009456-3, Penguin Bks) Viking Penguin.

Western Language Literature on Pre-Islamic Central Arabia: An Annotated Bibliography. Ed. by Stephen D. Ricks. (Bibliographic Ser.: No. 8). 163p. (Orig.). 1991. pap. text ed. 10.00 (0-933017-01-4) Am Inst Islamic.

Western Legacy. Erwin et al. 1993. pap. text ed. write for info. (0-07-019703-2) McGraw.

Western Life in the Stirrups. Ed. by Dwight L. Smith. 1965. 25.00 (0-940550-01-6) Caxton Club.

Western Lighthouses: Olympic Peninsula to San Diego. Photos by Bruce Roberts & Ray Jones. LC 92-32521. (Lighthouse Ser.). (Illus.). 128p. (Orig.). 1993. pap. 19.95 (1-56440-133-2) Globe Pequot.

Western Literature, 3 vols. Incl. Vol. I. Ancient World. Ed. by Heinrich Von Staden. 550p. (C). 1971. pap. text ed. 19.50 (0-15-595276-5); Vol. II. Middle Ages, Renaissance, Enlightenment. Ed. by Robert Hollander. 550p. (C). 1971. pap. text ed. 19.50 (0-15-595277-3); Vol. III. Modern World. Ed. by Peter Brooks. 552p. (C). 1971. pap. text ed. 19.50 (0-15-595278-1); (C). 1971. Set pap. text ed. write for info. (0-318-52977-7) HB Coll Pubs.

Western Literature Vol. 2: Five Novels. Davis. Date not set. pap. text ed. 59.40 (0-312-13279-4) St Martin.

Western Literature in Context, 2 vols., Vol. 1. Paul Davis et al. 2352p. 1994. pap. text ed. 32.50 (0-312-08124-3) St Martin.

Western Literature in Context, 2 vols., Vol. 2. Paul Davis et al. 2352p. 1994. pap. text ed. 29.50 (0-312-08125-1) St Martin.

Western Living: Coloring Book. large type ed. Loree Johnson & Alice L. Johnson. (Illus.). 32p. (Orig.). (J). (gr. 1-12). 1992. pap. 1.00 (0-9647690-1-8) Lorees Art.

***Western Long Island Geology: History Processes & Field Trips.** Les Sirkin. (Coastal Geology Ser.). (Illus.). viii, 180p. (Orig.). 1996. pap. 20.00 (0-910258-17-1) Book & Tackle.

***Western Long Island Geology, History, Processes & Field Trips.** Les Sirkin. (Illus.). 184p. 1996. 20.00 (0-614-30503-9) Book & Tackle.

Western Lore & Language: A Dictionary for Enthusiasts of the American West. Thomas L. Clark. (Illus.). 320p. (C). 1996. 24.95 (0-87480-510-4) U of Utah Pr.

Western Loving. 1994. mass mkt. 5.50 (0-373-20097-8, 1-20097-1) Harlequin Bks.

Western Man. Janet Dailey. 1993. mass mkt. 4.99 (0-671-87521-3) PB.

Western Man & the Modern World, 5 vols. Leonard F. James et al. Incl. Vol. 5. Africa, Latin America & the East. 1984. 2.20 (0-08-022619-1); 1979. Set pap. write for info. (0-318-55241-8) Elsevier.

Western Mandalas of Transformation: Astrological & Qabalistic Talismans & Tattwas. A. L. Soror. LC 95-44525. (Illus.). 272p. 1996. pap. 17.95 (1-56718-170-8) Llewellyn Pubns.

Western Marxism - A Critical Reader. Ed. by New Left Review Staff. 354p. 1977. pap. text ed. 16.95 (0-902308-29-7, A1021, Pub. by Verso NLB UK) Routledge Chapman & Hall.

Western Maryland: A Profile. Thomas H. Hattery. LC 79-65634. 208p. 1980. 29.75 (0-912338-21-0) Lomond.

***Western Maryland Diesel Locomotives.** Patrick H. Stakem. (Illus.). 128p. 1996. 24.95 (1-883089-24-7) TLC VA.

Western Maryland in Color. David R. Sweetland. 1995. 49.95 (1-878887-43-2) Morning NJ.

Western Maryland in the Revolution. Bernard C. Steiner. LC 78-63885. (Johns Hopkins University. Studies in the Social Sciences. Thirtieth Ser. 1912: 1). reprint ed. 29.50 (0-404-61140-0) AMS Pr.

Western Maryland Railway: Fireballs & Black Diamonds. Roger Cook & Karl Zimmermann. LC 92-25390. xii, 332p. 1992. 50.00 (0-9620844-4-1) Garrigues Hse.

Western Medical Pioneers in Feudal Japan. John Z. Bowers. LC 73-86098. (Josiah Macy Foundation Ser.). 256p. 1970. 42.00 (0-8018-1081-7) Johns Hopkins.

Western Medical Tradition: 800 B. C.-1800 A. D. Lawrence Conrad et al. (Illus.). 550p. (C). 1995. text ed. 90.00 (0-521-38135-5); pap. text ed. 35.95 (0-521-47564-3) Cambridge U Pr.

***Western Medicine: An Illustrated History.** Ed. by Irvine Loudon. (Illus.). 410p. 1997. 49.95 (0-19-820509-0) OUP.

***Western Medicine: Contest of Knowledge.** Cunningham. LC 96-34392. Date not set. text ed. 79.95 (0-7190-4673-4) St Martin.

Western Mediterranean. Ramon Margalef & John E. Treherne. LC 84-10993. (Key Environments Ser.). 275p. 1985. 169.00 (0-08-028870-7, Pub. by Pergamon Repr UK) Franklin.

***Western Mediterranean Kingdoms, 1200-1500: The Struggle for Dominion.** David Abulafia. LC 97-20258. (Medieval World Ser.). 1997. write for info. (0-582-07821-0, Pub. by Longman UK); pap. write for info. (0-582-07820-2, Pub. by Longman UK) Longman.

Western Mediterranean World: An Introduction to Its Regional Landscapes. James M. Houston. LC 65-87641. (Geographies for Advanced Study Ser.). 921p. reprint ed. pap. 180.00 (0-317-27875-4, 2025261) Bks Demand.

Western Memorabilia: Identification & Price Guide. Bill Ketchum. 408p. (Orig.). 1993. pap. 15.00 (0-380-77137-3, Confident Collect) Avon.

Western Memorabilia & Collectibles. Bob Ball. (Illus.). 160p. 1993. 29.95 (0-88740-484-7) Schiffer.

Western Merchant. John B. Jones. (Notable American Authors Ser.). 1992. reprint ed. lib. bdg. 90.00 (0-7812-3515-4) Rprt Serv.

Western Military Frontier 1815-1846. Henry P. Beers. LC 75-25798. (Perspectives in American History Ser.: No. 35). (Illus.). vi, 227p. 1975. reprint ed. lib. bdg. 35.00 (0-87991-359-2) Porcupine Pr.

Western Mining. O. J. Fargo. (Western History Ser.). (Illus.). 58p. (Orig.). 1990. pap. 1.50 (0-924702-25-7) Grn Valley Area.

Western Mining: An Informal Account of Precious-Metals Prospecting, Placering, Lode Mining, & Milling on the American Frontier from Spanish Times to 1893. Otis E. Young, Jr. LC 76-108800. (Illus.). 1977. pap. 18.95 (0-8061-1352-9) U of Okla Pr.

Western Montana Fair: A Pictorial Heritage. Stan Cohen. LC 95-70125. (Illus.). 68p. (Orig.). 1995. pap. 7.95 (1-57510-002-9) Pictorial Hist.

Western Mystical Tradition: An Intellectual History of Western Civilization, Vol. 1. Thomas Katsaros & Nathaniel Kaplan. 1969. 19.95 (0-8084-0316-8); pap. 15.95 (0-8084-0317-6) NCUP.

Western Mysticism: A Guide to the Basic Works. fac. ed. Mary A. Bowman. LC 78-18311. 121p. 1978. pap. 34.50 (0-7837-7318-8, 2047245) Bks Demand.

Western Mysticism: Neglected Chapters in the History of Religion. C. Butler. 1973. 250.00 (0-87968-244-2) Gordon Pr.

Western National Wildlife Refuges: Thirty-Six Havens from California to Texas. Dennis Wall. (Illus.). 288p. (Orig.). 1996. pap. 24.95 (0-89013-306-9) Museum NM Pr.

Western New Haven County. CCS Inc. Staff. (Street Directions Without a Map Ser.). 144p. 1992. pap. 14.95 (1-881638-04-9) CCS Inc.

Western New York Exhibition, No. 39. LC 82-70389. (Illus.). 40p. 1982. pap. 4.00 (0-914782-44-4) Buffalo Fine-Albrght-Knox.

Western New York Land Transactions, 1804-1824: Extracted from the Archives of the Holland Land Company. Karen E. Livsey. 472p. 1991. 35.00 (0-8063-1294-7, 3422) Genealog Pub.

***Western New York Land Transactions, 1825-1835.** Karen E. Livsey. 812p. 1996. text ed. 60.00 (0-8063-1522-9) Genealog Pub.

***Western New York Weather Guide: A Century of Sun, Snow, Sleet & Rain.** Tom Jolls et al. (Illus.). 108p. (Orig.). 1996. pap. 6.95 (1-879201-18-6) Meyer Enter.

Western North Atlantic Region. Ed. by P. R. Vogt & B. E. Tucholke. (DNAG, Geology of North America Ser.: Vol. M). (Illus.). 720p. 1986. 47.50 (0-8137-5202-7) Geol Soc.

***Western North Carolina: A History from 1730-1913.** John P. Arthur. (Illus.). 679p. 1996. 37.50 (1-57072-062-2) Overmountain Pr.

Western North Carolina: Its Mountains & Its People to 1880. 2nd ed. Ora Blackmun. LC 76-53030. (Illus.). (Orig.). 1977. 15.95 (0-913239-31-3) Appalach Consortium.

Western North Carolina Almanac. 2nd ed. Robert Beverley. (Living Almanacs Ser.). (Illus.). xii, 275p. 1993. pap. 12.95 (0-9629289-2-5) Sanctuary Pr.

Western North Carolina since the Civil War. Ina Van Noppen & John Van Noppen. LC 73-1241. 1973. 15.95 (0-913239-33-X); pap. 9.95 (0-913239-34-8) Appalach Consortium.

Western Ocean Packets. Basil Lubbock. (C). 1987. 120.00 (0-85174-118-5, Pub. by Brwn Son Ferg) St Mut.

W

An Asterisk (*) at the beginning of an entry indicates that the title is appearing in BIP for the first time.

Western Ocean Packets. Basil Lubbock. (Illus.). 192p. 1988. reprint ed. pap. 5.95 (0-486-25684-7) Dover.

Western Ocean Passenger Lines & Liners 1934-1969. C. R. Gibbs. (C). 1987. 27.00 (0-85174-056-1, Pub. by Brwn Son Ferg) St Mut.

Western Oil World Rocky Mountain Petroleum Directory see Hart Rocky Mountain Petroleum Directory, 1991

Western Oregon: Portrait of the Land & Its People. Marnie McPhee. LC 87-19341. (Oregon Geographic Ser.: No. 2). (Illus.). 104p. (Orig.). 1987. pap. 6.95 (0-938314-34-3) Am Wrld Geog.

Western Outlaws: The "Good Badman" in Fact, Film & Folklore. Kent L. Steckmesser. (Topics in American History & Culture Ser.). 161p. (C). 1983. 19.95 (0-941690-07-5); pap. 12.95 (0-941690-08-3) Regina Bks.

Western Pacific: Challenge of Sustainable Growth. Alan Burnett. 282p. (Orig.). 1992. 24.95 (1-85383-158-1, Pub. by Erthscan Pubns UK) Island Pr.

Western Pacific's Diesel Years. Joseph A. Strapac. LC 80-68133. (Overland Railbook Ser.). (Illus.). 208p. 1980. pap. 18.50 (0-916160-08-4) G R Cockle.

***Western Paradise: Greek & Hebrew Traditions.** James E. Miller. LC 96-44823. (Non Series Monograph). 144p. 1996. 69.95 (1-57309-127-8); pap. 49.95 (1-57309-126-X) Intl Scholars.

Western Paradise of Amitabha. Manly P. Hall. pap. 4.95 (0-89314-369-3) Philos Res.

Western Peace Officer: The Legacy of Law & Order. Frank R. Prassel. LC 71-39627. 304p. 1980. pap. 14.95 (0-8061-1694-3) U of Okla Pr.

Western Pennsylvania Symposium on World Literatures, 1974-1991: Selected Proceedings, a Retrospective. Pref. by Carla E. Lucente. LC 92-54567. (Humanities Ser.: No. 6). (Illus.). 266p. (C). 1992. text ed. 40.00 (0-929914-13-9) Eadmer Pr.

Western Pennsylvania Teen Challenge Presentation: A Biblical Treatise on Moral Integrity for Men & Its Challenges. Michael D. Juzwick. (J). 1989. 5.95 (1-887412-08-5) Light Eternal Pubns.

Western Perspective. Cannistrar. (C). 1998. text ed. 39.50 (0-03-045643-6) HarBrace.

***Western Perspective, Vol. I.** Cannistrar. (C). 1998. pap. text ed. 27.50 (0-03-045644-4) HB Coll Pubs.

***Western Perspective, Vol. II.** Cannistrar. (C). 1998. pap. text ed. 27.50 (0-03-045649-5) HB Coll Pubs.

***Western Perspective, Vol. C.** Cannistrar. (C). 1998. pap. text ed. 24.25 (0-03-045763-7) HarBrace.

***Western Perspective, Vol. A.** Cannistrar. (C). 1998. pap. text ed. 24.25 (0-03-045647-9) HB Coll Pubs.

***Western Perspective, Vol. B.** Cannistrar. (C). 1998. pap. text ed. 24.25 (0-03-045648-7) HB Coll Pubs.

Western Perspectives on Chinese Higher Education: A Model for Cross-Cultural Inquiry. Xiuwu R. Liu. LC 96-22432. 192p. 1996. 33.50 (0-8386-3709-4) Fairleigh Dickinson.

Western Philosophic Systems & Their Cyclic Transformations. Robert S. Brumbaugh. LC 91-28604. (Philosophical Explorations Ser.). 192p. (C). 1992. 29.95 (0-8093-1771-0) S Ill U Pr.

Western Philosophy: An Anthology. Ed. & Pref. by John Cottingham. 704p. (C). 1996. 74.95 (0-631-18626-3); pap. 26.95 (0-631-18627-1) Blackwell Pubs.

Western Philosophy: An Introduction. R. J. Hollingdale. 185p. pap. 12.95 (1-871082-46-3) Paul & Co Pubs.

Western Philosophy: From Antiquity to the Middle Ages. James N. Jordan. 887p. (C). 1987. pap. text ed. 51.00 (0-02-361450-1, Macmillan Coll) P-H.

Western Pioneer: Or, Incidents of the Life & Times of Rev. Alfred Brunson..., 2 Vols. Alfred Brunson. LC 75-89. (Mid-American Frontier Ser.). 1975. reprint ed. 66.95 (0-405-06856-5) Ayer.

Western Pleasure: Training & Showing to Win. Doug Carpenter & Carolyn Pryor. Ed. & Illus. by Robert Feinberg. (Masters Ser.). 190p. 1995. 29.95 (0-9625898-3-7) EquiMedia.

Western Political Theory: From Its Origins to the Present, 3 vols. Lee C. McDonald. Incl. Vol. 1. Ancient & Medieval. 228p. (C). 1970. pap. text ed. 18.00 (0-15-595297-8); Vol. 2. From Machiavelli to Burke. 297p. (C). 1970. pap. text ed. 18.00 (0-15-595298-6); Vol. 3. Nineteenth & Twentieth Centuries. 239p. (C). 1970. pap. text ed. 18.00 (0-15-595299-4); (C). 1970. Set pap. text ed. write for info. (0-318-52978-5) HB Coll Pubs.

Western Political Theory in the Face of the Future. 2nd ed. John Dunn. (Canto Book Ser.). 150p. (C). 1993. pap. text ed. 10.95 (0-521-43755-5) Cambridge U Pr.

Western Political Thought. R. P. Sharma. 340p. 1984. pap. text ed. 10.95 (0-86590-316-6, Pub. by Sterling Pubs II) Apt Bks.

Western Political Thought: A Bibliographical Guide to Post-War Research. Robert Eccleshall & Michael Kenny. LC 94-26466. 1995. text ed. 79.95 (0-7190-3569-4, Pub. by Manchester Univ Pr UK) St Martin.

Western Political Thought: From Socrates to the Age of Ideology. 2nd ed. Brian R. Nelson. LC 94-48427. 432p. (C). 1995. text ed. 49.00 (0-13-191172-4) P-H.

Western Populism: Studies in an Ambivalent Conservatism. Karel D. Bicha. (Illus.). 1976. 10.50 (0-87291-085-7) Coronado Pr.

Western Psychotherapy & Hindu-Sadhana: A Contribution to Comparative Studies in Psychology & Metaphysics. Hans Jacobs. LC 61-3343. (Illus.). 242p. reprint ed. pap. 69.00 (0-317-10274-5, 2010706) Bks Demand.

Western Public Lands: The Management of Natural Resources in a Time of Declining Federalism. Ed. by John G. Francis & Richard Ganzel. LC 83-19067. 320p. (C). 1984. 60.50 (0-86598-147-7, R3960) Rowman.

Western Public Lands & Environmental Politics. Charles Davis. LC 96-48499. (C). 1997. text ed. 59.95 (0-8133-8947-X) Westview.

***Western Public Lands & Environmental Politics.** Ed. by Charles Davis. LC 96-48499. (C). 1997. pap. text ed. 18.95 (0-8133-2970-1) Westview.

Western Pulp Hero. Nick Carr. LC 87-18370. (Starmont Popular Culture Studies: No. 3). (Illus.). 134p. 1989. lib. bdg. 39.00 (1-55742-033-5) Borgo Pr.

***Western Quest.** Clifford G. Kershner. Date not set. pap. 7.95 (0-9656015-3-6) C G Kershner.

Western Question in Greece & Turkey: A Study in the Contrast of Civilizations. 2nd ed. Arnold J. Toynbee. LC 68-9598. (Illus.). 1970. reprint ed. 47.50 (0-86527-209-3) Fertig.

Western Quotations: Famous Words from the American West. Ed. by Richard Dillon. LC 93-72249. 176p. (Orig.). 1993. pap. 9.95 (0-9632377-1-3) Four Peaks.

Western Races & the World. Unity Ser. 5. Ed. by Francis S. Marvin. LC 68-22929. (Essay Index Reprint Ser.). 1977. reprint ed. 19.95 (0-8369-0684-5) Ayer.

Western Rajputana States: A Medico-Topographical & General Account of Marwar, Sirohi, Jaisalmir. (C). 1990. reprint ed. 74.00 (81-85326-36-3, Pub. by Vintage II) S Asia.

***Western Ranch Houses by Cliff May: A Sunset Book.** Cliff May & Sunset Magazine & Books Staff. (California Architecture & Architects Ser.: No. 9). (Illus.). 176p. 1997. pap. 39.95 (0-940512-04-1) Hennessey.

Western Range. U. S. Senate Staff. Ed. by Stuart Bruchey. LC 78-53570. (Development of Public Land Law in the U. S. Ser.). (Illus.). 1979. reprint ed. lib. bdg. 47.95 (0-405-11390-0) Ayer.

Western Range Livestock Industry. Marion Clawson. Ed. by Stuart Bruchey. LC 78-56713. (Management of Public Lands in the U. S. Ser.). (Illus.). 1979. reprint ed. lib. bdg. 31.95 (0-405-11326-9) Ayer.

Western Reader's Guide: A Selected Bibliography of Nonfiction Magazines, 1953-91. Compiled by James A. Browning. LC 92-35419. 360p. 1993. 29.95 (0-935269-09-6, Barbed Wire Pr) Western Pubns.

Western Rediscovery of the Japanese Language, 8 vols., Set. Ed. by Stefan Kaiser. 4600p. (C). 1995. text ed. 995.00 (0-7007-0316-0, Pub. by Curzon Press UK) UH Pr.

Western Region see Audubon Society Field Guide to North American Wildflowers

***Western Region Directory of INS Offices.** Contrib. by Norman C. Plotkin & Amy R. Novick. 180p. 1995. 35.00 (1-878677-92-6, PT602) Amer Immi Law Assn.

Western Religion: A Country by Country Sociological Inquiry. Ed. & Intro. by Hans Mol. (Religion & Reason Ser.: No. 2). (Illus.). 642p. 1972. text ed. 86.15 (90-279-7004-1) Mouton.

Western Religions. J. Campbell. 1997. pap. 12.00 (0-06-092476-4) HarpC.

Western Reports on Taiping. Clarke & Gregory. (Australian National University Press Ser.). 1996. pap. text ed. 18.00 (0-08-033003-7, Pergamon Pr) Elsevier.

Western Reports on Taiping. Clarke & Gregory. (Australian National University Press Ser.). 1999. text ed. 29.50 (0-08-033004-5, Pergamon Pr) Elsevier.

***Western Reptiles & Amphibians.** Stebbins. (Peterson Field Guide Ser.). 1996. 16.95 (0-614-30004-5) Serpents Tale.

Western Republicanism & the Oriental Prince. Patricia Springborg. LC 92-60170. 359p. 1992. text ed. 50.00 (0-292-77664-0) U of Tex Pr.

***Western Republicanism & the Oriental Prince.** Patrucua Springborg. 350p. 1996. 50.00 (0-614-21502-1, 1301) Kazi Pubns.

Western Reserve: The Story of New Connecticut in Ohio (1949) Harlan H. Hatcher. LC 91-10987. (Black Squirrel Bks.: No. 2). (Illus.). 360p. 1991. reprint ed. pap. 14.00 (0-87338-449-0) Kent St U Pr.

Western Reserve & the Fugitive Slave Law: A Prelude to the Civil War. William C. Cochran. LC 71-127273. 1972. reprint ed. 29.50 (0-306-71212-1) Da Capo.

Western Response to State-Supported Terrorism. Geoffrey M. Levitt. LC 86-418. (Washington Papers: No. 134). (Illus.). 160p. 1988. text ed. 39.95 (0-275-93021-1, C3021, Praeger Pubs); pap. text ed. 9.95 (0-275-93022-X, B3022, Praeger Pubs) Greenwood.

Western Response to Zoroaster. J. Duchesne-Guillemin. LC 72-9593. 112p. 1973. reprint ed. text ed. 49.75 (0-8371-6590-3, DUWR, Greenwood Pr) Greenwood.

Western Responses to Human Rights Abuses in Cambodia, 1975-80. Jamie Frederic Metzl. 256p. 1996. text ed. 59.95 (0-312-12849-5) St Martin.

Western Responses to Tanzanian Socialism 1967-83. Susan C. Crouch. 300p. 1987. text ed. 48.95 (0-566-05455-8, Pub. by Dartmth Pub UK) Ashgate Pub Co.

Western Responses to Terrorism. Ed. by Alex P. Schmid & Ronald D. Crelinsten. LC 93-9572. (Studies in Terrorism). 363p. 1993. 45.00 (0-7146-4521-4, Pub. by F Cass Pubs UK); pap. 22.50 (0-7146-4090-5, Pub. by F Cass Pubs UK) Intl Spec Bk.

Western Rider: A Computerized Simulation. 5th ed. Kenton E. Ross. (BA-Accounting-First Year Ser.). 1992. 15.95 (0-538-60639-8) S-W Pub.

Western Rider, Simplified with Narrative: Century 21, First Year. 5th ed. Kenton E. Ross. (BA-Accounting-First Year Ser.). 1992. 19.95 (0-538-60637-1) S-W Pub.

Western Riding. Charlene Strickland. 240p. 1995. pap. 24.95 (0-88266-890-0, Storey Pub) Storey Comm Inc.

Western Rights? Post-Communist Application. Andras Sajo. LC 96-8669. 386p. 1996. 155.00 (90-411-0263-9) Kluwer Law Tax Pubs.

***Western River Transportation: The Era of Early Internal Development, 1810-1860.** Erik F. Haites & Gary M. Walton. LC 75-12568. (Johns Hopkins University Studies in Historical & Political Science: 93rd Series. No. 2). 224p. 1975. reprint ed. pap. 63.90 (0-608-03686-2, 2064512) Bks Demand.

Western Rivermen, 1763-1861: Ohio & Mississippi Boatmen & the Myth of the Alligator Horse. Michael Allen. LC 90-5860. (Illus.). 261p. 1994. pap. 12.95 (0-8071-1907-5) La State U Pr.

Western Rivers License Primer. Ed. by Richard A. Block. (Illus.). 382p. (Orig.). 1994. pap. text ed. 45.00 (1-879778-34-3) Marine Educ.

Western Rocks & Minerals. Stan Leaming & Chris Leaming. (Illus.). 33p. (Orig.). 1980. pap. 4.95 (0-88839-053-X) Hancock House.

***Western Rose.** Alan Markell. 2140p. (Orig.). 1998. mass mkt. 13.99 (1-889501-94-8, Appaloosa) Sovereign.

Western Rose (March Madness) Lynna Banning. (Historical Ser.). 1996. mass mkt. 4.50 (0-373-28910-3, 1-28910-7) Harlequin Bks.

Western Roundup. David L. Jarrett et al. Ed. by William T. Crowe & Michael X. Zelenak. (Seminar Textbook Ser.). (Illus.). vi, 119p. (Orig.). 1990. pap. text ed. 14.95 (0-911989-21-8) Philatelic Found.

***Western Sahara.** Anthony G. Pazzanita. (World Bibliographical Ser.: Vol. 190). 259p. 1996. 64.75 (1-85109-256-0, DT346) ABC-CLIO.

Western Sahara: No Alternative to Armed Struggle. S. C. Saxena. iii, 311p. 1995. 29.00 (81-85163-59-6, Pub. by Kalinga Pubns) Nataraj Bks.

Western San Juan Mountains: Their Geology, Ecology, & Human History. Ed. by Rob Blair. LC 95-41819. (Illus.). 416p. 1996. 39.95 (0-87081-377-3); pap. text ed. 22.95 (0-87081-378-1) Univ Pr Colo.

Western Scientific Gaze & Popular Imagery in Later Edo Japan: The Lens Within the Heart. Timon Screech. (Studies in New Art History & Criticism). (Illus.). 352p. (C). 1996. text ed. 80.00 (0-521-46106-5) Cambridge U Pr.

Western Security: The Formative Years. Ed. by Olav Riste. LC 85-7795. 410p. 1985. text ed. 59.50 (0-231-06168-4) Col U Pr.

Western Security Community, 1948-1950: Common Problems & Conflicting Interests During the Foundation Phase of the North Atlantic Treaty Organization. Ed. by Norbert Wiggershaus & Roland G. Foerster. LC 92-25569. (Studies in Military History). 448p. 1993. 45.95 (0-85496-692-7) Berg Pubs.

Western Sephardim: Sephardi Heritage, Vol. 11. Ed. by Richard Barnett & Walter Schwab. (C). 1988. text ed. 150.00 (0-948466-11-1, Pub. by Gibraltar Bks UK) St Mut.

Western Series & Sequels. 2nd ed. Bernard A. Drew. LC 92-22569. 304p. 1993. text ed. 49.00 (0-8240-9648-7, H1399) Garland.

Western Settlers. O. J. Fargo. (Western History Ser.). (Illus.). 52p. (Orig.). 1990. pap. 1.50 (0-924702-27-3) Grn Valley Area.

Western Shoshoni Grammar. Jon Dayley & Beverly Crum. 300p. (C). 1994. pap. text ed. 24.95 (0-9639749-0-4) Boise St U Dept Anthrop.

Western Skies: Bird Hunting in the Rockies & on the Plains. John C. Barsness. LC 94-11159. 160p. 1994. 18.95 (1-55821-307-4) Lyons & Burford.

Western Skyline. Noel Peattie. 120p. (Orig.). 1995. pap. 11.95 (0-916147-72-X) Regent Pr.

Western Slave Coast & Its Rulers: European Trade & Administration among the Yoruba & Adja-Speaking Peoples of Southwestern Nigeria, Southern Dahomey & Togo. Colin W. Newbury. LC 83-12619. ix, 234p. 1983. reprint ed. text ed. 55.00 (0-313-23967-3, NEWE) Greenwood.

Western Societies: A Documentary History, Vol. I. Brian Tierney & Joan Scott. 525p. 1984. pap. text ed. write for info. (0-07-554255-2) McGraw.

Western Societies: A Documentary History, Vol. 2. Brian Tierney & Joan Scott. 599p. (C). 1984. pap. text ed. 15.95 (0-07-554257-9) McGraw.

Western Societies: Primary Sources in Social History, 2 vols., Vol. 1. Richard M. Golden. Ed. by Thomas Kuehn. LC 92-50038. (Illus.). 330p. (C). 1992. pap. text ed. 21.00 (0-312-08032-8) St Martin.

Western Societies: Primary Sources in Social History, 2 vols., Vol. 2. Richard M. Golden. Ed. by Thomas Kuehn. LC 92-50038. (Illus.). 364p. (C). 1992. pap. text ed. 21.00 (0-312-08031-X) St Martin.

Western Societies Concept of Women Spirituality. Ranft. Date not set. text ed. write for info. (0-312-15911-0) St Martin.

Western Society & Church. R. W. Southerm. 1990. pap. 13.95 (0-14-013755-6) Viking Penguin.

Western Society & the Church in the Middle Ages. Richard W. Southern. (History of the Church Ser.). (Orig.). 1970. pap. 8.95 (0-14-020503-9, Penguin Bks) Viking Penguin.

Western Society in Transition. Volker Bornschier. LC 96-389. 453p. 1996. text ed. 49.95 (1-56000-227-1) Transaction Pubs.

Western Society Since 1400, 5 Vols. McKay. (C). Date not set. suppl. ed., teacher ed., pap. write for info. (0-395-71725-6) HM.

Western Speakers: Voices of the American Dream. Ed. by Susan Koester. (Illus.). 96p. 1989. pap. text ed. 15.00 (0-89745-119-8) Sunflower U Pr.

Western Spirit: Exploring New Territory in American Art. David P. Curry. Ed. by Marlene Chambers. LC 89-50092. (Illus.). 116p. (Orig.). 1989. pap. 14.95 (0-914738-38-0) Denver Art Mus.

Western Spirituality: Historical Roots, Ecumenical Routes. Matthew Fox. LC 81-67364. 454p. 1981. reprint ed. pap. 16.00 (0-939680-01-7) Bear & Co.

Western Star. Bonnie Bryant. (The Saddle Club Super Edition Ser.: Vol. 3). 208p. (J). (gr. 3-7). 1995. pap. 3.99 (0-553-48270-X, Skylark BDD) BDD Bks Young Read.

Western State Terrorism. Ed. by Alexander L. George. 240p. (C). 1991. pap. 17.95 (0-415-90473-0, A6329, Routledge NY) Routledge.

Western State University Law Review: 1972-1995/96, 23 vols., Set. Bound set. 805.00 (0-8377-9186-3) Rothman.

Western States see Encyclopedia of Associations: Regional

Western Steelhead Fishing Guide. Milt Keizer. (Illus.). 144p. (Orig.). 1988. pap. 14.95 (0-936608-76-5) F Amato Pubns.

***Western Story.** Jon Tuska. 1997. 9.99 (0-517-18659-4) Random Hse Value.

***Western Story: A Chronological Treasury.** Jon Tuska. LC 97-17588. 1997. write for info. (0-15-749009-2, Sagebrush LP West) T T Beeler.

Western Story: A Chronological Treasury. Jon Tuska. LC 94-46857. xl, 404p. 1995. 35.00 (0-8032-4428-2) U of Nebr Pr.

Western Story: The Recollections of Charley O'Kieffe, 1884-1898. Charley O'Kieffe. LC 60-5381. (Pioneer Heritage Ser.: No. 2). 239p. 1974. reprint ed. pap. 68.20 (0-608-01396-X, 2062159) Bks Demand.

Western Streamside Guide. 2nd ed. Dave Hughes. (Illus.). 159p. (Orig.). 1987. reprint ed. pap. 12.95 (0-936608-59-5) F Amato Pubns.

Western Subarctic Prehistory. Donald W. Clark. (Canadian Prehistory Ser.). (Illus.). 162p. 1991. pap. 16.95 (0-660-12920-5, Pub. by Can Mus Civil CN) U of Wash Pr.

Western Sudan: Ghana, Mali, Songhay. Kenny Mann. 128p. 1995. 15.95 (0-87518-656-4, Dillon Silver Burdett) Silver Burdett Pr.

Western Sudan: Ghana, Mali, Songhay. Kenny Mann. (African Kingdoms of the Past Ser.). 128p. (YA). (gr. 5 up). 1995. pap. 7.95 (0-382-39176-4, Dillon Silver Burdett) Silver Burdett Pr.

Western Sunrise: The Genesis & Growth of Britain's Major High Tech Corridor. P. Hall et al. 192p. (C). 1987. text ed. 47.95 (0-04-338142-1) Routledge Chapman & Hall.

Western Surface Coal Mining, Gillette, Wyoming, May 3-5, 1989. Ed. by Steven J. Kirk. LC 89-60830. 157p. reprint ed. pap. 44.80 (0-8357-3415-3, 2039672) Bks Demand.

***Western Swing.** Andrew Hager. 1997. pap. 16.98 (1-56799-507-1) M Friedman Pub Grp Inc.

***Western Swing.** Andrew G. Hager. LC 97-5486. (Life, Times, & Music Ser.). 1997. pap. write for info. (1-56799-506-3, Friedman-Fairfax) M Friedman Pub Grp Inc.

***Western Swing.** Tim Sandlin. 352p. 1997. pap. 13.00 (1-57322-631-9, Riverhd Trade) Berkley Pub.

Western Swing: Adventures with the Heretical Buddha. Andrew Greig et al. (Illus.). 112p. 9500. pap. 16.95 (1-85224-268-X, Pub. by Bloodaxe Bks UK) Dufour.

Western Systems of Juvenile Justice. Ed. by Malcolm W. Klein. LC 83-19150. 240p. 1984. reprint ed. pap. 68.40 (0-608-01519-9, 2059563) Bks Demand.

Western Tales of Southern Colorado: To Know the West. 2nd ed. Thomas Mariano. (Illus.). 312p. 1991. pap. 13.95 (1-877637-03-3) Mariano Pub.

Western Technology & Soviet Economic Development, 1917-1930. Antony C. Sutton. LC 68-2442. (Publication Ser.: No. 76). 381p. 1968. 36.95 (0-8179-1791-8) Hoover Inst Pr.

Western Technology & Soviet Economic Development, 1930-1945. Antony C. Sutton. (Publication Ser.: No. 90). 387p. 1971. 15.00 (0-8179-1901-5) Hoover Inst Pr.

Western Technology & Soviet Economic Development, 1945-1965. Antony C. Sutton. (Publication Ser.: No. 113). 482p. 1973. 18.00 (0-8179-6131-3) Hoover Inst Pr.

Western Territories in the Civil War. Ed. by Leroy H. Fischer. 1977. pap. 8.00 (0-686-00373-X) AG Pr.

Western Theology. Wes Seeliger. LC 72-96685. 103p. 1985. reprint ed. pap. 6.95 (0-915321-00-9) Pioneer Vent.

***Western Thunder.** Freeda Brown. 1996. mass mkt. 5.99 (1-55197-027-9, Pub. by Comnwlth Pub CN) Partners Pubs Grp.

Western Tibet & the British Border Land. Charles Sherring. (C). 1994. 28.50 (81-206-0854-2, Pub. by Asian Educ Servs II) S Asia.

Western Times & Water Wars: State, Culture, & Rebellion in California. John Walton. (Illus.). 360p. 1991. 30.00 (0-520-07245-6) U CA Pr.

Western Times & Water Wars: State, Culture, & Rebellion in California. John Walton. (C). 1993. pap. 15.00 (0-520-08453-5) U CA Pr.

Western Townbuilders. O. J. Fargo. (Western History Ser.). (Illus.). 50p. (Orig.). 1990. pap. 1.50 (0-924702-28-1) Grn Valley Area.

Western Trade Pressure on the Soviet Union: An Interdependence Perspective on Sanctions. David W. Hunter. LC 91-8531. 176p. 1991. text ed. 49.95 (0-312-06216-8) St Martin.

Western Tradition. Davis et al. 1994. teacher ed., pap. text ed. write for info. (0-312-08123-5) St Martin.

Western Tradition, 2 vols., Vol. I, From the Ancient World to Louis XIV. 4th ed. Eugen Weber. 484p. (C). 1990. pap. text ed. 29.56 (0-669-20146-4) HM College Div.

Western Tradition, 2 vols., Vol. II, From the Renaissance to the Present. 4th ed. Eugen Weber. 937p. (C). 1990. pap. text ed. 29.56 (0-669-20147-2) HM College Div.

Western Tradition: Study Guide, Semester I & II. WGBH Educational Foundation Staff & Ray Boggis. 384p. (C). 1989. pap. text ed. 27.20 (0-02-426620-5, Macmillan Coll) P-H.

Western Tradition Vol. 1: From the Ancient World to Louis XIV. 5th ed. Eugen Weber. 496p. (C). 1995. pap. text ed. 29.56 (0-669-39442-4) HM College Div.

An Asterisk (*) at the beginning of an entry indicates that the title is appearing in BIP for the first time.

Western Tradition Vol. 2: From the Renaissance to the Present. 5th ed. Eugen Weber. 654p. (C). 1995. pap. text ed. 29.56 (*0-669-39443-2*) HM College Div.

***Western Tradition Administrative Handbook & Faculty Guide, Semester I.** 2nd ed. Jay Boggis. 208p. (C). 1996. pap. text ed. 23.40 (*0-13-496779-8*, Prentice Hall) P-H.

***Western Tradition Administrative Handbook & Faculty Guide, Semester II.** 2nd ed. Jay Boggis. 200p. (C). 1996. pap. text ed. 23.40 (*0-13-496787-9*, Prentice Hall) P-H.

Western Trail. Ralph H. Compton. 1992. mass mkt. 5.50 (*0-312-92901-3*) St Martin.

Western Trail. large type ed. Ralph Compton. (Niagara Large Print Ser.). 1996. 27.99 (*0-7089-5819-2*) Ulverscroft.

Western Trails. Ed. by Gary Bowen. (Orig.). 1996. mass mkt. 6.50 (*1-56333-477-1*, Badboy) Masquerade.

***Western Trails: A Collection of Short Stories.** Mary H. Austin. Ed. by Melody Graulich. LC 87-16501. (Western Literature Ser.). reprint ed. pap. 90.40 (*0-608-04564-0*, 2065303) Bks Demand.

Western Trails: A Collection of Short Stories by Mary Austin. Selected by Melody Graulich. LC 87-16501. (Western Literature Ser.). 320p. 1987. 24.95 (*0-87417-127-X*) U of Nev Pr.

Western Training Theory & Practice. Jack Brainard. 1990. pap. 12.95 (*0-911647-16-3*) Western Horseman.

Western Transportation. O. J. Fargo. (Western History Ser.). (Illus.). 63p. (Orig.). 1990. pap. 1.50 (*0-924702-19-2*) Grn Valley Area.

Western Travellers to Constantinople: The West & Byzantium, 962-1204: Cultural & Political Relations. Krijnie N. Ciggaar. LC 96-19020. (Medieval Mediterranean, x0928-5520 Ser.). (Illus.). 368p. 1996. 116.25 (*90-04-10637-5*) E J Brill.

Western Tree Book. George Palmer & Martha Stuckey. Ed. by Ken Bierly. (Illus.). 144p. 1987. reprint ed. pap. 8.95 (*0-911518-75-4*) Touchstone Oregon.

Western Trout Fly Tying Manual I. 2nd ed. Jack Dennis. 1991. spiral bd. 24.95 (*0-937556-02-5*) Snake River Bk.

Western Trout Fly Tying Manual II, Vol. 2. rev. ed. Jack Dennis. 1995. spiral bd. 34.95 (*0-937556-00-9*) Snake River Bk.

Western Turkey. Dana Facaros & Michael Pauls. (Cadogan City Guides Ser.). (Illus.). 384p. (Orig.). 1995. pap. 17.95 (*0-86011-005-2*) Globe Pequot.

Western Turkey. Dana Facaros. (Illus.). 384p. 1995. pap. 17.95 (*1-86011-005-3*, Pub. by Cadogan Bks UK) Globe Pequot.

Western Union. Zane Grey. 320p. 1991. mass mkt. 3.99 (*0-06-100222-4*, Harp PBks) HarpC.

Western United States. Ed. by Christine J. Dillon. (My First Report Ser.). (Illus.). 53p. (J). (gr. 1-3). 1994. pap. 5.95 (*0-913717-63-0*, 1999) Hewitt Res Fnd.

Western University on Trial. Ed. by John W. Chapman. LC 82-20120. 256p. (C). 1983. 38.00 (*0-520-04940-3*) U CA Pr.

Western Vengeance. Don Hepler. 1993. 17.95 (*0-8034-9008-9*) Bouregy.

Western Views of Islam in the Middle Ages. Richard W. Southern. 1962. 22.25 (*0-674-95055-0*) HUP.

Western Views of Islam in the Middle Ages. Richard W. Southern. LC 62-13270. 128p. 1978. 19.00 (*0-674-99558-9*) HUP.

Western Visions. Roger Gibbins & Sonia Arrison. 185p. 1995. pap. 14.95 (*1-55111-073-3*) Broadview Pr.

Western Wagon Trains. Tim McNeese. LC 91-42076. (Americans on the Move Ser.). (Illus.). 48p. (J). (gr. 5). 1993. lib. bdg. 11.95 (*0-89686-734-X*, Crstwood Hse) Silver Burdett Pr.

Western Wall. Menachem M. Kasher. 172p. 1972. 7.95 (*0-910818-03-7*) Judaica Pr.

***Western Wall.** Roman Safdie. 1997. 40.00 (*0-88363-197-0*) H L Levin.

Western Wall (Hakotel) Meir Ben-Dov et al. 248p. (ENG & GER.). 1995. 19.00 (*965-05-0053-7*, Pub. by Israel Ministry Def IS) Gefen Bks.

Western Waltz. (Ballroom Dance Ser.). 1986. lib. bdg. 75.00 (*0-8490-3298-9*) Gordon Pr.

Western Waltz. (Ballroom Dance Ser.). 1985. lib. bdg. 58.00 (*0-87700-752-7*) Revisionist Pr.

Western Washington Treaty Proceedings. Robert B. Lane & Barbara Lane. (Treaty Manuscripts Ser.: No. 2). 67p. 12.50 (*0-944253-24-5*) Inst Dev Indian Law.

Western Water Made Simple. High Country News Staff. LC 87-17222. (Illus.). 231p. (Orig.). 1987. pap. 15.95 (*0-933280-39-4*) Island Pr.

Western Way. Caitlin Matthews & John Matthews. 480p. 1995. pap. 12.95 (*0-14-019462-2*, Arkana) Viking Penguin.

Western Way of Meditation: The Rosary Revisited. David B. Bryan. Ed. by Daniel Flaherty. LC 91-14245. 216p. 1991. pap. 10.95 (*0-8294-0715-4*) Loyola Pr.

Western Way of War: Infantry Battle in Classical Greece. Victor D. Hanson. 260p. 1990. pap. 12.95 (*0-19-506588-3*) OUP.

Western Ways to the Center: An Introduction to Religions of the West. 2nd ed. Denise L. Carmody & John T. Carmody. 296p. (C). 1991. pap. 37.95 (*0-534-13980-9*) Wadsworth Pub.

Western Whitewater from the Rockies to the Pacific: A River Guide for Raft, Kayak, & Canoe. Jim Cassady et al. (Illus.). 590p. (Orig.). 1994. pap. 34.95 (*0-9613650-4-8*) North Fork Pr.

Western Wind. Paula Fox. 208p. (J). (gr. 4-7). 1995. pap. 3.99 (*0-440-40991-8*) Dell.

Western Wind. Paula Fox. LC 93-9629. 208p. (YA). (gr. 5 up). 1993. 16.95 (*0-531-06802-1*); lib. bdg. 17.99 (*0-531-08652-6*) Orchard Bks Watts.

Western Wind: An Introduction to Poetry. 3rd ed. Ed. by John F. Nims. 1992. text ed. write for info. (*0-07-046574-6*) McGraw.

Western Window in the Arab World. Leon B. Blair. LC 78-131423. 350p. reprint ed. pap. 99.80 (*0-318-34942-6*, 2030736) Bks Demand.

Western Wizard. Mickey Z. Reichert. (Renshai Trilogy Ser.: Bk. 2). 640p. (Orig.). 1992. mass mkt. 5.99 (*0-88677-520-5*) DAW Bks.

Western Women: Their Land, Their Lives. Ed. by Lillian Schlissel et al. LC 88-10717. (Illus.). 360p. 1988. pap. 16.95 (*0-8263-1090-7*) U of NM Pr.

Western Women & Imperialism: Complicity & Resistance. Ed. by Nupur Chaudhuri & Margaret Strobel. LC 91-809. (Illus.). 288p. 1992. text ed. 39.95 (*0-253-31341-4*); pap. text ed. 15.95 (*0-253-20705-3*, MB-705) Ind U Pr.

Western Women in Colonial Africa. Caroline Oliver. LC 81-24194. (Contributions in Comparative Colonial Studies: No. 12). xv, 201p. 1982. text ed. 49.95 (*0-313-23388-8*, OWA/, Greenwood Pr) Greenwood.

Western Women Working in Japan: Breaking Corporate Barriers. Nancy K. Napier & Sully Taylor. LC 95-9841. 256p. 1995. text ed. 59.95 (*0-89930-901-1*, Quorum Bks) Greenwood.

Western Woods Use Book: Incl. 1996 Edition; Completely Revised & Updated. 3rd rev. ed. LC 73-77089. (Illus.). 314p. (C). 1996. 60.00 (*0-9600912-2-X*) Western Wood.

***Western Words: A Dictionary of the Old West.** Ramon Adams. (Illus.). 182p. 1997. pap. 11.95 (*0-7818-0590-2*) Hippocrene Bks.

Western World, Vol. 1. 2nd ed. Esler. 1996. pap. text ed. 21.33 (*0-13-495607-9*) P-H.

Western World, Vol. 2. Moczar. 1994. student ed., pap. text ed. 20.40 (*0-13-946740-8*) P-H.

Western World, Vol. 2. 2nd ed. Esler. 1996. pap. text ed. 21.33 (*0-13-495615-X*) P-H.

Western World: Or, Travels in the United States in 1846-47. Alexander Mackay. LC 68-55900. 1970. reprint ed. text ed. 45.00 (*0-8371-0549-8*, MAWF, Greenwood Pr) Greenwood.

Western World: Or, Travels in the United States in 1846-47, Vol. 2. Alexander Mackay. LC 68-55900. 1970. reprint ed. text ed. 45.00 (*0-8371-0823-3*, MAWG, Greenwood Pr) Greenwood.

Western World: Or, Travels in the United States in 1846-47, Vol. 3. Alexander Mackay. LC 68-55900. 1970. reprint ed. text ed. 45.00 (*0-8371-0824-1*, MAWH, Greenwood Pr) Greenwood.

Western World: Prehistory to the Present. Anthony Esler. LC 93-13253. 1148p. 1993. text ed. 69.33 (*0-13-946674-6*) P-H Gen Ref & Trav.

Western World: Volume 2, Vol. 1. Moczar. 1994. student ed., pap. text ed. 20.40 (*0-13-946724-6*) P-H.

Western World Vol. I: Prehistory to 1715. Anthony Esler. (Illus.). 544p. (C). 1993. pap. text ed. 53.00 (*0-13-946716-5*) P-H.

Western World Vol. II: 1600s to Present. Anthony Esler. (Illus.). 656p. (C). 1993. pap. text ed. 53.00 (*0-13-946732-7*) P-H.

Western World Combined. 2nd ed. Esler. LC 96-44445. 1996. pap. text ed. 28.00 (*0-13-495623-0*) P-H.

Western World, or Travels in the United States in 1846-47, 3 vols. 2nd ed. Alexander Mackay. LC 68-55900. (Illus.). 1970. reprint ed. text ed. 95.00 (*0-8371-2586-3*, MAWE, Greenwood Pr) Greenwood.

***Western Writers of America: A Saddlebag of Tales.** Ed. by Rutherford Montgomery. (Illus.). Date not set. write for info. (*0-8369-4140-3*) Ayer.

Western Zhou Ritaul Bronzes see Ancient Chinese Bronzes: In the Arthur M. Sackler Collections

***Westerners: A Roundup of Pioneer Reminiscences.** annot. ed. Anno. & Compiled by John M. Myers. LC 97-1510. xviii, 258p. 1997. pap. 13.00 (*0-8032-8236-2*, Bison Books) U of Nebr Pr.

Westerners in Gray: The Men & Missions of the Elite Fifth Missouri Infantry Regiment. Phillip T. Tucker. LC 94-27036. 341p. 1994. lib. bdg. 36.00 (*0-7864-0016-1*) McFarland & Co.

Westernization & Human Welfare. Maryam Jameelah. 95p. (Orig.). 1985. pap. 3.50 (*1-56744-423-7*) Kazi Pubns.

Westernization of Asia: A Comparative Political Analysis. Frank C. Darling. 320p. 1980. pap. text ed. 24.95 (*0-87073-971-9*) Transaction Pubs.

Westernization of the World: The Significance, Scope & Limits of the Drive Towards Global Uniformity. Serge Latouche. Tr. by Rosemary Morris from FRE. 160p. (C). 1996. text ed. 52.95 (*0-7456-1428-0*, Pub. by Polity Pr UK); pap. text ed. 23.95 (*0-7456-1429-9*, Pub. by Polity Pr UK) Blackwell Pubs.

Westernization vs. Muslims. Maryam Jameelah. 66p. (Orig.). 1985. pap. 3.50 (*1-56744-424-5*) Kazi Pubns.

Westernized Yankee: The Story of Cyrus Woodman. Larry Gara. LC 56-14602. (Illus.). 254p. 1956. 7.50 (*0-87020-032-1*) State Hist Soc Wis.

Westernizing the Third World: Eurocentricity of Economic Development Theories. Ozay Mehmet. LC 94-33805. (Illus.). 208p. (C). 1995. pap. 18.95 (*0-415-11829-8*, C0090) Routledge.

Westernizing the Third World: Eurocentricity of Economic Development Theories. Ozay Mehmet. LC 94-33805. (Illus.). 208p. (C). (gr. 13). 1995. text ed. 59.95 (*0-415-11828-X*, C0089) Routledge.

Westerns. Richard Dankleff. LC 83-21979. 96p. 1984. pap. 8.95 (*0-87071-340-X*) Oreg St U Pr.

Westerns: Making the Man in Fiction & Film. Lee C. Mitchell. 352p. 1996. 29.95 (*0-226-53234-8*) U Ch Pr.

Westerns of the Redrock Country: Forty-Three Movies Filmed in Sedona. Bob Bradshaw. 1991. 9.95 (*0-9629319-0-X*) Bradshaw Color.

Westerns of the 40's. Ed. by Damon Knight. LC 77-76880. 1977. 12.50 (*0-672-52036-2*, Bobbs) Macmillan.

Westerwald to America: Some Eighteenth Century German Immigrants. Annette K. Burgert & Henry Z. Jones, Jr. LC 89-60829. 284p. 1990. 29.95 (*0-929539-32-X*, 1132) Picton Pr.

Westfalians. Walter D. Kamphoefner. (Illus.). 240p. 1987. text ed. 45.00 (*0-691-04746-4*) Princeton U Pr.

Westfield, MA. Westfield Athenaeum Staff. (Images of America Ser.). 1996. pap. 16.99 (*0-7524-0451-2*, Arcdia) Chalford.

***Westfield, Mass., & Its Historical Influences, 1669-1919: The Life of an Early Town, with a Survey of Events in New England & Bordering Regions to Which It Was Related in Colonial & Revolutionary Times, 2 vols., Set.** John H. Lockwood. 1996. reprint ed. lib. bdg. 119.00 (*0-8328-5209-0*) Higginson Bk Co.

Westfield, NJ. Stan Lipson. (Images of America Ser.). 128p. 1996. pap. 16.99 (*0-7524-0406-7*, Arcdia) Chalford.

Westford, MA. E. Harde & B. Shaw. (Images of America Ser.). 128p. 1996. pap. 16.99 (*0-7524-0412-1*, Arcdia) Chalford.

***Westforth Architects: New York Calls Bucharest.** Maurizio Vitta. 1997. pap. text ed. 29.99 (*88-7838-018-0*, Pub. by Yeol-rin Munhwa KO) Consort Bk Sales.

Westgermanische Bodenfunde des Ersten bis Dritten Jahrhunderts N. Ch. aus Mittel-und Westdeutschland, 2 vols. Rafael Von Uslar. (Illus.). (C). 1978. 284.60 (*3-11-002250-8*) De Gruyter.

Westhill Project - Christians: Pupils Book 1. (C). 1987. text ed. 35.00 (*0-86158-694-8*, Pub. by S Thornes Pubs UK) St Mut.

Westhill Project - Christians: Pupils Book 2. G. Read. (C). 1987. text ed. 40.00 (*1-871402-34-4*, Pub. by S Thornes Pubs UK) St Mut.

Westhill Project - Christians: Pupils Book 3. G. Read. (C). 1987. text ed. 35.00 (*0-86158-696-4*, Pub. by S Thornes Pubs UK) St Mut.

Westhill Project - How Do I Teach R. E? G. Read. (C). 1986. text ed. 70.00 (*0-86158-894-0*, Pub. by S Thornes Pubs UK) St Mut.

Westhill Project - Islam: Photopack. G. Read. (C). 1988. text ed. 190.00 (*1-85234-072-X*, Pub. by S Thornes Pubs UK) St Mut.

Westhill Project - Islam: Teacher's Manual. G. Read. (C). 1988. text ed. 95.00 (*1-85234-071-1*, Pub. by S Thornes Pubs UK) St Mut.

Westhill Project - Jews: Pupils Book 1. M. Austerberry. (C). 1990. text ed. 45.00 (*1-871402-19-0*, Pub. by Stanley Thornes UK) Trans-Atl Phila.

Westhill Project - Jews: Pupils Book 2. M. Austerberry. (C). 1990. text ed. 35.00 (*0-685-39400-X*, Pub. by Stanley Thornes UK) Trans-Atl Phila.

Westhill Project - Jews: Pupils Book 3. G. Read. (C). 1990. text ed. 35.00 (*1-871402-20-4*, Pub. by Stanley Thornes UK) Trans-Atl Phila.

Westhill Project - Jews: Pupils Book 4. G. Read. (C). 1990. text ed. 50.00 (*1-871402-21-2*, Pub. by Stanley Thornes UK) Trans-Atl Phila.

Westhill Project - Judaism: Photopack. G. Read. (C). 1990. text ed. 190.00 (*1-871402-22-0*, Pub. by Stanley Thornes UK) Trans-Atl Phila.

Westhill Project - Life Themes in the Early Years - Pack 1. G. Read. (C). 1990. text ed. 350.00 (*1-871402-24-7*, Pub. by Stanley Thornes UK) Trans-Atl Phila.

Westhill Project - Life Themes in the Early Years - Pack 2. G. Read. (C). 1990. text ed. 350.00 (*1-871402-25-5*, Pub. by Stanley Thornes UK) Trans-Atl Phila.

Westhill Project - Life Themes in the Early Years - Pack 3. G. Read. (C). 1990. text ed. 350.00 (*1-871402-26-3*, Pub. by Stanley Thornes UK) Trans-Atl Phila.

Westhill Project - Muslims: Pupils Book 1. G. Read. (C). 1988. text ed. 42.00 (*1-85234-073-8*, Pub. by S Thornes Pubs UK) St Mut.

Westhill Project - Muslims: Pupils Book 2. G. Read. (C). 1988. text ed. 42.00 (*1-85234-074-6*, Pub. by S Thornes Pubs UK) St Mut.

Westhill Project - Muslims: Pupils Book 3. G. Read. (C). 1988. text ed. 42.00 (*1-85234-075-4*, Pub. by S Thornes Pubs UK) St Mut.

Westhill Project Judaism: Teacher's Manual. G. Read. (C). 1990. text ed. 95.00 (*1-871402-23-9*, Pub. by Stanley Thornes UK) Trans-Atl Phila.

Westies. T. J. English. 1991. mass mkt. 5.95 (*0-312-92429-1*) St Martin.

Westies: From Head to Tail. 2nd rev. ed. Ruth Faherty. (Illus.). 232p. 1986. 29.95 (*0-931866-44-8*) Alpine Pubns.

Westies Today. Derek Tattersall. (Illus.). 160p. 1992. pap. 25.95 (*0-87605-353-3*) Howell Bk.

Westing Game. Ellen Raskin. (Illus.). 192p. (YA). (gr. 7 up). 1984. pap. 3.50 (*0-380-67991-4*, Flare) Avon.

Westing Game. Ellen Raskin. (J). (gr. 5-9). 1978. pap. 15.99 (*0-525-42320-6*) Dutton Child Bks.

Westing Game. Ellen Raskin. 192p. (J). (gr. 5 up). 1992. pap. 4.99 (*0-14-034991-X*) Puffin Bks.

***Westing Game.** Ellen Raskin. (J). 1997. pap. 4.99 (*0-14-038664-5*) Viking Penguin.

Westing Game: A Study Guide. Beatrice G. Davis. (Novel-Ties Ser.). 1984. lab manual ed., teacher ed., pap. text ed. 15.95 (*0-88122-096-5*) Lrn Links.

Westinghouse Electric Corp. A Report on the Company's Environmental Policies & Practices. (Illus.). 50p. (C). 1994. reprint ed. pap. text ed. 250.00 (*0-7881-0932-4*, Coun on Econ) DIANE Pub.

Westinghouse Electric Railway Transportation: Bulletin No. 118. LC 78-74493. (Illus.). 384p. 1979. 23.00 (*0-915348-18-7*) Central Electric.

Westinghouse Equipped Cars. 1984. 6.95 (*0-912113-08-1*) Railhead Pubns.

Westinghouse Equipped Diesel-Electric. 100p. 10.95 (*0-912113-11-1*) Railhead Pubns.

***Westinghouse Roller & Gear Pitting Tests.** S. Way. (Technical Papers). 1940. pap. text ed. 30.00 (*1-55589-452-6*) AGMA.

Westland Aircraft since Nineteen-Fifteen. Derek N. James. LC 91-62369. (Putnam Aviation Ser.). (Illus.). 512p. 1992. 49.95 (*1-55750-921-2*) Naval Inst Pr.

Westlaw Access Guide for the IBM 3101 Terminal: Basic User Training. West Publishing Company Editorial Staff. 28p. 1981. write for info. (*0-314-62803-7*) West Pub.

Westlaw for Law Students. 2nd ed. West Publishing Company Editorial Staff. LC 85-228463. 1985. write for info. (*0-314-95833-9*) West Pub.

Westlaw Reference Manual. West Publishing Company Editorial Staff. 60p. 1981. pap. text ed. write for info. (*0-314-62801-0*) West Pub.

Westliche Hunsrueck-Eifel-Kultur: Text-Vol. & Vol. with Plates. A. Haffner. (Roemisch-Germanische Forschungen Ser.: Vol. 36). (Illus.). (C). 1976. 226.95 (*3-11-004889-2*) De Gruyter.

Westmark. Lloyd Alexander. 192p. (J). (gr. 5-9). 1982. pap. 3.99 (*0-440-99731-3*, LLL BDD) BDD Bks Young Read.

Westminster - Its Location & Advantages as a Place of Residence or for Business Including a Directory. By Vanderford. Publishers of the Democratic Advocate Jan. 1, 1887. Intro. by Jay A. Graybeal. LC 96-76304. 80p. 1996. reprint ed. pap. write for info. (*1-886742-25-1*) Hist Soc Carroll.

Westminster Abbey & Its People c.1050 - c.1216. Emma Mason. (Studies in the History of Medieval Religion: No. 9). (Illus.). 387p. 1996. 81.00 (*0-85115-396-8*) Boydell & Brewer.

Westminster Abbey & the King's Craftsmen. William R. Lethaby. LC 69-13243. (Illus.). 398p. 1972. reprint ed. 27.95 (*0-405-08745-4*, Pub. by Blom Pubns UK) Ayer.

Westminster Abbey & the Plantagenets: Kingship & the Representation of Power, 1200-1400. Paul Binski. 1995. 60.00 (*0-300-05980-9*) Yale U Pr.

Westminster Abbey Re-Examined. William R. Lethaby. LC 69-13244. (Illus.). 306p. 1972. reprint ed. 27.95 (*0-405-08744-6*, Pub. by Blom Pubns UK) Ayer.

Westminster Alice. Saki. 16.95 (*0-8488-0844-4*) Amereon Ltd.

Westminster & Europe: The Impact of the European Union on the Westminster Parliament. Ed. by Philip Giddings & Gavin Drewry. 378p. 1996. text ed. 75.00 (*0-312-15964-1*) St Martin.

Westminster Assembly: A Guide to Basic Bibliography. David W. Hall & J. Ligon Duncan, III. 24p. (C). 1994. reprint ed. pap. text ed. 4.95 (*1-884416-01-2*) A Press.

Westminster Benedictional: Variable Pontifical Blessings from the Missal of Abbot Nicholas of Westminster for the Hierarchical Celebration of Sarum Mass. Ed. by Francis. 64p. (Orig.). 1989. pap. 10.00 (*0-923864-02-4*) St Hilarion Pr.

***Westminster Bible Commentary Matthew.** Thomas G. Long. 1997. pap. text ed. 20.00 (*0-664-25257-5*) Westminster John Knox.

Westminster Catechism in Modern English. Douglas Kelly & Philip Rollinson. LC 86-22592. 1986. pap. 1.75 (*0-87552-548-2*, Pub. by Evangelical Pr) Presby & Reformed.

Westminster Cathedral 1895-1995. Peter Doyle. 192p. 1995. 25.95 (*0-225-66684-7*, Pub. by Geoffrey Chapman UK) Morehouse Pub.

Westminster Colony, California 1869-1879. Ivana F. Bollman. LC 83-82983. (Illus.). 152p. 1983. 13.50 (*0-943480-56-6*) Friis-Pioneer Pr.

Westminster Concise Bible Dictionary. Barbara Smith. LC 80-25771. (Illus.). 188p. 1981. pap. 12.00 (*0-664-24363-0*, Westminster) Westminster John Knox.

Westminster Confession of Faith: A Modern Study Edition. Ed. by John H. Ball, III & Philip Rollinson. v, 53p. (Orig.). 1991. pap. text ed. 4.00 (*0-9614303-4-6*) Summertown.

Westminster Confession of Faith: A Study Guide. G. I. Williamson. LC 65-13464. 1964. pap. 9.99 (*0-87552-538-5*, Pub. by Evangelical Pr) Presby & Reformed.

Westminster Confession of Faith: An Authentic Modern Version. 2nd rev. ed. Pref. by L. Edward Davis. x, 89p. 1985. pap. text ed. write for info. (*0-9614303-1-1*) Summertown.

Westminster Confession of Faith: An Authentic Modern Version. 3rd ed. Ed. by Douglas F. Kelly et al. xii, 107p. 1992. pap. text ed. 7.95 (*0-9614303-5-4*) Summertown.

Westminster Confession of Faith: The Preparation & Printing of Its Seven Leading Editions & a Critical Text. S. W. Carruthers. (C). pap. 8.95 (*1-884416-12-8*, Reformed Acad Pr) A Press.

Westminster Dictionary of Christian Ethics. rev. ed. Ed. by James F. Childress & John Macquarrie. LC 85-22539. 704p. 1986. 37.00 (*0-664-20940-8*, Westminster) Westminster John Knox.

Westminster Dictionary of Christian Spirituality. Ed. by Gordon S. Wakefield. LC 83-14527. 416p. 1983. 30.00 (*0-664-21396-0*, Westminster) Westminster John Knox.

Westminster Dictionary of Christian Theology. Ed. by Alan Richardson & John Bowden. LC 83-14521. 632p. 1983. 32.00 (*0-664-21398-7*, Westminster) Westminster John Knox.

Westminster Dictionary of Theological Terms. Donald K. McKim. LC 96-21588. 320p. (Orig.). 1996. pap. 20.00 (*0-664-25511-6*) Westminster John Knox.

***Westminster Dictionary of Theological Terms.** Donald K. McKim. 320p. (Orig.). 1996. 33.00 (*0-664-22089-4*) Westminster John Knox.

Westminster Guide to the Books of the Bible. William M. Ramsay. 608p. 1994. 30.00 (*0-664-22061-4*) Westminster John Knox.

W

Westminster Hall: Or Professional Relics & Anecdotes of the Bar, Bench, & Woolsack, 3 vols., Set. 944p. reprint ed. lib. bdg. 150.00 (*0-8377-2720-0*) Rothman.

Westminster Historical Maps of Bible Lands. Ed. by G. Ernest Wright & Floyd V. Filson. 24p. 1952. pap. 5.00 (*0-664-29077-9*, Westminster) Westminster John Knox.

Westminster Hymnal. Ed. by W. S. Bainbridge. (Illus.). 452p. 1996. pap. 12.95 (*0-912141-40-9*) Roman Cath Bks.

Westminster Hymnal. 468p. 1995. reprint ed. 29.95 (*0-912141-26-3*) Roman Cath Bks.

Westminster Inc. A Survey of Three States in the Eighties. Ed. by Allan Peachment. 225p. 1995. pap. 39.00 (*1-86287-164-7*, Pub. by Federation Pr AU) Gaunt.

Westminster Kennel Club Winners Book '96. Westminster Kennel Club Staff. (Illus.). 192p. 1996. 35.95 (*0-7938-1897-4*, TS264) TFH Pubns.

***Westminster Kennel Club Winners 1997.** (Illus.). 192p. 1997. 35.95 (*0-7938-1898-2*, TS-265) TFH Pubns.

Westminster Pulpit: Commemorative Edition, 5 vols. G. Campbell Morgan. 1995. 150.00 (*0-8010-1105-1*) Baker Bks.

Westminster Shorter Catechism with Cartoons. Vic Lockman. (Illus.). 140p. (Orig.). 1996. pap. 19.95 (*0-936175-28-1*) V Lockman.

Westminster West. Jessie Haas. LC 96-7096. 176p. (J). (gr. 5 up). 1997. 15.00 (*0-688-14883-2*) Greenwillow.

Westminster, Whitehall & the Vatican: The Role of Cardinal Hinsley 1935-43. Thomas Moloney. 264p. 1994. 36.00 (*0-86012-138-0*, Pub. by Srch Pr UK) St Mut.

Westminster Workshop: A Student's Guide to British Government. R. K. Mosley. 249p. 1985. pap. text ed. 20.00 (*0-08-031835-5*, Pergamon Pr) Elsevier.

Westminster's Confession: The Abandonment of Van Til's Legacy. Gary North. LC 91-7200. 385p. 1991. 14.95 (*0-930464-54-0*) Inst Christian.

Westminster's World: Understanding Political Roles. Donald D. Setting. LC 93-25088. 512p. 1994. text ed. 49.95 (*0-674-95072-0*) HUP.

Westmoreland: A Biography of General William C. Westmoreland. Samuel Zaffiri. 1995. pap. 15.00 (*0-688-14345-8*) Hearst Bks.

Westmoreland & Portland Places: The History & Architecture of America's Premier Private Streets, 1888-1988. Julius K. Hunter. LC 87-38079. (Illus.). 220p. (C). 1988. 49.95 (*0-8262-0677-8*) U of Mo Pr.

Westmoreland County: Virginia Publick Claims. Janice L. Abercrombie & Richard Slatten. (Virginia Publick Claims Ser.). ix, 21p. 1992. pap. 5.00 (*0-8095-8711-4*) Borgo Pr.

Westmoreland County: Virginia Publick Claims. Janice L. Abercrombie & Richard Slatten. (Virginia Publick Claims Ser.). ix, 21p. (C). 1992. reprint ed. lib. bdg. 25.00 (*0-8095-8367-4*) Borgo Pr.

Westmoreland County, PA Cemeteries, 7. Bob Closson & Mary Closson. 67p. per. 7.50 (*0-933227-15-9*) Closson Pr.

***Westmoreland County (PA) Court Rules.** Ed. by Thomas Davies. 176p. (Orig.). 1996. per. 52.50 (*1-57786-000-4*) Legal Communs.

Westmoreland County, PA in the American Revolution. Paul W. Myers. 263p. (Orig.). 1989. pap. text ed. 24.00 (*1-55856-001-7*) Closson Pr.

Westmoreland County, Pennsylvania, Deeds, 1773-1784. T. L.C. Genealogy Staff. 200p. (Orig.). 1995. spiral bd., pap. 16.00 (*1-57445-016-6*) TLC Genealogy.

Westmoreland County, Virginia: Records, Vol. 23. Beverly Fleet. 104p. 1985. reprint ed. pap. 15.00 (*0-89308-393-3*) Southern Hist Pr.

Westmoreland Glass: Identification & Value Guide. Charles W. Wilson. 256p. 1996. 24.95 (*0-89145-707-0*, 4656) Collector Bks.

***Westmoreland Glass (1888-1940)** Lorraine Kovar. (Illus.). 250p. 1997. write for info. (*1-57080-018-9*); pap. write for info. (*1-57080-017-0*) Antique Pubns.

Westmoreland Glass, 1950-1984, Vol. 2. Lorraine Kovar. (Illus.). 120p. (Orig.). 1992. 37.95 (*0-915410-81-8*, 4025); pap. 29.95 (*0-915410-80-X*, 4024) Antique Pubns.

Westmoreland Ne Neville. rev. ed. Mapes Monde Staff. (Illus.). 226p. (Orig.). 1995. pap. 32.00 (*0-7884-0261-7*) Heritage Bk.

Westmoreland Nee Neville. Olin V. Mapes. (Orig.). 1992. pap. 28.50 (*1-55613-615-3*) Heritage Bk.

Westmorelnd Glass: 1950-1984. Lorraine Kovar. (Illus.). 200p. (Orig.). 1991. 29.95 (*0-915410-79-6*, 4020); pap. 21.95 (*0-915410-78-8*, 4019) Antique Pubns.

Westmorland, a Bran New Wark see English Dialect Society Publications, No. 25: Specimens of English Dialects

Westnordisches Obligationenrecht see Nordgermanisches Obligationenrecht

***Weston: The Forging of a Connecticut Town.** rev. ed. Thomas J. Farnham. LC 79-14521. (Illus.). 1996. 30.00 (*0-614-30733-3*) Phoenix Pub.

Weston: Three Generations of American Photography. Photos by Edward Weston et al. (Illus.). 100p. 1995. 29.95 (*3-905514-40-0*) Dist Art Pubs.

***Weston - In Memoriam: My Father & Mother, Hon. Gershom Bradford Weston & Deborah Brownell Weston of Duxbury, Mass.: Memoirs of Capt. Ezra Weston (I), Ezra Weston (II), Gershom Bradford Weston, Alden Bradford Weston, Ezra Weston (IV) & Deborah Brownell Weston.** Edmund B. Weston. (Illus.). 93p. 1996. reprint ed. pap. 18.00 (*0-8328-5294-5*) Higginson Bk Co.

***Weston - In Memoriam: My Father & Mother, Hon. Gershom Bradford Weston & Deborah Brownell Weston of Duxbury, Mass.: Memoirs of Capt. Ezra Weston (I), Ezra Weston (II), Gershom Bradford Weston, Alden Bradford Weston, Ezra Weston (IV) & Deborah Brownell Weston.** Edmund B. Weston. (Illus.). 93p. 1996. reprint ed. lib. bdg. 28.00 (*0-8328-5293-7*) Higginson Bk Co.

Weston Manufacturing. Bettner. Date not set. pap. text ed. 12.00 (*0-314-03804-3*) West Pub.

***Weston Women.** Grace Thompson. (Pendragon Islan Ser.: No. 2). 320p. 1996. 24.00 (*0-7278-5176-4*) Severn Hse.

Weston's Weston: Portraits & Nudes. Theodore E. Stebbins, Jr. (Illus.). 140p. 1994. 60.00 (*0-8212-2142-6*) Bulfinch Pr.

Weston's Westons: California & the West. Theodore E. Stebbins, Jr. & Karen E. Quinn. (Illus.). 140p. 1994. 60.00 (*0-8212-2143-4*) Bulfinch Pr.

Weston's Westons: Portraits & Nudes. Theodore E. Stebbins, Jr. Ed. by Cynthia M. Purvis. (Illus.). 1990. text ed. 39.95 (*0-87846-317-8*); pap. text ed. 24.95 (*0-87846-312-7*) Mus Fine Arts Boston.

Westover Manuscripts. William Byrd. (Works of William Byrd). 1989. reprint ed. lib. bdg. 79.00 (*0-7812-2233-8*) Rprt Serv.

Westphal's "Die Agoraphobie" with Commentary: The Beginnings of Agoraphobia. Terry J. Knapp & Michael T. Schumacher. LC 88-56. (Illus.). 114p. (Orig.). (C). 1988. pap. text ed. 14.50 (*0-8191-6888-2*); lib. bdg. 32.00 (*0-8191-6887-4*) U Pr of Amer.

Westport: Missouri's Port of Many Returns. Patricia C. Miller. LC 83-17523. (Illus.). 128p. 1983. 15.00 (*0-913504-82-3*) Lowell Pr.

***Westport & Weston.** Ene T. Bonnyay. (Illus.). 80p. 1997. 24.95 (*0-9655360-0-9*) Drumgarth LLC.

***Westray: The Long Way Home.** Ken Schwartz & Chris O'Neill. 64p. 1997. 10.95 (*0-921368-68-2*, Pub. by Blizzard Pub CN) Genl Dist Srvs.

***West's American Government.** 2nd ed. Miller. (Social Studies). Date not set. pap. 69.95 (*0-314-14116-2*) S-W Pub.

Wests & the Rays & Allied Lines: Southern Families from the Colonies to Texas. Nan O. West. (Illus.). 476p. 1991. 40.00 (*0-9633463-1-8*) N O West.

West's Annotated California Codes. write for info. (*0-318-57491-8*) West Pub.

West's Annotated Indiana Code. write for info. (*0-318-57495-0*) West Pub.

West's Atlantic Digest. 2nd ed. West Publishing Company Editorial Staff. 1984. write for info. (*0-318-58312-7*) West Pub.

West's Business & Personal Law. Donald L. Carper et al. LC 92-45780. 1993. text ed. 53.25 (*0-314-01391-1*) West Pub.

***West's Business Law.** 7th ed. Clarkson. (LA - Business Law Ser.). (C). 1998. student ed., pap. 27.95 (*0-538-87980-7*); student ed., pap. 27.95 (*0-538-87981-5*) S-W Pub.

***West's Business Law.** 7th ed. Clarkson. LC 97-25028. (C). 1998. text ed. 137.25 (*0-538-87979-3*) Wadsworth Pub.

West's Business Law: Alternate Edition - Text, Summarized Cases, Legal, Ethical, Regulatory, & International Environment. 5th rev. ed. Gaylord A. Jentz et al. Ed. by Clyde Perlee. LC 92-24124. 900p. (C). 1993. text ed. 65.25 (*0-314-00997-3*) West Pub.

West's Business Law: Legal, Ethical, Regulatory, & International Environment. 6th alternate ed. Gaylord A. Jentz et al. 1500p. (C). Date not set. text ed. 68.50 (*0-314-06423-0*) West Pub.

West's Business Law: Text & Cases, Legal, Regulatory & International Environment. 6th ed. Kenneth W. Clarkson et al. LC 94-22665. 1530p. (C). 1995. text ed. 74.00 (*0-314-04220-2*) West Pub.

West's Business Law: Text, Cases, Legal & Regulatory Environment. 5th ed. Kenneth W. Clarkson et al. Ed. by Clyde Perlee. 1250p. (C). 1992. text ed. 66.00 (*0-314-88944-2*) West Pub.

West's California Basic Codes: Unannotated. write for info. (*0-318-57492-6*) West Pub.

West's California Code Forms, Corporation Code, the Limited Liability Company in California, the California Limited Liability Company Act. 96p. (C). 1995. pap. text ed. write for info. (*0-314-06747-7*) West Pub.

West's California Code Forms with Practice Commentaries-Public Utilities: Contains Pocket Parts. 3rd ed. Boris H. Lakusta. LC 82-50923. (Illus.). xi, 366p. 1984. 32.00 (*0-685-07262-2*) West Pub.

West's California Criminal Defense. Albert J. Menaster. LC 95-46982. 500p. (C). 1995. ring bd. 39.00 (*0-314-08726-5*) West Pub.

West's California Criminal Law. Douglas Dalton. LC 95-17931. 1995. text ed. write for info. (*0-314-06746-9*) West Pub.

West's California Criminal Procedure. Laurie L. Levenson. LC 95-24212. (West's Criminal Law Ser.). 1400p. (C). 1995. text ed. write for info. (*0-314-07049-4*) West Pub.

West's DOS 6.X & System. Bacon. (C). 1994. pap. text ed. 8.25 (*0-314-02864-1*) West Pub.

West's Education Law Reporter. write for info. (*0-318-57485-3*) West Pub.

Wests Encyclopedia of American Law. LC 96-34350. 1997. text ed. write for info. (*0-314-05538-X*) West Pub.

***West's Essentials of Microsoft Access.** 11th ed. Bruce J. McLaren. (DF - Computer Applications Ser.). 1994. pap. 8.00 (*0-314-02873-0*) West Pub.

West's Essentials of Microsoft Visual Basic. Jonathan C. Barron. LC 94-49431. (Microcomputing Ser.). 1995. pap. text ed. 17.75 (*0-314-05531-2*) West Pub.

***West's Essentials of Microsoft Windows 3.** 11th ed. Ross. (DF - Computer Applications Ser.). 1994. pap. 11.95 (*0-314-02636-3*) S-W Pub.

***West's Essentials of MS Access for Windows.** 21th ed. Ketcham. (DF - Computer Applications Ser.). (C). 1996. pap. 8.00 (*0-314-07232-2*) West Pub.

***West's Essentials of MS Access 2.0.** 11th ed. Bruce J. McLaren. (DF - Computer Applications Ser.). 1995. pap. 8.00 (*0-314-04633-X*) West Pub.

West's Essentials of Wordperfect 6.0. Bacon & Robert G. Sindt. (C). pap. text ed. 10.25 (*0-314-02867-6*) West Pub.

West's Federal Forms. write for info. (*0-318-57488-8*) West Pub.

West's Federal Forms, Vol. 2A: District Courts, Civil. 4th ed. Jay Grenig. 717p. 1994. text ed. write for info. (*0-314-04345-4*) West Pub.

West's Federal Forms, Vols. 5 & 5A: District Courts, Criminal, Vol. 5. 3rd ed. William A. Knox & Karol Prasifka. 567p. 1993. text ed. write for info. (*0-314-02342-9*) West Pub.

West's Federal Forms, Vols. 5 & 5A: District Courts, Criminal, Vol. 5A. 3rd ed. William A. Knox & Karol Prasifka. 579p. 1993. text ed. write for info. (*0-314-02343-7*) West Pub.

West's Federal Practice Digest. 2nd ed. write for info. (*0-318-57483-7*) West Pub.

West's Federal Practice Manual. 2nd ed. Ed. by Volz. write for info. (*0-318-57489-6*) West Pub.

West's Federal Tax Research. 3rd ed. William A. Raabe et al. LC 93-24109. 650p. (C). 1994. text ed. 61.50 (*0-314-02650-9*) West Pub.

***West's Federal Tax Research.** 4th ed. William A. Raabe et al. LC 96-36715. 1996. write for info. (*0-314-20182-3*) West Pub.

***West's Federal Tax 96 Comp.** 13th ed. Hoffman Willis. (Miscellaneous/Catalogs). (C). 1995. pap. 71.95 (*0-314-04547-3*) S-W Pub.

West's Federal Taxation: Comprehensive Volume, 1995. David J. Maloney et al. Ed. by Fenton. 1200p. (C). 1994. text ed. 71.25 (*0-314-03349-1*) West Pub.

West's Federal Taxation: Corporations, Partnerships, Estates, & Trusts, 1994 Edition. James E. Smith et al. Ed. by Fenton. 950p. (C). text ed. 67.00 (*0-314-03227-4*) West Pub.

West's Federal Taxation: Corporations, Partnerships, Estates, & Trusts, 1997. William H. Hoffman, Jr. et al. 1000p. 1996. text ed. write for info. (*0-314-08816-4*) West Pub.

West's Federal Taxation: Individual Income Taxes, 1995. William H. Hoffman, Jr. et al. Ed. by Fenton. 1000p. (C). text ed. 67.00 (*0-314-02992-3*) West Pub.

West's Federal Taxation: Individual Income Taxes, 1997. William H. Hoffman, Jr. et al. 1052p. 1996. text ed. write for info. (*0-314-08817-2*) West Pub.

West's Florida Criminal Laws & Rules, 1984. LC 84-248994. 1984. 23.50 (*0-317-18394-X*) West Pub.

West's Florida Digest. West Publishing Company Editorial Staff. write for info. (*0-318-59337-8*) West Pub.

West's Florida Probate Code with Related Laws & Court Rules. 544p. 1986. pap. 16.50 (*0-317-52102-0*) West Pub.

West's Florida Probate Code with Related Laws & Court Rules, 1984: Statutory Provisions & Rules & Guardianship Procedure. West Publishing Company Editorial Staff. LC 84-115068. 1983. pap. 14.00 (*0-317-13483-3*) West Pub.

West's Florida Statutes Annotated. write for info. (*0-318-57493-4*) West Pub.

West's Georgia Digest. 2nd ed. West Publishing Company Editorial Staff. 1985. write for info. (*0-318-60696-8*) West Pub.

West's Illinois Digest. 2nd ed. write for info. (*0-318-57055-6*) West Pub.

West's Intermediate Accounting. Vincent C. Brenner et al. (Illus.). 1336p. (C). 1983. Key figures. text ed. write for info. (*0-314-80324-6*) West Pub.

West's Intermediate Accounting, Pt. I, Working Papers. Vincent C. Brenner et al. (Illus.). 1336p. (C). 1983. Working papers, Pt. I. pap. text ed. write for info. (*0-314-72286-6*) West Pub.

West's Intermediate Accounting, Pt. II, Working Papers. Vincent C. Brenner et al. (Illus.). 1336p. (C). 1983. Working papers, Pt. II. write for info. (*0-314-72287-4*) West Pub.

***West's Intermediate Microsoft Access.** 11th ed. Bruce J. McLaren. (DF - Computer Applications Ser.). 1994. pap. 11.00 (*0-314-02872-2*) West Pub.

***West's Intermediate Microsoft Windows 3.** 11th ed. Ross. (DF - Computer Applications Ser.). 1994. pap. 15.95 (*0-314-02637-1*) S-W Pub.

***West's Intermediate MS Access 2.0.** 11th ed. Bruce J. McLaren. (DF - Computer Applications Ser.). (C). 1995. pap. 11.00 (*0-314-04642-9*) West Pub.

***West's Intermediate Paradox 4.5 for Window.** 11th ed. Smith. (DF-Computer Applications Ser.). 1994. pap. 15.95 (*0-314-02816-1*) S-W Pub.

***West's Intermediate Quattro Pro 6.0 for Windows.** 11th ed. Friedrichsen. (DF - Computer Applications Ser.). (C). 1995. pap. 11.00 (*0-314-04645-3*) West Pub.

West's Intermediate Wordperfect 6.0. Bacon & Robert G. Sindt. (C). 1995. pap. text ed. 14.50 (*0-314-02866-8*) West Pub.

***West's Internal Revenue Code of 1986 & Treasury Regulations: Annotated & Selected, 1997 Edition.** Smith. 1800p. 1997. pap. write for info. (*0-314-20018-5*) West Pub.

West's Kentucky Digest. 2nd ed. West Publishing Company Editorial Staff. write for info. (*0-318-59784-5*) West Pub.

West's Law & Commercial Dictionary. West & Zanchelli. 1856p. (ENG, FRE, ITA & SPA.). 1988. lib. bdg. 195.00 (*0-8288-3373-7*) Fr & Eur.

West's Law & Commercial Dictionary in Five Languages, 2 vols., Set. West Publishing Company Editorial Staff. text ed. write for info. (*0-314-80502-8*) West Pub.

West's Law & Commercial Dictionary in Five Languages, 2 vols., Vol. A-J, 1000p. West Publishing Company Editorial Staff. write for info. (*0-318-59110-3*) West Pub.

West's Law & Commercial Dictionary in Five Languages, 2 vols., Vol. K-Z, 950p. West Publishing Company Editorial Staff. write for info. (*0-318-59111-1*) West Pub.

West's Legal Environment of Business: Text, Cases, Ethical & Regulatory Issues. Frank B. Cross & Roger L. Miller. Ed. by Clyde Perlee. 676p. (C). 1992. text ed. 65.25 (*0-314-89333-4*) West Pub.

West's Legal Environment of Business: Text, Cases, Ethical & Regulatory Issues. 2nd ed. Frank B. Cross & Roger L. Miller. 1100p. (C). 1995. text ed. 68.50 (*0-314-04517-1*) West Pub.

West's Legal Forms. 2nd ed. write for info. (*0-318-57506-X*) West Pub.

West's Legal Forms: Business Organizations with Tax Analysis, Vol. 2A. 2nd rev. ed. Paul Lieberman. text ed. write for info. (*0-314-02897-8*) West Pub.

West's Legal Forms Vol. 26: Alternative Dispute Resolution. Jay E. Grenig. 800p. 1995. text ed. write for info. (*0-314-07590-9*) West Pub.

West's Legal Forms, Vol. 2: Business Organizations with Tax Analysis. 2nd rev. ed. Paul Lieberman. 800p. text ed. write for info. (*0-314-02102-7*) West Pub.

West's Legal Thesaurus-Dictionary. deluxe ed. William P. Statsky. 813p. 1985. text ed. 41.50 (*0-314-87755-X*) West Pub.

West's Massachusetts Civil Actions & Procedure, 1985: Statutory Provisions, Rules of Civil Procedure, Combined Index. West Publishing Company Editorial Staff. 1985. write for info. (*0-318-61250-X*) West Pub.

***West's Math Tutor IBM College Algebra.** 11th ed. Stevens. (Miscellaneous/Catalogs Ser.). (C). 1994. pap. 17.95 (*0-314-03818-3*) Brooks-Cole.

***West's Math Tutor Macintosh College Algebra.** 11th ed. Stevens. (Miscellaneous/Catalogs Ser.). (C). 1994. pap. 17.95 (*0-314-03819-1*) Brooks-Cole.

West's Paralegal Today: The Comprehensive Edition. unabridged ed. Roger L. Miller & Mary S. Urisko. LC 95-23789. 1000p. (C). 1996. text ed. 54.75 (*0-314-06588-1*) West Pub.

West's Paralegal Today: The Essentials: The Legal Team at Work. Roger L. Miller & Mary S. Urisko. LC 94-37656. 478p. (C). 1995. pap. text ed. 38.25 (*0-314-04595-3*) West Pub.

West's Paralegal Today: The Legal Team at Work. Roger L. Miller & Mary S. Urisko. LC 94-37650. 900p. (C). 1995. text ed. 52.75 (*0-314-04360-8*) West Pub.

West's Practice Digest. 3rd ed. West Publishing Company Editorial Staff. 1984. write for info. (*0-318-58313-5*) West Pub.

West's Tax Law Dictionary. Robert S. Smith. 798p. 1993. pap. text ed. write for info. (*0-314-01835-2*) West Pub.

West's Tax Law Dictionary: 1995 Edition. Robert S. Smith. 1134p. (C). 1995. pap. text ed. write for info. (*0-314-06461-3*) West Pub.

West's Texas Digest. 2nd ed. West Publishing Company Editorial Staff. write for info. (*0-318-57036-X*) West Pub.

West's Textbook of Cosmetology. 2nd ed. Jerry J. Ahern. (Illus.). 509p. (C). 1986. pap. text ed. 37.00 (*0-314-99125-5*) West Pub.

West's Textbook of Manicuring. Jerry J. Ahern. (Illus.). 107p. (Orig.). (C). 1986. pap. text ed. 24.50 (*0-314-99126-3*) West Pub.

West's Wisconsin Statutes Annotated. write for info. (*0-318-57502-7*) West Pub.

Westside Preschool Directory: A Guide to Childcare from Mulholland to Lax. Susan Scheding & Ayshe Ege. 192p. 1991. pap. text ed. 14.95 (*0-9629519-0-0*) Playdoughs Republic.

Westvaco Corp. A Report on the Company's Environmental Policies & Practices. (Illus.). 53p. (C). 1994. reprint ed. pap. text ed. 250.00 (*0-7881-0971-5*, Coun on Econ) DIANE Pub.

Westward. Amy Clampitt. 1990. pap. 15.00 (*0-679-72867-8*) Knopf.

Westward. Amy Clampitt. 1990. 18.95 (*0-394-58455-4*) Random.

Westward. Amanda MacLean. 289p. 1995. pap. 8.99 (*0-88070-751-8*, Multnomah Bks) Multnomah Pubs.

Westward! large type ed. Dana F. Ross. (General Ser.). 640p. 1992. pap. 16.95 (*0-8161-5449-X*, GK Hall); lib. bdg. 21.95 (*0-8161-5448-1*, GK Hall) Thorndike Pr.

Westward: The Epic Crossing of the American Landscape. Gerald Roscoe & David Larkin. LC 95-21909. (Illus.). 240p. 1995. 60.00 (*1-885254-09-1*) Monacelli Pr.

Westward: The Epic Crossing of the American Landscape, 4 vols., Set. Gerald Roscoe & David Larkin. LC 95-21909. (Illus.). 240p. 1995. 240.00 (*1-885254-19-9*) Monacelli Pr.

Westward Angel. Catherine Creel. 1995. mass mkt. 5.99 (*0-449-18280-0*) Fawcett.

Westward by Rail: The New Route to the East. William F. Rae. LC 72-9465. (Far Western Frontier Ser.). 412p. 1973. reprint ed. 25.95 (*0-405-04993-5*) Ayer.

Westward Expansion. (C. C. Publications Social Studies). (Illus.). 64p. 1985. 7.30 (*0-574-51761-8*) SRA.

***Westward Expansion.** Jim Haskins. Date not set. write for info. (*0-688-10264-6*); lib. bdg. write for info. (*0-688-10265-4*) Lothrop.

Westward Expansion. Sanford Wexler. (Eyewitness History Ser.). (Illus.). 432p. 1991. 45.00 (*0-8160-2407-3*) Facts on File.

W

An Asterisk (*) at the beginning of an entry indicates that the title is appearing in BIP for the first time.

Westward Expansion: Exploration & Settlement. Cheryl Edwards. LC 94-69883. (Perspectives on History Ser.). (Illus.). 64p. (Orig.). (YA). (gr. 5-12). 1995. pap. 5.95 (*1-878668-50-1*) Disc Enter Ltd.

Westward Expansion & the Frontier. Joyce Friedland & Rikki Kessler. (Novel-Ties Ser.). 1985. student ed., pap. text ed. 20.95 (*0-88122-039-6*) Lrn Links.

Westward Expansion to the Civil War: Significant Events & the People Who Shaped Them see Profiles in American History

Westward Extension, Eighteen Forty-One to Eighteen Fifty. George Garrison. LC 68-24978. (American History & Americana Ser.: No. 47). 1969. reprint ed. lib. bdg. 75.00 (*0-8383-0946-1*) M S G Haskell Hse.

Westward Extension, 1841-1850. George P. Garrison. (BCL1 - U. S. History Ser.). 366p. 1991. reprint ed. lib. bdg. 89.00 (*0-7812-6042-6*) Rprt Serv.

Westward H-O-O-O-o-o-o-o! The Olivers. Louise Morgan. LC 89-61486. (Illus.). 208p. 1989. 24.95 (*0-88323-0472-7*) Binford Mort.

***Westward Ha!** Jamie Gilson. Date not set. lib. bdg. write for info. (*0-688-14551-5*) Lothrop.

Westward Ho! Mike Flanagan. (Orig.). (J). 1993. pap. 5.00 (*0-87602-307-3*) Anchorage.

Westward Ho. Charles Kingsley. (Airmont Classics Ser.). (J). (gr. 8 up). 1968. mass mkt. 1.25 (*0-8049-0184-8*, CL-184) Airmont.

Westward Ho. Charles Kingsley. 1976. 24.95 (*0-8488-1069-4*) Amereon Ltd.

***Westward Ho!** Diana Waring. 1997. pap. 19.99 (*1-888306-25-4*) GCB.

Westward Ho! deluxe limited ed. Charles Kingsley. LC 20-18930. (Scribner's Illustrated Classics Ser.). (Illus.). 432p. (YA). (gr. 7 up). 1992. text ed. 26.95 (*0-684-19444-9*, C Scribner Sons Young) S&S Childrens.

Westward Ho. Thomas Dekker & John Webster. LC 79-133656. (Tudor Facsimile Texts. Old English Plays Ser.: No. 123). reprint ed. 59.50 (*0-404-53423-6*) AMS Pr.

Westward Ho' Charles Kingsley. 1982. reprint ed. lib. bdg. 18.95 (*0-89966-399-0*) Buccaneer Bks.

Westward Ho!, 2 vols., Set. James K. Paulding. (BCL1-PS American Literature Ser.). 1992. reprint ed. lib. bdg. 150.00 (*0-7812-6826-5*) Rprt Serv.

Westward Ho: A Tale, 2 vols., Set. James K. Paulding. LC 06-25598. 1968. reprint ed. 39.00 (*0-403-00066-1*) Scholarly.

Westward Ho: A Thematic Unit. Mary E. Sterling. (Thematic Units Ser.). (Illus.). 80p. (Orig.). 1992. student ed. 9.95 (*1-55734-282-2*) Tchr Create Mat.

Westward Ho! An Activity Guide to the Wild West. Laurie M. Carlson. LC 96-10841. (Illus.). 184p. (Orig.). (J). (gr. k-7). 1996. pap. 12.95 (*1-55652-271-1*) Chicago Review.

Westward Ho, Carlotta! Candace Fleming. 1997. 16.99 (*0-679-97182-3*) Random.

Westward Ho, Carlotta! Candace Fleming. LC 96-1922. (J). 1998. 16.00 (*0-689-81063-6*, Atheneum Bks Young) S&S Childrens.

Westward Ho, Carlotta. Candace Fleming. (J). 1997. 15.00 (*0-679-87182-9*) Random.

Westward, Ho, Ho, Ho! Peter Roop & Connie Roop. (Illus.). 48p. (J). (gr. 3-6). 1996. lib. bdg. 16.40 (*0-7613-0020-1*) Millbrook Pr.

Westward Ho! The Story of the Pioneers. Lucille R. Penner. LC 97-281. (Landmark Ser.). 1997. 13.00 (*0-679-84776-6*); lib. bdg. 14.99 (*0-679-94776-0*) Random.

Westward in Eden: The Public Lands & the Conservation Movement. William K. Wyant. LC 81-7519. (Illus.). 500p. 1982. pap. 13.00 (*0-520-06183-7*) U CA Pr.

Westward into Kentucky: The Narrative of Daniel Trabue. Daniel Trabue. Ed. by Chester R. Young. LC 80-51022. 224p. reprint ed. pap. 63.90 (*0-8357-8596-3*, 2034971) Bks Demand.

Westward March of American Settlement. Hamlin Garland. (Collected Works of Hamlin Garland). 1988. reprint ed. lib. bdg. 79.00 (*0-7812-1250-2*) Rprt Serv.

Westward March of American Settlement see Collected Works of Hamlin Garland

Westward Movement: The Colonies & the Republic West of the Alleghanies, 1763-1798. Justin Winsor. (BCL1 - United States Local History Ser.). 595p. 1991. reprint ed. lib. bdg. 99.00 (*0-7812-6305-0*) Rprt Serv.

Westward Movement & Abolitionism, 1815-1850. William L. Katz. LC 92-14965. (History of Multicultural America Ser.). (Illus.). 96p. (J). (gr. 7-8). 1992. lib. bdg. 25.68 (*0-8114-6276-5*) Raintree Steck-V.

Westward Movement & Abolitionism, 1815-1850. William L. Katz. 1995. pap. text ed. 6.95 (*0-8114-2913-X*) Raintree Steck-V.

Westward Movement of the Cotton Economy, 1840-1860: Perceived Interests & Economic Realities. Susan P. Lee. Ed. by Stuart Bruchey. LC 76-39832. (Nineteen Seventy-Seven Dissertations Ser.). (Illus.). 1977. lib. bdg. 24.95 (*0-405-09912-6*) Ayer.

Westward of Ye Laurall Hills, 1750-1850. 2nd ed. Helen E. Vogt. LC 75-21087. (Illus.). 1989. reprint ed. 20.00 (*0-87012-226-6*) H Vogt.

Westward the Texans: The Civil War Journal of Private William Randolph Howell. Ed. by Jerry D. Thompson. LC 89-50162. (Illus.). 184p. 1990. 20.00 (*0-87404-211-9*) Tex Western.

Westward the Tide. Louis L'Amour. 224p. (Orig.). 1984. pap. 3.99 (*0-553-24766-2*) Bantam.

Westward the Women. Nancy Ross. LC 76-117832. (Essay Index Reprint Ser.). 1977. 22.95 (*0-8369-1846-0*) Ayer.

Westward the Women. Nancy W. Ross. LC 84-62311. 208p. 1985. 10.95 (*0-86547-183-5*, North Pt Pr) FS&G.

***Westward the Women.** Nancy W. Ross. 196p. 1996. pap. 7.95 (*0-89174-063-5*) Comstock Edns.

Westward the Women: An Anthology of Western Stories by Women. Ed. by Vicki Piekarski. LC 87-34238. 186p. 1988. reprint ed. pap. 10.95 (*0-8263-1063-X*) U of NM Pr.

Westward They Rode. Theodore V. Olsen. 224p. 1996. reprint ed. mass mkt. 4.50 (*0-8439-4021-2*) Dorchester Pub Co.

Westward to a Cave-House Ranch. Frank Logan. write for info. (*0-89697-382-4*) Intl Univ Pr.

Westward to a High Mountain: The Colorado Writings of Helen Hunt Jackson. Ed. by Mark I. West. LC 94-19463. 1994. pap. 9.95 (*0-942576-35-7*) CO Hist Soc.

Westward Vision: The Story of the Oregon Trail. David Lavender. LC 84-20815. (Illus.). xx, 425p. 1985. reprint ed. pap. 15.00 (*0-8032-7915-9*, Bison Books) U of Nebr Pr.

Westward! Wagons West, the Trilogy. Dana F. Ross. 512p. 1992. mass mkt. 5.50 (*0-553-29402-4*) Bantam.

Westward Whoa. Hodding Carter. 1994. 21.00 (*0-671-79891-X*) S&S Trade.

Westward with Columbus. John Dyson. LC 90-15566. (Illus.). 64p. (J). (gr. 4-7). 1993. pap. 6.95 (*0-590-43847-6*) Scholastic Inc.

Westward with Columbus: A Time Quest Book. John Dyson. 64p. (J). 1991. 15.95 (*0-590-43846-8*, Scholastic Hardcover) Scholastic Inc.

***Westward Women.** C. Birch Pontius. 550p. (Orig.). 1997. pap. 24.95 (*1-881636-16-X*) Windsor Hse Pub Grp.

Westwood, California, a Company Town in Comparative Perspective, 1900-1930. Ruth V. Brydon. 59p. 1995. 8.00 (*0-614-15361-1*) Assn NC Records.

Westy the Hare Goes to the National Western Stock Show & Rodeo. Ann B. Pugh. (Illus.). (ENG & SPA.). (J). 1995. 5.00 (*0-9643660-0-2*) Diggy & Assocs.

***Wet: On Painting, Feminism & Art Culture.** Mira Schor. LC 96-29410. (Illus.). 280p. 1997. pap. 16.95 (*0-8223-1915-2*); lib. bdg. 49.95 (*0-8223-1910-1*) Duke.

Wet All Over: A Book about the Water Cycle. (Magic School Bus Ser.). (J). (gr. 1-2). 1996. pap. 2.99 (*0-590-50833-4*) Scholastic Inc.

Wet & Dry. Jack Challoner. LC 95-30014. (Start-up Science Ser.). (J). 1996. lib. bdg. 21.40 (*0-8172-4322-4*) Raintree Steck-V.

Wet & Dry Strength Short Course, Chicago, April 13-15, 1988. Technical Association of the Pulp & Paper Industry Staff. (TAPPI Notes Ser.). (Illus.). 75p. reprint ed. pap. 25.00 (*0-685-44404-X*, 2032271) Bks Demand.

***Wet & Operations Short Course, 1994: Omni Netherland Plaza, Cincinnati, OH, May 9-13.** Technical Association of the Pulp & Paper Industry Staff. (TAPPI Course Notes Ser.). (Illus.). 442p. pap. 126.00 (*0-608-05372-4*, 2082422) Bks Demand.

Wet & the Dry: Irrigation & Agricultural Intensification in Polynesia. Patrick V. Kirch. 408p. 1994. 49.95 (*0-226-43749-3*) U Ch Pr.

Wet & Wisdom Mad. 1992. 3.99 (*0-446-77615-7*) Warner Bks.

Wet & Wisdom of Mad. Mad Magazine Editors. 192p. (Orig.). 1987. mass mkt. 3.99 (*0-446-34366-8*) Warner Bks.

Wet Basement Manual. 62p. 1993. pap. 14.95 (*0-924659-68-8*, 1060) Aberdeen Group.

Wet Chemical Extinguishing Systems. National Fire Protection Association Staff. 1990. 16.75 (*0-317-63056-3*, 17A-90) Natl Fire Prot.

Wet Coastal Ecosystems. Ed. by Valentine J. Chapman. LC 77-342. (Ecosystems of the World Ser.: Vol. 1). 428p. 1977. 190.75 (*0-444-41560-2*) Elsevier.

***Wet Dreams.** 480p. 1997. mass mkt. 6.95 (*0-7867-0500-0*) Carroll & Graf.

Wet End Chemistry: An Introduction. William E. Scott. LC 92-31964. reprint ed. pap. 25.00 (*0-7837-4062-X*, 2044012) Bks Demand.

Wet End Operations Seminar, Nineteen Eighty-Five: Notes of TAPPI, Portland Marriott Hotel, Portland, OR, May 5-10. Technical Association of the Pulp & Paper Industry Staff. 387p. reprint ed. pap. 110.30 (*0-685-10712-4*, 2025289) Bks Demand.

Wet End Operations Seminar, Nineteen Eighty-Four Notes. Technical Association of the Pulp & Paper Industry Staff. 411p. reprint ed. pap. 117.20 (*0-317-27220-9*, 2024772) Bks Demand.

Wet End Operations Seminar, 1986: Notes of TAPPI, Marriott Copley Place, Boston, MA, May 4-9,1986. Technical Association of the Pulp & Paper Industry. 412p. pap. 117.50 (*0-685-17835-8*, 2029187) Bks Demand.

Wet End Operations Seminar, 1989: Ritz-Carlton, Buckhead, Atlanta, GA, May 8-12. Technical Association of the Pulp & Paper Industry Staff. (TAPPI Notes Ser.). (Illus.). 488p. reprint ed. pap. 139.10 (*0-8357-6346-3*, 2035619) Bks Demand.

Wet End Operations Short Course, 1990: Marriott City Center, Minneapolis, MN, May 14-18. Technical Association of the Pulp & Paper Industry Staff. (TAPPI Notes Ser.). (Illus.). 479p. reprint ed. pap. 136.60 (*0-8357-4230-X*, 2037017) Bks Demand.

Wet End Operations Short Course, 1991: Peabody Hotel, Orlando, FL, May 5-10. Technical Association of the Pulp & Paper Industry Staff. (TAPPI Notes Ser.). 533p. pap. 152.00 (*0-7837-0259-0*, 2040568) Bks Demand.

Wet End Operations Short Course, 1992: Hyatt Regency Hotel, Atlanta, GA, May 4-8. Technical Association of the Pulp & Paper Industry Staff. (TAPPI Notes Ser.). 501p. 1992. reprint ed. pap. 142.80 (*0-7837-3169-8*, 2042809) Bks Demand.

Wet Flies: Tying & Fishing Soft-Hackles, Winged & Wingless Wets, & Fuzzy Nymphs. Dave Hughes. LC 94-26502. (Illus.). 256p. 1995. 32.95 (*0-8117-1868-9*) Stackpole.

Wet Foot, Dry Foot, Low Foot, High Foot. Linda Haywood & Dr. Seuss. (J). 1996. pap. 3.99 (*0-679-87086-5*) Random Bks Yng Read.

Wet Forever. David A. Clark. (Orig.). 1993. mass mkt. 6.95 (*1-56333-117-9*, Rhinoceros) Masquerade.

Wet Hat: And Other Stories from Beyond the Black Stump. Ann Loder. (Illus.). 102p. (Orig.). (J). (gr. 4 up). 1993. pap. write for info. (*0-9636643-0-1*) A L Loder.

***Wet H2S Cracking of Carbon Steels & Weldments.** Russell D. Kane. 1042p. 1996. pap. 157.00 (*1-877914-97-5*) NACE Intl.

Wet-into-Wet: Watercolour Technique. Bryan A. Thatcher. 48p. (Orig.). 1995. pap. 11.95 (*0-85532-787-1*, 787-1, Pub. by Search Pr UK) A Schwartz & Co.

Wet-Into-Wet Watercolor: The Complete Guide to an Essential Watercolor Technique. Gail Speckmann. LC 94-46212. (Illus.). 144p. 1995. 29.95 (*0-8230-5715-1*) Watsn-Guptill.

***Wet Magic.** Edith Nesbit. (Illus.). 256p. (J). (gr. 3 up). 1996. reprint ed. 24.95 (*0-929605-63-2*); reprint ed. pap. 12.95 (*0-929605-54-3*) Books Wonder.

Wet Mind: The New Cognitive Neuroscience. Stephen M. Kosslyn & Olivier Koenig. (Illus.). 360p. 1992. 35.00 (*0-02-917595-X*, Free Press) Free Pr.

Wet Mind: The New Cognitive Neuroscience. Stephen M. Kosslyn & Olivier Koenig. 576p. 1995. pap. 19.95 (*0-02-874085-8*) Free Pr.

Wet Mountain Valley. Gayle Turk. 4.50 (*0-936564-14-8*) Little London.

Wet 'N' Wild. Alicia Baldwin. 176p. (YA). (gr. 5 up). 1996. pap. 3.99 (*0-679-88099-2*) Random.

Wet op die Hooggeregshof 59 van 1959 en die Wet Op Lannddroshowe 32 van 1944. 7th ed. H. J. Erasmus & Owen J. Barrow. 531p. 1992. pap. write for info. (*0-7021-2930-5*, Pub. by Juta SA) Gaunt.

Wet-Pavement Safety Programs. (National Cooperative Highway Research Program Report Ser.: No. 158). 54p. 1990. 8.00 (*0-309-04904-0*) Transport Res Bd.

***Wet Places at Noon.** Lee K. Abbott. 194p. 1997. 22.95 (*0-87745-605-4*) U of Iowa Pr.

Wet Rocks Seen from Above. John Berger. (Illus.). 48p. 1996. 32.95 (*3-9520497-3-5*, Pub. by Memory-Cage SZ) Dist Art Pubs.

***Wet-Scrape Braintanned Buckskin: A Practical Guide to Home Tanning & Use.** Steven Edholm & Tamara Wilder. LC 96-92705. (Illus.). 331p. (Orig.). 1997. pap. 17.95 (*0-9654965-4-6*) Paleotechnics.

Wet Scrubbers. rev. ed. Kenneth C. Schifftner & Howard E. Hesketh. LC 95-62014. 220p. 1995. pap. text ed. 59.95 (*1-56676-379-7*) Technomic.

Wet Site Archaeology. Ed. by Barbara A. Purdy. (Illus.). 450p. 1990. 55.00 (*0-936923-07-5*, Q); 55.00 (*0-936923-08-3*) CRC Pr.

Wet-Strength Resins & Their Application: A Project of the Papermaking Additives Committee of TAPPI's Paper & Board Manufacture Division. Lock L. Chan. LC 94-33119. (Illus.). 1994. 73.00 (*0-89852-060-6*) TAPPI.

Wet Wall Tattoos: Ben Long & the Art of Fresco. Richard Maschal. LC 93-13887. (Illus.). 212p. 1993. 12.95 (*0-89587-105-X*) Blair.

***Wet Way Home.** Lisa Steinman. 26p. 1996. 5.00 (*0-614-30122-X*) Skydog OR.

Wet Weather: Rain Showers & Snowfall. Jonathan Kahl. (How's the Weather? Ser.). (Illus.). 64p. (J). (gr. 4 up). 1992. lib. bdg. 19.95 (*0-8225-2526-7*, Lerner Publctns) Lerner Group.

Wet Wet Wet. Brian Beacom. (Illus.). 192p. 1996. 29.95 (*1-85158-739-X*, Pub. by Mnstream UK) Trafalgar.

Wet Wet Wet: Pictured. Mal Peachey. (Illus.). 128p. 1996. 21.95 (*1-85227-533-2*, Pub. by Virgin Pub UK) London Brdge.

Wet Wings & Drop Tanks: Recollections of American Transcontinental Air Racing 1928-1970. Birch Matthews. LC 93-84497. (Illus.). 268p. 1993. 45.00 (*0-88740-530-4*) Schiffer.

W.E.T. Workout: Water Exercise Techniques to Help You Tone Up & Slim Down Aerobically. Jane Katz. (Illus.). 192p. 1985. 18.95 (*0-8160-1159-1*); pap. 12.95 (*0-8160-1032-3*) Facts on File.

Wet World. Norma Simon. LC 94-25702. (Illus.). (J). (ps up). 1995. 12.95 (*1-56402-190-4*) Candlewick Pr.

Wet World. Norma Simon. LC 94-25702. (Illus.). 32p. (J). (ps up). 1997. reprint ed. pap. 5.99 (*0-7636-0114-4*) Candlewick Pr.

Wetherel Affair. John W. De Forest. (Collected Works of John W. De Forest). 1988. reprint ed. lib. bdg. 79.00 (*0-7812-1159-X*) Rprt Serv.

Wetherel Affair see Collected Works of John W. De Forest

Wetherfield Collection of Clocks: A Guide to Dating English Antique Clocks. Eric Bruton. (Illus.). 264p. 1981. 49.50 (*0-7198-0150-8*, Pub. by NAG Press UK) Antique Collect.

Wetherization Representative. (Career Examination Ser.). Date not set. pap. 27.95 (*0-8373-3784-4*, C3784) Nat Learn.

***Wethersfield & Her Daughters, Glastonbury, Rocky Hill, Newington. From 1634 to 1934.** Frances W. Fox et al. (Illus.). 123p. 1997. reprint ed. pap. 16.50 (*0-8328-5697-5*) Higginson Bk Co.

Wetland. April P. Sayre. (Exploring Earth's Biomes Ser.). (Illus.). 78p. (J). (gr. 5-8). 1996. lib. bdg. 16.98 (*0-8050-4086-2*) TFC Bks NY.

***Wetland Adaptations in the Great Basin.** Joel Janetski & Madsen. (Museum of Peoples & Cultures Occasional Papers: No. 1). Date not set. pap. 20.00 (*0-87480-495-7*) U of Utah Pr.

Wetland & Environmental Applications of GIS. Ed. by John G. Lyon & Jack McCarthy. LC 95-10772. (Mapping Sciences Ser.). 400p. 1995. 69.95 (*0-87371-897-6*, L897) Lewis Pubs.

Wetland Conservation: A Review of Current Issues & Required Action. Ed. by Patrick Dugan. 96p. (C). 1990. pap. 15.00 (*2-8317-0015-9*, Pub. by IUCN SZ) Island Pr.

Wetland Creation & Restoration: The Status of the Science. Jon Kusler & Mary E. Kentula. LC 90-4053. 591p. 1990. pap. 47.50 (*1-55963-044-2*) Island Pr.

Wetland Ecology & Management: Case Studies. Ed. by Dennis F. Whigham et al. (C). 1990. lib. bdg. 137.50 (*0-7923-0893-X*) Kluwer Ac.

Wetland Economics & Assessment: An Annotated Bibliography. Jay A. Leitch & Brenda L. Ekstrom. LC 88-30977. 203p. 1989. text ed. 35.00 (*0-8240-3648-4*, SS508) Garland.

Wetland Economics, 1989-1993: A Selected Annotated Bibliography. Jay A. Leitch & Herbert R. Ludwig. LC 94-39564. (Bibliographies & Indexes in Economics & Economic History Ser.: Vol. 17). 152p. 1995. text ed. 65.00 (*0-313-29286-8*, Greenwood Pr) Greenwood.

Wetland Functions & Values: The State of Our Understanding, Proceedings of the National Symposium of Wetlands Held in Disneyworld Village, Lake Buena Vista, Florida, November 7-10. National Symposium on Wetlands (1978: Lake Buena Vista, FL). LC 79-93316. (American Water Resources Association Technical Publication Ser.: TPS 79-2). 684p. reprint ed. pap. 180.00 (*0-685-15246-4*, 2027149) Bks Demand.

Wetland Heritage: The Louisiana Duck Decoy. Charles W. Frank, Jr. LC 84-9582. 192p. 1985. 49.95 (*0-88289-398-X*) Pelican.

Wetland Identification & Delineation. Lyon. 176p. 1993. 65.95 (*0-87371-590-X*, L590) Lewis Pubs.

Wetland Issues in Resources Development in the Western United States. (Mineral Law Ser.). 1993. student ed. 75.00 (*0-929047-39-7*) Rocky Mtn Mineral Law Found.

***Wetland Mitigation: Mitigation Banking & Other Strategies for Development & Compliance.** Mack S. Dennison & James A. Schmid. LC 96-30343. 305p. 1997. text ed. 75.00 (*0-86587-534-0*) Gov Insts.

Wetland Modelling. Ed. by Sven E. Jorgensen et al. (Developments in Environmental Modelling Ser.: Vol. 12). 238p. 1988. 148.25 (*0-444-42936-0*) Elsevier.

Wetland Planting Guide for the Northeastern United States: Plants for Wetland Creation, Restoration, & Enhancement. Gwendolyn A. Thunhorst. LC 93-71108. (Illus.). 184p. (Orig.). 1993. pap. 19.95 (*1-883226-02-3*) Environ Concern.

Wetland Plants Manual. U. S. EPA, Region 5 Staff et al. (Illus.). 58p. (Orig.). 1992. pap. 12.95 (*0-614-14306-3*) Terrene Inst.

***Wetland Plants of Ontario.** Alan G. Harris. 1996. pap. 19.95 (*1-55105-059-5*) Lone Pine.

Wetland Plants of Oregon & Washington, Vol. 1. B. Jennifer Guard. (Illus.). 240p. (Orig.). 1995. pap. 19.95 (*1-55105-060-9*, 1-55105) Lone Pine.

Wetland Riders. Robert Fritchey. LC 92-63214. (Illus.). (Orig.). 1993. pap. 14.95 (*0-9636215-0-5*) New Moon Pr.

***Wetland Systems for Water Pollution Control 1994.** R. H. Kadlec & H. Brix. (Water Science & Technology Ser.: Vol. 32). 376p. 1995. 109.25 (*0-08-042878-9*, Pergamon Pr) Elsevier.

Wetland Systems in Water Pollution Control. Bavor & Mitchell. (Water Science & Technology Ser.). 336p. 1994. pap. 173.00 (*0-08-042532-1*, Pergamon Pr) Elsevier.

Wetlands. David J. Hawke. (Illus.). 120p. 24.95 (*1-55046-046-3*, Pub. by Boston Mills Pr CN) Genl Dist Srvs.

Wetlands. Andrew Langley. LC 92-62551. (Nature Search Ser.). (Illus.). 32p. (J). (gr. 4-7). 1993. 14.00 (*0-89577-482-8*) RD Assn.

Wetlands. Emilie U. Lepthien & Joan Kalbacken. LC 92-35051. (New True Bks.). (Illus.). 48p. (J). (gr. k-4). 1993. pap. 5.50 (*0-516-41334-1*); lib. bdg. 19.00 (*0-516-01334-3*) Childrens.

Wetlands. Marylin Lisowski & Robert A. Williams. LC 96-25739. (Exploring Ecosystems Ser.). (J). 1997. lib. bdg. 22.00 (*0-531-11311-6*) Watts.

Wetlands. Downs Matthews. LC 93-3439. (J). 1994. pap. 15.00 (*0-671-86562-5*, S&S Bks Young Read) S&S Childrens.

Wetlands. William A. Niering. Ed. by Charles Elliott. LC 84-48672. (Audubon Society Nature Guides Ser.). (Illus.). 638p. 1985. pap. 19.95 (*0-394-73147-6*) Knopf.

***Wetlands.** Rose Pipes. LC 97-9072. (World Habitats Ser.). (J). 1998. write for info. (*0-8172-5001-8*) Raintree Steck-V.

Wetlands. Charles M. Rotter & Nicole Taylor. LC 92-41339. (Images Ser.). (J). 1994. 16.95 (*0-88682-594-6*) Creative Ed.

Wetlands. L. Stone. (Ecozones Ser.). (Illus.). 48p. (J). (gr. 4-8). 1989. 11.95 (*0-685-58569-7*); lib. bdg. 15.94 (*0-86592-447-3*) Rourke Corp.

Wetlands. Lynn M. Stone. LC 95-46183. (J). 1996. write for info. (*0-86593-425-8*) Rourke Corp.

Wetlands. Patti Tana. LC 93-24170. (Illus.). 115p. 1993. 12.00 (*0-918949-36-X*); pap. 8.00 (*0-918949-35-1*) Papier-Mache Press.

***Wetlands.** unabridged ed. Pamela Hickman. (Illus.). 96p. (J). (gr. 3-7). 1993. pap. 10.95 (*1-55074-126-8*, Pub. by Kids Can Pr CN) Genl Dist Srvs.

Wetlands. 2nd ed. William J. Mitsch. 1993. text ed. 65.95 (*0-442-00805-8*) Van Nos Reinhold.

***Wetlands.** 3rd ed. Mitschw. (General Science Ser.). Date not set. text ed. 64.95 (*0-442-02514-9*) Van Nos Reinhold.

Wetlands: A Global Perspective. Ed. by M. E. Moser & C. A. Finlayson. (Illus.). 224p. 1991. 45.00 (*0-8160-2556-8*) Facts on File.

W

An Asterisk (*) at the beginning of an entry indicates that the title is appearing in BIP for the first time.

Wetlands: A Threatened Landscape. Ed. by Michael Williams. (IBG Special Publications: No. 25). (Illus.). 400p. (C). 1993. pap. text ed. 32.95 (*0-631-19199-2*) Blackwell Pubs.

Wetlands: A World Conservation Atlas. Ed. by Patrick Dugan. LC 93-21729. 192p. (C). 1993. 39.95 (*0-19-520942-7*) OUP.

***Wetlands: All about Bogs, Bayous, Swamps, Sloughs & a Salt Marsh or Two.** Vicki Leon. LC 97-10936. (Close up Ser.). (J). 1998. pap. write for info. (*0-382-39724-X*); pap. write for info. (*0-382-39725-8*) Silver Burdett Pr.

Wetlands: An Approach to Improving Decision Making in Wetland Restoration & Creation. Mary E. Kentula et al. Ed. by Ann J. Hairston. LC 92-5675. (Illus.). 151p. (C). 1992. text ed. 40.00 (*1-55963-221-6*) Island Pr.

Wetlands: An Introduction to Ecology, the Law & Permitting. Theda Braddock & L. Reed Huppman. 185p. (Orig.). 1995. pap. text ed. 69.00 (*0-86587-467-0*) Gov Insts.

Wetlands: Characteristics & Boundaries. National Research Council Staff. 328p. (Orig.). (C). 1995. text ed. 37.95 (*0-309-05134-7*) Natl Acad Pr.

Wetlands: Concerns & Successes: Proceedings of the Symposium Held September 17-22, 1989, Tampa, FL. American Water Resources Association Staff. Ed. by David W. Fisk. LC 89-84352. (American Water Resources Association Technical Publication Ser.: Vol. TPS-89-3). (Illus.). 582p. 1989. reprint ed. pap. 165.90 (*0-7837-9218-2*, 2049969) Bks Demand.

Wetlands: Environmental Gradients, Boundaries, & Buffers: Proceedings of an International Symposium, April 22-23, 1994. Ed. by George Mulamoottil et al. LC 95-46404. 320p. 1996. 65.00 (*1-56670-147-3*) Lewis Pubs.

Wetlands: Guide to Science, Law, & Technology. Mark S. Dennison & James F. Berry. LC 93-5635. (Illus.). 439p. 1993. 64.00 (*0-8155-1333-X*) Noyes.

Wetlands: Mitigating & Regulating Development Impacts. 2nd ed. David Salvesen. LC 93-61896. 150p. 1994. pap. text ed. 54.95 (*0-87420-752-5*, W17) Urban Land.

Wetlands: Mitigating & Regulating Development Impacts. David Salvesen. LC 89-52209. (Illus.). 123p. 1990. reprint ed. pap. 35.10 (*0-7837-8927-0*, 2049637) Bks Demand.

Wetlands: Science, Politics & Geographic Relationships. John E. Benhart & Alex R. Margin, Jr. (Pathways in Geography Ser.: No. 9). (Illus.). 108p. (YA). (gr. 7 up). 1994. pap. text ed. 12.00 (*1-884136-01-X*) NCFGE.

Wetlands: Tealham Moor. Robin Williams. 296p. (C). 1995. 60.00 (*0-907151-92-2*, Pub. by IMMEL Pubng UK) St Mut.

Wetlands: The Web of Life. Paul Rezendes & Paulette M. Roy. LC 96-14942. (Illus.). 160p. 1996. pap. 25.00 (*0-87156-878-0*) Sierra.

Wetlands & Coastal Zone Regulation & Compliance. Steven M. Silverberg & Mark Dennison. (Environmental Law Ser.). 424p. 1993. text ed. 140.00 (*0-471-55513-4*) Wiley.

Wetlands & Real Estate Development Handbook. 2nd ed. Porter, Wright, Morris & Arthur Staff. 218p. 1991. pap. text ed. 79.00 (*0-86587-269-4*) Gov Insts.

Wetlands & Shallow Continental Water Bodies, Vol. 1: Natural & Human Relationships. Ed. by B. C. Patten. (Illus.). xiii, 759p. 1990. 190.00 (*90-5103-046-0*, Pub. by SPB Acad Pub NE) Balogh.

Wetlands & Shallow Continental Waters Bodies Vol. 2: Case Studies. Ed. by B. C. Patten. (Illus.). 732p. 1994. 190.00 (*90-5103-092-4*, Pub. by SPB Acad Pub NE) Balogh.

Wetlands & Water Quality: A Citizen's Handbook on How to Review & Comment on Section 404 Permits. Gerald A. Paulson. 47p. 1985. 3.00 (*0-318-18950-X*) Lake Mich Fed.

Wetlands Conservation: Emphasis in Pennsylvania. Ed. by Shyamal K. Majumdar et al. LC 89-61084. (Illus.). xiv, 395p. (C). 1989. text ed. 45.00 (*0-945809-01-8*) Penn Science.

Wetlands Delineation Manual: 1987 Edition. Environmental Protection Agency Staff. 170p. 1987. pap. text ed. 59.00 (*0-86587-367-4*) Gov Insts.

Wetlands Deskbook. Environmental Law Reporter Staff. 664p. 1993. pap. 85.00 (*0-911937-48-X*) Environ Law Inst.

Wetlands Identification, Delineation & Classification. Ralph W. Tiner. 1997. write for info. (*0-87371-892-5*, L892) Lewis Pubs.

Wetlands in Flanders: Contributions to Palaeohydrology of the Temperate Zone in the Last 15,000 Years. Ed. by F. Gullentops. (Aardkundige Mededelingen Ser.: No. 6). (Illus.). 209p. (Orig.). 1995. pap. 67.50 (*0-614-13002-6*, Pub. by Leuven Univ BE) Coronet Bks.

Wetlands Issue: What Should We Do with Our Bogs, Swamps & Marshes? Michele Archie. (Environmental Issues Forums Ser.: Vol. 2). (Illus.). 46p. (Orig.). 1992. pap. 6.00 (*1-884008-00-3*) NAAEE.

Wetlands Mitigation & Mitigation Banking. Cheryl C. Runyon & John Helland. 24p. 1995. 10.00 (*1-55516-403-X*, 4342) Natl Conf State Legis.

***Wetlands of American Midwest: An Historical Geography of Changing Attitudes.** Prince. LC 97-22226. 1998. pap. text ed. 19.95 (*0-226-68283-8*) U Ch Pr.

Wetlands of Connecticut. Kenneth J. Metzler & Ralph W. Tiner. (Report of Investigations Ser.: No. 13). (Illus.). 113p. (Orig.). 1992. pap. text ed. 12.95 (*0-942081-03-X*) CT DEP CGNHS.

***Wetlands of Greater Manchester.** David Hall et al. (Lancaster University Department of Archaeology Ser.). (Illus.). 188p. 1995. pap. 42.50 (*0-901800-80-5*, Pub. by Lancaster U Archaeol UK) David Brown.

***Wetlands of Merseyside.** R. W. Cowell & J. B. Innes. (North West Wetlands Survey 1; Lancaster Imprints Ser.: No. 2). (Illus.). 258p. 1995. pap. 45.00 (*0-901800-40-6*, Pub. by Lancaster U Archaeol UK) David Brown.

Wetlands of North America. William A. Niering. LC 91-9. (Illus.). 160p. 1991. 32.95 (*0-934738-81-5*); pap. 12.98 (*0-934738-93-9*) Lickle Pubng.

***Wetlands of North Lancashire.** Robert Middleton et al. (Illus.). 280p. 1995. pap. 45.00 (*0-901800-41-4*); pap. 45.00 (*0-614-22053-X*, Pub. by Lancaster U Archaeol UK) David Brown.

Wetlands of the Interior Southeastern United States. Ed. by Carl C. Trettin et al. LC 94-41173. 1994. lib. bdg. 172.00 (*0-7923-3294-6*) Kluwer Ac.

Wetlands of the World No. 1: Inventory, Ecology & Management. Ed. by Dennis F. Whigham. 768p. (C). 1993. lib. bdg. 351.50 (*0-7923-1685-1*) Kluwer Ac.

Wetlands Preservation Kit. Merryl Lambert. 1992. 19.95 (*0-614-06229-2*) Pequot Pubng.

Wetlands Protection: The Role of Economics. Paul F. Scodari. 89p. 1990. pap. 28.00 (*0-911937-32-3*) Environ Law Inst.

Wetlands Protection & the States. 26p. 1990. 10.00 (*1-55516-425-0*, 4325) Natl Conf State Legis.

Wetlands Regulation: A Complete Guide to Federal & California Programs. Paul D. Cylinder et al. (Illus.). 384p. 1995. pap. 40.00 (*0-923956-20-4*) Solano Pr.

***Wetlands Series.** Roger Rowley. 7.50 (*0-614-18207-7*) Visual Studies.

Wetmore Family of America & Its Collateral Branches. J. C. Wetmore. (Illus.). 672p. 1989. reprint ed. pap. 99.00 (*0-8328-1245-5*); reprint ed. lib. bdg. 107.00 (*0-8328-1244-7*) Higginson Bk Co.

Wets & Drys of Springdale. Rose M. Brown. (Illus.). 136p. (Orig.). 1987. pap. 9.95 (*0-940151-01-4*) Statesman-Exam.

Wetsuitleg - 'n Inleiding vir Studente. C. R. Botha. 132p. 1991. pap. write for info. (*0-7021-2604-7*, Pub. by Juta SA) Gaunt.

Wettability. John C. Berg. LC 93-12059. (Surfactant Science Ser.: Vol. 49). 552p. 1993. 235.00 (*0-8247-9046-4*) Dekker.

Wettability at High Temperatures. Ed. by Eustathopoulos & Nicholas. 1997. text ed. write for info. (*0-08-042146-6*, Pergamon Pr) Elsevier.

Wettbewerbsrecht. 7th ed. Wilhelm Nordemann. 495p. (GER.). 1993. pap. 53.00 (*3-7890-3120-8*, Pub. by Nomos Verlags GW) Intl Bk Import.

Wetter. (Meyers Kleine Kinderbibliothek Ser.). 24p. 1991. 13.25 (*3-411-08461-8*, Pub. by Bibliogr Inst Brockhaus GW) Langenscheidt.

Wetter. Thorsten Piske et al. (German Language Ser.). (Illus.). 42p. (Orig.). (GER.). (YA). (gr. 7 up). 1993. pap. 22.00 (*0-939990-86-5*) Intl Linguistics.

Wetting Agents. National Fire Protection Association Staff. 1990. 16.75 (*0-317-63057-1*, 18-90) Natl Fire Prot.

Wetting Phenomena. Ed. by J. De Coninck & F. Dunlop. (Lecture Notes in Physics Ser.: Vol. 354). viii, 112p. 1990. 40.00 (*0-387-52338-3*) Spr-Verlag.

Wetware. Rudy Rucker. 192p. 1988. mass mkt. 5.99 (*0-380-70178-2*, AvoNova) Avon.

Wetworks. Dave Stone. (Judge Dredd Ser.). 1995. pap. 5.95 (*0-352-32975-0*, Pub. by Virgin Pub UK) London Brdge.

***Wetworks TPB: Rebirth.** Whilce Pontacia & Brandon Choi. (Illus.). 96p. (Orig.). (YA). 1996. pap. 9.95 (*1-887279-33-4*) Image Comics.

***We've a Story to Tell: A History of First Baptist Church, Orlando, Florida, 1871-1996.** Pat Birkhead. LC 96-70690. 320p. 1996. 26.95 (*1-57736-020-6*) Providence Hse.

We've All Got Scars: What Boys & Girls Learn in Elementary School. Raphaela Best. LC 82-49198. 192p. 1983. 27.50 (*0-253-36420-5*) Ind U Pr.

We've All Got Scars: What Boys & Girls Learn in Elementary School. Raphaela Best. LC 82-49198. 192p. 1989. pap. 11.95 (*0-253-20510-7*, MB 510) Ind U Pr.

We've Been Had! Writings on Men's Issues. Roy U. Schenk. 60p. (Orig.). 1988. pap. 6.00 (*0-9613177-1-X*) Bioenergetics Pr.

We've Been Screwed: The Attorneys "Done" It. Clif Culp. 166p. (Orig.). 1994. pap. 19.94 (*0-9640840-0-7*) Clif Culp.

We've Been Through So Much Together, & Most of It Was Your Fault. Ashleigh Brilliant. LC 90-12357. (Brilliant Thoughts Ser.: No. 7). (Illus.). 168p. (Orig.). 1990. 17.95 (*0-88007-182-6*); pap. 9.95 (*0-88007-183-4*) Woodbridge Pr.

We've Climbed the Mountains. Shirley Dummer. 164p. 1992. pap. 8.00 (*0-9633479-0-X*) Dummer Pub.

We've Come a Long Way, Baby! Mary J. Pidgeon. 192p. 1994. pap. 8.99 (*0-89274-725-0*, HH-725) Harrison Hse.

We've Come, O Lord. 1990. 5.99 (*0-685-74842-1*, MB-627) Lillenas.

We've Got a Job to Do: Chicagoans & World War II. Perry Duis & Scott LaFrance. LC 92-14491. 152p. 1992. pap. 22.95 (*0-913820-17-2*) Chicago Hist.

We've Got Something to Say: Ihlgu Tenemos Que Decirles! Sheila L. Rinear & Megan A. Davis. (Scene Bks.). 42p. (YA). (gr. 7-12). 1994. pap. 6.95 (*1-57514-005-5*, 5014) Encore Perform Pub.

***We've Got the Beat: The New Pop of the Early Eighties.** Tim Frew. LC 97-13035. (Life, Times, & Music Ser.). 1997. pap. write for info. (*1-56799-498-9*) M Friedman Pub Grp Inc.

We've Got the Power: Skills for Democracy. Walter Enloe et al. (Illus.). 87p. 1992. pap. text ed. 15.00 (*1-877889-03-2*) League Wmn Voters MN.

We've Got the Power: Skills for Democracy. League of Women Voters of Minnesota Education Fund Staff. 1993. write for info. (*1-877889-06-7*) LWV MN.

We've Got to Start Meeting Like This! A Guide to Successful Business Meeting Management. Roger K. Mosvick & Robert B. Nelson. 312p. (Orig.). 1996. pap. 14.95 (*1-57112-069-6*, P0696) JIST Works.

We've Got to Start Meeting Like This, a Primer on Videoconferencing. rev. ed. Edward A. Daly. Ed. by Penny Luck. 1994. reprint ed. pap. text ed. 49.50 (*1-880145-02-2*) KJH Comm.

We've Had a Hundred Years of Psychotherapy - & the World's Getting Worse. James Hillman & Michael Ventura. LC 92-55294. 256p. 1993. reprint ed. pap. 13.00 (*0-06-250661-7*) Harper SF.

We've Laughed a Lot Together. Perry Tanksley. 2.50 (*0-686-15442-8*) Allgood Bks.

We've Never Done It Like This Before: 10 Creative Approaches to the Same Old Church Tasks. C. Jeff Woods. LC 93-74584. (Church Leader's Core Library). 106p. (Orig.). 1994. pap. 10.95 (*1-56699-124-2*, AL150) Alban Inst.

Wexford: An Omnibus. Date not set. write for info. (*0-09-956640-0*) Random.

Wexford Carols. Ed. by Diarmuid O'Muirithe. (Illus.). 96p. 8200. pap. 14.95 (*0-85105-376-9*, Pub. by Colin Smythe Ltd UK) Dufour.

Wexford County Michigan Cemeteries - Colfax Township. Cadillac Area Genealogical Society Staff. 76p. (Orig.). 1989. pap. 8.00 (*0-940133-22-9*) Kinseeker Pubns.

Wexford County Michigan Cemeteries - Wexford Township. Cadillac Area Genealogy Society Staff. (Illus.). 390p. 1989. pap. 20.00 (*0-940133-24-5*) Kinseeker Pubns.

Wexford Trilogy. Billy Roche. 192p. 1993. pap. 19.95 (*1-85459-265-3*, Pub. by N Hern Bks UK) Theatre Comm.

Wexner Center for the Visual Arts. Ed. by Maggie Toy. (Architectural Design Ser.: No. 82). (Illus.). 96p. (Orig.). 1989. pap. 21.95 (*1-85490-027-7*) Academy Ed UK.

Wexner Center for the Visual Arts: Philip Johnson, Charles Jencks, & Others Examine Peter Eisenman's "Deconstructionist Tour de Force" Philip Johnson et al. (Illus.). 96p. 1990. pap. 21.95 (*0-312-04471-2*) St Martin.

Weyerhaeuser Company: A Report on the Company's Environmental Policies & Practices. (Illus.). 54p. (C). 1994. reprint ed. pap. text ed. 250.00 (*0-7881-0972-3*, Coun on Econ) DIANE Pub.

Weygandt Prints. limited ed. David Swanger et al. (Illus.). 1991. pap. 18.00 (*0-939952-21-1*) Moving Parts.

Weyl Groups & Birational Transformations among Minimal Models. Kenji Matsuki. LC 95-15922. (Memoirs Ser.: No. 557). 133p. 1995. pap. 36.00 (*0-8218-0341-7*, MEMO/116/557) Am Math.

Weyland - Five Complete Novels: PepperTide, A New Dawn, The Understudy, Brenda at the Prom, & Kimberly. Jack Weyland. LC 94-72305. 806p. (J). (gr. 7-10). 1994. 18.95 (*0-87579-864-0*) Deseret Bk.

Weyland Duo: First Day of Forever, Punch & Cookies Forever, 2 bks., Set. Jack Weyland. 1994. 20.98 (*0-88290-459-0*) Horizon Utah.

Weyman's Brew. large type ed. Margery Forester. 384p. 1989. 25.99 (*0-7089-2024-1*) Ulverscroft.

Weymouth. Samuel T. Ragan. (Illus.). 152p. (Orig.). 1987. 14.00 (*0-932662-71-4*) St Andrews Pr.

Weymouth Yacht Log Book. Brown, Son & Ferguson Ltd. Staff. (C). 1987. 90.00 (*0-85174-180-0*, Pub. by Brwn Son Ferg) St Mut.

Weyward Sisters: Shakespeare & Feminist Politics. Dympna Callaghan et al. 192p. 1994. pap. 20.95 (*0-631-17798-1*) Blackwell Pubs.

WG Turbo C Bible. 2nd ed. Nabajyoti Barkakati. 1000p. 1990. 29.95 (*0-672-22742-8*, Bobbs) Macmillan.

WG&L Handbook of Financial Markets. Ed. by Dennis E. Logue. LC 94-20612. 1995. text ed. 23.95 (*0-538-84250-4*) S-W Pub.

WG&L Handbook of Financial Strategy & Policy. Ed. by Dennis E. Logue. LC 94-20887. 1995. text ed. 23.95 (*0-538-84252-0*) S-W Pub.

WG&L Handbook of International Finance. Ed. by Dennis E. Logue. LC 94-20613. 1995. text ed. 23.95 (*0-538-84253-9*) S-W Pub.

WG&L Handbook of Securities & Investment Management. Ed. by Dennis E. Logue. LC 94-20685. 1995. text ed. 23.95 (*0-538-84249-0*) S-W Pub.

WG&L Handbook of Short-Term & Long-Term Financial Management. Warren. 1995. pap. text ed. 39.95 (*0-583-84251-8*) Smithmark.

WG&L Handbook of Short-Time & Long-Term Financial Management. Ed. by Dennis E. Logue. LC 94-20686. 1995. text ed. 23.95 (*0-538-84251-2*) S-W Pub.

WG&L Pension & Benefits Fact Book. 1,992th ed. Nancy Asquith. 1991. per. 88.00 (*0-7913-0440-X*) Warren Gorham & Lamont.

WG&L Texas Real Estate Law Deskbook. Roger Beinhardt & Charles J. Jacobus. 816p. 99.50 (*0-7913-2005-7*) Warren Gorham & Lamont.

WGL Human Resources Checklists with Commentary. 2nd ed. Nancy Asquith. 1991. ring bd. 129.00 (*0-685-69676-6*, MPCK) Warren Gorham & Lamont.

WGL Tax Audio Alert. 225.00 (*0-685-69573-5*, WATA); 95.00 (*0-685-69574-3*, WATQ) Warren Gorham & Lamont.

WGL Tax Planning Checklists. annuals rev. ed. Ronald L. Bleich & Hal W. Mandel. Orig. Title: Modern Tax Planning Checklists. 1991. Supplemented annually; write for info. suppl. ed. 125.00 (*0-7913-0974-6*) Warren Gorham & Lamont.

WGS Linux Pro: Linux Compendium. (Linux-Flagship Ser.). 1200p. 1995. pap. 69.00 incl. disk (*0-9644309-1-6*) WrkGrp Solns.

W.H. Auden: The Life of a Poet. Charles Osborne. LC 95-34142. 352p. 1995. pap. 12.95 (*0-87131-788-5*) M Evans.

Whack on the Side of the Head. rev. ed. Roger Von Oech. 208p. (Orig.). 1993. pap. 12.99 (*0-446-77808-7*) Warner Bks.

Whack on the Side of the Head. rev. ed. Roger Von Olech. (Orig.). 1990. pap. 14.99 (*0-446-39158-1*) Warner Bks.

***Whaddaya Doin' in There? A Bathroom Companion (For Kids)** Planet Dexter Editors. (J). (gr. 4-8). Date not set. 10.00 (*0-614-19318-4*) Addison-Wesley.

Whaddaya Say? Nina Weinstein. (Orig.). (C). 1982. pap. text ed. 2.95 (*0-87789-214-8*, 1605); audio 14.95 (*0-87789-218-0*, 1606) ELS Educ Servs.

Whaddayah Mean Leave Home & Travel for the Rest of My Life! The Pre-Retirement Guide to RV Living. 2nd ed. Gene Townsend & Denne M. Townsend. (Illus.). 256p. 1995. pap. 13.95 (*0-923568-40-9*) Wilderness Adventure Bks.

Whadd'ya Gonna Do? 25 Secrets for Getting a Life. Joey O'Connor. LC 95-33147. 112p. (YA). (gr. 6-9). 1996. 9.99 (*0-8010-1103-5*) Baker Bks.

Whaiora: Maori Health Development. Mason Durie. (Illus.). 248p. 1995. pap. 35.00 (*0-19-558316-7*) OUP.

Whakairo: Maori Tribal Art. David Simmons. (Illus.). 192p. 1986. 55.00 (*0-19-558119-9*) OUP.

Whale. Judy Allen. LC 92-53019. (Illus.). 32p. (J). (ps up). 1993. 15.95 (*1-56402-160-2*) Candlewick Pr.

Whale. Judy Allen. LC 92-53019. (Illus.). 32p. (J). (ps up). 1994. pap. 4.99 (*1-56402-383-4*) Candlewick Pr.

Whale. Sabrina Crewe. LC 96-4846. (Life Cycles Bks.). (Illus.). (J). 1997. lib. bdg. 21.40 (*0-8172-4363-1*) Raintree Steck-V.

***Whale.** Sabrina Crewe. (Life Cycles Ser.). (Illus.). (J). (gr. 2-5). 1997. pap. 4.95 (*0-614-28912-2*) Raintree Steck-V.

Whale. Paula Z. Hogan. LC 79-13379. (Life Cycles Bks.). (Illus.). 32p. (J). (gr. 1-4). 1979. pap. 4.95 (*0-8114-8180-8*) Raintree Steck-V.

Whale. David Holman. (Methuen Young Drama Ser.). 46p. (YA). 1990. pap. 7.95 (*0-413-63090-0*, A0470, Pub. by Methuen UK) Heinemann.

Whale. Vasilli Papastavrov. (Eyewitness Bks.). (Illus.). 64p. (J). (gr. 5 up). 1993. 19.00 (*0-679-83884-8*); lib. bdg. 20.99 (*0-679-93884-2*) Knopf Bks Yng Read.

***Whale.** Adam Woog. LC 97-21349. (Overview Series). (Illus.). (J). (gr. 4-12). 1997. lib. bdg. 17.96 (*1-56006-460-9*) Lucent Bks.

***Whale: Giant of the Ocean.** Eric S. Grace. LC 97-7560. 1997. pap. write for info. (*1-57145-603-1*) Thunder Bay CA.

***Whale: The Anti-Moby Dick Edition.** Herman Melville. Ed. by Tom Darling. 300p. (Orig.). 1996. pap. 12.00 (*1-889543-02-0*) Beachchair Pr.

Whale: The Sovereigns of the Sea. Caroline Brett. Ed. by Rebecca Stefoff. LC 92-10242. (Wildlife Survival Library). (Illus.). 31p. (J). (gr. 3-6). 1992. lib. bdg. 17.26 (*1-56074-054-X*) Garrett Ed Corp.

Whale Adoption Kit. Merryl Lambert. (Friends of the Ocean Ser.). 1992. 19.95 (*0-9641742-3-5*) Pequot Pubng.

Whale Alert: An Integrated Activity Unit. Bev McKay. (Illus.). 32p. 1993. pap. text ed. 4.95 (*0-86530-238-3*) Incentive Pubns.

Whale & Dolphin. Vincent Serventy. LC 84-15118. (Animals in the Wild Ser.). (Illus.). 24p. (J). (gr. k-5). 1985. pap. 3.95 (*0-8114-6892-5*) Raintree Steck-V.

Whale & Its Captors, or, The Whaleman's Adventures. enl. ed. Henry T. Cheever. 315p. 1991. 24.95 (*0-87770-487-2*) Ye Galleon.

Whale & Other Uncollected Translations. Tr. by Richard Wilbur. (New American Translation Ser.: No. 3). 56p. (C). 1982. 18.00 (*0-918526-32-9*); pap. 10.00 (*0-918526-33-7*) BOA Edns.

Whale & the Reactor: A Search for Limits in an Age of High Technology. Langdon Winner. xiv, 200p. 1988. pap. text ed. 12.95 (*0-226-90211-0*) U Ch Pr.

Whale Brother. Barbara Steiner. (Illus.). (J). (ps-3). 1988. 12.95 (*0-8027-6804-0*); lib. bdg. 13.85 (*0-8027-6805-9*) Walker & Co.

Whale Brother. Barbara Steiner. LC 88-5565. (Illus.). 32p. (J). (gr. k-4). 1995. pap. 6.95 (*0-8027-7460-1*) Walker & Co.

Whale Called Trouble. Mary Ann Brittain. (Illus.). 24p. (J). (gr. 1-12). 1985. pap. 1.50 (*0-917134-08-7*) NC Natl Sci.

Whale Carton Craft. Hideharu Naitoh. (Illus.). 70p. (Orig.). 1993. pap. 13.00 (*0-87040-920-4*) Japan Pubns USA.

Whale Dancers. Anne E. Kafoure. (Illus.). 24p. (Orig.). (J). (gr. 5-9). 1995. pap. text ed. 8.95 (*1-884825-16-8*) Raspberry Pubns.

Whale Dancers: Relationship Between Dory & Humpback Whales. Anne E. KaFoure. (Illus.). 24p. (J). (gr. 1-8). 1995. lib. bdg. 14.95 (*1-884825-04-4*) Raspberry Pubns.

Whale Family Book. Cynthia D'Vincent. LC 91-41145. (Illus.). 60p. (J). (gr. 5 up). 1992. pap. 15.95 (*0-88708-148-7*, Picture Book Studio) S&S Childrens.

Whale for the Killing. Farley Mowat. 224p. 1984. mass mkt. 5.50 (*0-7704-2331-0*) Bantam.

Whale, Giant of the Seas. Valerie Tracqui. LC 95-8549. (Animal Close-Ups Ser.). 28p. (J). 1995. pap. 6.95 (*0-88106-435-1*) Charlesbridge Pub.

Whale Hunt: The Narrative of a Voyage in the Ship Charles W. Morgan, 1849-1853. Nelson C. Haley. (Illus.). 304p. 1990. pap. 17.95 (*0-913372-52-8*) Mystic Seaport.

Whale Hunters. Robert Smith. 180p. (C). 1996. pap. 27.00 (*0-85976-393-5*, Pub. by J Donald UK) St Mut.

Whale in Darkness. Brissenden. (Australian National University Press Ser.). 1980. text ed. 21.00 (*0-08-032933-0*, Pergamon Pr) Elsevier.

Whale in Lowell's Cove. Jane Robinson. LC 91-77670. (Illus.). 48p. (J). (gr. 1-4). 1992. 14.95 (*0-89272-308-4*) Down East.

Whale in the Sky. Anne Siberell. LC 82-2483. (Unicorn Paperbacks Ser.). (Illus.). 32p. (J). (ps-3). 1985. pap. 3.95 (*0-525-44197-2*) Dutton Child Bks.

Whale in the Sky. Anne Siberell. 1992. pap. 4.99 (*0-14-054792-4*) NAL-Dutton.

Whale Is Not a Fish - & Other Animal Mix-Ups. Melvin H. Berger. (J). 1995. pap. 4.99 (*0-590-47477-4*) Scholastic Inc.

***Whale Is Not a Fish & Other Animal Mix-Ups.** Melvin H. Berger & Marshall Peck, III. (Illus.). (FRE.). (J). pap. 6.99 (*0-590-16026-5*) Scholastic Inc.

Whale Is Stuck. Charles Fuge & Karen Hayles. LC 92-34078. (J). (ps-1). 1993. pap. 14.00 (*0-671-86587-0*, S&S Bks Young Read) S&S Childrens.

Whale Magic for Kids. Tom Wolpert. LC 90-50718. (Animal Magic for Kids Ser.). (Illus.). 48p. (J). (gr. 3-4). 1991. lib. bdg. 18.60 (*0-8368-0660-3*) Gareth Stevens Inc.

Whale of a Tale: A Historical Perspective of Virtual Enterprise. H. T. Goranson. (Perspectives on Agility Ser.). 6p. 1996. pap. 10.00 (*1-885166-10-9*, PA96-02) Agility Forum.

Whale of a Tale about a Guy Named Jonah. Joe Loesch. Ed. by Cheryl J. Hutchinson. (Parable Ser.: Vol. 2). (Illus.). 54p. (Orig.). (J). (gr. 1 up). 1996. 14.95 incl. audio (*1-887729-08-9*); 16.95 incl. audio compact disk (*1-887729-09-7*) Toy Box Prods.

***Whale Off! The Story of American Shore Whaling.** Rattray Edwards et al. Date not set. lib. bdg. 23.95 (*0-8488-1781-8*) Amereon Ltd.

***Whale on the Line.** Nuala Archer. 42p. 8100. 16.95 (*0-904011-21-6*) Dufour.

Whale Problem: A Status Report. Ed. by William E. Schevill. LC 73-88056. 384p. 1990. 38.95 (*0-674-95075-5*) HUP.

Whale Sharks. Sarah Palmer. (Shark Discovery Library). (Illus.). 24p. (J). (gr. k-5). 1988. lib. bdg. 11.94 (*0-86592-463-5*); lib. bdg. 8.95 (*0-685-58309-0*) Rourke Corp.

Whale Sharks. John F. Prevost. LC 95-6375. (Sharks Ser.). (J). (gr. k-3). 1995. lib. bdg. 13.98 (*1-56239-473-8*) Abdo & Dghtrs.

Whale Sharks. Anne Welsbacher. (Animals & the Environment Ser.). 48p. (J). (gr. 3-9). 1995. lib. bdg. 17.80 (*1-56065-271-3*) Capstone Pr.

***Whale Sharks.** Anne Welsbacher. (Sharks Ser.). (Illus.). 48p. (J). (gr. 3-7). 1995. 18.40 (*0-516-35271-7*) Childrens.

Whale Ships & Whaling. George F. Dow. (Illus.). 1967. reprint ed. 35.00 (*0-87266-007-9*) Argosy.

Whale Ships & Whaling: A Pictorial History. George F. Dow. (Antiques Series: Transportation). 288p. 1985. reprint ed. pap. 10.95 (*0-486-24808-9*) Dover.

Whale Song. Tony Johnston. (Illus.). 32p. (J). (ps-3). 1987. 14.95 (*0-399-21402-X*, Putnam) Putnam Pub Group.

Whale Songs. Phillis Thorpe. (C). 1990. pap. 30.00 (*0-646-11255-4*, Pub. by Boolarong Pubns AT) St Mut.

***Whale Tales.** P. Fromm. 1995. pap. 12.95 (*0-9648704-0-1*) Whale Tales.

Whale Tales. Wyland & Mark Doyle. LC 94-60366. (Illus.). 190p. 1995. 22.00 (*0-9631793-5-7*) Wyland Galleries.

Whale Watcher's Cookbook: Views from the Galley. Sharon M. Nogg. (Illus.). 224p. 1990. reprint ed. pap. 11.95 (*0-939644-66-5*) Actors Etc.

Whale Watchers' Guide. Robert Gardner. LC 83-17425. (Illus.). 170p. (YA). (gr. 7 up). 1984. pap. 5.95 (*0-671-49807-X*, Julian Messner) Silver Burdett Pr.

Whale Watcher's Guide: Whale-Watching Trips in North America. rev. ed. Patricia Corrigan. (Illus.). 328p. 1994. pap. 12.95 (*1-55971-436-0*) NorthWord.

Whale Who Wanted to Be Small. Gill McBarnet. (Illus.). 32p. (J). (gr. k-2). 1985. 8.95 (*0-9615102-0-X*) Ruwanga Trad.

Whaleboat: A Study of Design, Construction & Use from 1850-1970. 2nd rev. ed. Willits D. Ansel. (Illus.). vi, 147p. 1983. 17.95 (*0-913372-40-4*) Mystic Seaport.

Whaleghost. Howard L. Hipp. LC 87-71717. 141p. (Orig.). 1988. pap. 8.00 (*0-916383-35-0*) Aegina Pr.

Whalehead, Tales of Corolla, N.C. Suzanne Tate. LC 87-90489. (Illus.). 48p. 1987. pap. 4.95 (*0-9616344-1-3*) Nags Head Art.

Whalemen's Paintings & Drawings: Selections from the Kendall Whaling Museum Collection. Kenneth R. Martin. LC 81-50343. (Illus.). 172p. 1983. 30.00 (*0-87413-191-X*) Kendall Whaling.

Whalemen's Paintings & Drawings: Selections from the Kendall Whaling Museum Collection. Kenneth R. Martin. LC 81-50343. (Illus.). 176p. 1982. 30.00 (*0-685-07611-3*) U Delaware Pr.

Whaler & the Privateer: The Story of Two Ships, 1795-1807. Diana Brown & Colin Brown. LC 93-86010. (Illus.). 270p. (Orig.). 1993. pap. 23.50 (*0-9638208-0-X*) Letter of Marque.

***Whalers Encyclopedia: From Abrahamsson to Zuke.** (Illus.). 300p. (Orig.). 1997. pap. 24.95 (*0-9650315-3-5*) Glacier Publng.

***Whalers Trivia Compendium.** Jack Lautier. (Illus.). 72p. 1995. pap. 7.95 (*0-9650315-0-0*) Glacier Publng.

Whales. 1999. pap. write for info. (*0-590-73534-9*) Scholastic Inc.

***Whales.** Ariel Books Staff. 1996. 3.95 (*0-8362-1010-7*, Arie Bks) Andrews & McMeel.

Whales. Laura Bour. LC 92-41413. (First Discovery Bks.). (Illus.). 24p. (J). (ps-3). 1993. 11.95 (*0-590-47130-9*, Cartwheel) Scholastic Inc.

Whales. Cousteau Society Staff. LC 92-34176. (Illus.). (J). (ps-1). 1993. bds. 4.95 (*0-671-86564-1*, Litl Simon S&S) S&S Childrens.

Whales. Lesley Dow. (Great Creatures of the World Ser.). 72p. (J). (gr. 5-12). 1990. 17.95 (*0-8160-2271-2*) Facts on File.

Whales. Lesley A. DuTemple. LC 95-30803. (Early Bird Nature Bks.). 48p. (J). (gr. 1-3). 1996. lib. bdg. 18.95 (*0-8225-3008-2*, Lerner Publctns) Lerner Group.

Whales. Gail Gibbons. LC 91-4507. (Illus.). 32p. (J). (ps-3). 1991. lib. bdg. 15.95 (*0-8234-0900-7*) Holiday.

Whales. Gail Gibbons. (Illus.). (J). (gr. k-4). 1993. pap. 15.95 incl. audio (*0-87499-306-7*) Live Oak Media.

Whales. Gail Gibbons. (Illus.). (J). (gr. k-4). 1993. 22.95 incl. audio (*0-87499-307-5*) Live Oak Media.

Whales. Maura M. Gouck. (Nature Bks.). 32p. (J). (gr. 2-6). 1991. lib. bdg. 22.79 (*0-89565-717-1*) Childs World.

Whales. Tony Hall. (Fact Finders Ser.). (Illus.). 64p. (J). 1990. 7.99 (*0-517-05149-4*) Random Hse Value.

Whales. Tom Hill. 1973. pap. 5.00 (*0-685-37098-4*) Twowindows Pr.

***Whales.** Judith Hodge. LC 97-19630. (Animals of the Oceans Ser.). 1997. pap. text ed. 5.95 (*0-7641-0261-3*) Barron.

***Whales.** Kevin J. Holmes. LC 97-8240. (Animals Ser.). (J). 1998. write for info. (*1-56065-601-8*) Capstone Pr.

Whales. Casey Horton. (Endangered! Ser.). 32p. (J). (gr. 3-5). 1996. lib. bdg. 14.95 (*0-7614-0219-5*, Benchmark NY) Marshall Cavendish.

***Whales.** Marianne Johnston. LC 96-44024. (J). 1996. lib. bdg. 11.95 (*0-8239-5142-1*, PowerKids) Rosen Group.

Whales. Michael P. Jones. LC 86-74418. (Sealife Ser.: No. 1). (Illus.). 76p. 1984. 15.00 (*0-685-09702-1*); pap. text ed. 10.00 (*0-89904-096-9*) Crumb Elbow Pub.

Whales. L. Martin. (Wildlife in Danger Ser.). (Illus.). 24p. (J). (gr. k-5). 1988. lib. bdg. 11.94 (*0-86592-988-2*); lib. bdg. 8.95 (*0-685-67679-X*) Rourke Corp.

Whales. Jo E. Moore et al. (Illus.). 48p. (J). (gr. 3-6). 1990. pap. 5.95 (*1-55799-164-2*, EMC 239) Evan-Moor Corp.

Whales. Cynthia Rylant. LC 95-15298. (Illus.). 40p. (J). (gr. k). 1996. 14.95 (*0-590-58285-2*, Blue Sky Press) Scholastic Inc.

Whales. Joan Short & Bettina Bird. LC 96-15298. (Mondo Animals Ser.). (Illus.). (J). 1997. pap. write for info. (*1-57255-190-9*) Mondo Pubng.

Whales. Seymour Simon. LC 87-45285. (Illus.). 40p. (J). (gr. 2-5). 1989. 17.00 (*0-690-04756-8*, Crowell Jr Bks); lib. bdg. 16.89 (*0-690-04758-4*, Crowell Jr Bks) HarpC Child Bks.

Whales. Seymour Simon. LC 87-45285. (Trophy Nonfiction Bk.). (Illus.). 40p. (J). (gr. 2-5). 1992. pap. 6.95 (*0-06-446095-9*, Trophy) HarpC Child Bks.

Whales. Eileen Spinelli. (Childrens' Nature Library). (Illus.). 64p. (J). (gr. k-4). 1992. lib. bdg. 14.95 (*1-878363-90-5*, HTS Bks) Forest Hse.

Whales. Erik D. Stoops et al. LC 94-47278. (Illus.). 80p. (J). (gr. 3-7). 1995. 16.95 (*0-8069-0566-2*) Sterling.

Whales. Erik D. Stoops & Jeffrey L. Martin. (Illus.). 80p. (Orig.). (J). 1996. pap. 9.95 (*0-8069-0567-0*) Sterling.

Whales. Two Can Publishing Ltd. Staff. (Animal Bks.). (Illus.). 32p. (J). (gr. 2-7). 1991. pap. 2.95 (*0-87534-215-9*) Highlights.

Whales. John B. Wexo. (Zoobooks Ser.). 24p. (J). (gr. 4). 1989. lib. bdg. 14.95 (*0-88682-272-6*) Creative Ed.

***Whales.** John B. Wexo. (Zoobooks). (Illus.). 24p. (J). (gr. 1-7). 1997. 13.95 (*1-888153-34-2*, 272-6) Wildlife Educ.

Whales. Wildlife Education, Ltd. Staff. (Zoobooks Ser.). (Illus.). 20p. (Orig.). 1983. pap. 2.75 (*0-937934-10-0*) Wildlife Educ.

Whales. Barbara J. Zitwer. (Magic of the Ocean Ser.). (Illus.). 60p. 1995. write for info. (*0-446-51883-2*) Warner Bks.

Whales. deluxe ed. Michael P. Jones. LC 86-74418. (Sealife Ser.: No. 1). (Illus.). 76p. 1984. 25.00 (*0-89904-000-4*) Crumb Elbow Pub.

Whales. Gail Gibbons. (Illus.). (J). (ps-3). 1993. reprint ed. pap. 6.95 (*0-8234-1030-7*) Holiday.

Whales, 4 bks., Set. Gail Gibbons. (Illus.). (J). (gr. k-4). 1993. pap. 33.95 incl. audio (*0-87499-308-3*) Live Oak Media.

Whales: Activities Based on Research from the Center for Coastal Studies. Deborah Kovacs. 1992. pap. 9.95 (*0-590-49156-3*) Scholastic Inc.

Whales: An Educational Coloring Book. Spizzirri Publishing Co. Staff. Ed. by Linda Spizzirri. (Illus.). 32p. (J). (gr. 1-8). 1982. pap. 1.99 (*0-86545-039-0*) Spizzirri.

Whales: Giant Marine Mammals. Isidro Sanchez et al. (Secrets of the Animal World Ser.). (Illus.). 32p. (J). (gr. 3 up). 1996. lib. bdg. 18.60 (*0-8368-1398-7*) Gareth Stevens Inc.

***Whales: Killer Whales, Blue Whales & More.** unabridged ed. Deborah Hodge. (The Kid Can Press Wildlife Ser.). (Illus.). 32p. (J). (gr. 1-5). 1997. 10.95 (*1-55074-356-2*, Pub. by Kids Can Pr CN) Genl Dist Srvs.

Whales: Mighty Giants of the Sea, Set. Ed. by Donald J. Crump. (National Geographic Society Pop-ups Ser.: Set 5). (Illus.). 12p. (J). (ps up). 1996. 16.00 (*0-87044-810-2*) Natl Geog.

Whales: The Gentle Giants. Joyce Milton. LC 88-15616. (Step into Reading Bks.). (Illus.). 48p. (Orig.). (J). (gr. k-3). 1989. lib. bdg. 7.99 (*0-394-99809-X*) Random Bks Yng Read.

Whales: The Gentle Giants. Joyce Milton. LC 88-15616. (Step into Reading Bks.). (Illus.). 48p. (Orig.). (J). (gr. k-3). 1989. pap. 3.99 (*0-394-89809-5*) Random Bks Yng Read.

Whales--The Gentle Giants: Calendar 1988. Michael P. Jones. (Illus.). (Orig.). text ed. 10.00 (*0-89904-211-2*); pap. text ed. 5.00 (*0-89904-212-0*) Crumb Elbow Pub.

Whales--The Gentle Giants: Calendar 1988. limited ed. Michael P. Jones. (Illus.). (Orig.). 25.00 (*0-89904-213-9*) Crumb Elbow Pub.

Whales & Dolphins. (Information Ser.). 32p. (J). 3.50 (*0-7214-1743-4*, Ladybrd) Penguin.

***Whales & Dolphins.** (Eyes on Nature Ser.). (Illus.). 32p. (J). (gr. 1 up). write for info. (*1-56156-423-0*) Kidsbks.

Whales & Dolphins. Victor Cox. (Illus.). 128p. 1989. 15.99 (*0-517-69092-6*) Random Hse Value.

Whales & Dolphins. Jim Nollman. 1997. 30.00 (*0-8050-4575-9*) H Holt & Co.

***Whales & Dolphins.** Mark Oakley. (J). 1997. pap. 4.99 (*0-7214-5675-8*, Ladybrd) Penguin.

Whales & Dolphins. Steve Parker. LC 93-38518. (Look into Nature Ser.). (Illus.). 60p. (J). (gr. 3-6). 1994. 16.95 (*0-87156-465-3*) Sierra Club Childrens.

Whales & Dolphins: A Portrait of the Animal World. Andrew Cleave. 1995. 10.98 (*0-8317-0966-9*) Smithmark.

Whales & Dolphins - Shorelines of America: The Story Behind the Scenery. rev. ed. Peter C. Howorth. (Illus.). 48p. (Orig.). 1994. pap. 7.95 (*0-88714-083-1*) KC Pubns.

Whales & Dolphins Coloring Book. John Green. (Illus.). (J). (gr. k-3). 1990. pap. 2.95 (*0-486-26306-1*) Dover.

Whales & Dolphins of New Zealand & Australia: An Identification Guide. Alan A. Baker. (Illus.). 133p. (C). 1990. pap. text ed. 20.00 (*0-86473-099-3*, Pub. by Victoria Univ Pr NZ) Lubrecht & Cramer.

Whales & Giants of the Deep. Rupert Oliver. 1989. 4.99 (*0-517-69061-6*) Random Hse Value.

***Whales & Humans.** Nollman. Date not set. pap. 13.95 (*0-8050-5524-X*) H Holt & Co.

***Whales & Humans.** Nollman. 1998. 27.95 (*0-8050-5523-1*) H Holt & Co.

Whales & Other Creatures of the Sea. Joyce Milton. LC 92-2409. (Pictureback Ser.). (Illus.). 32p. (J). (ps-4). 1993. pap. 3.25 (*0-679-83899-6*) Random Bks Yng Read.

Whales & Other Marine Mammals. George S. Fichter. (Illus.). 160p. (J). 1990. pap. 5.50 (*0-307-24075-4*, Golden Pr) Western Pub.

Whales & Other Sea Mammals. Elsa Posell. LC 82-4451. (New True Bks.). (J). (gr. k-4). 1982. pap. 5.50 (*0-516-41663-4*); lib. bdg. 19.00 (*0-516-01663-6*) Childrens.

Whales & Other Wonders - Frozen Worlds. Querida L. Pearce. (Amazing Science Ser.). (Illus.). 64p. (J). (gr. 4-6). 1991. pap. 5.95 (*0-671-70694-2*, Julian Messner) Silver Burdett Pr.

Whales & People. Jason Cooper. LC 96-19194. (Read All About Whales Ser.). (J). 1996. write for info. (*0-86593-452-5*) Rourke Corp.

Whales, Dolphins & Porpoises. Mark Carwardine. LC 92-7624. (See & Explore Library). (Illus.). 64p. (J). (gr. 3 up). 1992. 12.95 (*1-56458-144-6*) DK Pub Inc.

Whales, Dolphins & Porpoises. Richard Harrison et al. 240p. 1988. 35.00 (*0-8160-1977-0*) Facts on File.

Whales, Dolphins & Porpoises. National Geographic Society Book Division Staff. LC 95-20916. 232p. 1995. 40.00 (*0-7922-2952-5*) Natl Geog.

***Whales, Dolphins & Porpoises.** Reader's Digest Association Staff. LC 97-3331. (Reader's Digest Explores Ser.). 1997. write for info. (*0-89577-976-5*) RD Assn.

Whales, Dolphins & Porpoises. deluxe ed. National Geographic Society Book Division Staff. 232p. 1995. 50.00 (*0-7922-2953-3*) Natl Geog.

Whales, Dolphins, & Porpoises in the Zoo. Roland Smith. LC 93-35425. (New Zoo Ser.). (Illus.). 64p. (J). (gr. 3-6). 1994. lib. bdg. 16.40 (*1-56294-318-9*) Millbrook Pr.

Whales, Dolphins, & Porpoises of the Eastern North Pacific & Adjacent Arctic Waters: A Guide to Their Identification. Stephen Leatherwood et al. (Illus.). 256p. 1988. reprint ed. pap. 12.95 (*0-486-25651-0*) Dover.

Whale's Footprints. Rick Boyer. 288p. 1989. mass mkt. 4.99 (*0-8041-0450-6*) Ivy Books.

Whale's Footprints. large type ed. Rick Boyer. (General Ser.). 392p. 1989. lib. bdg. 18.95 (*0-8161-4764-7*, GK Hall) Thorndike Pr.

Whales for Kids. (Illus.). 48p. (J). 1991. pap. 6.95 (*1-55971-125-6*) NorthWord.

Whales for Kids. Tom Wolpert. (Illus.). 48p. (J). 1991. 14.95 (*1-55971-088-8*, 0199) NorthWord.

Whales, Ice & Men: The History of Whaling in the Western Arctic. John R. Bockstoce. (Illus.). 400p. 1995. pap. 29.95 (*0-295-97447-8*) U of Wash Pr.

Whales in the Classroom Presents: Getting to Know the Whales. Larry Wade. (Illus.). 152p. (Orig.). (J). (gr. 4-8). 1995. pap. 16.95 (*0-9629395-2-8*) Singing Rock.

***Whales '93: Blue.** Bioacoutics Research Program Staff. 1995. pap. 19.95 incl. audio compact disk (*0-938027-27-1*) Crows Nest Bird.

***Whales '93: Finback.** Bioacoustics Research Program Staff. 1995. pap. 19.95 incl. audio compact disk (*0-938027-26-3*) Crows Nest Bird.

***Whales '93: Greatest Hits.** Bioacoustics Research Program Staff. 1995. pap. 14.95 incl. audio compact disk (*0-938027-25-5*) Crows Nest Bird.

***Whales '93: Minke.** Bioacoustics Research Program Staff. 1995. pap. 19.95 incl. audio compact disk (*0-938027-28-X*) Crows Nest Bird.

Whales of August. David Berry. 1984. pap. 5.25 (*0-8222-1234-X*) Dramatists Play.

Whales of Canada. Erich Hoyt. (Illus.). 128p. 1988. pap. 6.95 (*0-920656-33-1*, Pub. by Camden Hse CN) Firefly Bks Ltd.

Whales of Hawaii. Stanley M. Minasian. 1991. pap. 5.95 (*0-9627803-0-8*) Hamilton West.

Whales of Hawaii: Including All Species of Marine Mammals in Hawaiian & Adjacent Waters. Contrib. by Stanley M. Minasian et al. (Illus.). 100p. (Orig.). (YA). (gr. 9 up). 1991. pap. text ed. 7.00 (*0-9617803-0-4*) Marine Mammal Fund.

Whales of the Northwest: A Guide to Marine Mammals of Oregon, Washington & British Columbia. Chuck Flaherty. Ed. by Margaret Tarbert. (Illus.). 25p. (Orig.). 1990. pap. 5.95 (*0-9626750-0-8*) Cherry Lane Pr.

Whales of the Seas. Jason Cooper. LC 96-19193. (Read All About Whales Ser.). (J). 1996. write for info. (*0-86593-453-3*) Rourke Corp.

Whales of the World. June Behrens. LC 87-8046. (Sea Life Ser.). (Illus.). 48p. (J). (gr. 1-4). 1987. lib. bdg. 17.50 (*0-516-08877-7*) Childrens.

Whales of the World. Nigel Bonner. (Illus.). 191p. 1989. 25.95 (*0-8160-1734-4*) Facts on File.

***Whales of the World.** Phil Clapham. LC 97-1860. (Illus.). 120p. 1997. 29.95 (*0-89658-359-7*) Voyageur Pr.

Whales, Porpoises, & Dolphins. Mark Carwardine. LC 94-33301. (Eyewitness Handbks.). (Illus.). 256p. 1995. 29.95 (*1-56458-621-9*); pap. 17.95 (*1-56458-620-0*) DK Pub Inc.

Whales, Seals, Fish, & Man: Proceedings of the International Symposium on the Biology of Marine Mammals in the North East Atlantic, Troms, Norway, 29 November-1 December 1994. Ed. by Arnoldus Schytte-Blix et al. LC 95-9010. (Developments in Marine Biology Ser.: Vol. 4). 734p. 1995. 308.25 (*0-444-82070-1*) Elsevier.

Whales, Sharks, & Other Sea Creatures. Nina Kidd. (Draw Science Ser.). 64p. 1992. pap. 4.95 (*1-56565-013-1*) Lowell Hse.

Whales' Song. Dyan Sheldon. LC 90-46722. (Illus.). 32p. (J). (ps-3). 1991. pap. 16.99 (*0-8037-0972-2*) Dial Bks Young.

Whales Song. Dyan Sheldon. (J). 1997. pap. 5.99 (*0-14-055997-3*) Viking Penguin.

***Whales' Song.** Dyan Sheldon. (Illus.). 32p. (ARA & ENG.). (J). (ps-2). 1997. 16.95 (*1-85430-500-X*, Pub. by Global Bks UK) Talman.

***Whales' Song.** Dyan Sheldon. (Illus.). 32p. (CHI & ENG.). (J). (ps-2). 1997. 16.95 (*1-85430-502-6*, Pub. by Global Bks UK) Talman.

***Whales' Song.** Dyan Sheldon. (Illus.). 32p. (ENG & SPA.). (J). (ps-2). 1997. 16.95 (*1-85430-503-4*, Pub. by Global Bks UK) Talman.

***Whales' Song.** Dyan Sheldon. (Illus.). 32p. (VIE.). (J). (ps-2). 1997. 16.95 (*1-85430-505-0*, Pub. by Global Bks UK) Talman.

***Whale's Song.** Dyan Sheldon. (Illus.). (J). (ps-3). 1997. pap. 5.99 (*0-614-28894-0*, Puffin) Puffin Bks.

Whales Stained Glass Coloring Book. John Green. (Illus.). (J). (gr. k-3). 1993. pap. 1.00 (*0-486-27012-2*) Dover.

Whale's Tale. Charlie Beauchamp. 18p. (J). (gr. 1-4). 1995. pap. 4.95 (*0-9646498-4-5*) Pacific Tower.

Whale's Tale. Deborah Evans-Smith. LC 85-51791. (Illus.). 25p. (J). (gr. 2-6). 1986. 8.95 (*0-917507-02-9*) Sea Fog Pr.

Whale's Tale. Sally L. Jones. (Bible Playtime Bk.). (Illus.). 8p. (J). (ps). 1993. 8.49 (*0-7847-0048-6*, 03686) Standard Pub.

Whale's Tale. Gill McBarnet. (Illus.). 32p. (J). (gr. k-2). 1988. 8.95 (*0-9615102-4-2*) Ruwanga Trad.

***Whale's War.** Tom L. Eisenman. 228p. (YA). (gr. 5 up). 1997. pap. 12.99 (*0-8308-1364-0*, 1364) InterVarsity.

Whale's Way. Heather Kellerhals-Stewart. 120p. (YA). 1988. pap. 6.95 (*0-919591-30-2*, Pub. by Polestar Bk Pubs CN) Orca Bk Pubs.

Whale's World. Jason Cooper. LC 96-19189. (Read All About Whales Ser.). (J). 1996. write for info. (*0-86593-449-5*) Rourke Corp.

Whalesinger. Welwyn W. Katz. LC 90-34091. 224p. (YA). (gr. 7 up). 1991. lib. bdg. 14.95 (*0-689-50511-6*, McElderry) S&S Childrens.

Whalesong. Robert Siegel. 1995. 21.75 (*0-8446-6818-4*) Peter Smith.

Whalesong: A Novel. Robert Siegel. LC 90-55767. (Whale Song Trilogy Ser.). 144p. 1991. reprint ed. pap. 11.00 (*0-06-250798-2*) Harper SF.

Whalewatch! June Behrens. LC 78-7338. (Sea Life Ser.). (Illus.). 32p. (J). (gr. k-4). 1978. lib. bdg. 17.50 (*0-516-08873-4*) Childrens.

Whalewatchers Guide to the North Atlantic. Barry W. Van Dusen, pseud. (Habitat Ser.). (Illus.). 8p. 1988. 3.95 (*0-932691-06-4*) MA Audubon Soc.

Whalewatcher's Handbook: A Field Guide to the Whales, Dolphins, & Porpoises of North America. David Bulloch. (Illus.). 128p. 1993. pap. 13.95 (*1-55821-232-9*) Lyons & Burford.

Whaley: English Records of the Whaley Family & Its Branches in America. S. Whaley. (Illus.). 234p. 1991. reprint ed. pap. 36.50 (*0-8328-1840-2*); reprint ed. lib. bdg. 46.50 (*0-8328-1839-9*) Higginson Bk Co.

***Whaley & Wong's Essentials of Pediatric Nursing.** 5th ed. Murphy. 300p. (C). (gr. 13). 1996. student ed., pap. text ed. 19.95 (*0-8151-7470-5*, 28277, Yr Bk Med Pubs) Mosby Yr Bk.

Whaley & Wong's Nursing Care of Infants & Children. 5th ed. Donna L. Wong. 2112p. (C). (gr. 13). 1994. text ed. 69.00 (*0-8016-7882-X*) Mosby Yr Bk.

***Whaley & Wong's Nursing Care of Infants & Children: With Dynamic Human CD-ROM for Windows.** Wong Engineering Animation, Inc. Staff. (C). (gr. 13). 1996. pap. text ed. 79.00 incl. cd-rom (*0-8151-4627-2*, 30503, Yr Bk Med Pubs) Mosby Yr Bk.

Whaling & Old Salem: A Chronicle of the Sea. Frances D. Robotti. (Illus.). 292p. 1983. reprint ed. 17.95 (*0-685-41738-7*) Fountainhead.

Whaling Captain. Jon Zonderman. LC 94-4014. (How They Lived Ser.). (J). 1994. write for info. (*1-55916-041-1*) Rourke Bk Co.

Whaling Captains of New London County, Connecticut: For Oil & Buggy Whips. Barnard L. Colby. (Illus.). 256p. 1990. pap. 17.95 (*0-913372-54-4*) Mystic Seaport.

Whaling City: A History of New London. Robert O. Decker. LC 74-30794. (Illus.). 413p. 1976. 15.00 (*0-87106-053-1*) New London County.

Whaling Communities. Ed. by Elizabeth Vestergaard. (North Atlantic Studies: No. 2, Pts. 1 & 2). (Illus.). 217p. (C). 1990. pap. 40.00 (*87-983424-2-8*, Pub. by Aarhus Univ Pr DK) David Brown.

W

Whaling Days. Carol Carrick. (Illus.). 40p. (J). (gr. 4-7). 1993. 15.95 (*0-395-50948-3*, Clarion Bks) HM.
Whaling Days. Carol Carrick. (Illus.). 40p. (J). 1996. pap. 6.95 (*0-395-76480-7*, Clarion Bks) HM.
Whaling Masters. Federal Writers Project Editors. LC 87-872. (Stokvis Studies in Historical Chronology & Thought: No. 8). 314p. 1987. pap. 29.00 (*0-89370-933-6*, Sidewinder Press); lib. bdg. 39.00 (*0-89370-833-X*, Sidewinder Press) Borgo Pr.
Whaling Masters. Compiled by WPA, Federal Writers Project Staff. (Illus.). 314p. 1992. reprint ed. lib. bdg. 38.00 (*0-8328-2299-X*) Higginson Bk Co.
Whaling on the North Carolina Coast. Marcus B. Simpson, Jr. & Sallie W. Simpson. (Illus.). 51p. (Orig.). 1990. pap. 4.00 (*0-86526-242-X*) NC Archives.
Whaling Prints in the Francis B. Lothrop Collection. Elizabeth Ingalls. (Illus.). xxviii, 341p. 1987. 75.00 (*0-87577-154-8*, Peabody Museum) Peabody Essex Mus.
Whaling Voyage in the Pacific Ocean & Its Incidents. George A. Dodge. 30p. 1982. pap. 4.95 (*0-87770-243-8*) Ye Galleon.
Whaling Will Never Do for Me: The American Whaleman in the Nineteenth Century. Briton C. Busch. LC 93-10810. 280p. (C). 1993. 29.00 (*0-8131-1838-7*) U Pr of Ky.
Whalsay: Symbol, Segment & Boundary in the Shetland Community. Ed. by Anthony P. Cohen. LC 87-34004. 248p. 1989. text ed. 47.95 (*0-7190-2340-8*, Pub. by Manchester Univ Pr UK) St Martin.
***Wham - Make It Big.** Ed. by Michael Lefferts. 40p. (Orig.). (C). 1997. pap. text ed. 13.95 (*0-88188-397-2*, 00308571) H Leonard.
Whammy Bar & Fingergrease. 1993. pap. 24.95 incl. audio compact disk (*0-7935-1407-X*, 00660279) H Leonard.
Whammy Bar & Fingergrease. 1993. pap. 19.95 incl. audio (*0-7935-1408-8*, 00660280) H Leonard.
***Wharram Percy: The Memorial Stones of the Churchyard.** Philip Rahtz & L. Watts. (Wharram Ser.: Vol. II). 38p. 1983. 14.00 (*0-946722-00-5*, Pub. by U York Dept Archaeol UK) David Brown.
Wharton Annual: 1984, 8. Wharton School Staff. 185p. 1984. pap. 30.00 (*0-08-030929-1*) Elsevier.
Wharton Assembly Addresses Nineteen Thirty-Seven. William M. Lewis et al. LC 79-157969. (Essay Index Reprint Ser.). 1977. reprint ed. 15.95 (*0-8369-2258-1*) Ayer.
Wharton County Pictoral History, 1846-1946. Wharton County Historical Commission Staff. 256p. 1993. 35.00 (*0-89015-908-4*) Sunbelt Media.
***Wharton on Dynamic Competetive Strategies.** George S. Day. LC 96-53177. 1997. 29.95 (*0-471-17207-3*) Wiley.
Wharton's Criminal Evidence, 4 vols., Set. 14th ed. Charles E. Torcia. LC 85-81130. 1987. 385.00 (*0-685-59855-1*) Clark Boardman Callaghan.
Wharton's Criminal Law, 4 vols., Set. 15th ed. Charles E. Torcia. LC 93-72924. 1993. 430.00 (*0-685-59854-3*) Clark Boardman Callaghan.
Wharton's Criminal Procedure, 4 vols., Set. 13th ed. Charles E. Torcia. LC 89-63443. 1989. 430.00 (*0-685-59852-7*) Clark Boardman Callaghan.
Wharton's New England: Seven Stories & "Ethan Frome" Edith Wharton. Ed. by Barbara A. White. LC 94-42882. (Hardscrabble Classics Ser.). 286p. 1995. pap. 15.95 (*0-87451-715-X*) U Pr of New Eng.
***Wharton's Strengh Book.** Jim Wharton. 1998. pap. write for info. (*0-8129-2929-2*, Times Bks) Random.
Whartons' Stretch Book. Jim Wharton & Phil Wharton. 256p. 1996. pap. 15.00 (*0-8129-2623-4*) Random.
What? Gregory J. Rawlins. (C). 1995. text ed. write for info. (*0-7167-8279-0*) W H Freeman.
What. Ron Silliman. 1988. pap. 10.00 (*0-935724-30-3*) Figures.
***What?** Robert W. Wood. (Experiments for Young Scientists Ser.). (Illus.). 140p. (YA). (gr. 5 up). 1997. text ed. write for info. (*0-7910-4847-0*) Chelsea Hse.
What? A Touch of Humor for Those Who Need or Wear Hearing Aids. Ralph W. Ritchie & Fern J. Ritchie. (Illus.). 60p. (Orig.). 1992. pap. 9.95 (*0-939656-08-6*) Ritchie Unltd.
What? Experiments for the Young Scientists. Robert W. Wood. (J). (gr. 4-7). 1994. pap. text ed. 10.95 (*0-07-051636-7*) McGraw.
What a Bad Dream. Mercer Mayer. (Golden Look-Look Bks.). (Illus.). 24p. (J). (ps-3). 1992. 2.25 (*0-307-12685-4*, 12685, Golden Books) Western Pub.
What a Beautiful Day! Tilde Michels. (J). (ps-3). 1992. lib. bdg. 19.95 (*0-87614-739-2*, Carolrhoda) Lerner Group.
What a Book! Tom T. Hall. 192p. 1996. 20.00 (*1-56352-340-X*) Longstreet Pr Inc.
***What a Business College Can Do for You.** Norman C. Tognazzini. 8p. (Orig.). 1996. pap. 2.50 (*1-884241-24-7*, SPSO306) Energeia Pub.
What a Busy Day. Sally Brook. (Fun Board Books Ser.). (Illus.). 10p. (J). (ps-k). 1996. 2.99 (*0-88705-906-6*, Wshng Well Bks) Joshua Morris.
What a Canadian-Style Health Care System Would Cost U. S. Employers & Employees. Gary Robbins & Aldona Robbins. 1990. pap. 10.00 (*0-943802-48-2*, 145) Natl Ctr Pol.
What a Character! Twentieth-Century American Advertising Icons. Warren Dotz & Jim Morton. (Illus.). 132p. 1996. pap. 16.95 (*0-8118-0936-6*) Chronicle Bks.
What a Circus! Etienne Delessert. LC 93-27463. (Yok-Yok Ser.). (Illus.). 32p. (J). (gr. 1-8). 1994. 10.95 (*0-88682-640-3*, 97928-098) Creative Ed.
What a College Senior Should Know When the Barrel Is Empty & the Party Is Over. Charley Swayne. 140p. (Orig.). 1995. pap. 17.00 (*0-9642406-0-2*) C Swayne.
What a Computer Can Do for You. Widl. 1982. pap. 5.95 (*0-684-17804-4*) S&S Trade.
What a Country! Dry Bones Looks at Israel. Yaakov Kirschen. LC 96-942. (Illus.). 288p. 1996. pap. 24.95 (*0-8276-0572-2*) JPS Phila.
***What a Day for Flying!** (Get Ready...Get Set...Read! Ser.: Set 1). (J). lib. bdg. 11.95 (*1-56674-138-6*) Forest Hse.
What a Day for Flying! Gina C. Erickson. LC 92-42078. (Get Ready...Get Set...Read! Ser.). (Illus.). 32p. (J). (ps-2). 1993. pap. 3.95 (*0-8120-1557-6*) Barron.
***What a Difference a Day Makes: The Autobiography of Brian Irvine.** Brian Irvine & Stuart Weir. (Illus.). 192p. 1996. 34.95 (*1-85158-808-6*, Pub. by Mnstream UK) Trafalgar.
What a Dog. Sharon Gordon. (Illus.). 32p. (J). (gr. k-2). 1980. lib. bdg. 9.79 (*0-89375-393-9*) Troll Communs.
What a Dog. Sharon Gordon. (Illus.). 32p. (J). (gr. k-2). 1997. pap. 2.50 (*0-89375-293-2*) Troll Communs.
What a Doll! Sara Corbett. LC 95-39664. (World of Difference Ser.). (Illus.). 32p. (J). (gr. 3-7). 1996. lib. bdg. 19.50 (*0-516-08211-6*) Childrens.
What a Doll! Sara Corbett. LC 95-39664. (World of Difference Ser.). (Illus.). 32p. (J). (gr. 3-7). 1996. pap. 6.95 (*0-516-20080-1*) Childrens.
What a Duet! Roy K. Flanagan. Ed. by Ronald H. Bayes. 80p. (Orig.). 1977. pap. 10.00 (*0-932662-20-X*) St Andrews NC.
What a Fellowship: A Cartoon Collection. Jean Gralley. 96p. 1993. pap. 8.95 (*1-888493-09-7*) Chi Rho Pr.
What a Fifth Arab-Israeli War Might Look Like: An Exercise in Crisis Forecasting. Steven J. Rosen. (CISA Working Papers: No. 8). 46p. (Orig.). 1997. pap. 15.00 (*0-86682-007-8*) Ctr Intl Relations.
***What a Find! Using Archaeology to Unearth a System.** CGE (Van Tassel-Baska) Staff. 184p. (C). 1996. per., pap. text ed. 26.25 (*0-7872-2608-4*) Kendall-Hunt.
***What a Friend We Have in Jesus.** 100p. 1997. pap. 9.95 (*0-9652205-2-4*) H Martin.
What a Funny Bunny. Patricia Whitehead. LC 84-8833. (ABC Adventures Ser.). (Illus.). 32p. (J). (gr. k-2). 1997. pap. 3.50 (*0-8167-0362-0*) Troll Communs.
What a Go! The Life of Alfred Munnings. large type ed. Jean Goodman. (Charnwood Ser.). (Illus.). 1991. 27.99 (*0-7089-8619-6*) Ulverscroft.
***What a Goat!** Errol Broome. 74p. 1997. pap. 8.95 (*1-86368-171-X*, Pub. by Fremantle Arts AT) Intl Spec Bk.
What a Great Idea! Key Steps Creative People Take. Charles C. Thompson. LC 91-50522. 224p. 1992. pap. 14.00 (*0-06-096901-6*, PL) HarpC.
What a Guy: What's the Latest? Bill Hoest. 1990. pap. 2.95 (*0-8125-0222-1*) Tor Bks.
What a Haircut! Patricia Gray. LC 93-26931. (Voyages Ser.). (Illus.). (J). 1994. 4.25 (*0-383-03783-2*) SRA McGraw.
What a Hungry Puppy! Gail Herman. LC 92-24468. (All Aboard Reading Ser.: Level 1). (Illus.). 32p. (J). (ps-1). 1993. pap. 3.95 (*0-448-40536-9*, G&D) Putnam Pub Group.
What a Lesbian Looks Like: Writings by Lesbians on Their Lives & Lifestyles. National Lesbian & Gay Survey Staff. 192p. (C). 1992. pap. 16.95 (*0-415-08100-9*, A9591) Routledge.
What a Life. Clifford Goldsmith. 1943. pap. 5.25 (*0-8222-1235-8*) Dramatists Play.
***What a Life: One Man, One Mind, One Mistake after Another.** Brian Nessel. (Illus.). 163p. (Orig.). 1996. pap. 10.00 (*1-889934-00-3*) Bs Hive Pub.
What a Load of Trash! Rescue Your Household Waste. Steve Skidmore. (Lighter Look Bk.). (Illus.). 40p. (J). (gr. 2-6). 1991. pap. 5.95 (*1-878841-39-4*) Millbrook Pr.
What a Long Strange Trip It's Been: A Hippy's History of the 60's & Beyond. Lewis Sanders. 200p. (Orig.). (C). 1989. pap. 9.95 (*0-9623073-0-0*) Straight Hip.
***What a Lovely Day for an Airplane Ride.** William J. Lea. 109p. (Orig.). 1997. mass mkt. 4.99 (*1-55237-124-7*, Pub. by Comnwlth Pub CN) Partners Pubs Grp.
What a Man Weighs. Sherry Kramer. 1993. pap. 5.95 (*0-88145-104-5*) Broadway Play.
What a Man's Gotta Do: Masculine Myth in Popular Culture. Anthony Easthope. 208p. (C). 1990. pap. 17.95 (*0-415-90638-5*, Routledge NY) Routledge.
What a Man's Gotta Do: The Masculine Myth in Popular Culture. Anthony Easthope. (Illus.). 208p. (C). 1990. pap. text ed. 13.95 (*0-04-445738-3*) Routledge Chapman & Hall.
What a Mess: Sylvester & Tweety. Gina Ingoglia. (Illus.). (J). (ps-3). 1990. write for info. (*0-307-11595-X*, Golden Books) Western Pub.
What a Morning. John M. Langstaff. 1996. 4.99 (*0-689-80807-0*) S&S Childrens.
What a Morning! The Christmas Story in Black Spirituals. Illus. by Ashley Bryan. LC 87-750130. 32p. (J). 1987. lib. bdg. 14.95 (*0-689-50422-5*, McElderry) S&S Childrens.
What a Nightmare Charlie Brown. CharlesM. Schulz. (J). pap. 46.80 (*0-590-09458-0*) Scholastic Inc.
What a Noise: A Fun Book of Sounds. Neil Morris. (Fun Books of Learning). (Illus.). 32p. (J). (ps-2). 1991. lib. bdg. 13.50 (*0-87614-670-1*, Carolrhoda) Lerner Group.
***What a Novel Idea! Projects & Activities for Young Adult Literature.** Katherine W. Kuta. LC 97-279. (Illus.). 160p. 1997. lib. bdg. 21.50 (*1-56308-479-1*) Libs Unl.
What a One-World Government Will Mean for America. 1992. lib. bdg. 79.95 (*0-8490-5263-7*) Gordon Pr.
What a Pest! Maryann Cocca-Leffler. (All Aboard Reading Ser.). (Illus.). 32p. (J). (ps-1). 1994. pap. 3.95 (*0-448-40393-5*, G&D) Putnam Pub Group.
What a Piece of Work: Stories. Will Baker. LC 92-14336. 200p. 1992. 24.95 (*0-8262-0853-3*) U of Mo Pr.
What a Piece of Work I Am: A Novel. Eric Kraft. 288p. 1995. pap. 11.00 (*0-312-13211-5*, Picador USA) St Martin.
What a Piece of Work Is Man? Wesley D. Camp. 1989. pap. 12.95 (*0-13-952102-X*) P-H.
***What a Price!** 76p. 1987. pap. 4.99 (*0-8341-1210-8*) Nazarene.
What a Producer Does: The Art of Moviemaking (Not the Business) Buck Houghton. LC 92-6748. (Illus.). 200p. (Orig.). 1991. pap. 14.95 (*1-879505-05-3*) Silman James Pr.
***What a Riot: Comic Visions of Modern America.** David Marc. LC 88-10148. 1989. 16.95 (*0-385-23013-3*) Anchor Bks.
***What a Savior.** 1996. pap. 1.20 (*0-8341-9504-6*) Lillenas.
What a School. Lynn Salem & Josie Stewart. (Illus.). 16p. (J). (gr. k-1). 1992. pap. 3.50 (*1-880612-10-0*) Seedling Pubns.
What a Strange Way of Being Dead. Jack Collom. (Illus.). 65p. (Orig.). 1995. pap. 10.00 (*1-887289-09-7*) Rodent Pr.
***What a Tale: American Edition.** Brian Wildsmith. (Cat on the Mat Book). (Illus.). 16p. 1997. pap. 3.95 (*0-19-849009-7*) OUP.
***What a Technical College Can Do for You.** Norman C. Tognazzini. 8p. (Orig.). 1996. pap. 2.50 (*1-884241-34-4*, SPSO313) Energeia Pub.
What a Teddy Bear Needs. Marilyn Kaye. (Teddy Bear Tales Ser.: No. S897-2). (J). 1989. boxed 3.95 (*0-7214-5225-6*, Ladybrd) Penguin.
What a Teddy Bear Needs. Marilyn Kaye. (S Eight Hundred Ninety-Seven Ser.). (Illus.). 26p. (J). 1993. 2.95 (*0-7214-3510-6*, Ladybrd) Penguin.
What a Thing! Nona Freeman. Ed. by Nell Perry. 122p. 1993. pap. 6.00 (*1-878366-06-8*) Nonas Bk Sales.
What a Time to Live: The Autobiography of James B. Hamilton. James B. Hamilton. LC 95-46. 194p. 1995. 22.95 (*0-87013-353-5*) Mich St U Pr.
***What a Trip!** (Get Ready...Get Set...Read! Ser.: Set 2). (J). 1996. lib. bdg. 11.95 (*1-56674-155-6*) Forest Hse.
What a Trip! Gina Erickson & Kelli C. Foster. LC 94-15219. (Get Ready...Get Set...Read! Ser.). (Illus.). 24p. (J). (gr. k-3). 1994. pap. 3.95 (*0-8120-1923-7*) Barron.
What a University President Has Learned. Abbott L. Lowell. LC 77-93355. (Essay Index Reprint Ser.). 1977. 18.95 (*0-8369-1303-5*) Ayer.
What a Waste It Is to Lose One's Mind: The Unauthorized Autobiography of Dan Quayle. Deborah Werksman et al. (Illus.). 128p. (Orig.). 1992. pap. 6.95 (*0-9629162-2-6*) Rose Commns.
What a Way to Go: Northwest by Tent, Truck, & Tacklebox. Elizabeth F. Davis. 1995. 17.95 (*0-533-11339-3*) Vantage.
What a Way to Live & Make a Living: The Lyman P. Wood Story. Roger M. Griffith. 260p. pap. 19.95 (*0-9642295-0-1*) In Brief Pr.
***What a Way to Spend a War: Navy Nurse P. O. W.s in the Philippines.** Dorothy S. Danner. LC 96-44456. 1997. pap. 21.95 (*0-7838-2021-6*) G K Hall.
What a Way to Spend a War: Navy Nurse POWs in the Philippines. Dorothy S. Danner. LC 95-35862. (Illus.). 230p. 1995. 27.95 (*1-55750-154-8*) Naval Inst Pr.
What a Woman Ought to Be & to Do: Black Professional Women Workers During the Jim Crow Era. Stephanie J. Shaw. (Women in Culture & Society Ser.). xvi, 348p. 1996. pap. text ed. 16.95 (*0-226-75120-1*) U Ch Pr.
What a Woman Ought to Be & to Do: Black Professional Women Workers During the Jim Crow Era. Stephanie J. Shaw. (Women in Culture & Society Ser.). 360p. 1996. lib. bdg. 47.50 (*0-226-75119-8*) U Ch Pr.
***What a Woman Should Know about Protease Inhibitors.** Leslie R. Wolfe et al. 20p. (Orig.). 1996. pap. write for info. (*1-877966-34-7*) Ctr Women Policy.
What a Wonderful Day to Be a Cow. Carolyn Lesser. LC 93-13211. (Illus.). 36p. (J). (ps-2). 1995. 17.00 (*0-679-82430-8*); lib. bdg. 17.99 (*0-679-92430-2*) Knopf Bks Yng Read.
What a Wonderful World. George D. Weiss & Bob Thiele. (Sing-a-Song Storybooks Ser.). (Illus.). 24p. (J). 1993. 9.95 (*0-7935-1840-7*, 00183009) H Leonard.
What a Wonderful World. George D. Weiss & Bob Thiele. (Illus.). (J). (ps up). 1995. 16.00 (*0-689-80087-8*, Atheneum Bks Young) S&S Childrens.
What a Wonderful World: Poems for Nature-Loving Children. Carol J. Keck. (J). 1994. 7.95 (*0-533-10787-3*) Vantage.
What a Wonderful World: Precious Moments. (Golden Super Shape Bks.). (Illus.). 24p. (J). (ps). 1992. 1.95 (*0-307-10022-7*, 10022, Golden Pr) Western Pub.
***What a Wonderful World Intro - Animals! Animals!** Thomas-Cochran. (What a Wonderful World Intro Ser.). 1993. pap. text ed. write for info. (*0-582-91070-6*, Pub. by Longman UK) Longman.
What a Wonderful World This Could Be. Stanley S. Reyburn. (Illus.). 28p. (Orig.). 1990. pap. 7.50 (*0-910147-87-6*) World Poetry Pr.
What a Writer Needs. Ralph Fletcher. LC 92-24344. 182p. 1992. pap. text ed. 21.50 (*0-435-08734-7*, 08734) Heinemann.
***What a Year It Was - 1945.** Beverly Cohn. Date not set. 22.50 (*0-922658-02-1*) Nadel Wrldwide.
***What a Year It Was - 1947.** Beverly Cohn. Date not set. 22.50 (*0-922658-05-6*) Nadel Wrldwide.
***What a Year It Was - 1955.** Beverly Cohn. Date not set. 22.50 (*0-922658-01-3*) Nadel Wrldwide.
***What a Year It Was - 1956.** Beverly Cohn. Date not set. 22.50 (*0-922658-03-X*) Nadel Wrldwide.
***What a Year It Was - 1957.** Beverly Cohn. Date not set. 22.50 (*0-922658-06-4*) Nadel Wrldwide.
What about America's Homeless Children? Hide & Seek. Paul G. Shane. LC 96-10042. (Sage Sourcebooks for the Human Services Ser.: Vol. 32). 247p. 1996. 49.95 (*0-8039-4982-0*); pap. 24.95 (*0-8039-4983-9*) Sage.
What about Annie? Claudia Mills. LC 84-20862. 128p. (J). (gr. 5 up). 1985. 9.95 (*0-8027-6573-4*) Walker & Co.
What about Boy-Girl Friendships. Lester Showalter. 70p. 1982. pap. 3.00 (*0-686-35751-5*) Rod & Staff.
What about Charlie? Melodie Adams. (Romance Ser.). 1993. pap. 2.69 (*0-373-08934-1*, 5-08934-7) Silhouette.
What about Charlie? large type ed. Melodie Adams. LC 93-31003. 1994. lib. bdg. 14.95 (*0-7862-0124-X*) Thorndike Pr.
What about Christmas? Dora D. Flack. (Illus.). 87p. 1971. pap. 8.98 (*0-88290-000-5*) Horizon Utah.
What about Church? Guidelines for Fellowship for the Home Schooling Family. Jeff Barth. Ed. by Marge Barth. 140p. (Orig.). 1994. pap. write for info. (*0-9624067-4-0*) Parable Pub.
What about Divorce? rev. ed. Spiros Zodhiates. 442p. 1992. pap. 7.99 (*0-89957-574-9*) AMG Pubs.
What about Emma? Ken Rush. LC 95-53730. (Illus.). 32p. (J). (ps-2). 1996. 15.95 (*0-531-09534-7*); lib. bdg. 16.99 (*0-531-08884-7*) Orchard Bks Watts.
What about Flying? Ronald G. Adams. LC 93-93883. 144p. (Orig.). 1993. pap. 8.95 (*0-9637307-0-3*) Wrds For You Pub.
What about God Now That You're off to College: A Prayerguide for First-Year Students. Helen R. Neinast & Thomas C. Ettinger. LC 91-67171. 240p. 1992. text ed. 19.95 (*0-8358-0655-3*) Upper Room Bks.
What about Gods? Chris Brockman. (Young Readers Ser.). (Illus.). 32p. (J). (gr. 1-5). 1978. pap. 9.95 (*0-87975-106-1*) Prometheus Bks.
What about Grandma? Hadley Irwin. 176p. (YA). 1991. pap. 2.99 (*0-380-71138-9*, Flare) Avon.
***What about Her?** Beth Van Dyke, pseud. LC 96-62096. 144p. (Orig.). 1997. pap. 9.95 (*1-57921-000-7*) WinePress Pub.
What about Immunizations: Exposing the Vaccine Philosophy. Cynthia Cournoyer. 200p. (Orig.). 1995. pap. 12.95 (*0-9612188-5-1*) Nelsons Bks.
What about Jonah? Roger Barnett. 36p. (Orig.). 1997. pap. 3.00 (*1-880573-33-4*) Grace WI.
What about Kansas City? Dory DeAngelo. (Illus.). 168p. (Orig.). 1995. pap. 15.95 (*1-878686-19-4*) Two Lane Pr.
What about Ladybugs? Celia Godkin. LC 93-4202. (Illus.). 40p. (J). (ps-3). 1995. 14.95 (*0-87156-549-8*) Sierra Club Childrens.
What about Learning? Regional Laboratory for Education Improvement Staff. 17p. 1993. pap. text ed. write for info. incl. vhs (*1-878234-05-6*) Reg Lab Educ IOT NE Isls.
What about Me? Frank Endersby. (J). (gr. 4 up). 1981. 3.99 (*0-85953-232-1*) Childs Play.
***What about Me.** Joyce V. Howard. 246p. (Orig.). 1997. pap. 15.00 (*1-57502-520-5*, P01542) Morris Pubng.
What about Me? Joann Klusmeyer. (Illus.). (J). (gr. 4-7). 1987. 3.99 (*0-570-03641-0*, 39-1125) Concordia.
What About Me. Edward Koren. 1989. pap. 9.95 (*0-679-72636-5*) McKay.
What about Me? Illus. by Nina Paley. LC 93-8955. (Contemporary Health Ser.). (J). 1993. 3.00 (*1-56071-314-3*) ETR Assocs.
What about Me? Colby Rodowsky. 144p. (J). (gr. 3 up). 1989. pap. 3.50 (*0-374-48316-7*, Sunburst Bks) FS&G.
What about Me. B. Steinberg. (Middos Ser.). (J). 1990. 7.99 (*0-89906-506-6*) Mesorah Pubns.
What About Me? Growing Up with a Developmentally Disabled Sibling. B. Siegel & S. C. Silverstein. (Illus.). 316p. (C). 1994. 24.95 (*0-306-44650-2*, Plenum Insight) Plenum.
What about Me? When Brothers & Sisters Get Sick. Allan Peterkin. LC 92-20035. (Illus.). 32p. (J). 1992. pap. 8.95 (*0-945354-49-5*) Magination Pr.
What about Men: The Dark & Light Side of the Male. Luc De Schepper. (Illus.). 200p. 1995. pap. 12.95 (*0-942501-04-7*) Full of Life.
What about Mom & Dad? Leader's Guide. Patricia S. Bommarito & James L. Ramsey. 95p. (Orig.). 1988. pap. 49.95 (*0-941697-02-9*) ABT Inc.
What about Mom & Dad? Participant. Patricia S. Bommarito & James L. Ramsey. 75p. (Orig.). 1988. pap. 10.95 (*0-941697-03-7*) ABT Inc.
What About Murder? A Guide to Books about Mystery Detective Fiction. Jon L. Breen. LC 81-645. 175p. 1981. 25.00 (*0-8108-1413-7*) Scarecrow.
What about Murder? (1981-1991) A Guide to Books about Mystery & Detective Fiction. Jon L. Breen. 1992. 39.50 (*0-8108-2609-7*) Scarecrow.
What about Product Manager 6000? Dave Curtis. LC 94-125. 1994. 34.95 (*0-9633214-4-7*) Maximum Pr.
What about Religion? An Exploratory View. Wanda Cawein. LC 92-60737. (Illus.). 208p. (Orig.). 1992. pap. 10.00 (*0-9633488-1-7*) Midngt Oil.
***What about the Children? Sons & Daughters of Lesbian & Gay Parents Speak about Their Lives.** Lisa Saffron. (Sexual Politics Ser.). 224p. 1997. 75.00 (*0-304-33522-3*); pap. 17.95 (*0-304-33523-1*) Cassell.
What about the Children: The Ministry of the Sunday School. Curtis Redmon. (Practical Church Ser.). (Orig.). 1993. pap. text ed. 5.95 (*1-881685-01-2*) LUA Stand Minist.
What about the Holy Mandylion & Turin Shroud? An Orthodox Perspective. J. Kallos. 1991. pap. 4.95 (*0-937032-82-4*) Light&Life Pub Co MN.
What about the Holy Spirit? 1993. audio 19.99 (*1-884553-37-0*) Discipleshp.
What about the Holy Spirit? Gordon Ferguson. 24p. 1993. wbk. ed. 3.99 (*1-884553-11-7*) Discipleshp.
What about the Russians: A Christian Approach to U. S. - Soviet Conflict. Ed. by Dale W. Brown. LC 84-6169. 160p. reprint ed. pap. 45.60 (*0-7837-5927-4*, 2045726) Bks Demand.

What about the Workers? Making Employee Surveys Work. Michael Walters. 176p. (C). 1990. 60.00 (*0-85292-445-3*, Pub. by IPM Hse UK) St Mut.

What about the Workers? Workers & the Transition to Capitalism in Russia. Michael Burawoy et al. 240p. (C). 1993. pap. text ed. 19.00 (*0-86091-666-9*, B2515, Pub. by Vrso UK) Norton.

***What about Them Claymores? The Murrayfield Miracle.** Andy Colvin et al. (Illus.). 128p. 1997. 29.95 (*1-85158-925-2*, Pub. by Mnstream UK) Trafalgar.

What about Those Who Have Never Heard? Three Views on the Destiny of the Unevangelized. Gabriel Fackre et al. 184p. (Orig.). 1995. pap. 10.99 (*0-8308-1606-2*, 1606) InterVarsity.

What, Again Those Jews? H. Lantner. write for info. (*965-229-158-7*) Gefen Bks.

What Ails Me? Too Long, Don't Know Thyself. Kali Sichen. (Illus.). 45p. 1995. pap. 8.95 (*0-916299-50-3*) North Scale Co.

What All Good Dogs Should Know: The Sensible Way to Train. Jack Volhard & Melissa Bartlett. (Illus.). 128p. 1991. pap. 10.00 (*0-87605-832-2*) Howell Bk.

***What All the World's A-Seeking: Or The Vital Law of True Life, True Greatness, Power, & Happiness.** Ralph W. Trine. 224p. 1997. pap. 20.00 (*0-89540-359-5*) Sun Pub.

***What Am I?, 8 vols.** (What Am I? Ser.). (Illus.). (J). 111. 84 (*0-8172-4592-8*) Raintree Steck-V.

What Am I? Leo Dillion & Diane Dillion. LC 93-48835. (J). (gr. 1 up). 1994. 13.95 (*0-590-47885-0*, Blue Sky Press) Scholastic Inc.

What Am I? Margaret Hillert. (Illus.). (J). (ps). 1981. pap. 5.10 (*0-8136-5566-8*, TK2377); lib. bdg. 7.95 (*0-8136-5066-6*, TK2376) Modern Curr.

What Am I? Debbie MacKinnon. LC 94-44393. (Illus.). 24p. (J). (ps-k). 1996. pap. 10.99 (*0-8037-1826-8*) Dial Bks Young.

***What Am I?** large type ed. Deborah Williams. (Illus.). 12p. (Orig.). (J). (gr. k-1). 1997. pap. 4.95 (*1-879835-25-8*) Kaeden Corp.

What Am I? An Animal Guessing Game. Iza Trapani. LC 92-15029. (Illus.). 32p. (J). 1992. lib. bdg. 13.95 (*1-879085-76-3*) Whsprng Coyote Pr.

What Am I? An Animal Guessing Game. Iza Trapani. (Illus.). 32p. (J). (gr. k-2). 1996. pap. 5.95 (*1-879085-66-6*) Whsprng Coyote Pr.

What Am I? Easy Animal Reader. Brust. (Illus.). 16p. (J). (ps-1). 1996. pap. 2.49 (*1-57690-054-1*) Tchr Create Mat.

What Am I? Looking Through Shapes at Apples & Grapes. N. N. Charles. (Illus.). 32p. (J). (ps-4). 1994. 13.95 (*0-590-47891-5*, Blue Sky Press) Scholastic Inc.

What Am I? Very First Riddles. Stephanie Calmenson. LC 87-22959. (Illus.). 32p. (J). (ps-2). 1989. lib. bdg. 12.89 (*0-06-020998-4*) HarpC Child Bks.

What Am I Allergic To? J. J. Van Gasse. LC 95-71337. 124p. (C). 1995. 9.95 (*1-882792-17-3*) Proctor Pubns.

What Am I Doing Here? Bruce Chatwin. 384p. 1990. pap. 12.95 (*0-14-011577-3*, Penguin Bks) Viking Penguin.

What Am I Doing in a Foster Home? Terri Hunsicker. (Illus.). 24p. (Orig.). (J). (gr. 3 up). 1995. pap. text ed. 7.95 (*0-9647414-0-7*) Ranter Pr Pub.

What Am I Doing in a Step-Family? Claire G. Berman. (Illus.). 48p. (J). (gr. 2 up). 1982. 12.00 (*0-8184-0325-X*) Carol Pub Group.

What Am I Doing in a Stepfamily? Claire Berman. (Where Did I Come From Ser.). (Illus.). (J). (gr. k-7). 1992. pap. 8.95 (*0-8184-0563-5*, L Stuart) Carol Pub Group.

What Am I Doing in This Grade? A Book for Parents about School Readiness. Louise B. Ames. (Illus.). 31p. (Orig.). 1985. pap. 4.50 (*0-935493-00-X*, 156) Programs Educ.

What Am I That You Care for Me? Praying with the Psalms. Carlo M. Martini. 138p. (C). 1990. 49.00 (*0-85439-347-1*, Pub. by St Paul Pubns UK) St Mut.

What America Did Right: The Weapons Systems, Events, & Leaders That Brought Us to Victory in the Cold War. Herbert J. Friedman. 202p. (C). 1996. lib. bdg. 39.00 (*0-7618-0155-3*) U Pr of Amer.

What America Does Right: Lessons from Outstanding Enterprise. Robert H. Waterman, Jr. 196p. 1994. 23.00 (*0-393-03597-2*) Norton.

What America Does Right: Lessons from Today's Most Admired Corporate Role Models. Robert H. Waterman, Jr. 320p. 1995. pap. 12.95 (*0-452-27376-5*, Plume) NAL-Dutton.

What America Means to Me. Pearl S. Buck. LC 79-156622. (Essay Index Reprint Ser.). 1977. reprint ed. 18.95 (*0-8369-2387-1*) Ayer.

What America Wants, America Gets: Notes from the "G. O. P. Revolution" & Other Scary Stuff. Dan Sharpnack. LC 96-18520. 118p. 1996. pap. 10.00 (*0-86663-216-6*) Ide Hse.

***What Americans Know about Politics & Why It Matters.** Michael X. Carpini. 1997. pap. text ed. 18.00 (*0-300-07275-9*) Yale U Pr.

What Americans Know about Politics & Why It Matters. Michael X. Delli Carpini & Scott Keeter. 386p. 1996. 38.50 (*0-300-06256-7*) Yale U Pr.

***What America's Small Companies Pay Their Sales Forces: And How They Make It Pay Off.** Christen P. Heide. (Illus.). 276p. (Orig.). 1997. pap. 39.95 (*0-85013-270-3*) Dartnell Corp.

What America's Teachers Wish Parents Knew. Judy Privett & Tony Privett. LC 93-79657. 144p. 1993. pap. 5.95 (*1-56352-104-0*) Longstreet Pr Inc.

What an Abnormal Pap Smear Means. Margaret Wilson. (Living for Tomorrow Ser.). 137p. (Orig.). 1995. pap. 16.95 (*0-85572-243-6*, Pub. by Hill Content Pubng AT) Seven Hills Bk.

What an Art Director Does: An Introduction to Motion Picture Production Design. Ward Preston. LC 94-30605. (Illus.). 190p. (Orig.). 1994. pap. 21.95 (*1-879505-18-5*) Silman James Pr.

What & When to Sell During the Fall of Nineteen Eighty-Three. Frank Jakubowsky. 65p. 1983. pap. 5.00 (*0-932588-06-9*) Jesus Bks.

What & When to Sell During the Spring of Nineteen Eighty-Three. Frank Jakubowsky. 65p. (Orig.). 1983. pap. 5.00 (*0-932588-03-4*) Jesus Bks.

What & When to Sell During the Summer of Nineteen Eighty-Three. Frank Jakubowsky. 65p. 1983. pap. 5.00 (*0-932588-05-0*) Jesus Bks.

What & Where Is Religious Truth Today? Earth's Only Way Out! Donald J. Belknap. (Illus.). 512p. 1991. 18.95 (*0-9628767-0-4*) SERFI.

What & Why of History: Philosophical Essays. Leon J. Goldstein. LC 95-15082. (Philosophy of History & Culture Ser.: Vol. 15). 416p. 1996. 126.00 (*90-04-10308-2*) E J Brill.

What & Why of Magick. Frater Zarathustra, pseud. LC 82-91047. 48p. (Orig.). (C). 1982. pap. 5.00 (*0-939856-30-1*) Tech Group.

What Angela Needs. Rita Benson. LC 92-34266. (Voyages Ser.). (Illus.). (J). 1993. 14.00 (*0-383-03666-6*) SRA McGraw.

What Anglicans Believe. rev. ed. David L. Edwards. 136p. (Orig.). 1996. pap. 3.95 (*0-88028-170-7*, 503) Forward Movement.

What Animal Am I? Dot-to-Dot Coloring Book. Shirley Beegle. (Coloring & Activity Bks.). (Illus.). 16p. (J). 1993. pap. text ed. 1.69 (*0-7847-0124-5*, 02214) Standard Pub.

What Animal Is It? Tiziano Sclavi. LC 93-72525. (Illus.). 10p. (J). (ps). 1994. 4.95 (*1-56397-339-1*) Boyds Mills Pr.

What Animals Give Us: So Many Things. Donna Koren. LC 89-23991. (Discovery World Ser.). (Illus.). 32p. (J). (ps-2). 1990. lib. bdg. 21.36 (*0-89565-557-8*) Childs World.

What Animals Taught Me. Richard M. Shields. LC 94-73323. (Illus.). ix, 153p. (Orig.). 1995. pap. 7.95 (*1-882803-09-4*) Jerseydale Ranch.

What Answer? Anna E. Dickinson. LC 71-138646. (Black Heritage Library Collection). 1977. reprint ed. 22.95 (*0-8369-9004-8*) Ayer.

What Are Abraham's Blessings, Anyway?, Vol. 1: Christian's Healing & Prosperity Guaranteed by Abraham's Covenant. Jay S. Snell. 1990. pap. 7.00 (*0-685-67691-9*) J Snell Evangelistic.

***What Are Astrolocality Maps?** Maritha Pottenger. 31p. 1996. pap. 4.95 (*0-917086-67-8*) ACS Pubns.

***What Are Big Girls Made Of?** Marge Piercy. 1997. 25.00 (*0-614-29416-9*) Knopf.

***What Are Big Girls Made Of?** Marge Piercy. 1997. pap. 15.00 (*0-614-29417-7*) Knopf.

What Are Drugs. Gretchen Super. 48p. (J). (ps-3). 1996. pap. 3.95 (*0-8167-2364-8*) Troll Communs.

What Are Faces for? Jack Winder. Ed. by Alton Jordan. (Buppet Bks.). (Illus.). (J). (gr. 1-4). 1980. 9.95 (*0-89868-096-4*, Read Res); pap. 3.95 (*0-89868-107-3*, Read Res) ARO Pub.

What Are Feathers after All but Glory. Angela M. Elston. (Cleveland Poets Ser.: No. 25). 35p. (Orig.). 1980. pap. 2.50 (*0-914946-22-6*) Cleveland St Univ Poetry Ctr.

***What Are Food Chains & Webs?** Bobbie Kalman. (Science of Living Things Ser.). (Illus.). 32p. (J). 1997. lib. bdg. 18.64 (*0-86505-876-8*) Crabtree Pub Co.

***What Are Food Chains & Webs?** Bobbie Kalman. (Science of Living Things Ser.). (Illus.). 32p. (J). 1997. pap. 5.95 (*0-86505-888-1*) Crabtree Pub Co.

What Are Forests For? Catharine S. Roache. 44p. 1971. 2.00 (*0-913478-01-6*) Hermosa.

What are Freedoms For? John H. Garvey. LC 96-23282. 320p. 1996. 35.00 (*0-674-31929-X*) HUP.

What Are Friends For? (Kaleidoscope Ser.: Set A). 1993. 2.95 (*0-88336-174-4*) New Readers.

What Are Friends For? large type ed. Naomi Horton. (Silhouette Romance Ser.). 1995. 19.95 (*0-373-59626-X*) Harlequin Bks.

What Are Friends For? Feminist Perspectives on Personal Relationships & Moral Theory. Marilyn Friedman. 296p. 1993. 37.50 (*0-8014-2721-5*); pap. 14.95 (*0-8014-8004-3*) Cornell U Pr.

What Are Friends For? HIV Safe Coloring Book. Tim Jackson. (Illus.). 32p. (Orig.). (J). (gr. 3-6). 1990. pap. write for info. (*0-942675-08-8*, 0942675088) Creative License.

What Are Fronds For? Wendy Arbeit. LC 85-13940. (Illus.). 110p. (Orig.). 1985. pap. 14.95 (*0-8248-0999-8*, Kolowalu Bk) UH Pr.

What Are Human Needs? Vincent W. Kafka. 12p. 1986. pap. 3.95 (*0-913261-15-7*) Effect Learn Sys.

What Are Hyenas Laughing at, Anyway? An Imponderables Book. David Feldman. 304p. 1996. pap. text ed. 13.00 (*0-425-15451-3*) Berkley Pub.

What are Little Girls Made Of? Martin Yoseloff. 8.95 (*0-8453-2217-6*, Cornwall Bks) Assoc Univ Prs.

What Are Norms? A Study of Beliefs & Action in a Maya Community. Francesca M. Cancian. LC 74-77833. 222p. reprint ed. pap. 63.30 (*0-685-16313-X*, 2027284) Bks Demand.

What Are Numbers & What Should They Be? rev. ed. Richard Dedekind. Ed. by H. Pogorzelski et al. Tr. by W. Ryan & W. Snyder from GER. (Illus.). 90p. 1995. 49.00 (*0-9643023-1-4*) RIM.

What Are Opposites. (J). 1995. 8.99 (*0-88705-581-8*) Joshua Morris.

What Are People For? Wendell Berry. LC 89-29848. 224p. 1990. pap. 11.00 (*0-86547-437-0*, North Pt Pr) FS&G.

What Are Philosophical Systems? Jules Vuillemin. 240p. 1986. 64.95 (*0-521-30540-3*) Cambridge U Pr.

What Are Roses For? Sandol Stoddard. LC 95-2545. (Illus.). 32p. (J). (ps-2). 1996. 14.95 (*0-395-74277-3*) HM.

What Are Saints: Fifteen Chapters in Sanctity. Cyril C. Martindale. LC 68-16954. (Essay Index Reprint Ser.). 1977. 17.95 (*0-8369-0681-0*) Ayer.

What Are Schools For? Holistic Education in American Culture. 2nd rev. ed. Ron Miller. 208p. (Orig.). (C). 1992. pap. 16.95 (*0-9627232-0-7*) Holistic Educ Pr.

What Are the Chances? Risks & Odds in Everyday Life. James Burke. (Illus.). 128p. 1992. pap. 8.95 (*0-8065-1334-9*, Citadel Pr) Carol Pub Group.

What Are the Chances? Risks, Odds, & Likelihood in Everyday Life. David M. Rorvik et al. 224p. 1993. pap. 4.50 (*0-451-17488-7*, Sig) NAL-Dutton.

***What Are the Essentials of Christian Worship?** Ed. by G. Lathrop. 1996. pap. 5.95 (*0-8066-2797-2*) Augsburg Fortress.

***What Are the Ethical Implications of Worship?** Ed. by G. Lathrop. 1996. pap. 5.95 (*0-8066-2804-9*) Augsburg Fortress.

What Are the Five Senses? Dorine Barbey. (J). (ps-3). Date not set. 5.95 (*0-944589-48-0*) Young Discovery Lib.

What are the Gospels? A Comparison with Graeco-Roman Biography. Richard Burridge. (Society for New Testament Studies Monographs: No. 70). 306p. 1995. pap. text ed. 18.95 (*0-521-48363-8*) Cambridge U Pr.

***What Are the Hazards of Household Products?** unabridged ed. Ann M. Wolf & Anna H. Spitz. (Environmental Ser.). (Orig.). (J). (gr. 3-6). 1996. pap. 13.50 (*0-9651084-3-0*) Tyris Environ.

***What Are the Most Important Factors Shaping Return to Work? Evidence from Wisconsin.** Monica Galizzi et al. LC 96-3217. 1996. 75.00 (*0-935149-60-0*) Workers Comp Res Inst.

***What Are the Odds.** Paul Smith. Ed. by Tim Montgomery. ix, 128p. (Orig.). 1997. pap. 14.95 (*0-9658518-4-2*) PDB Pub.

What Are the Questions? Other Essays. Joan Robinson. LC 80-28062. 244p. (gr. 13). 1981. pap. text ed. 29.95 (*0-87332-200-2*) M E Sharpe.

What Are the Targums? Pierre Grelot. (Old Testament Message Ser.). 144p. (Orig.). 1992. pap. text ed. 12.95 (*0-8146-5644-7*) Liturgical Pr.

What Are They Doing in My World? Victor Westphall. LC 80-26459. 288p. 1981. 15.00 (*0-8453-4709-8*, Cornwall Bks) Assoc Univ Prs.

What Are They Doing to My Animal. Ivan Arguelles. 1985. pap. 1.50 (*0-317-19793-2*) Ghost Dance.

What Are They Saying about Acts? Mark A. Powell. LC 91-27685. (What Are They Saying about...Ser.). 160p. 1992. pap. 6.95 (*0-8091-3279-6*) Paulist Pr.

What Are They Saying about Biblical Archaeology? Leslie J. Hoppe. LC 83-63110. (What Are They Saying about... Ser.). (C). 1984. pap. 4.95 (*0-8091-2613-3*) Paulist Pr.

What Are They Saying about Dogma? William E. Reiser. LC 78-58955. (What Are They Saying about...Ser.). 1978. pap. 3.95 (*0-8091-2127-1*) Paulist Pr.

What Are They Saying about Genetic Engineering. Thomas A. Shannan. (What Are They Saying about...Ser.). 112p. (Orig.). 1986. pap. 4.95 (*0-8091-2743-1*) Paulist Pr.

What Are They Saying about John? Gerald S. Sloyan. (What Are They Saying about...Ser.). 1991. pap. 6.95 (*0-8091-3238-9*) Paulist Pr.

What Are They Saying about Luke. Mark A. Powell. (What Are They Saying about...Ser.). 1989. pap. 8.95 (*0-8091-3111-0*) Paulist Pr.

What Are They Saying about Masculine Spirituality? David C. James. LC 95-36345. 160p. 1996. pap. 9.95 (*0-8091-3632-5*, 3632-5) Paulist Pr.

What Are They Saying about Matthew? expanded rev. ed. Donald Senior. (W.A.T.S.about...Ser.). 144p. (Orig.). 1996. pap. 9.95 (*0-8091-3624-4*) Paulist Pr.

What Are They Saying about Matthew's Sermon on the Mount? Warren Carter. LC 94-2720. (What Are They Saying about...Ser.). 160p. (Orig.). 1994. pap. 7.95 (*0-8091-3473-X*) Paulist Pr.

What Are They Saying about Me? Maureen C. Wartski. 1996. mass mkt. 4.50 (*0-449-70451-3*) Fawcett.

What Are They Saying about Moral Norms? Richard M. Gula. LC 81-83188. (What Are They Saying about... Ser.). 128p. (Orig.). 1982. pap. 6.95 (*0-8091-2412-2*) Paulist Pr.

What Are They Saying about Papal Primacy? Michael Miller. (What Are They Saying about...Ser.). 128p. 1983. pap. 4.95 (*0-8091-2501-3*) Paulist Pr.

What Are They Saying about Peace & War? Thomas A. Shannon. (What Are They Saying about...Ser.). 128p. 1983. pap. 4.95 (*0-8091-2499-8*) Paulist Pr.

What Are They Saying about Salvation? Denis Edwards. (What Are They Saying about...Ser.). 100p. 1986. pap. 4.95 (*0-8091-2793-8*) Paulist Pr.

What Are They Saying about Scripture & Ethics. expanded rev. ed. William C. Spohn. LC 95-22768. (W.A.T.S. about...Ser.). 160p. (Orig.). 1996. pap. 8.95 (*0-8091-3609-0*) Paulist Pr.

What Are They Saying about Sexual Morality? James Hanigan. (What Are They Saying about...Ser.). 128p. (Orig.). 1982. pap. 7.95 (*0-8091-2451-3*) Paulist Pr.

***What Are They Saying about the Formation of the Pauline Churches?** Richard S. Ascough. 176p. 1998. 9.95 (*0-8091-3768-2*) Paulist Pr.

What Are They Saying about the Ministerial Priesthood? Daniel Donovan. LC 92-11649. (What Are They Saying about...Ser.). 160p. 1992. pap. 7.95 (*0-8091-3318-0*) Paulist Pr.

What Are They Saying about the Prophets? David P. Reid. LC 80-80869. (What Are They Saying about...Ser.). 112p. (Orig.). 1980. pap. 3.95 (*0-8091-2304-5*) Paulist Pr.

What Are They Saying about the Social Setting of the New Testament? enl. rev. ed. Carolyn A. Osiek. LC 92-16470. (What Are They Saying about...Ser.). 144p. (Orig.). 1992. pap. 7.95 (*0-8091-3339-3*) Paulist Pr.

What Are They Saying about the Theology of Suffering? Lucien J. Richard. LC 92-21583. (What Are They Saying about...Ser.). 176p. 1993. pap. 7.95 (*0-8091-3347-4*) Paulist Pr.

What Are They Saying about Theological Method? J. J. Mueller. LC 84-61031. (What Are They Saying about... Ser.). 88p. (Orig.). 1985. pap. 5.95 (*0-8091-2657-5*) Paulist Pr.

What Are They Trying to Do to Us? The Truth about the Animal Rights Movement & the New Age. Bernard Palmer. 207p. (Orig.). (C). 1994. pap. 9.95 (*0-9636072-1-9*) J Honea Pubs.

What Are They Trying to Do to Us? The Truth about the Animal Rights Movement & the New Age. Bernard Palmer. Ed. by M. L. Jones. LC 93-84736. 1994. pap. 9.95 (*1-882270-11-8*) Old Rugged Cross.

What Are Things Made Of? see **How Things Are Made**

What Are Those Crazy Americans Saying? An Easy Way to Understand Hundreds of American Expressions. 2nd rev. ed. Jarold A. Kieffer. LC 89-7553. 496p. 1990. reprint ed. pap. 8.00 (*1-877627-01-1*) SER Pubns.

What Are We? Watchman Nee. 26p. 1.00 (*0-87083-600-5*, 08034001) Living Stream Ministry.

What Are We Afraid Of? An Assessment of the "Communist Threat" in Central America. John Lamperti. Ed. by NARMIC-AFSC Staff. LC 88-6690. 125p. (Orig.). 1988. 25.00 (*0-89608-339-X*); pap. 8.00 (*0-89608-338-1*) South End Pr.

What Are We Doing Here? Associated Women's Organization, Mars Hill Bible School. 1972. pap. 6.25 (*0-89137-404-3*) Quality Pubns.

What Are We Doing in Gym Today? New Games & Activities for the Elementary Physical Education Class. Kenneth G. Tillman & Patricia R. Toner. LC 82-24606. 202p. 1983. 19.95 (*0-13-951822-3*, Parker Publishing Co) P-H.

What Are We Doing in Latin America? A Novel about Conneticut. Robert Riche. LC 90-53322. 208p. 1991. 22.00 (*1-877946-01-X*) Permanent Pr.

What Are We Feeding Our Kids? Michael F. Jacobson & Bruce Maxwell. LC 94-934. 320p. 1994. pap. 8.95 (*1-56305-632-1*) Workman Pub.

***What Are We Fighting For.** Russ. LC 96-36688. 1997. 27.95 (*0-312-15198-5*) St Martin.

What Are We Going to Do about David? Willo D. Roberts. LC 92-4726. 176p. (J). (gr. 3-7). 1993. lib. bdg. 16.00 (*0-689-31793-X*, Atheneum Bks Young) S&S Childrens.

What Are We Living For? J. G. Bennett. LC 91-27795. 124p. 1991. reprint ed. per. 11.00 (*0-9621901-8-7*) Bennett Bks.

What Are We Living for? A Practical Philosophy, 3 vols., Set. Chauncey D. Leake. Incl. Vol. 1. What Are We Living For? A Practical Philosophy Vol. 1: Ethics. LC 72-95448. 1973. 19.95 (*0-9600290-2-8*); Vol. 2. What Are We Living For? A Practical Philosophy Vol. 2: Logics. LC 72-95448. 1974. 19.95 (*0-9600290-5-2*); Vol. 3. What Are We Living For? A Practical Philosophy Vol. 3: Esthetics. LC 72-95448. 1976. 19.95 (*0-9600290-6-0*); LC 72-95448. (C). 40.00 (*0-685-73414-5*) PJD Pubns.

What Are We Living For? Vols. 1-3: A Practical Philosophy, Set. Chauncey D. Leake. Date not set. 50.00 (*0-685-76504-0*) PJD Pubns.

What Are We Living For? A Practical Philosophy, Vol. 1, Ethics see **What Are We Living for?: A Practical Philosophy**

What Are We Living For? A Practical Philosophy, Vol. 2, Logics see **What Are We Living for?: A Practical Philosophy**

What Are We Living For? A Practical Philosophy, Vol. 3, Esthetics see **What Are We Living for?: A Practical Philosophy**

What Are We Talking About: The Harper's Forum Book. Jack Hill. 1991. pap. 10.95 (*0-8065-1230-X*, Citadel Pr) Carol Pub Group.

What Are We Trying to Teach Them Anyway? A Father's Focus on School Reform. Ronald K. Pierce. LC 92-21143. 176p. 1993. 19.95 (*1-55815-239-3*) ICS Pr.

What Are We Up to, Herman? Jim Unger. 1985. pap. 1.95 (*0-451-13823-6*, Sig) NAL-Dutton.

What Are We Waiting For? A Commentary on Revelation. fac. ed. Robert H. Mounce. LC 91-45243. 151p. 1992. reprint ed. pap. 43.10 (*0-7837-7967-4*, 2047723) Bks Demand.

What Are Winds & What Are Waters. Hilda Morley. 72p. (Orig.). 1993. pap. 9.95 (*1-55921-089-3*, Asphodel Pr) Moyer Bell.

***What Are Winning Transits?** Joyce Wehrman. 15p. 1996. pap. 3.95 (*0-917086-68-6*) ACS Pubns.

What Are You? Imelda O. Shanklin. 168p. 1995. reprint ed. 11.95 (*0-87159-178-2*, 137) Unity Bks.

What Are You Called? Honey Anderson & Bill Reinholdt. LC 92-31953. (Voyages Ser.). (Illus.). (J). 1993. 3.75 (*0-383-03604-6*) SRA McGraw.

What Are You Doing? Robert D. Hoeft. 28p. (Orig.). 1987. pap. 3.00 (*0-916155-03-X*) Trout Creek.

What Are You Doing with the Rest of Your Life? Choices in Midlife. Paula P. Hardin. LC 91-42334. 272p. 1992. pap. 12.95 (*0-931432-89-8*) New Wrld Lib.

What Are You Figuring Now? A Story about Benjamin Banneker. Jeri Ferris. LC 88-7267. (Creative Minds Biographies Ser.). (Illus.). 56p. (J). (gr. 3-6). 1988. lib. bdg. 14.21 (*0-87614-331-1*, Carolrhoda) Lerner Group.

What Are You Figuring Now? A Story about Benjamin Banneker. large type ed. Jeri Ferris. (Illus.). 1993. 17.50 (*0-614-09860-2*, L-34120-00) Am Printing Hse.

What Are You Figuring Now? A Story about Benjamin Banneker. Jeri Ferris. (Creative Minds Biographies Ser.). (Illus.). 64p. (J). (gr. 3-6). 1988. reprint ed. pap. 5.95 (*0-87614-521-7*, Carolrhoda) Lerner Group.

What Are You Looking At? Queer Sex, Style & Cinema. Paul Burston. 179p. 1995. pap. 19.95 (*0-304-34300-5*, Pub. by Cassell Pubng UK) LPC InBook.

*__What Are You Planning to Do?__ Nannie Kuiper. LC 97-23387. (Illus.). (J). 1997. write for info. (*1-57379-026-5*) High-Scope.

What Are You Saying?, Bk. 2. Durlynn Aneman & Vickie Sanders. (Options: a Communication Skills Ser.: Bk. 2). 1994. pap. write for info. (*0-318-70141-3*) S-W Pub.

What Are You Touching? Mario Gomboli. LC 92-70229. (Illus.). 10p. (J). (ps-k). 1992. bds. 3.95 (*1-56397-150-X*) Boyds Mills Pr.

What Are You Waiting for? Jill Medvedow & Clive Phillpot. LC 84-9777. (Illus.). 32p. 1984. pap. 6.00 (*0-941104-11-7*) Real Comet.

What Are You Waiting For? Sermons on the Parables of Jesus. Mark Trotter. LC 92-20954. (Protestant Pulpit Exchange Ser.). 96p. (Orig.). 1992. pap. 8.95 (*0-687-44604-X*) Abingdon.

What Are Your Dreams Telling You? 2nd rev. ed. A La Lansun, pseud. (Solar Ser.: Bk. I). 136p. 1986. pap. 8.95 (*0-935861-00-9*) Solarium Analy.

*__What Are Your Goals?__ Gary R. Blair. 1997. pap. text ed. 14.95 (*1-889770-00-0*) Blair Publng.

What Are Your Goals? Powerful Questions to Discover What You Want Out of Life! Gary R. Blair. LC 93-61575. (Illus.). 189p. (Orig.). 1994. pap. 14.95 (*1-56912-096-X*) Wharton Pub.

*__What Astrology Can Do for You.__ Maritha Pottenger. 31p. 1996. pap. 4.95 (*0-935127-37-2*) ACS Pubns.

What Asylums Were, Are, & Ought to Be: Being the Substance of Five Lectures Delivered Before the Managers of the Montrose Royal Lunatic Asylum. W. A. Browne. LC 75-16691. (Classics in Psychiatry Ser.). 1976. reprint ed. 21.95 (*0-405-07421-2*) Ayer.

What Auditors Should Know about Data Processing. Donald L. Dawley. LC 83-17879. (Research for Business Decisions Ser.: No. 63). (Illus.). 250p. reprint ed. pap. 71.30 (*0-8357-1483-7*, 2070374) Bks Demand.

What Auto Mechanics Don't Want You To Know. 2nd ed. Mark Eskeldon. 210p. 1994. pap. 11.95 (*0-9640560-0-3*) Technews.

What Auto Mechanics Don't Want You to Know. 3rd ed. Mark Eskeldson. 204p. 1996. pap. 11.95 (*0-9640560-3-8*) Technews.

What Automation Does to Human Beings. George Soule. Ed. by Leon Stein. LC 77-70534. 1977. reprint ed. lib. bdg. 23.95 (*0-405-10202-X*) Ayer.

What Baptists Believe. Herschel H. Hobbs. LC 64-12411. 1964. bds. 4.25 (*0-8054-8101-X*, 4281-01) Broadman.

What Bass. Tony Bacon & L. Canty. 95p. (Orig.). 1989. pap. 12.95 (*0-685-47657-X*) Bold Strummer Ltd.

What Bass. 2nd ed. Tony Bacon & Laurence Canty. (Orig.). 1991. pap. 12.95 (*0-933224-54-0*) Bold Strummer Ltd.

*__What Bears Wear.__ Mouse Works Staff. (J). 1997. 7.98 (*1-57082-676-5*) Mouse Works.

What Became of Them & Other Stories from Franco-America. Denis Ledoux. 104p. (Orig.). 1988. pap. 8.95 (*0-9619373-0-0*) Soleil Pr.

What Became Words. Claes Andersson. Ed. by Stanley H. Barkan. Tr. by Rika Lesser. (Review Chapbook Ser.: No. 22: Swedish Poetry 2). 32p. (ENG & SWE.). 1991. 15.00 (*0-89304-890-9*); pap. 5.00 (*0-89304-891-7*) Cross-Cultrl NY.

What Became Words: A Bilingual Edition. Claes Andersson. Tr. by Rika Lesser from FIN. (Classics Ser.: No. 121). 165p. (Orig.). (ENG & SWE.). 1997. pap. 11.95 (*1-55713-302-6*) Sun & Moon CA.

What Became Words: Mini Book. Claes Andersson. Ed. by Stanley H. Barkan. Tr. by Rika Lesser. (Review Chapbook Ser.: No. 22: Swedish Poetry 2). 32p. (ENG & SWE.). 1991. 15.00 (*0-89304-892-5*); pap. 5.00 (*0-89304-893-3*) Cross-Cultrl NY.

W

What Beckoning Ghost. Douglas G. Browne. 265p. 1986. reprint ed. pap. 5.95 (*0-486-25055-5*) Dover.

*__What Becomes of a Broken Heart.__ Alan Duff. Date not set. pap. write for info. (*1-86941-310-5*) Random.

What Becomes of Pollution? Adversary Science & the Controversy on the Self-Purification of Rivers in Britain, 1850-1900. Christopher Hamlin. (Modern European History Ser.). 640p. 1987. text ed. 15.00 (*0-8240-7812-8*) Garland.

*__What Beethoven Heard: A Popular Guide to Classical Music.__ Anne Gray. LC 97-13247. 372p. 1997. pap. 16.95 (*0-8065-1884-7*, Citadel Pr) Carol Pub Group.

*__What Being Jewish Means.__ Bill Adler Books Staff. Date not set. write for info. (*0-688-13732-6*) Morrow.

What Being Responsible Means to Me. Donna Brook. 1988. 15.00 (*0-914610-50-3*); pap. 7.00 (*0-914610-49-X*) Hanging Loose.

What Belongs? Shereen G. Rutman. (Learn Today for Tomorrow Ser.). (Illus.). 32p. (J). (ps-1). 1992. student ed., pap. 2.25 (*1-56293-175-X*) McClanahan Bk.

*__What Belongs?__ Shereen G. Rutman. (J). 1997. wbk. ed., pap. text ed. 2.25 (*1-56293-956-4*) McClanahan Bk.

What Belongs?, Series, 4 bks., Set. (Illus.). (J). (ps-1). 1992. 23.80 (*0-382-31243-0*); lib. bdg. 39.92 (*0-382-31242-2*) Silver.

What Big Bird's Toes Knows. (Golden Shape 'n' Tape Ser.). (Illus.). 24p. (J). (ps-3). write for info. incl. audio (*0-307-14355-4*, 14355) Western Pub.

What Binds Us to This World. Robert Cording. LC 91-4688. 71p. (Orig.). 1991. pap. 9.95 (*0-914278-57-6*) Copper Beech.

What Bird Did That? Burton Silver & Peter Hansard. (Illus.). 64p. (Orig.). 1991. pap. 7.95 (*0-89815-427-8*) Ten Speed Pr.

What Bird Is This? Henry H. Collins, Jr. (Illus.). 1961. pap. 3.95 (*0-486-21490-7*) Dover.

What Bit Me? D. M. Souza. (Creatures All Around Us Ser.). (Illus.). 40p. (J). (gr. 1-4). 1991. lib. bdg. 14.96 (*0-87614-440-7*, Carolrhoda) Lerner Group.

What Bit Me? Identifying Hawai'i's Stinging & Biting Insects & Their Kin. Gordon M. Nishida & JoAnn M. Tenorio. LC 92-33673. (Illus.). 80p. (Orig.). 1993. pap. 11.95 (*0-8248-1492-4*) UH Pr.

*__What Black America Thinks.__ Manning Marable. 1998. write for info. (*0-395-85785-6*) HM.

What Black Librarians Are Saying. E. J. Josey. LC 72-5372. 324p. 1972. 27.50 (*0-8108-0530-8*) Scarecrow.

What Black People Should Do Now: Dispatches from Near the Vanguard. Ralph Wiley. 384p. 1994. reprint ed. pap. 12.00 (*0-345-38044-4*) Ballantine.

What Blind People Wish Sighted People Knew about Blindness. 190p. (Orig.). 1996. pap. 14.95 (*0-9652205-0-8*) H Martin.

*__What Book!? Mindful Poems from Beat to Hiphop.__ Ed. by Gary Gach. 225p. (Orig.). 1997. pap. 15.00 (*0-938077-92-9*) Parallax Pr.

*__What Book Publishers Won't Tell You: A Literary Agent's Guide to the Secrets of Getting Published.__ Bill Alder. 1997. pap. text ed. 12.95 (*0-8065-1926-6*, Citadel Pr) Carol Pub Group.

What Bunny Loves. Cyndy Szekeres. (Illus.). (J). (ps-1). 1990. write for info. (*0-318-68757-7*, Golden Pr) Western Pub.

What Bunny Loves. Cyndy Szekeres. (J). (ps-3). 1990. write for info. (*0-307-11590-9*) Western Pub.

What Business Leaders Can Do to Help Change Teacher Education. 1990. 5.00 (*0-89333-073-6*) AACTE.

What Business Must Know about the ADA: Compliance Guide. rev. ed. U. S. Chamber of Commerce Staff & Zachary D. Fasman. Ed. by Cheryl Nikos. 88p. (C). 1992. 21.00 (*0-89834-124-8*, 0320) Chamber Comm US.

What Calvin Says: On Introduction to the Theology of John Calvin. W. Gary Crampton. Ed. & Intro. by John W. Robbins. 160p. 1992. pap. 7.95 (*0-940931-35-4*) Trinity Found.

What Can a Man Do? A Selection of His Most Challenging Writings. Milton S. Mayer. Ed. by W. Eric Gustafson. LC 64-15801. 320p. reprint ed. pap. 91.20 (*0-317-09760-1*, 2020118) Bks Demand.

What Can a Police Officer Do: A Comparative Study: U. S. A. - German Federal Republic - Israel - Italy. (New York University Criminal Law Education & Research Center Monograph: Vol. 7). (Illus.). xiii, 272p. (Orig.). 1974. pap. text ed. 12.50 (*0-8377-0417-0*) Rothman.

What Can a Woman Do: or Her Position in the Business & Literary World. Martha L. Rayne. LC 74-3970. (Women in America Ser.). (Illus.). 584p. 1974. reprint ed. 44.95 (*0-405-06118-8*) Ayer.

What Can a Woman Do with a Camera? Ed. by Joan Solomon & Jo Spence. 1995. pap. 17.95 (*1-85727-077-0*) LPC InBook.

What Can a Woman Do with a Camera? Ed. by Joan Solomon & Jo Spence. 1997. 49.95 (*1-85727-082-7*) LPC InBook.

What Can Baby Do? Lauren Ariev. (My First Golden Board Bks.). (Illus.). 24p. (J). (ps). 1992. bds. 3.95 (*0-307-06140-X*, 6140, Golden Books) Western Pub.

What Can I Be? A Guide to Five Hundred Twenty-Five Liberal Arts & Business Careers. Leo Lieberman. LC 75-26001. 1976. 25.00 (*0-935198-03-2*) M M Bruce.

What Can I Be? Exercises, Prayers, Poetry, & Role-Playing to Help Kids Grow in Christ. John A. Flanagan. LC 94-79999. 160p. 1995. pap. 12.95 (*0-89243-582-8*) Liguori Pubns.

What Can I Do? - My Husband Has Prostate Cancer. Bev Farmer. 100p. 1995. pap. 9.95 (*0-9647936-0-1*) Pathfinder WA.

What Can I Do? Asked the Kangaroo. Ellie Rosenthal. (J). 1993. 7.95 (*0-533-10358-4*) Vantage.

What Can I Do in RE? Michael Grimmitt. 296p. (C). 1988. 40.00 (*0-85597-261-0*, Pub. by McCrimmon Pub) St Mut.

What Can I Do Today? Jodi Takhar. (Illus.). 14p. (J). (ps-3). 19.95 (*1-886000-03-4*) J Takhars.

What Can I Do Today? A Treasury of Crafts for Children. Joan F. Klimo. LC 73-15110. (Illus.). 64p. (J). (gr. k-3). 1974. reprint ed. pap. 2.95 (*0-394-82809-7*) Pantheon.

What Can I Do with a Major In...? How to Choose & Use Your College Major. Lawrence R. Malnig & Anita Malnig. LC 83-73269. (Illus.). 250p. 1984. 26.95 (*0-9612678-1-X*) Abbott Pr.

What Can I Do with My Bread Machine? Barbara Norman. 144p. 1995. mass mkt. 4.50 (*0-440-22048-3*) Dell.

What Can I Do with My Juicer? Barbara Norman. 144p. 1992. mass mkt. 3.99 (*0-440-21542-0*) Dell.

What Can I Learn? Mary L. George. (Illus.). 128p. (Orig.). 1983. pap. 5.25 (*0-9610930-0-5*) Sisters.

What Can I Say? How to Help Someone Who Is Grieving: A Guide. Kelly Osmont. Ed. by Marilyn McFarlane. 36p. 1988. pap. 3.95 (*0-941211-02-9*) Nobility Pr.

What Can I Say? How to Talk to People in Grief. Roger F. Miller. LC 86-26868. 96p. (Orig.). 1987. pap. 4.99 (*0-8272-4220-4*) Chalice Pr.

*__What Can I Say? How to Write Verse for All Occasions.__ Sadie Harris. 128p. 1996. 14.95 (*1-55821-502-6*) Lyons & Burford.

What Can It Be? Jacqueline A. Ball. (Illus.). 32p. (J). (gr. k-3). 1990. pap. 11.80 (*0-671-24920-7*, Silver Pr NJ) Silver Burdett Pr.

What Can It Be? Stephen White. Ed. by Linda C. Dowdy. LC 94-70489. (Illus.). 32p. (J). (ps-3). 1994. 4.95 (*1-57064-019-X*) Lyrick Pub.

What Can It Be? Stephen White. Ed. by Margie Larsen. LC 94-70489. (Barney Book & Tape Ser.). (Illus.). 32p. (J). (ps-3). 1996. pap. 6.95 incl. audio (*1-57064-071-8*) Lyrick Pub.

What Can It Be?, 8 bks., Set. Jacqueline A. Ball. (Illus.). 32p ea.p. (J). (gr. k-3). 1990. Set, 32p. ea. lib. bdg. 27.80 (*0-671-94103-8*, Silver Pr NJ) Silver Burdett Pr.

What Can King Do? see Take Along Stories

What Can Pinky Hear? Lucy Cousins. LC 96-85090. (Illus.). 16p. (J). (ps). 1997. reprint ed. pap. 5.99 (*0-7636-0109-8*) Candlewick Pr.

What Can Pinky See? Lucy Cousins. LC 96-85057. (Illus.). 16p. (J). (ps up). 1997. reprint ed. pap. 5.99 (*0-7636-0110-1*) Candlewick Pr.

What Can She Know? Feminist Theory & the Construction of Knowledge. Lorraine Code. LC 90-55755. 384p. 1991. 47.50 (*0-8014-2476-3*); pap. 16.95 (*0-8014-9720-5*) Cornell U Pr.

What Can the Matter Be & Other Stories. Ian Addis. 96p. 1992. pap. 21.00 (*1-85346-211-X*, Pub. by D Fulton UK) Taylor & Francis.

What Can Tribes Do? Strategies & Institutions in American Indian Economic Development. Ed. by Stephen Cornell & Joseph P. Kalt. LC 92-54417. (American Indian Hanbook & Manual Ser.: No. 4). 336p. 1992. pap. 15.00 (*0-935626-37-9*) U Cal AISC.

What Can We Do about Church Dropouts? C. Kirk Hadaway. LC 90-34749. (Creative Leadership Ser.). 1990. pap. 12.95 (*0-687-44605-8*) Abingdon.

What Can We Know? An Introduction to the Theory of Knowledge. Louis P. Pojman. LC 94-30155. 340p. 1995. pap. 26.95 (*0-534-24834-9*) Wadsworth Pub.

What Can We Know about Jesus. Howard C. Kee. (Understanding Jesus Today Ser.). 128p. (C). 1990. text ed. 31.95 (*0-521-36057-9*); pap. text ed. 11.95 (*0-521-36915-0*) Cambridge U Pr.

What Can We Play Today? Jane B. Moncure. LC 87-32565. (Magic Castle Readers Ser.). (Illus.). 32p. (J). (ps-2). 1987. lib. bdg. 21.36 (*0-89565-412-1*) Childs World.

What Can You Do with a Bagel? Harriet K. Feder. LC 91-60591. (Illus.). 12p. (J). (ps). 1992. bds. 4.95 (*0-929371-59-3*) Kar-Ben.

*__What Can You Do with a Law Degree? A Lawyer's Guide to Career Alternatives Inside, Outside & Around the Law.__ 3rd rev. ed. Deborah Arron. LC 96-49539. 373p. (Orig.). 1997. pap. 29.95 (*0-940675-46-3*) Niche Pr.

What Can You Do with a Shoe. Maurice Sendak. LC 96-20871. (J). 1997. 14.00 (*0-689-81231-0*) S&S Childrens.

What Can You Find. Tony Tallarico. (Tuffy Tiny Bks.). (Illus.). 28p. (J). (ps). 1992. bds. 2.95 (*0-448-40429-X*, G&D) Putnam Pub Group.

What Car Dealers Don't Want You to Know. Mark Eskeldson. 200p. 1995. pap. 11.95 (*0-9640560-1-1*) Technews.

*__What Car Dealers Don't Want You to Know.__ 2nd ed. Mark Eskeldson. 1997. pap. text ed. 11.95 (*0-9640560-5-4*) Technews.

What Car Dealers Won't Tell You: The Insider's Guide to Buying or Leasing a New or Used Car. Bob Elliston. LC 96-16018. 352p. 1996. pap. 13.95 (*0-452-27688-8*, Plume) NAL-Dutton.

What Cat Is That? Duncan Searl. (Real Reading Ser.). 32p. (J). 1989. pap. 3.95 (*0-8114-6705-8*) Raintree Steck-V.

What Cat Is That? Duncan Searl. (Real Readers Ser.: Level Red). 32p. (J). 1989. lib. bdg. 21.40 (*0-8172-3502-7*) Raintree Steck-V.

What Catholics Believe. Lawrence G. Lovasik. (Illus.). 1977. pap. 5.00 (*0-89555-027-X*) TAN Bks Pubs.

What Catholics Believe: A Primer of the Catholic Faith. Josef Pieper & Heinrich Raskop. Tr. by Jan Van Heurck. LC 82-1411. 110p. 1983. 7.95 (*0-8199-0796-0*, Frncscn Herld) Franciscan Pr.

What Catholics Really Believe: Setting the Record Straight - 52 Answers to Common Misconceptions about the Catholic Faith. Karl Keating. 170p. (Orig.). 1992. pap. 8.99 (*0-89283-711-X*, Charis) Servant.

What Catholics Really Believe: 52 Answers to Common Misconceptions about the Catholic Faith. Karl Keating. LC 95-75663. 155p. 1995. pap. 9.95 (*0-89870-553-3*) Ignatius Pr.

*__What Cats Are.__ Photos by Sharon Beals. LC 96-38609. (Illus.). 1997. 8.95 (*0-8118-1660-5*) Chronicle Bks.

What Causes Jesus to Work Miracles. Norvel Hayes. 112p. (Orig.). 1995. pap. 6.99 (*0-89274-788-9*, HH-788) Harrison Hse.

What Causes Our Teens to Take Their Lives? Dying to Live. Tim Faulk. 80p. (Orig.). (YA). (gr. 9 up). 1989. pap. text ed. 5.95 (*0-685-29873-6*) T Faulk Ministries.

What Causes War? An Introduction to Theories of International Conflict. Greg Cashman. LC 92-40643. 360p. pap. 18.95 (*0-669-21215-6*, Lexington) Jossey-Bass.

What Character Is That? An Easy-Access Dictionary of 5,000 Chinese Characters. Ping-Gam Go. 1995. pap. 18.95 (*0-9623113-2-4*) Simplex Pubns.

What Child Is This. 1982. 2.25 (*0-687-44610-4*) Abingdon.

What Child Is This? Rubel Shelly. 208p. 1992. pap. 8.99 (*1-878990-23-3*) Howard Pub LA.

What Child Is This? Rebecca York. (Intrigue Ser.: 253). 1993. mass mkt. 2.99 (*0-373-22253-X*, 1-22253-8) Harlequin Bks.

*__What Child Is This? A Christmas Story.__ Caroline B. Cooney. LC 96-54891. (J). 1997. write for info. (*0-385-32317-4*) Delacorte.

*__What Child Was This? Intro Pak.__ 1996. 19.95 (*0-687-01790-4*) Abingdon.

*__What Child Was This? Intro Pak.__ 1996. audio 29.95 (*0-687-01793-9*) Abingdon.

*__What Child Was This? Intro Pak.__ 1996. audio 11.95 (*0-687-01794-7*) Abingdon.

*__What Child Was This? Leader/Accompanist Edition.__ 1996. spiral bd., pap. 14.95 (*0-687-01791-2*) Abingdon.

*__What Child Was This? Preview Pak.__ 1996. 6.00 (*0-687-07185-2*) Abingdon.

*__What Child Was This? Singer's Edition.__ 1996. pap. 2.95 (*0-687-01792-0*) Abingdon.

What Children Bring to Light: A Constructivist Perspective on Children's Learning in Science. Bonnie Shapiro. (Ways of Knowing in Science Ser.). 240p. (C). 1994. text ed. 43.00 (*0-8077-3376-8*); pap. text ed. 19.95 (*0-8077-3375-X*) Tchrs Coll.

What Children Can Tell Us: Eliciting, Interpreting, & Evaluating Critical Information from Children. Erikson Institute Faculty et al. LC 92-1771. (Social & Behavioral Science Ser.). 405p. reprint ed. pap. 16.95 (*1-55542-465-1*) Jossey-Bass.

What Children Can Tell Us: Eliciting, Interpreting & Evaluating Information from Children. James Garbarino & Frances M. Stott. LC 89-8192. 401p. reprint ed. pap. 114.30 (*0-7837-6512-6*, 2045624) Bks Demand.

What Children Need to Know When Parents Get Divorced. William L. Coleman. LC 83-6006. 96p. (J). (gr. k-5). 1983. pap. 6.99 (*0-87123-612-5*) Bethany Hse.

What Children Tell Me about Angels. Charlie W. Shedd. LC 95-6837. 160p. (J). 1995. 12.99 (*0-89283-901-5*, Vine Bks) Servant.

What Chloe Wants. Emma Jensen. 1996. mass mkt. 4.50 (*0-449-22487-2*) Fawcett.

*__What Choice Do We Have? How States Manipulate Ballot Rules to Restrict Voter Choice, 2 vols.__ Alex M. Doty. LC 97-91750. Orig. Title: Military Counselors Manual. 650p. 1997. pap. 125.00 (*0-614-30326-5*) CCCO.

*__What Choice Do We Have? How States Manipulate Ballot Rules to Restrict Voter Choice.__ E. Joshua Rosenkranz & Richard Winger. 1997. write for info. (*0-614-30162-9*) Brennan Ctr.

What Christians & Muslims Should Know about Themselves. Robert W. Mond. 1994. write for info. (*0-9625301-4-X*) Forum Islamic.

What Christians Believe. Moody Press Editors. (C). 1951. mass mkt., pap. 4.99 (*0-8024-9378-5*) Moody.

What Christians Believe. Hubert J. Richards. 72p. (Orig.). 1992. pap. text ed. 4.95 (*0-8146-2198-8*) Liturgical Pr.

What Christians Believe. Hubert J. Richards. 72p. (Orig.). (C). 1993. 30.00 (*0-85597-481-8*, Pub. by McCrimmon Pub) St Mut.

What Christians Believe: A Biblical & Historical Summary. Alan F. Johnson & Robert E. Webber. 448p. 1993. pap. 22.99 (*0-310-36721-2*) Zondervan.

What Christmas Means to Me. J. L. Snyder. (Illus.). 45p. (YA). 1989. pap. text ed. 2.95 (*0-87227-134-X*, RBP5163) Reg Baptist.

What Church Members Wish Ministers Knew. Jan G. Linn. 160p. (Orig.). 1995. pap. 12.99 (*0-8272-4234-4*) Chalice Pr.

What Citizens Know about Their Schools. William H. Todd. LC 70-177700. (Columbia University. Teachers College. Contributions to Education Ser.: No. 279). reprint ed. 37.50 (*0-404-55279-X*) AMS Pr.

What Citizens Need to Know about Government. rev. ed. Eleanor C. Goldstein. LC 93-30248. (J). 1994. 16.00 (*0-89777-146-X*) Sirs Inc.

What Civilization Owes to Italy. J. J. Walsh. 1976. 250.00 (*0-87968-361-9*) Gordon Pr.

*__What Clients Need.__ 1996. pap. 70.00 (*1-879304-39-2*, J373) AIA DC.

What Clients Really Think About Consultants: 160 Turn-Ons & 169 Turn-Offs in 4 Phases of the Engagement. Ed. by James H. Kennedy. 1985. ring bd. 49.00 (*0-916654-39-7*) Kennedy Info.

What College & University Leaders Can Do to Help Change Teacher Education. 1990. 5.00 (*0-89333-074-4*) AACTE.

What College-Bound Students Abroad Are Expected to Know about Biology. 10.00 (*0-614-14063-3*) Natl Assn Bio Tchrs.

What College Students Know about Their World. Thomas S. Barrows et al. LC 80-69768. 56p. (Orig.). 1981. pap. 10.95 (*0-915390-30-2*, Pub. by Change Mag) Transaction Pubs.

What Color? Debbie MacKinnon. (Illus.). 24p. (J). (ps). 1991. pap. 10.99 (*0-8037-0909-9*) Dial Bks Young.

What Color? Photos by Anthea Sieveking. (Illus.). 24p. (J). (ps-k). 1995. pap. 4.99 (*0-14-055462-9*, Puff Pied Piper) Puffin Bks.

What Color? Que Color? Alan Benjamin. (Chubby Board Book in English & Spanish Ser.). (ENG & SPA.). (J). (ps). 1992. pap. 3.95 (*0-671-76930-8*, Litl Simon S&S) S&S Childrens.

What Color Are You? Darwin Walton. (Ebony Jr. Bks.). (Illus.). 64p. (J). (gr. 5 up). 1973. 10.95 (*0-87485-045-2*) Johnson Chi.

What Color Is Camouflage? Carolyn B. Otto. LC 95-32173. (Let's-Read-&-Find-Out Science Bk.). (Illus.). 32p. (J). (gr. k-4). 1996. lib. bdg. 14.89 (*0-06-027099-3*) HarpC Child Bks.

What Color Is Camouflage? Carolyn B. Otto. LC 95-32173. 32p. (J). 1996. pap. 4.95 (*0-06-445160-7*) HarpC.

What Color Is Camouflage? Carolyn B. Otto. LC 95-32173. (Let's-Read-&-Find-Out Science Bks.). (Illus.). 32p. (J). (gr. k-4). 1996. 14.95 (*0-06-027094-2*) HarpC.

What Color Is It. Elisabeth Ivanovsky. (Picture-Word Boards Bks.). (Illus.). (J). (ps). 1985. bds. 3.98 (*0-517-47342-9*) Random Hse Value.

What Color Is It? - What Shape Is It? (J). 1995. 8.99 (*0-88705-583-4*) Joshua Morris.

What Color is Newton's Apple. Smith. 1988. pap. 9.99 (*0-89824-105-7*) Trillium Pr.

What Color Is Saturday? Using Analogies to Enhance Creative Thinking in the Classroom. Jane D. Mcauliffe & Laura Stoskin. LC 93-8575. 144p. 1993. pap. 25.00 (*0-913705-87-X*) Zephyr Pr AZ.

What Color Is That Dinosaur? Questions, Answers, & Mysteries. Lowell Dingus. (Illus.). 80p. (J). (gr. 4-6). 1994. pap. 9.95 (*1-56294-728-1*); lib. bdg. 17.90 (*1-56294-365-0*) Millbrook Pr.

What Color Is the Sun. Ed. & Intro. by Kenneth Jernigan. (Kernel Bk.: No. 1). (Illus.). 120p. (Orig.). 1991. pap. 3.00 (*0-9624122-2-8*) Natl Fed Blind.

What Color Is Your Aura? Barbara Bowers. 1989. pap. 14.00 (*0-671-70763-9*) PB.

What Color Is Your God? Black Consciousness & the Christian Faith. Columbus Salley & Ronald Behm. 1988. pap. 5.95 (*0-8065-1111-7*, Citadel Pr) Carol Pub Group.

***What Color Is Your God? Multicultural Education in the Church.** James Breckenridge & Lillian Breckenridge. 288p. 1995. pap. 16.99 (*0-8010-5745-0*, Bridgept Bks) Baker Bks.

What Color Is Your Mind? Thubten Chodron. 91p. 1993. pap. 12.95 (*1-55939-015-8*) Snow Lion Pubns.

What Color Is Your Parachute, 1996? A Practical Manual for Job Hunters & Career Changers. Richard N. Bolles. 480p. 1995. pap. 14.95 (*0-89815-758-7*) Ten Speed Pr.

***What Color Is Your Parasite? (And Other Self-Help Near Misses)** Jonathan Bines. 128p. 1998. pap. 7.95 (*0-7868-8284-0*) Hyperion.

What Color Is Your Swimming Pool? The Guide to Trouble-Free Pool Maintenance. John O'Keefe. Ed. by Sarah M. Clarkson. LC 85-61479. 120p. (Orig.). 1987. pap. 12.95 (*0-88266-408-5*, Storey Pub) Storey Comm Inc.

What Color Is Your World. Bob Gill. (Illus.). (J). (gr. k-3). 1963. 10.95 (*0-8392-3042-7*) Astor-Honor.

What Color Was Jesus. William Mosley. 67p. 1987. pap. 6.95 (*0-913543-09-8*) African Am Imag.

What Color Was the Sky Today? Miela Ford. LC 96-10413. (Illus.). 24p. (J). 1997. 15.00 (*0-688-14558-2*); lib. bdg. 14.93 (*0-688-14559-0*) Greenwillow.

What Color Would You Choose? Koshiro Toda. (Kindercolor Ser.). (Illus.). 44p. (J). (gr. k-3). 1992. 11.95 (*1-881267-00-8*) Intercultural.

What Comes After Faith? Kenneth Hagin, Jr. 106p. 1992. pap. 3.95 (*0-89276-727-8*) Hagin Ministries.

What Comes after Pentecost? Robert Thompson. 240p. (C). pap. text ed. 7.99 (*0-86694-096-0*) Omega Pubns OR.

What Comes after You Say, "I Love You"? James R. Hine. LC 80-11277. (Illus.). 1980. 14.95 (*0-87015-231-9*) Pacific Bks.

What Comes First? Lyn Swanson-Natsues. LC 95-18651. (Illus.). (J). 1995. pap. write for info. (*1-57255-044-9*); pap. write for info. (*1-57255-045-7*) Mondo Pubng.

What Comes in Threes. Marlene Beierel & Anne Sylvan. (Emergent Reader Bk.). 8p. (J). (gr. k-2). 1995. 1.59 (*0-916119-85-8*) Creat Teach Pr.

What Comes in Threes? Marlene Beierel & Anne Sylvan. (Emergent Reader Big Bks.). (Illus.). 8p. (Orig.). (J). (gr. k-2). 1996. pap. 7.98 (*1-57471-096-6*) Creat Teach Pr.

What Comes in Twos, Threes & Fours? Suzanne Aker. LC 89-35482. (J). 1990. pap. 14.00 (*0-671-67173-1*, S&S Bks Young Read) S&S Childrens.

What Comes in Twos, Threes & Fours? Suzanne Aker. LC 89-3548. (J). (ps). 1992. pap. 5.95 (*0-671-79247-4*, S&S Bks Young Read) S&S Childrens.

What Comes Next: The End of Big Government - & the New Paradigm Ahead. James P. Pinkerton. LC 95-18432. 356p. 1995. 24.95 (*0-7868-6105-3*) Hyperion.

What Comes Uppermost: Byron's Letters & Journals, Supplementary Volume. Leslie A. Marchand. 128p. 1994. 29.50 (*0-87413-576-1*) U Delaware Pr.

What Compassionate Men Need to Know About Women. Jan Renfrow. 1991. pap. 7.00 (*0-9613072-5-0*) Jan Renfrow.

What Computers Can Do. 2nd ed. Donald D. Spencer. LC 81-21664. 256p. (YA). (gr. 9 up). 1982. pap. 6.95 (*0-89218-043-9*, 1003) Camelot Pub.

What Computers Still Can't Do: A Critique of Artificial Reason. Hubert L. Dreyfus. (Illus.). 420p. 1992. pap. 17.50 (*0-262-54067-3*) MIT Pr.

What Computing Is All About. Jan L. Van de Snepscheut. LC 93-12238. (Texts & Monographs in Computer Science). 1993. 59.95 (*0-387-94021-9*) Spr-Verlag.

What Connolly Said. Ed. by Proinsas Mac Aonghusa. 94p. (Orig.). 1995. pap. 9.95 (*1-874597-11-1*, Pub. by New Island Bks IE) Irish Bks Media.

What Constitutes the Patient in Psychotherapy: Alternative Approaches to Understanding Humans. Richard D. Chessick. LC 91-41341. 248p. 1993. 30.00 (*0-87668-549-1*) Aronson.

What Constitutes the State? A Lecture Before the Young Men's Association of the City of Albany. Henry James, Sr. LC 72-911. (Selected Works of Henry James, Sr.: Vol. 10). 1983. reprint ed. 27.50 (*0-404-10090-2*) AMS Pr.

What Cooks at Stillmeadow. Gladys Taber. 22.95 (*0-8488-1199-2*) Amereon Ltd.

What Cops Know. Connie Fletcher. Ed. by Julie Rubenstein. 352p. 1992. reprint ed. pap. 6.50 (*0-671-75040-2*) PB.

What Corporate & General Practitioners Should Know about Intellectual Property Litigation. Raphael V. Lupo & Donna M. Tanguay. LC 91-71727. 242p. 1991. text ed. 85.00 (*0-8318-0576-5*, B576) Am Law Inst.

What Could a Hippopotamus Be? Mike Thaler. LC 89-77080. (Illus.). 40p. (J). (ps-2). 1990. pap. 13.95 (*0-671-70847-3*, S&S Bks Young Read) S&S Childrens.

***What Could Be Keeping Santa?** Marilyn Janovitz. LC 97-15754. (J). 1997. write for info. (*1-55858-819-1*); lib. bdg. write for info. (*1-55858-820-5*) North-South Bks NYC.

What Could Be Simpler? Cooking for Good Health with Good Taste. Karen A. Farmelo. (Illus.). 168p. (Orig.). 1993. pap. 19.95 (*0-9635974-1-8*); Spiral bdg. spiral bd. 19.95 (*0-9635974-0-X*) Butcher Block.

What Could Go Wrong? Willo D. Roberts. LC 88-27484. 176p. (J). (gr. 3-7). 1989. lib. bdg. 15.00 (*0-689-31438-8*, Atheneum Bks Young) S&S Childrens.

What Could Go Wrong? Willo D. Roberts. LC 92-26177. 176p. (J). (gr. 3-6). 1993. reprint ed. pap. 3.95 (*0-689-71690-7*, Aladdin Paperbacks) S&S Childrens.

***What Crucified Jesus? Messianism, Pharisaism, & the Development of Christianity.** Ellis Rivkin. LC 97-11698. 192p. (Orig.). 1997. pap. 10.00 (*0-8074-0630-9*, 571214) UAHC.

What Curriculum for the Information Age? Ed. by Mary A. White. 112p. 1987. text ed. 19.95 (*0-89859-922-9*) L Erlbaum Assocs.

What Customers Value Most: How to Iprove the Processes That Touch Your Customers. Stanley A. Brown. 288p. 1996. text ed. 34.95 (*0-471-64123-5*) Wiley.

What Daddy Did. Neal Shusterman. (Trophy Keypoint Bk.). 240p. (YA). (gr. 7 up). 1993. pap. 4.50 (*0-06-447094-6*, Trophy) HarpC Child Bks.

What Daddy Did. Neal Shusterman. (YA). 1991. pap. 15.95 (*0-316-78906-2*) Little.

What Dante Did with Loss. Jan Conn. Ed. by Michael Harris. (Signal Editions Ser.). 104p. (Orig.). Date not set. pap. 9.95 (*1-55065-052-1*, Pub. by Vehicule Pr CN) Genl Dist Srvs.

What Darwin Really Said. Benjamin Farrington. 144p. 1996. reprint ed. pap. 12.00 (*0-8052-1062-8*) Schocken.

***What Death More Glorious: A Biography of General Strong Vincent.** James Nevins & William B. Styple. (Illus.). 195p. 1997. 21.95 (*1-883926-09-2*) Belle Grv Pub.

What Death Really Is: Questions We All Ask. G. De Purucker. Ed. by W. Emmett Small. 118p. (Orig.). 1986. 6.50 (*0-913004-48-0*) Point Loma Pub.

What Demons Can Do to Saints. Merrill F. Unger. 1991. pap. 10.99 (*0-8024-9418-8*) Moody.

What Did God Say? Ronald Wright. 48p. (Orig.). 1987. pap. 30.00 (*0-7212-0728-6*, Pub. by Regency Press UK) St Mut.

What Did I Do to Deserve a Sister Like You? Angela S. Medearis. LC 95-26358. (J). 1997. 14.00 (*0-689-31935-5*, Atheneum Bks Young) S&S Childrens.

What Did I Do Wrong?, What Can I Do Now? William Backus & Candace Backus. 176p. 1990. pap. 7.99 (*1-55661-154-4*) Bethany Hse.

What Did I Find? Brian Wildsmith & Rebecca Wildsmith. LC 92-17666. (J). 1993. pap. write for info. (*0-15-200689-3*) HarBrace.

What Did I Write? Beginning Writing Behaviour. Marie M. Clay. LC 79-17088. (Illus.). 78p. 1975. pap. text ed. 16.00 (*0-435-01120-0*, 01120) Heinemann.

What Did Jesus Say about That? rev. ed. Stanley C. Baldwin. LC 74-28510. 224p. 1975. pap. 9.99 (*0-88207-718-X*, 6-2718, Victor Bks) Chariot Victor.

***What Did Loonette Forget? A Book About Thoughtfulness.** Gavin Jackson. LC 96-43567. (Big Comfy Couch Ser.). (Illus.). (J). 1996. write for info. (*0-7835-4883-4*) Time-Life.

What Did Miss Darrington See? An Anthology of Feminist Supernatural Fiction. Ed. by Jessica A. Salmonson. LC 89-7506. 304p. 1989. pap. 14.95 (*1-55861-006-5*) Feminist Pr.

What Did Mommy Do Before You? Abby Levine. Ed. by Ann Fay. LC 87-27908. (Illus.). 32p. (J). (ps-3). 1988. lib. bdg. 14.95 (*0-8075-8819-9*) A Whitman.

What Did They Mean by That? A Dictionary of Historical Terms for Genealogists. Paul Drake. (Illus.). 234p. (Orig.). 1994. pap. text ed. 23.00 (*1-55613-944-6*) Heritage Bk.

What Did They Say About Gays? Allan Gould. 1995. pap. 12.95 (*1-55022-235-X*) LPC InBook.

What Did They Think of the Jews? Compiled by Allan Gould. LC 90-43139. 648p. 1991. 50.00 (*0-87668-751-6*) Aronson.

***What Did They Think of the Jews?** Ed. by Allan Gould. LC 90-43139. 648p. 1997. pap. 30.00 (*0-7657-9966-9*) Aronson.

What Did You Do in the War Auntie? The BBC at War 1939-45. Tom Hickman. LC 95-83727. (Illus.). 224p. 1996. 26.95 (*0-563-37116-1*, BBC-Parkwest) Parkwest Pubns.

***What Did You Do in the War, Mummy?** large type ed. Mavis Nicholson. (Large Print Ser.). (Illus.). 608p. 1996. 25.99 (*0-7089-3638-5*) Ulverscroft.

What Did You Do in the War, Mummy? Women in World War II. Mavis Nicolson. (Illus.). 272p. 1995. 35.00 (*0-7011-3356-2*, Pub. by Chatto & Windus UK) Trafalgar.

What Did You Do Today? Arquette. Date not set. write for info. (*0-15-201414-4*) HarBrace.

What Did You Learn in School Today? A Parent's Guide for Evaluating Your Children's Schools. Harlow G. Unger. 168p. 1991. 19.95 (*0-8160-2510-X*) Facts on File.

What Did You Really Say? Understanding the Destructive Effects of Profanity. Alfonzo K. Surrett, Jr. 128p. (Orig.). 1924. pap. 6.99 (*1-884369-30-8*, EBED Pubns) McDougal Pubng.

What Did You Say? Kathy M. Littlefield & Robert S. Littlefield. (Illus.). 32p. (Orig.). (J). (gr. 3-6). 1989. pap. text ed. 8.95 (*1-879340-01-1*, K0102) Kidspeak.

What Did You Sayeth? Carole M. Longmeyer. (Lost Colony Collection). (Illus.). (Orig.). (J). (gr. 4 up). 1994. pap. 19.95 (*0-935326-45-6*) Gallopade Pub Group.

What Difference Did the Deed of Christ Make? Jocelyn Beredene. 1979. reprint ed. pap. 2.95 (*0-88010-103-2*) Anthroposophic.

What Difference Did the War Make? Ed. by Brian Brivati & Harriet Jones. (Themes in Contemporary British History Ser.). 240p. 1995. pap. 19.95 (*0-7185-2263-X*, Pub. by Leicester Univ Pr) Bks Intl VA.

What Difference Did the War Make? The Impact of the Second World War on British Institutions & Culture. Ed. by Brian Brivati & Harriet Jones. (Contemporary British History Ser.). 240p. (C). 1993. text ed. 54.00 (*0-7185-1446-7*) St Martin.

What Difference Does Difference Make? Teacher Reflections on Diversity, Literacy, & the Urban Primary School. Anne H. Dyson. LC 96-23993. 158p. (Orig.). 1997. pap. text ed. 16.95 (*0-8141-5657-6*) NCTE.

What Dinah Thought. Deena Metzger. 1999. pap. 7.95 (*0-14-012054-8*) Viking Penguin.

What Do Animals Do in Winter? How Animals Survive the Cold. Melvin Berger & Gilda Berger. LC 95-10419. (Discovery Readers Ser.). (Illus.). 48p. (J). (gr. k-4). 1995. per., pap. 4.50 (*1-57102-041-1*, Ideals Child); lib. bdg. 12.00 (*1-57102-055-1*, Ideals Child) Hambleton-Hill.

What Do Animals Eat Colouring Book. (Illus.). (J). (ps-6). pap. 2.95 (*0-565-00808-0*, Pub. by Natural Hist Mus UK) Parkwest Pubns.

What Do Authors Do? Eileen Christelow. LC 94-19725. (J). (gr. k-3). 1995. 15.00 (*0-395-71124-X*, Clarion Bks) HM.

***What Do Authors Do?** Eileen Christelow. (Illus.). (J). 1997. pap. 4.95 (*0-395-86621-9*, Clarion Bks) HM.

***What Do Avoid Aids.** Earvin M. Johnson. 1997. 1.99 (*0-517-17990-3*) Random Hse Value.

What Do Babies Do. LC 84-61897. (Cuddle Bks.). (Illus.). 14p. (J). (ps). 1985. 3.99 (*0-394-87279-7*) Random Bks Yng Read.

What Do Bunnies Do All Day? Judy Mastrangelo. (Illus.). 32p. (J). (ps-1). 1991. per., pap. 4.95 (*0-8249-8509-5*, Ideals Child) Hambleton-Hill.

***What Do Calculated Gear Stresses Mean?** E. J. Wellauer. (Technical Papers). 1956. pap. text ed. 30.00 (*1-55589-271-X*) AGMA.

***What Do Children & Young Adults Read Next.** 2nd ed. 1997. 95.00 (*0-8103-6447-6*, 00004827, Gale Res Intl) Gale.

What Do Children & Young Adults Read Next, 2 Vols., Vol. 2. Candace Colborn & Pamela G. Spencer. 1994. Set. 95.00 (*0-8103-8885-5*, 022155) Gale.

What Do Children Read Next. Candace Colborn. 700p. 1994. 55.00 (*0-8103-8886-3*, 022180) Gale.

***What Do Children Read Next.** 2nd ed. LC 97-10560. 1997. 55.00 (*0-8103-6448-4*, 00002532, Gale Res Intl) Gale.

What Do Cowboys Like. Ann Tracy. LC 94-20260. 160p. 1995. 22.00 (*1-877946-52-4*) Permanent Pr.

***What Do Dogs Know?** Stanley Coren. 1997. pap. text ed. 16.95 (*0-684-84860-0*) Free Pr.

***What Do Dogs Know?** Stanley Coren. 1997. 14.95 (*0-87605-613-3*) Howell Bk.

What Do Draculas Do? Essays on Contemporary Writers of Fiction for Children & Young Adults. David Rees. LC 90-8669. 260p. 1990. 29.50 (*0-8108-2320-9*) Scarecrow.

***What Do Dreams Mean?** Maria F. Mahoney. LC 97-5628. 256p. 1997. pap. 12.95 (*0-8065-1867-7*, Citadel Pr) Carol Pub Group.

What Do Ducklings Do? Wishing Well Staff. (Illus.). 10p. 1995. 5.99 (*0-88705-561-3*, Wshng Well Bks) Joshua Morris.

***What Do Effective Team Leaders Really Do?** Jane Henry. 100p. 1997. 17.00 (*0-87389-382-4*) ASQC Qual Pr.

***What Do Fish Have to Do with Anything?** Avi. LC 97-1354. (YA). 1997. 17.99 (*0-7636-0329-5*); pap. write for info. (*0-7636-0412-7*) Candlewick Pr.

What Do High Performance Managers Really Do? Phil Hodgson & Stuart Crainer. (Financial Times Management Ser.). 224p. 1993. 37.50 (*0-273-60387-6*, Pub. by Pitman Pub Ltd UK) Trans-Atl Phila.

What Do I Do: English - Spanish Edition. Norma Simon. LC 74-79544. (Albert Whitman Concept Bks.). (Illus.). 40p. (J). (ps-2). 1969. lib. bdg. 14.95 (*0-8075-8823-7*) A Whitman.

What Do I Do along the Way? Polly Greenberg. 1996. pap. 3.95 (*0-590-94058-9*) Scholastic Inc.

What Do I Do? How to Care for, Comfort, & Commune with Your Nursing Home. Katherine L. Karr. LC 85-7649. (Activities, Adaptation & Aging Ser.: Vol. 7, No. 1). (Illus.). 130p. 1985. text ed. 19.95 (*0-86656-398-9*) Haworth Pr.

***What Do I Do If...? Practical Solutions to Common Parenting Problems.** Jay Colker & Dennis Niswonger. (Illus.). 120p. (Orig.). 1997. pap. 24.95 (*0-9657549-0-1*) InfoTele.

What Do I Do Monday? John Holt. LC 95-34036. (Innovators in Education Ser.). 292p. (Orig.). 1995. pap. 15.95 (*0-86709-368-4*, 0368) Boynton Cook Pubs.

What Do I Do Next? A Manual for People Just Entering Government Service. Albert J. Solnit. LC 80-67754. (Illus.). 128p. (Orig.). (C). 1980. pap. 15.95 (*0-918286-20-4*) Planners Pr.

***What Do I Do Now.** Ross. Date not set. pap. write for info. (*0-312-18208-2*) St Martin.

What Do I Do Now? Challenges & Choices for Camp Counselors & Other Youth Workers. rev. ed. Jerry Beker et al. 160p. (C). 1996. pap. 15.95 (*0-87603-151-3*) Am Camping.

What Do I Do Now? Making Sense of Today's Changing Workplace. Shena Crane. LC 93-94164. 296p. (Orig.). 1994. 21.95 (*0-9638247-0-8*); pap. 14.95 (*0-9638247-1-6*) Vista Mktg.

What Do I Do Now, Mom? Growing-up Guidance for Young Teen-age Girls. Jean D. Crowther. LC 80-82257. (Illus.). 86p. (J). (gr. 9-12). 1980. 10.98 (*0-88290-134-6*) Horizon Utah.

What Do I Do on a Boring Day in Great Falls? Jim Starbuck. LC 86-60897. (Illus.). 88p. (Orig.). 1986. pap. 5.95 (*0-9616479-2-2*) Med River Pub.

What Do I Do?: Patient's Guide see So in the Meantime

What Do I Do When...? How to Achieve Discipline with Dignity in the Classroom. Allen N. Mendler. 136p. (Orig.). 1992. pap. 19.95 (*1-879639-21-1*) Natl Educ Serv.

***What Do I Do When: The Answer Book on Individualized Education Programs.** Susan Gorn. LC 97-20412. 1997. write for info. (*1-57834-003-9*) LRP Pubns.

***What Do I Do When My Child Loses Control.** Polly Greenberg. (Family Bookshelf). 1997. pap. 3.95 (*0-590-94060-0*) Scholastic Inc.

***What Do I Do When My Child Won't Do As I Say?** Polly Greenberg. 1996. pap. text ed. 3.95 (*0-590-89926-0*) Scholastic Inc.

What Do I Do? Who Do I Call? Resources for Health Care Professionals Seeking Information Related to the Legal Profession. Barbara E. Calfee & David A. Calfee. 115p. (Orig.). 1995. pap. text ed. 10.00 (*0-9633540-4-3*) ARC Pub.

What Do I Eat? Shirley Greenway. LC 93-18592. (Animals Q & A Ser.). (Illus.). 32p. (J). (ps-2). 1993. per., pap. 3.95 (*0-8249-8602-4*, Ideals Child); lib. bdg. 11.00 (*0-8249-8627-X*, Ideals Child) Hambleton-Hill.

What Do I Have to Offer? Support for Laity in Their Ministries. C. A. Hahn et al. pap. 8.00 (*1-56699-099-8*, OD42) Alban Inst.

What Do I Hear? What Do I Hear? Sarah Albee. (J). 1996. pap. 4.99 (*0-689-80842-9*) S&S Childrens.

What Do I Know? Reading, Writing, & Teaching the Essay. Janis Forman. LC 95-24355. 144p. 1995. pap. text ed. 19.50 (*0-86709-370-6*, 0370) Boynton Cook Pubs.

What Do I Read Next? Ed. by Neil Barron et al. 600p. 1990. 105.00 (*0-8103-7555-9*) Gale.

What Do I Read Next? 2nd ed. Ramsdell. 1991. 105.00 (*0-8103-5405-5*) Gale.

What Do I Read Next? 3rd ed. Ramsdell. 1992. 105.00 (*0-8103-5406-3*) Gale.

What Do I Read Next? 4th ed. 1993. 105.00 (*0-8103-8235-0*) Gale.

What Do I Read Next? A Reader's Guide to Current Genre Fiction 1996. 7th ed. Steven A. Stilwell et al. 656p. 1996. 110.00 (*0-7876-1048-8*) Gale.

***What Do I Read Next? Historical Novels.** LC 97-10702. 1997. 125.00 (*0-7876-0388-0*, 00109602, Gale Res Intl) Gale.

***What Do I Read Next? Multicultural Literature.** LC 97-2044. 1997. 80.00 (*0-7876-0814-9*, 00153553, Gale Res Intl) Gale.

***What Do I Read Next 1994.** 5th ed. 1994. 105.00 (*0-8103-8597-X*, 00009969, Gale Res Intl) Gale.

What Do I Read Next 1995. 6th ed. Steven A. Stilwell et al. 1995. 105.00 (*0-8103-9146-5*) Gale.

***What Do I Read Next 1996.** 7th ed. 1996. 105.00 (*0-8103-6450-6*, 00009991, Gale Res Intl) Gale.

***What Do I Read Next 1997.** 8th ed. 1997. 110.00 (*0-7876-0058-X*, 00108706, Gale Res Intl) Gale.

What Do I Say Next? Talking Your Way to Business & Social Success. Susan RoAne. LC 96-43903. 288p. 1997. 20.00 (*0-446-52000-4*) Warner Bks.

What Do I Say When... Muriel Solomon. pap. 11.95 (*0-13-951617-4*) P-H.

What Do I Say When...A Guide Book for Getting Your Way with People on the Job. Muriel Solomon. 276p. 29.95 (*0-13-955782-2*) P-H.

What Do I See? What Do I See? Sarah Albee. (J). 1996. pap. 4.99 (*0-689-80841-0*) S&S Childrens.

***What Do I Take? The Nation's Leading Pharmacists Rate Non-Prescription Drugs.** American Pharmacists Association Staff. LC 97-2868. 208p. 1997. pap. 13.00 (*0-06-273422-9*, PL) HarpC.

What Do I Taste: The Five Senses. Harriet Ziefert. (Illus.). (J). (ps-1). 1988. pap. 3.95 (*0-317-69282-8*) Bantam.

What Do I Tell Them?: Doctor's Guide see So in the Meantime

What Do I Want in Prayer? William A. Barry. LC 94-17578. 144p. 1994. pap. 8.95 (*0-8091-3482-9*) Paulist Pr.

What Do Jews Believe? The Spiritual Foundations of Judaism. David S. Ariel. 304p. 1996. reprint ed. pap. 13.00 (*0-8052-1059-8*) Schocken.

What Do Kangaroo. (J). pap. 7.33 (*0-590-21036-X*) Scholastic Inc.

What Do Kangaroo. (J). pap. 69.33 (*0-590-21121-8*) Scholastic Inc.

What Do Kang/Lentil. pap. 7.50 (*0-590-20031-3*) Scholastic Inc.

***What Do Lions Know about Stress.** Majid Ali. 500p. Date not set. pap. 20.00 (*1-879131-10-2*) Inst of Prev Med.

What Do Mormons Believe? Rex E. Lee. LC 92-36087. vii, 118p. 1992. 11.95 (*0-87579-639-7*) Deseret Bk.

***What Do Numbers Dream Of?** D. A. Feinfeld. LC 96-90473. 80p. (Orig.). 1997. pap. 10.00 (*1-56002-688-X*, Univ Edtns) Aegina Pr.

***What Do People Do? A Learn-about Book.** Sarah Albee. (Fisher-Price Playbooks). (Illus.). 20p. (J). (ps up). 1997. bds. 10.99 (*1-57584-185-1*) Rdrs Dgst Yng Fam.

What Do Presbyterians Believe? Gordon H. Clark. LC 65-27481. 1965. pap. 9.99 (*0-87552-168-1*, Pub. by Evangelical Pr) Presby & Reformed.

W

What Do Professors of Education Profess? Harry S. Broudy. (DeGarmo Lectures: No. 4). 1979. 3.00 (0-933669-28-3) Soc Profs Ed.

What Do Psychoanalysts Want? The Problem of Aims in Psychoanalysts. Joseph Sandler & Anna U. Dreher. LC 95-9186. (New Library of Psychoanalysis: Vol. 24). 160p. (C). 1996. pap. 18.95 (0-415-13515-X); text ed. 59.95 (0-415-13514-1) Routledge.

What Do the Fairies Do with All Those Teeth. Michel Luppens. (Illus.). 24p. (J). (gr. k-3). 1996. 12.95 (1-55209-001-9); pap. 4.95 (1-55209-002-7) Firefly Bks Ltd.

***What Do the Fairies Do with All Those Teeth?** Michel Luppens & Phillipe Beha. (Illus.). (J). 15.95 (0-590-74050-4) Scholastic Inc.

***What Do the Fairies Do with All Those Teeth?** Michel Luppens & Phillipe Beha. (Illus.). (J). pap. 5.95 (0-590-74075-X) Scholastic Inc.

What Do They Do All Day in Heaven? Staci C. Thomas. (Illus.). 40p. (J). (gr. 3 up). 1995. 13.95 (0-9648203-0-7) Our Family Lines.

What Do They Do All Day in Heaven? Staci C. Thomas. (Illus.). 40p. (Orig.). (J). 1995. pap. 7.95 (0-9648203-1-5) Our Family Lines.

What Do They Expect of Me? Robert G. Davidson. 80p. (gr. 7-12). 1986. pap. 9.95 (0-940754-32-0) Ed Ministries.

What Do They Mean I'm Difficult. Louise B. Ames. (Illus.). 40p. (Orig.). 1986. teacher ed. 4.50 (0-935493-02-6, 302) Programs Educ.

What Do They Say When You Leave the Room? How to Increase Your Personal Effectiveness for Success at Work, at Home & in Your Life. Brigid M. Massie & John Waters. Ed. by Paula M. Lee. LC 91-22182. 215p. (Orig.). (C). 1991. pap. 10.95 (0-9629850-0-7) Eudemonia Pubns.

What Do They See When They See You Coming? The Power of Perception over Reality. Stephen M. Gower. 168p. 1993. 20.00 (1-880150-65-4) Lectern Pub.

***What Do Thin People Do Different?** Joannie Greggins. 1998. write for info. (0-375-50036-7, Villard Bks) Random.

What Do Toddlers Do? LC 84-61895. (Cuddle Bks.). (Illus.). 14p. (J). (ps). 1985. 3.99 (0-394-87280-0) Random Bks Yng Read.

What Do We Do Now? The Complete Guide for All New Parents & Parents-to-Be! Paul R. Feinsinger. Ed. by Cliff Carle. (Illus.). 112p. (Orig.). 1988. pap. 4.95 (0-918259-18-5) CCC Pubns.

What Do We Expect to Learn from Our History? The First Symposium on History in Landscape Architecture. Daniel J. Nadenicek. Ed. by Eliza Pennypacker. (Illus.). 156p. (Orig.). 1996. pap. write for info. (1-888901-00-4) PSU Ctr for SILH.

What Do We Know about Amazonian Indians? Anna Lewington. LC 93-1736. (What Do We Know about...? Ser.). (Illus.). 44p. (J). (gr. 3 up). 1993. pap. 8.95 (0-87226-262-6); lib. bdg. 18.95 (0-87226-367-3) P Bedrick Bks.

***What Do We Know about Buddhism?** Anita Ganeri. LC 96-52161. (What Do We Know about...? Ser.). (Illus.). 44p. (J). (gr. 3 up). 1997. lib. bdg. 18.95 (0-87226-389-4) P Bedrick Bks.

***What Do We Know about Christianity?** Carol Watson. LC 97-25302. (What Do We Know about...? Ser.). (Illus.). 44p. (J). (gr. 3 up). 1997. lib. bdg. 18.95 (0-87226-390-8) P Bedrick Bks.

What Do We Know about Hinduism? Anita Ganeri. LC 95-51827. (What Do We Know about...? Ser.). (Illus.). 44p. (J). (gr. 3 up). 1996. lib. bdg. 18.95 (0-87226-385-1) P Bedrick Bks.

What Do We Know about Islam? Shahrukh Hussein. LC 96-30873. (What Do We Know about...? Ser.). (Illus.). 44p. (J). (gr. 3 up). 1996. lib. bdg. 18.95 (0-87226-388-6) P Bedrick Bks.

What Do We Know about Judaism? Doreen Fine. (What Do We Know about...? Ser.). (Illus.). 44p. (J). (gr. 3 up). 1996. lib. bdg. 18.95 (0-87226-386-X) P Bedrick Bks.

***What Do We Know about Our Future? Heaven, Hell, Purgatory - A Conservative Space Age Approach.** Stephen A. Foglein. 160p. (Orig.). 1997. pap. 7.50 (1-884722-04-0) Two Hrts Bks.

What Do We Know about Prehistoric People? Mike Corbishley. LC 95-11224. (What Do We Know about...? Ser.). (Illus.). 44p. (J). (gr. 3 up). 1995. lib. bdg. 18.95 (0-87226-383-5) P Bedrick Bks.

What Do We Know about Rainforests? Brian Knapp. LC 92-5187. (Caring for Environments Ser.). (Illus.). 40p. (J). (gr. 4-6). 1992. lib. bdg. 15.95 (0-87226-358-4) P Bedrick Bks.

What Do We Know about Sikhism? Beryl Dhanjal. (What Do We Know about...? Ser.). (Illus.). 44p. (J). (gr. 3 up). 1996. lib. bdg. 18.95 (0-87226-387-8) P Bedrick Bks.

What Do We Know about the Aztecs? Joanna Defrates. LC 92-16997. (What Do We Know about...? Ser.). (Illus.). 44p. (YA). (gr. 3 up). 1993. lib. bdg. 18.95 (0-87226-357-6) P Bedrick Bks.

What Do We Know about the Celts? Hazel M. Martell. (What Do We Know about...? Ser.). (Illus.). 44p. (YA). (gr. 3 up). 1993. lib. bdg. 18.95 (0-87226-363-0) P Bedrick Bks.

What Do We Know about the Egyptians? Joanna Defrates. LC 91-25175. (What Do We Know about...? Ser.). (Illus.). 44p. (YA). (gr. 3 up). 1992. lib. bdg. 18.95 (0-87226-353-3) P Bedrick Bks.

What Do We Know about the Grasslands? Brian Knapp. LC 92-7888. (Caring for Environments Ser.). (Illus.). 40p. (J). (gr. 4-6). 1992. lib. bdg. 15.95 (0-87226-359-2) P Bedrick Bks.

What Do We Know about the Greeks? Anne Pearson. LC 92-9692. (What Do We Know about...? Ser.). (Illus.). 44p. (YA). (gr. 3 up). 1992. lib. bdg. 18.95 (0-87226-356-8) P Bedrick Bks.

What Do We Know about the Inuit? Brian Alexander & Cherry Alexander. (What Do We Know about...? Ser.). (Illus.). 44p. (J). (gr. 3 up). 1995. lib. bdg. 18.95 (0-87226-380-0) P Bedrick Bks.

What Do We Know about the Middle Ages? Sarah Howarth. LC 95-33280. (What Do We Know about...? Ser.). (Illus.). 44p. (J). (gr. 3 up). 1995. lib. bdg. 18.95 (0-87226-384-3) P Bedrick Bks.

What Do We Know about the Plains Indians? Colin Taylor. (What Do We Know about...? Ser.). (Illus.). 44p. (J). (gr. 3 up). 1993. pap. 10.95 (0-87226-261-8); lib. bdg. 18.95 (0-87226-368-1) P Bedrick Bks.

What Do We Know about the Romans? Mike Corbishley. LC 91-28763. (What Do We Know about...? Ser.). (Illus.). 44p. (YA). (gr. 3 up). 1992. lib. bdg. 18.95 (0-87226-352-5) P Bedrick Bks.

What Do We Know about the Vikings? Helen M. Martell. LC 92-7893. (What Do We Know about...? Ser.). (Illus.). 44p. (YA). (gr. 3 up). 1992. lib. bdg. 18.95 (0-87226-355-X) P Bedrick Bks.

***What Do We Need?** Trisha Callella. Ed. by Rozanne L. Williams. (Social Studies Learn to Read Ser.). (Illus.). 8p. (Orig.). (J). (ps-2). 1996. pap. 1.59 (1-57471-129-6, 3910) Creat Teach Pr.

***What Do We Need?** Trisha Callella. Ed. by Rozanne L. Williams. (Social Studies Big Bks.). (Illus.). 8p. (Orig.). (J). (ps-2). 1997. pap. 7.98 (1-57471-175-X, 3967) Creat Teach Pr.

What Do We Need a Union For? The TWUA in the South, 1945-1955. Timothy J. Minchin. LC 96-25419. (Fred W. Morrison Series in Southern Studies). 288p. (C). (gr. 13). 1997. 45.00 (0-8078-2317-1); pap. 16.95 (0-8078-4625-2) U of NC Pr.

What Do We Need to Know about the International Monetary System? Paul R. Krugman. LC 93-9099. (Essays in International Finance Ser.: No. 190). 32p. 1993. pap. 8.00 (0-88165-097-8) Princeton U Int Finan Econ.

What Do We Really Know about God? Kenneth McNeely. LC 86-91364. 1987. 12.00 (0-87212-201-8) Libra.

***What Do We Say.** Rich. LC 97-7858. 1997. pap. 12.95 (0-312-85433-1) St Martin.

What Do We Talk About When We Talk? Speculative Grammar & the Semantics & Pragmatics of Focus. Johan Van Der Auwera. (Pragmatics & Beyond Ser.: II: 3). vi, 122p. (Orig.). 1981. pap. 29.00 (90-272-2513-3) Benjamins North Am.

What Do We Want for Christmas? A Giving & Sharing Book. Andrea Doray. Ed. by Jonna Gress. LC 93-73679. (Illus.). 16p. (J). (ps-1). 1994. pap. 7.20 (0-944943-40-3, 23302-7) Current Inc.

What Do Women Want: Exploding the Myth of Dependency. Luise Eichenbaum & Susie Orbach. 240p. 1987. mass mkt. 5.50 (0-425-09912-1) Berkley Pub.

What Do You Ask for Your Child? Carol Luebering. 30p. (Orig.). 1980. pap. text ed. 1.35 (0-912228-64-4) St Anthony Mess Pr.

What Do You Call a Person From...? A Dictionary of Residential Terms. Paul Dickson. 1990. 19.95 (0-8160-1983-5) Facts on File.

What Do You Care What Other People Think? Further Adventures of a Curious Character. Richard P. Feynman. 256p. 1989. pap. 14.95 (0-553-34784-5) Bantam.

What Do You Communicate? Women's Practical Guide to Everyday Relationships. Sandra Humphrey. 1985. pap. 5.99 (0-89349-000-8) Gospel Advocate.

What Do You Do. (J). pap. 60.00 (0-590-21013-0) Scholastic Inc.

What Do You Do? Suzanne Hardin. (Let Me Read Ser.). (Illus.). (J). (ps-2). 1995. 2.95 (0-673-36282-5, GoodYrBooks) Addson-Wesley Educ.

What Do You Do after High School? Regina Skyer et al. 357p. (Orig.). 1982. pap. text ed. 24.95 (0-943106-00-1) Skyer Consul.

What Do You Do after High School? 1986-87 Edition. Regina Skyer & Gil Skyer. 444p. (Orig.). 1986. pap. text ed. 29.95 (0-943106-01-X) Skyer Consul.

What Do You Do, Dear? Sesyle Joslin. LC 84-43139. (Illus.). 48p. (J). 1958. lib. bdg. 13.89 (0-06-023075-4) HarpC Child Bks.

What Do You Do, Dear? Sesyle Joslin. LC 84-43139. (Trophy Picture Bk.). (Illus.). 48p. (J). (ps-3). 1986. reprint ed. pap. 4.95 (0-06-443113-4, Trophy) HarpC Child Bks.

What Do You Do Now? 72p. 1995. Minimum order of 3 copies. 3.00 (0-318-68050-5) LIMRA Intl.

***What Do You Do When Something Wants to Eat You?** Steve Jenkins. LC 96-44993. 1997. 16.00 (0-395-82514-8) HM.

***What Do You Do When You Can't Call a Cop?** Janice A. Seifert. Ed. by Billy D. Conley. (Illus.). xx, 208p. (Orig.). 1997. pap. 13.95 (0-9657443-0-2) Ultimate Survivors.

What Do You Do with a Cardboard Box on a Day When the Rain's Pourin' Down? R. Harris Sandling. Ed. by Mary C. Carter. (Illus.). 50p. (J). (gr. 3 up). 1993. write for info. (1-883194-00-8) Emerald Hummngbrd.

What Do You Do with a Child Like This? Creating Change in the Lives of Troubled Children. L. Tobin. LC 91-65948. 192p. (Orig.). 1991. pap. 14.95 (0-938586-44-0) Whole Person.

What Do You Do with a Grumpy Kangaroo? Jane B. Moncure. LC 87-11731. (Magic Castle Readers Ser.). (Illus.). 32p. (J). (ps-2). 1987. lib. bdg. 21.36 (0-89565-372-9) Childs World.

What Do You Do with a Kangaroo. Mercer Mayer. 48p. (J). (ps-3). 1987. pap. 5.99 (0-590-44850-1) Scholastic Inc.

What Do You Do with a Kangaroo. Mercer Meyer. (J). (ps-3). 1993. pap. 199.51 (0-590-21034-3) Scholastic Inc.

What Do You Do with a Potty? An Important Pop-up Book. Marianne Borgardt. (Illus.). 10p. (J). 1994. 7.95 (0-307-17610-X) Western Pub.

What Do You Do with an Ousted Liberal, Vol. 6. Merrill Matthews. (Salt Ser.). (Illus.). 48p. 1995. mass mkt. 3.49 (1-56384-112-6) Huntington Hse.

What Do You Eat? Rick Wetzel. LC 92-61623. (Sesame Street Little Pops Ser.). (Illus.). 6p. (J). (ps-1). 1993. 4.99 (0-679-83844-9) Random Bks Yng Read.

***What Do You Expect? Probability & Expected Value.** Glenda Lappan et al. Ed. by Catherine Anderson et al. (Connected Mathematics Ser.). (Illus.). 78p. (J). (gr. 7). 1996. wbk. ed. 5.95 (1-57232-174-1, 21469) Seymour Pubns.

***What Do You Expect? Probability & Expected Value.** Glenda Lappan et al. Ed. by Catherine Anderson et al. (Connected Mathematics Ser.). (Illus.). 161p. 1996. teacher ed. 16.50 (1-57232-175-X, 21470) Seymour Pubns.

***What Do You Expect? Probability & Expected Value.** rev. ed. Glenda Lappan et al. Ed. by Catherine Anderson et al. (Connected Mathematics Ser.). (Illus.). 179p. (J). (gr. 7). 1997. teacher ed., pap. text ed. 16.50 (1-57232-648-4, 45843) Seymour Pubns.

***What Do You Expect? Probability & Expected Value.** rev. ed. Glenda Lappan et al. Ed. by Catherine Anderson et al. (Connected Mathematics Ser.). (Illus.). 84p. (YA). (gr. 7 up). 1997. student ed., pap. text ed. 5.95 (1-57232-647-6, 45842) Seymour Pubns.

What Do You Get When You Cross a Dandelion with a Rose? The True Story of Psychoanalysis. Vamlk D. Volkan. LC 83-6332. 296p. 1984. 30.00 (0-87668-638-2) Aronson.

What Do You Give a Sick Tyrannosaurus Rex? Dick Dudley. (Dino Pop-up Joke Bks.). 12p. (J). (ps-3). 1992. 5.95 (1-56288-179-5) Checkerboard.

What Do You Hear? A Book about Animal Sounds. Anne M. Miranda. Ed. by Jean Crawford. (Snugglebug Bks.). (Illus.). 32p. (J). (ps). 1994. 4.95 (0-7835-4500-2) Time-Life.

What Do You Hear When Cows Sing? And Other Silly Riddles. Marco Maestro & Giulio Maestro. LC 94-18686. (I Can Read Bk.). (Illus.). 48p. (J). (gr. k-3). 1996. 14.95 (0-06-024948-X); lib. bdg. 14.89 (0-06-024949-8) HarpC Child Bks.

***What Do You Hear When Cows Sing? And Other Silly Riddles.** Marco Maestro & Giulio Maestro. LC 94-18686. (I Can Read Bk.). (Illus.). 48p. (J). (gr. 2-5). 1997. pap. 3.75 (0-06-444227-6, Trophy) HarpC Child Bks.

What Do You Know? Trivia Fun & Activities for Seniors. Teresa Sumrall. 72p. (Orig.). 1991. pap. text ed. 10.95 (1-879633-07-8) Eldersong.

What Do You Know about Accounting? Jack Rudman. (Test Your Knowledge Ser.: Q-1). 1994. pap. 23.95 (0-8373-7001-9) Nat Learn.

What Do You Know about Afro-American History? Jack Rudman. (Test Your Knowledge Ser.: Q-2). 1994. pap. 23.95 (0-8373-7002-7) Nat Learn.

What Do You Know about Air Conditioning, Refrigeration & Heating? Jack Rudman. (Test Your Knowledge Ser.: Q-3). 1994. pap. 29.95 (0-8373-7003-5) Nat Learn.

What Do You Know about American Government? Jack Rudman. (Test Your Knowledge Ser.: No. Q-4). 1994. pap. 23.95 (0-8373-7004-3) Nat Learn.

What Do You Know about American History? Jack Rudman. (Test Your Knowledge Ser.: No. Q-5). 1994. pap. 23.95 (0-8373-7005-1) Nat Learn.

What Do You Know about American Literature? Jack Rudman. (Test Your Knowledge Ser.: No. Q-6). 1994. pap. 23.95 (0-8373-7006-X) Nat Learn.

What Do You Know about Anatomic Sciences? Jack Rudman. (Test Your Knowledge Ser.: No. Q-7). 1994. pap. 23.95 (0-8373-7007-8) Nat Learn.

What Do You Know about Anthropology? Jack Rudman. (Test Your Knowledge Ser.: No. Q-8). 1994. pap. 23.95 (0-8373-7008-6) Nat Learn.

What Do You Know about Appliance Repair? Jack Rudman. (Test Your Knowledge Ser.: No. Q-9). 1994. pap. 23.95 (0-8373-7009-4) Nat Learn.

What Do You Know about Art History? Jack Rudman. (Test Your Knowledge Ser.: No. Q-10). 1994. pap. 23.95 (0-8373-7010-8) Nat Learn.

What Do You Know about Astronomy? Jack Rudman. (Test Your Knowledge Ser.: No. Q-11). 1994. pap. 23.95 (0-8373-7011-6) Nat Learn.

What Do You Know about Auto Mechanics? Jack Rudman. (Test Your Knowledge Ser.: No. Q-12). 1994. pap. 23.95 (0-8373-7012-4) Nat Learn.

What Do You Know? about Bacteriology? Jack Rudman. (Test Your Knowledge Ser.: No. Q-13). 1994. pap. 23.95 (0-8373-7013-2) Nat Learn.

What Do You Know about Biochemistry/Physiology? Jack Rudman. (Test Your Knowledge Ser.: No. Q-14). 1994. pap. 23.95 (0-8373-7014-0) Nat Learn.

What Do You Know about Biological Sciences? Jack Rudman. (Test Your Knowledge Ser.: No. Q-15). 1994. pap. 23.95 (0-8373-7015-9) Nat Learn.

What Do You Know about Biology? Jack Rudman. (Test Your Knowledge Ser.: No. Q-16). 1994. pap. 23.95 (0-8373-7016-7) Nat Learn.

What Do You Know about Building Maintenance? Jack Rudman. (Test Your Knowledge Ser.: No. Q-17). 1994. pap. 23.95 (0-8373-7017-5) Nat Learn.

What Do You Know about Business Law? Jack Rudman. (Test Your Knowledge Ser.: No. Q-18). 1994. pap. 23.95 (0-8373-7018-3) Nat Learn.

What Do You Know about Cabinet Making & Millwork? Jack Rudman. (Test Your Knowledge Ser.: No. Q-19). 1994. pap. 23.95 (0-8373-7019-1) Nat Learn.

What Do You Know about Calculus? Jack Rudman. (Test Your Knowledge Ser.: No. Q-20). 1994. pap. 23.95 (0-8373-7020-5) Nat Learn.

What Do You Know about Calculus with Analytical Geometry? Jack Rudman. (Test Your Knowledge Ser.: No. Q-21). 1994. pap. 23.95 (0-8373-7021-3) Nat Learn.

What Do You Know about Carpentry? Jack Rudman. (Test Your Knowledge Ser.: No. Q-22). 1994. pap. 23.95 (0-8373-7022-1) Nat Learn.

What Do You Know about Chemical Engineering? Jack Rudman. (Test Your Knowledge Ser.: No. Q-23). 1994. pap. 23.95 (0-8373-7023-X) Nat Learn.

What Do You Know about Chemistry? Jack Rudman. (Test Your Knowledge Ser.: No. Q-24). 1994. pap. 23.95 (0-8373-7024-8) Nat Learn.

What Do You Know about Civil Engineering? Jack Rudman. (Test Your Knowledge Ser.: No. Q-25). 1994. pap. 23.95 (0-8373-7025-6) Nat Learn.

What Do You Know about Civil Practice Law & Rules (CPLR)? Jack Rudman. (Test Your Knowledge Ser.: No. Q-26). 1994. pap. 23.95 (0-8373-7026-4) Nat Learn.

What Do You Know about Clinical Chemistry? Jack Rudman. (Test Your Knowledge Ser.: No. Q-27). 1994. pap. 23.95 (0-8373-7027-2) Nat Learn.

What Do You Know about College Algebra? Jack Rudman. (Test Your Knowledge Ser.: No. Q-28). 1994. pap. 23.95 (0-8373-7028-0) Nat Learn.

What Do You Know about College Algebra-Trigonometry? Jack Rudman. (Test Your Knowledge Ser.: No. Q-29). 1994. pap. 23.95 (0-8373-7029-9) Nat Learn.

What Do You Know about Commercial & Advertising Art? Jack Rudman. (Test Your Knowledge Ser.: No. Q-30). 1994. pap. 23.95 (0-8373-7030-2) Nat Learn.

What Do You Know about Computer Programming? Jack Rudman. (Test Your Knowledge Ser.: No. Q-31). 1994. pap. 23.95 (0-8373-7031-0) Nat Learn.

What Do You Know about Computer Science? Jack Rudman. (Test Your Knowledge Ser.: No. Q-32). 1994. pap. 23.95 (0-8373-7032-9) Nat Learn.

What Do You Know about Cooking? Jack Rudman. (Test Your Knowledge Ser.: No. Q-33). 1994. pap. 23.95 (0-8373-7033-7) Nat Learn.

What Do You Know about Cosmetology? Jack Rudman. (Test Your Knowledge Ser.: No. Q-34). 1994. pap. 23.95 (0-8373-7034-5) Nat Learn.

What Do You Know about Criminal Investigation? Jack Rudman. (Test Your Knowledge Ser.: No. Q-35). 1994. pap. 23.95 (0-8373-7035-3) Nat Learn.

What Do You Know about Criminal Procedure? Jack Rudman. (Test Your Knowledge Ser.: No. Q-36). 1994. pap. 23.95 (0-8373-7036-1) Nat Learn.

What Do You Know about Criminology? Jack Rudman. (Test Your Knowledge Ser.: No. Q-37). 1994. pap. 23.95 (0-8373-7037-X) Nat Learn.

What Do You Know about Data Processing? Jack Rudman. (Test Your Knowledge Ser.: No. Q-38). 1994. pap. 23.95 (0-8373-7038-8) Nat Learn.

What Do You Know about Dental Anatomy? Jack Rudman. (Test Your Knowledge Ser.: No. Q-39). 1994. pap. 23.95 (0-8373-7039-6) Nat Learn.

What Do You Know about Dental Pharmacology? Jack Rudman. (Test Your Knowledge Ser.: No. Q-40). 1994. pap. 23.95 (0-8373-7040-X) Nat Learn.

What Do You Know about Diesel Engine Repair? Jack Rudman. (Test Your Knowledge Ser.: No. Q-41). 1994. pap. 23.95 (0-8373-7041-8) Nat Learn.

What Do You Know about Drafting? Jack Rudman. (Test Your Knowledge Ser.: No. Q-42). 1994. pap. 23.95 (0-8373-7042-6) Nat Learn.

What Do You Know about Drama & Theatre? Jack Rudman. (Test Your Knowledge Ser.: No. Q-43). 1994. pap. 23.95 (0-8373-7043-4) Nat Learn.

What Do You Know about Dressmaking? Jack Rudman. (Test Your Knowledge Ser.: No. Q-44). 1994. pap. 23.95 (0-8373-7044-2) Nat Learn.

What Do You Know about Driving? Jack Rudman. (Test Your Knowledge Ser.: No. Q-45). 1994. pap. 23.95 (0-8373-7045-0) Nat Learn.

What Do You Know about Earth Science? Jack Rudman. (Test Your Knowledge Ser.: No. Q-46). 1994. pap. 23.95 (0-8373-7046-9) Nat Learn.

What Do You Know about Economics? Jack Rudman. (Test Your Knowledge Ser.: No. Q-47). 1994. pap. 23.95 (0-8373-7047-7) Nat Learn.

What Do You Know about Education? Jack Rudman. (Test Your Knowledge Ser.: No. Q-48). 1994. pap. 23.95 (0-8373-7048-5) Nat Learn.

What Do You Know about Educational Psychology? Jack Rudman. (Test Your Knowledge Ser.: No. Q-49). 1994. pap. 23.95 (0-8373-7049-3) Nat Learn.

What Do You Know about Electrical Engineering? Jack Rudman. (Test Your Knowledge Ser.: No. Q-50). 1994. pap. 23.95 (0-8373-7050-7) Nat Learn.

What Do You Know about Electrical Installation? Jack Rudman. (Test Your Knowledge Ser.: No. Q-51). 1994. pap. 23.95 (0-8373-7051-5) Nat Learn.

What Do You Know about Electrocardiography? Jack Rudman. (Test Your Knowledge Ser.: No. Q-52). 1994. pap. 39.95 (0-8373-7052-3) Nat Learn.

What Do You Know about Electronics? Jack Rudman. (Test Your Knowledge Ser.: No. Q-53). 1994. pap. 23.95 (0-8373-7053-1) Nat Learn.

What Do You Know about Endodontics/Periodontics? Jack Rudman. (Test Your Knowledge Ser.: No. Q-54). 1994. pap. 23.95 (0-8373-7054-X) Nat Learn.

An Asterisk (*) at the beginning of an entry indicates that the title is appearing in BIP for the first time.

What Do You Know about English Literature? Jack Rudman. (Test Your Knowledge Ser.: No. Q-55). 1994. pap. 23.95 (0-8373-7055-8) Nat Learn.

What Do You Know about First Aid? Jack Rudman. (Test Your Knowledge Ser.: No. Q-56). 1994. pap. 23.95 (0-8373-7056-6) Nat Learn.

What Do You Know about Food Service? Jack Rudman. (Test Your Knowledge Ser.: No. Q-57). 1994. pap. 23.95 (0-8373-7057-4) Nat Learn.

What Do You Know about French? Jack Rudman. (Test Your Knowledge Ser.: No. Q-58). 1994. pap. 23.95 (0-8373-7058-2) Nat Learn.

What Do You Know about Fundamentals of Nursing? Jack Rudman. (Test Your Knowledge Ser.: No. Q-59). 1994. pap. 23.95 (0-8373-7059-0) Nat Learn.

What Do You Know about Gardening? Jack Rudman. (Test Your Knowledge Ser.: No. Q-60). 1994. pap. 23.95 (0-8373-7060-4) Nat Learn.

What Do You Know about Geography? Jack Rudman. (Test Your Knowledge Ser.: No. Q-61). 1994. pap. 23.95 (0-8373-7061-2) Nat Learn.

What Do You Know about Geology? Jack Rudman. (Test Your Knowledge Ser.: No. Q-62). 1994. pap. 23.95 (0-8373-7062-0) Nat Learn.

What Do You Know about Geometry? Jack Rudman. (Test Your Knowledge Ser.: No. Q-63). 1994. pap. 23.95 (0-8373-7063-9) Nat Learn.

What Do You Know about Geophysics? Jack Rudman. (Test Your Knowledge Ser.: No. Q-64). 1994. pap. 23.95 (0-8373-7064-7) Nat Learn.

What Do You Know about German? Jack Rudman. (Test Your Knowledge Ser.: No. Q-65). 1994. pap. 23.95 (0-8373-7065-5) Nat Learn.

What Do You Know about Guidance & Counseling? Jack Rudman. (Test Your Knowledge Ser.: No. Q-66). 1994. pap. 23.95 (0-8373-7066-3) Nat Learn.

What Do You Know about Health? Jack Rudman. (Test Your Knowledge Ser.: No. Q-67). 1994. pap. 23.95 (0-8373-7067-1) Nat Learn.

What Do You Know about Hematology? Jack Rudman. (Test Your Knowledge Ser.: No. Q-68). 1994. pap. 23.95 (0-8373-7068-X) Nat Learn.

What Do You Know about History? Jack Rudman. (Test Your Knowledge Ser.: No. Q-69). 1994. pap. 23.95 (0-8373-7069-8) Nat Learn.

What Do You Know about Home Economics? Jack Rudman. (Test Your Knowledge Ser.: No. Q-70). 1994. pap. 23.95 (0-8373-7070-1) Nat Learn.

What Do You Know about Humanities? Jack Rudman. (Test Your Knowledge Ser.: No. Q-71). 1994. pap. 23.95 (0-8373-7071-X) Nat Learn.

What Do You Know about Immunohematology & Blood Banking? Jack Rudman. (Test Your Knowledge Ser.: No. Q-72). 1994. pap. 23.95 (0-8373-7072-8) Nat Learn.

What Do You Know about Inorganic Chemistry? Jack Rudman. (Test Your Knowledge Ser.: No. Q-73). 1994. pap. 23.95 (0-8373-7073-6) Nat Learn.

What Do You Know about Intermediate Algebra? Jack Rudman. (Test Your Knowledge Ser.: No. Q-74). 1994. pap. 23.95 (0-8373-7074-4) Nat Learn.

What Do You Know about Italian? Jack Rudman. (Test Your Knowledge Ser.: No. Q-75). 1994. pap. 23.95 (0-8373-7075-2) Nat Learn.

What Do You Know about Latin? Jack Rudman. (Test Your Knowledge Ser.: No. Q-76). 1994. pap. 23.95 (0-8373-7076-0) Nat Learn.

What Do You Know about Law Enforcement? Jack Rudman. (Test Your Knowledge Ser.: No. Q-77). 1994. pap. 23.95 (0-8373-7077-9) Nat Learn.

What Do You Know about Library Science? Jack Rudman. (Test Your Knowledge Ser.: No. Q-78). 1994. pap. 23.95 (0-8373-7078-7) Nat Learn.

What Do You Know about Literature? Jack Rudman. (Test Your Knowledge Ser.: No. Q-79). 1994. pap. 23.95 (0-8373-7079-5) Nat Learn.

What Do You Know about Machine Trades? Jack Rudman. (Test Your Knowledge Ser.: No. Q-80). 1994. pap. 23.95 (0-8373-7080-9) Nat Learn.

What Do You Know about Marketing? Jack Rudman. (Test Your Knowledge Ser.: No. Q-81). 1994. pap. 23.95 (0-8373-7081-7) Nat Learn.

What Do You Know about Masonry & Bricklaying. Jack Rudman. (Test Your Knowledge Ser.: No. Q-82). 1994. pap. 23.95 (0-8373-7082-5) Nat Learn.

What Do You Know about Mechanical Engineering? Jack Rudman. (Test Your Knowledge Ser.: No. Q-83). 1994. pap. 23.95 (0-8373-7083-3) Nat Learn.

What Do You Know about Meteorology? Jack Rudman. (Test Your Knowledge Ser.: No. Q-84). 1994. pap. 23.95 (0-8373-7084-1) Nat Learn.

What Do You Know about Microbiology/Pathology? Jack Rudman. (Test Your Knowledge Ser.: No. Q-85). 1994. pap. 23.95 (0-8373-7085-X) Nat Learn.

What Do You Know about Money & Banking? Jack Rudman. (Test Your Knowledge Ser.: No. Q-86). 1994. pap. 23.95 (0-8373-7086-8) Nat Learn.

What Do You Know about Music? Jack Rudman. (Test Your Knowledge Ser.: No. Q-87). 1994. pap. 23.95 (0-8373-7087-6) Nat Learn.

What Do You Know about Offset Lithography? Jack Rudman. (Test Your Knowledge Ser.: No. Q-88). 1994. pap. 23.95 (0-8373-7088-4) Nat Learn.

What Do You Know about Operative Dentistry? Jack Rudman. (Test Your Knowledge Ser.: No. Q-89). 1994. pap. 23.95 (0-8373-7089-2) Nat Learn.

What Do You Know about Oral Pathology/Radiography? Jack Rudman. (Test Your Knowledge Ser.: No. Q-90). 1994. pap. 23.95 (0-8373-7090-6) Nat Learn.

What Do You Know about Oral Surgery & Anaesthesia? Jack Rudman. (Test Your Knowledge Ser.: No. Q-91). 1994. pap. 23.95 (0-8373-7091-4) Nat Learn.

What Do You Know about Organic Chemistry? Jack Rudman. (Test Your Knowledge Ser.: No. Q-92). 1994. pap. 23.95 (0-8373-7092-2) Nat Learn.

What Do You Know about Orthodontics/Pedodontics? Jack Rudman. (Test Your Knowledge Ser.: No. Q-93). 1994. pap. 23.95 (0-8373-7093-0) Nat Learn.

What Do You Know about Penal Law? Jack Rudman. (Test Your Knowledge Ser.: No. Q-94). 1994. pap. 23.95 (0-8373-7094-9) Nat Learn.

What Do You Know about Pharmacology? Jack Rudman. (Test Your Knowledge Ser.: No. Q-95). 1994. pap. 23.95 (0-8373-7095-7) Nat Learn.

What Do You Know about Philosophy? Jack Rudman. (Test Your Knowledge Ser.: No. Q-96). 1994. pap. 23.95 (0-8373-7096-5) Nat Learn.

What Do You Know about Photography? Jack Rudman. (Test Your Knowledge Ser.: No. Q-97). 1994. pap. 23.95 (0-8373-7097-3) Nat Learn.

What Do You Know about Physical Education? Jack Rudman. (Test Your Knowledge Ser.: No. Q-98). 1994. pap. 23.95 (0-8373-7098-1) Nat Learn.

What Do You Know about Physical Sciences? Jack Rudman. (Test Your Knowledge Ser.: No. Q-99). 1994. pap. 23.95 (0-8373-7099-X) Nat Learn.

What Do You Know about Physics? Jack Rudman. (Test Your Knowledge Ser.: No. Q-100). 1994. pap. 23.95 (0-8373-7100-7) Nat Learn.

What Do You Know about Plumbing? Jack Rudman. (Test Your Knowledge Ser.: No. Q-102). 1994. pap. 23.95 (0-8373-7102-3) Nat Learn.

What Do You Know about Political Science? Jack Rudman. (Test Your Knowledge Ser.: No. Q-101). 1994. pap. 23.95 (0-8373-7101-5) Nat Learn.

What Do You Know about Printing? Jack Rudman. (Test Your Knowledge Ser.: No. Q-103). 1994. pap. 23.95 (0-8373-7103-1) Nat Learn.

What Do You Know about Prosthodontics? Jack Rudman. (Test Your Knowledge Ser.: No. Q-104). 1994. pap. 23.95 (0-8373-7104-X) Nat Learn.

What Do You Know about Psychology? Jack Rudman. (Test Your Knowledge Ser.: No. Q-105). 1994. pap. 23.95 (0-8373-7105-8) Nat Learn.

What Do You Know about Radio & TV Servicing? Jack Rudman. (Test Your Knowledge Ser.: No. Q-106). 1994. pap. 23.95 (0-8373-7106-6) Nat Learn.

What Do You Know about Shakespeare? Jack Rudman. (Test Your Knowledge Ser.: No. Q-107). 1994. pap. 23.95 (0-8373-7107-4) Nat Learn.

What Do You Know about Sheet Metal Work? Jack Rudman. (Test Your Knowledge Ser.: No. Q-108). 1994. pap. 23.95 (0-8373-7108-2) Nat Learn.

What Do You Know about Small Engine Repair? Jack Rudman. (Test Your Knowledge Ser.: No. Q-109). 1994. pap. 23.95 (0-8373-7109-0) Nat Learn.

What Do You Know about Social Sciences? Jack Rudman. (Test Your Knowledge Ser.: No. Q-110). 1994. pap. 23.95 (0-8373-7110-4) Nat Learn.

What Do You Know about Sociology? Jack Rudman. (Test Your Knowledge Ser.: No. Q-111). 1994. pap. 23.95 (0-8373-7111-2) Nat Learn.

What Do You Know about Spanish? Jack Rudman. (Test Your Knowledge Ser.: No. Q-112). 1994. pap. 23.95 (0-8373-7112-0) Nat Learn.

What Do You Know about Statistics? Jack Rudman. (Test Your Knowledge Ser.: No. Q-113). 1994. pap. 23.95 (0-8373-7113-9) Nat Learn.

What Do You Know about Succotash? Poems & Drawings. Diantha Ain. (Illus.). 75p. (Orig.). (J). (gr. 1-6). 1991. pap. 10.95 (0-925360-01-5) Geste Pub.

What Do You Know about Trigonometry? Jack Rudman. (Test Your Knowledge Ser.: No. Q-114). 1994. pap. 23.95 (0-8373-7114-7) Nat Learn.

What Do You Know about Welding? Jack Rudman. (Test Your Knowledge Ser.: No. Q-115). 1994. pap. 23.95 (0-8373-7115-5) Nat Learn.

What Do You Know about Western Civilization? Jack Rudman. (Test Your Knowledge Ser.: No. Q-116). 1994. pap. 23.95 (0-8373-7116-3) Nat Learn.

***What do You Like?** Michael Grejeniec. (Illus.). 32p. (J). 3.98 (0-8317-5977-1) Smithmark.

What Do You Like? Michael Grejniec. LC 92-3481. (Illus.). (J). (ps-3). Date not set. pap. 6.95 (1-55858-417-X) North-South Bks NYC.

What Do You Like about Yourself??? Developing a Positive Self Concept!!! Shirley Slater & Lee Cibrowski. 1982. pap. 6.00 (0-911365-21-4, A261-08456) Family & Consumer Sci Educ.

What Do You Mean? A Story about Noah Webster. Jeri Ferris. (Creative Minds Ser.). (Illus.). 56p. (J). (gr. 3-6). 1988. lib. bdg. 18.95 (0-87614-330-3, Carolrhoda) Lerner Group.

What Do You Mean-Christian Education? Fred Hughes. 180p. (Orig.). 1992. pap. 17.95 (0-85364-506-X, Pub. by Paternoster UK) Attic Pr.

What Do You Mean I Can't Write? John S. Fielden & Ronald E. Dulek. 96p. 1983. pap. 7.95 (0-13-952028-7, Busn) P-H.

What Do You Mean I Have a Learning Disability? Kathleen M. Dwyer. (Illus.). 32p. (YA). (gr. 5-9). 1991. 14.95 (0-8027-8102-0); lib. bdg. 15.85 (0-8027-8103-9) Walker & Co.

What Do You Mean I Have Attention Deficit Disorder? Kathleen M. Dwyer. LC 95-44556. (Illus.). 48p. (J). (gr. k-9). 1996. 14.95 (0-8027-8392-9); lib. bdg. 15.85 (0-8027-8393-7) Walker & Co.

What Do You Mean I'm Laid Off? How to Go from Pink Slip to Paycheck. Kathleen Marshall. (Illus.). 70p. (Orig.). 1995. pap. 9.95 (0-9649225-0-9) Career Solns.

***What Do You Mean It's Not Covered? A Practical Guide to Understanding Insurance in a High Risk.** 2nd ed. James Walsh. 1998. pap. text ed. 19.95 (1-56343-163-7) Merritt Pub.

What Do You Mean It's Not Covered? A Practical Guide to Understanding Insurance in a High Risk World. James Walsh. 402p. 1995. pap. 19.95 (1-56343-072-X) Merritt Pub.

What Do You Mean You Don't Want to Go to College? Turning Crisis into Opportunity for You & Your Child. Liliane Q. McCain & Larry Strauss. 160p. 1990. 17.95 (0-929923-16-2) Lowell Hse.

What Do You Mean You Don't Want to Go to College? Turning Crisis into Opportunity for You & Your Child. Liliane Q. McCain & Larry Strauss. 156p. 1991. pap. 9.95 (0-929923-36-7) Lowell Hse.

What Do You Really Want for Your Children? Wayne W. Dyer. 400p. 1986. mass mkt. 6.99 (0-380-69957-5) Avon.

***What Do You Really Want for Your Children?** Wayne W. Dyer. 1997. pap. text ed. 12.00 (0-380-73047-2) Avon.

What Do You Really Want for Your Children. Wayne W. Dyer. write for info. (0-318-60256-3) S&S Trade.

***What Do You Say?** Campbell. 8.90 (0-687-67009-8) Abingdon.

What Do You Say? Rick Wetzel. LC 91-61624. (Sesame Street Little Pops Ser.). (Illus.). 6p. (J). (ps-1). 1993. 4.99 (0-679-83845-7) Random Bks Yng Read.

What Do You Say? A Child's Guide to Manners. Nigel Snell. (Duets Ser.). (Illus.). 25p. (J). (gr. k-2). 1991. 13.95 (0-237-60294-6, Pub. by Evans Bros Ltd UK) Trafalgar.

What Do You Say, Dear? Sesyle Joslin. LC 84-43140. (Illus.). 48p. (J). 1958. lib. bdg. 14.89 (0-06-023074-6) HarpC Child Bks.

What Do You Say, Dear? Sesyle Joslin. LC 84-43140. (Trophy Picture Bk.). (Illus.). 48p. (J). (ps-3). 1986. reprint ed. pap. 4.95 (0-06-443112-6, Trophy) HarpC Child Bks.

What Do You Say to a Man Who Is Dying... Ann Rodier. LC 95-67828. 144p. (Orig.). 1995. pap. 13.95 (1-886036-06-3) Passages Pbg.

***What Do You Say to a Naked Icebox?** Pamela Connolly. (Illus.). 88p. 1997. pap. 10.00 (0-8059-4178-9) Dorrance.

What Do You Say When a Monkey Acts This Way? Jane B. Moncure. LC 87-11736. (Magic Castle Readers Ser.). (Illus.). 32p. (J). (ps-2). 1987. lib. bdg. 21.36 (0-89565-368-0) Childs World.

What Do You See? Patricia Lauber. LC 93-2388. (Illus.). 48p. (J). (gr. 3-7). 1994. 17.00 (0-517-59390-4) Crown Bks Yng Read.

What Do You See? Rozanne L. Williams. (Emergent Reader Bks.). 8p. (J). (gr. k-2). 1994. 1.59 (0-916119-59-9) Creat Teach Pr.

What Do You See? Rozanne L. Williams. (Emergent Reader Big Bks.). (Illus.). 8p. (Orig.). (J). (gr. k-2). 1995. pap. 7.98 (1-57471-071-0) Creat Teach Pr.

What Do You See? An Optical Illusion Slide Show. rev. ed. Theoni Pappas. 32p. 1988. pap. 29.95 incl. sl. (0-933174-78-0) Wide World-Tetra.

What Do You See? Phenomenology of Therapeutic Art Expression. Mala G. Betensky. LC 95-5939. 1995. pap. 29.95 (1-85302-261-6) Taylor & Francis.

What Do You See in a Cloud? Allan Fowler. LC 95-39676. (Rookie Read-about Science Ser.). (Illus.). 32p. (J). (ps-2). 1996. lib. bdg. 17.30 (0-516-06056-2) Childrens.

What Do You See in a Cloud? Allan Fowler. LC 95-39676. (Rookie Read-About Science Ser.). (Illus.). 32p. (J). (ps-2). 1996. pap. 3.95 (0-516-20222-7) Childrens.

What Do You See on Sesame Street? Illus. by Norman Gorbaty. (Cuddle Cloth Bks.). 12p. (J). (ps). 1988. 4.99 (0-394-80594-1) Random Bks Yng Read.

What Do You See under the Sea? Bobbie Kalman. (Crabapple Ser.). (Illus.). 32p. (J). (ps-3). 1995. pap. 5.95 (0-86505-721-4); lib. bdg. 18.08 (0-86505-621-8) Crabtree Pub Co.

What Do You See When You Look in the Mirror? The New Body-Image Therapy for Women & Men. Thomas F. Cash. LC 94-15548. 400p. 1995. pap. 11.95 (0-553-37450-8) Bantam.

***What Do You See When You Shut Your Eyes?** Cynthia Zarin. LC 97-12012. (Illus.). (J). 1998. write for info. (0-395-76507-2) HM.

***What Do You Stand For: A Kids Guide to Building Character.** Barbara Lewis. LC 97-13952. (J). 1997. pap. text ed. 21.95 (1-57542-029-5) Free Spirit Pub.

What Do You Think? L. Schwartz. LC 92-74103. (Values Clarification Ser.). 184p. (J). (gr. 3-7). 1993. 9.95 (0-88160-224-8, LW221) Learning Wks.

What Do You Think about God? Douglas A. Fox. 96p. 1985. pap. 7.50 (0-8170-1077-7) Judson.

What Do You Think about That? Maria D. Lekic et al. (C). 1994. pap. text ed. 29.90 (0-9643332-0-1) ACTR.

What Do You Think? Ideas & Opinions. Sandy Achterberg. (Illus.). 55p. (Orig.). (J). (gr. 3-10). 1995. pap. text ed. 11.00 (0-911943-40-4) Leadership Pub.

What Do You Want, Blood? Chuck Taylor. (Illus.). 120p. (Orig.). 1988. 14.95 (0-941720-61-6); pap. 7.95 (0-941720-60-8) Slough Pr TX.

What Do You Want to Be When You Grow Up? A Creative Approach to Choosing Your Life's Goals. Margo Chevers. (Illus.). 95p. (Orig.). 1993. pap. 14.95 (0-9636202-0-7) Grand Pub.

What Do You Want to Know about Gifted Education? Answers from Gifted Education News-Page. Ed. by Maurice D. Fisher. (J). (gr. k-12). 1995. 14.00 (0-910609-27-6) Gifted Educ Pr.

What Do Young Adults Read Next. Pamela G. Spencer. 700p. 1994. 55.00 (0-8103-8887-1, 022205) Gale.

***What Do Young Adults Read Next.** 2nd ed. LC 97-11643. 1997. 55.00 (0-8103-6449-2, 00000655, Gale Res Intl) Gale.

What Do Your Customers Really Want? Here's a Simple, Sure-Fire Way to Find Out. John F. Lytle. 250p. 1992. text ed. 24.95 (1-55738-456-8, 456) Irwin Prof Pubng.

What Do Your Customers Really Want? Here's a Sure-Fire Way to Find Out. John F. Lytle. 1994. per. 19.95 (1-55738-829-6) Irwin Prof Pubng.

What Does a Pastor Do Besides Preach? Understanding the Life of Your Pastor. Jeffrey B. Krall. 44p. (Orig.). 1996. pap. 3.75 (1-57688-006-0, 006-0) Branch & Vine.

What Does A Spider Do? Myrna Perkins. (Illus.). 20p. (Orig.). (J). (ps-3). 1985. pap. 3.95 (0-937729-00-0) Markins Enter.

What Does a Woman Want? Reading & Sexual Difference. Shoshana Felman. LC 92-47484. 208p. (C). 1993. text ed. 37.50 (0-8018-4617-X); pap. text ed. 13.95 (0-8018-4620-X) Johns Hopkins.

***What Does Amy Want? A Book about Shapes.** Barbara S. Hazen. (Fisher-Price Playbooks Ser.). (Illus.). 18p. (J). (ps up). 1997. bds. 10.99 (1-57584-191-6) Rdrs Dgst Yng Fam.

What Does Andrew Wear? Ed. by Amy Cohn. (Illus.). (J). 1999. pap. 12.95 (0-688-13591-9, Tupelo Bks) Morrow.

What Does Baby Fozzie Hear? Jennifer Mittelstadt. (Baby's First Bks.). (Illus.). 12p. (J). 1994. write for info. (0-307-06033-0) Western Pub.

What Does Baby Hear? Denise Lewis-Patrick. (My First Golden Board Bks.). (J). (ps). 1990. bds. 3.95 (0-307-06132-9, Golden Books) Western Pub.

What Does Baby Kermit Say? Illus. by Tom Brannon. (Deluxe Baby's First Bks.). 12p. (J). (ps). 1993. pap. 1.95 (0-307-06036-5, 6036, Golden Pr) Western Pub.

What Does Baby See? Denise Lewis-Patrick. (My First Golden Board Bks.). (Illus.). 24p. (J). (ps). 1990. bds. 3.95 (0-307-06130-2, Golden Books) Western Pub.

What Does Baby See? Margo Lundell. (Poke & Look Bks.). (Illus.). 16p. (J). (ps-k). 1990. bds. 9.95 (0-448-19098-2, G&D) Putnam Pub Group.

What Does Being Jewish Mean? Read-Aloud Responses to Questions Jewish Children Ask About History, Culture, and Religion. Freedman. 160p. 1991. pap. 9.00 (0-671-76574-4, Fireside) S&S Trade.

What Does Boots Hear? Sara James. (Boots Board Bks.). (Illus.). 6p. (J). 1993. 2.98 (1-56156-129-0) Kidsbks.

What Does Boots See? Sara James. (Boots Board Bks.). (Illus.). 6p. (J). 1993. 2.98 (1-56156-128-2) Kidsbks.

What Does Boots Smell? Sara James. (Boots Board Bks.). (Illus.). 6p. (J). 1993. lib. bdg. 2.98 (1-56156-130-4) Kidsbks.

What Does Boots Touch? Sara James. (Boots Board Bks.). (Illus.). 6p. (J). 1993. lib. bdg. 2.98 (1-56156-131-2) Kidsbks.

***What Does Dying Mean?** Lake P. Monhollon. (Illus.). 24p. (J). (ps-1). 1997. write for info. (0-9657561-1-4) Reflection TX.

***What Does God Know?** Frank E. Lasater, Jr. LC 96-92714. 150p. (Orig.). 1996. pap. 6.95 (0-9650559-9-X) Paloma TX.

What Does God Require? Sermons on Stewardship. Ed. by Henry R. Rust. 1992. pap. 8.95 (1-877871-31-1, 3543) Ed Ministries.

What Does God Want? A Practical Guide to Making Decisions. rev. ed. Michael Scanlan. LC 95-71709. 128p. (Orig.). 1996. pap. 7.95 (0-87973-584-8, UP190) Franciscan U Pr.

What Does It All Mean? Sarah A. Fifield. Ed. by Susan Carlton. (Illus.). 103p. (Orig.). 1983. pap. 2.50 (0-686-45384-0) SarSan Pub.

What Does It All Mean? A Very Short Introduction to Philosophy. Thomas Nagel. 120p. 1987. 22.00 (0-19-505292-7); pap. 11.95 (0-19-505216-1) OUP.

What Does It Do? Inventions Then & Now. Daniel Jacobs. (Ready-Set-Read Ser.). (Illus.). 24p. (J). (ps-2). 1990. lib. bdg. 21.40 (0-8172-3586-8) Raintree Steck-V.

What Does It Do? Inventions Then & Now. Daniel Jacobs. 1995. pap. text ed. 4.95 (0-8114-6748-1) Raintree Steck-V.

What Does It Mean to Be Black & Christian? Forrest E. Harris, Sr. & James T. Roberson. Ed. by Amos Jones, Jr. LC 94-18128. 130p. 1994. text ed. 10.50 (0-910683-26-3) Townsnd-Pr.

What Does It Mean to Be Born Again? Kirk Eland. 10p. (Orig.). 1992. pap. 0.50 (0-914271-31-8) Mnstry Wrd.

What Does It Mean to Be Filled with the Spirit? Richard S. Taylor. 72p. 1995. per., pap. 5.99 (0-8341-1561-1) Beacon Hill.

What Does It Mean to Grow Old: Reflections from the Humanities. Ed. by Thomas R. Cole & Sally A. Gadow. LC 85-27406. (Illus.). xiv, 302p. 1986. text ed. 53.00 (0-8223-0545-3); pap. text ed. 21.95 (0-8223-0817-7) Duke.

***What Does It Mean Today to Be a Feminist Theologian?** Ed. by Andrea Gunter & Ulrike Wagener. (Yearbook of the European Society of Women in Theological Research Ser.: Vol. 4/96). 192p. 1996. pap. 21.00 (90-390-0262-2, Pub. by KOK Pharos NE) Eisenbrauns.

What Does It Profit...? Christian Dialogue on the U. S. Economy. Shantilal P. Bhagat et al. LC 83-3687. 144p. (Orig.). 1983. reprint ed. pap. 41.10 (0-608-02153-9, 2062822) Bks Demand.

What Does Jesus Say? Linda J. Sattgast. (Getting to Know Jesus Ser.). 12p. (J). 1995. bds. 3.99 (0-88070-762-3, Gold & Honey) Multnomah Pubs.

What Does Joan Say? My Seven Years as White House Astrologer to Nancy & Ronald Reagan. Joan Quigley. 1990. 17.95 (1-55972-032-8, Birch Ln Pr) Carol Pub Group.

W

An Asterisk (*) at the beginning of an entry indicates that the title is appearing in BIP for the first time.

What Does Kitty See? Muff Singer. LC 92-62561. (Squeeze-&-Squeak Bks.). (Illus.). (J). (ps). 1993. 4.99 (*0-89577-486-0*) RD Assn.

What Does Mrs. Freeman Want. Petros Abatzoglou. Tr. by Kay Cicellis from GRE. (Modern Greek Writers Ser.). 124p. pap. 9.95 (*960-04-0482-8*, Pub. by Kedros Pubs GR) Paul & Co Pubs.

***What Does "Multicultural" Worship Look Like?** Ed. by G. Lathrop. 1996. pap. 5.95 (*0-8066-2799-9*) Augsburg Fortress.

***What Does Not Change: The Significance of Charles Olson's "The Kingfishers"** Ralph Maud. LC 97-14291. 1997. write for info. (*0-8386-3731-0*) Fairleigh Dickinson.

***What Does P. B. Bear Choose?** Lee Davis. LC 97-14044. (P. B. Bear Read-Alongs Ser.). 1997. write for info. (*0-7894-2223-9*) DK Pub Inc.

What Does Revelation Mean for the Modern Jew? Michael Oppenheim. LC 85-18929. (Symposium Ser.: Vol. 17). 152p. 1985. lib. bdg. 79.95 (*0-88946-708-0*) E Mellen.

***What Does She Want from Me, Anyway? Honest Answers to the Questions Men Ask about Women.** Holly F. Phillips. 208p. 1997. pap. 12.00 (*0-310-21659-1*) Zondervan.

***What Does She Want from Me, Anyway? Honest Answers to the Questions Men Ask about Women.** Holly F. Phillips. 208p. 1997. 20.00 (*0-310-21457-2*) Zondervan.

What Does That Mean? The Personal Stories Behind Vanity License Plates. Dennis R. Cowhey. Ed. by Julie A. Cowhey. 221p. 1994. 19.95 (*0-9642823-1-3*); pap. 9.95 (*0-9642823-0-5*) Key Answer Prods.

What Does the Angel Do in Our Astral Body. Rudolf Steiner. 12p. 1969. reprint ed. spiral bd. 3.50 (*0-7873-0833-1*) Hlth Research.

What Does the Bible Say About...? Howard F. Sugden. LC 87-33869. 219p. 1987. pap. 9.99 (*0-8254-3759-8*) Kregel.

What Does the Bible Say About...? Words of Wisdom That Can Lead to Happiness. Ed. by Patty Sleem. LC 94-66482. (Illus.). 172p. Date not set. 20.00 (*1-885288-02-6*) PREP Pubng.

What Does the Charpy Test Really Tell Us? Proceedings of a Symposium Held at the Annual Meeting of the American Institute of Mining, Metallurgical & Petroleum Engineers, 1978. Ed. by A. R. Rosenfield et al. LC 78-10109. 240p. reprint ed. pap. 68.40 (*0-317-26236-X*, 2052145) Bks Demand.

What Does the Crow Know? The Mysteries of Animal Intelligence. Margery Facklam. LC 93-17811. (Illus.). 48p. (J). (gr. 3-6). 1993. 15.95 (*0-87156-544-7*) Sierra Club Childrens.

What Does the Future Hold? Clarence H. Hewitt. 149p. 1954. pap. write for info. (*1-881909-19-0*) Advent Christ Gen Conf.

What Does the Lord Require? How American Christians Think about Economic Justice. Stephen Hart. 272p. 1992. 30.00 (*0-19-506762-2*) OUP.

What Does the Lord Require? How American Christians Think about Economic Justice. Stephen Hart. LC 95-52271. 288p. (C). 1996. pap. text ed. 17.95 (*0-8135-2325-7*) Rutgers U Pr.

What Does the Lord Require? The Old Testament Call to Social Witness. Bruce C. Birch. LC 85-610. 120p. 1985. pap. 12.00 (*0-664-24630-3*, Westminster) Westminster John Knox.

***What Does the Present Owe the Future: An Economic & Ethical Perspective on Climate Changes.** Kenneth J. Arrow. 12p. 1996. 7.50 (*0-910153-12-4*) E T Woolf.

What Does the Ruling Class Do When It Rules? State Apparatuses & State Power under Feudalism, Capitalism & Socialism. Goran Therborn. 290p. (C). 1985. pap. text ed. 20.00 (*0-86091-725-8*, Pub. by Vrso UK) Norton.

What Does this Mean? Principles of Biblical Interpretation in the Post-Modern World. James W. Voelz. LC 95-4147. (Scholarship Today Ser.). 368p. 1995. 18.99 (*0-570-04801-X*, 12-3255) Concordia.

***What Does This Mean? Principles of Biblical Interpretation in the Post-Modern World.** 2nd ed. James W. Voelz. LC 97-9141. 1997. 18.99 (*0-570-04983-0*) Concordia.

What Does This Say? Bil Keane. (Family Circus Ser.). (Illus.). (Orig.). 1994. mass mkt. 3.99 (*0-449-14814-9*) Fawcett.

***What Does Woman Want?** Timothy Leary. 288p. pap. 14.95 (*1-56184-086-6*) New Falcon Pubns.

What Does Woman Want. rev. ed. Timothy Leary. LC 87-83574. (Future History Ser.). (Illus.). 288p. 1987. reprint ed. pap. 9.95 (*0-941404-62-5*) New Falcon Pubns.

What Does Word Bird See? Jane B. Moncure. LC 81-21594. (Word Bird Library). (Illus.). 32p. (J). (ps-2). 1982. lib. bdg. 21.36 (*0-89565-220-X*) Childs World.

What Does Your Dog Do Everyday? Jill Arthur. LC 95-15324. (Illus.). (J). 1995. pap. 8.95 (*0-684-80044-6*, Fireside) S&S Trade.

What Does Your Wife Do? Gender Roles & the Transformation of Family Life. Leonard Beeghley. (New Perspectives in Sociology Ser.). (C). 1996. text ed. 49.95 (*0-8133-2634-6*) Westview.

What Does Your Wife Do? Gender Roles & the Transformation of Family Life. Leonard Beeghley. (New Perspectives in Sociology Ser.). (C). 1996. pap. text ed. 19.95 (*0-8133-2635-4*) Westview.

What Dogs Do. Photos by Sharon Beals. LC 94-44120. (Illus.). 64p. 1995. 7.95 (*0-8118-1023-2*) Chronicle Bks.

What Don't We Need Anymore? U. S. Land-Based Strategic Weapons Modernization & the End of the Cold War. Eric K. Graben. 270p. (Orig.). (C). 1992. lib. bdg. 57.00 (*0-8191-8779-8*) U Pr of Amer.

What Don't We Need Anymore? U. S. Land-Based Strategic Weapons Modernization & the End of the Cold War. Eric K. Graben. 270p. (Orig.). (C). 1992. pap. text ed. 29.00 (*0-8191-8780-1*) U Pr of Amer.

What Doth the Lord Require of Thee? Mildred B. Young. (C). 1966. pap. 3.00 (*0-87574-145-2*) Pendle Hill.

What Dread Hand. Sarah Kemp. 224p. 1988. mass mkt. 3.50 (*0-373-26005-9*) Harlequin Bks.

***What Dreams Remember.** Steve Leto. 24p. 1995. pap. 5.00 (*1-889806-09-9*) Devils Millhopper.

What Drives Third World City Growth? A Dynamic General Equilibrium Approach. Allen C. Kelley & Jeffrey G. Williamson. LC 84-2070. 292p. 1984. reprint ed. pap. 83.30 (*0-7837-9357-X*, 2060099) Bks Demand.

What Drum. 2nd ed. Geoff Nicholas & Andy Duncan. (Illus.). 113p. 1990. pap. 12.95 (*0-933224-52-4*) Bold Strummer Ltd.

What Earth Has Done to You: The Wisdom of Noel. Elgar Brom. Ed. by Patricia Moteka. (Brom Ser.: Vol. III). (Illus.). (Orig.). (C). 1989. pap. write for info. (*0-9624381-0-3*) Masters Ink.

What Editors Look For: How to Write Compelling Queries, Cover Letters, Synopses & Book Proposals. Sierra Adare. Ed. by Republic of Texas Press Staff. 160p. (Orig.). 1995. pap. 15.99 (*0-9646159-0-8*) Cougar Imprints.

What Educators Should Know about Copyright. Virginia M. Helm. LC 85-63688. (Fastback Ser.: No. 233). 50p. (Orig.). 1986. pap. 3.00 (*0-87367-233-X*) Phi Delta Kappa.

***What Einstein Didn't Know: Scientific Answers to Everyday Questions.** Robert L. Wolke. (Illus.). 256p. 1997. 19.95 (*1-55972-398-X*, Birch Ln Pr) Carol Pub Group.

What Else but Love? The Ordeal of Race in Faulkner & Morrison. Philip M. Weinstein. LC 96-17153. 296p. 1996. 15.50 (*0-231-10275-5*); pap. 42.00 (*0-231-10276-3*) Col U Pr.

What Else Should I Read? Guiding Kids to Good Books, Vol. 1. Matt Berman. LC 95-16213. xxi, 211p. (J). (gr. 3-8). 1995. pap. text ed. 24.50 (*1-56308-241-1*) Libs Unl.

What Else Should I Read? Guiding Kids to Good Books, Vol. 2. Matt Berman. 200p. 1996. pap. text ed. 24.00 (*1-56308-419-8*) Libs Unl.

***What Else You Can Do with a Library Degree: Career Options for the 90s & Beyond.** Betty-Carol Sellen. LC 97-18679. 300p. 1997. pap. 29.95 (*1-55570-264-3*) Neal-Schuman.

What Emily Wants. Fayrene Preston. (Loveswept Ser.: No. 620). 1993. pap. 3.50 (*0-553-44173-6*, Loveswept) Bantam.

***What Emotions Really Are: The Problem of Psychological Categories.** LC 96-48993. (Science & Its Conceptual Foundations Ser.). 1997. 26.95 (*0-226-30871-5*) U Ch Pr.

***What Emotions Really Are: The Problem of Psychological Categories.** LC 96-48993. (Science & Its Conceptual Foundations Ser.). 1997. pap. write for info. (*0-226-30872-3*) U Ch Pr.

What Employers Want: Job Prospects for Less-Educated Workers. Harry J. Holzer. LC 95-23154. (Illus.). 214p. (C). 1996. 32.50 (*0-87154-391-5*) Russell Sage.

What Engagement Ring?! Martha Schroeder. (Yours Truly Ser.). 1996. mass mkt. 3.50 (*0-373-52016-6*) Silhouette.

What Engineers Know & How They Know It: Analytical Studies from Aeronautical History. Walter G. Vincenti. (Studies in the History of Technology). (Illus.). 336p. 1993. reprint ed. pap. text ed. 15.95 (*0-8018-4588-2*) Johns Hopkins.

***What English Teachers Want.** Susan Vreeland. 92p. 1996. pap. 10.00 (*0-88092-224-9*) Royal Fireworks.

What Eric Knew. James Howe. 144p. 1986. pap. 3.50 (*0-380-70171-5*, Flare) Avon.

What Eric Knew. James Howe. 128p. (J). 1991. pap. 3.99 (*0-380-71330-6*, Camelot) Avon.

What Eric Knew. James Howe. (J). 1995. pap. 3.95 (*0-689-80340-0*, Aladdin Paperbacks) S&S Childrens.

What Eric Knew: A Sebastian Barth Mystery. 2nd ed. James Howe. LC 85-7418. 156p. (J). (gr. 4-6). 1990. lib. bdg. 15.00 (*0-689-31702-6*, Atheneum Bks Young) S&S Childrens.

What Europe Thinks: A Study of Western European Values. Sheena Ashford & Noel Timms. 168p. 1992. 54.95 (*1-85521-238-2*, Pub. by Dartmth Pub UK) Ashgate Pub Co.

What Ever Happened to Baby Jane? Henry Farrell. 256p. 1991. pap. 3.95 (*0-88184-725-9*) Carroll & Graf.

What Ever Happened to Baby Jane? Henry Farrell. 1995. reprint ed. lib. bdg. 24.95 (*1-56849-666-4*) Buccaneer Bks.

***What Ever Happened to Hope?** James McKeever. 24p. (C). pap. text ed. 2.99 (*0-86694-115-0*) Omega Pubns OR.

What Ever Happened to Robert Aldrich? His Life & Films. Alain Silver & James Ursini. (Illus.). 416p. 1995. 25.00 (*0-87910-185-7*) Limelight Edns.

What Ever Happened to the American Dream. Larry Burkett. 224p. 1993. text ed. 17.99 (*0-8024-7175-7*) Moody.

What Ever Happened to the Hall of Fame? Baseball, Cooperstown, & the Politics of Glory. Bill James. 1995. pap. 13.00 (*0-684-80088-8*, Fireside) S&S Trade.

What Every American Should Know about American History: Two Hundred Events That Shaped the Nation. Alan Axelrod & Charles Phillips. 384p. 1992. 15.00 (*1-55850-152-5*) Adams Media.

What Every American Should Know about American History: Two Hundred Events That Shaped the Nation. Alan Axelrod & Charles Phillips. 384p. 1993. pap. 10.95 (*1-55850-309-9*) Adams Media.

What Every American Should Know about Islam & the Muslims. Muhammad A. Nu'man. 74p. (Orig.). 1985. pap. 5.00 (*0-933821-04-2*) New Mind Prod.

What Every American Should Know about Women History: 200 Events That Shaped Our Destiny. Christine Lunardini. 416p. 1996. pap. text ed. 12.00 (*1-55850-687-X*) Adams Media.

What Every American Should Know about Women's History: Two Hundred Events That Shaped Our Destiny. Christine Lunardini. 1994. 16.00 (*1-55850-417-6*) Adams Media.

What Every Baby Knows. T. Berry Brazelton. (Illus.). 288p. 1988. pap. 11.00 (*0-345-34455-3*, Ballantine Trade) Ballantine.

What Every Banker Should Know about Broker-Dealers. 1988. 67.00 (*0-9603592-6-5*) MTA Financial Servs.

What Every Black African-American Should Know to Gain Financial Success in the 90's. Derek A. Broadnax. 60p. 1991. pap. 14.00 (*1-56028-007-7*) Blk Entrepreneurs.

What Every Boy & Girl Should Know see Works

What Every Business Needs to Know. Laddie F. Hutar. 51p. 1993. spiral bd. 24.95 (*0-614-06670-0*, 90900) Hutar.

What Every Busy Person Needs to Know about... Overcoming Difficult People at Work, Vol. 1. William White, Jr. 34p. (Orig.). 1989. pap. write for info. (*0-318-65785-6*) Concise Comns.

What Every Caregiver Ought to Know: Programs That Help - Meeting Needs - Nursing Care - Financial Concerns. Strauss et al. 96p. 1992. 5.00 (*0-685-67056-2*, 5492) Commerce.

What Every CEO Already Knows about Managing Diversity. John W. Work. LC 92-45797. 112p. (Orig.). 1993. pap. 14.95 (*0-935834-99-0*) Rainbow Books.

What Every Child Must Know about Grownups. Gail Elbek. Ed. by Jo Jaworski. LC 86-40333. (Illus.). 65p. (J). (gr. k-4). 1990. 5.95 (*1-55523-015-6*) Winston-Derek.

***What Every Child Needs: Daily Encouragement for Getting to the Heart of Mothering.** Elisa Morgan & Carol Kuykendall. 366p. (J). 1997. spiral bd. 9.99 (*0-310-97395-3*) Zondervan.

***What Every Child Needs: Getting to the Heart of Mothering.** Elisa Morgan & Carol Kuykendall. LC 97-21801. 208p. 1997. 15.99 (*0-310-21151-4*) Zondervan.

What Every Child Should Know & Do...for Surviving in the 90's: Picture Book. Judy A. Hall. (Illus.). 18p. (Orig.). (J). (ps-5). 1992. spiral bd. 12.00 (*0-9629597-0-7*) Personal Prods.

What Every Child Should Know & Do...for Surviving in the 90's Vol. 2: Super-Flash. unabridged ed. Judy A. Hall. (Illus.). 16p. (J). (ps-5). 1992. spiral bd. 25.00 (*0-9629597-3-1*) Personal Prods.

What Every Christian Should Know. large type ed. write for info. (*0-318-68667-8*, 8010) LBW.

What Every Church Member Should Know about Clergy. Robert G. Kemper. LC 84-22821. 180p. 1985. pap. 9.95 (*0-8298-0728-4*) Pilgrim OH.

What Every Condo Owner Should Know. Mark D. Bogen. 90p. pap. 4.95 (*0-9641154-0-9*) M D Bogen.

What Every Cook Should Know. Jessie Lindsay & Helen Tress. 1974. lib. bdg. 69.95 (*0-685-51386-6*) Revisionist Pr.

What Every Credit Union Executive Should Know about Marketing: The All in One Source for What... Michael P. Muckian. 1994. per. 149.00 (*1-55738-720-6*) Irwin Prof Pubng.

What Every Eighteen-Year-Old Needs to Know about Texas Law. L. Jean Wallace. LC 91-34295. 1992. 19.95 (*0-292-79069-4*); pap. 8.95 (*0-292-79070-8*) U of Tex Pr.

What Every Employee Should Know about Alcohol Abuse: Answers to 25 Good Questions. David H. Angeli. 20p. 1996. pap. 2.20 (*1-889437-07-7*) Inst Drug-Free Wrkpl.

What Every Employee Should Know about Drug Abuse: Answers to 20 Good Questions. Mark A. De Bernardo. 16p. 1995. reprint ed. pap. 1.80 (*1-889437-06-9*) Inst Drug-Free Wrkpl.

What Every Employer Should Be Doing About Sexual Harassment. rev. ed. Susan M. Omilian. 128p. 1986. per. 29.95 (*1-55645-443-0*, 443) Busn Legal Reports.

What Every Engineer Should Know about Artificial Intelligence. William A. Taylor. 350p. 1988. 30.00 (*0-262-20069-4*) MIT Pr.

WHAT Every Engineer Should Know about Ceramics. Solomon Musikant. (What Every Engineer Should Know Ser.: Vol. 28). 208p. 1991. 59.75 (*0-8247-8498-7*) Dekker.

What Every Engineer Should Know about Computer-Aided Design & Computer-Aided Manufacturing: The CAD-CAM Revolution. Ed. by John K. Krouse. (What Every Engineer Should Know Ser.: Vol. 10). 160p. 1982. 55.00 (*0-8247-1666-3*) Dekker.

What Every Engineer Should Know about Concurrent Engineering. Thomas A. Salomone. LC 95-13635. (What Every Engineer Should Know Ser.: Vol. 34). 280p. 1995. 55.00 (*0-8247-9578-4*) Dekker.

What Every Engineer Should Know about Data Communications. Clifton. (What Every Engineer Should Know Ser.: Vol. 19). 168p. 1986. 59.75 (*0-8247-7566-X*) Dekker.

What Every Engineer Should Know about Economic Decision Analysis. Dean S. Shupe. LC 80-22029. (What Every Engineer Should Know Ser.: No. 4). 150p. reprint ed. pap. 42.80 (*0-8357-2613-4*, 2039933) Bks Demand.

What Every Engineer Should Know about Inventing. Middendorf. (What Every Engineer Should Know Ser.: Vol. 7). 168p. 1981. 59.75 (*0-8247-7497-3*) Dekker.

What Every Engineer Should Know about Project Management. 2nd expanded rev. ed. Arnold M. Ruskin & W. Eugene Estes. LC 94-39689. (What Every Engineer Should Know Ser.: Vol. 33). 296p. 1994. 49.75 (*0-8247-8953-9*) Dekker.

What Every Executive Should Know about Chapter 11. 3rd ed. Benjamin Weintraub. LC 93-47559. 400p. 1994. text ed. 65.00 (*1-56425-032-6*) Juris Pubng.

What Every Executor Ought to Know: What to Expect - How to Prepare - Getting Professional Help. 48p. 1991. pap. 5.00 (*0-685-67057-0*, 4861) Commerce.

What Every Family Needs: Practical, Biblical Insights into All Areas of Family Life. Carl Breechen & Paul Faulkner. 1994. pap. 6.99 (*0-89225-424-6*) Gospel Advocate.

What Every Family Should Know. Carriage House Staff. 1993. Blue Green. 19.95 (*0-89786-098-5*); Green Burgundy. 19.95 (*0-89786-099-3*) CHP Ltd Redding.

What Every Female Should Know (Especially Teenagers) Linda D. Alston. 32p. 1993. pap. write for info. (*0-9636803-1-5*) Eagles Eye.

What Every Home Health Nurse Needs to Know: A Book of Readings. Ed. by Marjorie McHann. 200p. 1994. pap. 40.00 (*0-9640767-0-5*) Cnslts in Care.

What Every Husband & Wife Should Know: Before It's Too Late. Alvin B. Baranov & Esther Sirkin. 162p. pap. 8.00 (*0-685-47253-1*, AB27) Legal Pubns CA.

***What Every Investor Needs to Know: Ideas to Help You Protect Your Money from Bad Advice, Sales Tricks, & Fraud.** Julie Quintero-Joyce & Jonathan E. Joyce. 88p. (Orig.). 1996. pap. 19.95 (*0-9656808-1-9*, 96-2) Dynamic Pub IL.

What Every Jew Needs to Know about God. Michael Levin. LC 96-16444. 1997. 20.00 (*0-88125-537-8*) Ktav.

What Every Kid Should Know. Jonah Kalb & David Viscott. (Illus.). 128p. (J). (gr. 4-7). 1992. pap. 4.95 (*0-395-62983-7*, Sandpiper) HM.

***What Every Man Should Know about Seeding.** Donald F. Kaltenbach. (Illus.). 40p. (Orig.). 1996. pap. 5.00 (*0-9651827-2-X*) Proste Cancer.

What Every Man, Woman & Employer Should Know about Sexual Harassment: Your Rights & Responsibilities. Daniel K. Fee. 95p. (C). 1992. pap. text ed. 14.95 (*0-9636055-0-X*) EEO Cnslting.

What Every Manager Should Know About Financial Analysis. Alan S. Donnahoe. 224p. 1990. pap. 10.00 (*0-671-70640-3*) S&S Trade.

What Every Manager Should Know about Quality. Thomas Pyzdek. 248p. 1990. 69.75 (*0-8247-8401-4*) Dekker.

***What Every Manager Should Know about Training: Or I've Got a Training Problem & Other Odd Ideas.** Robert F. Mager. LC 91-78265. 160p. 1996. reprint ed. pap. 18.95 (*1-879618-08-7*) Ctr Effect Perf.

What Every Mom Needs. Elisa Morgan & Carol Kuykendall. 192p. 1995. 14.99 (*0-310-20097-0*); audio 14.99 (*0-310-20417-8*) Zondervan.

***What Every Mother-in-Law Wishes Her Daughter-in-Law Knew But Was Afraid to Tell Her.** Sue Verra. 1996. pap. text ed. 7.95 (*0-7880-0653-3*) CSS OH.

What Every Mother Needs to Know. deluxe ed. Brenda Hunter. 160p. 1993. pap. 5.99 (*0-88070-607-4*, Multnomah Bks) Multnomah Pubs.

What Every Mother Needs to Know about Babies. Brenda Hunter. 160p. 1994. pap. 5.99 (*0-88070-667-8*, Multnomah Bks) Multnomah Pubs.

***What Every Nazarene Board Member Needs to Know.** Ed. by David J. Felter. 86p. 1995. teacher ed. 8.99 (*0-8341-1560-3*) Beacon Hill.

What Every Orthodox Christian Should Know. George Nicozisin. 1992. pap. 4.95 (*0-937032-85-9*) Light&Life Pub Co MN.

***What Every Parent Needs to Know about 1st, 2nd & 3rd Grades: An Essential Guide to Your Child's Education.** Toni S. Bickart et al. LC 97-1802. (Illus.). 160p. (Orig.). 1997. pap. 12.95 (*1-57071-156-9*) Sourcebks.

What Every Parent Should Know about Child Care. Karla Satchwell. Ed. by Diane Parker. LC 92-50873. 100p. 1993. pap. 9.95 (*0-88247-974-1*) R & E Pubs.

What Every Parent Should Know about Childhood Immunization. Jamie Murphy. Ed. by Carol White. 192p. (Orig.). 1993. pap. 13.95 (*0-9630373-0-7*) Earth Healing.

***What Every Pastor Should Know... How to Protect the Children & Keep the Church Out of Court.** Richard D. Dobbins & Sharon K. Dobbins. 18p. (Orig.). 1988. pap. 3.00 (*1-890329-11-8*) Totally Alive.

What Every Person Wants to Know about Prayer. Marilyn Hickey. 1994. pap. 4.95 (*1-56441-052-8*) M Hickey Min.

What Every Potential Homeowner Should Know about Construction, Vol. I - General Construction: Residential Construction Information & Details That Every Potential Homeowner Should Be Familiar With. Douglas E. Hedlund. (Illus.). 162p. (Orig.). 1989. pap. 9.95 (*0-9621420-0-X*) Condata Co.

***What Every Principal Should Know about Teaching Reading: How to Raise Test Scores & Nurture a Love of Reading.** Richard W. Cole. (Illus.). 192p. (Orig.). 1997. pap. text ed. 19.95 (*1-883186-00-5*) Natl Read Styles Inst.

What Every Principal Should Know about Transforming Schools: The Mandate for New School Leadership. James Lewis, Jr. LC 95-26510. 1996. write for info. (*0-915253-49-6*) Wilkerson Pub Co.

What Every Programmer Should Know About Object-Oriented Design. Meilir Page-Jones. LC 95-22067. (Illus.). 392p. 1995. text ed. 40.00 (*0-932633-31-5*) Dorset Hse Pub Co.

What Every Prospective College Student Should Know. Archie W. Earl, Sr. (Higher Education Ser.). 85p. (YA). (gr. 11-12). 1994. pap. text ed. 13.95 (*1-884169-05-8*); lib. bdg. 25.95 (*1-884169-04-X*) Intl Educ Improve.

What Every Prospective Grad Student Should Know. Archie W. Earl, Sr. (Higher Education Ser.). 85p. (C). 1993. pap. text ed. 13.95 (*1-884169-01-5*); lib. bdg. 25.95 (*1-884169-00-7*) Intl Educ Improve.

What Every Senior Citizen Ought to Know: Taxes - Benefits - Health Care - Estate Planning Basics. 64p. 1992. pap. 5.00 (*0-685-67163-1*, 4718) Commerce.

What Every Software Manager Must Know. Williams & Sigs Books, Staff. 1995. pap. text ed. 35.00 (*0-13-227604-6*) P-H.

What Every Software Manager Must Know to Succeed with Object Technology. John D. Williams. LC 95-35598. (Managing Object Technology Ser.: Vol. 1). 300p. 1996. pap. 35.00 (*1-884842-14-3*) SIGS Bks & Multimedia.

***What Every Special Educator Must Know: The International Standards for the Preparation & Certification of Special Education Teachers.** 2nd ed. LC 95-39777. 145p. 1996. pap. text ed. 14.30 (*0-86586-287-7*, R5128R) Coun Exc Child.

What Every Student Athlete Must Know about Drugs - The Handbook. Marvin L. Sims. 112p. 1992. pap. 10.95 (*0-9634409-1-8*) M L Sims.

What Every Successful Lawyer Needs to Know about Accounting. (Corporate Law & Practice Course Handbook, 1985-86 Ser.). 376p. 1994. pap. 99.00 (*0-614-17183-0*, B4-7097) PLI.

What Every Supervisor Should Know. 5th ed. Lester R. Bittel. 672p. 1985. text ed. 37.65 (*0-07-005574-2*); Skills development Portfolio. student ed. 16.45 (*0-07-005575-0*) McGraw.

What Every Supervisor Should Know. 6th ed. Lester R. Bittle & John W. Newstrom. 1992. pap. text ed. 27.95 (*0-07-005589-0*) McGraw.

What Every Supervisor Should Know: Supervision-in-Action: An In-Basket Simulation by Reese & Manning. Lester R. Bittel & John W. Newstrom. 1989. write for info. (*0-07-051488-7*) McGraw.

What Every Supervisor Should Know: The Basics of Supervisory Management. 6th ed. Lester R. Bittel & John W. Newstrom. 1989. teacher ed. (*0-07-051489-5*) McGraw.

What Every Supervisor Should Know about Alcohol. (Illus.). 36p. 1995. pap. text ed. 12.50 (*0-88711-242-0*) Am Trucking Assns.

What Every Supervisor Should Know about Drug Abuse. 43p. 1995. pap. text ed. 12.50 (*0-88711-243-9*) Am Trucking Assns.

What Every Supervisor Should Know Study Guide: Based on the Text by Bittel & Newstrom. 6th ed. Davis Publishing Company Staff. Ed. by Robert Dahl. 144p. 1990. 26.95 (*1-56325-018-7*) Davis Pub Law.

What Every Teacher & Parent Should Know about Dyslexia. Dave Sargent & Laura Tirella. Ed. by Debbie Bowen. 103p. lib. bdg. 29.95 (*1-56763-128-2*) Ozark Pub.

What Every Teacher & Parent Should Know about Dyslexia. Dave Sargent & Laura Tirella. Ed. by Debbie Bowen. LC 96-6325. 1996. pap. text ed. 19.95 (*1-56763-127-4*) Ozark Pub.

What Every Teacher Should Know about How Students Think: A Survival Guide for Adults. Peter Ellsworth & Vincent Sindt. LC 91-42559. 112p. 1992. pap. 12.00 (*0-930599-74-8*) Thinking Pubns.

What Every Teacher Should Know about Student Rights. Eve Cary. LC 75-19038. 42p. reprint ed. pap. 25.00 (*0-317-29208-0*, 2022231) Bks Demand.

***What Every Teenager Really Wants to Know about Sex.** Sylvia Hacker. 10.95 (*0-7867-0969-3*) Carroll & Graf.

What Every Teenager Really Wants to Know about Sex: With Startling New Information Every Parent Should Read. Sylvia Hacker. 224p. 1993. pap. 10.95 (*0-88184-969-3*) Carroll & Graf.

What Every Therapist Should Know about AIDS. Samuel Knapp & Leon VandeCreek. Ed. by Harold H. Smith, Jr. LC 90-52652. (Practitioner's Resource Ser.). 80p. 1990. pap. 15.20 (*0-943158-58-3*, AIDSBP) Pro Resource.

What Every Union Free Supervisor Should Know About Unions. Gordon E. Jackson & Ted M. Yeiser, Jr. 1978. pap. text ed. 3.95 (*0-9607826-3-X*) Management Pr.

What Every Veteran Should Know: 1987. 1987. 6.00 (*0-346-32464-5*) Veterans Info.

What Every Well-Informed Person Should Know about Drug Addiction. David P. Ausubel. LC 79-16961. 1980. 36.95 (*0-88229-566-7*) Nelson-Hall.

***What Every Woman Can Learn from Cat.** Donna Hanbery. (Illus.). 64p. (Orig.). 1997. pap. 5.99 (*1-889647-11-X*) Boston Am.

***What Every Woman Knows.** James M. Barrie. LC 97-6902. (Dover Thrift Editions Ser.). 80p. 1997. reprint ed. pap. text ed. 1.50 (*0-486-29578-8*) Dover.

What Every Woman Knows & Other Plays see **Works of J. M. Barrie. Peter Pan Edition**

What Every Woman Must Know about Heart Disease: A No-Nonsense Approach to Diagnosing, Treating, & Preventing the Number 1 Killer of Women. Siegfried J. Kra. 224p. 1996. 22.95 (*0-446-51986-3*) Warner Bks.

What Every Woman Must Know about Heart Disease: A No-Nonsense Approach to Diagnosing, Treating, & Preventing the #1 Killer of Women. Siegfried J. Kra. 240p. (Orig.). 1997. pap. 14.99 (*0-446-39532-3*) Warner Bks.

***What Every Woman Needs to Know about Estrogen: Natural & Traditional Therapies for a Longer, Healthier Life.** Karen A. Hutchinson & Judith Sachs. LC 96-52948. 1997. pap. 12.95 (*0-452-27739-6*) NAL-Dutton.

What Every Woman Needs to Know about Menopause. Mary J. Minkin & Carol Wright. 1996. 25.00 (*0-614-96804-6*) Yale U Pr.

***What Every Woman Needs to Know about Menopause: The Years Before, During & After.** Mary J. Minkin. 1997. pap. text ed. 16.00 (*0-300-07261-9*) Yale U Pr.

What Every Woman Needs to Know about Sexual Assault. Richard W. Eaves. 80p. (Orig.). 1993. pap. 2.50 (*0-9632355-2-4*) Guardian Pr.

What Every Woman Needs to Know about Thru-Hiking. Dan W. Burce. LC 93-72959. 52p. 1996. pap. 7.95 (*0-9636342-2-4*) Ctr AT Studies.

What Every Woman Ought to Know about Love & Marriage. Joyce Brothers. 1985. mass mkt. 6.99 (*0-345-32113-8*) Ballantine.

What Every Woman Should Know: Staying Healthy after 40. Joan R. Heilman et al. 416p. 1995. 22.95 (*0-446-51731-3*) Warner Bks.

What Every Woman Should Know: Staying Healthy after 40. Lila Nachtigall et al. 1996. pap. write for info. (*0-446-67214-9*) Warner Bks.

What Every Woman Should Know about Child Support, Getting It! Mark A. Simpkins. LC 82-22597. 1985. pap. 14.95 (*0-87949-226-0*) Ashley Bks.

What Every Woman Should Know about Her Husband's Money. Shelby White. 1995. pap. 12.00 (*0-679-75816-X*) Random.

What Every Woman Should Know about Men. Joyce Brothers. 288p. 1987. mass mkt. 5.95 (*0-345-35372-2*) Ballantine.

What Every Woman Should Know about Retirement. Helen Franks. (C). 1989. 45.00 (*0-86242-054-7*, Pub. by Age Concern Eng UK) St Mut.

What Every Young Christian Should Know. William S. Deal. 1982. pap. 1.95 (*0-317-00333-X*) Crusade Pubs.

What Every Young Christian Should Know. William S. Deal. pap. 3.99 (*0-685-70972-8*) Schmul Pub Co.

What Every Young Girl Should Know Before She Marries a Naval Architect. Harry Benford. 48p. (Orig.). 1985. pap. text ed. 6.00 (*0-931781-01-9*) Jennings Pr.

***What Every Young Person Should Know about Cancer.** Anne Jordheim. (Orig.). (YA). (gr. 7-12). 1996. pap. write for info. (*1-57515-096-4*) PPI Pubng.

What Every Young Person Should Know & Be Able to Do in Dance: National Standards for Arts Education. 16p. (YA). 1995. pap. 1.95 (*0-88290-519-8*, 2982) Horizon Utah.

What Every Young Person Should Know & Be Able to Do in Music: National Standards for Arts Education. 16p. (YA). 1995. pap. 1.00 (*0-88290-520-1*, 2977) Horizon Utah.

What Every Young Person Should Know & Be Able to Do in Theatre: National Standards for Arts Education. 16p. (YA). 1995. pap. 1.00 (*0-88290-521-X*, 2987) Horizon Utah.

What Every Young Person Should Know & Be Able to Do in Visual Arts: National Standards for Arts Education. 16p. (YA). 1995. pap. 1.00 (*0-88290-522-8*, 2992) Horizon Utah.

What Every Young Wizard Should Know. Cal Roy. (Illus.). (J). (gr. 2 up). 1963. 8.95 (*0-8392-3043-5*) Astor-Honor.

What Every 18-Year-Old Needs to Know about California Law. L. Jean Wallace. LC 93-28844. 192p. (YA). (gr. 12). 1994. pap. 9.95 (*0-292-79085-6*); text ed. 25.00 (*0-292-79084-8*) U of Tex Pr.

***What Every 18-Year-Old Needs to Know about Texas Law.** 2nd rev. ed. Jean L. Wallace. LC 96-54799. (Illus.). 168p. 1997. pap. 11.95 (*0-292-79119-4*) U of Tex Pr.

What Everybody Needs to Know about Experiential Education. Joel D. Black. 200p. (Orig.). (C). 1996. pap. text ed. 23.95 (*0-910019-98-3*) Lghthse Pub Gp.

What Everyone Can Do to Fight AIDS. Anne Garwood & Ben Melnick. (Social & Behavioral Sciences Ser.). 205p. (Orig.). 14.00 (*0-7879-0044-3*) Jossey-Bass.

What Everyone Needs to Know about God. Richard Booker. 210p. (Orig.). 1992. pap. 8.99 (*1-56043-087-7*) Destiny Image.

What Everyone Should Know about Homosexuality: Homosexualidad: Lo que Es, Lo que Hace y Como Superarla. Tim LaHaye. Tr. by Hiram Duffer from ENG. (Una Respuesta Cristiana Ser.). 144p. (Orig.). (SPA.). 1991. pap. 5.99 (*0-311-46126-3*) Casa Bautista.

What Everyone Should Know about Islam & Muslims. S. Haneef. pap. 14.95 (*0-935782-00-1*) Kazi Pubns.

What Everyone Should Know about Patents, Trademarks, & Copyright. Donald M. Dible. LC 78-6780. 1982. pap. 29.95 (*0-8359-8640-3*, Reston) P-H.

What Everyone Should Know about the U. S. S. R. An Eyewitness Report of a Three-Year Visit. Joseph North. 1976. pap. 0.50 (*0-87898-121-7*) New Outlook.

What Everyone Should Know about the 20th Century: 200 Events That Shaped the World. Alan Axelrod & Charles Phillips. 300p. 1995. 16.00 (*1-55850-506-7*) Adams Media.

What Evil Lurks. James R. McCahery. 304p. 1995. 16.95 (*0-8217-4797-5*) Kensgtn Pub Corp.

What Evil Lurks. James R. McCahery. 256p. 1996. mass mkt. 4.99 (*1-57566-001-6*) Kensgtn Pub Corp.

***What Evil Means to Us.** Fredrick C. Alford. LC 97-10437. 200p. 1997. 22.50 (*0-8014-3430-0*) Cornell U Pr.

What Executive Officers Need to Know about Behavior Analysis. Linda J. Hayes et al. 1996. pap. 27.50 (*1-57654-007-3*, Creative Core) New Orient Media.

What Faith Is. 2nd ed. Kenneth E. Hagin. 1983. pap. 1.95 (*0-89276-002-8*) Hagin Ministries.

What Faith Really Means. Henry G. Graham. LC 82-74243. 94p. 1993. reprint ed. pap. 4.00 (*0-89555-204-3*) TAN Bks Pubs.

What Falls Away: A Memoir. Mia Farrow. LC 96-32868. 384p. 1997. 25.00 (*0-385-47187-4*, N A Talese) Doubleday.

***What Falls Away: A Memoir.** large type ed. Mia Farrow. LC 97-18659. (Americana Ser.). 518p. 1997. lib. bdg. 26.95 (*0-7862-1145-8*, Thorndike Lrg Prnt) Thorndike Pr.

What Falls Away: A Novel. Tracy Daugherty. 256p. 1996. 22.50 (*0-393-03837-8*) Norton.

What Faust Saw. Matt Ottley. (Illus.). 32p. (J). (gr. k-3). 1996. pap. 13.99 (*0-525-45650-3*) Dutton Child Bks.

What Feathers Are For. Maria Jacobs. 80p. 1995. lib. bdg. 27.00 (*0-8095-4592-6*) Borgo Pr.

What Feathers Are For. Maria Jacobs. 80p. pap. 8.95 (*0-88962-306-6*) Mosaic.

What Fiction Means: An Inquiry into the Nature of Fiction with a Study of Three Comic Novels. Bent Nordhjem. (University of Copenhagen Dept of English Ser.: No. 15). 144p. (Orig.). 1987. pap. 45.00 (*87-88648-22-2*) Coronet Bks.

What Finer Tradition: The Memoirs of Thomas O. Selfridge, Jr., Rear Admiral, U.S.N. Thomas O. Selfridge, Jr. & William J. Still, Jr. LC 86-30706. (Studies in Maritime History). 246p. 1987. reprint ed. text ed. 24.95 (*0-87249-507-8*) U of SC Pr.

What Fits What on Harley Davidson Nineteen Thirty-Six to Nineteen Eighty-Three. 6th ed. Mike Arman & Kurt Heinrichs. (Illus.). 1983. pap. 8.00 (*0-933078-11-0*) M Arman.

What Flower Is That? Stirling Macoboy. 1988. 24.99 (*0-517-66998-6*) Random Hse Value.

What Flowers When. Harry Oakman. 1995. pap. 29.95 (*0-7022-2839-7*, Pub. by Univ Queensland Pr AT) Intl Spec Bk.

What Flowers When: With Hints on Home Landscaping. Janice Glimn-Lacy. Ed. by Wendy Ford. LC 95-90129. (Illus.). 104p. (Orig.). 1995. pap. 19.95 (*0-9645162-2-5*) Flower & Leaf.

What Followers Expect from Leaders: How to Meet People's Expectations & Build Credibility. James M. Kouzes & Barry Z. Posner. (Management Ser.). 1988. Audiocassette program. audio 24.95 (*1-55542-908-4*) Jossey-Bass.

What Food is This? Rosmarie Hausherr. LC 93-17328. (Illus.). 40p. (J). (ps-3). 1994. 14.95 (*0-590-46583-X*) Scholastic Inc.

What Food Is This? Rosmarie Hausherr. 1995. pap. 4.95 (*0-590-46584-8*) Scholastic Inc.

What Foods Feed Us & How to Cook Them, with Recipes. Annie Mole. 1974. lib. bdg. 69.95 (*0-685-51381-5*) Revisionist Pr.

What Fools These Mortals Be: A Mediatation on Love Taken from the Works of Shakespeare. Anthony Powell. 19p. (Orig.). (YA). (gr. 6 up). 1995. pap. 3.00 (*1-57514-130-2*, 1111) Encore Perform Pub.

***What Freud Really Said.** David Stafford-Clark. 1997. pap. 12.00 (*0-8052-1080-6*) Schocken.

***What Fun!** Highlights Staff. LC 96-86538. (Illus.). (J). (gr. 2-7). 1997. pap. 7.95 (*1-56397-653-6*) Boyds Mills Pr.

***What Future for British Archaeology?** Martin Biddle. (Oxbow Lectures: No. 1, 1994). (Illus.). 20p. 1994. 4.95 (*0-946897-80-8*, Pub. by Oxbow Bks UK) David Brown.

What Future for Education? Simon. (C). 1992. pap. 18.50 (*0-85315-754-5*, Pub. by Lawrence & Wishart UK) NYU Pr.

What Future for Our Countryside? A Rural Development Policy. OECD Staff. 84p. (Orig.). 1993. pap. 20.00 (*92-64-13808-0*) OECD.

What Future for the U. N.? Lincoln P. Bloomfield & Charles W. Yost. 40p. (C). 1977. pap. 18.95 (*0-87855-741-5*) Transaction Pubs.

***What Future for Urban Environments in Europe? Contribution to Habitat, Vol. II.** 160p. 1996. pap. 25.00 (*92-827-7022-2*, SY95-96-495-ENC, Pub. by Europ Com UK) Bernan Associates.

What Future Professions - 1960, Vol. 23. Eugen Rosenstock-Huessy. (Eugen Rosenstock-Huessy Lectures). 93p. pap. 40.00 incl. audio (*0-614-05392-7*); pap. 20.00 (*0-912148-42-X*); audio 25.00 (*0-614-05391-9*) Argo Bks.

What Futurists Believe. Joseph F. Coates & Jennifer Jarratt. 1989. 19.50 (*0-930242-40-8*) World Future.

What Game Shall We Play? Pat Hutchins. LC 89-34621. (Illus.). 24p. (J). (ps up). 1995. reprint ed. pap. 4.95 (*0-688-13573-0*, Mulberry) Morrow.

***What Gardens Mean.** Ross. LC 97-22441. 1998. 40.00 (*0-226-72822-6*) U Ch Pr.

What Gets Measured & Rewarded Gets Done. 2nd ed. Peterson. (Industrial Health & Safety Ser.). 240p. 1996. text ed. 62.95 (*0-442-02179-8*) Van Nos Reinhold.

What Getting Drunk Doesn't Make You. Ed. by Michael P. Jones. (Alcohol Education Ser.). (Illus.). 20p. (J). 1984. text ed. 5.00 (*0-89904-027-6*); pap. text ed. 2.00 (*0-89904-197-3*) Crumb Elbow Pub.

What Girls Learn. Karin Cook. 1997. 23.00 (*0-679-44828-4*) Random.

What Girls Learn. Karin Cook. Date not set. pap. write for info. (*0-679-76944-7*) Random.

What Gives Me Strength: Reflections on the Basic Prayers & Truths of Christianity. Martin Gut. Tr. by John F. Laland, 2nd. LC 95-8781. 194p. 1995. pap. text ed. 7.95 (*0-8294-0861-4*) Loyola Pr.

What God Allows: The Crisis of Faith & Conscience in One Catholic Church. Ivor Shapiro. 304p. 1996. 23.95 (*0-385-47293-5*) Doubleday.

What God Does When Men Pray. Bill C. Peel. 96p. (Orig.). 1993. pap. 6.00 (*0-89109-729-5*) NavPress.

What God Has Joined: The Sacramentality of Marriage. Peter J. Elliot. LC 89-18533. 336p. (Orig.). 1990. pap. 15.95 (*0-8189-0568-9*) Alba.

What God Is Like. James D. Freeman. LC 73-87274. 1973. 7.95 (*0-87159-172-3*) Unity Bks.

What God Wants: A Novel. Lily Brett. LC 93-2497. (Illus.). 264p. 1993. 18.95 (*1-55972-193-6*, Birch Ln Pr) Carol Pub Group.

What God Was Doing When World Religions Were Born. Lester Sumrall. 50p. (C). 1981. pap. text ed. 12.00 (*0-937580-59-7*) LeSEA Pub Co.

***What God Wishes Christians Knew about Christianity: It Might Surprise You.** Bill Gillham. LC 96-41071. 225p. (Orig.). Date not set. pap. 9.99 (*1-56507-557-9*) Harvest Hse.

***What Goes Around.** David C. O'Neal. 180p. (Orig.). 1997. mass mkt. 4.99 (*1-55197-954-3*, Pub. by Comnwlth Pub CN) Partners Pubs Grp.

What Goes Around: Belts... Lois Ericson. Ed. by Barnard Bets. (Illus.). 144p. (Orig.). (C). 1993. pap. text ed. 18.00 (*0-911985-07-7*) Erics Pr.

What Goes Around Comes Around. Richard McGuire. LC 95-12337. (Illus.). 32p. (J). (gr. k up). 1995. pap. 13.99 (*0-670-86396-3*, Viking) Viking Penguin.

What Goes Around Comes Around: The Feedback Loop. Luis D. Pascual. LC 94-90701. (Illus.). 99p. (Orig.). 1994. pap. 12.95 (*0-9644398-3-2*) WGACA.

What Goes Around Comes Around: The Films of Jonathan Demme. Michael Bliss & Christiana Banks. LC 94-41204. (Illus.). 184p. (C). 1996. 24.95 (*0-8093-1983-7*); pap. 14.95 (*0-8093-1984-5*) S Ill U Pr.

What Goes into Your Book. Dahk Knox. (C). 1997. pap. 10.95 (*1-881116-66-2*) Black Forest Pr.

What Goes Without Saying: Collected Stories of Josephine Jacobsen. Josephine Jacobsen. LC 96-18654. (Johns Hopkins). 320p. 1996. 29.95 (*0-8018-5455-5*) Johns Hopkins.

What Good Is a Cactus? Peter Marchand. LC 94-65088. (Illus.). 24p. (Orig.). (J). (gr. 3-6). 1994. pap. 7.95 (*1-879373-83-1*) R Rinehart.

What Good Is a Line? see **Homeplay: Joyful Learning for Children & Adults, Series I**

What Good Is a Tail? Dorothy H. Patent. LC 92-45639. (Illus.). 32p. (J). (gr. 1-5). 1994. pap. 13.99 (*0-525-65148-9*, Cobblehill Bks) Dutton Child Bks.

***What Good Is Christianity...Anyhow?** John W. Clarke. 56p. 1992. pap. 9.95 (*1-877871-42-7*, 6710) Ed Ministries.

What Good Is Free Speech in a Closet: A Story of Cover-up in Planning for Our Grandchildren's Drinking Water. Joseph L. Miller, Jr. (Illus.). 68p. 1985. pap. 4.75 (*0-9614887-0-0*) DRC Graphics Serv.

What Good Is Religion to Me. Michael A. Polsky. 1993. pap. 0.50 (*0-89981-140-X*) Eastern Orthodox.

What Good Parents Have in Common: 13 Secrets for Success. Janis L. Harris. 224p. 1994. pap. 10.99 (*0-310-48191-0*) Zondervan.

What Got You Where You Are Today? Iris Acker. LC 90-86069. (Illus.). 192p. 1991. pap. 12.95 (*0-942963-08-3*) Distinctive Pub.

What Government Does. Ed. by Matthew Holden, Jr. & Dennis L. Dresang. (Organization Ser.). 320p. 1975. 15.00 (*0-317-35636-4*) Pol Studies.

What Government Does. Ed. by Matthew Holden, Jr. & Dennis L. Dresang. LC 73-77872. (Sage Yearbooks in Politics & Public Policy Ser.: No. 1). 320p. 1975. reprint ed. pap. 91.20 (*0-608-01520-2*, 2059564) Bks Demand.

What Grace They Received: Worship Commemorations for 12 Ancient & Modern Saints. Thomas A. Renquist. 1992. pap. 8.50 (*1-55673-567-7*, 9314) CSS OH.

What Grandmother Says. J. D. Whitney. Ed. by Robert Bixby. 22p. 1993. pap. 6.00 (*1-882983-07-6*) March Street Pr.

***What Great Chefs Know That You Don't.** (Non-Fiction Ser.: No. 80513). 1997. mass mkt. 5.99 (*0-373-80513-6*, 1-80513-4) Harlequin Bks.

What Great Men Have Said about Great Men. W. Wale. 1972. 75.00 (*0-8490-1284-8*) Gordon Pr.

What Great Men Think of Religion. Ira D. Cardiff. LC 71-161322. (Atheist Viewpoint Ser.). 504p. 1976. reprint ed. 31.95 (*0-405-03625-6*) Ayer.

***What Great Paintings Say, Vol. 2.** Rose-Marie Hagen. (Big Art Ser.). 1996. 19.99 (*3-8228-8904-0*) Taschen Amer.

What Growing Up Is All About: A Parent's Guide to Child & Adolescent Development. Ann Vernon & Radhi Al-Mabuk. LC 95-68368. 1995. 192p. (Orig.). 1995. pap. text ed. 13.95 (*0-87822-354-1*, 4845) Res Press.

What Gunpowder Plot Was. Samuel R. Gardiner. LC 73-131718. 1971. 9.00 (*0-403-00605-8*) Scholarly.

What Gunpowder Plot Was. Samuel Gardiner. LC 68-25234. (British History Ser.: No. 30). (Illus.). 1969. reprint ed. lib. bdg. 49.95 (*0-8383-0941-0*) M S G Haskell Hse.

What Gusto: Stories & Anecdotes about Justice Oliver Wendell Holmes. Harry C. Shriver. LC 79-132249. (Illus.). 36p. 1970. 5.00 (*0-685-88599-2*) Fox Hills Pr.

What Handwriting Indicates: An Analytical Graphology. John Rexford. 1991. lib. bdg. 79.95 (*0-8490-4528-2*) Gordon Pr.

What Handwriting Indicates: An Analytical Graphology. John Rexford. 142p. 1972. reprint ed. spiral bd. 8.50 (*0-7873-1082-4*) Hlth Research.

What Handwriting Tells You: About Yourself, Your Friends, & Famous People. M. N. Bunker. 1965. 23.95 (*0-911012-02-8*) Nelson-Hall.

What Happened? Rozanne L. Williams. (Emergent Reader Big Bks.). (Illus.). 16p. (Orig.). (J). (gr. k-2). 1995. pap. 11.98 (*1-57471-021-4*) Creat Teach Pr.

What Happened?, Level II. Rozanne L. Williams. (Emergent Reader Science Ser.). 16p. 1994. 2.49 (*0-916119-47-5*, 3537) Creat Teach Pr.

What Happened? American Politics, 1991. Robert Sherrill. 250p. (C). 1992. pap. text ed. write for info. (*0-318-69126-4*) HB Coll Pubs.

What Happened? My Experience with Divorce. Dorothy Miller. (Illus.). 61p. (Orig.). 1987. pap. 2.95 (*0-936625-10-4*, New Hope AL) Womans Mission Union.

W

What Happened at Christmas? Alan Parry & Linda Parry. (J). 1995. 12.99 (*0-8423-8377-8*) Tyndale.

What Happened at Midnight. Franklin W. Dixon. (Hardy Boys Ser.: Vol. 10). 180p. (J). (gr. 5-9). 1931. 5.95 (*0-448-08910-6*, G&D) Putnam Pub Group.

***What Happened Fisher?** Nancy J. Hopper. (J). 1998. pap. 4.99 (*0-14-038076-0*) Viking Penguin.

What Happened from the Cross to the Throne. E. W. Kenyon. 203p. (Orig.). (C). 1946. pap. 9.25 (*1-57770-001-5*) Kenyons Gospel.

What Happened in A. D. 70? rev. ed. Edward E. Stevens. (Illus.). 40p. (YA). 1997. reprint ed. pap. 4.95 (*0-9621311-0-5*) Kingdom Pubns.

What Happened in Hamelin. Gloria Skurzynski. 1995. 18.00 (*0-8446-6828-1*) Peter Smith.

What Happened in Hamelin. Gloria Skurzynski. LC 79-12814. (Illus.). 192p. (J). (gr. 5-9). 1993. pap. 3.99 (*0-679-83645-4*, Bullseye Bks) Random Bks Yng Read.

What Happened in Mr. Fisher's Room. Nancy J. Hopper. LC 94-41656. (J). 1995. pap. 14.99 (*0-8037-1841-1*) Dial Bks Young.

What Happened in Poland. Hyman Lumer. 1969. pap. 0.35 (*0-87898-035-0*) New Outlook.

What Happened in the Mooney Case. Ernest J. Hopkins. LC 73-107411. (Civil Liberties in American History Ser.). 1970. reprint ed. lib. bdg. 32.50 (*0-306-71891-X*) Da Capo.

What Happened in the Mooney Case. Ernest J. Hopkins. 1992. reprint ed. lib. bdg. 75.00 (*0-7812-5051-X*) Rprt Serv.

What Happened on Lexington Green? P. Bennett. 1970. pap. text ed. 7.90 (*0-201-00461-5*) Addison-Wesley.

***What Happened to Amy?** Jane Edwards. (J). Date not set. write for info. (*0-688-05499-4*); lib. bdg. write for info. (*0-688-05500-1*) Lothrop.

What Happened to Aunt Cordelia? Elizabeth Best. LC 93-167. (Voyages Ser.). (J). 1994. write for info. (*0-383-03725-5*) SRA McGraw.

What Happened to Benjamin: A True Story. Shirley B. Waring. LC 92-83949. (Illus.). 38p. (Orig.). (J). (gr. k-6). 1993. lib. bdg. 13.95 (*0-9622808-2-8*); Audio cass. audio 9.98 (*0-9622808-3-6*) S&T Waring.

What Happened to Coelophysis? J. Lynette Gillette. LC 94-46818. (Illus.). (J). 1997. pap. 15.89 (*0-8037-1722-9*) Dial Bks Young.

What Happened to France. Gordon Waterfield. LC 72-1303. (Select Bibliographies Reprint Ser.). 1977. reprint ed. 18.95 (*0-8369-6839-5*) Ayer.

What Happened to Grandma? Lenora B. Caldwell. LC 93-93902. 64p. (Orig.). 1994. pap. 8.00 (*1-56002-341-4*, Univ Edtns) Aegina Pr.

What Happened to Heather Hopkowitz? Charlotte Herman. LC 93-43628. 192p. (J). (gr. 4 up). 1994. pap. 8.95 (*0-8276-0520-X*) JPS Phila.

What Happened to Milly? Roger A. Faber. (Illus.). (J). (gr. 3 up). pap. write for info. (*1-880122-07-3*) White Stone.

What Happened to Mommy? Renee Fran. (Illus.). 32p. (Orig.). (J). (ps-6). 1994. pap. 7.95 (*0-9640250-0-0*) Eastman NY.

What Happened to Patrick's Dinosaurs? Carol Carrick. LC 85-13989. (Illus.). (J). (gr. k-3). 1986. 16.00 (*0-89919-406-0*, Clarion Bks) HM.

What Happened to Patrick's Dinosaurs? Carol Carrick. (Book & Cassette Favorites Ser.). (Illus.). (J). 1988. pap. 8.95 incl. audio (*0-89919-838-4*, Clarion Bks) HM.

What Happened to Patrick's Dinosaurs? Carol Carrick. LC 85-13989. (Illus.). (J). (gr. k-3). 1988. pap. 5.95 (*0-89919-797-3*, Clarion Bks) HM.

What Happened to Sherlock Holmes? as Set to Rest In... The Legend of Wilson-The Amazing Athlete. Terence White. Ed. by Francis Blackburn et al. LC 83-51870. (Illus.). 102p. (J). 1984. 9.95 (*0-9612698-0-4*) Seagull Pub Co.

What Happened to the Berkeley Co-Op. Ed. by Michael Fullerton. (Illus.). 107p. (Orig.). 1990. pap. 10.00 (*1-885641-02-8*, B1) U CA Ctr Cooperatives.

What Happened to the Dinosaurs? Franklyn M. Branley. LC 88-37626. (Let's-Read-&-Find-Out Science Bk.). (Illus.). 32p. (J). (gr. k-3). 1989. lib. bdg. 14.89 (*0-690-04749-5*, Crowell Jr Bks) HarpC Child Bks.

What Happened to the Dinosaurs? Franklyn M. Branley. LC 88-37626. (Trophy Let's-Read-&-Find-Out Bk.). (Illus.). 32p. (J). (gr. k-4). 1991. pap. 4.95 (*0-06-445105-4*, Trophy) HarpC Child Bks.

***What Happened to the Prince I Married? A Woman's Guide to Healing Herself & Her Mate.** Sirah Vettese. 240p. (Orig.). 1997. pap. 14.95 (*0-944031-76-5*) Aslan Pub.

What Happened to the Southern Baptist Convention? A Memoir of the Controversy. Grady C. Cothen. LC 93-14908. 390p. 1993. 24.95 (*1-880837-26-9*) Smyth & Helwys.

***What Happened to Those Boys?** Jay Devereaux. 1998. pap. write for info. (*0-614-30239-0*) Otter Crk Pr.

What Happened to You? Writings by Disabled Women. Lois Keith. LC 96-67347. 240p. 1996. pap. 12.95 (*1-56584-280-4*) New Press NY.

What Happened to You? Writings by Disabled Women. Ed. by Lois Keith. 240p. 1996. 22.50 (*0-614-16304-8*) New Press NY.

What Happened When. Anthony Barker. 504p. 1996. pap. 24.95 (*1-86373-986-6*, Pub. by Allen Unwin AT) Paul & Co Pubs.

What Happened When: A Chronology of Life & Events in America. Gorton Carruth. 1408p. (Orig.). 1991. pap. 8.99 (*0-451-16902-6*, Sig) NAL-Dutton.

What Happened When Grandma Died? Peggy Barker. (Illus.). 32p. 1984. 6.99 (*0-570-04090-6*, 56-1458) Concordia.

What Happened When He Went to the Store for Bread: Poems. Alden Nowlan. Ed. by Thomas R. Smith. LC 93-14682. 1993. pap. 10.00 (*1-883070-00-7*) Nineties Pr.

What Happened When the Hopi Hit New York. Wendy Rose. (Chapbook Ser.). (Illus.). 56p. (Orig.). (J). 1982. pap. 3.50 (*0-936556-08-0*) Contact Two.

***What Happened Where.** Chris Cook. LC 96-45597. 1997. text ed. 30.00 (*0-312-17278-8*) St Martin.

What Happens. Robert Long. LC 88-9423. 68p. (Orig.). 1988. pap. 9.95 (*0-913123-19-6*) Galileo.

What Happens: Poems by Jerry Thompson. Jerry Thompson. (Illus.). 50p. (Orig.). Date not set. pap. 7.48 (*0-9645361-9-6*) Cosmo Pr.

What Happens after Death? David Winter. (Pocketbooks Ser.). 48p. 1991. pap. 2.99 (*0-7459-2137-X*) Lion USA.

***What Happens after Death: Scientific & Personal Evidence for Survival.** Migene Gonzalez-Wippler. LC 97-1983. Orig. Title: Peregrinaje. 256p. (Orig.). 1997. pap. 7.95 (*1-56718-327-1*, K327-1) Llewellyn Pubns.

What Happens After Death? Some Musing on -- Is God Through with a Person After Death? John R. Richardson. LC 81-52115. 1981. 6.95 (*0-686-79843-0*) St Thomas.

What Happens after Death? see Life after Death

What Happens after I Die? Jewish Views of Life after Death. Rifat Sonsino & Daniel B. Syme. LC 94-13625. 160p. (Orig.). 1994. 22.50 (*1-56821-288-7*) Aronson.

What Happens after I Die? Jewish Views of Life after Death. Rifat Sonsino & Daniel B. Syme. (Orig.). 1990. pap. 8.95 (*0-8074-0356-3*, 571201) UAHC.

What Happens at Death & What Is Our Condition after Death. 3rd ed. Ernest R. Sill. 52p. 1970. reprint ed. spiral bd. 5.00 (*0-7873-0792-0*) Hlth Research.

***What Happens Drugs.** Rafaella Fletcher. 1997. pap. 6.99 (*0-14-038577-0*) Viking Penguin.

What Happens During Business Cycles? A Progress Report. Wesley C. Mitchell. (Studies in Business Cycles: No. 5). 427p. 1951. reprint ed. 111.10 (*0-87014-088-4*) Natl Bur Econ Res.

What Happens If I...Book: How to Make Action/Reaction Work for You Instead of Against You. Betsy O. Thompson. LC 95-20683. (Orig.). 1996. pap. 12.00 (*1-879023-05-9*) Ascension Pub.

What Happens in Art. Matthew Lipman. LC 66-27473. (Century Philosophy Ser.). (Orig.). 1967. pap. text ed. 9.95 (*0-89197-470-9*) Irvington.

What Happens in Book Publishing? 2nd ed. Ed. by Chandler B. Grannis. LC 67-19875. 477p. reprint ed. pap. 136.00 (*0-7837-0435-6*, 2040758) Bks Demand.

What Happens in Groups: Psychoanalysis, the Individual & the Community. R. D. Hinshelwood. 280p. (C). 1987. 47.00 (*0-946960-88-7*); pap. 18.00 (*0-946960-89-5*) NYU Pr.

What Happens in Hamlet. 3rd ed. John D. Wilson. 380p. (C). 1951. pap. text ed. 22.95 (*0-521-09109-8*) Cambridge U Pr.

What Happens in My Garden. rev. ed. Louise B. Wilder. LC 96-35489. (Illus.). 256p. 1997. pap. 14.95 (*0-88179-137-7*) Hartley & Marks.

What Happens in My Garden? Louise B. Wilder. (American Gardening Classics Ser.). 272p. 1991. reprint ed. pap. 10.95 (*0-02-040841-2*) Macmillan.

What Happens in Public Relations. Ed. by Gerald J. Voros & Paul H. Alvarez. LC 80-69700. (Illus.). 240p. reprint ed. pap. 68.40 (*0-317-08676-6*, 2022626) Bks Demand.

What Happens in the Autumn see Books for Young Explorers

What Happens in the Spring see Books for Young Explorers

What Happens Next? Ed. by Cheryl Christian. (Photo Flap Bks.). (Illus.). 12p. (J). (ps). 1991. 4.95 (*1-56288-131-0*) Checkerboard.

What Happens Next? Sandra Markle. (Illus.). 48p. (J). (gr. k-4). 1995. 14.95 (*1-56352-232-2*) Longstreet Pr Inc.

What Happens Next?, Vol. 2. Sandra Markle. (Illus.). (J). (gr. k-4). 1996. 14.95 (*1-56352-286-1*) Longstreet Pr Inc.

What Happens Sunday Morning: A Layperson's Guide to Worship. Carol M. Noren. 112p. (Orig.). 1992. pap. 9.00 (*0-664-25227-3*) Westminster John Knox.

What Happens to a Hamburger? rev. ed. Paul Showers. LC 84-48784. (Trophy Let's-Read-&-Find-Out Science Bk.). (Illus.). 32p. (J). (gr. k-3). 1985. pap. 4.95 (*0-06-445013-9*, Trophy) HarpC Child Bks.

What Happens to a Hamburger? rev. ed. Paul Showers. LC 84-45343. (Let's-Read-&-Find-Out Science Bk.). (Illus.). 32p. (J). (ps-3). 1985. lib. bdg. 14.89 (*0-690-04427-5*, Crowell Jr Bks) HarpC Child Bks.

What Happens to Good People When Bad Things Happen. Robert A. Schuller. LC 95-8642. 172p. (gr. 10). 1995. 14.99 (*0-8007-1712-0*) Revell.

What Happens to Good People When Bad Things Happen. large type ed. Robert A. Schuller. 256p. 1996. pap. 12.95 (*0-8027-2698-4*) Walker & Co.

What Happens to Homework: Poems by the JLS Middle School Poetry Club. Lisa Kepford et al. (Illus.). (Orig.). (J). (gr. 6-8). 1996. pap. 4.95 (*1-880964-15-5*) Zapizdat Pubns.

What Happens to Me When I Fish the Sea & a Fish Catches Me. Thelma Gilmartin. LC 76-12929. (Illus.). 36p. (Orig.). (J). (gr. 1-3). 1976. pap. 4.50 (*0-89317-009-7*) Windward Pub.

***What Happens to Your Food?** Alastaire Smith. (Flip Flap Ser.). 16p. (Orig.). (J). (ps-2). 1997. pap. 7.95 (*0-7460-2504-1*, Usborne) EDC.

***What Happens to Your Food?** Alastaire Smith. (Flip Flap Ser.). 16p. (J). (ps-2). 1997. lib. bdg. 15.95 (*0-88110-945-2*, Usborne) EDC.

What Happens When: A Poetic Record of Childhood Owies. Nancy Whyte. (Illus.). 32p. (J). (gr. k-4). 1995. 12.95 (*0-9643113-5-6*) KidLit Advent.

What Happens When: You Turn on the TV, Flick on a Light, Mail a Letter? John Farndon. LC 95-51718. (Illus.). (J). (gr. 1-5). 1996. 17.95 (*0-590-84754-6*) Scholastic Inc.

What Happens When...? you turn on the TV? switch on a light? mail a letter? John Farndon. 48p. (J). 1996. 17.95 (*0-590-84574-8*, Cartwheel) Scholastic Inc.

What Happens When a Christian Sins. Ken Parker. 18p. 1980. 0.50 (*0-89814-050-1*) Grace Publns.

What Happens When Flowers Grow? Daphne Butler. LC 95-10520. (What Happens When? Ser.). (J). 1995. lib. bdg. 21.40 (*0-8172-4150-7*) Raintree Steck-V.

What Happens When God Answers Prayer: Leaders Guide. Evelyn Christenson. 72p. (Orig.). 1994. pap. 6.50 (*1-56476-251-3*, 6-3251, Victor Bks) Chariot Victor.

What Happens When I Flush the Toilet? Isaac Asimov. (Ask Isaac Asimov Ser.). (Illus.). 24p. (J). (gr. 1-8). 1992. lib. bdg. 17.27 (*0-8368-0801-0*) Gareth Stevens Inc.

What Happens When People Talk? Daphne Butler. LC 95-12060. (What Happens When? Ser.). (J). 1996. lib. bdg. 21.40 (*0-8172-4154-X*) Raintree Steck-V.

What Happens When Rain Falls? Daphne Butler. LC 95-12061. (What Happens When? Ser.). (J). 1996. lib. bdg. 21.40 (*0-8172-4151-5*) Raintree Steck-V.

What Happens When Volcanoes Erupt? Daphne Butler. LC 95-10519. (What Happens When? Ser.). 31p. (J). (gr. k-3). 1995. lib. bdg. 21.40 (*0-8172-4157-4*) Raintree Steck-V.

What Happens When We Die? Carolyn Nystrom. (Children's Bible Basics Ser.). (Illus.). 32p. (J). (ps-2). 1981. text ed. 6.99 (*0-8024-7855-7*) Moody.

What Happens When We Pray for Our Families. Evelyn Christenson. LC 92-486. 204p. 1992. pap. 9.99 (*0-89693-541-8*, 6-1541, Victor Bks) Chariot Victor.

What Happens When Wheels Turn? Daphne Butler. LC 95-11782. (What Happens When? Ser.). (J). 1995. lib. bdg. 21.40 (*0-8172-4152-3*) Raintree Steck-V.

What Happens When Wind Blows? Daphne Butler. LC 95-13660. (What Happens When? Ser.). (J). 1995. lib. bdg. 21.40 (*0-8172-4153-1*) Raintree Steck-V.

What Happens When Women Pray. Evelyn Christenson. 144p. 1992. pap. 9.99 (*0-89693-975-8*, 6-1975, Victor Bks); teacher ed., pap. 6.50 (*0-89693-976-6*, 6-1976, Victor Bks) Chariot Victor.

***What Happens When Women Pray.** anniversary ed. 192p. 1997. write for info. (*1-56476-630-6*, Victor Bks) Chariot Victor.

What Happens When You Die: From Your Last Breath to the First Spadeful. Robert T. Hatch. LC 95-22526. Orig. Title: How to Embalm Your Mother-in-Law. 104p. 1995. reprint ed. pap. 8.95 (*0-8065-1667-4*, Citadel Pr) Carol Pub Group.

What Happpens When God Answers Prayer. Evelyn Christenson. 204p. (Orig.). 1994. pap. 9.99 (*1-56476-243-2*, 6-3243, Victor Bks) Chariot Victor.

What Has Archaeology to Do with Faith? Ed. by James H. Charlesworth & Walter P. Weaver. LC 92-5202. (Faith & Scholarship Colloquies Ser.). 128p. 1992. pap. 13.95 (*1-56338-038-2*) TPI PA.

***What Has Athens to Do with Jerusalem? Timaeus & Genesis in Counterpoint.** Jaroslav Pelikan. LC 97-4244. (C). 1997. 24.95 (*0-472-10807-7*) U of Mich Pr.

What Has Been Lost. David Eberly. 1982. pap. 4.95 (*0-914852-10-8*) Good Gay.

What Has Government Done to Our Health Care? Terree P. Wasley. LC 92-20121. 162p. 1992. pap. 10.95 (*0-932790-87-9*) Cato Inst.

What Has Government Done to Our Money? Murray N. Rothbard. 119p. (Orig.). 1990. reprint ed. pap. text ed. 6.95 (*0-945466-10-2*) Ludwig von Mises.

What Has Sociology Achieved? Ed. by Christopher G. Bryant & Henk A. Becker. 275p. 1990. text ed. 45.00 (*0-312-03671-X*) St Martin.

What Has the European Monetary System Achieved? M. P. Taylor & M. J. Artis. (Bank of England. Discussion Papers: No. 31). 47p. reprint ed. pap. 25.00 (*0-8357-8528-9*, 2034827) Bks Demand.

***What Have We Done? The Foundation for Global Sustainability's State of the Bioregion Report for the Upper Tennessee River Valley & Southern Appalachian Mountains.** John Nolt et al. LC 97-60066. 320p. (Orig.). 1997. pap. 19.95 (*0-9644659-2-2*) Earth Knows Publ.

What Have We Learned? Telling the Story & Teaching the Lessons of the Holocaust. Ed. by Franklin H. Littell et al. LC 93-24623. (Symposium Ser.: Vol. 30). 400p. 1994. text ed. 109.95 (*0-7734-9336-0*) E Mellen.

What Have You Done, Davy? Brigitte Weninger. (Illus.). 32p. (J). (ps-3). Date not set. lib. bdg. 15.88 (*1-55858-582-6*) North-South Bks NYC.

What Have You Done, Davy? Brigitte Weninger. LC 95-52221. (Illus.). 32p. (J). (gr. k-3). Date not set. 15.95 (*1-55858-581-8*) North-South Bks NYC.

What Have You Done to Your Homeless Brother? Veritas Publications Staff. 1989. pap. 15.00 (*1-85390-071-0*, Pub. by Veritas IE) St Mut.

What Have You Done to Your Homeless Brother? The Church & the Housing Problem. Pontifical Justice & Peace Commission Staff. 30p. (Orig.). 1987. pap. 1.95 (*1-55586-203-9*) US Catholic.

What Have You Done with Filbert MacFee? Roberta Karim. LC 94-43098. (Illus.). (J). 1997. write for info. (*0-395-72099-0*, Clarion Bks) HM.

What Have You Got to Lose. Jenny Craig. 1992. 19.50 (*0-679-40527-5*) McKay.

What He Says, Where He Sends. Philip Hacking. pap. 5.99 (*0-551-01634-5*) Zondervan.

What Hearts? Bruce Brooks. LC 92-5305. (Laura Geringer Bk.). 208p. (YA). (gr. 5 up). 1992. 14.95 (*0-06-021131-8*); lib. bdg. 14.89 (*0-06-021132-6*) HarpC Child Bks.

What Hearts? Bruce Brooks. LC 92-5305. 208p. (YA). 1995. pap. 4.50 (*0-06-447127-6*) HarpC Child Bks.

What Helped Me When My Loved One Died. Ed. by Earl A. Grollman. LC 80-68166. 168p. 1982. reprint ed. pap. 12.95 (*0-8070-3229-8*) Beacon Pr.

What Helps the Most...When Hope Is Hard to Find: 101 Insights from People Who Have Been There. Ed. by Lisa Engelhardt. LC 96-84538. 88p. (Orig.). 1996. pap. 4.95 (*0-87029-294-3*, 20158) Abbey.

What Helps the Most...When You Lose Someone Close: 101 Insights from People Who Have Been There. Ed. by Linus Mundy. LC 96-84550. 88p. (Orig.). 1996. pap. 4.95 (*0-87029-295-1*, 20159) Abbey.

What Henry James Knew. Cynthia Ozick. (Chapbooks in Literature Ser.). (Illus.). 40p. (Orig.). 1993. pap. text ed. 5.00 (*1-878603-05-1*) Bennington Coll.

***What Herb Is That? How to Grow & Use the Culinary Herbs.** John Hemphill. 1997. 32.95 (*0-8117-1634-1*) Stackpole.

What High School Students Should Know about Evolution. Kenneth N. Taylor. 70p. (YA). (gr. 9-12). 1983. mass mkt. 3.99 (*0-8423-7873-1*) Tyndale.

What Hinders You? Elizabeth S. Brengle. 112p. 1990. reprint ed. 5.95 (*0-86544-059-X*) Salv Army Suppl South.

What Holly Heard. R. L. Stine. (Fear Street Ser.: No. 34). (YA). (gr. 7 up). 1996. pap. 3.99 (*0-671-89427-7*, Pocket Books) PB.

What Home Buyers Want. Gopal Ahluwalia & Michael Carliner. 124p. 1989. pap. 115.00 (*0-86718-466-3*) Home Builder.

What, How & Do It! G. S. Miller. 205p. (C). 1989. text ed. 70.00 (*1-872795-41-2*, Pub. by Pentland Pr UK) St Mut.

What Husbands Expect of Wives. Brent A. Barlow. LC 83-70707. xii, 146p. 1989. reprint ed. pap. 6.95 (*0-87579-197-2*) Deseret Bk.

What I Am Pleased to Call My Education. Henry Kent. (American Autobiography Ser.). 208p. 1995. reprint ed. lib. bdg. 79.00 (*0-7812-8570-4*) Rprt Serv.

What I Believe: Kids Talk about Faith. Debbie H. Birdseye & Tom Birdseye. LC 96-11240. (Illus.). 32p. (J). (gr. 4-7). 1996. 15.95 (*0-8234-1268-7*) Holiday.

What I Believe Transpirations - Transpiring Minnesota. Robert Grenier. 1991. boxed 24.00 (*0-685-56984-5*) O Bks.

What I Came to Say. Raymond Williams. 1989. 21.95 (*0-09-175789-4*) Norton.

What I Cannot Say: Self, Word, & World in Whitman, Stevens, & Merwin. Thomas B. Byers. 160p. 1989. text ed. 24.95 (*0-252-01542-8*) U of Ill Pr.

What I Cannot Say - I Will Say. Monica Ochtrup. 80p. 1984. pap. 3.50 (*0-89823-059-4*) New Rivers Pr.

What I Did for Roman. Pam Conrad. LC 86-45497. (Trophy Bk.). 224p. (YA). (gr. 7 up). 1996. pap. 4.50 (*0-06-447164-0*, Trophy) HarpC Child Bks.

What I Did Last Summer. A. R. Gurney. 1983. pap. 5.25 (*0-8222-1236-6*) Dramatists Play.

What I Did on My Summer Vacation. Jean Van Leeuwen. LC 96-2380. (J). 1997. pap. 14.89 (*0-8037-1820-9*) Dial Bks Young.

What I Did Today. Linda F. Hatch. (Illus.). 1995. 7.95 (*0-533-11368-7*) Vantage.

What I Did with My Trash: Adventures with a TRS-80 Microcomputer. Eric Bagai. (Illus.). 80p. (Orig.). 1990. pap. text ed. 5.95 (*0-943292-24-7*, Flaming Sparrow) Forewords.

What I Didn't Learn in Flying School, Vol. 1. Vernon M. Foster. LC 95-92050. (Illus.). 204p. (Orig.). 1995. pap. text ed. 29.95 (*0-9644332-0-6*) Corona Pass.

What I Don't Know for Sure. deluxe ed. Phil Demise. (Burning Deck Poetry Chapbooks Ser.). 1978. pap. 15.00 (*0-930900-55-3*) Burning Deck.

What I Eat. Heidi Goennel. LC 95-60577. (Illus.). 12p. (J). (ps). 1995. pap. 3.95 (*0-688-14145-5*, Tambourine Bks) Morrow.

What I Eat. Christopher Wormell. LC 95-47655. 32p. (J). (ps-1). 1996. pap. 9.99 (*0-8037-2058-0*) Dial Bks Young.

What I Had Was Singing: The Story of Marian Anderson. Jeri Ferris. LC 93-28502. (Trailblazers Ser.). 96p. (J). (gr. 4-7). 1994. lib. bdg. 21.50 (*0-87614-818-6*, First Ave Edns) Lerner Group.

What I Had Was Singing: The Story of Marian Anderson. Jeri Ferris. (Trailblazers Ser.). 96p. (J). (gr. 4-7). 1994. pap. 6.95 (*0-87614-634-5*, First Ave Edns) Lerner Group.

What I Have Learned: Thinking about the Future Then & Now. Ed. by Michael Marien & Lane Jennings. LC 86-14958. 219p. 1987. text ed. 49.95 (*0-313-25071-5*, MWL/, Greenwood Pr) Greenwood.

What I Have Learned from Children. Michaelene P. Grassli. LC 93-13328. v, 121p. 1993. 11.95 (*0-87579-701-6*) Deseret Bk.

***What I Have Learned from Steelers Football.** Gene M. Bearer. LC 96-90372. (Orig.). 1996. pap. 6.95 (*0-533-12009-8*) Vantage.

What! I Have to Give a Speech? Thomas J. Murphy & Kenneth Snyder. LC 94-37438. 223p. (Orig.). (J). (gr. 6-9). 1995. pap. 12.95 (*1-883790-10-7*, EDINFO Pr) Grayson Bernard Pubs.

What I Hope to Leave Behind: The Essential Essays of Eleanor Roosevelt. Ed. by Allida M. Black. LC 95-38101. 683p. 1995. 75.00 (*0-926019-88-0*) Carlson Pub.

What I Know about Winchester. William G. Russell. 212p. 1953. write for info. (*0-318-64323-5*) Winchester-Frederick Cty Hist Soc.

What I Know Now. Rodger Larson. (J). 1997. 15.95 (*0-8050-4869-3*) H Holt & Co.

An Asterisk (*) at the beginning of an entry indicates that the title is appearing in BIP for the first time.

What I Know of Farming. Horace Greeley. LC 74-30631. (American Farmers & the Rise of Agribusiness Ser.). 1975. reprint ed. 33.95 (0-405-06800-X) Ayer.

What I Know of Farming: A Series of Brief & Plain Expositions of Practical Agriculture As an Art Based upon Science. Horace Greeley. LC 72-89058. (Rural America Ser.). 1973. reprint ed. 31.00 (0-8420-1484-5) Scholarly Res Inc.

What I Know So Far. 2nd ed. Gordon Lish. 176p. 1996. reprint ed. pap. 10.95 (1-56858-080-0) FWEW.

What I Learned Losing a Million Dollars. Jim Paul & Brendan Moynihan. 190p. 28.95 (0-9635794-9-5) Infrared Pr.

What I Like Best about Christmas. Julie Cassat. 12p. (J). 1989. 6.49 (1-55513-603-6) Cook.

What I Like Best about Christmas. Julie Cassat. (Illus.). 14p. (J). (gr. 4-7). 1989. pap. text ed. 5.95 (0-927106-02-7) Prod Concept.

What I Like to Eat. Jean-Paul Larocque. (Illus.). 18p. (J). (gr. k-3). 1995. pap. 10.95 (1-895583-74-8) MAYA Pubs.

What I Lived For. Joyce Carol Oates. 624p. 1995. pap. 14.95 (0-452-27269-6, Plume) NAL-Dutton.

What I Lived For. Joyce Carol Oates. 1995. pap. write for info. (0-451-18448-3, Sig) NAL-Dutton.

What I Love: Selected Poems of Odysseas Elytis 1943-1978. Odysseas Elytis. Tr. by Olga Broumas from GRE. LC 85-73081. 112p. (Orig.). 1985. 15.00 (0-914742-95-7) Copper Canyon.

What I Owe to My Father. Ed. by Sydney D. Strong. LC 69-17590. (Essay Index Reprint Ser.). 1977. reprint ed. 20.95 (0-8369-2672-2) Ayer.

What I Really Want to Do. Christopher C. Moore. 144p. (Orig.). 1989. pap. 10.99 (0-8272-4226-3) Chalice Pr.

***What I Really Want to Do Is Direct.** Billy Frolick. 1997. pap. 13.95 (0-452-27666-7, Plume) NAL-Dutton.

What I Really Want to Do Is Direct: Seven Film School Graduates Go to Hollywood. Billy Frolick. 384p. 1996. pap. 24.95 (0-525-93770-6) NAL-Dutton.

What I Really Want to Know Is -- Hard Questions about Christianity. David Willingham. LC 95-31595. 1995. 3.05 (1-56212-128-6) CRC Pubns.

What I Remember. Anne Kirby. 288p. 1995. text ed. 17.00 (0-8059-3708-0) Dorrance.

***What I Remember: 1924 Editions.** (Works of Henry & Millicent Garrett Fawcett). 278p. 1996. reprint ed. write for info. (1-85506-375-1) Bks Intl VA.

***What I Remember from My Time on Earth.** Patricia Young. 80p. 1997. 13.95 (0-88784-592-4, Pub. by Hse of Anansi Pr CN) Genl Dist Srvs.

What I Saw - Chto Ya Videl. Boris Zhitkov. Ed. & Anno. by Richard L. Leed. (Illus.). 70p. (Orig.). (ENG & RUS.). (C). 1988. pap. text ed. 12.95 (0-89357-183-0) Slavica.

What I Saw at the Dance: A Poem to A Friend. Joshua B. Lambee. Ed. by Daniel Y. Darden. LC 93-91549. 355p. (Orig.). (C). 1994. pap. 15.95 (0-9637078-3-3) HourGlass TX.

What I Saw at the Revolution: A Political Life in the Reagan Era. Peggy Noonan. 384p. 1991. mass mkt. 5.99 (0-8041-0760-2) Ivy Books.

What I Saw in California. Edwin Bryant. 1967. reprint ed. 20.00 (0-87018-004-5) Ross.

What I Saw in California. Edwin Bryant. LC 84-28003. xxii, 455p. 1985. reprint ed. pap. 16.00 (0-8032-6070-9, Bison Books) U of Nebr Pr.

***What I Saw in the Revolution.** Peggy Noonan. 1997. pap. 12.00 (0-449-00100-8) Fawcett.

What I See. Heidi Goennel. LC 95-60578. (Illus.). 12p. (J). (ps). 1995. pap. 3.95 (0-688-14146-3, Tambourine Bks) Morrow.

***What I (Should Have) Learned in Sunday School.** John Kincaid. 108p. 1996. pap. 5.95 (0-9651707-1-3) Kincaid Kountry.

What I Taught Mom about Football: The Easy Way to Learn about Football. Jason Henderson. (Illus.). 55p. (Orig.). 1992. pap. 5.95 (0-9633965-0-1) Aarons Bks.

What I Think. Adlai E. Stevenson. LC 74-12647. 240p. 1974. reprint ed. text ed. 59.75 (0-8371-7738-3, STIT, Greenwood Pr) Greenwood.

What I Think I Know: New & Selected Poems. Robert Dana. LC 90-85016. 176p. (Orig.). 1991. 18.95 (0-929968-23-9); pap. 10.95 (0-929968-18-2) Another Chicago Pr.

***What I Thought I Saw: New York-London.** Kelli Bickman & Neil Gaiman. Tr. by Connie Bickman. (Illus.). 64p. (Orig.). 1996. pap. 23.95 (1-889644-03-X) Yatra Publns.

What I Want to Be. P. Mignon Hinds. (Illus.). 24p. (J). (gr. k-3). 1996. 5.50 (0-307-11439-2, Golden Pr) Western Pub.

What I Want to Be When They Grow Up: The First Collection of Committed. Michael Fry. (Illus.). 128p. (Orig.). 1996. pap. 9.95 (0-8362-1308-4) Andrews & McMeel.

What I Wear. Heidi Goennel. LC 95-60580. (Illus.). 12p. (J). (ps). 1995. pap. 3.95 (0-688-14147-1, Tambourine Bks) Morrow.

***What I Wish I'd Known Before My Mission.** John Bytheway. LC 96-34139. 1996. pap. write for info. (1-57345-207-6) Deseret Bk.

What I Wish I'd Known in High School: A Crash Course in Teenage Survival. John Bytheway. LC 94-29540. x, 162p. (Orig.). (YA). (gr. 10-12). 1994. pap. 10.95 (0-87579-921-3) Deseret Bk.

What I Wish I'd Known in High School: The Second Semester. John Bytheway. LC 95-36686. 145p. (Orig.). (YA). (gr. 10-12). 1995. pap. 10.95 (1-57345-095-2) Deseret Bk.

What If. LC 85-80646. (Illus.). 672p. (Orig.). 1985. pap. 13.95 (0-935541-00-4) N C Hinds Pub.

What If? A. H. Benjamin. (Illus.). 32p. (J). (ps). 1996. 14.95 (1-888444-00-2) Little Tiger.

***What If?** A. H. Benjamin. 1997. pap. text ed. 5.95 (1-888444-14-2) Little Tiger.

What If. Charles Quivey. 191p. 1994. 16.00 (0-9641135-0-3) C Quivey.

What If. Peter Utton. LC 93-38511. (Illus.). 32p. (J). (gr. 3 up). 1994. lib. bdg. 18.60 (0-8368-1090-2) Gareth Stevens Inc.

What If... Louisa Von Dessau. 12p. 1992. pap. 2.95 (0-9624542-5-7) Hampshire Group.

What If... A Pondering. Kathleen Kerry. 278p. (Orig.). Date not set. pap. 14.95 (0-9630002-3-3) KMK Assocs.

***What If? Alternate Strategies of World War II.** Harold Deutsch & Dennis Showalter. (Illus.). 256p. 1997. 34.95 (1-883476-07-0) Emperors Pr.

What If... Daily Thoughts for Those Who Worry Too Much. A. J. Chevalier. 380p. 1995. pap. 8.95 (1-55874-342-1, 3421) Health Comm.

What If? Exploring the Paths Not Taken in American History. Ed. by Martin H. McKibbin. (Illus.). 1995. 20.00 (0-9641651-1-2) Sparrowhwk Pr.

What If? Just Wondering Poems. Joy N. Hulme. LC 92-60863. (Illus.). 32p. (J). (ps-1). 1993. 14.95 (1-56397-186-0, Wordsong) Boyds Mills Pr.

What If: Poems, 1969-1987. Andrew Hoyem. (Illus.). 92p. 1987. pap. 10.00 (0-910457-14-X) Arion Pr.

What If? Strange Occurrences. Jannay Valdez. (Illus.). 125p. 1995. write for info. (1-886709-04-1) Outlaw Publ.

What If...? Toward Excellence in Reasoning. Jaakko Hintikka & James Bachman. LC 90-44120. 465p. (C). 1991. pap. text ed. 42.95 (0-87484-964-0, 964) Mayfield Pub.

What If...? Turning Points in American History. 2nd rev. ed. Ed. by Martin H. McKibbin & Kenneth M. Deitch. (Illus.). 300p. 1997. pap. 19.95 (1-878668-59-5) Disc Enter Ltd.

What If? Writing Exercises For Fiction Writers. expanded rev. ed. Anne Bernays & Pamela Painter. 400p. 1995. pap. 16.95 (0-8230-5005-X) Watsn-Guptill.

What If? Writing Exercises for Fiction Writers. rev. ed. Anne Bernays & Pamela Painter. LC 94-9793. (C). 1995. text ed. 15.95 (0-673-99002-8) Addson-Wesley Educ.

What If? Writing Exercises for Fiction Writers. Anne Bernays & Pamela Painter. LC 89-46518. 256p. 1991. reprint ed. pap. 11.00 (0-06-272006-6, Harper Ref) HarpC.

***What If...? 450 Thought-Provoking Questions to Get Teenagers Talking, Laughing & Thinking.** Les Christie. 112p. (YA). 1996. pap. 7.99 (0-310-20776-2) Zondervan.

What If - Sixteen Physics Vignettes Kit. Robert G. Fuller & Dewey I. Dykstra. 1989. text ed. 115.50 incl. vhs (0-471-50934-5) Wiley.

What If Any Should Government's Role Be in Health Care: Selected Essays from the 1992 Harry Singer Foundation Essay Contest. Ed. by Margaret Bohannon-Kaplan. 128p. 1992. pap. 8.00 (0-915915-22-7) Wellington Pubns.

***What If Cruella de Vil Was Your Lunch Lady.** Illus. by Sparky Moore. (J). pap. 3.95 (0-614-19295-1) Disney Pr.

What If Dad Gets Lost at the Zoo? Florence Stevens & Ginette Lamont-Clarke. LC 91-65365. (Illus.). 24p. (J). (ps-2). 1991. 12.95 (0-88776-265-4) Tundra Bks.

What If Dad Gets Lost at the Zoo. Florence Stevens. (J). (ps-3). 1994. pap. 6.95 (0-88776-272-7) Tundra Bks.

What If I Married the Wrong Person? Help & Hope on the Question That at Some Time Every... Janis L. Harris & Richard L. Matteson. LC 96-45772. 256p. 1996. pap. 9.99 (1-55661-664-3) Bethany Hse.

***What If I Owned Everything?** Lauree Burkett & L. Allen Burkett. LC 97-24438. (Illus.). 32p. (J). (ps-2). 1997. 12.99 (0-8499-1509-0) Tommy Nelson.

What If? Instructor's Manual. Jaakko Hintikka & James Bachman. (C). 1991. teacher ed., pap. text ed. write for info. (0-87484-965-9, 965) Mayfield Pub.

What If It Never Stops Raining? Nancy Carlson. (Illus.). 32p. (J). (ps-3). 1994. pap. 4.99 (0-14-050774-4) Puffin Bks.

What If It Never Stops Raining? Nancy Carlson. (Illus.). 32p. (J). (ps-3). 1992. pap. 14.00 (0-670-81775-9) Viking Child Bks.

What if Jesus Had Never Been Born? D. James Kennedy & Jerry Newcombe. LC 93-42372. 288p. 1994. 18.99 (0-7852-8261-0) Nelson.

***What If Jesus Had Never Been Born?** D. James Kennedy & Jerry Newcombe. 288p. 1997. pap. 12.99 (0-7852-7178-3) Nelson.

What If the American Political System Were Different? Ed. by Herbert M. Levine. LC 91-26730. 308p. (gr. 13). 1992. text ed. 63.95 (1-56324-009-2); pap. text ed. 25.95 (1-56324-010-6) M E Sharpe.

What If the Bus Doesn't Come? Florence Stevens & Ginette Lamont-Clarke. LC 90-70135. (Illus.). 24p. (J). (ps-2). 1990. 12.95 (0-88776-251-4); pap. 6.95 (0-88776-259-X) Tundra Bks.

What If the Shark Wears Tennis Shoes? Winifred Morris. LC 89-38150. (Illus.). 32p. (J). (gr. k-3). 1990. lib. bdg. 13.95 (0-689-31587-2, Atheneum Bks Young) S&S Childrens.

What If the Shark Wears Tennis Shoes? Winifred Morris. (Illus.). (J). (ps-3). 1995. pap. 4.95 (0-689-71894-2, Aladdin Paperbacks) S&S Childrens.

***What If There Were No Significance Tests?** Ed. by Lisa L. Harlow & Stanley A. Mulaik. LC 97-20339. (Multivariate Applications Ser.). 375p. 1997. write for info. (0-8058-2634-3) L Erlbaum Assocs.

What If They Come for You? Arrest, Trial, Prison. Helen Maxwell & Connor Polk. (Illus.). 139p. (Orig.). 1996. per., pap. 15.00 (0-9652767-0-8) Raton Camp.

***What If They Gave a Crisis & Nobody Came? Interpreting International Crises.** Ron Hirschbein. 1997. text ed. write for info. (0-275-96043-9, Praeger Pubs) Greenwood.

What If You Could Unscramble an Egg? Robert Ehrlich. (Illus.). 250p. (C). 1996. 25.95 (0-8135-2254-4) Rutgers U Pr.

What If You Remembered Who You Are? Susan Buckley. LC 95-80367. 148p. 1998. pap. 12.95 (1-885221-16-9) BookPartners.

What If...Themes. Kenneth Craycraft & Laverne Warner. 144p. teacher ed. 13.99 (0-86653-717-1, GA1434) Good Apple.

What in Blazes. Glenhall Taylor. 1980. pap. 1.75 (0-686-37155-0) Eldridge Pub.

What in Sam Hill? (Kaleidoscope Ser.: Set B). 1993. 2.95 (0-88336-280-5) New Readers.

What in the Word? Origins of Words Dealing with People & Places. David Muschell. LC 95-42685. 216p. (Orig.). 1996. pap. 14.95 (1-881117-14-6, PE1596) McGuinn & McGuire.

***What in the World?** (Whizz Bang Bumper Bk.). (J). Date not set. text ed. write for info. (0-582-19329-X, Pub. by Longman UK) Longman.

***What in the World?** Eve Merriam. LC 96-42346. (Illus.). (J). write for info. (0-694-01036-7) HarpC Child Bks.

What in the World?! Exploring Global Issues. Bowers & Godfrey. (C). 1994. pap. text ed. 18.00 (0-13-180613-0) P-H.

What in the World Are We Going to Have for Dinner? Cookbook. rev. ed. Sarah E. Drummond. LC 88-82586. (Illus.). 192p. 1989. 11.95 (0-9621600-0-8) Essedee Enterprises.

What in the World Is a Homophone? Leslie Presson. 192p. (J). (gr. 3-7). 1996. 10.95 (0-8120-6585-9) Barron.

What in the World is God Doing? The Essentials of Global Missions. 3rd ed. C. Gordon Olson. (Illus.). 320p. 1994. pap. text ed. 11.95 (0-9624850-2-0) Global Gospel Pubs.

What in the World Is Going On? Pete DuPont. (Excellence in Education Ser.). 15p. (Orig.). 1992. pap. text ed. 3.00 (1-878802-03-8) J M Ashbrook Ctr Pub Affairs.

What in the World Is Going On? British Television & Global Affairs. Adrian Cleasby. 1995. pap. 7.95 (0-614-11425-X, Pub. by Oxfam UK) Humanities.

What in the World is Going On? British Television & Global Affairs. Adrian Cleasby. (Oxfam Research Discussion Papers). (C). 1995. pap. 7.95 (0-9525050-0-2) Humanities.

What in the World Is Going on Here? Coburn Tuller. LC 94-96508. 336p. (Orig.). 1995. pap. 17.50 (1-886322-17-1) Butterfly MO.

What in the World is Rolfing? Ida P. Rolf. 1975. pap. 4.00 (0-930422-05-8) Dennis-Landman.

What in the World Will Happen Next? Ivor C. Powell. LC 85-7579. 176p. 1985. pap. 7.99 (0-8254-3524-2) Kregel.

What Infants Know: The New Cognitive Science of Early Development. Jacques A. Mehler. LC 93-10147. 240p. 1994. pap. 21.95 (1-55786-370-9) Blackwell Pubs.

What Investing Is All About. 4th ed. John Barnes. (C). 1990. pap. 22.95 (0-538-70091-2, HM55DB) S-W Pub.

***What Investors Want to Know.** Maryland Public Television Staff. Date not set. write for info. (0-688-06383-7) Morrow.

***What IRS Doesn't Want You to Know.** Martin Kaplan. Date not set. pap. 3.99 (0-517-17827-3) Random Hse Value.

What Is A. A.? 6p. 1980. pap. 0.25 (0-89486-109-3, 1445) Hazelden.

What Is a Bellybutton? First Questions & Answers about the Human Body. Time Life Books Editors. Ed. by Neil Kagan. (Illus.). 48p. (J). (gr. k-2). 1993. 14.95 (0-7835-0854-9) Time-Life.

What Is a Bellybutton? First Questions & Answers about the Human Body. Time Life Books Editors. Ed. by Neil Kagan. (Library of First Questions & Answers). (Illus.). 48p. (J). (ps). 1993. lib. bdg. write for info. (0-7835-0855-7) Time-Life.

***What Is a Biome?** Bobbie Kalman. (Science of Living Things Ser.). (Illus.). 32p. (J). 1997. lib. bdg. 18.64 (0-86505-875-X) Crabtree Pub Co.

***What Is a Biome?** Bobbie Kalman. (Science of Living Things Ser.). (Illus.). 32p. (J). 1997. pap. 5.95 (0-86505-887-3) Crabtree Pub Co.

What Is a Bird? Ron Hirschi. (Illus.). (J). (ps-4). 1987. 10.95 (0-8027-6720-6); lib. bdg. 11.85 (0-8027-6721-4) Walker & Co.

What Is a Bird? Robert Snedden. (Illus.). 32p. (J). (gr. 2-5). 1993. 13.95 (0-87156-539-0) Sierra Club Childrens.

***What Is a Bird?** Robert Snedden. (Illus.). 32p. (J). (gr. 2-5). 1997. pap. 6.95 (0-87156-922-1) Sierra Club Childrens.

What Is a Bishop? Alexey Young. 16p. (Orig.). 1987. pap. 1.50 (0-912927-25-9, X024) St John Kronstadt.

***What Is a Book? Thoughts about Writing.** Dale Warren. 298p. Date not set. 20.95 (0-8369-2875-X) Ayer.

What Is a California Gray Whale? Jack A. Graves. (Illus.). 48p. (J). (gr. 1-4). 1991. pap. 4.95 (0-929526-13-9) Double B Pubns.

What Is a California Sea Otter? rev. ed. Jack A. Graves. (Illus.). (J). (gr. 3 up). 1996. pap. 4.95 (0-910286-61-2) Boxwood.

What Is a Case? Exploring the Foundations of Social Inquiry. Ed. by Charles C. Ragin & Howard S. Becker. (Illus.). 240p. (C). 1992. pap. text ed. 17.95 (0-521-42188-8) Cambridge U Pr.

What Is a Case? Exploring the Foundations of Social Inquiry. Ed. by Charles C. Ragin & Howard S. Becker. (Illus.). 240p. (C). 1992. text ed. 65.00 (0-521-42050-4) Cambridge U Pr.

What Is a Cat? Ron Hirschi. (Illus.). 32p. (J). (gr. 1-3). 1991. 13.95 (0-8027-8122-5); lib. bdg. 14.85 (0-8027-8123-3) Walker & Co.

***What Is a Christian?** John T. Ferrier. 64p. Date not set. pap. text ed. 6.00 (0-900235-00-4) Order Of The Cross.

What Is a Christian? Carolyn Nystrom. (Children's Bible Basics Ser.). (J). (ps). 1992. text ed. 6.99 (0-8024-7854-9) Moody.

What Is a Church: The Dilemma of the Parachurch. Center for Law & Religious Freedom Staff. 73p. (Orig.). (C). 1979. pap. text ed. 3.00 (0-944561-00-4) Chr Legal.

What Is a City: A Multi-Media Guide on Urban Living. Ed. by Rose Moorachian. 1969. 2.00 (0-89073-016-4) Boston Public Lib.

What Is a City: Young People Reply. Ed. by Ruth M. Hayes. (Illus.). 1969. 1.00 (0-89073-017-2) Boston Public Lib.

What Is a Classic? T. S. Eliot. LC 74-4089. (Studies in T. S. Eliot: No. 11). 1974. lib. bdg. 75.00 (0-8383-2059-7) M S G Haskell Hse.

What Is a Family? Gretchen Super. (Your Family Album Ser.). (Illus.). 56p. (J). (gr. k-3). 1991. lib. bdg. 15.98 (0-8050-3441-2) TFC Bks NY.

What Is a Family. Gretchen Super. 1997. pap. 4.95 (0-8167-2472-5) Troll Communs.

What Is a Family? Edith Schaeffer. 240p. (gr. 10). 1993. reprint ed. pap. 12.99 (0-8010-8365-6, Ravens Ridge) Baker Bks.

***What Is a Family?, Vol. 1.** Super. 1991. 15.98 (0-941477-63-0) TFC Bks NY.

What Is a Feast? Josef Pieper. 66p. (C). 1987. lib. bdg. 16.00 (0-921075-04-9) N Waterloo Acad Pr.

What Is a Feeling? David Kreuger. (Let's Talk about Feelings Ser.). (Illus.). 32p. (J). (ps-3). 1993. pap. 6.95 (0-943990-75-0); lib. bdg. 16.95 (0-943990-76-9) Parenting Pr.

What Is a Fish? David Eastman. LC 81-11373. (Now I Know Ser.). (Illus.). 32p. (J). (gr. k-2). 1982. pap. 3.50 (0-89375-661-X); lib. bdg. 12.95 (0-89375-660-1) Troll Communs.

What Is a Fish? Robert Snedden. LC 93-6495. (Illus.). 32p. (J). (gr. 2-5). 1993. 13.95 (0-87156-545-5) Sierra Club Childrens.

***What Is a Fish?** Robert Snedden. (Illus.). 32p. (J). (gr. 2-5). 1997. pap. 6.95 (0-87156-924-8) Sierra Club Childrens.

What is a Fossil? Meish Goldish. (Real Readers Ser.: Level Green). (Illus.). 32p. (J). (gr. 1-4). 1989. pap. 4.95 (0-8114-6734-1); lib. bdg. 21.40 (0-8172-3535-3) Raintree Steck-V.

What Is a Horoscope? J. I. Cox. 166p. 1985. 13.50 (0-86690-238-4, C2332-014) Am Fed Astrologers.

What Is a Horse? Ron Hirschi. (Illus.). 32p. (J). (ps-4). 1989. 11.95 (0-8027-6876-8); lib. bdg. 12.85 (0-8027-6877-6) Walker & Co.

What Is a Human Being? A Heideggerian View. Frederick A. Olafson. (Modern European Philosophy Ser.). 304p. (C). 1995. text ed. 59.95 (0-521-47395-0); pap. text ed. 19.95 (0-521-47937-1) Cambridge U Pr.

***What Is a Jew?** Kertzer. 1996. pap. 11.00 (0-684-84298-X) S&S Trade.

What Is a Jew? 5th rev. ed. Morris N. Kertzer. LC 92-35518. 336p. 1993. pap. 10.00 (0-02-033282-3) Macmillan.

What Is a Jewish Joke? An Excursion into Jewish Humor. Henry Eilbert. LC 90-22585. 304p. 1993. pap. 24.95 (0-87668-217-4) Aronson.

What Is a Law of Nature? D. M. Armstrong. (Studies in Philosophy). 190p. 1985. pap. 19.95 (0-521-31481-X) Cambridge U Pr.

***What Is a Life Cycle?** Bobbie Kalman. (Science of Living Things Ser.). (Illus.). 32p. (J). 1997. lib. bdg. 18.64 (0-86505-874-1) Crabtree Pub Co.

***What Is a Life Cycle?** Bobbie Kalman. (Science of Living Things Ser.). (Illus.). 32p. (J). 1997. pap. 5.95 (0-86505-886-5) Crabtree Pub Co.

What Is a Life Worth? Ethical Considerations in Healthcare Delivery. rev. ed. J. Hall. 212p. (C). 1995. 53.95 (0-933915-54-3) CA College Health Sci.

What Is a Logical System? Ed. by D. M. Gabbay. (Studies in Logic & Computation: No. 4). 464p. 1995. text ed. 85.00 (0-19-853859-6) OUP.

***What Is a Mammal?** Bobbie Kalman. (Science of Living Things Ser.). (Illus.). 32p. (J). 1997. lib. bdg. 18.64 (0-86505-878-4) Crabtree Pub Co.

***What Is a Mammal?** Bobbie Kalman. (Science of Living Things Ser.). (Illus.). 32p. (J). 1997. pap. 5.95 (0-86505-890-3) Crabtree Pub Co.

What Is a Mammal? Robert Snedden. LC 93-26145. (Illus.). 32p. (J). (gr. 2-5). 1994. 14.95 (0-87156-468-8) Sierra Club Childrens.

***What Is a Mammal?** Robert Snedden. (Illus.). 32p. (J). (gr. 2-5). 1997. pap. 6.95 (0-87156-929-9) Sierra Club Childrens.

What Is a New Mexico Santo? Eluid L. Martinez & James C. Smith, Jr. LC 77-78519. (Illus.). 1978. pap. 2.95 (0-913270-76-8) Sunstone Pr.

What Is a Patent? 2nd ed. 14p. 1982. pap. 1.00 (0-685-11099-0, 537-0021) Amer Bar Assn.

What Is a Pentecostal? Fred Smolchuck. 16p. 1996. pap. 0.99 (0-88243-849-2) Gospel Pub.

What Is a Person? Ed. by Michael Goodman. LC 86-21487. (Contemporary Issues in Biomedicine, Ethics, & Society Ser.). 320p. 1988. 39.50 (0-89603-117-9) Humana.

What Is a Person? Brain Function & Moral Status. James W. Walters. LC 96-9991. 1997. 23.95 (0-252-02278-5) U of Ill Pr.

W

What Is a Person? The Concept & the Implications for Ethics. Kevin Doran. LC 89-33546. (Studies in Health & Human Services: Vol. 14). 192p. 1989. lib. bdg. 79.95 (*0-88946-140-6*) E Mellen.

What Is a Poet? Ed. by Hank Lazer. LC 86-19234. 296p. 1987. text ed. 32.50 (*0-8173-0325-1*); pap. text ed. 21.50 (*0-8173-0326-X*) U of Ala Pr.

***What Is a Prayer Room?** Terry Teykl. 49p. (Orig.). 1997. 6.95 (*1-57892-023-X*) Prayer Pt Pr.

What Is a Reptile? Susan Kuchalla. LC 81-11364. (Now I Know Ser.). (Illus.). 32p. (J). (gr. k-2). 1982. pap. 3.50 (*0-89375-673-3*); lib. bdg. 12.95 (*0-89375-672-5*) Troll Communs.

What Is a Reptile? Robert Snedden. LC 94-14422. (Illus.). 32p. (J). (gr. 2-5). 1995. 14.95 (*0-87156-493-9*) Sierra Club Childrens.

***What Is a Reptile?** Robert Snedden. (Illus.). 32p. (J). (gr. 2-5). 1997. pap. 6.95 (*0-87156-930-2*) Sierra Club Childrens.

What Is a Scientist? Memorial Issue for Professor Oscar Bodansky. Ed. by Stacey B. Day. (Journal: Biosciences Communications: Vol. 4, No. 5). 1978. pap. 15.25 (*3-8055-2967-8*) S Karger.

What Is a Share of Stock. Jeffrey B. Little & Lucien Rhodes. 1977. pap. 2.95 (*0-8306-3001-5*, 30001, Liberty Hse) TAB Bks.

What is a Shooting Star? Isaac Asimov. LC 90-25922. (Ask Isaac Asimov Ser.). (Illus.). 24p. (J). (gr. 2-3). 1991. lib. bdg. 17.27 (*0-8368-0436-8*) Gareth Stevens Inc.

What Is a Spiritual Master? Omraam M. Aivanhov. (Izvor Collection: Vol. 207). 185p. 1989. pap. 7.95 (*2-85566-300-8*, Pub. by Prosveta FR) Prosveta USA.

What Is a Step? Linda D. Marshall. LC 91-67511. (Illus.). 48p. (Orig.). (J). (ps-5). 1992. pap. 10.00 (*1-879289-00-8*) Native Sun Pubs.

What Is a Wall, After All? Judy Allen. LC 92-54623. (Read & Wonder Bks.). (Illus.). 32p. (J). (ps up). 1993. 14.95 (*1-56402-218-8*) Candlewick Pr.

What Is a Wall, after All? Judy Allen. LC 92-54623. (Read & Wonder Bks.). (J). 1995. pap. 5.99 (*1-56402-492-X*) Candlewick Pr.

What Is Abstraction? Andrew Benjamin. (What Is? Ser.). 68p. 1996. pap. 16.95 (*1-85490-434-5*) Academy Ed UK.

What Is Acid Rain? Isaac Asimov. LC 91-50362. (Ask Isaac Asimov Ser.). (Illus.). 24p. (J). (gr. 2-3). 1992. lib. bdg. 17.27 (*0-8368-0741-3*) Gareth Stevens Inc.

What Is AIDS? Anna Forbes. LC 96-5879. (AIDS Awareness Library). (Illus.). 24p. (J). (gr. k-4). 1996. lib. bdg. 10.46 (*0-8239-2368-1*, PowerKids) Rosen Group.

What Is America Eating? Proceedings of a Symposium. National Research Council U. S. Staff. LC 85-62945. 183p. reprint ed. pap. 52.20 (*0-7837-2088-2*, 2042364) Bks Demand.

What Is an American? Abraham Lincoln & "Multiculturalism" Richard N. Current. (Klement Lecture Ser.: No. 2). 25p. (C). 1993. pap. 5.00 (*0-87462-326-X*) Marquette.

What Is an Amphibian? Robert Snedden. LC 93-11619. (Illus.). 32p. (J). (gr. 2-5). 1994. 14.95 (*0-87156-469-6*) Sierra Club Childrens.

***What Is an Amphibian?** Robert Snedden. (Illus.). 32p. (J). (gr. 2-5). 1997. pap. 6.95 (*0-87156-928-0*) Sierra Club Childrens.

What Is an Angel Doing Here? Ed. by Pat Rodegast & Judith Stanton. LC 94-16006. (Emmanuel's Bks.: 3). 272p. 1994. pap. 12.95 (*0-553-37412-5*) Bantam.

What Is an Animal? Ed. by T. M. Ingold. (One World Archaeology Ser.). 208p. (C). 1994. pap. 16.95 (*0-415-09556-5*, B3907) Routledge.

What Is an Animal? Ed. by Tim Ingold. LC 87-29005. 208p. (C). 1988. text ed. 59.95 (*0-04-445012-5*) Routledge Chapman & Hall.

What Is an Astrology Chart? Spiritual View. Gayle Bachicha. LC 95-21961. 1995. pap. text ed. write for info. (*1-885084-12-9*) Tickerwick.

What Is an Eclipse? Isaac Asimov. LC 90-26062. (Ask Isaac Asimov Ser.). (Illus.). 24p. (J). (gr. 2-3). 1991. lib. bdg. 17.27 (*0-8368-0440-6*) Gareth Stevens Inc.

What Is an Emotion? Classic Readings in Philosophical Psychology. Ed. by Cheshire Calhoun & Robert C. Solomon. 368p. 1984. pap. 18.95 (*0-19-503304-3*) OUP.

What Is an Evangelical? D. Martyn Lloyd-Jones. 91p. 1993. pap. 3.99 (*0-85151-626-2*) Banner of Truth.

What Is an Exchange? Automation & the Regulation of Trading Markets. Ruben Lee. 400p. 1997. 60.00 (*0-19-828840-9*) OUP.

What Is an Insect? Robert Snedden. LC 92-35060. (Illus.). 32p. (J). (gr. 2-5). 1993. 13.95 (*0-87156-540-4*) Sierra Club Childrens.

***What Is an Insect?** Robert Snedden. (Illus.). 32p. (J). (gr. 2-5). 1997. pap. 6.95 (*0-87156-923-X*) Sierra Club Childrens.

What Is Anarchism? An Introduction. Donald Rooum. 74p. (Orig.). 1992. pap. 3.50 (*0-900384-66-2*) Left Bank.

What Is Anglicanism? Urban T. Holmes, 3rd. LC 81-84715. (Anglican Studies Ser.). 112p. (Orig.). 1982. pap. 7.95 (*0-8192-1295-4*) Morehouse Pub.

What Is Anthroposophy? Otto Frankl-Lundborg. Tr. by Joseph Wetzl. 1977. pap. 3.95 (*0-916786-14-5*, Saint George Pubns) R Steiner Col Pubns.

***What Is Appropriate Care for the Children of Troubled Families.** Harry Nelson. 32p. (Orig.). 1996. pap. write for info. (*1-887748-06-7*) Milbank Memorial.

What Is Archaeology? An Essay on the Nature of Archaeological Research. Paul Courbin. Tr. by Paul Bahn. (Illus.). 224p. 1988. 29.95 (*0-226-11656-5*) U Ch Pr.

What Is Archaeology? An Essay on the Nature of Archaeological Research. Paul Courbin. LC 88-1727. (C). 1990. pap. text ed. 14.95 (*0-226-11657-3*) U Ch Pr.

What Is Architecture? An Essay on Landscapes, Buildings, & Machines. Paul Shepheard. LC 93-30168. (Illus.). 141p. 1994. pap. 9.95 (*0-262-69166-3*) MIT Pr.

What Is Art? Hugh Curtler. (World of Art Ser.). (Illus.). 220p. (Orig.). 1983. pap. text ed. 25.00 (*0-930586-17-4*) Haven Pubns.

What Is Art? Leo Tolstoy. Tr. by Richard Pevear & Larissa Volokhonsky. LC 60-9557. 240p. 1996. pap. 11.95 (*0-14-044642-7*) Penguin.

***What Is Art?** Leo N. Tolstoy. LC 96-77859. 213p. 1996. pap. 9.95 (*0-87220-295-X*, BH39) Hackett Pub.

What Is Art? An Introduction to Painting, Sculpture & Architecture. John E. Canaday. 1980. write for info. (*0-07-554329-X*) Knopf.

What Is Art? And Essays on Art. Len N. Tolstoi. LC 33-5715. 339p. 1959. reprint ed. 39.00 (*0-403-04330-1*) Somerset Pub.

What Is Art? And Essays on Art. Leo Tolstoy. 1988. reprint ed. lib. bdg. 59.00 (*0-7812-0533-6*) Rprt Serv.

What Is Art For? Ellen Dissanayake. LC 89-31648. (Illus.). 266p. 1990. pap. 17.95 (*0-295-97017-0*) U of Wash Pr.

What Is Art History? 2nd ed. Mark Roskill. LC 89-4749. (Illus.). 200p. 1989. pap. 14.95 (*0-87023-675-X*) U of Mass Pr.

What Is Asia to Us? Russia's Asian Heartland Yesterday & Today. Milan Hauner. 288p. (C). 1992. pap. text ed. 22.95 (*0-415-08109-2*, Routledge NY) Routledge.

What Is Asia to Us? Russia's Asian Heartland Yesterday & Today. Milan Hauner. 272p. 1990. text ed. 55.00 (*0-04-445623-9*) Routledge Chapman & Hall.

What Is Astrology? Colin Bennett. 124p. 1981. 12.00 (*0-89540-113-4*, SB-113, Sun Bks) Sun Pub.

What Is Auditory Processing? Susan Bell. 16p. 1993. pap. 14.95 (*0-937857-45-9*, 1545) Speech Bin.

What Is Beautiful? Maryjean W. Avery & David Avery. LC 95-1203. (Illus.). 20p. (J). (ps-2). 1995. 12.95 (*1-883672-27-9*) Tricycle Pr.

***What Is Beauty? New Definitions.** Schefer. 1997. 24.95 (*0-7893-0078-8*) Universe.

What Is Behavioralism? Thoughts on the Crisis in the Social Sciences. W. J. Stankiewicz. 1971. 8.50 (*0-686-09044-6*); 25.00 (*0-686-09045-4*) Girs Pr.

What Is Bendy? Sarah Warbrick. LC 95-41118. (What Is--? Ser.). (J). 1996. lib. bdg. write for info. (*1-57572-049-3*) Rigby Interact Libr.

What Is Bouncy & Stretchy? Sarah Warbrick. LC 95-41112. (What Is--? Ser.). (J). 1996. lib. bdg. write for info. (*1-57572-050-7*) Rigby Interact Libr.

What Is Calculus About? W. W. Sawyer. LC 61-6227. (New Mathematical Library: No. 2). 118p. 1961. pap. 19.00 (*0-88385-602-6*, NML-02) Math Assn.

What Is Called Thinking? Martin Heidegger. Tr. by J. Glenn Gray & Fred D. Wieck. 272p. 1976. pap. 13.00 (*0-06-090528-X*, CN528, PL) HarpC.

What Is Catholicism? An Anglican Responds to the Official Teaching of the Roman Catholic Church. David L. Edwards. 1995. pap. 19.95 (*0-264-67325-5*, Pub. by Mowbray-Cassell UK) Morehouse Pub.

***What Is Changing in Baptismal Practice?** Ed. by G. Lathrop. 1996. pap. 5.95 (*0-8066-2801-4*) Augsburg Fortress.

***What Is Changing in Eucharist Practice?** Ed. by G. Lathrop. 1996. pap. 5.95 (*0-8066-2802-2*) Augsburg Fortress.

What Is Child Abuse? Sharon F. Kissane. 137p. (YA). (gr. 7-12). 1993. pap. 6.95 (*1-57515-025-5*) PPI Pubng.

What Is Christianity? Adolf Von Harnack. LC 86-45209. (Texts in Modern Theology Ser.). 320p. 1986. pap. 24.00 (*0-8006-3201-X*, 1-3201, Fortress Pr) Augsburg Fortress.

What Is Christianity. Adolph Harnack. 1958. 18.00 (*0-8446-2208-7*) Peter Smith.

What Is Christianity? see IVP Booklets

What Is Christmas? Joy Dueland. (Illus.). 9p. 1976. pap. 1.50 (*0-685-43432-X*) Phunn Pubs.

What is Christmas? Illus. by Lillie James. 16p. (J). (ps-2). 1994. 5.95 (*0-694-00481-2*, Festival) HarpC Child Bks.

What Is Cinema?, Vol. 1. Andre Bazin. Tr. & Compiled by Hugh Gray. LC 67-18899. 1967. 35.00 (*0-520-00091-9*); pap. 12.00 (*0-520-00092-7*) U CA Pr.

What Is Cinema?, Vol. 2. Andre Bazin. Tr. & Compiled by Hugh Gray. 1971. 35.00 (*0-520-02034-0*); pap. 12.00 (*0-520-02255-6*) U CA Pr.

What Is Civilization? Ananda K. Coomaraswamy. Ed. by Brian Keeble. 194p. (Orig.). 1989. pap. 14.50 (*0-940262-06-1*) Lindisfarne Bks.

What Is Civilization. Maurice Maeterlinck et al. LC 68-57342. (Essay Index Reprint Ser.). 1977. 19.95 (*0-8369-0986-0*) Ayer.

What Is Classicism? Michael Greenhalgh. (What Is? Ser.). (Illus.). 72p. (Orig.). 1990. pap. 16.00 (*0-85670-970-0*) Academy Ed UK.

What Is Classicism? Michael Greenhalgh. (Illus.). 72p. (Orig.). 1990. pap. 16.00 (*0-312-04925-0*) St Martin.

What Is Clinical Psychology? 2nd ed. Ed. by John S. Marzillier & John Hall. (Illus.). 368p. 1992. 69.00 (*0-19-262169-6*) OUP.

What Is Cognitive Science? Barbara Von Eckardt. LC 92-10167. (Illus.). 440p. (C). 1992. 50.00 (*0-262-22046-6*, Bradford Bks) MIT Pr.

What is Cognitive Science? Barbara Von Eckardt. (Illus.). 478p. 1995. pap. 24.50 (*0-262-72023-X*, Bradford Bks) MIT Pr.

What Is Coming: A European Forecast. H. G. Wells. 1996. lib. bdg. 250.99 (*0-8490-5941-0*) Gordon Pr.

What Is Communism. 2nd enl. rev. ed. Alcander Longley. LC 73-8710. (Communal Societies in America Ser.). reprint ed. 55.00 (*0-404-10727-3*) AMS Pr.

What Is Communism & Other Anarchist Essays. J. A. Andrews. Ed. by Bob James. (Illus.). 190p. (Orig.). 1984. pap. 7.95 (*0-949300-00-4*) Left Bank.

What Is Communist Anarchism? Alexander Berkman. 118p. 1992. reprint ed. pap. 6.95 (*0-948984-11-2*, Pub. by Phoenix Pr UK) AK Pr Dist.

What Is Computer Equity? A Trainer's Workshop Guide. Jo Sanders & Mary McGinnis. LC 90-45787. (Computer Equity Ser.). (Illus.). 276p. 1991. ring bd. 19.95 (*0-8108-2367-5*) Scarecrow.

What Is Contemplation? Thomas Merton. (Illus.). 80p. 1981. pap. 9.95 (*0-87243-103-7*) Templegate.

***What Is "Contemporary" Worship?** Ed. by G. Lathrop. 1996. pap. 5.95 (*0-8066-2798-0*) Augsburg Fortress.

What Is Cool? Understanding Black Manhood in America. Marlene Connor. 1995. 20.00 (*0-517-79965-0*, Crown) Crown Pub Group.

What Is Cooperation? James P. Warbasse. 1980. 250.00 (*0-8490-1285-6*) Gordon Pr.

What Is Cost of Quality All About? Terry D. Stuck. 50p. 1993. pap. 14.95 (*1-883999-00-6*) Pressmark Intl.

What Is Counselling? The Promise & Problem of the Talking Therapies. Colin Feltham. 192p. 1995. 39.95 (*0-8039-8856-7*); pap. 18.95 (*0-8039-8857-5*) Sage.

What Is Creation Science. rev. ed. Henry M. Morris. LC 82-70114. (Illus.). 336p. 1987. pap. 11.95 (*0-89051-081-4*) Master Bks.

What Is Criticism? Ed. by Paul Hernadi. LC 80-8096. 347p. 1981. reprint ed. pap. 98.90 (*0-7837-6100-7*, 2059146) Bks Demand.

What Is Cultural Studies? A Reader. Ed. by John Storey. 234p. 1996. text ed. 49.95 (*0-340-65239-X*, Pub. by E Arnld UK); text ed. 18.95 (*0-340-65240-3*, Pub. by E Arnld UK) St Martin.

What Is Dance? Readings in Theory & Criticism. Roger Copeland & Marshall Cohen. (Illus.). 600p. 1983. pap. 17.95 (*0-19-503197-0*) OUP.

***What Is Death?** Etan Boritzer. (What Is? Ser.). (Illus.). 32p. (J). (gr. k-5). 1997. 14.95 (*0-9637597-4-4*) V Lane Bks.

***What Is Death?** Etan Boritzer. (What Is? Ser.). (Illus.). 32p. (J). (gr. k-5). 1997. pap. 5.95 (*0-9637597-5-2*) V Lane Bks.

What is Deconstruction? Christopher Norris & Andrew Benjamin. (Academy Editions Ser.). (Illus.). 56p. 1989. pap. 16.00 (*0-312-02711-7*) St Martin.

What Is Deconstruction? Christopher Norris & Andrew Benjamin. (What Is? Ser.). (Illus.). 56p. (Orig.). 1988. pap. 16.00 (*0-85670-961-1*) Academy Ed UK.

***What Is Democracy?** Alain Touraine. LC 96-52121. 1997. text ed. 69.00 (*0-8133-2706-7*) Westview.

***What Is Democracy?** Alain Touraine. LC 96-52121. (C). 1997. pap. text ed. 22.00 (*0-8133-2707-5*) Westview.

What Is Development? Jerry Segal. (Working Papers on Development & the National Interest). 1988. 2.50 (*0-317-01532-X*, DN1) IPPP.

What Is Diabetes? P. P. Foa. 104p. 1988. pap. 8.00 (*1-57235-075-X*) Piccin NY.

What Is Disease? Ed. by James M. Humber & Robert F. Almeder. LC 84-640015. (Biomedical Ethics Reviews Ser.). 372p. 1997. 49.50 (*0-89603-352-X*) Humana.

What Is Divine Love? James E. Padgett. 1989. pap. 0.50 (*1-887621-16-4*) Found Ch Divine Truth.

What Is Dramaturgy? Ed. by Bert Cardullo. LC 93-2357. (American University Studies: Vol. 20). 272p. (C). 1995. pap. text ed. 29.95 (*0-8204-2177-4*) P Lang Pubng.

What is Easter? Lillie James. (Lift-the-Flap Bk.). (Illus.). 16p. (J). (ps-2). 1994. 5.95 (*0-694-00480-4*, Festival) HarpC Child Bks.

What Is Ecology? 2nd ed. Denis F. Owen. (Illus.). 246p. 1980. pap. 16.95 (*0-19-289140-5*) OUP.

What Is Economics? 3rd rev. ed. James Eggert. LC 92-16627. 225p. (C). 1993. pap. text ed. 24.95 (*1-55934-212-9*) Mayfield Pub.

***What Is Economics?** 4th rev. ed. James Eggert. LC 96-41429. (Illus.). 225p. (C). 1996. pap. text ed. 24.95 (*1-55934-824-0*, 1824) Mayfield Pub.

What Is Economics? Student Study Guide. rev. ed. James Eggert. LC 92-16627. (C). 1993. student ed., pap. text ed. 10.95 (*1-55934-235-8*) Mayfield Pub.

***What Is Economics? Study Guide.** James Eggert & James V. Pinto. 115p. 1996. pap. text ed. write for info. (*1-55934-825-9*, 1825) Mayfield Pub.

What Is Effective in Psychoanalytic Therapy: The Move from Interpretation to Relation. William W. Meissner. LC 90-14509. 216p. 1991. 32.50 (*0-87668-572-6*) Aronson.

What Is Election? W. J. Ouweneel. pap. 2.25 (*0-88172-162-X*) Believers Bkshelf.

What Is Electricity? Eileen L. Corcoran & John Pavka. (Science Ser.). 32p. 1966. pap. 1.00 (*0-88323-080-1*, 177) Pendergrass Pub.

What Is Electricity. John T. Trowbridge. Ed. by I. Bernard Cohen. LC 79-8000. (Three Centuries of Science in America Ser.). (Illus.). 1980. reprint ed. lib. bdg. 30.95 (*0-405-12588-7*) Ayer.

What Is English? Peter Elbow. LC 90-44931. viii, 271p. 1990. pap. 15.50 (*0-87352-382-2*, W415P); lib. bdg. 37.50 (*0-87352-381-4*, W415C) Modern Lang.

What is English Teaching? Chris Davies. 160p. 1996. pap. 24.95 (*0-335-19478-8*, Open Univ Pr) Taylor & Francis.

What Is Enlightenment? Eighteenth-Century Answers & Twentieth-Century Questions. Ed. by James Schmidt. LC 95-46975. (Philosophical Tradition Ser.: Vol. 7). 500p. (C). 1996. pap. 24.95 (*0-520-20226-0*); text ed. 50.00 (*0-520-20225-2*) U CA Pr.

What Is Enlightenment? Exploring the Goal of the Spiritual Path. Ed. by John White. 256p. 1995. reprint ed. pap. 10.95 (*1-55778-726-3*) Paragon Hse.

What Is Eternal Life? W. J. Ouweneel. pap. 2.50 (*0-88172-149-2*) Believers Bkshelf.

What Is Europe? Rose. 384p. (C). 1996. text ed. 35.95 (*0-673-98087-1*) Addson-Wesley Educ.

***What Is Fair.** James H. Clinton. 1997. 19.95 (*0-614-29423-1*); pap. 11.95 (*0-614-29424-X*) La State U Pr.

***What Is Fair?** James H. Clinton. 64p. 1997. text ed. 19.95 (*0-8071-2195-9*) La State U Pr.

***What Is Fair?** James H. Clinton. 64p. 1997. pap. 11.95 (*0-8071-2196-7*) La State U Pr.

What Is Faith? J. Gresham Machen. 264p. 1991. pap. text ed. 9.99 (*0-85151-594-0*) Banner of Truth.

What Is Faith? Virginia Mueller. Ed. by Shirley Beegle. (Happy Day Bks.). (Illus.). 24p. (Orig.). (J). (ps-3). 1994. reprint ed. pap. 1.99 (*0-7847-0265-9*, 04215) Standard Pub.

What Is Family? Jaber F. Gubrium & James A. Holstein. 178p. (C). 1990. pap. text ed. 25.95 (*0-87484-878-4*, 878) Mayfield Pub.

***What Is Feng Shui?** Evelyn Lip. (What Is? Ser.: Vol. VI). (Illus.). 64p. (Orig.). 1997. pap. 16.95 (*1-85490-491-4*) Academy Ed UK.

***What Is Fiber Channel?** 3rd rev. ed. Jan Dedek. (Illus.). 1996. pap. 9.50 (*0-9637439-5-3*) Ancot Corp.

***What Is Focusing?** Edwin M. McMahon & Peter A. Campbell. 12p. 1996. 1.25 (*1-55612-500-3*, LL1500) Sheed & Ward MO.

What Is Found There: Notebooks On Poetry & Politics. Adrienne Rich. LC 93-9912. 1993. 20.00 (*0-393-03565-4*) Norton.

What Is Found There? Notebooks on Poetry & Politics. Adrienne Rich. 320p. 1994. pap. 11.00 (*0-393-31246-1*) Norton.

What Is Freedom of Choice? Harry Settanni. 50p. (Orig.). (C). 1992. pap. text ed. 8.95 (*0-8191-8674-0*) U Pr of Amer.

What Is Furlough? Jim Lo. (Illus.). 28p. (Orig.). (J). (gr. 3-5). Date not set. pap. 3.25 (*0-89827-060-X*, BKF99) Wesleyan Pub Hse.

What Is G. A.? 4p. 1985. 0.25 (*0-89486-266-9*) Hazelden.

What Is God? Etan Boritzer. (Illus.). 32p. (Orig.). (J). (gr. 1-7). 1990. 14.95 (*0-920668-89-5*); pap. 5.95 (*0-920668-88-7*) Firefly Bks Ltd.

What Is God? Joseph Girzone. (Illus.). 60p. 1996. 15.95 (*0-385-48261-2*) Doubleday.

***What Is God?** Joseph F. Girzone. (Illus.). 1996. 15.95 (*0-614-20415-1*) Doubleday.

What Is God? How to Think about the Divine. John F. Haught. 160p. (Orig.). 1986. pap. 11.95 (*0-8091-2754-7*) Paulist Pr.

What Is God? The Selected Essays of Richard LaCroix. Ed. by Kenneth G. Lucey. LC 93-20193. 200p. (C). 1993. Alk. paper. 35.95 (*0-87975-739-6*) Prometheus Bks.

What Is God Like? Mary Erickson. (Illus.). 32p. (J). (gr. k-3). 1990. 9.99 (*1-55513-273-1*) Chariot Victor.

What Is God Like? D. James Kennedy. LC 94-179918. (Life-Transforming Truths from a Never-Changing God Ser.). 192p. (Orig.). (gr. 10). 1995. pap. 9.99 (*0-8007-5558-8*) Revell.

What Is God Like? Lee O. Rohwer. (Illus.). 64p. (Orig.). (J). (gr. k-4). 1986. pap. 5.95 (*0-9617788-0-6*) Damon Pub.

What Is God Like? James V. Schall. 250p. (Orig.). 1992. pap. text ed. 14.95 (*0-8146-5020-1*, M Glazier) Liturgical Pr.

What is God Like? Joan C. Webb. LC 94-67875. (Illus.). 112p. (Orig.). (J). 1995. pap. 6.99 (*0-7847-0294-2*, 02754) Standard Pub.

What Is God Like? 2nd rev. ed. Lee O. Rohwer. (Illus.). 68p. (Orig.). (YA). (gr. 8 up). 1989. reprint ed. pap. 7.95 (*0-9617788-1-4*) Damon Pub.

What Is God Like, 4 vols., Set. Marie-Agnes Gaudrat. (Illus.). 10p. (J). 1992. 18.95 (*0-8146-2139-2*) Liturgical Pr.

***What Is God Like? The Biblical God for Contemporary Man.** Robert H. Lescelius. (Roadbuilding for Revival Ser.). 26p. (Orig.). 1996. pap. 1.99 (*1-56632-100-X*) Revival Lit.

What Is God Saying to America Today? Al Thomas. 80p. (Orig.). 1995. pap. 10.00 (*1-56167-200-9*) Am Literary Pr.

What Is Going On? Understanding the Powerful Evangelism of Pentecostal Churches. Vincent M. Walsh. LC 95-76638. 194p. 1995. pap. 8.00 (*0-943374-23-5*) Key of David.

What Is Good. Hilda Raz. 64p. (Orig.). 1988. pap. 5.95 (*0-939395-09-6*) Thorntree Pr.

What Is Good English? And Other Essays. Harry T. Peck. LC 72-39122. (Essay Index Reprint Ser.). 1977. reprint ed. 21.95 (*0-8369-2710-9*) Ayer.

What Is Good Instruction Now? Library Instruction in the 90s. Ed. by Linda Shirato. (Library Orientation Ser.: No. 23). 184p. 1993. pap. 35.00 (*0-87650-327-X*) Pierian.

What Is Good Music? William J. Henderson. LC 72-2485. (Select Bibliographies Reprint Ser.). 1977. reprint ed. 18.95 (*0-8369-6857-3*) Ayer.

What Is Halloween? Harriet Ziefert. (Lift-the-Flap Bk.). (Illus.). 16p. (J). (ps). 1992. 5.95 (*0-694-00381-6*, Festival) HarpC Child Bks.

What Is Hanukkah? Harriet Ziefert. (Illus.). 16p. (J). (ps-2). 1994. 5.95 (*0-694-00483-9*, Festival) HarpC Child Bks.

What Is Happening in the U. S. S. R.? Gorbachev & the Crisis of Stalinism. International Committee of the Fourth International Staff. 28p. 1987. pap. 2.00 (*0-929087-19-4*) Labor Pubns Inc.

What Is Happening to Our Children? How to Raise Them Right. Mardel E. Gustafson. Ed. by Diane Parker. LC 93-11322. 75p. 1993. pap. 7.95 (*1-56875-044-7*) R & E Pubs.

What Is Heaven Like? William W. Orr. (Bible Answers Ser.). 48p. reprint ed. pap. 3.50 (*0-944412-02-5*) Glad Tid.

W

An Asterisk (*) at the beginning of an entry indicates that the title is appearing in BIP for the first time.

***What Is Heaven Like? The Kingdom As Seen in the Beatitudes.** Morton Kelsey. LC 96-46246. (Today's Issues Ser.). 96p. (Orig.). 1997. pap. 6.95 (*1-56548-091-0*) New City.

What Is Hiding? Mario Gamboli. LC 91-70422. (Illus.). 10p. (J). (ps). 1991. bds. 3.95 (*1-878093-71-1*) Boyds Mills Pr.

What Is His Name. Ahmed Deedat. Ed. by Al I. Obaba. (Illus.). 49p. (Orig.) (YA). 1991. pap. text ed. 4.00 (*0-916157-74-1*) African Islam Miss Pubns.

What Is Historical Materialism? A Reader: A Reader. (C). 1997. pap. 33.99 (*1-899438-18-1*, Pub. by Porcupine Bks UK) Humanities.

What Is History. Edward H. Carr. 1967. pap. 7.16 (*0-394-70391-X*, V391, Vin) Random.

What Is History? & Other Late Unpublished Writings: The Collected Works of Eric Voegelin, Vol. 28. Eric Voegelin. Ed. by Thomas A. Hollweck & Paul Caringella. LC 90-35657. (Collected Works of Eric Voegelin). 280p. 1990. text ed. 35.00 (*0-8071-1603-3*) La State U Pr.

What Is History Teaching? Language, Ideas, & Meaning in Learning about the Past. Chris Husbands. LC 95-47333. 128p. (C). 1996. 85.00 (*0-335-19639-X*, Open Univ Pr); pap. 23.00 (*0-335-19638-1*, Open Univ Pr) Taylor & Francis.

What Is Household Hazardous Material? Anna H. Spitz & Ann M. Wolf. (Environmental Ser.). (Illus.). 132p. (Orig.). (J). (gr. 6-8). 1996. pap. text ed. 13.50 (*0-9651084-0-6*) Tyris Environ.

What Is Hypnosis? Current Theories & Research. Ed. by Peter L. Naish. 224p. 1987. 95.00 (*0-335-15338-0*, Open Univ Pr); pap. 39.00 (*0-335-15337-2*, Open Univ Pr) Taylor & Francis.

What Is Identity? C. J. Williams. 232p. 1990. 75.00 (*0-19-824808-3*) OUP.

What Is in the Closet? Ruth Tilden. (J). 1995. 9.95 (*0-689-80267-6*, Aladdin Paperbacks) S&S Childrens.

***What Is Information Warfare? The Struggle over Information Systems.** 1997. lib. bdg. 250.99 (*0-8490-6185-7*) Gordon Pr.

What Is Integrability? Ed. by V. E. Zakharov et al. (Nonlinear Dynamics Ser.). (Illus.). 344p. 1991. 93.95 (*0-387-51964-5*) Spr-Verlag.

What Is Intelligence? Ed. by Jean Khalfa. (Darwin College Lectures). (Illus.). 208p. (C). 1994. 33.95 (*0-521-43307-X*) Cambridge U Pr.

What Is Intelligence? Ed. by Jean Khalfa. (Darwin College Lectures). (Illus.). 213p. 1996. pap. text ed. 19.95 (*0-521-56685-1*) Cambridge U Pr.

What Is Intelligence? Contemporary Viewpoints on Its Nature & Definition. Robert J. Sternberg & Douglas K. Detterman. 176p. 1986. pap. 39.50 (*0-89391-389-8*) Ablex Pub.

What Is Intelligence? Contemporary Viewpoints on Its Nature & Definition. Ed. by Robert J. Sternberg & Douglas K. Detterman. 176p. 1986. text ed. 73.25 (*0-89391-373-1*) Ablex Pub.

What Is International Law & How Do We Tell It When We See It: Nulla Poena Sine Lege in English Criminal Law. R. J. Jennings & J. R. Spencer. (Cambridge-Tilburg Law Lectures: No. 3). 90p. pap. 16.00 (*90-6544-107-7*) Kluwer Ac.

What Is Investment Casting? (Illus.). 18p. 1990. 5.50 (*1-56061-047-6*, ICI-B-27) ICI Dallas.

What Is Iridology? Bernard Jensen. 1984. pap. 9.95 (*0-932615-22-8*) B Jensen.

What Is, Is: Encouraging Yourself to Accept What You Won't Change & Change What You Won't Accept. Lewis E. Losoncy & Diane G. Losoncy. 175p. (Orig.). 1996. pap. 14.95 (*1-57444-040-3*) St Lucie Pr.

What Is Islam? F. R. Ansari. pap. 3.00 (*0-933511-88-4*) Kazi Pubns.

What Is Islam? Montgomery Watt. 1968. 35.00 (*0-86685-555-6*) Intl Bk Ctr.

***What Is ISO 14000? Questions & Answers.** Ed. by Caroline E. Hemingway. 44p. (Orig.). 1996. pap. 24.95 (*1-883337-04-6*, H0923) ASQC Qual Pr.

What Is ISO 9000 All About? John J. Kirchesnstein. 42p. 1993. pap. 14.95 (*1-883999-01-4*) Pressmark Intl.

What Is It? Illus. by Pam Adams. (Motivation Ser.). (Orig.). (J). (ps-2). 1975. pap. 3.99 (*0-85953-044-2*, Pub. by Childs Play UK) Childs Play.

What Is It? Margaret Hillert. (Illus.). (J). (ps-2). 1978. pap. 5.10 (*0-8136-5556-0*); lib. bdg. 7.95 (*0-8136-5056-9*) Modern Curr.

What Is It? Tana Hoban. LC 84-13483. (Illus.). 12p. (J). (ps). 1985. pap. 4.95 (*0-688-02577-3*) Greenwillow.

What Is It? National Geographic Society Staff. Date not set. 3.00 (*0-7922-1969-4*) Natl Geog.

What Is It? Anne T. Perkins. (Big Books - Mini Bks.). (Illus.). 8p. (J). 1993. 12.00 (*1-884204-03-1*) Teach Nxt Door.

***What Is It about Me You Can't Teach? An Instructional Guide for the Urban Educator.** Eleanor R. Rodriguez & James Bellanca. LC 96-78752. (Illus.). 208p. (Orig.). 1996. pap. 29.95 (*1-57517-066-3*, 1444) IRI-SkyLght.

What Is It, Dainty Dinosaur? (Illus.). (J). (ps-2). 1991. pap. 5.10 (*0-8136-5722-9*); lib. bdg. 7.95 (*0-8136-5222-7*) Modern Curr.

***What Is It Then Between Us? Traditions of Love in American Poetry.** Eric M. Selinger. 264p. 1997. 39.95 (*0-8014-3262-6*) Cornell U Pr.

***What Is It Then Between Us? Traditions of Love in American Poetry.** Eric M. Selinger. 264p. 1997. pap. 15.95 (*0-8014-8466-9*) Cornell U Pr.

What Is It, Tink, Is Pan in Trouble? Garry B. Trudeau. (Doonesbury Bk.). (Illus.). 96p. 1992. pap. 7.95 (*0-8362-1886-8*) Andrews & McMeel.

What Is It to Be Human: New Perspectives in Philosophy. Ed. by David Holbrook. 185p. 1990. text ed. 68.95 (*1-85628-055-1*, Pub. by Avebury Pub UK) Ashgate Pub Co.

What Is It? What Do I Do with It? Beth Tartan & Fran Parker. 141p. 1978. 4.00 (*0-686-40980-9*) TarPar.

What Is Japan? Contradictions & Transformations. Taichi Sakaiya. Tr. by Steven Karpa. 320p. 1995. pap. 13.00 (*1-56836-087-8*) Kodansha.

What Is Japanese Architecture? A Survey of Traditional Japanese Architecture. Kazuo Nishi & Kazuo Hozumi. (International Ser.). (Illus.). 144p. 1996. pap. text ed. 28.00 (*4-7700-1992-0*, Pub. by Kodansha Int JA) OUP.

What Is Japanese Architecture: A Survey of Traditional Japanese Architecture with a List of Sites & a Map. Kazuo Nishi. Tr. by Mack H. Horton. LC 84-48695. (Illus.). 144p. (C). 1985. 35.00 (*0-87011-711-4*) Kodansha.

What Is Japan's Advantage in the Commercialization of Technology? (Illus.). 121p. (Orig.). (C). 1994. pap. text ed. 30.00 (*1-56806-218-4*) DIANE Pub.

What Is Jewish Literature? Ed. by Hana Wirth-Nesher. LC 94-2270. 1994. pap. 18.95 (*0-8276-0538-2*) JPS Phila.

What Is John? Readers & Readings of the Fourth Gospel. Ed. by Fernando F. Segovia. LC 96-2495. (SBL Symposium Ser.: No. 3). 286p. 1996. 49.95 (*0-7885-0239-5*, 06 07 03); pap. 29.95 (*0-7885-0240-9*, 06 07 03) Scholars Pr GA.

What Is Justice? Classic & Contemporary Readings. Robert C. Solomon & Mark C. Murphy. 394p. (C). 1990. pap. text ed. 20.95 (*0-19-506050-4*) OUP.

What Is Life. 1995. write for info. (*0-684-81326-2*) S&S Trade.

What Is Life? Lynn Margulis & Sagan. 1995. 40.00 (*0-684-81087-5*, S&S) S&S Trade.

What Is Life? Kalamu Y. Salaam. 1992. pap. 12.95 (*0-88378-083-6*) Third World.

What Is Life? A Bowl of Cherries & Nearly 800 Other Answers. Compiled by Ronald B. Shwartz. LC 94-45482. 128p. 1995. pap. 7.95 (*0-8065-1606-2*, Citadel Pr) Carol Pub Group.

What Is Life? Reclaiming the Black Blues Self. Kalamu Y. Salaam. 1994. 14.95 (*0-88378-119-0*) Third World.

What Is Life? The Next Fifty Years: Speculations on the Future of Biology. Ed. by Michael P. Murphy & Luke A. O'Neil. (Illus.). 179p. (C). 1995. 24.95 (*0-521-45509-X*) Cambridge U Pr.

***What Is Life? the Next Fifty Years: Speculations on the Future of Biology.** Ed. by Michael P. Murphy & Luke A. O'Neill. 208p. 1997. pap. text ed. 15.95 (*0-521-59939-3*) Cambridge U Pr.

What is Life? with Mind & Matter & Autobiographical Sketches. Erwin Schrodinger. (Canto Book Ser.). (Illus.). 200p. (C). 1992. pap. text ed. 10.95 (*0-521-42708-8*) Cambridge U Pr.

What Is Lightbody? Archangel Ariel, Channeled by Tashira Tachi-ren. Tashira Tachi-ren. LC 94-31333. 172p. 1995. pap. 12.95 (*1-880666-25-1*) Oughten Hse.

What Is Literary Language? Jeremy Tambling. (Open Guides to Literature Ser.). 128p. 1988. pap. 22.00 (*0-335-09015-X*, Open Univ Pr) Taylor & Francis.

What Is Literature? Ed. by Arthur Gibson. LC 88-51311. 448p. 9200. 65.00 (*1-85224-084-9*, Pub. by Bloodaxe Bks UK); pap. 25.00 (*1-85224-085-7*, Pub. by Bloodaxe Bks UK) Dufour.

What Is Literature? Ed. by Paul Hernadi. LC 77-23640. 283p. 1978. reprint ed. pap. 80.70 (*0-7837-1505-6*, 2057290) Bks Demand.

What Is Literature? & Other Essays. Jean-Paul Sartre. Tr. by Bernard Frechtman & Jeffrey Mehlman from FRE. LC 87-37931. 376p. 1988. reprint ed. 47.00 (*0-674-95083-6*); reprint ed. pap. text ed. 12.50 (*0-674-95084-4*) HUP.

What Is Literature? France, 1100-1600. Ed. by Francois Cornilliat et al. LC 91-73983. (Edward C. Armstrong Monographs on Medieval Literature: No. 7). 231p. (Orig.). 1993. pap. 17.95 (*0-917058-84-4*) French Forum.

What Is Liturgical Theology? A Study in Methodology. David W. Fagerberg. 344p. (Orig.). 1992. pap. 22.95 (*0-8146-6122-X*, Pueblo Bks) Liturgical Pr.

What Is Logo? Ed. by Peter Evans. (C). 1986. 23.00 (*0-7300-0446-5*, Pub. by Deakin Univ AT) St Mut.

What Is Lonergan up to in "Insight"? A Primer. Terry J. Tekippe. LC 96-4761. 170p. (Orig.). 1996. pap. 13.95 (*0-8146-5782-6*, M Glazier) Liturgical Pr.

What Is Love? Etan Boritzer. LC 93-94066. (Illus.). 32p. (J). (gr. k-5). 1994. pap. 5.95 (*0-9637597-3-6*) V Lane Bks.

What Is Love? Etan Boritzer. LC 93-94066. (Illus.). 32p. (J). (gr. k-5). 1996. 14.95 (*0-9637597-2-8*) V Lane Bks.

***What Is Love?** Richard Carlile. Date not set. 15.00 (*1-85984-851-6*, Pub. by Verso UK) Routledge Chapman & Hall.

What Is Love? Jack Dawson. 110p. 1993. pap. 15.00 (*0-9635888-0-X*) Loverly Pubs.

What Is Love? Sarah Eberle. (Happy Day Ser.). (Illus.). 24p. (Orig.). (J). (ps-2). 1996. pap. 1.99 (*0-7847-0555-0*, 04245) Standard Pub.

What Is Love? Joseph A. Labadie. (Men & Movements in the History & Philosophy of Anarchism Ser.). 1979. lib. bdg. 250.00 (*0-87700-311-4*) Revisionist Pr.

***What Is Love?** Deidre S. Laiken. (J). Date not set. write for info. (*0-688-05556-7*) Lothrop.

***What Is Love?** Deidre S. Laiken. (J). Date not set. lib. bdg. write for info. (*0-688-05557-5*) Lothrop.

What Is Love. Alana Willoughby. Ed. by Alton Jordan. (I Can Eat an Elephant Ser.). (Illus.). (J). (gr. k-3). 1984. 7.95 (*0-89868-018-2*, Read Res); pap. 3.95 (*0-89868-051-4*, Read Res) ARO Pub.

What Is Love? Sarah Eberle. Ed. by Shirley Beegle. (Happy Day Bks.). (Illus.). 24p. (Orig.). (J). (ps-3). 1994. reprint ed. pap. 1.99 (*0-7847-0266-7*, 04216) Standard Pub.

What Is Love? A Coloring Book for Kids. Gyeorgos C. Hatonn & L-L Research Staff. (Illus.). 34p. (J). (ps-2). 1984. pap. 6.95 (*0-945007-05-1*) L-L Resrch.

What Is Loving? Mabel McCaw. (Good Little Books for Good Little Children). (Illus.). 12p. (J). (ps). 1987. 3.25 (*0-8378-5208-0*) Gibson.

***What Is Maggie Eating?** Lieve Baeten. (Tom & Maggie Ser.). (J). 1997. 3.95 (*0-7641-5021-9*) Barron.

***What is Maggie Wearing?** Lieve Baeten. (Tom & Maggie Ser.). 1997. 3.95 (*0-7641-5022-7*) Barron.

What Is Man. Leslie B. Flynn. Tr. by Lorna Y. Chao. (CHI.). 1985. pap. write for info. (*0-941598-27-6*) Living Spring Pubns.

What Is Man? Harry Settanni. LC 91-19617. (American University Studies: Philosophy: Ser. V, Vol. 113). 123p. 1991. 29.95 (*0-8204-1463-8*) P Lang Pubng.

What Is Man? A Book of Interpretations. 2nd ed. Bernard J. Fleury. LC 87-27836. 208p. (C). 1988. pap. text ed. 21.50 (*0-8191-6726-6*); lib. bdg. 41.50 (*0-8191-6725-8*) U Pr of Amer.

What Is Man? And Other Essays. Mark Twain, pseud. LC 71-167326. (Essay Index Reprint Ser.). 1977. reprint ed. 28.95 (*0-8369-2762-1*) Ayer.

What Is Man? And Other Essays. Mark Twain, pseud. (BCL1-PS American Literature Ser.). 375p. 1992. reprint ed. lib. bdg. 89.00 (*0-7812-6688-2*) Rprt Serv.

What Is Man? Leader's Guide. James Long. Tr. by Lorna Y. Chao. (Basic Doctrine Ser.). 1986. pap. write for info. (*0-941598-36-5*) Living Spring Pubns.

What Is Man? & Other Philosophical Writings. Mark Twain. Ed. & Intro. by Paul Baender. LC 78-104109. (Iowa-California Edition of the Works of Mark Twain: No. 19). 1973. 35.00 (*0-520-01621-1*) U CA Pr.

***What Is Man? (1906)** Ed. by Shelley F. Fishkin. (Oxford Mark Twain). 224p. 1997. lib. bdg. 28.00 (*0-19-511421-3*) OUP.

What Is Martin Luther King, Jr. Day? Margot Parker. LC 89-29254. (Understanding Holidays Ser.). (Illus.). 48p. (J). (ps-3). 1990. pap. 4.95 (*0-516-43784-4*); lib. bdg. 17.10 (*0-516-03784-6*) Childrens.

What Is Marxism All about. Workers World Newspaper Staff. 51p. 1977. pap. 1.50 (*0-89567-015-1*) World View Forum.

What Is Mathematical Logic. J. N. Crossley. 1990. pap. 4.95 (*0-486-26404-1*) Dover.

What is Mathematics? An Elementary Approach to Ideas & Methods. 2nd ed. Richard Courant et al. (Illus.). 592p. (C). 1996. pap. 18.95 (*0-19-510519-2*) OUP.

***What Is Mathematics, Really?** Reuben Hersh. LC 96-38483. (Illus.). 384p. 1997. 35.00 (*0-19-511368-3*) OUP.

What Is Meditation? Osho. 1995. pap. 10.95 (*1-85230-726-9*) Element MA.

***What Is Midrash? & a Midrash Reader.** 2nd ed. Jacob Neusner. 294p. 1994. 74.95 (*1-55540-982-2*, 240106) Scholars Pr GA.

What Is Missing? Mario Gamboli. LC 91-70414. (Illus.). 10p. (J). (ps). 1991. bds. 3.95 (*1-878093-70-3*) Boyds Mills Pr.

What Is Modern Mathematics. Gustave Choquet. 46p. 1963. pap. 5.00 (*0-87825-250-9*) Ed Solutions.

What Is Modern Painting? Alfred H. Barr, Jr. (Illus.). 48p. 1975. pap. 6.95 (*0-87070-631-4*, 0-8109-6083-4) Mus of Modern Art.

What is Modernism? Ian B. Whyte. 1996. pap. 16.95 (*1-85490-389-6*) Academy Ed UK.

What Is Money: An Original Arno Press Compilation. Murray N. Rothbard & Isaiah W. Sylvester. LC 74-172227. (Right Wing Individualist Tradition in America Ser.). 1972. reprint ed. 13.95 (*0-405-00447-8*) Ayer.

What Is Money for? Ezra Pound. 1983. lib. bdg. 250.00 (*0-87700-459-5*) Revisionist Pr.

What Is Money For? A Sane Man's Guide to Economics. Ezra Pound. 1982. lib. bdg. 250.00 (*0-87700-408-0*) Revisionist Pr.

What Is Morality? Questions in Search of Answers. Harry Settanni. 72p. (Orig.). (C). 1992. pap. text ed. 9.95 (*0-8191-8616-3*) U Pr of Amer.

***What Is Morality? The Light Through Different Windows.** Donal Harrington. 240p. (Orig.). 1996. pap. 15.95 (*1-85607-149-9*, Pub. by Columba Pr IE) Twenty-Third.

What Is Music? An Introduction to the Philosophy of Music. Ed. by Philip A. Alperson. (C). 1994. reprint ed. pap. text ed. 20.00 (*0-271-01318-4*) Pa St U Pr.

What Is Mutualism. Clarence L. Swartz. 1972. 250.00 (*0-8490-1286-4*) Gordon Pr.

What Is Mutualism: A Challenge to Downsizing. Clarence L. Swartz. 1996. lib. bdg. 253.95 (*0-8490-5869-4*) Gordon Pr.

What Is My Antique Stove Worth? Clifford Boram. 9p. 1987. reprint ed. pap. 2.00 (*0-9612204-3-0*) Autonomy Hse.

What Is My Shadow Made Of? Questions Kids Ask about Everyday Science. Neil Morris. LC 94-14120. (Tell Me Why Ser.). (Illus.). 32p. (J). (ps-2). 1995. 7.99 (*0-89577-609-X*, Rdrs Dig Kids) RD Assn.

What Is Narrative Criticism? Mark A. Powell. LC 90-13863. (Guides to Biblical Scholarship Ser.). 144p. (Orig.). 1991. pap. 11.00 (*0-8006-0473-3*, 1-473, Fortress Pr) Augsburg Fortress.

What Is Nature? Kate Soper. 200p. (C). 1995. 58.95 (*0-631-18889-4*); pap. 20.95 (*0-631-18891-6*) Blackwell Pubs.

What Is Neorealism? A Critical English-Language Bibliography of Italian Cinematic Neorealism. Bert Cardullo. 158p. (C). 1991. lib. bdg. 36.50 (*0-8191-7756-3*) U Pr of Amer.

What Is Neostructuralism? Manfred Frank. Tr. by Sabine Wilke & Richard T. Gray from GER. (Theory & History of Literature Ser.: Vol. 41). 500p. 1989. text ed. 49.95 (*0-8166-1599-3*) U of Minn Pr.

What is New Historicism? Gallagher. 1993. 19.95 (*0-226-27934-0*) U Ch Pr.

What Is News in India? A Content Analysis of the Elite Press. S. M. Haque. LC 88-5470. 198p. (C). 1988. lib. bdg. 31.00 (*0-8191-5712-0*) U Pr of Amer.

***What Is Normal?** Hazelden Staff. 1996. pap. 2.50 (*0-89486-485-8*) Hazelden.

What Is Occultism? Papus. 104p. 1981. pap. 10.00 (*0-89540-073-1*, SB-073) Sun Pub.

What Is Orange? Mary O'Neill. (J). (gr. k-2). 1993. pap. 8.95 incl. audio (*0-7608-0500-8*); pap. 4.95 (*0-88741-933-X*) Sundance Pub.

What Is Orange?, Big bk. Mary O'Neill. (J). (gr. k-2). 1993. pap. 17.95 (*0-88741-932-1*) Sundance Pub.

What Is Our Future, America? Vladimir Mare. (Illus.). 1985. 24.95 (*0-933517-00-9*) V & M World Wide.

What Is Our Message? Shaheed H. Al-Banna. 46p. (Orig.). 1985. pap. 3.00 (*1-56744-416-4*) Kazi Pubns.

***What Is P. B. Bear Doing?** Lee Davis. LC 97-14042. (P. B. Bear Read-Alongs Ser.). 1997. write for info. (*0-7894-2224-7*) DK Pub Inc.

What Is Painting? "Winslow Homer" & Other Essays. Kenyon Cox. (Classical America Series in Art & Architecture). (Illus.). 1988. pap. 12.50 (*0-393-30545-7*) Norton.

What Is Passover? Harriet Ziefert. (Lift-the-Flap Bk.). (Illus.). 16p. (J). (ps-2). 1994. 5.95 (*0-694-00482-0*, Festival) HarpC Child Bks.

***What Is Past Is Prologue: Cost Accounting in the British Industrial Revolution, 1760-1850.** Richard K. Fleischman & Lee D. Parker. LC 97-25287. (New Works in Accounting History). 368p. 1997. 64.00 (*0-8153-3015-4*) Garland.

What Is Pastoral? Paul J. Alpers. LC 95-35356. 448p. (C). 1996. 34.95 (*0-226-01516-5*) U Ch Pr.

***What Is Pastoral?** Paul J. Alpers. 1997. pap. text ed. 14.95 (*0-226-01517-3*) U Ch Pr.

What is Philosophy? Gilles Deleuze & Felix Guattari. Tr. by Hugh Tomlinson & Graham Burchell. LC 93-40801. (European Perspectives Ser.). 256p. 1994. 29.95 (*0-231-07988-5*) Col U Pr.

What Is Philosophy? Gilles Deleuze & Felix Guattari. 256p. 1996. pap. 17.00 (*0-231-07989-3*) Col U Pr.

What Is Philosophy? Martin Heidegger. (Masterworks of Literatute Ser.). 1956. pap. 12.95 (*0-8084-0319-2*) NCUP.

What Is Philosophy? Dietrich Von Hildebrand. LC 73-9988. 252p. reprint ed. pap. 71.90 (*0-317-09325-8*, 2019098) Bks Demand.

What Is Political Economy. Martin Staniland. LC 84-13193. 240p. 1987. pap. 14.00 (*0-300-03936-0*, Y-630) Yale U Pr.

What Is Political Philosophy? Leo Strauss. LC 73-1408. 315p. 1973. reprint ed. text ed. 59.75 (*0-8371-6802-3*, STPP, Greenwood Pr) Greenwood.

What Is Political Philosophy? And Other Studies. Leo Strauss. 316p. 1988. pap. text ed. 15.95 (*0-226-77713-8*) U Ch Pr.

What Is Post-Modernism? (What Is? Ser.). 1996. 16.95 (*1-85490-428-0*) Academy Ed UK.

What Is Post-Modernism? Charles Jencks. (Illus.). 48p. 1986. pap. 12.95 (*0-312-86603-8*) St Martin.

What Is Post-Modernism? 2nd enl. rev. ed. Charles Jencks. (Academy Editions Ser.). (Illus.). 56p. 1988. pap. 12.95 (*0-312-01699-9*) St Martin.

What Is Post-Modernism? 3rd ed. Charles Jencks. (Illus.). 64p. 1990. pap. 16.00 (*0-312-03988-3*) St Martin.

What Is Postmodern Biblical Criticism? Andrew K. Adam. LC 95-3485. (Guides to Biblical Scholarship Ser.). 9p. 1995. 11.00 (*0-8006-2879-9*, Fortress Pr) Augsburg Fortress.

What Is Pragmatism? James B. Pratt. LC 75-3327. reprint ed. 36.00 (*0-404-59322-4*) AMS Pr.

What Is Prayer. Carolyn Nystrom. (Children's Bible Basics Ser.). (J). (ps-3). 1993. text ed. 6.99 (*0-8024-7859-X*) Moody.

What Is Property. P. J. Proudhon. 1972. 300.00 (*0-8490-1287-2*) Gordon Pr.

What Is Property? Pierre-Joseph Proudhon et al. LC 93-16214. (Cambridge Texts in the History of Political Thought Ser.). 260p. (C). 1994. text ed. 59.95 (*0-521-40555-6*); pap. text ed. 18.95 (*0-521-40556-4*) Cambridge U Pr.

What Is Protected in a Computer Program? Copyright Protection in the United States & Europe. Josef Drexl. (IIC Studies: Vol. 15). 124p. 1995. 60.00 (*3-527-28688-8*, VCH) Wiley.

What Is Psychoanalysis? enl. rev. ed. Ernest Jones. LC 48-2924. 126p. reprint ed. pap. 36.00 (*0-317-10263-X*, 2010707) Bks Demand.

What Is Psychoanalysis? Isador H. Coriat. LC 73-2393. (Mental Illness & Social Policy; the American Experience Ser.). 1973. reprint ed. 14.95 (*0-405-05201-4*) Ayer.

What Is Psychoanalysis? Ernest Jones. LC 72-11478. 126p. 1973. reprint ed. text ed. 49.75 (*0-8371-6670-5*, JOWP, Greenwood Pr) Greenwood.

What Is Psychology? The Inside Story. 2nd ed. Andrew M. Colman. 196p. 1989. pap. 14.95 (*0-09-172989-0*) Routledge Chapman & Hall.

***What Is Psychology Inside.** (C). 1988. pap. text ed. 14.95 (*0-04-172989-7*) Routledge.

What Is Psychotherapy? Contemporary Perspectives. Ed. by Jeffrey K. Zeig & Michael Munion. LC 90-5010. (Social & Behavioral Sciences Ser.). 477p. 45.95 (*1-55542-283-7*) Jossey-Bass.

What Is Psychotherapy? Proceedings of the International Congress of Psychotherapy, 9th, Oslo, June, 1973, 3 pts. International Congress of Psychotherapy Staff. Ed. by T. E. Mogstad & F. Magnussen. (Journal: Psychotherapy & Psychosomatics: Vol. 24, Nos. 4-6). 600p. 1975. reprint ed. 118.50 (*3-8055-2057-3*) S Karger.

What Is Punishment for & How Does It Relate to the Concept of Community? H. R. H. the Princess Anne. 12p. (C). 1991. pap. text ed. 7.95 (*0-521-42416-X*) Cambridge U Pr.

What Is Qigong: Self-Healing in Chinese Medicine. (Alternative Medicine Ser.). 1992. lib. bdg. 90.00 (*0-8490-5392-7*) Gordon Pr.

What Is Quakerism? A Primer. George T. Peck. LC 87-63556. (Orig.). 1988. pap. 3.00 (*0-87574-277-7*) Pendle Hill.

What Is Quality Child Care? Bettye M. Caldwell & Asa G. Hilliard, III. 33p. 1985. pap. text ed. 3.00 (*0-912674-89-X*, NAEYC #117) Natl Assn Child Ed.

What Is Quality in Higher Education? Ed. by Diana Green. LC 93-10117. 160p. 1993. 90.00 (*0-335-15741-6*, Open Univ Pr); pap. 27.50 (*0-335-15740-8*, Open Univ Pr) Taylor & Francis.

What Is Quantum Mechanics? A Physics Adventure. Transnational College of LEX Staff. Tr. by John Nambu from JPN. LC 95-80427. (Illus.). 592p. (Orig.). (JPN.). (C). 1996. pap. 29.95 (*0-9643504-1-6*) Lang Res Fnd.

***What Is Quantum Mechanics? A Physics Adventure.** 2nd ed. Transnational College of LEX Staff. Ed. by Japanese Language Services Staff. Tr. by John Nambu from JPN. (Illus.). 592p. (Orig.). 1997. pap. 29.95 (*0-9643504-4-0*) Lang Res Fnd.

What Is Real Love? George B. Eager. (Illus.). (Orig.). (YA). (gr. 6-12). 1993. pap. 3.00 (*1-879224-06-2*) Mailbox.

***What Is Reality?** Allen G. Viduka. LC 97-67135. 224p. (Orig.). 1997. pap. 15.95 (*1-57197-073-8*) Pentland Pr.

What Is Reality. Alan Watts. Ed. by Mark Watts. 125p. (Orig.). Date not set. pap. 8.95 (*0-89708-167-6*) And Bks.

***What Is Red?** Suzanne Gottlie. (J). Date not set. write for info. (*0-688-05505-2*); lib. bdg. write for info. (*0-688-05506-0*) Lothrop.

What Is Redaction Criticism? Norman Perrin. Ed. by Dan O. Via, Jr. LC 72-81529. (Guides to Biblical Scholarship Ser.). 96p. (Orig.). 1969. pap. 9.00 (*0-8006-0181-5*, 1-181, Fortress Pr) Augsburg Fortress.

What Is Religion? An Introduction. John F. Haught. 320p. 1990. pap. 14.95 (*0-8091-3117-X*) Paulist Pr.

What Is Religion? An Introduction to Religion & Ethics. William Wade. 1979. teacher ed. 24.00 (*1-881678-25-3*) CRIS.

What Is Revealed When One Looks Back into Repeated Lives on Earth (Plus) Michael & the Dragon. Rudolf Steiner. 14p. 1993. reprint ed. spiral bd. 3.50 (*0-7873-0832-3*) Hlth Research.

What Is Revelation? Frederick D. Maurice. LC 76-173061. reprint ed. 49.50 (*0-404-04276-7*) AMS Pr.

What Is Right? Biblical Principles for Decision-Making. Elmer L. Towns. Ed. by Timothy J. Pierce. (Video Curriculum Ser.). 62p. 1995. text ed. 49.95 incl. vhs (*1-57052-041-0*) Chrch Grwth VA.

What Is Safe: Corporate Aviation Safety Seminar Proceedings, 28th Annual Meeting, April 17-19, 1983, Fairmont Hotel, New Orleans, Louisiana. Flight Safety Foundation Staff. 212p. reprint ed. pap. 60.50 (*0-317-29629-9*, 2021549) Bks Demand.

What Is Sahaj Marg. rev. ed. Parthasarathi Rajagopalachari. 248p. 1994. 12.00 (*0-945242-26-3*) Shri Ram Chandra.

What Is Said: A Theory of Indirect Speech Reports. Rod Bertolet. 266p. (C). 1990. lib. bdg. 118.50 (*0-7923-0792-5*, Pub. by Klwr Acad Pubs NE) Kluwer Ac.

What is Salvation of the Soul? see Lay Counseling Series

What Is Sanctification. Leslie Parrott. 48p. 1979. pap. 3.99 (*0-8341-0077-0*) Beacon Hill.

What Is Saving Faith? Beyond Salvation. Lance B. Johnson. LC 94-94301. 386p. (Orig.). 1992. 10.00 (*0-9631328-2-2*) Come & See Minist.

What Is Schizophrenia? Ed. by William F. Flack et al. xii, 270p. 1991. 59.95 (*0-387-97642-6*) Spr-Verlag.

What Is Science? Norman R. Campbell. 1921. pap. 5.95 (*0-486-60043-2*) Dover.

What Is Science? An Introduction to the Structure & Methodology of Science. V. James Mannoia, Jr. LC 79-47988. (Illus.). 149p. 1980. pap. text ed. 15.00 (*0-8191-0989-4*) U Pr of Amer.

What Is Scientology? L. Ron Hubbard. 624p. pap. 19.95 (*0-88404-850-0*) Bridge Pubns Inc.

What Is Scientology? The Comprehensive Reference on the World's Fastest Growing Religion. 834p. (YA). 1992. 85.00 (*0-88404-633-8*) Bridge Pubns Inc.

What is Scripture? A Comparative Approach. Wilfred C. Smith. LC 93-27795. 1993. pap. 20.00 (*0-8006-2608-7*, 1-2608, Fortress Pr) Augsburg Fortress.

What Is Secret No. 9: Short Stories by Chilean Women. Ed. by Marjorie Agosin. (Secret Weaver Ser.: Vol. 9). 302p. (Orig.). 1996. pap. 17.00 (*1-877727-41-5*) White Pine.

What Is See-Through? Sarah Warbrick. LC 95-41115. (What Is--? Ser.). (J). 1996. lib. bdg. write for info. (*1-57572-051-5*) Rigby Interact Libr.

What Is Self? A Study of the Spiritual Journey in Terms of Consciousness. 2nd ed. Bernadette Roberts. LC 89-91249. 216p. (Orig.). 1996. reprint ed. pap. 17.00 (*0-9623993-0-2*) M Goens Pub.

***What Is Sex?** Lynn Margulis & Dorion Sagan. LC 97-19220. 1997. write for info. (*0-684-82691-7*) S&S Trade.

What Is Sex. Abraham Smith. 100p. (Orig.). 1986. write for info. (*0-9615763-0-8*) Pussy Willow.

What Is Sex Education All About? A Guide for Parents. Sidney S. Ross. LC 78-64612. 1979. pap. 7.95 (*0-9602028-0-3*) Sidney Scott Ross.

What Is Sexual Harassment? (At Issue Ser.). 96p. (C). 1995. pap. text ed. 8.96 (*1-56510-266-5*) Greenhaven.

What Is Sexual Harassment? (At Issue Ser.). 96p. 1995. lib. bdg. 14.96 (*1-56510-299-1*) Greenhaven.

What Is Sexual Harassment. Terry Gooche, Jr. LC 92-60809. 80p. 1993. pap. 5.95 (*1-55523-545-X*) Winston-Derek.

What Is She Like? Lesbian Identities from 1950s to 1990s. Rosa Ainley. Date not set. pap. 16.95 (*0-304-32900-2*, Pub. by Cassell Pubng UK) LPC InBook.

What Is Shiny? Sarah Warbrick. LC 95-41114. (What Is--? Ser.). (J). 1996. lib. bdg. write for info. (*1-57572-053-1*) Rigby Interact Libr.

***What Is Sinan Going to Do?** Dagmar Stam. LC 97-23386. (J). 1997. write for info. (*1-57379-025-7*) High-Scope.

What Is Situationism? A Reader. Ed. by Stewart Home. (Illus.). 208p. (Orig.). 1996. pap. 14.95 (*1-873176-13-9*) AK Pr Dist.

What Is Social Case Work: An Introductory Description. Mary E. Richmond. LC 70-137185. (Poverty U. S. A. Historical Record Ser.). 1977. reprint ed. 23.95 (*0-405-03123-8*) Ayer.

What Is Social-Scientific Criticism? John H. Elliott. LC 93-22407. 1993. 17.00 (*0-8006-2678-8*, 1-2678) Augsburg Fortress.

What Is Society? Reflections on Freedom, Order, & Change. Earl R. Babbie. LC 93-15178. 172p. 1993. pap. 16.95 (*0-8039-9015-4*) Pine Forge.

What Is Sociology? Norbert Elias. LC 78-2386. 187p. 1978. text ed. 45.00 (*0-231-04550-6*) Col U Pr.

What Is Sociology? Norbert Elias. LC 78-2386. 187p. 1984. pap. text ed. 15.00 (*0-231-04551-4*) Col U Pr.

***What Is South America?** Ed. by Meacham. (C). 1998. text ed. write for info. (*0-321-01052-3*) Addson-Wesley Educ.

What Is Special Education? John Fish. (Children with Special Needs Ser.). 128p. 1989. 80.00 (*0-335-09536-4*, Open Univ Pr); pap. 27.00 (*0-335-09535-6*, Open Univ Pr) Taylor & Francis.

***What Is Spiritual about Focusing?** Edwin M. McMahon & Peter A. Campbell. 12p. 1996. pap. text ed. 1.25 (*1-55612-501-1*, LL1501) Sheed & Ward MO.

What Is Spiritual Freedom? Harold Klemp. (Mahanta Transcripts Ser.: No. 11). 201p. 1995. pap. 14.00 (*1-57043-101-9*) ECKANKAR.

What Is Spiritualism, Who Are These Spiritualists, & What Has Spiritualism Done for the World? J. M. Peebles. 131p. 1972. reprint ed. spiral bd. 5.50 (*0-7873-0663-0*) Hlth Research.

What Is Spirituality? Paul Bjorklund. 15p. (Orig.). 1983. pap. 1.75 (*0-89486-182-4*, 1451B) Hazelden.

What Is Squishy? Sarah Warbrick. LC 95-41113. (What Is--? Ser.). (J). 1996. lib. bdg. write for info. (*1-57572-054-X*) Rigby Interact Libr.

What Is Sticky? Sarah Warbick. LC 95-41111. (What Is--? Ser.). (J). 1996. lib. bdg. write for info. (*1-57572-052-3*) Rigby Interact Libr.

***What Is Sufism?** Martin Lings. 135p. 1996. pap. 10.50 (*0-614-21381-9*, 1308) Kazi Pubns.

What Is Sufism? Martin Lings. 136p. 1988. pap. 9.95 (*0-04-297039-3*) Routledge Chapman & Hall.

What Is Sufism? Martin Lings. (Golden Palm Ser.). 134p. 1996. reprint ed. pap. text ed. 19.95 (*0-946621-41-1*, Pub. by Islamic Texts UK) Intl Spec Bk.

What Is Surrealism. Andre Breton. LC 74-6446. (Studies in Comparative Literature: No. 35). (C). 1973. reprint ed. lib. bdg. 75.00 (*0-8383-1709-X*) M S G Haskell Hse.

What Is Surrealism? Selected Writings. Andre Breton. Ed. by Franklin Rosemont. LC 71-186691. (Illus.). 557p. (C). 1978. reprint ed. lib. bdg. 60.00 (*0-913460-59-1*) Pathfinder NY.

What Is Surrealism? Selected Writings. Andre Breton. Ed. by Franklin Rosemont. LC 71-186691. (Illus.). 557p. (C). 1978. reprint ed. pap. 30.95 (*0-87348-822-9*) Pathfinder NY.

What Is Taoism? And Other Studies in Chinese Cultural History. Herrlee G. Creel. LC 77-102905. (Midway Reprint Ser.). viii, 200p. (C). 1982. pap. text ed. 18.00 (*0-226-12047-3*) U Ch Pr.

What Is Thanksgiving? Harriet Ziefert. (Lift-the-Flap Bk.). (Illus.). 16p. (J). (ps). 1992. 5.95 (*0-694-00408-1*, Festival) HarpC Child Bks.

What Is Thanksgiving Day? Margot Parker. LC 88-11112. (Understanding Holidays Ser.). (Illus.). 48p. (J). (ps-3). 1988. pap. 4.95 (*0-516-43783-6*) Childrens.

What Is That? Tana Hoban. LC 93-33645. (Illus.). 12p. (J). (ps up). 1994. pap. 4.95 (*0-688-12920-X*) Greenwillow.

"What Is That?" Said the Cat. Grace Maccarone. LC 94-39100. (Hello Reader! Ser.). (Illus.). (J). 1995. 2.95 (*0-590-25945-8*, Cartwheel) Scholastic Inc.

What Is That, That Is So Controversial of & about the Lord Jesus & His Life? (Walk with Jesus Ser.). 12p. 1987. pap. 5.00 (*1-57277-205-0*) Script Rsch.

***What Is the Animal Kingdom?** Bobbie Kalman. (Science of Living Things Ser.). (Illus.). 32p. (J). 1997. lib. bdg. 18.64 (*0-86505-877-6*) Crabtree Pub Co.

***What Is the Animal Kingdom?** Bobbie Kalman. (Science of Living Things Ser.). (Illus.). 32p. (J). 1997. pap. 5.95 (*0-86505-889-X*) Crabtree Pub Co.

What Is the Best Life? An Introduction to Ethics. Brad Art. 310p. (C). 1993. pap. 31.95 (*0-534-17652-6*) Wadsworth Pub.

What Is the Best Thing about God? Christine H. Tangvald. (Big Picture Bks.). (Illus.). 32p. (J). (ps-2). 1994. 10.99 (*0-7847-0163-6*, 03633) Standard Pub.

What Is the Best Thing about Jesus? Christine H. Tangvald. (Big Picture Bks.). (Illus.). 32p. (J). (ps-2). 1994. 10.99 (*0-7847-0164-4*, 03634) Standard Pub.

What is the Bible? Carl Lofmark. 118p. (C). 1992. 22.95 (*0-87975-781-7*) Prometheus Bks.

What Is the Bible? Carolyn Nystrom. (Children's Bible Basics Ser.). 32p. (J). (ps-2). 1994. text ed. 6.99 (*0-8024-7864-6*) Moody.

What Is the Christian's Hope? W. J. Ouweneel. 53p. pap. 2.95 (*0-88172-116-6*) Believers Bkshelf.

What Is "The Church" Eddie Cloer. 216p. 1993. pap. write for info. (*0-945441-16-9*) Res Pubns AR.

What Is "the Church"? Eddie Cloer. (RUS.). 1993. write for info. (*0-945441-20-7*) Res Pubns AR.

What Is the Church, Bk. 3. Bruce L. Shelly. Tr. by Lorna Y. Chao. (Basic Doctrine Ser.). (CHI.). 1985. pap. write for info. (*0-941598-25-X*) Living Spring Pubns.

What Is the Church? Leader's Guide. S. P. Publications Editors. Tr. by Lorna Y. Chao. (Basic Doctrine Ser.). 1986. pap. write for info. (*0-941598-35-7*) Living Spring Pubns.

What Is the Church Coming To? LaFayette Scales. 296p. 1996. pap. 8.99 (*1-56043-169-5*) Destiny Image.

***What Is the Church of the Nazarene?** 24p. 1973. pap. 1.99 (*0-8341-0433-4*) Nazarene.

What Is the Difference? see Cual Es la Diferencia?

***What Is the Emperor Wearing? Truth-Telling in Business Relationships.** Laurie Weiss. LC 97-17512. 1998. write for info. (*0-7506-9872-1*) Buttrwrth-Heinemann.

What Is the Father Like? A Devotional Look at How God Cares for His Children. W.T. Phillip Keller. 176p. (Orig.). 1996. pap. 8.99 (*1-55661-722-4*, Hampshire MN) Bethany Hse.

What Is the Fear of the Lord? Billy J. Daugherty. 32p. (Orig.). 1991. pap. 0.50 (*1-56267-005-0*) Victory Ctr OK.

***What Is the Future for a Primary Care-Led NHS?** Robert Boyd. LC 96-53158. (National Primary Care Research & Development Centre Ser.). 1997. write for info. (*1-85775-265-1*, Radcliffe Med Pr) Scovill Paterson.

What is the Future for Defined Benefit Pension Plans? 1989. pap. 19.95 (*0-86643-065-2*) Empl Benefit Res Inst.

What Is the Gift? Poetry & a Little Prose. Judy McGorray. 94p. 1994. pap. text ed. write for info. (*1-888200-01-4*) JayMac Commun.

What Is the Iona Community? Wild Goose Publications Staff. (C). 1990. 40.00 (*0-947988-07-6*, Pub. by Wild Goose Pubns UK) St Mut.

What Is the Meaning of "This"? A Puzzle about Demonstrative Belief. David F. Austin. LC 89-22110. 192p. 1990. 29.95 (*0-8014-2409-7*) Cornell U Pr.

What Is the Moon? Caroline Dunant. (Illus.). 32p. (J). (ps). 1994. 18.95 (*0-370-31811-0*, Pub. by Bodley Head UK) Trafalgar.

***What is the Moon Full Of?** Shulamith L. Oppenheim. LC 96-80399. (Illus.). 32p. (J). (ps-3). 1997. 14.95 (*1-56397-479-7*) Boyds Mills Pr.

What Is the Name of This Book? The Riddle of Dracula & Other Logical Puzzles. Raymond Smullyan. LC 77-18692. 1978. pap. 5.95 (*0-13-955062-3*) P-H.

What Is the Nature of Authority in the Church? Menco A. Afonso. LC 96-10255. 108p. 1996. pap. text ed. 19.50 (*0-7618-0286-X*) U Pr of Amer.

What Is the New Age? Defining Third Millennium Consciousness. William P. Frost. LC 92-32767. 404p. 1992. text ed. 109.95 (*0-7734-9192-9*) E Mellen.

What Is the New Birth of Soul? F.C.D.T. Trustees Staff. 1989. pap. write for info. (*1-887621-17-2*) Found Ch Divine Truth.

***What Is the Optimal Size of Government in the United States.** Gerald W. Scully. 15p. 1994. pap. 10.00 (*1-56808-051-4*, 188) Natl Ctr Pol.

What Is the Origin of Man. Maurice Bucaille. pap. 14.50 (*0-933511-89-2*) Kazi Pubns.

What Is the Point of Community Architecture? Ed. by J. Scott & M. Jenks. (C). 1986. 45.00 (*0-685-30255-5*, Pub. by Oxford Polytechnic UK) St Mut.

What Is the Purpose of Creation? A Jewish Anthology. Ed. by Michael J. Alter. LC 90-48734. 346p. 1996. pap. 24.95 (*1-56821-515-0*) Aronson.

What Is the Reformed Faith? John R. DeWitt. (Orig.). 1981. pap. text ed. 2.00 (*0-85151-326-3*) Banner of Truth.

What Is the Sonship of Christ? W. J. Ouweneel. pap. 2.25 (*0-88172-167-0*) Believers Bkshelf.

What Is the Sun? Reeve Lindbergh. LC 93-3557. (Illus.). 32p. (J). (ps up). 1994. 14.95 (*1-56402-146-7*) Candlewick Pr.

What Is the Sun? Reeve Lindbergh. LC 93-3557. (J). (ps up). 1996. pap. 4.99 (*1-56402-609-4*) Candlewick Pr.

What Is the Time? Lynne Bradbury. (Series 921). (Illus.). 28p. (J). (ps). 1992. Series 921. 3.50 (*0-7214-1511-3*, Ladybrd) Penguin.

What is Theatre? An Introduction & Exploration. John R. Brown. LC 96-41113. (Illus.). 320p. 1997. pap. 34.95 (*0-240-80232-2*, Focal) Buttrwrth-Heinemann.

What Is Theological Exegesis? Interpretation & Use of Scripture in Barth's Doctrine of Election. Mary K. Cunningham. LC 95-6389. 96p. (Orig.). (C). 1995. pap. text ed. 10.00 (*1-56338-115-X*) TPI PA.

***What is Theology?** Rudolf Bultmann. LC 96-40256. (Fortress Texts in Modern Theology Ser.). 1997. pap. 22.00 (*0-8006-3088-2*, Fortress Pr) Augsburg Fortress.

What Is Theology? J. J. Mueller. (Zacchaeus Studies: Theology). 103p. (Orig.). 1988. pap. 7.95 (*0-8146-5681-1*) Liturgical Pr.

What Is Theosophy? A General View of Occult Doctrine. rev. ed. Charles J. Ryan. Ed. by W. Emmett Small & Helen Todd. (Theosophical Manual Ser.: No. 1). 92p. 1975. pap. 4.00 (*0-913004-18-9*) Point Loma Pub.

What Is There to Do in the Country? Ben Douglas. (Life in the Country Ser.). (Illus.). 32p. (J). (ps-2). 1994. write for info. (*1-885483-00-7*) Sontag Pr.

What Is This? Myrna Perkins. (Illus.). 36p. (Orig.). (J). (ps-3). 1986. pap. 4.95 (*0-937729-01-9*) Markins Enter.

What Is This Book? Norman Pedersen. LC 89-61804. (Illus.). 104p. (Orig.). 1989. pap. text ed. 5.95 (*0-685-26789-X*) Sol-Earth.

What Is This Madness? Bud Johns. LC 85-12710. (Illus.). 192p. (Orig.). 1985. pap. 7.95 (*0-912184-05-1*) Synergistic Pr.

What Is This Thing Called Love? Irwin M. Bloom. LC 89-60773. 288p. (Orig.). 1989. pap. 12.95 (*0-915677-44-X*) Roundtable Pub.

What Is This Thing Called Love? Edward T. Dunn. LC 95-90975. (Orig.). 1996. pap. 8.95 (*0-533-11804-2*) Vantage.

What Is This Thing Called Love? Fogiel. 192p. Date not set. pap. text ed. 12.95 (*0-87891-972-4*) Res & Educ.

***What Is This Thing Called Preaching? An Authentic Collection of Sermons by Rev. Leon Johnson, 2 vols.** Leon Johnson & Leonidas A. Johnson. Incl. Vol. 1. . LC 96-85843. 176p. 1997. 16.95 (*1-889561-01-0*); Vol. 2. . 175p. 1997. 16.95 (*1-889561-02-9*); write for info. (*1-889561-03-7*) Crystal Fntn.

***What Is This Thing Called Science? An Assessment of the Nature & Status of Science & Its Methods.** 2nd ed. Alan F. Chalmers. 200p. 1982. pap. 11.99 (*0-335-10107-0*, Open Univ Pr) Taylor & Francis.

What Is This Thing Called Science: An Assessment of the Nature & Status of Science & Its Methods. 2nd ed. Alan F. Chalmers. LC 94-44831. 179p. (C). 1995. pap. text ed. 12.95 (*0-87220-149-X*); lib. bdg. 34.95 (*0-87220-199-6*) Hackett Pub.

What Is to Be Done? Nikolai G. Chernyshevsky. Tr. by Michael R. Katz. LC 88-21676. 488p. 1989. pap. 15.95 (*0-8014-9547-4*) Cornell U Pr.

What Is to Be Done? Robert W. Service. 262p. 1990. pap. 10.95 (*0-14-018126-1*, 468, Penguin Classics) Viking Penguin.

What Is to Be Done? Burning Questions of Our Movement. Vladimir I. Lenin. Ed. by James S. Allen. LC 69-18884. 200p. (C). 1969. pap. text ed. 5.75 (*0-7178-0218-3*) Intl Pubs Co.

What Is to Be Done? Proposals for the Soviet Transition to the Market. Merton J. Peck & Thomas J. Richardson. 224p. (Orig.). 1992. pap. 15.00 (*0-300-05468-8*); text ed. 32.50 (*0-300-05466-1*) Yale U Pr.

What Is to Be Done: The Enlightened Thinkers & an Islamic Renaissance. Ali Shariati. 200p. 1987. 25.95 (*0-932625-04-5*); pap. text ed. 11.95 (*0-932625-01-0*) Inst Res Islam.

What Is to Be Done about Law & Order? Crisis in the Nineties. John Lea & Jock Young. (C). 65.00 (*0-7453-0735-3*, Pub. by Pluto Pr UK) LPC InBook.

What Is to Be Done about Law & Order? Crisis in the Nineties. 2nd ed. John P. Lea & Jock Young. 284p. (C). pap. 20.95 (*0-7453-0398-6*, Pub. by Pluto Pr UK) LPC InBook.

What Is Told. Askold Melnuczuk. 216p. 1995. pap. 11.95 (*0-571-19865-1*) Faber & Faber.

What Is Total Quality Control? Kaoru Ishikawa. 1991. pap. 17.95 (*0-13-952441-X*, Busn) P-H.

What is Toxemia? J. H. Tilden. 1996. pap. 9.95 (*1-56459-870-5*) Kessinger Pub.

What Is Toxemia & Tumors. J. H. Tilden. 29p. 1975. reprint ed. spiral bd. 9.00 (*0-7873-0875-7*) Hlth Research.

What Is Transfiguration? Jan Van Rijckenborgh. 40p. 1987. pap. 4.00 (*0-317-56232-0*) Rosycross Pr.

***What Is Translation? Centrifugal Theories, Critical Interventions.** Douglas Robinson. LC 97-11216. (Translation Studies). 1997. write for info. (*0-87338-573-X*) Kent St U Pr.

What Is Transylvania? S. Mehedinti. 124p. 1986. write for info. (*0-937019-02-X*); pap. 15.00 (*0-937019-03-8*) Romanian Hist.

What Is True Forgiveness? Gene Steiner. 78p. (Orig.). 1993. pap. 5.95 (*1-886045-10-0*) Covenant Marriages.

***What Is Truth?** Edo Pivcevic. (Avebury Series in Philosophy). 220p. 1997. text ed. 59.95 (*1-85972-701-8*, Pub. by Ashgate UK) Ashgate Pub Co.

What Is Truth? James E. White. 248p. (Orig.). 1994. pap. 19.99 (*0-8054-1156-9*, 4211-56) Broadman.

What Is Truth? Christopher J. Williams. LC 75-23533. 118p. reprint ed. pap. 33.70 (*0-685-20579-7*, 2030629) Bks Demand.

What Is Two Plus Two. Jean-Paul Larocque. (Illus.). 12p. (J). (gr. k-3). 1993. pap. 10.95 (*1-895583-63-2*) MAYA Pubs.

What Is User Friendly? Ed. by F. W. Lancaster. (Clinic on Library Applications of Data Processing, Proceedings: 1977). (C). 1988. text ed. 10.00 (*0-87845-076-9*) U of Ill Grad Sch.

What Is Valentine's Day? Harriet Ziefert. (Lift-the-Flap Bk.). (Illus.). 16p. (J). (ps). 1993. 5.95 (*0-694-00413-8*, Festival) HarpC Child Bks.

What Is Vocal Hoarseness? Julie A. Blonigen. 24p. 1995. pap. text ed. 16.95 (*0-937857-55-6*, 1547) Speech Bin.

What Is War? Fifty Questions & Answers for Kids. Richard Rabinowitz. (J). (gr. 4-7). 1991. pap. 2.95 (*0-380-76704-X*, Camelot) Avon.

What is White? April Gohier. 1995. pap. 9.95 (*0-88494-986-9*) Bookcraft Inc.

What Is Wisdom? Cyril Upton. 148p. 1959. pap. 20.00 (*0-8464-0967-4*) Beekman Pubs.

What Is Wisdom? The World's Oldest Question Posed in the Light of Contemporary Perplexity. Cyril. Upton. 247p. reprint ed. pap. 70.40 (*0-317-08824-6*, 2015627) Bks Demand.

What Is World & Family Enlightenment? Marie B. Hall. 1977. pap. 9.98 (*0-938760-04-1*) Veritat Found.

W

An Asterisk (*) at the beginning of an entry indicates that the title is appearing in BIP for the first time.

What Is Worth Teaching? Krishna Kumar. 1993. pap. 4.95 (0-86311-175-0, Pub. by Orient Longman Ltd II) Apt Bks.

What Is Worth While? Anna R. Brown. 32p. pap. 9.95 (1-56849-515-3) Buccaneer Bks.

What Is Written Remains: Historical Essays on the Libraries of Notre Dame. Ed. by Maureen Gleason & Katharina J. Blackstead. LC 93-40670. (C). 1994. text ed. 28.00 (0-268-01949-5) U of Notre Dame Pr.

What Is Wrong with Jung. Don McGowan. 217p. 1994. 29.95 (0-87975-859-7) Prometheus Bks.

What Is Wrong with Marxism? On Capitalists & State in India & Indonesia. Olle Tornquist. (C). 1989. 22.50 (81-85054-92-4, Pub. by Manohar II) S Asia.

What Is Wrong with Modern Banking & Full Service Banks. 1992. lib. bdg. 154.95 (0-8490-5565-2) Gordon Pr.

What is Wrought in the Craftsman Workshops. 96p. pap. 15.00 (0-940326-18-3) Turn of Cent.

***What Is Your Destiny?** Michael Howard. Ed. by Roz Heyns. 84p. (Orig.). 1996. pap. 6.00 (1-888529-03-2) Out of Africa Pub.

What Is Your Language? Debra Leventhal. LC 93-10156. (Illus.). 32p. (J). (ps-1). 1994. pap. 12.99 (0-525-45133-1) Dutton Child Bks.

***What Is Your Language.** Debra Leventhal. 1998. pap. 4.99 (0-14-056315-6) Viking Penguin.

What Is Your Name? Book of Eritrean & Ethiopian Names. Zeray Habte-Sillasie. LC 95-51098. 140p. 1997. 29.95 (0-86543-446-8) Africa World.

What Is Your Will, O God? A Casebook for Studying Discernment of God's Will. Jules J. Toner. LC 95-80588. (Original Studies Composed in English: Series III, Vol. 13). vi, 110p. (Orig.). 1995. pap. 14.95 (1-880810-14-X) Inst Jesuit.

What Islam Gave to Humanity? Abdul H. Siddiqui. pap. 3.95 (0-933511-90-6) Kazi Pubns.

What it Costs - 1996: Survey of Revenue, Costs & Profits. rev. ed. Ed. by Thomas A. McCoy. (Illus.). 40p. 1996. pap. 39.75 (1-56461-164-7, 30179) Rough Notes.

What It Feels Like to Be a Building. rev. ed. Forrest Wilson. LC 88-22382. (Landmark Reprint Ser.). (Illus.). 80p. (J). (gr. 1 up). 1995. reprint ed. pap. text ed. 10.95 (0-471-14433-9) Wiley.

What It Is? Frank S. Jenkins. LC 81-90546. (Illus.). 48p. (Orig.). 1982. pap. 4.00 (0-942048-00-8) Shockley Pr.

What It Is, & How It Is Done: The Life of a Man As Told in First, Second, & Third Person in Reverse. 25.00 (0-9622997-3-1) Volcanic Eruptions.

What It Is & What It Is Not see Notes on Nursing

What It Is to Be Human: Hope Lies in Our Ability to Bring Back to Awareness. Robert J. Wolff. (Orig.). 1994. pap. 12.00 (0-9641638-1-0) Periwinkle WA.

What It Means to Be a Bad Boy. Alex N. Holland. (Illus.). 13p. (J). (gr. k-3). 1992. pap. 4.95 (1-895583-51-9) MAYA Pubs.

What It Means to Be a Christian. William L. Ludlow. LC 85-73080. 1988. pap. 8.95 (0-8158-0434-2) Chris Mass.

What It Means to Be a Church Leader: A Biblical Point of View. Norman Shawchuck. (Illus.). 71p. (Orig.). (C). 1984. pap. 12.95 (0-938180-13-4) Spiritual Growth.

***What It Means to be a Libertarian: A Personal Interpretation.** Charles Murray. LC 96-33531. 192p. 1997. 20.00 (0-553-06928-4) Broadway BDD.

***What It Means to Be a Libertarian: A Personal Interpretation.** Charles Murray. 192p. 1997. reprint ed. pap. 12.00 (0-7679-0039-1) Broadway BDD.

What It Means to Be an American. Michael Walzer. LC 92-82641. 124p. 1992. 18.00 (0-941419-66-5) Marsilio Pubs.

What It Means to Be Avant-Garde. David Antin. LC 93-9189. 256p. (Orig.). 1993. pap. 15.95 (0-8112-1238-6, NDP760) New Directions.

What It Means to Be Born Again. Johnnie Godwin. 144p. 1994. mass mkt. 1.99 (1-55748-542-9) Barbour & Co.

What It Means to Be Catholic. Joseph M. Champlin. 1995. pap. text ed. 4.95 (0-86716-245-7) St Anthony Mess Pr.

What It Means to Be Crucified with Christ. Harold D. Vaughan. (Illus.). 39p. (Orig.). (C). 1985. pap. text ed. 2.25 (0-942889-03-7) Christ Life Pubns.

What It Means to Be Free. Calvin B. Hanson. LC 89-81719. 1990. 12.95 (0-911802-66-5) Free Church Pubns.

What It Means to Be Human. Fitzgerald. 1979. text ed. 40.00 (0-08-023356-2, Pergamon Pr) Elsevier.

What It Means to Be Human. Molly Marshall. 160p. (Orig.). 1995. pap. 12.95 (1-880837-85-4) Smyth & Helwys.

What It Means to Forgive. Ivan A. Beals. (Christian Living Ser.). 48p. (Orig.). 1987. pap. 3.25 (0-8341-1185-3) Beacon Hill.

What It Might Be Like If There Were a Tax on Intelligence. Marji Gold-Vukson. (J). (gr. 4-9). 1990. pap. text ed. 6.97 (0-937659-42-8) GCT.

***What It Takes.** Ron Hostettler. LC 97-19576. 180p. 1997. pap. 10.99 (1-57673-174-X, Multnomah Bks) Multnomah Pubs.

What It Takes: A Survival Guide for Young & Teen Dads-to-Be. Connie Nykiel. LC 95-90854. (Illus.). 80p. (Orig.). (YA). (gr. 7 up). 1995. pap. 5.00 (1-888231-02-5) For Teen Moms.

What It Takes: The ABC's of Excelling. Keith Bell. LC 94-29303. 121p. 1995. 19.95 (0-945609-22-1) Keel Pubns.

What It Takes: The Way to the White House. Richard B. Cramer. LC 92-50848. 1993. pap. 19.00 (0-679-74649-8, Vin) Random.

What It Takes: To Get Children to Memorize Scripture. N. A. Woychuk. 40p. (Orig.). 1980. pap. 2.50 (1-880960-23-0) Script Memory Fl.

What It Takes to Succeed in Sales: Selecting & Retaining Top Producers. Jeanne Greenberg & Herbert Greenberg. 275p. 1989. text ed. 17.00 (1-55623-218-7) Irwin Prof Pubng.

What It Takes to Succeed in Sales: Selecting and Retaining Top Producers. Jeanne Greenberg. 1992. pap. 17.50 (1-55623-883-5) Irwin Prof Pubng.

What It Takes to Win. Charles R. Swindoll. (Swindoll Bible Study Guide Ser.). 1993. pap. 5.99 (0-8499-8475-0) Word Pub.

What It Takes to Write a Winning Grant Proposal. Lynnette R. Porter & William O. Coggin. 175p. 1993. pap. write for info. (1-883868-02-5) Am Vision Pub.

What It Was Was Rockabilly: A History of Rock 'n' Roll. Richard E. Jandrow. Ed. by Nancy A. DeFalco. (Illus.). 315p. (Orig.). 1995. pap. 15.95 (1-886791-01-5) Box Car Pub.

What Italy Has Given to the World. Gaetano Cipolla. (Illus.). 32p. (C). 1994. pap. 2.00 (1-881901-04-1) LEGAS.

What Italy Owes to Mussolini. Mario Missiroli. 1976. lib. bdg. 250.00 (0-8490-2817-5) Gordon Pr.

What It's All About: Being a Reporter's Story of the Early Campaign. William A. White. (History - United States Ser.). 146p. 1993. reprint ed. lib. bdg. 69.00 (0-7812-4806-X) Rprt Serv.

What It's Like to Be Me. 2nd ed. Helen Exley. (Illus.). 127p. (J). (gr. 4-11). 1984. pap. 10.95 (0-377-00144-9) Friendship Pr.

What It's Like to Live Now. Meredith Maran. 352p. 1996. reprint ed. pap. 11.95 (0-553-37493-1, Bantam Trade Bks) Bantam.

What Ivan Knows That Johnny Doesn't. Arthur S. Trace. LC 78-622. 213p. 1978. reprint ed. text ed. 55.00 (0-313-20276-1, TRWI, Greenwood Pr) Greenwood.

What I've Learned from Life's Little Giants. Lee Buddy. 114p. 1994. pap. write for info. (0-9643230-0-1) Achieve Unltd.

What I've Learned So Far. 160p. 1993. pap. write for info. (0-9636353-0-1) Sprngfld Pub Schls.

What Jamie Saw. Carolyn Coman. LC 95-23545. 128p. (YA). (gr. 5 up). Date not set. 13.95 (1-886910-02-2) Front Str.

What Jamie Saw. Carolyn Coman. 128p. 1997. pap. 3.99 (0-14-038335-2) Viking Penguin.

What Jane Austen Ate & Charles Dickens Knew: From Fox Hunting to Whits-The Facts of Daily Life in Nineteenth-Century England. Daniel Pool. 416p. 1994. pap. 14.00 (0-671-88236-8, Touchstone Bks) S&S Trade.

***What Jazz Is: An Insider's Guide to Understanding & Listening to Jazz.** Jonny King. 176p. 1997. 22.95 (0-8027-1328-9) Walker & Co.

***What Jazz Is: Listening & Hearing with Soul.** Jonny King. LC 97-8139. 250p. 1997. pap. 12.95 (0-8027-7519-5) Walker & Co.

What Jesus & the Bible Really Said about Drugs, Sex, Gays, Gambling, Prostitution, Alternative Healing, Assisted Suicide, & Other Consensual "Sins" Peter McWilliams. pap. 5.95 (0-931580-59-5) Prelude Press.

What Jesus Likes to Do Through You. Roberts Liardon. 1995. pap. text ed. 4.00 (1-879993-01-5) Albury Pub.

What Jesus Means to Me. Herman W. Gockel. 142p. 1968. 6.99 (0-570-03021-8, 06-1008) Concordia.

What Jesus Means to Me. large type ed. write for info. (0-318-68668-6, 7015) LBW.

What Jesus Said About. (Dialog Ser.). 44p. 1989. teacher ed., pap. 5.25 (0-8341-1221-3) Beacon Hill.

What Jesus Said About. Ed. by Stephen M. Miller. (Dialog Ser.). 112p. 1989. student ed., pap. 6.25 (0-8341-1171-3) Beacon Hill.

What Jesus Said about Successful Living: Principles from the Sermon on the Mount for Today. Haddon W. Robinson. 300p. 1991. pap. 12.99 (0-929239-43-1) Discovery Hse Pubs.

***What Jesus Saw from the Cross.** A. G. Sertillanges. LC 94-42378. (Illus.). 252p. 1997. pap. 15.95 (0-918477-37-9) Sophia Inst Pr.

What Jesus Taught. Hubert J. Richards. 48p. (Orig.). 1992. pap. text ed. 3.95 (0-8146-2197-X) Liturgical Pr.

What Jesus Taught. Hubert J. Richards. (Orig.). (C). 1993. 40.00 (0-85597-482-6, Pub. by McCrimmon Pub) St Mut.

What Jesus Taught about Manifesting Abundance. John Ayanzini. 130p. 1996. pap. 5.99 (0-89274-941-5, HH-941) Harrison Hse.

What Jesus Taught in Secret. Max F. Long. (Illus.). 137p. 1983. pap. 8.95 (0-87516-510-9) DeVorss.

What Jesus Would Say. Lee Strobel. 160p. 1994. pap. 10.99 (0-310-48511-8) Zondervan.

What Joe Saw. Anna G. Hines. LC 93-26583. 32p. 1994. 15.00 (0-688-13123-9); lib. bdg. 14.93 (0-688-13124-7) Greenwillow.

What Johnny Shouldn't Read: Textbook Censorship in America. Joan DelFattore. 224p. (C). 1992. 30.00 (0-300-05709-1) Yale U Pr.

What Johnny Shouldn't Read: Textbook Censorship in America. Joan DelFattore. 218p. 1994. pap. 13.00 (0-300-06050-5) Yale U Pr.

What Judaism Says about Politics: The Political Theology of the Torah. Martin Sicker. LC 92-35705. 272p. 1994. pap. 29.95 (0-87668-776-1) Aronson.

What Jung Really Said. E. A. Bennet. 192p. 1995. pap. 12.00 (0-8052-1046-6) Schocken.

What Justice Holmes Wrote, & What Has Been Written About Him, a Bibliography 1866-1976. Harry C. Shriver. LC 77-89073. 67p. 1978. 5.00 (0-685-01672-2) Fox Hills Pr.

What Kansas Means to Me: Twentieth-Century Writers on the Sunflower State. Ed. by Thomas F. Averill. LC 90-41688. (Illus.). 256p. 1995. pap. 12.95 (0-7006-0710-2) U Pr of KS.

***What Katy Did.** Susan Coolidge. (J). 1997. pap. 3.99 (0-14-036697-0) Viking Penguin.

What Katy Did. Susan Coolidge. 190p. (J). 1988. reprint ed. lib. bdg. 19.95 (0-89966-585-3) Buccaneer Bks.

What Katy Read: Feminist Re-Readings of 'Classic' Stories for Girls, 1850-1920. Shirley Foster & Judy Simons. LC 94-61440. 256p. 1995. text ed. 19.95 (0-87745-493-0) U of Iowa Pr.

What Keeps a House Warm? (Library of First Questions & Answers). (Illus.). 48p. (J). (gr. k-2). 14.95 (0-7835-0894-8) Time-Life.

What Keeps Me Here: Stories. Rebecca Brown. LC 96-12310. 160p. 1996. 20.00 (0-06-017440-4) HarpC.

What Keeps Us Here. Allison Joseph. LC 92-73325. 1992. pap. 10.00 (0-935331-11-5) Ampersand RI.

What Keynes Means. Anatol Murad. 1962. pap. 15.95 (0-8084-0320-6, B18) NCUP.

***What Kids Buy - & Why: Psychological Secrets to Creating the Products That Kids Love.** Daniel Acuff. 1997. 28.00 (0-684-83448-0) Free Pr.

What Kids Like to Do. Edward Stautberg. 1993. pap. 7.95 (0-942361-70-9) MasterMedia Pub.

What Kids Need Most in a Dad. Tim Hansel. LC 83-22902. 1988. pap. 8.99 (0-8007-5293-7) Revell.

What Kids Need Most in a Mom. Patricia H. Rushford. LC 83-3964. 1988. pap. 8.99 (0-8007-5294-5) Revell.

What Kids Need to Succeed: Proven, Practical Ways to Raise Good Kids. Peter L. Benson et al. LC 94-36533. 176p. (Orig.). 1995. mass mkt. 4.99 (0-915793-78-4) Free Spirit Pub.

***What Kids Need to Succeed: Proven Practical Ways to Raise Good Kids.** rev. ed. Peter L. Benson et al. 1997. pap. text ed. 5.95 (1-57542-030-9) Free Spirit Pub.

What Kids Really Want to Know about Sex. Phillip Hodson. 228p. (J). 1995. 10.95 (0-86051-882-5, Robson-Parkwest) Parkwest Pubns.

What Kids Say When They Write. Beverly Doyle. LC 92-83877. 1992. 12.95 (0-932881-17-3) Regulus Bks.

What Killed Leanita McClain? Essays on Living in Both Black & White Worlds. Leanita McClain & Clarence Page. 1995. 21.95 (1-879360-38-1) Noble Pr.

What Kind. Priscilla L. McQueen. (Illus.). (J). (gr. k). 1968. pap. 2.07 (0-685-16726-7) McQueen.

What Kind of a God Would Allow a Thing Like This to Happen?!! John Callahan. LC 94-11351. (Illus.). 1994. pap. 8.95 (0-688-13337-1, Quill) Morrow.

What Kind of Baby-Sitter Is This? Dolores Johnson. LC 90-42860. (Illus.). 32p. (J). (gr. k-3). 1991. lib. bdg. 15.00 (0-02-747846-7, Mac Bks Young Read) S&S Childrens.

***What Kind of Criminal Policy for Europe?** Mireille Delmas-Marty et al. LC 96-41628. 1996. 225.00 (90-411-0310-4) Kluwer Law Tax Pubs.

What Kind of God? Essays in Honor of Richard L. Rubenstein, Vol. 11. Betty R. Rubenstein et al. Ed. by Hannah R. Feibel et al. LC 95-23284. (Studies in the Shoah: Vol. 11). 524p. (C). 1995. lib. bdg. 64.50 (0-7618-0036-0) U Pr of Amer.

What Kind of God Is God? George E. Drew. 65p. (Orig.). 1986. pap. 7.95 (0-940754-33-9) Ed Ministries.

What Kind of Life: The Limits of Medical Progress. Daniel Callahan. LC 94-34440. 320p. 1995. pap. 15.95 (0-87840-573-9) Georgetown U Pr.

What Kind of Love? The Diary of a Pregnant Teenager. Sheila Cole. 144p. (YA). (gr. 7 up). 1996. pap. 4.50 (0-380-72575-4, Flare) Avon.

What Kind of Love? The Diary of a Pregnant Teenager. Sheila Cole. LC 94-78938. (Illus.). 192p. (YA). (gr. 5 up). 1995. 15.00 (0-688-12848-3) Lothrop.

What Kind of Love Is This. Sandra K. Musser. Ed. by Steve Zimmerman. LC 82-84236. (Orig.). 1982. pap. 7.95 (0-934896-43-7) Adopt Aware Pr.

What Kind of Man? The Life of Henry Smith Leiper. William J. Schmidt & Edward Quellette. LC 86-12012. 323p. 1986. reprint ed. pap. 92.10 (0-608-01654-3, 2062306) Bks Demand.

What Kind of Name Is Juan? Marilyn H. McClaskey. Ed. by Roger Rosen. (Flipside Fiction Ser.). (YA). (gr. 7-12). 1989. lib. bdg. 12.95 (0-8239-0830-5) Rosen Group.

What Kind of Truck? (J). 1995. 1.59 (0-307-10154-1, Golden Pr) Western Pub.

What Kind of Weather? Rice & Cerbu. (Easy Theme Reader Ser.). (Illus.). 16p. (J). (ps-1). 1996. pap. 2.49 (1-55734-898-7) Tchr Create Mat.

What Kwanzaa Means to Me. Sauda Oni. (Illus.). 36p. (J). (gr. k-3). 1992. pap. 3.95 (0-912444-38-X) DARE Bks.

What Language Shall I Borrow? God-Talk in Worship: A Male Response to Feminist Theology. Brian Wren. 276p. 1990. reprint ed. pap. 15.95 (0-8245-1055-0) Crossroad NY.

What Latter-Day Stripling Warriors Learn from Their Mothers. Ardeth G. Kapp. LC 96-10503. 86p. 1996. 9.95 (1-57345-164-9) Deseret Bk.

What Law Now for the Seas? ABA, International Law & Practice Section Staff. LC 84-70164. 73p. 1984. pap. 8.00 (0-89707-132-8, 521-0034) Amer Bar Assn.

***What Law School Administrators Should Know about the ABA/AALS Law Library Inspection Process.** 2nd rev. ed. Donald J. Dunn & Roy M. Mersky. (Law Library Information Reports: Vol. 1). pap. 100.00 (0-87802-098-5) Glanville.

What Law There Was. Al Dempsey. 1992. mass mkt. 3.99 (0-8125-8184-9) Tor Bks.

What Lawyers Earn... TBA Staff. 1997. pap. text ed. 17.95 (0-15-900183-8) HB Legal.

What Legislators Need to Know about Children's Mental Health. 50p. 1990. 15.00 (1-55516-688-1, 6627) Natl Conf State Legis.

What Legislators Need to Know about the National Board of Professional Teaching Standards. Constance L. Koprowicz. (State Legislative Reports: Vol. 19, No. 1). 6p. 1994. 5.00 (1-55516-340-8, 7302-1901) Natl Conf State Legis.

What Legislators Need to Know about Traumatic Brain Injury. Barbara Wright. 56p. 1993. 10.00 (1-55516-660-1, 6639) Natl Conf State Legis.

What Lies Behind It...! Herbert Vollmann. 1977. pap. 6.00 (3-87860-083-6) Grail Fndtn-Amer.

What Life Could Mean to You. Alfred Adler. Tr. by Colin Brett from GER. 256p. (Orig.). (C). 1994. pap. 13.95 (1-85168-022-5) Onewrld Pubns.

What Life Means to Me & the Dreams of Debs. Jack London. (Illus.). 42p. 1991. pap. 1.95 (0-932458-15-7) Star Rover.

What Life Was Like: On the Banks of the Nile, Ancient Egypt (4000-30 B. C.) Time-Life Books Editors. 1996. write for info. (0-8094-9378-0) Time-Life.

***What Life Was Like in the Age of Chivalry: Medieval Europe, 800-1500 AD.** Ed. by Time-Life Books Editors. LC 97-13092. (What Life Was Like Ser.). (Illus.). 168p. 1997. write for info. (0-7835-5451-6) Time-Life.

***What Life Was Like When Rome Ruled the World.** Time-Life Books Staff. LC 97-23245. 1997. write for info. (0-7835-5452-4) Time-Life.

What Light Through Yonder Window Breaks: More Experiments in Atmospheric Physics. Craig F. Bohren. LC 00-90. 190p. 1991. pap. text ed. 12.95 (0-471-52915-X) Wiley.

What Lisa Knew. Joyce Johnson. 416p. 1991. mass mkt. 4.95 (0-8217-3387-7, Zebra Kensgtn) Kensgtn Pub Corp.

What Little I Remember. Otto Frisch. (Canto Book Ser.). (Illus.). 238p. (C). 1991. pap. text ed. 11.95 (0-521-40583-1) Cambridge U Pr.

What Lives in a Shell? Kathleen W. Zoehfeld. LC 93-12428. (Trophy Let's-Read-&-Find-Out Science Bk.). (Illus.). 32p. (J). (ps-1). 1994. pap. 4.95 (0-06-445124-0, Trophy) HarpC Child Bks.

What Lives in a Shell? Kathleen W. Zoehfeld. LC 93-12428. (Let's-Read-&-Find-Out Science Bk.: Stage 1). (Illus.). 32p. (J). (ps-1). 1994. 15.00 (0-06-022998-5); lib. bdg. 14.89 (0-06-022999-3) HarpC Child Bks.

What Lives in the Sea. Peter Seymour. (Science Action Book Ser.). (Illus.). 10p. (J). (gr. 2-5). 1985. lib. bdg. 8.95 (0-02-782170-6, Mac Bks Young Read) S&S Childrens.

***What Lives in the Trees Bk. 7.** Danielle Ponsolle. (Life with Sylvie Ser.: Bk. 7). (Illus.). 24p. (J). (ps-k). 1997. 12.95 (0-9655782-6-7, Tern Bks) Tern Bk Co.

***What Lives in the Water Bk. 6.** Danielle Ponsolle. (Life with Sylvie Ser.: Bk. 6). (Illus.). 24p. (J). (ps-k). 1997. 12.95 (0-9655782-5-9, Tern Bks) Tern Bk Co.

***What Logos Do & How They Do It.** Jared Brown & Anistatia R. Miller. (Illus.). 144p. 1997. 29.99 (1-56496-382-9) Rockport Pubs.

***What Looks Like Crazy on an Ordinary Day: A Novel.** Pearl Cleage. LC 97-17708. 1997. write for info. (0-380-97584-X) Avon.

***What Losing Taught Me about Winning.** Fran Tarkenton. 1997. 23.00 (0-684-83413-8) S&S Trade.

What Love. Maria Madison. 254p. 1996. mass mkt. 7.95 (0-929654-86-2, 117) Blue Moon Bks.

What Love Sees: A Biographical Novel. large type ed. Susan Vreeland. LC 96-11831. 608p. 1996. lib. bdg. 22.95 (0-7862-0696-9, Thorndike Lrg Prnt) Thorndike Pr.

What Lovemaking Means to a Man: Practical Advice to Married Men About Sex. Tim LaHaye & Beverly LaHaye. LC 83-18338. 64p. 1984. pap. 4.99 (0-310-27102-9, 18338P) Zondervan.

What Lovemaking Means to a Woman: Practical Advice to Married Women About Sex. Tim LaHaye & Beverly LaHaye. LC 83-18339. 64p. 1984. pap. 4.99 (0-310-27052-9, 18339P) Zondervan.

What Luther Says: A Practical-in-Home Anthology for the Active Christian. Ewald Plass. 1696p. 1987. 40.99 (0-570-04240-2, 15-1232) Concordia.

What Maastricht Meant for Business: Opportunities & Regularities in the EC Internal Market. Brian Rothery. 200p. 1993. 49.95 (0-566-07430-3, Pub. by Gower UK); pap. 21.95 (0-566-07431-1, Pub. by Gower UK) Ashgate Pub Co.

What Machines Can't Do: Politics & Technology in the Industrial Enterprise. Robert J. Thomas. LC 93-15746. 1994. 35.00 (0-520-08131-5); pap. 16.00 (0-520-08701-1) U CA Pr.

What Mad Universe? Fredric Brown. 1993. reprint ed. lib. bdg. 18.95 (0-89968-333-9, Lghtyr Pr) Buccaneer Bks.

What Made Gertie Gallop. Jeffrey K. Pinto & O. P. Kharbanda. (Industrial Engineering Ser.). 336p. 1996. text ed. 34.95 (0-442-02158-5) Van Nos Reinhold.

What Made Pistachio Nuts? Early Sound Comedy & the Vaudeville Aesthetic. Henry Jenkins. (Film & Culture Ser.). (Illus.). 416p. 1992. text ed. 49.50 (0-231-07854-4) Col U Pr.

What Made Pistachio Nuts? Early Sound Comedy & the Vaudeville Aesthetic. Henry Jenkins. 1993. pap. 16.50 (0-231-07855-2) Col U Pr.

What Made the South Different? Ed. by Kees Gispen. LC 90-12611. 1990. 35.00 (0-87805-454-5); pap. 16.95 (0-87805-455-3) U Pr of Miss.

What Made Them Great Series, 5 bks., Set. Claudio Solarino et al. (Illus.). 832p. (J). (gr. 5-8). 1990. pap. 29.75 (0-382-09984-2); lib. bdg. 90.65 (0-382-09983-4) Silver Burdett Pr.

What Made Them So Brave? deluxe ed. Basilea M. Schlink. (Illus.). (J). (gr. 3 up). 1978. 2.25 (3-87209-655-9) Evang Sisterhood Mary.

What Madness Brought Me Here: New & Selected Poems, 1968-1988. Colleen J. McElroy. LC 89-37803. (Wesleyan Poetry Ser.). 118p. 1990. pap. 12.95 (0-8195-1188-9, Wesleyan Univ Pr) U Pr of New Eng.

What Magnets Can Do. Allan Fowler. LC 94-35628. (Rookie Read-About Science Ser.). (Illus.). 32p. (J). (ps-2). 1995. lib. bdg. 17.30 (0-516-06034-1) Childrens.

What Magnets Can Do. Allan Fowler. (Rookie Read-About Science Ser.). (Illus.). 32p. (J). (ps-2). 1995. pap. 3.95 (0-516-46034-X) Childrens.

***What Mailman Brought.** Carolyn Craven. (J). Date not set. pap. 4.95 (0-399-21307-4) Putnam Pub Group.

What Maisie Knew. Henry James. Ed. & Intro. by Paul Theroux. (Classics Ser.). 288p. 1986. pap. 8.95 (0-14-043248-5, Penguin Classics) Viking Penguin.

What Maisie Knew. Henry James. (Sun & Moon Classics Ser.: No. 80). 300p. 1995. pap. 11.95 (1-55713-201-1) Sun & Moon CA.

What Maisie Knew. Henry James. Ed. & Intro. by Adrian Poole. (World's Classics Ser.). 316p. 1996. pap. 4.95 (0-19-282428-7) OUP.

What Maisie Knew. Henry James, Jr. (Notable American Authors Ser.). 1992. reprint ed. lib. bdg. 75.00 (0-7812-3414-X) Rprt Serv.

What Maisie Knew. Henry James. (BCL1-PS American Literature Ser.). 240p. 1993. reprint ed. lib. bdg. 79.00 (0-7812-6977-6) Rprt Serv.

What Maisie Knew; In the Cage; The Pupil. Henry James. LC 72-158790. (Novels & Tales of Henry James Ser.: Vol. 11). xxi, 576p. 1979. reprint ed. 45.00 (0-678-02811-7) Kelley.

What Makes a Bird a Bird? May Garelick. (Illus.). 32p. (Orig.). (J). (gr. 1-5). 25.95 (1-57255-009-0) Mondo Pubng.

What Makes a Bird a Bird? May Garelick. (Illus.). 32p. (Orig.). (J). (ps-5). pap. 4.95 (1-57255-008-2) Mondo Pubng.

What Makes a Bruegel a Bruegel? Text by Richard Muhlberger. (Illus.). 48p. (J). (gr. 5 up). 1993. pap. 9.95 (0-670-85203-1) Viking Child Bks.

What Makes a Car Go? S. Tanta. (Starting Point Science Ser.). (Illus.). 24p. (J). (gr. k up). 1994. pap. 3.95 (0-7460-1650-6, Usborne); lib. bdg. 12.95 (0-88110-704-2, Usborne) EDC.

What Makes a Cassatt a Cassatt? Metropolitan Museum Of Art Staff. (Illus.). 48p. (YA). (gr. 5 up). 1994. pap. 11.99 (0-670-85742-4) Viking Child Bks.

What Makes a Degas a Degas? Text by Richard Muhlberger. (Illus.). 48p. (J). (gr. 5 up). 1993. pap. 9.95 (0-670-85205-8) Viking Child Bks.

What Makes a Flower Grow? Susan Mayes. (Starting Point Science Ser.). (Illus.). 24p. (J). (gr. 1-4). 1989. pap. 3.95 (0-7460-0275-0, Usborne); lib. bdg. 12.95 (0-88110-381-0, Usborne) EDC.

***What Makes a Good Teacher.** Greg Anderson. (Illus.). 8p. (Orig.). 1996. pap. 2.50 (1-884241-74-3, AN1021) Energeia Pub.

What Makes a Goya a Goya? Metropolitan Museum Of Art Staff. (Illus.). 48p. (YA). (gr. 5 up). 1994. pap. 11.99 (0-670-85743-2) Viking Child Bks.

What Makes a Leonardo a Leonardo? Metropolitan Museum Of Art Staff. (Illus.). 48p. (YA). (gr. 5 up). 1994. pap. 11.99 (0-670-85744-0) Viking Child Bks.

What Makes a Magnet? Franklyn M. Branley. LC 95-23181. (Let's-Read-&-Find-Out Science Ser.: Stage 2). (Illus.). 32p. (J). (gr. k-4). 1996. 14.95 (0-06-026441-1); lib. bdg. 14.89 (0-06-026442-X) HarpC Child Bks.

What Makes a Magnet? Franklyn M. Branley. LC 95-32181. (Let's-Read-&-Find-Out Science Ser.: Stage 2). (Illus.). 32p. (J). (gr. k-4). 1996. pap. 4.95 (0-06-445148-8, Trophy) HarpC Child Bks.

What Makes a Man? Twelve Promises That Will Change Your Life. Bill McCartney et al. LC 92-61235. 240p. 1992. 18.00 (0-89109-707-4) NavPress.

What Makes a Man a Man. Dan Jones. 103p. 1993. pap. 9.95 (0-9638104-0-5) Mandala B & T.

What Makes a Man? Study Guide. Steve Griffith. 127p. (Orig.). 1993. pap. 7.00 (0-89109-730-9) NavPress.

What Makes a Master. Harriet L. McCollum. 114p. 1975. reprint ed. spiral bd. 11.00 (0-7873-0596-0) Hlth Research.

What Makes a Master? Being & Outline of the Law of Life & the Process of Its Development & Unfoldment Towards Self Conscious Awareness & Mastery of Destiny (1932) Harriet L. McCollum. 114p. 1996. pap. 16.95 (1-56459-841-1) Kessinger Pub.

What Makes a Minister? Duane Magnani. 1986. 4.95 (1-883858-23-2) Witness CA.

What Makes a Monet a Monet? Text by Richard Muhlberger. (Illus.). 48p. (J). (gr. 5 up). 1993. pap. 11.99 (0-670-85200-7) Viking Child Bks.

What Makes a Picasso a Picasso? Metropolitan Museum Of Art Staff. (Illus.). 48p. (YA). (gr. 5 up). 1994. pap. 11.99 (0-670-85741-6) Viking Child Bks.

What Makes a Project Marginal. Tom S. Radford. (C). 1989. 140.00 (0-89771-730-9, Pub. by Lorne & MacLean Marine) St Mut.

What Makes a Project "Marginal?" Tom S. Radford. 1989. 140.00 (90-6314-862-3, Pub. by Lorne & MacLean Marine) St Mut.

What Makes a Raphael a Raphael? Text by Richard Muhlberger. (Illus.). 48p. (J). (gr. 5 up). 1993. pap. 9.95 (0-670-85204-X) Viking Child Bks.

What Makes a Rembrandt a Rembrandt? Text by Richard Muhlberger. (Illus.). 48p. (J). (gr. 5 up). 1993. pap. 9.95 (0-670-85199-X) Viking Child Bks.

What Makes a School Catholic? William J. O'Malley et al. 47p. (Orig.). 1991. pap. 5.00 (1-55833-102-6) Natl Cath Educ.

***What Makes a Shadow?** Clyde R. Bulla. LC 92-36350. 32p. (J). (ps-1). 1996. pap. 7.95 incl. digital audio (0-694-70081-9) HarpC.

What Makes a Shadow? rev. ed. Clyde R. Bulla. LC 92-36350. (Let's-Read-&-Find-Out Science Bk.: Stage 1). (Illus.). 32p. (J). (ps-1). 1994. lib. bdg. 14.89 (0-06-022916-0) HarpC Child Bks.

What Makes a Sicilian? Gaetano Cipolla. (Illus.). 32p. (Orig.). 1996. 3.00 (1-881901-11-4) LEGAS.

What Makes a Successful Transition? Ed. by David Clinton & Daniel G. Lang. (Papers on Presidential Transitions & Foreign Policy: Vol. IX). 172p. (Orig.). (C). 1993. pap. text ed. 22.50 (0-8191-8929-4, Pub. by White Miller Center); lib. bdg. 48.50 (0-8191-8928-6, Pub. by White Miller Center) U Pr of Amer.

What Makes a Woman Beautiful. Joan Logghe. (Green Ser.). 6.00 (0-938631-15-2) Pennywhistle Pr.

What Makes Airplanes Fly? History, Science, & Applications of Aerodynamics. Peter P. Wegener. (Illus.). x, 225p. 1994. 32.00 (0-387-97513-6) Spr-Verlag.

What Makes Airplanes Fly? History, Science & Applications of Aerodynamics. 2nd ed. Peter P. Wegener. LC 96-23154. 250p. 1996. 32.50 (0-387-94784-1) Spr-Verlag.

What Makes an Effective School? A Monograph from the Nineteen Eighty Journalism Fellowship Program. 112p. 7.50 (0-318-03010-1) Inst Educ Lead.

What Makes Boys Town So Special? Val J. Peter. 150p. (Orig.). (C). 1986. pap. 5.95 (0-938510-36-3, 19-003) Boys Town Pr.

What Makes Churches Grow? The Best of Action Information. Ed. by Celia A. Hahn. pap. 11.25 (1-56699-100-5, OD76) Alban Inst.

What Makes Danny Run? Carolyn M. Erwin. (Illus.). 32p. (Orig.). (J). (gr. k-6). 1991. pap. 8.95 (0-9630903-0-5) Little Gems.

***What Makes Day & Night.** Franklyn M. Branley & Arthur Dorros. (Illus.). (J). (gr. 1-5). 7.66 (0-690-04523-9, 147013) HarpC Child Bks.

What Makes Day & Night? rev. ed. Franklyn M. Branley. LC 85-40657. (Trophy Let's-Read-&-Find-Out Bk.). (Illus.). 32p. (J). (gr. k-3). 1986. pap. 4.95 (0-06-445050-3, Trophy) HarpC Child Bks.

What Makes Day & Night? rev. ed. Franklyn M. Branley. LC 85-47903. (Let's-Read-&-Find-Out Science Bk.). (Illus.). 32p. (J). (ps-3). 1986. lib. bdg. 14.89 (0-690-04524-7, Crowell Jr Bks) HarpC Child Bks.

What Makes Everything Go? Michael E. Ross. 94p. (J). (gr. k-2). 1979. pap. 4.95 (0-939666-19-7) Yosemite Assn.

***What Makes Exports Boom?** pap. 10.00 (0-8213-3667-3, 13667) World Bank.

What Makes Honey? Myrna Perkins. (Illus.). 32p. (Orig.). (J). (ps-3). pap. 3.95 (0-937729-03-5) Markins Enter.

***What Makes Industries Strategic.** (Illus.). 92p. 1990. pap. text ed. 40.00 (1-57979-170-0) BPI Info Servs.

***What Makes Industries Strategic: A Perspective on Technology, Economic Development, & Defense.** 1997. lib. bdg. 255.75 (0-8490-6101-6) Gordon Pr.

What Makes Industries Strategic: A Perspective on Technology, Economic Development, & Defense. Martin C. Libicki. (Illus.). 93p. (Orig.). 1990. per. 2.75 (0-16-025888-X, 008-020-01225-4) USGPO.

***What Makes Industries Strategic: A Perspective on Technology, Economic Development, & Defense.** Martin C. Libicki. (Illus.). 89p. (Orig.). (C). 1996. reprint ed. pap. 30.00 (0-7881-3155-9) DIANE Pub.

What Makes It Rain? Keith Brandt. LC 81-7495. (Illus.). 32p. (J). (gr. 2-4). 1982. lib. bdg. 12.95 (0-89375-582-6) Troll Communs.

What Makes It Rain? Keith Brandt. LC 81-7495. (Illus.). 32p. (J). (gr. 2-4). 1996. pap. 3.50 (0-89375-583-4) Troll Communs.

What Makes It Rain? Susan Mayes. (Starting Point Science Ser.). (Illus.). 24p. (J). (gr. 1-4). 1989. pap. 3.95 (0-7460-0274-2, Usborne); lib. bdg. 12.95 (0-88110-379-9, Usborne) EDC.

What Makes Life Worth Living? How Japanese & Americans Make Sense of Their Worlds. Gordon Mathews. LC 95-22263. (Illus.). 296p. 1996. pap. 16.95 (0-520-20133-7) U CA Pr.

What Makes Life Worth Living? How Japanese & Americans Make Sense of Their Worlds. Gordon Mathews. LC 95-22263. (Illus.). 296p. (C). 1996. 45.00 (0-520-20132-9) U CA Pr.

What Makes Me Happy. B. B. Precious. Ed. by Dewilda M. Williams. (Byrant Series). (Illus.). 16p. (J). (gr. k-2). 1996. 10.95 (1-886493-03-0) NBC Study Pub.

What Makes Me Happy? Catherine Anholt & Laurence Anholt. LC 94-5144. (Illus.). 32p. (J). 1996. reprint ed. pap. 5.99 (1-56402-828-3) Candlewick Pr.

***What Makes Me Me: A Small Group Counseling & Classroom Guidance on Self Esteem & Decision Make Skills.** Lagretta M. Walker. (Illus.). 59p. (Orig.). (J). (gr. 5-9). 1991. pap. 3.95 (1-57543-012-6) Mar Co Prods.

***What Makes Music Work.** 3rd ed. Philip Seyer et al. (Understanding Music Ser.: Vol. 1). (Illus.). 256p. 1996. reprint ed. 14.95 (0-9651344-0-7) Forest Hill Mus.

What Makes Musicians So Sarcastic? Charles M. Schulz. LC 76-8677. 192p. 1976. pap. 4.95 (0-03-018111-9, Owl) H Holt & Co.

What Makes Musicians So Sarcastic? Charles M. Schulz. (Illus.). 128p. 1992. pap. 6.95 (0-8050-2060-8, Owl) H Holt & Co.

What Makes My Daddy Best? Albert. (J). 1998. pap. 3.99 (0-689-81230-2) S&S Childrens.

What Makes Nature Tick? Roger G. Newton. LC 93-9507. 269p. 1993. text ed. 27.95 (0-674-95085-2) HUP.

What Makes Nature Tick? Roger G. Newton. (Illus.). 269p. 1994. pap. text ed. 14.95 (0-674-95082-8, NEWWHX) HUP.

What Makes New York City Run? A Citizen's Guide to How City Government Works. rev. ed. Adrienne Kivelson. Ed. by Patricia Young. LC 79-88289. (Illus.). 100p. (C). 1990. pap. text ed. 4.00 (0-916130-02-9) LWV NYC.

What Makes People Buy. Donald A. Laird. LC 75-39254. (Getting & Spending: The Consumer's Dilemma Ser.). 1976. reprint ed. 23.95 (0-405-08027-1) Ayer.

***What Makes People Click: Advertise on the Web.** Jim Sterne. 1997. 24.99 (0-7897-1235-0) Que.

What Makes People Cook with Improved Biomass Stoves? A Comparative International Review of Stove Programs. Douglas F. Barnes & Keith Openshaw. LC 94-10830. (World Bank Technical Paper Ser.: No. 242). 56p. 1994. 6.95 (0-8213-2800-X, 12800) World Bank.

What Makes Popcorn Pop? And Other Questions about the World Around Us. Jack Myers. LC 90-85912. (Illus.). 64p. (J). (gr. 1-5). 1991. 12.95 (1-878093-33-9) Boyds Mills Pr.

What Makes Popcorn Pop? First Questions & Answers about Food. Ed. by Elizabeth Ward. (Library of First Questions & Answers). (Illus.). 48p. (J). (gr. k-2). 1994. 14.95 (0-7835-0862-X) Time-Life.

What Makes Popcorn Pop? First Questions & Answers about Food. Ed. by Elizabeth Ward. (Library of First Questions & Answers). (Illus.). 48p. (J). (ps). 1994. lib. bdg. write for info. (0-7835-0863-8) Time-Life.

What Makes Pornography "Sexy"? John Stoltenberg. LC 94-3812. (Thistle Series of Chapbooks). 80p. 1994. pap. 4.95 (1-57131-201-3) Milkweed Ed.

What Makes Ryan Tick: A Family's Triumph over Tourette Syndrome & Attention Deficit Disorder. Susan Hughes. Date not set. pap. 15.95 (1-878267-35-3) Hope Pr CA.

What Makes Sammy Run? Budd Schulberg. LC 93-10497. 1993. pap. 14.00 (0-679-73422-8, Vin) Random.

What Makes Sammy Run. Budd Schulberg. 1990. 19.95 (0-394-57618-7) Random.

What Makes Sammy Run? Budd Schulberg. 1994. reprint ed. lib. bdg. 32.95 (1-56849-333-9) Buccaneer Bks.

What Makes Sammy Run? Budd Schulberg. LC 79-10457. 1979. reprint ed. lib. bdg. 16.00 (0-8376-0435-4) Bentley.

What Makes Sammy Run - Vocal Selections. (Classic Broadway Shows Ser.). 28p. (Orig.). 1993. pap. 10.95 (0-89724-075-8, VF2074) Warner Brothers.

What Makes Sound Patterns Expressive? The Poetic Mode of Speech Perception. Reuven Tsur. LC 91-585. (Sound & Meaning: The Roman Jakobson Series in Linguistics & Poetics). 188p. 1992. text ed. 37.95 (0-8223-1164-X); pap. text ed. 18.95 (0-8223-1170-4) Duke.

What Makes the Great Great: Strategies for Extraordinary Achievement. Dennis Kimbro. 352p. 1997. 23.95 (0-385-48268-X) Doubleday.

What Makes the Public Schools Work? A Monograph from the Nineteen Eighty-One Journalism Fellowship Program. 112p. 7.50 (0-318-03009-8) Inst Educ Lead.

What Makes the Weather. Janet Palazzo. LC 81-11383. (Now I Know Ser.). (Illus.). 32p. (J). (gr. k-2). 1982. pap. 3.50 (0-89375-655-5) Troll Communs.

What Makes the Wind? Laurence Santrey. LC 81-7486. (Illus.). 32p. (J). (gr. 2-4). 1982. lib. bdg. 12.95 (0-89375-584-2) Troll Communs.

What Makes the Wind? Laurence Santrey. LC 81-7486. (Illus.). 32p. (J). (gr. 2-4). 1996. pap. 3.50 (0-89375-585-0) Troll Communs.

***What Makes the World Go Round? A Question & Answer Encyclopedia.** Jinny Johnson. LC 96-41111. (Henry Holt Reference Bk.). 1997. 18.95 (0-8050-5086-8) H Holt & Co.

What Makes Things Move? Althea. LC 90-10924. (First Science Ser.). (Illus.). 32p. (J). (gr. k-3). 1991. lib. bdg. 12.95 (0-8167-2124-6) Troll Communs.

What Makes Things Move? Althea. LC 90-10924. (First Science Ser.). (Illus.). 32p. (J). (gr. k-3). 1997. pap. 3.95 (0-8167-2125-4) Troll Communs.

What Makes Us Episcopalians? John E. Booty. LC 82-80468. 48p. (Orig.). 1982. pap. 3.95 (0-8192-1302-0) Morehouse Pub.

***What Makes Winners Win: Over 100 Athletes, Coaches, & Managers Tell You the Secrets of Success.** Compiled by Charlie Jones. 188p. 1997. 18.95 (1-55972-399-8, Birch Ln Pr) Carol Pub Group.

What Makes Women Sick: Gender & the Political Economy of Health. Lesley Doyal. 320p. 1995. text ed. 50.00 (0-8135-2206-4); pap. text ed. 15.95 (0-8135-2207-2) Rutgers U Pr.

What Makes Workers Learn: The Role of Incentives in Workplace Education & Training. Donald Hirsch & Daniel A. Wagner. LC 94-28030. (National Center on Adult Literacy Series on Literacy Studies). 224p. 1995. text ed. 47.50 (1-881303-23-3) Hampton Pr NJ.

What Makes Workers Learn: The Role of Incentives in Workplace Education & Training. Ed. by Donald Hirsch & Daniel A. Wagner. LC 94-28030. (National Center on Adult Literacy Series on Literacy Studies). 224p. 1995. pap. text ed. 21.95 (1-881303-24-1) Hampton Pr NJ.

What Makes Writing Good: A Multiperspective. William E. Coles, Jr. & James Vopat. LC 84-80295. 360p. (C). 1985. pap. text ed. 35.96 (0-669-06614-1) HM College Div.

What Makes You Feel Like Shouting. Libby Collen. 1987. 3.45 (0-89741-026-2) Gila River.

What Makes You Ill? (Starting Point Science Ser.). (Illus.). 24p. (J). (gr. 1 up). 1993. lib. bdg. 12.95 (0-88110-653-4, Usborne) EDC.

What Makes You Ill? (Starting Point Science Ser.). (Illus.). 24p. (J). (gr. 1 up). 1994. pap. 3.95 (0-7460-0692-6, Usborne) EDC.

What Makes You So Strong? Sermons of Joy & Strength from Jeremiah A. Wright, Jr. Jeremiah A. Wright. Ed. by Jini K. Ross. 176p. 1993. pap. 14.00 (0-8170-1198-6) Judson.

What Makes You Think You're Happy? Charles M. Schulz. 128p. 1990. pap. 5.95 (0-8050-1483-7, Owl) H Holt & Co.

What Makes You What You Are? A First Look at Genetics. Sandy Bornstein. Ed. by Jane Steltenpohl. (Illus.). 128p. (J). (gr. 7 up). 1989. pap. 6.95 (0-671-68650-X, Julian Messner) Silver Burdett Pr.

What Makes Your Teen Tick? William Coleman. 160p. (Orig.). 1993. pap. 7.99 (1-55661-322-9) Bethany Hse.

What Man Can Make of Man. William E. Hocking. LC 75-3191. reprint ed. 27.50 (0-404-59192-2) AMS Pr.

What Managed Care Is Doing to Outpatient Mental Health: A Look Behind the Veil of Secrecy. Ivan J. Miller. 49p. 1994. pap. 6.00 (0-9645263-0-1) Boulder Psychother.

What Management Should Know about Industrial Advertising. Emil Hofsoos. LC 70-114692. 134p. reprint ed. pap. 38.20 (0-685-23786-9, 2032873) Bks Demand.

What Managers & Supervisors Need to Know about the ADA. 55p. 1992. pap. 18.50 (0-685-56813-X, PB14B) Soc Human Resc Mgmt.

What Managers & Supervisors Need to Know about the ADA: Trainer's Guide. Richard Pimentel et al. 113p. (C). 1992. 395.00 (0-942071-18-2) M Wright & Assocs.

What Manner of Love. Raymond H. Woolsey. LC 94-46262. 1995. write for info. (0-8280-0932-5) Review & Herald.

What Manner of Man: A Biography of Martin Luther King Jr, 1929-1968. Lerone Bennett, Jr. 251p. 1968. 19.95 (0-87485-027-4) Johnson Chi.

What Manner of Man? Sermons on Christ by St. Bonaventure. 2nd ed. St. Bonaventure. 135p. 1989. reprint ed. pap. 6.95 (0-8199-0497-X, 0497-X, Frncscn Herld) Franciscan Pr.

What Manner of Man Is This? Earl E. Cummings. 1992. pap. 10.00 (1-56186-515-X) Pilgrim Pubns.

***What Manner of Men? A Reconsideration Across the Synapses of Art History of Three Paintings & Their Images of Men of African Descent.** Thomas M. Shaw. LC 97-21317. 1997. write for info. (0-7618-0821-3); pap. write for info. (0-7618-0822-1) U Pr of Amer.

What Manner of Woman: Essays on English & American Life & Literature. Ed. by Marlene Springer. LC 76-53876. (Gotham Library). 357p. (C). 1977. text ed. 32.00 (0-8147-7777-5); pap. text ed. 18.00 (0-8147-7779-1) NYU Pr.

What Marx Really Meant. George D. Cole. LC 79-90489. 309p. 1971. reprint ed. text ed. 59.75 (0-8371-3082-4, COWM, Greenwood Pr) Greenwood.

What Mary Jo Shared. Janice M. Udry. LC 66-16082. (Illus.). 40p. (J). (gr. k-2). 1966. lib. bdg. 14.95 (0-8075-8842-3) A Whitman.

What Mary Jo Shared. Janice M. Udry. (Illus.). 32p. (J). (ps-3). 1991. pap. 3.99 (0-590-43757-7) Scholastic Inc.

What Masonry Means. 5th ed. William E. Hammond. 173p. 1994. reprint ed. pap. 8.50 (0-88053-051-0, M-311) Macoy Pub.

What Matisse Is After. Diana Chang. (Poetry Ser.). (Illus.). 60p. (Orig.). (C). 1985. pap. 4.00 (0-936556-12-9) Contact Two.

What Matrimonial Lawyers Need to Know about Bankruptcy, Tax, & Corporate Law Issues. (Tax Law & Estate Planning Course Handbook Ser.). 210p. 1992. pap. 70.00 (0-685-69513-1) PLI.

What Matters? A Primer for Teaching Reading. Joan Gillette et al. Ed. by Diane Stephens. LC 90-35949. (Illus.). 76p. (Orig.). (C). 1990. pap. text ed. 16.50 (0-435-08524-7, 08524) Heinemann.

What Matters: No Expanding Universe, No Big Bang. J. L. Riley. (Illus.). 227p. 1993. pap. 19.00 (0-9636842-1-3); lib. bdg. 29.00 (0-9636842-0-5) J L Riley.

What Matters in College? Four Critical Years Revisited. Alexander W. Astin. LC 92-20581. (Higher & Adult Education Ser.). 512p. text ed. 36.00 (1-55542-492-9) Jossey-Bass.

***What Matters in College? Four Critical Years Revisited.** Alexander W. Astin. 1997. pap. 24.00 (0-7879-0838-X) Jossey-Bass.

***What Matters Most.** 1997. pap. 6.99 (0-451-18603-6, Sig) NAL-Dutton.

***What Matters Most.** Paul S. Dolman. Ed. by Mark Kaufman. 240p. (Orig.). 1996. pap. 20.00 (0-614-30446-6) South Beach.

What Matters Most. Cynthia Victor. 320p. 1996. pap. 23.95 (0-525-94033-2, Dutton) NAL-Dutton.

What Matters Most. large type ed. Cynthia Victor. 1996. pap. 23.95 (1-56895-352-6) Wheeler Pub.

***What Matters Most: Four Absolute Necessities in Following Christ.** Tony Evans. 352p. 1997. 18.99 (0-8024-3923-3) Moody.

***What May Be Expected from Non-Metallic Gears?** C. W. Mansur. (Technical Papers). 1931. pap. text ed. 30.00 (1-55589-323-6) AGMA.

What McGillicuddy Said. pap. 1.95 (0-590-08849-1) Scholastic Inc.

What Me Befell. Jean J. Jusserand. (Select Bibliographies Reprint Ser.). 1977. reprint ed. 24.95 (0-8369-6831-X) Ayer.

What, Me Pregnant? A for Better or for Worse Collection. Lynn Johnston. (Illus.). 128p. (Orig.). 1991. pap. 9.95 (0-8362-1876-0) Andrews & McMeel.

What? Me Teach Music? A Classroom Teacher's Guide to Music in Early Childhood. Marjorie Lawrence. 140p. (Orig.). 1982. pap. text ed. 24.95 (0-88284-213-7, 2075) Alfred Pub.

W

What Mean These Bones? Studies in Southeastern Bioarchaeology. Ed. by Mary L. Powell et al. LC 89-20455. (Illus.). 243p. 1991. reprint ed. pap. 69.30 (*0-608-01678-0*, 2062334) Bks Demand.

What Medicine Is About: Using Its Past to Improve Its Future. Mark D. Altschule. (Countway Library Associates Historical Publication: No. 3). 100p. 1975. 7.95 (*0-686-15547-5*) F A Countway.

What Men Are Asking. Henry S. Coffin. LC 70-117770. (Essay Index Reprint Ser.). 1977. 15.95 (*0-8369-1791-X*) Ayer.

What Men Are Like. John Sanford & George Lough. 320p. 1988. pap. 12.95 (*0-8091-2996-5*) Paulist Pr.

What Men or Gods Are These? A Genealogical Approach to Classical Mythology. Fred Boswell & Jeanetta Boswell. LC 80-13780. 324p. 1980. 39.50 (*0-8108-1314-9*) Scarecrow.

What Men Really Think: About Women, Love, Sex, Themselves. Mark Baker. Ed. by Julie Rubenstein. 352p. 1993. reprint ed. mass mkt. 5.99 (*0-671-79592-9*) PB.

What Men Really Want. Herb Goldberg. 1991. pap. 5.99 (*0-451-16972-7*, Sig) NAL-Dutton.

What Men Really Want: Straight Talk from Men about Sex. Susan C. Bakos. 256p. 1991. mass mkt. 3.99 (*0-312-92638-3*) St Martin.

What Men Say. Joan Smith. 1995. mass mkt. 5.99 (*0-449-22297-7*, Crest) Fawcett.

What Men Want: Mothers, Fathers, & Manhood. John M. Ross. LC 93-46057. 252p. 1994. text ed. 29.95 (*0-674-95080-1*) HUP.

What Men Want: Why Men Think, Feel & Act the Way They Do. H. Norman Wright. 192p. 1996. pap. 11.99 (*0-8307-1818-4*, 5422747) Regal.

What Men Want from the Women They Love. Ken Carlton. 240p. (Orig.). 1996. mass mkt. 4.99 (*0-380-77497-6*) Avon.

What Men Won't Tell You But Women Need to Know. Bob Berkowitz & Roger Gittines. 192p. 1991. mass mkt. 5.99 (*0-380-71364-0*) Avon.

***What Mennonites Are Thinking, 1998.** Ed. by Merle Good & Phyllis P. Good. 160p. 1997. pap. 11.95 (*1-56148-241-2*) Good Bks PA.

What Mennonites Believe. rev. ed. John C. Wenger. LC 90-84719. 96p. 1991. pap. 4.99 (*0-8361-3542-3*) Herald Pr.

What Might Have Been. Glenda Sanders. 1994. mass mkt. 2.99 (*0-373-25593-4*, 1-25593-4) Harlequin Bks.

What Might Have Been: The Social Psychology of Counterfactual Thinking. Ed. by Neal J. Roese & James M. Olson. 416p. 1995. text ed. 89.95 (*0-8058-1613-5*); pap. text ed. 39.95 (*0-8058-1614-3*) L Erlbaum Assocs.

What Might Have Been Expected: With Illustrations by Col Eytinge, Sheppard, Hallock, Beard & Others. Frank R. Stockton. LC 72-3103. (Black Heritage Library Collection). (Illus.). 1977. reprint ed. 30.95 (*0-8369-9080-3*) Ayer.

***What Minds Can Do: Intentionality in a Non-Intentional World.** Pierre Jacob. (Studies in Philosophy). 305p. (C). 1997. 59.95 (*0-521-57401-3*); pap. 21.95 (*0-521-57436-6*) Cambridge U Pr.

What Ministers Can't Learn in Seminary: A Survival Manual for the Parish Ministry. R. Robert Cueni. LC 88-6325. 160p. 1988. pap. 4.78 (*0-687-44652-X*) Abingdon.

What Ministers Know: A Qualitative Study of Pastors as Information Professionals. Thomas M. Tanner. LC 94-16609. (ATLA Monographs: No. 34). (Illus.). 406p. 1994. 52.00 (*0-8108-2916-9*) Scarecrow.

What Ministers Wish Church Members Knew. Jan G. Linn. LC 92-32944. 144p. (Orig.). 1993. pap. 12.99 (*0-8272-4230-1*) Chalice Pr.

What Model for Europe? Michael Emerson. 100p. (Orig.). 1988. 22.50 (*0-262-05036-6*); pap. 10.95 (*0-262-55016-4*) MIT Pr.

***What Mommy Said: An Arlene Flynn Mystery.** H. Paul Jeffers. LC 97-8808. 1997. 21.95 (*0-312-15687-1*) St Martin.

What Mona Lisa Knew: A Woman's Guide to Getting Ahead in Business by Lightening Up. Barbara Mackoff. 168p. 1991. reprint ed. pap. 9.95 (*0-929923-68-5*) Lowell Hse.

What Money Can't Buy: Conquer Financial Stress. Bruce Eaton. Date not set. write for info. (*0-8129-6376-8*, Times Bks) Random.

***What Money Can't Buy: Family Income & Children's Life Chances.** Susan E. Mayer. LC 96-34429. 1997. write for info. (*0-674-58733-2*) HUP.

What More Is There to Say but Amen: The Autobiography of Dr. Oswald C. J. Hoffmann As Told to Ronald J. Schlegel. Oswald C. Hoffmann. LC 96-13788. 368p. 1996. 21.99 (*0-570-04876-1*, 12-3298) Concordia.

What Mother Never Told Ya about Retail: A Small Store Survival Guide. 2nd rev. ed. T. J. Reid. Ed. by Carolyn Porter. (Illus.). 119p. (C). 1994. pap. 29.95 (*1-880522-24-1*) Retail Res.

What Motivates People. Harold McAlindon. Ed. by Mac Anderson. 77p. (Orig.). 1988. pap. 7.50 (*1-880461-11-0*) Celebrat Excell.

What Moves the Heavens? Christian Van Devere. 70p. (Orig.). 1996. pap. 7.99 (*1-57502-156-0*) Morris Pubng.

What Mrs. Fisher Knows about Old Southern Cooking: Soups, Pickles, Preserves, Etc. Abby Fisher. LC 94-42998. 80p. 1995. pap. 8.95 (*1-55709-403-9*) Applewood.

What Mrs. McGillicuddy Saw! large type ed. Agatha Christie. (Agatha Christie Ser.). 342p. 1990. lib. bdg. 12.95 (*0-8161-4617-9*, GK Hall) Thorndike Pr.

What Mrs. McGillicuddy Saw! see Four Fifty from Paddington

What Museum Guides Need to Know: Access for Blind & Visually Impaired Visitors. Gerda Groff & Laura Gardner. LC 88-35009. 64p. 1989. pap. 16.95 (*0-89128-158-4*) Am Foun Blind.

What Must I Do? Morality & the Challenge of God's Word. Daniel E. Pilavczyk. 83p. 1993. pap. 4.95 (*0-86716-209-0*) St Anthony Mess Pr.

What Must I Do to Be Lost. Jack Van Impe. 49p. 1986. pap. 2.00 (*0-934803-57-9*) J Van Impe.

What Must I Do to Be Saved? What Do the Scriptures Say? A Catholic Perspective. Joseph C. Kindel. LC 95-92598. 96p. (Orig.). 1995. pap. 5.00 (*1-877678-39-2*) Riehle Found.

What Must the Church Do? Robert S. Bilheimer. LC 70-134053. (Essay Index Reprints - Interseminary Ser.: Vol. 5). 1977. reprint ed. 19.95 (*0-8369-2384-7*) Ayer.

What Must We Do? A Blueprint for Releasing God's Power. Larry Huch. Ed. by Margaret J. Kinney. 96p. 1993. pap. text ed. 7.95 (*1-880563-04-5*) FAME Pub.

What Must We Do to Be Saved? Robert G. Ingersoll. (Notable American Authors Ser.). 1992. reprint ed. lib. bdg. 75.00 (*0-685-59996-5*) Rprt Serv.

***What My Cat Has Taught Me about Life: Meditations for Cat Lovers.** Niki Anderson. 1997. 15.99 (*1-56292-366-8*) Honor Bks OK.

What My Father Believed. Robert Wrigley. 72p. (Orig.). 1991. 11.95 (*0-252-06168-3*) U of Ill Pr.

What My Heart Wants to Tell. Verna M. Slone. LC 87-23046. 160p. 1987. pap. 12.95 (*0-8131-0174-3*) U Pr of Ky.

What My Parents Did Right. Gloria Gaither. 400p. 1994. mass mkt. 5.99 (*0-8423-8136-8*) Tyndale.

What My Parents Did Right. Ed. by Gloria Gaither. Tr. by Lily Yang. 356p. 1994. pap. write for info. (*1-885216-00-9*) Evan Formosan.

What My Parents Did Right. Shirley Tyree. 298p. (Orig.). 1995. pap. write for info. (*1-885591-87-X*) Morris Pubng.

What My Sister Remembered. Marilyn Sachs. LC 91-32263. 120p. (J). (gr. 5-9). 1992. pap. 15.00 (*0-525-44953-1*) Dutton Child Bks.

What My Sister Remembered. Marilyn Sachs. 128p. (J). (gr. 5 up). 1994. pap. 3.99 (*0-14-036944-9*) Puffin Bks.

***What Mystery Do I Read Next? A Reader's Guide.** Charles Montney. LC 96-47713. 1996. 79.00 (*0-7876-1592-7*) Gale.

What Nature Suffers to Groe: Life, Labor, & Landscape on the Georgia Coast, 1680-1910. Mart A. Stewart. LC 95-36581. 1996. 45.00 (*0-8203-1808-6*) U of Ga Pr.

***What Nell Knows.** Barbara L. Greenberg. (Orig.). 1997. pap. 10.00 (*0-9638099-2-X*) SPSHR.

What Neural Networks Can Do. J. A. Anderson. 144p. 1988. lab manual ed. write for info. (*1-56321-003-7*); lab manual ed. 295.00 incl. vhs (*1-56321-000-2*); vhs 235.00 (*1-56321-004-5*); vhs 15.00 (*1-56321-002-9*) L Erlbaum Assocs.

What Neural Networks Can Do, Demo. J. A. Anderson. 1988. vhs 35.00 (*1-56321-001-0*) L Erlbaum Assocs.

What Never to Say to a Pregnant Woman: The #1 Guide to Pregnancy Etiquette. Barbara S. Glazier et al. (Illus.). 96p. 1996. pap. 7.95 (*0-930753-18-6*) Spect Ln Pr.

What News? The Market, Politics & the Local Press. Bob Franklin & David Murphy. (Communication & Society Ser.). (Illus.). 240p. (C). 1991. pap. text ed. 22.95 (*0-415-04049-3*, A5786) Routledge.

What News? The Market, Politics & the Local Press. Bob Franklin & David Murphy. (Communication & Society Ser.). (Illus.). 240p. (C). (gr. 13). 1991. text ed. 89.95 (*0-415-06172-5*, A5782) Routledge.

What Newt Could Do for Turtle. Jonathan London. LC 95-52361. (Illus.). 40p. (J). (ps-2). 1996. 16.99 (*1-56402-259-5*) Candlewick Pr.

***What Next?** JoAnne Nelson. LC 91-35731. (Primarily Health Ser.). (Illus.). 24p. (J). (ps-2). 1995. pap. 6.00 (*0-7802-3247-X*) Wright Group.

What Next?, 4 bks., Set. Marcia Leonard. (Illus.). 24 pgs ea.p. (J). (ps-1). 1990. 19.80 (*0-671-94102-X*, Julian Messner); lib. bdg. 27.80 (*0-671-94101-1*, Julian Messner) Silver Burdett Pr.

What Next? Creation. M. Simon. 24p. 1990. pap. text ed. 2.49 (*0-570-04175-9*, 56-1634) Concordia.

What Next? Futuristic Scenarios for Creative Problem Solving. Robert E. Myers & E. Paul Torrance. LC 94-3990. 1994. 29.00 (*1-56976-001-2*) Zephyr Pr AZ.

What Next? Provocative Tales of Faith & Morals. Laurence Housman. LC 77-167452. (Short Story Index Reprint Ser.). 1977. reprint ed. 19.95 (*0-8369-3978-6*) Ayer.

What Next? Understanding Your Child at Each Age & Stage. Robert E. Ripley & Marie J. Ripley. LC 93-70691. (Illus.). 186p. 1993. pap. 19.95 (*0-9621133-4-4*, B010) Carefree Pr.

What Next, Baby Bear! Jill Murphy. LC 83-7316. (Pied Piper Bks.). (Illus.). 32p. (J). (ps-2). 1986. pap. 3.95 (*0-685-37306-1*) Dial Bks Young.

What Next, Baby Bear! 7. Murphy. 1992. pap. 5.99 (*0-14-054982-X*) NAL-Dutton.

What Next Doctor? large type ed. Robert Clifford. (General Ser.). 288p. 1993. 25.99 (*0-7089-2874-9*) Ulverscroft.

What Next? Exploring the Future of High-Energy Physics: Proceedings of the 16th Annual Montreal. J. R. Cudell et al. 332p. 1994. text ed. 106.00 (*981-02-2073-1*) World Scientific Pub.

What Next in Mission? Nancy Heisey & Paul Longacre. 48p. (Orig.). 1990. pap. 1.50 (*1-877736-05-8*) MB Missions.

What Next? More Leverage for Teachers. 50p. 1986. 8.00 (*0-318-22546-8*, TR-86-3) Ed Comm States.

What Nietzsche Means. George A. Morgan, Jr. LC 74-2555. 408p. 1975. reprint ed. text ed. 35.00 (*0-8371-7404-X*, MOWN, Greenwood Pr) Greenwood.

***What Night Do the Angels Wander?** Phoebe Stone. LC 97-10178. (J). 1997. write for info. (*0-316-81439-3*) Little.

What? No Chili? Rose-Mary Rumbley. LC 94-39639. (Illus.). (J). (gr. 6-8). 1994. 14.95 (*0-89015-992-0*, Eakin Pr) Sunbelt Media.

***What No One Told You about Health Care: A Look at Some Health Care Problems & Some Possible Solutions.** Donald L. Price. 160p. 1997. text ed. 49.95 (*1-85972-569-4*, Pub. by Avebury Pub UK) Ashgate Pub Co.

What Noise? Debbie MacKinnon. LC 92-43651. (Illus.). (J). (gr. 4 up). 1994. pap. 10.99 (*0-8037-1510-2*) Dial Bks Young.

What Not to Name Your Baby. Darold B. Cummings & Gary Johnson. (Illus.). 64p. (Orig.). 1982. pap. 2.95 (*0-914743-01-5*) Matrix Design Pubns.

What Not to Name Your Baby. Billy Frolick. Date not set. pap. 7.95 (*0-452-27624-1*, Plume) NAL-Dutton.

What Not to Name Your Baby. Andy Meisler & Michael Rey. (Illus.). 64p. (Orig.). 1996. pap. 7.95 (*0-89815-814-1*) Ten Speed Pr.

What Now? Pat O'Neil. 60p. (Orig.). 1989. pap. text ed. 7.95 (*0-9627243-0-0*) Pat Pubns.

What Now?! (This Book Is User Friendly) Pat O'Neil. 61p. 1991. Tchr's. ed. 7.95 (*0-9627243-1-9*) Pat Pubns.

***What Now? Help for Pregnant Teens.** Linda I. Shands. 120p. 1997. pap. 8.99 (*0-8308-1967-3*, 1967) InterVarsity.

What Now My Love. Floyd Salas. LC 93-47654. 154p. 1994. pap. 9.95 (*1-55885-112-7*) Arte Publico.

What Now Skipper? Forty Fiendish Challenges to Your Seamanship Skills. Des Sleightholme. 1989. pap. 16.50 (*0-924486-18-X*) Sheridan.

What Number Is God? Metaphors, Metaphysics, Metamathematics, & the Nature of Things. Sarah Voss. LC 94-18260. (SUNY Series in Western Esoteric Traditions). 214p. (C). 1995. text ed. 49.50 (*0-7914-2417-0*); pap. text ed. 16.95 (*0-7914-2418-9*) State U NY Pr.

What Nuns Read: Books & Libraries in Medieval English Nunneries. David N. Bell. LC 94-27837. (Cistercian Studies: No. 158). 1995. 49.95 (*0-87907-558-9*) Cistercian Pubns.

What Nursery School Teachers Ask Us About: Psychoanalytic Consultations in Preschools. Erna Furman. LC 86-4346. (Emotions & Behavior Monographs: No. 5). 250p. 1986. 37.50 (*0-8236-6830-4*, BN#06830) Intl Univs Pr.

What of the Night? A Journey Through Depression & Anxiety. Jeffrey J. Knowles. LC 92-37499. 144p. (Orig.). 1993. pap. 8.99 (*0-8361-3617-9*) Herald Pr.

What of Tomorrow. Challoner. 1976. pap. 4.95 (*0-7229-5046-2*) Theos Pub Hse.

What Older Americans Think: Interest Groups & Aging Policy. Christine L. Day. (Illus.). 179p. (C). 1990. text ed. 29.95 (*0-691-07825-4*) Princeton U Pr.

What on Earth. Pam Adams. LC 90-45581. (J). 1989. 9.99 (*0-85953-165-1*) Childs Play.

What On Earth? Making Personal Decisions on Controversial Issues. Harvey Seifert. (Orig.). (C). 1986. pap. 7.25 (*0-9613222-1-7*, CS1014) General Board.

What on Earth? Poems with a Conservation Theme. Ed. by Judith Nicholls. (Illus.). 132p. (J). (gr. 2 up). 1989. pap. 8.95 (*0-571-15262-7*) Faber & Faber.

What on Earth Are We Doing? Finding Our Place As Christians in the World. John Fischer. LC 96-46559. 220p. (Orig.). 1997. pap. 12.99 (*0-89283-976-7*, Vine Bks) Servant.

What on Earth Are We Here for? Keith Butler. 128p. (Orig.). 1996. pap. 6.99 (*0-89274-947-4*, HH-947) Harrison Hse.

What on Earth Are You Doing? Michael Griffiths. 96p. 1992. reprint ed. pap. 10.95 (*1-57383-004-6*) Regent College.

What on Earth Are You Doing for Heaven's Sake? (J). 1990. 5.95 (*0-8378-2061-8*) Gibson.

What on Earth Can You Do? Making Your Church a Creation Awareness Center. Donna Lehman. LC 93-600. 192p. (Orig.). 1993. pap. 10.99 (*0-8361-3632-2*) Herald Pr.

What on Earth For. Kimi Mitchell. 1994. pap. 3.95 (*1-55673-929-X*) CSS OH.

What on Earth Is a Pout? Edward R. Ricciuti. Ed. by Bruce Glassman. LC 95-43326. (What on Earth Is...? Ser.). (Illus.). 32p. (J). (gr. 2-5). 1996. lib. bdg. 14.95 (*1-56711-103-3*) Blackbirch.

What on Earth Is a Quokka? Jenny E. Tesar. LC 95-43327. (What on Earth Is...? Ser.). (Illus.). 32p. (J). (gr. 2-5). 1996. lib. bdg. 14.95 (*1-56711-104-1*) Blackbirch.

What on Earth Is an Atheist! Madalyn M. O'Hair. LC 71-88701. (Fifty-Two Programs from the American Atheist Radio Ser.). 288p. 1969. pap. 12.00 (*0-911826-00-9*, 5412) Am Atheist.

What on Earth Is an Atheist. Madalyn M. O'Hair. LC 74-161339. (Atheist Viewpoint Ser.). 288p. 1976. reprint ed. 20.95 (*0-405-03802-X*) Ayer.

What on Earth Is God Doing? Satan's Conflict with God. Renald E. Showers. LC 73-81551. 128p. 1973. pap. 7.99 (*0-87213-784-8*) Loizeaux.

What on Earth Is the Church? An Exploration in New Testament Theology. Kevin S. Giles. LC 95-42909. 310p. 1995. 16.99 (*0-8308-1868-5*, 1868) InterVarsity.

What on Earth Can You Do with Kids? Robyn Spizman. 352p. (gr. 1-5). 1991. 25.99 (*0-86653-623-X*, GA1342) Good Apple.

What Once Was White. Samantha Abeel. Ed. by Roberta Williams. LC 93-77359. (Illus.). 48p. 1993. text ed. 19.95 (*0-941653-13-7*) Village Pr Pubns.

What One Beholds of a Woman Is the Least Part of Her: Collections of Poems by Writers in Delaware, Maryland, Virginia & the District of Columbia. Ed. & Compiled by Joseph D. Adams. (Poet's Domain Ser.: Vol. 12). 128p. 1995. pap. 8.00 (*1-880016-21-4*) Road Pubs.

What One Man Said to Another: Talks with Richard Selzer. Peter Josyph. LC 94-23233. 1994. 27.95 (*0-87013-362-4*) Mich St U Pr.

What Only a Mother Can Tell You about Child Sexual Abuse. Karen L. Schaefer. 1993. 14.95 (*0-87868-508-1*) Child Welfare.

***What Our Families Need: Toward a Policy Agenda for Lesbian & Gay Families.** John Demilio. 1997. pap. text ed. 10.00 (*0-9652779-3-3*) Natl Gay & Lesbian.

What Ownership's All About. Karel Polacek. Tr. & Intro. by Peter Kussi. LC 92-33558. 240p. 1993. 21.95 (*0-945774-19-2*, PG5038.P64D813) Catbird Pr.

***What Parents Can Do.** Music Educators National Conference Staff. (Implementing the Arts Education Standards Ser.). 6p. (Orig.). (C). 1994. pap. write for info. (*1-56545-061-2*, 4020) Music Ed Natl.

What Parents Need to Know about Dating Violence. Barrie Levy & Patricia Griggans. LC 94-42614. 196p. (Orig.). 1995. pap. 10.95 (*1-878067-47-8*) Seal Pr WA.

What Parents Should Know about Juvenile Delinquency & Juvenile Justice. Waln K. Brown. 20p. 1989. 2.95 (*1-56456-007-4*, 201) W Gladden Found.

***What Parish Are You From? A Chicago Irish Community & Race Relations.** Eileen M. McMahon. (Illus.). 240p. 1995. pap. 19.95 (*0-8131-0894-2*) U Pr of Ky.

What Part of No Don't You Understand? Avoiding & Defending Against Rape. Dennis G. Korby. 150p. 1994. pap. text ed. 14.95 (*0-9642425-0-8*) Koto Pr.

***What Part Will I Play?** Mary H. Surface. 31p. (Orig.). (YA). 1992. pap. 3.00 (*1-57514-277-5*, 1173) Encore Perform Pub.

***What Passes for Love: Short Stories.** Stan Rogal. 144p. pap. 14.99 (*1-895837-34-0*, Pub. by Insomniac Pr CN) Login Pubs Consort.

What Paul Really Said about Women: The Apostle's Liberating Views on Equality in Marriage, Leadership & Love. John T. Bristow. LC 87-46200. 144p. 1991. reprint ed. pap. 12.00 (*0-06-061063-8*) Harper SF.

What People Ask about the Church: Answers to Your Questions Concerning Today's Church. Dale A. Robbins. LC 95-90611. 212p. (Orig.). 1995. pap. 9.95 (*0-9648022-0-1*) Victorious Pubns.

What People Call Pessimism: Sigmund Freud, Arthur Schnitzler & Nineteenth-Century Controversy at the University of Vienna Medical School. Mark Luprecht. (Studies in Austrian Literature, Culture, & Thought). 172p. 1990. pap. 23.00 (*0-929497-28-7*) Ariadne CA.

What People Expect from Church: Why Meeting the Needs of People Is More Important Than Church Meetings. Lyle E. Shaller. LC 92-33162. (Ministry for the Third Millennium Ser.). 128p. (Orig.). 1993. pap. 12.95 (*0-687-13387-4*) Abingdon.

What People Say. 5th ed. Kathryn A. Ordman & Mary P. Ralli. LC 76-6143. 1976. pap. text ed. 10.95 (*0-88200-073-X*, B0990) Alexander Graham.

What People Say They Do with Words. Jef Verschueren. Ed. by Roy O. Freedle. LC 85-6211. (Advances in Discourse Processes Ser.: Vol. 14). 276p. 1985. pap. 42.50 (*0-89391-197-6*); text ed. 78.50 (*0-89391-196-8*) Ablex Pub.

What People Wore: One Thousand Eight Hundred Illustrations from Ancient Times to the Early Twentieth Century. unabridged ed. Douglas Gorsline. LC 94-10460. (Illus.). 269p. 1994. pap. 11.95 (*0-486-28162-0*) Dover.

***What Perennials Where.** Roy Lancaster. 160p. 1997. 24.95 (*0-7894-2087-2*) DK Pub Inc.

What Planners Do. Charles Hoch. LC 93-74203. 330p. (Orig.). 1995. pap. 34.95 (*0-918286-90-5*); lib. bdg. 45.00 (*0-918286-91-3*) Planners Pr.

What Plant Where. Roy Lancaster. LC 95-8172. (Illus.). 256p. 1995. 24.95 (*0-7894-0151-7*, 6-70482) DK Pub Inc.

What Plants Give Us: The Gift of Life. Janet Riehecky. LC 90-30374. (Discovery World Ser.). (Illus.). 32p. (J). (ps-2). 1990. lib. bdg. 21.36 (*0-89565-570-5*) Childs World.

What Plants Need: The Rabbit Who Knew. Jane B. Moncure. LC 89-24001. (Discovery World Ser.). (Illus.). 32p. (J). (ps-2). 1990. lib. bdg. 21.36 (*0-89565-559-4*) Childs World.

What Plato Said. Paul Shorey. LC 33-11964. (Midway Reprint Ser.). 694p. reprint ed. pap. 180.00 (*0-685-15474-2*, 2026743) Bks Demand.

What Poetry Is. Harry Mulisch. Ed. by Stanley H. Barkan. Tr. by Claire Nicolas White. (Cross-Cultural Review Chapbook Ser.: No. 9:). 40p. (DUT & ENG.). 1981. 15.00 (*0-89304-875-5*, CCC133); pap. 5.00 (*0-89304-808-9*) Cross-Cultrl NY.

What Poetry Is All About. Greg Kuzma. LC 96-19979. 128p. (Orig.). 1997. pap. 13.95 (*0-914061-62-3*) Orchises Pr.

What Political Economy Is All About: An Exposition & Critique. Ezra J. Mishan. LC 82-12880. 256p. 1982. text ed. 69.95 (*0-521-25072-2*); pap. text ed. 18.95 (*0-521-27195-9*) Cambridge U Pr.

What Predicts Divorce? The Relationship Between Marital Processes & Marital Outcomes. John M. Gottman. 536p. 1993. pap. 49.95 (*0-8058-1402-7*) L Erlbaum Assocs.

W

What Predicts Divorce? The Relationship Between Marital Processes & Marital Outcomes. John M. Gottman. 536p. 1993. text ed. 99.95 (*0-8058-1285-7*) L Erlbaum Assocs.

What Present-Day Theologians Are Thinking. rev. ed. Daniel D. Williams. LC 78-16410. 190p. 1978. reprint ed. text ed. 49.75 (*0-313-20587-6*, WIWP, Greenwood Pr) Greenwood.

What Prevents Christian Adults from Learning. rev. ed. John M. Hull. LC 91-23520. 256p. (C). 1991. pap. 15.95 (*1-56338-027-7*) TPI PA.

What Price. William J Baumol. Ed. by Klaus E. Knorr. LC 77-781. (Illus.). 1977. reprint ed. text ed. 65.00 (*0-8371-9356-7*, KNWP, Greenwood Pr) Greenwood.

What Price Alliance? Black Radicals Confront White Labor, 1918-1938. Keith P. Griffler. LC 94-32944. (Studies in African American History & Culture). (Illus.). 272p. 1995. text ed. 57.00 (*0-8153-1921-5*) Garland.

What Price Clean Air? A Market Approach to Energy & Environmental Policy. Ed. by Julie Won. 120p. 1993. pap. 15.00 (*0-87186-097-X*) Comm Econ Dev.

What Price Food? Agricultural Price Policies in Developing Countries. Paul Streeten. LC 88-47773. 128p. 1988. pap. 13.95 (*0-8014-9533-4*) Cornell U Pr.

What Price Freedom. (Illus.). 56p. 1995. 35.00 (*0-87104-440-4*) NY Pub Lib.

What Price Freedom. (Illus.). 56p. 1995. pap. 19.95 (*0-87104-441-2*) NY Pub Lib.

What Price Glory. Marianne Shock. (Special Edition Ser.). 1995. mass mkt. 3.75 (*0-373-09952-5*, 1-09952-2) Silhouette.

What Price Glory-In Translation? 80p. Date not set. 15.00 (*0-614-11327-X*) Bagehot Council.

What Price Incentives? Economists & the Environment. Steven Kelman. LC 81-7883. 170p. 1981. text ed. 24.95 (*0-86569-082-0*, Auburn Hse) Greenwood.

What Price Love. Alice L. Covert. (Orig.). 1979. mass mkt. 2.25 (*0-89083-491-1*, Zebra Kensgtn) Kensgtn Pub Corp.

What Price Mental Health? The Ethics & Politics of Setting Priorities. Ed. by Philip J. Boyle & Daniel Callahan. LC 94-37059. (Hastings Center Studies in Ethics). 256p. 1995. 45.00 (*0-87840-576-3*) Georgetown U Pr.

What Price Mink? Edward J. Ohanian. (Illus.). 240p. (Orig.). 1983. pap. 9.95 (*0-317-13105-2*) Ohanian.

What Price PACS? Report of the Twentieth Century Fund Task Force on Political Action Committees. 129p. (Orig.). 1984. pap. text ed. 10.00 (*0-87078-152-9*) TCFP-PPP.

What Price Parenthood? Ethics & Assisted Reproduction. Ed. by Courtney Campbell. 120p. 1992. text ed. 62.95 (*1-85521-224-2*, Pub. by Dartmth Pub UK) Ashgate Pub Co.

*__What Price Religion?__ Christoph Turcke. 112p. 1997. pap. 17.00 (*0-334-02688-1*, SCM Pr) TPI PA.

What Price Vaccination? Simone Delarue. 1995. pap. 15.00 (*0-916508-22-6*) Happiness Pr.

What Price Vigilance? The Burdens of National Defense. Bruce M. Russett. LC 75-119475. (Yale Fastback Ser.: No. YF-5). (Illus.). 274p. reprint ed. pap. 78.10 (*0-317-09345-2*, 2022036) Bks Demand.

What Prize Awaits Us: Letters from Guatemala. Bernice Kita. LC 88-17842. 200p. (Orig.). 1988. pap. 14.00 (*0-88344-273-6*) Orbis Bks.

What Process Is Due? Courts & Science-Policy Disputes. David M. O'Brien. LC 87-43100. 190p. 1988. text ed. 29.95 (*0-87154-623-X*) Russell Sage.

*__What Profit for Us? Remembering the Story of Joseph.__ Barbara Green. LC 96-34951. 240p. 1996. pap. text ed. 28.50 (*0-7618-0511-7*); lib. bdg. 65.00 (*0-7618-0510-9*) U Pr of Amer.

What Proper Person? An Anthology of Latin Verse. H. H. Huxley. 64p. 1984. 14.95 (*0-86292-109-0*, Pub. by Brstl Class Pr UK) Focus Pub-R Pullins.

*__What Public Schools Need to Know about Discipline Their Mamas Should Have Taught Them.__ Deborah A. Murphy. (Sound-Off Ser.). 16p. 1997. pap. 2.95 (*0-9646811-7-X*) Stardust PA.

What "R" Big Girls Made. Marge Piercy. LC 96-29207. 1997. pap. 15.00 (*0-679-76594-8*) McKay.

What "R" Big Girls Made Of. Marge Piercy. LC 96-29207. 1997. 25.00 (*0-679-45065-3*) McKay.

What Racists Believe: Race Relations in South Africa & the United States. Gerhard Schutte. (Sage Series on Race & Ethnic Relations: Vol. 8). 320p. 1994. 58.00 (*0-8039-5785-8*); pap. 26.95 (*0-8039-5786-6*) Sage.

What Radiology Professionals Won't Tell You: X-Ray - the Dark Side of the Revolving Door. Ricardo A. Scott. (Techwise Ser.). (Illus.). 70p. (Orig.). pap. write for info. (*1-883427-30-4*) Crnerstone GA.

W

What Really Goes on in Sophocles' Theban Plays. Charles B. Daniels & Sam Scully. LC 96-6787. 160p. 1996. lib. bdg. 36.50 (*0-7618-0304-1*) U Pr of Amer.

What Really Happened at the Battle of the Little Big Horn. 20.00 (*0-9630113-2-4*) G&C.

What Really Happened? JFK: Five Hundred & One Questions & Answers. Joan Hubbard-Burrell. Ed. by Douglas H. Hubbard & Frances C. Hubbard. LC 92-62333. (Illus.). 320p. (Orig.). 1995. pap. 14.95 (*0-9634795-9-8*) Ponderosa TX.

What Really Happened to Jesus: A Historical Approach to the Resurrection. Gerd Ludemann & Alf Ozen. Tr. by John Bowden from GER. LC 95-35036. 160p. (Orig.). 1996. pap. 13.00 (*0-664-25647-3*) Westminster John Knox.

What Really Happened to the Dinosaurs? John Morris et al. (Illus.). 32p. (J). (ps-2). 1990. 10.95 (*0-89051-159-4*) Master Bks.

What Really Happens in Bed: A Demystification of Sex. Steven Carter & Julia Sokol. LC 89-1561. 352p. 1989. 17.95 (*0-87131-562-9*) M Evans.

What Really Happens in Bed? A Demystification of Sex. Steven Carter & Julia Sokol. 352p. 1990. pap. 8.95 (*0-440-50330-2*) Dell.

What Really Happens When You Cut Chemicals? New Farm Staff et al. Ed. by Christopher Shirley & Greg Bowman. LC 92-41471. 1993. write for info. (*0-913107-16-6*) Rodale Inst.

What Really Helps (Or Hurts) the Company's Bottom Line? 1983. 30.00 incl. audio (*0-318-19180-6*) Assn Equip Distrs.

What Really Killed Rosebud? Claire Burch. 120p. 1996. pap. 14.00 (*0-916147-69-X*) Regent Pr.

What Really Matters: Passing on Your Family Values. Cliff Bajema. (Issues Ser.). 1995. pap. 7.15 (*1-56212-098-0*) CRC Pubns.

What Really Matters: Searching for Wisdom in America. Tony Schwartz. 496p. 1996. pap. 12.95 (*0-553-37492-3*, Bantam Trade Bks) Bantam.

What Really Matters at Home? Susan A. Yates & John Yates. 196p. 1992. pap. 10.99 (*0-8499-3416-8*) Word Pub.

What Really Works with Men: Solve Ninety-Five Percent of Your Relationship Problems (& Cope with the Rest) A. Justin Sterling. 288p. 1993. mass mkt. 5.99 (*0-446-36439-8*) Warner Bks.

What Reason Demands: On Justifications of Morality & Autonomy. Rudiger Bittner. Tr. by Theodore Talbot. 240p. (C). 1989. text ed. 59.95 (*0-521-35215-0*); pap. text ed. 19.95 (*0-521-37710-2*) Cambridge U Pr.

*__What Religion Is: 1920 Edition.__ Bernard Bosanquet. 96p. 1996. reprint ed. write for info. (*1-85506-183-X*) Bks Intl VA.

What Religion Is in the Words of Vivekananda. Swami Vivekananda. Ed. by John Yale. 1972. pap. 5.95 (*0-87481-213-5*, Pub. by Advaita Ashrama II) Vedanta Pr.

What Religious Science Is. Tom Johnson. 18p. (YA). (gr. 7-12). 1989. reprint ed. 2.00 (*0-941992-19-5*) Los Arboles Pub.

What Religious Science Teaches. Ernest Holmes. 93p. 1974. pap. 7.95 (*0-917849-23-X*) Sci of Mind.

What Remains & Other Stories. Christa Wolf. Tr. by Heike Schwarzbauer & Rick Takvorian. LC 90-27906. 288p. 1993. 25.00 (*0-374-28888-7*) FS&G.

What Remains & Other Stories. Christa Wolf. viii, 296p. 1995. pap. 14.95 (*0-226-90495-4*) U Ch Pr.

What Remains of a Rembrandt Torn into Four Equal Parts & Flushed Down the Toilet. Jean Genet. 90p. (Orig.). 1989. 5.95 (*0-937815-21-7*) Hanuman Bks.

What Remains to Be Discovered. John Maddox. 1996. 25.00 (*0-684-82292-X*) Free Pr.

What Research Has to Say about Reading Instruction. 2nd ed. Ed. by S. J. Samuels & Alan E. Farstrup. 368p. 1992. pap. 20.95 (*0-87207-495-1*) Intl Reading.

What Research Has to Say about Reading Instruction. Ed. by S. Jay Samuels. LC 78-4573. (Illus.). 185p. reprint ed. pap. 52.80 (*0-685-23679-X*, 2027914) Bks Demand.

What Research Says about Learning in Science Museums. Association of Science-Technology Centers Staff. 31p. 1990. pap. 14.00 (*0-944040-20-9*) AST Ctrs.

What Research Says about Learning in Science Museums, Vol. 2. Ed. by Patty McNamara et al. 44p. (Orig.). 1993. pap. 14.00 (*0-944040-31-4*, 68-0) AST Ctrs.

What Research Says to the Science Teacher Vol. 7: The Science, Technology, Society Movement. Ed. by Robert E. Yager. (Illus.). 184p. 1993. pap. text ed. 16.50 (*0-87355-113-3*) Natl Sci Tchrs.

*__What Researchers Say on Sri Shirdi Sai Baba.__ Ed. & Compiled by S. P. Ruhela. 137p. 1995. pap. 40.00 (*81-85880-85-9*, Pub. by Print Hse II) St Mut.

What Return Can I Make? The Dimensions of the Christian Experience. M. Scott Peck et al. LC 85-11945. 96p. 1985. 24.95 (*0-317-38030-3*) S&S Trade.

What Rhymes with Eel? Harriet Ziefert. (Illus.). 16p. (J). (ps-1). 1996. pap. 12.99 (*0-670-86670-9*) Viking Child Bks.

What Rhymes with "Secret"? Sandy Brownjohn. 104p. (Orig.). 1990. pap. text ed. 15.00 (*0-340-28271-1*, Pub. by Hodder & Stoughton Ltd UK) Lubrecht & Cramer.

What Rhymes with Snake? A Word & Picture Flap Book. Rick Brown. LC 92-37870. (Illus.). 24p. (J). 1994. 11.95 (*0-688-12328-7*, Tambourine Bks) Morrow.

What Right Does Ethics Have? Public Philosophy in a Pluralistic Culture. Sander Griffioen & Karl-Otto Apel. 168p. 1993. pap. 28.50 (*90-6256-945-5*, Pub. by VU Univ Pr NE) Paul & Co Pubs.

What Robots Can & Can't Be. Selmer Bringsjord. 394p. (C). 1992. lib. bdg. 145.00 (*0-7923-1662-2*, Pub. by Klwr Acad Pubs NE) Kluwer Ac.

What Role Does & What Role Should the Media Play in Choosing Our Candidates for National Office? Excerpts from the 1993 Harry Singer Foundation Essay Contest. Ed. by Margaret Bohannon-Kaplan. 1993. 8.00 (*0-915915-23-5*) Wellington Pubns.

What Role for Currency Boards. John Williamson. (Policy Analyses in International Economics Ser.: Vol. 40). 1995. pap. 12.95 (*0-88132-222-9*) Inst Intl Eco.

What Role for Government? Lessons from Policy Research. Ed. by Richard F. Zeckhauser & Derek Leebaert. LC 82-21074. (Duke Press Policy Studies). (Illus.). x, 365p. (C). 1983. text ed. 53.00 (*0-8223-0481-3*) Duke.

*__What Romance Do I Read Next? A Reader's Guide to Recent Romance Fiction.__ Kristen Ramsdell. 650p. 1997. 79.00 (*0-7876-1867-5*) Gale.

What Rose Doesn't Know. Gina C. Erickson & Kelli C. Foster. LC 93-36071. (Get Ready...Get Set...Read! Ser.). (Illus.). 24p. (J). (ps-3). 1994. pap. 3.50 (*0-8120-1672-6*) Barron.

What Rose Doesn't Know: A First Book: Second Reading Level. Kelli C. Foster & Gina C. Erickson. (Get Ready, Get Set, Read! Ser.). (Illus.). 24p. (J). 1995. lib. bdg. 11.95 (*1-56674-117-3*) Forest Hse.

What Rot! Nature's Mighty Recycler. Elizabeth Ring. LC 95-353. (Illus.). 32p. (J). (gr. k-3). 1996. lib. bdg. 17.40 (*1-56294-671-4*) Millbrook Pr.

What Rough Book: Dark Poems & Light. Keith A. Daniels. LC 91-76733. 144p. (Orig.). 1992. pap. 10.95 (*0-9631203-2-8*) Anamnesis Pr.

What Rules America? James W. Lamare. 203p. (C). 1988. pap. text ed. 30.00 (*0-314-64228-5*) West Pub.

*__What Saint Paul Really Said.__ Tom Wright. 192p. (Orig.). 1997. pap. 14.00 (*0-8028-4445-6*) Eerdmans.

*__What Saint Paul Really Said: Was Paul of Tarsus the Real Founder of Christianity.__ N. T. Wright. 192p. (Orig.). 1997. pap. 14.00 (*0-88028-181-2*, 1427) Forward Movement.

What Saves Us. Bruce Weigl. 80p. 1992. pap. 11.95 (*0-8101-5013-1*) Northwestern U Pr.

What Saves Us. Bruce Weigl. 80p. 1992. 17.00 (*0-916384-08-X*) TriQuarterly.

*__What Savvy Investors Know That You Don't.__ Alison Smith. 1997. mass mkt. 5.99 (*0-373-80514-4*, 1-80514-2) Harlequin Bks.

*__What School Administrators Can Do.__ Music Educators National Conference Staff. (Implementing the Arts Education Standards Ser.). 6p. (Orig.). (C). 1994. pap. write for info. (*1-56545-059-0*, 4018) Music Ed Natl.

*__What School Boards Can Do.__ Music Educators National Conference Staff. (Implementing the Arts Education Standards Ser.). 6p. (Orig.). (C). 1994. pap. write for info. (*1-56545-058-2*, 4017) Music Ed Natl.

*__What School Boards Don't Understand about Music, Budgets & Reverse Economics.__ Deborah A. Murphy. (Sound-Off Ser.). 12p. 1996. pap. 2.95 (*0-9646811-9-6*) Stardust PA.

What Schools Are For. 2nd ed. John I. Goodlad. LC 94-66515. 144p. 1994. pap. 14.50 (*0-87367-467-7*) Phi Delta Kappa.

What Schools Can Do: Critical Pedagogy & Practice. Ed. by Kathleen Weiler & Candace Mitchell. LC 91-30790. (SUNY Series, Teacher Empowerment & School Reform). 301p. (C). 1992. text ed. 59.50 (*0-7914-1127-3*); pap. text ed. 19.95 (*0-7914-1128-1*) State U NY Pr.

*__What Schools Forget to Tell Parents about Their Rights.__ Reed Martin. 48p. (Orig.). (C). 1997. pap. 14.95 (*1-885477-35-X*) Fut Horizons.

*__What Science Fiction/Fantasy/Horror Do I Read Next? A Reader's Guide to Recent Fantastic Fiction.__ Neil Barron. 1997. 89.00 (*0-7876-1866-7*) Gale.

What Science Stands For. J. B. Orr et al. LC 72-134157. (Essay Index Reprint Ser.). 1977. 17.95 (*0-8369-1938-6*) Ayer.

What Scouts Can Do: More Yarns. Robert Baden-Powell. (Illus.). 173p. 1992. pap. 14.95 (*0-9632054-5-5*) Stevens Pub.

What Shall I Be? Robert Donahue. 16p. 1993. pap. text ed. 4.95 (*0-87487-669-9*) Summy-Birchard.

*__What Shall I Be?__ Ray Gibson. Ed. by Fiona Watt & Jenny Tyler. (What Shall I Do Today? Ser.). (Illus.). 32p. (Orig.). (J). (gr. 1-6). 1997. pap. 6.95 (*0-7460-2717-6*, Usborne) EDC.

*__What Shall I Be?__ Ray Gibson. Ed. by Fiona Watt & Jenny Tyler. (What Shall I Do Today? Ser.). (Illus.). 32p. (Orig.). (J). (gr. 1-6). 1997. lib. bdg. 14.95 (*0-88110-946-0*, Usborne) EDC.

*__What Shall I Cook.__ Ray Gibson. (What Shall I Do Today Ser.). (Illus.). 32p. (J). (gr. k-6). 1997. pap. 6.95 (*0-7460-2853-9*, Usborne); lib. bdg. 14.95 (*0-88110-915-0*, Usborne) EDC.

What Shall I Cook? Nika Hazelton. 1999. pap. 19.95 (*0-670-81360-5*) Viking Penguin.

*__What Shall I Do to Inherit Life?__ 2nd rev. ed. Margaret Davis. (Illus.). 224p. 1997. pap. 5.95 (*0-614-30871-2*) Hartland Pubns.

What Shall I Do Today? Ray Gibson. (Illus.). 96p. (J). (gr. k-6). 1996. 17.95 (*0-7460-2029-5*, Usborne) EDC.

What Shall I Do with Jesus Kit. Tim H. Gumm & Bryan Gerlach. 40p. (Orig.). 1996. pap. 19.99 (*0-614-16399-4*) NW Pub Co WA.

What Shall I Draw? R. Gee & A. Barlow. (What Shall I Do Today? Ser.). (Illus.). 32p. (J). (gr. k-6). 1995. pap. 6.95 (*0-7460-2024-4*, Usborne); lib. bdg. 14.95 (*0-88110-735-2*, Usborne) EDC.

What Shall I Dream? Laura M. Kvasnosky. LC 95-30890. (Illus.). 32p. (J). (gr. k-3). 1996. pap. 14.99 (*0-525-45207-9*) Dutton Child Bks.

What Shall I Feed the Family Tonight: Short Cuts & Other Ways to Cheat. Monica Benderly. 107p. 1993. 19.95 (*0-9638157-0-9*) Gourmet Comp.

*__What Shall I Grow?__ Ray Gibson. Ed. by Fiona Watt & Jenny Tyler. (What Shall I Do Today? Ser.). (Illus.). 32p. (Orig.). (J). (gr. 1-6). 1997. pap. 6.95 (*0-7460-2715-X*, Usborne) EDC.

*__What Shall I Grow?__ Ray Gibson. Ed. by Fiona Watt & Jenny Tyler. (What Shall I Do Today? Ser.). (Illus.). 32p. (J). (gr. 1-6). 1997. lib. bdg. 14.95 (*0-88110-947-9*, Usborne) EDC.

What Shall I Make? Ray Gibson. (What Shall I Do Today Ser.). (Illus.). 32p. (J). (gr. k-6). 1996. lib. bdg. 14.95 (*0-88110-782-4*, Usborne) EDC.

What Shall I Make? Ray Gibson. (What Shall I Do Today Ser.). (Illus.). (J). (gr. k-6). 1996. pap. 6.95 (*0-7460-2030-9*, Usborne) EDC.

What Shall I Paint? Ray Gibson. (What Shall I Do Today? Ser.). (Illus.). 32p. (J). (ps-6). 1995. pap. 6.95 (*0-7460-2026-0*, Usborne); lib. bdg. 14.95 (*0-88110-769-7*, Usborne) EDC.

What Shall I Say? Discerning God's Call to Ministry. Sue M. Setzer. 1995. pap. 5.95 (*0-9636630-1-1*) Evang Luth Church.

What Shall I Say? How to Write Eulogies. Celeste Walters. 48p. (Orig.). 1995. pap. 11.95 (*1-86407-110-9*, Pub. by JBCE AT) Morehouse Pub.

*__What Shall I Wear?__ Meredith Dunham. (J). Date not set. write for info. (*0-688-04661-4*); lib. bdg. write for info. (*0-688-04662-2*) Lothrop.

What Shall I Write Handbook: For Editors of Family & Genealogy Society Newsletters. Corinne Earnest. LC TX 3-259-169. (Illus.). 80p. (Orig.). 1992. pap. 16.00 (*1-879311-04-6*) R D Earnest.

What Shall This Man Do? Watchman Nee. 1979. pap. 5.95 (*0-87508-427-3*) Chr Lit.

What Shall This Man Do? see Que Hare, Senor?

What Shall We Defend? Denham Sutcliffe. Ed. by Harley Henry. 92p. 1973. pap. 1.50 (*0-911028-24-2*) Newberry.

*__What Shall We Do Tomorrat at Lak Tahoe: A Complete Activities Guide for Lake Tahoe, Truckee & Carson Pass.__ 3rd rev. ed. Ellie Huggins. Ed. by Laurel H. Lipert. LC 95-83873. (What Shall We Do Tomorrow at Lake Tahoe Ser.: Vol. 4). (Illus.). 300p. (Orig.). 1997. pap. 12.95 (*0-9633056-4-6*) Coldstream Pr.

What Shall We Do Tomorrow at Lake Tahoe, 1996 Edition: A Complete Activities Guide for Lake Tahoe, Truckee & Carson Pass. rev. ed. Ellie Huggins. Ed. by Laurel H. Lippert. LC 95-83873. (Illus.). 296p. 1996. pap. 12.95 (*0-9633056-3-8*) Coldstream Pr.

What Shall We Do Tomorrow in Mammoth Lakes Sierra. Don Douglas & Ellie Huggins. 1994. pap. 10.95 (*0-938665-30-8*) Fine Edge Prods.

What Shall We Do When We All Go Out? Ed. by Philip H. Bailey. LC 94-38573. (Illus.). 32p. (J). (ps-3). 1995. 14.95 (*1-55858-424-2*); lib. bdg. 14.88 (*1-55858-425-0*) North-South Bks NYC.

*__What Shall We Do When We All Go Out?__ Illus. by Shari Halpern. 32p. (J). (gr. k-1). 1997. pap. 6.95 (*1-55858-705-5*) North-South Bks NYC.

What Shall We Do Without Us? Kenneth Patchen. LC 84-4891. (Illus.). 112p. (Orig.). 1984. 25.00 (*0-87156-843-8*); pap. 12.95 (*0-87156-818-7*) Sierra.

What Shall We Name the Baby? Winthrop Ames. 1990. pap. 5.99 (*0-671-70962-3*) S&S Trade.

*__What Shall We Pray About?__ Andy Robb. (Illus.). 32p. (J). (ps-3). Date not set. 10.99 (*1-56507-753-9*) Harvest Hse.

What Shall We Tell Our Children? Priscilla White. 1991. 14.95 (*0-8187-0127-7*) Harlo Press.

What Shall We Tell the Children: Talking with Your Children about Sex. Nancy Kohner. (Illus.). 172p. (Orig.). 1994. pap. 9.95 (*0-563-36762-8*, BBC-Parkwest) Parkwest Pubns.

What Shape? Debbie MacKinnon. LC 91-34700. (Illus.). 24p. (J). (ps). 1992. pap. 10.99 (*0-8037-1244-8*) Dial Bks Young.

What Shape? Debbie MacKinnon. Date not set. pap. 4.99 (*0-14-055744-X*) NAL-Dutton.

What Shape Is This? Mario Gomboli. LC 92-70230. (Illus.). 10p. (J). (ps-k). 1992. bds. 3.95 (*1-56397-149-6*) Boyds Mills Pr.

*__What Shape Is This?__ Ingrid Van der Leeden. (Teething Time Bks.). (J). 1997. 3.99 (*0-689-81446-1*, Litl Simon S&S) S&S Childrens.

What She Could Not Name. Nancy Shiffrin. Ed. by Kathleen Iddings. LC 87-90546. (Illus.). 67p. (Orig.). 1987. per. 6.95 (*0-931721-04-0*) La Jolla Poets.

What She Did on Her Summer. Tracy Sinclair. (Special Edition Ser.). 1995. mass mkt. 3.75 (*0-373-09976-2*, 1-09976-1) Silhouette.

*__What She Knew.__ Peter Filkins. LC 97-25370. 1998. write for info. (*0-914061-66-6*) Orchises Pr.

What She Means. Clayton Eshleman. LC 78-7502. 180p. (Orig.). 1978. pap. 10.00 (*0-87685-346-7*) Black Sparrow.

*__What She Wanted.__ Nicky Singer. 320p. 1997. pap. 17.95 (*0-7528-0491-X*, Pub. by Orion Bks UK) Trafalgar.

What She Wants. Curtis Pesman. 1992. pap. 10.00 (*0-345-36653-0*) Ballantine.

What She Wants for Christmas. Janice K. Johnson. 1996. pap. 3.99 (*0-373-70720-7*, 1-70720-7) Harlequin Bks.

What Ship Is That? Bob Basnight. (Illus.). 160p. (Orig.). 1996. pap. 15.95 (*1-55821-433-X*, 1433X) Lyons & Burford.

What Should Banks Do? Robert E. Litan. LC 87-18235. 207p. 1987. 29.95 (*0-8157-5270-9*); pap. 12.95 (*0-8157-5269-5*) Brookings.

What Should Be Taxed, Income or Expenditure? A Report of a Conference Sponsored by the Fund for Public Policy Research & the Brookings Institution. Ed. by Joseph A. Pechman. LC 79-22733. (Studies of Government Finance). 344p. reprint ed. pap. 98.10 (*0-8357-7072-9*, 2033591) Bks Demand.

What Should Economists Do? James Buchanan. LC 79-19511. 1979. 14.00 (*0-913966-64-9*); pap. 7.00 (*0-913966-65-7*) Liberty Fund.

What Should I Be? Beth Esh. (HRL Big Bks.). (Illus.). 8p. (Orig.). (J). (ps-k). 1995. pap. text ed. 10.95 (*1-57332-067-6*) HighReach Lrning.

What Should I Bring? Great Gifts for Every Occasion. Alison Boteler. (Illus.). 250p. 1992. spiral bd. 13.95 (*0-8120-4941-1*) Barron.

What Should I Do? Barbara L. McCombs & Linda Brannan. (Skills for Job Success Ser.). 32p. (Orig.). 1990. student ed., pap. 4.95 (*1-56119-031-4*) Educ Pr MD.

What Should I Do? Barbara L. McCombs & Linda Brannan. (Skills for Job Success Ser.). (Illus.). 32p. (Orig.). (YA). (gr. 7-12). 1990. teacher ed. 1.95 (*1-56119-032-2*); disk 39.95 (*1-56119-116-7*) Educ Pr MD.

An Asterisk (*) at the beginning of an entry indicates that the title is appearing in BIP for the first time.

What Should I Do?, Set. Barbara L. McCombs & Linda Brannan. (Skills for Job Success Ser.). (Illus.). 32p. (Orig.). (YA). (gr. 7-12). 1990. teacher ed., wbk. ed. 44. 95 (*1-56119-074-8*) Educ Pr MD.

What Should I Do? Safety & Emergency Care Handbook. rev. ed. Judith K. Schneider et al. (Competent Caregiver Ser.). (Illus.). 63p. 1986. student ed., pap. 8.95 (*0-944454-07-0*); pap. text ed. 8.95 (*0-944454-00-3*) CAPE Center.

What Should I Do? Six True Adventures from Orleans History. June C. Fletcher. 64p. (J). (gr. 5-6). 1996. pap. 9.95 (*0-9651393-1-X*) Snow Lib.

What Should I Feed My Kids? Ronald Kleinman et al. 304p. 1996. pap. 11.00 (*0-449-90709-0*) Fawcett.

What Should I Feed My Kids? Ronald Kleinmen & Michael S. Jellinek. 1996. pap. 11.00 (*0-614-12607-X*, Columbine) Fawcett.

What Should I Know about Someone Who Abuses Alcohol & Other Drugs. Charles Dodgen. 1994. pap. 5.95 (*1-55691-115-7*, 157) Learning Pubns.

What Should I Tell the Kids? A Parent's Guide to Real Problems in the Real World. Ava L. Siegler. 336p. 1994. pap. 10.95 (*0-452-27247-5*, Plume) NAL-Dutton.

What Should I Write My Report On? Joyce Senn. 88p. 1994. pap. 9.95 (*0-590-49648-4*) Scholastic Inc.

What Should Legal Analysis Become? Roberto M. Unger. 192p. (C). 1996. text ed. 55.00 (*1-85984-969-5*, Pub. by Vrso UK); pap. text ed. 17.00 (*1-85984-100-7*, Pub. by Vrso UK) Norton.

***What Should Methodists.** Meeks. 23.75 (*0-687-44912-X*) Abingdon.

What Should Political Theory Be Now? Ed. by John S. Nelson. LC 82-19167. (SUNY Series in Political Theory: Contemporary Issues). 607p. (C). 1984. text ed. 19.95 (*0-87395-694-X*) State U NY Pr.

What Should We Do about Mom? A New Look at Growing Old. Richard T. Conard. (Illus.). 160p. 1992. pap. 8.95 (*0-8306-3957-8*, 4145, TAB-Human Servs Inst) TAB Bks.

What Should We Do about Mom? A New Look at Growing Old. Richard T. Conrad. 1992. pap. text ed. 8.95 (*0-07-012352-7*) McGraw.

What Should We Tell Our Children about Vietnam? Bill McCloud. LC 89-40218. 144p. 1989. 19.95 (*0-8061-2229-3*) U of Okla Pr.

What Should You Do If You Are Arrested or Framed by the Cops? Al-Hajj I. Muhammad. 32p. (Orig.). 1990. pap. 4.95 (*1-56411-034-6*) Untd Bros & Sis.

What Shrub Is That. Stirling Macoboy. 1989. 24.99 (*0-517-69211-2*) Random Hse Value.

What Sign Is Your Pet? Donald D. Wolf. 1990. pap. 3.95 (*0-312-92342-2*) St Martin.

What Silence Equals: Poems. Tory Dent. LC 93-3466. 80p. (Orig.). 1993. pap. 9.95 (*0-89255-196-8*) Persea Bks.

***What Single Flank Measurement Can Do for You.** Robert E. Smith. (1984 Fall Technical Meeting Ser.). 11p. 1984. pap. text ed. 30.00 (*1-55589-084-9*) AGMA.

What Size? Debbie MacKinnon. LC 93-40103. (J). 1995. pap. 10.99 (*0-8037-1745-8*) Dial Bks Young.

What Smart Students Know: Maximum Grades Optimum Learning, Minimum Time. Adam Robinson. LC 93-20437. 1993. pap. 16.00 (*0-517-88085-7*, Crown) Crown Pub Group.

What Smart Women Know: Wisdom for the Thinking Woman. Steven Carter & Julia Sokol. LC 90-13826. 216p. 1991. pap. 11.95 (*0-440-50389-2*, Dell Trade Pbks) Dell.

What Social Class Is in America: The American Dream & Social Class. W. Lloyd Warner. (Reprint Series in Sociology). (C). 1993. reprint ed. pap. text ed. 2.30 (*0-8290-2654-1*, S-302) Irvington.

What Social Classes Owe to Each Other. William G. Sumner. 1952. pap. 6.95 (*0-87004-166-5*) Caxton.

What Social Classes Owe to Each Other. William G. Sumner. LC 70-172234. (Right Wing Individualist Tradition in America Ser.). 1978. reprint ed. 20.95 (*0-405-00443-5*) Ayer.

What Social Workers Do. Margaret Gibelman. (Illus.). 387p. (Orig.). (C). 1995. lib. bdg. 32.95 (*0-87101-242-1*, 2421) Natl Assn Soc Wkrs.

What Socrates Began: An Examination of the Intellect, Vol. 1. Libby G. Cohen. (Orig.). (C). 1988. pap. write for info. (*0-939561-01-8*) Univ South ME.

What Socrates Began: An Examination of the Intellect, Vol. 2. Libby G. Cohen. (Orig.). 1989. write for info. (*0-939561-04-2*) Univ South ME.

What Songwriters Need to Know about Getting Their Songs Published. Peggy Bradley. 1993. 9.95 (*0-9639326-0-8*) Music Sq Cnslts.

What Spacetime Explains: Metaphysical Essays on Space & Time. Graham Nerlich. LC 93-27336. 272p. (C). 1994. text ed. 54.95 (*0-521-45261-9*) Cambridge U Pr.

What Spilled When the Door of Life Was Left Ajar. Willard L. Hartshorn. 100p. 1991. pap. 9.95 (*0-9629603-0-6*) Summit CT.

What Spot? Crosby N. Bonsall. LC 63-8005. (Harper I Can Read Bk.). (Illus.). 64p. (J). (gr. k-3). 1963. lib. bdg. 14. 89 (*0-06-020611-X*) HarpC Child Bks.

What Squashes Your Spirit. Lewis C. Parker. 1992. pap. 7.95 (*1-55673-493-X*, 7943) CSS OH.

***What State Education Agencies Can Do.** Music Educators National Conference Staff. (Implementing the Arts Education Standards Ser.). 6p. (Orig.). (C). 1994. pap. write for info. (*1-56545-060-4*, 4019) Music Ed Natl.

What State Leaders Can Do to Help Change Teacher Education. 1990. 5.00 (*0-89333-072-8*); 5.00 (*0-89333-075-2*) AACTE.

What Stimulation Your Baby Needs to Become Smart: Birth to Eight Months. William H. Staso. (Illus.). 150p. 1995. pap. 19.95 (*0-9644245-0-9*) Great Beginnings.

What Stories Are: Narrative Theory & Interpretation. Thomas M. Leitch. LC 85-43559. 232p. 1986. 20.00 (*0-271-00431-2*) Pa St U Pr.

What Strategies Can Support the Evolutionary Emergence of Cooperation? Jack Hirshleifer & Juan C. Coll. (CISA Working Papers: No. 58). 44p. (Orig.). 1987. pap. 15.00 (*0-86682-075-2*) Ctr Intl Relations.

What Students Can Tell Us about the Multicultural Classroom. Carol Miller. Ed. by Lillian Bridwell-Bowles & Susan Batchelder. (Technical Reports: No. 1). 7p. (Orig.). (C). 1992. pap. 2.00 (*1-881221-04-0*) U Minn Ctr Interdis.

***What Students Really Think of Professors: An Analysis of Classroom Evaluation Forms at an American University.** Ed. by Linda A. Jackson & Michael Murray. LC 97-12633. 1997. text ed. 79.95 (*0-7734-8610-0*) E Mellen.

What Style Is It? A Guide to American Architecture. 2nd ed. John C. Poppeliers et al. LC 83-19278. (Building Watchers Ser.). (Illus.). 112p. (C). 1995. pap. text ed. 8.95 (*0-471-14434-7*) Wiley.

***What Successful Performers Know.** Keith M. Johnson. 96p. 1997. pap. 15.00 (*1-890833-04-5*) KMJ Educ.

***What Sucks about South Florida: A Travel-To Move-To Guide.** Scott Marcus. (Illus.). 208p. (Orig.). 1997. pap. 12.95 (*0-9640354-8-0*) Fender Pubng.

What Survives. Gary Doore. 1990. pap. 13.95 (*0-87477-583-3*, Tarcher Putnam) Putnam Pub Group.

What Teachers Do: Developments in Special Education. Philip Garner et al. 208p. 1995. pap. 26.95 (*1-85396-285-6*, Pub. by Paul Chapman UK) Taylor & Francis.

What Teachers Need to Know: The Knowledge, Skills & Values Essential to Good Teaching. David D. Dill et al. LC 89-48337. (Education-Higher Education Ser.). 276p. 34.95 (*1-55542-226-8*) Jossey-Bass.

What Teenagers Want to Know. Shideler Harpe & Wesley W. Hall. (Illus.). 1992. pap. 6.00 (*0-318-37517-6*) Budlong.

***What Teens Need to Succeed: Proven, Practical Ways to Shape Your Own Future.** Pamela Espeland. 1997. pap. text ed. 14.95 (*1-57542-027-9*) Free Spirit Pub.

What the AFS Literature Says About...Gas Defects in Gray & Ductile Iron Castings. 243p. 1987. ring bd. 100.00 (*0-317-59871-6*, LS4) Am Foundrymen.

What the AFS Literature Says About...Gas Porosity in Aluminum Castings. 131p. 1987. ring bd. 60.00 (*0-317-59870-8*, LS3) Am Foundrymen.

What the AFS Literature Says About...Gating & Risering of Copper-Base Alloys. 137p. 1987. ring bd. 60.00 (*0-317-59873-2*, LS5) Am Foundrymen.

What the AFS Literature Says About...Inclusions in Cast Iron. 112p. 1987. ring bd. 50.00 (*0-317-59866-X*, LS1) Am Foundrymen.

What the AFS Literature Says About...Inclusions in Steel. 159p. 1987. ring bd. 70.00 (*0-317-59868-6*, LS2) Am Foundrymen.

What the AFS Literature Says About...Sand Reclamation. 142p. 1987. 70.00 (*0-317-59876-7*, LS7) Am Foundrymen.

What the AFS Literature Says About...The Evaporative Casting Process. 127p. 1987. 60.00 (*0-317-59874-0*, LS6) Am Foundrymen.

What the Ancient Wisdom Expects of Its Disciples. Manly P. Hall. 1982. pap. 5.95 (*0-89314-811-3*) Philos Res.

What the Angels Would Feed There Babies. Tammi Adair. 50p. 1995. pap. 6.95 (*0-9649833-1-1*) T Adair.

***What the Animals Tell Me: Developing Your Innate Telepathic Skills to Understand and Communicate With Your Pets.** Sonya Fitzpatrick & Patricia Burkhart Smith. 1997. 19.95 (*0-7868-6259-9*) Hyperion.

What the Anti-Federalists Were for: The Political Thought of the Opponents of the Constitution: Volume I of the Complete Anti-Federalist. Herbert J. Storing. LC 81-11395. 120p. (C). 1981. pap. text ed. 6.95 (*0-226-77574-7*) U Ch Pr.

***What the Arts Community Can Do.** Music Educators National Conference Staff. (Implementing the Arts Education Standards Ser.). 6p. (Orig.). 1994. pap. write for info. (*1-56545-062-0*, 4021) Music Ed Natl.

What the Authorities Will Never Tell You: How to Make Your Life Better Now. Tracy W. Humble. Ed. by Sheila A. Nicholson. 96p. (Orig.). 1993. pap. 12.95 (*1-882799-05-4*) Edutainment.

***What the Aztecs Told Me.** 1997. 15.95 (*0-88899-305-6*, Pub. by Groundwood-Douglas & McIntyre CN); pap. 6.95 (*0-88899-306-4*, Pub. by Groundwood-Douglas & McIntyre CN) Firefly Bks Ltd.

What the Banks Did to Poland. Sam Marcy. 26p. 1988. pap. 0.50 (*0-89567-090-9*) World View Forum.

What the Bee Knows: Reflections on Myth, Symbol & Story. Pamela L. Travers. 304p. 1994. pap. 11.95 (*0-14-019466-5*, Arkana) Viking Penguin.

What the Bible Actually Teaches. Bill Scheidler. (Illus.). 144p. 1992. teacher ed., pap. 8.95 (*0-914936-78-6*) BT Pub.

What the Bible Is All About. rev. ed. Henrietta C. Mears. 642p. 1987. pap. 12.99 (*0-8423-7902-9*) Tyndale.

***What the Bible Is All About.** 2nd ed. Henrietta C. Mears. LC 97-22327. 1997. write for info. (*0-8307-1893-1*); pap. write for info. (*0-8307-1896-6*) Regal.

What the Bible Really Says. Ed. by Morton Smith & R. Joseph Hoffmann. 256p. 1989. 28.95 (*0-87975-468-0*) Prometheus Bks.

What the Bible Really Says: Casting New Light on the Book of Books. Manfred Barthel. Tr. by Mark Howson from GER. LC 83-3001. (Illus.). 416p. 1983. pap. 13.20 (*0-688-01979-X*, Quill) Morrow.

What the Bible Really Says? Top Scholars Put Homosexuality in Perspective. Daniel A. Helminiak. 128p. (Orig.). 1994. pap. 9.95 (*0-9624751-9-X*) Alamo Sq Pr.

What the Bible Really Says about Love, Marriage, & Family. John T. Bristow. 152p. (Orig.). 1994. pap. 12.99 (*0-8272-4232-8*) Chalice Pr.

What the Bible Really Says about Women. Sheri Adams. LC 94-28. 108p. (Orig.). 1994. pap. 9.95 (*1-880837-88-9*) Smyth & Helwys.

What the Bible Says about Angels. Arno C. Gaebelein. 118p. (YA). (gr. 10). 1975. pap. 5.99 (*0-8010-3810-3*) Baker Bks.

What the Bible Says about Angels. David Jeremiah. 232p. 1996. 18.99 (*0-88070-902-2*, Multnomah Bks) Multnomah Pubs.

***What the Bible Says about Angels - Booklet.** David Jeremiah. 160p. (Orig.). 1996. pap. 5.99 (*1-57673-027-1*, Multnomah Bks) Multnomah Pubs.

What the Bible Says about Child Training. J. Richard Fugate. (What the Bible Says about...Ser.). (Illus.). 287p. 1980. reprint ed. pap. 5.95 (*0-86717-000-X*) Aletheia Pubs.

What the Bible Says about Civil Government. Paul Butler. 466p. 1990. 13.99 (*0-89900-266-8*) College Pr Pub.

What the Bible Says about Cremation. Billy J. Turnage. 24p. (Orig.). 1995. pap. 2.99 (*1-880726-08-4*) Turnage Pub.

What the Bible Says about Leadership. Arthur Harrington. LC 85-72670. (What the Bible Says Ser.). 446p. 1988. reprint ed. text ed. 13.99 (*0-89900-250-1*) College Pr Pub.

What the Bible Says about Marriage, Divorce, & Remarriage. John Coblentz. 1992. pap. 4.95 (*0-87813-544-8*) Christian Light.

What the Bible Says about Muhammad? A. Deedat. 3.00 (*0-933511-12-4*) Kazi Pubns.

What the Bible Says about Muhammad. Ahmed Deedat. 49p. 1970. pap. text ed. 2.50 (*0-916157-71-7*) African Islam Miss Pubns.

What the Bible Says about Prehistoric Man. W. Fred Conway, Sr. (Illus.). 96p. (Orig.). 1993. pap. 4.99 (*0-925165-13-1*) Fire Buff Hse.

What the Bible Says about Salvation. Virgil Warren. LC 82-73345. (What the Bible Says Ser.). 622p. 1982. pap. 13.99 (*0-89900-088-6*) College Pr Pub.

What the Bible Says about Salvation: Question & Answers. Virgil Warren. 78p. pap. 4.99 (*0-89900-654-X*) College Pr Pub.

What the Bible Says about Sex. Friend Stuart. 40p. 1985. pap. 4.95 (*0-912132-17-5*) Dominion Pr.

What the Bible Says about Sin. Brant L. Doty. 361p. 13.99 (*0-89900-418-0*) College Pr Pub.

What the Bible Says about Stewardship. A. Q. Van Benschoten, Jr. 96p. 1983. pap. 10.00 (*0-8170-0993-0*) Judson.

What the Bible Says about the Heart. Gary Carpenter. 308p. (C). 1991. text ed. 13.99 (*0-89900-267-6*) College Pr Pub.

What the Bible Says about the Holy Spirit. Russell Boatman. LC 88-63252. (What the Bible Says Ser.). 380p. (C). 1989. text ed. 13.99 (*0-89900-262-5*) College Pr Pub.

What the Bible Says about the Holy Spirit. Stanley M. Horton. LC 75-43154. 320p. (YA). (gr. 12). 1976. kivar 9.95 (*0-88243-647-3*, 02-0647) Gospel Pub.

What the Bible Says about Tongues. Robert E. Picirilli. 1981. pap. 0.95 (*0-89265-071-0*) Randall Hse.

***What the Bible Says about Tongues-Speaking.** 40p. 1988. pap. 2.99 (*0-8341-1267-1*) Nazarene.

What the Bible Says to Emotionally Hurting People. Bob Snyder. 132p. 1994. pap. 5.95 (*1-883624-04-5*) Hope Hurt Minist.

What the Bible Says to the Hurting Jew. Bob Snyder. 132p. 1994. pap. 5.95 (*1-883624-08-8*) Hope Hurt Minist.

What the Bible Says to the Minister: The Minister's Personal Handbook. 400p. (Orig.). (C). 1992. pap. 15. 95 (*0-945863-33-0*) Ldrship Minist Wrldwide.

What the Bible Says to the Minister Chapter 7: About False Teaching. (C). 1992. pap. write for info. (*0-945863-32-2*) Ldrship Minist Wrldwide.

What the Bible Says...to the Minister: The Minister's Personal Handbook. (SPA.). 1995. pap. text ed. 9.95 (*0-945863-79-9*) Ldrship Minist Wrldwide.

What the Bible Teaches. James McRobbie. pap. 8.99 (*0-88019-122-8*) Schmul Pub Co.

What the Bible Teaches. F. G. Smith. 1970. pap. 6.95 (*0-87162-104-5*, D8850) Warner Pr.

What the Bible Teaches. R. A. Torrey. 1995. pap. 12.99 (*0-551-05558-8*) Zondervan.

What the Bible Teaches. R. A. Torrey. LC 97-110. 560p. 1996. pap. 9.99 (*0-88368-400-4*) Whitaker Hse.

What the Bible Teaches. F. G. Smith. 576p. reprint ed. 5.50 (*0-686-29174-3*) Faith Pub Hse.

What the Bible Teaches, 2 vols., 1. Leslie G. Thomas. 1962. 5.95 (*0-88027-023-3*) Firm Foun Pub.

What the Bible Teaches, 2 vols., II. Leslie G. Thomas. 1962. write for info. (*0-88027-024-1*) Firm Foun Pub.

***What the Bible Teaches Vol. 1: Galatians, Ephesians.** 414p. 1996. 24.99 (*0-946351-01-5*, Pub. by John Ritchie UK) Loizeaux.

***What the Bible Teaches Vol. 2: Matthew, Mark.** 588p. 1996. 24.99 (*0-946351-02-3*, Pub. by John Ritchie UK) Loizeaux.

***What the Bible Teaches Vol. 3: Thess., Timothy, Titus.** 454p. 1996. 24.99 (*0-946351-03-1*, Pub. by John Ritchie UK) Loizeaux.

***What the Bible Teaches Vol. 4: Corinthians.** 427p. 1996. 24.99 (*0-946351-06-6*, Pub. by John Ritchie UK) Loizeaux.

***What the Bible Teaches Vol. 5: Epis., Peter, John, Jude.** 338p. 1996. 24.99 (*0-946351-09-0*, Pub. by John Ritchie UK) Loizeaux.

***What the Bible Teaches Vol. 6: Gospel of John.** 349p. 1996. 24.99 (*0-946351-12-0*, Pub. by John Ritchie UK) Loizeaux.

***What the Bible Teaches Vol. 7: Gospel of Luke.** 416p. 1996. 24.99 (*0-614-19123-8*, Pub. by John Ritchie UK) Loizeaux.

***What the Bible Teaches Vol. 8: Hebrews.** 315p. 1996. 24. 99 (*0-946351-30-9*, Pub. by John Ritchie UK) Loizeaux.

***What the Bible Teaches Vol. 9: Acts, James.** 332p. 1996. 24.99 (*0-946351-35-X*, Pub. by John Ritchie UK) Loizeaux.

What the Bible Teaches about the Promised Messiah. James E. Smith. LC 93-4591. 544p. 1993. reprint ed. 24. 99 (*0-8407-4239-8*) Nelson.

What the Black Box Said: Poems. Terry Wright. LC 96-14249. 116p. 1996. pap. 19.95 (*0-7734-2694-9*, Mellen Poetry Pr) E Mellen.

***What the Blues Is All About: Black Women Overcoming Stress & Depression.** Angela Mitchell & Gladys Croom. LC 97-24482. 1998. pap. write for info. (*0-399-52376-6*, Perigee Bks) Berkley Pub.

What the Body Remembers. Adele Slaughter. 96p. pap. 11. 95 (*0-934257-99-X*) Story Line.

What the Body Told. Rafael Campo. LC 95-36519. 136p. 1996. text ed. 35.95 (*0-8223-1733-8*); pap. text ed. 12.95 (*0-8223-1742-7*) Duke.

What the Buddha Never Taught. Tim Ward. LC 92-39702. 256p. 1995. reprint ed. pap. 14.95 (*0-89087-687-8*) Celestial Arts.

What the Buddha Taught. rev. ed. Walpola Rahula. LC 73-21017. (Illus.). 192p. 1987. pap. 11.00 (*0-8021-3031-3*, Grove) Grove-Atltic.

What the Butler Saw: Selected Writings by Stuart Morgan. Ian Hunt & Stuart Morgan. 300p. 1996. pap. 22.95 (*0-9527414-0-7*, 610342, Pub. by Durian-Frieze UK) Dist Art Pubs.

What the Catholic Faithful Can Do. Gerard Morrissey. 128p. (Orig.). 1987. pap. 5.95 (*0-931888-23-9*) Christendom Pr.

What the Church Fathers Say. George Grube. 148p. (Orig.). 1996. pap. 10.95 (*1-880971-16-X*) Light&Life Pub Co MN.

What the Church of England Stands For. J. W. Wand. LC 76-106700. 131p. 1972. reprint ed. text ed. 55.00 (*0-8371-3382-3*, WACE, Greenwood Pr) Greenwood.

What the Church of God Means. 1990. pap. 0.75 (*0-87162-600-4*, D8855) Warner Pr.

What the Church Teaches: A Guide for the Study of Veritatis Splendor. William F. Maestri. 87p. 1994. pap. 1.50 (*0-8198-3072-0*) Pauline Bks.

What the Cow Said to the Calf: Native American Historical Biography. Helen P. Neilson. LC 93-84752. 200p. (Orig.). (C). 1993. pap. text ed. 17.95 (*1-880222-15-9*) Red Apple Pub.

What the Cults Believe. expanded rev. ed. Irvine G. Robertson. 1991. pap. 10.99 (*0-8024-9414-5*) Moody.

What the Darkness Proposes: Poems. Charles Martin. LC 96-18437. (Johns Hopkins). 80p. 1996. 16.95 (*0-8018-5487-3*) Johns Hopkins.

What the Deaf-Mute Heard. G.D. Gearino. 224p. 1996. 21. 00 (*0-684-81337-8*) S&S Trade.

What the Dickens! Jane L. Curry. LC 90-26864. 160p. (J). (gr. 4-7). 1991. lib. bdg. 13.95 (*0-689-50524-8*, McElderry) S&S Childrens.

***What the Dinosaurs Saw.** Miriam Schlein & Carol Schwartz. LC 97-12892. (Hello Science Reader Ser.). (J). 1998. write for info. (*0-590-37128-2*) Scholastic Inc.

What the Dogs Have Taught Me: And Other Amazing Things I've Learned. Merrill Markoe. 256p. 1993. pap. 10.00 (*0-14-016682-3*, Penguin Bks) Viking Penguin.

***What the Earth Taught Us.** Arnold Johnston. Ed. by Robert Bixby. 47p. (Orig.). 1996. pap. 6.00 (*0-614-30175-0*) March Street Pr.

What the Establishment Doesn't Want You to Know about Government & Politics. John Bryant. 95p. (Orig.). 1995. pap. 9.95 (*1-886739-23-4*) Socratic Pr.

What the Eye Reveals. rev. ed. Denny Johnson. Ed. by Erik Ness. LC 94-68709. (Illus.). 128p. 1995. pap. text ed. 29.95 (*0-917197-04-6*) Rayid Pubns.

***What the Face Reveals: Basic & Applied Studies of Spontaneous Expression Using the Facial Action Coding System (FACS)** Ed. by Paul Ekman & Erika Rosenberg. LC 96-36655. (Series in Affective Science). (Illus.). 432p. 1997. pap. 39.95 (*0-19-510447-1*) OUP.

***What the Face Reveals: Basic & Applied Studies of Spontaneous Expression Using the Facial Action Coding System (FACS)** Ed. by Paul Ekman & Erika Rosenberg. LC 96-36655. (Series in Affective Science). (Illus.). 432p. 1997. 65.00 (*0-19-510446-3*) OUP.

What the General Practitioner Should Know about Patent Law & Practice. 4th ed. Arthur H. Seidel. LC 84-71268. (Illus.). xvi, 252p. 1984. 41.50 (*0-8318-0457-2*, B457) Am Law Inst.

What the General Practitioner Should Know about Patent Law & Practice. 5th ed. Arthur H. Seidel et al. LC 93-70658. 331p. 1993. text ed. 95.00 (*0-8318-0651-6*, B651) Am Law Inst.

What the General Practitioner Should Know about Trade Secrets & Employment Agreements. 2nd ed. Arthur H. Seidel. LC 83-73153. (Illus.). xiv, 166p. 1984. 68.00 (*0-8318-0461-0*, B461) Am Law Inst.

What the General Practitioner Should Know about Trade Secrets & Employment Agreements. 3rd ed. Arthur H. Seidel & David R. Crichton. (Ali-Aba's Ser.). 215p. 1995. 120.00 incl. disk (*0-8318-0700-8*, B700/B747) Am Law Inst.

W

What the General Practitioner Should Know about Trademarks & Copyrights. 5th ed. Arthur H. Seidel. LC 86-70229. 300p. 1986. 38.00 (*0-8318-0517-X*, B517) Am Law Inst.

What the General Practitioner Should Know about Trademarks & Copyrights. 6th ed. Arthur H. Seidel et al. LC 92-71394. (Ali-Aba's Ser.). 383p. 1992. 95.00 (*0-8318-0652-4*, B652) Am Law Inst.

What the Good Parent Knows: The Six Rules for Treating Yourself Like a Child. Steve Harrelson. 168p. (Orig.). 1996. pap. 12.00 (*1-888174-88-9*) Am PressWrks.

What the Great Religions Believe. Joseph Gaer. pap. 3.95 (*0-451-14320-5*, AE1978, Sig) NAL-Dutton.

What the Gunpowder Plot Was. Samuel R. Gardiner. LC 76-89457. (BCL Ser.: I). reprint ed. 21.50 (*0-404-02677-X*) AMS Pr.

What the Hands Reveal about the Brain. Howard Poizner et al. (Studies in the Biology of Language & Cognition). 264p. 1990. reprint ed. pap. 17.50 (*0-262-66066-0*) MIT Pr.

What the Heart Keeps. Rosalind Laker. 1986. pap. 3.95 (*0-8217-1810-X*) NAL-Dutton.

What the Heart Knows. William W. Johnstone. 304p. 1995. 17.95 (*0-8217-5028-3*, Zebra Kensgtn) Kensgtn Pub Corp.

What the Heart Knows. William W. Johnstone. 256p. 1996. mass mkt. 4.99 (*1-57566-028-8*) Kensgtn Pub Corp.

What the Heck Are Ethics? Carole Marsh. (Quantum Leap Ser.). (J). (gr. 4-9). 1994. 29.95 (*1-55609-342-X*) Gallopade Pub Group.

What the Heck Are Ethics? Carole Marsh. (Quantum Leap Ser.). (J). (gr. 4-9). 1997. pap. 19.95 (*1-55609-244-X*) Gallopade Pub Group.

What the Heck's Goin' on at the Rodeo? Ed. by Robin Williams. (Illus.). 28p. 1994. pap. 3.00 (*0-9642268-0-4*) Red Hen Ent.

What the Hell Do Women Really Want: A Guide for Men in the 90's. Jama Clark. 154p. 1995. pap. 13.95 (*0-9642254-0-9*) Islnd Flower.

What the Hell for You Left Your Heart in San Francisco. Bienvenido N. Santos. 192p. (Orig.). 1987. pap. 15.00 (*971-10-0319-8*, Pub. by New Day Pub PH) Cellar.

What the Hell Is Homeopathy? 2nd rev. ed. Jacob I. Mirman. (Illus.). 65p. (Orig.). (YA). 1996. wbk. ed. 4.95 (*0-9651950-0-7*) New Hope Pubs.

***What the Hidden Monster Did to O. J. & Nicole.** Edmond Locklear, Jr. LC 95-60789. 164p. 1995. pap. 12.95 (*0-9614336-6-3*) WFCPr.

What the Holy Spirit Does in a Believer's Life. Charles H. Spurgeon. (Believer's Life Ser.). 180p. (Orig.). 1993. pap. 9.99 (*1-883002-01-X*) Emerald WA.

What the Informed Citizen Needs to Know. Ed. by Bruce Bliven, Jr. & Avrahm G. Mezerik. LC 72-1244. (Essay Index Reprint Ser.). 1977. reprint ed. 26.95 (*0-8369-2833-4*) Ayer.

What the International Bankers Are Doing with Your Money. 1992. lib. bdg. 79.95 (*0-8490-5428-1*) Gordon Pr.

What the IRS Doesn't Want You to Know. Martin Kaplan. LC 96-41874. 1996. pap. 13.95 (*0-679-77371-1*, Villard Bks) Random.

***What the IRS Dosen't Want You to Know.** Marty Kaplan. 1997. pap. 13.95 (*0-375-75045-2*, Villard Bks) Random.

What the Jews Believe. Philip S. Bernstein. LC 77-28446. (Illus.). 100p. 1978. reprint ed. text ed. 35.00 (*0-313-20228-1*, BEWJ, Greenwood Pr) Greenwood.

What the Judge Thought. Edward A. Parry. LC 68-29237. (Essay Index Reprint Ser.). 1977. 20.95 (*0-8369-0772-8*) Ayer.

What the Kite Thinks: A Linked Poem. Makoto Ooka et al. 88p. 1994. pap. text ed. 11.00 (*0-8248-1599-8*) UH Pr.

What the Lady Wants. Jennifer Crusie. (Temptation Ser.). 1995. mass mkt. 3.25 (*0-373-25644-2*, 1-25644-5) Harlequin Bks.

What the Land Gave. Phyllis Thompson. (QRL Poetry Bks.: XXII). 1981. 20.00 (*0-614-06390-6*) Quarterly Rev.

***What the Light Has Shown: Poems.** Marilyn Shelton. LC 96-50138. 52p. 1996. pap. 12.95 (*0-7734-2697-3*, Mellen Poetry Pr) E Mellen.

What the Light Was Like. Amy Clampitt. Ed. by Alice Quinn. LC 84-48652. (Poetry Ser.: No. 18). 111p. 1985. pap. 12.95 (*0-394-72937-4*) Knopf.

***What the Living Do.** Marie Howe. 1997. 21.00 (*0-393-04560-9*) Norton.

What the Maid Saw. Yasutaka Tsutsui. Tr. by Adam Kabat from JPN. 192p. 1990. 18.95 (*0-87011-992-3*) Kodansha.

***What the Moon Is Like.** Franklyn M. Branley & True Kelley. (Illus.). (J). (gr. 1-3). 7.66 (*0-06-04511-5*, 147023) HarpC Child Bks.

What the Moon Saw. Brian Wildsmith. (Illus.). 32p. (J). (ps-3). 1987. pap. 11.95 (*0-19-272157-7*) OUP.

What the Moon Saw: Early Intermediate Piano Solos. K. Beard. 16p. 1991. pap. 5.95 (*0-7935-0602-6*, 00290305) H Leonard.

What the Movies Made Me Do. Susan Braudy. LC 85-40117. 234p. 1985. 15.95 (*0-394-53246-5*) Knopf.

What the New Testament Says about Holiness. unabridged ed. J. Harold Greenlee. 52p. (Orig.). 1994. pap. 3.99 (*0-88019-326-3*) Schmul Pub Co.

What the Night Tells the Day. Hector Bianciotti. Tr. by Linda Coverdale from FRE. LC 94-43354. 272p. 1995. 22.00 (*1-56584-240-5*) New Press NY.

What the Night Tells the Day: A Novel. Hector Bianciotti. Tr. by Linda Coverdale. (International Fiction Ser.). 272p. Date not set. pap. 11.00 (*1-56584-241-3*) New Press NY.

What the Night Told Me: Poems. Bill Brown. LC 92-40363. 64p. 1993. pap. 12.95 (*0-7734-0035-4*, Mellen Poetry Pr) E Mellen.

W

What the Orthodox Church Owes to the West. Emilianos Timiades. LC 91-37169. 271p. (Orig.). (C). 1991. pap. 14.95 (*0-917651-96-0*) Holy Cross Orthodox.

What the Painter's Sees: Portraits, Still Lifes, Landscapes, Trick Painting, Animals, Water, & Light. Scholastic Staff. (Voyages of Discovery Ser.). 48p. (YA). (gr. 3 up). 1996. 19.95 (*0-590-47648-3*, Scholastic Voy Discov) Scholastic Inc.

What the Parrot Told Alice. Dale Smith. LC 96-96118. (Illus.). 128p. (Orig.). (J). (gr. 5-11). 1996. pap. 11.95 (*0-9651452-7-1*) Deer Creek Pubng.

What the People Should See: A History of Movie Censorship in America. Koppes. 1994. 24.95 (*0-02-917565-8*) S&S Trade.

What the Philosophy of Biology Is: Essays for David Hull. Ed. by Michael Ruse. 348p. (C). 1989. lib. bdg. 158.50 (*90-247-3778-8*) Kluwer Ac.

What the Poor Eat. Alice W. Gray. LC 92-70730. (CSU Poetry Ser.: XXXIX). 105p. (Orig.). 1993. pap. 8.00 (*0-914946-99-4*) Cleveland St Univ Poetry Ctr.

What the President Will Say & Do!! Madeline Gins. 160p. (Orig.). 1984. 14.95 (*0-930794-93-1*); pap. 7.95 (*0-930794-92-3*) Station Hill Pr.

What the Printer Should Know about Paper. 3rd ed. William Bureau. Ed. by Deborah L. Stevenson. LC 94-73206. (Illus.). 356p. 1995. text ed. 60.00 (*0-88362-175-4*) Graphic Arts Tech Found.

What the Public School Doesn't Tell You. Margie Doran. 219p. 1991. pap. 5.95 (*0-9629270-7-4*) Doran Prods.

What the Public Wants. Arnold Bennett. LC 74-16478. (Collected Works of Arnold Bennett: Vol. 86). 1977. reprint ed. 21.95 (*0-518-19167-2*) Ayer.

What the River Knows: An Angler in Midstream. Wayne Fields. 256p. 1996. pap. 14.95 (*0-226-24857-7*) U Ch Pr.

***What the River Reveals: Understanding & Restoring Healthy Watersheds.** Valerie Rapp. 1997. pap. text ed. 16.95 (*0-89886-527-1*) Mountaineers.

What the River Says: Whitewater Journeys along the Inner Frontier. Jeff Wallach. LC 96-21364. 192p. (Orig.). 1996. pap. 12.95 (*0-936085-35-5*) Blue Heron OR.

***What the Sam Hill.** Toby Swanson. 231p. (Orig.). 1996. pap. 10.00 (*0-9654116-0-5*) Main Menu Pr Now.

What the Scarecrow Said: A Novel. Stewart D. Ikeda. LC 96-2244. (Illus.). 464p. 1996. 24.00 (*0-06-039164-2*) HarpC.

***What the Scarecrow Said: A Novel.** Stewart D. Ikeda. 1997. pap. text ed. 13.50 (*0-06-098718-9*, ReganBooks) HarpC.

What the Sea Left Behind. Mimi G. Carpenter. LC 81-66251. (Illus.). 32p. (J). (gr. 1-4). 1981. pap. 9.95 (*0-89272-123-5*) Down East.

What the Seeker Needs: Essays & Glossary on Sufism. Muhyiddin Ibn 'Arabi. Tr. by Tosun Bayrak & Rabia T. Harris. 138p. 1992. pap. 10.00 (*0-939660-41-5*) Threshold VT.

What the Self-Publishing Manuals Don't Tell You & You Didn't Know to Ask. Gene Corpening. LC 95-94210. 94p. (Orig.). 1995. pap. 19.95 (*1-887108-95-5*) Alice Pub.

What the Soul Teaches. Harriet Mohr. 170p. 1994. pap. 6.95 (*0-9629467-1-0*) New Focus Pr.

What the Spirit Says to the Churches: An Exposition of the Letters of Jesus Christ to the Churches in Asia As Revealed to the Apostle John (Revelation 2 & 3) Jerome M. Julien. 1996. write for info. (*0-921100-76-0*) Inhtce Pubns.

What the Stars Reveal About the Men in Your Life. Thelma White. 1980. pap. 3.00 (*0-87980-378-9*) Wilshire.

What the Stones Say. Charles H. Spurgeon. 1975. mass mkt. 5.00 (*1-56186-322-X*) Pilgrim Pubns.

What the Storyteller Brings. Robyn Demby. LC 93-94372. 128p. (Orig.). (YA). 1995. pap. 10.00 (*1-56002-427-5*, Univ Edtns) Aegina Pr.

What the Sun Sees, What the Moon Sees. Nancy Tafuri. LC 96-20976. (Illus.). 32p. (J). (ps up). 1997. 16.00 (*0-688-14493-4*) Greenwillow.

***What the Sun Sees, What the Moon Sees.** Nancy Tafuri. (Illus.). 32p. (J). (ps up). 1997. lib. bdg. 15.93 (*0-688-14494-2*) Greenwillow.

What the Tax Practitioner Should Know about the Supreme Court's Baggot & Sells Decisions. Marvin J. Garbis et al. 36p. 1984. 2.75 (*0-685-08923-1*, 95520-9) P-H.

What the Thunder Really Said: A Retrospective Essay on the Making of the Waste Land. Anne C. Bolgan. LC 73-79500. 202p. reprint ed. pap. 57.60 (*0-7837-6936-9*, 2046765) Bks Demand.

What the Trout Said. rev. ed. Datus Proper. (Illus.). 304p. 1989. reprint ed. 35.00 (*1-55821-014-8*) Lyons & Burford.

What the Water Gave Me. Tania Elizov. (Poetry Ser.). (Orig.). 1992. pap. 10.00 (*1-880855-00-3*) Fifth Planet.

What the Wind Told. Betty Roegehold. Date not set. pap. 1.95 (*0-590-05406-6*) Scholastic Inc.

What the World Is Coming To. rev. ed. Chuck Smith. LC 77-3186. 224p. 1993. pap. 4.99 (*0-936728-48-5*) Word for Today.

What Therapists Learn about Themselves & How They Learn It: Autognosis. Ed. by Edward Messner et al. LC 93-74196. 166p. 1994. pap. 25.00 (*1-56821-188-0*) Aronson.

What They Always Wanted. Christopher G. Janus. LC 88-62489. 1989. pap. 9.95 (*0-934831-01-7*) Sheffield Bks.

What They Always Were. Norita Dittberner-Jax. 76p. 1995. pap. 9.95 (*0-89823-160-4*) New Rivers Pr.

What They Did: Public Activities of German Immigrants in Missouri. Anita M. Mallinckrodt. 20p. 1995. 4.00 (*0-931227-09-7*) Mallinckrodt Comm.

What They Did Not Teach You in Seminary. Paul Meier et al. LC 92-27058. 1993. 12.99 (*0-8407-7708-6*) Nelson.

What They Did to Princess Paragon. Robert Rodi. 1995. pap. 10.95 (*0-452-27163-0*, Plume) NAL-Dutton.

***What They Didn't Teach You about the Civil War.** Mike Wright. LC 96-32970. 1996. 24.95 (*0-89141-596-3*) Presidio Pr.

What They Didn't Teach You in School about Programming. Russell F. Jacobs. 1998. pap. 39.99 incl. disk (*0-672-30502-X*) Sams.

What They Don't Always Teach You at a Christian College. Keith R. Anderson. 192p. (Orig.). 1995. pap. 9.99 (*0-8308-1611-9*, 1611) InterVarsity.

What They Don't Teach You about History. Tim Wood. 1990. 7.99 (*0-517-03704-1*) Random Hse Value.

What They Don't Teach You at Harvard Business School: Notes from a Street-Smart Executive. Mark H. McCormack. 272p. 1986. pap. 14.95 (*0-553-34583-4*) Bantam.

What They Don't Teach You at Harvard Business School about Executive Travel: Hit the Ground... Mark H. McCormack. 1996. pap. 12.95 (*0-7871-0684-4*, Dove Bks) Dove Audio.

What They Don't Tell You in Schools of Education about School Administration. John A. Black & Fenwick W. English. LC 86-50183. 339p. 1986. 39.95 (*0-87762-461-5*) Technomic.

What They Fought for, 1861-1865. James M. McPherson. LC 93-36934. (Walter Lynwood Fleming Lectures in Southern History). 96p. (C). 1994. 16.95 (*0-8071-1904-0*) La State U Pr.

What They Fought for 1861-1865. James M. McPherson. LC 94-38423. 96p. 1995. pap. 10.00 (*0-385-47634-5*, Anchor NY) Doubleday.

What They Heard: Music in America, 1852-1881, from the Pages of "Dwight's Journal of Music" Irving Sablosky. LC 85-13016. (Illus.). x, 317p. 1986. text ed. 40.00 (*0-8071-1258-5*) La State U Pr.

What They Never Told Me When I Became a Christian. Verne Becker et al. 128p. 1991. pap. 8.99 (*0-310-71171-1*) Zondervan.

What They Never Told You about Boston - or What They Did That Were Lies. Walt Kelley. LC 93-71411. (Illus.). 128p. 1993. pap. 12.95 (*0-89272-333-5*) Down East.

What They Said in 1987: The Yearbook of World Opinion, Vol. 19. Ed. by Alan F. Pater & Jason R. Pater. LC 74-111080. 600p. 1988. 37.50 (*0-917734-17-3*) Monitor Bk.

What They Said in 1988: The Yearbook of World Opinion, Vol. 20. Ed. by Alan F. Pater & Jason R. Pater. LC 74-111080. 592p. 1989. 37.50 (*0-917734-18-1*) Monitor Bk.

What They Said in 1989: The Yearbook of World Opinion, Vol. 21. Ed. by Alan F. Pater & Jason R. Pater. 576p. 1990. 37.95 (*0-917734-20-3*) Monitor Bk.

What They Said in 1990: The Yearbook of World Opinion, Vol. 22. Ed. by Alan F. Pater & Jason R. Pater. LC 74-111080. 556p. 1991. 39.75 (*0-917734-21-1*) Monitor Bk.

What They Said in 1991: The Yearbook of World Opinion, Vol. 23. Ed. by Alan F. Pater & Jason R. Pater. 480p. 1992. 41.00 (*0-917734-24-6*) Monitor Bk.

What They Said in 1994: The Yearbook of World Opinion, Vol. 26. Ed. by Alan F. Pater & Jason R. Pater. 559p. 1995. 42.90 (*0-917734-27-0*) Monitor Bk.

***What They Said in 1995 Vol. 27: The Yearbook of World Opinion.** Ed. by Alan F. Pater & Jason R. Pater. 529p. 1996. 42.90 (*0-917734-28-9*) Monitor Bk.

***What They Saw...at the Hour of Death: A New Look at Evidence for Life after Death.** Karlis Osis & Erlendur Haraldsson. 260p. 1997. pap. 14.95 (*0-8038-9386-8*, 702563) Hastings.

What They Still Don't Teach You at Harvard Business School: Selling More, Managing Better, & Getting the Job Done in the '90s. Mark H. McCormack. 320p. 1990. pap. 14.95 (*0-553-34961-9*) Bantam.

What They Tell You to Forget: A Novella & Stories. Fred Pfeil. 277p. 1996. 25.00 (*0-916366-49-9*) Norton.

What They Thought Vol. I: Missouri's German Immigrants Assess Their World, 1850s. Abr. by Anita M. Mallinckrodt. 44p. 1995. 6.00 (*0-931227-07-0*) Mallinckrodt Comm.

What They Thought Vol. II: Missouri's German Immigrants Assess Their World 1860s. Anita M. Mallinckrodt. 32p. 1995. 5.00 (*0-931227-08-9*) Mallinckrodt Comm.

What This Awl Means: Feminist Archaeology at a Wahpeton Dakota Village. Janet D. Spector. LC 92-46737. vii, 161p. 1993. 32.50 (*0-87351-277-4*); pap. 15.95 (*0-87351-278-2*) Minn Hist.

What This Modern Jew Believes. Isaiah Z. Rabb. (Illus.). 200p. (Orig.). 1996. pap. text ed. 18.00 (*0-914615-01-7*) I Nathan Pub Co.

What Thoreau Said: Walden & the Unsayable. William C. Johnson, Jr. LC 90-49358. 156p. (C). 1991. 15.95 (*0-89301-146-0*) U of Idaho Pr.

What Those People Need Is a Puppy! More Cartoons by Pat Oliphant. Patrick Oliphant. (Illus.). 160p. (Orig.). 1989. pap. 8.95 (*0-8362-1857-4*) Andrews & McMeel.

What Thou Lovest Well Remains: 100 Years of Ezra Pound. limited ed. Ezra Pound et al. Ed. by Richard Ardinger. 1986. pap. 15.00 (*0-931659-01-9*) Limberlost Pr.

What Though the Odds... The Story of Notre Dame Tennis. Thomas W. Fallon. LC 94-26482. 1994. 34.95 (*0-912083-79-4*) Diamond Communications.

What Time Does. Klaus Wagn. 1976. 4.50 (*0-686-17603-0*) Caann Verlag.

What Time Does the Rally Start & Other Poems. Edilberto P. Dagot. (Illus.). 102p. (Orig.). (C). 1990. pap. 9.50 (*971-10-0409-7*, Pub. by New Day Pub PH) Cellar.

***What Time Is It?** Clegg & Hughes. (J). Date not set. pap. text ed. write for info. (*0-05-004265-3*) Addison-Wesley.

What Time Is It? Judith Grey. LC 81-5113. (Illus.). 32p. (J). (gr. k-2). 1997. pap. 3.95 (*0-89375-510-9*) Troll Communs.

What Time Is It? Elisabeth Ivanovsky. (Picture-Word Boards Bks.). (Illus.). (J). (ps). 1985. bds. 3.98 (*0-517-47343-7*) Random Hse Value.

***What Time Is It?** Jo E. Moore. (Mathematics Ser.). (Illus.). 32p. (J). (gr. k-1). 1997. teacher ed., pap. 2.95 (*1-55799-443-9*, 4045) Evan-Moor Corp.

What Time Is It? Rozanne L. Williams. (Emergent Reader Bks.). (Illus.). 8p. (Orig.). (J). (gr. k-2). 1995. pap. 1.59 (*0-916119-98-X*) Creat Teach Pr.

What Time Is It? Rozanne L. Williams. (Emergent Reader Big Bks.). (Illus.). 8p. (Orig.). (J). (gr. k-2). 1996. pap. 7.98 (*1-57471-102-4*) Creat Teach Pr.

What Time Is It? unabridged ed. A. G. Smith. (Illus.). 96p. (Orig.). (YA). (gr. 4 up). 1995. pap. 12.95 (*0-7737-5525-X*, Pub. by Stoddart Kids CN) Genl Dist Srvs.

***What Time Is It? It's My Time to Reach Success!** Danyelle Bachand. 128p. 1996. per., pap. text ed. 19.95 (*0-7872-3018-9*) Kendall-Hunt.

What Time Is It Around the World? Hans Baumann. LC 75-24710. (Illus.). (J). (gr. k-5). 1979. 6.95 (*0-87592-061-6*) Scroll Pr.

What Time Is It, Mr. Wolf? Bob Beeson. (Illus.). 32p. (J). (ps-1). 1994. 12.95 (*0-8249-8649-0*, Ideals Child) Hambleton-Hill.

What Time Is Recess? Jeannie S. Williams. (A Classroom Teacher Collection). (Illus.). 32p. (Orig.). 1994. pap. 6.95 (*1-886648-00-X*) Craftmasters Bks.

What Time Is This Place? Kevin Lynch. LC 72-7059. 1976. pap. 15.95 (*0-262-62032-4*) MIT Pr.

What Time of Night Is It? Mary Stolz. (J). 1994. 17.75 (*0-8446-6777-3*) Peter Smith.

***What to Ask When You Don't Know What to Say.** Sam Deep & Lyle Sussman. 1997. 8.98 (*1-56731-190-3*, MJF Bks) Fine Comms.

What to Ask When You Don't Know What to Say: Seven Hundred Twenty Powerful Questions to Use for Getting Your... Sam Deep. LC 93-9657. 29.95 (*0-13-953977-8*) P-H.

What to Ask When You Don't Know What to Say: Seven Hundred Twenty Powerful Questions to Use for Getting Your... Sam Deep. LC 93-9657. 1993. pap. 14.95 (*0-13-953985-9*) P-H.

What to Believe & Why. Clarence Blasier. 96p. 1994. mass mkt. 1.99 (*1-55748-433-3*) Barbour & Co.

What to Cook When You Think There's Nothing in the House to Eat: More Than 175 Recipes & Meal Ideas. Arthur Schwartz. LC 91-55141. (Illus.). 304p. 1992. pap. 16.00 (*0-06-096432-4*, PL) HarpC.

What to Do? Creative Problem-Solving Level A. Kathryn T. Hegeman. (J). (gr. 1-2). 1984. teacher ed., pap. 15.00 (*0-89824-045-X*); student ed., pap. 4.99 (*0-89824-043-3*) Trillium Pr.

What to Do? Creative Problem-Solving Level B. Kathryn T. Hegeman. (J). (gr. 3-4). 1985. teacher ed., pap. 15.00 (*0-89824-088-3*); student ed., pap. 4.99 (*0-89824-089-1*) Trillium Pr.

What to Do? Level C. 1988. student ed., pap. 4.99 (*0-89824-701-2*); teacher ed., pap. 15.00 (*0-89824-700-4*) Trillium Pr.

What to Do About... A Collection of Essays from Commentary Magazine. Ed. by Neal Kozodoy. LC 95-23212. 320p. 1995. 25.00 (*0-06-039154-5*, HarpT) HarpC.

What to Do About: A Collection of Essays from Commentary Magazine. Neal Kozodoy. 320p. 1996. pap. 13.50 (*0-06-098708-1*) HarpC.

What to Do about AIDS: Physicians & Mental Health Professionals Discuss the Issues. Ed. by Leon McKusick. 224p. (C). 1986. 30.00 (*0-520-05935-2*); pap. 13.00 (*0-520-05936-0*) U CA Pr.

***What to Do about Baby.** Martha Hix. (That's My Baby! Ser.). 1997. mass mkt. 3.99 (*0-373-24093-7*, 1-24093-6) Silhouette.

What to Do about Equal Pay for Women in the United Kingdom. G. L. Buckingham. 144p. 1973. 23.00 (*0-8464-0968-2*) Beekman Pubs.

What to Do about Nuclear Waste. Tricia Andryszewski. LC 94-44662. (Illus.). 128p. (YA). (gr. 7 up). 1995. lib. bdg. 16.90 (*1-56294-577-7*) Millbrook Pr.

What to Do about Performance Appraisal. rev. ed. Marion S. Kellogg. LC 75-8604. 221p. reprint ed. pap. 63.00 (*0-317-26907-0*, 2023555) Bks Demand.

What to Do about Personnel Problems in Your State, 2 vols., Set. rev. ed. Diane L. Cantor & Jeani Thomson. 1983. ring bd. 295.00 (*1-55645-001-X*) Busn Legal Reports.

What to Do About Race. Henry Louis Gates, Jr. 1997. write for info. (*0-679-45210-9*) Random.

What to Do about Race. Henry Louis Gates, Jr. Date not set. pap. write for info. (*0-679-77351-7*) McKay.

What to Do about Toxic Chemicals in Your Water. 1991. lib. bdg. 65.95 (*0-8490-4683-1*) Gordon Pr.

What to Do about Worry - Chinese Edition. Jay E. Adams. Tr. by Cheuk Choy. 29p. (CHI.). 1983. pap. 1.60 (*1-56582-078-9*) Christ Renew Min.

What to Do about Your Brain-Injured Child. Glenn Doman. 1990. 19.95 (*0-944349-24-2*) Better Baby.

What to Do about Your Brain-Injured Child. 3rd ed. Glenn Doman. 320p. pap. 11.95 (*0-89529-598-9*) Avery Pub.

What to do about Youth Dropouts? A Summary of Solutions. Margaret T. Orr. Ed. by Mary L. O'Connor. 32p. (Orig.). 1987. pap. 5.00 (*0-943567-00-9*) SEEDCO.

***What to Do after You Say "I Do" A Couple's Guide to the First Year of Marriage.** Prima Publishing Staff. 256p. 1997. per. 15.00 (*0-7615-1159-8*) Prima Pub.

What To Do, Ask Moose: 365 Alternatives to Addiction, Boredom & Television. Lisa Johnson. 1993. 5.25 (*0-9634399-0-1*) Funmakers.

An Asterisk (*) at the beginning of an entry indicates that the title is appearing in BIP for the first time.

What to Do Before the Money Runs Out: A Roadmap for America's Automobile Dealers. James J. Kaufman. LC 92-76051. 160p. 1993. pap. 24.95 (*0-942963-37-7*) Distinctive Pub.

What to Do Between Birth & Death: The Art of Growing Up. Charles Spezzano. 192p. 1993. reprint ed. pap. 8.00 (*0-380-71406-X*) Avon.

What to Do for Healing. Norvel Hayes. (Mini-Bks.). 32p. 1988. pap. 0.99 (*0-89274-216-X*, HH-216) Harrison Hse.

What to Do If: A Guide for Parents of Teenagers. American Assoc. of School Administrators Staff. 24p. 1987. 2.50 (*0-87652-151-0*, 021-00299); Spanish ed. write for info. (*0-87652-161-8*, 021-00318) Am Assn Sch Admin.

What To Do if You Get Breast Cancer: Two Breast Cancer Specialists Help You Take Charge & Make Informed Choices. Lydia Komarnicky et al. LC 94-15964. 1995. pap. 10.95 (*0-316-09289-4*) Little.

***What to Do If You Get Colon Cancer: A Specialist Helps You Take Charge & Make Informed Choices.** Paul F. Miskovitz & Marian Betancourt. LC 97-10074. 256p. 1997. pap. text ed. 15.95 (*0-471-15984-0*) Wiley.

What to Do If You Have an Auto Accident: 50 Questions & Answers with Accident Scene Forms. Jon R. Abele. (Illus.). 32p. 1993. pap. text ed. 1.80 (*0-88450-613-4*, 6114) Lawyers & Judges.

What to Do If You Or Someone You Know Is under 18 & Pregnant. Arlene K. Richards & Irene Willis. LC 82-12698. (Illus.). 256p. (J). (gr. 7 up). 1983. pap. 8.95 (*0-688-01044-X*) Morrow.

***What to Do in a Pediatric Emergency.** Ed. by Phil Monroe et al. 60p. (Orig.). (C). 1996. pap. text ed. 20.00 (*0-7279-1032-9*, Pub. by BMJ Pubng Grp UK) Amer Coll Phys.

What to do in an Emergency: Action Guide. Reader's Digest Editors. LC 88-18537. (Illus.). 354p. 1988. 24.95 (*0-89577-319-8*) RD Assn.

What to Do Next: Consider the Book of Transfinity: The Mystery of Leadership & Its Magnitudes. Shiloh H. Theriault. Ed. by Leslie D. Stahl. 1022p. (Orig.). 1989. pap. 35.00 (*0-930909-13-5*) World Faith Ex.

What to Do on Thursday: A Layman's Guide to the Practical Use of the Scriptures. rev. ed. Jay E. Adams. 144p. 1995. reprint ed. pap. 8.95 (*0-9643556-7-1*) Timeless Texts.

What to Do until Enlightenment: Healing Ourselves ... Healing the Earth. Stuart W. Alpert. Ed. by Edward Tick. (Frontiers in Psychotherapy Ser.). 168p. (C). 1991. pap. 39.50 (*0-89391-804-0*); text ed. 73.25 (*0-89391-805-9*) Ablex Pub.

***What to Do until Love Finds You: Preparing Yourself for Your Perfect Mate.** Michelle McKinney-Hammond. 250p. (Orig.). 1997. pap. 8.99 (*1-56507-531-5*) Harvest Hse.

What to Do until the Grownup Arrives: The Art & Science of Raising Teenagers. Joseph R. Novello. LC 91-18659. 360p. 1993. 24.50 (*0-88937-040-0*) Hogrefe & Huber Pubs.

What to Do Until the Psychiatrist Comes: How to Counsel Yourself & Others. Bob Phillips. (Orig.). 1995. pap. 9.99 (*1-56507-231-6*) Harvest Hse.

What to Do When --it Happens. 2nd ed. Debbie Gallagher & Sharon Willen. (Illus.). 50p. 1991. reprint ed. pap. 4.95 (*1-878131-00-1*) Brght Ideas Make Diff.

What to Do When a Bug Climbs in Your Mouth: And Other Poems to Drive You Buggy. Rick Walton. LC 94-79124. (Illus.). 32p. (J). (ps up). 1995. 16.00 (*0-688-13658-3*); lib. bdg. 15.93 (*0-688-13659-1*) Lothrop.

What to Do When a Loved One Dies: A Practical & Compassionate Guide to Dealing with Death on Life's Terms. Eva Shaw. LC 93-9995. 1994. pap. 18.95 (*1-880741-10-5*) Dickens Pr.

What to Do When & Why: At Parties, at Home, at School, in Your Growing World. Marjabelle Y. Stewart & Ann Buchwald. 1988. 14.95 (*0-88331-105-4*) Luce.

What to Do When Everyone's Doing It. Harold C. Warlick. 1991. pap. 7.95 (*1-55673-409-3*, 9222) CSS OH.

What to Do When Faith Seems Weak & Victory Lost. Kenneth E. Hagin. 1979. pap. 3.95 (*0-89276-501-1*) Hagin Ministries.

What to Do When It Hurts: Self-Diagnosis & Rehabilitation of Common Aches & Pains. Malcolm Read & Paul Wade. LC 96-14912. (Illus.). 192p. (Orig.). 1996. pap. 14.95 (*1-882606-66-3*) Peoples Med Soc.

What to Do When It Hurts So Bad. Ed Montgomery. 240p. 1993. text ed. 14.95 (*1-56043-770-7*) Destiny Image.

What to Do When It Hurts So Bad. Ed Montgomery. 240p. 1994. pap. 8.95 (*1-56043-124-5*) Destiny Image.

***What to Do When Kids Are Mean to Your Child.** Elin McCoy. LC 97-2464. (What to Do Parenting Guides Ser.). 1997. write for info. (*0-89577-984-6*) RD Assn.

What to Do When Leaded Fuel Becomes Extinct. Timothy P. Banse. (Illus.). 64p. 1986. pap. 4.95 (*0-934523-21-5*) Middle Coast Pub.

What to Do When Leaded Fuel Becomes Extinct. rev. ed. Timothy P. Banse. LC 86-5459. (Illus.). 71p. 1989. pap. 9.95 (*0-934523-20-7*) Middle Coast Pub.

***What to Do When Life Is Driving You Crazy!** Barbara A. Berg. LC 96-93010. (Illus.). 251p. 1997. pap. 14.95 (*0-9654014-0-5*) Creat Options.

***What to Do When Love Turns Violent.** Marian Betancourt. 1997. pap. 12.00 (*0-614-27643-8*, Harper Ref) HarpC.

***What to Do When Mom Moves In.** Betty Kuhn. LC 96-79219. 192p. 1997. pap. 14.95 (*1-885221-65-7*) BookPartners.

***What to Do When Nothing Works Vol. 2: The Manual for the Work.** 4th rev. ed. Byron Katie & Linda Sharpe. Ed. by Val Green & Maxine Hanks. (Illus.). 88p. 1996. reprint ed. pap. text ed. 10.00 (*1-890246-01-8*) Work.

What to Do When Psychotherapy Goes Wrong. Shirley J. Siegel. 176p. (Orig.). 1991. pap. write for info. (*0-9629397-4-9*) Stop Abuse.

What to do When Someone You Love Is Depressed. 1997. 21.00 (*0-679-45154-4*) Random.

What to Do When the Bill Collector Calls: Know Your Rights. David L. Kelcher. 192p. 1991. pap. 9.95 (*0-914984-32-2*) Starburst.

What to Do When the Dot Hazardous Materials Inspector Calls. Lawrence W. Bierlein. 1986. 24.95 (*0-940394-20-0*) Labelmaster.

***What to Do When the Honeymoon Is Over: Guerrilla Mating Tactics for Keeping Your Love Alive.** Sharyn Wolf. LC 96-39772. 1997. write for info. (*0-525-94287-4*, Dutton) NAL-Dutton.

What to Do When the Numbers Are In. Joan W. DiLeonardi & Patrick A. Curtis. (Illus.). 175p. (C). 1988. pap. text ed. 19.95 (*0-8304-1145-3*) Nelson-Hall.

What to Do When the Stock Market Falls: Learn from the Financial Experts Who Saw It Coming. A. Jane Archer. LC 95-90960. 128p. (Orig.). 1996. pap. 12.95 (*0-9649573-0-2*) Touchstone Advent.

What to Do When the Suit Comes. Eugene B. Waggoner. 5.00 (*0-614-05199-1*, WTD12732M) ASFE.

***What to Do When the Tempter Comes.** John Osteen. Date not set. mass mkt. 1.99 (*0-912631-16-3*) J O Pubns.

What to Do When the Wine Runs out of Your Marriage. Mack Timberlake. 64p. 1990. pap. 2.95 (*0-88144-151-1*) Christian Pub.

What to Do When Things Go Wrong When Using a Lawyer. 1992. lib. bdg. 77.95 (*0-8490-5355-2*) Gordon Pr.

What to Do When You Can't Afford Health Care. Matthew Lesko & Mary A. Martello. Ed. by Andrew Naprawa. 769p. (Orig.). 1993. pap. 24.95 (*1-878346-16-4*) Info USA.

What to Do When You Can't Pay Your Taxes. Gregory A. Diggins. 14p. (Orig.). 1995. pap. text ed. 14.95 (*0-7811-0126-3*) Res Inst Am.

What to Do When You Don't Know What to Do. Neil Eskelin. 189p. 1995. pap. 10.99 (*0-9641058-5-5*) Western Front.

What to Do When You Don't Know What to Do: A Christian Teen's Guide to Coping. Randy Simmons. 1994. pap. 6.99 (*0-89225-423-8*) Gospel Advocate.

***What to Do When You Don't Know What to Do: Braille Adult Journal.** Chapel of the Air Ministries Staff. (Nineteen Ninety-Six 50-Day Spiritual Adventure Ser.). (Orig.). 1996. pap. 12.00 (*1-879050-96-X*) Chapel of Air.

***What to Do When You Don't Know What to Do: Church Leader's Manual.** Illus. by John McPherson. (Nineteen Ninety-Six 50-Day Spiritual Adventure Ser.). 320p. 1995. ring bd. 50.00 (*1-879050-87-0*) Chapel of Air.

***What to Do When You Don't Know What to Do: Church Leader's Manual with Samples.** (Nineteen Ninety-Six 50-Day Spiritual Adventure Ser.). 1996. 65.00 (*1-879050-86-2*) Chapel of Air.

***What to Do When You Don't Know What to Do: Church Starter Kit.** (Nineteen Ninety-Six 50-Day Spiritual Adventure Ser.). 1995. 65.00 (*1-879050-85-4*) Chapel of Air.

***What to Do When You Don't Know What to Do: Small Group Leader's Guide.** Marilyn Moravec. Ed. by Brian Hayes. (Nineteen Ninety-Six 50-Day Spiritual Adventure Ser.). (Illus.). 64p. (Orig.). 1995. wbk. ed., pap. 7.00 (*1-879050-75-7*) Chapel of Air.

***What to Do When You Don't Know What to Do: Small Group Starter Kit.** (Nineteen Ninety-Six 50-Day Spiritual Adventure Ser.). 1995. 49.00 (*1-879050-89-7*) Chapel of Air.

***What to Do When You Don't Know What to Do: Trusting Christ When Life Gets Confusing.** Chapel of the Air Ministries, Inc. Staff. Ed. by Marian Oliver & Mitchell Vander Vorst. (Nineteen Ninety-Six 50-Day Spiritual Adventure Ser.). (Illus.). 80p. (Orig.). 1995. wbk. ed., pap. 6.00 (*1-879050-70-6*) Chapel of Air.

***What to Do When Your Child Has Trouble in School.** Karen Levine. LC 97-2469. (What to Do Parenting Guides Ser.). 1997. write for info. (*0-89577-985-4*) RD Assn.

What to Do When Your Child Hates to Read. Lee Canter. (Illus.). 48p. (Orig.). 1994. pap. 5.95 (*0-939007-84-3*) Lee Canter & Assocs.

What to Do When Your Child Won't Behave. Lee Canter. (Illus.). 48p. 1995. pap. 5.95 (*0-939007-85-1*) Lee Canter & Assocs.

What to Do When Your Child Won't Study. Lee Canter. (Illus.). 48p. (Orig.). 1994. pap. 5.95 (*0-939007-83-5*) Lee Canter & Assocs.

What to Do When Your Friends Reject Christ. C. S. Lovett. 1966. pap. 6.25 (*0-938148-06-0*) Prsnl Christianity.

***What to Do When Your Kids Talk Dirty.** Timothy Jay. 160p. (Orig.). 1997. pap. 14.95 (*0-89390-412-0*) Resource Pubns.

What to Do When Your Spouse Dies: Decisions to Make - Legal & Financial Considerations - Planning Ahead. David L. Gibberman. 48p. 1991. pap. 5.00 (*0-685-67061-9*, 4862) Commerce.

What to Do When Your Students Talk Dirty. Timothy Jay. LC 96-11898. 224p. (Orig.). 1996. pap. 15.95 (*0-89390-363-9*) Resource Pubns.

What to Do When You're Angry. E. Dean Bevan. LC 94-5581. 74p. (Orig.). 1994. pap. 9.95 (*1-56825-016-9*) Rainbow Books.

What to Do Where There Is No Doctor or Dentist, 2 vols., Set. 1991. lib. bdg. 129.95 (*0-8490-4679-3*) Gordon Pr.

What to Do with a Dead Lawyer. Bill Berger & Ricardo Martinez. (Illus.). 128p. (Orig.). 1988. pap. 9.95 (*0-89815-285-2*) Ten Speed Pr.

What to Do With a Squirt of Glue: And Paper, Paint & Scissors, Too! Lori A. Howard. (Illus.). 96p. (J). (gr. k-6). 1987. pap. text ed. 9.95 (*0-86530-086-0*, IP 86-0) Incentive Pubns.

What to Do with the Gifted Child: Meeting the Needs of the Gifted Child in the Regular Classroom. Judith Cochran. (Illus.). 80p. 1992. pap. text ed. 9.95 (*0-86530-174-3*) Incentive Pubns.

What to Do with the Kid Who... Developing Cooperation, Self-Discipline, & Responsibility in the Classroom. Kay Burke. LC 92-64102. 352p. 1992. pap. 39.95 (*0-932935-42-7*) IRI-SkyLght.

What to Do with the Kids. Kathy Shaeffer & Jan Sevier. Ed. by Sylvia E. Schmidt. (Illus.). 80p. (Orig.). 1990. pap. 7.95 (*1-882043-01-4*) Nanel Unlimited.

What to Do with the Kids on a Rainy Day: Or in a Car, or on a Train, or When They're Sick... Adrienne Katz. 128p. (Orig.). 1989. pap. 8.95 (*0-312-03451-2*) St Martin.

What to Do with the Second Shepherd on the Left. Deborah Craig-Claar. 1992. 19.99 (*0-685-68558-6*, MP-671) Lillenas.

***What to Do with Wishes That Don't Come True: All about Wishing, Mourning, & Joy.** Maribeth Ekey. 1997. pap. text ed. 10.99 (*1-56955-012-3*) Servant.

What to Do with Your Bad Car. Ralph Nader et al. 175p. 1971. pap. 2.95 (*0-686-36552-6*) Ctr Responsive Law.

What to Eat If You Have Cancer: A Guide to Adding Nutritional Therapy to Your Treatment Plan. Maureen B. Keane & Daniella Chace. (Illus.). 224p. 1996. pap. 14. 95 (*0-8092-3261-8*) Contemp Bks.

***What to Eat if You Have Cancer Cookbook: Over 100 Easy-to-Prepare Recipes for Patients & Their Families Caregivers.** Maureen B. Keane & Daniella Chace. LC 96-33483. 1997. pap. write for info. (*0-8092-3129-8*) Contemp Bks.

What to Eat Now: The Cancer Lifeline Cookbook. Rachel Keim & Ginny Smith. 160p. (Orig.). 1996. pap. 14.95 (*1-57061-073-8*) Sasquatch Bks.

What to Eat When You're Expecting. Arlene Eisenberg et al. LC 85-40903. 352p. 1986. pap. 8.95 (*0-89480-015-9*, 1015) Workman Pub.

***What to Expect.** D. Peoples. Date not set. 25.00 (*0-393-04104-2*) Norton.

What to Expect from College: A University President's Guide for Students & Parents. George D. O'Brien. 224p. 1993. pap. 10.95 (*0-312-09412-4*, Thomas Dunne Bks) St Martin.

What to Expect in the First Year of Marriage. Curtis Pesmen. LC 95-17631. 1995. pap. 11.00 (*0-684-80246-5*, Fireside) S&S Trade.

What to Expect in the Toddler Years. Arlene Eisenberg et al. LC 93-8932. (What to Expect Ser.). (Illus.). 704p. (Orig.). 1994. pap. 15.95 (*0-89480-994-6*, 1994) Workman Pub.

What to Expect in the Year 2000. Eric Lefcowitz. 300p. 1995. pap. 12.95 (*1-879682-64-8*, Behind-the-News-Pr) Earth Works.

What to Expect of Shakespeare. Jean J. Jusserand. LC 70-128889. (Select Bibliographies Reprint Ser.). 1977. reprint ed. 13.95 (*0-8369-5509-9*) Ayer.

What to Expect the First Year. Arlene Eisenberg et al. LC 87-40647. (Illus.). 704p. 1988. pap. 12.95 (*0-89480-577-0*, 1577) Workman Pub.

What to Expect the First Year. Arlene Eisenberg. LC 87-40647. 704p. 1994. 22.00 (*1-56305-876-6*, 3876) Workman Pub.

What to Expect When Your Wife Is Expanding: A Reassuring Month-by-Month Guide for the Father-to-Be, Whether He Wants Advice or Not. Thomas Hill. (Illus.). 144p. 1993. pap. 9.95 (*0-8362-8018-0*) Andrews & McMeel.

What to Expect When You're Expecting. Arlene Eisenberg et al. LC 90-50951. 504p. (Orig.). 1994. 20.00 (*1-56305-875-8*, 3875) Workman Pub.

What to Expect When You're Expecting. enl. rev. ed. Arlene Eisenberg et al. LC 90-50951. 256p. (Orig.). 1991. pap. 10.95 (*0-89480-829-X*, 1829) Workman Pub.

What to Expect When You're Expecting Pregnancy Organizer. Arlene Eisenberg et al. 256p. 1995. spiral bd. 12.95 (*1-56305-872-3*) Workman Pub.

What to Feed Your Baby: How to Give Your Baby the Best of Health & Vitality. Sara Lewis. (Books from Paul Anness Ser.). 1996. 16.95 (*0-8317-7180-1*) Smithmark.

***What to Feed Your Toddler: How to Give Your Growing Child the Best of Health And Vitality.** Sara Lewis. 1996. 12.98 (*0-8317-7176-3*) Smithmark.

What to Fix for Dinner Cookbook. Heidi Rabel. LC 95-79402. 356p. 1995. pap. 21.95 (*1-883697-91-3*) Hara Pub.

What to Give Your Agent for Christmas & 100 Other Tips for the Working Actor. Ed. by Glenn Alterman. 128p. 1995. pap. 8.95 (*1-880399-57-1*) Smith & Kraus.

What to Have for Dinner. Martha Stewart Living Editors. 144p. 1996. pap. 20.00 (*0-517-88681-2*, C P Pubs) Crown Pub Group.

What to Listen for in Beethoven. Robert Harris. (What to Listen for Ser.). 288p. 1996. 22.95 (*1-55199-001-6*, Pub. by Macfarlane Walter & Ross CN) Genl Dist Srvs.

***What to Listen for in Jazz.** Barry Kernfeld. 1997. pap. text ed. 22.50 incl. cd-rom (*0-300-07259-7*) Yale U Pr.

What to Listen for in Jazz. Barry D. Kernfeld. LC 94-18324. 1995. 40.00 (*0-300-05902-7*) Yale U Pr.

What to Listen for in Music. rev. ed. Aaron Copland & William Schuman. 192p. 1988. pap. 5.99 (*0-451-62735-0*, Ment) NAL-Dutton.

What to Listen for in Music. rev. ed. Aaron Copland. 192p. (YA). (gr. 9-12). 1989. pap. 4.95 (*0-451-62687-7*, Ment) NAL-Dutton.

What to Listen for in the World. Bruce Adolphe. LC 96-27066. (Illus.). 112p. (Orig.). 1996. 17.95 (*0-87910-085-0*) Limelight Edns.

What to Name Your African-American Baby. Benjamin Faulkner. 1995. mass mkt. 4.50 (*0-312-95449-2*) St Martin.

What to Name Your African-American Baby. 6th ed. Faulkner. Date not set. pap. 47.70 (*0-312-11572-5*) St Martin.

What to Name Your African-American Baby: Names of Significance, Dignity & Tenderness to Reflect Your Child's Heritage. Benjamin Faulkner. 208p. 1994. pap. 7.95 (*0-312-11348-X*) St Martin.

What to Name Your Baby: From Adam to Zoe. 2nd ed. Maxwell Nurnberg & Morris Rosenblum. 352p. 1984. pap. 4.95 (*0-02-081010-5*) Macmillan.

What to Name Your Dog. Carrie Shook. (Illus.). 151p. 1989. pap. 10.95 (*0-87605-807-1*) Howell Bk.

What to Read. Mickey Pearlman. LC 93-44807. 192p. (Orig.). 1994. pap. 9.00 (*0-06-095061-7*, PL) HarpC.

What to Really Say When the Customer Complains: Nobody Knows You're Swimming Naked Till the Tide Goes Out. Bernice Johnston. 100p. (Orig.). 1993. pap. write for info. (*0-9625747-7-5*) Niche OR.

What to Say. enl. rev. ed. v, 154p. 1993. reprint ed. pap. 7.50 (*0-88053-324-2*, S-072) Macoy Pub.

What to Say & How to Say It. David Belson. 1985. 4.98 (*0-89009-602-3*) Bk Sales Inc.

What to Say & How to Say It: For All Occasions. David Belson. 1961. pap. 8.95 (*0-8065-0891-4*, 98, Citadel Pr) Carol Pub Group.

What to Say & How to Say It: Model Speeches, Letters & Remarks for Every Occasion. David Belson. 192p. 1993. pap. 8.95 (*0-8065-1447-7*, Citadel Pr) Carol Pub Group.

What to Say to Get What You Want: Strong Words for 40 Types of Bosses, Employees, Coworkers & Customers. Sam Deep & Lyle Sussman. 256p. 1991. pap. 9.95 (*0-201-57712-7*) Addison-Wesley.

What to Say When-- A Complete Resource for Speakers, Trainers & Executives. Lilly Walters. LC 94-34198. 1995. text ed. 39.95 (*0-07-068038-8*) McGraw.

What to Say When: A Guide to More Effective Communication. 2nd ed. Rachel L. Leeds. 192p. (C). 1996. per. 17.79 (*0-8403-9315-6*) Kendall-Hunt.

What to Say When They Say "I'm Jewish" Fenton Ward. 208p. 1993. pap. 10.00 (*0-939513-86-2*) Joy Pub SJC.

What to Say When They Say I'm Jewish: Sharing the Gospel with the Original Messengers. Fenton Ward. (C). 1993. pap. text ed. 10.00 (*0-942115-16-3*) California State Univ at Long.

What to Say When You Talk to Your Self. Shad Helmstetter. 1990. pap. 6.50 (*0-671-70882-1*) PB.

What to Say When You Talk to Yourself. Shad Helmstetter. 1994. 6.98 (*1-56731-002-8*, MJF Bks) Fine Comms.

What to Say When You Talk to Yourself. Shad Helmstetter. LC 86-91140. 228p. 1986. 16.95 (*0-937065-05-6*) Grindle Pr.

What to Say When You're Dying on the Platform: A Complete Resource for Speakers, Trainers, & Executives. Lilly Walters. LC 94-33609. 1995. pap. text ed. 14.95 (*0-07-068039-6*) McGraw.

***What to See & Do in the Lost River & South Branch Valleys.** Nancy H. Powell. (Illus.). viii, 204p. 1997. pap. 12.95 (*0-9655938-0-0*) Lost River Educ.

***What to Serve the Goddess When She Comes for Dinner-- An Environmental, Historical, & Semi-Autobiographical Food Book, Goddess Recipes Included.** James R. Deal. 220p. 1997. pap. 18.95 (*1-884949-10-X*) Great Ideas.

What to Solve? Problems & Suggestions for Young Mathematicians. Judita Cofman. (Illus.). 268p. 1990. pap. 35.00 (*0-19-853294-6*) OUP.

***What to Study: Generating & Developing Research Questions.** John P. Campbell. LC 82-10720. (Studying Organizations Ser.: No. 6). 168p. 1982. reprint ed. pap. 47.90 (*0-608-02988-2*, 2063482) Bks Demand.

***What to Study: 101 Fields in a Flash.** Freedman. LC 97-21904. 1997. 18.00 (*0-684-84388-9*) S&S Trade.

What to Take Backpacking--& Why. Robert Follett. (Illus.). 1978. pap. 3.95 (*0-931712-01-7*) Alpine Guild.

What to Tell the People about the Public Schools: A Study of the Content of the Public School Publicity Program. Belmont M. Farley. LC 73-176763. (Columbia University. Teachers College. Contributions to Education Ser.: No. 355). reprint ed. 37.50 (*0-404-55355-9*) AMS Pr.

What to Tell Your Children. Ed. by Mac Anderson. 78p. (Orig.). 1991. pap. 7.95 (*1-56245-014-X*) Great Quotations.

What to Tell Your Children about Cults. Kevin R. O'Neil. 52p. (Orig.). 1982. pap. 9.95 (*0-86627-001-9*) Crises Res Pr.

What Tolstoy Taught. Ed. by Bolton Hall. 1977. lib. bdg. 59.95 (*0-8490-2818-3*) Gordon Pr.

What Tom Sawyer Learned from Dying. Sidney S. Farr. 272p. 1993. pap. 11.95 (*1-878901-66-4*) Hampton Roads Pub Co.

***What Tomorrow Brings.** John P. Jones, Jr. (Illus.). 230p. 1996. 19.95 (*0-9655225-0-4*) Old Mariners Pr.

What Touched His Life. Mark Grover. Ed. by Denise Broms. 200p. (Orig.). 1994. pap. 13.95 (*0-9640114-2-5*) Noble Crown.

What Trouble I Have Seen: A History of Violence Against Wives. David P. Del Mar. LC 95-46974. 240p. (C). 1996. text ed. 39.95 (*0-674-95076-3*) HUP.

W

What Trudy Knows & Other Poems. Knute Skinner. 103p. 9500. pap. 13.95 (*1-897648-22-7*, Pub. by Salmon Poetry IE) Dufour.

What Turns Men On? Brigitte Nioche. 224p. (Orig.). 1989. pap. 5.99 (*0-451-16054-1*, Sig) NAL-Dutton.

What Turns Us On. Iris Finz & Steven Finz. LC 96-25640. 240p. 1996. 21.95 (*0-312-14758-9*) St Martin.

What Type of Financial Institutions Would Be Needed to Incorporate the Northwest Territories into the Canadian Federation? Fiscal Policies for the Future. James M. Dean. LC 96-17497. (Canadian Studies: Vol. 18). 232p. 1996. text ed. 89.95 (*0-7734-8813-8*) E Mellen.

What Uncle Sam Really Wants. Noam Chomsky. LC 92-23824. (Real Story Ser.). 112p. (Orig.). 1992. pap. 7.00 (*1-878825-01-1*) Odonian Pr.

What United Methodists Believe about the Church. Henry Young. (We Believe Ser.). 144p. (Orig.). 1993. pap. 8.95 (*0-687-44914-6*) Abingdon.

***What Unites Presbyterians? Common Ground for Troubled Times.** Clifton Kirkpatrick & William H. Hopper. LC 97-19427. 1997. write for info. (*0-664-50007-2*) Westminster John Knox.

What Use Is a Moose? Martin Waddell. LC 95-36138. (Illus.). 32p. (J). (gr. k-3). 1996. 14.99 (*1-56402-933-6*) Candlewick Pr.

What Viewers Should Know about the Oberammergau Passion Play. Judith H. Banki. 20p. 1980. pap. 1.50 (*0-87495-024-4*) Am Jewish Comm.

What Volunteers Should Know for Successful Fund Raising. Maurice G. Gurin. LC 81-48508. (Illus.). 144p. (C). 1982. pap. 7.95 (*0-8128-6150-7*, Scrbrough Hse) Madison Bks UPA.

What Waiting Really Means. June A. Seese. LC 89-27251. 96p. 1990. pap. 7.95 (*0-916583-58-9*) Dalkey Arch.

What Was & Could Be: Narrative Poems. J. S. Olga. 48p. 1993. pap. 5.95 (*1-883683-06-8*) Metropolis Pubs.

What Was Communism, Pt. 1. Ed. by Thompson. (Socialist History Ser.: 2). Date not set. pap. 9.99 (*0-7453-0806-6*, Pub. by Pluto Pr UK) LPC InBook.

What Was Communism, Pt. Two. Ed. by Thompson. (Socialist History Ser.: 3). Date not set. pap. 9.99 (*0-7453-0807-4*, Pub. by Pluto Pr UK) LPC InBook.

What Was Freedom's Price? Ed. by David G. Sansing. LC 78-3736. (Chancellor's Symposium on Southern History Ser.). 126p. 1978. pap. 12.95 (*0-87805-048-5*) U Pr of Miss.

What Was God Doing on the Cross? Alister E. McGrath. 128p. 1993. pap. 10.99 (*0-310-59451-0*) Zondervan.

What Was Hot. Julian Biddle. 192p. 1994. mass mkt. 4.50 (*1-55817-894-5*, Pinncle Kensgtn) Kensgtn Pub Corp.

What Was I Like? Childhood Memory Book Series, 5 bks., Set. Jennifer Harris. (Illus.). (J). (gr. k-4). 1992. boxed 49.95 (*1-879956-13-6*) Tintern Abbey.

What Was I Like? Childhood Memory Book Series, 6 bks., Set. Jennifer Harris. (Illus.). (J). (ps). 1992. boxed 49.95 (*1-879956-12-8*) Tintern Abbey.

What Was I Like You & Your... Harris. 1992. pap. text ed. 9.95 (*1-879956-08-X*) Tintern Abbey.

***What Was I Scared Of?** Dr. Seuss. LC 96-47709. (J). 1997. 7.99 (*0-679-88540-4*) Random Bks Yng Read.

***What Was I Scared Of.** Dr. Seuss. (J). 1997. lib. bdg. 9.99 (*0-679-98540-9*) Random Bks Yng Read.

***What Was in Jeremy's Egg? & Other Stories.** Ida M. Kempel. (Illus.). 81p. 1997. mass mkt. 10.00 (*0-614-29357-X*, 3) Nascent Pr.

What Was It Like Before Electricity. Paul Bennett. LC 94-28575. (Read All about It Ser.). (Illus.). (J). (gr. 1-8). 1995. lib. bdg. 21.40 (*0-8114-5734-6*) Raintree Steck-V.

What Was It Like Before Electricity. Paul Bennett. 1995. pap. text ed. 4.95 (*0-8114-3786-8*) Raintree Steck-V.

What Was It Like Before Telephone. Paul Humphrey. (J). 1995. pap. text ed. 4.95 (*0-8114-3781-7*) Raintree Steck-V.

What Was It Like Before Television? Rosie Hankin. LC 94-28574. (Read All about It Ser.). (Illus.). (J). 1995. lib. bdg. 21.40 (*0-8114-5735-4*) Raintree Steck-V.

What Was It Like Before Television? Rosie Hankin. (J). 1996. pap. text ed. 4.95 (*0-8114-3788-4*) Raintree Steck-V.

What Was It Like Before the Telephone? Paul Humphrey. LC 94-28402. (Read All about It Ser., Social Studies, Level B). (Illus.). (J). 1995. lib. bdg. 21.40 (*0-8114-5736-2*) Raintree Steck-V.

What Was It Like in Vietnam? Honest Answers from Those Who Were There. Linda Calvin & Sandy Strait. 160p. (Orig.). (YA). (gr. 7 up). 1994. pap. 10.00 (*0-88092-049-1*) Royal Fireworks.

What Was Mine. Ann Beattie. 1992. pap. 12.00 (*0-679-73903-3*, Vin) Random.

What was Shakespeare? Renaissance Plays & Changing Critical Practice. Edward Pechter. LC 94-25366. 216p. 1995. 32.50 (*0-8014-3065-8*); pap. 12.95 (*0-8014-8229-1*) Cornell U Pr.

What Was Socialism, & What Comes Next? Katherine Verdery. 256p. 1996. pap. text ed. 17.95 (*0-691-01132-X*) Princeton U Pr.

What Was Socialism, & What Comes Next? Princeton Studies in Culture - Power - History. Katherine Verdery. LC 95-32123. 256p. (C). 1996. text ed. 49.50 (*0-691-01133-8*) Princeton U Pr.

What Was That? (Golden Story Book 'n Tape Ser.). (Illus.). 24p. (J). (ps-3). 1991. write for info. (*0-307-14175-6*, 14175) Western Pub.

What Was the First Rock 'n Roll Record? Jim Dawson & Steve Propes. 228p. (Orig.). 1992. pap. 12.95 (*0-571-12939-0*) Faber & Faber.

What Was the Original Gospel in 'Buddhism'? C. Rhys Davids. LC 78-72416. reprint ed. 17.00 (*0-404-17277-6*) AMS Pr.

What Was Watergate. Pamela Kilian. (J). 1990. 16.95 (*0-312-04446-1*) St Martin.

***What Water Says.** James Bertolino. (Tanbark Ser.). 32p. (Orig.). 1997. pap. 8.00 (*1-887853-15-4*) Radiolarian.

What We Are about to Receive. John F. Carter. LC 68-29196. (Essay Index Reprint Ser.). 1977. reprint ed. 20.95 (*0-8369-0280-7*) Ayer.

What We Believe: A Biblical Catechism of the Apostles Creed. Pheme Perkins. 144p. (Orig.). 1986. pap. 7.95 (*0-8091-2764-4*) Paulist Pr.

***What We Believe: An Exposition of the Apostles Creed.** Cornelis P. Venema. 136p. (Orig.). 1996. pap. write for info. (*0-9653981-1-0*) Reformed Fellowship.

What We Believe: Gospel Principles for Young Latter-Day Saints, Vol. 1. Loa T. Jenkins. 48p. (Orig.). 1982. pap. 6.98 (*0-88290-201-6*, 4524) Horizon Utah.

What We Believe: Understanding & Applying the Basics of the Christian Life. John Walvoord. LC 90-35531. 240p. 1990. pap. 10.99 (*0-929239-31-8*) Discovery Hse Pubs.

What We Believe...What We Do... A Pocket Guide for Reform Jews. Simeon J. Maslin. (Orig.). 1993. pap. 1.00 (*0-8074-0531-0*, 164030) UAHC.

What We Bought: The New World. Robert Adams. (Illus.). 202p. 1996. 40.00 (*3-89169-094-0*, 610591, Pub. by Sprengel Mus GW) Dist Art Pubs.

What We Call Smart: A New Narrative for Intelligence & Learning. Lynda Miller. LC 92-40680. (School-Age Children Ser.). (Illus.). 191p. (Orig.). (C). 1993. pap. text ed. 34.95 (*1-879105-44-6*, 0228) Singular Publishing.

What We Can Do about Litter. Donna Bailey. LC 90-45006. (What We Can Do about Ser.). (Illus.). 32p. (J). (gr. k-4). 1991. lib. bdg. 18.00 (*0-531-11016-8*) Watts.

What We Can Do about Noise & Fumes. Donna Bailey. (What We Can Do about Ser.). (Illus.). 48p. (J). (gr. k-4). 1992. lib. bdg. 18.00 (*0-531-11018-4*) Watts.

What We Can Do about Protecting Nature. Donna Bailey. Ed. by Marjory Kline. LC 91-11534. (What We Can Do about Ser.). (Illus.). 48p. (J). (gr. 3-5). 1992. lib. bdg. 18.00 (*0-531-11080-X*) Watts.

What We Can Do about Recycling Garbage. Donna Bailey. (What We Can Do about Ser.). (Illus.). 48p. (J). (gr. k-4). 1991. lib. bdg. 18.00 (*0-531-11017-6*) Watts.

What We Can Learn from the East. Beatrice Bruteau. LC 94-46868. 132p. (Orig.). 1995. pap. 11.95 (*0-8245-1457-2*) Crossroad NY.

What We Carry. Dorianne Laux. (American Poets Continuum Ser.). 80p. 1994. pap. 12.50 (*1-880238-07-1*) BOA Edns.

What We Did after Rain: Poems. Art Homer. (Illus.). 1984. 25.00 (*0-317-40771-6*) Abattoir.

***What We Do for Love.** Ilene Beckerman. LC 97-16640. 1997. write for info. (*1-56512-180-5*) Algonquin Bks.

What We Do for Music. Michael J. Bugeja. (Amelia Chapbooks Ser.). 48p. (Orig.). 1991. pap. 10.95 (*0-936545-17-8*) Amelia.

What We Don't Know about Each Other. Lawrence Raab. LC 93-2664. 96p. (Orig.). 1993. pap. 12.00 (*0-14-058701-2*, Penguin Bks) Viking Penguin.

***What We Eat: A First Look at Food.** Sara Lynn & Diane James. LC 96-51092. (Play & Discover Ser.). (Illus.). (J). 1997. write for info. (*0-7166-4800-8*); pap. write for info. (*0-7166-4801-6*) World Bk.

What We Go By. Russell Hardin. LC 73-78029. (Illus.). 101p. 1973. 4.50 (*0-941179-44-3*) Latitudes Pr.

What We Have Learned since the Big Thompson Flood: Proceedings of the 10th Anniversary Conference, Boulder, CO, July 17-19, 1986. Ed. by Eve C. Gruntfest. (Special Publications: No. 16). 271p. (Orig.). (C). 1987. pap. 10.00 (*0-685-28097-7*) Natural Hazards.

What We Have Seen & Heard: A Pastoral Letter on Evangelization from the Black Bishops of the United States. James P. Lyke. 40p. (Orig.). 1984. pap. text ed. 1.95 (*0-86716-040-3*) St Anthony Mess Pr.

What We Have to Live With. Marilyn Krysl. 64p. (Orig.). (C). 1989. pap. write for info. (*0-9646331-0-8*) KRYSL.

What We Have to Live With. Marilyn Krysl. 64p. (Orig.). 1993. pap. 7.00 (*0-317-05633-6*) KRYSL.

What We Know about Acquisition of Adult Literacy: Is There No Hope? Helen Abadzi. LC 94-20038. 1994. 8.95 (*0-8213-2862-X*, 12862) World Bank.

What We Know about Jewish Education: A Handbook of Today's Research for Tomorrow's Jewish Education. Ed. by Stuart L. Kelman. 348p. (Orig.). 1992. pap. text ed. 24.95 (*0-933873-67-0*) Torah Aura.

What We Know So Far. Ed. by Beth Benatovich. 272p. 1996. pap. 11.95 (*0-312-14759-7*) St Martin.

What We Know So Far. large type ed. Ed. by Beth Benatovich. 355p. 1996. 25.95 (*0-7838-1598-0*, GK Hall) Thorndike Pr.

What We Know So Far: Wisdom among Women in Their Own Words. Ed. by Beth Benatovich. 320p. 1995. 22.95 (*0-312-13618-8*) St Martin.

What We Like. Anne Rockwell. LC 91-4990. (Illus.). 24p. (J). (ps-1). 1992. lib. bdg. 13.95 (*0-02-777274-8*, Mac Bks Young Read) S&S Childrens.

What We May Be: Techniques for Psychological & Spiritual Growth Through Psychosynthesis. Piero Ferrucci. LC 81-51107. (Illus.). 256p. 1983. pap. 12.95 (*0-87477-262-1*, Tarcher Putnam) Putnam Pub Group.

What We Mean by Religion. Willard L. Sperry. LC 78-128316. (Essay Index Reprint Ser.). 1977. reprint ed. 19.95 (*0-8369-2370-7*) Ayer.

What We Owe Children. Caleb Gattegno. LC 72-106612. 1970. 9.95 (*0-87825-175-8*) Ed Solutions.

What We Owe the Reader: A Resource Workbook for Writers. 2nd ed. Larry Edgerton. 272p. (C). 1996. pap. text ed. 25.14 (*0-7872-2148-1*) Kendall-Hunt.

What We Really Want to Know... Answers to 101 Questions Teens Always Ask. Michael F. Pennock. LC 95-83180. 224p. (Orig.). (YA). (gr. 9-12). 1996. pap. 8.95 (*0-87793-573-4*) Ave Maria.

What We Save for Last. Corinne D. Bliss. LC 91-45688. 128p. (Orig.). 1992. pap. 11.00 (*0-915943-69-7*) Milkweed Ed.

What We Say to Strangers. Barbara Drake. LC 86-8300. 76p. 1987. 14.95 (*0-932576-34-6*); pap. 6.95 (*0-932576-35-4*) Breitenbush Bks.

What We See & Hear in a Greek Eastern Orthodox Church. G. Polyzoides. 92p. 6.00 (*0-686-83965-X*) Divry.

What We Talk about When We Talk about Love. Raymond Carver. 168p. 1989. pap. 9.00 (*0-679-72305-6*, Vin) Random.

What We Told Our Kids about Sex. Betsy A. Weisman & Michael H. Weisman. 80p. (Orig.). 1987. pap. 4.95 (*0-15-696050-8*, Harvest Bks) HarBrace.

***What We Wear: A First Look at Clothes.** Diane James & Sara Lynn. LC 96-49560. (Play & Discover Ser.). 1997. write for info. (*0-7166-4802-4*); pap. write for info. (*0-7166-4803-2*) World Bk.

What We Will Give Each Other: Poems. Sidney Hall, Jr. LC 93-91470. 50p. (Orig.). 1993. pap. 9.95 (*0-9636413-0-1*) Hobblebush Bks.

What We Women Know. 3rd ed. Juan F. Maura. (Vagrom Chap Bk.: No. 15). 41p. 1981. 3.95 (*0-935552-05-7*) Sparrow Pr.

What We Wore: An Exhibit Catalogue Celebrating 150 Years of Summit County Costume. Ed. by Stephen H. Paschen. (Illus.). 31p. (Orig.). 1990. pap. 9.50 (*0-9621895-4-5*) Summit Cty Hist Soc.

***What Wells Up: Poems.** Michelle M. Paulsen. LC 96-53098. 64p. 1997. pap. 12.95 (*0-7734-2713-9*, Mellen Poetry Pr) E Mellen.

What Went Right in the Nineteen Eighties. Richard B. McKenzie. LC 93-7236. (Illus.). 250p. (Orig.). 1993. pap. 21.95 (*0-936488-71-9*) PRIPP.

What Went Wrong? Case Histories of Process Plant Disasters. 2nd ed. Trevor A. Kletz. LC 88-16283. 256p. 1988. reprint ed. pap. 73.00 (*0-608-00826-5*, 2061615) Bks Demand.

What Went Wrong? Case Histories of Process Plant Disasters. 3rd ed. Trevor A. Kletz. LC 93-43441. (Illus.). 331p. 1994. 65.00 (*0-88415-027-5*) Gulf Pub.

What Went Wrong? The Creation & Collapse of the Black-Jewish Alliance. Murray Friedman. LC 92-22616. (Illus.). 423p. 1994. 24.95 (*0-02-910910-8*, Free Press) Free Pr.

***What Went Wrong? The Paradox of Progress, Social Problems & the Crisis of Liberalism.** Christopher Hurn. 1997. 56.00 (*0-8133-2919-1*) Westview.

What Went Wrong with Perestroika? Marshall I. Goldman. 256p. 1992. pap. 8.95 (*0-393-30904-5*) Norton.

What Went Wrong with the 20th Century? James Bennett & William Bonner. 228p. 1995. 22.00 (*1-886414-02-5*) Shot Tower.

What Were Castles For? P. Roxbee-Cox. (Starting Point History Ser.). (Illus.). 24p. (J). (gr. k up). 1995. pap. 4.95 (*0-7460-1341-8*, Usborne); lib. bdg. 12.95 (*0-88110-729-8*, Usborne) EDC.

***What Were They Thinking? Lessons I've Learned from 80, 000 Other New Product Innovations, Idiosyncrasies, & Idiocies.** Robert McMath. LC 97-20804. 1998. 23.00 (*0-8129-2950-0*, Times Bks) Random.

***What Western Do I Read Next? A Reader's Guide to Recent Western Fiction.** Wayne Barton. 500p. 1997. 69.00 (*0-7876-1865-9*) Gale.

What, When, Where in Knoxville: A Kid's Activity Sourcebook. Rene Waibel. 200p. 1994. pap. 9.95 (*1-882194-08-X*) TN Valley Pub.

What, Where, When of Theater Props: An Illustrated Chronology from Arrowheads to Video Games. Thurston James. (Illus.). 224p. (Orig.). 1992. 29.95 (*1-55870-258-X*, Betrwy Bks); pap. 19.95 (*1-55870-257-1*, Betrwy Bks) F & W Pubns Inc.

What? Where? Why? Robert McLaughlin. 336p. 1982. lib. bdg. 112.00 (*90-277-1337-5*, D Reidel) Kluwer Ac.

What, Why, & How of High-Quality Early Childhood Education: A Guide for on-Site Supervision. Derry G. Koralek et al. LC 93-85077. (Illus.). 132p. (Orig.). 1993. pap. text ed. 7.00 (*0-935989-56-0*, 336) Natl Assn Child Ed.

What, Why, & How of High-Quality Early Childhood Education: A Guide for On-Site Supervision. rev. ed. Derry G. Koralek et al. LC 93-85077. (Illus.). 172p. (Orig.). 1995. pap. text ed. 7.00 (*0-935989-67-6*, 336) Natl Assn Child Ed.

***What Widow's Face: Sudden Death of Spouse.** Anne B. Brauer. 120p. (Orig.). (C). 1997. pap. 18.00 (*1-887648-07-0*) A-A Bks Pub.

What Wild Ecstasy: The Rise & Fall of the Sexual Revolution. John Heidenry. 448p. 1997. 26.00 (*0-684-81037-9*) S&S Trade.

***What Wild Ecstasy: The Rise & Fall of the Sexual Revolution.** John Heidenry. 1997. 25.00 (*0-614-28186-5*) S&S Trade.

***What Will Be: How the New World of Information Will Change Our Lives.** Michael Dertouzos. LC 96-37301. 1997. 25.00 (*0-06-251479-2*) Harper SF.

What Will Dr. Newman Do? John Henry Newman & Papal Infallibility, 1865-1875. John R. Page. LC 94-5538. (John Henry Newman & Papal Infallibility Ser.). 464p. 1994. pap. 24.95 (*0-8146-5027-9*, M Glazier) Liturgical Pr.

What Will Happen If... Young Children & the Scientific Method. Barbara Sprung et al. LC 85-687. 1985. pap. text ed. 14.95 (*0-931629-02-0*) Educ Equity Con.

What Will Happen to God? Feminism & the Reconstruction of Christian Belief. William Oddie. LC 88-81091. 179p. 1988. pap. 9.95 (*0-89870-211-9*) Ignatius Pr.

What Will Have Happened: A Philosophical & Technical Essay on Mystery Stories. Robert Champigny. LC 77-74446. 183p. 1977. 18.95 (*0-253-36515-5*) Boulevard.

What Will Have Happened: A Philosophical & Technical Essay on Mystery Stories. Robert Champigny. 191p. reprint ed. pap. 54.50 (*0-317-27937-8*, 2056028) Bks Demand.

What Will Heaven Be Like? Jack Hartman. 160p. 1991. pap. text ed. 6.95 (*0-915445-19-0*) Lamplight FL.

What Will Hell Be Like? John Schaefer. 24p. 1988. reprint ed. pap. 0.75 (*0-89555-341-4*) TAN Bks Pubs.

What Will Help Me?/How Can I Help? 12 Things to Remember When You Have Suffered a Loss/12 Things to Do When Someone You Know Suffers a Loss. James E. Miller. LC 94-96346. 64p. 1994. reprint ed. pap. 5.95 (*1-885933-20-7*) Willowgreen Pubng.

What Will I Be When I Grow Up? Whole-Brain Guide to Deciding the Best Path Forward. Ned Herrmann. Ed. by Michele Wolf. (Illus.). 232p. (Orig.). Date not set. write for info. (*0-944850-04-9*); pap. write for info. (*0-944850-03-0*) N Herrmann Grp.

What Will I Do Tomorrow? Probing Depression. Barbara Condron. 111p. (C). 1987. reprint ed. pap. 4.95 (*0-944386-02-4*) SOM Pub.

What Will It Be? Mario Gamboli. LC 91-70413. (Illus.). 10p. (J). (ps). 1991. bds. 3.95 (*1-878093-73-8*) Boyds Mills Pr.

What Will Mommy Do When I'm at School? Dolores Johnson. LC 90-5559. (Illus.). 32p. (J). (ps-1). 1990. lib. bdg. 15.00 (*0-02-747845-9*, Mac Bks Young Read) S&S Childrens.

What Will My Mother Say: A Tribal African Girl Comes of Age in America. Dympna Ugwu-Oju. (Illus.). 414p. 1995. 24.95 (*1-56625-042-0*) Bonus Books.

What Will Suffice: Contemporary American Poets on the Art of Poetry. Ed. by Christopher Buckley & Christopher Merrill. LC 95-14830. 200p. 1995. pap. 17.95 (*0-87905-692-4*) Gibbs Smith Pub.

What Will the Children Think? Trisha Alexander. (Special Edition Ser.). 1994. mass mkt. 3.50 (*0-373-09906-1*, 1-09906-8) Harlequin Bks.

What Will the Weather Be? Lynda DeWitt. LC 90-1446. (Let's-Read-&-Find-Out Science Bk.). (Illus.). 32p. (J). (gr. k-4). 1991. lib. bdg. 14.89 (*0-06-021597-6*) HarpC Child Bks.

What Will the Weather Be? Lynda DeWitt. LC 90-1446. (Trophy Let's-Read-&-Find-Out Science Bk.: Stage 2). (Illus.). 32p. (J). (gr. k-4). 1993. pap. 4.95 (*0-06-445113-5*, Trophy) HarpC Child Bks.

What Will the Weather Be Like Today? Paul Rogers. LC 88-32736. (Illus.). (J). (ps up). 1990. 13.95 (*0-688-08950-X*); lib. bdg. 13.88 (*0-688-08951-8*) Greenwillow.

What Will the Weather Be?, No. 1: A Folk Weather Calendar. Hubert J. Davis. LC 88-17869. (Illus.). 36p. (Orig.). (J). (gr. k-12). 1988. pap. 4.95 (*0-936015-11-X*) Pocahontas Pr.

What Will the Weather Be?, No. 2: Animal Signs. Hubert J. Davis. LC 90-22327. (Illus.). 56p. (Orig.). (J). (gr. k-12). 1991. pap. 5.95 (*0-936015-12-8*) Pocahontas Pr.

What Will the World Be Like? Adel Lebovics. (Illus.). 32p. (J). (ps-1). 1993. 9.95 (*0-922613-56-7*); Russian translation. 8.95 (*0-922613-58-3*); Italian translation. 8.95 (*0-922613-59-1*); pap. 6.95 (*0-922613-57-5*) Hachai Pubns.

What Will the World Be Like. Adel Lebovics. (Illus.). 32p. (SWE.). (J). (ps-1). 1994. 8.95 (*0-922613-60-5*) Hachai Pubns.

What Will Tomorrow Bring? Betty M. Hockett. LC 85-70504. (Illus.). 80p. (J). (gr. 3-8). 1985. pap. 4.95 (*0-943701-10-4*) George Fox Pr.

What Will We Do? Preparing a School Community to Cope with Crises. Ed. by Robert G. Stevenson. LC 94-5217. (Death, Value & Meaning Ser.). 224p. 1994. pap. 20.96 (*0-89503-152-3*); text ed. 27.95 (*0-89503-151-5*) Baywood Pub.

What Will We Do with the Children? David Merritt & Muriel Porter. 1992. pap. 8.50 (*0-85819-785-5*, Pub. by JBCE AT) Morehouse Pub.

What Will We Do Without Grandpa? Nancy L. Jensen. (Illus.). 32p. (J). (ps-6). 1995. pap. 6.25 (*0-9649196-0-5*) Heather Hill.

What Will We Play Today? Judy Mullican. (HRL Big Bks.). (Illus.). 8p. (J). (ps-k). 1995. pap. text ed. 10.95 (*1-57332-019-6*) HighReach Lrning.

***What Will You Be?** Carolyn Owens. 32p. (J). (ps-2). 1996. 3.99 (*0-570-04795-1*, 56-1815) Concordia.

What Will You Do for an Encore? Robert Drake. 168p. (Orig.). 1996. pap. 19.95 (*0-86554-523-5*, MUP/P147) Mercer Univ Pr.

What Wind Will Do. Debra Bruce. LC 96-29068. (Poetry Ser.). 1997. 19.95 (*1-881163-18-0*); pap. 11.95 (*1-881163-19-9*) Miami Univ Pr.

What Winston Saw. Francine Pascal. (Sweet Valley University Thriller Ser.: 7). 288p. (YA). 1997. mass mkt. 4.50 (*0-553-57050-1*) Bantam.

What Witches Do. 2nd ed. Stewart Farrar. (Illus.). 193p. 1983. reprint ed. pap. 9.95 (*0-919345-17-4*) Phoenix WA.

What Wives Expect of Husbands. Brent A. Barlow. LC 82-70919. xi, 164p. 1989. reprint ed. pap. 8.95 (*0-87579-198-0*) Deseret Bk.

What Wives Wish Their Husbands Knew about Women. James Dobson. 192p. 1977. pap. 9.99 (*0-8423-7889-8*) Tyndale.

What Wives Wish Their Husbands Knew about Women. James Dobson. 192p. 1979. mass mkt. 5.99 (*0-8423-7896-0*) Tyndale.

What, Woman, & Who, Myself, I Am. Ed. by Rosalie Sorrels. (Illus.). 1974. pap. 4.95 (*0-8256-9905-3*) Wooden Shoe.

What Women & Men Really Want: Creating Deeper Understanding & Love in Our Relationships. rev. ed. Aaron Kipnis & Elizabeth Herron. LC 95-16835. 208p. 1995. write for info. (*1-882591-24-0*) Nataraj Pub.

What Women Don't Understand about Men: And Vice Versa. John Carmody. LC 91-66987. 120p. (Orig.). 1992. pap. 7.95 (*0-89622-500-3*) Twenty-Third.

What Women Know, What Men Believe. Wyatt Prunty. LC 85-24095. (Poetry & Fiction Ser.). 80p. 1986. text ed. 14.95 (*0-8018-3327-2*) Johns Hopkins.

What Women Need to Know: From Headaches to Heart Disease & Everything in Between. Marianne Legato. 1997. 23.00 (*0-684-80773-4*) S&S Trade.

What Women Say about Men. Ariel Books Staff. (Illus.). 80p. 1993. 4.95 (*0-8362-3030-2*, Arie Bks) Andrews & McMeel.

What Women Should Know: Information for Wives & Mothers. Eliza B. Duffey. LC 73-20620. (Sex, Marriage & Society Ser.). 324p. 1974. reprint ed. 24.95 (*0-405-05825-X*) Ayer.

What Women Should Know about Menopause. Judith Sachs. 160p. 1991. mass mkt. 4.99 (*0-440-20643-X*) Dell.

What Women Thought: The Creation of Feminist Consciousness, 700 A.D.-1870. Gerda Lerner. LC 92-20411. (Women & History Ser.: Vol. 2). 320p. 1993. 30.00 (*0-19-506604-9*) OUP.

***What Women Want.** Ellen Hawkes. Date not set. write for info. (*0-688-06554-6*) Morrow.

What Women Want. Patricia Ireland. 320p. 1996. pap. 23.95 (*0-525-93857-5*) NAL-Dutton.

***What Women Want: A Journey to Personal & Political Power.** Patricia Ireland. 1997. pap. 12.95 (*0-452-27249-1*, Plume) NAL-Dutton.

What Women Want: The Ideologies of the Movement. Gayle G. Yates. 235p. 1980. pap. text ed. 6.95 (*0-674-95079-8*) HUP.

What Women Want Most. Thomas J. Hatton & Geoffrey Chaucer. 1982. pap. 3.00 (*0-87129-378-1*, W51) Dramatic Pub.

What Women Want to Know about Breast Implants. Karen Berger & John Bostwick, III. (Illus.). 40p. 1994. pap. 6.00 (*0-942219-61-9*) Quality Med Pub.

What Women Want to Know about Breast Self-Examination. Karen Berger & John Bostwick, III. (Illus.). 8p. 1996. pap. 1.95 (*0-942219-99-6*) Quality Med Pub.

What Women Want to Know about Men: What Men Need to Know about Themselves. Nick Durso. 89p. 1994. pap. 9.95 (*0-87012-524-9*) McClain.

***What Wonderous Love.** Jay C. Rochelle. LC 96-44814. 64p. 1996. pap. 5.99 (*0-8066-2983-5*) Augsburg Fortress.

What Wood Is That? A Manual of Wood Identification. Herbert L. Edlin. (Illus.). 1969. pap. 26.95 (*0-670-75907-4*) Viking Penguin.

What Work Is. Philip Levine. 1991. 19.00 (*0-679-40166-0*) McKay.

What Work Is. Philip Levine. 1992. pap. 13.00 (*0-679-74058-9*) McKay.

What Work Requires of Schools: A Scans Report for America 2000. 52p. (Orig.). (C). 1993. pap. text ed. 25.00 (*1-56806-386-5*) DIANE Pub.

What Working People Should Know about the Dangers of Nuclear Power. 2nd ed. Fred Halstead. 39p. 1981. pap. 3.00 (*0-87348-429-0*) Pathfinder NY.

What Works? An Annotated Bibliography of Case Studies of Sustainable Development. D. Scott Slocombe et al. LC 93-31077. (Working Papers, IUCN Commission on Environmental Strategy & Planning: No. 5). 56p. (Orig.). 1993. pap. 20.00 (*0-912102-99-3*) Cal Inst Public.

***What Works? An International Survey of Research on School Effectiveness.** Charles Teddie & David Reynolds. 304p. 1997. pap. 29.95 (*0-7507-0607-4*, Falmer Pr) Taylor & Francis.

What Works: Instructional Strategies for Music Education. Ed. by Margaret Merrion & Clifford Madsen. (Illus.). 144p. (Orig.). (C). 1989. pap. 18.25 (*0-940796-61-9*, 1501) Music Ed Natl.

What Works: Research about Teaching & Learning Through the School's Library Resource Center. Ken Haycock. 1993. write for info. (*0-920175-06-6*) Rockland Pr.

What Works? Synthesizing Effective Bio-Medical & Psychosocial Strategies for Healthy Families in the 21st Century. Ed. by Lorraine C. Blackman. (Illus.). 172p. (Orig.). (C). 1994. pap. text ed. 29.95 (*0-9643817-0-2*) IN U Schl Soc Wrk.

***What Works: William J. Bennett's Research about Teaching & Learning.** 3rd ed. Ed. by Dana B. Ciccoue. LC 96-41073. 112p. 1996. pap. 6.00 (*1-888683-27-9*) Wooster Bk.

What Works at Work: Lessons from the Masters. George Dixon. 328p. 1988. 39.95 (*0-943210-05-4*) Lakewood Pubns.

What Works for Whom? A Critical Review of Psychotherapy Research. Anthony Roth & Peter Fonagy. 484p. 1996. lib. bdg. 48.95 (*1-57230-125-2*) Guilford Pr.

What Works in Children's Mental Health Services? Uncovering Answers to Critical Questions. Krista Kutash & Vestena R. Rivera. (Systems of Care for Children's Mental Health Ser.: Vol. 3). 208p. (Orig.). 1996. pap. text ed. 30.00 (*1-55766-254-1*) P H Brookes.

What Works in Drug Abuse Epidemiology. Ed. by Blanche Frank & Ronald Simeone. LC 91-23375. (Journal of Addictive Diseases: Vol. 11, No. 1). (Illus.). 150p. 1992. 39.95 (*1-56024-185-3*) Haworth Pr.

What Works in Drug Abuse Epidemiology. Ed. by Blanche Frank & Ronald Simeone. LC 91-23375. (Journal of Addictive Diseases: Vol. 11, No. 1). 150p. 1996. pap. 15.95 (*0-7890-6043-4*) Haworth Pr.

***What Works in Fashion Advertising.** Ed. by Peggy F. Winters & Arthur A. Winters. 160p. (C). 1996. 39.95 (*0-934590-89-3*) Retail Report.

***What Works in Policing.** Ed. by David H. Bayley. (Readings in Crime & Punishment Ser.). (Illus.). 288p. (C). 1997. pap. text ed. 19.95 (*0-19-510821-3*) OUP.

***What Works in Policing.** Ed. by David H. Bayley. (Readings in Crime & Punishment Ser.). (Illus.). 288p. (C). 1997. text ed. 45.00 (*0-19-510820-5*) OUP.

What Works in Policing? Operations & Administration Examined. Gary W. Cordner & Donna C. Hale. LC 91-70612. (ACJS - Anderson Monographs). 198p. (C). 1991. pap. text ed. 18.95 (*0-87084-015-0*) Anderson Pub Co.

What Works in Preventing Rural Violence: Strategies, Risk Factors, & Assessment Tools. Barbara R. Monsey et al. LC 94-49041. 1995. pap. 17.00 (*0-940069-04-0*) A H Wilder.

What Works on Wall Street: A Guide to the Best-Performing Investment Strategies of All Time. James P. O'Shaughnessy. (Illus.). 400p. 1996. text ed. 29.95 (*0-07-047985-2*) McGraw.

***What Works on Wall Street: A Guide to the Best-Performing Investment Strategies of All Time.** James P. O'Shaughnessy. 1997. text ed. 29.95 (*0-07-048246-2*) McGraw.

What Works Report No. 1: Air Pollution Solutions. Mark Malaspina et al. (What Works Ser.). (Illus.). 113p. (Orig.). (C). 1992. pap. text ed. 17.00 (*0-9638613-0-1*) Environ Exchange.

What Works Report No. 2: Local Solutions to Toxic Pollution. Kristin Schafer et al. (What Works Ser.). 160p. (C). 1993. pap. text ed. 17.00 (*0-9638613-5-2*) Environ Exchange.

***What Would Barney Say?** Sheryl Leach. Ed. by Margie Larsen. LC 96-86262. (Illus.). 24p. (J). (ps-3). 1996. pap. 2.95 (*1-57064-121-8*) Lyrick Pub.

What Would Happen If... Linda P. Silbert & Alvin J. Silbert. (Little Twirps Creative Thinking Workbook Ser.). (Illus.). (J). (gr. 3-9). 1976. student ed. 4.98 (*0-89544-018-0*, 018) Silbert Bress.

What Would I Be. Shirley R. Wachtel. LC 94-60455. (Illus.). 44p. (J). (gr. k-3). 1995. 10.95 (*1-55523-692-8*) Winston-Derek.

What Would It Be? A. Child. (Cityscapes Ser.). 13p. (J). (gr. k). 1992. pap. text ed. 4.50 (*1-56843-061-2*) BGR Pub.

What Would It Be? Big Book. A. Child. (Cityscapes Ser.). 13p. (J). (gr. k). 1992. pap. text ed. 23.00 (*1-56843-011-6*) BGR Pub.

***What Would Jesus Do?** pap. 12.50 (*0-8054-6099-3*) Broadman.

What Would Jesus Do? Glenn Clark. pap. 9.95 (*0-910924-20-1*) Macalester.

***What Would Jesus Do? Charles M. Sheldon's Classic "In His Stpes" Retold for Children.** Ed. by Helen Haidle. LC 96-40118. (Illus.). 256p. (J). (gr. k-5). 1997. 12.99 (*1-57673-053-0*, Gold & Honey) Multnomah Pubs.

What Would Jesus Do? see Sheldon Collection

What Would Jesus Say about Your Church? Richard L. Mayhue. 10.99 (*1-85792-150-X*, Pub. by Christian Focus UK) Spring Arbor Dist.

What Would Mama Do? Judith R. Enderle & Stephanie G. Tessler. LC 94-79153. (Illus.). 32p. (J). (ps-1). 1995. 14.95 (*1-56397-418-5*) Boyds Mills Pr.

What Would the Zoo Do? Lynn Salem. (Illus.). 8p. (Orig.). (J). (gr. k-1). 1996. pap. 3.50 (*1-880612-49-6*) Seedling Pubns.

What Would They Say? The Founding Fathers on the Current Issues. Glen Gorton. 270p. (Orig.). 1996. pap. 12.95 (*1-57502-194-3*, P0822) Morris Pubng.

What Would You Do? Mel Poretz. 112p. (Orig.). 1994. pap. 5.99 (*0-449-90762-7*, ExPress) Fawcett.

***What Would You Do?** Debra Raisner et al. (Illus.). 374p. (Orig.). 1997. pap. 5.95 (*0-8362-5076-1*) Andrews & McMeel.

What Would You Do? John H. Yoder. LC 92-15726. 144p. 1992. pap. 7.99 (*0-8361-3603-9*) Herald Pr.

What Would You Do? A Kid's Guide to Tricky & Sticky Situations. Linda Schwartz. LC 90-63597. (Illus.). 184p. (J). (gr. 3-7). 1991. pap. 9.95 (*0-88160-196-9*, LW294) Learning Wks.

***What Would You Do? Bk. A-1: Developing &/or Applying Ethical Standards.** Michael O. Baker. (J). (gr. 7-8). 1989. pap. text ed. 11.00 (*0-89455-348-8*) CRIS.

***What Would You Do? Bk. B-1: Developing &/or Applying Ethical Standards.** Michael O. Baker. (YA). (gr. 9-12). 1989. 11.00 (*0-614-24448-X*) CRIS.

What Would You Do If...? Marilyn Kile & Kristin Baird. (BodyRights: a DUSO Approach to Preventing Sexual Abuse of Children Ser.). (J). 1986. pap. text ed. 19.95 (*0-88671-172-X*, 7205) Am Guidance.

What Would You Do If...? Anecdote Joke Book. 2nd ed. Jack Anglestoff. (Illus.). 52p. 1995. pap. 6.95 (*0-9626963-0-7*) Acrus Pubng.

What Would You Do If...? 101 Five-Minute Devotions for the Family. Greg Johnson. 173p. 1995. pap. 10.99 (*0-89283-855-8*, Vine Bks) Servant.

***What Would You Do If a Worm Was Your Mother?** Ralph Sexton, Sr. (Illus.). 102p. (Orig.). 1997. pap. 9.95 (*1-57090-064-7*) Alexander Bks.

What Would You Do If You Lived at the Zoo? Nancy W. Carlstrom. LC 93-7036. (J). 1994. 13.95 (*0-316-12867-8*) Little.

***What Would You Give Baby Jesus?** 4.15 (*0-687-44917-0*) Abingdon.

What Would You Like on Your Mashed Potatoes? Thomas Davis, III. 124p. 1993. pap. text ed. 10.00 (*1-884778-00-3*) Old Mountain.

What Would You Like to Be? Velma Bright. (Illus.). 32p. (J). (gr. 1). 1976. reprint ed. lib. bdg. 10.00 (*0-9605968-0-1*) Bright Bks.

What Would You Say? see Phonics Is My Way Series

What Writers Know: The Language Process & Structure of Written Discourse. Ed. by Martin Nystrand. 1981. text ed. 59.00 (*0-12-523480-5*) Acad Pr.

What Wrongdoers Deserve: The Moral Reasoning Behind Responses to Misconduct. R. Murray Thomas & Ann Diver-Stamnes. LC 93-9322. (Contributions in Psychology Ser.: No. 21). 192p. 1993. text ed. 47.95 (*0-313-28630-2*, TTJ/, Greenwood Pr) Greenwood.

What You Always Wanted to Know about CRAPS but Were Afraid to Bet. Hugh Heritage. (Illus.). 216p. (Orig.). 1985. pap. 5.95 (*0-913651-01-X*) Inst Sci Res.

What You Always Wanted to Know about Football but Were Afraid to Ask: The Beginner's Guide. Carole Leigh. Ed. by Kristi K. Berg. (Illus.). 65p. (Orig.). 1994. pap. 6.90 (*0-9638943-1-5*) Leigh Enter.

What You Always Wanted to Know about Operating a Small Business but Didn't Know Who to Ask. Kathryn A. Erskine. (Illus.). 69p. (Orig.). (C). 1980. pap. 9.95 (*0-9605058-0-6*) Erskine.

What You Always Wanted to Know about the Card Catalog but Were Afraid to Ask. 1,988th rev. ed. Sherry S. DuPree. LC 77-87133. (Illus.). (J). (gr. k-6). 1988. pap. 6.95 (*0-9600962-3-X*) Displays Sch.

What You Aren't Supposed to Know about the Legal Profession: An Expose of Lawyers, Judges, Law Schools & More. Laurens R. Schwartz. 206p. 1990. pap. 9.95 (*1-56171-023-7*) Sure Seller.

What You Aren't Supposed to Know about the Legal Profession: An Expose of Lawyers, Law Schools, Judges & More: An Insider's Report. Laurens R. Schwartz. LC 88-16910. 206p. 1988. 14.95 (*0-685-74003-X*) Sure Seller.

What You Aren't Supposed to Know about Writing & Publishing: An Expose of Editors, Agents, Publishing Houses & More: An Insider's Report. Laurens R. Schwartz. LC 88-16909. 1988. 14.95 (*0-944007-03-1*) Sure Seller.

What You Can Change & What You Can't: The Ultimate Guide to Self-Improvement. Martin E. Seligman. LC 93-14757. 1994. 23.00 (*0-679-41024-4*) Knopf.

What You Can Change...& What You Can't: The Complete Guide to Successful Self-Improvement. Martin G. Seligman. 336p. 1995. pap. 12.00 (*0-449-90971-9*) Fawcett.

What You Can Do about AIDS, 8, Set. Anna Forbes. (AIDS Awareness Library). (Illus.). 24p. (J). (gr. k-4). 1996. lib. bdg. 10.46 (*0-8239-2370-3*, PowerKids) Rosen Group.

What You Can Do about Allergy. William Pierpont. 6p. 1965. reprint ed. spiral bd. 5.50 (*0-7873-1107-3*) Hlth Research.

What You Can Do about Asthma. Nathaniel Altman. 176p. 1991. mass mkt. 4.99 (*0-440-20641-3*) Dell.

What You Can Do about Diabetes. Nora Tannenhaus. 144p. 1991. mass mkt. 4.99 (*0-440-20640-5*) Dell.

What You Can Do for the Environment. Mike Wald. (Earth at Risk Ser.). (Illus.). 112p. (J). (gr. 5 up). 1993. lib. bdg. 19.95 (*0-7910-1587-4*) Chelsea Hse.

What You Can Do for You. K. Schwarz. pap. 3.98 (*0-8317-4347-6*) Smithmark.

What You Can Do for Your Country: Report of the Commission on National & Community Service. (Illus.). 130p. (Orig.). (C). 1993. pap. text ed. 35.00 (*0-7881-0004-1*) DIANE Pub.

What You Can Do to Avoid AIDS. Earvin Johnson. 204p. (YA). 1992. pap. 3.99 (*0-8129-2063-5*, Times Bks) Random.

What You Can Do to Avoid AIDS. Ervin Johnson. 1996. pap. 4.99 (*0-8129-2844-X*, Times Bks) Random.

What You Can Do to Help the Hungry Feed Themselves. Gregg Hoffmann & Robert Spitzer. (Illus.). 96p. (Orig.). (C). 1994. pap. 8.50 (*0-9637643-1-4*) M&T Communs.

What You Can Do to Prevent Fetal Alcohol Syndrome: A Professional's Guide. Sheila B. Blume. LC 92-15315. 64p. 1992. pap. 6.95 (*1-56246-043-9*, P219) Johnsn Inst.

What You Can Expect from an Interim Pastor & an Interim Consultant. Philip G. Porcher, Jr. pap. 6.75 (*1-56699-101-3*, OD71) Alban Inst.

What You Can Learn from Things That Go Wrong: A Guidebook to the Root Causes of Failure. C. Robert Nelms. (Illus.). 192p. (Orig.). 1996. pap. text ed. 35.00 (*1-886118-10-8*) Failsafe Netwrk.

What You Can See, You Can Be! David A. Anderson. (Illus.). 48p. (Orig.). (J). (gr. 3-8). 1988. 12.95 (*0-87516-603-2*) DeVorss.

What You Didn't Think to Ask Your Obstetrician: Answers to 1000 Questions about Your Pregnancy. Raymond I. Poliakin. 320p. 1994. pap. 11.95 (*0-8092-3658-3*) Contemp Bks.

What You Do Best: In the Body of Christ. Bruce L. Bugbee. Orig. Title: Your Perfect Fit. 176p. 1995. pap. 10.99 (*0-310-49431-1*) Zondervan.

What You Do Is Easy, What I Do Is Hard. Jake Wolf. LC 95-5467. (Illus.). (J). Date not set. lib. bdg. write for info. (*0-688-13441-6*) Greenwillow.

What You Do Is Easy, What I Do Is Hard. Jake Wolf. LC 95-5467. (Illus.). (J). 1996. 15.00 (*0-688-13440-8*) Greenwillow.

***What You Don't Know about Having Babies.** Armor. 1997. pap. 6.00 (*0-671-57682-8*) S&S Trade.

***What You Don't Know about Having Babies: The Pregnancy Question & Answer Book.** Joyce Armor. LC 97-20567. 1997. write for info. (*0-88166-292-5*) Meadowbrook.

What You Don't Know about Health Insurance Will Cost You. Heidi H. Hale. 67p. (Orig.). 1991. pap. 12.95 (*0-9631623-0-6*, 3160337) MediPro Mgmt.

What You Don't Know Can Heal You: The Missing Link of Wholistic Medicine. David Waldman. Ed. by Bob Owen. LC 93-80599. (Orig.). pap. 12.95 (*1-882657-04-7*) Health Hope.

What You Don't Know Can Heal You: The Missing Link of Wholistic Medicine. David Waldman. Ed. by Bob Owen. LC 94-76251. 232p. (Orig.). 1994. pap. text ed. 12.95 (*1-882657-09-8*) Health Hope.

What You Don't Know Can Hurt You: A Guide to the Medical Literature. A. J. Longley. (Orig.). (C). 1981. pap. 3.00 (*0-937038-00-8*) Star Pr.

What You Don't Know Can Kill You. Fran Arrick. 160p. (YA). 1994. mass mkt. 3.99 (*0-440-21894-2*) Dell.

What You Feel You Can Heal: A Guide for Enriching Relationships. 4th rev. ed. John Gray. LC 84-82045. (Illus.). 213p. 1984. pap. 12.95 (*0-931269-01-6*) Heart Pub CA.

***What You Knead.** Mary A. Esposito. LC 97-11279. 1997. write for info. (*0-688-15010-1*) Morrow.

What You Know First. Patricia MacLachlan. LC 94-38341. (Joanna Cotler Bks.). (Illus.). 32p. (J). (gr. k up). 1995. 14.95 (*0-06-024413-5*); lib. bdg. 14.89 (*0-06-024414-3*) HarpC Child Bks.

What You Must Know about Home Lenders: Seventeen Answers - the Answer Book, Vol. I. Larry Oxenham. (Illus.). 40p. (Orig.). 1987. pap. 4.75 (*0-943813-00-X*) Page One Pub.

What You Must Know about Social Security & Medicare. Eric R. Kingson. 112p. 1986. pap. 4.95 (*0-345-34397-2*) Newspaper Ent.

What You Must Know to Get the Job You Want. Kenneth H. Kuehne. LC 83-90472. (Illus.). 160p. 1983. pap. 10.00 (*0-916041-84-0*) Kenco Pub Co.

What You Need Is What You've Got: Rediscovering, Developing & Using Your Inner Resources. Larry Althouse & Valere Althouse. LC 88-13100. 208p. 1989. pap. 9.95 (*0-87728-691-4*) Weiser.

What You Need to Know about Business Law. Laurence J. Pino. 1991. write for info. (*0-318-68780-1*) Open U FL.

***What You Need to Know about Cancer: A Scientific American Special Issue.** LC 97-3663. (Illus.). 160p. 1997. pap. 16.95 (*0-7167-3102-9*) W H Freeman.

What You Need to Know about Developing Study Skills, Taking Notes & Tests, Using Dictionaries & Libraries. Marcia Conan & Kathy Heavers. (NTC's Skill Builders Ser.). (Illus.). 96p. 1994. pap. 6.95 (*0-8442-5175-5*, Natl Textbk) NTC Pub Grp.

***What You Need to Know about Developing Study Skills, Taking Notes & Tests, Using Dictionaries & Libraries.** 2nd ed. Marcia J. Coman & Kathy L. Heavers. 96p. 1997. pap. 7.95 (*0-8442-5888-1*) NTC Pub Grp.

What You Need to Know about Developing Your Test-Taking Skills: Reading Comprehension. Robert S. Boone. 64p. 1995. pap. 6.95 (*0-8442-5896-2*) NTC Pub Grp.

What You Need to Know about Developing Your Test-Taking Skills: Standard English. Robert S. Boone. 64p. 1995. pap. 6.95 (*0-8442-5894-6*) NTC Pub Grp.

What You Need to Know about Developing Your Test-Taking Skills: Writing Assessment. Robert S. Boone. 64p. 1995. pap. 6.95 (*0-8442-5895-4*) NTC Pub Grp.

What You Need to Know about Drug Testing in the Workplace: How to Protect Your Job, Your Career, & Your Reputation. Andrea Huxford. 50p. 1994. pap. 12.95 (*0-9641940-7-4*) Steinhatchee Trad.

What You Need to Know about Getting a Job & Filling Out Forms. Carolyn M. Starkey & Norgina W. Penn. (Essential Life Skills Ser.). 80p. 1993. pap. 5.95 (*0-8442-5657-9*, Natl Textbk) NTC Pub Grp.

What You Need to Know about Improving Basic English Skills. Jerry D. Reynolds. 228p. 1994. pap. 12.95 (*0-8442-5285-9*, Natl Textbk) NTC Pub Grp.

***What You Need to Know about Improving Basic English Skills.** 2nd ed. Jerry D. Reynolds & Marion L. Steet. LC 97-12336. (NTC's Skill Builders Ser.). (J). 1997. write for info. (*0-8442-5967-5*) NTC Pub Grp.

What You Need to Know about Improving Basic English Skills: Intermediate Through Advanced. Jerry D. Reynolds et al. 256p. (YA). 1994. pap. text ed. 15.95 (*0-8442-5283-2*, Natl Textbk) NTC Pub Grp.

What You Need to Know about Improving Basic English Skills: Intermediate Through Advanced. annot. ed. Jerry D. Reynolds et al. 256p. (YA). 1994. teacher ed. 19.95 (*0-8442-5284-0*, Natl Textbk) NTC Pub Grp.

What You Need to Know about Jehovah's Witnesses. rev. ed. Lorri MacGregor. (Conversations with the Cults Ser.). 160p. 1992. pap. 6.99 (*0-89081-944-0*) Harvest Hse.

What You Need to Know about Masons. Ed Decker. (Conversations with the Cults Ser.). 160p. (Orig.). 1992. pap. 7.99 (*0-89081-945-9*) Harvest Hse.

What You Need to Know about Me: How to Organize Your Important Categories of Personal Information. Arthur Esbin. 148p. (Orig.). 1996. pap. 19.95 (*0-9651854-0-0*) Plan Ahead.

What You Need to Know about Menopause: Answers to the Questions Women Ask Most. Paul C. Reisser & Teri K. Reisser. 212p. 1994. pap. 10.99 (*0-89283-880-9*, Vine Bks) Servant.

What You Need to Know about Mormons. rev. ed. Ed Decker. (Conversations with the Cults Ser.). 160p. 1992. pap. 6.99 (*0-89081-968-8*) Harvest Hse.

What You Need to Know about Psychiatric Drugs. Stuart C. Yudofsky et al. 672p. 1992. pap. 14.00 (*0-345-37334-0*, Ballantine Trade) Ballantine.

What You Need to Know about Reading Comprehension & Speed, Skimming & Scanning, Reading for Pleasure. Marcia J. Coman & Kathy Heavers. (NTC's Skill Builders Ser.). (Illus.). 112p. 1994. pap. 6.95 (*0-8442-5176-3*, Natl Textbk) NTC Pub Grp.

W

*What You Need to Know about Reading Comprehension & Speed, Skimming & Scanning, Reading for Pleasure. 2nd ed. Marcia J. Coman & Kathy L. Heavers. 112p. 1997. pap. 7.95 (0-8442-5887-3) NTC Pub Grp.

What You Need to Know about Reading Newspapers, Labels & Directions. 2nd ed. Carolyn M. Starkey & Norgina W. Penn. (Essential Life Skills Ser.). 1993. pap. 5.95 (0-8442-5655-2, Natl Textbk) NTC Pub Grp.

What You Need to Know about Reading Signs, Directories, Schedules, Maps, Charts & Utility Bills. 2nd ed. Carolyn M. Starkey & Norgina W. Penn. (Essential Life Skills Ser.). 64p. 1993. pap. 5.95 (0-8442-5658-7, Natl Textbk) NTC Pub Grp.

What You Need to Know about Roman Catholicism: Quick Reference Guide. James G. McCarthy. 10p. 1995. pap. 1.99 (1-56507-429-7) Harvest Hse.

What You Need to Know about Salvation. Peter Jeffery. 96p. (Orig.). 1996. pap. 4.99 (0-85234-347-7, Pub. by Evangelical Pr) Presby & Reformed.

What You Need to Know about the New Age Movement. F. LaGard Smith. LC 93-7345. (Conversations with the Cults Ser.). 1993. pap. 6.99 (1-56507-124-7) Harvest Hse.

What You Need to Know Before You Fall in Love. David Nicholson. LC 94-40598. 1995. pap. text ed. 10.99 (0-7852-8143-6) Nelson.

What You Need to Know Before You Invest: An Introduction to the Stock Market & Other Investments. Rod Davis. LC 95-16623. 272p. 1996. pap. 8.95 (0-8120-9466-2) Barron.

What You Need to Know Before You Win the Lottery. Tom Reilly. Ed. by Rosa Glenn-Reilly. Tr. by Lillian De Tuite. 50p. (Orig.). 1996. pap. 10.00 (0-9651636-0-1) OdysseyPtrns.

What You Need to Know to Avoid: Auto Repair Rip-Offs. H. Lee Stone. (Illus.). 48p. (Orig.). (C). 1990. pap. write for info. (0-9625465-0-X) H L Stone Pubns.

What You Need to Know to Settle with Insurance Companies. Thomas H. Veitch. (Business Practice Library: No. 1692). 120p. 1993. ring bd. 58.00 (0-471-59726-0) Wiley.

What You Need to Know to Settle with Insurance Companies. Thomas H. Veitch. (Business Practice Library: No. 1692). 544p. 1993. ring bd. 130.00 (0-471-58788-5) Wiley.

What You Need to Know to Settle with Insurance Companies. Thomas H. Veitch. 136p. 1994. spiral bd. 60.00 (0-471-05192-6) Wiley.

*What You Need to Know to Settle with Insurance Companies. 2nd ed. (Personal Injury Library Ser.). text ed. 120.00 (0-471-13512-7) Wiley.

*What You Need to Know to Settle with Insurance Companies: 1995 Supplement. Thomas H. Veitch. 1995. suppl. ed., text ed. 65.00 (0-471-12312-9) Wiley.

What You Need to Know When You Can't Find Your UNIX System Administrator. Linda Mui. 156p. 1995. pap. text ed. 17.95 (1-56592-104-6) OReilly & Assocs.

*What You Need to Know When...Your Child Is Learning to Read. Sara Wilford. 1997. pap. text ed. 6.95 (0-590-31073-9) Scholastic Inc.

What You Never Learned in Graduate School (Norton Professional Books) A Survival Guide for Therapists. Jeffrey A. Kottler & Richard J. Hazler. LC 96-41947. 256p. (C). 1997. 32.00 (0-393-70242-1) Norton.

What You Ought to Know about Family & Medical Leave: What Are the Rules - Who Is Eligible - What Is Required. 48p. 1993. pap. 5.00 (0-685-67148-8, 5414) Commerce.

What You Ought to Know about Hiring a Domestic: Avoiding Tax Pitfalls - Checking Immigration Status - Keeping Good Records. 32p. 1993. pap. 5.00 (0-685-67058-9, 5459) Commerce.

What You Ought to Know about Living Trusts: How They Work - What They Accoomplish - What Is Involved. 32p. 1992. pap. 5.00 (0-685-67059-7, 4808) Commerce.

What You Ought to Know about Medicare Supplement Insurance Plans: What Are the Model Plans - Understanding Coverage - Descriptive Charts of Model Plans. 32p. 1993. pap. 5.00 (0-685-67164-X, 5468) Commerce.

What You Ought to Know about Mutual Funds: Their Advantages - Selecting Funds - Investment Returns. Auster. 56p. 1992. pap. 5.00 (0-685-67060-0, 4705) Commerce.

*What You Ought to Know about Natural Disasters & Your Taxes. Miller. 64p. 1994. pap. 5.00 (0-614-26831-1, BLS-3295) Commerce.

What You Ought to Know about New Pension Withholding Rules: What Are the Rules - How to Avoid Withholding - IRS Withholding Notice. Auster. 32p. 1993. pap. 5.00 (0-685-67165-8, 5470) Commerce.

What You Ought to Know about the ADA: Who Must Comply - Employment - Accommodation - Accessibility. 64p. 1992. pap. 5.00 (0-685-67147-X, 4728) Commerce.

What You Pay For. C. J. Henderson. Ed. by Michael Cantalupo. 225p. 1990. pap. 10.95 (0-936071-18-4) Gryphon Pubns.

*What You Really Need to Know about Cancer: A Comprehensive Guide for Patients & Their Families. Robert Buckman. LC 97-5203. 1997. write for info. (0-8018-5594-2); pap. write for info. (0-8018-5593-4) Johns Hopkins.

*What You Really Need to Know about Cancer: A Comprehensive Guide for Patients & Their Families. Robert Buckman. 485p. 1996. 52.50 (0-333-61866-1, Pub. by Macmlln UK) Trans-Atl Phila.

What You Say Is What You Get. Don Gossett. 192p. 1976. mass mkt. 5.99 (0-88368-066-1) Whitaker Hse.

What You See: Drawings by Gail Geltner. Illus. by Gail Geltner. 156p. 1992. pap. 12.95 (0-929005-29-5, Pub. by Second Story Pr CN) LPC InBook.

What You See Is What... (Illus.). (J). (ps-2). 1991. pap. 5.10 (0-8136-5584-6); lib. bdg. 7.95 (0-8136-5084-4) Modern Curr.

What You Should Know about a Parent Who Drinks Too Much. William L. Coleman. LC 92-18314. 96p. (Orig.). (J). (gr. 3-8). 1992. pap. 5.99 (0-8066-2610-0, 9-2610, Augsburg) Augsburg Fortress.

What You Should Know about AIDS. Raymond Beshara et al. (Illus.). 72p. (YA). (gr. 6-10). 1989. teacher ed. 3.00 (0-9623161-3-X); pap. text ed. 9.85 (0-9623161-2-1) ERN Inc.

What You Should Know about Angels. Charlene Altemose. LC 95-40228. 80p. (Orig.). 1996. pap. 4.95 (0-89243-906-8) Liguori Pubns.

What You Should Know about Earthquakes: It Could Save Your Life. Joseph W. Foraker. (Illus.). 64p. (Orig.). 1983. pap. 5.95 (0-912287-00-4) SJB Pub Co.

What You Should Know about Federal Taxes When You Sell Your House. 32p. 1983. 2.00 (0-685-07392-0) P-H.

What You Should Know about Ghosts...But Were Afraid to Ask. Norma Edwards. LC 87-72592. 256p. (C). 1988. 16.95 (0-944534-00-7) Diamond Stockton.

What You Should Know about Herbs for Your Health. Earl R. Mindell & Virginia L. Hopkins. 96p. 1996. pap. text ed. 4.95 (0-87983-749-7) Keats.

*What You Should Know about Hydraulic Cylinders. James E. Anders, Sr. 1995. spiral bd. 30.00 (0-9636737-2-6) Hydraulics.

What You Should Know about Jewelry: Buyer's Guide. Simon Beylin. Ed. by Lisa Hant & Jake Carpenter. (Illus.). 81p. 1995. 12.99 (0-9648865-0-2) Romans Pubng.

What You Should Know about Jewish Religion, History, Ethics & Culture. Sidney L. Markowitz. 240p. 1992. pap. 8.95 (0-8065-0811-6, Citadel Pr) Carol Pub Group.

What You Should Know about Jews & Judaism see How Firm a Foundation: A Gift of Jewish Wisdom for Christians & Jews

What You Should Know about Living with One Parent. William L. Coleman. LC 93-31851. (Grubstake Adventure Ser.). 96p. (J). 1993. pap. 5.99 (0-8066-2636-4, 9-2636) Augsburg Fortress.

What You Should Know about Parents - Chinese Edition. Ed. by Jay Kesler. Tr. by May-Chun Kam. 192p. (CHI.). 1993. pap. 8.50 (1-56582-018-5) Christ Renew Min.

What You Should Know about Prophecy. C. M. Ward. LC 75-22610. (Radiant Life Ser.). 127p. 1975. pap. 3.95 (0-88243-890-5, 02-0890) Gospel Pub.

What You Should Know about Prophecy. C. M. Ward. LC 75-22610. (Radiant Life Ser.). 1975. teacher ed., pap. 5.50 (0-88243-164-1, 32-0164) Gospel Pub.

*What You Should Know about Psychics. Keith C. Smith. 49p. (Orig.). 1997. pap. 5.98 (0-9657627-7-7) I-Can Minist.

What You Should Know about Sports & Drugs. John J. Bowman. (Family Forum Library Ser.). 16p. 1992. 1.95 (1-56688-020-3) Bur For At-Risk.

What You Should Know about Taxes & Marital Split-Ups. 36p. 1983. 2.15 (0-685-07393-9) P-H.

What You Should Know about Teaching & Learning Styles. Claudia E. Cornett. LC 82-63062. (Fastback Ser.: No. 191). 50p. 1983. pap. 3.00 (0-87367-191-0) Phi Delta Kappa.

What You Should Know about Teenagers - Chinese Edition. Ed. by Jay Kesler. Tr. by May-Chun Kam. 92p. (CHI.). 1993. pap. 5.00 (1-56582-019-3) Christ Renew Min.

What You Should Know about the American Flag. rev. ed. Earl P. Williams, Jr. (Illus.). 68p. (J). (gr. 4-6). 1989. reprint ed. pap. text ed. 4.95 (0-939631-10-5) Thomas Publications.

What You Should Know about the Bible: A Practical Guide to Bible Basics. Stanford Herlick. LC 85-82137. (Illus.). 255p. 1985. 12.50 (0-9616026-0-0) FBF Pubns.

What You Should Know about the Catechism of the Catholic Church. Charlene Altemose. LC 93-79929. 64p. (Orig.). 1994. pap. 1.95 (0-89243-647-6) Liguori Pubns.

What You Should Know about the Flags of the Confederacy. Earl P. Williams, Jr. (Illus.). 40p. (C). 1994. pap. text ed. 4.95 (0-939631-39-3) Thomas Publications.

What You Should Know about the Golden Dawn. 6th rev. ed. Israel Regardie. LC 83-81663. (Illus.). 248p. 1993. pap. 12.95 (1-56184-064-5) New Falcon Pubns.

What You Should Know about the Mass. Charlene Altemose. LC 92-72595. (Illus.). 64p. (Orig.). 1992. pap. text ed. 2.95 (0-89243-462-7) Liguori Pubns.

What You Should Know about the Pension Law. (Illus.). 60p. (C). 1994. pap. text ed. 15.00 (0-7881-0255-9) DIANE Pub.

What You Should Know about the Pension Law. 1990. lib. bdg. 75.00 (0-87700-913-9) Revisionist Pr.

What You Should Know about the Sacraments. Charlene Altemose. LC 94-75243. 64p. (Orig.). 1994. pap. 2.95 (0-89243-629-8) Liguori Pubns.

*What You Should Know about the Saints. Charlene Altemose. 80p. (Orig.). 1997. pap. 4.95 (0-7648-0047-7) Liguori Pubns.

What You Should Know about UFO's. J. Allen Hynek. reprint ed. spiral bd. 6.50 (0-7873-1073-5) Hlth Research.

What You Should Know about Your Child. 1990. write for info. (81-900106-5-4, Pub. by Kalakshetra Pubns II) N Montessori.

What You Should Know about Your Ultrasound Examinations: Abdomen. Date not set. 1.50 (0-614-14616-X) Am Inst Ultrasound.

What You Should Know about Your Ultrasound Examinations: Doppler. Date not set. 1.50 (0-685-27245-1) Am Inst Ultrasound.

What You Should Know about Your Ultrasound Examinations: Obstetrics. Date not set. 1.50 (0-685-72218-X) Am Inst Ultrasound.

What You Should Know about Your Ultrasound Examinations: Safety. Date not set. 1.50 (0-614-14954-1) Am Inst Ultrasound.

What You Should Know Before Buying a Wheelchair Lift: Tips for the Prospective Buyer. Mark Hittson & Carol Hirsch. 16p. (Orig.). 1995. pap. 4.95 (1-888349-02-6) Katydid.

What You Should Know If You're Accused of a Crime. rev. ed. Joyce B. David. 32p. (Orig.). 1989. pap. 4.00 (0-9617121-1-2) Balaban Pub.

What You Think of Me Is None of My Business. Terry Cole-Whittaker. (Orig.). 1988. mass mkt. 5.99 (0-515-09479-X) Jove Pubns.

What You Thought You Knew about Judaism: 341 Common Misconceptions about Jewish Life. Reuven P. Bulka. LC 89-171. 448p. 1995. reprint ed. pap. 25.00 (1-56821-407-3) Aronson.

What You Want Wants You: How to Get Out of Your Rut. Debra Jones. 175p. (Orig.). 1995. pap. 9.95 (1-55874-367-7, 3677) Health Comm.

What Young Chimpanzees Know about Seeing. Daniel J. Povinelli & Timothy J. Eddy. 216p. 1996. pap. text ed. 14.00 (0-226-67675-7) U Ch Pr.

What Your Astrologer Never Told You. Maxine Taylor. 56p. 1976. 9.00 (0-86690-216-3, T1476-014) Am Fed Astrologers.

What Your Boss Doesn't Tell You Until Its Too Late: How to Correct Personal Trait. Robert Bramson. 176p. 1996. pap. 10.00 (0-684-81146-4, Fireside) S&S Trade.

*What Your Broker Never Tells You: A Guide to Becoming a Better Player. (Illus.). 120p. (Orig.). 1997. pap. write for info. (0-9656976-0-6) R A Groth.

What Your Car Is Trying to Tell You. Peter Novellino. LC 81-730689. 1982. student ed. 5.00 (0-8064-0153-2, 445); audio, vhs 179.00 (0-8064-0154-0) Bergwall.

*What Your Child Needs to Know about God. Ron Rhodes. 304p. (Orig.). 1997. pap. 9.99 (1-56507-556-0) Harvest Hse.

What Your Dentist Does to Keep the Dental Office Safe. Michael Glick & Brian C. Muzyka. LC 95-45830. (Illus.). 32p. 1996. pap. 20.00 (0-86715-314-8) Quint Pub Co.

What Your Doctor Can't Tell You about Cosmetic Surgery. Joyce D. Nash. LC 95-69485. (Illus.). 240p. (Orig.). 1995. pap. 13.95 (1-57224-032-6) New Harbinger.

What Your Doctor Didn't Learn in Medical School . . . & What You Can Do About It! Stuart M. Berger. 352p. 1989. reprint ed. mass mkt. 4.95 (0-380-70319-X) Avon.

*What Your Doctor Doesn't Know Can Kill You: Advice on Health & Long Life from the Top Medical Scientists of the World. William A. Kent. 1997. 24.95 (0-9654622-1-8) C A Inc.

What Your Doctor May Not Tell You about Menopause: The Breakthrough Book on Natural Progesterone. John R. Lee & Virginia L. Hopkins. 320p. (Orig.). 1996. pap. 12.99 (0-446-67144-4) Warner Bks.

What Your Doctor Should Do for You: A Symptom-by-Symptom Guide to Getting Proper Treatment from Your Physician. Joel Goldberg. LC 95-50687. 368p. (Orig.). 1996. pap. 18.95 (0-89733-430-2) Academy Chi Pubs.

What Your Doctor Won't Tell You. Jane Heimlich. LC 89-46097. 288p. 1990. pap. 14.00 (0-06-096539-8, PL); pap. 10.95 (0-00-002911-4, PL) HarpC.

*What Your Dreams Can Teach You. Alex Lukeman. LC 90-45793. 288p. 1990. pap. 14.95 (1-56718-475-8) Llewellyn Pubns.

What Your Dreams Can Teach You. 2nd ed. Alex Lukeman. LC 97-23110. 288p. 1997. pap. 14.95 (0-87542-475-9) Llewellyn Pubns.

What Your Fifth Grader Needs to Know: Fundamentals of a Good Fifth-Grade Education. Ed. by E. D. Hirsch, Jr. LC 92-30548. (Core Knowledge Ser.: Bk. 5). 416p. 1993. 22.50 (0-385-41119-7) Doubleday.

What Your First Grader Needs to Know: The Fundamentals of a Good First Grade Education. Ed. by E. D. Hirsch, Jr. 272p. 1993. pap. 10.95 (0-385-31026-9, Delta) Dell.

What Your First Grader Needs to Know: The Fundamentals of a Good First Grade Education. Ed. by E. D. Hirsch, Jr. LC 96-24454. (Core Knowledge Ser.). 304p. 1997. 24.95 (0-385-48119-5) Doubleday.

What Your Fourth Grader Needs to Know. E. D. Hirsch, Jr. 416p. 1992. 22.50 (0-385-41118-9) Doubleday.

What Your Handwriting Reveals. Albert E. Hughes. 1978. 4.00 (0-87980-365-7) Wilshire.

*What Your Horoscope Doesn't Tell You. 2nd rev. ed. Charles Strohmer. Ed. by Tomm Knutson. 150p. 1997. pap. 8.99 (1-889893-10-2) Emerald House Group Inc.

What Your Kids Are up to & in For. Bill Sanders. LC 96-8628. 224p. (gr. 10). 1996. pap. 9.99 (0-8007-5604-5) Revell.

*What Your Kindergartner Needs To Know. E. D. Hirsch. 1997. pap. 12.95 (0-385-31841-3, Delta) Dell.

What Your Kindergartner Needs to Know: Preparing Your Child for a Lifetime of Learning. Ed. by E. D. Hirsch, Jr. & John Holdren. LC 95-47000. (Core Knowledge Ser.). (Illus.). 304p. 1996. 24.95 (0-385-48117-9) Doubleday.

What Your Lenses Can Do. Herb Taylor et al. LC 81-71225. (Modern Photo Guides Ser.). (Illus.). 120p. (Orig.). 1982. pap. 7.95 (0-385-18146-9) Avalon Comm.

*What Your Little Black Book Reveals: The Incredible Secret Power of the Addresses You Keep. Judith M. Baldwin. Ed. by Merry Clark. LC 96-92434. (Illus.). 112p. 1997. pap. 9.95 (0-9652969-0-3) SFC Communs.

*What Your Mother Couldn't Teach You Cause Your Father Wasn't Home: And Other Vital Life Lessons. Angelo Ellerbee. 1997. pap. text ed. 12.00 (0-06-098807-X) HarpC.

What Your Mother Couldn't Tell You & Your Father Didn't Know: Advanced Relationship Skills for Lasting Intimacy. John Gray. LC 94-18713. 256p. 1994. 23.00 (0-06-017162-6) HarpC.

What Your Parents Don't Know. Francine Pascal. (Sweet Valley University Ser.: No. 3). 240p. (YA). 1994. pap. 3.99 (0-553-56307-6) Bantam.

*What Your Parents Never Told You. Stan Berenstain & Jan Berenstain. Date not set. 2.99 (0-517-17611-4) Random Hse Value.

What Your Parents Never Told You About Being a Mom Or Dad. Stan Berenstain & Jan Berenstain. LC 94-30746. 1995. 15.00 (0-517-59671-7) Crown Pub Group.

What Your Parents Never Told You about Being a Mom or Dad. Stan Berenstain & Jan Berenstain. (Illus.). 128p. 1996. reprint ed. pap. 10.00 (0-517-88622-7) Crown Pub Group.

What Your Sixth Grader Needs to Know: Fundamentals of a Good Sixth-Grade Education. Ed. by E. D. Hirsch, Jr. LC 92-42136. (Core Knowledge Ser.: Bk. 6). 416p. 1993. 22.50 (0-385-41120-0) Doubleday.

What Your Stockbroker Doesn't Want You to Know. Bruce N. Sankin. LC 90-86108. 265p. (Orig.). 1991. pap. 29.95 (0-9629811-0-9) Business Pub.

What Your Stockbroker Doesn't Want You To Know. rev. ed. Bruce N. Sankin. 180p. 1991. pap. 20.00 (0-9629811-1-7) Business Pub.

What Your Third Grader Needs to Know. E. D. Hirsch, Jr. 368p. 1992. 22.50 (0-385-41117-0) Doubleday.

*What Your Travel Agent Knows That You Don't. 1997. mass mkt. 5.99 (0-373-80510-1, 1-80510-0) Harlequin Bks.

*What Your Tutor May Never Tell You. Howard S. Barrows. 45p. (Orig.). 1996. pap. 9.95 (0-931369-29-0) Southern IL Univ Sch.

What Your Wedding Can Be. William J. Peters. LC 80-65402. 136p. (Orig.). 1980. pap. 2.95 (0-87029-163-7, 20350-5) Abbey.

What Your 2nd Grader Needs to Know: Fundamentals of a Good Second Grade Education. Ed. by E. D. Hirsch, Jr. 336p. 1993. pap. 10.95 (0-385-31027-7, Delta) Dell.

What Your 3rd Grader Needs to Know: Fundamentals of a Good Third-Grade Education. Ed. by E. D. Hirsch, Jr. 368p. 1994. pap. 10.95 (0-385-31257-1, Delta) Dell.

What Your 4th Grader Needs to Know: Fundamentals of a Good Fourth-Grade Education. Ed. by E. D. Hirsch, Jr. 416p. 1994. pap. 10.95 (0-385-31260-1, Delta) Dell.

What Your 5th Grader Needs to Know. Ed. by E. D. Hirsch, Jr. (The Core Knowledge Series). 416p. 1995. pap. 10.95 (0-385-31464-7, Delta) Dell.

What Your 6th Grader Needs to Know. Ed. by E. D. Hirsch, Jr. (The Core Knowledge Series). 416p. 1995. pap. 10.95 (0-385-31467-1, Delta) Dell.

What You've Always Wanted to Know about Your "." Ed. by Susie Shellenberger. ("Let's Talk About Life Ser." by Brio: Vol. 1). (Orig.). (YA). 1996. pap. 3.99 (1-56179-446-5) Focus Family.

What Zeesie Saw on Delancey Street. Elsa O. Rael. LC 95-11321. (Illus.). (J). 1996. 16.00 (0-689-80549-7, S&S Bks Young Read) S&S Childrens.

Whatchagot Stew & the Troll's Idaho Cookbook. Patrick F. McManus & Patricia M. Gass. 288p. 1989. 16.95 (0-8050-0922-1) H Holt & Co.

Whatcom County Bike Book. Patrick Vala. (Illus.). 1977. pap. 2.95 (0-913140-22-8) Signpost Bk Pub.

Whatcom County in Maps, 1832-1937. Scott & Turbeville. (Special Papers: Vol. 2). 1986. pap. 9.95 (0-318-23341-X) WWU CPNS.

Whatcom Images. Koert & Scott. 1986. pap. 12.50 (0-318-23344-4) WWU CPNS.

*Whatcom Places. Ivan Doig & Wendy Walker. Ed. by Robert H. Keller. (Illus.). 96p. Date not set. pap. 25.00 (0-9657053-0-7) Whatcom Land.

Whatcom Scenes. Koert. 1986. pap. 9.95 (0-318-23343-6) WWU CPNS.

What...Dead Again? 1979. 50.00 (0-918784-52-2) N Shulman.

*What'D'Ya Wanna Do? Songbook. Ed. by Frank Metis. (J). 1986. 11.00 (1-877942-02-2) Moose Schl Records.

*Whatever. Julian Sheppard. 1997. pap. 5.25 (0-8222-1610-8) Dramatists Play.

Whatever Alex Wants... Carla Cassidy. (Romance Ser.: No. 856). 1992. pap. 2.69 (0-373-08856-6, 5-08856-2) Silhouette.

Whatever Alex Wants. large type ed. Carla Cassidy. 217p. 1992. reprint ed. lib. bdg. 13.95 (1-56054-460-0) Thorndike Pr.

Whatever Became of...? rev. ed. Richard Lamparski. 1989. pap. 10.95 (0-517-57151-X, Crown) Crown Pub Group.

Whatever Became of...? 11th rev. ed. Richard Lamparski. 1989. 21.95 (0-517-57150-1, Crown) Crown Pub Group.

Whatever Became of Holiness? The Urgency of Holiness in the Post-Modern Age. Steve DeNeff. Ed. by Keith Drury et al. 150p. (Orig.). 1996. pap. 9.95 (0-89827-156-8, BK978) Wesleyan Pub Hse.

Whatever Comes. Lass Small. 1995. mass mkt. 3.25 (0-373-05963-9, 1-05963-3) Silhouette.

Whatever Happaned to Sherlock Holmes? Detective Fiction, Popular Theology, & Society. Robert S. Paul. LC 90-23719. 256p. (C). 1991. 24.95 (0-8093-1722-2) S Ill U Pr.

*Whatever Happend to the Man of Tomorrow? Alan Moore. 1997. pap. text ed. 5.95 (1-56389-315-0) DC Comics.

Whatever Happened - Class Reunions. Maryln Schwartz. 1995. 15.00 (0-517-70141-3) Random.

W

Whatever Happened to Baby Peggy? The Autobiography of Hollywood's Pioneer Child Star. Diana S. Cary. LC 96-23290. 352p. 1996. 25.95 (*0-312-14760-0*) St Martin.

Whatever Happened to Billy the Kid? Helen L. Airy. LC 92-9629. (Illus.). (Orig.). 1992. pap. 12.95 (*0-86534-185-0*) Sunstone Pr.

Whatever Happened to Curtiss-Wright. Robert W. Fausel. (Illus.). 88p. (Orig.). 1989. pap. 14.95 (*0-89745-080-9*) Sunflower U Pr.

Whatever Happened to Divine Grace? (An Alexander Book) Ramon Stevens. LC 87-63015. 385p. (Orig.). 1988. pap. 14.95 (*0-913299-46-4*) Stillpoint.

Whatever Happened to Epperson Springs? Vernon Roddy. 1974. pap. 10.00 (*0-686-40797-0*) Upper Country.

Whatever Happened to "Eureka"? Cartoons on Science. Nick Downes. (Illus.). 155p. (Orig.). (C). 1994. pap. 10.95 (*0-8135-2146-7*) Rutgers U Pr.

***Whatever Happened to God's Country.** Joseph N. Tlaga. 126p. (Orig.). 1997. pap. 13.00 (*0-9657277-0-X*) J N Tlaga.

Whatever Happened to Happily Ever After? Sandra R. Fujita. (Uplook Ser.). 1981. pap. 0.99 (*0-8163-0378-9*) Pacific Pr Pub Assn.

Whatever Happened to Hell? John Blanchard. LC 94-39192. 336p. 1995. pap. 14.99 (*0-89107-837-1*) Crossway Bks.

***Whatever Happened to High School History?** Bob Davis. pap. 19.95 (*1-55028-486-X*, Pub. by J Lorimer CN) Formac Dist Ltd.

Whatever Happened to Hope: Mini Book. Roy H. Hicks. 31p. 1978. pap. 0.99 (*0-89274-074-4*) Harrison Hse.

***Whatever Happened to Humpty Dumpty? And Other Subversive Verses Inspired by Mother Goose.** David Greenberg. LC 97-14173. (Illus.). (J). 1998. write for info. (*0-316-32767-0*) Little.

***Whatever Happened to Jacy Farrow?** Ceil Cleveland. LC 97-22946. 352p. 1997. 26.50 (*1-57441-030-X*) UNTX Pr.

Whatever Happened to Janie? Caroline B. Cooney. LC 92-32334. 208p. (J). 1993. 15.95 (*0-385-31035-8*) Delacorte.

Whatever Happened to Janie? Caroline B. Cooney. 176p. (J). 1994. mass mkt. 4.99 (*0-440-21924-8*) Dell.

Whatever Happened to Jennifer Steele? A Cat Wilde Mystery. Jean Ruryk. LC 95-40806. 208p. 1996. 20.95 (*0-312-14067-3*, Thomas Dunne Bks) St Martin.

Whatever Happened to Justice? Richard J. Maybury. Ed. by Jane A. Williams. (Uncle Eric Bks.). (Illus.). 256p. (Orig.). (J). (gr. 7 up). 1993. pap. 14.95 (*0-942617-10-X*) Blstckng Pr.

Whatever Happened to Local Government? Allan Cochrane. LC 92-42634. 1993. pap. 25.00 (*0-335-19011-1*, Open Univ Pr) Taylor & Francis.

Whatever Happened to Margo? Margaret Durrell. (Illus.). 226p. 1996. 29.95 (*0-233-98917-X*, Pub. by A Deutsch UK) Trafalgar.

***Whatever Happened to Monetarism? Economic Policy Making & Social Learning in the United Kingdom since 1979.** Michael J. Oliver. LC 97-14589. (Modern Social & Economic History Ser.: Vol. 2). (Illus.). 224p. 1997. text ed. 68.95 (*1-85928-433-7*, Pub. by Scolar Pr UK) Ashgate Pub Co.

Whatever Happened to Mother? A Primer for Those Who Care about Children. James Kimmel. LC 93-93641. 70p. 1993. pap. 7.50 (*0-9638503-0-X*) Sweet & Simple.

Whatever Happened to Penny Candy? A Fast, Clear, & Fun Explanation of the Economics You Need for Success in Your Career, Business, & Investments. 3rd enl. rev. ed. Uncle Eric, pseud. LC 92-36378. (Uncle Eric Bks.). 125p. (J). (gr. 5 up). 1993. 9.95 (*0-942617-15-0*) Blstckng Pr.

Whatever Happened to Peter Downstairs? Ed. by Peter G. Cranford. (Illus.). 400p. (Orig.). 1991. pap. write for info. (*0-9605822-2-3*) Great Pyramid.

Whatever Happened to Planning? Peter Ambrose. 224p. 1987. text ed. 59.50 (*0-416-37100-0*, 1121) Routledge Chapman & Hall.

Whatever Happened to Professor Potts? Phil R. Cox. (Solve It Yourself Ser.). 48p. (J). (gr. 4 up). 1995. pap. 6.95 (*0-7460-2051-1*, Usborne); lib. bdg. 14.95 (*0-88110-780-8*, Usborne) EDC.

Whatever Happened to Randolph Scott? C. H. Scott. LC 94-61282. (Illus.). 230p. 1994. pap. 12.95 (*0-944019-16-1*) Empire NC.

Whatever Happened to Randolph Scott. large type ed. C. H. Scott. LC 96-20238. 344p. 1996. 23.95 (*0-7838-1861-0*, GK Hall) Thorndike Pr.

Whatever Happened to Sandy Fowler? Gary Gabriel. Ed. by Jean A. McConochie. (Regents Readers Ser.). 80p. (gr. 7-12). 1987. pap. text ed. 3.50 (*0-13-952052-X*, 20987) Prentice ESL.

***Whatever Happened to Shame.** Twitchell. LC 97-15787. 1997. 22.95 (*0-312-15543-3*) St Martin.

Whatever Happened to Sin? The Truth about Catholic Morality. Charles E. Bouchard. LC 95-80151. 144p. (Orig.). 1995. pap. 5.95 (*0-89243-849-5*) Liguori Pubns.

Whatever Happened to Teamwork? see Teamwork & Team Sabotage

Whatever Happened to the Dinosaurs? Bernard Most. LC 84-3779. (Illus.). 32p. (J). (ps-3). 1984. 16.00 (*0-15-295295-0*, HB Juv Bks) HarBrace.

Whatever Happened to the Dinosaurs? Bernard Most. LC 84-37795. (Voyager Picture Bks.). (Illus.). 32p. (J). (ps-3). 1987. pap. 5.00 (*0-15-295296-9*, Voyager Bks) HarBrace.

Whatever Happened to the Dinosaurs? Bernard Most. LC 84-37795. (Illus.). 32p. (J). (ps). 1995. pap. 5.00 (*0-15-200378-9*, Red Wagon Bks) HarBrace.

Whatever Happened to the Good Sisters. Kathleen W. FitzGerald & Claire Breault. (Finding Our Voice Ser.). 1992. pap. 14.95 (*1-882195-00-0*) Whales Tale Pr.

Whatever Happened to the Hippies? Mary S. Anderson. LC 90-91784. (Illus.). 192p. (Orig.). 1990. pap. 10.95 (*0-936810-19-X*) M & M.

Whatever Happened to the Human Race? C. Everett Koop & Francis A. Schaeffer. LC 83-70955. 168p. 1983. pap. 11.99 (*0-89107-291-8*) Crossway Bks.

Whatever Happened to the Human Race?, 5 vols., 3 cass., Set. 1990. 149.95 (*1-55568-117-4*) Gospel Films.

Whatever Happened to the Kids from Pierce? Delores Stacy. 1985. pap. 4.95 (*0-317-89498-6*) Delcy Bks.

***Whatever Happened to the "Paper Rex" Man? & Other Stories of Cleveland's New West Side.** 1993. pap. 15.95 (*0-9630760-1-9*) M Dugan Ctr.

Whatever Happened to the Peace Dividend? The Post-Cold War Armaments Momentum. Marek Thee. 113p. (Orig.). 1992. 50.00 (*0-85124-532-3*, Pub. by Spkesman UK) Dufour.

Whatever Happened to the Peace Dividend? The Post-Cold War Armaments Momentum. Marek Thee. 113p. (Orig.). 9200. pap. 21.00 (*0-85124-533-1*, Pub. by Spkesman UK) Dufour.

Whatever Happened to the Power of God. Michael L. Brown. 210p. (Orig.). 1991. pap. 8.99 (*1-56043-042-7*) Destiny Image.

Whatever Happened to "the Smiths" J. T. Wilson. 40p. 1994. pap. 10.00 (*1-885513-00-3*) Press Club.

Whatever Happened to the Wrath of God? John Muncy. 112p. (Orig.). 1995. pap. 6.95 (*0-9629625-5-4*) Ethnos.

***Whatever Happened to the Year of the Woman? Why Women Still Aren't Getting to the Top in Politics.** Amy H. Handlin. (Illus.). 200p. (Orig.). 1997. pap. 24.50 (*0-912869-22-4*) Arden Pr.

Whatever Happened to Uncle Albert? Sue Alexander. (Illus.). 128p. (J). (gr. 3-6). 1900. 14.95 (*0-395-29104-6*, Clarion Bks) HM.

Whatever Happened to Worship? Aiden W. Tozer. Ed. by Gerald B. Smith. LC 85-71185. 128p. (Orig.). 1985. pap. 8.99 (*0-87509-367-1*) Chr Pubns.

Whatever Happens to Little Women? Gender & Primary Schooling. Ed. by Christine Skelton. (Gender & Education Ser.). 160p. 1990. pap. 27.00 (*0-335-09239-X*, Open Univ Pr) Taylor & Francis.

Whatever It Takes. Jean L. Buchan. 398p. (Orig.). 1996. mass mkt. 5.99 (*1-55197-049-X*, Pub. by Comnwlth Pub CN) Partners Pubs Grp.

Whatever It Takes: A Journey into the Heart of Human Achievement Thoughts to Inspire & Celebrate Your Commitment to Excellence. Bob Moawad. (Gift of Inspiration Ser.). 172p. 1996. 12.95 (*0-9640178-3-0*) Compendium Inc.

Whatever It Takes: Decision Makers at Work. Morgan W. McCall, Jr. & Robert K. Kaplan. (Illus.). 144p. 1985. text ed. 27.00 (*0-13-952086-4*) P-H.

Whatever It Takes! Excellence in Family Support: When Families Experience a Disability. Susan B. Covert. LC 95-7831. (Illus.). 89p. (Orig.). 1995. pap. 25.00 (*1-883302-08-0*) Trning Res.

***Whatever It Takes: The Real Struggle for Political Power in America.** Elizabeth Drew. LC 97-10423. 1997. pap. 25.95 (*0-670-87536-8*) Viking Penguin.

Whatever It Takes: The Realities of Managerial Decision Making. 2nd ed. McCall. 1989. pap. text ed. 36.40 (*0-13-952136-4*) P-H.

Whatever Mother Says. Clarkson. 1995. mass mkt. 5.99 (*0-312-95542-1*) St Martin.

Whatever Next. Adam McLean. (Illus.). 193p. (Orig.). 1992. pap. 9.95 (*0-948747-09-9*) Grosvenor USA.

Whatever Next? Thomson. (J). 10.95 (*0-7136-3062-0*, 91522, Pub. by A&C Black UK) Talman.

***Whatever! Notes.** Running Press Staff. 1996. pap. text ed. 3.95 (*1-56138-694-4*) Running Pr.

Whatever Possessed the President? Academic Experts & Presidential Policy, 1960-1988. Robert C. Wood. LC 92-41985. 224p. (C). 1993. pap. 15.95 (*0-87023-863-9*) U of Mass Pr.

Whatever Tomorrow Brings. Lori Wick. 250p. 1992. pap. 8.99 (*0-89081-969-6*) Harvest Hse.

Whatever You Resolve to Be: Essays on Stonewall Jackson. A. Wilson Greene. (Illus.). 186p. (C). 1992. 22.50 (*0-935523-27-8*) Butternut & Blue.

Whatever's Happening to Women? Julia Neuberger. 218p. 1992. pap. 19.95 (*1-85626-046-1*) Trafalgar.

Whatley's Quest. Bruce Whatley & Rosie Smith. (Illus.). 56p. (J). (ps-2). 1995. 14.95 (*0-06-026291-5*) HarpC Child Bks.

***Whatley's Quest: A Magical Word Adventure.** Bruce Watley. (Illus.). (J). (gr. 1-5). 39.95 incl. cd-rom (*0-06-264013-5*) HarpC.

***What'll We Do with the Baby-O?** Lockman. Date not set. pap. 15.95 (*0-8050-4286-5*) St Martin.

What'll We Do with This Life? Selected Poems by Karl Krolow, 1950-1990. Karl Krolow. Tr. by Stuart Friebert from GER. LC 92-54881. 128p. (ENG.). 1993. 26.50 (*0-8386-3509-1*) Fairleigh Dickinson.

What'll We Do with Weird Uncle Will? VeraLee Wiggins. LC 92-26310. 1993. pap. 5.99 (*0-8280-0695-4*) Review & Herald.

What'll We Watch Tonight? Edward Kunnes. 256p. (Orig.). 1995. pap. 9.95 (*1-884550-05-3*) Wide World-Tetra.

What'll You Have: Fifty Plus Non-Alcoholic Drinks for Brunch, Lunch & Dinner. Ed. by Cynthia Parsons. 52p. (Orig.). 1986. pap. 5.00 (*0-9617872-0-1*) VT Schoolhse Pr.

***What's a Bear Supposed to Do?** Illus. by Linda Worrall. (Toddlers' First Stories Ser.). 12p. (J). (ps up). 1997. bds. 2.98 (*1-85854-662-1*) Brimax Bks.

***What's a Bear Supposed to Wear?** Illus. by Linda Worrall. (Toddlers' First Stories Ser.). 12p. (J). (ps up). 1997. bds. 2.98 (*1-85854-661-3*) Brimax Bks.

What's a Coal Miner to Do? The Mechanization of Coal Mining. Keith Dix. LC 88-1337. (Social & Labor History Ser.). (Illus.). 272p. 1988. 49.95 (*0-8229-3585-6*) U of Pittsburgh Pr.

***What's a Commie Ever Done to Black People? A Korean War Memoir of Fighting in the U.S. Army's Last All Negro Unit.** Curtis Morrow. LC 97-35102. (Illus.). 138p. 1997. 23.95 (*0-7864-0333-0*) McFarland & Co.

***What's a Daring Detective Like Me Doing in the Dog House?** Linda Bailey. LC 97-25358. (Stevie Diamond Mysteries Ser.: Vol. 5). 200p. (J). (gr. 4-7). 1997. pap. 4.50 (*0-8075-8835-0*) A Whitman.

***What's a Daring Detective Like Me Doing in the Dog House?, Vol. 5.** Linda Bailey. LC 97-25358. (Stevie Diamond Mysteries Ser.: Vol. 5). 200p. (J). (gr. 4-7). 1997. lib. bdg. 13.95 (*0-8075-8834-2*) A Whitman.

What's a Diurnal? Maxine Taylor. 64p. 1976. 8.00 (*0-86690-204-X*, T1474-014) Am Fed Astrologers.

What's a Duck Like You Doing in a Place Like This? Deborah Lanni. (Illus.). iv, 23p. (Orig.). (J). (gr. 3-6). 1984. pap. 2.00 (*0-942788-12-5*) Iris Visual.

What's a Girl Gotta Do? Sparkle Hayter. LC 93-17896. 270p. 1994. 19.95 (*1-56947-000-6*) Soho Press.

What's a Girl Gotta Do? Sparkle Hayter. 288p. 1995. pap. 5.95 (*0-14-024481-6*, Penguin Bks) Viking Penguin.

What's a Heaven For? Juanita Kirk. LC 92-45559. 64p. 1993. pap. 12.95 (*0-7734-2798-8*, Mellen Poetry Pr) E Mellen.

***What's a Kid Like Me.** (YA). 1992. pap. write for info. (*0-89693-114-5*, Chariot Bks) Chariot Victor.

What's a Kid Like Me Doing in a Family Like This? Leader's Book. Karen Dockrey. 72p. (YA). (gr. 7-9). 1992. pap. 1.00 (*0-89693-113-7*, 6-1113) SP Pubns.

***What's a Nice Girl Like You Doing in a Place Like This?** Joan Lunden. Date not set. write for info. (*0-688-04944-3*) Morrow.

What's a Nice God Like You Doing in a Place Like This? Ron Birk. 110p. 1991. pap. 10.00 (*0-9629331-0-4*) Golden Goat.

What's a Nice God Like You Doing in a Place Like This? Wesley D. Tracy. 120p. (J). 1990. pap. 7.99 (*0-8341-1371-6*) Beacon Hill.

What's a Nice Harvard Boy Like You. Wolff. 24.95 (*0-8488-1545-9*) Amereon Ltd.

***What's a Nice Republican Girl Like Me Doing in the ACLU?** Sheila S. Kennedy. 1997. pap. 16.95 (*1-57392-143-2*) Prometheus Bks.

What's a Parent to Do? C. S. Lovett. 1971. pap. 8.45 (*0-938148-27-3*) Prsnl Christianity.

***What's a Parent to Do? Becoming a Christlike Mom or Dad.** Glenn Latham. 1997. 15.95 (*0-614-27499-0*) Deseret Bk.

***What's a Penguin Doing in a Place Like This?** Miriam Schlein. LC 96-28803. (Illus.). 64p. (J). (gr. 2-4). 1997. lib. bdg. 17.90 (*0-7613-0003-1*) Millbrook Pr.

What's a Relocated Chart? Maxine Taylor. 11p. 1976. 6.00 (*0-86690-205-8*, T1475-014) Am Fed Astrologers.

What's a Right Turn. Matthew V. Smith. (Illus.). 13p. (J). (gr. k-3). 1993. pap. 12.95 (*1-895583-56-X*) MAYA Pubs.

What's a Saint, Brother? Paula Fitzgerald & Edwrd Fitzgerald. 115p. 1991. pap. 7.50 (*0-935915-13-3*) Corinth Pub.

What's a Sampler. Freff. 48p. 1989. pap. 5.95 (*0-88188-883-4*, 00330004) H Leonard.

***What's a Schwa Sound Anyway & Why Should I Care? A Holistic Guide to Phonetics, Phonics & Spelling.** LC 97-602. 1997. pap. text ed. write for info. (*0-435-08865-3*, 08865) Heinemann.

What's a Sequencer: A Basic Guide to Their Features & Use. Greg R. Starr. Ed. by Jon Eiche. LC 90-53369. (Hi Tech Bks.). 64p. (Orig.). 1990. pap. 5.95 (*0-7935-0083-4*, 00330045) H Leonard.

What's a Smart Woman Like You Doing at Home? 2nd rev. ed. Linda Burton et al. LC 92-22259. 170p. (Orig.). 1993. pap. 8.95 (*0-9631188-1-1*) Mothers at Home.

What's a Synthesizer? J. Eiche. 64p. (SPA.). 1992. per. 5.95 (*0-7935-1926-8*, 00183854) H Leonard.

What's a Synthesizer: Simple Answers to Common Questions about the New Technology. Jon F. Eiche. 64p. (Orig.). 1987. pap. 5.95 (*0-88188-671-8*, 00183855) H Leonard.

What's a Teen to Do? Developing Helping Skills with 14 to 16 Year Olds. John A. Flanagan. 135p. (Orig.). 1989. pap. 6.95 (*0-86716-119-1*) St Anthony Mess Pr.

What's a Virus, Anyway? The Kids' Book about AIDS. David Fassler & Kelly McQueen. LC 89-40719. (Illus.). 85p. (Orig.). (J). (ps-6). 1990. pap. 8.95 (*0-914525-15-8*); spiral bd. 10.95 (*0-914525-14-X*) Waterfront Bks.

***What's a Woman Doing Here?** Dickey Chapelle. Date not set. write for info. (*0-688-04453-0*) Morrow.

What's a Woman to Do in Church? David R. Nicholas. 148p. 1979. 7.99 (*0-88469-123-3*) BMH Bks.

***What's a Zubble-Wump?** Dr. Seuss. (Lift-&-Peek-a-Board Bks.). (J). 1997. 4.99 (*0-679-88615-X*) Random Bks Yng Read.

What's above the Sky? A Book about the Planets. Caroline A. Glyman. LC 92-10247. (First Ser.). (Illus.). 32p. (J). (gr. k-3). 1992. lib. bdg. 12.95 (*1-878363-76-X*) Forest Hse.

What's Age Got to Do With It? Changing Lifestyles in the 90s. Shirley Zarrilli. 176p. (Orig.). 1996. pap. 19.95 (*0-931673-07-0*) J March Pub Grp.

What's Ahead? Charles Harris. LC 80-84173. (Radiant Life Ser.). 128p. (Orig.). 1982. pap. 3.95 (*0-88243-897-2*, 02-0897) Gospel Pub.

What's Ahead? W. Charles Harris. LC 80-84173. (Radiant Life Ser.). 128p. (Orig.). 1982. teacher ed., pap. 5.50 (*0-88243-195-1*, 32-0195) Gospel Pub.

What's Ahead & Meanwhile. Edward S. Martin. LC 74-156688. (Essay Index Reprint Ser.). 1977. reprint ed. 23.95 (*0-8369-2325-1*) Ayer.

***What's Alice Up to?** Harley Jessup. LC 97-8822. 1997. pap. 14.99 (*0-670-87396-9*) Viking Penguin.

What's Alive? Kathleen W. Zoehfeld. LC 94-11450. (Let's-Read-&-Find-Out Science Ser.). (Illus.). 32p. (J). (ps-1). 1995. 14.95 (*0-06-023443-1*); pap. 4.95 (*0-06-445132-1*, Trophy); lib. bdg. 14.89 (*0-06-023444-X*) HarpC Child Bks.

What's Anarchism. Hippolyte Havel. 1973. 59.95 (*0-8490-1288-0*) Gordon Pr.

What's at the Beach? Peter Seymour. LC 84-81819. (Illus.). 18p. (J). (ps). 1985. 7.95 (*0-03-002557-5*, Bks Young Read) H Holt & Co.

What's at the Beach? A Lift-the-Flap, Pop-up Book. rev. ed. Peter Seymour. LC 84-81819. (Illus.). 18p. (J). (ps-2). 1993. 11.95 (*0-8050-2869-2*, Bks Young Read) H Holt & Co.

What's (Bad) Good about Divorce? 1977. James R. Snyder. LC 77-84446. (Illus.). 23p. (J). 1977. 6.95 (*0-9601452-1-4*) FIG Ltd.

What's Become of Eden: Poems of Family at Century's End. Ed. by Stephanie Strickland. 80p. (Orig.). 1994. pap. 10.00 (*0-9624178-4-X*) Slapering Hol.

What's Behind the Research? Discovering Hidden Assumptions in the Behavioral Sciences. Brent D. Slife & Richard N. Williams. 232p. (C). 1995. 38.00 (*0-8039-5862-5*); pap. 17.95 (*0-8039-5863-3*) Sage.

What's Best for Kids: A Guide to Developmentally Appropriate Practices for Teacher & Parents of Children. Anthony Coletta. 175p. (Orig.). 1991. pap. text ed. 14.95 (*0-935493-23-9*, RRB 456) Modern Learn Pr.

What's Best for Kids: A Guide to Developmentally Appropriate Practices for Teachers & Parents. Anthony J. Coletta. 1992. pap. 14.95 (*0-935493-43-3*) Programs Educ.

***What's Best for Me: An Anger Control Program for Young Children.** Ken Smith. LC 95-75126. (Illus.). 24p. (J). (ps-2). 1995. pap. 14.95 (*1-884063-49-7*) Mar Co Prods.

What's Black & White & Came to Visit? Evan Levine. LC 93-46418. (Illus.). 32p. (J). (ps-2). 1994. 15.95 (*0-531-06852-8*) Orchard Bks Watts.

What's Bothering You? George Rich. (New Life Ser.). 24p. 1991. teacher ed. 1.95 (*0-87227-162-5*, RBP5186); student ed., pap. text ed. 1.95 (*0-87227-155-2*, RBP5187) Reg Baptist.

What's Bred in the Bone. Robertson Davies. 348p. 1986. pap. 11.95 (*0-14-009711-2*, Penguin Bks) Viking Penguin.

***What's Brewing in New England.** Kate Cone. LC 97-313. (Illus.). 224p. (Orig.). 1997. pap. 12.95 (*0-89272-387-4*) Down East.

What's Brewing in the East Bay, Vol. 1: Espresso Guide & Coupon Book. Thomas P. Steinbrecher. Ed. by Kathleen M. Ladra. (Orig.). 1993. pap. 9.95 (*0-9639291-0-0*) K C Pubng.

What's Bugging Me? Identifying & Controlling Household Pests in Hawai'i. JoAnn M. Tenorio & Gordon M. Nishida. LC 95-10158. (Illus.). 160p. (Orig.). 1995. pap. 18.95 (*0-8248-1742-7*) UH Pr.

***What's Bugging You?** James Preller. (Kratts' Creatures Ser.). 1997. pap. 3.50 (*0-590-53742-3*) Scholastic Inc.

What's Called Love: A Real Romance. Jim Paul. 1993. 19.00 (*0-685-63495-7*, Villard Bks) Random.

What's Cheap & Free in Michigan. 2nd rev. ed. Bill Bailey. 400p. 1995. pap. 12.95 (*1-881139-05-0*) Glovebox Guidebks.

What's Claude Doing? Dick Gackenbach. LC 83-14983. (Illus.). 32p. (J). (ps-3). 1986. pap. 5.95 (*0-89919-464-8*, Clarion Bks) HM.

What's Conscience For? Robert Hodge. 320p. 1994. pap. 35.00 (*0-85439-504-0*, Pub. by St Paul Pubns UK) St Mut.

What's Cookin'? A Collection of Recipes & Nostalgia. Kathleen Freeman. 742p. 1989. pap. text ed. write for info. (*0-9624259-0-7*) K Freeman.

What's Cookin' at Bell: The Bell Family's Cookbook. Becky Ownby. 269p. 1995. 16.95 (*0-9649191-0-9*) Beckys Busn.

What's Cookin' in Alabama! (Orig.). pap. text ed. write for info. (*1-56944-085-9*) Terrell Missouri.

What's Cookin' in Arizona! More than 240 Recipes from Arizona Celebrities & Personalities. Sandy Bruce. LC 93-37691. 256p. 1993. pap. 9.95 (*0-914846-88-4*) Golden West Pub.

***What's Cookin' up on Capitol Hill: Recipes from Congress.** Ed. by J. David Schenken. (Illus.). 136p. (Orig.). 1996. pap. 12.95 (*1-889783-00-5*) Pennythrift.

What's Cooking. Beth Esh. (HRL Little Bks.). (Illus.). 8p. (Orig.). (J). (ps-1). 1996. pap. text ed. 10.95 (*1-57332-035-8*) HighReach Lrning.

What's Cooking? Shelley Harwayne. LC 95-35352. (Illus.). (J). 1996. pap. write for info. (*1-57255-122-4*) Mondo Pubng.

What's Cooking. John Light. LC 90-34355. (Light Reading Ser.). (J). (gr. 4 up). 1991. 3.99 (*0-85953-337-9*) Childs Play.

***What's Cooking?** John Light. (ITA.). (J). 1991. 3.99 (*0-85953-601-7*) Childs Play.

What's Cooking. large type ed. Beth Esh. (HRL Big Bks.). (Illus.). 8p. (Orig.). (J). (ps-1). 1996. pap. text ed. 10.95 (*1-57332-036-6*) HighReach Lrning.

What's Cooking? Favorite Recipes from Around the World. Ruth A. Hayward & Margaret B. Warner. (J). (gr. 4 up). 1981. 16.95 (*0-316-35252-7*) Little.

What's Cooking? Italian Style. Anne Fraulo. 136p. 1986. pap. 6.00 (*0-9616577-0-7*) A Fraulo.

W

What's Cooking - Que Se Cocina en Puerto Rico: An English-Spanish Cookbook. Ed. by Barbara Ezratty. Tr. by Sonia Hirsch from ENG. (Illus.). 222p. 1994. spiral bd. 14.95 (0-942929-06-3) Omni Arts.

***What's Cooking America.** 2nd ed. Linda Stradley & Andra Cook. LC 95-92570. (Illus.). 434p. 1997. reprint ed. pap. 21.95 (1-885221-55-X) BookPartners.

What's Cooking at Moody's Diner: 60 Years of Recipes & Reminiscences. Nancy Genthner. (Illus.). 128p. 1989. pap. 8.95 (0-88448-075-5) Tilbury Hse.

What's Cooking at the Cooper Clinic. Cooper Clinic, Nutrition Department Staff. 1992. pap. 14.95 (0-9633862-0-4) Its Cooking.

What's Cooking "Down Home" Eileen Mears. (Illus.). 494p. (Orig.). 1994. spiral bd. 16.50 (0-9641341-0-1) E Mears.

What's Cooking in Congress?, Vol. I. Ed. by Harry Barba & Marian Barba. LC 79-83777. (Illus.). 144p. (J). (gr. 5 up). 1979. pap. 9.95 (0-911906-15-0) Harian Creative Bks.

What's Cooking in Congress?, Vol. II. Ed. by Harry Barba & Marian Barba. LC 79-83777. (What's Cooking Ser.). (Illus.). 250p. 1982. 24.95 (0-911906-20-7, 0278-4947); pap. 11.95 (0-911906-21-5) Harian Creative Bks.

What's Cooking in Kentucky. 4th ed. Irene Hayes. 416p. 1994. spiral bd. 19.95 (0-938402-10-2) T I Hayes Pub Co.

What's Cooking in Multicultural America? An Annotated Bibliographic Guide to over Four Hundred Ethnic Cuisines. Vladimir F. Wertsman. 164p. 1996. 37.50 (0-8108-3127-9) Scarecrow.

What's Cooking in Our National Parks? Cookbook Committee, National Park Service, Western Region Staff. LC 89-8541. (Illus.). 254p. 1989. reprint ed. pap. 12.95 (0-89646-081-9) Vistabooks.

What's Cooking in Philadelphia: A Collection of Favorites Recipes-Cookbook. Philadelphia Rotary Club Members & Wives. Ed. by Claudie Brock. (Illus.). 224p. 1987. write for info. (0-9619470-0-4) Rotary Club Phila.

What's Cooking in the Zonta World. Zonta Club of Tampa Staff. 1994. text ed. 30.00 (0-9640759-0-3); pap. text ed. 15.00 (0-9640759-1-1) Zonta Club.

What's Cooking in Towne & Country U. S. A., Vol. I. Lois A. Weist. (Special Collectors' Keepsake Ser.). (Illus.). 240p. 1979. 14.99 (0-938166-00-X) Weist Pub OH.

What's Cooking in Towne & Country U. S. A., Vol. 2. Lois A. Weist. (Special Collectors' Keepsake Ser.). (Illus.). 14.99 (0-685-57249-8) Weist Pub OH.

What's Cooking in Westchester. 192p. 1986. 10.00 (0-318-20546-7) Am Cancer Westchester.

What's Cooking in Western Colorado, Vol. 1. Crossroads United Methodist Church Congregation Staff. Ed. by Mildred J. Groen & Rosalee Holton. LC 89-85767. (Illus.). 300p. (Orig.). 1989. pap. 12.95 (0-9624514-0-1) Crossroads United Meth Ch.

***What's Cooking Inn Arizona: A Recipe Guidebook of the Arizona Association of Bed & Breakfast Innkeepers.** Tracy Winters & Phyllis Winters. LC 96-60992. (Illus.). 96p. (Orig.). 1996. pap. 12.95 (1-883651-03-4) Winters IN.

What's Cooking, Jenny Archer? Ellen Conford. (J). (ps-3). 1991. mass mkt. 3.95 (0-316-15357-5) Little.

What's Creative about Creative Writing? John E. Westburg. pap. 8.00 (0-87423-018-7) Westburg.

What's Different? (Look & Learn Ser.). (Illus.). 24p. (J). 1993. 7.98 (1-56173-907-3, Anchor NY) Pubns Intl Ltd.

What's Different? Istar Schwager. (Look & Learn Ser.). (Illus.). 24p. (J). (ps-3). 1993. lib. bdg. 12.95 (1-56674-070-3, HTS Bks) Forest Hse.

What's "Drunk," Mama? (Illus.). 30p. (J). (ps-5). 1977. 1.25 (0-910034-64-8) Al-Anon.

What's Eating Gilbert Grape? Peter Hedges. 1994. mass mkt. 5.99 (0-671-87080-7) PB.

What's English in Departments of English? Pepper Worthington. (Illus.). 77p. (Orig.). 1994. pap. 15.00 (1-880994-20-8) Mt Olive Coll Pr.

What's Ethical in Business? Verne E. Henderson. 232p. 1992. text ed. 19.95 (0-07-028173-4) McGraw.

What's Fair? American Beliefs about Distributive Justice. Jennifer L. Hochschild. 357p. 1986. pap. 15.95 (0-674-95087-9) HUP.

What's Fair? America's Beliefs about Distributive Justice. Jennifer L. Hochschild. LC 81-6272. (Illus.). 357p. (C). 1981. 37.00 (0-674-95086-0) HUP.

***What's Faster Than a Speeding Cheetah?** Robert E. Wells. LC 96-54491. (J). 1997. pap. write for info. (0-8075-2281-3) A Whitman.

***What's Faster Than a Speeding Cheetah?** Robert E. Wells. LC 96-54491. (J). (gr. 1-4). 1997. 14.95 (0-8075-2280-5) A Whitman.

***What's Food Got to Do with It? 101 Natural Remedies for Learning Disabilities.** Sandra Hills & Pat Wyman. LC 96-92935. (Illus.). 128p. (Orig.). 1997. pap. 12.95 (1-890047-24-4) Ctr New Discv Lrng.

What's for Breakfast? Light & Easy Morning Meals for Busy People. Donna S. Roy & Kathleen Flores. Ed. by Faith Winchester & Linda Hachfeld. (Illus.). 286p. 1994. pap. 13.95 (0-9620471-4-7) Appletree MN.

What's for Dinner? Lynn Salem & Josie Stewart. (Illus.). 12p. (J). (gr. k-1). 1992. pap. 3.50 (1-880612-09-7) Seedling Pubns.

What's for Dinner? James Schuyler. LC 78-16914. 180p. (Orig.). 1978. pap. 10.00 (0-87685-381-5) Black Sparrow.

What's for Dinner? A Family Meal Planner. Trisha Wadle. 135p. 1995. 12.95 (0-9644995-0-9) Kitchen Cupboard.

What's for Dinner? A Guide to Preparing 30 Meals in One Day. Brenda Bennett. (Illus.). vii, 108p. 1996. reprint ed. ring bd. 18.95 (0-9651526-0-X, WFD-011) Natural Selections.

What's for Dinner? And Other Stories. 140p. (J). (ps-1). 1994. 17.95 (0-340-58988-4, Pub. by H & S UK); pap. 6.95 (0-340-58996-5, Pub. by H & S UK) Trafalgar.

***What's for Dinner: 200 Delicious Recipes That Work Every Time.** Maryana Vollstedt. LC 96-37107. 1997. pap. 11.95 (0-8118-1395-9) Chronicle Bks.

***What's for Lunch?** Arch Books Staff. 1997. 1.99 (0-570-07537-8) Concordia.

What's for Lunch? Cindy Chang. 1996. 3.99 (0-679-87822-X) Random.

What's for Lunch? John Schindel. LC 93-48621. (Illus.). 1994. lib. bdg. 14.93 (0-688-13599-4) Lothrop.

What's for Lunch? John Schindel. LC 93-48621. (Illus.). (J). 1994. 15.00 (0-688-13598-6) Lothrop.

What's for Lunch Charley? A Study Guide. Joyce Friedland & Rikki Kessler. (Novel-Ties Ser.). 1982. teacher ed., wbk. ed., pap. text ed. 15.95 (0-88122-011-6) Lrn Links.

What's God Have to Do with It? 384p. (Orig.). 1993. pap. 14.99 (0-929239-76-8) Discovery Hse Pubs.

What's Going On? Ed. by Francis E. Abernethy. (Texas Folklore Society Publications: Vol. 40). (Illus.). 1976. 20.00 (0-88426-049-6) Encino Pr.

What's Going On? Rozanne L. Williams. (Emergent Reader Big Bks.). (Illus.). 8p. (Orig.). (J). (gr. k-2). 1995. pap. 7.98 (1-57471-010-9) Creat Teach Pr.

What's Going On?, Level 1. Rozanne L. Williams. (Emergent Reader Science Ser.). 8p. 1994. 1.59 (0-916119-24-6, 3500) Creat Teach Pr.

What's Going On? Language Learning Episodes in British & American Classrooms, Grades 4-13. Ed. by Mary Barr et al. LC 81-18119. (Illus.). 240p. (C). 1982. pap. text ed. 18.50 (0-86709-013-8, 0013) Boynton Cook Pubs.

***What's Going On? Personal Essays.** Nathan McCall. LC 97-18520. 1997. 21.00 (0-679-45589-2) Random.

***What's Going On: Stories of Life.** Greg Lopez. 1996. pap. 17.95 (0-9654695-0-6) Bohland Pub.

What's Going on among the Lutherans? A Comparison of Beliefs. Patsy A. Leppien & J. Kincaid Smith. LC 92-80393. 400p. (Orig.). 1992. pap. 11.99 (0-8100-0427-5, 15N0544) Northwest Pub.

What's Going on Here? Complementary Studies of Professional Talk. Allen D. Grimshaw et al. Ed. by Roy O. Freedle. (Advances in Discourse Processes Ser.: Vol. 43). 576p. (C). 1994. pap. 42.50 (0-89391-929-2); text ed. 89.95 (0-89391-746-X) Ablex Pub.

***What's Going on Here? Complementary Studies of Professional Talk.** (Advances in Discourse Processes Ser.: Vol. 43). 1994. text ed. 78.50 (0-614-30972-7) Ablex Pub.

What's Going to Happen? Answering Your Prophetic Questions. Carl G. Johnson. LC 92-6597. 216p. (Orig.). 1992. pap. text ed. 11.95 (0-87227-173-0, RBP5206) Reg Baptist.

What's Going to Happen: Stories about Neglect, Physical Abuse & Sexual Abuse. Eunice H. Hannah. LC 93-81152. (Illus.). 28p. (Orig.). (J). (gr. 1-4). 1993. pap. 6.95 (1-884063-17-9) Mar Co Prods.

***What's Going to Happen in 1997 in Hong Kong? Everything You Wanted to Know.** Thomas & Nicole Turner. 1997. pap. 19.95 (0-13-647223-0) P-H.

What's Good: Describing Your Public Library's Effectiveness. Thomas A. Childers & Nancy A. Van House. LC 93-3683. (Illus.). 94p. (Orig.). 1993. pap. text ed. 25.00 (0-8389-0617-6) ALA.

What's Good About the Good News? The Plan of Salvation in a New Light. Neal Punt. LC 87-63576. 156p. (Orig.). 1988. pap. 8.95 (0-945315-07-4) Northland Bks.

What's Good to Eat: The Best of Northwest Ohio. Public Broadcasting Foundation of Northwest Ohio Staff. 200p. 1995. 24.95 (0-9649111-0-8) Public Broadcsting.

What's Growing under Your Bed? Martha Bolton. (YA). 1986. 8.99 (0-685-68720-1, MP-634) Lillenas.

***What's Growing under Your Bed? A Collection of Sketches & Monologues for Children & Young Teens.** 75p. 1986. 8.99 (0-8341-9621-2) Lillenas.

What's Happening. Jimmy S. Baca. LC 82-5089. 36p. (Orig.). 1982. pap. 5.95 (0-915306-27-1) Curbstone.

What's Happening: A Manifesto for the Future: a Human Affairs Manifesto of Individual & Social Behaviors with Two Hundred Questions & Answers to Help People Adapt to Changes in the Twenty-First Century. Edward M. Cummings. LC 93-3722. 1993. 34.95 (0-9636276-0-0) Cummings Assocs.

What's Happening in Math Class, Vol. 1. Deborah Schifter. (Series on School Reform: Vol. 1). 240p. (C). 1995. text ed. 42.00 (0-8077-3482-9); pap. text ed. 18.95 (0-8077-3481-0) Tchrs Coll.

What's Happening in Math Class Vol. II: Reconstructing Professional Identities. Deborah Schifter. (Series on School Reform). 216p. (C). 1995. pap. text ed. 18.95 (0-8077-3483-7) Tchrs Coll.

What's Happening in Math Class Vol. II: Reconstructing Professional Identities. Deborah Schifter. (Series on School Reform: Vol. II). 216p. (C). 1995. text ed. 42.00 (0-8077-3484-5) Tchrs Coll.

***What's Happening in Utah Schools? Our Children in Crisis.** Ruth B. Lehenbauer. (Illus.). 80p. (Orig.). 1996. pap. 5.98 (0-9656244-0-4) R B Lehenbauer.

***What's Happening to Americans' Income?, BG138.** W. Michael Cox & Beverly J. Fox. 11p. 1996. pap. 5.00 (1-56808-069-7) Natl Ctr Pol.

What's Happening to India? Punjab, Ethnic Conflict & the Test for Federalism. 2nd ed. Robin Jeffrey. 252p. (C). 1994. text ed. 45.00 (0-8419-1350-1); pap. text ed. 20.00 (0-8419-1351-X) Holmes & Meier.

What's Happening to Me? Peter Mayle. LC 75-14410. (Illus.). 56p. (J). (gr. 3 up). 1975. 12.00 (0-8184-0221-0); pap. 6.95 (0-8184-0312-8) Carol Pub Group.

What's Happening to My Body? Book for Boys: A Growing Up Guide for Parents & Sons. rev. ed. Lynda Madaras & Dane Saavedra. LC 87-28116. (Illus.). 288p. 1991. pap. 11.95 (0-937858-99-4) Newmarket.

What's Happening to My Body? Book for Boys: A Growing Up Guide for Parents & Sons. 2nd rev. ed. Lynda Madaras & Dane Saavedra. LC 87-28116. (Illus.). 288p. 1991. 18.95 (1-55704-002-8) Newmarket.

What's Happening to My Body? Book for Girls: A Growing Up Guide for Parents & Daughters. rev. ed. Lynda Madaras & Area Madaras. LC 87-28117. (Illus.). 304p. 1991. pap. 11.95 (0-937858-98-6) Newmarket.

What's Happening to My Body? Book for Girls: A Growing Up Guide for Parents & Daughters. rev. ed. Lynda Madaras & Area Madaras. LC 87-28117. (Illus.). 304p. 1997. 18.95 (1-55704-001-X) Newmarket.

What's Happening to My Junior Year? Judith S. St. George. 176p. 1987. pap. 2.50 (0-380-70376-9, Flare) Avon.

What's Happening to the American Family? Tensions, Hopes, Realities. rev. ed. Sar A. Levitan et al. LC 87-46304. (Illus.). 240p. 1988. reprint ed. pap. 68.40 (0-8357-8374-X, 2034132) Bks Demand.

What's Happening to the Ozone Layer? Isaac Asimov. LC 92-5347. (Ask Isaac Asimov Ser.). (Illus.). 24p. (J). (gr. 1-8). 1993. lib. bdg. 17.27 (0-8368-0795-2) Gareth Stevens Inc.

What's Happening to U. S. Banking? ...How You Can Be Protected. Marshall E. Surratt. (Illus.). 280p. 1993. 24.95 (0-9635525-0-3) Comm Pubs.

***What's Hazardous in Our Home?** unabridged ed. Ann M. Wolf & Anna H. Spitz. (Environmental Ser.). (Illus.). 93p. (Orig.). (J). (gr. 6-8). 1996. pap. 9.50 (0-9651084-1-4) Tyris Environ.

***What's He So Angry About?** David Stoop. 1996. pap. 9.99 (0-345-40780-6, Moorings) Ballantine.

***What's Hecuba To Him? Fictional Events & Actual Emotions.** E. M. Dadlez. LC 96-42211. 1997. 35.00 (0-271-01650-7); pap. 16.95 (0-271-01651-5) Pa St U Pr.

What's Hecuba to Him or He to Hecuba? Nanni Cagnone. Tr. by David Verzoni. LC 75-4969. 183p. (ENG & ITA.). 1975. 7.95 (0-915570-01-7) Oolp Pr.

What's Hiding Here? (Lift the Flap Bks.). 12p. (J). 1995. 4.95 (0-7894-0221-1, 5-70634) DK Pub Inc.

What's In. Tony Tallarico. (Tuffy Tiny Bks.). (Illus.). 28p. (J). (ps). 1992. bds. 3.95 (0-448-40427-3, G&D) Putnam Pub Group.

What's in a Box? Kelly Boivin. LC 91-4062. (Rookie Reader Ser.). (Illus.). 32p. (J). (ps-2). 1991. pap. 3.50 (0-516-42010-0); lib. bdg. 15.00 (0-516-02010-2) Childrens.

What's in a Doctor's Bag. Neil B. Shulman. (Illus.). (Orig.). (J). (ps-3). 1994. pap. 8.95 (0-9639002-3-4) N Shulman.

What's in a Name? Peter Filichia. 224p. (YA). (gr. 7 up). 1988. pap. 2.75 (0-380-75536-X, Flare) Avon.

What's in a Name? Linda Francis et al. (Orig.). 1982. mass mkt. 4.99 (0-8423-7935-5) Tyndale.

What's in a Name? Advertising & the Concept of Brands. John P. Jones. LC 85-45039. 292p. 27.95 (0-669-11142-2, Lexington) Jossey-Bass.

What's in a Name? An Engaging & Whimsical Look at the Lore, Legends, Symbolism & Psychology of Names. Paul Dixon. LC 96-50257. 1996. pap. 14.95 (0-87779-613-0) Merriam-Webster Inc.

What's in a Name? Everything You Wanted to Know. rev. ed. Leonard Ashley. 265p. 1996. pap. 17.95 (0-8063-1261-0) Genealog Pub.

***What's in a Name? Including African Names & Their Meanings.** Reuben O. Perechi. 102p. (Orig.). 1996. pap. 14.95 (0-9653372-0-0) Sina Invest.

What's in a Name? Unaitwaje? A Swahili Book of Names. Sharifa M. Zawawi. LC 93-14859. (Illus.). 98p. 1993. 24.95 (0-86543-290-2); pap. 9.95 (0-86543-291-0) Africa World.

***What's in a Name...Calgary?, Vol. II.** Donna M. Humber. 200p. (Orig.). 1997. pap. 18.95 (1-55059-154-1, Pub. by Detselig CN) Temeron Bks.

What's in a Nickname? Ray Franks. LC 82-90195. (Illus.). 208p. (Orig.). 1982. pap. 12.95 (0-943976-00-6) R Franks Ranch.

What's in a Number? Numerology Tells It All. George Pierson. LC 96-15844. (Illus.). 24p. 1996. bds., pap. 12.95 (0-7892-0168-2) Abbeville Pr.

***What's in a Prehistoric Forest.** Peter Seymour. (GRE.). (J). 1991. 11.99 (0-85953-850-8) Childs Play.

What's in a Relative? Household & Family in Formentera. Joan Bestard-Camps. (Explorations in Anthropology Ser.). 230p. 1991. 24.95 (0-85496-586-6) Berg Pubs.

What's in a Word? Reading & Vocabulary Building. S. Eckstut & K. Sorensen. 1992. pap. text ed. 20.67 (0-8013-0624-8, 78563); audio 24.95 (0-8013-0923-9, 79188) Longman.

***What's in a Word: 40 Words of Jesus for the 40 Days of Lent.** David Winter. 144p. 1996. pap. 8.95 (0-687-00250-8) Abingdon.

What's in an Ambulance. Sue Kassirer. (J). 1996. pap. 2.50 (0-679-87153-5) Random Bks Yng Read.

***What's in an Ocean.** Sandra J. Geisel-Churchill. (Illus.). 15p. (Orig.). (J). (gr. 1-3). 1997. pap. 8.99 (1-55197-709-5, Pub. by Comnwlth Pub CN) Partners Pubs Grp.

What's in Aunt Mary's Room? Elizabeth F. Howard. LC 94-4985. (Illus.). 32p. (J). 1996. 14.95 (0-395-69845-6, Clarion Bks) HM.

***What's in Dickie's House?** unabridged ed. Ann M. Wolf & Anna H. Spitz. (Environmental Ser.). (Illus.). 47p. (Orig.). (J). (ps-2). 1996. pap. 5.50 (0-9651084-4-9) Tyris Environ.

What's in Disguise? Mario Gomboli. LC 92-70227. (Illus.). 10p. (J). (ps-k). 1992. bds. 3.95 (1-56397-151-8) Boyds Mills Pr.

What's in Doctor's Bag? Hautzig. 1995. 2.50 (0-679-87152-7) Random.

What's in Fox's Sack? Paul Galdone. LC 81-10251. (Illus.). (J). (gr. 1-3). 1987. pap. 6.95 (0-89919-491-5, Clarion Bks) HM.

What's in It? The Busy Cook's Diet & Nutrition Guide to... Chef Paul Prudhomme's Louisiana Kitchen. Nutrinfo Corporation Staff. LC 91-62643. (Orig.). 1991. pap. text ed. 4.95 (1-56503-012-5) Nutrinfo.

What's in It? The Busy Cook's Diet & Nutrition Guide to... Crockery Cookery. Nutrinfo Corporation Staff. LC 91-62644. (Orig.). 1991. pap. text ed. 4.95 (1-56503-013-3) Nutrinfo.

What's in It? The Busy Cook's Diet & Nutrition Guide to... the Frugal Gourmet. Nutrinfo Corporation Staff. LC 91-62631. (Orig.). 1991. pap. text ed. 4.95 (1-56503-000-1); pap. text ed. 4.95 (1-56503-001-X); pap. text ed. 4.95 (1-56503-002-8); pap. text ed. 4.95 (1-56503-003-6); pap. text ed. 4.95 (1-56503-004-4); pap. text ed. 4.95 (1-56503-005-2); pap. text ed. 4.95 (1-56503-006-0); pap. text ed. 4.95 (1-56503-007-9); pap. text ed. 4.95 (1-56503-008-7); pap. text ed. 4.95 (1-56503-009-5); pap. text ed. 4.95 (1-56503-010-9); pap. text ed. 4.95 (1-56503-011-7); pap. text ed. 4.95 (1-56503-014-1) Nutrinfo.

***What's in It for Me.** Joseph Stedino & Dary Matera. 336p. 3.98 (0-8317-8041-X) Smithmark.

What's in It for Me: A Marketer's Guide to Establishing an Equal Partnership with Customers. Robin Woods. 224p. 1993. 24.95 (0-8144-5147-0) AMACOM.

What's in It for Us? A Guide to Chambers of Commerce. Pat Crockett. Ed. by David Dawson. 56p. (Orig.). 1993. pap. text ed. 10.95 (1-881096-06-8) Towery Pub.

What's in My Food: A Book of Nutrients. Xandria Williams. (Illus.). 320p. (Orig.). pap. write for info. (1-85327-017-2, Pub. by Prism Pr UK) Assoc Pubs Grp.

What's in My Garden? Book of Many Colors. (J). 1996. 5.98 (1-57082-429-0) Mouse Works.

***Whats in My Poc Riser.** Carter. (J). Date not set. write for info. (0-399-22267-7) Putnam Pub Group.

What's in My Pocket? Rozanne L. Williams. (Emergent Reader Big Bks.). 16p. (J). (gr. k-2). 1995. 11.98 (0-916119-83-1) Creat Teach Pr.

What's in My Pocket? Rozanne L. Williams. (Spanish Emergent Reader Bks.). (Illus.). 16p. (Orig.). (SPA.). (J). (gr. k-2). 1995. pap. 2.49 (1-57471-037-0) Creat Teach Pr.

What's in My Pocket?, Level 2. Rozanne L. Williams. (Emergent Reader Science Ser.). 16p. 1994. 2.49 (0-916119-45-9, 3535) Creat Teach Pr.

What's in My Pocket? A Pop-up & Peek-in Book. David A. Carter. (Illus.). 10p. (J). (ps). 1989. 10.95 (0-399-21685-5, Putnam) Putnam Pub Group.

What's in My Toy Box? Book of Many Colors. (J). 1996. 5.98 (1-57082-428-2) Mouse Works.

What's in My Tree. Ginny L. Winter. (Illus.). (J). (gr. k-1). 1962. 8.95 (0-8392-3044-3) Astor-Honor.

What's in Oscar's Trash Can? And Other Good-Night Stories. Michaela Muntean. (Sesame Street Good-Night Stories Ser.). (Illus.). (J). (ps-1). 1991. 3.25 (0-307-12342-1, Golden Pr) Western Pub.

What's in Our Food: Fact & Fiction about Fat & Fiber, Vitamins & Minerals, Nutrients & Contaminants. Mia Parsonnet. 145p. 1996. pap. 14.95 (1-56833-049-9) Madison Bks UPA.

What's in the Bible? A Concise Look at the 39 Books of the Hebrew Bible. Lillian C. Freudmann. LC 96-4776. 200p. 1996. 24.95 (1-56821-602-5) Aronson.

What's in the Box? (Lift the Flap Bks.). 12p. (J). 1995. 4.95 (0-7894-0305-6, 5-70665) DK Pub Inc.

What's in the Box? Bridget Gibbs. (J). 1990. 9.95 (1-55782-334-0, Warner Juvenile Bks) Little.

What's in the Cave? Peter Seymour. LC 84-81820. 18p. (J). (ps-2). 1985. 7.95 (0-03-002554-0, Bks Young Read) H Holt & Co.

What's in the Cave? A Lift-the-Flap, Pop-up Book. rev. ed. Peter Seymour. LC 84-81820. (Illus.). 18p. (J). (ps-2). 1993. 11.95 (0-8050-2868-4, Bks Young Read) H Holt & Co.

What's in the Dark? Charles Shaw. (Illus.). 32p. (J). (gr. k-4). 1991. 11.95 (0-938349-66-X); pap. 5.95 (0-938349-67-8) State House Pr.

What's in the Deep. Alese Pecther. 1991. 14.95 (0-87491-247-4) Acrpls Bks CO.

What's in the Deep: An Underwater Adventure for Children. rev. ed. Alese Pechter. (J). 1991. 14.95 (0-87491-983-5) Acrpls Bks CO.

***What's in the Deep Blue Sea?** Peter Seymour. (GRE.). (J). 1991. 11.99 (0-85953-851-6) Childs Play.

What's in the Deep Blue Sea? Peter Seymour. LC 90-80884. (What's in the... Ser.). (Illus.). 18p. (J). (ps-2). 1990. 10.95 (0-8050-1449-7, Bks Young Read) H Holt & Co.

What's in the Fridge. Ruth Tilden. (J). 1994. 8.95 (0-671-89554-0, Litl Simon S&S) S&S Childrens.

What's in the House? (Lift the Flap Bks.). 12p. (J). 1995. 4.95 (0-7894-0222-X, 5-70635) DK Pub Inc.

What's in the Jungle. Peter Seymour. LC 87-81818. (Illus.). 18p. (J). (ps-2). 1988. 10.95 (0-8050-0688-5, Bks Young Read) H Holt & Co.

What's in the Prehistoric Forest? Peter Seymour. LC 90-80885. (What's in the... Ser.). (Illus.). 18p. (J). (ps-2). 1990. 10.95 (0-8050-1450-0, Bks Young Read) H Holt & Co.

What's in the Rainforest? One Hundred Six Answers from A to Z. Suzanne Ross. LC 91-72682. (Illus.). 48p. (Orig.). (J). (gr. 1-7). 1991. pap. 5.95 (0-9629895-0-9) Enchanted Rain Pr.

What's in the Thicket? see Take Along Stories

W

An Asterisk (*) at the beginning of an entry indicates that the title is appearing in BIP for the first time.

What's in the Trunk? Michele S. Spirn. (J). (ps-1). 1988. 8.49 (*0-87386-057-8*); 16.99 incl. audio (*0-685-25202-7*); pap. 1.95 (*0-87386-053-5*); pap. 9.95 incl. audio (*0-685-25203-5*) Jan Prods.

What's in the Woods? An Outdoor Activity Book. Sara S. Miller. (Illus.). (J). (gr. 3-6). 1995. pap. 11.95 (*0-9646246-0-5*) Cygnet Mill Bks.

What's in Wodehouse: A Quiz Book. Charles E. Gould, Jr. & P. G. Wodehouse. (Illus.). 163p. 1995. 14.95 (*0-87008-106-3*) JAS Heineman.

***What's in Your Basket?** Gerver. (J). 1998. mass mkt. 4.99 (*0-689-81732-0*) S&S Childrens.

What's in Your Cosmetics? A Complete Consumer's Guide to Natural & Synthetic Ingredients. Aubrey Hampton. LC 95-11514. (Illus.). 320p. (Orig.). 1995. pap. 11.00 (*1-878825-45-3*) Odonian Pr.

What's in your Food. Ed Blonz. 1998. pap. 10.95 (*0-452-27437-0*, Plume) NAL-Dutton.

What's in Your Name: The Science of Letters & Numbers. Clifford W. Cheasley. 105p. 1968. spiral bd. 5.00 (*0-7873-1228-2*) Hlth Research.

What's in Your Name: The Science of Letters & Numbers. Clifford W. Cheasley. 1991. lib. bdg. 65.75 (*0-8490-4516-9*) Gordon Pr.

What's in Your Name: The Science of Letters & Numbers. Clifford W. Cheasley. 105p. 1993. reprint ed. pap. 14.95 (*1-56459-402-5*) Kessinger Pub.

What's Inside? Satoshi Kitamura. (Sunburst Ser.). (Illus.). 32p. (J). (ps up). pap. 4.95 (*0-374-48324-8*) FS&G.

What's Inside? Anthea Sieveking. LC 89-11897. (J). 1990. pap. 9.95 (*0-8037-0719-3*) Dial Bks Young.

What's Inside? Anthea Sieveking. (Illus.). 24p. (J). (ps). 1994. pap. 4.50 (*0-14-050353-6*, Puff Pied Piper) Puffin Bks.

What's Inside? A Lift the Flap Book. Eric Hill. 16p. (J). 1996. pap. 4.99 (*0-14-054965-X*) Puffin Bks.

What's Inside: The Alphabet Book. Satoshi Kitamura. LC 84-73117. (Illus.). 32p. (J). (ps up). 1985. 12.95 (*0-374-38306-5*) FS&G.

***What's Inside a Mud Dauber's Nest? A Teachers' Guide with Identification Keys.** Janice R. Matthews. (Illus.). 32p. 1996. 4.95 (*1-888499-07-9*) Riverview GA.

What's Inside Airplanes? Steve Parker. LC 94-48544. (What's Inside? Ser.). (Illus.). 44p. (J). (gr. 3 up). 1995. 17.95 (*0-87226-394-0*) P Bedrick Bks.

What's Inside Buildings? Steve Parker. LC 94-48543. (What's Inside? Ser.). (Illus.). 44p. (J). (gr. 3 up). 1995. 17.95 (*0-87226-395-9*) P Bedrick Bks.

What's Inside Everyday Things? Peter Lafferty. LC 95-2060. (What's Inside Series). (Illus.). 44p. (J). (gr. 3 up). 1995. 17.95 (*0-87226-396-7*) P Bedrick Bks.

What's Inside? Planes. (Lift the Flap Bks.). 12p. (J). 1995. 4.95 (*0-7894-0223-8*, 5-70636) DK Pub Inc.

What's Inside Plants? Anita Ganeri. LC 94-48545. (What's Inside? Ser.). (Illus.). 44p. (J). (gr. 3 up). 1995. 17.95 (*0-87226-397-5*) P Bedrick Bks.

***What's Inside the Human Body.** Barbara Drillsma. (Illus.). 44p. (YA). (gr. 5 up). 1997. 17.95 (*0-87226-398-3*) P Bedrick Bks.

What's Inside the Magic Box: Using Computers in the 21st Century. Jay Johnson. (J). pap. 3.95 (*0-590-24007-2*) Scholastic Inc.

What's Inside the Magic Box? Using Personal Computers in the 21st Century. Jay Johnson. (J). (gr. 4 up). 1991. 14.00 (*0-910609-24-1*) Gifted Educ Pr.

What's Inside Us? Anita Ganeri. LC 94-19406. (How Do We Know? Ser.). (J). (gr. 1 up). 1995. lib. bdg. 24.26 (*0-8114-3885-6*) Raintree Steck-V.

What's Inside You? Susan Mayes. (Starting Point Science Ser.). (Illus.). 24p. (J). (gr. 1 up). 1991. pap. 3.95 (*0-7460-0602-0*, Usborne); lib. bdg. 12.95 (*0-88110-550-3*, Usborne) EDC.

What's Inside Your Body? Robert De Weese. (Science Mini Unit Intermediate Ser.). (Illus.). 16p. (J). (gr. 1-3). 1994. pap. text ed. 5.95 (*1-55799-290-8*, EMC 830) Evan-Moor Corp.

What's It All About? Michael Caine. 1994. reprint ed. mass mkt. 6.99 (*0-345-38680-9*) Ballantine.

What's It All About: A Novel of Life, Love, & Key Lime Pie. William Van Wert. 240p. 1996. 20.00 (*0-684-81872-8*, S&S) S&S Trade.

What's It All About? Letters of Reflection on Human Freedom, Mercy & Humility. George W. Kosicki. LC 90-81274. 60p. (Orig.). 1990. pap. 3.00 (*0-9625975-1-1*) Faith Pub OH.

***What's It For?** Claudette C. Mitchell et al. (Visions: African-American Experiences: Vol. 39). (Illus.). 8p. (Orig.). (J). (gr. k-1). 1996. pap. text ed. 3.00 (*1-57518-081-2*) Arborlake.

***What's It Like Being Jewish? Besides Having Heartburn?** Jerry Cooper. 24p. (Orig.). 1996. pap. 3.95 (*1-889419-13-3*) J Cooper.

What's It Like to Be a Chef. Susan C. Poskanzer. LC 89-34390. (What's It Like to Be a...Ser.). (Illus.). 32p. (J). (gr. k-3). 1994. pap. 3.95 (*0-8167-1797-4*) Troll Communs.

What's It Like to Be a Dentist. Judith B. Stamper. LC 89-34392. (What's It Like to Be a...Ser.). (Illus.). 32p. (J). (gr. k-3). 1989. lib. bdg. 12.95 (*0-8167-1799-0*) Troll Communs.

What's It Like to Be a Doctor. Judith Bauer. LC 89-34398. (What's It Like to Be a...Ser.). (Illus.). 32p. (J). (gr. k-3). 1990. lib. bdg. 12.95 (*0-8167-1801-6*) Troll Communs.

What's It Like to Be a Doctor. Judith Bauer. LC 89-34398. (What's It Like to Be a...Ser.). (Illus.). 32p. (J). (gr. k-3). 1996. pap. 3.95 (*0-8167-1802-4*) Troll Communs.

What's It Like to be a Fish? Wendy Pfeffer. LC 94-6543. (Let's-Read-&-Find-Out Science Ser.). (Illus.). 32p. (J). (ps-1). 1996. 14.95 (*0-06-024428-3*); lib. bdg. 14.89 (*0-06-024429-1*) HarpC Child Bks.

What's It Like to Be a Fish? Wendy Pfeffer. LC 94-6543. (Trophy Let's-Read-&-Find-Out Bk.). (Illus.). 32p. (J). (ps-3). 1996. pap. 4.95 (*0-06-445151-8*, Trophy) HarpC Child Bks.

What's It Like to Be a Grocer. Shelley Wilks. LC 89-34394. (What's It Like to Be a...Ser.). (Illus.). 32p. (J). (gr. k-3). 1997. pap. 3.95 (*0-8167-1806-7*) Troll Communs.

What's It Like to Be a Newspaper Reporter. Janet Craig. LC 89-34384. (What's It Like to Be a...Ser.). (Illus.). 32p. (J). (gr. k-3). 1989. lib. bdg. 12.95 (*0-8167-1807-5*) Troll Communs.

What's It Like to Be a Newspaper Reporter. Janet Craig. LC 89-34384. (What's It Like to Be a...Ser.). (Illus.). 32p. (J). (gr. k-3). 1997. pap. 3.95 (*0-8167-1808-3*) Troll Communs.

What's It Like to Be a Nurse. Judith Bauer. LC 89-34387. (What's It Like to Be a...Ser.). (Illus.). 32p. (J). (gr. k-3). 1994. lib. bdg. 12.95 (*0-8167-1809-1*) Troll Communs.

What's It Like to Be a Police Officer. Michael J. Pellowski. LC 89-34395. (What's It Like to Be a...Ser.). (Illus.). 32p. (J). (gr. k-3). 1990. lib. bdg. 12.95 (*0-8167-1811-3*) Troll Communs.

What's It Like to Be a Postal Worker. Morgan Matthews. LC 89-34385. (What's It Like to Be a...Ser.). (Illus.). 32p. (J). (gr. k-3). 1997. pap. 3.95 (*0-8167-1814-8*) Troll Communs.

What's It Like to Be a Puppeteer. Susan C. Poskanzer. LC 88-10042. (What's It Like to Be a...Ser.). (Illus.). 32p. (J). (gr. 1-3). 1997. pap. 3.95 (*0-8167-1433-9*) Troll Communs.

What's It Like to Be a Railroad Worker. Morgan Matthews. LC 89-34389. (What's It Like to Be a...Ser.). (Illus.). 32p. (J). (gr. k-3). 1989. lib. bdg. 12.95 (*0-8167-1815-6*) Troll Communs.

What's It Like to Be a Railroad Worker. Morgan Matthews. LC 89-34389. (What's It Like to Be a...Ser.). (Illus.). 32p. (J). (gr. k-3). 1997. pap. 3.95 (*0-8167-1816-4*) Troll Communs.

What's It Like to Be a Sanitation Worker. Susan C. Poskanzer. LC 88-10044. (What's It Like to Be a...Ser.). (Illus.). 32p. (J). (gr. k-3). 1989. lib. bdg. 11.50 (*0-8167-1436-3*) Troll Communs.

What's It Like to Be a Teacher. Kira Daniel. LC 88-10041. (What's It Like to Be a...Ser.). (Illus.). 32p. (J). (gr. k-3). 1989. lib. bdg. 11.50 (*0-8167-1430-4*) Troll Communs.

What's It Like to Be a Truck Driver. Judith B. Stamper. LC 88-10039. (What's It Like to Be a...Ser.). (Illus.). 32p. (J). (gr. k-3). 1997. pap. 3.95 (*0-8167-1425-8*) Troll Communs.

What's It Like to Be a Veterinarian. Judith B. Stamper. LC 89-34391. (What's It Like to Be a...Ser.). (Illus.). 32p. (J). (gr. k-3). 1990. lib. bdg. 12.95 (*0-8167-1817-2*) Troll Communs.

What's It Like to Be a Zoo Worker. Judith B. Stamper. LC 88-10046. (What's It Like to Be a...Ser.). (Illus.). 32p. (J). (gr. k-3). 1989. lib. bdg. 12.95 (*0-8167-1440-1*) Troll Communs.

What's It Like to Be an Airline Pilot. Judith Bauer. LC 89-34397. (Illus.). 32p. (J). (gr. k-3). 1990. lib. bdg. 12.95 (*0-8167-1791-5*) Troll Communs.

What's It Like to Be an Astronaut. Susan C. Poskanzer. LC 89-34393. (Illus.). 32p. (J). (gr. k-3). 1990. lib. bdg. 12. 95 (*0-8167-1793-1*) Troll Communs.

What's It Like to Be an Astronaut. Susan C. Poskanzer. LC 89-34393. (Illus.). 32p. (J). (gr. k-3). 1997. pap. 3.95 (*0-8167-1794-X*) Troll Communs.

What's It Like to Be Me? Directed Discovery Journal. Patsy R. Booth. 100p. (YA). (gr. 4 up). 1994. pap. 10.95 (*1-884393-25-X*) Cedar Tree.

***What's It Worth? A Guide to Personal Injury Awards & Settlements.** James P. Munger. 1096p. 1996. pap. 80.00 (*1-55834-348-2*, 68439-14) MICHIE.

What's It Worth? A Guide to Personal Injury Awards & Settlements, 1993 Edition. Michie Butterworth Editorial Staff. 979p. 1993. pap. 75.00 (*1-55834-096-3*) MICHIE.

What's It Worth? Educational Background & Economic Status. 75p. (Orig.). (C). 1993. pap. text ed. 30.00 (*1-56806-405-5*) DIANE Pub.

What's It Worth? Probing Our Values with Questions Jesus Asked. Margaret Ragland. 1977. pap. 6.25 (*0-89137-409-4*) Quality Pubns.

What's It Worth? A Guide to Current Personal Injury Awards & Settlements, 1991: A Guide to Current Personal Injury Awards & Settlements. Stephan H. Peskin. (Kluwer Damages Library). 1066p. 1991. 70.00 (*0-87473-819-9*) MICHIE.

***What's Japanese about Japan.** J. Condon. 1996. 23.95 (*4-07-972039-4*) Shufu no Tomo-Sha.

What's Left: A New Vision for Democrats. Robert S. McElvaine. 240p. 1996. 20.00 (*1-55850-629-2*) Adams Media.

What's Left? Radical Politics & the Radical Psyche. Michael Neumann. 240p. 1988. pap. 7.95 (*0-921149-22-0*) Broadview Pr.

What's Left? Radical Politics in the Postcommunist Era. Charles Derber et al. LC 94-36925. 240p. (C). 1995. 40. 00 (*0-87023-953-8*) U of Mass Pr.

What's Left? Radical Politics in the Postcommunist Era. Charles Derber et al. LC 94-36925. 240p. (C). 1995. pap. 15.95 (*0-87023-954-6*) U of Mass Pr.

What's Left? The Ecole Normale Superieure & the Right. Diane Rubenstein. LC 90-50096. (Rhetoric of the Human Sciences Ser.). 256p. (Orig.). (C). 1991. text ed. 40.00 (*0-299-12560-2*); pap. text ed. 19.75 (*0-299-12564-5*) U of Wis Pr.

What's Left to Eat? Sue Gebo. (Illus.). 294p. 1992. pap. text ed. 15.95 (*0-07-023534-1*) McGraw.

***What's Left? Who's Left? The Layman's Handbook for Estate Property Management, with Accounting Records & Survivor's Guide to Personal & Financial Well-Being.** Teresa Pedicino. (Illus.). xviii, 274p. (Orig.). 1996. pap. 24.95 (*0-9652846-0-3*) Tristus Pub.

What's Legally Required: A Guide to the Legal Rules for Making Local Land-Use Decisions in Connecticut. 5th ed. Michael A. Zizka. (Bulletin Ser.: No. 16). 116p. 1993. pap. text ed. 10.00 (*0-942085-03-5*) DEP Nat Resc Ctr.

What's Love Got to Do with It? Nancy M. Pollard. 180p. (Orig.). 1993. pap. 12.95 (*0-9637705-1-9*) Benchmark UT.

What's Love Got to Do with It: The Evolution of Human Mating. Meredith Small. (Illus.). 272p. 1996. pap. 14.00 (*0-385-47702-3*) Doubleday.

***What's Luck Got to Do with It? 12 Entrepreneurs Reveal the Secrets behind Their Success.** Ernst & Young Staff. LC 96-53187. 256p. 1997. 24.95 (*0-471-17998-1*) Wiley.

What's Made in The U. S. A. George Vargish. 112p. 1987. 34.95 (*0-88738-187-1*) Transaction Pubs.

What's Michael, Bk. 1. Makoto Kobayashi. (Illus.). 1990. 29.95 (*1-56060-005-5*); pap. 9.95 (*1-56060-006-3*) Eclipse Bks.

What's Michael, Bk. 2. Makoto Kobayashi. (Illus.). 1991. 29.95 (*1-56060-077-2*); pap. 9.95 (*1-56060-078-0*) Eclipse Bks.

What's Midi? J. Eiche. 64p. (SPA.). 1992. per. 5.95 (*0-7935-1912-8*, 00183523) H Leonard.

What's Midi. 2nd ed. A. Honeybone et al. 132p. 1990. pap. 12.95 (*0-933224-53-2*) Bold Strummer Ltd.

What's MIDI? Making Musical Instruments Work Together. Jon F. Eiche. (Illus.). 64p. 1990. pap. 5.95 (*0-7935-0082-6*, 00330044) H Leonard.

What's Mine's Mine. George MacDonald. 1994. 33.50 (*0-940652-64-1*) Sunrise Bks.

What's Mine's Mine. George MacDonald. (George MacDonald Original Works: Series I). 387p. 1991. reprint ed. 18.00 (*1-881084-00-0*) Johannesen.

What's Missing. Niki Yektai. LC 87-784. 32p. (J). (ps-1). 1989. pap. 4.95 (*0-317-04349-8*, Clarion Bks) HM.

What's Modern Painting. 1990. pap. 6.95 (*0-8109-6083-4*) Abrams.

What's Music All about? Libby Hobson. (Music Ser.). 24p. (gr. 3-6). 1977. student ed. 5.00 (*0-8209-0272-1*, MU-1) ESP.

What's My Name? New Testament Coloring Book. Shirley Beegle. (Coloring & Activity Bks.). (Illus.). 16p. (J). 1993. pap. text ed. 1.69 (*0-7847-0126-1*, 02216) Standard Pub.

What's My Name: Old Testament Coloring Book. Shirley Beegle. (Coloring & Activity Bks.). (Illus.). 16p. (J). 1993. pap. text ed. 1.69 (*0-7847-0125-3*, 02215) Standard Pub.

What's My Style? Create a Look & Build a Wardrobe with Universal Style. rev. ed. Alyce Parsons & Allison Better. (Illus.). 120p. (C). Date not set. pap. 14.95 (*0-9627405-2-7*) A Parsons.

What's My Type? Kathleen V. Hurley & Theodore E. Dobson. LC 91-55279. 208p. 1992. pap. 15.00 (*0-06-250421-5*) Harper SF.

***What's New for the 6.09 Enhanced Release of SAS Software: Changes & Enhancements.** 224p. (C). 1996. pap. 15.00 (*1-55544-753-8*) SAS Inst.

What's New in Allergy & Asthma: New Developments & How They Help You to Overcome Allergy & Asthma. 4th rev. ed. Stephen Astor. LC 96-90200. (Illus.). 288p. (Orig.). 1996. pap. 14.95 (*0-915001-12-8*) Two As.

What's New in Anesthesiology. Ed. by Theodore H. Stanley. (Developments in Critical Care, Medicine, & Anesthesiology Ser.). (C). 1988. lib. bdg. 122.00 (*0-89838-367-6*) Kluwer Ac.

What's New in Barrier Packaging for Food & Non-Food Packaging, No. P-085N. Business Communications Co., Inc. Staff. 213p. 1990. 2,650.00 (*0-89336-793-1*) BCC.

What's New in Cardiac Imaging? SPECT, PET & MRI. Ed. by Ernst E. Van der Wall. (Developments in Cardiovascular Medicine Ser.). 580p. (C). 1992. lib. bdg. 275.00 (*0-7923-1615-0*) Kluwer Ac.

What's New in Medicine - More Than 250 of the Biggest Health Issues of the Decade. L. A. Chotkowski. LC 90-4347. (Illus.). 286p. (Orig.). 1991. pap. 14.95 (*0-929173-04-X*) Health Press.

What's New in Nevada Schools? A Case Study: Jacobson Elementary School. Susan Balkenbush. 7p. 1993. 7.00 (*1-886306-01-X*) Nevada Policy.

What's New in Wedding Food. Beth Tartan. 102p. 1985. 7.95 (*0-933193-00-9*) TarPar.

What's News: A Game Simulation of TV News, Participant's Manual. William A. Gamson. 1984. Instr's. manual. teacher ed. 4.95 (*0-02-911200-1*, Free Press); pap. 16.95 (*0-02-911110-2*, Free Press) Free Pr.

What's News? High Interest, Skills-Based Activities to Strengthen Reading Interest & Global Awareness. Dorothy Michener. Ed. by Anna Quinn. (Illus.). 96p. (Orig.). 1995. pap. text ed. 9.95 (*0-86530-337-1*, IP 337-1) Incentive Pubns.

What's News: The Media in American Society. Ed. by Eli Abel. 300p. 1981. 39.95 (*0-87855-448-3*) Transaction Pubs.

What's News in Coos County, Vol. 1. viii, 381p. (Orig.). 1996. pap. 32.00 (*0-7884-0396-6*, K155) Heritage Bk.

***What's News in Coos County, Vol. 2.** Milli S. Kenney. ix, 441p. (Orig.). 1996. pap. 25.00 (*0-7884-0575-6*, K156) Heritage Bk.

What's Next? Becky Daniel & Charlie Daniel. 64p. (J). (gr. k-6). 1979. 5.99 (*0-916456-41-2*, GA116) Good Apple.

What's Next? Barbara L. McCombs & Linda Brannan. (Skills for Job Success Ser.). (Illus.). 32p. (Orig.). 1990. student ed., pap. 4.95 (*1-56119-019-5*) Educ Pr MD.

What's Next? Barbara L. McCombs & Linda Brannan. (Skills for Job Success Ser.). (Illus.). 32p. (Orig.). (YA). (gr. 7-12). 1990. Set. teacher ed., wbk. ed. 44.95 (*1-56119-068-3*); teacher ed. 1.95 (*1-56119-020-9*); disk 39.95 (*1-56119-110-8*) Educ Pr MD.

What's Next? A Guide to Valued Aging & Other High-Wire Adventures. Richard Griffin et al. xx, 211p. (Orig.). 1996. pap. 14.95 (*0-9651530-0-2*) Eldercorps Pr.

What's Next? A Non-Biased Study of Eschatology. Keith J. Walsworth. 100p. (Orig.). 1993. pap. 6.95 (*1-879366-39-8*) Hearthstone OK.

What's Next? A Perceptive Study of the End Times & Christ's Second Coming. C. E. Colton. 138p. (Orig.). 1995. pap. 7.95 (*0-9646448-0-0*) Colton Bks.

What's Next? New Life in Christ Guidebook for Children. Ralph W. Harris. 24p. 1971. pap. 0.59 (*0-88243-559-0*, 02-0559) Gospel Pub.

***What's Next? Preparing the Student with Autism or Other Developmental Disabilities for Success in the Community.** Carol Gray. 196p. (Orig.). 1992. pap. 29.95 (*1-885477-18-X*) Fut Horizons.

What's Next? Vol. 1: A Pattern Discovery Approach to Problem Solving. Wilbert Reimer. Ed. by Elaine Reimer. (What's Next Ser.: Vol. 1). (Illus.). 60p. (Orig.). 1995. teacher ed., wbk. ed. 16.95 (*1-881431-54-1*, 1660) AIMS Educ Fnd.

What's Next? Vol. 2: A Pattern Discovery Approach to Problem Solving. Wilbert Reimer. Ed. by Elaine Reimer. (What's Next Ser.: No. 2). (Illus.). 60p. (Orig.). 1996. teacher ed., wbk. ed. 16.95 (*1-881431-55-X*, 1665) AIMS Educ Fnd.

What's Next? Vol. 3: A Pattern Discovery Approach to Problem Solving, 3 vols. Wilbert Reimer. Ed. by Elaine Reimer. (What's Next Ser.: No. 3). (Illus.). 60p. (Orig.). 1996. teacher ed., wbk. ed. 16.95 (*1-881431-56-8*, 1670) AIMS Educ Fnd.

***What's Next, Billy & Jodie?** (Ready Readers Series II Stage II). (Illus.). 32p. (J). (gr. 1-3). 1996. pap. write for info. (*1-56144-955-5*, Honey Bear Bks) Modern Pub NYC.

What's Next? Career Strategies after 35. Jack Falvey. Ed. by Susan Williamson. LC 87-10553. 192p. (Orig.). 1987. pap. 9.95 (*0-913589-26-8*) Williamson Pub Co.

What's Next on Your Spiritual Path? Nancy R. Feldman. (Illus.). 100p. 1995. wbk. ed. 19.95 (*0-9649696-0-2*) Rainbows Three.

What's Next, PJ Funnybunny? Judith Conaway. (J). 1998. pap. 3.99 (*0-679-88166-2*) McKay.

***What's Noteworthy on Learners, Learning & Schooling.** 1996. lib. bdg. 252.75 (*0-8490-6060-5*) Gordon Pr.

What's Novel in the Novel. (Yale French Studies: No. 8). 1951. pap. 25.00 (*0-527-01716-7*) Periodicals Srv.

What's Nude? Fred Gwynne & Peter Basch. (Illus.). 1960. pap. 10.95 (*0-8392-1129-5*) Astor-Honor.

What's on My Mind? Becoming Inspired with New Perception. Swami Anantananda. LC 96-9267. 176p. (Orig.). 1996. pap. 11.95 (*0-911307-47-8*) SYDA Found.

***What's on Satellite.** Date not set. write for info. (*0-936361-64-6*) Design Pubs.

What's on the Internet. 3rd ed. Eric Gagnon. (Illus.). 440p. (C). 1996. pap. text ed. 19.95 (*0-201-88627-8*) Peachpit Pr.

What's on the Menu? Illus. by Chris L. Demarest. 32p. (J). (ps-3). 1995. pap. 4.99 (*0-14-055483-1*) Puffin Bks.

What's on the Other Side? Tiziano Sclavi. LC 93-72524. (Illus.). 10p. (J). (ps). 1994. bds. 4.95 (*1-56397-345-6*) Boyds Mills Pr.

What's on the Web Fall/Winter 1996. 3rd ed. Eric Gagnon. 1996. pap. text ed. 29.95 (*1-884640-20-6*) Internet Media.

What's on the Web Spring/Summer 1997. Ed. by Eric Gagnon. (Illus.). 500p. 1996. 23.95 (*1-884640-21-4*) Internet Media.

What's on the Worker's Mind: By One Who Put on Overalls to Find Out. Whiting Williams. LC 73-156441. (American Labor Ser., No. 2). 1971. reprint ed. 24.95 (*0-405-02949-7*) Ayer.

What's on Your Mind. Merlin R. Carothers. 1984. 6.95 (*0-943026-13-X*) Carothers.

What's Opposite? Illus. by Tony Tallarico. (Tiny Bks.). 28p. (J). (ps-1). 1984. bds. 2.95 (*0-448-48824-8*, Tuffy) Putnam Pub Group.

What's Out in Space? Susan Mayes. (Starting Point Science Ser.). (Illus.). 24p. (J). (gr. 1-4). 1990. pap. 3.95 (*0-7460-0430-3*, Usborne); lib. bdg. 12.95 (*0-88110-443-4*, Usborne) EDC.

What's Out There? A Book about Space. Lynn Wilson. LC 92-24469. (All Aboard Bks.). (Illus.). 32p. (J). (ps-3). 1993. pap. 2.95 (*0-448-40517-2*, G&D) Putnam Pub Group.

What's Past Is Prologue. Mary B. Gilson. Ed. by Annette K. Baxter. LC 79-8793. (Signal Lives Ser.). 1980. reprint ed. lib. bdg. 35.95 (*0-405-12842-8*) Ayer.

What's Polite. Harriet Ziefert. (Illus.). 20p. (Orig.). (J). 1995. pap. 5.99 (*0-14-055349-5*) Puffin Bks.

What's Pretend? Harriet Ziefert. (Lift-the-Flaps Ser.). (Illus.). 16p. (J). (ps-1). 1995. pap. 5.99 (*0-14-055348-7*) Puffin Bks.

What's Real, What's Not? Insights from Luke 19-24. Norman D. Stolpe. (Prime-Time Bible Studies). 58p. 1991. teacher ed. 8.45 (*1-56212-004-2*) CRC Pubns.

What's Really Going On? Marcus Brown. 50p. (Orig.). 1995. pap. 8.95 (*0-9645118-0-0*) Consc Pub Co.

What's Really Happening in Central America: The Facts about the Crisis. Lawrence L. Tracy. (Illus.). 104p. (Orig.). 1989. pap. write for info. (*0-318-65544-6*) Amer Dem Latin Amer.

***What's Really Happening in Education: A Case Study Approach.** James J. Van Patten. LC 96-51878. 1997. 49. 50 (*0-7618-0666-0*); pap. 29.50 (*0-7618-0667-9*) U Pr of Amer.

W

What's Really Important in Princeton. Mary Lou K. Stevenson. 50p. 1990. write for info. (*0-9624277-0-5*) Passage Hse.

What's Really in Our Food: Facts Everyone Should Know about Foods & Vitamins. Mia Parsonnet. 1991. pap. 12.95 (*1-56171-034-2*) Sure Seller.

***What's Really Said in the Teachers' Lounge: Provocative Ideas about Cultures & Classrooms.** Jeffrey A. Kottler. LC 96-51211. (Illus.). 208p. 1997. pap. 22.95 (*0-8039-6338-6*) Corwin Pr.

***What's Really Said in the Teachers' Lounge: Provocative Ideas about Cultures & Classrooms.** Jeffrey A. Kottler. (Illus.). 208p. 1997. 49.95 (*0-8039-6337-8*) Corwin Pr.

What's Really Wrong with You? A Revolutionary Look at How Muscles Affect Your Health. Thomas Griner & Maxine Nunes. LC 95-35289. (Illus.). 226p. pap. 10.95 (*0-89529-658-6*) Avery Pub.

What's Remembered: A Critical Analysis. Jill Beck. (Educational Performance Collection). 52p. (C). 1986. pap. text ed. write for info. (*0-932582-45-1*) Dance Notation.

What's Remembered: Labanotation Score. Rachel Lampert & Leslie Rotman. (Educational Performance Collection). 231p. 1986. pap. write for info. (*0-932582-46-X*) Dance Notation.

***What's Right: The New Conservative Majority & the Remaking of America.** David Frum. 224p. 1997. pap. 14.00 (*0-465-04198-1*) Basic.

What's Right for Roxy Independent Reader 5-Pack, Unit 8. (Networks Ser.). 1991. 15.00 (*0-88106-767-9*, N248) Charlesbridge Pub.

***What's Right? What's Wrong? Director's Manual.** William Callaghan. Ed. by Kieran Sawyer. (Developing Faith Ser.). (Orig.). (YA). 1997. pap. text ed. 16.95 (*0-87793-609-9*) Ave Maria.

***What's Right? What's Wrong? Participant Book.** William Callaghan. Ed. by Kieran Sawyer. (Developing Faith Ser.). 80p. (Orig.). (YA). (gr. 9-12). 1997. pap. text ed. 5.95 (*0-87793-608-0*) Ave Maria.

What's Right with America. Sam Johnson & Chris Marcil. (Illus.). 128p. 1996. pap. 9.00 (*0-385-48425-9*, Anchor NY) Doubleday.

What's Right with Football. John D. Bridgers. 1995. 24.95 (*1-57168-016-0*, Eakin Pr) Sunbelt Media.

What's Right with Our Schools. Silberman. 1994. 22.95 (*0-02-928755-3*) S&S Trade.

***What's Roaming in My Home?** unabridged ed. Ann M. Wolf & Anna H. Spitz. (Environmental Ser.). (Illus.). 47p. (Orig.). (J). (gr. 3-6). 1996. pap. 5.50 (*0-9651084-2-2*) Tyris Environ.

***What's Size Got to Do with It? Understanding Rightsizing.** John Blyler. 352p. 1997. pap. 39.95 (*0-7803-1096-9*, PP4499) Inst Electrical.

What's Smaller Than a Pygmy Shrew? Robert E. Wells. LC 94-27150. (Illus.). 32p. 1995. 13.95 (*0-8075-8837-7*) A Whitman.

What's Smaller Than a Pygmy Shrew? Robert E. Wells. (J). (gr. 4-7). 1995. pap. 6.95 (*0-8075-8838-5*) A Whitman.

***What's So Amazing about Grace.** Philip Yancey. 336p. 19.99 (*0-310-21327-4*) Zondervan.

What's So Funny? The Comic Conception of Culture & Society. Murray S. Davis. LC 93-10217. (Illus.). 400p. 1993. 29.95 (*0-226-13810-0*) U Ch Pr.

What's So Funny? Wit & Humor in American Children's Literature. Michael Cart. LC 94-15583. 210p. (J). 1995. 25.00 (*0-06-024453-4*) HarpC.

What's So Funny about Being Catholic? A (Slightly Irreverent) Book of Holy Jokes, Strange but True Stories, Weird Nun Names, & Much More. Karen Warner. LC 93-39547. (Illus.). 160p. (Orig.). 1994. pap. 7.99 (*0-06-095023-4*, PL) HarpC.

***What's So Funny about Business Now?** Sidney Harris. (Illus.). 1997. pap. 12.95 (*0-614-20782-7*) Crisp Fulfillment Ctr.

What's So Funny about Getting Old. Jane T. Nolan. LC 94-25971. 1994. pap. 6.00 (*0-88166-223-2*, 0671511521) Meadowbrook.

What's So Funny about Getting Old. Jane T. Noland. 1994. pap. 7.00 (*0-671-51152-1*) S&S Trade.

What's So Funny about Ninth Grade? Catherine Clark. LC 91-2494. (Midway Junior High Ser.). 128p. (J). (gr. 6-9). 1996. pap. 2.95 (*0-8167-2397-4*) Troll Communs.

What's So Funny, Ketu? Verna Aardema. LC 82-70195. (Pied Piper Paperback Ser.). (Illus.). 32p. (J). (ps-3). 1989. pap. 4.95 (*0-8037-0646-4*) Dial Bks Young.

***What's So Great about Cindy Snappleby.** Barbara Samuels. 32p. (J). 3.98 (*0-8317-2477-3*) Smithmark.

What's So Important about Self-Esteem. Peggy P. Ehling. Ed. by Kieran Sawyer. (Developing Faith Ser.). (Orig.). (YA). (gr. 9-12). 1996. teacher ed., pap. 16.95 (*0-87793-584-X*); pap. text ed. 5.95 (*0-87793-583-1*) Ave Maria.

What's So Lucky about a Four-Leaf Clover. Claudia De Lys. 528p. 1989. 8.99 (*0-517-69424-7*) Random Hse Value.

What's So Special about Nantucket? Mary Miles. LC 98-71418. (Illus.). 36p. (J). (ps up). 1993. lib. bdg. 17.00 (*0-9636885-0-2*) Faraway Pub.

What's So Terrible about Swallowing an Apple Seed? Harriet G. Lerner & Susan H. Goldhor. LC 94-2769. (Illus.). 40p. (J). (ps-1). 1996. 14.95 (*0-06-024523-9*); lib. bdg. 14.89 (*0-06-024524-7*) HarpC Child Bks.

What's Social about Social Cognition? Social Cognition Research in Small Groups. Ed. by Judith L. Nye & Aaron M. Brower. 328p. (C). 1996. 58.00 (*0-8039-7204-0*); pap. 27.95 (*0-8039-7205-9*) Sage.

What's Special about Being Catholic? William Odell. Ed. by Kieran Sawyer. (Developing Faith Ser.). (Illus.). 80p. (Orig.). (YA). (gr. 9-12). 1996. student ed., pap. text ed. 5.95 (*0-87793-568-8*) Ave Maria.

What's Special about Being Catholic?, Director manual. William Odell. Ed. by Kieran Sawyer. (Developing Faith Ser.). (Illus.). 128p. (Orig.). (YA). (gr. 8-12). 1996. teacher ed., pap. 16.95 (*0-87793-567-X*) Ave Maria.

What's Stopped Happening to Me? Dale Burg & Mary J. Minkin. LC 92-37548. (Illus.). 1993. 9.95 (*0-8065-1417-5*) Carol Pub Group.

What's Stopped Happening to Me? Gail Parent et al. 1990. 12.00 (*0-8184-0522-8*, L Stuart) Carol Pub Group.

What's Stopping You? Attitude Adjustment for the About-to-Be Entrepreneur. William A. Remas. (Know How Now Ser.). 55p. 1995. pap. 5.00 (*0-9639557-0-5*, Know How Now) A R K Co.

What's That From? The Ultimate Quiz Book of Memorable Movie Lines since 1969. Jai Nanda. 208p. 1996. pap. 9.95 (*0-312-14145-9*) St Martin.

***What's That Noise?** Gill Davies. (Little Spooky Window Book Ser.). (Illus.). 13p. (J). (ps-1). 1997. bds. 3.99 (*1-57584-168-1*) Rdrs Dgst Yng Fam.

What's That Noise? Gillian Lui. (Early Words Ser.). (Illus.). 24p. (J). (gr. 1-3). 1996. 9.95 (*0-237-51429-X*, Pub. by Evans Bros Ltd UK) Trafalgar.

What's That Noise? Francesca Simon. (J). (ps-3). 1996. pap. 5.95 (*0-8120-9783-1*) Barron.

***What's That Noise? A Book about Farm Sounds.** Susan Hood. (Fisher-Price Playbooks). (Illus.). 18p. (J). (ps up). 1997. bds. 10.99 (*1-57584-187-8*) Rdrs Dgst Yng Fam.

What's That Pig Outdoors? A Memoir of Deafness. Henry Kisor. 288p. 1991. pap. 10.95 (*0-14-014899-X*, Penguin Bks) Viking Penguin.

What's That Pig Outdoors? A Memoir of Deafness. large type ed. Henry Kisor. (General Ser.). 345p. 1991. lib. bdg. 21.95 (*0-8161-5113-X*, GK Hall) Thorndike Pr.

What's That Sound? Stewart Cowley. LC 94-67214. (Tiny Magic Window Bks.). (Illus.). 14p. (J). (ps). 1994. 2.99 (*0-89577-596-4*) RD Assn.

***What's That Sound? The Audible Audio Dictionary.** Michael Molenda. 1997. pap. 14.95 incl. audio compact disk (*0-7935-6853-6*) H Leonard.

What's That Sound, Woolly Bear? Philemon Sturges. LC 95-5427. (Illus.). 32p. (J). (ps-3). 1996. 14.95 (*0-316-82021-0*) Little.

What's That You Say? A Viewpoint Challenge. David W. Abel. 167p. (Orig.). 1990. pap. 6.95 (*0-9627711-0-4*) D W Abel.

What's the Best Way to Deal with Hyperactivity? New Update on the Attention Deficit Disorders. C. Thomas Wild. LC 83-71951. (Illus.). 52p. (Orig.). 1983. pap. 3.95 (*0-9606990-1-5*) Attent Span Advan.

What's the Big Deal? Your Changing Body. Stan L. Jones & Brenna B. Jones. LC 94-67237. (Gods Design for Sex Ser.: No. 3). (Illus.). 93p. (Orig.). (J). (gr. 3-6). 1995. pap. 9.00 (*0-89109-845-3*) NavPress.

***What's the Big Idea?** Margaret Snyder. (Big Bag Bks.). (Illus.). 24p. (J). (ps-k). 1997. pap. 2.99 (*0-307-10206-8*, 10206, Golden Books) Western Pub.

***What's the Big Idea?** Margaret Snyder. (Golden Super Shape Bks.). (Illus.). (J). (ps-k). 1997. pap. 2.99 (*0-614-28789-8*, Golden Books) Western Pub.

What's the Big Idea? How to Win with Outrageous Ideas (That Sell) George Lois & Bill Pitts. LC 92-21351. (Illus.). 304p. 1993. pap. 12.95 (*0-452-26938-5*, Plume) NAL-Dutton.

What's the Big Idea, Ben Franklin? Jean Fritz. (Illus.). 48p. (J). (gr. 2-6). 1982. pap. 7.95 (*0-698-20543-X*, Coward) Putnam Pub Group.

What's the Big Idea, Ben Franklin? Jean Fritz. LC 75-25902. (Illus.). 48p. (J). (gr. 3-6). 1996. pap. 5.95 (*0-698-11372-1*, Paperstar) Putnam Pub Group.

What's the Big Secret, Dinosaurs? A Guide to Sex for Girls & Boys. Laurie K. Brown & Marc Brown. LC 96-15521. (J). 1997. 15.95 (*0-316-10915-0*) Little.

What's the Color of Your Underwear. George W. Poole. 100p. 1995. pap. 29.95 (*0-9648565-0-6*) Career Resrcs.

What's the Diagnosis? Race Foster & Marty Smith. LC 95-21877. (Illus.). 1302p. 1995. 19.95 (*0-87605-788-1*) Howell Bk.

What's the Difference. Edward G. Klemm. 75p. 1988. per. 6.95 (*0-89697-298-4*) Intl Univ Pr.

What's the Difference? A Footbridge over the Chasm Between Science & Religion. Peter Wilson. (Illus.). 192p. (Orig.). 1995. pap. 15.00 (*0-9646509-5-9*) Stone Hemp Enter.

What's the Difference? Manhood & Womanhood According to the Bible. John Piper. 64p. (Orig.). (YA). 1990. pap. 4.99 (*0-89107-562-3*) Crossway Bks.

What's the Difference Between...Apes & Monkeys & Other Living Things? GAry Soucie. LC 95-6585. (What's the Difference? Ser.). 96p. 1995. pap. text ed. 9.95 (*0-471-08625-8*) Wiley.

What's the Difference Between...Lenses & Prisms & Other Scientific Things? Gary Soucie. LC 95-10235. (What's the Difference? Ser.). (Illus.). 85p. (J). (gr. 3-6). 1995. pap. text ed. 9.95 (*0-471-08626-6*) Wiley.

What's the Earth Made Of? Susan Mayes. (Starting Point Science Ser.). (Illus.). 24p. (J). (ps up). 1995. pap. 3.95 (*0-7460-1709-X*, Usborne); lib. bdg. 12.95 (*0-88110-752-2*, Usborne) EDC.

What's the Economy Trying to Tell You? Everyone's Guide to Understanding & Profiting from the Economy. David M. Blitzer. LC 97-7891. (Illus.). 256p. 1997. text ed. 22.95 (*0-07-005939-X*) McGraw.

What's the Good Word. William Safire. 1983. mass mkt. 5.95 (*0-380-64550-5*) Avon.

***What's the Matter, Habibi?** LC 96-52440. (J). 1997. 15.00 (*0-395-85816-X*, Clarion Bks) HM.

What's the Matter, Kelly Beans? Judith R. Enderle & Stephanie G. Tessler. LC 95-11337. (Illus.). 112p. (J). (gr. 1-3). 1996. 14.99 (*1-56402-534-9*) Candlewick Pr.

What's the Matter with Carruthers? James Marshall. LC 72-75607. (Illus.). 32p. (J). (gr. k-3). 1972. 16.95 (*0-395-13895-7*) HM.

What's the Matter with Christmas? Phyllis Futer. 1992. pap. 4.25 (*1-55673-459-X*, 9252) CSS OH.

What's the Matter with Herbie Jones? Suzy Kline. 1987. pap. 3.99 (*0-14-032324-4*, Puffin) Puffin Bks.

What's the Matter with Herbie Jones? Suzy Kline. (Illus.). (J). (gr. 3-7). reprint ed. pap. 3.95 (*0-317-62246-3*, Puffin) Puffin Bks.

What's the Matter with Liberalism? Ronald S. Beiner. 208p. (C). 1992. 30.00 (*0-520-07793-8*) U CA Pr.

What's the Matter with Liberalism? Ronald S. Beiner. LC 91-29453. 205p. 1995. pap. 13.95 (*0-520-20335-6*) U CA Pr.

What's the Matter with Today's Experimental Music? Organized Sound Too Rarely Heard. Leigh Landy. (Contemporary Music Studies). 308p. 1991. pap. text ed. 27.00 (*3-7186-5168-8*, Harwood Acad Pubs) Gordon & Breach.

What's the Monster Making? (Magic Corner Bks.). (Illus.). 14p. (J). 1995. bds. 8.95 (*0-307-76027-8*, Golden Pr) Western Pub.

***What's the Name of That Rock?** Hoyt Johnson. (Illus.). 20p. (Orig.). 1996. pap. 3.95 (*1-890195-02-2*, SPC 051296) Sedona Pub.

What's the Next Move? George Kane. LC 74-12618. (Encore Editions Ser.). (Illus.). (J). (gr. 4-6). 1974. 1.79 (*0-684-15841-8*) S&S Trade.

What's the Opposite? A Lift the Flap Book. Eric Hill. 16p. (J). 1996. pap. 4.99 (*0-14-054966-8*) Puffin Bks.

What's the Opposite of a Best Friend? A. Bates. 160p. (J). (gr. 4-7). 1993. pap. 2.95 (*0-590-44145-0*) Scholastic Inc.

What's the Proper Way? Barbara L. McCombs & Linda Brannan. (Skills for Job Success Ser.). (Illus.). 32p. (Orig.). 1990. student ed., pap. 4.95 (*1-56119-017-9*) Educ Pr MD.

What's the Proper Way? Barbara L. McCombs & Linda Brannan. (Skills for Job Success Ser.). (Illus.). 32p. (Orig.). (YA). (gr. 7-12). 1990. Set. teacher ed., wbk. ed. 44.95 (*1-56119-067-5*); teacher ed. 1.95 (*1-56119-018-7*); disk 39.95 (*1-56119-109-4*) Educ Pr MD.

***What's the Shape? Big Book.** Judy Nayer. Ed. by Linette Ellis. (Newbridge Early Math Ser.). (Illus.). 16p. (J). (ps-1). 1997. pap. 16.95 (*1-56784-950-4*) Newbridge Comms.

***What's the Shape? Mini-Book.** Judy Nayer. Ed. by Linette Ellis. (Newbridge Early Math Ser.). (Illus.). 16p. (J). (ps-1). 1997. pap. 3.16 (*1-56784-975-X*) Newbridge Comms.

What's the Story? Photographs for Language Practice, 4 bks. Linda R. Markstein & Dorien Grunbaum. (English As a Second Language Bk.). 1981. pap. text ed. 9.50 (*0-685-73375-0*, 75037); Teacher's manual. teacher ed. 10.95 (*0-582-79787-X*, 75042); 95.00 (*0-582-79788-8*) Longman.

What's the Story? Photographs for Language Practice, 4 bks., Bk. 2, Low-Intermediate. Linda R. Markstein & Dorien Grunbaum. (English As a Second Language Bk.). 1981. Bk. 2: Low-Intermediate. write for info. (*0-582-79784-5*, 75039) Longman.

What's the Story? Photographs for Language Practice, 4 bks., Bk. 3, High-Intermediate. Linda R. Markstein & Dorien Grunbaum. (English As a Second Language Bk.). 1981. Bk. 3: High-Intermediate. write for info. (*0-582-79785-3*, 75040) Longman.

What's the Story? Photographs for Language Practice, 4 bks., Bk. 4, Advanced. Linda R. Markstein & Dorien Grunbaum. (English As a Second Language Bk.). 1981. Bk. 4: Advanced. write for info. (*0-582-79786-1*, 75041) Longman.

What's the Story? Photographs for Language Practice, 4 bks., Bk.1 , Beginning. Linda R. Markstein & Dorien Grunbaum. (English As a Second Language Bk.). 1981. Bk. 1: Beginning. write for info. (*0-582-79783-7*, 75038) Longman.

What's the Time? Lara Tankel. LC 94-28972. 24p. (J). (ps-3). 1994. write for info. (*1-56458-726-6*) DK Pub Inc.

***What's the Time? Benjamin Learns to Tell Time.** Sterling Publishing Company, Inc. Staff. (Balloon Bks.). 1997. 7.95 (*0-8069-0382-1*) Sterling.

What's the Verdict? Mark Riddoch. LC 93-24237. 1993. pap. 3.95 (*1-56420-000-0*) New Readers.

What's the Verdict? Real Life Court Cases to Test Your Legal IQ. Ted LeValliant & Marcel Theroux. LC 90-28616. (Illus.). 128p. 1991. pap. 5.95 (*0-8069-7466-4*) Sterling.

What's the Weather Like Today? Rozanne L. Williams. (Emergent Reader Big Bks.). 16p. (J). (gr. k-2). 1995. 11.98 (*0-916119-80-7*) Creat Teach Pr.

What's the Weather Like Today?, Level II. Rozanne L. Williams. (Emergent Reader Science Ser.). 16p. 1994. 2.49 (*0-916119-41-6*, 3531) Creat Teach Pr.

What's the Weather Today? Allan Fowler. LC 91-3125. (Rookie Read-about Science Ser.). (Illus.). 32p. (J). (ps-2). 1991. pap. 3.95 (*0-516-44918-4*); lib. bdg. 17.30 (*0-516-04918-6*) Childrens.

What's the Weather Today? Big Book. Allan Fowler. LC 91-3125. (Rookie Read-about Science Ser.). (Illus.). 32p. (J). (ps-2). 1991. lib. bdg. 32.40 (*0-516-49478-3*) Childrens.

What's the Word? (Sesame Street Ser.: No. 17). (J). 1989. pap. 1.49 (*0-553-18400-8*) Bantam.

What's the Word that Means . . . George S. Welsh. 300p. (Orig.). 1989. pap. write for info. (*0-318-65812-7*) Algee Bks.

What's the Word That Means...? How to Find the Word That You Can't Remember-or One That You Don't Know but Would Like To. George S. Welsh. LC 89-81812. 344p. (Orig.). 1990. pap. 14.95 (*0-9624698-0-7*) Algee Bks.

What's the Worst That Could Happen? Donald E. Westlake. LC 96-12770. 384p. 1996. 22.00 (*0-89296-586-X*) Mysterious Pr.

***What's the Worst That Could Happen?** Donald E. Westlake. 336p. 1997. mass mkt. 6.50 (*0-446-60471-2*) Warner Bks.

***What's the Worst That Could Happen?** large type ed. Donald E. Westlake. LC 96-34448. (Cloak & Dagger Ser.). 536p. 1996. 23.95 (*0-7862-0862-7*, Thorndike Lrg Prnt) Thorndike Pr.

What's There to Write. (J). 1993. pap. 7.95 (*0-590-73354-0*) Scholastic Inc.

What's This Green Stuff, Flo? Chriss McNaught. (Flo's Cooking Ser.). (Illus.). 64p. (Orig.). 1993. pap. 6.95 (*1-879894-05-X*) Stargaze Pub.

What's This World Coming To? Stan Campbell. (Biblelog Ser.: Bk. 4). 144p. (YA). (gr. 8 up). 1988. pap. text ed. 6.50 (*0-89693-865-4*, 6-2865, Victor Bks) Chariot Victor.

What's This World Coming To? Leader's Guide. Stan Campbell. (BibleLog Ser.: Bk.4). 1988. pap. 5.99 (*0-89693-866-2*) SP Pubns.

What's to Be Scared of, Suki? C. S. Adler. LC 95-50141. (J). (gr. 3-7). 1996. 13.95 (*0-395-77600-7*, Clarion Bks) HM.

What's to Become of the Boy? or, Something to Do with Books. Heinrich Boll. Tr. by Leila Vannewitz. LC 95-51551. 82p. (C). 1996. pap. 13.95 (*0-8101-1208-6*) Northwestern U Pr.

What's to Eat? Edith Down. 1981. teacher ed. 9.32 (*0-02-666160-8*); text ed. 16.60 (*0-02-666150-0*) Glencoe.

What's under My Bed? (Glow in the Dark Bks.). (Illus.). (J). (ps-3). 1991. write for info. (*0-307-06254-6*, Golden Books) Western Pub.

***What's under My Bed?** Patricia T. Cousin et al. (Visions: African-American Experiences: No. 22). (Illus.). 8p. (Orig.). (J). (gr. k-1). 1995. pap. text ed. 3.00 (*1-57518-021-9*) Arborlake.

What's under My Bed? James Stevenson. LC 83-1454. (Illus.). 32p. (J). (gr. k-3). 1983. 16.00 (*0-688-02325-8*); lib. bdg. 15.93 (*0-688-02327-4*) Greenwillow.

What's under My Bed? James Stevenson. LC 83-1454. (Illus.). 32p. (J). (ps up). 1990. reprint ed. pap. 4.95 (*0-688-09350-7*, Mulberry) Morrow.

What's under that Shell? D. M. Souza. (Creatures All Around Us Ser.). (Illus.). 40p. (J). (gr. 1-4). 1992. lib. bdg. 14.96 (*0-87614-712-0*, Carolrhoda) Lerner Group.

***What's under the Bed?** Mick Manning & Brita G. Om. LC 97-16326. (Wonderwise Ser.). 1997. pap. write for info. (*0-531-15327-4*) Watts.

***What's under the Bed?** Mick Manning & Brita G. Om. LC 97-16326. (Wonderwise Ser.). (Illus.). (J). 1997. write for info. (*0-531-14489-5*) Watts.

What's under the Ground? Susan Mayes. (Starting Point Science Ser.). (Illus.). 24p. (J). (gr. 1-4). 1989. pap. 3.95 (*0-7460-0357-9*, Usborne) EDC.

What's under the Ocean. Janet Craig. LC 81-11425. (Now I Know Ser.). (Illus.). 32p. (J). (gr. k-2). 1996. pap. 3.50 (*0-89375-653-9*) Troll Communs.

What's under the Sea? Sophy Tahta. (Starting Point Science Ser.). (Illus.). 24p. (J). (gr. 1 up). 1994. pap. 3.95 (*0-7460-0968-2*, Usborne); lib. bdg. 11.95 (*0-88110-663-1*, Usborne) EDC.

***What's Up?** Mick Manning & Brita G. Om. LC 97-14014. (Wonderwise). (J). 1997. write for info. (*0-531-14485-2*); pap. write for info. (*0-531-15323-1*) Watts.

What's Up. McPartland. 1989. pap. text ed. 15.25 (*0-13-955766-0*) P-H.

***What's Up?** William Scheller. 1998. spiral bd. write for info. (*0-201-15833-7*) Addison-Wesley.

What's Up? Roxanne Vallet. (Illus.). 12p. (J). (gr. k-3). 1994. pap. 9.95 (*1-56606-028-1*) Bradley Mann.

What's Up Girlfriend? Elsaida Peltier-Draine. (Illus.). 170p. (Orig.). 1994. 17.95 (*0-9643320-1-9*); per., pap. 11.95 (*0-9643320-0-0*) Zenon Pubn.

What's Up Girlfriend? large type ed. Elsaida Peltier-Draine. (Illus.). 170p. (Orig.). 1994. 17.95 (*0-9643320-2-7*) Zenon Pubn.

What's up in the Attic? Sesame Street. (Golden Story Book 'n Tape Ser.). (Illus.). 24p. (J). (ps-3). 1991. write for info. (*0-307-14171-3*, 14171, Golden Books) Western Pub.

What's Up? Know How to Repair & Fabricate Antennas. 1995. lib. bdg. 250.95 (*0-8490-6619-0*) Gordon Pr.

What's up the Coconut Tree? A. Benjamin. (Illus.). 32p. (J). (ps up). 1992. bds. 11.95 (*0-19-279896-0*) OUP.

***What's up with You, Taquandra Fu?** Matt Cibula. (Illus.). (J). (ps up). 1997. 16.95 (*0-614-29157-7*) Zino Pr.

***What's up with You, Taquandra Fu?** Matt S. Cibula. LC 97-13617. (Illus.). (J). 1997. write for info. (*1-55933-212-3*) Zino Pr.

***What's What.** Barbara Bader. Date not set. write for info. (*0-688-05152-9*); lib. bdg. write for info. (*0-688-05153-7*) Greenwillow.

What's What. Arlene D. Miller. Ed. by Carol Gilbert. (Illus.). 21p. (Orig.). (J). (ps-6). 1985. pap. 4.00 (*0-9614209-0-1*) Adam Pub Co.

What's What. Julie O'Callaghan. 77p. (Orig.). 9100. pap. 15.95 (*1-85224-161-6*, Pub. by Bloodaxe Bks UK) Dufour.

What's What? A Guessing Game. Mary Serfozo. (Illus.). (J). 1996. 15.00 (*0-689-80653-1*, McElderry) S&S Childrens.

What's What: A Visual Glossary of the Physical World. Reginald Bragonier. 1994. 15.98 (*0-8317-9469-0*) Smithmark.

What's What & Who's Who in Europe. Harry Drost. LC 94-6211. 1995. 75.00 (*0-13-955030-5*) S&S Trade.

An Asterisk (*) at the beginning of an entry indicates that the title is appearing in BIP for the first time.

What's What & Who's Who in Europe. Harry Drost. LC 94-6211. 1995. 25.00 (0-13-955097-6) S&S Trade.

What's What in Japanese Restaurants: A Guide to Ordering, Eating, & Enjoying. Robb Satterwhite. LC 87-82865. (Illus.). 144p. 1988. pap. 12.00 (0-87011-867-6) Kodansha.

What's What in Japanese Restaurants: A Guide to Ordering, Eating & Enjoying. Robb Satterwhite. (Illus.). 180p. 1996. pap. 9.95 (4-7700-2086-4) Kodansha.

What's What in the Nineteen Eighty's: A Dictionary of Contemporary History, Literature, Arts, Technology, Medicine, Cinema, Theatre, Controversies, Fads, Movements & Events, Vol. 1. Ed. by Christopher Pick. 399p. 1982. 58.00 (0-8103-2035-5) Gale.

***What's Whole in Whole Language.** Ken Goodman. (FRE.). pap. 12.99 (0-590-71985-8) Scholastic Inc.

What's Whole in Whole Language? A Parent/Teacher Guide to Children's Learning. Kenneth Goodman. LC 85-27154. 80p. (Orig.). 1986. pap. text ed. 10.50 (0-435-08254-X, 08254) Heinemann.

Whats, Whys, & Hows of Quality of Improvement. George L. Miller & La Rue Krumm. 283p. 1992. pap. 16.00 (0-87389-183-X, H0720) ASQC Qual Pr.

What's Working & What's Not: A Summary of Research of the Economic Impact of Employment & Training Programs. 1996. lib. bdg. 251.99 (0-8490-6871-1) Gordon Pr.

What's Worrying Gus. Henry Beard & J. Boswell. Date not set. pap. 12.00 (0-679-77012-7) McKay.

What's Worrying Gus? The True Story of a Big City Bear. Henry Beard & John Boswell. 80p. 1995. 12.00 (0-679-44950-7, Villard Bks) Random.

***What's Worth Fighting for in Headship? Strategies for Taking Charge of the Headship.** Michael Fullan. 80p. 1992. pap. 8.99 (0-335-15754-8, Open Univ Pr) Taylor & Francis.

What's Worth Fighting for in Your School? Michael Fullan & Andy Hargreaves. 128p. (C). 1996. pap. text ed. 9.95 (0-8077-3554-X) Tchrs Coll.

***What's Worth Fighting for in Your School? Working Together for Improvement.** Michael Fullan & Andy Hargreaves. 160p. 1992. pap. 8.99 (0-335-15755-6, Open Univ Pr) Taylor & Francis.

What's Wrong: American Satisfaction & Complaint. Everett C. Ladd & Karlyn H. Bowman. 100p. 1996. text ed. 19.95 (0-8447-3954-5, AEI Pr) Am Enterprise.

***What's Wrong: American Satisfaction & Complaint.** Everett C. Ladd & Karlyn H. Bowman. 100p. 1997. pap. write for info. (0-8447-3955-3) Am Enterprise.

What's Wrong Here. Elvira Gamiello. (Illus.). (Orig.). (J). (gr. 4-6). 1989. pap. 1.95 (0-942025-91-1) Kidsbks.

What's Wrong Here?, No. 2. Anthony Tallarico. (Illus.). 64p. (Orig.). (J). 1990. pap. 1.95 (0-942025-92-X) Kidsbks.

What's Wrong Here? At School. Tony Tallarico. (What's Wrong Here? Ser.). (Illus.). 24p. (J). 1991. pap. 2.95 (1-56156-034-0) Kidsbks.

What's Wrong Here? At School. Tony Tallarico. (What's Wrong Here? Ser.). (Illus.). 24p. (J). 1991. 9.95 (1-56156-005-7) Kidsbks.

What's Wrong Here? At the Amusement Park. Tony Tallarico. (What's Wrong Here? Ser.). (Illus.). 32p. (J). 1991. pap. 2.95 (1-56156-032-4) Kidsbks.

What's Wrong Here? At the Amusement Park. Tony Tallarico. (What's Wrong Here? Ser.). (Illus.). 24p. (J). 1991. 9.95 (1-56156-003-0) Kidsbks.

What's Wrong Here? At the Movies. Tony Tallarico. (What's Wrong Here? Ser.). (Illus.). 24p. (J). 1991. pap. 2.95 (1-56156-035-9) Kidsbks.

What's Wrong Here? At the Movies. Tony Tallarico. (What's Wrong Here? Ser.). (Illus.). 24p. (J). 1991. 9.95 (1-56156-004-9) Kidsbks.

What's Wrong Here? In the Haunted House. Tony Tallarico. (What's Wrong Here? Ser.). (Illus.). 24p. (J). 1991. 9.95 (1-56156-002-2); pap. 2.95 (1-56156-033-2) Kidsbks.

What's Wrong in Washington? Illus. by John Holladay. 24p. 1992. pap. 9.95 (1-56288-317-8) Checkerboard.

What's Wrong Now, Millicent? David S. Meier. LC 95-38291. (Illus.). 32p. (J). (ps-3). 1996. 13.00 (0-689-80680-9, S&S Bks Young Read) S&S Childrens.

What's Wrong? What's Wrong? What's Wrong? Carol Hamoy. (Illus.). (J). (gr. k-3). 1965. 8.95 (0-685-00564-X) Astor-Honor.

What's Wrong, Who's Right in Central America? 2nd ed. Richard A. Nuccio. 170p. 1989. pap. 14.95 (0-8419-1177-0) Holmes & Meier.

What's Wrong, Who's Right in Central America: A Citizen's Guide. Richard A. Nuccio. LC 85-31093. (Illus.). Np. reprint ed. pap. 43.90 (0-318-39769-2, 2033168) Bks Demand.

What's Wrong with America. Scott Bradfield. LC 94-12803. 1994. 18.95 (0-312-11349-8) St Martin.

What's Wrong with America. Scott Bradfield. LC 94-12803. 1995. pap. 10.00 (0-312-13619-6, Picador USA) St Martin.

What's Wrong with Being Crabby? Charles M. Schulz. LC 75-29872. 192p. 1976. pap. 4.95 (0-03-017486-4, Owl) H Holt & Co.

What's Wrong with Being Crabby? Charles M. Schulz. (Peanuts Classics Ser.). 128p. (J). (ps-2). 1992. pap. 7.95 (0-8050-2400-X, Owl) H Holt & Co.

What's Wrong with Being Happy. Y. Miller. 1994. 18.99 (0-89906-121-4); pap. 15.99 (0-89906-122-2) Mesorah Pubns.

What's Wrong with Being Human. Y. Miller. 1992. 18.99 (0-89906-544-9); pap. 15.99 (0-89906-545-7) Mesorah Pubns.

What's Wrong with Christian Rock? Jeff Godwin. LC 90-85347. (Illus.). 1990. pap. 9.95 (0-937958-36-0) Chick Pubns.

What's Wrong with Eating Meat? Vistara Parham. LC 79-52319. (Illus.). (Orig.). (J). 1979. pap. 3.50 (0-88476-009-X) Ananda Marga.

What's Wrong with Eddie? Elizabeth Janoski. 92p. (Orig.). (J). (gr. 5-8). 1995. pap. 5.00 (0-88092-040-8) Royal Fireworks.

What's Wrong with Ethnography? Martyn Hammersley. 240p. (C). (gr. 13). 1991. pap. 16.95 (0-415-05477-X, A6206) Routledge.

What's Wrong with God. T. Steeman. Ed. by Fitan McNamee. (Synthesis Ser.). pap. 1.00 (0-8199-0233-0, Frncscn Herld) Franciscan Pr.

What's Wrong with Grandma? A Family's Experience with Alzheimer's. Margaret Shawver. (Young Readers Ser.). (Illus.). 50p. (J). (gr. 2 up). 1996. 14.95 (1-57392-107-6) Prometheus Bks.

What's Wrong with Human Rights. T. Robert Ingram. LC 78-68732. (Orig.). 1979. pap. 5.95 (0-686-24267-X) St Thomas.

What's Wrong with Japan, Anyway? Dorothy Robins-Mowry. 112p. (Orig.). 1993. pap. text ed. 9.95 (1-883223-00-8) Pacific NY.

What's Wrong with Marxism? On Peasants & Workers in India & Indonesia. Olle Tournquist. (C). 1991. 24.00 (0-685-59778-4, Pub. by Manohar II) S Asia.

What's Wrong with Me? Learning Disabilities at Home & School. Regina Cicci. LC 95-40227. 253p. 1995. pap. 26.50 (0-912752-38-6) York Pr.

What's Wrong with My Car? Ed. by Mort Schultz. 240p. 1990. pap. 16.95 (0-89043-068-3) Consumer Reports.

What's Wrong with My Car? A Quick & Easy Guide to the Most Common Symptoms of Car Trouble. Bob Cerullo. 160p. (Orig.). 1993. pap. 11.95 (0-452-26993-8, Plume) NAL-Dutton.

***What's Wrong with My Horse?** Colin J. Vogel. (Illus.). 144p. 1997. pap. 14.95 (0-7153-0489-5, Pub. by D & C Pub UK) Sterling.

What's Wrong with My Snake? John Rossi & Roxanne Rossi. LC 96-15432. (Illus.). 150p. 1996. 14.95 (1-882770-35-8) Adv Vivarium.

What's Wrong with Postmodernism: Critical Theory & the Ends of Philosophy. Christopher Norris. (Parallax). 256p. 1991. text ed. 48.50 (0-8018-4136-4); pap. text ed. 15.95 (0-8018-4137-2) Johns Hopkins.

What's Wrong with Preaching? Albert N. Martin. 32p. 1992. pap. 1.95 (0-85151-632-7) Banner of Truth.

What's Wrong with Public Education - From A to Z. Carl W. Salser, Jr. LC 78-68114. 1978. pap. 13.95 (0-89420-049-6, 110060, Halcyon) Natl Book.

What's Wrong with Rights? Elizabeth Kingdom. 1991. text ed. 42.50 (0-7486-0250-X, Pub. by Edinburgh U Pr UK) Col U Pr.

What's Wrong with Rights? Problems for Feminist Politics of Law. Elizabeth Kingdom. (Edinburgh Law & Society Ser.). 192p. 1992. pap. text ed. 27.50 (0-7486-0322-0, Pub. by Edinburgh U Pr UK) Col U Pr.

What's Wrong with Sex Education? Preteen & Teenage Sexual Development & Environmental Influences. Melvin Anchell. Ed. by Bobbie H. Ames. (Illus.). 108p. (Orig.). 1993. pap. 7.00 (0-9626257-4-4) CBCCU Amer.

What's Wrong with Tamara? D. A. Fowler. Ed. by Eric Toblias. 304p. (Orig.). 1992. mass mkt. 4.99 (0-671-73805-4) PB.

What's Wrong with the Girls? Manuscript Edition. Conrad Seiler. 1956. pap. 13.00 (0-8222-1237-4) Dramatists Play.

What's Wrong with the Mental Health System. 1991. pap. 3.00 (0-913937-53-3) Rational Isl.

What's Wrong with the Mental Health System. 1995. pap. 3.00 (1-885357-20-6) Rational Isl.

What's Wrong with the Mental Health System: Spanish Translation. 1994. pap. 3.00 (1-885357-01-X) Rational Isl.

What's Wrong with the Movies? Tamar Lane. LC 78-160237. (Moving Pictures Ser.). 254p. 1971. reprint ed. lib. bdg. 29.95 (0-89198-038-5) Ozer.

What's Wrong with the Social Sciences? The Perils of the Postmodern. Michael A. Faia. 260p. (Orig.). (C). 1993. pap. text ed. 22.50 (0-8191-9236-8); lib. bdg. 49.50 (0-8191-9235-X) U Pr of Amer.

What's Wrong with the U. S. A., Anyway? Ed. by Dorothy Robins-Mowry. LC 93-47930. 1994. 9.50 (1-883223-03-2) Pacific NY.

What's Wrong with the U. S. Economy? A Popular Guide for the Rest of Us. Institute for Labor Education & Research Staff. LC 82-80690. (Illus.). 399p. 1982. pap. 10.00 (0-89608-010-2) South End Pr.

What's Wrong with the World. Gilbert K. Chesterton. LC 93-80844. 205p. 1996. pap. 12.95 (0-89870-489-8) Ignatius Pr.

What's Wrong with the World. Gilbert K. Chesterton. 224p. 1992. reprint ed. pap. 10.95 (0-89385-037-3) Sugden.

What's Wrong with This Book? Richard McGuire. 1997. pap. 14.99 (0-670-86852-3) Viking Penguin.

***What's Wrong with This Country Anyway?** Morton J. Kessler. LC 96-69831. 80p. (Orig.). 1997. pap. 12.95 (1-57197-040-1) Pentland Pr.

What's Wrong with This Picture. Donald Margulies. 75p. (Orig.). 1988. pap. 5.95 (0-88145-059-6) Broadway Play.

What's Wrong with This Picture? Coloring Book. Anna Pomaska. (Illus.). (J). (gr. k-3). 1983. pap. 2.50 (0-486-24485-7) Dover.

***What's Wrong with Uncle Johnny?** Illus. by John M. Doherty. 36p. (J). (gr. 3-5). 1997. write for info. (0-614-28392-2, Power Hse) MYD Pubns.

Whats Wrong with Wall Street. Louis Lowenstein. 1989. pap. 10.53 (0-201-51796-5) Addison-Wesley.

What's Wrong with Wall Street: Short-Term Gain & the Absentee Shareholder. Louis Lowenstein. 1988. 17.26 (0-201-17169-4) Addison-Wesley.

What's Wrong with Your Life Insurance? Norman F. Dacey. 448p. 1989. 24.95 (0-02-529350-8) Macmillan.

What's Wrong with Your Life Insurance. Dacy. 1994. pap. 5.00 (0-02-009471-X) Macmillan.

***What's Your Agatha Christie I. Q. 1001 Puzzling Questions about the World's Most Beloved Mystery.** Kathleen Kaska. 1996. pap. text ed. 10.95 (0-8065-1819-7, Citadel Pr) Carol Pub Group.

What's Your "Cheers" IQ? 750 Questions & Answers for Fans. Mark Wenger. 160p. 1996. pap. 9.95 (0-8065-1780-8, Citadel Pr) Carol Pub Group.

What's Your Excuse. Barbara Arnstein. 1991. 4.98 (1-55521-645-5) Bk Sales Inc.

What's Your Favorite Flower? Allan Fowler. LC 92-7404. (Rookie Read-about Science Ser.). (Illus.). 32p. (J). (ps-2). 1993. pap. 3.95 (0-516-46007-2) Childrens.

What's Your Favorite Flower? Big Book. Allan Fowler. LC 92-7404. (Rookie Read-about Science Big Bks.). (Illus.). 32p. (J). (ps-2). 1992. pap. 32.40 (0-516-49634-4) Childrens.

What's Your Frasier IQ? 501 Questions & Answers for Fans. Robert Bly. LC 95-19778. (Illus.). 160p. 1995. pap. 8.95 (0-8065-1732-8, Citadel Pr) Carol Pub Group.

What's Your "Friends" IQ? 501: Questions & Answers for Fans. Stephen J. Spignesi. 144p. 1996. pap. 9.95 (0-8065-1776-X, Citadel Pr) Carol Pub Group.

What's Your Game? Michael Cornelius & Alan Parr. (Illus.). 160p. (C). 1991. pap. text ed. 18.95 (0-521-38625-X) Cambridge U Pr.

What's Your Literacy IQ? Over 1,000 Questions on Subjects from Abacus to Zygotes. Norma Gleason. LC 92-39178. 1993. 6.95 (0-8065-1389-6, Citadel Pr) Carol Pub Group.

Whats Your Mad about You IQ? Six Hundred & One Questions & Answers for Fans. Stephen J. Spignesi. (Illus.). 160p. 1995. pap. 8.95 (0-8065-1682-8, Citadel Pr) Carol Pub Group.

What's Your Name: A Book of Eritrean & Ethiopian Names. Zeray Habte-Sillasie. LC 95-51098. 140p. 1997. pap. 9.95 (0-86543-447-6) Africa World.

What's Your Name? And Other Poems. Hilary Weisman. LC 94-71901. (Illus.). 32p. (J). (gr. 1-6). 1995. pap. 8.95 (1-878668-42-0) Disc Enter Ltd.

What's Your Name? From Ariel to Zoe. Eve Sanders. LC 95-9771. (Illus.). 32p. (J). (gr. k-3). 1995. lib. bdg. 15.95 (0-8234-1209-1) Holiday.

What's Your Objection to Holy Spirit Baptism? Robert B. Burnette. 90p. 1992. student ed. 9.95 (1-881202-11-9) Anointed Pubns.

What's Your Opera I. Q. A Quiz Book for Opera Lovers. Iris Bass. 1991. pap. 8.95 (0-8065-1211-3, Citadel Pr) Carol Pub Group.

***What's Your Opera I.Q.? A Quiz Book for Opera Lovers.** Iris Bass. LC 96-50272. 208p. 1997. pap. 12.00 (0-8065-1862-6, Citadel Pr) Carol Pub Group.

What's Your Point? Bob Boylan. 176p. 1990. pap. 15.99 (0-446-39102-6) Warner Bks.

What's Your Point? Kathy M. Littlefield & Robert S. Littlefield. (Illus.). 32p. (Orig.). (J). (gr. 3-6). 1990. pap. text ed. 8.95 (1-879340-05-4, K0106) Kidspeak.

What's Your Point? A Proven Method for Giving Crystal Clear Presentations! Bob Boylan. Ed. by Norine Larson. (Illus.). 160p. 1989. pap. 12.95 (0-941755-00-2) Point Pubns MN.

What's Your Problem? Karen Dockrey. 96p. (YA). (gr. 7 up). 1987. pap. 2.80 (0-89693-381-4, Victor Bks) Chariot Victor.

What's Your Problem? Posing & Solving Mathematical Problems, K-2. Penny Skinner. LC 91-20373. 128p. 1991. pap. text ed. 18.50 (0-435-08326-0, 08326) Heinemann.

What's Your S. Q.? (Spiritual Quotient) Maralene Wesner & Miles Wesner. LC 86-71133. 100p. 1986. pap. 4.95 (0-936715-04-9) Diversity Okla.

What's Your Story? A Young Person's Guide to Writing Fiction. Marion Dane Bauer. 144p. (YA). (gr. 5 up). 1992. 14.95 (0-395-57781-0, Clarion Bks); pap. 6.95 (0-395-57780-2, Clarion Bks) HM.

***What's Your Type? How Blood Types Are the Keys to Unlocking Your Personality.** Peter Constantine. LC 97-587. 1997. pap. 10.95 (0-452-27802-3, Plume) NAL-Dutton.

***What's Your X-Files I. Q. 501 Questions & Answers for Fans.** Marc Shapiro. 1997. pap. text ed. 9.95 (0-8065-1927-4, Citadel Pr) Carol Pub Group.

What's Yr Hair Like after U Wash It? Natural Poems by Valerie Lawrence. Valerie Lawrence. LC 90-6188. 100p. (J). (gr. 6 up). 1990. 10.95 (0-929917-01-4) Magnolia PA.

Whatsoever Things Are True. Compiled by Harold Whaley. LC 79-67283. 64p. 1980. 4.95 (0-87159-100-6) Unity Bks.

Whatsoever You Doeth Shall Prosper! Betty P. Peebles. 96p. (Orig.). 1989. pap. text ed. 3.95 (0-918925-00-2) Jericho Chr Trng.

Whattaya Do? Business English Book. Nina Weinstein. (Illus.). 104p. (Orig.). 1989. pap. text ed. 11.50 (0-937354-29-5); audio 29.95 (0-937354-30-9) Delta Systems.

Whattaya Hear? Listening Strategies & Culture Through American Jokes. Nina Weinstein. (Illus.). 90p. (Orig.). 1989. pap. text ed. 10.95 (0-937354-27-9); audio 29.95 (0-937354-28-7) Delta Systems.

Whattizit? Nature Pun Quizzes. Allan Eckert. (Illus.). 48p. (Orig.). 1981. pap. 2.95 (0-913428-30-2) Landfall Pr.

What've They Done with Abraham's Blessings?, Vol. 2. Jay S. Snell. (Orig.). 1990. pap. 8.00 (0-685-67692-7) J Snell Evangelistic.

Wheat. Ed. by Y. P. Bajaj. (Biotechnology in Agriculture & Forestry Ser.: Vol. 13). (Illus.). 704p. 1991. 398.95 (0-387-51809-6) Spr-Verlag.

***Wheat.** Denise DeVries. (Premier Ser.: Vol. 9). (Illus.). 25p. 1997. 5.00 (0-9654421-8-7) Mica Press.

Wheat. Sylvia A. Johnson. (Natural Science Ser.). (Illus.). 48p. (J). (gr. 4 up). 1990. lib. bdg. 21.50 (0-8225-1490-7, Lerner Publctns) Lerner Group.

Wheat: Chemistry & Technology, Vol. I. 3rd ed. Ed. by Y. Pomeranz. LC 88-71636. (Monograph Ser.). 514p. 1988. write for info. (0-913250-65-1) Am Assn Cereal Chem.

Wheat: Chemistry & Technology, Vol. II. 3rd ed. Ed. by Y. Pomeranz. LC 88-71636. (Monograph Ser.). 562p. 1988. write for info. (0-913250-73-2) Am Assn Cereal Chem.

Wheat: Humor & Wisdom of J. Golden Kimball. Mikal Lofgren. LC 80-81556. 95p. 1980. 6.50 (0-936718-04-8) Moth Hse.

Wheat: Production, Properties & Quality. W. Bushuk. 1994. 114.95 (0-7514-0181-1, Pub. by Blackie Acad & Prof UK) Routledge Chapman & Hall.

Wheat among Bones. Mary Baron. LC 79-90839. 94p. 1979. 11.95 (0-935296-04-2) Sheep Meadow.

Wheat & Politics. J. W. Brinton. Ed. by Dan C. McCurry & Richard E. Rubenstein. LC 74-30621. (American Farmers & the Rise of Agribusiness Ser.). 1975. reprint ed. 26.95 (0-405-06768-2) Ayer.

Wheat & the AAA. Joseph S. Davis. LC 76-172868. (FDR & the Era of the New Deal Ser.). 468p. 1973. reprint ed. 59.50 (0-306-70375-0) Da Capo.

Wheat & the Chaff. Francois Mitterrand. LC 82-3156. 284p. 1982. 16.95 (0-86579-022-1) Seaver Bks.

Wheat & the Chaff. Francois Mitterrand. LC 82-3156. 284p. 1982. pap. 7.95 (0-86579-026-4) Seaver Bks.

Wheat & Weeds & the Wolf of Gubbio: Stories & Prayers for People Who Pray & for People Who Don't. Graziano Marcheschi. (Illus.). 140p. (Orig.). 1993. pap. 9.95 (1-55612-661-1) Sheed & Ward MO.

Wheat & Wheat Improvement. 2nd ed. Ed. by E. G. Heyne. (Illus.). 766p. 1987. 44.00 (0-89118-091-5) Am Soc Agron.

Wheat & Wheat Quality in Australia. David H. Simmonds. 1989. 70.00 (0-643-04799-9, Pub. by CSIRO AT) Aubrey Bks.

Wheat & Wine. Arlene H. Honeycutt. LC 92-82587. 296p. 1993. pap. 12.00 (1-56002-202-7, Univ Edtns) Aegina Pr.

Wheat & Women. Georgina Binnie-Clark. LC 80-463250. (Social History of Canada Ser.: No. 30). 364p. reprint ed. pap. 103.80 (0-685-16244-3, 2026424) Bks Demand.

Wheat, Barley, Rice, Rye & Oat Genome Mapping: Sponsored CRIS/ICAR Projects & Bibliography. Sarah Ranck. 74p. (Orig.). (C). 1996. pap. text ed. 35.00 (0-7881-2728-4) DIANE Pub.

Wheat Boards: How Canada & Australia Market Grain Worldwide. (Illus.). 60p. (Orig.). (C). 1992. pap. text ed. 30.00 (1-56806-007-6) DIANE Pub.

Wheat Breeding & Its Scientific Basis. F. G. Lupton. 580p. 1987. lib. bdg. 145.00 (0-412-24470-5) Chapman & Hall.

Wheat End Uses Around the World. Ed. by Hamed Faridi & Jon M. Faubion. LC 95-75074. (Illus.). xv, 292p. 1995. 99.00 (0-913250-87-2) Am Assn Cereal Chem.

Wheat, Europe & the GATT: A Political Economy Analysis. Peter W. Phillips. LC 90-37799. 272p. 1990. text ed. 49.95 (0-312-05038-0) St Martin.

Wheat Field. Stephanie H. Adkins. LC 92-75006. (Orig.). 1992. pap. 9.95 (0-9635140-0-8) Atrax Pub.

***Wheat Flour Messiah: Eric Jansen of Bishop Hill.** Paul Elmen. LC 76-28380. (Illus.). 178p. 1997. pap. 15.95 (0-8093-2118-1) S Ill U Pr.

***Wheat Flour Milling.** E. S. Posner & A. N. Hibbs. LC 96-79927. (Illus.). 341p. 1997. text ed. 139.00 (0-913250-93-7) Am Assn Cereal Chem.

***Wheat-Free Cooking: Practical Help for the Home Cook.** Rita Greer. (Illus.). 128p. 1996. pap. text ed. 9.95 (0-285-63238-8, Pub. by Souvenir UK) IPG Chicago.

***Wheat-Free Dairy-Free Baking.** Mary Mauksch. LC 97-19003. 1997. 24.00 (0-02-862002-X) Macmillan.

Wheat-Free Recipes & Menus. Carol Fenster. 300p. (Orig.). 1995. pap. 19.95 (1-57502-049-1) Morris Pubng.

Wheat Genetic Resources: Meeting Diverse Needs. International Center for Agricultural Research in the Dry Areas - ICARDA Staff. LC 90-45855. 391p. 1991. text ed. 195.00 (0-471-92880-1) Wiley.

Wheat Gluten & Seitan - Bibliography & Sourcebook, A.D. 535 to 1993: Detailed Information on 462 Published Documents (Extensively Annotated Bibliography), 363 Commercial Gluten & Seitan Products, 208 Original Interviews... Ed. by Akiko Aoyagi. (Vegetable Proteins Ser.). 347p. (Orig.). 1994. spiral bd. 99.00 (0-933332-86-6) Soyfoods Center.

Wheat Growth & Modeling. Ed. by W. Day & R. K. Atkin. LC 85-3691. (NATO ASI Series A, Life Sciences: Vol. 86). 420p. 1985. 95.00 (0-306-41933-5, Plenum Pr) Plenum.

Wheat Health Management. R. James Cook & Roger J. Veseth. LC 90-85253. (Plant Health Management Ser.). (Illus.). 168p. 1991. pap. 45.00 (0-89054-111-6) Am Phytopathol Soc.

Wheat in India. A. Howard. 288p. 1979. 175.00 (0-685-44167-9, Pub. by Intl Bk Distr II) St Mut.

Wheat in India. Ed. by A. Howard. 288p. (C). 1979. text ed. 275.00 (0-89771-644-2, Pub. by Intl Bk Distr II) St Mut.

Wheat Is Unique: Structure, Composition, Processing, End-Use Properties, & Products. Ed. by Y. Pomeranz. LC 89-84430. (Illus.). 715p. 1989. 89.00 (0-913250-68-6) Am Assn Cereal Chem.

Wheat Lines & Super Freights. Joe McMillan. (Illus.). 1992. 64.95 (0-934228-17-5) McMillan Pubns.

Wheat Market & the Farmer in Minnesota, 1858-1900. Henrietta M. Larson. LC 70-82232. (Columbia University. Studies in the Social Sciences: No. 269). reprint ed. 29.50 (0-404-51269-0) AMS Pr.

W

Wheat of Christ. St. Nectarios Press Staff. (Orig.). 1988. pap. 3.00 (0-913026-68-9) St Nectarios.

Wheat Plant: Its Origin, Culture, Growth, Development, Composition, Varieties Together with Information on Corn & Its Culture, 2 vols. John H. Klippart. 1980. Set. lib. bdg. 200.00 (0-8490-3119-2) Gordon Pr.

Wheat Pricing: Information on Transition to New Tests for Protein. (Illus.). 39p. (Orig.). (C). 1995. pap. text ed. 20.00 (0-7881-2214-2) DIANE Pub.

Wheat Problem. William Crookes. LC 75-27633. (World Food Supply Ser.). (Illus.). 1976. reprint ed. 25.95 (0-405-07775-0) Ayer.

*__Wheat Production & Utilization: Systems, Quality, & the Environment.__ Mike J. Gooding & W. Paul Davies. LC 97-8472. 320p. 1997. 90.00 (0-85199-155-6) CAB Intl.

Wheat Revolution in India: Constraints & Prospects. Aswwini Pal. 1990. 58.00 (81-7099-198-6, Pub. by Mittal II) S Asia.

Wheat Rusts: An Atlas of Resistance Genes. Ed. by R. A. McIntosh et al. LC 95-7869. (Illus.). 200p. (C). 1995. lib. bdg. 92.50 (0-7923-3430-2) Kluwer Ac.

*__Wheat Rusts: An Atlas of Resistance Genes.__ R. A. McIntosh et al. (Illus.). 250p. 1995. 120.00 (0-643-05428-6, Pub. by CSIRO AT) Aubrey Bks.

Wheat Science-Today & Tomorrow. Ed. by L. T. Evans & W. J. Peacock. LC 80-41871. (Illus.). 300p. 1981. text ed. 74.95 (0-521-23793-9) Cambridge U Pr.

Wheat Support: The Impact of Target Prices vs. Export Subsidies. (Illus.). 50p. (Orig.). (C). 1995. pap. text ed. 25.00 (0-7881-1854-4) DIANE Pub.

Wheat That Springeth Green. J. F. Powers. LC 87-46104. 352p. 1988. 18.95 (0-394-49609-4) Knopf.

Wheat Trading & Hedging. William Grandmill. 1989. pap. 34.95 (0-930233-34-4) Windsor.

Wheat Varieties for Kansas: Your Best Choices for 1995. Steve Watson. 92p. (Orig.). 1994. pap. 9.95 (0-943861-10-1) Lone Tree.

Wheat, Wheat Flour, & Semolina: An International Trade Investigation. Jonathan Seiger. (Illus.). 250p. (Orig.). (C). 1994. pap. text ed. 65.00 (0-7881-1554-5) DIANE Pub.

Wheater's Basic Histopathology: A Colour Atlas & Text. 3rd ed. Paul R. Wheater & H. George Burkitt. LC 96-26701. 1996. write for info. (0-443-05088-0) Churchill.

Wheater's Functional Histology: A Text & Colour Atlas. 3rd ed. H. George Burkitt et al. LC 93-7323. (Illus.). 416p. 1993. pap. text ed. 42.95 (0-443-04691-3) Churchill.

Wheatfree Recipes. Julia A. Fletcher. LC 90-107035. (Illus.). 85p. 1989. spiral bd. 8.95 (0-9625877-0-2) Jay-Reflection Pub.

Wheatgrass: Nature's Finest Medicine. 3rd ed. Steve Meyerowitz. 60p. 1992. reprint ed. pap. 5.95 (1-878736-72-8) Sprout Hse.

Wheatgrass Book: How to Grow & Use Wheatgrass to Maximize Your Health & Vitality. Ann Wigmore. LC 84-24194. 144p. (Orig.). pap. 8.95 (0-89529-234-3) Avery Pub.

Wheatgrass Juice-Gift of Nature. rev. ed. Ed. by Betsy Russell-Manning. 1988. pap. 2.95 (0-930165-06-3) Greensward Pr.

*__Wheatland, Monroe County: A Brief Sketch of Its History.__ George E. Slocum. (Illus.). 138p. 1997. reprint ed. lib. bdg. 27.50 (0-8328-6280-0) Higginson Bk Co.

*__Wheatland, Monroe County: A Brief Sketch of Its History.__ George E. Slocum. (Illus.). 138p. 1997. reprint ed. pap. 17.50 (0-8328-6281-9) Higginson Bk Co.

Wheatless Cooking. Lynette Coffey. LC 85-17289. (Illus.). 96p. 1986. pap. 12.95 (0-89815-156-2) Ten Speed Pr.

*__Wheatley, Banneker & Horton.__ William G. Allen. Date not set. write for info. (0-88143-148-6) Ayer.

Wheatley, Banneker & Horton. William G. Allen. LC 77-133145. (Black Heritage Library Collection). 1949. reprint ed. 7.00 (0-8369-8657-1) Ayer.

Wheatley Manuscript: A Collection of Middle English Verse & Prose. (EETS, OS Ser.: No. 155). 1932. reprint ed. 40.00 (0-527-00152-X) Periodicals Srv.

Wheaton College Collection of Greek & Roman Coins. David Bishop & R. Ross Holloway. (Ancient Coins in North American Collections 4). (Illus.). 64p. 1981. 30.00 (0-89722-190-7) Am Numismatic.

Wheatstone English Concertina in Victorian England. Allan W. Atlas. LC 96-13333. (Illus.). 160p. 1996. 65.00 (0-19-816580-3, Clarendon Pr) OUP.

Whedon's Commentary on Acts, Romans, Vol. 3. 19.99 (0-88019-125-2) Schmul Pub Co.

Whedon's Commentary on First Corinthians, Vol. 4. 19.99 (0-88019-126-0) Schmul Pub Co.

Whedon's Commentary on Luke, Vol. 2. 19.99 (0-88019-124-4) Schmul Pub Co.

Whedon's Commentary on Matthew, Vol. 1. 19.99 (0-88019-123-6) Schmul Pub Co.

Whedon's Commentary on Psalms. F. G. Hibbard & D. D. Whedon. 1979. 21.99 (0-88019-130-9) Schmul Pub Co.

Whedon's Commentary on the Old Testament, Vol. 1: Genesis-Exodus. Fales H. Newhall & Milton S. Terry. 1987. 21.99 (0-88019-216-X) Schmul Pub Co.

Whedon's Commentary on the Old Testament, Vol. 2: Leviticus-Deuteronomy. John W. Lindsay & D. Steele. 21.99 (0-88019-129-5) Schmul Pub Co.

Whedon's Commentary on Titus & Revelations, Vol. 5. 19.99 (0-88019-127-9) Schmul Pub Co.

Whedon's Commentary Revised, 2 vols., Vol. Luke John. D. D. Whedon. 1981. pap. 7.65 (0-87813-918-4) Christian Light.

Whedon's Commentary Revised, 2 vols., Vol. Matthew Mark. D. D. Whedon. 1981. pap. 7.65 (0-87813-917-6) Christian Light.

Whedon's New Testament Commentary, 5 vols., Set. D. D. Whedon. 1979. 99.79 (0-88019-128-7) Schmul Pub Co.

Whee! We, Wee All the Way Home: A Guide to Sensual, Prophetic Spirituality. Matthew Fox. LC 81-67365. (Illus.). 264p. 1981. reprint ed. pap. 14.00 (0-939680-00-9) Bear & Co.

*__Wheel.__ Patricia Armentrout. LC 97-15151. (Simple Machines Ser.). (J). 1997. write for info. (1-57103-180-4) Rourke Pr.

Wheel. Ed. by Jim Bodeen & Tom Moore. (Illus.). 1995. 35.00 (0-911287-18-3) Blue Begonia.

Wheel: Poems. Wendell Berry. LC 82-81482. 72p. 1982. pap. 6.95 (0-86547-079-0, North Pt Pr) FS&G.

Wheel, a Kansas Tradition. Bill Venable. (Illus.). 128p. (Orig.). 1994. pap. 10.95 (1-882907-03-5) Old Market.

Wheel Alignment Specifications, Nineteen Ninety. 56p. 1990. 7.95 (0-13-129727-9, H M Gousha) P-H Gen Ref & Trav.

Wheel & Handwriting Analysis. Joseph Zmuda. (Illus.). 48p. (Orig.). 1985. pap. text ed. 20.00 (0-941572-02-1) Z Graphic Pubns.

Wheel & How It Changed the World. Ian Locke. LC 94-15228. (History & Invention Ser.). (Illus.). 48p. 1995. 14.95 (0-8160-3143-6) Facts on File.

Wheel & the Diamond: The Life of Dhardo Tulku. Suvajra. (Illus.). 160p. (Orig.). 1996. pap. 12.00 (0-904766-48-9) Windhorse Pubns.

Wheel Away! Dayle A. Dodds. LC 87-27091. (Trophy Picture Bk.). (Illus.). 32p. (J). (ps-1). 1991. pap. 4.95 (0-06-443267-X, Trophy) HarpC Child Bks.

*__Wheel Estate: The Rise & Decline of Mobile Homes.__ Allan D. Wallis. LC 96-53492. 1997. pap. 16.95 (0-8018-5641-8) Johns Hopkins.

Wheel Estate: The Rise & Decline of Mobile Homes. Allan D. Wallis. (Illus.). 304p. 1991. 24.95 (0-19-506183-7) OUP.

Wheel Excitement: The Official Rollerblade Guide to In-Line Skating. Neil Feineman. (Illus.). 144p. 1991. pap. 9.00 (0-688-10814-8) Hearst Bks.

Wheel of Becoming: Personal Growth Through the Liturgical Year. Augustin Belisle. LC 87-26493. 87p. (Orig.). 1987. pap. 5.95 (0-932506-57-7) St Bedes Pubns.

*__Wheel of Change Tarot.__ Alexandra Genetti. LC 97-2103. (Illus.). 320p. 1997. pap. 29.95 (0-89281-609-0) Inner Tradit.

Wheel of Destiny. Wilhelmina McKerron. 1981. 20.00 (0-7223-1408-6, Pub. by A H S Ltd UK) St Mut.

Wheel of Destiny: The Tarot Reveals Your Master Plan. Patricia Mclaine. LC 90-28371. (Illus.). 480p. 1991. pap. 17.95 (0-87542-490-2) Llewellyn Pubns.

Wheel of Dreams. Salinda Tyson. (Orig.). 1996. mass mkt. 4.99 (0-345-39430-5, Del Rey) Ballantine.

Wheel of Eternity. Helen Greaves. 152p. (Orig.). pap. 20.95 (0-8464-4313-9) Beekman Pubs.

Wheel of Eternity. Helen Greaves. 191p. 1974. pap. 13.95 (0-85435-192-2, Pub. by C W Daniel UK) Natl Bk Netwk.

Wheel of Fire. G. Wilson Knight. 1986. 12.95 (0-416-50930-4) Routledge Chapman & Hall.

*__Wheel of Fire.__ 4th ed. G. Wilson Knight. 364p. (C). 1949. pap. 17.95 (0-415-05096-0) Routledge.

Wheel of Fire: Interpretations of Shakespearean Tragedy. 4th ed. G. Wilson Knight. 350p. 1949. pap. 13.95 (0-416-67620-0, NO. 2276) Routledge Chapman & Hall.

Wheel of Fortune. Susan Howatch. 1280p. 1985. mass mkt. 6.99 (0-449-20624-6, Expression) Fawcett.

Wheel of Fortune. Ed. by Roger Zelazny. 400p. (Orig.). 1995. mass mkt. 5.99 (0-380-77423-2, AvoNova) Avon.

Wheel of Fortune. large type ed. James A. Pattinson. (Adventure Suspense Ser.). 1991. 25.99 (0-7089-2376-3) Ulverscroft.

Wheel of Fortune: The History of a Poor Community in Jakarta. Lea Jellinek. LC 89-46274. 236p. 1991. pap. text ed. 19.00 (0-8248-1381-2) UH Pr.

Wheel of God. George Egerton, pseud. LC 79-8263. reprint ed. 44.50 (0-404-61843-X) AMS Pr.

Wheel of Health: Preventive Medicine for the Family. H. James Beecham. (Illus.). 96p. (Orig.). 1990. pap. 9.95 (0-929894-01-4) K-W Pubns.

Wheel of Justice. William A. Holland. 1996. mass mkt., pap. 5.99 (0-671-79954-1) PB.

Wheel of Justice. William E. Holland. Ed. by Bill Grose. LC 94-22916. 352p. 1995. 22.00 (0-671-79954-3) PB.

*__Wheel of Life.__ Elisabeth Kbler-Ross. LC 97-6435. 1997. 22.00 (0-684-19361-2) S&S Trade.

Wheel of Life. Dorothy M. Lyon. 1989. 75.00 (0-7223-2167-8, Pub. by A H S Ltd UK) St Mut.

Wheel of Life. large type ed. Mary Munro. 330p. 1989. 25.99 (0-7089-1964-2) Ulverscroft.

*__Wheel of Life: A Memoir of Living & Dying.__ Elisabeth Kubler-Ross. 1997. 22.00 (0-614-28028-1, Scribners PB Fict) S&S Trade.

Wheel of Life & Death: A Practical & Spiritual Guide to Death, Dying & Beyond. Roshi P. Kapleau. 400p. 12.95 (0-385-23413-9, Anchor NY) Doubleday.

Wheel of Rebirth. Douglas M. Baker. 1978. pap. 12.00 (0-906006-16-3, Pub. by Baker Pubns UK) New Leaf Dist.

Wheel of Seasons. (Illus.). 178p. pap. 13.50 (0-9619384-1-2) Purple Mnt Pr.

Wheel of Servitude: Black Forced Labor after Slavery. Daniel A. Novak. LC 77-76334. 144p. 1978. 15.00 (0-8131-1371-7) U Pr of Ky.

Wheel of Stars. Andre Norton. (Orig.). 1991. mass mkt. 3.99 (0-8125-1678-8) Tor Bks.

Wheel of Tarot: A New Revolution. Angeles Arrien. Ed. by James Wanless. 303p. 1992. pap. 4.95 (0-9615079-7-7) Merrill-West Pub.

Wheel of the Year: Living the Magical Life. Pauline Campanelli. LC 89-38809. (Practical Magick Ser.). (Illus.). 172p. (Orig.). 1989. pap. 12.95 (0-87542-091-5) Llewellyn Pubns.

*__Wheel of the Year: Myth & Magic Through the Seasons.__ Teresa Moorey & Jane Brideson. (Illus.). 160p. 1997. pap. 17.95 (0-340-68386-4, Pub. by Headway UK) Trafalgar.

Wheel of Things: Lucy Maud Montgomery. Mollie Gillen. (Illus.). 224p. 1995. pap. 5.95 (0-88780-109-9) Formac Dist Ltd.

Wheel of Time. Robert Jordan. (Wheel of Time Ser.). 1995. boxed 17.97 (0-8125-3836-6) Tor Bks.

Wheel of Time. David Patt. 1983. pap. write for info. (0-318-62752-3) Deer Park Bks.

Wheel of Time: The Kalachakra in Context. Geshe L. Sopa et al. 96p. 1991. reprint ed. pap. 12.95 (1-55939-001-8) Snow Lion Pubns.

Wheel of Time Sand Mandala: Visual Scripture of Tibetan Buddhism. Barry Bryant. LC 91-59044. 288p. 1994. pap. 24.00 (0-06-250088-0) Harper SF.

Wheel on the Chimney. Margaret Wise Brown. LC 84-48379. (Illus.). 32p. (J). (ps-3). 1954. 14.00 (0-397-30288-6, Lipp Jr Bks); lib. bdg. 13.89 (0-397-30296-7, Lipp Jr Bks) HarpC Child Bks.

Wheel on the School. Meindert DeJong. LC 54-8945. (Illus.). 256p. (J). (gr. 4-7). 1954. lib. bdg. 14.89 (0-06-021586-0) HarpC Child Bks.

Wheel on the School. Meindert DeJong. LC 54-8945. (Illus.). 256p. (J). (gr. 4-7). 1954. 15.00 (0-06-021585-2) HarpC Child Bks.

Wheel on the School. Meindert DeJong. LC 54-8945. (Trophy Bk.). (Illus.). (J). (gr. 4-7). 1972. pap. 3.95 (0-06-440021-2, Trophy) HarpC Child Bks.

*__Wheel Selection Technique for Form Gear Grinding.__ R. W. Schwartz & S. B. Rao. (1985 Fall Technical Meeting Ser.: Vol. 7). 1p. 1985. pap. text ed. 30.00 (1-55589-100-4) AGMA.

Wheel to Storm. Barlow. Date not set. pap. 19.95 (0-670-83902-7) Viking Penguin.

Wheel to Wheel: The Great Rivalries of Formula One Racing. Alan Henry. (Illus.). 120p. 1996. 24.95 (0-7603-0269-3) Motorbooks Intl.

*__Wheel Within a Wheel.__ Frances E. Willard. LC 97-1615. (Illus.). 96p. 1997. reprint ed. pap. 8.95 (1-55709-449-7) Applewood.

Wheelbarrowful of Gold & More. Rosetta G. Bell. 1994. pap. 12.95 (0-533-10645-1) Vantage.

*__Wheelchair.__ Mickey Mongiovi. 96p. (YA). (gr. 9-12). 1997. pap. 9.00 (0-8059-4060-X) Dorrance.

*__Wheelchair Around the World.__ Patrick Simpson. LC 96-71069. (Illus.). 400p. (Orig.). 1997. pap. 24.95 (1-57197-054-1) Pentland Pr.

*__Wheelchair Basketball.__ Stan Labanowich. LC 97-19254. (Wheelchair Sports Ser.). (J). 1998. write for info. (1-56065-614-X) Capstone Pr.

Wheelchair Basketball. 2nd ed. Brad Hedrick et al. (Illus.). 120p. (Orig.). (C). 1994. pap. write for info. (0-929819-05-5) Paralyzed Vets.

Wheelchair Batteries. Betty Garee. LC 87-71478. 32p. (Orig.). 1987. reprint ed. pap. 3.50 (0-915708-22-1) Cheever Pub.

Wheelchair Gourmet: A Cookbook for the Disabled. Mary E. Blakeslee. LC 81-4547. 192p. 1981. spiral bd. 8.95 (0-8253-0063-0) Beaufort Bks NY.

Wheelchair Posture & Pressure Sores. Dennis Zacharkow. (Illus.). 108p. (C). 1983. 27.95 (0-398-04892-4) C C Thomas.

Wheelchair Recipes from the Collection of Momma Wheels. Maxine Smolen. Ed. by Debbie Hammond. LC 80-11153. pap. 12.95 (0-87949-171-X) Ashley Bks.

*__Wheelchair Road Racing.__ James R. Little. LC 97-15071. (Wheelchair Sports Ser.). (J). 1998. write for info. (1-56065-615-8) Capstone Pr.

Wheelchair Tennis: Myth to Reality. Ballard J. Moore & Randy Snow. 256p. 1994. per., pap. text ed. 21.95 (0-8403-9581-7) Kendall-Hunt.

*__Wheelchair Track Events.__ Stan Labanowich. LC 97-19255. (Wheelchair Sports Ser.). 1998. write for info. (1-56065-616-6) Capstone Pr.

*__Wheelchair Users & Postural Seating: A Clinical Approach.__ R. Ham et al. LC 97-17576. 1997. write for info. (0-443-05472-X) Churchill.

Wheelchair Vagabond. John G. Nelson. 1975. 14.95 (0-933261-10-1); pap. 9.95 (0-933261-07-1) Twin Peaks Pr.

Wheelchair Willie & Other Plays: Brown Ale with Gertie & O'Conner. Alan Brown. (Orig.). 1980. pap. 6.95 (0-7145-3655-5) Riverrun NY.

Wheeler: Trail in the Dust. braille ed. Richard G. Hubler. LC 70-91859. 772p. 1970. 9.95 (0-685-24689-2) Creek Hse.

Wheeler & Woolsey: The Vaudeville Comic Duo & Their Films, 1929-1937. Edward Watz. LC 94-26995. (Illus.). 336p. 1994. lib. bdg. 42.50 (0-89950-894-4) McFarland & Co.

Wheeler Dealers. adapted ed. Geroge Goodman. 1966. pap. 5.25 (0-8222-1238-2) Dramatists Play.

Wheeler's Atlas of Tooth Form. 5th ed. Major M. Ash, Jr. (Illus.). 158p. 1984. text ed. 48.00 (0-7216-1277-6) Saunders.

Wheeler's Choice. Jerry Buck. LC 89-17228. (Novel of the West Ser.). 192p. 1989. 14.95 (0-87131-597-1) M Evans.

Wheeler's Deluxe Atlas 1992. Gousha. 1992. 10.00 (0-671-84364-8) S&S Trade.

Wheeler's Dental Anatomy, Physiology & Occlusion. 7th ed. Major M. Ash, Jr. (Illus.). 490p. 1992. text ed. 51.00 (0-7216-4374-4) Saunders.

Wheeler's Photographic Survey of the American West, 1871-1873: With Fifty Landscape Photographs by Timothy O'Sullivan & Willia Bell. Ed. by George M. Wheeler. LC 82-19773. (Illus.). 50p. 1983. reprint ed. pap. 7.95 (0-486-24466-0) Dover.

*__Wheelers RV Resort & Campground Guide.__ rev. ed. Gloria Telander et al. 800p. 1997. pap. 14.95 (0-942398-15-7) Print Med Serv Ltd.

Wheeling: An Illustrated History. Doug Fethering. 1983. 19.95 (0-89781-071-6) Am Historical Pr.

Wheeling: Options for Industries. 25p. 1984. 10.00 (0-317-01259-2) Elec Consumers Res.

Wheeling & Dealing: An Ethnography of Upper-Level Drug Dealing & Smuggling Community. Patricia A. Adler. 224p. (C). 1993. pap. 14.00 (0-231-08133-2) Col U Pr.

Wheeling & Dealing: An Ethnography of Upper-Level Drug Dealing & Smuggling Community. Patricia A. Adler. 224p. (C). 1993. text ed. 49.50 (0-231-08132-4) Col U Pr.

Wheeling & Dealing for Dummies. Deanna Sclar. 400p. (Orig.). 1997. pap. 14.95 (0-89815-770-6) Ten Speed Pr.

Wheeling & Transmission Manual. Scott A. Spiewak. 1991. pap. 95.00 (0-88173-113-7) Fairmont Pr.

Wheeling & Whirling-Around Book. Judy Hindley. LC 93-28125. (Read & Wonder Bks.). (J). (ps-3). 1994. 14.95 (1-56402-490-3) Candlewick Pr.

Wheeling & Whirling-Around Book. Judy Hindley. LC 93-28125. (Read & Wonder Bks.). (Illus.). 32p. (J). (gr. 1-4). 1996. reprint ed. pap. 5.99 (1-56402-989-1) Candlewick Pr.

Wheeling Bridge Case: Its Significance in American Law & Technology. Elizabeth B. Monroe. 256p. 1992. text ed. 50.00 (1-55553-130-X) NE U Pr.

Wheeling Glass 1829-1939: Collection of the Oglebay Institute Glass Museum. James Measell et al. (Illus.). 177p. 1994. pap. 34.95 (1-57080-002-2) Antique Pubns.

*__Wheelmaking: Wooden Wheel Design & Construction.__ Ed. by Don Peloubet. (Illus.). 248p. (Orig.). 1996. pap. 29.95 (1-879335-73-5) Astragal Pr.

Wheelock's Latin. 5th ed. Frederic M. Wheelock. 1995. pap. 13.00 (0-06-467179-8, Harper Ref) HarpC.

Wheels. Pamela C. Beall & Susan H. Nipp. (Wee Sing Sounds & Songs Board Book & Cassette Ser.). (Illus.). 10p. (J). (ps). 1996. bds. 8.95 incl. audio (0-8431-3986-2, Wee Sing) Price Stern Sloan.

Wheels. Isabel Bissett. LC 92-21399. (Voyages Ser.). (Illus.). (J). 1993. 3.75 (0-383-03605-4) SRA McGraw.

Wheels! Annie Cobb. LC 94-48884. (Early Step into Reading Ser.). (Illus.). (J). 1996. lib. bdg. 11.99 (0-679-96445-2) Random.

Wheels! Annie Cobb. LC 94-48884. (Early Step into Learning Ser.). (Illus.). (J). (gr. k-1). 1996. pap. 3.99 (0-679-86445-8) Random.

Wheels. Annie Cobb. (J). 1996. pap. write for info. (0-679-88161-1) McKay.

Wheels. Michael Evans. (Little Surprises Ser.). (Illus.). 24p. (J). (ps-2). 1992. bds. 2.95 (0-8249-8527-3, Ideals Child) Hambleton-Hill.

Wheels. Susin Nielsen. (Degrassi Book Ser.). (J). (gr. 6-9). 1995. pap. 4.95 (1-55028-360-X) Formac Dist Ltd.

Wheels. Susin Nielsen. (Degrassi Book Ser.). (J). (gr. 6-9). 1995. bds. 16.95 (1-55028-362-6) Formac Dist Ltd.

*__Wheels.__ Brenda Parkes. Ed. by Susan Evento. (Newbridge Links Ser.). 8p. (J). 1997. pap. 2.75 (1-56784-900-8) Newbridge Comms.

Wheels. Jan Pienkowski. (Illus.). 24p. (J). (ps). 1992. pap. 2.95 (0-671-74517-4, Litl Simon S&S) S&S Childrens.

Wheels. Jane R. Thomas. LC 85-18404. (J). (ps-3). 1986. 12.95 (0-317-39001-5, Clarion Bks) HM.

*__Wheels: A Season on Nascar's Winston Cup Circuit.__ Paul Hemphill. LC 97-19242. 1997. 25.00 (0-684-83017-5) S&S Trade.

Wheels: First Readers. Jacqueline Harding. (Series 929). (Illus.). 28p. (J). (ps-1). 1992. 3.50 (0-7214-1483-4, Ladybird) Penguin.

*__Wheels & Axels.__ Michael Dahl. (Early-Reader Science Simple Machines Ser.). (Illus.). 24p. (J). (gr. k-3). 1996. 13.25 (0-516-20273-1) Childrens.

Wheels & Axles. Michael S. Dahl. LC 96-27771. (Early Reader Science Ser.). 24p. (J). (gr. 1-2). 1996. 13.25 (1-56065-446-5) Capstone Pr.

*__Wheels & Cars.__ John Williams. LC 97-1262. (Design & Create Ser.). (J). 1998. write for info. (0-8172-4887-0) Raintree Steck-V.

Wheels & Cogs. Caroline Rush. LC 96-21231. (Simple Science Ser.). (Illus.). (J). 1997. lib. bdg. 18.54 (0-8172-4500-6) Raintree Steck-V.

Wheels & Cranks. David Glover. LC 96-15814. (Simple Machines Ser.). (J). 1997. lib. bdg. write for info. (1-57572-081-7) Rigby Interact Libr.

Wheels & Paddles in the Sudan: Nineteen Twenty-Three to Nineteen Forty-Six. C. R. Williams. 1986. 45.00 (0-946270-24-4, Pub. by Pentland Pr UK) St Mut.

Wheels & Pinions & How to Determine Their Exact Size. H. Shouffelberger. (Illus.). 20p. 1988. pap. 5.00 (0-930163-15-X) Arlington Bk.

Wheels & Wings. Gakken Co. Ltd. Editors. Tr. by Time-Life Books Editors. (Child's First Library of Learning). (Illus.). 90p. (J). (gr. k-3). 1988. lib. bdg. 21.27 (0-8094-4862-9) Time-Life.

Wheels & Wings. Gakken Co. Ltd. Editors. Tr. by Time-Life Books Editors. (Child's First Library of Learning). (Illus.). 88p. (J). (gr. 1-4). 1988. 14.95 (0-8094-4861-0) Time-Life.

*__Wheels & Wings: Exploring the Word of Transportation & Travel.__ Raymond C. Clark & Susannah J. Clark. (Vocabureader Workbook Ser.: No. 6). (Illus.). 104p. (Orig.). 1992. pap. text ed. 10.50 (0-86647-053-0) Pro Lingua.

Wheels Around. Shelley Rotner. (Illus.). 32p. (J). (ps-3). 1995. 13.95 (0-395-71815-5) HM.

Wheels at Work. Bernie Zubrowski. LC 86-12500. (Illus.). 112p. (J). (gr. 3-7). 1986. pap. 6.95 (0-688-06349-7); lib. bdg. 11.93 (0-688-06348-9) Morrow.

W

Wheels for Rent: An Information Process. Boyce. (DF - Computer Applications Ser.). 1988. pap. 19.95 (*0-538-10640-9*) S-W Pub.

Wheels for Sale: A Computer Application. 2nd ed. Boyce. (DF - Computer Applications Ser.). 1992. pap. 20.95 (*0-538-60845-5*) S-W Pub.

Wheels for Walking. Sandra Richmond. Ed. by Melanie Kroupa. LC 85-70855. 196p. (YA). (gr. 6 up). 1985. 13.95 (*0-316-74439-5*, Joy St Bks) Little.

Wheels Go Round. (Poke & Look Bks.). (Illus.). 16p. (J). (ps-k). 1989. 9.95 (*0-448-21030-4*, G&D) Putnam Pub Group.

***Wheels Go Round.** Photos by Margaret Miller. (Illus.). (J). (ps-k). 1997. 4.99 (*0-614-29108-9*, Litl Simon S&S) S&S Childrens.

Wheels Go Round. W. Nikola-Lisa. LC 93-38595. (Illus.). 32p. (J). 1994. 12.95 (*0-385-32069-8*) Doubleday.

Wheels in Motion: The American Automobile Industry's First Century. Gerald Perschbacher. 1996. 19.95 (*0-87341-453-5*) Krause Pubns.

Wheels in the Head: Educational Philosphies of Authority, Freedom, & Culture from Socrates to Paulo Freire. Joel H. Spring. LC 93-17348. 1993. pap. text ed. write for info. (*0-07-060529-7*) McGraw.

Wheels, Life & Other Mathematical Amusements. Martin Gardner. LC 83-11592. (Illus.). 261p. 1995. pap. text ed. write for info. (*0-7167-1589-9*) W H Freeman.

Wheels 'Ninety-Two. Intro. by John Lessels. (Illus.). 259p. (Orig.). 1992. pap. 57.75 (*0-85825-584-7*, Pub. by Inst Engrs Aust-EA Bks AT) Accents Pubns.

Wheels of a Soul. Philip S. Berg. 160p. (HEB.). 1986. 11.95 (*0-943688-41-8*); pap. 11.95 (*0-943688-42-6*) Res Ctr Kabbalah.

Wheels of a Soul. Philip S. Berg. 256p. (SPA.). 1987. 13.95 (*0-943688-45-0*); 13.95 (*0-943688-71-X*); pap. 13.95 (*0-943688-46-9*); pap. 13.95 (*0-943688-72-8*) Res Ctr Kabbalah.

Wheels of a Soul. Philip S. Berg. 256p. (PER.). 1989. 13.95 (*0-924457-16-3*); 11.95 (*0-924457-06-6*); pap. 13.95 (*0-924457-17-1*); pap. 11.95 (*0-924457-07-4*) Res Ctr Kabbalah.

Wheels of a Soul. Philip S. Berg. (Mandarin Ser.). 288p. 1992. write for info. (*0-924457-44-9*); pap. write for info. (*0-924457-45-7*); pap. write for info. (*0-318-70264-9*) Res Ctr Kabbalah.

Wheels of a Soul. rev. ed. Philip S. Berg. 224p. 1991. write for info. (*0-318-70381-5*) Res Ctr Kabbalah.

***Wheels of Chance: A Bicycling Idyll.** H. G. Wells. (Illus.). 320p. 1997. reprint ed. pap. 12.95 (*1-55821-564-6*) Lyons & Burford.

Wheels of Eternity: A Comparative Study of William Blake & W. B. Yeats. Rachel V. Billigheimer. 240p. 1990. text ed. 45.00 (*0-312-03563-2*) St Martin.

Wheels of Farm Progress. Marvin McKinley. LC 80-68925. (Illus.). 160p. 1980. pap. 13.95 (*0-916150-24-0*, HO680) Am Soc Ag Eng.

Wheels of Fire. Mercedes Lackey & Mark Shepherd. (Serrated Edge Ser.). 400p. 1992. mass mkt. 5.99 (*0-671-72138-0*) Baen Bks.

Wheels of Fortune. Francis A. Seufert. Ed. by Thomas Vaughan. LC 80-81719. (Illus.). 284p. 1981. 19.95 (*0-87595-083-3*); pap. 12.95 (*0-87595-069-8*) Oregon Hist.

Wheels of Learning - Core Curricula. Construction Education Foundation Staff. (Wheels of Learning Ser.). 398p. (Orig.). (C). 1992. pap. 50.00 (*1-886831-01-7*) Constrct Educ.

Wheels of Life: A User's Guide to the Chakra System. Anodea Judith. LC 87-45110. (New Age Ser.). (Illus.). 549p. 1987. pap. 17.95 (*0-87542-320-5*) Llewellyn Pubns.

Wheels of Light: A Study of the Chakras, Vol. 1. Rosalyn L. Bruyere. Ed. by Jeanne Farrens. (Illus.). 282p. (Orig.). 1989. pap. 19.95 (*0-923808-01-9*) Bon Prodns.

Wheels of Light: A Study of the Chakras, Vol. 2. Rosalyn L. Bruyere. Ed. by Jeanne Farrens. (Illus.). 364p. (Orig.). 1992. pap. write for info. (*0-923808-02-7*) Bon Prodns.

Wheels of Light: Chakras, Auras, & the Healing Energy of the Body. Rosalyn Bruyere. Ed. by Jeanne Farrens. 288p. 1994. pap. 14.00 (*0-671-79624-0*, Fireside) S&S Trade.

Wheels of Progress? Motor Transport, Pollution & the Environment. Ed. by Rose. x, 160p. 1973. text ed. 105.00 (*0-677-15425-9*) Gordon & Breach.

***Wheels of Thunder.** P. J. Richardson & Robert Darden. LC 96-37194. (Illus.). 192p. (Orig.). 1997. pap. 14.99 (*0-7852-7223-2*) Nelson.

***Wheels of Time: A Picture Biography of Henry Ford.** Catherine Gourley. (Illus.). 48p. (J). (gr. 2-4). 1997. lib. bdg. 15.90 (*0-7613-0214-X*) Millbrook Pr.

Wheels on the Bus. (Play - a - Sound Ser.). (Illus.). 24p. (J). 1993. 12.98 (*1-56173-752-6*) Pubns Intl Ltd.

Wheels on the Bus. (My Big Beanstalk Bks.). 24p. (J). 1996. write for info. (*1-57719-076-9*) GT Pubng Corp.

Wheels on the Bus. Ellen Appleby. (Little Golden Sound Story Bks.). (Illus.). 24p. (J). (ps-3). 1993. 6.95 (*0-307-74815-4*, 64815, Golden Books) Western Pub.

Wheels on the Bus. Illus. by Susan Banta. (Hear! Hear! Ser.). 20p. (J). (ps-3). 1994. 3.95 (*0-307-17353-4*, Golden Books) Western Pub.

Wheels on the Bus. Golden Books Staff. (First Little Golden Bks.). (Illus.). 24p. (J). 1995. 1.09 (*0-307-10245-9*, Golden Pr) Western Pub.

Wheels on the Bus. Maryann Kovalski. (J). (ps-4). 1990. mass mkt. 4.95 (*0-316-50259-6*, Joy St Bks) Little.

Wheels on the Bus. Raffi. LC 87-30126. (Raffi Songs to Read Ser.). (Illus.). 32p. (J). (ps-2). 1990. pap. 5.99 (*0-517-57645-7*) Crown Bks Yng Read.

***Wheels on the Bus.** Raffi. 1998. 6.99 (*0-517-70999-6*) Crown Pub Group.

Wheels on the Bus. Dana Regan. (Wheel Bks.). 12p. (J). (ps-k). 1996. 5.95 (*0-590-54316-4*, Cartwheel) Scholastic Inc.

Wheels on the Bus. Illus. by Sylvie K. Wickstrom. (Raffi Songs to Read Ser.). 32p. (J). (ps-2). 1988. lib. bdg. 13.00 (*0-517-56784-9*) Crown Bks Yng Read.

Wheels on the Bus. Harriet Ziefert. LC 89-38100. (Pictureback Ser.). (Illus.). 24p. (Orig.). (J). (ps-2). 1990. pap. 2.25 (*0-394-84870-5*) Random Bks Yng Read.

Wheels on the Bus: With Pictures that Move. Paul O. Zelinsky. 16p. (J). (ps). 1990. pap. 15.99 (*0-525-44644-3*) Dutton Child Bks.

Wheels on the Bus Big Book. Illus. by Dale Champlin. (J). (ps-2). 1988. pap. text ed. 14.00 (*0-922053-15-4*) N Edge Res.

Wheels Still Turn: A History of Australian Paddleboats. Peter Plowman. (Illus.). 160p. 1993. 32.50 (*0-86417-428-4*, Pub. by Kangaroo Pr AT) Seven Hills Bk.

Wheels That Work. (Chubby Board Bks.). (Illus.). 16p. (J). (ps). 1988. pap. 2.95 (*0-671-64872-1*, Litl Simon S&S) S&S Childrens.

Wheels Went Around: The Story of Camborne Town. Janet Thomas. (C). 1989. 45.00 (*1-85022-026-3*, Pub. by Dyllansow Truran UK) St Mut.

Wheels, Wheels, & More Wheels. Edward Radlauer. (Ed Radlauer Bks.). (Illus.). 32p. (J). 1991. lib. bdg. 11.95 (*1-878363-36-0*) Forest Hse.

***Wheels, Wings, & Moving Things.** Moira Butterfield & Jan Lewis. LC 97-19102. (Can You Find? Ser.). 1999. write for info. (*0-382-39987-0*) Silver Burdett Pr.

Wheelwork. Marilyn R. Rosenberg. 14p. 1986. pap. 100.00 (*0-913615-11-0*) Marilyn R Rosenberg.

Wheelwright's Shop. George Sturt. (C). 1934. 75.00 (*0-521-06570-4*) Cambridge U Pr.

Wheelwright's Shop. George Sturt. (Canto Book Ser.). (Illus.). 256p. (C). 1993. pap. text ed. 10.95 (*0-521-44772-0*) Cambridge U Pr.

Whelan Lake (CA-SDI-6010) A La Jollan Campsite on the Lower San Luis Rey River, San Diego County, California. Rein Vanderpot et al. (Statistical Research Technical Ser.: No. 40). (Illus.). 222p. 1993. spiral bd. 15.00 (*1-879442-38-8*) Stats Res.

Whelping & Rearing of Puppies: A Complete & Practical Guide. 4th ed. Muriel P. Lee. LC 84-60962. (Illus.). 126p. 1984. pap. 11.95 (*0-9612546-0-2*) Plantin Pr.

When? Margaret W. Hudson. 1965. 1.50 (*0-88323-081-X*, 178) Pendergrass Pub.

***When?** Robert W. Wood. (Experiments for Young Scientists Ser.). (Illus.). 140p. (YA). (gr. 5 up). 1997. text ed. write for info. (*0-7910-4850-0*) Chelsea Hse.

When? Experiments for the Young Scientists. Robert W. Wood. (J). (gr. 4-7). 1995. pap. text ed. 10.95 (*0-07-051640-5*) McGraw.

***When: Poems.** Baron Wormser. LC 96-44929. 96p. 1997. 20.95 (*1-889330-03-5*); pap. 12.95 (*1-889330-04-3*) Sarabande Bks.

When a Baby Dies: A Handbook for Healing & Helping. Rana K. Limbo & Sara R. Wheeler. 168p. 1986. pap. 8.95 (*0-9612310-3-3*) Harsand Pr.

When a Baby Dies: Psychotherapy for Pregnancy & Newborn Loss. Irving G. Leon. LC 89-22706. 248p. (C). 1990. 15.00 (*0-300-04575-1*) Yale U Pr.

When a Baby Dies: Psychotherapy for Pregnancy & Newborn Loss. Irving G. Leon. 248p. (C). 1992. reprint ed. pap. text ed. 15.00 (*0-300-05230-8*) Yale U Pr.

When a Baby Dies: The Experiences of Late Miscarriage, Stillbirth & Neonatal Death. Nancy Kohner & Alix Henley. 1995. pap. 16.00 (*0-04-440934-6*) Harper SF.

When a Baby Is New: Reading Level 2-3. 1993. 2.75 (*0-88336-517-0*) New Readers.

When a Baby Suddenly Dies: Cot Death - the Impact & Effects. Janet D. Lord. 291p. (Orig.). 1994. pap. 13.95 (*0-85572-162-6*, Pub. by Hill Content Pubng AT) Seven Hills Bk.

When a Bear Bakes a Cake. Jasper Tomkins. (Orig.). (J). (ps-3). 1991. pap. 7.95 (*0-671-75277-4*, Green Tiger S&S) S&S Childrens.

***When a Believer Marries a Nonbeliever: How to Grow Together in Love, Faith & Joy.** Bebe Nicholson. 312p. 1997. pap. write for info. (*0-9655127-1-1*) Priority Pub.

***When a Believer Marries a Nonbeliever: How to Grow Together in Love, Faith & Joy.** unabridged ed. Bebe Nicholson. 336p. 1997. 19.95 (*0-9655127-0-3*) Priority Pub.

***When a Believer Marries a Nonbeliever: How to Grow Together in Love, Faith, & Joy.** unabridged ed. Bebe Nicholson. 336p. (Orig.). 1997. pap. 12.95 (*0-9655127-9-7*) Priority Pub.

When a Building Calls in Sick: Consequences, Cures & Prevention. Sue Whittle. Ed. by Madeleine Havlick. 1995. 23.00 (*1-882403-20-7*) The Innovation Grps.

When a Child Dies. Carol Pregent. LC 92-72923. 120p. (Orig.). 1992. pap. 7.95 (*0-87793-487-8*) Ave Maria.

When a Child Dies: Stories of Survival & Hope. Richard S. Hipps. 96p. (Orig.). 1996. pap. 10.95 (*1-57312-032-4*, Peake Road) Smyth & Helwys.

***When a Child Has Been Murdered: Ways You Can Help the Grieving Parents.** Bonnie H. Conrad. (Death, Value & Meaning Ser.). 164p. 1997. text ed. write for info. (*0-89503-182-5*) Baywood Pub.

When a Child Has Cancer. A. Faulkner & G. Peace. 128p. 1995. pap. 24.95 (*1-56593-331-1*, 0661) Singular Publishing.

When a Child Has Died: Ways You Can Help a Bereaved Parent. Bonnie H. Conrad. 64p. (Orig.). 1995. pap. 8.95 (*1-56474-141-9*) Fithian Pr.

When a Child Kills. Paul Mones. Ed. by Claire Zion. 416p. 1992. reprint ed. pap. 6.99 (*0-671-67421-8*) PB.

When a Child Misbehaves. IEC Staff. 102p. 1996. pap. text ed., spiral bd. 15.95 (*0-7872-2179-1*) Kendall-Hunt.

When a Child Wanders. Robert L. Millet. LC 95-51313. xii, 164p. 1996. 13.95 (*1-57345-142-8*) Deseret Bk.

When a Classmate Dies. Julie Berg. 63p. 1991. 5.00 (*0-685-54284-X*) Prairie Hse.

When a Congregation Cares. 2nd ed. Abraham Schmitt & Dorothy Schmitt. LC 85-27335. (Illus.). 122p. 1986. reprint ed. pap. 34.80 (*0-608-01755-8*, 2062413) Bks Demand.

***When a Crisis Hits: Will Your School Be Ready?** Robert H. Decker. LC 97-4896. (Illus.). 208p. 1997. pap. 29.95 (*0-8039-6304-1*) Corwin Pr.

***When a Crisis Hits: Will Your School Be Ready?** Robert H. Decker. LC 97-4896. (Illus.). 208p. 1997. text ed. 69.95 (*0-8039-6615-6*) Corwin Pr.

When a Death Occurs: A Handbook for Counsellors. Alan A. Watson & Jeannette A. Watson. (Aberdeen University Press Bks.). 160p. 1992. pap. text ed. 14.21 (*0-08-041216-5*, Pub. by Aberdeen U Pr) Macmillan.

When a Doctor Hates a Patient: Chapters from a Young Physicians Life. Richard E. Peschel & Enid R. Peschel. (C). 1986. pap. 12.00 (*0-520-06343-0*) U CA Pr.

When a Drunk Driver Kills: A Widow's Survival. Judy Mardorf. Ed. by LaRue Krumm. LC 94-96787. (Illus.). 128p. (Orig.). 1994. pap. 7.95 (*0-9643936-3-8*) Taleteller.

When a Family Is in Trouble: Children Can Cope with Grief from Drug & Alcohol Addictions. Marge E. Heegaard. 32p. (J). (gr. 1-6). 1993. pap. 6.95 (*0-9620502-7-X*) Woodland Pr.

When a Father Abandons His Children. Ron Ballard. (Christian Living Ser.). pap. 1.49 (*0-87509-596-8*) Chr Pubns.

When a Friend Dies: A Book for Teens about Grieving & Healing. Marilyn E. Gootman. Ed. by Pamela Espeland. LC 93-37992. 120p. (Orig.). (YA). (gr. 5 up). 1994. pap. 7.95 (*0-915793-66-0*) Free Spirit Pub.

When a Grandparent Dies: A Kid's Own Remembering Workbook for Dealing with Shiva & the Year Beyond. Nechama Liss-Levinson. LC 95-5379. 48p. (J). (gr. 2-6). 1995. 14.95 (*1-879045-44-3*) Jewish Lights.

When a Hurricane Strikes: A Survival Guide. John Klein. Ed. by Louise McRovie. (Illus.). 138p. (Orig.). 1993. pap. 9.95 (*1-883626-05-6*) Image Grp.

When a Hyena Laughs: A Somalian Novel. Abdi Abdulkadir Sheik-Abdi. (Illus.). 275p. (Orig.). 1994. 29.95 (*0-9638802-5-X*); pap. 14.95 (*0-9638802-6-8*) Dr Leisure.

When a Jew Celebrates. Harry Gersh. LC 70-116678. (Jewish Values Ser.). (Illus.). 256p. (J). (gr. 5-6). 1971. pap. text ed. 8.95 (*0-87441-091-6*) Behrman.

When a Jew Celebrates. Harry Gersh et al. LC 70-116678. (Jewish Values Ser.). (Illus.). 256p. (J). 1971. teacher ed., pap. 14.95 (*0-87441-092-4*) Behrman.

When a Jew Celebrates. Morris J. Sugarman. (J). (gr. 5-6). 1995. wbk. ed., pap. 4.95 (*0-87441-431-8*) Behrman.

When a Jew Prays. Laura Karp. (J). (gr. 4-5). 1995. wbk. ed., pap. 4.95 (*0-87441-098-3*) Behrman.

When a Jew Prays. Seymour Rossel. (Illus.). 192p. (J). (gr. 4-5). pap. 8.95 (*0-87441-093-2*) Behrman.

When a Jew Prays. Seymour Siegel & David Bamberger. 1995. teacher ed., pap. 14.95 (*0-87441-094-0*) Behrman.

When a Jew Seeks Wisdom: The Sayings of the Fathers. Seymour Rossel et al. LC 75-14119. (Jewish Values Ser.). (J). (gr. 7). pap. 8.95 (*0-87441-089-4*) Behrman.

When a Jew Seeks Wisdom: The Sayings of the Fathers: Encounter Book. Laura Karp. (J). (gr. 7-8). 1995. student ed., pap. 4.95 (*0-87441-255-2*) Behrman.

When a Lady: Prose - 1982. Mark Insingel et al. Tr. by Dixon et al. 95p. (DUT, FRE, GER & RUS.). 1982. 8.95 (*0-87376-038-7*) Red Dust.

***When a Life Mate Dies: Stories of Love, Loss, & Healing.** Ed. by Susan Heinlein et al. 256p. 1997. pap. 14.95 (*1-57749-056-8*) Fairview Press.

When a Line Bends - a Shape Begins. Rhonda G. Greene. LC 96-13717. (Illus.). 1997. 16.00 (*0-395-78606-1*) HM.

When a Loose Cannon Flogs a Dead Horse There's the Devil to Pay: Seafaring Words in Everyday Speech. Olivia A. Isil. (Illus.). 115p. 1996. pap. text ed. 9.95 (*0-07-032877-3*) McGraw.

***When a Love Dies...or Merely Grows Away: A Poetic Odyssey from Divorce to Healing.** limited ed. Edmond Frank & Judie Penton. Ed. by Laurel A. Duffy. (Illus.). 164p. (Orig.). 1997. spiral bd. 19.95 (*0-9655836-0-0*) Bell Toll Bks.

When a Loved One Dies: Meditations for the Journey Through Grief. Philip W. Williams. 1994. pap. 7.99 (*0-8066-2777-8*) Augsburg Fortress.

***When a Man Love a Woman.** Patrick Augustus. 192p. 1996. pap. 9.95 (*1-874509-24-7*) LPC InBook.

***When a Man Loves a Walnut.** Edwards. 1997. pap. 9.95 (*0-684-84567-9*) S&S Trade.

When a Man Loves a Woman. Bonnie K. Winn. (American Romance Ser.). 1996. mass mkt. 3.75 (*0-373-16646-X*, 1-16646-1) Harlequin Bks.

When a Man Marries. Mary R. Rinehart. 24.95 (*0-8488-0315-9*) Amereon Ltd.

***When a Man's Fancy Turns to Cooking.** G. Wesley Rice. (Illus.). 136p. 1996. pap. 13.95 (*0-89745-988-1*) Sunflower U Pr.

***When a Man's Fancy Turns to Cooking. G. Wesley Rice. (Illus.). 144p. 1996. spiral bd. 13.95 (*0-9656644-1-4*) Pecan Creek.**

More than a recipe collection, this book includes enhancements in the form of essays & explanatory notes on family living, food preparation, & memories that sketch a good life. "A good read even if you never sample a recipe." 144 pages, color photos, illustrations. Plastic coil binding book lays flat. Essays include: Dog Katie - who received her Ph.D. in begging at age one, Walnut Baseball, World War II Remembrances, That Turkey Carcass - Yuk, & more. Twelve chapters each describe different cooking styles. Learn to make nine herbal blends used extensively in the book's recipes. The author's fondness for New Mexico is illustrated with essays, sketches & unique cooking know-how from northern New Mexico. Rice, author of a leading pecan book, provides an expert's recipes & culinary aspects of this favorite nut. Ten select soup recipes round out "soup to nuts." Wild edibles, historic Swedish recipes, smokery cooking & barbecue, holiday tradition, traditional favorites - including the best-ever herbal chili & more. A must for the cookbook collector & all who love to read & cook. $13.95 (quantity discounts available). Order from Pecan Creek Publications, 9704 Braden School Road, Ponca City, OK 74604. 405- 767-1195 or Hervey's (1-800-413-3300, orders only). ***Publisher Provided Annotation.***

When a Man's Single see **Works of J. M. Barrie. Peter Pan Edition**

When a Mate Wants Out: Secrets for Saving a Marriage. Sally Conway & Jim Conway. 224p. 1992. 15.99 (*0-310-57370-X*) Zondervan.

When a Monkey Speaks: And Other Stories from Australia. Damian Sharp. LC 92-54817. 224p. 1994. 15.00 (*0-06-258500-2*) Harper SF.

When a New Baby Comes. Martha Alexander. 1992. pap. 3.99 (*0-14-054723-1*) NAL-Dutton.

***When a Parent Has a Brain Injury: Sons & Daughters Speak Out.** Marilyn Lash. 41p. 1996. reprint ed. pap. 20.00 (*0-7881-2787-X*) DIANE Pub.

***When a Parent Has Cancer: A Guide to Caring for Your Children.** Wendy S. Harpham. LC 96-32529. (Illus.). 176p. 1997. 24.00 (*0-06-018709-3*) HarpC.

When a Parent Marries Again. Marge E. Heegaard. 32p. (J). (ps-3). 1993. pap. 6.95 (*0-9620502-6-1*) Woodland Pr.

When a Storm Comes Up. Allan Fowler. LC 94-35627. (Rookie Read-About Science Ser.). (Illus.). 32p. (J). (ps-2). 1995. lib. bdg. 17.30 (*0-516-06035-X*) Childrens.

When a Storm Comes Up. Allan Fowler. (Rookie Read-About Science Ser.). (Illus.). 32p. (J). (ps-2). 1995. pap. 3.95 (*0-516-46035-8*) Childrens.

When a Teenager Chooses You - As Friend, Confidante, Confirmation Sponsor: Practical Advice for Any Adult. rev. ed. Joseph Moore. 82p. 1989. pap. text ed. 4.95 (*0-86716-139-6*) St Anthony Mess Pr.

When a Writer Can't Write: Studies in Writer's Block & Other Composing Problems. Ed. by Mike Rose. LC 84-19304. (Guilford Perspectives in Writing Research Ser.). 272p. 1985. pap. text ed. 15.00 (*0-89862-904-7*); lib. bdg. 35.00 (*0-89862-251-4*) Guilford Pr.

When AA Doesn't Work for You: Rational Steps to Quitting Alcohol. Albert Ellis & Emmett Velten. LC 91-38539. 330p. 1992. pap. 14.95 (*0-942637-53-4*) Barricade Bks.

When Abortion Was a Crime: Women, Medicine, & Law in the United States, 1867-1973. Leslie J. Reagan. LC 96-22568. (Illus.). 384p. (C). 1997. 29.95 (*0-520-08848-4*) U CA Pr.

When Acceptance Is Denial: A Handbook for People Who Are Confused about Confusion. Gil Eriksen. (Illus.). 248p. (Orig.). 1993. pap. 12.95 (*0-9638868-7-8*) G Eriksen Communs.

When Acting out Isn't Acting: Understanding Child & Adolescent Temper, Anger & Behavior Disorders. Lynne W. Weisberg & Rosalie Greenberg. 128p. (Orig.). 1988. pap. 7.95 (*0-929162-03-X*) PIA Pr.

When Ads Work. John P. Jones. 240p. 30.00 (*0-02-916662-4*, Free Press) Free Pr.

When Africa Awakes. Hubert H. Harrison. (African Studies). reprint ed. 25.00 (*0-938818-89-9*) ECA Assoc.

When Africa Awakes: The Inside Story of the Stirrings & Strivings of the New Negro in the Western World. Hubert H. Harrison. 152p. reprint ed. 29.95 (*0-933121-88-1*) Black Classic.

When Africa Was Home. Karen L. Williams. LC 90-7684. (Illus.). 32p. (J). (ps-2). 1991. 15.95 (*0-531-05925-1*); lib. bdg. 16.99 (*0-531-08525-2*) Orchard Bks Watts.

When Africa Was Home. Karen L. Williams. LC 90-7684. (Illus.). 32p. (J). (ps-2). 1994. pap. 5.95 (*0-531-07043-3*) Orchard Bks Watts.

When Age Grows Young. Clare H. Kirk. Ed. by Robert J. Kastenbaum. LC 78-22204. (Aging & Old Age Ser.). 1979. reprint ed. lib. bdg. 23.95 (*0-405-11819-8*) Ayer.

***When AIDS Comes Home: Answers to the Most Commonly Asked Questions: What to Say, What to Do, & How to Live with AIDS.** Mignon Zylstra & David B. Beibel. LC 96-28813. 1997. 12.99 (*0-7852-7714-5*) Nelson.

When AIDS Comes to the Church. William E. Amos, Jr. LC 87-30875. 132p. 1988. pap. 11.00 (*0-664-25009-2*, Westminster) Westminster John Knox.

When AIDS Strikes. Peter A. Mozeleski. Ed. by Paul M. Mozeleski & Rosie Dominguez. (Illus.). 8p. (Orig.). 1991. pap. 1.75 (*1-880058-85-5*) Rubbers Bros Comics.

When AIDS Strikes, Vol. 1, Nos. 1 & 2. Peter A. Mozeleski. Ed. by Paul M. Mozeleski & Rosie Dominguez. Tr. by Rosie Dominguez. (Illus.). 8p. (Orig.). 1991. pap. 1.75 (*1-880058-84-7*) Rubbers Bros Comics.

W

When Alaska Was Free. Knut D. Peterson. Ed. by Sylvia Ashton. LC 77-70299. 1977. 21.95 (*0-87949-081-0*) Ashley Bks.

When Alcohol Abuses Our Marriage. Dave Jackson et al. LC 94-69840. (Recovering Hope in Your Marriage Ser.). 128p. 1995. pap. 4.95 (*0-89221-285-3*) New Leaf.

When All Else Fails: Finding Solutions to Your Most Persistent Management Problems. Kevin E. O'Connor & Frank C. Bucaro. 154p. 1992. 19.95 (*0-9631170-4-1*) Ritmar Pub.

When All Else Fails, Read the Instructions. James W. Moore. LC 92-24122. 144p. (Orig.). 1993. pap. 10.00 (*0-687-44918-9*) Dimen for Liv.

When All Hell Breaks Loose...You May Be Doing Something Right! Steven J. Lawson. LC 93-24957. 256p. 1993. 17.00 (*0-89109-732-5*) NavPress.

When All the Doors Close, Look to the Windows. Angela Brown. 200p. 1995. 16.95 (*0-8059-3505-3*) Dorrance.

When All the Wild Summer. Gene Detro. (Kestrel Ser.: No. 7). 28p. 1983. pap. 3.00 (*0-914974-39-4*) Holmgangers.

***When All the World Was Browns Town.** Pluto. LC 97-14358. 1997. 25.00 (*0-684-82246-6*) S&S Trade.

When All the World Was Young. Ferrol Sams. LC 91-61938. 610p. 1991. 23.95 (*1-56352-001-X*) Longstreet Pr Inc.

When All the World Was Young. Ferrol Sams. (Contemporary American Fiction Ser.). 624p. 1992. reprint ed. pap. 12.95 (*0-14-017227-0*, Penguin Bks) Viking Penguin.

When All You Ever Wanted Isn't Enough. Harold S. Kushner. 1990. mass mkt. 6.50 (*0-671-73212-9*, PB Trade Paper) PB.

When Allah Reigns Supreme. Susi Schalit. (Studies in Austrian Literature, Culture, & Thought). 194p. 1992. pap. 19.00 (*0-929497-49-X*) Ariadne CA.

When Allies Differ: Anglo-American Relations During the Suez & Falklands Crises. Louise Richardson. LC 95-38641. 352p. 1996. text ed. 45.00 (*0-312-15852-1*) St Martin.

When Alzheimer's Disease Strikes. Stephen Sapp. 56p. (Orig.). 1996. pap. 5.95 (*0-914733-12-5*) Desert Min.

When Alzheimer's Hits Home. Jo Danna. Ed. by Carl Danna. LC 94-65719. (Illus.). 208p. (Orig.). 1995. pap. 14.95 (*0-9610036-4-2*) Palomino Pr.

When Am I Going to Be Happy? Penelope Russianoff. 304p. 1989. mass mkt. 6.50 (*0-553-28215-8*) Bantam.

When America Does It Right: Case Studies in Service Quality. Ed. by Jay W. Spechler. 615p. 1991. 27.00 (*0-89806-100-8*) Eng Mgmt Pr.

When America Was Young. Mabel A. Murphy. LC 72-38326. (Biography Index Reprint Ser.). (Illus.). 1977. reprint ed. 22.95 (*0-8369-8126-X*) Ayer.

When Americans Complain: Governmental Grievance Procedures. Walter Gellhorn. LC 66-23466. 251p. 1966. reprint ed. pap. 71.60 (*0-7837-4149-9*, 2057997) Bks Demand.

***When an Aging Loved One.** pap. 2.95 (*0-687-61190-3*) Abingdon.

When an Aging Loved One Needs Care. Ron DelBene et al. (Times of Change, Times of Challenge Ser.). 32p. (Orig.). 1991. pap. 2.95 (*0-8358-0636-7*) Upper Room Bks.

When an Angel Dies. Kent Cahill & Kathleen Cahill. Ed. by Bob Moog. (Murder Mystery Parties Ser.). 50p. 1986. 8.00 (*0-935145-05-2*) Univ Games.

When an Employee Has AIDS. Victor Schachter & Susan Von Seeburg. 1989. pap. 19.95 (*1-55840-168-7*) Exec Ent Pubns.

When & How to Ask for a Raise from Your Boss. Travis Young. (Orig.). 1997. pap. 12.95 (*0-9650566-6-X*, F-006) Active Edit.

When & Where I Enter: The Impact of Black Women on Race & Sex in America. Paula Giddings. LC 96-19349. 1996. pap. 14.00 (*0-688-14650-3*, Quill) Morrow.

When & Where Was Ol'ga Baptized? Omeljan Pritsak. 24p. 1994. write for info. (*0-940465-01-9*) Ukrainian Studies Fund.

When Andy's Father Went to Prison. rev. ed. Martha W. Hickman. Ed. by Abby Levine. LC 89-77318. (Albert Whitman Concept Bks.). Orig. Title: When Can Daddy Come Home?. (Illus.). 40p. (J). (gr. 2-5). 1990. lib. bdg. 12.95 (*0-8075-8874-1*) A Whitman.

When Angels Appear. Hope MacDonald. 128p. (Orig.). 1982. pap. 6.99 (*0-310-28531-3*, 10047P) Zondervan.

When Angels Appear. Hope MacDonald. (Orig.). 1994. 4.99 (*0-310-96278-1*) Zondervan.

When Angels Appear. Hope MacDonald. 188p. (Orig.). 1995. mass mkt. 5.50 (*0-06-104380-X*) Zondervan.

When Angels Come Near: 101 Thoughts About Angels. Brownlow. (Easelette Miniatures Ser.). (Illus.). 1995. spiral bd. 4.99 (*1-57051-047-4*) Brownlow Pub Co.

When Angels Cry. Rudolph A. Peart. 1994. 15.95 (*0-533-10523-4*) Vantage.

When Angels Intervene. Hartt Wixom. 1995. pap. 12.95 (*1-55517-144-3*) CFI Dist.

***When Angels Speak.** Williamson. LC 97-7694. 1997. pap. 9.00 (*0-684-84356-0*) S&S Trade.

***When Angels Speak: Messages from the Keepers of the Lion's Gate.** Donna Wolfe & Nadira Duran. (Illus.). 144p. (Orig.). 1997. pap. 9.95 (*0-9658290-0-6*) I Am Pub OR.

When Anger Hits Home: Taking Care of Your Anger Without Taking It Out on Your Family. H. Norman Wright & Gary J. Oliver. (Healing for the Heart Ser.). 1992. text ed. 18.99 (*0-8024-9237-1*) Moody.

When Anger Hurts. Matthew McKay et al. 1994. 7.98 (*1-56731-028-1*, MJF Bks) Fine Comms.

When Anger Hurts: Quieting the Storm Within. Matthew McKay et al. 325p. (Orig.). 1989. pap. 13.95 (*0-934986-76-2*) New Harbinger.

***When Anger Hurts Your Kids.** Matthew McKay et al. 1997. 5.98 (*1-56731-208-X*, MJF Bks) Fine Comms.

When Anger Hurts Your Kids: A Parent's Guide. Matthew Mckay et al. LC 95-72228. 161p. 1996. pap. 12.95 (*1-57224-045-8*) New Harbinger.

When Antibiotics Fail: Restoring the Ecology of the Body. rev. ed. Marc Lappe. 288p. (Orig.). 1987. reprint ed. pap. 12.95 (*0-938190-74-1*) North Atlantic.

When Antibiotics Fail: Restoring the Ecology of the Body. 2nd ed. Marc Lappe. LC 94-48258. 320p. (Orig.). (C). 1995. pap. 14.95 (*1-55643-191-0*) North Atlantic.

When Anxiety Attacks: What the Health Care Community Does Not Know about Anxiety Attacks. Stan H. Looper & Cynthia M. Scott. 152p. (Orig.). (C). 1993. 11.95 (*0-943629-08-X*) Swan Pub.

When Any Time Was Train Time. Elizabeth A. Willmot. Ed. by Noel Hudson. (Illus.). 96p. 29.95 (*1-55046-056-0*, Pub. by Boston Mills Pr CN) Genl Dist Srvs.

When Are Pteranodons Sad? Dick Dudley & Emilie Kong. (Dino Pop-up Joke Bks.). (Illus.). 12p. (J). (ps-2). 1992. 5.95 (*1-56288-180-9*) Checkerboard.

***When Are We Going to Get There? A Guide to Help Travelers Answer That Question.** Anita Almich & Dan Almich. (Illus.). 100p. (Orig.). 1997. pap. 11.95 (*0-9650570-1-1*) Evergreen Creations.

When Are You Entitled to New Underwear & Other Major Financial Decisions: Making Your Money Dreams Come True. Eileen Michaels. 1997. 24.00 (*0-684-81534-6*) S&S Trade.

***When Are You Entitled to New Underwear & Other Major Financial Decisions: Making Your Money Dreams Come True.** Eileen Michaels. LC 97-2317. 459p. 1997. 24.95 (*0-7838-8116-9*, GK Hall) Thorndike Pr.

When Art Became Fashion: Kosode in Edo-Period Japan. Dale C. Gluckman & Sharon S. Takeda. (Illus.). 352p. 1992. 60.00 (*0-8348-0266-X*) Weatherhill.

When Artie Was Little. Harriet B. Schwartz. 40p. (J). (ps-4). 1996. 15.00 (*0-679-83236-X*) McKay.

When Artie Was Little. Harriet B. Schwartz. 40p. (J). (ps-4). 1996. lib. bdg. 16.99 (*0-679-93236-4*) McKay.

When Aunt Lena Did the Rhumba. Eileen Kurtis-Kleinman. LC 94-35489. (Illus.). 32p. (J). 1997. 14.95 (*0-7868-0082-8*); lib. bdg. 14.89 (*0-7868-2067-5*) Hyprn Child.

When Autumn Comes. Robert Maass. LC 90-32069. (Illus.). 32p. (J). (ps-2). 1992. pap. 5.95 (*0-8050-2349-6*, Owlet BYR) H Holt & Co.

When Autumn Leaves. Timothy E. Stinson. 1993. pap. 9.95 (*1-878852-01-9*) Standard Hse.

***When Axioms Collide.** (Torg Ser.). 12.00 (*0-87431-347-3*, 20580) West End Games.

***When Baby Boom Women Retire.** Nancy Dailey. 1998. text ed. write for info. (*0-275-96070-6*, Praeger Pubs) Greenwood.

When Baby Makes Two. Helen C. Keen. LC 86-83412. (Illus.). 260p. (Orig.). pap. 9.95 (*0-89896-341-9*) Larksdale.

When Baby Makes Two: Single Mothers by Chance or by Choice. Jene Stonesifer. 216p. 1994. 22.95 (*1-56565-158-8*) Lowell Hse.

When Baby Makes Two: Single Mothers by Chance or by Choice. Jene Stonsifer. 216p. 1995. pap. 14.00 (*1-56565-346-7*) Lowell Hse.

When Bad Things Happen. Harold S. Kushner. 1990. pap. 3.99 (*0-517-05997-5*) Random Hse Value.

***When Bad Things Happen in Good Organizations.** Art Dykstra. 175p. 1998. 24.50 (*0-9653744-2-4*) High Tide Pr.

When Bad Things Happen to Good People. Harold S. Kushner. 144p. 1983. pap. 10.00 (*0-380-67033-X*) Avon.

When Bad Things Happen to Good People. Harold S. Kushner. LC 81-40411. 176p. 1989. 22.00 (*0-8052-4089-6*) Schocken.

When Bad Things Happen to Good People. Harold S. Kushner. 160p. 1983. reprint ed. mass mkt. 5.50 (*0-380-60392-6*) Avon.

When Bar Harbor Was Eden, ME. L. Turner. (Images of America Ser.). 1995. pap. 16.99 (*0-7524-0086-X*, Arcdia) Chalford.

When Basildon Was Farms & Fields. Jessie Payne. 1993. pap. 16.00 (*0-86025-416-X*, Pub. by Ian Henry Pubns UK) Empire Pub Srvs.

When Battered Women Kill. Angela Browne. 240p. 1989. pap. 12.95 (*0-02-903881-2*, Free Press) Free Pr.

When Bear Stole Chinook: A Blackfoot Tale. Illus. & Retold by Harriet P. Taylor. LC 96-33843. 1997. write for info. (*0-374-10947-8*) FS&G.

***When Bear Stole the Chinook.** Harriet P. Taylor. 1997. 16.00 (*0-374-30589-7*) FS&G.

When Beauty Fires the Blood: Love & the Arts in the Age of Dryden. James A. Winn. LC 91-43619. (Illus.). 476p. (C). 1992. text ed. 44.50 (*0-472-10339-3*) U of Mich Pr.

When Beaver Was Very Great: Stories to Live by. Anne M. Dunn. LC 95-75453. (Illus.). 224p. 1995. 18.95 (*1-883953-08-1*); pap. 13.95 (*1-883953-07-3*) Midwest Trad.

When Being Good Isn't Good Enough. Steve Brown. LC 95-36568. 224p. (Orig.). (YA). (gr. 10). 1995. reprint ed. pap. 12.99 (*0-8010-5446-X*, Ravens Ridge) Baker Bks.

When Best Doesn't Equal Good: Educational Reform & Teacher Recruitment - a Longitudinal Study. James Sears & J. Dan Marshall. 320p. (C). 1994. text ed. 48.00 (*0-8077-3346-6*); pap. text ed. 23.95 (*0-8077-3345-8*) Tchrs Coll.

When Birds Could Talk & Bats Could Sing: The Adventures of Bruh Sparrow, Sis Wren & Their Friends. Virginia Hamilton. LC 95-15307. (Illus.). 72p. (J). (gr. 2-5). 1996. 17.95 (*0-590-47372-7*, Blue Sky Press) Scholastic Inc.

When Black Folks Was Colored. 1994. pap. text ed. write for info. (*0-9643592-0-0*) African AHS.

When Black Folks Was Colored Vol. 3. (Illus.). 158p. (Orig.). 1995. pap. 10.00 (*0-9643592-1-9*) African AHS.

***When Black Men Stand up for God: Reflections on the Million Man March.** Frank M. Reid, 3rd et al. 240p. (Orig.). 1996. pap. text ed. 12.95 (*0-913543-48-9*) African Am Imag.

When Black Roses Bloom. 1995. 9.95 (*0-7869-0101-2*) TSR Inc.

***When Blossoms Opened in the Sun.** 110p. (Orig.). 1994. pap. 8.95 (*0-9637154-9-6*) Flagg Mtn Pr.

When Bluebell Sang. Lisa C. Ernst. LC 88-22262. (Illus.). 32p. (J). (ps-1). 1989. lib. bdg. 15.00 (*0-02-733561-5*, Bradbury S&S) S&S Childrens.

When Bluebell Sang. Lisa C. Ernst. LC 91-15552. (Illus.). 40p. (J). (ps-1). 1992. reprint ed. pap. 4.95 (*0-689-71584-6*, Aladdin Paperbacks) S&S Childrens.

When Bobby Kennedy Was a Moving Man. Robert Gordon. 180p. (Orig.). 1993. pap. 10.95 (*0-930773-28-4*); lib. bdg. 20.95 (*0-930773-27-6*) Black Heron Pr.

When Bombay Burned: Reportage & Comments on the Riots & Blasts from the Times of India. Ed. by Dileep Padgaonkar. (C). 1993. 22.50 (*81-85944-55-5*, Pub. by UBS Pubs Dist II) S Asia.

When Bonding Fails: Clinical Assessment of High-Risk Families. Frank G. Bolton, Jr. LC 83-4425. (Sage Library of Social Research: No. 151). 224p. 1983. reprint ed. pap. 63.90 (*0-608-01521-0*, 2059565) Bks Demand.

When Borders Don't Divide: Labor Migration & Refugee Movements in the Americas. Ed. by Patricia R. Pessar. LC 87-20856. 300p. 1988. 19.50 (*0-934733-26-0*); pap. 14.50 (*0-934733-27-9*) CMS.

When Bosses Ruled Philadelphia: The Emergence of the Republican Machine, 1867-1933. Peter McCaffery. LC 92-42467. (Illus.). 304p. 1993. 35.00 (*0-271-00923-3*) Pa St U Pr.

When Boundaries Betray Us: Beyond Illustrations of What is Ethical in Therapy & Life. Carter Heyward. LC 92-54536. 1994. pap. 10.00 (*0-06-063896-6*, PL) HarpC.

When Breaks the Dawn. Janette Oke. LC 86-3405. (Canadian West Ser.). 224p. (Orig.). 1986. pap. 8.99 (*0-87123-882-9*) Bethany Hse.

When Breaks the Dawn. large type ed. Janette Oke. LC 86-3405. (Canadian West Ser.: Vol. 3). 224p. (Orig.). 1986. pap. 10.99 (*0-87123-895-0*) Bethany Hse.

When Brooklyn Was the World 1920-1957. Elliot Willensky. (Illus.). 1986. 24.00 (*0-517-55858-0*, Harmony) Crown Pub Group.

When Brothers Dwell Together: The Preeminence of Younger Siblings in the Hebrew Bible. Frederick E. Greenspahn. 224p. (C). 1994. 35.00 (*0-19-508253-2*, 154) OUP.

When Buffalo Ran. George B. Grinnell. LC 66-13429. (Western Frontier Library: No. 31). (Illus.). 1966. pap. 8.95 (*0-8061-1271-9*) U of Okla Pr.

When Buffalo Ran. George B. Grinnell. 86p. 1993. reprint ed. pap. 9.95 (*0-88839-258-3*) Hancock House.

When Bunny Grows Up. Golden Staff & Richard Scarry. (Illus.). 24p. (J). (ps-2). 1995. bds. 1.59 (*0-307-00311-6*, Golden Books) Western Pub.

When Business East Meets Business West: The Pacific Rim Guide to Practice & Protocol. Christopher Engholm. LC 91-12204. 368p. 1991. text ed. 60.00 (*0-471-53033-6*); pap. text ed. 14.95 (*0-471-53034-4*) Wiley.

When Business Gets Personal. Jonathan L. Alder. 1993. 135.00 incl. disk (*0-250-48604-0*) MICHIE.

When Businesses Cross International Borders: Strategic Alliances & Their Alternatives. Harvey S. James, Jr. & Murray L. Weidenbaum. LC 92-36013. (Washington Papers: No. 161). 135p. (Orig.). 1993. text ed. 47.95 (*0-275-94577-4*, C4577, Praeger Pubs); pap. text ed. 16.95 (*0-275-94578-2*, B4578, Praeger Pubs) Greenwood.

When California Was an Island. Barbara Haas. 160p. (Orig.). 1993. 15.00 (*0-934257-11-6*); pap. 8.00 (*0-934257-10-8*) Story Line.

When Calls the Heart. Janette Oke. LC 82-24451. (Canadian West Ser.: Vol. 1). (Illus.). 224p. (Orig.). 1983. pap. 8.99 (*0-87123-611-7*) Bethany Hse.

When Calls the Heart. large type ed. Janette Oke. LC 82-24451. (Canadian West Ser.). 226p. (Orig.). 1985. pap. 10.99 (*0-87123-885-3*) Bethany Hse.

When Can a Child Believe? Eugene Chamberlain. LC 73-80778. 80p. 1973. pap. 5.99 (*0-8054-6208-2*, 4262-08) Broadman.

When Can Daddy Come Home? see When Andy's Father Went to Prison

***When Can I Get a Tattoo? And 94 More Questions (& Answers) about Teen Rights & the Law.** Tom Jacobs. LC 97-8599. (J). 1997. pap. text ed. 14.95 (*1-57542-028-7*) Free Spirit Pub.

When Cancer Comes: Mobilizing Physical, Emotional, & Spiritual Resources to Combat One of Life's Most Dreaded Diseases. Don Hawkins et al. (Healing for the Heart Ser.). 208p. 1993. text ed. 18.99 (*0-8024-0949-0*) Moody.

When Cancer Returns: Meeting the Challenge Again. 28p. 1995. pap. text ed. 10.00 (*0-7881-2115-4*) DIANE Pub.

When Capitalists Collide: Business Conflict & the End of Empire in Egypt. Robert Vitalis. LC 94-16550. 1995. 50.00 (*0-520-08593-0*); pap. 20.00 (*0-520-08594-9*) U CA Pr.

***When Catfish Had Ticks: Texas Drought Humor.** Rana Williamson. LC 97-4267. (Illus.). 64p. (Orig.). 1997. pap. 5.95 (*1-57168-159-0*, 159-0, Eakin Pr) Sunbelt Media.

When Catholics Speak about Jews: Notes for Homilists & Catechists. John T. Pawlikowski & James A. Wilde. 88p. 1987. pap. 5.95 (*0-930467-60-4*, CAJEW) Liturgy Tr Pubns.

When Cats Dream. Dave Pilkey. LC 91-31355. 32p. (J). (ps-2). 1992. 15.95 (*0-531-05997-9*); lib. bdg. 16.99 (*0-531-08597-X*) Orchard Bks Watts.

When Cats Dream. Dave Pilkey. LC 91-31355. (Illus.). 32p. (J). (ps-2). 1996. pap. 5.95 (*0-531-07075-1*) Orchard Bks Watts.

***When 'CCO Was Cookin' Book.** Dick Chapman. (Illus.). 210p. (Orig.). 1996. pap. 14.95 (*0-9655087-0-6*) Chapman Ent.

When Chemicals Come to School: The Core Team Model of Student Assistance Programs. 3rd rev. ed. Gary L. Anderson. (Illus.). 452p. (Orig.). 1993. pap. 34.95 (*0-9618023-5-9*) Community Rec Pr.

When Chester Lost Maybelle. David W. Babson. LC 96-60274. (Illus.). 14p. (Orig.). (J). (gr. k-5). 1996. pap. 2.95 (*0-940787-09-1*) Winstead Pr.

When Chickens Grow Teeth: A Story from the French of Guy de Maupassant. Illus. & Retold by Wendy A. Halperin. 32p. (J). (ps-2). 1996. 15.95 (*0-531-09526-6*); lib. bdg. 16.99 (*0-531-08876-6*) Orchard Bks Watts.

When Child Abuse Comes to Church. Bill Anderson. 176p. (Orig.). 1992. pap. 8.99 (*1-55661-286-9*) Bethany Hse.

When Children Abuse: Group Treatment Strategies for Children with Impulse Control Problems. rev. ed. Carolyn Cunningham & Kee MacFarlane. (Illus.). 272p. 1995. pap. text ed. 28.00 (*1-884444-23-7*) Safer Soc.

When Children Ask about God. Harold S. Kushner. LC 76-155714. 176p. 1971. 7.95 (*0-935457-25-9*) Reconstructionist Pr.

When Children Ask about God: A Guide for Parent's Who Don't Always Have All the Answers. Harold S. Kushner. 1995. pap. 12.00 (*0-8052-1033-4*) Schocken.

***When Children Can Be Children: Adults Must Help.** unabridged ed. Augustine A. Amanzeh. (Illus.). 15p. (YA). (gr. 8-12). 1997. 8.00 (*1-890606-02-2*) A A Amanzeh.

When Children Invite Child Abuse. Svea J. Gold. (Illus.). 276p. 1986. 15.95 (*0-9615332-0-X*) Fern Ridge Pr.

When Children Kill. Charles P. Ewing. 171p. 35.00 (*0-669-21883-9*, Lexington) Jossey-Bass.

When Children Molest Children: Group Treatment Strategies for Young Sexual Abusers. Carolyn Cunningham & Kee McFarlane. 240p. 1991. pap. 28.00 (*1-884444-06-7*) Safer Soc.

When Children Play: Proceedings of International Conference on Play & Play Environments. Ed. by Joe L. Frost & Sylvia Sunderlin. LC 84-20477. (Illus.). 365p. 1985. 34.75 (*0-87173-107-X*) ACEI.

When Children Play: Proceedings of the International Conference on Play & Play Environments. International Conference on Play & Play Environments Staff. Ed. by Joe L. Frost & Sylvia Sunderlin. LC 84-20477. (Illus.). 367p. reprint ed. pap. 104.60 (*0-7837-6160-0*, 2045882) Bks Demand.

When Children Suffer: A Sourcebook for Ministry with Children in Crisis. Ed. by Andrew D. Lester. LC 87-8165. 210p. (C). 1987. 16.00 (*0-664-21327-8*, Westminster) Westminster John Knox.

When Children Think: Using Journals to Encourage Creative Thinking. Gabriel H. Jacobs. LC 71-78837. 77p. reprint ed. pap. 25.00 (*0-8357-3029-8*, 2039276) Bks Demand.

When Children Use Drugs. Waln K. Brown. 20p. 1989. 2.95 (*1-56456-001-5*, 216) W Gladden Found.

When Children Want Children: An Inside Look at the Crisis of Teenage Parenthood. Leon Dash. 272p. 1990. pap. 11.95 (*0-14-011789-X*, Penguin Bks) Viking Penguin.

When Children Write: Critical Re-Visions of the Writing Workshop. Timothy J. Lensmire. LC 93-44983. 192p. (C). 1994. text ed. 38.00 (*0-8077-3329-6*); pap. text ed. 17.95 (*0-8077-3328-8*) Tchrs Coll.

When China Ruled the Seas: The Treasure Fleet of the Dragon Throne 1403-1433. Louise Levathes. LC 93-42773. (Illus.). 256p. 1994. 23.00 (*0-671-70158-4*) S&S Trade.

***When China Ruled the Seas: The Treasure Fleet of the Dragon Throne, 1405-1433.** Louis Levathes. (Illus.). 264p. 1997. pap. 14.95 (*0-19-511207-5*) OUP.

When Christ & His Saints Slept. Sharon K. Penman. (Eleanor of Aquitaine Trilogy Ser.: Bk. 1). 768p. 1996. pap. 14.00 (*0-345-39668-5*) Ballantine.

When Christ & His Saints Slept. Sharon K. Penman. LC 94-22593. 757p. 1995. 25.00 (*0-8050-1015-7*) H Holt & Co.

***When Christ Comes & Comes Again.** Thomas F. Torrance. 192p. 1996. pap. 16.00 (*1-57910-009-0*) Wipf & Stock.

When Christ Lives in Us. Justo L. Gonzalez. 96p. 1996. student ed., pap. text ed. 5.95 (*0-687-01560-X*); teacher ed., pap. text ed. 5.95 (*0-687-01562-6*) Abingdon.

When Christ Meets Christ: Homilies on the Just Word. Walter J. Burghardt. LC 92-46434. 256p. 1993. pap. 14.95 (*0-8091-3373-3*) Paulist Pr.

***When Christ Returns.** Charles H. Spurgeon. 176p. (Orig.). 1997. mass mkt. 4.99 (*0-88368-433-0*) Whitaker Hse.

When Christ Was Preached to Christ. Basil Overton. 1983. pap. 6.95 (*0-89137-545-7*) Quality Pubns.

When Christians Disagree. Harvey Seifert & Lois Seifert. 58p. 1991. pap. 9.95 (*1-877871-20-6*, 6607) Ed Ministries.

When Christians Face Death. George R. Bruggemann. (Stepping Stones Ser.). 32p. (Orig.). 1992. pap. 1.95 (*0-8100-0453-4*, 15N2000) Northwest Pub.

When Christians Gather: Issues in the Celebration of the Eucharist. Neil Darragh. 176p. (Orig.). 1997. pap. 11.95 (*0-8091-3678-3*) Paulist Pr.

When Churches Mind the Children: A Study of Day Care in Local Parishes. Eileen W. Lindner et al. LC 83-22545. 192p. (Orig.). 1983. pap. 15.95 (*0-931114-23-3*) High-Scope.

W

When Citizens Complain: Reforming Justice & Administration. Norman Lewis & Patrick Birkinshaw. LC 92-21161. (Law & Political Change Ser.). 1993. 85. 00 (*0-335-15745-9*, Open Univ Pr); pap. 34.00 (*0-335-15744-0*, Open Univ Pr) Taylor & Francis.

When Civil Law Fails. Robert S. Rankin. LC 39-16186. reprint ed. 29.50 (*0-404-05224-X*) AMS Pr.

***When Civilians Manned the Ships - Life in the Amphibious Fleet During World War II.** James A. Kehl. (Illus.). 198p. (Orig.). 1997. pap. 13.95 (*1-883911-15-X*) Brandylane.

***When Clauses & Temporal Structure.** Renaat H. Declerck. (Routledge Studies in Germanic Linguistics Ser.: No. 2). 304p. (C). 1997. text ed. 89.95 (*0-415-15488-X*, Routledge NY) Routledge.

When Clay Sings. Byrd Baylor. LC 86-20587. (Illus.). 32p. (J). (gr. 1-4). 1987. reprint ed. pap. 4.95 (*0-689-71106-9*, Aladdin Paperbacks) S&S Childrens.

When Clay Sings. Byrd Baylor. LC 70-180758. (Illus.). 32p. (J). (ps-3). 1987. reprint ed. lib. bdg. 15.00 (*0-684-18829-5*, C Scribner Sons Young) S&S Childrens.

When Coal Was King. (Americana Bks.). (Illus.). 1970. 3.00 (*0-911410-26-0*) Applied Arts.

When Coffee Was a Nickel. Ardyce H. Samp. Ed. by Randy J. Califf. LC 89-92279. (Illus.). 94p. (Orig.). 1989. reprint ed. pap. 9.95 (*0-9624593-0-5*) Rushmore Hse Pub.

When Colleges Lobby States: The Higher Education-State Government Connection. Ed. by Leonard E. Goodall. 264p. 1987. pap. text ed. 26.50 (*0-88044-115-1*) AASCU Press.

When Colombia Bled: A History of the Violencia in Tolima. James D. Henderson. LC 83-18027. (Illus.). 365p. 1985. pap. 104.10 (*0-7837-8377-9*, 2059187) Bks Demand.

When Comes the Spring. Janette Oke. LC 85-11261. (Canadian West Ser.: Vol. 2). 256p. (Orig.). 1985. pap. 8.99 (*0-87123-795-4*) Bethany Hse.

When Comes the Spring. large type ed. Janette Oke. LC 85-11261. (Canadian West Ser.: Vol. 2). 254p. (Orig.). 1985. pap. 10.99 (*0-87123-884-5*) Bethany Hse.

When Computers Take Over. Rochlin. Date not set. 24.95 (*0-02-926647-5*, Free Press) Free Pr.

When Conscience & Politics Meet: A Catholic View. Ed. by Eugene Clark. LC 93-78818. 104p. (Orig.). 1993. pap. 8.95 (*0-89870-477-4*) Ignatius Pr.

When Conservation Reserve Program Contracts Expire - the Policy Options: Conference Proceedings. LC 94-18051. 143p. 1994. pap. 25.00 (*0-935734-36-8*) Soil & Water Conserv.

When Consumers Complain. Arthur Best. LC 80-21789. 256p. 1981. text ed. 45.00 (*0-231-05124-7*) Col U Pr.

When Consumers Complain. Arthur Best. LC 80-21789. 256p. 1986. pap. text ed. 17.50 (*0-231-06397-0*) Col U Pr.

When Corporations Rule the World. David C. Korten. LC 95-18853. (Kumarian Press Books for a World That Works). (Illus.). 386p. 1995. 29.95 (*1-887208-00-3*) Berrett-Koehler.

When Corporations Rule the World. David C. Korten. LC 95-18853. (Kumarian Press Books for a World That Works). (Illus.). x, 376p. (C). 1996. pap. 19.95 (*1-887208-01-1*) CoPublns.

When Corporations Rule the World. David C. Korten. 384p. 1995. write for info. (*1-85383-313-4*, Pub. by Erthscan Pubns UK) Island Pr.

***When Cosmic Cultures Meet: The Proceedings.** LC 96-79629. (Illus.). 400p. (Orig.). 1997. pap. 35.00 (*1-882658-03-5*) Human Potent Fnd.

When Counting to 10 Isn't Enough: Defusing Anger. Kathy C. Miller. LC 96-3838. 96p. 1996. pap. 7.99 (*0-87788-745-4*) Shaw Pubs.

When Cowboys Die. large type ed. Patrick Dearen. 253p. 1995. 19.95 (*0-7838-1514-X*, GK Hall) Thorndike Pr.

When Cowboys Die: An Evans Novel of the West. Patrick Dearen. 196p. 1994. 18.95 (*0-87131-756-7*) M Evans.

When Cows Come Home. David L. Harrison. LC 93-70870. (Illus.). 32p. (J). (ps-3). 1994. 15.95 (*1-56397-143-7*) Boyds Mills Pr.

When Coyote Howls: A Lavaland Fable. Robert F. Gish. LC 94-819. 152p. 1994. 13.95 (*0-8263-1528-3*) U of NM Pr.

When Crisis Strikes on Campus. Ed. by Wendy A. Larson. 254p. 1994. boxed 79.95 incl. vdisk (*0-89964-297-7*, 24902S) Coun Adv & Supp Ed.

***When Critics Ask: A Popular Handbook on Bible Difficulties.** Norman Geisler & Thomas Howe. 608p. 1992. 26.99 (*0-8010-1142-6*) Baker Bks.

***When Crocodile Is Happy.** Illus. by Terry Burton. (My Big Little Fat Bks.). 20p. (J). (ps up). 1997. bds. 3.49 (*1-85854-598-6*) Brimax Bks.

***When Cultists Ask: A Popular Handbook on Cultic Misinterpretations.** Norman L. Geisler & Ron Rhodes. LC 97-23217. 320p. 1997. 23.99 (*0-8010-1149-3*) Baker Bks.

When Cultures Clash: Case Studies in Multiculturalism. 2nd ed. John W. Friesen. 208p. (Orig.). (C). 1993. pap. text ed. 21.95 (*1-55059-069-3*) Temeron Bks.

When Cultures Collide: Managing Successfully Across Cultures. Richard D. Lewis. LC 95-47015. (Illus.). 331p. 1996. reprint ed. 28.00 (*1-85788-086-2*) Nicholas Brealey.

When Cultures Meet: Remembering San Gabriel del Yunge Oweenge. LC 86-14466. (Illus.). 96p. (Orig.). 1987. pap. 9.95 (*0-86534-091-9*) Sunstone Pr.

When Cupid's Arrow Is a Pain in the Ass: Freedom from Destructive Relationship Syndrome. Steven Heller. LC 96-94302. (Orig.). 1996. pap. 12.95 (*0-9639994-5-1*) H I Ent.

When Daddy Came to School. Julie Brillhart. LC 94-25981. (Illus.). 32p. (J). (ps-k). 1995. lib. bdg. 12.95 (*0-8075-8878-4*) A Whitman.

When Daddy Comes to Visit. Margaret M. Burke. LC 95-61846. (Illus.). 44p. (J). (gr. k-3). 1996. pap. 6.95 (*1-55523-764-9*) Winston-Derek.

***When Daddy Took Us Camping.** Julie Brillhart. LC 96-27302. (Illus.). 24p. (J). 1997. lib. bdg. 13.95 (*0-8075-8879-2*) A Whitman.

When Dallas Became a City: Letters of John Milton McCoy, 1870-1881. Elizabeth Y. Enstam. 1988. 22.95 (*0-932018-02-5*) Dallas His Soc.

When Dana Was the Sun. Charles J. Rosebault. LC 77-103657. (Select Bibliographies Reprint Ser.). 1977. 30.95 (*0-8369-5157-3*) Ayer.

When Dana Was the Sun: A Story of Personal Journalism. Charles J. Rosebault. 1970. reprint ed. text ed. 69.50 (*0-8371-4009-9*, RODS, Greenwood Pr) Greenwood.

When Darkness Calls. Janet E. Gill. 160p. (Orig.). (J). 1996. pap. 3.99 (*0-380-78283-6*, Flare) Avon.

When Darkness Falls. Sydney Williams. 384p. 1992. mass mkt. 4.50 (*1-55817-621-7*, Pinncle Kensgtn) Kensgtn Pub Corp.

***When Darkness Falls: Tales of San Antonio Ghosts & Hauntings.** Docia S. Williams. LC 97-9192. 234p. 1997. pap. 16.95 (*1-55622-536-9*, Rep of TX Pr) Wordware Pub.

***When Dawn Stole the Dark.** deluxe large type ed. Donna Joerg. LC 96-92939. (Illus.). iii, 29p. (J). (gr. k-5). 1997. lib. bdg. 18.95 (*0-9653018-0-X*) Cadence Pr.

***When Dawn Stole the Dark.** large type ed. Donna Joerg. LC 96-92939. (Illus.). iii, 29p. (J). (gr. k-6). 1997. 17.95 (*0-9653018-1-8*) Cadence Pr.

When Day Is Done. Edgar Guest. 191p. 1981. reprint ed. lib. bdg. 20.95 (*0-89968-219-7*, Lghtyr Pr) Buccaneer Bks.

When Daylight Comes. Howard Murphet. LC 74-18958. (Orig.). 1987. pap. 7.50 (*0-8356-0459-4*) Theos Pub Hse.

When Dead Kings Speak. Tony Ortzen. 144p. (C). 1988. pap. 40.00 (*0-7212-0785-5*, Pub. by Regency Press UK) St Mut.

When Death Comes Stealing. Valerie W. Wesley. 320p. 1995. reprint ed. mass mkt. 5.99 (*0-380-72491-X*) Avon.

When Death has Touched Your Life. John E. Biegert. (Looking up Ser.). 1981. pap. 1.95 (*0-8298-0455-2*) Pilgrim OH.

When Death is Imminent. Greg D. Hardegree. Ed. by James A. Milstead. LC 95-69774. 80p. (Orig.). 1995. pap. 7.99 (*0-9647177-6-X*) SHM Pub.

When Death Is Sought: Assisted Suicide & Euthanasia in the Medical Context. NYS Task Force on Life & the Law Staff. 234p. 1994. pap. 9.00 (*1-881268-01-2*) NYS Task Force.

When Death Touches Your Life. large type ed. Mervin E. Thompson. (Large Print Inspirational Ser.). 1988. pap. 14.95 (*0-8027-2592-9*) Walker & Co.

When Death Touches Your Life: Practical Help in Preparing for Death. Mervin E. Thompson. LC 86-544. 224p. 1986. 5.95 (*0-933173-02-4*) Chging Church Forum.

When Dempsey Fought Tunney: Heroes, Hokum & Storytelling in the Jazz Age. Bruce J. Evensen. LC 95-32483. (Illus.). 240p. 1996. pap. 16.95 (*0-87049-918-1*); text ed. 34.00 (*0-87049-919-X*) U of Tenn Pr.

When Descanso Was Young: Early Settlers & Ranchers Descanso, 1845-1947. Beryl Newman. (Illus.). 204p. (Orig.). 1994. pap. 12.00 (*0-938711-25-3*) Tecolote Pubns.

***When Diabetes Complicates Your Life: Controling Diabetes & Related Complications.** 2nd rev. ed. Joseph Juliano. 208p. 1998. pap. 12.95 (*1-56561-127-6*) Chronimed.

When Did I Begin? Conception of the Human Individual in History, Philosophy & Science. Norman Ford. (Illus.). 220p. (C). 1991. pap. text ed. 20.95 (*0-521-42428-3*) Cambridge U Pr.

When Did I Start to Love You? Mini-Book. Gloria Gaither. 32p. 1996. 9.50 (*0-687-01585-5*) Dimen for Liv.

When Did I Stop Being Twenty & Other Injustices. Judith Viorst. (Illus.). 112p. 1987. 10.95 (*0-671-64328-2*) S&S Trade.

When Did the Buddha Live? Controversy on the Dating of the Historical Buddha. Ed. by Heinz Bechert. (C). 1995. 98.50 (*81-7030-469-5*, Pub. by Sri Satguru Pubns II) S Asia.

When Did the Shoshoni Begin to Occupy Southern Idaho: Essays on Late Prehistoric Cultural Remains from the Upper Snake & Salmon River Countries. B. Robert Butler. (Occasional Papers of the Idaho Museum of Natural History: No. 32). 27p. 1981. pap. 5.00 (*0-686-30007-6*) Idaho Mus Nat Hist.

When Did We Get That Lawn Mower? Our Home Improvements. Mae Mary. 1995. pap. 14.95 (*1-887679-57-X*) Foxglove Found.

***When Did We Lose Harriet?** Patricia H. Sprinkle. LC 97-13722. (MacLaren Yarbrough Mysteries Ser.). 1997. pap. write for info. (*0-310-21294-4*) Zondervan.

When Did We See You? Sixty Creative Activities to Help Fourth to Eighth Graders Recognize Jesus Today. Colleen A. Wiessner. LC 94-71582. (Illus.). 192p. (J). (gr. 4-8). 1994. teacher ed., spiral bd. 14.95 (*0-87793-535-1*) Ave Maria.

When Dinosaurs Die: A Guide to Understanding Death. Laurie K. Brown. (Illus.). 32p. (J). (ps-3). 1996. 14.95 (*0-316-10917-7*) Little.

When Dinosaurs Go Visiting. Linda Martin. LC 93-10207. 32p. (J). 1993. 11.95 (*0-8118-0122-5*) Chronicle Bks.

***When Dinosaurs Go Visiting.** Linda Martin. 1997. pap. 5.95 (*0-8118-1707-5*) Chronicle Bks.

When Dinosaurs Roamed. Alice Jablonsky. (Pop 'N Hear Ser.). 12p. (J). (ps-2). 1994. write for info. (*1-883366-58-5*) YES Ent.

When Dinosaurs Roamed New Jersey. William B. Gallagher. LC 96-22044. (Illus.). 250p. 1997. pap. 17.95 (*0-8135-2349-4*); text ed. 47.00 (*0-8135-2348-6*) Rutgers U Pr.

When Dinosaurs Ruled the Basement. William L. DeAndrea & Matthew DeAndrea. 128p. (Orig.). (J). 1995. pap. 3.99 (*0-380-77932-3*, Camelot) Avon.

When Dinosaurs Ruled the Earth. Martha Morss. (Really Reading Ser.: Level 1). (Illus.). 32p. (J). (gr. 1-2). 1991. pap. 2.99 (*0-87406-560-7*) Willowisp Pr.

When Dinosaurs Ruled the Earth. David Norman. (J). 1985. 6.98 (*0-671-07522-5*) S&S Trade.

When Dinosaurs Ruled the Screen. Marc Shapiro. (Illus.). 200p. (Orig.). 1991. pap. 14.95 (*0-685-50336-4*) Image NY.

When Disaster Strikes: Preparing Schools for Bus Accidents, Murders, Suicides, Tornados & Other Community Catastrophes. Alan W. McEvoy. 1992. pap. 6.95 (*1-55691-053-3*, 533x) Learning Pubns.

When Disaster Strikes Series, 6 vols., Set. (Illus.). 64p. (J). (gr. 5-8). 1994. lib. bdg. 95.88 (*0-8050-3459-5*) TFC Bks NY.

***When Divas Get Ready.** John B. Jones. 1997. 21.95 (*1-879360-49-7*) Noble Pr.

When Divorce Happens: A Guide for Family & Friends. James Greteman & Joseph Dunne. LC 90-81942. 128p. (Orig.). 1990. pap. 5.95 (*0-87793-427-4*) Ave Maria.

When Divorce Hits Home: Keeping Yourself Together When Your Family Comes Apart. Beth B. Joselow & Thea Joselow. 160p. (Orig.). 1996. pap. 11.00 (*0-380-77957-9*) Avon.

When Do Fish Sleep? And Other Imponderables of Everyday Life. David Feldman. LC 89-45038. (Illus.). 272p. 1990. reprint ed. pap. 10.00 (*0-06-092011-4*, PL) HarpC.

***When Do I Start? A Memoir.** Karl Malden. LC 97-18104. 1997. 25.00 (*0-684-84309-9*, S&S) S&S Trade.

When Do I Start? A Nine-Point Strategy for Getting the Job You Want. Richard F. Olson. 272p. 1995. pap. 10. 00 (*0-688-14073-4*, Quill) Morrow.

When Do the Good Things Start? Abraham J. Twerski. LC 95-3541. (Illus.). 1995. pap. 8.95 (*0-312-13212-3*) St Martin.

When Do We Eat?, What Can We Do? Wenham et al. LC 91-41354. 1994. spiral bd., pap. 10.00 (*0-87197-324-3*) Favorite Recipes.

When Doctors Get Sick. Ed. by Harvey Mandell & Howard Spiro. LC 87-14104. (Illus.). 484p. 1987. 29.50 (*0-306-42653-6*, Plenum Med Bk) Plenum.

When Doctors Join Unions. Gladys Budrys. LC 96-32596. (IRL Press Book). (Illus.). 224p. 1996. 35.00 (*0-8014-3277-4*) Cornell U Pr.

When Doctors Join Unions. Gladys Budrys. (IRL Press Book). (Illus.). 224p. 1996. pap. 14.95 (*0-8014-8354-9*) Cornell U Pr.

When Does a Twig Become a Limb? History, Imagination, Autobiography, & Humor in the Writings of a Fifth-Generation Adirondack Lad. Clarence Jones. LC 87-82824. 196p. (Orig.). 1988. pap. 14.95 (*0-944962-00-9*) Frankfort Pub.

When Does Discipline Become Abuse? Answers for Parent & Teachers. Chris M. Gove. Ed. by Edward Mycue. 50p. (Orig.). 1992. pap. 10.00 (*1-879457-00-8*) Norton Coker Pr.

When Does the Fun Start? Jean Thesman. 160p. (Orig.). (YA). 1991. mass mkt. 3.50 (*0-380-76129-7*, Flare) Avon.

When Doing Business in Russia, It Pays to Speak Russian. 80p. (RUS.). 1992. pap. 65.00 incl. audio (*0-88432-501-6*, SRU250) Audio-Forum.

***When Drag Is Not a Car Race.** Karen Rauch & Jeff Fessler. LC 97-11165. 1997. pap. 8.95 (*0-684-83081-7*, Fireside) S&S Trade.

When Dragons Dream. Kathleen O'Brien. (Presents Plus Ser.). 1993. mass mkt. 2.99 (*0-373-11600-4*, 1-11600-3) Harlequin Bks.

When Dreams & Heroes Died: A Portrait of Today's College Student. Arthur Levine. LC 80-8005. (Higher & Adult Education Ser.). 29.95p. text ed. 29.95 (*0-87589-481-X*) Jossey-Bass.

When Dreams Came True. Calvin Miles. Ed. by Literacy Volunteers of New York City Staff. (New Writers' Voices Ser.). (Illus.). 64p. (Orig.). 1990. pap. text ed. 3.50 (*0-929631-18-8*, Signal Hill) New Readers.

When Dreams Came True: The GI Bill & the Making of Modern America. Michael J. Bennett. 352p. 1996. 27. 95 (*1-57488-041-1*) Brasseys Inc.

***When Dreams Come True.** Judi Lind. 256p. 1997. mass mkt. 5.50 (*0-7860-0393-6*, Pinncle Kensgtn) Kensgtn Pub Corp.

When Dreams Come True. large type ed. Margaret A. Carr. 320p. 1992. pap. 15.99 (*0-7089-7186-5*) Ulverscroft.

When Dreams Come True: A Story of Emotional Life. Edgar E. Saltus. LC 78-115005. reprint ed. 37.50 (*0-404-05535-4*) AMS Pr.

***When Dreams Cross.** Terri Blackstock. LC 96-35255. (Second Chances Ser.: Vol. 2). 256p. (Orig.). 1997. pap. 9.99 (*0-310-20709-6*) Zondervan.

***When Dreams Don't Work: Professional Caregivers & Burnout.** Ronna F. Jevne & Donna R. Williams. (Death, Value & Meaning Ser.). 1997. text ed. write for info. (*0-89503-179-5*) Baywood Pub.

When Drug Addicts Have Children: Reorienting Child Welfare Response. Ed. by Douglas Besharov. (Orig.). 1994. pap. 26.95 (*0-87868-561-8*) Child Welfare.

***When Drummers Were Women: A Spiritual History of Rhythm.** Layne Redmond. 1997. pap. 18.00 (*0-609-80128-7*) Random Hse Value.

When Duty Called: The Journal of an Enlisted Man, British Isles to Northwest France-April 1944-June 1945. James B. Denney. (Illus.). 180p. 1994. pap. text ed. 19.95 (*0-89745-176-7*) Sunflower U Pr.

When Duty Calls. R.P. Hendrick. 1988. pap. 4.50 (*0-8217-3168-8*) NAL-Dutton.

When Duty Calls. Richard P. Henrick. 384p. 1988. mass mkt. 3.95 (*0-8217-2256-5*, Zebra Kensgtn) Kensgtn Pub Corp.

When Each Leaf Shines: Voices of Women's Ministry. Mary E. Giles. 1986. pap. 4.95 (*0-87193-246-6*) Dimension Bks.

When East Meets West: Indian Thought in Anglo-Indian & Indo-English Fiction. Ed. by Adapa R. Rao & M. Sivaramkrishna. (C). 1995. 20.00 (*81-207-1513-6*, Pub. by Sterling Plns Pvt II) S Asia.

When East Met West: Sociolinguistics in the Former Socialist Bloc. Ed. by Jeffrey Harlig & Csaba Pleh. (Contributions to the Sociology of Language Ser.: No. 68). viii, 208p. 1995. lib. bdg. 106.15 (*3-11-014585-5*) Mouton.

When Eastern Michigan Rode the Rails, Bk. 2. Mac Sebree et al. LC 84-19180. (Special Ser.: No. 105). (Illus.). 232p. 1986. 39.95 (*0-916374-75-0*) Pentrex Pub.

When Eastern Michigan Rode the Rails, Bk. III. William Andres et al. LC 84-19180. (Special Ser.: No. 109). 224p. 1988. 39.95 (*0-916374-80-7*) Pentrex Pub.

When Eastern Michigan Rode the Rails Bk. 4: Detroit to Wyandotte, Monroe & Toledo Including the Windsor, Canada Area. Jack E. Schramm et al. Ed. by Marion Harris. LC 84-19180. (Illus.). 232p. 1994. text ed. 59.00 (*0-933449-23-2*) Transport Trails.

When Economic Crises Endure. Jacques Mazier et al. 320p. (C). (gr. 13-13). 1998. text ed. 62.95 (*1-56324-568-X*) M E Sharpe.

When Economic Crises Endure. Jacques Mazier et al. 320p. (C). (gr. 13-13). 1998. pap. text ed. 26.95 (*1-56324-569-8*) M E Sharpe.

When Ego Dies: A Compilation of Near-Death & Mystical Conversion Experiences. Ed. by Christopher Carson. 196p. (Orig.). 1996. pap. 9.95 (*1-885373-07-4*) Emerald Ink.

When Egypt Ruled the East. rev. ed. George Steindorff & Keith C. Seele. LC 57-5276. 304p. 1963. pap. 13.95 (*0-226-77199-7*, P125) U Ch Pr.

When Elephants Last in Dooryard Bloomed. Ray Bradbury. 1973. 14.95 (*0-394-47931-9*) Knopf.

When Elephants Weep: The Emotional Lives of Animals. Jeffrey M. Mason & Susan McCarthy. LC 94-23819. 320p. 1995. 23.95 (*0-385-31425-6*) Delacorte.

When Elephants Weep: The Emotional Lives of Animals. Jeffrey M. Masson & Susan McCarthy. 320p. 1996. pap. 19.95 (*0-385-31428-0*, Delta) Dell.

When Elephants Weep: The Emotional Lives of Animals. large type ed. Jeffrey M. Masson & Susan McCarthy. (Large Print Bks.). 1995. 25.95 (*1-56895-267-8*) Wheeler Pub.

When Elijah Knocks: A Religious Response to Homelessness. Charles A. Kroloff. LC 92-508. 1992. 14.95 (*0-87441-516-0*) Behrman.

When Elvis Died: Media Overload & the Origins of the Elvis Cult. Neal Gregory & Janice Gregory. 304p. 1992. pap. 12.95 (*0-88687-663-X*, Pharos) Wrld Almnc.

***When Emily Was Sick.** Holly Keller. (J). Date not set. write for info. (*0-688-05211-8*); lib. bdg. write for info. (*0-688-05212-6*) Greenwillow.

When Emily Woke up Angry. Riana Duncan. (Illus.). 32p. (J). (ps-1). 1989. 12.95 (*0-8120-5985-9*) Barron.

***When Empty Arms Become a Heavy Burden: Encouragement for Couples Facing Infertility.** Sandra Glahn & William Cutrer. LC 96-3414. 240p. 1997. pap. 12.99 (*0-8054-6127-2*, 4261-27) Broadman.

When End of Summer is Near. 1998. pap. 14.99 (*0-525-65218-3*) NAL-Dutton.

When Enemies Marry. large type ed. Lindsay Armstrong. 288p. 1995. 21.50 (*0-263-14315-5*, Pub. by M & B UK) Ulverscroft.

When ENFP & INFJ Interact. William D. Murray & Rosalie R. Murray. (When Types Interact Ser.). 56p. 1987. pap. text ed. 9.95 (*1-878287-00-1*, BTAA) Type & Temperament.

When Enough Is Enough. David Augsburger. LC 84-81255. 192p. 1984. pap. 7.99 (*0-8361-3375-7*) Herald Pr.

When Eric's Mom Fought Cancer. Judith Vigna. 32p. (J). (ps-3). 1993. lib. bdg. 14.95 (*0-8075-8883-0*) A Whitman.

When Europe Speaks with One Voice: The External Relations of the European Community. Phillip Taylor. LC 78-57767. (Contributions in Political Science Ser.: No. 22). 235p. 1979. text ed. 55.00 (*0-313-20614-7*, TES/, Greenwood Pr) Greenwood.

When Even the Cows Were Up: Kate's Book of Childhood in the Early 1900s & After. Kate Pedigo. LC 90-71867. (Illus.). 64p. (Orig.). 1990. pap. text ed. 6.95 (*1-877675-06-7*) Midmarch Arts-WAN.

When Evensong & Morrowsong Accord: Three Essays on the Proverb by Bartlett Jere Whiting. Bartlett Jere Whiting. Ed. by Joseph Harris. (Illus.). 138p. 1995. 14. 95 (*0-674-95109-3*, WHIWHE) HUP.

When Every Hour's a Rush Hour. Cristine Bolley & Joann C. Webster. 288p. Date not set. pap. 9.99 (*1-56292-056-1*) Honor Bks OK.

When Every Moment Counts, Count on Provision. Leon Revien. 16p. 1987. pap. text ed. 4.95 (*0-940429-02-0*) M B Glass Assocs.

When Everyone's a Volunteer: The Effective Functioning of All-Volunteer Groups. Ivan H. Scheier. LC 92-82929. (Illus.). 63p. (Orig.). 1992. pap. 15.75 (*0-940576-12-0*) Energize.

W

When Everyone's Looking at You. Karen Dockrey. 136p. 1989. teacher ed., pap. 2.80 (*0-89693-663-5*, 6-1663) SP Pubns.

When Everyone's Looking at You. Karen Dockrey. 96p. (YA). 1989. student ed., pap. 0.60 (*0-89693-664-3*, 6-1664) SP Pubns.

When Evil Strikes. Lila W. Shelburne. 200p. 1992. pap. 9.95 (*0-929292-25-1*) Hannibal Bks.

When Fairy Tale Romances Break Real Hearts: A Guide to Creating Loving Lasting Relationships. Kimberley Heart. Ed. by Nancy Carleton. LC 91-58573. 252p. 1992. pap. 12.95 (*0-915811-39-1*) H J Kramer Inc.

When Faith Crumbles: Hard Evidence for Rock-Solid Faith. Mark Finley & Steven R. Mosley. LC 93-3818. 1993. pap. 1.99 (*0-8163-1160-9*) Pacific Pr Pub Assn.

***When Faith Is Not Enough.** Kelly J. Clark. LC 97-17758. 1997. write for info. (*0-8028-4354-9*) Eerdmans.

***When Faith Is Tested: Pastoral Responses to Suffering & Tragic Death.** Jeffrey R. Zurheide. LC 97-21560. (Creative Pastoral Care & Counseling Ser.). 1997. pap. text ed. 15.00 (*0-8006-2978-7*, Fortress Pr) Augsburg Fortress.

When Faith Meets Faith. David M. Stowe. LC 67-10834. 194p. reprint ed. pap. 55.30 (*0-7837-1959-0*, 2042176) Bks Demand.

When Families Fail...the Social Costs. Ed. by Bryce J. Christensen. 162p. (C). 1991. pap. text ed. 21.75 (*0-8191-8141-2*); lib. bdg. 36.75 (*0-8191-8140-4*) Rockford Inst.

When Families Made Memories Together. Ed. by Mike Beno. LC 94-66341. 164p. 1994. 14.95 (*0-89821-124-7*, 19503) Reiman Pubns.

When Farmers Voted Red: The Gospel of Socialism in the Oklahoma Countryside, 1910-1924. Garin Burbank. LC 76-5259. (Contributions in American History Ser.: No. 53). (Illus.). 225p. 1977. text ed. 49.95 (*0-8371-8903-9*, BSO/, Greenwood Pr) Greenwood.

When Father Kills Mother: Helping Children Move from Trauma to Grief. Dora Black et al. LC 92-48528. 240p. (C). 1993. pap. 16.95 (*0-415-07663-3*, B0873); text ed. 69.95 (*0-415-07662-5*, B0869) Routledge.

When Fathers Rape: Socio-Psyco-Legal-Global Study. Manish Sharma. (C). 1996. 44.00 (*81-7024-739-X*, Pub. by Ashish II) S Asia.

When Fathers Ruled: Family Life in Reformation Europe. Steven Ozment. LC 83-6098. (Illus.). 256p. (C). 1983. 29.95 (*0-674-95120-4*) HUP.

When Fathers Ruled: Family Life in Reformation Europe. Steven Ozment. (Studies in Cultural History). 256p. 1985. pap. 13.95 (*0-674-95121-2*) HUP.

When Federalism Works. Paul E. Peterson et al. LC 86-24467. 243p. 1987. 36.95 (*0-8157-7020-0*); pap. 15.95 (*0-8157-7019-7*) Brookings.

When Feeling Bad. (J). 4.98 (*0-8317-5246-7*) Smithmark.

When Feeling Bad Is Good: An Innovative Self-Help Program for Women to Convert Healthy Depression into New Sources of Growth & Power. Ellen H. McGrath. 432p. 1994. mass mkt. 5.99 (*0-553-56513-3*) Bantam.

When First We Deceive. Charles Wilson. 272p. 1994. 19.95 (*0-7867-0058-0*) Carroll & Graf.

When Fish Go Peopling. Paul Borgese. LC 95-82030. (Illus.). 48p. (J). (ps-4). 1996. 11.95 (*1-886489-07-6*) Laugh & Learn.

When Fishermen Cook Fish: Recipes from America's Best & Best-Known Anglers. Rebecca Gray. (Illus.). 144p. 1996. 24.95 (*1-57223-067-3*, 0673) Idyll Arbor.

When Food Is Love: Exploring the Relationship Between Eating & Intimacy. Geneen Roth. 224p. 1992. pap. 10.00 (*0-452-26818-4*, Plume) NAL-Dutton.

When Food's a Foe: How to Confront & Conquer Eating Disorders. rev. ed. Nancy J. Kolodny. 192p. (YA). (gr. 7 up). 1992. pap. 9.95 (*0-316-50181-6*) Little.

When Football Is Funny! Raymond Berry. (Illus.). 64p. (Orig.). 1996. mass mkt. 5.95 (*0-934651-04-3*) Colony Pub.

When Fox Is a Thousand. Larissa Lai. 1995. pap. 14.95 (*0-88974-041-0*, Pub. by Press Gang CN) LPC InBook.

When Frank Was Four. Alison Lester. LC 95-50979. (Illus.). 32p. (J). (gr. k-3). 1996. 15.00 (*0-395-74275-7*) HM.

When Freedom Bleeds: Journey Through Indian Emergency. Brij M. Toofan. (C). 1989. 26.00 (*81-202-0202-3*, Pub. by Ajanta II) S Asia.

W

When Freedom Is Lost: The Dark Side of Relationship Between Government & the Fort Hope Band. Paul Driben & Robert S. Trudeau. LC 84-165129. 143p. reprint ed. pap. 40.80 (*0-7837-1046-1*, 2041358) Bks Demand.

When Freedom Is Lost: The Dark Side of the Relationship Between Government & the Fort Hope Band. Paul Driben & Robert S. Trudeau. 128p. 1983. pap. 15.95 (*0-8020-6526-0*) U of Toronto Pr.

When Freedom Was Lost: The Unemployed, the Agitator & the State. Lorne Brown. 200p. 1986. 36.95 (*0-920057-75-6*, Pub. by Black Rose Bks CN); pap. 14.95 (*0-920057-77-2*, Pub. by Black Rose Bks CN) Consort Bk Sales.

When French Women Cook. Madeleine Kamman. 372p. 1996. 16.95 (*0-02-861016-4*) Macmillan.

When Friday Isn't Payday: A Complete Guide to Starting, Running - & Surviving in - a Very Small Business. Randy W. Kirk. 352p. 1993. pap. 13.99 (*0-446-39398-3*) Warner Bks.

When Friends Ask about Adoption: A Question & Answer Guide for Non-Adoptive Parents & Other Caring Adults. rev. ed. Linda Bothun. 96p. (Orig.). 1996. pap. 5.95 (*0-9619559-0-2*) Swan Pubns.

When Friends Cook. Friends of the Institute Staff. 1992. 19.95 (*0-9634248-0-7*) Frnds of the Inst.

When Gallantry Was Commonplace: The History of the Michigan Eleventh Volunteer Infantry, 1861-1864. Leland W. Thornton. LC 91-3693. (American University Studies: History: Ser. IX, Vol. 90). 257p. 1991. 42.95 (*0-8204-1259-7*) P Lang Pubng.

***When Geologists Were Historians, 1665-1750.** Rhoda Rappaport. (Illus.). 336p. 1997. 39.95 (*0-8014-3386-X*) Cornell U Pr.

When Giants Converge: The Role of U. S. - Japan Direct Investment. Dorothy B. Christelow. LC 94-28479. 274p. (C). (gr. 13). 1995. text ed. 62.95 (*1-56324-114-5*); pap. text ed. 27.95 (*1-56324-115-3*) M E Sharpe.

When Giants Fall. Vernelle B. Allen. 70p. pap. write for info. (*1-885984-02-2*) Wings of Healing.

When Giants Learn to Dance. Rosabeth M. Kanter. 416p. 1990. pap. 14.00 (*0-671-69625-4*) S&S Trade.

***When Giants Learn to Dance: Mastering the Challenges of Strategy, Management, & Careers in the 1990s.** Rosabeth M. Kanter. 16.45 (*0-671-68355-1*) S&S Trade.

When God Asks for an Undivided Heart: Choosing Celibacy in Love & Freedom. Andrew Apostoli. LC 95-37944. 200p. 1995. pap. 7.95 (*0-8198-8272-0*) Pauline Bks.

When God Became Human. Owen Crouch. 808p. 1991. pap. 19.99 (*0-89900-374-5*) College Pr Pub.

When God Became Man. Burt Groves. 1991. pap. 6.25 (*0-89137-127-3*) Quality Pubns.

When God Becomes a Drug: Breaking the Chains of Religious Addiction & Abuse - Attaining Healthy Spirituality. Leo Booth. 288p. 1992. pap. 12.95 (*0-87477-703-8*, Tarcher Putnam) Putnam Pub Group.

When God Becomes Goddess: The Transformation of American Religion. Richard Grigg. 190p. 1995. 22.95 (*0-8264-0864-8*) Continuum.

When God Began in the Middle. Joseph J. Juknialis. LC 81-52597. (Illus.). 104p. (Orig.). 1982. pap. text ed. 7.95 (*0-89390-027-3*) Resource Pubns.

***When God Calls.** Mary Jessup. LC 97-6389. (Covenant Bible Studies). 1997. pap. 5.95 (*0-87178-009-7*) Brethren.

***When God Calls: A Biography of Bishop Arthur M. Brazier.** Sammie M. Dortch. LC 96-41883. 1996. pap. 14.00 (*0-8028-4299-2*) Eerdmans.

When God Calls, He Annoints. Cheryl Ingram. 111p. 1996. mass mkt. 4.99 (*0-88368-429-2*) Whitaker Hse.

When God Calls, He Anoints. Cheryl Ingram. 100p. (Orig.). 1990. pap. 7.00 (*0-9626900-0-7*) IMI Pub.

When God Can't Answer (Divine Limitations) Maralene Wesner & Miles E. Wesner. LC 86-70753. 100p. 1986. pap. 4.95 (*0-936715-26-X*) Diversity Okla.

When God Chooses: The Life of David. Keith Kaynor. LC 88-32550. 332p. 1989. kivar 9.95 (*0-87227-126-9*, RBP5156) Reg Baptist.

When God Comes Close: A Journey Through Scripture. rev. ed. Rea McDonnell. LC 94-1614. 208p. 1994. pap. 5.25 (*0-8198-8271-2*) Pauline Bks.

When God Cries: Portrait of a Child Slayer. Sherri Jilek. (Illus.). 190p. (Orig.). 1996. pap. 14.95 (*1-56072-330-0*) Nova Sci Pubs.

When God Doesn't Answer: Removing the Roadblocks to Answered Prayer. Woodrow M. Kroll. LC 96-19389. 192p. (YA). (gr. 10). 1997. pap. 11.99 (*0-8010-5726-4*) Baker Bks.

When God Doesn't Make Sense. James Dobson. LC 93-24631. 250p. 1993. 18.99 (*0-8423-8227-5*) Tyndale.

When God Doesn't Make Sense. James Dobson. 64p. 1994. student ed., pap. 5.99 (*0-8423-8239-9*) Tyndale.

When God Doesn't Make Sense. James Dobson. (Mini Bk.). 80p. 1996. 4.99 (*0-8499-5141-0*) Word Pub.

When God Doesn't Make Sense. large type ed. James Dobson. 1994. 19.99 (*0-8423-8242-9*) Tyndale.

When God Gives a Sign: A Response to Objections Made Against Vassula's Testimony on True Life in God. Rene Laurentin. 139p. (Orig.). 1993. pap. 7.00 (*1-883225-14-0*) Trinitas.

***When God Gives You Glimpses...** Pam Vredebelt. 1998. 9.99 (*1-57673-250-9*) Multnomah Pubs.

When God Interrupts: Finding New Life Through Unwanted Change. M. Craig Barnes. LC 95-50979. 160p. (Orig.). 1996. pap. 9.99 (*0-8308-1979-7*, 1979) InterVarsity.

When God Is a Customer: Telugu Courtesan Songs by Ksetrayya & Others. Ed. by A. K. Ramanujan et al. LC 93-28264. (C). 1994. 25.00 (*0-520-08068-8*); pap. 12.00 (*0-520-08069-6*) U CA Pr.

When God Is Silent: How to Hear When He Seems Far Away. Elmer L. Towns. Ed. by Cindy G. Spear & Timothy J. Pierce. (Video Curriculum Ser.: Vol. 2). 60p. 1995. boxed, pap. 49.95 incl. vhs (*1-57052-027-5*); pap. text ed. 2.95 (*1-57052-042-9*) Chrch Grwth VA.

When God Laughs. Jack London. 272p. 1992. pap. write for info. (*0-932458-40-8*) Star Rover.

***When God Laughs.** Jack London. lib. bdg. 24.95 (*0-8488-1999-3*) Amereon Ltd.

When God Lived in a Tent. Susan Davis. (My Church Teaches Ser.). (Illus.). (J). (ps-1). 1978. 1.95 (*0-8127-0181-X*) Review & Herald.

When God Provides. (Living Testimony Ser.: No. 3). 1986. pap. 4.99 (*9971-972-44-1*) OMF Bks.

When God Says I Do. Don Krow. pap. 2.00 (*1-881541-11-8*, 402) A Wommack.

***When God Says No.** Judith Briles. LC 96-47560. 1997. pap. 8.99 (*0-8007-5618-5*) Revell.

When God Says No: Finding the "Yes" in Pain & Disappointment. Judith Briles. 160p. 1994. per., pap. text ed. 12.95 (*0-8403-9820-4*) Kendall-Hunt.

When God Says No: Making Sense of Unanswered Prayer. Leith Anderson. 1996. pap. text ed. 10.99 (*1-55661-599-X*) Bethany Hse.

When God Says No: Twenty-Five Reasons Why Some Prayers Aren't Answered. John H. Hampsch. 24p. (Orig.). 1993. pap. 1.50 (*0-87973-178-8*, 178) Our Sunday Visitor.

When God Says "Well Done!" R. T. Kendall. 10.99 (*1-85792-017-1*, Pub. by Christian Focus UK) Spring Arbor Dist.

***When God Scrambles Your Plans-- And 49 Other Complete Lessons for Youth Bible Study.** Ed. by Ann B. Cannon. LC 96-24114. (Essentials for Christian Youth Ser.). 224p. (YA). 1997. pap. 19.95 (*0-687-02599-0*) Abingdon.

When God Seems Far Away: How to Break Down the Barriers & Embrace the One Who Is All You Need. Joy Jacobs. 217p. pap. 8.99 (*0-87509-403-1*) Chr Pubns.

When God Sheds Tears: A Christian Looks at the Mystery of Suffering. Richard W. Coffen. LC 93-17785. 1993. 8.99 (*0-8280-0721-7*) Review & Herald.

***When God Steps In: Divine Resources for Life's Situations.** A. B. Simpson. 1996. 7.99 (*0-87509-590-9*) Chr Pubns.

When God Was a Woman. Merlin Stone. LC 77-16262. (Illus.). 265p. 1978. pap. 11.00 (*0-15-696158-X*, Harvest Bks) HarBrace.

***When God Weeps: Why Our Sufferings Matter to the Almighty.** Joni Eareckson Tada & Steven Estes. LC 97-25826. 256p. 1997. 19.99 (*0-310-21186-7*) Zondervan.

When, God, When? Joyce Meyer. 64p. (Orig.). 1995. mass mkt. 4.99 (*0-89274-846-X*, HH-846) Harrison Hse.

***When God Whispers.** Carole Mayhall. 1997. pap. text ed. 8.00 (*0-89109-948-4*) NavPress.

When God Whispers Your Name. Max Lucado. LC 94-17302. 1994. 19.99 (*0-8499-1099-4*) Word Pub.

When God Whispers Your Name. Max Lucado. 1995. 4.99 (*0-8499-5108-9*) Word Pub.

When God Whispers Your Name. large type ed. Max Lucado. 272p. 1996. pap. 14.99 (*0-8499-3945-3*, 2437) Word Dist.

When Godly Robes Unravel. Randall Massie. 164p. (Orig.). 1990. pap. 5.99 (*0-89900-386-9*) College Pr Pub.

When God's Children Suffer. Horatius Bonar. 144p. 1992. pap. 8.99 (*0-8254-2294-9*, Kregel Class) Kregel.

When Gods Die: An Introduction to St. John of the Cross. John W. Welch. 1990. 11.95 (*0-8091-3183-8*) Paulist Pr.

When God's People Let You Down: How to Rise above the Hurts That Often Occur Within the Church. Jeff Van Vonderen. 208p. 1995. pap. 9.99 (*1-55661-348-2*) Bethany Hse.

When God's People Pray: Pastorial Prayers for the Congregation First United Methodist Church, Dallas. Susan B. Mohts. Ed. by Margaret Hale. 96p. (Orig.). 1989. pap. 4.95 (*0-685-26559-5*) First United Meth Ch.

When Good-Bye Is Forever: Learning to Live Again after the Loss of a Child. John Bramblett. 1991. mass mkt. 5.99 (*0-345-36399-X*) Ballantine.

When Good Dogs Do Bad Things. Mordecai Siegal. 1993. pap. 12.95 (*0-316-79012-5*) Little.

When Good Kids Do Bad Things. Katherine G. Levine. Ed. by Julie Rubenstein. 272p. 1993. reprint ed. pap. 10.00 (*0-671-79296-2*) PB.

When Good People Quarrel. Robert S. Kreider & Rachel W. Goossen. LC 88-35688. 200p. 1989. pap. 11.99 (*0-8361-3469-9*) Herald Pr.

When Good People Throw Bad Parties. Terri Mandell. Ed. by James Mandell. 100p. (Orig.). 1994. pap. 8.95 (*0-9623062-7-4*) First Hse Pr.

When Good Things Become Addictions. Grant Martin. 192p. 1991. pap. 1.80 (*0-89693-933-2*) SP Pubns.

When Government Regulates Itself: EPA, TVA & Pollution Control in the 1970s. Robert F. Durant. LC 84-22058. 224p. 1985. text ed. 29.00 (*0-87049-458-9*) U of Tenn Pr.

***When Government Regulates Itself: EPA, TVA, & Pollution Control in the 1970s.** Robert F. Durant. LC 84-22058. 210p. pap. 59.90 (*0-608-05194-2*, 2065731) Bks Demand.

When Governments Collide: Coercion & Diplomacy in the Vietnam Conflict, 1964-1968. Wallace J. Thies. 500p. 1980. pap. 13.00 (*0-520-04646-3*) U CA Pr.

***When Grammie Was Little.** Margot S. Bieshman. (Grammie Stories Ser.: Vol. 1). (Illus.). 24p. (Orig.). (J). (gr. k-6). 1992. pap. 7.95 (*0-614-29578-5*) Pergot Pr.

When Grampa Kissed His Elbow. Cynthia C. DeFelice. LC 90-6696. (Illus.). 32p. (J). (gr. k-3). 1992. 16.00 (*0-02-726455-6*, Mac Bks Young Read) S&S Childrens.

When Grandfather Sailed Away. Mike Sackett. (Illus.). 27p. (Orig.). (J). (gr. 3-5). 1996. pap. 3.00 (*0-88092-077-7*, 0777) Royal Fireworks.

When Grandma Came. Jill P. Walsh. (Illus.). 32p. (J). (ps-3). 1994. pap. 4.99 (*0-14-054527-9*) Puffin Bks.

When Grandma Came. Jill P. Walsh. (Illus.). 32p. (J). (ps-3). 1992. pap. 13.00 (*0-670-83581-1*) Viking Child Bks.

When Grapes Turn to Wine. Jelaluddin Rumi. Tr. by Robert Bly. (Illus.). 24p. (PER.). 1986. reprint ed. pap. 6.00 (*0-938756-16-8*) Yellow Moon.

When Gravity Fails. David Ackerman et al. Ed. by Derek Quintanar & Michael MacDonald. (Cyberpunk Ser.). (Illus.). 88p. (C). 1991. pap. 12.00 (*0-937279-12-9*, CP3601) R Talsorian.

When Greek Meets Greek. George Demetrios. LC 76-116949. (Short Story Index Reprint Ser.). (Illus.). 1977. 20.95 (*0-8369-3452-0*) Ayer.

When Grief Breaks your Heart. Jim Moore. LC 94-19609. 80p. (Orig.). 1995. pap. 4.95 (*0-687-00791-7*) Abingdon.

When Grief Visits School: Organizing a Successful Response. John Dudley. LC 95-60209. 176p. (Orig.). (C). 1995. pap. text ed. 14.95 (*0-932796-71-0*) Ed Media Corp.

When Grover Moved to Sesame Street. (Golden Story Book 'n' Tape Ser.). (Illus.). 24p. (J). (ps-3). write for info. incl. audio (*0-307-14291-4*, 14291) Western Pub.

When Growing up Hurts Too Much: A Parent's Guide to Knowing When & How to Choose a Therapist for Your Teenager. Scott O. Harris & Edward N. Reynolds. 141p. pap. 10.95 (*0-02-914055-2*, Free Press) Free Pr.

***When Grown-Ups Fall in Love: A Book for Very Young Children & Rush Limbaugh.** Barbara L. Edmonds. LC 96-91015. (Illus.). 20p. (Orig.). (J). (ps). 1997. pap. 10.00 (*0-9656700-0-7*) Barbys Hse Bks.

When Grownups Drive You Crazy. Eda LeShan. LC 87-22005. 128p. (J). (gr. 3-7). 1988. lib. bdg. 14.00 (*0-02-756340-5*, Mac Bks Young Read) S&S Childrens.

When Hamtramck & I Were Young. Arthur J Majewski. LC 86-62351. 120p. 1987. 11.00 (*0-9617557-0-9*) Maryt Pub.

When Harlem Was in Vogue. David L. Lewis. (Illus.). 400p. 1989. pap. 15.95 (*0-19-505969-7*) OUP.

***When Harlem Was in Vogue.** David L. Lewis. 1997. pap. 14.95 (*0-14-026334-9*) Viking Penguin.

When Harlem Was Jewish, 1870-1930. Jeffrey S. Gurock. LC 79-14768. (Illus.). 234p. reprint ed. pap. 66.70 (*0-8357-3729-2*, 2036451) Bks Demand.

When He Is Come: The Personality & Work of the Holy Spirit. Reader Harris. 56p. 1994. pap. 4.99 (*0-88019-321-2*) Schmul Pub Co.

***When He Leaves.** 224p. 1998. write for info. (*1-56476-699-3*, Victor Bks) Chariot Victor.

When Health Care Is Not Enough: Support Services for Pregnant Women & Infants. Jennifer Laman. (State Legislative Report Ser.: Vol. 19, No. 8). 9p. 1994. 5.00 (*1-55516-226-6*, 7302-1908) Natl Conf State Legis.

When Health Is Lost: Providing for Long-Term Nursing Care. F. Bentley Mooney, Jr. Ed. by Lee Perry. 183p. 1989. 24.95 (*0-943637-04-X*) Amer Commerce Pub.

When Heaven & Earth Changed Place: A Vietnamese Woman's Journey from War to Peace. Le L. Hayslip. 368p. 1993. pap. 12.00 (*0-452-26417-0*, Plume) NAL-Dutton.

When Heaven & Earth Changed Places: A Vietnamese Woman's Journey from War to Peace. Le L. Hayslip. 1993. pap. 12.95 (*0-452-27168-1*, Plume) NAL-Dutton.

When Heaven Fell. William Barton. 352p. (Orig.). 1995. mass mkt. 5.50 (*0-446-60166-7*, Aspect) Warner Bks.

When Heaven Is Silent. Ronald Dunn. LC 94-5604. 1994. 14.99 (*0-8407-4895-7*) Nelson.

***When Hell Freezes Over... The Gift.** Sharrye Farlow-Schlerf. 300p. (Orig.). 1997. per. 17.95 (*0-9649406-1-2*) Spiritual Realities.

When Hello Means Goodbye: A Guide for Parents Whose Child Dies before Birth, at Birth or Shortly after Birth. 2nd rev. ed. Pat Schwiebert & Paul Kirk. Ed. by Perinatal Loss Project Staff. 48p. 1993. Eng. pap. 2.20 (*0-9615197-0-3*); Span. pap. 2.20 (*0-9615197-1-1*) Perinatal Loss.

When Helping Starts to Hurt: A New Look at Burnout among Psychotherapists. William N. Grosch & David C. Olsen. 180p. (C). 1994. 23.00 (*0-393-70167-0*) Norton.

When Hens Crow: The Women's Rights Movements in Antebellum America. Sylvia D. Hoffert. LC 94-44083. 168p. 1995. 25.00 (*0-253-32880-2*) Ind U Pr.

When Heroes Die. Peggy R. Durant. LC 91-48267. (J). 1995. pap. 3.95 (*0-689-71835-7*, Aladdin Paperbacks) S&S Childrens.

When Heroes Die. Penny R. Durant. LC 91-48267. 144p. (YA). (gr. 5 up). 1992. lib. bdg. 15.00 (*0-689-31764-6*, Atheneum Bks Young) S&S Childrens.

***When Heroes Pass Away: The Invention of a Chinese Communist Pantheon.** Dachang Cong. LC 97-21811. 1997. write for info. (*0-7618-0809-4*); pap. write for info. (*0-7618-0810-8*) U Pr of Amer.

When Hippo Was Hairy & Other Tales from Africa. Nick Greaves. (Illus.). 144p. (J). (gr. 3-12). 1988. 12.95 (*0-8120-4131-3*) Barron.

When Hippo Was Hairy & Other Tales from Africa. Nick Greaves. (Illus.). 144p. (J). (gr. k up). 1991. pap. 10.95 (*0-8120-4548-3*) Barron.

When History Accelerates: Essays on Social Change, Complexity & Creativity. Ed. by C. M. Hann. 224p. (C). 1994. text ed. 75.00 (*0-485-11464-X*, Pub. by Athlone Pr UK) Humanities.

***When History Enters the House: Essays from Eastern Europe.** unabridged ed. Michael Blumenthal. (Illus.). 180p. (Orig.). 1997. pap. 15.95 (*0-614-30226-9*) Pleasure Boat.

When History Was Made: The Women of 1916. Ruth Tailln. (Illus.). 180p. (Orig.). 1996. pap. 13.95 (*0-9514229-8-7*, Pub. by Beyond the Pale IE) Irish Bks Media.

When Hitler Stole Pink Rabbit. Judith Kerr. 192p. (Orig.). (J). (gr. 3 up). 1987. mass mkt. 3.99 (*0-440-49017-0*, YB BDD) BDD Bks Young Read.

***When Hitler Stole Pink Rabbit.** Judith Kerr. (Illus.). 192p. (Orig.). (J). (gr. 3-7). 1997. pap. 5.95 (*0-698-11589-9*, Paperstar) Putnam Pub Group.

When Hitler Stole the Pink Rabbit - Cuando Hitler Robo el Conejo Rosa. Judith Kerr. (SPA.). 11.95 (*84-204-3201-6*) Santillana.

***When Holidays Are Hell...! A Guide to Surviving Family Gatherings.** Mariana Caplan. (Illus.). 120p. (Orig.). 1997. pap. 7.95 (*0-934252-77-7*) Hohm Pr.

When Hollywood Was Fun: Snapshots of an Era. Gene Lester & Peter Laufer. (Illus.). 224p. 1993. 24.95 (*1-55972-197-9*, Birch Ln Pr) Carol Pub Group.

When Home Is No Haven: Child Placement Issues. Albert J. Solnit et al. 176p. (C). 1992. pap. 12.00 (*0-300-05931-0*); text ed. 30.00 (*0-300-05091-7*) Yale U Pr.

When Hope Springs New. Janette Oke. LC 86-13664. (Canadian West Ser.). 224p. (Orig.). 1986. pap. 8.99 (*0-87123-657-5*) Bethany Hse.

When Hope Springs New. large type ed. Janette Oke. LC 86-13664. (Canadian West Ser.: Vol. 4). 224p. (Orig.). 1986. pap. 10.99 (*0-87123-675-3*) Bethany Hse.

An Asterisk (*) at the beginning of an entry indicates that the title is appearing in BIP for the first time.

When Hopi Children Were Bad: A Monster Story. Tawa Mana & Youyouseyah. (Illus.). 41p. (Orig.). (J). (gr. k-5). 1989. pap. 46.95 (*0-940113-20-1*) Sierra Oaks Pub.

When Horses Pulled Boats. William H. Shank. 1994. reprint ed. 6.00 (*0-933788-43-6*) Am Canal & Transport.

When Hunger Calls. Bert Kitchen. LC 93-32360. (Illus.). 32p. (J). (ps up). 1994. 15.95 (*1-56402-316-8*) Candlewick Pr.

When Hunger Calls. Bert Kitchen. LC 93-32360. (Illus.). 32p. (J). (gr. k-4). 1996. reprint ed. pap. 5.99 (*1-56402-971-9*) Candlewick Pr.

When Hurts Go Deep: Helping Each Other in Times of Crisis. Thomas L. Haan. LC 95-16263. 1995. student ed. 7.35 (*1-56212-106-5*) CRC Pubns.

When Husbands Come Out of the Closet. Ed. by Jean S. Gochros. LC 88-36884. (Haworth Series on Women: No. 1). 267p. 1989. pap. text ed. 14.95 (*0-918393-61-2*) Harrington Pk.

When Husbands Come Out of the Closet. Ed. by Jean S. Gochros. LC 88-36883. (Haworth Series on Women: Vol. 1). 267p. 1989. text ed. 39.95 (*0-86656-868-9*) Haworth Pr.

***When I Am a Sister.** Robin Ballard. LC 97-6326. (J). (ps up). 1998. 15.00 (*0-688-15397-6*); lib. bdg. 14.93 (*0-688-15398-4*) Greenwillow.

When I Am an Old Coot. Roy English. LC 95-13153. (Illus.). 144p. 1995. pap. 6.95 (*0-87905-695-9*) Gibbs Smith Pub.

When I Am an Old Woman: Reading Card. Ed. by Sandra H. Martz. (Illus.). 24p. 1995. per. 5.00 (*0-918949-70-X*) Papier-Mache Press.

***When I Am an Old Woman I Shall Wear Purple.** Ed. by Sandra H. Martz. (Illus.). 64p. 1997. text ed. 6.95 (*1-57601-052-X*) Papier-Mache Press.

When I Am an Old Woman I Shall Wear Purple. large type ed. Ed. by Sandra H. Martz. LC 95-44938. 224p. (Orig.). 1996. 17.00 (*0-918949-83-1*) Papier-Mache Press.

When I Am an Old Woman I Shall Wear Purple. 2nd ed. Ed. by Sandra H. Martz. LC 91-13828. (Illus.). 181p. (Orig.). 1991. 18.00 (*0-918949-15-7*); pap. 11.00 (*0-918949-16-5*) Papier-Mache Press.

When I Am Dictator of the U. S. A. A Plan to Save America. Gene McPherson. 231p. 1994. pap. 9.95 (*0-9640797-0-4*) Mt Adams Media.

When I am Eight. Joan L. Nixon. LC 93-20023. (J). (gr. 1-3). 1994. pap. 13.99 (*0-8037-1499-8*) Dial Bks Young.

When I Am Eight. Joan L. Nixon. LC 93-20023. (J). (ps-3). 1994. pap. 14.89 (*0-8037-1500-5*) Dial Bks Young.

When I Am Little Again & the Child's Right to Respect. Janusz Korczak. Tr. by E. P. Kulawiec. 208p. (Orig.). (C). 1991. pap. text ed. 28.00 (*0-8191-8307-5*); lib. bdg. 47.50 (*0-8191-8306-7*) U Pr of Amer.

When I Am Old with You. Angela Johnson. LC 89-70928. (Illus.). 32p. (J). (ps-2). 1990. 15.95 (*0-531-05884-0*); lib. bdg. 16.99 (*0-531-08484-1*) Orchard Bks Watts.

When I Am Old with You. Angela Johnson. LC 89-70928. (Illus.). 32p. (J). (ps-2). 1993. pap. 5.95 (*0-531-07035-2*) Orchard Bks Watts.

When I Am Queen of the World. Muriel R. Kulwin. 21p. 1995. pap. 10.00 (*1-889080-05-5*) Doublem Bks.

When I Am Weak Then I Am Strong. Elijah Richards. 67p. (Orig.). 1994. pap. write for info. (*0-913183-04-0*) Lantern Lght.

***When I Awaken.** Marion Forderbrugen. (Orig.). 1997. pap. write for info. (*1-57553-463-0*) Watermrk Pr.

When I Become a Functionnaire-School Knowledge in French Colonial Africa. Gail P. Kelly. (Special Studies in Comparative Education: No. 11). 76p. (Orig.). 1984. pap. text ed. 10.00 (*0-937033-01-4*) SUNY GSE Pubns.

When I Become King. Terry Page. (Illus.). 24p. (J). (gr. 2-6). 1977. pap. text ed. 4.00 (*1-887864-62-8*) Boo Bks.

When I Become King. Terry Page. (Illus.). 24p. (J). (gr. 2-6). 1997. lib. bdg. 7.00 (*1-887864-24-5*) Boo Bks.

When I Become King Coloring Book. Terry Page. (Illus.). 32p. (J). (ps-5). 1997. pap. 3.00 (*1-887864-25-3*) Boo Bks.

When I Call for Help: A Pastoral Response to Domestic Violence Against Women. Secretariat for Family, Laity, Women & Youth Staff. 1992. pap. 0.99 (*1-55586-547-X*); pap. 0.99 (*1-55586-548-8*) US Catholic.

When I Can Read My Title Clear: Literacy, Slavery & Religion in the Antebellum South. Janet D. Cornelius. (Illus.). 228p. (C). 1995. pap. text ed. 16.95 (*0-87249-871-9*) U of SC Pr.

***When I Can't Pray.** Rob Frost. 216p. Date not set. 12.99 (*1-56476-712-4*, Victor Bks) Chariot Victor.

When I Die see Basic Truths

When I Die, Will I Get Better? Joeri Breebaart & Piet Breebaart. LC 93-2713. (Illus.). 32p. (J). (gr. k-4). 1993. 11.95 (*0-87226-375-4*) P Bedrick Bks.

When I Do, I Learn: A Guide to Creative Planning for Teachers & Parents of Preschool Children. rev. ed. Barbara J. Taylor. LC 74-2122. (Illus.). 250p. 1977. pap. 9.95 (*0-8425-1023-0*) Frnds of the Libry.

When I Dream I Hear Hoof Beats. Jamie Mayhew. 187p. (Orig.). 1996. mass mkt. 4.99 (*1-55197-101-1*, Pub. by Comnwlth Pub CN) Partners Pubs Grp.

When I Eat. Mandy Suhr. (J). (ps-1). 1992. lib. bdg. 18.95 (*0-87614-737-6*, Carolrhoda) Lerner Group.

When I Eat. Mandy Suhr. (J). (ps-1). 1993. pap. 5.95 (*0-87614-596-9*, First Ave Edns) Lerner Group.

***When I First Came to This Land.** Harriet Ziefert. LC 97-9612. 1998. 15.95 (*0-399-23044-0*, Putnam) Putnam Pub Group.

When I Get Bigger. Mercer Mayer. (Golden Look-Look Bks.). (Illus.). 24p. (J). (ps-3). 1985. reprint ed. pap. 2.25 (*0-307-11943-2*, Golden Pr) Western Pub.

When I Get Old, This Will Be Funny: A Nostalgic Look at the One-Room School. Robert Haney. (Illus.). 247p. 1979. 12.95 (*0-9609552-0-8*) Haney Bks.

When I Give My Love. Antoinette Wrighton. 1996. mass mkt. 5.99 (*0-671-56115-4*, PB Trade Paper) PB.

When I Go Camping with Grandma. Marion Dane Bauer. LC 93-33809. (Illus.). 32p. (J). (gr. k-3). 1996. pap. 4.95 (*0-8167-3449-6*) BrdgeWater.

When I Go Camping with Grandma. Marion Dane Bauer. LC 93-33809. (Illus.). 32p. (J). (gr. k-3). 1997. pap. 14.95 (*0-8167-3448-8*) BrdgeWater.

When I Go to Bed at Night: A Modern Tale of Fear, Magic & Healing. Susan Bassett. LC 94-713772. (Illus.). 48p. 1994. 14.95 (*1-885221-00-2*) BookPartners.

When I Grow Bigger. Trish Cooke. LC 93-42601. (Illus.). 32p. (J). (ps up). 1994. 13.95 (*1-56402-430-X*) Candlewick Pr.

When I Grow Old I'll Be a Tree, Vol. 1500. Illus. by Khrys Roybal. 40p. (Orig.). (J). (gr. 1-8). 1996. pap. write for info. (*0-9652600-0-3*) Misheeka.

When I Grow Up. P. K. Hallinan. LC 95-8293. (Illus.). 24p. (J). (ps-3). 1995. per., pap. 4.95 (*1-57102-046-2*, Ideals Child); lib. bdg. 11.00 (*1-57102-061-6*, Ideals Child) Hambleton-Hill.

When I Grow Up. Candri Hodges. (Turtle Bks.). (Illus.). 32p. (J). (gr. k-4). 1995. pap. 8.95 (*0-944727-26-3*); lib. bdg. 14.95 (*0-944727-27-1*) Jason & Nordic Pubs.

When I Grow Up. Annie Kubler. LC 91-27125. (J). 1992. 5.99 (*0-85953-505-3*) Childs Play.

***When I Grow Up.** Shelly D. Lekven. (J). Date not set. 15.95 (*0-399-23124-2*) Putnam Pub Group.

When I Grow Up. Bernice Stebbing. Ed. by William Schulz. (Options Ser.). 80p. (Orig.). (J). (gr. 1-8). 1989. pap. 8.00 (*0-920541-57-7*) Peguis Pubs Ltd.

When I Grow Up. Dayle M. Timmons & Kerry Rogers. (J). (ps-1). 1996. 23.99 (*0-86653-861-5*, FE3861) Fearon Teach Aids.

***When I Grow Up.** Sreven Walker. 1998. pap. 5.99 (*0-14-056243-5*) Viking Penguin.

When I Grow Up. Jodi L. Wilson. LC 90-90465. (Illus.). 32p. (Orig.). (J). (gr. 1-3). 1990. pap. 4.95 (*0-9628335-0-9*) Wilander Pub.

When I Grow up, Ea. Ediba Kezzeiz. (Illus.). 20p. (Orig.). (J). (ps-1). 1991. pap. 3.50 (*0-89259-116-1*) Am Trust Pubns.

When I Grow Up: Mercer Mayer. (Golden Little Look-Look Bks.). (Illus.). 24p. (J). (ps). 1991. 1.49 (*0-307-11520-8*, Golden Pr) Western Pub.

When I Grow Up: Structured Experiences for Expanding Male & Female Roles, Vol. I. Illus. by Susan Fritts. LC 78-56486. 206p. (J). (ps-8). 1979. pap. 14.95 (*0-89334-016-2*) Humanics Ltd.

When I Grow Up: Structured Experiences for Expanding Male & Female Roles, Vol. II. Illus. by Susan Fritts. LC 78-56486. 183p. (YA). (gr. 9-12). 1981. pap. 14.95 (*0-89334-017-0*) Humanics Ltd.

When I Grow up, I Want to Be... Blaise Douglas. (Illus.). 32p. (J). 1996. 9.99 (*1-56402-866-6*) Candlewick Pr.

***When I Grow up I Want to Be...** Blaise Douglas. LC 95-70914. (Illus.). 32p. (J). (ps-3). 1997. reprint ed. pap. 5.99 (*0-7636-0230-2*) Candlewick Pr.

***When I Grow up I Want to Be a Doctor.** Charles H. Ripp. (Illus.). 11p. (J). (gr. 3-6). 1996. pap. 6.00 (*0-8059-4056-1*) Dorrance.

***When I Grow up, I'm Going to Be a Superhero!** Tom Le Blanc. LC 96-90866. (Illus.). (Orig.). (J). (gr. k-3). 1997. pap. 7.95 (*0-533-12201-5*) Vantage.

When I Grow up...I Want to Be an Adult: Christ-Centered Recovery Workbook for Adult Children. rev. ed. Ron Ross. LC 90-60660. (Illus.). 197p. (Orig.). 1990. student ed., pap. 12.95 (*0-941405-15-X*) RPI Pubng.

When I Have a Little Girl. Charlotte Zolotow. LC 65-24656. (Trophy Picture Bk.). (Illus.). 32p. (J). (ps-3). 1988. pap. 4.95 (*0-06-443175-4*, Trophy) HarpC Child Bks.

When I Hear a Tale. Beach. 1996. text ed. 48.00 (*0-02-307081-1*, Macmillan Coll) P-H.

When I Hear Music. Libby Roderick. (Illus.). 118p. (Orig.). 1994. pap. write for info. (*0-9641114-1-1*) Turtle Islnd.

When I Kept Silence. Naomi Clark. LC 88-71363. (CSU Poetry Ser.: No. XXVI). 80p. (Orig.). 1988. 12.00 (*0-914946-68-4*); pap. 6.00 (*0-914946-69-2*) Cleveland St Univ Poetry Ctr.

When I Know the Power of My Black Hand. Lance Jeffers. 1975. 4.95 (*0-910296-04-9*) Broadside Pr.

***When I Leave & You Are Left.** Mary M. Drakesmith & Jane R. Moerschel. 68p. 1996. pap. 12.95 (*0-9655020-7-4*) M & J Enter.

When I Left My Village. Maxine R. Schur. LC 94-45799. (Illus.). 64p. (J). (gr. 1-5). 1996. pap. 14.99 (*0-8037-1561-7*); pap. 14.89 (*0-8037-1562-5*) Dial Bks Young.

When I Listen: A Listener's Little Book. Marilyn Gatlin & Mary L. Cook. LC 85-60794. (Illus.). 68p. 1985. per. 6.50 (*0-943734-03-7*) Ocean Tree Bks.

When I Look in the Mirror. Sopoeia Greywolf. (Illus.). 24p. 1993. pap. text ed. 6.95 (*1-881316-28-9*) A&B Bks.

When I Looked Back You Were Gone: Poems. Cary Waterman. LC 92-52505. 1992. pap. 8.85 (*0-930100-47-6*) Holy Cow.

When "I Love You" Turns Violent: Abuse in Dating Relationships. Scott A. Johnson. LC 92-63127. 176p. 1993. pap. 12.95 (*0-88282-124-5*) New Horizon NJ.

When I Prayed for Patience...God Let Me Have It! Jeanne Zornes. 150p. 1995. pap. 7.99 (*0-87788-254-1*) Shaw Pubs.

When I Relax I Feel Guilty. Tim Hansel. LC 78-73460. 156p. 1979. pap. 9.99 (*0-89191-137-5*, LifeJourney) Chariot Victor.

When I Remember. Debra W. Alexander. 24p. (YA). (gr. 6-12). 1993. 3.95 (*1-56688-068-8*) Bur For At-Risk.

When I Remember. Natalie Kinsey-Warnock. 1998. pap. 14.99 (*0-525-65200-0*) NAL-Dutton.

When I Rise Cryin' Holy: Afro-American Denominationalism on the Georgia Coast. Peter D. Goldsmith. LC 88-36496. (Immigrant Communities & Ethnic Minorities in the U. S. & Canada Ser.: No. 45). 1989. 49.50 (*0-404-19455-9*) AMS Pr.

When I Saw Him. Roy Hession. 1993. pap. 4.95 (*0-87508-239-4*) Chr Lit.

When I Say No, I Feel Guilty. Manuel J. Smith. 352p. 1985. 6.99 (*0-553-26390-0*) Bantam.

When I Sleep, Then I See Clearly: Selected Poems of J. V. Foix. Tr. & Intro. by David H. Rosenthal. (Illus.). 1988. pap. 12.95 (*0-89255-130-5*) Persea Bks.

When I Stood on Mt. Sinai. Joel L. Grishaver et al. (Illus.). 32p. (Orig.). (J). (gr. 6 up). 1992. pap. text ed. 2.45 (*0-933873-70-0*) Torah Aura.

When I Think about My Father: Sons & Daughters Remember. Ed. by Mary K. Shanley. (Illus.). 50p. 1996. 14.95 (*1-882835-35-2*) STA-Kris.

When I Think about You, My Friend. Ed. by Susan P. Schutz. LC 83-71748. (Illus.). 93p. 1983. text ed. 16.95 (*0-88396-196-2*) Blue Mtn Pr CO.

***When I Think of You.** Zannah. 64p. (Orig.). 1997. pap. 6.95 (*1-890613-04-5*) West Coast Media.

When I Turned Six. David Drew. LC 93-26929. (Voyages Ser.). (Illus.). (J). 1994. 4.25 (*0-383-03784-0*) SRA McGraw.

When I Visit Yosemite. Mary Arrigo & Connie Hargreaves. (Illus.). 43p. (Orig.). (J). (ps). pap. 2.95 (*0-318-21253-6*) Arrigo CA.

When I Walk I Change the Earth. deluxe limited ed. Ruth Krauss. (Burning Deck Poetry Chapbooks Ser.). 1978. pap. 20.00 (*0-930900-51-0*) Burning Deck.

***When I Was a Boy: One Year in Vietnam. Robert L. Ordonez. Ed. by Lenda Ziegler. LC 96-96065. (Illus.). 320p. (Orig.). 1997. pap. 13.95 (*0-9656070-0-3*) CIMA Pub.**

This book is an account of the author's experiences as young Marine Corps Corpsman serving with a combat platoon in Vietnam from 1970 to 1971. The reader is carried through the initial experiences of a fresh green replacement as he undergoes a metamorphosis evolving into a hardened, experienced veteran. The language is geared for all readers which is void of the abrasive language so common in most war novels. This is intended to involve many individuals who would not otherwise read such material but have a genuine interest in the conflict that so divided our country. The story centers around this corpsman as he engages in the intensity & horrors of war down to the everyday mundane activities that are curiously typical of a frontline grunt. There is both heart-pounding drama & hysterical humor intertwined in each page. Admiral E. R. Zumwalt, Jr., stated in his critique of the book, "The manner in which Dr. Ordonez ties in the tragedy, the humor & the pathos & his revealing insights about its impact on his religious perspective makes it a worthwhile as well as a most enjoyable read." To order contact: CIMA Publishing Co., P.O. Box 6494, Lubbock, TX 79493-6494. Phone: (806) 797-2616. ***Publisher Provided Annotation.***

When I Was a Boy in Boston. Charles Angoff. LC 70-132111. (Short Story Index Reprint Ser.). (Illus.). 1977. 18.95 (*0-8369-3668-X*) Ayer.

When I Was a Boy in Palestine. Mousa J. Kaleel. LC 77-876440. (Illus.). reprint ed. 32.50 (*0-404-16429-3*) AMS Pr.

When I Was a Boy in Persia. Youel B. Mirza. LC 77-87650. (Illus.). reprint ed. 37.50 (*0-404-16419-6*) AMS Pr.

When I Was a Boy in Turkey. Ahmed Sabri. LC 77-87624. (Illus.). reprint ed. 24.50 (*0-404-16450-1*) AMS Pr.

When I Was a Child. V. Moberg. 1976. 26.95 (*0-8488-0302-7*) Amereon Ltd.

When I Was a Child in Minnesota. Neil Hutchison. 156p. 1996. pap. 10.00 (*0-9648232-2-5*) L E Frith.

When I Was a Girl I Used to Scream & Shout: When We Were Women: The Brave. Sharman Macdonald. 256p. (Orig.). 1990. pap. 8.95 (*0-571-14348-2*) Faber & Faber.

When I Was a Girl in the Martin Box. Orra Phelps. (American Autobiography Ser.). 157p. 1995. reprint ed. lib. bdg. 69.00 (*0-7812-8618-2*) Rprt Serv.

When I Was a Little Girl. Gilmore & Davies. 1994. pap. 5.95 (*0-929005-01-5*, Pub. by Second Story Pr CN) LPC InBook.

When I Was a Little Girl. Susie Jenkin-Pearce. (Illus.). 32p. (J). (gr. k-2). 1993. 17.95 (*0-09-176359-2*, Pub. by Hutchinson UK) Trafalgar.

When I Was First Alone: A Journey from Hurt to Healing. Jan J. Stennes. Ed. by Renee Hermanson. LC 93-14794. (Illus.). 136p. 1993. 12.95 (*1-880292-08-4*) LangMarc.

When I Was Five. Arthur Howard. LC 94-43987. (J). (ps-3). 1996. 14.00 (*0-15-200261-8*) HarBrace.

When I Was in Prison You Visited Me. Ronald S. Bourne. 42p. (Orig.). 1991. pap. 2.00 (*0-9630569-2-1*) Follow Me Comm.

When I Was Just Your Age. Robert Flynn & Susan Russell. LC 92-15460. (Illus.). 175p. (Orig.). (J). (gr. 1-7). 1992. pap. text ed. 14.95 (*0-929398-39-4*) UNTX Pr.

When I was Listening. Anabel Edwards. 8.95 (*0-533-11553-1*) Vantage.

When I Was Little. Toyomi Igus. LC 92-72006. (Illus.). 32p. (Orig.). (J). (gr. 1 up). 1992. 14.95 (*0-940975-32-7*); pap. 6.95 (*0-940975-33-5*) Just Us Bks.

When I Was Little: A Four-Year-Old's Memoir of Her Youth. Jamie L. Curtis. LC 91-46188. (Illus.). 32p. (J). (gr. k-3). 1993. 14.95 (*0-06-021078-8*); lib. bdg. 14.89 (*0-06-021079-6*) HarpC Child Bks.

When I Was Little: A Four-Year-Old's Memoir of Her Youth. Jamie L. Curtis. LC 91-46188. (Trophy Picture Bk.). (Illus.). 32p. (J). (gr. k-3). 1995. pap. 4.95 (*0-06-443423-0*, Trophy) HarpC Child Bks.

When I Was Little Like You. Jane Porett. LC 93-13974. (Illus.). (J). 1993. 14.95 (*0-87868-530-8*) Child Welfare.

***When I Was Little Like You.** Jill P. Walsh. (J). 1997. pap. 13.99 (*0-670-87608-9*) Viking Child Bks.

When I Was Nine. James Stevenson. LC 85-9777. (Illus.). 32p. (J). (gr. k-3). 1986. 16.00 (*0-688-05942-2*); lib. bdg. 15.93 (*0-688-05943-0*) Greenwillow.

When I Was on Horseback. Compiled by Stefan Grossman. 5.95 (*1-56222-664-9*, 94829); audio 10.98 (*1-56222-673-8*, 94829C) Mel Bay.

***When I Was on Horseback.** Compiled by Stefan Grossman. 20.95 incl. audio compact disk (*0-7866-1132-4*, 94829CDP) Mel Bay.

When I Was on Horseback. Martin Simpson. cd-rom 15.98 (*0-7866-1131-6*, 94829CD) Mel Bay.

When I Was Puerto Rican. Esmeralda Santiago. (Illus.). 208p. 1993. 20.00 (*0-201-58117-5*) Addison-Wesley.

When I Was Puerto Rican. Esmeralda Santiago. 288p. 1994. pap. 12.00 (*0-679-75676-0*, Vin) Random.

When I Was Short. Michael Fry & Guy Vasilovich. 128p. (Orig.). 1991. pap. 5.95 (*0-380-76434-2*) Avon.

When I Was Straight. Janet Mason. 35p. (Orig.). 1995. pap. 7.00 (*1-882827-06-6*) Insight to Riot.

When I Was Ten: Of McLoud, Oklahoma. Letha Campbell. Ed. by Glenda P. Kuhn. (Our Heritage Ser.: Vol. II). (Illus.). 29p. (J). 1995. pap. 4.99 (*0-9643029-2-6*) SpritSBo.

When I Was Twelve. Noemi Weygant. (Illus.). (Orig.). pap. 8.00 (*0-936773-08-1*) Priory Bks.

When I Was White. Jim E. Foote & Johnnie M. Foote. 349p. (Orig.). 1991. pap. 10.95 (*0-9628752-0-1*) Fifty-Six Palms.

When I Was Young. Cynthia Rylant. 1993. pap. 4.99 (*0-14-054875-0*) NAL-Dutton.

When I Was Young I Loved School: Dropping Out & Hanging In. Ed. by Anne Sheffield & Bruce Frankel. (YA). (gr. 7 up). 1989. 18.00 (*0-9621641-2-7*) CEF Inc.

When I Was Young in Indiana: A Country Life. Dorothy Hinshaw. LC 95-80437. (Illus.). 60p. (J). 1994. 14.95 (*1-878208-38-1*) Guild Pr IN.

When I Was Young in the Mountains. Cynthia Rylant. LC 81-5359. (Unicorn Paperbacks Ser.). (Illus.). 32p. (J). (ps-3). 1982. pap. 14.99 (*0-525-42525-X*, 0966-290); pap. 3.99 (*0-525-44198-0*) Dutton Child Bks.

When I Was Your Age: Original Stories about Growing Up. Ed. & Intro. by Amy Ehrlich. 160p. (J). (gr. 4-8). 1996. 15.99 (*1-56402-306-0*) Candlewick Pr.

When I Was Your Age, We Didn't Even HAVE Church: Chronicles of a Catholic Parent. Kevin Cowherd. 144p. 1995. pap. 7.95 (*0-87973-672-0*) Our Sunday Visitor.

When I Was Your Age...Sports: Remarkable Achievements of Famous Athletes at Every Age from 1-100. David Lewman. (Illus.). 192p. 1997. pap. 10.95 (*1-57243-145-8*) Triumph Bks.

When I Was Your Age...the Arts: Remarkable Achievements of Famous Athletes at Every Age from 1-100. David Lewman. (Illus.). 192p. (Orig.). 1997. pap. 10.95 (*1-57243-144-X*) Triumph Bks.

When I Whistle. Shusaku Endo. Tr. by Van C. Gessel from JPN. LC 79-13183. Orig. Title: Kuchibue wo Fuku Toki. 273p. 1980. pap. 9.95 (*0-8008-8244-X*) Taplinger.

***When I Woke.** Rusted Root. pap. 19.95 (*0-7935-6555-3*) H Leonard.

When Illness Comes: Seeking Strength Through Prayer. Margaret A. Huffman. LC 95-11991. 144p. 1995. pap. 12.00 (*0-8170-1232-X*) Judson.

When Illness Strikes the Leader: The Dilemma of the Captive King. Jerrold M. Post & Robert S. Robins. LC 92-25302. 320p. (C). 1993. 30.00 (*0-300-05683-4*) Yale U Pr.

When Illness Strikes the Leader: The Dilemma of the Captive King. Jerrold M. Post & Robert S. Robins. 1995. pap. 17.00 (*0-300-06314-8*) Yale U Pr.

***When I'm Alone.** Delbene. 5.95 (*0-687-61316-7*) Abingdon.

When I'm Alone. Ron DelBene et al. 24p. 1988. pap. 3.95 (*0-8358-0579-4*) Upper Room Bks.

When I'm Alone. Carol P. Ochs. (Illus.). 32p. (J). (ps-3). 1993. lib. bdg. 14.96 (*0-87614-752-X*, Carolrhoda) Lerner Group.

When I'm Alone. Carol P. Ochs. (Illus.). 32p. (J). (ps-3). 1993. pap. 6.95 (*0-87614-620-5*, Carolrhoda) Lerner Group.

***When I'm an Old Man, I'll Wear Mixed Plaids.** 96p. 1996. pap. 7.00 (*1-887317-10-4*) Bad Dog Pr.

When I'm Bad I'm Better: Mae West, Sex & American Entertainment. Marybeth Hamilton. LC 92-54716. (Illus.). 256p. 1995. 25.00 (*0-06-019031-0*, A Asher Bks) HarpC.

***When I'm Bad, I'm Better: Mae West, Sex, & American Entertainment.** Marybeth Hamilton. LC 97-8277. 1997. write for info. (*0-520-21094-8*) U CA Pr.

When I'm Big. Debi Gliori. LC 92-43346. (Illus.). 32p. (J). (ps up). 1994. 4.99 (*1-56402-241-2*) Candlewick Pr.

***When I'm on My Knees: Devotional Thoughts on Prayer for Women.** Anita C. Donihue. 1997. pap. text ed. 4.97 (*1-55748-976-9*) Barbour & Co.

***When I'm Sick.** JoAnne Nelson. LC 93-9348. (Primarily Health Ser.). (Illus.). (J). (ps-2). 1995. 6.00 (*0-7802-3259-3*) Wright Group.

W

When I'm Sleepy Board Book. Jane R. Howard. LC 84-25895. (Illus.). (J). (ps). 1996. pap. 7.99 (*0-525-45561-2*) Dutton Child Bks.

When in Disgrace. Budd Boetticher. Ed. by Dirk Summers & Corene Adams. (Illus.). 450p. 1997. 25.95 (*1-882747-69-0*) Fallbrook Pub.

When in Doubt, Check Him Out: A Women's Survival Guide for the 90's. rev. ed. Joseph J. Culligan. LC 93-83775. (Illus.). 344p. 1997. reprint ed. pap. 19.95 (*0-9630621-2-3*) FJA.

When in Doubt, Do Both: The Times of My Life. Kay Macpherson. (Illus.). 298p. 1994. 50.00 (*0-8020-0454-7*); pap. 18.95 (*0-8020-7473-1*) U of Toronto Pr.

When in Doubt, Roll. B. Bruford. 136p. 1988. pap. 13.95 (*0-7935-3529-8*, 06630298) H Leonard.

***When in Doubt, Sing: Experiencing Prayer in Everyday Life.** Jane Redmont. 288p. 1997. 23.00 (*0-06-017439-0*) HarpC.

***When in Doubt, Tell the Truth, & Other Quotations.** Mark Twain, pseud. 224p. (C). 1997. 19.95 (*0-231-10498-7*) Col U Pr.

When in Rome: An Introduction to Relativism & Knowledge. Nancy L. Gifford. LC 82-10374. (SUNY Series in Philosophy). 159p. (C). 1983. text ed. 39.50 (*0-87395-667-2*); pap. text ed. 12.95 (*0-87395-668-0*) State U NY Pr.

When in Rome... Living & Working in A Foreign Country. Beverly D. Roman. Ed. by Cathleen Lawson. LC 93-90795. (Personal & Professional Management Ser.). (Illus.). 96p. (Orig.). 1993. pap. text ed. 12.95 (*0-9627470-5-X*) BR Anchor.

When Incumbency Fails: The Senate Career of Mark Andrews. 309p. 1992. pap. text ed. 22.95 (*0-87187-700-7*) Congr Quarterly.

When Incumbency Fails: The Senate Career of Mark Andrews. Richard F. Fenno. 309p. 1992. 33.95 (*0-87187-701-5*) Congr Quarterly.

***When Indians Became Cowboys: Native Peoples & Cattle Ranching in the American West.** Peter Iverson. LC 97-10314. (Illus.). 288p. 1997. pap. 15.95 (*0-8061-2884-4*) U of Okla Pr.

When Indians Became Cowboys: Native Peoples & Cattle Ranching in the American West. Peter J. Iverson. LC 94-10314. (Illus.). 288p. 1994. 26.95 (*0-8061-1867-9*) U of Okla Pr.

When Internal Transfer Prices & Costs Differ: How Stock Funding of Depot-Level Reparables Affects Decision Making in the Air Force. Frank Camm & H. L. Shulman. LC 93-23292. 1993. pap. 13.00 (*0-8330-1440-4*, MR-307-AF) Rand Corp.

***When Irish Eyes Are Crying.** Stephen D. Manning. LC 96-90583. 128p. (Orig.). 1997. pap. 8.00 (*1-56002-693-6*, Univ Edtns) Aegina Pr.

When Iron Was King in Dodge County, Wisconsin: 1845-1928. George G. Frederick. LC 93-86025. (Illus.). 750p. 1993. 39.95 (*0-9638443-0-X*) G G Frederick.

***When Is a Bug Really a Bug?** Sara S. Miller. LC 97-15720. (Animals in Order Ser.). (J). 1998. write for info. (*0-531-11479-1*) Watts.

When Is a Dose Not a Dose? Victor Bond. LC 91-46381. (Taylor Lectures: No. 15). 41p. (Orig.). 1991. pap. text ed. 25.00 (*0-929600-21-3*) NCRP Pubns.

When Is a Kiva? And Other Questions about Southwestern Archaeology. Watson Smith. Ed. by Raymond H. Thompson. LC 89-29089. (Illus.). 273p. 1994. reprint ed. pap. 18.95 (*0-8165-1498-4*) U of Ariz Pr.

When Is a Kiva? & Other Questions about Southwestern Archaeology. Watson Smith. Ed. by Raymond H. Thompson. LC 89-29089. 260p. 1990. 45.00 (*0-8165-1155-1*) U of Ariz Pr.

***When Is a Pig a Hog? A Guide to Confoundingly Related English Words.** Bernice Randall. 1997. 9.99 (*0-88365-977-8*) Galahad Bks.

***When Is a Pig a Hog? A Guide to Confoundingly Related English Words.** Bernice Randall. 328p. pap. 3.98 (*0-7651-0008-8*) Smithmark.

When Is an Example Binding? Thomas B. Warren. (Biblical Hermeneutics Ser.). 1975. pap. 8.00 (*0-934916-43-8*) Natl Christian Pr.

When Is Enough Enough? What You Can Do If You Never Feel Satisfied. Laurie Ashner & Mitch Meyerson. Ed. by Steve Lehman. 275p. 1996. 21.95 (*1-56838-102-6*) Hazelden.

When Is It My Turn. Audrey E. Holland. (Illus.). 15p. (J). (gr. k-3). 1992. pap. 15.95 (*1-895583-11-X*) MAYA Pubs.

W

When Is It Right to Fight? Robert A. Morey. 1994. reprint ed. pap. 8.99 (*0-87552-361-7*, Pub. by Evangelical Pr) Presby & Reformed.

When Is My Birthday? Ray Sipherd. LC 88-80284. (Sesame Street Growing-up Bks.). (Illus.). 32p. (J). (ps-1). 1988. write for info. (*0-307-12028-7*) Western Pub.

When It Comes to the Crunch: The Mechanics of Car Collections. Noel W. Murray. (Series on Engineering Machines). 180p. 1995. text ed. 43.00 (*981-02-2096-0*) World Scientific Pub.

When It Grows up You Say Goodbye to It. Ed. by Margot Kriel & Terry Sophn. (Illus.). 164p. 1981. pap. 5.00 (*0-927663-10-4*) COMPAS.

When-It-Happened Bible Timeline: New Testament. 1993. pap. text ed. 8.99 (*1-55945-194-7*) Group Pub.

When-It-Happened Bible Timeline: Old Testament. 1993. pap. text ed. 8.99 (*1-55945-193-9*) Group Pub.

When It Hurts to Live: Devotions for Difficult Times. Kathleen Kern. LC 94-61647. 208p. 1995. pap. 11.95 (*0-87303-233-0*) Faith & Life.

When It Hurts to Say Good-Bye: Welcome to My World. Vernelle B. Allen. 48p. 1994. pap. write for info. (*1-885984-00-6*) Wings of Healing.

***When It Hurts Too Much to Quit: Smoking & Depression.** Gerald S. Mayer. (Quit Smoking Cessation Ser.). 12p. 1997. pap. 2.95 (*0-9642504-1-1*) Desert City Pr.

When It Is Dark Enough: Sermons for Advent, Christmas & Epiphany - Gospel. Charles H. Bayer. LC 93-51080. (Orig.). 1994. pap. 9.75 (*0-7880-0000-4*) CSS OH.

When It Is Night & When It Is Day. Jenny Tyers. LC 94-19925. (Illus.). 32p. (J). (gr. k-2). 1996. 14.95 (*0-395-71546-6*) HM.

When It Rains. Jan Millicer. LC 92-31136. (Voyages Ser.). (Illus.). (J). 1993. 2.50 (*0-383-03667-4*) SRA McGraw.

When It Rains: Papago & Pima Poetry. Ed. by Ofelia Zepeda. LC 82-10967. (Sun Tracks, An American Indian Literary Ser.: Vol. 7). 88p. reprint ed. pap. 25.10 (*0-317-28046-5*, 2025557) Bks Demand.

When It Rains see Set 8

***When It Snowed That Night.** Norma Farber. (Trophy Book Ser.). (Illus.). 40p. 1997. pap. 5.95 (*0-06-443486-9*, Trophy) HarpC Child Bks.

***When It Starts to Snow.** Gershator. 1998. pap. 15.95 (*0-8050-5404-9*) H Holt & Co.

When It's Hard to Trust. Steve Wilke et al. 144p. 1992. mass mkt. 3.99 (*0-8423-7955-X*) Tyndale.

When It's Right to Die: Conflicting Voices, Difficult Choices. Dick Westley. LC 94-60475. 224p. (Orig.). 1995. pap. 14.95 (*0-89622-609-3*) Twenty-Third.

When It's Time For Bed. Nick Butterworth. (Illus.). (J). (ps). 1995. pap. 4.95 (*0-316-11902-4*) Little.

When It's Twilight Time: Thirty Worship Services for Health Care Centers, Retirement Homes, & Other Special Life Settings. Clement E. Lewis. LC 93-42515. 1994. pap. 10.75 (*1-55673-837-4*) CSS OH.

When Jane-Marie Told My Secret. Gina Willner-Pardo. LC 94-12820. (Illus.). (J). (gr. 1-8). 1995. 14.95 (*0-395-66382-2*, Clarion Bks) HM.

When Jeremiah Found Mrs. Ming. Sharon Jennings. (Illus.). 24p. (J). (ps). 1992. pap. 5.95 (*1-55037-234-3*, Pub. by Annick CN); lib. bdg. 15.95 (*1-55037-237-8*, Pub. by Annick CN) Firefly Bks Ltd.

***When Jessie Came Across the Sea.** Amy Hest. LC 97-6250. (Illus.). 40p. (J). 1997. 16.99 (*0-7636-0094-6*) Candlewick Pr.

When Jesus Came, the Corn Mothers Went Away: Marriage, Sexuality & Power in New Mexico, 1500-1846. Ramon A. Gutierrez. LC 90-9512. 456p. 1991. 55.00 (*0-8047-1816-4*); pap. 17.95 (*0-8047-1832-6*) Stanford U Pr.

When Jesus Comes. Charles R. Taylor. (Illus.). 76p. (Orig.). 1985. pap. 4.95 (*0-937682-08-X*) Today Bible.

When Jesus Comes Back. Carolyn Nystrom. (Children's Bible Basics Ser.). (J). (ps-3). 1994. text ed. 6.99 (*0-8024-7861-1*) Moody.

When Jesus Holds Our Hand. Audrey Carli. 72p. (Orig.). 1987. pap. 3.95 (*0-9618664-0-3*) AMC Pub.

When Jesus Said Good-Bye. Frank G. Carver. 134p. (Orig.). 1996. kivar 16.99 (*0-8341-1570-0*) Beacon Hill.

When Jesus Smiled. Giorgio Conconi. Tr. by Jordan Aumann from ITA. (Orig.). 1997. mass mkt. write for info. (*0-8189-0768-1*) Alba.

When Jesus Walked: A Story of the Christ. Glenn Barnett. 253p. (Orig.). 1991. pap. 12.00 (*0-9629405-0-X*) Wide Awake Pr.

When Jesus Was a Lad. Rae Oetting. LC 68-56816. (Illus.). 32p. (J). (gr. 2-3). 1968. lib. bdg. 9.95 (*0-87783-047-9*) Oddo.

When Jesus Was a Lad. Rae Otting. (Illus.). (J). (gr. 1-2). 1978. pap. 1.25 (*0-89508-055-9*) Rainbow Bks.

When Jesus Was Born. Maryann Dotts. LC 93-49667. 32p. (J). 1994. pap. 1.49 (*0-687-45019-5*) Abingdon.

***When Jesus Was Born.** Maryann J. Dotts. 1996. pap. text ed. 5.95 (*0-687-02004-2*) Abingdon.

When Jews & Christians Meet. Ed. by Jakob J. Petuchowski. LC 87-9981. 160p. 1988. text ed. 59.50 (*0-88706-631-3*) State U NY Pr.

When Jews & Christians Meet: A Guide for Christian Teaching & Preaching. Clark M. Williamson. 128p. (Orig.). 1989. pap. 9.99 (*0-8272-4224-7*) Chalice Pr.

When Jo Louis Won the Title. Belinda Rochelle. LC 93-34317. (Illus.). (J). (gr. 4 up). 1994. 14.95 (*0-395-66614-7*) HM.

***When Jo Louis Won the Title.** Belinda Rochelle. (Illus.). 32p. (J). (ps-3). 1996. pap. 5.95 (*0-395-81657-2*) HM.

When Joel Comes Home. Susi G. Fowler. LC 92-7979. (Illus.). 24p. (J). (ps up). 1993. 14.00 (*0-688-11064-9*); lib. bdg. 13.93 (*0-688-11065-7*) Greenwillow.

When Jonathan Died. Duvert. 1995. per. 12.95 (*0-85449-154-6*, Pub. by Gay Mens Pr UK) LPC InBook.

When Justice Failed: The Fred Korematsu Story. Steven A. Chin. LC 92-18086. (Stories of America Ser.). (Illus.). 105p. (J). (gr. 2-5). 1992. lib. bdg. 25.68 (*0-8114-7236-1*) Raintree Steck-V.

When Kids Are Mad, Not Bad: A Guide to Recognizing & Handling Children's Anger. Henry A. Paul. 256p. (Orig.). 1995. mass mkt. 5.99 (*0-425-14648-0*) Berkley Pub.

When Kids Get into Trouble: A Guide for Parents & Children, Teachers & Professionals, Including the Young Offenders Act. Priscilla Platt. 208p. 1987. pap. 14.95 (*0-7737-5104-1*) Genl Dist Srvs.

When Kids Go to College: A Parent's Guide to Changing Relationships. Barbara Newman & Philip Newman. 166p. 1992. 45.00 (*0-8142-0561-5*); pap. 21.95 (*0-8142-0562-3*) Ohio St U Pr.

When Kingdoms Clash: The Christian & Ideologies. Calvin E. Shenk. LC 88-14719. (Peace & Justice Ser.: Vol. 6). 104p. (Orig.). 1988. pap. 6.99 (*0-8361-3481-8*) Herald Pr.

When Kings Speak: Royal Speech & Royal Prayer in Chronicles. Mark A. Throntveit. LC 86-15497. (Society of Biblical Literature Dissertation Ser.). 162p. 1987. pap. 12.95 (*0-89130-999-3*) Scholars Pr GA.

When Knighthood Was in Flower. Charles Major. LC 70-126656. reprint ed. 45.00 (*0-404-04169-8*) AMS Pr.

When Knighthood Was in Flower. Charles Major. (BCL1-PS American Literature Ser.). 295p. 1992. reprint ed. lib. bdg. 79.00 (*0-7812-6792-7*) Rprt Serv.

When Knowledge Is Power: Three Models of Change in International Organizations. Ernst B. Haas. (Studies in International Political Economy: Vol. 22). (Illus.). 278p. 1991. pap. 15.00 (*0-520-07402-5*) U CA Pr.

When Knowledge is Power: Three Models of Change in International Organizations. Ernst B. Haas. LC 89-31643. (Studies in International Political Economy). (Illus.). 278p. reprint ed. pap. 79.30 (*0-7837-4821-3*, 2044468) Bks Demand.

***When Kumbaya Is Not Enough: Practical Theology for Youth Ministry.** Dean Borgman. LC 97-20785. 175p. 1997. pap. 12.95 (*1-56563-247-8*) Hendrickson MA.

When Labor Organizes. Robert R. Brooks. LC 76-156407. (American Labor Ser., No. 2). (Illus.). 1971. reprint ed. 25.95 (*0-405-02916-0*) Ayer.

When Labor Trouble Strikes: An Action Handbook. Gordon E. Jackson. LC 81-556. 255p. 1981. 44.95 (*0-13-956128-5*, Busn) P-H.

When Labor Votes. Arthur W. Kornhauser & Harold L. Sheppard. LC 76-2533. (Illus.). 352p. 1976. reprint ed. text ed. 65.00 (*0-8371-8787-7*, KOWL, Greenwood Pr) Greenwood.

When Ladies Go A-Thieving: Middle-Class Shoplifters in the Victorian Department Store. Elaine S. Abelson. 304p. 1992. pap. 19.95 (*0-19-507142-5*) OUP.

When Land Becomes Scarce. Ornulf Gulbrandsen. (Bergen Studies in Social Anthropology: No. 33). 128p. (C). 1990. pap. text ed. 13.95 (*0-936508-74-4*, Pub. by Bergen Univ Dept Social Anthro NO) Barber Pr.

When Last I Saw You: Poems. Patricia C. Peters. Ed. by Patricia Schultz. LC 91-34456. (Lewiston Poetry Ser.: Vol. 18). 78p. 1992. pap. 12.95 (*0-7734-9619-X*) E Mellen.

***When Last Seen Alive.** Gar A. Haywood. 240p. 1998. 22.95 (*0-399-14303-3*) Putnam Pub Group.

When Lawyers Write. Richard H. Weisberg. 350p. 1987. 55.00 (*0-316-92871-2*) Little.

When Leadership Fails: Desegregation & Demoralization in the San Francisco Schools. Doris Fine. Ed. by Ray C. Rist. (Observations in Education Ser.). 242p. (Orig.). 1986. 34.95 (*0-88738-079-4*) Transaction Pubs.

When Lean Enterprises Collide: Competing Through Confrontation. Robin Cooper. 400p. 1995. 35.00 (*0-87584-540-1*) Harvard Busn.

When Lean Enterprises Collide: Competing Through Confrontation. Robin Cooper. 1996. text ed. 35.00 (*0-07-103632-6*) McGraw.

When Learned Men Murder. David Patterson. LC 95-71479. (Illus.). 181p. 1996. 32.00 (*0-87367-484-7*) Phi Delta Kappa.

When Learning Is Tough: Kids Talk about Learning Disabilities. Cynthia Roby. (J). (ps-3). 1993. lib. bdg. 13.95 (*0-8075-8892-X*) A Whitman.

***When Liberty & Justice Were Won.** Marc Levy. LC 97-8188. 112p. 1997. 12.95 (*0-944957-92-7*) Rivercross Pub.

When Life & Choice Collide: Essays on Rhetoric & Abortion, Vol. 1 To Set the Dawn Free. Ed. by David Mall. LC 93-20573. (Words in Conflict Ser.). (Illus.). 368p. 1994. 30.00 (*0-9608410-3-2*); pap. 15.00 (*0-9608410-2-4*) Kairos Bks.

When Life Becomes a Maze: Discovering Christ's Resources for Times of Confusion. David R. Mains & Laurie Mains. (Nineteen Ninety-Six 50-Day Spiritual Adventure Ser.). 192p. (Orig.). 1995. pap. 6.00 (*1-879050-77-3*) Chapel of Air.

***When Life Becomes Precious: A Guide for Loved Ones & Friends of Cancer Patients.** Elise N. Babcock. LC 96-30256. 320p. 1997. pap. 13.95 (*0-553-37869-4*) Bantam.

***When Life Doesn't Make Sense.** Joseph Breighner. LC 97-8650. 152p. (Orig.). 1997. pap. 10.00 (*1-885938-08-X*) Cathdrl Fndtn Pr.

When Life Doesn't Seem Fair. Bruce Erickson & Joyce Erickson. 1995. 12.95 (*0-88494-971-0*) Bookcraft Inc.

When Life Doesn't Turn Out Like You Planned. Bill Butterworth. LC 95-37259. 252p. 1996. pap. 16.99 (*0-7852-7561-4*) Nelson.

When Life Ends: Legal Overviews, Medicolegal Forms & Hospital Policies. Arthur S. Berger. LC 94-43173. 208p. 1995. text ed. 59.95 (*0-275-94620-7*, Praeger Pubs) Greenwood.

***When Life Gets Complicated, Look for Simple Solutions.** Dick Sutphen. 144p. (Orig.). 1996. pap. 5.95 (*0-87554-603-X*, B941) Valley Sun.

When Life Gets Rough. Ed. by Stephen M. Miller. (Dialog Ser.). 108p. 1986. student ed., pap. 5.95 (*0-8341-1116-0*) Beacon Hill.

When Life Gets Rough. Ed. by Stephen M. Miller & Stephen M. MIller. 44p. 1986. teacher ed., pap. 4.95 (*0-8341-1117-9*) Beacon Hill.

When Life Gives You Lemons: And Other Recipes for Living & Loving Life. Meiji Stewart. (Illus.). 160p. 1996. pap. 6.95 (*0-9647349-4-X*) Keep Coming Back.

When Life Is Changed Forever. Rick Taylor. 1993. pap. 7.99 (*0-89081-971-8*) Harvest Hse.

When Life Is Lovable & Love Is Livable. Adnan Sarhan. 80p. 1991. pap. 5.00 (*1-884328-02-4*) Sufi Fnd Amer.

***When Life Kicks - Kick Back: Survival Lesson for Personal Crisis & Life's Challenges.** Tamara Hall. Ed. by Phyllis Rigg. 172p. (Orig.). 1997. pap. 13.95 (*0-9653683-0-0*) Commns Plus.

***When Life Meets Death: Stories of Death & Dying.** Thomas W. Shane. LC 97-19562. 1997. write for info. (*0-7890-0289-2*); pap. write for info. (*0-7890-0290-6*) Haworth Pr.

When Life Takes More Than It Gives: A Devotional Daybook. Neva Coyle. 160p. 1996. pap. text ed. 8.99 (*1-55661-589-2*) Bethany Hse.

When Life Takes What Matters: Devotions to Comfort You Through Crisis & Change. Susan Lenzkes. LC 92-31268. 128p. 1993. pap. 8.99 (*0-929239-70-9*) Discovery Hse Pubs.

When Life Throws You a Curveball, Hit It: Simple Wisdom about Lifes Ups & Downs. Criswell Freeman. 1994. 14.95 (*0-9640955-0-5*) Walnut Gr Pr.

When Life Tumbles In: A Handbook for Coping. C. Welton Gaddy. 128p. (Orig.). 1993. pap. 10.00 (*0-664-25458-6*) Westminster John Knox.

***When Life Went Hectic: The Incredible Journey of Quentin Borg a True Story.** Quentin Borg & JoLouise McNally. (Illus.). 208p. (Orig.). 1996. pap. 10.00 (*0-9652309-0-2*) Crex Land.

***When Life's Pieces Don't Fit.** Joan D. James et al. (Illus.). 72p. (Orig.). 1996. pap. 5.95 (*0-9654456-0-7*) Womens Retreat.

When Light Pierced the Darkness: Christian Rescue of Jews in Nazi-Occupied Poland. Nechama Tec. (Illus.). 288p. 1987. pap. 12.95 (*0-19-505194-7*) OUP.

When Lightning Strikes. Rexanne Becnel. 416p. 1995. mass mkt. 5.99 (*0-440-21568-4*) Dell.

When Lightning Strikes. Kristin Hannah. 1994. mass mkt. 4.99 (*0-449-14908-0*, GM) Fawcett.

When Lightning Strikes. large type ed. Kristin Hannah. LC 94-36996. 455p. 1995. 21.95 (*0-7838-1167-5*, GK Hall) Thorndike Pr.

When Lightning Strikes a Hummingbird: The Awakening of a Healer. Foster Perry. LC 93-10285. 224p. (Orig.). 1993. pap. 10.95 (*1-879181-10-X*) Bear & Co.

When Lilacs Bloom. Anne Scherer. Ed. by Larry Fortner. (Illus.). 160p. (Orig.). 1995. pap. 11.95 (*0-9645557-0-0*, Fortner BkWorks) Fortner WordWorks.

When Lilacs Bloom Again: A Novel Based on the Life & Times of Lincoln. Henry K. DuGarm. LC 87-63213. 358p. (Orig.). 1988. pap. 5.50 (*0-942323-01-7*) N Amer Heritage Pr.

When Lines Are Drawn: A Guide to Resolving Conflict in the Church. E. Steve Edison. 111p. pap. 7.99 (*0-89900-685-X*) College Pr Pub.

When Lion Could Fly: And Other Tales from Africa. Nick Greaves. LC 93-21841. (Illus.). 144p. (J). (gr. 3 up). 1993. 13.95 (*0-8120-6344-9*); pap. 8.95 (*0-8120-1625-4*) Barron.

When Lions Could Fly. Gamal Koram. (Illus.). 42p. (J). (gr. 4-12). 1989. pap. 5.00 (*1-877610-01-1*) Sea Island.

***When Listening Comes Alive: A Guide to Effective Learning & Communication.** Paul Madaule. (Illus.). 224p. pap. 14.95 (*0-9697079-0-8*, Pub. by Moulin Pub CN) Genl Dist Srvs.

***When Listening Comes Alive: A Guide to Effective Learning & Communication.** Paul Madaule. 1997. pap. text ed. 14.95 (*0-9697079-1-6*, Pub. by Moulin Pub CN) Genl Dist Srvs.

When Literacy Empowers: Navajo Language in Print. Daniel McLaughlin. LC 92-377. 224p. 1992. 32.50 (*0-8263-1366-3*) U of NM Pr.

When Little Ones Die: Angel Children, Before Birth, Beyond Death, 2 bks., Set. Mary V. Hill & Connie R. Taylor. 1994. pap. 15.98 (*0-88290-477-9*) Horizon Utah.

When Living Alone Means Living at Risk: A Guide for Caregivers & Families. Robert W. Buckingham. (Golden Age Books - Perspectives on Aging Ser.). 165p. (Orig.). 1993. 24.95 (*0-87975-844-9*); pap. 16.95 (*0-87975-873-2*) Prometheus Bks.

When Living Hurts. Sol Gordon. 160p. 1989. mass mkt. 5.99 (*0-440-20389-9*) Dell.

When Living Hurts: Directives for Treating Depression. Michael D. Yapko. LC 87-22437. 240p. 1988. text ed. 37.95 (*0-87630-485-4*) Brunner-Mazel.

When Living Hurts: Directives for Treating Depression. Michael D. Yapko. LC 87-22437. 240p. 1994. pap. 13.95 (*0-87630-757-8*) Brunner-Mazel.

When Living Hurts: For Teenagers & Young Adults. rev. ed. Sol Gordon. LC 94-14153. (Illus.). 128p. (YA). (gr. 10-12). 1994. pap. 10.00 (*0-8074-0505-1*, 160003) UAHC.

When Love Awaits. Johanna Lindsey. 368p. 1986. mass mkt. 6.99 (*0-380-89739-3*) Avon.

When Love Comes Along. Elaine Coffman. 358p. (Orig.). 1995. mass mkt. 6.50 (*0-446-60212-4*, Warner Vision) Warner Bks.

When Love Commands. Jennifer Wilde. 608p. 1984. mass mkt. 4.95 (*0-380-89193-X*) Avon.

When Love Dies. Francine Pascal. (Sweet Valley High Ser.: No. 12). 144p. (Orig.). (YA). 1984. mass mkt. 3.99 (*0-553-27755-3*) Bantam.

When Love Dies: The Process of Marital Disaffection. Karen Kayser. LC 93-10227. (Perspectives on Marriage & the Family Ser.). 191p. 1993. lib. bdg. 28.50 (*0-89862-086-4*) Guilford Pr.

When Love Filled the Gap. LaJoyce Martin. LC 87-37241. 150p. (Orig.). 1988. pap. 7.99 (*0-932581-30-7*) Word Aflame.

When Love Gets Tough. Doug Manning. LC 85-42783. 1990. pap. 11.00 (*0-06-250561-0*) Harper SF.

When Love Had a Face. Klaus Luthardt. LC 90-62547. 1996. write for info. (*0-943512-31-X*) Linwood Pub.

When Love is Forever. Ed. by Helen Exley. (Miniature Square Bks.). (Illus.). 64p. 1996. 6.00 (*1-85015-711-1*) Exley Giftbooks.

When Love Is Not Enough. Stephen F. Arterburn & Jim Burns. LC 92-14651. 1992. 14.99 (*1-56179-098-2*) Focus Family.

An Asterisk (*) at the beginning of an entry indicates that the title is appearing in BIP for the first time.

When Love Is Not Enough: A Childs View of Parenting. Cecil R. Benoit. 1990. pap. 12.95 (*0-939298-77-5*) J M Prods.

When Love Is Not Enough: How Mental Health Professionals Can Help Special-Needs Adoptive Families. 96p. 1988. pap. 9.95 (*0-87868-346-1*) Child Welfare.

***When Love Is Not Enough: The Management of Covert Dynamics in Organizations That Treat Children & Adolescents.** Ed. by Donna P. Piazza. LC 95-44786. (Residential Treatment for Children & Youth Ser.: Vol. 13, No. 1). 105p. (C). 1996. pap. 14.95 (*0-7890-0223-X*) Haworth Pr.

When Love Is Not Enough: The Management of Covert Dynamics in Organizations That Treat Children & Adolescents. Ed. by Donna P. Piazza. LC 95-44786. (Residential Treatment for Children & Youth Ser.: Vol. 13, No. 1). 105p. (C). 1996. 29.95 (*1-56024-778-9*) Haworth Pr.

When Love Isn't Easy. Phyllis L. Hobe. 1985. 12.95 (*0-02-551900-X*) Macmillan.

***When Love Meets Fear: Becoming Defense-Less & Resource-Full.** David Richo. 1997. pap. 11.95 (*0-614-27651-9*) Paulist Pr.

***When Love Meets Fear: How to Become Defense-Less & Resource-Ful.** David Richo. LC 96-39729. 240p. (Orig.). 1997. pap. 12.95 (*0-8091-3702-X*) Paulist Pr.

When Love Returns. Vanessa Grant. (Presents Ser.). 1994. mass mkt. 2.99 (*0-373-11622-5*, 1-11622-7) Harlequin Bks.

When Love Speaks, Are You Listening? Joseph A. Mills. (Illus.). 100p. 1985. pap. 7.95 (*0-943454-02-6*) Jotarian.

When Love Takes Wing. large type ed. Sharon Sanders. 237p. 1993. reprint ed. lib. bdg. 13.95 (*1-56054-600-X*) Thorndike Pr.

When Love Was Like That. large type ed. Marie Joseph. (Charnwood Library). 288p. 1993. 27.99 (*0-7089-8732-X*, Trail West Pubs) Ulverscroft.

When Loved Ones Are Called Home. Herbert H. Wernecke. 64p. (gr. 10). 1950. pap. 3.99 (*0-8010-9513-1*) Baker Bks.

When Loved Ones Are Taken in Death. Lehman Strauss. 32p. 1973. pap. 3.99 (*0-310-33102-1*, 6340P) Zondervan.

***When Loving Meets Love.** Lydia F. Williams. (Orig.). 1997. pap. write for info. (*0-9648045-2-2*) LFW Ent.

***When Loving You Is Wrong.** George G. Bloomer. LC 97-24811. 1997. write for info. (*0-88368-504-3*) Whitaker Hse.

When Lucifer & Jezebel Join Your Church. Dick Bernal. 97p. (Orig.). 1994. pap. 6.95 (*1-884920-00-4*) Jubilee Christian Ctr.

When Lucifer Cometh: The Autobiographical Discourse of Writers & Intellectuals Exiled During the Third Reich. Richard Critchfield. LC 93-42551. (Literature & the Sciences of Man Ser.: Vol. 7). 250p. (C). 1994. text ed. 41.95 (*0-8204-2313-0*) P Lang Pubng.

When Luck Runs Out: Help for Compulsive Gamblers & Their Families. Robert L. Custer & Harry Milt. LC 84-26055. 247p. reprint ed. pap. 70.40 (*0-8357-3445-5*, 2039705) Bks Demand.

When Mac Met Hailey. Celeste Hamilton. (Yours Truly Ser.). 1996. mass mkt. 3.50 (*0-373-52024-7*, 1-52024-6) Silhouette.

When Madmen Speak: The Observations of a Modern Day Fool of God. Shaykh A. Elbisani. 188p. 1996. 60.00 (*0-614-16279-3*, Pub. by Curzon Pr UK); pap. 25.00 (*0-614-16280-7*, Pub. by Curzon Pr UK) Paul & Co Pubs.

***When Madness Comes Home: Help & Hope for the Children, Siblings, & Partners of the Mentally Ill.** Victoria Secunda. LC 96-28612. 384p. 1997. 23.95 (*0-7868-6171-1*) Hyperion.

When Malindy Sings. Paul L. Dunbar. LC 79-83916. (Black Heritage Library Collection). (Illus.). 1903. 14.25 (*0-8369-8568-0*) Ayer.

When Malindy Sings. (Illus.). 1991. reprint ed. pap. 22.95 (*0-88143-134-6*) Ayer.

When Malindy Sings. Paul L. Dunbar. LC 71-164805. (Illus.). reprint ed. 19.50 (*0-404-00039-8*) AMS Pr.

When Mama Comes Home from Work. Eileen Spinelli. LC 96-53141. (J). 1997. 13.00 (*0-689-81065-2*) S&S Childrens.

***When Mama Gets Home.** Marisabina Russo. LC 96-46617. (Illus.). 32p. (J). 1998. 15.00 (*0-688-14985-5*); lib. bdg. 14.93 (*0-688-14986-3*) Greenwillow.

When Man Becomes God: Humanism & Hubris in the Old Testament. Donald E. Gowan. LC 75-17582. (Pittsburgh Theological Monographs: No. 6). 1975. pap. 8.75 (*0-915138-06-9*) Pickwick.

When Mankind Was Young. Frederick B. Austin. LC 71-125201. (Short Story Index Reprint Ser.). 1977. 19.95 (*0-8369-3568-3*) Ayer.

When Mark Was a Widdle Boy...& Before Mark, There Was Lauren... Robert E. Fishbain. 1994. pap. 8.95 (*0-533-11022-X*) Vantage.

When Markets Quake: The Management Challenge of Restructuring Industry. Joseph L. Bower. 1986. text ed. 27.95 (*0-07-103213-4*) McGraw.

When Martha's Away. Bruce Ingman. LC 94-36582. (Illus.). 32p. (J). (gr. k-3). 1995. 14.95 (*0-395-72360-4*) HM.

When Marxists Do Research. Pauline M. Vaillancourt. LC 85-27254. (Contributions in Political Science Ser.: No. 150). (Illus.). 222p. 1986. text ed. 55.00 (*0-313-24703-X*, VMX/, Greenwood Pr) Greenwood.

When Mashiach Comes. R. Grossblatt. 1994. 9.99 (*0-89906-129-X*) Mesorah Pubns.

When MBAs Rule the Newsroom: How the Marketers & Managers Are Reshaping Today's Media. Doug Underwood. LC 92-40020. (Illus.). 272p. (C). 1993. 35.00 (*0-231-08048-4*) Col U Pr.

When MBAs Rule the Newsroom: How the Marketers & Managers Are Reshaping Today's Media. Doug Underwood. 259p. 1995. pap. 16.50 (*0-231-08049-2*) Col U Pr.

When Medicine Went Mad: Bioethics & the Holocaust. Ed. by Arthur L. Caplan. LC 92-11687. (Contemporary Issues in Biomedicine, Ethics, & Society Ser.). 359p. 1992. 39.50 (*0-89603-235-3*) Humana.

When Memory Comes. Saul Friedlander. 192p. 1980. mass mkt. 3.50 (*0-380-50807-9*, 60139-7, Discus) Avon.

When Memory Comes. Saul Friedlander. Tr. by Helen R. Lane from FRE. 192p. 1991. pap. 8.95 (*0-374-52272-3*, Noonday) FS&G.

When Memory Fails: Helping the Alzheimer's & Dementia Patient. A. J. Edwards. (Illus.). 296p. (C). 1994. 27.95 (*0-306-44648-0*, Plenum Pr) Plenum.

***When Memory Speaks: The Holocaust in Art.** Nelly Toll. LC 97-1746. 1997. text ed. write for info. (*0-275-95534-6*, Praeger Pubs) Greenwood.

When Men & Mountains Meet: The Explorers of the Western Himalayas, 1820-1875. John Keay. (Illus.). 278p. (C). 1994. pap. 11.95 (*0-19-577465-5*, 6922) OUP.

When Men & Women Mattered: A History of Gender Relations among the Owan of Nigeria. Onaiwu W. Ogbomo. LC 97-1501. 232p. 1997. 49.50 (*1-878822-78-0*) Univ Rochester Pr.

When Men Are Gods. G. Cope Schellhorn. LC 91-72270. 307p. (Orig.). 1991. pap. 12.95 (*1-881852-05-9*) Horus Hse Pr.

When Men are Pregnant: Needs & Concerns of Expectant Fathers. Jerrold L. Shapiro. 288p. 1993. pap. 12.95 (*0-385-30921-X*, Delta) Dell.

When Men Believe in Love: A Book for Men Who Love Women & the Women They Love. Susan Edwards. 1995. pap. 19.95 (*1-85230-619-X*) Element MA.

When Men Believe in Love: A Book for Men Who Love Women & the Women They Love. Susan Edwards. 1996. pap. 7.95 (*1-85230-795-1*) Element MA.

When Men Kill: Scenarios of Masculine Violence. Kenneth Polk. LC 94-8969. (Illus.). 288p. (C). 1994. text ed. 54.95 (*0-521-46267-3*); pap. text ed. 18.95 (*0-521-46808-6*) Cambridge U Pr.

***When Men Meet: Homosexualiity & Modernity.** Henning Bech. LC 96-46557. 1997. pap. 18.95 (*0-226-04022-4*); lib. bdg. 42.00 (*0-226-04021-6*) U Ch Pr.

When Men Play God: The Fallacy of Capital Punishment. Eugene B. Block. LC 81-15143. 1984. 14.95 (*0-89666-015-X*) Cragmont Pubns.

When Men Revolt & Why. James Davies. LC 96-38938. 360p. (Orig.). 1996. pap. text ed. 24.95 (*1-56000-939-X*) Transaction Pubs.

When Men Think Private Thoughts. Gordon MacDonald. 272p. 1996. 19.99 (*0-7852-7839-7*) Nelson.

***When Men Think Private Thoughts.** Gordon MacDonald. 288p. 1997. pap. 12.99 (*0-7852-7163-5*) Nelson.

***When Men Think Private Thoughts.** Gordon MacDonald. 1996. audio 15.99 (*0-7852-7428-6*) Nelson.

When Men Walk Dry: Portuguese Messianism in Brazil. Carol A. Myscofski. LC 88-24015. (American Academy of Religion Academy Ser.). 211p. 1989. pap. 15.95 (*1-55540-257-7*, 01-01-61) Scholars Pr GA.

When Messiah Comes. Paul Hegele. Ed. by Michael L. Sherer. (Orig.). 1986. pap. 6.50 (*0-89536-823-4*, 6832) CSS OH.

When Midnight Turns to Dawn. Ralph E. Paries & Merrit Corp. Staff. 308p. (Orig.). 1994. pap. 9.99 (*1-56043-822-3*) Destiny Image.

When Midwifery Became the Male Physician's Province: The Sixteenth Century Handbook "The Rose Garden for Pregnant Women & Midwives," Newly Enlisted. Eucharius Rosslin. Tr. & Intro. by Wendy Arons. LC 93-42981. (Illus.). 143p. 1994. lib. bdg. 35.00 (*0-89950-934-7*) McFarland & Co.

When Minds Go Wrong. John M. Grimes. 1954. 6.95 (*0-8159-7206-7*) Devin.

When Ministers Sin: Sexual Abuse in the Churches. Neal Ormerod & Thea Ormerod. 178p. (Orig.). pap. 12.95 (*1-86429-011-0*, Pub. by Millennium Bks AT) Morehouse Pub.

When Molly Was in the Hospital: A Book for Brothers & Sisters of Hospitalized Children. Debbie Duncan. LC 94-67525. (Minimed Ser.: Vol. 1). (Illus.). 40p. (J). (ps-7). 1994. 12.95 (*1-877810-44-4*) Rayve Prodns.

When Mom & Dad Separate: Children Can Learn to Cope with Grief from Divorce. Marge E. Heegaard. (Drawing Out Feelings Ser.). (Illus.). 32p. (Orig.). (J). (gr. k-6). 1990. student ed., pap. 5.95 (*0-9620502-2-9*) Woodland Pr.

When Mom or Dad Has Seizures: A Guide for Young People. Epilepsy Foundation of America Staff. 100p. (YA). (gr. 7 up). 1994. pap. 12.95 (*0-916570-15-0*) Epilepsy Foundation of America.

When Mom Turned into a Monster. Joanna Harrison. 1996. 14.95 (*1-57505-013-7*, Carolrhoda) Lerner Group.

When Mommy Is Sick. Ferne Sherkin-Langer. (J). (ps-3). 1995. lib. bdg. 12.95 (*0-8075-8894-6*) A Whitman.

When Money Is King: How Ron Perelman Mastered the World of Finance to Create One of America's Greatest Business Empires & Found Glamour, Beauty & the High Life in the Bargain. Richard Hack. 288p. 1996. pap. 23.95 (*0-7871-1033-7*, Dove Bks) Dove Audio.

When Money Is Not Enough: Fulfillment in Work. 2nd ed. Eileen R. Hannegan. LC 94-44136. (Business of Life Ser.). 123p. (C). 1995. reprint ed. pap. 10.95 (*1-885223-14-5*) Beyond Words Pub.

When More Is Less: The Paradox of American Health Care & How to Resolve It. Arnold S. Relman. 224p. 1993. 19.95 (*0-393-03579-4*) Norton.

When Morning Comes. Patricia Calvert. 160p. 1992. pap. 3.50 (*0-380-71186-9*, Flare) Avon.

When Morning Comes. Robin L. Wiete. 384p. (Orig.). 1993. pap. 4.99 (*0-451-40336-3*, Onyx) NAL-Dutton.

When Moshiach Comes: Halachic & Aggadic Perspectives. Yehudah Chayoun. Tr. by Yaakov M. Rapoport & Mushe Grossman from HEB. 288p. 1994. 14.95 (*1-56871-065-8*) Targum Pr.

When Mothers & Fathers Work: Creative Strategies for Balancing Career & Family. Renee Y. Magid & Nancy E. Fleming. LC 86-47817. 208p. reprint ed. pap. 59.30 (*0-7837-4240-1*, 2043929) Bks Demand.

When Mothers & Fathers Work: Creative Ways to Succeed with Both Family & Career. Renee Y. Magid & Nancy E. Fleming. 224p. 1989. reprint ed. pap. 3.95 (*0-380-70753-5*) Avon.

***When Mothers Pray.** Cheri Fuller. LC 97-17188. 200p. 1997. pap. 9.99 (*1-57673-040-9*, Multnomah Bks) Multnomah Pubs.

When Mothers Work, Who Pays? Martha H. Sugar. LC 93-43727. 168p. 1994. text ed. 45.00 (*0-89789-383-2*, Bergin & Garvey) Greenwood.

***When Mountains Walked.** Wheeler. 1999. write for info. (*0-395-85991-3*) HM.

When Mourning Comes: A Book of Comfort for the Grieving. William B. Silverman & Kenneth Cinnamon. LC 89-17771. 160p. 1994. pap. 20.00 (*1-56821-184-8*) Aronson.

When Mr. Pickwick Went Fishing. Samuel W. Lambert. LC 74-3271. (Studies in Dickens: No. 52). 1974. lib. bdg. 47.95 (*0-8383-2063-5*) M S G Haskell Hse.

When Muscle Pain Won't Go Away: The Relief Handbook for Fibromyalgia & Chronic Muscle Pain. Gayle Backstrom. LC 92-3289. 168p. 1992. pap. 12.95 (*0-87833-794-6*) Taylor Pub.

When Muscle Pain Won't Go Away: The Relief Handbook for Fibromyalgia & Chronic Muscle Pain. rev. ed. Gayle Backstrom. 208p. 1995. pap. 12.95 (*0-87833-891-8*) Taylor Pub.

When Music Sings on the Wind. Audrey H. Winkler. (Illus.). 64p. 1987. pap. 6.50 (*0-9603312-2-0*) Wynaud Pr.

When My Dad Died: A Child's View of Death. Janice M. Hammond. (Illus.). 48p. (Orig.). (J). (gr. k-6). 1981. pap. 8.95 (*0-9604690-3-6*) Cranbrook Pub.

When My Grandmother Was a Child. Leigh W. Rutledge. Date not set. pap. 8.95 (*0-452-27438-9*, Plume) NAL-Dutton.

When My Grandmother Was a Child. Leigh W. Rutledge. 128p. 1996. pap. 12.95 (*0-525-94105-3*, Dutton) NAL-Dutton.

When My Love Returns from the Ladies' Room Will I Be Too Old to Care? Lewis Gizzard. 1989. mass mkt. 5.99 (*0-345-35785-X*) Ballantine.

When My Love Returns from the Ladies Room, Will I Be Too Old to Care? Lewis Grizzard. LC 87-40183. 256p. 1987. 14.95 (*0-394-56418-9*, Villard Bks) Random.

When My Mommy Died: A Child's View of Death. Janice M. Hammond. (Illus.). 27p. (Orig.). (J). (ps-5). 1980. pap. 8.95 (*0-9604690-0-1*) Cranbrook Pub.

When My Parents Were My Age, They Were Old: Who Are You Calling Middle -Aged? Cathy Crimmins. 1995. pap. 10.00 (*0-684-80289-9*, Fireside) S&S Trade.

When My Parents Were My Age, They Were Old: Who Are You Calling Middle-Aged. Crimmins. 1995. pap. 10.00 (*0-671-89944-9*, Fireside) S&S Trade.

When Nancy Lived on Chestnut Street. Virginia Muldoon. Ed. by Marilynn C. Muldoon. (Illus.). 52p. 1982. pap. 3.95 (*0-940930-00-5*) Forsythe & Cromwell.

When Nations Die. Jim N. Black. 1995. pap. 10.99 (*0-8423-8007-8*) Tyndale.

When Nature Heals: The Greening of Rocky Mountain Arsenal. Chris Madson. 80p. 1990. pap. 14.95 (*0-911797-71-8*) R Rinehart.

When New Flowers Bloomed: Short Stories by Women Writers from Costa Rica & Panama. Ed. by Enrique J. Levi. LC 91-26038. (Discoveries Ser.). 208p. 1988. pap. 14.95 (*0-935480-47-1*) Lat Am Lit Rev Pr.

When New Time Folds Up. Kathleen Fraser. LC 93-35570. 1993. pap. 11.00 (*0-925904-14-7*) Chax Pr.

***When Nick Returns.** Dee Holmes. 384p. (Orig.). 1997. mass mkt. 5.99 (*0-380-79161-7*) Avon.

***When Nickels Were Indians: An Urban, Mixed-Blood Story.** Patricia P. Hilden. (Series of Studies in Native American Literatures). (Illus.). 260p. 1997. pap. 16.95 (*1-56098-747-2*) Smithsonian.

When Nicki Went Away. Fay Robinson. LC 92-13835. (Bear & Alligator Tales Ser.). (Illus.). 32p. (J). (ps-2). 1992. lib. bdg. 17.00 (*0-516-02376-4*) Childrens.

When Nietzsche Wept: A Novel of Obsession. Irvin D. Yalom. LC 91-59014. 320p. 1993. pap. 13.00 (*0-06-097550-4*, PL) HarpC.

When Night Falls. Cheryln Biggs. (Loveswept Ser.: No. 813). 240p. 1996. mass mkt. 3.50 (*0-553-44552-9*, Loveswept) Bantam.

When Night Falls. Jenna Ryan. (Intrigue Ser.). 1994. mass mkt. 2.99 (*0-373-22265-3*, 1-22265-2) Harlequin Bks.

When Night the Moon Awakes. Kenneth M. Kelly. 1994. 8.95 (*0-533-11037-8*) Vantage.

When Night Turns to Day: Take Heed My Children. Ricardo A. Scott. (Ras Cardo Speaks on the Issues Ser.). (Illus.). 100p. (Orig.). Date not set. pap. write for info. (*1-883427-54-1*) Crnerstone GA.

When Nine to Five Isn't Enough: A Guide to Finding Fulfillment at Work. Marcia A. Perkins-Reed. LC 90-80052. 304p. (Orig.). 1990. pap. 10.00 (*0-937611-93-X*, 126) Hay House.

***When "No" Gets You Nowhere: Teaching Your Toddler & Child Self-Control.** Mark Brenner. LC 97-1560. 176p. 1997. per. 12.00 (*0-7615-0954-2*) Prima Pub.

When No Majority Rules: The Electoral College & Presidential Succession. Michael J. Glennon. LC 92-40267. 162p. 1993. pap. 19.95 (*0-87187-875-5*) Congr Quarterly.

When No Means No: A Guide to Sexual Harassment by a Woman Who Won a Million Dollar Verdict. Cheryl Preston-Gomez & Randi Reisfeld. 224p. 1992. 17.95 (*1-55972-143-X*, Birch Ln Pr) Carol Pub Group.

When No One Was Looking. Pipikwass. 50p. (Orig.). 1990. pap. 7.00 (*0-9621498-4-5*, Robin Hood) R Hood Little.

***When No One Was Watching.** Conly. 1997. pap. 14.95 (*0-8050-3934-1*) St Martin.

When Nobody's Home: Fifteen Baby-Sitting Tales of Terror. Judith Gorog. LC 93-34595. 95p. (YA). (gr. 7 up). 1996. 15.95 (*0-590-46862-6*) Scholastic Inc.

When Nomads Settle. Philip C. Salzman. (Praeger Special Studies). 192p. 1980. text ed. 49.95 (*0-275-90543-8*, C0543, Praeger Pubs) Greenwood.

When Not to Borrow: Unconventional Financial Wisdom to Set Your Church Free. Ray Bowman & Eddy Hall. LC 96-33859. (Illus.). 144p. (C). 1996. pap. 9.99 (*0-8010-9021-0*) Baker Bks.

When Not to Build: An Architect's Unconventional Wisdom for the Growing Church. Ray Bowman & Eddy Hall. 160p. (C). 1992. pap. 9.99 (*0-8010-1031-4*) Baker Bks.

When Not to Say Help. Matthew V. Smith. (Illus.). 16p. (J). (gr. k-3). 1992. pap. 11.95 (*1-895583-34-9*) MAYA Pubs.

***When Nothing Else Works: Innovative Interventions with Intractable Individuals.** Herbert S. Strean. LC 97-5663. 1997. pap. text ed. 25.00 (*0-7657-0074-3*) Aronson.

When Nothing Makes Sense: Disaster, Crisis, & Their Effects on Children. Gerald Deskin & Greg Steckler. 224p. 1996. 19.95 (*0-925190-95-0*) Fairview Press.

***When Nothing Makes Sense: Disaster, Crisis, & Their Effects on Children.** Gerald Deskin & Greg Steckler. 1997. reprint ed. pap. 12.95 (*1-57749-027-4*) Fairview Press.

When Old Gods Die. William Alex. 1971. pap. 3.00 (*0-317-13544-9*) C G Jung Frisco.

When Old Men Die. Bill Crider. 192p. 1994. 19.95 (*0-8027-3195-3*) Walker & Co.

When Old Technologies Were New. Carolyn Marvin. 272p. 1990. reprint ed. pap. 18.95 (*0-19-506341-4*) OUP.

When Old Town Was Young: The Early Decades of Old Pasadena. Kirk Myers. 24p. 1994. pap. 6.95 (*0-9642429-0-7*) K Myers.

When Old Worlds Meet. Peter Wood. Ed. by Eric R. Bates. (Illus.). 64p. (Orig.). 1992. pap. 5.00 (*0-943810-52-3*) Inst Southern Studies.

When on the Edge. Edith Shiffert. 1991. pap. 10.00 (*0-934834-95-4*) White Pine.

When Once Is Not Enough: Help for Obsessive Compulsive. Gail Steketee & Kerrin White. 240p. (Orig.). 1990. 24.95 (*0-934986-88-6*); pap. 13.95 (*0-934986-87-8*) New Harbinger.

When One Door Closes. Joan Jonker. 448p. 1995. pap. 9.95 (*0-7472-4551-7*, Pub. by Headline UK) Trafalgar.

***When One Door Closes.** Joan Jonker. 528p. write for info. (*0-7505-1025-0*, Pub. by Magna Print Bks UK) Ulverscroft.

When One Has Lived a Long Time Alone. Galway Kinnell. 1990. pap. 15.00 (*0-679-73281-0*) Knopf.

***When One Partner Is Willing & the Other Is Not.** Ed. by Barbara J. Brothers. LC 96-51966. (Journal of Couples Therapy Monograph Ser.: Vol. 7, No. 1). 122p. (C). 1996. 29.95 (*0-7890-0038-5*) Haworth Pr.

***When One Partner Is Willing & the Other Is Not.** Ed. by Barbara J. Brothers. LC 96-51966. 106p. 1997. pap. 9.95 (*0-7890-0342-2*) Haworth Pr.

When One Wants Out & the Other Doesn't: Doing Therapy with Polarized Couples. Ed. by John F. Crosby. LC 88-7444. 240p. 1989. text ed. 36.95 (*0-87630-527-3*) Brunner-Mazel.

When Only a Miracle Will Do. Marilyn Hickey. 1994. pap. 4.95 (*1-56441-051-X*) M Hickey Min.

When Only the Best Will Do. large type ed. Lillian H. Lalumandier. (Illus.). 190p. 1996. spiral bd. 14.95 (*0-9656047-0-5*) Lillians LA Kitchen. This cookbook was written by a native Louisianian who has presented recipes in a way to delight even the most experienced cooks. Elegance at its best - for those with gourmet taste. The book includes classic Cajun & Creole recipes, & recipes of the 90s. A must for those who entertain. Buyers have been delighted with the large print & easy-to-read directions. The collection of recipes includes hors d'oeuvres, appetizers, salads, entrees' & after-dinner liqueurs. The author is the daughter of the first Mayor-President of Baton Rouge. The presentation encourages readers to "make their home the best restaurant in town!" One page brochure available which includes a picture of the book & the Table of Contents. To order: Lillian's Louisiana Kitchen, 8988 Baker Drive, Baton Rouge, LA 70809. 504-925-0156, E-mail: llalumandi@aol.com.** ***Publisher Provided Annotation.

When Opponents Cooperate: Great Power Conflict & Collaboration in World Politics. Benjamin Miller. 376p. 1994. text ed. 49.50 (*0-472-10458-6*) U of Mich Pr.

When Opportunity Knocks. Susan Hecht. (Inter Acta Ser.). (Illus.). 6p. (C). 1996. teacher ed., ring bd. 1.25 (*1-57334-026-X*, 741-072t, Inter Acta); student ed., ring bd. 3.25 (*1-57334-025-1*, 741-072s, Inter Acta) WSN Pr.

W

When Opposites Attract: Right Brain/Left Brain Relationships & How to Make Them Work. Rebecca Cutter. 285p. 1996. pap. 12.95 (*0-452-27114-2*, Plume) NAL-Dutton.

*__When Oracles Speak.__ Skafte. 23.00 (*0-06-251444-X*); pap. 12.00 (*0-06-251445-8*) HarpC.

When Orchids Were Flowers. Kate K. Johnson. LC 86-13435. 64p. 1986. 14.00 (*0-937872-34-2*); pap. 7.00 (*0-937872-35-0*) Dragon Gate.

When Oscar Was a Little Grouch & Other Good-Night Stories. Liza Alexander. (Illus.). 24p. (J). (ps-1). 1989. write for info. (*0-318-65332-X*) Western Pub.

*__When Our Bad Season Comes: A Cultural Account of Subsistence Harvesting & Harvest Disruption on the Yukon Delta.__ Ann Fienup-Riordan. (Aurora Ser.: Vol. 1). (Illus.). xii, 377p. 1986. reprint ed. pap. 28.00 (*1-890396-01-X*) AK Anthropological.

When Our Days Go to the Dogs: We Don't Have to Step in Their S..t! Leonard M. Foley, Ill. 64p. (YA). (gr. 9-12). 1992. pap. 1.95 (*0-9630314-2-2*) One World SC.

When Our Love Is Charity. Chiara Lubich. Ed. by New City Press Editorial Staff. 152p. 1991. 8.95 (*0-911782-93-1*) New City.

When Our Parents Need Us Most: Loving Care for the Aging Years. David L. McKenna. LC 93-42150. 150p. 1994. pap. 8.99 (*0-87788-902-3*) Shaw Pubs.

When Our Words Return: Writing, Hearing, & Remembering Oral Traditions of Alaska & the Yukon. Ed. by Phyllis Morrow & William Sshneider. LC 95-32445. (C). 1995. 36.95 (*0-87421-199-9*); pap. 19.95 (*0-87421-195-6*) Utah St U Pr.

*__When Papa Snores.__ Long. (J). Date not set. pap. 16.00 (*0-689-81943-9*) S&S Childrens.

When Pappy Goes Hunting. Kurt L. Bonello. LC 94-72497. (Illus.). 24p. (J). (ps-3). 1994. 12.95 (*0-9642248-0-1*) Bonello Studios.

When Parents Age: What Children Can Do. Tom Adams & Kathryn Armstrong. 208p. (Orig.). 1996. reprint ed. pap. text ed. 5.99 (*0-425-15262-6*) Berkley Pub.

When Parents Die. Edward Myers. LC 96-28999. 1997. pap. 11.95 (*0-14-026231-8*) Viking Penguin.

When Parents Die: A Guide for Adults. Edward Myers. 224p. 1987. pap. 11.95 (*0-14-009211-0*, Penguin Bks) Viking Penguin.

When Parents Face the Schools. Judy-Arin Krupp & Robert Pauker. (Illus.). 192p. (Orig.). 1984. pap. 10.00 (*0-9613245-0-3*) Adult Dev Learn.

When Parents Grow Old. Julie Johnson. (Lifestyle Ser.). 31p. 1986. pap. 0.89 (*0-8163-0658-3*) Pacific Pr Pub Assn.

When Parents Have Problems: Teens & Older Children with an Abusive, Alcoholic or Mentally Ill Parent. Susan B. Miller. LC 94-45929. 94p. (C). 1995. text ed. 31.95 (*0-398-05989-6*); pap. text ed. 18.95 (*0-398-05990-X*) C C Thomas.

When Parents Kidnap: The Families Behind the Headlines. Geoffrey L. Greif & Rebecca L. Hegar. LC 92-23855. 322p. 1992. 27.95 (*0-02-912975-3*, Free Press) Free Pr.

When Parents Love Too Much: What Happens When Parents Won't Let Go. Laurie Ashner & Mitch Meyerson. 384p. 1991. reprint ed. mass mkt. 5.95 (*0-380-70813-2*) Avon.

When Part of the Self Is Lost: Helping Clients Heal after Sexual & Reproductive Losses. Constance H. Shapiro. LC 92-17610. (Social & Behavioral Science - Health Ser.). 287p. 32.95 (*1-55542-485-6*) Jossey-Bass.

*__When Parties Fail: Emerging Alternative Organizations.__ Ed. by Kay Lawson & Peter H. Merkl. LC 87-22566. 605p. 1988. reprint ed. pap. 172.50 (*0-608-03755-9*, 2064578) Bks Demand.

When Passion Reigned: Sex & Victorians. Patricia Anderson. 224p. 1996. pap. text ed. 15.00 (*0-465-08992-5*) Basic.

When Patterns Change: Turning Points in International Politics. Ed. by Nissan Oren. LC 83-40614. 250p. 1985. text ed. 29.95 (*0-312-86666-6*) St Martin.

When Peanut Butter Is Not Enough. Mary D. Beachy & Kristie Wolferman. (Illus.). 100p. (J). (gr. 2-7). 1986. pap. 7.95 (*0-9616883-0-0*) Petit Appetit.

*__When People Are Big & God Is Small: Overcoming Peer Pressure, Codependency, & the Fear of Man.__ Edward T. Welch. LC 97-18713. (Resources for Changing Lives Ser.). 224p. (Orig.). 1997. pap. 9.99 (*0-87552-600-4*) Presby & Reformed.

*__When People Could Fly.__ Morton Marcus. 1997. 22.00 (*0-614-29401-0*) Hanging Loose.

*__When People Could Fly.__ Morton Marcus. 1997. pap. 13.00 (*0-614-29402-9*) Hanging Loose.

When People Die. Jessie Schut. (Friendship Ser.). 1995. teacher ed. 3.15 (*1-56212-095-6*) CRC Pubns.

When People Do You Wrong. Horace L. Patterson. 98p. 1996. pap. 7.95 (*1-55523-768-1*) Winston-Derek.

When People Matter: Nordic Industrial Architecture & Engineering Design. Ed. by Anders Tornqvist & Peter Ullmark. (Swedish Council for Building Research Ser.). (Illus.). 224p. (Orig.). 1989. pap. 97.50 (*91-540-5059-6*, Pub. by Umea U Bibl SW) Coronet Bks.

When People Play People: Development Communications Through Theatre. Zakes Mda. LC 93-18987. 288p. (C). 1993. pap. 25.00 (*1-85649-200-1*, Pub. by Zed Bks Ltd UK); text ed. 55.00 (*1-85649-199-4*, Pub. by Zed Bks Ltd UK) Humanities.

When Philadelphia Was the Capital of Jewish America. Ed. by Murray Friedman. LC 92-54949. 1993. 35.00 (*0-944190-13-8*) Balch IES Pr.

When Physicians Fail As Managers: An Exploratory Analysis of Career Change Problems. Robert M. Peters. 48p. (Orig.). 1994. pap. text ed. 25.00 (*0-924674-31-8*) Am Coll Phys Execs.

*__When Pigs Fly.__ Ian Boyd. (J). 1997. pap. 5.95 (*0-8167-4212-X*) Troll Communs.

When Pigs Fly. June R. Wood. LC 94-42110. 224p. (Orig.). (J). (gr. 5-9). 1995. 16.95 (*0-399-22911-6*, Putnam) Putnam Pub Group.

*__When Pigs Fly.__ June R. Wood. 272p. (Orig.). (J). (gr. 3-7). 1997. pap. 5.95 (*0-698-11570-8*, Paperstar) Putnam Pub Group.

*__When Pigs Fly: An Omnium-Gatherum of Double Dactyls (Poems in Dactylic Meter)__ Ed. by William J. Middleton. LC 97-90229. (Illus.). 64p. (Orig.). 1997. pap. 6.00 (*1-886467-16-1*) WJM Press.

*__When Pioneer Wagons Rumbled West.__ Christine Graham. LC 97-15210. (Illus.). (J). 1997. write for info. (*1-57345-272-6*) Deseret Bk.

When Plague Strikes: The Black Death, Smallpox, AIDS. James C. Giblin. LC 94-39881. (Illus.). 240p. (YA). (gr. 5 up). 1995. 14.95 (*0-06-025854-3*); lib. bdg. 14.89 (*0-06-025864-0*) HarpC Child Bks.

*__When Plague Strikes: The Black Death, Smallpox, AIDS.__ James C. Giblin. LC 94-39881. (Nonfiction Bks.). (Illus.). 240p. (YA). (gr. 5 up). 1997. pap. 6.95 (*0-06-446195-5*, Trophy) HarpC Child Bks.

*__When Praise Demands a Sacrifice.__ 1993. 1.20 (*0-8341-9006-0*) Nazarene.

When Prayer Seems Not to Work. Harry E. Jessop. 1987. pap. 4.99 (*0-88019-217-8*) Schmul Pub Co.

When Prayers Are Answered. John Holmstrom. LC 95-7695. 1995. pap. 12.00 (*0-399-52159-3*, Perigee Bks) Berkley Pub.

When Pregnancy Isn't Perfect: A Layperson's Guide to Complications in Pregnancy. Albert Sassoon. 496p. 1991. pap. 19.95 (*0-525-24961-3*, Dutton) NAL-Dutton.

*__When Pregnancy Isn't Perfect: A Layperson's Guide to Complications in Pregnancy.__ 3rd ed. Laurie A. Rich. 349p. 1996. reprint ed. pap. 12.00 (*0-9654985-0-6*) Larata Pr.

When Presidents Are Great. Marcia L. Whicker & Raymond A. Moore. 192p. (C). 1988. pap. text ed. write for info. (*0-13-956228-1*) P-H.

*__When Prince Charming Falls off His Horse.__ 204p. 1997. write for info. (*1-56476-628-4*, Victor Bks) Chariot Victor.

When Prophets Die: The Postcharismatic Fate of New Religious Movements. Ed. by Timothy Miller. LC 90-44859. (SUNY Series in Religious Studies). 251p. (C). 1991. text ed. 21.50 (*0-7914-0717-9*) State U NY Pr.

*__When Psychological Problems Mask Medical Disorders: A Guide for Psychotherapists.__ LC 97-17253. 1997. lib. bdg. 35.00 (*1-57230-180-5*, C0180) Guilford Pr.

When Public Sector Workers Unionize. Richard B. Freeman & Casey Ichniowski. (National Bureau of Economic Research Project Report Ser.). (Illus.). 440p. 1988. lib. bdg. 59.00 (*0-226-26166-2*) U Ch Pr.

When Push Comes to Shove: A Practical Guide to Mediating Disputes. Karl A. Slaikeu. (Conflict Resolution Ser.). 320p. text ed. 28.95 (*0-7879-0161-X*) Jossey-Bass.

When Rabbit Howls. Truddi Chase. 1990. mass mkt. 6.50 (*0-515-10329-2*) Jove Pubns.

When Race Counts: The Morality of Racial Preference in Britain & America. John Edwards. LC 94-13286. 272p. (C). 1995. pap. 18.95 (*0-415-07293-X*, B4860) Routledge.

When Race Counts: The Morality of Racial Preference in Britain & America. John Edwards. LC 94-13286. 272p. (C). (gr. 13). 1995. text ed. 62.95 (*0-415-07292-1*, B4856) Routledge.

When Ragtime Was Young & Grandma Did the Cooking. Elsa Altshool. Ed. by Mary Eberhardt. (Illus.). 206p. (Orig.). 1993. pap. 10.00 (*0-9633372-0-3*) Centurys End.

When Rain Clouds Gather. Bessie Head. (African Writers Ser.). 188p. (C). 1987. pap. 9.95 (*0-435-90726-3*, 90726) Heinemann.

*__When Rain Clouds Gather.__ Bessie Head. 1996. pap. text ed. 10.95 (*0-435-90961-4*) Heinemann.

When Reality Shines. Susan L. Majette. LC 94-61158. 205p. 1995. pap. 10.95 (*1-55523-723-1*) Winston-Derek.

When Reason Sleeps. Tom Sehler. Date not set. pap. 4.95 (*0-14-015449-3*) Viking Penguin.

When Refugees Go Home: African Experiences. Ed. by Tim Allen & Hubert Morsink. 400p. (C). 1994. 59.95 (*0-86543-432-8*); pap. 18.95 (*0-86543-433-6*) Africa World.

When Rich Men Die. Harold Adams. 256p. 1988. pap. 3.50 (*0-380-70539-7*) Avon.

When Riding a Dead Horse, for Heavens Sake...Dismount! Barry Asmus. 243p. 1995. 19.95 (*0-9640421-3-4*); pap. 12.95 (*0-9649421-4-3*); pap. text ed. 12.95 (*0-9640421-4-2*) Ameripress.

When Right Is Wrong: Fundamentalists & the Public Schools. Richard Manatt. LC 94-61497. 150p. 1994. pap. text ed. 24.95 (*1-56676-222-7*) Technomic.

When Rio Grande City Was Young. Shirley B. Green. Ed. by Pan American University Press. (Illus.). (Orig.). (C). 1986. 10.00 (*0-318-21749-X*); pap. 6.00 (*0-318-21750-3*) S B Greene.

When Rocks Dance. Elizabeth Nunez-Harrell. 320p. 1992. pap. 10.00 (*0-345-38068-1*, One World) Ballantine.

When Romeo Wrote Juliet: Your Inspirational Guide to the Art of Writing Love Letters. Brian Holtcamp & Paula Hilton. 136p. 1994. 15.95 (*1-884327-17-6*) Stylus Pubng.

When Roots Die: Endangered Traditions on the Sea Islands. Patricia Jones-Jackson. LC 85-20912. (Brown Thrasher Bks.). (Illus.). 206p. 1989. pap. 14.95 (*0-8203-1121-9*) U of Ga Pr.

When Rover Just Won't Do: Over Two Thousand Suggestions for Naming Your Puppy. Danny Scalisi & Libby Moses. (Illus.). 224p. 1993. pap. 9.95 (*0-87605-691-5*) Howell Bk.

When Sacred & Secular Mix: Religious Nonprofit Organizations & Public Money. Stephen V. Monsma. (Religious Forces in the Modern Political World Ser.). 240p. (C). 1996. pap. 27.95 (*0-8476-8182-3*) Rowman.

*__When Saints Are Lovers: The Spirituality of Maryknoll Founder Thomas F. Price.__ John T. Sedden, Ill. 184p. (Orig.). 1997. pap. 14.95 (*0-8146-2228-3*) Liturgical Pr.

When Santa Was a Shaman: Ancient Origins of Santa Claus & the Christmas Tree. Tony Van Renterghem. LC 95-20306. (Illus.). 208p. 1995. pap. 16.95 (*1-56718-765-X*) Llewellyn Pubns.

When Santa Was Late. Frank R. Leet. (Illus.). 24p. (J). (ps-2). 1990. pap. 3.95 (*0-8249-8483-8*, Ideals Child) Hambleton-Hill.

When School Bells Rang. Florence Langley. LC 76-50006. (Illus.). 80p. 1976. 6.95 (*0-914016-34-2*) Phoenix Pub.

When School Districts Become Entrepreneurs: Opportunity or Danger? Paul Bauman & Faith E. Crampton. 8p. 1995. 5.00 (*1-55516-396-3*, 7302-2011) Natl Conf State Legis.

When Science Becomes Culture. Ed. by Bernard Schiele. 455p. 1994. pap. 35.00 (*0-7766-0388-4*, Pub. by Univ Ottawa Pr CN) Paul & Co Pubs.

When Science Meets the Public. Ed. by Bruce Lewinstein. 164p. 1992. 14.00 (*0-87168-440-3*, 92-06S) AAAS.

When Scripture Changes Lives. Frank Borcham. 155p. 1995. pap. 7.99 (*1-884543-03-0*) O M Lit.

When Sea & Sky Are Blue. Letitia Parr. LC 78-151272. (Illus.). 32p. (J). (ps-3). 7.95 (*0-87592-059-4*) Scroll Pr.

When Seconds Count: Everyone's Guide to Self-Defense. Sammy Franco. (Illus.). 144p. 1994. pap. 22.00 (*0-87364-762-9*) Paladin Pr.

When Self-Help Isn't Enough: Overcoming Addiction & Psychiatric Disorders. A. Scott Winter. 144p. (Orig.). 1990. pap. 7.95 (*0-929162-19-6*) PIA Pr.

When Servants Ride Horses: One Version of the David Dickson Story. rev. ed. Dorothy H. Morgan. (Illus.). 208p. (Orig.). 1992. Perfect bdg. per. 15.00 (*0-9632936-0-5*) D H Morgan.

When Servants Suffer: Finding Purpose in Pain. Ron Rhodes. (Fisherman Bible Studyguide Ser.). 79p. (Orig.). 1989. pap. text ed. 4.99 (*0-87788-929-5*) Shaw Pubs.

*__When Shadows Fall.__ Brian S. Smith. 320p. (Orig.). 1997. mass mkt. 4.99 (*0-8439-4313-0*, Leisure Bks) Dorchester Pub Co.

When Shakespeare's Ladies Meet. Charles George. 1942. pap. 3.25 (*0-8222-1239-0*) Dramatists Play.

When Shannon Came Home. Marlene E. McFadden. (Rainbow Romances Ser.). 160p. 1994. 14.95 (*0-7090-5432-7*, 919, Hale-Parkwest) Parkwest Pubns.

When She Hollers. Cynthia Voigt. LC 93-43519. 192p. (YA). (gr. 7-9). 1994. 13.95 (*0-590-46714-X*) Scholastic Inc.

When She Hollers. Cynthia Voigt. 176p. (YA). (gr. 7 up). 1996. pap. 3.99 (*0-590-46715-8*, Scholastic Hardcover) Scholastic Inc.

When She Was Bad. Corey. 1995. pap. 3.25 (*0-373-05950-7*) Harlequin Bks.

When She Was Bad. Ron Faust. 384p. 1995. 5.99 (*0-8125-1380-0*) Forge NYC.

*__When She Was Bad.__ large type ed. Kate O'Mara. (Black Satin Romance Ser.). 464p. 1996. 25.99 (*1-86110-022-1*) Ulverscroft.

When She Was Bad: The Story of Bess, Hortense, Sukhreet & Nancy. Shana Alexander. (Illus.). 1990. 19.95 (*0-394-57606-3*) Random.

*__When She Was Bad... Violent Women & the Myth of Innocence.__ Patricia Pearson. 1997. pap. 23.95 (*0-670-85925-7*, Viking) Viking Penguin.

When She Was Good. Philip Roth. LC 94-31360. 1995. pap. 12.00 (*0-679-75925-5*, Vin) Random.

When She Was the Good Time Girl. Katharyn M. Aal. 24p. (Orig.). 1987. pap. 2.00 (*0-936563-11-7*) Signpost.

When Sheep Cannot Sleep. Satoshi Kitamura. (Sunburst Ser.). (Illus.). 32p. (J). (ps up). 1988. pap. 4.95 (*0-374-48359-0*) FS&G.

When Sheep Cannot Sleep. Satoshi Kitamura. LC 86-45000. (Illus.). 32p. (J). (ps up). 1986. 14.00 (*0-374-38311-1*) FS&G.

When Sheep Can't Sleep: (Cuando los Borregos no Pueden Dormir) Satoshi Kitamura. (SPA.). (J). (gr. 1-6). 19.95 (*84-372-6605-X*) Santillana.

When Shepherds Bleed: A Study Guide for Wounded Pastors. T. D. Jakes & Stanley Miller. student ed. 11.99 (*1-56229-446-6*) Pneuma Life Pub.

When Shlemiel Went to Warsaw & Other Stories. Isaac B. Singer. (Sunburst Ser.). (Illus.). 161p. (J). (gr. 3-7). 1986. pap. 4.95 (*0-374-48365-5*) FS&G.

*__When Shopping Heals.__ April Benson. 1998. pap. write for info. (*0-609-80033-7*) Crown Pub Group.

When Should the Watchdogs Bark? Media Coverage of the Clinton Scandals. Larry J. Sabato & S. Robert Lichter. 120p. 1995. pap. text ed. 12.95 (*0-9643877-0-0*) Ctr for Media.

When Should We Confirm? The Order of Christian Initiation. Frank D. Almade et al. (Font & Table Ser.). 96p. 1989. pap. 5.95 (*0-930467-84-1*, WSWC) Liturgy Tr Pubns.

When Silence Becomes Singing. Helen Kylin. LC 84-61827. 32p. (Orig.). 1984. pap. 3.00 (*0-87574-258-0*) Pendle Hill.

When Silver Turns to Gold. Mildred J. Katemopoulos. (Orig.). 1996. pap. write for info. (*1-57553-146-1*) Watermrk Pr.

When Singapore Fell: Evacuations & Escapes, 1941-42. Joseph Kennedy. LC 88-23364. 244p. 1989. text ed. 45.00 (*0-312-02506-8*) St Martin.

When Six-Guns Ruled: Outlaw Tales of the Southwest. Marc Simmons. LC 89-82081. (Illus.). 140p. (Orig.). 1990. pap. 11.95 (*0-941270-63-7*) Ancient City Pr.

*__When Skeptics Ask.__ Norman L. Geisler & Ronald M. Brooks. 348p. 1990. 23.99 (*0-8010-1141-8*) Baker Bks.

When Sleeping Beauty Wakes Up: A Woman's Tale of the Healing of the Immune System & the Awakening of the Feminine. Patricia Lind-Kyle. LC 92-93335. 46p. 1992. pap. 14.95 (*0-9632310-1-4*) Swan Raven.

When Slow Is Fast Enough: Educating the Delayed Preschool Child. Joan F. Goodman. LC 92-1416. 306p. 1992. lib. bdg. 38.95 (*0-89862-793-1*) Guilford Pr.

When Slow Is Fast Enough: Educating the Delayed Preschool Child. Joan F. Goodman. LC 92-1416. 306p. 1993. pap. text ed. 18.95 (*0-89862-491-6*) Guilford Pr.

When Smart People Fail: Rebuilding Yourself for Success. rev. ed. Carole Hyatt & Linda Gottlieb. 256p. 1993. pap. 12.95 (*0-14-017811-2*, Penguin Bks) Viking Penguin.

When Snow Lay Soft on the Mountains. Patricia Hermes. (Illus.). 32p. (J). (ps-3). 1996. 15.95 (*0-316-36005-8*) Little.

When Snow Turns to Rain: One Family's Struggle to Solve the Riddle of Autism. Craig B. Schulze. LC 93-10209. 216p. (Orig.). (C). 1993. pap. 14.95 (*0-933149-63-8*) Woodbine House.

When Social Services Are Local. Roger Hadley & Morag McGrath. 1984. 50.00 (*0-317-40564-0*, Pub. by Natl Inst Soc Work) St Mut.

When Society Becomes an Addict. Anne W. Schaef. LC 86-46828. 176p. 1988. pap. 11.00 (*0-06-254854-9*) Harper SF.

When Socks Went to the White House. Harold Stearns. (Yes: When Socks...Ser.). (Illus.). 64p. (Orig.). (YA). (gr. 5 up). 1994. pap. 5.95 (*0-924799-15-3*) Am Articulat.

When Soldiers March Through Town: Wenn die Soldaten Durch die Stadt Marchieren. Hermann Siegmann. Tr. by Ray R. Cowdery from GER. (Illus.). 16p. (J). 1995. reprint ed. pap. 10.00 (*0-910667-37-3*) USM.

When Soldiers Quit: Studies in Military Disintegration. Bruce A. Watson. LC 96-28568. 208p. 1997. text ed. 59.95 (*0-275-95223-1*) Greenwood.

When Solomon Was King. Sheila MacGill-Callahan. LC 93-28058. (Illus.). (J). 1995. pap. 15.99 (*0-8037-1589-7*) Dial Bks Young.

When Somebody Loves You. Trisha Alexander. (Special Edition Ser.: No. 748). 1992. mass mkt. 3.39 (*0-373-09748-4*, 5-09748-0) Harlequin Bks.

When Somebody Wants You. Trisha Alexander. (Special Edition Ser.). 1993. mass mkt. 3.50 (*0-373-09822-7*, 5-09822-3) Silhouette.

When Someday Comes. Faith E. Garner. 1995. 17.95 (*0-8034-9103-4*, 095122) Bouregy.

When Someone Asks for Help: A Practical Guide to Counseling. Everett L. Worthington, Jr. LC 82-81. (Illus.). 239p. (Orig.). 1982. pap. 14.99 (*0-87784-375-9*, 375) InterVarsity.

When Someone Dies. Sharon Greenlee. (Illus.). 40p. (J). (gr. 1-7). 1992. 13.95 (*1-56145-044-8*) Peachtree Pubs.

When Someone Dies: A Children's Grief Workbook. Ed. by Joanne M. Pearring. (Illus.). 16p. (Orig.). 1995. student ed., pap. 1.50 (*0-89622-644-1*) Twenty-Third.

*__When Someone Dies: What You Can Do.__ Phyllis Davies. (Illus.). 56p. (Orig.). 1997. pap. 6.50 (*0-941343-32-4*) Sunnybank.

When Someone Has a Very Serious Illness: Children Learn to Cope with Loss & Change Workbook. Marge E. Heegaard. 36p. (J). (gr. 1-6). 1992. pap. 6.95 (*0-9620502-4-5*) Woodland Pr.

When Someone in the Family Drinks Too Much. Richard C. Langsen. LC 94-39449. (Illus.). 32p. (J). (gr. 1-5). 1996. pap. 14.89 (*0-8037-1687-7*) Dial Bks Young.

When Someone in the Family Drinks Too Much: A Guide for Children. Richard C. Langsen. LC 94-39449. (Illus.). 32p. (J). (gr. 1-5). 1996. pap. 14.99 (*0-8037-1686-9*) Dial Bks Young.

*__When Someone in Your Family Has Cancer.__ rev. ed. (Illus.). 27p. 1996. pap. 10.00 (*0-7881-3004-8*) DIANE Pub.

When Someone Is Dying: The Words You Both Need. Ed. by Martin Hall. 54p. (Orig.). 1988. pap. 9.95 (*0-9621163-0-0*) Writeside Pub Co.

*__When Someone Is Seriously Ill or Injured: What You Can Do.__ Phyllis Davies. (Illus.). 56p. (Orig.). 1997. pap. 6.50 (*0-614-29952-7*) Sunnybank.

When Someone Is Very Sick. Jim Boulden & Joan Boulden. Ed. by JoAnn Farness. (Illus.). 32p. (Orig.). (J). (gr. 3-5). 1995. pap. 5.95 (*1-878076-43-4*) Boulden Pub.

When Someone Very Special Dies: Children Can Learn to Cope with Grief. Marge E. Heegaard. (Illus.). 32p. (J). (gr. 1-6). 1988. student ed., pap. 6.95 (*0-9620502-0-2*) Woodland Pr.

When Someone Wants to Die. S. J. Anderson. (PathFinder Pamphlets Ser.). 32p. (Orig.). 1988. pap. 3.99 (*0-87784-220-5*, 220) InterVarsity.

When Someone You Know Has AIDS, 8, Set. Anna Forbes. LC 96-1507. (AIDS Awareness Library). (Illus.). 24p. (J). (gr. k-4). 1996. lib. bdg. 10.46 (*0-8239-2369-X*, PowerKids) Rosen Group.

When Someone You Know Has AIDS: A Practical Guide. Leonard J. Martelli et al. 256p. 1987. 15.97 (*0-317-52879-3*, Crown); pap. 12.00 (*0-517-56556-0*, Crown) Crown Pub Group.

When Someone You Know Has AIDS: A Practical Guide. rev. ed. Leonard J. Martelli et al. LC 93-2740. 1993. pap. 16.00 (*0-517-88039-3*, Crown) Crown Pub Group.

When Someone You Know Is Depressed: What You Need to Know about Depression & Its Effects on Relationships. Laura E. Rosen & Xavier F. Amador. LC 96-5899. 272p. 1996. 22.00 (*0-684-82407-8*) Free Pr.

When Someone You Know Is Hurting: What You Can Do to Help. M. Gregory Richards. 256p. 1994. mass mkt. 5.99 (*0-06-104305-2*) Zondervan.

An Asterisk (*) at the beginning of an entry indicates that the title is appearing in BIP for the first time.

When Someone You Know Is Sexually Abused. Susie Shellenberger. ("Let's Talk About Life Ser." by Brio: Vol. 3). (Orig.). (YA). 1996. pap. 3.99 (*1-56179-448-1*) Focus Family.

When Someone You Love Dies. William L. Coleman. (Grubstake Adventure Ser.). 128p. (J). (gr. 4-7). 1994. pap. 5.99 (*0-8066-2670-4*, 9-2670, Augsburg) Augsburg Fortress.

When Someone You Love Dies. Robert V. Dodd. 1986. pap. text ed. 2.95 (*0-687-45025-X*) Abingdon.

***When Someone You Love Gambles.** Hazelden Staff. 1996. pap. 2.50 (*0-89486-535-8*) Hazelden.

When Someone You Love Has a Mental Illness: A Handbook for Family, Friends, & Caregivers. Rebecca Woolis. 256p. 1992. pap. 11.95 (*0-87477-695-3*, Tarcher Putnam) Putnam Pub Group.

When Someone You Love Has a Stroke. Lynn Sonberg. 256p. 1995. mass mkt. 4.99 (*0-440-21666-4*) Dell.

When Someone You Love Has AIDS. Sachs. 1995. mass mkt. 4.99 (*0-440-77891-3*) Dell.

When Someone You Love Has Aids. Lynn Sonberg. 256p. 1995. mass mkt. 4.99 (*0-440-21663-X*) Dell.

When Someone You Love Has AIDS: A Book of Hope for Family & Friends. Bettyclare Moffatt. LC 87-721. 154p. (Orig.). 1986. reprint ed. lib. bdg. 29.00 (*0-8095-6551-X*) Borgo Pr.

When Someone You Love Has Alzheimers. Lynn Sonberg. 256p. 1995. mass mkt. 4.99 (*0-440-21660-5*) Dell.

***When Someone You Love Has Alzheimer's.** large type ed. Earl A. Grollman & Kenneth S. Kosik. LC 96-44094. (Spec-Hall Ser.). 163p. 1997. lib. bdg. 23.95 (*0-7838-2049-6*, GK Hall) Thorndike Pr.

When Someone You Love Has Alzheimer's: The Caregiver's Journey. Earl A. Grollman & Kenneth S. Kosik. LC 96-15884. 192p. 1996. 22.00 (*0-8070-2720-0*) Beacon Pr.

***When Someone You Love Has Alzheimer's: The Caregiver's Journey.** Earl A. Grollman & Kenneth S. Kosik. LC 96-15884. 192p. 1997. reprint ed. pap. 12.00 (*0-8070-2721-9*) Beacon Pr.

When Someone You Love Has Cancer. Le. 1995. mass mkt. 4.99 (*0-440-77889-1*) Dell.

When Someone You Love Has Cancer. Danarae Pomeroy. 176p. (Orig.). 1996. mass mkt. 5.99 (*0-425-15129-8*) Berkley Pub.

When Someone You Love Has Cancer. Lynn Sonberg. 1995. mass mkt. 4.99 (*0-440-21664-8*) Dell.

When Someone You Love Is Depressed. Rosen & Amador. 1996. 23.00 (*0-02-874131-5*) Free Pr.

***When Someone You Love Is Depressed.** Rosen & Amador. 1997. pap. 12.00 (*0-684-83407-3*, Fireside) S&S Trade.

When Someone You Love Is in Therapy. Michael Gold & Marie Scampini. 256p. (Orig.). (C). 1992. lib. bdg. 31.00 (*0-8095-6334-7*) Borgo Pr.

When Someone You Love Is in Therapy. Michael Gold & Marie Scampini. LC 92-26422. 256p. (Orig.). 1993. pap. 10.95 (*0-89793-114-9*) Hunter Hse.

When Something Changes Everything: How to Recover from the Zero Zone of Loss & Change. Peter M. McGugan. (Illus.). 200p. (Orig.). 1991. pap. text ed. 12.95 (*0-9694312-1-X*) Potentls Pr.

When Something Terrible Happens: Children Can Learn to Cope with Grief Workbook. Marge E. Heegaard. 32p. (J). (gr. 1-6). 1992. pap. 6.95 (*0-9620502-3-7*) Woodland Pr.

When Sons & Daughters Choose Alternative Lifestyles. Mariana Caplan. 200p. (Orig.). 1996. 14.95 (*0-934252-69-6*) Hohm Pr.

When Sorrow-Song Descends on You. Vinoko Akpalu. Ed. by Stanley H. Barkan. Tr. by Kofi Awoonor. (Cross-Cultural Review Chapbook Ser.: No. 14). 16p. (ENG & EWE.). 1992. 15.00 (*0-89304-876-3*); pap. 5.00 (*0-89304-877-1*) Cross-Cultrl NY.

When Sorrow-Song Descends on You. Vinoko Akpalu. Ed. by Stanley H. Barkan. Tr. by Kofi Awoonor. (Cross-Cultural Review Chapbook Ser.: No. 14: African Ghanaian Poetry 1). 16p. (ENG & EWE.). 1992. 15.00 (*0-89304-813-5*); pap. 5.00 (*0-89304-838-0*) Cross-Cultrl NY.

When Soul & Spirit Agree: Anchoring the Soul to the Spirit to Achieve Ultimate Success & Prosperity. Leo Natale. 115p. (Orig.). 1994. pap. 6.95 (*0-88270-683-7*) Bridge-Logos.

When South Yarmouth Was Quaker Village. Laurence Barber. (Illus.). 52p. 1988. pap. 4.00 (*0-9625068-2-6*) Hist Soc Yarmouth.

When Spirit Soared. Mike Smith. 160p. per., pap. text ed. 9.95 (*0-9643429-1-X*) Concord Pubs.

***When Spirit Speaks: A Woman's Mystical Journey & Her Transformation Through the Power of Prayer.** Susanne S. Blake. Ed. by John A. Blake. 300p. 1997. pap. 18.95 (*1-890247-00-6*) Yellow Bird Commun.

When Spring Comes. Natalie Kinsey-Warnock. LC 92-14066. (Illus.). (J). (ps-3). 1993. pap. 14.99 (*0-525-45008-4*) Dutton Child Bks.

When Spring Comes. Robert Maass. LC 93-29816. (J). 1994. 14.95 (*0-8050-2085-3*, Bks Young Read) H Holt & Co.

When Spring Comes. Robert Maass. (Illus.). 32p. (J). (gr. k-3). 1996. pap. 5.95 (*0-8050-4705-0*, Owlet BYR) H Holt & Co.

When Stars Came Down to Earth: Cosmology of the Skidi Pawnee Indians of North America. Von Del Chamberlain. LC 82-16390. (Anthropological Papers: No. 26). (Illus.). 260p. (Orig.). 1982. pap. 17.95 (*0-87919-098-1*) Ballena Pr.

When Stars Collide. Patricia Coughlin. (Special Edition Ser.). 1994. mass mkt. 3.50 (*0-373-09867-7*, 5-09867-8) Silhouette.

When Stars Come Out. Linda J. Sattgast. 128p. (J). (ps). 1994. 9.99 (*0-88070-641-4*, Gold & Honey) Multnomah Pubs.

When Steam Ran the Clinchfield. 2nd ed. James A. Goforth. (Illus.). 108p. 1996. pap. 14.95 (*1-57072-029-0*) Overmountain Pr.

When Stories Come to School: Telling, Writing, & Performing Stories in the Early Childhood Classroom. Patsy Cooper. (Illus.). 144p. (Orig.). 1993. pap. 12.95 (*0-915924-77-3*) Tchrs & Writers Coll.

When Stories Fell Like Shooting Stars. V. Gregory. (J). 1996. 16.00 (*0-689-80012-6*, S&S Bks Young Read) S&S Childrens.

When Strangers Cooperate: Using Social Conventions to Govern Ourselves. David W. Brown. 1995. 25.00 (*0-02-904875-3*, Free Press) Free Pr.

When Strikes Make Sense - & Why: Lessons from Third Republic French Coal Miners. Samuel Cohn. LC 93-28082. (Studies in Work & Industry). (Illus.). 254p. (C). 1993. 39.50 (*0-306-44445-3*, Plenum Pr) Plenum.

When Students Choose Content: A Guide to Increasing Motivation, Autonomy, & Achievement. Jeff Passe. LC 96-18455. (1-Off Ser.). (Illus.). 112p. 1996. 37.00 (*0-8039-6448-X*); pap. 17.00 (*0-8039-6449-8*) Corwin Pr.

When Students Have Power: Negotiating Authority in a Critical Pedagogy. Ira Shor. LC 96-15983. 224p. 1996. pap. text ed. 13.95 (*0-226-75355-7*); lib. bdg. 34.00 (*0-226-75354-9*) U Ch Pr.

When Students Have Time to Talk... Creating Contexts for Learning Language. Curtis Dudley-Marling & Dennis Searle. LC 91-12786. 147p. 1991. pap. text ed. 20.00 (*0-435-08588-3*, 08588) Heinemann.

When Summer Comes. Robert Maass. (Illus.). 32p. (J). (gr. k-3). 1996. pap. 5.95 (*0-8050-4706-9*, Owlet BYR) H Holt & Co.

When Summer's in the Meadow. Niall Williams & Christine Breen. LC 88-30265. 256p. 1990. pap. 11.00 (*0-939149-37-0*) Soho Press.

When Sun Ruled the Land: A Story from Cuba. Janet Palazzo-Craig. (First-Start Legends Ser.). (Illus.). 32p. (Orig.). (J). (gr. k-2). 1997. pap. 4.95 (*0-8167-4002-X*) Troll Communs.

***When Susie Sings.** Muriel Vallet. (Illus.). 18p. (J). (gr. 1-4). 1997. pap. 12.95 (*1-895583-83-7*) MAYA Pubs.

When Sweet Birds Sing. Robert A. Bowen. (Illus.). 1967. pap. 2.00 (*0-912462-03-5*) Foun Hist Rest.

When Symptoms Return. Dennis Daley & Loren Roth. 1992. pap. 5.95 (*1-55691-090-8*, 908) Learning Pubns.

When Talk Works: Profiles of Mediators. Deborah M. Kolb et al. LC 93-48667. (Business-Management Ser.). (Illus.). 535p. text ed. 33.95 (*1-55542-640-9*) Jossey-Bass.

***When Talk Works: Profiles of Mediators.** Deborah M. Kolb. 1997. pap. 24.95 (*0-7879-1090-2*) Jossey-Bass.

When Talking Makes Things "Worse!" Resolving Problems When Communication Fails. David Stiebel. LC 96-23674. (Illus.). 288p. 1997. 24.95 (*1-888430-42-7*) Whitehall & Nolton.

When Teachers Do Teach see Maestro Eficiente

When Teachers Face Themselves. Arthur Jersild. 169p. 1984. pap. text ed. 16.95 (*0-8077-1575-1*) Tchrs Coll.

When Teachers Lead. Cooper et al. Ed. by David L. Clark. 84p. (Orig.). (C). 1993. pap. text ed. 7.00 (*1-55996-157-0*) Univ Council Educ Admin.

When Teaching Becomes Learning: Entitlement & Provision. Eric Sotto. (Education Ser.). (Illus.). 150p. 1993. 75.00 (*0-304-32792-1*); pap. 25.00 (*0-304-32790-5*) Weidner & Sons.

When Technology Fails. Nell Y. Schlager. 575p. 1993. 59.95 (*0-8103-8908-8*, 101569) Gale.

When Telephones Reach the Village: The Role of Telecommunications in Rural Development. Heather Hudson. Ed. by Melvin J. Voigt. LC 84-18409. (Communication & Information Science Ser.). 160p. 1984. text ed. 73.25 (*0-89391-207-7*) Ablex Pub.

When Television Was Young: Primetime Canada 1952-1967. Paul Rutherford. 638p. 1990. 65.00 (*0-8020-5830-2*); pap. 29.95 (*0-8020-6647-X*) U of Toronto Pr.

When the Aardvark Parked on the Ark. Calvin Miller. LC 95-13082. 190p. (J). (gr. 3 up). 1995. pap. 9.99 (*0-8499-3699-3*) Word Pub.

***When the Air Hits Your Brain.** Frank T. Vertosick. 1997. mass mkt. 5.99 (*0-449-22713-8*, Crest) Fawcett.

When the Air Hits Your Brain: Tales of Neurosurgery. Frank T. Vertosick, Jr. LC 95-9790. 288p. 1996. 23.00 (*0-393-03894-7*) Norton.

***When the Airlines Went to War.** Robert J. Serling. 304p. 1997. 24.00 (*1-57566-246-9*, Knsington) Kensgtn Pub Corp.

When the Almond Tree Blossoms. David Aikman. 1995. mass mkt. 5.99 (*0-8499-3641-1*) Word Pub.

When the Animals Leave. Peggy Rambach. LC 86-70220. 48p. 1986. pap. 4.00 (*0-935331-00-X*) Ampersand RI.

When the Animals Left. P. L. Chestney. (Illus.). 52p. (J). (gr. 1-6). 1994. pap. 12.95 (*1-883533-00-7*) PL&R Chestney.

When the Animals Were People. Kay Sanger. 1983. 7.50 (*0-939046-32-6*) Malki Mus Pr.

When the Animals Were People: Stories Told by the Chumash Indians of California. Ed. by Kay Sanger. Tr. by Tom Sanger. (Illus.). vi, 41p. (C). 1993. reprint ed. lib. bdg. 25.00 (*0-8095-6201-4*) Borgo Pr.

When the Apricots Bloom. large type ed. Roberta Forrest. 1990. 25.99 (*0-7089-2135-3*) Ulverscroft.

When the Arabs Attack Jerusalem see World War III When the Arabs Attack Jerusalem

***When the Army Still Wore Blue.** William L. Ewers. 242p. (Orig.). 1997. mass mkt. 4.99 (*1-55237-008-9*, Pub. by Comnwlth Pub CN) Partners Pubs Grp.

When the Band Plays Dixie. Cohodas. 1997. 23.00 (*0-02-874011-4*) Free Pr.

When the Bank Says No! Creative Financing for Closely Held Businesses. Lawrence W. Tuller. 288p. 1991. 22.95 (*0-8306-3590-4*, 3590, Liberty Hall Pr) TAB Bks.

When the Barrage Lifts: A Topographical History & Commentary on the Battle of the Somme 1916. Gerald Gliddon. 496p. 1988. 150.00 (*0-947893-02-4*, Pub. by Gliddon Bks UK) St Mut.

When the Barred Owl Calls. Demetra Mihevic. 189p. (Orig.). (YA). 1995. pap. 5.00 (*0-88092-131-5*) Royal Fireworks.

When the Bell was Rung. Walter Irwin. Date not set. pap. 5.99 (*0-451-45464-2*, ROC) NAL-Dutton.

When the Big Dog Barks. Munzee Curtis. LC 96-10412. (Illus.). 24p. (J). 1997. 15.00 (*0-688-09539-9*); lib. bdg. 14.93 (*0-688-09540-2*) Greenwillow.

When the Birds Fly South. Stanton A. Coblentz. Ed. by R. Reginald & Douglas Melville. LC 77-84212. (Lost Race & Adult Fantasy Ser.). 1978. reprint ed. lib. bdg. 23.95 (*0-405-10967-9*) Ayer.

When the Black Lotus Blooms. Ed. by Elizabeth A. Saunders. (Illus.). 320p. (Orig.). 1990. pap. 12.95 (*0-934227-05-5*) Unnameable Pr.

When the Black Lotus Blooms. deluxe limited ed. Ed. by Elizabeth A. Saunders. (Illus.). 320p. (Orig.). 1990. 120.00 (*0-934227-07-1*); 65.00 (*0-934227-06-3*) Unnameable Pr.

***When the Bluebird Sings.** (Ready Readers Series II Stage 1). (Illus.). 32p. (J). (ps-1). 1996. pap. write for info. (*1-56144-947-4*, Honey Bear Bks) Modern Pub NYC.

When the Body Speaks: Psychological Meanings in Kinetic Clues. Ed. by Selma Kramer & Salman Akhtar. LC 91-45288. 224p. 1992. 30.00 (*0-87668-461-4*) Aronson.

When the Borders Bleed: The Struggle of the Kurds. Ed Kashi. LC 93-50156. 1994. 40.00 (*0-679-43337-6*) Pantheon.

When the Bottom Drops: How Any Business Can Survive & Thrive in the Coming Hard Times. A. David Silver. 240p. 1991. 18.95 (*0-914629-46-8*) Prima Pub.

When the Bottom Line Is Faithfulness: Management of Christian Service Organizations. Thomas H. Jeavons. LC 93-30292. (Philanthropic Studies). 260p. 1994. 27.50 (*0-253-33089-0*) Ind U Pr.

When the Bough Breaks. Jonathan Kellerman. 448p. 1994. mass mkt. 6.99 (*0-553-56961-9*) Bantam.

When the Bough Breaks. Jonathan Kellerman. 1986. pap. 5.99 (*0-451-16862-3*, Sig); pap. 5.99 (*0-451-17803-3*, Sig) NAL-Dutton.

When the Bough Breaks. Mercedes Lackey & Holly Lisle. (Serrated Edge Ser.). 288p. 1993. mass mkt. 5.99 (*0-671-72154-2*) Baen Bks.

When the Bough Breaks: A Helping Guide for Parents of Sexually Abused Children. Aphrodite Matsakis. LC 90-63758. 272p. (Orig.). 1991. pap. 11.95 (*1-879237-00-8*) New Harbinger.

***When the Bough Breaks: Forever after the Death of a Son or Daughter.** Judith R. Bernstein. LC 96-33993. 256p. 1997. 19.95 (*0-8362-2576-7*) Andrews & McMeel.

When the Bough Breaks: Metaphors & Meanings about Institutional Problems & Dysfunctional Organizations. E. Gene Rooney. (Illus.). 384p. (Orig.). 1995. student ed. 35.00 (*1-881596-05-2*) L E A D Cnslts.

When the Bough Breaks: Pregnancy & the Legacy of Addiction. Kira Corser & Frances P. Adler. 112p. 1993. 39.95 (*0-939165-20-1*); pap. 22.95 (*0-939165-19-8*) NewSage Press.

When the Bough Breaks: The Cost of Neglecting Our Children. Sylvia A. Hewlett. LC 91-58461. 368p. 1992. reprint ed. pap. 14.00 (*0-06-097479-6*, PL) HarpC.

When the Bough Breaks, & Other Stories. Naomi M. Mitchison. LC 71-160944. (Short Story Index Reprint Ser.). 1977. reprint ed. 20.95 (*0-8369-3923-9*) Ayer.

When the Boys Came Back: Baseball & 1946. Frederick J. Turner. LC 95-37707. (Illus.). 320p. 1996. 27.50 (*0-8050-2645-2*) H Holt & Co.

When the Brave Ones Cried. Lee Dalton. LC 86-81778. 176p. 1986. 10.98 (*0-88290-282-2*) Horizon Utah.

When the Buzzard Blows. large type ed. Ed. by Kenneth Jernigan. (Kernel Bk.: No. 7). (Illus.). 84p. (Orig.). 1994. pap. 3.00 (*0-9624122-9-5*) Natl Fed Blind.

When the Canary Stops Singing: Women's Perspectives on Transforming Business. Ed. by Pat Barrentine. LC 93-27145. (Illus.). 235p. 1994. 24.95 (*1-881052-41-9*) Berrett-Koehler.

***When the Candle Burned Its Last.** R. J. Williams. (Illus.). 19p. (Orig.). 1997. pap. 6.50 (*0-9652226-1-6*) Borderline Arts.

When the Century Was Young: A Writer's Notebook. Dee Brown. LC 93-25232. 223p. 1993. 23.00 (*0-87483-267-5*); audio 18.00 (*0-87483-273-X*) August Hse.

When the Chestnuts Bloom. large type ed. Marjorie Warby. 1989. 25.99 (*0-7089-2099-3*) Ulverscroft.

When the Church Was Young. Ernest Loosley. LC 88-63264. 92p. (Orig.). 1989. pap. 7.95 (*0-940232-32-4*) Seedsowers.

When the Church Was Young: Studies in Thessalonians. David Ewert. (Luminaire Studies: No. 4). 152p. 1993. pap. 8.95 (*0-921788-18-5*) Kindred Prods.

When the Circus Came to Town. Polly Horvath. LC 96-11591. 112p. (J). (gr. 3-7). 1996. 14.00 (*0-374-38308-1*) FS&G.

***When the City Leans Against the Sky.** Allan De Fina. LC 94-79159. (Illus.). 64p. (YA). (gr. 5 up). 1997. pap. text ed. 8.95 (*1-56397-137-2*, Wordsong) Boyds Mills Pr.

When the Clock Struck Zero: Science's Ultimate Limits. John Taylor. 211p. (Orig.). 1994. pap. 19.95 (*0-330-32525-6*, Pub. by Picador UK) Trans-Atl Phila.

When the Cloud Lifted. Bruno Hussar. 128p. (Orig.). 1989. pap. 9.95 (*1-85390-048-6*, Pub. by Veritas Publns IE) Ignatius Pr.

When the Colts Belonged to Baltimore. William Gildea. 1994. 21.95 (*0-395-62145-3*) HM.

When the Colts Belonged to Baltimore: A Father & a Son, a Team & a Time. William Gildea. (Maryland Paperback Bookshelf Ser.). (Illus.). 320p. (C). 1996. reprint ed. pap. 14.95 (*0-8018-5379-6*) Johns Hopkins.

***When the Comet Runs: Prophecies for the Millennium.** Tom Kay. 248p. (Orig.). 1997. pap. 12.95 (*1-57174-059-7*) Hampton Roads Pub Co.

When the Comforter Came: Thirty-One Daily Devotionals on the Holy Spirit. A. B. Simpson. LC 91-73585. 134p. 1991. pap. 7.99 (*0-87509-469-4*) Chr Pubns.

When the Cook Camps Out. Marilyn Meredith. (Illus.). 112p. (Orig.). 1990. pap. 7.95 (*0-929935-03-9*) Countrywomans Pr.

When the Corn Grows Tall in Texas. Archie McDonald. (Illus.). 96p. (J). (gr. 4-8). 1991. 12.95 (*0-89015-808-8*) Sunbelt Media.

***When the Creature Strikes.** Fingeroth. 1997. mass mkt. 3.99 (*0-671-01172-3*) PB.

When the Crying Stops. Harold L. Senkbeil. LC 91-67779. 200p. (Orig.). 1992. pap. 9.99 (*0-8100-0420-8*, 12N1756) Northwest Pub.

When the Crying's Done: A Journey Through Widowhood. Jeannette Kupfermann. LC 94-77109. 205p. 1995. 23.95 (*0-86051-787-X*, Robson-Parkwest) Parkwest Pubns.

When the Crying's Done: A Journey Through Widowhood. Jeannette Kupfermann. LC 94-77109. 206p. 1996. pap. 11.95 (*0-86051-904-X*, Robson-Parkwest) Parkwest Pubns.

When the Dancing Ends. Judy L. Hairfield. LC 95-83549. 163p. (Orig.). (YA). (gr. 7-12). 1996. pap. text ed. 8.95 (*0-943864-79-8*) Davenport.

When the Dancing Ends, Tchr's. Guidance Daily Lesson Plans. Judy L. Hairfield. LC 95-83549. 47p. (Orig.). 1996. spiral bd. 5.00 (*0-943864-80-1*) Davenport.

***When the Dancing Stops: The First Brett Higgins Mystery.** Therese Szymanski. LC 97-10804. (Orig.). 1997. pap. 11.95 (*1-56280-186-4*) Naiad Pr.

When the Dark Comes Dancing. Illus. by John Wallner. (J). (ps-8). 1990. 17.99 (*0-399-61288-2*, Philomel Bks) Putnam Pub Group.

***When the Dark Man Calls.** Stuart M. Kaminsky. 3.95 (*0-7867-0977-4*) Carroll & Graf.

When the Dark Man Calls. Stuart M. Kaminsky. 240p. 1993. pap. 3.95 (*0-88184-977-4*) Carroll & Graf.

***When the Devil Came Down to Dixie: Ben Butler in New Orleans.** Chester G. Hearn. LC 97-16092. (Illus.). 272p. 1997. 26.95 (*0-8071-2180-0*) La State U Pr.

When the Devil Came to Endless. Charles Boeckman. LC 95-96224. 192p. 1996. 17.95 (*0-8034-9171-9*, Avalon Bks) Bouregy.

***When the Devil Makes an Offer: How to Escape Satan's Plan to Trap You.** David B. Smith. LC 97-23175. 1997. pap. write for info. (*0-8163-1397-0*) Pacific Pr Pub Assn.

***When the Doctor Drops the Bomb.** Christopher Brookes. 104p. (Orig.). 1997. pap. 9.95 (*0-9655207-0-6*) Cutters Rig Bks.

***When the Drug War Hits Home: Healing the Family Torn Apart by Teenage Drug Abuse.** 2nd ed. Laura Stamper. LC 97-18752. 160p. 1997. pap. 11.95 (*1-57749-051-7*) Fairview Press.

When the Drumbeat Changes. Ed. by Carolyn Parker & Stephen Arnold. 293p. (Orig.). 1981. 22.00 (*0-89410-262-1*); pap. 14.00 (*0-89410-263-X*) Cornell AS&RC.

When the Drummer Falls. Spencer Kope. 191p. 1995. 17.95 (*0-9647183-0-8*) Willow Crk Pr.

When the Drummers Were Women. Layne Redmond. 1997. 21.00 (*0-517-70389-0*, Harmony) Crown Pub Group.

When the Drums Speak of Love. Shirley Boje. (Heartbeats Ser.). (YA). (gr. 7 up). 1995. pap. write for info. (*0-7910-2931-X*) Chelsea Hse.

When the Eagle Screams: America's Vulnerability to Terrorism. Stephen Bowman. LC 93-47233. 1994. 21.95 (*1-55972-228-2*, Birch Ln Pr) Carol Pub Group.

***When the Earth Explodes! Volcanos & the Environment.** Buck Dawson. (Illus.). 200p. 1997. pap. 17.95 (*1-56072-450-1*, Nova Kroshka Bks) Nova Sci Pubs.

When the Earth Nearly Died see Asteroid: Compelling Evidence of a Global Catastrophe in 9500 B. C.

When the Earth Quakes. James B. Macelwane. LC 76-29402. reprint ed. 32.50 (*0-404-15340-2*) AMS Pr.

***When the Earth Wakes.** Ani Rucki. LC 97-8187. (J). 1998. write for info. (*0-590-05951-3*) Scholastic Inc.

When the Earth Was Bare. Judith Witters. LC 93-26930. (Voyages Ser.). (Illus.). (J). 1994. 4.25 (*0-383-03785-9*) SRA McGraw.

When the Earth Was Like New: Western Apache Songs & Stories. Chesley G. Wilson et al. LC 94-41700. (Illus.). 128p. (Orig.). 1995. pap. 29.95 incl. audio (*0-937203-56-4*); pap. 29.95 incl. audio compact disk (*0-937203-57-2*) World Music Pr.

***When the Earth Was New.** Leia Stinnett. 1996. pap. text ed. 6.95 (*0-929385-91-8*) Light Tech Comns Servs.

When the Earth Was New: An Experience in Healing Our Planet. Leia A. Greene. (Little Angel Bks..). (Illus.). 20p. (J). (gr. k-9). 1991. student ed., pap. text ed. 4.95 (*1-880737-02-7*) Crystal Jrns.

When the Eiffel Tower Was New: French Visions of Progress at the Centennial of the Revolution. Miriam R. Levin. LC 88-63428. (Illus.). 128p. 1989. pap. 18.95 (*0-87023-673-3*) U of Mass Pr.

***When the Elephant Walks.** Keiko Kasza. (Illus.). 32p. (J). (ps-1). 1997. pap. 5.95 (*0-698-11430-2*, Paperstar) Putnam Pub Group.

When the Family Gathers: An International Cookbook & Calendar for Special Times. Beverly Reilman. (Illus.). 176p. 1996. pap. 16.95 (*1-56352-288-8*) Longstreet Pr Inc.

W

When the Fat Lady Sings: Opera History As It Ought to Be Taught. David W. Barber. (Illus.). 164p. (Orig.). 1990. pap. 12.95 (*0-920151-11-6*, Pub. by Sound & Vision CN) Firefly Bks Ltd.
*When the Fighting is All Over: The Memoir of a Marine Corps General's Daughter.** Katie L. Lyle. 1997. 21.95 (*1-56352-426-0*) Longstreet Pr Inc.
When the Fire Fell: The Great Welsh Revival of 1904 & Its Meaning for Revival Today. R. Maurice Smith. 160p. (Orig.). 1996. pap. 9.95 (*0-9650735-1-3*) Preparedness.
When the Fire Fell & Rent the Heavens. pap. 6.99 (*0-88019-197-X*) Schmul Pub Co.
When the Fires Burn High & the Wind Is from the North: The Pastoral Fiction of Clifford D. Simak. Robert J. Ewald. (Milford Series: Popular Writers of Today: Vol. 71). (Orig.). lib. bdg. write for info. (*1-55742-218-4*) Borgo Pr.
When the Fires Burn High & the Wind Is from the North: The Pastoral Fiction of Clifford D. Simak. Robert J. Ewald. (Milford Series: Popular Writers of Today: Vol. 71). (Orig.). pap. write for info. (*1-55742-217-6*) Borgo Pr.
When the French Were Here. Fritz Reuter. Tr. by Carl F. Bayerschmidt. 200p. 1984. 28.50 (*0-8386-3230-0*) Fairleigh Dickinson.
When the Frost Is on the Punkin. James W. Riley. (Illus.). 1993. pap. 8.95 (*0-87923-988-3*) Godine.
When the Game Was Black & White: The Illustrated History of Baseball's Negro Leagues. Bruce Chadwick. LC 92-13673. (Illus.). 192p. 1992. 29.95 (*1-55859-372-1*) Abbeville Pr.
*When the Game Was Black & White: The Illustrated History of Baseball's Negro Leagues.** Bruce Chadwick. (Illus.). 1997. 14.98 (*0-89660-091-2*) Abbeville Pr.
*When the Geese Come: The Journals of a Moravian Missionary Ella Mae Ervin Romig 1898-1905, Southwest Alaska.** Ella M. Romig & Phyllis D. Movius. LC 96-51588. 1997. pap. 20.00 (*0-912006-89-7*) U of Alaska Pr.
When the Giant Lies Down. Dick Foth & Ruth Foth. 200p. 1995. pap. 9.99 (*1-56476-388-9*, 6-3388, Victor Bks) Chariot Victor.
When the Giants Were Giants: Bill Terry & the Golden Age of New York Baseball. Peter Williams. LC 94-1019. 300p. 1994. 24.95 (*0-945575-02-5*) Algonquin Bks.
When the Goblins Came Knocking. Anna G. Hines. LC 94-19366. (Illus.). 24p. (J). (ps up). 1995. 16.00 (*0-688-13735-0*); lib. bdg. 15.93 (*0-688-13736-9*) Greenwillow.
*When the Gods Are Silent.** Jane Lindskold. 1997. mass mkt. 5.99 (*0-380-78848-9*) Avon.
When the Gods Are Silent. Mikhail Soloviev. Tr. by Harry C. Stevens from RUS. LC 74-27185. 506p. 1975. reprint ed. text ed. 89.50 (*0-8371-7891-6*, SOGS, Greenwood Pr) Greenwood.
*When the Gods Shoot.** unabridged ed. Augustine A. Amanzeh. 50p. (Orig.). 1997. pap. 12.00 (*1-890606-03-0*) A A Amanzeh.
*When the Going Gets Tough.** Richard Higgings. 144p. (Orig.). 1997. mass mkt. 4.99 (*1-55237-311-8*, Pub. by Comnwlth Pub CN) Partners Pubs Grp.
*When the Going Gets Tough: Need for Early Progress in the Uruguay Round.** Duck-Woo Nam. LC 88-25198. (Special Reports). 1988. pap. write for info. (*0-566-05781-6*, Pub. by Gower UK) Ashgate Pub Co.
*When the Going Gets Tough the Tough Lighten Up! How to Be Happy in Spite of It All.** unabridged ed. Terry Braverman. Ed. by Vicki St. George. LC 97-93424. (Illus.). 185p. (Orig.). 1997. pap. 12.95 (*0-9657395-1-1*) Mental Floss.
When the Going Gets Tough, the Tough Start Laughing. Martha Bolton. (Orig.). 1996. pap. 9.99 (*0-8024-9185-5*) Moody.
When the Going Was Good. Evelyn Waugh. LC 75-16612. (Illus.). 318p. 1976. reprint ed. text ed. 35.00 (*0-8371-8253-0*, WAWG, Greenwood Pr) Greenwood.
When the Going Was Good, Vol. 1. Evelyn Waugh. 1985. pap. 14.95 (*0-316-92647-7*) Little.
When the Government Breaks the Law: A Practical Guide for Enforcing Environmental Laws Against Federal Facilities. 72p. 1993. 15.00 (*0-317-05909-2*, PB11) Natl Attys General.
When the Grass Was Taller: Autobiography & the Experience of Childhood. Richard N. Coe. LC 84-3517. 331p. reprint ed. pap. 94.40 (*0-7837-2790-9*, 2043182) Bks Demand.
When the Great Canoes Came. Mary L. Clifford. LC 92-27913. (Illus.). (J). 1993. 12.95 (*0-88289-926-0*) Pelican.
When the Ground Fails: Planning & Engineering Response to Debris Flows. Martha Blair et al. (Program on Environment & Behavior Monograph Ser.: No. 40). 110p. (Orig.). (C). 1985. pap. 8.00 (*0-685-28114-0*) Natural Hazards.
When the Guayacans Were in Bloom. Nelson E. Bass. Tr. by Henry J. Richards from SPA. LC 87-72081. 230p. (Orig.). (C). 1987. pap. 15.00 (*0-939423-01-4*) Afro Hispanic Inst.
When the Half-Gods Go. Benjamin Laskin. LC 94-12045. 384p. 1997. pap. 14.95 (*0-9649600-0-1*) Phx Prime.
When the Hearing Gets Hard: Winning the Battle Against Hearing Impairments. Elaine Suss. 282p. 1993. 24.95 (*0-306-44505-0*, Plenum Insight) Plenum.
When the Hearing Gets Hard: Winning the Batttle Against Hearing Impairment. Elaine Suss. 288p. (Orig.). 1996. mass mkt. 5.99 (*0-553-57469-8*) Bantam.
When the Heart Beckons. Jill Gregory. 416p. 1995. mass mkt. 5.99 (*0-440-21857-8*) Dell.
When the Heart Has Healed Again: A Memoir of Tragedy & Forgiveness. Julie White. LC 87-20929. (Illus.). 104p. (Orig.). 1988. pap. 11.00 (*0-937897-87-6*) Centerpoint Pr.
When the Heart Remembers. large type ed. Constance Walker. LC 93-27243. 1994. lib. bdg. 13.95 (*0-7862-0043-X*) Thorndike Pr.
When the Heart Speaks. large type ed. Kathleen Treves. 368p. 1987. 25.99 (*0-7089-1718-6*) Ulverscroft.
When the Heart Waits. Sue M. Kidd. LC 89-45961. 1991. teacher ed., pap. 4.95 (*0-06-064577-6*) Harper SF.
When the Heart Waits: Spiritual Direction for Life's Sacred Questions. Sue M. Kidd. LC 91-58175. 240p. 1992. reprint ed. pap. 12.00 (*0-06-064587-3*) Harper SF.
*When the Heavens Are Brass: Keys to Genuine Revival.** John Kilpatrick. 168p. 1997. pap. 9.99 (*1-56043-190-3*) Destiny Image.
When the Heavens Frowned: American Autobiography. Joseph Cline. 221p. 1995. lib. bdg. 79.00 (*0-7812-8485-6*) Rprt Serv.
When the Hippos Crashed the Dance. Phil Kern et al. (Illus.). 125p. (J). (gr. 1-6). 1991. pap. 69.95 (*1-56516-008-8*) H Leonard.
When the Holy Ghost Is Come. Samuel L. Brengle. 1980. reprint ed. pap. 4.95 (*0-86544-009-3*) Salv Army Suppl South.
When the Holy Ghost Is Come. Samuel L. Brengle. 144p. 1997. reprint ed. pap. 6.99 (*0-88019-131-7*) Schmul Pub Co.
*When the Honeymoon's Over: Building a Real-Life Marriage.** Kathy C. Miller & D. Larry Miller. LC 97-10278. 1997. write for info. (*0-87788-565-6*) Shaw Pubs.
When the Iron Eagle Flies: Buddhism for the West. Ayya Khema. 208p. 1991. pap. 11.95 (*0-14-019300-6*, Arkana) Viking Penguin.
When the Italians Came to My Home Town. Thom Tammaro. (Illus.). 80p. 1995. pap. 6.95 (*0-944024-28-9*) Spoon Riv Poetry.
When the Jaguar's Ate the Moon: And Other Stories about Animals & Plants of the Americas. Maria C. Brusca. (Illus.). (J). (gr. 1-4). 1995. 16.95 (*0-8050-2797-1*) H Holt & Co.
When the Kids Come First: Enhancing Self-Esteem. James A. Beane & Richard P. Lipka. 86p. 1987. 5.00 (*1-56090-036-9*) Natl Middle Schl.
When the King Loses His Head, & Other Stories. Leonid N. Andreev. Tr. by Archibald J. Wolfe. LC 74-116927. (Short Story Index Reprint Ser.). 1977. 21.95 (*0-8369-3429-6*) Ayer.
When the King Rides By. Margaret Mahy. (Illus.). 16p. (Orig.). (J). (ps-2). 1995. 21.95 (*1-57255-003-1*); pap. 4.95 (*1-57255-002-3*) Mondo Pubng.
When the King Was Carpenter. Maria Von Trapp. LC 75-46021. 142p. 1976. 4.50 (*0-89221-018-4*) New Leaf.
When the Knead Rises: Creative Breads & More. Jackie E. Guice. (Illus.). 256p. 1992. 14.95 (*0-9634026-0-9*) Gingerbrd Pr.
When the Ku Klux Rode. Eyre Damer. LC 79-37588. (Black Heritage Library Collection). 1977. reprint ed. 23.95 (*0-8369-8964-3*) Ayer.
When the Lamp Is Shattered: Desire & Narrative in Catullus. Micaela Janan. LC 92-43064. 256p. (C). 1993. 34.95 (*0-8093-1765-6*) S Ill U Pr.
When the Land Calls. Mary E. Pourchot. LC 91-77561. (Illus.). 272p. 1992. pap. 8.95 (*0-87341-195-1*, LC01) Krause Pubns.
When the Land Calls: A Celebration of Country Living. Mary E. Pourchot. 224p. (Orig.). 1992. pap. write for info. (*0-9628635-0-5*) Krause Pubns.
When the Land Was Young: Reflections on American Archaeology. Sharman Russell. 224p. 1996. 23.00 (*0-201-40698-5*) Addison-Wesley.
When the Last Acorn Is Found. Deborah Latzke. 64p. 1993. 12.95 (*0-9643956-1-4*) Legacy of Love.
When the Latch Is Lifted. Frances J. Roberts. 1970. pap. 4.99 (*0-932814-18-2*) Kings Farspan.
When the Legends Die. Hal Borland. 224p. (YA). (gr. 6-12). 1984. mass mkt. 5.50 (*0-553-25738-2*) Bantam.
When the Legends Die. Hal Borland. Date not set. pap. 1.95 (*0-590-03172-4*) Scholastic Inc.
When the Legends Die. Barbara Reeves. Ed. by J. Friedland & R. Kessler. (Novel-Ties Ser.). 1993. student ed., pap. text ed. 15.95 (*0-88122-898-2*) Lrn Links.
When the Levee Breaks: The Patronage Crisis at the Pennsylvania Turnpike, the General Assembly & the State Supreme Court. William Keisling. LC 93-5117. 183p. 1993. 18.95 (*1-882611-00-4*); pap. 11.95 (*1-882611-01-2*) Yardbird Bks.
When the Lights Go Down. Pauline Kael. LC 79-19067. 608p. 1980. pap. 9.95 (*0-03-056842-0*) H Holt & Co.
When the Lights Go Out. Margaret R. MacDonald. (Illus.). 176p. 1988. 35.00 (*0-8242-0770-X*); pap. 20.00 (*0-8242-0823-4*) Wilson.
When the Lights Go Out, & Never Come Back On: Nuclear Terrorism in America. (International Security & Terrorism Ser.: No. 4). 192p. (Orig.). 1991. pap. 35.00 (*0-941375-05-6*) DIANE Pub.
When the Line Is Straight: Jack Oakie's Comedy in Motion Pictures. Jack Oakie & Victoria H. Oakie. LC 96-20391. (Illus.). 128p. 1997. 13.95 (*0-89407-140-8*, 1408) Strawberry Hill.
When the Lion Feeds. Wilbur Smith. 1989. mass mkt. 6.99 (*0-7493-2292-6*) Heinemann.
When the Luvenders Came to Merrick Town. June Considine. LC 89-82487. 240p. (Orig.). (YA). (gr. 8-12). 1990. pap. 6.95 (*0-685-46916-6*, Pub. by Poolbeg Pr IE) Dufour.
When the Luvenders Came to Merrick Town. June Considine. 240p. (Orig.). 1990. pap. 6.95 (*1-85371-055-5*) Dufour.
When the Machine Stopped: A Cautionary Tale from Industrial America. Max Holland. 1991. pap. text ed. 14.95 (*0-07-103287-8*) McGraw.
When the Machine Stopped: A Cautionary Tale from Industrial America. Max Holland. 355p. 1989. reprint ed. pap. 14.95 (*0-87584-244-5*) Harvard Busn.
When the Many Become One: Three Lectures. 2nd ed. Swami Ashokananda. 104p. (C). 1987. pap. 4.95 (*0-9612388-1-X*) Vedanta Soc N Cal.
When the Marching Stopped: The Politics of Civil Rights Regulatory Agencies. Hanes Walton, Jr. LC 87-7081. (SUNY Series in Afro-American Studies). 263p. 1988. text ed. 64.50 (*0-88706-687-9*); pap. text ed. 21.95 (*0-88706-688-7*) State U NY Pr.
When the Master Relents: The Neglected Short Fictions of Henry James. George Bishop. Ed. by A. Walton Litz. LC 87-25543. (Studies in Modern Literature: No. 80). 128p. reprint ed. 36.50 (*0-8357-1826-3*, 2070693) Bks Demand.
When the Meat Loaf Explodes, It's Done! Martha Bolton. 72p. (Orig.). 1993. pap. 6.99 (*0-8341-1509-3*) Beacon Hill.
When the Mind Fails: A Guide to Dealing with Incompetency. Michel Silberfeld & Arthur Fish. LC 93-94593. 184p. (C). 1994. 45.00 (*0-8020-0463-6*); pap. 14.95 (*0-8020-6780-8*) U of Toronto Pr.
When the Mind Hears. Harlan Lane. 1989. pap. 15.96 (*0-679-72023-5*) McKay.
When the Mind Hears: A History of the Deaf. Harlan Lane. LC 83-43201. 608p. 1984. 29.95 (*0-394-50878-5*) Random.
When the Mind Hears: A History of the Deaf. Harlan Lane. 1989. pap. 16.95 (*0-685-27139-0*, Vin) Random.
When the Mockingbird Sings. Ed. by Richard S. Danbury, III. 100p. (Orig.). 1986. 19.95 (*0-89754-059-X*); pap. 9.95 (*0-89754-058-1*) Dan River Pr.
When the Mongols Return. Nicola Vulpe. 64p. 1995. lib. bdg. 35.00 (*0-8095-4846-1*) Borgo Pr.
When the Mongols Return. Nicola Vulpe. 64p. pap. 12.95 (*0-88962-569-7*) Mosaic.
When the Monkeys Came Back. Kristine L. Franklin. LC 92-33684. (Illus.). 32p. (J). 1994. text ed. 14.95 (*0-689-31807-3*, Pub. by Ctrl Bur voor Schimmel NE) Macmillan.
When the Monkeys Came Back: Spanish. Franklin. (J). 1998. 4.95 (*0-689-31951-7*, Atheneum Bks Young) S&S Childrens.
When the Monster Comes Out of the Closet: Westley Allan Dodd in His Own Words. Lori Steinhorst & John Rose. 264p. (Orig.). 1994. pap. 12.95 (*1-881170-06-3*) Rose Pub OR.
When the Moon Is Full: Supernatural Stories from the Pennsylvania Mountains. Robin Moore. 128p. (J). (gr. 5-9). 1994. 15.00 (*0-679-85642-0*) Knopf Bks Yng Read.
When the Moon Peeps In. Pamela I. Phillips. (J). 1994. 7.95 (*0-533-10982-5*) Vantage.
When the Moon Shines Brightly on the House. Hans Poppel & Ilona Bodden. 24p. (J). (ps). 1985. 5.95 (*0-8120-5669-8*) Barron.
When the Moon Waxes Red: Representation, Gender & Cultural Politics. Trinh T. Minh-Ha. (Illus.). 240p. (gr. 13). 1991. pap. 16.95 (*0-415-90431-5*, A5631, Routledge NY) Routledge.
When the Moon Waxes Red: Representation, Gender & Cultural Politics. Trinh T. Minh-Ha. (Illus.). 240p. (C). (gr. 13). 1991. text ed. 59.95 (*0-415-90430-7*, A5627, Routledge NY) Routledge.
When the Morning Came. Piet Prins. Tr. by Gertrude Deboer from DUT. (Struggle for Freedom Ser.: No. 1). (Illus.). 158p. (Orig.). (J). 1989. pap. 8.90 (*0-921100-12-4*) Inhtce Pubns.
When the Morning Comes. large type ed. Christine Flynn. (Silhouette Ser.). 1996. 19.95 (*0-373-59666-9*) Thorndike Pr.
When the Mountain Sings. John MacLean. LC 91-26720. 212p. (J). (gr. 5-9). 1992. 14.95 (*0-395-59917-2*) HM.
When the Movies Were Young. Linda A. Griffith. 1972. 19.95 (*0-405-09119-2*, 1724) Ayer.
When the Music Is Over. Elaine Hutchison. 1993. 10.95 (*0-533-10646-X*) Vantage.
When the Music Stopped. large type ed. Elisabeth Ogilvie. LC 89-77193. 560p. 1990. lib. bdg. 18.95 (*0-89621-966-6*) Thorndike Pr.
When the Music Stopped: The Big Band Era Remembered. Bernie Woods. LC 94-25364. 272p. 1994. 24.95 (*1-56980-022-7*) Barricade Bks.
When the Music Stopped I Kept on Dancing: A Story of Courage, Hope & the Magnificence of the Human Spirit. Angela Riggs. LC 94-78434. 184p. 1995. pap. 12.95 (*1-885221-19-3*) BookPartners.
When the Music Stops. Jonnie Stinson. 534p. (Orig.). 1994. pap. 6.95 (*0-9639047-1-X*) J Stinson.
When the Music's Over: My Journey into Schizophrenia. Ross D. Burke. Ed. by Richard Gates & Robin Hammond. LC 95-44253. 256p. 1996. reprint ed. pap. 10.95 (*0-452-27584-9*, Plume) NAL-Dutton.
When the Nation Was in Need: Blacks in the Women's Army Corps During World War II. Martha S. Putney. LC 92-24084. (Illus.). 245p. 1992. 35.00 (*0-8108-2531-7*) Scarecrow.
When the New Age Gets Old: Looking for a Greater Spirituality. Vishal Mangalwadi. LC 92-36926. 287p. (Orig.). 1993. pap. 12.99 (*0-8308-1770-0*, 1770) InterVarsity.
When the North Was Red: Aboriginal Education in Soviet Siberia. Dennis A. Bartels & Alice L. Bartels. (McGill-Queen's Native & Northern Ser.: No. 11). 126p. 1995. 39.95 (*0-7735-1336-1*, LA1391, Pub. by McGill CN) U of Toronto Pr.
When the Nursing Home Is the Only Choice. Donna Du Bois. 76p. 1991. pap. text ed. 5.00 (*1-877735-17-5*, 130) M&H Pub Co TX.
When the Odds Are Against Us. Dave Jackson et al. LC 94-69842. (Recovering Hope in Your Marriage Ser.). 128p. 1995. pap. 4.95 (*0-89221-287-X*) New Leaf.
When the Odds Were Even: The Vosges Mountains Campaign, October 1944-January 1945. Keith E. Bonn. LC 94-5062. 320p. 1996. pap. text ed. 16.95 (*0-89141-602-1*) Presidio Pr.
*When the Old Left Was Young: Student Radicals & America's First Mass Student Movement, 1929-1941.** Robert Cohen. 456p. 1997. reprint ed. pap. 24.95 (*0-19-511136-2*) OUP.
When the One You Love Wants to Leave: Guidance & Comfort for Surviving Marital Crisis. 2nd ed. Donald R. Harvey. LC 89-8427. 224p. (Orig.). (YA). (gr. 10). 1993. pap. 9.99 (*0-8010-4385-9*, Ravens Ridge) Baker Bks.
When the Other Guy's Price Is Lower: You Can Still Make the Sale. James M. Bleech & David G. Mutchler. 288p. 1995. pap. 14.95 (*0-8119-0811-9*) LIFETIME.
When "The Other Woman" is His Mother: Book I: Boys and Incest Victims, & Male Multiple Personality Disorder. Faithe Brodie. LC 90-70218. 181p. 1992. pap. 13.95 (*0-9626009-0-3*) Winged Eagle Pr.
When the Owl Cries, Indians Die. J. W. Rivers. LC 85-47624. 112p. 1986. 14.95 (*0-8453-4509-5*) VA Ctr Creative Arts.
When the Parrot Boy Sings. John Champagne. 1990. pap. 8.95 (*0-8216-2009-6*, Univ Books) Carol Pub Group.
When the Pentagon Was for Sale: Inside America's Biggest Defense Scandal. Andy Pasztor. (Illus.). 416p. 1995. 25.00 (*0-684-19516-X*) S&S Trade.
When the People Are Away. Ann Jungman. LC 92-73988. (Illus.). 32p. (J). (ps-3). 1993. 12.95 (*1-56397-202-6*) Boyds Mills Pr.
When the Phone Rang. Harry Mazer. 192p. (YA). (gr. 7-9). 1986. pap. 4.50 (*0-590-44773-4*) Scholastic Inc.
When the Phone Rings, My Bed Shakes: The Memoirs of a Deaf Doctor. Philip Zazove. LC 93-6384. 312p. 1993. 22.95 (*1-56368-024-6*) Gallaudet Univ Pr.
When the Pines Grew Tall. Guy Croom. 1991. 12.95 (*1-878096-10-9*) Best E TX Pubs.
When the Plow Cuts. Katherine Andraski. 64p. (Orig.). 1988. pap. 5.95 (*0-939395-11-8*) Thorntree Pr.
When the Poor Boys Dance. G. F. Borden. 272p. 1997. mass mkt. 6.50 (*0-446-60407-0*) Warner Bks.
When the Pressure Is on see Vivendo Sob Pressao
When the Railroad Was King. Frank N. Elliot. 73p. write for info. (*0-935719-06-7*) MI Hist Mag.
When the Rain Came. Eleanor Watkins. (J). 1996. 4.99 (*1-85792-210-7*, Pub. by Christian Focus UK) Spring Arbor Dist.
When the Rainbow Goddess Wept. Cecilia M. Brainard. 224p. 1995. pap. 10.95 (*0-452-27471-0*, Plume) NAL-Dutton.
When the Rainbow Touches Down. Tryntje Van Ness Seymour. LC 87-82906. (Illus.). 396p. 1989. pap. 50.00 (*0-295-96858-3*) U of Wash Pr.
When the Rainbow Touches Down: The Articles & Stories Behind the Apache, Navajo, Rio Grande Pueblo & Hopi Paintings in the William & Leslie Van Ness Denman Collection. Tryntje Van Ness Seymour. LC 87-82906. (Illus.). 377p. (Orig.). 1988. pap. 50.00 (*0-934351-01-5*) Heard Mus.
When the Rains Came: And Other Legends of the Salish People. Illus. by D. Johnnie Seletze. 128p. 1992. 9.95 (*0-920501-87-7*) Orca Bk Pubs.
When the Ripe Pears Fell: The Battle of Richmond, Kentucky. Dean W. Lambert. LC 95-14688. (Illus.). 325p. 1996. lib. bdg. 32.50 (*0-9615162-3-2*) Madison Cty KY Hist.
When the River Rises: Flood Control on the Boise River. Susan M. Stacy. LC 92-31277. (Special Publications: No. 27). 209p. 1993. 15.00 (*1-877943-08-8*) Natural Hazards.
When the Road Ends. Jean Thesman. 192p. (YA). 1993. pap. 3.99 (*0-380-72011-6*, Camelot) Avon.
When the Road Ends. Jean Thesman. 192p. (J). (gr. 5-9). 1992. 14.95 (*0-395-59507-X*) HM.
When the Roof Caves in. (Living Testimony Ser.: No. 2). 1985. pap. 4.99 (*9971-972-31-X*) OMF Bks.
When the Root Children Wake Up. Helen D. Fish. LC 91-22577. (Illus.). 24p. (J). 1991. reprint ed. 12.95 (*0-671-75216-2*, Green Tiger S&S) S&S Childrens.
When the Root Children Wake Up. Illus. by Mark A. Weatherby. LC 93-32737. (J). reprint ed. 14.95 (*0-590-42517-X*) Scholastic Inc.
*When the Roses Start Stinking, It's Time to Throw Them Out.** Venus Andrecht. Ed. by Summer Andrecht. LC 96-72083. 200p. 1997. write for info. (*0-941903-22-2*) Ransom Hill.
*When the Sacred Ginmill Closes.** Lawrence Block. 1997. mass mkt. 5.99 (*0-380-72825-7*) Avon.
*When the Sacred Ginmill Closes.** Lawrence Block. 1997. mass mkt. 5.99 (*0-614-27706-X*) Avon.
When the Sacred Marriage Ends. Tom Meehan. LC 95-94377. 271p. (Orig.). 1995. pap. 14.40 (*0-9646166-0-2*) Dollar Spec Pubns.
*When the Sandman Meets the Reaper: 12 Tales of Magic & Terror.** Jeff Dennis. (Illus.). 260p. (Orig.). 1996. pap. 13.00 (*0-9655522-0-9*) Wordcraft Res.
When the Season Is Dry: A Promise & a Wilderness. J. Timothy Allen. 160p. (Orig.). 1995. pap. 12.95 (*1-57312-010-3*) Smyth & Helwys.
When the Shooting Stops... The Cutting Begins: A Film Editor's Story. Ralph Rosenblum & Robert Karen. (Illus.). 304p. 1986. pap. 12.95 (*0-306-80272-4*) Da Capo.
When the Sleeper Wakes. Intro. by John Lawton. 352p. 1994. pap. 7.95 (*0-460-87499-3*, Everyman's Classic Lib) C E Tuttle.

W

An Asterisk (*) at the beginning of an entry indicates that the title is appearing in BIP for the first time.

*When the Smoke Clears, Families Are Baptized! Illus. by Kent Jeppson. 66p. 1997. pap. 9.95 (1-890828-01-7) Camden Ct.

When the Sons of Heaven Meet the Daughters of the Earth. Fernanda Eberstadt. LC 96-38579. 1997. 25.00 (0-679-44514-5) Knopf.

When the South Was Southern. Michael A. Grissom. LC 94-5239. (Illus.). 400p. 1994. 22.95 (1-56554-092-1) Pelican.

When the Soviet Union Entered World Politics. Jon Jacobson. LC 94-4959. 1994. 40.00 (0-520-08332-6); pap. 18.00 (0-520-08976-6) U CA Pr.

When the Spider Danced: Notes from an African Village. rev. ed. Alexander Alland, Jr. (Illus.). 269p. (C). 1990. reprint ed. pap. text ed. 11.50 (0-88133-553-3) Waveland Pr.

*When the Spirit Comes: An Overview of Acts. Jack Hayford et al. (Bible Book-a-Month Ser.: Vol. 2). (Illus.). 71p. 1996. pap. 3.95 (0-916847-19-5) Living Way.

When the Spirit Comes with Power: Signs & Wonders Among God's People. John White. LC 88-6841. 247p. (Orig.). 1988. pap. 11.99 (0-8308-1222-9, 1222) InterVarsity.

When the Spirit Is Willing. Margaret Chittenden. (Superromance Ser.). 1993. mass mkt. 3.50 (0-373-70575-1, 1-70575-5) Harlequin Bks.

When the Spirit Moves You: The Autobiography of Tammy Faye Bakker. Tammy F. Bakker & David Rudnitsky. 1996. pap. 22.00 (0-614-15433-2, Villard Bks) Random.

When the Spirit Says Sing: A Read-along, Sing-along, Coloring Book. Sandy Paton & Caroline Paton. (Illus.). 40p. (Orig.). (J). (gr. k-8). 1989. pap. 13.98 (0-938702-06-8) Folk-Legacy.

When the Spirit Says Sing! The Role of Freedom in the Civil Rights Movement. Kerran L. Sanger. LC 95-40853. (Studies in American Popular History & Culture). 951207p. 1996. text ed. 50.00 (0-8153-2164-3) Garland.

When the Spirits Come Back. Janet Dallett. pap. 16.00 (0-919123-32-5, Pub. by Inner City CN) BookWorld Dist.

*When the Spirit's Fire Swept Korea. Jonathan Goforth. 32p. pap. 1.99 (0-934998-65-5, B319) Bethel Pub.

When the Splendor Falls. Laurie McBain. 1985. mass mkt. 4.95 (0-380-89826-8) Avon.

When the Squeeze Is On: Growing Through Pressure. Martha Thatcher. 96p. (Orig.). 1987. pap. 6.00 (0-89109-182-3) NavPress.

When the Stakes Are Too High: A Spouse's Struggle to Live with a Compulsive Gambler. Loraine Allison. LC 91-75429. pap. 6.95 (0-87029-240-4) Abbey.

When the Stars Sing: A Good Night Story. Mariah T. Deans. (Kuumba Ser.). (Illus.). 28p. (J). (gr. k-2). 1997. 12.95 (0-937913-09-X) W Stery.

When the State Kills. 280p. (ARA & SPA.). 1989. 10.00 (0-939994-45-3) Amnesty Intl USA.

When the Stones Fly Up. Dale Zieroth. 95p. (Orig.). 1985. pap. 8.95 (0-88784-145-7, Pub. by Hse of Anansi Pr CN) Genl Dist Srvs.

When the Summer Ends. D. T. Gilbert. 182p. (C). 1989. text ed. 40.00 (1-872795-92-7, Pub. by Pentland Pr UK) St Mut.

When the Sun Moves Northward. Mabel Collins. LC 86-40402. 195p. (Orig.). 1987. pap. 5.95 (0-8356-0614-7, Quest) Theos Pub Hse.

When the Sun Rose. Barbara H. Berger. LC 86-2484. (Illus.). 32p. (J). (ps-2). 1986. 14.95 (0-399-21360-0, Philomel Bks) Putnam Pub Group.

*When the Sun Rose. Barbara H. Berger. (Illus.). 32p. (J). (ps-3). 1997. pap. 5.95 (0-698-11434-5, Paperstar) Putnam Pub Group.

When the Sun Set. Jake Behringer. 156p. (Orig.). 1994. pap. text ed. 14.95 (0-930401-74-3) Artex Pub.

When the Teddy Bears Came. Martin Waddell. LC 94-10580. (Illus.). 32p. (J). (ps). 1995. 15.99 (1-56402-529-2) Candlewick Pr.

When the Tempter Comes: Victory over Habits. Randall W. Needham. 60p. (Orig.). 1994. pap. 4.95 (0-9636067-0-0) Grace TX.

When the Theater Turns to Itself: The Aesthetic Metaphor in Shakespeare. Sidney Homan. LC 80-65453. 240p. 1981. 34.50 (0-8387-5009-5) Bucknell U Pr.

When the Third World Matters: Latin America & United States Grand Strategy. Michael C. Desch. LC 92-36818. 224p. 1993. text ed. 38.50 (0-8018-4552-1) Johns Hopkins.

When the Thornbush Blooms. I. Howat. 5.99 (1-85792-009-0, Pub. by Christian Focus UK) Spring Arbor Dist.

When the Tide Is Low. Sheila Cole. LC 84-10023. (Illus.). 32p. (J). (ps-1). 1985. 16.00 (0-688-04066-7); lib. bdg. 15.93 (0-688-04067-5) Lothrop.

When the Tide Is Right. William H. Davis. (Illus.). 64p. 1993. 10.00 (0-8233-0488-4) Golden Quill.

When the Time Comes. Maurice Blanchot. Tr. by Lydia Davis from FRE. LC 84-12373. Orig. Title: Au Moment Voulu. 80p. (Orig.). 1984. 12.95 (0-930794-96-6); pap. 7.95 (0-930794-95-8) Station Hill Pr.

When the Time Was Fulfilled. Eberhard Arnold et al. LC 65-17599. 256p. 1965. 6.00 (0-87486-104-7) Plough.

When the Tom-Tom Beats: Selected Poems. Jacques Roumain. Ed. by Joann Fungaroli. LC 94-72476. 96p. (Orig.). pap. 11.95 (0-9632363-8-5) Azul Edits.

When the Tree Flowered: The Story of Eagle Voice, a Sioux Indian. John G. Neihardt. LC 90-19669. xxii, 248p. 1991. reprint ed. pap. 10.95 (0-8032-8363-6, Bison Books) U of Nebr Pr.

When the Tripods Came. John Christopher. LC 90-1436. (Prequel to the Tripods Trilogy Ser.). 160p. (YA). (gr. 7 up). 1990. reprint ed. pap. 3.95 (0-02-042575-9) Macmillan.

When the Trumpet Sounds: Today's Foremost Authorities Speak Out on End-Time Controversy. Ed. by Thomas Ice & Timothy Demy. (Orig.). 1995. pap. 16.99 (1-56507-313-4) Harvest Hse.

When the Tulips Bloom. Susan E. Miller. Ed. by Jereng Burdge-Rezvan. LC 93-60937. (Illus.). 152p. (Orig.). 1993. pap. text ed. 12.95 (1-880254-08-5) Vista.

When the Tunnels Meet: Contemporary Romanian Poetry. Ed. by John Fairleigh. (Illus.). 116p. 9600. pap. 16.95 (1-85224-305-8, Pub. by Bloodaxe Bks UK) Dufour.

When the Turtles Sing & Other Unusual Tales. Don Marquis. LC 70-130065. (Short Story Index Reprint Ser.). 1977. reprint ed. 19.95 (0-8369-3664-7) Ayer.

When the TV Broke Level 1, Blue. Harriet Ziefert. LC 88-62153. (Easy-to-Read Ser.). (Illus.). (J). (ps-2). 1993. pap. 3.50 (0-14-036540-0, Puffin) Puffin Bks.

*When the Twin Meet: The Rise of Western Medicine in Japan. John Z. Bowers. LC 80-22356. (Henry E. Sigerist Supplements to the Bulletin of the History of Medicine Ser.: No. 5). 187p. 1980. reprint ed. pap. 53.30 (0-608-03642-0, 2064468) Bks Demand.

When the Unthinkable Happens: A Father's Journey Through Grief. Thomas G. Crouthamel. LC 94-24127. 1995. 19.95 (0-940701-44-8) Keystone Pr.

When the Victim Is a Child. 2nd ed. Debra Whitcomb. (Illus.). 176p. (C). 1994. pap. text ed. 30.00 (0-7881-0594-9) DIANE Pub.

When the Vow Breaks: A Survival & Recovery Guide for Christians Facing Divorce. Joseph W. Kniskern. LC 93-13955. 1993. pap. 13.99 (0-8054-6084-5, 4260-84) Broadman.

***When the Vows Break: Living Through Separation & Divorce, Vol. 1. Maria Costa & Rob Grogan. Ed. by Rob Grogan. LC 96-92843. (Illus.). 176p. (Orig.). 1996. pap. 16.95 (0-9654990-0-6) M Costa & Assocs.**

Truly LIVE Through Separation & Divorce? New Book says, "Yes you can!" & Tells How! Thinking about divorce? In the midst of one now? Been there, done that & wonder what happened? If you say "yes" to any of these questions, then WHEN THE VOWS BREAK: LIVING THROUGH SEPARATION & DIVORCE by Maria Costa with Rob Grogan, is a book that can help you. This new self-help book, authored by a prominent Fredericksburg woman with the help of a local writer, aims to inform, support & give practical, common sense advice to anyone going through the pain of broken marriage vows, all in a non-judgmental way. Author Costa, who has been through the rigors of separation & divorce, holds your hand, slaps your wrist & sends you skipping down the road to recovery. According to Costa, who is the current President of the Board of the Fredericksburg Area Women's Resource Center, as well as a motivational speaker & corporate trainer, "Most people go through divorce just hoping to survive." Costa shows you how to "Live through it, come out whole, happy & ready to move forward with your life!" WHEN THE VOWS BREAK combines her personal story with extensive research & interviews with divorced men & women. Its pages are filled with emotion, a sense of humor, useful information, guidance & resources. Chapters include such topics as: How to Handle Finances (or the lack of), Collecting Child Support, Counseling & New Relationships, Coping & Stress, Children as Pawns in Divorce, Decision-Making, & much more. Co-writer Grogan (Best of the 'Burg, NewComers Guide, The Journal newspapers), works his craft on every page, helping men & women smile through their tears, as they learn how to handle every aspect of this difficult process. WHEN THE VOWS BREAK is published by Maria Costa & Associates. The cover price is $16.95. To order now, call toll free, at 1-800-879-4214. Major credit cards accepted.

Publisher Provided Annotation.

When the Wall Came Down: Reactions to German Unification. Ed. by Harold James & Marla Stone. 464p. (C). (gr. 13). 1992. pap. 18.95 (0-415-90590-7, A7221, Routledge NY) Routledge.

When the Walls Are Closing In. M. Scott Miles. 132p. (Orig.). 1993. pap. 6.50 (1-56476-104-5, 6-3104, Victor Bks) Chariot Victor.

When the War Was Over. Elizabeth Becker. (Illus.). 502p. 1986. 19.95 (0-671-41787-8) S&S Trade.

When the War Was Over: The Failure of Self-Reconstruction in the South, 1865-1867. Dan T. Carter. LC 84-21315. 285p. 1985. pap. text ed. 14.95 (0-8071-1204-6) La State U Pr.

When the Water Closes over My Head. Donna J. Napoli. LC 93-14486. (Illus.). 60p. (J). (gr. 2-5). 1994. pap. 13.99 (0-525-45083-1) Dutton Child Bks.

When the Water Closes over My Head. Donna J. Napoli. (Illus.). 144p. (J). (gr. 3-7). 1996. pap. 3.99 (0-14-037996-7) Puffin Bks.

When the Water Smokes: Tides & Seasons on a Wooden Boat. Bob Simpson. 198p. 1990. pap. 8.95 (0-945575-44-0) Algonquin Bks.

When the Waters Recede: Rescue & Recovery During the Great Flood. Dan Guillory. (Illus.). 150p. (Orig.). 1996. pap. 14.95 (0-935153-16-0) Stormline Pr.

*When the Well Runs Dry. Broadman & Holman Publishers Staff. 1995. mass mkt. 6.99 (0-8054-7892-2) Broadman.

When the Well Runs Dry. large type ed. Thomas H. Green. (Large Print Inspirational Ser.). 288p. 1986. pap. 15.95 (0-8027-2545-7) Walker & Co.

When the Well Runs Dry: Prayer Beyond the Beginnings. Thomas H. Green. LC 79-52404. 176p. (Orig.). 1979. pap. 5.95 (0-87793-182-8) Ave Maria.

*When the Well Runs Dry Again: Preschool Teaching Centers. Broadman Staff. 1996. pap. text ed. 6.99 (0-8054-0020-6) Broadman.

When the Whale Came. 2nd ed. Charles Jones. (Illus.). 40p. pap. 7.95 (0-936646-01-2) Studio Pr AZ.

When the Whalers Were up North: Inuit Memories from the Eastern Arctic. Dorothy H. Eber. (Illus.). 1989. 45.00 (0-7735-0702-7, Pub. by McGill CN) U of Toronto Pr.

When the Whalers Were up North: Inuit Memories from the Eastern Arctic. Dorothy H. Eber. LC 95-42214. (Illus.). 208p. (Orig.). 1996. pap. 19.95 (0-8061-2852-6) U of Okla Pr.

*When the Wheels Fly Off. unabridged ed. Ernest Solivan. 130p. 1995. 24.95 (0-9653920-1-5); pap. 19.95 (0-9653920-0-7) E Solivan.

When the Whip Comes Down: A Novel about De Sade. Jeremy Reed. 136p. 9300. 30.00 (0-7206-0857-0, Pub. by P Owen Ltd UK); pap. 18.95 (0-7206-0858-9, Pub. by P Owen Ltd UK) Dufour.

When the Whippoorwill Calls. Candice F. Ransom. LC 94-41567. (Illus.). 32p. (J). (gr. 2-5). 1995. 16.00 (0-688-12729-0, Tambourine Bks); lib. bdg. 15.93 (0-688-12730-4, Tambourine Bks) Morrow.

When the Wicked Rise: American Public Opinion & the Manchurian Crisis. Justus D. Doenecke. LC 82-45619. (Illus.). 192p. 1984. 29.50 (0-8387-5048-6) Bucknell U Pr.

When the Wind Bears Go Dancing. Phoebe Stone. LC 95-52930. (J). 1997. 15.95 (0-316-81701-5) Little.

*When the Wind Blows. Booth. 1984. pap. text ed. 21.25 (0-03-921404-4) HR&W Schl Div.

When the Wind Blows. Judith Marshall. 1992. mass mkt. 4.50 (1-55817-613-6, Pinncle Kensgtn) Kensgtn Pub Corp.

When the Wind Blows. John Saul. 384p. (Orig.). 1990. mass mkt. 6.99 (0-440-19490-3) Dell.

*When the Wind Blows. Kyle Shiver. 1997. mass mkt. 5.99 (1-55197-318-9, Pub. by Comnwlth Pub CN) Partners Pubs Grp.

When the Wind Is Blue. Jennifer L. Cohen. (Illus.). 24p. 1995. 15.00 (0-9650549-0-X) Barking at the Moon.

When the Wind Is in the South & Other Stories by O. E. Rolvaag. Solveig Zempel. LC 84-72484. (Illus.). 110p. 1984. 7.95 (0-931170-25-7) Ctr Western Studies.

When the Wind Stops. Ed. by Laura Sargent. LC 92-74753. (Illus.). 70p. (Orig.). 1992. pap. 8.95 (1-878149-19-9) Counterpoint Pub.

When the Wind Stops. Charlotte Zolotow. LC 94-14477. (Trophy Picture Bk.). (Illus.). 32p. (J). (ps-3). 1997. pap. 4.95 (0-06-443472-9, Trophy) HarpC Child Bks.

When the Wind Stops. rev. ed. Charlotte Zolotow. LC 94-14477. (Illus.). 32p. (J). (ps-3). 1995. 14.95 (0-06-025425-4); lib. bdg. 14.89 (0-06-025426-2) HarpC Child Bks.

When the Wind Was a River: Aleut Evacuation in World War II. Dean Kohlhoff. 248p. 1995. 24.95 (0-295-97403-6) U of Wash Pr.

When the Wine Runs Out of Your Marriage. Mack Timberlake. 64p. (Orig.). 1990. pap. 4.99 (0-89274-763-3, HH763) Harrison Hse.

When the Wolves Return. Ron Hirschi. LC 94-16307. (J). 1995. pap. 14.99 (0-525-65144-6) Dutton Child Bks.

When the Womb Is Empty. Ray Larson & Rebecca Larson. 200p. 1988. pap. 8.99 (0-88368-198-6) Whitaker Hse.

*When the Women You Love Has Breast Cancer. Larry Eiler. 1996. pap. text ed. 9.95 (0-9641757-0-3) Queen Bee.

*When the Word Comes Alive: An Overview of John. Jack Hayford et al. (Bible Book-a-Month Ser.: Vol. 3). 71p. 1997. pap. 3.95 (0-916847-20-9) Living Way.

When the Word Is Given... A Report on Elijah Muhammad, Malcolm X, & the Black Muslim World. Louis E. Lomax. LC 78-14002. (Illus.). 192p. 1979. reprint ed. text ed. 45.00 (0-313-21002-0, LOWW, Greenwood Pr) Greenwood.

When the Work's All Done This Fall: Voices of Early Canada the Opening of the Land. Dave McIntosh. (Illus.). 320p. 1989. 29.95 (0-7737-2323-4) Genl Dist Srvs.

*When the World Began. Standard Publishing Staff. (Collect-a-Bible Story Bks.). 26p. (J). 1996. pap. 1.99 (0-7847-0469-4, 21509) Standard Pub.

When the World Ended: The Diary of Emma LeConte. Emma LeConte. Ed. by Earl S. Miers. LC 87-5937. xxxii, 124p. 1987. reprint ed. pap. 8.95 (0-8032-8151-X, Bison Books) U of Nebr Pr.

When the World Ended, How Hummingbird Got Fire, How People Were Made: Rumsien Ohlone Stories. Linda Yamane. (Illus.). 48p. (Orig.). (J). 1995. pap. 10.00 (0-9625175-1-8) Oyate.

When the World Shook. H. Rider Haggard. 25.95 (0-8488-0101-6) Amereon Ltd.

When the World Shook: Account of the Great Adventure of Bastin, Bickley, & Arbuthnot. H. Rider Haggard. LC 74-15980. (Science Fiction Ser.). (Illus.). 424p. 1975. reprint ed. 30.95 (0-405-06296-6) Ayer.

When the World Was Flat: Memoirs of Old Baltimore. Mildred T. Hicks. LC 82-82037. (Illus.). 163p. (Orig.). 1985. pap. 6.95 (0-935680-13-6) Kentucke Imprints.

When the World Was New. Linda J. Sattgast. 80p. (J). 1996. 13.99 (0-88070-915-4, Gold & Honey) Multnomah Pubs.

When the World Was New. Jurg Schubiger. (Illus.). 72p. (J). (gr. 2-5). 1996. 12.95 (1-55037-500-8, Pub. by Annick CN) Firefly Bks Ltd.

When the World Was Steady. Clare Messud. 270p. 1995. 19.95 (0-9645611-0-7) Granta USA.

When the World Was Steady. Claire Messud. 270p. 1996. reprint ed. pap. 11.95 (0-9645611-3-1) Granta USA.

When the World Was Young: Creation & Pourquois Tale. Margaret Mayo. (J). 1996. 19.95 (0-689-80867-4, S&S Bks Young Read) S&S Childrens.

*When the World's Foundation Shifts. T. H. Wallace. 61p. (Orig.). 1997. mass mkt. 5.99 (1-55237-013-5, Pub. by Comnwlth Pub CN) Partners Pubs Grp.

When the Wrong Thing Is Right: How to Overcome Conventional Wisdom, Popular Opinion. Sylvia Bigelsen. 1994. pap. 9.95 (0-942361-99-7) MasterMedia Pub.

When the Yankees Came. George B. West. Ed. by Parke Rouse, Jr. (Civil War & Reconstruction on the Virginia Peninsula Ser.). 1978. 7.00 (0-87517-049-8) Dietz.

When the Yankees Came: Chaos & Conflict in the Occupied South, 1861-1865. Stephen V. Ash. LC 94-49525. (Civil War America Ser.). 1995. 29.95 (0-8078-2223-X) U of NC Pr.

When the Zebras Came for Lunch. Barbara Van Curen. (Illus.). 64p. (J). (ps-2). 1989. pap. text ed. 5.95 (0-922510-01-6) Lucky Bks.

When Therapy Isn't Enough: The Healing Power of Prayer & Psychology. Samuel E. Menahem. Ed. by Ryan Elliott & Joe Hauser. 250p. (Orig.). 1995. pap. 14.95 (0-9615140-4-3) Relaxed Bks.

When There Are No Secrets. C. G. Hanzlicek. LC 85-71691. (Poetry Ser.). 1986. 20.95 (0-88748-052-7); pap. 11.95 (0-88748-053-5) Carnegie-Mellon.

When There Are No Words. Charlie Walton. 1996. 29.00 (0-8095-5920-X) Borgo Pr.

When There Are No Words: Finding Your Way to Cope with Loss & Grief. Charlie Walton. LC 95-38853. 96p. 1996. pap. 9.95 (0-934793-57-3) Pathfinder CA.

When There is Hope. Jane Goodger. 360p. 1996. mass mkt. 5.99 (0-312-95860-9) St Martin.

*When There's a Will There's a Way: Refocusing Child Care Practice: A Guide for Team Managers. Sheryl Burton. 114p. 1997. pap. 16.00 (1-900990-07-5, Pub. by Natl Childrens Bur UK) Paul & Co Pubs.

When There's No Mechanic: One Hundred Twenty-Seven Important Things to Know about Your Car. 2nd rev. ed. Jim Gaston. LC 91-71419. (Illus.). 277p. 1994. pap. 12.95 (1-879699-23-0) CoNation Pubns.

When There's No More Room in Heck the Darned Will Walk the Earth. Chris Trian. 24p. (Orig.). 1990. pap. 3.00 (0-929730-27-5) Zeitgeist Pr.

When There's No Place Like Home: Options for Children Living Apart from Their Natural Families. Ed. by Jan B. Blacher. LC 93-49692. 384p. 1994. 29.00 (1-55766-145-6) P H Brookes.

When There's Work to Do. Nick Butterworth. (Illus.). (J). (ps). 1995. pap. 4.95 (0-316-11906-7) Little.

When They All Go Home. Robert V. Dodd. 1989. pap. text ed. 2.50 (0-687-45042-X) Abingdon.

*When They Call My Name. 1988. pap. 1.20 (0-8341-9108-3) Lillenas.

When They Came to Take My Father: Voices of the Holocaust. Ed. by Leora Kahn & Rachel Hager. LC 95-17852. (Illus.). 180p. 1996. 35.00 (1-55970-305-9) Arcade Pub Inc.

*When They Came to Take My Father: Voices of the Holocaust. Ed. by Leora Kahn & Rachel Hager. LC 95-17852. (Illus.). 176p. 1997. pap. 19.95 (1-55970-404-7) Arcade Pub Inc.

When They Invited Me to Fellowship I Thought They Meant a Cruise. Mark Littleton. LC 92-81349. 166p. (Orig.). (YA). 1992. pap. 8.99 (0-87509-496-1) Chr Pubns.

When They Read What We Write: The Politics of Ethnography. Ed. by Caroline B. Brettell. LC 92-43386. 216p. 1993. text ed. 55.00 (0-89789-325-5, H325, Bergin & Garvey) Greenwood.

When They Read What We Write: The Politics of Ethnography. Ed. by Caroline B. Brettell. LC 92-43386. 208p. 1996. pap. text ed. 18.95 (0-89789-492-8, Bergin & Garvey) Greenwood.

When They Say You Are Going to Die. Carl Asbury & Linda Asbury. 112p. 1995. pap. 6.99 (0-89274-784-6, HH-784) Harrison Hse.

When They Think They Have Nothing to Write About: Cottonwood Composition Book. Cheryl M. Thurston. 62p. (Orig.). (YA). (gr. 5-12). 1986. pap. text ed. 14.95 (1-877673-00-5, C) Cottonwood Pr.

When They Took Away the Man in the Moon. large type ed. Kate Lehrer. LC 93-30904. 1993. lib. bdg. 17.95 (0-7862-0042-1) Thorndike Pr.

*When Things Fall Apart: Heart Advice for Difficult Times. Pema Chodron. 144p. 1997. 18.00 (1-57062-160-8) Shambhala Pubns.

When Things Get Back to Normal. Constance Pierce. LC 86-27870. 256p. 1987. 15.95 (0-932511-00-7); pap. 7.95 (0-932511-01-5) Fiction Coll.

When Things Get Worse: The Problem of Negative Effects in Psychotherapy. Hans H. Strupp et al. LC 94-33810. 366p. 1994. pap. text ed. 35.00 (1-56821-372-7) Aronson.

When Things Were Doing. C. A. Steere. LC 77-154464. (Utopian Literature Ser.). 1976. reprint ed. 23.95 (0-405-03546-2) Ayer.

W

When This Box Is Full. Patricia Lillie. LC 92-28743. (Illus.). 24p. (J). 1993. 14.00 (*0-688-12016-4*); lib. bdg. 13.93 (*0-688-12017-2*) Greenwillow.

When This Box is Full. Patricia Lillie. 1997. pap. 4.99 (*0-14-055831-4*) Viking Penguin.

When This Cruel War Is Over: The Civil War Home Front. Duane Damon. LC 95-11740. (J). 1996. lib. bdg. 19.95 (*0-8225-1731-0*, Lerner Publctns) Lerner Group.

When This Cruel War Is Over: The Civil War Letters of Charles Harvey Brewster. Charles H. Brewster. Ed. by David W. Blight. LC 91-38861. (Illus.). 376p. (C). 1992. lib. bdg. 37.50 (*0-87023-773-X*) U of Mass Pr.

When Thou Walkest Thru the Waters. 2nd rev. ed. Josephine Fitzgerald. Ed. by Nita Scoggan. LC 90-60867. 128p. 1992. pap. 5.95 (*0-910487-24-3*) Royalty Pub.

When Thought Is Young: Reflections on Teaching & the Poetry of the Child. Richard Lewis. LC 91-61262. (Illus.). 80p. 1992. pap. 7.95 (*0-89823-137-X*) New Rivers Pr.

When Thunders Spoke. Virginia D. Sneve. LC 93-10953. (Illus.). 95p. (J). (gr. 5 up). 1993. pap. 7.95 (*0-8032-9220-1*, Bison Books) U of Nebr Pr.

When Time Began. Zecharia Sitchin. (Earth Chronicles Bks.: Bk. 5). 416p. (Orig.). 1993. mass mkt. 6.99 (*0-380-77071-7*) Avon.

When Time Began: The First New Age. Zecharia Sitchin. (Earth Chronicles Ser.: Bk. 5). (Illus.). 416p. 1994. reprint ed. 22.95 (*1-879181-16-9*) Bear & Co.

When Time Breaks Down: The Three-Dimensional Dynamics of Electorchemical Waves & Cardiac Arrhythmias. Arthur T. Winfree. (Illus.). 340p. 1987. pap. text ed. 35.00 (*0-691-02402-2*) Princeton U Pr.

When Time Shall Be No More: Prophecy Belief in Modern American Culture. Paul Boyer. (Studies in Cultural History). (Illus.). 468p. 1992. text ed. 35.00 (*0-674-95128-X*) HUP.

When Time Shall Be No More: Prophecy Belief in Modern American Culture. Paul Boyer. (Studies in Cultural History). 468p. (C). 1994. pap. text ed. 14.95 (*0-674-95129-8*) HUP.

When Time Was Born. James T. Farrell. LC 66-16296. (Illus.). 64p. 1966. 7.50 (*0-912292-04-0*) Smith.

When Time Was Born. deluxe limited ed. James T. Farrell. LC 66-16296. (Illus.). 64p. 1966. 75.00 (*0-912292-05-9*) Smith.

When Titans Clashed: How the Red Army Stopped Hitler. David M. Glantz & Jonathan M. House. LC 95-24588. (Modern War Studies). (Illus.). 448p. (C). 1995. 29.95 (*0-7006-0717-X*) U Pr of KS.

When to Buy Stocks, Bonds, & Gold see Beating the Market: How to Win the Wall Street Game

When to Count by Race: Affirmative Action, Quotas & Equal Opportunity. Lawrence H. Fuchs. LC 86-71979. 32p. (Orig.). 1986. pap. 3.50 (*0-87495-082-1*) Am Jewish Comm.

When to Refuse Treatment: A Practical Guide for Dying in Peace. Joseph F. Bentivegna. (Illus.). 190p. (Orig.). (C). 1992. 13.95 (*0-9626001-1-3*) Michelle Pub.

When to Say Help. Matthew V. Smith. (Illus.). 18p. (J). (gr. k-3). 1992. pap. 12.95 (*1-895583-33-0*) MAYA Pubs.

When to Say Yes & Make More Friends. Sharon Scott. 118p. (Orig.). (J). (gr. 4-10). 1988. pap. text ed. 7.95 (*0-87425-066-8*) HRD Press.

When To Screen In Obstetrics-Gynecology. Wildschut. 1996. pap. text ed. 42.50 (*0-7020-1874-0*) HarBrace.

When to Sell for the 90's: Inside Strategies for Stock-Market Profits. Justin Mamis. LC 94-22970. (Illus.). 335p. (C). 1994. pap. 20.00 (*0-87034-116-2*) Fraser Pub Co.

When Tolerance Is No Virtue: PC, Multiculturalism & the Future of Truth & Justice. S. D. Gaede. LC 93-41903. 120p. (Orig.). 1994. pap. 10.99 (*0-8308-1699-2*, 1699) InterVarsity.

***When Tolerance Was on Trial: The Life & Times of Hanserd Krollys: Baptist Hero of the Seventeenth Century.** Muriel James. (Illus.). 224p. (Orig.). 1997. pap. 12.95 (*1-57736-048-6*) Providence Hse.

When Tomorrow Comes: A Novel. Jennie L. Hansen. LC 94-29731. 1994. pap. 9.95 (*1-55503-725-9*) Covenant Comms.

When Toys Come Alive: Narratives of Animation, Metamorphosis, & Development. Lois R. Kuznets. LC 93-40849. (Illus.). 352p. 1994. 35.00 (*0-300-05645-1*) Yale U Pr.

When Trees Become the Enemy - Wenn Baume die Gegner Sind: Military Use of Defoliants - Militarische Verwendung von Entlaubungsmitteln. Burkhard Luber. (Anstoesse Zur Friedensarbeit Ser.: Vol. 2). 136p. 1990. 11.57 (*0-685-66491-0*) G Olms Pubs.

When Trees Become the Enemy (Wenn Baeume Die Gegner Sind), Military Use of Defoliants. Burkhard Luber. 128p. (ENG & GER.). 1990. pap. text ed. 13.50 (*3-487-09372-3*) G Olms Pubs.

***When Trouble Comes.** H. C. Chiles. LC 97-8992. 80p. 1997. reprint ed. 11.95 (*1-57736-038-9*) Providence Hse.

When Trouble Comes: Sermons for the Sundays after Pentecost (Last Third), Cycle B, First Lesson Texts. Zan W. Holmes. LC 96-20273. 1996. pap. 5.95 (*0-7880-0785-8*) CSS OH.

When True Night Falls. C. S. Friedman. (Coldfire Trilogy Ser.: Bk. II). 624p. (Orig.). 1993. 22.00 (*0-88677-569-8*) DAW Bks.

When True Night Falls. C. S. Friedman. (Coldfire Trilogy Ser.: Bk. II). 624p. (Orig.). 1994. mass mkt. 6.99 (*0-88677-615-5*) DAW Bks.

***When True Simplicity Is Gained.** Martin Marty. 1997. pap. text ed. 15.00 (*0-8028-4237-2*) Eerdmans.

When Trust Breaks Down: Alliance Norms & World Politics. Charles W. Kegley, Jr. & Gregory A. Raymond. Ed. by Donald J. Puchala. (Studies in International Relations). 356p. 1989. pap. text ed. 21.95 (*0-87249-688-0*) U of SC Pr.

When Trust Breaks Down: Alliance Norms & World Politics. Charles W. Kegley, Jr. & Gregory A. Raymond. Ed. by Donald J. Puchala. (Studies in International Relations). 356p. 1990. text ed. 39.95 (*0-87249-644-9*) U of SC Pr.

When Truth Is Known. Ed. by Ken Morrice. 72p. 1986. pap. text ed. 5.75 (*0-08-032451-7*, R140, K150, Pergamon Pr) Elsevier.

When Truth Was Treason: German Youth Against Hitler: the Story of the Helmuth Hubener Group. Ed. by Blair R. Holmes & Alan F. Keele. Tr. & Compiled by Alan F. Keele. LC 95-3567. 1995. pap. write for info. (*0-252-06498-4*) U of Ill Pr.

When Truth Was Treason: German Youth Against Hitler: the Story of the Helmuth Hubener Group. Ed. by Blair R. Holmes & Alan F. Keele. Tr. & Compiled by Alan F. Keele. LC 95-3567. 496p. 1995. 34.95 (*0-252-02201-7*) U of Ill Pr.

When Turtles Come to Town. Cary B. Ziter. LC 88-37843. (First Bks.). (Illus.). 64p. (J). (gr. 3-5). 1989. lib. bdg. 21.00 (*0-531-10691-8*) Watts.

When Tutor Meets Student. 2nd ed. Ed. by Martha Maxwell. 226p. (C). 1993. text ed. 32.50 (*0-472-09532-3*); pap. text ed. 16.95 (*0-472-06532-7*) U of Mich Pr.

When Two Saints Meet. Bill Hunger. Ed. by Jill Ripley. (Illus.). 100p. (Orig.). (YA). (gr. 6-12). pap. 9.95 (*0-9625782-0-7*) Two Saints Pub.

When Vegetables Go Bad. Don Gilmor & Gay. 32p. 1994. 14.95 (*0-385-25451-2*) Doubleday.

When Vegetables Go Bad. Don Gilmor. 32p. 1996. pap. 6.95 (*0-385-25554-3*) Doubleday.

When Victims Marry: Building a Stronger Marriage by Breaking Destructive Cycles. Don Frank & Jan Frank. LC 89-26984. 208p. (Orig.). 1990. pap. 10.99 (*0-8407-4442-0*) Nelson.

***When Violence Begins At Home: A Comprehensive Guide to Understanding & Ending Domestic Abuse.** Karen Wilson. 384p. 1997. 29.95 (*0-89793-228-5*); pap. 19.95 (*0-89793-227-7*) Hunter Hse.

When Violence Erupts: A Survival Guide for Emergency Responders. Krebs et al. (Illus.). 256p. (gr. 13). 1990. pap. text ed. 26.00 (*0-8016-6195-1*) Mosby Yr Bk.

***When Wallflowers Die.** Sandra W. Prowell. 1997. mass mkt. 5.99 (*0-553-56970-8*, Crimeline) Bantam.

When Wallflowers Die: A Phoebe Siegel Mystery. Sandra W. Prowell. 336p. 1996. 22.95 (*0-8027-3254-2*) Walker & Co.

When Walls Are High. Elizabeth V. Hamilton. LC 72-93195. (Illus.). 1973. 10.00 (*0-937684-09-0*) Tradd St Pr.

When Walls Come Tumbling Down: Experiencing God's Power to Break Through Barriers. Deborah P. Brunt. Ed. by Susan Hansen. 163p. (Orig.). 1994. pap. text ed. 8.95 (*1-56309-093-7*, New Hope) Womans Mission Union.

When War Becomes a Crime: The Case of My Lai. rev. ed. Jerold M. Starr & Christopher W. Wilkens. (Lessons of the Vietnam War Ser.). (Illus.). 32p. (C). 1991. pap. text ed. 5.00 (*0-945919-06-9*) Ctr Social Studies.

When War Is Unjust: Being Honest in Just-War Thinking. rev. ed. John H. Yoder. LC 96-527. 125p. (Orig.). 1996. pap. 14.00 (*1-57075-070-X*) Orbis Bks.

When Wars Were Won. Hugh Aaron. Ed. by Barbara Feller-Roth. LC 95-69538. 280p. (Orig.). 1995. pap. text ed. 16.00 (*1-882521-02-1*) Stones Pt Pr.

***When Was the Last Time You Felt Healthy?** Marilu Henner. 224p. Date not set. 24.00 (*0-06-039216-9*, ReganBooks) HarpC.

When Waves Sprout Birds. Peter Jensen. (Illus.). 68p. (Orig.). 1985. pap. 7.95 (*0-9615387-0-8*) Walking Bird OR.

When We Are Free. 3rd ed. Lawrence W. Reed & Dale M. Haywood. 403p. 17.50 (*0-87359-054-6*) Northwood Univ.

When We Belonged to Spain. Susan M. Gregory. Ed. by John D. Short. (Illus.). 80p. 1989. 85.00 (*0-933861-08-7*) H Berliner.

When We Can't Talk Anymore. Steve Wilke et al. 144p. 1992. mass mkt. 3.99 (*0-8423-7987-8*) Tyndale.

When We Dead Awake see Ghosts & Other Plays

When We Dead Awaken. Henrik Ibsen. (Plays for Performance Ser.). 72p. 1992. pap. 7.95 (*0-929587-90-1*, Elephant Paperbacks) I R Dee.

When We Dead Awaken. Henrik Ibsen. (Plays for Performance Ser.). 72p. 1992. text ed. 15.95 (*0-929587-91-X*) I R Dee.

When We Dead Awaken see Ibsen: Plays Four

When We Deal with Children: Selected Writings. Fritz Redl. 1972. pap. 16.95 (*0-02-925880-4*, Free Press) Free Pr.

When We Die - A Unique, Authentic Account. Geoffrey A. Farthing. 120p. 1994. pap. 8.50 (*0-913004-88-X*) Point Loma Pub.

When We Don't Remember: A Book about Discovering Incest. Lyda W. Hersloff. LC 93-34351. 112p. 1994. pap. 9.95 (*0-942963-42-3*) Distinctive Pub.

When We Don't Understand. John Legg. 1992. pap. 6.99 (*0-85234-291-8*) Presby & Reformed.

When We Fight All the Time. Dave Jackson et al. LC 94-69841. (Recovering Hope in Your Marriage Ser.). 128p. 1995. pap. 4.95 (*0-89221-286-1*) New Leaf.

When We Gather: A Book of Prayers for Worship, Year B. James G. Kirk. LC 83-14221. (Illus.). 144p. 1984. pap. 10.00 (*0-664-24553-6*, Geneva Pr) Westminster John Knox.

When We Gather: A Book of Prayers for Worship, Year C. James G. Kirk. LC 83-14221. (Illus.). 142p. 1985. pap. 10.00 (*0-664-24652-4*, Geneva Pr) Westminster John Knox.

When We Go Shopping. Nick Butterworth. (J). (ps). 1995. pap. 4.95 (*0-316-11900-8*) Little.

When We Grow Up. Bahiyyih Nakhjavani. 120p. 1979. 11.50 (*0-85398-085-3*); pap. 6.00 (*0-85398-086-1*) G Ronald Pub.

When We Married Gary. Anna G. Hines. LC 95-1627. (Illus.). 24p. (J). 1996. 15.00 (*0-688-14276-1*) Greenwillow.

When We Married Gary. Anna G. Hines. LC 95-1627. (Illus.). 24p. (J). 1999. lib. bdg. write for info. (*0-688-14277-X*) Greenwillow.

When We Play Together. Nick Butterworth. (J). (ps). 1995. pap. 4.95 (*0-316-11901-6*) Little.

When We Practice to Deceive. Gloria Mallette. 224p. 1995. mass mkt. 4.95 (*0-87067-865-5*) Holloway.

***When We Pray: A Prayer Journal for Pastors & Worship Leaders, Year C.** Ed. by Lavon Bayler & Bob Bayler. 120p. (Orig.). 1997. pap. 16.95 (*0-8298-1159-1*) Pilgrim OH.

When We Pray: A Prayer Journal for Pastors & Worship Leaders, Year A. Lavon Bayler & Bob Bayler. LC 94-39950. 136p. (Orig.). 1995. pap. 16.95 (*0-8298-1103-6*) Pilgrim OH.

When We Pray: A Prayer Journal for Pastors & Worship Leaders, Year B. Lavon Bayler & Bob Bayler. LC 94-39950. 144p. (Orig.). 1995. pap. 16.95 (*0-8298-1028-5*) Pilgrim OH.

When We Pray for Other. Carrol J. Shewmake. LC 95-19378. 1995. 7.99 (*0-8280-0933-3*) Review & Herald.

When We Ride the School Bus. Muriel Vallet. (Illus.). 17p. (J). (gr. k-3). 1994. pap. 8.95 (*1-895583-68-3*) MAYA Pubs.

***When We Say, "Our Father"** Ralph B. Johnson. LC 97-65929. 64p. (Orig.). 1997. pap. 9.95 (*1-57736-037-0*) Providence Hse.

When We Start Having Fun. Audrey E. Holland. (Illus.). 13p. (J). (gr. k-3). 1992. pap. 10.95 (*1-895583-12-8*) MAYA Pubs.

When We Talk about God...Let's Be Honest. R. Kirby Godsey. 224p. 1996. 19.95 (*1-57312-028-6*) Smyth & Helwys.

When We Went First Class: A Recollection of Good Times. Ellen Williamson. LC 90-4825. (Iowa Heritage Collection). 262p. (Orig.). 1990. reprint ed. pap. 10.95 (*0-8138-1083-3*) Iowa St U Pr.

When We Went to the Mountains. Hap Gilliland et al. 36p. (CHY, CRO, ENG, NAV & SPA.). (J). (gr. 1-9). 1991. pap. 5.95 (*0-89992-103-5*) Coun India Ed.

When We Went to the Zoo. Jan Ormerod. (Illus.). (J). (ps-3). 1991. lib. bdg. 13.88 (*0-688-09879-7*) Lothrop.

When We Were Colored. Clifton L. Taulbert. LC 95-4994. 160p. 1995. pap. 9.95 (*0-14-024477-8*, Penguin Bks) Viking Penguin.

When We Were Colored: A Poetic Look at How It Was Before We Overcame. Big Mama. LC 85-63502. 88p. (Orig.). (C). 1986. pap. 8.95 (*0-88100-052-3*) Cultral Alliance Foundation.

***When We Were God: The Folk Revival.** Robert S. Cantwell. 1997. pap. text ed. 15.95 (*0-674-95133-6*) HUP.

When We Were Good: The Folk Revival. Robert S. Cantwell. LC 95-20954. (Illus.). 416p. 1996. 24.95 (*0-674-95132-8*) HUP.

***When We Were Ten.** Judy Gelles. (Artists' Bks.). (Illus.). 40p. (Orig.). 1997. pap. 15.00 (*0-89822-120-X*) Visual Studies.

When We Were Very Young. A. A. Milne. (Illus.). 112p. (J). (ps up). 1988. pap. 10.99 (*0-525-44445-9*) Dutton Child Bks.

When We Were Very Young. A. A. Milne. (Illus.). 112p. (J). 1992. pap. 3.99 (*0-14-036123-5*, Puffin) Puffin Bks.

When We Were Very Young. deluxe ed. A. A. Milne. (Illus.). 112p. (J). (ps-6). 1992. pap. 20.00 (*0-525-44961-2*) Dutton Child Bks.

When We Were Very Young see Treasury of Winnie-the-Pooh

When We Were Young. Eddy Memorial Geriatric Ctr Residents Staff. (Illus.). 36p. (Orig.). (J). (gr. 1-4). 1994. pap. 7.00 (*0-9643410-0-X*) J A Eddy.

***When We Were Young: A Baby-Boomer Yearbook.** Rita L. Kleinfelder. 760p. 8.98 (*0-7651-0009-6*) Smithmark.

***When We Were Young & Other Poems.** Patricia S. Spicer. 102p. 1996. pap. 8.50 (*0-9619118-2-4*) Wooded Hill Pr.

***When Well Runs Dry Again: Four & Five Year Olds.** Broadman & Holman Publishing Staff. 1997. pap. text ed. 6.99 (*0-8054-7890-6*) Broadman.

When Were You Born. Cheiro. 122p. 1996. pap. 10.00 (*0-89540-233-5*, SB-233, Sun Bks) Sun Pub.

When Whales Exhale & Other Poems. Constance Levy. (J). 1996. 15.00 (*0-689-80946-8*, S&S Bks Young Read) S&S Childrens.

When, Where, Why & How It Happened: History's Most Dramatic Events & How They Changed the World. Reader's Digest Editors. (Illus.). 448p. 1996. 35.00 (*0-276-42105-1*, Pub. by RD Assn UK) RD Assn.

When Will I, Dainty Dinosaur? (Illus.). (J). (ps-2). 1991. pap. 5.10 (*0-8136-5723-7*); lib. bdg. 7.95 (*0-8136-5223-5*) Modern Curr.

When Will I Read? Miriam Cohen. LC 76-28320. (Illus.). 32p. (J). (ps-3). 1977. lib. bdg. 16.93 (*0-688-84073-6*) Greenwillow.

When Will I Read? Welcome to First Grade! Miriam Cohen. 32p. (J). 1996. pap. 4.99 (*0-440-41158-0*) Dell.

When Will I Stop Hurting? Dealing with a Recent Death. June C. Kolf. 62p. (Orig.). 1990. pap. 5.99 (*0-8010-5487-7*) Baker Bks.

When Will It Snow? Bruce Hiscock. LC 94-9385. (Illus.). (J). (ps-1). 1995. text ed. 15.00 (*0-689-31937-1*, Atheneum S&S) S&S Trade.

When Will Summer Come? Art Rollini. LC 90-70904. (Illus.). 21p. (J). (ps-6). 1991. pap. 5.95 (*1-55523-354-6*) Winston-Derek.

When Will This Cruel War Be Over? The Civil War Diary of Emma Simpson, Gordonsville, Virginia, 1864. Barry Denenberg. (Dear America Ser.: Vol. 1). 160p. (J). (gr. 4-9). 1996. 9.95 (*0-590-22862-5*) Scholastic Inc.

When Will We Laugh Again? Living & Dealing with Anorexia Nervosa & Bulimia. Ed. by Barbara P. Kinoy & Estelle B. Miller. LC 83-26230. 1984. pap. text ed. 16.00 (*0-231-05639-7*) Col U Pr.

When Will Ye Be Wise? Stephen Neill et al. Ed. by C. A. Kilmister. 208p. (Orig.). 1984. reprint ed. pap. 6.95 (*0-685-09580-0*) St Thomas.

When Will You Marry? Your Romantic Destiny Through Astrology. Rose Murray. LC 95-2101. 224p. 1995. pap. 12.95 (*1-56718-479-0*) Llewellyn Pubns.

When Will You Rage? Stewart Wieck & White Wolf Staff. 400p. 1994. pap. 4.99 (*1-56504-087-2*, 11002) White Wolf.

***When Willard Met Babe Ruth.** Hall. (J). 1997. write for info. (*0-15-201445-4*) HarBrace.

When Willard Met Babe Ruth. Donald Hall. LC 94-30798. (Illus.). 41p. (J). (gr. 3-5). 1996. 16.00 (*0-15-200273-1*) HarBrace.

When William Came. Saki. 18.95 (*0-8488-0845-2*) Amereon Ltd.

When Winter Comes. Robert Maass. (Illus.). 32p. (J). (gr. k-3). 1996. pap. 5.95 (*0-8050-4926-6*, B Martin BYR) H Holt & Co.

When Winter Comes. Pearl Neuman. (Real Readers Ser.: Level Blue). (Illus.). 32p. (J). (gr. 1-4). 1989. lib. bdg. 21.40 (*0-8172-3519-1*) Raintree Steck-V.

When Winter Comes. Pearl Neuman. (Real Readers Ser.: Level Blue). (Illus.). 32p. (J). (gr. 1-4). 1989. pap. 4.95 (*0-8114-6723-6*) Raintree Steck-V.

When Winter Comes to Main Street. Grant M. Overton. LC 72-37798. (Essay Index Reprint Ser.). 1977. reprint ed. 26.95 (*0-8369-2616-1*) Ayer.

When Wish Replaces Thought: Why So Much of What You Believe Is False. Steven Goldberg. 216p. 1992. 28.95 (*0-87975-711-6*) Prometheus Bks.

When Wolves Cry. Chris N. Africa. 270p. (Orig.). 1996. mass mkt. 4.99 (*1-55197-076-7*, Pub. by Comnwlth Pub CN) Partners Pubs Grp.

When Wolves Return. Ron Hirschi. 1998. pap. 4.99 (*0-14-054972-2*) Viking Penguin.

***When Women Call the Shots.** Seger. 1997. pap. 12.95 (*0-8050-5505-3*) H Holt & Co.

When Women Call the Shots: The Developing Power & Influence of Women in Television & Film. Linda Seger. LC 96-15016. (Illus.). 320p. 1996. 25.00 (*0-8050-3891-4*) H Holt & Co.

When Women Choose to Be Single. Rita Robinson. (Orig.). 1992. pap. 9.95 (*0-87877-170-0*) Newcastle Pub.

When Women Dive: A Female's Guide to Both Diving & Snorkeling. Erin O'Neill & Ella J. Morgan. 1992. pap. 12.95 (*0-922769-11-7*) Watersport Pub.

When Women Kill. Coramae R. Mann. LC 95-15374. (SUNY Series in Violence). 215p. 1996. text ed. 59.50 (*0-7914-2811-7*); pap. text ed. 19.95 (*0-7914-2812-5*) State U NY Pr.

When Women Played Hardball. Susan E. Johnson. LC 93-23645. (Illus.). 300p. (Orig.). 1994. pap. 14.95 (*1-878067-43-5*) Seal Pr WA.

When Women Rebel: The Rise of Popular Feminism in Peru. Carol Andreas. LC 85-27244. 356p. (C). 1986. pap. 12.95 (*1-55652-127-8*) L Hill Bks.

When Women Stop Hating Their Bodies: Freeing Yourself from Food & Weight Problems. Jane R. Hirschmann & Carol Munter. 1997. pap. 12.00 (*0-449-91058-X*) Fawcett.

When Women Were Priests: Women's Leadership in the Early Church & the Scandal of Their Subordination in the Rise of Christianity. Karen J. Torjesen. LC 91-58916. 288p. 1995. pap. 12.00 (*0-06-068661-8*) Harper SF.

When Women Work Together: Using Our Strengths to Overcome Our Challenges. Carolyn Duff & Barbara Cohen. 300p. (Orig.). 1993. lib. bdg. 35.00 (*0-8095-5876-9*) Borgo Pr.

When Women Work Together: Using Our Strengths to Overcome Our Challenges. Carolyn Duff & Barbara Cohen. 300p. (Orig.). 1993. pap. 12.95 (*0-943233-53-4*) Conari Press.

***When Words Are Not Enough: The Women's Prescription for Depression & Anxiety.** Valerie D. Raskin. LC 96-38081. 336p. 1997. pap. 16.00 (*0-553-06713-3*) Broadway BDD.

When Words Collide. 2nd ed. Kessler. (Mass Communication Ser.). 1988. pap. 8.50 (*0-534-08575-X*) Wadsworth Pub.

When Words Collide. 4th ed. Kessler. (Mass Communication Ser.). 1996. suppl. ed., pap. 13.95 (*0-534-25741-0*) Wadsworth Pub.

When Words Collide: A Media Writer's Guide to Grammar & Style. 3rd ed. Lauren Kessler & Duncan McDonald. 242p. (C). 1992. pap. 19.50 (*0-534-17028-5*) Wadsworth Pub.

When Words Collide: A Media Writer's Guide to Grammar & Style. 4th ed. Lauren Kessler & Duncan McDonald. LC 95-8439. 221p. 1996. pap. 27.95 (*0-534-25740-2*) Wadsworth Pub.

When Words Fail: God & the World of Beauty. David Shearlock. 183p. (Orig.). 1996. pap. 21.00 (*1-85311-131-7*, Pub. by Canterbury Press Norwich UK) Morehouse Pub.

W

An Asterisk (*) at the beginning of an entry indicates that the title is appearing in BIP for the first time.

*__When Words Hurt.__ Mary L. Heldmann. 1997. pap. 11.00 (0-345-41932-4) Ballantine.

When Words Hurt: How to Keep Criticism from Undermining Your Self-Esteem. Mary L. Heldmann. 240p. 1990. mass mkt. 4.99 (0-345-35893-7) Ballantine.

When Words Lose Their Meaning: Constitutions & Reconstitutions of Language, Character & Community. James B. White. LC 83-9191. xvi, 398p. 1985. pap. text ed. 17.95 (0-226-89502-5) U Ch Pr.

When Words Matter Most. Robyn F. Spizman. 128p. 1996. 14.00 (0-517-70406-4, Crown) Crown Pub Group.

*__When Work Disappears.__ William J. Wilson. 1997. pap. 13.00 (0-679-72417-6, Vin) Random.

When Work Disappears: The World of the New Urban Poor. William J. Wilson. 322p. 1996. 26.00 (0-394-57935-6) Random.

*__When Work Disappears: The World of the New Urban Poor.__ William J. Wilson. 322p. Date not set. 26.00 (0-614-21929-9) Knopf.

*__When Work Doesn't Work Anymore.__ Elizabeth McKenna. LC 96-38071. 1997. mass mkt. 23.95 (0-385-31795-6) Doubleday.

When Work Is Not Enough. Sarri. 1994. 19.18 (0-02-929330-8) S&S Trade.

When Workers Call the Shots: Can They Achieve Retirement Security? Ed. by Dallas L. Salisbury. 1995. write for info. (0-86643-084-9) Empl Benefit Res Inst.

When Workers Fight: The Politics of Industrial Relations in the Progressive Era, 1898-1916. Bruno Ramirez. LC 77-83895. (Contributions in Labor History Ser.: No. 2). 241p. 1978. text ed. 55.00 (0-8371-9826-7, RAW/, Greenwood Pr) Greenwood.

When Workers Organize: New York City in the Progressive Era. Melvyn Dubofsky. LC 68-19669. 240p. 1968. 30.00 (0-87023-042-5) U of Mass Pr.

When World Views Collide: A Study in Imagination & Evolution. John J. Pierce. LC 88-7708. (Contributions to the Study of Science Fiction & Fantasy Ser.). 255p. 1989. text ed. 55.00 (0-313-25457-5, PWH, Greenwood Pr) Greenwood.

When Worlds Collide: Communication Between the Sexes. Tim Downs & Kent Kramer. (Life Skills Ser.). (Illus.). 4p. (C). 1994. teacher ed., ring bd. 1.25 (1-885702-19-1, 742-010t); student ed., ring bd. 3.25 (1-885702-18-3, 742-010s) WSN Pr.

When Worlds Collide: The Bellagio Papers. Ed. by T. L. Markey & John A. Greppin. xii, 478p. 1989. pap. 65.00 (0-89720-090-X) Karoma.

When Wounds Won't Heal. George E. Vandeman. (Outreach Ser.). 48p. 1985. pap. 1.49 (0-8163-0632-X) Pacific Pr Pub Assn.

When Writers Read. Jane Hansen. LC 86-29556. 242p. (Orig.). 1987. pap. 22.95 (0-435-08438-0, 08438) Heinemann.

When Writers Write. 2nd ed. Kathleen MacDonald. (Illus.). 320p. (C). 1987. pap. text ed. 43.00 (0-13-956509-4) P-H.

When Writing Teachers Teach Literature: Bringing Writing to Reading. Ed. by Art Young & Toby Fulwiler. LC 95-18517. 338p. 1995. text ed. 32.00 (0-86709-363-3, 0363) Boynton Cook Pubs.

When Ye Fast. Joy Haney. 1991. pap. write for info. (1-880969-10-6) Schl Prophet.

When Ye Give. Joy Haney. 1992. pap. write for info. (1-880969-01-7) Schl Prophet.

When Ye Pray. Joy Haney. 1992. pap. write for info. (1-880969-05-X) Schl Prophet.

When You & I Were Young Whitefish. 2nd ed. Dorothy M. Johnson. LC 97-7548. 200p. 1997. reprint ed. pap. 10.95 (0-917298-43-8) MT Hist Soc.

When You & Your Mother Can't be Friends: Resolving the Most Complicated Relationship Of....... Victoria Secunda. 432p. 1991. pap. 12.95 (0-385-30423-4, Delta) Dell.

*__When You Are at a Loss for Words.__ Daryl W. Lewis. (Illus.). 166p. 1997. 17.95 (0-89896-429-6, Am Intl Bk) Larksdale.

When You Are Baptized. John A. Braun. (Stepping Stones Ser.). 40p. (Orig.). 1992. pap. 1.95 (0-8100-0454-2, 12N2009) Northwest Pub.

When You Are Confirmed. (Stepping Stones Ser.). 32p. (Orig.). 1992. pap. 1.95 (0-8100-0457-7, 12N2004) Northwest Pub.

When You Are Facing Change: Resources for Living. J. Bill Ratliff. 132p. (Orig.). 1989. pap. 10.00 (0-664-25048-3) Westminster John Knox.

*__When You Are Facing Surgery.__ pap. 2.95 (0-687-61193-8) Abingdon.

When You Are Facing Surgery. Ron DelBene et al. (Times of Change, Times of Challenge Ser.). 31p. (Orig.). 1991. pap. 2.95 (0-8358-0639-1) Upper Room Bks.

*__When You Are Getting Married.__ pap. 2.95 (0-687-61191-1) Abingdon.

When You Are Getting Married. Ron DelBene et al. (Times of Change, Times of Challenge Ser.). 32p. (Orig.). 1991. pap. 2.95 (0-8358-0637-5) Upper Room Bks.

*__When You Are Living.__ Delbene. pap. 2.95 (0-687-61187-3) Abingdon.

When You Are Living with an Illness That Is Not Your Own. Ron DelBene et al. (Times of Change, Times of Challenge Ser.). 32p. 1992. pap. 2.95 (0-8358-0653-7) Upper Room Bks.

*__When You Are Terminally Ill.__ Dodd. pap. 2.95 (0-687-45044-6) Abingdon.

When You Are the Partner of a Rape or Incest Survivor: A Workbook for You. Robert B. Levine. 104p. pap. 14.95 (0-89390-329-9) Resource Pubns.

When You Ask Why. Daniel Johnson. LC 92-80703. 80p. (Orig.). 1992. pap. 5.95 (0-89221-220-9) New Leaf.

*__When You Became She.__ Imre Oravecz. Tr. by Bruce Berlind from HUN. Date not set. write for info. (0-614-24578-8) Xenos Riverside.

When You Became She. Imre Oravecz. Tr. by Bruce Berlind. LC 93-6265. xii, 113p. 1994. pap. 13.00 (1-879378-09-4) Xenos Riverside.

When You Become an Adult. Jason M. Nelson. (Stepping Stones Ser.). 32p. (Orig.). 1992. pap. 1.95 (0-8100-0460-7, 12N2007) Northwest Pub.

When You Buy or Sell a Company. rev. ed. Paul B. Baron. 396p. 1986. ring bd. 85.00 (0-936936-50-9) Ctr Busn Info.

When You Call My Name. Sharon Sala. (Intimate Moments Ser.). 1996. mass mkt. 3.75 (0-373-07687-8, 1-07687-6) Silhouette.

When You Can Walk on Water, Take the Boat. John Harricharan. 1991. mass mkt. 4.99 (0-425-12499-1) Berkley Pub.

When You Can You Will: Why You Can't Always Do What You Want to Do & What to Do about It. Lynne Bernfield. 240p. 1994. pap. 10.00 (0-425-14375-9, Berkley Trade) Berkley Pub.

When You Can You Will: Why You Can't Always Do What You Want to Do...& What to Do about It. Lynne Bernfield. 224p. 1992. 21.95 (1-56565-008-5) Lowell Hse.

When You Can't Come Back. Dravecky. 240p. 1994. mass mkt. 5.99 (0-06-104307-9, Harp PBks) HarpC.

When You Can't Have a Child: Personal Stories of Living Through Infertility & Childlessness. Susan Powell. 160p. 1993. pap. 11.95 (1-86373-295-0, Pub. by Allen & Unwin Aust Pty AT) IPG Chicago.

When You Can't Hide Your Mistakes. Max Lucado. 32p. 1995. pap. 2.99 (0-8499-5149-6) Word Pub.

When You Can't See a Way. Theta Burke. LC 85-72772. 80p. (Orig.). 1987. pap. 5.95 (0-916872-08-4) Delafield Pr.

When You Care Enough: The Story of Hallmark Cards & Its Founder. Joyce C. Hall & Curtiss Anderson. 260p. 1992. 40.00 (0-87529-655-6) Hallmark.

When You Comin' Back, Red Ryder? Mark Medoff. 1974. pap. 5.25 (0-8222-1240-4) Dramatists Play.

When You Consider the Alternative. William Cole. 144p. 1996. pap. 8.95 (0-312-14445-8) St Martin.

*__When You Divorce.__ Jacksack. 96p. 1994. pap. 5.00 (0-614-26832-X, BLS-3370) Commerce.

When You Don't Agree. James G. Fairfield. LC 77-3133. 248p. 1977. reprint ed. pap. 70.70 (0-7837-9053-8, 2049804) Bks Demand.

When You Feel Like Screaming: Help for Frustrated Mothers. Pat Holt & Grace H. Ketterman. LC 88-4978. 84p. (Orig.). 1988. pap. 6.99 (0-87788-940-6) Shaw Pubs.

When You Feel Like Your Out of Luck. Robert F. Brunner et al. (Illus.). 58p. (Orig.). (J). (ps-3). 1991. teacher ed. write for info. (0-318-68318-0); lib. bdg. 24.95 (1-879209-01-2) Saundras Story Bks.

When You Get Really Mad! - Cuando Estas Muy Enojado! Sharon Landeen. 36p. (ENG & SPA.). (J). (gr. 3-4). 1996. 14.95 (1-887342-00-1); pap. 7.95 (1-887342-01-X); lib. bdg. 11.96 (0-614-15963-6) Ol Stone Pr.

*__When You Get to the End of Yourself.__ 72p. 1986. pap. 5.99 (0-8341-1141-1) Nazarene.

When You Go Back to Work. Robert I. Ward. 14p. (Orig.). 1984. pap. 1.25 (0-89486-235-9, 1417B) Hazelden.

When You Go to Kindergarten. James Howe. LC 93-48152. (Illus.). 48p. (J). (ps up). 1995. pap. 5.95 (0-688-14387-3, Mulberry) Morrow.

When You Go to Kindergarten. rev. ed. James Howe. LC 93-48152. (Illus.). (J). 1994. 16.00 (0-688-12912-9, Morrow Junior); lib. bdg. 15.93 (0-688-12913-7, Morrow Junior) Morrow.

When You Graduate. rev. ed. Charles L. Allen. LC 88-38571. 1989. 7.95 (0-687-45043-8) Abingdon.

*__When You Graduate: Living a Life That Makes a Difference.__ Charles L. Allen. 1997. 6.99 (0-88486-166-X, Bristol Park Bks) Arrowood Pr.

*__When You Have a Decision to Make.__ Delbene. pap. 2.95 (0-687-61189-X) Abingdon.

When You Have a Decision to Make. Ron DelBene et al. (Times of Change, Times of Challenge Ser.). 32p. 1992. pap. 2.95 (0-8358-0652-9) Upper Room Bks.

When You Haven't Got a Prayer. S. Sacks. 9.99 (1-85792-092-9, Pub. by Christian Focus UK) Spring Arbor Dist.

When You Hear Hoof. Elaine Lafferty. 1992. pap. 18.95 (0-13-957440-9) P-H.

*__When You Hear Hoofbeats Think of a Zebra.__ Shems Friedlander. 162p. 1996. pap. 9.95 (0-614-21382-7, 1498) Kazi Pubns.

When You Hear Hoofbeats Think of a Zebra. Shems Friedlander. 176p. 1992. pap. 7.95 (0-939214-06-7) Mazda Pubs.

*__When You Know You're Dying: 12 Thoughts to Guide You Through the Days Ahead.__ James E. Miller. (Illus.). 64p. (Orig.). Date not set. pap. text ed. 5.95 (1-885933-24-X) Willowgreen Pubng.

When You Lick a Slug, Your Tongue Goes Numb. H. Jackson Brown, Jr. LC 95-2626. (Illus.). 150p. 1995. pap. 7.95 (1-55853-326-5) Rutledge Hill Pr.

When You Live Alone: More Things Dedicated Singles Do. Don-Paul Benjamin. (Illus.). (Orig.). 1983. pap. 5.00 (0-932624-06-5) Elevation Pr.

When You Live Alone: Things Dedicated Singles Do. Don-Paul Benjamin. (Illus.). 1979. pap. 5.00 (0-932624-00-6) Elevation Pr.

When You Live with a Messie. Sandra Felton. LC 94-17694. (Illus.). 208p. (Orig.). (YA). (gr. 10). 1994. pap. 8.99 (0-8007-5546-4) Revell.

When You Look Like Your Passport Photo, It's Time to Go Home. Erma Bombeck. 288p. 1992. mass mkt. 5.99 (0-06-109981-3, Harp PBks) HarpC.

When You Look up at the Moon. Allan Fowler. LC 93-38589. (Rookie Read-about Science Ser.). (Illus.). 32p. (J). (ps-2). 1994. lib. bdg. 17.30 (0-516-06025-2) Childrens.

When You Look up at the Moon. Allan Fowler. (Rookie Read-About Science Ser.). (Illus.). 32p. (J). (ps-2). 1994. pap. 3.95 (0-516-46025-0) Childrens.

When You Lose a Loved One/Life Is Forever. Charles L. Allen & Helen Steiner Rice. LC 59-5995. 122p. (YA). (gr. 10). 1988. pap. 6.99 (0-8007-5031-4) Revell.

When You Lose Someone. Richard M. Cromie. 64p. (Orig.). 1993. pap. 6.95 (0-914733-18-4) Desert Min.

*__When You Lose Someone You Love.__ Susan Florence. 1997. 6.95 (0-7667-0952-3) Gibson.

When You Lose Someone You Love: Comfort for Those Who Grieve. Richard Exley. 96p. (Orig.). 1991. 4.95 (1-56292-006-5, HH006) Honor Bks OK.

When You Lose Someone You Love: Comfort for Those Who Grieve. Richard Exley. 1995. pap. 4.99 (1-56292-116-9, HB-116) Honor Bks OK.

When You Lose Someone You Love: Gift Edition. Richard Exley. Date not set. 9.99 (1-56292-111-8, HB-111) Honor Bks OK.

When You Lose Touch. Lawrence O. Olson. (Stepping Stones Ser.). 32p. (Orig.). 1992. pap. 1.95 (0-8100-0455-0, 12N2002) Northwest Pub.

When You Lose Your Job: Laid off, Fired, Early Retired, Relocated, Demoted, Unchallenged. Cliff Hakim. LC 93-2707. 272p. (Orig.). 1993. pap. 14.95 (1-881052-25-7) Berrett-Koehler.

When You Love a Child: For the Times When Caring for Kids is Difficult. Harriet Hodgson. 384p. 1992. pap. 9.95 (0-925190-51-9) Fairview Press.

When You Make the Two One: A Dream of the True Reality...or Perhaps the Reality of a True Dream. Claudia Gasparrini. LC TX-3-897-82. 350p. (Orig.). 1994. pap. text ed. 29.95 (0-9627647-3-6) Space Eagle.

When You Make the Two One: A Dream of the True Reality...or Perhaps the Reality of a True Dream. 2nd rev. ed. Claudia Gasparrini. 374p. 1996. pap. 29.95 (0-9627647-7-9) Space Eagle.

When You Marry. James P. Becher. (Stepping Stones Ser.). 32p. (Orig.). 1992. pap. 1.95 (0-8100-0458-5, 12N2005) Northwest Pub.

When You Marry a Man with Children. Barbara Keenan. 320p. (Orig.). 1992. pap. 9.00 (0-671-72704-4) PB.

When You Need Incredible Answers to Prayer. Roger J. Morneau. LC 95-19379. 1995. 7.99 (0-8280-0976-7) Review & Herald.

When You Need to Take a Stand. Carolyn S. Bohler. 120p. (Orig.). 1990. pap. 10.00 (0-664-25051-3) Westminster John Knox.

When You Owe the IRS. Wade. 1983. 12.95 (0-02-622230-2) Macmillan.

When You Place A Child. . . Erwin H. Plumer. (Illus.). 258p. (C). 1992. text ed. 47.95 (0-398-05770-2) C C Thomas.

When You Place a Child... Erwin H. Plumer. (Illus.). 258p. 1992. pap. 32.95 (0-398-06326-5) C C Thomas.

When You Pray. Johannes M. Lee. 80p. (Orig.). 1995. pap. 4.99 (0-89274-970-9, HH-970) Harrison Hse.

When You Pray: Going Everywhere with Jesus. E. Dee Freeborn. 108p. (Orig.). 1992. pap. 6.99 (0-8341-1442-9) Beacon Hill.

When You Pray: Thinking Your Way Into God's World. Douglas J. Hall. 176p. 1987. pap. 12.00 (0-8170-1105-6) Judson.

When You Pray - Chinese Edition. Harold Lindsell. Tr. by Jonathan Liu. 288p. (CHI.). 1991. pap. 5.50 (1-56582-092-4) Christ Renew Min.

When You Preside. 5th ed. John D. Lawson. 1980. 19.95 (0-8134-2036-9, 2036) Interstate.

When You Really Embarrass Yourself Nobody Ever Forgets. Stephen D. Williford. LC 94-77968. 143p. 1994. 16.95 (1-879111-06-3) Lincoln-Bradley.

When You Relocate. Larry Zessin. (Stepping Stones Ser.). 40p. (Orig.). 1992. pap. 1.95 (0-8100-0461-5, 12N2008) Northwest Pub.

When You See Me You Know Me. Samuel Rowley. LC 70-133730. (Tudor Facsimile Texts. Old English Plays Ser.: No. 106). reprint ed. 59.50 (0-404-53406-6) AMS Pr.

*__When You See the Emu in the Sky: My Journey of Self-Discovery in the Outback.__ Elizabeth Fuller. LC 97-16194. 1997. 21.50 (0-688-14895-6) Morrow.

When You Should Really Know - It's Over! 100+ Ways to Let You Know Your Relationship Is Headed Toward Destruction. Talibah F. Modupe et al. 34p. (Orig.). 1995. pap. 3.00 (1-887442-03-0) Modupe Pr.

When You Stop Believing... Words of Confidence & Power. Raymond C. Brantley. Ed. by Mark Weisser & Nancy Brown. 275p. (Orig.). (C). 1996. pap. 12.95 (0-9638758-8-4) Brockton Pubng.

When You Walk Alone. Dale Jackson. 138p. (C). 1990. 60.00 (0-86439-152-8, Pub. by Boolarong Pubns AT) St Mut.

When You Walk Through the Storm. Jeris Bragen. 127p. 1991. pap. 7.99 (0-8163-0936-1) Pacific Pr Pub Assn.

*__When You Want Your Wish.__ Delbene. pap. 2.95 (0-687-61195-4) Abingdon.

When You Want Your Wishes Known. Ron DelBene et al. (Times of Change, Times of Challenge Ser.). 32p. 1993. pap. 2.95 (0-8358-0679-0) Upper Room Bks.

When You Were a Baby. Ann Jonas. LC 81-12800. (Illus.). 24p. (J). (ps-1). 1982. 16.00 (0-688-00863-1); lib. bdg. 15.93 (0-688-00864-X) Greenwillow.

When You Were a Baby. Photos by Deborah S. Lewis & Gregg A. Lewis. LC 94-44691. (J). 1995. 13.95 (1-56145-102-9) Peachtree Pubs.

When You Were Just a Little Girl. B. G. Hennessy. (Illus.). 32p. (J). (ps-3). 1994. pap. 4.99 (0-14-054172-1) Puffin Bks.

When You Were Little & I Was Big. H. Collins. (Illus.). 32p. (J). (ps-8). 1984. pap. 4.95 (0-920236-71-5, Pub. by Annick CN) Firefly Bks Ltd.

When You Were Young: A Memory Book for the First Two Years. Illus. by Emily Boland. 64p. 1985. 14.95 (0-89659-603-6) Abbeville Pr.

When You Were Young: A Memory Book for the Toddler Years. Emily Boland. (Illus.). 72p. 1991. 7.98 (1-55859-164-8) Abbeville Pr.

*__When You Wish.__ Jane Feather. 1997. mass mkt. 5.99 (0-553-57643-7) Bantam.

When You Wish upon a Star. Ed. & Compiled by Liesl Vazquez. (Charming Petites Ser.). (Illus.). 80p. 1995. 4.95 (0-88088-792-3) Peter Pauper.

When You Wish Upon a Star. Washington. (J). 15.95 incl. lp (0-671-74904-8, S&S Bks Young Read) S&S Childrens.

When You Wish upon a Star: A Musical Pop-Up Book. Illus. by Sparky Moore. 10p. (J). (ps-1). 1996. 11.95 (0-7868-3058-1) Disney Pr.

When You Wish/ Upon a Star & Other Disney Movie Songs. 1990. pap. 4.95 (0-7935-0202-0, 00001325) H Leonard.

When You Wish upon a Star & Other Disney Movie Songs. 1990. pap. 5.95 (0-7935-0140-7, 00001237) H Leonard.

*__When You Wonder Why.__ R. W. Schambach. (Legacy Ser.). 110p. 1995. pap. 5.00 (1-888361-02-6) Power Publns.

When You Work Outside the Home. Judy Hamlin. (Searching for Answers Ser.). 64p. (Orig.). 1993. pap. 1.00 (1-56476-074-X, 6-3074, Victor Bks) Chariot Victor.

*__When You Worry about the Child.__ Hallowell. 1997. pap. 11.00 (0-684-83268-2, Fireside) S&S Trade.

When You Worry about the Child You Love: Emotional & Learning Problems in Children. Edward E. Hallowell. 352p. 1996. 23.00 (0-684-80090-X, S&S) S&S Trade.

*__When Your Best Is Never Good Enough: The Secret of Measuring Up.__ LC 97-25997. 256p. 1997. pap. 9.99 (0-8007-5636-3) Revell.

When Your Child... John M. Drescher et al. LC 86-4831. 144p. (Orig.). 1986. pap. 8.99 (0-8361-3416-8) Herald Pr.

When Your Child Asks: A Handbook for Jewish Parents. rev. ed. Simon Glustrom. LC 91-14423. 165p. 1991. pap. 10.95 (0-8197-0571-3) Bloch.

When Your Child Begins School. Joel A. Nelson. (Stepping Stones Ser.). 32p. (Orig.). 1992. pap. 1.95 (0-8100-0456-9, 12N2003) Northwest Pub.

When Your Child Drives You Crazy. Eda Leshan. 1992. mass mkt. 5.99 (0-312-92930-7) St Martin.

When Your Child Flies Alone: A Guide for Parents. Helen Murray & Donald C. Leavens. 44p. 1990. pap. text ed. 6.95 (1-879668-00-9) Info Finders.

When Your Child Has a Chronic Illness. Lynn Sonberg. 208p. 1995. mass mkt. 4.99 (0-440-21667-2) Dell.

When Your Child Has Been Molested: A Parent's Guide to Healing & Recovery. Kathryn B. Hagans & Joyce Case. LC 87-46364. 159p. pap. 12.95 (0-669-17981-7, Lexington) Jossey-Bass.

When Your Child Has LD (Learning Differences) A Survival Guide for Parents. Gary Fisher & Rhoda Cummings. Ed. by Pamela Espeland. LC 95-5583. (Illus.). 160p. (Orig.). 1995. pap. 12.95 (0-915793-87-3) Free Spirit Pub.

*__When Your Child Is Baptized.__ pap. 2.95 (0-687-61192-X) Abingdon.

When Your Child Is Baptized. Ron DelBene et al. (Times of Change, Times of Challenge Ser.). 32p. (Orig.). 1991. pap. 2.95 (0-8358-0638-3) Upper Room Bks.

When Your Child Is Chemically Dependent. Dennis C. Daley & Judy Miller. 16p. 1995. pap. 4.95 (1-56246-026-9, P182) Johnsn Inst.

When Your Child Is Deaf: A Guide for Parents. David M. Luterman & Mark Ross. LC 91-3239. (Illus.). 182p. 1991. pap. text ed. 19.95 (0-912752-27-0) York Pr.

When Your Child Is Difficult: Solve Your Toughest Child-Raising Problems with a Four-Step Plan That Works. Mel Silberman. LC 95-70413. 128p. (Orig.). 1995. reprint ed. pap. text ed. 12.95 (0-87822-361-4, 4850) Res Press.

When Your Child Is Gone: Learning to Live Again. Francine A. Toder. LC 85-72304. (Illus.). 215p. (Orig.). 1986. pap. 12.95 (0-9615703-7-7) Capital Pub Co.

When Your Child Is Ready to Return to School. 1982. write for info. (0-9616451-8-0) Am Brain Tumor.

When Your Child Is Ready to Return to School. 1994. write for info. (0-944093-32-9) Am Brain Tumor.

When Your Child Is Ready to Return to School. rev. ed. 1989. write for info. (0-944093-13-2) Am Brain Tumor.

When Your Child Is Ready to Return to School. rev. ed. 1992. write for info. (0-944093-21-3) Am Brain Tumor.

When Your Child Is Six to Twelve. John M. Drescher. LC 93-23558. 128p. (Orig.). 1993. pap. 8.95 (1-56148-094-0) Good Bks PA.

When Your Child Needs Help: A Parent's Guide to Therapy for Children. Norma Doft. 1994. pap. 12.00 (0-517-88169-1, Crown) Crown Pub Group.

When Your Child Needs Testing. Milton F. Shore. 192p. 1996. pap. 15.95 (0-8245-1542-0) Crossroad NY.

When Your Child Struggles: The Myths of 20/20. 4th ed. David L. Cook. (Illus.). 173p. (Orig.). 1991. reprint ed. pap. text ed. 15.00 (0-9632657-0-9) Cook Vision.

When Your Children Divorce. Elaine R. Seppa. LC 94-45526. (Saltshaker Bks.). 162p. (Orig.). 1995. pap. 8.99 (0-8308-1644-5, 1644, Saltshaker Bk) InterVarsity.

When Your Comfort Zone Gets the Squeeze. Charles R. Swindoll. (Swindoll Booklets Ser.). 40p. pap. 3.99 (0-310-20094-6) Zondervan.

When Your Daughter Marries. Rayburn W. Ray & Rose A. Ray. 96p. (Orig.). 1982. pap. 7.95 (*0-939298-14-7*, 147) J M Prods.

When Your Doctor Doesn't Know Best: Medical Mistakes That Even the Best Docotrs Make-and How to Protect Yourself. William Proctor & Richard N. Podell. 416p. 1995. 23.50 (*0-671-87112-9*) S&S Trade.

When Your Dreams Die: Finding Strength & Hope Through Life's Disappointments. Marilyn W. Heavilin. LC 93-6966. 144p. (Orig.). 1993. pap. 10.99 (*0-8407-4592-3*) Nelson.

When Your Dreams Don't Come True. David Shibley. LC 92-63374. 176p. 1993. reprint ed. pap. 7.95 (*0-89221-232-2*) New Leaf.

When Your Ex Won't Pay: Getting Your Kids the Financial Support They Deserve. Nancy S. Palmer & Ana Tangel-Rodriguez. LC 94-38141. 176p. (Orig.). 1995. pap. 12.00 (*0-89109-879-8*) Pinon Press.

***When Your Family Fights: Eight Lifeskills for Improving Family Health & Harmony.** Redford Williams. 1997. 24.00 (*0-8129-2424-X*, Times Bks) Random.

When Your Friend Gets Cancer: How You Can Help. Amy Harwell & Kristine Tomasik. LC 87-9547. 128p. (Orig.). 1987. pap. 8.99 (*0-87788-934-1*) Shaw Pubs.

When Your Friend Is Grieving: Building a Bridge of Love. Paula D'Arcy. 114p. (Orig.). 1990. pap. 7.99 (*0-87788-088-3*) Shaw Pubs.

When Your Jewish Child Asks Why: Answers for Tough Questions. Kerry M. Olitzky et al. LC 92-37176. 1992. 19.95 (*0-88125-452-5*); pap. 12.95 (*0-88125-451-7*) Ktav.

When Your Kids Go to College. Lucantoni Salvi & Michael J. Hunt. LC 94-19323. 80p. 1994. pap. 5.95 (*0-8091-3502-7*) Paulist Pr.

When Your Library Budget Is Almost Zero. Lesley S. Farmer. (Illus.). xi, 125p. 1993. pap. text ed. 23.00 (*0-87287-990-9*) Libs Unl.

When Your Long-Term Marriage Ends: A Workbook for Divorced Women. Elaine Newell. LC 94-405. 234p. 1994. pap. 14.95 (*0-89390-291-8*) Resource Pubns.

When Your Money Fails. 1992. lib. bdg. 79.00 (*0-8490-5274-2*) Gordon Pr.

When Your Money Fails. Mary S. Relfe. 234p. (Orig.). 1981. pap. text ed. 5.95 (*0-9607986-0-9*) League Prayer.

When Your Ox Is in the Ditch: Genealogical How-To Letters. Vera McDowell. 161p. 1995. pap. 19.95 (*0-8063-1484-2*, 3515) Genealog Pub.

When Your Parent Dies. Cathleen L. Curry. LC 93-71436. 152p. (Orig.). 1993. pap. 7.95 (*0-87793-511-4*) Ave Maria.

When Your Parent Drinks Too Much: A Book for Teenagers. Eric Ryerson. 144p. 1985. 16.95 (*0-8160-1259-8*) Facts on File.

When Your Parents Need You: A Caregiver's Guide. Rita Robinson. LC 90-4138. 224p. (Orig.). pap. 9.95 (*1-877880-01-9*) Borgo Pr.

When Your Pet Dies: Dealing with Your Grief & Helping Your Children Cope. Christine Adamec. 192p. 1996. mass mkt. 4.99 (*0-425-15253-7*) Berkley Pub.

When Your Phone Doesn't Ring, It Will Be Me. Cynthia Heimel. 208p. 1996. pap. 11.00 (*0-87113-634-1*, Atlntc Mnthly) Grove-Atltic.

When Your Problems Create Problems: Counseling for Survival. Roz Klein & Thelma R. Miller. LC 89-48214. 160p. 1990. pap. 16.95 (*0-914783-40-8*) Charles.

When Your Rope Breaks. Stephen W. Brown. 192p. (YA). (gr. 10). 1996. pap. 11.99 (*0-8010-5729-9*, Ravens Ridge) Baker Bks.

***When Your Son or Daughter Divorces.** DelBene. pap. 2.95 (*0-8358-0678-2*) Upper Room Bks.

***When Your Son or Daughter Is Baptized.** Delbene. pap. 2.95 (*0-687-61198-9*) Abingdon.

When Your Spouse Dies: A Concise & Practical Source of Help & Advice. Cathleen L. Curry. LC 89-81539. 128p. (Orig.). 1990. pap. 6.95 (*0-87793-416-9*) Ave Maria.

When Your Wife Says No: Forced Sex in Marriage. Fay H. Knopp. 40p. (Orig.). 1994. pap. text ed. 7.00 (*1-884444-10-5*) Safer Soc.

***When You're a Christian, the Whole World is from Missouri: Living the Life of Faith in a Show Me Way.** James W. Moore. 1997. pap. text ed. 10.00 (*0-687-00786-0*) Abingdon.

When You're a Widow. 3rd ed. Clarissa Start. (Illus.). 138p. 1990. reprint ed. pap. 5.95 (*0-935284-76-1*) Patrice Pr.

When You're from Brooklyn, Everything Else Is Tokyo. large type ed. Larry King & Marty Appel. LC 92-42517. (General Ser.). 316p. 1993. reprint ed. lib. bdg. 18.95 (*1-56054-661-1*) Thorndike Pr.

When You're Happy. Elizabeth Crary & Shari Steelsmith. (Feelings for Little Children Ser.). (Illus.). 10p. (J). (ps-1). 1997. bds. 5.95 (*1-884734-12-X*) Parenting Pr.

When You're Ill or Incapacitated/When You're the Caregiver: 12 Things to Remember in Times of Sickness, Injury or Disability/12 Things to Do if Someone You Care For is Ill or Incapacitated. James E. Miller. LC 95-90163. 64p. 1995. reprint ed. pap. 5.95 (*1-885933-21-5*) Willowgreen Pubng.

When You're Mad. Elizabeth Crary & Shari Steelsmith. (Feelings for Little Children Ser.). (Illus.). 10p. (J). (ps-1). 1997. bds. 5.95 (*1-884734-10-3*) Parenting Pr.

When You're Not Looking: A Storytime Counting Book. Maggie Kneen. (J). (ps-1). 1996. 15.00 (*0-689-80026-6*, S&S Bks Young Read) S&S Childrens.

When You're on Your Own: Ten Things Every Young Woman Needs to Know As She Faces an Adult World. Ruth Senter. 160p. 1993. pap. 9.99 (*0-310-57641-5*) Zondervan.

When You're Ready: A Woman's Healing from Childhood Physical & Sexual Abuse by Her Mother. Kathy Evert. LC 87-82076. 194p. 1987. pap. 9.95 (*0-9613205-4-0*) Launch Pr.

When You're Serious about Love. Kay Kuzma. LC 93-579. 1993. pap. 10.99 (*0-8407-4597-4*) Nelson.

When You're Shy. Elizabeth Crary & Shari Steelsmith. (Feelings for Little Children Ser.). (Illus.). 10p. (J). (ps-1). 1997. bds. 5.95 (*1-884734-11-1*) Parenting Pr.

When You're Silly. Elizabeth Crary & Shari Steelsmith. (Feelings for Little Children Ser.). (Illus.). 10p. (J). (ps-1). 1997. bds. 5.95 (*1-884734-13-8*) Parenting Pr.

When You're Teaching Adults. rev. ed. Intro. by James R. Dorland. LC 59-15148. 1970. pap. text ed. 1.00 (*0-686-00786-7*, 751-00798) A A A C E.

When You're up to Your Ass in Alligators: More Urban Folklore from the Paperwork Empire. Alan Dundes & Carl R. Pagter. LC 87-3056. (Humor in Life & Letters Ser.). (Illus.). 272p. 1987. 34.95 (*0-8143-1866-5*); pap. 16.95 (*0-8143-1867-3*) Wayne St U Pr.

***When You're up to Your Eyeballs in Alligators.** Larry Wilde. Ed. by Mary Poulos. LC 97-22849. (Illus.). x, 246p. 1997. 30.00 (*0-945040-02-4*) Jester Pr CA.

***When You've Been There.** Estella M. Pitt. 68p. (Orig.). 1996. pap. 5.95 (*0-9642764-2-9*) E Pitt.

When You've Made It Your Own. . . Teaching Poetry to Young People. Gregory A. Denman. LC 88-2989. 201p. (Orig.). (C). 1988. pap. text ed. 22.00 (*0-435-08462-3*, 08462) Heinemann.

Whence & Whither. Paul Carus. 1972. 59.95 (*0-8490-1289-9*) Gordon Pr.

Whence Came Our Early Place-Names? David B. Skillman. (Illus.). 12p. (Orig.). 1960. pap. text ed. 3.00 (*1-877701-02-5*) NCH&GS.

Whence Comes Evil? An Essay on Man in Action. Jossef Kratzenstein. Ed. by Stephen Konowalow. 88p. (Orig.). (C). 1991. pap. 7.95 (*0-9631929-0-6*) Atara-Brahman Ent.

Whence Comes the Rain. Bethany Chaffin. LC 83-81724. 114p. 1983. 8.98 (*0-88290-230-X*) Horizon Utah.

Whence the Goddesses: A Source Book. Miriam R. Dexter. (Athene Ser.). 384p. 1990. text ed. 47.50 (*0-08-037279-1*, Pergamon Pr); pap. text ed. 18.95 (*0-08-037281-3*, Pergamon Pr) Elsevier.

Whence the Goddesses: A Source Book. Miriam R. Dexter. (Athene Ser.). 304p. (C). 1990. pap. text ed. 20.95 (*0-8077-6234-2*) Tchrs Coll.

Whence They Came: Deportation from Canada, 1900-1935. Barbara Roberts. 246p. 1988. pap. 25.00 (*0-7766-0163-6*, Pub. by Univ Ottawa Pr CN) Paul & Co Pubs.

Whence? Where? Whither? & Occasional Verse. Hugh R. Lupton. 120p. 1984. 40.00 (*0-7212-0678-6*, Pub. by Regency Press UK) St Mut.

Whene'er You Make a Promise: A Paper Doll History of the Girl Scout Uniform, Vol. 2. Kathryn M. Hunt. (Illus.). 32p. (Orig.). 1996. pap. 9.95 (*0-89672-361-5*) Tex Tech Univ Pr.

Whenever the Wind Is High. (Strategies Program Ser.). 1991. pap. 23.24 (*0-8123-6914-9*); pap. 7.76 (*0-8123-6915-7*); text ed. 20.12 (*0-8123-6913-0*) McDougal-Littell.

***When's This Place Gonna Get Smooth? Twenty-Nine Parenting Lessons We Learned the Hard Way.** Rod Kennedy & Johnelle Kennedy. 66p. 1996. pap. text ed. 9.00 (*1-886901-06-6*) Up With Youth.

Where? Margaret W. Hudson. 1965. 1.50 (*0-88323-082-8*, 179) Pendergrass Pub.

***Where?** Robert W. Wood. (Experiments for Young Scientists Ser.). (Illus.). 140p. (YA). (gr. 5 up). 1997. text ed. write for info. (*0-7910-4848-9*) Chelsea Hse.

Where? Experiments for the Young Scientists. Robert W. Wood. (J). (gr. 4-7). 1995. pap. text ed. 10.95 (*0-07-051638-3*) McGraw.

Where a Nickel Cost a Dime. Willie Perdomo. Date not set. write for info. (*0-393-31415-4*, Norton Paperbks) Norton.

Where a Nickel Costs a Dime. Willie Perdomo. LC 95-13225. 128p. 1996. pap. 14.95 (*0-393-31383-2*) Norton.

Where All Roads End. Robert A. Diskin. 72p. (Orig.). 1996. pap. 6.95 (*0-9647582-1-0*) R A Diskin.

Where Am I? Clue-by-Clue Descriptive Sketches of American Historical Places. Marsha L. Beeman. LC 96-4227. 319p. (Orig.). 1997. pap. 29.95 (*0-7864-0243-1*) McFarland & Co.

***Where Am I? The Story of Maps & Navigation.** A. G. Smith. (Illus.). 96p. (YA). (gr. 4 up). 1997. pap. 13.95 (*0-7737-5836-4*, Pub. by Stoddart Kids CN) Genl Dist Srvs.

Where Am I? ADV & OMNI (VOR) Instruction Manual. 2nd ed. Ken Stremming. Ed. by Harold J. Holmes. (Illus.). 75p. 1984. spiral bd. 15.95 (*0-940766-07-8*) Haldon Bks.

Where Am I Now? Where Am I Going? Career Manual. William Lareau. LC 92-3981. 1992. pap. 12.95 (*0-8329-0500-3*) New Win Pub.

Where Am I Now? Where Am I Going? The Career Manual. William Lareau. LC 92-3981. 256p. 1991. 17.95 (*0-8329-0464-3*) New Win Pub.

Where America Stands in 1996: The Gallup Guide to the State of the Nation. Gallup Poll Staff & Michael Golay. LC 96-5486. 304p. 1996. pap. text ed. 16.95 (*0-471-14526-2*) Wiley.

Where America Stands, 1997. Michael Golay. 1997. pap. text ed. 16.95 (*0-471-16183-7*) Wiley.

Where America's Black Leaders Learned to Lead: The Black College Career Guide. Joan Carroll. 144p. (YA). (gr. 9-12). 1995. pap. text ed. 6.95 (*1-881223-05-1*) Zulema Ent.

Where & How to Find Personal Contacts Fast: A Complete Directory of Singles Publications, National Organizations, Pen Pals, Correspondence Clubs, International Contacts with Current Addresses for Love, Marriage & Companionship. 1992. lib. bdg. 300.00 (*0-8490-8881-X*) Gordon Pr.

Where & How to Find the Law. Frank H. Childs. LC 85-60261. (Legal Bibliographic & Research Reprint Ser.: Vol. 4). vi, 119p. 1985. reprint ed. lib. bdg. 37.50 (*0-89941-397-8*, 303640) W S Hein.

Where & Why. Susan S. Swartz. (Illustrator Is...Ser.). (Illus.). 24p. (Orig.). (J). (ps-6). 1987. student ed., pap. 4.50 (*0-943901-00-6*) Creare Pubns.

***Where Angels Dared to Tread.** Victor F. Calverton. 381p. Date not set. 24.95 (*0-8369-0009-X*) Ayer.

Where Angels Dwell. Hilde L. Scheffler. (Illus.). 175p. 20.00 (*1-888106-02-6*) Custom Fmly.

Where Angels Dwell: A Treasury of Hope, Inspiration, & Blessings. (Cherished Moments Ser.). (Illus.). 1995. 9.99 (*1-57051-065-2*) Brownlow Pub Co.

Where Angels Fear to Tread. E. M. Forster. 1976. 22.95 (*0-8488-1329-4*) Amereon Ltd.

Where Angels Fear to Tread. E. M. Forster. 192p. 1992. pap. 9.00 (*0-679-73634-4*, Vin) Random.

Where Angels Fear to Tread. E. M. Forster. 320p. (J). 1996. mass mkt. 4.50 (*0-553-21446-2*, Bantam Classics) Bantam.

Where Angels Fear to Tread. E. M. Forster. 1986. reprint ed. lib. bdg. 21.95 (*0-89968-224-3*, Lghtyr Pr) Buccaneer Bks.

Where Angels Fear to Tread. E. M. Forster. 128p. 1993. reprint ed. pap. text ed. 1.00 (*0-486-27791-7*) Dover.

Where Angels Fear to Tread: Descriptive Bibliography & Alexander Pope. David L. Vander Meulen. LC 88-600137. (Engelhard Lecture on the Book). 29p. 1988. 3.95 (*0-8444-0608-2*) Lib Congress.

Where Angels Fear to Tread, & Other Tales of the Sea. Morgan Robertson. LC 79-122733. (Short Story Index Reprint Ser.). 1977. 19.95 (*0-8369-3566-7*) Ayer.

Where Angels Glide at Dawn. Lori M. Carlson & Cynthia L. Ventura. LC 90-6697. (Trophy Bk.). 128p. (J). (gr. 5 up). 1993. pap. 3.95 (*0-06-440464-1*, Trophy) HarpC Child Bks.

Where Angels Walk: True Stories of Heavenly Visitors. Joan W. Anderson. 224p. 1992. 16.95 (*0-9631981-0-6*) Barton & Brett.

Where Angels Walk: True Stories of Heavenly Visitors. large type ed. Joan W. Anderson. LC 93-10047. 1993. lib. bdg. 22.95 (*0-8161-5818-5*, GK Hall) Thorndike Pr.

Where Angels Walk: True Stories of Heavenly Vistors. Joan W. Anderson. 224p. 1993. pap. 12.00 (*0-345-38338-9*, Ballantine Epiphany) Ballantine.

***Where Another Light Has Been.** Ed. by Demitra Flanagan. (Illus.). 90p. (C). 1996. pap. text ed. 22.99 (*1-886352-13-5*) Natl Poets Assn.

Where Are All the Angels? Heavenly Host Handbook. Richard E. Leffler. (Illus.). 192p. 1994. pap. 8.95 (*0-9640465-1-2*) Del King Pubng.

Where Are All the Children. Matthew V. Smith. (Illus.). 10p. (J). (gr. 1-2). 1992. pap. 12.95 (*1-56606-002-8*) Bradley Mann.

Where Are All the Dinosaurs? Mary O'Neill. LC 89-31165. (Illus.). 32p. (J). (gr. 2-6). 1996. pap. 3.95 (*0-8167-1638-2*) Troll Communs.

Where Are Kermit's Keys? Alison Inches. (Muppet Lift-the-Flaps Ser.). (Illus.). 16p. (J). (ps-k). 1995. 5.99 (*0-14-055692-3*) Puffin Bks.

Where Are Kermit's Keys? Alison Inches. (Lift-the-Flaps Ser.). (Illus.). 16p. (J). (gr. k). 1995. pap. 5.99 (*0-14-055569-2*) Puffin Bks.

Where Are Momma, Poppa, & Sister June. Dick Gackenbach. LC 93-40809. (J). 1994. 13.95 (*0-395-67323-2*, Hills Med) HM.

Where Are My Birth Parents? A Guide for Teenage Adoptees. Karen Gravelle & Susan Fischer. LC 92-34586. 112p. (YA). (gr. 5 up). 1993. 14.95 (*0-8027-8257-4*); lib. bdg. 15.85 (*0-8027-8258-2*) Walker & Co.

Where Are My Birth Parents? A Guide for Teenage Adoptees. Karen Gravelle & Susan Fischer. LC 92-34586. 112p. (YA). 1995. pap. 8.95 (*0-8027-7453-9*) Walker & Co.

Where Are My Children. Cassie Kimbrough. 1991. mass mkt. 4.95 (*0-8217-3563-2*, Zebra Kensgtn) Kensgtn Pub Corp.

Where Are My People? Eydith I. Johnson. LC 95-95147. 300p. 1996. 10.99 (*1-888188-50-2*); pap. 8.99 (*1-888188-51-0*) E Johnsn.

Where Are My Prairie Dogs & Black-Footed Ferrets? Ron Hirschi. (Illus.). 48p. (J). (ps-3). 1992. pap. 8.00 (*0-553-35471-X*) Bantam.

Where Are My Shoes? Mary A. Dudko & Margie Larsen. Ed. by Linda Hartley. LC 93-77013. (Illus.). 24p. (J). (ps-1). 1993. pap. 2.25 (*1-57064-004-1*) Lyrick Pub.

Where Are My Stripes? Gillian Liu. (Early Words Ser.). (Illus.). 24p. (J). (gr. 1-3). 1996. 9.95 (*0-237-51431-1*, Pub. by Evans Bros Ltd UK) Trafalgar.

Where Are Percy's Friends? Anna Nilsen. LC 95-72153. (Illus.). 16p. (J). (ps). 1996. 7.99 (*0-7636-0017-2*) Candlewick Pr.

Where Are the Babies? Diane Iverson. (Illus.). 48p. (Orig.). (J). (ps). 1995. 14.95 (*0-9623349-1-X*); pap. 8.95 (*0-9623349-2-8*) MS Pub.

***Where Are the Bears?** Kay Winters. LC 96-34388. (Illus.). (J). 1998. pap. write for info. (*0-440-41308-7*) Dell.

Where Are the Black Men? Roosevelt Wright, Jr. 62p. (Orig.). (C). 1994. pap. 4.95 (*0-943751-01-2*) Free Pr LA.

Where Are the Champions? A Simple Approach to Effective Criminal Justice & Social Reform. Arnold A. Gibbs. Ed. by A.A. Gibbs Publishing Staff. 91p. (Orig.). 1994. pap. 8.95 (*0-9643497-0-1*) A A Gibbs.

Where Are the Children. Herb Brin. 200p. 1991. 17.95 (*0-8246-0351-6*) Jonathan David.

Where Are the Children? Mary Higgins Clark. Ed. by Julie Rubenstein. 1992. mass mkt. 6.99 (*0-671-74118-7*) PB.

Where Are the Children. Mary Higgins Clark. 192p. 1991. reprint ed. lib. bdg. 27.95 (*0-89966-780-5*) Buccaneer Bks.

***Where Are the Children? - The Cradle Will Fall - A Stranger Is Watching.** Mary Higgins Clark. 1996. mass mkt. 22.50 (*0-671-85157-8*) PB.

Where Are the Customers' Yachts?, or A Good Hard Look at Wall Street. Fred Schwed. (Investment Classics Ser.). 215p. 1995. text ed. 45.00 (*0-471-11979-2*); pap. text ed. 16.95 (*0-471-11978-4*) Wiley.

Where Are the Dead? Arnold Bennett. LC 74-17034. (Collected Works of Arnold Bennett: Vol. 87). 1977. reprint ed. 21.95 (*0-518-19168-0*) Ayer.

Where Are the Dead? see Donde Estan los Muertos?

***Where Are the Elephants?** Budd Boetticher. Ed. by Dirk Summers & Corene Adams. (Illus.). 445p. 1998. 25.95 (*1-882747-71-2*) Fallbrook Pub.

Where Are the Jobs? 40p. (Orig.). 1994. pap. text ed. 8.00 (*1-55877-186-7*) Natl Governor.

Where Are the Love Poems for Dictators? E. Ethelbert Miller. LC 86-62885. (Illus.). (Orig.). (YA). (gr. 10 up). 1987. pap. 7.95 (*0-940880-16-4*) Open Hand.

Where Are the Stars During the Day? A Book about Stars. Melvin Berger & Gilda Berger. LC 92-18200. (Discovery Readers Ser.). (Illus.). 48p. (J). (gr. k-4). 1993. per., pap. 4.50 (*0-8249-8607-5*, Ideals Child); lib. bdg. 12.00 (*0-8249-8644-X*, Ideals Child) Hambleton-Hill.

Where Are They? Tony Tallarico. (Illus.). 96p. (J). 1992. 14.95 (*1-56156-139-8*) Kidsbks.

Where Are They? Where's the Bunny? (Illus.). 32p. (J). (ps-3). 1993. reprint ed. 5.98 (*0-8317-7728-1*) Smithmark.

Where Are We Going Besides Crazy? Kathleen C. Null. 1989. 8.95 (*0-88494-693-2*) Bookcraft Inc.

Where Are We Going Today? Sylvia R. Tester. (Illus.). 12p. (J). (ps). 1992. bds. 4.99 (*0-87403-996-7*, 03116) Standard Pub.

Where Are We Going? Who Will Lead Us There? Gary D. Fenstermacher. 1993. 12.00 (*0-89333-102-3*) AACTE.

Where Are You? Coming to Terms with the Death of My Child. Karin Von Schilling. 88p. (Orig.). 1988. pap. 7.95 (*0-88010-268-3*) Anthroposophic.

Where Are You, Ernest & Celestine? Gabrielle Vincent. LC 85-17595. (Illus.). 28p. (J). (gr. k-3). 1986. lib. bdg. 15.93 (*0-688-06235-0*) Greenwillow.

Where Are You God? Bible Studies about the Presence of God. Nigel Watson. 48p. 1995. pap. 7.50 (*1-86407-041-2*, Pub. by JBCE AT) Morehouse Pub.

Where Are You Going? Rozanne L. Williams. (Emergent Reader Big Bks.). (Illus.). 16p. (Orig.). (J). (gr. k-2). 1995. pap. 11.98 (*1-57471-016-8*) Creat Teach Pr.

Where Are You Going?, Level 2. Rozanne L. Williams. (Emergent Reader Science Ser.). 16p. 1994. 2.49 (*0-916119-36-X*, 3526) Creat Teach Pr.

Where Are You Going? A Guide to the Spiritual Journey. 2nd ed. Swami Muktananda. Ed. by Swami Durgananda. LC 88-37035. 240p. (Orig.). 1989. pap. 10.95 (*0-914602-99-3*) SYDA Found.

Where Are You Going, Emma? Jeanne Titherington. (Illus.). 24p. (J). (ps-1). 1988. 12.95 (*0-688-07081-7*); lib. bdg. 12.88 (*0-688-07082-5*) Greenwillow.

***Where Are You Going, Kermit?** Illus. by Tammie Speer-Lyon. (Muppet Lift & Look Board Bks.). 12p. (J). (ps). 1997. bds. 5.95 (*0-448-41578-X*, G&D) Putnam Pub Group.

Where Are You Going, Little Mouse? Robert Kraus. LC 84-25868. (Illus.). 32p. (J). (ps-1). 1986. 16.00 (*0-688-04294-5*) Greenwillow.

Where Are You Going, Little Mouse? Robert Kraus. LC 84-25868. (Illus.). 32p. (J). (ps-1). 1986. lib. bdg. 15.93 (*0-688-04295-3*) Greenwillow.

Where Are You Going, Little Mouse? Robert Kraus. LC 84-25868. (Illus.). (J). (ps up). 1989. pap. 4.95 (*0-688-08747-7*, Mulberry) Morrow.

Where Are You Going, Manyoni? Catherine Stock. LC 92-29793. (Illus.). 48p. (J). (ps up). 1993. 15.00 (*0-688-10352-9*, Morrow Junior); lib. bdg. 14.93 (*0-688-10353-7*, Morrow Junior) Morrow.

Where Are You Going, Where Have You Been? Joyce Carol Oates. LC 94-11284. (Women Writers: Texts & Contexts Ser.). 160p. (C). 1995. text ed. 30.00 (*0-8135-2134-3*); pap. text ed. 14.00 (*0-8135-2135-1*) Rutgers U Pr.

Where Are You Going, Where Have You Been? Selected Early Stories. Joyce Carol Oates. LC 92-44899. 522p. 1993. 24.95 (*0-86538-077-5*) Ontario Rev NJ.

Where Are You Going, Where Have You Been? Selected Early Stories. Joyce Carol Oates. LC 92-44899. 522p. 1994. pap. 12.95 (*0-86538-078-3*) Ontario Rev NJ.

Where Are You Going, Where Have You Been? Stories of Young America. Joyce Carol Oates. 352p. 1976. pap. 1.75 (*0-449-30795-6*, Prem) Fawcett.

Where Are You Hashem. Y. Ganz. (Middos Ser.). 1989. 7.99 (*0-89906-504-X*) Mesorah Pubns.

***Where Are You Henry?** Anna Yeomans. 256p. 1997. pap. 17.95 (*0-7528-0160-0*, Pub. by Orion Bks UK) Trafalgar.

Where Are You, Little Green Dragon? Klaus Baumgart. LC 92-72026. (Little Green Dragon Ser.). (Illus.). 32p. (J). (ps-3). 1993. 12.95 (*1-56282-344-2*) Hyprn Child.

Where Are You, Little Green Dragon? Klaus Baumgart. LC 92-72026. (Little Green Dragon Ser.). (Illus.). 32p. (J). (ps-3). 1995. pap. 4.95 (*0-7868-1073-4*) Hyprn Child.

Where Are You, Little Zack? Judith R. Enderle & Stephanie G. Tessler. LC 96-15381. (Illus.). (J). 1997. 14.95 (*0-395-73092-9*) HM.

Where Are You Mrs. Caterpillar?, Vol. 3: Pasitos English Language Development Books. Darlyne F. Schott. (Pasitos Hacia la Lectura Ser.). 14p. (J). (gr. k-1). 1990. pap. text ed. 11.00 (*1-56537-062-7*) D F Schott Educ.

Where Are You When I Need You? Suzanne Newton. LC 92-31360. 208p. (YA). (gr. 7 up). 1993. pap. 3.99 (*0-14-034454-3*) Puffin Bks.

Where Are You When I Need You? Befriending God When Life Hurts. Robert N. Levine. LC 95-25507. 112p. 1996. 15.00 (*0-06-251351-6*); pap. 10.00 (*0-06-251352-4*) Harper SF.

Where Art Is Joy: Haitian Art--The First Forty Years. Selden Rodman. 1988. 60.00 (*0-938291-01-7*) R deLatour.

Where Art Thou Black Man: A Guide to Empower Black Men to Reach Their Potential. Henry Abraham. Ed. by Tamara Shaffer. (Illus.). 112p. (Orig.). 1996. pap. 12.00 (*0-9651167-0-0*) Proj Restoration.

Where Artists Live, 1980. (Research Division Reports: No. 19). 48p. 1987. pap. 8.00 (*0-317-62787-2*) Natl Endow Arts.

Where Bald Eagles Gather. Dorothy H. Patent. 1990. pap. 5.95 (*0-395-53464-X*) Ticknor & Fields.

Where Bible & Life Connect: Reflections of a Spiritual Director. Lester Bach. 256p. (Orig.). 1995. pap. 17.95 (*0-8146-2247-X*) Liturgical Pr.

***Where Bigfoot Walks.** Robert M. Pyle. 1997. pap. 13.00 (*0-395-85701-5*) HM.

Where Bigfoot Walks: Crossing the Dark Divide. Robert M. Pyle. (Illus.). 331p. 1995. 21.95 (*0-395-44114-5*); (*0-395-44144-7*) HM.

Where Black Rules White. Hesketh Prichard. LC 70-161272. (Black Heritage Library Collection). 1977. reprint ed. 27.95 (*0-8369-8831-0*) Ayer.

Where Blind Fish Swim. Joan Hunt. 44p. 1996. 6.95 (*1-885206-34-8*, Iliad Pr) Cader Pubng.

Where Blue Begins. Janice Deaner. 464p. 1994. pap. 4.99 (*0-451-17919-6*, Sig) NAL-Dutton.

Where Bluebirds Fly. Ann Gasser. (Illus.). 74p. (Orig.). 1994. pap. 3.95 (*1-884257-01-1*) AGEE Keyboard.

Where Bluebirds Sing. Ida M. Kempel. 147p. (Orig.). 1991. pap. 9.95 (*0-9628132-1-4*) Nascent Pr.

Where Bobby Learned to Play. Lindon C. Hopkins. 159p. 1996. write for info. (*0-9628381-1-X*) McGuire Pub.

Where Buffalo Roam. Milo J. Schult & Arnold O. Haugen. (Illus.). 1979. pap. 2.00 (*0-912410-07-8*) Badlands Natl Hist.

Where Buffalo Roam: A Pictorial History of Kandiyohi County. Kandiyohi County Historical Society Staff. LC 94-30779. (Illus.). 1994. write for info. (*0-89865-914-0*) Donning Co.

Where Bugles Called & Rifles Gleamed. William A. Spedale. 174p. 1986. 17.95 (*0-685-36257-4*); pap. 10.77 (*0-935545-06-9*) Land & Land.

Where Butterflies Grow. Joanne Ryder. LC 88-37989. (Illus.). 32p. (J). (ps-3). 1989. pap. 15.99 (*0-525-67284-2*, Lodestar Bks) Dutton Child Bks.

Where Butterflies Grow. Joanne Ryder. (Illus.). 32p. (J). (ps-3). 1996. pap. 4.99 (*0-14-055858-6*, Puff Unicorn) Puffin Bks.

Where Can Daniel Be? Leah Komaiko. LC 93-49393. (Illus.). 32p. (J). (ps-1). 1994. 15.95 (*0-531-06850-1*); lib. bdg. 16.99 (*0-531-08700-X*) Orchard Bks Watts.

Where Can We Turn: A Parent's Guide to Evaluating Treatment Programs for Troubled Youth. Jacki Allred & Claudia Olsen. 48p. 1995. pap. 4.99 (*1-56684-092-9*) Pubs Dist Ctr Inc.

Where Cats Sleep. Liz Ross. LC 95-35900. (Illus.). 48p. 1996. 7.95 (*0-8118-1201-4*) Chronicle Bks.

Where China Meets Burma: Life & Travel in the Burma-China Border Lands. Beatrix Metford. LC 77-87047. reprint ed. 29.50 (*0-404-16844-2*) AMS Pr.

Where Colleges Fail: A Study of the Student As a Person. Nevitt Sanford. LC 67-13279. (Jossey-Bass Behavioral Science Ser.). 252p. reprint ed. 71.90 (*0-8357-9354-0*, 2013865) Bks Demand.

Where Communism Works. Douglas M. Kenrick. pap. 8.95 (*0-8048-1671-9*) C E Tuttle.

Where Could I Go. Melvin Jackson. (Illus.). 97p. (Orig.). 1995. pap. 9.95 (*1-883893-20-8*) WinePress Pub.

Where Could the Dark Matter Be. Louise O. Neaderland. (Illus.). 1992. 5.00 (*0-942561-21-X*) Bone Hollow.

***Where Courage Is Like a Wild Horse.** Sharon Skolnick & Manny Skolnick. LC 97-2094. 144p. 1997. 25.00 (*0-8032-4263-8*) U of Nebr Pr.

Where Coverage Ends: Catastrophic Illness & Long-Term Health Care Costs. LC 88-16237. 1988. pap. 19.95 (*0-86643-061-X*) Empl Benefit Res Inst.

Where Coyotes Howl. Thelma M. Anderson. 336p. (Orig.). 1995. pap. 16.95 (*1-57502-102-1*) Morris Pubng.

Where Coyotes Howl & Wind Blows Free: Growing Up in the West. Ed. by Alexandra R. Haslam & Gerald W. Haslam. LC 94-38567. (Illus.). 224p. (YA). 1995. text ed. 18.50 (*0-87417-255-1*) U of Nev Pr.

Where Crawls the Lizard? Marvel Comics Staff. (Spiderman Ser.: No. 2). (J). (gr. 5). 1996. mass mkt. 3.99 (*0-8125-4345-9*) Tor Bks.

Where Credit Is Due: A Guide to Proper Citing of Sources - Print & Nonprint. Nancy E. Shields & Mary E. Uhle. LC 85-1701. 258p. 1985. 22.50 (*0-8108-1788-8*) Scarecrow.

***Where Credit Is Due: A Guide to Proper Citing of Sources - Print & Nonprint.** 2nd rev. ed. Nancy E. Shields & Mary E. Uhle. LC 96-6523. 272p. 1997. 32.50 (*0-8108-3211-9*) Scarecrow.

Where Cross the Crowded Ways. Gary Forbes. Ed. by Michael L. Sherer. 1987. pap. 8.25 (*1-55673-034-9*, 8819) CSS OH.

Where Crows & Men Collide. Kate Gale. 72p. 1995. pap. 7.95 (*0-9639528-4-6*, Red Hen Press) Valentine CA.

Where Cultures Meet: Frontiers in Latin American History. Ed. by David J. Weber & Jane M. Rausch. LC 94-1788. (Jaguar Books on Latin America: No. 6). 226p. 1994. 40.00 (*0-8420-2477-8*) Scholarly Res Inc.

Where Cultures Meet: The Story of the Jews of Czechoslovakia. 224p. 1993. 39.95 (*965-05-0503-2*, Pub. by Israel Ministry Def IS) Gefen Bks.

Where D. H. Lawrence Was Wrong about Women. David Holbrook. LC 90-56165. 384p. 1993. 55.00 (*0-8387-5207-1*) Bucknell U Pr.

Where Darkness Sleeps. Brian Riselman. 1995. mass mkt. 5.99 (*0-312-95682-7*) Tor Bks.

Where Dawn Lingers. Ed. by Melissa Mitchell. 1996. 69.95 (*1-57553-065-1*) Watermrk Pr.

Where Death Lies. Ann C. Fallon. Ed. by Dana Isaacson. 256p. (Orig.). 1991. mass mkt. 4.99 (*0-671-70624-1*) PB.

Where Deregulation Went Wrong. 210p. 1988. 7.95 (*0-929097-32-7*, 19638) Sav & Comm Bank.

Where Did AIDS Come From?, 8, Set. Anna Forbes. LC 96-1518. (AIDS Awareness Library). (Illus.). 24p. (J). (gr. k-4). 1996. lib. bdg. 10.46 (*0-8239-2365-7*, PowerKids) Rosen Group.

Where Did All the Dragons Go? Fay Robinson. LC 95-3620. (Illus.). 32p. (J). (gr. k-3). 1996. pap. 14.95 (*0-8167-3808-4*) BrdgeWater.

***Where Did Birdie Go?** Michaela Friends. (Illus.). 36p. 1995. pap. 10.95 (*1-880812-20-7*) S Ink WA.

Where Did Christmas Come From? Al Remson. LC 96-7821. 96p. 1996. pap. 8.00 (*0-399-52247-6*) Berkley Pub.

Where Did Dinosaurs Go? (Starting Point Science Ser.). (Illus.). 24p. (J). (gr. 1-6). 1992. pap. 3.95 (*0-7460-1016-8*); lib. bdg. 12.95 (*0-88110-582-1*) EDC.

Where Did God Come From? Harvey Jackins. 1981. pap. 2.00 (*0-913937-08-8*) Rational Isl.

Where Did I Come From. Peter Mayle. (Illus.). 48p. (J). (gr. 3 up). 1973. 12.00 (*0-8184-0161-3*); pap. 9.95 (*0-8184-0253-9*) Carol Pub Group.

Where Did I Come From? Special 20th Anniversary Gift Edition. anniversary ed. Peter Mayle. (Illus.). 48p. (J). 1996. 13.95 (*0-8184-0581-3*, L Stuart) Carol Pub Group.

Where Did I Come From; Why Am I Here. Hilton Hotema. 97p. 1969. reprint ed. spiral bd. 10.00 (*0-7873-0447-6*) Hlth Research.

Where Did I Go Wrong? Rosalyn Rushbrook. (Illus.). 96p. (C). 1990. 29.00 (*0-85439-418-4*, Pub. by St Paul Pubns UK) St Mut.

Where Did I Put It? The Here's Where Registry & Guide. Joseph A. Ecclesine. 60p. 1989. pap. text ed. 5.00 (*0-9606814-1-8*) Wry Idea.

Where Did I Put My Glasses? How You Can Improve Your Memory As You Grow Older. Ralph Mendelson. 348p. 1993. 24.95 (*0-9635556-0-X*) Segno Bks.

Where Did I Wake up? The Poetry of Stanislaw Baranczak. Tr. by Frank Kujawinski. (Poetry Chapbook Ser.). 1978. 2.00 (*0-932191-00-2*) Mr Cogito Pr.

Where Did Mary Go? A Loving Husband's Struggle with Alzheimers. Frank A. Wall. (Illus.). 148p. 1996. 19.95 (*1-57392-070-3*) Prometheus Bks.

Where Did My Feather Pillow Come From? Audilee B. Taylor. LC 81-71027. (Illus.). 32p. (J). (ps-3). 1982. 10.00 (*0-942250-00-1*) Castlemarsh.

Where Did Our Love Go? The Rise & Fall of the Motown Sound. Nelson George. (Illus.). 256p. 1985. pap. 9.95 (*0-685-43290-4*) St Martin.

Where Did Our Love Go? The Rise & Fall of the Motown Sound. Nelson George. 256p. 1987. pap. 9.95 (*0-312-01109-1*) St Martin.

Where Did Papa Go: Looking at Death from a Young Child's Perspective. Judy E. Laufer. (Illus.). 32p. (Orig.). (J). (ps-2). 1991. pap. 9.95 (*1-881669-00-9*) Little Egg Pub.

Where Did the Bible Come From? Gregory Williams. 16p. (Orig.). 1989. pap. 1.00 (*0-912927-36-4*, X036) St John Kronstadt.

Where Did the Dinosaurs Go? C. Vance Cast. (Clever Calvin Ser.). (Illus.). 40p. (J). (ps-2). 1994. pap. 4.95 (*0-8120-1573-8*) Barron.

Where Did the Reindeer Come From? Alaska Experience the First Fifty Years. Alice E. Postell. Ed. by Susan P. York. LC 90-146. (Illus.). 144p. (YA). (gr. 9 up). 1990. write for info. (*0-9626090-0-5*) Amaknak Pr.

Where Did the Time Go? The Working Woman's Guide to Time Management. Ruth Klein. 272p. 1992. 19.95 (*1-55958-222-7*) Prima Pub.

Where Did the Time Go: The Working Woman's Guide to Time Management. Ruth Klein. 1994. pap. 10.95 (*1-55958-492-0*) Prima Pub.

Where Did They Go When They Came to America: Over a Century of Jewish Life in America. Marilyn Conn & Ori Z. Soltes. (Illus.). 32p. pap. text ed. write for info. (*1-881456-14-5*) B B K Natl Jew Mus.

Where Did Those Dudes Come From? James R. Granger, Jr. Ed. by Richard Morris. (Illus.). 30p. (Orig.). 1990. pap. 3.95 (*0-945023-03-0*) Uraeus Pub.

Where Did You Get Those Eyes: A Guide to Discovering Your Family History. Kay Cooper. (American History Series for Young People). (Illus.). (J). (gr. 5 up). 1988. 13.95 (*0-8027-6802-4*); lib. bdg. 14.85 (*0-8027-6803-2*) Walker & Co.

Where Did You Get Your Moccasins? Bernelda Wheeler. (Illus.). 24p. (J). (gr. k-2). 1992. pap. 6.00 (*1-895411-50-5*) Peguis Pubs Ltd.

Where Did You Go? "Out" "What Did You Do? "Nothing" 2nd ed. Robert P. Smith. (Illus.). 144p. pap. 5.95 (*0-938530-23-2*) Lexikos.

Where Did You Put Your Sleep? Marcia Newfield. LC 83-2785. (Illus.). 32p. (J). (gr. k-4). 1983. lib. bdg. 13.95 (*0-689-50286-5*, McElderry) S&S Childrens.

Where Did You Spend the Night? Richard Booth. LC 93-4583. 1993. pap. 6.00 (*0-88734-273-6*) Players Pr.

Where Did Your Family Come From? A Book about Immigrants. Melvin Berger & Gilda Berger. LC 92-28626. (Discovery Readers Ser.). (Illus.). 48p. (J). (gr. k-4). 1993. per., pap. 4.50 (*0-8249-8610-5*, Ideals Child); lib. bdg. 12.00 (*0-8249-8647-4*, Ideals Child) Hambleton-Hill.

Where Dinosaurs Still Rule: A Guide to Dinosaur Areas of the West. Debbie Tewell & Gayle C. Shirley. LC 92-55078. (Interpreting the Great Outdoors Ser.). (Illus.). 48p. (Orig.). (J). 1993. pap. 6.95 (*1-56044-177-1*) Falcon Pr MT.

Where Divinity Begins. Deborah DeNicola. 80p. (Orig.). 1994. pap. 9.95 (*1-882295-02-1*) Alicejamesbooks.

Where Do Angels Buy Their Clothes? Starr Hall. Ed. by Heidi Borchers. LC 96-92164. (Illus.). 48p. (J). (ps-6). 1996. 13.95 (*0-9651678-0-1*) Simply Angels.

Where Do Ants Live? Questions Kids Ask about Backyard Nature. Neil Morris. LC 94-14122. (Tell Me Why Ser.). (Illus.). 32p. (J). (ps-2). 1995. 7.99 (*0-89577-607-3*, Rdrs Dig Kids) RD Assn.

Where Do Babies Come From? Ruth Hummel. (Learning about Sex Ser.: Bk. 2). 32p. (J). (gr. 1-3). 1995. 8.99 (*0-570-03553-8*, 14-2102) Concordia.

Where Do Babies Come From? Susan Mayes. (Starting Point Science Ser.). (Illus.). 24p. (J). (gr. 1 up). 1992. pap. 3.95 (*0-7460-0690-X*, Usborne); lib. bdg. 12.95 (*0-88110-547-3*, Usborne) EDC.

Where Do Babies Come From? Angela Royston. (J). 1996. 9.95 (*0-7894-0579-2*) DK Pub Inc.

***Where Do Bears Sleep?** Barbara S. Hazen. LC 96-43071. (Illus.). (J). 1997. write for info. (*0-694-01037-5*) HarpC.

Where Do Birds Live? Ron Hirschi. (Illus.). (J). (ps-4). 1987. 10.95 (*0-8027-6722-2*); lib. bdg. 11.85 (*0-8027-6723-0*) Walker & Co.

Where Do Bumblebees Live? Lucille Quinitchette. (Illus.). 13p. (Orig.). (J). (gr. 4). 1994. pap. 5.95 (*0-9640122-1-9*) Pen & Pr Unltd.

Where Do Cats Live? Ron Hirschi. (Illus.). 32p. (J). (gr. 1-3). 1991. 13.95 (*0-8027-8109-8*); lib. bdg. 14.85 (*0-8027-8110-1*) Walker & Co.

***Where Do Falling Stars Go?** Melanie Friedersdorf. (Illus.). 48p. (J). (ps-1). 1997. 14.95 (*0-9658061-6-2*) Peaceful Village.

Where Do Grandmothers Come From? And Where Do They Go? 2nd ed. Frances Weaver. (Illus.). 140p. 1992. pap. text ed. 10.00 (*0-9617930-4-X*) Midlife Musings.

Where Do Horses Live? Ron Hirschi. (J). 1989. 11.95 (*0-8027-6878-4*); lib. bdg. 12.85 (*0-8027-6879-2*) Walker & Co.

Where Do I Draw the Line. Michael P. Farris. 224p. 1992. pap. 8.99 (*1-55661-229-X*) Bethany Hse.

Where Do I Go for Strength. Max Lucado. 32p. 1995. pap. 2.99 (*0-8499-5151-8*) Word Pub.

Where Do I Go from Here? (Now That I'm a Christian Ser.). 24p. 1985. pap. 0.59 (*0-88243-561-2*, 02-0561) Gospel Pub.

Where Do I Go from Here? Valerie W. Wesley. 144p. (J). (gr. 7-9). 1996. pap. 3.50 (*0-590-45607-5*) Scholastic Inc.

Where Do I Go from Here? Understanding & Living Your Christian Faith. Dave Branon. LC 93-41779. 224p. 1993. pap. 10.99 (*0-929239-80-6*) Discovery Hse Pubs.

***Where Do I Go from Here - After Divorce.** Joseph B. Stingley. LC 96-94795. 130p. (Orig.). 1996. pap. 9.95 (*0-9654956-0-4*) Gift of God.

Where Do I Go from Here with My Life? John C. Crystal & Richard N. Bolles. LC 78-61867. (Illus.). 272p. 1980. pap. 17.95 (*0-89815-084-1*) Ten Speed Pr.

Where Do I Go to Get a Life? Nicholas Comninellis. 182p. 1995. student ed., pap. 9.99 (*0-88070-732-1*, Multnomah Bks) Multnomah Pubs.

Where Do I Grow from Here. Greg Glassford. 96p. 1993. mass mkt. 3.99 (*0-88368-248-6*) Whitaker Hse.

Where Do I Live? Neil Chesanow. LC 95-8463. (Illus.). 48p. (J). (gr. k-4). 1995. 11.95 (*0-8120-6541-7*) Barron.

Where Do I Live? Neil Chesanow. LC 95-8463. (Illus.). 48p. (J). (gr. k-4). 1995. pap. 5.95 (*0-8120-9241-4*) Barron.

Where Do I Live? Shirley Greenway. LC 92-7739. (Animals Q & A Ser.). (Illus.). 32p. (J). (ps-2). 1992. per., pap. 3.95 (*0-8249-8561-3*, Ideals Child); lib. bdg. 11.00 (*0-8249-8576-1*, Ideals Child) Hambleton-Hill.

***Where Do I Live?** Claudette C. Mitchell et al. (Visions: African-American Experiences: Vol. 40). (Illus.). 8p. (Orig.). (J). (gr. k-1). 1996. pap. text ed. 3.00 (*1-57518-082-0*) Arborlake.

Where Do I Look? Jacque Franklin. LC 83-82861. (Illus.). 40p. (Orig.). 1983. pap. 7.95 (*0-938216-20-1*) GCA.

Where Do I Put My Purse While I Preach. Mary B. Craft. LC 88-64024. (Miss Father Ser.). (Illus.). 64p. (Orig.). 1990. pap. 6.00 (*0-938991-40-X*) Colonial Pr AL.

Where Do I Put the Decimal Point? How to Conquer Math Anxiety & Let Numbers Work for You. Elisabeth Ruedy & Sue Nirenberg. 1992. pap. 9.00 (*0-380-71596-1*) Avon.

Where Do Judges Come From? Cynthia Owen Philip et al. 132p. 1976. 3.50 (*0-318-14448-4*) IJA NYU.

Where Do Little Girls Grow? Milly J. Limmer. Ed. by Abby Levine. LC 92-22936. (Illus.). 32p. (J). (ps-2). 1993. lib. bdg. 15.95 (*0-8075-8924-1*) A Whitman.

Where Do Monsters Hide? The Story of Magical Monster Dust. Tracy L. Mitropoulos. (Button Bks.). (Illus.). 32p. (J). (ps-3). 1992. 9.95 (*1-886250-01-4*) Belly Buttons.

Where Do Monsters Live? Rozanne L. Williams. (Emergent Reader Bks.). 8p. 1994. 1.59 (*0-916119-52-1*) Creat Teach Pr.

Where Do Monsters Live? Rozanne L. Williams. (Emergent Reader Big Bks.). (Illus.). 8p. (Orig.). (J). (gr. k-2). 1995. pap. 7.98 (*1-57471-064-8*) Creat Teach Pr.

Where Do People Take Their Troubles? Lee R. Steiner. LC 45-6876. 279p. reprint ed. pap. 79.60 (*0-317-10255-9*, 2010708) Bks Demand.

Where Do Puddles Go? Fay Robinson. LC 94-35629. (Rookie Read-About Science Ser.). (Illus.). 32p. (J). (ps-2). 1995. lib. bdg. 17.30 (*0-516-06036-8*) Childrens.

Where Do Puddles Go? Fay Robinson. (Rookie Read-About Science Ser.). (Illus.). 32p. (J). (ps-2). 1995. pap. 3.95 (*0-516-46036-6*) Childrens.

Where Do the Animals Live? Melvin Berger. Ed. by Lisa Trumbauer. (Early Science Big Bks.). (Illus.). 16p. (J). (ps-2). 1994. pap. 14.95 (*1-56784-019-1*) Newbridge Comms.

Where Do the Animals Live? Mini Book. Melvin Berger. Ed. by Lisa Trumbauer. (Early Science Big Bks.). 16p. (J). (ps-2). 1995. pap. 2.95 (*1-56784-044-2*) Newbridge Comms.

Where Do the Animals Live? Theme Pack. Melvin Berger. Ed. by Susan Evento. (Macmillan Early Science Big Bks.). (Illus.). (J). (ps-2). 1995. pap. write for info. (*1-56784-176-7*) Newbridge Comms.

Where Do the Birds Go When It Storms. Ed. by J. Grubbs. (Science Ser.). (Illus.). (J). (gr. 1-3). 1992. 32.00 (*1-56611-143-9*); pap. 28.00 (*1-56611-042-4*); lib. bdg. 28.00 (*1-56611-012-2*) Jones.

Where Do the Ducks Go? Barbara Seuling. LC 95-52259. (Illus.). (J). 1998. write for info. (*0-15-201403-9*) HarBrace.

Where Do We Come From? What Are We? Where Are We Going? An Annotated Bibliography of Aging & the Humanities. Donna Polisar et al. LC 88-24578. (C). 1988. pap. 15.00 (*0-929596-01-3*) Gerontological Soc.

***Where Do We Draw the Line? The Seductive Power of New Age.** J. William Smit. LC 96-33505. (Issues in Christian Living Ser.). 127p. (Orig.). 1996. pap. 7.15 (*1-56212-225-8*, 1344-0470) CRC Pubns.

Where Do We Go from Here? Isaac Asimov. 1976. pap. 1.75 (*0-449-22849-5*, X2849, Crest) Fawcett.

Where Do We Go from Here? H. A. Gardner. 1995. 16.95 (*0-533-11334-2*) Vantage.

Where Do We Go from Here? Kenneth Hagin, Jr. 1982. pap. 0.75 (*0-89276-712-X*) Hagin Ministries.

***Where Do We Go from Here?** R. Neighbor. 1996. pap. 14.95 (*1-880828-54-5*) Touch Pubns.

Where Do We Go from Here? Tom Sabella & Michael Pachell. 36p. 1983. pap. 5.00 (*0-9612786-0-9*) Positive Notes.

Where Do We Go from Here? Matthew V. Smith. (Illus.). 15p. (J). (gr. k-3). 1992. pap. 11.95 (*1-895583-35-7*) MAYA Pubs.

Where Do We Go from Here: The Place of the Artist & the NEA. Michael Brenson. 22p. (Orig.). 1995. pap. 3.00 (*0-9637817-2-3*) Schl Art Inst.

Where Do We Live? Annie Kubler. (J). 1985. 4.99 (*0-85953-256-9*) Childs Play.

Where Do We Sleep? Nicola Smee. Ed. by Amy Cohn. (Illus.). (J). 1995. pap. write for info. (*0-318-72967-9*, Tupelo Bks) Morrow.

Where Do Words Come From? Gary Bevington. 96p. (C). 1995. per., pap. text ed. 21.99 (*0-7872-1013-7*) Kendall-Hunt.

Where Do You Draw the Line? Steve Benson & Bill Keane. Ed. by Richard Lessner. (Illus.). 170p. 1992. pap. 10.95 (*0-938448-72-2*) Wide World Maps.

Where Do You Get Your Ideas? Sandy Asher. (Illus.). 96p. (J). (gr. 5 up). 1987. 12.95 (*0-8027-6690-0*); lib. bdg. 13.85 (*0-8027-6691-9*) Walker & Co.

Where Do You Get Your Ideas? Sandy Asher. 96p. (J). (gr. 4-7). 1994. pap. 6.95 (*0-8027-7421-0*) Walker & Co.

***Where Do You Go after You've Been to the Moon? A Case Study of NASA's Pioneer Effort at Change.** Francis T. Hoban et al. LC 96-46071. (Orbit Ser.). (Illus.). 240p. (C). 1997. 29.50 (*0-89464-060-7*) Krieger.

Where Do You Go to Give Up? Building a Community of Grace. C. Welton Gaddy. 182p. (Orig.). 1993. pap. 12.95 (*1-880837-73-0*) Smyth & Helwys.

Where Do You Go to Give Up: Building a Community of Grace. C. Welton Gaddy. 182p. 1994. pap. text ed. 12.95 (*1-57312-005-7*) Smyth & Helwys.

Where Do You Go When Love Dies? Gene E. Nelson. (Illus.). (Orig.). 1991. pap. 7.95 (*0-9623810-5-5*) White Plume Pr.

Where Do You Put the Horse? Essays. Paul Metcalf. LC 86-71074. 168p. 1986. 20.00 (*0-916583-16-3*) Dalkey Arch.

Where Do You Put the Horse? Essays. deluxe limited ed. Paul Metcalf. LC 86-71074. 165p. 1986. 40.00 (*0-916583-95-3*) Dalkey Arch.

Where Do You Stand? Eight Moral Issues Confronting Today's Christians. Gregory C. Higgins. LC 95-31454. 128p. (Orig.). 1996. pap. 8.95 (*0-8091-3608-2*) Paulist Pr.

Where Do You Stand with the Church? The Dilemma of Divorced Catholics. John T. Catoir. LC 96-33124. 124p. (Orig.). 1996. pap. 7.95 (*0-8189-0776-2*) Alba.

Where Do You Stop? The Personal History, Adventures, Experiences & Observations of Peter. Eric Kraft. 1995. pap. 10.00 (*0-312-11932-1*) St Martin.

Where Do You Stop? The Personal History, Adventures, Experiences, & Observations of Peter Leroy. Eric Kraft. (Illus.). 192p. 1992. 15.00 (*0-517-58544-8*, Crown) Crown Pub Group.

Where Do You Think Sex Came From? Richard Dunn. 48p. (YA). 1991. student ed., pap. 0.60 (*0-89693-195-1*, Victor Bks) Chariot Victor.

Where Do You Think Sex Came From? Richard Dunn. 96p. 1991. teacher ed. 1.00 (*0-89693-194-3*, Victor Bks) Chariot Victor.

Where Do You Think You're Going, Christopher Columbus? Jean Fritz. (Illus.). 48p. (J). (gr. 2-6). 1980. 13.95 (*0-399-20723-6*, Putnam) Putnam Pub Group.

Where Do You Think You're Going, Christopher Columbus? Jean Fritz. (Illus.). 80p. (J). (gr. 3-7). 1980. pap. 8.95 (*0-399-20734-1*, Putnam) Putnam Pub Group.

W

***Where Do You Think You're Going, Christopher Columbus?** Jean Fritz. (Illus.). 80p. (J). (gr. 2-5). 1997. pap. 5.95 (*0-698-11580-5*, Paperstar) Putnam Pub Group.

Where Does a Mother Go to Resign? Barbara Johnson. LC 79-12686. 160p. 1979. pap. 8.99 (*0-87123-606-0*) Bethany Hse.

Where Does All the Garbage Go? Melvin Berger. Ed. by Natalie Lunis. (Early Science Big Bks.). (Illus.). 16p. (J). (ps-2). 1992. pap. 14.95 (*1-56784-002-7*) Newbridge Comms.

Where Does All the Garbage Go? Mini Book. Melvin Berger. Ed. by Natalie Lunis. (Early Science Big Bks.). (Illus.). 16p. (J). (ps-2). 1993. pap. 2.95 (*1-56784-027-2*) Newbridge Comms.

Where Does All the Garbage Go? Theme Pack. Melvin Berger. Ed. by Susan Evento. (Macmillan Early Science Big Bks.). (Illus.). (J). (ps-2). 1995. pap. write for info. (*1-56784-134-1*) Newbridge Comms.

Where Does All the Money Go? Jim Becker. Date not set. pap. 69.80 (*0-393-30900-2*) Norton.

Where Does All the Money Go? Taking Control of Your Personal Expenses. Jim Becker & Andy Mayer. 1992. pap. 3.49 (*0-393-30899-5*) Norton.

Where Does Christian Freedom End? First Corinthians 8. (First Corinthians Commentary Ser.). 1985. pap. 7.99 (*0-89957-469-6*) AMG Pubs.

Where Does Christian Freedom End? First Corinthians 8. Spiros Zodhiates. (Exegetical Commentary Ser.). 118p. 1995. ring bd. 15.99 (*0-89957-466-1*) AMG Pubs.

Where Does Electricity Come From? C. Vance Cast. (Clever Calvin Ser.). (Illus.). 40p. (J). (ps-2). 1992. pap. 5.95 (*0-8120-4835-0*) Barron.

Where Does Electricity Come From? Susan Mayes. (Starting Point Science Ser.). (Illus.). 24p. (J). (gr. 1-4). 1989. pap. 3.95 (*0-7460-0358-7*, Usborne) EDC.

Where Does Garbage Go? Isaac Asimov. LC 91-50361. (Ask Isaac Asimov Ser.). (Illus.). 24p. (J). (gr. 2-3). 1992. lib. bdg. 17.27 (*0-8368-0742-1*) Gareth Stevens Inc.

***Where Does God Live?** Holly Bea. (Illus.). 32p. (J). (gr. k-2). 1997. 14.00 (*0-915811-73-1*, Starseed) H J Kramer Inc.

Where Does God Live? Marc Gellman & Thomas Hartman. 112p. 1992. mass mkt. 4.99 (*0-345-37795-8*) Ballantine.

Where Does God Live? Fifty Eight More "Something for the Kids" Children's Sermons for Worship. Ted Lazicki. Ed. by Arthur L. Zapel & Rhonda Wray. LC 91-8734. (Illus.). 144p. (Orig.). (J). (ps-5). 1991. pap. 9.95 (*0-916260-77-1*, B189) Meriwether Pub.

Where Does God Live? Questions & Answers for Parents & Children. Marc Gellman & Thomas Hartman. LC 90-25458. (Illus.). 144p. 1991. reprint ed. 13.95 (*0-89243-510-0*, Triumph Books) Liguori Pubns.

Where Does God Live? Questions & Answers for Parents & Children. Marc Gellman & Thomas Hartman. LC 90-25458. (Illus.). 144p. 1996. reprint ed. pap. 10.00 (*0-89243-927-0*) Liguori Pubns.

***Where Does God Sleep, Momma?** Nancy Bestmann. (Illus.). 18p. (J). 1997. 12.99 (*0-89900-664-7*) College Pr Pub.

Where Does It Belong? Interactive Language Activities Featuring Vocabulary & Question Forms. Marilyn M. Toomey. (Illus.). 1989. student ed. 16.95 (*0-923573-13-5*) Circuit Pubns.

Where Does It Go? Margaret Miller. LC 91-30160. (Illus.). 40p. (J). (ps-4). 1992. 16.00 (*0-688-10928-4*); lib. bdg. 15.93 (*0-688-10929-2*) Greenwillow.

Where Does It Hurt? A Guide to Symptoms & Illnesses. Susan C. Pescar & Christine A. Nelson. LC 83-5663. 323p. reprint ed. pap. 92.10 (*0-7837-1573-0*, 2041865) Bks Demand.

Where Does It Hurt? Life Story of New England Country Doctor. Aubrey V. Gould. (Illus.). 86p. (Orig.). 1987. pap. 7.95 (*0-9619628-0-1*) Fieldside Pub.

Where Does It Hurt? The Story of a New England Country Doctor. 2nd rev. ed. Aubrey V. Gould. LC 90-82594. 123p. 1996. write for info. (*0-9619628-5-2*) Fieldside Pub.

Where Does Kissing End? Kate Pullinger. (Masks Ser.). 129p. 1995. pap. 12.99 (*1-85242-277-7*) Serpents Tail.

Where Does My Spaghetti Go When I Eat? Questions Kids Ask about the Human Body. Neil Morris. LC 94-14121. (Illus.). 32p. (J). (ps-2). 1995. 7.99 (*0-89577-608-1*, Rdrs Dig Kids) RD Assn.

Where Does Oil Come From? C. Vance Cast. (Clever Calvin Ser.). (Illus.). 40p. (J). (ps-2). 1993. pap. 4.95 (*0-8120-1467-7*) Barron.

***Where Does One Go When There's No Place Left to Go.** deluxe limited ed. Harry Crews. 92p. 1997. 75.00 (*0-940941-09-0*) Blood & Guts Pr.

Where Does Paper Come From? C. Vance Cast. (Clever Calvin Ser.). (Illus.). 40p. (J). (ps-2). 1993. pap. 4.95 (*0-8120-1468-5*) Barron.

Where Does Pollution Come From? C. Vance Cast. (Clever Calvin Ser.). (Illus.). 40p. (J). (ps-2). 1994. pap. 4.95 (*0-8120-1571-1*) Barron.

Where Does Rubbish Go? Susan Mayes. (Starting Point Science Ser.). (Illus.). 24p. (J). (gr. 1 up). 1992. pap. 3.95 (*0-7460-0627-6*, Usborne); lib. bdg. 12.95 (*0-88110-551-1*, Usborne) EDC.

Where Does the Brown Bear Go? Nicki Weiss. LC 87-36980. (Illus.). 24p. (J). (ps up). 1989. 16.00 (*0-688-07862-1*); lib. bdg. 15.93 (*0-688-07863-X*) Greenwillow.

Where Does the Brown Bear Go? Nicki Weiss. (J). (ps). 1990. pap. 5.99 (*0-14-054181-0*, Puffin) Puffin Bks.

***Where Does the Butterfly Go When It Rains?** May Garelick. LC 96-27575. (Illus.). (J). 1997. write for info. (*1-57255-165-8*); pap. write for info. (*1-57255-162-3*) Mondo Pubng.

Where Does the Garbage Go? rev. ed. Paul Showers. LC 91-46115. (Trophy Let's-Read-&-Find-Out Science Bk.: Stage 2). (Illus.). 32p. (J). (gr. k-4). 1994. pap. 4.95 (*0-06-445114-3*, Trophy) HarpC Child Bks.

Where Does the Garbage Go? rev. ed. Paul Showers. LC 91-46115. (Let's-Read-&-Find-Out Science Bk.: Stage 2). (Illus.). 32p. (J). (gr. k-4). 1994. 15.00 (*0-06-021054-0*); lib. bdg. 14.89 (*0-06-021057-5*) HarpC Child Bks.

Where Does the Mail Go? A Book about the Postal System. Melvin Berger & Gilda Berger. LC 94-6254. (Discovery Readers Ser.). (Illus.). 48p. (J). (gr. k-4). 1994. per., pap. 4.50 (*1-57102-006-3*, Ideals Child); lib. bdg. 12.00 (*1-57102-022-5*, Ideals Child) Hambleton-Hill.

Where Does the Marine Corps Go from Here? Martin Binkin & Jeffrey Record. LC 75-45068. (Studies in Defense Policy). 105p. reprint ed. pap. 30.00 (*0-317-30403-8*, 2024962) Bks Demand.

Where Does the Money Go? Resource Allocation in Elementary & Secondary Schools. Lawrence O. Picus & James L. Wattenbarger. (Yearbook of the American Education Finance Association Ser.). (Illus.). 296p. 1996. 46.95 (*0-8039-6162-6*) Corwin Pr.

Where Does the Moon Go? Sidney Rosen. (Question of Science Book). (Illus.). 40p. (J). (gr. k-3). 1992. lib. bdg. 14.96 (*0-87614-685-X*, Carolrhoda) Lerner Group.

Where Does the Night Hide? Nancy W. Carlstrom. LC 89-32910. (Illus.). 32p. (J). (ps-1). 1990. lib. bdg. 13.95 (*0-02-717390-9*, Mac Bks Young Read) S&S Childrens.

***Where Does the Night Hide.** Nancy W. Carlstrom. (Illus.). 32p. (J). 3.98 (*0-8317-6784-7*) Smithmark.

Where Does the Sky End, Grandpa? M. Alexander. 32p. (J). (ps-3). 1992. 13.00 (*0-15-295603-4*, HB Juv Bks) HarBrace.

Where Does the Sun Go at Night? Mirra Ginsburg. LC 79-16151. (Illus.). 32p. (J). (ps up). 1987. reprint ed. pap. 4.95 (*0-688-07041-8*, Mulberry) Morrow.

Where Does the Sun Sleep? First Questions & Answers about Bedtime. Time-Life Books Editors. Ed. by Neil Kagan. (Library of First Questions & Answers). (Illus.). 48p. (J). (gr. k-2). 1993. 14.95 (*0-7835-0866-2*) Time-Life.

Where Does the Sun Sleep? First Questions & Answers about Bedtime. Time-Life Books Editors. Ed. by Neil Kagan. (Library of First Questions & Answers). (Illus.). 48p. (J). (ps). 1993. lib. bdg. write for info. (*0-7835-0867-0*) Time-Life.

Where Does the Teacher Live? Paula K. Feder. (Illus.). 48p. 1996. pap. 3.50 (*0-14-038119-8*) Viking Penguin.

Where Does the Teacher Live? Paula K. Feder. 1999. pap. 3.50 (*0-14-054854-8*) NAL-Dutton.

Where Does the Teacher Sleep? Kathleen Gibson & Kristine Dillard. (Illus.). 8p. (Orig.). (J). (gr. k-1). 1994. pap. text ed. 3.50 (*1-880612-45-3*) Seedling Pubns.

Where Does the Trail Lead? Burton Albert. (J). (gr. k-3). 1991. pap. 15.00 (*0-671-73409-1*, S&S Bks Young Read) S&S Childrens.

Where Does the Trail Lead? Burton Albert. LC 90-21450. (Illus.). 40p. (J). (ps-3). 1993. pap. 5.95 (*0-671-79617-8*, S&S Bks Young Read) S&S Childrens.

Where Does the Weirdness Go? Why Quantum Mechanics Is Strange but Not As Strange As You Think. David Lindley. 176p. 1996. 20.00 (*0-465-06785-9*) Basic.

***Where Does the Weirdness Go? Why Quantum Mechanics is Strange, But Not as Strange as you Think.** David Lindley. 272p. 1997. pap. 13.00 (*0-465-06786-7*) Basic.

Where Does the Wind Go? Marcia Vaughan. (Illus.). (J). 1996. pap. write for info. (*1-57255-007-4*) Mondo Pubng.

Where Does the World End? Elizabeth Kontoyiannaki. (Illus.). 14p. (J). (gr. k-3). 1992. pap. 12.95 (*1-895583-45-4*) MAYA Pubs.

Where Does Water Come From? C. Vance Cast. (Clever Calvin Ser.). (Illus.). 40p. (J). (ps-2). 1992. pap. 5.95 (*0-8120-4642-0*) Barron.

Where Domino Fell. 2nd ed. Olson. 326p. 1996. pap. 26.95 (*0-312-14784-8*) St Martin.

Where Dreams Are Born. Mitchell D. Tolle. 128p. 1994. pap. 29.95 (*0-9644951-1-2*) Painted Treas.

***Where Dreams Have Been.** Penny Richards. (Silhouette Romance Ser.). 1996. 19.95 (*0-373-59748-7*) Thorndike Pr.

Where Dreams Have Been... (That Special Woman!) Penny Richards. (Special Edition Ser.). 1995. mass mkt. 3.75 (*0-373-09949-5*, 1-09949-8) Silhouette.

***Where Duty Calls: Growing up in the Marine Corps.** Charlie Romine. 1997. pap. text ed. 12.95 (*1-887269-31-2*) J Culler & Sons.

Where Dwarfs Reign: A Tropical Rainforest in Puerto Rico. Kathryn Robinson. LC 96-22091. 1996. write for info. (*0-8477-0255-3*) U of PR Pr.

***Where Eagles Dare.** (Nelson Readers Ser.). (J). Date not set. pap. text ed. write for info. (*0-17-557049-3*) Addison-Wesley.

Where Eagles Dare. Alistair MacLean. 1987. mass mkt. 5.99 (*0-449-21581-4*) Fawcett.

Where Eagles Fall. Lorri Martinez. 1983. pap. 2.50 (*0-942396-32-4*) Blackberry ME.

Where Eagles Fly. Jack D. Countryman. (Illus.). 20p. 1992. pap. 4.00 (*1-878149-13-X*) Counterpoint Pub.

***Where Eagles Fly: Jan Opperman: The Rest of the Story.** Harvey Shapiro. (Illus.). 272p. 1996. 30.00 (*0-9627653-6-8*) Witness Prods.

Where Eagles Fly: The Shamanic Way to Inner Wisdom. Kenneth Meadows. 1995. pap. 14.95 (*1-85230-620-3*) Element MA.

Where Eagles Land: Planning & Development of U. S. Army Airfields, 1910-1941. Jerold E. Brown. LC 89-23256. (Contributions in Military Studies: No. 94). 232p. 1990. text ed. 59.95 (*0-313-26800-2*, BUF/, Greenwood Pr) Greenwood.

Where Eagles Rest. Hyrum M. Smith. pap. 5.95 (*1-55503-217-6*, 0111821) Covenant Comms.

Where Eagles Soar: An Alternative to Negative Religion. William E. Cameron. LC 94-71044. 270p. (Orig.). 1994. pap. 17.95 (*0-940121-16-6*, P214, Cross Roads Bks) Cross Cultural Pubns.

Where East Meets West: The West on the Agenda of the Islamic Revival. Mona Abul-Fadl. LC 90-45360. (Islamization of Knowledge Ser.: No. 10). 117p. (Orig.). 1992. pap. 6.00 (*0-912463-73-2*) IIIT VA.

Where Echoes Live. Marcia Muller. 368p. 1992. mass mkt. 3.99 (*0-446-40161-7*, Mysterious Paperbk) Warner Bks.

Where Every Breath Is a Prayer: A Photographic Pilgrimage into the Spiritual Heart of Asia. Jon Ortner. LC 96-16630. (Illus.). 248p. 1996. 50.00 (*1-55670-439-9*) Stewart Tabori & Chang.

Where Everything Points to Him. Karel Deddens. Tr. & Intro. by Theodore Plantinga. LC 93-24061. 170p. (Orig.). 1993. pap. 11.90 (*0-921100-39-6*) Inhtce Pubns.

***Where Evil Sleeps.** Valerie W. Wesley. 1997. mass mkt. 6.50 (*0-380-72908-3*) Avon.

Where Evil Sleeps. Valerie W. Wesley. 224p. 1996. 21.95 (*0-399-14145-6*, Putnam) Putnam Pub Group.

***Where Evil Sleeps.** Valerie W. Wesley. 1997. mass mkt. 6.50 (*0-614-27696-9*) Avon.

Where Exactly Is Heaven: Science, God & Common Sense. Bennett Litwin. LC 89-69867. (Illus.). 184p. (Orig.). 1990. pap. 8.95 (*0-9615743-7-2*) SunShine CO.

Where Fate Leads. large type ed. Harry Howarth. (Charnwood Library). 432p. 1993. 27.99 (*0-7089-8739-7*, Trail West Pubs) Ulverscroft.

Where Feminists Come From. Peacock & Martin. 1995. per. 7.95 (*0-920813-75-5*, Pub. by Sister Vision CN) LPC InBook.

***Where Fireflies Dance.** Lucha Corpi. LC 96-29355. (Illus.). (J). 1997. 15.95 (*0-89239-145-6*) Childrens Book Pr.

Where Fish Go in Winter: And Answers to Other Great Mysteries. Amy G. Koss. LC 87-25867. (Illus.). 32p. (J). (ps-5). 1987. 9.95 (*0-8431-2218-8*) Price Stern Sloan.

Where Flaubert Lies: Mythology & History. Claire Addison. (Studies in French: No. 48). 348p. (C). 1996. text ed. 64.95 (*0-521-42016-4*) Cambridge U Pr.

Where Flowers Grow. Belle B. Broadbent. 16p. 1982. pap. 1.95 (*0-939298-04-X*) J M Prods.

Where Food Comes From. J. Cook. (Explainers Ser.). 1989. pap. 4.50 (*0-7460-0280-7*, Usborne) EDC.

Where Food Comes From. Dorothy H. Patent. LC 90-49833. (Illus.). 40p. (J). (gr. 3-7). 1991. lib. bdg. 14.95 (*0-8234-0877-9*) Holiday.

Where Freedom Begins. Teresa A. Pitts. 27p. (Orig.). (J). (gr. 5 up). 1990. pap. 10.00 (*0-9618600-1-4*) T A Pitts.

Where Gardens Grow: An Adoption Story for Children. Sherry Simon & Debra Fischman. (J). 1994. 7.95 (*0-533-10829-2*) Vantage.

Where Giants Trod: The Saga of Kenya's Desert Lake. Monty Brown. 1992. 35.00 (*1-870948-25-4*, Pub. by Quiller Pr UK) St Mut.

Where God Begins to Be: A Woman's Journey into Solitude. Karen Karper. 127p. (Orig.). 1994. pap. 10.00 (*0-8028-0718-6*) Eerdmans.

Where God May Be Found. L. Patrick Carroll. LC 93-48993. 112p. (Orig.). 1994. pap. 7.95 (*0-8091-3472-1*) Paulist Pr.

Where God Meets Man: Luther's Down-to-Earth Approach to the Gospel. Gerhard O. Forde. LC 72-78569. 128p. 1972. pap. 10.99 (*0-8066-1235-5*, 10-7060, Augsburg) Augsburg Fortress.

Where God Put the West: A Moab-Monument Valley Movie History. Bette L. Stanton. Ed. by Jeanie Reynolds & Jean Akens. LC 89-80710. (Illus.). 192p. (Orig.). 1994. pap. 19.95 (*0-944123-02-3*) Four Crnrs UT.

Where God Weeps. rev. ed. Werenfried Van Straaten. LC 88-83744. (Illus.). 269p. 1989. reprint ed. pap. 9.95 (*0-89870-234-8*) Ignatius Pr.

***Where God's People Meet: A Guide to Significant Religious Places in Indiana.** Joseph M. White. LC 96-79138. 200p. (Orig.). 1996. pap. 19.95 (*1-878208-57-8*) Guild Pr IN.

Where Golfers Buy Their Pants: And Other Collected Cartoons. Steve Moore. LC 94-593. (Illus.). 96p. 1994. pap. 8.00 (*0-02-035127-5*) Macmillan.

Where Has Ireland Come From? Frank Mitchell. (Illus.). 64p. 1995. pap. 9.95 (*0-946172-43-9*, Pub. by Town Hse IE) R Rinehart.

Where Has Tommy Flowers Gone? Terrence McNally. 1972. pap. 5.25 (*0-8222-1241-2*) Dramatists Play.

Where Has Tommy Gone? Cedric Vallet. (Illus.). 21p. (J). (gr. k-4). 1995. pap. 9.95 (*1-895583-75-6*) MAYA Pubs.

Where Have All the Adjectives Gone & Other Essays on Semantics & Syntax. R. M. W. Dixon. (Janua Linguarum, Series Major: No. 107). 256p. 1982. text ed. 52.35 (*90-279-3309-X*) Mouton.

Where Have All the Birds Gone? Essays on the Biology & Conservation of Birds that Migrate to the American Tropics. John Terborgh. (Illus.). 224p. (C). 1990. pap. text ed. 16.95 (*0-691-02428-6*) Princeton U Pr.

Where Have All the Bluebirds Gone? Transforming Ability-Based Reading Classrooms. Ed. by JoAnne Caldwell & Michael P. Ford. 117p. (Orig.). 1996. pap. text ed. 8.00 (*1-888714-01-8*) Wiscon St Rding.

Where Have All the Children Gone? Gone to Grown Ups Everyone! Karen K. Clark. (Illus.). 67p. 1977. reprint ed. pap. 7.95 (*0-9626467-0-9*) Ctr Exec Planning.

Where Have All the Colours Gone? Jane Courtney. (Illus.). (J). 1990. 29.00 (*0-85439-407-9*, Pub. by St Paul Pubns UK) St Mut.

Where Have All the Flowers Gone: A Musical Autobiography. rev. ed. Pete Seeger. Ed. by Peter Blood. LC 97-5151. (Illus.). 288p. 1997. pap. 25.00 (*1-881322-10-6*) Sing Out.

Where Have All the Good Fathers Gone? Bk. 2: Child Support & Custody. Douglas O'Brien. 256p. (Orig.). 1997. pap. 16.95 (*0-9637496-2-5*) Skid Eighteen Pr.

Where Have All the Little Girls Gone? Bagz Costello. 320p. (Orig.). 1987. mass mkt. 3.50 (*0-87067-838-8*) Holloway.

Where Have All the Nephites Gone? Pat Bagley. (Illus.). 28p. (J). (gr. 3-12). 1993. 12.95 (*0-87579-757-1*) Deseret Bk.

Where Have All the Parents Gone? M. T. Coffin. (Spinetinglers Ser.). 160p. (Orig.). (J). (gr. 4-5). 1995. pap. 3.50 (*0-380-78117-4*, Camelot) Avon.

***Where Have All the Profits Gone? An Analysis of the Major U. S. Defense Contractors: 1950-1985.** David E. Kaun. (IGCC Research Papers: No. 4). 50p. (Orig.). 1988. pap. 3.50 (*0-934637-09-1*) U of CA Inst Global.

Where Have All the Sardines Gone? Randall A. Reinstedt. LC 79-101716. (Illus.). 168p. 1978. pap. 8.95 (*0-933818-05-X*) Ghost Town.

***Where Have All the Smart Women Gone?** Alice Rowe. Ed. by Margaret D. Smith. LC 96-76263. 84p. (Orig.). 1996. pap. 11.95 (*1-883697-50-6*) Hara Pub.

Where Have All the Tigers Gone? Lynn Hall. LC 88-28835. 144p. (YA). (gr. 7 up). 1989. lib. bdg. 13.95 (*0-684-19003-6*, C Scribner Sons Young) S&S Childrens.

***Where Have I Been All My Life.** Penn. 20.00 (*0-06-251349-4*); pap. 10.00 (*0-06-251350-8*) HarpC.

***Where Have the Wild Geese Gone?** Miriam Elle. LC 94-90272. 136p. (Orig.). 1996. pap. 9.00 (*1-56002-478-X*, Univ Edtns) Aegina Pr.

***Where Have You Been?** Delma Morton. (Illus.). (J). (gr. k-3). 1989. write for info. (*1-57842-113-6*) Delmas Creat.

Where Have You Been? Margaret Wise Brown. (Illus.). 32p. (J). (ps). 1990. reprint ed. 8.95 (*0-8038-8018-9*) Hastings.

Where Have You Gone, Davy? Brigitte Weninger. (Illus.). (J). Date not set. lib. bdg. 15.88 (*1-55858-665-2*) North-South Bks NYC.

Where Have You Gone, Davy? Brigitte Weninger. (Illus.). (J). (gr. k-3). Date not set. 15.95 (*1-55858-664-4*) North-South Bks NYC.

Where Have You Gone, Michelangelo? The Loss of Soul in Catholic Culture. Thomas Day. LC 93-20674. 192p. 1993. 19.95 (*0-8245-1396-7*) Crossroad NY.

Where Have You Gone Mickey Mantle? Robert Kravetz. Ed. by Maurine Johnson & Ralph Hyman. (Illus.). 130p. (Orig.). 1996. pap. 5.95 (*0-9652026-0-7*) GK Creations.

Where He Stands: Albert Shanker of the American Federation of Teachers. Dickson A. Mungazi. LC 94-25964. 280p. 1995. text ed. 55.00 (*0-275-94929-X*, Praeger Pubs) Greenwood.

Where Healing Waters Meet. Clyde W. Ford. 1992. pap. 12.95 (*0-88268-137-0*) Station Hill Pr.

Where Heat Looms. Andre Du Bouchet. Tr. by David Mus from FRE. (Sun & Moon Classics Ser.: No. 87). 110p. 1995. pap. 12.95 (*1-55713-238-0*) Sun & Moon CA.

Where Heaven & Earth Touch: An Anthology of Midrash & Halachah. Danny Siegel. LC 88-35010. 352p. 1995. pap. 24.95 (*1-56821-514-2*) Aronson.

Where Heavens Hide. Dolores Dahl. LC 84-51375. (Illus.). 48p. (Orig.). 1984. pap. 9.95 (*0-9608960-2-3*) Single Vision.

Where Helen Lies. large type ed. Rae Foley. 307p. 1980. 25.99 (*0-7089-0506-4*) Ulverscroft.

Where Honor Dwells. Gilbert Morris. LC 92-36469. (Appomattox Ser.: No. 3). 355p. 1993. pap. 10.99 (*0-8423-6799-3*) Tyndale.

Where Hope Shines Through. Noreen Riols. LC 94-4323. (House of Annanbrae Ser.). 320p. 1994. pap. 10.99 (*0-89107-790-1*) Crossway Bks.

***Where Hope Shines Through.** Noreen Riols. LC 97-18506. (House of Annanbrae Ser.). 1997. 21.95 (*0-7838-8225-4*) G K Hall.

Where I Belong: A Forest of Dean Childhood in the 1930s. Joyce Latham. LC 93-30086. 1993. 29.00 (*0-7509-0386-4*, Pub. by Sutton Pubng UK) Bks Intl VA.

Where I Come From: Selected & New Poems. Maria M. Gillan. (Essential Poets Ser.: No. 64). 150p. 1995. pap. 15.00 (*1-55071-005-2*) Guernica Editions.

Where I Come from! Songs & Poems from Mary Coltores. Illus. by Teresa Flavin. 24p. (J). (gr. k-6). 1991. pap. 25.00 incl. audio (*0-944941-04-4*) Talking Stone Pr.

Where I Hang My Hat. Dick Gallup. 1970. 12.50 (*0-06-011398-7*) Ultramarine Pub.

Where I Live. Heidi Goennel. LC 95-60580. (Illus.). 12p. (J). (ps). 1995. pap. 3.95 (*0-688-14148-X*, Tambourine Bks) Morrow.

Where I Live. Christopher Wormell. LC 95-44730. (Illus.). 32p. (J). (ps-1). 1996. pap. 9.99 (*0-8037-2056-4*) Dial Bks Young.

Where I Live: Selected Essays. Tennessee Williams. Ed. by Christine R. Day & Bob Woods. LC 78-19046. 1978. pap. 9.95 (*0-8112-0706-4*, NDP468) New Directions.

***Where I Stopped: Remembering Rape at Thirteen.** Martha Ramsey. LC 96-47488. (Harvest Book Ser.). 1997. pap. 13.00 (*0-15-600493-3*) HarBrace.

Where I Stopped: Remembering Rape at Thirteen. Martha Ramsey. LC 95-17415. 336p. 1996. 24.95 (*0-399-14107-3*, Putnam) Putnam Pub Group.

Where I Was Born & Raised. David L. Cohn. (History - United States Ser.). 380p. 1993. reprint ed. lib. bdg. 89.00 (*0-7812-4834-5*) Rprt Serv.

Where Ickes Went Right or Reason & Rationality in Environmental Law. Mark Sagoff. 1987. 1.50 (*0-318-33309-0*) IPPP.

W

An Asterisk (*) at the beginning of an entry indicates that the title is appearing in BIP for the first time.

Where Illinois Began: A Pictorial History of Randolph County. Carol Pirtle. LC 95-11610. (Illus.). 1995. write for info. (*0-89865-939-6*) Donning Co.

Where I'm Bound. Sidonie Smith. LC 73-20973. 194p. 1974. text ed. 49.95 (*0-8371-7337-X*, SPS/, Greenwood Pr) Greenwood.

Where I'm Calling From. Raymond Carver. (Contemporaries Ser.). 1989. pap. 13.00 (*0-679-72231-9*, Vin) Random.

Where I'm Coming From. Barbara Brandon. (Illus.). 96p. 1993. pap. 8.95 (*0-8362-8016-4*) Andrews & McMeel.

Where I'm Still Coming From. Barbara Brandon. (Illus.). 96p. 1994. pap. 8.95 (*0-8362-8051-2*) Andrews & McMeel.

Where in America Is Carmen Sandiego? John Peel. (Golden Favorites Ser.). (Illus.). 32p. (J). (gr. 2-5). 1992. 8.50 (*0-307-15859-4*, 15859, Golden Pr) Western Pub.

Where in America's Past Is Carmen Sandiego? John Peel. (Carmen Sandiego Ser.). (Illus.). 96p. (J). (gr. 3-7). 1992. pap. 2.95 (*0-307-22205-5*, 22205, Golden Pr) Western Pub.

Where in Europe Is Carmen Sandiego? (Carmen Sandiego Ser.). (Illus.). 96p. (J). (gr. 3-7). 1991. pap. 2.95 (*0-307-22203-9*, 22203, Golden Pr) Western Pub.

Where in Moscow. 6th ed. Scott D. McDonald. 1996. pap. 10.00 (*1-880100-31-2*) Russian Info Srvs.

Where in Space Is Carmen Sandiego? John Peel. (You Are the Detective Ser.). (Illus.). 96p. (J). (gr. 4-7). 1993. pap. 3.25 (*0-307-22207-1*, Golden Pr) Western Pub.

Where in Space Is Carmen Sandiego? A Mark & See Book with Marker. John Peel. (J). (gr. 4-7). 1993. pap. 3.95 (*0-307-22305-1*, Golden Pr) Western Pub.

Where in St. Petersburg. 3rd ed. Scott D. McDonald. 174p. 1995. pap. 13.50 (*1-880100-29-0*) Russian Info Srvs.

Where in St. Petersburg. 4th ed. Ed. by Scott D. McDonald. 128p. 1996. pap. 10.00 (*1-880100-32-0*) Russian Info Srvs.

Where in the U. S. A. Is Carmen Dandiego?, Pt. II. John Peel. (You Are the Detective Ser.). 96p. (J). 1994. 3.25 (*0-307-22208-X*, Golden Pr) Western Pub.

Where in the U. S. A. Is Carmen Sandiego? (Carmen Sandiego Ser.). (Illus.). 96p. (J). (gr. 3-7). 1991. pap. 2.95 (*0-307-22202-0*, 22202, Golden Pr) Western Pub.

Where in the U. S. A. Is Carmen Sandiego? John Peel. (J). (gr. 4-7). 1991. pap. 3.95 (*0-307-22304-3*, Golden Pr) Western Pub.

***Where in the World? Travels & Travails in Search of the Good Life.** Tony Del Prete. LC 97-9685. 196p. (Orig.). 1996. reprint ed. pap. 13.95 (*1-887969-02-0*) Cathedral PA.

***Where in the World & What? An Introduction to Global Positioning Systems.** Richard Oderwald & Britt Boucher. 80p. (C). 1996. pap. text ed. 20.94 (*0-7872-2840-0*) Kendall-Hunt.

Where in the World Are We Now? (J). 14.95 (*1-56156-274-2*) Kidsbks.

Where in the World Are You? Kay Cooper. (Illus.). 80p. (J). (gr. 3-7). 1990. 13.95 (*0-8027-6912-8*); lib. bdg. 14. 85 (*0-8027-6913-6*) Walker & Co.

Where in the World Are You Going? Judith M. Blohm. (Illus.). 64p. (Orig.). (J). (gr. 1-5). 1996. pap. 9.95 (*1-877864-44-7*) Intercult Pr.

Where in the World Are You Going? Connecting Faith & Daily Life. Norma C. Everist & Nelvin Vos. 1996. pap. 12.95 (*1-56699-167-6*) Alban Inst.

Where in the World Did You Come From? Paul Nichols. (Illus.). 26p. (J). (ps-4). 1993. 17.95 (*1-884507-00-X*) Boyer-Caswell.

Where in the World Do Muslims Live: Grade 4. Kasule. 266p. 1996. ring bd. 19.95 (*0-7872-1684-4*) Kendall-Hunt.

Where in the World Is Carmen San Diego? John Peel. 48p. (J). (gr. 4-7). 1991. pap. 3.95 (*0-307-22301-9*, 22301) Western Pub.

Where in the World Is Carmen Sandiego? (Carmen Sandiego Ser.). (Illus.). 96p. (J). (gr. 3-7). 1991. pap. 2.95 (*0-307-22201-2*, 22201, Golden Pr) Western Pub.

***Where in the World Is Carmen Sandiego? Sticker Book.** James Buckley. 1997. pap. 3.95 (*0-8167-4223-5*) Troll Communs.

Where in the World Is Geo? A Child's First Atlas. Susanna Ronchi. (Illus.). 12p. (J). (ps-4). 1991. bds. 15.95 (*0-8120-6251-5*) Barron.

***Where in the World Is Odessa?** Kather Polizzi. (Illus.). 20p. (Orig.). (J). (ps-3). 1997. pap. 8.99 (*1-55237-171-9*, Pub. by Comnwlth Pub CN) Partners Pubs Grp.

Where in the World Is the Church? A Christian View of Culture & Your Role in It. Michael S. Horton. 1995. text ed. 17.99 (*0-8024-9239-8*) Moody.

Where in the World Is the Coverage? Extraterritorial Coverages in United States Insurance Policies. John O'Connell. (Orig.). (C). 1990. pap. text ed. 10.00 (*1-878204-15-7*) APIS Inc.

Where in the World to Learn: A Guide to Library & Information Science for International Education Advisers. Edward A. Riedinger. LC 94-42728. (Educators' Reference Collection). 176p. 1995. text ed. 57.95 (*0-313-28703-1*, Greenwood Pr) Greenwood.

Where in the World, When in the World? Ben George. (Illus.). 125p. (Orig.). (C). 1988. pap. text ed. 15.00 (*0-935920-37-4*, Ntl Pubs Blck) P-H.

Where in Time Is Carmen San Diego? John Peel. 48p. (J). (gr. 4-7). 1991. pap. 3.95 (*0-307-22302-7*, 22302) Western Pub.

Where in Time is Carmen Sandiego? (Carmen Sandiego Ser.). (Illus.). 96p. (YA). (gr. 3-7). 1991. pap. 2.95 (*0-307-22204-7*, 22204, Golden Pr) Western Pub.

Where in Time Is Carmen Sandiego!, Pt. II. John Peel. (You Are the Detective Ser.). (Illus.). 96p. (J). (gr. 3-7). 1993. pap. 3.25 (*0-307-22206-3*, 22206-00, Golden Pr) Western Pub.

Where Indians Live: American Indian Houses. Nashone. (Illus.). 38p. (Orig.). (J). (gr. k-6). 1989. pap. 6.95 (*0-940113-16-3*) Sierra Oaks Pub.

Where Is All the Honey? Matthew V. Smith. (Illus.). 17p. (J). (gr. k-3). 1992. pap. 13.95 (*1-895583-31-4*) MAYA Pubs.

Where Is Baby Bear? Jane B. Moncure. LC 87-12840. (Magic Castle Readers Ser.). (Illus.). 32p. (J). (ps-2). 1987. lib. bdg. 21.36 (*0-89565-405-9*) Childs World.

Where Is Baby Bear? Magic Castle Reader. Jane B. Moncure. (Magic Castle Ser.). (J). 1993. pap. text ed. 3.95 (*1-56189-381-1*) Amer Educ Pub.

Where Is Baby Natasha? Sesame Street. Liza Alexander. (J). (ps). 1996. 4.95 (*0-307-12443-6*, Golden Pr) Western Pub.

Where Is Batool? Susheila Stone. (Duets Ser.). (Illus.). 25p. (J). (gr. 2-4). 1991. 15.95 (*0-237-60157-5*, Pub. by Evans Bros Ltd UK) Trafalgar.

Where Is Bernardino? A. L. Staveley. (Illus.). 96p. 1982. 8.95 (*0-89756-011-6*) Two Rivers.

Where Is Calvin? Fay G. Oden. (Illus.). 48p. (Orig.). (J). (gr. 2-6). 1994. pap. text ed. 6.95 (*0-9638946-0-9*) Tennedo Pubs.

Where Is Carmen Sandiego? License Plate Sticker Book. Morgan Michaels & Michael Teitelbaum. (Illus.). 64p. (Orig.). (J). (gr. 3-7). 1996. pap. 3.95 (*0-8167-3965-X*) Troll Communs.

Where Is Carmen Sandiego? U. S. Sticker Book. James Buckley, Jr. & Michael Teitelbaum. (Illus.). 64p. (Orig.). (J). (gr. 3-7). 1996. pap. 3.95 (*0-8167-4134-4*) Troll Communs.

Where Is Clifford? A Lift-a-Flap Book. Norman Bridwell. 10p. (J). 1989. 11.95 (*0-590-42925-6*) Scholastic Inc.

Where Is Crystal Martin? large type ed. C. K. Cambray. (Orig.). 1989. 25.99 (*0-7089-2186-8*) Ulverscroft.

***Where Is DNA? A Biology Adventure.** Transnational College of LEX Staff. Ed. by Japanese Language Services Staff. Tr. by Alan Gleason from JPN. (Illus.). 420p. (Orig.). 1998. pap. 24.95 (*0-9643504-2-4*) Lang Res Fnd.

Where Is Duckling Three? I. Green. LC 68-16402. (Illus.). 32p. (J). (gr. 1-2). 1967. lib. bdg. 9.95 (*0-87783-048-7*) Oddo.

Where Is Everybody? Eve Merriam. LC 88-19800. (Illus.). (J). (ps-1). 1989. pap. 14.95 (*0-671-64964-7*, S&S Bks Young Read) S&S Childrens.

Where Is Everybody? The Search for Extra-Terrestial Intelligence. Edward Ashpole. 250p. (Orig.). 1996. pap. 19.95 (*1-85058-576-8*, Pub. by Sigma Press UK) Coronet Bks.

Where Is Gah-Ning? Robert Munsch. (Illus.). 32p. (J). (gr. 3 up). 1994. pap. 4.95 (*1-55037-982-8*, Pub. by Annick CN); lib. bdg. 14.95 (*1-55037-983-6*, Pub. by Annick CN) Firefly Bks Ltd.

Where Is Giraffe? Illus. by Peter Rutherford. (You Can Read It Ser.). 24p. (J). (ps-1). 1996. 3.49 (*1-85854-468-8*) Brimax Bks.

***Where Is God?** Heidi Bratton. LC 97-7463. (Walking with God Ser.). (J). 1997. write for info. (*0-8091-6641-0*) Paulist Pr.

Where Is God? Leia A. Greene. (Little Angel Bks.). (Illus.). 40p. (J). (gr. k-12). 1991. pap. text ed. 4.95 (*1-880737-05-1*) Crystal Jrns.

***Where Is God?** Leia Stinnett. 1996. pap. text ed. 6.95 (*0-929385-90-X*) Light Tech Comns Servs.

Where Is God in All This? Leonard Cheshire. 144p. (C). 1990. 75.00 (*0-85439-380-3*, Pub. by St Paul Pubns UK) St Mut.

Where Is God When-- Joey O'Connor. LC 93-17942. 1993. pap. 9.99 (*0-8407-9184-4*) Nelson.

Where Is God When a Child Suffers? Penny R. Giesbrecht. (Illus.). 180p. 1988. pap. 8.95 (*0-929292-02-2*) Hannibal Bks.

Where Is God When Bad Things Happen? Horace O. Duke. LC 91-75428. pap. 7.95 (*0-87029-239-0*) Abbey.

Where Is God When It Hurts? expanded rev. ed. Philip Yancey. 320p. 1996. student ed., mass mkt. 4.99 (*0-06-104428-8*, Harp PBks) HarpC.

Where Is God When It Hurts? large type ed. Philip Yancey. LC 96-22273. 320p. 1996. pap. 14.95 (*0-8027-2709-3*) Walker & Co.

Where Is God When It Hurts? rev. ed. Philip Yancey. (Tiny Treasures Ser.). 192p. 1977. pap. 10.99 (*0-310-35411-0*, 9992P) Zondervan.

Where Is God When It Hurts? & Disappointment with God. rev. ed. Philip Yancey. (Treasures Ser.). 560p. 1996. 24.99 (*0-310-21176-X*) Zondervan.

Where Is God When You Need Him? Sharing Stories of Suffering with Job & Jesus. Karl A. Schultz. LC 91-35603. 204p. (Orig.). 1992. pap. 9.95 (*0-8189-0623-5*) Alba.

Where Is Grandma Rabbit? (Rabbit Tales Ser.: No. S899-2). (J). 1989. boxed 3.95 (*0-7214-5231-0*, Ladybrd) Penguin.

Where Is Heaven? Children's Wisdom on Facing Death. Theodore Menten. 128p. 1995. 12.95 (*1-56138-525-5*) Running Pr.

Where Is Hell? Marshall J. Gauvin. 18p. 1991. reprint ed. 4.00 (*0-911826-53-X*, 5116) Am Atheist.

Where Is Here? Joyce Carol Oates. 1992. 18.95 (*0-88001-283-8*) Ecco Pr.

Where Is Here? Cedric Vallet. (Illus.). 19p. (J). (gr. k-3). 1992. pap. 12.95 (*1-895583-29-2*) MAYA Pubs.

Where Is Here: Stories. Joyce Carol Oates. 1993. pap. 10. 00 (*0-88001-338-9*) Ecco Pr.

Where Is Home? Basic Elements. deluxe ed. Louise O. Neaderland. (Illus.). 1986. boxed 10.00 (*0-942561-09-0*) Bone Hollow.

Where Is Home? Living Through Foster Care. E. P. Jones. LC 89-39770. (Illus.). 184p. 1989. 17.95 (*0-941423-34-4*); pap. 9.95 (*0-941423-53-0*) FWEW.

Where Is Home Papa? Isaacson. 382p. 1992. pap. 9.95 (*0-931714-45-1*) Nodin Pr.

Where Is It? Tana Hoban. LC 73-8573. (Illus.). 32p. (J). (ps-1). 1974. lib. bdg. 15.00 (*0-02-744070-2*, Mac Bks Young Read) S&S Childrens.

Where Is It? Dee Lillegard. LC 84-7005. (Rookie Readers Ser.). (Illus.). 32p. (J). (ps-2). 1984. pap. 3.50 (*0-516-42065-8*); lib. bdg. 15.00 (*0-516-02065-X*) Childrens.

***Where Is It?** Karen B. Mole. LC 96-38741. (Science Buzzwords Ser.). (Illus.). 32p. (J). (gr. 1 up). 1997. lib. bdg. 18.60 (*0-8368-1729-X*) Gareth Stevens Inc.

Where Is It? Questions & Answers. Simon & Schuster Staff. (J). 1989. pap. 7.95 (*0-671-68468-X*, S&S Bks Young Read) S&S Childrens.

Where Is It, Dainty Dinosaur? (Illus.). (J). (ps-2). 1991. pap. 5.10 (*0-8136-5274-5*); lib. bdg. 7.95 (*0-8136-5224-3*, TK7285) Modern Curr.

Where Is It Written? An Introductory, Annotated Bibliography in Spirituality. John Weborg. 1978. pap. 1.00 (*0-8199-0739-1*, Frncscn Herld) Franciscan Pr.

Where Is Jake? Mary Packard. (My First Reader Ser.). (Illus.). 28p. (J). (ps-2). 1990. pap. 3.95 (*0-516-45361-0*); lib. bdg. 15.50 (*0-516-05361-2*) Childrens.

Where Is Jeffrey's Yo-Yo? Mildred S. Smith. (Illus.). 56p. (J). (ps-12). 1988. 8.50 (*0-9612296-5-9*) Williams SC.

***Where Is Jesus?** Sharilyn S. Adair. 24p. (J). 1997. pap. text ed. 4.95 (*0-687-45869-2*) Abingdon.

Where Is Jesus? An Interactive Bible Storybook. Rhona Pipe. (J). (ps-3). 1993. 7.99 (*1-56507-146-8*) Harvest Hse.

Where Is Jesus? Easter. Mary M. Simon. (Hear Me Read Ser.). (Illus.). 24p. (Orig.). (J). (ps-1). 1991. pap. 2.49 (*0-570-04703-X*, 56-1662) Concordia.

Where Is Joe Merchant? Jimmy Buffett. 416p. 1993. mass mkt. 6.99 (*0-380-72118-X*) Avon.

Where Is Joe Merchant? large type ed. Jimmy Buffett. LC 93-10397. 1993. 22.95 (*1-56895-011-X*) Wheeler Pub.

Where Is Joe Merchant? A Novel Tale. Jimmy Buffett. 1992. 19.95 (*0-15-196296-0*); 75.00 (*0-15-196297-9*) HarBrace.

***Where Is Joey Garcia? Griggs Anthology.** annuals unabridged ed. Fred Norman. Ed. by Richard Griggs. (Illus.). 108p. (C). 1997. 11.00 (*0-922530-05-X*) Manfit Pubns.

***Where is Jonah?** Broadman & Holman Staff. (Rainbow Ser.). 1997. pap. 4.99 (*0-8054-0009-5*) Broadman.

Where Is Michael? Duane Magnani. 1984. 6.95 (*1-883858-24-0*) Witness CA.

***Where Is Mind? Building on Piaget & Vygotsky.** Ed. by Deanna Kuhn. (Journal Ser.: Vol. 39, No. 5). (Illus.). 76p. 1996. pap. 21.75 (*3-8055-6428-7*) S Karger.

Where Is Miss Piggy? Alison Inches. (Muppet Lift-the-Flaps Ser.). (Illus.). 16p. (J). (ps-k). 1995. pap. 5.99 (*0-14-055693-1*) Puffin Bks.

Where Is Mittens? Kelly Boivin. LC 90-2220. (Rookie Reader Ser.). (Illus.). 32p. (J). (ps-2). 1990. pap. 3.50 (*0-516-42060-7*); lib. bdg. 15.00 (*0-516-02060-9*) Childrens.

Where Is Moses When We Need Him? Teaching Your Kids the 10 Values That Matter Most. Bill C. Peel & Kathy Peel. LC 95-3390. 256p. 1995. pap. 12.99 (*0-8054-6181-7*, 4261-81) Broadman.

Where Is Moses When We Need Him? Teaching Your Kids the 10 Values That Matter Most. William C. Peel & Kathy Peel. LC 95-3390. 256p. 1995. 21.99 (*0-8054-6180-9*, 4261-80) Broadman.

Where Is Mr. Mole? Ivan Gantschev. LC 89-8778. (Illus.). 28p. (J). (ps up). 1991. pap. 15.95 (*0-88708-109-6*, Picture Book Studio) S&S Childrens.

Where Is Muffy Hiding? Rachel N. Luna. 10p. (J). (ps). 1994. pap. 7.95 (*1-886551-01-4*) R N Luna.

***Where Is My Baby?** Harriet Ziefert. (Illus.). 16p. (J). (ps-2). 1997. 5.95 (*0-694-00855-9*, Festival) HarpC Child Bks.

Where Is My Baby? A Portfolio of Prints. Harriet Ziefert. (Illus.). 10p. (J). (ps-2). 1995. 8.95 (*0-694-00807-9*, Festival) HarpC Child Bks.

***Where Is My Broom?** Margaret A. Hartelius. (Picture Readers Ser.). (Illus.). (J). 1997. pap. text ed. 3.95 (*0-448-41614-X*, Grosset-Putnam) Putnam Pub Group.

Where Is My Dad? Donde Esta Mi Papa? George Waintrub. (Illus.). 48p. (ENG & SPA.). (J). (ps-1). 1996. write for info. (*1-884083-47-1*) Maval Pub.

***Where is Noah?** Broadman & Holman Staff. 1997. pap. 4.99 (*0-8054-0012-5*) Broadman.

Where Is Our Responsibility? Unions & Economic Change in the New England Textile Industry, 1870-1960. William F. Hartford. LC 95-45291. 268p. (C). 1996. text ed. 35.00 (*1-55849-022-1*) U of Mass Pr.

***Where Is P. B. Bear?** Lee Davis. LC 97-14177. (P. B. Bear Picture Bks.). (J). 1997. write for info. (*0-7894-2222-0*) DK Pub Inc.

Where Is Papa Now? Celeste Conway. LC 92-74584. (Illus.). 32p. (J). (ps-1). 1994. 14.95 (*1-56397-130-5*) Boyds Mills Pr.

***Where Is P.B. Bear Going?** Lee Davis. LC 97-14178. (P. B. Bear Read-Alongs Ser.). 1997. write for info. (*0-7894-2221-2*) DK Pub Inc.

Where Is Percy's Dinner? Anna Nilsen. LC 95-83547. (Illus.). 16p. (J). (ps). 1996. 7.99 (*0-7636-0019-9*) Candlewick Pr.

Where Is Science Going? Max Planck. Tr. by James Murphy from GER. LC 80-84974. 224p. 1981. reprint ed. 26.00 (*0-918024-21-8*); reprint ed. pap. 14.00 (*0-918024-22-6*) Ox Bow.

Where Is Science Going? Max K. Planck. Tr. by James Murphy. LC 75-41215. reprint ed. 18.50 (*0-404-14696-1*) AMS Pr.

***Where Is She?** (Young Dragon Readers 3 Ser.). (J). 1995. pap. text ed. write for info. (*962-359-538-7*) Addison-Wesley.

***Where Is That Fish?** Barbara Brenner et al. (Illus.). (FRE.). (J). pap. 6.99 (*0-590-24226-1*) Scholastic Inc.

Where Is That Music Coming From? A Path to Creativity. Jeannine W. Hamburg. LC 89-92059. (Illus.). 172p. (Orig.). 1989. pap. 11.95 (*0-9623501-0-9*) Myrte Pr.

Where is the Afikomen. Rosalyn Schanzer. LC 89-63254. (Illus.). 12p. (J). (ps). 1989. bds. 4.95 (*0-929371-06-2*) Kar-Ben.

Where Is the Bear? Richard Hefter. LC 83-6296. (Stickybear Bks.). (Illus.). 32p. (J). (gr. 3-6). 1983. 5.95 (*0-911787-06-2*) Optimum Res Inc.

Where Is the Bear at School? Bonnie L. Nims. Ed. by Kathy Tucker. LC 89-37903. (Illus.). 24p. (J). (ps-1). 1989. lib. bdg. 12.95 (*0-8075-8935-7*) A Whitman.

Where Is the Bear in the City? Bonnie L. Nims. Ed. by Judith Mathews. LC 92-3390. (Illus.). 24p. (J). (ps-1). 1992. lib. bdg. 12.95 (*0-8075-8937-3*) A Whitman.

Where Is the Cat? Stella Blackstone. (Illus.). 24p. (J). (ps-1). 1996. 8.95 (*0-7892-0290-5*, Abbeville Kids) Abbeville Pr.

Where Is the Church Heading? Franz Koenig. (C). 1988. 39.00 (*0-85439-251-3*, Pub. by St Paul Pubns UK) St Mut.

Where Is the Light. Dorothy M. Arnold. 244p. (C). 1988. 55.00 (*0-85335-236-4*, Pub. by Stuart Titles Ltd UK) St Mut.

Where Is the Night Train Going? Vol. 1: Bedtime Poems. Eileen Spinelli. LC 94-79162. (Illus.). 32p. (J). (ps-3). 1996. 14.95 (*1-56397-171-2*, Wordsong) Boyds Mills Pr.

Where Is the Pirate's Treasure? Rupert Heath. (Solve It Yourself Ser.). 48p. (YA). (gr. 6 up). 1996. lib. bdg. 14. 95 (*0-88110-828-6*, Usborne) EDC.

Where Is the Pirate's Treasure? Rupert Heath. (Solve It Yourself Ser.). (YA). (gr. 6 up). 1996. pap. 6.95 (*0-7460-2055-4*, Usborne) EDC.

***Where Is the Treasure?** (Get Ready...Get Set...Read! Ser.: Set 2). (J). 1996. lib. bdg. 11.95 (*1-56674-156-4*) Forest Hse.

Where Is the Treasure? Kelli C. Foster & Gina C. Erickson. LC 94-38559. (Get Ready--Get Set--Read! Ser.). 1995. pap. 3.95 (*0-8120-1098-1*) Barron.

Where Is Theology Going? Issues & Perspectives on the Future of Theology. Millard J. Erickson. LC 94-13404. 232p. (C). 1994. pap. 14.99 (*0-8010-3224-5*) Baker Bks.

Where Is Thumbkin? Five Hundred Activities to Use with Songs You Already Know. Pam Schiller & Thomas Moore. (Illus.). 252p. (Orig.). 1993. pap. text ed. 19.95 (*0-87659-164-0*) Gryphon Hse.

Where Is Tibet? Gina Halpern. Tr. by Ngawang Jorden. (Illus.). 165p. (J). (gr. k-4). 1991. pap. 12.95 (*0-937938-93-9*) Snow Lion Pubns.

***Where Is Tom?** Lieve Baeten. (Tom & Maggie Ser.). 1997. 3.95 (*0-7641-5024-3*) Barron.

Where Is Wes? John W. White. (Orig.). 1996. pap. 7.99 (*1-56043-271-3*) Destiny Image.

Where Is Your Body? And Other Essays on Race, Gender & the Law. Mari J. Matsuda. LC 96-25498. 208p. 1996. 22.00 (*0-8070-6780-6*) Beacon Pr.

***Where Is Your Body? And Other Essays on Race, Gender, & the Law.** Mari J. Matsuda. LC 96-25498. 224p. 1997. reprint ed. pap. 12.50 (*0-8070-6781-4*) Beacon Pr.

***Where Is Your Mommy?** Illus. by Tammie Speer-Lyon. (Muppet Lift & Look Board Bks.). 12p. (J). (ps). 1997. bds. 5.95 (*0-448-41577-1*, G&D) Putnam Pub Group.

***Where Is Your Nose? A Peekaboo Book with Flaps & a Mirror!** Trisha L. Shappie. (Illus.). 24p. (J). (ps). 1997. bds. 6.99 (*0-590-87727-5*, Cartwheel) Scholastic Inc.

***Where Is Zoga Bird?** Victoria Davis. 20p. (Orig.). (J). (gr. 1-2). 1997. pap. 8.99 (*0-614-29757-5*, Pub. by Comnwlth Pub CN) Partners Pubs Grp.

Where It All Begins: A Vivid Portrait of Antebellum America...the Story of the Old South & Its Civilization (1825-60's) LC 96-94274. 114p. 1996. 21.95 (*0-9652632-0-7*) Hummngway Metro.

Where It Stops, Nobody Knows. Amy Ehrlich. 224p. (J). (gr. 6 up). 1990. pap. 4.99 (*0-14-034266-4*, Puffin) Puffin Bks.

Where It's At: Geography for the Quick. (J). (gr. 4-8). 1987. pap. 1.95 (*0-685-57931-X*) Trillium Pr.

Where Jamaica Go? Dale Gottlieb. LC 96-3997. (Illus.). 32p. (J). (ps-2). 1996. 14.95 (*0-531-09525-8*); lib. bdg. 15.99 (*0-531-08875-8*) Orchard Bks Watts.

Where Jesus Walked: The Land & Culture of New Testament Times. D. Kelly Ogden. LC 91-11411. 171p. 1991. 16.95 (*0-87579-530-7*) Deseret Bk.

Where Jesus Walked: Through the Holy Land with the Master. Frank M. Field. Ed. by Moshe Davis. LC 77-70681. (America & the Holy Land Ser.). (Illus.). 1977. reprint ed. lib. bdg. 23.95 (*0-405-10244-5*) Ayer.

Where Joy Resides: A Christopher Isherwood Reader. Ed. by Don Bachardy & James P. White. 1989. 25.00 (*0-374-12332-2*) FS&G.

Where Joy Resides: A Christopher Isherwood Reader. Christopher Isherwood. Ed. by Don Bachardy & James P. White. 1991. pap. 12.95 (*0-374-52255-3*, Noonday) FS&G.

Where Kings & Gods Meet: The Royal Centre at Vijayanagara India. John Fritz et al. LC 85-1117. (Illus.). 158p. 1985. 33.50 (*0-8165-0927-1*) U of Ariz Pr.

Where Land & Water Interwine: An Architectural History of Talbot County, Maryland. Ed. by Christopher Weeks. LC 84-7186. (Illus.). 280p. (Orig.). 1984. pap. 14.95 (*0-8018-3165-2*) Johns Hopkins.

***Where Land Is Mostly Sky: Essays on the American West.** Richard F. Fleck. (Illus.). 1997. 24.00 (*1-57889-073-X*) Passeggiata.

W

***Where Land Is Mostly Sky: Essays on the American West.** Richard F. Fleck. (Illus.). 1997. pap. 14.00 (*1-57889-074-8*) Passeggiata.

***Where Land Meets Sea.** Allan Fowler. LC 96-26984. (Rookie Read-about Science Ser.). (J). 1997. lib. bdg. 17.50 (*0-516-20322-3*) Childrens.

***Where Land Meets Sea.** Allan Fowler. (Rookie Read-About Science Ser.). 1997. pap. 4.95 (*0-516-26155-X*) Childrens.

Where Land Meets Sea: The Enduring Cape Cod. Clare Leighton. LC 54-7922. (Illus.). 208p. 1973. reprint ed. pap. 14.95 (*0-85699-056-6*) Chatham Pr.

Where Laugh Touches Tears. Ed. by Sigrid Bergie. (Illus.). 165p. (Orig.). 1991. pap. 8.00 (*0-927663-17-1*) COMPAS.

Where Laughter Stops: Pinter's Tragicomedy. Bernard F. Dukore. LC 76-15590. (Literary Frontiers Ser.). 80p. 1976. pap. 9.95 (*0-8262-0208-X*) U of Mo Pr.

Where Lawyers Fear to Tread. Lia Matera. (Willa Jansson Ser.). 1991. mass mkt. 5.99 (*0-345-37125-9*) Ballantine.

Where Legends Live. Douglas A. Rossman. (Illus.). 48p. (Orig.). 1988. pap. 4.95 (*0-935741-10-0*) Cherokee Pubns.

Where Liberals Go to Die: The End of Let's Pretend. James T. Evans. 200p. 1994. pap. write for info. (*0-9640388-0-3*) Commonwlth TX.

***Where Light & Shadow Meet: A Memoir.** Emilie W. Schindler & Erika Rosenberg. (Illus.). 144p. (C). 1997. 22.00 (*0-393-04123-9*) Norton.

Where Lilith Dances. Darl M. Boyle. LC 70-144713. (Yale Series of Younger Poets: No. 6). reprint ed. 18.00 (*0-404-53806-1*) AMS Pr.

***Where Lincoln Walked.** Raymond Bial. LC 97-9922. (J). 1997. write for info. (*0-8027-8630-8*); lib. bdg. write for info. (*0-8027-8631-6*) Walker & Co.

Where Lionel Lies. large type ed. Well. (Dales Large Print Ser.). 1995. pap. 17.99 (*1-85389-557-1*, Dales) Ulverscroft.

Where Love Begins. Donna F. Crow. LC 94-5286. (Cambridge Chronicles Ser.: No. 3). 224p. 1995. reprint ed. pap. 9.99 (*0-89107-808-8*) Crossway Bks.

***Where Love Endures.** Noreen Riols. (House of Annanbrae Ser.). 304p. (Orig.). 1997. pap. 10.99 (*0-89107-779-0*) Crossway Bks.

Where Love Goes. Joyce Maynard. 352p. 1995. 23.00 (*0-517-70177-4*) Random Hse Value.

Where Love Goes. Joyce Maynard. 352p. 1996. pap. 12.00 (*0-679-77102-6*) Random.

Where Love Goes. Joyce Maynard. 1995. 23.00 (*0-614-15472-3*, Crown) Crown Pub Group.

Where Love Goes. Peggy Warren. LC 91-77292. (Illus.). 36p. (J). (gr. k-3). 1992. 5.95 (*0-9628710-3-6*) Art After Five.

Where Love Goes. large type ed. Joyce Maynard. LC 95-50400. (Large Print Ser.). 432p. 1995. lib. bdg. 22.95 (*1-57490-031-5*, Beeler LP Bks) T T Beeler.

Where Love Has Gone. Harold Robbins. 1994. mass mkt. 5.99 (*0-671-87498-5*) PB.

Where Love Is. Peggy Warren. LC 91-77294. (Illus.). (J). (gr. k-3). 1992. 5.95 (*0-9628710-2-8*) Art After Five.

Where Love Is, There God Is Also. Leo Tolstoy. 1993. 10.99 (*0-8407-6792-7*) Nelson.

Where Love Is, There Is God Also. large type ed. Leo Tolstoy. (Illus.). 36p. (Orig.). 1987. pap. 7.00 (*0-9603748-4-1*) Sandpiper OR.

Where Love Leaves Us. Renee Manfredi. LC 93-28456. (Iowa Short Fiction Award Ser.). 158p. 1994. 22.95 (*0-87745-444-2*) U of Iowa Pr.

Where Love Resides: Reflections on Love & Life. Ed. by Greg Sharp et al. LC 95-46917. (Illus.). 64p. 1996. 16.95 (*1-56477-145-8*, B280) That Patchwork.

Where Love Starts. Peggy Warren. LC 91-77291. (Illus.). 36p. (J). (gr. k-3). 1992. 5.95 (*0-9628710-4-4*) Art After Five.

Where Magic Dwells. Roxanne Becnel. 416p. 1994. mass mkt. 5.99 (*0-440-21565-X*) Dell.

Where Many Rivers Meet. David Whyte. 120p. 1996. reprint ed. pap. 13.00 (*0-9621524-1-2*) Many Rivers Pr.

Where Masks Still Dance: New Guinea. Chris Rainier. LC 96-7327. (Illus.). 1996. 60.00 (*0-8212-2261-9*) Bulfinch Pr.

Where Medicine Fails. 4th ed. Ed. by Anselm L. Strauss. 400p. 1984. pap. text ed. 18.95 (*0-87855-951-5*) Transaction Pubs.

Where Medicine Fails. 5th ed. Anselm L. Strauss. 460p. 1996. pap. text ed. 24.95 (*1-56000-869-5*) Transaction Pubs.

Where Memories Linger Silver Birds Will Someday Land: From Quiet Farm Life of Box Elder, Adams County, Colorado to Denver International Airport. Gladys M. Forshee. 503p. 1994. per. 29.95 (*0-9632251-0-3*) A Appletree.

Where Miracles Happen. Joan W. Anderson. 1995. pap. 12.00 (*0-345-39305-8*) Ballantine.

Where Miracles Happen: True Stories of Heavenly Encounters. Joan W. Anderson. LC 94-878. 256p. 1994. 17.95 (*0-9636620-1-5*) Brett Bks.

Where Miracles Happen: True Stories of Heavenly Encounters. large type ed. Joan W. Anderson. LC 94-41966. 329p. 1995. lib. bdg. 21.95 (*0-7838-1202-7*, GK Hall) Thorndike Pr.

Where Moth & Rust Do Not Consume. Anthony M. Coniaris. 1983. pap. 9.95 (*0-937032-30-1*) Light&Life Pub Co MN.

Where Mountains Live: Twelve Great Treks of the World. Leo Le Bon. (Illus.). 144p. 1988. 40.00 (*0-89381-242-0*) Aperture.

Where Mountains Meet the Sea: Alaska's Gulf Coast. Ed. by Alaska Geographic Staff. LC 72-92087. (Alaska Geographic Ser.: Vol. 13, No. 1). (Illus.). 192p. (Orig.). 1972. pap. 19.95 (*0-88240-175-0*) Alaska Geog Soc.

Where Mountains Touch Heaven. Ena K. Powell. 222p. (Orig.). 1995. pap. 14.95 (*0-88839-365-2*) Hancock House.

Where Mountains Wait. Frances E. Wilson. 1980. pap. 1.50 (*0-373-58001-0*) Harlequin Bks.

***Where Muses Dwell.** Photos by Massimo Listri. LC 96-71418. (Illus.). 192p. 1997. 55.00 (*0-8478-2027-0*) Rizzoli Intl.

***Where Music Comes From.** Photos by Nubar Alexanian. (Illus.). 96p. 1996. 39.95 (*1-899235-06-X*, 620403, Pub. by Dewi Lewis UK) Dist Art Pubs.

Where My Heart Is Turning Ever: Civil War Stories & Constitutional Reform, 1861-1876. Kathleen Diffley. LC 92-7048. 264p. 1992. 35.00 (*0-8203-1445-5*) U of Ga Pr.

Where Mystery Dwells: A Psychiatrist Studies Psychical Phenomena. B. J. Laubscher. 272p. 1972. 11.50 (*0-227-67801-X*) Attic Pr.

Where Nature Ends: The Designation of Landscape in Arnold, Swinburne, Hardy, Conrad & Woolf. Susan E. Lorsch. LC 81-72056. 240p. 1983. 26.50 (*0-8386-3162-2*) Fairleigh Dickinson.

***Where Nature Reigns: The Wilderness Areas of the Southern Appalachians.** Jack Horan. (Illus.). 248p. (Orig.). 1997. pap. 14.95 (*1-878086-58-8*) Down Home NC.

***Where Nests the Water Hen.** Gabrielle Roy. 1996. pap. text ed. 5.95 (*0-7710-9854-5*) McCland & Stewart.

Where Next, Columbus? The Future of Space Exploration. Ed. by Valerie Neal. (Illus.). 256p. 1994. 39.95 (*0-19-509277-5*) OUP.

Where Nights Are Longest: Travels by Car Through Western Russia. Colin Thubron. LC 87-14455. (Travel Ser.). 224p. 1987. reprint ed. pap. 7.95 (*0-87113-167-6*, Atlntc Mnthly) Grove-Atltic.

Where No Man Has Gone Before: A History of Apollo Lunar Exploration Missions. William D. Compton. LC 88-600242. (NASA History Ser.: No. SP-2414). (Illus.). 429p. 1989. per. 25.00 (*0-16-004253-4*, S/N 033-000-01047-8) USGPO.

***Where No Man Has Gone Before: A History of Apollo Lunar Exploration Missions.** William D. Compton. (Illus.). 415p. 1996. reprint ed. pap. 45.00 (*0-7881-3633-X*) DIANE Pub.

Where No Man Has Gone Before: A History of Apollo Lunar Exploration Missions, 2 vols., Set. 1994. lib. bdg. 629.95 (*0-8490-6448-1*) Gordon Pr.

Where No Man Has Gone Before: Essay on Woman & Science Fiction. Ed. by Lucie Armitt. 240p. (C). 1990. pap. 18.95 (*0-415-04448-0*, A4867) Routledge.

Where No One Has Gone Before: A History in Pictures. J. M. Dillard. (Illus.). 1994. 45.00 (*0-671-51149-1*) PB.

Where No One Stands Alone. Evelyn Hege. 146p. 1992. 5.05 (*0-317-05257-8*) Rod & Staff.

Where No Road Goes. Bob Mossel. 104p. (C). 1989. text ed. 75.00 (*0-89771-017-7*, Pub. by Bob Mossel AT) St Mut.

***Where No Wind Blows.** unabridged ed. Thompson Lennox. 74p. (Orig.). 1997. pap. 12.00 (*1-890283-04-5*, 9701) L Thompson NY.

Where Nobody Dies. Carolyn Wheat. 272p. 1996. mass mkt. 5.99 (*0-425-15408-4*, Prime Crime) Berkley Pub.

Where North Meets South: Cities, Space, & Politics on the United States - Mexico Border. Lawrence A. Herzog. 304p. 1990. pap. 16.95 (*0-292-79053-8*) U of Tex Pr.

Where, Oh, Where? A Sesame Street Book. Anna Ross. (Chunky Flap Bks.). (Illus.). 22p. (J). (ps). 1994. 3.99 (*0-679-85303-0*) Random Bks Yng Read.

Where, Oh Where, Is Kipper's Bear? Mick Inkpen. LC 94-73252. (Illus.). 16p. (J). (ps). 1995. 16.00 (*0-15-200394-0*, Red Wagon Bks) HarBrace.

Where, Oh, Where's My Underwear? Barney Saltzberg. LC 93-61051. (Illus.). 12p. (J). (ps-3). 1994. 9.95 (*1-56282-694-8*) Hyprn Child.

Where Old Bones Lie. Ann Granger. (New Meredith & Markby Mystery Ser.: No. 5). 288p. 1995. mass mkt. 4.99 (*0-380-72477-4*) Avon.

Where Old Bones Lie: A Mitchell & Markby Village Mystery. Ann Granger. 224p. 1994. 19.95 (*0-312-11097-9*) St Martin.

Where Old Trails Meet the New. Ramona Turmon & Lona Burkhart. (Illus.). 90p. (Orig.). (C). 1988. pap. 7.50 (*0-9620746-0-8*) R Turmon.

Where on Earth? Irol W. Balsley. 144p. (J). (gr. 4-8). 1986. student ed. 11.99 (*0-86653-336-2*, GA 691) Good Apple.

Where on Earth: A Geografunny Guide to the Globe. Paul Rosenthal. LC 92-1227. (Illus.). 112p. (Orig.). (J). (gr. 3-7). 1992. pap. 11.00 (*0-679-80833-7*); lib. bdg. 15.99 (*0-679-90833-1*) Knopf Bks Yng Read.

***Where on Earth: A Guide to Specialty Nurseries & Other Resources for California Gardeners.** 3rd rev. ed. Nancy Conner & Barbara Stevens. 400p. 1997. pap. 12.95 (*0-930588-92-4*) Heyday Bks.

Where on Earth Am I? Robert Gardner. LC 96-12128. 128p. (YA). (gr. 7-12). 1996. lib. bdg. 22.70 (*0-531-11297-7*) Watts.

***Where on Earth Am I?** Robert Gardner. 160p. (J). 1997. pap. 9.95 (*0-531-15827-6*) Watts.

Where on Earth Are We Going? Jonathon Porritt. (Illus.). 241p. 1992. pap. 17.95 (*0-563-20847-3*, BBC-Parkwest) Parkwest Pubns.

Where on Earth Is Jean? Muriel Vallet. (Illus.). 17p. (J). (gr. k-3). 1992. pap. 8.95 (*1-895583-49-7*) MAYA Pubs.

Where Once There Was a Wood. Denise Fleming. LC 95-18906. 32p. (J). (gr. k-5). 1996. 15.95 (*0-8050-3761-6*, Bks Young Read) H Holt & Co.

Where Once They Toiled: A Visit to the Former Mennonite Homelands in the Vistula River Valley. Edward R. Brandt. 28p. 1992. pap. 4.50 (*1-883294-04-5*) Olde Sprgfld.

Where Once We Walked: A Guide to the Jewish Communities Destroyed in the Holocaust. Gary Mokotoff & Sallyann A. Sack. LC 91-70405. (Illus.). xxviii, 544p. 1991. 69.50 (*0-9626373-1-9*) Avotaynu.

We're (One Issue) see Work (Four Issues)

Where Only Love Can Go: A Journey of the Soul into the Cloud of Unknowing. John Kirvan. LC 96-19549. (30 Days with a Great Spiritual Teacher Ser.). 216p. (Orig.). 1996. pap. 6.95 (*0-87793-591-2*) Ave Maria.

Where Or When. Anita Shreve. LC 92-39392. 1993. 19.95 (*0-15-131461-6*) HarBrace.

Where or When. Anita Shreve. 304p. 1994. pap. 5.99 (*0-451-40478-5*, Sig) NAL-Dutton.

Where Our Children Play: Community Park Playground Equipment. Ed. by Donna Thompson & Louis Bowers. (Illus.). 121p. (Orig.). 1989. pap. text ed. 10.80 (*0-88314-411-5*, A4115) AAHPERD.

***Where Our Children Play Vol. 1: Elementary School Playground Equipment.** Ed. by Lawrence D. Bruya & Stephen J. Langerdorfer. (Illus.). 261p. (Orig.). 1988. pap. text ed. 9.50 (*0-88314-390-9*, A3909) AAHPERD.

Where Our Lives Touch. Mary H. Johnson. 35p. (Orig.). 1985. pap. 3.00 (*0-914631-00-4*) Questpr.

Where Paradise Lay. John Holt. (Orig.). 1997. pap. write for info. (*0-87108-863-0*) Pruett.

Where Past Meets Present: Modern Colorado Short Stories. Ed. by James B. Hemesath. 184p. (C). 1994. pap. 17.50 (*0-87081-331-5*) Univ Pr Colo.

Where Peachtree Meets Sweet Auburn: A Lisa Drew Book. Gary M. Pomerantz. (Illus.). 608p. 1996. 27.00 (*0-684-80717-3*) S&S Trade.

***Where Peachtree Meets Sweet Auburn: A Saga of Race and Family.** Gary M. Pomerantz. 1997. pap. 14.95 (*0-14-026509-0*) Viking Penguin.

***Where Peachtree Meets Sweet Auburn: A Saga of Race & Family.** Gary M. Pomerantz. 1997. pap. 14.95 (*0-614-27379-X*) Penguin.

Where Peachtree Meets Sweet Auburn: The Saga of Two Families & the Making of Atlanta. Gary M. Pomerantz. LC 96-10399. 1996. write for info. (*0-02-597985-X*) Schirmer Bks.

Where People Fly & Water Runs Uphill: Using Dreams to Tap the Wisdom of the Unconscious. Jeremy Taylor. 304p. 1993. pap. 14.99 (*0-446-39462-9*) Warner Bks.

Where Peoples Meet: Racial & Ethnic Frontiers. Everett C. Hughes & Helen M. Hughes. LC 80-27901. 204p. 1981. reprint ed. text ed. 49.75 (*0-313-22785-3*, HUWP, Greenwood Pr) Greenwood.

***Where Pheasants & Meadowlarks Nest.** Lois Bogue. Ed. by Janet Leih. (Illus.). 58p. (Orig.). 1997. pap. 7.00 (*1-877649-29-5*) Tesseract SD.

Where? Place in Recent North American Fiction: Place in Recent North American Fictions. Ed. by Karl-Heinz Westarp. (The Dolphin Ser.: No. 20). 160p. (C). 1991. pap. 19.95 (*87-7288-370-7*, Pub. by Aarhus Univ Pr DK) David Brown.

Where Prosperity Appears. 6th rev. ed. Harvest Economic Research Department Staff. 1997. pap. 17.95 (*0-939074-13-3*) Harvest Pubns.

Where Puddles Go: Investigating Science with Kids. Michael Strauss. LC 95-15174. (Illus.). 224p. (J). 1995. pap. 16.95 (*0-435-08367-8*, 08367) Heinemann.

***Where Queen Elizabeth Slept.** Durant. LC 97-11287. 1997. 24.95 (*0-312-15688-X*) St Martin.

***Where R the Billabongs.** McVeity. (Clipper Fiction Ser.). 1994. pap. text ed. write for info. (*0-582-80270-9*, Pub. by Longman UK) Longman.

Where Rainbows Wait for Rain: The Big Bend Country. Sandra Lynn. LC 89-39975. (Illus.). 90p. 1989. 22.00 (*0-940352-06-0*) Mesa Hse.

Where Ratas Twine. large type ed. Ivy Preston. (Linford Romance Library). 336p. 1993. pap. 15.99 (*0-7089-7326-4*, Linford) Ulverscroft.

Where Real Worship Begins: Lessons from the Life of Job. James T. Draper, Jr. LC 95-51512. 1996. pap. 9.99 (*0-87213-126-2*) Loizeaux.

Where Reincarnation & Biology Intersect. Ian Stevenson. LC 95-34442. 240p. 1997. text ed. 59.95 (*0-275-95188-X*, Auburn Hse) Greenwood.

Where Reincarnation & Biology Intersect. Ian Stevenson. LC 95-34442. 240p. 1997. pap. text ed. 17.95 (*0-275-95189-8*, Praeger Pubs) Greenwood.

Where Resident Aliens Live: Exercises for Christian Practice. Stanley Hauerwas & William H. Willimon. 128p. 1996. pap. 12.95 (*0-687-01605-3*) Abingdon.

Where River Turns to Sky. Gregg Kleiner. LC 96-22024. 400p. 1996. 23.00 (*0-380-97347-2*) Avon.

***Where River Turns to Sky.** large type ed. Gregg Kleiner. LC 97-15893. 1997. write for info. (*1-56895-458-1*) Wheeler Pub.

Where Rivers Meet: Lore From The Colorado Frontier. Muriel Marshall. LC 95-40368. (Elma Dill Russell Spencer Series in the West & Southwest: No. 14). (Illus.). 232p. 1996. 32.95 (*0-89096-686-9*); pap. 16.95 (*0-89096-687-7*) Tex A&M Univ Pr.

***Where Rivers Run.** Gary McGuffin. 1996. pap. text ed. 14.50 (*0-7737-5352-4*, Pub. by Boston Mills Pr CN) Genl Dist Srvs.

Where Rivers Run: A Six Thousand Mile Exploration of Canada by Canoe. Gary McGuffin & Joanie McGuffin. (Illus.). 272p. 1989. 23.95 (*0-913276-54-5*) Stone Wall Pr.

Where Rolls the Oregon. Rick Steber & Jerry Gildemeister. LC 85-9181. (Illus.). 212p. 1985. 42.50 (*0-936376-03-1*) Bear Wallow Pub.

Where Salmon Come to Die: An Autumn on Alaska's Raincoast. Leon Kolankiewicz. LC 93-2167. (Illus.). 126p. 1993. pap. 16.95 (*0-87108-855-X*) Pruett.

Where Science Magic Meet: Quantum Physics & Parapsychology: the Reunion of Intellect Intuition. rev. ed. Serena Roney-Dougal. 272p. 1993. pap. 19.95 (*1-85230-446-4*) Element MA.

***Where Science Went Wrong: Tracking Four Centuries of Misconceptions.** Peter Bros. Staff. (Copernican Ser.: Vol. 7). 215p. (Orig.). 1997. pap. 16.95 (*0-9627769-7-1*) Fin Bk Partners.

Where Seldom Was Heard a Discouraging Word ... Bill Guy Remembers. William L. Guy. LC 92-6056. 275p. 1992. 25.00 (*0-911042-42-3*) NDSU Inst Reg.

***Where Serpents Lie.** T. Jefferson Parker. LC 97-2633. 448p. 1998. 23.95 (*0-7868-6287-4*) Hyperion.

Where Shadows Fall. Nicholas A. Patricca. Ed. by Robert Sturm. 50p. (Orig.). 1994. pap. 12.00 (*0-9640343-9-5*) Traditional Arts.

Where Shadows Fall. Judith Kelman. 352p. 1987. reprint ed. mass mkt. 5.99 (*0-425-10181-9*) Berkley Pub.

Where Shadows Go. Eugenia Price. LC 92-38400. 656p. 1993. 22.50 (*0-385-26702-9*) Doubleday.

Where Shadows Go. Eugenia Price. 1996. mass mkt. 6.99 (*0-312-95969-9*) St Martin.

Where Shakespeare Set His Stage. Elise L. Lathrop. LC 70-128571. (Studies in Shakespeare: No. 24). 1970. reprint ed. lib. bdg. 59.95 (*0-8383-0907-0*) M S G Haskell Hse.

Where Shall We Go This Summer? 2nd ed. Anita Desai. 157p. 1982. reprint ed. pap. 4.50 (*0-86578-125-7*) Ind-US Inc.

Where Shall We Meet? 2nd ed. Ed. by Maureen Lally & Cynthia Stimpson. 54p. pap. 11.95 (*0-685-44384-1*) WOW Pub.

Where Shall We Meet? In Seattle & King County. 2nd rev. ed. Ed. by Where Shall We Meet Group Staff & Cynthia Stimpson. 64p. (Orig.). 1989. pap. 11.95 (*0-923051-02-3*) WOW Pub.

Where Shall Wisdom Be Found? Calvin's Exegesis of Job from Medieval & Modern Perspectives. Susan E. Schreiner. 274p. 1994. 39.95 (*0-226-74043-9*) U Ch Pr.

***Where She Came From: A Daughter's Search for Her Mother's History.** Helen Epstein. LC 97-13845. 1997. write for info. (*0-316-24608-5*) Little.

Where She Danced: The Birth of American Art-Dance. Elizabeth Kendall. (Illus.). 254p. (C). 1984. pap. 13.00 (*0-520-05173-4*) U CA Pr.

Where Should I Run To? Robert Kaminski. (Kid Safe Ser.). (Illus.). 16p. (Orig.). (J). (ps-3). 1995. pap. 5.00 (*0-9644142-2-8*) Open Book Pubng.

Where Should We Take the Kids? California: Fresh, Most-Fun-for-the-Money, Anything but Boring Getaways for You & Your Children, Complete with Family-Friendly Places to Stay & Eat. Fodor's Travel Staff. (Illus.). 1997. pap. 18.00 (*0-679-03300-9*) Fodors Travel.

Where Should We Take the Kids? Northeast. 2nd ed. Fodor's Travel Staff. (Illus.). 1997. pap. 18.00 (*0-679-03301-7*) Fodors Travel.

Where Silence Reigns: Selected Prose. Rainer M. Rilke. LC 78-9079. 1978. pap. 8.95 (*0-8112-0697-1*, NDP464) New Directions.

Where Silence Rules: The Suppression of Dissent in Malawi. Africa Watch Staff. LC 90-84931. 104p. 1990. pap. 10.00 (*0-929692-73-X*, Africa Watch) Hum Rts Watch.

Where Silence Speaks: Feminism, Social Theory, & Religion. Victoria L. Erickson. LC 92-26577. 240p. 1992. pap. 24.00 (*0-8006-2635-4*, 1-2635, Fortress Pr) Augsburg Fortress.

Where Skies Are Not Cloudy. Walter McDonald. LC 93-14496. (Texas Poets Ser.: Vol. 4). 84p. 1993. 14.95 (*0-929398-61-0*); pap. 10.95 (*0-929398-60-2*) UNTX Pr.

Where "Something Catches" Work, Love, & Identity in Youth. Victoria I. Munoz. LC 94-44800. (SUNY Series, Identities in the Classroom). 282p. (C). 1995. text ed. 49.50 (*0-7914-2685-8*); pap. text ed. 16.95 (*0-7914-2686-6*) State U NY Pr.

Where Stands Democracy? Fabian Society Staff. LC 76-117788. (Essay Index Reprint Ser.). 1977. 17.95 (*0-8369-1651-4*) Ayer.

Where Stars May Lead. large type ed. Ivy Preston. (Romance Ser.). 304p. 1995. pap. 15.99 (*0-7089-7668-9*, Linford) Ulverscroft.

Where Still the Source Endures. Pearl N. Rook. 64p. 1987. 7.50 (*0-8233-0426-4*) Golden Quill.

Where the Action Is. Randal E. Denny. 128p. 1981. pap. 6.99 (*0-8341-0723-6*) Beacon Hill.

Where the Air Is Clear. Carlos Fuentes. Tr. by Sam Hileman from SPA. 376p. 1988. pap. 14.00 (*0-374-50919-0*) FS&G.

Where the Angels Come Toward Us: Selected Essays, Reviews & Interviews. David St. John. 240p. (Orig.). 1995. pap. 15.00 (*1-877727-46-6*) White Pine.

Where the Animals Are: A Guide to the Best Zoos, Aquariums, & Wildlife Attractions in North America. Tim O'Brien. LC 92-20081. (Illus.). 320p. (Orig.). 1992. pap. 12.95 (*1-56440-077-8*) Globe Pequot.

Where the Ashes Are: The Odyssey of a Vietnamese Family. Qui Duc Nguyen. LC 93-25869. 1994. 21.95 (*0-201-63202-0*) Addison-Wesley.

Where the Bald Eagles Gather. Dorothy H. Patent. (Illus.). 56p. (J). (gr. 3-7). 1990. pap. 5.95 (*0-395-52598-5*) HM.

Where the Balloons Go: For Loss of a Grandparent. Paul Coleman. LC 95-26335. (Illus.). 56p. (J). 1995. pap. 10.95 (*1-56123-089-8*) Centering Corp.

***Where the Bears Live.** Jim Arnosky. (J). Date not set. write for info. (*0-688-05447-1*); lib. bdg. write for info. (*0-688-05448-X*) Lothrop.

Where the Bee Sucks: Workers, Drones & Queens of Contemporary American Poetry. Robert Peters. LC 94-70673. 300p. (Orig.). 1994. pap. 14.95 (*1-878580-63-9*) Asylum Arts.

W

Where the Big Bottom Begins: Randle History. Irma Boyer & LaVonne M. Sparkman. LC 95-67170. (Illus.). 256p. 1995. 24.95 (0-9645570-0-2) Sparkman Pub.

Where the Big River Runs. Carol T. Plum. (I Am Special Story Bks.). (Illus.). 32p. (J). (gr. k-3). 1991. 6.95 (0-87973-010-2, 10); pap. 3.95 (0-87973-011-0, 11) Our Sunday Visitor.

Where the Birds Sing Bass. Reginald Lockett. LC 88-93046. (Illus.). 109p. (Orig.). 1995. pap. 10.95 (0-932693-05-9) Jukebox Press.

Where the Bluebird Sings to the Lemonade Springs: Living & Writing in the West. Wallace Stegner. 240p. 1993. pap. 11.00 (0-14-017402-8, Penguin Bks) Viking Penguin.

Where the Bluebird Sings to the Lemonade Springs: Living & Writing in the West. Wallace Stegner. LC 95-13086. 1995. 7.99 (0-517-12408-4) Random.

***Where the Body Meets Memory.** David Mura. 1997. pap. 14.95 (0-385-47184-X, Anchor NY) Doubleday.

Where the Body Meets the Memory: An Odyssey of Race, Sexuality, & Identity. David Mura. LC 95-40950. 304p. 1996. 22.95 (0-385-47183-1, Anchor NY) Doubleday.

Where the Books Are: History & Architecture of Vermont's Public Libraries with Photos & Anecdotes. Patricia W. Belding. LC 95-92807. (Illus.). 184p. 1996. pap. 22.50 (0-9650699-0-7) Potash Brook.

***Where the Boys Are: A Step-by-Step Guide to Finding Mr. Right.** Gloria Brame. 1997. mass mkt. 5.99 (0-380-79179-X) Avon.

Where the Boys Are: Cuba, Cold War America, & the Making of a New Left. Van Gosse. (Haymarket Ser.). 260p. (C). 1993. pap. text ed. 20.00 (0-86091-690-1, B2522, Pub. by Vrso UK) Norton.

Where the Boys Are: Cuba, Cold War America, & the Making of a New Left. Van Gosse. (Haymarket Ser.). 260p. (C). (gr. 13). 1993. text ed. 60.00 (0-86091-416-X, B2518, Pub. by Vrso UK) Norton.

Where the Broken Heart Still Beats: The Story of Cynthia Ann Parker. Carolyn Meyer. LC 92-257. (Great Episodes Ser.). 192p. (J). (gr. 3-7). 1992. 17.00 (0-15-200639-7, Gulliver Bks); pap. 7.00 (0-15-295602-6, Gulliver Bks) HarBrace.

***Where the Buf Fellows Roamed.** James Hoopaw. 363p. (Orig.). 1997. mass mkt. 4.99 (1-55197-616-1, Pub. by Comnwlth Pub CN) Partners Pubs Grp.

Where the Buffalo Roam. Illus. & Adapted by Jacqueline Geis. LC 92-7733. 32p. (J). (gr. k-3). 1992. 13.95 (0-8249-8570-2, Ideals Child); lib. bdg. 14.00 (0-8249-8584-2, Ideals Child) Hambleton-Hill.

Where the Buffalo Roam. Anne Matthews. LC 91-33637. 1992. pap. 9.95 (0-8021-3339-8, Grove) Grove-Atltic.

Where the Buffalo Roam. Jacqueline Geis. LC 92-7733. (Illus.). 32p. (J). (gr. k-3). 1994. reprint ed. per., pap. 4.95 (0-8249-8661-X, Ideals Child) Hambleton-Hill.

Where the Buffaloes Begin. Olaf Baker. LC 85-5682. (Illus.). 48p. (J). (ps-4). 1985. pap. 5.99 (0-14-050560-1) Viking Child Bks.

Where the Buffaloes Roam: Building a Team for Life Challenges. Bob Stone & Jenny Stone Humphries. LC 93-15917. 1993. 19.95 (0-201-62641-1) Addison-Wesley.

Where the Cars Are: Color Photos & Stories from Owners of Classic Thunderbird Cars, Plus Restoration Section in Color. LC 90-92042. (Illus.). 308p. 1990. 59.95 (0-945334-00-1) Craftsman Print.

Where the Cinnamon Winds Blow - Donde Soplan los Vientos de Canela: A Bilingual English - Spanish Book. Jim Sagel. (Illus.). 168p. (ENG & SPA.). 1993. pap. 12.95 (1-878610-32-5) Red Crane Bks.

Where the Clouds Can Go: The Autobiography of Conrad Kain. 3rd ed. Ed. by J. Monroe Thorington. LC 79-55308. (Illus.). 456p. 1979. reprint ed. 17.50 (0-930410-09-2) Amer Alpine Club.

Where the Dark Streets Go. Dorothy S. Davis. 192p. 1986. mass mkt. 2.95 (0-380-70131-6) Avon.

***Where the Dead Walk: The Haunted History of Greenwood Cemetery.** Troy Taylor. (Haunted Decatur Ser.: Vol. 4). (Illus.). 158p. (Orig.). 1997. pap. 12.95 (0-9651497-3-0) Whitechapel.

Where the Deer & the Antelope Play. Stephen A. Bly. LC 95-14510. (Code of the West Ser.: Bk. 3). 192p. (Orig.). 1995. pap. 8.99 (0-89107-850-9) Crossway Bks.

Where the Deer & the Antelope Play. large type ed. Stephen Bly. LC 96-11959. (West-Hall Ser.: Bk. 3). 280p. (Orig.). 1997. lib. bdg. 22.95 (0-7838-1789-4, GK Hall) Thorndike Pr.

Where the Deer Were. Kate Barnes. (Illus.). 110p. 1994. 20.95 (0-87923-984-0) Godine.

***Where the Dogs Bark: What Poor Countries Will Need to Make Their Markets Work.** Hernando De Soto. 288p. 1997. 25.00 (0-06-017152-9) HarpC.

Where the Domino Fell. 2nd ed. Olson. 1996. pap. text ed. 18.00 (0-312-08431-5) St Martin.

Where the Dove Calls: The Political Ecology of a Peasant Corporate Community in Northwestern Mexico. Thomas E. Sheridan. LC 87-30139. (Arizona Studies in Human Ecology). (Illus.). 237p. 1988. 39.00 (0-8165-1055-5) U of Ariz Pr.

***Where the Dove Calls: The Political Ecology of a Peasant Corporate Community in Northwestern Mexico.** Thomas E. Sheridan. (Illus.). 237p. 1996. pap. text ed. 19.95 (0-8165-1703-7) U of Ariz Pr.

Where the Eagles Fly. Ruth N. Moore. LC 94-630. 104p. (Orig.). (J). (gr. 4-7). 1994. pap. 5.99 (0-8361-3664-0) Herald Pr.

***Where the Fellow Went.** Eisenberg & McCall. Date not set. write for info. (0-688-04532-4) Morrow.

Where the Ferry Crosses: Ferry. B. J. Woods. Ed. by Bowling & Quertermous. (Illus.). 431p. (Orig.). 1993. pap. text ed. 6.99 (0-9636901-0-8) R C W Pub.

***Where the Fire Burns: A Novel, Vol. 2.** Anne De Graaf. LC 97-21026. (Hidden Harvest Ser.). Date not set. pap. text ed. 9.99 (1-55661-619-8) Bethany Hse.

Where the Flame Trees Bloom. Ada. (SPA.). (J). 1998. 14.00 (0-689-80018-5, Atheneum Bks Young) S&S Childrens.

Where the Flame Trees Bloom. Ada. (J). 1998. 15.00 (0-689-80631-0) S&S Childrens.

Where the Flame Trees Bloom. Alma F. Ada. (J). 1994. 14.95 (0-689-31900-2, Atheneum Bks Young) S&S Childrens.

Where the Forest Meets The Sea. Jeannie Baker. LC 87-7551. (Illus.). 32p. (J). (ps-3). 1988. 16.00 (0-688-06363-2); lib. bdg. 15.93 (0-688-06364-0) Greenwillow.

Where the Forest Murmurs. William Sharp. LC 73-111865. (Essay Index Reprint Ser.). 1977. 23.95 (0-8369-1627-1) Ayer.

Where the Four Winds Blow. Philippe Soupault. Tr. by Pat Nolan. 40p. 1993. pap. 4.00 (0-944550-32-0) Pygmy Forest Pr.

***Where the Game Matters Most.** William Gildea. 1998. 22.95 (0-316-51967-7) Little.

Where the Ghost Horse Runs. Alfred Silver. 1994. mass mkt. 5.99 (0-345-38670-1) Ballantine.

Where the Ghosts Are: Favorite Haunted Houses in America & the British Isles. Hans Holzer. 220p. 1986. 15.95 (0-13-957093-4, Busn); 7.95 (0-13-957077-2, Busn) P-H.

Where the Ghosts Are: The Ultimate Guide to Haunted Houses. Hans Holzer. (Citadel Library of the Mystic Arts). (Illus.). 224p. 1995. pap. 9.95 (0-8065-1626-7, Citadel Pr) Carol Pub Group.

Where the Giants Trod. M. J. Brown. (Illus.). 431p. 1989. 35.00 (0-940143-25-9) Safari Pr.

Where the Girls Are. Nikolaus Heidelbach. (Illus.). 56p. (J). (gr. k up). 1994. pap. 8.95 (1-55037-974-7, Pub. by Annick CN) Firefly Bks Ltd.

Where the Girls Are: Growing Up Female with the Mass Media. Susan Douglas. 1995. pap. 15.00 (0-8129-2530-0, Times Bks) Random.

Where the Gods Reign. Richard E. Schultes. (Illus.). 125p. 1988. pap. 20.00 (0-907791-13-1) Synerg AZ.

Where the Grapevines Grow. Gabriel Donner. 1995. 12.95 (0-533-11049-1) Vantage.

Where the Grass Is Greener: Living in an Unequal World. David M. Smith. LC 82-47979. 392p. (C). 1982. reprint ed. pap. 15.95 (0-8018-2883-X) Johns Hopkins.

Where the Healing Waters Meet. Clyde W. Ford. 228p. 19.95 (0-88268-080-3) Station Hill Pr.

***Where the Heart Is.** Robin L. Hatcher. 448p. 1997. mass mkt. 5.99 (0-8439-4334-3, Leisure Bks) Dorchester Pub Co.

Where the Heart Is. Billie Letts. LC 94-43079. 358p. 1995. 17.95 (0-446-51972-3) Warner Bks.

Where the Heart Is. Billie Letts. 1996. pap. write for info. (0-446-67221-1) Warner Bks.

Where the Heart Is. Billie Letts. 336p. 1996. mass mkt. 5.99 (0-446-60365-1) Warner Bks.

***Where the Heart Is.** Elizabeth Lowell. 384p. (Orig.). 1997. mass mkt. 6.50 (0-380-76763-5) Avon.

***Where the Heart Is.** Ann Mitchell. 1997. 24.00 (1-55046-193-1, Pub. by Boston Mills Pr CN) Genl Dist Srvs.

Where the Heart Is. large type ed. Julia Ashwell. 336p. 1996. 25.99 (0-7089-3459-5) Ulverscroft.

Where the Heart Is. large type ed. Rowan Edwards. (Linford Romance Library). 1991. pap. 15.99 (0-7089-7061-3) Ulverscroft.

Where the Heart Is: (Nine Months) Patricia Keelyn. (Superromance Ser.). 1995. mass mkt. 3.75 (0-373-70631-6, 1-70631-6) Harlequin Bks.

Where the Heart Is: A Celebration of Home. Ed. by Julienne Bennett & Mimi Luebbermann. (Illus.). 224p. (Orig.). 1995. pap. 14.00 (1-885171-00-5) Wldcat Canyon.

Where the Heart Is: A Novel. large type ed. Billie Letts. LC 95-30936. 427p. 1995. 23.95 (0-7838-1478-X, GK Hall) Thorndike Pr.

Where the Heart Is: Stories of Home & Family. Chick Moorman. Ed. by Nancy Lewis. 323p. (Orig.). 1996. pap. text ed. 14.95 (0-9616046-3-8) Prsnl Power Pr.

Where the Highway Ends. Geneva Hamilton. LC 74-77228. (Illus.). 1977. pap. 8.95 (0-914598-25-2) Bear Flag Bks.

Where the Hills Reply. Christina Laffeaty. 359p. 1992. 24.95 (0-340-54674-3, Pub. by H & S UK) Trafalgar.

Where the Indian Walks... Jean Van Hamme. Tr. by Jean-Jacques Surbeck from FRE. (Code XIII Ser.). (Illus.). 49p. (Orig.). 1989. pap. 6.95 (0-87416-081-2, Comcat Comics) Catalan Communs.

Where the Information Is: A Guide to Electronic Research for Nonprofit Organizations. Helen J. Bergan. LC 96-96139. (Illus.). 257p. (Orig.). 1996. pap. 29.95 (0-9615277-2-2) BioGuide Pr.

Where the Jobs Are. John W. Wright. 1992. mass mkt. 5.99 (0-380-77052-0) Avon.

Where the Jobs Are. 2nd ed. Joyce Hadley. 312p. 1995. pap. 9.99 (1-56414-160-8) Career Pr Inc.

***Where the Jobs Are: How Labor Market Conditions in the New York Area Will Affect the Employment Prospects of Public Assistance Recipients.** Hugh O'Neill et al. 83p. (Orig.). Date not set. mass mkt. 12.00 (0-88156-201-7) Comm Serv Soc NY.

Where the Jobs Are: Identification & Analysis of Local Employment Opportunities. William L. McKee & Richard C. Froeschle. LC 85-10570. 175p. 1985. pap. text ed. 12.00 (0-88099-029-5) W E Upjohn.

Where the Kissing Never Stops. Ronald Koertge. 224p. (J). 1993. mass mkt. 3.99 (0-380-71796-4, Flare) Avon.

Where the Laurel Grows. Evelyn P. Graham. LC 86-51075. 96p. (YA). (gr. 7 up). 1987. 6.95 (1-55523-056-3) Winston-Derek.

Where the Law Ends: The Social Control of Corporate Behavior. Christopher D. Stone. 273p. (C). 1991. reprint ed. pap. text ed. 10.95 (0-88133-632-7) Waveland Pr.

Where the Law Stopped & Grace Began. Vernelle B. Allen. 170p. 1994. pap. text ed. write for info. (1-885984-04-9) Wings of Healing.

Where the Lilies Bloom. Vera Cleaver & Bill Cleaver. 1977. 5.00 (0-87129-546-6, W40) Dramatic Pub.

Where the Lilies Bloom: A Study Guide. Mary Medland. Ed. by Joyce Friedland & Rikki Kessler. (Novel-Ties Ser.). 30p. (YA). (gr. 9-12). 1990. pap. text ed. 15.95 (0-88122-399-9) Lrn Links.

Where the Lillies Bloom. Bill Cleaver. LC 75-82402. (Trophy Keypoint Bk.). 224p. (YA). (gr. 7 up). 1989. pap. 3.95 (0-06-447005-9, Trophy) HarpC Child Bks.

Where the Lillies Bloom. Vera Cleaver. (J). 1969. 21.00 (0-397-31111-7) Lppncott-Raven.

***Where the Locals Eat: A Guide to the Best Restaurants in America.** Ed. by L. Lee Wilson et al. 1200p. (Orig.). 1996. pap. 19.95 (0-9634403-1-4) Magellan Pr.

Where the Long Grass Blows. Louis L'Amour. 192p. 1985. mass mkt. 3.99 (0-553-28172-0) Bantam.

Where the Meanings Are: Feminism & Cultural Spaces. Catherine R. Stimpson. 256p. 1989. 29.50 (0-416-01941-2, A1445, Routledge NY) Routledge.

Where the Meanings Are: Feminism & Cultural Spaces. Catherine R. Stimpson. 256p. (C). 1989. pap. 12.95 (0-415-90148-0, A1449, Routledge NY) Routledge.

Where the Men Are: Perfectly Proper Places to Meet with Style. D. C. Sands. Ed. by Ruth Sholes. (Orig.). 1988. pap. 9.95 (0-9620661-0-9) Ladys Bks Inc.

***Where the Men Are: 99 Ways to Meet Men.** C. Tomaso. (Illus.). (Orig.). 1997. pap. 4.95 (0-9632121-3-3) CNC Prods.

***Where the Money Grows.** Garet Garrett. (Investment Classics Ser.). 128p. 1997. text ed. 34.95 (0-471-23897-X) Wiley.

***Where the Money Grows.** Garet Garrett. (Investment Classics Ser.). 128p. 1997. pap. text ed. 16.95 (0-471-23898-8) Wiley.

Where the Money Grows. Garet Garrett. LC 66-30517. 1966. reprint ed. pap. 10.00 (0-87034-024-7) Fraser Pub Co.

Where the Money Is: A Fund Raiser's Guide to the Rich. 2nd enl. rev. ed. Helen J. Bergan. LC 91-76590. (Illus.). 257p. (Orig.). 1992. pap. 29.95 (0-9615277-6-5) BioGuide Pr.

Where the Money Is: A Novel of Las Vegas. Ivan G. Goldman. LC 95-24377. 192p. 1995. 22.00 (1-56980-052-9) Barricade Bks.

***Where the Money Is... America's Strongest Local Economies.** William H. Fruth. LC 96-92912. (Illus.). 416p. 1997. 37.97 (0-9655479-1-4) Policom Corp.

Where the Mopane Bloom: A Biologist in Ngamiland, Botswana. Frank L. Lambrecht. LC 89-8101. 1990. 25.00 (0-89341-577-4, Longwood Academic) Hollowbrook.

Where the Morning Light's Still Blue: Personal Essays About Idaho. Ed. by William Studebaker & Rick Ardinger. LC 93-35584. 200p. (Orig.). (C). 1994. pap. 15.95 (0-89301-170-3) U of Idaho Pr.

Where the Music Was: Stories. Charles East. LC 95-16011. (Brown Thrasher Bks.). 1995. pap. 12.95 (0-8203-1778-0) U of Ga Pr.

Where the Oceans Meet. Bhargavi C. Mandava. LC 96-34887. 272p. (Orig.). 1996. 22.95 (1-878067-86-9) Seal Pr WA.

Where the Passion Is: A Reading of Kierkegaard's Philosophical Fragments. H. A. Nielsen. LC 83-6923. 209p. 1983. 39.95 (0-8130-0742-9) U Press Fla.

Where the Past Has Been Preserved: Hollis, New Hampshire Eighteen Seventy-Nine to Nineteen Seventy-Nine. Hollis History Committee. LC 79-27118. (Illus.). 1980. 15.00 (0-914016-65-2) Phoenix Pub.

Where the Pavement Ends. John Russell. LC 73-144170. (Short Story Index Reprint Ser.). 1977. reprint ed. 21.95 (0-8369-3785-6) Ayer.

Where the People Gather: Carving a Totem Pole. Vickie Jensen. LC 92-23937. (Illus.). 194p. 1992. 29.95 (0-295-97220-3) U of Wash Pr.

Where the Pirates Are. Townsend. 96p. 1988. 11.95 (0-89015-500-3) Sunbelt Media.

Where the Pirates Are. Townsend. 96p. 1988. pap. 5.95 (0-89015-553-4) Sunbelt Media.

Where the Potomac Begins: A History of the North Branch Valley. Gilbert Gude. LC 84-14120. (Illus.). 208p. 1985. 26.95 (0-932020-32-1) Lomond.

Where the Queens All Strayed. Barbara Hanrahan. (Paperbacks Ser.). 182p. 1984. pap. 16.95 (0-7022-1305-5, Pub. by Univ Queensland Pr AT) Intl Spec Bk.

Where the Red Fern Grows. Holt & Company Staff. 1989. student ed., pap. 10.00 (0-03-023433-6) HR&W Schl Div.

Where the Red Fern Grows. Wilson Rawls. 256p. (J). 1984. mass mkt. 5.50 (0-553-27429-5) Bantam.

***Where the Red Fern Grows.** Wilson Rawls. (J). 1996. 16.95 (0-385-32330-1, Delacorte Pr Bks) BDD Bks Young Read.

Where the Red Fern Grows. Wilson Rawls. 208p. (J). 1996. pap. 4.99 (0-440-41267-6) Dell.

***Where the Red Fern Grows.** Scholastic Staff. (Literature Guide Ser.). (J). 1997. pap. text ed. 3.95 (0-590-37357-9) Scholastic Inc.

Where the Red Fern Grows: A Literature Unit. John Carratello & Patty Carratello. (Illus.). 48p. (Orig.). (gr. 5-8). 1991. student ed. 7.95 (1-55734-400-0) Tchr Create Mat.

Where the Red Fern Grows - Study Guide. Michael Golden. Ed. by Joyce Friedland & Rikki Kessler. (Novel-Ties Ser.). (YA). (gr. 6-8). 1993. pap. text ed. 15.95 (0-88122-034-5) Lrn Links.

Where the Rhododendrons Grow: A History of Camping & Leisure Ministries in the Holston Conference. Charles W. Maynard. (Illus.). 130p. 1988. 14.95 (0-932807-31-3); pap. 9.95 (0-932807-32-1) Overmountain Pr.

Where the River Begins. Thomas Locker. LC 84-1709. (Illus.). 32p. (J). (gr. k-3). 1984. pap. 17.99 (0-8037-0089-X); lib. bdg. 14.89 (0-8037-0090-3) Dial Bks Young.

Where the River Begins. Thomas Locker. (Illus.). 32p. (J). 1993. pap. 5.99 (0-14-054595-6) Puffin Bks.

Where the River Begins. Patricia M. St. John. LC 80-12304. (Patricia St. John Bks.). 127p. (Orig.). (J). (gr. 5-8). 1980. mass mkt. 5.99 (0-8024-8124-8) Moody.

Where the River Begins see Donde Nace el Rio

***Where the River Flows.** 96p. 1997. 6.50 (0-8341-1645-6) Nazarene.

Where the River Flows: Tales of Love & Romance in the Glorious Steamboat Era. Helen Colby. (Illus.). 130p. (Orig.). 1993. pap. write for info. (0-9639817-0-6) H C Swiers.

Where the River Rises. Max Marlow. 1994. 22.00 (0-7278-4583-7) Severn Hse.

Where the River Rises. large type ed. Joyce Marlow. 520p. 1995. 25.99 (0-7505-0803-5, Pub. by Magna Print Bks UK) Ulverscroft.

Where the River Runs. Richard S. Wheeler. 1992. mass mkt. 3.99 (0-8125-1298-7) Tor Bks.

Where the River Runs. large type ed. Richard Wheeler. LC 90-38613. 353p. 1990. reprint ed. lib. bdg. 15.95 (1-56054-035-4) Thorndike Pr.

Where the River Runs: A Portrait of a Refugee Family. Nancy P. Graff. LC 92-24184. (Illus.). 80p. (J). 1993. 17.95 (0-316-32287-3) Little.

Where the River Runs Deep: The Story of a Mississippi River Pilot. Joy J. Jackson. LC 93-7019. (Illus.). xviii, 352p. 1993. 29.95 (0-8071-1797-8) La State U Pr.

Where the River Shannon Flows. Richard Hayward. (Illus.). 331p. 8900. reprint ed. 32.00 (0-85221-114-7) Dufour.

Where the Rivers Converge: Roosevelt Platform Mound Study. Owen Lindauer et al. LC 95-45382. (Roosevelt Monograph Ser.: Vol. 4). 1995. write for info. (1-886067-04-X) ASU Office Cultural Res.

Where the Rivers Flow North. Howard F. Mosher. (Contemporary American Fiction Ser.). 224p. 1989. pap. 10.95 (0-14-007748-0, Penguin Bks) Viking Penguin.

Where the Rivers Join. Beckylane. 1995. pap. 14.95 (0-88974-043-7, Pub. by Press Gang CN) LPC InBook.

***Where the Rivers Meet.** large type ed. Ailie Scullion. (Dales Large Print Ser.). 257p. 1997. pap. 18.99 (1-85389-724-8, Dales) Ulverscroft.

Where the Road Bottoms Out: Stories. Victoria Redel. 1995. 20.00 (0-679-42071-1) Knopf.

Where the Road Ends: From Self Through Sai to Self. Howard Murphet. 227p. 1994. reprint ed. pap. 12.00 (0-9629835-3-5) Leela Pr.

Where the Road Ends: Havasu Palms, Recipes & Remembrances. Bobbi Holmes. Ed. by Caroline Johnson. (Illus.). 120p. 1995. pap. 9.35 (0-9649956-0-3) Robeth Pubng.

***Where the Road Goes.** Greenberg. Date not set. write for info. (0-8050-5163-5) H Holt & Co.

Where the Road Leads. Charles E. Miller. LC 94-90225. 320p. (Orig.). 1995. pap. 10.00 (1-56002-473-9, Univ Edtns) Aegina Pr.

Where the Rocks Float. Mary O'Malley. 78p. 9300. pap. 11.95 (1-897648-02-2, Pub. by Salmon Poetry IE) Dufour.

Where the Saints Have Trod: The Life of Helen Gougar. Robert C. Kriebel. LC 85-3633. (Illus.). 250p. 1985. 17.25 (0-911198-73-3) Purdue U Pr.

Where the Saints Meet, Nineteen Eighty-Four. 1979. pap. text ed. 10.00 (0-686-25231-4) Firm Foun Pub.

Where the Sea Breaks Its Back: The Epic Story of Early Naturalist Georg W. Steller & the Russian Exploration of Alaska. 2nd ed. Corey Ford. LC 92-3387. (Illus.). 224p. 1992. reprint ed. pap. 12.95 (0-88240-394-X) Alaska Northwest.

Where the Ships Die. William C. Dietz. 1996. mass mkt. 5.99 (0-441-00354-0) Ace Bks.

Where the Sidewalk Ends: Poems & Drawings. Shel Silverstein. LC 70-105486. (Illus.). 176p. (J). (gr 4 up). 1974. 15.95 (0-06-025667-2) HarpC Child Bks.

Where the Sidewalk Ends: Poems & Drawings. Shel Silverstein. LC 70-105486. (Illus.). 176p. (J). (gr. 4 up). 1974. lib. bdg. 15.89 (0-06-025668-0) HarpC Child Bks.

Where the Sky Began: Land of the Tallgrass Prairie. John Madson. LC 95-38585. (Illus.). 338p. 1995. pap. 21.95 (0-8138-2515-6) Iowa St U Pr.

***Where the Sky Begins.** Jill Creighton. (Illus.). 94p. (J). (gr. 4-6). 1996. pap. 4.95 (1-55037-270-X, Pub. by Annick CN) Firefly Bks Ltd.

Where the Spirit Breathes: Prophetic Dissent in the Church. Jose I. Faus Gonzalez. Tr. by Robert R. Barr. LC 88-36925. 160p. 1989. reprint ed. pap. 45.60 (0-7837-9823-7, 2060552) Bks Demand.

Where the Spirit Is Lord. Kristin Plummer. 89p. (Orig.). 1995. pap. write for info. (0-9645112-0-7) Jeremiah.

Where the Spirits Dwell: An Odyssey in the Jungle of New Guinea. Tobias Schneebaum. LC 88-10715. (Illus.). 240p. 1989. pap. 10.95 (0-8021-3166-2, Grove) Grove-Atltic.

Where the Spirits Ride the Wind: Trance Journeys & Other Ecstatic Experiences. Felicitas D. Goodman. LC 89-45567. (Illus.). 258p. 1990. 35.00 (0-253-32764-4); pap. 13.95 (0-253-20566-2) Ind U Pr.

W

Where the Strange Roads Go Down. Mary Del Villar & Fred Del Villar. LC 91-16622. 244p. 1991. reprint ed. pap. 16.95 (*0-8165-1273-6*) U of Ariz Pr.

Where the Suckers Moon: An Advertising Story. Randall Rothenberg. LC 94-496. 1994. 25.00 (*0-679-41227-1*) Knopf.

Where the Suckers Moon: The Life & Death of an Advertising Campaign. Randall Rothenberg. 1995. pap. 15.00 (*0-679-74042-2*) Random.

Where the Sun Stood Still. Donald Richter. LC 92-61189. 432p. 1992. text ed. 19.95 (*0-9611696-3-X*) Toucan Pub.

Where the Tall Grass Grows. John J. Sabuco & Marikay P. Witlock. (Illus.). 117p. (Orig.). (C). pap. text ed. 9.95 (*1-887619-02-X*) Plantsmans Pubns.

Where the Talmud Comes From: A Talmudic Phenomenology: Identifying the Free-Standing Building Blocks of Talmudic Discourse. Jacob Neusner. LC 95-25545. (South Florida Studies in the History of Judaism: Vol. 120). 176p. (C). 1995. 74.95 (*0-7885-0184-4*, 240120) Scholars Pr GA.

Where the Trails Are - Ashland - Medford & Beyond. 4th ed. Bill Williams. (Illus.). 224p. (Orig.). 1996. pap. 7.95 (*0-9622114-4-3*) B Williams.

Where the Trains Are! Wonderful North American Train Attractions for Kids of All Ages. Heather R. Taylor. LC 96-223. 416p. 1996. per. 16.95 (*0-7615-0408-7*) Prima Pub.

Where the Trilliums Bloom. C. H. Malesis. 192p. 1991. pap. 11.95 (*0-9631266-0-1*) Poon Crick Pub.

Where the Trout Are All As Long As Your Leg. John Gierach. 96p. Date not set. 16.95 (*1-55821-098-9*) Lyons & Burford.

Where the Trout Are All As Long As Your Leg. John Gierach. (Illus.). 96p. 1993. pap. 9.00 (*0-671-75455-6*, Fireside) S&S Trade.

Where the Truth Lies: Franz Moewus & the Origins of Molecular Biology. Jan Sapp. (Illus.). 349p. (C). 1990. pap. text ed. 24.95 (*0-521-36751-4*) Cambridge U Pr.

Where the Truth Lies: Franz Moewus & the Origins of Molecular Biology. Jan Sapp. (Illus.). 350p. (C). 1990. text ed. 65.00 (*0-521-36550-3*) Cambridge U Pr.

Where the Twilight Never Ends. John Haines. 28p. (Orig.). 1994. pap. 12.00 (*0-931659-21-3*) Limberlost Pr.

Where the Twilight Never Ends. deluxe limited ed. John Haines. 28p. (Orig.). 1994. 35.00 (*0-931659-22-1*) Limberlost Pr.

Where the Two Came to Their Father: A Navaho War Ceremonial. J. E. King & M. Oakes. Ed. by J. Campbell. (Mythos: The Princeton - Bollingen Series in World Mythology: No. I). (Illus.). 72p. 1991. pap. text ed. 14.95 (*0-691-02069-8*) Princeton U Pr.

***Where the Two Came to Their Father: A Navaho War Ceremonial.** J. E. King & M. Oakes. Ed. by J. Campbell. (Bollinger Ser.). 72p. 1991. text ed. 90.00 (*0-691-09974-X*, Bollingen) Princeton U Pr.

***Where the Water Buffalo Roam: The Assault on Free Speech on American's Campuses.** Alan C. Kors & Harvey Silverglate. 288p. 1997. 24.95 (*0-89526-444-7*) Regnery Pub.

Where the Water Hits the Wheel: Fifteen Sermons on the Great Beliefs of the Christian Faith. William G. Benton. LC 93-3849. 136p. 1993. pap. 9.95 (*1-880837-34-X*) Smyth & Helwys.

Where the Waters Begin: The Traditional Nisqually Indian History of Mount Rainier. Cecelia S. Carpenter. (Illus.). 108p. (Orig.). 1994. pap. text ed. 10.95 (*0-914019-33-3*, 5339) NW Interpretive.

***Where the Waters Divide: A 3,000-Mile Trek Along America's Continental Divide.** Karen Berger & Daniel R. Smith. LC 97-23823. (Illus.). 356p. 1997. reprint ed. pap. 17.95 (*0-88150-403-3*) Countryman.

Where the Waters Flow: A Half-Century of Regional Development, 1941-91. Michael J. Goc. (Illus.). 152p. 1991. 24.95 (*0-938627-15-5*) New Past Pr.

Where the Waters Gather & the Rivers Meet. Paul C. Durand. (Illus.). 165p. 1994. 14.95 (*0-9641469-0-8*) P C Durand.

Where the Waters Run - Chinese Edition. Moody Institute of Science Staff. Tr. by CRM Staff. 15p. (CHI.). 1980. 0.40 (*1-56582-056-8*) Christ Renew Min.

Where the Waves Break: Life at the Edge of the Sea. Anita Malnig. LC 84-9614. (Nature Watch Bks.). (Illus.). 48p. (J). (gr. 2-5). 1985. lib. bdg. 14.96 (*0-87614-226-9*, Carolrhoda) Lerner Group.

Where the Waves Break: Life at the Edge of the Sea. Anita Malnig. (Nature Watch Bks.). (Illus.). 48p. (J). (gr. 2-5). 1987. reprint ed. pap. 6.95 (*0-87614-477-6*, First Ave Edns) Lerner Group.

Where the Waves Fall: A New South Sea Islands History from First Settlement to Colonial Rule. K. R. Howe. LC 83-18295. (Pacific Islands Monographs: No. 2). (Illus.). 424p. 1988. reprint ed. pap. text ed. 24.00 (*0-8248-1186-0*) UH Pr.

Where the Weather Suits My Clothes. John Godfrey. Ed. by Kenward Elmslie. 32p. 1985. pap. 6.00 (*0-915990-25-3*) Z Pr.

Where the West Begins: America's Plains & Prairies. Karen Kent. 1995. 15.98 (*0-8317-8172-6*) Smithmark.

Where the West Meets the East. V. Chandra Mowli. 1993. 25.00 (*81-207-1459-8*, Pub. by Sterling Pubs II) Apt Bks.

Where the Whippoorwill Sings. Barbara Chambers. LC 94-90531. 120p. (Orig.). 1995. pap. 7.00 (*1-56002-507-7*, Univ Edtns) Aegina Pr.

Where the Wild Birds Sing. Oberdorfer. LC 97-19302. 1997. write for info. (*0-201-40927-5*) Addison-Wesley.

Where the Wild Goose Goes: B. D. White, Preservationist; Includes Gleanings in the History of Princess Anne County. Benjamin D. White. Ed. by Calvert W. Tazewell. LC 91-75147. (Illus.). 64p. (Orig.). 1993. reprint ed. pap. 8.00 (*1-878515-69-1*) W S Dawson.

Where the Wild Horses Roam. Dorothy H. Patent. (J). (gr. 4-7). 1993. pap. 6.95 (*0-395-66506-X*, Clarion Bks) HM.

Where the Wild Horses Roam. Dorothy H. Patent. (J). 1989. 15.95 (*0-89919-507-5*) Ticknor & Fields.

Where the Wild Rose Blooms. Lori Wick. (Rocky Mountain Memories Ser.: No. 1). (Orig.). 1996. pap. 9.99 (*1-56507-391-6*) Harvest Hse.

Where the Wild Strawberries Grow. David Arp & Claudia Arp. 224p. 1996. 16.99 (*0-7814-0291-3*) Chariot Victor.

Where the Wild Things Are. Garrett Christopher. Ed. by J. Friedland & R. Kessler. (Novel-Ties Ser.). 1992. student ed., pap. text ed. 14.95 (*0-88122-737-4*) Lrn Links.

Where the Wild Things Are. Maurice Sendak. LC 63-21253. (Trophy Picture Bk.). (Illus.). 48p. (J). (ps up). 1988. pap. 4.95 (*0-06-443178-9*, Trophy) HarpC Child Bks.

Where the Wild Things Are. Maurice Sendak. Tr. by Teresa Mlawer from SPA. LC 95-80605. (Trophy Picture Bk.). (Illus.). 48p. (SPA.). (J). (ps up). 1996. pap. 5.95 (*0-06-443422-2*, HpArco Iris) HarpC Child Bks.

Where the Wild Things Are. Maurice Sendak. (J). Date not set. pap. write for info. (*0-590-04537-7*) Scholastic Inc.

Where the Wild Things Are. 25th anniversary ed. Maurice Sendak. LC 63-21253. (Illus.). 48p. (J). (ps up). 1988. 15.00 (*0-06-025492-0*); lib. bdg. 14.89 (*0-06-025493-9*) HarpC Child Bks.

Where the Wild Things Are. Maurice Sendak. 1995. reprint ed. lib. bdg. 29.95 (*1-56849-659-1*) Buccaneer Bks.

Where the Wild Things Are: (Donde Viven los Monstruos) Maurice Sendak. (SPA.). (J). (gr. 1-6). 22.95 (*84-204-3022-6*) Santillana.

Where the Wilds Thing Are: Literature Unit. Kilpatrick. (Illus.). 48p. 1995. wbk. ed., pap. text ed. 7.95 (*1-55734-525-2*) Tchr Create Mat.

Where the Wind Blows Free. Lyle Rishell. 230p. 1993. 19.95 (*0-913969-63-X*, G Mason Univ Pr) Univ Pub Assocs.

Where the Wind Lives. Linda Hussa. LC 94-12402. 64p. 1994. pap. 9.95 (*0-87905-607-X*) Gibbs Smith Pub.

Where the Wind Lives: A Trilogy. Jack Walker. 480p. (Orig.). (YA). (gr. 12). 1995. pap. 19.95 (*1-881825-07-8*) Hist Pubns TX.

Where the Windrush Flows. Mollie Harris. (Illus.). 160p. 1990. 30.00 (*0-86299-680-5*, Pub. by Sutton Pubng UK) Bks Intl VA.

Where the Winds Blow Free: The History of Dunbarton, N.H. Alice M. Hadley. LC 76-47005. (Illus.). 1977. 15.00 (*0-914016-33-4*) Phoenix Pub.

Where the Wolf Sings. Mary Low. (Illus.). 64p. (Orig.). 1994. pap. 12.00 (*0-614-06074-5*) Black Swan Pr.

Where the Word Ends: The Life of Louis Moreau Gottschalk. fac. ed. Vernon Loggins. LC 58-7553. 289p. 1958. reprint ed. pap. 82.40 (*0-7837-7804-X*, 2047560) Bks Demand.

Where the Words Are Valid: T.S. Eliot's Communities of Drama. Randy Malamud. LC 94-22018. (Contributions in Drama & Theatre Studies: Vol. 58). 224p. 1994. text ed. 49.95 (*0-313-27818-0*, Greenwood Pr) Greenwood.

Where Their Feet Dance: Englishwomen's Sexual Fantasies. Rachel Silver. 166p. 1995. pap. 16.95 (*0-7126-6000-3*, Pub. by Century UK) Trafalgar.

Where There Is Light: Insight & Inspiration for Meeting Life's Challenges. Paramahansa Yogananda. LC 88-63330. 215p. 1988. 10.50 (*0-87612-275-6*); pap. 6.50 (*0-87612-276-4*) Self Realization.

Where There Is Love. Annette Broadrick. (Desire Ser.: No. 714). 1992. pap. 2.89 (*0-373-05714-8*, 5-05714-6) Harlequin Bks.

Where There Is No Dentist. Murray Dickson. Ed. by Michael Blake. LC 82-84067. (Illus.). 192p. (Orig.). 1983. pap. 9.00 (*0-942364-05-8*) Hesperian Found.

Where There Is No Doctor: A Village Health Care Handbook. rev. ed. David B. Werner et al. Orig. Title: Donde No Hay Doctor. (Illus.). 504p. 1992. reprint ed. pap. 17.00 (*0-942364-15-5*) Hesperian Found.

Where There Is No Name for Art: The Art of Tewa Pueblo Children. Bruce Hucko. (Illus.). 128p. (Orig.). 1996. pap. 20.00 (*0-933452-44-6*) Schol Am Res.

***Where There Is No Name for Art: The Art of Tewa Pueblo Children.** Bruce Hucko. (Orig.). 1996. pap. 20.00 (*0-614-20453-4*) U of Wash Pr.

Where There Is Nothing & the Unicorn from the Stars. William Butler Yeats & Lady Gregory. Ed. by Katharine Worth. LC 86-24434. (Irish Dramatic Texts Ser.). 176p. 1987. reprint ed. pap. 50.20 (*0-7837-9124-0*, 2049925) Bks Demand.

Where There's a Wall--There's a Way (101 Ways to "Dress" a Naked Wall. Barbara Jennings. (Illus.). 128p. 1986. pap. write for info. (*0-9618026-0-X*) Natl Design Assocs.

Where There's a Will, There's a Wag. Marilyn Singer. LC 85-24837. (Illus.). 96p. (J). (gr. 2-4). 1986. 11.95 (*0-03-005747-7*, Bks Young Read) H Holt & Co.

Where There's a Will, There's a Way. Joe Hayes. (Illus.). 32p. (Orig.). (J). (gr. 3-6). 1995. pap. 5.95 (*0-939729-25-3*) Trails West Pub.

Where There's Hope: There's Life & Laughter. Hope Mihalap. Ed. by Judith A. Johnson. (Illus.). 215p. (Orig.). 1994. pap. 15.00 (*0-9611354-6-8*) T Knox Pub.

***Where There's Love There's Life! An Easter Play in One Act.** John B. Wintermute. (Illus.). 12p. (Orig.). 1996. pap. 3.00 (*0-88680-431-0*) I E Clark.

***Where There's Smoke...** Laura Abbot. (Women Who Dare Ser.). 1997. mass mkt. 3.99 (*0-373-70747-9*, 1-70747-0) Harlequin Bks.

Where There's Smoke. Sandra Brown. 512p. 1994. mass mkt. 6.99 (*0-446-60034-2*) Warner Bks.

***Where There's Smoke.** Sandra Brown. 418p. 5.98 (*0-7651-0140-8*) Smithmark.

Where There's Smoke. Patricia Lakin. LC 94-19706. (My Community Ser.). (Illus.). (J). 1995. lib. bdg. 21.40 (*0-8114-8262-6*) Raintree Steck-V.

Where There's Smoke. Ed McBain. 192p. 1987. pap. 3.50 (*0-380-70372-6*) Avon.

Where There's Smoke. Ed McBain. 224p. 1997. mass mkt. 6.99 (*0-446-60483-6*) Warner Bks.

Where There's Smoke. Janet Munsil. (Illus.). 24p. (ENG & FRE.). (J). (ps-2). 1993. 14.95 (*1-55037-291-2*, Pub. by Annick CN); English ed. pap. 4.95 (*1-55037-290-4*, Pub. by Annick CN) Firefly Bks Ltd.

Where There's Smoke. Doreen Roberts. 1994. 3.50 (*0-373-07567-7*) Silhouette.

Where There's Smoke. large type ed. Sandra Brown. LC 93-23766. 1993. Alk. paper. 22.95 (*1-56054-781-2*) Thorndike Pr.

Where There's Smoke. large type ed. Sandra Brown. LC 93-23766. 1994. Alk. paper. lib. bdg. 15.95 (*1-56054-782-0*) Thorndike Pr.

Where There's Smoke: Problems & Policies Concerning Smoking in the Workplace. (Special Report Ser.). 140p. 1986. 25.00 (*0-87179-907-3*, LDSR46) BNA Plus.

Where There's Smoke: Problems & Policies Concerning Smoking in the Workplace. 2nd ed. (Special Report Ser.). 184p. 1987. 35.00 (*0-87179-925-1*, BSP71) BNA Plus.

Where There's Smoke There's Flavor: The Tastier Alternative to Grilling. Richard W. Langer. 256p. 1996. pap. 13.95 (*0-316-51301-6*) Little.

***Where They Ain't: A Cautionary Tale of Baseball at the Century's End.** Burt Solomon. 304p. Date not set. pap. write for info. (*0-465-09155-9*) Basic.

***Where They Ain't: A Cautionary Tale of Baseball at the Century's End.** Burt Solomon. 304p. 1998. write for info. (*0-465-09154-7*) Basic.

Where They Lie: The Story of the Jewish Soldiers of the North & South Whose Deaths - Killed, Mortally Wounded or Died of Disease or Other Causes - Occurred During the Civil War, 1861-1865 - Someone Should Say Kaddish. Mel Young. (Illus.). 330p. (C). 1991. lib. bdg. 39.00 (*0-8191-8109-9*) U Pr of Amer.

***Where Things Come From.** Time Life Inc. Editors. Ed. by Allan Fallow. LC 97-3636. (Child's First Library of Learning). (Illus.). 88p. (J). (ps-3). 1997. write for info. (*0-8094-9484-1*) Time-Life.

***Where This Lake Is.** Jeff Lodge. (New American Voices Ser.: Vol. 1). 184p. (Orig.). 1997. pap. 14.00 (*1-877727-68-7*) White Pine.

Where Thousands Fell. William J. Leonard. 256p. (Orig.). 1995. pap. 15.95 (*1-55612-755-3*); pap. 29.95 (*1-55612-756-1*) Sheed & Ward MO.

Where Three Empires Meet: A Narrative of Recent Travel in Kashmir, Western Tibet, Gilgit, & the Adjoining Countries. E. F. Knight. (C). 1993. reprint ed. 28.00 (*81-206-0828-3*, Pub. by Asian Educ Servs II) S Asia.

Where Tigers Roar in Silence: Mini Book. Lynn Hess. (Illus.). 32p. 1981. Miniature Bk. 27.50 (*0-915998-11-4*) Lime Rock Pr.

Where Time Becomes Space. Judith Antony. 147p. 1978. 4.95 (*0-8199-0699-9*, Frncscn Herld) Franciscan Pr.

Where Time Stood Still: A Portrait of Oman. Dutchess of St. Albans. (Illus.). 160p. 1982. 11.95 (*0-7043-2247-1*, Pub. by Quartet UK) Charles River Bks.

Where To? A Soft Skull Anthology. Ed. by Sander Hicks. 1995. pap. 6.00 (*1-887128-09-3*) Soft Skull Pr.

Where to Begin: A Guide to Teaching Secondary English. Jane Kearns. LC 96-20719. 143p. (Orig.). 1997. pap. text ed. 18.50 (*0-86709-406-0*, 0406) Boynton Cook Pubs.

Where to Borrow Money Without Expenses Or Interest Charges of Any Kind. (How to Manage in a Depression & Recession Ser.). 1992. lib. bdg. 79.95 (*0-8490-8780-5*) Gordon Pr.

Where to Buy Chemicals & Chemical Plant. British Chemical Dist. & Trade Association Directory Staff. (C). 1989. 200.00 (*0-685-36826-2*, Pub. by Fuel Metallurgical Jrnl UK) St Mut.

Where to Buy Everything Wholesale. 1987. lib. bdg. 175.00 (*0-8490-3868-5*) Gordon Pr.

Where to Buy Everything Wholesale: A Book of Lifetime Savings. Ben Carter. 32p. 1984. pap. 7.95 (*0-934650-06-3*) Sunnyside.

Where to Buy Hardwood Plywood & Veneer: 1993 Membership Directory. 100p. 1992. 5.00 (*0-317-04140-1*) Hardwd Ply.

***Where to Eat in Budapest.** Judit Acsay. 100p. 1989. 30.00 (*963-13-3495-3*, Pub. by Corvina Bks HU) St Mut.

Where to Eat in Canada, 1995-1996. Anne Hardy. 432p. 1995. pap. 12.95 (*1-55832-108-X*) Harvard Common Pr.

Where to Eat in Canada, 1996-1997. Anne Hardy. 1996. pap. text ed. 12.95 (*1-55832-122-5*) Harvard Common Pr.

***Where to Eat in Northern Ireland 1997.** NITB Staff. (Northern Ireland Tourist Board Ser.). (Illus.). 200p. (Orig.). 1997. pap. 7.95 (*1-86193-010-0*, Pub. by Jarrold Pub UK) Seven Hills Bk.

Where to Find Adoption Records: A Guide for Counsellors. G. Stafford. (C). 1989. 39.00 (*0-903534-61-4*, Pub. by Brit Ag for Adopt & Fost UK) St Mut.

Where to Find Birds in New York State: The Top 500 Sites. Susan R. Drennan. LC 81-16744. (New York State Bks.). (Illus.). 532p. 1981. pap. text ed. 24.95 (*0-8156-0173-5*) Syracuse U Pr.

Where to Find Dinosaurs Today. Daniel Cohen & Susan Cohen. LC 91-32084. (Illus.). 224p. (J). 1992. pap. 15.00 (*0-525-65098-9*, Cobblehill Bks) Dutton Child Bks.

Where to Find Everything for Practically Nothing in Chicagoland: A Bargain Hunters Guide to Resale & Thrift Shops. Trudy Miller. LC 87-82215. 170p. 1987. pap. 6.95 (*0-913587-02-8*) Second T Pub.

Where to Find Gold & Gems in Nevada. James Klein. (Illus.). 110p. 1992. 7.95 (*0-935182-15-2*) Gem Guides Bk.

Where to Find Gold in Southern California. James Klein. LC 93-73444. (Illus.). 112p. (Orig.). 1994. pap. 7.95 (*0-935182-68-3*) Gem Guides Bk.

Where to Find Gold in the Desert. 2nd ed. James Klein. LC 95-75456. (Illus.). 144p. (Orig.). 1995. pap. 7.95 (*0-935182-81-0*) Gem Guides Bk.

Where to Find It, Buy It, Eat It in New York. 8th rev. ed. Gerry Frank. LC 80-7802. (Illus.). 600p. 1993. pap. 12.95 (*1-879333-03-1*) Gerrys Frank.

Where to Find It in the Bible: The Ultimate A to Z Resource. Ken Anderson. 608p. 1996. pap. 19.99 (*0-7852-1157-8*) Nelson.

Where to Find Products Made in the U. S. A. A Guide to American Made Products. Karen Jackson. Ed. by Ohara Smith. 195p. (Orig.). 1992. pap. 7.95 (*0-9632642-7-3*) Plum Pubns.

Where to Find the Best of Huntsville. Mike Kaylor. LC 83-83209. (Illus.). 128p. (Orig.). 1984. pap. text ed. 3.95 (*0-916039-00-5*) Kaylor & Kaylor.

Where to Find the Best of Huntsville. 2nd ed. Mike Kaylor. (Illus.). 150p. (Orig.). (YA). (gr. 9-12). 1985. pap. text ed. 4.95 (*0-916039-01-3*) Kaylor & Kaylor.

Where to Find the General Register Office & International Genealogical Indexes. (C). 1987. 30.00 (*0-317-89814-0*, Pub. by Birmingham Midland Soc UK) St Mut.

Where to Find the Oregon in Oregon: A Guide to Oregon's Local, Natural, & Cultural Resources. 8th rev. ed. Bridget-Beattie McCarthy. (Illus.). 182p. 1994. pap. 10.95 (*0-9616696-6-7*) B B McCarthy.

Where to Find the Oregon in Oregon, 1989-1990. 5th rev. ed. Bridget-Beattie McCarthy. (Illus.). 128p. (Orig.). 1989. pap. 6.95 (*0-9616696-3-2*) B B McCarthy.

Where to Find Venture Capital: A Resource Guide. Philip C. Paul. LC 95-815. 296p. (Orig.). 1995. pap. 19.95 (*1-56825-028-2*) Rainbow Books.

Where to Find What: A Handbook to Reference Service. 3rd ed. James M. Hillard. LC 91-9025. 351p. 1991. 39.50 (*0-8108-2404-3*) Scarecrow.

***Where to Find What: A Handbook to Reference Service.** 4th ed. James M. Hillard. 512p. 1998. 45.00 (*0-8108-3402-2*) Scarecrow.

***Where to Gamble.** 1997. 18.95 (*1-57859-022-1*, 00157352) Visible Ink Pr.

***Where to Gamble in America.** Jacqueline A. Galati. 1996. pap. text ed. 9.95 (*0-9637194-0-8*) Galati Pr.

Where to Get the Money & Management Help for New Business Start-Ups & Small-Business Growth: EastNorth Central Region, IL, IN, MI, OH, WI. Richard S. Guyer & Frank J. Domeracki. 1995. ring bd. 197.00 (*1-884404-05-7*) Special Reports.

Where to Get the Money & Management Help for New Business Start-Ups & Small-Business Growth: EastSouth Central Region, AL, KY, MS, TN. Richard S. Guyer & Frank J. Domeracki. 1995. ring bd. 197.00 (*1-884404-09-X*) Special Reports.

Where to Get the Money & Management Help for New Business Start-Ups & Small-Business Growth: Middle Atlantic Region, NJ, NY, PA. Richard S. Guyer & Frank J. Domeracki. (Illus.). 200p. 1995. ring bd. 197.00 (*1-884404-01-4*) Special Reports.

Where to Get the Money & Management Help for New Business Start-Ups & Small-Business Growth: Mountain Region, AZ, CO, ID, MT, NV, NM, UT, WY. Richard S. Guyer & Frank J. Domeracki. 1995. ring bd. 197.00 (*1-884404-07-3*) Special Reports.

Where to Get the Money & Management Help for New Business Start-Ups & Small-Business Growth: New England Region, CT, ME, MA, NH, RI, VT. Richard S. Guyer & Frank J. Domeracki. 1995. ring bd. 197.00 (*1-884404-02-2*) Special Reports.

Where to Get the Money & Management Help for New Business Start-Ups & Small-Business Growth: Pacific Region, AK, CA, HI, OR, WA. Richard S. Guyer & Frank J. Domeracki. 1995. ring bd. 197.00 (*1-884404-04-9*) Special Reports.

Where to Get the Money & Management Help for New Business Start-Ups & Small-Business Growth: South Atlantic Region, DE, DC, FL, GA, MD, NC, SC, VA, WV. Richard S. Guyer & Frank J. Domeracki. 1995. ring bd. 197.00 (*1-884404-03-0*) Special Reports.

Where to Get the Money & Management Help for New Business Start-Ups & Small-Business Growth: WestNorth Central Region, IA, KS, MN, MO, NE, ND, SD. Richard S. Guyer & Frank J. Domeracki. 1995. ring bd. 197.00 (*1-884404-08-1*) Special Reports.

Where to Get the Money & Management Help for New Business Start-Ups & Small-Business Growth: WestSouth Central Region, AR, LA, OK, TX. Richard S. Guyer & Frank J. Domeracki. 1995. ring bd. 197.00 (*1-884404-06-5*) Special Reports.

Where to Go & What to Do on Long Island. SCOPE (Suffolk County Organization for the Promotion of Education) Staff. (Illus.). 256p. (Orig.). 1992. pap. 7.95 (*0-486-27162-5*) Dover.

***Where to Go for Career Training in South Florida: A Guide to Public & Private Vocational, Technical, Business & Health Training Programs.** (Where to Go for Career Training Ser.). 104p. (Orig.). 1996. pap. 14.95 (*0-9652536-0-0*) Resource Media.

***Where to Go from Here.** Birren. LC 97-22499. 1997. 22.00 (*0-684-83057-4*) S&S Trade.

Where to Go in Britain. Automobile Association of Great Britain Staff. (Illus.). 192p. 1993. 35.00 (*0-393-03459-3*) Norton.

Where to Go in Los Angeles. Ed. by Jeffrey Kaufman. (Illus.). 656p. (Orig.). 1985. pap. 17.95 (*0-912785-01-2*) Where To Go.

Where to Go in Minneapolis & St. Paul. 2nd ed. Ed. by Jeffrey Kaufman. 352p. 1985. pap. 14.95 (*0-317-27038-9*) Where To Go.

W

An Asterisk (*) at the beginning of an entry indicates that the title is appearing in BIP for the first time.

Where to Go Really Four-Wheelin' in California. Casey Smith. Ed. by Lori Smith. (Illus.). 122p. (Orig.). 1988. pap. 9.95 (0-945294-00-X) Cloud Nine Pubns.

Where to Go, What to Do, When You Are Bern Porter: A Personal Biography. James Schevill. LC 91-67866. (Illus.). 256p. 1992. 27.50 (0-88448-125-5); pap. 16.95 (0-88448-126-3) Tilbury Hse.

Where to Go with Kids in the Capital District. Patricia Dahl et al. (Illus.). 50p. (Orig.). 1982. pap. text ed. 2.50 (0-9611292-0-4) With Kids.

Where to Have Affairs: Unique Locations for Business & Private Special Events in California's Historic Gold Country. Carol C. Nelson. (Illus.). 152p. (Orig.). 1996. pap. 14.95 (0-9648292-6-6) Riba Commun.

Where to Look for a Dinosaur. Bernard Most. LC 92-19443. (Illus.). 32p. (J). (PS-3). 1993. 13.00 (0-15-295616-6, HB Juv Bks) HarBrace.

***Where to Look for a Dinosaur.** Bernard Most. 1997. pap. 5.00 (0-15-201504-3, Voyager Bks) HarBrace.

***Where to Look for a Dinosaur: Mini-Book.** Most. (J). 1995. write for info. (0-15-200379-7, HB Juv Bks) HarBrace.

Where to Look for Hard-To-Find German-Speaking Ancestors in Eastern Europe: Index to 19,720 Surnames in 13 Books, with Historical Background on Each Settlement. 2nd ed. Bruce Brandt & Edward R. Brandt. 148p. 1996. reprint ed. pap. 18.50 (0-614-16615-2, 9042) Clearfield Co.

Where to Make Money: A Rating Guide to Opportunities in America's Metro Areas. G. Scott Thomas. 327p. (Orig.). (C). 1993. 38.95 (0-87975-762-0); pap. 20.95 (0-87975-795-7) Prometheus Bks.

Where to Now? Australia's Identity in the Nineties. Ed. by J. Beaumont. 216p. 1993. pap. 29.00 (1-86287-124-8, Pub. by Federation Pr AU) Gaunt.

Where to Play in the U. S. A. The Gaming Guide. Ed. by Michael Sankey & Timothy Russell. 344p. 1997. pap. 19. 95 (1-889150-03-7) Facts on Demand.

***Where to Prospect for Gold in Alaska Without Getting Shot!** Ronald R. Wendt. (Illus.). 70p. (Orig.). 1996. pap. text ed. 9.95 (1-886574-12-X) Goldstream Pubns.

Where to Retire: America's Best & Most Affordable Places. 2nd ed. John Howells. (Illus.). 372p. 1994. pap. 14.95 (0-933469-19-5) Gateway Bks.

Where to Retire in Florida: America's Most Complete Guide to Retirement Areas in the Sunshine State. Richard Fox & Betty Fox. Ed. by Karen Northridge. LC 94-61753. 224p. (Orig.). 1995. pap. 16.95 (0-9644216-0-7) Vacation Pubns.

Where to Sell Anything & Everything Book. Henry A. Hyman. 288p. 1986. pap. 8.95 (0-685-08151-6, World Almanac) Newspaper Ent.

Where to Sell It! How to Find the Best Buyers of Antiques, Collectibles, & Other Undiscovered Treasures. Tony Hyman. 512p. (Orig.). 1993. pap. 16. 95 (0-399-51817-7, Perigee Bks) Berkley Pub.

***Where to Sell-It Directory: 1997-1998 Edition.** rev. ed. LC 78-31582. 62p. 1997. pap. 7.95 (0-87576-198-4) Pilot Bks.

***Where to Ski.** Ed. by Chris Gill & Dave Watts. (Illus.). 520p. 1997. pap. 24.95 (0-7522-1689-9, Pub. by Boxtree UK) Trafalgar.

Where to Start & What to Ask: The Assessment Handbook. Susan Lukas. 220p. (C). 1992. 22.94 (0-393-70148-4) Norton.

Where to Start & What to Ask: The Assessment Handbook. Susan Lukas. 220p. (C). 1993. pap. 14.95 (0-393-70152-2) Norton.

Where to Stay. Amoco Pathfinder Staff. 1992. pap. 2.25 (0-671-84037-1) S&S Trade.

***Where to Stay in England, 1997: Families Welcome.** English Tourist Board Staff. (Where to Stay Ser.). 1997. pap. text ed. 10.95 (0-7117-0873-8, Pub. by Jarrold Pub UK) Seven Hills Bk.

***Where to Stay in England, 1997: Hotels & Guesthouses.** English Tourist Board Staff. (Where to Stay Ser.). 1997. pap. text ed. 16.95 (0-86143-198-7, Pub. by Jarrold Pub UK) Seven Hills Bk.

Where to Stay in Florida. 2nd ed. Phil Philcox. 1995. pap. 12.95 (1-55650-682-1) Hunter NJ.

Where to Stay in France. 3rd ed. Meg Jump. 1996. pap. text ed. 18.95 (0-9521500-2-6, Pub. by Parasol Pubns UK) Seven Hills Bk.

***Where to Stay in Northern Ireland 1997.** NITB Staff. (Northern Ireland Tourist Board Ser.). (Illus.). 264p. (Orig.). 1997. pap. 8.95 (1-86193-015-1, Pub. by Jarrold Pub UK) Seven Hills Bk.

***Where to Stay Self-Catering Holiday Homes in England 1997.** English Tourist Board Staff. (Where to Stay Ser.). 1997. pap. text ed. 10.95 (0-86143-200-2, Pub. by Jarrold Pub UK) Seven Hills Bk.

***Where to Stay Somewhere Special in England, 1997.** English Tourist Board Staff. (Where to Stay Ser.). 1997. pap. text ed. 12.95 (0-7117-0872-X, Pub. by Jarrold Pub UK) Seven Hills Bk.

Where to, Tarapada-Babu? Tarapada Roy. Tr. by Shyamasree Devi & P. Lal from BEN. (Saffronbird Ser.). 51p. 1975. 10.00 (0-88253-839-X); pap. 4.80 (0-88253-840-3) Ind-US Inc.

Where to Turn: The Directory of Health, Welfare & Community Services in Allegheny County. rev. ed. Ed. by Anne Walsh Fogoros. 598p. (Orig.). 1994. pap. 40.00 (0-930053-01-X) United Way HelpLine.

***Where to Turn: 1997.** 300p. (Orig.). 1997. pap. 40.00 (0-9657581-0-9) Info Line.

Where to Turn for Help for Older Persons: A Guide for Action on Behalf of an Older Person. 54p. 1988. write for info. (1-55672-029-7) US HHS.

***Where to Turn for Help for Older Persons: A Guide for Action on Behalf of an Older Person.** 41p. (Orig.). 1997. pap. 15.00 (0-7881-3624-0) DIANE Pub.

Where to Walk Your Dog in San Francisco & Marin Counties. Cheryl S. Smith. LC 93-7035. (Illus.). 160p. (Orig.). 1993. pap. 11.95 (0-89997-159-8) Wilderness Pr.

Where to Walk Your Dog in Santa Clara & San Mateo Counties. Cheryl S. Smith. (Illus.). 160p. (Orig.). 1991. pap. 11.95 (0-89997-127-X) Wilderness Pr.

Where to Watch Birds in Africa. Nigel Wheatley. 432p. 1996. text ed. 35.00 (0-691-02140-6) Princeton U Pr.

***Where to Watch Birds in Asia.** Nigel Wheatley. LC 96-27112. 464p. 1997. text ed. 35.00 (0-691-01214-8) Princeton U Pr.

Where to Watch Birds in Britain & Europe. John Gooders. 254p. 1992. pap. 17.95 (0-8442-9544-2, Passport Bks) NTC Pub Grp.

***Where to Watch Birds in Bulgaria.** Peter Yankov. (Illus.). 120p. 1996. pap. 29.95 (954-642-011-5) Intl Scholars.

Where to Watch Birds in Ireland. Clive Hutchinson. (Illus.). 200p. (Orig.). 1995. pap. 19.95 (0-7171-2204-2, Pub. by Gill & MacMill IE) Irish Bks Media.

Where to Watch Birds in South America. Nigel Wheatley. LC 94-26773. 432p. 1995. text ed. 35.00 (0-691-04337-X) Princeton U Pr.

Where to Write for Confederate Pension Records. 2nd ed. Desmond Walls Allen. (Illus.). 16p. 1994. pap. 5.95 (1-56546-588-1) Arkansas Res.

Where to Write for County Maps. 2nd ed. Desmond W. Allen. 20p. 1995. pap. 5.95 (1-56546-062-6) Arkansas Res.

Where to Write for Vital Records: Births, Death, Marriages, & Divorces. National Center for Health Statistics Staff. Ed. by Klaudia Cox. 29p. pap. text ed. 1.75 (0-8406-0375-4) Natl Ctr Health Stats.

Where to Write for Vital Statistics. 1982. 5.00 (0-89593-652-6) Accelerated Index.

Where Tomorrow Waits. Jane Peart. (Westward Dreams Ser.: Vol. 3). 256p. 1995. reprint ed. pap. text ed. 9.99 (0-310-41291-9) Zondervan.

Where Town Meets Country: Problems of Peri-Urban Areas of Scotland, Royal Scottish Geographical Society Symposium May 1981. Ed. by A. B. Cruickshank. (Illus.). 140p. 1982. 23.00 (0-08-028442-6, R130, Pergamon Pr); pap. 16.00 (0-08-028443-4, R145, Pergamon Pr) Elsevier.

Where Trdition Began: The Centennial History of Auburn Football. Wayne Hester. (Illus.). 240p. (Orig.). 1991. pap. 15.00 (1-878561-06-5) Seacoast AL.

***Where Trouble Sleeps: A Novel.** Clyde Edgerton. LC 97-3151. 1997. write for info. (1-56512-061-2) Algonquin Bks.

Where Two Are Gathered. April Yamasaki. 128p. (Orig.). 1988. pap. 9.95 (0-87178-943-4) Brethren.

***Where Two Are Gathered: Stories of 12 Small Christian Communities.** Margaret O. Bisgrove. Ed. by Carl Koch. 192p. (Orig.). 1997. pap. 14.95 (0-88489-499-1) St Marys.

Where Two Oceans Meet. James Cowan. 1992. pap. 13.95 (1-85230-330-1) Element MA.

Where Two or Three Are Gathered. David Williams & Ruth Williams. 168p. (Orig.). 1994. pap. 7.99 (1-56043-833-9) Destiny Image.

Where Two or Three Are Gathered: Community Life for the Contemporary Religious. Barbara Fiand. 108p. 1992. pap. 12.95 (0-8245-1151-4) Crossroad NY.

Where Two or Three Are Gathered: Liturgy & the Moral Life. Harmon L. Smith. LC 94-39961. 224p. (Orig.). 1995. pap. 15.95 (0-8298-1024-2) Pilgrim OH.

Where Two or Three Are Gathered, Someone Spills the Milk. Tom Mullen. LC 86-14322. 126p. 1986. reprint ed. pap. 4.50 (0-913408-95-6) Friends United.

Where Two Ways Meet. Grace L. Hill. (Grace Livingston Hill Ser.: Vol. 1). 1990. pap. 4.99 (0-8423-8203-8) Tyndale.

Where Two Ways Met. Grace L. Hill. 23.95 (0-8488-0089-3) Amereon Ltd.

Where Two Worlds Meet: The Great Lakes Fur Trade. Carolyn Gilman. LC 82-2089. (Museum Exhibit Ser.: No. 2). (Illus.). 136p. (Orig.). 1982. pap. 18.95 (0-87351-156-5) Minn Hist.

Where Two Worlds Met: The Russian State & the Kalmyk Nomads, 1600-1771. Michael Khodarkovsky. LC 92-5282. (Illus.). 280p. 1992. 37.50 (0-8014-2555-7) Cornell U Pr.

Where Two Worlds Touch: Spiritual Rites of Passage. Gloria Karpinski. 450p. (Orig.). 1990. pap. 11.50 (0-345-35331-5, Ballantine Trade) Ballantine.

Where Virgins Abound. Harold L. Crist. LC 88-92740. 112p. (Orig.). 1989. pap. text ed. 6.95 (0-9621743-0-0) H L Crist.

***Where Wagons Could Go: Narcissa Whitman & Eliza Spaulding.** Ed. & Intro. by Clifford M. Drury. LC 96-38594. (Illus.). 280p. 1997. pap. 12.00 (0-8032-6606-5, Bison Books) U of Nebr Pr.

Where Was George Washington? Carla Heymsfeld. LC 92-17341. (Illus.). (J). 1992. 9.95 (0-931917-20-4); pap. 5.95 (0-931917-21-2) Mt Vernon Ladies.

Where Was God at 9:02 A. M.? Miraculous Stories of Faith & Love from Oklahoma City. Robin L. Jones & Sandy Dengler. LC 95-31358. (Illus.). 288p. 1995. pap. 5.99 (0-7852-7577-0) Nelson.

Where Was Patrick Henry on the 29th of May? Jean Fritz. (Illus.). 48p. (J). (gr. 3-5). 1975. 13.95 (0-698-20307-0, Coward) Putnam Pub Group.

Where Was Patrick Henry on the 29th of May? Jean Fritz. (Illus.). 48p. (J). (gr. 3-5). 1982. pap. 7.95 (0-698-20544-8, Coward) Putnam Pub Group.

***Where Was Patrick Henry on the 29th of May?** Jean Fritz. (Illus.). 48p. (J). (gr. 2-6). 1997. pap. 5.95 (0-698-11439-6, Paperstar) Putnam Pub Group.

Where Was the Sexual Revolution When I Needed It? (Playscript) Lew Riley. LC 92-56436. 68p. (Orig.). 1992. pap. 6.00 (0-88734-204-3) Players Pr.

Where Water Comes Together with Other Water. Raymond Carver. 1985. 13.95 (0-394-54470-6) Random.

Where Water Comes Together with Other Water: Poems. Raymond Carver. 1986. pap. 11.00 (0-394-74327-X, Vin) Random.

Where Water Falls. Clarence C. Dill. LC 73-140147. 276p. 1970. 7.50 (0-614-16725-6) Ye Galleon.

***Where Water Meets Land.** Lucian Niemeyer. (Illus.). 96p. (Orig.). 1996. pap. 16.95 (0-9651966-0-7) York Graphic.

Where Waves Were. 3rd rev. ed. Robert F. Mainone. (Haiku: Vol. 3). (Illus.). 60p. 1986. pap. 7.00 (1-888693-03-7) Wnderlnd MI.

Where We Are At. Thomas H. Barber. (Right Wing Individualist Tradition in America Ser.). 1972. reprint ed. 21.95 (0-405-00412-5, 71-172202) Ayer.

Where We Came In: Poems. David Adams. (Wild Dog Ser.). 64p. (Orig.). 1993. pap. 5.95 (0-933087-26-8) Bottom Dog Pr.

Where We Go. (Key Words Readers Ser.: A Series, No. 641-5a). (Illus.). (J). (ps-5). 3.50 (0-7214-0005-1, Ladybrd) Penguin.

Where We Go. (Series S705: No. 5). (Illus.). (J). (ps-5). Ser. S705, No. 5. student ed. 1.95 (0-7214-3066-X, Ladybrd) Penguin.

Where We Got the Bible... Our Debt to the Catholic Church. Henry G. Graham. 153p. 1994. reprint ed. pap. 6.00 (0-89555-137-3) TAN Bks Pubs.

Where We Live. Walter Cummins. LC 82-22922. (Short Stories Ser.: Vol. 2). 94p. (Orig.). 1983. pap. text ed. 7.50 (0-89924-037-2) Lynx Hse.

Where We Live. Peter Makuck. (New Poets of America Ser.). 80p. (C). 1982. 14.00 (0-918526-40-X); pap. 7.00 (0-918526-41-8) BOA Edns.

Where We Live. Judy Mullican. (HRL Little Bks.). (Illus.). 8p. (Orig.). (J). (ps-1). 1996. pap. text ed. 10.95 (1-57332-040-4) HighReach Lrning.

Where We Live. large type ed. Judy Mullican. (HRL Big Bks.). (Illus.). 8p. (Orig.). (J). (ps-1). 1996. pap. text ed. 10.95 (1-57332-041-2) HighReach Lrning.

Where We Live: A Citizen's Guide to Conducting a Community Environmental Inventory. Donald F. Harker & Elizabeth U. Natter. LC 94-32180. 336p. (C). 1995. pap. text ed. 18.95 (1-55963-377-8) Island Pr.

Where We Live: A Guide to St. Louis Communities. Ed. by Tim Fox. LC 95-45700. 225p. 1995. 22.95 (1-883982-12-X) MO Hist Soc.

Where We Live: Essays about Indiana. Ed. by David Hoppe. LC 89-2002. 126p. 1989. 24.95 (0-253-32801-2); pap. 5.95 (0-253-20540-9, MB-540) Ind U Pr.

***Where We Once Belonged.** Sia Figiel. 236p. 1997. pap. text ed. 20.00 (0-908597-27-4) UH Pr.

***Where We Park.** Edward Locke. 78p. (Orig.). 1996. pap. 7.00 (0-9646587-2-0) Harlequinade.

Where We Sleep. Nancy Tafuri. LC 86-27115. (Illus.). (J). (ps). 1987. pap. 3.95 (0-688-07189-9) Greenwillow.

Where We Stand. Mark E. Braun. 72p. (Orig.). 1988. pap. text ed. 3.50 (0-938272-60-8, 22N2201) WELS Board.

Where We Stand. Sharon Bryan. 1994. pap. 11.00 (0-393-31209-7) Norton.

***Where We Stand: Jewish Consciousness on Campus.** Ed. by Alan L. Smith. 1997. pap. 10.95 (0-8074-0539-6, 243875) UAHC.

***Where We're Bound.** Bonnie Kahn. 1997. write for info. (0-201-13294-X) Addison-Wesley.

***Where Were You in 1968? The Year That Changed Our World.** Patricia L. Iverson & Steven C. Parker. (Illus.). 304p. (Orig.). 1997. pap. 19.95 (1-889528-45-5) White Star Pub.

Where Were You When I Needed You, Dad? A Guide for Healing Your Father Wound. Jane M. Drew. LC 91-68455. (Illus.). 216p. (Orig.). 1992. pap. 16.95 (1-880883-00-7) Tiger Lily Pub.

Where Were You When President Kennedy Was Shot? Memories & Tributes to a Slain President As Told to Dear Abby. Abigail Van Buren. (Illus.). 160p. (Orig.). 1993. pap. 6.95 (0-8362-6246-8) Andrews & McMeel.

Where We've Been. William Greenway. LC 87-888. 80p. 1987. 14.95 (0-932576-45-1); pap. 7.95 (0-932576-46-X) Breitenbush Bks.

***Where White Men Fear to Tread.** Means. 1996. pap. 16. 95 (0-312-14761-9) St Martin.

Where White Men Fear to Tread: The Autobiography of Russell Means. Russell Means & Marvin J. Wolf. LC 95-23289. (Illus.). 608p. 1995. 26.95 (0-312-13621-8) St Martin.

Where Wigwams Stood: A History of Muncey. Katherine Yurchak. (Illus.). 128p. (Orig.). 1994. pap. 12.95 (0-942991-01-X) Spectrum PA.

Where Wild Rivers Run. Howard L. Norskog. 40p. (Orig.). pap. 6.00 (0-9625171-7-8) H L Norskog.

Where Wilderness Preservation Began: The Adirondack Writings of Howard Zahniser. Edward Zahniser. 82p. 1992. pap. 9.95 (0-685-74773-5) North Country.

Where Will the Animals Stay? Stephanie Calmenson. LC 83-13479. (Illus.). 48p. (J). (ps-3). 1984. 5.95 (0-8193-1119-7) Parents.

Where Will This Shoe Take You? A Walk Through the History of Footwear. Laurie Lawlor. (Illus.). 128p. (YA). (gr. 5 up). 1996. lib. bdg. 18.85 (0-8027-8435-6) Walker & Co.

Where Will This Shoe Take You? A Walk Through the History of Footwear. Laurie Lawlor. (Illus.). 132p. (YA). (gr. 5 up). 1997. 17.95 (0-8027-8434-8) Walker & Co.

Where Will You Be in 300 Years? James McKeever. 36p. (C). pap. text ed. 3.99 (0-86694-119-3) Omega Pubns OR.

Where Will You Swim Tonight? Milly J. Limmer. Ed. by Ann Fay. LC 90-38938. (Illus.). 32p. (J). (ps-1). 1991. 15.95 (0-8075-8949-7) A Whitman.

***Where Willows Weed.** Bonita Rivas. Ed. by Victoria Rivas. (Illus.). 36p. (Orig.). 1996. pap. 4.00 (1-889289-08-6) Ye Olde Font Shoppe.

Where Wisdom Shines. Ed. & Intro. by Robert A. Norman. (Illus.). 160p. (Orig.). 1994. pap. text ed. 7.95 (0-9637802-0-4) Medford Sr Citizens.

Where Wizards Stay up Late: The Origins of the Internet. Katie Hafner & Matthew Lyon. LC 96-19533. (Illus.). 320p. 1996. 24.00 (0-684-81201-0, S&S) S&S Trade.

***Where Wizards Stay up Late: The Origins of the Internet.** Katie Hafner. 1998. pap. text ed. 13.00 (0-684-83267-4, Touchstone Bks) S&S Trade.

Where Women Are Leaders: The SEWA Movement in India. Kalima Rose. (Illus.). 288p. (C). 1993. pap. 19.95 (1-85649-084-X, Pub. by Zed Bks Ltd UK) Humanities.

***Where Women Have No Doctor: A Health Guide for Women.** A. August Burns & Sandy Niemann. LC 97-19421. 1997. pap. write for info. (0-942364-25-2) Hesperian Found.

***Where Women Stand: An International Report on the Status of Women in Over 140 Countries 1997 - 1998.** N. Neft & A. Levine. LC 97-1728. 1997. pap. 20.00 (0-679-78015-7, Random Ref) Random.

Where Women Work: A Study of Yoruba Women in the Marketplace & in the Home. Niara Sudarkasa. LC 74-175945. (University of Michigan, Museum of Anthropology, Anthropological Papers: No. 53). 186p. reprint ed. pap. 53.10 (0-317-29764-3, 2017305) Bks Demand.

***Where Wonders Prevail.** Joan W. Anderson. 1997. pap. 12.00 (0-345-40910-8) Ballantine.

Where Wonders Prevail: True Accounts That Bear Witness to the Existence of Heaven. Joan W. Anderson. 304p. 1996. 21.00 (0-345-39731-2) Ballantine.

***Where Wonders Prevail: True Accounts That Bear Witness to the Existence of Heaven.** Joan W. Anderson. LC 97-22183. 1997. write for info. (0-7838-8263-7) G K Hall.

***Where Worlds Collide: The Wallace Line.** Penny Van Oosterzee. LC 97-25861. (Illus.). 234p. 1997. pap. 17.95 (0-8014-8497-9) Cornell U Pr.

***Where Writers Become Authors II.** Albert R. Steward, III. LC 96-61316. 1997. pap. 14.95 (1-881180-09-3) Trebla Pr.

Where Ya' Been, Mate? Herb Wharton. 136p. 1996. pap. 16.95 (0-7022-2803-6, Pub. by Univ Queensland Pr AT) Intl Spec Bk.

Where You Are. George Constable. LC 95-49348. 320p. 1997. 21.95 (0-385-48438-0) Doubleday.

Where You Belong. Mary A. McGuigan. (J). 1997. 16.00 (0-689-81250-7) S&S Childrens.

Where You Belong: Government & Black Culture. Alrick Cambridge et al. 160p. 1992. 59.95 (1-85628-394-1, Pub. by Avebury Pub UK) Ashgate Pub Co.

Where You First Saw the Eyes of Coyote. Linda Noel. 16p. (Orig.). 1983. pap. 2.00 (0-936574-09-7) Strawberry Pr NY.

Where You Live. Michael Rawcliffe. (Changing Britain Ser.). (Illus.). 48p. (J). (gr. 6-9). 1994. 19.95 (0-7134-6714-2, Pub. by Batsford UK) Trafalgar.

Where You Live Is What You Learn: How the Number of Your Residence Affects Your Life. Kathleen Jacoby. 60p. (Orig.). 1995. pap. 12.00 (0-9650576-0-7) Mouse the Pub.

Where You'll Find Me: And Other Stories. Ann Beattie. 224p. 1996. pap. 10.00 (0-684-81510-9) S&S Trade.

Where Your Money Goes: America's Entitlements - The 1994-95 Green Book. U. S. House of Representatives Staff. 1312p. 1995. 35.95 (0-02-881130-5) Brasseys Inc.

Where Your Money Goes: America's Entitlements: The 1996-97 Green Book. U. S. House of Representatives Staff. 1312p. 1997. 35.95 (1-57488-015-2) Brasseys Inc.

Where Your Treasure Is: Psalms That Summon You from Self to Community. 2nd ed. Eugene H. Peterson. 190p. 1993. reprint ed. pap. 13.00 (0-8028-0115-3) Eerdmans.

Where Your Treasure Is: Your Attitude on Finances. Larry Burkett. (Stewardship Ser.: Bk. 2). (Orig.). 1996. pap. 5.99 (0-8024-2804-5) Moody.

Where You've Seen Her. Grace Bauer. (Green Ser.). 6.00 (0-938631-11-X) Pennywhistle Pr.

Whereabouts: Notes on Being a Foreigner. Alastair Reid. 1990. reprint ed. pap. 10.00 (1-877727-10-5) White Pine.

Whereabouts of Some American Refugees, 1784-1800: The Nova Scotian Land Grants, Pt. 2: Surnames Clark - Furnay. Clifford N. Smith. (British-American Genealogical Research Monographs: No. 12, Pt. 2). i, 54p. (Orig.). 1993. pap. 20.00 (0-915162-42-3) Westland Pubns.

Whereabouts of Some American Refugees, 1784-1800 Pt. 1: The Nova Scotian Land Grants, Surnames Aarons - Clapper. Clifford N. Smith. (British-American Genealogical Research Monograph Ser.: No. 12). iv, 54p. (Orig.). 1992. pap. 20.00 (0-915162-41-5) Westland Pubns.

Whereabouts of Some American Refugees, 1784-1800 Pt. 3: The Nova Scotian Land Grants, Surnames Gabriel - Jingo. Clifford N. Smith. (British-American Genealogical Research Monograph: No. 12). i, 56p. (Orig.). 1994. pap. 20.00 (0-915162-43-1) Westland Pubns.

Whereabouts of Some American Refugees, 1784-1800. The Nova Scotia Land Grants Pt. 5: Surnames Mead-Rivers. Clifford N. Smith. (British-American Genealogical Research Monographs: Vol. 12, Pt. 5). i, 54p. 1995. pap. 20.00 (0-915162-45-8) Westland Pubns.

Whereabouts of Some American Refugees, 1784-1800. The Nova Scotia Land Grants Pt. 6: Surnames Roach-Smyth. Clifford N. Smith. (British-American Genealogical Research Monographs: Vol. 12, Pt. 6). i, 59p. 1995. pap. 20.00 (0-915162-46-6) Westland Pubns.

Whereabouts of Some American Refugees, 1784-1800. The Nova Scotia Land Grants Pt. 7: Surnames Snarlock-Way. Clifford N. Smith. (British-American Genealogical Research Monographs: Vol. 12, Pt. 7). i, 57p. 1995. pap. 20.00 (*0-915162-69-5*) Westland Pubns.

Whereabouts of Some American Refugees, 1784-1800. The Nova Scotia Land Grants Pt. 8: Surnames Wear-Zeneva. Clifford N. Smith. (British-American Genealogical Research Monographs: Vol. 12, Pt. 8). i, 23p. 1995. pap. 20.00 (*0-915162-70-9*) Westland Pubns.

Whereabouts of Some American Refugees, 1784-1800, The Nova Scotian Land Grants Pt. 4: Surnames Johallen-McVie. Clifford N. Smith. (British-American Genealogical Research Monographs: No. 12, Pt. 4). i, 50p. (Orig.). 1995. pap. 20.00 (*0-915162-44-X*) Westland Pubns.

Whereas... a Judge's Premises: Essays in Judgement, Ethics, & the Law. Charles E. Wyzanski. LC 76-43310. xvi, 312p. 1977. reprint ed. text ed. 59.75 (*0-8371-9298-6*, WYWH, Greenwood Pr) Greenwood.

Whereby We Thrive: A History of American Farming, 1607 to 1972. John T. Schlebecker. LC 74-19455. 352p. reprint ed. pap. 100.40 (*0-685-15322-3*, 2026658) Bks Demand.

Wherein! see Me Han Defraudado!

Whereon to Stand: The Acts of the Apostles & Ourselves. Daniel Berrigan. 300p. (Orig.). (C). 1991. pap. 17.95 (*1-879175-08-8*) Fortkamp.

***Where're the Bears?** Martin Kratt. (Kratts' Creatures Ser.). (J). 1997. pap. text ed. 3.50 (*0-590-06740-0*) Scholastic Inc.

Where's Al? Byron Barton. LC 78-171866. (Illus.). 32p. (J). (ps). 1989. pap. 6.95 (*0-395-51582-3*, Clarion Bks) HM.

***Where's Arthur's Gerbil?** Marc Brown. (Chunky Flap Bks.). (J). 1998. pap. 3.99 (*0-679-88460-2*) Random Bks Yng Read.

Where's Baby? Wendy C. Lewison. (J). 1992. 4.95 (*0-685-53516-9*) Scholastic Inc.

Where's Bill? Missing in Action. Danial Reagan. 24p. 1994. pap. 10.95 (*1-886504-00-8*) Funny Bone FL.

Where's Billy. Nancy Yeager & Doug Yeager. 32p. (J). (ps). 1991. pap. 4.95 (*1-879911-00-0*) Rams Horn Bks.

Where's Brooke? Ellen Javernick. LC 92-11097. (Rookie Readers Ser.). (Illus.). 32p. (J). (ps-2). 1993. pap. 3.50 (*0-516-42012-7*) Childrens.

Where's Bunny's Mommy? Charlotte Doyle. (Illus.). (J). (ps). 1995. 14.00 (*0-671-89984-8*, Litl Simon S&S) S&S Childrens.

Where's Caesar: The Story of Caesar, King Edward VII's Terrier. (Dog Ser.). 1992. lib. bdg. 75.00 (*0-8490-5233-5*) Gordon Pr.

Where's Caterpillar? A Hide-&-Seek Peephole Book. Sarah Godwin & Louise Batchelor. LC 94-41055. (Illus.). 32p. 1995. 11.95 (*0-8120-6510-7*) Barron.

Where's Charley? (Vocal Score Ser.). 144p. 1982. pap. 40.00 (*0-88188-213-5*, 00448785) H Leonard.

Where's Charley? Vocal Selections. Frank Loesser. 32p. 1983. pap. 7.95 (*0-7935-4290-1*, 00447285) H Leonard.

Where's Chimpy? Berniece Rabe. Ed. by Kathleen Tucker. LC 87-37259. (Illus.). 32p. (J). (ps-2). 1988. pap. 5.95 (*0-8075-8927-6*); lib. bdg. 14.95 (*0-8075-8928-4*) A Whitman.

Where's Columbus? Smithmark Staff. (J). 1992. 4.98 (*0-8317-9284-1*) Smithmark.

Where's Columbus? Tony Tallarico. (Where Are They? Ser.). (Illus.). 24p. (J). 1992. 9.95 (*1-56156-098-7*); pap. 2.95 (*1-56156-097-9*) Kidsbks.

Where's Cupid? Tony Tallarico. (Where Are They? Ser.). (Illus.). 32p. (J). 1991. 10.95 (*1-56156-048-0*); pap. 3.95 (*1-56156-043-X*) Kidsbks.

Where's Curley Q. Ida Agee. (Illus.). 32p. (Orig.). (J). (gr. k-4). 1995. pap. 3.50 (*0-9648344-0-5*) LCQ.

Where's Dad Now That I Need Him? Surviving Away from Home. B. R. Frandsen. 350p. pap. 7.77 (*0-9615390-3-8*) Aspen West Pub.

Where's Dad Now That I Need Him? Surviving Away from Home. Betty R. Frandsen. (Illus.). 1988. vinyl bd. 21.95 (*0-9615390-2-X*) Aspen West Pub.

Where's Daddy? William Inge. 1966. pap. 5.25 (*0-8222-1242-0*) Dramatists Play.

Where's Daddy? Claudette Wassil-Grimm. 304p. 1995. pap. 11.95 (*0-87951-627-5*) Overlook Pr.

Where's Daddy? How Divorced, Single, & Widowed Mothers Can Provide What's Missing When Dad's Missing. Ed. by Claudette Wassil-Grimm. 280p. 1994. 21.95 (*0-87951-541-4*) Overlook Pr.

Where's Daddy When It Hurts? Leland O. Clarke. 254p. 1993. pap. 12.95 (*0-9638413-9-4*) Educ & Psychol.

Where's Elmo? 1992. pap. write for info. (*0-679-83067-7*) McKay.

Where's Elvis? 1992. pap. 8.95 (*1-56288-260-0*) Checkerboard.

***Where's Elvis? Documented Sightings Through the Ages.** Hans Teensma & Daniel Klein. 1997. pap. 14.95 (*0-670-87635-6*) Viking Penguin.

***Where's Flit? Level 1.** Bettina Ling. LC 96-85712. (Disney's First Readers Ser.). (J). 1997. pap. text ed. 2.95 (*0-7868-4075-7*) Disney Pr.

Where's God? Karen King. (Illus.). (J). 1995. 1.80 (*1-56476-467-2*, 6-3467, Victor Bks) Chariot Victor.

***Where's Grandpa.** Tom Barron. Date not set. 15.95 (*0-399-23037-8*) Putnam Pub Group.

***Where's Home?** Jonathan London. 1997. pap. 3.99 (*0-14-037513-9*) Penguin.

Where's Home? Jonathan London. LC 94-39237. (J). 1995. pap. 13.99 (*0-670-86028-X*, Viking) Viking Penguin.

Where's Jenna? Margaret Miller. LC 93-13981. (J). 1994. pap. 15.00 (*0-671-79167-2*, S&S Bks Young Read) S&S Childrens.

Where's Jess? Sibling Loss/S.I.D.S. (Sudden Infant Death Syndrome) Ray Goldstein & Jody Goldstein. (Illus.). 24p. (Orig.). (J). (ps-1). 1982. pap. 3.75 (*1-56123-009-X*) Centering Corp.

***Where's Jonah?** Linda Parry. (Illus.). 1997. 4.99 (*0-614-27568-7*) Broadman.

Where's Kimo? Jeff Langcaon. (Illus.). 24p. (J). (gr. k-2). 1993. pap. 4.95 (*1-880188-65-1*) Bess Pr.

Where's Kitty. Cherie Rayburn. Ed. by Jonna Gress. (Illus.). 12p. (J). (ps-5). 1994. pap. 8.25 (*0-944943-45-4*, 23304-5) Current Inc.

Where's Little Mole? 2nd ed. Inez Greene. (Let Me Read Ser.). (Illus.). (J). (ps). 1995. bds. 2.95 (*0-673-36266-3*, GoodYrBooks) Addison-Wesley Educ.

Where's Lulu? Byron Preiss. 32p. (J). (ps-3). 1991. pap. 3.99 (*0-553-35211-3*) Bantam.

***Where's Mittens?** JoAnne Nelson. LC 91-9373. (Primarily Health Ser.). (Illus.). 24p. (J). (ps-2). 1995. pap. 6.00 (*0-7802-3239-9*) Wright Group.

Where's Molly? Uli Waas. Tr. by Rosemary Lanning from GER. LC 93-19736. (Illus.). 48p. (J). (gr. 1-3). 1993. lib. bdg. 12.88 (*1-55858-230-4*) North-South Bks NYC.

Where's Molly? Uli Waas. LC 93-19736. (Illus.). 48p. (J). (gr. 2-3). 1994. pap. 4.95 (*1-55858-354-8*) North-South Bks NYC.

Where's Molly? A Book about Taking Care of Your Things. Ellen Weiss. Ed. by Sara Mark. LC 95-49362. (Big Comfy Couch Ser.). (Illus.). 32p. (J). (ps-1). 1996. 4.95 (*0-7835-4507-X*) Time-Life.

Where's Mom? Libby Gleeson. (J). 1996. pap. 4.99 (*0-590-46961-4*) Scholastic Inc.

Where's Mom Now That I Need Her? Surviving Away from Home. Betty R. Frandsen et al. (Illus.). 1983. vinyl bd. 21.95 (*0-9615390-0-3*, TX 1-504-973) Aspen West Pub.

***Where's Mommy?** Cathryn Falwell. (J). Date not set. write for info. (*0-688-09277-2*); lib. bdg. write for info. (*0-688-09278-0*) Lothrop.

***Where's Mommy?** Steve Metzger. LC 97-9118. (Dinofours Ser.). (Illus.). (J). 1997. write for info. (*0-590-37456-7*) Scholastic Inc.

Where's Mommy Now? Rochelle M. Krich. 1990. mass mkt. 4.50 (*1-55817-366-8*, Pinncle Kensgtn) Kensgtn Pub Corp.

Where's Moo Cow? Tig's Tale. Paul B. Ricchiuti. LC 94-23758. (J). (ps-2). 1994. pap. 6.99 (*0-8280-0890-6*) Review & Herald.

Where's Murray Ross? Mick Zatarain. 272p. 1994. 21.95 (*0-9643558-0-9*, TXU 510 718) Alarion Press.

Where's My AFV (Alternative Fuel Vehicle)? Steve McCrea. (Illus.). 1995. pap. text ed. write for info. (*1-57074-251-0*) Greyden Pr.

***Where's My Baby?** Ashworth & Clark. (Footsteps Big Bk.). (J). 1991. pap. text ed. write for info. (*0-17-556759-X*) Addison-Wesley.

Where's My Baby? Elizabeth Ergas. 384p. 1994. mass mkt. 4.50 (*0-8217-4721-5*, Zebra Kensgtn) Kensgtn Pub Corp.

Where's My Baby? H. A. Rey. (Illus.). 24p. (J). (ps-3). 1943. pap. 2.95 (*0-395-07069-4*, Sandpiper) HM.

Where's My Christmas Stocking. Noelle Carter. (Lift and Touch Bks.). (Illus.). 14p. (J). (ps-k). 1995. 6.95 (*0-590-56870-1*, Cartwheel) Scholastic Inc.

Where's My Easter Egg? Harriet Ziefert. LC 84-62004. (Illus.). (J). (gr. 2-6). 1985. pap. 5.99 (*0-14-050537-7*, Puffin) Puffin Bks.

Where's My Frog. Mercer Mayer. 1995. 3.99 (*0-679-87344-9*) Random.

Where's My Kitten? Michele Coxon. 16p. (J). 1996. pap. 5.99 (*0-14-055907-8*) Puffin Bks.

Where's My Kitty. Mercer Mayer. 1995. 3.99 (*0-679-87343-0*) Random.

Where's My Mom? Leon Rosselson. LC 93-32383. (Illus.). 32p. (J). 1996. pap. 5.99 (*1-56402-835-6*) Candlewick Pr.

Where's My Other Sock? How to Get Organized & Drive Your Parents & Teachers Crazy. Claudine G. Wirths & Mary Bowman-Kruhm. LC 88-39338. (Illus.). 128p. (J). (gr. 5 up). 1989. lib. bdg. 14.89 (*0-690-04667-7*, Crowell Jr Bks) HarpC Child Bks.

Where's My Sneaker? Mercer Mayer. 22p. (J). 1996. 3.99 (*0-679-87370-8*) Random Bks Yng Read.

Where's My Stocking? Jane Walker. (Little Christmas Window Book Ser.). (Illus.). 14p. (J). (gr. k-3). 1996. bds. 3.99 (*1-57584-046-4*) Rdrs Dgst Yng Fam.

Where's My Teddy? Jez Alborough. LC 91-58765. (Illus.). 32p. (J). (ps up). 1992. 15.95 (*1-56402-048-7*) Candlewick Pr.

Where's My Teddy? Jez Alborough. LC 91-58765. (Illus.). 32p. (J). (ps up). 1993. 4.95 (*1-56402-255-2*) Candlewick Pr.

Where's My Teddy? Jez Alborough. LC 91-58765. (Illus.). 32p. (J). (ps up). 1994. pap. 4.99 (*1-56402-280-3*) Candlewick Pr.

***Where's My Teddy?** Jez Alborough. (Little Book Cards Ser.). (Illus.). (J). 1997. pap. 3.29 (*0-7636-0220-5*) Candlewick Pr.

***Where's My Teddy?** Illus. by Stephanie Longfoot. (Interactive Push-Pull Ser.). 14p. (J). (ps up). 1997. bds. 4.98 (*1-85854-701-6*) Brimax Bks.

Where's My Teddy? Big Book. Jez Alborough. LC 91-58765. (J). 1995. pap. 19.99 (*1-56402-468-7*) Candlewick Pr.

Where's My Web. Terry Page. (Illus.). 24p. (J). (gr. 2-6). 1996. pap. text ed. 4.00 (*1-887864-60-1*); lib. bdg. 7.00 (*1-887864-20-2*) Boo Bks.

Where's My Web Coloring Book. Terry Page. (Illus.). 32p. (J). (ps-5). 1996. pap. 3.00 (*1-887864-21-0*) Boo Bks.

Where's My Wife. Jennifer Blowdryer. 24p. (Orig.). 1989. pap. 3.00 (*0-929730-15-1*) Zeitgeist Pr.

Where's Nicky? Cathryn Falwell. Ed. by Cathryn Briley. (Illus.). 24p. (J). (ps). 1991. 5.95 (*0-395-56936-2*, Clarion Bks) HM.

***Where's Nicky?** Cathryn Falwell. (J). Date not set. write for info. (*0-688-09275-6*); lib. bdg. write for info. (*0-688-09276-4*) Lothrop.

***Where's Noah?** Linda Parry. (Illus.). 1997. 4.99 (*0-614-27569-5*) Broadman.

Where's Our Dinner? Gillian Liu. (Early Words Ser.). (Illus.). 24p. (J). (gr. 1-3). 1996. 9.95 (*0-237-51427-3*, Pub. by Evans Bros Ltd UK) Trafalgar.

Where's Our Mama? Diane Goode. LC 91-2158. (Illus.). 32p. (J). (ps-2). 1991. pap. 13.95 (*0-525-44770-9*) Dutton Child Bks.

Where's Our Mama? Diane Goode. (Illus.). 32p. (J). (ps-2). 1995. pap. 4.99 (*0-14-055555-2*) Puffin Bks.

Where's Our Teacher? Fourth Graders at Rio Bravo-Greeley Elem. Staff. (Kids Are Authors Picture Book Ser.). (Illus.). 24p. 1995. 5.99 (*0-87406-742-1*) Willowisp Pr.

Where's Ours? Natalie McKelvy. 200p. 1987. pap. 9.00 (*0-89733-277-6*) Academy Chi Pubs.

Where's Percy: Where's Percy? Mouse Works Staff. (J). 1995. 7.98 (*1-57082-270-0*) Mouse Works.

Where's Peter Rabbit? Beatrix Potter. (Illus.). (J). (ps-3). 1988. pap. 6.95 (*0-7232-3519-8*) Warne.

Where's Piglet? Mouse Works Staff. (J). 1995. 6.98 (*1-57082-262-X*) Mouse Works.

***Where's Prancer?** rev. ed. Syd Hoff. LC 96-45028. (Illus.). 32p. (J). (ps-2). 1997. 13.95 (*0-06-027600-2*); lib. bdg. 13.89 (*0-06-027601-0*) HarpC.

Where's Rufus. (Parents Magazine Press Read-Aloud Library). (J). 1994. lib. bdg. 17.27 (*0-8368-0990-4*) Gareth Stevens Inc.

Where's Rufus? Stephanie Calmenson. LC 88-4092. (Illus.). 48p. (J). (ps-3). 1988. 5.95 (*0-8193-1177-4*) Parents.

Where's Spot? Eric Hill. (Lift-the-Flap Ser.). (Illus.). 24p. (ARA & ENG.). (J). (ps-2). 1988. 11.95 (*0-940793-04-0*, Crocodile Bks) Interlink Pub.

Where's Spot? Eric Hill. (Illus.). 16p. (J). (ps-1). 1994. pap. 5.99 (*0-14-050740-X*) Puffin Bks.

Where's Spot? Eric Hill. (Lift-the-Flap Bks.). (Illus.). 22p. (J). (ps-1). 1980. 12.95 (*0-399-20758-9*, Putnam) Putnam Pub Group.

Where's Spot? A Lift-the-Flap Book Miniature Edition. Eric Hill. (Illus.). 22p. (J). (ps-k). 1990. 5.95 (*0-399-21822-X*, Putnam) Putnam Pub Group.

Where's That Cat? Barbara Brenner & Bernice Chardiet. LC 93-40722. (Hide & Seek Science Ser.). (Illus.). 32p. (J). (gr. k-3). 1995. 10.95 (*0-590-45216-9*, Cartwheel) Scholastic Inc.

Where's That Cat? Barbara Brenner & Bernice Chardiet. (Hide & Seek Science Ser.). (J). 1996. pap. text ed. 4.95 (*0-590-45217-7*) Scholastic Inc.

***Where's That Cat?** Barbara Brenner et al. (Illus.). (FRE.). (J). pap. 6.99 (*0-590-24534-1*) Scholastic Inc.

Where's That Fish? Barbara Brenner & Bernice Chardiet. LC 93-2929. (Illus.). 32p. (J). (ps-3). 1994. 10.95 (*0-590-45214-2*, Cartwheel) Scholastic Inc.

Where's That Fish: A Hide & Seek Science Book. Barbara Brenner. (J). 1995. pap. 4.95 (*0-590-45215-0*) Scholastic Inc.

Where's That Insect: A Hide & Seek Science Book. Barbara Brenner. 32p. (J). 1995. pap. 4.95 (*0-590-45211-8*) Scholastic Inc.

Where's That Reptile. 32p. (J). 1995. pap. 4.95 (*0-590-45213-4*) Scholastic Inc.

Where's That Tune? An Index to Songs in Fakebooks. William D. Goodfellow. LC 90-20847. 457p. 1990. 47.50 (*0-8108-2391-8*) Scarecrow.

Where's That Turkey Lurking? Book & Cookie Cutter Pack. Stephanie St. Pierre. 16p. (Orig.). (J). (gr. k-3). 1990. pap. 3.95 (*0-590-68984-3*) Scholastic Inc.

Where's the Baby? Ed. by Cheryl Christian. (Illus.). 12p. (J). (ps). 1992. 4.95 (*1-56288-128-0*) Checkerboard.

Where's The Baby? Pat Hutchins. LC 86-33566. (Illus.). 32p. (J). (ps-3). 1988. 12.95 (*0-688-05933-5*); lib. bdg. 12.88 (*0-688-05934-1*) Greenwillow.

Where's the Baby? Tom Paxton. LC 92-39875. (Illus.). 32p. (J). (ps up). 1993. 16.00 (*0-688-10692-7*, Morrow Junior) Morrow.

Where's the Ball? Catarina Kruuval. 28p. (J). 6.95 (*91-29-63076-2*) FS&G.

Where's the Bear? Charlotte Pomerantz. LC 83-1697. (Illus.). 32p. (J). (ps-1). 1984. 16.00 (*0-688-01752-5*); lib. bdg. 15.93 (*0-688-01753-3*) Greenwillow.

Where's the Bear. Charlotte Pomerantz. LC 83-1697. (Illus.). 32p. (J). (ps up). 1991. reprint ed. pap. 3.95 (*0-688-10999-3*, Mulberry) Morrow.

***Where's the Bear? A Look-And-Find Book.** Jan Brueghel & J. Paul Getty Museum Staff. LC 96-39856. (Illus.). 60p. (J). (gr. 1-3). 1997. 16.95 (*0-89236-378-9*, J P Getty Museum) J P Getty Trust.

Where's the Big Dipper. Sidney Rosen. LC 94-39379. (Illus.). 40p. (J). (gr. 2-4). 1995. 14.96 (*0-87614-883-6*, Carolrhoda) Lerner Group.

Where's the Bunny? Tony Tallarico. (Illus.). 32p. (Orig.). (J). 1991. pap. 3.95 (*1-56156-011-1*) Kidsbks.

Where's the Bunny? Tony Tallarico. (Where Are They? Ser.). (Illus.). 28p. (Orig.). (J). 1991. pap. 2.95 (*1-56156-096-0*) Kidsbks.

Where's the Bunny? Tony Tallarico. (Where Are They? Ser.). (Illus.). 24p. (Orig.). (J). 1992. 10.95 (*1-56156-101-0*) Kidsbks.

Where's the Chicken in Kiev? An American's Adventures & Heartwarming Encounters in the Former Soviet Union. Cliff Schimmels. LC 94-1076. 176p. 1994. pap. 8.99 (*0-87788-901-5*) Shaw Pubs.

Where's the Ducky? Stef De Reuver. (J). 1996. pap. 4.99 (*0-614-15833-8*) Random.

Where's the Fire? Allard. Date not set. write for info. (*0-395-33069-6*) HM.

Where's the Fire? American Firefighters in Picture Postcards Circa 1910. Geoffrey N. Stein. LC 90-26048. (Illus.). 112p. (Orig.). 1992. pap. 11.95 (*0-911572-91-0*) Madison Bks UPA.

Where's the Fly? Caron L. Cohen. LC 95-962. (Illus.). 32p. (J). Date not set. lib. bdg. write for info. (*0-688-14045-9*) Greenwillow.

Where's the Fly? Caron L. Cohen. LC 95-962. (Illus.). 32p. (J). (ps up). 1996. 15.00 (*0-688-14044-0*) Greenwillow.

Where's the Green Pea? Michael Greene. LC 91-91536. (Illus.). 32p. (J). (ps-1). 1992. lib. bdg. 19.95 incl. audio (*1-881134-00-8*) Tues Child.

Where's the Halloween Treat? Harriet Ziefert. LC 85-3632. (Illus.). 20p. (J). (ps). 1985. pap. 5.99 (*0-14-050556-3*, Puffin) Puffin Bks.

Where's the Kitten? Ed. by Cheryl Christian. (Photo Flap Bks.). (Illus.). 12p. (J). (ps). 1992. 4.95 (*1-56288-130-2*) Checkerboard.

Where's the Manual. Richard Mcgrath. 1991. pap. 39.95 (*0-442-00425-7*) Van Nos Reinhold.

Where's the Me in Museum? Going to Museums with Children. Mildred Waterfall & Sarah Grusin. LC 88-17190. (Illus.). 128p. 1988. pap. 7.95 (*0-918339-08-1*) Vandamere.

Where's the Mouse? Cindy Chang. 1996. 3.99 (*0-679-87819-X*) Random.

Where's the Picnic? Disney Studios Staff. (Mickey Mouse Ser.). (Illus.). 14p. (J). (ps-3). 1994. 5.98 (*1-57082-096-1*) Mouse Works.

Where's the Puppy? Ed. by Cheryl Christian. (Photo Flap Bks.). (Illus.). 12p. (J). (ps). 1992. 4.95 (*1-56288-129-9*) Checkerboard.

Where's the Puppy? Deborah Shine. (Whole-Language Big Bks.). 16p. (J). (ps-2). 1992. pap. 14.95 (*1-56784-052-3*) Newbridge Comms.

Where's the Shortage? A Nontechnical Guide to Petroleum Economics. Bob Tippee. LC 93-5826. 200p. 1993. 69.95 (*0-87814-403-X*) PennWell Bks.

Where's Tom Kitten? Beatrix Potter. (Lift-the-Flap Bks). 24p. (J). (ps-3). 1990. pap. 6.95 (*0-7232-3597-X*) Warne.

***Where's Waldo?** 2nd ed. Martin Handford. LC 97-14990. (Illus.). (J). 1997. 9.99 (*0-7636-0310-4*) Candlewick Pr.

Where's Waldo? The Completely Crazy Activity Book. Martin Hanford. (Illus.). 24p. (Orig.). (J). (gr. 1-6). 1996. pap. 4.99 (*1-56402-973-5*) Candlewick Pr.

Where's Waldo? The Really Remarkable Activity Book. Martin Hanford. (Illus.). 24p. (Orig.). (J). (gr. 1-6). 1996. pap. 4.99 (*1-56402-972-7*) Candlewick Pr.

Where's Waldo? Waldo in Dinoland. Where's Waldo, Inc. Staff. (Comes to Life Bks.). 16p. (J). (ps-2). 1993. write for info. (*1-883366-13-5*) YES Ent.

Where's Waldo? in Hollywood. Martin Handford. LC 91-71819. (Illus.). 32p. (J). (ps up). 1994. 14.95 (*1-56402-044-4*); lib. bdg. 14.88 (*1-56402-294-3*) Candlewick Pr.

Where's Waldo? in Hollywood. Martin Handford. (Illus.). (J). 1995. pap. 7.99 (*1-56402-659-0*) Candlewick Pr.

***Where's Waldo Now?** Martin Handford. LC 97-13734. (Illus.). (J). 1997. 9.99 (*0-7636-0308-2*) Candlewick Pr.

***Where's Waldo Pillow Book.** (J). 1990. 19.95 (*1-55923-128-9*) Wicklow Ltd.

Where's Waldo-Spaer Adventure: The Great Space Adventure. Martin Handford. (Illus.). 24p. (J). (gr. k up). text ed. 19.95 (*0-9627001-4-2*) Futech Educ Prods.

Where's Waldo? The Dazzling Deep-Sea Divers Sticker Book! Martin Handford. (J). 1994. pap. 7.99 (*1-56402-553-5*) Candlewick Pr.

Where's Waldo? The Fabulous Flying Carpets Sticker Book! Martin Handford. (J). 1994. pap. 7.99 (*1-56402-552-7*) Candlewick Pr.

Where's Waldo? The Simply Sensational Activity Book. Martin Handford. (Illus.). 24p. (Orig.). (J). (gr. 1 up). 1995. pap. 4.99 (*1-56402-576-4*) Candlewick Pr.

Where's Waldo? The Wildly Wonderful Activity Book. Martin Handford. (Illus.). 24p. (Orig.). (J). (gr. 1 up). 1995. pap. 4.99 (*1-56402-575-6*) Candlewick Pr.

***Where's Waldo? The Wonder Book.** Martin Handford. (Illus.). (J). 1997. write for info. (*0-614-29199-2*) Candlewick Pr.

Where's Wendy? Tony Tallarico. (Where Are They? Ser.). (Illus.). 24p. (Orig.). (J). 1991. pap. 2.95 (*1-56156-040-5*) Kidsbks.

Where's Wendy? Tony Tallarico. (Where Are They? Ser.). (Illus.). 24p. (Orig.). (J). 1992. 9.95 (*1-56156-069-3*) Kidsbks.

Where's Willy? Martha Alexander. LC 92-53006. (Illus.). 14p. (J). (ps). 1993. 4.95 (*1-56402-161-0*) Candlewick Pr.

Where's Your Tooth? Rozanne L. Williams. (Emergent Reader Bks.). 8p. 1994. 1.59 (*0-916119-49-1*) Creat Teach Pr.

Where's Your Tooth? Rozanne L. Williams. (Emergent Reader Big Bks). (Illus.). 8p. (Orig.). (J). (gr. k-2). 1995. pap. 7.98 (*1-57471-061-3*) Creat Teach Pr.

Wherever Home Begins: 100 Contemporary Poems. Selected by Paul B. Janeczko. LC 94-48740. 128p. (YA). (gr. 6 up). 1996. 15.95 (*0-531-09481-2*); lib. bdg. 16.99 (*0-531-08781-6*) Orchard Bks Watts.

Wherever I Looked. Gary Young. (Illus.). 23p. 1993. boxed 200.00 (*0-924433-03-5*) R Price.

Wherever Men Trade: The Romance of the Cash Register. Isaac F. Marcosson. LC 72-5062. (Technology & Society Ser.). (Illus.). 310p. 1972. reprint ed. 21.95 (*0-405-04713-4*) Ayer.

Wherever That Great Heart May Be: Stories. W. D. Wetherell. LC 95-19680. 196p. 1996. 21.95 (*0-87451-721-4*) U Pr of New Eng.

Wherever You Go, There You Are. John Hampel. 352p. 1991. 19.95 (*0-9627992-0-3*) BZFF Bks.

Wherever You Go, There You Are. Jon Kabat-Zinn. 1994. 16.95 (*1-55927-262-7*) St Martin.

W

An Asterisk (*) at the beginning of an entry indicates that the title is appearing in BIP for the first time.

Wherever You Go, There You Are: Mindfulness Meditation in Everyday Life. Jon Kabat-Zinn. 304p. 1994. 19.95 (*1-56282-769-3*) Hyperion.
Wherever You Go, There You Are: Mindfulness Meditation in Everyday Life. Jon Kabat-Zinn. 304p. 1995. pap. 13. 95 (*0-7868-8070-8*) Hyperion.
Wherries & Waterways. Robert Malster. 176p. 1994. 36.00 (*0-86138-042-8*, Pub. by T Dalton UK) St Mut.
Whet. Michael Chitwood. 64p. (Orig.). 1995. pap. 13.00 (*0-942148-16-9*) Ohio Review.
Whether or Not. Marie L. Kaschnitz. Tr. by Lisel Mueller. (Juniper Bk. Ser.: No. 46). 1984. pap. 5.00 (*1-55780-045-6*) Juniper Pr WI.
Whether White or Black, a Man. Edith S. Davis. LC 77-37590. (Black Heritage Library Collection). (Illus.). 1977. reprint ed. 19.95 (*0-8369-8966-X*) Ayer.
Whetstone. Joanne Allred. 24p. 1996. pap. 7.00 (*1-886226-01-6*) Flume Pr.
Whetstones: Mostly Frontier Grit & Spun-funnery. Robert E. Enlow. LC 95-71671. 256p. 1996. pap. 9.95 (*1-887750-11-8*) Rutledge Bks.
***Whetton Developing Management Skills for Europe.** D. Whetton. (C). 1994. pap. text ed. write for info. (*0-201-17559-2*) Addison-Wesley.
Which Ad Pulled Best? 8th ed. Philip W. Burton & Scott C. Purvis. LC 95-39651. (Illus.). 256p. 1995. 19.95 (*0-8442-3315-3*, NTC Busn Bks) NTC Pub Grp.
***Which AD Pulled Best? Answer Key.** 8th ed. Philip W. Burton & Scott C. Purvis. pap. 3.95 (*0-8442-3316-1*) NTC Pub Grp.
Which Apostle Are You Most Like? Terry Deffenbaugh. 1988. pap. 6.50 (*0-940754-53-3*, 8411) Ed Ministries.
Which Babies Shall Live? Humanistic Dimensions of the Care of Imperiled Newborns. Ed. by Thomas H. Murray & Arthur L. Caplan. LC 85-18058. (Contemporary Issues in Biomedicine, Ethics, & Society Ser.). 240p. 1985. 39.95 (*0-89603-086-5*) Humana.
Which, Being Interpreted, Means... Jack Taylor. (Illus.). 180p. (Orig.). 1996. pap. 7.95 (*0-940232-54-5*) Seedsowers.
Which Bible? rev. ed. Ed. by David O. Fuller. 350p. reprint ed. pap. 11.95 (*0-944355-24-2*) IBTS.
Which Bible? Elton A. Jones. 50p. 1960. reprint ed. spiral bd. 9.00 (*0-7873-0482-4*) Hlth Research.
Which Bible Is God's Word? Gail A. Riplinger. 150p. (Orig.). 1994. pap. 8.95 (*1-879366-81-9*) Hearthstone OK.
Which Business? Help in Selecting Your New Venture. Nancy Drescher. LC 96-47509. (Successful Business Library). 376p. (Orig.). 1996. pap. 18.95 (*1-55571-390-4*) Oasis Pr OR.
Which Business? Tested Ideas for Profitable Business. Stephen Halliday. 160p. 1990. 44.95 (*0-8464-1383-3*) Beekman Pubs.
Which Business Structure Is Best for You? Brian T. Regan. 40p. (Orig.). (C). 1995. pap. text ed. 15.00 (*1-878630-69-5*) CA Chamber Commerce.
Which Church. Carl W. Ketcherside. pap. 0.99 (*0-87377-063-3*) GAM Pubns.
Which Comes First? Honey Andersen. LC 93-18113. (J). 1994. write for info. (*0-383-03726-3*) SRA McGraw.
Which Dog for Me? James Johnson & Andrew DePrisco. (KW Ser.). (Illus.). 96p. 1992. text ed. 9.95 (*0-86622-442-4*, KW227) TFH Pubns.
***Which Executive Programme.** 2nd ed. 1997. 245.00 (*0-614-25443-4*, M517) Econ Intel.
Which Father Are You Following? Robert Palmer. 64p. 1987. pap. text ed. 1.95 (*0-937580-11-2*) LeSEA Pub Co.
***Which form of Building Contract?** David Chappell. (C). 1991. pap. text ed. write for info. (*1-85454-950-2*) Addison-Wesley.
Which Hand Holds the Brother. Simon Perchik. 1969. 4.00 (*0-685-01009-0*) Elizabeth Pr.
Which Is Witch. (Spider Tales Ser.). (J). (gr. 3-7). 1995. 14. 00 (*0-922242-91-7*) Bepuzzled.
Which Map Is Best? Projections for World Maps. American Cartographic Association Staff. 14p. 1988. pap. 12.00 (*0-614-06091-5*, C167) Am Congrs Survey.
Which Map Is Best? Projections for World Maps. Committe of Maps Projections of the American Cartographic Association Staff. 1986. 6.40 (*0-913459-1-8*, C167) Am Congrs Survey.
Which MBA? 6th ed. George Bickerstaffe. (C). 1994. pap. text ed. 17.25 (*0-201-42784-2*) Addison-Wesley.
Which MBA? 7th ed. George Bickerstaffe. 1995. pap. 16.95 (*0-201-87755-4*) Addison-Wesley.
***Which MBA.** 8th ed. 1996. 39.95 (*0-201-41997-1*, M515) Economist Intell.
***Which MBA.** 9th ed. 1997. write for info. (*0-614-25446-9*) Econ Intel.
***Which MBA?** 9th ed. George Bickerstaffe. 1997. pap. write for info. (*0-201-33129-2*) Addison-Wesley.
Which MBA? A Critical Guide to the World's Best Programs. 5th ed. George Bickerstaffe. (C). 1994. pap. text ed. 17.25 (*0-201-59378-5*) Addison-Wesley.
***Which Mrs. Turner?** Betty W. Davis. 416p. (Orig.). 1997. mass mkt. 5.99 (*1-55197-741-9*, Pub. by Comnwlth Pub CN) Partners Pubs Grp.
Which One. Priscilla L. McQueen. (Illus.). (J). (gr. k). 1968. pap. 6.15 (*0-685-16727-5*) McQueen.
Which One? & Other Ante Bellum Days. Mary M. Pleasants. LC 72-4620. (Black Heritage Library Collection). 1977. reprint ed. 19.95 (*0-8369-9121-4*) Ayer.
Which One Is Whitney? James Stevenson. LC 89-34614. (Illus.). 40p. (J). (gr. k up). 1990. lib. bdg. 12.88 (*0-688-09062-1*) Greenwillow.
Which One of You Is Interracial? & Other Stories. Ira Lunan-Ferguson. LC 78-79431. 1969. 6.95 (*0-685-03133-0*) Lunan-Ferguson.
Which One Would You Choose? Edith Kunhardt. LC 91-32500. Date not set. write for info. (*0-688-11218-8*) Morrow.
Which Paper? Silvie Turner. 144p. 1992. pap. 24.95 (*0-8306-3967-5*) McGraw-Hill Prof.
Which Phone System Should I Buy? 9th ed. Teleconnect Staff & Harry Newton. 41.95 (*0-936648-59-7*) Flatiron Pubng.
Which Process? A Guide to the Selection of Welding & Related Processes. P. T. Houldcroft. (Illus.). 97p. 1990. 95.00 (*1-85573-008-1*, Pub. by Woodhead Pubng UK) Am Educ Systs.
***Which Psychotherapy? Lending Exponents Explain Their Differences.** Ed. by Colin Feltham. 240p. 1997. text ed. 69.95 (*0-8039-7478-7*) Sage.
***Which Psychotherapy? Lending Exponents Explain Their Differences.** Ed. by Colin Feltham. 240p. 1997. pap. text ed. 23.95 (*0-8039-7479-5*) Sage.
Which Reminds Me: A Memoir. Mitchell Sharp. LC 93-94384. (Illus.). 300p. (C). 1994. 35.00 (*0-8020-0545-4*) U of Toronto Pr.
Which Rite Is Right? The Eucharistic Prayer in the Anglican Tradition. Peter Toon. LC 94-69807. 160p. (Orig.). 1995. pap. 8.95 (*1-886412-03-0*) Preserv Press.
Which Road to the Past? Two Views of History. Robert W. Fogel & G. R. Elton. LC 83-3573. 160p. 1983. 27.00 (*0-300-03011-8*) Yale U Pr.
Which Road to the Past? Two Views of History. Robert W. Fogel & G. R. Elton. LC 83-3573. 160p. 1984. reprint ed. pap. 13.00 (*0-300-03278-1*, Y-512) Yale U Pr.
Which Shakespeare? A User's Guide to Editions. Ann Thompson et al. 224p. 1991. 120.00 (*0-335-09035-4*, Open Univ Pr) Taylor & Francis.
Which Side Are You On? The Harlan County Coal Miners, 1931-39. John W. Hevener. LC 78-16417. 240p. reprint ed. pap. 68.40 (*0-8357-3295-9*, 2039518) Bks Demand.
Which Side Are You On: Trying to Be for Labor When It's Flat on Its Back. Thomas Geoghegan. 1991. 19.95 (*0-374-28919-0*) FS&G.
Which Side Are You On? Trying to Be for Labor When It's Flat on Its Back. Thomas Geoghegan. 320p. 1992. pap. 12.95 (*0-452-26891-5*, Plume) NAL-Dutton.
Which Side Were You On? The American Communist Party During the Second World War. Maurice Isserman. LC 92-37087. 328p. (C). 1993. reprint ed. pap. text ed. 15. 95 (*0-252-06336-8*) U of Ill Pr.
***Which Stitch?** Sallie J. Russell. (Illus.). 28p. 1997. pap. 6.00 (*1-883777-01-1*) SJR Sew.
Which Tests for My Unborn Baby? A Guide to Prenatal Diagnosis. Lachlan De Crespigny & Rhonda Dredge. (Illus.). 200p. 1997. pap. 19.95 (*0-19-553954-0*) OUP.
Which Things Belong to Caesar? Bradford W. Chaney. 87p. (Orig.). 1986. pap. 4.95 (*0-9615151-0-4*) Anatello.
Which Three Till Now. P. M. Beaven. 231p. 1978. 75.00 (*0-906204-04-6*) St Mut.
Which Tools to Use. Barbara L. McCombs & Linda Brannan. (Skills for Job Success Ser.). (Illus.). 32p. (Orig.). 1990. student ed., pap. 4.95 (*1-56119-049-7*) Educ Pr MD.
Which Tools to Use? Barbara L. McCombs & Linda Brannan. (Skills for Job Success Ser.). (Illus.). 32p. (Orig.). (YA). (gr. 7-12). 1990. Set. teacher ed., wbk. ed. 44.95 (*1-56119-083-7*); teacher ed. 1.95 (*1-56119-050-0*); disk 39.95 (*1-56119-125-6*) Educ Pr MD.
Which Translation Do You Prefer. Carol E. Mille. 1975. pap. 1.95 (*0-915374-52-8*, 52-8) Rapids Christian.
Which Way? (J). 1981. pap. 1.75 (*0-671-30750-9*) PB.
Which Way Are You Leading Me, Lord? Bible Devotions for Boys. Nathan Aaseng. LC 84-21562. (Augsburg Young Readers Ser.). 112p. (Orig.). (J). (gr. 3-7). 1996. pap. 5.99 (*0-8066-2113-3*, 10-7099, Augsburg) Augsburg Fortress.
Which Way Ben Bunny? A Lift-the-Flap Book about Left & Right. Mavis Smith. (Lift-the-Flap Concept Bks.). (Illus.). 24p. (J). (ps-1). 1996. 7.95 (*0-590-62245-5*, Cartwheel) Scholastic Inc.
Which Way, Democracy? Wilfrid Parsons. LC 72-5747. (Essay Index Reprint Ser.). 1977. reprint ed. 21.95 (*0-8369-7296-1*) Ayer.
Which Way Did He Go? The Private Eye in Dashiell Hammett, Raymond Chandler, Chester Himes, & Ross MacDonald. Edward Margolies. LC 81-1061. 130p. 1982. 25.00 (*0-8419-0436-7*); pap. 15.00 (*0-8419-0790-0*) Holmes & Meier.
***Which Way Did the Bicycle Go? And Other Intriguing Mathematical Mysteries.** Joseph D. Konhauser et al. LC 95-81495. (Dolciani Mathematical Expositions Ser.). (Illus.). 256p. (Orig.). 1996. pap. text ed. 27.50 (*0-88385-325-6*) Math Assn.
Which Way for the Ecology Movement. Murray Bookchin. LC 93-40416. 76p. (Orig.). 1994. pap. 6.00 (*1-873176-26-0*, AK Pr San Fran) AK Pr Dist.
Which Way Freedom? Joyce Hansen. 128p. (J). 1992. pap. 4.50 (*0-380-71408-6*, Camelot) Avon.
Which Way, Hugo? Morgan Matthews. LC 85-14132. (Illus.). 48p. (Orig.). (J). (gr. 1-3). 1997. pap. 3.50 (*0-8167-0649-2*) Troll Communs.
Which Way Is Home? Celeste Hamilton. 1994. mass mkt. 3.50 (*0-373-09897-9*, 1-09897-9) Harlequin Bks.
***Which Way Is Ireland?** James Savage. LC 96-90183. 1996. 16.00 (*0-533-11936-7*) Vantage.
Which Way Is Right? Barbara L. McCombs & Linda Brannan. (Skills for Job Success Ser.). (Illus.). 32p. (Orig.). 1990. student ed., pap. 4.95 (*1-56119-051-9*) Educ Pr MD.
Which Way Is Right? Barbara L. McCombs & Linda Brannan. (Skills for Job Success Ser.). (Illus.). 32p. (Orig.). (YA). (gr. 7-12). 1990. Set. teacher ed., wbk. ed. 44.95 (*1-56119-084-5*); teacher ed. 1.95 (*1-56119-052-7*); disk 39.95 (*1-56119-126-4*) Educ Pr MD.
Which Way Is South Africa Going? Gwendolen M. Carter. LC 79-3658. 174p. reprint ed. pap. 49.60 (*0-317-27941-6*, 2056026) Bks Demand.
Which Way Is the Sky Falling? Global Warming: Forecast for the Future. Thomas G. Kyle. LC 93-19628. 197p. 1993. 16.95 (*1-55971-216-3*) NorthWord.
Which Way Is Up? R. W. Connell. 224p. 1984. pap. 12.95 (*0-86861-374-6*) Routledge Chapman & Hall.
Which Way Israel? Hyman Lumer. 1966. pap. 0.20 (*0-87898-010-5*) New Outlook.
Which Way Now? - Small Book. J. Croser & M. Quick. 8p. (J). 1987. 3.95 (*0-88679-539-7*) Educ Insights.
Which Way Now? - Tall Book. J. Croser & M. Quick. 8p. (J). 1987. 19.95 (*0-88679-538-9*) Educ Insights.
Which Way Out? And Other Essays. Arthur M. Young. (Illus.). 206p. 1980. pap. 15.95 (*0-9609850-0-X*) Rob Briggs.
Which Way the Wind Blows, Valley of Many Winds: Part II of Valley of Many Winds, Pt. II. Mario Edlosi. 183p. 1978. 8.00 (*0-682-49073-3*) Tesseract SD.
***Which Way to Grow: Poverty & Development in Southeast Asia.** James B. Goodno. (C). 1997. pap. 19.95 (*1-85649-500-0*, Pub. by Zed Bks Ltd UK); text ed. 59. 95 (*1-85649-499-3*, Pub. by Zed Bks Ltd UK) Humanities.
Which Way to Improvement? A Catalog of Programs for Discipline, Drugs, Achievement & Attendence. Michele A. Woods-Houston. 90p. 1985. pap. 17.95 (*1-56602-009-3*) Research Better.
Which Way to Jesus? Cycle B: Sermons for Lent-Easter: Gospel Texts. Harry N. Huxhold. LC 96-10704. 123p. (Orig.). 1996. pap. 9.95 (*0-7880-0793-9*) CSS OH.
Which Way to Look. Susan Hauser. 120p. (Orig.). 1992. pap. 9.95 (*0-926147-03-X*) Loonfeather.
Which Way to the Dojo? Caryn Andrews. (Illus.). 60p. (Orig.). 1986. pap. text ed. 5.95 (*0-9617494-0-7*) Laughing Stock.
***Which Way to the Dragon? Poems for the Coming on Strong.** Sara Holbrook. LC 96-85176. (Illus.). 48p. (J). (gr. 1-9). 1997. 6.95 (*1-56397-641-2*, Wordsong) Boyds Mills Pr.
Which Way to the Milky Way? Sidney Rosen. (J). (gr. k-3). 1992. lib. bdg. 19.95 (*0-87614-709-0*, Carolrhoda) Lerner Group.
Which Way Yaweh: The Story of Our Son, James Schmidt Thimm, & His Death by the Rulo Cult. Hilda N. Schmidt. 143p. 1993. pap. write for info. (*0-9637362-3-X*) James Pub NE.
***Which Wine? At-a-Glance Listings of the Five Best Wines for Every Menu, Every Occasion, Every Budget.** Robert Finigan. 176p. (Orig.). 1997. pap. 12.99 (*1-56530-278-8*) Summit TX.
Which Witch. (J). pap. write for info. (*0-590-38042-7*) Scholastic Inc.
Which Witch Is Which? (Illus.). 26p. (J). (ps-1). 1988. pap. 2.95 (*0-671-66868-4*, Litl Simon S&S) S&S Childrens.
Which Witch Is Which? Pat Hutchins. LC 88-18781. (Illus.). 24p. (J). (ps up). 1989. 16.00 (*0-688-06357-8*); lib. bdg. 15.93 (*0-688-06358-6*) Greenwillow.
***Which Witch Is Which?** Michaela Muntean. (Little Golden Bks.). (Illus.). 24p. (J). (ps). 1996. write for info. (*0-307-98770-1*, 98770, Golden Books) Western Pub.
***Whichaway.** Glendon Swarthout & Kathryn Swarthout. LC 97-19585. 136p. (J). (gr. 3 up). 1997. pap. 6.95 (*0-87358-676-X*, Rising Moon Bks) Northland AZ.
***Whichaway.** Glendon Swarthout & Kathryn Swarthout. LC 97-19585. 136p. (YA). (gr. 3 up). 1997. 12.95 (*0-87358-675-1*, Rising Moon Bks) Northland AZ.
Whidbey Island Sketchbook. Dixie Rushmer. LC 84-14629. (Illus.). 64p. (Orig.). 1985. spiral bd., pap. 9.95 (*0-88240-266-8*) Alaska Northwest.
Whiff of Danger. Nancy H. Wilson. 96p. (Orig.). (J). (gr. 4-7). 1996. pap. 3.50 (*0-380-78276-6*, Camelot) Avon.
Whiffle. Ed. & Intro. by Don Thornton. (Illus.). 52p. (J). (gr. 4-8). 1986. pap. write for info. (*0-933727-02-X*) Cajun Pubs.
Whiffle Squeek. Caron L. Cohen. (Illus.). 32p. (J). (ps-3). 1994. pap. 4.99 (*0-14-050448-6*) Puffin Bks.
Whiffy's Wish Comes True. Lynne F. Willard. (J). pap. 3.50 (*0-9647497-1-8*) Whiffy.
Whig in Power: The Political Career of Henry Pelham. John W. Wilkes. LC 64-10854. (Studies in History Ser.: No. 3). 312p. reprint ed. 89.00 (*0-8357-9476-8*, 2013682) Bks Demand.
Whig Interpretation of History. Herbert Butterfield. LC 75-41043. (BCL Ser. II). reprint ed. 32.50 (*0-404-14515-9*) AMS Pr.
Whig Loyalism: An Aspect of Political Ideology in the American Revolutionary Era. William A. Benton. LC 69-19433. 231p. 1975. 32.50 (*0-8386-7338-4*) Fairleigh Dickinson.
Whig Party in Pennsylvania. Henry R. Mueller. LC 74-82233. (Columbia University. Studies in the Social Sciences: No. 230). reprint ed. 27.50 (*0-404-51230-5*) AMS Pr.
Whig Party in the South. Arthur C. Cole. 1959. 14.50 (*0-8446-1126-3*) Peter Smith.
Whig Party, 1807-1812. Michael Roberts. 453p. 1965. 45. 00 (*0-7146-1512-9*, Pub. by F Cass Pubs UK) Intl Spec Bk.
Whig Press: Death Notices-1851 to 1865. Ed. by George Gardner & Virginia Gardner. 158p. (Orig.). 1978. 22.00 (*0-9604116-3-1*) Orange County Genealog.
Whig Press: Marriages, 1851-1865, Names & Dates. Orange County Genealogical Society Staff. 1986. 22.00 (*0-9604116-9-0*) Orange County Genealog.
Whig Supremacy, 1714-1760. 2nd ed. Basil Williams. Ed. by C. H. Stuart. (Oxford History of England Ser.: Vol. 11). 1962. 70.00 (*0-19-821710-2*) OUP.
Whiggery & Reform, 1830-41: The Politics of Government. Ian Newbould. LC 89-62180. 410p. 1991. 49.50 (*0-8047-1759-1*) Stanford U Pr.
Whigs & Cities: Popular Politics in the Age of Walpole & Pitt. Nicholas Rogers. 456p. 1990. 95.00 (*0-19-821785-4*) OUP.
Whigs of Florida, 1845-1854. Herbert J. Doherty. LC 59-62570. (University of Florida Monographs: Social Sciences: No. 1). 79p. reprint ed. pap. 25.00 (*0-7837-4936-8*, 2044602) Bks Demand.
While a Tree Was Growing. Jane Bosveld. LC 96-46862. (Illus.). 64p. (J). (gr. 1 up). 1997. bds. 13.95 (*0-7611-0540-9*, 10540) Workman Pub.
While Ago in Brewster. Bernice H. Hunt. (Illus.). 96p. (Orig.). 1994. pap. 11.95 (*1-883613-03-5*) Byte Size.
While Angels Dance: The Life & Times of Jeston Nash. Ralph W. Cotton. 1995. mass mkt. 5.50 (*0-312-95461-1*) St Martin.
While Angels Sleep. Judith Kelman. 352p. 1988. reprint ed. mass mkt. 5.99 (*0-425-11093-1*) Berkley Pub.
While Back: Essays in Celebration of the Past. Mary L. Turner. LC 88-51454. (Illus.). 328p. (Orig.). 1988. pap. 13.95 (*0-934955-13-1*) Watercress Pr.
While Beyond the Forest. Randy Rinkwich. Ed. by Stanley H. Barkan. (Review Chapbook Ser.: No. 24: Yiddish Poetry 1). 40p. (ENG & YID.). 1991. 15.00 (*0-89304-762-7*); pap. 5.00 (*0-89304-763-5*) Cross-Cultrl NY.
While Beyond the Forest: Mini Book. Randy Rinkwich. Ed. by Stanley H. Barkan. (Review Chapbook Ser.: No. 24: Yiddish Poetry 1). 40p. (ENG & YID.). 1991. 15.00 (*0-89304-764-3*); pap. 5.00 (*0-89304-765-1*) Cross-Cultrl NY.
***While Breath Persist.** Gael Turnbull. 160p. 1992. pap. 10. 95 (*0-88984-133-0*, Pub. by Porcupines Quill CN) Genl Dist Srvs.
While China Faced West: American Reformers in Nationalist China, 1928-1937. James C. Thomson, Jr. LC 76-82298. (East Asian Monographs: No. 38). 328p. 1969. reprint ed. pap. 13.95 (*0-674-95137-9*) HUP.
While Courting the Sergeant's Daughter. Nathan Whiting. 63p. 1969. 4.00 (*0-913219-04-5*); pap. 2.00 (*0-913219-05-3*) Pym-Rand Pr.
While Courting the Sergeant's Daughter. deluxe ed. Nathan Whiting. 63p. 1969. 7.50 (*0-913219-06-1*) Pym-Rand Pr.
While Dancing Feet Shatter the Earth. Keith Wilson. LC 77-13792. 76p. reprint ed. pap. 25.00 (*0-685-75297-6*, 2046880) Bks Demand.
While Dragons Sleep: How to Solve a Chemical Dependence Problem. Tom Kwasnik. LC 90-83989. (Illus.). 272p. (Orig.). 1991. pap. 12.95 (*0-9627555-0-8*) Able Pr.
While Drowning in the Desert: A Neal Carey Mystery. Don Winslow. LC 96-1249. 192p. 1996. 20.95 (*0-312-14446-6*) St Martin.
While England Sleeps. rev. ed. David Leavitt. LC 95-30964. 324p. 1995. 24.95 (*0-395-75937-4*); pap. 11.95 (*0-395-75286-8*) HM.
While England Slept: A Survey of World Affairs 1932-1938. Winston S. Churchill. LC 76-165621. (Select Bibliographic Reprint Ser.). 415p. 1982. reprint ed. lib. bdg. 22.00 (*0-8290-0804-7*) Irvington.
While I Am Here: One Woman's Journey to Freedom. rev. ed. Jan Goethel & Mai Holter. 200p. 1994. pap. 7.00 (*1-885474-07-5*) Chipp Valley.
While I Sleep. Mary Calhoun. LC 90-25488. (Illus.). 32p. (J). (ps up). 1992. 14.00 (*0-688-08200-9*, Morrow Junior) Morrow.
***While I was Making Soup: A Widow Remembers.** Florine C. Everett. Ed. by John J. Schmidt. LC 95-85296. 110p. 1996. 14.95 (*0-9626185-0-0*) Brookcliff Pubs.
While I Was Praying... Gloria Gold. pap. 5.95 (*0-614-13894-9*) Gold Pubs.
While I'm Dead Feed the Dog: CDZeene, Bk. 1. Ric Browde. 240p. (Orig.). 1996. pap. 19.95 incl. audio compact disk (*1-57787-099-9*) ComEnt Media.
While It Is Day. Elton Trueblood. 163p. 1983. reprint ed. pap. write for info. (*0-932970-36-2*) Yokefellow Pr.
While It Was Still Dark: One Person's Pilgrimage Through Grief. rev. ed. Adaline Bjorkman. 1993. pap. 7.95 (*0-910452-77-6*) Covenant.
While Lincoln Lay Dying: A Facsimile Reproduction of the First Testimony Taken in Connection with the Assassination of President Abraham Lincoln. Intro. by Maxwell Whiteman. LC 68-19803. (Illus.). 1971. 10.00 (*0-915810-02-6*) Union League PA.
While Martha Told the Hours. Bridge Publications Staff. (C). 1989. 75.00 (*0-947934-18-9*, Pub. by Bridge Pubns UK); pap. 45.00 (*0-947934-17-0*, Pub. by Bridge Pubns UK) St Mut.
While Morning Stars Sang. Dorothy Bennett et al. Ed. by Linda G. Salisbury. LC 91-66376. (Illus.). 104p. (Orig.). 1991. pap. 7.95 (*0-9627974-4-8*) Tabby Hse Bks.
While My Country Is in Danger: The Life & Letters of Lieutenant Colonel Richard S. Thompson, Twelfth New Jersey Volunteers. Gerry H. Poriss & Ralph G. Poriss. LC 94-11305. (Illus.). 251p. 1994. 22.95 (*0-9622393-6-4*) Edmonston Pub.
While My Pretty One Sleeps. Mary Higgins Clark. 1991. reprint ed. lib. bdg. 25.95 (*1-56849-072-0*) Buccaneer Bks.
While My Pretty One Sleeps. Mary Higgins Clark. Ed. by Julie Rubenstein. 320p. 1990. reprint ed. mass mkt. 6.99 (*0-671-67368-8*) PB.
While on the Way Home. Diane Moomey. LC 87-72319. (Illus.). 64p. 1988. 18.00 (*0-9619714-0-1*) Dayseye Pr.
While Passion Sleeps. Shirlee Busbee. 496p. 1983. mass mkt. 5.50 (*0-380-82297-0*) Avon.
While Six Millon Died: A Chronicle of American Apathy. Arthur D. Morse. LC 82-22291. 432p. 1985. pap. 9.95 (*0-87951-973-8*) Overlook Pr.

W

While Standing on One Foot: Puzzle Stories & Wisdom Tales from the Jewish Tradition. Nina Jaffe & Steve Zeitlin. (Illus.). 128p. (J). (gr. 3-7). 1993. 14.95 (*0-8050-2594-4*, Bks Young Read) H Holt & Co.

While Standing on One Foot: Puzzle Stories & Wisdom Tales from the Jewish Tradition. Nina Jaffe. (Illus.). 128p. (J). (gr. 3-7). 1996. pap. 6.95 (*0-8050-5073-6*, B Martin BYR) H Holt & Co.

While Still We Live. Helen MacInnes. 448p. 1985. mass mkt. 5.95 (*0-449-20835-4*, Crest) Fawcett.

While Still We Live. Helen MacInnes. LC 44-2182. 1971. 24.95 (*0-15-196090-9*) HarBrace.

While Still We Live. large type ed. Helen MacInnes. LC 92-27926. 830p. 1992. reprint ed. lib. bdg. 20.95 (*1-56054-456-2*) Thorndike Pr.

While Story-Log Burns. Thornton W. Burgess. (J). 18.95 (*0-8488-0401-5*) Amereon Ltd.

While the Candles Burn: Eight Stories for Hanukkah. Barbara D. Goldin. LC 95-50310. (Illus.). 64p. (J). 1996. pap. 15.99 (*0-670-85875-7*, Viking) Viking Penguin.

***While the Cannons Roared: The Civil War Behind the Lines.** John M. Taylor. (Illus.). 192p. 1997. 22.95 (*1-57488-150-7*) Brasseys Inc.

While the City Sleeps. (J). (ps-3). 1995. 6.98 (*1-57082-282-4*) Mouse Works.

While the Clock Ticked. Franklin W. Dixon. (Hardy Boys Ser.: Vol. 11). 180p. (J). (gr. 5-9). 1932. 5.95 (*0-448-08911-4*, G&D) Putnam Pub Group.

While the Distance Widens. Elizabeth Herron. 1992. pap. 12.00 (*0-912449-42-X*) Floating Island.

While the Earth Endures. Ed. by St. Andrew Press Staff. 122p. (C). 1989. 30.00 (*0-86153-085-3*, Pub. by St Andrew UK) St Mut.

While the Fire Rages. Amii Lorin. 288p. 1992. reprint ed. mass mkt., pap. text ed. 3.99 (*0-8439-3369-0*) Dorchester Pub Co.

While the Gods Play. Alain Danielou. 288p. (Orig.). 1987. pap. 12.95 (*0-89281-115-3*) Inner Tradit.

While the Heart Heals. Helen Wingo. 192p. 1992. 17.95 (*0-8034-8970-6*) Bouregy.

***While the Light Lasts: An International Anthology of Twenty-Four Poets.** Vassar W. Smith. LC 96-61858. 156p. 1996. pap. 10.00 (*1-880964-19-8*, Lapiz #20) Zapizdat Pubns.

***While the Messiah Tarries.** Melvin J. Bukiet. LC 97-25580. (Library of Modern Jewish Literature). 208p. 1997. pap. 16.95 (*0-8156-0497-1*) Syracuse U Pr.

While the Messiah Tarries: Stories. Melvin J. Bukiet. LC 94-38038. 1995. 20.00 (*0-15-100083-2*) HarBrace.

***While the Moon Looked up to Heaven.** Terry Stellini. 300p. (Orig.). 1997. pap. 12.95 (*0-9649272-1-7*) Cielo Pubng.

While the Music Lasts: My Life in Politics. William M. Bulger. LC 95-46803. 320p. 1996. 22.95 (*0-395-72041-9*) HM.

While the Music Plays. Diane Austell. 448p. 1996. mass mkt. 5.99 (*0-553-29916-6*, Fanfare) Bantam.

While the Pasta Cooks. Andrew Schloss & Ken Bookma. 192p. 1996. 22.00 (*0-02-860989-1*) Macmillan.

While the Patient Slept. Mignon G. Eberhart. LC 94-44360. xvii, 315p. 1995. pap. 11.00 (*0-8032-6726-6*, Bison Books) U of Nebr Pr.

While the Rivers Run. Wynema McGowan. 304p. 1996. mass mkt. 5.99 (*0-7860-0340-5*, Pinncle Kensgtn) Kensgtn Pub Corp.

***While the Shepherd Slept.** Matt Novak. (Illus.). 32p. (J). 3.98 (*0-8317-6778-2*) Smithmark.

While the Sun is High. Marjorie Palmer & Bernard Palmer. LC 83-83388. (Heritage Ser.: Vol. 7). 1984. 10.95 (*0-911802-60-6*) Free Church Pubns.

While the Sun Shines: Making Hay in Vermont, 1789-1990. Allen R. Yale, Jr. 88p. 1991. pap. 14.95 (*0-934720-35-5*) VT Hist Soc.

While the United States Slept. Nasrollah S. Fatemi. LC 81-65538. 480p. 1982. 25.00 (*0-8453-4721-7*, Cornwall Bks) Assoc Univ Prs.

While the Women Only Wept: Loyalist Refugee Women in Eastern Ontario. Janice Potter-MacKinnon. 216p. 1993. 49.95 (*0-7735-0962-3*, Pub. by McGill CN) U of Toronto Pr.

While the Women Only Wept: Loyalist Refugee Women in Eastern Ontario. Janice Potter-MacKinnon. 216p. 1995. pap. 17.95 (*0-7735-1317-5*, Pub. by McGill CN) U of Toronto Pr.

While Waiting. rev. ed. George E. Verrilli & Anne M. Mueser. (Illus.). (Orig.). 1993. pap. 6.95 (*0-312-09938-X*) St Martin.

While Waiting: A Prenatal Handbook. George E. Verrilli & Anne M. Mueser. LC 81-9008. (Illus.). 89p. 1981. pap. 5.95 (*0-312-86773-5*) St Martin.

While Waiting to Win the Lottery! The Baby Boomers' Money Manual. Luki Vail. (Illus.). 192p. (Orig.). 1992. pap. 12.95 (*0-9632536-9-7*) Pendleton Pr.

While Washington Burned: The Battle for Fort Erie, 1814. Joseph Whitehorne. LC 92-50541. (Illus.). 227p. 1992. 29.95 (*1-877853-18-6*) Nautical & Aviation.

While We Run This Race: Confronting the Power of Racism in a Southern Church. Gibson Stroupe & Inez Fleming. LC 95-5183. 192p. (Orig.). 1995. pap. 13.00 (*1-57075-000-9*) Orbis Bks.

While You Are Asleep. Gwynne L. Isaacs. (Illus.). 32p. (J). (gr. 4-8). 1991. 12.95 (*0-8027-6985-3*); lib. bdg. 13.85 (*0-8027-6986-1*) Walker & Co.

***While You Are Expecting: Your Own Prenatal Classroom.** 2nd rev. ed. F. Rene Van De Carr & Marc Lehrer. LC 96-5908. (Illus.). 142p. 1997. lib. bdg. 26.95 (*0-89334-268-8*, Humanics Trade) Humanics Ltd.

While You Are Expecting: Your Own Prenatal Classroom. 2nd rev. ed. Rene Van De Carr. LC 96-5908. Orig. Title: Prenatal Classroom (A Parents' Guide for Teaching Your Baby in the Womb). (Illus.). 142p. (Orig.). 1997. pap. 16.95 (*0-89334-251-3*, Humanics Trade) Humanics Ltd.

While You Can. Palmer Gedde. (Orig.). 1987. pap. 4.25 (*0-89536-890-0*, 7876) CSS OH.

While You Can: Participant. Palmer Gedde. (Orig.). 1987. pap. 4.75 (*0-89536-891-9*, 7877) CSS OH.

While You Sleep. Julia Moore. LC 95-45812. (Illus.). 32p. (J). (ps). 1996. pap. 11.99 (*0-525-45462-4*) Dutton Child Bks.

***While You Sleep.** Julia Moore. 1998. pap. 5.99 (*0-14-055982-5*) Viking Penguin.

While You Slept: Our Tragedy in Asia & Who Made It. John T. Flynn. 1951. 10.00 (*0-8159-7207-5*) Devin.

While You Were Gone: A Handbook for Returning Catholics, & Those Thinking about It. William J. Bausch. LC 93-60817. 112p. (Orig.). 1994. pap. 5.95 (*0-89622-575-5*) Twenty-Third.

While You Were Gone: A Report on Wartime Life in the United States. Ed. by Jack Goodman. LC 73-19969. (FDR & the Era of the New Deal Ser.). 625p. 1974. reprint ed. lib. bdg. 69.50 (*0-306-70605-9*) Da Capo.

Whillan's Tax Tables 1994-95. 47th ed. Ed. by Sheila Parrington. 1994. pap. 3.50 (*0-406-03644-6*, UK) MICHIE.

Whillans's Tax Office Directory 1996. 2nd ed. 66p. 1996. pap. write for info. (*0-406-00106-5*) MICHIE.

Whillans's Tax Tables 1994-1995. 48th ed. Ed. by Sheila Parrington. 1994. pap. write for info. (*0-406-04979-3*) MICHIE.

Whillans's Tax Tables 1996-1997. 51th ed. Sheila Parrington. 100p. 1996. pap. 7.00 (*0-406-06448-2*) MICHIE.

Whilomville Stories. Stephen Crane. 1991. 65.00 (*0-403-00013-0*) Scholarly.

Whilomville Stories. Stephen Crane. (Works of Stephen Crane Ser.). 1990. reprint ed. lib. bdg. 79.00 (*0-7812-0378-3*) Rprt Serv.

Whilton Dispute, 1264-1380: A Social-Legal Study of Dispute Settlement in Medieval England. Robert C. Palmer. LC 83-13858. 318p. reprint ed. pap. 90.70 (*0-8357-7073-7*, 2033377) Bks Demand.

Whimbey Writing Program: How to Analyze, Organize, & Write Effectively, Sample bklt. Arthur Whimbey. 1995. student ed., wbk. ed., pap. write for info. (*1-57004-029-X*) L Erlbaum Assocs.

Whimbey Writing Program: How to Analyze, Organize, & Write Effectively, 10 bks., Set. Arthur Whimbey. 1995. student ed., wbk. ed., pap. 129.95 (*1-57004-030-3*) L Erlbaum Assocs.

Whimbey Writing Program: How to Analyze, Organize, & Write Effectively, 10 bks., Set incl. instr's. manual. Arthur Whimbey. 1995. student ed., wbk. ed., pap. 149.95 (*1-57004-026-5*) L Erlbaum Assocs.

W.H.I.M.P.U.R. Map: Where Is My Public Radio. Maxwell Cutler & Marjory L. Robinson-Cutler. 1986. write for info. (*0-9643131-1-1*) Snicker Pub.

Whims of Creation, Bk. II. Simon Hawke. 224p. (Orig.). 1995. mass mkt. 5.50 (*0-446-36518-1*, Aspect) Warner Bks.

Whims of Time: Stories. Mary A. Guerrero-Levin. 100p. (Orig.). (C). 1990. pap. 8.75 (*971-10-0402-X*, Pub. by New Day Pub PH) Cellar.

Whimsey, Wit & Wisdom: For the Wonderful Years after Fifty. Robert O. Redd & Ann Redd. LC 90-90119. 128p. 1990. pap. text ed. 8.95 (*1-877756-03-2*) Thornapple Pub.

Whimsical Critters. Lori Ohlson. 100p. 1990. pap. text ed. 7.50 (*1-56770-228-7*) S Scheewe Pubns.

Whimsical Look at Kids. S. J. Preston. (C). 1989. 25.00 (*0-7223-2255-0*, Pub. by A H S Ltd UK) St Mut.

Whimsical, Quizzical Bible Trivia Book. J. Stephen Lang. LC 94-40271. 496p. 1995. pap. 11.99 (*0-8423-8001-9*) Tyndale.

Whimsical Woodcrafts to Make & Paint. Patrick Lose. LC 95-11545. (Illus.). 144p. 1995. 24.95 (*0-8069-1395-9*, Chapelle) Sterling.

***Whimsies & Whynots: A Playful Approach to Quiltmaking.** Mary L. Weidman. Ed. by Melissa Lowe. LC 96-37092. (Illus.). 96p. (Orig.). 1997. pap. 22.95 (*1-56477-180-6*, B294) That Patchwork.

Whimsy with Words. Mary K. Allton. (Illus.). 68p. (Orig.). (YA). (gr. 7 up). 1996. pap. 8.00 (*0-9625217-2-8*) M E K A.

***Whine Out.** Pawnee (Illinois) Elem. School, Mrs. Kern's 1996-97 Third-Grade Class. (Wee Write Bks.: No. 36). (Illus.). 50p. (J). (ps-4). 1997. pap. 8.95 (*1-57635-012-6*) WeWrite.

Whing Ding Dilly. Bill Peet. 1994. pap. 8.95 incl. audio (*0-395-68981-3*) Ticknor & Flds Bks Yng Read.

Whingdingdilly. Bill Peet. 1977. pap. 4.95 (*0-395-44785-2*) HM.

Whingdingdilly. Bill Peet. LC 71-98521. (Illus.). (J). (gr. k-3). 1977. 16.00 (*0-395-24729-2*) HM.

Whingdingdilly. Bill Peet. LC 71-98521. (Illus.). (J). (gr. k-3). 1982. pap. 6.95 (*0-395-31381-3*) HM.

***Whining.** Tamara Eberlein. (Child's Magazine Guide To... Ser.). 1997. mass mkt. 5.99 (*0-671-88042-X*) PB.

Whinnie the Lovesick Dragon. Mercer Mayer. LC 85-18886. (Illus.). 32p. (J). (gr. k-3). 1986. lib. bdg. 14.95 (*0-02-765180-0*, Mac Bks Young Read) S&S Childrens.

Whinny Moor Crossing. Judith Moffett. LC 83-43055. (Contemporary Poets Ser.). 100p. 1984. pap. 9.95 (*0-691-01410-8*) Princeton U Pr.

Whinorrhea & Other Nursing Diagnoses: Best of Journal of Nursing Jocularity 1991-1993. Ed. by Fran London. (Illus.). 244p. 1995. pap. 18.95 (*0-9649276-0-8*) JNJ Pubng.

Whinosaurus Rex. Eve R. Beutler & Bryce D. Beutler. (Illus.). 36p. (J). (ps-3). 1993. pap. 6.95 (*0-9637262-0-X*) Evening Pearl.

Whip & Spur: The Memoirs of a Civil War Officer. George E. Waring, Jr. (Borgo Bioviews Ser.: No. 9). 144p. pap. write for info. (*0-89370-253-6*); lib. bdg. write for info. (*0-89370-153-X*) Borgo Pr.

Whip Angels. (Velvet Ser.: Vol. 5). 192p. (Orig.). 1995. pap. 9.95 (*1-871592-53-4*) Creation Bks.

Whip Hand. Dick Francis. 1987. mass mkt. 5.99 (*0-449-21274-2*) Fawcett.

***Whip Hand.** Dick Francis. 1996. pap. 5.99 (*0-449-45617-X*) Fawcett.

Whip Hand. large type ed. Dick Francis. LC 94-29436. 376p. 1995. 21.95 (*0-8161-5785-5*, GK Hall) Thorndike Pr.

Whip, Hoe & Sword. George H. Hepworth. LC 73-37305. (Black Heritage Library Collection). 1977. reprint ed. 27.95 (*0-8369-8942-2*) Ayer.

Whip, Hoe & Sword. George H. Hepworth. Ed. by Joe G. Taylor. LC 78-10596. (Louisiana Bicentennial Reprint Ser.). xxiv, 312p. 1979. reprint ed. 32.50 (*0-8071-0490-6*, HMWHIPH) Claitors.

Whip-Poor-Will's Song. Marjorie H. Russell. 120p. (Orig.). (J). 1995. pap. 5.75 (*0-9614745-2-1*) Arcadia Ministry Pubns.

***Whipers on the Wind.** Donna Fletcher. 352p. 1997. mass mkt. 5.99 (*0-515-12029-4*) Jove Pubns.

Whiplash: Mechanisms & Management. Larry S. Nordhoff. LC 92-49445. 608p. 1992. 64.95 (*0-8016-6821-2*) Mosby Yr Bk.

Whiplash & the Jaw Joint: TMJ Injury. 2nd rev. ed. Dale M. Foreman & Donald Rolfs. (Illus.). 1991. 85.00 (*0-939737-01-9*) Bk Pub Co WA.

Whiplash Handbook. Monique B. Harriton. (Illus.). 108p. 1989. 29.95 (*0-398-05598-X*); pap. 17.95 (*0-398-06380-X*) C C Thomas.

***Whiplash Injuries: Current Concepts in Prevention, Diagnosis & Treatment of the Cervical Whiplash Syndrome.** Marek Szpalski. 1998. text ed. write for info. (*0-397-51856-0*) Lppncott-Raven.

Whiplash Injuries: Medical Subject Analysis & Research Guide with Bibliography. Rosa M. Madrigana. LC 83-45539. 140p. 1985. 44.50 (*0-88164-094-8*); pap. 39.50 (*0-88164-095-6*) ABBE Pubs Assn.

Whiplash Injuries: The Cervical Acceleration/Deceleration Syndrome. 2nd ed. Stephen Foreman & Arthur C. Croft. (Illus.). 500p. 1994. 95.00 (*0-683-03315-8*) Williams & Wilkins.

Whiplash Injuries & Disequilibrium: Diagnosis & Treatment. D. Alpini & N. Cesarini. (Illus.). 220p. 1996. 125.00 (*3-540-75015-0*) Spr-Verlag.

Whiplash on the Couch. John Bennett. Ed. by Kirk Robertson. LC 77-73210. (Orig.). 1979. pap. 3.00 (*0-916918-06-8*) Duck Down.

Whipped Faster Pussycat. (Guitar-Vocal Ser.). 17.95 (*0-89524-730-5*, 02501210) Cherry Lane.

Whipped into Glory: Abraham Lincoln & the White Dream. Lerone Bennett, Jr. 1996. 29.95 (*0-87485-085-1*) Johnson Chi.

Whippet Champions: 1981-1986. Camino E. E. & Bk. Co. Staff. (Illus.). 158p. 1984. pap. 32.95 (*0-940808-29-3*) Camino E E & Bk.

Whippet Champions, 1952-1980. Jan L. Pata. (Illus.). 187p. 1987. pap. 36.95 (*0-940808-03-X*) Camino E E & Bk.

Whippet Champions, 1987-1995. Camino E. E. & Bk. Co. Staff. (Illus.). 118p. 1997. pap. 32.95 (*1-55893-048-5*) Camino E E & Bk.

***Whippets.** Christine Cormany. (Illus.). 224p. 1997. pap. 9.95 (*0-7938-2394-3*, KW-179S) TFH Pubns.

Whippets: An Owners Companion. Shirley Rawlings. (Illus.). 1992. 39.95 (*1-85223-279-X*, Pub. by Crowood Pr UK) Trafalgar.

Whippets Today. Patsy Gilmour. LC 94-9643. (Illus.). 160p. 1994. pap. 25.95 (*0-87605-359-2*) Howell Bk.

Whipping Boy. Sid Fleischman. LC 85-17555. (Illus.). 96p. (J). (gr. 2-6). 1986. 16.00 (*0-688-06216-4*) Greenwillow.

***Whipping Boy.** Sid Fleischman. (Illus.). (J). (gr. 5). 1995. 8.64 (*0-395-73260-3*) HM.

***Whipping Boy.** HarBrace Staff. (J). 1995. pap. 11.00 (*0-15-305608-8*) HarBrace.

Whipping Boy. Houghton Mifflin Company Staff. (Literature Experience 1993 Ser.). (J). (gr. 5). 1992. pap. 9.16 (*0-395-61818-5*) HM.

Whipping Boy. Houghton Mifflin Company Staff. (Literature Experience 1991 Ser.). (J). (gr. 5). 1990. pap. 9.16 (*0-395-55164-1*) HM.

***Whipping Boy.** large type ed. Sid Fleischman. (Illus.). 116p. 1996. 29.50 (*0-614-20627-8*, L-38200-00 APHB) Am Printing Hse.

Whipping Boy. 93th ed. 1993. pap. text ed. 12.00 (*0-15-300357-X*, HB Juv Bks) HarBrace.

Whipping Boy. Sid Fleischman. (Illus.). (J). (gr. 2-5). 1996. reprint ed. pap. 3.95 (*0-8167-1038-4*) Troll Communs.

Whipping Boy: A Study Guide. Rosemary Villanella. (Novel-Ties Ser.). 1989. teacher ed., wbk. ed., pap. text ed. 15.95 (*0-88122-054-X*) Lrn Links.

Whipping Boy - Nino Que Pagaba el Pato. Sid Fleischman. (SPA.). (J). 9.95 (*84-204-4641-6*) Santillana.

Whipping Hidden Allergies. Harris Hosen. 1994. pap. text ed. 17.75 (*0-9622762-2-7*) Non-Fictitious.

Whipping Song. Leonard A. Slade, Jr. LC 93-28609. 64p. 1993. pap. 12.95 (*0-7734-2771-6*, Mellen Poetry Pr) E Mellen.

Whipple: The John Whipple House in Ipswich, Massachusetts, & the People Who Have Owned & Lived in It. T. F. Waters. (Illus.). 55p. 1993. reprint ed. pap. 12.50 (*0-8328-3428-9*) Higginson Bk Co.

Whipple - Wright & Allied Families, Whipple- Wright, Wager, Ward-Pell, McLean-Burnett Families, with Record of Allied Families. Charles H. Whipple. (Illus.). 117p. 1993. reprint ed. pap. 22.00 (*0-8328-3757-1*); reprint ed. lib. bdg. 32.00 (*0-8328-3756-3*) Higginson Bk Co.

Whipple & Black: Commercial Photographers in Boston. Sally Pierce. (Illus.). 132p. 1987. 45.00 (*0-934552-49-5*, Northeastern Univ Ctr for International); pap. 18.00 (*0-934552-50-9*, Northeastern Univ Ctr for International) Boston Athenaeum.

Whips. Victor Terry. (Orig.). 1995. mass mkt. 4.95 (*1-56333-254-X*, Badboy) Masquerade.

Whips & Kisses: Parting the Leather Curtain. Mistress Jacqueline. (Illus.). 236p. (C). 1991. 25.95 (*0-87975-656-X*) Prometheus Bks.

Whips & Whipmaking: With a Practical Introduction to Braiding. David Morgan. LC 72-78240. (Illus.). 139p. 1972. pap. 9.95 (*0-87033-270-8*) Cornell Maritime.

Whipsaw Trail. large type ed. Ray Hogan. 1996. 20.00 (*0-7862-2081-3*, Thorndike Lrg Prnt) Thorndike Pr.

Whipsaw Trail. large type ed. Ray Hogan. (Western Ser.). 275p. 1996. 18.95 (*0-7862-0813-9*, Thorndike Lrg Prnt) Thorndike Pr.

***Whipsaw Trail.** Ray Hogan. 192p. 1997. reprint ed. mass mkt. 3.99 (*0-8439-4258-4*, Leisure Bks) Dorchester Pub Co.

Whipt 'Em Everytime: The Diary of Bartlett Yancey Malone Co H 6th North Carolina Regiment. Bartlett Y. Malone. Ed. by William W. Pierson, Jr. & Bell I. Wiley. (Illus.). 131p. 1992. reprint ed. 25.00 (*0-916107-37-X*) Broadfoot.

***Whiptail of Blackshale Trail.** (Get Ready...Get Set...Read! Ser.: Set 4). (J). 1996. lib. bdg. 11.95 (*1-56674-160-2*) Forest Hse.

Whiptale of Blackshale Trail. Gina C. Erickson & Kelli C. Foster. (Get Ready...Get Set...Read! Ser.). (Illus.). 24p. (J). (ps-3). 1993. pap. 3.50 (*0-8120-1733-1*) Barron.

Whirl Around the World. Daniel A. Marino. 180p. pap. 9.95 (*0-9633159-0-0*) Jemet Bks.

***Whirled: A Performance Quartet.** Marion Kimes. (Illus.). 16p. (Orig.). 1996. pap. 5.00 (*1-890654-00-0*) Wood Work.

***Whirled Views: Tracking Today's Culture Storms.** Marvin N. Olasky & Joel Belz. LC 96-51913. 243p. (Orig.). 1997. pap. 12.99 (*0-89107-938-6*) Crossway Bks.

***Whirligig.** Paul Fleischman. LC 97-24429. (J). 1997. write for info. (*0-8050-5582-7*) H Holt & Co.

Whirligig. Russell J. Smith. LC 94-40034. 1995. pap. 9.95 (*0-910155-29-1*) Bartleby Pr.

Whirligig Book: How to Make Action Mechanical Whirligigs. Jack Wiley. LC 89-92026. (Illus.). 121p. 1990. pap. 19.95 (*0-913999-17-2*) Solipaz Pub Co.

Whirligigs & Weathervanes: A Celebration of Wind Gadgets with Dozens of Creative Projects to Make. David Schoonmaker & Bruce Woods. LC 91-12145. (Illus.). 128p. 1992. pap. 14.95 (*0-8069-8365-5*) Sterling.

***Whirling Around: Helicopters Then & Now.** Paul Otfinoski. LC 97-13163. (Here We Go! Ser.). (Illus.). 32p. (J). (gr. 1 up). 1998. lib. bdg. 14.95 (*0-7614-0610-7*, Benchmark NY) Marshall Cavendish.

Whirling Dervishes: Being an Account of the Sufi Order Known As the Mevlevis & Its Founder the Poet & Mystic Mevlana Jalalu'ddin Rumi. Shems Friedlander. LC 91-34969. (SUNY Series in Islam). 160p. 1992. pap. 27.95 (*0-7914-1156-7*); text ed. 54.50 (*0-7914-1155-9*) State U NY Pr.

Whirling Mass of Space - Time. Ian McCrimmon. (C). 1992. text ed. 40.00 (*1-874686-00-9*, Pub. by Cosmatom UK) St Mut.

Whirling Round the Sun. Suzanne Noguere. LC 96-76462. (Poetry Ser.). (Illus.). 96p. (Orig.). 1996. pap. 12.00 (*1-877675-22-9*) Midmarch Arts-WAN.

Whirlpool. Aleister Crowley. 1973. lib. bdg. 250.00 (*0-87968-507-7*) Krishna Pr.

Whirlpool. Barry Estabrook. LC 95-30627. 1995. 21.95 (*0-312-13622-6*, Thomas Dunne Bks) St Martin.

Whirlpool. Colin Forbes. 542p. 1991. pap. 15.95 (*0-330-31880-2*, Pub. by Pan Books UK) Trans-Atl Phila.

***Whirlpool.** Gissing. 1997. pap. 8.95 (*0-460-87781-X*, Everyman's Classic Lib) C E Tuttle.

Whirlpool. George R. Gissing. Ed. by Patrick Parinder. LC 77-80329. 467p. 1978. 24.50 (*0-8386-2172-4*) Fairleigh Dickinson.

Whirlpool. Madeleine Ker. (Presents Ser.). 1993. mass mkt. 2.99 (*0-373-11590-3*, 1-11590-6) Harlequin Bks.

Whirlpool. Junichiro Tanizaki. Tr. by Howard S. Hibbett, Jr. from JPN. LC 93-20582. (ENG.). 1994. 22.00 (*0-394-58547-X*) Knopf.

Whirlpool. Ethel Archer. 1993. reprint ed. 27.50 (*1-55818-215-2*, First Impress) Holmes Pub.

Whirlpool. George Gissing. LC 71-80632. reprint ed. 39.50 (*0-404-02812-8*) AMS Pr.

Whirlpool. Jane Urquhart. LC 89-45383. 238p. 1989. reprint ed. 18.95 (*0-87923-806-2*) Godine.

Whirlpool: U. S. Foreign Policy Toward Latin America & the Caribbean. Robert A. Pastor. (Studies in International History & Politics). 353p. 1992. pap. text ed. 16.95 (*0-691-02561-4*) Princeton U Pr.

***Whirlpool of Passion.** large type ed. Emma Darcy. (Magna Large Print Ser.). (Illus.). 245p. 1996. 25.99 (*0-7505-0997-X*) Ulverscroft.

Whirlwind. Marolyn Caldwell-Wilson. (Judy Sullivan Romance Ser.). 1985. 14.95 (*0-8027-0850-1*) Walker & Co.

Whirlwind. James Clavell. 1280p. 1987. mass mkt. 6.99 (*0-380-70312-2*) Avon.

***Whirlwind.** Drumbeat Publishing Staff. Date not set. pap. text ed. write for info. (*0-582-78543-X*, Drumbeat) Longman.

An Asterisk (*) at the beginning of an entry indicates that the title is appearing in BIP for the first time.

Whirlwind. Nancy Martin. (Tyler Ser.: No. 501). 1992. mass mkt. 3.99 (0-373-82501-3, 1-82501-7) Harlequin Bks.

Whirlwind. Bill Myers. (Journeys to Fayrah Ser.: Vol. 3). 144p. (Orig.). (J). (gr. 3-8). 1992. pap. 5.99 (1-55661-258-3) Bethany Hse.

Whirlwind - A Doctor's Odyssey from Addiction: Recovery & Help for Others. Richard Turner & Thomas E. Butcher. Ed. by Barbara Reitt. 156p. (Orig.). 1992. 14.95 (1-877652-07-5); pap. 9.95 (1-877652-06-7) Valet Pub.

Whirlwind Alchemy. Douglas W. Clark. 320p. (Orig.). 1993. mass mkt. 4.99 (0-380-76309-5, AvoNova) Avon.

Whirlwind in Culture: Frontiers in Theology. Murse. LC 88-42731. 288p. (Orig.). 1988. pap. 22.95 (0-940989-39-5) Meyer Stone Bks.

Whirlwind in Culture: Frontiers in Theology. Murse. Ed. by Donald W. Musser & Joseph L. Price. LC 88-42731. 288p. (Orig.). 1988. 33.95 (0-940989-43-3) Meyer Stone Bks.

Whirlwind in Dublin: The Plough & the Stars Riots. Ed. by Robert G. Lowery. LC 83-22652. (Contributions to Drama & Theatre Studies: No. 11). xiii, 121p. 1984. text ed. 29.95 (0-313-23764-6, LOW/, Greenwood Pr) Greenwood.

Whirlwind in the Danube Valley. Laszlo Gorgenyi. (Illus.). (C). 25.00 (1-882785-05-3) Matthias Corvinus.

Whirlwind War: The U. S. Army in Operations Desert Shield & Desert Storm. Ed. by Frank N. Schubert & Theresa L. Kraus. (Illus.). 312p. 1996. 55.00 (0-7881-2829-9) DIANE Pub.

*__Whirlwind War: The United States Army in Operations Desert Shield & Desert Storm.__ 1996. lib. bdg. 251.99 (0-8490-6362-0) Gordon Pr.

Whirlwinds of Danger: The Memoirs of Mary Gosman Scarborough. Mary G. Scarborough. LC 89-51437. (Illus.). 208p. 1990. 14.95 (0-912135-03-4) D Walker Pr.

Whirr Pop Click Clang. Carol MacKenzie. LC 94-8525. (Illus.). (J). Date not set. 15.00 (0-688-13292-8, Tambourine Bks) Morrow.

Whirr Pop Click Clang. limited ed. Carol MacKenzie. LC 94-8525. (Illus.). (J). Date not set. Limited Ed. lib. bdg. 14.93 (0-688-13293-6, Tambourine Bks) Morrow.

Whisked Away: Poems for More Than One Voice. Richard Brown. LC 93-17849. (C). 1992. pap. 9.50 (0-521-44588-4) Cambridge U Pr.

Whiskers, a Kitten's Story. Roma N. Burke. LC 87-62417. 120p. (J). (gr. 3-8). 1988. pap. 8.95 (0-88100-058-2) Natl Writ Pr.

Whiskers & Paws. Ed. by Fiona Waters. LC 89-77349. (Illus.). 32p. (J). 1990. 9.95 (0-940793-51-2, Crocodile Bks) Interlink Pub.

Whiskers & Rhymes. Arnold Lobel. LC 83-25424. (Illus.). 48p. (J). (gr. k-3). 1985. 13.00 (0-688-03835-2); lib. bdg. 12.88 (0-688-03836-0) Greenwillow.

Whiskers & Rhymes. Arnold Lobel. LC 83-25424. (Illus.). 48p. (J). 1988. pap. 4.95 (0-688-08291-2, Mulberry) Morrow.

*__Whiskers & Smoke.__ Marian Babson. 1997. mass mkt. 5.99 (0-312-96181-2) St Martin.

Whisker's Great Adventure. Meryl Doney. (Illus.). 32p. (J). (gr. k-1). 1996. 15.00 (0-8028-5124-X); pap. 7.50 (0-8028-5064-2) Eerdmans.

Whiskers in the Sink: And Other Family Matters. Bradley B. Williams. (Orig.). 1991. pap. 5.95 (0-9620486-1-5) B B Williams.

Whiskers, the Bank Mouse. Claudia E. Wells. LC 77-10823. (Illus.). (J). (gr. 1-4). 1981. 4.50 (0-930506-00-6); pap. write for info. (0-930506-01-4) Popcorn Pubs.

*__Whiskerville Bakery.__ Joanne Barkan. (GRE.). (J). 1990. 5.99 (0-85953-857-5); 5.99 (0-85953-645-9) Childs Play.

*__Whiskerville Firestation.__ Joanne Barkan. (GRE.). (J). 1990. 5.99 (0-85953-858-3); 5.99 (0-85953-646-7) Childs Play.

*__Whiskerville Post Office.__ Joanne Barkan. (GRE.). (J). 1990. 5.99 (0-85953-856-7); 5.99 (0-85953-647-5) Childs Play.

*__Whiskerville School.__ Joanne Barkan. (GRE.). (J). 1990. 5.99 (0-85953-855-9); 5.99 (0-85953-644-0) Childs Play.

Whiskey. Terrence McNally. 1973. pap. 3.25 (0-8222-1243-9) Dramatists Play.

Whiskey Dan & Me. Earl A. Monaghan. LC 95-92281. 162p. (Orig.). (YA). (gr. 8-12). 1995. pap. text ed. 7.50 (0-9622840-1-7) NEB Pr.

Whiskey Distillers of Scotland, 1887. Picton Publishing Staff & Alfred Barnard. (Illus.). 160p. (C). 1987. reprint ed. 60.00 (0-317-90428-0, Pub. by Picton UK) St Mut.

Whiskey Gulch. large type ed. Marshall Grover. (Linford Western Library). 1989. pap. 15.99 (0-7089-6770-1) Ulverscroft.

Whiskey Insurrection. Reed B. Day. 33p. 1992. pap. 6.00 (1-55856-117-X) Closson Pr.

*__Whisk(e)y Lexicon: Lexicon.__ Stefan Gabanyi. LC 97-3339. (Illus.). 368p. 1997. 24.95 (0-7892-0383-9) Abbeville Pr.

Whiskey Peddler: Johnny Healy, North Frontier Trader. William R. Hunt. Ed. by Daniel Greer. (Illus.). 263p. (Orig.). 1992. pap. 12.00 (0-87842-284-6) Mountain Pr.

Whiskey Rebellion: Frontier Epilogue to the American Revolution. Thomas P. Slaughter. LC 85-3095. 304p. 1988. reprint ed. pap. 11.95 (0-19-505191-2) OUP.

Whiskey Rebellion: Past & Present Perspectives. Ed. by Steven R. Boyd. LC 84-22437. (Contributions in American History Ser.: No. 109). (Illus.). xii, 212p. 1985. text ed. 55.00 (0-313-24534-7, BWH/, Greenwood Pr) Greenwood.

Whiskey Rebels: The Story of a Frontier Uprising. Leland D. Baldwin. LC 39-11763. 336p. (C). 1968. reprint ed. pap. 14.95 (0-8229-5151-7) U of Pittsburgh Pr.

Whiskey River. Patrick E. Andrews. 256p. 1993. mass mkt. 3.50 (0-8217-4409-7, Zebra Kensgtn) Kensgtn Pub Corp.

Whiskey, Six-Guns & Red-Light Ladies: George Hand's Saloon Diary, Tucson, 1875-1878. Ed. by Neil B. Carmony. LC 94-77781. (Illus.). 268p. 1994. 22.95 (0-944383-24-6) High-Lonesome.

*__Whiskey Tax.__ large type ed. K. Vernon Davis. 280p. (Orig.). 1997. pap. 12.50 (1-878431-11-0) Artist Profile Pub.

Whiskey Trade of the Northwestern Plains: A Multidisciplinary Study. Margaret A. Kennedy. LC 94-30659. (American University Studies, Series IX, History: Vol. 171). 1995. write for info. (0-8204-2596-6) P Lang Pubng.

*__Whiskey Trails: A Traveller's Guide to Scotch Whisky.__ Gordon Brown. (Illus.). 224p. 1997. pap. 19.95 (1-85375-227-4, Pub. by Prion UK) Trafalgar.

*__Whiskey's Children.__ Erdmann & Kearney. 256p. 1997. 21.50 (1-57566-215-9, Knsington) Kensgtn Pub Corp.

Whiskey's Children. Jack Erdmann & Larry Kearney. (Illus.). 248p. (Orig.). 1995. pap. 12.95 (0-9646416-0-7) Vernal Pr.

Whiskeytown National Recreation Area. Gregory Gnesios. Ed. by Ronald J. Foreman & T. J. Priehs. LC 92-62153. (Illus.). 16p. (Orig.). (YA). 1993. pap. 3.95 (1-877856-23-1) SW Pks Mnmts.

Whiskies of Scotland. rev. ed. R. J. McDowall. LC 87-21962. (Illus.). 192p. 1987. pap. 11.95 (0-941533-06-9) New Amsterdam Bks.

*__Whisky: Collins Pocket Reference.__ Carol Shaw. (Orig.). 1997. pap. write for info. (0-00-472018-0) HarperColl Wrld.

Whisky Murders. Richard Grindal. 192p. 1987. 15.95 (0-8027-5661-1) Walker & Co.

Whisky Trails: A Geographical Guide to Scotch Whisky. Gordon Brown. (Illus.). 224p. 1994. 24.95 (1-56138-490-9) Running Pr.

Whisper: A Novel. Carolyn Doty. 288p. 1992. text ed. 21.95 (0-684-19287-X) S&S Trade.

Whisper Again. Dorothy N. Morrison. 208p. (J). (gr. 2-9). 1989. reprint ed. pap. 2.95 (0-8167-1307-3) Troll Communs.

Whisper & a Wish. Robin J. Gunn. (Christy Miller Ser.: Vol. 2). 176p. (Orig.). (YA). (gr. 7-11). 1989. pap. 5.99 (0-929608-29-1) Focus Family.

Whisper Behind the Wind. Walkin J. Stoltz. 52p. (Orig.). 1988. pap. 6.00 (0-9620228-0-2) Lone Coyote Pubns.

Whisper from the Woods. Victoria Wirth. (J). (gr. 4-7). 1991. 17.00 (0-671-74790-8, S&S Bks Young Read) S&S Childrens.

Whisper Goodbye. Dorothy N. Morrison. 192p. (J). (gr. 2-9). 1997. reprint ed. pap. 2.95 (0-8167-1045-7) Troll Communs.

Whisper in the Attic. Gloria Murphy. 352p. 1992. 4.99 (0-451-17315-5, Sig) NAL-Dutton.

Whisper in the Wind. Madeline Baker. 432p. 1996. mass mkt. 5.99 (0-8439-4035-2) Dorchester Pub Co.

*__Whisper in the Wind.__ Anthony Demarcantonio. 36p. (Orig.). 1996. pap. 3.95 (0-9646450-4-1) DeeMar Commun.

Whisper into My Good Ear - Mrs. Dally Has a Lover: Two Plays. William Hanley. 1963. pap. 5.25 (0-8222-1244-7) Dramatists Play.

Whisper Is Quiet. Carolyn Lunn. LC 88-11968. (Rookie Readers Ser.). (Illus.). 32p. (J). (ps-2). 1988. pap. 3.50 (0-516-42087-9); lib. bdg. 15.00 (0-516-02087-0) Childrens.

Whisper Is Quiet Big Book. (Rookie Readers Big Bks.). (Illus.). 32p. (J). (ps-2). 1990. pap. 32.40 (0-516-49457-0) Childrens.

Whisper My Name. Raine Cantrell. 384p. (Orig.). 1995. mass mkt. 4.99 (0-451-40605-2, Topaz) NAL-Dutton.

Whisper My Name. Fern Michaels. (Best of the Best Ser.). 1993. mass mkt. 4.50 (0-373-48273-6, 5-48273-2) Silhouette.

*__Whisper of a Captive Dreamer.__ Yogendrasinh H. Rathod. LC 96-92450. (Whisper Ser.: No. 1). Date not set. write for info. (0-9656129-0-2) Rathod Pub.

*__Whisper of Black.__ Clay Harvey. LC 96-46252. 240p. 1997. 23.95 (0-399-14232-0, Putnam) Putnam Pub Group.

Whisper of Blood. Ed. by Ellen Dallow. 288p. 1995. mass mkt. 5.50 (0-441-00266-8) Ace Bks.

Whisper of Death. Christopher Pike. Ed. by Patricia MacDonald. 256p. (Orig.). (YA). (gr. 9 up). pap. 3.99 (0-671-69058-2, Archway) PB.

*__Whisper of Doubt.__ large type ed. Rachael Croft. (Linford Romance Large Print Ser.). 224p. 1997. pap. 16.99 (0-7089-5078-7, Linford) Ulverscroft.

*__Whisper of Dreams.__ Stephen F. Cox. (Orig.). 1997. mass mkt. 5.99 (1-55237-080-1, Pub. by Comnwlth Pub CN) Partners Pubs Grp.

Whisper of Dreams: A Collection of Poetry. Ed. by Rebecca S. Bell & C. Sherman Severin. (Collection of National Poetry Ser.). (Illus.). 232p. 1982. pap. 9.95 (0-942170-04-0) CSS Pubns.

Whisper of Espionage: Wolfgang Kohler & the Apes of Tenerife. Ronald Ley. LC 89-36061. (Illus.). 284p. 19.95 (0-89529-432-X) Avery Pub.

*__Whisper of Fans.__ 2nd ed. Leslie Cameron. 1997. reprint ed. mass mkt. 6.50 (1-56333-542-5, Rosebud) Masquerade.

Whisper of Love. Jewel Miller. LC 91-30828. 176p. (Orig.). 1991. pap. 7.99 (0-8361-3570-9) Herald Pr.

Whisper of Rage. Timothy Hemlin. 1997. mass mkt. 5.50 (0-345-40319-3) Ballantine.

Whisper of Romance. Alice Sharpe. LC 95-95227. 192p. 1996. 17.95 (0-8034-9154-9, Avalon Bks) Bouregy.

Whisper of Roses. Teresa Medeiros. 416p. 1993. mass mkt. 5.99 (0-553-29408-3) Bantam.

Whisper of Roses. large type ed. Teresa Medeiros. LC 93-33801. 1994. lib. bdg. 21.95 (0-7862-0070-7) Thorndike Pr.

Whisper of Scandal. Janis Laden. 448p. 1993. mass mkt. 3.99 (0-8217-4106-3, Zebra Kensgtn) Kensgtn Pub Corp.

*__Whisper of Scandal.__ Kathryn Ross. (Presents Ser.: No. 1898). 1997. mass mkt. 3.50 (0-373-11898-8, 1-11898-3) Harlequin Bks.

Whisper of Scandal. large type ed. Kathryn Ross. 1995. 21.50 (0-263-14129-2, Pub. by M & B UK) Ulverscroft.

Whisper of the Muse: The Overstone Album & Other Photographs by Julia Margaret Cameron. Mike Weaver. LC 86-20939. (Illus.). 104p. 1986. 49.95 (0-89236-088-7, J P Getty Museum) J P Getty Trust.

Whisper of the River. Ferrol Sams. LC 84-42777. 528p. 1984. 21.95 (0-931948-60-6) Peachtree Pubs.

Whisper of the River. Ferrol Sams. (Contemporary American Fiction Ser.). 544p. 1986. pap. 11.95 (0-14-008387-1, Penguin Bks) Viking Penguin.

Whisper of the Wolf. Terry C. Johnston. (Sons of the Plains Ser.: No. 03). 464p. 1991. mass mkt. 6.50 (0-553-29179-3) Bantam.

*__Whisper of Violets.__ Linda Mehl. 384p. 1997. mass mkt. 4.99 (0-8217-5633-8, Zebra Kensgtn) Kensgtn Pub Corp.

*__Whisper of Waves.__ Barbara Stevens. (Illus.). 58p. 1993. per. 4.00 (0-614-24782-9) Tesseract SD.

*__Whisper on the Water.__ Earl P. Murray. 1996. mass mkt. 5.99 (0-8125-3887-0) Forge NYC.

Whisper to Me of Love. Shirlee Busbee. 528p. 1991. mass mkt. 4.95 (0-380-75211-5) Avon.

Whisper Whisper Jesse, Whisper Whisper Josh: A Story about AIDS. Kristine H. Templeman. LC 92-72471. (Illus.). 32p. (J). (ps up). 1992. pap. 5.95 (0-9624828-3-8); lib. bdg. 16.95 (0-9624828-4-6) Advantage-Aurora.

Whisperd Kisses. Janelle Taylor. 1996. pap. 5.99 (0-8217-5454-8) Kensgtn Pub Corp.

Whispered Beginnings. Joann M. Everett. Ed. by Ave J. Zettlemoyer. (Illus.). 63p. (Orig.). 1984. pap. 5.00 (0-930069-00-5) Jasmine Pr.

Whispered in the Dark. Lars Eighner. (Orig.). 1995. mass mkt. 5.95 (1-56333-286-8, Badboy) Masquerade.

Whispered Kisses. Janelle Taylor. 1990. mass mkt. 4.95 (0-8217-2912-8, Zebra Kensgtn) Kensgtn Pub Corp.

Whispered Kisses. Janelle Taylor. 512p. 1993. mass mkt. 4.99 (0-8217-3830-5, Zebra Kensgtn) Kensgtn Pub Corp.

Whispered Meanings: Selected Essays of Simon O. Lesser. Robert W. Sprich. LC 77-73480. 248p. 1977. pap. 17.95 (0-87023-244-4) U of Mass Pr.

Whispered Promises. Brenda Jackson. 256p. 1996. mass mkt. 4.99 (0-7860-0307-3, Pinncle Kensgtn) Kensgtn Pub Corp.

Whispered Secrets: The Couple's Guide to Erotic Fantasy. Iris Finz & Steven Finz. 256p. 1990. pap. 5.99 (0-451-16401-6, Sig) NAL-Dutton.

Whispered Silences: Japanese Americans & World War II. Gary Y. Okihiro. LC 95-21895. (Samuel & Althea Stroum Bks.). (Illus.). 256p. 1996. pap. 29.95 (0-295-97498-2) U of Wash Pr.

Whispered Silences: Japanese Americans & World War II. Gary Y. Okihiro. LC 95-21895. (Samuel & Althea Stroum Bks.). (Illus.). 256p. 1996. text ed. 60.00 (0-295-97497-4) U of Wash Pr.

Whispered Thunder. E. M. Adkins. (Orig.). 1995. pap. write for info. (1-57553-092-9) Watermrk Pr.

Whispered Wisdom: Portraits of Grandmother Earth. Mary S. Rain. 160p. 1992. pap. 18.95 (1-878901-49-4) Hampton Roads Pub Co.

Whisperer. Diane Hoh. (Nightmare Hall Ser.: No. 12). 176p. (YA). (gr. 7-9). 1994. pap. 3.50 (0-590-48154-1) Scholastic Inc.

Whisperer Mystery. Daniel Torres. Ed. by Bernd Metz. Tr. by David Rosenthal from SPA. (Astral Adventures of Rocco Vargas Ser.). (Illus.). 49p. (Orig.). 1990. pap. 9.95 (0-87416-096-0) Catalan Communs.

*__Whisperers Book One of the Gate of Time.__ Dan Parkinson. (Whisperers Ser.: Bk. 1). 1998. mass mkt. 5.99 (0-345-41380-6, Del Rey) Ballantine.

Whisper...He Might Hear You. William Appel. 256p. 1992. reprint ed. mass mkt. 4.50 (1-55817-641-1, Pinncle Kensgtn) Kensgtn Pub Corp.

Whispering. large type ed. Jane A. Hodge. LC 95-7910. 313p. 1995. pap. 20.95 (0-7862-0457-5) Thorndike Pr.

Whispering Bluffs. Mary H. Talken. (Illus.). 208p. 1992. reprint ed. pap. 4.95 (0-9619510-2-8) M Talken.

Whispering Brook Farm. Carrie Bender. LC 94-39706. (Whispering Brook Ser.: Bk. 1). (Illus.). 224p. (Orig.). (J). (gr. 4 up). 1995. pap. 7.99 (0-8361-9011-4) Herald Pr.

*__Whispering Brook Series, 3 vols.__ Carrie Bender. Date not set. pap. 23.97 (0-8361-9068-8) Herald Pr.

Whispering Clay. Kathleen L. Mendel. Ed. by Candy K. Brethauer. LC 92-71598. (Illus.). 30p. (Orig.). (J). 1992. pap. 6.10 (1-878142-29-1) Telstar FL.

Whispering Cloth: A Refugee's Story. Pegi D. Shea. LC 94-71025. (Illus.). 32p. (J). (ps-2). 1995. 16.95 (1-56397-134-8) Boyds Mills Pr.

Whispering Cloth: A Refugee's Story. Pegi D. Shea. LC 94-71025. (Illus.). 32p. (J). (ps-3). 1996. pap. 7.95 (1-56397-623-4) Boyds Mills Pr.

Whispering Dark. large type ed. Jean Saunders. (Dales Large Print Ser.). 288p. 1995. pap. 17.99 (1-85389-544-X, Dales) Ulverscroft.

Whispering Death: The Life & Times of Michael Holding. Michael Holding & Tony Cozier. (Illus.). 208p. 1996. pap. 17.95 (0-233-98855-6, Pub. by A Deutsch UK) Trafalgar.

Whispering Hope. Phil Bosmans. 128p. (C). 1990. text ed. 39.00 (0-85439-328-5, Pub. by St Paul Pubns UK) St Mut.

Whispering Land. Gerald Durrell. (Illus.). 224p. 1975. pap. 7.95 (0-14-002083-7, Penguin Bks) Viking Penguin.

Whispering Land. large type ed. Gerald Durrell. 334p. 1980. 25.99 (0-7089-0474-2) Ulverscroft.

Whispering Leaves. Ed Davis. 28p. 1989. 4.00 (0-945251-02-5) Great Elm.

Whispering Master. large type ed. Frank Gruber. (Linford Mystery Library). 352p. 1994. pap. 15.99 (0-7089-7474-0, Linford) Ulverscroft.

*__Whispering Moments: Inspiration.__ 2nd ed. Molana S. Ali. LC 95-81158. (Illus.). 23p. (Orig.). 1997. reprint ed. pap. 25.00 (0-910735-83-2) MTO Printing & Pubn Ctr.

Whispering of Angels. John Marcovic. 147p. (Orig.). 1996. mass mkt. 4.99 (1-55197-097-X, Pub. by Comnwlth Pub CN) Partners Pubs Grp.

Whispering Outlaw. Max Brand. 320p. 1994. reprint ed. mass mkt., pap. text ed. 3.99 (0-8439-3678-9) Dorchester Pub Co.

Whispering Pines: Photographs by Birney Imes. Birney Imes. (Illus.). 96p. 1994. 49.95 (0-87805-695-5); pap. 29.95 (0-87805-696-3) U Pr of Miss.

Whispering Pines: Photographs by Birney Imes. limited ed. Birney Imes. (Illus.). 96p. 1994. 150.00 (0-87805-708-0) U Pr of Miss.

Whispering Pond: A Personal Guide to the Emerging Vision of Science. Ervin Laszlo. 208p. 1996. pap. 24.95 (1-85230-899-0) Element MA.

Whispering Rabbit. Margaret Wise Brown. (Favorite Sound Story Bks.). (Illus.). 24p. (J). (ps-2). 1992. bds. write for info. (0-307-00138-5, 312-03, Golden Books) Western Pub.

Whispering Range. Ernest Haycox. 1976. 25.95 (0-89190-979-6) Amereon Ltd.

Whispering Range. large type ed. Ernest Haycox. LC 94-5670. 1994. lib. bdg. 19.95 (0-7862-0200-9) Thorndike Pr.

Whispering River. A. Westcott & C. Symons. LC 78-108727. (Illus.). 48p. (J). (gr. 3-5). 1970. lib. bdg. 10.95 (0-87783-049-5) Oddo.

Whispering River. deluxe ed. A. Westcott & C. Symons. LC 78-108727. (Illus.). 48p. (J). (gr. 3-5). 1970. pap. 3.94 (0-87783-116-5) Oddo.

Whispering Room: Haunted Poems. Illus. by Justin Todd. LC 96-3387. 72p. (J). (gr. 1 up). 1996. 15.95 (0-7534-5024-0, Kingfisher LKC) LKC.

Whispering Roots. large type ed. Valerie Georgeson. 592p. 1988. 27.99 (0-7089-8487-8, Charnwood) Ulverscroft.

Whispering Rose. Joseph L. Kavanaugh. 159p. (Orig.). 1996. pap. 14.95 (0-9650463-0-3) J L Kavanaugh.

Whispering Sands. large type ed. Mary Munro. 400p. 1988. 25.99 (0-7089-1869-7) Ulverscroft.

Whispering Sands & Other Poems. Jack Shiner. LC 88-38045. 144p. (Orig.). 1989. 11.95 (0-922224-09-9); pap. 6.95 (0-922224-10-2) Stargazer Music.

Whispering Smith. unabridged ed. Frank H. Spearman. (Illus.). 420p. 1996. reprint ed. 34.95 (1-889439-02-9) Paper Tiger NJ.

Whispering Smith. Frank H. Spearman. 1995. reprint ed. lib. bdg. 24.95 (1-56849-592-7) Buccaneer Bks.

Whispering Statue. Carolyn Keene. LC 72-106316. (Nancy Drew Ser.: Vol. 14). (Illus.). 180p. (J). (gr. 4-7). 1937. 5.95 (0-448-09514-9, G&D) Putnam Pub Group.

Whispering Surgeon. 2nd ed. Edward Mycue et al. Ed. by Joseph A. Uphoff, Jr. (Illus.). 32p. 1986. pap. text ed. 2.00 (0-943123-01-1) Arjuna Lib Pr.

Whispering the Lyrics. Thomas Long. 1995. pap. 11.25 (0-7880-0492-1) CSS OH.

Whispering to Fool the Wind. Alberto A. Rios. LC 82-3269. 72p. (C). 1982. pap. 10.95 (0-935296-31-X) Sheep Meadow.

Whispering Veils: Poems on Christo's Art. Cyril Christo. (Illus.). 24p. 1988. 15.00 (0-88363-023-0) H L Levin.

Whispering Wall. Patricia Carlon. LC 96-20040. 212p. 1996. 20.00 (1-56947-066-9) Soho Press.

*__Whispering Wall.__ Patricia Carlon. 1998. pap. 12.00 (1-56947-111-8) Soho Press.

Whispering Well. large type ed. Mary Mackie. (Nightingale Ser.). 1996. pap. 17.95 (0-7838-1622-7, GK Hall) Thorndike Pr.

*__Whispering Willow Vol. 2: Sleuth Edition.__ Elizabeth Lawrence et al. (Whispering Willow Mystery Magazine Ser.). (Illus.). 112p. 1997. pap. 9.95 (0-9653990-3-6) Whispering Willows.

Whispering Wind. Sukey Gross. (Illus.). 128p. (J). (gr. 6-8). 1991. 10.95 (1-56062-068-4); pap. 7.95 (1-56062-069-2) CIS Comm.

Whispering Winds of Change. Stuart Wilde. 310p. pap. 12.95 (1-56170-160-2, 193) Hay House.

Whispering Winds of Change. Stuart Wilde. 309p. 1993. pap. 12.95 (0-930603-45-1) White Dove NM.

Whispering Winds of Chapel Road. Marie H. O'Neil. LC 91-77625. (Illus.). 114p. (Orig.). 1993. pap. 6.50 (1-56002-184-5) Aegina Pr.

Whispering Wings of Autumn. limited ed. William J. Schaldach. (Illus.). 1994. lthr. 95.00 (1-885106-01-7) Wild Adven Pr.

Whispering Wings of Autumn. William J. Schaldach. (Illus.). 1994. reprint ed. 29.00 (1-885106-00-9) Wild Adven Pr.

*__Whispering Women.__ large type ed. Christine Hainsworth. (Dales Large Print Ser.). 304p. 1996. pap. 17.99 (1-85389-692-6, Dales) Ulverscroft.

Whisperings of Life. Esther Corrigan. 98p. (Orig.). 1993. pap. 9.95 (0-9638825-0-3) SUESTA.

Whisperings of Self. 6th ed. Validivar. LC 68-57028. 86p. 1969. 16.95 (0-912057-40-8, 501660) RO AMORC.

Whisperings on the Nile (Saraarah Fouk el Nil) Arabic Novel. Naguib Mahfouz. (ARA.). 1976. 8.95 (0-86685-160-7) Intl Bk Ctr.

Whisperings on the Porch: A Collection of Haiku. Anthony Navarra. (Illus.). 128p. (Orig.). 1992. pap. 6.95 (0-9632041-3-0) Japan Am Comm.

*__Whispers.__ 424p. 1996. 45.00 (1-885206-44-5, Iliad Pr) Cader Pubng.

Whispers. Kenneth R. Berry. LC 91-67339. 115p. 1993. 19.95 (1-56002-138-1, Univ Edtns) Aegina Pr.

W

An Asterisk (*) at the beginning of an entry indicates that the title is appearing in BIP for the first time.

Whispers. Kris Bruyer. 224p. 1995. pap. 10.95 (*1-56280-082-5*) Naiad Pr.

Whispers. B. H. Friedman. LC 73-151219. (Ithaca House Fiction Ser.). 154p. 1972. 3.95 (*0-87886-021-5*, Greenfld Rev Pr) Greenfld Rev Lit.

***Whispers.** Lydia Goings. (Orig.). 1997. pap. write for info. (*1-57553-488-6*) Watermrk Pr.

Whispers. Robin J. Gunn. 1995. pap. 8.99 (*0-88070-755-0*, Multnomah Bks) Multnomah Pubs.

Whispers. Lisa Jackson. 1996. pap. text ed. 5.99 (*0-8217-5360-6*) Kensgtn Pub Corp.

Whispers. Dean R. Koontz. 512p. 1986. mass mkt. 7.50 (*0-425-09760-9*) Berkley Pub.

Whispers. Belva Plain. LC 92-36572. 336p. 1993. 22.95 (*0-385-29928-1*) Delacorte.

Whispers. Belva Plain. 480p. 1994. mass mkt. 6.99 (*0-440-21674-5*) Dell.

Whispers. large type ed. Belva Plain. 1994. 90.95 (*0-7862-9990-8*, GK Hall) Thorndike Pr.

Whispers: Prayers & Poems for Personal Growth. Ross Kingham. 158p. 1995. pap. 16.95 (*1-86407-037-4*, Pub. by JBCE AT) Morehouse Pub.

Whispers: The Voices of Paranoia. Ronald K. Siegel. LC 93-34558. 1994. 23.00 (*0-517-59239-8*, Crown) Crown Pub Group.

Whispers: The Voices of Paranoia. Ronald K. Siegel. 320p. 1996. pap. 13.00 (*0-684-80285-6*, Touchstone Bks) S&S Trade.

Whispers along the Mission Trail. Gail Faber & Michele Lasagna. (California History Ser.). (Illus.). 331p. (Orig.). 1986. teacher ed., ring bd. 34.95 (*0-936480-05-X*) Magpie Pubns.

Whispers along the Mission Trail. Gail Faber & Michele Lasagna. (California History Ser.). (Illus.). 216p. (Orig.). (J). (gr. 4-8). 1986. student ed. 17.95 (*0-936480-04-1*); student ed., pap. 14.95 (*0-936480-03-3*) Magpie Pubns.

***Whispers & Chants Primarily Inspirational.** Ruth Goldfarb. (Orig.). 1997. pap. write for info. (*1-57553-535-1*) Watermrk Pr.

Whispers & Wonders. Jo Denson. LC 96-13451. 144p. 1996. 14.95 (*1-56554-143-X*) Pelican.

***Whispers at Dusk.** Ed. by Diana Zeiger. Date not set. 69.95 (*1-57553-161-5*) Watermrk Pr.

Whispers at Midnight. Peggy Roberts. 352p. 1994. mass mkt. 4.50 (*0-8217-4529-8*, Zebra Kensgtn) Kensgtn Pub Corp.

Whispers Down the Lane. Beverly Lewis. (Summerhill Secrets Ser.: Bk. 1). 144p. (J). (gr. 6-9). 1995. pap. 5.99 (*1-55661-476-4*) Bethany Hse.

Whispers from Eternity. Paramahansa Yogananda. (Illus.). 240p. 1980. 12.00 (*0-87612-100-8*) Self Realization.

Whispers from Eternity. 9th ed. Paramahansa Yogananda. LC 86-60584. (Illus.). 239p. 1986. 12.00 (*0-87612-103-2*) Self Realization.

Whispers from Eternity. Paramahansa Yogananda. LC 85-71375. 256p. 1978. reprint ed. pap. 18.95 (*0-937134-03-1*) Amrita Found.

Whispers from Eternity: First Version. Paramahansa Yogananda. 1977. 9.00 (*0-87612-102-4*) Self Realization.

Whispers from Heaven. Sarah Hart. 1996. mass mkt. 5.99 (*0-515-11892-3*) Jove Pubns.

Whispers from Heaven: On An Ordinary Day You Can Hear. Dayle Allen-Shockley. LC 94-27730. 128p. 1994. pap. 8.99 (*0-8163-1237-0*) Pacific Pr Pub Assn.

Whispers from Old Genesee & Echoes of the Salmon River. John A. Platt. (Illus.). 184p. 1975. 14.95 (*0-87770-143-1*) Ye Galleon.

Whispers from the Caribbean: I Going Away, I Going Home. Wilfred G. Cartey. (Afro-American Culture & Society Monograph Ser.: Vol. 11). 503p. (C). 1991. 43.00 (*0-934934-35-5*); pap. text ed. 25.95 (*0-934934-36-3*) CAAS Pubns.

Whispers from the Dead. Joan L. Nixon. 192p. (YA). 1991. pap. 3.50 (*0-440-20809-2*, LLL BDD) BDD Bks Young Read.

Whispers from the First Californians: A Story of California's First People. rev. ed. Gail Faber & Michele Lasagna. (California History Ser.). (Illus.). 355p. (J). 1994. teacher ed., ring bd. 34.95 (*0-936480-11-4*) Magpie Pubns.

Whispers from the First Californians: A Story of California's First People. rev. ed. Gail Faber & Michele Lasagna. (California History Ser.). (Illus.). 268p. (J). (gr. 4-8). 1994. student ed. 17.95 (*0-936480-10-6*); student ed., pap. text ed. 14.95 (*0-936480-09-2*) Magpie Pubns.

Whispers from the Grave. Leslie Rule. 272p. (Orig.). (YA). 1995. mass mkt. 5.99 (*0-425-14777-0*) Berkley Pub.

Whispers from the Heart. Alice L. Bowens. (Orig.). 1996. pap. write for info. (*1-57553-177-1*) Watermrk Pr.

Whispers from the Other Shore. Ravi Ravindra. LC 84-40164. 170p. (Orig.). 1984. pap. 6.50 (*0-8356-0589-2*, Quest) Theos Pub Hse.

Whispers from the Sea. Sally Sharp. (Illus.). 80p. Date not set. write for info. (*0-9634910-6-7*) Sharp Sallys Pr.

Whispers from Wildlife. Marcus Bach. LC 90-61424. (Illus.). 108p. 1990. 12.95 (*0-87516-628-8*) DeVorss.

Whispers from Within. 2nd ed. Yog D. Ahuja. 108p. (YA). 1996. reprint ed. pap. 5.95 (*0-9637230-1-4*) Y D Ahuja.

Whispers from Within, Vol. II. Madeleine S. Gary. Ed. by Stephen M. Stigler. 150p. 1986. pap. 7.95 (*0-913459-04-6*) New Writers Guild.

***Whispers in the Dark.** B. J. James. (Desire Ser.: No. 1081). 1997. mass mkt. 3.50 (*0-373-76081-7*, 1-76081-8) Silhouette.

Whispers in the Dark. Heather McCann. (Intrigue Ser.). 1993. mass mkt. 2.99 (*0-373-22236-X*, 1-22236-3) Harlequin Bks.

Whispers in the Dark: The Fiction of Louisa May Alcott. Elizabeth L. Keyser. LC 93-17587. 288p. (C). 1995. pap. text ed. 17.00 (*0-87049-906-8*) U of Tenn Pr.

Whispers in the Darkness. Sam Goldenberg. LC 88-61624. (Illus.). 140p. 1988. 16.95 (*0-88400-130-X*) Shengold.

Whispers in the Moonlight. Lori Wick. LC 96-20622. (Rocky Mountain Memories Ser.: Vol. 2). 1996. pap. 9.99 (*1-56507-483-1*) Harvest Hse.

***Whispers in the Moonlight.** large type ed. Lori Wick. LC 97-16237. (Christian Ser.). 599p. 1997. lib. bdg. 23.95 (*0-7862-1139-3*, Thorndike Lrg Prnt) Thorndike Pr.

Whispers in the Sand. Laflorya Gauthier. 1994. pap. 4.99 (*1-885478-01-1*) Genesis Press.

Whispers in the Valley. Lance Wubbels. (Gentle Hills Ser.: Bk. 2). 304p. 1995. pap. 9.99 (*1-55661-419-5*) Bethany Hse.

Whispers in the Valley. large type ed. Lance Wubbels. (Gentle Hills Ser.: No. 2). 464p. 1995. pap. 15.99 (*1-55661-630-9*) Bethany Hse.

Whispers in the Wind. Katherine Compton. 368p. 1995. mass mkt. 4.99 (*0-380-77455-0*) Avon.

Whispers in the Wind. Debbi Dickinson. 20p. 1995. pap. text ed. 4.00 (*0-9647108-5-4*) D Dickinson.

Whispers in the Wind. Madeleine S. Gary. Ed. by Stephen M. Stigler. 150p. (Orig.). 1986. Set. pap. write for info. (*0-913459-05-4*) New Writers Guild.

***Whispers in the Wind.** Betty R. Headapohl. 158p. (Orig.). 1996. pap. 7.99 (*0-88092-297-4*) Royal Fireworks.

Whispers in the Wind. John Muniz. LC 95-61621. 100p. 1995. pap. text ed. 10.00 (*0-9638455-4-3*) Warwick Hse.

Whispers in the Wind. Dottlee D. Reid. LC 91-68089. 65p. 1992. pap. 5.95 (*1-55523-502-6*) Winston-Derek.

Whispers in the Wind, Vol. I. Madeleine S. Gary. Ed. by Stephen M. Stigler. 150p. (Orig.). 1986. pap. 7.95 (*0-913459-03-8*) New Writers Guild.

Whispers in the Wings. Frank Chipasula. (African Writers Ser.). 112p. (Orig.). (C). 1991. pap. 8.95 (*0-435-91192-9*, 91192) Heinemann.

Whispers in the Woods. Helen R. Myers. (Shadows Ser.). 1994. mass mkt. 3.50 (*0-373-27023-2*, 5-27023-6) Silhouette.

***Whispers in Williamsburg.** 208p. (J). 1997. write for info. (*0-7814-3008-9*, Chariot Bks) Chariot Victor.

Whispers Near Niagara. S. Santhi. 5.00 (*0-89253-731-0*); text ed. 4.00 (*0-89253-732-9*) Ind-US Inc.

***Whispers of Comfort: A Devotional.** Lois A. Roosa. LC 96-69299. 100p. (Orig.). 1996. spiral bd., pap. 9.95 (*0-9653265-0-0*) Sandstone Ent.

***Whispers of Fear.** large type ed. Brenda Castle. (Dales Large Print Ser.). 245p. 1996. pap. 17.99 (*1-85389-668-3*, Dales) Ulverscroft.

Whispers of Generations. Bettye T. Spinner. (Illus.). 32p. (Orig.). 1988. pap. 4.00 (*0-9622614-0-8*) Luke Pr.

Whispers of God: Liturgical Resources for Year B. Lavon Bayler. LC 87-23596. 276p. 1987. pap. 14.95 (*0-8298-0758-6*) Pilgrim OH.

Whispers of His Power. Amy Carmichael. 288p. 1993. pap. 8.95 (*0-87508-317-X*) Chr Lit.

***Whispers of His Word: Food for the Soul.** Dean Bauman. 210p. (Orig.). 1997. pap. 17.77 (*0-614-18959-4*, PO977) Morris Pubng.

***Whispers of Joy.** Garborg's Publishing Staff. 1997. 9.99 (*1-881830-65-9*) Garborgs.

***Whispers of Love.** Clip Art & Belinda A. Landtroop. (Illus.). 24p. 1997. 6.99 (*0-9658553-0-9*) Whispers TN.

Whispers of Love. Shirley Hailstock. 416p. 1994. mass mkt. 4.99 (*0-7860-0055-4*, Pinncle Kensgtn) Kensgtn Pub Corp.

Whispers of Love: Encounters with Deceased Relatives & Friends. Mitch Finley. 180p. 1995. 19.95 (*0-8245-1491-2*) Crossroad NY.

Whispers of Love on Wings of Light. Ruth E. Norman. (Tesla Speaks Ser.: No. 10). (Illus.). 241p. 1975. 17.00 (*0-932642-33-0*); pap. 12.00 (*0-932642-44-6*) Unarius Acad Sci.

Whispers of Madmen: Collected Poems. Matt Fontana & R. G. Bell. 80p. 1995. 10.00 (*0-9646231-0-2*) DMM Intl.

Whispers of Nature. Vijay. (Orig.). pap. 5.75 (*0-89744-009-9*) Auromere.

Whispers of the Angel (Nawa-E-Sarosh) Mirza A. Ghalib. (Illus.). 56p. 1969. 3.00 (*0-88253-384-3*) Ind-US Inc.

Whispers of the Heart. 400p. 1995. 49.95 (*0-9647617-0-X*) Valory-Hetzel.

Whispers of the Heart for the One I Love. Richard Exley. 80p. 1996. 10.99 (*1-56292-287-4*) Honor Bks OK.

***Whispers of the Heart for the One I Love.** Richard Exley. 80p. 1996. 10.99 (*1-57757-200-9*) Trade Life.

Whispers of the Moon: The Life & Work of Scott Cunningham, Philosopher-Magician, Modern-Day Pagan. David Harrington & De Traci Regula. LC 96-62724. (Illus.). 288p. 1996. pap. 15.00 (*1-56718-559-2*) Llewellyn Pubns.

Whispers of the Mountain. Tom Hron. 352p. 1996. pap. 5.99 (*0-451-18794-6*, Sig) NAL-Dutton.

Whispers of the River. Tom Hron. 352p. 1996. pap. 5.99 (*0-451-18780-6*, Sig) NAL-Dutton.

Whispers of the Spirit. Charlotte Campbell. (Orig.). 1996. pap. write for info. (*1-57553-127-5*) Watermrk Pr.

Whispers Shouting Glory. Duane L. Herrmann. 40p. 1989. pap. text ed. 3.00 (*1-879448-02-5*) Buffalo Pr KS.

Whispers under the Wharf. Vincent DiGirolamo. LC 90-331073. 144p. (Orig.). (J). 1990. pap. 8.95 (*0-931832-52-7*) Fithian Pr.

Whistle: Chapter One of a Work-in-Progress. limited ed. James Jones. 1974. 35.00 (*0-89723-017-5*) Bruccoli.

Whistle Down the Valley: One Hundred Years of Green River Railroading. Kurt E. Armbruster. LC 91-61795. (Illus.). 78p. (Orig.). 1991. pap. 10.95 (*0-9629725-3-3*) NW Railway Loco Pres.

Whistle for the Crows. large type ed. Dorothy Eden. 1977. 15.95 (*0-7089-0023-2*) Ulverscroft.

Whistle for Willie. Ezra Jack Keats. LC 64-13595. (Illus.). (J). (ps-1). 1977. pap. 4.99 (*0-14-050202-5*, Puffin) Puffin Bks.

Whistle for Willie. Ezra Jack Keats. (Illus.). (J). (ps-1). 1964. pap. 14.99 (*0-670-76240-7*) Viking Child Bks.

Whistle for Willie: A Study Guide. Garrett Christopher. Ed. by Joyce Friedland & Rikki Kessler. (Little Novel-Ties Ser.). (J). (gr. k-3). 1991. pap. text ed. 14.95 (*0-88122-596-7*) Lrn Links.

***Whistle in the Dark.** large type ed. Elizabeth Elgin. LC 96-38770. 1997. 20.95 (*0-7862-0921-6*, Thorndike Lrg Prnt) Thorndike Pr.

Whistle Me Home. Barbara Wersba. (J). 1997. 14.95 (*0-8050-4850-2*) H Holt & Co.

Whistle over the Mountain: Timber, Track & Trails in the Tennessee Smokies. Ronald G. Schmidt & William S. Hooks. LC 94-76724. (Illus.). 192p. (Orig.). 1994. pap. 16.95 (*0-9641734-0-9*) Graphicom Pr.

Whistle Punk. Alice Ross et al. LC 93-14187. (Chaparral Books for Young Readers). 142p. (J). (gr. 5-8). 1994. pap. 9.95 (*0-87565-123-2*) Tex Christian.

***Whistle Stop.** Lisa Higdon. 304p. 1997. mass mkt. 5.99 (*0-515-12085-5*) Jove Pubns.

Whistle-Stop Puppet Plays. Taffy Jones. LC 82-23931. (Illus.). 142p. (Orig.). 1983. pap. 18.95 (*0-89950-075-7*) McFarland & Co.

Whistle-Stop West. Arleta Richardson. LC 92-46260. (Orphan Journey Ser.: Bk. 2). 144p. (J). 1993. pap. 4.99 (*0-7814-0922-5*, Chariot Bks) Chariot Victor.

Whistle Stops: Adventures in Public Life. Wilson W. Wyatt, Sr. LC 85-15066. (Illus.). 248p. 1985. 27.00 (*0-8131-1537-X*) U Pr of Ky.

Whistle up the Chimney. Nancy Hunt. (J). (ps-3). 1994. pap. 7.00 (*0-207-17606-X*, Pub. by Angus & Robertson AT) HarpC.

***Whistle up the Dead.** Janice Steinberg. 256p. 1997. mass mkt. 5.99 (*0-425-16037-8*, Prime Crime) Berkley Pub.

Whistleblower Litigation Handbook: Environmental, Health & Safety Claims. Stephen M. Kohn. LC 91-22751. (Employment Law Library). 442p. 1991. text ed. 135.00 (*0-471-55330-1*) Wiley.

Whistleblower Litigation Handbook: Environmental, Healthy & Safety Claims. S. M. 104p. 1994. suppl. ed., pap. text ed. 48.00 (*0-471-11173-2*) Wiley.

Whistleblower Protection: Reasons for Whistleblower Complainants' Dissatisfaction Need to Be Explored. (Illus.). 44p. (Orig.). (C). 1995. pap. text ed. 25.00 (*0-7881-2375-0*) DIANE Pub.

Whistleblowing: Managing Dissent in the Workplace. Frederick A. Elliston et al. LC 85-13294. 176p. 1985. text ed. 49.95 (*0-275-90091-6*, C0091, Praeger Pubs) Greenwood.

Whistleblowing: Subversion of Corporate Citizenship? Gerald Vinten. 1994. text ed. 39.95 (*0-312-12422-8*) St Martin.

Whistleblowing: Subversion or Corporate Citizenship? Ed. by Gerald Vinten. 224p. 1994. pap. 29.50 (*1-85396-238-4*, Pub. by Paul Chapman UK) Taylor & Francis.

Whistleblowing: The Law of Retaliatory Discharge. Daniel P. Westman. LC 90-23947. 348p. 1991. reprint ed. pap. 99.20 (*0-608-00712-9*, 2061485) Bks Demand.

Whistleblowing in the Federal Government: An Update. (Illus.). 52p. (Orig.). (C). 1994. pap. text ed. 25.00 (*0-7881-0645-7*) DIANE Pub.

Whistleblowing in the Health Service: Accountability, Law & Professional Practice. Ed. by Geoffrey Hunt. 170p. 1995. pap. 32.95 (*0-340-59234-6*, Pub. by E Arnold UK) Routledge Chapman & Hall.

Whistleblowing in the Health Service: Accountability, Law & Professional Practice. Ed. by Geoffrey Hunt. 192p. 1994. pap. text ed. 32.95 (*1-56593-502-0*, 1162) Singular Publishing.

Whistleblowing Research: Methodological & Moral Issues. Frederick A. Elliston et al. LC 84-13294. 192p. 1985. text ed. 49.95 (*0-275-90092-4*, C0092, Praeger Pubs) Greenwood.

Whistlecraft. John H. Frere. LC 90-37030. 138p. 1992. reprint ed. 43.00 (*1-85477-122-1*, Pub. by Woodstock Bks UK) Cassell.

***Whistled Like a Bird: The Untold Story of Dorothy Putnam, George Putnam & Amelia Earhart.** Sally P. Chapman. LC 97-9456. 224p. 1997. 22.00 (*0-446-52055-1*) Warner Bks.

***Whistlejacket.** Jack Hawkes. 208p. 1997. reprint ed. pap. 12.95 (*1-56478-176-3*) Dalkey Arch.

Whistler. Pierre Cabanne. (CAL Art Ser.). 1985. 14.95 (*0-517-55726-6*, Crown) Crown Pub Group.

Whistler. Pierre Cabanne. (Illus.). 1995. pap. 12.00 (*0-517-88411-9*) Random.

Whistler. Frances Spalding. (Color Library). (Illus.). 128p. (C). 1994. pap. 14.95 (*0-7148-3186-7*, Pub. by Phaidon Press UK) Chronicle Bks.

Whistler. John Walker. (Library of American Art). (Illus.). 160p. 1987. 45.00 (*0-8109-1786-6*) Abrams.

Whistler: Masterworks. Robin Spencer. 1990. 15.99 (*0-517-01506-4*) Random Hse Value.

Whistler: Themes & Variations. Betsy Fryberger. LC 77-28083. (Illus.). 1978. pap. 6.50 (*0-937031-08-9*) Stanford Art.

Whistler - the Etched Work: Catalogue Raisonne. rev. ed. Edward G. Kennedy. LC 75-27621. (Illus.). 352p. 1978. 95.00 (*0-915346-06-0*) A Wofsy Fine Arts.

Whistler & Montesquiou: The Butterfly & the Bat. Edgar Munhall. (Illus.). Date not set. 45.00 (*0-615-00826-7*) Frick Collection.

Whistler & Montesquiou: The Butterfly & the Bat. Edgar Munhall. (Illus.). 176p. 1996. 45.00 (*2-08-013577-5*, Pub. by Flammarion FR) Abbeville Pr.

***Whistler & the Sea to Sky Country.** Constance Brissenden. 1995. pap. text ed. 16.95 (*1-55153-029-5*, Pub. by Paperblank Bk CN) Consort Bk Sales.

Whistler at the Plough: Containing Travels, Statistics & Descriptions of Scenery & Agricultural Customs in Most Parts of England. Alexander Somerville. LC 89-15532. xxxi, 432p. 1989. reprint ed. lib. bdg. 49.50 (*0-678-08082-8*) Kelley.

Whistler in His Time. Anne Koval. (Illus.). 80p. 1995. pap. 19.95 (*1-85437-146-0*) U of Wash Pr.

Whistler Landscapes & Seascapes. Donald Holden. (Great Artists Ser.). (Illus.). 88p. 1984. pap. 16.95 (*0-8230-5726-7*, Watsn-Guptill) Watsn-Guptill.

Whistler-Mode Waves in a Hot Plasma. Sergei Sazhin. (Atmospheric & Space Science Ser.: No. 7). (Illus.). 300p. (C). 1993. text ed. 80.00 (*0-521-40165-8*) Cambridge U Pr.

Whistler on Art: Selected Letters & Writings, 1849-1903, of James McNeill Whistler. Ed. & Intro. by Nigel Thorp. (Illus.). 192p. 1994. pap. 15.95 (*1-56098-508-9*) Smithsonian.

***Whistler Outdoor Guide.** Jack Christie. 224p. 1997. pap. 12.95 (*1-55054-478-0*) Orca Bk Pubs.

Whistler Peacock Room. rev. ed. Susan Hobbs. LC 80-20516. (Illus.). 1980. pap. 2.00 (*0-934686-34-3*) Freer.

Whistlers & Related Ionospheric Phenomena. Robert A. Helliwell. LC 63-14128. (Illus.). 359p. reprint ed. pap. 102.40 (*0-7837-4068-9*, 2044024) Bks Demand.

Whistler's London: A Bridge Through Time. Shelia Foley & J. M. Pellerin. (Illus.). 32p. (Orig.). 1995. pap. 7.00 (*0-9646709-0-9*) Pellerin.

Whistler's Mother's Cook Book. 2nd ed. Margaret F. MacDonald. LC 94-67328. (Illus.). 152p. 1995. pap. 10.95 (*0-87654-108-2*) Pomegranate Calif.

Whistler's Pocket Companion. Dona Gilliam & Mizzy McCaskill. (Orig.). 1993. 9.95 (*1-56222-008-X*, 93820); audio 9.98 (*1-56222-604-5*, 93820C) Mel Bay.

***Whistler's Pocket Companion.** Dona Gilliam & Mizzy McCaskill. (Orig.). 1993. pap. 18.95 incl. audio (*0-7866-0941-9*, 93820P) Mel Bay.

Whistles Across the Land: A Love for Affair with Trains. Richard Steinheimer. 96p. 1994. pap. 19.95 (*1-55912-505-5*) CEDCO Pub.

***Whistles Echo on the Bay.** Edwin L. Dunbaugh. Ed. by Linda Eppich & Marta V. Martinez. (Illus.). 20p. (Orig.). 1996. 5.00 (*0-932840-12-4*) RI Hist Soc.

Whistles of Silver, & Other Stories. Helen Eden. LC 72-152939. (Short Story Index Reprint Ser.). (Illus.). 1977. reprint ed. 18.95 (*0-8369-3798-8*) Ayer.

Whistley. Yvonne Childs. LC 95-90334. 304p. (Orig.). 1996. pap. 10.00 (*1-56002-547-6*) Aegina Pr.

Whistlin' Dixie: A Dictionary of Southern Expressions. Robert Hendrickson. (Dictionary of American Regionalisms Ser.). 288p. 1992. 24.95 (*0-8160-2110-4*) Facts on File.

Whistlin' Dixie: A Tale of the South. Karoleigh K. Nitchman. 191p. (Orig.). 1993. pap. 12.95 (*1-883962-01-3*) Kristalex Pr.

Whistling & Other Stories. Myra Goldberg. LC 92-43938. 192p. 1993. 19.95 (*0-944072-26-7*) Zoland Bks.

Whistling & Other Stories. Myra Goldberg. LC 92-43938. 192p. 1994. pap. 12.95 (*0-944072-27-5*) Zoland Bks.

Whistling at a Deaf Horse. Calvin Bowden. 1990. 16.95 (*1-878096-04-4*) Best E TX Pubs.

***Whistling Bird: Women Writers from the Caribbean.** Ed. by Pierrette Frickey & Elaine Campbell. 1997. 36.50 (*0-614-27329-3*) Lynne Rienner.

***Whistling Bird: Women Writers from the Caribbean.** Ed. by Pierrette Frickey & Elaine Campbell. 1997. pap. 16.95 (*0-614-27330-7*) Lynne Rienner.

Whistling Bombs & Bumpy Trains: The Life-Story of Anna Nixon. Betty M. Hockett. LC 89-84572. (Life-Story Mission Ser.). (Illus.). 80p. (Orig.). (J). (gr. 3-6). 1989. pap. 4.95 (*0-943701-15-5*) George Fox Pr.

Whistling Death: The Test Pilot's Story of the F4U Corsair. Bonne T. Guyton. (Illus.). 272p. 1991. 25.00 (*0-517-57526-4*, Orion Bks) Crown Pub Group.

Whistling Death: The Test Pilot's Story of the F4U Corsair. Boone T. Guyton. LC 90-7529. (Illus.). 288p. 1995. 25.00 (*0-88740-732-3*) Schiffer.

Whistlin' Dixie. Robert Hendrickson. 288p. 1995. pap. 12.00 (*0-671-52291-4*, PB Trade Paper) PB.

Whistling Dixie. Marcia K. Vaughan. LC 91-45831. (Illus.). 32p. (J). (ps-3). 1995. lib. bdg. 14.89 (*0-06-021029-X*, HarpT) HarpC.

Whistling Dixie. Marcia K. Vaughan. LC 91-45831. (Illus.). 32p. (J). (ps-3). 1995. 15.00 (*0-06-021030-3*, HarpT) HarpC.

Whistling Dixie: Dispatches from the South. John S. Reed. 1992. pap. 9.95 (*0-15-696174-1*, Harvest Bks) HarBrace.

Whistling Dixie: Dispatches from the South. John S. Reed. 200p. 1990. 29.95 (*0-8262-0758-8*) U of Mo Pr.

Whistling-Ducks: Zoogeography, Ecology, Anatomy. Eric G. Bolen & Michael K. Rylander. (Special Publications: No. 20). (Illus.). 67p. 1983. pap. 12.00 (*0-89672-111-6*) Tex Tech Univ Pr.

Whistling Hunters: Field Studies of the Asiatic Wild Dog (Cuon Alpinus) Michael W. Fox. LC 84-2442. (SUNY Series on Animal Behavior). 150p. 1985. text ed. 64.50 (*0-87395-842-X*); pap. text ed. 21.95 (*0-87395-843-8*) State U NY Pr.

Whistling in the Dark. Agnes Garrett. 1992. 19.95 (*0-15-191313-7*) HarBrace.

Whistling in the Dark: An ABC Theologized. Frederick Buechner. LC 87-45690. 128p. 1993. reprint ed. pap. 11.00 (*0-06-061140-5*) Harper SF.

Whistling in the Dark: The Story of Fred Lowery, the Blind Whistler. Fred Lowery. LC 83-4085. (Illus.). 416p. 1983. 25.00 (*0-88289-298-3*) Pelican.

Whistling Jigs to the Moon: Tales of Irish & Scottish Pipers - Folklore about Bagpipers. Ed. by Joanne Asala. 144p. (Orig.). 1993. pap. 9.95 (*1-880954-02-8*) Kalevala Bks.

W

Whistling Song. Stephen Beachy. 416p. 1992. pap. 9.95 (*0-393-30949-5*) Norton.
Whistling Stallion. Stephen Holt. 1976. 21.95 (*0-8488-0134-2*) Amereon Ltd.
Whistling the Morning in New Poems by Lillian Morrison: New Poems. Lillian Morrison. LC 91-91409. (Illus.). 40p. (J). 1992. lib. bdg. 16.95 (*1-56397-035-X*, Wordsong) Boyds Mills Pr.
Whistling Thorn: An Anthology of South Asian Canadian Fiction. Ed. by Suwanda Sugunasiri. 220p. 1995. lib. bdg. 39.00 (*0-8095-4823-2*) Borgo Pr.
Whistling Thorn: An Anthology of South Asian Canadian Fiction. Ed. by Suwanda Sugunasiri. 220p. 1994. pap. 14.95 (*0-88962-547-6*) Mosaic.
Whistling Thorns. Helen Cowcher. LC 92-39533. (J). (gr. 6 up). 1993. 14.95 (*0-590-47299-2*) Scholastic Inc.
Whistling Toilets. Randy Powell. LC 96-10475. 256p. (YA). (gr. 7 up). 1996. 17.00 (*0-374-38381-2*) FS&G.
Whistling Wings: Dove Chronicles. Elliot McClure. 1991. 9.95 (*0-940168-19-7*) Boxwood.
Whistling Wings: The Beauty of Ducks in Flight. Stephen Kirkpatrick. LC 89-50221. (Illus.). 112p. (C). 1989. 38.00 (*0-9619353-3-2*) Thy Marvelous Works.
Whistling Wings: The Beauty of Ducks in Flight. deluxe ed. Stephen Kirkpatrick. LC 89-50221. (Illus.). 112p. (C). 1989. 85.00 (*0-9619353-4-0*) Thy Marvelous Works.
Whistling with Olives. Robin Hansen. (Illus.). 128p. (Orig.). 1996. pap. 7.95 (*0-89815-797-8*) Ten Speed Pr.
Whistling Woman. Louise Shivers. LC 93-79654. 160p. 1993. 15.00 (*1-56352-085-0*) Longstreet Pr Inc.
Whistling Woman Is up to No Good: Finding Your Wild Woman. Laurel King. LC 93-7867. 240p. 1995. pap. 12.95 (*0-89087-696-7*) Celestial Arts.
Whistling Women: Poems. Denise Harvey. (Illus.). 30p. (C). 1995. reprint ed. pap. 15.00 (*0-934172-41-2*) WIM Pubns.
Whitaker's Alamack, 1996. 96th ed. 1279p. 1995. 80.00 (*0-85021-254-5*, Pub. by Whitaker UK) Gale.
***Whitaker's Almanac 1981.** 113th ed. 1980. 46.00 (*0-8103-0947-5*, 00001321, Gale Res Intl) Gale.
***Whitaker's Almanac 1982.** 114th ed. 1982. 46.00 (*0-8103-0967-X*, 00001245, Gale Res Intl) Gale.
***Whitaker's Almanac 1984.** 116th ed. 1983. 46.00 (*0-8103-0672-7*, 00003103, Gale Res Intl) Gale.
Whitaker's Almanack, 1983. 83th ed. (Illus.). 1220p. 1982. 46.00 (*0-8103-0671-9*) Gale.
Whitaker's Almanack 1985. 85th ed. 1220p. 1985. 50.00 (*0-8103-0673-5*) Gale.
Whitaker's Almanack 1986. 86th ed. 1986. 52.00 (*0-85021-161-1*) Gale.
Whitaker's Almanack, 1988. 88th ed. 1987. 57.00 (*0-85021-178-6*) Gale.
Whitaker's Almanack, 1989. 89th ed. 1236p. 1988. 57.00 (*0-85021-188-3*, 70813-02604) Gale.
Whitaker's Almanack, 1990. 90th ed. 1240p. 1989. 60.00 (*0-85021-197-2*, Pub. by Whitaker UK) Gale.
Whitaker's Almanack 1991. 91th ed. 1990. 65.00 (*0-85021-205-7*, Pub. by Whitaker UK) Gale.
Whitaker's Almanack 1992. 2nd ed. 1995. 18.95 (*0-8103-9887-7*, Pub. by Whitaker UK) Gale.
Whitaker's Almanack, 1992. 92th ed. 1991. 70.00 (*0-85021-220-0*, 070845, Pub. by Whitaker UK) Gale.
Whitaker's Almanack 1993. 93th ed. 1992. 72.00 (*0-85021-231-6*, 070846, Pub. by Whitaker UK) Gale.
Whitaker's Almanack 1994. 94th ed. 1200p. 1993. 75.00 (*0-85021-238-3*) Gale.
Whitaker's Almanack 1995. 95th ed. 1280p. 1994. 78.00 (*0-85021-245-6*) Gale.
Whitaker's Almanack 1995. 127th ed. 1280p. 1994. lib. bdg. 110.00 (*0-85021-246-4*) Gale.
***Whitaker's Almanack 1997.** 129th ed. 1300p. 1996. 90.00 (*0-85021-260-X*, GML00197-110556, Pub. by Whitaker UK) Gale.
Whitaker's Books in Print 1994 (British), 4 vols. 10000p. 1994. Set. 450.00 (*0-85021-241-3*) Bowker.

***Whitaker's Books in Print 1997 (British), 5 vols. Whitaker, J. & Sons Ltd. Staff. 12800p. 1997. 640.00 (*0-85021-263-4*, Pub. by J Whitaker UK) Bowker.**
The latest edition of this one-of-a-kind bibliographic guide will help you identify & order any of the more than 800,000 titles available from some 30,000 publishers & distributors in the United Kingdom. Books are listed in one alphabetical sequence of authors, titles, & subjects. A Publishers ISBN Prefix Listing, a Directory of Publishers, & a Book Trade Bibliography are also included. ***Publisher Provided Annotation.***

Whitaker's British Books in Print 1996. 1996. 500.00 (*0-85021-257-X*) Bowker-Saur.
Whitcomb Family in America, a Biographical Genealogy. C. Whitcomb. (Illus.). 621p. 1989. reprint ed. pap. 93.00 (*0-8328-1247-1*); reprint ed. lib. bdg. 101.00 (*0-8328-1246-3*) Higginson Bk Co.
White. Richard Dyer. LC 96-11485. 284p. 1997. pap. write for info. (*0-415-09537-9*) Routledge.
White. Richard Dyer. LC 96-11485. 284p. (C). 1997. text ed. write for info. (*0-415-09536-0*) Routledge.
***White, 2 vols.** Mary E. Weems. LC 96-38232. (Wick Poetry Chapbook Ser.: No. 2). 1997. pap. 4.75 (*0-87338-571-3*) Kent St U Pr.
White: Descendants of Thomas White, Sudbury, MA, 1638. E. W. Ford. (Illus.). 93p. 1991. reprint ed. pap. 17.00 (*0-8328-1755-4*); reprint ed. lib. bdg. 27.00 (*0-8328-1754-6*) Higginson Bk Co.
***White: I&T Shop Manual - Models 2-30, 2-35.** (Illus.). Date not set. reprint ed. pap. 22.95 (*0-87288-440-6*, W-3) Intertec Pub.
***White: I&T Shop Manual - White Collection Models 2-70, 2-85, 2-105, 2-150 - Models 2-135, 2-155 - 2-30, 2-35 - Models 45, 2-62 - Models 2-55, 2-65, 2-75.** (Illus.). Date not set. reprint ed. pap. 29.95 (*0-87288-488-0*, W-201) Intertec Pub.
White: Irish Law of Damages for Personal Injuries & Death, 2 vols. 2nd ed. John P. White. 1989. Set. 219.00 (*1-85475-026-7*) MICHIE.
White: Norman White, His Ancestors & Descendants. Erskine N. White. (Illus.). 155p. 1993. reprint ed. pap. 25.00 (*0-8328-2977-3*); reprint ed. lib. bdg. 35.00 (*0-8328-2976-5*) Higginson Bk Co.
White: The White Genealogy: A History of the Descendants of Matthew & Elizabeth (Given) White of Co. Tyrone, Ireland & Albany, N.Y. Vol. I: The Line of Joseph & Elizabeth (White) Strain. Harold P. White, Jr. (Illus.). 236p. 1991. reprint ed. pap. 35.00 (*0-8328-1958-1*) Higginson Bk Co.
White: The White Genealogy: A History of the Descendants of Matthew & Elizabeth (Given) White of Co. Tyrone, Ireland & Albany, N.Y. Vol. I: The Line of Joseph & Elizabeth (White) Strain. Harold P White, Jr. (Illus.). 236p. 1991. reprint ed. lib. bdg. 45.00 (*0-8328-1957-3*) Higginson Bk Co.
White Abacus. Damien Broderick. LC 96-23764. 1997. 23.00 (*0-380-97476-2*); pap. 12.50 (*0-380-78559-5*) Avon.
White Acre vs. Black Acre. William M. Burwell. LC 72-83941. (Black Heritage Library Collection). 1977. 15.95 (*0-8369-8514-1*) Ayer.
***White African: An Early Autobiography.** Louis S. Leakey. LC 67-7042. (Illus.). 320p. reprint ed. pap. 91.20 (*0-608-05349-X*, 2065054) Bks Demand.
White Album. Joan Didion. 224p. 1990. pap. 10.00 (*0-374-52221-9*, Noonday) FS&G.
White Album. Floyd Domino. 1989. 10.95 (*0-938971-29-8*) JTG Nashville.
White Americans Who Cared. John Favors & Kathryne Favors. (Illus.). 28p. 1973. pap. text ed. 4.95 (*0-614-03623-2*) Jonka Enter.
White Americans Who Cared. John Favors & Kathryne Favors. 26p. (J). (gr. 4 up). 1973. reprint ed. 4.95 (*1-878794-01-9*) Jonka Enter.
White & Black in East Africa. Hermann Norden. LC 74-15074. reprint ed. 49.50 (*0-404-12124-1*) AMS Pr.
White & Black Under the Old Regime. Victoria V. Clayton. LC 70-119928. (Select Bibliographies Reprint Ser.). 1977. 25.95 (*0-8369-5371-1*) Ayer.
White & Coloured: The Behavior of the British People Towards Coloured Immigrants. Michael P. Banton. LC 76-43335. 223p. 1977. reprint ed. text ed. 55.00 (*0-8371-9290-0*, BAWAC, Greenwood Pr) Greenwood.
White Angel. Libby Elis. (Critic's Choice Paperbacks Ser.). 1988. pap. 2.95 (*0-318-37655-5*, Univ Books) Carol Pub Group.
White Angel. Gary Gottesfeld. 1995. mass mkt. 5.99 (*0-449-14879-3*, GM) Fawcett.
White Apache. Frank Burleson. 1996. mass mkt. 5.99 (*0-451-18729-6*) NAL-Dutton.
White Apache's Woman. Shirl Henke. 448p. (Orig.). 1993. mass mkt. pap. text ed. 4.99 (*0-8439-3498-0*) Dorchester Pub Co.
White Apos: American Governors on the Cordillera Central. Frank L. Jenista. (Illus.). 321p. (Orig.). 1987. pap. 17.50 (*971-10-0318-X*, Pub. by New Day Pub PH) Cellar.
White April. Harold Vinal. LC 78-144718. (Yale Series of Younger Poets: No. 11). reprint ed. 18.00 (*0-404-53811-8*) AMS Pr.
***White Aprons: Near Impeachment of Andy Jackson, Cmdr.** Grubbs. Ed. & Photos by Abell. (Illus.). 60p. 1997. 40.00 (*0-614-31008-3*) Jones.
***White Aprons: Near Impeachment of Andy Jackson, Cmdr.** Grubbs. Ed. & Photos by Abell. (Illus.). 60p. 1997. pap. 20.00 (*0-614-31009-1*) Jones.
***White Aprons: Near Impeachment of Andy Jackson, Cmdr.** Grubbs. Ed. & Photos by Abell. (Illus.). 60p. 1997. lib. bdg. 50.00 (*0-614-31010-5*) Jones.
White Archer. Houghton Mifflin Company Staff. (Literature Experience 1993 Ser.). (J). (gr. 7). 1992. pap. 9.84 (*0-395-61853-3*) HM.
White Armies' Orders & Badges in the Civil War 1917-1922. P. Pashkov. Tr. by G. N. Budzilovich & R. Zander from RUS. (Illus.). vi, 31p. (Orig.). 1983. pap. 8.50 (*0-912671-04-1*) Russian Numis.
White Army. Anton Denikin. 1973. lib. bdg. 59.95 (*0-8490-1290-2*) Gordon Pr.
White Attitudes Toward Black People. Angus Campbell. LC 74-161548. 177p. 1971. pap. 8.00 (*0-87944-006-6*) Inst Soc Res.
White Awareness: A Handbook for Anti-Racism Training. Judy H. Katz. LC 77-18610. 1978. pap. 12.95 (*0-8061-1466-5*) U of Okla Pr.
White Badge: A Novel of Korea. Ahn Junghyo. LC 88-38506. 337p. 1993. pap. 13.00 (*1-56947-004-9*) Soho Press.
White Banners. Lloyd C. Douglas. 1990. reprint ed. lib. bdg. 23.95 (*0-89968-502-1*) Buccaneer Bks.
White Bead Ceremony. Sherrin Watkins. LC 93-50735. (Greyfeather Ser.). (Illus.). 40p. (J). (gr. 3-6). 1995. 16.95 (*0-933031-92-0*) Coun Oak Bks.
***White Bead Ceremony.** Sherrin Watkins. (Illus.). 40p. (J). (gr. 1-3). 1997. pap. 9.95 (*1-57178-056-4*) Coun Oak Bks.
White Bean Lama. Sid Hite. 1996. 15.95 (*0-8050-5054-X*, Bks Young Read) H Holt & Co.
White Bear. Daniel Besnehard. Tr. by Stephen J. Vogel from FRE. 78p. (Orig.). 1992. pap. 7.95 (*0-913745-35-9*) Ubu Repertory.
White Bear. deluxe limited ed. William I. Yeagy, Sr. Ed. by Rodney L. Cron. 403p. (Orig.). 1991. pap. 20.00 (*1-880159-05-8*) Crossroads Pubns.
White Bear: Robert Dudley, the Elizabethan Earl of Leicester. Alan Haynes. LC 87-60974. (Illus.). 240p. 8700. 40.00 (*0-7206-0672-1*, Pub. by P Owen Ltd UK) Dufour.
White Bear, Ice Bear. Joanne Ryder. LC 87-36781. (Just for a Day Book). (Illus.). 32p. (J). (gr. k-3). 1989. 16.00 (*0-688-07174-0*, Morrow Junior) Morrow.
White Bear, Ice Bear. Joanne Ryder. Ed. by Amy Cohn. LC 87-36781. (Illus.). 32p. (J). (gr. k-3). 1994. reprint ed. pap. 4.95 (*0-688-13111-5*, Morrow Junior) Morrow.
White Bears & Other Unwanted Thoughts: Suppression, Obsession & the Psychology of Mental Control. Daniel M. Wegner. 207p. 1994. pap. 16.95 (*0-89862-223-9*) Guilford Pubns.
***White Bear's Woman.** Candace McCarthy. 352p. 1998. mass mkt. 4.99 (*0-8217-5823-3*, Zebra Kensgtn) Kensgtn Pub Corp.
White Bicycle. Rob Lewis. LC 88-45092. (Illus.). 32p. (J). (ps up). 1988. 12.00 (*0-374-38384-7*) FS&G.
White Bird. Clyde R. Bulla. LC 89-70231. (Stepping Stone Bks.). (Illus.). 64p. (J). (gr. 2-4). 1990. pap. 3.99 (*0-679-80662-8*); lib. bdg. 6.99 (*0-679-90662-2*) Random Bks Yng Read.
White Bird. large type ed. Lauran Paine. LC 96-43958. (Five Star Ser.). 219p. 1997. 17.95 (*0-7862-0735-3*, Five Star) Mac Lib Ref.
White Bird. large type ed. Paino. Date not set. 20.00 (*0-7862-0758-2*, Thorndk Lrg Prnt) Thorndike Pr.
White Bird Flying. Bess S. Aldrich. LC 87-30057. ii, 222p. 1988. pap. 9.95 (*0-8032-5915-8*, Bison Books) U of Nebr Pr.
White Bird of Tao. Manly P. Hall. pap. 6.95 (*0-89314-371-5*) Philos Res.
***White Biting Dog.** Judith Thompson. LC 84-12939. 1997. pap. text ed. 9.95 (*0-88754-369-3*, Pub. by Playwrights CN Pr CN) Theatre Comm.
***White Blackbird.** Honor Moore. 1997. pap. 14.95 (*0-14-024920-6*) Viking Penguin.
White Blackbird: A Granddaughter's Life of the Painter Margarett Sargent. Honor Moore. LC 95-23912. (Illus.). 384p. 1996. pap. 29.95 (*0-670-80563-7*, Viking) Viking Penguin.
White Blood Cells. U. Bagge & G. V. Born. 1982. lib. bdg. 93.00 (*90-247-2681-6*) Kluwer Ac.
White Bolts Black Locks: Participation in the Inner City. David N. Thomas. (C). 1986. 65.00 (*0-685-28597-9*, Pub. by Natl Inst Soc Work) St Mut.
White Bones of the Year Are Scattered among Jonquils. Lee Perron. (Illus.). 52p. 1988. pap. 35.00 (*0-9620634-0-1*) Sun Moon Bear Pr.
White Bones of Truth. 2nd ed. Cris Newport. 200p. (Orig.). 1996. pap. 10.95 (*1-886383-15-4*) Pride OH.
White Book. Abbeville Press. 1994. 10.95 (*1-55859-916-9*) Abbeville Pr.
White Book: Cerithous. Michael T. Bucci & Cerithous. (Illus.). 100p. 1991. pap. 12.50 (*0-9630824-5-0*) M T Grp.
White Book Mabinogion. Ed. by John G. Evans. LC 78-72670. (Series of Old Welsh Texts: Vol. 7). reprint ed. 52.50 (*0-404-60587-7*) AMS Pr.
White Book of Ski Areas. 18th ed. Robert Enzel. 360p. 1993. pap. 15.95 (*0-931636-18-3*) Inter-Ski.
White Book of Ski Areas. 20th ed. Robert Enzel. 360p. 1995. pap. 18.95 (*0-931636-20-5*) Inter-Ski.
***White Book of Ski Areas: U. S. & Canada.** 22th rev. ed. Photos by Fred McKinney. (Illus.). 360p. 1997. pap. 18.95 (*0-614-30204-8*) Inter-Ski.
White Book of Ski Areas: U. S. & Canada 1996-97. 21th rev. ed. Ed. by R. Enzel. (Illus.). 360p. 1996. pap. 18.95 (*0-931636-21-3*) Inter-Ski.
***White Book of Ski Areas Vol. 22: U. S. & Canada.** Ed. by R. Enzel. Date not set. pap. 21.95 (*0-931636-22-1*) Inter-Ski.
White Book of Ski Areas, 1980-81. 5th ed. 448p. 1980. 8.95 (*0-528-84111-4*) Inter-Ski.
White Book of Ski Areas, 1981-82. 6th ed. 448p. 1981. 9.95 (*0-931636-06-X*) Inter-Ski.
White Book of Ski Areas, 1982-83. 7th ed. 448p. 1982. 9.95 (*0-931636-03-5*) Inter-Ski.
White Book of Ski Areas, 1983-84. 8th ed. 416p. 1983. 10.95 (*0-931636-08-6*) Inter-Ski.
White Book of Ski Areas, 1984-85. 9th ed. Ed. by Robert G. Enzel. 430p. 1984. 10.95 (*0-931636-09-4*) Inter-Ski.
White Book of Ski Areas, 1985-86. 10th ed. Ed. by Robert G. Enzel. 450p. 1985. 12.95 (*0-931636-10-8*) Inter-Ski.
White Book of Ski Areas, 1986-87. 11th ed. 416p. 1986. 12.95 (*0-931636-11-6*) Inter-Ski.
White Book of Ski Areas, 1994-95. 19th ed. 360p. 1994. pap. text ed. 16.95 (*0-931636-19-1*) Inter-Ski.
"White Book" on the 1992 General Election in Indonesia: Body for the Protection of the People's Political Rights Facing the 1992 General Election (BPHPR) Tr. by Dwight Y. King from IND. (Indonesia Project Ser.: No. 73). 70p. (Orig.). (C). 1994. pap. 10.00 (*0-87763-039-9*, CMIP-73) Cornell Mod Indo.
White Boy Papers. Paul Weinman. Ed. by Chris Winkler. (Illus.). 10p. 1989. pap. write for info. (*0-929611-08-X*) Plutonium Pr.
White Boy Shuffle. Paul Beatty. LC 96-1994. 223p. 1996. 19.95 (*0-395-74280-3*) HM.
***White Boy Shuffle.** Paul Beatty. 1997. pap. 10.00 (*0-8050-5351-4*) H Holt & Co.
White Boy Singin' the Blues: The Black Roots of White Rock. rev. ed. Michael Bane. (Illus.). 286p. 1992. reprint ed. pap. 12.95 (*0-306-80479-4*) Da Capo.
White-Boy, the Proud Horse. large type ed. William O. Beazley. (Illus.). 44p. (J). (gr. k-5). 1993. reprint ed. spiral bd., pap. 7.95 (*1-884758-05-3*) W O Beazley.
White Boys & River Girls. Paula K. Gover. 1996. pap. 11.00 (*0-684-82518-X*) S&S Trade.
White Boys & River Girls: Stories. Paula Gover. LC 94-40901. 238p. 1995. 17.95 (*1-56512-049-3*) Algonquin Bks.
***White Bread Competition.** JoAnn Y. Hernandez. LC 97-22159. (J). 1997. pap. write for info. (*1-55885-210-7*, Pinata Bks) Arte Publico.
White Brothers: Jack, Jules & Sam White. Jack White et al. Ed. by David N. Bruskin. LC 90-30123. (Directors Guild of American Oral History Ser.: No. 10). (Illus.). 531p. 1990. 49.50 (*0-8108-2314-4*) Scarecrow.
White Bucks & Black-Eyed Peas: Coming of Age Black in White America. Marcus Mabry. 303p. 1995. 23.00 (*0-684-19669-7*) S&S Trade.
White Buddhist: The Asian Odyssey of Henry Steel Olcott. Stephen Prothero. LC 95-22092. (Religion in North America Ser.). 256p. 1996. 35.00 (*0-253-33014-9*) Ind U Pr.
White Buffalo Poems. Laura M. Larbig. Ed. by Evelyn Sharenov. 24p. (Orig.). 1994. pap. 5.50 (*0-9627791-4-8*) Willamette Bks OR.
White Buffalo Woman. Christine Crowl. (American Heritage Ser.). (Illus.). 18p. (Orig.). (YA). (gr. 6 up). 1990. pap. 3.95 (*1-877976-10-5*, 406-0014) Tipi Pr.
White Buildings. Hart Crane. 1986. pap. 3.95 (*0-87140-272-6*) Liveright.
White Butcher Block. 1989. 120.00 (*0-394-58542-9*) Random.
White Butterflies & Other Stories. Kate Clark. LC 75-103505. (Short Story Index Reprint Ser.). 1977. 20.95 (*0-8369-3247-1*) Ayer.
White Butterfly. large type ed. Walter Mosley. LC 93-16668. 1993. lib. bdg. 20.95 (*1-56054-724-3*) Thorndike Pr.
White Butterfly. Walter Mosley. Ed. by Jane Chelius. 394p. 1993. reprint ed. mass mkt. 6.50 (*0-671-86787-3*) PB.
White Butterfly: An Easy Rawlins Mystery. Walter Mosley. 256p. 1992. 19.95 (*0-393-03366-X*) Norton.
White by Definition: Social Classification in Creole Louisiana. Virginia R. Dominguez. 256p. (C). 1986. text ed. 40.00 (*0-8135-1109-7*) Rutgers U Pr.
White by Definition: Social Classification in Creole Louisiana. Virginia Dominguez. 325p. (C). 1994. reprint ed. pap. text ed. 17.00 (*0-8135-2088-6*) Rutgers U Pr.
White by Definition: Social Classification in Creole Louisiana. Virginia R. Dominguez. LC 85-14609. 343p. reprint ed. pap. 97.80 (*0-7837-5666-6*, 2059092) Bks Demand.
White by Design. Bo Niles. LC 84-228. (Illus.). 200p. 1984. 40.00 (*0-941434-54-0*); pap. 24.95 (*1-55670-277-9*) Stewart Tabori & Chang.
***White by Law.** Lopez. 1998. pap. 17.95 (*0-8147-5137-7*) NYU Pr.
White by Law: The Legal Construction of Race. Ian F. Lopez. (Critical America Ser.). 296p. (C). 1996. 24.95 (*0-8147-5099-0*) NYU Pr.
White Camellias. large type ed. Anne T. Brooks. (Romance Ser.). 256p. 1993. 25.99 (*0-7089-2889-7*) Ulverscroft.
White Canada Forever: Popular Attitudes & Public Policy Toward Orientals in British Columbia. 2nd ed. W. Peter Ward. (McGill-Queen's Studies in Ethnic History). 205p. (C). 1990. reprint ed. pap. text ed. 19.95 (*0-7735-0824-4*, Pub. by McGill CN) U of Toronto Pr.
White Canary: An Illustrated Tale. Caleb Gattegno. 31p. 1968. 6.95 (*0-85225-550-0*) Ed Solutions.
***White Cane Religion: And Other Messages from the Brownsville Revival.** Stephen Hill. 182p. 1997. pap. 8.99 (*1-56043-186-5*) Destiny Image.
White Canoe & Other Legends of the Ojibways. E. Monckton. 1977. lib. bdg. 59.95 (*0-8490-2819-1*) Gordon Pr.
White Captain, Black Troops: Stories of World War II. Redman Callaway. LC 93-79330. 144p. 1993. 19.95 (*0-932845-60-6*) Lowell Pr.
White Captives: Gender & Ethnicity on the American Frontier. June Namias. LC 92-31235. (Illus.). xxii, 378p. (C). 1993. pap. text ed. 17.95 (*0-8078-4408-X*) U of NC Pr.
White Cargo. Stuart Woods. 320p. 1989. mass mkt. 6.50 (*0-380-70783-7*) Avon.
White Cargo. large type ed. Stuart Woods. 1990. 25.99 (*0-7089-2249-X*) Ulverscroft.
White Castle. Orhan Pamuk. Tr. by Victoria Holbrook from TUR. 162p. 1991. 17.50 (*0-8076-1264-2*) Braziller.
***White Castle.** Orhan Pamuk. 1998. pap. write for info. (*0-375-70161-3*, Vin) Random.
White Cat. Rabbit. (J). 1996. pap. 19.95 (*0-689-80140-8*, Rabbit) S&S Childrens.
White Cat. Robert D. San Souci. LC 88-19698. (Illus.). 32p. (J). (ps-3). 1990. lib. bdg. 17.99 (*0-531-08409-4*) Orchard Bks Watts.
White Cats & Lilacs: Essays from an American Garden. Teresa Keene. (Illus.). 112p. 1996. pap. 10.95 (*1-57427-060-5*) Howell Pr VA.
White Cell. Martin J. Cline. LC 74-25998. (Commonwealth Fund Publications). (Illus.). 616p. 1975. 50.00 (*0-674-95142-5*) HUP.
***White Cell Manual.** 5th ed. Alan Winkelstein & Ronald A. Sacher. (Illus.). 130p. (C). 1998. pap. text ed. 20.00 (*0-8036-0305-3*) Davis Co.
White Cell Rheology & Inflammation. Ed. by K. Messmer & F. Hammersen. (Mikrozirkulation in Forschung und Klinik; Progress in Applied Microcirculation Ser.: Vol. 7). (Illus.). x, 124p. 1985. pap. 57.00 (*3-8055-4040-X*) S Karger.
White Chameleon. Christopher Hampton. 96p. (Orig.). 1991. pap. 9.95 (*0-571-16305-X*) Faber & Faber.

W

White Chief: A Legend of North Mexico. Thomas M. Reid. LC 68-23726. (Americans in Fiction Ser.). (Illus.). 401p. reprint ed. pap. text ed. 5.95 (*0-89197-975-1*); reprint ed. lib. bdg. 29.50 (*0-8398-1752-5*) Irvington.

White Chip. large type ed. Nelson C. Nye. (Five Star Western Ser.). 1997. 20.00 (*0-7838-1542-5*) Thorndike Pr.

***White Chip.** large type ed. Nelson C. Nye. 317p. 1997. 17.95 (*0-7862-0902-X*, Thorndike Lrg Prnt) Thorndike Pr.

White Chip: A Western Story. Nelson C. Nye. (Five-Star Western Ser.). 220p. 1996. 16.95 (*0-7862-0565-2*) Thorndike Pr.

***White Christmas: Decorating & Entertaining for the Holiday Season.** Tricia Foley. 1997. write for info. (*0-517-70411-0*, Harmony) Crown Pub Group.

White Cities. Ben Mazer. LC 95-75261. (Illus.). 52p. (Orig.). 1995. pap. 10.00 (*0-9645516-0-8*) B Matteau.

White City: The History of an Early Copper Country Recreational Area. (Copper Country Local History Ser.: Vol. 4). (Illus.). 65p. 1975. 3.00 (*0-942363-03-5*) C J Monette.

White Clam: A Northwest Adventure. Gary K. Cowart. LC 92-75271. 300p. 1992. 19.95 (*0-9635169-0-6*) Cascade Hse.

White Clapboard. Mary A. Larkin. (Illus.). 12p. (Orig.). (C). 1988. pap. 7.00 (*0-9620840-0-X*) C O Allen.

White Cliffs. Alice D. Miller. 74p. 1987. reprint ed. lib. bdg. 19.95 (*0-89966-615-9*) Buccaneer Bks.

***White Cliffs of Dover Songbook.** Ed. by Carol Cuellar. 228p. (Orig.). (C). 1994. pap. text ed. 24.95 (*0-943748-57-7*, VF1832) Warner Brothers.

White Cloud - Lakota Spirit. Cecelia F. Brownlow & Leslie S. Wilner. LC 92-16827. 1992. 10.95 (*0-86534-166-4*) Sunstone Pr.

White Cloud the First Hundred Years, 1873-1973: White Cloud Area. Newaygo County Bicentennial Committee. (Illus.). 166p. 1995. reprint ed. pap. 22.00 (*0-8328-5046-2*); reprint ed. lib. bdg. 29.50 (*0-8328-5045-4*) Higginson Bk Co.

White Coat, Purple Coat: Collected Poems 1948-1988. Dannie Abse. 304p. 1991. 29.95 (*0-89255-153-4*) Persea Bks.

White Coat, Purple Coat: Collected Poems 1948-1988. Dannie Abse. 288p. 1992. pap. 12.95 (*0-89255-177-1*) Persea Bks.

White Cockade: A Book of Poetry & Verse. Charles A. Coulombe. Ed. by J. Fred Farrell. (Illus.). 100p. (Orig.). (C). 1990. pap. text ed. 10.00 (*0-685-45128-3*) Charlemagne Pr.

White Cockatoo. large type ed. Mignon G. Eberhart. LC 93-29320. 1993. lib. bdg. 21.95 (*0-7862-0083-9*) Thorndike Pr.

White Collar: American Middle Classes. C. Wright Mills. 398p. 1956. pap. 12.95 (*0-19-500677-1*) OUP.

White Collar & Professional Stress. Ed. by Cary L. Cooper & Judi Marshall. LC 79-41779. (Wiley Series on Studies in Occupational Stress). 271p. reprint ed. pap. 77.30 (*0-685-23756-7*, 2032830) Bks Demand.

White Collar Crime. Hazel Croall. 176p. 1992. 80.00 (*0-335-09657-3*, Open Univ Pr); pap. 23.00 (*0-335-09656-5*, Open Univ Pr) Taylor & Francis.

White Collar Crime. Ed. by David Nelken. (International Library of Criminology & Criminal Justice). 656p. 1994. 168.95 (*1-85521-376-1*, Pub. by Dartmth Pub UK) Ashgate Pub Co.

White Collar Crime. 2nd ed. Brickey. 1995. 52.00 (*0-316-10880-4*) Little.

White Collar Crime. Edwin H. Sutherland. LC 83-12987. xvi, 272p. 1983. reprint ed. text ed. 59.75 (*0-313-24227-5*, SUWC, Greenwood Pr) Greenwood.

White Collar Crime: A Bibliography. Dorothy L. Thompkins. LC 72-77488. 93p. reprint ed. pap. 26.60 (*0-317-10522-1*, 2002383) Bks Demand.

White Collar Crime: Business & Regulatory Offenses. Ed. by Otto G. Obermaier & Robert G. Morvillo. 800p. 1990. ring bd. 110.00 (*0-317-05403-1*, 00610) NY Law Pub.

White Collar Crime: Cases & Materials On. Pamela H. Bucy. (American Casebook Ser.). 688p. 1992. pap. text ed. 48.50 (*0-314-00658-3*) West Pub.

White-Collar Crime: Offenses in Business, Politics and the Professions. 3rd ed. Ed. by Gilbert Geis et al. LC 94-31736. 1994. pap. 19.95 (*0-02-911601-5*, Free Press) Free Pr.

White Collar Crime: The Uncut Version. Edwin H. Sutherland. Ed. by Gilbert Geis & Colin Goff. LC 82-48911. 294p. 1983. 42.00 (*0-300-02921-7*) Yale U Pr.

White Collar Crime: The Uncut Version. Edwin H. Sutherland. 320p. 1985. reprint ed. pap. text ed. 19.00 (*0-300-03318-4*, Y-527) Yale U Pr.

White Collar Crime, Cases & Materials: Teacher's Manual to Accompany. Pamela H. Bucy. (American Casebook Ser.). 217p. (C). 1992. pap. text ed. write for info. (*0-314-01146-3*) West Pub.

White Collar Crime, Cases & Materials: 1994 Supplement. Pamela H. Bucy. (American Casebook Ser.). 127p. 1994. pap. text ed. 10.00 (*0-314-04389-6*) West Pub.

White-Collar Crime Explosion: How to Protect Yourself & Your Company from Prosecution. Roger J. Magnuson. 1992. text ed. 24.95 (*0-07-039520-9*) McGraw.

White Collar Crime in a Nutshell. Ellen S. Podgor. (Nutshell Ser.). 303p. 1993. pap. text ed. 16.00 (*0-314-02349-6*) West Pub.

White Collar Crime in America. Jay S. Albanese. LC 94-2292. 320p. (C). 1994. pap. text ed. 32.00 (*0-02-301261-7*, Macmillan Coll) P-H.

White-Collar Crime in Modern England: Financial Fraud & Business Morality, 1845-1929. George Robb. 264p. (C). 1992. text ed. 59.95 (*0-521-41234-X*) Cambridge U Pr.

White Collar Crime Law & Practice. Jerold H. Israel et al. (American Casebook Ser.). 890p. 1996. text ed. write for info. (*0-314-06773-6*) West Pub.

White-Collar Crime Reconsidered. Ed. by Kip Schlegel & David Weisburd. 400p. 1992. text ed. 50.00 (*1-55553-141-5*) NE U Pr.

White-Collar Crime Reconsidered. Ed. by Kip Schlegel & David Weisburd. 384p. 1994. reprint ed. pap. text ed. 20.00 (*1-55553-199-7*) NE U Pr.

White Collar Criminality. Edwin H. Sutherland. (Reprint Series in Social Sciences). (C). 1993. reprint ed. pap. text ed. 1.00 (*0-8290-2924-9*, S-284) Irvington.

***White Collar Ethos.** Siegfried Kracauer. Date not set. pap. 15.00 (*1-85984-187-2*, Pub. by Verso UK) Routledge Chapman & Hall.

***White Collar Ethos.** Siegfried Kracauer. (C). Date not set. text ed. 500.00 (*1-85984-881-8*, Pub. by Verso UK) Routledge Chapman & Hall.

White Collar Fictions: Class & Social Representation in American Literature, 1885-1925. Christopher P. Wilson. LC 91-19791. (Illus.). 344p. 1992. 40.00 (*0-8203-1367-X*) U of Ga Pr.

White Collar Hobo: The Travels of Whiting Williams. Daniel A. Wren. LC 87-4048. 177p. 1987. reprint ed. pap. 50.50 (*0-608-00009-4*, 2060775) Bks Demand.

White-Collar Knowledge Worker: Measuring & Improving Productivity & Effectiveness. Marvin E. Mundel. 355p. 1989. pap. text ed. 36.00 (*92-833-1092-6*, 92-833-1092-0) Qual Resc.

White Collar Politics. Martin Oppenheimer. 288p. 1985. 26.00 (*0-85345-659-3*); pap. 12.00 (*0-85345-660-7*) Monthly Rev.

White Collar Power: Changing Patterns of Interest Group Behavior in Sweden. Christopher Wheeler. LC 75-15541. 222p. reprint ed. pap. 63.30 (*0-317-39627-7*, 2020862) Bks Demand.

White Collar Productivity, Vol 23. William A. Ruch. (Studies in Productivity: Highlights of the Literature Ser.). (Orig.). pap. 55.00 (*0-89361-033-X*) Work in Amer.

White-Collar Stress. Louis C. Feuer. Ed. by Susan Y. Snider. 178p. 1988. 12.95 (*0-8119-0727-9*) LIFETIME.

White Collar Unemployment: Impact & Stress. Stephen Fineman. LC 82-8590. (Wiley Series on Organizational Change & Development). (Illus.). 166p. reprint ed. pap. 47.40 (*0-7837-4398-X*, 2044138) Bks Demand.

White Collar Workers in America, 1890-1940: A Social-Political History in International Perspective. Jurgen Kocka. Tr. by Maura Kealey. LC 80-40572. (Sage Studies in 20th Century History: No. 10). 421p. reprint ed. pap. 120.00 (*0-8357-4813-8*, 2037750) Bks Demand.

White Collar Workers in Transition: The Boom Years, 1940-1970. Mark D. McColloch. LC 83-5546. (Contributions in Labor History Ser.: No. 15). xii, 193p. 1983. text ed. 42.95 (*0-313-23785-9*, MCW/, Greenwood Pr) Greenwood.

White Collar Working Class: From Structure to Politics. Richard Sobel. LC 88-38720. 208p. 1989. text ed. 55.00 (*0-275-93026-2*, C3026, Praeger Pubs) Greenwood.

White Columns in Hollywood: Reports from the GWTW Sets. Susan Myrick. LC 82-18881. (Illus.). 345p. 1982. pap. 14.95 (*0-86554-245-7*, MUP/P037) Mercer Univ Pr.

White Company. Arthur Conan Doyle. LC 87-62625. (Books of Wonder). (Illus.). 362p. (J). 1988. 22.00 (*0-688-07817-6*, Morrow Junior) Morrow.

White Company. Arthur Conan Doyle. 1986. reprint ed. lib. bdg. 24.95 (*0-89966-517-9*) Buccaneer Bks.

White Conquest, 2 Vols. William H. Dixon. LC 70-138335. (Black Heritage Library Collection). 1977. Set. 42.95 (*0-8369-8727-6*) Ayer.

***White Cottage Mystery.** Margery Allingham. 3.50 (*0-7867-0666-X*) Carroll & Graf.

White Cottage Mystery. Margery Allingham. 139p. 1990. pap. 3.50 (*0-88184-666-X*) Carroll & Graf.

***White Crane Spreads Wings.** Gary Hyland. 1997. pap. 9.95 (*1-55050-106-2*, Pub. by Coteau CN) Genl Dist Srvs.

***White Crosses.** Larry Watson. 1997. 23.00 (*0-671-56771-3*, PB Hardcover) PB.

White Curtain. Daniel A. Birchmore. Ed. by Melinda B. Musick. LC 96-7762. (Illus.). 32p. (J). (ps-3). 1997. 15.95 (*1-887813-09-8*) Cucumber Island.

White Darkness: & Other Stories of the Great Northwest. Lawrence Mott. LC 74-150554. (Short Story Index Reprint Ser.). (Illus.). 1977. reprint ed. 23.95 (*0-8369-3851-8*) Ayer.

White Dawn: An Eskimo Saga. James R. Houston. LC 82-23236. 275p. 1989. pap. 8.00 (*0-15-696256-X*, Harvest Bks) HarBrace.

White Death. 1989. pap. 5.25 (*0-19-421646-2*) OUP.

White Death. Georges Bettembourg & Michael Brame. (Illus.). 300p. 1981. 13.95 (*0-685-03582-4*) Reynard Hse.

White Death. William C. Knott. 1993. mass mkt. 3.99 (*0-312-92831-9*) St Martin.

White Deer. James Thurber. LC 45-35191. (Illus.). 115p. (J). 1968. reprint ed. pap. 7.00 (*0-15-696264-0*, Harvest Bks) HarBrace.

White Deer: And Other Stories Told by the Lenape. Ed. by John Bierhorst. LC 94-30962. (Illus.). 160p. (YA). (gr. 7 up). 1995. 15.00 (*0-688-12900-5*, Morrow Junior) Morrow.

White Devil. John Webster. (Study Texts Ser.). (Orig.). 1988. pap. 5.95 (*0-582-33188-9*) Longman.

White Devil. John Webster. Ed. by John R. Brown. LC 95-21693. (Revels Student Editions Ser.). (Orig.). 1996. text ed. write for info. (*0-7190-4354-9*, Pub. by Manchester Univ Pr UK) St Martin.

White Devil. John Webster. Ed. by John R. Brown. LC 95-21693. (Revels Student Editions Ser.). 176p. (Orig.). 1996. text ed. 12.95 (*0-7190-4355-7*, Pub. by Manchester Univ Pr UK) St Martin.

***White Devil.** John Webster. Ed. by Simon Trussler. (Drama Classics Ser.). 160p. (Orig.). 1996. pap. 8.95 (*1-85459-345-5*, Pub. by N Hern Bks UK) Theatre Comm.

White Devil. John Webster. Ed. by J. R. Mulryne. LC 68-20771. (Regents Renaissance Drama Ser.). 186p. (Orig.). reprint ed. pap. 53.10 (*0-7837-7046-4*, 2046857) Bks Demand.

White Devil. John Webster. Ed. by John R. Brown. (Revels Plays Ser.). 205p. (Orig.). 1988. reprint ed. text ed. 22.95 (*0-7190-1611-8*, Pub. by Manchester Univ Pr UK) St Martin.

White Devil: The Duchess of Malfi. Ed. by David Gunby et al. LC 93-24457. (C). 1994. write for info. (*0-521-22009-2*) Cambridge U Pr.

White Devil see Three Jacobean Tragedies

White Devil Discover'd: Backgrounds & Foregrounds to Webster's Tragedy. Frederick O. Waage. LC 83-48766. (American University Studies: English Language & Literature: Ser. IV, Vol. 5). 197p. (Orig.). (C). 1984. pap. text ed. 19.70 (*0-8204-0055-6*) P Lang Pubng.

White Diamonds. Shirley Hailstock. 416p. 1996. mass mkt. 4.99 (*0-7860-0296-4*, Pinncle Kensgtn) Kensgtn Pub Corp.

White Doe of Rylstone: Or, The Fate of the Nortons. William Wordsworth. Ed. by Kristine Dugas. LC 87-9265. (Cornell Wordsworth Ser.). (Illus.). 392p. 1988. 55.00 (*0-8014-1946-8*) Cornell U Pr.

White Dogs. William P. Murphy. 334p. (Orig.). 1996. mass mkt. 5.99 (*1-55197-202-6*, Pub. by Comnwlth Pub CN) Partners Pubs Grp.

White Dolphin. large type ed. Geoffrey Morgan. 1996. pap. 17.99 (*1-85389-607-1*, Dales) Ulverscroft.

White Dominican. Gustav Meyrink. Tr. by Michael Mitchell. (Studies in Austrian Literature, Culture, & Thought. Translation Ser.). 1994. pap. 12.95 (*0-929497-88-0*) Ariadne CA.

White Dove. M. B. Keckeis. Tr. by Anne Beaubeau & Frank Steiner. (Illus.). 286p. (ENG, FRE, GER & SPA.). (J). (gr. 6-10). 1993. 23.50 (*1-879870-56-8*) Pro Lingua Pr.

***White Dove Other.** 1996. pap. 6.95 (*0-7871-0641-0*, Dove Bks) Dove Audio.

White Dove Review, Nos. 1-5. Ed. by Ron Padgett. (Avant-Garde Magazines Ser.). 1974. reprint ed. 18.95 (*0-405-01757-X*) Ayer.

***White Dragon.** Anne McCaffrey. 1997. pap. 12.95 (*0-345-41940-5*, Del Rey) Ballantine.

White Dragon, No. 3. Anne McCaffrey. 368p. 1986. mass mkt. 6.99 (*0-345-34167-8*, Del Rey) Ballantine.

White Dreams, Black Africa: The Antislavery Expedition to the Niger, 1841-1842. Howard Temperley. (Illus.). 224p. (C). 1991. text ed. 40.00 (*0-300-05021-6*) Yale U Pr.

***White Dress.** Mignon G. Eberhart. 1997. write for info. (*0-7862-1131-8*) Thorndike Pr.

***White Dress.** Catherine Lynn. Ed. by Marilyn Johnson. (Illus.). (Orig.). 1996. pap. 15.00 (*0-943795-30-3*) Chiron Rev.

***White Dwarfs.** 1997. lib. bdg. 340.00 (*0-7923-4585-1*) Kluwer Ac.

White Dwarfs. Ed. by Gerard Vauclair & Edward Sion. (C). 1991. lib. bdg. 194.00 (*0-7923-1266-X*) Kluwer Ac.

White Dwarfs. Ed. by G. Wegner. (Lecture Notes in Physics Ser.: Vol. 328). xiv, 524p. 1989. 74.95 (*0-387-51031-1*) Spr-Verlag.

White Dwarfs: Proceedings of the NATO Advanced Research Workshop Eight European Workshop on White Dwarfs, Leicester, United Kingdom, July 20-24, 1992. Ed. by Martin A. Barstow. LC 93-1727. (NATO Advanced Study Institutes Series C, Mathematical & Physical Sciences: Vol. 403). 588p. (C). 1993. lib. bdg. 284.50 (*0-7923-2332-7*) Kluwer Ac.

White Dwarfs: Proceedings of the 9th European Workshop on White Dwarfs Held at Kiel, Germany, 29 August-1 September 1994. K. Werner. (Lecture Notes in Physics Ser.: Vol. 443). xii, 346p. 1995. 92.95 (*3-540-59157-5*) Spr-Verlag.

White Dynamite & Curly Kidd. Bill Martin, Jr. & John Archambault. LC 85-27214. (Illus.). 32p. (J). (ps-2). 1986. 12.95 (*0-8050-0658-3*, Bks Young Read) H Holt & Co.

White Dynamite & Curly Kidd. Bill Martin, Jr. & John Archambault. LC 85-27214. (Illus.). 32p. (J). (ps-2). 1989. pap. 5.95 (*0-8050-1018-1*, Bks Young Read) H Holt & Co.

***White Eagle.** James Forte. 51p. (Orig.). 1995. pap. 13.95 (*1-889560-09-X*) Wildflower Pub.

White Eagle Lodge Book of Health & Healing. Joan Hodgson. 240p. 1983. text ed. 12.50 (*0-85487-063-6*, Pub. by White Eagle UK) DeVorss.

***White Eagle Medicine Wheel.** Harvey. Date not set. 24.95 (*0-312-15689-8*) St Martin.

***White Eagle Medicine Wheel.** Harvey. 1997. 24.99 (*0-312-14533-0*) St Martin.

White Eagles Over Serbia. Lawrence Durrell. LC 58-7779. 1958. 24.95 (*0-87599-030-4*) S G Phillips.

White Eagles over Serbia. Lawrence Durrell. LC 95-17743. 200p. 1995. 19.95 (*1-55970-312-1*) Arcade Pub Inc.

White Earth Tragedy: Ethnicity & Dispossession at a Minnesota Anishinaabe Reservation, 1889-1920. Melissa L. Meyer. LC 93-23456. (Illus.). xviii, 333p. (C). 1994. text ed. 43.00 (*0-8032-3154-7*) U of Nebr Pr.

White Elephants. Reetika Vazirani. LC 95-45057. 112p. 1996. pap. 12.00 (*0-8070-6833-0*) Beacon Pr.

***White Etching on Case-Hardened Gears in Connection with Flank Damage.** Hans Winter & G. Knauer. (1987 Fall Technical Meeting). 1987. pap. text ed. 30.00 (*1-55589-486-0*) AGMA.

White Eye. Blanche D'Alpuget. 1994. pap. 22.00 (*0-671-62005-3*) S&S Trade.

White Eyes, Dark Ages. Deborah Randall. (Illus.). 64p. 9400. pap. 12.95 (*1-85224-222-1*, Pub. by Bloodaxe Bks UK) Dufour.

White Eyes Long Knives & Renegade Indians. V. Keith Thorne. Ed. by Aliza Caillou. (Illus.). 35p. (Orig.). 1993. pap. 4.95 (*0-9628329-8-7*) Thorne Enterprises.

White Face. Carl R. Offord. LC 73-18596. reprint ed. 32.50 (*0-404-11407-5*) AMS Pr.

White Faculty, Black Students: Exploring Assumptions & Practices. Carolyn D. Spatta. (Illus.). 23p. 1984. pap. 7.00 (*0-911696-37-7*) Assn Am Coll.

White Falcon: The House of Godeffroy & Its Commercial & Scientific Role in the Pacific. Florence M. Spoehr. LC 63-18693. (Illus.). 1963. 14.95 (*0-87015-119-3*) Pacific Bks.

White Fang. (J). 9.95 (*1-56156-306-4*) Kidsbks.

White Fang. Jack London. (Airmont Classics Ser.). (J). (gr. 6 up). 1964. mass mkt. 2.95 (*0-8049-0036-1*, CL-36) Airmont.

White Fang. Jack London. 1976. 22.95 (*0-8488-0567-4*) Amereon Ltd.

***White Fang.** Jack London. (Illustrated Classics Collection 3). 64p. 1994. pap. 4.95 (*0-7854-0728-6*, 40471) Am Guidance.

White Fang. Jack London. 1995. pap. 16.95 (*0-7871-0422-1*, Dove Bks) Dove Audio.

White Fang. Jack London. 208p. pap. 14.95 (*0-88839-260-5*) Hancock House.

White Fang. Jack London. (Illustrated Classics Ser.). (Illus.). 240p. (J). (ps-6). Date not set. text ed. 9.95 (*1-56987-396-8*); pap. text ed. 2.95 (*1-56987-406-9*); pap. text ed. 3.95 (*1-56987-413-1*) Landoll.

White Fang. Jack London. LC 85-42971. (Classics Ser.). 272p. (J). (gr. 4-6). 1985. pap. 3.99 (*0-14-035045-4*, Puffin) Puffin Bks.

White Fang. Jack London. (Classics Ser.). 272p. (J). (gr. 5 up). 1994. pap. 3.99 (*0-14-036667-9*) Puffin Bks.

White Fang. Jack London. 256p. (J). (gr. 6 up). 1986. pap. 4.50 (*0-590-42591-9*) Scholastic Inc.

White Fang. Jack London. 224p. (J). 1989. pap. 2.50 (*0-8125-0512-3*) Tor Bks.

White Fang. Jack London. (J). pap. 4.95 (*0-8167-2893-3*) Troll Communs.

White Fang. Jack London. 1996. pap. 10.95 (*0-14-086220-X*) NAL-Dutton.

White Fang. Jack London. 1996. pap. 3.95 (*0-89375-346-7*) NAL-Dutton.

***White Fang.** Jack London. Ed. by Joshua Hanft. (Great Illustrated Classics Ser.: Vol. 34). (Illus.). 240p. (J). (gr. 3-6). 1994. 9.95 (*0-86611-985-X*) Playmore Inc.

White Fang. Illus. by Van Gool Studio Staff. (Classic Ser.). 64p. (J). (ps-1). 1995. 4.98 (*0-8317-1669-X*) Smithmark.

White Fang. abr. ed. Jack London. Ed. by Naunerle Farr. (Now Age Illustrated III Ser.). (Illus.). (J). (gr. 4-12). 1977. pap. text ed. 2.95 (*0-88301-271-5*) Pendulum Pr.

White Fang. large type ed. Jack London. LC 93-32332. 1993. lib. bdg. 20.95 (*0-8161-5889-4*, GK Hall) Thorndike Pr.

White Fang. large type ed. Jack London. LC 93-32332. 1994. pap. 15.95 (*0-8161-5892-4*, GK Hall) Thorndike Pr.

White Fang. Jack London. (Thrift Editions Ser.). 160p. reprint ed. pap. 1.00 (*0-486-26968-X*) Dover.

White Fang: Illustrated Classics. Jack London. Ed. by D. J. Arneson. (Illus.). 128p. (Orig.). (J). 1990. pap. 2.95 (*0-942025-84-9*) Kidsbks.

White Fang: Student Activity Book. Marcia Sohl & Gerald Dackerman. (Now Age Illustrated Ser.). (Illus.). (gr. 4-12). 1976. student ed. 1.25 (*0-88301-295-2*) Pendulum Pr.

White Fang & The Call of the Wild. Jack London. 288p. 1991. pap. 4.95 (*0-451-52558-2*, Sig Classics) NAL-Dutton.

White Fang & the Call of the Wild. large type ed. Jack London. 502p. 1995. lib. bdg. 24.00 (*0-939495-87-2*) North Bks.

White Fang II: Myths of the White Wolf. Elizabeth Faucher. 184p. (YA). 1994. pap. 3.50 (*0-590-48611-X*) Scholastic Inc.

***White Fang Readalong.** Jack London. (Illustrated Classics Collection 3). (Illus.). 64p. 1994. pap. 14.95 incl. audio (*0-7854-0744-8*, 40473) Am Guidance.

***White Fang/Call of the Wild.** Jack London. (Classic Library Collection). 1996. 12.98 (*0-7651-9879-7*) Smithmark.

White Farms, Black Labour: Agrarian Transition in Southern Africa, 1910-1950. Jeeves & Crush. LC 97-3133. (Social History of Africa Ser.). 1996. write for info. (*0-435-08991-9*, 08991); pap. write for info. (*0-435-08993-5*, 08993) Heinemann.

White Feather. Ruth Eitzen. LC 86-31786. (Illus.). 64p. (J). (gr. 2-5). 1995. pap. 7.99 (*0-8361-9025-4*) Herald Pr.

White Figure, White Ground. Hugh Hood. 246p. 1983. pap. 3.95 (*0-7736-7059-9*) Genl Dist Srvs.

***White Fire.** Edwards Cassie. 1997. pap. 5.99 (*0-451-40756-3*, Onyx) NAL-Dutton.

***White Fire.** Fern Michaels. 352p. 1997. mass mkt. 6.99 (*0-8217-5638-9*, Zebra Kensgtn) Kensgtn Pub Corp.

White Fire. large type ed. Jan Maclean. (Linford Romance Library). 368p. 1985. pap. 15.99 (*0-7089-6051-0*) Ulverscroft.

White Fire: The Influence of Emerson on Melville. John B. Williams. 208p. (C). 1991. lib. bdg. 37.50 (*1-878981-02-1*) CSULB Univ Pr.

W

White Fire: The Life & Works of Jessie Sampter. Bertha Badt-Strauss. Ed. by Moshe Davis. LC 77-70663. (America & the Holy Land Ser.). (Illus.). 1977. reprint ed. lib. bdg. 23.95 (*0-405-10224-0*) Ayer.

White Flag. Gene S. Porter. 30.95 (*0-89190-943-5*) Amereon Ltd.

White Flame. James Grady. 304p. 1996. pap. 22.95 (*0-7871-0903-7*, Dove Bks); pap. 24.95 (*0-7871-0876-6*, Dove Bks) Dove Audio.

*__White Flame.__ James Grady. 1997. mass mkt. 5.99 (*0-7871-1420-0*, Dove Bks) Dove Audio.

White Flash - Black Rain: Women of Japan Relive the Bomb. Ed. by Lequita Vance-Watkins & Aratani Mariko. Tr. by Aratani Mariko. LC 95-7560. 175p. (Orig.). 1995. pap. 12.95 (*1-57131-402-4*) Milkweed Ed.

White Flower. Grace L. Hill. reprint ed. lib. bdg. 24.95 (*0-89190-051-9*, Rivercity Pr) Amereon Ltd.

White Flower, No. 82. Grace L. Hill. 1995. pap. 4.99 (*0-8423-8149-X*) Tyndale.

White Flower Farm Garden Book. rev. ed. Amos Pettingill. (Illus.). 376p. 1995. 20.00 (*0-9647440-0-7*) White Flower.

White Footed Doe & Other Poems. William C. Bryant. (Works of William Cullen Bryant). 1989. reprint ed. lib. bdg. 79.00 (*0-7812-2129-3*) Rprt Serv.

WHITE. "From the Dim & Misty Past" Genealogy of the White Family (Descendants of Alexander White, b. Ireland & Emigrated to Pa. in 18th Century. L. B. White. 50p. 1995. reprint ed. pap. 10.00 (*0-8328-4861-1*) Higginson Bk Co.

White. "From the Dim & Misty Past" Genealogy of the White Family (Descendants of Alexander White, Born Ireland & Emigrated to Pennsylvania in 18th Century. L. B. White. 50p. 1995. reprint ed. lib. bdg. 20.00 (*0-8328-4860-3*) Higginson Bk Co.

White Fury. Dulci Nemec. 150p. (Orig.). 1989. pap. 3.49 (*0-9618998-4-0*) Nemec Pub.

White Gamma. David Chacko. 1989. pap. 3.95 (*0-312-91577-2*) St Martin.

White Garden. Carmel Bird. 232p. 1995. pap. 16.95 (*0-7022-2821-4*, Pub. by Univ Queensland Pr AT) Intl Spec Bk.

White German Shepherd Book. Paul D. Strang et al. (Illus.). 119p. 17.50 (*0-911039-00-7*) Medea DC.

*__White Ghetto.__ Hope. 1997. 17.95 (*0-8059-3992-X*) Dorrance.

White Girl in Search of the Party. Pauline Podbrey. (Illus.). 216p. 1993. 23.00 (*0-86980-904-0*, Pub. by Univ Natal Pr SA) Intl Spec Bk.

White Girls. Lynn Lauber. LC 91-50012. (Vintage Contemporaries Ser.). 192p. 1991. pap. 9.00 (*0-679-73411-2*, Vin) Random.

White Gloves: How Our Memories Tell Us Who We Are. John Kotre. 288p. 1996. pap. 14.00 (*0-393-31525-8*) Norton.

White Gloves: How We Create Ourselves Through Memory. John Kotre. 1995. 22.00 (*0-02-918464-9*, Free Press) Free Pr.

White Gloves & Party Manners. Marjabelle Y. Young & Ann Buchwald. LC 65-25830. (YA). (gr. 7 up). 1988. 14.95 (*0-88331-054-6*) Luce.

*__White Gloves & Raised Fists.__ Marie Cantlon. 1998. pap. 29.95 (*0-670-86743-8*) Viking Penguin.

White Gloves & Red Bricks: APVA 1889-1989. Nancy E. Packer. (Illus.). 87p. 1989. pap. 9.95 (*0-917565-02-9*) Assn Preserv VA.

White Goats & Black Bees. Donald Grant. 316p. 1990. reprint ed. pap. 10.95 (*0-911797-86-6*) R Rinehart.

White Goblin. Ul De Rico et al. LC 96-60140. (Illus.). 36p. (J). 1996. 19.95 (*0-500-01724-7*) Thames Hudson.

White God & Other Poems. Thomas C. Chubb. LC 76-144712. (Yale Series of Younger Poets: No. 5). reprint ed. 18.00 (*0-404-53805-3*) AMS Pr.

*__White Goddess: A Historical Grammar of Poetic Myth.__ Robert Graves. 1997. pap. 14.00 (*0-614-27334-X*, Noonday) FS&G.

White Goddess (amended & enlarged edition) Robert Graves. 1983. 25.25 (*0-8446-5983-5*) Peter Smith.

White Gold. Curtiss A. Matlock. (Historical Ser.). 1995. pap. 3.99 (*0-373-28851-4*, 1-28851-3) Harlequin Bks.

White Gold. John C. Yungjohann. Ed. by Ghillean T. Prance. (Illus.). 108p. 1989. pap. 7.95 (*0-907791-16-6*) Synerg AZ.

White Gold: A Brief History of the Louisiana Sugar Industry, 1795-1995. Glenn R. Conrad & Ray F. Lucas. LC 94-74142. (Louisians Life Ser.: No. 8). (Illus.). 102p. (Orig.). 1995. pap. 5.00 (*0-940984-92-X*) U of SW LA Ctr LA Studies.

*__White Gold & Other Stories.__ Thompson. 1993. pap. text ed. write for info. (*0-17-555983-X*) Addison-Wesley.

*__White Gold Wielder.__ Stephen R. Donaldson. 1997. pap. 12.00 (*0-345-41848-4*) Ballantine.

White Gold Wielder. Stephen R. Donaldson. 526p. 1987. mass mkt. 6.99 (*0-345-34870-2*, Del Rey) Ballantine.

White Goods in Europe. Euromonitor Staff. 110p. 1987. 825.00 (*0-86338-212-6*, Pub. by Euromonitor Pubns UK) Gale.

White Grease Paint on Black Performers: A Study of the Federal Theatre, 1935-1939. Glenda E. Gill. (American University Studies: History: Ser. IX, Vol. 40). 220p. 1988. text ed. 36.00 (*0-8204-0682-1*) P Lang Pubng.

White Grubs & Their Allies: A Study of North American Scarabaeoid Larvae. Paul O. Ritcher. LC 66-63008. (Illus.). 216p. 1966. 27.95 (*0-87071-054-0*) Oreg St U Pr.

White Gryphon. Mercedes Lackey & Larry Dixon. 400p. 1995. 21.95 (*0-88677-631-7*) DAW Bks.

White Gryphon. Mercedes Lackey & Larry Dixon. 384p. 1996. mass mkt. 5.99 (*0-88677-682-1*) DAW Bks.

White Guard. Mikhail Bulgakov. Tr. by Michael Gleeny from RUS. 319p. 1994. reprint ed. pap. 12.95 (*0-89733-246-6*) Academy Chi Pubs.

White Guinea-Pig. Ursula Dubosarsky. 190p. (YA). (gr. 5 up). 1995. pap. 14.99 (*0-670-85738-6*) Viking Child Bks.

White Guns. Douglas Reeman. Date not set. mass mkt. 6.99 (*0-7493-2407-4*) Heinemann.

White Guys: Studies in Postmodern Domination & Difference. Fred Pfeil. 240p. 1995. pap. 19.00 (*1-85984-032-9*, C0538, Pub. by Vrso UK) Norton.

White Guys: Studies in Postmodern Domination & Difference. Fred Pfeil. 240p. (C). (gr. 13). 1995. text ed. 65.00 (*1-85984-937-7*, C0537, Pub. by Vrso UK) Norton.

*__White-Haired Girl.__ Jaia Sun-Childers & Doug Childers. 1997. pap. 14.00 (*0-614-28146-6*, Picador USA) St Martin.

White-Haired Girl: Bittersweet Adventures of a Little Red Soldier. Jaia S. Childers & Douglas Childers. LC 95-44498. 318p. 1996. 23.00 (*0-312-14093-2*) St Martin.

White Haired Girl see Supplementary Readers for Intermediate Chinese Reader

White Hand. Jean Warmbold. LC 87-60782. 224p. 1988. 22.00 (*0-932966-79-9*) Permanent Pr.

*__White Hart Lane Encyclopedia: An A-Z of Tottenham Hotspur.__ Dean Hayes. (Illus.). 192p. 1996. pap. 17.95 (*1-85158-802-7*, Pub. by Mnstream UK) Trafalgar.

*__White Harvest.__ large type ed. Louis Charbonneau. 576p. 31.50 (*0-7089-3681-4*) Ulverscroft.

White Hats: People Who Are Trying to Make a Difference: Submitted to the Harry Singer Foundation by Students across the Nation. Harry Singer Foundation Staff. Ed. by Margaret Bohannon-Kaplan. LC 94-60870. 140p. (Orig.). 1994. pap. 8.00 (*0-915915-28-6*) Wellington Pubns.

White Hats & Silver Spurs: Interviews with 24 Stars of Film & Television Westerns of the Thirties Through the Sixties. Herb Fagen. LC 96-22997. (Illus.). 253p. 1996. lib. bdg. 38.50 (*0-7864-0200-8*) McFarland & Co.

White-Headed Eagle: John McLoughlin, Builder of an Empire. Richard G. Montgomery. LC 76-164616. (Select Bibliographies Reprint Ser.). 1977. reprint ed. 26.95 (*0-8369-5900-0*) Ayer.

White Heat. Steve James. 60p. (C). 1990. pap. 30.00 (*0-7223-2484-7*, Pub. by A H S Ltd UK) St Mut.

White Heat. Ed. by Patrick McGilligan. LC 83-40257. (Warner Bros. Screenplay Ser.). 1984. 11.95 (*0-299-09670-X*) U of Wis Pr.

White Heat. C. C. Risenhoover. LC 91-77072. 362p. 1992. 20.00 (*0-9627509-3-X*) Baskerville.

White Heat: People & Technology. Carroll Pursell. 1994. pap. 18.00 (*0-520-08905-7*) U CA Pr.

*__White Heat: The Leeds United Dream Team.__ Jason Tomas. (Illus.). 192p. 1997. 34.95 (*1-85158-886-8*, Pub. by Mnstream UK) Trafalgar.

White Heather. Helene Lehr. 416p. (Orig.). 1995. mass mkt., pap. text ed. 4.99 (*0-8439-3795-5*) Dorchester Pub Co.

*__White Heather.__ Jaclyn Reding. 1997. mass mkt. 5.99 (*0-451-40650-8*, Onyx) NAL-Dutton.

*__White Heron.__ Sarah Orne Jewett. LC 96-46638. (Candlewick Treasures Ser.). (Illus.). (J). (gr. 3-9). 1997. 9.99 (*0-7636-0205-1*) Candlewick Pr.

White Heron. Sarah Orne Jewett. LC 83-71791. (Creative's Classic Short Stories Ser.). 40p. (YA). (gr. 6 up). 1983. lib. bdg. 13.95 (*0-87191-966-4*) Creative Ed.

*__White Heron.__ large type ed. Evo Findlow. (Linford Romance Library). 256p. 1996. pap. 15.99 (*0-7089-7919-X*, Linford) Ulverscroft.

*__White Heron & Other Stories.__ Sarah Orne Jewett. (Collected Works of Sarah Orne Jewett). 1988. reprint ed. lib. bdg. 59.00 (*0-7812-1308-8*) Rprt Serv.

White Heron & Other Stories see Collected Works of Sarah Orne Jewett

"White Heron" & the Question of Minor Literature. Louis A. Renza. LC 84-40157. (Wisconsin Project on American Writers Ser.: No. 1). 256p. 1984. text ed. 25.00 (*0-299-09960-1*) U of Wis Pr.

White Heron & the Question of Minor Literature. Louis A. Renza. LC 84-40157. (Wisconsin Project on American Writers Ser.: No. 1). 256p. 1985. pap. text ed. 12.95 (*0-299-09964-4*) U of Wis Pr.

White Hibiscus. large type ed. Rosemary Pollack. (Linford Romance Library). 295p. 1984. pap. 15.99 (*0-7089-6020-0*) Ulverscroft.

White-Hmong English Dictionary. rev. ed. Compiled by Ernest E. Heimbach. (Linguistics Ser.: No. 4). 523p. 1969. pap. 18.00 (*0-87727-075-9*, DP 75) Cornell SE Asia.

White Hole in Time. Peter Russell. 230p. 1995. 30.00 (*1-885261-03-9*) Global Brain.

White Horse. Margaret E. Frere. (C). 1989. 23.00 (*0-7223-2362-X*, Pub. by A H S Ltd UK) St Mut.

White Horse, Dark Dragon. Robert C. Fleet. 224p. (Orig.). 1993. mass mkt. 4.50 (*0-441-88571-3*) Ace Bks.

*__White Horse, Red Rider.__ Barry Brierley. 188p. (Orig.). 1996. pap. 11.95 (*1-889657-27-1*); pap. 11.95 (*0-933025-49-1*) Bear Bks AZ.

White Horses. Alice Hoffman. 1993. mass mkt. 6.99 (*0-425-13980-8*) Berkley Pub.

White Horses & Other Hill Figures. Morris Marples. (Illus.). 224p. 1991. pap. 16.00 (*0-86299-759-3*, Pub. by Sutton Pubng UK) Bks Intl VA.

White Horses & Shooting Stars: A Book of Wishes. David Greer. 156p. (Orig.). 1994. lib. bdg. 29.00 (*0-8095-5885-8*) Borgo Pr.

White Horses & Shooting Stars: A Book of Wishes. David Greer. (Illus.). 160p. (Orig.). 1994. pap. 9.95 (*0-943233-74-7*) Conari Press.

White Horses over France. large type ed. Robin Hanbury-Tenison. (Illus.). 320p. 1987. 25.99 (*0-7089-1574-4*) Ulverscroft.

White Hotel. D. M. Thomas. 240p. 1993. pap. 11.95 (*0-14-023173-0*, Penguin Bks) Viking Penguin.

White Hound of the Mountain. Thomas J. Kiernan. (Illus.). 1962. 9.95 (*0-8159-7208-3*) Devin.

White House. Leonard E. Fisher. LC 89-1990. (Illus.). 96p. (J). (gr. 3-7). 1989. lib. bdg. 16.95 (*0-8234-0774-8*) Holiday.

White House. Paula Guzzetti. LC 95-13275. (Places in American History Ser.). 72p. (YA). (gr. 4 up). 1995. pap. 7.95 (*0-382-39175-6*, Dillon Silver Burdett) Silver Burdett Pr.

White House. Paula Guzzetti. LC 95-13275. (Places in American History Ser.). 72p. (YA). (gr. 4 up). 1995. lib. bdg. 14.95 (*0-87518-650-5*, Dillon Silver Burdett) Silver Burdett Pr.

White House. Deborah Kent. LC 94-9489. (Cornerstones of Freedom Ser.). (Illus.). 32p. (J). (gr. 3-6). 1994. pap. 4.95 (*0-516-46684-4*); lib. bdg. 18.00 (*0-516-06684-6*) Childrens.

White House. Patricia R. Quiri. LC 95-44444. (First Bks.). (Illus.). 64p. (J). (gr. 4-7). 1996. lib. bdg. 21.00 (*0-531-20221-6*) Watts.

White House. Lynda Sorensen. LC 94-7055. (American Symbols Ser.). (J). 1994. write for info. (*1-55916-050-0*) Rourke Bk Co.

White House: An Historic Guide. 160p. 1987. pap. 6.95 (*0-912308-10-9*) Natl Geog.

White House: An Historic Guide. National Geographic Society Staff. 160p. 1996. 12.95 (*0-912308-61-3*) White House Hist.

White House: An Historic Guide. 17th ed. 160p. 1991. 12.95 (*0-912308-43-5*); pap. 9.95 (*0-912308-42-7*) White House Hist.

*__White House: An Historic Guide.__ 17th ed. Ed. by Elizabeth W. Fisher. (Illus.). 161p. 1996. pap. 30.00 (*0-7881-3486-8*) DIANE Pub.

White House: An Historic Guide. 19th ed. National Geographic Society Staff. 160p. 1996. pap. 9.95 (*0-912308-60-5*) White House Hist.

White House: An Historical Guide. 18th ed. National Geographic Society Editorial Staff. 1995. 12.95 (*0-912308-53-2*); pap. 9.95 (*0-912308-52-4*) White House Hist.

White House: Organization & Operations. R. Gordon Hoxie. LC 72-160151. 218p. 1971. 11.00 (*0-317-39576-9*) Ctr Study Presidency.

White House: Resources for Research at the Library of Congress. John Guidas. LC 92-12623. 150p. 1992. 18.00 (*0-8444-0755-0*) Lib Congress.

White House: The First Two Hundred Years. Ed. by Frank Freidel & William Pencak. (Illus.). 288p. 1993. text ed. 24.95 (*1-55553-170-9*) NE U Pr.

White House: The History of an American Idea. William Seale. (Illus.). 350p. 1992. boxed 55.00 (*1-55835-048-9*) AIA Press.

White House Autumn. Ellen E. White. (Orig.). (YA). (gr. 7 up). 1985. mass mkt. 2.95 (*0-380-89780-6*, Flare) Avon.

White House Collection of American Crafts. Michael W. Monroe & Barbaralee Diamonstein. LC 95-75050. (Illus.). 128p. 1995. 35.00 (*0-8109-4035-3*) Abrams.

White House Cookbook. Hugo Ziemann. (Illus.). 640p. 1995. 9.98 (*0-8317-9427-5*) Smithmark.

White House Cookbook: Centennial Edition. rev. ed. Hugo Ziemann et al. 1996. pap. 13.95 (*1-56561-083-0*) Chronimed.

White House Daze: The Unmaking of Domestic Policy in the Bush Years. Charles Kolb. 377p. 1993. text ed. 24.95 (*0-02-917495-3*, Free Press) Free Pr.

White House Diary. Henrietta Nesbitt. (American Autobiography Ser.). 314p. 1995. reprint ed. lib. bdg. 89.00 (*0-7812-8600-X*) Rprt Serv.

*__White House Doctor.__ William A. Lukash. Date not set. write for info. (*0-688-05266-5*) Morrow.

White House Doctor. T. Burton Smith & Carter Henderson. LC 92-31506. 224p. 1992. 24.95 (*0-8191-8625-2*) Madison Bks UPA.

White House E-Mail: The Top-Secret Messages the Reagan/Bush White House Thought They Had Destroyed. Ed. by Tom Blanton. 256p. (Orig.). 1995. pap. 14.95 (*1-56584-276-6*) New Press NY.

White House Ethics: The History of the Politics of Conflict of Interest Regulation. Robert N. Roberts. LC 87-24962. (Contributions in Political Science Ser.: No. 204). 224p. 1988. text ed. 55.00 (*0-313-25934-8*, RWH/, Greenwood Pr) Greenwood.

White House Family Cookbook. Henry Haller & Virginia Aronson. LC 87-9674. (Illus.). 464p. 1987. 30.00 (*0-394-55657-7*) Random.

*__White House Garden: A History.__ William Seale. LC 95-39086. (Illus.). 128p. 1996. pap. 7.95 (*0-912308-65-6*) White House Hist.

White House Glassware: Two Centuries of Entertaining. 148p. 1989. 34.95 (*0-912308-41-9*) White House Hist.

White House Glassware: Two Centuries of Presidential Entertaining. Jane S. Spillman. 148p. 1989. pap. 19.95 (*0-912308-36-2*) White House Hist.

White House Hand-Book of Oratory. Ed. by Charles E. Chadman. LC 77-88075. (Granger Poetry Library). 1977. reprint ed. 25.00 (*0-89609-062-0*) Roth Pub Inc.

White House Horrors. 1996. pap. 5.99 (*0-88677-659-7*) DAW Bks.

White House in Gascony. large type ed. Rex Grizell. 448p. 1994. 25.99 (*0-7089-3076-X*) Ulverscroft.

White House in Miniature: Based on the White House Replica by John & Jan Zweifel. Gail Buckland. LC 94-4193. 1994. 29.95 (*0-393-03663-4*) Norton.

White House Kids. Rose Blue & Corinne J. Naden. (Illus.). 80p. (J). (gr. 5-8). 1995. lib. bdg. 18.90 (*1-56294-447-9*) Millbrook Pr.

White House Ladies. Webb Garrison. LC 96-44333. (Illus.). 256p. 1996. pap. 9.95 (*1-55853-417-2*) Rutledge Hill Pr.

White House Landscapes: Horticultural Achievements of American Presidents. Barbara McEwan. 224p. 1992. 24.95 (*0-8027-1192-8*) Walker & Co.

White House Mess. Christopher Buckley. 320p. 1995. pap. 9.95 (*0-14-009793-7*, Penguin Bks); pap. 11.95 (*0-14-024928-1*, Penguin Bks) Viking Penguin.

White House Mouse. Byron Preiss. (J). Date not set. pap. 14.99 (*0-670-85272-4*) Viking Penguin.

White House on the Pamunkey & the Peninsula Campaign in Virginia, 1862, 6 vols., Set. William A. Dervishian. 1659p. 1995. pap. text ed. 119.70 (*1-887667-00-8*) Pamunkey River Pub.

White House on the Pamunkey & the Peninsula Campaign in Virginia, 1862 Vol I: On to White House, 2nd Part. William A. Dervishian. 260p. 1995. pap. text ed. 19.95 (*1-887667-02-4*) Pamunkey River Pub.

White House on the Pamunkey & the Peninsula Campaign in Virginia, 1862 Vol. I: On to Yorktown, 1st Part. William A. Dervishian. 260p. 1995. pap. text ed. 19.95 (*1-887667-01-6*) Pamunkey River Pub.

White House on the Pamunkey & the Peninsula Campaign in Virginia, 1862 Vol. III: White House Depot, 3rd Part. William A. Dervishian. 1995. pap. text ed. 19.95 (*1-887667-03-2*) Pamunkey River Pub.

White House on the Pamunkey & the Peninsula Campaign in Virginia, 1862 Vol. IV: On to Harrison's Landing, 4th Part. William A. Dervishian. 275p. 1995. pap. text ed. 19.95 (*1-887667-04-0*) Pamunkey River Pub.

White House on the Pamunkey & the Peninsula Campaign in Virginia, 1862 Vol. V: On Back to Washington, D. C., 5th Part. William A. Dervishian. 275p. 1995. pap. text ed. 19.95 (*1-887667-05-9*) Pamunkey River Pub.

White House on the Pamunkey & the Peninsula Campaign in Virginia, 1862 Vol. VI: Cumulative Supplement. William A. Dervishian. 250p. 1995. pap. text ed. 19.95 (*1-887667-06-7*) Pamunkey River Pub.

White House Operations: The Johnson Presidency. Emmette S. Redford & Richard T. McCulley. LC 85-26437. (Administrative History of the Johnson Presidency Ser.). 261p. 1986. text ed. 30.00 (*0-292-79033-3*) U of Tex Pr.

White House Pantry Murder. Elliott Roosevelt. 224p. 1988. mass mkt. 4.50 (*0-380-70404-8*) Avon.

*__White House Press Corp.__ L. H. Whittemore. Date not set. write for info. (*0-688-05106-5*) Morrow.

White House Speaks: Presidential Leadership as Persuasion. Craig A. Smith & Kathy B. Smith. LC 93-23468. (Praeger Series in Political Communication). 288p. 1994. text ed. 59.95 (*0-275-94394-1*, Praeger Pubs) Greenwood.

White House Staff & The National Security Assistant: Friendship & Friction at the Water's Edge. Joseph G. Bock. LC 86-29619. (Contributions in Political Science Ser.: No. 170). 226p. 1987. text ed. 55.00 (*0-313-25698-5*, BFF, Greenwood Pr) Greenwood.

White House Sucks. Chris Musun. (Orig.). 1986. pap. 8.95 (*0-936729-00-7*) Dare Co.

White House to Your House: Media & Politics in Virtual America. Edwin Diamond & Robert A. Silverman. (Illus.). 168p. (C). 1995. 20.00 (*0-262-04150-2*) MIT Pr.

*__White House to Your House: Media & Politics in Virtual America.__ Edwin Diamond & Robert A. Silverman. (Illus.). 192p. 1997. reprint ed. pap. 12.50 (*0-262-54086-X*) MIT Pr.

White House Travel Office Operations. (Illus.). 93p. (Orig.). (C). 1994. pap. text ed. 40.00 (*0-7881-1091-8*) DIANE Pub.

*__White House Trivia.__ Karr. (J). 1998. 15.95 (*0-7868-2319-4*) Hyprn Child.

White Hyacinths. Elbert Hubbard. (DeYoung Classic Reprint Ser.). reprint ed. 25.00 (*0-936128-31-3*) De Young Pr.

White Ibis: Wetland Wanderer. Keith L. Bildstein. LC 92-38961. (Illus.). 272p. 1993. 22.50 (*1-56098-223-3*) Smithsonian.

White Indian Boy. Duane R. Lund. 1981. pap. 8.95 (*0-934860-17-3*) Adventure Pubns.

White Indian Boy. Charles A. Wilson. Ed. by John Stewart & Trilba N. Redding. Bd. with Return of the White Indian. LC 86-127837. LC 86-127837. (Illus.). 395p. 1985. 32.50 (*0-9616261-0-0*) C A Wilson.

White Indian Boy. rev. ed. Ed. by Charles A. Wilson & Trilba N. Redding. Bd. with Return of the White Indian. LC 86-127837. LC 86-127837. (Illus.). 395p. 1988. 32.50 (*0-317-89517-6*) C A Wilson.

White Indians of Colonial America. James Axtell. 38p. 1991. reprint ed. pap. 5.95 (*0-87770-210-1*) Ye Galleon.

White Ink: Essays on Twentieth-Century Feminine Fiction in Spain & Latin America. Stephen Hart. (Monagrafias A Ser.: Vol. 156). 170p. (C). 1993. 63.00 (*1-85566-031-8*, Pub. by Tamesis Bks Ltd UK) Boydell & Brewer.

*__White Ironstone.__ LC 95-76091. (Illus.). 240p. 1996. pap. text ed. 25.95 (*0-930625-38-2*, Antque Trdr Bks) Antique Trader Bks.

White Ironstone: A Collector's Guide. Jean Wetherbee. LC 95-76091. (Illus.). 240p. (Orig.). 1996. pap. 20.95 (*0-930625-36-6*, Antque Trdr Bks) Antique Trader Bks.

*__White Ironstone: A Survey of Its Many Forms Undecorated, Flow Blue, Mulberry, Copper Lustre.__ Dawn Stoltzfus & Jeffrey B. Snyder. LC 97-20246. 1997. pap. write for info. (*0-7643-0326-0*) Schiffer.

White Is the Moon. Valerie Greeley. LC 90-40522. (Illus.). 32p. (J). (ps-1). 1991. text ed. 13.95 (*0-02-736915-3*, Mac Bks Young Read) S&S Childrens.

W

White Isle. Darrell Schweitzer. (Weird Tales Library). (Illus.). viii, 139p. 1989. lib. bdg. 18.95 (*0-913896-26-8*) Owlswick Pr.

***White Issue, Vol. 6, No. 4.** Ed. by K. Anthony Appiah et al. 200p. 1997. pap. 10.00 (*0-8223-6442-5*) Duke.

White Jacket. Herman Melville. 1979. mass mkt. 4.95 (*0-452-00955-3*, Meridian Bks MD) NAL-Dutton.

White-Jacket. Herman Melville. Ed. by Harrison Hayford et al. LC 67-21603. (Northwestern-Newberry Edition of the Writings of Herman Melville: Vol. 5). 499p. 1970. 59.95 (*0-8101-0257-9*); pap. 19.95 (*0-8101-0258-7*) Northwestern U Pr.

White-Jacket. Herman Melville. LC 88-2650. (Classics of Naval Literature Ser.). 736p. 1988. reprint ed. 32.95 (*0-87021-788-7*) Naval Inst Pr.

White-Jacket: Or the World in a Man of War. Herman Melville. 488p. 1991. pap. 7.95 (*0-19-281828-7*) OUP.

White Jazz. James Ellroy. (Los Angeles Mysteries Ser.). 1993. mass mkt. 5.99 (*0-449-14841-6*, GM) Fawcett.

***White Jazz.** James Ellroy. 1997. pap. 12.00 (*0-449-00088-5*) Fawcett.

White Jazz. Charles Newman. LC 86-46072. 213p. (Orig.). 1984. pap. 7.95 (*0-385-18863-3*) Ultramarine Pub.

White Junk of Love, Again. Sibyl James. LC 86-20772. 75p. (Orig.). 1986. 14.95 (*0-934971-05-6*) Calyx Bks.

***White Knights & Ascending Shadows: An Oral History of the San Francisco AIDS Epidemic.** Benjamin H. Shepard. LC 97-6629. (Illus.). 320p. 1997. pap. 29.95 (*0-304-70126-2*) Cassell.

***White Knights & Ascending Shadows: An Oral History of the San Francisco AIDS Epidemic.** Benjamin H. Shepard. LC 97-6629. (Illus.). 320p. 1997. 79.50 (*0-304-70125-4*) Cassell.

White Knuckle Ride. 1996. 14.99 (*0-517-15945-7*) Random Hse Value.

White Knuckles: Thrillers & Other Stories by American Teen Writers. Ed. by R. James Stahl & Jo-Ann Langseth. LC 94-42352. (American Teen Writer Ser.). 144p. (Orig.). (YA). (gr. 7-12). 1995. pap. 9.75 (*1-886427-01-1*) Merlyns Pen.

White Knuckles & Wishful Thinking: Breaking the Chain of Compulsive Reaction & Relapse in Alcoholism & Other Addictions. George DuWors. LC 91-35428. (Illus.). 288p. 1992. 22.50 (*0-88937-092-3*) Hogrefe & Huber Pubs.

White Labyrinth: Cocaine & Political Power. Rensselaer W. Lee. 256p. 1989. 39.95 (*0-88738-285-1*) Transaction Pubs.

White Labyrinth: Cocaine & Political Power. Rensselaer W. Lee, III. 262p. (C). 1991. pap. text ed. 24.95 (*1-56000-565-3*) Transaction Pubs.

***White Lace & Promices, Vol. 842.** Marcia Evanick. (Loveswept Ser.). 1997. mass mkt. 3.50 (*0-553-44586-3*) Bantam.

White Lace, Black Leather, & the Immaculate Conception of Edmund, Earl of Gloucester. Brendan Tripp. 36p. 1980. pap. 5.00 (*1-57353-002-6*) Eschaton Prods.

White Lady. Grace L. Hill. 1976. reprint ed. lib. bdg. 23.95 (*0-89190-025-X*, Rivercity Pr) Amereon Ltd.

White Lady Doing Nothing in the Tropics: The Story of Herman & Mary Dixon. Mary Dixon. LC 95-71782. (Jaffray Collection Of Missionary Portraits: No. 15). 1996. pap. 8.99 (*0-87509-641-7*) Chr Pubns.

***White Lady Doing Nothing in the Tropics: The Story of Herman & Mary Dixon.** Carol S. Wedeven. (Junior Jaffray Collection of Missionary Stories: Bk. 15). (Illus.). (J). 1996. 3.99 (*0-87509-649-2*) Chr Pubns.

White Lady War. William Costopoulos. LC 89-328. 1990. 21.95 (*0-87949-301-1*) Ashley Bks.

White Lake Township Cemeteries, Oakland County, Michigan. Intro. by Joan Pate. 109p. (Orig.). 1990. pap. 8.00 (*1-879766-13-2*) OCG Society.

White Land, Black Labor: Caste & Class in Late Nineteenth-Century Georgia. Charles L. Flynn. LC 83-721. (Illus.). 210p. 1983. reprint ed. pap. 59.90 (*0-608-00864-8*, 2061656) Bks Demand.

White Leaves. Joy Balyeat Nash. LC 90-71567. (Illus.). 80p. (Orig.). 1990. pap. 8.95 (*0-9623026-1-9*) Stonehaven TX.

White Leg. Max Martinez. LC 95-33396. 257p. 1996. 19.95 (*1-55885-098-8*) Arte Publico.

White Leopard. Inglis Fletcher. 304p. reprint ed. lib. bdg. 23.95 (*0-89244-013-9*, Queens House) Amereon Ltd.

***White Lie.** Bird & Falk, (New Trend Fiction B Ser.). (J). 1993. pap. text ed. write for info. (*0-582-80039-0*, Pub. by Longman UK) Longman.

White Lie. Walter T. Rea. LC 81-83353. (Illus.). 409p. (Orig.). 1982. 16.95 (*0-9607424-0-9*); pap. 13.95 (*0-9607424-1-7*) M & R Pubns.

White Lies. David Axelrod. Ed. by Kathleen Iddings. LC 87-83063. (Illus.). 48p. (Orig.). 1988. per. write for info. (*0-931721-08-3*) La Jolla Poets.

***White Lies.** Linda Howard. 1997. mass mkt. 5.50 (*1-55166-274-4*, 1-66274-1, Mira Bks) Harlequin Bks.

***White Lies.** H. F. Saint. Date not set. write for info. (*0-688-11817-8*) Morrow.

White Lies. Trevor Shearston. LC 85-8756. 206p. 1988. pap. 14.95 (*0-7022-2026-4*, Pub. by Univ Queensland Pr AT) Intl Spec Bk.

***White Lies.** Sara Wood. 1997. mass mkt. 3.50 (*0-373-11910-0*, 1-11910-6) Harlequin Bks.

White Lies. large type ed. Francine Pascal. (Sweet Valley High Ser.: No. 52). 137p. (J). (gr. 5-8). 1989. reprint ed. 9.50 (*1-55905-007-1*); reprint ed. lib. bdg. 10.50 (*1-55905-017-9*) Grey Castle.

***White Lies.** large type ed. Sara Wood. (Mills & Boon Large Print Ser.). 288p. 1996. 21.50 (*0-263-14753-3*, Pub. by M & B UK) Ulverscroft.

White Lies: Melville's Narratives of Facts. John Samson. LC 88-43324. 272p. 1989. 39.95 (*0-8014-2280-9*) Cornell U Pr.

White Lies: Race, Class, Gender & Sexuality in White Supremacist Discourse. Jessie Daniels. 256p. 1996. pap. 15.95 (*0-415-91290-3*) Routledge.

White Lies: Race, Class, Gender, & Sexuality in White Supremacist Discourse. Jessie Daniels. 256p. (C). (gr. 13 up). 1997. text ed. 55.00 (*0-415-91289-X*, Routledge NY) Routledge.

White Lies: Rape, Murder & Justice Texas Style. Nick Davies. 432p. 1993. mass mkt. 4.99 (*0-380-71845-6*) Avon.

White Lies, White Power: The Fight Against White Supremacy & Reactionary Violence. Michael Novick. Ed. by Greg Bates. 330p. (C). 1995. lib. bdg. 29.95 (*1-56751-051-5*) Common Courage.

White Lies, White Power: The Fight Against White Supremacy & Reactionary Violence. Michael Novick. Ed. by Greg Bates. 330p. (C). 1995. pap. 16.95 (*1-56751-050-7*) Common Courage.

White Light. Wendy Haley. 1995. pap. 4.99 (*0-8217-4998-6*) NAL-Dutton.

***White Light.** Rudy Rucker. LC 97-15079. 1997. pap. text ed. 12.95 (*1-888869-17-8*) HardWired.

White Light Meditation: The Shekinah Experience. Richard L. Harding. (Illus.). 137p. (Orig.). 1996. pap. 9.95 (*0-614-14201-6*) Internet Bks.

White Lightning. Sharon Brondos. (Crystal Creek Ser.). 1993. mass mkt. 3.99 (*0-373-82516-1*, 1-82516-5) Harlequin Bks.

***White Lightning.** Candice Poarch. 1997. mass mkt. 4.99 (*0-7860-0365-0*, Pinncle Kensgtn) Kensgtn Pub Corp.

White Lightning. Sherryl Woods. 320p. (Orig.). 1995. pap. 5.99 (*0-446-60090-3*) Warner Bks.

White Lilacs. Carolyn Meyer. LC 92-30503. 256p. (J). (gr. 3-7). 1993. 11.00 (*0-15-200641-9*, Gulliver Bks) HarBrace.

White Lilacs. Carolyn Meyer. LC 92-3050. 256p. (J). (gr. 3-7). 1993. pap. 4.00 (*0-15-295876-2*, Gulliver Bks) HarBrace.

White Lilacs. large type ed. Carolyn Meyer. 1993. 63.00 (*0-614-09861-0*, L-34182-00) Am Printing Hse.

White Lily. Linda Ladd. 384p. (Orig.). 1993. pap. 4.99 (*0-451-40363-0*, Topaz) NAL-Dutton.

***White Line.** G. Brender a Brandis. 108p. 1990. pap. 14.95 (*0-88984-117-9*, Pub. by Porcupines Quill CN) Genl Dist Srvs.

***White Lion - Big Game.** Ed. by Aaron Stang. 140p. (Orig.). (C). 1989. pap. text ed. 17.95 (*0-7692-0950-5*, GF0400) Warner Brothers.

White Logic: Alcoholism & Gender in American Modernist Fiction. John W. Crowley. LC 94-14809. 216p. (C). 1994. pap. 15.95 (*0-87023-944-9*) U of Mass Pr.

White Logic: Jack London's Short Stories see Jack London's Strong Truths

White Lotus. John Hersey. LC 89-40134. 1994. reprint ed. lib. bdg. 35.95 (*1-56849-532-3*) Buccaneer Bks.

White Lotus Teachings in Chinese Religious History. B. J. Ter Haar. LC 91-18963. (Sinica Leidensia Ser.: Vol. 26). (Illus.). ix, 343p. 1992. 121.50 (*90-04-09414-8*) E J Brill.

***White Magic.** Mary Stanton. (Magical Mystery Ser.). 160p. (J). 1997. mass mkt. 3.99 (*0-425-15904-3*) Berkley Pub.

***White Magic.** Mary Stanton. (Magical Mystery Ser.). (J). 1997. write for info. (*0-614-29183-6*) Berkley Pub.

White Magic. David C. Phillips. (Collected Works of David G. Phillips). 1988. reprint ed. lib. bdg. 79.00 (*0-7812-1340-1*) Rprt Serv.

White Magic. David G. Phillips. (American Author Ser.). 1981. reprint ed. lib. bdg. 49.00 (*0-686-71946-8*) Scholarly.

White Magic: The Origins & Ideas of Black Mental & Cultural Colonialism. Chukwudi O. Maduno. 279p. (Orig.). 1994. pap. 12.00 (*1-56411-085-0*) Untd Bros & Sis.

White Magic Book. John LeBreton. 100p. 1970. reprint ed. spiral bd. 7.00 (*0-7873-0546-4*) Hlth Research.

White Magic Book: The Correct Answers to Your Problems. J. LeBreton. 1991. lib. bdg. 79.95 (*0-8490-4553-3*) Gordon Pr.

White, Male & Middle Class: Explorations in Feminism & History. Catherine Hall. 320p. (C). 1992. pap. 17.95 (*0-415-90663-6*, A9507, Routledge NY) Routledge.

White Man: A Study of the Attitudes of Africans to Europeans in Ghana before Independence. Gustav Jahoda. LC 83-5655. xii, 144p. 1983. reprint ed. text ed. 49.75 (*0-313-23963-0*, JAWH, Greenwood Pr) Greenwood.

White Man Got No Dreaming. Stanner. (Australian National University Press Ser.). 1979. text ed. 64.00 (*0-08-032921-7*, Pergamon Pr) Elsevier.

White Man in a Rickshaw: Famous & Forgotten Pre-War Writings on Japan. John Ashburne. (Illus.). 352p. 1996. pap. 12.00 (*4-7700-2031-7*) Kodansha.

White Man, Listen! Richard A. Wright. LC 94-44808. 224p. 1995. pap. 12.00 (*0-06-092564-7*, PL) HarpC.

White Man, Listen! Richard A. Wright. LC 78-17905. 190p. 1978. reprint ed. text ed. 49.50 (*0-313-20533-7*, WRWM, Greenwood Pr) Greenwood.

White Man of God. Kenjo Jumbam. (African Writers Ser.). 151p. (Orig.). (C). 1981. pap. 8.95 (*0-435-90231-8*, 90231) Heinemann.

White Man Returns. large type ed. Agnes N. Keith. 1979. 25.99 (*0-7089-0344-4*) Ulverscroft.

White-Man-Runs-Him. 2nd ed. Dennis W. Harcey & Brian Croone. (Illus.). 224p. (Orig.). 1995. pap. 15.50 (*1-879260-36-0*) Evanston Pub.

White Man, We Want to Talk to You. Denis Herbstein. LC 78-26133. 270p. 1979. 28.00 (*0-8419-0455-3*, Africana) Holmes & Meier.

White Man Will Eat You! An Anthropologist among the Imbonggu of New Guinea. George D. Spindler. LC 92-81264. (Case Studies in Cultural Anthropology). 140p. (C). 1993. pap. text ed. 13.50 (*0-15-500196-5*) HB Coll Pubs.

White Man's Burden: A Satirical Forecast. Roger S. Tracy, pseud. LC 72-4597. (Black Heritage Library Collection). 1977. reprint ed. 25.95 (*0-8369-9130-3*) Ayer.

White Man's Burden: An Anthology of British Poetry of the Empire. Ed. by Brooks & Faulkner. 176p. 1996. text ed. 50.00 (*0-85989-492-4*, Pub. by Univ Exeter Pr UK) Northwestern U Pr.

White Man's Burden: An Anthology of British Poetry of the Empire. Ed. by Chris Brooks & Faulkner. 176p. 1996. pap. text ed. 19.95 (*0-85989-450-9*, Pub. by Univ Exeter Pr UK) Northwestern U Pr.

White Man's Burden: Historical Origins of Racism in the United States. Winthrop D. Jordan. 246p. 1974. pap. 10.95 (*0-19-501743-9*) OUP.

White Man's Dilemma: Climax of the Age of Imperialism. Nathaniel Peffer. LC 72-4288. (World Affairs Ser.: National & International Viewpoints). 320p. 1972. reprint ed. 23.95 (*0-405-04580-8*) Ayer.

White Man's Dreaming: Killalpaninna Mission 1866-1915. Christine Stevens. (Illus.). 312p. 1994. 55.00 (*0-19-553574-X*) OUP.

White Man's Grave. Richard Dooling. LC 93-37427. 1994. 22.00 (*0-374-28951-4*) FS&G.

White Man's Grave: A Novel. Richard Dooling. 400p. 1995. pap. 13.00 (*0-312-13214-X*) St Martin.

White Man's Indian: Images of the American Indian from Columbus to the Present. Robert F. Berkhofer, Jr. LC 78-11047. (Illus.). 1979. pap. 8.76 (*0-394-72794-0*, V-794, Vin) Random.

White Man's Justice. Donald Goines. 240p. 1995. mass mkt. 4.95 (*0-87067-955-4*) Holloway.

White Man's Justice: South African Political Trials in the Black Consciousness Era. Michael Lobban. 304p. 1996. 65.00 (*0-19-825809-7*) OUP.

White Man's Road. Benjamin Capps. LC 88-42633. (Southwest Life & Letters Ser.). 328p. 1988. reprint ed. 22.50 (*0-87074-281-7*); reprint ed. pap. 10.95 (*0-87074-272-8*) SMU Press.

White Man's Wicked Water: The Alcohol Trade & Prohibition in Indian Country, 1802-1892. William E. Unrau. LC 95-51317. (Illus.). 200p. 1996. 25.00 (*0-7006-0779-X*) U Pr of KS.

White Mask. G. Turner Howard. 1996. 13.95 (*0-533-11630-9*) Vantage.

White Men & My Stuff. Karol Finley. 248p. (Orig.). 1993. pap. 13.95 (*0-9637106-0-5*) Crystal Hse.

White Men Don't Have Juju: An American Couple's Adventure Through Africa from the Forbidden Zone to Timbuktu. Pam Ascanio. LC 91-51220. (Illus.). 345p. (Orig.). 1992. pap. 12.95 (*1-879360-12-8*) Noble Pr.

***White Men, Women & Minorities in the Changing Work Force: Race, Innovation, Sex, Technology, Power, Global Markets.** Anthony J. Ipsaro. (Orig.). 1997. mass mkt. 19.95 (*0-9645723-3-8*) Meridian Assocs.

White Merc with Fins. James Hawes. 1997. pap. 12.00 (*0-679-77615-X*) Random.

White Merc with Fins: A Novel. James Hawes. LC 95-33078. 304p. 1996. 22.00 (*0-679-44225-1*) Pantheon.

White Mercedes. Sandra Agricola. (Ohio Review Bks.). 72p. 1988. 11.95 (*0-942148-09-6*); pap. 7.95 (*0-942148-08-8*) Ohio Review.

***White Mercedes.** Philip Pullman. 1997. pap. 4.99 (*0-679-88623-0*) Knopf.

White Mercedes. Phillip Pullman. LC 92-11072. 160p. (J). (gr. 7 up). 1993. 16.00 (*0-679-83198-3*) Knopf Bks Yng Read.

White Mercedes. Phillip Pullman. 1992. pap. write for info. (*0-679-93198-8*) McKay.

White Metal Universe: Navajo Silver from the Fred Harvey Collection. Byron Harvey, III et al. Ed. by Cynthia J. Davies. LC 81-171386. (Illus.). 53p. (Orig.). 1981. pap. 5.00 (*0-934351-20-1*) Heard Mus.

White Mirror. Johannes Bobrowski. Ed. by Constance Hunting. Tr. by Muska Nagel. 100p. 1993. pap. 12.95 (*0-913006-55-6*) Puckerbrush.

White Mists of Power. Kristine K. Rusch. 304p. (Orig.). 1991. pap. 3.99 (*0-451-45120-1*, ROC) NAL-Dutton.

White Monk: An Essay on Dostoevsky & Melville. F. D. Reeve. LC 89-35562. 192p. 1990. 22.95 (*0-8265-1234-8*) Vanderbilt U Pr.

White Monkey King: A Chinese Fable. Sally Wriggins. LC 76-44281. (Illus.). (J). (gr. 1-5). 1977. 5.95 (*0-394-83450-X*) Pantheon.

White Moon, Red Dragon. David Wingrove. LC 95-39571. (Chung Kuo Ser.: No. 6). 576p. 1996. pap. 14.95 (*0-440-50731-6*, Dell Trade Pbks) Dell.

White Moon Tree, Vol. 3. Paul A. Hawkins. (Ben Tree Saga Ser.). 352p. 1994. 5.99 (*0-451-17828-9*, Sig) NAL-Dutton.

White Morning. Judith Berke. LC 88-38537. (Wesleyan New Poets Ser.). 62p. 1989. 12.95 (*0-8195-2173-6*, Wesleyan Univ Pr) U Pr of New Eng.

White Motif: The Cyclades Islands of Greece. Howard Bond. (Illus.). 84p. 1991. 32.00 (*0-9612734-2-9*) Goodrich Pr.

White Mountain: Chung Kuo III. David Wingrove. 624p. 1992. mass mkt. 6.50 (*0-440-21356-8*) Dell.

White Mountain Murders. Steve Sherman. 176p. 1989. 17.95 (*0-8027-5735-9*) Walker & Co.

***White Mountain Redware: A Pottery Tradition of East-Central Arizona & Western New Mexico.** Roy L. Carlson. (Anthropological Papers: No. 19). 130p. 1970. write for info. (*0-8165-1731-2*) U of Ariz Pr.

White Mountain Sports & Activities. Chris Stewart. (Illus.). 275p. 1990. pap. 14.95 (*0-9623199-3-7*) Dirigo Bks.

White Mountains. John Christopher. LC 67-10362. 192p. (J). (gr. 5-9). 1967. lib. bdg. 16.00 (*0-02-718360-2*, Mac Bks Young Read) S&S Childrens.

White Mountains. 2nd ed. John Christopher. LC 88-16119. (Tripods Trilogy Ser.). (Illus.). 224p. (YA). (gr. 7 up). 1988. pap. 3.95 (*0-02-042711-5*) Macmillan.

White Mountains: A Study Guide. Gloria Levine. (Novel-Ties Ser.). 1987. teacher ed., wbk. ed., pap. text ed. 15.95 (*0-88122-097-3*) Lrn Links.

White Mountains: Names, Places, & Legends. 2nd ed. John T. Mudge. (Illus.). 222p. 1995. pap. 13.95 (*0-9633560-6-2*) Durand Pr.

White Mountains Hotels. David Emerson. (Images of America Ser.). 128p. 1996. pap. 16.99 (*0-7524-0289-7*, Arcdia) Chalford.

White Mountains, NH. R. Bennett. (Images of America Ser.). 1994. pap. 14.99 (*0-7524-0077-0*, Arcdia) Chalford.

White Mountains-West. Philip Preston & Jonathan A. Kannair. LC 79-66098. (Illus.). (Orig.). 1979. pap. 7.50 (*0-9603106-0-6*) Waumbek.

White Mule. William C. Williams. LC 37-11249. (Stecher Trilogy Ser.: Vol. 1). 1967. pap. 11.95 (*0-8112-0238-0*, NDP226) New Directions.

White Museum. Lynne Dreyer. LC 86-6180. (Roof Bks.). 125p. (Orig.). 1986. pap. 7.50 (*0-937804-21-5*) Segue NYC.

White Mutiny. Edwin Hirschmann. 1980. 24.00 (*0-8364-0639-7*) S Asia.

***White Mutiny: British Military Culture in India.** Peter Stanley. LC 97-716. 1997. 40.00 (*0-8147-8083-0*) NYU Pr.

White Mythologies: Writing, History & the West. Robertd Young. 256p. (C). (gr. 13). 1991. pap. 17.95 (*0-415-05372-2*, A4851) Routledge.

***White Narcissus.** Raymond Knister. 1996. pap. text ed. 5.95 (*0-7710-9963-0*) McCland & Stewart.

White, New York Corporation, 8 vols. 13th ed. Isidore Kantrowitz & Sol Slutsky. 1963. Updates. ring bd. write for info. (*0-8205-1812-3*) Bender.

White Niggers of America: The Precocious Autobiography of a Quebec "Terrorist" Pierre Vallieres. LC 76-142986. 288p. reprint ed. pap. 82.10 (*0-7837-6996-2*, 2046809) Bks Demand.

White Nights. Boris Sokoloff. 9.95 (*0-8159-7209-1*) Devin.

White Nights & Other Stories see Notes from the Underground

White Nights, Red Morning. Judith Pella. (Russians Ser.: Bk. 6). 416p. 1996. pap. 10.99 (*1-55661-360-1*) Bethany Hse.

***White Nile.** Alan Moorehead. lib. bdg. 27.95 (*0-8488-2006-1*) Amereon Ltd.

White Nile. rev. ed. Alan Moorehead. LC 95-75324. (Adventure Library: Vol. 4). (Illus.). 424p. 1995. reprint ed. lib. bdg. 25.00 (*1-885283-03-2*) Advent Library.

White Nile Arabs: Political Leadership & Economic Change. Abbas A. Mohamed. (London School of Economics Monographs on Social Anthropology: No. 53). (Illus.). 193p. (C). 1980. text ed. 42.50 (*0-485-19553-4*, Pub. by Athlone Pr UK) Humanities.

White Nineteens. David Christiana. (Illus.). 32p. (J). (ps-3). 1992. 15.00 (*0-374-38390-1*) FS&G.

White Ninja. Eric Van Lustbader. 1991. mass mkt. 5.95 (*0-449-21851-1*, Crest) Fawcett.

White Noise. Don DeLillo. (Contemporary American Fiction Ser.). 336p. 1986. pap. 11.95 (*0-14-007702-2*, Penguin Bks) Viking Penguin.

White Noise. Don DeLillo. (Contemporary American Fiction Ser.). 336p. 1991. pap. 8.95 (*0-14-099704-0*, Penguin Bks) Viking Penguin.

***White Noise.** Eve Zaremba. 1997. pap. 9.95 (*0-929005-97-X*, Pub. by Second Story Pr CN) LPC InBook.

White Noise: An Infinite Dimensional Calculus. T. Hida. (Mathematics & Its Applications Ser.). 532p. (C). 1993. lib. bdg. 251.50 (*0-7923-2233-9*) Kluwer Ac.

White Noise Analysis. Ed. by Ludwig Streit et al. 436p. (C). 1990. text ed. 130.00 (*981-02-0242-3*) World Scientific Pub.

White Noise Calculus & Fock Space. N. Obata. (Lecture Notes in Mathematics Ser.: No. 1577). 183p. 1994. 35.95 (*0-387-57985-0*) Spr-Verlag.

White Noise Distribution Theory. Hui-Hsiung Kuo. 400p. 1996. 69.95 (*0-8493-8077-4*) CRC Pr.

White Noise on Bialgebras. Michael Schurmann. LC 93-18938. (Lecture Notes in Bialgebras Ser.: Vol. 1544). 1993. 37.95 (*0-387-56627-9*) Spr-Verlag.

White Noise Theory of Prediction, Filtering & Smoothing, Vol. 3. G. Kallianpur & R. L. Karandikar. (Stochastics Monographs: Vol. 3). xiv, 598p. 1988. text ed. 275.00 (*2-88124-685-0*) Gordon & Breach.

White on Black. Tana Hoban. LC 92-20092. (Illus.). 12p. (J). (ps up). 1993. pap. 4.95 (*0-688-11919-0*) Greenwillow.

White on Black: Contemporary Literature about Africa. John Gruesser. 200p. (C). 1992. text ed. 29.95 (*0-252-01916-4*) U of Ill Pr.

White on Black: Images of Africa & Blacks in Western Popular Culture. Jan N. Pieterse. LC 91-41603. (C). 1992. 40.00 (*0-300-05020-8*) Yale U Pr.

White on Black: Images of Africa & Blacks in Western Popular Culture. Jan N. Pieterse. (Illus.). 242p. 1995. 20.00 (*0-300-06311-3*) Yale U Pr.

White on Black see Blanco en Negro

White on Black in South Africa: A Study of English-Language Inscriptions of Skin Color. Michael Wade. LC 90-32845. 240p. 1993. text ed. 45.00 (*0-312-04712-6*) St Martin.

White on Black on White. Coleman Dowell. 1991. pap. 14.95 (*1-85242-160-6*) Serpents Tail.

An Asterisk (*) at the beginning of an entry indicates that the title is appearing in BIP for the first time.

W

White on White. Eugenio De Andrade. Tr. by Levitin. (QRL Poetry Bks.: Vol. XXVII). (POR.). 1987. 35.00 (*0-614-06420-1*) Quarterly Rev.

White Orchid. Linda Ladd. 384p. (Orig.). 1995. mass mkt. 5.99 (*0-451-40555-2*, Topaz) NAL-Dutton.

White Orchids. Grace L. Hill. 24.95 (*0-8488-0090-7*) Amereon Ltd.

White Orchids. large type ed. Grace L. Hill. 384p. 1992. lib. bdg. 19.95 (*1-56054-366-3*) Thorndike Pr.

White Orchids, No. 28. Grace L. Hill. (Grace Livingston Hill Ser.: Vol. 28). 288p. 1995. mass mkt., pap. 4.99 (*0-8423-8150-3*) Tyndale.

***White Out.** Alexander Cockburn. Date not set. pap. 17.00 (*1-85984-139-2*, Pub. by Verso UK) Routledge Chapman & Hall.

***White Out.** Alexander Cockburn. (C). Date not set. text ed. 60.00 (*1-85984-897-4*, Pub. by Verso UK) Routledge Chapman & Hall.

White over Black: American Attitudes Toward the Negro, 1550-1812. Winthrop D. Jordan. LC 68-13295. (Institute of Early American History & Culture Ser.). (Illus.). xx, 671p. 1968. 50.00 (*0-8078-1055-X*) U of NC Pr.

White over Black: American Attitudes Toward the Negro, 1550-1812. Winthrop D. Jordan. LC 68-13295. (Published for the Institute of Early American History & Culture Ser.). 671p. (C). 1995. pap. 16.95 (*0-8078-4550-7*) U of NC Pr.

White Owl & Blue Mouse. Jean Joubert. Tr. by Denise Levertov from FRE. LC 90-70710. (Illus.). 64p. (J). (gr. 1-3). 1990. 13.95 (*0-944072-13-5*) Zoland Bks.

White Paper & Beyond: One Year On. Ed. by E. J. Beck & S. A. Adam. (Illus.). 160p. 1991. 49.95 (*0-19-262048-7*) OUP.

White Paper International Trade in Japan, 89. 1990. 85.00 (*4-8224-0473-0*) Taylor & Francis.

White Paper on International Trade: Japan 1993. Ministry on International Trade & Industry Staff. 410p. 1993. 105.00 (*4-8224-0633-4*, Pub. by Japan External Trade JA) Gale.

White Paper on International Trade: Japan 1995. Ministry on International Trade & Industry Staff. 400p. 1995. pap. 143.00 (*4-8224-0711-X*, Pub. by JETRO JA) Taylor & Francis.

White Paper on International Trade, Japan, 1992. Ed. by Japan External Trade Organization (JETRO) Staff. 430p. 1992. pap. 130.00 (*4-8224-0595-8*, Pub. by JETRO JA) Taylor & Francis.

***White Paper on International Trade 1996.** Ministry on International Trade & Industry Staff. 400p. 1996. pap. 113.00 (*4-8224-0757-8*, Pub. by JETRO JA) Taylor & Francis.

***White Papers.** James White. Ed. by Mark L. Olson & Bruce Pelz. LC 96-69493. 397p. 1996. 25.00 (*0-915368-71-4*) New Eng SF Assoc.

White Papers for White Americans. Calvin C. Hernton. LC 82-6101. x, 155p. 1982. reprint ed. text ed. 49.75 (*0-313-22325-4*, HEWP, Greenwood Pr) Greenwood.

White Papers of an Outraged Conservative. John P. Cohane. LC 72-190112. 1972. 10.00 (*0-672-51280-7*, Bobbs) Macmillan.

***White Papers on Club Management.** Bridgette M. Redman et al. LC 97-25551. (Topical Reference Ser.). 1997. write for info. (*0-86612-164-1*) Educ Inst Am Hotel.

White Papers on Facility Topics Vol. I. John L. Stanley et al. (Illus.). 78p. (Orig.). 1994. pap. 25.00 (*1-883176-01-8*) Intl Facility Mgmt Assn.

***White Papers on Today's Vietnam: How the World Can Help the People of Vietnam Reach a Better Life.** Pham Kim Vinh. 164p. (Orig.). 1996. pap. 10.00 (*1-882273-28-1*) P K Vinh Res.

White Pass: Gateway to the Klondike. Roy Minter. (Illus.). 394p. 1987. 24.95 (*0-912006-26-9*) U of Alaska Pr.

White Pass: Gateway to the Klondike. Roy Minter. (Illus.). 394p. 1988. pap. 15.95 (*0-912006-33-1*) U of Alaska Pr.

White Pass & Yukon Route: A Pictorial History. Stan B. Cohen. LC 79-90884. (Illus.). 120p. 1980. pap. text ed. 9.95 (*0-933126-08-5*) Pictorial Hist.

White Paternoster, & Other Stories. Theodore F. Powys. LC 70-178455. (Short Story Index Reprint Ser.). 1977. reprint ed. 18.95 (*0-8369-4056-3*) Ayer.

White Peace among the Willows. 274p. 1968. lib. bdg. 70.50 (*90-247-0200-3*, Pub. by M Nijhoff NE) Kluwer Ac.

***White Peacock.** D. H. Lawrence. Ed. by David Bradshaw. (World's Classics). 416p. 1997. pap. 9.95 (*0-19-283087-2*) OUP.

White Peacock. D. H. Lawrence. 432p. 1990. pap. 9.95 (*0-14-018219-5*, Penguin Classics) Viking Penguin.

White Peacock. D. H. Lawrence. (Twentieth Century Classics Ser.). 416p. 1995. pap. 10.95 (*0-14-018778-2*, Penguin Classics) Viking Penguin.

White Peak Farm. Berlie Doherty. LC 89-23060. 128p. (YA). (gr. 5 up). 1990. 15.95 (*0-531-05867-0*); lib. bdg. 16.99 (*0-531-08467-1*) Orchard Bks Watts.

White Pebbles in the Dark Forests. Tr. by Klein & Jovette Marchessault. (NFS Canada Ser.). pap. 9.95 (*0-88922-280-0*) LPC InBook.

White People. Frances Hodgson Burnett. 72p. 1987. pap. 6.50 (*0-910458-61-8*) Select Bks.

White People. Allan Gurganus. 1991. 21.95 (*0-394-58841-X*) Knopf.

***White People.** Allan Gurganus. 1996. pap. 11.00 (*0-449-91187-X*) Fawcett.

***White People.** Paul Mooney. Date not set. write for info. (*0-688-14488-8*) Morrow.

White People: Stories & Novellas. Allan Gurganus. 1992. reprint ed. mass mkt. 6.99 (*0-8041-0851-X*) Ivy Books.

White Peril: Foreign Relations & Asian Immigration to Australasia & North America 1875-1910. Sean Brawley. 1995. pap. 35.95 (*0-86840-278-8*, Pub. by New South Wales Univ Pr AT) Intl Spec Bk.

White Pillars see Plantation Houses & Mansions of the Old South

White Pine: Poems & Prose Poems. Mary Oliver. LC 94-20112. 1994. 20.00 (*0-15-100131-6*); pap. 13.00 (*0-15-600120-9*) HarBrace.

White Pine on the Saco River: An Oral History of River Driving in Southern Maine. Michael Chaney. Ed. by Edward D. Ives & Pauleena M. MacDougall. (Northeast Folklore Ser.: Vol. XXIX). (Illus.). 88p. 1993. pap. 15.00 (*0-943197-21-X*) ME Folklife Ctr.

White Pine Sucker River: Collected Prose Poems. Robert Alexander. LC 91-61261. 72p. (Orig.). 1993. pap. 8.95 (*0-89823-136-1*) New Rivers Pr.

White Pines Chronicles. Hilda Stahl. 792p. 1996. 24.99 (*0-7852-7405-7*) Nelson.

White Plague, Black Labor: Tuberculosis & the Political Economy of Health & Disease in South Africa. Randall M. Packard. 1989. 52.00 (*0-520-06574-3*); pap. 17.00 (*0-520-06575-1*) U CA Pr.

***White Plague, Black Labor: Tuberculosis & the Political Economy of Health & Disease in South Africa.** Randall M. Packard. 416p. 1990. pap. write for info. (*0-86980-733-1*, Pub. by Univ Natal Pr SA) Intl Spec Bk.

White Plains Friends Meeting, 1850-1982. Frederic R. Crownfield. 1983. pap. 6.00 (*0-614-04686-6*) NC Frnds Hist Soc.

White Planet. 2nd ed. Frank E. Stranges. 30p. 1982. 4.95 (*0-933470-04-5*) Intl Evang.

White Plum: A Biography of Ume Tsuda. Yoshiko Furuki. (Illus.). 204p. 1991. 24.95 (*0-8348-0243-0*) Weatherhill.

White Plume. Charles Bowman. (Illus.). 160p. 10.00 (*0-8092-7911-8*, Pub. by Boston Mills Pr CN) Genl Dist Srvs.

White Plume Mountain. Gary Gygax. 1980. 4.50 (*0-394-51184-0*) Random.

White Poem. Ed. by Jay Ramsay. (Illus.). 48p. (C). 1988. 60.00 (*0-947612-29-7*, Pub. by Rivelin Grapheme Pr); pap. 39.00 (*0-947612-30-0*, Pub. by Rivelin Grapheme Pr) St Mut.

White Political Women: Paths from Privilege to Empowerment. Diane L. Fowlkes. LC 91-10605. 276p. (C). 1992. text ed. 40.00 (*0-87049-717-0*); pap. text ed. 16.00 (*0-87049-718-9*) U of Tenn Pr.

White Poppy. large type ed. Margaret Gaan. 435p. 1989. 25.99 (*0-7089-1973-1*) Ulverscroft.

White Porcupine. Carol J. Howard. 1996. 10.00 (*0-533-11912-X*) Vantage.

White Powder. Mary S. Plowman. 9.99 (*0-9639882-6-3*) Goodfellow Pr.

White Powder, Black Death. Dan Matthews. (Slam Ser.). 1993. mass mkt. 3.50 (*0-373-63408-0*, 1-63408-8) Harlequin Bks.

***White Power.** unabridged ed. George L. Rockwell. (Illus.). 482p. 1996. reprint ed. 25.00 (*0-9656492-8-8*) J McLaughlin.

White Power Movement: America's Racist Hate Groups. Elaine Landau. LC 92-40920. (Illus.). 96p. (YA). (gr. 7 up). 1993. lib. bdg. 17.90 (*1-56294-327-8*) Millbrook Pr.

White Press & Black America. Carolyn A. Martindale. LC 85-27219. (Contributions in Afro-American & African Studies: No. 97). 215p. 1986. text ed. 55.00 (*0-313-25103-7*, MWP/, Greenwood Pr) Greenwood.

White Prison. large type ed. Eva Burfield. 352p. 1986. 25.99 (*0-7089-1498-5*) Ulverscroft.

White Puma. R. D. Lawrence. 1991. mass mkt. 4.95 (*1-55817-532-6*, Pinncle Kensgtn) Kensgtn Pub Corp.

White Python: Adventure & Mystery in Tibet. Mark Channing. Ed. by R. Reginald & Douglas Melville. LC 77-84208. (Lost Race & Adult Fantasy Ser.). 1978. reprint ed. lib. bdg. 29.95 (*0-405-10964-4*) Ayer.

White Queen. Gwyneth Jones. 320p. 1994. pap. 12.95 (*0-312-89013-3*) Orb NYC.

White Queen Psychology & Other Essays for Alice. Ruth G. Millikan. LC 92-24024. (Illus.). 420p. (C). 1993. 45.00 (*0-262-13288-5*, Bradford Bks) MIT Pr.

White Queen Psychology & Other Essays for Alice. Ruth G. Millikan. (Illus.). 400p. 1995. pap. 17.50 (*0-262-63162-8*, Bradford Bks) MIT Pr.

White Rabbit. Kate Phillips. 192p. 1996. 21.95 (*0-395-74285-4*) HM.

White Rabbit. Bruce Marshall. LC 87-8663. 256p. 1987. reprint ed. text ed. 59.75 (*0-313-25322-6*, MRWR, Greenwood Pr) Greenwood.

***White Rabbit.** Kate Phillips. 224p. 1997. reprint ed. pap. 12.00 (*0-06-097719-1*, PL) HarpC.

White Rabbit: A Psychedelic Reader. Randall Koral. Ed. by John Miller. LC 94-7317. 304p. 1995. pap. 13.95 (*0-8118-0666-9*) Chronicle Bks.

White Rabbit & Other Delights: East Totem West, a Hippie Company, 1967-1969. Alan Bisbort. LC 96-26464. (Illus.). 88p. (Orig.). 1996. pap. 26.95 (*0-7649-0011-0*) Pomegranate Calif.

White Rabbit's Color Book. Alan Baker. LC 93-32316. (Little Rabbit Bks.: No. 4). (Illus.). 24p. (J). (ps). 1994. 7.95 (*1-85697-953-9*, Kingfisher LKC) LKC.

White Racism. Joel Kovel. LC 83-20961. 301p. 1984. pap. text ed. 17.00 (*0-231-05797-0*) Col U Pr.

White Racism: Causes, Character, & Cures. Joe R. Feagin & Hernan Vera. LC 94-12232. 224p. (gr. 13). 1994. pap. 16.95 (*0-415-90919-8*, B3856) Routledge.

White Radiance: Collected Poems, 1958-1993. Nicholas Hagger. 1994. pap. 30.00 (*1-85230-489-8*) Element MA.

White Rat. Gayl Jones. (Northeastern Library of Black Literature). 200p. 1991. reprint ed. pap. text ed. 12.95 (*1-55553-100-8*) NE U Pr.

White Raven. Diana L. Paxson. 480p. 1989. reprint ed. mass mkt. 4.99 (*0-380-75229-8*, AvoNova) Avon.

White Reflections on Black Power. Charles E. Fager. LC 67-13982. 118p. reprint ed. pap. 33.70 (*0-317-10004-1*, 2012961) Bks Demand.

White Regiment. John Dalmas. (Orig.). 1990. mass mkt. 4.99 (*0-671-69880-X*) Baen Bks.

***White Reign.** Kincheloe. Date not set. write for info. (*0-312-17716-X*) St Martin.

White Rhino Hotel. Bartle Bull. 448p. 1993. pap. 5.99 (*0-451-17583-2*, Sig) NAL-Dutton.

White River, Brown Water: A Record-Making Kayak Journey down the Amazon. large type ed. Alan Holman. (Illus.). 384p. 1987. 25.99 (*0-7089-1597-3*) Ulverscroft.

White River Chronicles of S. C. Turnbo: Man & Wildlife on the Ozarks Frontier. Ed. by Lynn Morrow. LC 93-49518. 400p. 1994. 40.00 (*1-55728-307-9*) U of Ark Pr.

White River Junction. Pat Schneider. (Amherst Writers & Artists Chapbook Ser.). 48p. (Orig.). 1987. pap. 9.00 (*0-941895-00-9*) Amherst Wri Art.

***White River Light Station.** Thomas A. Tag. (Illus.). 61p. (Orig.). 1997. pap. 9.95 (*0-9649980-2-5*) Data Image.

***White River National Forest.** Outdoor Books & Maps Inc. Staff. 96p. 1997. 9.95 (*0-930657-16-0*) Outdr Bks & Maps.

White River Quarterly, Annual I. Ed. by Fadely et al. (Illus.). 95p. (Orig.). pap. 6.95 (*0-934293-08-2*) Huber-Copeland Pub.

White Road. Claude Esteban. Tr. by David Cloutier. LC 78-64433. 1979. 7.50 (*0-910350-04-3*) Charioteer.

White Romance. Virginia Hamilton. 240p. (YA). (gr. 7 up). 1989. pap. 4.00 (*0-15-295888-6*, Odyssey) HarBrace.

White Rook. J. Madison Davis. 224p. 1989. 18.95 (*0-8027-1096-4*) Walker & Co.

White Rooster & Other Stories. Robert Bausch. 168p. 1995. 19.95 (*0-87905-721-1*) Gibbs Smith Pub.

White Roots: A Nichols Genealogy. M. Q. Nichols. (Illus.). 377p. 1983. 25.00 (*0-9612516-0-3*) M Q Nichols.

White Roots & the Mysteries of God. Lena E. Rudder. (Illus.). 144p. (Orig.). 1986. pap. write for info. (*0-937581-00-3*) Zarathustrotemo Pr.

White Roots of Peace: Iroquois Book of Life. Paul Wallace. LC 93-24297. 1993. pap. 12.95 (*0-940666-36-7*) Clear Light.

White Roots of Peace: Iroquois Book of Life. rev. ed. Paul Wallace. LC 93-24297. 98p. 1993. 19.95 (*0-940666-30-8*) Clear Light.

White Rose. Glen Cook. 320p. 1990. pap. 3.95 (*0-8125-0844-0*) Tor Bks.

White Rose. Lillian Garrett-Groag. 1993. pap. 5.25 (*0-8222-1352-4*) Dramatists Play.

White Rose. Linda Ladd. 384p. (Orig.). 1994. pap. 4.99 (*0-451-40479-3*, Topaz) NAL-Dutton.

White Rose: Munich, 1942-1943. 2nd ed. Inge Scholl. Tr. by Arthur R. Schultz. LC 83-16828. (Illus.). 176p. 1983. pap. 13.95 (*0-8195-6086-3*, Wesleyan Univ Pr) U Pr of New Eng.

White Rose Ensnared. Juliet Hastings. (Black Lace Ser.). 272p. (Orig.). 1996. mass mkt. 5.95 (*0-352-33052-X*, Pub. by Virgin Pub UK) London Brdge.

White Rose Murders. Michael Clynes. LC 92-43889. 1993. 18.95 (*0-312-08920-1*) St Martin.

White Rose Murders. large type ed. Michael Clynes. 464p. 1995. 25.99 (*0-7089-3218-5*) Ulverscroft.

***White Rose, Sparrow & Unicorn.** Stephen Running-Bear. (Illus.). 36p. (J). 14.95 (*0-9653175-0-1*) Voices of Wellness.

White Roses. Rebecca D. Larson. 1996. write for info. (*0-614-17877-0*) Thomas Publications.

***White Roses: Women Nurses in the Civil War.** (Illus.). 80p. 1997. pap. 6.95 (*1-57747-011-7*) Thomas Publications.

White Roses of Brambledene. Joyce C. Ware. 1992. mass mkt. 3.99 (*0-8217-3700-7*, Zebra Kensgtn) Kensgtn Pub Corp.

White Rule in South Africa 1830-1910. Edgar H. Brookes. 230p. 1974. 14.95 (*0-86980-031-0*, Pub. by Univ Natal Pr SA) Intl Spec Bk.

White Rush - Green Fire. Mark McGarrity. 464p. 1992. mass mkt. 4.99 (*0-380-71097-8*) Avon.

White Saddle. Ethel H. Miller. (J). 1934. 5.95 (*0-912142-02-2*); pap. 3.95 (*0-912142-03-0*); lib. bdg. 6.95 (*0-912142-01-4*) White S Bks.

White Sail: Crossing the Serene Waves of Ocean Mind to the Serene Continent of the Triple Gems. Thinley Norbu. LC 92-50129. 280p. (Orig.). 1992. pap. 15.00 (*0-87773-693-6*) Shambhala Pubns.

White Sambo: Novel in Stories. Robert B. Sweet. 235p. (Orig.). 1993. pap. 12.95 (*1-879194-12-0*) GLB Pubs.

***White Sands.** Simon Gandolfi. mass mkt. write for info. (*0-06-109576-1*, Harp PBks) HarpC.

***White Sands.** Simon Gandolfi. 272p. 1997. 22.50 (*0-06-018720-4*) HarpC.

***White Sands: The History of a National Monument.** Dietmar Schneider-Hector. LC 92-33665. (Illus.). 294p. 1993. reprint ed. pap. 83.80 (*0-608-04153-X*, 2064886) Bks Demand.

White Sands Incident Including an Extraterrestrial Statement. Daniel W. Fry & Rolf Telano. LC 92-73366. 211p. 1992. reprint ed. pap. 12.95 (*1-881852-00-8*) Horus Hse Pr.

White Sands National Monument. Rose Houk & Michael Collier. Ed. by Sandra Scott. LC 94-67912. 68p. 1994. pap. 9.95 (*1-877856-50-9*) SW Pks Mnmts.

White Savages in the South Seas. Mel Kernahan. (C). 1995. text ed. 65.00 (*1-85984-978-4*, Pub. by Vrso UK) Norton.

White Savages in the South Seas. Mel Kernahan. 288p. 1995. pap. 19.00 (*1-85984-004-3*, Pub. by Vrso UK) Norton.

White Savannahs. William E. Collin. LC 73-92516. (Literature of Canada, Poetry & Prose in Reprint Ser.: No. 15). 383p. reprint ed. pap. 109.20 (*0-317-26932-1*, 2023604) Bks Demand.

White Scholar & the Black Community, 1945-1965: Essays & Reflections. August Meier. LC 92-3205. 248p. 1992. 40.00 (*0-87023-809-4*); pap. 17.95 (*0-87023-810-8*) U of Mass Pr.

***White Scourge: Mexicans, Blacks, & Poor Whites in the Cotton Culture of Central Texas.** Neil Foley. LC 97-10222. (American Crossroads Ser.). 1997. write for info. (*0-520-20723-8*); pap. write for info. (*0-520-20724-6*) U CA Pr.

White Screen, Poetry & Graphics. John M. Bennett. 1976. pap. 6.00 (*0-935350-95-0*) Luna Bisonte.

White Screens - Black Images: Hollywood from the Dark Side. James A. Snead. 200p. (Orig.). (gr. 13). 1994. pap. 16.95 (*0-415-90574-5*, A7149, Routledge NY) Routledge.

White Sects & Black Men in the Recent South. David E. Harrell. LC 72-157742. 180p. reprint ed. pap. 51.60 (*0-7837-6198-8*, 2045920) Bks Demand.

White Servitude & Black Slavery in Barbados, 1627-1715. Hilary M. Beckles. LC 88-27788. 238p. 1989. text ed. 34.95 (*0-87049-601-8*) U of Tenn Pr.

White Servitude in Colonial America: An Economic Analysis. David W. Galenson. LC 81-7682. (Illus.). 320p. 1984. pap. 16.95 (*0-521-27379-X*) Cambridge U Pr.

White Servitude in Maryland, 1634-1820. Eugene I. McCormac. LC 78-63901. (Johns Hopkins University. Studies in the Social Sciences. Thirtieth Ser. 1912: 3-4). reprint ed. 29.50 (*0-404-61154-0*) AMS Pr.

White Servitude in Pennsylvania: Indentured & Redemption Labor in Colony & Commonwealth. Cheesman A. Herrick. LC 78-124238. (Select Bibliographies Reprint Ser.). 1977. reprint ed. 34.95 (*0-8369-5426-2*) Ayer.

***White Servitude in Pennsylvania: Indentured & Redemption Labor in Colony & Commonwealth.** Cheesman A. Herrick. (Illus.). 340p. 1996. reprint ed. pap. 35.00 (*0-614-23498-0*, 9182) Clearfield Co.

White Servitude in Pennsylvania: Indentured & Redemption Labor in Colony & Commonwealth. Cheesman A. Herrick. LC 70-99480. 330p. 1970. reprint ed. text ed. 45.00 (*0-8371-2373-9*, HWS&, Greenwood Pr) Greenwood.

White Servitude in the Colony of Virginia: A Study of the System of Indentured Labor in the American Colonies. James C. Ballagh. LC 78-63840. (Johns Hopkins University. Studies in the Social Sciences. Thirtieth Ser. 1912: 6-7). reprint ed. 39.50 (*0-404-61098-6*) AMS Pr.

White Settlers: The Impact of Rural Repopulation in Scotland. Charles Jedrej. 210p. 1995. text ed. 56.00 (*3-7186-5752-X*, Harwood Acad Pubs) Gordon & Breach.

White Settlers: The Impact of Rural Repopulation in Scotland. Charles Jedrej & Mark Nuttall. 1995. pap. text ed. 22.00 (*3-7186-5753-8*) Gordon & Breach.

White Settlers & Native Peoples: An Historical Study of Racial Contacts Between English-Speaking Whites & Aboriginal Peoples in the United States, Canada, Australia, & New Zealand. Archibald G. Price. LC 71-142320. (Illus.). 232p. 1972. reprint ed. text ed. 59.75 (*0-8371-5923-7*, PRWH) Greenwood.

White Settlers in the Tropics. Archibald G. Price. LC 75-41217. reprint ed. 72.50 (*0-404-14731-3*) AMS Pr.

White Settlers in Tropical Africa. Lewis H. Gann & Peter Duignan. LC 76-49445. 169p. 1977. reprint ed. text ed. 48.50 (*0-8371-9394-X*, GAWH, Greenwood Pr) Greenwood.

White Shadows. Intro. by Carroll Yoder. LC 86-51308. 180p. (Orig.). 1991. pap. 14.00 (*0-914478-79-6*, Three Contnts) Lynne Rienner.

White Shaman: Selected Poems. H. C. Ten Berge. Ed. & Tr. by Theo Hermans from DUT. Tr. by Great Kilburn et al. from DUT. LC 90-85576. (Illus.). 85p. (Orig.). 1992. pap. 16.95 (*1-85610-004-9*, Pub. by Forest Bks UK) Dufour.

White Shark. Peter Benchley. 1995. pap. 6.50 (*0-312-95573-1*) St Martin.

White Shark. large type ed. Peter Benchley. 1994. pap. 22.00 (*0-679-75388-5*) Random Hse Lrg Prnt.

White Sheets. Rebekka Whetstyne. (Illus.). 24p. (Orig.). 1985. pap. text ed. 1.50 (*1-879594-08-0*) Androgyne Bks.

White Ship: Estonian Tales. Aino J. Kallas. Tr. by Alex Matson from FIN. LC 73-163034. (Short Story Index Reprint Ser.). 1977. reprint ed. 19.95 (*0-8369-3948-4*) Ayer.

White Shirts. Ellen Field. 72p. reprint ed. pap. 25.00 (*0-7837-3545-6*, AU00432) Bks Demand.

White Shroud: Poems 1980-1985. Allen Ginsberg. LC 86-45104. (Illus.). 112p. 1987. pap. 13.00 (*0-06-091429-7*, PL/1429, PL) HarpC.

***White Siberia: The Politics of Civil War.** N. G. Pereira. (Illus.). 280p. 1995. 44.95 (*0-7735-1349-3*, Pub. by McGill CN) U of Toronto Pr.

White-Sided Dolphin. John F. Prevost. LC 95-8121. (Dolphins Ser.). (J). (gr. k-3). 1995. lib. bdg. 13.98 (*1-56239-494-0*) Abdo & Dghtrs.

White Sister. Francis M. Crawford. (Works of Francis Marion Crawford Ser.). 1990. reprint ed. lib. bdg. 79.00 (*0-7812-2560-4*) Rprt Serv.

White Skin, Black Masks: Representation & Colonialism. Gail Ching-Liang. 280p. (C). 1996. pap. 18.95 (*0-415-08148-3*, Routledge NY) Routledge.

White Skins/Black Masks: Representation, Colonialism & Cultural Cross-Dressing. Gail C. Low. LC 95-8889. 280p. (C). (gr. 13). 1995. text ed. 69.95 (*0-415-08147-5*) Routledge.

White Skull: The Book of Captain Mission. James Havoc. 128p. (Orig.). 1996. pap. 12.95 (*1-871592-48-8*) Creation Bks.

W

White Slave: Or, Memoirs of a Fugitive. Richard Hildreth. LC 71-82200. (Anti-Slavery Crusade in America Ser.). (Illus.). 1970. reprint ed. 18.95 (*0-405-00639-X*) Ayer.
White Slave Market. A. Mackirdy & W. N. Willis. 1972. 59.95 (*0-8490-1291-0*) Gordon Pr.
White Slave Traffic. Emma Goldman. 1972. 250.00 (*0-8490-1292-9*) Gordon Pr.
White Slavery in the Barbary States. Charles Sumner. LC 74-89443. (Black Heritage Library Collection). 1977. 13.95 (*0-8369-8663-6*) Ayer.
White Slaves in Early America. 1991. lib. bdg. 69.95 (*0-8490-4731-5*) Gordon Pr.
***White Smoke.** Andrew M. Greeley. 1997. mass mkt. 6.99 (*0-8125-9055-4*, Fortress Pr) Augsburg Fortress.
White Smoke. Robert Herz. LC 77-92110. 50p. 1977. per. 3.75 (*0-934332-01-0*) LEpervier Pr.
White Smoke. large type ed. Andrew M. Greeley. 752p. 1996. 26.95 (*0-7862-0788-4*) Thorndike Pr.
White Smoke: A Novel about the Next Papal Conclave. Andrew M. Greeley. 384p. 1996. 24.95 (*0-312-85814-0*) Forge NYC.
White Snake. Leon Whiteson. 247p. 1995. lib. bdg. 35.00 (*0-8095-4593-4*) Borgo Pr.
White Snake. Leon Whiteson. 247p. pap. 12.95 (*0-88962-402-X*) Mosaic.
White Snow - Blue Feather. Julie Downing. LC 89-815. (Illus.). 32p. (J). (ps-1). 1989. text ed. 14.95 (*0-02-732530-X*, Bradbury S&S) S&S Childrens.
White Snow, Bright Snow. Alvin R. Tresselt. (Illus.). (J). (ps-3). 1947. 16.00 (*0-688-41161-4*); lib. bdg. 15.93 (*0-688-51161-9*) Lothrop.
White Snow Bright Snow. Alvin R. Tresselt. LC 88-10018. (Illus.). 32p. (J). (ps up). 1988. reprint ed. pap. 4.95 (*0-688-08294-7*, Mulberry) Morrow.
***White Society in Africa.** Asiwaju Tarikh. Date not set. pap. text ed. write for info. (*0-582-60960-7*, Pub. by Longman UK) Longman.
White Society in Black Africa: The French of Senegal. Rita C. O'Brian. LC 74-183533. 320p. reprint ed. pap. 91.20 (*0-317-11345-3*, 2006875) Bks Demand.
White Society in the Antebellum South. Bruce Collins. (Studies in Modern History). 216p. (C). 1985. pap. text ed. 18.95 (*0-582-49194-0*, 73519) Longman.
White Socks Only. Evelyn Coleman. LC 95-38324. (Illus.). (J). (gr. k-4). 1996. lib. bdg. 15.95 (*0-8075-8955-1*) A Whitman.
White Song & a Black One. Joseph S. Cotter. LC 73-18568. reprint ed. 19.50 (*0-404-11382-6*) AMS Pr.
***White South.** Innes. Date not set. pap. text ed. write for info. (*0-17-556587-2*) Addison-Wesley.
White South. large type ed. Hammond Innes. 1971. 25.99 (*0-85456-063-7*) Ulverscroft.
White Southerners. rev. ed. Lewis M. Killian. LC 85-5844. 216p. (Orig.). 1986. reprint ed. pap. text ed. 15.95 (*0-87023-488-9*); reprint ed. lib. bdg. 27.50 (*0-87023-487-0*) U of Mass Pr.
White Sow's Sons. Norene Berry & Jennifer Heath. (Illus.). 10p. (J). (gr. 2-6). 1994. pap. 5.00 (*1-887997-01-6*) Baksun Bks.
***White Sox: The Illustrated Story.** Richard Whittingham. Ed. by Susan Smith. (Illus.). 208p. 1997. 29.50 (*1-885758-09-X*) Quality Sports.
White Sox Encyclopedia. Richard C. Lindberg. LC 95-48446. (Baseball Encyclopedias of North America Ser.). 1344p. (C). 1997. 59.95 (*1-56639-449-X*) Temple U Pr.
White Spaces. Paul Auster. 1980. pap. 10.00 (*0-930794-27-3*) Station Hill Pr.
White Spaces in Shakespeare. Paul Bertram. 112p. 1981. 12.50 (*0-934958-01-7*); pap. 8.50 (*0-934958-02-5*) Bellflower.
White Specks on Dark Shores. J. Lergessner. 80p. (C). 1990. pap. 30.00 (*0-86439-147-1*, Pub. by Boolarong Pubns AT) St Mut.
White Squaw, Adventures of a Lady Woodsman. Dolores Brown. 19.95 (*1-879356-13-9*) Wolfe Pub Co.
White Squaw, No. 22: Desert Climax. E. J. Hunter. 224p. 1991. mass mkt. 3.50 (*0-8217-3376-1*, Zebra Kensgtn) Kensgtn Pub Corp.
White Squaw 8-Horn. E. J. Hunter. 1985. pap. 2.50 (*0-8217-1649-2*) Kensgtn Pub Corp.
White Stag. Kate Seredy. (Storybooks Ser.). (J). (gr. 4-7). 1979. pap. 4.99 (*0-14-031258-7*, Puffin) Puffin Bks.
White Stag. Kate Seredy. (Illus.). (J). (gr. 7 up). 1937. pap. 14.99 (*0-670-76375-6*) Viking Child Bks.
White Stag Adventure. Rennie McOwan. 160p. (C). 1992. pap. 32.00 (*0-685-60702-X*, Pub. by St Andrew UK) St Mut.
White Stag Adventure. Rennie McOwan. 160p. 1993. pap. 30.00 (*0-7152-0665-6*, Pub. by St Andrew UK) St Mut.
White Stains. A. Crowley. 134p. 1973. 39.95 (*0-7156-0680-8*, Pub. by Duckworth UK) Focus Pub-R Pullins.
***White Stallion.** Elizabeth Shub. 64p. (J). 1997. pap. 3.50 (*0-440-91308-X*) BDD Bks Young Read.
White Stallion. Elizabeth Shub. LC 81-20308. (Greenwillow Read-Alone Bks.). (Illus.). 56p. (J). (gr. 1-3). 1982. 16.00 (*0-688-01210-8*); lib. bdg. 15.93 (*0-688-01211-6*) Greenwillow.
White Stallion. Elizabeth Shub. 64p. (J). 1996. pap. 3.50 (*0-440-41292-7*) BDD Bks Young Read.
White Stallion of Lipizza. Marguerite Henry. LC 93-86024. (Illus.). 112p. (J). (gr. 3-7). 1994. reprint ed. 14.95 (*0-02-743628-4*, Mac Bks Young Read) S&S Childrens.
White Stallion of Lipizza. Marguerite Henry. LC 93-34065. (Illus.). 112p. (J). (gr. 3-7). 1994. reprint ed. pap. 9.95 (*0-689-71824-1*, Aladdin Paperbacks) S&S Childrens.
White Stallion, Red Mare. large type ed. J. T. Edson. 1982. 15.95 (*0-7089-0827-6*) Ulverscroft.
White Stallions: The Story of the Dancing Horses of Lipizza. Laurel Van der Linde. LC 93-18919. (Timestop Bks.). (Illus.). 72p. (YA). (gr. 6 up). 1994. lib. bdg. 14.95 (*0-02-759055-0*, New Dscvry Bks) Silver Burdett Pr.
White Star. James Thayer. 1996. mass mkt. 5.99 (*0-671-52817-3*, Pocket Books) PB.
White Star. James S. Thayer. LC 94-19678. 1995. 22.00 (*0-671-79814-6*) S&S Trade.
White Star Line. P. Louden-Brown. 1990. 59.00 (*0-9516038-2-5*, Pub. by Ship Pictorial Pubng UK) St Mut.
White Star of the East. Thedra. 76p. 1990. pap. 7.95 (*0-941131-06-8*) ASSK Pub.
White Stone. P. Lewis. Date not set. 3.99 (*1-871676-20-7*, Pub. by Christian Focus UK) Spring Arbor Dist.
White Stone. Wilfred H. Weeks. LC 85-51932. (Illus.). 37p. (Orig.). (J). (gr. 4-9). 1990. pap. 5.25 (*0-9615677-0-8*) Three Riv Ctr.
White Stone: A Mystical Novel from Early Ireland. Alcott Allison. LC 92-17296. 155p. (Orig.). 1992. pap. 8.95 (*0-9620507-2-5*) Cosmic Concepts Pr.
White Stone: The Spiritual Theology of John Henry Newman. Vincent F. Blehl. LC 93-31998. 187p. 1993. pap. 12.95 (*1-879007-03-7*) St Bedes Pubns.
White Stone in the Castle Wall. Sheldon Oberman. LC 93-61791. (Illus.). 24p. (J). (gr. k-3). 1995. 14.95 (*0-88776-333-2*) Tundra Bks.
***White Stone In The Castle Wall.** Sheldon Oberman. (Illus.). 1996. pap. 10.95 (*0-88776-379-0*) Tundra Bks.
White Stones & Fir Trees: An Anthology of Contemporary Slavic Literature. Ed. by Vasa D. Mihailovich. LC 74-32519. 603p. 1977. 50.00 (*0-8386-1194-X*) Fairleigh Dickinson.
White Supremacist Movement in Contemporary Africa: The KKK, Neo-Nazis & Skinheads. Dobratz. 1997. 14.95 (*0-8057-3866-5*, Twayne) Scribnrs Ref.
White Supremacist Movement in Contemporary America: KKK Neo Nazis & Skinhead. Dobratz. 1997. 24.95 (*0-8057-3865-7*, Twayne) Scribnrs Ref.
White Supremacy: A Comparative Study in American & South African History. George M. Fredrickson. 400p. 1982. pap. 14.95 (*0-19-503042-7*) OUP.
White Supremacy: A Comparative Study of American & South African History. George M. Fredrickson. (Illus.). 400p. 1981. 45.00 (*0-19-502759-0*) OUP.
White Supremacy & Black Resistance in Pre-Industrial South Africa: The Making of the Colonial Order in the Eastern Cape, 1770-1865. Clifton C. Crais. (African Studies: No. 72). (Illus.). 288p. (C). 1992. text ed. 80.00 (*0-521-40479-7*) Cambridge U Pr.
White Supremacy & Negro Subordination. John H. Van Evrie. 1991. lib. bdg. 66.76 (*0-8490-4414-6*) Gordon Pr.
***White Supremacy Myth in Juvenile Books about Blacks, 1830-1900.** Jack D. Zipes. (Children's Literature & Culture Ser.). 250p. 1998. text ed. 50.00 (*0-8153-2056-6*) Garland.
White Sustenance. Kat S. Blackbird. LC 93-35959. (Wick Poetry Chapbook Ser.: No. 1). 38p. (Orig.). 1994. pap. 4.75 (*0-87338-503-9*) Kent St U Pr.
White Swan. large type ed. Prudence Bebb. (Linford Romance Library). 1996. pap. 15.99 (*0-7089-7834-7*, Linford) Ulverscroft.
White Swan. large type ed. Frances Turk. 448p. 1984. 25.99 (*0-7089-1218-4*) Ulverscroft.
White Sweaters. Nihon Vogue Staff. (Illus.). 61p. (Orig.). 1987. pap. 17.00 (*0-87040-652-3*) Japan Pubns USA.
White T. Alice Harris. 144p. 1996. 45.00 (*0-06-270166-5*) HarpC.
White Tablecloths. Lynne McMahon. (International Poetry Chapbook Ser.). 11p. (Orig.). (C). 1984. pap. 4.00 (*0-936600-04-7*) Riverstone Foothills.
***White-Tailed Dear.** Michael Zwaschka. (Wildlife of North America Ser.). (Illus.). (J). 1997. 18.40 (*0-516-20543-9*) Childrens.
***White-Tailed Deer.** LC 96-48685. (Wildlife of North America Ser.). (J). 1997. write for info. (*1-56065-470-8*) Capstone Pr.
White-Tailed Deer. Gary Clancy & Larry R. Nelson. LC 91-16959. (Hunting & Fishing Library). 160p. 1991. 19.95 (*0-86573-036-9*) Cowles Creative.
White-Tailed Deer. Ilo Hiller. LC 95-47480. (Louise Lindsey Merrick Natural Environment Ser.: Vol. 25). (Illus.). 128p. (C). 1996. pap. 9.95 (*0-89096-697-4*) Tex A&M Univ Pr.
White-Tailed Deer. Joan Kalbacken. LC 91-35277. (New True Bks.). (Illus.). 48p. (J). (gr. k-4). 1992. pap. 5.50 (*0-516-41138-1*); lib. bdg. 19.00 (*0-516-01138-3*) Childrens.
White-Tailed Deer: Ecology & Management. Ed. by Lowell K. Halls. LC 84-2626. 864p. 1984. 79.95 (*0-8117-0486-6*) Stackpole.
White Tales & Other Hunting Stories. Duncan Dobie. (Illus.). 229p. (YA). (gr. 8 up). 1989. 15.95 (*0-939801-01-9*) Bucksnort.
White Talk, Black Talk: Inter-Racial Friendship & Communication Amongst Adolescents. Roger Hewitt. (Comparative Ethnic & Race Relations Ser.). 272p. 1986. text ed. 59.95 (*0-521-26239-9*); pap. text ed. 19.95 (*0-521-33824-7*) Cambridge U Pr.
White Teacher. Vivian G. Paley. 156p. 1989. reprint ed. pap. text ed. 9.95 (*0-674-95186-7*) HUP.
White Teacher in a Black School. Robert Kendall. 1980. 9.95 (*0-8159-7210-5*) Devin.
***White Tecumseh: A Biography of William T. Sherman.** Stanley P. Hirshson. LC 96-29477. 400p. 1997. text ed. 30.00 (*0-471-17578-1*) Wiley.
White Terror: The Ku Klux Klan Conspiracy & Southern Reconstruction. Allen W. Trelease. 557p. 1995. pap. text ed. 17.95 (*0-8071-1953-9*) La State U Pr.
White Terror: The Ku Klux Klan Conspiracy & Southern Reconstruction. Allen W. Trelease. LC 78-12864. 557p. 1979. reprint ed. text ed. 55.00 (*0-313-21168-X*, TRWT, Greenwood Pr) Greenwood.
White Terror & the Political Reaction After Waterloo. Daniel P. Resnick. LC 66-18254. (Historical Studies: No. 77). 161p. 1966. 15.00 (*0-674-95190-5*) HUP.
White Terror & the Red: A Novel of Revolutionary Russia. Abraham Cahan. LC 74-27969. (Modern Jewish Experience Ser.). 1975. reprint ed. 37.95 (*0-405-06699-6*) Ayer.
White Thighs. 240p. 1986. pap. 4.50 (*0-88184-244-3*) Carroll & Graf.
White Thighs. 1992. mass mkt. 4.95 (*1-56333-009-1*) Masquerade.
White Thighs. Alexander Trocchi. 1994. pap. 9.95 (*0-922233-14-4*) Blast Bks.
White Thunder. Dave Sargent & Pat L. Sargent. (Animal Pride Ser.: No. 6). (Illus.). 32p. (J). (gr. 2-8). 1996. pap. 2.95 (*1-56763-007-3*) Ozark Pub.
White Thunder. Dave Sargent & Pat L. Sargent. LC 96-1495. (Animal Pride Ser.). (Illus.). 32p. (J). 1996. 12.95 (*1-56763-087-1*) Ozark Pub.
***White Thunder & Kokopelli.** Illus. by Owen Richardson. 186p. (Orig.). 1997. pap. 9.95 (*1-890828-02-5*) Pubs Dist Ctr Inc.
White Tide. Ruth Dunbar. 256p. (Orig.). 1993. pap. 8.95 (*1-878903-07-1*) Nosado Pr.
White Tie & Decorations: Sir John & Lady Hope Simpson in Newfoundland, 1934-1936. Ed. by Peter Neary. (Illus.). 392p. 1996. 39.95 (*0-8020-0719-8*) U of Toronto Pr.
White Tigers: My Secret War in North Korea. Ben S. Malcom & Ron Martz. (Association of the U.S. Army). (Illus.). 288p. 1996. 24.95 (*1-57488-016-0*) Brasseys Inc.
White to White on Black - White. Toni E. Weaver. 116p. 1993. pap. 9.95 (*0-9636543-7-3*) Voices Pub.
***White Trail.** 24p. (J). 1997. pap. write for info. (*0-7814-3027-5*, Chariot Bks) Chariot Victor.
White Trail. Barbara Davoll. (Illus.). 24p. (J). 1988. audio 11.99 (*0-89693-615-5*, 3-1615, Victor Bks) Chariot Victor.
White Trail. Barbara Davoll. (Christopher Churchmouse Classics Ser.). (Illus.). 24p. (J). 1988. 8.99 (*0-89693-404-7*, 6-1404, Victor Bks) Chariot Victor.
White Trash. Katie Carothers. 200p. (C). 1994. pap. 10.95 (*0-9639528-0-3*, Blue Beg Pub) Valentine CA.
White Trash: An Anthology of Contemporary Southern Poets. Ed. by Nancy Stone & Robert W. Grey. (Illus.). 128p. 1976. 25.00 (*0-917990-01-3*) New South Co.
White Trash: An Anthology of Contemporary Southern Poets. Ed. by Nancy Stone & Robert W. Grey. (Illus.). 128p. 1986. pap. 7.95 (*0-917990-06-4*) New South Co.
***White Trash: Race & Class in America.** Matt Wray & Annalee Newitz. LC 96-28339. 272p. 1996. pap. 17.95 (*0-415-91692-5*) Routledge.
***White Trash: Race & Class in America.** Matt Wray & Annalee Newitz. LC 96-28339. 272p. (C). 1997. text ed. 65.00 (*0-415-91691-7*) Routledge.
White Trash: The Eugenics Family Studies, 1877-1919. Ed. by Nicole H. Rafter. 428p. 1988. text ed. 55.00 (*1-55553-030-3*) NE U Pr.
White Trash Cooking. Ernest M. Mickler. 192p. 1986. spiral bd. 14.95 (*0-89815-189-9*) Ten Speed Pr.
***White Trash Cooking II.** Ernest M. Mickler. LC 96-48635. (Illus.). 192p. 1997. spiral bd. 17.95 (*0-89815-892-3*) Ten Speed Pr.
White Trash Gardening. Mike Benton & Rufus T. Firefly. LC 95-45772. (Illus.). 160p. (Orig.). 1996. pap. 14.95 (*0-87833-907-8*) Taylor Pub.
White Trash Velvet. (*0-8317-5444-3*) Smithmark.
White Tribe. Robin Moore. 550p. 1991. 24.95 (*1-879915-03-0*) Affil Writers America.
***White Tribunal.** Paula Volsky. LC 97-12378. 400p. 1997. mass mkt. 13.95 (*0-553-37846-5*, Spectra) Bantam.
White Umbrella: Indian Political Thought from Manu to Ghandi. Donald M. Brown. LC 81-13391. (Illus.). xii, 204p. 1982. reprint ed. text ed. 55.00 (*0-313-23210-5*, BRWU, Greenwood Pr) Greenwood.
White v. Reliable Realtors, Inc. K. Byron McCoy. 128p. 1989. pap. 18.95 (*1-55681-192-6*, FBA0192) Natl Inst Trial Ad.
White v. Reliable Realtors, Inc., et al (Pretrial Casefile) K. Byron McCoy. 100p. 1993. pap. 18.95 (*1-55681-380-5*) Natl Inst Trial Ad.
White v. Reliable Realtors, Inc. Teaching Notes. K. Byron McCoy. 11p. 1989. teacher ed., pap. 8.95 (*1-55681-193-4*, FBA0193) Natl Inst Trial Ad.
White Violence & Black Response: From Reconstruction to Montgomery. Herbert Shapiro. LC 87-6009. (Illus.). 584p. (C). 1988. pap. text ed. 19.95 (*0-87023-578-8*) U of Mass Pr.
White, Vol. 1: Genealogy of Descendants of John White of Wenham & Lancaster, MA, 1638-1900. A. L. White. (Illus.). 931p. 1991. reprint ed. pap. 115.00 (*0-8328-1844-5*); reprint ed. lib. bdg. 125.00 (*0-8328-1843-7*) Higginson Bk Co.
White, Vol. 2: Genealogy of Descendants of John White of Wenham & Lancaster, MA, 1638-1903. A. L. White. (Illus.). 924p. 1991. reprint ed. pap. 113.00 (*0-8328-1846-1*); reprint ed. lib. bdg. 123.00 (*0-8328-1845-3*) Higginson Bk Co.
White, Vol. 3: Genealogy of Descendants of John White of Wenham & Lancaster, MA, 1638-1905. A. L. White. (Illus.). 754p. 1991. reprint ed. pap. 105.00 (*0-8328-1848-8*); reprint ed. lib. bdg. 115.00 (*0-8328-1847-X*) Higginson Bk Co.
White, Vol. 4: Genealogy of Descendants of John White of Wenham & Lancaster, MA, 1638-1909. A. L. White. (Illus.). 210p. 1991. reprint ed. pap. 32.00 (*0-685-38994-4*); reprint ed. lib. bdg. 42.00 (*0-8328-1849-6*) Higginson Bk Co.
White, Vols. 1-4: Genealogy of Descendants of John White of Wenham & Lancaster, MA, 1638-1909, 4 vols. A. L. White. (Illus.). 2819p. 1991. reprint ed. Set. pap. 325.00 (*0-8328-1852-6*); reprint ed. Set. lib. bdg. 365.00 (*0-8328-1851-8*) Higginson Bk Co.
White Waits. Robert Ronnow. LC 83-71219. 64p. (Orig.). 1984. pap. 6.95 (*0-935306-27-7*) Barnwood Pr.
White Wake: A Collection of Photographs. Virgil D. Haynes. Ed. by Cynthia Haynes. (Illus.). 144p. 1991. write for info. (*0-9623243-1-0*) Haynes Studio.
White Wall of Spain: The Mysteries of Andalusian Culture. Allen Josephs. 208p. (C). 1990. reprint ed. pap. text ed. 16.95 (*0-8130-1013-6*) U Press Fla.
White Walls, Designer Dresses: The Fashioning of Modern Architecture. Mark Wigley. (Illus.). 500p. (C). 1996. 40.00 (*0-262-23185-9*) MIT Pr.
***White Water.** (Destroyer Ser.). 1997. 5.50 (*0-373-63221-5*, 1-63221-5, Wrldwide Lib) Harlequin Bks.
White Water. Joyce R. Kornblatt. 10.95 (*0-931848-85-7*) Dryad Pr.
White Water. P. J. Peterson. (YA). 1997. 15.00 (*0-689-80664-7*, S&S Bks Young Read) S&S Childrens.
White Water. large type ed. Pamela Oldfield. 550p. 1995. 25.99 (*0-7505-0622-9*) Ulverscroft.
White Water Europe: The North Alps, Bk. 1. Peter Bandtock & Peter Knowles. (Illus.). 256p. Date not set. pap. 24.95 (*0-89732-212-6*) Menasha Ridge.
White Water Kayaking. Ray Rowe. (Illus.). 128p. 1989. pap. 18.95 (*0-8117-2284-8*) Stackpole.
White Water, Pebbles & Love. Faith T. Allum. (Illus.). 48p. (Orig.). 1984. pap. 3.00 (*0-9613349-0-8*) F T Allum.
White Water Rafting. Martin Nabhan. (Action Sports Ser.). 48p. (J). (gr. 3-4). 1991. lib. bdg. 17.80 (*1-56065-053-2*) Capstone Pr.
White Water Terror: The Nancy Drew Files, Case 6. large type ed. Carolyn Keene. 149p. (J). (gr. 5-10). 1988. reprint ed. 9.50 (*0-942545-37-0*); reprint ed. lib. bdg. 10.50 (*0-942545-32-X*) Grey Castle.
White Wave. Kate Daniels. LC 83-40341. (Poetry Ser.). 64p. 1984. 19.95 (*0-8229-3493-0*); pap. 10.95 (*0-8229-5359-5*) U of Pittsburgh Pr.
White Wave: A Chinese Tale. Illus. by Ed Young. LC 95-451. 32p. (J). 1996. 16.00 (*0-15-200293-6*) HarBrace.
White Wealth & Black Poverty: American Investments in Southern Africa. Barbara R. Rogers. LC 75-35353. (Studies in Human Rights: No. 2). 288p. 1976. text ed. 55.00 (*0-8371-8277-8*, RWW/, Greenwood Pr) Greenwood.
White Whale: A Novel about Friendship & Courage in the Deep. Robert Siegel. (Whale Song Trilogy Ser.). 240p. 1994. pap. 10.00 (*0-06-251017-7*) Harper SF.
***White Whores & Black Whoremongers: A Bonafide Racial Holocaust.** Marsha Stewart. Ed. by Mary Jackson. (Orig.). reprint ed. pap. write for info. (*1-56411-140-7*) Untd Bros & Sis.
***White Widow.** Jim Lehrer. LC 97-1178. (Basic Ser.). 312p. 1997. 24.95 (*0-7862-1088-5*) Thorndike Pr.
White Widow: A Novel. Jim Lehrer. LC 96-1877. 1997. 21.00 (*0-679-45236-2*) Random.
White Wind. Susan Edwards. 400p. (Orig.). 1996. mass mkt. 5.50 (*0-8439-3933-8*) Dorchester Pub Co.
White Wind. Joseph P. Kent. LC 89-91662. 64p. (Orig.). 1989. pap. 6.95 (*0-9623751-0-1*) Sunlight SF.
White Wine for Dummies. Ed McCarthy. 256p. 1996. pap. 12.99 (*0-7645-5011-X*, Dummies Tech) IDG Bks.
White Wing. Gordon Kendall. 320p. (Orig.). 1991. mass mkt. 3.99 (*0-8125-1770-9*) Tor Bks.
White Wing: A Joe Bass Adventure. Christopher Barry. (Illus.). 94p. (Orig.). (YA). (gr. 8 up). 1994. pap. 5.00 (*0-88092-087-4*) Royal Fireworks.
White Wing: A Joe Bass Adventure. Christopher Barry. (Illus.). 94p. (Orig.). (YA). (gr. 8 up). 1994. lib. bdg. 15.00 (*0-88092-088-2*) Royal Fireworks.
***White Wings.** Daniel F. Montague. LC 96-29874. 1997. pap. 23.95 (*0-525-94303-X*) NAL-Dutton.
White Wings: And Other Stories. Marie Powell. 176p. (Orig.). 1993. pap. 9.95 (*1-56474-055-2*) Fithian Pr.
White Wolf. Max Brand. 208p. 1995. mass mkt., pap. text ed. 4.50 (*0-8439-3870-6*) Dorchester Pub Co.
***White Wolf.** Lindsay McKenna. 1997. mass mkt. 3.99 (*0-373-24135-6*, 1-24135-5) Silhouette.
White Wolf: Living with an Arctic Legend. Jim Brandenburg. 160p. 1988. 40.00 (*0-942802-95-0*) NorthWord.
White Wolf: Living with an Arctic Legend. Jim Brandenburg. 1991. 19.95 (*1-55971-093-4*) NorthWord.
White Wolf Woman: And Other Native American Transformation Myths. Teresa Pijoan. 160p. 1992. 17.95 (*0-87483-201-2*); pap. 11.95 (*0-87483-200-4*) August Hse.
White Woman. Liam Davidson. 1995. pap. text ed. 14.95 (*0-7022-2680-7*, Pub. by Univ Queensland Pr AT) Intl Spec Bk.
White Woman Witchdoctor: Tales of the African Life of Rae Graham. Told to Taffy G. McCallum. LC 92-72451. 248p. 1992. 22.95 (*0-9633721-8-1*, Coun Oak Bks) Fielden Bks.
White Woman's Blues: A Contemporary Musical. Gail Erwin. 40p. (Orig.). 1993. pap. 4.50 (*1-57514-128-0*, 0066) Encore Perform Pub.
White Woman's "Other" Burden: Western Women & South Asia During British Rule. Kumari Jayawardena. LC 94-28881. 300p. (C). 1995. pap. 17.95 (*0-415-91105-2*, B4829, Routledge NY) Routledge.

An Asterisk (*) at the beginning of an entry indicates that the title is appearing in BIP for the first time.

***White Women, Black Men: Illicit Sex in the Nineteenth-Century South.** Martha E. Hodes. LC 97-9320. 1997. write for info. (0-300-06970-7) Yale U Pr.
White Women, Coloured Men. H. Champly. 1972. 59.95 (0-8490-1293-7) Gordon Pr.
White Women Got Flat Butts. I. M. Blacque. Ed. by C & C Publishing, Inc. Staff. 182p. (Orig.). 1993. pap. 12.95 (0-9639017-0-2) C & C Pubng.
White Women, Race Matters: The Social Construction of Whiteness. Ruth Frankenberg. LC 92-43433. 297p. 1993. pap. 17.95 (0-8166-2258-2) U of Minn Pr.
White Women's Christ & Black Women's Jesus: Feminist Christology & Womanist Response. Jacquelyn Grant. 225p. 1989. pap. 21.95 (1-55540-303-4, 01 01 64) Scholars Pr GA.
White Wonderful Winter. Elaine W. Good. LC 91-74052. (Seasonal Ser.). (Illus.). 32p. (J). (ps-1). 1991. 12.95 (1-56148-018-5) Good Bks PA.
White Wonderful Winter. Elaine W. Good. LC 91-74052. (J). (ps-3). 1994. pap. 6.95 (1-56148-143-2) Good Bks PA.
White Wool. large type ed. Naomi Jacob. 400p. 1983. 25.99 (0-7089-0932-9) Ulverscroft.
White Work: Techniques & 180 Designs. Ed. by Carter Houck. (Illus.). 1979. pap. 3.95 (0-486-23695-1) Dover.
White World: Life & Adventures Within the Arctic Circle. Ed. by Rudolf Kersting. LC 74-5851. reprint ed. 57.50 (0-404-11658-2) AMS Pr.
White Zombie: Astro-Creep 2000. Ed. by Aaron Stang. (Illus.). 76p. (Orig.). 1995. pap. text ed. 21.95 (0-89724-720-5, PG9535) Warner Brothers.
Whiteboy. Stan Rice. 1975. pap. 3.00 (0-685-52155-9) Mudra.
***Whitecaps.** Danny Wadsworth. Date not set. write for info. (0-614-29850-4) Sterling Hse.
***Whitecaps.** Danny Wadsworth. 1997. 19.95 (1-56315-048-4) Sterling Hse.
Whitecaps in the Ice Box. Lynn O. Mortensen. 114p. 1990. spiral bd. 9.95 (0-945265-10-7) Evergreen Pacific.
Whitechapel Horrors. Edward B. Hanna. 384p. 1992. 19.95 (0-88184-861-1) Carroll & Graf.
Whitechapel Horrors. Edward B. Hanna. 400p. 1993. pap. 10.95 (0-7867-0019-X) Carroll & Graf.
Whited Sepulchres: An Expose of Corruption in Church Hierarchies. Aimee D. Anderson & Albert E. Anderson. (Illus.). 352p. (Orig.). 1996. pap. 15.95 (0-9650875-0-6) A & A Anderson.
Whitefella Comin' Aboriginal Response to Colonialism in North Australia. David S. Trigger. (Illus.). 256p. (C). 1992. text ed. 59.95 (0-521-40181-X) Cambridge U Pr.
Whitefield & Wesley on the New Birth. Timothy L. Smith. 1986. pap. 8.99 (0-685-70969-8) Schmul Pub Co.
Whitefield in Print: A Bibliographic Record. Richard O. Roberts. xlii, 765p. 1988. lib. bdg. 75.00 (0-940033-28-3) R O Roberts.
***Whitefire.** Michaels. LC 97-23467. 1997. 20.00 (0-7862-1208-X) Mac Lib Ref.
***Whitefire.** Gern Michaels. 1996. mass mkt. 6.99 (0-614-27813-9, Zebra Kensgtn) Kensgtn Pub Corp.
Whitefish Can't Jump: And Other Tales of Gamefish on the Fly. E. Donnall Thomas, Jr. LC 94-13837. (Illus.). 160p. 1994. pap. text ed. 19.95 (0-07-064248-6, Ragged Mntn) Intl Marine.
Whitefish Will Rides Again! Arthur Yorinka. LC 93-79562. (Michael di Capua Bks.). (Illus.). 32p. (YA). 1996. pap. 5.95 (0-06-205921-1, Trophy) HarpC Child Bks.
Whitefish Will Rides Again! Arthur Yorinks. LC 93-79562. (Michael di Capua Bks.). (Illus.). 32p. (J). (gr. 1 up). 1994. 15.00 (0-06-205037-0) HarpC Child Bks.
Whitefolks: Seeing America Through Black Eyes, Vol. 1. Lowell Thompson. 190p. 1995. 20.00 (0-9647616-0-2) L Thompson.
Whitefoot the Wood Mouse. Thornton W. Burgess. (J). 18.95 (0-8488-0395-7) Amereon Ltd.
Whitefoot the Wood Mouse. Thornton Burgess. (J). 1992. reprint ed. lib. bdg. 17.95 (0-89966-980-8) Buccaneer Bks.
Whitefriars Glass: The Art of James Powell & Sons. Lesley Jackson. (Illus.). 160p. 1996. pap. 60.00 (0-903685-40-X, Pub. by R Dennis UK) Antique Collect.
***Whitehaired Girl.** Sun-Childers. Date not set. pap. 14.00 (0-312-15691-X) St Martin.
Whitehall. Peter Hennessy. 1989. 45.00 (0-02-914441-8, Free Pr) Free Pr.
Whitehall & the Labour Problem in Late Victorian & Edwardian Britain: A Study in Official Statistics & Social Control. Roger Davidson. LC 84-21424. 294p. 1985. 32.50 (0-7099-0832-6, Pub. by Croom Helm UK) Routledge Chapman & Hall.
Whitehall & the Wilderness: The Middle West in British Colonial Policy, 1760 to 1775. Jack M. Sosin. LC 80-21061. (Illus.). xi, 307p. 1981. reprint ed. text ed. 69.50 (0-313-22678-4, SOWW, Greenwood Pr) Greenwood.
Whitehall, Cheam: A Brief History & Guide to the 16th Century Timber-Framed House in Cheam. Cynthia Bradley. 24p. 1985. pap. 40.00 (0-9503224-4-X, Pub. by Sutton Libs & Arts) St Mut.
Whitehall Companion, 1994-1995. 5th ed. 1174p. 1994. 295.00 (1-872110-46-0) Gale.
Whitehall Reader: The U. K.'s Administrative Machine in Action. Peter Barberis. LC 95-24921. 256p. 1996. 95.00 (0-335-19312-9, Open Univ Pr); pap. 29.00 (0-335-19311-0, Open Univ Pr) Taylor & Francis.
Whitehaven. Richard Holland. Ed. by Paula Cunningham. LC 87-60373. (Illus.). 140p. 1988. 12.95 (0-913383-07-4) McClanahan Pub.
Whitehead & Bradley: A Comparative Analysis. Leemon B. McHenry. LC 91-12725. (SUNY Series in Philosophy). 213p. (C). 1991. pap. text ed. 21.95 (0-7914-0916-3) State U NY Pr.
Whitehead & Bradley: A Comparative Analysis. Leemon B. McHenry. LC 91-12725. (SUNY Series in Philosophy). 213p. (C). 1991. text ed. 64.50 (0-7914-0915-5) State U NY Pr.
Whitehead & the Modern World: Science, Metaphysics, & Civilization. Victor Lowe et al. LC 72-5738. (Essay Index Reprint Ser.). 1977. reprint ed. 18.95 (0-8369-7281-3) Ayer.
Whitehead Encyclopedia of Deer. G. Kenneth Whitehead. (Illus.). 704p. 1993. boxed 140.00 (0-940143-76-3) Safari Pr.
Whitehead Encyclopedia of Deer. G. Kenneth Whitehead. (Illus.). 597p. 1993. 140.00 (1-85310-362-4) Voyageur Pr.
Whitehead Groups of Finite Groups. R. Oliver. (London Mathematical Society Lecture Note Ser.: No. 132). 360p. 1988. pap. text ed. 52.95 (0-521-33646-5) Cambridge U Pr.
Whitehead, Process Philosophy, & Education. Robert S. Brumbaugh. 154p. (C). 1992. pap. text ed. 22.50 (0-8191-8484-5) U Pr of Amer.
Whitehead's American Essays in Social Philosophy. Alfred N. Whitehead. Ed. by A. H. Johnson. LC 74-11997. 206p. 1975. reprint ed. text ed. 59.50 (0-8371-7716-2, WHAE, Greenwood Pr) Greenwood.
Whitehead's Four Principles from West-East Perspectives. Anil K. Sarkar. (C). 1994. 24.00 (81-7003-180-X, Pub. by S Asia Pubs II) S Asia.
Whitehead's Four Principles from West-East Perspectives: Ways & Prospects of Process Philosophy. 2nd enl. ed. Anil K. Sarkar. 188p. 1994. reprint ed. pap. 53.60 (0-608-01604-7, AU00476) Bks Demand.
Whitehead's Metaphysics of Creativity. Ed. by Friedrich Rapp & Reiner Wiehl. LC 89-4479. 223p. 1990. pap. text ed. 21.95 (0-7914-0203-7) State U NY Pr.
Whitehead's Metaphysics of Creativity. Ed. by Friedrich Rapp & Reiner Wiehl. LC 89-4479. 223p. 1990. text ed. 64.50 (0-7914-0202-9) State U NY Pr.
Whitehead's Metaphysics of Extension & Solidarity. Jorge L. Nobo. LC 85-25040. 437p. (Orig.). 1986. text ed. 74.50 (0-88706-261-X); pap. text ed. 24.95 (0-88706-262-8) State U NY Pr.
Whitehead's Ontology. John W. Lango. LC 78-171184. 102p. 1972. text ed. 28.50 (0-87395-093-3) State U NY Pr.
Whitehead's Ontology. John W. Lango. LC 78-741184. 112p. reprint ed. pap. 32.00 (0-317-09030-5, 2010958) Bks Demand.
Whitehead's Organic Philosophy of Science. Ann L. Plamondon. LC 78-7350. 174p. 1979. text ed. 29.50 (0-87395-387-8) State U NY Pr.
Whitehead's Philosophical Development. Nathaniel M. Lawrence. LC 68-23306. 370p. 1968. reprint ed. text ed. 35.00 (0-8371-0139-5, LAWD, Greenwood Pr) Greenwood.
Whitehead's Philosophy: Primary Texts in Dialogue. Arthur H. Jentz, Jr. LC 85-698. 88p. (Orig.). 1985. pap. 13.50 (0-8191-4577-7); lib. bdg. 34.50 (0-8191-4576-9) U Pr of Amer.
Whitehorn's Woman. Barbara McCauley. (Desire Ser.). 1993. mass mkt. 2.99 (0-373-05803-9, 5-05803-7) Silhouette.
***Whitehorse & Area Hikes & Bikes: Yukon Conservation Society.** Yukon Conservation Society Staff. 1996. pap. text ed. 14.95 (0-9694612-5-9, Pub. by Stoddart Pubng CN) Genl Dist Srvs.
***Whiteness: A Critical Reader.** Mike Hill. LC 97-4575. 1997. 55.00 (0-8147-3544-4); pap. 21.95 (0-8147-3545-2) NYU Pr.
***Whiteness: A Critical Reader.** Mike Hill. 1997. pap. 21.95 (0-614-28101-6) NYU Pr.
Whiteness of Bones. Susanna Moore. 288p. 1990. pap. 11.95 (0-14-013020-9, Penguin Bks) Viking Penguin.
***Whiteness Visible.** Babb. 1998. 50.00 (0-8147-1302-5); pap. 17.95 (0-8147-1312-2) NYU Pr.
Whiteoak Brothers. large type ed. Mazo De la Roche. (Whiteoak Chronicles Ser.). 1973. 25.99 (0-85456-678-3) Ulverscroft.
Whiteoaks. large type ed. Mazo De la Roche. (Whiteoak Chronicles Ser.). 1973. 25.99 (0-85456-680-5) Ulverscroft.
***Whiteout.** Walker. 1997. pap. 13.95 (0-312-86302-0) St Martin.
Whiteout. Sage Walker. 352p. 1996. 23.95 (0-312-85765-9) Tor Bks.
***Whiteout.** Sage Walker. 1997. pap. 13.95 (0-614-27319-6) Tor Bks.
Whiter Than Snow. Pete Finch & Gretchen Finch. 52p. 1991. pap. write for info. (0-9629877-0-0) Fir Creek Min.
Whites: Stories. Norman Rush. LC 92-50099. 1992. pap. 11.00 (0-679-73816-9, Vin) Random.
White's Conspectus of American Biography. 2nd enl. rev. ed. (BCL1 - U. S. History Ser.). 455p. 1991. reprint ed. lib. bdg. 99.00 (0-7812-6032-9) Rprt Serv.
White's Conspectus of American Biography. J. T. White. 1971. reprint ed. 59.00 (0-403-01271-6) Scholarly.
***Whites Crossing.** Donald J. Rowland. LC 96-92135. (Illus.). viii, 231p. 1996. 20.00 (0-9653407-0-8) Sunset Publns.
White's Edition for Clarinet & Piano, 1027. Ed. by Phillip Rehfeldt. (Editions for Clarinet Ser.). 1983. 16.50 (0-933251-03-3) Mill Creek Pubns.
Whites in Desegregated Schools. Center for Equal Education Staff. LC 76-24186. 1976. 4.50 (0-912008-11-3) Equity & Excel.
Whites in Skullyville County, Choctaw Nation Vol. 222: Permit Register 1889 - February 19, 1905; Choctaw. Sandra McKim. (Orig.). 1995. pap. 25.00 (0-7884-0327-3) Heritage Bk.
White's Law Dictionary. Ed. by D. Robert White. 128p. 1985. mass mkt. 5.95 (0-446-38259-0) Warner Bks.
Whites Only: A Pastor's Retrospective on Signs of the New South. Robert E. Seymour. 160p. 1991. pap. 13.00 (0-8170-1178-1) Judson.
White's Tree Frogs. J. Coborn. (Illus.). 1995. pap. text ed. 9.95 (0-7938-0282-2, RE114) TFH Pubns.
Whiteside Island Story-Emerald Isle of St. Louis Bay. 3rd ed. Claire W. Schumacher. LC 74-29021. (Illus.). 65p. 1993. 5.00 (0-917378-04-0) Zenith City.
Whitesmiths of Taunton: A History of Reed & Barton, 1824-1943. George S. Gibb. LC 75-41755. (Companies & Men: Business Enterprises in America Ser.). (Illus.). 242p. 1976. reprint ed. 51.95 (0-405-08071-9) Ayer.
***Whitesnake: Selections for "Slip of the Tongue"** Ed. by Aaron Stang. 124p. 1990. pap. text ed. 18.95 (0-7692-1350-2) Warner Bros.
Whitestone. Philip Holmes. (Illus.). 208p. (Orig.). 1989. pap. 14.95 (0-940151-14-6) Statesman-Exam.
Whitetail: The Ultimate Challenge. Charles J. Alsheimer. LC 95-76857. (Illus.). 223p. 1995. pap. text ed. 14.95 (0-87341-338-5, WVC01) Krause Pubns.
Whitetail Autumn. John J. Ozoga. LC 94-32654. (Seasons of the Whitetail Ser.). (Illus.). 160p. 1994. 29.50 (1-57223-007-X) Idyll Arbor.
Whitetail Behavior Through the Seasons. Charles J. Alsheimer. 208p. 1996. 34.95 (0-87341-449-7) Krause Pubns.
Whitetail Country. Photos by Daniel J. Cox. (Illus.). 176p. 1990. 39.00 (1-55971-081-0, 1494) NorthWord.
Whitetail Country. John Ozaga. (Illus.). 1993. pap. 19.95 (1-55971-207-4) NorthWord.
Whitetail Country. John J. Ozoga. Ed. & Frwd. by Chuck Petrie. (Illus.). 144p. 1988. 39.00 (0-932558-43-7) Willow Creek Pr.
Whitetail Deer Hunting. Mike Lapinski. (Illus.). 64p. 1988. pap. 3.50 (0-912299-34-7) Stoneydale Pr Pub.
Whitetail Hunter Education: A Complete Guide to Whitetail Hunting from Scouting to Butchering. Dodman J. Nobel. LC 94-90454. 184p. (Orig.). 1995. pap. 15.95 (1-56002-489-5, Univ Edtns) Aegina Pr.
Whitetail Hunter's Almanac: An Introduction to Whitetail Hunting. Ken Nordberg. 150p. 1988. pap. 8.95 (1-886422-01-X) Shingle Creek.
Whitetail Hunter's Almanac: An Introduction to Whitetail Hunting. 2nd ed. Ken Nordberg. 153p. 1989. pap. 8.95 (1-886422-02-8) Shingle Creek.
Whitetail Hunter's Almanac: An Introduction to Whitetail Hunting. 3rd ed. Ken Nordberg. 151p. 1990. pap. 8.95 (1-886422-03-6) Shingle Creek.
Whitetail Hunter's Almanac: An Introduction to Whitetail Hunting. 4th ed. Ken Nordberg. 147p. 1991. pap. 8.95 (1-886422-04-4) Shingle Creek.
Whitetail Hunter's Almanac: An Introduction to Whitetail Hunting. 5th ed. Ken Nordberg. 166p. 1992. pap. 8.95 (1-886422-05-2) Shingle Creek.
Whitetail Hunter's Almanac: An Introduction to Whitetail Hunting. 6th ed. Ken Nordberg. 186p. 1993. pap. 8.95 (1-886422-06-0) Shingle Creek.
Whitetail Hunter's Almanac: An Introduction to Whitetail Hunting. 7th ed. Ken Nordberg & Jennifer J. O'Donnell. Ed. by M. C. O'Donnell et al. (Illus.). 150p. 1994. pap. 8.95 (1-886422-07-9) Shingle Creek.
Whitetail Hunter's Almanac: First-Seventh Edition. 7th ed. Ken Nordberg. (Illus.). (Orig.). 1994. pap. 62.65 (1-886422-00-1) Shingle Creek.
Whitetail Magic for Kids. Tom Wolpert. LC 90-50719. (Animal Magic for Kids Ser.). (Illus.). 48p. (J). (gr. 2-3). 1991. lib. bdg. 18.60 (0-8368-0661-1) Gareth Stevens Inc.
***Whitetail Medicine.** Craig Boddington. (Whitetail Secrets Ser.: No. 6). (Illus.). 196p. 1995. 17.95 (1-56416-156-0) Derrydale Pr.
***Whitetail Movement.** John Wootters. Ed. by Craig Boddington. (Whitetail Secrets Ser.: No. 1). (Illus.). 183p. (YA). (gr. 10 up). 1994. 17.95 (1-56416-151-X) Derrydale Pr.
Whitetail Spring. John J. Ozoga. LC 96-6030. (Seasons of the Whitetail Ser.). (Illus.). 144p. 1996. 29.50 (1-57223-039-8, 0398) Idyll Arbor.
***Whitetail Summer.** John J. Ozoga. LC 97-1060. (Seasons of the Whitetail Ser.). 1997. pap. write for info. (1-57223-044-4) Idyll Arbor.
Whitetail Tactics with Recurves & Longbows. Jim Hamm. (Illus.). 176p. (Orig.). 1996. pap. 16.95 (0-9645741-1-X) Bois dArc Pr.
Whitetail Winter. Text by John J. Ozoga. LC 95-10901. (Seasons of the Whitetail Ser.). (Illus.). 160p. 1995. 29.50 (1-57223-027-4) Idyll Arbor.
Whitetail X Two. Norm Jolliffe & Ben Lee. LC 91-20440. (Illus.). 1991. pap. 12.95 (0-945980-31-0) Nrth Country Pr.
Whitetails: Behavior, Ecology, & Conservation. Erwin A. Bauer. LC 93-17728. (Illus.). 160p. 1993. 35.00 (0-89658-196-9) Voyageur Pr.
Whitetails: Behavior, Ecology, Conservation. Erwin A. Bauer. LC 93-17728. (Illus.). 160p. 1995. pap. text ed. 19.95 (0-89658-308-2) Voyageur Pr.
***Whitetails: Behavior, Ecology, Conservation.** Erwin A. Bauer. (Illus.). 160p. 1998. reprint ed. pap. 19.95 (0-89658-375-9) Voyageur Pr.
Whitetails: Phantoms of the Forest. Michael Furtman. LC 96-13249. (Wildlife Ser.). (Illus.). 144p. (Orig.). 1996. pap. 14.95 (1-55971-572-3) NorthWord.
Whitetails for Kids. (Illus.). 48p. (J). 1991. pap. 6.95 (1-55971-122-1) NorthWord.
Whitetails for Kids. Tom Wolpert. (Illus.). 48p. (J). 1991. 14.95 (1-55971-086-1, 0197) NorthWord.
***Whitetails in Action.** unabridged ed. Mike Biggs. (Illus.). 192p. 1996. 39.95 (0-9642915-2-5) T P W.
***Whitewash.** Ntozake Shange. LC 97-8184. (Illus.). 32p. (J). (gr. 1-5). 1997. 15.95 (0-8027-8490-9); lib. bdg. 16.85 (0-8027-8491-7) Walker & Co.
Whitewash: Exposing the Health & Environmental Dangers of Women's Sanitary Products & Disposable Diapers - What You Can Do about It. Liz Armstrong & Adrienne Scott. 194p. 1993. pap. 11.00 (0-00-637709-2, Pub. by HarpC CN) HarpC.
Whitewash: Selections from Volumes I to IV. Harold Weisberg. 408p. 1993. pap. 16.95 (0-7867-0016-5) Carroll & Graf.
Whitewash: The Report on the Warren Report. Harold Weisberg. 1965. 25.00 (0-911606-01-7) Weisberg.
Whitewash II: The FBI-Secret Service Cover-Up. Harold Weisberg. 1966. pap. 12.00 (0-911606-02-5) Weisberg.
Whitewash IV: Top Secret JFK Assassination Transcript. Harold Weisberg. 1974. per. 12.00 (0-911606-07-6) Weisberg.
***Whitewashing Britain: Race & Citizenship in the Postwar Era.** Kathleen Paul. LC 97-5410. (Illus.). 288p. 1996. 39.95 (0-8014-3348-7); pap. 16.95 (0-8014-8440-5) Cornell U Pr.
Whitewashing of the Yellow Badge: Antisemitism & Philosemitism in Postwar Germany 1945-1952. Frank Stern. Tr. by William Templer. (Studies in Antisemitism). 482p. 1991. 57.95 (0-08-040653-X, Prgamon Press) Buttrwrth-Heinemann.
Whitewater. large type ed. Bill Knox. 1978. 25.99 (0-7089-0097-6) Ulverscroft.
Whitewater: From the Editorial Pages of The Wall Street Journal. Ed. by Robert L. Bartley. LC 94-79762. 550p. 1994. pap. 14.95 (1-881944-02-6) Dow Jones & Co.
***Whitewater Europe Bk. 2: The South Alps.** Peter Knadis. (Illus.). 240p. (Orig.). 1996. pap. 24.95 (0-9519413-1-3) Menasha Ridge.
Whitewater Gems of the Alps. Joseph Haas. (Illus.). 173p. 1994. text ed. 29.95 (0-89732-070-0) Menasha Ridge.
Whitewater Handbook. 3rd ed. Bruce Lessels. LC 93-21066. (Illus.). 288p. 1994. pap. 14.95 (1-878239-01-5) AMC Books.
Whitewater Home Companion Vol. 2: Southeastern Rivers. William Nealy. LC 81-9854. (Illus.). 176p. (Orig.). 1984. pap. 12.95 (0-89732-025-5) Menasha Ridge.
Whitewater Home Companion, Southeastern Rivers, Vol. 1. William Nealy. LC 81-9854. (Illus.). 176p. (Orig.). 1981. pap. 14.95 (0-89732-028-X) Menasha Ridge.
Whitewater Kayaking. Jeremy Evans. LC 91-39142. (Adventurers Ser.). (Illus.). 48p. (J). (gr. 5-6). 1992. lib. bdg. 13.95 (0-89686-685-8, Crstwood Hse) Silver Burdett Pr.
***Whitewater Kayaking.** David Harrison. LC 97-18079. (Canoe & Kayak Techniques Ser.). 1998. write for info. (0-8117-2723-8) Stackpole.
Whitewater Nepal: A Rivers Guidebook for Rafting & Kayaking. Peter Knowles & Dave Allardice. (Illus.). 280p. 1993. pap. 18.95 (0-9519413-0-5) Menasha Ridge.
Whitewater; Quietwater: A Guide to the Rivers of Wisconsin, Upper Michigan & Northeast Minnesota. Bob Palzer & Jody Palzer. LC 83-80899. (Illus.). 160p. 1983. pap. 12.95 (0-89732-086-7) Menasha Ridge.
Whitewater; Quietwater: A Guide to the Wild Rivers of Wisconsin, Upper Michigan, & Northeast Minnesota. 5th ed. Bob Palzer & Jody Palzer. LC 83-80899. (Illus.). 160p. 1983. pap. 9.95 (0-916166-04-X) Evergreen WI.
Whitewater; Quietwater: A Guide to the Wild Rivers of Wisconsin, Upper Michigan, & Northeast Minnesota. 5th ed. Bob Palzer & Jody Palzer. (Illus.). 160p. 1985. suppl. ed. (0-318-51868-6) Evergreen WI.
Whitewater Rafting. William McGinnis. LC 74-24280. (Illus.). 1978. pap. 12.95 (0-8129-6301-6, Times Bks) Random.
Whitewater Rafting: An Introductory Guide. Cecil Kuhne. (Illus.). 176p. 1995. pap. 16.95 (1-55821-317-1) Lyons & Burford.
***Whitewater Rafting in North America: More Than 100 Rafting Adventures in the U. S. & Canada.** 2nd rev. ed. Lloyd D. Armstead. LC 96-47037. (Illus.). 288p. 1997. pap. 16.95 (0-7627-0083-1) Globe Pequot.
Whitewater Rafting Manual: Tactics & Techniques for Great River Adventures. Jimmie Johnson. (Illus.). 256p. 1994. pap. 16.95 (0-8117-3098-0) Stackpole.
Whitewater Rescue Manual: New Techniques for Canoers, Kayakers, & Rafters. Wayne A. Sundmacher & Charles C. Walbridge. (Illus.). 208p. 1995. pap. text ed. 16.95 (0-07-067790-5, Ragged Mntn) Intl Marine.
Whitewater Sourcebook. rev. ed. Richard Penny. LC 88-16932. (Illus.). 400p. 1990. pap. 19.95 (0-89732-078-6) Menasha Ridge.
Whitewater Tales of Terror. William Nealy. LC 83-22051. (Illus.). 120p. (Orig.). 1983. pap. 6.95 (0-89732-024-7) Menasha Ridge.
Whitewater Tidal Wave: Every American Taxpayer Is Affected. A. K. Karsky. 92p. 1995. 7.95 (1-883740-25-8) Pebble Bch Pr Ltd.
Whitewater Trips & Hot Springs in the Kootenays of British Columbia: For Kayakers, Canoeists & Rafters. Betty Pratt-Johnson. LC 89-85596. (Illus.). 185p. (Orig.). 1989. pap. 16.95 (0-921009-18-6) Adventure WA.
Whitewater Trips for Kayakers, Canoeists & Rafters in British Columbia: Greater Vancouver Through Whistler, Okanagan & Thompson River Regions. Betty Pratt-Johnson. (Illus.). 215p. (Orig.). 1986. pap. 16.95 (0-931397-08-1) Adventure WA.
Whitewater Trips for Kayakers, Canoeists & Rafters on Vancouver Island. Betty Pratt-Johnson. LC 83-26190. (Illus.). 127p. (Orig.). 1984. pap. 8.95 (0-914718-90-8) Adventure WA.
Whitey. David Muller. (Writers Ser.). 120p. 1995. reprint ed. pap. text ed. 12.95 (0-86975-468-8, Pub. by Ravan Pr ZA) Ohio U Pr.

W

Whitfield History & Genealogy of Tennessee. 2nd ed. Vallie J. Whitfield. Ed. by Joanne V. Whitfield. LC 79-64403. (Illus.). 315p. 1979. reprint ed. 15.00 (0-930920-12-0) Whitfield Bks.

Whitfield Records of United States, 1620-1995. Vallie J. Whitfield. Ed. by Joanne V. Whitfield. (Illus.). 568p. 1997. 30.00 (0-930920-20-1) Whitfield Bks.

Whitfield's University Rhyming Dictionary: English Language Rime. Frances Stillman. 283p. 1964. pap. 3.95 (0-8152-0080-3, M-9049) Fr & Eur.

Whither African Economies? Ed. by Jean-Claude Berthelemy. (Development Centre Seminars Ser.). 168p. (Orig.). (ENG & FRE.). 1995. pap. 27.00 (92-64-14647-4, Pub. by Org for Econ FR) OECD.

Whither America: Will There be a Tricentennial? Arthur W. Munk. 1984. 9.75 (0-8158-0419-9) Chris Mass.

***Whither APEC? Progress to Date & the Agenda for the Future: A Conference Hosted by the Institute for International Economics.** Institute for International Economics (U.S.) Staff. LC 97-19897. 1997. write for info. (0-88132-248-2) Inst Intl Eco.

Whither China? R. Palme Dutt. 1967. pap. 0.40 (0-87898-021-0) New Outlook.

Whither Environmental Archaeology? Ed. by Rosemary Luff & Peter Rowley-Conwy. (Oxbow Monographs in Archaeology: No. 38). (Illus.). 224p. 1994. pap. 50.00 (0-946897-69-7, Pub. by Oxbow Bks UK) David Brown.

Whither EU-Israeli Relations? Common & Divergent Interests. Ed. by Ephraim Ahiram & Alfred Tovias. LC 95-18748. (Ethnien, Regionen, Konflikte Ser.: Vol. 6). 297p. 1995. pap. 57.95 (3-631-47549-7) P Lang Pubng.

Whither India: India & the Changing Geopolitics of Asia. Shekhar Gupta. (Adelphi Papers). 1995. pap. text ed. 26.00 (0-19-828021-1) OUP.

Whither India's Democracy? Ed. by Bidyut Chakrabarty. 1993. 22.00 (81-7074-126-2, Pub. by KP Bagchi IA) S Asia.

Whither Islam? A Survey of Modern Movements in the Moslem World. Ed. by Hamilton A. Gibb. LC 73-180338. reprint ed. 32.50 (0-404-56263-9) AMS Pr.

Whither Israel? The Domestic Challenge. Ed. by Keith Kyle & Joel Peters. 350p. 1993. text ed. 59.50 (1-85043-643-6, Pub. by I B Tauris UK) St Martin.

Whither Israel? The Domestic Challenge, Vol. 1. Keith Kyle. 1994. text ed. 19.95 (1-85043-868-4, Pub. by I B Tauris UK) St Martin.

Whither Jerusalem? Proposals & Petitions Concerning the Future of Jerusalem. Moshe Hirsch et al. Tr. by Ralph Mandel from HEB. LC 95-20417. 1995. lib. bdg. 92.00 (90-411-0077-6, Pub. by M Nijhoff NE) Kluwer Ac.

Whither Jerusalem? 1995. pap. text ed. write for info. (90-411-0078-4) Kluwer Ac.

Whither Mankind. Ed. by Charles A. Beard. LC 78-109708. 408p. 1973. reprint ed. text ed. 69.50 (0-8371-4199-0, BEWM, Greenwood Pr) Greenwood.

Whither Mankind: A Panorama of Modern Civilization. Ed. by Charles A. Beard. LC 72-128206. (Essay Index Reprint Ser.). 1977. reprint ed. 26.95 (0-8369-2344-8) Ayer.

Whither Marxism? Global Crises in International Perspective. Ed. by Bernd Magnus & Stephen Cullenberg. 288p. (C). (gr. 13). 1994. pap. 17.95 (0-415-91043-9, B4463) Routledge.

Whither, O Ship: Adventures in a Tramp Steamer. Stanley R. Green. 208p. 8900. 27.00 (0-7206-0743-4, Pub. by P Owen Ltd UK) Dufour.

Whither Public Policy? Liberalism, Conservatism, & Social Change. Ed. by Gary Mucciaroni. (Orig.). 1990. pap. 15.00 (0-944285-21-X) Pol Studies.

Whither Socialism? Joseph E. Stiglitz. (Wicksell Lectures Ser.). (Illus.). 352p. 1996. reprint ed. pap. 15.00 (0-262-69182-5) MIT Pr.

Whither South Africa? Ed. by Bernard M. Magubane & Ibbo Mandaza. LC 86-73224. 250p. (C). 1988. 29.95 (0-86543-048-9); pap. 9.95 (0-86543-049-7) Africa World.

Whither the American Empire: Expansion or Contraction? Ed. by Marvin E. Wolfgang. (Annals Ser.: Vol. 500). 1988. 26.00 (0-8039-3171-9); pap. 17.00 (0-8039-3172-7) Sage.

Whither the U. S. Church? Context, Gospel, Planning. John A. Grindel. LC 91-19427. 280p. (Orig.). 1991. pap. 17.00 (0-88344-776-2) Orbis Bks.

Whither Thou Goest. Carolyn S. Hind. LC 85-51991. (Illus.). 192p. 1985. 12.50 (0-936029-00-5) Western Bk Journ.

Whither Thou Goest. Mary L. Kellar. (Illus.). 77p. (Orig.). 1989. pap. 3.95 (0-89114-171-5) Baptist Pub Hse.

***Whither Thou Goest.** Al Lacy. (Angel of Mercy Ser.: No. 5). 300p. 1997. pap. 9.99 (1-57673-078-6, Multnomah Bks) Multnomah Pubs.

Whither Thou Goest. large type ed. Peggy L. Jones. (Linford Romance Library). 320p. 1996. pap. 15.99 (0-7089-7831-2, Linford) Ulverscroft.

Whither WAC? Reflections on the Silver Anniversary of Writing Across the Curriculum. Susan McLeod. Ed. by Lillian Bridwell-Bowles & Kim Donehower. (Technical Reports: Vol. 14). 11p. (Orig.). 1996. pap. 2.00 (1-881221-22-9) U Minn Ctr Interdis.

Whither Willow. Peter J. Ponzo. 440p. 1996. mass mkt. 4.99 (1-896329-94-2, Pub. by Comnwlth Pub CN) Partners Pubs Grp.

***Whithorn & St. Ninian: The Excavations of a Monastic Town 1984-91.** Ed. by Peter Hill. (Illus.). 1997. 62.95 (0-7509-0912-9, Pub. by Sutton Pubng UK) Bks Intl VA.

Whitley County, Kentucky. Turner Publishing Company Staff. LC 93-61560. 352p. 1993. 48.00 (1-56311-124-1) Turner Pub KY.

Whitman. Edgar L. Masters. LC 68-22695. 1968. reprint ed. 30.00 (0-8196-0210-8) Biblo.

Whitman: A Study. John Burroughs. LC 72-131652. 1979. reprint ed. 29.00 (0-403-00539-6) Scholarly.

Whitman: An Interpretation in Narrative. Emory Holloway. LC 70-79953. (Illus.). 1969. reprint ed. 30.00 (0-8196-0236-1) Biblo.

Whitman: An Interpretation in Narrative. Emory Holloway. (BCL1-PS American Literature Ser.). 330p. 1992. reprint ed. lib. bdg. 89.00 (0-7812-6898-2) Rprt Serv.

***Whitman: Unpublished Prose.** Grier. (C). 1984. text ed. 72.00 (0-8147-2996-7) NYU Pr.

Whitman: Unpublished Prose, Vol. 1. Grier. (C). 1984. text ed. 72.00 (0-8147-2991-6) NYU Pr.

Whitman: Unpublished Prose, Vol. 2. Grier. (C). 1984. text ed. 72.00 (0-8147-2992-4) NYU Pr.

Whitman: Unpublished Prose, Vol. 3. Grier. (C). 1984. text ed. 72.00 (0-8147-2993-2) NYU Pr.

Whitman: Unpublished Prose, Vol. 4. Grier. (C). 1984. text ed. 72.00 (0-8147-2994-0) NYU Pr.

Whitman: Unpublished Prose, Vol. 5. Grier. (C). 1984. text ed. 72.00 (0-8147-2995-9) NYU Pr.

Whitman a Study. John Burroughs. (Works of John Burroughs). 1989. reprint ed. lib. bdg. 79.00 (0-7812-0010-5) Rprt Serv.

Whitman & Nietzsche: A Comparative Study of Their Thought. C. N. Stavrou. LC 64-65034. (North Carolina. University. Studies in the Germanic Languages & Literatures: No. 48). reprint ed. 27.00 (0-404-50948-7) AMS Pr.

Whitman & the American Idiom. Mark Bauerlein. LC 91-10929. 191p. 1991. text ed. 25.00 (0-8071-1681-5) La State U Pr.

***Whitman & the Romance of Medicine.** Robert L. Davis. LC 96-39258. 1997. 35.00 (0-520-20760-2) U CA Pr.

Whitman & Tradition: The Poet in His Century. Kenneth M. Price. LC 89-27380. 208p. (C). 1990. text ed. 22.50 (0-300-04683-9) Yale U Pr.

Whitman & Traubel. William Walling. LC 76-95452. (Studies in Whitman: No. 28). 1970. reprint ed. lib. bdg. 49.95 (0-8383-1209-8) M S G Haskell Hse.

Whitman as Editor of the Brooklyn Daily Eagle. Thomas L. Brasher. LC 70-91872. 264p. reprint ed. 75.30 (0-685-16207-9, 2027595) Bks Demand.

Whitman at Auction: 1899-1972. Ed. by Gloria A. Francis & Artem Lozynsky. LC 77-16647. (Authors Auction Ser.). (Illus.). 504p. 1978. 44.00 (0-8103-0921-1) Gale.

Whitman Between Impressionism & Expressionism: Language of the Body, Language of the Soul. Erik I. Thurin. LC 94-28805. 1995. 35.00 (0-8387-5297-7) Bucknell U Pr.

Whitman Explorations in Form. Howard J. Waskow. 289p. reprint ed. pap. 82.40 (0-318-58058-6, 2020174) Bks Demand.

Whitman in His Own Time: A Biographical Chronicle of His Life, Drawn from Recollections, Memoirs, Interviews by His Friends & Associates. Ed. by Joel Myerson. (Writers in Their Own Time Ser.). (Illus.). 1991. lib. bdg. 65.00 (1-55888-424-6) Omnigraphics Inc.

Whitman in the Light of Vedantic Mysticism: An Interpretation. V. K. Chari. LC 64-19853. 192p. reprint ed. pap. 54.80 (0-7837-1899-3, 2042103) Bks Demand.

Whitman Juvenile Books: Reference & Value Guide. David Brown & Virginia Brown. (Illus.). 744p. (Orig.). 1996. pap. 17.95 (0-89145-740-2, 4733) Collector Bks.

Whitman Massacre. Mary Saunders. 1978. 9.95 (0-87770-188-1); pap. 4.95 (0-87770-189-X) Ye Galleon.

Whitman Massacre of 1847. Catherine Sager et al. (Illus.). 208p. 19.95 (0-87770-260-8) Ye Galleon.

Whitman Portrait. Paul Shyre. 1967. pap. 5.25 (0-8222-1246-3) Dramatists Play.

Whitman Revisited. Frank Jakubowsky. 61p. 1989. pap. 5.95 (0-932588-12-3) Jesus Bks.

Whitman, Slavery, & the Emergence of Leaves of Grass. Martin Klammer. LC 93-33495. 192p. 1995. 32.50 (0-271-01315-X) Pa St U Pr.

***Whitman, Slavery, & the Emergence of Leaves of Grass.** Martin Klammer. 188p. 1997. pap. 16.95 (0-271-01642-6) Pa St U Pr.

***Whitman the Political Poet.** Betsy Erkkila. (Illus.). 384p. 1996. reprint ed. pap. 18.95 (0-19-511380-2) OUP.

***Whitmanism, Imagism & Modernism in China & America.** Guiyou Huang. LC 97-17139. 1997. write for info. (1-57591-011-X) Susquehanna U Pr.

Whitman's & Dickinson's Contemporaries: An Anthology of Their Verse. Ed. by Robert Bain. LC 95-9867. 504p. (C). 1996. 49.95 (0-8093-1721-4); pap. 19.95 (0-8093-2031-2) S Ill U Pr.

Whitman's Chocolate Cookbook. (From America's Favorite Kitchens Ser.). (Illus.). 128p. 1991. 9.99 (0-517-64157-7) Random Hse Value.

Whitman's Drama of Consensus. Kerry C. Larson. 296p. 1988. pap. text ed. 18.95 (0-226-46908-5); lib. bdg. 54.00 (0-226-46907-7) U Ch Pr.

Whitman's Journeys into Chaos: A Psychoanalytic Study of the Poetic Process. Stephen A. Black. LC 75-2979. 272p. 1975. pap. 77.60 (0-7837-7446-X, 2010547) Bks Demand.

Whitman's Manuscripts: Leaves of Grass (1860): A Parallel Text. Walt Whitman. Ed. by Fredson Bowers. LC 55-7313. 342p. reprint ed. pap. 97.50 (0-317-26648-9, 2024084) Bks Demand.

Whitman's Men: Walt Whitman's Famous Poems Celebrated by Contemporary Photographers. David Groff & Richard Berman. (Illus.). 80p. 1996. 18.95 (0-7893-0022-2) Universe.

Whitman's Poetry of the Body: Sexuality, Politics, & the Text. M. Jimmie Killingsworth. LC 88-20579. xxii, 196p. (C). 1991. reprint ed. pap. 12.95 (0-8078-4314-8) U of NC Pr.

Whitman's Presence: Body, Voice, & Writing in Leaves of Grass. Tenney Nathanson. 528p. (C). 1992. 60.00 (0-8147-5770-7) NYU Pr.

Whitman's Presence: Body, Voice & Writing in Leaves of Grass. Tenney Nathanson. (C). 1994. pap. 18.50 (0-8147-5779-0) NYU Pr.

Whitman's "Song of Myself" Thirty-Four & Its Background. Daniel M. McKeithan. (Essays & Studies on American Language & Literature: Vol. 18). (Orig.). 1969. pap. 25.00 (0-8115-0198-1) Periodicals Srv.

***Whitman's Tomb: Stories from the Pines.** Robert Bateman. 215p. Date not set. 21.95 (0-937548-32-4) Plexus Pub.

Whitman's Wild Children. Neeli Cherkovski. (Illus.). 225p. 1988. 19.95 (0-932499-57-0); pap. 12.95 (0-932499-56-2) Lapis Pr.

Whitney. Dennis Eichhorn. (Illus.). 76p. (Orig.). (YA). (gr. 7-12). 1987. pap. 4.25 (0-89872-211-X) Turman Pub.

Whitney Cousins: Amelia. Jean Thesman. 144p. (J). (gr. 4-5). 1990. pap. 2.95 (0-380-75874-1, Flare) Avon.

Whitney Cousins: Erin. Jean Thesman. 144p. (J). (gr. 4-5). 1990. pap. 2.95 (0-380-75875-X, Flare) Avon.

Whitney Cousins: Heather. Jean Thesman. 160p. (J). (gr. 4-5). 1990. pap. 2.95 (0-380-75869-5, Flare) Avon.

Whitney Cousins: Triple Trouble. Jean Thesman. 160p. (Orig.). (YA). 1992. mass mkt. 3.50 (0-380-76464-4, Flare) Avon.

***Whitney Guide to Twentieth Century American Architecture: Two Hundred Key Buildings.** rev. ed. Sydney Le Blanc. (Illus.). 224p. 1996. pap. text ed. 19.95 (0-8230-2173-4) Watsn-Guptill.

***Whitney Houston.** Jeff Savage. LC 97-2713. (Taking Part Bks.). 1998. write for info. (0-382-39798-3, Dillon Silver Burdett); lib. bdg. write for info. (0-382-39797-5, Dillon Silver Burdett) Silver Burdett Pr.

Whitney Houston. Rosemary Wallner. LC 94-19029. (Reaching for the Stars Ser.). (J). (gr. 4-8). 1994. lib. bdg. 13.98 (1-56234-337-8) Abdo & Dghtrs.

***Whitney Houston: Singer-Actress.** Chelsea House Publishers Staff. LC 97-21869. (Junior Black Americans of Achievement Ser.). (Illus.). 72p. (J). (gr. 3-6). 1997. lib. bdg. 14.95 (0-7910-4565-X) Chelsea Hse.

***Whitney Houston: Singer/Actress.** Ted Cox. (Black Americans of Achievement Ser.). (Illus.). 104p. (YA). (gr. 5 up). 1997. pap. 8.95 (0-7910-4456-4); lib. bdg. 19.95 (0-7910-4455-6) Chelsea Hse.

Whitney M. Young, Jr., & the Struggle for Civil Rights. Nancy J. Weiss. (Illus.). 302p. (C). 1989. 37.50 (0-691-04757-X) Princeton U Pr.

Whitney My Love. Judith McNaught. Ed. by Linda Marrow. 1991. mass mkt. 6.99 (0-671-73764-3) PB.

Whitney, My Love. large type ed. Judith McNaught. LC 94-17376. 1994. 25.95 (1-56895-107-8) Wheeler Pub.

Whitney's New Glasses. Linda P. Silbert & Alvin J. Silbert. (Little Twirps Understanding People Bks.). (Illus.). (J). (gr. k-4). 1978. pap. 4.98 (0-89544-052-0) Silbert Bress.

Whitney's Star Finder. 5th ed. Charles A. Whitney. LC 85-40349. (Illus.). 1989. pap. 16.95 (0-679-72582-2) Knopf.

***Whitout 96: The Blizzard of 1996.** Ivan Schoone. 110p. (Orig.). 1996. pap. write for info. (1-57502-299-0, P1028) Morris Pubng.

Whitsun Weddings. Philip Larkin. 46p. 1971. pap. 9.95 (0-571-09710-3) Faber & Faber.

***Whittaker Chambers: A Biography.** Sam Tanenhaus. LC 96-36087. (Illus.). 638p. 1997. 35.00 (0-394-58559-3) Random.

Whittaker's Theatricals. Herbert Whittaker. Ed. by Marian M. Wilson. 264p. 1993. pap. text ed. 19.00 (0-88924-239-9, Pub. by Simon & Pierre Pub CN) Empire Pub Srvs.

Whitten's Flying Fables: How Not to Fly Or How to Crash Or How Not to Crash. Louis G. Whitten. (Illus.). 357p. 1994. pap. 14.95 (0-9622166-8-2) Honoribus Pr.

Whittier: Notes of His Life & of His Friendship. Annie Fields. (Notable American Authors Ser.). 1992. reprint ed. lib. bdg. 75.00 (0-7812-2824-7) Rprt Serv.

Whittier & His Poetry. William H. Hudson. LC 77-120993. (Poetry & Life Ser.). reprint ed. 16.00 (0-404-52523-7) AMS Pr.

Whittier & Whittierland: Portrait of a Poet & His World. Ed. by Donald C. Freeman et al. (Illus.). 92p. 1987. reprint ed. pap. 10.00 (1-878651-07-2) HPL Pr.

Whittier College: The First Century on the Poet Campus. Charles Elliott, Jr. (Illus.). 240p. 1986. 50.00 (0-9608808-3-6) Legends Pr.

Whittier-Land: A Handbook of North Essex. Samuel T. Pickard. LC 73-7511. (American Literature Ser.: No. 49). 1973. reprint ed. lib. bdg. 62.95 (0-8383-1698-0) M S G Haskell Hse.

Whittier on Writers & Writing. John Greenleaf Whittier. LC 76-128329. (Essay Index Reprint Ser.). 1977. 20.95 (0-8369-2089-9) Ayer.

Whittier's Unknown Romance: Letters to Elizabeth Lloyd. John Greenleaf Whittier. LC 73-8938. (American Biography Ser.: No. 32). 1973. reprint ed. lib. bdg. 42.95 (0-8383-1707-3) M S G Haskell Hse.

Whittier's Unknown Romance: Letters to Elizabeth Lloyd. John Greenleaf Whittier. (American Biography Ser.). 91p. 1991. reprint ed. lib. bdg. 59.00 (0-7812-8417-1) Rprt Serv.

Whittingham: The Story of a Thoroughbred Racing Legend. Jay Hovdey. (Illus.). 210p. 1993. 29.95 (0-939049-61-9) Blood-Horse.

Whittington's Dictionary of Plastics. 3rd expanded rev. ed. Ed. by James F. Carley. LC 93-60943. 575p. (Orig.). (C). 1993. 89.95 (1-56676-090-9) Technomic.

Whittlesworth Comes to Christmas. Gerald R. Toner. LC 91-23134. (Illus.). 144p. 1991. 15.95 (0-88289-877-9) Pelican.

Whittlin, Whistlin & Thingama Jigs see Pioneer Book of Nature Crafts

Whittling. Bill Higginbotham. LC 81-85041. (Home Craftsman Bks.). (Illus.). 128p. 1982. pap. 10.95 (0-8069-7598-9) Sterling.

Whittling & Woodcarving. Elmer J. Tangerman. 1936. pap. 5.95 (0-486-20965-2) Dover.

Whittling Simplified: Everything You Need to Know. Herb Reinecke. LC 85-11136. (Illus.). 162p. (Orig.). 1985. pap. 11.95 (0-930256-14-X) Almar.

Whittling the Old Sea Captain & His Mates with Mike Shipley. Mike Shipley. (Illus.). 48p. (Orig.). 1996. pap. 12.95 (1-56523-075-2) Fox Chapel Pub.

***Whiz Bang Web Site FX.** Graeme Bennett. 400p. 1996. 34.99 (0-7897-0938-4) Mac Comp Pub.

***Whiz Kid of Wall Street.** Matt Seto. 1997. pap. write for info. (0-688-15383-6, Quill) Morrow.

Whiz Kid of Wall Street: How I Returned 34 Percent on My Portfolio, & You Can Too. Matthew Seto & Steven Levingston. 1996. 22.00 (0-688-14567-1) Morrow.

Whiz Kid Starter Kit: Plugging Your Child into the 21st Century. Calvin Ross. 127p. (Orig.). 1995. pap. 7.95 (0-9642658-8-5) Small Wonder.

Whiz Kids & the 1950 Pennant. Robin Roberts & C. Paul Rogers, 3rd. (Baseball in America Ser.). (Illus.). 288p. (C). 1996. 29.95 (1-56639-466-X) Temple U Pr.

Whiz Mob. David W. Maurer. 1964. 21.95 (0-8084-0321-4) NCUP.

***Whiz, Zip & Zap.** Peggy Hausheer & Alice Lindgren. (Illus.). 116p. (J). (gr. 2-9). 1996. spiral bd. 11.95 (0-9654230-0-X) Nutra-Net.

Whizz for Atoms. Geoffrey Willans & Ronald Searle. (Molesworth Ser.). (Illus.). 104p. 1995. pap. 8.95 (1-85145-960-X, Pub. by Pavilion UK) Trafalgar.

***Whizzer Bat.** Gill Davies. (Little Spooky Window Book Ser.). (Illus.). 13p. (J). (ps-1). 1997. bds. 3.99 (1-57584-167-3) Rdrs Dgst Yng Fam.

WHMIS Pocket Dictionary. Joseph O. Accrocco & Jon Mayo. 70p. 1991. 41.80 (0-931690-28-5) Genium Pub.

Who. Chris Charlesworth. (Complete Guides to the Music Of...Ser.). (Illus.). 136p. (Orig.). pap. 7.95 (0-7119-4306-0, OP 47740, Pub. by Omnibus Press UK) Omnibus NY.

Who? Joan Hutson. LC 92-31811. (Illus.). 32p. (J). (ps-2). 1992. 3.50 (0-8198-8266-6) Pauline Bks.

Who. Richard Thompson. (Illus.). 32p. (J). (gr. 1-4). 1993. 9.95 (0-920501-98-2) Orca Bk Pubs.

***Who?** Robert W. Wood. (Experiments for Young Scientists Ser.). (Illus.). 140p. (YA). (gr. 5 up). 1997. text ed. write for info. (0-7910-4851-9) Chelsea Hse.

***Who: Concert File.** Irish Jack & Joe McMichael. 160p. pap. 27.95 (0-7119-6316-9) Omnibus NY.

Who? Famous Experiments for the Young Scientist. Robert W. Wood. LC 94-29632. (J). (gr. 1-8). 1995. pap. text ed. 10.95 (0-07-051634-0) McGraw-Hill Prof.

Who: Maximum R&B. rev. ed. Richard Barnes. 168p. 1995. pap. 24.95 (0-85965-186-X, Pub. by Plexus UK) Publishers Group.

Who: Sixty Years of American Eminence. Cedric Larson. (Illus.). 1958. 25.00 (0-8392-1131-7) Astor-Honor.

Who: The Last Tour. Peter Goddard. (Illus.). 128p. 1983. pap. 9.95 (0-8253-0137-8) Beaufort Bks NY.

Who Adjusts? Domestic Sources of Foreign Economic Policy During the Interwar Years. Beth A. Simmons. LC 93-2272. (Studies in International History & Politics). 348p. 1994. text ed. 39.50 (0-691-08641-9) Princeton U Pr.

***Who Adjusts? Domestic Sources of Foreign Economic Policy During the Interwar Years.** Beth A. Simmons. (Princeton Studies in International History & Politics). 1997. pap. text ed. 19.95 (0-691-01710-7) Princeton U Pr.

Who Am I? (Shorewood Art Programs for Education Ser.). 8p. teacher ed. 107.00 (0-88185-023-3); 143.00 (0-685-07221-5) Shorewood Fine Art.

Who Am I? Pamela Allardice. (Illus.). 112p. 1995. 7.98 (0-8317-3588-0) Smithmark.

Who Am I? Betty Birney. (Riddle Flap Bks.). (Illus.). 16p. (J). (ps). 1992. pap. 5.95 (0-671-76914-6, Litl Simon S&S) S&S Childrens.

Who Am I? Nancy Christensen. LC 92-36006. (Illus.). 32p. (J). 1993. pap. 3.99 (0-590-46192-3) Scholastic Inc.

Who Am I. Sherrilyn Henning. (J). Date not set. pap. 5.99 (0-14-037692-5, Viking) Viking Penguin.

Who Am I? Sherrilyn Henning. (Illus.). 16p. (J). (ps-1). 1996. pap. 5.99 (0-14-055846-2, Puffin) Puffin Bks.

Who Am I. Anthony Hill. Ed. by Henry Anderson. (Orig.). 1995. pap. text ed. 10.00 (1-887333-03-7) Touch Down Prodns.

***Who Am I?** Mary Lawrence. (Illus.). 80p. 1997. pap. 8.00 (0-8059-4078-2) Dorrance.

Who Am I? Robert A. Meyering. LC 95-49452. (Open Door Bks.). 1996. 3.95 (0-56212-151-0) CRC Pubns.

Who Am I? Judy Mullican. (HRL Little Bks.). (Illus.). 8p. (J). (ps-k). 1995. pap. text ed. 10.95 (1-57332-017-X) HighReach Lrning.

Who Am I? Judy Mullican. (HRL Big Bks.). (Illus.). 8p. (J). (ps-k). 1995. pap. text ed. 10.95 (1-57332-018-8) HighReach Lrning.

Who Am I? Katherine Paterson. (Illus.). 96p. (Orig.). (J). 1992. pap. 8.00 (0-8028-5072-3) Eerdmans.

Who Am I? Illus. by Tony Tallarico. (Tiny Bks.). 28p. (J). (ps-1). 1984. bds. 2.95 (0-448-48825-6, Tuffy) Putnam Pub Group.

Who Am I?, Bk. 1. Durlynn Aneman & Vickie Sanders. (Options: a Communication Skills Ser.: Bk. 1). 1994. pap. write for info. (0-318-70140-5) S-W Pub.

Who Am I? A Genealogical Study of the Bower, Taylor, & Related Families. Mary B. Carpenter. 208p. 1986. pap. 11.95 (0-9617470-0-5) McClain.

Who Am I? A Jeter Family Saga. Loren E. Jeter, Sr. Ed. & Illus. by Marjorie A. Harbath. 467p. (Orig.). 1989. write for info. (0-9623339-0-5) L E Jeter.

An Asterisk (*) at the beginning of an entry indicates that the title is appearing in BIP for the first time.

Who Am I? A Key to Your Inner Nature & Personality. Pamela Allardice. 1995. 7.98 (1-86302-373-9) Smithmark.

Who Am I? Activity Coloring Book. (Illus.). 16p. (J). 1992. pap. 1.49 (0-87403-950-9, 02500) Standard Pub.

Who Am I? Clue-by-Clue Biographical Sketches of American Historical Figures. Marsha L. Beeman. LC 92-56629. (Illus.). 212p. 1993. pap. 23.50 (0-89950-899-5) McFarland & Co.

Who Am I? History, Vol. 1. Nathan Levy et al. (J). (gr. 4-8). 1990. pap. 7.50 (1-878347-04-7) NL Assocs.

Who Am I? Identity, Adoption & Human Fertilisation. C. Walby & B. Symons. (C). 1989. 39.00 (0-903534-87-8, Pub. by Brit Ag for Adopt & Fost UK) St Mut.

Who Am I? Inventors, Vol. 5. Nathan Levy & Steven Pastis. (J). (gr. 4-8). 1992. pap. 7.50 (1-878347-19-5) NL Assocs.

Who Am I? Journal for Discovering My Personal Worth. Laurel Edison & Kelly Peavey. (Discovery Ser.). (YA). 1994. pap. 9.99 (0-7814-5134-5, 21725) Cook.

***Who Am I? Kindergarten.** (Image of God Ser.). (J). 1996. pap. text ed. 7.95 (0-614-24906-6) Ignatius Pr.

Who Am I? Leader's Guide. Elizabeth S. Stickney. 36p. 1994. pap. 10.00 (0-8028-5093-6) Eerdmans.

Who Am I? Literature Authors, Vol. 2. Nathan Levy et al. (J). (gr. 4-8). 1991. pap. 7.50 (1-878347-12-8) NL Assocs.

Who Am I? Literature Characters, Vol. 4. Nathan Levy et al. (J). (gr. 2-8). 1991. pap. 7.50 (1-878347-14-4) NL Assocs.

Who Am I? Music, Vol. 3. Nathan Levy et al. (J). (gr. 4-8). 1991. pap. 7.50 (1-878347-13-6) NL Assocs.

Who Am I? Personality Types for Self-Discovery. Ed. by Robert Frager. LC 93-32401. (New Consciousness Reader Ser.). 288p. (Orig.). 1994. pap. 13.95 (0-87477-761-5, Tarcher Putnam) Putnam Pub Group.

***Who Am I? Pre-School B.** (Image of God Ser.). (J). 1996. pap. text ed. 4.95 (0-614-24905-8) Ignatius Pr.

***Who Am I? Pre-School Workbook A.** (Image of God Ser.). (J). 1996. pap. text ed. 4.95 (0-614-24904-X) Ignatius Pr.

Who Am I? Sesame Street. Normand Chartier. (Golden Sturdy Bks.). (Illus.). 22p. (J). (ps). 1978. bds. 3.95 (0-307-12124-0, 12124, Golden Books) Western Pub.

***Who Am I? Teacher's Manual.** (Image of God Ser.). 1996. pap. text ed. 15.95 (0-614-24907-4) Ignatius Pr.

Who Am I? The Mysterious Search for My Identity. Vincent O'Neil. (Illus.). 182p. 1994. 19.95 (0-9644938-1-0) RVON Enter.

Who Am I? The Sacred Quest. Jean Klein. 1993. pap. 13.95 (1-85230-029-9) Element MA.

Who Am I? see Hewitt Early Readers: Level I

Who Am I among So Many? An Autobiography Plus Special Articles: The Biggest Exception in the Bible, Paul's Thorn in the Flesh, & Not Discerning the Lord's Body. Carl Chapman. LC 88-92635. 132p. (Orig.). (YA). (gr. 9-12). 1989. pap. 4.99 (0-9621529-0-0) C Chapman.

Who Am I & Can I Love Me? Vincent Judge. Ed. by Gwen Costa. LC 91-34689. 1990. 19.95 (0-87949-357-7) Ashley Bks.

Who Am I & Why Am I in Treatment? A Guided Workbook for Clients in Evaluation & Beginning Treatment. R. Freeman-Congo & L. Bays. Ed. by Fay H. Knopp. (Illus.). 80p. (Orig.). 1988. wbk. ed., pap. 12.00 (1-884444-24-5) Safer Soc.

Who Am I & Why Am I in Treatment? see Porque Estoy en Tratamiento: Una Guia para Clientes en Evaluacion y Empezando Tratamiento

Who Am I in the Lives of Children: An Introduction to Teaching Young Children. 5th ed. Stephanie Feeney et al. 1995. text ed. 58.00 (0-02-336631-1, Macmillan Coll) P-H.

Who Am I Now That I Am Alone? 3rd ed. James L. Ramsey. (Orig.). 1994. pap. 49.95 (0-614-04768-4); pap. 10.95 (0-614-04769-2) ABT Inc.

Who Am I Really?, 1. Daryl Sharp. (Studies in Jungian Psychology by Jungian). 1995. pap. 15.00 (0-919123-68-6, Pub. by Inner City CN) BookWorld Dist.

Who Am I This Time? Kurt Vonnegut. 1970. pap. 3.00 (0-87129-351-X, W41) Dramatic Pub.

Who Am I? What Am I? Where Do I Belong? The Storytale about the Search for Meaning, Identity & Purpose. Shinan N. Barclay. (Illus.). 40p. (J). (ps-4). 1990. 5.95 (0-317-89505-2); pap. write for info. (0-945086-08-3) Sunlight Prodns.

Who Am I? Who Are They? Robert S. Littlefield & Jane A. Ball. (Illus.). 28p. (Orig.). (J). (gr. 3-6). 1990. pap. text ed. 8.95 (1-879340-06-2, K0107) Kidspeak.

Who & How in Planning for Large Companies: Generalizations from the Experiences of Oil Companies. Leslie E. Grayson. 256p. 1987. text ed. 45.00 (0-312-87005-1) St Martin.

Who & What Is God? James E. Padgett. 1989. pap. 0.50 (1-887621-05-9) Found Ch Divine Truth.

Who Anthology. 208p. 1981. per. 19.95 (0-7935-0269-1, 00358565) H Leonard.

Who Anthology: Easy Guitar. (Easy Play Ser.). 160p. 1983. per. 16.95 (0-7935-2301-X, 00704300) H Leonard.

Who Are Baby's Friends? Lauren Ariev. (My First Golden Board Bks.). (Illus.). 24p. (J). (ps). 1992. bds. 3.95 (0-307-06142-6, 6142, Golden Books) Western Pub.

***Who Are God's Guerillas?** Stuart Gramenz. 160p. (C). pap. text ed. 5.99 (1-85240-020-X) Omega Pubns OR.

Who Are My Sisters & Brothers? A Catholic Educational Guide for Understanding & Welcoming Immigrants & Refuges. 280p. (Orig.). 1996. pap. 14.95 (1-57455-006-3) US Catholic.

Who Are My Sisters & Brothers? Reflections on Understanding & Welcoming Immigrants & Refugees. 64p. (Orig.). 1996. pap. 6.95 (1-57455-057-8) US Catholic.

Who Are the Anglicans? Charles H. Long et al. 88p. (Orig.). 1988. pap. 2.75 (0-88028-080-8, 940) Forward Movement.

Who Are the Finns? A Study in Prehistory. Robert E. Burnham. LC 76-44701. reprint ed. 32.50 (0-404-15913-3) AMS Pr.

Who Are the Guilty? A Study of Education & Crime. David Abrahamsen. LC 70-143306. 340p. 1972. reprint ed. text ed. 65.00 (0-8371-5807-9, ABWG, Greenwood Pr) Greenwood.

Who Are the Macedonians? Hugh Poulton. LC 94-10136. 244p. 1995. 31.50 (0-253-34598-7) Ind U Pr.

Who Are the Mennonite Brethren? Katie F. Wiebe. LC 84-82049. 107p. (Orig.). 1984. pap. 6.95 (0-919797-31-8) Kindred Prods.

Who Are the People of God? Early Christian Models of Community. Howard C. Kee. LC 94-13883. 1995. 35.00 (0-300-05952-3) Yale U Pr.

***Who Are the People of God? Early Christian Models of Community.** Howard C. Kee. 288p. 1997. pap. 16.00 (0-300-07063-2) Yale U Pr.

Who Are the Poor? The Beatitudes As a Call to Community. John S. Pobee. (Risk Book Ser.: No. 32). 74p. (Orig.). 1987. pap. 5.50 (2-8254-0884-0) Wrld Coun Churches.

***Who Are the Promise Keepers?** Ken Abraham. LC 97-1777. 1997. 19.95 (0-385-48699-5) Doubleday.

***Who Are These Good People? An Analysis of Mormonism.** Kerby Anderson. 22p. pap. 1.75 (0-614-25150-8) Probe Bks.

Who Are These Spiritualists? J. M. Peebles. 129p. 1972. reprint ed. spiral bd. 9.00 (0-7873-1080-8) Hlth Research.

Who Are They? Tana Hoban. LC 93-33644. (Illus.). 12p. (J). (ps up). 1994. pap. 4.95 (0-688-12921-8) Greenwillow.

***Who Are We? Building a Knowledge Base of the Different Ethnic, Racial & Cultural Groups in America.** Avaneda Hobbs et al. LC 92-97001. (Orig.). 1997. pap. 24.95 (1-878898-14-0, 97B094001) Christian Star.

Who Are You? Stella Blackstone. (Illus.). 24p. (J). (ps-1). 1996. 8.95 (0-7892-0291-3, Abbeville Kids) Abbeville Pr.

***Who Are You?** John Charnesky. 127p. (Orig.). 1997. mass mkt. 4.99 (1-55197-703-6, Pub. by Comnwlth Pub CN) Partners Pubs Grp.

***Who Are You?** Carole O. Cole. (Illus.). 24p. (J). (gr. k-2). 1997. 9.95 (0-945767-09-9) Write Place.

Who Are You? Alan Fensin. (Illus.). 116p. 1989. 15.75 (0-9622183-0-8) Way Enterprises.

Who Are You? William Hornaday. 1972. pap. 2.50 (0-87516-146-4) DeVorss.

***Who Are You?** Anna Kavan. write for info. (0-614-20082-2, Pub. by P Owen Ltd UK) Dufour.

Who Are You? Sidney Lecker. 1979. 4.95 (0-671-24750-6, Fireside) S&S Trade.

Who Are You? Edward Packard. (Choose Your Own Adventure Ser.: No. 150). 128p. (J). (gr. 4-7). 1994. pap. 3.50 (0-553-56398-X) Bantam.

Who Are You? And What Are You All About? Arlene T. Dyer. LC 95-69130. 328p. 1996. pap. 14.95 (1-57464-000-3) Reyd Pubns.

Who Are You? Discovering Your Real Identity. unabridged ed. Chris Butler. LC 83-80825. (Who Are You Ser.: Vol. 1). (Illus.). 489p. 1984. 11.95 (0-912093-00-5) Identity Inst.

***Who Are You? Knowing Your True Identity in Christ.** Corbin N. Nash. 48p. 1997. pap. 5.00 (0-9649747-1-1) Chrstian Outreach.

Who Are You? Poems. Sally Gibbs. LC 96-14246. 76p. 1996. pap. 12.95 (0-7734-2696-5, Mellen Poetry Pr) E Mellen.

Who Are You: The Life of St. Cecilia. Marie C. Buehrle. LC 70-158918. 85p. 1971. pap. 2.95 (0-913382-07-8, 101-7) Marytown Pr.

Who Are You Calling Stupid? The Revolution That's Changing Education. Dan Hull. Ed. by Margaret M. Leary. LC 95-70035. 234p. Date not set. 26.00 (1-55502-705-9) CORD Commns.

Who Are You Calling Stupid? The Revolution That's Changing Education. Dan Hull. Ed. by Margaret M. Leary. LC 95-70035. 234p. 1995. pap. 16.00 (1-55502-706-7) CORD Commns.

Who Are You, Filipino Youth? Messages & Meditations. William H. Scott. 44p. (C). 1990. reprint ed. pap. 5.00 (971-10-0345-7, Pub. by New Day Pub PH) Cellar.

Who Are You, God? Dawson McAllister & Rich Miller. (Illus.). (J). (gr. 5-12). 1988. pap. 7.95 (0-923417-11-7) Shepherd Minst.

Who Are You God? Dawson McAllister & Rich Miller. (J). (gr. 5-12). 1990. teacher ed., pap. 5.95 (0-923417-13-3) Shepherd Minst.

Who Are You, Jesus? Dawson McAllister. (Illus.). (J). (gr. 5-12). 1986. pap. 7.95 (0-923417-05-2) Shepherd Minst.

Who Are You Jesus? Dawson McAllister & Tom May. (J). (gr. 5-12). 1986. teacher ed., pap. 7.95 (0-923417-03-6) Shepherd Minst.

Who Are You, Really? Understanding Your Life's Energy. Gary Null. LC 96-19282. 144p. 1996. pap. 9.95 (0-7867-0326-1) Carroll & Graf.

Who Are You Really? 20 Fun Quizzes to Help You Find Out! Catherine Daly-Weir. 80p. (J). (gr. 4-9). 1996. pap. text ed. 3.95 (0-448-41137-7, G&D) Putnam Pub Group.

***Who Are You, Sue Snue?** Dr. Seuss. (Wubbulous World of Reading Ser.). (J). 1997. 7.99 (0-679-88636-2) Random Bks Yng Read.

***Who Are You, Sue Snue.** Dr. Seuss. LC 96-49448. (J). 1997. lib. bdg. 11.99 (0-679-98636-7) Random Bks Yng Read.

Who Are You This Morning? Don Harrold. (Cleveland Poets Ser.: No. 45). 28p. (Orig.). 1989. pap. 4.00 (0-914946-71-4) Cleveland St Univ Poetry Ctr.

Who Are Your Today? A Survivors Handbook for Substitute Teachers. Tom Quinlan. (Illus.). vi, 82p. 1985. pap. 6.95 (0-9615691-0-7) Queue Prodns.

Who Ate It? Taro Gomi. (J). (ps). 1992. pap. 5.44 (0-395-65834-9) HM.

Who Ate It? Taro Gomi. (Illus.). 24p. (J). (ps-k). 1991. lib. bdg. 10.40 (1-56294-010-4) Millbrook Pr.

Who Ate It? Taro Gomi. (Illus.). 24p. (J). (ps-k). 1992. pap. 4.95 (1-56294-842-3) Millbrook Pr.

***Who Ate the Brocolli: Level 2.** Catherine Peters. (Special Times, Little Readers Ser.). (J). 1997. pap. text ed. 2.50 (0-395-88290-7) HM.

Who Audits America. Compiled by Spencer P. Harris. (Corporations & Accountants Ser.). 1982. 62.00 (0-933088-03-5); pap. 54.00 (0-685-90844-5) Data Financial.

Who Audits the World: Trends in the Worldwide Accounting Profession. Vinod B. Bavishi & Harold E. Wyman. 900p. 1983. pap. 75.00 (0-913795-01-1) Ctr Trans Acct Fin.

Who Bears the Lifetime Tax Burden? Don Fullerton & Diane L. Rogers. 246p. (C). 1993. 38.95 (0-8157-2992-8); pap. 18.95 (0-8157-2993-6) Brookings.

Who Belongs Here? An American Story. Margy B. Knight & Anne S. O'Brien. (Illus.). 40p. (J). (gr. 3-8). 1993. 16.95 (0-88448-110-7) Tilbury Hse.

Who Belongs Here? An American Story. Margy B. Knight. (Illus.). 40p. (J). (gr. 3-8). 1996. pap. 8.95 (0-88448-169-7) Tilbury Hse.

Who Belongs Here? Teacher's Activity Guide. Margy B. Knight & Thomas Chan. (Illus.). 80p. 1994. teacher ed., pap. 9.95 (0-88448-111-5) Tilbury Hse.

***Who Benefits & Who Pays for Minimum Wage Increases in California? A Perspective on Proposition 210.** Thomas E. Macurdy et al. LC 97-18745. (Essays in Public Policy Ser.). 1997. write for info. (0-8179-5832-0) Hoover Inst Pr.

***Who Benefits from Public Education Spending in Malawi? Results from the Recent Education Reform.** Florencia Castro-Leal. (World Bank Discussion Paper Ser.: No. 350). 60p. 1996. pap. 7.95 (0-8213-3837-4, 13837) World Bank.

Who Benefits from State & Local Economic Development Policies? Timothy J. Bartik. LC 91-27375. 354p. 1991. text ed. 29.00 (0-88099-114-3); pap. text ed. 19.00 (0-88099-113-5) W E Upjohn.

Who Benefits from the Nonprofit Sector? Ed. by Charles T. Clotfelter. LC 91-41221. 296p. 1992. 26.50 (0-226-11052-4) U Ch Pr.

Who Benefits from the Nonprofit Sector? Ed. by Charles T. Clotfelter. (Illus.). x, 296p. 1994. pap. text ed. 13.95 (0-226-11053-2) U Ch Pr.

***Who Betrayed the African World Revolution?** John H. Clarke. 1996. 32.00 (0-88378-183-2) Third World.

Who Brings Forth the Wind. Lori Wick. LC 94-10718. (Kensington Chronicles Ser.). 1994. pap. 9.99 (1-56507-229-4) Harvest Hse.

Who Broke the Baby? Jean S. Garton. LC 79-22683. 112p. (Orig.). 1979. pap. 6.99 (0-87123-608-7) Bethany Hse.

Who Brought the Bread? Bob Hartman. Ed. by Diane Stortz. (Big Picture Bks.). (Illus.). 32p. (J). (gr. 1-3). 1994. 10.99 (0-7847-0188-1, 03638) Standard Pub.

Who Built America? American Social History Project Staff. 1990. pap. 24.00 (0-679-72699-3) McKay.

Who Built America? Working People & the Nation's Economy, Politics, Culture & Society, Vol. 2: From the Rise of Industrial Capitalism to the Contemporary Era, Vol. 2. American Social History Project Staff. LC 89-43240. (Illus.). 624p. 1992. pap. 24.00 (0-679-73022-2) Pantheon.

Who Built That? Quintet Books Staff. 1993. 12.98 (1-55521-927-6) Bk Sales Inc.

Who Built the Ark? Pamela Paparone. LC 93-31383. (J). 1994. 15.00 (0-671-87129-3, S&S Bks Young Read) S&S Childrens.

Who Built the Pyramids? Stuart Reid. (Starting Point History Ser.). (Illus.). 32p. (J). (gr. k up). 1996. lib. bdg. 12.95 (0-88110-796-4, Usborne) EDC.

Who Built the Pyramids? Stuart Reid & Chisholm Reid. (Starting Point History Ser.). (Illus.). (J). (gr. k up). 1996. pap. 4.95 (0-7460-2036-8, Usborne) EDC.

Who Built This Home? Easy Animal Reader. Freeman. (Illus.). 16p. (J). (ps-1). 1996. pap. 2.49 (1-57690-056-8) Tchr Create Mat.

Who by Fire. Chaya M. Abramson & Esther Tscholkowsky. 1995. 16.95 (0-87306-742-8); pap. 13.95 (0-87306-746-0) Feldheim.

Who Called That Lady a Skipper? The Strange Voyage of a Woman Navigator. Marion R. Hart. (American Biography Ser.). 313p. 1991. reprint ed. lib. bdg. 79.00 (0-7812-8169-5) Rprt Serv.

Who Calls? David Campton. 28p. 1980. pap. 3.00 (0-87129-177-0, W46) Dramatic Pub.

Who Calls the Shots on the New York Stages?, Vol. 4. Kalina Stefanov-Peteva. LC 93-34934. (Contemporary Theatre Studies, 1049-6513: Vol. 4). 256p. 1994. text ed. 46.00 (3-7186-5437-7); pap. text ed. 23.00 (3-7186-5438-5) Gordon & Breach.

Who Calls the Tune? A Psychodramtic Approach to Child Therapy. Bernadette Hoey. LC 96-6387. 152p. (C). 1997. pap. 16.95 (0-415-14573-2); text ed. 55.00 (0-415-14572-4) Routledge.

Who Came Down That Road? George E. Lyon. LC 91-20742. (Illus.). 32p. (J). (ps-2). 1992. 16.95 (0-531-05987-1) Orchard Bks Watts.

Who Came Down That Road? George E. Lyon. LC 91-20742. (Illus.). 32p. (J). (ps-2). 1996. pap. 5.95 (0-531-07073-5) Orchard Bks Watts.

Who Can? Houghton Mifflin Company Staff. (Literature Experience 1993 Ser.). (C). 1993. pap. 4.00 (0-395-62571-8) HM.

Who Can? Judy Mullican. (HighReach Learning Big Bks.). 8p. (J). (ps-k).-1994. pap. text ed. 10.95 (1-57332-001-3) HighReach Lrning.

Who Can? - Quien Puede? Judy Mullican. Tr. by Linda Loomis. (HRL Big Bks.). (Illus.). 8p. (Orig.). (SPA.). (J). (ps). 1995. pap. text ed. 10.95 (1-57332-056-0) HighReach Lrning.

Who Can Be Happy & Free in Russia. Nikolai A. Nekrasov. LC 72-120571. reprint ed. 39.50 (0-404-04677-0) AMS Pr.

Who Can Compete Against the World? Power-Protection & Buddhism in Shan Worldview. Nicola B. Tannenbaum. LC 95-43510. (Monograph & Occasional Papers: No. 51). 1996. 32.00 (0-924304-29-4) Assn Asian Studies.

Who Can Fix It? Leslie A. MacKeen. Ed. by Nancy R. Thatch. LC 89-31819. (Books for Students by Students). (Illus.). 26p. (J). (gr. k-3). 1989. lib. bdg. 14.95 (0-933849-19-2) Landmark Edns.

Who Can Fix the Dragon's Wagon? R. Eugene Jackson. 52p. (J). (ps up). 1966. pap. 3.50 (0-88680-202-4); Director's Production Script. teacher ed., pap. 10.00 (0-88680-203-2) I E Clark.

Who Can Help. Barbara L. McCombs & Linda Brannan. (Skills for Job Success Ser.). (Illus.). 32p. (Orig.). 1990. student ed., pap. 4.95 (1-56119-035-7) Educ Pr MD.

Who Can Help? Barbara L. McCombs & Linda Brannan. (Skills for Job Success Ser.). (Illus.). 32p. (Orig.). (YA). (gr. 7-12). 1990. Set. teacher ed., wbk. ed. 44.95 (1-56119-076-4); teacher ed. 1.95 (1-56119-036-5); disk 39.95 (1-56119-118-3) Educ Pr MD.

Who Can Not Read about Crocodiles? Miv Schaaf. 28p. 1988. pap. 5.25 (0-929722-16-7) CA State Library Fndtn.

Who Can Speak? Authority & Critical Identity. Judith Roof & Robyn Wiegman. LC 95-4115. 264p. 1995. pap. text ed. 13.95 (0-252-06487-9) U of Ill Pr.

Who Can Speak? Authority & Critical Identity. Ed. by Judith Roof & Robyn Wiegman. LC 95-4115. 264p. 1995. text ed. 32.50 (0-252-02191-6) U of Ill Pr.

Who Can You Trust? Reading Level 3-4. (Stormy Night Stories Ser.). 16p. 1993. 2.50 (0-88336-074-8) New Readers.

Who Can't Follow an Ant? Michael J. Pellowski. LC 85-14009. (Illus.). 48p. (Orig.). (J). (gr. 1-3). 1997. pap. 3.50 (0-8167-0593-3) Troll Communs.

Who Cares? "A Wake up Call for Service & Leadership" Peter Burwash. 160p. 1993. pap. 14.95 (1-883743-00-1) P Burwash Int.

Who Cares? A Handbook of Christian Counselling. Evelyn H. Peterson. 181p. 1982. pap. text ed. 11.95 (0-85364-272-9) Attic Pr.

Who Cares? Compassion. Cynthia Hagen. (Inter Acta Ser.). (Illus.). 6p. (C). 1995. teacher ed., ring bd. 1.25 (1-885702-09-4, 741-015t, Inter Acta); student ed., ring bd. 3.25 (1-885702-08-6, 741-015s, Inter Acta) WSN Pr.

Who Cares? Health Issues for Lesbian, Gay & Bisexual Persons. Michele Eliason. LC 96-17319. 180p. 1996. pap. 22.95 (0-88737-676-2) Natl League Nurse.

Who Cares? Millions Do-- Milton Meltzer. LC 94-4082. (J). 1994. 15.95 (0-8027-8324-4); Reinforced. lib. bdg. 16.85 (0-8027-8325-2) Walker & Co.

***Who Cares? Rediscovering Community.** David B. Schwartz. LC 96-3462. 1997. text ed. 50.00 (0-8133-3207-9) Westview.

***Who Cares? Rediscovering Community.** David B. Schwartz. LC 96-3462. (C). 1997. pap. text ed. 17.95 (0-8133-3208-7) Westview.

***Who Cares? Simple Ways You Can Reach Out.** Marcy Heidish. LC 96-45032. 160p. (Orig.). 1997. pap. 9.95 (0-87793-599-8) Ave Maria.

Who Cares? Social Service Organizations & Their Users. Ed. by Hans-Joachim Schulze & Wolfgang Wirth. LC 96-517. (Illus.). 192p. 1996. pap. 23.95 (0-304-33081-7); text ed. 65.00 (0-304-33079-5) Cassell.

Who Cares: The Church & Older People. Leslie Underwood. 46p. 1995. pap. 7.95 (1-86407-036-6, Pub. by JBCE AT) Morehouse Pub.

Who Cares? Theory, Research & Educational Implications of the Ethic of Care. Ed. by Mary M. Brabeck. LC 89-3911. 268p. 1989. text ed. 55.00 (0-275-93253-2, C3253, Praeger Pubs) Greenwood.

Who Cares? Women, Care, & Culture. Julia T. Wood. LC 93-16226. 208p. (C). 1993. 29.95 (0-8093-1816-4); pap. 19.95 (0-8093-1948-9) S Ill U Pr.

Who Cares about Animal Rights? Michael Twinn. LC 92-10852. (One World Ser.). (Illus.). (J). 1992. 7.99 (0-85953-358-1, Pub. by Childs Play UK) Childs Play.

Who Cares about Health? Caleb Gattegno. 166p. 1979. pap. text ed. 14.95 (0-87825-149-9) Ed Solutions.

Who Cares about Law & Order? Pam Adams. 1995. 7.95 (0-85953-364-6) Childs Play.

Who Cares about the Inner City? Bud Weidenthal. 1989. pap. 5.00 (0-87117-208-9, 1213) Am Assn Comm Coll.

Who Cares about the Weather? Melvin Berger. Ed. by Natalie Lunis. (Early Science Big Bks.). (Illus.). 16p. (J). (ps-2). 1992. pap. 14.95 (1-56784-004-3) Newbridge Comms.

Who Cares about the Weather? Mini Book. Melvin Berger. Ed. by Natalie Lunis. (Early Science Big Bks.). (Illus.). 16p. (J). (ps-2). 1993. pap. 2.95 (1-56784-029-9) Newbridge Comms.

Who Cares about the Weather Theme Pack. Melvin Berger. Ed. by Susan Evento. (Macmillan Early Science Big Bks.). (Illus.). (J). (ps-2). 1995. pap. write for info. (1-56784-136-8) Newbridge Comms.

W

Who Cares for America's Children? M. J. Zaslow et al. 388p. 1990. 29.95 (0-309-04032-9) Natl Acad Pr.

Who Cares for the Caregiver: Learning to Take Care of Yourself While Caring for Others. Sunny Ba-tor. (In-Service Sourcebook Ser.). 64p. 1995. pap. text ed. 29.95 (1-888343-03-6) Hartman Pub.

Who Cares for the Children: A Case Study of Policies & Practices. Ed. by Allen W. Imershein et al. LC 95-77753. 232p. (Orig.). 1995. text ed. 35.95 (1-882289-32-3); pap. text ed. 22.95 (1-882289-31-5) Gen Hall.

Who Cares for the Elderly? Public Policy & the Experiences of Adult Daughters. Emily K. Abel. (Women in the Political Economy Ser.). 220p. 1991. 44.95 (0-87722-814-0) Temple U Pr.

Who Cares for the Elderly? Public Policy & the Experiences of Adult Daughters. Emily K. Abel. (Women in the Political Economy Ser.). 220p. 1992. pap. 18.95 (0-87722-950-3) Temple U Pr.

Who Cares for Them? Workers in the Home Care Industry. Penny H. Feldman et al. LC 89-17234. (Contributions to the Study of Aging Ser.: No. 16). 256p. 1990. text ed. 49.95 (0-313-26837-1, FWH/, Greenwood Pr) Greenwood.

Who Cares If Its a Choice? Snappy Answers to 101 Nosey, Intrusive & Highly Personal Questions about Lesbians & Gays. Ellen Orleans. 96p. (Orig.). 1994. pap. 7.50 (0-9632526-4-X) Laugh Lines.

Who Cares What I Think? American Teens Talk about Their Lives & Their Country. Ed. by Marcia A. Thompson. LC 93-35903. 204p. (YA). (gr. 7-12). 1994. pap. 10.95 (0-932765-49-1, 1341-94) Close Up Fnd.

Who Cares When I Hurt? Help from the Bible for Those Who Are Hurting. Edwin D. Roels. (Friendship Ser.). (Illus.). 48p. (Orig.). 1993. pap. write for info. (1-882536-05-3, A100-0020) Bible League.

Who Chooses? Who Loses? Culture, Institutions, & the Unequal Effects of School Choice. Ed. by Bruce Fuller et al. (Sociology of Education Ser.: Vol. 2). 224p. (C). 1996. text ed. 43.00 (0-8077-3538-8); pap. text ed. 19.95 (0-8077-3537-X) Tchrs Coll.

Who Comes? Deborah Chandra. LC 94-47193. (Illus.). 32p. (J). (ps-3). 1995. 16.95 (0-87156-407-6) Sierra Club Childrens.

Who Comes after the Subject? Ed. by Eduardo Cadava et al. 256p. (C). 1991. pap. 16.95 (0-415-90360-2, A4950, Routledge NY) Routledge.

Who Comes with Cannons? Patricia Beatty. LC 92-6317. 192p. (YA). (gr. 5 up). 1992. 15.00 (0-688-11028-2, Morrow Junior) Morrow.

***Who Conquers Me.** L. C. Burton. (Staples South West Region Publication Ser.). 1996. pap. write for info. (1-875560-83-1, Pub. by Staples AT) Intl Spec Bk.

Who Controls Public Lands? Mining, Forestry, & Grazing Policies, 1870-1990. Christopher M. Klyza. LC 95-23352. 256p. (C). 1996. lib. bdg. 34.95 (0-8078-2264-7) U of NC Pr.

Who Controls Public Lands? Mining, Forestry, & Grazing Policies, 1870-1990. Christopher M. Klyza. LC 95-23352. 256p. (C). 1996. pap. text ed. 14.95 (0-8078-4567-1) U of NC Pr.

***Who Controls the Local Hospital?** Mary Gabay & Sidney M. Wolfe. 39p. (Orig.). 1996. pap. 15.00 (0-937188-11-5) Pub Citizen Inc.

Who Controls the Whiskey Trust? 1991. lib. bdg. 75.00 (0-8490-4464-2) Gordon Pr.

Who Cried for Pie. (J). 1997. pap. 2.95 (0-8167-0036-2) Troll Communs.

Who Cries for the Hurting. Michael D. Evans. 323p. 1995. pap. 8.00 (0-935199-01-2) Bedfrd Books.

***Who Dared? Joshua Dared!** Ellen Shepard. (Great Big Bks.). (Illus.). 16p. (J). (gr. k-3). 1996. pap. 14.95 (0-687-06687-5) Abingdon.

Who Decides? A State-by-State Review of Abortion Rights. 4th ed. 147p. (C). 1994. pap. text ed. 30.00 (0-7881-1109-4) DIANE Pub.

Who Decides? Conflicts of Rights in Health Care. Ed. by Nora K. Bell. LC 81-83908. (Contemporary Issues in Biomedicine, Ethics, & Society Ser.). 240p. 1982. 39.50 (0-89603-034-2) Humana.

Who Defends America? Race, Sex, & Class in the Armed Forces. Joint Center for Political Studies Press Staff. Ed. by Edwin Dorn. 176p. (Orig.). (C). pap. text ed. 20.50 (0-941410-78-1); lib. bdg. 32.25 (0-941410-77-3) Jt Ctr Pol Studies.

W

Who Deliberates? Mass Media in Modern Democracy. Benjamin I. Page. (Illus.). 136p. 1996. pap. text ed. 10.95 (0-226-64473-1); lib. bdg. 29.00 (0-226-64472-3) U Ch Pr.

Who Destroyed the Jews? Hitler: The Scapegoat? - The Final Solutions? James M. DeVone. LC 90-93013. (Illus.). 50p. (Orig.). (C). 1989. pap. text ed. 9.95 (0-9625092-0-5) Schl Univ Studies.

Who Did Jesus Think He Was? J. C. O'Neill. (Biblical Interpretation Ser.: Vol. 11). 1995. 81.50 (90-04-10429-1) E J Brill.

Who Did That? Jill B. Bruce. (Illus.). 48p. (Orig.). (J). (gr. 2-6). 1994. pap. text ed. 7.95 (0-86417-575-2, Pub. by Kangaroo Pr AT) Seven Hills Bk.

Who Did This, Dainty Dinosaur? (Illus.). (J). (ps-2). 1991. pap. 5.10 (0-8136-5721-0); lib. bdg. 7.95 (0-8136-5221-9, TK7283) Modern Curr.

Who Dies? An Investigation of Conscious Living & Conscious Dying. Stephen Levine. 336p. 1996. pap. 10.95 (0-385-26221-3, Anchor NY) Doubleday.

Who Discovered America? Jo E. Moore. (Illus.). 48p. (J). (gr. 3-6). 1992. pap. 5.95 (1-55799-218-5, EMC 258) Evan-Moor Corp.

Who Discovered the Straits of Juan de Fuca? Don Marshall. 27p. 1991. pap. 6.95 (0-87770-493-7) Ye Galleon.

Who Discriminates Against Women? Ed. by Florence Denmark. LC 74-78560. (Sage Contemporary Social Science Issues Ser.: No. 15). (Illus.). 144p. reprint ed. pap. 41.10 (0-317-08953-6, 2021887) Bks Demand.

Who Do People Say I Am? The Interpretation of Jesus in the New Testament Gospels. Marvin W. Meyer. LC 82-24229. 95p. reprint ed. pap. 27.10 (0-317-30155-1, 2025337) Bks Demand.

Who Do You Love? Janet Quin-Harkin. (Love Stories Ser.: 13). 192p. (J). 1996. mass mkt. 3.99 (0-553-57043-9) Bantam.

***Who Do You Say I Am? Concilium Journal.** Ed. by Werner Jeanrond & Christoph Theobald. 150p. 1997. pap. 15.00 (1-57075-126-9) Orbis Bks.

Who Do You Say I Am? Introduction to Christology. Jacques Dupuis. LC 93-45599. 200p. (Orig.). 1994. pap. 18.00 (0-88344-940-4) Orbis Bks.

Who Do You Say I Am? Meeting the Historical Jesus in Prayer. William A. Barry. LC 95-48160. 152p. (Orig.). 1996. pap. 7.95 (0-87793-575-0) Ave Maria.

Who Do You Say That I Am? An Adult Inquiry Into the First Three Gospels. 2nd rev. ed. Edward J. Ciuba. LC 92-37734. 172p. 1993. pap. 7.95 (0-8189-0638-3) Alba.

***Who Do You Say That I Am? Christians Encounter Other Religions.** Calvin E. Shenk. LC 97-19784. 304p. (Orig.). 1997. pap. 19.99 (0-8361-9060-2) Herald Pr.

Who Do You Say That I Am? Reflections on Jesus in Our World Today. Robert Sullivan & Joshua Simon. 96p. 1996. 14.95 (0-02-861323-6) Macmillan.

***Who Do You Think You Are?** Hjorth & Bakalis. 1997. pap. text ed. 10.67 (0-13-621624-2) P-H.

Who Do You Think You Are? Explore Your Many-Sided Self with the Berkeley Personality Profile. Keith Harary & Eileen Donahue. LC 94-4814. 224p. 1994. pap. 16.00 (0-06-250278-6) Harper SF.

Who Do You Think You Are? How to Build Self-Esteem. Joel Wells. 1989. pap. 10.95 (0-88347-240-6) Res Christian Liv.

Who Do You Think You Are? Stories of Friends & Enemies. Hazel Rochman. (YA). 1993. 16.95 (0-316-75355-6) Little.

***Who Do You Think You Are? Stories of Friends & Enemies.** Hazel Rochman. 1997. pap. text ed. 7.95 (0-316-75320-3) Little.

***Who Do You Think You Are? The Healing Power of Your True Identity.** Carlos Warter. LC 97-24738. 1998. write for info. (0-553-10494-2) Bantam.

Who Do You Trust? Hiring & Firing an Investment Advisor. Noreen Gonce. 55p. (Orig.). pap. 8.95 (0-9629252-0-9) Ampersand OR.

Who Do You Want to Be? The Art of Presenting Yourself with Ease. Glynn Bedington. 155p. (Orig.). 1995. pap. 10.95 (0-9624945-9-3) Silvercat Pubns.

Who Does What & Why in Book Publishing: Writers, Editors, & Money Men. Clarkson N. Potter. 1990. 12.95 (1-55972-056-5, Birch Ln Pr) Carol Pub Group.

Who Done Did It? A Crime Reader for Students of English. Carlos A. Yorio & L. A. Morse. 192p. 1981. pap. text ed. write for info. (0-13-958207-X) P-H.

Who Done It? Gail Roper. LC 94-11889. 48p. (J). 1996. pap. 3.99 (0-7814-0079-1, Chariot Bks) Chariot Victor.

***Who Downed the Aces in WWI? Facts, Figures & Photos on the Fate of Over 300 Top Pilots Flying.** Norman Franks. 1996. 32.95 (1-898697-51-5, Pub. by Grub St Pubns UK) Seven Hills Bk.

Who Drives This? Charles Reasoner. (Sliding Surprise Ser.). (J). (ps up). 1996. 9.95 (0-8431-3939-0) Price Stern Sloan.

***Who Dropped down the Chimney?** 2nd ed. Isabel Ferguson. LC 96-71936. (Illus.). iii, 14p. (Orig.). (J). (ps-2). 1997. pap. 9.95 (0-9655317-0-8, 1) Small Rain.

Who Dropped Peter Pan? A Jocelyn O'Roarke Mystery. Jane Dentinger. LC 95-6768. 273p. 1995. pap. 21.95 (0-670-86070-0, Viking) Viking Penguin.

Who Dropped Peter Pan? A Jocelyn O'Roarke Mystery. Jane Dentinger. 288p. 1996. pap. 5.95 (0-14-024554-5, Penguin Bks) Viking Penguin.

Who Dwelt By a Churchyard. Berry Fleming. LC 88-92465. 160p. 1988. 22.00 (0-932966-88-8) Permanent Pr.

Who Eats What? Food Chains & Food Webs. Patricia Lauber. LC 93-10609. (Let's Read-&-Find-Out Science Bk.). 32p. (J). (ps-3). 1995. pap. 4.95 (0-06-445130-5) HarpC Child Bks.

Who Eats What? Food Chains & Food Webs. Patricia Lauber. LC 93-10609. (Let's-Read-&-Find-Out Science Bk.). (Illus.). 32p. (J). (gr. k-4). 1995. 15.00 (0-06-022981-0); lib. bdg. 14.89 (0-06-022982-9) HarpC Child Bks.

***Who Elected the Bankers? Surveillance & Control in the World Economy.** Louis M. Pauly. LC 96-45087. (Cornell Studies in Political Economy). 176p. 1996. 25.00 (0-8014-3322-3) Cornell U Pr.

***Who Elected the Bankers? Surveillance & Control in the World Economy.** Louis W. Pauly. LC 96-45087. 1997. pap. write for info. (0-8014-8375-1) Cornell U Pr.

***WHO Expert Committee on Addiction-Producing Drugs.** (Technical Report Ser.: No. 273). 20p. 1964. pap. text ed. 3.00 (92-4-120273-4) World Health.

***WHO Expert Committee on Bilharziasis.** (Technical Report Ser.: No. 299). 56p. 1965. pap. text ed. 5.00 (92-4-120299-8) World Health.

***WHO Expert Committee on Biological Standardization.** (Technical Report Ser.: No. 658). 325p. 1981. pap. text ed. 21.00 (92-4-120658-6) World Health.

***WHO Expert Committee on Biological Standardization.** (Technical Report Ser.: No. 673). 180p. 1982. pap. text ed. 13.00 (92-4-120673-X) World Health.

***WHO Expert Committee on Biological Standardization.** (Technical Report Ser.: No. 687). 184p. 1983. pap. text ed. 13.00 (92-4-120687-X) World Health.

***WHO Expert Committee on Biological Standardization.** (Technical Report Ser.: No. 700). 75p. 1984. pap. text ed. 7.00 (92-4-120700-0) World Health.

WHO Expert Committee on Biological Standardization: Fortieth Report. (Technical Report Ser.: No. 800). 221p. (ENG, FRE, RUS & SPA.). 1990. pap. text ed. 26.00 (92-4-120800-7, 1100800) World Health.

WHO Expert Committee on Biological Standardization: Forty-First Report. (Technical Report Ser.: No. 814). v, 79p. (ENG, FRE, RUS & SPA.). 1991. pap. text ed. 11.00 (92-4-120814-7, 1100814) World Health.

WHO Expert Committee on Biological Standardization: Forty-Fourth Report. (WHO Technical Report Ser.: No. 848). vi, 88p. (CHI, ENG, FRE & SPA.). 1994. pap. text ed. 14.00 (92-4-120848-1, 1100848) World Health.

WHO Expert Committee on Biological Standardization: Forty-Second Report. (Technical Report Ser.: No. 822). v, 84p. (ENG, FRE & SPA.). 1992. pap. text ed. 10.80 (92-4-120822-8, 1100822) World Health.

WHO Expert Committee on Biological Standardization: Forty-Third Report. WHO Staff. (Technical Report Ser.: No. 840). v, 218p. (CHI, ENG, FRE & SPA.). 1994. pap. text ed. 31.00 (92-4-120840-6, 1100840) World Health.

WHO Expert Committee on Biological Standardization: Proceedings of the WHO Expert Committee, 24th, Geneva, 1971. WHO Staff. (Technical Report Ser.: No. 486). 1972. pap. text ed. 5.00 (92-4-120486-9, 1100486) World Health.

WHO Expert Committee on Biological Standardization: Proceedings of the WHO Expert Committee, 26th, Geneva, 1974. WHO Staff. (Technical Report Ser.: No. 565). 1975. pap. text ed. 7.00 (92-4-120565-2, 1100565) World Health.

***WHO Expert Committee on Biological Standardization: Thirtieth Report of the WHO Expert Committee.** (Technical Report Ser.: No. 638). 199p. 1979. pap. text ed. 20.00 (92-4-120638-1, 1100638) World Health.

WHO Expert Committee on Biological Standardization: Thirty-Eighth Report. (Technical Report Ser.: No. 771). 221p. (C). 1988. pap. text ed. 26.00 (92-4-120771-X, 110771) World Health.

WHO Expert Committee on Biological Standardization: Thirty-Fifth Report. (Technical Report Ser.: No. 725). 140p. 1985. pap. text ed. 11.00 (92-4-120725-6, 1100725) World Health.

WHO Expert Committee on Biological Standardization: Thirty-Ninth Report. (Technical Report Ser.: No. 786). 184p. (C). 1989. pap. text ed. 22.00 (92-4-120786-8, 1100786) World Health.

WHO Expert Committee on Biological Standardization: Thirty-Seventh Report. (Technical Report Ser.: No. 760). 203p. (C). 1987. pap. text ed. 28.00 (92-4-120760-4, 1100760) World Health.

***WHO Expert Committee on Biological Standardization: Twenty-Eighth Report of the WHO Expert Committee.** (Technical Report Ser.: No. 610). 133p. 1977. pap. text ed. 11.00 (92-4-120610-1, 1100610) World Health.

***WHO Expert Committee on Biological Standardization: Twenty-Ninth Report of the WHO Expert Committee.** (Technical Report Ser.: No. 626). 147p. 1978. pap. text ed. 14.00 (92-4-120626-8, 1100626) World Health.

WHO Expert Committee on Biological Standardization: 45th Report. (Technical Report Ser.: Vol. 858). 102p. (FRE & SPA.). (C). 1995. pap. 17.00 (92-4-120858-9, 1100858) World Health.

WHO Expert Committee on Biological Standardization Thirty Sixth Report. (Technical Report Ser.: No. 745). 149p. 1987. pap. text ed. 20.00 (92-4-120745-0, 1100745) World Health.

***WHO Expert Committee on Cholera: Second Report of a WHO Expert Committee.** (Technical Report Ser.). 0028p. 1967. pap. text ed. 3.00 (92-4-120352-8, 1100352) World Health.

***WHO Expert Committee on Dependence-Producing Drugs.** (Technical Report Ser.: No. 312). 16p. 1965. pap. text ed. 3.00 (92-4-120312-9) World Health.

***WHO Expert Committee on Dependence-Producing Drugs: Fifteenth Report of the WHO Expert Committee.** (Technical Report Ser.: No. 343). 0018p. 1966. pap. text ed. 3.00 (92-4-120343-9, 1100343) World Health.

***WHO Expert Committee on Diabetes Mellitus: Second Report of the WHO Expert Committee.** (Technical Report Ser.: No. 646). 79p. 1980. pap. text ed. 5.00 (92-4-120646-2, 1100646) World Health.

WHO Expert Committee on Drug Dependence: Proceedings of the WHO Expert Committee, 17th, Geneva, 1969. WHO Staff. (Technical Report Ser.: No. 437). 1970. pap. text ed. 5.00 (92-4-120437-0, 1100437) World Health.

WHO Expert Committee on Drug Dependence: Proceedings of the WHO Expert Committee, 19th, Geneva, 1972. WHO Staff. (Technical Report Ser.: No. 526). 1973. pap. text ed. 4.00 (92-4-120526-1, 1100526) World Health.

WHO Expert Committee on Drug Dependence: Twenty-Eighth Report. (Technical Report Ser.: No. 836). vi, 44p. (ENG, FRE & SPA.). 1993. pap. text ed. 10.00 (92-4-120836-8, 1101836) World Health.

***WHO Expert Committee on Drug Dependence: Twenty-Fifth Report.** WHO Staff. (Technical Report Ser.: No. 775). 48p. 1989. 6.00 (92-4-120775-2) World Health.

***WHO Expert Committee on Drug Dependence: Twenty-First Report of the WHO Expert Committee.** (Technical Report Ser.: No. 618). 0049p. 1978. pap. text ed. 6.00 (92-4-120618-7, 1100618) World Health.

***WHO Expert Committee on Drug Dependence: Twenty-Fourth Report.** WHO Staff. (Technical Report Ser.: No. 761). 34p. 1988. 6.00 (92-4-120761-2) World Health.

WHO Expert Committee on Drug Dependence: Twenty-Second Report. (Technical Report Ser.: No. 729). 31p. 1985. pap. text ed. 4.00 (92-4-120729-9, 1100729) World Health.

WHO Expert Committee on Drug Dependence: Twenty-Seventh Report. (Technical Report Ser.: No. 808). 17p. (ENG, FRE & SPA.). 1991. pap. text ed. 6.00 (92-4-120808-2, 1100808) World Health.

***WHO Expert Committee on Drug Dependence: Twenty-Sixth Report, 1987.** WHO Staff. (Technical Report Ser.: No. 787). 32p. 1989. 4.00 (92-4-120787-6) World Health.

WHO Expert Committee on Drug Dependence: 29th Report. (Technical Report Ser.: No. 856). iv, 17p. (FRE & SPA.). (C). 1995. pap. text ed. 6.00 (92-4-120856-2, 1100856) World Health.

WHO Expert Committee on Drug Dependence Twenty-Third Report. (Technical Report Ser.: No. 741). 64p. 1987. pap. text ed. 9.00 (92-4-120741-8, 1100741) World Health.

WHO Expert Committee on Filariasis: Proceedings of the WHO Expert Committee, 3rd, Athens, 1973. WHO Staff. (Technical Report Ser.: No. 542). 1974. pap. text ed. 5.00 (92-4-120542-3, 1100542) World Health.

***WHO Expert Committee on Filariasis (Wuchereria & Brugia Infections)- Second Report of the WHO Expert Committee.** (Technical Report Ser.: No. 359). 0047p. 1967. pap. text ed. 5.00 (92-4-120359-5, 1100359) World Health.

***WHO Expert Committee on Hepatitis.** (Technical Report Ser.: No. 285). 25p. 1964. pap. text ed. 3.00 (92-4-120285-8) World Health.

WHO Expert Committee on Insecticides: Proceedings of the WHO Expert Committee, 19th, Geneva, 1971. WHO Staff. (Technical Report Ser.: No. 475). 1971. pap. text ed. 3.00 (92-4-120475-3, 1100475) World Health.

***WHO Expert Committee on Leprosy: Fifth Report of the WHO Expert Committee.** (Technical Report Ser.: No. 607). 48p. 1977. pap. text ed. 6.00 (92-4-120607-1, 1100607) World Health.

WHO Expert Committee on Leprosy: Proceedings of the WHO Expert Committee, 4th, Geneva, 1970. WHO Staff. (Technical Report Ser.: No. 459). 1970. pap. text ed. 5.00 (92-4-120459-1, 1100459) World Health.

***WHO Expert Committee on Leprosy: Sixth Report.** WHO Staff. (Technical Report Ser.: No. 768). 51p. 1988. 8.00 (92-4-120768-X) World Health.

***WHO Expert Committee on Malaria.** (Technical Report Ser.: No. 291). 46p. 1964. pap. text ed. 5.00 (92-4-120291-2) World Health.

***WHO Expert Committee on Malaria.** (Technical Report Ser.: No. 324). 48p. 1966. pap. text ed. 5.00 (92-4-120324-2) World Health.

WHO Expert Committee on Malaria: Eighteenth Report. (Technical Report Ser.: No. 735). 104p. 1986. pap. text ed. 14.00 (92-4-120735-3, 1100735) World Health.

***WHO Expert Committee on Malaria: Seventeenth Report of the WHO Expert Committee.** (Technical Report Ser.: No. 640). 71p. 1979. pap. text ed. 5.00 (92-4-120640-3, 1100640) World Health.

WHO Expert Committee on Medical Rehabilitation: Proceedings of the WHO Expert Committee, 2nd, Geneva, 1968. WHO Staff. (Technical Report Ser.: No. 419). 1969. pap. text ed. 3.00 (92-4-120419-2, 1100419) World Health.

***WHO Expert Committee on Nursing: Fifth Report of the WHO Expert Committee.** (Technical Report Ser.). 0032p. 1966. pap. text ed. 3.00 (92-4-120347-1, 1100347) World Health.

WHO Expert Committee on Onchocerciasis Third Report. (Technical Report Ser.: No. 752). 167p. 1987. pap. text ed. 21.60 (92-4-120752-3, 1100752) World Health.

WHO Expert Committee on Plague: Proceedings of the WHO Expert Committee, 4th, Geneva, 1969. WHO Staff. (Technical Report Ser.: No. 447). 1970. pap. text ed. 3.00 (92-4-120447-8, 1100447) World Health.

***WHO Expert Committee on Rabies.** (Technical Report Ser.: No. 321). 38p. 1966. pap. text ed. 5.00 (92-4-120321-8) World Health.

WHO Expert Committee on Rabies: Eighth Report. (Technical Report Ser.: No. 824). vii, 84p. (ENG, FRE & SPA.). 1992. pap. text ed. 12.00 (92-4-120824-4, 1100824) World Health.

WHO Expert Committee on Rabies: Proceedings of the WHO Expert Committee, 6th, Geneva, 1972. WHO Staff. (Technical Report Ser.: No. 523). 1973. pap. text ed. 4.00 (92-4-120523-7, 1100523) World Health.

***WHO Expert Committee on Rabies: Seventh Report of the WHO Expert Committee.** WHO Staff. (Technical Report Ser.: No. 709). 104p. 1984. 9.00 (92-4-120709-4) World Health.

***WHO Expert Committee on Smallpox.** (Technical Report Ser.: No. 283). 37p. 1964. pap. text ed. 5.00 (92-4-120283-1) World Health.

***WHO Expert Committee on Specifications for Pharmaceutical Preparations.** (Technical Report Ser.: No. 307). 31p. 1965. pap. text ed. 3.00 (92-4-120307-2) World Health.

***WHO Expert Committee on Specifications for Pharmaceutical Preparations.** (Technical Report Ser.: No. 681). 33p. 1982. pap. text ed. 4.00 (92-4-120681-0) World Health.

WHO Expert Committee on Specifications for Pharmaceutical Preparations: Proceedings of the WHO Expert Committee, 22nd, Geneva, 1968. WHO Staff. (Technical Report Ser.: No. 418). 1969. pap. text ed. 5.00 (92-4-120418-4, 1100418) World Health.

An Asterisk (*) at the beginning of an entry indicates that the title is appearing in BIP for the first time.

WHO Expert Committee on Specifications for Pharmaceutical Preparations: Proceedings of the WHO Expert Committee, 24th, Geneva, 1971. WHO Staff. (Technical Report Ser.: No. 487). 1972. pap. text ed. 6.00 (*92-4-120487-7*, 1100487) World Health.

WHO Expert Committee on Specifications for Pharmaceutical Preparations: Thirty-Second Report. (Technical Report Ser.: No. 823). vi, 134p. (ENG, FRE & SPA.). 1992. pap. text ed. 17.00 (*92-4-120823-6*, 1100823) World Health.

WHO Expert Committee on Specifications for Pharmaceutical Preparations: Thirty-Third Report. (Technical Report Ser.: No. 834). v, 30p. (ENG, FRE & SPA.). 1993. pap. text ed. 7.00 (*92-4-120834-1*, 1100834) World Health.

***WHO Expert Committee on Specifications for Pharmaceutical Preparations: Twenty-Sixth Report of the WHO Expert Committee.** (Technical Report Ser.: No. 614). 53p. 1977. pap. text ed. 7.00 (*92-4-120614-4*, 1100614) World Health.

***WHO Expert Committee on Specifications for Pharmaceutical Preparations: 34th Report of a WHO Expert Committee.** (WHO Technical Report Ser.: Vol. 863). 194p. 1996. pap. 35.00 (*92-4-120863-5*, 1100863) World Health.

WHO Expert Committee on Specifications for Pharmaceutical Preparations Thirtieth Report. (Technical Report Ser.: No. 748). 50p. 1987. pap. text ed. 9.00 (*92-4-120748-5*, 1100748) World Health.

WHO Expert Committee on Venereal Diseases & Treponematoses: Sixth Report. (Technical Report Ser.: No. 736). 141p. 1986. pap. text ed. 18.00 (*92-4-120736-1*, 1100736) World Health.

Who Farted Now? (Illus.). 68p. (Orig.). 1990. pap. 5.95 (*0-312-03952-2*) St Martin.

***Who Financed Hitler?** Pool. LC 97-15509. 1997. pap. 14.00 (*0-671-76083-1*, PB Trade Paper) PB.

Who Fought for the U. S. rev. ed. Jerold M. Starr. (Lessons of the Vietnam War Ser.). (Illus.). 32p. (C). 1991. pap. text ed. 5.00 (*0-945919-04-2*) Ctr Social Studies.

Who Founded Christianity: Jesus or Jewry? W. J. Sheard. 24p. (Orig.). 1990. pap. 3.50 (*1-56744-417-2*) Kazi Pubns.

***Who Framed Art Decco?** Margaret Benoit. (Illus.). 112p. (YA). (gr. 5 up). 1997. text ed. 10.95 (*0-07-006309-5*); pap. text ed. 5.95 (*0-07-006274-9*) McGraw.

Who Framed Roger Rabbit? Daan Jippes & Dan Spiegle. 48p. 1988. 6.95 (*0-87135-464-0*) Marvel Entmnt.

Who Framed Roger Rabbit?, No. 2. Bob Foster & Dan Spiegle. 64p. 1989. 8.95 (*0-87135-593-0*) Marvel Entmnt.

Who from Their Labours Rest? Conflict & Practice in Rural Tourism. Mary Bouquet & Michael Winter. 160p. 1987. text ed. 63.95 (*0-566-05330-6*, Pub. by Avebury Pub UK) Ashgate Pub Co.

Who Gathered & Whispered Behind Me. Albert Goldbarth. LC 80-21309. 53p. (Orig.). 1980. pap. 4.25 (*0-934332-27-4*) LEpervier Pr.

***Who Gave My Orangutan a Paintbrush?** Mallory Tarcher. (J). (gr. 2-5). 1997. pap. 2.95 (*0-8167-4278-2*) Troll Communs.

***Who Gave Pinta to the Santa Maria? Tropical Diseases in a Temperate Climate.** Robert S. Desowitz. LC 96-44741. 288p. 1997. 25.00 (*0-393-04084-4*) Norton.

***Who Gets Grants: Foundation Grants to Nonprofit Organizations.** 4th ed. 1997. write for info. (*0-614-29891-1*) Foundation Ctr.

***Who Gets Grants: Foundation Grants to Nonprofit Organizations.** 4th ed. 1469p. 1997. write for info. (*0-87954-704-9*) Foundation Ctr.

Who Gets Health Care? An Arena for Nursing Action. Ed. by Barbara Kos-Munson. LC 92-48981. 80p. 1992. 22.95 (*0-8261-8240-2*) Springer Pub.

Who Gets In? A Guide to College Selection - 1988. Ed. by Dan Tyson. 120p. 1988. pap. 37.50 (*0-945871-34-1*) Graphic Pub KS.

***Who Gets It When You Go? Wills, Probates, & Inheritance Taxes for the Hawaii Resident.** 3rd rev. ed. David C. Larsen. 128p. 1997. pap. 14.95 (*0-8248-1940-3*, Latitude Twenty) UH Pr.

Who Gets Sick: Thinking & Health. Blair Justice. LC 86-61576. 408p. 1987. 17.95 (*0-9605376-1-9*) Peak Pr.

Who Gets the Antelope's Liver? W. George Bourland. 12.95 (*0-686-37633-1*) Harp & Thistle.

Who Gets the Past? Competition for Ancestors among Non-Russian Intellectuals in Russia. Victor A. Shnirelman. 100p. 1996. text ed. 23.00 (*0-8018-5221-8*) Johns Hopkins.

Who Gets the Sun Out of Bed? Nancy W. Carlstrom. (Illus.). 32p. (J). (ps-3). 1996. pap. 4.95 (*0-316-12829-5*) Little.

***Who Gets to Go?** Ann Bateman. 25p. 1996. pap. 5.75 (*1-57438-005-2*, 2564) Ed Ministries.

Who Gets to the Top? Executive Suite Discrimination in the Eighties. Richard L. Zweigenhaft. LC 84-70044. 48p. 1984. pap. 3.00 (*0-87495-059-7*) Am Jewish Comm.

Who Gets What? The Hardening of Class Inequality in the Late Twentieth Century. John Westergaard. 216p. (C). 1995. text ed. 49.95 (*0-7456-0107-3*) Blackwell Pubs.

Who Gets What from Government. Benjamin I. Page. LC 82-13454. 264p. 1983. pap. 14.00 (*0-520-04703-6*) U CA Pr.

WHO Global Programme on AIDS: 1991 Progress Report. ix, 136p. 1992. pap. text ed. 26.00 (*92-4-156156-4*, 1150391) World Health.

Who God Is Not. Mac Hammond. Ed. by David Holland. 24p. (Orig.). 1995. pap. 1.00 (*1-57399-001-9*) Mac Hammond.

Who Goes First? The Story of Self-Experimentation in Medicine. Lawrence K. Altman. LC 84-18807. 416p. 1987. 24.95 (*0-394-50382-1*) Random.

Who Goes Home? Elizabeth Lemarchand. 192p. 1987. 15.95 (*0-8027-5675-1*) Walker & Co.

Who Goes Home? large type ed. Elizabeth Lemarchand. 304p. 1987. 25.99 (*0-7089-1599-X*) Ulverscroft.

Who Goes Moo? (Big Board Bks.). (Illus.). 10p. (J). (ps). 1994. 4.95 (*1-56458-737-1*) DK Pub Inc.

Who Goes Out on Halloween-Bank Street? Sue Alexander. 32p. (J). (ps-3). 1990. pap. 3.99 (*0-553-34922-8*, Litl Rooster) BDD Bks Young Read.

Who Goes There. Fergus Allen. 96p. 1996. pap. text ed. 10.95 (*0-571-17782-4*) Faber & Faber.

Who Goes There? Susan E. McCloud. 1995. pap. 8.95 (*0-88494-973-7*) Bookcraft Inc.

Who Goes There. John W. Campbell, Jr. 152p. 1990. reprint ed. lib. bdg. 16.95 (*0-89966-734-1*) Buccaneer Bks.

Who Goes There - Friend or Foe? Friendly Fire Casualties. (Illus.). 84p. (Orig.). (C). 1993. pap. text ed. 30.00 (*0-7881-0149-8*) DIANE Pub.

Who Goes to School? Margaret Hillert. (Illus.). (J). (ps-k). 1981. pap. 5.10 (*0-8136-5575-7*, TK2383); lib. bdg. 7.95 (*0-8136-5075-5*, TK2382) Modern Curr.

Who Got Einstein's Office? Eccentricity & Genius at the Institute for Advanced Study. Edward Regis. LC 87-11568. (Illus.). 320p. 1988. pap. 15.00 (*0-201-12278-2*) Addison-Wesley.

Who Got In? College Boards National Survey of Admissions. 10th rev. ed. Ed. by R. Craig Sautter. 175p. (Orig.). (C). 1996. pap. 16.95 (*1-882794-96-6*) Coll Bound.

Who Got In? College Board's 1995 National Survey of Admissions Trends. 9th ed. Ed. by R. Craig Sautter. 102p. (Orig.). 1995. pap. 14.95 (*1-882794-95-8*) Coll Bound.

***Who Got In? College Bounds National Survey of Admissions Trends.** rev. ed. R. Craig Sautter. Ed. by Connie Amon & Irma Gonzalez Hider. 128p. 1997. mass mkt. 14.95 (*1-882794-97-4*) VB Document.

Who Governs? Democracy & Power in an American City. Robert A. Dahl. LC 61-16913. (Studies in Political Science: No. 4). (Illus.). 1963. pap. 18.00 (*0-300-00051-0*, Y73) Yale U Pr.

Who Growls in Your Jungle: A Safari into Understanding People. J. G. Sibley. (Illus.). 178p. (Orig.). 1991. pap. 11.95 (*0-913507-21-0*) New Forums.

Who Guards the Guardians: Judicial Control of Administration. Martin Shapiro. LC 87-5927. (Richard B. Russell Lecture Ser.: No. 6). 208p. 1988. 12.00 (*0-8203-0963-X*) U of Ga Pr.

***WHO Handbook for Reporting Results of Cancer Treatment.** WHO Staff. (WHO Offset Publications: No. 48). 45p. 1979. 6.00 (*92-4-170048-3*) World Health.

WHO Handbook for Standardized Cancer Registries. (Offset Publication Ser.: No. 25). 1976. pap. text ed. 9.00 (*92-4-170025-4*, 1120025) World Health.

Who Harnessed the Horse? The Story of Animal Domestication. Margery Facklam. (Illus.). 176p. (J). (gr. 2-5). 1992. 15.95 (*0-316-27381-3*) Little.

Who Has Been Tampering with These Pianos? Montagu O'Reilly. 1988. pap. 10.00 (*0-947757-18-X*, Pub. by Atlas Pr UK) Serpents Tail.

***Who Has God's Life?** (Image of God Ser.). (J). (gr. 1). 1996. pap. text ed. 8.95 (*0-614-24896-5*) Ignatius Pr.

Who Has Seen a Blood Sugar? Reflections on Medical Education. Frank Davidoff et al. LC 96-2019. 200p. 1996. 46.00 (*0-943126-47-9*) Amer Coll Phys.

Who Has the Courage to Stand Alone in the Truth? Andrew Cohen. 48p. (Orig.). 1992. pap. 3.50 (*0-9622678-6-4*) Moksha Found.

Who Has the Youth, Has the Future: The Campaign to Save Young Workers in Imperial Germany. Derek S. Linton. 256p. (C). 1991. text ed. 69.95 (*0-521-38537-7*) Cambridge U Pr.

***Who Hid Honey.** Mouse Works Staff. (J). 1997. 3.98 (*1-57082-565-3*) Mouse Works.

Who Hid It? Taro Gomi. (J). (ps). 1992. pap. 5.44 (*0-395-65835-7*) HM.

Who Hid It? Taro Gomi. (Illus.). 24p. (J). (ps-k). 1991. lib. bdg. 10.40 (*1-56294-011-2*) Millbrook Pr.

Who Hid It? Taro Gomi. (Illus.). 24p. (J). (ps-k). 1992. pap. 4.95 (*1-56294-841-5*) Millbrook Pr.

Who Hides in the Park. Warabe Aska. (Illus.). 36p. (CHI, ENG, FRE & JPN.). (J). (gr. k up). 1990. reprint ed. pap. 7.95 (*0-88776-244-1*) Tundra Bks.

Who Holds the Balance? 62p. 1986. pap. 6.00 (*0-949667-58-7*, Pub. by Veritas Pub AT) Legion Survival.

Who Hunts the Hunter. Nyx Smith. (Shadowrun Ser.: No. 16). 288p. (Orig.). 1995. mass mkt. 4.99 (*0-451-45369-7*, ROC) NAL-Dutton.

Who I Am Depends on Me! Patty Hendrickson. 202p. 1990. pap. 8.00 (*0-9639095-0-9*) P Hendrickson.

***Who I Am Depends on Me! A Smorgasbord of Tidbits for the Head & the Heart.** 3rd ed. Patty Hendrickson. 202p. 1992. reprint ed. pap. 10.95 (*0-9639095-1-7*) P Hendrickson.

Who I Will Be: Is There Joy & Suffering in God? Robert Wild. 1974. pap. 5.95 (*0-87193-089-7*) Dimension Bks.

Who If I Cry Out. Gustavo Corcao. Tr. by Clotilde Wilson. LC 67-64317. (Texas Pan-American Ser.). 229p. reprint ed. pap. 65.30 (*0-8357-7733-2*, 2036090) Bks Demand.

WHO in a New Europe. (WHO Regional Publications: No. 50). 17p. (ENG, FRE, GER & RUS.). 1993. pap. text ed. 12.00 (*92-890-1314-1*, 1310050) World Health.

WHO in Europe: Meeting the Challenges. WHO Regional Office for Europe Staff. (WHO Regional Publications, European Ser.: No. 57). (Illus.). 17p. 1995. pap. 10.80 (*92-890-1321-4*, 1310057) World Health.

***WHO in Europe 1991.** (WHO Regional Publications, European Ser.: No. 41). 17p. 1991. pap. text ed. 12.00 (*92-890-1304-4*) World Health.

Who in Hell: A Guide to the Whole Damned Bunch. Sean Kelly & Rosemary Rogers. (Illus.). 256p. 1996. pap. 12.95 (*0-679-76484-4*, Villard Bks) Random.

Who in Hell Is Wanda Fuca? G. M. Ford. 320p. 1996. mass mkt. 5.99 (*0-380-72761-7*) Avon.

Who in Hell Is Wanda Fuca: A Leo Waterman Mystery. G. M. Ford. 244p. 1995. 21.95 (*0-8027-3255-0*) Walker & Co.

Who Invented Baseball? Paul R. Walker. LC 93-50898. (J). (gr. 4 up). 1994. 10.99 (*0-679-84137-7*) Random Bks Yng Read.

Who Invented Running? HeartPower! Student Reader - Level 3-5. American Heart Association Staff. (HeartPower! American Heart Association Schoolsite Program Ser.). (Illus.). 32p. 1996. pap. write for info. (*0-87493-305-6*) Am Heart.

Who Invented What 1992: With a Focus on Top Ten Technologies: Advanced Materials, Biotechnology, Computer-Aided Manufacturing, & Robotics, Computer Software, Electronics, Environmental Remediation, Medical Products, Photonics, Scientific & Technical Instrumentation, & Telecommunications. Malcolm M. Dickinson. LC 93-12095. (Who Invented What Ser.). (Illus.). 160p. (Orig.). 1993. pap. 9.95 (*0-940983-03-6*); pap. 199.00 incl. cd-rom (*0-940983-04-4*) OPUS Pubns.

***Who Invited Aliens to My Slumber Party?** George E. Stanley. LC 96-30511. (Scaredy Cats Ser.). (Illus.). (J). 1997. pap. 3.99 (*0-689-81348-1*, Aladdin Paperbacks) S&S Childrens.

Who Is a Campbell? More Than Most Campbells Ever Learn about Their Famous (and Infamous) Scottish Family. Jack Campbell. LC 88-42581. (Illus.). 144p. (Orig.). 1988. 17.00 (*0-945508-00-X*); pap. 12.00 (*0-945508-01-8*) Deertrail Bks.

Who Is a Christian? John H. Newman. 1985. pap. 16.95 (*0-87193-188-5*) Dimension Bks.

Who Is a Christian? A Study in Pauline Ethics. Robert F. O'Toole. (Zacchaeus Studies: New Testament). 167p. (C). 1990. pap. 10.95 (*0-8146-5678-1*) Liturgical Pr.

Who Is a Daisy Girl Scout? Girl Scouts of the U. S. A. Staff. (Big Book Ser.). (Illus.). 32p. (J). 1993. 14.95 (*0-88441-275-X*, 20-905) Girl Scouts USA.

Who Is a Daisy Girl Scout? Girl Scouts of the U. S. A. Staff. (Girls' Book Ser.). (Illus.). 32p. (J). (gr. k-1). 1993. 2.95 (*0-88441-276-8*, 20-906) Girl Scouts USA.

***Who Is a Jew?** Meryl Hyman. 288p. 1998. 24.95 (*1-879045-76-1*) Jewish Lights.

Who Is a Stranger & What Should I Do? Linda W. Girard. Ed. by Abby Levine. LC 84-17313. (Albert Whitman Concept Bks.). (Illus.). 32p. (J). (gr. 2-6). 1985. pap. 4.95 (*0-8075-9016-9*); lib. bdg. 12.95 (*0-8075-9014-2*) A Whitman.

***Who Is Al Gore? The Ideas That Make the Man.** (Illus.). 100p. (Orig.). 1997. pap. 9.95 (*0-9647446-9-4*) Great Albany.

Who Is Alex Best? Trudy J. Morgan. LC 93-35925. (J). 1994. pap. 5.99 (*0-8280-0736-5*) Review & Herald.

Who Is Alex Best? Trudy J. Morgan. LC 95-51102. 1996. write for info. (*0-8280-1063-3*) Review & Herald.

***Who Is Alf Thompson? The Biography of a Centenarian Who Has Really Lived - Not Merely Existed.** (Illus.). 243p. 1996. 17.95 (*0-9655389-0-7*) G Wheaton.

Who is Alice? Phyllis Stowell. (Red Ser.). (Illus.). 32p. (Orig.). 1989. pap. 6.00 (*0-938631-04-7*) Pennywhistle Pr.

Who is Angelina? Al Young. (California Fiction Ser.). 280p. (C). 1996. pap. 12.95 (*0-520-20712-2*) U CA Pr.

Who Is Ben? Charlotte Zolotow. LC 96-2382. (Illus.). 32p. (J). (gr. k up). 1997. 14.95 (*0-06-027351-8*); lib. bdg. 14.89 (*0-06-027352-6*) HarpC Child Bks.

Who Is Black? One Nations's Definition. F. James Davis. 216p. 1991. pap. 13.95 (*0-271-00749-4*) Pa St U Pr.

Who Is Blaming Who. Will Clark. LC 93-72225. (Illus.). 320p. (Orig.). 1993. pap. 12.95 (*1-56883-008-4*) Colonial Pr AL.

Who Is Bruce Simonds. Virginia Gaburo. 44p. 1978. boxed 13.95 incl. lp (*0-939044-22-6*) Lingua Pr.

Who Is Calling? Barbara Esbensen. Date not set. 15.95 (*0-8050-4899-5*) H Holt & Co.

Who Is Carrie? James L. Collier & Christopher Collier. 176p. (J). (gr. k-6). 1987. mass mkt. 3.99 (*0-440-49536-9*, YB BDD) BDD Bks Young Read.

Who Is Chauncey Spencer? Chauncey E. Spencer. 1975. 7.95 (*0-685-00874-6*) Broadside Pr.

Who Is Christ? A Theology of the Incarnation. Galot. Tr. by M. Angeline Bouchard. 408p. 1981. 6.95 (*0-8199-0813-4*, Frncscn Herld) Franciscan Pr.

Who Is Coming? Patricia McKissack. LC 86-11805. (Rookie Readers Ser.). (Illus.). 32p. (J). (ps-3). 1990. pap. 3.50 (*0-516-42073-9*); lib. bdg. 15.00 (*0-516-02073-0*) Childrens.

Who Is Coming? Big Book. Patricia McKissack. LC 86-11805. (Rookie Readers Big Bks.). (Illus.). 32p. (J). (ps-3). 1990. pap. 32.40 (*0-516-49458-9*) Childrens.

Who Is Coming to Our House? Joseph Slate. LC 77-16336. (Illus.). 32p. (J). (ps-3). 1996. pap. 5.95 (*0-698-11415-9*, Paperstar) Putnam Pub Group.

Who Is Deborah? Elise Title. (Shadows Ser.: No. 2). 1993. mass mkt. 3.50 (*0-373-27002-X*) Silhouette.

Who Is Delivering the Goods in a Changing Economy: An Opportunity to Redefine the Social Contract. Jenice L. View. 37p. (Orig.). 1994. pap. 5.00 (*1-886949-00-X*) Union Inst.

Who Is Eddie Leonard? Harry Mazer. 240p. (YA). 1995. mass mkt. 3.99 (*0-440-21922-1*) Dell.

Who Is for Liberty. H. R. Williamson. 1972. 250.00 (*0-8490-1294-5*) Gordon Pr.

Who Is Fourier? A Mathematical Adventure. Transnational College of LEX Staff. Tr. by Alan Gleason from JPN. LC 94-979684. (Illus.). 429p. 1995. pap. 24.95 (*0-9643504-0-8*) Lang Res Fnd.

***Who Is Fourier? A Mathematical Adventure.** 2nd ed. Transnational College of LEX Staff. Ed. by Japanese Language Services Staff. Tr. by Alan Gleason from JPN. (Illus.). 430p. 1997. pap. 24.95 (*0-9643504-3-2*) Lang Res Fnd.

Who Is God? Morris Greidanus. LC 93-19846. (Open Door Bks.). 1993. 3.95 (*1-56212-034-4*) CRC Pubns.

Who Is God? Carolyn Nystrom. (Children's Bible Basics Ser.). 30p. (J). 1992. 6.99 (*0-8024-7857-3*) Moody.

Who Is God? David P. Seemuth. (Fisherman Bible Studyguide Ser.). 80p. 1996. pap. 4.99 (*0-87788-852-3*) Shaw Pubs.

Who Is God? A Four Week Study to Help Teenagers Understand Who God Is. Phil Stevenson. Ed. by Gary Swyers et al. (Bibles Basics Ser.). (Illus.). 32p. (YA). (gr. 6-12). 1991. wbk. ed., pap. 8.95 (*0-89827-085-5*, BKS01) Wesleyan Pub Hse.

Who Is God? Who Am I? Who Are You? Introduction to Basic Christian Psychology. Dee Pennock. (Illus.). 160p. (Orig.). 1973. pap. 4.95 (*1-878997-08-4*) St Tikhons Pr.

Who Is Gribich? Marcus Porus & Shirley Porus. LC 95-92141. (Gribich & Friends Ser.). (Illus.). 32p. (J). (ps). 1995. 14.95 (*0-9646125-0-X*) Doog Pub Grp.

Who Is He, What Is He Doing: Religious Rhetoric & Performances in Sri Lanka During R. Premadasa's Presidency (1989-1993) Josine Van der Horst. 300p. 1996. pap. 32.00 (*90-5383-417-6*, Pub. by VU Univ Pr NE) Paul & Co Pubs.

Who Is in the House? A Psychological Study of Two Centuries of Women's Fiction in America, 1795 to the Present. Sally A. McNall. LC 80-26601. 153p. 1981. text ed. 39.95 (*0-444-99081-X*, MWH/) Greenwood.

Who Is Insane? Stephen Smith. Ed. by Gerald N. Grob. LC 78-22590. (Historical Issues in Mental Health Ser.). 1980. reprint ed. lib. bdg. 23.95 (*0-405-11941-0*) Ayer.

Who Is Jane Williams? M. J. Rodgers. (Intrigue Ser.). 1994. mass mkt. 2.99 (*0-373-22290-4*, 1-22290-0) Harlequin Bks.

Who Is Jesus? (Bible Adventure Bks.). (J). (gr. 4-6). 1990. 2.19 (*0-89636-117-9*, JB 2C) Accent CO.

Who Is Jesus? Aza Baxter. (Cosmology Ser.: No. 3). (Orig.). 1996. student ed., pap. 3.00 (*0-9643205-8-4*) Intuitive Psy.

Who Is Jesus. Bruce A. Demarest. Tr. by Ruth T. Chen. (Basic Doctrine Ser.: Bk. 1). 1985. pap. write for info. (*0-941598-26-8*) Living Spring Pubns.

***Who Is Jesus?** Raul G. Fonsica. 17p. (Orig.). 1988. pap. 1.00 (*0-940999-38-2*, C-2150) Star Bible.

Who Is Jesus? Mary Hollingsworth. (Getting to Know Jesus Ser.). 12p. (J). 1995. bds. 3.99 (*0-88070-761-5*, Gold & Honey) Multnomah Pubs.

Who Is Jesus? Dugan McDonald. 163p. (Orig.). 1989. pap. 6.95 (*0-685-27181-1*) Bible Key Pubns.

Who Is Jesus? Robert A. Meyering. LC 93-49845. 1993. 3.95 (*1-56212-035-2*) CRC Pubns.

Who Is Jesus? Carolyn Nystrom. (Children's Bible Basics Ser.). 30p. (J). 1992. 6.99 (*0-8024-7856-5*) Moody.

Who Is Jesus? Answers to Your Questions about the Historical Jesus. John D. Crossan & Richard G. Watts. 208p. 1996. mass mkt. 5.99 (*0-06-104427-X*, Harp PBks) HarpC.

Who Is Jesus? In His Own Words. Ruth E. Van Reken. (Fisherman Bible Studyguide Ser.). 96p. (Orig.). 1993. pap. 4.99 (*0-87788-914-7*) Shaw Pubs.

Who Is Jesus? Leader's Guide. Robert Clark. Tr. by Lorna Y. Chao. (Basic Doctrine Ser.). 1986. pap. write for info. (*0-941598-33-0*) Living Spring Pubns.

Who Is Jesus Christ? Bob E. Patterson. 144p. (Orig.). 1996. pap. 12.95 (*1-57312-027-8*) Smyth & Helwys.

***Who Is Joint? Reevaluating the Joint Duty Assignment List.** John F. Schank et al. 108p. (Orig.). 1996. pap. text ed. 13.00 (*0-8330-2302-0*, MR-574-JS) Rand Corp.

Who Is Kissinger? Henry Paolucci. 1980. pap. 4.00 (*0-918680-13-1*) Bagehot Council.

Who Is Man? Abraham J. Heschel. LC 65-21491. x, 119p. 1965. reprint ed. 22.50 (*0-8047-0265-9*); reprint ed. pap. 10.95 (*0-8047-0266-7*) Stanford U Pr.

Who Is Most Vulnerable to Macroeconomic Shocks? Hypotheses Tests Using Panel Data from Peru. Paul Glewwe & Gillette Hall. LC 95-13479. (LSMS Working Papers: No. 17). 40p. 1995. 6.95 (*0-8213-3244-9*, 13244) World Bank.

***Who Is Mr. Right?** Susan H. Grant & Michael Levin. LC 96-86588. 96p. (Orig.). 1997. pap. 4.95 (*0-8362-2789-1*) Andrews & McMeel.

Who Is My Father. E. L. Brooke. (Illus.). 80p. 1996. write for info. (*1-887922-06-7*) Orange Cty Univ Pr.

Who Is My Neighbor? A Parable. Bettie P. Mitchell. (Illus.). 333p. 1990. pap. 16.00 (*1-885193-00-9*) Good Samaritan.

Who Is My Neighbor? A Primer for Group Discussion. Lila Hensel. 32p. (Orig.). (YA). 1989. pap. 3.95 (*0-932727-29-8*) Hope Pub Hse.

Who Is My Neighbor? Economics As If Values Matter. Sojourners Editors. 180p. 1994. pap. 10.00 (*0-9641109-1-1*) Sojrners.

Who Is My Neighbor? The Christian Response to Human Tragedy. William G. Johnson. (Illus.). 125p. (Orig.). 1995. pap. 10.95 (*0-9648134-0-8*) ADRAI.

***Who Is My Self? A Guide to Buddhist Meditation.** Ayya Khema. LC 97-2606. 1997. write for info. (*0-86171-127-0*) Wisdom MA.

***Who Is Our Example?** (Image of God Ser.). (J). (gr. 3). 1996. pap. text ed. 10.95 (*0-614-24898-1*) Ignatius Pr.

Who Is Padre Pio? Tr. by Laura C. White. (Illus.). 45p. 1994. reprint ed. pap. 1.50 (*0-89555-101-2*) TAN Bks Pubs.

Who Is Responsible for My Old Age? Ed. by Robert N. Butler & Kenzo Kiikuni. LC 92-25181. 288p. 1992. 36.95 (*0-8261-8140-6*) Springer Pub.

W

An Asterisk (*) at the beginning of an entry indicates that the title is appearing in BIP for the first time.

Who Is Responsible for Sickness. Elbert Willis. 1978. 1.95 (*0-89858-010-2*) Fill the Gap.

Who Is Robin? Jon Dijon. LC 93-84590. 248p. 1993. 21.95 (*0-938539-77-9*) Newmark Pub.

Who Is Simon Warwick? Patricia Moyes. LC 78-53951. 176p. 1982. pap. 5.95 (*0-8050-0719-9*, Owl) H Holt & Co.

Who Is Sleeping? A Book about Bedtime. Andrew M. Gutelle. Ed. by Jean Crawford. (Snugglebug Bks.). (Illus.). 32p. (J). (ps). 1994. lib. bdg. 4.95 (*0-7835-4503-7*) Time-Life.

Who Is Sleeping in Aunty's Bed? unabridged ed. Kathy Stinson. (Illus.). 32p. (J). (gr. k-2). 1991. pap. 6.95 (*0-19-540852-7*, Pub. by Stoddart Kids CN) Genl Dist Srvs.

Who Is Sylvia? Tom Clark. LC 79-19070. 1979. 29.95 (*0-912652-54-3*); pap. 9.95 (*0-912652-53-5*) Blue Wind.

Who Is Sylvia? deluxe limited ed. Tom Clark. LC 79-19070. 1979. 49.95 (*0-912652-55-1*) Blue Wind.

Who Is Tapping at My Window? A. G. Deming. (Illus.). 24p. (J). (ps). 1994. pap. 4.99 (*0-14-054553-0*, Puff Unicorn) Puffin Bks.

Who Is Tapping at My Window? large type ed. A. G. Demig. (Illus.). 24p. (J). (ps up). 1994. pap. 17.99 (*0-14-050303-X*) Puffin Bks.

Who Is That? Warren B. Meyers. (Illus.). 1976. pap. 7.95 (*0-8065-0535-4*, Citadel Pr) Carol Pub Group.

Who Is That Peeking in My Windows. Donald Babisch. Ed. by Mary Caroland. LC 90-83590. (Illus.). 44p. (J). 1991. pap. 5.95 (*1-55523-374-0*) Winston-Derek.

Who Is the Afflictor? - Is God Glorified in Sickness? Phillip G. Goudeaux. 99p. 1992. pap. text ed. 9.95 (*1-56550-003-2*) Vis Bks Intl.

Who Is the Beast? Keith Baker. LC 89-29365. (Illus.). 32p. (J). (ps-2). 1990. 14.95 (*0-15-296057-0*) HarBrace.

Who Is the Beast? Keith Baker. LC 89-29365. (Illus.). 32p. (J). (ps-3). 1994. pap. 5.00 (*0-15-200122-0*) HarBrace.

Who Is the Beast? Keith Baker. (Big Bks.). (Illus.). 32p. (J). (ps-3). 1991. reprint ed. pap. 20.00 (*0-15-296059-7*) HarBrace.

Who Is the Buddha? Sangharakshita. (Illus.). 176p. (Orig.). 1996. pap. 11.95 (*0-904766-24-1*) Windhorse Pubns.

Who Is the Faithful & Wise Servant? rev. ed. Duane Magnani. 1992. 11.95 (*1-883858-25-9*) Witness CA.

Who Is the Federal Reserve System. 1992. lib. bdg. 79.95 (*0-8490-8718-X*) Gordon Pr.

Who Is the God of Israel? Richard Honorof. 1995. pap. 2.95 (*0-9632375-1-9*) Feed My Sheep.

Who Is the Holy Ghost. Hughes. 1992. pap. 9.99 (*0-87148-925-2*) Pathway Pr.

***Who Is the Holy Spirit?** Morris Greidanus. LC 96-26330. (Open Door Bks.). 64p. 1996. 3.95 (*1-56212-240-1*, 1740-9015) CRC Pubns.

Who Is the Holy Spirit? Barbara Knuckles & Ruth E. Van Reken. (Fisherman Bible Studyguide Ser.). 80p. 1996. pap. 4.99 (*0-87788-853-1*) Shaw Pubs.

Who Is the King of Glory? A Critical Study of the Christos-Messiah Tradition. Alvin B. Kuhn. 500p. 1992. pap. 30.00 (*1-56459-176-X*) Kessinger Pub.

Who Is the Master Omraam Mikhael Aivanhov. (Testimonials Ser.). (Illus.). 156p. (Orig.). 1982. pap. 11.95 (*2-85566-190-0*, Pub. by Prosveta FR) Prosveta USA.

Who Is the Messiah? David Hocking. Ed. by M. B. Steele. 32p. (Orig.). 1988. pap. 2.95 (*0-939497-15-8*) Promise Pub.

Who Is the Mona Lisa. Ruth E. Norman & Vaughn Spaegal. (Illus.). 88p. 1973. pap. 5.00 (*0-932642-18-7*) Unarius Acad Sci.

Who Is the New Afrikan? Zolo A. Azania. (Illus.). 13p. (Orig.). 1991. pap. 2.00 (*1-56411-007-9*) Untd Bros & Sis.

Who Is the Widow's Muse? Ruth Stone. (Illus.). 59p. 1991. pap. 10.95 (*0-938756-32-X*) Yellow Moon.

Who Is There to Mourn for Logan? Boen Hallum. (Illus.). 144p. (Orig.). 1982. pap. 6.95 (*0-685-05776-3*) B Hallum.

Who Is Theresa Neumann? Charles M. Carty. 1992. reprint ed. pap. 2.00 (*0-89555-093-8*) TAN Bks Pubs.

***Who Is This 'Cut-Off' Man & Why Do They All Want to Hit Him? The Parents Guide to Baseball.** Doug Luthanen. (Illus.). 88p. (Orig.). 1997. pap. 8.00 (*0-9656366-0-7*) Picadilly Pr.

***Who Is This Ghost Called Holy? The Ministry of the Holy Spirit.** Arnold Prater. Orig. Title: The Presence. 147p. 1995. write for info. (*1-888874-01-5*) Marno Bks.

***Who Is This Jesus.** Green. 6.95 (*0-340-54610-7*, Pub. by H & S UK) Trafalgar.

Who Is This Jesus? Michael Green. 144p. 1994. pap. 5.99 (*0-7852-8249-1*) Nelson.

Who Is This King of Glory? A Critical Study of the Christos - Messiah Tradition. Alvin B. Kuhn. (African Studies). 493p. reprint ed. 50.00 (*0-938818-83-X*) ECA Assoc.

Who Is This "We" Absence of Community. Ed. by Eleanor M. Godway & Geraldine Finn. 185p. 1994. pap. 19.99 (*1-55164-004-X*, Pub. by Black Rose Bks CN) Consort Bk Sales.

Who Is This "We" Absence of Community. Ed. by Eleanor M. Godway & Geraldine Finn. 250p. 1996. 48.99 (*1-55164-005-8*, Pub. by Black Rose Bks CN) Consort Bk Sales.

Who Is to Be Master of the World? an Introduction to the Philosophy of Friedrich Nietzsche. A. M. Ludovici. 1972. 99.95 (*0-8490-1295-3*) Gordon Pr.

Who Is to Blame? Alexander Herzen. Tr. by Michael R. Katz from RUS. LC 84-7666. 288p. 1984. 42.50 (*0-8014-1460-1*); pap. 16.95 (*0-8014-9286-6*) Cornell U Pr.

Who Is Uncle Sam? Taffy Jones. LC 91-52615. (Illus.). 64p. (Orig.). (J). 1991. pap. write for info. (*0-917882-32-6*) MD Hist Pr.

Who Is Who? Patricia McKissack. LC 83-7361. (Rookie Reader Ser.). (Illus.). 32p. (J). (ps-2). 1983. pap. 3.50 (*0-516-42042-9*); lib. bdg. 15.00 (*0-516-02042-0*) Childrens.

Who Is Who in Freemasonry, Vol. 1. Ed. by Allen E. Roberts. 188p. 1984. 36.00 (*0-935633-00-6*) Anchor Comm.

Who Is Who in Freemasonry, Vol. 2. Ed. by Allen E. Roberts. 203p. 1986. 36.00 (*0-935633-02-2*) Anchor Comm.

Who Is Who in Freemasonry, Vol. 3. Ed. by Allen E. Roberts. 300p. 1996. 36.00 (*0-935633-16-2*) Anchor Comm.

Who Is Who in Service to the Earth. 2nd ed. Ed. by Hans J. Keller. 370p. 1993. lib. bdg. 195.00 (*3-598-11160-6*) K G Saur.

Who Is Witter Bynner? A Biography. James Kraft. LC 94-18764. (Illus.). 128p. 1995. 19.95 (*0-8263-1626-3*) U of NM Pr.

Who Is Worth Following? see Who Really Has the Answer?

Who Is Your Doctor & Why? Alonzo J. Shadman. LC 80-82320. 446p. 1980. reprint ed. pap. 3.95 (*0-87983-227-4*) Keats.

Who Judges the Judges? A Study of Procedures for Removal & Retirement. William T. Braithwaite. LC 72-179947. (American Bar Foundation Publications). xviii, 167p. 1972. pap. 20.00 (*1-57588-379-1*, 305070) W S Hein.

***Who Keeps the Water Clean? Ms. Schindler!** Jill Duvall. LC 96-34908. (Our Neighborhood Ser.). (Illus.). (J). 1997. lib. bdg. 18.00 (*0-516-20315-0*) Childrens.

***Who Keeps the Water Clean? Ms. Schindler!** Jill D. Duvall. (Our Neighborhood Ser.). 1997. pap. 5.95 (*0-516-26152-5*) Childrens.

***Who Kidnapped Jesus?** Vicki B. Erwin. LC 97-5517. (Elizabeth Bryan Mysteries Ser.). (J). 1997. 4.99 (*0-570-04971-7*) Concordia.

Who Kidnapped the Sheriff? Larry Callen. (Illus.). 176p. (J). (gr. 4 up). 1985. 14.95 (*0-316-12499-0*, Joy St Bks) Little.

Who Kids Turn to When They're in Trouble: Will Kids Choose You? 32p. 1992. pap. 4.95 (*1-56246-060-9*, P234) Johnsn Inst.

Who Killed Alaska. Dave Brown & Paula Crane. LC 90-50876. 336p. 1991. 21.95 (*0-88282-069-9*) New Horizon NJ.

Who Killed Candida? Vicki Glassburn. LC 89-51934. (Illus.). 255p. (Orig.). 1991. pap. 17.95 (*0-945383-12-6*, 945-5923) Teach Servs.

Who Killed Carmen? Rose Weite. 237p. 1995. Perfect bdg. per. 11.95 (*0-9636043-1-7*) Clementine Bks.

***Who Killed Classical Music? Maestros, Managers & Corporate Politics.** Norman Lebrecht. LC 97-9667. 448p. 1997. 24.95 (*1-55972-415-3*, Birch Ln Pr) Carol Pub Group.

Who Killed Cock Robin? Kevin O'Malley. LC 92-40340. (Illus.). (J). (gr. k-3). 1993. 15.00 (*0-688-12430-5*); lib. bdg. 14.93 (*0-688-12431-3*) Lothrop.

***Who Killed Confederation Life? The Inside Story.** Rod McQueen. 1997. 26.95 (*0-7710-5631-1*) McCland & Stewart.

Who Killed Father Christmas? And Other Unseasonable Demises. Patricia Moyes. 248p. (Orig.). 1996. pap. 16.00 (*1-885941-09-9*) Crippen & Landru.

Who Killed Father Christmas? And Other Unseasonable Demises. deluxe limited ed. Patricia Moyes. 248p. (Orig.). 1996. 40.00 (*1-885941-08-0*) Crippen & Landru.

Who Killed George Polk? The Press Covers up a Death in the Family. Elias Vlanton & Zak Mettger. LC 95-39362. 322p. (C). 1996. 27.95 (*1-56639-367-1*) Temple U Pr.

Who Killed Harlowe Thrombey?, No. 9. large type ed. Edward Packard. (Choose Your Own Adventure Ser.). 121p. (J). (gr. 3-7). 1987. reprint ed. 8.95 (*0-942545-13-3*); reprint ed. lib. bdg. 9.95 (*0-942545-18-4*) Grey Castle.

Who Killed James Dean? Warren N. Beath. (Orig.). 1995. 4.99 (*0-8125-3873-0*) Tor Bks.

***Who Killed Jesus.** Crossan. 1995. pap. 12.00 (*0-06-061671-7*) HarpC.

Who Killed Jesus? Exposing the Roots of Anti-Semitism in the Gospel Story of the Death of Jesus. John D. Crossan. LC 95-40200. 256p. 1996. pap. 14.00 (*0-06-061480-3*) Harper SF.

Who Killed JFK? Carl Oglesby. LC 91-46501. (Real Story Ser.). (Illus.). 96p. (Orig.). 1992. pap. 5.00 (*1-878825-10-0*) Odonian Pr.

Who Killed JFK? The Kennedy Assassination Cover-up. James R. Duffy. LC 89-6035. 1990. 14.95 (*0-944007-39-2*) Sure Seller.

***Who Killed Kennedy.** James Stevens & David Bishop. (Dr. Who Ser.). 320p. 1996. mass mkt. 5.95 (*0-426-20467-0*, Pub. by Virgin Pub UK) London Brdge.

Who Killed Kurt? The Cobain Dossier. 144p. 1995. per. 19.95 (*0-85965-225-4*, Pub. by Plexus UK) Publishers Group.

Who Killed Martin Luther King? Philip Melanson. LC 93-19961. (Real Story Ser.). (Illus.). 96p. (Orig.). 1993. pap. 5.00 (*1-878825-11-9*) Odonian Pr.

Who Killed Martin Luther King? The True Story by the Alleged Assassin. James E. Ray. 285p. 1993. pap. 12.95 (*1-882605-02-0*) Natl Pr Bks.

***Who Killed Martin Luther King? The True Story by the Alleged Assassin.** James Earl Ray. 1997. pap. text ed. 13.95 (*1-56924-711-0*) Marlowe & Co.

Who Killed Mr. Boddy? Created by A. E. Parker. (Clue Ser.: No. 1). 160p. (J). (gr. 4-6). 1992. pap. 3.50 (*0-590-46110-9*, Apple Paperbacks) Scholastic Inc.

Who Killed Mr. Chippendale? A Mystery in Poems. Mel Glenn. 112p. (YA). (gr. 7 up). 1996. pap. 14.99 (*0-525-67530-2*) NAL-Dutton.

Who Killed My Daughter: The True Story of a Mother's Search for Her Daughter's Murderer. Lois Duncan. 368p. 1994. mass mkt. 5.99 (*0-440-21342-8*) Dell.

Who Killed Netta Maul? large type ed. Frank Arthur. (Large Type Ser.). 480p. 1994. 25.99 (*0-7089-2999-0*) Ulverscroft.

***Who Killed Olive Souffle?** Margaret Benoit. 1997. text ed. 10.95 (*0-07-006310-9*) McGraw.

***Who Killed Olive Souffle?** Margaret Benoit. (Illus.). 112p. (YA). (gr. 5 up). 1997. pap. text ed. 5.95 (*0-07-006275-7*) McGraw.

Who Killed Polly?, Vol. 1. Frank Spiering. (Illus.). 256p. (Orig.). 1995. mass mkt. 5.99 (*0-9647612-0-3*) Monterey CA.

Who Killed Robert Kennedy? Philip Melanson. LC 93-15398. (Real Story Ser.). (Illus.). 96p. (Orig.). 1993. pap. 5.00 (*1-878825-12-7*) Odonian Pr.

Who Killed Stutz Bearcat? Stories of Finding Faith after Loss. Kristen Johnson Ingram. LC 93-23775. 104p. (Orig.). (C). 1993. pap. text ed. 8.95 (*0-89390-264-0*) Resource Pubns.

Who Killed the Congo? Philippa Schuyler. (Illus.). 1962. 9.50 (*0-8159-7212-1*) Devin.

Who Killed the Constitution: The Judges vs. the Law. William Eaton. LC 88-4207. 1988. pap. 10.95 (*0-89526-776-4*) Regnery Pub.

***Who Killed the Homecoming Queen?** R. L. Stine. (Fear Street Ser.: No. 48). (YA). 1997. mass mkt. 3.99 (*0-671-52964-1*) PB.

Who Killed Virginia Woolf? A Psychobiography. Alma H. Bond. (Insight Book Ser.). (Illus.). 194p. 1989. 23.95 (*0-89885-427-X*) Human Sci Pr.

Who Knew There'd Be Ghosts? Bill Brittain. LC 84-48496. (Illus.). 128p. (J). (gr. 4-7). 1985. lib. bdg. 14.89 (*0-06-020700-0*) HarpC Child Bks.

Who Knew There'd Be Ghosts? Bill Brittain. LC 84-48496. (Trophy Bk.). (Illus.). 128p. (J). (gr. 4-7). 1992. pap. 3.95 (*0-06-440224-X*, Trophy) HarpC Child Bks.

***Who Knows?** Britten. 1992. pap. text ed. write for info. (*0-17-555894-9*) Addison-Wesley.

Who Knows. Francis Picabia. Tr. by Remy Hall from FRE. 168p. (Orig.). 1987. pap. 5.95 (*0-937815-04-7*) Hanuman Bks.

Who Knows: From Quine to a Feminist Empiricism. Lynn H. Nelson. 336p. (C). 1990. 34.95 (*0-87722-647-4*) Temple U Pr.

Who Knows: From Quine to a Feminist Empiricism. Lynn H. Nelson. 336p. 1992. pap. 18.95 (*1-56639-007-9*) Temple U Pr.

Who Knows: Information in the Age of the Fortune 500. Herbert I. Schiller. LC 81-3572. (Communication & Information Science Ser.). 192p. 1981. pap. 39.50 (*0-89391-135-6*); text ed. 73.25 (*0-89391-069-4*) Ablex Pub.

Who Knows: Safeguarding Your Privacy in a Networked World. Ann Cavoukian & Don Tapscott. (Illus.). 240p. 1996. text ed. 24.95 (*0-07-063320-7*) McGraw.

Who Knows One? A Book of Jewish Numbers. Yaffa Ganz. (J). (gr. k-4). 1981. 13.95 (*0-87306-285-X*) Feldheim.

Who Knows Ten? Children's Tales of the Ten Commandments. Molly Cone. (Illus.). (Orig.). (J). (gr. k-3). 1997. pap. 10.00 (*0-8074-0080-7*, 102551) UAHC.

Who Knows What: A Guide to Experts. 13th ed. (Business Research Ser.). 340p. 1994. 195.00 (*1-56365-025-8*) Wash Res.

Who Knows Who. 2nd ed. 950p. 1994. 150.00 (*0-9638874-1-6*) Gale.

Who Knows Who: Networking Through Corporate Boards. 5th ed. Jeannette E. Glynn. 906p. 1994. pap. 150.00 (*0-9638874-0-8*) Who Knows Who.

Who Knows Who: Networking Through Corporate Boards 3. 3rd ed. 1995. 150.00 (*0-9638874-2-4*) Gale.

***Who Knows Who 1997.** 8th ed. 900p. 1996. 165.00 (*0-9638874-3-2*, GML00197-109807) Who Knows Who.

WHO Laboratory Manual for the Examination of Human Semen & Sperm-Cervical Mucus Interaction. 3rd ed. World Health Organization Staff. (Illus.). 90p. (C). 1993. pap. text ed. 35.95 (*0-521-42168-3*) Cambridge U Pr.

Who Laughs Last? Nellie McCaslin. (Illus.). 50p. (Orig.). 1996. pap. 5.00 (*0-88734-449-6*) Players Pr.

Who Let Girls in the Boys' Locker Room? Elaine Moore. LC 94-820. (Illus.). 144p. (J). (gr. 3-6). 1996. pap. 3.95 (*0-8167-3439-9*) Troll Communs.

Who Lies Inside. Ireland. 1995. per. 10.95 (*0-907040-30-6*, Pub. by Gay Mens Pr UK) LPC InBook.

Who Likes That Stuff? ETR Associates Staff. LC 92-8356. (Contemporary Health Ser.). (Illus.). (YA). 1992. 2.00 (*1-56071-101-9*) ETR Assocs.

Who Likes to Play? Easy Animal Reader. Freeman. (Illus.). 16p. (J). (ps-1). 1996. pap. 2.49 (*1-57690-048-7*) Tchr Create Mat.

Who Likes Wolfie? Ragnhild Scamell. LC 94-73588. (Illus.). 32p. (J). (gr. 1-3). 1996. 14.95 (*0-316-77243-7*) Little.

***Who Lived at Alfoxton? Virginia Woolf & English Romanticism.** Ellen Tremper. LC 97-16907. 1997. write for info. (*0-8387-5365-5*) Bucknell U Pr.

Who Lived in This House? A Study of Koyukuk River Semisubterranean Houses. A. McFadyen Clark. (Mercury Ser.: No. 153). (Illus.). 282p. 1996. pap. 24.95 (*0-660-15958-9*, Pub. by Can Mus Civil CN) U of Wash Pr.

Who Lives Happily Ever After? For Families Whose Child Has Died Violently. Sharon Turnbull. Ed. by Joy Johnson. (Illus.). 24p. (Orig.). 1990. pap. 3.25 (*1-56123-000-6*) Centering Corp.

Who Lives Here? (J). 1995. 8.99 (*0-88705-582-6*) Joshua Morris.

Who Lives Here? Maggie Silver. LC 95-913. (J). (ps-3). 1995. 10.95 (*0-87156-371-1*) Sierra Club Childrens.

Who Lives Here? Rozanne L. Williams. (Spanish Emergent Reader Bks.). (Illus.). 16p. (ENG & SPA.). (J). (gr. k-2). 1995. pap. 2.49 (*1-57471-038-9*) Creat Teach Pr.

Who Lives Here? Rozanne L. Williams. (Emergent Reader Big Bks.). 16p. (J). (gr. k-2). 1995. 11.98 (*0-916119-78-5*) Creat Teach Pr.

Who Lives Here?, Bk. 1. Dawn B. Brunke. (Illus.). (Orig.). (J). (gr. k-6). 1993. pap. 6.95 (*1-55971-152-3*) NorthWord.

Who Lives Here?, Bk. 2. Dawn B. Brunke. (Illus.). (Orig.). (J). (gr. k-6). 1993. pap. 6.95 (*1-55971-153-1*) NorthWord.

Who Lives Here?, Bk. 3. Dawn B. Brunke. (Illus.). (Orig.). (J). (gr. k-6). 1993. pap. 6.95 (*1-55971-154-X*) NorthWord.

Who Lives Here?, Bk. 4. Dawn B. Brunke. (Illus.). (Orig.). (J). (gr. k-6). 1993. pap. 6.95 (*1-55971-155-8*) NorthWord.

Who Lives Here?, Level 2. Rozanne L. Williams. (Emergent Reader Science Ser.). 16p. 1994. 2.49 (*0-916119-37-8*, 3527) Creat Teach Pr.

***Who Lives in a Tree?** Lisa Trumbauer. Ed. by Susan Evento. (Newbridge Links Ser.). 8p. (J). 1997. pap. 2.75 (*1-56784-901-6*) Newbridge Comms.

Who Lives in the Country? Robert Crowther. LC 91-58766. (Illus.). 10p. (J). (ps). 1992. 6.95 (*1-56402-090-8*) Candlewick Pr.

Who Lives in the Field? Diana D. Hearn. (Illus.). (J). (ps-3). 1992. 4.95 (*0-87483-244-6*) August Hse.

Who Lives in the Forest? Diana D. Hearn. (Illus.). (J). (ps-3). 1992. 4.95 (*0-87483-245-4*) August Hse.

Who Lives in the Garden? Robert Crowther. LC 91-58767. (Illus.). 10p. (J). (ps). 1992. 6.95 (*1-56402-091-6*) Candlewick Pr.

Who Lives in the Garden? Diana D. Hearn. (Illus.). (J). (ps-3). 1992. 4.95 (*0-87483-246-2*) August Hse.

Who Lives in the Lake? Diana D. Hearn. (Illus.). (J). (ps-3). 1992. 4.95 (*0-87483-247-0*) August Hse.

Who Lives in the Oceans, Lakes & Rivers: Baby Animal Sticker Books. Ann Hardy. (J). 1995. 2.95 (*0-689-80352-4*) S&S Childrens.

Who Lives in the Rain Forest: Baby Animal Sticker Books. Ann Hardy. (J). 1995. 2.95 (*0-689-80351-6*) S&S Childrens.

Who Lives in the Woods? Pat Upton. LC 90-85721. (Illus.). 32p. (J). (ps-1). 1991. 7.95 (*1-878093-19-3*) Boyds Mills Pr.

Who Lives There? Jane Norman & Frank Beazley. 24p. (J). (ps-3). 1993. pap. write for info. (*1-883585-13-9*) Pixanne Ent.

Who Lives? Who Dies? Ethical Criteria in Patient Selection. John F. Kilner. 373p. (C). 1992. reprint ed. pap. text ed. 18.00 (*0-300-05220-0*) Yale U Pr.

Who Lost a Shoe? Barbara S. Hazen. (Whole-Language Big Bks.). 16p. (J). (ps-2). 1992. pap. 14.95 (*1-56784-050-7*) Newbridge Comms.

Who Loves Brian. Love. Date not set. 19.95 (*0-312-08335-1*) St Martin.

***Who Loves Me Always?** (Image of God Ser.). (J). (gr. 2). 1996. pap. text ed. 8.95 (*0-614-24897-3*) Ignatius Pr.

Who Loves Patti. Mary E. Lebar. (J). 1985. pap. text ed. 1.95 (*0-88207-073-8*) SP Pubns.

Who Loves the Children. Mary E. Lebar. (J). 1985. pap. text ed. 1.95 (*0-88207-074-6*) SP Pubns.

***Who Loves You Little Beetle?** Carla Dijs. (Flap Bks.). (Illus.). (J). 1997. 11.99 (*0-85953-961-X*) Childs Play.

***Who Made Baby Animals?** Standard Publishing Staff. (Happy Day Coloring Bks.). 12p. (J). 1996. pap. 0.99 (*0-7847-0436-8*, 22206) Standard Pub.

Who Made God. Emmy L. Murphy. (J). (ps-3). 1978. pap. 3.25 (*0-915374-07-2*, 07-2) Rapids Christian.

Who Made Stevie Cry? Michael Bishop. LC 84-9251. (Illus.). 325p. 1984. 15.95 (*0-87054-099-8*) Arkham.

Who Made the Lamb. Charlotte Painter. LC 88-72025. 224p. (Orig.). 1988. reprint ed. pap. 8.95 (*0-88739-063-3*) Creat Arts Bk.

Who Made the Morning? Jane Godfrey. (Illus.). 32p. (J). 1995. 7.99 (*1-56476-472-9*, 6-3472, Victor Bks) Chariot Victor.

Who Made This Big Mess? Andrew Gutelle. Ed. by Sara Mark. LC 95-39254. (Big Comfy Couch Ser.). (Illus.). 32p. (J). (ps-1). 1996. 4.95 (*0-7835-4505-3*) Time-Life.

Who Made This Nest? Easy Animal Reader. Brust. (Illus.). 16p. (J). (ps-1). 1996. pap. 2.49 (*1-57690-053-3*) Tchr Create Mat.

Who Made You? Theology, Science, & Human Responsibility. Alfred H. Howell. LC 89-30018. (Convergence Ser.). 200p. 1989. text ed. 49.95 (*0-275-93293-1*, C3293, Praeger Pubs); pap. text ed. 16.95 (*0-275-93294-X*, B3294, Praeger Pubs) Greenwood.

Who Makes Our Money: How Our Financial System Creates Poverty & War. F Irsigler. 1982. lib. bdg. 69.95 (*0-87700-447-1*) Revisionist Pr.

Who Makes Public Policy? The Struggle for Control Between Congress & the Executive. Robert S. Gilmour et al. LC 93-34362. (Illus.). 400p. (Orig.). (C). 1994. pap. text ed. 29.95 (*1-56643-004-6*) Chatham Hse Pubs.

Who Makes the Laws? Creativity & Power in Senate Committees. David E. Price. 380p. 1972. boxed, ring bd. 34.95 (*0-87073-298-6*) Transaction Pubs.

WHO Manual for the Standardized Investigation & Diagnosis of the Infertile Couple. Patrick J. Rowe et al. (Illus.). 65p. (C). 1993. pap. text ed. 26.95 (*0-521-43136-0*) Cambridge U Pr.

WHO Manual of Radiotherapy in Cancer Management. Hanson. 192p. 1996. pap. 34.50 (*0-412-63580-1*) Chapman & Hall.

W

WHO Manual on Environmental Management for Mosquito Control. 283p. 1982. 13.50 (*92-4-170066-1*) Am Mosquito.
WHO Manual on Larval Control Operations in Malaria Programmes. 199p. 1973. 20.00 (*0-318-12865-9*) Am Mosquito.
Who, Me? Ely J. Kahn, Jr. LC 77-179731. (Biography Index Reprint Ser.). 1977. reprint ed. 18.95 (*0-8369-8099-9*) Ayer.
Who Me? A Missionary? Daniel W. Bacon. 1985. pap. 1.25 (*9971-972-32-8*) Ashgate Pub Co.
Who-Me? Do a Program? Cynthia E. Cowen. LC 95-12243. 1995. 12.95 (*0-7880-0590-1*) CSS OH.
Who? Me?! Exercise? Safe Exercise for People over 50. Sara Harris & Olga Hurley. (Illus.). 42p. 1995. pap. 3.95 (*0-937829-08-0*) Ctr Study Aging.
Who Me? Go Where? Do What? The Missionary & the Mission. Macklyn W. Hubbell. LC 94-48646. 1995. 10.00 (*0-914520-31-8*) Insight Pr.
Who, Me Lead a Group? Jean I. Clarke. 128p. (Orig.). 1985. pap. 10.00 (*0-86683-724-8*, AY8284) Harper SF.
Who Ministers to Ministers? A Study of Support Systems for Clergy & Spouses. Roy M. Oswald & Otto Kroeger. LC 87-72687. 104p. (Orig.). 1987. pap. 10.95 (*1-56699-022-X*, AL101) Alban Inst.
WHO Model Prescribing Information: Drugs Used in Anaesthesia. 53p. (ENG & FRE.). 1989. pap. text ed. 11.00 (*92-4-140101-X*, 1150333) World Health.
WHO Model Prescribing Information: Drugs Used in Mycobacterial Diseases. 40p. (ENG, FRE & SPA.). 1991. pap. text ed. 9.00 (*92-4-140103-6*, 1150363) World Health.
Who Model Prescribing Information: Drugs Used in Parasitic Diseases. 2nd ed. (WHO Model Prescribing Information Ser.). 146p. (FRE & SPA.). (C). 1995. pap. 35.00 (*92-4-140104-4*, 1152343) World Health.
WHO Model Prescribing Information: Drugs Used in Sexually Transmitted Diseases & HIV Infection. 97p. (FRE & SPA.). (C). 1995. pap. 25.00 (*92-4-140105-2*, 1150429) World Health.
*__Who Moved the Line.__ AmieBeth Dickinson & Denise George. Ed. by William Buck et al. (Illus.). 175p. (Orig.). 1996. pap. 12.95 (*0-934530-10-6*) Buck Pub.
Who Moved the Stone? Frank Morison. 193p. 1987. pap. 10.99 (*0-310-29561-0*, 10373P) Zondervan.
Who Named My Street Magnolia? First Questions & Answers about Neighborhoods. Time-Life Book Editors. Ed. by Sara Mark. (Library of First Questions & Answers). (Illus.). 48p. (J). (gr. k-2). 1995. 14.95 (*0-7835-0898-0*) Time-Life.
Who Need Las Vegas: Gambling & Its Impacts in a Southwestern Minnesota Agricultural Community. Mikal J. Aasved & James M. Schaefer. (Illus.). 63p. (Orig.). (C). 1994. pap. 30.00 (*0-7881-0862-X*) DIANE Pub.
Who Needs a Boat? The Story of Moses. Marilyn Lashbrook. LC 87-83295. (Me Too! Bks.). (Illus.). 32p. (J). (ps). 1988. 5.95 (*0-86606-431-1*, 862) Treasure Pub.
Who Needs a Boat? (Moses) see No Les Hizo Falta Un Barco (Moises)
*__Who Needs Credit: Poverty & Finance in Bangladesh.__ Geoffrey D. Wood. (C). 1997. pap. 27.50 (*1-85649-524-8*, Pub. by Zed Bks Ltd UK); text ed. 62.50 (*1-85649-523-X*, Pub. by Zed Bks Ltd UK) Humanities.
Who Needs Feminism. Richard Holloway. 1991. pap. text ed. 12.95 (*0-281-04543-7*) Abingdon.
Who Needs Feminism? Men Respond to Sexism in the Church. Richard Holloway. 1991. pap. write for info. (*0-687-86493-3*) Abingdon.
Who Needs God? Harold J. Kushner. Ed. by Julie Rubenstein. 208p. 1991. reprint ed. mass mkt. 6.50 (*0-671-68027-7*) PB.
Who Needs Headaches? Why Suffer if You Don't Have To? Cass Igram. 1991. write for info. (*0-911119-36-1*); pap. 13.95 (*0-911119-32-9*) Knowledge Hse.
Who Needs the Negro? Sidney M. Wilhelm. (Illus.). 266p. (Orig.). 1993. pap. 14.95 (*1-56411-069-9*) Untd Bros & Sis.
Who Needs the Past? Indigenous Values & Archaeology. Ed. by Robert Layton. LC 88-15598. (One World Archaeology Ser.: No. 5). 256p. (C). 1988. text ed. 62.95 (*0-04-445020-6*) Routledge Chapman & Hall.
Who Needs the Past? Indigenous Values in Archaeology. Ed. by R. Layton. (One World Archaeology Ser.). 240p. (C). 1994. pap. 19.95 (*0-415-09558-1*, B4706) Routledge.
Who Needs Theology? An Invitation to the Study of God. Stanley J. Grenz & Roger E. Olson. LC 96-19405. 168p. (Orig.). 1996. pap. 12.99 (*0-8308-1878-2*, 1878) InterVarsity.
Who Needs Third Grade? Candice F. Ransom. LC 92-30754. (Tales from Third Grade Ser.). 128p. (J). (gr. 2-4). 1996. pap. 3.95 (*0-8167-2989-1*) Troll Communs.
*__Who Needs to Sleep Anyway! How Animals Sleep.__ Colin H. Shapiro. (Illus.). 32p. (J). (gr. 2 up). 1996. 19.95 (*0-88753-288-8*, Pub. by Black Moss Pr CN); pap. 6.95 (*0-88753-281-0*, Pub. by Black Moss Pr CN) Firefly Bks Ltd.
*__Who of Pooh: Finding Your Personality Type in the Hundred Acre Wood.__ A. A. Milne. 1997. pap. 13.99 (*0-525-45761-5*) NAL-Dutton.
Who Offended You: And Stopped You from Receiving Your Miracle? Phillip G. Goudeaux. Ed. by Debra S. Pappas. 96p. (Orig.). (C). 1994. pap. 12.95 (*1-56550-018-0*) Vis Bks Intl.
Who Only England Know: Conservatives & Foreign Policy. Ed. by Christopher Coker. (C). 1990. 35.00 (*0-907967-18-3*, Pub. by Inst Euro Def & Strat UK) St Mut.
Who Only Stand & Wait. Helene C. Phelan. (Illus.). 406p. (Orig.). 1990. pap. 16.95 (*0-9605836-6-1*) Phelan.
Who or What Are You Referring to? David Blot. 64p. (Orig.). (C). 1987. pap. text ed. 4.00 (*0-317-93604-2*) D Blot Pubns.
Who or What Is Man, Who or What Are You? Alan C. Walter. Ed. by Beverly Miles. 25p. (Orig.). 1995. pap. text ed. 24.97 (*1-57569-006-3*) Wisdom Pubng.
Who Owns America. Ed. by Herbert Agar & Allen Tate. LC 71-99616. (Essay Index Reprint Ser.). 1977. 25.95 (*0-8369-1540-2*) Ayer.
Who Owns Appalachia. (Southern Exposure Ser.). 88p. 1982. pap. 3.00 (*0-943810-33-7*) Inst Southern Studies.
Who Owns Appalachia? Landownership & Its Impact. Appalachian Land Ownership Task Force Staff. LC 82-40173. 260p. reprint ed. pap. 74.10 (*0-685-23450-9*, 2032705) Bks Demand.
Who Owns Corporate America, 1993: A Comprehensive Listing of More than 75,000 Officers, Directors, & Ten Percent Principal Stockholders & Their Holdings of Securities Issued by U. S. Public Companies. 93th ed. Ed. by Mark W. Scott & Catherine M. Ehr. 1716p. 1992. 275.00 (*1-879784-36-X*, 600357) Taft Group.
Who Owns Corporate America, 1994. 94th ed. 1775p. 1993. 285.00 (*0-930807-48-0*, 600471) Taft Group.
Who Owns Corporate America 1997. Mark W. Scott. 285.00 (*1-56995-060-1*) Taft Group.
Who Owns English? Ed. by Mike Hayhoe & Stephen Parker. LC 93-42511. (English, Language & Education Ser.). 1994. pap. 27.50 (*0-335-19266-1*, Open Univ Pr) Taylor & Francis.
Who Owns Information? From Privacy to Public Access. Anne W. Branscomb. 256p. 1995. pap. 13.00 (*0-465-09144-X*) Basic.
Who Owns Learning? Questions of Autonomy, Choice, & Control. Curt Dudley-Marling & Dennis Searle. LC 94-27338. 213p. 1994. pap. text ed. 21.50 (*0-435-08827-0*, 08827) Heinemann.
*__Who Owns Our Bodies? Making Moral Choices in Health Care.__ John Spiers & Institute of Health Services Management Staff. 1997. write for info. (*1-85775-210-4*, Radcliffe Med Pr) Scovill Paterson.
*__Who Owns St. Bartholomew?__ Brent C. Brolin. Date not set. write for info. (*0-688-05939-2*) Morrow.
Who Owns Scotland Now? The Use & Abuse of Private Land. Auslan Cramb. (Illus.). 224p. 1996. 35.00 (*1-85158-728-4*, Pub. by Mnstream UK) Trafalgar.
Who Owns the Blue Chips in Great Britain. R. A. Vernon et al. 200p. 1973. 29.00 (*0-8464-0971-2*) Beekman Pubs.
Who Owns the Children? Public Compulsion, Private Responsibility & the Dilemma of Ultimate Authority: Public Compulsion, Private Responsibility, & the Dilemma of Ultimate Authority. enl. rev. ed. Blair Adams & Joel Stein. LC 84-50087. 1991. pap. 16.95 (*0-916387-24-0*) Truth Forum.
Who Owns the Children? Public Compulsion, Private Responsibility & the Dilemma of Ultimate Authority: Public Compulsion, Private Responsibility, & the Dilemma of Ultimate Authority. 5th enl. rev. ed. Blair Adams & Joel Stein. LC 84-50087. 1991. 26.95 (*0-916387-25-9*) Truth Forum.
Who Owns the Corporation? Management vs. Shareholders - A Twentieth Century Fund Paper. Edward J. Epstein. 69p. (Orig.). (C). 1986. pap. text ed. 8.00 (*0-87078-208-8*) TCFP-PPP.
Who Owns the Cow? Andrew Clements. LC 94-19308. (Illus.). 32p. (J). (ps-2). 1995. 14.95 (*0-395-70145-7*) HM.
Who Owns the Federal Reserve System? 1992. lib. bdg. 79.95 (*0-8490-8729-5*) Gordon Pr.
Who Owns the Sun? Stacy Chbosky. LC 88-12694. (Books for Students by Students). (Illus.). 26p. (J). (gr. 3-12). 1988. lib. bdg. 14.95 (*0-933849-14-1*) Landmark Edns.
Who Owns the Sun? Preparing for the New Solar Economy. Daniel M. Berman & John T. O'Connor. LC 96-43593. 356p. 1996. 24.95 (*0-930031-86-5*) Chelsea Green Pub.
Who Owns the West? William Kittredge. 176p. (Orig.). 1996. pap. 14.95 (*1-56279-078-1*) Mercury Hse Inc.
Who Owns the Wildlife? The Political Economy of Conservation in Nineteenth-Century America. James A. Tober. LC 80-23482. (Contributions in Economics & Economic History Ser.: No. 37). (Illus.). 300p. 1981. text ed. 49.95 (*0-313-22597-4*, TOW/) Greenwood.
Who Owns Welfare? Questions on the Social Services Agenda. Tessa Harding. (Social Services Policy Forum Papers: No. 2). 1992. pap. 24.00 (*0-902789-80-5*, Pub. by Natl Inst Soc Work) St Mut.
Who Owns What Is in Your Head? A Guide for Entrepreneurs, Inventors & Creative Employees. Stanley H. Lieberstein. 1995. pap. 14.95 (*0-941968-04-9*) Wildcat Pubs.
*__Who Owns Whom Directories, 6 vols.__ Dun & Bradstreet Staff. Incl. Vol. 1 Australia & Far East. 939p. 1995. 395.00 (*0-901491-24-1*); Vol. 2 North America. 1032p. 1995. 445.00 (*0-901491-19-5*); Vols. 3 & 4 United Kingdom. , 2 vols. 1376p. 1995. 395.00 (*0-901491-09-8*); Vols. 5 & 6 Continental Europe. , 2 vols. 1885p. 1995. 395.00 (*0-901491-14-4*); 1,300.00 (*0-614-25163-X*) Dun & Bradstreet.
Who Packed Your Parachute? Practical Advice from the Chronically Unemployed. Tony X. & Danny Y. (Illus.). 96p. 1995. pap. 7.00 (*1-887317-00-7*) Bad Dog Pr.
*__Who Paid for Modernism? Art, Money & the Fiction of Conrad, Joyce & Lawrence.__ Joyce P. Wexler. LC 96-33005. 1997. 24.00 (*1-55728-445-8*) U of Ark Pr.
Who Paid the Taxes, 1966-85? Joseph A. Pechman. LC 84-45845. (Studies of Government Finance). 84p. 1985. 26.95 (*0-8157-6998-9*); pap. 9.95 (*0-8157-6997-0*) Brookings.
Who Pays? Casino Gambling, Hidden Interests, & Organized Crime. Craig A. Zendzian. LC 93-19981. 162p. (C). 1993. lib. bdg. 42.50 (*0-911577-25-4*) Harrow & Heston.
Who Pays? The Burden of Environmental Cleanup & Pollution Control. Debra W. Struhsacker. 21p. 1994. pap. text ed. 10.00 (*1-886306-12-5*) Nevada Policy.
*__Who Pays for Development Fees & Exactions?__ Marla Dresch & Steven M. Sheffrin. LC 97-23718. 1997. write for info. (*0-9653184-7-8*) Pub Policy Inst.
Who Pays for Student Diversity? Population Changes & Educational Policy. Ed. by James G. Ward & Patricia Anthony. LC 91-35594. 280p. 1992. 49.95 (*0-8039-4019-X*, D1478) Corwin Pr.
Who Pays for the Kids? Gender & the Structure of Constraint. Nancy Folbre. LC 93-17207. (Economics As Social Theory Ser.). 336p. (C). (gr. 13). 1994. pap. 19.95 (*0-415-07565-3*); text ed. 74.95 (*0-415-07564-5*) Routledge.
Who Pays the Cost. Louis R. Rivera. (Illus.). 40p. (Orig.). 1977. pap. 2.00 (*0-917886-03-8*) Shamal Bks.
Who Pays the Price? The Sociocultural Context of the Environmental Crisis. Barbara R. Johnston. LC 94-14152. 1994. text ed. 45.00 (*1-55963-302-6*); pap. text ed. 19.00 (*1-55963-303-4*) Island Pr.
Who Pays the Price? The Cost of War in the Guatemalan Highlands. Washington Office on Latin America Staff. 107p. (Orig.). 1988. pap. 6.00 (*0-9613249-9-6*) WOLA.
Who Pays the Property Tax? A New View. Henry J. Aaron. LC 75-19270. (Studies of Government Finance). 122p. reprint ed. pap. 34.80 (*0-8357-7074-5*, 2033587) Bks Demand.
Who Pays? Who Profits? The Truth about the American Tax System: A Dialogue Between Rip Van Winkle VIII & Professor Derrick Van Bummel. Ralph W. Estes. LC 93-8024. (Illus.). 160p. (Orig.). 1993. pap. 8.95 (*0-89758-048-6*) Inst Policy Stud.
Who Plays? Who Pays? Who Cares? A Case Study in Applied Sociology, Political Economy, & the Community Mental Health Centers Movement. Sylvia Kenig. (Critical Approaches in the Health Social Sciences Ser.). 235p. 1992. text ed. 33.00 (*0-89503-093-4*); pap. text ed. 24.75 (*0-89503-092-6*) Baywood Pub.
Who Pocket Guide to Classification of Mental & Behavioural Disorders: With Glossary & Diagnostic Criteria for Research. Compiled by J. E. Cooper. 422p. 1994. pap. text ed. 26.95 (*0-88048-983-9*, 8983) Am Psychiatric.
Who Pretends? Charles Reasoner. (Sliding Surprise Ser.). (J). (ps up). 1996. 9.95 (*0-8431-3940-4*) Price Stern Sloan.
Who Profits from Profits? rev. ed. (Private Enterprise Market System Program Ser.). (Illus.). 66p. 1993. reprint ed. student ed. 4.00 (*0-614-13406-4*) Free Ent Partner.
Who Profits from Profits? rev. ed. (Private Enterprise Market System Program Ser.). (Illus.). 66p. 1993. reprint ed. teacher ed. 14.00 (*0-943447-14-3*) Free Ent Partner.
Who Prospers? How Cultural Values Shape Economic & Political Success. Lawrence E. Harrison. LC 91-58597. 288p. 1993. pap. text ed. 14.00 (*0-465-09167-9*) Basic.
*__WHO Psychiatric Disability Assessment Schedule (WHO/DAS) with a Guide to Its Use.__ WHO Staff. 88p. 1988. 16.00 (*92-4-156111-4*) World Health.
Who Publish in China? China Machine Pr. Staff. (C). 1988. 75.00 (*0-685-30237-7*, Pub. by China Machine Pr CH) St Mut.
*__Who Put All These Cucum.__ Wilson. 11.85 (*0-687-61321-3*) Abingdon.
Who Put All These Cucumbers in My Garden? Patricia F. Wilson. LC 83-51398. 144p. (Orig.). 1984. pap. 9.95 (*0-8358-0475-5*) Upper Room Bks.
Who Put Jesus on the Cross? Aiden W. Tozer. LC 95-67401. 1996. pap. 8.99 (*0-87509-599-2*) Chr Pubns.
Who Put That Hair in My Toothbrush. Jerry Spinelli. (J). (gr. 4-7). 1994. 5.95 (*0-316-80841-5*) Little.
Who Put the Butter in Butterfly? And Other Fearless Investigations into Our Illogical Language. David Feldman. LC 88-45575. 224p. 1990. reprint ed. pap. 10.00 (*0-06-091661-3*, PL) HarpC.
Who Put the Cannon in the Courthouse Square: A Guide to Uncovering the Past. Kay Cooper. LC 84-17251. (Illus.). (J). (gr. 4 up). 1984. lib. bdg. 12.85 (*0-8027-6561-0*) Walker & Co.
Who Put the Con in Consumer? David Sanford. 1972. 5.95 (*0-87140-550-4*) Liveright.
Who Put the Con in Consumer? David Sanford. 1972. pap. 2.95 (*0-87140-270-X*) Liveright.
Who Put the Pepper in the Pot? Joanna Cole. (Parents Magazine Press Read-Aloud Library). (Illus.). 42p. (J). (ps-3). 1992. lib. bdg. 17.27 (*0-8368-0883-5*) Gareth Stevens Inc.
*__Who Put the Pepper in the Pot?__ Joanna Cole. (Illus.). (J). (gr. 3). 1995. 7.92 (*0-395-73232-8*) HM.
Who Put the Pepper in the Pot? Joanna Cole. LC 88-36625. (Illus.). 48p. (J). (ps-3). 1989. 5.95 (*0-8193-1189-8*) Parents.
*__Who Put the Pepper in the Pot?__ large type ed. Joanna Cole. (Illus.). 62p. (J). (gr. 3). 15.50 (*0-614-20628-6*, L-38217-00 APHB) Am Printing Hse.
Who Put the Pizza in the VCR? Laughing Your Way Through Life's Little Emergencies. Martha Bolton. (Illus.). 140p. (Orig.). 1996. pap. 10.99 (*0-89283-958-9*, Vine Bks) Servant.
Who Put the Rainbow in the Wizard of Oz. Yip Harburg. 1995. pap. 18.95 (*0-472-08312-0*) U of Mich Pr.
Who Put the Rainbow in The Wizard of Oz? Yip Harburg, Lyricist. Harold Meyerson & Ernie Harburg. (Illus.). 550p. (C). 1993. 35.00 (*0-472-10482-9*) U of Mich Pr.
Who Reads Literature? The Future of the U. S. As a Nation of Readers. Nicholas Zill & Marianne Winglee. LC 90-33699. 104p. (Orig.). 1990. pap. 9.95 (*0-932020-86-0*) Seven Locks Pr.
Who Reads What? Charles H. Compton. LC 69-18923. (Essay Index Reprint Ser.). 1977. 17.95 (*0-8369-0012-X*) Ayer.
Who Really Discovered America? Stephen Krensky. (Illus.). 64p. (Orig.). (J). (gr. 4-6). 1987. pap. 2.50 (*0-590-40854-2*) Scholastic Inc.
Who Really Discovered America? Stephen Krensky. Ed. by Judy Donnelly. (Illus.). 64p. (Orig.). (J). (gr. 3-7). 1991. reprint ed. 12.95 (*0-8038-9306-X*) Hastings.
Who Really Has the Answer? Spiros Zodhiates. Orig. Title: Who Is Worth Following?. 153p. 1982. pap. 4.99 (*0-89957-514-5*) AMG Pubs.
*__Who Really Invented the Automobile: Skulduggery at the Crossroads.__ 2nd rev. ed. David Beasley. LC HD9710. A2B42 1966. (Illus.). 192p. 1997. pap. 13.95 (*0-915317-08-7*) Davus Pub.
Who Really Killed Chief Paulina? An Oregon Documentary. Dorsey Griffin. (Illus.). (Orig.). pap. 13.75 (*0-9640768-3-7*) C & P Press.
Who Really Killed Cock Canada. George. (J). 1991. 19.95 (*0-06-023874-7*, HarpT) HarpC.
Who Really Killed Cock Robin? Estelle Kleinman. Ed. by J. Friedland & R. Kessler. (Novel-Ties Ser.). 1995. student ed., pap. text ed. 15.95 (*1-56982-301-4*) Lrn Links.
Who Really Killed Cock Robin? An Ecological Mystery. Jean Craighead George. LC 90-38659. 176p. (J). (gr. 3-7). 1991. 15.00 (*0-06-021980-7*); lib. bdg. 14.89 (*0-06-021981-5*) HarpC Child Bks.
Who Really Killed Cock Robin? An Ecological Mystery. Jean Craighead George. LC 90-38659. (Trophy Bk.). 192p. (J). (gr. 3-7). 1992. pap. 4.50 (*0-06-440405-6*, Trophy) HarpC Child Bks.
Who Really Rules? New Have & Community Power Reexamined. G. William Domhoff. 190p. (C). 1978. pap. 32.95 (*0-87620-965-7*) Transaction Pubs.
Who Really Said. Michael Ryan. 78p. (Orig.). 1993. pap. 7.95 (*1-56245-032-8*) Great Quotations.
Who Remembers the Sea. Mohammed Dib. Tr. by Louis Tremaine from FRE. LC 85-50529. 122p. 1985. 18.00 (*0-89410-444-6*, Three Contnts) Lynne Rienner.
Who Rides a Tiger? Doris M. Disney. 1989. mass mkt. 3.50 (*0-8217-2799-0*, Zebra Kensgtn) Kensgtn Pub Corp.
*__Who Rides with Wyatt.__ Will Henry. 208p. 1997. mass mkt. 3.99 (*0-8439-4292-4*, Leisure Bks) Dorchester Pub Co.
Who Robbed America? A Citizen's Guide to the Savings & Loan Scandal. Michael Waldman. 160p. 1990. pap. 10.95 (*0-679-73482-1*) Random.
Who Rock Score. (Illus.). 80p. 1989. pap. 15.95 (*0-7119-2096-6*, AM77793) Music Sales.
Who Rules America? J. McConaughey. 1980. lib. bdg. 150.00 (*0-8490-3205-9*) Gordon Pr.
*__Who Rules America Now?__ G. William Domhoff. 230p. (C). 1997. reprint ed. pap. text ed. 10.95 (*0-88133-938-5*) Waveland Pr.
Who Rules America Now? A View for the Eighties. G. William Domhoff. 230p. (Orig.). (YA). (gr. 9-12). 1983. pap. 7.95 (*0-13-958405-6*, Spectrum IN) Macmillan Gen Ref.
Who Rules Britain? John Scott. 200p. (C). 1991. 52.95 (*0-7456-0302-5*); pap. 27.95 (*0-7456-0563-X*) Blackwell Pubs.
Who Rules Japan? The Inner Circles of Economic & Political Power. Harold R. Kerbo & John A. McKinstry. LC 95-7988. 256p. 1995. text ed. 24.95 (*0-275-94903-6*, Praeger Pubs) Greenwood.
Who Runs for Congress: Ambition, Context, & Candidate Emergence. Ed. by Thomas Kazee. 209p. 1994. 38.95 (*0-87187-985-9*); pap. text ed. 23.95 (*0-87187-984-0*) Congr Quarterly.
Who Runs Our Schools? The Changing Face of Educational Leadership. George Kaplan. 98p. 1989. 12.00 (*0-937846-68-6*) Inst Educ Lead.
Who Runs Professional Sports: The NFL. Ed. by Marie T. Finn & Jeffrey E. Long. LC 92-12044. 350p. (Orig.). 1995. pap. 21.95 (*0-931398-33-9*) Forster-Long.
Who Runs the Rivers: Dams & Decisions in the New West. Andrews & Sansone. 452p. 1983. 12.00 (*0-318-04411-0*) Stanford Enviro.
Who Runs the University? The Politics of Higher Education in Hawaii, 1985-1992. David Yount. LC 95-43780. 1996. 29.95 (*0-8248-1786-9*) UH Pr.
Who Runs the University? The Politics of Higher Education in Hawaii, 1985-1992. David Yount. LC 95-43780. 1996. pap. 19.95 (*0-8248-1821-0*) UH Pr.
Who Said Boo? Halloween Poems for the Very Young. Nancy W. Carlstrom. (J). 1995. 14.00 (*0-689-80308-7*, Aladdin Paperbacks) S&S Childrens.
Who Said It Would Be Easy? One Woman's Life in the Political Arena. Elizabeth Holtzman & Cynthia C. Holtzman. (Illus.). 288p. 1996. lib. bdg. 24.95 (*1-55970-302-4*) Arcade Pub Inc.
Who Said Life Is Fair? Jean Thesman. 160p. 1987. mass mkt. 3.50 (*0-380-75088-0*, Flare) Avon.
Who Said Meow? Maria Polushkin. LC 87-28073. (Illus.). 32p. (J). (ps). 1988. lib. bdg. 13.95 (*0-02-774770-0*, Bradbury S&S) S&S Childrens.
*__Who Said Moo?__ Harriet Ziefert. (Illus.). 16p. (J). (ps-1). 1997. 5.95 (*0-694-00854-0*, Festival) HarpC Child Bks.
Who Said Moo? A Lift-the-Flap Book. Harriet Ziefert. (Illus.). 16p. (J). (ps-1). 1996. 11.95 (*0-694-00846-X*, Festival) HarpC Child Bks.
Who Said Red? Mary Serfozo. LC 88-9345. (Illus.). 32p. (J). (ps-1). 1988. lib. bdg. 15.00 (*0-689-50455-1*, McElderry) S&S Childrens.

W

Who Said Red? Mary Serfozo. LC 91-21160. (Illus.). 32p. (J). (ps-1). 1992. reprint ed. pap. 4.95 (0-689-71592-7, Aladdin Paperbacks) S&S Childrens.

Who Said Red? Big Book. Mary Serfozo. LC 91-21160. (Illus.). 32p. (J). (ps-1). 1992. reprint ed. pap. 18.95 (0-689-71651-6, Aladdin Paperbacks) S&S Childrens.

Who Said That? (Illus.). (J). (ps-2). 1991. lib. bdg. 7.95 (0-8136-5142-5) Modern Curr.

Who Said That? Robert Burleigh. LC 96-19985. (J). 1996. 15.95 (0-8050-4394-2) H Holt & Co.

Who Said That? A Book of Irish Lists. Robert Duffy. 104p. 8700. pap. 8.95 (0-905169-99-9, Pub. by Poolbeg Pr IE) Dufour.

Who Said That? More Than 2500 Usable Quotes & Illustrations. George Sweeting. 1995. pap. 15.99 (0-8024-9199-5) Moody.

***Who Said That? The Remarkable True Stories Behind the Most Familiar Quotations in the English Language.** Joey West. LC 96-38923. 1997. write for info. (0-517-18212-2) Crown Pub Group.

***Who Said That Mexican Food Is Fattening? Take the Fear & Fat Out of Mexican Food.** Julie Loera. Ed. by Robby Johnson. 100p. 1996. pap. 9.95 (0-9655256-0-0) RJL Bks.

Who Said Women Can't Teach? Charles Trombley. LC 85-72150. 235p. 1986. pap. 7.95 (0-88270-584-9) Bridge-Logos.

Who Sank the Boat? Pamela Allen. (Illus.). 32p. (J). (ps-3). 1996. pap. 4.95 (0-698-11373-X, Paperstar) Putnam Pub Group.

Who Saw Him Die? J. P. Gregson. 1994. 19.00 (0-7278-4606-X) Severn Hse.

Who Says? Kirsten Hall & Jessica Flaxman. (My First Reader Ser.). (Illus.). 28p. (J). (ps-2). 1990. pap. 3.95 (0-516-45362-9); lib. bdg. 15.50 (0-516-05362-0) Childrens.

Who Says: Essays on Pivotal Issues in Contemporary Storytelling. Carol L. Birch & Melissa A. Heckler. 1996. pap. text ed. 16.95 (0-87483-454-6) August Hse.

Who Says: Essays on Pivotal Issues in Contemporary Storytelling. Carol L. Birch & Melissa A. Heckler. 1996. 26.95 (0-87483-453-8) August Hse.

***Who Says a Dog Goes Bow-Wow?** Hank De Zutter. (Illus.). 32p. (J). 1997. pap. 5.99 (0-440-41338-9) Dell.

Who Says Girls Can't? The Girl's Guide to Women's Issues. Catherine Dee. LC 96-27958. 1997. write for info. (0-316-17979-5) Little.

Who Says Homework Can't Be Fun? Grade 1-4. Carol George et al. (Illus.). 110p. (Orig.). 1989. pap. 9.95 (0-673-38742-9, GoodYrBooks) Addson-Wesley Educ.

Who Says I Can't? Mary C. Ryan. 160p. (YA). (gr. 12 up). 1990. mass mkt. 2.95 (0-380-70804-3, Flare) Avon.

Who Says I Can't? Mary C. Ryan. 160p. (YA). (gr. 12 up). 1988. 12.95 (0-316-76374-8) Little.

Who Says It's a Woman's Job to Clean? Don A. Aslett. LC 86-1717. (Illus.). 116p. (Orig.). 1986. pap. 5.95 (0-89879-215-0) Marsh Creek Pr.

Who Says Men Don't Talk or Listen? Safe-Talk Guidelines. Richard B. Austin, Jr. Ed. by Connie L. Schmidt. 46p. (Orig.). (C). 1993. pap. text ed. 9.95 (0-614-11344-X) Brockton Pubng.

Who Says Moo? Ruth Young. LC 94-11878. (Illus.). 32p. (J). (ps-3). 1994. pap. 13.99 (0-670-85162-0) Viking Child Bks.

***Who Says Moo?** Ruth Young. 1997. pap. 4.99 (0-14-050113-4) Viking Penguin.

Who Says Moo? A Beginner's Book of Rhymes. Muriel Kalish & Lionel Kalish. LC 92-10145. (Illus.). 12p. (J). (ps-1). 1993. 7.95 (0-590-44917-6) Scholastic Inc.

Who Says So? Bob Jones, 3rd. (Orig.). 1996. pap. 3.25 (0-89084-875-0, 097840) Bob Jones Univ Pr.

Who Says So? Communication Skills. Ed. by P. Pepperell. (C). 1989. 70.00 (0-09-173060-0, Pub. by S Thornes Pubs UK) St Mut.

Who Says There Are No Jobs Out There? 25 Irreverent Rules for Getting a Job. Bob Weinstein. LC 96-33055. (Illus.). 256p. 1996. pap. text ed. 12.95 (0-07-069209-2) McGraw.

Who Says This? The Authority of the Author, the Discourse, & the Reader. Welsh D. Everman. LC 87-19285. (Crosscurrents-Modern Critiques, Third Ser.). 160p. 1988. text ed. 19.95 (0-8093-1444-4) S Ill U Pr.

Who Says This Is Cheating? Anybody's Sport Ethics Book. Sharon K. Stoll. 128p. 1993. per. 12.95 (0-8403-8521-8) Kendall-Hunt.

***Who Says What & the Question of Voice.** Denis Donoghue. 48p. 9200. pap. 8.95 (0-86140-365-7, Pub. by Colin Smythe Ltd UK) Dufour.

Who Says You Can't Teach Science? Grades K-6. Alan Ticotsky. (Illus.). 80p. (Orig.). 1985. pap. 9.95 (0-673-18107-3, GoodYrBooks) Addson-Wesley Educ.

"Who Set You Flowin'" The African-American Migration Narrative. Fara J. Griffin. (Race & American Culture Ser.). (Illus.). 248p. (C). 1996. pap. 14.95 (0-19-508897-2) OUP.

Who Set You Flowin? The African-American Migration Narrative. Farah J. Griffin. (Race & American Culture Ser.). (Illus.). 248p. 1995. 35.00 (0-19-508896-4) OUP.

Who Sets Prices? (Illus.). 60p. (YA). (gr. 9-12). 1996. teacher ed. 14.00 (0-943447-10-0) Free Ent Partner.

Who Sets Prices? rev. ed. (Illus.). 60p. (YA). (gr. 9-12). 1996. reprint ed. student ed. 4.00 (0-614-13407-2) Free Ent Partner.

***Who Shall Live: Health, Economics & Social Choice.** 2nd ed. 200p. 1997. text ed. 26.00 (981-02-3201-2) World Scientific Pub.

Who Shall Live? Medicine, Technology, Ethics. Houston Conference on Ethics in Medicine & Technology Staff. Ed. by Kenneth Vaux. LC 70-99463. 213p. reprint ed. pap. 60.80 (0-685-16039-4, 2026841) Bks Demand.

Who Shall Live? The Wilhelm Bachner Story. Samuel P. Oliner & Kathleen M. Lee. LC 96-24750. 277p. 1996. 25.00 (0-89733-437-X) Academy Chi Pubs.

Who Shall Live, Who Shall Die. Daniel Stern. LC 94-13178. (First Rediscovered Modern Masterpieces Edition Ser.). 319p. 1994. 22.50 (0-89263-329-8); pap. 11.95 (0-89263-330-1) Tex A&M Univ Pr.

Who Shares? Ed. by Donald W. Attwood & B. S. Baviskar. (Oxford India Paperbacks Ser.). 442p. 1993. pap. 15.95 (0-19-563200-1) OUP.

Who Shares Your Birthday? Famous Birthdays Listed for Each Day of the Year. Glenn Anton & Debra Anton. LC 94-18202. 176p. 1994. pap. 12.95 (0-9637195-2-1, Kingsley Pr) Anton Enterprises.

Who Shot the President? The Death of John F. Kennedy. Judy Donnelly. LC 88-4418. (Step into Reading Bks.). (Illus.). 48p. (Orig.). (J). (gr. 2-4). 1988. lib. bdg. 7.99 (0-394-99944-4) Random Bks Yng Read.

Who Shot the President? The Death of John F. Kennedy. Judy Donnelly. LC 88-4418. (Step into Reading Bks.). (Illus.). 48p. (Orig.). (J). (gr. 2-4). 1988. pap. 3.99 (0-394-89944-X) Random Bks Yng Read.

***Who Shot the Sheriff.** Phil R. Cox. (Solve It Yourself Ser.). (Illus.). 48p. (J). (gr. 6 up). 1997. pap. 6.95 (0-7460-2695-1, Usborne); lib. bdg. 14.95 (0-88110-912-6, Usborne) EDC.

Who Shot the Sheriff? The Rise & Fall of the Television Western. J. Fred MacDonald. LC 86-18230. 172p. 1986. text ed. 42.95 (0-275-92326-6, C2326, Praeger Pubs) Greenwood.

Who Should Be Liable: A Guide to Policy for Dealing with Risk, 1989. 1989. pap. 10.50 (0-87186-089-9) Comm Econ Dev.

Who Should Decide? Paternalism in Health Care. James F. Childress. 264p. 1985. pap. text ed. 19.95 (0-19-503976-9) OUP.

Who Should I Listen To: Readings for Early Teens on Identifying Truth from Lies. Kevin W. Johnson. (J). (gr. 6-9). 1993. pap. 6.99 (1-55661-283-4) Bethany Hse.

Who Should Melissa Marry? Bruce Cassiday. LC 94-12616. 1994. 18.95 (1-55972-259-2) Carol Pub Group.

***Who Should Run the Health Service? Realignment & Reconstruction.** Olusola O. Oni. LC 96-33577. 1996. write for info. (1-85775-169-8, Radcliffe Med Pr) Scovill Paterson.

Who Should We Treat? Law, Patients, & Resources in the NHS. Christopher Newdick. 320p. 1995. 74.00 (0-19-825924-7); pap. 26.00 (0-19-825925-5) OUP.

Who Shrank My Grandmother's House? Poems of Discovery. Barbara J. Esbensen. LC 90-39631. (Illus.). 48p. (J). (gr. 3-7). 1992. 15.00 (0-06-021827-4) HarpC Child Bks.

Who Sleeps in the City? Lynne Bertrand. (Illus.). 26p. (J). (ps). 1994. 9.95 (1-881527-48-4) Chapters Pub.

Who Speaks for Earth? Barbara Ward. Ed. by Maurice F. Strong. 160p. 1973. pap. 1.95 (0-393-09341-7) Norton.

Who Speaks for Earth? Barbara Ward. Ed. by Maurice F. Strong. 160p. 1973. 6.95 (0-393-06392-5) Norton.

Who Speaks for God? Charles Colson. 283p. 1994. mass mkt. 5.99 (0-8423-8033-7) Tyndale.

***Who Speaks for God? An Alternative to the Religious Right: a New Politics of Compassion, Community, & Civility.** Jim Wallis. 240p. 1997. pap. 10.95 (0-385-31693-3) Doubleday.

Who Speaks for God? Confronting the World with Real Christianity. Charles Colson. LC 85-71892. 192p. (Orig.). 1985. pap. 10.99 (0-89107-372-8) Crossway Bks.

Who Speaks for God? The New Spiritual Politics Beyond the Religious Right. Jim Wallis. 144p. 1996. 17.95 (0-385-31690-9) Delacorte.

Who Speaks for the Child? The Problems of Proxy Consent. Ed. by Willard Gaylin & Ruth Macklin. (Hastings Center Series in Ethics). 328p. 1982. 52.50 (0-306-40860-0, Plenum Pr) Plenum.

Who Speaks for the Children? Kids in the System. Peter Silverman. 224p. 1989. pap. 14.95 (0-7737-5257-9) Genl Dist Srvs.

Who Speaks for the Children? The Handbook of Individual & Class Child Advocacy. Ed. by Jack C. Westman. LC 90-52847. 392p. 1991. 39.20 (0-943158-48-6, WSCBP) Pro Resource.

Who Speaks for the Vanquished? American Jewish Leaders & the Holocaust. Leon W. Wells. Ed. by Michael Ryan. 350p. (Orig.). (C). 1988. text ed. 56.00 (0-8204-0728-3) P Lang Pubng.

Who Speaks for the Witch? Gavin Frost & Yvonne Frost. (Illus.). 60p. (Orig.). 1992. pap. text ed. 5.00 (0-9630657-3-4) Godolphin Hse.

Who Speaks for Tokyo Bay? Ed. by Blair T. Bower & Takao Katsuki. (IFIAS Coastal Waters Ser.: No. 3). (Illus.). 156p. (C). 1993. text ed. 70.00 (90-5410-130-X, Pub. by A A Balkema NE) Ashgate Pub Co.

Who Speaks for Wolf: A Native American Learning Story. 2nd rev. ed. Paula Underwood. Ed. by Jeanne L. Slobod. LC 91-65522. (Three Learning Stories Ser.). (Illus.). 51p. 1991. reprint ed. pap. 12.00 (1-879678-01-2) Tribe Two Pr.

Who Spilled That Stuff? The Muffin Family Learns about Forgiving. Gilbert V. Beers. (J). 1995. pap. 2.99 (1-56476-316-1, 6-3316, Victor Bks) Chariot Victor.

Who Spirits This Place? P. Nabokov. LC 90-55770. 20.00 (0-06-250646-3, HarpT); pap. 10.00 (0-06-250722-2, PL) HarpC.

Who Spoke Up? American Protest Against the War in Vietnam 1963-1975. Nancy Zaroulis & Gerald Sullivan. LC 85-8474. 480p. 1985. pap. 10.95 (0-03-005603-9) H Holt & Co.

Who Started the First World War? Harry E. Barnes. 1985. lib. bdg. 79.95 (0-87700-651-2) Revisionist Pr.

Who Stole a Bloater? Frances Thomas. 71p. 1991. 21.00 (1-85411-066-7, Pub. by Seren Bks UK) Dufour.

Who Stole Feminism? How Women Have Betrayed Women. Christina H. Sommers. 320p. 1994. 23.00 (0-671-79424-8) S&S Trade.

Who Stole Feminism? How Women Have Betrayed Women. Christina H. Sommers. 1995. pap. 12.00 (0-684-80156-6, Touchstone Bks) S&S Trade.

Who Stole Home Plate? Steven Otfinoski. (Southside Sluggers Ser.). (Illus.). 112p. (J). (gr. 2-6). 1992. pap. 2.95 (0-671-72932-2, S&S Bks Young Read) S&S Childrens.

Who Stole the American Dream: The Book Your Boss Doesn't Want You to Read. Burke Hedges. 1992. pap. 9.95 (0-9632667-0-5) Intl Netwk Train.

Who Stole the Black Diamond? Phil Roxbee-Cox. (Solve It Yourself Ser.). 48p. (YA). (gr. 6 up). 1996. lib. bdg. 14.95 (0-88110-829-4, Usborne) EDC.

Who Stole the Black Diamond? Phil Roxbee-Cox. (Solve It Yourself Ser.). (YA). (gr. 6 up). 1996. pap. 6.95 (0-7460-2053-8, Usborne) EDC.

Who Stole the Cookies? Judith Moffatt. LC 95-20847. (All Aboard Reading Ser.: Level 1). 32p. (J). (ps-1). 1996. pap. 3.95 (0-448-41127-X, G&D) Putnam Pub Group.

Who Stole the News? Why We Can't Keep Up with What Happens in the World & What We Can Do About It. Mort Rosenblum. LC 93-15559. 298p. 1995. pap. text ed. 14.95 (0-471-12032-4) Wiley.

Who Stole the Wizard of Oz? Avi. LC 81-884. (Illus.). 128p. (J). (gr. 3-6). 1990. reprint ed. pap. 4.99 (0-394-84992-2) Random Bks Yng Read.

***Who Stole the 2134.** D. R. Ayres. (Railroad Fiction Ser.: Vol. 2). (Illus.). 266p. 1997. pap. 8.95 (0-943857-09-0) D R Ayres.

Who Stole Wizard. Houghton Mifflin Company Staff. (Literature Experience 1993 Ser.). (J). (gr. 4). 1992. pap. 9.16 (0-395-61806-1) HM.

Who Stopped the Clock? The Seventy Weeks of Daniel. Vic Lockman. (Illus.). 24p. 1993. 3.00 (0-936175-21-4) V Lockman.

Who Succeeds in Science: The Gender Dimension. Gerhard Sonnert. LC 95-8598. 248p. (C). 1995. text ed. 50.00 (0-8135-2219-6); pap. text ed. 16.95 (0-8135-2220-X) Rutgers U Pr.

***Who Supports the Family: Gender & Breadwinning in Dual-Earner Marriages.** Jean L. Potuchek. LC 96-34115. 1997. write for info. (0-8047-2835-6); pap. write for info. (0-8047-2836-4) Stanford U Pr.

Who Survives Cancer? Howard P. Greenwald. 1992. 30.00 (0-520-07725-3) U CA Pr.

Who Switched the Price Tags? Anthony Campolo. 200p. 1987. pap. 10.99 (0-8499-3088-X) Word Pub.

Who Talks Funny? A Book about Languages for Kids. Brenda S. Cox. LC 94-5379. xii, 202p. 1995. lib. bdg. 25.00 (0-208-02378-X, Linnet Bks) Shoe String.

Who Tampered with the Bible? Patricia G. Eddy. LC 92-59949. 200p. 1993. pap. 10.95 (1-55523-573-5) Winston-Derek.

Who Taught Frogs to Hop? A Child's Book about God. Robert D. Ingram. LC 89-82552. (Illus.). 32p. (J). (ps). 1990. pap. 5.99 (0-8066-2457-4, 9-2457) Augsburg Fortress.

Who Taught You about Money? Richard Harris. 48p. (Orig.). 1994. pap. 8.95 (1-878901-91-5) Hampton Roads Pub Co.

Who Tells the Truth? A Collection of Logical Puzzles to Make You Think. Adam Case. 39p. (J). 1991. 4.95 (0-906212-77-4, Pub. by Tarquin UK) Parkwest Pubns.

***Who the Devil Made It.** Peter Bogdanovich. LC 96-36442. (Illus.). 847p. 1997. 39.95 (0-679-44706-7) Knopf.

***Who the Hell Is Brandon Freels.** Frandon Freels. 28p. 1996. 3.00 (0-9653194-2-3) Future Tense.

Who Told You That You Were Naked? Freedom from Judgement, Guilt & Fear of Punishment. John J. Raub. 160p. (C). 1990. 49.00 (0-85439-423-0, Pub. by St Paul Pubns UK) St Mut.

Who Told You That You Were Naked? Freedom from Judgment, Guilt, & Fear of Punishment. John J. Raub. 128p. (Orig.). 1992. pap. 11.95 (0-8245-1203-0) Crossroad NY.

Who Took Apple Frapple's Cookbook? Professor Glugg. LC 92-73242. (Galactic Glue Glugg Stories Ser.). (Illus.). 32p. (Orig.). (J). (ps up). 1992. pap. 3.95 (1-881905-00-4) Glue Bks.

***Who Took Henry & Mr. Z?** Dave Glaze. (J). 1997. pap. 5.95 (1-55050-107-0, Pub. by Coteau CN) Genl Dist Srvs.

Who Took the Cookies from the Cookie Jar? Rozanne L. Williams. (Emergent Reader Bks.). 8p. (J). (gr. k-2). 1995. 1.59 (0-916119-87-4) Creat Teach Pr.

Who Took the Cookies from the Cookie Jar? Rozanne L. Williams. (Emergent Reader Big Bks.). (Illus.). 8p. (Orig.). (J). (gr. k-2). 1995. pap. 7.98 (1-57471-059-1) Creat Teach Pr.

Who Took the Farmer's Hat? Joan L. Nodset. LC 62-17964. (Illus.). 32p. (J). (ps-3). 1963. lib. bdg. 14.89 (0-06-024566-2) HarpC Child Bks.

Who Took the Farmer's Hat? Joan L. Nodset. LC 62-17964. (Trophy Picture Bk.). (Illus.). 32p. (J). (ps-2). 1988. pap. 5.95 (0-06-443174-6, Trophy) HarpC Child Bks.

***Who Took the Farmer's Hat?** Joan L. Nodset. (Illus.). (J). (ps-3). 1963. 7.79 (0-06-024565-4, 678598) HarpC.

Who Touched the Remote Control? Television & Christian Choices for Children & Adults Who Care about Children. Mary Duckert. 1990. pap. 9.95 (0-377-00210-0) Friendship Pr.

Who Uses Drugs? Nancy K. Mello. (Encyclopedia of Psychoactive Drugs Ser.: No. 2). 112p. (YA). (gr. 7 up). 1988. lib. bdg. 19.95 (1-55546-223-5) Chelsea Hse.

Who Uses This? Margaret Miller. LC 89-30456. (Illus.). 40p. (J). (ps up). 1990. lib. bdg. 14.93 (0-688-08279-3) Greenwillow.

Who Voted? The Dynamics of Electoral Turnout, 1870-1980. Paul Kleppner. Ed. by Gerald M. Pomper. LC 82-3740. (American Political Parties & Elections Ser.). 254p. 1981. text ed. 52.95 (0-275-90661-2, C0661, Praeger Pubs) Greenwood.

Who Votes? Raymond E. Wolfinger & Steven J. Rosenstone. LC 79-48068. 160p. 1980. pap. 12.00 (0-300-02552-1) Yale U Pr.

Who Wakes Rooster? Clare H. Meeker. LC 95-19192. (Illus.). (J). (ps-1). 1996. 13.00 (0-689-80541-1, S&S Bks Young Read) S&S Childrens.

Who Walk with the Earth. Dorsha Hayes. LC 74-26112. (Labor Movement in Fiction & Non-Fiction Ser.). reprint ed. 45.00 (0-404-58438-1) AMS Pr.

Who Wants a Cheap Rhinoceros? rev. ed. Shel Silverstein. LC 82-23945. (Illus.). 64p. (J). (ps-3). 1983. lib. bdg. 15.00 (0-02-782690-2, Mac Bks Young Read) S&S Childrens.

Who Wants an Old Teddy Bear? Ginnie Hofmann. LC 80-10445. (Pictureback Ser.). (Illus.). 32p. (J). (ps-3). 1980. pap. 3.25 (0-394-83925-0) Random Bks Yng Read.

Who Wants Arthur? (J). (gr. 2 up). 1995. 39.93 incl. cd-rom (0-8368-1334-0) Gareth Stevens Inc.

Who Wants Arthur? Amanda Graham. LC 86-42812. (Illus.). 32p. (J). (gr. 2-3). 1987. lib. bdg. 18.60 (1-55532-868-7) Gareth Stevens Inc.

Who Wants One? Mary Serfozo. LC 88-26614. (Illus.). 32p. (J). (ps-1). 1989. lib. bdg. 15.00 (0-689-50474-8, McElderry) S&S Childrens.

Who Wants One? Mary Serfozo. LC 92-4341. (Illus.). 32p. (J). (ps-1). 1992. reprint ed. pap. 4.95 (0-689-71642-7, Aladdin Paperbacks) S&S Childrens.

Who Wants One? Big Book. Mary Serfozo. LC 92-4341. (Illus.). 32p. (J). (ps-1). 1992. reprint ed. pap. 18.95 (0-689-71652-4, Aladdin Paperbacks) S&S Childrens.

Who Wants to Be a Prairie Dog? Haisha'taa K'ad Dloo' Silii? Ann N. Clark. 64p. (J). (gr. 2-4). 1994. pap. 9.00 (0-9644189-0-8) Salina Bkshelf.

***Who Wants to Buy a Water Company? From Public to Private Control in New Haven.** Dorothy McCluskey & Claire Bennitt. 144p. 1996. 13.95 (1-887750-39-8) Rutledge Bks.

Who Wants to Live. Mendel Weinbach. 202p. 1993. 12.95 (1-56871-002-X); pap. 9.95 (1-56871-003-8) Targum Pr.

Who Wants to Nap? E. Greenleaf. LC 68-56820. (Illus.). 32p. (J). (gr. 2-3). lib. bdg. 9.95 (0-87783-050-9) Oddo.

Who Was a Jew? Rabbinic & Halakhic Perspectives on the Jewish-Christian Schism. Lawrence H. Schiffman. (Illus.). 140p. 1985. 19.95 (0-88125-053-8); pap. 14.95 (0-88125-054-6) Ktav.

Who Was David Weiser? Pawel Huelle. Tr. by Michael Kandel. 1992. 17.95 (0-685-51157-X) HarBrace.

Who Was David Weiser? Pawel Huelle. 1994. pap. 12.95 (0-15-600127-6) HarBrace.

***Who Was Eleanor Rigby: And 908 More Questions & Answers about the Beatles.** Brandon Toropov. LC 96-24982. 224p. 1997. pap. 60.00 (0-06-273141-6, PL) HarpC.

Who Was Eleanor Rigby? And 998 More Questions & Answers about the Beatles. Brandon Toropov. LC 96-24982. 224p. (Orig.). 1997. pap. 10.00 (0-06-273442-3, Harper Ref) HarpC.

Who Was I? Creating a Living History Persona. Cathy Johnson. (Illus.). 52p. (Orig.). 1995. pap. 8.95 (0-9638158-1-4) Graphics-Fine Art.

Who Was Jesus? Diana Bohn. (Great Big Bks.). (Illus.). 16p. (J). 1995. pap. 14.95 (0-687-07067-8) Abingdon.

Who Was Jesus? N. T. Wright. 116p. (Orig.). (C). 1993. pap. 9.00 (0-8028-0694-5) Eerdmans.

Who Was Jesus? The Historical Jesus & the Synoptic Gospel. Hendrikus Boers. 1996. 37.95 (0-06-060809-9) Bks Intl VA.

Who Was Jolly Holiday? Ted C. Hindmarsh. LC 86-81774. 80p. 1986. pap. 5.50 (0-88290-281-4) Horizon Utah.

***Who Was Nancy?** McRae. 1992. pap. text ed. write for info. (0-17-556000-5) Addison-Wesley.

Who was Responsible? & Stories, Vol. 9. Maggie S. Fullilove & Mary E. Spencer. LC 94-12994. (African American Women Writers 1910-1940 Ser.). 1996. 30.00 (0-8161-1630-X) G K Hall.

Who Was Shakespeare? Hilda Amphlett. LC 72-126768. reprint ed. 32.50 (0-404-00325-7) AMS Pr.

Who Was That Lady I Saw You With? Manuscript Edition. Norman Krasna. 1959. pap. 13.00 (0-8222-1247-1) Dramatists Play.

Who Was That Man? A Present for Mr. Oscar Wilde. Neil Bartlett. 256p. 1992. pap. 14.95 (1-85242-123-1) Serpents Tail.

Who Was That Masked Man, Anyway? Avi. 176p. (J). 1994. pap. 3.99 (0-380-72113-9, Camelot) Avon.

Who Was That Masked Man, Anyway? Avi. LC 92-7942. 176p. (J). (gr. 4 up). 1992. 15.95 (0-531-05457-8); lib. bdg. 16.99 (0-531-08607-0) Orchard Bks Watts.

Who Was That Masked Man Anyway? large type ed. Avi. 1995. 45.50 (0-614-09615-4, L-81864-00) Am Printing Hse.

Who Was That Masked Woman. Noretta Koertge. 256p. 1981. pap. 8.95 (0-312-87033-7) St Martin.

Who Was the Pharoah of the Exodus? Jeff J. Williams. 144p. 1994. 11.98 (0-88290-488-4, 1042) Horizon Utah.

Who Was When? 3rd ed. Ed. by Miriam A. De Ford & Joan S. Jackson. LC 76-2404. 184p. 1976. 53.00 (0-8242-0532-4) Wilson.

Who Was Who, Vol. 8. 1992. text ed. 99.95 (0-312-06818-2) St Martin.

Who Was Who, 13 vols., Vol. 11. Ed. by Marquis Who's Who Staff. 1996. 90.00 (0-8379-0225-8) Marquis.

***Who Was Who: A Past Life Directory Based on the Edgar Cayce Discourses.** Elyse Curtis. xiv, 454p. (Orig.). 1997. pap. 49.95 (0-9657282-1-8, 101) Astral Projections.

W

Who Was Who: Companion to Who's Who, 7 vols., Set. Incl. 1897-1915. 4th ed. 790p. 1969. 99.95 (0-312-87570-3); 1916-1928. 3rd ed. 2640p. 1969. 99.95 (0-312-87605-X); 1941-1950. rev. ed. 2640p. 1969. text ed. 99.95 (0-312-87675-0); 1951-1960. 2640p. 1969. 99.95 (0-312-87710-2); 1961-1970. 1972. 99.95 (0-312-87745-5); 1971-1980. 950p. 1981. 99.95 (0-312-87746-3); 1970. 599.00 (0-312-87535-5) St Martin.

Who Was Who: Cumulative Index. 1992. 99.95 (0-312-06817-4) St Martin.

Who Was Who: Index 1607 - 1996. Ed. by Marquis Who's Who Staff. 1996. 45.00 (0-8379-0226-6) Marquis.

Who Was Who among English & European Authors, 1931-1949, 3 vols. LC 77-280. (Composite Biographical Dictionary Ser.: No. 2). 1584p. 1978. 240.00 (0-8103-0400-7) Gale.

Who Was Who at Ellis Island: A Survey. Barry Moreno. (Illus.). 150p. (Orig.). 1995. pap. 17.95 (0-9646079-0-5) Bellona Pr.

Who Was Who During the American Revolution. Compiled by Who's Who in America Editors. LC 75-34514. (Illus.). 448p. 1976. 19.95 (0-672-52216-0, Bobbs) Macmillan.

Who Was Who in America: A Series Providing Concise Biographies of the Outstanding Individuals of America's Past...from 1607 to the Present, 13 vols., Set, Set. Incl. Vol. 1. 1897-1942. Ed. by Marquis Who's Who Staff. 1408p. 1966. reprint ed. 90.00 (0-8379-0201-0, 030103); Vol. 2. 1943-1950. Ed. by Marquis Who's Who Staff. 614p. 1966. 90.00 (0-8379-0213-4, 030104); Vol. 3. 1951-1960. Ed. by Marquis Who's Who Staff. 959p. 1966. 90.00 (0-8379-0203-7, 030105); Vol. 4. 1961-1968. Marquis Who's Who Staff. 1236p. 1969. 90.00 (0-8379-0204-5, 030106); Vol. 5. 1969-1973. Ed. by Marquis Who's Who Staff. 1031p. 1973. 90.00 (0-8379-0205-3, 030131); Vol. 6. 1974-1976. Ed. by Marquis Who's Who Staff. 673p. 1976. 90.00 (0-8379-0207-X, 030185); Vol. 7. 1977-1981. Ed. by Marquis Who's Who Staff. 636p. 1981. 90.00 (0-8379-0210-X, 030209); Vol. 8. 1982-1985. Ed. by Marquis Who's Who Staff. 441p. 1985. 90.00 (0-8379-0214-2, 030301); Vol. 9. 1985-1989. 392p. 1989. 90.00 (0-8379-0217-7, 030491); Historical Vol. 1607-1896. Ed. by Marquis Who's Who Staff. 1966. 90.00 (0-8379-0200-2, 0437); Index Vol. 1607-1996. 1989. 37.50 (0-8379-0218-5, 030492); Vol. 10. 1989-1993. 402p. 1993. 90.00 (0-8379-0220-7); 999.95 (0-8379-0224-X, 030451) Marquis.

***Who Was Who in America Vol. XI & Index.** Marquis Who's Who Staff. 1996. 135.00 (0-8379-0227-4) Marquis.

Who Was Who in America, 1607-1993, 12 vols. 10th ed. 1993. Set. 767.50 (0-8379-0222-3) Marquis.

Who Was Who in America, 1607-1993, 2 vols., Index vol., 283p. 10th ed. 1993. 42.50 (0-8379-0221-5) Marquis.

Who Was Who in American Art. Ed. by Peter H. Falk. LC 85-50119. (Illus.). 744p. 1985. lib. bdg. 115.00 (0-932087-00-0) Sound View Pr.

Who Was Who in Journalism: Nineteen Twenty-Five to Nineteen Twenty-Eight. LC 78-13580. (Composite Biographical Dictionary Ser.: No. 4). 672p. 1978. 98.00 (0-8103-0401-5) Gale.

Who Was Who in Literature: Nineteen Six to Nineteen Thirty-Four, 2 vols., Set. LC 78-25583. (Composite Biographical Dictionary Ser.: No. 5). 1328p. 1979. 210.00 (0-8103-0402-3) Gale.

Who Was Who in Native American History: Indians & Non-Indians from First Contacts Through 1900. Ed. by Carl Waldman. (Illus.). 416p. 1989. 50.00 (0-8160-1797-2) Facts on File.

Who Was Who in the American Revolution. L. Edward Purcell. 560p. 1993. lib. bdg. 60.00 (0-8160-2107-4) Facts on File.

Who Was Who in the Civil War. John Bowman. 1994. 19.99 (0-517-10330-3) Random Hse Value.

Who Was Who in the Civil War, 2 vols., Set. Stewart Sifakis. (Illus.). 832p. 1989. pap. 41.00 (0-8160-2202-X) Facts on File.

Who Was Who in the Confederacy. Stewart Sifakis. (Illus.). 336p. 1989. pap. 22.95 (0-8160-2204-6) Facts on File.

Who Was Who in the Greek World. Ed. by Diana Bowder. 240p. 1982. 45.00 (0-8014-1538-1) Cornell U Pr.

***Who Was Who in the People's Republic of China, 2 vols.** Wolfgang Bartke. 850p. 1997. 350.00 (3-598-11331-5) K G Saur.

Who Was Who in the Soviet Union. Ed. by Ulrich-Joachim Schulz-Torge. 464p. 1992. lib. bdg. 300.00 (3-598-10810-9) K G Saur.

Who Was Who in the Theatre, 1912-1976, 4 vols. 76th ed. Incl. Vol. 1-4. Biographical Dictionary of Actors, Actresses, Directors, Playwrights, & Producers of the English Speaking Theatre. LC 78-9634. 1978. (0-318-52363-9); LC 78-9634. (Composite Biographical Dictionary Ser.: No. 3). 2680p. 1978. 400.00 (0-8103-0406-6) Gale.

Who Was Who in the Twentieth Century? Brompton Books Staff. 1993. 17.98 (1-55521-929-2) Bk Sales Inc.

Who Was Who in the Union. Stewart Sifakis. (Illus.). 496p. 1989. pap. 22.95 (0-8160-2203-8) Facts on File.

Who Was Who in Twentieth-Century Romania. Serban N. Ionescu. 318p. 1994. 59.00 (0-88033-292-1) East Eur Monographs.

Who Was Who in World Exploration. Carl Waldman & Alan Wexler. (Illus.). 720p. 1991. lib. bdg. 65.00 (0-8160-2172-4) Facts on File.

***Who Was Who 1991-1995, Vol. IX.** 675p. 1996. text ed. 99.95 (0-312-16246-4) St Martin.

***Who Was William Shakespeare? New Evidence.** A. D. Wraight & Peter Farey. 1996. 30.00 (1-897763-08-5, Pub. by Drake Intl Serv UK); pap. 14.95 (1-897763-09-3, Pub. by Drake Intl Serv UK) Intl Spec Bk.

Who Was Zwingli? A Journal of Archetype & Culture. Ed. by James Hillman et al. (Journal Ser.: Vol. 56). 176p. (Orig.). 1994. pap. 17.50 (1-882670-04-3) Spring Jrnl.

Who We Are: A Portrait of America. Sam Roberts. 1995. pap. 13.00 (0-8129-2526-2, Times Bks) Random.

Who We Are: A Second Look. Margaret Gibelman & Philip H. Schervish. 192p. (C). 1996. pap. text ed. 27.95 (0-614-11916-2) Natl Assn Soc Wkrs.

***Who We Are: A Second Look.** 2nd ed. Margaret Gibelman & Philip H. Schervish. LC 96-29546. 192p. (C). 1996. pap. text ed. 27.95 (0-87101-261-8, 2618) Natl Assn Soc Wkrs.

Who We Are: Our Dignity As Human. Paul Jewett. Ed. by Marguerite Shuster. 496p. 1996. pap. text ed. 32.00 (0-8028-4075-2) Eerdmans.

Who We Are: What Some Educators Say About Their Characteristics, Competencies & Roles. Alexander N. Charters & R. Hilton. (MS Ser.). 1977. 5.00 (0-686-52212-5, MSS 5) Syracuse U Cont Ed.

Who We Are & How We Relate see Understanding Who You Are: What Your Relationships Tell You about Yourself

Who We Are Is How We Pray: Matching Personality & Spirituality. Charles J. Keating. LC 86-50245. 168p. (Orig.). 1987. 13.95 (0-89622-292-6); pap. 9.95 (0-89622-321-3) Twenty-Third.

Who We Could Be at Work. Margaret A. Lulic. 261p. 1994. 19.95 (0-9638526-3-9) Blue Edge Pub.

Who We Could Be at Work. rev. ed. Margaret A. Lulic. LC 95-46389. 248p. 1996. pap. 17.95 (0-7506-9739-3) Buttrwrth-Heinemann.

Who Wears Shoes? Judy Nayer. Ed. by Janet Reed. (Newbridge Early Learning Program Ser.). (Illus.). 16p. (J). (ps-1). 1996. pap. 14.95 (1-56784-303-4) Newbridge Comms.

Who Wears Shoes? Mini Book. Judy Nayer. Ed. by Janet Reed. (Early Learning Program Ser.). (Illus.). 16p. (J). (ps-1). 1996. pap. 2.95 (1-56784-328-X) Newbridge Comms.

Who Were the First North Americans. Stuart Reid & Philippa Wingate. (Starting Point History Ser.). (Illus.). (J). (gr. k up). 1996. pap. 4.95 (0-7460-2040-6, Usborne); lib. bdg. 12.95 (0-88110-786-7, Usborne) EDC.

Who Were the First People? P. Roxbee-Cox. (Starting Point History Ser.). (Illus.). 24p. (J). 1995. pap. 4.95 (0-7460-1343-4, Usborne); lib. bdg. 12.95 (0-88110-730-1, Usborne) EDC.

Who Were the Founding Fathers? Two Hundred Years of Reinventing American History. Steve H. Jaffe. (Illus.). 160p. (YA). (gr. 6 up). 1996. 16.95 (0-8050-3102-2) H Holt & Co.

Who Were the Pharaohs: A History of Their Names. Stephen Quirke. 1991. pap. 6.95 (0-486-26586-2) Dover.

Who Were the Pre-Columbians? Mysteries, Adventures & Challenges for Today's World. Bernard B. Kaufman. LC 92-62495. (Illus.). 189p. (C). 1993. 22.95 (0-9635235-0-3) New Wrld Art.

Who Were the Romans? Roxbee Cox. (Starting Point History Ser.). (Illus.). 24p. (J). (gr. 1 up). 1994. pap. 4.95 (0-7460-1339-6, Usborne); lib. bdg. 12.95 (0-88110-669-0, Usborne) EDC.

Who Were the Vikings? Phil R. Cox. (Starting Point History Ser.). (Illus.). 32p. (J). (ps up). 1995. pap. 4.95 (0-7460-2038-4, Usborne); lib. bdg. 12.95 (0-88110-770-0, Usborne) EDC.

***Who Were Those Celts?** Kevin Duffy. xviii, 250p. (Orig.). 1996. pap. 24.00 (0-7884-0505-5, D822) Heritage Bk.

Who Were Those Strangers in My Dream? Barbara Condron. 129p. (C). 1988. reprint ed. pap. 4.95 (0-944386-08-3) SOM Pub.

Who, What & Where in Communications Security. Marketing Consultants International Inc. Staff. Ed. by J. Michael Nye. (Illus.). 124p. 1986. pap. 75.00 (0-937195-25-1) Mktg Consult Intl.

Who, What, & Why. Jackie Susnik. (Illus.). 169p. 1995. spiral bd. 24.00 (1-884135-16-1) Mayer-Johnson.

Who, What, When, Where, Why?... in the World of American History. Andy Seamans. 144p. 1991. pap. 5.95 (0-8120-4547-5) Barron.

Who, What, When, Where, Why?... in the World of Geography. Wilbur Cross. 144p. 1991. pap. 5.95 (0-8120-4480-0) Barron.

Who, What, When, Where, Why?... in the World of Literature. Ceil Cleveland. 144p. 1991. pap. 5.95 (0-8120-4478-9) Barron.

Who, What, When, Where, Why? in the World of History. Andy Seamans. (Whiz Quiz Ser.). (Illus.). 300p. 1991. pap. 5.95 (0-8120-4408-8) Barron.

Who, What, When, Where, Why? in the World of Music & Art. Benjamin Griffith. (Whiz Quiz Ser.). (Illus.). 300p. 1991. pap. 5.95 (0-8120-4479-7) Barron.

Who, What, When, Where, Why? in the World of Nature. Andy Seamans. (Whiz Quiz Ser.). (Illus.). 300p. (Orig.). (J). (gr. 6 up). 1992. pap. 5.95 (0-8120-4699-4) Barron.

Who, What, When, Where, Why in the World of Science. John Carlisle. 1992. pap. 5.95 (0-8120-4854-7) Barron.

Who? What? Where? Resources for Women's Health & Aging. 82p. (Orig.). (C). 1993. pap. text ed. 30.00 (1-56806-943-X) DIANE Pub.

Who, Where & What Is "Israel"? Zionist Perspectives on Israeli & American Judaism. Jacob Neusner. LC 88-33976. (Studies in Judaism). 176p. (C). 1989. lib. bdg. 35.00 (0-8191-7360-6, Studies in Judaism) U Pr of Amer.

Who Whispered Near Me. Killarney Clary. 80p. 1989. 14.95 (0-374-28983-2) FS&G.

Who Whispered Near Me. Killarney Clary. 1990. pap. 8.95 (0-374-52240-5, Noonday) FS&G.

Who Will Be Miss Unicorn. Francine Pascal. (Unicorn Club Ser.: No. 13). 144p. (J). (gr. 3-7). 1996. pap. 3.50 (0-553-48399-4, Sweet Valley) BDD Bks Young Read.

Who Will Be My Friends? Syd Hoff. (Harper Early I Can Read Bk.). (Illus.). 32p. (J). (gr. k-2). 1960. lib. bdg. 14.89 (0-06-022556-4) HarpC Child Bks.

***Who Will Be My Friends?** Syd Hoff. (Illus.). (J). (ps-3). 1960. 17.02 (0-06-022555-6, 452049) HarpC.

Who Will Be My Friends? Syd Hoff. LC 60-14096. (Trophy Early I Can Read Bk.). (Illus.). 32p. (J). (ps-2). 1985. reprint ed. pap. 3.50 (0-06-444072-9, Trophy) HarpC Child Bks.

Who Will Be My Teacher? Marjory G. Ward. LC 91-9649. 160p. (gr. 10). 1991. 10.99 (0-8007-1654-X) Revell.

***Who Will Be the Role Model for Tomorrow's Teens?** Virginia Fogle. 16p. 1996. pap. 6.00 (0-8059-3872-9) Dorrance.

***Who Will Believe the Report?** Elizabeth R. Visland. 144p. 1996. pap. 9.95 (0-9633106-2-3) E R Visland.

Who Will Break the Silence? Liturgical Resources for the Healing of AIDS. Pernessa C. Seele. 100p. 1995. pap. text ed. 20.00 (0-9649799-0-X) Balm In Gilead.

Who Will Buy a Poem? Seventeenth Century. Ed. & Tr. by Malachi McCormick. (Miniatures Ser.). 24p. 1991. 7.00 (0-943984-41-6); 7.00 (0-685-65461-3) Stone St Pr.

Who Will Care for Us? Aging & Long-Term Care in Multicultural America. Ronald J. Angel & Jacqueline L. Angel. 304p. (C). 1997. 29.95 (0-8147-0629-0) NYU Pr.

Who Will Cross the Jordan: A Call to Holiness. Doug Stringer. LC 91-78268. (Orig.). 1992. pap. 7.95 (0-88270-675-6) Bridge-Logos.

Who Will Cry for Staci? The True Story of a Grieving Father's Quest for Justice. Milton Shapiro. (Illus.). 352p. 1995. pap. 5.99 (0-451-40604-4, Onyx) NAL-Dutton.

Who Will Deliver Us? large type ed. Paul Zahl. 170p. (Orig.). 1985. reprint ed. pap. 7.95 (0-8027-2487-6) Walker & Co.

Who Will Do Science? Educating the Next Generation. Ed. by Willie Pearson, Jr. & Alan Fechter. LC 94-9005. 208p. 1994. text ed. 31.95 (0-8018-4857-1) Johns Hopkins.

Who Will Feed China? Wake-up Call for a Small Planet. Lester Brown. 160p. 1995. pap. write for info. (1-85383-316-9, Pub. by Erthscan Pubns UK) Island Pr.

Who Will Feed China? Wake-Up Call for a Small Planet. Lester R. Brown. (Illus.). 160p. 1995. 19.95 (0-393-03897-1); pap. 8.95 (0-393-31409-X, Norton Paperbks) Norton.

Who Will Fight the Next War? The Changing Face of the American Military. Martin Binkin. 224p. (C). 1993. 31.95 (0-8157-0956-0); pap. 14.95 (0-8157-0955-2) Brookings.

Who Will Fill Our Shoes? Thirteen Dramatic Sketches for Missions Awareness. Glen D. Post. Ed. by Gina Howard. 43p. (Orig.). 1991. pap. text ed. 4.95 (1-56309-011-2, New Hope AL) Womans Mission Union.

Who Will Fly with Butterfly? Lorice Hartmann. (Illus.). 48p. (YA). (gr. 7-11). 1979. pap. 8.95 (0-912760-51-6) Valkyrie Pub Hse.

Who Will Go for Us? An Invitation to Ordained Ministry. Dennis M. Campbell. LC 93-23623. 128p. (Orig.). 1994. pap. 7.95 (0-687-46775-6) Abingdon.

Who Will Help? Rozanne L. Williams. (Emergent Reader Bks.). 16p. (J). (gr. k-2). 1994. 2.49 (0-916119-69-6) Creat Teach Pr.

Who Will Help? Rozanne L. Williams. (Emergent Reader Big Bks.). (Illus.). 16p. (Orig.). (J). (gr. k-2). 1995. pap. 11.98 (1-57471-081-2) Creat Teach Pr.

Who Will Help? The Good Samaritan. Mary M. Simon. 24p. 1990. pap. text ed. 2.49 (0-570-04180-5, 56-1639) Concordia.

Who Will It Hurt When I Die? A Primer on the Living Trust. Nan L. Goodart. (Illus.). 176p. (Orig.). 1992. pap. 19.95 (0-9631531-0-2) Honor Bound.

Who Will Lead? Senior Leadership in the United States Army. Edward C. Meyer et al. LC 94-34319. 296p. 1995. text ed. 59.95 (0-275-95041-7, Praeger Pubs) Greenwood.

Who Will Lead Kiddush? Barbara Pomerantz. (Illus.). 32p. (Orig.). (J). (gr. 1-3). 1985. pap. 6.00 (0-8074-0306-7, 102000) UAHC.

Who Will Mind the Baby? Geographies of Childcare & Working Mothers. Ed. by Kim England. LC 95-52129. (International Studies of Women & Place). 224p. (C). 1996. pap. 18.95 (0-415-11741-0); text ed. 59.95 (0-415-11740-2) Routledge.

Who Will Pay for Your Retirement? The Looming Crisis: A Statement. Ed. by Research & Policy Committee of the Economic Development Committee. LC 95-3345. 1995. 20.00 (0-87186-119-4) Comm Econ Dev.

Who Will Roll Away This Stone? Discipleship Queries for First World Christians. Ched Myers. LC 94-4445. 425p. (Orig.). 1994. pap. 22.00 (0-88344-947-1) Orbis Bks.

Who Will Run the Frog Hospital? Lorrie Moore. LC 94-278. 1994. 20.00 (0-679-43484-4) Knopf.

Who Will Run the Frog Hospital? Lorrie Moore. 1994. 20.00 (0-679-43482-8) Knopf.

Who Will Run the Frog Hospital? Lorrie Moore. 160p. 1995. pap. 11.99 (0-446-67191-6) Warner Bks.

***Who Will Save Our Schools? Teachers As Constructivist Leaders.** Linda Lambert et al. (Illus.). 232p. 1996. 49.95 (0-8039-6462-5); pap. 22.95 (0-8039-6463-3) Corwin Pr.

Who Will Save the Forests? Knowledge, Power & Environmental Destruction. Ed. by Tariq Banuri & Frederique A. Marglin. LC 93-2788. 224p. (C). 1993. pap. 17.50 (1-85649-160-9, Pub. by Zed Bks Ltd UK); text ed. 59.95 (1-85649-159-5, Pub. by Zed Bks Ltd UK) Humanities.

Who Will Speak for the Victim? A Practical Treatise on Plaintiff's Jury Argument. Jim M. Perdue. LC 88-63945. 420p. 1989. 74.00 (0-938160-54-0, 6231) State Bar TX.

Who Will Stop the Bomb? A Primer on Nuclear Proliferation. Roger C. Molander & Robbie Nichols. LC 85-10362. 160p. reprint ed. pap. 45.60 (0-7837-5341-1, 2045083) Bks Demand.

Who Will Take the Children? A New Custody Option for Divorced Mothers & Fathers. Susan Meyers & Joan Lakin. LC 82-17847. 228p. 1983. write for info. (0-672-52739-1) Macmillan.

Who Will Teach? Policies That Matter. Richard J. Murnane et al. 182p. (C). 1991. 28.00 (0-674-95192-1) HUP.

Who Will Teach Me? A Handbook for Parents. Joseph F. Girzone. Ed. by Laurine M. Easton. 96p. (Orig.). 1989. pap. 3.95 (1-55588-179-3) St Michael Guild.

Who Will Teach Me? A Handbook for Parents. rev. ed. Joseph F. Girzone. LC 82-80555. 88p. 1995. 9.95 (0-911519-69-6) Richelieu Court.

Who Will Teach the Children? Progress & Resistance in Teacher Education. Harriet Tyson. LC 93-36595. (Jossey-Bass Education Ser.). 230p. text ed. 29.95 (1-55542-600-X) Jossey-Bass.

Who Will Tell the People? The Betrayal of the American Democracy. William Greider. 464p. 1993. pap. 13.00 (0-671-86740-7, Touchstone Bks) S&S Trade.

Who Will Tell the People? The Breakdown of American Democracy. William Greider. 416p. 1992. 25.00 (0-671-68891-X) S&S Trade.

Who Will Win? A Key to the Puzzle of Revolutionary War. George K. Tanham & Douglas Blaufarb. 176p. 1989. 32.00 (0-8448-1636-1, Crane Russak); pap. 21.00 (0-8448-1637-X, Crane Russak) Taylor & Francis.

Who Won What When: The Nineteen Eighty Edition of the Record Book of Winners. Ed. by Sandra L. Stuart. 1980. pap. 8.95 (0-8184-0293-8) Carol Pub Group.

Who Wore What? Women's Wear 1861-1865. Juanita Leisch. (Illus.). 128p. (C). 1995. text ed. 29.95 (0-939631-81-4) Thomas Publications.

Who Would Have Thought. Sheri Shepherd. 1995. pap. 12.95 (0-9647475-0-2) Shepherd Mktg.

Who Would Have Thought It? Maria A. Ruiz de Burton. Ed. by Rosaura Sanchez & Beatrice Pita. LC 95-11585. 367p. 1995. pap. 12.95 (1-55885-081-3) Arte Publico.

Who Would I Be If I Weren't So Afraid? Ginger Grancagnolo. 1995. 17.95 (0-533-11524-8) Vantage.

Who Would Want Those Apples Anyway? Laura Griscom & Pam Griscom. (Illus.). 24p. (Orig.). (J). (ps up). 1993. pap. 4.95 (0-9633705-3-7) Share Pub CA.

Who Wrecked the Roof? Bob Hartman. Ed. by Diane Stortz. (Big Picture Bks.). (Illus.). 32p. (J). (gr. 1-8). 1994. 10.99 (0-7847-0189-X, 03639) Standard Pub.

Who Writes Science Fiction. Charles Platt. 400p. (Orig.). 1981. pap. 3.95 (0-86130-048-3, Pub. by Savoy Bks UK) AK Pr Dist.

Who Wrote Shakespeare? John Michell. LC 95-62460. (Illus.). 272p. 1996. 24.95 (0-500-01700-X) Thames Hudson.

Who Wrote That Song? Dick Jacobs & Harriet Jacobs. (Illus.). 448p. (Orig.). 1994. pap. 19.99 (0-89879-639-3, Wrtrs Digest Bks) F & W Pubns Inc.

Who Wrote That Song? Popular Songs in America & Their Composers. W. Colbert. 1974. lib. bdg. 250.00 (0-87700-216-9) Revisionist Pr.

***Who Wrote the Bible?** Richard E. Friedman. 1997. pap. text ed. 14.00 (0-06-063035-3) Harper SF.

Who Wrote the Bible? A Book for the People. Washington T. Gladden. LC 72-5435. (Select Bibliographies Reprint Ser.). 1977. reprint ed. 31.95 (0-8369-6909-X) Ayer.

Who Wrote the Book of Love? Thomas Farber. LC 84-45096. 127p. 1984. pap. 6.95 (0-916870-69-3) Creat Arts Bk.

Who Wrote the Dead Sea Scrolls? Norman Golb. 464p. 1996. pap. 15.00 (0-684-80692-4, Touchstone Bks) S&S Trade.

Who Wrote the Dead Sea Scrolls? The Search for the Secret of Qumran. Norman Golb. (Illus.). 320p. 1995. 25.00 (0-02-544395-X) S&S Trade.

***Who Wrote the Gospels?** Randel Helms. (Illus.). 200p. 1997. 21.95 (0-9655047-2-7) Millennium Pr.

***Who Wrote the Gospels?** Randel Helms. (Illus.). 200p. 1998. pap. 11.95 (0-9655047-3-5) Millennium Pr.

Who Wrote the Mozart Four-Wind Concertante? Authenticity, Origin & Reconstruction. Robert D. Levin. LC 84-26365. 1989. 62.00 (0-918728-31-2) Pendragon NY.

Who Wrote the New Testament? The Making of the Christian Myth. Burton L. Mack. LC 95-8937. 336p. 1996. pap. 15.00 (0-06-065518-6) Harper SF.

Who Wrote This Story? (Illus.). (J). (ps-2). 1991. pap. 5.10 (0-8136-5663-X); lib. bdg. 7.95 (0-8136-5163-8) Modern Curr.

Who Wrote What? W. A. Wheeler. 1972. 250.00 (0-87968-367-8) Gordon Pr.

Who You Are: Personality & Its Development. Robert S. Feldman & Joel Feinman. LC 92-25494. (Venture Bks.). (Illus.). 112p. (YA). (gr. 9-12). 1992. lib. bdg. 22.00 (0-531-12544-0) Watts.

Who You Are When No One's Looking: Christian Character for All of Life. Bill Hybels. LC 87-16856. 113p. (Orig.). 1987. pap. 8.99 (0-87784-945-5, 945) InterVarsity.

W

An Asterisk (*) at the beginning of an entry indicates that the title is appearing in BIP for the first time.

Whoa Guido! Nancy Leflar. LC 93-94980. (Illus.). 64p. (Orig.). 1995. pap. 5.00 (1-56002-398-8, Univ Edtns) Aegina Pr.

***Whoa, Nellie!** Hope Benton. LC 96-92562. (Illus.). 102p. (J). (gr. 3-8). 1996. 14.95 (1-888927-01-1, WNB); pap. 4.50 (1-888927-79-8, WNB) Open Minds.

***Whoa, Nellie! Parent & Teacher Guide.** Beatrice H. Benton-Borghi et al. LC 96-92558. (Illus.). 60p. (Orig.). 1996. teacher ed., pap. 14.95 (1-888927-26-7, WNG) Open Minds.

***Whoa There, Wanda Wilson!** Linda L. Maifair. (Winners! Ser.). 64p. (Orig.). (J). (gr. 2-5). 1997. pap. 3.99 (0-310-20703-7) Zondervan.

Whoa...Yuh Sonsabitches. Edgar R. Potter. (Illus.). 1977. pap. 6.95 (0-918292-00-X) Griggs Print.

Who'd Say That? Outrageous Celebrity Quotes. Ronald L. Smith. 256p. (Orig.). 1993. pap. 4.99 (1-56171-228-0, S P I Bks) Sure Seller.

Who'd Stay a Missionary? Helen Morgan. 1979. pap. 1.95 (0-87508-366-8) Chr Lit.

Whodunit? Alice G. Dow. (Illus.). (Orig.). (J). (gr. 1-4). 1996. pap. 6.95 (0-533-11851-4) Vantage.

Whodunit. rev. ed. Anne C. Martens. 1981. pap. 3.00 (0-87129-328-5, W25) Dramatic Pub.

***Whodunit? A Reader's Companion for Mystery Lovers.** Bruce Murphy. 464p. 1998. 35.00 (0-06-271604-2, Harper Ref); pap. 20.00 (0-06-273433-4, PL) HarpC.

Whodunit? Science Solves the Crime. Steven Otfinoski. LC 95-11961. (Mysteries of Science Ser.). (Illus.). 80p. (J). 1995. pap. 13.95 (0-7167-6559-4, Sci Am Yng Rdrs) W H Freeman.

Whodunit? Science Solves the Crime. Steven Otfinoski. LC 95-11961. (Mysteries of Science Ser.). (Illus.). 80p. (J). 1996. 19.95 (0-7167-6515-2, Sci Am Yng Rdrs) W H Freeman.

Whodunit - You Decide! Mini-Mysteries for You to Solve. Hy Conrad. LC 96-25416. (Illus.). 96p. 1996. pap. 5.95 (0-8069-6150-3) Sterling.

Whodunnit. Debra McKillop. 1997. write for info. (0-679-44143-3) Random.

Whodunnits (Blu) Emma Fischel & M. Oliver. (Illus.). 144p. (J). (gr. 3 up). 1994. pap. 9.95 (0-7460-0729-9, Usborne) EDC.

Whoever Fights Monsters: A Brilliant FBI Detective's Career-Long War Against Serial Killers. Robert K. Ressler & Tom Shachtman. (Illus.). 256p. 1992. 22.95 (0-312-07883-8) St Martin.

Whoever Fights Monsters: A Brilliant FBI Detective's Career-Long War Against Serial Killers. Robert K. Ressler & Thomas Schachtman. 1993. mass mkt. 5.99 (0-312-95044-6) St Martin.

Whoever Finds This: I Love You. Faye Moskowitz. 1992. pap. 11.95 (0-87923-936-0) Godine.

***Whoever Has the Heart.** Jennie Melville. 218p. 3.95 (0-8317-5152-5) Smithmark.

Whoever Has the Heart. large type ed. Jennie Melville. LC 94-7116. 330p. 1994. lib. bdg. 17.95 (0-7862-0207-6) Thorndike Pr.

Whoever You Are. Mem Fox. LC 95-17887. (Illus.). (J). 1997. write for info. (0-15-200787-3) HarBrace.

Whole Act: Immigration & Nationality Act, As Amended, 1992. 1992. 59.00 (0-9609346-4-2) Legal Res Bureau.

Whole Again Resource Guide. Tim Ryan. LC 83-641044. 380p. 1986. pap. 24.95 (0-915051-01-X) SourceNet.

***Whole & Divided Self: The Bible & Theological Anthropology.** Ed. by John McCarthy. LC 97-6807. 300p. 1997. 29.95 (0-8245-1668-0, Crossrd Herd) Crossroad NY.

Whole & Holy Sexuality. William F. Kraft. LC 88-83364. 134p. (Orig.). 1989. pap. 5.95 (0-87029-222-6, 20212-7) Abbey.

Whole Armor. Rhoda L. Seoane. 1965. 6.95 (0-8315-0023-9) Speller.

Whole Art of the Stage. Francois H. Aubignac. LC 68-21218. 1972. 36.95 (0-405-08227-4, Pub. by Blom Pubns UK) Ayer.

Whole Arts Directory. Cynthia Navaretta. LC 87-62289. (Directories Ser.). (Illus.). 172p. (Orig.). pap. 12.95 (0-9602476-7-X) Midmarch Arts-WAN.

Whole-Body Computed Tomography. 2nd enl. rev. ed. Otto H. Wegener. Tr. by Suzyon O. Wandrey from GER. LC 92-35853. 632p. 1992. 135.00 (0-86542-223-0) Blackwell Sci.

Whole Body Computed Tomography CD-ROM. Otto H. Wegener. 1994. 195.00 (0-86542-947-2) Blackwell Sci.

Whole Body Hyperthermia: Biological & Clinical Aspects. Ed. by M. Gautherie. (Clinical Thermology Ser.). (Illus.). 104p. 1992. 100.00 (0-387-54560-3) Spr-Verlag.

***Whole-Body Irradiation.** 1997. lib. bdg. 250.95 (0-8490-7707-9) Gordon Pr.

Whole Book: Cultural Perspectives on the Medieval Miscellany. Ed. by Stephen G. Nichols & Siegfried Wenzel. (C). 1995. 37.50 (0-472-10696-1) U of Mich Pr.

Whole Book of Guitar Chords. D. Fox. 160p. 1986. otabind 19.95 (0-7935-0700-6, 50333370) H Leonard.

Whole Brain Business Book: Unlocking the Power of the Whole Brain Organization & the Whole. Ned Herrmann. 1996. text ed. 24.95 (0-07-028462-8) McGraw.

Whole Brain Education. Michael P. Grady. LC 90-60218. (Fastback Ser.: No. 301). 40p. (Orig.). (C). 1990. pap. 3.00 (0-87367-301-8) Phi Delta Kappa.

Whole Car Catalog. Consumer Guide Editors. (Illus.). 1978. pap. 7.95 (0-671-23022-0, Fireside) S&S Trade.

Whole Child: Developmental Education for the Early Years. 6th ed. Joanne Hendrick. LC 95-10898. 1995. text ed. 55.00 (0-02-353164-9, Macmillan Coll) P-H.

Whole Child Bk. III: How Music Fits In, Bk. III. Elizabeth L. Mayer. (Music Makes a Difference Ser.). 12p. 1994. pap. 1.95 (1-886380-02-3) Langstaff Vid.

Whole Child-Whole Parent. Polly B. Berends. LC 81-48029. (Illus.). 384p. (Orig.). 1987. pap. 16.00 (0-06-091427-0, PL1427, PL) HarpC.

***Whole Child, Whole Parent.** 4th ed. Polly Berends. LC 97-9532. 384p. 1997. pap. 16.00 (0-06-092818-2, PL) HarpC.

Whole Chile Pepper Book. Dave Dewitt. 1990. pap. 19.95 (0-316-18223-0) Little.

Whole Christmas Catalogue: The Complete Compendium of Christmas Traditions, Recipes, Crafts, Carols, Lore & More. (Illus.). 176p. 1994. 14.98 (1-56138-438-0) Courage Bks.

Whole Church Body Book. Jean Gralley. 24p. 1993. pap. 4.95 (1-888493-08-9) Chi Rho Pr.

Whole City Catalogue: Greater Rochester's Guide to Personal Excellence. Ed. by Blair H. Hornbuckle et al. (Illus.). 160p. (Orig.). 1988. pap. 5.00 (0-922636-00-1) Metaview Comns.

Whole Cloth: A History of the Greater Boston Council of Girl Scouts, 1913-1969. Nancy H. Hannan. 136p. (Orig.). 1987. pap. 12.95 (0-913553-04-2) Albert Hse Pub.

Whole Computer Catalog. Narda L. Schwartz. 1984. pap. 35.00 (0-9609254-0-6) Designs Three.

Whole Cosmos Catalog of Science Activities for Kids of All Ages. Joseph Abruscato & Jack Hassard. LC 76-46463. (Illus.). 1977. pap. 12.95 (0-673-16459-4, ScottFrsmn) Addson-Wesley Educ.

Whole Cosmos Catalog of Science Activities, Grades 4-8. 2nd ed. Joe Abruscato & Jack Hassard. 1990. pap. 14.95 (0-673-16753-4, GoodYrBooks) Addson-Wesley Educ.

***Whole Costumer's Catalogue.** 13th rev. ed. Ed. by Karen L. Dick. 224p. 1997. pap. 15.00 (1-888288-01-9) CBTB Pr.

Whole Counsel of God. Carl E. Braaten. LC 73-88345. 176p. reprint ed. pap. 50.20 (0-685-16036-X, 2026840) Bks Demand.

Whole Cowboy Catalog: An Entertaining Guide to Everything Western. Ed. by Rod McQueary & Sue Wallis. LC 95-13702. (Illus.). 1995. pap. 16.95 (0-87905-689-4) Gibbs Smith Pub.

Whole Craft of Spinning from the Raw Material to the Finished Yarn. Carol Kroll. 1981. pap. 3.50 (0-486-23968-3) Dover.

Whole Crop Cereals. 2nd ed. B. A. Stark & J. M. Wilkinson. (Illus.). 176p. 1992. pap. text ed. 32.50 (0-948617-25-X, Pub. by Chalcombe Pubns UK) Scholium Intl.

Whole-Crop Cereals: Making & Feeding Cereal Silage. Ed. by J. M. Wilkinson & B. A. Stark. (Illus.). 92p. (Orig.). 1990. pap. text ed. 25.00 (0-948617-21-7, Pub. by Chalcombe Pubns UK) Scholium Intl.

Whole Different Ballgame: The Sport & Business of Baseball. Marvin Miller. 1991. 21.95 (1-55972-067-0, Birch Ln Pr) Carol Pub Group.

***Whole Dog Catalog: More Than 800 Terrific Toys.** John Reed. 1997. pap. 19.95 (0-609-80037-X) Random Hse Value.

Whole Earth Geography Book, Grades 4-6. Anthony D. Fredericks. 1990. pap. 8.95 (0-673-38639-2, GoodYrBooks) Addson-Wesley Educ.

Whole Earth Holiday Book: Grades 4-6. Linda Polon & Aileen Cantwell. (Illus.). 218p. (Orig.). 1983. pap. 13.95 (0-673-16585-X, GoodYrBooks) Addson-Wesley Educ.

Whole Earth Meditation: Ecology for the Spirit. Joan Sauro. LC 91-45190. 96p. (Orig.). 1992. pap. 10.95 (0-931055-89-X) Innisfree Pr.

Whole-Earth Security: A Geopolitics of Peace. Daniel Deudney. 1983. pap. write for info. (0-916468-54-2) Worldwatch Inst.

Whole Earth Shall Cry Glory. George F. MacLeod. 1987. 35.00 (0-947988-04-1, Pub. by Wild Goose Pubns UK); pap. 21.00 (0-947988-01-7, Pub. by Wild Goose Pubns UK) St Mut.

Whole Education: A New Direction to Fill the Relevance Gap. Raja T. Nasr. LC 94-21380. 138p. (Orig.). (C). 1994. reprint ed. pap. text ed. 24.50 (0-8191-9610-X); reprint ed. lib. bdg. 42.00 (0-8191-9609-6) U Pr of Amer.

Whole Effluent Toxicity Testing - an Evaluation of Methods & Prediction of Receiving System Impacts: Proceedings of the Pellston Workshop on Whole Effluent Toxicity, September 16-21, 1995, University of Michigan Biological Station, Douglas Lake, Pellston, Michigan. Donald R. Grothe et al. LC 96-22107. (SETAC Special Publications). 1996. write for info. (1-880611-06-6) SETAC.

Whole Emergency Department Catalog. Michael S. Jastremski et al. (Illus.). 416p. 1985. text ed. 62.00 (0-7216-1175-3) Saunders.

Whole Enchilada: A Spicy Collection of Sylvia. Nicole Hollander. 208p. 1986. pap. 11.95 (0-312-87757-9) St Martin.

Whole Family Cookbook. Carol Gillis. 1997. 19.95 (0-02-860996-4) Macmillan.

Whole Family Handbook for Unifying Mind, Body & Spirit. Debra Hockenberry. (Christina Davis Ser.). (Orig.). 1992. pap. write for info. (1-878056-07-7) D Hockenberry.

Whole Food Bible: How to Select & Prepare Safe, Healthful Foods. Christopher S. Kilham. LC 96-47742. 304p. 1996. reprint ed. pap. 19.95 (0-89281-626-0, Heal Arts VT) Inner Tradit.

Whole Food Facts: The Complete Reference Guide. Evelyn Roehl. LC 96-3961. (Illus.). 192p. 1996. pap. 19.95 (0-89281-635-X, Heal Arts VT) Inner Tradit.

Whole Foods Companion: A Guide for Adventurous Cooks, Curious Shoppers, & Lovers of Natural Foods. Diane Orstad. LC 96-33441. (Illus.). 400p. 1996. pap. 25.00 (0-930031-83-0) Chelsea Green Pub.

Whole Foods Companion: A Guide for Adventurous Cooks, Curious Shoppers, & Lovers of Natural Foods. Diane Orstad. 1996. 42.00 (0-930031-89-X) Chelsea Green Pub.

Whole Foods Encyclopedia. Rebecca Wood. 1998. pap. 14.95 (0-14-025032-8) Viking Penguin.

Whole Foods Experience. Ellen S. Spivack. (Illus.). 248p. 1985. pap. 9.95 (0-89496-042-3) Ross Bks.

Whole Foods for Kids to Cook. Judy Torgus. LC 95-77518. (Illus.). 96p. 1995. spiral bd. 7.50 (0-912500-46-8, 261) La Leche.

Whole Foods for the Whole Family. 2nd ed. La Leche League International Staff. LC 93-80166. (Illus.). 306p. 1993. spiral bd. 16.95 (0-912500-43-3) La Leche.

Whole Foods for the Whole Family: La Leche League International Cookbook. Ed. by Roberta B. Johnson. LC 84-2128. (Illus.). 340p. 1984. pap. 15.95 (0-452-25503-1, Plume) NAL-Dutton.

Whole Foods for Whole People. rev. ed. Lucy Fuller. LC 93-61495. (Illus.). 112p. 1994. spiral bd. 10.95 (0-945383-64-9) Teach Servs.

Whole Foods from the Whole World Cookbook. Ed. by Virginia S. Halonen. LC 93-80165. (Illus.). 223p. 1993. spiral bd. 12.50 (0-912500-44-1) La Leche.

Whole Gospel, Whole World: The Foreign Mission Board of the Southern Baptist Convention, 1845-1995. William R. Estep. LC 94-8237. 456p. 1994. 29.99 (0-8054-1041-4, 4210-41) Broadman.

Whole Grain: Collected Poems 1958-1989. James A. Emanuel. LC 90-61082. (Illus.). 400p. (YA). (gr. 9-12). 1991. 25.00 (0-916418-79-0) Lotus.

Whole-Grain Health Saver Cookbook. Miriam Polunin. LC 81-84465. (Illus.). 1982. pap. 2.95 (0-87983-270-3) Keats.

Whole Grain Sampler. Jan Siegrist. (Illus.). 48p. (Orig.). 1990. pap. 3.95 (0-933050-83-6) New Eng Pr VT.

***Whole Grains.** 2nd ed. Martha Mapes & Jennifer Morrill. (Illus.). 100p. 1989. reprint ed. teacher ed. 3.50 (1-57753-034-9, 399R202) Corn Coop Ext.

***Whole Healing.** 1997. pap. 11.95 (0-452-27665-9, Plume) NAL-Dutton.

Whole Healing: A Step-by-Step Guide to Reclaim Your Power to Heal. Elliott S. Dacher. LC 95-47671. (Illus.). 256p. 1996. pap. 23.95 (0-525-94155-X, Dutton) NAL-Dutton.

Whole Health: The Guide to Wellness of Body & Mind. Joseph Keon. LC 95-70987. (Illus.). 380p. (Orig.). 1997. pap. 24.00 (0-9648974-8-2) Parissound.

Whole Health Shiatsu: Health & Vitality for Everyone. Shizuko Yamamoto & Patrick McCarty. (Illus.). 288p. (Orig.). 1992. pap. 25.00 (0-87040-874-7) Japan Pubns USA.

Whole Heart: Poems about Abraham Lincoln. Mary A. Malone. (Marigold Poetry Ser.). 50p. 1995. pap. 9.95 (1-887888-00-4) Marigold Ent.

***Whole Hog.** Michael Kenyon. 1996. 18.50 (0-7451-8688-2, Black Dagger) Chivers N Amer.

Whole Horse Catalogue: Revised & Updated for the 1990's. 2nd ed. Steven D. Price & David A. Spector. (Illus.). 288p. 1993. pap. 18.00 (0-671-86681-8, Fireside) S&S Trade.

Whole House Remodeling Guide. S. Blackwell Duncan. (Illus.). 340p. 1989. 28.95 (0-8306-9281-9); pap. 19.95 (0-8306-3281-6) McGraw-Hill Prof.

Whole Houses Shaking. Jim Bodeen. (Illus.). 88p. 1993. pap. 10.00 (0-912887-30-3) Blue Begonia.

***Whole Houses Shaking.** Jim Bodeen. 1996. pap. text ed. 10.00 (0-911287-30-2) Blue Begonia.

Whole Internal Universe: Imitation & the New Defense of Poetry in British Criticism, 1660-1830. John L. Mahoney. LC 85-80479. 176p. reprint ed. pap. 50.20 (0-7837-5878-2, 2045598) Bks Demand.

Whole Internet for Windows 95. Ed Krol & Paula Ferguson. 1995. pap. text ed. 24.95 (1-56592-155-0) OReilly & Assocs.

Whole Internet User's Guide & Catalog. 2nd ed. Ed Krol. Ed. by Mike Loukides. (Illus.). 574p. (Orig.). 1994. pap. 9.99 (1-56592-063-5) OReilly & Assocs.

Whole Is More: Living the Travel Experience. Heide Gondek. 1993. 10.00 (0-533-10398-3) Vantage.

Whole Journey: Shakespeare's Power of Development. C. L. Barber & Richard P. Wheeler. LC 85-20712. 425p. 1986. 45.00 (0-520-05432-6); pap. 14.00 (0-520-06622-7) U CA Pr.

Whole Kitt & Caboodle: A Painless Journey to Investment Enlightenment. Susan Laubach. 188p. (Orig.). 1996. reprint ed. pap. 16.95 (0-9631246-1-7) Bancroft MD.

Whole Kitty Catalog: More than 800 Terrific Toys, Treats, & True Cat Facts--for You & Your Kitty. John A. Reed. 1996. pap. 19.95 (0-517-88689-8) Crown Pub Group.

Whole Knowledge Scoreboard Management Series. Alan C. Walter. Ed. by Beverly Miles. 28p. (Orig.). 1995. pap. text ed. 2.79 (1-57569-027-6) Wisdom Pubng.

Whole Language. 1993. pap. 8.95 (0-590-73371-0) Scholastic Inc.

Whole Language: Beliefs & Practices, K-8. Ed. by Maryann M. Manning & Gary L. Manning. 240p. 1989. pap. 16.95 (0-8106-1482-0) NEA.

Whole Language: Getting Started . . . Moving Forward. Linda K. Crafton. LC 90-7977. 336p. (Orig.). (C). 1991. pap. text ed. 22.95 (0-913461-19-9) R Owen Pubs.

Whole Language: History, Philosophy, & Practice. Sandra Brady & Toni M. Sills. 240p. (C). 1993. per. 39.84 (0-8403-8763-6) Kendall-Hunt.

Whole Language: Literature, Learning, & Literacy - A Workshop in Print. Lou W. Stanek. LC 92-29691. 244p. 1992. 39.00 (0-8242-0837-4) Wilson.

Whole Language: Practical Ideas. Mayling Chow et al. (Pippin Teacher's Library). 114p. 1995. pap. text ed. 14.50 (0-88751-032-9, 00711) Heinemann.

Whole-Language: Practice & Theory. 2nd ed. Ed. by Victor Froese. LC 95-32108. 493p. 1995. pap. text ed. 50.00 (0-205-15779-3) Allyn.

Whole Language: The Debate. Ed. by Warren W. Lewis. 350p. (Orig.). 1994. pap. 24.95 (0-927516-39-X) ERIC-REC.

Whole Language: Theory in Use. Ed. by Judith M. Newman. LC 85-17636. 204p. (Orig.). 1985. pap. text ed. 23.50 (0-435-08244-2, 08244) Heinemann.

Whole Language - Whole Learning. Claudia E. Cornett & Lesley Blankenship. LC 90-62022. (Fastback Ser.: No. 307). (Orig.). (C). 1990. pap. 3.00 (0-87367-307-7) Phi Delta Kappa.

Whole Language Across the Curriculum. Ed. by Shirley C. Raines. (Language & Literacy Ser.). 240p. (J). (gr. 1-3). 1995. pap. text ed. 19.95 (0-8077-3446-2) Tchrs Coll.

***Whole Language Action-Learning Manual: An Integrated Approach to Reading & Writing.** (Literacy Linkage Series Manuals). 67p. (Orig.). 1996. pap. 6.50 (0-614-23139-6) Ctr Intl Ed U of MA.

Whole Language & Literature: A Practical Guide. Alma F. Ada. (Hagamos Caminos Ser.). (Illus.). 64p. 1989. pap. text ed. 7.25 (0-201-50069-8) Addison-Wesley.

Whole Language & the Bilingual Learner. Ed. by Angela Carrasquillo & Carolyn N. Hedley. LC 92-10595. 240p. (C). 1993. text ed. 49.50 (0-89391-767-2); pap. text ed. 24.50 (0-89391-861-X) Ablex Pub.

Whole Language Approach to Enhancing Self-Esteem: Learn How to Develop Literature Based Esteem Building Thematic Units. John Gust. 162p. (Orig.). 1993. pap. 14.95 (0-9635008-7-2) Summit Seminar.

Whole Language Approach to Reading. Gordon S. Anderson. LC 84-13229. (Illus.). 642p. (Orig.). 1984. pap. text ed. 43.50 (0-8191-4197-6) U Pr of Amer.

Whole Language Big Books, 12 units, Set. 1994. pap. 178.00 (1-56784-828-1) Newbridge Comms.

Whole Language Big Books, 20 units, Set. (Illus.). (J). (ps-2). 1994. pap. 296.00 (1-56784-826-5) Newbridge Comms.

Whole Language Big Books, 6 units, Set. (Illus.). (J). (ps-2). 1994. pap. 89.00 (1-56784-827-3) Newbridge Comms.

Whole Language Celebrations. Flora Joy. (Illus.). 176p. (J). (gr. k-4). 1992. student ed. 13.99 (0-86653-690-6, 1424) Good Apple.

Whole Language Companion, Grades 4-8. David C. Yeager. 1990. pap. 12.95 (0-673-46188-2, GoodYrBooks) Addson-Wesley Educ.

Whole Language Discovery Activities for the Primary Grades. Margaret C. Riley. 1992. pap. text ed. 27.95 (0-87628-616-3) Ctr Appl Res.

Whole Language Evaluation Book. Ed. by Kenneth S. Goodman et al. LC 88-16593. 280p. 1988. pap. text ed. 25.00 (0-435-08484-4) Heinemann.

Whole Language for Second Language Learners. Yvonne S. Freeman & David E. Freeman. LC 92-765. (Illus.). 257p. 1992. pap. text ed. 24.50 (0-435-08723-1, 08723) Heinemann.

Whole Language for the Holidays. Flora Joy. (Illus.). 144p. (J). (gr. k-4). 1992. student ed. 13.99 (0-86653-689-2, 1423) Good Apple.

Whole Language in Middle & Secondary Classrooms: Becoming a Classroom Archaeologist. Harry R. Noden & Richard Vacca. LC 93-31908. (C). 1994. text ed. 32.95 (0-06-500071-4) Addson-Wesley Educ.

Whole Language Intervention for School-Age Children. Janet Norris & Paul Hoffman. LC 92-40679. (School-Age Children Ser.). (Illus.). 361p. (Orig.). (C). 1993. pap. text ed. 45.00 (1-56593-070-3, 0374) Singular Publishing.

Whole Language Journey. Rebecca Harlin et al. (Pippin Teacher's Library). 112p. 1991. pap. text ed. 14.50 (0-88751-034-5, 00709) Heinemann.

Whole Language Kindergarten. Shirley C. Raines & Robert J. Canady. (Early Childhood Education Ser.: No. 30). 304p. (C). 1990. pap. text ed. 19.95 (0-8077-3049-1) Tchrs Coll.

Whole Language Language. Kenneth Gaburo. (Illus.). 48p. 1988. pap. 10.25 (0-939044-21-8) Lingua Pr.

Whole Language Literature Activities for Young Children. Bonnie N. Bogen & Mary A. Sobut. LC 93-2429. 418p. 1996. pap. 28.95 (0-87628-973-1) Ctr Appl Res.

Whole Language Plus: Essays on Literacy in the United States & New Zealand. Courtney B. Cazden. LC 92-17657. (Language & Literacy Ser.). 328p. (C). 1992. text ed. 46.00 (0-8077-3210-9); pap. text ed. 21.95 (0-8077-3209-5) Tchrs Coll.

Whole Language Prime. 1993. pap. 7.95 (0-590-73295-1) Scholastic Inc.

Whole-Language Reading: A Comprehensive Teaching Guide. Emerald Dechant. LC 93-60365. 225p. 1993. 29.95 (1-56676-007-0) Technomic.

Whole Language Research: For Mainstream & High-Ability Elementary Students. M. Lynne Wilson. 104p. 1993. 27.00 (0-9638431-0-9) Growth In Process.

Whole Language Source. 1993. pap. 52.50 (0-590-71637-9) Scholastic Inc.

Whole Language Strategies for Secondary Students. Ed. by Carol Gilles et al. LC 87-24725. 208p. (Orig.). (C). 1989. pap. text ed. 21.95 (0-913461-84-9) R Owen Pubs.

Whole Language Unit. Nancy Polette. (Illus.). 32p. 1989. pap. 4.95 (0-913839-79-5) Pieces of Lrning.

Whole Language Voices in Teacher Education. Ed. by Kathryn F. Whitmore & Yetta M. Goodman. (Illus.). 360p. 1996. pap. text ed. 32.50 (1-57110-028-8) Stenhse Pubs.

Whole Language, What's the Difference? What's the Difference? Carole Edelsky et al. LC 90-42804. (Illus.). 120p. (Orig.). (C). 1990. pap. 11.95 (0-435-08537-9, 08537) Heinemann.

W

Whole Language, Whole Learners: Creating a Literature-Centered Classroom. Laura Robb. (Illus.). 480p. 1994. 30.00 (*0-688-11957-3*) Morrow.

Whole Language 3-4. 1993. pap. 52.50 (*0-590-71756-1*) Scholastic Inc.

Whole Language/OBE Fraud. Samuel L. Blumenfeld. LC 95-26059. 351p. (Orig.). 1996. pap. 19.95 (*0-941995-09-7*) Paradigm ID.

Whole Learning: Whole Language & Content in the Upper Elementary Grades. Pat Cordeiro. LC 91-39407. 288p. (C). 1992. pap. 19.95 (*1-878450-15-8*) R Owen Pubs.

Whole Learning - Whole Child. Joy Cowley. 58p. (Orig.). 1994. pap. 4.95 (*0-7802-1484-6*) Wright Group.

Whole Learning in the Middle School: Evolution & Transition. Ed. by Glennellen Pace. 320p. 1994. pap. text ed. 28.95 (*0-926842-44-7*) CG Pubs Inc.

Whole Library Handbook: Current Data, Professional Advice & Curiosa about Libraries & Library Services. 2nd ed. Compiled by George M. Eberhart. LC 94-42091. 521p. 1995. pap. 30.00 (*0-8389-0646-X*, 0659-1-2045) ALA.

Whole Life Adoption Book: Realistic Advice for Building a Healthy Adoptive Family. Jayne Schooler. LC 93-17998. 219p. (Orig.). 1993. pap. 12.00 (*0-89109-722-8*) Pinon Press.

Whole Life Cookbook: Concept, Principles & Fundamentals of Whole Life Health & Nutrition Using Whole Fresh & Natural Foods. W. David Goines, Sr. (Guide for Total Living Ser.). (Illus.). 60p. 1995. spiral bd. 12.95 (*0-929153-06-5*) Royal Pub NC.

Whole Life Diet: An Integrated Program of Nutrition & Exercise for a Lifestyle of Total Health. Thomas J. Bassler & Robert E. Burger. LC 79-19375. 204p. 1979. 9.95 (*0-87131-305-7*) M Evans.

Whole Life Economics: Revaluing Daily Life. Barbara Brandt. 224p. 1995. pap. 14.95 (*0-86571-266-2*) New Soc Pubs.

Whole Life Economics: Revaluing Daily Life. Barbara Brandt. 256p. 1995. lib. bdg. 39.95 (*0-86571-265-4*) New Soc Pubs.

Whole Lives: Shapers of Modern Biography. Reed Whittemore. LC 89-31338. 192p. 1989. 19.95 (*0-8018-3817-7*) Johns Hopkins.

Whole Lotta Shakin' Goin' On. Campbell & Brody. 1997. 33.00 (*0-02-864727-0*) Mac Lib Ref.

Whole Mac: Solution for the Creative Professional. Giordan. 600p. 1996. 39.99 (*1-56830-298-3*) Mac Comp Pub.

Whole Man & a Half Century, 1890-1940. Rockwell Hereford. (Illus.). 1985. 19.50 (*0-910286-97-3*) Boxwood.

Whole Marriages in a Broken World: God's Design for a Healthy Marriage. Gary Inrig. LC 96-18449. 224p. 1996. pap. 12.99 (*1-57293-015-2*, 0152) Discovery Hse Pubs.

Whole Matter: The Poetic Evolution of Thomas Kinsella. Thomas H. Jackson. LC 94-47563. (Irish Studies). 1995. 39.95 (*0-8156-2659-2*); pap. 17.95 (*0-8156-2660-6*) Syracuse U Pr.

Whole-Meal Salads. Norman Kolpas. 184p. 1992. pap. 9.95 (*0-8092-3995-7*) Contemp Bks.

Whole Meals. Marcea Weber. 160p. pap. 9.95 (*0-89529-606-3*) Avery Pub.

Whole Megillah. Shoshana Silberman. LC 90-5137. (Illus.). 40p. (J). (gr. k-6). 1991. pap. 3.95 (*0-929371-23-2*) Kar-Ben.

Whole Memory Recovery. Beverly Sheridan. 154p. 1993. pap. text ed. 11.95 (*0-913412-68-6*) Brandon Hse.

Whole Men: The Masculine Tradition in New Zealand Literature. Kai Jensen. 208p. 1996. pap. 29.95 (*1-86940-145-X*, Pub. by Auckland Univ NZ) Paul & Co Pubs.

Whole Motion: Collected Poems, 1945-1992. James Dickey. LC 91-50811. (Wesleyan Poetry Ser.). 494p. (C). 1992. pap. 19.95 (*0-8195-1218-4*, Wesleyan Univ Pr) U Pr of New Eng.

Whole Music of Passion: New Essays on Swinburne. Ed. by Rikky Rooksby & Nicholas Shrimpton. 300p. 1993. 67.95 (*0-85967-925-X*, Pub. by Scolar Pr UK) Ashgate Pub Co.

Whole Mystery of Art: Pattern into Poetry in the Work of W. B. Yeats. Giorgio Melchiori. LC 72-12553. (Illus.). 306p. 1978. text ed. 35.00 (*0-8371-6719-1*, MEMA, Greenwood Pr) Greenwood.

Whole New Ball: The Story of the All-American Girls Professional Baseball League. large type ed. Sue Macy. 1995. 42.50 (*0-614-09616-2*, L-81917-00) Am Printing Hse.

Whole New Ball Game: An Interpretation of American Sports. Allen Guttmann. LC 87-26131. x, 233p. (C). 1988. pap. 15.95 (*0-8078-4220-6*) U of NC Pr.

Whole New Ball Game: The Story of the All-American Girls Professional Baseball League. Sue Macy. LC 92-31813. (Illus.). 160p. (YA). (gr. 5 up). 1993. 14.95 (*0-8050-1942-1*, Bks Young Read) H Holt & Co.

Whole New Ball Game: The Story of the All-American Girls Professional Baseball League. Sue Macy. LC 94-46789. (J). 1995. pap. 4.99 (*0-14-037423-X*) Puffin Bks.

Whole New Life. Reynolds Price. 224p. 1994. 20.00 (*0-689-12197-0*, Pub. by Ctrl Bur voor Schimmel NE) Macmillan.

Whole New Life. large type ed. Reynolds Price. LC 94-48471. 1995. pap. 11.95 (*0-452-27473-7*, Plume) NAL-Dutton.

Whole New Light. Sandra Brown. 304p. 1992. mass mkt. 5.99 (*0-553-29783-X*) Bantam.

Whole New Light. large type ed. Sandra Brown. 244p. 1993. reprint ed. lib. bdg. 21.95 (*1-56054-564-X*) Thorndike Pr.

Whole New World & Other Top Recorded Hits. 64p. 1993. pap. 7.95 (*0-7935-2366-4*, 00311623) H Leonard.

Whole Number Book. Bunson. 1995. 84.00 (*0-517-88445-3*) Random Hse Value.

Whole Numbers. Carson & Dellosa. (Home Workbooks Ser.). (Illus.). 64p. (Orig.). (J). (gr. 3-6). 1995. wbk. ed., pap. 2.49 (*0-88724-351-7*, CD6848) Carson-Dellos.

Whole Numbers. Glenn Shepherd. (Power Math Tutor Ser.). (Illus.). 76p. (YA). (gr. 6-12). 1994. pap. text ed. 5.75 (*1-885120-01-X*) F E Braswell.

Whole Numbers. 4th ed. Mary S. Charuhas. (Essential Mathematics for Life Ser.: No. 1). 1995. pap. text ed. 7.95 (*0-02-802608-X*) Glencoe.

Whole Numbers & Money. Jan Phillips. (Smart Solutions Ser.). 1995. pap. 9.64 (*1-56420-118-X*) New Readers.

Whole of Their Lives: Communism in America - a Personal History & Intimate Portrayal of Its Leaders. Benjamin Gitlow. LC 78-179726. (Biography Index Reprint Ser.). 1977. reprint ed. 24.95 (*0-8369-8094-8*) Ayer.

*__Whole Organ Approaches to Cellular Metabolism: Permeation, Cellular Uptake & Product Formation.__ James Bassingthwaighte et al. LC 97-19015. 1998. write for info. (*0-387-94975-5*) Spr-Verlag.

*__Whole Other Ball Game: Women's Literature on Women's Sport.__ Joli Sandoz. LC 97-19260. 1997. pap. write for info. (*0-374-52521-8*) FS&G.

Whole Paddler's Catalog: Views, Reviews, & Resources. Ed. by Zip Kellogg. LC 96-37339. (Illus.). 256p. 1997. pap. text ed. 19.95 (*0-07-033901-5*, Ragged Mntn) Intl Marine.

Whole Parent - Whole Child: A Parents Guide to Raising the Child with a Chronic Illness. Broatch Haig & Patricia M. Moynihan. LC 88-30988. (Orig.). 1989. pap. 9.95 (*0-937721-53-0*) Chronimed.

Whole People Whole Earth: Shalom Lifestyles. Jerry L. Holsopple. 52p. (YA). (gr. 9-12). 1991. Grades 9-12., teacher ed. 59.95 incl. vhs (*1-877736-12-0*) MB Missions.

Whole Picture. Richard Walter. LC 97-23568. 1997. pap. 12.95 (*0-452-27179-7*, Plume) NAL-Dutton.

Whole Plant Perspective on Carbon-Nitrogen Interactions. Ed. by Jacques Roy & Eric Garnier. (Illus.). 1994. 95.00 (*90-5103-086-X*, Pub. by SPB Acad Pub NE) Balogh.

Whole Pop Catalog. Berkeley Pop Culture Project Staff. 608p. (Orig.). 1991. pap. 20.00 (*0-380-76094-0*) Avon.

*__Whole Prayer.__ Walter Wangerin. LC 97-21635. (Spiritual Directions Ser.). 1997. write for info. (*0-310-20197-7*) Zondervan.

*__Whole Psychology Catalog.__ 5th ed. Michael B. Reiner. 366p. (C). 1996. pap. text ed. write for info. (*0-15-504153-3*) HB Coll Pubs.

Whole Realm of Rebellion. Noah W. Hutchings. 34p. (Orig.). 1994. pap. 2.50 (*1-879366-61-4*) Hearthstone OK.

Whole Regolith Pedology: Proceedings of a Symposium Sponsored by Committee S880, Divisions S-5 & S-9 of the Soil Science Society of America & the Clay Minerals Society in Minneapolis, Minnesota, 3 Nov. 1992. Ed. by David L. Cremeens et al. LC 93-47659. (Special Publications: No. 34). 136p. 1994. pap. 24.00 (*0-89118-805-3*) Soil Sci Soc Am.

Whole-School Approaches: Meeting the Special Educational Needs of All Children - A Guide to Teachers. Ed. by Arlene Ramasut. 280p. 1989. 75.00 (*1-85000-569-9*, Falmer Pr); pap. 35.00 (*1-85000-570-2*, Falmer Pr) Taylor & Francis.

Whole School Curriculum: Development in the Primary School. Jennifer Nias & Geoff Southworth. 270p. 1992. 80.00 (*0-7507-0064-5*, Falmer Pr); pap. 29.00 (*0-7507-0065-3*, Falmer Pr) Taylor & Francis.

*__Whole Shebang: The State of the Universe Report.__ Timothy Ferris. LC 96-49768. 393p. 1997. 25.00 (*0-684-81020-4*) S&S Trade.

Whole Sky. Pamela Kircher. LC 95-61372. 80p. 1996. pap. 11.95 (*1-884800-10-6*) Four Way Bks.

*__Whole Soy Cookbook.__ P. Greenberg & Helen N. Hartung. LC 97-19011. 1997. pap. write for info. (*0-517-88813-0*, Crown) Crown Pub Group.

Whole Spy Catalog: A Research Encyclopedia for Researchers, PIs, Spies & Generally Nosy People. Lee Lapin. (Illus.). 440p. (Orig.). 1995. pap. 44.95 (*1-880231-10-7*) Intelligence.

Whole Story. (J). 1993. pap. 19.95 (*0-590-21976-6*) Scholastic Inc.

Whole Story. Elizabeth Bibesco. LC 75-403493. (Short Story Index Reprint Ser.). 1977. 21.95 (*0-8369-3235-8*) Ayer.

*__Whole Story.__ Briane Cambourne. pap. 17.50 (*0-908643-49-7*) Scholastic Inc.

Whole Story: Short Stories for Pleasure & Language Improvement. Richard Rossner. (YA). (gr. 9-12). 1988. audio 22.95 (*0-582-01887-0*, 78325) Longman.

Whole Story: Short Stories for Pleasure & Language Improvement. Richard Rossner. (YA). (gr. 9-12). 1988. pap. text ed. 16.93 (*0-582-79109-X*, 78326) Longman.

Whole Story: 3000 Years of Series & Sequels, 2 vols., Set. John Simkin. 1600p. 1996. 135.00 (*1-875589-26-0*) D W Thorpe.

Whole Story - Editors on Fiction: A Collection of Essays & Stories. Ed. by Warren Slesinger. LC 94-21549. 302p. 1995. pap. 19.95 (*0-930769-12-0*) Bench Pr SC.

Whole Surgery Handbook. David Mclanahan. 1998. pap. 23.95 (*0-525-93798-6*) Viking Penguin.

Whole System Architecture: Beyond Reengineering: A Guidebook for Designing Work Processes & Human Systems for High Performance Capabilities. 2nd ed. Lawrence Miller. (Illus.). 320p. 1994. student ed., spiral bd. 49.95 (*0-9629679-2-0*) Miller Howard Cnslt.

*__Whole-Systems Shared Governance: Architecture for Integration.__ Timothy Porter-O'Grady et al. LC 97-10153. 300p. 1997. 49.00 (*0-8342-0951-9*, 20951) Aspen Pub.

Whole Ten Yards. large type ed. Frank Gifford & Harry Waters. LC 94-161. 1994. lib. bdg. 22.95 (*0-7862-0196-7*) Thorndike Pr.

Whole Ten Yards. Frank Gifford & Harry Waters, Jr. 1994. reprint ed. mass mkt. 5.99 (*0-8041-1284-3*) Ivy Books.

Whole Thing. Catherine Mumaw & Marilyn H. Voran. 24p. (J). (gr. 6-11). 1981. pap. 2.99 (*0-8361-1962-2*) Herald Pr.

*__Whole Tooth.__ Marvin Schissel. 1997. 23.95 (*0-312-15229-9*) St Martin.

Whole Treatise of the Cases of Conscience. William Perkins. LC 74-38218. (English Experience Ser.: No. 482). 690p. 1972. reprint ed. 75.00 (*90-221-0482-6*) Walter J Johnson.

Whole Truth. Janice Kaplan. 304p. (Orig.). 1997. mass mkt. 5.99 (*0-614-17551-8*) Berkley Pub.

*__Whole Truth.__ Janice Kaplan. 304p. 1997. mass mkt. 5.99 (*0-425-15603-6*) Berkley Pub.

Whole Truth. Anthony Robinson. 480p. 1992. mass mkt. 5.99 (*0-8217-3792-9*, Zebra Kensgtn) Kensgtn Pub Corp.

Whole Truth about Contraception: A Guide to Safe & Effective Choices. Beverly Winikoff & Suzanne Wymelenberg. (Illus.). 260p. (Orig.). 1997. pap. 14.95 (*0-309-05494-X*, Joseph Henry Pr) Natl Acad Pr.

Whole Truth About Mexico: President Wilson's Responsibility. Francisco Bulnes. 1976. lib. bdg. 59.95 (*0-8490-1296-1*) Gordon Pr.

Whole Truth About SWAPO: Idealistic Christians & Heroes of Freedom & Justice? or Instruments of International Communist Aggression? American Society for the Defense of Tradition, Family, & Property (TFP) Staff. LC 84-71115. (Illus.). 66p. (Orig.). (C). 1984. pap. 2.50 (*1-877905-23-2*) Am Soc Defense TFP.

*__Whole Truth about the Tithe: What the Church Never Told You.__ Marque Payne. (Illus.). 40p. (Orig.). 1996. pap. 5.99 (*1-889208-97-3*) Glad Tidngs Pub.

*__Whole Truth & Other Myths: Retelling Ancient Tales.__ H. M. Hoover et al. LC 96-47313. (J). 1996. pap. write for info. (*0-89468-267-9*) Natl Gallery Art.

Whole vs. Part Methods in Motor Learning see Scientific Study of the College Student

Whole Waitress Handbook. Lynn Schiavi. (Illus.). 90p. 1985. pap. 4.95 (*0-937269-00-X*) Midnight Oil Pr.

Whole Way to Allergy Relief & Prevention: A Doctor's Complete Guide to Treatment & Self-Care. 2nd rev. ed. Jacqueline Krohn. LC 96-29185. 320p. 1996. pap. 24.95 (*0-88179-134-2*) Hartley & Marks.

Whole Way to Natural Detoxification: Clearing Your Body of Toxins. Jacqueline Krohn. LC 96-22512. (Illus.). 280p. (Orig.). 1996. pap. 24.95 (*0-88179-127-X*) Hartley & Marks.

Whole Wheat Bread Making: Secrets of the Masters Made Easy. Diana Ballard. 1993. pap. 9.95 (*1-55517-120-6*) CFI Dist.

Whole Wheat Bread Recipes. Daniel D. Stuhlman. (Illus.). (Orig.). 1979. pap. 1.25 (*0-934402-00-0*) BYLS Pr.

Whole Wheat Cookery: Treasures from the Wheat Bin. Howard Beck & Anna R. Beck. 166p. 1993. spiral bd., pap. 12.95 (*1-882420-00-4*) Hearth KS.

Whole Woman: Fashioned in His Image. Faye C. Stowe. 136p. 1984. pap. 8.99 (*0-8341-0913-1*) Beacon Hill.

Whole Word Catalogue 1: A Handbook of Writing Ideas for Teachers. Ed. by Rosellen Brown et al. 72p. (Orig.). 1975. pap. 10.95 (*0-915924-02-1*) Tchrs & Writers Coll.

Whole Word Catalogue 2: A Unique Collection of Ideas & Materials to Stimulate Creativity in the Classroom. Ed. by Bill Zavatsky & Ron Padgett. 352p. 1987. pap. 21.95 (*0-915924-67-6*) Tchrs & Writers Coll.

Whole Works, 2 vols. in 1. William Browne. Ed. by W. Carew Hazlitt. (Anglistica & Americana Ser.: No. 66). xxxix, 579p. 1970. reprint ed. 130.00 (*0-685-66437-6*, 05102767) G Olms Pubs.

Whole Works, 3 vols. in 4 pts., Set. Roger Ascham. Ed. by J. A. Giles. LC 70-121837. reprint ed. 265.00 (*0-404-00490-3*) AMS Pr.

Whole Works: With a Life of the Author, & a Critical Examination of His Writings, 10 vols., Set. Jeremy Taylor. Ed. by Reginald Heber. (Anglistica & Americana Ser.: No. 67). 1970. reprint ed. 897.00 (*0-685-66523-2*, 05102770) G Olms Pubs.

Whole Works of Alfred the Great, 3 Pts. in 2 Vols, Set. Alfred The Great. Ed. by J. A. Giles. LC 73-86832. reprint ed. 175.00 (*0-404-00380-X*) AMS Pr.

Whole Works of John Howe, 6 Vols, Set. John Howe. Ed. by H. Rogers. LC 71-169450. reprint ed. lib. bdg. write for info. (*0-404-03360-1*) AMS Pr.

Whole Works of John Lightfoot, 13 Vols, Set. John Lightfoot. Ed. by John Pitman. LC 79-172318. reprint ed. write for info. (*0-404-04010-1*) AMS Pr.

Whole Works This Our Home Record Keeping & Joy of Dicscovery Workbook. Charles Peach. (Illus.). 200p. 1987. student ed. 30.00 (*0-942751-33-7*) Whole Works.

Whole Works Wine Tasting & Record Book. 2nd ed. Charles Peach. (Illus.). 100p. 1987. student ed. 13.00 (*0-942751-01-9*) Whole Works.

Whole World: Books & Manuscripts on Many Subjects. Jenkins Company Staff. (Illus.). 368p. 1980. 10.00 (*0-685-23197-6*, VI5-35-8110) Jenkins.

Whole World Book of Quotations: Wisdom from Women & Men Around the Globe Throughout the Centuries. Ed. by Kathryn Petras & Ross Petras. 576p. 1995. 25.00 (*0-201-62258-0*) Addison-Wesley.

Whole-World Cookbook. Veronica Vezza. LC 96-50409. (J). 1997. 19.95 (*0-689-80155-6*, S&S Bks Young Read) S&S Childrens.

Whole World Cookbook: International Macrobiotic Cuisine. Ed. by East West Journal Staff. (Macrobiotic Home Library). (Illus.). 144p. pap. 6.95 (*0-89529-231-9*) Avery Pub.

Whole World Done Gone Crazy! Ralph Wing. Ed. by Pangaea Press Staff. (Convenience Bks.). 214p. (YA). (gr. 10 up). 1990. pap. text ed. 7.95 (*0-9625534-1-7*, P101) Pangaea Pr.

Whole World Guide to Culture Learning. J. Daniel Hess. LC 94-28819. 280p. (Orig.). 1994. pap. text ed. 22.95 (*1-877864-19-6*) Intercult Pr.

Whole World Guide to Language Learning. Terry Marshall. LC 88-45727. 176p. 1990. pap. 15.95 (*0-933662-75-0*) Intercult Pr.

Whole World in His Hands: A Pictoral Biography of Paul Robeson. Susan Robeson. (Illus.). 256p. 1981. 17.95 (*0-8065-0754-3*, Citadel Pr) Carol Pub Group.

Whole World in His Hands: A Pictorial Biography of Paul Robeson. Susan Robeson. (Illus.). 256p. 1985. reprint ed. pap. 14.95 (*0-8065-0977-5*, Citadel Pr) Carol Pub Group.

Whole World in Your Hands: Looking at Maps. Melvin Berger & Gilda Berger. LC 92-18199. (Discovery Readers Ser.). (Illus.). 48p. (J). (gr. k-4). 1993. per., pap. 4.50 (*0-8249-8609-1*, Ideals Child); lib. bdg. 12.00 (*0-8249-8646-6*, Ideals Child) Hambleton-Hill.

Whole World Is a Single Flower: 365 Kong-ans for Everyday Life. Seung Sahn. LC 91-67336. 288p. (Orig.). 1992. pap. 16.95 (*0-8048-1782-0*) C E Tuttle.

Whole World Is Watching: Mass Media in the Making & Unmaking of the New Left. Todd Gitlin. LC 78-68835. 1980. pap. 14.00 (*0-520-04024-4*) U CA Pr.

Whole World Kit: American Dream Activity Cards. Nikki B. Schreiner et al. (Illus.). 1800p. (J). (gr. 4-8). 1990. pap. text ed. 265.00 (*1-879218-29-1*) Touch & See Educ.

Whole World Over. adapted ed. K. Simonov. Tr. & Adapted by Thelma Schnee. 1947. pap. 5.25 (*0-8222-1248-X*) Dramatists Play.

Whole World Pours Down: Remembering William Stafford, Consultant in Poetry to the Library of Congress, 1970-1971: An Occasion at the Library of Congress, October 13, 1994. William Stafford. LC 94-24646. 1994. write for info. (*0-8444-0844-1*) Lib Congress.

Whole Writer's Catalog: An Introduction to Advanced Composition. Rodney Simard & Susan Stone. LC 92-28588. 280p. 1992. pap. 29.95 (*0-7734-9926-1*) E Mellen.

*__Wholehearted Way: A Translation of Eibei Dogen's Bendowa.__ Kosho U. Roshi. 1997. pap. text ed. 14.95 (*0-8048-3105-X*) C E Tuttle.

Wholeistic Diet Book. 2nd ed. Loretta H. Kurban. LC 85-90057. (Illus.). 50p. 1991. reprint ed. pap. 8.00 (*0-938863-03-7*) Libra Press Chi.

Wholeness. Warren W. Wiersbe. LC 94-7623. (Thirty-Day Devotional Ser.). 72p. (Orig.). 1994. pap. 3.50 (*1-56476-263-7*, 6-3263, Victor Bks) Chariot Victor.

Wholeness & the Implicate Order. Daivd Bohm. 240p. 1996. pap. 16.95 (*0-415-11966-9*) Routledge.

*__Wholeness & the Implicate Order.__ David Bohm. Date not set. pap. 14.95 (*0-7448-0000-5*) Routledge.

Wholeness in Interaction. Community Service Editors. 1976. pap. 1.00 (*0-910420-10-6*) Comm Serv OH.

Wholeness Lost & Wholeness Regained: Forgotten Tales of Individuation from Ancient Tibet. Herbert V. Guenther. LC 93-27380. (SUNY Series in Buddhist Studies). 169p. (C). 1994. pap. text ed. 14.95 (*0-7914-1990-8*) State U NY Pr.

Wholeness Lost & Wholeness Regained: Forgotten Tales of Individuation from Ancient Tibet. Herbert V. Guenther. LC 93-27380. (SUNY Series in Buddhist Studies). 169p. (C). 1994. text ed. 44.50 (*0-7914-1989-4*) State U NY Pr.

Wholeness of Life. Jiddu Krishnamurti. 254p. 1987. 8.95 (*0-318-37035-2*) Asia Bk Corp.

Wholeness of Nature: Goethe's Way Toward a Science of Conscious Participation in Nature. Henri Bortoft. (Goethean Science Ser.). (Illus.). 212p. (Orig.). 1996. pap. 24.95 (*0-940262-79-7*) Lindisfarne Bks.

Wholeness or Transcendence: Ancient Lessons for the Emerging Global Civilization. rev. ed. Georg Feuerstein. 312p. 1992. pap. 15.95 (*0-943914-58-2*) Larson Pubns.

Wholeness Principle: Dynamics of Unity Within Science, Religion & Society. 2nd ed. Anna F. Lemkow. LC 94-34924. 355p. 1995. pap. 14.00 (*0-8356-0715-1*, Quest) Theos Pub Hse.

Wholesale & Retail Trade U. S. A. Industry Analyses, Statistics, & Leading Organizations. Ed. by Arsen J. Darnay & Gary Alampi. 993p. 1995. 195.00 (*0-7876-0865-3*, HG) Gale.

Wholesale Arrangement. large type ed. Day Leclaire. LC 93-20048. 247p. 1993. reprint ed. Alk. paper. 13.95 (*1-56054-681-6*) Thorndike Pr.

Wholesale Book Sources & Moneymaking Book Selling Ideas. Lee Howard. 1988. 10.00 (*0-317-01695-4*) AC Enterp OH.

Wholesale-by-Mail Catalog 1997: The Consumer's Bible to Shopping by Mail, Phone, or On-Line... Print Project Staff. 656p. 1996. pap. 18.00 (*0-06-273339-7*) HarpC.

Wholesale Distribution Channels: New Insights & Perspectives. Intro. by Bert Rosenbloom. LC 93-44293. (Journal of Marketing Channels). (Illus.). 167p. 1994. pap. text ed. 14.95 (*1-56024-618-9*); lib. bdg. 39.95 (*1-56024-617-0*) Haworth Pr.

Wholesale Distributor: Purpose & Function. Don A. Rice. 246p. 1990. pap. 19.00 (*1-881154-01-7*) Darco Pr.

Wholesale Marketing of Fruits & Vegetables in Baltimore. Robert G. Deupree. LC 78-64175. (Johns Hopkins University. Studies in the Social Sciences. Thirtieth Ser. 1912: 2). 128p. 1982. reprint ed. 39.50 (*0-404-61284-9*) AMS Pr.

*__Wholesale Markets: Planning & Design Manual.__ 209p. 1992. 19.00 (*92-5-103107-X*, Pub. by FAO IT) Bernan Associates.

W

An Asterisk (*) at the beginning of an entry indicates that the title is appearing in BIP for the first time.

Wholesaling & Physical Distribution. Kenneth Ertel & Lawrence A. Walsh. Ed. by Eugene L. Dorr. (Occupational Manuals & Projects in Marketing Ser.). 1978. text ed. 12.28 (*0-07-019627-3*) Glencoe.

Wholesaling in Marketing Organization. David A. Revzan. Ed. by Henry Assael. LC 78-256. (Century of Marketing Ser.). 1979. reprint ed. lib. bdg. 58.95 (*0-405-11181-9*) Ayer.

Wholesaling in the U. K. Nineteen Ninety. Euromonitor Staff. (C). 1990. 1,800.00 (*0-86338-393-9*, Pub. by Euromonitor Pubns UK) Gale.

Wholesight. Frederick Parker-Rhodes. LC 77-95406. 30p. (Orig.). 1978. pap. 3.00 (*0-87574-217-3*) Pendle Hill.

Wholesome Communication. J. A. Knepper. Tr. by Theodore Plantinga from DUT. (Pastoral Perspectives Ser.). 104p. (Orig.). 1989. pap. 8.90 (*0-921100-13-2*) Inhtce Pubns.

Wholesome Country Cooking. Don Holm & Myrtle Holm. LC 84-22975. (Orig.). 1985. pap. 7.95 (*0-87004-302-1*) Caxton.

Wholesome Example. Ed Prichard. 172p. 1993. pap. 9.95 (*0-917851-71-4*) Bristol Hse.

Wholesome Nutrition for Mind, Body, & Microflora: The Goal of Lacto-Vegetarianism (Recipes of Udipi Cuisine Included) Yamuna Lingappa & B. T. LIngappa. 416p. 1992. pap. 16.00 (*0-9634999-0-4*) Ecobiol Fnd.

Wholesome Ways of Our Olden Days. Lucretia Larsen. 116p. 1985. 14.95 (*0-87770-360-4*) Ye Galleon.

***Wholesomeness of Irradiated Food.** (Technical Report Ser.: No. 659). 34p. 1981. pap. text ed. 3.00 (*92-4-120659-4*) World Health.

Wholesomeness of Irradiated Food with Special Reference to Wheat, Potatoes & Onions: Report of the FAO-IAEA-WHO Expert Committee, Geneva, 1969. FAO-IAEA-WHO Expert Committee Staff. (Technical Report Ser.: No. 451). 1970. pap. text ed. 5.00 (*92-4-120451-6*, 1100451) World Health.

Wholism & Wholistic Health: The Individual in a Personal Context: Ecology: Our Home & Heritage Held in Trust. Richard L. Crews. 40p. (C). 1988. pap. text ed. write for info. (*0-945864-09-4*) Columbia Pacific U Pr.

Wholism & Wholistic Health: The Individual in a Personal Context: Health & Healing: Ultimate Perspectives & Practicalities. Richard L. Crews. 45p. (C). 1988. pap. text ed. write for info. (*0-945864-10-8*) Columbia Pacific U Pr.

Wholism & Wholistic Health: The Individual in a Personal Context: Wholism: The Concept, Its Origins & Implications. Richard L. Crews. 29p. (C). 1988. pap. text ed. write for info. (*0-945864-08-6*) Columbia Pacific U Pr.

Wholistic Christianity. fac. ed. David O. Moberg. LC 84-29216. 243p. 1985. pap. 69.30 (*0-7837-7348-X*, 2047301) Bks Demand.

Wholistic Hands-On Science. 336p. teacher ed. 20.99 (*0-86653-855-0*, GA1537) Good Apple.

***Wholistic Taxes: Good Advice You Never Thought You Would Hear from a CPA.** Mark Maugnan & Daniel Wilson. LC 96-94805. (Illus.). 240p. (Orig.). 1996. pap. 11.95 (*1-57502-319-9*, P01083) Morris Pubng.

Who'll Sing for Me. Mac McMillion. LC 87-91267. 122p. (Orig.). (J). 1987. pap. 6.00 (*0-9619399-0-7*) M McMillion Pub.

Wholly Animals: A Book of Beastly Tales. David N. Bell. (Cistercian Studies). (Illus.). 300p. 1992. 28.95 (*0-87907-328-4*); pap. 12.95 (*0-87907-628-3*) Cistercian Pubns.

Wholly Bible: What I Intended. Jesus, the Christed. 131p. 1995. 17.95 (*0-9642866-9-6*) HeartHse.

Wholly Cow. Photos by Niki Berg. (Illus.). 96p. 1988. 27.50 (*0-89659-816-0*) Abbeville Pr.

Wholly Cowboy. Rick Walton. 64p. (Orig.). (J). 1995. pap. 3.99 (*1-885628-07-2*) Buckaroo Bks.

Wholly Frijoles: The Whole Bean Cook Book. Shayne Fischer. LC 95-49. 128p. (Orig.). 1995. pap. 6.95 (*1-885590-01-6*) Golden West Pub.

Wholly Hank! Student Activity & Teacher Guides for Hank, Unit 1. Cecilia Boswell. 40p. (J). (gr. k-2). 1991. pap. 12.95 (*0-87719-203-0*, 9203) Gulf Pub.

Wholly Hank! Student Activity & Teacher Guides for Hank, Unit 2. Cecilia Boswell. 40p. (J). (gr. 3-6). 1991. teacher ed., pap. 12.95 (*0-87719-204-9*, 9204) Gulf Pub.

Wholly Holy. Herb Brokering. 96p. (Orig.). 1981. pap. 3.95 (*0-942562-00-3*) Brokering Pr.

Wholly Human: Essays on the Theory & Language of Morality. Bruno Schuller. LC 85-12682. Orig. Title: Der Menschliche Mensch. 224p. (Orig.). reprint ed. pap. 63.90 (*0-7837-6338-7*, 2046050) Bks Demand.

***Wholly Mother Jones: Her Full-to-Bursting Life with Songs & Pictures.** Peter Agnos. (Illus.). 110p. (Orig.). 1997. 24.95 (*0-914018-05-1*, 7270); pap. 16.95 (*0-914018-08-6*, 7271) Green Eagle Pr.

Wholly Sanctified: Living a Life Empowered by the Holy Spirit. rev. ed. A. B. Simpson. LC 82-72739. 128p. 1991. pap. 7.99 (*0-87509-455-4*) Chr Pubns.

Whom Does the Constitution Command? A Conceptual Analysis with Practical Implications. Larry L. Alexander & Paul Horton. LC 87-32272. (Contributions in Legal Studies: No. 42). 181p. 1988. text ed. 49.95 (*0-313-26216-0*, AWC/, Greenwood Pr) Greenwood.

***Whom God Has Joined Together: Words to Stay Married By.** Helen Caswell. (Illus.). 48p. 1997. 15.00 (*0-687-01009-8*) Abingdon.

Whom God Hath Joined. Arnold Bennett. (Pocket Classics Ser.). 235p. 1985. reprint ed. pap. 7.00 (*0-86299-207-9*) Academy Chi Pubs.

Whom God Hath Joined. Arnold Bennett. LC 74-17007. (Collected Works of Arnold Bennett: Vol. 88). 1977. reprint ed. 34.95 (*0-518-19169-9*) Ayer.

Whom God Hath Joined Together: The Work of Marriage Guidance. Ed. by Jane Lewis & David Clark. 320p. (C). (gr. 13 up). 1991. text ed. 79.95 (*0-415-05553-9*, Routledge NY) Routledge.

Whom God Wishes to Destroy... Francis Coppola & the New Hollywood. Jon Lewis. LC 94-44270. (Illus.). 208p. Date not set. pap. 12.95 (*0-8223-1889-X*) Duke.

Whom God Wishes to Destroy... Francis Coppola & the New Hollywood. Jon Lewis. LC 94-44270. (Illus.). 216p. 1995. text ed. 23.95 (*0-8223-1602-1*) Duke.

Whom Gods Destroy: Elements of Greek & Tragic Madness. Ruth Padel. LC 94-25529. 276p. 1995. text ed. 39.50 (*0-691-03360-9*) Princeton U Pr.

Whom Gods Destroy: Elements of Greek & Tragic Madness. Ruth Padel. 296p. 1995. pap. text ed. 14.95 (*0-691-02588-6*) Princeton U Pr.

Whom Has God Joined Together? A Biblical Examination of Miscegenation. Dallas Jackson. 240p. (Orig.). 1990. pap. 10.00 (*0-9624412-0-1*) Jackson MI.

Whom Have We Welcomed? The Adequacy & Quality of United States Immigration Data for Policy Analyses & Evaluation. Silvano M. Tomasi & Charles B. Keely. LC 75-27815. 115p. (C). 1975. pap. text ed. 9.95 (*0-913256-19-6*) CMS.

Whom Shall I Fear? Kendra Burkholder. (Illus.). 228p. (J). 1996. 7.65 (*0-614-17646-8*, 2469) Rod & Staff.

Whom Shall I Fear? A Garr Reed Mystery. Athol Dickson. (Garr Reed Ser.). 352p. 1996. pap. 12.99 (*0-310-20760-6*) Zondervan.

Whom Shall I Marry. Andrew Swanson. 30p. 1995. pap. 2.00 (*0-85151-688-2*) Banner of Truth.

Whom Shall I Send? Watchman Nee. Tr. by Stephen Kaung. 89p. 1979. pap. 3.50 (*0-935008-45-4*) Christian Fellow Pubs.

Whom the Gods Destroyed. Josephine D. Bacon. LC 70-116931. (Short Story Index Reprint Ser.). 1977. 19.95 (*0-8369-3433-4*) Ayer.

Whom the Gods Love. Kate Ross. 400p. 1996. pap. 5.95 (*0-14-024767-X*, Penguin Bks) Viking Penguin.

Whom We Shall Welcome. Naturalization Staff & President's Commission on Immigration. LC 73-146270. (Civil Liberties in American History Ser.). 1971. reprint ed. lib. bdg. 45.00 (*0-306-70145-6*) Da Capo.

Whom We Would Never More See: History & Archaeology Recover the Lives & Deaths of African American Civil War Soldiers on Folly Island, South Carolina. Steven D. Smith. Ed. by Judith M. Andrews. (Topics in African American History Ser.). 52p. 1993. pap. 5.00 (*1-880067-19-6*) SC Dept of Arch & Hist.

Whomp & Moonshiver. Thomas Whitbread. (New Poets of America Ser.). 72p. (C). 1982. pap. 7.00 (*0-918526-31-0*) BOA Edns.

Whoo Done It? Gayle Roper. (Adventures of Scooter & Jake Ser.). (Illus.). 48p. (Orig.). (J). (gr. 3-6). 1996. pap. 3.99 (*0-614-11766-6*) Chariot Victor.

Whoo-oo Is It? Megan McDonald. LC 91-18494. (Illus.). 32p. (J). (ps-1). 1992. lib. bdg. 16.99 (*0-531-08574-0*) Orchard Bks Watts.

***Whoo-oo Is It?** Megan McDonald. LC 91-18494. (Illus.). 32p. (J). (ps-1). 1997. pap. 5.95 (*0-531-07094-8*) Orchard Bks Watts.

Whooo's There? Lily Jones. (Light-&-Sound Bks.). 16p. (J). (ps-3). 1992. 9.95 (*0-89577-439-9*) RD Assn.

Whooosh! Went the Wish. Toby Speed. LC 95-10592. (Illus.). (J). 1996. 15.95 (*0-399-23000-9*, Putnam) Putnam Pub Group.

Whoop for Joy: A Christmas Wish. Jane Briggs-Bunting. LC 95-95152. (Barnyard Tales Ser.). (Illus.). 32p. (J). (gr. 1-5). 1995. 13.95 (*0-9649083-0-1*) Blck Riv Trad.

Whoopee John Wilfahrt Old Time Dance Band: The German-Bohemian Roots of the Whoopee John Wilfahrt Dance Band. La Vern J. Rippley. (Illus.). 22p. (Orig.). 1992. pap. write for info. (*0-9622931-1-3*) St Olaf German.

***Whoopi.** Whoopi Goldberg. 1997. write for info. (*0-688-15252-X*, R Weisbach Bks) Morrow.

Whoopi Goldberg. Mary A. Adams. 1996. pap. text ed. 7.95 (*0-382-39497-6*) Silver Burdett Pr.

Whoopi Goldberg: Entertainer. Rose Blue. Ed. by Nathan I. Huggins. (Black Americans of Achievement Ser.). (Illus.). 144p. (YA). (gr. 5 up). 1994. lib. bdg. 19.95 (*0-7910-2152-1*) Chelsea Hse.

***Whoopi Goldberg: Entertainer.** Rose Blue. Ed. by Nathan I. Huggins. (Black Americans of Achievement Ser.). (Illus.). 144p. (YA). (gr. 5 up). 1995. pap. 8.95 (*0-7910-2153-X*) Chelsea Hse.

Whoopi Goldberg: Entertainer. Chelsea House Publishers Staff. LC 96-17829. (Junior Black Americans of Achievement Ser.). 1996. 15.95 (*0-7910-2396-6*) Chelsea Hse.

Whoopi Goldberg: From Street to Stardom. Mary A. Adams. LC 92-23766. (Taking Part Ser.). (Illus.). 64p. (J). (gr. 3 up). 1993. lib. bdg. 13.95 (*0-87518-562-2*) Silver Burdett Pr.

***Whoopi Goldberg: Her Journey from Poverty to Mega-Stardom.** James R. Parish. 1997. 22.50 (*1-55972-431-5*, Birch Ln Pr) Carol Pub Group.

Whooping Crane. Dorothy H. Patent. (J). (gr. 4-7). 1993. pap. 6.95 (*0-395-66505-1*, Clarion Bks) HM.

Whooping Crane: North America's Symbol of Conservation. Jerome J. Pratt. Ed. by Susan Stevens. (Illus.). 171p. 1996. pap. 12.95 (*0-9640308-3-7*) Castle R Pubng.

***Whooping Crones: God-Songs for Women.** Nancy Williams. (Illus.). 116p. 1996. spiral bd. 35.00 (*0-9655467-0-5*) Catherine Joseph.

Whoops! Jonah & the Fish. Mary M. Simon. (Hear Me Read Ser.). (Illus.). 24p. (Orig.). (J). (ps-1). 1992. pap. 2.49 (*0-570-04704-8*, 56-1663) Concordia.

Whooptie Whooptie Whatie Whatiee Bird. Richard Ivy. 28p. (J). (ps-6). 1993. pap. 8.50 (*1-884095-00-3*) Ivy Hill Pubs.

Whoosh. C. Paul Willis. 48p. (Orig.). 1994. pap. 4.50 (*1-885857-04-7*) Four Wnds Pubng.

Whoosher, the Happy Little Whale. Christine H. Tangvald. (Illus.). 24p. (J). (ps-k). 1995. pap. 3.99 (*0-7847-0166-0*, 03926) Standard Pub.

Whopper! Idella F. Bodie. LC 88-36243. (Illus.). (J). (gr. 4-7). 1989. pap. 6.95 (*0-87844-086-0*) Sandlapper Pub Co.

Whoppers: Tall Tales & Other Lies Collected from American Folklore. Ed. by Alvin Schwartz. LC 74-32024. (Trophy Nonfiction Bk.). (Illus.). 128p. (J). (gr. 4 up). 1990. reprint ed. pap. 3.95 (*0-06-446091-6*, Trophy) HarpC Child Bks.

Whoppi Goldberg. Judy DeBoer. LC 93-50691. (Ovations Ser.). (Illus.). 32p. (YA). (gr. 4 up). 1998. lib. bdg. 14.95 (*0-88682-696-9*) Creative Ed.

Whore Carnival. Shannon Bell. 287p. Date not set. 8.00 (*1-57027-022-8*) Autonomedia.

Whore Stories. Kurt Brecht. 54p. (Orig.). (C). 1994. pap. 6.00 (*1-879188-03-1*) Dirty Rotten Pr.

***Whoredom: God's Unfaithful Wife in Biblical Theology.** Raymond C. Ortlund, Jr. LC 96-45363. (New Studies in Biblical Theology Ser.). 200p. 1996. pap. 18.00 (*0-8028-4285-2*) Eerdmans.

Whoredom in Kimmage: Irish Women Coming of Age. Rosemary Mahoney. LC 94-11848. 336p. 1994. pap. 12.95 (*0-385-47450-4*, Anchor NY) Doubleday.

Whorehouse Bells Were Ringing & Other Songs Cowboys Sing. Ed. by Guy Logsdon. LC 88-19931. (Music in American Life Ser.). (Illus.). 416p. 1989. text ed. 24.95 (*0-252-01583-5*) U of Ill Pr.

Whorehouse Bells Were Ringing & Other Songs Cowboys Sing. Guy Logsdon. (Illus.). 416p. 1995. 15.95 (*0-252-06488-7*) U of Ill Pr.

***Whores & Other Feminists.** Ed. by Jill Nagle. 256p. 1997. pap. 17.95 (*0-415-91822-7*, Routledge NY) Routledge.

***Whores & Other Feminists.** Ed. by Jill Nagle. 256p. (C). 1997. text ed. 65.00 (*0-415-91821-9*, Routledge NY) Routledge.

Whores Before Descartes: Assorted Poetry & Sordid Prose. Stuart L. Burns. LC 80-54381. 96p. (Orig.). (C). 1980. pap. 4.50 (*0-9605326-0-9*) Wash Launderan.

Whores for Gloria. William T. Vollmann. 176p. 1991. 18.50 (*0-679-40342-6*, Penguin Bks) Viking Penguin.

Whores for Gloria. William T. Vollmann. 144p. 1994. pap. 9.95 (*0-14-023157-9*, Penguin Bks) Viking Penguin.

Whores from Samarkand. A. Grenier. LC 92-74972. 64p. (Orig.). 1993. pap. 8.95 (*1-877978-46-9*, FLF Pr) Woldt.

Whores in History. Nickie Roberts. (Illus.). 384p. 1992. 28.00 (*0-246-13234-5*, Pub. by HarpC UK) HarpC.

Whores in History. Nickie Roberts. (Illus.). 384p. 1993. pap. 12.00 (*0-586-20029-0*, Pub. by HarpC UK) HarpC.

Whores of Lost Atlantis. Charles Busch. 304p. 1995. pap. 10.95 (*0-14-024391-7*, Penguin Bks) Viking Penguin.

Whores of Lost Atlantis: A Novel. Charles Busch. LC 93-1399. 304p. 1993. 21.95 (*1-56282-780-4*) Hyperion.

***Whores of the Court: The Fraud of Psychiatric Testimony & the Rape of American Justice.** Margaret A. Hagen. LC 96-52972. 224p. 1997. 23.00 (*0-06-039197-9*, ReganBooks) HarpC.

Whore's Rhetorick. Ferrante Pallavicino. 1961. 10.95 (*0-8392-1132-5*) Astor-Honor.

Whores Rhetorick, Calculated to the Meridian of London, & Conformed to the Rules of Art. LC 79-17643. 1979. 50.00 (*0-8201-1338-7*) Schol Facsimiles.

Whoreson. Donald Goines. 320p. (Orig.). 1995. mass mkt. 4.95 (*0-87067-954-6*) Holloway.

Whorf Theory Complex: A Critical Reconstruction. Penny Lee. LC 96-21119. (Studies in the History of the Language Sciences: No. 81). x, 324p. 1996. pap. 29.95 (*1-55619-619-9*); lib. bdg. 79.00 (*1-55619-618-0*) Benjamins North Am.

Who's a Goblin? (Little Landoll Halloween Ser.). 32p. (J). (ps-6). Date not set. text ed. 1.29 (*1-56987-329-1*) Landoll.

Who's a Hero. Allen Gerry. (Illus.). 250p. 1992. pap. write for info. (*0-9629660-0-2*) A Gerry.

***Who's a Pest?** Crosby N. Bonsall. (Illus.). (J). (ps-3). 6.93 (*0-06-020620-9*, 133597) HarpC Child Bks.

Who's a Pest? Crosby N. Bonsall. LC 62-13310. (Harper I Can Read Bk.). (Illus.). 64p. (J). (gr. k-3). 1962. lib. bdg. 14.89 (*0-06-020621-7*) HarpC Child Bks.

Who's a Pest? Crosby N. Bonsall. LC 62-13310. (Trophy I Can Read Bk.). (Illus.). 64p. (J). (gr. k-3). 1986. pap. 3.50 (*0-06-444099-0*, Trophy) HarpC Child Bks.

Who's a Pretty Boy Then? Vol. 1: One Hundred & Fifty Years of Gay Life in Pictures. James Gardiner. LC 96-67904. (Illus.). 240p. (Orig.). (C). 1997. 40.00 (*1-85242-513-X*) Serpents Tail.

Who's a Silly Egg? Bob Reese. Ed. by Alton Jordan. (Buppet Bks.). (Illus.). (J). (gr. 1-4). 1980. 9.95 (*0-89868-092-1*, Read Res); pap. 3.95 (*0-89868-103-0*, Read Res) ARO Pub.

Who's Afraid? A Pop-Up Counting Book. Carla Dijs. LC 95-78339. (Illus.). 12p. (J). (ps-1). 1996. 9.95 (*0-8050-4398-5*, B Martin BYR) H Holt & Co.

Who's Afraid ...? Facing Children's Fears with Folktales. Norma J. Livo. (Learning Through Folklore Ser.). (Illus.). xxxii, 176p. 1994. pap. text ed. 18.50 (*0-87287-950-X*) Teacher Ideas Pr.

Who's Afraid? The Phobic's Handbook. rev. ed. Barbara Fried. LC 84-28671. (Illus.). 100p. 1985. reprint ed. 16.95 (*0-89876-104-2*) Gardner Pr.

Who's Afraid? & Other Strange Stories. Philippa Pearce. LC 86-14299. 160p. (J). (gr. 5-9). 1987. 11.95 (*0-688-06895-2*) Greenwillow.

***Who's Afraid Ernestine.** Marjorie W. Sharmat. (J). Date not set. 9.95 (*0-399-21007-5*) Putnam Pub Group.

Who's Afraid of a Hinged-Tail Bingbuffer? Object Lessons for Children. Ed. by King Duncan. LC 87-90466. 144p. (Orig.). 1987. pap. 7.50 (*0-936497-02-5*) Seven Worlds.

Who's Afraid of Beowulf? Tom Holt. 1991. mass mkt. 5.50 (*0-441-88591-8*) Ace Bks.

Who's Afraid of Beowulf? Tom Holt. 224p. 1996. mass mkt. 5.50 (*0-614-13604-0*) Ace Bks.

Who's Afraid of C Plus Plus: Programming Primer for the PC. Steve Heller. (Illus.). 508p. 1996. pap. 39.95 (*0-12-339097-4*) Acad Pr.

Who's Afraid of Classical Music? Michael Walsh. 224p. 1989. pap. 11.00 (*0-671-66751-3*, Fireside) S&S Trade.

***Who's Afraid of Feminism.** Ann Oakley. Date not set. 30.00 (*1-56584-384-3*) New Press NY.

***Who's Afraid Of Feminism Pa.** Ann Oakley. Date not set. pap. 15.95 (*1-56584-385-1*) New Press NY.

Who's Afraid of Freedom: Korean-American Artists in California. Sarah Lee. Ed. by Lorna Price. (Illus.). 56p. (Orig.). 1996. pap. 14.95 (*0-917493-22-2*) Newport Harbor.

Who's Afraid of Freemasons? Alexander Piatigorsky. 380p. 1996. 30.00 (*1-86046-029-1*) Harvill Pr UK.

Who's Afraid of Indian Cooking? Book of Menus. Lali Nayar & Rajul Suxena. (C). 1994. 22.50 (*81-86112-64-2*, Pub. by UBS Pubs Dist II) S Asia.

***Who's Afraid of Java.** Steve Heller. (Who's Afraid Ser.). (Illus.). 350p. 1997. pap. 39.95 (*0-12-339101-6*, AP Prof) Acad Pr.

Who's Afraid of Opera? Michael Walsh. 1994. pap. 12.00 (*0-671-88402-6*, Fireside) S&S Trade.

***Who's Afraid of Perl.** Morgan Davis. (Who's Afraid Ser.). (Illus.). 350p. 1997. pap. 39.95 (*0-12-206355-4*, AP Prof) Acad Pr.

Who's Afraid of Schrodinger's Cat? All the New Science Ideas You Need to Keep up with the New Thinking. Danah Zohar et al. LC 96-20769. 1997. 30.00 (*0-688-11865-8*) Morrow.

***Who's Afraid of Schrodinger's Cat? All the New Science Ideas You Need to Keep up with the New Thinking.** Danah Zohar et al. (Illus.). Date not set. write for info. (*0-614-19436-9*) Morrow.

Who's Afraid of the Big Bad Bully. Teddy Slater. LC 94-3323. (Hello Reader! Ser.). (Illus.). 48p. (J). (gr. 1-2). 1995. 3.50 (*0-590-47879-6*, Cartwheel) Scholastic Inc.

Who's Afraid of the Dark? Crosby N. Bonsall. LC 79-2700. (Harper Early I Can Read Bk.). (Illus.). 32p. (J). (ps-3). 1980. lib. bdg. 14.89 (*0-06-020599-7*) HarpC Child Bks.

Who's Afraid of the Dark. Cynthia Carosella. 1994. pap. 12.00 (*0-06-095072-2*, HarpT) HarpC.

Who's Afraid of the Dark? Leia A. Greene. (Little Angel Bks.). (Illus.). 32p. (J). (gr. k-12). 1992. pap. text ed. 4.95 (*1-880737-09-4*) Crystal Jrns.

***Who's Afraid of the Dark?** Leia Stinnett. 1996. pap. text ed. 6.95 (*0-929385-89-6*) Light Tech Comns Servs.

Who's Afraid of the Dark? Crosby N. Bonsall. LC 79-2700. (Trophy Early I Can Read Bk.). (Illus.). 32p. (J). (ps-2). 1985. reprint ed. pap. 3.50 (*0-06-444071-0*, Trophy) HarpC Child Bks.

Who's Afraid of the Ghost Train? Frank Rodgers. (Illus.). 32p. (J). (ps-1). 1989. 13.00 (*0-15-200642-7*, Gulliver Bks) HarBrace.

***Who's Afraid of the Holy Ghost?** Stevan Williamson. Date not set. 8.99 (*0-89274-916-4*) Harrison Hse.

Who's Afraid of the Holy Ghost? Steven Williamson. 192p. 1994. pap. 8.99 (*0-88144-916-4*, HH-916) Harrison Hse.

Who's Afraid of the Religious Right? Don Feder. 300p. 1996. 19.95 (*0-89526-456-0*) Regnery Pub.

Who's Afraid of Virginia Woolf? (Book Notes Ser.). 1985. pap. 2.50 (*0-8120-3549-6*) Barron.

Who's Afraid of Virginia Woolf? Edward Albee. 1962. pap. 5.25 (*0-8222-1249-8*) Dramatists Play.

Who's Afraid of Virginia Woolf? Edward Albee. 256p. 1983. pap. 5.99 (*0-451-15871-7*, Sig) NAL-Dutton.

Who's Afraid of Virginia Woolf? Notes. Cynthia C. McGowan. (Orig.). 1979. pap. text ed. 4.50 (*0-8220-1383-5*) Cliffs.

Who's Afraid of Wole Soyinka: Essays on Censorship. Adewale Maja-Pearce. (Studies in African Literature). 128p. (C). 1991. pap. 17.50 (*0-435-90977-0*, 90977) Heinemann.

Who's at Shining Time Station. Bill Kispert. (Shining Time Station Classics Ser.). (Illus.). 22p. (J). (ps-2). 1993. bds. 4.95 (*1-884336-02-7*) Qual Family.

Who's at the Firehouse? Illus. by Bettina Paterson. LC 95-77544. (Life & Look Board Bks.). 12p. (J). (ps). 1996. bds. 4.95 (*0-448-41281-0*, G&D) Putnam Pub Group.

Who's Bashing Whom? Trade Conflict in High-Technology Industries. Laura D. Tyson. LC 92-15646. 324p. 1992. pap. 25.00 (*0-88132-106-0*) Inst Intl Eco.

***Who's Been Sleeping in My Bed?** Jule McBride. (Love & Laughter Ser.: No. 23). 1997. mass mkt. 3.50 (*0-373-44023-5*, 1-44023-9) Harlequin Bks.

Who's Been Sleeping in My Grave? R. L. Stine. (Ghosts of Fear Street Ser.: Vol. 2). (J). (gr. 3-6). Date not set. pap. 3.50 (*0-671-52942-0*, PB Trade Paper) PB.

Who's Behind Our Farm Policy. Wesley McCune. LC 75-14699. 374p. 1975. reprint ed. text ed. 65.00 (*0-8371-8238-7*, MCWB, Greenwood Pr) Greenwood.

Whom's Behind the New World Order. 1992. lib. bdg. 75.00 (*0-8490-5434-6*) Gordon Pr.

Who's Boss? Training Your Pre-Schooler in Self-Management. Francis H. Wise. Ed. & Intro. by Joyce M. Wise. LC 82-91074. (Illus.). 220p. (Orig.). (C). 1982. pap. 5.95 (*0-915766-58-2*) Wise Pub.

Who's Bringing Them Up? Television & Child Development: How to Break the T. V. Habit. Martin Large. (Illus.). 192p. 1990. pap. 14.95 (*1-869890-24-8*, 317, Pub. by Hawthorn Press UK) Anthroposophic.

***Who's Bugging You?** Charles Reasoner. (Sliding Surprise Ser.). (Illus.). 12p. (J). (ps). 1997. bds. 9.95 (*0-8431-7989-9*) Price Stern Sloan.

Who's Buried in Grandmother's Garden? Marion J. Dickerson. 1995. 15.95 (*0-533-11205-2*) Vantage.

W

An Asterisk (*) at the beginning of an entry indicates that the title is appearing in BIP for the first time.

Who's Buried Where in England. 2nd ed. Douglas Greenwood. (Illus.). 352p. 1990. pap. 33.50 (*0-09-474040-2*, Pub. by Constable Pubs UK) Trans-Atl Phila.

*__Who's Buying Food & Drink.__ Marcia Mogelonsky. 292p. 1996. 69.95 (*1-885070-04-7*) New Strategist.

*__Who's Buying for the Home.__ Alison S. Wellner. 502p. 1996. 89.95 (*1-885070-05-5*) New Strategist.

Who's Calling the Shots: How to Respond Effectively to Children's Fascination with War Play & War Toys. Nancy Carlsson-Paige & Diane E. Levin. (Illus.). 204p. 1990. pap. 14.95 (*0-86571-165-8*); lib. bdg. 41.95 (*0-86571-164-X*) New Soc Pubs.

Who's Coming to Stay? Jane Walker. (Little Christmas Window Book Ser.). (Illus.). 14p. (J). (gr. k-3). 1996. bds. 3.99 (*1-57584-044-8*) Rdrs Dgst Yng Fam.

Who's Counting. (Little Remembrance Gift Editions Ser.). (J). 6.95 (*0-87741-006-2*) Makepeace Colony.

Who's Counting? Nancy Tafuri. LC 85-17702. (Illus.). 24p. (J). (ps-1). 1986. 16.00 (*0-688-06130-3*); lib. bdg. 15.93 (*0-688-06131-1*) Greenwillow.

Who's Counting? Nancy Tafuri. LC 92-24604. (Illus.). 32p. (J). (ps up). 1993. reprint ed. pap. 4.95 (*0-688-12266-3*, Mulberry) Morrow.

Who's Doing What in Development Education. 274p. 1991. pap. 20.00 (*0-944675-50-6*) Amer Forum.

Who's Endangered on Noah's Ark? Literary & Scientific Activities for Teachers & Parents. Glenn McGlathery & Norma J. Livo. LC 92-19570. (Learning Through Folklore Ser.). (Illus.). 173p. 1992. pap. text ed. 22.00 (*0-87287-949-6*) Teacher Ideas Pr.

Who's Fit to Be A Parent? Mukti J. Campion. LC 94-8500. 288p. (C). (gr. 13). 1994. text ed. 59.95 (*0-415-06683-2*, A7818) Routledge.

Who's Fit to Be A Parent? Mukti J. Campion. LC 94-8500. 336p. (C). 1995. pap. 18.95 (*0-415-06684-0*, A7822) Routledge.

Who's Following Directions? Beverly Armstrong. (Skill Builder Ser.). (Illus.). 32p. (J). (gr. 4-7). 1979. student ed. 4.95 (*0-88160-072-5*, LW 805) Learning Wks.

Who's Getting Ready for Christmas? Maggie Kneen. LC 93-11061. (Illus.). (J). (gr. 4-7). 1993. 13.95 (*0-8118-0470-4*) Chronicle Bks.

*__Who's Going to Bury Me When I'm Gone?__ Robin A. Clark. Ed. by Tammy Maksen. 150p. (Orig.). 1997. pap. 9.99 (*0-9656425-9-3*) Fly Robin.

Who's Going to Run General Motors? Green. 1995. pap. text ed. write for info. (*0-13-185257-4*) P-H.

Who's Going to Run General Motors? What College Students Need to Learn Today to Become the Business Leaders of Tomorrow. Kenneth C. Green & Daniel T. Seymour. LC 90-49064. 218p. (Orig.). 1990. pap. 10.95 (*1-56079-037-7*) Petersons.

*__Who's Gonna Tie My Shoes?__ Susan Staff. (Illus.). 80p. 1997. pap. 8.00 (*0-8059-4147-9*) Dorrance.

Who's Got Big Googly Eyes? Playskool Staff. (J). 1996. pap. 7.99 (*0-525-45552-3*) Dutton Child Bks.

Who's Got Gertie? & How Can We Get Her Back? Linda Bailey. Ed. by Christy Grant. LC 96-13692. (Stevie Diamond Mystery Ser.: Vol. 3). 176p. (J). (gr. 4-7). 1996. lib. bdg. 13.95 (*0-8075-9062-2*) A Whitman.

Who's Got Gertie? & How Can We Get Her Back? Linda Bailey. Ed. by Christy Grant. LC 96-13692. (Stevie Diamond Mystery Ser.: Vol. 3). 176p. (J). (gr. 4-7). 1996. pap. 4.50 (*0-8075-9063-0*) A Whitman.

Who's Got the Ball? (& Other Nagging Questions about Team Life) A Player's Guide for Work Teams. Maureen O'Brien. LC 94-23535. (Management Ser.). 207p. 22.00 (*0-7879-0057-5*) Jossey-Bass.

*__Who's Got the Compass? I Think I'm Lost.__ Sherry Buffington. LC 96-79217. 216p. 1997. pap. 14.95 (*1-885221-67-3*) BookPartners.

Who's Had Who. Simon Bell et al. 1990. pap. 9.95 (*0-446-39042-9*) Warner Bks.

Who's Happy Now? Oliver Hailey. 1970. pap. 5.25 (*0-8222-1250-1*) Dramatists Play.

Who's Hatching? Charles Reasoner. LC 93-87680. (Sliding Surprise Bks.). (Illus.). 12p. (J). (ps). 1994. bds. 9.95 (*0-8431-3717-7*) Price Stern Sloan.

Who's Hatching Here? - Quien Nacera Aqui? Alma F. Ada. (Libros para Contar Ser.). (Illus.). 24p. (ENG & SPA.). (J). (gr. k-2). 1989. English ed. 3.95 (*0-88272-811-3*); Spanish ed. 3.95 (*0-88272-800-8*) Santillana.

*__Who's Haunting the House of Horror.__ Rupert Heath. (Solve It Yourself Ser.). (Illus.). (J). (gr. 6 up). 1997. pap. 6.95 (*0-7460-2699-4*, Usborne); lib. bdg. 14.95 (*0-88110-913-4*, Usborne) EDC.

Who's He & Who's Out. Cathy Hope. LC 92-21396. (Voyages Ser.). (Illus.). (J). 1993. 4.25 (*0-383-03607-0*) SRA McGraw.

Who's He When He's at Home: A James Joyce Directory. Shari Benstock & Bernard Benstock. LC 79-17947. 251p. reprint ed. pap. 71.60 (*0-7837-5731-X*, 2045392) Bks Demand.

Who's Helping Out: Support Networks among American Families. 1995. lib. bdg. 250.99 (*0-8490-6860-6*) Gordon Pr.

Who's Here. Dan Rattiner. 1994. pap. 15.00 (*0-916366-91-X*) Pushcart Pr.

Who's Hiding? Lynette Ruschak. (J). (ps). 1991. pap. 8.95 (*0-671-73957-3*, S&S Bks Young Read) S&S Childrens.

Who's Hiding? Rozanne L. Williams. (Emergent Reader Big Bks.). (Illus.). 16p. (J). (gr. k-2). 1995. pap. 11.98 (*1-57471-017-6*) Creat Teach Pr.

Who's Hiding?, Level 2. Rozanne L. Williams. (Emergent Reader Science Ser.). 16p. 1994. 2.49 (*0-916119-39-4*, 3529) Creat Teach Pr.

Who's Hiding? Sesame Street. Children's Television Workshop Staff. LC 84-81602. (Golden Touch & Feel Bks.). (Illus.). 14p. (J). (ps). 1986. 6.50 (*0-307-12157-7*, Golden Books) Western Pub.

Who's Hiding Here? Yoshi. LC 86-25455. (Illus.). 36p. (J). (ps up). 1991. pap. 16.00 (*0-88708-041-3*, Picture Book Studio) S&S Childrens.

Who's Hiding Here? Mini Book. Yoshi. LC 86-25455. (Illus.). 32p. (J). (ps up). 1992. pap. 4.95 (*0-88708-277-7*, Picture Book Studio) S&S Childrens.

*__Who's Hiring in Atlanta: 1997 Edition.__ Stephen Hines. (Who's Hiring Ser.). 336p. (Orig.). 1996. pap. 14.95 (*0-929255-19-4*) CareerSource.

Who's Hiring in Hospitality. Joseph E. Witzman & Jack Block. (Illus.). 200p. (Orig.). 1987. pap. write for info. (*0-935423-02-8*) Educ Pubns.

Who's Hiring Who. rev. ed. Richard Lathrop. (Illus.). 268p. 1989. pap. 9.95 (*0-89815-298-4*) Ten Speed Pr.

Who's His Buddy? Easy Animal Reader. Shiotsu. (Illus.). 16p. (J). (ps-1). 1996. pap. 2.49 (*1-57690-051-7*) Tchr Create Mat.

Who's Holding the Baby? Day Leclaire. 1994. mass mkt. 2.99 (*0-373-03338-9*, 1-03338-0) Harlequin Bks.

Who's Home? Keith Faulkner. (Illus.). 12p. (J). (ps). 6.99 (*1-881445-33-X*) Sandvik Pub.

Who's Hungry? Keith Faulkner. (Illus.). 12p. (J). (ps). 1994. 6.99 (*1-881445-34-8*) Sandvik Pub.

Who's Important to You?, Bk. 3. Durlynn Aneman & Vickie Sanders. LC 92-84129. (Options: a Communication Skills Ser.: Bk. 3). 1994. pap. write for info. (*0-318-70142-1*) S-W Pub.

Who's in a Family? Robert Skutch. LC 94-29635. (Illus.). 32p. (J). (ps-2). 1995. 12.95 (*1-883672-13-9*) Tricycle Pr.

Who's in Charge? Harvey Jackins. 1965. pap. 2.00 (*0-911214-10-0*) Rational Isl.

Who's in Charge? A Biblical Approach to Parenting. Norman D. Stolpe. LC 93-9613. (Issues in Christian Living Ser.). 1993. 7.15 (*1-56212-029-8*) CRC Pubns.

Who's in Charge? A Teacher Speaks Her Mind. Susan Ohanian. LC 94-5586. 249p. 1994. pap. 19.95 (*0-86709-339-0*, 0339) Boynton Cook Pubs.

Who's in Charge? How to Take Back Control of Your Health & Life. Irvin Miller. 358p. 1992. pap. 14.95 (*0-89716-454-7*) P B Pubng.

Who's in Charge? Leadership Skills for Clergy & Others in Ministry. James E. Harvey. LC 95-12792. (Illus.). 141p. (Orig.). 1995. pap. 13.95 (*0-8294-0863-0*) Loyola Pr.

*__Who's in Charge? Putting the Pieces Together to Build Confidence, Conquer Fears, & Develop a Successful Classroom.__ Sharon A. Barnes & Denise A. VanWormer. LC 96-94794. (Illus.). 85p. (Orig.). 1996. pap. 19.95 (*0-9653495-0-0*) In Charge Pub.

Who's in Charge? Standing up to Leadership Pressures. Leith Anderson et al. (Pressure Points Ser.). 169p. 1993. 15.99 (*0-88070-541-8*, Multnomah Bks) Multnomah Pubs.

Who's in Charge? A Positive Parenting Approach to Disciplining Children. Charles D. Spielberger. LC 89-92329. (Illus.). 144p. (Orig.). 1990. pap. 12.50 (*0-9624728-0-8*) Lindsay FL.

Who's in Charge Here? Charles Gallagher. (Celebrate Love Ser.). 72p. (Orig.). 1990. pap. text ed. 3.95 (*0-911905-39-1*) Past & Mat Rene Ctr.

Who's in Charge Here? A Guidebook for the Long Term Care Charge Nurse. Sharon Baker. 132p. (Orig.). (C). 1990. pap. text ed. 10.50 (*1-877735-26-4*, 157) M&H Pub Co TX.

*__Who's in Charge Here? Overcoming Power Struggles with Your Kids.__ Robert G. Barnes. LC 97-3343. 1997. pap. write for info. (*0-310-21743-1*) Zondervan.

Who's in Charge Here? The Patient As Primary Caregiver. Jimmie R. Rankin. (Literature of Patient Response Ser.: Vol. II). 70p. 1993. pap. 12.95 (*1-883938-05-8*) Dry Bones Pr.

*__Who's in Charge Here, 1996.__ Gerald Gardner. 1996. pap. 5.95 (*0-7871-1300-X*, Dove Bks) Dove Audio.

Who's in Control? The Polarization of American Politics & the Revival for a Sensible Center. Richard Darman. 384p. 1996. 25.00 (*0-684-81123-5*) S&S Trade.

Who's in Control? Thinking Through the Authority of Christ, the Thinking Through Discipleship. Karen Lee-Thorp. (Thinking Through Discipleship Ser.). 80p. (Orig.). 1993. pap. 5.00 (*0-89109-739-2*) NavPress.

Who's in My Christmas Tree? Christopher Santoro. (J). 1995. 4.99 (*0-679-86933-6*) Random.

Who's in My Gingerbread House. Christopher Santoro. (J). 1995. 4.99 (*0-679-86947-6*) Random.

Who's In Rabbit's House? Verna Aardema. 1992. pap. 5.99 (*0-14-054724-X*) NAL-Dutton.

Who's in Rabbit's House? Illus. by Leo D. Dillon & Diane Dillon. LC 77-71514. (Pied Piper Bks.). 32p. (J). (ps-3). 1979. reprint ed. pap. 4.95 (*0-8037-9549-1*) Dial Bks Young.

Who's in the Box? see Homeplay: Joyful Learning for Children & Adults, Series I

Who's in the Sea? Charles Reasoner. LC 94-68514. (Sliding Surprise Bks.). (Illus.). 1995. 9.95 (*0-8431-3912-9*) Price Stern Sloan.

Who's in the Shell? (Squeaky Suprise Ser.). (Illus.). 14p. (J). (ps up). 1996. bds. 7.99 (*0-89577-688-X*) Rdrs Dgst Yng Fam.

Who's in the Shoe? Le Rap. (Nursery Rhymes Ser.). 15p. (J). (gr. k-2). 1991. pap. text ed. 23.00 (*1-56843-041-8*); pap. text ed. 4.50 (*1-56843-088-4*) BGR Pub.

Who's in the Truck? (Squeaky Surprise Ser.). (Illus.). 14p. (J). (ps up). 1996. bds. 7.99 (*0-89577-691-X*) Rdrs Dgst Yng Fam.

Who's In? Who's Out? A Look at Jonah & Ruth. Steve Clapp. (Generation Why Ser.: Vol. 1:1). 32p. (YA). (gr. 9-12). 1995. pap. 12.95 (*0-87303-257-8*) Faith & Life.

Who's Inventing What? 1990: Patents Granted in the United States as Reported in the Official Gazette of the United States Patent & Trademark Office: Patents from January Through March 1990, Set, 750p ea. 90th ed. 1990. Three quarterlies, 750p. ea. & cum. 2950p. teacher ed. 195.00 (*0-8103-5445-4*) Gale.

Who's Inventing What 1990 Issue 2. 1990. write for info. (*0-8103-5447-0*) Gale.

Who's Inventing What 1990 Issue 3. 1990. write for info. (*0-8103-5448-9*) Gale.

Who's Inventing What 1990 Issue 4, Vol. 4. 1991. write for info. (*0-8103-5547-7*) Gale.

Who's Involved with Hunger: An Organization Guide for Education & Advocacy. 6th ed. Patricia L. Kutzner et al. 54p. (Orig.). 1995. pap. 12.50 (*0-9645644-0-8*) Wld Hunger Ed Serv.

Who's Listening? Bev Armstrong. (Skill Builder Ser.). (Illus.). 32p. (gr. 1-3). 1981. student ed. 4.95 (*0-88160-079-2*, LW 812) Learning Wks.

Who's Listening? Leonard E. Read. 208p. 1973. 12.95 (*0-910614-48-2*) Foun Econ Ed.

Who's Listening - Handbook of the Listening Activity. Franklin H. Ernst, Jr. LC 73-84380. 1973. 15.95 (*0-916944-15-8*) Addressoset.

Who's Making That Mess? J. Tyler. (Flap Bks.). (Illus.). 16p. (J). (ps up). 1994. pap. 6.95 (*0-7460-0848-1*, Usborne) EDC.

Who's Making That Noise? J. Tyler & Philip Hawthorne. (Flap Bks.). (Illus.). 16p. (J). (ps up). 1995. pap. 6.95 (*0-7460-0850-3*, Usborne) EDC.

Who's Making That Smell? J. Tyler & P. Hawthorn. (Flap Bks.). (Illus.). 16p. (J). (ps up). 1995. pap. 6.95 (*0-7460-1681-6*, Usborne) EDC.

*__Who's Minding Main Street? A Political Primer for Future Leaders of America's Hometowns.__ Alan J. Palmer. LC 97-13506. 1997. pap. write for info. (*1-880090-48-1*) Gabriel Pr.

Who's Minding the Kids: Child Care Arrangements. 1995. lib. bdg. 251.95 (*0-8490-6859-2*) Gordon Pr.

Who's Minding the Kids? Child Care Arrangements, Fall 1991. Lynne M. Casper et al. (Illus.). 61p. (Orig.). (C). 1994. pap. text ed. 30.00 (*0-7881-0867-0*) DIANE Pub.

Who's Minding Your Minerals? A Comprehensive Guide to Understanding Mineral Ownership. Amy J. Love-Meeh. 84p. 1996. 14.95 (*1-57502-223-0*, P0884) Morris Pubng.

Who's Mining the Farm: A Report on the Energy Corporation's Ownership of Illinois Land & Coal Reserves & its Implications for Rural People & Their Communities. Janet M. Smith et al. 76p. (Orig.). 1978. 4.00 (*0-943724-02-3*) Illinois South.

Who's My Baby? (Big Board Bks.). (Illus.). 10p. (J). (ps). 1994. 4.95 (*1-56458-735-5*) DK Pub Inc.

Who's My Friend? (Big Board Bks.). (Illus.). 10p. (J). (ps). 1994. 4.95 (*1-56458-736-3*) DK Pub Inc.

Who's New at the Zoo. Janette Oke. (Illus.). 152p. (J). (gr. 3 up). pap. 4.99 (*0-934998-55-8*) Bethel Pub.

Who's New at the Zoo? Jack Winder. Ed. by Dan Wasserman. (Ten Word Book Ser.). (Illus.). (J). (gr. k-1). 1979. 9.95 (*0-89868-074-3*); pap. 3.95 (*0-89868-085-9*) ARO Pub.

Who's New Wave in Music: An Illustrated Encyclopedia 1976-1982. David Bianco. (Rock & Roll Reference Ser.: No. 14). (Illus.). 430p. 1989. reprint ed. 55.00 (*1-56075-008-1*) Popular Culture.

*__Who's on First.__ William F. Buckley, Jr. LC 96-51933. 320p. 1997. reprint ed. pap. 10.95 (*1-888952-28-8*) Cumberland Hse.

Who's on Second Beach? Paula Buehler. (Geronimo Pack Ser.). 8p. (J). (gr. k-2). 1993. pap. write for info. (*1-882563-07-7*) Lamont Bks.

Who's on Top, Who's on Bottom: How Couples Can Learn to Share Power. Robert Schwebel. LC 93-46313. 256p. 1994. 19.95 (*1-55704-197-0*) Newmarket.

Who's on What? Basketball Trading Cards Reference Book, 1990-1991. B. J. Garrett. 100p. (Orig.). (J). (gr. 3 up). 1993. pap. write for info. (*1-882816-00-5*) Eyes of August.

Who's Orp's Girlfriend? Suzy Kline. 112p. (J). (gr. 3-6). 1993. 13.95 (*0-399-22431-9*, Putnam) Putnam Pub Group.

Who's Peeking? Charles Reasoner. (Sliding Surprise Bks.). (Illus.). 12p. (J). (ps). 1993. 9.95 (*0-8431-3478-X*) Price Stern Sloan.

Who's Raising Whom? A Parent's Guide to Effective Child Discipline. Larry Waldman. LC 87-13759. (Illus.). 144p. (Orig.). 1987. pap. 6.95 (*0-943247-00-4*) UCS Press.

Who's Running America? The Clinton Years. 6th ed. Thomas R. Dye. LC 94-9675. 320p. 1994. pap. text ed. 30.40 (*0-13-123241-X*) P-H.

*__Who's Running the Asylum? Inside the Insane World of Sports Today.__ Wilt Chamberlain. (Illus.). 360p. (Orig.). Date not set. pap. 19.95 (*1-57901-005-9*) Intl Promotions.

Who's Running This Country Anyhow? Ottawa Unbuttoned. Dave McIntosh. 256p. 1987. 21.95 (*0-7737-2115-0*) Genl Dist Srvs.

Who's Running This Kingdom? Pam Campbell & Stan Campbell. (BibleLog Ser.). 180p. (Orig.). 1992. pap. 7.99 (*0-89693-872-7*, 6-1872, Victor Bks) Chariot Victor.

*__Who's Running Your Career? Creating Stable Work in Unstable Times.__ Caela Farren. LC 97-23791. (Illus.). 300p. 1997. text ed. 24.95 (*1-885167-16-4*) Bard Press.

*__Who's Running Your Career? Creating Stable Work in Unstable Times.__ Caela Farren. LC 97-23791. (Illus.). 300p. 1997. pap. 14.95 (*1-885167-17-2*) Bard Press.

Who's Scaring Alfie Atkins? Gunilla Bergstrom. Tr. by Joan Sandin from SWE. (Illus.). 32p. (J). (ps up). 1987. 6.95 (*91-29-58318-7*, Pub. by R & S Bks) FS&G.

Who's Searching for Whom: 1986. Victoria Wilson. 10p. (Orig.). 1986. pap. 2.00 (*0-940133-01-6*) Kinseeker Pubns.

Who's Searching for Whom: 1987. Victoria Wilson. 28p. 1987. pap. 3.00 (*0-940133-05-9*) Kinseeker Pubns.

Who's Searching for Whom, 1988. 62p. 1988. pap. 5.00 (*0-940133-17-2*) Kinseeker Pubns.

Who's Searching for Whom, 1989. 50p. 1989. pap. 5.00 (*0-940133-21-0*) Kinseeker Pubns.

Who's Sick Today? Lynne Cherry. (Illus.). 24p. (J). (ps-1). 1993. pap. 4.99 (*0-14-054839-4*) Puffin Bks.

Who's Susan. Elsie Hayden. 182p. (Orig.). 1996. mass mkt. 4.99 (*1-55197-182-8*, Pub. by Comnwlth Pub CN) Partners Pubs Grp.

Who's Telling the Story. Ed. by Cunningham. 1995. pap. 12.95 (*0-614-11373-3*, Pub. by Oxfam UK) Humanities.

Who's That Baby? Kristin Morgan. (Romance Ser.). 1993. pap. 2.69 (*0-373-08929-5*, 5-08929-7) Silhouette.

Who's That Banging on the Ceiling? Colin McNaughton. LC 91-58768. (Illus.). 32p. (J). (ps up). 1994. pap. 5.99 (*1-56402-384-2*) Candlewick Pr.

Who's That Knocking at My Door? Tilde Michels. (Illus.). 28p. (J). (ps-3). 1986. 10.95 (*0-8120-5732-5*) Barron.

Who's That Knocking at My Door? Tilde Michels. (Illus.). 28p. (J). (ps-3). 1992. pap. 4.95 (*0-8120-1486-3*) Barron.

Who's That Stepping on Plymouth Rock? Jean Fritz. LC 74-30593. (Illus.). 32p. (J). (gr. 2-6). 1975. 15.95 (*0-698-20325-9*, Coward) Putnam Pub Group.

*__Who's That Whale?__ Trisha Cole. (Illus.). 15p. (J). (ps-3). 1994. 4.95 (*1-56550-026-1*) Vis Bks Intl.

*__Who's the Boss?__ Barbara Boswell. (Man of the Month Ser.). 1997. mass mkt. 3.50 (*0-373-76069-8*, 1-76069-3) Silhouette.

*__Who's the Boss?__ Linda Turner. (Silhouette Ser.). 1997. 20.95 (*0-373-59816-5*) Harlequin Bks.

Who's the Boss? Linda Turner. (Intimate Moments Ser.). 1995. mass mkt. 3.75 (*0-373-07649-5*, 1-07649-6) Silhouette.

Who's the Boss in Israel: Israel at the Polls 1988-1989. Ed. by Daniel J. Elazar & Shmuel Sandler. LC 92-9029. 313p. (C). 1992. 39.95 (*0-8143-2397-9*) Wayne St U Pr.

Who's the Daddy? (New Arrival) Judy Christenberry. (American Romance Ser.). 1995. mass mkt. 3.50 (*0-373-16579-X*, 1-16579-3) Harlequin Bks.

Who's the Funny-Looking Kid? Charles M. Schulz. (Illus.). 128p. 1993. pap. 6.95 (*0-8050-2889-7*) H Holt & Co.

*__Who's the Man?__ Hank Herman. (Super Hoops Ser.: No. 14). 96p. (Orig.). (J). (gr. 2-5). 1997. pap. 3.50 (*0-553-48477-X*) BDD Bks Young Read.

Who's the Matter with Me? Alice T. Steadman. (Illus.). 1977. reprint ed. pap. 10.95 (*0-87516-225-8*) DeVorss.

*__Who's the Prisoner of Portcullis Castle.__ Rhil Roxbee-Cox. (Solve It Yourself Ser.). (Illus.). 48p. (Orig.). (YA). (gr. 7 up). 1997. pap. 6.95 (*0-7460-2697-8*, Usborne) EDC.

*__Who's the Prisoner of Portcullis Castle.__ Rhil Roxbee-Cox. (Solve It Yourself Ser.). (Illus.). 48p. (YA). (gr. 7 up). 1997. lib. bdg. 14.95 (*0-88110-948-7*, Usborne) EDC.

Who's the Savage? Ed. by David R. Wrone & Russell S. Nelson. LC 81-17167. 186p. (Orig.). (C). 1982. lib. bdg. 22.50 (*0-89874-452-0*) Krieger.

Who's the Target? large type ed. Margaret A. Carr. (Linford Mystery Library). 256p. 1988. pap. 15.99 (*0-7089-6500-8*) Ulverscroft.

Who's There? Tim Archbold. (J). (gr. 1-5). 1995. 2.95 (*1-85697-570-3*, Kingfisher LKC) LKC.

Who's There? Porter Gold. (Real Readers Ser.: Level Blue). (Illus.). 32p. (J). (gr. 1-4). 1989. lib. bdg. 21.40 (*0-8172-3514-0*) Raintree Steck-V.

Who's There? Porter Gold. (Real Reading Ser.). (Illus.). 32p. (J). (gr. 1-4). 1989. pap. 3.95 (*0-8114-6717-1*) Raintree Steck-V.

Who's There? Charles Reasoner. (Sliding Surprise Bks.). (Illus.). 12p. (J). (ps). 1993. 9.95 (*0-8431-3479-8*) Price Stern Sloan.

Who's There? Stephanie S. Tolan. LC 94-15384. 240p. (YA). (gr. 5 up). 1994. 15.00 (*0-688-04611-8*, Morrow Junior) Morrow.

*__Who's There?__ Stephanie S. Tolan. 1997. pap. 4.95 (*0-688-15289-9*, Mulberry) Morrow.

Who's There? The Life & Career of William Hartnell. Jessica Carney. (Illus.). 224p. 1996. 22.95 (*1-85227-514-6*, Pub. by Virgin Pub UK) London Brdge.

Who's to Blame? How to Deal with a Victim Without Becoming One Yourself. Carmen R. Berry & Mark W. Baker. 240p. (Orig.). 1996. pap. 14.00 (*0-89109-915-8*) Pinon Press.

Who's to Know? Information, the Media & Public Awareness. Ann E. Weiss. 192p. (J). (gr. 5-9). 1990. 14.95 (*0-395-49702-7*) HM.

Who's to Pay for the Arts? The International Search for Models of Support. Ed. by Milton Cummings & J. Mark Davidson-Schuster. LC 88-27288. (ACA Arts Research Seminar Ser.). 128p. 1989. pap. 9.95 (*0-915400-74-X*, ACA Bks) Am Council Arts.

Who's to Say: A Dialogue on Relativism. Norman Melchert. LC 94-21086. 96p. (C). 1994. pap. text ed. 4.95 (*0-87220-271-2*); lib. bdg. 24.95 (*0-87220-272-0*) Hackett Pub.

*__Who's under Grandma's Quilt.__ Rachel Waterstone. LC 97-60090. (Illus.). 32p. (J). (ps-1). 1997. 13.95 (*1-890326-08-9*) First Story Pr.

Who's Upside Down? Crockett Johnson. LC 89-28059. (Illus.). 32p. (J). (ps-3). 1990. reprint ed. lib. bdg. 16.50 (*0-208-02276-7*, Linnet Bks) Shoe String.

Who's Uptown: Harlem 'Eighty-Seven. Ed. by Glenderlyn Johnson. (Illus.). 56p. (Orig.). 1988. 8.00 (*0-87104-406-4*) NY Pub Lib.

Who's Watching the Playpen. David Benoit. 1995. pap. 10.95 (*1-57558-000-4*) Hearthstone OK.

W

Who's Wealthy in America, 2 Vols. 94th ed. Ed. by Catherine M. Ehr. 1993. 380.00 (*0-930807-51-0*, 600474) Taft Group.

Who's Wealthy in America? A Directory of the 50,000 Richest People in America. 90th ed. 2000p. 1990. 295.00 (*0-914756-68-0*, 100867-99584) Taft Group.

*Who's Wealthy in America 1991, 2 vols. 91th ed. 1991. 349.00 (*1-879784-05-X*, 00000763) Taft Group.

Who's Wealthy in America, 1993: A Prospecting List & Directory of 102,000 Affluent Americans, 2 vols. 93th ed. Ed. by Mark W. Scott. 2140p. 1992. Set. 365.00 (*1-879784-62-9*, 600341) Taft Group.

Who's Wealthy in America 1995, Vol. 2. 95th ed. Romaniuk. 1994. write for info. (*0-930807-56-1*) Fund Raising.

Who's Wealthy in America 1995: A Prospect List & Directory of Nearly 100,000 Affluent Americans, 2 vols. 95th ed. Bohdan R. Romaniuk. 2300p. 1994. 415.00 (*0-930807-54-5*) Taft Group.

Who's Wealthy in America 1996, Vol. 2. 96th ed. Ed. by Taghrid Barron. 1995. 425.00 (*0-930807-57-X*) Taft Group.

Who's Wealthy in America 1997, 2 vol., 1. Mark W. Scott. (Who's Wealthy in America Ser.). write for info. (*1-56995-066-0*) Taft Group.

Who's Wealthy in America 1997, 2 vol., 2. Mark W. Scott. (Who's Wealthy in America Ser.). write for info. (*1-56995-067-9*) Taft Group.

Who's Wealthy in America 1997, 2 vol., Set. 97th ed. Mark W. Scott. (Who's Wealthy in America Ser.). 1996. 435.00 (*1-56995-065-2*) Taft Group.

*Who's Wealthy in America 1998, 2 vols. 1997. 435.00 (*1-56995-245-0*, 00156564) Taft Group.

Who's Wealthy in American 1995, Vol. 1. 95th ed. Romaniuk. 1994. write for info. (*0-930807-55-3*) Fund Raising.

Who's What & Where: A Directory & Reference Book on America's Minority Journalists. Ben Johnson & Mary Bullard-Johnson. (Illus.). 600p. (Orig.). (C). 1988. pap. text ed. 34.95 (*0-9614418-2-8*) Whos What Where.

Who's What & Where: A Directory of America's Black Journalists. Ben Johnson & Mary Bullard-Johnson. (Illus.). 480p. (Orig.). 1985. pap. 24.95 (*0-9614418-0-1*) Whos What Where.

Who's Where in the American Theatre. 3rd ed. 208p. 1992. pap. 7.50 (*0-937657-10-7*) Feedbk Theabks & Prospero.

Who's Who: American Law Students, Vol. 15. unabridged ed. Ed. by Joanne R. Desotelle. 402p. 1996. write for info. (*0-614-16496-6*) Summa Pub Bur.

*Who's Who - Famous People, Set 3. (Questivities Ser.). 1995. 9.95 (*1-880505-64-9*, CLC0176) Pieces of Lrning.

Who's Who African American History. John Bowman. 160p. 1994. 14.98 (*0-8317-9190-X*) Smithmark.

Who's Who among African Americans 1996-97. 9th ed. Ed. by Shirelle Phelps. 1995. 140.00 (*0-8103-5728-3*) Gale.

*Who's Who among African Americans 1998/99. 10th ed. Ed. by Shirelle Phelps. 1855p. 1997. 140.00 (*0-7876-0109-8*, 00108813, Gale Res Intl) Gale.

*Who's Who among American High School Students, 18 vols. 31th ed. 1997. write for info. (*1-56244-150-7*) Educ Comm.

Who's Who among American High School Students, 16 vols., Set. annuals 28th ed. LC 68-43796. 1994. 34.95 (*1-56244-057-8*) Educ Comm.

Who's Who among American High School Students, 15 vols., Set, Vols. I-XV. 25th ed. Compiled by Educational Communications, Inc. Staff. 1991. Set. 28.95 (*1-56244-000-4*) Educ Comm.

Who's Who among American High School Students, Vol. I. LC 68-43796. 1993. 34.95 (*1-56244-048-9*) Educ Comm.

Who's Who among American High School Students, Vol. 1. annuals 28th ed. LC 68-43796. 1994. 34.95 (*1-56244-058-6*) Educ Comm.

*Who's Who among American High School Students, Vol. I. 31th ed. 1997. 44.95 (*1-56244-151-5*) Educ Comm.

Who's Who among American High School Students, Vol. II. LC 68-43796. 1993. 34.95 (*1-56244-049-7*) Educ Comm.

Who's Who among American High School Students, Vol. 2. annuals 28th ed. LC 68-43796. 1994. 34.95 (*1-56244-059-4*) Educ Comm.

*Who's Who among American High School Students, Vol. II. 31th ed. 1997. 44.95 (*1-56244-152-3*) Educ Comm.

Who's Who among American High School Students, Vol. III. LC 68-43796. 1993. 34.95 (*1-56244-075-6*) Educ Comm.

Who's Who among American High School Students, Vol. 3. annuals 28th ed. LC 68-43796. 1994. 34.95 (*1-56244-060-8*) Educ Comm.

*Who's Who among American High School Students, Vol. III. 31th ed. 1997. 44.95 (*1-56244-153-1*) Educ Comm.

Who's Who among American High School Students, Vol. IV. LC 68-43796. 1993. 34.95 (*1-56244-076-4*) Educ Comm.

Who's Who among American High School Students, Vol. 4. annuals 28th ed. LC 68-43796. 1994. 34.95 (*1-56244-061-6*) Educ Comm.

*Who's Who among American High School Students, Vol. IV. 31th ed. 1997. 44.95 (*1-56244-154-X*) Educ Comm.

Who's Who among American High School Students, Vol. V. LC 68-43796. 1993. 34.95 (*1-56244-077-2*) Educ Comm.

Who's Who among American High School Students, Vol. 5. annuals 28th ed. LC 68-43796. 1994. 34.95 (*1-56244-062-4*) Educ Comm.

*Who's Who among American High School Students, Vol. V. 31th ed. 1997. 44.95 (*1-56244-155-8*) Educ Comm.

Who's Who among American High School Students, Vol. VI. LC 68-43796. 1993. 34.95 (*1-56244-078-0*) Educ Comm.

W

Who's Who among American High School Students, Vol. 6. annuals 28th ed. LC 68-43796. 1994. 34.95 (*1-56244-063-2*) Educ Comm.

*Who's Who among American High School Students, Vol. VI. 31th ed. 1997. 44.95 (*1-56244-156-6*) Educ Comm.

Who's Who among American High School Students, Vol. VII. LC 68-43796. 1993. 34.95 (*1-56244-079-9*) Educ Comm.

Who's Who among American High School Students, Vol. 7. annuals 28th ed. LC 68-43796. 1994. 34.95 (*1-56244-064-0*) Educ Comm.

*Who's Who among American High School Students, Vol. VII. 31th ed. 1997. 44.95 (*1-56244-157-4*) Educ Comm.

Who's Who among American High School Students, Vol. VIII. LC 68-43796. 1993. 34.95 (*1-56244-080-2*) Educ Comm.

Who's Who among American High School Students, Vol. 8. annuals 28th ed. LC 68-43796. 1994. 34.95 (*1-56244-065-9*) Educ Comm.

*Who's Who among American High School Students, Vol. VIII. 31th ed. 1997. 44.95 (*1-56244-158-2*) Educ Comm.

Who's Who among American High School Students, Vol. IX. LC 68-43796. 1993. 34.95 (*1-56244-081-0*) Educ Comm.

Who's Who among American High School Students, Vol. 9. annuals 28th ed. LC 68-43796. 1994. 34.95 (*1-56244-066-7*) Educ Comm.

*Who's Who among American High School Students, Vol. IX. 31th ed. 1997. 44.95 (*1-56244-159-0*) Educ Comm.

Who's Who among American High School Students, Vol. X. LC 68-43796. 1993. 34.95 (*1-56244-082-9*) Educ Comm.

Who's Who among American High School Students, Vol. 10. annuals 28th ed. LC 68-43796. 1994. 34.95 (*1-56244-067-5*) Educ Comm.

*Who's Who among American High School Students, Vol. X. 31th ed. 1997. 44.95 (*1-56244-160-4*) Educ Comm.

Who's Who among American High School Students, Vol. XI. LC 68-43796. 1993. 34.95 (*1-56244-083-7*) Educ Comm.

Who's Who among American High School Students, Vol. 11. annuals 28th ed. LC 68-43796. 1994. 34.95 (*1-56244-068-3*) Educ Comm.

*Who's Who among American High School Students, Vol. XI. 31th ed. 1997. 44.95 (*1-56244-161-2*) Educ Comm.

Who's Who among American High School Students, Vol. 12. annuals 28th ed. LC 68-43796. 1994. 34.95 (*1-56244-069-1*) Educ Comm.

*Who's Who among American High School Students, Vol. XII. 31th ed. 1997. 44.95 (*1-56244-162-0*) Educ Comm.

Who's Who among American High School Students, Vol. XIII. LC 68-43796. 1993. 34.95 (*1-56244-085-3*) Educ Comm.

Who's Who among American High School Students, Vol. 13. annuals 28th ed. LC 68-43796. 1994. 34.95 (*1-56244-070-5*) Educ Comm.

*Who's Who among American High School Students, Vol. XIII. 31th ed. 1997. 44.95 (*1-56244-163-9*) Educ Comm.

Who's Who among American High School Students, Vol. XIV. LC 68-43796. 1993. 34.95 (*1-56244-086-1*) Educ Comm.

Who's Who among American High School Students, Vol. 14. annuals 28th ed. LC 68-43796. 1994. 34.95 (*1-56244-071-3*) Educ Comm.

*Who's Who among American High School Students, Vol. XIV. 31th ed. 1997. 44.95 (*1-56244-164-7*) Educ Comm.

Who's Who among American High School Students, Vol. 15. annuals 28th ed. LC 68-43796. 1994. 34.95 (*1-56244-072-1*) Educ Comm.

*Who's Who among American High School Students, Vol. XV. 31th ed. 1997. 44.95 (*1-56244-165-5*) Educ Comm.

Who's Who among American High School Students, Vol. XVI. LC 68-43796. 1993. 34.95 (*1-56244-088-8*) Educ Comm.

Who's Who among American High School Students, Vol. 16. annuals 28th ed. LC 68-43796. 1994. 34.95 (*1-56244-073-X*) Educ Comm.

*Who's Who among American High School Students, Vol. XVI. 31th ed. 1997. 44.95 (*1-56244-166-3*) Educ Comm.

*Who's Who among American High School Students, Vol. XVII. 31th ed. 1997. 44.95 (*1-56244-167-1*) Educ Comm.

*Who's Who among American High School Students, Vol. XVIII. 31th ed. 1997. 44.95 (*1-56244-168-X*) Educ Comm.

Who's Who among American High School Students: 1994-95, 18 vols., Set. annuals 29th ed. LC 68-43796. 1995. 765.00 (*1-56244-095-0*) Educ Comm.

Who's Who among American High School Students: 1995-96, 18 vols. 30th ed. LC 68-43796. 1996. 42.50 (*1-56244-119-1*) Educ Comm.

Who's Who among American High School Students: 1995-96, 18 vols., Set. 30th ed. LC 68-43796. 1996. 765.00 (*1-56244-117-5*) Educ Comm.

Who's Who among American High School Students Vol. 1: 1994-95, 18 vols., Vol. 1. annuals 29th ed. LC 68-43796. 1995. 42.50 (*1-56244-096-9*) Educ Comm.

Who's Who among American High School Students Vol. 1: 1995-96, 18 vols. 30th ed. LC 68-43796. 1996. 42.50 (*1-56244-118-3*) Educ Comm.

Who's Who among American High School Students Vol. 2: 1994-95, 18 vols., Vol. 2. annuals 29th ed. LC 68-43796. 1995. 42.50 (*1-56244-097-7*) Educ Comm.

Who's Who among American High School Students Vol. 3: 1994-95, 18 vols., Vol. 3. annuals 29th ed. LC 68-43796. 1995. 42.50 (*1-56244-098-5*) Educ Comm.

WHo's Who among American High School Students Vol. 3: 1995-96, 18 vols. 30th ed. LC 68-43796. 1996. 42.50 (*1-56244-120-5*) Educ Comm.

Who's Who among American High School Students Vol. 4: 1994-95, 18 vols., Vol. 4. annuals 29th ed. LC 68-43796. 1995. 42.50 (*1-56244-099-3*) Educ Comm.

Who's Who among American High School Students Vol. 4: 1995-96, 18 vols. 30th ed. LC 68-43796. 1996. 42.50 (*1-56244-121-3*) Educ Comm.

Who's Who among American High School Students Vol. 5: 1994-95, 18 vols., Vol. 5. annuals 29th ed. LC 68-43796. 1995. 42.50 (*1-56244-100-0*) Educ Comm.

Who's Who among American High School Students Vol. 5: 1995-96, 18 vols. 30th ed. LC 68-43796. 1996. 42.50 (*1-56244-122-1*) Educ Comm.

Who's Who among American High School Students Vol. 6: 1994-95, 18 vols., Vol. 6. annuals 29th ed. LC 68-43796. 1995. 42.50 (*1-56244-101-9*) Educ Comm.

Who's Who among American High School Students Vol. 6: 1995-96, 18 vols. 30th ed. LC 68-43796. 1996. 42.50 (*1-56244-123-X*) Educ Comm.

Who's Who among American High School Students Vol. 7: 1994-95, 18 vols., Vol. 7. annuals 29th ed. LC 68-43796. 1995. 42.50 (*1-56244-102-7*) Educ Comm.

Who's Who among American High School Students Vol. 7: 1995-96, 18 vols. 30th ed. LC 68-43796. 1996. 42.50 (*1-56244-124-8*) Educ Comm.

Who's Who among American High School Students Vol. 8: 1994-95, 18 vols., Vol. 8. annuals 29th ed. LC 68-43796. 1995. 42.50 (*1-56244-103-5*) Educ Comm.

Who's Who among American High School Students Vol. 9: 1994-95, 18 vols., Vol. 9. annuals 29th ed. LC 68-43796. 1995. 42.50 (*1-56244-104-3*) Educ Comm.

Who's Who among American High School Students Vol. 9: 1995-96, 18 vols. 30th ed. LC 68-43796. 1996. 42.50 (*1-56244-126-4*) Educ Comm.

Who's Who among American High School Students Vol. 10: 1994-95, 18 vols., Vol. 10. annuals 29th ed. LC 68-43796. 1995. 42.50 (*1-56244-105-1*) Educ Comm.

Who's Who among American High School Students Vol. 10: 1995-96, 18 vols. 30th ed. LC 68-43796. 1996. 42.50 (*1-56244-127-2*) Educ Comm.

Who's Who among American High School Students Vol. 11: 1994-95, 18 vols., Vol. 11. annuals 29th ed. LC 68-43796. 1995. 42.50 (*1-56244-106-X*) Educ Comm.

Who's Who among American High School Students Vol. 11: 1995-96, 18 vols. 30th ed. LC 68-43796. 1996. 42.50 (*1-56244-128-0*) Educ Comm.

Who's Who among American High School Students Vol. 12: 1994-95, 18 vols., Vol. 12. annuals 29th ed. LC 68-43796. 1995. 42.50 (*1-56244-107-8*) Educ Comm.

Who's Who among American High School Students Vol. 12: 1995-96, 18 vols. 30th ed. LC 68-43796. 1996. 42.50 (*1-56244-129-9*) Educ Comm.

Who's Who among American High School Students Vol. 13: 1994-95, 18 vols., Vol. 13. annuals 29th ed. LC 68-43796. 1995. 42.50 (*1-56244-108-6*) Educ Comm.

Who's Who among American High School Students Vol. 13: 1995-96, 18 vols. 30th ed. LC 68-43796. 1996. 42.50 (*1-56244-130-2*) Educ Comm.

Who's Who among American High School Students Vol. 14: 1994-95, 18 vols., Vol. 14. annuals 29th ed. LC 68-43796. 1995. 42.50 (*1-56244-109-4*) Educ Comm.

Who's Who among American High School Students Vol. 14: 1995-96, 18 vols. 30th ed. LC 68-43796. 1996. 42.50 (*1-56244-131-0*) Educ Comm.

Who's Who among American High School Students Vol. 15: 1994-95, 18 vols., Vol. 15. annuals 29th ed. LC 68-43796. 1995. 42.50 (*1-56244-110-8*) Educ Comm.

Who's Who among American High School Students Vol. 15: 1995-96, 18 vols. 30th ed. LC 68-43796. 1996. 42.50 (*1-56244-132-9*) Educ Comm.

Who's Who among American High School Students Vol. 16: 1994-95, 18 vols., Vol. 16. annuals 29th ed. LC 68-43796. 1995. 42.50 (*1-56244-111-6*) Educ Comm.

Who's Who among American High School Students Vol. 16: 1995-96, 18 vols. 30th ed. LC 68-43796. 1996. 42.50 (*1-56244-133-7*) Educ Comm.

Who's Who among American High School Students Vol. 17: 1994-95, 18 vols. 29th ed. LC 68-43796. 1995. 42.50 (*1-56244-112-4*) Educ Comm.

Who's Who among American High School Students Vol. 17: 1995-96, 18 vols. 30th ed. LC 68-43796. 1996. 42.50 (*1-56244-134-5*) Educ Comm.

Who's Who among American High School Students Vol. 18: 1994-95, 18 vols. 29th ed. LC 68-43796. 1995. 42.50 (*1-56244-113-2*) Educ Comm.

Who's Who among American High School Students Vol. 18: 1995-96, 18 vols. 30th ed. LC 68-43796. 1996. 42.50 (*1-56244-135-3*) Educ Comm.

*Who's Who among American High School Students Vol. VIII: 1995-96. 30th ed. Educational Communications Staff. 1996. 42.50 (*1-56244-125-6*) Educ Comm.

Who's Who among American High School Students, 1992-93, 16 vols., Set. 27th ed. LC 68-43796. 1993. write for info. (*1-56244-047-0*) Educ Comm.

Who's Who among American Law Students. 4th ed. Ed. by Joanne R. Desotelle. LC 81-645742. 364p. 1984. 35.00 (*0-317-19181-0*) Summa Pub Bur.

Who's Who among American Law Students. 5th ed. Ed. by Joanne R. Desotelle. 366p. 1985. 35.00 (*0-317-52484-4*) Summa Pub Bur.

Who's Who among American Law Students. 6th ed. Ed. by Joanne R. Desotelle. 350p. 1986. 39.95 (*0-04-396000-6*) Summa Pub Bur.

Who's Who among American Law Students, 1983. Ed. by Joanne R. Desotelle. LC 81-645742. 160p. 1982. 30.00 (*0-685-05964-2*) Summa Pub Bur.

Who's Who among American Law Students, 1984. 3rd ed. Ed. by Joanne R. Desotelle. LC 81-645742. 321p. 1983. 35.00 (*0-685-08313-6*) Summa Pub Bur.

Who's Who among America's Teachers, 1 vol. LC 90-662490. 1990. 59.95 (*0-930315-77-4*) Educ Comm.

Who's Who among America's Teachers, 2 vols., Set. 3rd ed. LC 90-662490. 1994. 159.90 (*1-56244-054-3*) Educ Comm.

Who's Who among America's Teachers, 2 vols., Vol. 1. 3rd ed. LC 90-662490. 1994. 79.95 (*1-56244-055-1*) Educ Comm.

Who's Who among America's Teachers, 2 vols., Vol. 2. 3rd ed. LC 90-662490. 1994. 79.95 (*1-56244-056-X*) Educ Comm.

Who's Who among America's Teachers: 1996, 4 vols. 4th ed. LC 90-662490. 1996. 319.80 (*1-56244-138-8*) Educ Comm.

Who's Who among America's Teachers Vol. 1: 1996. 4th ed. LC 90-662490. 1996. 79.95 (*1-56244-139-6*) Educ Comm.

Who's Who among America's Teachers Vol. 2: 1996. 4th ed. LC 90-662490. 1996. 79.95 (*1-56244-140-X*) Educ Comm.

Who's Who among America's Teachers Vol. 3: 1996. 4th ed. LC 90-662490. 1996. 79.95 (*1-56244-141-8*) Educ Comm.

Who's Who among America's Teachers Vol. 4: 1996. 4th ed. LC 90-662490. 1996. 79.95 (*1-56244-142-6*) Educ Comm.

*Who's Who among Asian Americans. 2nd ed. 1998. 75.00 (*0-8103-9328-X*, 00002705, Gale Res Intl) Gale.

Who's Who among Asian Americans, 1994-95. Amy L. Unterburger. 779p. 1994. 75.00 (*0-8103-9433-2*) Gale.

Who's Who among Bible Women. Peggy Musgrove. LC 81-81126. (Radiant Life Ser.). 128p. (Orig.). 1981. pap. 3.95 (*0-88243-883-2*, 02-0883) Gospel Pub.

Who's Who among Black Americans, 1990. 6th ed. Iris Lloyd. 870p. 1989. 110.00 (*0-8103-2243-9*) Gale.

Who's Who among Black Americans 1992. 7th ed. 1991. 115.00 (*0-8103-5404-7*) Gale.

Who's Who among Black Americans 1994. 8th ed. 1993. 140.00 (*0-8103-5461-6*) Gale.

Who's Who among Hispanic Americans. Ed. by Amy L. Unterburger & Jane L. Delgado. 550p. 1990. 89.95 (*0-8103-7451-X*) Gale.

*Who's Who among Hispanic Americans. 2nd ed. 1992. 96.00 (*0-8103-7604-0*, 00001314, Gale Res Intl) Gale.

Who's Who among Hispanic Americans. 3rd ed. Amy L. Unterburger. 1994. 100.00 (*0-8103-8550-3*) Gale.

*Who's Who among Hispanic Americans. 4th ed. 1998. 100.00 (*0-8103-9327-1*, 00003496, Gale Res Intl) Gale.

Who's Who Among Human Services Professionals. 3rd ed. 1992. 125.00 (*0-940863-47-2*); 125.00 (*0-940863-49-9*) Marquis.

Who's Who among Living Authors of Older Nations. A. Lawrence. 1973. 59.95 (*0-8490-1297-X*) Gordon Pr.

Who's Who among Play-by-Mail Gamers, 1990-1991. Ed. by Kieron B. Mitchell. 167p. (Orig.). 1990. pap. text ed. 12.95 (*0-9620846-2-X*) K & C Enterp.

Who's Who among the Colored Baptists of the United States. Samuel W. Bacote. Ed. by Edwin S. Gaustad. LC 79-52588. (Baptist Tradition Ser.). (Illus.). 1980. reprint ed. lib. bdg. 25.95 (*0-405-12455-4*) Ayer.

***Who's Who among Top Executives. Ed. by Laura Matteo. (Illus.). 415p. 1997. 39.95 (*0-9652836-1-5*) Kaleo Publns.**
Welcome to WHO'S WHO AMONG TOP EXECUTIVES, the largest & most prestigious publication honoring business leaders & entrepreneurs throughout the world. Recognizing the need for a comprehensible, user-friendly directory that would offer high-level business executives exposure & recognition as well as a forum for networking, this source-book was created. Each year more than 250,000 candidates are reviewed for inclusion in WHO'S WHO AMONG TOP EXECUTIVES, & approximately ten percent are selected. Biographies are submitted by our honorees & compiled by our editorial department. These entries, written in clear, complete sentences, are listed first by industry & then by state, province or commonwealth, to facilitate the search for colleagues or contacts. It is our intention to provide our honorees with an invaluable resource from which they can expand their base of business & make new contacts. For those in the midst of a career change, we offer a diverse range of potential opportunities, & to college graduates & entrants into the field of business, we present a veritable smorgasbord of key players in the industry internationally. In an ever-changing corporate environment, WHO'S WHO AMONG TOP EXECUTIVES will become an essential resource & invaluable means for keeping abreast of these changes, & will also serve as a lasting tribute to those whose achievements we acknowledge & congratulate here. To order WHO'S WHO AMONG TOP EXECUTIVES please contact the publisher directly: Kaleo Publications, 1208 East Broadway Road, #208, Tempe, AZ 85282. 602-736-8400 or 800-965-2536. Feel free to Fax your order: 602-736-8939.
Publisher Provided Annotation.

Whos Who among Werewolves: Garou Saga. Russ Quanide. 96p. 1994. per., pap. 12.00 (*1-56504-140-2*, 3401) White Wolf.

Who's Who & Resource Guide, 1994. Ed. by JoAnn Roberts. 84p. 1993. pap. 10.00 (*1-880715-14-7*) Creat Des Srvs.

Who's Who & What's What in Shakespeare: Over 6,000 Factual & Analytical Entries. Evangeline M. O'Connor. 1996. 9.99 (*0-517-25923-0*) Random Hse Value.

***Who's Who & What's What in Wagner.** Jonathan Lewsey. LC 96-41353. 400p. 1997. text ed. 76.95 (*1-85928-280-6*, Pub. by Scolar Pr UK) Ashgate Pub Co.

***Who's Who & What's What in Wagner.** Jonathan Lewsey. LC 96-41353. 400p. (C). 1997. pap. 42.95 (*1-85928-285-7*, Pub. by Scolar Pr UK) Ashgate Pub Co.

Who's Who at Electric Power Plants. 6th ed. Utility Data Institute Staff. Ed. by Kathy Brown. 700p. (Orig.). 1995. pap. 175.00 (*1-56760-035-2*) Utility Data Inst.

Who's Who at the Frankfurt Book Fair 1994. 25th ed. 550p. 1994. pap. 40.00 (*3-598-21894-X*) K G Saur.

Who's Who at the Frankfurt Book Fair 1995. 26th ed. 550p. 1995. pap. 45.00 (*3-598-21895-8*) K G Saur.

Who's Who at the Frankfurt Book Fair 1996: An International Publisher's Guide. 550p. 1996. 45.00 (*3-598-21896-6*) K G Saur.

Who's Who at the Zoo? (Big Board Bks.). (Illus.). 10p. (J). (ps). 1994. 4.95 (*1-56458-738-X*) DK Pub Inc.

Who's Who at the Zoo. (Golden Story Book 'n' Tape Ser.). (Illus.). 24p. (J). (ps-3). write for info. incl. audio (*0-307-14182-9*, 14182-01) Western Pub.

***Who's Who from MACV-SOG.** LC 96-71710. (Special Forces Reference Resources). 580p. 1996. pap. 60.00 (*0-9624009-8-X*) Radix Pr.

Who's Who in Advertising, 1990-1991. 708p. 1989. 210.00 (*0-8379-1350-0*) Marquis.

Who's Who in Africa: Leaders for the Nineteen Nineties. Alan Rake. LC 92-8166. 456p. 1992. 59.50 (*0-8108-2557-0*) Scarecrow.

***Who's Who in African American History.** (Twentieth Century Ser.). (Illus.). (YA). (gr. 6 up). 24.95 (*0-614-21970-1*) Random.

Who's Who in African Heritage Book Publishing. Ed. by E. Curtis Alexander. LC 87-82649. 160p. 1988. 21.95 (*0-938818-13-9*); pap. 11.95 (*0-938818-12-0*) ECA Assoc.

Who's Who in African Heritage Book Publishing, 1989-90. 2nd ed. Ed. by Mwalimu I. Mwadilifu. LC 89-647142. 300p. 1990. 24.95 (*0-938818-16-3*) ECA Assoc.

Who's Who in African Heritage Book Publishing, 1990-1991. 3rd ed. Ed. by Mwalimu I. Mwadilifu. LC 89-647142. 1990. 25.95 (*0-938818-51-1*) ECA Assoc.

Who's Who in African Heritage Book Publishing, 1991-1992. 4th ed. Ed. by Mwalimu I. Mwadilifu. LC 89-647142. 325p. 1992. spiral bd. 34.95 (*0-938818-95-3*) ECA Assoc.

Who's Who in AI - Update 'Eighty-Eight. Ed. by Di Schwartz. 200p. 1988. 87.95 (*0-937287-04-0*) WWAI.

Who's Who in AI-A Guide to People, Products, Companies, Resources, Schools & Jobs. Ed. by Alan Kernoff. 330p. (Orig.). 1986. pap. 95.00 (*0-937287-00-8*); lib. bdg. 125.00 (*0-937287-01-6*) WWAI.

Who's Who in Alaskan Arts & Crafts, 1990. 3rd ed. 340p. 1990. pap. 25.95 (*0-924663-04-9*) Alaskan Viewpoint.

Who's Who in Alaskan Arts & Crafts, 1991, Vol. IV. (Illus.). 400p. 1991. 72.50 (*0-924663-08-1*) Alaskan Viewpoint.

Who's Who in Alaskan Politics: A Biographical Dictionary of Alaskan Political Personalities, 1884-1974. Compiled by Evangeline Atwood & Robert N. De Armond. LC 77-76025. 1977. 10.00 (*0-8323-0287-2*) Binford Mort.

Who's Who in America, 3 vols., 1. 48th ed. 1993. 429.95 (*0-8379-0152-9*) Marquis.

Who's Who in America, 3 vols., 2. 48th ed. 1993. 429.95 (*0-8379-0153-7*) Marquis.

Who's Who in America, 3 vols., Set. Classic Ed. 48th ed. 1993. Set, classic ed. 429.95 (*0-8379-0151-0*) Marquis.

Who's Who in America, 3 vols., Vol. 1. 51th ed. Marquis Who's Who Staff. 1996. write for info. (*0-8379-0176-6*) Marquis.

Who's Who in America, 3 vols., Vol. 2. 51th ed. Marquis Who's Who Staff. 1996. write for info. (*0-8379-0177-4*) Marquis.

Who's Who in America, 3 vols., Vol. 3. 51th ed. Marquis Who's Who Staff. 1996. write for info. (*0-8379-0178-2*) Marquis.

Who's Who in America, 3 vols., Vol 3, Geographic Professional Index. 48th ed. 1993. Vol. 3: Geographic Professional Index. 429.95 (*0-8379-0154-5*) Marquis.

Who's Who in America: Junior & Senior High School Version, 1989-1991, 4 vols., Set, Vols. 1-4. 4946p. 1989. Set. 89.50 (*0-8379-1250-4*) Marquis.

Who's Who in America: Junior & Senior High School Version, 1991-1993, 4 vols., Vols. 5 - 8. 4946p. 1991. Set. 89.50 (*0-8379-1251-2*) Marquis.

Who's Who in America Geographic - Professional Index, 1990-1991. rev. ed. 486p. 1990. 79.00 (*0-8379-1506-6*) Marquis.

Who's Who in America 1992-1993, 2 vols. 47th rev. ed. 3981p. 1992. 399.00 (*0-8379-0147-2*) Marquis.

Who's Who in America 1992-1993 Geographic-Professional Index. 47th ed. 486p. 1992. 89.00 (*0-8379-1507-4*) Marquis.

Who's Who in America, 1993-1995: Junior & Senior High Version, 4 vols. 4946p. 1993. Set. text ed. 89.50 (*0-8379-1252-0*) Marquis.

Who's Who in America, 1993-1995: Junior & Senior High Version, 4 vols., 1. 1993. text ed. write for info. (*0-8379-1253-9*) Marquis.

Who's Who in America, 1993-1995: Junior & Senior High Version, 4 vols., 2. 1993. text ed. write for info. (*0-8379-1254-7*) Marquis.

Who's Who in America, 1993-1995: Junior & Senior High Version, 4 vols., 3. 1993. text ed. write for info. (*0-8379-1255-5*) Marquis.

Who's Who in America, 1993-1995: Junior & Senior High Version, 4 vols., 4. 1993. text ed. write for info. (*0-8379-1256-3*) Marquis.

Who's Who in America 1995, 3 vols. 49th ed. Ed. by Marquis Who's Who Staff. 5000p. 1994. 450.00 (*0-8379-0159-6*) Marquis.

Who's Who in America 1996, 3 vols. 50th ed. Ed. by Marquis Who's Who Staff. 5258p. 1995. 459.95 (*0-8379-0167-7*) Marquis.

Who's Who in America 1997, 3 vols. 51th ed. Ed. by Marquis Who's Who Staff. 5100p. 1996. 489.95 (*0-8379-0175-8*) Marquis.

***Who's Who in America, 1998. 52th ed. Marquis Who's Who Staff. 1997. 509.95 (*0-8379-0183-9*) Marquis.**
"We make very heavy use of WHO'S WHO IN AMERICA in our library. It's used daily to check biographical facts on people of distinction." --MARIE WATERS, HEAD OF COLLECTION DEVELOPMENT, UNIVERSITY OF CALIFORNIA AT LOS ANGELES. This, the world's preeminent biographical resource, keeps pace with a changing America with thousands of new entries each year. AND it speeds research with the Geographic/Professional Indexes. ANNUAL UPDATING enables Marquis Who's Who to bring users more new names & to update more existing entries each year. Every entry is selected & researched to ensure the most current, accurate biographical data for Who's Who users. The Geographical/Professional Indexes makes WHO'S WHO IN AMERICA an even more useful research tool. Now users can identify & locate prospective partners & new clients by profession, as well as by country, state, or province, or city. Essential for quickly finding the entries you need. More than 92,000 leaders decision-makers, & innovators from every important field - business, finance, government, education, science & technology, the arts & more - are profiled in this 51st Edition. Entries include name, occupation, vital statistics, parents, marriage, children, education, career, civic & political activities, writings & creative works, awards, professional memberships, & office address. When you need authoritative, accurate facts on our nation's leaders, go to the preeminent record of American achievement that offers new information EVERY year: Marquis WHO'S WHO IN AMERICA. ***Publisher Provided Annotation.***

Who's Who in American Art. 24th ed. 600p. 1990. 95.00 (*0-900083-13-1*) Gale.

***Who's Who in American Art 1997-1998.** 22th ed. Marquis Who's Who Staff. 1997. 210.00 (*0-8379-6300-1*) Marquis.

Who's Who in American Education, 1992-93. rev. ed. 979p. 1991. 129.95 (*0-940863-46-4*) Marquis.

Who's Who in American Education, 1992-93. 3rd rev. ed. 979p. 1991. 129.95 (*0-940863-45-6*) Marquis.

Who's Who in American Education, 1994-1995. 4th deluxe ed. 1993. Deluxe ed. 150.00 (*0-8379-2703-X*) Marquis.

Who's Who in American Education, 1994-1995. 4th limited ed. 1244p. 1993. Classic ed. 150.00 (*0-8379-2702-1*) Marquis.

Who's Who in American Education 1996-1997. 5th ed. Ed. by Marquis Who's Who Staff. 1092p. 1995. 159.95 (*0-8379-2704-8*) Marquis.

Who's Who in American Film Now. James Monaco. (Illus.). 600p. 1984. 39.95 (*0-918432-63-4*); pap. 19.95 (*0-918432-62-6*) Baseline Bks.

Who's Who in American Law, 1992-1993. 7th rev. ed. 1084p. 1991. 229.00 (*0-8379-3507-5*, 030650) Marquis.

Who's Who in American Law, 1994-1995. 8th ed. 1157p. 1994. 249.95 (*0-8379-3509-1*) Marquis.

Who's Who in American Law 1996-1997. 9th deluxe ed. Ed. by Marquis Who's Who Staff. 980p. 1996. 269.95 (*0-8379-3511-3*) Marquis.

***Who's Who in American Law, 1998-1999.** 10th ed. Marquis Who's Who Staff. 1998. 285.00 (*0-8379-3513-X*) Marquis.

Who's Who in American Nursing, 1993-1994. 5th ed. 893p. 1993. 139.00 (*0-8379-1002-1*) Marquis.

Who's Who in American Nursing 1996-1997. 6th ed. Ed. by Marquis Who's Who Staff. 806p. 1995. 149.95 (*0-8379-1004-8*) Marquis.

Who's Who in American Politics 1995-96, 2 vols. Ed. by Bowker, R. R., Staff. 2100p. 1995. 239.95 (*0-8352-3666-8*) Bowker.

Who's Who in American Politics 1995-96, Vol. 1. Ed. by Bowker, R. R., Staff. 1995. write for info. (*0-8352-3667-6*) Bowker.

Who's Who in American Politics 1995-96, Vol. 2. Ed. by Bowker, R. R., Staff. 1995. write for info. (*0-8352-3668-4*) Bowker.

***Who's Who in American Politics, 1997-1998, Set, 2 vols.** 16th ed. Marquis Who's Who Staff. 1997. 259.95 (*0-8379-6900-X*) Marquis.

***Who's Who in American Politics 1997-1998, Vol. 1.** 16th ed. Marquis Staff. 1997. write for info. (*0-8379-6901-8*) Marquis.

***Who's Who in American Politics 1997-1998, Vol. 2.** Marquis Staff. 1997. write for info. (*0-8379-6902-6*) Marquis.

***Who's Who in American Quilting.** American Quilter's Society Staff. LC 96-44771. 1996. write for info. (*0-89145-886-7*, Am Quilters Soc) Collector Bks.

Who's Who in Art. 21th ed. 600p. 1984. 90.00 (*0-8103-0533-X*, Pub. by Art Trade Pr UK) Gale.

Who's Who in Art. 23th ed. 600p. 1988. 90.00 (*0-8103-2744-9*) Gale.

Who's Who in Art. 25th ed. 1992. 105.00 (*0-900083-14-X*, Pub. by Art Trade Pr UK) Gale.

Who's Who in Art. 26th ed. 566p. 1994. 110.00 (*0-900083-15-8*, Pub. by Art Trade Pr UK) Gale.

Who's Who in Art. 27th ed. 1996. 120.00 (*0-900083-16-6*, Gale Res Intl) Gale.

Who's Who in Asian & Australasian Politics. 496p. 1991. lib. bdg. 175.00 (*0-86291-593-7*) Bowker-Saur.

Who's Who in Asian Equities. 455p. 1996. write for info. (*962-7982-06-7*, Pub. by Edinburgh Finan HK) Am Educ Systs.

Who's Who in Australasia & the Far East 1991-92. 2nd ed. 766p. 1991. 175.00 (*0-948875-55-0*, Pub. by Melrose UK) Intl Pubns Serv.

***Who's Who in Australasia & the Pacific Nations 1996/97.** 3rd ed. 600p. 1997. 165.00 (*0-948875-42-9*, Pub. by Melrose UK) Taylor & Francis.

Who's Who in Aviation. LC 73-88547. 311p. 1973. 140.00 (*0-08-018205-4*, Pub. by Pergamon Repr UK) Franklin.

Who's Who in Aviation History: 500 Biographies. William H. Longyard. LC 95-21493. 1995. 29.95 (*0-89141-556-4*) Presidio Pr.

Who's Who in Bible. Consumer Guide Staff. 1997. pap. 7.99 (*0-451-19064-5*, Sig) NAL-Dutton.

Who's Who in Biblical Studies & Archaeology. 2nd ed. 360p. 1993. 39.95 (*1-880317-06-0*) Biblical Arch Soc.

Who's Who in Bloomsbury. Alan Palmer & Veronica Palmer. LC 87-28467. 225p. 1988. text ed. 35.00 (*0-312-01630-1*) St Martin.

Who's Who in British Economics: A Directory of Economists in Higher Education, Business & Government. Ed. by Paul Sturges & Claire Sturges. 640p. 1990. text ed. 140.00 (*1-85278-105-X*) E Elgar.

Who's Who in British History: Geoffrey Treasure, 8 vols., Set. (Illus.). 1990. 360.00 (*1-55862-139-3*) St James Pr.

Who's Who in British Opera. Nicky Adam. LC 93-12314. 600p. 1993. 59.95 (*0-85967-894-6*, Pub. by Scolar Pr UK); pap. text ed. 34.95 (*1-85928-044-7*, Pub. by Scolar Pr UK) Ashgate Pub Co.

Who's Who in Burns. John D. Ross. LC 75-144480. reprint ed. 34.50 (*0-404-08547-4*) AMS Pr.

Who's Who in Business & Industry in the U. K. Ed. by Juliet Margetts. 1000p. 1991. 250.00 (*1-55862-155-5*) St James Pr.

***Who's Who in California.** Edna L. Barrett. 503p. 1996. lib. bdg. 205.00 (*1-880142-05-8*) Whos Who Hist Soc.

Who's Who in California. 21th ed. Sarah A. Vitale. LC 56-1715. 500p. 1991. text ed. 165.00 (*1-880142-00-7*) Whos Who Hist Soc.

Who's Who in California. 22th ed. Sarah A. Vitale. 1993. text ed. 185.00 (*1-880142-01-5*) Whos Who Hist Soc.

Who's Who in California. 23th ed. Ed. by Edna L. Barrett. 1994. lib. bdg. 195.00 (*1-880142-02-3*) Whos Who Hist Soc.

Who's Who in California. 24th ed. Edna L. Barrett. 1995. lib. bdg. 195.00 (*1-880142-03-1*) Whos Who Hist Soc.

Who's Who in California. 25th ed. Edna L. Barrett. 1995. lib. bdg. 205.00 (*1-880142-04-X*) Whos Who Hist Soc.

Who's Who in Canada: 1989. 992p. 1989. 130.00 (*0-7715-3961-4*) Taylor & Francis.

Who's Who in Canada 1996. 87th ed. 960p. 1996. text ed. 130.00 (*0-7715-3963-0*) Taylor & Francis.

Who's Who in Chemical Plants. unabridged ed. Victoria Hull. 400p. 1995. pap. 195.00 (*1-56760-065-4*, 2470-95) Utility Data Inst.

Who's Who in China. 6th ed. Who's Who Staff. LC 78-38093. (China Classic & Contemporary Works in Reprint Ser.). 1995. reprint ed. 45.00 (*0-404-56968-4*) AMS Pr.

Who's Who in Chiropractic International. 2nd ed. Fern L. Dzaman. Ed. by Sidney Scheiner et al. LC 80-51366. 1980. 55.00 (*0-918336-02-3*) Chiropractic.

Who's Who in Chiropractic, International 1976-78. Ed. by Fern L. Dzaman et al. LC 77-79754. (Illus.). 1977. 49.50 (*0-918336-01-5*) Chiropractic.

***Who's Who in Christian Hip-Hop Resource Directory.** Lady J, pseud. (Illus.). 64p. (Orig.). 1997. 6.95 (*1-889133-02-7*) Rising Son Media.

Who's Who in Christian History. J. D. Douglas. 768p. 1992. 24.99 (*0-8423-1014-2*) Tyndale.

***Who's Who in Christianity.** Lavinia Cohn-Sherbok. LC 97-22310. 1998. write for info. (*0-415-13582-6*); pap. write for info. (*0-415-13583-4*) Routledge.

Who's Who in Classical Mythology. Michael Grant & John Hazel. (Who's Who Ser.). 352p. (C). 1993. pap. 16.95 (*0-19-521030-1*, 3771) OUP.

Who's Who in Classical Mythology. Michael H. Grant. 367p. (gr. 13). 1994. pap. write for info. (*0-415-11937-5*, B4950) Routledge.

Who's Who in Classical Mythology. Jessica Hodge. 1995. 15.98 (*0-8317-9362-7*) Smithmark.

Who's Who in Classical Mythology. Adrian Room. 352p. 1996. pap. 16.95 (*0-8442-5469-X*) NTC Pub Grp.

Who's Who in Cogeneration & Independent Power. 4th ed. Utility Data Institute Staff. (Illus.). 500p. 1995. pap. 150.00 (*1-56760-053-0*) Utility Data Inst.

Who's Who in Comedy: Comedians, Comics, Jokesters & Clowns from Vaudeville to Today's Standups. Ron Smith. (Illus.). 544p. 1992. lib. bdg. 55.00 (*0-8160-2338-7*) Facts on File.

Who's Who in Comic Book Publishers: Guide for Creative Talent. Dan Stewart. LC 95-94870. 140p. 1995. spiral bd. 24.95 (*0-9648654-0-8*) Art Pubns AZ.

Who's Who in Commercial Real Estate: San Diego County Edition: Winter 1992-1993 Issue. Ed. by Jean S. Field. 103p. (Orig.). 1992. pap. 24.95 (*0-9635875-0-1*) Whos Who CA.

Who's Who in Computer Education & Research: U. S. Edition. Ed. by T. C. Hsiao. LC 74-18169. 330p. 1975. 35.00 (*0-912291-01-X*) Sci & Tech Pr.

Who's Who in Congress 1994: 103rd Congress, 2nd Session. 352p. 1994. spiral bd. 14.95 (*1-56802-021-X*) Congr Quarterly.

Who's Who in Congress, 1995. Congressional Quarterly, Inc. Staff. 345p. 1995. pap. 15.95 (*0-87187-903-4*) Congr Quarterly.

Who's Who in Congress 1995: 104th Congress, 1st Session, Preview Edition. Congressional Quarterly, Inc. Staff. 350p. 1994. pap. 14.95 (*1-56802-062-7*) Congr Quarterly.

Who's Who in Congress 1996: 104th Congress, 2nd Session. 200p. 1996. pap. 15.95 (*1-56802-071-6*) Congr Quarterly.

Who's Who in Consulting: A Reference Guide to Professional Personnel Engaged in Consultation for Business, Industry & Government. 2nd ed. Ed. by Paul Wasserman & Janice McLean. LC 73-16373. 216p. 1973. 180.00 (*0-8103-0360-4*) Gale.

***Who's Who in Democracy.** Ed. by Seymour M. Lipset. LC 96-48342. 247p. 1996. 85.00 (*1-56802-121-6*) Congr Quarterly.

***Who's Who in Dickens.** Donald Hawes. LC 97-12735. (Who's Who Ser.). 256p. 1998. pap. write for info. (*0-415-13605-9*) Routledge.

***Who's Who in Dickens.** Donald Hawes. LC 97-12735. (Who's Who Ser.). 256p. (C). 1998. text ed. write for info. (*0-415-13604-0*) Routledge.

Who's Who in Dickens: A Complete Dickens Repertory in Dickens' Own Words. Ed. by Alexander Fyfe. 1998. reprint ed. 39.00 (*1-55888-178-6*) Omnigraphics Inc.

Who's Who in Dickens: A Complete Dickens Repertory in Dickens Own Words. T. Fyfe. LC 75-152551. (Studies in Dickens: No. 52). 1971. reprint ed. lib. bdg. 75.00 (*0-8383-1236-5*) M S G Haskell Hse.

***Who's Who in Dogs.** Connie Vanacore. 1997. 25.95 (*0-87605-591-9*) Howell Bk.

Who's Who in Early Hanoverian England. Ed. by Geoffrey Treasure. LC 90-64266. (Who's Who in British History Ser.). (Illus.). 450p. 1992. 59.95 (*1-55862-136-9*) St James Pr.

Who's Who in Earth Service: People Working for the New Age. 1992. lib. bdg. 245.95 (*0-8490-5294-7*) Gordon Pr.

Who's Who in Egyptian Mythology. 2nd ed. Anthony S. Mercatante. Ed. by Robert Steven Bianchi. 256p. 1995. 32.50 (*0-8108-2967-3*) Scarecrow.

Who's Who in Electric Transmission & Distribution. Utility Data Institute Staff. 700p. 1995. pap. 150.00 (*1-56760-056-5*) Utility Data Inst.

Who's Who in Engineering. 9th ed. Gordon Davis. 1995. 220.00 (*0-87615-017-2*, 0149-7537) AAES.

Who's Who in Entertainment, 1992-1993. 2nd rev. ed. Ed. by Marquis Who's Who Staff. 702p. 1992. 235.00 (*0-8379-1851-0*) Marquis.

***Who's Who in Entertainment, 1998-1999.** 3rd ed. Marquis Who's Who Staff. 1997. 259.95 (*0-8379-1857-X*) Marquis.

***Who's Who in Environmental Engineering.** annuals AAEE Staff. 460p. 1997. write for info. (*0-614-30722-8*) Am Acad Environ.

Who's Who in European Institutions & Enterprises. (Sutters International Red Ser.). 1993. 230.00 (*88-85246-18-4*, Pub. by Whos Who Italy IT) Informatica.

Who's Who in European Integration Studies: European Community Studies Association - Europe. 155p. 1989. pap. 26.00 (*3-7890-1809-0*, Pub. by Nomos Verlags GW) Intl Bk Import.

Who's Who in European Politics. 2nd ed. 850p. 1993. 285.00 (*1-85739-021-0*) Bowker-Saur.

***Who's Who in European Politics.** 3rd ed. 873p. 299.95 (*1-85739-163-2*) Bowker-Saur.

Who's Who in European Research & Development, 3 vols., Set. 832p. 1996. pap. 400.00 (*1-85739-097-0*) Bowker-Saur.

Who's Who in European Research & Development 1996. Ed. by Bowker-Saur Staff. 1996. 450.00 (*1-85739-122-5*) Bowker-Saur.

Who's Who in Fashion. 3rd ed. Ann Stegemeyer. LC 95-61081. (Illus.). 300p. 1995. pap. 43.00 (*1-56367-040-2*) Fairchild.

Who's Who in Federal Regulation 1995. Congressional Quarterly, Inc. Staff. 300p. 1995. pap. 15.95 (*1-56802-135-6*) Congr Quarterly.

Who's Who in Film. Taub. Date not set. write for info. (*0-312-01130-X*) St Martin.

***Who's Who in Finance.** deluxe ed. 1997. write for info. (*0-8379-0333-5*) Marquis.

Who's Who in Finance & Industry, 1992-1993. 27th rev. ed. 942p. 1991. 220.00 (*0-8379-0327-0*) Marquis.

Who's Who in Finance & Industry, 1994-1995. 28th ed. 920p. 1993. 249.95 (*0-8379-0328-9*) Marquis.

Who's Who in Finance & Industry 1996-1997. 29th ed. Ed. by Marquis Who's Who Staff. 950p. 1995. 259.95 (*0-8379-0330-0*) Marquis.

W

***Who's Who in Finance & Industry 1998-1999.** 30th ed. Marquis Who's Who Staff. 1997. 279.95 (*0-8379-0332-7*) Marquis.

Who's Who in Food Chemistry-Europe. Richard A. Battaglia et al. 256p. 1996. 74.95 (*3-540-60239-9*) Spr-Verlag.

Who's Who in Foreign Trade. Ed. by Kristin Murphy. 150p. 1995. pap. 25.00 (*0-318-14134-5*) Foreign Trade.

***Who's Who in France.** 18th ed. 1986. 190.00 (*2-85784-018-7*, 00004383, Gale Res Intl) Gale.

Who's Who in France, 1991-1992 Edition. 23th ed. (FRE.). 1990. 795.00 (*0-685-60777-1*) Fr & Eur.

Who's Who in France 1995-1996. 1995. 1,095.00 (*0-7859-9952-3*) Fr & Eur.

***Who's Who in France 1996-1997.** 28th ed. 1997. 1,195.00 (*0-7859-9365-7*) Fr & Eur.

Who's Who in Genealogy. Ed. by Mary K. Meyer & P. William Filby. LC 81-69203. 1982. 70.00 (*0-8103-1630-7*) Gale.

Who's Who in Gerontology. 175p. 1986. pap. 5.00 (*0-318-20326-X*) Gerontological Soc.

Who's Who in Hollywood, 2 vols., Set, 1400p ea. David P. Ragan. 1920p. 1992. Set, 1400p. ea. 195.00 (*0-8160-2011-6*) Facts on File.

Who's Who in Intellectual Property. Pref. by Quentin N. Burdich. (Annual Ser.). 441p. 1989. text ed. 239.00 (*0-929432-00-2*) WWIP NY.

Who's Who in Interior Design: 1994-1995 Edition. Ed. by John L. Pellam. 512p. 1994. 175.00 (*1-882292-02-2*) Barons Whos Who.

Who's Who in Interior Design: 1996-1997 Edition. Ed. by John L. Pellam. 540p. 1996. 210.00 (*1-882292-07-3*) Barons Whos Who.

Who's Who in International Banking. 6th ed. 625p. 1992. 225.00 (*1-85739-040-7*) Bowker-Saur.

Who's Who in International Organizations, 3 Vols. 2nd ed. Ed. by Jon J. Jenkins & Union of International Associations Staff. 1280p. 1995. 385.00 (*3-598-11239-4*) K G Saur.

Who's Who in International Organizations, 3 vols., 1. Ed. by Union of International Associations Staff & Jon J. Jenkins. 1600p. 1992. lib. bdg. write for info. (*3-598-10909-1*) K G Saur.

Who's Who in International Organizations, 3 vols., 2. Ed. by Union of International Associations Staff & Jon J. Jenkins. 1600p. 1992. lib. bdg. write for info. (*3-598-10910-5*) K G Saur.

Who's Who in International Organizations, 3 vols., 3. Ed. by Union of International Associations Staff & Jon J. Jenkins. 1600p. 1992. lib. bdg. write for info. (*3-598-10911-3*) K G Saur.

Who's Who in International Organizations, 3 vols., Set. Ed. by Union of International Associations Staff & Jon J. Jenkins. 1600p. 1992. lib. bdg. 475.00 (*3-598-10908-3*) K G Saur.

Who's Who in Israel & Jewish Personalities Abroad, 1990-91. 21th ed. 1990. 130.00 (*0-8002-4277-7*) Intl Pubns Serv.

Who's Who in Isshinryu Karate. Harold Long et al. 110p. (Orig.). 1981. pap. 3.95 (*0-89826-007-8*) Natl Paperback.

Who's Who in Japan. Asia Press Staff. 1991. 236.00 (*4-900618-01-2*) CRC Pr.

Who's Who in Japan. Ed. by Japan Travel Bureau Staff. (JTB's Illustrated Japan in Your Pocket Ser.: No. 9). (Illus.). 192p. 1987. pap. 17.95 (*4-533-00798-8*, Pub. by Japan Trvl Bur JA) Bks Nippan.

Who's Who in Japan 1991-1992. Asia Press Co., Ltd. Staff. 800p. 1991. 225.00 (*0-685-54324-2*, AP1801, CRC Reprint) Franklin.

Who's Who in Jewish History. Joan Comay. (Who's Who Ser.). 400p. 1995. pap. 15.95 (*0-19-521079-4*) OUP.

Who's Who in Jewish History. 2nd rev. ed. Joan Comay. 400p. (gr. 13). 1995. pap. write for info. (*0-415-11887-5*, B4893) Routledge.

Who's Who in Jewish History. 2nd rev. ed. Joan Comay. 400p. (C). (gr. 13). 1995. text ed. write for info. (*0-415-12583-9*, B4953) Routledge.

Who's Who in Karate: 1982-83. Ed. by Dale Brooks. (Illus.). 112p. 1983. pap. 17.95 (*0-931981-00-X*) Am Martial Arts Pub.

Who's Who in Korean Literature. Korean Culture & Arts Foundation Staff. LC 95-82080. 557p. 1996. lib. bdg. 46.50 (*1-56591-066-4*) Hollym Intl.

W

Who's Who in Labor. LC 75-7962. 1976. 78.95 (*0-405-06651-1*) Ayer.

Who's Who in Late Medieval England. Ed. by Michael Hicks. LC 90-64267. (Who's Who in British History Ser.). (Illus.). 400p. 1991. 59.95 (*1-55862-135-0*) St James Pr.

Who's Who in Latin America: Government, Politics, Banking & Industry, 2 vols., Set. 4th rev. ed. Ed. by Bettina Corke. 1997. lib. bdg. 149.00 (*0-88354-225-0*) N Ross.

***Who's Who in Latin America Vol. 1: South America, 2 vols., Set.** 4th rev. ed. Ed. by Bettina Corke. 1997. lib. bdg. 99.00 (*0-88354-226-9*) N Ross.

***Who's Who in Latin America Vol. 2: Central America & the Caribbean, 2 vols., Set.** 4th rev. ed. Ed. by Bettina Corke. 1997. lib. bdg. 99.00 (*0-88354-227-7*) N Ross.

Who's Who in Lebanon. 12th ed. 500p. 1993. 140.00 (*2-903188-10-6*, 071200, Pub. by Publitec LB) Gale.

Who's Who in Lebanon. 14th ed. 1996. 160.00 (*2-903188-14-9*, Gale Res Intl) Gale.

Who's Who in Lebanon, Vol. 2. 12th ed. 1995. write for info. (*0-8103-9723-4*, Pub. by Publitec LB) Gale.

Who's Who in Lebanon, 1995-1996. 13th ed. 496p. 1994. 155.00 (*2-903188-12-2*) Gale.

Who's Who in Lebanon 1997 - 1998. Ed. by Publitec Publications Staff. 482p. 1996. 245.00 (*3-598-07647-9*) K G Saur.

***Who's Who in Luxury Real Estate.** John B. Losh. Ed. by Emily E. Burns. 400p. 1997. 19.95 (*1-886020-05-1*) Whos Who Lux Real Est.

Who's Who in Luxury Real Estate, No. IX. 9th rev. ed. John B. Losh. Ed. by Emily Burns. 365p. 1996. 19.95 (*1-886020-04-3*) Whos Who Lux Real Est.

Who's Who in Luxury Real Estate, Vol. VIII. 8th rev. ed. John B. Losh. Ed. by Emily E. Burns. 344p. 1995. 19.95 (*1-886020-00-0*) Whos Who Lux Real Est.

Who's Who in Luxury Real Estate Vol. rev. ed. John B. Losh. Ed. by Emily E. Burns. 279p. 1992. 19.95 (*1-886020-03-5*) Whos Who Lux Real Est.

Who's Who in Luxury Real Estate Vol. rev. ed. John B. Losh. Ed. by Emily E. Burns. 311p. 1993. 19.95 (*1-886020-02-7*) Whos Who Lux Real Est.

Who's Who in Luxury Real Estate Vol. rev. ed. John B. Losh. Ed. by Emily E. Burns. 336p. 1994. 19.95 (*1-886020-01-9*) Whos Who Lux Real Est.

Who's Who in Mail: A Directory of Women & Minorities in Business. Ed. by SDiane Bogus. 50p. (Orig.). 1990. reprint ed. 4.00 (*0-934172-18-8*) WIM Pubns.

Who's Who in Malaysia & Singapore, 1983-84, 2 vols. 15th ed. 700p. 1983. 144.00 (*0-8002-3685-8*) Taylor & Francis.

Who's Who in Marketing in Great Britain. Ed. by Gower Publications Staff. 500p. 1974. 50.00 (*0-8464-0972-0*) Beekman Pubs.

Who's Who in Mass Communication Research. 2nd ed. Ed. by Press Research Center Staff et al. 191p. 1990. lib. bdg. 135.00 (*3-598-10884-2*) K G Saur.

Who's Who in Medicine & Healthcare 1997-1998. Ed. by Marquis Who's Who Staff. 700p. 1996. 249.95 (*0-8379-0000-X*) Marquis.

Who's Who in Mexico Today. 2nd ed. Roderic A. Camp. LC 92-35773. 206p. 1993. text ed. 82.00 (*0-8133-8452-4*) Westview.

***Who's Who in Middle East Bank & Trade.** 3rd ed. 1986. 220.00 (*0-8103-6940-0*, 00006656, Gale Res Intl) Gale.

Who's Who in Military History: From 1453 to the Present Day. 2nd ed. John Keegan & Andrew Wheatcroft. (Illus.). 352p. (C). 1996. text ed. 49.95 (*0-415-12722-X*, Routledge NY) Routledge.

Who's Who in Military History: From 1453 to the Present Day. 2nd rev. ed. John Keegan. (Illus.). 352p. (C). 1996. pap. 16.95 (*0-415-11884-0*) Routledge.

Who's Who in Mozart's Operas: From Don Alfonso to Zerlina. Joachim Kaiser. Tr. by Charles Kessler. (Illus.). 212p. 1987. text ed. 21.95 (*0-02-873380-0*) Schirmer Bks.

Who's Who in My Family. Loreen Leedy. LC 94-16611. (Illus.). 32p. (J). (ps-3). 1995. lib. bdg. 15.95 (*0-8234-1151-6*) Holiday.

Who's Who in Mythology, 2 vols. 1996. pap. 29.90 (*0-19-521149-9*) OUP.

Who's Who in Natural Gas: Spring & Fall, 2 vols., Set. 1997. pap. text ed. 125.00 (*0-911299-84-X*) Oil Price Info Serv.

Who's Who in Nazi Germany. Robert S. Wistrich. 1982. 17.07 (*0-02-630600-X*) Macmillan.

Who's Who in New Country Music. Andrew Vaughan. (Illus.). 128p. (Orig.). 1990. pap. 9.95 (*0-312-03953-0*) St Martin.

Who's Who in Nineteen Ninety-Two. 144th ed. St. Martin's Press Staff. 2069p. 1992. text ed. 175.00 (*0-312-07513-8*) St Martin.

Who's Who in Non-Classical Mythology. Egerton Sykes. (Who's Who Ser.). 304p. 1993. pap. 14.95 (*0-19-521032-8*) OUP.

Who's Who in Non-Classical Mythology. 3rd ed. (Who's Who Ser.). 235p. (gr. 13). 1994. pap. write for info. (*0-460-86136-0*) Routledge.

Who's Who in Nuclear Weapons. Patrick Burke. LC 88-30078. 750p. 1989. text ed. 105.00 (*0-313-26590-9*, BWW/, Greenwood Pr) Greenwood.

Who's Who in Ocean & Freshwater Science. Ed. by Allen Varley. LC 79-301729. 336p. reprint ed. pap. 95.80 (*0-317-27839-8*, 2025251) Bks Demand.

Who's Who In Oceania: 1980-1981. Compiled by Robert D. Craig & Russell T. Clement. 1981. 12.95 (*0-939154-13-7*); pap. 7.95 (*0-939154-14-5*) Inst Polynesian.

Who's Who in Opera: An International Biographical Directory of Singers, Conductors, Directors, Designers & Administers. Maria F. Rich. 1976. 12.95 (*0-405-06652-X*, 19119) Ayer.

Who's Who in Pacific Navigation. John Dunmore. 328p. 1993. pap. 19.95 (*0-522-84558-4*, Pub. by Melbourne Univ Pr AT) Paul & Co Pubs.

Who's Who in Pacific Navigation. John Dunmore. LC 91-19280. (Illus.). 320p. (C). 1992. text ed. 34.00 (*0-8248-1350-2*) UH Pr.

Who's Who in Philosophy, Vol. 1. Ed. by Dagobert D. Runes. LC 79-88971. 293p. 1969. reprint ed. text ed. 35.00 (*0-8371-2095-0*, WWIP, Greenwood Pr) Greenwood.

Who's Who in Photography: An Illustrated Biographical Directory - 1991-1992. Ed. by H. Donald Kroitzsh et al. (Illus.). 300p. 1990. 89.95 (*0-9627262-0-6*) Five Corners.

Who's Who in Pipelining. 11th rev. ed. Ed. by Paula Jepperson. 400p. 1994. pap. 77.00 (*0-912553-46-4*) Hart Pubns.

Who's Who in Pipelining. 12th rev. ed. Ed. by Paula Jepperson. 400p. 1995. pap. text ed. 79.00 (*0-912553-53-7*) Hart Pubns.

***Who's Who in Polish America.** Hippocrene Books Staff. 1996. 60.00 (*0-7818-0520-1*) Hippocrene Bks.

Who's Who in Polish America: A Biographical Directory of Polish-American Leaders & Distinguished Poles Resident in the Americas. Ed. by Francis Bolek. LC 75-129390. (American Immigration Collection. Series 2). 1970. reprint ed. 34.95 (*0-405-00545-8*) Ayer.

Who's Who in Polish America: 1995-96. Ed. by Boleslaw Wierzbianski. LC 96-7273. 1996. 60.00 (*0-614-13387-4*) Bicenten.

Who's Who in Powder Metallurgy. 184p. (Orig.). 1997. pap. 75.00 (*1-878954-29-6*) Metal Powder.

Who's Who in Prepaid Legal Services: 1991 Membership Directory. 215p. 1991. write for info. (*0-318-64381-2*) Am Prepaid.

Who's Who in Professional Speaking. 320p. 1987. 25.00 (*0-318-15873-6*) Natl Speakers.

Who's Who in Public Relations. 6th ed. Ed. by Otto Lerbinger. 762p. 1992. 50.00 (*0-9632901-0-X*) P R Pub Co.

Who's Who in Religion, 1992-1993. 4th ed. Ed. by Marquis Who's Who Staff. 580p. 1992. 129.00 (*0-8379-1604-6*) Marquis.

Who's Who in Residential Real Estate in North America. 2nd ed. Ed. by S. Doniece Welch. 350p. 95.99 (*0-9645705-0-5*) Real Trends.

Who's Who in Rhode Island Jazz: c. 1925-1988. Lloyd S. Kaplan & Robert E. Petteruti. (Illus.). 112p. 1992. pap. 19.95 (*0-940139-26-X*) Consortium RI.

Who's Who in Roman Britain & Anglo-Saxon England. Ed. by Richard Fletcher. LC 90-63659. (Who's Who in British History Ser.). (Illus.). 270p. 1990. 59.95 (*1-55862-131-8*) St James Pr.

Who's Who in Russia. Geron. Date not set. text ed. 185.00 (*1-85043-744-0*, Pub. by I B Tauris UK) St Martin.

***Who's Who in Russia & the Soviet Union: From 1900-1991.** Martin McCauley. LC 96-42009. 280p. 1997. pap. write for info. (*0-415-13898-1*) Routledge.

***Who's Who in Russia & the Soviet Union: From 1900-1991.** Martin McCauley. LC 96-42009. 296p. (C). 1997. text ed. write for info. (*0-415-13897-3*) Routledge.

Who's Who in Russia Today: A Biographical Dictionary of more than 2,100 Individuals from the Russian Federation Including the Other Fourteen Former USSR Republics. Ed. by Ulrich-Joachim Schulz-Torge. 412p. 1994. 325.00 (*3-598-11184-3*) K G Saur.

Who's Who in Science & Engineering. 3rd ed. Ed. by Marquis Who's Who Staff. 1300p. 1996. 259.95 (*0-8379-5754-0*) Marquis.

Who's Who in Science & Engineering: Premier Edition, 1992-1993. 1098p. 1992. 199.00 (*0-8379-5751-6*) Marquis.

Who's Who in Science & Engineering, 1994-1995. 2nd limited ed. 1269p. 1994. Classic ed. 249.95 (*0-8379-5752-4*) Marquis.

***Who's Who in Science & Engineering, 1998-1999.** 4th ed. Marquis Who's Who Staff. 1997. 272.95 (*0-8379-5756-7*) Marquis.

Who's Who in Science in Europe: A Biograhical Guide in Science, Technology, Agriculture & Medicine. 9th ed. 2752p. 1995. 950.00 (*1-56159-132-7*, Stockton Pr) Groves Dictionaries.

***Who's Who in Scottish History.** Gordon Donaldson & Robert Morpeth. 254p. 1997. pap. 19.95 (*1-86057-005-4*, Pub. by Welsh Acad UK) Intl Spec Bk.

Who's Who in Scuba Diving: Academy of Marine Sciences & Undersea Research. Ed. by Harry Bachstein. 436p. (C). 1992. 14.95 (*0-941332-28-4*, D500) Best Pub Co.

Who's Who in Security. Stephen S. Burns & David A. Marston. 398p. 1989. 145.00 (*0-9623775-0-3*) Natl Sec Inst.

Who's Who in Shakespeare. Wendy Nelson-Cave. 1995. 7.98 (*0-7858-0222-3*) Bk Sales Inc.

Who's Who in Shakespeare. Peter Quennell & Hamish Johnson. (Who's Who Ser.). 240p. 1995. pap. 14.95 (*0-19-521081-6*) OUP.

Who's Who in Shakespeare. Peter Quennell & Hamish Johnson. LC 94-26058. (Who's Who Ser.). 256p. (gr. 13). 1995. pap. write for info. (*0-415-11883-2*, B4951, Routledge NY) Routledge.

Who's Who in Shakespeare. Frances G. Stokes. 1990. 7.99 (*0-517-69684-3*) Random Hse Value.

Who's Who in Shakespeare's England. Alan Palmer & Veronica Palmer. (Illus.). 350p. 1981. 32.50 (*0-312-87096-5*) St Martin.

***Who's Who in Skulls: Ethnic Identification of Crania from Measurements.** William W. Howells. (Illus.). 120p. 1995. pap. 22.00 (*0-87365-209-6*) Peabody Harvard.

Who's Who in South African Politics. Shelagh Gastrow. (Illus.). 356p. (Orig.). (C). 1995. pap. 24.95 (*0-89675-458-8*, Pub. by Ravan Pr ZA) Ohio U Pr.

Who's Who in South African Politics. 4th ed. Ed. by Shelagh Gastrow. 371p. (Orig.). 1993. 95.00 (*1-873836-06-6*, Pub. by H Zell Pubs UK) Bowker-Saur.

Who's Who in Southern African Law. 1991. boxed 112.00 (*0-409-06743-1*, SA) MICHIE.

Who's Who in Space. 2nd ed. Michael Cassutt. 439p. 1993. 90.00 (*0-02-897092-6*) Macmillan.

Who's Who in Space: The First Twenty-Five Years. Michael Cassutt. (Illus.). 336p. 1987. text ed. 40.00 (*0-8161-8801-7*, Hall Reference) Macmillan.

Who's Who in Stuart Britain. Ed. by C. P. Hill. LC 90-63660. (Who's Who in British History Ser.). (Illus.). 508p. 1990. 59.95 (*1-55862-132-6*) St James Pr.

Who's Who in Technology. 6th ed. Amy L. Unterburger. 1900p. 1989. 95.00 (*0-8103-4951-5*) Gale.

Who's Who in Technology: Bio & Index. 7th ed. Amy L. Unterburger. 1995. 195.00 (*0-8103-7467-6*) Gale.

Who's Who in Technology: Biograph. 7th ed. Amy L. Unterburger. 1995. 95.00 (*0-8103-7468-4*) Gale.

Who's Who in Technology: Index. 7th ed. Amy L. Unterburger. 1995. 220.00 (*0-8103-7469-2*) Gale.

Who's Who in Technology, Biography & Index, 2 vols., Set. 6th ed. Ed. by Amy L. Unterburger. 1995. 380.00 (*0-8103-4950-7*) Gale.

Who's Who in Technology Index. 6th ed. Ed. by Amy L. Unterburger. 1995. 285.00 (*0-8103-4952-3*) Gale.

Who's Who in the Ancient World. Betty Radice. (Reference Ser.). 336p. (Orig.). 1973. pap. 13.95 (*0-14-051055-9*, Penguin Bks) Viking Penguin.

Who's Who in the Arab World. 11th ed. 1000p. 1992. 280.00 (*2-903188-09-2*, 071099, Pub. by Publitec LB) Gale.

Who's Who in the Arab World. 13th ed. 1996. 325.00 (*2-903188-13-0*) Gale.

Who's Who in the Arab World, 1990-1991. 10th ed. 1000p. 1990. 200.00 (*2-903188-07-6*, Pub. by Publitec LB) Gale.

Who's Who in the Arab World, 1995-1996. 12th ed. 980p. 1994. 325.00 (*2-903188-11-4*) Gale.

Who's Who in the Arab World 1997 - 1998. Ed. by Publitec Publications Staff. 978p. 1996. 425.00 (*3-598-07646-0*) K G Saur.

Who's Who in the Bible, 2 vols. in 1. Ronald Brownrigg. 1993. 19.99 (*0-517-32170-X*) Random Hse Value.

Who's Who in the Bible. Peter Calvocoressi. 1988. 19.95 (*0-670-81188-2*) Grossman.

Who's Who in the Bible. Ed. by Peter Calvocoressi. 304p. 1989. pap. 13.95 (*0-14-051212-8*, Penguin Bks) Viking Penguin.

Who's Who in the Bible. Albert E. Sim & George Dent. 176p. (Orig.). 1995. pap. 9.95 (*0-572-01648-4*, Pub. by Foulsham UK) Assoc Pubs Grp.

Who's Who in the Bible. Albert E. Sims & George Dent. 1979. pap. 2.95 (*0-8065-0705-5*, Citadel Pr) Carol Pub Group.

***Who's Who in the California Legislature - 1997-98: W1998 Supplement.** 5th rev. ed. Ed. by Ted Fourkas. (Illus.). 280p. 1997. ring bd. 74.95 (*0-917982-59-2*, WB7) Capitol Enquiry.

Who's Who in the California Legislature, 1993-94 with 1994 Supplement. (Illus.). 280p. 1993. ring bd. 25.00 (*0-917982-44-4*) Capitol Enquiry.

Who's Who in the California Legislature, 1995-96 & 1996 Supplement. Ed. by Ted Fourkas. (Illus.). 280p. (C). 1996. 35.00 (*0-917982-50-9*) Capitol Enquiry.

Who's Who in the Classical World. John Warrington. (Who's Who Ser.). 576p. 1998. pap. 18.95 (*0-19-521082-4*) OUP.

***Who's Who in the Doctrine & Covenants.** Susan E. Black. 1997. 19.95 (*1-57008-292-8*) Bookcraft Inc.

Who's Who in the East, 1991-92. 23th rev. ed. 1000p. 1990. 245.00 (*0-8379-0623-7*, 030591) Marquis.

Who's Who in the East, 1993-1994. 24th ed. 1040p. 1992. 259.00 (*0-8379-0624-5*) Marquis.

Who's Who in the East, 1995-1996. 25th ed. 1328p. 1994. 275.00 (*0-8379-0626-1*) Marquis.

Who's Who in the East 1997-1998 Classic ed. 26th ed. Ed. by Marquis Who's Who Staff. 900p. 1996. 279.95 (*0-8379-0628-8*) Marquis.

Who's Who in the Federal Executive Branch 1994. 207p. 1994. 15.95 (*0-87187-994-8*) Congr Quarterly.

Who's Who in the Federal Executive Branch 1995. Congressional Quarterly, Inc. Staff. 209p. 1995. pap. 16.95 (*1-56802-084-8*) Congr Quarterly.

Who's Who in the Federal Executive Branch 1996. 400p. 1996. pap. 16.95 (*1-56802-085-6*) Congr Quarterly.

Who's Who in the Film World of 1914. Fred C. Justice & T. R. Smith. 1976. lib. bdg. 59.95 (*0-8490-2820-5*) Gordon Pr.

Who's Who in the History of Punjab, 1800-1849. Balraj Saggar. (C). 1993. 48.00 (*81-85135-60-6*, National Bk Ctr) S Asia.

***Who's Who in the Irish War of Independence & the Civil War.** 2nd rev. ed. Padraic O'Farrell. Orig. Title: Who's Who in the Irish War of Independence, 1916-1921. 240p. 1997. pap. 19.95 (*1-874675-85-6*, Pub. by Lilliput Pr Ltd IE) Irish Bks Media.

Who's Who in the Irish War of Independence, 1916-1921 see Who's Who in the Irish War of Independence & the Civil War

Who's Who in the Jewelry Industry. Ed. by Donald S. McNeil. LC 79-27501. 231p. 1980. 24.95 (*0-931744-02-4*) Jewlrs Circular-Keystone.

Who's Who in the JFK Assassination: An A-to-Z Encyclopedia. Michael Benson. (Illus.). 452p. 1993. pap. 18.95 (*0-8065-1444-2*, Citadel Pr) Carol Pub Group.

Who's Who in the Martial Arts. Ed. by Dale Brooks. (Illus.). 180p. (Orig.). 1985. pap. 12.95 (*0-931981-04-2*) Am Martial Arts Pub.

Who's Who in the Martial Arts & Directory of Black Belts. Bob Wall. LC 75-22880. (Illus.). 275p. (Orig.). 1975. pap. 7.95 (*0-685-62677-6*) R A Wall.

***Who's Who in the Media & Communications, 1998-1999.** Marquis Who's Who. 1997. 259.95 (*0-8379-3950-X*) Marquis.

Who's Who in the Midwest. 24th deluxe ed. 1994. Deluxe ed. 249.95 (*0-8379-0725-X*) Marquis.

Who's Who in the Midwest. 24th limited ed. 969p. 1994. Classic ed. 249.95 (*0-8379-0724-1*) Marquis.

Who's Who in the Midwest, 1992-1993. 23th rev. ed. 832p. 1992. 220.00 (*0-8379-0723-3*, 030654) Marquis.

Who's Who in the Midwest, 1996-1997 Classic ed. 25th ed. Ed. by Marquis Who's Who Staff. 1000p. 1996. 259.95 (*0-8379-0726-8*) Marquis.

Who's Who in the Motion Picture Industry, 1996: Producers, Directors, Writers, Cinematographers, & Studio Executives. 9th rev. ed. Ed. by Rodman W. Gregg. LC 81-64574. (Illus.). 275p. 1996. pap. 24.95 (*0-941710-09-2*) Packard.

Who's Who in the New Testament. 1998. 17.99 (*0-517-15934-1*) Random Hse Value.

Who's Who in the New Testament. Ronald Brownrigg. (Who's Who Ser.). 288p. (C). 1993. pap. 15.95 (*0-19-521031-X*, 3952) OUP.

Who's Who in the New Testament. 2nd ed. (Who's Who Ser.). 286p. (gr. 13). 1994. pap. 0.01 (*0-460-86133-6*, B4949) Routledge.

An Asterisk (*) at the beginning of an entry indicates that the title is appearing in BIP for the first time.

Who's Who in the Old Testament. Joan Comay. (Who's Who Ser.). 384p. (C). 1993. pap. 16.95 (*0-19-521029-8*, 3778) OUP.

Who's Who in the Old Testament. Donald Sommerville. (Illus.). 160p. 1996. 17.99 (*0-517-14022-5*) Random Hse Value.

Who's Who in the Old Testament. 2nd ed. (Who's Who Ser.). 398p. (gr. 13). 1994. pap. write for info. (*0-460-86134-4*, B4952) Routledge.

Who's Who in the Peace Corps. Ed. by Cheryl K. Lacoff. 725p. 1994. 95.00 (*1-879583-03-8*); pap. 75.00 (*1-879583-02-X*) Ref Pr Intl.

Who's Who in the People's Republic of China. Wolfgang Bartke. Tr. by Franciscus Verellen. LC 80-27599. 743p. 1981. reprint ed. pap. 180.00 (*0-7837-9933-0*, 2060660) Bks Demand.

Who's Who in the People's Republic of China, 2 vols., Set. 3rd ed. Wolfgang Bartke. (Illus.). 900p. 1991. lib. bdg. 325.00 (*3-598-10771-4*) K G Saur.

Who's Who in the Safety Profession. Ed. by Stephen S. Burns & David A. Marston. 413p. 1990. pap. text ed. 145.00 (*0-9623775-1-1*) Natl Sec Inst.

Who's Who in the Second World War. John Keegan. (Who's Who Ser.). 208p. 1995. pap. 14.95 (*0-19-521080-8*) OUP.

Who's Who in the Socialist Countries of Europe: Albania, Bulgaria, CSSR, Hungary, Poland, Romania & Yugoslavia, 3 vols., Set. Ed. by Juliusz Stroynowski. 1369p. 1989. lib. bdg. 375.00 (*3-598-10636-X*) K G Saur.

Who's Who in the South & Southwest, 1991-92. 22th rev. ed. 848p. 1991. 189.00 (*0-8379-0822-1*) Marquis.

Who's Who in the South & Southwest, 1993-1994. 23th ed. 920p. 1993. 210.00 (*0-8379-0823-X*) Marquis.

Who's Who in the South & Southwest, 1995-1996. 24th ed. 1250p. 1995. 239.95 (*0-8379-0825-6*) Marquis.

***Who's Who in the South & Southwest 1997-1998.** 25th ed. Marquis Who's Who Staff. 1997. 249.95 (*0-8379-0827-2*) Marquis.

Who's Who in the Talmud. Shulamis Frieman. LC 94-22067. 488p. 1995. 40.00 (*1-56821-113-9*) Aronson.

Who's Who in the Theatre, 2 vols. 17th ed. Ed. by Ian Herbert. 768p. 1981. Set. 200.00 (*0-8103-0234-9*) Gale.

Who's Who in the United Nations & Related Agencies. LC 75-4105. 1975. 65.00 (*0-405-06490-X*) Ayer.

Who's Who in the United Nations & Related Agencies. 1975. 25.95 (*0-405-00490-7*, 19120) Ayer.

Who's Who in the United Nations & Related Agencies. 2nd ed. Ed. by Stanley R. Greenfield. 800p. 1992. lib. bdg. 185.00 (*1-55888-762-8*) Omnigraphics Inc.

Who's Who in the West, 1992-93. 23th rev. ed. 816p. 1992. 220.00 (*0-8379-0923-6*) Marquis.

Who's Who in the West, 1994-1995. 24th limited ed. 939p. 1993. Classic ed. 255.00 (*0-8379-0924-4*) Marquis.

Who's Who in the West 1996-1997. 25th ed. Ed. by Marquis Who's Who Staff. 1055p. 1995. 259.95 (*0-8379-0926-0*) Marquis.

Who's Who in the World, 1993-1994. 11th ed. 1299p. 1992. 319.00 (*0-8379-1111-7*) Marquis.

Who's Who in the World 1995. 12th ed. Ed. by Marquis Who's Who Staff. 1567p. 1995. 329.95 (*0-8379-1113-3*) Marquis.

Who's Who in the World 1996. 13th ed. Ed. by Marquis Who's Who Staff. 1496p. 1995. 339.95 (*0-8379-1115-X*) Marquis.

Who's Who in the World 1997 Classic ed. 14th ed. Ed. by Marquis Who's Who Staff. 1400p. 1996. 359.95 (*0-8379-1117-6*) Marquis.

***Who's Who in the World,1998.** 15th ed. Marquis Who's Who Staff. 1998. 369.95 (*0-8379-1119-2*) Marquis.

Who's Who in Theology & Science: A Templeton Foundation Book. rev. ed. Ed. by Robert L. Herrmann. 500p. 1996. 59.50 (*0-8264-0845-1*) Continuum.

Who's Who in Tudor England. Ed. by C. R. Routh. LC 90-63661. (Who's Who in British History Ser.). (Illus.). 494p. 1990. 59.95 (*1-55862-133-4*) St James Pr.

Who's Who in U. S. Writers, Editors & Poets, 1986-87. Ed. by Curt Johnson. 600p. 1987. 35.00 (*0-913204-18-8*) December Pr.

Who's Who in U. S. Writer's, Editors & Poets, 1988. 2nd ed. Ed. by Curt Johnson. LC 87-648220. 704p. 1988. 35.00 (*0-913204-21-8*) December Pr.

Who's Who in Washington Non-Profit Groups, 1994. 313p. 1994. 12.95 (*0-87187-971-9*) Congr Quarterly.

Who's Who in Washington Non-Profit Groups 1995. Congressional Quarterly, Inc. Staff. 313p. 1995. pap. 15.95 (*1-56802-131-3*) Congr Quarterly.

Who's Who in Washington Non-Profit Groups 1996. 200p. 1996. pap. 15.95 (*1-56802-089-9*) Congr Quarterly.

Who's Who in Wodehouse. Daniel Garrison. (Illus.). 219p. (C). 1987. text ed. 32.50 (*0-8204-0517-5*) P Lang Pubng.

Who's Who in Wodehouse. Daniel Garrison. LC 91-70594. 218p. 1991. reprint ed. pap. 10.95 (*1-55882-087-6*, Lib Crime Classics) Intl Polygonics.

***Who's Who in World Agriculture.** 2nd ed. 1985. 340.00 (*0-582-90111-1*, 00007503, Pub. by Longman Grp UK) Gale.

Who's Who in World Oil & Gas. 10th ed. 506p. 1991. 150.00 (*1-55862-103-2*) St James Pr.

Who's Who in World Politics: From 1860 to the Present Day. Alan Palmer. LC 95-53055. 424p. 1996. pap. 17.95 (*0-415-13162-6*) Routledge.

Who's Who in World Politics: From 1860 to the Present Day. Alan Palmer. LC 95-53055. 424p. (C). 1996. text ed. 65.00 (*0-415-13161-8*) Routledge.

Who's Who in World War II. John Keegan. 216p. (gr. 13). 1995. pap. write for info. (*0-415-11889-1*, C0555) Routledge.

Who's Who in Writers, Editors & Poets: United States & Canada, 1989-1990. 3rd ed. Ed. by Curt Johnson. 640p. 1990. 35.00 (*0-913204-22-6*) December Pr.

Who's Who in Writers, Editors & Poets: United States & Canada, 1995-1996. 5th ed. Ed. by Curt Johnson. LC 87-648220. (Biennial Ser.). 544p. 1995. 35.00 (*0-913204-30-7*) December Pr.

Who's Who Nepal. NRA Staff. (C). 1992. 240.00 (*0-7855-0220-3*, Pub. by Ratna Pustak Bhandar) St Mut.

Who's Who of American Inventors. Ed. by Roger B. Hooper. 320p. 1990. 79.95 (*0-929956-04-4*) Hooper Group.

Who's Who of American Inventors: 1992-93. Ed. by Roger B. Hooper. (Illus.). 192p. 1992. 99.95 (*0-929956-06-0*) Hooper Group.

Who's Who of American Women, 1991-1992. 17th rev. ed. 1160p. 1991. 210.00 (*0-8379-0417-X*) Marquis.

Who's Who of American Women, 1993-1994. 18th rev. ed. Ed. by Marquis Who's Who Staff. 1083p. 1993. 225.00 (*0-8379-0418-8*) Marquis.

Who's Who of American Women 1995-1996. 19th ed. Ed. by Marquis Who's Who Staff. 1150p. 1995. 239.00 (*0-8379-0420-X*) Marquis.

Who's Who of American Women 1997-1998. 20th ed. Ed. by Marquis Who's Who Staff. 1996. 249.00 (*0-8379-0422-6*) Marquis.

Who's Who of Australian & New Zealand Film Actors: The Sound Era. Scott Palmer. LC 87-32215. 179p. 1988. 22.50 (*0-8108-2090-0*) Scarecrow.

Who's Who of Australian Children's Writers. 2nd ed. 200p. 1996. pap. 30.00 (*1-875589-77-5*) D W Thorpe.

Who's Who of Australian Visual Artists. 356p. 1991. 39.95 (*0-909532-78-8*) D W Thorpe.

Who's Who of Australian Visual Artists. 2nd ed. 400p. 1995. 40.00 (*1-875589-82-1*) D W Thorpe.

Who's Who of Australian Writers. 2nd ed. Compiled by National Centre for Australian Studies Staff. 700p. 1995. 80.00 (*1-875589-20-1*) D W Thorpe.

Who's Who of Ballooning: 1783-1983. Robert J. Rechs. 362p. (Orig.). 1982. 35.00 (*0-937568-26-0*, TL 615 R43); pap. text ed. 20.00 (*0-937568-27-9*) Rechs Pubns.

Who's Who of Black Millionaires. Frank J. Johnson. LC 83-82591. (Illus.). 182p. 1984. pap. 9.95 (*0-915021-00-5*) Who's Black Mill.

Who's Who of British Engineers 1980. 352p. 1981. 55.00 (*0-312-87413-8*) St Martin.

***Who's Who of British Jazz.** John Chilton. (Cassell Jazz Ser.). 512p. 1997. 89.95 (*0-304-33909-1*); pap. 29.95 (*0-304-33910-5*) Cassell.

Who's Who of British Scientists 1980-81. 650p. 1981. 75.00 (*0-312-87433-2*) St Martin.

Who's Who of Cats. Ed. by John R. F. Breen. LC 94-1330. 500p. 1994. pap. 7.95 (*1-56305-629-1*, 3629) Workman Pub.

Who's Who of Dogs. Ed. by John R. Breen. LC 94-44826. 504p. 1995. pap. 7.95 (*1-56305-871-5*, 3871) Workman Pub.

Who's Who of Emerging Leaders in America, 1991-92. 3rd ed. 736p. 1991. 220.00 (*0-8379-7202-7*) Marquis.

Who's Who of Emerging Leaders in America, 1993-1994. 4th ed. Ed. by Marquis Who's Who Staff. 758p. 1992. 229.00 (*0-8379-7203-5*) Marquis.

Who's Who of Entrepreneurs in the U. S. Ed. by Roger B. Hooper. 320p. 1991. 99.95 (*0-929956-05-2*) Hooper Group.

Who's Who of Heaven: Saints for All Seasons. John P. Kleinz. LC 87-71420. 220p. (Orig.). 1987. pap. 12.95 (*0-87061-136-4*) Chr Classics.

***Who's Who of Indian Writers: Supplementary Volume 1990.** Ed. by K. Satchidanandan. (C). 1993. 16.00 (*81-7201-514-3*, Pub. by Sahitya Akademi II) S Asia.

Who's Who of Institutions & Mutual Funds. Carson Publications Staff. Ed. by Ian Sax. 1996. ring bd. write for info. (*0-615-00871-2*) Carson Grp.

Who's Who of Jazz. 4th ed. John Chilton. LC 84-20062. (Roots of Jazz Ser.). (Illus.). 362p. 1985. 29.50 (*0-306-76271-4*); pap. 13.95 (*0-306-80243-0*) Da Capo.

Who's Who of Nobel Prize Winners 1901-1995. 3rd ed. Bernard S. Schlessinger & June H. Schlessinger. LC 96-14746. 288p. (YA). 1996. boxed 49.95 (*0-89774-899-9*) Oryx Pr.

Who's Who of Sanskrit Scholars in India 1991. Ed. by K. C. Dutt. (C). 1995. 32.00 (*81-7201-689-1*, Pub. by Sahitya Akademi II) S Asia.

Who's Who of Southern Africa, 1987. 70th ed. 1628p. 1987. write for info. (*0-8002-4201-7*) Taylor & Francis.

Who's Who of Southern Africa 1995/96 Edition. 1600p. 1995. 130.00 (*0-9583902-3-1*, Pub. by Whos Who So Africa SA) Taylor & Francis.

***Who's Who of Southern Africa 1996/97.** 1600p. 1996. 135.00 (*0-9583902-5-8*, Pub. by Whos Who So Africa SA) Taylor & Francis.

Who's Who of Sports Champions: Their Stories & Records. Ralph Hickok. LC 94-49144. 928p. 1995. pap. 19.95 (*0-395-73312-X*) HM.

Who's Who of (the) American Teachers Association of the Martial Arts: 1995 Directory. Bernd W. Weiss. LC 94-72838. (Illus.). 185p. (Orig.). 1995. pap. 50.00 (*0-931373-05-0*) Hiles & Hardin Pubs.

Who's Who of the Asian Pacific Rim: 1993-1994 Edition. Ed. by John L. Pellam. 403p. 1993. 175.00 (*1-882292-01-4*) Barons Whos Who.

Who's Who of the Asian Pacific Rim: 1995-1996 Edition. Ed. by John L. Pellam. 381p. 1995. 210.00 (*1-882292-05-7*) Barons Whos Who.

***Who's Who of the Asian Pacific Rim: 1997-1998 Edition.** John L. Pellam. 464p. 1996. 210.00 (*1-882292-09-X*) Barons Whos Who.

Who's Who of the Elite: Elite Organizations Dominating the United States. 1996. lib. bdg. 259.95 (*0-8490-6915-7*) Gordon Pr.

Who's Who of the Elite: Members of the Bilderbergs, Council on Foreign Relations, Trilateral Commission & Skull & Bones Society. Robert G. Ross, Sr. 243p. 1995. pap. text ed. 25.95 (*0-9649888-0-1*) RIE.

***Who's Who of the South & Southwest, 1997.** deluxe ed. Marquis Who's Who Staff. 1997. write for info. (*0-8379-0828-0*) Marquis.

Who's Who of Unsolved Murders. James Morton. (Illus.). 300p. 1996. 24.95 (*1-85626-163-8*, C Kyle) Trafalgar.

Who's Who of Unsolved Murders. James Morton. (Illus.). 304p. 1996. pap. 11.95 (*1-85626-203-0*, C Kyle) Trafalgar.

***Who's Who of Victorian Cinema: A Worldwide Survey.** Ed. by Stephen Herbert & Luke McKernan. (Distributed for the British Film Institute Ser.). (Illus.). 184p. 1996. 59.95 (*0-85170-539-1*, Pub. by British Film Inst UK) Ind U Pr.

Who's Who of Women in World Politics: Biographies of Women Currently in Government or Legislatures. Ed. by Yolanda Dolling & Polly Cooper. 320p. 1991. 95.00 (*0-86291-627-5*) Bowker-Saur.

Who's Who of World Religions. Ed. by John R. Hinnells. 656p. 1992. 60.00 (*0-13-952946-2*) S&S Trade.

***Who's Who on Big Bag.** Golden Books Staff. (Illus.). (J). 1997. pap. text ed. 1.09 (*0-307-08646-1*, Golden Books) Western Pub.

Who's Who on the Moon: A Biographical Dictionary of Lunar Nomenclature. Elijah E. Cocks & Josiah Cocks. (Illus.). 599p. (C). 1995. lib. bdg. 45.00 (*0-936389-27-3*) Tudor Pubs.

Who's Who on the Postage Stamps of the World, 1840-1984: A Master Index. Paul G. Partington. 1989. lib. bdg. 45.00 (*0-685-26477-7*) P G Partington.

Who's Who on the Screen. C. D. Fox & Milton L. Silver. 1976. 300.00 (*0-87968-277-9*) Gordon Pr.

Who's Who on U. S. Stamps. Richard L. Thomas. 450p. 1991. 30.00 (*0-940403-43-9*); pap. 14.95 (*0-940403-42-0*) Linns Stamp News.

***Who's Who West 1998-1999.** 26th ed. Marquis Who's Who Staff. 1997. 272.95 (*0-8379-0928-7*) Marquis.

***Who's Who West 1998-99.** deluxe ed. Marquis Who's Who Staff. 1997. write for info. (*0-8379-0929-5*) Marquis.

Who's Who 1979-1980. 131th ed. 1979. 69.95 (*0-312-87468-5*) St Martin.

Who's Who, 1989. 141th ed. LC 04-16933. 2000p. 1989. 145.00 (*0-312-02678-1*) St Martin.

Who's Who 1990. LC 04-16933. 2020p. 1990. pap. 150.00 (*0-312-04040-7*) St Martin.

Who's Who, 1991. 143th ed. LC 04-16933. 1950p. 1991. 165.00 (*0-312-05797-0*) St Martin.

Who's Who 1993: An Annual Biographical Dictionary One Hundred & Forty-Fifth Year of Issue. 2070p. 1993. text ed. 185.00 (*0-312-09426-4*) St Martin.

Who's Who, 1994: An Annual Biographical Dictionary. 146th ed. 2093p. 1994. 185.00 (*0-312-10581-9*) St Martin.

Who's Who, 1995: An Annual Biographical Dictionary. 147th ed. St. Martin's Press Staff. 2300p. 1995. 195.00 (*0-312-12413-9*) St Martin.

Who's Who 1996: An Annual Biographical Dictionary. 148th ed. 2100p. 1996. text ed. 200.00 (*0-312-12949-1*) St Martin.

Whos Who 1997 149th Edition. 1997. text ed. 210.00 (*0-312-16366-5*) St Martin.

Who's Whodunit. Lenore S. Gribbin. LC 71-627563. (North CArolina University Library Studies: No. 5). 184p. reprint ed. pap. 52.50 (*0-317-09228-6*, 2004350) Bks Demand.

Who's Whose. Jan Ormerod. LC 96-27998. (J). Date not set. write for info. (*0-688-14678-3*); lib. bdg. write for info. (*0-688-14679-1*) Lothrop.

Who's Writing This? Notations on the Authorial I, with Self-Portraits. Ed. by Daniel Halpern. LC 94-17421. (Illus.). 1994. 22.00 (*0-88001-377-X*) Ecco Pr.

Who's Writing This? Notations on the Authorial I, with Self-Portraits. Ed. by Daniel Halpern. (Illus.). 208p. 1996. pap. 15.00 (*0-88001-446-6*) Ecco Pr.

Who's Your County Named For? And Other Hoosier County Facts. Glenda S. Shull. (Illus.). 248p. (Orig.). (J). (gr. 4-7). 1990. pap. 12.95 (*0-938682-20-2*) River Rd Pubns.

***Who's Your Fave Rave? Who's Your Fave Rave?** Randi Reisfeld & Danny Fields. 256p. (YA). 1997. pap. 14.00 (*1-57297-253-X*) Blvd Books.

Who's Your Hoosier Ancestor? Genealogy for Beginners. Mona Robinson. LC 91-39969. (Illus.). 240p. 1992. 29.95 (*0-253-34996-6*); pap. 13.95 (*0-253-20731-2*, MB-771) Ind U Pr.

Who's Your Mama, Are You Catholic & Can You Make a Roux? rev. ed. Marcelle Bienvenu. Ed. by Susan C. Dore. 112p. 1993. 22.95 (*0-9631637-1-X*) Times Acadiana.

Whose Are You? Identity & Ethnicity among the Toronto Macedonians. Peter Vasiliadis. LC 88-84005. (Immigrant Communities & Ethnic Minorities in the U. S. & Canada Ser.: No. 58). 1989. 69.50 (*0-404-19468-0*) AMS Pr.

Whose Art Is It? Jane Kramer. LC 94-11528. (Public Planet Bks.). (Illus.). 144p. 1994. text ed. 24.95 (*0-8223-1535-1*); pap. text ed. 10.95 (*0-8223-1549-1*) Duke.

Whose Baby? Suzanne Carey. (Intimate Moments Ser.). 1996. mass mkt. 3.99 (*0-373-07715-7*, 1-07715-5) Silhouette.

Whose Baby Am I? Shirley Greenway. LC 92-6133. (Animals Q & A Ser.). 32p. (J). 1992. per., pap. 3.95 (*0-8249-8562-1*, Ideals Child); lib. bdg. 11.00 (*0-8249-8577-X*, Ideals Child) Hambleton-Hill.

Whose Backyard, Whose Risk: Fear & Fairness in Toxic & Nuclear Waste Siting. Michael B. Gerrard. LC 94-18925. 1994. 42.00 (*0-262-07160-6*) MIT Pr.

Whose Backyard, Whose Risk: Fear & Fairness in Toxic & Nuclear Waste Siting. Michael B. Gerrard. (Illus.). 352p. 1996. reprint ed. pap. 17.50 (*0-262-57113-7*) MIT Pr.

Whose Body? Dorothy L. Sayers. 746p. 1992. Not sold separately (*0-615-00014-2*) Random Hse Value.

Whose Body? A Lord Peter Wimsey Mystery. Dorothy L. Sayers. 224p. 1995. mass mkt. 4.99 (*0-06-104357-5*, Harp PBks) HarpC.

Whose Broad Stripes & Bright Stars? The Trivial Pursuit of the Presidency 1988. Jack W. Germond & Jules Witcover. 1990. pap. 12.95 (*0-446-39187-5*) Warner Bks.

***Whose Business Is It Anyway? Is Owning & Operating God's Business "the Life to Which You Were Called"?** Sherri Jefferson. 50p. (Orig.). (ENG, JPN & SPA.). 1997. pap. 12.00 (*0-9654656-4-0*, CH-01-100) S Jefferson.

***Whose Business Values? Some Asian & Cross-Cultural Perspectives.** Ed. by Sally Stewart & Gabriel Donleavy. 310p. (Orig.). 1995. pap. 39.50 (*962-209-386-8*, Pub. by Hong Kong Univ Pr HK) Coronet Bks.

Whose Chick Is That? Jill B. Bruce. (Illus.). 48p. (Orig.). (J). (gr. 3-7). 1995. pap. 7.95 (*0-86417-576-0*, Pub. by Kangaroo Pr AT) Seven Hills Bk.

Whose Child Is This? Bill Wilson. 178p. 1994. pap. 9.99 (*0-88419-382-9*) Creation House.

***Whose Child Is This? A Biblical View of Adoption.** Luther B. McIntyre, Jr. 28p. (Orig.). (YA). (gr. 8 up). 1997. pap. 0.95 (*0-9652285-9-2*) Good Life Pub.

Whose Choice: Population Controllers' or Yours? Robert Whelan. 1992p. 3.95 (*0-946680-42-6*) Human Life Intl.

Whose Common Future: Reclaiming the Commons. Ecologist Magazine Editors. 224p. 1993. pap. write for info. (*1-85383-149-2*) New Soc Pubs.

Whose Common Future: Reclaiming the Commons. Ecologist Magazine Staff. 1993. pap. 14.95 (*0-86571-277-8*); lib. bdg. 39.95 (*0-86571-276-X*) New Soc Pubs.

***Whose Daddy Does This?** Charles Reasoner. (Sliding Surprise Ser.). (Illus.). 12p. (J). (ps). 1997. bds. 9.95 (*0-8431-7988-0*) Price Stern Sloan.

Whose Death Is It, Anyway? Elizabeth D. Squire. 256p. (Orig.). 1997. mass mkt. 5.99 (*0-425-15627-3*, Prime Crime) Berkley Pub.

***Whose Democracy? Nationalism, Religion, & the Doctrine of Collective Rights in Post-1989 Eastern Europe.** Sabrina P. Ramet. LC 97-7819. 224p. (Orig.). 1997. 49.50 (*0-8476-8323-0*) Rowman.

***Whose Democracy? Nationalism, Religion, & the Doctrine of Collective Rights in Post-1989 Eastern Europe.** Sabrina P. Ramet. LC 97-7819. 224p. (Orig.). 1997. pap. 17.95 (*0-8476-8324-9*) Rowman.

Whose Experience Counts in Theological Reflection? Monika Hellwig. LC 82-80331. (Pere Marquette Lectures). 112p. 1982. 15.00 (*0-87462-537-8*) Marquette.

***Whose Eyes Are These?** Illus. by Elizabeth Burman. (J). 1997. 14.99 (*0-8499-1464-7*) Tommy Nelson.

Whose Eyes Are These? Byalick. 1997. write for info. (*0-15-201430-6*) HarBrace.

Whose Eyes Are These? Byalick. 1997. pap. write for info. (*0-15-201431-4*) HarBrace.

Whose File Is It Anyway? Ruth Cohen. (C). 1988. 40.00 (*0-901108-97-9*, Pub. by NCCL UK) St Mut.

Whose Forest Is It? Rozanne L. Williams. (Emergent Reader Big Bks.). 8p. (J). (gr. k-2). 1995. 7.98 (*0-916119-74-2*) Creat Teach Pr.

Whose Forest Is It?, Level 1. Rozanne L. Williams. (Emergent Reader Science Ser.). 8p. 1994. 1.59 (*0-916119-29-7*, 3506) Creat Teach Pr.

Whose Hands Are These? A Gifted Healer's Miraculous True Story. Gene Egidio. 256p. 1997. 22.00 (*0-446-52045-4*) Warner Bks.

Whose Hat? Margaret Miller. LC 86-18324. (Illus.). 40p. (J). (ps-1). 1988. 16.00 (*0-688-06906-1*); lib. bdg. 15.93 (*0-688-06907-X*) Greenwillow.

***Whose Hat?** Margaret Miller. 1997. pap. 4.95 (*0-688-15279-1*, Mulberry) Morrow.

Whose Hat Is That? Ronald Roy. (Illus.). 40p. (J). (ps-3). 1990. pap. 6.95 (*0-395-54778-4*, Clarion Bks) HM.

Whose Hat Is That? A Little People Book. Peter Trumbull. (J). 1995. pap. 2.99 (*0-88743-437-1*) Sch Zone Pub Co.

Whose Hat Was That? Brian Wildsmith & Rebecca Wildsmith. LC 92-17237. (J). 1993. pap. write for info. (*0-15-200690-7*) HarBrace.

***Whose Historical Jesus?** Ed. by William E. Arnal & Michel Desjardins. (Studies in Christianity & Judaism Ser.: Vol. 7). vi, 337p. 1997. pap. 27.95 (*0-88920-295-8*) Wilfrid Laurier.

Whose House Is This? Charles Reasoner. (Sliding Surprise Bks.). (Illus.). 12p. (J). 1995. bds. 9.95 (*0-8431-3911-0*) Price Stern Sloan.

Whose India? The Independence Struggle in British & Indian Fiction & History. Teresa Hubel. LC 95-30470. 256p. 1996. text ed. 46.95 (*0-8223-1708-7*) Duke.

Whose India? The Independence Struggle in British & Indian Fiction & History. Teresa Hubel. LC 95-30470. 256p. (C). 1996. pap. text ed. 16.95 (*0-8223-1718-4*) Duke.

***Whose Interests Are Supreme? Organizational Politics in the Civil Courts in India.** Robert S. Moog. LC 96-36657. (Monograph & Occasional Papers). 1996. write for info. (*0-924304-30-8*) Assn Asian Studies.

Whose Is the Hidden Hand? J. Schoeman. 1984. lib. bdg. 79.95 (*0-87700-604-0*) Revisionist Pr.

Whose Is the Kingdom? A Nine-Part Radio Series. John Arden & Margaretta D'Arcy. 212p. (Orig.). (C). 1988. pap. 13.95 (*0-413-18710-1*, AO337, Pub. by Methuen UK) Heinemann.

Whose Jerusalem? A 3000 Year History. Eliyahu Tal. (Illus.). 336p. 1994. text ed. 38.00 (*965-229-123-4*, Pub. by Gefen Pub Hse IS) Gefen Bks.

W

Whose Justice? Which Rationality? A. MacIntyre. 65.95 (*0-7156-2198-X*, Pub. by Duckworth UK) Focus Pub-R Pullins.
Whose Justice? Which Rationality? A. MacIntyre. pap. 24.95 (*0-7156-2199-8*, Pub. by Duckworth UK) Focus Pub-R Pullins.
Whose Justice? Which Rationality? Alasdair MacIntyre. LC 87-40354. 432p. (C). 1989. text ed. 26.50 (*0-268-01942-8*); pap. text ed. 17.50 (*0-268-01944-4*) U of Notre Dame Pr.
Whose Keeper? Social Science & Moral Obligation. Alan Wolfe. (Illus.). 388p. 1991. pap. 14.00 (*0-520-07426-2*) U CA Pr.
Whose Knees Are These? Anna Ross. (Illus.). 12p. (J). (ps). 1994. write for info. (*0-318-72490-1*) Random Bks Yng Read.
Whose Language: A Study in the Linguistic-Pragmatics. Jacob L. Mey. LC 85-6123. (Pragmatics & Beyond Companion Ser.: Vol. 3). ix, 412p. 1985. 84.00 (*0-915027-61-5*); pap. 27.95 (*0-915027-57-7*) Benjamins North Am.
Whose Language? What Power? A Universal Conflict in a South African Setting. Frank Smith. 192p. (C). 1993. text ed. 38.00 (*0-8077-3282-6*); pap. text ed. 18.95 (*0-8077-3281-8*) Tchrs Coll.
Whose Life Is It Anyhow? The Doctor's Dilema in Intensive Care - an Insiders View. Simon L. Cohen. 206p. 1995. 26.95 (*0-86051-806-X*, Robson-Parkwest) Parkwest Pubns.
Whose Life Is It, Anyway? Female Version. Brian Clark. 1980. Female Version. pap. 5.95 (*0-87129-371-4*, W48) Dramatic Pub.
Whose Life Is It, Anyway? Male Version. Brian Clark. 1980. pap. 5.95 (*0-87129-329-3*, W43) Dramatic Pub.
Whose List Is This?, Level 1. Andrea Butler. (Let Me Read Ser.). (J). 1996. 2.95 (*0-673-36334-1*, GoodYrBooks) Addson-Wesley Educ.
Whose Master's Voice? The Development of Popular Music in Thirteen Cultures. Ed. by Alison J. Ewbank & Fouli T. Papageorgiou. LC 95-46060. (Contributions to the Study of Music & Dance Ser.: No. 41). 280p. 1997. text ed. 69.50 (*0-313-27772-9*, Greenwood Pr) Greenwood.
Whose Mommy Is This? Charles Reasoner. LC 93-87681. (Sliding Surprise Bks.). (Illus.). 12p. (J). (ps). 1994. bds. 9.95 (*0-8431-3718-5*) Price Stern Sloan.
Whose Mouse Are You? Robert Kraus. LC 70-89931. (Illus.). 40p. (J). (ps-k). 1970. lib. bdg. 15.00 (*0-02-751190-1*, Mac Bks Young Read) S&S Childrens.
Whose Mouse Are You? Robert Kraus. LC 70-89931. (Illus.). 32p. (J). (ps). 1986. pap. 4.95 (*0-689-71142-5*, Aladdin Paperbacks) S&S Childrens.
Whose New World Order? What Role for the United Nations? Ed. by Mara R. Bustelo & Philip Alston. xiv, 157p. 1991. pap. 32.50 (*1-86287-067-5*, Pub. by Federation Pr AU) Gaunt.
Whose News? The Media & Women's Issues. Ed. by Ammu Joseph & Kalpana Sharma. LC 94-8044. 316p. 1994. 36.00 (*0-8039-9152-5*) Sage.
***Whose Pet Is Best?, Vol. 17.** Carolyn Keene. (Nancy Drew Notebooks Ser.). (J). 1997. pap. 3.99 (*0-671-56861-2*, Minstrel Bks) PB.
***Whose Reality Counts? Putting the First Last.** Robert Chambers. 256p. (Orig.). 1996. pap. 6.50 (*1-85339-386-X*) Women Ink.
Whose Report Will You Believe? Marilyn Phillipps. 60p. 1993. pap. text ed. write for info. (*1-884794-04-1*) Eden Pubng.
Whose Right It Is. Kelley Varner. 350p. (Orig.). 1995. pap. 9.99 (*1-56043-151-2*) Destiny Image.
Whose School Is It Anyway? Parent-Teacher Conflict Over an Innovative School. Barry A. Gold & Matthew B. Miles. LC 81-8562. 416p. 1981. text ed. 65.00 (*0-275-90633-7*, C0633, Praeger Pubs) Greenwood.
Whose Science? Whose Knowledge? Thinking from Women's Lives. Sandra Harding. LC 90-55724. 336p. 1991. 39.95 (*0-8014-2513-1*); pap. 15.95 (*0-8014-9746-9*) Cornell U Pr.
***Whose Science? Whose Knowledge? Thinking from Women's Lives.** Sandra Harding. 336p. 1991. pap. 13.99 (*0-335-09760-X*, Open Univ Pr) Taylor & Francis.
Whose Second Self? Gender & (Ir)rationality in Computer Culture. Ed. by Zoe Sofia. 149p. 1995. pap. 46.00 (*0-7300-1635-8*, ECS814, Pub. by Deakin Univ AT) St Mut.
Whose Service Is Perfect Freedom. C. H. Douglas. 157p. 1986. pap. 6.00 (*0-949667-64-1*, Noontide Pr) Legion Survival.
Whose Shoe? Margaret Miller. LC 90-38491. (Illus.). 40p. (J). (ps up). 1991. 16.00 (*0-688-10008-2*); lib. bdg. 15.93 (*0-688-10009-0*) Greenwillow.
***Whose Shoes?** Hines. Date not set. write for info. (*0-15-201773-9*) HarBrace.
Whose Shoes? Brian Wildsmith. (Illus.). 16p. (J). 1987. pap. 3.95 (*0-19-272145-3*) OUP.
Whose Side Are You On? Emily Moore. 128p. (J). (gr. 3-7). 1988. 14.00 (*0-374-38409-6*) FS&G.
Whose Side Are You On? Emily Moore. 128p. (J). (gr. 3-7). 1990. pap. 3.95 (*0-374-48373-6*, Sunburst Bks) FS&G.
Whose Slippers Are Those? Marilyn Kahalewai. LC 87-92272. (Illus.). 16p. (J). (ps-6). 1988. 8.95 (*0-935848-58-4*) Bess Pr.
***Whose Song Is Sung.** Frank Schaefer. 1997. mass mkt. 5.99 (*0-8125-5012-9*) Tor Bks.
Whose Song Is Sung: A Novel of Beowulf. Frank Schaefer. LC 95-39744. 304p. 1996. 23.95 (*0-312-85756-X*) Tor Bks.
Whose Standards: Consumer & Professional Standards in Health Care. Charlotte Williamson. LC 92-13012. 1992. 90.00 (*0-335-09721-9*, Open Univ Pr); pap. 27.50 (*0-335-09720-0*, Open Univ Pr) Taylor & Francis.
Whose Story? Reporting the Developing World after the Cold War. Gerald B. Sperling. (Illus.). 242p. (Orig.). (C). 1993. pap. text ed. 17.95 (*1-55059-077-4*) Temeron Bks.
Whose Toes Are Those? Joyce Elias. LC 92-8603. (Illus.). (J). (ps). 1992. 11.95 (*0-8120-6215-9*) Barron.
Whose Tracks Are These? Morrell Gipson & Paul Mangold. Ed. by Rebecca Stefoff. LC 90-13798. (Magic Mountain Fables Ser.). (Illus.). 24p. (J). (gr. k-3). 1990. lib. bdg. 14.60 (*0-944483-93-3*) Garrett Ed Corp.
Whose Tracks Are These? A Clue Book of Familiar Forest Animals. James T. Nail. LC 94-65087. (Illus.). 32p. (J). (gr. k-4). 1994. 13.95 (*1-879373-89-0*) R Rinehart.
Whose Tracks Are These? A Clue Book of Familiar Forest Animals. 2nd ed. James D. Nail. LC 94-65087. (Illus.). 32p. (J). 1996. reprint ed. pap. 7.95 (*1-57098-078-0*) R Rinehart.
Whose Utility? The Social Impact Of Public Utility Privatization & Regulations in Britain. John Ernst. LC 93-38812. 1994. 85.00 (*0-335-19268-8*, Open Univ Pr); pap. 34.00 (*0-335-19267-X*, Open Univ Pr) Taylor & Francis.
Whose Votes Count: Affirmative Action & Minority Voting Rights. Abigail M. Thernstrom. LC 87-7406. (Twentieth Century Fund Study). 336p. 1987. 36.00 (*0-674-95195-6*) HUP.
Whose Votes Count: Affirmative Action & Minority Voting Rights. Abigail M. Thernstrom. (Twentieth Century Fund Study). 336p. 1989. pap. 17.50 (*0-674-95196-4*) HUP.
Whose Water Is It, Anyway? Anatomy of the Water Battle Between El Paso, Texas & New Mexico. Linda G. Harris et al. (Illus.). 50p. (Orig.). (C). 1990. pap. 12.95 (*0-9623682-1-0*) Arroyo Pr.
***Whose Welfare?** Tony Cole. 156p. (C). 1990. pap. text ed. 13.95 (*0-422-60220-5*) Routledge.
Whose Welfare? AFDC & Elite Politics. Steven M. Teles. LC 96-12351. (Studies in Government & Public Policy). 232p. 1996. 29.95 (*0-7006-0801-X*) U Pr of KS.
Whose Woods These Are. Ed. by Karren L. Alenier. LC 83-50101. 176p. 1983. pap. 8.00 (*0-915380-18-8*) Word Works.
Whose Woods These Are: A History of the Bread Loaf Writers' Conference, 1926-1990. Ed. by Mary S. Duffy. LC 92-43688. 1993. 40.00 (*0-88001-323-0*) Ecco Pr.
Whose World Order? Uneven Globalization & the End of the Cold War. George Sorensen. LC 94-24014. 246p. (C). 1995. pap. text ed. 21.50 (*0-8133-2187-5*) Westview.
Whose World to Lose? Ours. Ed. by Alden Bryant & Fred B. Wood. (Illus.). 102p. (Orig.). 1992. 18.00 (*0-9602410-2-7*); pap. 5.00 (*0-9602410-0-0*); spiral bd. 8.00 (*0-9602410-1-9*) Earth Regnrtn.
***Whoso Knoweth Himself...** Muhyiddin I. Arabi. Tr. by T. H. Weir from ARA. 27p. (Orig.). 1988. reprint ed. 11.00 (*0-904975-14-2*, Pub. by Beshara Pubns UK); reprint ed. pap. 6.00 (*0-904975-06-1*, Pub. by Beshara Pubns UK) New Leaf Dist.
Whosoever Shall Offend. Francis M. Crawford. (Works of Francis Marion Crawford Ser.). 1990. reprint ed. lib. bdg. 79.00 (*0-7812-2555-8*) Rprt Serv.
Whump. Gail Chislett. (Annikin Ser.: No. 12). (Illus.). (J). (ps-1). 1992. 0.99 (*1-55037-253-X*, Pub. by Annick CN) Firefly Bks Ltd.
Whuppity Stoorie. Carolyn White. LC 95-16032. (Illus.). 1997. 15.95 (*0-399-22903-5*, Putnam) Putnam Pub Group.
***Why.** Leroy Fritz, Jr. LC 97-90000. 160p. (Orig.). 1997. pap. 8.95 (*0-9656518-0-0*) OC Pub.
Why? William L. Murphy. (Orig.). 1996. pap. 8.95 (*0-533-11764-X*) Vantage.
Why? Nikolai Popov. LC 95-45957. (Illus.). 32p. (J). (ps-3). Date not set. 15.95 (*1-55858-534-6*); lib. bdg. 15.88 (*1-55858-535-4*) North-South Bks NYC.
***Why?** Robert W. Wood. (Experiments for Young Scientists Ser.). (Illus.). 140p. (YA). (gr. 5 up). 1997. text ed. write for info. (*0-7910-4849-7*) Chelsea Hse.
***Why? A Guide to Answering Life's Toughest Questions.** Robin Norwood. 250p. 1997. pap. 12.95 (*1-55874-522-X*) Health Comm.
Why? Experiments for the Young Scientist. Dave Prochnow & Kathy Prochnow. (Illus.). 160p. (J). (gr. 4-7). 1992. 16.95 (*0-8306-4015-0*, 4176); pap. 9.95 (*0-8306-4023-1*, 4176) McGraw-Hill Prof.
Why: Science Unveiling the Mind. R. Colin Johnson. 381p. 1995. pap. 17.00 (*0-9639899-2-8*) Cognizer.
Why: Staples. abr. ed. Paul E. Johnson. (Illus.). (Orig.). Date not set. pap. text ed. write for info. (*1-878230-88-3*) P E Johnson.
Why? The Road from There to Here was Tough but Now I'm on the Highway. Kathy M. Moonbeam. LC 91-76844. (Illus.). 192p. (Orig.). 1992. pap. 9.95 (*1-880601-07-9*) Danon Pub.
Why: The Serial Killer in America. Margaret Cheney. Ed. by Diane Parker. LC 92-54172. 230p. 1992. pap. 11.95 (*0-88247-924-5*) R & E Pubs.
Why a Budget Based on Debt-Money Cannot Be Balanced. 1996. lib. bdg. 250.95 (*0-8490-5871-6*) Gordon Pr.
Why a Disguise? Laura J. Numeroff. LC 93-19025. (Illus.). (J). 1995. pap. 14.00 (*0-671-87006-8*, S&S Bks Young Read) S&S Childrens.
Why a Disguise? Laura J. Numeroff. LC 93-19025. (J). (ps-1). 1996. 14.00 (*0-689-80513-6*) S&S Childrens.
Why a Friends School. Douglas Heath. LC 75-81158. (Orig.). 1969. pap. 3.00 (*0-87574-164-9*) Pendle Hill.
Why? A Study of Christian Standards. Ed. by R. M. Davis & P. D. Buford. 160p. reprint ed. pap. 5.99 (*1-56722-043-6*) Word Aflame.
Why a Swan? Essays, Interviews, & Conversations on "Swan Lake" Stephen C. Steinberg & Janice Ross. (Journals: No. 1). 92p. 1989. pap. 15.00 (*1-881106-00-4*) SF Perf Arts Lib.
***Why a Wave of Frustration Is Sweeping the Nation: The Pulse of the People Speaks Out on Issues.** Ricardo A. Scott. (Ras Cardo Speaks on the Issues of Life Ser.). (Illus.). 150p. (Orig.). 1996. pap. write for info. (*1-883427-89-4*, RAS9949) Crnerstone GA.
Why a Woman Should Not Preach: Victory Collection. Robert H. Prince. Ed. by Jean Randolph. 20p. 1993. reprint ed. pap. 3.50 (*1-882821-02-5*) DPK Pubns.
Why Abstract? William Saroyan et al. LC 74-6407. (Studies in Comparative Literature: No. 35). 1974. lib. bdg. 59.95 (*0-8383-1837-1*) M S G Haskell Hse.
Why Adults Use the Public Library: A Research Perspective. Maurice P. Marchant. LC 93-31053. x, 134p. 1994. pap. text ed. 24.00 (*1-56308-193-8*) Libs Unl.
***Why Africa Failed to Develop.** Ayittey. LC 97-11236. 1997. 29.95 (*0-312-16400-9*) St Martin.
Why Airplanes Crash: Aviation Safety in a Changing World. Clinton V. Oster, Jr. et al. 192p. 1992. 35.00 (*0-19-507223-5*) OUP.
Why Alaska? Poems of the Aleutians. Faye Denton. (Illus.). 92p. 1990. pap. 8.95 (*0-939116-21-9*) Frontier OR.
Why All Church-Age Endtime Prophets Are False: A Scriptural Thesis That Endures. Raymond A. Waugh, Sr. LC 94-90179. 140p. 1994. pap. write for info. (*0-9631249-6-X*) Morris Pubng.
Why All the Fuss over Certified Raw Milk for Infant? The Certified Raw Milk Helps This Baby Well & Strong. rev. ed. Harry C. Gibbens, Sr. (Illus.). 39p. 1989. 8.95 (*0-685-29787-X*) H C Gibbens.
Why All the Fuss over Certified Raw Milk for Infants? This Certified Raw Milk Keeps This Baby Well & Strong Along with His Family. 3rd ed. Harry C. Gibbens, Sr. (Illus.). 51p. 1991. pap. 10.95 (*0-9624921-0-8*) H C Gibbens.
Why Alliances Endure: The United States-Pakistan Alliance. Rekha Datta. (C). 1994. 22.00 (*81-7003-169-9*, Pub. by S Asia Pubs II) S Asia.
Why Alligator Hates Dog: A Cajun Folktale. J. J. Reneaux. LC 94-46965. (Illus.). (J). (ps-2). 1995. 15.95 (*0-87483-412-0*) August Hse.
Why Alligators Don't Have Wings. Martin Camp. (Illus.). 32p. (J). (ps-5). 1994. 13.95 (*1-880092-06-9*) Bright Bks TX.
Why Althusser Killer His Wife: Essays on Discourse & Violence. Geraldine Finn. LC 95-8841. 224p. (C). 1996. pap. 17.50 (*0-391-03908-3*); text ed. 49.95 (*0-391-03907-5*) Humanities.
Why Am I Afraid to Love? Overcoming Rejection & Indifferences. John Powell. (John Powell Library). (Illus.). 112p. (Orig.). 1995. reprint ed. pap. 9.50 (*0-88347-322-4*, 7322) Res Christian Liv.
Why Am I Afraid to Tell You Who I Am? John Powell. (John Powell Library). (Illus.). 153p. (Orig.). 1995. reprint ed. pap. 9.50 (*0-88347-323-2*, 7323) Res Christian Liv.
Why Am I Always Broke: How to Be Sure about Money. Albert Ellis. 1991. pap. 8.95 (*0-8184-0547-3*) Carol Pub Group.
Why Am I Crying? A Helpful & Honest Look at Depression. Martha Maughon. LC 89-19681. 128p. 1989. pap. 8.99 (*0-929239-17-2*) Discovery Hse Pubs.
Why Am I Different? Norma Simon. Ed. by Caroline Rubin. LC 76-41172. (Albert Whitman Concept Bks.). (Illus.). 32p. (J). (gr. k-2). 1976. lib. bdg. 12.95 (*0-8075-9074-6*) A Whitman.
Why Am I Different? Norma Simon. (J). (ps-3). 1993. pap. 4.95 (*0-8075-9076-2*) A Whitman.
Why Am I Going to the Hospital? Claire Ciliotta & Carole Livingston. (Where Did I Come From Ser.). (Illus.). (J). (gr. k-7). 1992. pap. 8.95 (*0-8184-0568-6*, L Stuart) Carol Pub Group.
Why Am I Going to the Hospital? Carole Livingston & Claire Ciliotta. (Illus.). (J). (gr. 1 up). 1981. 12.00 (*0-8184-0316-0*) Carol Pub Group.
Why Am I Here? The Meaning of God in the Aquarian Age. Loy Young. Ed. by Kathryn Hall. (Illus.). 386p. (Orig.). 1993. pap. 24.95 (*1-882888-39-1*) Aquarius Hse.
***Why Am I Laughing?** Colleen Dewhurst. Date not set. write for info. (*0-688-05841-8*) Morrow.
Why Am I So Brown? Contrib. by Trinidad Sanchez, Jr. 98p. 1995. reprint ed. pap. 10.00 (*1-877636-03-7*) March Abrazo.
Why Am I So Miserable If These Are the Best Years of My Life? Andrea B. Eagan. (YA). (gr. 7 up). 1988. pap. 2.95 (*0-380-46136-6*, Flare) Avon.
Why Am I Still Addicted? A Holistic Approach to Recovery. Richard Plagenhoef & Carol Adler. 1991. pap. text ed. 9.95 (*0-07-050280-3*) McGraw.
Why Am I Still Addicted? A Holistic Approach to Recovery. Richard Plagenhoef & Carol Adler. 252p. 1991. 17.95 (*0-8306-3361-8*, 2307, TAB-Human Servs Inst); pap. 9.95 (*0-8306-2135-0*, TAB-Human Servs Inst) TAB Bks.
Why America Needs Religion: Secular Modernity & Its Discontents. Guenter Lewy. LC 96-9149. 172p. (Orig.). 1996. pap. 18.00 (*0-8028-4162-7*) Eerdmans.
Why America Should Re-Elect Bill Clinton in '96. Margo J. Fraser. 96p. (Orig.). 1995. mass mkt. write for info. (*0-9650785-0-7*, S0019) Fraser.
Why Americans Don't Vote: Turnout Decline in the United States, 1960-1984. Ruy A. Teixeira. LC 86-33585. (Contributions in Political Science Ser.: No. 172). 149p. (C). 1987. text ed. 45.00 (*0-313-25532-6*, Greenwood Pr) Greenwood.
Why Americans Hate Politics: The Death of the Democratic Process. rev. ed. E. J. Dionne, Jr. 432p. 1992. pap. 12.00 (*0-671-77877-3*, Touchstone Bks) S&S Trade.
Why Americans Read or Spell Poorly: Problem, Cause, & Correction of 80 Years of Educational Decline. Edward L. Tottle. LC 92-70457. Orig. Title: Spelling Scores for Five Thousand Five Hundred Six Words: Grade & Age Scores for Common English Words. (Illus.). 256p. (Orig.). (J). (gr. 8). 1993. pap. text ed. 20.00 (*0-937117-08-0*) Educ Materials.
Why an Electron? Gail B. Marsella. 100p. (Orig.). (C). Date not set. pap. text ed. 10.00 (*0-9646155-8-4*) Branch Text Pr.
Why & How: Some Problems & Methods in Historical Biology. George G. Simpson. LC 79-42774. (Illus.). 263p. 1980. pap. text ed. 50.00 (*0-08-025784-4*, Pergamon Pr) Elsevier.
Why & How of Burial & Death of a Muslim. Abdullah & Al I. Obaba. (Illus.). 24p. (Orig.). (YA). 1985. pap. 1.50 (*0-916157-03-2*) African Islam Miss Pubns.
Why & How of Home Horticulture. 2nd ed. Darrel R. Bienz. LC 92-46400. (C). 1995. pap. text ed. write for info. (*0-7167-2286-0*) W H Freeman.
Why & How of Home Horticulture. 2nd ed. Darrel R. Bienz. LC 92-46400. (C). 1995. text ed. write for info. (*0-7167-2353-0*) W H Freeman.
Why & How Should We Assess Students? The Competing Measures of Student Performance. James E. McLean & Robert E. Lockwood. LC 95-44371. (Roadmaps to Success Ser.). 1996. pap. 15.00 (*0-8039-6074-3*) Sage.
Why & How to Become a Successful Student. James L. Warner. 64p. 1991. 7.95 (*0-8403-6942-5*) Kendall-Hunt.
Why & How Was I Born, Vol. 3. Lou Austin. (J). (gr. 1-6). 1963. 4.95 (*0-934538-28-X*) Partnership Foundation.
***Why & How We Work in a Political Party.** Philip J. Dodge et al. (Illus.). 130p. (Orig.). 1997. 12.00 (*0-9657747-0-8*) P & N Dodge.
Why Angels? Are They Real...Really Needed? Bernard Cooke. LC 95-62068. 96p. (Orig.). 1996. pap. 9.95 (*0-89622-686-7*) Twenty-Third.
***Why Angels Have Wings: A Pneumatological Assay of Beings from the Spirit Realms.** G. James Olsen. 96p. (Orig.). 1997. pap. 7.50 (*1-57353-114-6*, Eschaton Bks) Eschaton Prods.
Why Animals Don't Get Heart Attacks. Matthias Rath. (Illus.). (Orig.). (YA). 1994. pap. 7.95 (*0-9638768-1-3*) Health Now.
Why Antisemitism? A Translation of "The Remnant of Israel" by Rabbi Naphtali Zvi Yehuda Berlin, the Neziv. Tr. by Howard S. Joseph. LC 95-15046. 152p. 1996. 20.00 (*1-56821-521-5*) Aronson.
Why Architects Draw. Edward Robbins. (Illus.). 323p. 1994. 45.00 (*0-262-18157-6*) MIT Pr.
***Why Architects Draw.** Edward Robbins. (Illus.). 328p. 1997. reprint ed. pap. 25.00 (*0-262-68098-X*) MIT Pr.
***Why Are All the Black Kids Sitting Together in the Cafeteria? And Other Conversations about Race.** Beverly D. Tatum. 224p. 1997. 22.00 (*0-465-09127-X*) Basic.
Why Are Animals Endangered? Isaac Asimov. LC 92-5346. (Ask Isaac Asimov Ser.). (Illus.). 24p. (J). (gr. 1-8). 1993. lib. bdg. 17.27 (*0-8368-0798-7*) Gareth Stevens Inc.
Why Are Boys So Weird? Candice F. Ransom. LC 93-6222. (Tales from the Third Grade Ser.). (Illus.). 128p. (J). (gr. 2-6). 1994. pap. text ed. 3.95 (*0-8167-2991-3*); lib. bdg. 11.89 (*0-8167-2990-5*) Troll Communs.
Why Are People Beating up on Higher Education. Chester E. Finn, Jr. (Excellence in Education Ser.). 16p. (Orig.). 1992. pap. text ed. 3.00 (*1-878802-07-0*) J M Ashbrook Ctr Pub Affairs.
Why Are People Different? Sue Meredith. (Starting Point Science Ser.). (Illus.). 24p. (J). (gr. 1-5). 1993. pap. 3.95 (*0-7460-1014-1*, Usborne); lib. bdg. 12.95 (*0-88110-642-9*, Usborne) EDC.
***Why Are Pineapples Prickly?** LC 96-45927. (Why Bks.). (Illus.). 24p. (J). 1997. 9.95 (*0-7894-1530-5*) DK Pub Inc.
***Why Are Pineapples Prickly?** Christopher Mainard. (Why Bks.). (J). (ps up). 1997. 9.95 (*0-614-28704-9*) DK Pub Inc.
Why Are Some Beaches Oily? Isaac Asimov. LC 92-5345. (Ask Isaac Asimov Ser.). (YA). 1992. lib. bdg. 17.27 (*0-8368-0796-0*) Gareth Stevens Inc.
Why Are Some People Healthy & Others Not? The Determinants of Health of Populations. Ed. by Robert G. Evans et al. (Social Institutions & Social Change Ser.). 399p. 1994. pap. text ed. 26.95 (*0-202-30490-6*); lib. bdg. 56.95 (*0-202-30489-2*) Aldine de Gruyter.
***Why Are Still Here.** Roberto Hernandez. Ed. by Janett Camps. 112p. Date not set. pap. text ed. 12.95 (*0-9641506-6-2*) Edit Interamerica.
Why Are the Casseroles Always Tuna? A Loving Look at the Lighter Side of Grief. 2nd ed. Darcie D. Sims. LC 90-82575. (Illus.). 96p. (Orig.). 1992. reprint ed. pap. 9.95 (*0-9618995-1-4*) Big A & Co.
Why Are the Dandelions Weeds? Stories for Growing Faith. Kathleen O. Chesto. 160p. (Orig.). 1995. pap. 8.95 (*1-55612-610-7*, LL1610) Sheed & Ward MO.
Why are the Heroes Always White? Sheryl McCarthy. 160p. 1995. pap. 8.95 (*0-8362-7049-5*) Andrews & McMeel.
Why Are the Rain Forests Vanishing? Isaac Asimov. LC 92-5348. (Ask Isaac Asimov Ser.). (YA). 1992. lib. bdg. 17.27 (*0-8368-0797-9*) Gareth Stevens Inc.
Why Are the Whales Vanishing? Isaac Asimov. (Ask Isaac Asimov Ser.). (Illus.). 24p. (J). (gr. 2-3). 1992. lib. bdg. 17.27 (*0-8368-0745-6*) Gareth Stevens Inc.

An Asterisk (*) at the beginning of an entry indicates that the title is appearing in BIP for the first time.

Why Are There No Tall Grandma's: A Guide to Assist You in Researching Your Family History. Scott B. Chase. LC 90-4741. (Illus.). 1990. pap. 12.95 (1-55787-072-1, SR01001) Hrt of the Lakes.

***Why Are There Waves?** LC 96-45928. (Why Bks.). (Illus.). 24p. (J). 1997. 9.95 (0-7894-1531-3) DK Pub Inc.

***Why Are There Waves?** Christopher Mainard. (Why Bks.). (J). (ps up). 1997. 9.95 (0-614-28705-7) DK Pub Inc.

Why Are They Here - Spaceships from Other Worlds: UFO Experiences with Friend & Associate George Adamskin 1963-1965. 3rd ed. Fred Steckling. (Illus.). 148p. 1975. reprint ed. pap. 16.95 (0-614-12951-6) GAF Intl.

Why are Things the Way They Are? G. Venkataraman. (Vignettes in Physics Ser.). 1993. pap. 5.95 (0-86311-312-5, Pub. by Universities Pr II) Apt Bks.

Why Are Wagons Red? First Questions & Answers about Transportation. Time-Life Books Editors. Ed. by Sara M. Lesk. (Library of First Questions & Answers). (Illus.). 48p. (J). (gr. k-2). 1994. 14.95 (0-7835-0878-6) Time-Life.

Why Are Wagons Red? First Questions & Answers about Transportation. Time-Life Books Editors. Ed. by Sara M. Lesk. (Library of First Questions & Answers). (Illus.). 48p. (J). (ps). 1994. lib. bdg. write for info. (0-7835-0879-4) Time-Life.

Why Are We Getting a Divorce? Peter Mayle. LC 87-12105. (Illus.). 32p. (J). (gr. k-3). 1988. 16.00 (0-517-56527-7, Harmony) Crown Pub Group.

Why Are We Here? The Scientific Answer to This Age-Old Question. Dennis Marcellino. LC 96-9440. 304p. 1997. pap. 14.50 (0-945272-10-3) Lighthouse.

Why Are We in Vietnam? A Novel. Norman Mailer. LC 81-7261. 216p. 1982. pap. 5.95 (0-03-059977-6, Owl); pap. 13.00 (0-8050-1880-8, Owl) H Holt & Co.

Why Are You Calling Me LD? Manual. Holly G. Parzych. (Orig.). 1989. student ed. write for info. (0-944791-90-5, CS102) Peekan Pubns.

***Why Are You So Mad?** Larry Hampton. LC 96-79218. 196p. 1997. pap. 14.95 (1-885221-60-6) BookPartners.

Why Are You Worrying? Joseph W. Ciarrocchi. LC 95-3039. (Illumination Bks.). (Illus.). 80p. (Orig.). 1995. pap. 4.95 (0-8091-3561-2) Paulist Pr.

Why Are Your Fingers Cold? Larry McKaughan. LC 92-16549. (Illus.). 32p. (Orig.). (J). (ps-1). 1992. 14.99 (0-8361-3604-7) Herald Pr.

Why Are Zebras Black & White? Questions about Color. LC 96-13956. (Why Bks.). (Illus.). 24p. (J). 1996. 9.95 (0-7894-1122-9) DK Pub Inc.

***Why Are Zebras Black & White? Questions Children Ask about Colour.** (Why Bks.). (Illus.). (J). 10.99 (0-590-24946-0) Scholastic Inc.

***Why Aren't Black Holes Black? The Unanswered Questions at the Frontiers of Space.** Robert M. Hazen & Maxine Singer. LC 96-29856. 304p. (Orig.). 1997. pap. 12.95 (0-385-48014-8, Anchor NY) Doubleday.

Why Aren't Economists As Important As Garbagemen? Essays on the State of Economics. David C. Colander. LC 90-8841. 200p. (gr. 13). 1991. text ed. 52.95 (0-87332-776-4); pap. text ed. 23.95 (0-87332-777-2) M E Sharpe.

Why Aren't More Women Running the Show? How Women Can Stop Being Their Own Worst Enemies, Unblock Their Paths to Power Positions & Break Through Glass Ceilings. Eve Cappello. 84p. (Orig.). 1994. pap. text ed. 12.95 (0-9639037-0-5) ACT Intl.

Why Aren't They Screaming? Joan Smith. 224p. 1990. mass mkt. 4.99 (0-449-21777-9, Crest) Fawcett.

Why Aren't You More Like Me? Everett T. Robinson. 1994. pap. 12.95 (0-87425-970-3) HRD Press.

Why Art? Florence M. Daniels. LC 77-28084. (Illus.). 236p. 1978. 31.95 (0-88229-173-4) Nelson-Hall.

***Why Art?** Lazzari. (C). Date not set. pap. text ed. 29.00 (0-15-505796-0) HB Coll Pubs.

Why Art Education? write for info. (0-937652-29-6) Natl Art Ed.

Why Arthritis? Searching for the Cause & Cure of Rheumatoid Disease. Harold W. Clark. Ed. by Karen L. Jacob. LC 95-80337. (Illus.). 272p. (Orig.). 1997. pap. 18.95 (0-936417-51-X) Axelrod Pub.

Why Artists' Books? Ed. by Anne Anninger. (Illus.). 32p. (Orig.). 1993. pap. 15.00 (0-914630-12-1) Houghton Lib.

Why Astrology Endures. Theodore Rosak. (Broadside Editions Ser.). 20p. (C). 1986. pap. 3.95 (0-9609850-9-3) Rob Briggs.

Why Authors Go Wrong, & Other Explanations. Grant M. Overton. LC 68-22936. (Essay Index Reprint Ser.). 1977. 19.95 (0-8369-0757-4) Ayer.

***Why Bad Things Happen to Good People.** Brent L. Top. 1997. pap. 9.95 (1-57008-321-5) Bookcraft Inc.

Why Bank Regulation Failed: Designing a Bank Regulatory Strategy for the 1990's. Helen A. Garten. LC 91-30. 192p. 1991. text ed. 55.00 (0-89930-580-6, GBR, Quorum Bks) Greenwood.

Why Baptism? see IVP Booklets

Why Be a Priest? Bartholomew J. O'Brien. Ed. by Riehle Foundation Staff. 58p. (Orig.). 1993. pap. 0.50 (0-685-72757-2) Riehle Found.

Why Be a Vegetarian? Tej Sheth & Tarang Sheth. LC 94-238710. (Illus.). 160p. (Orig.). 1995. pap. 12.95 (0-87573-035-3) Jain Pub Co.

Why Be Catholic? William J. O'Malley. LC 93-17605. 169p. (Orig.). 1993. pap. 11.95 (0-8245-1362-2) Crossroad NY.

Why Be Catholic? Understanding Our Experience & Tradition. Richard Rohr & Joseph Martos. 146p. (Orig.). 1989. pap. 6.95 (0-86716-101-9) St Anthony Mess Pr.

Why Be Different? A Look Into Judaism. Eric S. Gurvis. 1995. teacher ed., pap. 14.95 (0-87441-507-1) Behrman.

Why Be Different: A Look into Judaism. Janice Prager & Arlene LePoff. 118p. (J). (gr. 6-8). 1986. pap. text ed. 8.50 (0-87441-427-X) Behrman.

Why Be Jewish? David J. Wolpe. LC 94-48199. 104p. 1995. pap. 9.95 (0-8050-3927-9) H Holt & Co.

Why Be Jewish? Intermarriage, Assimilation, & Alienation. Meir Kahane. LC 77-8774. 264p. 1982. pap. 7.95 (0-8128-6129-9, Scrbrough Hse) Madison Bks UPA.

Why Be Moral? Kai Nielsen. 300p. 1989. pap. 20.95 (0-87975-519-9) Prometheus Bks.

Why Be Moral? 2nd ed. Archie J. Bahm. LC 92-90090. 447p. 1992. pap. 20.00 (0-911714-19-7, World Bks) Bahm.

Why Be Moral? The Egoist Challenge. John F. Van Ingen. LC 93-36873. (American University Studies, V, Philosophy: Vol. 156). 200p. (C). 1994. text ed. 29.95 (0-8204-2357-2) P Lang Pubng.

Why Be Quantitative about Radiation Risk Estimates? Edward E. Pochin. LC 78-61402. (Taylor Lectures: No. 2). 1978. 20.00 (0-913392-42-1) NCRP Pubns.

***Why Beauty Matters.** Karen Lee-Thorp & Cynthia Hicks. 1997. pap. 14.00 (0-89109-979-4) NavPress.

Why? Because You Are Annointed. T. D. Jakes. 1995. pap. 8.99 (1-56229-434-2) Pneuma Life Pub.

Why Believe? Reason & Mystery As Pointers to God. C. Stephen Evans. 164p. (Orig.). 1996. pap. 13.00 (0-8028-0127-7) Eerdmans.

Why Believe? God Exists! Rethinking the Case for God & Christianity. Terry L. Miethe & Gary Habermas. 400p. pap. 13.99 (0-89900-699-X) College Pr Pub.

Why Benny Barks: A Step One Book. David Milgrin. LC 93-47102. (Step into Reading Bks.: Step 1). (Illus.). 32p. (Orig.). (J). (ps-1). 1994. pap. 3.99 (0-679-86157-2); lib. bdg. 11.99 (0-679-96157-7) Random Bks Yng Read.

Why Big Fierce Animals Are Rare: An Ecologist's Perspective. Paul Colinvaux. LC 77-71977. 264p. 1978. pap. text ed. 12.95 (0-691-02364-6) Princeton U Pr.

Why Black People Tend to Shout: Cold Facts & Wry Views from a Black Man's World. Ralph Wiley. 1991. 15.95 (1-55972-073-5, Birch Ln Pr) Carol Pub Group.

Why Black People Tend to Shout: Cold Facts & Wry Views from a Black Man's World. Ralph Wiley. 208p. 1992. pap. 10.95 (0-14-016853-2, Penguin Bks) Viking Penguin.

Why Blacks, Women, & Jews Are Not Mentioned in the Constitution, & Other Unorthodox Views. Robert A. Goldwin. 194p. (C). 1990. 24.75 (0-8447-3693-7) Am Enterprise.

Why Blame the Organization? A Pragmatic Analysis of Collective Moral Responsibility. Raymond S. Pfeiffer. 178p. (C). 1995. pap. text ed. 22.95 (0-8226-3045-1); lib. bdg. 48.50 (0-8226-3044-3) Littlefield.

***Why Bob Marley & Peter Tosh Were Killed: Why Babylon Targets Our Reggae Phophets.** Ricardo A. Scott. (Ricardo Reggae Archives). (Illus.). 75p. (Orig.). 1996. pap. write for info. (1-883427-83-5) Crnerstone GA.

Why? Boddah You? A Collection of Cartoons & Illustrations. James Mercado. (Illus.). 120p. (Orig.). 1996. pap. 9.95 (0-913611-07-7) W E C Plant.

Why Book of Golf: Two Hundred Practical Tips & Fascinating Facts about Golf Traditions, Rules & Etiquette! William C. Kroen. (Illus.). 152p. 1992. pap. 8.95 (0-8431-2982-4) Putnam Pub Group.

Why Bosnia? Writings on the Balkan War. Ed. by Rabia Ali & Lawrence Lifschultz. 416p. (Orig.). 1993. 35.00 (0-9630587-8-9); pap. 19.95 (0-9630587-9-7) Pamphleteers.

***Why Bother with Jesus.** Green. 4.95 (0-340-56312-5, Pub. by H & S UK) Trafalgar.

Why Boys & Girls Are Different. Carol Greene. (Learning about Sex Ser.: Bk. 1). 32p. (J). (ps up). 1995. 7.99 (0-570-03552-X, 14-2101) Concordia.

Why Bright Kids Get Poor Grades: And What You Can Do about It. Sylvia B. Rimm. 1996. pap. 15.00 (0-517-88687-1) Crown Bks Yng Read.

Why Bright Kids Get Poor Grades & What You Can Do about It. Sylvia B. Rimm. 1995. 23.00 (0-517-70062-X, Crown) Crown Pub Group.

Why Buffalo Roam. L. Michael Kershen. (Illus.). 32p. (J). (gr. k-4). 1992. lib. bdg. 15.00 (0-88045-043-6) Stemmer Hse.

Why Buildings Fall Down. Matthys Levy. 1994. pap. 13.00 (0-393-31152-X) Norton.

Why Buildings Stand Up: The Strength of Architecture. Mario G. Salvadori. 1990. pap. 12.95 (0-393-30676-3) Norton.

Why Bush Lost the Election: Ten Lessons for the Clinton Administration. Aldona Robbins & Gary Robbins. (Illus.). 24p. 1993. pap. 5.00 (1-56808-007-7, BG 120) Natl Ctr Pol.

Why Call Them Back from Heaven? Clifford D. Simak. 192p. 1980. mass mkt. 3.50 (0-380-50575-4) Avon.

Why Calories Don't Count. rev. ed. Paul A. Stitt. (Illus.). (Orig.). 1983. pap. text ed. 7.00 (0-939956-05-5) Natural Pr.

Why Canadians Get the Politicians & Governments They Don't Want. Heward Grafftey. 216p. 1991. 22.95 (0-7737-2519-9) Genl Dist Srvs.

Why Canadians Get the Politicians & Governments They Don't Want. Heward Grafftey. 208p. 1992. pap. 14.95 (0-7737-5542-X) Genl Dist Srvs.

Why Can't a Man Be More Like a Cat: Notes, Observations, & Ruminations Providing Paws for Thought. Linda Konner & Antonia Van Der Meer. LC 95-41922. (Illus.). 144p. 1996. pap. 7.95 (0-440-50582-8) Dell.

Why Can't a Man Be More Like a Woman? Sandra Beckwith. 1995. pap. 10.00 (0-8217-4926-9, Pinncle Kensgtn) Kensgtn Pub Corp.

Why Can't a Woman be More Like a Man: A Woman's Guide to Revitalizing Her Natural Sex Drive. Michael P. Bonaventura. 1996. pap. 16.95 (1-56530-184-6) Summit TX.

Why Can't Anyone Hear Me? A Guide for Surviving Adolescence. 2nd rev. ed. Monte Elchoness. LC 86-737. (Illus.). 200p. (YA). (gr. 5-12). 1989. pap. 10.95 (0-936781-06-8) Monroe Pr.

Why Can't Grownups Believe in Angels? Marsha Sinetar. LC 93-12906. (Illus.). 48p. (J). 1993. text ed. 14.95 (0-89243-551-8, Triumph Books) Liguori Pubns.

Why Can't I Be Me? Understanding How Personality Type Affects Emotional Healing, Relationships, & Spiritual Growth. Mark A. Pearson. LC 92-20526. 224p. (Orig.). 1992. pap. 9.99 (0-8007-9195-9) Chosen Bks.

Why Can't I Be the Leader? Bailey Griscom & Pam Griscom. (Illus.). 24p. (Orig.). (J). (ps up). 1992. pap. 4.95 (0-9633705-2-9) Share Pub CA.

***Why Can't I Breathe Underwater? And Other Questions about the Respiratory System.** Sharon Cromwell. LC 97-22212. (Bodywise Ser.). (Illus.). (J). 1997. lib. bdg. write for info. (1-57572-158-9) Rigby Interact Libr.

Why Can't I Eat That? Helping Kids Obey Medical Diets. John F. Taylor & R. Sharon Latta. Ed. by Diane Parker. LC 92-50875. 250p. 1993. pap. 11.95 (0-88247-981-4, 981) R & E Pubs.

Why Can't I Fly? Rita G. Gelman. (J). (ps-3). 1986. pap. 2.95 (0-590-40506-3) Scholastic Inc.

***Why Can't I Fly? And Other Questions about the Motor System.** Sharon Cromwell. LC 97-22227. (Bodywise Ser.). (Illus.). (J). 1997. lib. bdg. write for info. (1-57572-159-7) Rigby Interact Libr.

Why Can't I Forgive You. Joan Mueller. 1996. pap. text ed. 9.95 (0-88347-331-3, 7331) Res Christian Liv.

Why Can't I Live Forever? And Other Not Such Dumb Questions about Life. Vicki Cobb. (J). 1997. pap. 13.99 (0-525-67505-1) NAL-Dutton.

***Why Can't I Live Forever! & Other Not Such Dumb Questions about Life.** Vicki Cobb. (Illus.). (J). (gr. 2-5). 1997. 13.99 (0-614-28850-9, Lodestar Bks) Dutton Child Bks.

Why Can't I See the Wind? First Questions & Answers about Weather. Time-Life Books Editors. Ed. by Pat Daniels. (Library of First Questions & Answers). (Illus.). 48p. (J). (gr. k-2). 1994. 14.95 (0-7835-0890-5) Time-Life.

Why Can't I See the Wind? First Questions & Answers about Weather. Time-Life Books Editors. Ed. by Pat Daniels. (Library of First Questions & Answers). (Illus.). 48p. (J). (ps). 1994. lib. bdg. write for info. (0-7835-0891-3) Time-Life.

Why Can't My Child Behave? Why Can't She Cope? Why Can't He Learn? Jane H. Hersey. 500p. (Orig.). 1996. pap. 22.00 (0-9651105-0-8, PTP-96-01) Pear Tree VA.

Why Can't My Life Be a Summer Vacation? Kevin W. Johnson. 112p. (J). (gr. 6-9). 1994. pap. 6.99 (1-55661-284-2) Bethany Hse.

Why Can't Sharon Kowalski Come Home? Karen Thompson & Julie Andrzejewski. LC 88-18502. 280p. (Orig.). 1988. 20.95 (0-933216-56-4); pap. 10.95 (0-933216-46-7) Spinsters Ink.

Why Can't They Be Like Us? Facts & Fallacies About Ethnic Differences & Group Conflicts in America. Andrew M. Greeley. LC 73-81091. (Institute of Human Relations Press Paperback Ser.). x, 76p. (Orig.). 1980. pap. 1.50 (0-87495-009-0) Am Jewish Comm.

Why Can't We? DPK Publications. 2nd ed. Dorothy P. Koger. Ed. by Rebecca E. Oduba. (Illus.). 88p. 1992. pap. 10.00 (1-882821-01-7) DPK Pubns.

Why Can't We Say Goodbye? Nat Roman. 516p. 1981. pap. 21.95 (0-686-32931-7) Roman Enter.

Why Can't We Talk? Prayers for Parents & Teenagers. Mobby Larson. LC 90-70621. 72p. (Orig.). 1990. pap. 5.95 (0-89622-475-9) Twenty-Third.

Why Can't You Tickle Yourself? And Other Bodily Curiosities. Ingrid Johnson. LC 93-10192. 128p. 1993. pap. 8.99 (0-446-39395-9) Warner Bks.

Why Catholics Can't Sing: The Culture of Catholicism & the Triumph of Bad Taste. Thomas Day. 248p. 1992. pap. 12.95 (0-8245-1153-0) Crossroad NY.

Why Catholics Pray to the Blessed Virgin Mary: An Incident in Catholic Life. Canon Moyes. (Compact Study Ser.). 15p. (Orig.). 1993. pap. 1.95 (0-935952-94-2) Angelus Pr.

Why Cats Chase Mice: A Story of the 12 Zodiac Signs. Mina H. Eimon. (Japanese Fairy Tale Ser.). (Illus.). 32p. (J). (gr. k-6). 1993. 12.95 (0-89346-533-X) Heian Intl.

Why Cats Meow. Abbie Miller. 23p. (J). (gr. 4-7). 1996. pap. text ed. 1.95 (1-56763-166-5) Ozark Pub.

Why Cats Paint. Heather Busch & Burton Silver. 96p. 1994. 18.95 (0-89815-623-8); pap. 16.95 (0-89815-612-2) Ten Speed Pr.

Why Cats Paint Address Book. Burton Silver & Heather Busch. (Illus.). 112p. 1996. spiral bd. 14.95 (0-89815-858-3) Ten Speed Pr.

***Why Change? Making Changes to Get Ahead.** Howard E. Ovist. LC 97-91527. 146p. (Orig.). 1997. pap. 7.50 (1-57502-431-4, PO1316) Morris Pubng.

Why Change Doesn't Work: Why Initiatives Go Wrong & How to Try Again & Succeed. Harvey Robbins & Michael Finley. 240p. 1996. 24.95 (1-56079-675-8, Petersons Pacesetter) Petersons.

Why Chemistry? Thomas Gilbert & Rein Kirss. 104p. (C). 1996. spiral bd. 23.04 (0-8403-8192-1) Kendall-Hunt.

Why Child Care Matters: Preparing Young Children for a More Productive America. Committee for Economic Development Staff. Ed. by Sandra K. Hamburg. 144p. 1993. pap. 14.50 (0-87186-096-1) Comm Econ Dev.

Why Children? Ed. by Stephanie Dowrick & Sibyl Grundberg. LC 80-84688. 272p. 1981. pap. 6.95 (0-15-696362-0, Harvest Bks) HarBrace.

Why Children End up Muslims. Yuhaayaa L. Kaahena. Ed. by Latifa Ismail. 56p. 1993. pap. 5.00 (1-883781-03-5) Yuhaaya.

Why Children Misbehave: And What to Do About It. Christine Adams & Ernest Fruge. LC 96-67939. (Illus.). 176p. (Orig.). 1996. pap. 14.95 (1-57224-051-2) New Harbinger.

Why Children Reject School: Views from Seven Countries. Colette Chiland & J. Gerald Yound. (International Association for Child & Adolescent Psychiatry & Allied Prefessions Yearbook Ser.: Vol. 10). 256p. (C). 1990. text ed. 37.50 (0-300-04828-9) Yale U Pr.

Why Choose the Episcopal Church? 2nd rev. ed. John M. Krumm. 184p. 1996. pap. 4.95 (0-88028-169-3, 531) Forward Movement.

Why Christ Can't Be Pictured: God Is Not Like Art. Virgil Dunbar. 244p. 1994. pap. 14.95 (1-886096-00-7) Priceless Prnting.

***Why Christian Kids Leave the Faith.** Tom Bisset. LC 97-20794. 1997. write for info. (1-57293-026-8) Discovery Hse Pubs.

***Why Christian Men Don't Date.** Otto Haugland. 192p. 1996. 16.99 (1-883893-70-4) WinePress Pub.

Why Christianity? Michael Azkoul. LC 93-85955. 54p. (Orig.). 1994. pap. 2.50 (0-913026-41-7) St Nectarios.

Why Christians Are Sick. Gordon Lindsay. 1960. per. 3.95 (0-89985-029-4) Christ for the Nations.

Why Christians Cannot Be Demon Possessed. Everitt M. Fjordbak. 53p. 1986. pap. text ed. 1.25 (1-882449-11-8) Messenger Pub.

Why Christians Can't Trust Psychology. Ed Bulkley. LC 93-31617. 1994. pap. 10.99 (1-56507-026-7) Harvest Hse.

Why Christians Get Sick. George H. Malkmus. 154p. (Orig.). 1995. pap. 7.99 (1-56043-849-5) Destiny Image.

Why Christmas Trees Aren't Perfect. Richard H. Schneider. LC 87-20571. (Illus.). 1988. 13.95 (0-687-45363-1) Abingdon.

Why Civilizations Self-Destruct. Elmer Pendell. LC 76-40801. 196p. 1977. 13.00 (0-914576-07-0) Howard Allen.

***Why Climb the Corporate Ladder When You Can Take the Elevator?** 144p. 1997. 17.95 (0-9656410-1-5) JMC Industries.

Why Climb the Corporate Ladder When You Can Take the Elevator? 500 Secrets for Success in Business. John M. Capozzi. 1994. 15.00 (0-679-43249-3, Villard Bks) Random.

Why Climb the Corporate Ladder When You Can Take the Elevator? 500 Secrets for Success in Business. John M. Capozzi. 144p. 1995. pap. 8.95 (0-14-024973-7, Penguin Bks) Viking Penguin.

Why Colored Americans Need an Abraham Lincoln in 1992. Edward L. Jones & Frederick Douglass. 24p. (Orig.). 1992. pap. text ed. 8.00 (1-881533-01-8) Ed-Lynne Jones.

Why Computers Are Computers: A Personal Account of How an Early Computer Was Like Today's PC. David Rutland. LC 94-62225. 208p. 1995. 24.95 (1-885391-05-6) Wren Pubs.

Why Conservative Churches Are Growing: A Study in Sociology of Religion. Dean M. Kelley. LC 86-5347. (Reprints of Scholarly Excellence Ser.: No. II). 184p. (Orig.). (C). 1995. reprint ed. pap. text ed. 19.95 (0-86554-224-4, MUP-P029) Mercer Univ Pr.

Why Cow Protection? Panduranga R. Malyala. 1.99 (0-938924-01-X) Sri Shirdi Sai.

Why Cowboys Need a Brand. Laurie L. Knowlton. (Illus.). 32p. (J). (gr. k-5). 1996. 14.95 (1-56554-228-2) Pelican.

Why Cowboys Sleep with Their Boots On. Laurie L. Knowlton. LC 94-24803. (Illus.). 32p. (J). (gr. 4-8). 1995. 14.95 (1-56554-094-8) Pelican.

Why Coyote Sings to the Moon 001673. Ellen Jackson. (Illus.). 32p. (J). 1995. pap. 6.95 (1-56189-398-6) Amer Educ Pub.

Why Cucumbers Are Better Than Men. Cucumber Group Staff. LC 82-24194. (Illus.). 32p. 1983. pap. 3.95 (0-87131-483-5) M Evans.

Why Customers Don't Do What You Want Them to Do & What to Do about It. Ferdinand F. Fournies. LC 93-22717. 1993. pap. text ed. 12.95 (0-07-021701-7) McGraw.

Why, Dainty Dinosaur? (Illus.). (J). (ps-2). 1991. pap. 5.10 (0-8136-5725-3); lib. bdg. 7.95 (0-8136-5225-1) Modern Curr.

Why Damien Oh Why. Bridget Briar. 152p. 1984. 39.00 (0-7212-0662-X, Pub. by Regency Press UK) St Mut.

***Why David Was a Threat to Goliath.** Roland A. Coulson. LC 96-90991. (Orig.). 1997. pap. 14.95 (0-533-12240-6) Vantage.

Why Day Care? Research Highlights in Social Work. Gordon Horobin. 1987. text ed. 29.95 (0-312-00241-6) St Martin.

Why Daycare? Research Highlights in Social Work. Ed. by Gordon Horobin. 192p. 1987. 25.00 (0-685-17607-X) St Martin.

Why Delinquency? Maurice Cusson. LC 84-167472. 203p. (Orig.). reprint ed. pap. 57.90 (0-8357-3636-9, 2036364) Bks Demand.

Why Design? Jens Bernsen. (C). 1989. pap. text ed. 35.00 (0-85072-227-6) St Mut.

Why Design? Projects from the National Building Museum. Anna Slafer & Kevin Cahill. LC 95-12376. (Illus.). 208p. (Orig.). (YA). (gr. 7 up). 1995. pap. 19.95 (1-55652-249-5) Chicago Review.

***Why Did Blacks Demonstrate for Freedom on Grounds Honoring Abraham Lincoln?** Herbert Davis. 54p. 1998. pap. 6.00 (0-8059-4162-2) Dorrance.

Why Did Christ Die? F. E. Marsh. LC 85-18093. Orig. Title: The Greatest Theme in the World. 204p. 1985. reprint ed. pap. 8.99 (0-8254-3249-9) Kregel.

W

Why Did Daddy Die? Helping a Child Cope with the Loss of a Parent. Linda Alderman. 1991. pap. 8.95 (*0-671-74670-7*) PB.

***Why Did Elijah Hide?** Pauline Youd. LC 96-26816. (Illus.). (J). 1996. pap. 2.95 (*0-8198-8287-9*) Pauline Bks.

Why Did God Make Bugs & Other Icky Things: Questions Kids Ask. Kel Groseclose. LC 93-3670. 96p. (Orig.). 1992. pap. 7.00 (*0-687-46583-4*) Dimen for Liv.

Why Did God Make Zits & Other Disgusting Stuff? Questions Preteens Ask. Kel Groseclose. LC 92-47417. 96p. (Orig.). 1993. pap. 7.00 (*0-687-46586-9*) Dimen for Liv.

***Why Did God Say That He Would Dwell in the Thick Darkness?** Ralph Sexton, Sr. (Illus.). 52p. (Orig.). 1997. pap. 9.95 (*1-57090-056-6*) Alexander Bks.

Why Did Grandma Die? Trudy Madler. LC 79-23892. (Life & Living from a Child's Point of View Ser.). (Illus.). 32p. (J). (gr. k-6). 1980. lib. bdg. 21.40 (*0-8172-1354-6*) Raintree Steck-V.

Why Did Grandma Die? Trudy Madler. (Life & Living from a Child's Point of View Ser.). (J). (ps-3). 1993. pap. 4.95 (*0-8114-7156-X*) Raintree Steck-V.

Why Did Grandma Have to Die? Kristen D. Randle. (J). 1987. pap. 5.95 (*0-88494-621-5*) Bookcraft Inc.

***Why Did Grandpa Die? Questions Children Ask about Families.** Christopher Maynard. LC 97-14463. (Why Bks.). (J). 1997. write for info. (*0-7894-2055-4*) DK Pub Inc.

***Why Did I Do It?** (Young Dragon Readers 3 Ser.). (J). 1995. pap. text ed. write for info. (*962-359-539-5*) Addison-Wesley.

Why Did I Do It Again? Understanding My Cycle of Problem Behaviors. L. Bays & R. Freeman-Longo. Ed. by Ewan Bear & Fay H. Knopp. (Illus.). 80p. (Orig.). 1989. wbk. ed., pap. 12.00 (*1-884444-25-3*) Safer Soc.

Why Did I Marry You? Warwick W. Hartin. 121p. (Orig.). 1994. pap. 11.95 (*0-85572-183-9*, Pub. by Hill Content Pubng AT) Seven Hills Bk.

Why Did I Say I Do? Stephen Schwambach. LC 92-12395. 1992. pap. 12.95 (*0-89081-987-4*) Hundredth Century.

Why Did It Happen? Helping Children Cope in a Violent World. Janice I. Cohn. LC 93-1573. (Illus.). 32p. (J). (ps up). 1994. 15.00 (*0-688-12312-0*, Morrow Junior); lib. bdg. 14.93 (*0-688-12313-9*, Morrow Junior) Morrow.

Why Did It Happen on a School Day? My Family's Experience with Brain Injury. Maryland Head Injury Foundation Staff. (Illus.). 40p. (Orig.). (J). (gr. k-6). 1995. pap. 10.00 (*0-927093-02-2*) Brain Injury Assoc.

Why Did Jesus Fast? Herman Arndt. 87p. (Orig.). 1962. reprint ed. spiral bd. 6.50 (*0-7873-0041-1*) Hlth Research.

Why Did Jesus Walk? (Walk with Jesus Ser.). 52p. 1994. pap. 15.00 (*1-57277-203-4*) Script Rsch.

Why Did My Baby Die: The Phenomenon of Sudden Infant Death Syndrome & How to Cope with It. Abraham Bergman & Judith Choate. LC 73-92794. 1975. 20.00 (*0-89388-146-5*) Okpaku Communications.

Why Did Nehemiah Work So Hard? Pauline Youd. LC 96-20215. (I Wonder...Bks.). (Illus.). 16p. (Orig.). (J). (gr. 2-4). 1996. pap. 2.95 (*0-8198-8279-8*) Pauline Bks.

Why Did Sarah Laugh? Pauline Youd. LC 96-20219. (I Wonder...Bks.). (Illus.). 16p. (Orig.). (J). (gr. 2-4). 1996. pap. 2.95 (*0-8198-8275-5*) Pauline Bks.

Why Did the Chicken Cross the Road? And Other Riddles, Old & New. Joanna Cole & Stephanie Calmenson. LC 94-2582. (Illus.). 64p. (J). (gr. 2 up). 1994. 16.00 (*0-688-12202-7*, Morrow Junior); lib. bdg. 14.93 (*0-688-12203-5*, Morrow Junior) Morrow.

Why Did the Chicken Cross the Road? And Other Riddles Old & New. Joanna Cole & Stephanie Calmenson. Ed. by Amy Cohn. LC 94-2582. (Illus.). 64p. (J). (gr. 2 up). 1994. reprint ed. pap. 6.95 (*0-688-12204-3*) Morrow.

Why Did the Dinosaurs Disappear? The Great Dinosaur Mystery. Melvin Berger & Gilda Berger. LC 94-29806. (Discovery Readers Ser.). (Illus.). 48p. (J). (gr. k-4). 1995. per., pap. 4.50 (*1-57102-026-8*, Ideals Child); lib. bdg. 12.00 (*1-57102-033-0*, Ideals Child) Hambleton-Hill.

***Why Did the Underwear Cross the Road?** Gordon Korman. (J). 1997. pap. text ed. 3.99 (*0-590-47502-9*) Scholastic Inc.

***Why Did We Have to Move Here?** Sally Davies. LC 96-44995. (J). 1997. write for info. (*1-57505-046-3*, Carolrhoda) Lerner Group.

Why Did You Do That? Understand Why Your Family Members Act As They Do. W. Lee Carter. LC 96-520. 304p. 1996. pap. 10.99 (*0-8423-7174-5*) Tyndale.

Why Didn't I Just Raise Radishes? Finding God in the Everyday. Melodie M. Davis. LC 93-31064. 176p. (Orig.). 1994. pap. 8.99 (*0-8361-3659-4*) Herald Pr.

Why Didn't I Say That?! What to Say & How to Say It in Tough Situations on the Job. Donald H. Weiss. LC 94-18556. 208p. 1994. 21.95 (*0-8144-0209-7*) AMACOM.

Why Didn't I Say That?! What to Say & How to Say It in Tough Situations on the Job. Donald H. Weiss. Ed. by Adrienne Hickey. 224p. 1996. pap. 17.95 (*0-8144-7937-5*) AMACOM.

Why Didn't I Think of That? Lee Towe. Ed. by Bonnie Sanford. LC 95-75607. (AMI How-to Ser.). 100p. 1996. per. 12.95 (*1-884926-37-1*) Amer Media.

***Why Didn't I Think of That? Bizarre Origins of Ingenious Inventions We Couldn't Live Without.** Allyn Freeman & Bob Golden. LC 97-7700. 224p. 1997. pap. 14.95 (*0-471-16511-5*) Wiley.

Why Didn't I Think of That? Improving Reading Comprehension. Patricia Williams & Zenobia Verner. (Illus.). 84p. (Orig.). 1988. pap. 9.95 (*0-673-18247-9*, GoodYrBooks) Addson-Wesley Educ.

***Why Didn't I Think of That? 1,198 Hints from 222 Cruisers on 120 Boats from 9 Countries.** John Roberts & Susan Roberts. LC 97-5422. (Illus.). 224p. 1997. text ed. 24.95 (*0-07-053222-2*); pap. text ed. 19.95 (*0-07-053221-4*) McGraw.

Why Didn't Noah Swat Both Mosquitoes? Plus Other Humorous Stories for Clergy. Hoover Rupert. LC 93-44439. 100p. 1994. pap. 10.25 (*1-55673-519-7*) CSS OH.

Why Didn't She Keep Me: The Question Every Adopted Child Asks. Barbara Burlingham-Brown. LC 93-29241. 1993. 19.95 (*0-912083-66-2*, Langford Bks) Diamond Communications.

Why Didn't They Tell Me. rev. ed. Donald G. Moss. 50p. 1989. pap. 3.00 (*0-9623251-1-2*) Laryngectomee.

***Why Didn't You Get Me Out? The Story of Vietnam's Longest Held P. O. W.** Frank Anton & Tommy Denton. LC 97-4897. 240p. 1997. 22.99 (*1-56530-251-6*) Summit TX.

Why Didn't You Say That in the First Place? How to Be Understood at Work. Richard Heyman. LC 93-48663. (Management Ser.). 213p. 1994. 25.00 (*1-55542-653-0*) Jossey-Bass.

***Why Didn't You Say That in the First Place? How to Be Understood at Work.** Richard Heyman. 1997. pap. text ed. 16.00 (*0-7879-0344-2*) Jossey-Bass.

***Why Die? A Beginner's Guide to Living Forever.** Herbert H. Bowie. LC 97-66499. xiv, 306p. (Orig.). 1998. pap. 12.95 (*1-890457-07-8*, B02) PowerSurge.

Why Do Africans Hate Cats. Polo Kamba. Ed. by Paula Scalist. (Illus.). 98p. (YA). 1990. pap. 7.95 (*0-685-28131-0*) Backwards & Backwards.

Why Do Animals Breathe? Diana L. Hall. Ed. by I. Bernard Cohen. LC 80-2089. (Development of Science Ser.). (Illus.). 1981. lib. bdg. 27.95 (*0-405-13855-5*) Ayer.

***Why Do Animals Do That?** Bobbie Kalman. LC 96-43341. (Crabapple Ser.). 32p. 1996. pap. 5.95 (*0-86505-736-2*) Crabtree Pub Co.

***Why Do Animals Do That?** Bobbie Kalman & Greg Nickles. LC 96-43341. (Crabapple Ser.). 32p. (J). 1996. lib. bdg. 18.08 (*0-86505-636-6*) Crabtree Pub Co.

Why Do Balls Bounce? First Questions & Answers about How Things Work. Time-Life Books Editors. Ed. by Allan Fallow. LC 95-3746. (The Time-Life Library of First Questions & Answers). (Illus.). 48p. (J). (gr. k-2). 1995. 14.95 (*0-7835-0901-4*) Time-Life.

Why Do Batteries Die? Scientific Answers to Everyday Questions. Robert L. Wolke. 256p. 1996. pap. 14.95 (*0-8065-1756-5*, Citadel Pr) Carol Pub Group.

Why Do Bees Hum: And 265 Other Great Jokes for Kids. Gary Chmielewski. (J). 1990. 4.99 (*0-517-02536-1*) Random Hse Value.

Why Do Birds. Damon Knight. 272p. 1994. pap. 9.95 (*0-312-89009-5*) Orb NYC.

Why Do Birds. Damon Knight. 288p. 1994. pap. 9.95 (*0-8125-1434-3*) Tor Bks.

Why Do Bugs Bite & Sting? Steve Parker. LC 96-17667. (Ask about Animals Ser.). (Illus.). (J). (gr. 2 up). 1996. lib. bdg. 14.95 (*0-7614-0498-8*, Benchmark NY) Marshall Cavendish.

Why Do Catholics Do That? Kevin O. Johnson. 304p. 1995. pap. 12.00 (*0-345-39726-6*) Ballantine.

***Why Do Cats Do That? Facts about Real Cats & Why They Act the Way They Do.** Nancy White. (J). 1997. pap. text ed. 4.99 (*0-590-95942-5*) Scholastic Inc.

Why Do Christians Shoot Their Wounded? Helping (Not Hurting) Those with Serious Emotional Difficulties. Dwight L. Carlson. LC 93-43019. 180p. (Orig.). 1994. pap. 10.99 (*0-8308-1666-6*, 1666) InterVarsity.

Why Do Clocks Run Clockwise? David Feldman. LC 87-45045. 1988. pap. 10.00 (*0-06-091515-3*, PL) HarpC.

Why Do Clowns Smile? Matthew V. Smith. (Illus.). 14p. (J). (gr. k-3). 1992. pap. 14.95 (*1-895583-06-3*) MAYA Pubs.

Why Do Dogs Do That: Facts about Real Dogs & Why They Act the Way They Do. Nancy White. (J). 1995. pap. 4.99 (*0-590-26597-0*) Scholastic Inc.

Why Do Dogs Have Wet Noses? And Other Imponderables. David Feldman. LC 89-46529. (Imponderables Ser.). (Illus.). 272p. 1991. reprint ed. pap. 10.00 (*0-06-092111-0*, PL) HarpC.

Why Do I Daydream? Betty R. Wright. LC 80-25561. (Life & Living from a Child's Point of View Ser.). (Illus.). 32p. (J). (gr. k-6). 1981. lib. bdg. 21.40 (*0-8172-1371-6*) Raintree Steck-V.

Why Do I Do Things Wrong? Carolyn Nystrom. (Children's Bible Basics Ser.). 32p. (J). (ps-2). 1994. 6.99 (*0-8024-7862-X*) Moody.

Why Do I Do What I Do? How to Understand Yourself & Others. Virginia Dunstone. (Illus.). 348p. (Orig.). 1995. pap. 15.95 (*0-9638282-0-7*) Gate Pubng.

Why Do I Do What I Don't Want to Do? William Backus & Marie Chapian. LC 84-6336. 144p. 1984. pap. 7.99 (*0-87123-625-7*) Bethany Hse.

Why Do I Drink More Than I Want? Five Came Back; Three Did Not. Juanita M. Ferrey. LC 88-72476. 200p. (Orig.). 1987. pap. 13.00 (*0-939339-03-X*, 662-4685) AFCOM Pub.

Why Do I Eat More Than I Want Diet Book. Juanita M. Ferrey. LC 88-72476. 214p. (Orig.). 1987. pap. 13.00 (*0-939339-02-1*, 662-4685) AFCOM Pub.

Why Do I Eat When I'm Not Hungry? Roger Callahan & Paul J. Perry. 240p. 1993. reprint ed. mass mkt. 5.99 (*0-380-71872-3*) Avon.

Why Do I Feel Like Hiding? How to Overcome Shame & Guilt. Daniel Green & Mel Lawrenz. LC 93-41807. (Strategic Christian Living Ser.). 128p. (C). 1994. pap. 8.99 (*0-8010-3862-6*) Baker Bks.

Why Do I Feel So Bad (When the Doctor Says I'm O.K.)? 2nd ed. Howard E. Hagglund. Ed. by Pam Mauldin. (Illus.). 48p. 1984. pap. 6.00 (*0-9614173-0-7*) Metabolic Trans OK.

Why Do I Feel This Way? What Every Woman Needs to Know about Depression. Brenda Poinsett. 180p. (Orig.). 1996. pap. 12.00 (*0-89109-924-7*, 99247) NavPress.

Why Do I Feel Uneasy? Patrick Oliphant. (Illus.). 160p. (Orig.). 1993. pap. 9.95 (*0-8362-1719-5*) Andrews & McMeel.

Why Do I Have to Learn This? Teaching the Way People Learn Best. Dale P. Parnell. Ed. by Margaret M. Leary. LC 95-70034. 144p. 1995. 16.00 (*1-55502-704-0*) CORD Commns.

Why Do I Have to Wear Glasses? Sandra L. Stuart. (Illus.). 48p. (J). 1989. 12.00 (*0-8184-0477-9*) Carol Pub Group.

***Why Do I Laugh or Cry? And Other Questions about the Nervous System.** Sharon Cromwell. LC 97-25172. (Bodywise Ser.). (Illus.). (J). 1997. lib. bdg. write for info. (*1-57572-161-9*) Rigby Interact Libr.

Why Do I Shout at My Wife? Dick Jewett. (Uplook Ser.). 1978. pap. 0.99 (*0-8163-0300-2*, 23617-4) Pacific Pr Pub Assn.

Why Do I Write? Elizabeth Bowen et al. LC 75-22190. (English Literature Ser.: No. 33). 1975. lib. bdg. 75.00 (*0-8383-2094-5*) M S G Haskell Hse.

Why Do Kids Need Feelings? A Guide to Healthy Emotions. Monte Elchoness. LC 92-188. (Illus.). 96p. (Orig.). (J). (gr. 3-8). 1992. pap. 9.95 (*0-936781-07-6*) Monroe Pr.

Why Do Kids Need Feelings? Parent-Teacher Guide. Monte Elchoness. LC 92-188. 40p. (Orig.). 1992. pap. 4.95 (*0-936781-08-4*) Monroe Pr.

Why Do Leaves Change Color? Betsy Maestro. LC 93-9611. (Let's-Read-&-Find-Out Science Bk.). (Illus.). 32p. (J). (gr. k-3). 1994. pap. 4.95 (*0-06-445126-7*, Trophy) HarpC Child Bks.

Why Do Leaves Change Color? Betsy Maestro. LC 93-9611. (Let's-Read-&-Find-Out Science Bk.). (Illus.). 32p. (J). (gr. k-4). 1994. 15.00 (*0-06-022873-3*); lib. bdg. 14.89 (*0-06-022874-1*) HarpC Child Bks.

***Why Do Leaves Change Color?** Betsy Maestro. LC 93-9611. 32p. (J). (ps-4). 1996. pap. 7.95 incl. digital audio (*0-694-70080-0*) HarpC.

Why Do Men Have Nipples? And Other Low-Life Answers to Real-Life Questions. Katherine Dunn. 1992. reprint ed. mass mkt. 6.99 (*0-446-39412-2*) Warner Bks.

Why Do Mice Celebrate Christmas? And Other Fun Questions of the Season. Andrea Alexander. (Illus.). 64p. (Orig.). (J). (ps-5). 1991. pap. 13.95 (*0-9628006-0-0*) Zenon Pub.

Why Do Mullet Jump? And Other Puzzles & Possibilities of God's Creation. Gene Zimmerman. 128p. (Orig.). 1986. pap. 6.95 (*0-935311-01-7*) Post Horn Pr.

Why Do Music Conductors Live into their 90s? The Simple, Revolutionary Discovery that Can Make You Live Longer, Increase Your Stamina & Stretch & Normalize Your Blood Pressure in Minutes. Steve Rochlitz. LC 93-33432. (Illus.). 140p. (Orig.). 1994. pap. 12.95 (*0-945262-42-6*) HEBS Inc.

***Why Do My Feet Fall Asleep? And Other Questions about the Circulatory System.** Sharon Cromwell. LC 97-22213. (Bodywise Ser.). (Illus.). (J). 1997. lib. bdg. write for info. (*1-57572-162-7*) Rigby Interact Libr.

Why Do People Come in Different Colors? Isaac Asimov & Carrie Dierks. LC 93-20157. (Ask Isaac Asimov Ser.). (J). 1993. lib. bdg. 17.27 (*0-8368-0808-8*) Gareth Stevens Inc.

Why Do People Do What They Do? Insights into the Human Behaviors That Achieve Excellence. Clifford I. Sears & Carol A. Schneier. (Illus.). 250p. (Orig.). 1992. pap. 12.95 (*0-9634993-0-0*) Corp Int Assocs.

Why Do People Eat? Kate Needham. (Starting Point Science Ser.). (Illus.). 24p. (J). (gr. 1-5). 1993. pap. 3.95 (*0-7460-1302-7*, Usborne); lib. bdg. 12.95 (*0-88110-638-0*, Usborne) EDC.

Why Do People Fall under the Power? Kenneth E. Hagin. 1981. pap. 0.75 (*0-89276-254-3*) Hagin Ministries.

Why Do People Get Sick: The New Science of Psychoneuroimmunology & What It Can Do for You. 1992. lib. bdg. 88.00 (*0-8490-5402-8*) Gordon Pr.

Why Do Roosters Crow? First Questions & Answers about the Farm. Time-Life Books Editors. Ed. by Allan Fallow. (Time-Life Library of First Questions & Answers). (Illus.). 48p. (J). (gr. k-2). 1995. 14.95 (*0-7835-0899-9*) Time-Life.

***Why Do Ruling Classes Fear.** Kaye. Date not set. pap. 15.95 (*0-312-17227-3*) St Martin.

Why Do Ruling Classes Fear History? And Other Questions. Harvey J. Kaye. LC 95-25548. 256p. 1995. 23.95 (*0-312-12691-3*) St Martin.

***Why Do Seasons Change?** LC 96-45926. (Why Bks.). (Illus.). 24p. (J). 1997. 9.95 (*0-7894-1529-1*) DK Pub Inc.

***Why Do Seasons Change?** Christopher Mainard. (Why Bks.). (J). (ps up). 1997. 9.95 (*0-614-28703-0*) DK Pub Inc.

***Why Do Some People Use Wheelchairs? Questions Children Ask about Disabled People.** LC 97-14462. (Why Bks.). (J). 1997. write for info. (*0-7894-2057-0*) DK Pub Inc.

Why Do Some People Wear Glasses? Isaac Asimov & Carrie Dierks. LC 93-20156. (Ask Isaac Asimov Ser.). (J). 1993. lib. bdg. 17.27 (*0-8368-0809-6*) Gareth Stevens Inc.

Why Do Stars Twinkle? Isaac Asimov. (Ask Isaac Asimov Ser.). (Illus.). 24p. (J). (gr. 2-3). 1991. lib. bdg. 17.27 (*0-8368-0437-6*) Gareth Stevens Inc.

Why Do Stars Twinkle? And Other Nighttime Questions. Catherine Ripley. (Illus.). 32p. (J). (ps-3). 1996. 17.95 (*1-895688-41-8*, Pub. by Owl Bks CN); pap. 6.95 (*1-895688-42-6*, Pub. by Owl Bks CN) Firefly Bks Ltd.

Why Do Sunflowers Face the Sun? Questions about Nature. (Why Bks.). (Illus.). 24p. (J). 1996. 9.95 (*0-7894-1120-2*) DK Pub Inc.

***Why Do Sunflowers Face the Sun? Questions Children Ask about Nature.** (Why Bks.). (Illus.). (J). 10.99 (*0-590-24954-1*) Scholastic Inc.

Why Do the Jews Need a Land of Their Own? Ed. by Joseph Leftwich & Mordecai S. Chertoff. LC 83-45297. 242p. 1984. 19.95 (*0-8453-4774-8*, Cornwall Bks) Assoc Univ Prs.

Why Do the Right Words Always Come Out of the Wrong Mouth? Cathy Guisewite. (Illus.). 128p. (Orig.). 1988. pap. 9.95 (*0-8362-1808-6*) Andrews & McMeel.

Why Do the Righteous Suffer? Gordon Lindsay. 1963. 2.95 (*0-89985-032-4*) Christ for the Nations.

***Why Do They Call It a Birdie? 1,001 Fascinating Facts about Golf.** Frank Coffey. LC 97-21506. 1997. 14.95 (*1-55972-429-3*, Birch Ln Pr) Carol Pub Group.

Why Do They Call It Topeka? How Places Got Their Names. John W. Pursell. LC 94-17790. 1994. 9.95 (*0-8065-1588-0*, Citadel Pr) Carol Pub Group.

Why Do They Do It? Gordon Lindsay. 1971. 1.00 (*0-89985-120-7*) Christ for the Nations.

***Why Do They Dress That Way?** rev. ed. Stephen Scott. LC 86-81058. (People's Place Book Ser.: No. 7). (Illus.). 160p. 1997. pap. 7.95 (*1-56148-240-4*) Good Bks PA.

Why Do Tigers Have Stripes? M. Unwin. (Encyclopedias Ser.). (Illus.). 24p. (J). (gr. 1 up). 1993. pap. 3.95 (*0-7460-1300-0*); lib. bdg. 12.95 (*0-88110-625-9*) EDC.

Why Do Vegetarians Eat Like That? Everything You Wanted to Know (& Some Things You Didn't) about Vegetarianism. David A. Gabbe. LC 94-66410. (Illus.). 288p. (Orig.). 1994. pap. 11.95 (*0-9640190-0-0*) Prime Imprints.

***Why Do Volcanoes Erupt?** LC 96-45924. (Why Bks.). (Illus.). 24p. (J). 1997. 9.95 (*0-7894-1532-1*) DK Pub Inc.

***Why Do Volcanoes Erupt?** Christopher Mainard. (Why Bks.). (J). (ps up). 1997. 9.95 (*0-614-28706-5*) DK Pub Inc.

Why Do We Age? Hilton Hotema. 58p. 1959. reprint ed. spiral bd. 6.50 (*0-7873-0435-2*) Hlth Research.

***Why Do We Americans Submit to This?** LC 97-66393. (Illus.). 200p. (Orig.). 1997. pap. 20.00 (*0-9649531-1-0*) Newcomb Pub.

Why Do We Celebrate That? Jane Wilcox. (Why Do We? Ser.). 32p. (J). 1996. lib. bdg. 18.00 (*0-531-14393-7*) Watts.

Why Do We Do That? Mark Kirtland. (Why Do We? Ser.). 32p. (J). 1996. lib. bdg. 18.00 (*0-531-14394-5*) Watts.

Why Do We Dream. J. Everett Irion. 240p. (Orig.). 1990. 15.95 (*0-87604-238-8*, 345) ARE Pr.

Why Do We Exist. Gordis. 1997. 24.00 (*0-684-80389-5*) S&S Trade.

Why Do We Fall in Love: The Psychology of Choosing a Partner. Cathy Troupp. 288p. 1995. 22.95 (*0-312-13215-8*) St Martin.

Why Do We Gotta Do This Stuff, Mr. Nehring? Notes from a Teacher's Day in School. James Nehring. LC 89-1352. 204p. 1989. 15.95 (*0-87131-574-2*) M Evans.

Why Do We Have Different Seasons? Isaac Asimov. LC 90-26061. (Ask Isaac Asimov Ser.). (Illus.). 24p. (J). (gr. 2-3). 1991. lib. bdg. 17.27 (*0-8368-0439-2*) Gareth Stevens Inc.

Why Do We Have To? Learning Why We Have to with the Alphabet Pals. World Book Editors. LC 90-71689. (Illus.). 24p. (J). (ps). 1991. bds. write for info. (*0-7166-1905-9*) World Bk.

Why Do We Have to Move? Helping Your Child Adjust with Love & Illustrations. Cynthia MacGregor. LC 96-26092. (Illus.). 1996. 14.95 (*0-8184-0583-X*, L Stuart) Carol Pub Group.

Why Do We Laugh? Stephen Gregg. 1983. pap. 3.00 (*0-87129-282-3*, W58) Dramatic Pub.

Why Do We Laugh? Questions about the Human Body. LC 95-47848. (Why Bks.). (Illus.). 24p. (J). 1996. 9.95 (*0-7894-1121-0*) DK Pub Inc.

Why Do We Laugh? Questions about the Human Body. Illus. by Susan Jacoby. LC 95-47848. (Geotrivia Ser.). (J). 1996. pap. 3.95 (*0-528-83760-5*) Rand McNally.

***Why Do We Laugh? Questions Children Ask about the Human Body.** (Why Bks.). (Illus.). (J). 10.99 (*0-590-24955-X*) Scholastic Inc.

Why Do We Need Another Baby? Helping Your Child Welcome a New Arrival. Cynthia MacGregor. (Illus.). (J). 1996. pap. 13.95 (*0-8065-1757-3*, Citadel Pr) Carol Pub Group.

Why Do We Need Another Baby? Helping Your Child Welcome a New Arrival - with Love & Illustrations. Cynthia MacGregor. (Illus.). 1996. 13.95 (*0-8184-0578-3*, L Stuart) Carol Pub Group.

Why Do We Need Railways? International Seminar 19-20 January 1995. ECMT Staff. 210p. (Orig.). (ENG & FRE.). 1995. pap. 62.00 (*92-821-1207-1*, Pub. by Org for Econ FR) OECD.

Why Do We Need Sleep? Isaac Asimov & Carrie Dierks. LC 92-20154. (Ask Isaac Asimov Ser.). (J). 1993. lib. bdg. 17.27 (*0-8368-0806-1*) Gareth Stevens Inc.

Why Do We Need to Brush Our Teeth. Isaac Asimov & Carrie Dierks. LC 93-20155. (Ask Isaac Asimov Ser.). (J). 1993. lib. bdg. 17.27 (*0-8368-0807-X*) Gareth Stevens Inc.

Why Do We Recycle? Markets, Values, & Public Policy. Frank Ackerman. 180p. (C). 1996. pap. text ed. 16.95 (*1-55963-505-3*) Island Pr.

An Asterisk (*) at the beginning of an entry indicates that the title is appearing in BIP for the first time.

*Why Do We Recycle? Markets, Values, & Public Policy. Frank Ackerman. 180p. (C). 1996. 29.95 (1-55963-504-5) Island Pr.

Why Do We Say It. 1991. 4.98 (1-55521-010-4, Castle Bks Inc) Bk Sales Inc.

*Why Do We Struggle So. Carol Richardson. 168p. (Orig.). 1997. pap. 7.99 (1-884369-44-8, EBED Pubns) McDougal Pubng.

Why Do We Suffer? New Ways of Understanding. Daniel Liderbach. LC 92-12767. 160p. 1992. pap. 11.95 (0-8091-3319-9) Paulist Pr.

Why Do We Use That? Jane Wilcox. (Why Do We? Ser.). 32p. (J). 1996. lib. bdg. 18.00 (0-531-14395-3) Watts.

Why Do We Wear Ashes? Paul L. Larsen. 1991. pap. 5.50 (1-55673-284-8, 9117) CSS OH.

Why Do We Wear That? Franklin Watts. (Why Do We? Ser.). 32p. 1996. lib. bdg. 18.00 (0-531-14396-1) Watts.

Why Do Winners Win? Can Anyone Be a Winner? Alyce P. Cornyn-Selby. 64p. (Orig.). (C). 1990. pap. 8.95 (0-941383-12-1) Beynch Pr.

Why Do Winners Win? see Why Winners Win

*Why Do Women Write More Letters Than They Send? A Meditation on the Loneliness of the Sexes. Darian Leader. LC 96-34933. 192p. 1997. 20.00 (0-465-09169-5) Basic.

Why Do You Call Me Chocolate Boy? Carol Parker. LC 93-79098. (Illus.). 28p. (Orig.). (J). (gr. 2-6). 1993. pap. 7.95 (0-9637267-0-6) Gull Crest.

Why Do You Force Me to Talk to a Chemical When All I Want is Your Heart? Bertie Ryan Synowiec. (Illus.). 40p. 1993. pap. 9.97 (1-885335-07-5) Positive Support.

Why Do You Love Me? Martin Baynton. LC 89-1861. (Illus.). 32p. (J). (ps up). 1990. 16.00 (0-688-09156-3); lib. bdg. 15.93 (0-688-09157-1) Greenwillow.

Why Do You Speak As You Do? A Guide to Learning about Language - A Discovery Book. Kay Cooper. 66p. 1992. 13.95 (0-8027-8164-0); lib. bdg. 14.85 (0-8027-8165-9) Walker & Co.

*Why Doctors Need Asset Protection: The 10 Greatest Threats to Your Financial Security. David B. Mandell. (Illus.). 58p. (Orig.). 1997. spiral bd., pap. write for info. (1-890415-01-4) Finacial Inst.

Why Does a B Look Like a D. Jennifer L. Chan. LC 93-45793. (J). 12.95 (1-879965-06-2) Polychrome Pub.

Why Does a Brachiosaurus Have Such a Long Neck? Dick Dudley. (Dino Pop-up Joke Bks.). (J). (ps-3). 1992. 5.95 (1-56288-178-7) Checkerboard.

Why Does an Apatosaurus Get Its Way? Dick Dudley & Emilie Kong. (Dino Pop-up Joke Bks.). (Illus.). 12p. (J). 1992. 5.95 (1-56288-181-7) Checkerboard.

Why Does Baby Cry? Feagin. 1990. pap. 6.06 (0-8092-4140-4) Contemp Bks.

Why Does Crime Pay? Morgan O. Reynolds. 1991. pap. 5.00 (0-943802-89-X, BG110) Natl Ctr Pol.

Why Does Crime Pay? rev. ed. Morgan O. Reynolds. (Illus.). 15p. 1992. pap. 5.00 (1-56808-006-9, BG 123) Natl Ctr Pol.

Why Does God Allow It? A. E. Wilder-Smith. 60p. 1990. pap. 2.99 (0-614-11246-X) Word for Today.

Why Does God Allow Suffering? D. Martyn Lloyd-Jones. 128p. (Orig.). 1994. pap. 8.99 (0-89107-776-6) Crossway Bks.

Why Does God Allow Suffering? And Other Essays on the Spiritual Quest. Robert Powell. LC 88-83535. 158p. reprint ed. pap. 45.10 (0-7837-5211-3, 2044942) Bks Demand.

*Why Does He Say One Thing. Mcnaughton. 1997. pap. 5.99 (0-671-00207-4) PB.

Why Does Language Matter to Philosophy. Ian Hacking. LC 75-13832. 180p. 1975. pap. text ed. 19.95 (0-521-09998-6) Cambridge U Pr.

Why Does Lightning Strike? Questions about Weather. (Why Bks.). (Illus.). 24p. (J). 1996. 9.95 (0-7894-1123-7) DK Pub Inc.

*Why Does Lightning Strike? Questions Children Ask about Weather. (Why Bks.). (Illus.). (J). 10.99 (0-590-24945-2) Scholastic Inc.

Why Does Litter Cause Problems? Isaac Asimov. LC 92-5349. (Ask Isaac Asimov Ser.). (YA). 1992. lib. bdg. 17.27 (0-8368-0799-5) Gareth Stevens Inc.

Why Does Muhammad & Any Muslim Murder the Devil? Amir Fatir. 54p. 1995. reprint ed. pap. 15.00 (1-56411-096-6) Untd Bros & Sis.

*Why Does My Cat...? Sarah Heath. (Illus.). 224p. 1997. 18.95 (0-285-63147-0, Pub. by Souvenir UK) IPG Chicago.

Why Does My Dog...? John Fisher. (Illus.). 240p. 1992. pap. 21.95 (0-87605-792-X) Howell Bk.

*Why Does My Dog Do That? Randy A. Jacobs. LC 97-93387. (Illus.). 92p. 1997. pap. 9.95 (0-9658680-0-1) Essex Pub.

*Why Does My Dog Drink Out of the Toilet: Answers & Advice for All Kinds of Dog Dilemmas. John Ross. LC 96-6552. 1997. 14.95 (0-312-15692-8, Griffin) St Martin.

Why Does My Horse...? Paul McGreevy. (Illus.). 256p. 1996. 16.95 (1-57076-067-5) Trafalgar.

*Why Does My Tummy Rumble When I'm Hungry? And Other Questions about the Digestive System. Sharon Cromwell. LC 97-25170. (Bodywise Ser.). (Illus.). (J). 1997. lib. bdg. write for info. (1-57572-163-5) Rigby Interact Libr.

*Why Does Popcorn Pop? And Other Kitchen Questions. Catherine Ripley. (Question & Answer Storybook Ser.). 1997. 17.95 (1-895688-70-1, Pub. by Owl Bks CN); pap. 6.95 (1-895688-71-X, Pub. by Owl Bks CN) Firefly Bks Ltd.

Why Does Popcorn Pop? And Two Hundred & One Other Fascinating Facts about Food. Donald A. Voorhees. 240p. 1995. pap. 8.95 (0-8065-1690-9, Citadel Pr) Carol Pub Group.

Why Does Santa Celebrate Christmas? Cheryl Gimbel & Wendelin Maners. Ed. by Janet Lovelady. (Illus.). 36p. (J). (gr. k up). 1990. 12.95 (0-915190-67-2, JP9067-2) Jalmar Pr.

Why Does Software Cost So Much? And Other Puzzles of the Information Age. Tom DeMarco. LC 95-35656. 237p. 1995. pap. 32.50 (0-932633-34-X, QA76.754) Dorset Hse Pub Co.

Why Does That Man Have Such a Big Nose? Mary B. Quinsey. LC 85-63760. (Illus.). 32p. (Orig.). (J). (ps-1). 1986. pap. 5.95 (0-943990-24-6); lib. bdg. 16.95 (0-943990-25-4) Parenting Pr.

Why Does the Moon Change Shape? Isaac Asimov. LC 90-25430. (Ask Isaac Asimov Ser.). (Illus.). 24p. (J). (gr. 2-3). 1991. lib. bdg. 17.27 (0-8368-0438-4) Gareth Stevens Inc.

Why Doesn't God Intervene? Basilea M. Schlink. 32p. 1982. pap. 0.50 (3-87209-629-X) Evang Sisterhood Mary.

Why Doesn't Russian Industry Work. L. Kosals. Tr. by John Crowfoot & Igor Poluyan. (Second World Ser.). 256p. 1994. text ed. 59.50 (1-85043-190-6, Pub. by I B Tauris UK) St Martin.

Why Doesn't the Earth Fall Up? And Other Not Such Dumb Questions about Motion. Vicki Cobb. LC 88-11108. (Illus.). 40p. (J). (gr. 2-5). 1989. pap. 14.99 (0-525-67253-2, Lodestar Bks) Dutton Child Bks.

Why Dogs Are Better Than Men. Jennifer Berman. Ed. by Eric Tobias. (Illus.). 80p. (Orig.). 1993. pap. 10.00 (0-671-86488-2) PB.

Why Dogs Are Better Than Republicans...& Other Political Animals: ...And Other Political Animals. Jennifer Berman. 96p. 1996. pap. text ed. 10.00 (0-06-092772-0) HarpC.

Why Dolphins Call: A Story of Dionysus. Scott Simons & Jamie Simons. (Gods of Olympus Ser.). (Illus.). 32p. (J). (gr. 2-5). 1992. 5.95 (0-671-69125-2, Silver Pr. NJ); lib. bdg. 10.95 (0-671-69121-X, Silver Pr NJ) Silver Burdett Pr.

*Why Don't Cats Lay Eggs? Olivia Long. (Our Precious Planet Ser.). (Illus.). 32p. (J). (ps-4). Date not set. write for info. (1-880042-12-6) Shelf-Life Bks.

*Why Don't Dogs Go Bald? Lois Sayritch-Procko & George Procko, Jr. LC 96-90042. (Illus.). 64p. (J). 1997. 9.00 (1-56002-652-9, Univ Edtns) Aegina Pr.

Why Don't I Get What I Pray For? John W. Cowart. LC 93-3527. 180p. (Orig.). 1993. pap. 8.99 (0-8308-1344-6, 1344, Saltshaker Bk) InterVarsity.

Why Don't I Listen to My Parents? Wayne H. Miller. Ed. by Denise M. Smith. (Sandy Dallas Series of Books for Children, Parents, & Teachers). (Illus.). 100p. (Orig.). (YA). (gr. 6-12). 1995. pap. text ed. 4.95 (0-9634735-1-4) Hiram Charles.

Why Don't the Stars Fall Down? Jan Godfrey. (Illus.). 32p. (J). (ps-3). 1994. pap. 6.99 (0-8066-2743-3, Augsburg) Augsburg Fortress.

Why Don't They Give Them Guns? The Great American Indian Myth. Stephen E. Feraca. LC 89-39411. (Illus.). 250p. (Orig.). (C). 1990. pap. text ed. 24.00 (0-8191-7625-7); lib. bdg. 45.00 (0-8191-7624-9) U Pr of Amer.

Why Don't They Teach This in Bible School? 31 Master Secrets Rarely Discovered. 2nd ed. Sherman Owens. LC 94-96199. 68p. (Orig.). 1994. reprint ed. pap. 7.00 (0-9642305-0-X) Ldrship Pubng.

Why Don't They Write Plays Like They Used To? A Memoir of Two Lifetimes. Howard Stein. 256p. 24.95 (1-55783-176-9) Applause Theatre Bk Pubs.

Why Don't You Believe What We Tell You? 39p. (Orig.). 1992. pap. 1.00 (0-939482-47-9, 0509, Noontide Pr) Legion Survival.

Why Don't You Get a Horse, Sam Adams? Jean Fritz. (Illus.). 48p. (J). (gr. 2-5). 1996. pap. 5.95 (0-698-11416-7, Paperstar) Putnam Pub Group.

Why Don't You Get a Horse, Sam Adams? Jean Fritz. (Illus.). 48p. (J). (gr. 2-6). 1974. reprint ed. 14.95 (0-698-20292-9, Coward) Putnam Pub Group.

Why Don't You Have Wings to Fly With? Marianna D. Dahl. 1995. 10.95 (0-533-11251-6) Vantage.

Why Don't You Play Loud? A Guide for Teaching Music to Young Children. Marilyn M. Helminiak. Ed. by Karen Faster. (Illus.). 71p. (Orig.). 1994. pap. 12.95 (1-878569-23-6) Badger Bks Inc.

Why Don't You Send Somebody? Sermons for Advent, Christmas, & Epiphany: First Lesson. Frederick C. Edwards. LC 93-19941. 1993. pap. 9.50 (1-55673-611-8, 9336) CSS OH.

Why Don't You Talk Right? Multicultural Communication Perspectives. Aprele Elliott. 288p. (C). 1992. per., pap. text ed. 25.14 (0-8403-8167-0) Kendall-Hunt.

Why Don't You...701 Ways to Jumpstart Your Life: 701 Ways to Jumpstart Your Life. Elizabeth Nix. 1996. mass mkt. 5.99 (0-380-78671-0, Cosmopolitan) Avon.

Why Duchamp: An Essay on Aesthetic Impact. Gianfranco Baruchello & Henry Martin. LC 85-11544. 160p. 1985. 20.00 (0-914232-71-1); pap. 10.00 (0-914232-73-8) McPherson & Co.

Why Duchamp: An Essay on Aesthetic Impact. deluxe ed. Gianfranco Baruchello & Henry Martin. LC 85-11544. 160p. 1985. 200.00 (0-914232-72-X) McPherson & Co.

*Why Economics Doesn't Work. Mark D. Greenfield. 400p. Date not set. 35.00 (0-9641115-2-7, VMS-2) Unherd Opinions.

Why Economics Is Not Yet a Science. Ed. by Alfred S. Eichner. LC 83-12859. 264p. (gr. 13). 1983. text ed. 51.95 (0-87332-249-5) M E Sharpe.

Why Economics Is Not Yet a Science. Ed. & Intro. by Alfred S. Eichner. LC 83-12859. 264p. (gr. 13). 1983. pap. text ed. 28.95 (0-87332-265-7) M E Sharpe.

*Why Economists Disagree: An Introduction to the Alternative Schools of Thought. Ed. by David L. Prychitko. LC 97-1725. (SUNY Series, Diversity in Contemporary Economics). 320p. (C). 1997. text ed. 65.50 (0-7914-3569-5) State U NY Pr.

*Why Economists Disagree: An Introduction to the Alternative Schools of Thought. Ed. by David L. Prychitko. LC 97-1725. (SUNY Series, Diversity in Contemporary Economics). 320p. (C). 1997. pap. text ed. 21.95 (0-7914-3570-9) State U NY Pr.

*Why Economists Disagree: The Political Economy of Economics. 2nd ed. Ken Cole et al. LC 90-13461. 1991. pap. text ed. write for info. (0-582-06400-7) Longman.

Why Educational Policies Can Fail: An Overview of Sellected African Experiences. George Psacharopoulos. (Discussion Paper Ser.: No. 82). 34p. 1990. 6.95 (0-8213-1549-8, 11549) World Bank.

Why Elephants & Fleas Don't Sweat: A Zoological Miscellany. Gideon Louw. (Illus.). 224p. (Orig.). (YA). (gr. 7 up). 1996. pap. 15.95 (1-55059-125-8, Pub. by Detselig CN) Temeron Bks.

Why Employees Don't Do What They're Supposed to Do: And What to Do about It. Ferdinand F. Fournies. 1991. text ed. 15.95 (0-07-156149-8) McGraw.

Why Employees Don't Do What They're Supposed to Do: And What to Do About It. Ferdinand F. Fournies. 1991. pap. text ed. 9.95 (0-07-157969-9) McGraw.

Why Employees Don't Do What They're Supposed to Do & What to Do about It. Ferdinand F. Fournies. (Illus.). 120p. 1989. 14.95 (0-8306-3064-3, Liberty Hse); pap. 8.95 (0-8306-9834-5, Liberty Hse) TAB Bks.

Why England Slept. John F. Kennedy. LC 81-6296. xxviii, 252p. 1981. reprint ed. text ed. 45.00 (0-313-22874-4, KEWE, Greenwood Pr) Greenwood.

Why Entrepreneurs Fail: Avoid the 20 Fatal Pitfalls of Running Your Business. James W. Halloran. 1991. pap. text ed. 14.95 (0-07-155125-5) McGraw.

Why Entrepreneurs Fail: Avoid the 20 Fatal Pitfalls of Running Your Business. James W. Halloran. 220p. 1991. pap. 14.95 (0-8306-3511-4, 3511) McGraw-Hill Prof.

Why ERA Failed: Politics, Women's Rights, & the Amending Process of the Constitution. Mary F. Berry. LC 85-45985. (Everywoman: Studies in History, Literature & Culture; Blacks in the Diaspora Ser.). 160p. 1986. 27.50 (0-253-36537-6) Ind U Pr.

Why ERA Failed: Politics, Women's Rights, & the Amending Process of the Constitution. Mary F. Berry. LC 85-45985. (Everywoman: Studies in History, Literature & Culture; Blacks in the Diaspora Ser.). 160p. 1988. pap. 7.95 (0-253-20459-3) Ind U Pr.

Why Europe Leaves Home: A True Account of the Reasons Which Cause Central Europeans to Overrun America. Kenneth L. Roberts. Ed. by Gerald Grob. LC 76-46100. (Anti-Movements in America Ser.). 1977. reprint ed. lib. bdg. 34.95 (0-405-09971-1) Ayer.

Why Eve Doesn't Have an Adam's Apple: A Dictionary of Sex Differences. Carol A. Rinzler. LC 95-43133. 1996. write for info. (0-8160-3356-0) Facts on File.

*Why Eve Doesn't Have an Adam's Apple: A Dictionary of Sex Differences. Carol A. Rinzler. 256p. 1996. pap. 24.95 (0-8160-3352-8) Facts on File.

Why Everyone Hates You. Steven Ochs. 96p. 1996. mass mkt. 5.99 (0-7860-0223-9, Pinncle Kensgtn) Kensgtn Pub Corp.

Why Executives Lose Their Balance. Joan R. Kofodimos. (Technical Reports: No. 137). 46p. 1989. pap. 20.00 (0-912879-35-1) Ctr Creat Leader.

Why Exports Really Matter: More. David Richardson & Karin Rindal. 1996. 40.00 (0-88132-229-6) Inst Intl Eco.

Why Exports Really Matter! What We Know. J. David Richardson & Karin Rindal. 1995. pap. 40.00 (0-88132-221-0) Inst Intl Eco.

Why Fakes Matter. Mark Jones. (Illus.). 200p. 1992. 70.00 (0-7141-1721-8) Antique Collect.

Why Families Move. Peter H. Rossi. LC 79-25370. 243p. reprint ed. pap. 69.30 (0-7837-4558-3, 2044086) Bks Demand.

Why Farmers Are Poor: The Agricultural Crisis in the United States. Anne Rochester. Ed. by Dan C. McCurry & Richard E. Rubenstein. LC 74-30649. (American Farmers & the Rise of Agribusiness Ser.). 1975. reprint ed. 31.95 (0-405-06821-2) Ayer.

Why Fascism? Ellen C. Wilkinson & Edward Conze. LC 78-177843. reprint ed. 39.50 (0-404-56169-1) AMS Pr.

Why Fear Death? see I Tell You a Mystery: Life, Death, & Eternity

*Why Feeling Bad Is Good: How Women Can Use Depression to Make Positive Changes in Their Lives. Lindsay Knight. 200p. 1997. pap. 15.95 (0-340-62594-5, Pub. by H & S UK) Trafalgar.

Why Fingerprint? 3rd ed. National Notary Association Editors. LC 92-83795. 101p. 1995. pap. 10.95 (0-933134-48-7) Natl Notary.

Why Firms Succeed. John A. Kay. (Illus.). 334p. (C). 1995. 30.00 (0-19-508767-4, 13738) OUP.

Why Flannery O'Connor Stayed Home. Marion Montgomery. (Prophetic Poet & the Spirit of the Age Ser.: Vol. I). 486p. 1981. pap. 14.95 (0-89385-033-0) Sugden.

*Why Flip a Coin? The Art & Science of Good Decisions in Everyday Life. H. W. Lewis. LC 96-29444. 200p. 1997. text ed. 22.95 (0-471-16597-2) Wiley.

*Why Flip a Coin? The Art & Science of Good Decisions in Everyday Life. H. W. Lewis. 1997. 24.95 (0-614-28190-3) Wiley.

Why Flowers Bloom. Janet C. Chandler. LC 93-39967. (Illus.). 115p. 1994. 12.00 (0-918949-38-6); pap. 8.00 (0-918949-37-8) Papier-Mache Press.

Why Fly? A Philosophy of Creativity. E. Paul Torrance. (Creavitity Research Monographs). (Illus.). 402p. 1995. pap. 39.50 (1-56750-173-7); text ed. 73.25 (1-56750-172-9) Ablex Pub.

Why Flying Endangers Your Health: Hidden Health Hazards of Air Travel. F. S. Kahn. LC 92-70860. (Illus.). 305p. (Orig.). 1992. pap. 14.00 (0-943358-36-1) Aurora Press.

Why Food Aid? Ed. by Vernon W. Ruttan. LC 92-25476. 320p. 1993. text ed. 45.00 (0-8018-4471-1); pap. text ed. 15.95 (0-8018-4472-X) Johns Hopkins.

Why Foreign Aid. Ed. by Robert A. Goldwin. LC 71-134083. (Essay Index Reprint Ser.). 1977. 17.95 (0-8369-2036-8) Ayer.

Why Forget. Dorothy M. Obe. 122p. (C). 1989. text ed. 50.00 (0-946270-54-6, Pub. by Pentland Pr UK) St Mut.

Why Four Gospels? unabridged ed. Donald Bridge. 208p. 1996. 15.99 (1-85792-225-5, Pub. by Christian Focus UK) Spring Arbor Dist.

Why Frau Frohman Raised Her Prices & Other Stories. Anthony Trollope. Ed. by N. John Hall. LC 80-1900. (Selected Works of Anthony Trollope). 1981. reprint ed. lib. bdg. 49.95 (0-405-14189-0) Ayer.

Why Frau Frohmann Raised Her Prices. Anthony Trollope. Ed. by John K. Shannon. (Harting Grange Library). (Illus.). 1978. pap. 5.95 (0-932282-05-9); lib. bdg. 9.95 (0-932282-06-7) Caledonia Pr.

Why Free Enterprise Is in Deep Trouble. 1992. lib. bdg. 75.00 (0-8490-8734-1) Gordon Pr.

Why Freud Was Wrong: Sin, Science, & Psychoanalysis. Richard Webster. LC 95-22640. 688p. 1995. 35.00 (0-465-09579-8) Basic.

Why Freud Was Wrong: Sin, Science, & Psychoanalysis. Richard Webster. 688p. 1996. pap. 22.50 (0-465-09128-8) Basic.

Why Friends Are Friends. Jack L. Willcuts. 90p. (Orig.). 1984. pap. 5.95 (0-913342-45-9) Barclay Pr.

Why Frogs Go to School & Other Weird Facts You Never Learned. Robin Keats. (Illus.). 96p. (Orig.). (J). 1992. pap. 3.50 (0-380-76718-X, Camelot) Avon.

Why Futures Traders Change Brokers. John Walsh. 4p. 1989. pap. 2.00 (0-915513-34-X) Ctr Futures Ed.

Why Gay Guys Are a Girl's Best Friend. Jeff Fessler & Karen Rauch. LC 95-2045. 1995. pap. 7.95 (0-684-80053-5, Fireside) S&S Trade.

Why Genocide? The Armenian & Jewish Experiences in Perspective. Florence Mazian. LC 89-15268. 306p. 1990. reprint ed. pap. 87.30 (0-608-00182-1, 2060964) Bks Demand.

Why George Should Eat Broccoli. Paul A. Stitt. Ed. by Terry L. Firkins & Barbara R. Stitt. (Illus.). 399p. (Orig.). (C). 1991. pap. 12.95 (1-878150-00-6) Natural Pr.

Why Germany? National Socialist Antisemitism & the European Context. John Milfull. 264p. 1993. 45.95 (0-85496-315-4) Berg Pubs.

Why Girls Ride Sidesaddle. Dennis Lynds. LC 79-50801. (Illus.). 115p. (C). 1980. pap. 12.50 (0-913204-13-7) December Pr.

Why Give "Gifts" to the Gifted? Investing in a National Resource. Lita L. Schwartz. LC 93-40547. 160p. 1994. 42.95 (0-8039-6103-0); pap. 18.95 (0-8039-6104-9) Corwin Pr.

Why Go to Confession? Questions & Answers about Sacramental Reconciliation. rev. ed. Joseph M. Champlin. 32p. 1996. pap. text ed. 1.95 (0-86716-263-5) St Anthony Mess Pr.

Why Go to Mass: Reasons & Resources to Motivate Teenagers. Greg Dues. LC 94-60478. 72p. (Orig.). 1994. pap. 9.95 (0-89622-604-2) Twenty-Third.

*Why Go Vo-Tech? Norman C. Tognazzini. (Illus.). 16p. (Orig.). 1996. pap. 3.00 (1-884241-33-6, SPSO312) Energeia Pub.

*Why Goats Smell Bad: And Other Stories from Benin. Ed. by Raouf Mama. (Illus.). 128p. (J). (gr. 3-6). 1997. lib. bdg. write for info. (0-208-02469-7) Shoe String.

Why God? Burton Z. Cooper. LC 87-21499. 132p. 1988. pap. 14.00 (0-8042-0731-3, John Knox) Westminster John Knox.

Why, God? James M. Tarter. 156p. 1995. pap. 9.95 (0-925591-35-1) Covenant Hse Bks.

Why God Allows Trials & Disappointments. Gerald R. Nash. (Uplook Ser.). 31p. 1972. pap. 0.99 (0-8163-0082-8, 23618-2) Pacific Pr Pub Assn.

Why God Became Man & the Virgin Conception & Original Sin. Anselm of Canterbury. Tr. & Intro. by Joseph M. Colleran. LC 71-77166. 256p. (Orig.). 1982. pap. text ed. 6.95 (0-87343-025-5) Magi Bks.

Why God Gave Me Pain. Shirley Holdren. 128p. 1984. pap. 1.00 (0-8294-0469-4) Loyola Pr.

*Why God Hates Dirty Underwear! Ralph Sexton, Sr. (Illus.). 80p. (Orig.). 1997. pap. 9.95 (1-57090-061-2) Alexander Bks.

*Why God Makes Bald Guys. Paul Della Valle. Ed. by Cliff Carle. (Illus.). 96p. (Orig.). 1997. pap. 5.95 (1-57644-043-5) CCC Pubns.

Why God Permits Accidents. Spiros Zodhiates. LC 79-51340. 87p. 1982. pap. 3.99 (0-89957-537-4) AMG Pubs.

Why God Permits Evil: Poems. fac. ed. Miller Williams. LC 77-8711. 69p. 1977. reprint ed. pap. 25.00 (0-7837-7760-4, 2047516) Bks Demand.

Why, God, Why? Joyce Meyer. 64p. (Orig.). 1995. mass mkt. 4.99 (0-89274-845-1, HH-845) Harrison Hse.

Why God Why? Sermons on the Problem of Pain. Justin Tull. (Protestant Pulpit Exchange Ser.). 96p. (Orig.). 1996. pap. 8.95 (0-687-00702-X) Abingdon.

Why Good Girls Don't Get Ahead...but Gutsy Girls Do: Nine Secrets Every Career Woman Must Know. Kate White. 288p. 1996. pap. 12.99 (0-446-67215-7) Warner Bks.

W

Why Good People Do Bad Things. Gerard A. Vanderhaar. LC 93-60403. 160p. (Orig.). 1993. pap. 9.95 (*0-89622-571-2*) Twenty-Third.

Why Good People Do Bad Things: How to Make Moral Choices in an Immoral World. Bruce Hamstra. 272p. 1995. 19.95 (*1-55972-324-6*, Birch Ln Pr) Carol Pub Group.

Why Government Doesn't Work: How Reducing Government Will Bring Us Safer Cities, Better Schools, Lower Taxes, More Freedom, & Prosperity for All. Harry Browne. LC 95-20251. 1995. 19.95 (*0-312-13623-4*) St Martin.

Why Government Is the Problem. Milton Friedman. LC 93-6673. (Essays in Public Policy Ser.: No. 39). 1993. pap. 5.00 (*0-8179-5442-2*) Hoover Inst Pr.

Why Government Programs Fail: Improving Policy Implementation. James S. Larson. LC 79-26917. 140p. 1980. text ed. 45.00 (*0-275-90511-X*, C0511, Praeger Pubs) Greenwood.

Why Governments Grow: Measuring Public Sector Size. Ed. by Charles L. Taylor. LC 83-14390. (Advances in Political Science: An International Ser.: No. 3). (Illus.). 288p. reprint ed. pap. 82.10 (*0-8357-8395-2*, 2034669) Bks Demand.

Why Grace Changes Everything. Chuck Smith. (Orig.). 1995. pap. 8.99 (*1-56507-373-8*) Harvest Hse.

***Why Grow Old?** large type ed. Orison S. Marden. 50p. 1997. pap. 3.50 (*0-89540-340-4*) Sun Pub.

Why Growth Rates Differ: Postwar Experience in Nine Western Countries. Edward F. Denison. LC 67-27682. 1967. pap. 16.95 (*0-8157-1805-5*) Brookings.

Why Growth Rates Differ: Postwar Experience in Nine Western Countries. Edward F. Denison & Jean-Pierre Poullier. LC 67-27682. 516p. 1967. reprint ed. pap. 147.10 (*0-608-01998-4*, 2062654) Bks Demand.

Why Has Japan Succeeded? Western Technology & the Japanese Ethos. Michio Morishima. LC 81-15544. (Illus.). 219p. 1984. pap. text ed. 17.95 (*0-521-26903-2*) Cambridge U Pr.

Why Have I Accepted Islam? A. Chattopadhya. pap. 2.00 (*0-933511-92-2*) Kazi Pubns.

Why Have (More) Children? rev. ed. James Park. (Love among Authentic Persons Ser.: No. 5). 1995. pap. 3.75 (*0-89231-505-9*) Existential Bks.

Why Haven't You Written? Selected Stories, 1950-1970. Nadine Gordimer. 240p. 1993. pap. 11.00 (*0-14-017657-8*, Penguin Bks) Viking Penguin.

Why Hawthorne Was Melancholy. Marion Montgomery. (Prophetic Poet & the Spirit of the Age Ser.: Vol. III). 576p. (Orig.). 1984. 26.95 (*0-89385-027-6*) Sugden.

***Why Healing Happens.** O. T. Bonnett. 209p. (Orig.). 1996. pap. 14.95 (*1-878448-70-6*) MacMurray & Beck.

Why Her Why Now: A Man's Journey Through Love & Death & Grief. Lon Elmer. LC 87-62939. 213p. 1994. pap. 10.00 (*0-944844-47-2*) Signal Elm Pr.

Why Him, Why Now? A Mother, Her Son & AIDS. Louise Walker. 144p. 1995. pap. 12.95 (*0-9646361-0-7*) Rare Visions.

***Why History.** M. Reeves. 1980. text ed. write for info. (*0-582-36119-2*, Pub. by Longman UK) Longman.

Why History? Marjorie Reeves. LC 81-111881. 159p. reprint ed. pap. 45.40 (*0-7837-1597-8*, 2041889) Bks Demand.

***Why History Matters: Life & Thought.** Gerda Lerner. 272p. 1997. text ed. 30.00 (*0-19-504644-7*) OUP.

Why Hitler? The Genesis of the Nazi Reich. Samuel W. Mitcham, Jr. LC 96-16246. 232p. 1996. text ed. 24.95 (*0-275-95485-4*, Praeger Pubs) Greenwood.

Why Hitler Came into Power. Theodore Abel. 352p. 1986. pap. 15.95 (*0-674-95200-6*) HUP.

Why Honor Thy Father & Mother? Class, Mobility, & Family Ties in Later Life. rev. ed. Stephen S. Kulis. LC 91-37723. (Studies on Elderly in America). 288p. 1992. text ed. 70.00 (*0-8153-0526-5*) Garland.

Why Houses, Mrs. K? Blanche Kloman. Ed. by Carol Spelius. (Illus.). (Orig.). 1995. pap. 14.95 (*0-941363-35-X*) Lake Shore Pub.

Why Humanae Vitae Was Right: A Reader. Ed. by Janet Smith. 464p. 1993. pap. 24.95 (*0-89870-433-2*) Ignatius Pr.

Why Humans Have Cultures: Explaining Anthropology & Social Diversity. Ed. by Michael Carrithers. 240p. 1992. 59.00 (*0-19-219227-2*); pap. 16.95 (*0-19-289211-8*) OUP.

Why Humans Vary in Intelligence. Seymour W. Itzkoff. LC 87-8861. (Evolution of Human Intelligence Ser.: Vol. 3). 392p. 1987. 25.00 (*0-913993-09-3*) Paideia MA.

Why Humans Vary in Intelligence. Seymour W. Itzkoff. (Evolution of Human Intelligence Ser.: Vol. III). 392p. 1989. 25.00 (*0-8204-1304-6*) P Lang Pubng.

Why I Am a Bachelor. Conrad Seiler. 1946. pap. 3.25 (*0-8222-1251-X*) Dramatists Play.

Why I Am a Conscientious Objector. John M. Drescher. LC 82-894. (Christian Peace Shelf Ser.). 80p. (Orig.). 1991. reprint ed. pap. 4.99 (*0-8361-1993-2*) Herald Pr.

Why I Am a Democrat. Theodore C. Sorensen. 160p. 1996. 20.00 (*0-8050-4414-0*) H Holt & Co.

Why I Am a Jew. 2nd ed. Edmond Fleg. Tr. by Louise W. Wise from FRE. LC 74-27984. (Modern Jewish Experience Ser.). 1975. reprint ed. 16.95 (*0-405-06711-9*) Ayer.

Why I Am a Jew. Edmond Fleg. Tr. by Louise W. Wise from FRE. LC 75-4124. 1985. reprint ed. pap. 4.95 (*0-8197-0009-6*) Bloch.

Why I Am a Mennonite: Essays on Mennonite Identity. Ed. by Harry Loewen. LC 87-62522. 352p. (Orig.). 1988. pap. 15.99 (*0-8361-3463-X*) Herald Pr.

Why I Am a Monster (Pourquoi Je Suis un Monstre) limited ed. Hughes-Alain Dal. Tr. by Thomas R. Crowe from FRE. 44p. 1990. pap. 4.50 (*0-685-64798-6*) New Native Pr.

***Why I Am a Nazarene.** 144p. 1981. pap. 7.99 (*0-8341-0070-3*) Nazarene.

Why I Am a Separatist. Marcel Chaput. Tr. by Robert Taylor from FRE. LC 75-9634. 101p. 1975. reprint ed. text ed. 59.75 (*0-8371-8107-0*, CHWI, Greenwood Pr) Greenwood.

Why I Am a United Methodist. William H. Willimon. LC 89-27339. 112p. 1990. pap. 7.95 (*0-687-45356-9*) Abingdon.

Why I Am an Abortion Doctor. Suzanne T. Poppema & Mike Henderson. 266p. 1996. 25.95 (*1-57392-045-2*) Prometheus Bks.

Why I Am An Agnostic. Robert G. Ingersoll. (Notable American Authors Ser.). 1992. reprint ed. lib. bdg. 90.00 (*0-685-59998-1*) Rprt Serv.

Why I Am An Agnostic & Other Essays. Clarence Darrow. (Freethought Library). 109p. (C). 1994. pap. 14.95 (*0-87975-940-2*) Prometheus Bks.

Why I Am an Anarchist. Benjamin R. Tucker. 1980. 250.00 (*0-87700-232-0*) Revisionist Pr.

Why I Am an Atheist. Carl Shapiro. 14p. (Orig.). 1979. Incl. audio cass. 15.00 incl. audio (*0-914937-02-2*) Ind Pubns.

Why I Am an Atheist, Including a History of Materialism. 2nd rev. ed. Madalyn M. O'Hair. LC 91-26426. 56p. 1991. pap. 9.00 (*0-910309-98-1*, 5416) Am Atheist.

Why I Am an Infidel. Luther Burbank. (Little Blue Bk.). pap. 5.00 (*0-936128-77-1*) De Young Pr.

Why I Am Catholic: 21 People Give Their Own Reasons. George R. Szews. 48p. (Orig.). 1996. pap. 3.95 (*0-87946-136-5*) ACTA Pubns.

Why I Am Not a Christian. Bertrand Russell. 268p. (C). 1967. pap. 12.00 (*0-671-20323-1*, Touchstone Bks) S&S Trade.

Why I Am Not a Muslim. Ibn Warraq. LC 95-6342. 350p. 1995. 25.95 (*0-87975-984-4*) Prometheus Bks.

Why I Became a Buddhist. William Constandse. 130p. (Orig.). (C). 1985. pap. 6.95 (*0-911527-02-8*) Utama Pubns Inc.

***Why I Became a Catholic.** Eugenio Zolli. 209p. 1997. reprint ed. 19.95 (*0-912141-46-8*) Roman Cath Bks.

Why I Believe. Jake Garn. LC 92-26486. 1992. 11.95 (*1-56236-200-3*) Aspen Bks.

Why I Believe. D. James Kennedy. 164p. 1982. pap. 10.99 (*0-8499-2943-1*) Word Pub.

Why I Believe in a Personal God: The Credibility of Faith in a Doubting Culture. George Carey. 152p. 1991. per. 8.99 (*0-87788-947-3*) Shaw Pubs.

Why I Believe in Christ see IVP Booklets

Why I Believe These Are the Last Days. rev. ed. 180p. (C). 1990. pap. 6.95 (*0-9624517-7-0*) Hearthstone OK.

Why I Came to Alaska. Ray Rebarchek. 1994. pap. 7.95 (*0-533-10726-1*) Vantage.

Why I Came to Judevine. David Budbill. 1987. 7.00 (*0-934834-14-8*) White Pine.

Why I Can Say I Am God. rev. ed. Herbert L. Beierle. 1995. pap. 2.00 (*0-940480-33-6*) UNI Press.

Why I Can't Read Wallace Stegner & Other Essays: A Tribal Voice. Elizabeth Cook-Lynn. LC 96-18557. 172p. 1996. 45.00 (*0-299-15140-9*); pap. 17.95 (*0-299-15144-1*) U of Wis Pr.

Why I Chose to Believe in My Marriage Healing. 2nd rev. ed. Bob Christensen. 76p. 1993. pap. 5.95 (*1-886045-04-6*) Covenant Marriages.

Why I Cough, Sneeze, Shiver, Hiccup, & Yawn. Melvin Berger. LC 82-45587. (Let's-Read-&-Find-Out Science Bk.). (Illus.). 40p. (J). (gr. k-3). 1983. lib. bdg. 14.89 (*0-690-04254-X*, Crowell Jr Bks) HarpC Child Bks.

Why I Couldn't Fight. Lloy A. Kniss. 1974. pap. 2.50 (*0-87813-507-3*) Christian Light.

Why I Don't Eat Faces: The Hierarchical Principle Behind Vegetarianism. David C. Lane. (Occam's Razor Ser.). 54p. (Orig.). 1992. pap. 4.95 (*1-56543-019-0*) Mt SA Coll Philos.

Why I Embraced Islam. Maryam Jameelah. 24p. (Orig.). 1985. pap. 3.00 (*1-56744-418-0*) Kazi Pubns.

Why I Hate Saturn. Kyle Baker. Ed. by Mark Nevelow. (Illus.). 208p. 1990. pap. 14.95 (*0-930289-72-2*, Piranha Pr) DC Comics.

Why I Have Not Written Any of My Books. Marcel Benabou. Tr. by David Kornacker. LC 95-4887. (French Modernist Library). xvii, 111p. 1996. text ed. 25.00 (*0-8032-1239-9*) U of Nebr Pr.

Why I Left America & Other Essays. Oliver W. Harrington. LC 93-25039. (Illus.). 114p. 1994. pap. 12.95 (*0-87805-739-0*); text ed. 25.00 (*0-87805-655-6*) U Pr of Miss.

***Why I Left Boston Movement: (Diary 1984-1992) the Emperor's New Clothes.** Sue Condon. (Orig.). 1995. pap. 3.00 (*1-56794-103-6*, C-2403) Star Bible.

Why I Left Canada: Reflections on Science & Politics. Leopold Infeld. Ed. by Lewis Pyenson. (Illus.). 1978. lib. bdg. 34.95 (*0-7735-0272-6*, Pub. by McGill CN) U of Toronto Pr.

Why I Left Canada: Reflections on Science & Politics. Leopold Infeld. Ed. by Lewis Pyenson. Tr. by Helen Infeld. LC 78-392900. (Illus.). 224p. reprint ed. pap. 63.90 (*0-7837-6911-3*, 2046741) Bks Demand.

Why I Left Orthodox Medicine: Healing for the 21st Century. Derrick Lonsdale. 256p. (Orig.). 1994. pap. 10.95 (*1-878901-98-2*) Hampton Roads Pub Co.

Why I Left Scofieldism. William E. Cox. 1975. pap. 1.50 (*0-87552-154-1*, Pub. by Evangelical Pr) Presby & Reformed.

Why I Left the Roman Catholic Church: Charles Davis: Includes Letters from a Roman Catholic. 2nd ed. Carolynne Simms. 22p. 1987. 4.00 (*0-910309-45-0*, 5080) Am Atheist.

Why I Love This Guy. Tracey Bernstein. 96p. 1995. mass mkt. 4.99 (*0-8217-0108-8*, Zebra Kensgtn); mass mkt. 4.99 (*0-7860-0108-9*, Pinncle Kensgtn) Kensgtn Pub Corp.

***Why I May Never See the Walls of China.** Anthony Howell. 128p. 1986. 24.95 (*0-85646-159-8*, Pub. by Anvil Press UK); pap. 17.95 (*0-85646-160-1*, Pub. by Anvil Press UK) Dufour.

Why I Preach that the Bible is Literally True. W. A. Criswell. Ed. by Timothy George & Denise George. LC 94-47061. (Library of Baptist Classics: Vol. 10). 288p. 1995. 24.99 (*0-8054-1260-3*, 4212-60) Broadman.

***Why I Quit the Baby-Sitters Club.** Betsy Haynes. 1997. mass mkt. 3.99 (*0-06-106449-1*, Harp PBks) HarpC.

Why I Still Believe These Are the Last Days: Are We Rapidly Approaching the End of This Age? I. D. Thomas et al. (Illus.). 250p. (Orig.). 1993. pap. 12.95 (*1-879366-38-X*) Hearthstone OK.

Why I Survived the A-Bomb. Akira Kohchi. (Illus.). 230p. 1989. 13.95 (*0-939484-31-5*) Legion Survival.

Why I Waited: Successful Women Talk about Their Pregnancy Choices, 8 vols. Patricia Sunderland. LC 96-44797. (Teen Pregnancy Prevention Library). (Illus.). 64p. (YA). (gr. 7-12). 1997. lib. bdg. 16.95 (*0-8239-2252-9*) Rosen Group.

Why I'm Afraid of Bees. R. L. Stine. (Goosebumps Ser.: No. 17). 160p. (J). (gr. 4-6). 1994. pap. 3.99 (*0-590-47739-0*) Scholastic Inc.

***Why I'm Not Afraid.** R. L. Stine. (Ghosts of Fear Street Ser.: No. 23). (YA). 1997. mass mkt. 3.99 (*0-671-00852-8*) PB.

Why in the World. Ed. by Donald J. Crump. LC 85-18862. (Books for World Explorers Series 7: No. 1). (Illus.). 104p. 1985. lib. bdg. 12.50 (*0-87044-578-2*) Natl Geog.

Why in the World. National Geographic Staff. Ed. by Donald J. Crump. LC 85-18862. (Books for World Explorers Series 7: No. 1). (Illus.). 104p. 1994. 12.50 (*0-87044-573-1*) Natl Geog.

Why in the World: Adventures in Geography. George Demko & Eugene Boe. 416p. 1992. pap. 14.00 (*0-385-26629-4*, Anchor NY) Doubleday.

Why Information Systems Fail. Henry C. Lucas. LC 74-18395. (Illus.). 141p. reprint ed. pap. 40.20 (*0-317-10726-7*, 2021970) Bks Demand.

***Why Inheritance Taxes Are Illegal.** Max. 50p. (Orig.). 1997. pap. 30.00 (*0-922070-45-8*) M Tecton Pub.

Why Invest in America. Pat Cody. 50p. (Orig.). 1989. pap. write for info. (*0-318-65069-X*) Cristal Globe.

Why Ireland Starved: A Quantitative & Analytical History of the Irish Economy, 1800-1850. Joel Mokyr. (Illus.). 344p. 1985. pap. text ed. 24.95 (*0-04-941014-8*) Routledge Chapman & Hall.

Why Is a Frog Not a Toad? Querida L. Pearce. 32p. 1992. 11.95 (*1-56565-025-5*) Lowell Hse.

Why Is Everybody Always Picking on Me? A Guide to Handling Bullies. Terrence Webster-Doyle. (Education for Peace Ser.). (Illus.). 144p. (J). (gr. 3-9). 1991. pap. 14.95 (*0-942941-22-5*) Atrium Soc Educ.

Why Is God Looking for Friends? Kevin W. Johnson. 112p. (Orig.). (J). (gr. 6-9). 1993. pap. 6.99 (*1-55661-282-6*) Bethany Hse.

Why Is It Called Whitewoman Street? Roscoe's Pre-Canal History. M. Ruth Norton. (Illus.). 80p. (Orig.). 1992. pap. 4.00 (*1-880443-06-6*) Roscoe Village.

Why Is It Raining? Jan Godfrey. (J). (ps-3). 1994. pap. 6.99 (*0-8066-2744-1*, Augsburg) Augsburg Fortress.

***Why Is Mommy's Tummy So Big? Questions Children Ask about Growing Up.** LC 97-14464. (Why Bks.). (J). 1997. write for info. (*0-7894-2058-9*); write for info. (*0-7894-2175-5*) DK Pub Inc.

Why Is My Baby Crying? A Practical Guide to What Bothers Babies & Worries Parents During the First Six Months of Life. Evelyn M. Shukat & Angela Haines. LC 86-40104. (Illus.). 144p. 1987. pap. 6.95 (*0-394-74642-2*, Villard Bks) Random.

Why Is My Child Having Trouble at School? A Parent's Guide to Learning Disabilities. Barbara Z. Novick & Maureen M. Arnold. LC 90-28508. (Illus.). 256p. 1991. 18.50 (*0-394-58509-7*, Villard Bks) Random.

Why Is My Child Having Trouble in School: A Parent's Guide to Learning Disabilities. Barbara Z. Novick & Maureen M. Arnold. LC 95-13772. 272p. 1995. pap. 12.95 (*0-87477-817-4*, Tarcher Putnam) Putnam Pub Group.

Why Is My Name Marisol? A Dominican Children's Story. Josefina Baez. (Marisol Ser.: Vol. 1). (Illus.). 24p. (Orig.). (J). (gr. k-3). 1993. pap. 12.95 (*1-882161-02-5*) Latinarte.

Why Is Night Dark? Susan Mayes. (Starting Point Science Ser.). (Illus.). 24p. (J). (gr. 1-4). 1990. pap. 3.95 (*0-7460-0428-1*, Usborne); lib. bdg. 12.95 (*0-88110-442-6*, Usborne) EDC.

***Why Is Sex Fun? The Evolution of Human Sexuality.** Jared M. Diamond. LC 96-44065. 1997. write for info. (*0-465-03127-7*) HarpC.

***Why Is Snow So White?** F. H. Low-Beer. 64p. 1992. pap. 12.95 (*1-55082-057-5*, Pub. by Quarry Pr CN) LPC InBook.

Why Is Soap So Slippery? And Other Bathtime Questions. Catherine Ripley. (Question & Answer Storybook Ser.). (Illus.). 32p. (J). (ps-3). 1995. 14.95 (*1-895688-34-5*, Pub. by Owl Bks CN); pap. 5.95 (*1-895688-39-6*, Pub. by Owl Bks CN) Firefly Bks Ltd.

Why Is the Air Dirty? Isaac Asimov. (Ask Isaac Asimov Ser.). (Illus.). 24p. (J). (gr. 2-3). 1992. lib. bdg. 17.27 (*0-8368-0743-X*) Gareth Stevens Inc.

Why Is the Grass Green? First Questions & Answers about Nature. Time-Life Books Editors. Ed. by Neil Kagan. (Library of First Questions & Answers). (Illus.). 48p. (J). (gr. k-2). 1993. 14.95 (*0-7835-0858-1*) Time-Life.

Why Is the Grass Green? First Questions & Answers about Nature. Time-Life Books Editors. Ed. by Neil Kagan. (Library of First Questions & Answers). (Illus.). 48p. (J). (ps). 1993. lib. bdg. write for info. (*0-7835-0859-X*) Time-Life.

Why Is the Negro Lynched. Frederick Douglass. Ed. by Al I. Obaba. 49p. (Orig.). (YA). 1991. pap. text ed. 7.95 (*0-916157-78-4*) African Islam Miss Pubns.

***Why Is the Sky Blue?** Sally Grindley. LC 96-35362. (J). 1997. 16.00 (*0-689-81486-0*, S&S Bks Young Read) S&S Childrens.

***Why Is the Sky Blue? And Other Outdoor Questions, Vol. 4.** Catherine Ripley. (Question & Answer Storybook Ser.). (Illus.). 32p. (J). (gr. k-5). 1997. 17.95 (*1-895688-43-4*, Pub. by Owl Bks CN); pap. 6.95 (*1-895688-44-2*, Pub. by Owl Bks CN) Firefly Bks Ltd.

Why Is the Third World Poor? Piero Gheddo. Tr. by Kathryn Sullivan. LC 72-85793. 159p. reprint ed. pap. 45.40 (*0-8357-7075-3*, 2033554) Bks Demand.

Why Is There No Socialism in the United States. Werner Sombart. Tr. by Patricia M. Hocking & C. T. Husbands from GER. LC 76-8031. Orig. Title: Warum Gibt Es in Den Vereinigten Staaten Keinen Sozialismus. 221p. (gr. 13). 1976. text ed. 48.95 (*0-87332-083-2*) M E Sharpe.

Why Is There Salt in the Sea? - Wie Kommt das Salz Ins Meer. Brigitte Schwaiger. LC 87-21934. (European Women Writers Ser.). 134p. 1988. reprint ed. pap. 38.20 (*0-608-02372-8*, 2063014) Bks Demand.

Why Is This Country Dancing? A No-Hope Samba Through Brazil. John Krich. 256p. 1993. 22.00 (*0-671-76814-X*) S&S Trade.

***Why Is This Happening to Me...Again?! ...And What You Can Do About It -- The Primer. Michael Ryce. 1996. pap. 15.00 (*1-886562-29-6*) M Ryce.**

James Redfield, author of THE CELESTINE PROPHESY, says IN THE INTRODUCTION, "A new & original understanding of relationship dynamics...an amazing journey through the world of inner healing...Michael has the gift of being able to synthesize the many diverse elements of human experience & bring them into a clear picture...a coherent system for change!" A synthesis of the ancient Aramaic language & culture that integrates physics, psychology, Naturopathic Medicine & theology into a profound, life-changing event! The techniques taught are easy to grasp & assimilate--& they work! A dialogue between Michael & the troubled Richard is fast paced & enlightening. You will be gripped by the way Richard unravels the blocks that keep him from the love for which he yearns, & rebuilds his understanding of life & relationships. The deep, heartfelt learning that happens for Richard becomes available to the reader through the insights & the wisdom he gains. This unusually intimate conversation between two men, cover topics equally illuminating for both sexes including: * Communication * The Cause of Health * How the Mind Works * The Cause of Pain * The Human Energy System * Healing Inherited Patterns * How to: - Truly Forgive, - Form & Maintain Healing Relationships, - Heal Guilt, Blame, Fear, & Other Wounds. Available for product support such as booksignings & workshops, also a wide variety of tapes. Contact dr. ryce at Heartland 417-273-4838. We want to be on your team! ***Publisher Provided Annotation.***

Why Is Welfare So Hard to Reform? Henry J. Aaron. LC 72-13543. (Studies in Social Economics). 71p. 1973. pap. 10.95 (*0-8157-0019-9*) Brookings.

Why Isaac Laughed: The Biblical Plays of Yehuda Hanegbi. Yehuda Hanegbi. LC 93-50949. 272p. 1994. pap. 25.00 (*1-56821-177-5*) Aronson.

Why Isn't Becky Twitchell Dead? Mark R. Zubro. 1991. pap. 8.95 (*0-312-05996-5*) St Martin.

Why Isn't God Giving Cash Prizes? Lorraine Peterson. LC 82-17866. (Devitional for Teens Ser.: No. 3). (Illus.). 176p. (YA). (gr. 8-12). 1982. pap. 7.99 (*0-87123-626-5*) Bethany Hse.

Why Isn't Johnny Crying? Coping with Depression in Children. Donald H. McKnew, Jr. et al. 1985. pap. 5.95 (*0-393-30240-7*) Norton.

Why It's Great to Be a Girl: Fifty Eye-Opening Things You Can Tell Your Daughter to Increase Her Pride in Being Female. Jacqueline Shannon. 128p. (Orig.). 1994. mass mkt. 8.99 (*0-446-39539-0*) Warner Bks.

Why Jesus: Exploring Relationship with Jesus. 2nd ed. David M. Knight. (Spiritual Growth Through Matthew's Gospel Ser.). 160p. 1987. reprint ed. pap. 6.95 (*0-942971-01-9*) His Way.

Why Jesus Never Had Ulcers: Collected Sermons of Robert M. Holmes. 2nd ed. Robert M. Holmes. Ed. by Krys L. Holmes. (Illus.). 100p. 1988. reprint ed. pap. 7.95 (*0-937017-00-0*) Rainforest Pub.

Why Jesus Taught Reincarnation: A Better News Gospel. Herbert B. Puryear. Ed. by Pat Merrill. 262p. (Orig.). 1993. pap. 14.95 (*0-9634964-9-2*) N Paradigm.

Why Jesus Waits: How the Sanctuary Message Explains the Mission of the Seventh-Day Adventist Church. rev. ed. Herbert E. Douglass. LC 76-10925. 96p. (YA). (gr. 10 up). 1987. pap. 3.95 (*0-945460-00-7*) Upward Way.

Why Jesus Wept: Together with, "The Child of Ephraim" Aleister Crowley. 1993. 45.00 (*1-55818-223-3*, First Impress) Holmes Pub.

Why Jobs Die & What to Do about It: Job Redesign & Future Productivity. Robert N. Ford. LC 79-11307. 238p. reprint ed. pap. 67.90 (*0-317-26950-X*, 2023583) Bks Demand.

Why Johnny Ain't Never Gonna Read! A Challenge to the Nation. Mary F. Pecci. (Illus.). 148p. (Orig.). 1995. pap. 6.95 (*0-943220-10-6*) Pecci Educ Pubs.

Why Johnny Can't Concentrate: Coping with Attention Deficit Problems. rev. ed. Robert A. Moss & Helen D. Dunlap. LC 95-35807. 240p. 1996. pap. 12.95 (*0-553-37541-5*) Bantam.

Why Johnny Can't Putt... Jack Ohman. 144p. 1994. 9.00 (*0-671-87298-2*, Fireside) S&S Trade.

Why Johnny Can't Read. Rudolf Flesch. 1993. reprint ed. lib. bdg. 25.95 (*1-56849-138-7*) Buccaneer Bks.

Why Johnny Can't Read: And What You Can Do about It. Rudolf Flesch. LC 85-45729. 256p. 1986. reprint ed. pap. 11.00 (*0-06-091340-1*, PL 1340, PL) HarpC.

Why Johnny Can't Run, Swim, Pull, Dig, Slither, Etc. Jason Alexander. Ed. by Deirdre J. G. Porter. LC 78-58309. (Illus.). 206p. 1978. pap. text ed. 9.95 (*0-931826-00-4*) Sitnalta Pr.

Why Johnny Can't Tell Right from Wrong. William Kilpatrick. 1993. pap. 12.00 (*0-671-87073-4*, Touchstone Bks) S&S Trade.

Why Johnny Can't Write: How to Improve Writing Skills. Myra J. Linden & Arthur Whimbey. 136p. 1990. 19.95 (*0-8058-0852-3*) L Erlbaum Assocs.

Why Johnny Can't Write: How to Improve Writing Skills. Myra J. Linden & Arthur Whimbey. 136p. 1990. pap. 10.95 (*0-8058-0853-1*) L Erlbaum Assocs.

Why Johnny Still Can't Read: A New Look at the Scandal of Our Schools. Rudolf Flesch. LC 80-8686. 224p. 1983. pap. 10.00 (*0-06-091031-3*, CN 1031, PL) HarpC.

Why Jonathan Doesn't Cry. Shula Modan. (Illus.). (J). (ps-2). 1988. 7.95 (*1-55774-022-4*, Watts) Hemed Bks.

***Why Just Me?** Martyn Godfrey. (YA). pap. 5.99 (*0-590-24919-3*) Scholastic Inc.

Why Kids Kill Parents: Child Abuse & Adolescent Homicide. Kathleen M. Heide. 224p. 1992. lib. bdg. 35.00 (*0-8142-0563-1*) Ohio St U Pr.

Why Kids Kill Parents: Child Abuse & Adolescent Homicide. Kathleen M. Heide. 200p. 1994. pap. 17.95 (*0-8039-7060-9*) Sage.

Why Kill Yourself? My Heart Attack & How to Prevent Yours. Bernard Falk & Roger Blackwood. (Illus.). 192p. 1988. 22.95 (*0-575-04006-8*, Pub. by V Gollancz UK) Trafalgar.

Why Kosher? An Anthology of Answers. Irving Welfeld. LC 96-11441. 224p. 1996. 22.50 (*1-56821-606-8*) Aronson.

Why L. A. Happened: Implications of the '92 Los Angeles Rebellion. Intro. by Haki R. Madhubuti. LC 92-63015. 287p. (Orig.). 1993. pap. 14.95 (*0-88378-094-1*) Third World.

***Why Lapin's Ears Are Long & Other Stories of the Louisiana Bayou.** Illus. by David Catrow. LC 96-53304. 64p. (J). (gr. k up). 1997. 18.95 (*0-531-30041-2*); lib. bdg. 19.99 (*0-531-33041-9*) Orchard Bks Watts.

***Why Leaders Can't Lead.** Bennis. 1997. pap. 20.00 (*0-7879-0943-2*) Jossey-Bass.

Why Leaders Can't Lead: The Unconscious Conspiracy Continues. Warren Bennis. LC 88-46091. (Management Ser.). 192p. text ed. 28.00 (*1-55542-152-0*) Jossey-Bass.

Why Leaders Can't Lead: The Unconscious Conspiracy Continues. Warren Bennis. LC 88-46091. (Management Ser.). 191p. 1990. pap. 20.00 (*1-55542-282-9*) Jossey-Bass.

Why Lenin? Why Stalin? Why Gorbachev? The Rise & Fall of the Soviet System. 3rd ed. Theodore H. Von Laue. LC 92-15870. (C). 1993. text ed. 16.95 (*0-06-501111-2*) Addson-Wesley Educ.

Why Literary Criticism Is Not an Exact Science. abr. ed. Harry T. Levin. LC 68-7221. 27p. 1967. pap. 3.00 (*0-674-95235-9*) HUP.

Why Live the Christian Life? T. B. Maston. LC 96-23690. 200p. 1996. reprint ed. pap. 16.00 (*0-914520-36-9*) Insight Pr.

Why Lord? Suffering & Evil in Black Theology. Anthony B. Pinn. 256p. 1995. 24.95 (*0-8264-0854-0*) Continuum.

Why Love Is Not Enough. 2nd ed. Sol Gordon. 168p. 1990. pap. 6.95 (*1-55850-850-3*) Adams Media.

Why Mammals Have Fur. Dorothy H. Patent. LC 94-28064. (Illus.). 26p. (J). 1995. pap. 14.99 (*0-525-65141-1*, Cobblehill Bks) Dutton Child Bks.

Why Managers Have Trouble Empowering: A Theoretical Perspective Based on Concepts of Adult Development. Wilfred H. Drath. LC 93-70892. 1993. pap. 15.00 (*0-912879-96-3*, 155) Ctr Creat Leader.

Why Margaret Fuller Ossoli Is Forgotten, Vol. II. 1988. pap. 8.50 (*0-944382-01-0*) Golden Heritage Pr.

Why Marijuana Should Be Legal. Ed Rosenthal. LC 96-16079. 1996. pap. 9.95 (*1-56025-110-7*) Thunders Mouth.

Why Market Socialism? Voices from Dissent. Frank Roosevelt & David Belkin. LC 94-19803. 412p. (C). (gr. 13). 1994. text ed. 65.95 (*1-56324-465-9*); pap. text ed. 25.95 (*1-56324-466-7*) M E Sharpe.

***Why Marriage Matters: Reasons to Believe Marriage in a Postmodern Society.** Glenn T. Stanton. LC 97-17776. 1997. pap. text ed. 14.00 (*1-57683-018-7*) NavPress.

Why Marriages Succeed or Fail. Gottman. 1995. pap. 11.00 (*0-671-89932-5*, Pocket Books) PB.

Why Marriages Succeed or Fail. John Gottman & Nan Silver. 1994. 21.00 (*0-671-86748-2*) S&S Trade.

Why Marriages Succeed or Fail: And How You Can Make Yours Last. John Gottman. 1995. pap. 12.00 (*0-684-80241-4*, Fireside) S&S Trade.

Why Marry Her? Society & Symbolic Structures. Luc de Heusch. LC 80-41710. (Cambridge Studies in Social Anthropology: No. 33). 226p. reprint ed. pap. 64.50 (*0-318-34779-2*, 2031640) Bks Demand.

Why Math? Undergraduate Texts in Mathematics. R. D. Driver. (Undergraduate Texts in Mathematics Ser.). (Illus.). 248p. 1996. 24.00 (*0-387-94427-3*) Spr-Verlag.

***Why Me?** Lillian Allen. (Illus.). 24p. (J). pap. 4.95 (*1-895248-02-7*, Pub. by Wmns Pr CN) LPC InBook.

Why Me? Ellen Conford. 156p. (J). (gr. 5 up). 1985. 14.95 (*0-316-15326-5*) Little.

***Why Me?** Jacob Damkani. LC 97-5104. 256p. (Orig.). 1997. pap. 10.99 (*0-88368-440-3*) Whitaker Hse.

Why Me? Sammy Davis, Jr. et al. 1990. mass mkt. 5.95 (*0-446-36025-2*) Warner Bks.

Why Me? Deborah Kent. (J). (gr. 4-7). 1992. pap. 3.50 (*0-590-44179-5*) Scholastic Inc.

Why Me. Pesach Krauss. 192p. 1990. mass mkt. 5.99 (*0-553-28228-X*) Bantam.

Why Me? A Philosophical Inquiry into Fate. Michael Gelven. LC 91-17447. 211p. 1991. 22.00 (*0-87580-164-1*) N Ill U Pr.

Why Me? Help for Victims of Child Sexual Abuse (Even If They Are Adults Now) Lynn B. Daugherty. LC 84-61863. 112p. (Orig.). 1985. pap. 8.95 (*0-941300-01-3*) Mother Courage.

Why Me? How to Heal What's Hurting You. Arleen Lorrance. LC 77-88151. 186p. 1982. 11.95 (*0-916192-19-9*) L P Pubns.

Why Me? Learning to Harness the Healing Power of the Human Spirit. Garrett Porter & Patricia Norris. LC 84-52877. 169p. (Orig.). 1985. pap. 10.95 (*0-913299-19-7*) Stillpoint.

Why Me? The Story of Jenny. Patricia Dizeno. (J). (gr. 7 up). 1976. pap. 3.50 (*0-380-00563-8*, Flare) Avon.

Why Me, God? A Jewish Guide for Coping with Suffering. Lisa Aiken. LC 95-19572. 304p. 1996. 30.00 (*1-56821-535-5*) Aronson.

***Why Me God? A Jewish Guide for Coping & Suffering.** Lisa Aiken. LC 95-19572. 304p. 1997. pap. 24.95 (*0-7657-9954-5*) Aronson.

***Why Me Lord? When Will It Be? If Men Could Really See the Future Today.** Ricardo A. Scott. (Only One Life, One God, One Spirituality Ser.). (Illus.). 200p. (Orig.). Date not set. pap. text ed. write for info. (*1-883427-98-3*, GRTS/RAS 949) Crnerstone GA.

***Why Me, Why This, Why Now?** Norwood. 1995. 2.99 (*0-517-16551-1*) Random Hse Value.

Why Me, Why This, Why Now: A Guide to Answering Life's Toughest Questions. Robin Norwood. 1994. 22.00 (*0-517-59850-7*, Carol Southern Bks) Crown Pub Group.

Why Meddle in Europe & the Orient?, 2 vols., Set. Boake Carter. 1972. 250.00 (*0-8490-1298-8*) Gordon Pr.

Why Meditation? Vimala Thakar. 1994. 9.95 (*81-208-0047-8*) Asia Bk Corp.

Why Men & Women Don't Get Along. Carol L. Rhodes & Norman S. Goldner. 288p. 1992. pap. 13.95 (*0-9632309-6-4*) Somerset MI.

Why Men Are Clueless. Jan B. King. Ed. by Cliff Carle. 1995. pap. text ed. 5.95 (*0-918259-83-5*) CCC Pubns.

Why Men Are the Way They Are. Warren Farrell. 1988. mass mkt. 5.99 (*0-425-11094-X*) Berkley Pub.

Why Men Cheat & What to Do about It. Paul Blanchard. (Why Men Ser.). 1996. pap. 6.95 (*1-884942-02-4*) Carmichael Pubns.

Why Men Commit: Men Explain What It Takes to Turn a Casual Relationship into the Love of a Lifetime. rev. ed. Susan C. Kelley. 192p. 1992. pap. 6.95 (*1-55850-159-2*) Adams Media.

Why Men Don't Date. Otto Haugland. LC 95-80405. 114p. 1995. pap. 10.95 (*1-883697-41-7*) Hara Pub.

Why Men Don't Have a Clue: Resolve Relationship Problems You Once Thought Were Insurmountable. Jan B. King. Ed. by Cliff Carle. 1995. pap. text ed. 7.99 (*0-918259-86-X*) CCC Pubns.

Why Men Fight: A Method of Abolishing the International Duel. Bertrand Russell. LC 72-164623. (Select Bibliographies Reprint Ser.). 1977. reprint ed. 23.95 (*0-8369-5906-X*) Ayer.

Why Men Marry: Insights from Marrying Men. A. T. Langford. LC 94-42508. 1995. 18.95 (*1-57101-008-4*) MasterMedia Pub.

Why Men Marry: Insights from Marrying Men. A. T. Langford. (Illus.). 224p. 1996. 18.95 (*1-57101-022-X*) MasterMedia Pub.

Why Men Rule: A Theory of Male Dominance. Steven Goldberg. LC 93-23346. 266p. 1993. 39.95 (*0-8126-9236-5*); pap. 18.95 (*0-8126-9237-3*) Open Court.

Why Men Shouldn't Marry. Jim Moran. LC 69-10633. 1969. 3.00 (*0-8184-0094-3*) Carol Pub Group.

Why Men Stray, Why Men Stay: What Every Woman Needs to Know about Making the Commitment Last. Susan C. Kelley. LC 96-26130. 1996. pap. text ed. 8.95 (*1-55850-634-9*) Adams Media.

Why Men Watch Football: A Report from the Couch. Bob Andelman. Ed. by Trent Angers. (Illus.). 176p. 1993. 14.95 (*0-925417-14-9*) Acadian Hse Pub.

Why Men Work. Alexander R. Heron. Ed. by Leon Stein. LC 77-70502. 1977. reprint ed. lib. bdg. 23.95 (*0-405-10174-0*) Ayer.

Why Metals Fail-Selected Case Histories. R. D. Barer & B. F. Peters. 346p. 1970. text ed. 176.00 (*0-677-02630-7*) Gordon & Breach.

Why Michael Couldn't Hit: And Other Tales of the Neurology of Sports. Harold L. Klawans. (Illus.). 225p. 1996. text ed. 22.95 (*0-7167-3001-4*) W H Freeman.

Why Milk Pasteurization? Plowing under the Truth. Jean B. Darlington. 18p. 1994. reprint ed. spiral bd. 5.00 (*0-7873-1030-1*) Hlth Research.

***Why Millions Believe.** 20p. 1976. pap. 1.50 (*0-8341-0976-X*) Nazarene.

***Why Millions Tithe.** 28p. 1981. pap. 1.50 (*0-8341-1032-6*) Nazarene.

Why Mine? A Book for Parents Whose Child Is Seriously Ill. Joy Johnson & Marv Johnson. (Illus.). (Orig.). 1981. pap. 3.25 (*1-56123-057-X*) Centering Corp.

Why Mona Lisa Smiles & Other Tales by Vasari. Paul Barolsky. 128p. 1991. 25.00 (*0-271-00719-2*) Pa St U Pr.

***Why Money Was Invented.** Neal S. Godfrey. (One & Only Common Cents Ser.). 32p. (J). 1996. pap. 5.95 (*0-382-39313-9*) Silver Burdett Pr.

Why Money Was Invented. Neale S. Godrey. LC 94-39823. (One & Only Common Sense Ser.). (Illus.). (J). (gr. k-4). 1995. lib. bdg. 15.95 (*0-382-24914-3*) Silver Burdett Pr.

Why Money Was Invented. Neale S. Godrey. LC 94-39823. (One & Only Common Sense Ser.). (Illus.). 32p. (J). (gr. k-3). 1995. 13.95 (*0-382-24913-5*) Silver Burdett Pr.

Why Monkeys Live in Trees. Shirley Climo. (J). 15.00 (*0-06-020773-6*, HarpT); lib. bdg. 14.89 (*0-06-020774-4*, HarpT) HarpC.

Why More English Instruction Won't Mean Better Grammar. Charles-James N. Bailey. (Grammar Ser.: No. 1). (Orig.). (C). 1992. pap. write for info. (*1-881309-01-0*) Orchid Land.

Why Mosquitoes Buzz. (J). Date not set. pap. 3.95 (*0-590-20789-X*) Scholastic Inc.

Why Mosquitoes Buzz in People's Ears. Garrett Christopher. Ed. by J. Friedland & R. Kessler. (Novel-Ties Ser.). 1993. pap. text ed. 14.95 (*0-88122-946-6*) Lrn Links.

Why Mosquitoes Buzz in People's Ears: A West African Tale. Verna Aardema. LC 74-2886. (Illus.). 32p. (J). (ps-3). 1975. pap. 15.99 (*0-8037-6089-2*) Dial Bks Young.

Why Mosquitoes Buzz in People's Ears: A West African Tale. Verna Aardema. Ed. by Leo D. Dillon. LC 77-71514. (Pied Piper Bks.). (Illus.). (J). (ps-3). 1978. pap. 4.95 (*0-8037-6088-4*, Puff Pied Piper) Puffin Bks.

Why Mosquitoes Buzz in People's Ears: A West African Tale. Illus. by Leo D. Dillon & Diane Dillon. 32p. (J). (ps-3). 1992. pap. 4.99 (*0-14-054905-6*) Puffin Bks.

Why Mosquitoes Buzz in People's Ears: A West African Tale. Ed. by Leo D. Dillon. (Illus.). 32p. (J). (ps-3). 1993. pap. 19.99 (*0-14-054589-1*) Puffin Bks.

Why Mosquitos Buzz. (J). Date not set. pap. 2.25 (*0-590-10294-X*) Scholastic Inc.

Why Mosquitos Buzz/Flat Stan. (J). pap. 7.50 (*0-590-20032-1*) Scholastic Inc.

Why Most Investors Are Mostly Wrong Most of the Time. 2nd ed. William X. Scheinman. LC 90-84332. (Illus.). 352p. 1991. pap. 21.00 (*0-87034-099-9*) Fraser Pub Co.

Why Movements Matter: The West. Steven Breyman. (C). 1997. text ed. 42.00 (*0-8133-8811-2*) Westview.

Why Movements Succeed or Fail: Opportunity, Culture, & the Struggle for Woman Suffrage. Lee A. Banaszak. LC 96-2190. (Studies in American Politics). 296p. 1996. text ed. 49.50 (*0-691-02640-8*); pap. text ed. 19.95 (*0-691-02639-4*) Princeton U Pr.

Why Must I Choose? June O'Connell. 143p. (J). (gr. 5-8). 1992. pap. 2.75 (*0-87406-631-X*) Willowisp Pr.

Why My Mother Likes Liberace; A Musical Selection. Diane Wakoski. (Illus.). 76p. (Orig.). 1985. pap. 6.95 (*0-933313-01-2*) SUN Gemini Pr.

Why Nations Act: Theoretical Perspectives for Comparative Foreign Policy Studies. Ed. by Maurice A. East et al. LC 77-22119. (Sage Focus Editions Ser.: No. 2). (Illus.). 234p. reprint ed. pap. 66.70 (*0-8357-4783-2*, 2037720) Bks Demand.

Why Nations Arm. James L. Payne. LC 88-21684. 247p. (C). 1995. 39.95 (*0-915728-11-7*) Lytton Pub.

Why Nations Cooperate: Circumstance & Choice in International Relations. Arthur A. Stein. LC 90-55132. 232p. 1990. 37.50 (*0-8014-2417-8*) Cornell U Pr.

Why Nations Cooperate: Circumstance & Choice in International Relations. Arthur A. Stein. LC 90-55132. 232p. 1993. pap. 14.95 (*0-8014-9781-7*) Cornell U Pr.

Why Nations Go to War. 6th ed. John G. Stoessinger. 239p. (C). 1992. pap. text ed. write for info. (*0-318-70020-4*) St Martin.

Why Nations Go to War. 6th ed. John G. Stoessinger. 1992. pap. text ed. 16.00 (*0-312-08035-2*) St Martin.

***Why Nations Go to War.** 7th ed. Stoessinger. Date not set. text ed. 49.95 (*0-312-17637-6*) St Martin.

***Why Nations War, Vol. 1.** 7th ed. Stoessinger. Date not set. pap. text ed. write for info. (*0-312-11609-8*) St Martin.

Why Nietzsche Now? Ed. by Daniel T. O'Hara. LC 84-48455. (Illus.). 460p. 1985. 31.50 (*0-253-36530-9*) Ind U Pr.

Why No Gospels in Talmudic Judaism? Jacob Neusner. (Brown Judaic Studies). 100p. 1987. 31.95 (*1-55540-198-8*, 14-01-35); pap. 12.95 (*1-55540-199-6*) Scholars Pr GA.

Why Nobody Learns Much of Anything at Church: And How to Fix It. Date not set. mass mkt. 5.99 (*1-55945-902-6*) Group Pub.

Why Not? Sylvia A. Hofsepian. LC 89-39333. (Illus.). 32p. (J). (gr. k-3). 1991. lib. bdg. 13.95 (*0-02-743980-1*, Four Winds Pr) S&S Childrens.

Why Not? Cecily Matthews. LC 93-9280. (Voyages Ser.). (Illus.). (J). 1994. write for info. (*0-383-03727-1*) SRA McGraw.

Why Not. Joel Oppenheimer. 1987. 7.00 (*0-934834-32-6*) White Pine.

Why Not! A Picture Out of Life. Ed. by Sven H. Rossel. Tr. & Intro. by Lori A. Ingalsbe. 120p. (Orig.). (C). 1994. pap. 9.95 (*1-880755-08-4*) Mermaid Pr.

Why Not? Daring to Live the Challenge of Christ. William J. O'Malley. LC 86-14059. 169p. (Orig.). 1986. pap. 6.95 (*0-8189-0504-2*) Alba.

Why Not? The Art of Ginny Ruffner. Bonnie J. Miller. LC 95-36629. (Samuel & Althea Stroum Bks.). (Illus.). 112p. 1996. pap. 29.95 (*0-295-97508-3*) U of Wash Pr.

Why Not? a Book for Every Woman, Boston, 1868 see Proper Bostonian or Sex & Birth Control

***Why Not Abolish the Welfare State?** John C. Goodman et al. 41p. 1994. pap. 10.00 (*1-56808-050-6*, 187) Natl Ctr Pol.

Why Not An Answering Service? Telephone Answering Service Suggestions. rev. ed. 1991. student ed., ring bd. 25.95 (*0-939476-65-7*, Bibliotheca Pr) Prosperity & Profits.

Why Not Be a Mystic. Frank Tuoti. 144p. (Orig.). 1995. pap. 12.95 (*0-8245-1453-X*) Crossroad NY.

Why Not Bunnies at Christmas? Jack N. White. Ed. by Debbie Cavalier. (Illus.). 32p. (Orig.). (J). 1994. pap. text ed. 8.95 (*0-910957-61-4*, BMR05200) Warner Brothers.

Why Not Call It Cow Juice? Steven Krasner. LC 94-96228. 32p. (J). (gr. 2-6). 1994. pap. text ed. 4.95 (*0-9642721-0-5*) Gorilla Prodns.

Why Not Celebrate! Sara W. Shenk. LC 87-80804. 192p. 1987. pap. 9.95 (*0-934672-45-8*) Good Bks PA.

Why Not Eat Insects? A. V. Holt. 1885. 50.00 (*0-317-07183-1*) St Mut.

Why Not Fly Right? Dick Hanley. LC 94-45686. (Illus.). 73p. 1996. pap. 9.95 (*1-56327-108-7*) Prod Press.

Why Not Freedom! America's Revolt Against Big Government. James R. Kennedy & Walter D. Kennedy. LC 95-16936. 400p. 1995. 19.95 (*1-56554-152-9*) Pelican.

Why Not Go to West Africa. Stuart J. Faber. 79p. (Orig.). 1974. pap. 1.95 (*0-89074-006-2*) Charing Cross.

***Why Not Here? Teaching Geography to a New Standard.** Philip J. Gersmehl. (Illus.). 249p. 1996. pap. 15.95 (*1-884136-09-5*) NCFGE.

Why Not? How to Be Doing What You Really Like...& Getting Paid. Jim Ballard. LC 76-14016. (Mandala Series in Education). 180p. (Orig.). 1976. pap. 8.95 (*0-916250-10-5*) Irvington.

Why Not? Jesse Jackson for President 1988: A Voter's Guide. E. Herbert & Kathleen Wright-Bland. 49p. (Orig.). 1987. pap. text ed. 4.95 (*0-944855-00-8*) Tudor Hse Classics.

Why Not Love All of Me? Richard Dunn. 72p. 1991. teacher ed. 1.00 (*0-89693-182-X*, 6-1182, Victor Bks) Chariot Victor.

Why Not Love All of Me? Richard Dunn. 48p. (YA). 1991. student ed., pap. 0.60 (*0-89693-183-8*, 6-1183, Victor Bks) Chariot Victor.

Why Not Me? The Story of Gladys Milton, Midwife. Gladys Milton. LC 92-38694. (Illus.). 128p. 1993. 9.95 (*0-913990-97-3*) Book Pub Co.

Why Not Say It Clearly: A Guide to Expository Writing. 2nd ed. Lester S. King. 1991. 28.95 (*0-316-49353-8*) Little.

Why Not Say It Clearly: A Guide to Scientific Writing. Lester S. King. 1978. pap. 15.50 (*0-316-49346-5*, Little Med Div) Little.

Why Not Speak in Tongues? Tom Thompson. 106p. pap. 4.95 (*0-936369-19-1*) Son-Rise Pubns.

Why Not the Best? The First Fifty Years. Jimmy Carter. LC 96-17579. 1996. pap. 20.00 (*1-55728-418-0*) U of Ark Pr.

Why Not Victory? A Fresh Look at American Foreign Policy. Barry M. Goldwater. LC 79-28300. 201p. 1980. reprint ed. text ed. 38.50 (*0-313-22316-5*, GOWN, Greenwood Pr) Greenwood.

Why Not Write a Little Poetry? Nick Kayafas. Ed. by Helen Graves. LC 85-40889. 64p. 1986. pap. 5.95 (*1-55523-002-4*) Winston-Derek.

Why Nothing Can Travel Faster Than Light....& Other Explorations in Nature's Curiosity Shop. Barry E. Zimmerman & David J. Zimmerman. LC 93-27837. 320p. 1993. pap. 14.95 (*0-8092-3821-7*) Contemp Bks.

Why Nothing Works: The Anthropology of Daily Life. Marvin Harris. Orig. Title: America Now: The Anthropology of a Changing Culture. 208p. 1987. pap. 11.00 (*0-671-63577-8*, Touchstone Bks) S&S Trade.

Why Now? Changes & Turmoil in U. S. Banking. Lawrence J. White. (Orig.). pap. text ed. write for info. (*1-56708-081-2*) Grp of Thirty.

***Why Numbers Count: Quantitative Literacy for Tomorrow's America.** Lynn A. Steen. 1997. 29.95 (*0-87447-503-1*); pap. text ed. 19.95 (*0-87447-577-5*) College Bd.

Why Nutrition: The Nutritional Path to a Vigorus & Healthy Life. Mitchell P. Pries. LC 92-72195. 125p. (Orig.). 1992. pap. 14.95 (*1-879560-13-5*) Harbor Hse West.

Why of Albert Schweitzer. large type ed. Jeanne F. Montague. 16p. 1967. 25.99 (*0-85456-575-2*) Ulverscroft.

Why of Life: Answers Beyond Organized Religion. James Muth. Ed. by Mary Westheimer. 112p. (Orig.). 1994. pap. 6.95 (*1-885001-02-9*) Via Press.

Why? Oh Why Do I Do What I Do (Quotes from Bible or Scriptures) Coming to Christ. Dolores M. Eichler. (Happy Heart Ser.: No. 1-882283-09-0). (Illus.). 48p. (Orig.). pap. 3.00 (*1-882283-02-3*) D M Eichler.

Why? Oh Why Do I Do What I Do (Quotes from Scriptures or Bible) Coming to Christ. Dolores M. Eichler. (Happy Heart Ser.: No. 1-882283-09-0). (Illus.). 45p. (Orig.). reprint ed. pap. 3.00 (*1-882283-00-7*) D M Eichler.

Why, Oh, Why Do You Laugh At Me? Ellie Rosenthal. (J). 1994. 7.95 (*0-533-10765-2*) Vantage.

W

Why, Oh Why? Oh Me, Oh My! The Story of Job. Phil A. Smouse. (Perfect in His Sight Ser.). 32p. 1995. 5.97 (1-55748-651-4) Barbour & Co.

Why on Earth? Jane R. McCauley & National Geographic Society Staff. LC 88-25486. (Books for World Explorers). (Illus.). 96p. (J). (gr. 3-6). 1993. 12.50 (0-87044-701-7) Natl Geog.

Why on Earth. Joan Hodgson. 144p. 1949. reprint ed. pap. 6.95 (0-85487-043-1, Pub. by White Eagle UK) DeVorss.

Why Opossum Is Gray: A Story from Mexico. Janet Palazzo-Craig. (First-Start Legends Ser.). (Illus.). 32p. (Orig.). (J). (gr. k-2). 1997. pap. 4.95 (0-8167-4004-6) Troll Communs.

Why Organizations? How - & Why - People Organize. Bengt Abrahamsson. (Illus.). 312p. (C). 1993. text ed. 45.00 (0-8039-5040-3); pap. text ed. 22.95 (0-8039-5041-1) Sage.

Why Ostriches Don't Fly & Other Tales from the African Bush. I. Murphy Lewis. (World Folklore Ser.). 120p. 1997. lib. bdg. 21.50 (1-56308-402-3) Libs Unl.

Why Our Children Are Killing Themselves. 2nd ed. Mauri Saalakhan. LC 92-85134. 132p. 1993. pap. 10.00 (0-9627854-4-X) Writers Inc.

***Why Our Children Can't Read & What We Can Do About It.** Diane McGuiness. LC 96-24112. 1997. 25.00 (0-684-83161-9) Free Pr.

***Why Our Food Is Safer Through Science: Fallacies of the "Chemical Threat"** Jim E. Riviere. LC 96-70835. 192p. (Orig.). 1997. pap. 12.95 (1-884570-62-3) Research Triangle.

***Why Our Jury System Doesn't Work.** Hunter R. Clark. 224p. 1997. 22.50 (1-55972-410-2, Birch Ln Pr) Carol Pub Group.

Why Our Kids Don't Study: An Economic Analysis of Causes & Proposed Remedies. John D. Owen. 136p. 1995. text ed. 29.95 (0-8018-4925-X) Johns Hopkins.

Why Owl Comes Out at Night: A Story from Haiti. Janet Palazzo-Craig. (First-Start Legends Ser.). (Illus.). 32p. (Orig.). (J). (gr. k-2). 1997. pap. 4.95 (0-8167-4006-2) Troll Communs.

Why Papa Went Away & Other Stories. Phyllis Marten. 112p. (YA). (gr. 8 up). 1988. pap. 4.95 (0-919797-45-8) Kindred Prods.

Why Parents Disagree & What You Can Do about It: Working Together to Raise Healthy Children. Ron Taffel & Roberta Israeloff. 256p. 1995. reprint ed. pap. 10.00 (0-380-72046-9) Avon.

Why Parties? The Origin & Transformation of Political Parties in America. John H. Aldrich. LC 94-36879. (American Politics & Political Economy Ser.). 360p. 1995. pap. text ed. 16.95 (0-226-01272-7); lib. bdg. 48.00 (0-226-01271-9) U Ch Pr.

Why Peace Breaks Out: Great Power Rapprochement in Historical Perspective. Stephen R. Rock. LC 88-33824. xii, 220p. (C). 1989. 37.50 (0-8078-1857-7) U of NC Pr.

Why Pear? limited ed. Denise Newman. (Illus.). 1996. 25.00 (0-9632085-9-4) Em Pr.

***Why People Believe Weird Things: Pseudoscience, Superstition & Other Confusions of Our Time.** Michael Shermer. LC 97-3387. (Illus.). 352p. 1997. 22.95 (0-7167-3090-1) W H Freeman.

Why People Buy. John O'Shaughnessy. (Illus.). 208p. (C). 1989. reprint ed. pap. text ed. 17.95 (0-19-504087-2) OUP.

Why People Do Bad Things in the Name of Religion. Richard E. Wentz. LC 93-32630. 106p. 1992. 15.95 (0-86554-431-X, MUP-H344) Mercer Univ Pr.

***Why People Don't Heal & How.** Caroline Myss. 1997. 25.00 (0-609-60090-7, Harmony) Crown Pub Group.

***Why People Don't Trust Goverment.** Joseph S. Nye. LC 97-20363. 1997. pap. text ed. 18.95 (0-674-94057-1) HUP.

***Why People Don't Trust Government.** Joseph S. Nye et al. LC 97-20363. 1997. write for info. (0-674-94056-3) HUP.

Why People Drink: Parameters of Alcohol As a Reinforcer. Ed. by Miles Cox. LC 87-19775. 336p. 1991. text ed. 34.95 (0-89876-132-8) Gardner Pr.

Why People Kill Themselves: A 1990s Summary of Research Findings on Suicidal Behavior. 3rd ed. David Lester. 464p. 1992. pap. 42.95 (0-398-06236-6) C C Thomas.

Why People Kill Themselves: A 1990s Summary of Research Findings on Suicidal Behavior. 3rd ed. David Lester. 464p. (C). 1992. text ed. 68.95 (0-398-05767-2) C C Thomas.

W

Why People Lack Confidence in Chairs. Norman Fischer. (Morning Coffee Chapbook Ser.). (Illus.). 20p. (Orig.). 1984. pap. 7.50 (0-918273-07-2) Coffee Hse.

Why People Move: Migration in African History. unabridged ed. Philip D. Curtin. (Charles Edmondson Historical Lectures: Vol. 16). 50p. (Orig.). (C). 1995. pap. 5.95 (0-918954-61-4) Baylor Univ Pr.

Why People Obey the Law. Tom R. Tyler. 280p. (C). 1992. reprint ed. pap. text ed. 17.00 (0-300-05235-9) Yale U Pr.

Why People Pay Taxes: Tax Compliance & Enforcement. Ed. by Joel Slemrod. LC 92-28163. 376p. (C). 1992. text ed. 59.50 (0-472-10338-5) U of Mich Pr.

Why People Photograph. Robert Adams. (Illus.). 192p. 1994. 16.95 (0-89381-597-7) Aperture.

Why People Photograph. Robert Adams. (Illus.). 192p. 1996. pap. 12.95 (0-89381-603-5) Aperture.

Why People Recreate: An Overview of Research. David H. Smith & Nancy Theberge. LC 82-83933. 192p. 1987. text ed. 31.00 (0-87322-902-9, BSMI0902) Human Kinetics.

Why Perestroika Failed: The Politics & Economics of Socialist Transformation. Peter J. Boettke. LC 92-18067. 192p. (C). (gr. 13). 1993. 29.95 (0-415-08514-4, A9924, Routledge NY) Routledge.

Why Persimmons & Other Poems. Stanley R. Hopper. LC 86-13913. (Studies in Humanities). 192p. 1987. 27.95 (1-55540-043-4, 00-01-12) Scholars Pr GA.

Why Play Bridge. Marty Bergen. Date not set. pap. 14.95 (0-670-86416-1) Viking Penguin.

Why Poe Drank Liquor. Marion Montgomery. (Prophetic Poet & the Spirit of the Age Ser.: Vol. II). 442p. 1982. pap. 14.95 (0-89385-036-5) Sugden.

Why Police Organizations Change: A Study of Community-Oriented Policing. Jihong Zhao. LC 96-68262. 140p. (Orig.). (C). 1996. pap. 18.50 (1-878734-45-8) Police Exec Res.

Why Policies Succeed or Fail. Ed. by Helen M. Ingram & Dean E. Mann. LC 79-26317. (Sage Yearbooks in Politics & Public Policy Ser.: No. 8). (Illus.). 312p. reprint ed. pap. 89.00 (0-8357-8432-0, 2034695) Bks Demand.

Why Posterity Matters: Environmental Policies & Future Generations. Avner De-Shalit. LC 94-19023. (Environmental Philosophies Ser.). 176p. (C). 1995. pap. 15.95 (0-415-10019-4, C0377) Routledge.

Why Posterity Matters: Environmental Policies & Future Generations. Avner De-Shalit. LC 94-19023. (Environmental Philosophies Ser.). 176p. (C). (gr. 13). 1995. text ed. 49.95 (0-415-10018-6, C0376) Routledge.

Why Potocki? R. T. Risk. (Illus.). 60p. 1981. 50.00 (0-930126-07-6) Typographeum.

Why Poverty Persists in India: A Framework for Understanding the Indian Economy. Mukesh Eswaran & Ashok Kotwal. (Oxford India Paperbacks Ser.). (Illus.). 136p. 1994. pap. 6.95 (0-19-563238-9) OUP.

Why Pray? Spiros Zodhiates. LC 82-71266. 176p. 1995. pap. 5.99 (0-89957-554-4) AMG Pubs.

***Why Pray When You Can.** Wilson. 11.85 (0-687-61391-4) Abingdon.

Why Pray When You Can Take Pills & Worry? Patricia Wilson. 112p. 1994. pap. 9.95 (0-8358-0694-4) Upper Room Bks.

Why Preserve Natural Variety? Bryan G. Norton. 1987. 35.00 (0-317-05526-7); pap. 13.95 (0-317-05216-0) IPPP.

Why Preserve Natural Variety? Bryan G. Norton. Ed. by Marshall Cohen. (Studies in Moral, Political, & Legal Philosophy). 295p. (C). 1988. pap. text ed. 18.95 (0-691-02507-X) Princeton U Pr.

Why Presidents Succeed. Dean K. Simonton. LC 86-28088. 292p. 1987. 35.00 (0-300-03836-4) Yale U Pr.

Why Priests Don't Marry. Edward K. Taylor. (Compact Study Ser.). 14p. (Orig.). 1993. reprint ed. pap. 1.95 (0-935952-93-4) Angelus Pr.

***Why Property Taxes Are Illegal.** Max. 50p. (Orig.). 1997. pap. 30.00 (0-922070-48-2) M Tecton Pub.

Why Psychiatry Is a Branch of Medicine. Samuel B. Guze. 160p. 1992. 26.50 (0-19-507420-3) OUP.

Why? Psychic Development & How! Ed. by Mystic Jhamon Publishers Staff. (Conversations with a Mystic Ser.: No. 2). (Illus.). 176p. 1985. pap. 11.75 (0-933961-05-7) Mystic Jhamom.

Why? Psychic Development & How! Illustration Booklet, Supplement. Ed. by Mystic Jhamon Publishers Staff. (Conversations with a Mystic Ser.: No. 2). (Illus.). 12p. 1985. pap. 1.75 (0-933961-06-5) Mystic Jhamom.

Why Psychology? Adrian Furnham & David Oakley. 128p. 1995. pap. text ed. 14.95 (1-85728-298-1) Taylor & Francis.

Why Psychotherapists Fail. Richard D. Chessick. LC 84-45108. 203p. 1983. 25.00 (0-87668-700-1) Aronson.

Why Psychotherapy? Nini Herman. 165p. (C). 1987. 35.00 (0-946960-71-2); pap. 16.00 (0-946960-72-0) NYU Pr.

Why Punish? Nigel Walker. 184p. 1991. pap. 15.95 (0-19-289219-3) OUP.

Why Punish the Children? A Study of Children of Women Prisoners. Brenda G. McGowan & Karen L. Blumenthal. 124p. 1978. 6.50 (0-318-15376-9) Natl Coun Crime.

Why Race Riots? Earl L. Brown. LC 74-22734. (Labor Movement in Fiction & Non-Fiction Ser.). reprint ed. 29.50 (0-404-58486-1) AMS Pr.

Why Racism Is Used Against Welfare Programs: Why Workers Should Join Welfare Recipients' Struggles. Julia Barnes. 1971. pap. 0.10 (0-87898-068-7) New Outlook.

Why Rat Comes First: The Story of the Chinese Zodiac. Clara Yen. LC 90-26536. (Illus.). 32p. (J). (gr. 3-4). 1991. lib. bdg. 14.95 (0-89239-072-7) Childrens Book Pr.

Why Reaganomics & Keynesian Economics Failed. James E. Sawyer. LC 87-9578. 256p. 1987. text ed. 35.00 (0-312-00532-6) St Martin.

Why Recall? An Example of Politics in the Public Schools. Vera W. Frederickson. (Orig.). 1987. pap. 9.95 (0-9619247-0-5) V W Fredrickson.

Why Record Keeping & Financial Feedback Is Not an Option but a Requirement of Success: How to Conquer the Financial Side of Your Business. Business Development Systems, Inc. Staff. (Self-Improvement Business Ser.). 37p. 1994. pap. text ed. 8.95 (1-884392-08-3) Busn Develop.

Why Recycle? Proceedings of the Recycling Council Annual Seminar, Birmingham, U. K., February 1994. A. K. Rainbow. (Illus.). (C). 1994. text ed. 95.00 (90-5410-367-1, Pub. by A A Balkema NE) Ashgate Pub Co.

Why Regulate Utilities? The New Institutional Economics & the Chicago Gas Industry, 1849-1921. Werner Troesken. LC 96-10150. (C). 1996. 37.50 (0-472-10739-9) U of Mich Pr.

Why Remain Jewish? David C. Gross. (Judaica Ser.). 171p. (YA). (gr. 8 up). 1993. pap. 9.95 (0-7818-0216-4) Hippocrene Bks.

Why Replace a Missing Back Tooth? 2nd ed. Joel M. Berns. LC 93-21223. (Illus.). 24p. 1994. pap. 20.00 (0-86715-231-1) Quint Pub Co.

Why Revival Tarries. Leonard Ravenhill. 176p. 1979. pap. 7.99 (0-87123-607-9) Bethany Hse.

Why Revolution? Theories & Analyses. Clifford T. Paynton & Robert Blackey. 294p. 1971. pap. 22.95 (0-87073-133-5) Schenkman Bks Inc.

Why Rimbaud Went to Africa. David Lerner. 76p. (Orig.). 1990. pap. 5.95 (0-929730-12-7) Zeitgeist Pr.

Why Root Canal Therapy. 2nd ed. Joel M. Berns. LC 93-36688. (Illus.). 1993. pap. 28.00 (0-86715-284-2) Quint Pub Co.

Why Rush Limbaugh Is Wrong: A Look at the Man & the Issues Surrounding Him. Michael Reinhold. LC 95-77891. 275p. (Orig.). 1996. 24.95 (0-9647470-0-6); pap. write for info. (0-9647470-1-4) Mighty Pen.

Why S. A.? Ernst Rohm. 1982. lib. bdg. 59.95 (0-87700-368-8) Revisionist Pr.

Why Salvation. David I. Eatmon. (Illus.). 95p. (Orig.). 1989. pap. write for info. (0-318-65823-2) Hope Homes Pubs.

Why Santa Needs Helpers. William Fletcher. 32p. 1993. 12.95 (0-930753-13-5) Spect Ln Pr.

Why Sarah Ran Away with the Veterinarian. Liz Newell. LC 93-27524. 171p. 1994. 22.00 (1-877946-45-1) Permanent Pr.

Why Satan Wants To Steal God's Word from You. Curtis A. Merriweather. 29p. (Orig.). 1993. pap. 2.95 (0-9623431-4-5) Faith Christ Ch.

Why Say No When the World Says Yes. iii, 204p. (YA). (gr. 8-12). 1993. 12.95 (0-87579-736-9) Deseret Bk.

Why School Health. Kristen Amundson. 16p. 1987. pap. text ed. 0.75 (0-87652-121-9, 021-00211) Am Assn Sch Admin.

Why Schools Fail: The Denial of Individuality & the Decline of Learning. Bruce Goldberg. LC 96-39244. 1996. 19.95 (1-882577-39-6); pap. text ed. 9.95 (1-882577-40-X) Cato Inst.

Why Scots Matters. J. Derrick McClure. 1989. 40.00 (0-685-31783-8, Pub. by Saltire Soc) St Mut.

Why Scottish History Matters. Rosalind Mitchinson. (C). 1989. 39.00 (0-85411-048-8, Pub. by Saltire Soc) St Mut.

Why Scotty? Wynell Hunt. Ed. by Terry Hill. (Illus.). 126p. (Orig.). 1992. pap. 5.99 (0-9634057-3-X) Full Court MI.

Why Seals Blow Their Noses: North American Wildlife in Fact & Fiction. Illus. by Douglas Penhale. LC 94-14816. 70p. 1994. pap. 4.95 (0-89658-250-7) Voyageur Pr.

Why Seashells Sing. Scott Simons & Jamie Simons. (Gods of Olympus Ser.). (Illus.). 32p. (J). (gr. 2-5). 1992. 13.95 (0-382-69122-9); lib. bdg. 14.98 (0-382-69118-0) Silver.

***Why Sex is Fun: The Evolution of Human Sexuality.** Jared Diamond. 1997. 20.00 (0-614-28201-2) Basic.

Why Shoot a Butler. Georgette Heyer. reprint ed. lib. bdg. 22.95 (0-89190-649-5, Rivercity Pr) Amereon Ltd.

Why Should Anyone Believe Anything at All? James W. Sire. LC 94-18632. 220p. (Orig.). 1994. pap. 11.99 (0-8308-1397-7, 1397, Saltshaker Bk) InterVarsity.

Why Should I? Karon Peterson. 29p. 1983. pap. 2.95 (0-913923-47-8) Woodland UT.

Why Should I Be the First to Change? rev. ed. Nancy Missler. (King's High Way Ser.). 124p. 1994. reprint ed. pap. text ed. 4.25 (1-880532-70-0) Koinonia Hse.

Why Should I Eat Better? Simple Answers to All Your Nutritional Questions. Lisa Messinger. LC 92-33752. 224p. (Orig.). pap. 9.95 (0-89529-508-3) Avery Pub.

Why Should I Hire You? How to Do Well in Job Interviews. J. Michael Farr & Susan Christophersen. Ed. by Sara Hall. (Living Skills Ser.). (Illus.). 64p. 1992. pap. 5.95 (1-56370-039-5, HIREU) JIST Works.

Why Should I Nurse My Baby? Pamela K. Wiggins. 64p. 1993. pap. 4.95 (0-9623529-7-7) Prof Pr NC.

Why Should I Speak in Tongues? Aglow. (Booklet Ser.). 32p. 1991. pap. 1.25 (0-932305-97-0, 542004) Aglow Communs.

Why Should "I" Speak in Tongues. Charles Hunter & Frances Hunter. 1976. pap. 6.95 (0-917726-02-2) Hunter Bks.

Why Should Jews Survive? Looking Past the Holocaust Toward a Jewish Future. Michael Goldberg. 224p. 1995. 27.50 (0-19-509109-4) OUP.

Why Should Jews Survive? Looking Past the Holocaust Toward a Jewish Future. Michael Goldberg. 208p. 1996. reprint ed. pap. 12.95 (0-19-511126-5) OUP.

***Why Should Lawyers Have All the Fun? How to File a Lawsuit in 20 Easy to Follow Steps.** Timothy L. Williams. LC 97-60223. v, 150p. (Orig.). 1996. mass mkt. 12.50 (0-9656597-0-4) T Wayne Mgmt.

***Why Should Someone Do Business with You... Rather Than Someone Else?** Sam Geist. 336p. 1997. 24.95 (1-896984-00-2, Pub. by Add & Went CN) ACCESS Pubs Network.

Why Should We Care? Ed. by Donald Evans. LC 89-77583. (Professional Studies in Health Care Ethics). 200p. 1990. text ed. 39.95 (0-312-04481-X) St Martin.

Why Should We Change Our Form of Government: Studies in Practical Politics. Nicholas M. Butler. LC 73-167321. (Essay Index Reprint Ser.). 1977. reprint ed. 19.95 (0-8369-2758-3) Ayer.

Why Should White Guys Have All the Fun? How Reginald Lewis Created a Billion-Dollar Business Empire. Reginald F. Lewis & Blair S. Walker. 336p. 1994. text ed. 22.95 (0-471-04227-7) Wiley.

"Why Should White Guys Have All the Fun?" How Reginald Lewis Created a Billion-Dollar Business Empire. Reginald F. Lewis & Blair S. Walker. LC 94-17864. 1995. pap. text ed. 12.95 (0-471-14560-2) Wiley.

***Why Should White Guys Have All the Fun? How Reginald Lewis Created a Billion-Dollar Business Empire.** Reginald F. Lewis & Blair S. Walker. 336p. 1997. pap. text ed. 6.99 (0-471-17689-3) Wiley.

Why Should You Doubt Me Now? Mary Breasted. LC 93-3561. 1993. 23.00 (0-374-29007-5) FS&G.

Why Shouldn't I. Christopher Howell. LC 77-94479. 63p. 1977. per. 3.75 (0-934332-02-9) LEpervier Pr.

Why Sing? Toward a Theology of Catholic Church Music. Miriam T. Winter. 346p. (Orig.). 1984. pap. 11.95 (0-912405-07-4) Pastoral Pr.

Why Small Businesses Fail: Don't Make the Same Mistake Once. William A. Delaney. 204p. 1984. 16.95 (0-13-959016-1, Busn); pap. 9.95 (0-13-959008-0, Busn) P-H.

Why Small Christian Communities Work. Timothy J. O'Brien & Margaret Gunnell. LC 96-7045. 72p. (Orig.). 1996. pap. 7.95 (0-89390-371-X) Resource Pubns.

Why Small Groups? Ed. by Greg Somerville & C. J. Mahaney. 112p. (Orig.). 1996. pap. 7.00 (1-881039-06-4) People of Destiny.

Why Smart People Do Dumb Things: The Greatest Business Blunders- How They Happened, & How They Could Have Been Prevented. Mortimer Feinberg. 304p. 1995. pap. 12.00 (0-671-89258-4, Fireside) S&S Trade.

Why Snails Have Shells: Minority & Han Folktales of China. Tr. by Jay Han from CHI. LC 93-25769. (Illus.). 80p. (J). (gr. 3-8). 1993. 14.95 (0-8248-1505-X, Kolowalu Bk) UH Pr.

Why So Many Churches? Noah W. Hutchings. 150p. (Orig.). 1992. pap. 7.95 (1-879366-28-2) Hearthstone OK.

Why So Many Churches? Victor H. Prange. 71p. (Orig.). 1985. pap. 4.50 (0-8100-0188-8, 15N0413) Northwest Pub.

Why So Many Denominations? Revelation's Four Horseman Provide an Answer. Mark Finley. LC 93-47907. 1994. pap. 1.99 (0-8163-1218-4) Pacific Pr Pub Assn.

***Why So Slow? The Advancement of Women.** Virginia Valian. LC 96-37029. 1997. 35.00 (0-262-22054-7) MIT Pr.

Why Socialism Works in Cuba. Fidel Castro. 26p. 1988. pap. 0.50 (0-89567-092-5) World View Forum.

Why Some Are Not Healed. Gordon Lindsay. 1967. 1.95 (0-89985-033-2) Christ for the Nations.

Why Some Children Succeed Despite the Odds. Ed. by Warren A. Rhodes & Waln K. Brown. LC 90-49203. 208p. 1991. text ed. 49.95 (0-275-93705-4, C3705, Praeger Pubs) Greenwood.

Why Some Christians Commit Adultery. John L. Sandford. 220p. (Orig.). 1989. pap. 9.95 (0-932081-22-3) Victory Hse.

Why Some Churches Don't Grow: Factors That Might Motivate Those Not Interested in Growth. Roy M. Oswald & Martin Saarinen. pap. 9.50 (1-56699-127-7, OD103) Alban Inst.

Why Some Get Snared in Sexual Traps. Howard Collier. 32p. 1995. pap. 5.00 (1-887939-00-8) VisionQuest Media.

Why Some People Are More Unemployed Than Others: The Strange Paradox of Growth & Unemployment. Goran Therborn. 181p. 1986. text ed. 49.95 (0-86091-109-8, A1065, Pub. by Verso UK); pap. text ed. 14.95 (0-86091-817-3, A1069, Pub. by Verso UK) Routledge Chapman & Hall.

Why Some Positive Thinkers Get Powerful Results. Norman Vincent Peale. 224p. 1987. mass mkt. 5.99 (0-449-21359-5, Crest) Fawcett.

***Why Some Positive Thinkers Get Powerful Results.** Norman Vincent Peale. 1996. pap. 10.00 (0-449-91213-2) Fawcett.

Why Some Positive Thinkers Get Powerful Results. large type ed. Norman Vincent Peale. (Large Print Inspirational Ser.). 320p. 1987. pap. 12.95 (0-8027-2569-4) Walker & Co.

Why Some Therapies Don't Work: The Dangers of Transpersonal Psychology. Albert Ellis & Raymond Yeager. 189p. 1989. 25.95 (0-87975-471-0) Prometheus Bks.

Why South Africa Will Survive. Lewis H. Gann & Peter Duignan. 329p. 1981. text ed. 32.50 (0-312-87878-8) St Martin.

Why Speak in Tongues? The Christian's Three-Fold Ministry Through Prayer in the Spirit. Hobart E. Freeman. 40p. (Orig.). 1969. pap. 1.50 (1-878725-25-4) Faith Min & Pubns.

Why Speak in Tongues & Prophesy see Receiving Power

Why Spider Spins Tales: A Story from Africa. Janet Palazzo-Craig. (First-Start Legends Ser.). (Illus.). 32p. (Orig.). (J). (gr. k-2). 1997. pap. 4.95 (0-8167-4008-9) Troll Communs.

Why Spiders Spin: A Story of Arachne. Scott Simons & Jamie Simons. (Gods of Olympus Ser.). (Illus.). 32p. (J). (gr. 2-5). 1992. 5.95 (0-671-69124-4, Silver Pr NJ); lib. bdg. 10.95 (0-671-69120-1, Silver Pr NJ) Silver Burdett Pr.

Why Squander Illness? Charles M. Carty. 1992. reprint ed. pap. 2.00 (0-89555-051-2) TAN Bks Pubs.

Why Start a Business When You Can Steal One Instead! John Phillips, Sr. 48p. 1994. pap. 7.95 (0-8059-3481-2) Dorrance.

***Why Stay Married? Is It Time for a New Contract?** Ernest F. Pecci. (Illus.). 224p. 1997. per., pap. 12.95 (0-9642637-7-7) Pavior Pubng.

Why Stocks Go up & Down: A Guide to Sound Investing. 2nd ed. Pike & William H. Pike. LC 95-40724. (Investments Ser.). 260p. 1996. text ed. 28.95 (0-538-86138-X) S-W Pub.

An Asterisk (*) at the beginning of an entry indicates that the title is appearing in BIP for the first time.

Why Stress Keeps Returning: A Spiritual Response. Douglas C. Vest. Ed. by Maureen Callaghan. LC 91-13250. 176p. 1991. pap. 11.95 (*0-8294-0713-8*) Loyola Pr.

Why Students Fail. Austin Hill. LC 91-91927. 68p. (Orig.). 1992. pap. 8.00 (*0-9635009-0-2*) A Hill TX.

Why Study Christian Science as a Science? Max Kappeler. 30p. 1973. reprint ed. pap. 4.50 (*0-85241-040-9*) Kappeler Inst Pub.

Why Sue: A Journey Through Life's Darkest Days. Herb Mayes. 142p. (Orig.). 1995. pap. write for info. (*1-885591-93-4*) Morris Pubng.

Why Suffer? How I Overcame Illness & Pain Naturally. 2nd ed. Ann Wigmore. LC 85-1332. 200p. pap. 5.95 (*0-89529-286-6*) Avery Pub.

Why Suffer? The Answer of Jesus. Marck G. Boyer. (Orig.). 1994. pap. text ed. 11.95 (*1-56929-019-9*) Pastoral Pr.

Why Suffer in Silence? How to Control Those Tension Headaches. William W. Won. (Illus.). 88p. 1995. pap. 9.00 (*0-8059-3600-9*) Dorrance.

Why Suffering? Paul W. Nisly. 1980. pap. text ed. 1.99 (*0-8361-1914-2*) Herald Pr.

Why Suicide? Answers to 200 of the Most Frequently Asked Questions about Suicide, Attempted Suicide, & Assisted Suicide. Eric Marcus. LC 95-33431. 240p. 1996. pap. 11.00 (*0-06-251166-1*) Harper SF.

***Why Sun & Moon Live in the Sky.** Shannon Dugan. (Illus.). (J). 1997. pap. 11.95 (*1-57532-082-7*) Press-Tige Pub.

***Why Sun & Moon Live in the Sky: Folktales from Highlights.** Highlights for Children Staff. (J). Date not set. pap. 3.95 (*1-56397-610-2*) Boyds Mills Pr.

Why Switzerland? 2nd ed. Jonathan Steinberg. (Illus.). 250p. (C). 1996. text ed. 59.95 (*0-521-48170-8*) Cambridge U Pr.

Why Switzerland? 2nd ed. Jonathan Steinberg. (Illus.). 250p. (C). 1996. pap. text ed. 19.95 (*0-521-48453-7*) Cambridge U Pr.

Why Syria Goes to War: Thirty Years of Confrontation. Fred H. Lawson. LC 96-17769. (Studies in Political Economy). (Illus.). 224p. 1996. 29.95 (*0-8014-2373-2*) Cornell U Pr.

Why Systems Fail: And How to Make Sure Yours Doesn't. David A. Turbide. LC 95-44985. 1996. 42.95 (*0-8311-3059-8*) Indus Pr.

Why Tax Employee Benefits? Intro. by Dallas L. Salisbury. LC 84-1683. 120p. (Orig.). 1984. pap. 15.95 (*0-86643-036-9*) Empl Benefit Res Inst.

***Why Taxes on Tobacco Are Illegal.** Max. 50p. (Orig.). 1997. pap. 30.00 (*0-922070-47-4*) M Tecton Pub.

Why Teach? A First Look at Working with Young Children. Joanne Hendrick. LC 87-60267. 32p. 1987. pap. 3.00 (*0-935989-05-6*, NAEYC #220) Natl Assn Child Ed.

***Why Teach? Why Music? Why Me?** Ira Collins & Music Educators National Conference Staff. 8p. (Orig.). (C). 1992. pap. write for info. (*1-56545-070-1*, 4007) Music Ed Natl.

Why Teachers Organized. Wayne J. Urban. LC 82-11160. 203p. reprint ed. pap. 57.90 (*0-318-39793-5*, 2033196) Bks Demand.

Why Teams Can Fail & What to Do about It: Essential Tools for Anyone Implementing Self-Directed Work Teams. Marsha L. Willard. 225p. 1995. text ed. 30.00 (*0-7863-0423-5*) Irwin Prof Pubng.

Why Teams Don't Work: What Went Wrong & How to Make It Right. Harvey Robbins & Michael Finley. LC 95-3270. 240p. 1995. 24.95 (*1-56079-497-6*, Petersons Pacesetter) Petersons.

Why Teams Don't Work: What Went Wrong & How to Make It Right. Harvey Robbins. 229p. 1996. pap. text ed. 14.95 (*1-56079-704-5*) Petersons.

Why Term Limits? Because They Have It Coming. John Armor. 174p. 1995. pap. write for info. (*0-915463-70-9*) Jameson Bks.

Why Terrorism. Joe E. Pierce. 160p. (Orig.). 1991. pap. 8.50 (*0-913244-25-2*) Hapi Pr.

Why Test? 1983. 0.50 (*0-939418-52-5*) Ferguson-Florissant.

***Why the Allies Won.** Richard Overy. 428p. 1997. pap. 15.95 (*0-393-31619-X*) Norton.

Why the Baal Shem Tov Laughed: Fifty-Two Stories about Our Great Chasidic Rabbis. Sterna Citron. LC 92-39644. 320p. 1993. 27.50 (*0-87668-350-2*) Aronson.

Why the Bible Is the Word of God. Gordon Lindsay. (Literature Crusade Ser.). 1965. pap. 0.95 (*0-89985-356-0*) Christ for the Nations.

Why the Bible Is the Word of God (La Biblia el la Palabrade Dios Por Que? Gordon Lindsay. (Literature Crusade Ser.). (SPA.). 1965. pap. 0.95 (*0-89985-369-2*) Christ for the Nations.

Why the Boom Went Bust: An Analysis of the Saudi Government. Mohammed H. Siddig. 120p. (Orig.). 1995. pap. write for info. (*1-57502-004-1*) Morris Pubng.

Why the Boundary of a Round Drop Becomes a Curve of Order Four. A. N. Varchenko & P. I. Etingof. LC 92-20985. (University Lectures: Vol. 3). 72p. 1992. 15.00 (*0-8218-7002-5*, ULECT/3) Am Math.

Why the Chicken Crossed the Road. David Macaulay. (Illus.). 32p. (J). (gr. 4-6). 1987. 13.95 (*0-395-44241-9*, Clarion Bks) HM.

Why the Chicken Crossed the Road. David Macaulay. (J). 1991. pap. 6.95 (*0-395-58411-6*) HM.

Why the Chimes Rang. Raymond M. Alden. (Illus.). 44p. 1989. reprint ed. lib. bdg. 17.95 (*0-89966-595-0*) Buccaneer Bks.

Why the Chimes Rang. Raymond M. Alden. LC 94-78669. (Illus.). 38p. 1994. reprint ed. 14.95 (*1-878208-46-2*) Guild Pr IN.

Why the Church Must Teach. Lucien E. Coleman, Jr. LC 84-4966. 1994. pap. 6.99 (*0-8054-3234-5*, 4232-34) Broadman.

Why the Church Will Not Go Through the Great Tribulation. Rob Lindsted & Emil Gaverluk. 40p. (Orig.). 1994. pap. 2.50 (*1-879366-58-4*) Hearthstone OK.

Why the Civil War Came. Ed. by Gabor S. Boritt. 256p. 1996. 25.00 (*0-19-507941-8*) OUP.

***Why the Civil War Came.** Ed. by Gabor S. Boritt. 272p. 1997. reprint ed. pap. 13.95 (*0-19-511376-4*) OUP.

Why the Cold War Ended: A Range of Interpretations. Ed. by Ralph Summy & Michael E. Salla. LC 94-47428. (Contributions in Political Science Ser.: No. 353). 288p. 1995. text ed. 59.95 (*0-313-29569-7*, Greenwood Pr) Greenwood.

Why the Confederacy Lost. Gabor S. Boritt. 160p. 1992. 25.00 (*0-19-507405-X*) OUP.

Why the Confederacy Lost. Ed. by Gabor S. Boritt. 224p. (C). 1993. reprint ed. pap. 11.95 (*0-19-508549-3*, 11094) OUP.

***Why the Coqui Sings Little Book Level B.** Pals. (J). 1996. ring bd. 4.33 (*0-201-85359-0*) Addison-Wesley.

Why the Crab Has No Head: An African Folktale. Barbara Knutson. (Carolrhoda Picture Bks.). (Illus.). 24p. (J). (ps-3). 1987. pap. 4.95 (*0-87614-489-X*, Carolrhoda); lib. bdg. 13.13 (*0-87614-322-2*, Carolrhoda) Lerner Group.

Why the Dragon Breathes Fire. Ciwa Griffiths. (Illus.). 70p. (J). (gr. 3-12). 1995. 18.00 (0-9630709-1-6) Wide Range. Meet Lafalotchu, Luvmetoochoo, Whatsrongkee, Efalotum, & other characters in these fourteen stories by Ciwa Griffiths, who knows that writing is about poetry & imagination & reading out loud. Griffiths is in touch with the vital concerns of children as she spins tales of Spider, who cries because she feels ugly & unwanted; Gotabagtee, who gets in trouble because he forgets his chores; & a whole pantheon of friends who sometimes argue but eventually all work together to solve problems. Generously & brightly illustrated with appealing watercolors, WHY THE DRAGON BREATHES FIRE is a welcome addition to any child's library. "This delightful book answers all those questions you never thought to ask -- Who DOES OWN the Pot of Gold? Why do mortals have itchy feet? How DID angels earn their halos? And more. Much more. Ciwa Griffith's explanation of the cosmos will delight both young & old. Beautifully written. Imaginative. Fun to read."--Mary Jane Roberts. To order: Wide Range Press, 4000-3B Calle Sonora W., Laguna Hills, CA 92653. ***Publisher Provided Annotation.***

Why the Earth Quakes: The Story of Earthquakes & Volcanoes. Matthys Levy & Mario G. Salvadori. (Illus.). 256p. 1995. 25.00 (*0-393-03774-6*) Norton.

Why the Earth Quakes: The Story of Earthquakes & Volcanoes. Matthys Levy. 224p. 1997. pap. 13.00 (*0-393-31527-4*) Norton.

Why the Green Nigger? Re-Mything Genesis. Elizabeth Dodson Gray. LC 79-89193. x, 166p. 1979. 14.95 (*0-934512-01-9*) Roundtable Pr.

Why the Groundhog Fears Her Shadow. Ava L. Haymon. Ed. by Robert Bixby. 27p. 1994. pap. text ed. 6.00 (*1-882983-14-9*) March Street Pr.

Why the Homeless Don't Have Homes & What to Do about It. Micheal Elliott. LC 93-4208. 152p. (Orig.). 1993. pap. 9.95 (*0-8298-0965-1*) Pilgrim OH.

***Why the Income Tax Is Illegal.** Max. 50p. (Orig.). 1997. pap. 30.00 (*0-922070-46-6*) M Tecton Pub.

Why the Jews? The Reason for Anti-Semitism. Dennis Prager & Joseph Telushkin. 340p. 1985. pap. 12.00 (*0-671-55624-X*, Touchstone Bks) S&S Trade.

Why the Left Is Not Right: The Religious Left - Who They Are & What They Believe. Ronald H. Nash. 208p. 1996. pap. 10.99 (*0-310-21015-1*) Zondervan.

Why the Moon Only Glows. Dina Rosenfeld. (Illus.). 32p. (J). (ps-1). 1992. 8.95 (*0-922613-00-1*); pap. 6.95 (*0-922613-01-X*) Hachai Pubns.

Why the North Star Stands Still. William R. Palmer. LC 57-11627. (Illus.). 118p. 1978. pap. 6.50 (*0-915630-12-5*) Zion.

Why the North Won the Civil War. David H. Donald. 1996. pap. 9.00 (*0-684-82506-6*) S&S Trade.

Why the North Won the Civil War. Ed. by David Herbert Donald. (Paperbook Series in History). (Illus.). 128p. 1993. reprint ed. pap. text ed. 2.25 (*1-877891-12-6*) Paperbook Pr Inc.

Why the Novel Matters: A Postmodern Perplex. Ed. by Mark Spilka & Caroline McCracken-Flesher. LC 89-45857. 400p. 1990. 14.95 (*0-253-35554-0*) Ind U Pr.

Why the Pina Has a Hundred Eyes & Other Classic Philippine Folk Tales about Fruits. Neni S. Romana-Cruz. (Illus.). (J). (gr. 3-7). 1995. 11.95 (*971-630-026-3*, Pub. by Tahanan Pacific PH) Paperworks.

Why the Poor Get Richer & the Rich Slow Down: Essays in the Marshallian Long Period. Walt W. Rostow. 394p. 1980. text ed. 25.00 (*0-292-73012-8*) U of Tex Pr.

Why the Possum's Tail Is Bare: And Other North American Indian Nature Tales. Ed. by James E. Connolly. LC 84-26871. (Illus.). 64p. (J). (gr. 4-8). 1992. reprint ed. 15.95 (*0-88045-069-X*); reprint ed. pap. 7.95 (*0-88045-107-6*) Stemmer Hse.

Why the Possum's Tail Is Bare & Other Classic Southern Stories. Jimmy N. Smith. 224p. (Orig.). 1993. pap. 10.00 (*0-380-76857-7*) Avon.

Why the Religious Right Is Wrong: About the Separation of Church & State. Robert Boston. 257p. (C). 1994. pap. 17.95 (*0-87975-834-1*) Prometheus Bks.

***Why the Righteous Are Afflicted: Job, the Mystery Revealed.** R. M. Marinari. 152p. (Orig.). 1996. pap. 8.99 (*1-57502-367-9*, PO1176) Morris Pubng.

Why the River Disappears. Marcia Southwick. LC 89-61328. (Poetry Ser.). 1989. pap. 11.95 (*0-88748-099-3*) Carnegie-Mellon.

Why the Sea Is Salt. Illus. by Patrice Aggs. LC 92-53138. 32p. (J). (ps up). 1993. 14.95 (*1-56402-183-1*) Candlewick Pr.

Why the Sky Is Far Away: A Nigerian Folktale. Mary-Joan Gerson. (J). (ps-3). 1992. 15.95 (*0-316-30852-8*, Joy St Bks) Little.

Why the Sky Is Far Away: A Nigerian Folktale. Illus. by Carla Golembe. (J). (ps-3). 1995. pap. 4.95 (*0-316-30874-9*) Little.

Why the South Lost the Civil War. Richard E. Beringer et al. LC 85-8638. (History Book Club Selection). (Illus.). 608p. (C). 1991. text ed. 34.95 (*0-8203-0815-3*) U of Ga Pr.

Why the South Lost the Civil War. Richard E. Beringer et al. LC 85-8638. (Brown Thrasher Bks.). (Illus.). 608p. (C). 1991. pap. 22.95 (*0-8203-1396-3*) U of Ga Pr.

Why the South Lost the War: And Other Things I Don't Understand. Bo Whaley. LC 92-5854. (Illus.). 160p. (Orig.). 1992. pap. 6.95 (*1-55853-161-0*) Rutledge Hill Pr.

Why the Stars Come Out at Night. Jeanne Daniels. (J). (ps up). 1995. 14.95 (*1-885108-05-2*) Armstrong CT.

Why the Sun & Moon Live. Daynell. 14.95 (*0-395-29609-9*) HM.

Why the Sun & Moon Live in the Sky. Illus. & Retold by Niki Daly. LC 93-47304. 32p. (J). (ps up). 1995. 15.00 (*0-688-13331-2*); lib. bdg. 14.93 (*0-688-13332-0*) Lothrop.

Why the Sun & Moon Live in the Sky. Elphinstone Dayrell. (Illus.). 32p. (J). (gr. k-3). 1990. pap. 5.95 (*0-395-53963-3*) HM.

Why the Sun Cannot Set: New & Selected Poems. Mary Ferrari. 1994. 20.00 (*1-882413-05-9*); pap. 12.00 (*1-882413-04-0*) Hanging Loose.

Why the Tides Ebb & Flow. Joan Bowden. (J). (gr. k-3). 1979. 16.00 (*0-395-28378-7*) HM.

Why the Tides Ebb & Flow. Joan Bowden. (Illus.). 48p. (J). (gr. k-3). 1990. pap. 5.95 (*0-395-54952-3*) HM.

Why the Tithe? Edward L. Haygood. (Mini-Bks.). 32p. 1982. pap. 0.99 (*0-89274-128-7*, HH-128) Harrison Hse.

***Why the Tree Loves the Ax.** Jim Lewis. LC 97-16010. 1998. write for info. (*0-609-60109-1*) Crown Pub Group.

Why the United States Does Not Have a National Health Program. Ed. by Vicente Navarro. (Policy, Politics, Health & Medicine Ser.). 266p. 1992. pap. text ed. 26.00 (*0-89503-105-1*) Baywood Pub.

Why the United States Lacks a National Health Insurance Program. Nicholas Laham. 216p. 1993. pap. text ed. 18.95 (*0-275-94779-3*, Praeger Pubs) Greenwood.

Why the United States Lacks a National Health Program. Nicholas Laham. LC 93-3167. (Contributions in Political Science Ser.: No. 331). 216p. 1993. Alk. paper. text ed. 59.95 (*0-313-28745-7*, GM8745) Greenwood.

Why the Vietcong Fought: A Study of Motivation & Control in a Modern Army in Combat. William D. Henderson. LC 79-7062. (Contributions in Political Science Ser.: No. 31). 163p. 1980. text ed. 45.00 (*0-313-20708-9*, HVC/, Greenwood Pr) Greenwood.

Why the Wealthy Give: The Culture of Elite Philanthropy. Francie Ostrower. LC 95-2854. 208p. 1996. text ed. 35.00 (*0-691-04434-1*) Princeton U Pr.

***Why the Wealthy Give: The Culture of Elite Philanthropy.** Francie Ostrower. 203p. 1996. pap. text ed. 14.95 (*0-691-01588-0*) Princeton U Pr.

Why the Worst Sinners Make the Best Saints: When Sin Is Grace - When Grace Is Sin. Michael Lister. 100p. 1996. pap. 9.95 (*1-888146-00-1*) St Matthews.

Why Theology? Ed. by Werner Jeanrond & Jean-Pierre Joshua. (Concilium Ser.). 135p. (Orig.). 1994. pap. 15.00 (*0-88344-881-5*) Orbis Bks.

Why There Are No Clitics. Daniel Everett. LC 95-78751. (Publications in Linguistics). (Orig.). fiche write for info. (*1-55671-980-9*) Summer Instit Ling.

Why There Are No Clitics. Daniel Everett. LC 95-78751. (Publications in Linguistics). (Orig.). 1996. pap. 25.00 (*1-55671-004-6*) Summer Instit Ling.

Why? There Is More to You Than Meets the Eye. Jean E. Beckman. (Illus.). 50p. (Orig.). (J). (gr. 9-12). 1981. pap. 4.25 (*0-941992-00-4*) Los Arboles Pub.

Why There Is No Arguing in Heaven: A Mayan Myth. Deborah N. Lattimore. LC 87-35045. (Illus.). 40p. (J). (gr. 1-5). 1989. lib. bdg. 14.89 (*0-06-023718-X*) HarpC Child Bks.

Why There Must Be a Revolution in Quebec. Leandre Bergeron. (Illus.). 144p. pap. 4.95 (*0-919600-16-6*, Pub. by NC Press CN) U of Toronto Pr.

Why There Never Was a "Talmud of Caesarea" Saul Lieberman's Mistake. Jacob Neusner. LC 94-35372. (South Florida Studies in the History of Judaism: No. 108). 193p. 1994. 69.95 (*0-7885-0047-3*, 240108) Scholars Pr GA.

Why They Are Criminals. William A. Grable. 220p. 1995. pap. 9.50 (*1-887508-01-5*) MGM Sahara.

Why They Buy: American Consumers Inside & Out. Robert B. Settle & Pamela Allreck. 351p. 1989. pap. text ed. 19.95 (*0-471-62127-7*) Wiley.

Why They Call It Politics: A Guide to America's Government. 5th ed. Robert T. Sherrill. 579p. (C). 1990. pap. text ed. 20.00 (*0-15-596004-0*) HB Coll Pubs.

Why They Fear Nation of Islam & Rasta Fari: The Truth Is No Offense, Nor Is It a Shame. Ricardo A. Scott. (Ras Cardo Speaks Truths & Rights Ser.). 75p. Date not set. pap. write for info. (*1-883427-61-4*) Crnerstone GA.

***Why They Killed Big Boy: And Other Stories.** Michael Perry. (Orig.). 1996. pap. 9.95 (*0-9631695-3-X*) Whist & Jugg.

Why They Left: German Immigration from Prussia to Missouri. rev. ed. Anita M. Mallinckrodt. (Illus.). 34p. 1989. reprint ed. pap. 5.25 (*0-931227-03-8*) Mallinckrodt Comm.

Why They Scratch Themselves: How to Understand Baseball. John W. Hood. LC 94-94184. (Illus.). (Orig.). 1994. pap. 9.95 (*0-9640870-4-9*) Forward Press.

Why Things Are: Answers to Every Essential Question in Life. Joel Achenbach. 336p. 1991. pap. 9.00 (*0-345-36224-1*, Ballantine Trade) Ballantine.

Why Things Are & Why Things Aren't: The Answers to Life's Greatest Mysteries. Joel Achenbach. (Illus.). 416p. 1996. pap. 11.00 (*0-345-39288-4*) Ballantine.

***Why Things Are the Way They Are.** B. S. Chandrasekhar. (Illus.). 272p. (C). 1997. text ed. 59.95 (*0-521-45039-X*) Cambridge U Pr.

***Why Things Are the Way They Are.** B. S. Chandrasekhar. (Illus.). 272p. (C). 1997. pap. text ed. 24.95 (*0-521-45660-6*) Cambridge U Pr.

Why Things Are the Way They Are: Self-Direction vs. the System. Erica Carle. 168p. 1996. 16.00 (*0-8059-3944-X*) Dorrance.

***Why Things Bite Back.** Edward Tenner. 1997. pap. 13.00 (*0-679-74756-7*, Vin) Random.

Why Things Bite Back: Technology & the Revenge of Unintended Consequences. Edward Tenner. LC 95-38036. 352p. 1996. 26.00 (*0-679-42563-2*) Knopf.

Why Things Go Wrong: Deming Philosophy in Dozen Ten-Minute Sessions. Gary Fellers. LC 94-4769. 112p. 1994. 13.95 (*1-56554-070-0*) Pelican.

Why Things Work: Case Histories in Development. Ed. by Scott B. Halstead & Julia A. Walsh. (Illus.). 234p. (C). 1990. pap. text ed. 39.00 (*0-944903-05-3*) Adams Pub Group.

Why This Horse Won't Drink: How to Win - & Keep - Employee Commitment. Ken Matejka. LC 90-53215. 256p. 1990. 22.95 (*0-8144-5005-9*) AMACOM.

Why This Skeptic Is a Christian. Claud C. Crawford. LC 88-92019. 100p. (Orig.). 1989. pap. 9.95 (*0-933697-06-6*) Claud Crawford.

***Why Toast Falls Jelly-Side Down: Zen & the Art of Physics Demonstrations.** Robert Ehrlich. LC 96-42053. 224p. 1997. text ed. 35.00 (*0-691-02891-5*); pap. text ed. 14.95 (*0-691-02887-7*) Princeton U Pr.

***Why Toast Lands Jelly-Side Down: Zen & the Art of Physics Demonstrations.** Robert Ehrlich. 1997. 14.95 (*0-614-27636-5*) Princeton U Pr.

***Why Toast Lands Jelly-Side Down: Zen & the Art of Physics Demonstrations.** Robert Ehrlich. 1997. 35.00 (*0-614-27637-3*) Princeton U Pr.

Why Tongues? Kenneth E. Hagin. 1975. pap. 0.75 (*0-89276-051-6*) Hagin Ministries.

Why TQM Fails & What to Do about It. Mark G. Brown et al. 252p. 25.00 (*0-614-04831-1*, DJ20H) Assn Qual & Part.

Why TQM Fails & What to Do about It. Mark G. Brown et al. 276p. 1994. text ed. 30.00 (*0-7863-0140-6*) Irwin Prof Pubng.

Why Trade It In? 4th ed. George Fremon & Suzanne Fremon. (Illus.). 176p. 1991. pap. 8.95 (*0-89709-194-9*) Liberty Pub.

Why Traders Lose, How Traders Win: Timing Futures Trades with Daily Market Sentiment. Jake Bernstein. 250p. 1992. 37.50 (*1-55738-252-2*) Irwin Prof Pubng.

Why Turtles Have Shells. Gerrie L. Cockburn. Ed. by Ian Cockburn. (Friendship Ser.). (Illus.). 31p. (Orig.). (J). (gr. k-4). pap. 5.95 (*1-887461-00-0*) Cockburn Pub.

Why Us? When Bad Things Happen to God's People. Warren W. Wiersbe. LC 83-19117. 160p. (Orig.). (YA). (gr. 10). 1987. pap. 7.99 (*0-8007-5208-2*) Revell.

Why Vegan: The Ethics of Eating & the Need for Change. rev. ed. Kath Clements. 128p. 1995. pap. 10.95 (*0-946097-30-5*) LPC InBook.

***Why Vegetarian? A Healthy, Humane, & Environmentally Friendly Approach to Food.** Lynda Dickinson. 111p. (Orig.). 1997. pap. 11.95 (*0-919574-89-0*) Gordon Soules Bk.

Why Vegetarianism? write for info. (*0-938924-19-2*) Sri Shirdi Sai.

Why Video Works: New Applications for Management. John A. Bunyan. LC 86-21106. (Professional Librarian Ser.). (Illus.). 203p. 1988. 40.00 (*0-86729-079-X*, Hall Reference) Macmillan.

Why Vietnam? Prelude to America's Albatross. Archimedes L. Patti. LC 80-51242. (Illus.). 700p. 1980. pap. 15.00 (*0-520-04783-4*) U CA Pr.

Why Viewers Watch: A Reappraisal of Television's Effects. Jib Fowles. 253p. (C). 1992. 52.00 (*0-8039-4076-9*); pap. 23.50 (*0-8039-4077-7*) Sage.

***Why Violence? A Philosophical Interpretation.** Sergio Cotta. LC 84-25779. 164p. reprint ed. pap. 46.80 (*0-608-04511-X*, 2065256) Bks Demand.

Why Waco? Cults & the Battle for Religious Freedom in America. James D. Tabor & Eugene V. Gallagher. LC 95-3553. (Illus.). 266p. 1995. 27.50 (*0-520-20186-8*) U CA Pr.

***Why Waco? Cults & the Battle for Religious Freedom in America.** James D. Tabor & Eugene V. Gallagher. LC 95-3553. (Illus.). 1997. pap. 15.95 (*0-520-20899-4*) U CA Pr.

Why Waikiki? Chris Fairman. (Illus.). 68p. (Orig.). 1991. pap. 10.95 (*0-9630900-3-8*) Kilikina Prods.

Why Wait? What You Need to Know About the Teen Sexuality Crisis. Josh McDowell & Dick Day. LC 87-194. 1987. pap. 14.99 (*0-8407-4282-7*) Nelson.

Why Wait for Detroit? Drive an Electric Car Today! Ed. by Steve McCrea & R. Minner. (Illus.). 224p. 1995. pap. text ed. 25.00 (*1-57074-236-7*) Greyden Pr.

Why Wait 'Til I'm Dead? Buy This Book Now. M. Agrelius. 64p. (Orig.). 1986. pap. 4.95 (*0-936805-00-5*) Happy Val Whittier.

Why Wait till Marriage? see Por Que Esperar Hasta el Matrimonio?

Why War? Albert Einstein & Sigmund Freud. 15p. 1991. pap. 3.99 (*1-56226-043-X*) CT Pub.

Why War? Frederic C. Howe. LC 73-125179. (Americana Library Ser.: No. 16). 394p. 1970. reprint ed. 20.00 (*0-295-95091-9*) U of Wash Pr.

Why War? Ideology, Theory, & History. Keith L. Nelson & Spencer C. Olin. LC 78-51746. 1980. pap. 13.00 (*0-520-04279-4*) U CA Pr.

Why War? Psychoanalysis, Politics & the Return to Melanie Klein. Jacqueline Rose. Ed. by Harold Schweizer. (Bucknell Lectures in Literary Theory). 144p. 1993. 30.95 (*0-631-18923-8*); pap. 17.95 (*0-631-18924-6*) Blackwell Pubs.

***Why Was Andrew Surprised?** Pauline Youd. LC 96-26817. (Illus.). (J). 1996. pap. write for info. (*0-8198-8285-2*) Pauline Bks.

Why Was Daniel Scared? Pauline Youd. LC 96-22770. (I Wonder...Bks.). (Illus.). 16p. (Orig.). (J). (gr. 2-4). 1996. pap. 2.95 (*0-8198-8282-8*) Pauline Bks.

Why Was David Brave? Pauline Youd. LC 96-21548. (I Wonder...Bks.). (Illus.). 16p. (Orig.). (J). (gr. 2-4). 1996. pap. 2.95 (*0-8198-8280-1*) Pauline Bks.

***Why Was Deborah Mad?** Pauline Youd. LC 96-26819. (Illus.). (J). 1996. pap. 2.95 (*0-8198-8286-0*) Pauline Bks.

***Why Was Gideon Worried?** Pauline Youd. LC 96-26815. (Illus.). (J). 1996. pap. 2.95 (*0-8198-8283-6*) Pauline Bks.

Why Was I Adopted? Carole Livingston. (Illus.). (J). (gr. 1 up). 1978. text ed. 12.00 (*0-8184-0257-1*) Carol Pub Group.

Why Was I Adopted? Carole Livingston. (Illus.). 48p. 1986. pap. 8.95 (*0-8184-0400-0*) Carol Pub Group.

***Why Was I Adopted?** Carole Livingston. (Illus.). 1997. pap. 9.95 (*0-8184-0588-0*, L Stuart) Carol Pub Group.

***Why Was I Born? Bridging Birth & Justice.** Richard Steinpach. Orig. Title: Warum Geburten Doch Gerecht Sind. 96p. (Orig.). 1997. pap. 7.95 (*1-57461-013-9*) Grail Found Pr.

Why Was Jeremiah Sad? Pauline Youd. LC 96-20220. 1996. pap. 2.95 (*0-8198-8277-1*) Pauline Bks.

***Why Was Mary Embarrassed?** Pauline Youd. LC 96-26820. (Illus.). (J). 1996. pap. 2.95 (*0-8198-8284-4*) Pauline Bks.

Why Was Pharoah Puzzled? Pauline Youd. LC 96-21547. (I Wonder...Bks.). (Illus.). 16p. (Orig.). (J). (gr. 2-4). 1996. pap. 2.95 (*0-8198-8278-X*) Pauline Bks.

Why Was the Shepherd Glad? Pauline Youd. LC 96-20221. (I Wonder...Bks.). (Illus.). 16p. (Orig.). (J). (gr. 2-4). 1996. pap. 2.95 (*0-8198-8276-3*) Pauline Bks.

Why Waste a Second Chance? A Small Town Guide to Recycling. National Association of Towns & Townships Staff. (Illus.). 48p. (Orig.). 1989. pap. text ed. 10.00 (*0-925532-00-2*) Natl Assn Town & Twps.

***Why We Age: What Science Is Discovering about the Bodies' Journey Through Life.** Steven N. Austad. LC 97-5542. 1997. text ed. 24.95 (*0-471-14803-2*) Wiley.

Why We Are Baptized. Kathleen England. LC 78-19180. (Illus.). 27p. (J). (gr. 2-5). 1978. pap. 6.95 (*0-87747-893-7*) Deseret Bk.

Why We Are Conscientious Objectors to War. William McGrath. 1991. pap. 1.50 (*0-935409-02-5*) Amish Mennonite.

Why We Are Happily Married. Compiled by Harold Critcher & June Critcher. 1979. pap. 1.95 (*0-89265-054-0*) Randall Hse.

Why We Are Here. J. David King. (Illus.). 148p. (Orig.). 1993. pap. 8.00 (*0-9617359-1-0*) Friend Man Assn.

Why We Are Here. Gloria Lee. 183p. 1974. reprint ed. spiral bd. 12.00 (*0-7873-0547-2*) Hlth Research.

Why We Are Not Like Bears: And Other Poems. Mather T. Schneider. 183p. (Orig.). 1996. pap. 10.00 (*0-9652195-1-8*) OBanan Pr.

Why We Are Not Nietzschiennes. Ferry. 1997. pap. text ed. 15.95 (*0-226-24481-4*) U Ch Pr.

Why We Are Not Nietzschiennes. Ferry. 1997. lib. bdg. 45.00 (*0-226-24480-6*) U Ch Pr.

Why We Can't Wait. Martin Luther King, Jr. (Illus.). 160p. 1964. pap. 5.99 (*0-451-62754-7*, Ment) NAL-Dutton.

Why We Do It. Edwin D. Wolff. LC 68-16990. (Essay Index Reprint Ser.). 1977. 19.95 (*0-8369-1006-0*) Ayer.

Why We Do What We Do: The Dynamics of Personal Autonomy. Edward L. Deci & Richard Flaste. LC 95-1901. 1995. 24.95 (*0-399-14047-6*, Grosset-Putnam) Putnam Pub Group.

Why We Do What We Do: Understanding Self-Motivation. Edward Deci & Richard Flaste. 240p. 1996. pap. 11.95 (*0-14-025526-5*, Penguin Bks) Viking Penguin.

***Why We Dream.** James M. Carroll. 16p. (Orig.). 1996. pap. 9.95 (*0-89826-062-0*) Natl Paperback.

Why We Eat What We Eat: The Psychology of Eating. Ed. by Elizabeth P. Capaldi. (Illus.). 339p. 1996. 49.95 (*1-55798-366-6*, 4318500) Am Psychol.

Why We Fought. C. H. Grattan. Ed. by Keith L. Nelson. LC 70-84163. 1969. 37.50 (*0-8290-1392-X*) Irvington.

Why We Garden: Cultivating A Sense of Place. Jim Nollman. 320p. 1996. pap. 14.00 (*0-8050-4561-9*, Owl) H Holt & Co.

Why We Get Sick: How Darwinian Medicine is Revolutionizing the Science of Healing. Randolph M. Neese & George C. Williams. 304p. 1996. pap. 13.00 (*0-679-74674-9*, Vin) Random.

***Why We Go to Zoos.** Noah Leznoff. 112p. pap. 11.99 (*1-895837-03-0*, Pub. by Insomniac Pr CN) Login Pubs Consort.

Why We Grow Old. Austad. (C). 1998. write for info. (*0-201-40968-2*) Addison-Wesley.

***Why We Have a Body.** Claire Chafee. 57p. 1996. pap. 5.25 (*0-87129-690-X*, W79) Dramatic Pub.

Why We Have Thanksgiving. Margaret Hillert. (Illus.). (J). (ps). 1962. pap. 5.10 (*0-8136-5604-4*, TK2385); lib. bdg. 7.95 (*0-8136-5104-2*, TK2384) Modern Curr.

Why We Laugh. 2nd enl. ed. Samuel S. Cox. LC 67-13325. 1972. reprint ed. 29.95 (*0-405-08379-3*, Pub. by Blom Pubns UK) Ayer.

Why We Learn the Arabic Language. S. Inayatulla. pap. 4.00 (*0-933511-93-0*) Kazi Pubns.

Why We Live after Death. Richard Steinpach. LC BL535. 575. 96p. 1995. pap. 7.95 (*1-57461-005-8*) Grail Found Pr.

Why We Live in Community: With Two Interpretive Talks by Thomas Merton. Eberhard Arnold & Thomas Merton. Ed. by Bruderhof. 96p. 1995. pap. 5.00 (*0-87486-068-7*) Plough.

Why We Live with Animals. Alvin Greenberg. LC 90-40518. (Illus.). 60p. (Orig.). 1990. pap. 8.95 (*0-918273-78-1*) Coffee Hse.

Why We Lost the E. R. A. Jane J. Mansbridge. LC 86-6954. (Illus.). xii, 336p. 1986. pap. text ed. 15.95 (*0-226-50358-5*); lib. bdg. 42.00 (*0-226-50357-7*) U Ch Pr.

***Why We Must Abolish the Income Tax & the IRS: A Special Report on the National Sales Tax.** Nelson Hultberg. 128p. (Orig.). 1996. pap. 9.95 (*0-9654276-0-9*) AFR Pubns.

Why We Nap: Evolution, Chronobiology, & Functions of Polyphasic & Ultrashort Sleep. Ed. by Claudio Stampi. LC 92-23206. xxiii, 279p. 1992. 98.00 (*0-8176-3462-2*) Birkhauser.

Why We Need Ideologies in American Foreign Policy: Democratic Politics & World Order. Edward H. Alden & Franz Schurmann. LC 89-82374. (Policy Papers in International Affairs: No. 37). 92p. 1990. pap. text ed. 8.50 (*0-87725-537-7*) U of Cal IAS.

Why We Need the Arts: Eight Quotable Speeches by Leaders in Education, Government, Business, & the Arts. LC 89-6698. 80p. (Orig.). 1989. pap. 9.95 (*0-915400-79-0*, ACA Bks) Am Council Arts.

Why We Serve: A Sampler of Quotations from School People. 1990. 8.00 (*0-614-13439-0*) CRIS.

Why We Should Abolish the Income Tax: A Guide to the Principal Proposals. William W. Oliver. 142p. (Orig.). 1995. pap. 15.95 (*0-940121-33-6*) Cross Cultural Pubns.

Why We Should Read. Stuart P. Mais. LC 67-26760. (Essay Index Reprint Ser.). 1977. 20.95 (*0-8369-0669-1*) Ayer.

Why We Shouldn't Call Our Foreparents Slaves. LaRue E. Nedd. 20p. pap. 5.00 (*1-883762-02-2*) HomeBased Comm.

Why We Spend Too Much on Health Care. Joseph L. Bast et al. 10p. 1992. pap. 8.95 (*0-9632027-0-7*) Heartland Inst.

Why We Spend Too Much on Health Care...& What We Can Do about It. Joseph L. Bast et al. (Illus.). 176p. (Orig.). (C). 1993. 41.00 (*0-9632027-1-5*); pap. text ed. 8.95 (*0-9632027-2-3*) Heartland Inst.

Why We Still Need Public Schools: Church - State Relations & Visions of Democracy. Ed. by Art Must. 311p. (Orig.). (C). 1992. pap. 18.95 (*0-87975-758-2*) Prometheus Bks.

Why We Still Need the United Nations: The Collective Management of International Conflict, 1945-1984. Ernst B. Haas. LC 86-84126. (Policy Papers in International Affairs: No. 26). (Illus.). x, 115p. 1986. pap. text ed. 8.95 (*0-87725-526-1*) U of Cal IAS.

Why We Watch: Killing the Gilligan Within. Will Miller. 1996. pap. 11.00 (*0-684-83106-6*) S&S Trade.

Why We Went to War. Newton D. Baker. LC 72-1278. (Select Bibliographies Reprint Ser.). 1977. reprint ed. 15.95 (*0-8369-6820-4*) Ayer.

Why Weight. Earl W. Wharton. LC 89-51040. 230p. 1990. pap. 9.95 (*1-55523-238-8*) Winston-Derek.

Why Weight? A Guide to Ending Compulsive Eating. Geneen Roth. (Illus.). 224p. 1989. pap. 11.95 (*0-452-26254-2*, Plume) NAL-Dutton.

Why We're Here. R. Joshua Murry. LC 88-51384. 56p. 1989. 5.95 (*1-55523-198-5*) Winston-Derek.

Why Were You Created? James McKeever. 24p. (C). pap. text ed. 2.99 (*0-86694-083-9*) Omega Pubns OR.

Why, What & How of Interest Development Centers. Berdine Stoltz & Pamela Saloom. 1978. pap. text ed. 3.95 (*0-936386-02-9*) Creative Learning.

Why, Who & How of the Editorial Page. 2nd ed. Kenneth Rystrom. LC 93-84254. 336p. (C). 1994. pap. text ed. write for info. (*0-9634489-1-9*) Strata Pub Co.

Why Winners Win. rev. ed. Alyce P. Cornyn-Selby. Orig. Title: Why Do Winners Win?. (Illus.). 64p. pap. 8.95 (*0-941383-23-7*) Beynch Pr.

Why Winners Win. 2nd ed. Art Garner. LC 95-2872. 184p. 1995. 16.95 (*1-56554-148-0*) Pelican.

Why Women? Gender Issues & Eating Disorders. Ed. by Bridget Dolan & Inez Gitzinger. 120p. (C). 1994. pap. 15.00 (*0-485-12106-9*, Pub. by Athlone Pr UK) Humanities.

***Why Women & Power Don't Mix: The Perils of Feminism.** J. P. McDermott. Date not set. 18.95 (*0-9654987-0-0*) Patriarchic Pub Co.

Why Women Are Oppressed. Anna G. Jonasdottir. LC 93-24039. Orig. Title: Love, Power, & Political Interests. 288p. 1994. reprint ed. 59.95 (*1-56639-110-5*); reprint ed. pap. 18.95 (*1-56639-111-3*) Temple U Pr.

Why Women Are So. Mary R. Coolidge. LC 72-2595. (American Women Ser.: Images & Realities). 376p. 1974. reprint ed. 25.95 (*0-405-04452-6*) Ayer.

Why Women Kill Themselves. Ed. by David Lester. 160p. (C). 1988. text ed. 37.95 (*0-398-05508-4*) C C Thomas.

Why Women Kill Themselves. Ed. by David Lester. 160p. 1988. pap. 23.95 (*0-398-06237-4*) C C Thomas.

***Why Women Live Longer Than Men: And What Men Can Do about It.** Royda Crose. LC 96-50433. 1997. 24.00 (*0-7879-0340-X*) Jossey-Bass.

Why Women Need Chocolate: Eat What You Crave to Look & Feel Great. Debra Waterhouse. LC 94-14966. 288p. 1995. 19.95 (*0-7868-6051-0*) Hyperion.

Why Women Need Chocolate: How to Get the Body You Want by Eating the Foods You Crave. Debra Waterhouse. 288p. 1996. pap. 10.95 (*0-7868-8134-8*) Hyperion.

Why Women Pay More: How to Avoid Marketplace Perils. Frances C. Whittelsey. 1993. pap. 10.00 (*0-936758-34-1*) Ctr Responsive Law.

Why Women Shouldn't Marry: A Guidebook for Women of the 80's. Cynthia S. Smith. 224p. 1988. 15.95 (*0-8184-0467-1*) Carol Pub Group.

Why Women Wear Clothes. C. W. Cunnington. 1979. lib. bdg. 250.00 (*0-8490-2821-3*) Gordon Pr.

Why Women Win at Bridge. Daniel Roth. (Illus.). 192p. (Orig.). 1994. pap. 10.95 (*0-571-16748-9*) Faber & Faber.

Why Women Worry & How to Stop. Jane Handly et al. 1992. reprint ed. mass mkt. 5.99 (*0-449-22061-3*, Crest) Fawcett.

Why Won't Anyone Tell Me the Price? Finally, a Straight Forward Book That Puts You in the Driver's Seat When Buying a New or Used Car. Training Mark, pseud. 102p. 1991. per. 9.95 (*0-9631803-0-4*) Bookmark AZ.

Why Work? Judi Jennings. LC 89-38086. (Illus.). 64p. 1989. pap. 4.50 (*0-8131-0904-3*) U Pr of Ky.

Why Work? Arguments for the Leisure Society. Ed. by Vernon Richards. (Illus.). 210p. (Orig.). (C). 1983. pap. 8.00 (*0-900384-25-5*) Left Bank.

Why Work? Arguments for the Leisure Society. B. Russell et al. 1984. lib. bdg. 250.00 (*0-87700-644-X*) Revisionist Pr.

Why Work? Motivating the New Workforce. 2nd ed. Michael Maccoby. 155p. 1995. pap. 24.95 (*0-917917-05-7*) Miles River.

Why Workers Behave the Way They Do. Duane Beeler et al. 240p. (Orig.). 1983. pap. 7.95 (*0-317-12241-X*) Union Rep.

Why Worlds Are Made. John Croff. LC 89-62982. 192p. 1990. 15.95 (*0-9624793-0-6*) Light Hse Bks.

Why Worry. S. Breton. 1994. pap. 9.95 (*1-85230-556-8*) Element MA.

Why Worry? Laird. 1993. pap. 9.95 (*1-883748-01-1*) Chrstian Stewardshp.

Why Worry? large type ed. write for info. (*0-318-68669-4*, 6004) LBW.

Why Worry? Conquering a Common Inclination. James R. Beck & David T. Moore. LC 94-20699. (Strategic Christian Living Ser.). 96p. (Orig.). (C). 1994. pap. 7.99 (*0-8010-1092-6*) Baker Bks.

Why Worry about Global Warming? Kent Jeffreys. 1991. pap. 10.00 (*0-943802-60-1*, 157) Natl Ctr Pol.

Why Would Matthew Do Crack? Henny Wenkart. (J). (gr. 3-7). 1990. write for info. (*0-911612-00-9*) Wenkart.

Why Write? Paul Auster. LC 96-5350. (Illus.). 64p. 1996. 20.00 (*1-886224-15-3*); pap. 10.00 (*1-886224-14-5*) Burning Deck.

Why Write Letters: Ten Ways to Simplify--& Enjoy--Your Life. Donna E. Schaper. LC 95-51673. 112p. (Orig.). 1996. pap. 9.95 (*0-8298-1084-6*) Pilgrim OH.

Why You Act the Way You Do. Tim LaHaye. 342p. 1988. mass mkt. 5.99 (*0-8423-8212-7*) Tyndale.

Why You Are Who You Are: A Conversation with Richard. Graham Bernard. 208p. (Orig.). 1985. pap. 9.95 (*0-89281-100-5*, Destiny Bks) Inner Tradit.

***Why You Behave in Ways You Hate: And What You Can Do about It.** Irwin Gootnick. 208p. 1997. 19.95 (*1-883955-08-4*) Penmarin Bks.

Why You Can Disagree & Remain a Faithful Catholic. Phillip S. Kaufman. 224p. 1995. pap. 16.95 (*0-8245-1472-6*) Crossroad NY.

Why You Can Never Get to the End of the Rainbow & Other Moments of Science. Ed. by Don Glass. LC 92-34770. 192p. (J). 1993. 31.50 (*0-253-32591-9*); pap. 10.95 (*0-253-20780-0*) Ind U Pr.

Why You Cannot Die! The Continuity of Life. Lao Russell. (Illus.). 253p. 1972. text ed. 18.00 (*1-879605-18-X*) U Sci & Philos.

Why You Do What You Do. Bobb Biehl. LC 93-10149. 1993. 17.99 (*0-8407-9154-2*) Nelson.

Why You Get Sick, How You Get Well: How Feelings Affect Your Health. Arthur Janov. 288p. 1996. pap. 24.95 (*0-7871-0685-2*, Dove Bks) Dove Audio.

Why You Lose at Bridge. Simon. 11.95 (*0-939460-75-0*, 0790) Devyn Pr.

Why You Say It. rev. ed. Webb Garrison. LC 92-26951. 320p. 1992. 16.95 (*1-55853-147-5*); pap. 12.95 (*1-55853-128-9*) Rutledge Hill Pr.

Why You Should: The Pragmatics of Deontic Speech. James W. Forrester. LC 88-40111. 256p. 1988. text ed. 35.00 (*0-87451-453-3*) U Pr of New Eng.

Why You Should Believe in the Trinity: An Answer to Jehovah's Witnesses. Robert M. Bowman, Jr. LC 89-39309. (Christian Research Institute Ser.). 160p. (Orig.). (gr. 10). 1989. pap. 9.99 (*0-8010-0981-2*) Baker Bks.

Why You Should Speak in Tongues. Norvel Hayes. (Mini-Bks.). 32p. 1979. pap. 0.99 (*0-89274-244-5*, HH-244) Harrison Hse.

***Why You Should Take Your Travel Agent to Lunch: 101 Timely Tips for Travelers.** Harry Knitter & L. William Chiles. (Illus.). 176p. (Orig.). 1997. pap. 9.95 (*0-9652333-1-6*) Kordene Publns.

Why You Should Use a Pet Sitter: A Guide to Using Professional Pet Sitting Services. National Association of Professional Pet Sitters Staff. 12p. (Orig.). 1995. pap. text ed. 5.00 (*0-938369-21-0*) Greeting Card Assn.

Why You Win or Lose. Fred C. Kelly. LC 62-22236. 177p. 1962. reprint ed. pap. 13.00 (*0-87034-002-6*) Fraser Pub Co.

Why You Won't Go to Heaven: Though a Murderer Might. Stephen Schwambach. 128p. 1994. pap. 12.95 (*0-9639172-7-7*) Hundredth Century.

Why Your Child Can Read! Lea-Ruth C. Wilkens. LC 80-51610. 104p. (Orig.). 1980. pap. 3.95 (*0-9604638-0-1*) Readon Pub.

Why Your Child Is Hyperactive. Ben F. Feingold. 271p. 1985. pap. 12.00 (*0-394-73426-2*) Random.

Why Your Corporate Culture Isn't Working: And What to Do About It. Michael Ward. 160p. 1994. 44.95 (*0-566-07434-6*, Pub. by Gower UK) Ashgate Pub Co.

Why Your Ears Are Crooked. T. Cahill & J. Gallagher. pap. write for info. (*0-345-37096-1*) Ballantine.

Why Zebras Don't Get Ulcers: A Guide to Stress, Stress-Related Diseases, & Coping. Robert M. Sapolsky. LC 93-27078. 368p. 1995. pap. text ed. 12.95 (*0-7167-2718-8*) W H Freeman.

Why Zoos? UFAW Staff. (UFAW Courier Ser.: No. 24). (C). 1988. 65.00 (*0-900767-49-9*) St Mut.

Why'd He Have to Go & Do That. Marc Swan. 16p. (Orig.). 1994. pap. 5.00 (*1-885141-01-7*) Harlequin Ink.

Why'd They Name It That? A Look at Some Peculiar Missouri Towns. C. H. Curtis. LC 92-90469. 1992. pap. 24.95 (*0-9633863-3-6*) Curtis Ent.

Whylah Falls. George E. Clarke. 160p. (Orig.). 1990. pap. 9.95 (*0-919591-57-4*, Pub. by Polestar Bk Pubs CN) Orca Bk Pubs.

Whys & Ways of Science: Introducing Philosophical & Sociological Theories of Science. Peter J. Riggs. 248p. (Orig.). (C). 1992. pap. 19.95 (*0-522-84471-5*, Pub. by Melbourne Univ Pr AT) Paul & Co Pubs.

Whys Behind Testing Standards for Solid Fuel Burning Appliances. Ben A. Zimmer. 1981. 3.50 (*0-686-31891-9*, TR 81-4) Society Fire Protect.

Why's of Social Policy: Perspective on Policy Preferences. Hobart A. Burch. LC 91-10856. 256p. 1991. text ed. 55.00 (*0-275-94006-3*, C4006, Praeger Pubs) Greenwood.

Whyte Tropical Grazing Lands. 1974. pap. text ed. 80.50 (*90-6193-020-0*) Kluwer Ac.

***Why...Thank You! How to Have FUN Writing Fantastic Notes & More...** Cat Wagman. LC 96-90575. (Illus.). 128p. 1997. 15.95 (*0-9652670-4-0*); pap. 12.95 (*0-9652670-6-7*) Wrking Words.

Why...the Brooklyn Center High School Bible Challenge Pt. I: The Evidence, 2 vols., Set. Gene Kasmar. LC 95-94289. 500p. (Orig.). 1995. pap. 9.95 (*0-9645995-4-6*) Kas-Mark.

Wi-Ne-Ma the Woman-Chief & Her People. Alfred B. Meacham. LC 76-43773. reprint ed. 27.50 (*0-404-15628-2*) AMS Pr.

Wibbly Pig Can Dance! Mick Inkpen. (Illus.). 16p. (J). 1995. bds. 3.95 (*0-307-16626-0*) Western Pub.

Wibbly Pig Can Make a Tent. Mick Inkpen. (Illus.). 16p. (J). 1995. bds. 3.95 (*0-307-16628-7*) Western Pub.

Wibbly Pig Is Upset. Mick Inkpen. (Illus.). 16p. (J). 1995. bds. 3.95 (*0-307-16629-5*) Western Puo.

Wibbly Pig Likes Bananas. Mick Inkpen. (Illus.). 16p. (J). 1995. bds. 3.95 (*0-307-16630-9*) Western Pub.

Wibbly Pig Makes Pictures. Mick Inkpen. (Illus.). 16p. (J). 1995. bds. 3.95 (*0-307-16625-2*) Western Pub.

Wibbly Pig Opens His Presents. Mick Inkpen. (Illus.). 16p. (J). 1995. bds. 3.95 (*0-307-16627-9*) Western Pub.

WIBC Championship Tournament Program. Women's International Bowling Congress Staff. Ed. by Karen L. Sytsma. (Illus.). 80p. 1987. 1.00 (*0-318-21985-9*) WIBC.

WIC Nutrition Risk Criteria: A Scientific Evaluation. Institute of Med., Food & Nutrition Board, Committee on Scientific Eval. of WIC Nutrition Risk Criteria. 377p. (Orig.). 1996. pap. text ed. 39.00 (*0-309-05385-4*) Natl Acad Pr.

Wicca: A Guide for the Solitary Practitioner. Scott Cunningham. LC 88-45279. (Practical Magick Ser.). (Illus.). 240p. 1988. pap. 9.95 (*0-87542-118-0*) Llewellyn Pubns.

Wicca: Satan's Little White Lie. William Schnoebelen. LC 90-82581. (Illus.). 224p. 1990. pap. 8.95 (*0-937958-34-4*) Chick Pubns.

Wicca: The Old Religion in the New Age. Vivianne Crowley. (Illus.). 272p. 1989. pap. 15.00 (*0-85030-737-6*, Pub. by Aquarian Pr UK) Thorsons SF.

***Wicca A to Z: A Modern Witch's Encyclopedia.** Gerina Dunwich. LC 97-25999. 1997. pap. text ed. 10.95 (*0-8065-1930-4*, Citadel Pr) Carol Pub Group.

Wicca Awakens. Keith Morgan. (Orig.). 1995. pap. 7.95 (*1-872189-20-2*, Pub. by Mandrake Pr UK) Holmes Pub.

Wicca Book of Days: Legend & Lore for Every Day of the Year. Gerina Dunwich. (Illus.). 176p. 1995. pap. 9.95 (*0-8065-1685-2*, Citadel Pr) Carol Pub Group.

***Wicca Candle Magick.** Gerina Dunwich. Date not set. pap. 9.95 (*0-8065-1831-6*, Citadel Pr) Carol Pub Group.

Wicca Course: Ten Lessons in Witchcraft, 10 lessons, Set. Steven Brynes. (Illus.). 135p. 1994. 120.00 (*1-57179-007-1*); spiral bd. 100.00 (*1-57179-006-3*) Intern Guild ASRS.

Wicca Craft: The Book of Herbs, Magick & Dreams. Gerina Dunwich. 192p. Date not set. pap. 9.95 (*0-8065-1238-5*, Citadel Pr) Carol Pub Group.

W

Wicca Garden: A Modern Witch's Book of Magickal & Enchanted Herbs & Plants. Gerina Dunwich. (Citadel Library of the Mystic Arts). 192p. 1996. pap. 10.95 (0-8065-1777-8, Citadel Pr) Carol Pub Group.

Wicca Love Spells: How to Attract a Lover, Make a Former Lover Return to You...& Much, Much More. Gerina Dunwich. LC 95-50273. 216p. 1996. pap. 10.95 (0-8065-1782-4) Carol Pub Group.

***Wicca Source Book: Complete Guide for the Modern Witch.** Gerina Dunwich. Date not set. pap. 10.95 (0-8065-1830-8, Citadel Pr) Carol Pub Group.

Wicca Spellbook. Gerina Dunwich. LC 93-43436. 204p. Date not set. pap. 10.95 (0-8065-1476-0, Citadel Pr) Carol Pub Group.

WiccaCraft for Families. Margie McArthur. (Illus.). 272p. (Orig.). 1994. pap. 14.95 (0-919345-52-2) Phoenix WA.

***Wiccan Herbal.** Marie Rodway. 1997. pap. text ed. 14.95 (0-572-02340-5, Pub. by W Foulsham UK) Trans-Atl Phila.

***Wiccan Mysteries: Ancient Origins & Teachings.** Raven Grimassi. LC 97-11937. 1997. pap. text ed. 14.95 (1-56718-254-2) Llewellyn Pubns.

Wiccan Path: A Guide to Solitary Practice. Rae Beth. 192p. 1995. pap. 12.95 (0-89594-744-7) Crossing Pr.

***Wiccan Prophecy: A Practical Guide to the Mystical Guide of Divination.** Gerina Dunwich. LC 97-8641. (Illus.). 200p. 1997. pap. 10.95 (0-8065-1864-2, Citadel Pr) Carol Pub Group.

Wiccan Resources: A Guide to the Witchcraft Community. Michael Thorn. 1983. pap. 3.95 (0-9635647-0-6) Liquid Lght.

Wichita: The Early Years, 1865-80. H. Craig Miner. LC 81-23138. 215p. 1982. reprint ed. pap. 61.30 (0-608-01395-1, 2062158) Bks Demand.

Wichita: The Magic City. H. Craig Miner. LC 88-62144. (Illus.). 210p. 1988. 24.95 (0-9621250-0-8) Wichita-Sedgwick Hist Mus.

Wichita Falls, Texas. Gousha, H.M., Editors. 1992. pap. 2.25 (0-13-962028-1, H M Gousha) P-H Gen Ref & Trav.

Wichita, Kansas. San Antonio Cartographers Staff. 1995. 2.95 (0-671-56284-3) Macmillan.

***Wichita Mysteries Vol. 1: Three Complete Novels.** 2nd ed. Gaylord Dold. 640p. 1996. reprint ed. pap. 13.95 (0-922820-17-1) Watermrk Pr.

***Wichita Poems.** Robert K. Headley & Rafael Zepeda. 44p. (Orig.). 1996. pap. 6.00 (1-888219-04-1) Pearl Edit.

Wichita Poems. Michael Van Walleghen. LC 75-19257. 66p. 1975. 9.95 (0-252-00570-8); text ed. 14.95 (0-252-00447-7) U of Ill Pr.

Wichita Poems. fac. ed. Michael Van Walleghen. LC 75-19257. 59p. 1975. reprint ed. pap. 25.00 (0-7837-8064-8, 2047817) Bks Demand.

Wichita Reader: A Collection of Writing about a Prairie City. Ed. by Craig Miner. (Illus.). 160p. 1992. 19.95 (1-880652-13-7) Wichita Eagle.

Wichtigsten PC-Begriffe. Bernhard Kopp. 63p. (GER.). 1991. 19.95 (0-7859-8492-5, 3806843678) Fr & Eur.

Wickcliffe's Way: A Memoir. Robert Wickcliffe. (Illus.). 1994. 17.95 (1-881116-35-2) Black Forest Pr.

Wicked. Susan Johnson. 336p. 1997. mass mkt. 5.99 (0-553-57214-8, Fanfare) Bantam.

Wicked. Gregory Maguire. 1995. 24.00 (0-614-15470-7) HarpC.

***Wicked.** Gregory Maguire. 1996. pap. 14.00 (0-614-20736-3, ReganBooks) HarpC.

Wicked. Evelyn Rogers. 448p. (Orig.). 1996. mass mkt. 5.99 (0-505-52082-6) Dorchester Pub Co.

Wicked: The Life & Times of the Wicked Witch of the West. Gregory Maguire. LC 95-669. (Illus.). 448p. 1995. 24.00 (0-06-039144-8, HarpT) HarpC.

Wicked: The Life & Times of the Wicked Witch of the West. Gregory Maguire. 416p. 1996. pap. text ed. 14.00 (0-06-098710-3) HarpC.

Wicked: The Life & Times of the Wicked Witch of the West. large type ed. Gregory Maguire. 697p. 1996. 24.95 (0-7862-0643-8, Thorndike Lrg Prnt) Thorndike Pr.

Wicked Acts of Sacrilege. Neil Steinberg. 1992. pap. 9.95 (0-312-07810-2) St Martin.

Wicked Acts of Sacrilege: The Book of College Pranks. Neil Steinberg. (Illus.). 256p. (Orig.). 1992. pap. 79.60 (0-312-07928-1) St Martin.

Wicked at Heart. Danelle Harmon. 400p. 1996. mass mkt. 5.50 (0-380-78004-6) Avon.

***Wicked Caprice.** Anne Mather. (Presents Ser.). 1997. mass mkt. 3.50 (0-373-11869-4, 1-11869-4) Harlequin Bks.

***Wicked Caprice.** Anne Mather. (Harlequin Ser.). 1997. 20.95 (0-263-15068-2) Thorndike Pr.

Wicked Cat. Christopher Pike. (Spooksville Ser.: No. 10). (J). (gr. 4-7). 1996. pap. 3.99 (0-671-55069-1) PB.

Wicked City Chicago: From Kenna to Capone. Curt Johnson. LC 93-73785. (Illus.). 400p. 1994. pap. 19.95 (0-913204-31-5) December Pr.

Wicked Count. Emily Maxwell. 1990. mass mkt. 2.95 (0-8217-2994-2, Zebra Kensgtn) Kensgtn Pub Corp.

Wicked Day. Mary Stewart. 384p. 1984. mass mkt. 5.95 (0-449-20519-3, Crest) Fawcett.

***Wicked Day.** Mary Stewart. 1996. pap. 12.95 (0-449-91185-3) Fawcett.

Wicked Designs: A Mici Anhalt Mystery. large type ed. Lillian O'Donnell. LC 92-19379. 341p. 1992. reprint ed. lib. bdg. 17.95 (1-56054-373-6) Thorndike Pr.

***Wicked for a Weekend.** Keene. (YA). 1997. mass mkt. 3.99 (0-671-00748-3) PB.

Wicked French for the Traveler. Howard Tomb. LC 88-40229. 80p. 1988. pap. 3.95 (0-89480-616-5, 1616) Workman Pub.

Wicked Games. Barbara Boswell. 384p. (Orig.). 1994. mass mkt. 5.99 (0-515-11487-1) Jove Pubns.

Wicked Generation. Alison Johnson. 262p. 9300. pap. 12.95 (0-85640-398-9, Pub. by Blackstaff Pr IE) Dufour.

Wicked German for the Traveler. Howard Tomb. LC 92-50289. 64p. 1992. pap. 3.95 (1-56305-294-6, 3294) Workman Pub.

Wicked Greek for the Traveler. Howard Tomb. LC 94-33026. (Illus.). 64p. (Orig.). 1995. pap. 3.95 (1-56305-707-7, 3707) Workman Pub.

Wicked Groom. April Kihlstrom. (Regency Romance Ser.). 224p. 1996. mass mkt. 4.99 (0-451-18750-4, Sig) NAL-Dutton.

Wicked Hand. Titian Beresford. (Orig.). 1995. mass mkt. 5.95 (1-56333-343-0) Masquerade.

Wicked Heart. Christopher Pike. Ed. by Patricia MacDonald. 224p. (Orig.). (YA). (gr. 9 up). 1993. pap. 3.99 (0-671-74511-5, Archway) PB.

***Wicked in Bed.** Sheri Campbell. 192p. 1996. pap. 9.95 (1-874509-14-X) LPC InBook.

***Wicked in Silk.** Andrea Young. 400p. (Orig.). 1997. mass mkt. 3.99 (1-85487-719-4, Pub. by Scarlet Bks UK); mass mkt. 3.99 (1-85487-179-X, Pub. by Scarlet Bks UK) London Brdge.

Wicked Italian for the Traveler. Howard Tomb. LC 88-40247. 80p. 1988. pap. 3.95 (0-89480-617-3, 1617) Workman Pub.

Wicked Jack. Illus. by Will Hilldenbrand. 32p. (J). (ps-3). 1995. lib. bdg. 15.95 (0-8234-1101-X) Holiday.

***Wicked Jack.** Illus. by Will Hillenbrand. 1997. pap. text ed. 6.95 (0-8234-1292-X) Holiday.

***Wicked Japanese.** H. Tomb. 1996. pap. 6.50 (0-8348-0267-8) Weatherhill.

Wicked Japanese: For the Business Traveler. Howard Tomb. LC 90-21100. (Illus.). 64p. (Orig.). 1991. pap. 3.95 (0-89480-862-1, 1862) Workman Pub.

Wicked Lady. Inglis Fletcher. (Carolina Ser.). 245p. reprint ed. lib. bdg. 25.95 (0-89244-009-0, Queens House) Amereon Ltd.

***Wicked Liaisons.** Laura Bradley. (Orig.). 1997. mass mkt. 3.99 (1-85487-711-9, Pub. by Scarlet Bks UK) London Brdge.

***Wicked Little Book of Quotes.** Ed. by Helen Exley. (Miniature Square Bks.). (Illus.). 64p. 1996. 6.00 (1-85015-798-7) Exley Giftbooks.

Wicked Loving Lies. Rosemary Rogers. 672p. 1983. mass mkt. 6.50 (0-380-00776-2) Avon.

Wicked Mate: The Antarctic Diary of Victor Campbell. Victor Campbell. Ed. & Intro. by Harry King. (Antarctic Classics Ser.). (Illus.). 192p. (C). 1989. 105.00 (1-85297-030-8, Pub. by Archival Facs UK) St Mut.

Wicked One. Mollie Hunter. 1995. 18.00 (0-8446-6817-6) Peter Smith.

Wicked Pack of Cards: The Origins of the Occult Tarot. Ronald Decker. LC 96-24391. 1997. 29.95 (0-312-16294-4) St Martin.

Wicked Pavilion. Dawn Powell. 246p. 1996. pap. 14.00 (1-883642-39-6) Steerforth Pr.

Wicked Pavilion. Dawn Powell. 1990. pap. 8.95 (0-685-29464-1, Vin) Random.

Wicked Prince. Hans Christian Andersen. LC 94-45650. (Illus.). (J). 1995. 18.00 (1-56846-107-0) Creative Ed.

Wicked Prince. Hans Christian Andersen. (Illus.). 40p. (J). (gr. 3-6). 1995. 18.00 (0-15-200958-2, Red Wagon Bks) HarBrace.

Wicked Problems, Righteous Solutions: Modern Paradigms in Software Engineering. Peter Degrace. 1990. pap. text ed. 52.00 (0-13-590126-X) P-H.

***Wicked Queen: The Origins of the Myth of Marie Antoinette.** LC 96-50157. 1998. write for info. (0-942299-39-6) Zone Bks.

Wicked Rebellion & the Republic: Henry Tuckerman's Civil War. Robert W. Johannsen. LC 94-78790. (Klement Lecture Ser.: No. 3). 40p. (C). 1994. pap. 5.00 (0-87462-327-8) Marquette.

Wicked Secrets. Justine Davis. (Intimate Moments Ser.). 1994. mass mkt. 3.50 (0-373-07555-3, 5-07555-1) Silhouette.

Wicked Sisters: Women Poets, Literary History, & Discord. Betsy Erkkila. (Illus.). 320p. 1992. pap. 19.95 (0-19-507212-X) OUP.

Wicked Slice. Charlotte Elkins & Aaron J. Elkins. 192p. 1990. mass mkt. 4.99 (0-449-14686-3, GM) Fawcett.

Wicked Sounds. Axel Stolz. 1993. pap. 29.95 incl. disk (1-55755-168-5) Abacus MI.

Wicked Spanish for the Traveler. Howard Tomb. LC 90-20799. (Illus.). 64p. (Orig.). 1991. pap. 3.95 (0-89480-861-3, 1861) Workman Pub.

Wicked Stepdog. Carol L. Benjamin. 128p. (YA). (gr. 5 up). 1986. mass mkt. 2.50 (0-380-70089-1, Flare) Avon.

Wicked Tenants & Gethsemane: Isaiah in the Wicked Tenants' Vineyard, & Moses & the High Priest in Gethsemane: Judaic Traditions in Mark 12: 1-9 & 14: 32-42. Roger D. Aus. LC 96-13044. (South Florida International Studies in Formative Christianity & Judaism: Vol. 4). 224p. (C). 1996. 79.95 (0-7885-0261-1, 242504) Scholars Pr GA.

***Wicked Truth.** Lyn Stone. (March Madness Ser.). 1997. mass mkt. 4.99 (0-373-28958-8, 1-28958-6) Harlequin Bks.

Wicked Uncle. Patricia Wentworth. 288p. 1996. mass mkt. 4.99 (0-06-104401-6, Harp PBks) HarpC.

Wicked Uncles: The Father of Queen Victoria - His Brothers. Roger Fulford. LC 68-8461. (Essay Index Reprint Ser.). 1977. reprint ed. 21.95 (0-8369-0466-4) Ayer.

***Wicked Vows.** Clarica Burns. 160p. (Orig.). 1997. mass mkt. 4.99 (1-55237-034-8, Pub. by Comnwlth Pub CN) Partners Pubs Grp.

Wicked Ways. Kate Hoffmann. (Temptation Ser.). 1996. mass mkt. 3.50 (0-373-25699-X, 1-25699-9) Harlequin Bks.

Wicked Ways. Carolyn Keene. (Nancy Drew Files Ser.: No. 113). (YA). (gr. 6 up). 1996. pap. 3.99 (0-671-50353-7) PB.

Wicked Wazir. Juwairiah J. Simpson. (Illus.). 48p. (Orig.). (J). (gr. 3-6). 1990. pap. 6.50 (0-89259-084-X) Am Trust Pubns.

Wicked Wicks of the West. Randy Wicks. 60p. 1995. 9.95 (0-9648977-9-2) The Signal.

Wicked Willie's Guide to Women: A Worm's-Eye View of the Fair Sex. Peter Mayle. (Illus.). 64p. 1987. pap. 8.95 (0-517-56652-4, CPT Corp) Crown Pub Group.

Wicked Windows Comes Alive. S. Schlomer & Gulich. 180p. 1993. 29.95 incl. disk (1-55755-186-3) Abacus MI.

***Wicked Witch Is at It Again!** Hanna Kraan. LC 97-454. 108p. 1997. 14.95 (1-886910-18-9) Front Str.

***Wicked Women.** Fay Weldon. LC 96-37499. 304p. 1997. 23.00 (0-87113-681-3, Atlntc Mnthly) Grove-Atltic.

***Wicked Women: Stories.** Fay Weldon. LC 96-37499. 1997. write for info. (0-87113-701-1, Atlntc Mnthly) Grove-Atltic.

Wicked Words. Hugh Rawson. 1989. 24.95 (0-517-57334-2, Crown) Crown Pub Group.

Wicked Words: A Treasury of Curses, Insults, Put-Downs, & Other Formerly Unprintable Terms from Anglo-Saxon Times to the Present. Hugh Rawson. 448p. 1992. pap. 14.00 (0-517-59089-1, Crown) Crown Pub Group.

***Wicked Words: Racism in the Dictionary.** Firpo Carr. (Illus.). 144p. 1997. 24.95 (0-9631293-5-X) Prof Pr NC.

Wicked Work. (Black Lace Ser.). 1995. mass mkt. 5.95 (0-352-32958-0, Pub. by Virgin Pub UK) London Brdge.

Wicked Wynsleys. large type ed. Alanna Knight. 1990. 25.99 (0-7089-2139-6) Ulverscroft.

Wickedness. Mary Midgley. 232p. 1986. pap. 9.95 (0-7448-0053-6, 0053W) Routledge Chapman & Hall.

Wickedness: A Philosophical Essay. Mary Midgley. 208p. 1984. 35.00 (0-7100-9759-X, RKP) Routledge.

Wickenburg! The Ultimate Guide to the Ultimate Western Town. Alan Korwin. (Illus.). 176p. (Orig.). 1994. pap. 9.95 (0-9621958-1-2) Bloomfield Pr.

Wicker. Lyn Hejinian & Jack Collom. 40p. (Orig.). 1996. pap. 5.00 (1-887289-21-6) Rodent Pr.

Wicker Basketry. Flo Hoppe. LC 89-7618. (Illus.). 166p. (Orig.). 1989. pap. 17.95 (0-934026-49-1) Interweave.

Wicker Furniture. Richard Saunders. 1990. pap. 18.95 (0-517-57185-4, Crown) Crown Pub Group.

Wickerby. Charles Siebert. 1997. write for info. (0-517-70688-1) Random Hse Value.

Wicker's Wishes. Carol B. Kaplan. Ed. by Janet L. Bolinske. LC 87-63001. (Animal Tales Ser.). (Illus.). 24p. (Orig.). (J). (ps). 1988. 17.95 (0-88335-757-7); pap. 4.95 (0-88335-075-0) Milliken Pub Co.

Wickersham Commission, National Commission on Law Observance & Enforcement: Complete Reports, Including the Mooney-Billings Report, 14 Vols. Wickersham Commission. LC 68-55277. (Criminology, Law Enforcement, & Social Problems Ser.: No. 6). (Illus.). 1968. reprint ed. 250.00 (0-87585-006-5) Patterson Smith.

Wicket Women: Cricket & Women in Australia. Amanda Weaver & Richard Cashman. (Illus.). 240p. 42.95 (0-86840-364-4, Pub. by New South Wales Univ Pr AT) Intl Spec Bk.

Wickford Anthology. Ed. by Peter C. Crolius. LC 85-7265. (Illus.). 160p. (Orig.). 1985. pap. 6.95 (0-934881-00-6) Dutch Island.

Wickford Point. John P. Marquand. 1990. 14.50 (0-8446-2666-X) Peter Smith.

Wickham: Ancestors of James Wickham & His Wife Cora Prudence Billard. J. C. Frost. (Illus.). 207p. 1994. reprint ed. pap. 32.50 (0-8328-4248-6); reprint ed. lib. bdg. 42.50 (0-8328-4247-8) Higginson Bk Co.

Wickham - Ancestors of James Wickham & His Wife Cora Prudence Billard. J. C. Frost. (Illus.). 207p. 1994. reprint ed. pap. 32.50 (0-8328-4518-3); reprint ed. lib. bdg. 42.50 (0-8328-4517-5) Higginson Bk Co.

Wickham Claim: Being an Inquiry into the Attainder of Parker Wickham. Dwight Holbrook. LC 86-6040. 1986. lib. bdg. 21.50 (0-938769-00-6, KEN5078.W52H65 1986) Suffolk Cnty Hist Soc.

Wickizer Annals. Mary W. Burgess. LC 80-11075. (Borgo Family Histories Ser.: No. 2). xviii, 125p. 1983. lib. bdg. 27.00 (0-89370-802-X) Borgo Pr.

Wicks & the Wacks. Louis Reed. LC 85-70443. (J). (ps-2). 1985. pap. 5.00 (0-916383-00-8, Univ Edtns) Aegina Pr.

Wicksell's Monetary Theory. Guglielmo Chiodi. LC 90-8932. 144p. 1991. text ed. 69.95 (0-312-05369-X) St Martin.

Wiclif & Hus. Johann Loserth. Tr. by M. J. Evans. LC 78-63198. (Heresies of the Early Christian & Medieval Era Ser.: Second Ser.). 1979. reprint ed. 61.50 (0-404-16236-3) AMS Pr.

Wid Dis Ring. French. Date not set. per. 8.95 (0-920813-83-6, Pub. by Sister Vision CN) LPC InBook.

Widdershins. George Oliver. Ed. by R. Reginald & Douglas Manville. LC 75-46297. (Supernatural & Occult Fiction Ser.). 1976. reprint ed. lib. bdg. 25.95 (0-405-08157-X) Ayer.

Widdershins. Oliver Onions. 1993. reprint ed. lib. bdg. 18.95 (0-89968-438-6, Lghtyr Pr) Buccaneer Bks.

Wide Acre. Philippa Gregory. Ed. by Claire Zion. 1990. pap. 6.99 (0-671-73036-3) PB.

Wide & Dark. large type ed. Netta Muskett. 480p. 1981. 25.99 (0-7089-0664-8) Ulverscroft.

Wide-Angle Lens Photography. Joseph Paduano. (Illus.). 110p. 1996. pap. 15.95 (0-936262-43-5) Amherst Media.

Wide-Angle Vision: Beat Your Competition by Focusing on Fringe Competitors, Lost Customers & Rogue Employees. Wayne Burkan. LC 96-10239. 288p. 1996. text ed. 27.95 (0-471-13416-3) Wiley.

Wide-Area Network Essentials. Ed Tittel. 1995. pap. text ed. 21.00 (0-12-784833-9) Acad Pr.

Wide Area Networks: Performance & Optimization. Robert Lloyd-Evans. (C). 1995. text ed. 38.95 (0-201-42270-0) Addison-Wesley.

***Wide Awake.** Michaels. (J). 1997. pap. 4.95 (0-7868-1235-4) Hyprn Child.

Wide Awake! Clara Vulliamy. (Illus.). (J). (ps). 1996. bds. 4.99 (1-56402-816-X) Candlewick Pr.

Wide Awake at Three A. M. By Choice or by Chance. Richard M. Coleman. LC 86-7665. (Psychology Ser.). (Illus.). 195p. 1995. pap. text ed. 14.95 (0-7167-1796-4) W H Freeman.

Wide Awake, Clear Headed & Refreshed: Medical Hypnoanalysis in Action. Ryan Elliott. Ed. by Gene Owens. (Illus.). 300p. (Orig.). 1991. pap. 12.95 (0-9615140-0-0) Relaxed Bks.

Wide Awake in Seattle: Success Stories of Outstanding Leaders Who Learned to Share Leadership. Kristine Sullivan & Johnna L. Howell. LC 96-75557. 210p. 1996. 25.00 (1-886671-01-X) Integrty Pub.

***Wide-Awake Wesley.** (Little Monsters Ser.). (J). 1997. write for info. (0-614-21794-6, Pub. by Splash UK) Assoc Pubs Grp.

Wide Band Gap Electronic Materials: Proceedings of the NATO Advanced Research Workshop on "Wide Band Gap Electronic Materials-Diamond, Aluminum Nitride & Boron Nitride", Minsk, Belarus, May 4-6, 1994. Ed. by Mark A. Prelas et al. LC 95-7367. (NATO Advanced Science Institutes - Partnership Sub Series 3: Vol. 1). 552p. (C). 1995. lib. bdg. 247.00 (0-7923-3405-1) Kluwer Ac.

Wide Band-Gap Semiconductors. Ed. by Y. Hamakawa et al. (Symposium Proceedings Ser.: Vol. 242). 789p. 1992. text ed. 65.00 (1-55899-136-0) Materials Res.

Wide-Band-Gap Semiconductors. Ed. by C. G. Van de Walle. 634p. 1993. 279.75 (0-444-81573-2, North Holland) Elsevier.

***Wide Bandgap Semiconductors & Devices: State-of-the-Art Program on Compound Semiconductors XXIII.** Ed. by F. Ren et al. (Illus.). 510p. 1995. 53.00 (1-56677-116-1, PV95-21) Electrochem Soc.

Wide Bandwidth, Low Power Operational Amplifiers. R. G. Eschauzier. 272p. 1994. pap. 62.50 (90-407-1056-2, Pub. by Delft U Pr NE) Coronet Bks.

Wide Components in Double & Multiple Stars. Ed. by J. Dommanget et al. (C). 1988. lib. bdg. 127.00 (90-277-2737-6) Kluwer Ac.

***Wide Eyed & Legless.** Rosenthal. 1995. pap. text ed. write for info. (0-582-24950-3, Pub. by Longman UK) Longman.

***Wide-Field Spectroscopy: Proceedings of the 2nd Conference of the Working Group of IAU Commission 9 on "Wide-Field Imaging" Held in Athens, Greece, May 20-25, 1996.** E. Kontizas & IAU Commission 9 Staff. LC 97-8153. (Astrophysics & Space Science Library). 1997. lib. bdg. 182.00 (0-7923-4518-5) Kluwer Ac.

Wide Field Spectroscopy & the Distant Universe: Proceedings of the 35th Herstmonceux Conference. S. Maddox & A. Aragon-Salamanca. 400p. 1995. text ed. 99.00 (981-02-2031-6) World Scientific Pub.

***Wide-Gap Luminescent Materials: Theory & Applications.** Ed. by Stanley R. Rotman. LC 96-39299. (Electronic Materials, Science & Technology Ser.). 384p. 1996. lib. bdg. 155.00 (0-7923-9837-8) Kluwer Ac.

Wide Horizon. Anna Brinton. (C). 1947. pap. 3.00 (0-87574-038-3) Pendle Hill.

Wide House. Taylor Caldwell. 1993. reprint ed. lib. bdg. 28.95 (1-56849-153-0) Buccaneer Bks.

***Wide Mouthed Frog.** Keith Faulkner. 1996. pap. 10.95 (0-8037-2145-5) Dial Bks Young.

Wide-Mouthed Frog. Rex Schneider. LC 80-13449. (Illus.). 32p. (J). (gr. k up). 1980. 13.95 (0-916144-58-5) Stemmer Hse.

Wide-Mouthed Frog: A Pop-Up Book. Keith Faulkner. LC 94-49340. (Illus.). 14p. (J). (ps-1). 1996. pap. 10.95 (0-8037-1875-6) Dial Bks Young.

Wide Neighborhoods: A Story of the Frontier Nursing Service. Mary Breckinridge. LC 81-50181. (Illus.). 400p. 1981. reprint ed. 35.00 (0-8131-1453-5); reprint ed. pap. 15.00 (0-8131-0149-2) U Pr of Ky.

Wide Net & Other Stories. Eudora Welty. LC 73-12880. 214p. 1974. reprint ed. pap. 7.95 (0-15-696610-7, Harvest Bks) HarBrace.

Wide-Ons. Diane Christian. LC 81-8979. 64p. 1981. 9.00 (0-912184-00-0); pap. 4.00 (0-912184-01-9) Synergistic Pr.

Wide Open to Terrorism. Tony Lesce. LC 95-81596. (Illus.). 248p. (Orig.). 1996. pap. 18.95 (1-55950-138-3, 32059) Loompanics.

Wide Open Town: A Novel. rev. ed. Myron Brinig. LC 93-4645. (Sweetgrass Bks.). 192p. 1993. reprint ed. pap. 12.95 (1-56037-034-3) Am Wrld Geog.

Wide Places in the California Roads: The Encyclopedia of California's Small Towns & the Roads that Lead to Them, 4 vols., Set. David W. Kean. (Illus.). 1386p. (Orig.). 1996. pap. text ed. 85.00 (1-884261-04-3) Concord Pr CA.

Wide Places in the California Roads: The Encyclopedia of California's Small Towns & the Roads That Lead to Them, Vol. 1: Southern California. David W. Kean. (Illus.). 334p. (Orig.). 1993. pap. 21.00 (1-884261-00-0) Concord Pr CA.

Wide-Point: The Photography of John Chamberlain. Donna De Salvo. LC 93-83245. (Illus.). 44p. 1993. pap. 18.00 (0-943526-24-8) Parrish Art.

***Wide Range Reading Index.** Longman Publishing Staff. Date not set. pap. text ed. write for info. (0-05-003817-6) Addison-Wesley.

***Wide Ruins.** S. Wagner. LC 96-45821. 1997. pap. 16.95 (0-8263-1805-3) U of NM Pr.

Wide Sargasso Sea. Jean Rhys. 192p. 1992. pap. 11.00 (0-393-30880-4) Norton.

W

An Asterisk (*) at the beginning of an entry indicates that the title is appearing in BIP for the first time.

Wide Sargasso Sea. Jean Rhys. (Critical Edition Ser.). (C). Date not set. pap. text ed. write for info. (*0-393-96012-9*) Norton.

Wide Sargasso Sea. large type ed. Jean Rhys. LC 93-35502. 1994. lib. bdg. 21.95 (*0-7862-0073-1*) Thorndike Pr.

Wide Screen Movies: A History & Filmography of Wide Gauge Filmmaking. Robert E. Carr & R. M. Hayes. LC 86-43093. (Illus.). 516p. 1988. lib. bdg. 49.95 (*0-89950-242-3*) McFarland & Co.

***Wide Skies: Finding a Home in the West.** Gary Holthaus. LC 97-4568. 1997. 45.00 (*0-8165-1672-3*); pap. 18.95 (*0-8165-1673-1*) U of Ariz Pr.

Wide Sleeve of Kwannon. Bruce Lancaster. (Illus.). 307p. 1975. reprint ed. lib. bdg. 24.95 (*0-89190-884-6*, Rivercity Pr) Amereon Ltd.

Wide Spot in the Road. Bob Budd. (Illus.). 280p. 1990. 14.95 (*0-943255-28-7*); pap. 9.95 (*0-943255-29-5*) Saratoga Pub.

Wide White Space. 400p. 1996. 75.00 (*3-928762-38-9*, Pub. by Richter Verlag GW) Dist Art Pubs.

Wide White Space: 1966-1976. Yves Aupetitallot. (Illus.). 400p. 85.00 (*3-928762-31-1*) Dist Art Pubs.

Wide, Wide World. Susan Warner. LC 86-27062. 608p. (C). 1987. reprint ed. text ed. 35.00 (*0-935312-65-X*); reprint ed. pap. text ed. 19.95 (*0-935312-66-8*) Feminist Pr.

Wide, Wide World. Susan Warner. LC 72-78850. 1851. reprint ed. 69.00 (*0-403-01989-3*) Somerset Pub.

Wide, Wonderful World As I Saw It. Georgia P. Gates. LC 90-80491. (Illus.). 321p. 1990. 19.95 (*0-940591-10-3*) Basin Pub.

Wide World of Arbitration - An Anthology. Ed. by Charlotte Gold & Susan Mackenzie. LC 78-51449. 230p. 1978. 15.00 (*0-685-25772-X*) Am Arbitration.

Wide World of John Steinbeck. Peter Lisca. 338p. (C). 1981. 50.00 (*0-87752-217-0*) Gordian.

***WideBand Networking.** 2nd rev. ed. Roger E. Billings. (Illus.). 128p. (C). 1996. pap. text ed. 19.95 (*0-9631634-6-9*) Intl Acad Science.

WideBand Second Generation Networking. Roger E. Billings. (Illus.). 144p. (Orig.). (C). 1996. pap. 19.95 (*0-9631634-5-0*) Intl Acad Science.

Widegap II-VI Compounds for Opto-Electronic Applications. Ed. by Harry E. Ruda. (Electronic Materials Ser.). (Illus.). 352p. (C). (gr. 13). 1992. text ed. 109.95 (*0-412-39100-7*, A6530) Chapman & Hall.

Widener Experience. Andrew Bushko. 232p. (C). 1995. ring bd. 27.24 (*0-7872-1380-2*) Kendall-Hunt.

Wideness in God's Mercy: The Finality of Jesus Christ in a World of Religions. Clark H. Pinnock. 208p. 1992. pap. 16.99 (*0-310-53591-3*) Zondervan.

Wideness of God's Mercy: Litanies to Enlarge Our Prayer. rev. ed. Jeffery W. Rowthorn. LC 95-2357. 256p. 1995. pap. 19.95 (*0-8192-1606-2*) Morehouse Pub.

Widening Atlantic: Domestic Changes & Foreign Policy. Ed. by Andrew J. Pierre. 144p. (C). 1986. text ed. 24.00 (*0-8147-6597-1*) NYU Pr.

Widening Breach: Evolutionism in the Mirror of Cosmology. Whitall N. Perry. (Illus.). 111p. (Orig.). 1995. pap. 9.95 (*1-870196-13-9*, Pub. by Islamic Texts UK) Intl Spec Bk.

***Widening Breach: Evolutionism in the Mirror of Cosmology.** Whitall N. Perry. 110p. 1996. pap. 9.95 (*0-614-21613-3*, 1403) Kazi Pubns.

Widening Circle. Polly Murray. 336p. 1996. 23.95 (*0-312-14068-1*) St Martin.

Widening Circle: Extension & Continuing Education at the University of Alabama, 1904-1992. Jeanie Thompson. LC 92-61798. 256p. 1993. text ed. 35.00 (*0-9634589-0-6*) U AL Coll Cont Stu.

***Widening Circle: The Consequences of Modernism in Contemporary Art.** Barry Schwabsky. (Contemporary Artists & Their Critics Ser.). (Illus.). 240p. (C). 1997. text ed. 54.95 (*0-521-56282-1*); pap. text ed. 17.95 (*0-521-56569-3*) Cambridge U Pr.

Widening Circle of Genocide. Ed. by Israel W. Charney. (Genocide: A Critical Bibliographic Review Ser.: Vol. 3). 430p. (C). 1994. 49.95 (*1-56000-172-0*) Transaction Pubs.

Widening Circles 83: Level 8. Earley. 1983. 32.50 (*0-15-331258-0*) HB Schl Dept.

Widening Gate: Bristol & the Atlantic Economy, 1450-1700. David H. Sacks. LC 90-19878. (New Historicism: Studies in Cultural Poetics: No. 15). (Illus.). 450p. 1991. 45.00 (*0-520-07148-4*); pap. 18.00 (*0-520-08449-7*) U CA Pr.

Widening Gulf: Northern Attitudes to the Independent Irish State, 1919-49. Dennis Kennedy. 266p. 8900. 27.00 (*0-85640-396-2*, Pub. by Blackstaff Pr IE) Dufour.

Widening Gyre. Robert B. Parker, Jr. 192p. 1984. mass mkt. 6.50 (*0-440-19535-7*) Dell.

Widening Gyre: Class & Nation in Yugoslavia. Branca Magas. 256p. 1990. 50.00 (*0-86091-262-0*, A3750); pap. 17.95 (*0-86091-975-7*, A3754) Routledge Chapman & Hall.

Widening Light. Luci Shaw. 143p. 1994. reprint ed. pap. 12.95 (*1-57383-024-0*) Regent College.

Widening Pathway. Early. 1983. text ed. 48.00 (*0-15-331270-X*) HB Schl Dept.

Widening Scope of Self Psychology. Ed. by Arnold Goldberg. (Progress in Self Psychology Ser.: Vol. 9). 304p. 1993. text ed. 39.95 (*0-88163-163-9*) Analytic Pr.

Widening Scope of Shame. Ed. by Andrew Morrison & Melvin R. Lansky. LC 97-11431. 1997. write for info. (*0-88163-169-8*) Analytic Pr.

Widening Spell of the Leaves. Larry Levis. LC 90-21308. (Poetry Ser.). 77p. (C). 1991. 19.95 (*0-8229-3675-5*); pap. 10.95 (*0-8229-5454-0*) U of Pittsburgh Pr.

Widening Sphere: Changing Roles of Victorian Women. Ed. by Martha Vicinus. LC 76-26433. (Illus.). 345p. reprint ed. pap. 98.70 (*0-685-23901-2*, 2056723) Bks Demand.

Widening Sphere of Usefulness: Newark Academy 1774-1993. Suzanne Geissler. LC 93-23268. (Illus.). 320p. 1993. 40.00 (*0-914659-65-0*) Phoenix Pub.

Widening the Field: Continuing Education in Higher Education. Ed. by Colin J. Titmus. 121p. 1985. pap. 38.00 (*1-85059-012-5*, Open Univ Pr) Taylor & Francis.

Widening Witness. Fredrick H. Shively. (Eagle Bible Ser.). 1989. pap. 0.99 (*0-87162-498-2*, D9150) Warner Pr.

***Wider Application & Diffusion of Bioremediation Technologies: The Amsterdam '95 Workshop.** Ed. by S. Wald & T. Hirakawa. 460p. (Orig.). 1996. pap. 72.00 (*92-64-14869-8*, 93-96-03-1, Pub. by Org for Econ FR) OECD.

Wider Domain of Evolutionary Thought. Ed. by David R. Oldroyd & Ian G. Langham. (Australasian Studies in History & Philosophy of Science: 2). 336p. 1983. lib. bdg. 146.00 (*90-277-1477-0*, D Reidel) Kluwer Ac.

Wider European Market: The European Economic Area. Alastair Sutton. 1995. pap. write for info. (*0-406-02131-7*, U.K.) MICHIE.

Wider Families: New Traditional Family Forms. Ed. by Theresa D. Marciano & Marvin B. Sussman. LC 91-19686. (Marriage & Family Review Ser.). (Illus.). 182p. 1993. pap. 19.95 (*1-56024-271-X*); lib. bdg. 39.95 (*1-56024-167-5*) Haworth Pr.

Wider Giving: Women Writing after a Long Silence. Intro. by Sondra Zeidenstein. LC 87-72314. 344p. (Orig.). 1988. pap. 14.95 (*0-9619111-0-7*) Chicory Blue.

***Wider Horizon: Selected Messages of the Universal House of Justice 1983-1992.** Compiled by Paul Lample. x, 257p. (Orig.). 1992. pap. 10.00 (*1-890101-11-7*) Palabra Pubns.

Wider Horizons in Christian Adult Education. Lawrence C. Little. LC 62-14381. 348p. reprint ed. pap. 99.20 (*0-8357-9763-5*, 2017871) Bks Demand.

Wider Range: Travel Writing by Women in Victorian England. Maria H. Frawley. LC 92-55127. 1994. 38.50 (*0-8386-3544-X*) Fairleigh Dickinson.

Wider Sea of Love. large type ed. Frederick E. Smith. (Romance Ser.). 336p. 1992. 25.99 (*0-7089-2580-4*) Ulverscroft.

Wider Sky. Kyffin Williams. 255p. (C). 1991. 50.00 (*0-86383-757-3*, Pub. by Gomer Pr UK) St Mut.

Wider Uses for Foreign Languages see Language Teaching: Broader Contexts

***Wider View of the Universe: Henry Thoreau's Study of Nature.** Robert K. Mcgregor. LC 96-45799. 1997. 16.95 (*0-252-06620-0*); text ed. 29.95 (*0-252-02318-8*) U of Ill Pr.

Wider Vision. Marcus Braybrooke. 1996. pap. 16.95 (*1-85168-119-1*) Onewrld Pubns.

Wider Western Europe. Ed. by Helen Wallace. 1991. text ed. 59.00 (*0-86187-069-7*) St Martin.

Wider Western Europe: Reshaping the EC - EFTA Relationship. Ed. by Helen Wallace. 285p. 1992. pap. text ed. 19.95 (*1-85567-088-7*) St Martin.

Wider World: Collections of Foreign Ethnography in Scotland. Ed. by Elizabeth Kwasnik. (Illus.). 96p. 1995. pap. 19.95 (*0-948636-56-4*, 6564, Woodstocker Bks) A Schwartz & Co.

***Widerstand als Sprachliche Gemeinschaft: Die Romane von Kingsley Amis als Selbstreflexive Texte.** Wilfried Ladewig. (Europaische Hochschulschriften, Reihe 14: Bd. 324). 387p. (GER.). 1997. 63.95 (*3-631-30696-2*) P Lang Pubng.

***Widerstand Gegen das Dritte Reich: Im Raum der Katholischen Kirche.** Marc Steinhoff. (Elementa Theologiae Ser.: Bd. 9). 188p. (GER.). 1997. 42.95 (*3-631-31164-8*) P Lang Pubng.

***Widerstande bei Organisatorischem Wandel: Mechanismen bei Veranderungsprozessen in Unternehmensorganisationen.** Margit Schmidt. (Europaische Hochschulschriften: Reihe 6: Bd. 567). 207p. (GER.). 1996. pap. 42.95 (*3-631-30885-X*) P Lang Pubng.

Widescreen Cinema. John Belton. (Harvard Film Studies). (Illus.). 300p. 1992. 37.50 (*0-674-95260-X*); pap. 21.00 (*0-674-95261-8*) HUP.

Widmann's Clinical Interpretation of Laboratory Tests. 10th ed. Ronald A. Sacher & Richard A. McPherson. LC 89-71420. (Illus.). 841p. 1991. pap. text ed. 44.95 (*0-8036-7694-8*) Davis Co.

***Widmann's Clinical Interpretation of Laboratory Tests.** 11th ed. Ronald A. Sacher & Richard A. McPherson. (Illus.). 825p. 1998. pap. 48.00 (*0-8036-0270-7*) Davis Co.

Widow. Billie S. Mosiman. 384p. (Orig.). 1995. mass mkt. 5.99 (*0-425-14683-9*) Berkley Pub.

Widow: Rebuilding Your Life. Genevieve D. Ginsburg. LC 94-48279. 240p. (Orig.). 1995. pap. 12.95 (*1-55561-075-7*) Fisher Bks.

Widow & the Colonel. Rochelle Owens. 1977. pap. 3.25 (*0-8222-1252-8*) Dramatists Play.

Widow & the Parrot. Virginia Woolf. (Illus.). 32p. (J). (ps up). 1988. 12.95 (*0-15-296783-4*) HarBrace.

Widow & the Rodeo Man. Jackie Merritt. (Montana Mavericks Ser.). 1994. mass mkt. 3.99 (*0-373-50166-8*, 1-50166-7) Silhouette.

Widow & the Wastrel. Janet Dailey. (Americana Ser.: No. 885). 1992. mass mkt. 3.59 (*0-373-89885-1*) Harlequin Bks.

Widow Barnaby, 3 vols. in 2, Set. Frances E. Trollope. LC 79-8208. reprint ed. 84.50 (*0-404-62141-4*) AMS Pr.

Widow Claire. Horton Foote. 1987. pap. 5.25 (*0-8222-1253-6*) Dramatists Play.

Widow Directed to the Widow's God. John A. James. 260p. 1996. 24.95 (*1-57358-035-X*) Soli Deo Gloria.

Widow LeRouge. Emile Gaboriau. Tr. by Fred Williams & George A. Ernst from FRE. LC 75-32746. (Literature of Mystery & Detection Ser.). 1976. reprint ed. 19.95 (*0-405-07872-2*) Ayer.

Widow LeRouge. Emile Gaboriau. 293p. 1980. reprint ed. lib. bdg. 12.50 (*0-89968-184-0*, Lghtyr Pr) Buccaneer Bks.

Widow Makers. Robert Kammen. 1989. mass mkt. 2.95 (*0-8217-2765-6*, Zebra Kensgtn) Kensgtn Pub Corp.

Widow, Nun & Courtesan: Three Novelettes from the Chinese. Lin Yu-T'ang. LC 75-112328. vi, 266p. 1971. reprint ed. text ed. 38.50 (*0-8371-4716-6*, LIWN, Greenwood Pr) Greenwood.

Widow of Borley: A Psychical Investigation. R. Wood. 178p. 1992. 31.95 (*0-7156-2419-9*, Pub. by Duckworth UK) Focus Pub-R Pullins.

Widow of the Waves. Bev Jamison. 1994. pap. 15.95 (*1-886028-06-0*) Savage Pr.

Widow of Windsor. large type ed. Jean Plaidy. (Shadows of the Crown Ser.). 1975. 15.95 (*0-85456-602-3*) Ulverscroft.

***Widow Traditions in Luke - Acts: A Feminist - Critical Scrutiny.** Robert M. Price. LC 96-53453. (SBL Dissertation Ser.). 281p. 1997. 29.95 (*0-7885-0224-7*, 062155) Scholars Pr GA.

Widow Woman. Parris A. Bonds. 1992. mass mkt., pap. text ed. 3.99 (*0-8439-3297-X*) Dorchester Pub Co.

Widowed. Joyce Brothers. 1992. mass mkt. 5.99 (*0-345-37400-2*) Ballantine.

Widowed. Philip Jebb. LC 83-11160. 90p. 1984. pap. 4.95 (*0-932506-30-5*) St Bedes Pubns.

Widowed. Frances H. Mulliken. 1983. pap. 6.25 (*0-8309-0361-5*) Herald Hse.

Widowed. large type ed. Joyce Brothers. 274p. 1991. reprint ed. lib. bdg. 21.95 (*1-56054-165-2*) Thorndike Pr.

Widowed Beaver. Michael P. Jones. (Illus.). 150p. (Orig.). 1986. pap. 9.95 (*0-317-67925-2*); text ed. 14.95 (*0-89904-201-5*) Crumb Elbow Pub.

Widowed Beaver. limited ed. Michael P. Jones. (Illus.). 150p. (Orig.). 1986. 25.00 (*0-89904-203-1*) Crumb Elbow Pub.

Widowed Priest. Joseph Allen. 176p. (Orig.). 1994. pap. 9.95 (*1-880971-01-1*) Light&Life Pub Co MN.

Widower: When Men Are Left Alone. Scott Campbell & Phyllis R. Silverman. (Death, Value & Meaning Ser.). 247p. 1996. 34.95 (*0-89503-140-X*) Baywood Pub.

Widower & Some Spinsters: Short Stories. Maria L. Pool. LC 78-101288. (Short Story Index Reprint Ser.). 1977. 21.95 (*0-8369-3225-0*) Ayer.

Widowers' Houses. Ed. by Jerald Bringle. LC 79-56699. (Bernard Shaw Early Texts: Play Manuscripts in Facsimile). 245p. 1981. text ed. 20.00 (*0-8240-4575-0*) Garland.

Widowers' Houses (Playscript) George Bernard Shaw. LC 79-56699. 1990. pap. 7.00 (*0-88734-225-6*) Players Pr.

Widowhood. A. Rhodes. 1995. 16.95 (*1-879041-20-0*) Sigo Pr.

Widowhood: A Socio-Psychiatric Study. Sandhya. (C). 1995. 30.00 (*81-7445-002-5*, Pub. by UBS Pubs Dist II) S Asia.

Widowhood in an American City. Helena Z. Lopata. 369p. 1973. pap. text ed. 24.95 (*0-87073-091-6*) Transaction Pubs.

Widowing: Surviving the First Year. rev. ed. Nancy Brown & Jane C. Krimbill. LC 95-68228. 96p. 1995. reprint ed. wbk. ed., pap. 9.95 (*0-9652809-0-X*) Magoo Ltd.

Widowmaker. William Appel. LC 94-15362. 1994. 19.95 (*0-8027-3193-7*) Walker & Co.

Widowmaker: A Mystery Thriller. Lizz Raines. 1994. pap. 5.95 (*0-9625632-4-2*) NUVENTURES Pub.

Widowmaker in Spring. Mike Resnick. (Widowmaker Trilogy: Bk. 1). 304p. 1996. mass mkt. 5.99 (*0-553-57160-5*) Bantam.

***Widowmaker Reborn.** Mike Resnick. (Widowmaker Trilogy: Bk. 2). 1997. mass mkt. 5.99 (*0-553-57161-3*, Spectra) Bantam.

Widows. Ed McBain. 336p. 1992. reprint ed. mass mkt. 6.50 (*0-380-71383-7*) Avon.

Widows' Adventures. Charles Dickinson. 400p. 1990. reprint ed. pap. 10.00 (*0-380-70847-7*) Avon.

Widows & Destitute Women in India. Ed. by Pramila Dandavate et al. 145p. 1989. text ed. 15.95 (*81-7027-139-8*, Pub. by Radiant Pubs II) S Asia.

Widows Are Not for Burning. A. K. Ray. 1985. 24.95 (*0-318-37316-5*) Asia Bk Corp.

Widows Are Special: They Know the Sun Will Rise Again. Kathleen L. Peabody et al. LC 94-17856. 128p. (Orig.). (C). 1994. pap. 10.95 (*0-929350-7-7*) Sharp Pub.

Widow's Beads. large type ed. Cyril Joyce. (Linford Mystery Library). 304p. 1994. pap. 15.99 (*0-7089-7483-X*, Linford) Ulverscroft.

Widow's Blind Date. Israel Horovitz. 1990. pap. 5.25 (*0-8222-1254-4*) Dramatists Play.

Widow's Broom. Chris Van Allsburg. LC 92-7110. (Illus.). 32p. (J). (gr. k-4). 1992. 17.95 (*0-395-64051-2*) HM.

Widows Club. Dorothy A. Cannell. 352p. 1989. mass mkt. 5.50 (*0-553-27794-4*) Bantam.

***Widow's Dilemma: It Can Happen to Anyone.** Eleanor B. Burns. Ed. & Illus. by Ann Robertson. 92p. (Orig.). 1995. pap. 6.00 (*0-9652990-0-7*) E B Burns.

Widow's End. large type ed. John Penn. 352p. 1995. 25.99 (*0-7089-3246-0*) Ulverscroft.

Widow's Gambit. Anthea Malcolm. 256p. 1988. pap. 2.95 (*0-8217-2357-X*, Zebra Kensgtn) Kensgtn Pub Corp.

Widow's Gambit. Anthea Malcolm. 352p. 1993. mass mkt. 3.99 (*0-8217-4075-X*, Zebra Kensgtn) Kensgtn Pub Corp.

Widow's Handbook: A Guide for Living. Charlotte Foehner & Carol Cozart. LC 88-3619. 320p. (C). 1987. 8.99 (*1-55591-014-9*); pap. 6.99 (*1-55591-023-8*) Fulcrum Pub.

Widow's House by the Great Water. William Morris. Ed. by Helen Timo. 64p. (Orig.). (C). 1991. pap. 8.50 (*0-931332-07-9*) Wm Morris Soc.

Widows in African Societies: Choices & Constraints. Ed. by Betty Potash. 336p. 1986. 42.50 (*0-8047-1299-9*) Stanford U Pr.

Widows in India. T. N. Kitchlu. (Illus.). xxviii, 341p. (C). 1993. 42.00 (*81-7024-529-X*, Pub. by Ashish Pub Hse II) Nataraj Bks.

Widow's Might. large type ed. Rosamond Fitzroy. 397p. 1982. 25.99 (*0-7089-0755-5*) Ulverscroft.

***Widow's Might: Strength from the Rock.** Leona Choy. 156p. 1996. pap. 14.95 (*1-889283-01-0*) Golden Morning.

***Widow's Might: Three Plays.** Ned Conquest. LC 97-71095. 115p. (Orig.). 1997. pap. 9.95 (*0-9627485-3-6*) Apollonian Pr.

Widow's Mite. large type ed. Emma Goldrick. (Harlequin Ser.). 1993. reprint ed. lib. bdg. 18.95 (*0-263-13275-7*, Pub. by Mills & Boon UK) Thorndike Pr.

Widow's Mite: One-Act Play. adapted ed. C. B. Gilford. 1967. pap. 3.25 (*0-8222-1255-2*) Dramatists Play.

Widow's Mite & Other Stories. Ferrol Sams. 224p. 1989. pap. 10.95 (*0-14-011250-2*, Penguin Bks) Viking Penguin.

Widow's Mite Presents Plus. Emma Goldrick. (Presents Ser.). 1993. mass mkt. 2.99 (*0-373-11576-8*, 1-11576-5) Harlequin Bks.

Widows of Broome: An Inspector Napoleon Bonaparte Mystery. Arthur W. Upfield. 256p. 1985. pap. 5.95 (*0-684-18389-7*) S&S Trade.

Widows of Russia. Carl R. Proffer. 1992. pap. 12.00 (*0-679-74262-X*, Vin) Random.

Widows of Thornton. Stories. Peter Taylor. LC 53-7839. (Voices of the South Ser.). 320p. 1994. pap. 11.95 (*0-8071-1930-X*) La State U Pr.

Widow's Quilt. Fran Castan. 84p. 1996. pap. 12.00 (*1-886435-04-9*) Canios Edit.

***Widow's Resource: How to Solve the Financial & Legal Problems That Occur Within the First Six to Nine Months of Your Husband's Death.** Julie Calligaro. LC 96-61700. 124p. 1997. pap. 12.95 (*1-890117-03-X*) Womens Source.

Widow's Story. Bertha E. Piercey. LC 92-23311. (Orig.). 1992. pap. 8.95 (*0-9627635-4-3*) Brandylane.

Widow's Tale, 1822. Caroline B. Southey. (Revolution & Romanticism, 1789-1834 Ser.). 1996. 48.00 (*1-85477-177-9*, Pub. by Woodstock Bks UK) Cassell.

Widow's Tears. fac. ed. George Chapman. Ed. by Ethel M. Smeak. LC 68-24305. 145p. 1966. pap. 41.40 (*0-7837-7335-8*, 2047288) Bks Demand.

Widow's Topical Bible. Michael D. Murdock. Ed. by Joy A. Loy. 165p. (Orig.). 1991. pap. text ed. 4.95 (*1-56394-005-1*) Wisdom Intl.

Widows, Vol. I: The Middle East, Asia, & the Pacific. Ed. by Helena Z. Lopata. LC 87-5410. xiii, 258p. (C). 1987. 48.00 (*0-8223-0680-8*); pap. text ed. 22.95 (*0-8223-0768-5*) Duke.

Widows, Vol. II: North America. Ed. by Helena Z. Lopata. LC 87-5410. xii, 313p. (C). 1987. text ed. 53.00 (*0-8223-0724-3*); pap. text ed. 22.95 (*0-8223-0770-7*) Duke.

Widow's Watch. Nancy Herndon. 304p. (Orig.). 1995. pap. text ed. 5.50 (*0-425-14900-5*) Berkley Pub.

***Widows Wear Weeds.** A. A. Fair, pseud. 1997. 18.50 (*0-7451-8699-8*, Black Dagger) Chivers N Amer.

Widow's Web. Gene Lyons. 1994. mass mkt. 5.99 (*0-8041-1268-1*) Ivy Books.

***Widow's Windows.** Elmer A. Spiezio, 2nd. 70p. (Orig.). 1996. pap. 10.95 (*1-57502-292-3*, PO1002) Morris Pubng.

Wid's Year Book: 1919-20. 1971. 35.95 (*0-405-02563-7*, 57) Ayer.

Wid's Year Book 1918. 1971. 27.95 (*0-405-02562-9*, 58) Ayer.

Wid's Year Book 1918-1922. 1971. 110.95 (*0-405-02557-2*, 128) Ayer.

Wid's Year Book 1920-1921. 1971. 35.95 (*0-405-02564-5*, 56) Ayer.

Wid's Year Book 1921-1922. 1971. 27.95 (*0-405-02565-3*, 55) Ayer.

Widsith, A Study in Old English Heroic Legend. Raymond W. Chambers. (BCL1-PR English Literature Ser.). 263p. 1992. reprint ed. lib. bdg. 79.00 (*0-7812-7166-5*) Rprt Serv.

***Widsom from the Bible for Women: A Daily Devotional for Women.** Carol Fitzpatrick. 1997. pap. text ed. 4.97 (*1-55748-937-8*) Barbour & Co.

Width of a Vibrato. Edith A. Jenkins. (Blue Ser.). 32p. (Orig.). 6.00 (*0-938631-10-1*) Pennywhistle Pr.

Wie Alles Anfing see How It All Began: A Personal Account of a West German Urban Guerrilla

Wie Baut Amerika? Baubucher, Vol. 1. Richard J. Neutra. (Bauhaus Ser.). 1990. reprint ed. 37.00 (*3-601-00289-2*) Periodicals Srv.

WIE Computer Architecture: Synthesis, Vol. 1. 377p. (Orig.). 1988. pap. 17.95 (*0-471-61277-4*) Wiley.

Wie Gebraucht Fremdworter? (Duden-Taschenbucher Ser.: No. 9). 368p. 1970. 15.95 (*3-411-01139-4*, Pub. by Bibliogr Inst Brockhaus GW) Langenscheidt.

Wie Geht's? 4th annot. ed. Dieter H. Sevin et al. 544p. (C). 1991. teacher ed. write for info. (*0-03-049494-X*) HB Coll Pubs.

Wie Geht's? 4th ed. Dieter H. Sevin et al. 544p. (C). 1991. text ed. 45.25 (*0-03-049493-1*); write for info. (*0-318-69161-2*) HB Coll Pubs.

***Wie Geht's?** 5th ed. Sevin. (C). 1995. lab manual ed., wbk. ed. write for info. (*0-15-501062-X*) HB Coll Pubs.

Wie Geht's? An Introductory German Course. Dieter H. Sevin et al. (Illus.). 480p. (GER.). (C). 1994. text ed. write for info. (*0-15-501060-3*) HB Coll Pubs.

W

*Wie Gertrud Ihre Kinder Lehrt: 1801 Edition. Johann H. Pestalozzi. Ed. & Intro. by Jeffrey Stern. (Classics in Education Ser.). 392p. 1996. reprint ed. write for info. (1-85506-304-2) Bks Intl VA.

Wie Geschrieben Steht: Studien zu Einer Besonderen Art Fruehchristlichen Schriftbezuges. Reinhold Liebers. viii, 445p. (GER.). (C). 1993. lib. bdg. 136.95 (3-11-013859-X) De Gruyter.

*Wie New York Paris die Idee der Modernen Kunst Stahl Abstrakter Expressionismus, Freiheit und Kalter Krieg. Sege Guilbaut. (GER.). 1996. text ed. 40.00 (90-5705-022-6) Gordon & Breach.

Wie Niet Weg Is Word Gezien see Hide & Seek

Wie Politisch war Jesus Christus? A. Von Juechen. (Anstoesse Zur Friedensarbeit Ser.: No. 1). 132p. (GER.). 1990. pap. text ed. 12.50 (3-487-09371-5) G Olms Pubs.

Wie Sage Ichs Den Patienten: German, Turkish, Italian, Spanish, Serbocroatian. Pia M. Guardiola. 71p. 1986. lib. bdg. 45.00 (0-8288-3591-8, F105160) Fr & Eur.

Wie Sagt der Arzt? (Duden-Taschenbucher Ser.: No. 10). 176p. 1970. 12.25 (3-411-01140-8, Pub. by Bibliogr Inst Brockhaus GW) Langenscheidt.

Wie Sagt Man Anderswo? (Duden-Taschenbucher Ser.: No. 15). 190p. 1983. 12.25 (3-411-01978-6, Pub. by Bibliogr Inst Brockhaus GW) Langenscheidt.

Wie Sagt Man Im Osterreich? (Duden-Taschenbucher Ser.: No. 8). 252p. 1980. 14.00 (3-411-01794-5, Pub. by Bibliogr Inst Brockhaus GW) Langenscheidt.

Wie Sagt Man Inder Schweiz? (Duden-Taschenbucher Ser.: No. 22). 380p. 1989. 17.50 (3-411-04131-5, Pub. by Bibliogr Inst Brockhaus GW) Langenscheidt.

Wie Sagt Man Noch? (Duden-Taschenbucher Ser.: No. 2). 219p. 1968. 12.25 (3-411-01132-7, Pub. by Bibliogr Inst Brockhaus GW) Langenscheidt.

Wie Sah das Erste Sternenbanner Aus? What Did the First U. S. Flag Look Like? Arnold Rabbow. 1980. 1.50 (0-934021-36-8) Natl Flag Foun.

Wie Schreibt Man Gutes Deutsch? (Duden-Taschenbucher Ser.: No. 7). 163p. 1969. 12.25 (3-411-01137-8, Pub. by Bibliogr Inst Brockhaus GW) Langenscheidt.

Wie Verfast Man Wissenschaftliche Arbeiten? (Duden-Taschenbucher Ser.: No. 21). 216p. 1988. 12.25 (3-411-02751-7, Pub. by Bibliogr Inst Brockhaus GW) Langenscheidt.

*Wie Werdet Ihr Die Gleichnisse Verstehen? Empirisch-Theologische Forschung Zur Gleichnisdidaktik. Chris Hermans. (Theologie & Empirie Ser.: Vol. 12). 236p. 1990. pap. 34.95 (90-242-3110-8, Pub. by KOK Pharos NE) Eisenbrauns.

Wiederholte Spiegelungen: Funktion und Bedeutung der Verseinlage in Goethes Iphigenie auf Tauris und Wilhelm Meisters Lehrjahre. Ingrid Winter. (Studies in Modern German Literature: Vol. 21). 351p. 1988. 43.00 (0-8204-0603-1) P Lang Pubng.

Wiedza Powszechna Compact Polish & English Dictionary. Wiedza Powszechna et al. 720p. 1994. 16.95 (0-8442-8366-5, 8366-5, Natl Textbk) NTC Pub Grp.

Wiedza Powszechna Compact Polish & English Dictionary. Wiedza Powszechna et al. 720p. 1994. pap. 12.95 (0-8442-8367-3, Natl Textbk) NTC Pub Grp.

Wiegand Models of Matter. Date not set. student ed., pap. text ed. 16.75 (0-314-05510-X) West Pub.

Wiehnachtsstern. Marcus Pfister. (Illus.). (J). 1993. 16.95 (3-314-00601-2) North-South Bks NYC.

*Wiel Arets: Strange Bodies. Stan Allen. (Illus.). 116p. 1996. 48.00 (3-7643-5411-9) Birkhauser.

Wieland. Charles B. Brown. 22.95 (0-8488-0922-X) Amereon Ltd.

*Wieland: A Cultural Biography. James M. Skidmore. (GERM Ser.). Date not set. write for info. (1-57113-137-X) Camden Hse.

Wieland: Or, the Transformation. Charles B. Brown. Ed. by F. L. Pattee. LC 58-13328. 351p. 1969. reprint ed. pap. 10.95 (0-15-696680-8, Harvest Bks) HarBrace.

Wieland: Or the Transformation. Charles B. Brown. (Works of Charles Brockden Brown). 1989. reprint ed. lib. bdg. 79.00 (0-7812-2066-1) Rprt Serv.

Wieland & Carwin the Biloquist. Charles Brockton Brown. Ed. by Emory Elliott. (World's Classics Ser.). 336p. 1994. pap. text ed. 8.95 (0-19-282876-2) OUP.

Wieland & "Memoirs of Carwin" Charles B. Brown. Ed. by Sydney J. Krause & S. W. Reid. LC 78-15330. 310p. 1978. pap. 14.00 (0-87338-220-X) Kent St U Pr.

Wieland & Memoirs of Carwin the Biloquist. Charles B. Brown. Ed. & Intro. by Jay Fliegelman. 416p. 1991. pap. 10.95 (0-14-039079-0, Penguin Classics) Viking Penguin.

*Wieland, or the Transformation. Charles B. Brown. (Literary Classics Ser.). 1997. pap. text ed. 7.95 (1-57392-175-0) Prometheus Bks.

Wieland und die Weidmannsche Buchhandlung. Karl Buchner. viii, 168p. reprint ed. write for info. (0-318-71748-4) G Olms Pubs.

*Wielands Geschichtsphilosophische Reflexionen. Susanne Wipperfurth. (GER.). 1995. 42.95 (3-631-48971-4) P Lang Pubng.

Wielding a Red Sword. Piers Anthony. (Incarnations of Immortality Ser.). 320p. 1987. mass mkt. 5.95 (0-345-32221-5, Del Rey) Ballantine.

*Wielki Slownik Angielsko-Polski - The Great English-Polish Dictionary, 2 vols. Jan Stanislawski. (ENG & POL.). 1993. pap. 98.00 (83-85840-34-6) Szwede Slavic.

Wielki Slownik Polsko-Angielsi - The Great Polish-English Dictionary: Great, 2 vols. Jan Stanislawski. (ENG & POL.). 1993. Set. pap. 98.00 (83-214-0956-3) Szwede Slavic.

Wielki Slownik Polsko-Rosyjski, 2 vols., Set. Mirowicz & R. Stypula. 1331p. (POL & RUS.). 1980. 150.00 (0-8288-1037-0, M9131) Fr & Eur.

Wielki Slownik Techni Rosyjsko - Polski. M. Martin. 1151p. (POL & RUS.). 1980. 95.00 (0-8288-2142-9, M14452) Fr & Eur.

Wielkopolski Slownik Biograficzny. Ed. by Antoni Gasiorowski. 890p. (POL.). 1981. 80.00 (0-614-02652-0) Szwede Slavic.

Wielopole-Wielopole. Tadeusz Kantor. Tr. by Mariusz Tchorek & George Hyde from POL. (Illus.). 192p. 1988. 24.95 (0-7145-2782-3) M Boyars Pubs.

Wiener Dog Art: A Far Side Collection. Gary Larson. (Illus.). 112p. 1990. pap. 7.95 (0-8362-1865-5) Andrews & McMeel.

Wiener Werkstaette. (Illus.). 1966. pap. 7.00 (0-910810-10-9) Johannes.

*Wiener Werkstaette. Benedik Taschen GW Staff. 1996. pap. text ed. 29.99 (3-8228-8571-1) Taschen Amer.

*Wiener Werkstatte. Gabriele Fahr-Becker. 1995. 39.99 (3-8228-8880-X) Taschen Amer.

Wier & Pouce. Steve Katz. LC 83-40578. (New American Fiction Ser.: No. 1). 368p. 1984. 16.95 (0-940650-33-9); pap. 10.95 (0-940650-47-9) Sun & Moon CA.

Wier & Pouce. deluxe ed. Steve Katz. LC 83-40578. (New American Fiction Ser.: No. 1). 368p. 1984. 30.00 (0-940650-35-5) Sun & Moon CA.

*Wierd & Wonderful. Dennett. LC 97-4880. 1998. 45.00 (0-8147-1885-X); pap. 15.95 (0-8147-1886-8) NYU Pr.

*Wierd Wide Web. Erfert Fenton & David Pogue. 140p. (Orig.). 1997. pap. write for info. (0-614-26299-2) IDG Bks.

Wierix Family Prints (Les Estampes des Wierix), Catalogue Raisonne, 4 vols. Marie Mauquoy-Hendrickx. (Illus.). 1983. pap. 295.00 (1-55660-225-1) A Wofsy Fine Arts.

Wiersbe's Expository Outlines on the New Testament. Warren W. Wiersbe. LC 92-5611. 864p. 1992. 34.99 (0-89693-848-4, 6-1848, Victor Bks) Chariot Victor.

Wiersbe's Expository Outlines on the Old Testament. Warren W. Wiersbe. LC 92-40776. 640p. 1993. 28.99 (0-89693-847-6, 6-1847, Victor Bks) Chariot Victor.

Wiersbe's Expository Sermon Outlines on the Old Testament. Warren W. Wiersbe. (To Be Ser.). 1991. 25.99 (0-89693-876-X, Victor Bks) Chariot Victor.

Wiersze na dwu Strunach (Two String Poems) Leszek Czuchajowski. 80p. (Orig.). (POL.). 1989. pap. text ed. 7.00 (0-930401-23-9) Artex Pub.

Wiersze Sercem Pisane. Jan Skupien. 64p. 1992. pap. text ed. 7.00 (0-930401-51-4) Artex Pub.

Wiesengesellschaften des Mittleren Schwarzwaldes: Standort - Nutzung - Naturschutz. F. Kretzschmar. (Dissertationes Botanicae Ser.: Vol. 189). (Illus.). 146p. (GER.). 1992. pap. text ed. 75.00 (3-443-64101-6, Pub. by Cramer-Borntraeger GW) Lubrecht & Cramer.

WIFB's QRP Notebook. DeMaw. 1991. pap. 10.00 (0-87259-365-7) Am Radio.

Wife. Jim Cory. 29p. 1993. pap. 6.00 (1-882827-01-5) Insight to Riot.

Wife. Stephen Emerson. 96p. 1985. 6.00 (0-942986-02-4) LongRiver Bks.

Wife. Bharati Mukherjee. 1992. reprint ed. mass mkt. 5.99 (0-449-22098-2, Crest) Fawcett.

Wife: A Libretto (For an Opera in Three Acts) 2nd ed. Janet Lewis. LC 88-11720. 64p. 1988. pap. 8.95 (0-936784-63-6) J Daniel.

Wife & Other Stories. Anton P. Chekhov. Tr. by Constance Garnett from RUS. (Tales of Chekhov Ser.: Vol. 5). 200p. 1985. reprint ed. pap. 8.50 (0-88001-052-5) Ecco Pr.

Wife & Widow in Medieval England. Ed. by Sue S. Walker. (Studies in Medieval & Early Modern Civilization). 300p. (C). 1993. text ed. 44.50 (0-472-10415-2) U of Mich Pr.

Wife Battering, a Systems Theory Approach. Jean Giles-Sims. LC 82-15555. (Perspectives on Marriage & the Family Ser.). 207p. reprint ed. pap. 59.00 (0-7837-1205-7, 2041737) Bks Demand.

*Wife by Contract. Raye Morgan. 1997. mass mkt. 3.50 (0-373-76100-7, 1-76100-6) Silhouette.

Wife for a Night. Angela Devine. (Presents Ser.). 1993. pap. 2.89 (0-373-11538-5, 1-11538-5) Harlequin Bks.

Wife for a While. Donna Clayton. 1994. pap. 2.75 (0-373-19039-5, 1-19039-6) Harlequin Bks.

*Wife for Christmas. Kaye & Bauer. 1997. mass mkt. 3.25 (0-373-03485-7) Harlequin Bks.

*Wife for Christmas. large type ed. Kaye & Bauer. 1997. mass mkt. 3.25 (0-373-15731-2) Harlequin Bks.

*Wife for Dr. Sam. Phyllis Halldorson. 1997. mass mkt. 3.25 (0-373-19219-3, 1-19219-4) Silhouette.

Wife for My Son. Ali Ghalem. Tr. by G. Kazolias. LC 84-20414. 211p. 1984. pap. 7.95 (0-916650-17-0) Banner Pr.

Wife for My Son. 3rd ed. Ali Ghalem. 211p. reprint ed. pap. 7.95 (0-86543-116-7) Africa World.

Wife for My Son. Ali Ghalem. Tr. by G. Kazolias from FRE. LC 84-20414. 211p. 1986. reprint ed. 14.95 (0-916650-33-2) Banner Pr.

*Wife For Winter Man. large type ed. Linda Acaster. (Large Print Ser.). 496p. 1996. 25.99 (0-7089-3641-5) Ulverscroft.

Wife He Wanted. Elizabeth August. (Romance Ser.: No. 881). 1992. pap. 2.69 (0-373-08881-7) Silhouette.

Wife-in-Law! Your Ex-Husband Married Her or Your Present Husband Divorced Her. rev. ed. Jocelyn Regina. 208p. (Orig.). 1995. pap. 21.00 (0-914345-02-8) Bereny Bear.
The first book to directly address the emotionally charged relationship faced by millions of today's women. Based on hundreds of interviews, coast to coast. PREMIERE edition sold out! This is a new UPDATED edition. WIVES-IN-LAW & blended families want this book! Your readers need the advantage of understanding the hidden angers, fears & vulnerabilities that fuel domestic strife, the better to cope with them. They meet wise & foolish WIVES-IN-LAW, the MAN-IN-THE-MIDDLE, children, step-children, ADULT CHILDREN OF DIVORCE, in-laws, out-laws & more. An inside perspective reveals taboos, jealousies, guilt & games of the EX, FUTURE, INCUMBENT, VIRTUAL, DOUBLE WIFE-IN-LAW & THE MAN-IN-THE-MIDDLE. Secret dynamics & motivations of gossip, court actions, money problems, holidays, weddings, funerals, presents, telephone conversations, encounters, & hidden agendas are explored. Practical BETTER WAYS are suggested. 50% of marriages end in divorce. Most re-marry. Hand sell WIFE-IN-LAW! Your customers will thank you. TV/radio, promotions. Website: www.wife-in-law.com/ Orders: B&T, your distributor. Special Orders: info 212-679-7935. Established accounts & libraries: FAX 212-679-0506 or e-mail: dept29@wife-in-law.com. Mail Orders/ Payments to: BERENY-BEAR Books, P.O. Box 1601, FDR Station, New York, NY 10150. Editorial: Bereny-Bear Books, 4 Park Ave., New York, NY 10016. *Publisher Provided Annotation.*

Wife in Name Only. Carolyn Zane. (Silhouette Romance Ser.). 1994. pap. 2.75 (0-373-19035-2, 1-19035-4) Harlequin Bks.

Wife in Training. Susan Meier. (Romance Ser.). 1996. mass mkt. 3.25 (0-373-19184-7, 1-19184-0) Silhouette.

Wife in Waiting. Jessica Steele. (Harlequin Romance Ser.: No. 3416). 1996. mass mkt. 3.25 (0-373-03416-4, 1-03416-4) Harlequin Bks.

*Wife in Waiting. Jessica Steele. (Harlequin Romance Ser.). 1996. 19.95 (0-263-14671-5) Thorndike Pr.

Wife Is Many People & Other Poems. Charles R. Hayes. 53p. (Orig.). 1981. pap. text ed. write for info. (0-9621710-0-X) C R Hayes.

Wife Most Unlikely: (Mr. Right, Inc.) Linda Varner. (Romance Ser.). 1995. pap. 2.99 (0-373-19068-9, 1-19068-5) Silhouette.

Wife, Mother & Mystic: Blessed Anna Maria Taigi. Albert Bessieres. Ed. by Douglas Newton. Tr. by Stephen Rigby from FRE. 1977. reprint ed. pap. 8.00 (0-89555-058-X) TAN Bks Pubs.

*Wife, Mother...Lover? Sally T. Hayes. 1997. mass mkt. 3.99 (0-373-07818-8, 1-07818-7) Silhouette.

Wife Next Door. Carolyn Zane. 1994. pap. 2.75 (0-373-19011-5, 5-19011-1) Harlequin Bks.

Wife Next Door. Carolyn Zane. 1994. 2.75 (0-373-91011-8) Silhouette.

Wife Number Nineteen: The Story of a Life in Bondage, Being a Complete Expose of Mormonism, & Revealing the Sorrows, Sacrifices & Sufferings of Women in Polygamy. Ann E. Young. LC 72-2634. (American Women Ser.: Images & Realities). (Illus.). 632p. 1978. reprint ed. 40.95 (0-405-04488-7) Ayer.

*Wife of a Preacher. Al Tarvin. 310p. 1998. pap. 12.95 (0-9643250-9-8) CJH Ent.

Wife of Bath. Beidler. 1995. pap. text ed. 6.00 (0-312-11128-2) St Martin.

Wife of Bath. Geoffrey Chaucer. 240p. 1996. pap. 9.95 (0-312-14201-3) St Martin.

Wife of Bath's Prologue & Tale. Geoffrey Chaucer. Ed. by J. Winny. (Selected Tales from Chaucer Ser.). 1966. pap. 9.95 (0-521-04630-0) Cambridge U Pr.

Wife of Bath's Prologue & Tale. Geoffrey Chaucer. Ed. by Peter G. Beidler. (Case Studies in Contemporary Criticism). 304p. 1996. text ed. 35.00 (0-312-15859-9) St Martin.

Wife of Bath's Prologue & Tale. 2nd ed. Geoffrey Chaucer. Ed. by J. Winny. (Selected Tales from Chaucer Ser.). (Illus.). 144p. (C). 1995. pap. text ed. 9.95 (0-521-46689-X) Cambridge U Pr.

Wife of Bath's Prologue & Tale & the Clerk's Prologue & Tale from the Canterbury Tales. Geoffrey Chaucer. Ed. by Gloria Cigman. LC 75-17976. (London Medieval & Renaissance Ser.). 94p. (C). 1976. 17.95 (0-8419-0225-9) Holmes & Meier.

Wife of Bath's Tale: Its Sources & Analogues. Gustavus H. Maynadier. LC 71-144526. (Grimm Library: No. 13). reprint ed. 27.50 (0-404-53556-9) AMS Pr.

Wife of Bath's Tale, Its Sources & Analogues. G. H. Maynadier. 1972. 200.00 (0-8490-1299-6) Gordon Pr.

Wife of His Youth & Other Stories. Charles W. Chesnutt. (Illus.). (C). 1968. reprint ed. pap. 13.95 (0-472-06134-8, 134, Ann Arbor Bks) U of Mich Pr.

Wife of Martin Guerre. Janet Lewis. LC 82-70548. 109p. 1967. reprint ed. pap. 7.95 (0-8040-0321-1) Ohio U Pr.

Wife of Riley, Vol. I. 2nd ed. Marjorie Riley. Ed. by Wyman Riley. LC 88-886235. (Illus.). 173p. reprint ed. 16.95 (0-9623624-0-9) Levee Hse Bks.

Wife on the Farm. Louise Cleland. 86p. (Orig.). 1995. pap. write for info. (0-9645637-1-1) Belrock Printing.

Wife Rape: Understanding the Response of Survivors & Service Providers. Raquel K. Bergen. (Sage Series on Violence Against Women: Vol. 2). 208p. (C). 1996. 42.00 (0-8039-7240-7); pap. 18.95 (0-8039-7241-5) Sage.

Wife, Son, Daughter: A Father's Poems. Bruce Linton. 24p. (Orig.). 1995. pap. 6.95 (0-9649441-3-8) Fathers Forum.

*Wife to Be. Hart. 1997. mass mkt. 3.25 (0-373-15693-6) Harlequin Bks.

*Wife-to-Be. Jessica Hart. (Romance Ser.). 1997. mass mkt. 3.50 (0-373-03447-4, 1-03447-9) Harlequin Bks.

*Wife to Mr. Wilde. Thomas Kilroy. 80p. 1996. 24.95 (1-85235-194-2); pap. 14.95 (1-85235-193-4) Dufour.

Wife Unravelled. Philip Brown. 1989. pap. 30.00 (1-873812-01-9, Pub. by Icon Pr UK) St Mut.

*Wife Wanted. Christine Rimmer. (Fortune's Children Ser.). 1997. 4.50 (0-373-50184-6, 1-50184-0) Harlequin Bks.

Wife Who Spoke Japanese in Her Sleep. Vivienne Plumb. 113p. 1993. pap. 24.95 (0-908569-74-2, Pub. by U Otago Pr NZ) Intl Spec Bk.

*Wife Without a Past. Elizabeth Harbison. 1997. mass mkt. 3.25 (0-373-19258-4, 1-19258-2) Silhouette.

Wife Worth Waiting For: This Side of Heaven. Arlene James. (Romance Ser.). 1993. pap. 2.75 (0-373-08974-0, 5-08974-3) Silhouette.

Wife's Little Instruction Book: Your Survival Guide to Marriage Without Bloodshed. Diana Jordan & Paul Seaburn. 176p. (Orig.). 1994. pap. 6.50 (0-380-77598-0) Avon.

Wife's Role in Initiating Divorce in Jewish Law & the Agunah Problem: A Halakhic Solution. Shlomo Riskin. 1989. 22.95 (0-88125-122-4) Ktav.

Wifey. Judy Blume. 1989. mass mkt. 5.99 (0-671-69381-6) PB.

Wifie & Hubby: Incidents in the Life of a New York Couple. LC 76-49356. 1976. 3.50 (0-9601182-1-7) R Smith.

Wifredo Lam: And His Contemporaries, 1938-1952. Ed. by Maria R. Balderrama. (Illus.). 176p. 1993. pap. 34.95 (0-8109-2548-6) Abrams.

Wig! B-52s. LC 94-33486. (Illus.). 32p. (J). (ps-3). 1995. 14.95 (0-7868-0079-8); lib. bdg. 14.89 (0-7868-2064-0) Hyprn Child.

Wig Wam Bam. Jaime Hernandez. 128p. 1993. per. 14.95 (1-56097-120-7) Fantagraph Bks.

Wig Wam Bam, Vol. 11. Jaime Hernandez. (Love & Rockets Ser.). 128p. 1993. 35.00 (1-56097-121-5) Fantagraph Bks.

Wigalois, the Knight of Fortune's Wheel. Von Grafenberg Wirnt. LC 76-44239. 244p. 1977. reprint ed. pap. 69.60 (0-7837-8310-8, 2049096) Bks Demand.

Wigger. Lawrence Braithwaite. 1995. pap. text ed. 9.95 (1-55152-020-6, Pub. by Arsenal Pulp CN) LPC InBook.

*Wiggins for President. Walter R. Brooks. Date not set. lib. bdg. 22.95 (0-8488-1707-9) Amereon Ltd.

Wiggle-Butts & Up-Faces: A Child's Primer for Beginning Swimming. Irene M. Kolbisen. Ed. by John Reiter. (I Can Swim Ser.: Vol. 1). (Illus.). 32p. (J). (ps). 1989. lib. bdg. 14.95 (1-877863-00-9) I Think I Can.

Wiggle Worm. Mary Buckman. LC 89-63502. (One in a Series of Predictable Books). (Illus.). (Orig.). (J). (gr. k-2). 1989. pap. text ed. 12.95 (1-879414-06-6) Mary Bee Creat.

Wiggle Worm's Surprise (Playscript) Judith Martin & Donald Ashwander. 16p. (Orig.). (J). (ps up). 1977. 4.00 (0-87602-218-2) Anchorage.

*Wiggle Worthy: Affective Fingere Plays, Energizers & Dramatizations. Judy B. Williams. (Illus.). 26p. (Orig.). (J). (ps-2). 1993. pap. 4.95 (1-884063-55-1) Mar Co Prods.

Wiggle Your Words: Exploring Poetry with Children. Alison Odell. 1990. pap. text ed. 26.40 (0-201-25121-3) Addison-Wesley.

Wiggler's Worms: Stories about God's Green Earth. Paulette Nehemias. LC 92-28486. (God's Green Earth Ser.). (Illus.). 96p. (Orig.). (J). (gr. 3-5). 1993. pap. 4.99 (0-570-04731-5, 56-1697) Concordia.

Wiggles. Linda T. Brandon. (Illus.). 24p. (J). (gr. k-3). 1995. pap. 1.99 (0-87406-780-4) Willowisp Pr.

Wiggles & Giggles: Short Vowel I Sequence. Ellis Richardson. (Read Aloud Ser.: Bk. 6). 32p. (Orig.). 1988. pap. text ed. 4.00 (1-56775-020-6, SVIS6-5) ISM Teach Systs.

Wigglesworth Standard. P. J. Madden. 242p. 1993. mass mkt. 4.99 (0-88368-261-3) Whitaker Hse.

Wiggling Wishbone: Stories of Patasexual Speculation. Bart Plantenga. 160p. Date not set. 7.00 (1-57027-009-0) Autonomedia.

*Wigglits Theater: Contraducktions. (J). 1997. 5.99 (0-8289-0983-0) Penguin.

*Wigglits Theater: Dog-Tired Pussycat. (J). 1997. 5.99 (0-8289-0985-7) Penguin.

*Wigglits Theater: Spin Your Partner. (J). 1997. 5.99 (0-8289-0984-9) Penguin.

Wiggly Tooth Book. Linda P. Pohl. (Illus.). 16p. (J). (ps-2). 1991. 3.95 (0-9625453-1-7) L P Pohl.

*Wiggly Worms Bk. 3. Groves. (J). Date not set. pap. text ed. write for info. (0-582-18764-8, Pub. by Longman UK) Longman.

Wight Magic: Tales of the Isle of Wight, Its Islanders & Overners. Philip Ward. (Travel Bks.: Vol. 17). (Illus.). 240p. (Orig.). 1989. pap. 19.95 (0-900891-98-X) Oleander Pr.

Wightman. M. R. Whitman. 486p. 1991. reprint ed. pap. 73.50 (0-8328-2050-4); reprint ed. lib. bdg. 83.50 (0-8328-2049-0) Higginson Bk Co.

Wights: Thomas Wight of Dedham & Medfield, & His Descendants, 1635-1890. W. W. Wight. (Illus.). 368p. 1989. reprint ed. pap. 55.00 (0-8328-1267-6); reprint ed. lib. bdg. 63.00 (0-8328-1266-8) Higginson Bk Co.

Wigmaker in Eighteenth-Century Williamsburg. Colonial Williamsburg Foundation Staff. (Historic Trades Ser.). (Illus.). 36p. (Orig.). 1959. pap. 2.95 (0-910412-22-7) Colonial Williamsburg.

Wigmaking Step by Step, Pt. 1: Weft Work. Jean Anderson. 138p. 1992. 125.00 (0-9519080-0-6, Pub. by JA Pubns UK) St Mut.

Wigmaking Step by Step, Pt. 2: Foundation Work. Jean Anderson. 250p. 1992. 150.00 (0-9519080-1-4, Pub. by JA Pubns UK) St Mut.

Wigmore, Vol. 2. 4th ed. Chadbourn. 1979. 145.00 (0-316-13567-4) Little.

W

Wigmore, Vol. 3. 4th ed. Chadbourn. 1970. 145.00 (*0-316-13560-7*) Little.

Wigmore, Vol. 3A. 4th ed. Chadbourn. 1970. 145.00 (*0-316-13561-5*) Little.

Wigmore, Vol. 4. 4th ed. Chadbourn. 1972. 145.00 (*0-316-13562-3*) Little.

Wigmore, Vol. 5. 4th ed. Chadbourn. 1974. 145.00 (*0-316-13563-1*) Little.

Wigmore, Vol. 7. 4th ed. Chadbourn. 1978. 145.00 (*0-316-13566-6*) Little.

Wigmore, Vol. 8. 4th ed. McNaughton. 1961. 145.00 (*0-316-93978-1*) Little.

Wigmore, Vol. 9. 4th ed. Chadbourn. 1981. 145.00 (*0-316-13568-2*) Little.

Wigmore: On Evidence, 2 vols., I. Peter Tillers. 1983. 145.00 (*0-316-84559-0*) Little.

Wigmore: On Evidence, 2 vols., IA. Peter Tillers. 1983. 145.00 (*0-316-84560-4*) Little.

Wigmore on Evidence, 11 vols. 4th ed. John H. Wigmore et al. 9800p. 1988. Set. 595.00 (*0-316-93970-6*) Little.

Wigmore on Evidence: Indexes, Vol. XI. Emma Tenant. LC 84-939. 1985. 145.00 (*0-316-84093-9*) Little.

Wigner Distribution Functions. Francis J. Narcowich & Stephen A. Fulling. (Discourses in Mathematics & Its Applications Ser.). iii, 45p. (Orig.). 1994. pap. 6.00 (*0-9630728-1-1*) TX A&M Dept Math.

Wigs & Make-up for Theatre, TV & Film. Patsy Baker. (Illus.). 240p. 1993. 49.95 (*0-7506-0431-X*) Buttrwrth-Heinemann.

Wigstock. Marc Wilkins. LC 96-8684. 64p. 1996. pap. 9.95 (*0-312-14762-7*) St Martin.

Wigwam & the Cabin. rev. ed. W. Gilmore Simms. LC 72-116014. reprint ed. 37.50 (*0-404-06038-2*) AMS Pr.

Wigwam & the Cabin. William G. Simms. LC 68-23729. (Americans in Fiction Ser.). 311p. reprint ed. pap. text ed. 12.95 (*0-89197-976-X*); reprint ed. lib. bdg. 14.50 (*0-8398-1861-0*) Irvington.

Wigwam Evenings: Sioux Tales Retold. Charles A. Eastman & Elaine G. Eastman. LC 90-35728. (Illus.). xii, 253p. 1990. reprint ed. pap. 9.95 (*0-8032-6717-7*, Bison Books) U of Nebr Pr.

Wigwam Stories. M. C. Judd. 1977. lib. bdg. 59.95 (*0-8490-2825-6*) Gordon Pr.

Wii-Kon-Ge Inizan Maazina 'Igans: Ojibwa for "to Have a Feast Cooking Recipes" Tom Whitecloud. (Illus.). 160p. 1996. spiral bd. 9.95 (*1-57166-064-X*) Black Iron.

Wijhat al-lam al-Islami. Malik Bin-Nabi. (Mushkilat al-Hadarah Ser.). 200p. 1986. pap. 4.95 (*1-57547-039-X*) Dar Al-Fikr.

Wikchamni Grammar. Geoffrey Gamble. LC 77-85666. (University of California Publications in Social Welfare: No. 89). 156p. reprint ed. pap. 44.50 (*0-685-23992-6*, 2031575) Bks Demand.

***Wilber Winkle Has a Complaint! Consumer Advocate or Nut with Too Much Time on His Hands?** John Homans. LC 96-79742. 202p. (Orig.). 1997. pap. 12.95 (*0-9631246-4-1*) Bancroft MD.

Wilberforces & Henry Manning: The Parting of Friends. David H. Newsome. LC 67-2. (Illus.). 498p. 1966. 42.50 (*0-674-95280-4*) Belknap Pr.

Wilbur: The Wildbores in America: A Family Tree, 5 vols. rev. ed. J. R. Wilbour & B. F. Wilbour. (Illus.). 1513p. 1990. reprint ed. Set. pap. 199.00 (*0-8328-1573-X*) Higginson Bk Co.

Wilbur: The Wildbores in America: A Family Tree, 5 vols. 2nd rev. ed. J. R. Wilbour & B. F. Wilbour. (Illus.). 1513p. 1990. reprint ed. Set. lib. bdg. 235.00 (*0-8328-1572-1*) Higginson Bk Co.

Wilbur & Orville Wright: The Flight to Adventure. Louis Sabin. LC 82-15879. (Illus.). 48p. (J). (gr. 4-6). 1983. pap. 3.95 (*0-89375-852-3*); lib. bdg. 12.95 (*0-89375-851-5*) Troll Communs.

Wilbur & Orville Wright: Young Fliers. Augusta Stevenson. LC 86-10747. (Childhood of Famous Americans Ser.). (Illus.). 192p. (J). (gr. 2-6). 1986. reprint ed. pap. 4.95 (*0-02-042170-2*) Macmillan.

Wilbur Daniel Steele. Martin Bucco. Ed. by Sylvia E. Bowman. LC 77-161826. (Twayne's United States Authors Ser.). 181p. (C). 1972. 17.95 (*0-8290-1708-9*) Irvington.

***Wilbur Daniel Steele: Great American Short Stories III.** Illus. by James Balkovek. LC 95-76754. (Classic Short Stories Ser.). 80p. (YA). (gr. 6-12). 1995. pap. 5.95 (*0-7854-0629-8*, 40090) Am Guidance.

Wilbur, Orville & the Flying Machine. Max Marquardt. (Real Readers Ser.: Level Green). (Illus.). 32p. (J). (gr. 1-4). 1989. lib. bdg. 21.40 (*0-8172-3530-2*) Raintree Steck-V.

Wilbur, Orville & the Flying Machine. Max Marquardt. (Real Readers Ser.: Level Green). (Illus.). 32p. (J). (gr. 1-4). 1989. pap. 4.95 (*0-8114-6735-X*) Raintree Steck-V.

Wilbur, Vol. 1: The Wildbores in America: A Family Tree. rev. ed. J. R. Wilbour & B. F. Wilbour. (Illus.). 304p. 1990. reprint ed. pap. 44.00 (*0-8328-1563-2*) Higginson Bk Co.

Wilbur, Vol. 1: The Wildbores in America: A Family Tree. 2nd rev. ed. J. R. Wilbour & B. F. Wilbour. (Illus.). 304p. 1990. reprint ed. lib. bdg. 52.00 (*0-8328-1562-4*) Higginson Bk Co.

Wilbur, Vol. 2: The Wildbores in America: A Family Tree. rev. ed. J. R. Wilbour & B. F. Wilbour. (Illus.). 320p. 1990. reprint ed. pap. 44.00 (*0-8328-1565-9*) Higginson Bk Co.

Wilbur, Vol. 2: The Wildbores in America: A Family Tree. 2nd rev. ed. J. R. Wilbour & B. F. Wilbour. (Illus.). 320p. 1990. reprint ed. lib. bdg. 52.00 (*0-8328-1564-0*) Higginson Bk Co.

Wilbur, Vol. 3: The Wildbores in America: A Family Tree. rev. ed. J. R. Wilbour & B. F. Wilbour. (Illus.). 287p. 1990. reprint ed. pap. 44.00 (*0-8328-1567-5*) Higginson Bk Co.

Wilbur, Vol. 3: The Wildbores in America: A Family Tree. 2nd rev. ed. J. R. Wilbour & B. F. Wilbour. (Illus.). 287p. 1990. reprint ed. lib. bdg. 52.00 (*0-8328-1566-7*) Higginson Bk Co.

Wilbur, Vol. 4: The Wildbores in America: A Family Tree. rev. ed. J. R. Wilbour & B. F. Wilbour. (Illus.). 298p. 1990. reprint ed. pap. 44.00 (*0-8328-1569-1*) Higginson Bk Co.

Wilbur, Vol. 4: The Wildbores in America: A Family Tree. 2nd rev. ed. J. R. Wilbour & B. F. Wilbour. (Illus.). 298p. 1990. reprint ed. lib. bdg. 52.00 (*0-8328-1568-3*) Higginson Bk Co.

Wilbur, Vol. 5: The Wildbores in America: A Family Tree. rev. ed. J. R. Wilbour & B. F. Wilbour. (Illus.). 304p. 1990. reprint ed. pap. 44.00 (*0-8328-1571-3*) Higginson Bk Co.

Wilbur, Vol. 5: The Wildbores in America: A Family Tree. 2nd rev. ed. J. R. Wilbour & B. F. Wilbour. (Illus.). 304p. 1990. reprint ed. lib. bdg. 52.00 (*0-8328-1570-5*) Higginson Bk Co.

Wilbur's Book. Parker & Parker Staff. Ed. by Ruby P. Goodwin. (Illus.). 128p. reprint ed. pap. 9.00 (*0-934482-02-0*) Hathor House Bks.

Wilbur's Last Book. Parker & Parker Staff. Ed. by Ruby P. Goodwin-Layman. (Illus.). 130p. Date not set. pap. 9.00 (*0-934482-04-7*) Hathor House Bks.

Wilbur's Poetry: Music in a Scattering Time. Bruce Michelson. LC 90-20353. 272p. (C). 1991. lib. bdg. 35.00 (*0-87023-741-1*) U of Mass Pr.

Wilbur's Space Machine. Lorna Balian. LC 90-55095. (Illus.). 32p. (J). (gr. k-5). 1990. lib. bdg. 14.95 (*0-8234-0836-1*) Humbug Bks.

***Wilco - Being There: Being There.** Ed. by Aaron Stang. (Illus.). 120p. (Orig.). (C). 1997. pap. text ed. 24.95 (*1-57623-943-8*, 0024B) Warner Brothers.

Wilcox County, Alabama, Records Of. Marilyn D. Barefield. (Illus.). 219p. 1988. 22.50 (*0-89308-636-3*, BH 17) Southern Hist Pr.

Wilcox Guide to the Best Watercolor Paints. Michael Wilcox. (Illus.). 285p. (Orig.). 1991. pap. 27.95 (*0-89134-409-8*, 30350, North Lght Bks) F & W Pubns Inc.

Wilcox Sandstone Reservoirs in the Deep Subsurface along the Texas Gulf Coast, Their Potential for Production of Geopressured Geothermal Energy. Don G. Bebout et al. (Report of Investigations Ser.: RI 117). (Illus.). 125p. 1982. pap. 5.00 (*0-318-03251-1*) Bur Econ Geology.

***Wild.** Fabio. 320p. 1997. mass mkt. 6.99 (*0-7860-0411-8*, Pinncle Kensgtn) Kensgtn Pub Corp.

Wild. Whitley Strieber. 1991. mass mkt. 5.95 (*0-8125-1277-4*) Tor Bks.

Wild. David Zindell. (Requiem for Homo Sapiens Ser.: No. 2). 560p. 1996. mass mkt. 5.99 (*0-553-28966-7*, Spectra) Bantam.

Wild Abandon. 1993. pap. 4.95 (*0-8216-5099-8*, Univ Books) Carol Pub Group.

Wild Abandon. Cassie Edwards. 384p. (Orig.). 1994. pap. 4.99 (*0-451-40465-3*, Topaz) NAL-Dutton.

***Wild about Austin: A Guide to Children's Adventures.** Janie Fox & Randy Fox. 180p. (Orig.). 1997. per. 12.95 (*0-9657976-0-0*) Fox Hollow Designs.

Wild about Birds: The DNR Bird Feeder Guide. Carrol Henderson. (Illus.). 288p. 1995. spiral bd. write for info. (*0-9647451-0-0*) MN Bkstore.

Wild about Brownies. Barbara Albright & Jerry Weiner. (Wild about Ser.). 1985. pap. 9.95 (*0-8120-2911-9*) Barron.

Wild about Chili. Dotty Griffith. (Wild about Ser.). (Illus.). 96p. 1985. pap. 8.95 (*0-8120-3498-8*) Barron.

Wild about Color. Christopher Carrie. (Illus.). 40p. (J). (gr. k up). 1990. 1.99 (*0-86696-234-4*) Binney & Smith.

Wild about Harry. Linda L. Miller. 1995. mass mkt. 5.99 (*0-373-15310-4*, 1-15310-5) Harlequin Bks.

Wild about Harry. Linda L. Miller. 1996. pap. 5.99 (*0-373-48340-6*, 1-48340-3) Harlequin Bks.

Wild about Ice Cream. Sue Spitler. (Wild about Ser.). 1985. pap. 6.95 (*0-8120-2916-X*) Barron.

Wild about Muffins. Angela Clubb. 1985. 9.95 (*0-8120-2910-0*) Barron.

Wild about Munchies. Dotty Griffith. (Wild about Ser.). 96p. 1989. spiral bd. 7.95 (*0-8120-4096-1*) Barron.

Wild about Mushrooms. Louise Freedman & Bill Freedman. (Illus.). 224p. 1987. pap. 12.45 (*0-201-19188-1*) Addison-Wesley.

Wild about Mushrooms: The Cookbook of the Mycological Society of San Francisco. Louise Freedman. 1987. pap. 12.95 (*0-685-18085-9*) Aris Bks.

Wild about Mushrooms: The Cookbook of the Mycological Society of San Francisco. Louise Freedman. 1986. 21.45 (*0-671-62312-5*) S&S Trade.

Wild about Pasta & Pizza. Christofano. (Wild about Ser.). 1985. pap. 6.95 (*0-8120-2912-7*) Barron.

Wild about Potatoes. Marie Bianco. (Wild about Ser.). 1985. pap. 6.95 (*0-8120-2914-3*) Barron.

Wild about Rice. Marie Bianco. 96p. 1989. spiral bd. 7.95 (*0-8120-4263-8*) Barron.

Wild about Salads. Marie Bianco. (Wild about Ser.). 96p. 1989. spiral bd. 9.95 (*0-8120-4092-9*) Barron.

Wild about Texas: A Bouquet of Recipes, Wild Flowers & Wines. Cypress Woodlands Junior Forum Staff. (Illus.). 244p. 1989. reprint ed. write for info. (*0-9622009-0-5*) Cypress-Woodlands.

Wild about Turkey. National Wild Turkey Federation Staff. Ed. by Carol Boker. 288p. 1996. 19.95 (*1-879958-30-9*) Tradery Hse.

***Wild about Weather.** (Illus.). 96p. 1997. teacher ed., pap. text ed. 12.95 (*0-07-047098-7*) McGraw.

***Wild about Weather.** (Ranger Rick's Naturescope Ser.). (Illus.). 96p. (J). (gr. 1-7). 1997. text ed. 19.95 (*0-7910-4838-1*) Chelsea Hse.

Wild about Weather. National Wildlife Federation Staff. (J). (gr. k-8). 1991. pap. 7.95 (*0-945051-45-X*, 75003) Natl Wildlife.

***Wild about Wool: Designs for Embroiderers.** Liz Walsh. 1997. pap. text ed. 14.95 (*1-86351-204-7*, Pub. by S Milner AT) Sterling.

***Wild Action.** Dawn Stewardson. 1997. mass mkt. 3.99 (*0-373-70748-7*, 1-70748-8) Harlequin Bks.

Wild Africa. Tony Elliott. LC 94-11876. (TimberTrails Bks.). (J). 1994. pap. 3.95 (*0-914565-42-7*) Capstan Pubns.

Wild Africa: Three Centuries of Nature Writing from Africa. John A. Murray. LC 92-10672. (Illus.). 256p. 1993. 30.00 (*0-19-507377-0*) OUP.

***Wild America.** Peterson. LC 97-12874. 1997. pap. 14.00 (*0-395-86497-6*) HM.

***Wild America: MTV.** Troll Communications Staff. 1997. pap. 3.95 (*0-8167-4327-4*) Troll Communs.

Wild & Crafty. National Wildlife Federation Staff. (J). (gr. k-8). 1991. pap. 7.95 (*0-945051-46-8*, 75043) Natl Wildlife.

Wild & Famous Fish & Game Cookbook. George Manthei. Ed. by Vernon Taylor. (Illus.). 140p. 1992. spiral bd. 9.95 (*1-878816-01-2*) Schildge Pub.

Wild & Free: A Cookbook & Guide to Northwest Blackberries. Kaethe Fulton. (Illus.). 108p. (Orig.). 1994. pap. 9.95 (*0-9641900-0-1*) Grace & Loie.

Wild & Free: Living with Wildlife in Canada's North. Ian Wilson & Sally Wilson. (Illus.). 192p. (Orig.). 1989. pap. 16.95 (*0-919574-87-4*) Gordon Soules Bk.

Wild & Free: On the High Plains. Karyn Stansbery. (Illus.). 136p. (Orig.). 1992. pap. 12.95 (*0-9634396-0-X*) K Stansbery.

Wild & Free: The Story of a Black-Footed Ferret. Jo-Ellen Bosson. LC 92-22797. (Smithsonian Wild Heritage Collection). (Illus.). 32p. (J). (gr. k-3). 1992. 11.95 (*0-924483-68-7*); 16.95 incl. audio (*0-924483-67-9*); 25.95 incl. audio (*0-924483-72-5*); audio write for info. (*0-924483-75-X*) Soundprints.

Wild & Free: The Story of a Black-Footed Ferret. Jo-Ellen Bosson. (Smithsonian Wild Heritage Collection). (Illus.). 32p. (J). (gr. k-3). 1995. pap. 4.95 (*1-56899-197-5*) Soundprints.

Wild & Free: The Story of a Black-Footed Ferret, Incl. toy. Jo-Ellen Bosson. (Smithsonian Wild Heritage Collection). (Illus.). 32p. (J). (gr. k-3). 1995. pap. 14.95 (*1-56899-203-3*) Soundprints.

Wild & Free Cookbook. Tom Squier. LC 95-79302. (Illus.). 360p. (Orig.). 1995. pap. 19.95 (*1-55950-128-6*, 14178) Loompanics.

Wild & Lonely Place: A Sharon McCone Mystery. Marcia Muller. 336p. 1996. mass mkt. 6.50 (*0-446-60328-7*) Warner Bks.

Wild & Outside: How a Renegade Minor League Revived the Spirit of Baseball in America's Heartland. Stefan Fatsis. (Illus.). 288p. (Orig.). 1995. 22.95 (*0-8027-1297-5*) Walker & Co.

Wild & Outside: How a Renegade Minor League Revived the Spirit of Baseball in America's Heartland. Stefan Fatsis. 288p. (Orig.). 1996. pap. 12.95 (*0-8027-7497-0*) Walker & Co.

Wild & Scenic California: The Natural Landscape. Carr Clifton. (Illus.). 128p. 1995. 39.95 (*1-56313-640-6*) BrownTrout Pubs Inc.

Wild & Scenic Florida: A Photographic Portfolio. Photos by James Randklev. LC 95-35810. (Illus.). 128p. 1995. write for info. (*1-56313-702-X*) BrownTrout Pubs Inc.

Wild & Scenic Rivers of America. Tim Palmer. LC 92-32660. (Illus.). 339p. 1993. pap. 22.95 (*1-55963-144-9*); text ed. 45.00 (*1-55963-145-7*) Island Pr.

Wild & the Innocent: A Story & Photographs. Peter De Lory. (CMP Bulletin Ser.). (Illus.). 48p. (Orig.). 1987. pap. 10.00 (*0-9619038-2-1*) Cal Mus Photo.

***Wild & the Sown: Agriculture & Botany in Western Europe, 1350-1850.** Mauro Ambrosoli. Tr. by Mary Salvatorelli. LC 96-300. (Past & Present Publications). (Illus.). 512p. (C). 1997. text ed. 69.95 (*0-521-46509-5*) Cambridge U Pr.

Wild & Whacky Lompoc! A Collection of Colorful Characters & Stories. Harry J. Crompe. LC 92-10640. 144p. (Orig.). 1992. pap. 9.95 (*1-56474-026-9*) Fithian Pr.

Wild & Wonderful. 1993. mass mkt. 3.59 (*0-373-89898-3*, 1-89898-0) Harlequin Bks.

Wild & Wonderful Santee Cooper Country. W. Horace Carter. LC 01-67210. (Illus.). 392p. (Orig.). 1983. pap. 9.95 (*0-937866-03-2*) Atlantic Pub Co.

Wild & Woolly Clean Jokes for Kids. Bob Phillips & Steve Russo. (Orig.). 1996. mass mkt. 3.99 (*1-56507-412-2*) Harvest Hse.

Wild & Woolly Mammoths. Aliki. LC 76-18082. (Let's-Read-&-Find-Out Science Bk.). (Illus.). 40p. (J). (gr. k-3). 1977. lib. bdg. 14.89 (*0-690-01276-4*, Crowell Jr Bks) HarpC Child Bks.

Wild & Woolly Mammoths. Aliki. LC 76-18082. (Trophy Let's-Read-&-Find-Out Bk.). (Illus.). 40p. (J). (ps-3). 1983. pap. 4.50 (*0-06-445005-8*, Trophy) HarpC Child Bks.

Wild & Woolly Mammoths. Aliki. LC 94-48217. (Illus.). 32p. (J). (ps-3). 1996. 14.95 (*0-06-026276-1*); lib. bdg. 14.89 (*0-06-026277-X*) HarpC Child Bks.

Wild Animal Care & Rehabilitation Manual. 4th ed. Vicki Johnson et al. Ed. by Monica Evans. (Illus.). 137p. (C). 1991. pap. text ed. 24.95 (*0-939294-16-8*) Beech Leaf.

Wild Animal Fun. (Animal Fun Bks.). 48p. (J). (gr. 3 up). 1990. 1.95 (*0-88679-810-8*) Educ Insights.

Wild Animal Go-Round. Mary Ling. (Illus.). 18p. (J). 1995. 12.95 (*0-7894-0213-0*, 5-70626) DK Pub Inc.

Wild Animal Paperchains. Stewart Walton & Sally Walton. (Illus.). 32p. (J). (gr. 3 up). 1993. reprint ed. pap. 6.95 (*0-688-12608-1*) Morrow.

Wild Animal Ways. Ernest T. Seton. (Illus.). 242p. (YA). 1994. pap. 16.95 (*1-885529-17-1*) Stevens Pub.

Wild Animals. (Science Safari Ser.). (Illus.). 20p. (Orig.). (J). (gr. k up). 1990. 4.95 (*0-88679-822-1*) Educ Insights.

Wild Animals. (Giant Step Picture Library). (Illus.). 16p. (Orig.). (J). (gr. 3 up). 1990. 9.95 (*0-88679-660-1*) Educ Insights.

Wild Animals. (Child's First Library of Learning). (Illus.). 88p. (Orig.). (J). (gr. 1-4). 1989. 14.95 (*0-8094-4877-7*) Time-Life.

Wild Animals. (Child's First Library of Learning). (Illus.). 88p. (Orig.). (J). (ps-3). 1989. lib. bdg. 21.27 (*0-8094-4878-5*) Time-Life.

Wild Animals. (Sticker Puzzle Bks.). (Illus.). 16p. (J). (ps-3). 1995. pap. 4.95 (*0-7894-0006-5*) DK Pub Inc.

Wild Animals. 1996. 4.99 (*0-517-14260-0*) Crown Pub Group.

***Wild Animals.** (Illus.). 8p. (J). 1997. pap. 3.95 (*0-7894-1534-8*) DK Pub Inc.

Wild Animals. Monika Baierlacher. LC 95-13964. (Animals at a Glance Ser.). (Illus.). 32p. (J). (gr. 1 up). 1996. lib. bdg. 18.60 (*0-8368-1355-3*) Gareth Stevens Inc.

***Wild Animals.** Helen Bateman. (Nature Company Discoveris Library Sticker Bks.). (Illus.). (J). (ps-3). 1997. pap. 7.95 (*0-614-29122-4*) Time-Life.

Wild Animals. Moira Butterfield. LC 92-53114. (One-Thousand Facts about . . . Ser.). (Illus.). 48p. (Orig.). (J). (gr. 3-8). 1992. pap. 6.95 (*1-85697-809-5*, Kingfisher LKC) LKC.

Wild Animals. Cork. (First Nature Bks.). (J). (gr. 2-5). 1982. lib. bdg. 11.95 (*0-88110-077-3*, Usborne) EDC.

Wild Animals. Barbara Cork. (First Nature Bks.). (J). (gr. 2-5). 1982. pap. 3.95 (*0-86020-628-9*, Usborne) EDC.

Wild Animals. Ellen Dreyer. LC 90-11163. (Illus.). 96p. (J). (gr. 2-5). 1991. pap. 6.95 (*0-8167-2243-9*) Troll Communs.

Wild Animals. Gabriele. (J). 1986. pap. 1.95 (*0-911211-60-8*) Penny Lane Pubns.

Wild Animals. Nina Kidd. (Draw Science Ser.). 64p. (J). (ps-3). 1992. pap. 4.95 (*0-929923-90-1*) Lowell Hse.

Wild Animals. Barb McKean. (Discover Nature Ser.). (Illus.). 32p. (J). (gr. 3-7). 1985. pap. 3.50 (*0-88625-117-6*) Durkin Hayes Pub.

Wild Animals. Lorna Read. (Look & Learn Ser.). (Illus.). 12p. (J). (ps). 1996. bds. 4.98 (*1-85854-387-8*) Brimax Bks.

Wild Animals. Philip Steele. LC 90-42014. (Pocket Facts Ser.). (Illus.). 32p. (J). (gr. 5-6). 1991. lib. bdg. 11.95 (*0-89686-584-3*, Crstwood Hse) Silver Burdett Pr.

Wild Animals. Brian Wildsmith. (Illus.). (J). (ps). 1979. pap. 11.50 (*0-19-272103-8*) OUP.

Wild Animals: A Novel of Suspense. Robert S. Reid. 304p. 1996. 22.00 (*0-7867-0257-5*) Carroll & Graf.

Wild Animals: Animal-Shaped Book. 14p. (J). 1996. 3.95 (*0-7894-0619-5*) DK Pub Inc.

***Wild Animals: First Picture Book.** Lorenz Books Staff. 24p. (J). 1996. 3.95 (*1-85967-251-5*, Lorenz Bks) Anness Pub.

***Wild Animals: Sticker Activity Book.** Time Life Books Staff. (The Nature Company Discoveries Library). 1997. pap. text ed. 7.95 (*0-7835-4899-0*) Time-Life.

Wild Animals: 1000 or More Places to See & Photograph Birds & Wildlife in the United States & Canada. Julia K. Miller. (Illus.). 400p. 1990. pap. 18.95 (*0-937480-11-8*) Intl Resources.

Wild Animals & American Environmental Ethics. Lisa Mighetto. LC 91-16910. (Illus.). 209p. (Orig.). 1991. pap. 19.95 (*0-8165-1266-3*); lib. bdg. 39.95 (*0-8165-1160-8*) U of Ariz Pr.

Wild Animals & Settlers on the Great Plains. Eugene D. Fleharty. LC 94-23240. (Illus.). 315p. 1995. 27.95 (*0-8061-2709-0*) U of Okla Pr.

Wild Animals at Home. Ernest T. Seton. (Illus.). 226p. (YA). 1994. pap. 16.95 (*1-885529-15-5*) Stevens Pub.

***Wild Animals Charted Designs.** Celeste Plowden. (Illus.). pap. 3.50 (*0-486-25991-9*) Dover.

Wild Animals Coloring Book. John Green. (Illus.). (J). (gr. k-3). 1989. pap. 2.95 (*0-486-25476-3*) Dover.

Wild Animals I Have Known. Robert Burton. Ed. by William A. Kottmeyer et al. 1962. pap. 7.96 (*0-07-009288-5*) McGraw.

***Wild Animals I Have Known.** Ernest T. Seton. 1996. pap. text ed. 6.95 (*0-7710-9873-1*) McCland & Stewart.

Wild Animals I Have Known. Ernest T. Seton. (Illus.). 354p. (YA). 1994. pap. 18.95 (*1-885529-14-7*) Stevens Pub.

Wild Animals I Have Known. rev. ed. Ernest T. Seton. LC 87-71147. (Illus.). 368p. (J). (gr. 5 up). 1987. reprint ed. pap. 9.95 (*0-88739-053-6*) Creat Arts Bk.

Wild Animals I Have Known. Ernest T. Seton. 1986. reprint ed. lib. bdg. 18.95 (*0-89966-548-9*) Buccaneer Bks.

Wild Animals Masks: Six Punch-Out Designs. Anthony Roa. (Illus.). (J). (gr. k-3). 1993. pap. 2.95 (*0-486-27653-8*) Dover.

Wild Animals of California & the West: Mountains & Desert, Vol. 1. Jack Wilburn. LC 76-29497. (Nature's Wild Ser.). (Illus.). 1980. pap. 7.95 (*0-917982-12-6*, Cougar Books) Capitol Enquiry.

Wild Animals of North America. deluxe rev. ed. National Geographic Society Book Division Staff. 406p. 1995. write for info. (*0-7922-2960-6*) Natl Geog.

Wild Animals of North America. rev. ed. (Illus.). 406p. 1988. 29.95 (*0-87044-700-9*) Natl Geog.

Wild Animals of North America. rev. ed. National Geographic Society, Book Division Staff. 406p. 1995. 40.00 (*0-7922-2958-4*) Natl Geog.

Wild Animals of the Far West. Stouten. Date not set. write for info. (*0-395-27710-8*) HM.

W

An Asterisk (*) at the beginning of an entry indicates that the title is appearing in BIP for the first time.

***Wild Animals of Western Canada.** Kevin Van Tighem. Date not set. pap. text ed. 9.95 (*1-55153-800-8*) Consort Bk Sales.

***Wild Animals on the Moon: And Other Poems.** Naomi Ayala. LC 96-45140. 64p. (Orig.). 1997. pap. 10.95 (*1-880684-44-6*) Curbstone.

Wild Animals Punch-Out Stencils. John E. Cymerman. (Illus.). (J). (gr. k-3). 1994. pap. 3.95 (*0-486-27971-5*) Dover.

Wild Animals Stained Glass Pattern Book: 60 Full-Page Designs. Connie C. Eaton. LC 96-25713. (Pictorial Archive Ser.). 64p. 1996. pap. 5.95 (*0-486-29337-8*) Dover.

Wild Apples. Lucinda Franks. 352p. 1993. mass mkt. 4.99 (*0-380-71923-1*) Avon.

Wild Apples. Henry David Thoreau. 48p. 1989. pap. 4.95 (*1-55709-130-7*) Applewood.

***Wild Arms: Unauthorized Game Secrets.** Ed. by Judie Svabik. 96p. 1997. per. 14.99 (*0-7615-1130-X*) Prima Pub.

Wild Ass of the Ozarks: Jeff Davis & the Social Bases of Southern Politics. Raymond Arsenault. LC 87-25461. 352p. (C). 1988. pap. 19.50 (*0-87049-569-0*) U of Tenn Pr.

Wild Asses: A Journey Through Persia. W. V. Emanuel. LC 76-180336. reprint ed. 49.50 (*0-404-56248-5*) AMS Pr.

Wild Ass's Skin. Honore De Balzac. Tr. by Herbert J. Hunt. (Classics Ser.). 288p. 1977. pap. 9.95 (*0-14-044330-4*, Penguin Classics) Viking Penguin.

***Wild at Heart.** Susan Fox. 1997. pap. 3.25 (*0-373-15714-2*, 1-15714-8) Harlequin Bks.

***Wild at Heart.** Susan Fox. 1997. pap. 3.25 (*0-373-03468-7*, 1-03468-5) Harlequin Bks.

Wild at Heart. Patricia Gaffney. 1997. pap. 5.99 (*0-451-40536-6*, Onyx) NAL-Dutton.

***Wild at Heart.** Patricia Gaffney. 1997. mass mkt. 5.99 (*0-614-20531-X*, Topaz) NAL-Dutton.

Wild at Heart. Barry Gifford. 112p. 1996. reprint ed. pap. 12.00 (*0-8021-3453-X*, Grove) Grove-Atltic.

***Wild Australians.** Wendy L. Jennings. (Illus.). 32p. (Orig.). (J). (gr. 2 up). 1997. pap. 8.95 (*0-86417-784-4*, Pub. by Kangaroo Pr AT) Seven Hills Bk.

Wild Babies. Seymour Simon. LC 96-14558. (Illus.). 32p. (J). (gr. k-3). 1997. 15.95 (*0-06-023033-9*) HarpC Child Bks.

Wild Babies. Seymour Simon. LC 96-14558. (Illus.). 32p. (J). (gr. k-3). 1997. lib. bdg. 15.89 (*0-06-023034-7*) HarpC Child Bks.

***Wild Baron.** Catherine Coulter. 384p. 1997. mass mkt. 6.99 (*0-515-12044-8*) Jove Pubns.

***Wild Baron.** large type ed. Catherine Coulter. LC 97-17236. 1997. write for info. (*0-7862-1117-2*, Thorndike Lrg Prnt) Thorndike Pr.

Wild Beach. Helena Goscillo. 1993. pap. 16.00 (*0-679-74893-8*, Vin) Random.

Wild Beach & Other Stories. Ed. by Helena Goscilo & Byron Lindsey. 390p. 1992. 39.95 (*0-87501-097-0*) Ardis Pubs.

Wild Bears. Laycock. 1988. pap. 19.95 (*1-55654-038-8*) Times Mir Mag Bk Div.

Wild Bears of the World. Paul Ward & Suzanne Kynaston. LC 95-12487. 192p. 1995. 25.95 (*0-8160-3245-9*) Facts on File.

Wild Beasts & Idle Humours: The Insanity Defense from Antiquity to the Present. Daniel N. Robinson. 320p. 1996. 29.95 (*0-674-95289-8*) HUP.

Wild Beasts & Their Ways. Samuel Baker. 1988. 35.00 (*0-935632-75-1*) Wolfe Pub Co.

Wild Bells to the Wild Sky. Laurie McBain. 592p. 1984. mass mkt. 4.95 (*0-380-87387-7*) Avon.

Wild Berry Book: Romance. Recipes & Remedies. Katie L. Lyle. LC 93-48078. (Camp & Cottage Ser.). (Illus.). 144p. 1994. pap. 16.95 (*1-55971-221-X*) NorthWord.

Wild Berry Magic: Pick the Berries. Marge Davenport. (Illus.). (Orig.). 1981. pap. 3.95 (*0-938274-01-5*) Paddlewheel.

Wild Bill & Intrepid: Bill Donovan, Bill Stephenson & the Origins of CIA. Thomas F. Troy. 1996. 30.00 (*0-300-06563-9*) Yale U Pr.

Wild Bill Hickok. Carl R. Green & William R. Sanford. LC 91-29856. (Outlaws & Lawmen of the Wild West Ser.). (Illus.). 48p. (J). (gr. 4-10). 1992. lib. bdg. 14.95 (*0-89490-366-7*) Enslow Pubs.

Wild Bill Hickok. John Hamilton. LC 95-36370. (Heroes & Villains of the Wild West Ser.). (J). 1996. lib. bdg. 14.98 (*1-56239-562-9*) Abdo & Dghtrs.

Wild Bill Hickok. Maryann N. Weidt. LC 92-9732. (Illus.). (J). Date not set. lib. bdg. write for info. (*0-688-10090-2*) Lothrop.

Wild Bill Hickok: The Man & His Myth. Joseph G. Rosa. (Illus.). 272p. 1996. 24.95 (*0-7006-0773-0*) U Pr of KS.

Wild Bill Hickok & the Rebel Raiders. Ron Fontes & Justine Korman. LC 92-56159. (Disney's American Frontier Ser.: Bk. 10). (Illus.). 80p. (Orig.). (J). (gr. 1-4). 1993. pap. 3.50 (*1-56282-493-7*) Disney Pr.

Wild Bill Neely & the Pagan Brothers' Golden Goat Winery. William L. Neely. Ed. by Allan Shields. LC 92-74907. 125p. 1992. pap. 7.95 (*1-882803-02-7*) Jerseydale Ranch.

Wild Bill Sullivan: King of the Hollow. Ann R. Hammons. 160p. 1992. pap. 12.95 (*0-87805-568-1*) U Pr of Miss.

Wild Bird & Other Poems. Donald Lawder. Ed. by Shirley Warren. 40p. (Orig.). 1992. pap. 5.00 (*1-877801-20-8*) Still Waters.

Wild Bird Photography: A Full Color Guide. Tim Gallagher. (Illus.). 176p. 1994. pap. 15.95 (*1-55821-310-4*) Lyons & Burford.

Wild Bird Photography: National Audubon Society Guide. Tim Fitzharris. (Illus.). 112p. (Orig.). 1996. pap. 19.95 (*1-55209-018-3*) Firefly Bks Ltd.

Wild Birds: Six Stories of the Port William Membership. Wendell Berry. LC 85-72988. 160p. 1989. pap. 9.00 (*0-86547-217-3*, North Pt Pr) FS&G.

Wild Birds: Six Stories of the Port William Membership. Wendell Berry. LC 85-72988. 160p. 1986. 13.95 (*0-86547-216-5*) Gnomon Pr.

Wild Blood. Nancy A. Collins. 304p. (Orig.). 1994. pap. 4.99 (*0-451-45432-4*, ROC) NAL-Dutton.

Wild Blood. Naomi Horton. (Intimate Moments Ser.: No. 721). 243p. 1996. mass mkt. 3.99 (*0-373-07721-1*, 1-07721-3) Silhouette.

Wild Blood. Anne Logston. 240p. (Orig.). 1995. mass mkt. 4.99 (*0-441-00243-9*) Ace Bks.

Wild Blue & the Gray. William Sanders. 1991. mass mkt. 4.50 (*0-446-36142-9*) Warner Bks.

Wild Blue Yonder: A Wartime Romance Remembered. Dorothy C. Sheahan. (Illus.). 176p. (Orig.). 1995. pap. 10.95 (*1-56474-145-1*) Fithian Pr.

Wild Blue Yonder: An Adventure of Hitler's Hostages. Leslie J. Tyler. 160p. (Orig.). 1992. pap. 12.95 (*0-9631159-0-1*) Crystal Pub.

Wild Blue Yonder: Money, Politics, & the B-1 Bomber. Nick Kotz. 322p. 1989. pap. text ed. 17.95 (*0-691-02306-9*) Princeton U Pr.

Wild Boar. Felix Mettler. Tr. by Edna McCown from GER. 224p. (GER.). 1993. 18.95 (*0-88064-134-7*) Fromm Intl Pub.

Wild Boar. Felix Mettler. Tr. by Edna McCown from GER. 224p. 1993. pap. 8.95 (*0-88064-153-3*) Fromm Intl Pub.

Wild Boars. Darrell Nicholson. (Nature Watch Bks.). (Illus.). 48p. (J). (gr. 2-5). 1987. lib. bdg. 14.96 (*0-87614-308-7*, Carolrhoda) Lerner Group.

Wild Body. Wyndham Lewis. LC 70-137666. (Studies in Poetry: No. 38). 1971. reprint ed. lib. bdg. 75.00 (*0-8383-1225-X*) M S G Haskell Hse.

Wild Bouquet: Nature Poems. Harry Martinson. Tr. by William J. Smith & Leif Sjoberg from SWE. LC 84-73437. (International Ser.). (Illus.). 80p. 1985. 10.95 (*0-933532-48-2*) BkMk.

Wild Boy. Joan Tate. (J). Date not set. pap. 1.75 (*0-590-02580-5*) Scholastic Inc.

Wild Boy of Aveyron. Jean-Marc-Gaspard Itard. Tr. by George Humphrey & Muriel Humphrey. 1962. pap. text ed. 19.20 (*0-13-959494-9*) P-H.

Wild Boy of Aveyron. Harlan Lane. (Illus.). 384p. 1979. pap. 15.95 (*0-674-95300-2*) HUP.

Wild Boys: A Book of the Dead. William S. Burroughs. LC 92-19273. 184p. 1992. pap. 9.95 (*0-8021-3331-2*, Grove) Grove-Atltic.

***Wild Bride.** Jeanne Montague. (Black Satin Romance Ser.). 487p. 1997. 25.99 (*1-86110-039-6*) Ulverscroft.

Wild Brides. Laura Kasischke. 108p. (Orig.). (C). 1991. pap. 12.95 (*0-8147-4621-7*); text ed. 20.00 (*0-8147-4620-9*) NYU Pr.

Wild Britain. 2nd ed. Douglas Botting. LC 93-28699. (Natural Traveler Ser.). (Illus.). 224p. 1994. reprint ed. pap. 16.00 (*0-87156-475-0*) Sierra.

***Wild Bull, Vol. 178.** J. R. Roberts. (Gunsmith Ser.: No. 178). 1996. mass mkt. 4.99 (*0-515-11957-1*) Jove Pubns.

Wild Bull & the Sacred Forest: Form, Meaning & Change in Senegambian Initiation Masks of the Diola. Peter A. Mark. (RES Monographs on Anthropology & Aesthetics). (Illus.). 208p. (C). 1992. text ed. 85.00 (*0-521-41346-X*) Cambridge U Pr.

Wild Bull of Blue River: A Hoosier Christmas Tale. Daniel M. Williams. 200p. 1995. 27.50 (*1-887495-00-2*) Coiny Pub.

Wild Bunch. Ernest Haycox. 1976. 23.95 (*0-89190-973-7*) Amereon Ltd.

Wild Bunch. Ernest Haycox. 1992. mass mkt. 3.50 (*1-55817-616-0*, Pinncle Kensgtn) Kensgtn Pub Corp.

***Wild Bunch.** Dee Lillegard. (Illus.). 32p. (J). (gr. k-3). 1997. 15.95 (*0-399-22826-8*) Putnam Pub Group.

Wild Bunch. large type ed. Ernest Haycox. LC 93-44663. 344p. 1994. lib. bdg. 17.95 (*1-56054-702-2*) Thorndike Pr.

Wild Bunch: An Annotated Bibliography. F. Bruce Lamb. LC 93-77747. (Illus.). 160p. 1993. 23.50 (*1-881019-05-5*) High Plns WY.

Wild Bunch at Robbers Roost. Pearl Baker. LC 88-38635. (Illus.). x, 224p. 1989. reprint ed. pap. 8.95 (*0-8032-6089-X*, Bison Books) U of Nebr Pr.

***Wild Bunch Wanton.** large type ed. David Horsley. (Dales Large Print Ser.). 203p. 1997. pap. 18.99 (*1-85389-733-7*, Dales) Ulverscroft.

Wild Bush Tribes of Tropical Africa. G. Cyril Claridge. LC 74-90111. (Illus.). 314p. 1969. reprint ed. text ed. 52.50 (*0-8371-2029-2*, CLB&, Greenwood Pr) Greenwood.

Wild By Law: The Sierra Club Legal Defense Fund & the Places It Has Saved. Tom Turner. LC 89-78349. 1990. 50.00 (*0-87156-627-3*) Sierra.

Wild Cactus. Photos by George H. Huey. LC 95-47808. (Illus.). 128p. 1996. 25.00 (*1-885183-20-8*) Artisan.

Wild California: Vanishing Lands, Vanishing Wildlife. A. Starker Leopold et al. Ed. by Raymond F. Dasmann. 150p. 1985. 50.00 (*0-520-05293-5*); pap. 25.00 (*0-520-06024-5*) U CA Pr.

Wild Camp Tales. Mike Blakely. LC 95-32. 208p. 1995. pap. 12.95 (*1-55622-383-8*, Rep of TX Pr) Wordware Pub.

Wild Canaries. deluxe limited ed. Joyce James. (New Texas Poetry Sampler Ser.). 32p. (Orig.). 1992. pap. 10.00 (*0-930324-21-8*) Wings Pr.

***Wild Card.** Susan Amarillas. 1997. mass mkt. 4.99 (*0-373-28988-X*, 1-28988-3) Harlequin Bks.

Wild Card. Martin Galvin. LC 88-26869. 72p. (Orig.). 1989. pap. 7.00 (*0-931846-34-X*) Wash Writers Pub.

Wild Card. Assumpta Margenat. Tr. by Sheila McIntosh from CAT. 165p. (Orig.). 1992. pap. 8.95 (*1-879679-04-3*) Women Translation.

Wild Card Bride. Joy Tucker. 384p. (Orig.). 1991. mass mkt. 4.50 (*0-380-76445-8*) Avon.

Wild Card of Design: A Perspective on Architecture in a Project Management Environment. Kenneth Allinson. (Illus.). 458p. 1993. pap. 36.95 (*0-7506-2329-2*) Buttrwrth-Heinemann.

Wild Card Wedding. Jule McBride. (American Romance Ser.). 1993. mass mkt. 3.50 (*0-373-16500-5*, 1-16500-0) Harlequin Bks.

Wild Cards, No. 1. 48p. 1990. 4.50 (*0-87135-696-1*) Marvel Entmnt.

Wild Cards, No. 2. 48p. 1990. 4.50 (*0-87135-716-X*) Marvel Entmnt.

Wild Cards, No. 3. 48p. 1990. 4.50 (*0-87135-717-8*) Marvel Entmnt.

Wild Cards, No. 4. 48p. 1990. 4.50 (*0-87135-718-6*) Marvel Entmnt.

Wild Cat. Mary Hoffman. LC 86-10007. (Animals in the Wild Ser.). (Illus.). 24p. (J). (gr. k-5). 1986. pap. 3.95 (*0-8114-6893-3*) Raintree Steck-V.

Wild Cat Species of the World. Ed. by Richard Green. (C). 1989. 80.00 (*0-946873-93-3*, Pub. by Basset Pubns UK) St Mut.

Wild Cats. Lynn M. Stone. LC 92-34499. (Predators Ser.). (J). 1993. 12.67 (*0-86625-441-2*); 9.50 (*0-685-66272-1*) Rourke Pubns.

***Wild C.A.T.S. A Gathering of Eagles.** Chris Claremont. (Illus.). 112p. (Orig.). (YA). 1997. pap. write for info. (*1-887279-45-8*) Image Comics.

Wild Cats: A Status Survey & Conservation Action Plan. Ed. by Peter Jackson & Kristin Nowell. 406p. (C). 1996. pap. text ed. 40.00 (*2-8317-0045-0*, Pub. by IUCN SZ) Island Pr.

***Wild Cats: Cougars, Bobcats & Lynx.** unabridged ed. Deborah Hodge. (The Kid Can Press Wildlife Ser.). (Illus.). 32p. (J). (gr. 1-5). 1997. 10.95 (*1-55074-267-1*, Pub. by Kids Can Pr CN) Genl Dist Srvs.

Wild Cats: Lynx, Bobcats, Mountain Lions. Candace C. Savage. LC 93-2821. (Illus.). 144p. 1994. pap. 20.00 (*0-87156-424-6*) Sierra.

Wild Cats see Books for Young Explorers

Wild Cats & Their Relatives. David Stone. 32p. (C). pap. text ed. 6.00 (*2-8317-0050-7*, Pub. by IUCN SZ) Island Pr.

Wild Cats of the World. David Alderton. LC 92-38774. (Illus.). 192p. 1993. 25.95 (*0-8160-2736-6*) Facts on File.

Wild Cats of the World. Barbara Sleeper. LC 94-28413. (Illus.). 1995. 50.00 (*0-517-79978-2*, Crown) Crown Pub Group.

Wild Caught Discus. Bernd Degen. (Illus.). 1995. 29.95 (*0-7938-0296-2*, TS244) TFH Pubns.

***Wild Champagne.** large type ed. Kate Kingston. (Magna Large Print Ser.). 272p. 1997. 27.50 (*0-7505-1053-6*) Ulverscroft.

Wild Cherries. Dale Herd. 100p. (Orig.). 1980. pap. 5.00 (*0-939180-16-2*) Tombouctou.

***Wild Cherry.** Marcella Chester. 1998. 19.95 (*1-888675-52-7*) Wlking Brdge.

***Wild Child.** Masson. LC 96-37744. 1997. pap. 13.00 (*0-684-83096-5*, Fireside) S&S Trade.

Wild Children. Felice Holman. LC 85-3541. 152p. (J). (gr. 5-9). 1985. pap. 4.99 (*0-14-031930-1*, Puffin) Puffin Bks.

Wild Children: A Zine for Kids. Ed. by Dave Mandl & Peter L. Wilson. 64p. Date not set. 5.00 (*0-936756-83-7*) Autonomedia.

***Wild Children: Growing up Without Human Contact.** LC 96-53587. (First Bk.). (J). 1997. write for info. (*0-531-20256-9*) Watts.

Wild China. John MacKinnon. LC 96-16953. (Illus.). 208p. (C). 1996. 40.00 (*0-262-13329-6*) MIT Pr.

Wild Christmas Reindeer. Jan Brett. (Illus.). 32p. (J). (ps-3). 1990. 15.95 (*0-399-22192-1*, Putnam) Putnam Pub Group.

Wild Civility: Interactions in the Poetry & Thought of Robert Graves. Patrick J. Keane. LC 79-5428. 120p. 1980. pap. 12.95 (*0-8262-0296-9*) U of Mo Pr.

Wild Coast: An Account of Politics in West Indies. Reynold A. Burrowes. 350p. 1984. pap. 16.95 (*0-87073-127-0*); text ed. 22.95 (*0-87073-037-1*) Schenkman Bks Inc.

Wild Coast & Lonely: Big Sur Pioneers. 2nd ed. Rosalind S. Wall. 1992. pap. 9.95 (*0-933174-83-7*) Wide World-Tetra.

Wild Cold State. Debra Monroe. 272p. 1995. 21.00 (*0-671-89717-9*) S&S Trade.

Wild, Cold State: Stories. Debra Monroe. 272p. 1996. pap. 11.00 (*0-684-81511-7*) S&S Trade.

Wild Colonial Boy. James Hynes. Ed. by Jane Rosenman. 368p. 1992. reprint ed. pap. 9.00 (*0-671-74186-1*, WSP) PB.

Wild Colonial Boy: Bushranger Jack Donahoe, 1806-1830. John Meredith. (Studies in Australian Folklore: No. 3). (Illus.). 102p. (Orig.). 1985. reprint ed. pap. 12.95 (*0-908247-04-4*) Legacy Books.

***Wild Colorado.** Richard Maurer. 1997. 18.00 (*0-517-70945-7*, C P Pubs) Crown Pub Group.

Wild Concerto. Anne Mather. (Bestsellers Ser.). 384p. 1983. mass mkt. 4.95 (*0-373-97006-4*) Harlequin Bks.

Wild Conquest. Hannah Howell. 400p. (Orig.). 1993. mass mkt. 4.50 (*0-380-77182-9*) Avon.

Wild Country. Dean Ing. 320p. (Orig.). 1993. mass mkt. 4.99 (*0-8125-1171-9*) Tor Bks.

Wild Country Companion. Will Harmon. LC 94-20531. (Falcon Guides Ser.). (Illus.). 195p. (Orig.). 1994. pap. 9.95 (*1-56044-169-0*) Falcon Pr MT.

Wild Country of Mexico. John Annerino. LC 94-6199. (Illus.). 144p. 1994. 25.00 (*0-87156-536-6*) Sierra.

Wild Cow Tales. Ben K. Green. (Illus.). 1969. 25.00 (*0-394-45188-0*) Knopf.

***Wild Cowboys: Urban Marauders & the Forces of Order.** Robert Jackall. LC 97-11739. 1997. write for info. (*0-674-95310-X*) HUP.

Wild Critters. Tim Jones. Ed. by Kent Sturgis. LC 91-7308. (Illus.). 48p. (Orig.). (J). 1992. pap. 7.95 (*0-945397-25-9*) Epicenter Pr.

Wild Critters. Tim Jones. Ed. by Kent Sturgis. LC 91-7308. (Illus.). 48p. (Orig.). (J). 1992. 15.95 (*0-945397-10-0*) Epicenter Pr.

Wild Cry of Love. large type ed. Barbara Cartland. 268p. 1995. 25.99 (*0-7505-0655-5*) Ulverscroft.

Wild Culpepper Cruise, No. 14. Gary Paulsen. 80p. (J). 1993. pap. 3.50 (*0-440-40883-0*) Dell.

Wild Days. McClendon. LC 89-62912. pap. 12.95 (*0-916990-23-0*) META Pubns.

***Wild Designs.** Katie Fforde. LC 97-11290. 1997. 22.95 (*0-312-15693-6*) St Martin.

Wild Desire. Karen Brennan. LC 91-11114. 184p. (C). 1991. pap. 13.95 (*0-87023-752-7*) U of Mass Pr.

Wild Desire. Cassie Edwards. 384p. (Orig.). 1994. pap. 4.99 (*0-451-40464-5*, Sig) NAL-Dutton.

Wild Desires & Mistaken Identities: Lesbianism & Psychoanalysis. Noreen O'Connor & Joanna Ryan. LC 93-43814. (Between Men - Between Women Ser.). 1994. 31.50 (*0-231-10022-1*) Col U Pr.

Wild Dog. (Animals in the Wild Ser.). (Illus.). 24p. (J). (gr. k-5). 1987. pap. 3.95 (*0-8114-6894-1*) Raintree Steck-V.

***Wild Dog.** Bird & Falk. (New Trend Fiction B Ser.). (J). 1993. pap. text ed. write for info. (*0-582-80040-4*, Pub. by Longman UK) Longman.

Wild Dog & Loan. Dan Crawford. 368p. (Orig.). 1995. mass mkt. 5.50 (*0-441-00183-1*) Ace Bks.

Wild Dog Running. large type ed. Alan Scholefield. 544p. 1996. 25.99 (*0-7089-3525-7*) Ulverscroft.

Wild Dogs. Timothy L. Biel. (Zoobooks Ser.). 24p. (J). (gr. 1-7). 1995. 13.95 (*1-888153-04-0*) Wildlife Educ.

Wild Dogs. Timothy L. Biel. (Zoobooks Ser.). (Illus.). 24p. (J). (gr. 3 up). 1996. lib. bdg. 14.95 (*0-88682-780-9*) Creative Ed.

Wild Dogs. Steve Maurer. 24p. (Orig.). 1981. pap. 3.50 (*0-940846-01-2*) Hastings Bks.

Wild Dogs. Peter Skrzynecki. LC 85-15888. 202p. 1988. 14.95 (*0-7022-2014-0*, Pub. by Univ Queensland Pr AT) Intl Spec Bk.

Wild Dogs. Wildlife Education, Ltd. Staff. (Illus.). 20p. (Orig.). 1985. pap. 2.75 (*0-937934-40-2*) Wildlife Educ.

Wild Dogs: The Wolves, Coyotes, & Foxes of North America. Photos by Erwin A. Bauer & Peggy Bauer. LC 93-29205. (Illus.). 120p. 1994. 27.50 (*0-8118-0690-1*); pap. 16.95 (*0-8118-0405-4*) Chronicle Bks.

***Wild Dogs: Wolves, Coyotes & Foxes.** unabridged ed. Deborah Hodge. (The Kid Can Press Wildlife Ser.). (Illus.). 32p. (J). (gr. 1-5). 1997. 10.95 (*1-55074-360-0*, Pub. by Kids Can Pr CN) Genl Dist Srvs.

Wild Dogs & Their Relatives. Peter Jackson & Olga Sheean-Stone. (Illus.). 32p. 1991. pap. 6.00 (*2-8317-0047-7*, Pub. by IUCN SZ) Island Pr.

***Wild Dream.** Alice Duncan. 1997. mass mkt. 5.50 (*0-440-22361-X*) Dell.

Wild Dreams of a New Beginning: Including Landscapes of Living & Dying & Who Are We Now? Lawrence Ferlinghetti. LC 88-5304. 144p. 1988. reprint ed. 18.95 (*0-8112-1074-X*); reprint ed. pap. 9.95 (*0-8112-1075-8*, NDP663) New Directions.

Wild Duck. Henrik Ibsen. (C). 1969. pap. text ed. 8.95 (*0-393-09825-7*) Norton.

Wild Duck. Henrik Ibsen. Ed. by Kai Jurgensen & Robert Schenkkan. (Crofts Classics Ser.). 184p. 1966. pap. text ed. write for info. (*0-88295-046-0*) Harlan Davidson.

***Wild Duck.** Henrik Ibsen. (Plays for Performance Ser.). 112p. 1997. 15.95 (*1-56663-169-6*) I R Dee.

***Wild Duck.** Henrik Ibsen. (Plays for Performance Ser.). 112p. 1997. pap. 7.95 (*1-56663-170-X*) I R Dee.

***Wild Duck.** Henrik Ibsen. Ed. by William-Alan Landes. 85p. 1997. pap. 7.00 (*0-88734-747-9*) Players Pr.

Wild Duck see Hedda Gabler & Other Plays

Wild Duck see Eight Plays

Wild Duck see Four Major Plays

Wild Duck & Hedda Gabler. Henrik Ibsen. Tr. by Michael Meyer. 256p. (J). 1997. pap. 12.00 (*0-393-31449-9*, Norton Paperbks) Norton.

Wild Ducks & Geese of North America. Sandra D. Romashko. LC 77-81167. (Illus.). 1978. pap. 3.95 (*0-89317-018-6*) Windward Pub.

Wild Dunedin: Enjoying the Natural History of New Zealand's Wildlife Capital. Neville Peat & Brian Patrick. (Illus.). 136p. 1995. 45.00 (*0-908569-94-7*, Pub. by U Otago Pr NZ) Intl Spec Bk.

Wild Ecstasy. Cassie Edwards. 352p. (Orig.). 1992. pap. 5.99 (*0-451-40306-1*, Onyx) NAL-Dutton.

Wild Edible Fruits & Berries. Marjorie Furlong & Virginia Pill. LC 74-32015. (Illus.). 64p. 1974. pap. 8.95 (*0-87961-032-8*) Naturegraph.

Wild Edible Plants of Mother Nature: A Guide to Eating Hardy on Plants Common to 48 States. Ronald E. Ross. (Illus.). 92p. (Orig.). 1991. pap. 7.50 (*0-9632601-0-3*) Ronald Ross.

Wild Edible Plants of Western North America. rev. ed. Donald R. Kirk. LC 75-5998. (Illus.). 343p. 1975. pap. 7.95 (*0-87961-036-0*) Naturegraph.

Wild Edibles, Identification for Living off the Land. rev. ed. Marian Van Atta. LC 84-62805. (Living off the Land Ser.). (Illus.). 64p. 1985. pap. text ed. 6.95 (*0-938524-01-1*) Geraventure.

Wild Embers. Anita R. Bunkley. 448p. 1996. mass mkt., pap. 5.99 (*0-451-17974-9*, Sig) NAL-Dutton.

Wild Embers. large type ed. Anita R. Bunkley. 653p. 1996. 23.95 (*0-7862-0594-6*, Thorndike Lrg Prnt) Thorndike Pr.

Wild Embrace. Cassie Edwards. 384p. (Orig.). 1993. pap. 5.99 (*0-451-40361-4*, Topaz) NAL-Dutton.

W

An Asterisk (*) at the beginning of an entry indicates that the title is appearing in BIP for the first time.

Wild Empire. Richard R. Searight. (Orig.). 1994. pap. 8.95 (*0-9633548-2-5*) Iroquois Pr.

***Wild Enchantment.** large type ed. Marianne Harvey. (Large Print Ser.). 320p. 1996. 25.99 (*0-7089-3570-2*) Ulverscroft.

Wild Escapade. Lisa Bingham. 1996. mass mkt. 5.99 (*0-671-52804-1*) PB.

***Wild Faces.** Snazaroo Staff. LC 96-50914. (J). 1997. write for info. (*0-7534-5055-0*, Kingfisher LKC) LKC.

***Wild Feasts: A Duck's Unlimited Game & Fish Cookbook.** Ed. by Diane Jolie. 264p. 1997. 24.50 (*1-57223-130-0*, 1300) Willow Creek Pr.

Wild Field. Rita B. Gabis. 80p. (Orig.). 1994. pap. 9.95 (*1-882295-01-3*) Alicejamesbooks.

***Wild Fiordland: Exploring the Natural History of New Zealand's World Heritage Area.** Neville Peat & Brian Patrick. (Illus.). 144p. 1996. 39.95 (*1-877133-17-5*, Pub. by U Otago Pr NZ) Intl Spec Bk.

***Wild Fire.** Liz Fielding. (Scarlet Ser.). (Orig.). 1997. mass mkt. 3.99 (*1-85487-977-4*, Pub. by Scarlet Bks UK) London Brdge.

***Wild Fish & Game Cookbook.** John Manikowski. LC 97-16187. (Illus.). 192p. 1997. 35.00 (*1-885183-50-X*) Artisan.

Wild Fish Gourmet Style, Vol. 1. Tim J. Burrow. 60p. 1996. pap. text ed. 9.95 (*0-9641654-3-0*) G W Teal.

***Wild Flamingos.** Bruce McMillan. LC 97-1521. 1997. 15.00 (*0-395-84545-9*) HM.

Wild Flora of the Northeast. Photos by Anita Barbour. (Illus.). 196p. 1991. 35.00 (*0-87951-344-6*) Overlook Pr.

Wild Flora of the Northeast. Spider Barbour & Anita Barbour. (Illus.). 196p. 1995. 19.95 (*0-87951-584-8*) Overlook Pr.

Wild Flower. Jill M. Landis. 1989. mass mkt. 6.50 (*0-515-10102-8*) Jove Pubns.

Wild Flower. Donna Stephens. 384p. (Orig.). 1994. mass mkt. 4.50 (*0-380-77577-8*) Avon.

Wild Flower by Any Other Name: Sketches of Pioneer Naturalists Who Named Our Western Plants. Karen B. Nilsson. LC 93-44015. (Illus.). 162p. 1994. pap. 14.95 (*0-939666-76-6*) Yosemite Assn.

Wild Flower Lover Album. Nancy S. Taylor. 25p. 1990. 4.50 (*0-937745-08-1*) Traditions Pr.

Wild Flowering of Chastity. Dutton Foster. 1973. 3.00 (*0-87129-406-0*, W33) Dramatic Pub.

Wild Flowering Plants of Bahrain: An Illustrated Guide. M. D. Cornes & C. D. Cornes. (Illus.). 272p. (C). 1995. pap. 51.00 (*0-907151-41-8*, Pub. by IMMEL Pubng UK) St Mut.

Wild Flowering Plants Relation to Insects. John Lubbock. 194p. 1989. 100.00 (*81-7041-178-5*, Pub. by Scientific Pubs II) St Mut.

Wild Flowers. Busch. 1977. 10.00 (*0-684-14820-X*) S&S Trade.

Wild Flowers. Pam Forey. Ed. by Angela Royston. LC 93-46146. (Science Nature Guides Ser.). (Illus.). 81p. (J). (gr. 3-6). 1994. 12.95 (*1-85028-266-8*) Thunder Bay CA.

Wild Flowers. C. Humphries. (Spotter's Guides Ser.). (Illus.). 64p. (YA). (gr. 10 up). 1993. pap. 4.95 (*0-7460-1628-X*) EDC.

Wild Flowers. Snowdon. 96p. 1996. 14.50 (*0-517-70565-6*, C P Pubs) Crown Pub Group.

Wild Flowers: Along Mt. McKinley Park Road. Louise Potter & Jerryne Cole. LC 79-52424. (Illus.). (Orig.). 1979. pap. 5.95 (*0-9602792-0-2*) Camp Denali.

Wild Flowers & How They Grew. Barbara Oaks. Tr. by Robin Wollman. LC 95-92150. (Illus.). 210p. (Orig.). 1995. pap. 7.95 (*0-9618582-4-9*) Barbara Oaks.

Wild Flowers in Their Seasons: A Gower Flora. Lois Wilson. 208p. (C). 1989. 350.00 (*0-905928-76-8*, Pub. by D Brown & Sons Ltd UK) St Mut.

Wild Flowers of America. Intro. by Harold W. Rickett. LC 92-40132. (Tiny Folios Ser.). (Illus.). 448p. 1996. pap. 11.95 (*1-55859-564-3*) Abbeville Pr.

Wild Flowers of Britain: Over a Thousand Species by Photographic Identification. Roger Phillips. (Illus.). 192p. (Orig.). 1994. pap. 37.50 (*0-330-25183-X*, Pub. by Pan Books UK) Trans-Atl Phila.

Wild Flowers of California. Mary E. Parsons. 1992. reprint ed. lib. bdg. 75.00 (*0-7812-5074-9*) Rprt Serv.

Wild Flowers of Central Saudi Arabia. Betty A. Vincett. 114p. 1977. 60.00 (*0-317-07184-X*) St Mut.

Wild Flowers of Japan: A Field Guide. Ran Levy. Ed. by Barry Lancet. 224p. 1995. pap. 25.00 (*4-7700-1809-6*) Kodansha.

***Wild Flowers of Maine.** Ruth G. Grierson. Ed. by Jane Weinberger. (Illus.). 200p. 1997. pap. 18.00 (*1-883650-38-0*) Windswept Hse.

Wild Flowers of Majorca, Minorca & Ibiza: With Keys to the Flora of the Balearic Islands. Elspeth Beckett. (Illus.). 224p. (C). 1987. text ed. 70.00 (*90-6191-634-8*, Pub. by A A Balkema NE) Ashgate Pub Co.

Wild Flowers of Marin: A Layman's Handbook. Lilian McHoul. LC 79-51455. (Illus.). 1979. pap. 4.95 (*0-912908-08-4*) Tamal Land.

Wild Flowers of New York, 2 vols. Homer D. House. 1993. reprint ed. Set. lib. bdg. 150.00 (*0-7812-5147-8*) Rprt Serv.

Wild Flowers of North Alabama. Bonnie P. Tondera et al. 250p. 1987. 12.00 (*0-9619472-0-9*) I H Paul.

Wild Flowers of North Carolina. William S. Justice & C. Ritchie Bell. LC 68-18051. (Illus.). xxviii, 217p. 1987. reprint ed. pap. 15.95 (*0-8078-4192-7*) U of NC Pr.

Wild Flowers of Pakistan. Ed. by T. J. Roberts et al. (Illus.). 442p. 1996. 65.00 (*0-19-577584-8*) OUP.

Wild Flowers of the Big Thicket, East Texas, & Western Louisiana. Geyata Ajilvsgi. LC 78-21781. (W. L. Moody, Jr. Natural History Ser.: NO. 4). (Illus.). 448p. 1979. 24.95 (*0-89096-064-X*); pap. 14.95 (*0-89096-065-8*) Tex A&M Univ Pr.

Wild Flowers of the Canary Islands. D. Bramwell & Z. Bramwell. (C). 1974. text ed. 120.00 (*0-85950-227-9*, Pub. by S Thornes Pubs UK) St Mut.

Wild Flowers of the North York Moors National Park. Sylvia Arnold. 120p. 1986. 36.00 (*0-907033-42-3*) St Mut.

Wild Flowers of the United States Vol. 1: Northeastern States. Harold W. Rickett. LC 66-17920. (Illus.). 559p. 1966. 70.00 (*0-89327-274-4*) NY Botanical.

Wild Flowers of the United States Vol. 2: Southeastern States. Harold W. Rickett. (Illus.). 688p. 1967. 70.00 (*0-89327-277-9*) NY Botanical.

Wild Flowers of the United States Vol. 4: Southwestern States. Harold W. Rickett. (Illus.). 801p. 1970. 70.00 (*0-89327-280-9*) NY Botanical.

Wild Flowers of the United States Vol. 5: Northwestern States. Harold W. Rickett. LC 66-17920. (Illus.). 666p. 1971. 70.00 (*0-89327-284-1*) NY Botanical.

Wild Food Cookbook. 2nd ed. Frances Hamerstrom. (Illus.). 144p. 1994. reprint ed. pap. 12.95 (*0-942495-37-3*) Amherst Pr.

***Wild Food from Land & Sea.** Marco P. White. 176p. 1997. pap. 16.95 (*0-09-181415-4*, Pub. by Ebury Pr UK) Trafalgar.

Wild Food Plants of Indiana & Adjacent States. 2nd ed. Alan McPherson & Sue A. Clark. (Illus.). 215p. 1994. reprint ed. pap. 12.50 (*0-9636978-1-1*) A McPherson.

Wild Food Trailguide. Alan Hall. LC 75-21466. (Illus.). 240p. 1990. pap. 12.95 (*0-8050-1345-8*, Owl) H Holt & Co.

Wild Foods Cookery. John Tomikel. LC 78-57184. 1978. pap. 4.00 (*0-910042-34-9*) Allegheny.

Wild Foods Field Guide & Cookbook. Billy J. Tatum. LC 85-5360. (Illus.). 276p. 1985. pap. 7.95 (*0-911104-77-1*, 067) Workman Pub.

Wild Foods of Appalachia. rev. ed. William H. Gillespie. (Illus.). 200p. (Orig.). 1995. pap. 15.95 (*0-89092-020-6*) Seneca Bks.

Wild Foods of the Sonoran Desert. Kevin Dahl. LC 95-78196. (Illus.). 24p. (Orig.). 1995. pap. 4.95 (*1-886679-03-7*) Ariz-Sonora Des Mus.

Wild Foods, What's Worth Eating? Phil King. 50p. 1987. write for info. (*0-9601900-4-X*) Phil King.

Wild for Kicks. John Nemec. 160p. (Orig.). 1991. pap. 3.49 (*0-9618998-6-7*) Nemec Pub.

Wild Forests: Conservation Biology & Public Policy. William Alverson et al. LC 94-8950. 1994. text ed. 49.95 (*1-55963-187-2*); pap. text ed. 25.95 (*1-55963-188-0*) Island Pr.

Wild Fowl Decoys. Joel D. Barber. (Illus.). pap. 14.95 (*0-486-20011-6*) Dover.

Wild Fox: A True Story. Cherie Mason. LC 92-74622. (Illus.). 32p. (J). (gr. 2-5). 1993. 15.95 (*0-89272-319-X*) Down East.

Wild France. Ed. by Douglas Botting. LC 93-28771. (Natural Traveler Ser.). (Illus.). 224p. (Orig.). 1994. reprint ed. pap. 16.00 (*0-87156-476-9*) Sierra.

Wild Frontier: Adventures of Jean Baptiste Du Sable. Pepper Bird Staff. (Multicultural Historical Fiction Ser.). (Illus.). 48p. (Orig.). (J). (gr. 4-7). 1993. pap. 4.95 (*1-56817-003-3*) Pepper Bird.

Wild Frontier: Scotland's Roman Wall. Anne Johnstone. (Illus.). (C). 1989. 45.00 (*0-948473-03-7*) St Mut.

Wild Game. Frank Bergon. LC 94-41278. (Western Literature Ser.). 336p. 1995. 22.00 (*0-87417-257-8*) U of Nev Pr.

Wild Game Cookbook. Illus. by Wayne Horne. LC 87-16225. 156p. (Orig.). 1987. pap. 8.95 (*0-943247-01-2*) UCS Press.

***Wild Game Cookbook.** Blanche Johnson & Chuck Johnson. Date not set. 29.95 (*1-885106-49-1*) Wild Adven Pr.

Wild Game Cookbook. Ed. by L. W. Johnson. LC 70-114972. (Remington Sportsmen's Library). pap. 3.95 (*0-87502-907-8*) Benjamin Co.

***Wild Game Cookbook.** Doug Kazulak. 1996. pap. 5.50 (*1-55105-066-8*) Lone Pine.

Wild Game Cookbook. Mary R. Pitzer. (Illus.). ix, 54p. (Orig.). 1993. pap. 5.50 (*0-9650698-0-X*) M R Pitzer.

Wild Game Cookbook. Dennis Rohde. LC 96-8354. (Illus.). 176p. (Orig.). 1996. spiral bd. 14.95 (*0-87358-641-7*) Northland AZ.

Wild Game Cookbook. John A. Smith. 64p. (Orig.). 1986. pap. 4.95 (*0-486-25127-6*) Dover.

Wild Game Cookery: The Hunter's Home Companion. expanded rev. ed. Carol V. Wary. LC 88-2728. 208p. 1984. pap. 15.00 (*0-88150-111-5*) Countryman.

Wild Game Cuisine. George Politis. (Illus.). 160p. 1996. 35.00 (*1-55209-052-3*) Firefly Bks Ltd.

Wild Game Gourmet Style. Tim J. Burrow. Ed. by Kelli J. Burrow. (Illus.). (Orig.). 1992. pap. 9.95 (*0-9641654-0-6*) G W Teal.

Wild Garden. Violet Stevenson. 1993. 25.50 (*0-8446-6710-2*) Peter Smith.

Wild Garden. Violet Stevenson. (Illus.). 168p. 1985. pap. 19.95 (*0-14-025153-7*, Penguin Bks) Viking Penguin.

Wild Garden. 5th ed. William Robinson. LC 93-44917. (Illus.). 318p. 1994. reprint ed. 24.95 (*0-88192-284-6*) Sagapr.

Wild Garden: The Monterey Peninsula. Ron Mackie. (Illus.). 1985. pap. 7.95 (*0-910286-99-X*) Boxwood.

Wild Gardener: On Flowers & Foliage for the Natural Border. Peter H. Loewer. LC 91-15394. 256p. 1991. 19.95 (*0-8117-0885-3*) Stackpole.

Wild Gardener: The Life & Selected Writings of Eloise Butler. Martha Hellander. LC 92-3664. (Illus.). 208p. 1992. pap. 19.95 (*0-87839-064-2*) North Star.

Wild Gardener in the Wild Landscape: The Art of Naturalistic Landscaping. rev. ed. Warren G. Kenfield. (Illus.). xii, 232p. 1991. reprint ed. pap. 25.95 (*1-878899-00-7*) CT Coll Arboretum.

Wild Garlic Islands: A Genealogical Account of the Ramsey Family. Robert H. Stone. LC 82-90342. (Illus.). 191p. (Orig.). 1982. 22.50 (*0-9609192-0-1*) R H Stone.

Wild Garlic Islands: A Genealogical Account of the Ramsey Family--Updated Version. 158p. 1986. 24.95 (*0-9609192-3-6*) R H Stone.

Wild Geese. Ogai Mori. Tr. by Sanford Goldstein & Kingo Ochiai from JPN. LC 59-14087. 119p. 1974. pap. 8.95 (*0-8048-1070-2*) C E Tuttle.

Wild Geese. Malcolm A. Ogilvie. LC 77-94181. (Illus.). 1978. 35.00 (*0-931130-00-X*) Harrell Bks.

***Wild Geese.** Martha Ostenso. 1996. pap. text ed. 6.95 (*0-7710-9994-0*) McCland & Stewart.

Wild Geese. large type ed. Daniel Carney. 512p. 1986. 25.99 (*0-7089-1442-X*) Ulverscroft.

Wild Geese. large type ed. Eilis Dillon. 512p. 1983. 25.99 (*0-7089-1052-1*) Ulverscroft.

Wild Geese. Theodore H. Banks. LC 73-144741. (Yale Series of Younger Poets: No. 7). reprint ed. 18.00 (*0-404-53807-X*) AMS Pr.

Wild Geese & Other Poems. Barker Fairley. 64p. 1984. 39.95 (*0-920806-63-5*, Pub. by Penumbra Pr CN); pap. 6.95 (*0-920806-51-1*, Pub. by Penumbra Pr CN) U of Toronto Pr.

Wild Geese & Tea: An Asian-American Wedding Planner. Shu S. Costa. (Illus.). 208p. 1997. 27.50 (*1-57322-040-X*, Riverhead Books) Putnam Pub Group.

Wild Geese & the Water. Rajneesh Osho Staff. Ed. by Swami K. Prabhu. LC 85-43053. (Responses to Questions Ser.). 416p. (Orig.). 1985. pap. 4.95 (*0-88050-673-3*) Osho America.

Wild Geese of the Antrim MacDonnells. Hector MacDonnell. 176p. 1996. 37.50 (*0-7165-2609-3*, Pub. by Irish Acad Pr IE) Intl Spec Bk.

Wild Ghost Chase. R. A. Noonan. (Monsterville Ser.). (J). (gr. 3-7). 1996. pap. 3.95 (*0-614-15781-1*, Aladdin Paperbacks) S&S Childrens.

Wild Girls Club: Tales from below the Belt. Anka Radakovich. 1994. 18.00 (*0-517-59631-8*) Crown Pub Group.

Wild Girls Club: Tales from below the Belt. Anka Radakovich. 240p. 1995. pap. 10.00 (*0-449-90985-9*) Fawcett.

Wild Good: Lesbian Photographs & Writings on Love. Ed. by Beatrix Gates. LC 96-15994. (Illus.). 256p. 1996. pap. 19.95 (*0-385-48172-1*, Anchor NY) Doubleday.

Wild Goose Chase. Anne George. (Illus.). 48p. (Orig.). 1985. reprint ed. pap. 5.00 (*0-945301-00-6*) Druid Pr.

Wild Goose Chase. Rex Warner. (Radical Fiction Ser.). 442p. 1990. reprint ed. lib. bdg. 27.50 (*0-929587-38-3*) I R Dee.

Wild Goose Country. Michael Furtman. 160p. 1992. 39.00 (*1-55971-177-9*) NorthWord.

Wild Goose (Gan) Mori Ogai. Tr. by Burton Watson. LC 95-17764. (Michigan Monographs in Japanese Studies: No. 14). xiv, 166p. 1995. 28.95 (*0-939512-70-X*); pap. 14.95 (*0-939512-71-8*) U MI Japan.

Wild Goose Songs, Vol. 1. Wild Goose Publications Staff. (C). 1990. 25.00 (*0-947988-23-8*, Pub. by Wild Goose Pubns UK) St Mut.

Wild Goose Songs, Vol. 2. Wild Goose Publications Staff. (C). 1990. 30.00 (*0-947988-27-0*, Pub. by Wild Goose Pubns UK) St Mut.

Wild Gourmet. Babette Brackett & Maryann Lash. 1992. pap. 13.25 (*0-87923-142-4*) Peter Smith.

***Wild Grapes.** Gally Marchmont. 352p. 1997. pap. 17.95 (*0-7528-0490-1*, Pub. by Orion Bks UK) Trafalgar.

Wild Gratitude. Edward Hirsch. LC 85-40348. (Poetry Ser.). 1986. pap. 16.00 (*0-394-74153-6*) Knopf.

Wild Grow the Lilies. Christy Brown. 304p. (C). 1991. pap. 9.95 (*0-7493-9183-9*, A0574) Heinemann.

Wild Grow the Lilies. Christy Brown. LC 75-37905. 304p. 1976. reprint ed. pap. 9.95 (*0-8128-2470-9*, Scrbrough Hse) Madison Bks UPA.

Wild Harp. Jacqueline La Tourrette. 576p. (Orig.). 1981. pap. 2.95 (*0-449-14408-9*, GM) Fawcett.

Wild Harvest. Leonard Wiley. LC 66-13394. (Illus.). 1966. 15.00 (*0-911742-01-8*) L Wiley.

Wild Harvest: Edible Plants of The Pacific Northwest. Terry Domico. (Illus.). 88p. 1979. reprint ed. pap. 8.95 (*0-88839-022-X*) Hancock House.

Wild Harvest: Poems from the Land. Michael Whitt. 1995. pap. 15.00 (*0-912449-48-9*) Floating Island.

Wild Harvest Cookbook. Dan Small & Nancy Frank. 144p. 1991. pap. 14.95 (*1-55971-111-3*) NorthWord.

Wild Hawk. Justine Dare. 1996. mass mkt. 5.50 (*0-451-40657-5*, Topaz) NAL-Dutton.

Wild Heart. (Orig.). 1992. mass mkt. 4.95 (*1-56333-007-5*) Masquerade.

Wild Heart. Jane Bonander. 1995. mass mkt. 5.99 (*0-671-52983-8*) PB.

Wild Hearts. Cherrie Bennett. Ed. by Patricia MacDonald. 224p. (Orig.). (J). (gr. 3-6). pap. 3.99 (*0-671-86513-7*, Archway) PB.

***Wild Hearts.** Garda Parker. 1997. mass mkt. 4.99 (*0-8217-5645-1*) Kensgtn Pub Corp.

***Wild Hearts.** Garda Parker. 384p. 1997. mass mkt. 4.99 (*0-8217-5646-X*, Zebra Kensgtn) Kensgtn Pub Corp.

Wild Hearts. Virginia Henley. (Avon Romance Ser.). 400p. 1985. reprint ed. mass mkt. 5.99 (*0-380-89536-6*) Avon.

Wild Hearts Dancing: A Personal One-Day Quest to Liberate the Artist & Lover Within. Elliot Sobel. LC 93-36248. 176p. 1994. pap. 11.00 (*0-671-86965-5*, Fireside) S&S Trade.

Wild Hearts Forever. Cherrie Bennett. Ed. by Patricia MacDonald. 224p. (Orig.). (J). (gr. 3-6). 1994. pap. 3.50 (*0-671-86515-3*, Archway) PB.

Wild Hearts on Fire. Cherie Bennett. (YA). (gr. 3-6). 1994. pap. 3.50 (*0-671-86514-5*, Archway) PB.

Wild Heather. Millie Criswell. 352p. 1995. mass mkt. 5.99 (*0-446-60171-3*) Warner Bks.

Wild Herbs in Your Backyard: A Pocket Guide for Identifying & Using Common Plants of Exceptional Medicinal & Nutritional Value. Brigitte Miner et al. (Illus.). 80p. (Orig.). 1996. pap. 6.95 (*0-9632814-1-0*) N Wrld CA.

Wild Heritage. large type ed. Williams. (Dales Large Print Ser.). 1995. pap. 17.99 (*1-85389-486-9*, Dales) Ulverscroft.

Wild Heritage: The History & Nature of the New Forest. Terry Heathcote. (C). 1989. 39.00 (*0-685-52530-9*, Pub. by Ensign Pubns & Print UK) St Mut.

Wild Honey. Anton P. Chekhov. Tr. by Michael Frayn. 104p. (C). 1988. pap. 8.95 (*0-413-55160-1*, A0318, Pub. by Methuen UK) Heinemann.

Wild Honey. Fern Michaels. Ed. by Carolyn Tolley. 336p. 1992. mass mkt. 5.99 (*0-671-79390-X*) PB.

***Wild Honey.** Veronica Sattler. 1997. mass mkt. 3.99 (*0-373-70731-2*, 1-70731-4) Harlequin Bks.

Wild Honey. large type ed. Fern Michaels. (Large Print Ser.). 352p. 1996. lib. bdg. 24.95 (*1-57490-041-2*, Beeler LP Bks) T T Beeler.

Wild Honey. large type ed. Alison Uttley. (Isis Reminiscence Ser.). 164p. 1992. 20.95 (*1-85089-524-4*, Pub. by ISIS UK) Transaction Pubs.

Wild Honey. Cynthia Stockley. LC 71-150564. (Short Story Index Reprint Ser.). 1977. reprint ed. 24.95 (*0-8369-3862-3*) Ayer.

Wild Honey: Man of the Month, Something Wild. Ann Major. (Desire Ser.). 1993. mass mkt. 2.99 (*0-373-05805-5*, 5-05805-2) Silhouette.

Wild Honeysuckle. Betsy B. Bancroft. (Illus.). 20p. 1972. reprint ed. 12.95 (*0-911116-73-7*) Pelican.

Wild Horse - (Musical) Charles E. Pascoe. 1993. pap. 5.00 (*0-87129-272-6*, W08) Dramatic Pub.

***Wild Horse Family Book.** Sybille Kalas. LC 96-47344. (Illus.). 56p. (J). (gr. 1-5). 1997. pap. 8.95 (*1-55858-698-9*) North-South Bks NYC.

Wild Horse Family Book. Sybille Kalas. Tr. by Patricia Crampton. LC 89-3929. (Illus.). (J). (ps up). 1991. pap. 15.95 (*0-88708-110-X*, Picture Book Studio) S&S Childrens.

Wild Horse Mesa. large type ed. Zane Grey. LC 93-35503. (Large Type Ser.). 1993. lib. bdg. 20.95 (*0-7862-0075-8*) Thorndike Pr.

Wild Horse Rider. Rick Steber. 1984. pap. text ed. 8.95 (*0-945134-96-7*) Bonanza Pub.

Wild Horse Shorty - Blood of Kings. Nelson Nye. 416p. 1995. mass mkt., pap. text ed. 4.99 (*0-8439-3751-3*) Dorchester Pub Co.

Wild Horse Summer. Hope Ryden. LC 96-14221. (YA). 1997. 15.00 (*0-395-77519-1*, Clarion Bks) HM.

Wild Horse Winter. Tetsuya Honda. (Illus.). 40p. (J). (ps-3). 1992. 12.95 (*0-8118-0251-5*) Chronicle Bks.

Wild Horse Winter. Tetsuya Honda. 40p. (J). 1995. pap. 6.95 (*0-8118-1211-1*) Chronicle Bks.

Wild Horses. Bonnie Bryant. (Saddle Club Ser.: No. 58). 144p. (J). (gr. 4-7). 1996. pap. 3.99 (*0-553-48371-4*, Skylark BDD) BDD Bks Young Read.

Wild Horses. Eve Bunting. (Author's Signature Collection). (Illus.). 64p. (J). (gr. 3-8). 1992. lib. bdg. 12.79 (*0-89565-778-3*) Childs World.

Wild Horses. Ruth J. Dale. 1994. 2.99 (*0-373-03313-3*) Harlequin Bks.

Wild Horses. Dick Francis. 352p. 1995. mass mkt. 5.99 (*0-515-11789-7*) Jove Pubns.

Wild Horses. Dick Francis. 352p. (Orig.). 1995. pap. 5.99 (*0-515-11723-4*) Jove Pubns.

Wild Horses. Carol A. Moorhead. (Wonder Ser.). (Illus.). 64p. (Orig.). (J). (gr. 1-6). 1994. pap. 7.95 (*1-879373-51-3*) R Rinehart.

Wild Horses. Glen Rounds. LC 92-73608. (Illus.). 32p. (J). (ps-3). 1993. lib. bdg. 14.95 (*0-8234-1019-6*) Holiday.

Wild Horses. John B. Wexo. (Zoobooks Ser.). (Illus.). 24p. (J). (gr. 3 up). 1996. lib. bdg. 14.95 (*0-88682-781-7*) Creative Ed.

Wild Horses. John B. Wexo. (Zoobooks Ser.). 24p. (J). (gr. 1-7). 1995. 13.95 (*1-888153-00-8*) Wildlife Educ.

Wild Horses. Wildlife Education, Ltd. Staff. (Zoobooks Ser.). (Illus.). 20p. (Orig.). (YA). (gr. 5 up). 1982. pap. 2.75 (*0-937934-08-9*) Wildlife Educ.

Wild Horses, Vols. 7-12. Rick Steber. (Tales of the Wild West Ser.). (Illus.). 360p. 1995. 27.50 (*0-945134-48-7*) Bonanza Pub.

Wild Horses: A Spirit Unbroken. Elwyn H. Edwards. LC 95-3272. (Illus.). 112p. 1995. 24.95 (*0-89658-271-X*) Voyageur Pr.

Wild Horses: Wild Horse Magic for Kids. Mark Henckel. LC 95-16312. (Animal Magic for Kids Ser.). (Illus.). (J). 1995. lib. bdg. 18.60 (*0-8368-1378-2*) Gareth Stevens Inc.

Wild Horses & Angry Bulls: The Lonely Life of the Rodeo Cowboy. Dirk Johnson. 1994. 22.00 (*0-671-79221-0*) S&S Trade.

Wild Horses for Kids. Mark Henckel. (Wildlife for Kids Ser.). (Illus.). 48p. (Orig.). (J). (gr. 3-7). 1995. pap. write for info. (*1-55971-465-4*) NorthWord.

Wild Horses of Hidden Valley. Ronald P. Westmoreland. Ed. by Melissa Roberts. (Illus.). 96p. (J). (gr. 4-7). 1990. 8.95 (*0-89015-717-0*) Sunbelt Media.

Wild Horses of Sweetbriar. Natalie Kinsey-Warnock. LC 89-32280. (Illus.). (J). (ps-3). 1990. pap. 14.99 (*0-525-65015-6*, Cobblehill Bks) Dutton Child Bks.

Wild Horses, Turn of the Century Prairie Girlhood. Eva P. Henderson. LC 82-10631. (Illus.). 96p. (Orig.). 1983. pap. 8.95 (*0-86534-013-7*) Sunstone Pr.

Wild Horses, Wild Men. Ann Williams. (Intimate Moments Ser.). 1994. mass mkt. 3.50 (*0-373-07585-5*, 1-07585-2) Harlequin Bks.

Wild Hunger. Charlotte Lamb. (Presents Ser.). 1996. mass mkt. 3.50 (*0-373-11834-1*, 1-11834-8) Harlequin Bks.

An Asterisk (*) at the beginning of an entry indicates that the title is appearing in BIP for the first time.

Wild Hunger. large type ed. Charlotte Lamb. (Harlequin Romance Ser.). 1996. 19.95 (*0-263-14450-X*, Pub. by Mills & Boon UK) Thorndike Pr.

Wild Hunt. Jane Yolen. LC 94-30105. (Illus.). 160p. (YA). (gr. 5 up). 1995. 17.00 (*0-15-200211-1*) HarBrace.

***Wild Hunt.** Jane Yolen. 160p. (YA). (gr. 7 up). 1997. mass mkt. 3.99 (*0-590-52836-X*) Scholastic Inc.

Wild Hunter in the Bush of the Ghosts: Standard Edition. 2nd ed. Amos Tutuola. LC 84-51444. 150p. 1989. reprint ed. 20.00 (*0-89410-452-7*, Three Contnts); reprint ed. pap. 10.00 (*0-89410-453-5*, Three Contnts) Lynne Rienner.

Wild Hunters: Predators in Peril. Monte Hummel et al. Tr. by Robert Bateman. (Illus.). 251p. 1992. pap. 16.95 (*1-879373-27-0*) R Rinehart.

Wild Ice: Antarctic Journeys. Ron Naveen et al. (Illus.). 224p. 1990. 35.00 (*0-87474-395-8*) Smithsonian.

Wild Ideas. Ed. by David Rothenberg. LC 94-49620. 280p. 1995. text ed. 49.95 (*0-8166-2614-6*); pap. text ed. 19.95 (*0-8166-2615-4*) U of Minn Pr.

***Wild Imaginings.** Bob Weir. 228p. (Orig.). 1997. mass mkt. 4.99 (*1-55237-110-7*, Pub. by Comnwlth Pub CN) Partners Pubs Grp.

Wild Impressions: Prints from the Collection of the Adirondack Museum. Georgia B. Barnhill. (Imago Mundi Ser.). (Illus.). 200p. 1996. 40.00 (*1-56792-041-1*) Godine.

Wild Impressions: The Adirondacks on Paper. Georgia B. Barnhill. (Illus.). 144p. 1995. pap. 20.00 (*0-910020-45-0*) Adirondack Mus.

Wild in Bed Together. Graham Masterton. 256p. (Orig.). 1992. pap. 5.99 (*0-451-17212-4*, Sig) NAL-Dutton.

***Wild in the City.** Jan Thornhill. (Illus.). 32p. (YA). (gr. 3 up). 1996. 14.95 (*1-895688-33-7*, Pub. by Greey dePencier CN) Firefly Bks Ltd.

Wild in the City. Jan Thornhill. (Illus.). 32p. (J). (PS-3). 1996. 16.95 (*0-87156-910-8*) Sierra Club Childrens.

Wild in the City: The Best of Zoonooz. Ed. by Robert Wade & Marjorie B. Shaw. LC 85-51709. (Illus.). 1985. 24.50 (*0-911461-12-4*); 37.50 (*0-911461-13-2*) Zoological Soc.

Wild in the City: The Best of Zoonooz. Ed. by Robert Wade & Marjorie B. Shaw. (Illus.). 192p. 1988. reprint ed. pap. 6.95 (*0-911461-14-0*) Zoological Soc.

***Wild in the Kitchen.** Martin Wild. 250p. 1996. pap. 13.50 (*0-9653378-0-4*) M Wild.

Wild India: The Wild Life & Scenery of India & Nepal. G. Mountfort. (C). 1991. 105.00 (*0-7855-0222-X*, Pub. by Ratna Pustak Bhandar) St Mut.

Wild India: The Wildlife & Scenery of India & Nepal. Guy Mountfort. (Illus.). 208p. 1991. 39.95 (*0-262-13276-1*) MIT Pr.

***Wild Indians & Other Creatures.** Adrian Louis. (Western Literature Ser.). 200p. 1997. reprint ed. pap. 17.00 (*0-87417-303-5*) U of Nev Pr.

Wild Indians & Other Creatures. Adrian C. Louis. LC 95-47239. (Western Literature Ser.). 200p. (C). 1997. reprint ed. 20.00 (*0-87417-279-9*) U of Nev Pr.

Wild Indonesia: The Wildlife & Scenery of the Indonesian Archipelago. Tony Whitten & Jane Whitten. LC 92-14891. (Illus.). 208p. 1992. 39.95 (*0-262-23165-4*) MIT Pr.

Wild Injustice. large type ed. Margaret Mayo. 18.95 (*0-263-14041-5*) Thorndike Pr.

Wild Innocence: (Man of the Month, Something Wild) Ann Major. (Desire Ser.). 1994. mass mkt. 2.99 (*0-373-05835-7*, 5-05835-9) Silhouette.

Wild Ireland. Brendan Lehane. LC 94-34011. (Orig.). 1995. pap. 16.00 (*0-87156-427-0*) Sierra.

Wild Iris. Louise Gluck. 72p. 1992. 19.95 (*0-88001-281-1*) Ecco Pr.

Wild Iris: Poems. Louise Gluck. 1993. pap. 11.00 (*0-88001-334-6*) Ecco Pr.

Wild Irish Boy. Charles R. Maturin. Ed. by Devendra P. Varma. LC 77-2043. (Gothic Novels Ser.: No. III). 1977. lib. bdg. 72.95 (*0-405-10141-4*) Ayer.

Wild Irish Girl: A National Tale. Sydney O. Morgan. LC 79-8177. reprint ed. 44.50 (*0-404-62064-7*) AMS Pr.

Wild Irish Girl, 1807. Sidney Owenson. LC 94-44534. (Revolution & Romanticism, 1789-1834 Ser.). 1995. 85.00 (*1-85477-189-2*, Pub. by Woodstock Bks UK) Cassell.

***Wild Irish Rose.** Lisa A. Verge. 416p. 1997. mass mkt. 4.99 (*0-8217-5598-6*, Zebra Kensgtn) Kensgtn Pub Corp.

***Wild Irish Skies.** Nancy Richards-Akers. 1997. mass mkt. 5.99 (*0-380-78948-5*) Avon.

Wild Is My Love. Janelle Taylor. 432p. (Orig.). 1994. mass mkt. 4.99 (*1-55817-781-7*, Pinncle Kensgtn) Kensgtn Pub Corp.

***Wild Is the Day.** Christine M. Fraser. 224p. 1996. 22.00 (*0-7278-4943-3*) Severn Hse.

Wild Is the Wind. Laurie Paige. 1994. 3.50 (*0-373-09887-1*) Silhouette.

Wild Island Sands. Sonya T. Pelton. 1983. mass mkt. 3.75 (*0-8217-1135-0*, Zebra Kensgtn) Kensgtn Pub Corp.

Wild Italy. Tim Jepson. LC 93-28770. (Natural Traveler Ser.). (Illus.). 224p. (Orig.). 1994. pap. 16.00 (*0-87156-478-5*) Sierra.

Wild Jake Hiccup: The History of America's First Frontiersman. Sol M. Davidson. LC 91-19499. (Illus.). 160p. (Orig.). (J). (gr. 3-10). 1992. 19.95 (*1-56412-003-1*); pap. 14.95 (*1-56412-004-X*); audio 9.95 (*1-56412-001-5*) Hse Nine Muses.

Wild Jasmine. Bertrice Small. 704p. 1992. pap. 10.00 (*0-345-36862-2*) Ballantine.

Wild Jasmine. Bertrice Small. 1996. mass mkt. 5.99 (*0-345-40134-4*) Ballantine.

***Wild Justice.** Liz Fielding. 400p. (Orig.). 1996. mass mkt. 3.99 (*1-85487-487-X*, Pub. by Scarlet Bks UK) London Brdge.

Wild Justice. Margret Pierce. 192p. 1995. 19.95 (*0-312-13216-6*) St Martin.

Wild Justice. Ruth M. Sprague. LC 93-60721. 171p. 1993. pap. 5.99 (*1-883889-05-7*) TWanda.

Wild Justice. Craig Thomas. 368p. 1996. mass mkt. 6.50 (*0-06-109169-3*) HarpC.

Wild Justice. large type ed. Lesley Grant-Adamson. 413p. 1989. 25.99 (*0-7089-1931-6*) Ulverscroft.

Wild Justice. large type ed. James A. Pattinson. (Linford Mystery Library). 1989. pap. 15.99 (*0-7089-6752-3*, Trailtree Bookshop) Ulverscroft.

Wild Justice. large type ed. Craig Thomas. LC 95-30746. 581p. 1995. 25.95 (*0-7862-0527-X*) Thorndike Pr.

Wild Justice: A Study in Euripides' Hecuba. Judith Mossman. (Oxford Classical Monographs). (Illus.). 304p. 1995. text ed. 59.00 (*0-19-814789-9*) OUP.

Wild Justice: The People of Geronimo vs. the United States. M. Lieder & Jake Page. 1997. 25.00 (*0-679-45183-8*) Random.

Wild Justice, Not Fade Away & Gimme Shelter. Barrie Keeffe. (Methuen Modern Plays Ser.). 216p. (Orig.). (C). 1990. pap. 13.95 (*0-413-64180-5*, A0483, Pub. by Methuen UK) Heinemann.

Wild Kat. Karen Kijewski. 384p. 1995. mass mkt. 5.99 (*0-553-56877-9*) Bantam.

Wild Kingdom. Vampyre M. Kassel. 25p. (Orig.). 1992. pap. 3.00 (*0-929730-40-2*) Zeitgeist Pr.

Wild Kingdom. Judy Klass. 56p. (Orig.). 1994. pap. 7.50 (*1-880286-15-7*) Singular Speech Pr.

Wild Kingdom. Vijay Seshadri. LC 95-80895. 64p. (Orig.). 1996. pap. 12.95 (*1-55597-236-5*) Graywolf.

Wild Kingdoms. Reader's Digest Editors. LC 96-1917. (Explore America Ser.). 1996. write for info. (*0-89577-902-1*) RD Assn.

Wild Kittens. Photos by Peggy Bauer & Erwin A. Bauer. (Illus.). 80p. 1995. pap. 10.95 (*0-8118-1012-7*) Chronicle Bks.

Wild Knowledge: Science, Language, & Social Life in a Fragile Environment. Will Wright. 240p. (C). 1992. text ed. 39.95 (*0-8166-2050-4*); pap. text ed. 14.95 (*0-8166-2051-2*) U of Minn Pr.

***Wild Lady.** Liz Fielding. 400p. (Orig.). 1997. mass mkt. 3.99 (*1-85487-718-6*, Pub. by Scarlet Bks UK) London Brdge.

Wild Lake Michigan. John Mahan & Ann Mahan. LC 90-24427. (Illus.). 128p. 1991. 29.95 (*0-89658-132-2*) Voyageur Pr.

Wild Lake Michigan. John Mahan & Ann Mahan. LC 92-24427. (Illus.). 128p. 1993. pap. 19.95 (*0-89658-184-5*) Voyageur Pr.

***Wild Land Shrub & Arid Land Restoration Symposium: Proceedings.** Ed. by Bruce A. Roundy et al. (Illus.). 384p. (Orig.). (C). 1996. pap. text ed. 50.00 (*0-7881-3067-6*) DIANE Pub.

Wild Lands for Wildlife: America's National Refuges. Noel Grove. Ed. by Donald J. Crump. LC 84-16539. (Special Publications Series 19: No. 2). (Illus.). 200p. 1984. 12.95 (*0-87044-477-8*) Natl Geog.

***Wild Lawn Handbook.** Stevie Daniels. 1997. pap. text ed. 17.95 (*0-02-862004-6*) Macmillan.

Wild Lawn Handbook: Alternatives to the Traditional Front Lawn. Steve Daniels. LC 94-5369. 1995. pap. 22.00 (*0-02-529445-8*) Macmillan.

Wild Leaves. Patty Smith. (Illus.). 106p. 1995. 17.95 (*0-393-03743-6*) Norton.

Wild Leaves. limited ed. Patty Smith. (Illus.). 106p. write for info. (*0-393-03751-7*) Norton.

Wild Life: The Guide to Unusual Oregon. Mark Christensen. LC 97-9948. 256p. (Orig.). 1997. pap. 18.95 (*1-57061-050-9*) Sasquatch Bks.

Wild Life: The Remarkable Lives of Ordinary Animals. Edward Kanze. LC 95-2500. (Illus.). 224p. 1995. 21.00 (*0-517-70169-3*, Crown) Crown Pub Group.

Wild Life A-B-C: A Natural Alphabet Book. Jan Thornhill. LC 89-19711. (J). (ps-3). 1994. pap. 7.95 (*0-671-88614-2*, Half Moon Paper) S&S Childrens.

Wild Life Conservation in Theory & Practice. William T. Hornaday. LC 72-2843. (Use & Abuse of America's Natural Resources Ser.). 280p. 1972. reprint ed. 20.95 (*0-405-04510-7*) Ayer.

Wild Life of Sailor & Lula. Barry Gifford. 304p. 1996. reprint ed. pap. 12.00 (*0-8021-3454-8*, Grove) Grove-Atltic.

Wild Life on the Plains & Horrors of Indian Warfare. George A. Custer. LC 79-90403. (Mass Violence in America Ser.). (Illus.). 1978. reprint ed. 54.95 (*0-405-01300-0*) Ayer.

Wild Life on the Rockies. fac. ed. Enos A. Mills. LC 87-30203. (Illus.). 373p. 1988. reprint ed. pap. 106.40 (*0-7837-8105-9*, 2047908) Bks Demand.

Wild Life Watcher's Guide to San Luis Obispo County. Anthony Krause. (Illus.). 128p. (Orig.). 1991. pap. 8.95 (*0-945092-20-2*) EZ Nature.

Wild Life 1-2-3: A Nature Counting Book. Jan Thornhill. LC 89-5970. (J). (ps-3). 1994. pap. 5.95 (*0-671-88613-4*, Half Moon Paper) S&S Childrens.

Wild Light: Selected Poems of Yona Wallach. Yona Wallach. Tr. by Linda Zisquit from HEB. LC 96-27458. 110p. (Orig.). 1997. pap. 12.95 (*1-878818-54-6*) Sheep Meadow.

Wild Like the Wind: Passion's Quest. Janice Kaiser. (Temptation Ser.). 1994. mass mkt. 2.99 (*0-373-25577-2*, 1-25577-7) Harlequin Bks.

Wild Lilies. Walt McLaughlin. (Illus.). 17p. (Orig.). 1995. pap. 3.00 (*0-944048-07-2*) Timberline Missouri.

Wild Lily, Prairie Fire: China's Road to Domocracy, Yan'an to Tian'anmen, 1942-1989. Gregor Benton & Alan Hunter. LC 95-5200. 400p. 1995. text ed. 55.00 (*0-691-04359-0*) Princeton U Pr.

Wild Lily, Prairie Fire: China's Road to Domocracy, Yan'an to Tian'anmen, 1942-1989. Ed. by Gregor Benton & Alan Hunter. LC 95-5200. 400p. 1995. pap. text ed. 19.95 (*0-691-04358-2*) Princeton U Pr.

Wild Lives: The Animal Kingdom fo Charles Lynn Bragg. Charles L. Bragg. 1995. 19.95 (*1-57036-065-0*) Turner Pub GA.

Wild Lonesome. large type ed. Harry Whittington. (Linford Western Library). 1991. pap. 15.99 (*0-7089-7016-8*) Ulverscroft.

Wild Love. David A. Grebner. (Illus.). 60p. (Orig.). 1995. pap. 5.95 (*0-9626273-3-X*) Grebner Bks Pub.

Wild Magic. Tamora Pierce. LC 96-42023. (J). 1997. pap. 4.99 (*0-679-88288-X*, Bullseye Bks) Random Bks Yng Read.

Wild Magic. Angus Wells. (Godwars Ser.: Vol. 3). 544p. 1993. mass mkt. 5.99 (*0-553-29130-0*) Bantam.

Wild Magic. large type ed. Tamora Pierce. LC 93-8427. (Immortals Ser.). (J). 1993. pap. 15.95 (*1-56054-796-0*) Thorndike Pr.

Wild Magic: The Immortals. Tamora Pierce. LC 91-43909. 272p. (YA). (gr. 5 up). 1992. lib. bdg. 17.00 (*0-689-31761-1*, Atheneum Bks Young) S&S Childrens.

Wild Majesty: Encounters with Caribs from Columbus to the Present Day, an Anthology. Ed. by Peter Hulme & Neil L. Whitehead. (Illus.). 416p. 1992. pap. 21.00 (*0-19-812274-8*) OUP.

Wild Malaysia: The Wildlife & Scenery of Peninsular Malaysia, Sarawak & Sabah. Junaidi Payne. (Illus.). 210p. 1990. 39.95 (*0-262-16078-1*) MIT Pr.

Wild Mammals in Captivity: Principles & Techniques. Devra G. Kleiman. LC 95-21376. 640p. 1996. 70.00 (*0-226-44002-8*) U Ch Pr.

Wild Mammals in Captivity: Principles & Techniques. Ed. by Devra G. Kleiman et al. LC 95-21376. 1997. pap. text ed. 29.95 (*0-226-44003-6*) U Ch Pr.

Wild Mammals of Missouri. rev. ed. Charles W. Schwartz & Elizabeth R. Schwartz. LC 80-24138. (Illus.). 368p. (C). 1981. text ed. 35.00 (*0-8262-0324-8*) U of Mo Pr.

Wild Mammals of North America: Biology, Management, & Economics. Ed. by Joseph A. Chapman & George A. Feldhamer. LC 81-8209. 1184p. 1982. text ed. 110.00 (*0-8018-2353-6*) Johns Hopkins.

***Wild Man.** Wells. Date not set. write for info. (*0-312-17719-4*) St Martin.

Wild Man at the Wheel. Marcia Leonard. (The Kids on Bus 5 Ser.: No. 2). (J). (gr. 2-4). 1996. mass mkt. 3.50 (*0-671-54191-9*) PB.

Wild Man Within: An Image in Western Thought from the Renaissance to Romanticism. Ed. by Edward J. Dudley & Maximillian E. Novak. LC 72-77191. 345p. reprint ed. pap. 98.40 (*0-318-34981-7*, 2030794) Bks Demand.

Wild Man's Journey: Reflections on Male Spirituality. Richard Rohr & Joseph Martos. 225p. 1991. 17.95 (*0-86716-128-0*) St Anthony Mess Pr.

Wild Man's Journey: Reflections on Male Spirituality. rev. ed. Richard Rohr & Joseph Martos. (Fifty-Two Weekends Ser.). 1996. pap. 10.95 (*0-86716-279-1*, B2791) St Anthony Mess Pr.

***Wild Masquerade.** Bingham. 1997. mass mkt. 5.99 (*0-671-52811-4*) PB.

Wild Meat. Carolyn B. Whitlow. LC 86-20814. (Lost Roads Ser.: No. 30). 64p. (Orig.). 1986. pap. 6.95 (*0-918786-34-7*) Lost Roads.

***Wild Meat & the Bully Burgers.** Lois A. Yamanaka. 1997. pap. 12.00 (*0-15-600483-6*) HarBrace.

Wild Meat & the Bully Burgers. Lois-Ann Yamanaka. LC 95-14121. 240p. 1996. 20.00 (*0-374-29020-2*) FS&G.

Wild Men in the Looking-Glass: The Mythic Origins of European Otherness. Roger Bartra. Tr. by Carl T. Berrisford from SPA. (Illus.). 276p. (C). 1994. text ed. 49.50 (*0-472-10477-2*) U of Mich Pr.

Wild Men of St. Helena. Jarvis Finger. (C). 1990. pap. 21.00 (*0-86439-023-8*, Pub. by Boolarong Pubns AT) St Mut.

Wild Men of the Wild West. Edwin L. Sabin. 1977. 19.95 (*0-8369-6952-9*, 7833) Ayer.

Wild Menu: National Wild Game Cooking Competition Recipes. Christopher Ray. (Illus.). 141p. 1995. 24.50 (*1-57223-037-1*, 0371) Idyll Arbor.

Wild Michigan. Jim DuFresne et al. 128p. 1992. 24.95 (*1-55971-141-8*) NorthWord.

Wild Midnight: Something Wild. Ann Major. (Desire Ser.). 1993. mass mkt. 2.99 (*0-373-05819-5*, 5-05819-3) Silhouette.

Wild Mind: Living the Writer's Life. Natalie Goldberg. 256p. 1990. pap. 11.95 (*0-553-34775-6*) Bantam.

Wild Minnesota. Greg Breining. LC 93-49599. (Wild State Ser.). (Illus.). 144p. 1994. 24.95 (*1-55971-226-0*) NorthWord.

Wild Mississippi: A Natural View. Stephen Kirkpatrick. Ed. by Ann Becker. (Illus.). 128p. 1993. 29.95 (*0-9619353-6-7*) Thy Marvelous Works.

Wild Montana: A Recreation Guide to 55 Roadless Areas. Bill Cunningham. LC 95-52631. (Illus.). 326p. (Orig.). 1995. pap. 14.95 (*1-56044-393-6*) Falcon Pr MT.

***Wild Moose Country.** Paul Strong. LC 97-5959. (Illus.). 160p. 1997. write for info. (*1-55971-638-X*) NorthWord.

Wild Mother. Elizabeth Cunningham. LC 93-2998. 1993. 19.95 (*0-88268-147-8*) Station Hill Pr.

Wild Mother. Elizabeth Cunningham. 1995. pap. 12.95 (*0-88268-197-4*) Station Hill Pr.

***Wild Mountain Thyme.** Rosamunde Pilcher. 1996. mass mkt. 5.99 (*0-312-96123-5*) St Martin.

Wild Mountain Thyme. Rosamunde Pilcher. 304p. 1989. reprint ed. mass mkt. 5.50 (*0-440-20250-7*) Dell.

Wild Muir: Twenty-Two of John Muir's Greatest Adventures. Lee Stetson. (Illus.). 216p. 1994. pap. 9.95 (*0-939666-75-8*) Yosemite Assn.

Wild Mushroom. George McCarthy. (Illus.). 144p. 1996. 34.95 (*0-86343-386-3*, Pub. by Fountain Pr UK) Fisher Bks.

***Wild Mushroom & Toadstool Poisoning.** S. G. Oldridge et al. 23p. 1989. pap. 10.00 (*0-947643-18-4*, Pub. by Royal Botnic Grdns UK) Balogh.

Wild Mushrooms: How to Find, Identify & Cook Them. Nigel Addinall & Marie F. Addinall. (Illus.). 96p. (C). 1992. 49.00 (*0-7154-0724-4*, Pub. by C Davies Pubs) St Mut.

Wild Mustang. (J). Date not set. pap. 3.95 (*0-590-20748-2*) Scholastic Inc.

Wild Mustang. Joanna Campbell. 144p. (J). (gr. 3-5). 1989. pap. 3.50 (*0-553-15698-5*, Skylark BDD) BDD Bks Young Read.

Wild Mustang Sponsorship Kit. Merryl Lambert. pap. 19.95 (*1-886738-01-7*) Pequot Pubng.

Wild Mustangs. Parley J. Paskett. LC 86-13165. (Western Experience Ser.). 151p. 1986. reprint ed. pap. 43.10 (*0-7837-9256-5*, 2049996) Bks Demand.

***Wild Neighbors: The Humane Approach to Living with Wildlife.** Humane Society of the United States Staff. Ed. by John Hadidian et al. LC 96-47459. (Illus.). 288p. (Orig.). 1997. pap. 16.95 (*1-55591-309-1*) Fulcrum Pub.

Wild New York. M. Mittlebach & Crewdson. LC 96-53915. 1997. 30.00 (*0-517-70484-6*) Random.

Wild New Zealand. Les Molloy. LC 94-27175. 1994. 39.95 (*0-262-13304-0*) MIT Pr.

Wild Night. large type ed. Rae Foley. LC 94-717. 1994. lib. bdg. 20.95 (*0-7862-0184-3*) Thorndike Pr.

Wild Night in Widow's Peak. large type ed. Marshall Grover. (Western Ser.). 1994. pap. 15.99 (*0-7089-7589-5*, Linford) Ulverscroft.

Wild Nights. deluxe limited ed. Joyce Carol Oates. 56p. 1985. 45.00 (*0-912348-13-5*) Croissant & Co.

Wild Northland, Being the Story of a Winter Journey, with Dogs, Across Northern North America. William F. Butler. LC 72-2824. (American Explorers Ser.). reprint ed. 59.50 (*0-404-54904-7*) AMS Pr.

Wild Oakie. George Martin. LC 92-85412. 76p. (J). (gr. 2-6). 1993. 6.95 (*1-55523-552-2*) Winston-Derek.

Wild Oats. Pamela Morsi. 336p. (Orig.). 1993. mass mkt. 5.99 (*0-515-11185-6*) Jove Pubns.

Wild Oats. John O'Keeffe. 96p. (Orig.). 1996. pap. 12.95 (*1-85459-229-7*, Pub. by N Hern Bks UK) Theatre Comm.

Wild Oats. large type ed. Pamela Morsi. LC 93-37210. (Orig.). 1994. lib. bdg. 17.95 (*0-7862-0099-5*) Thorndike Pr.

Wild Oats: A Romance of the Old West. James McLure. 1985. pap. 5.25 (*0-8222-1257-9*) Dramatists Play.

Wild of Canada. John Cadiz. 96p. 1995. pap. 12.95 (*0-385-25537-3*) Doubleday.

Wild Ohio. Art Weber. LC 95-14868. (Wild State Ser.). (Illus.). 128p. 1995. 24.95 (*1-55971-473-5*) NorthWord.

Wild Olive Tree, 2 vols. in one. Bert Meyers. Bd. with Blue Cafe. 118p. 1982. reprint ed. Set pap. 6.95 (*0-915572-67-2*) Panjandrum.

***Wild on Wheels: Motorcycles Then & Now.** Paul Otfinoski. LC 97-3540. (Here We Go! Ser.: Group 2). (Illus.). 32p. (J). (gr. 1 up). 1997. lib. bdg. 14.95 (*0-7614-0607-7*, Benchmark NY) Marshall Cavendish.

Wild One. John Reese. 1981. pap. 1.75 (*0-449-13953-0*, GM) Fawcett.

***Wild One: The Life of Marlon Brando.** Donald Spoto. mass mkt. write for info. (*0-06-109303-3*, Harp PBks) HarpC.

***Wild Onions.** Karla Andersdatter. 295p. 1997. write for info. (*0-911051-89-9*) Plain View.

Wild Orchids. Eric Hansen. pap. write for info. (*0-679-45141-2*) Random.

Wild Orchids. Eric Hansen. (J). (gr. 8-8). pap. write for info. (*0-679-77183-2*) Random.

Wild Orchids. Karen Robards. 384p. 1986. mass mkt. 5.99 (*0-446-32692-5*) Warner Bks.

***Wild Orchids.** large type ed. Karen Robards. LC 97-3572. 1997. 25.95 (*1-56895-421-2*, Compass) Wheeler Pub.

Wild Orchids of Arkansas. Carl R. Slaughter. LC 93-93586. (Illus.). 101p. 1993. 17.50 (*0-9638497-0-0*) C R Slaughter.

Wild Orchids of California. Ronald A. Coleman. (Comstock Bk.). (Illus.). 264p. 1995. 45.00 (*0-8014-3012-7*) Cornell U Pr.

Wild Orchids of Crete. C. Alibertis & A. Alibertis. (Illus.). 176p. 1989. pap. 32.50 (*0-945345-41-0*) Lubrecht & Cramer.

Wild Orchids of the Middle Atlantic States. Oscar W. Gupton & Fred C. Swope. LC 86-4349. (Illus.). 132p. 1987. 16.95 (*0-87049-509-7*) U of Tenn Pr.

***Wild Orchids of the Northeastern United States: A Field Guide.** Paul M. Brown. LC 96-34508. (Comstock Bk.). (Illus.). 224p. 1996. pap. 17.95 (*0-8014-8341-7*, Comstock Pub) Cornell U Pr.

Wild Origami: Amazing Animals You Can Make. P. D. Tuyen. LC 96-28264. (Illus.). 80p. 1996. pap. 12.95 (*0-8069-1380-0*) Sterling.

Wild Orphan. (J). Date not set. pap. 3.50 (*0-590-20760-1*) Scholastic Inc.

Wild Otters: Predation & Populations. Hans Kruuk. (Illus.). 300p. 1995. 65.00 (*0-19-854070-1*) OUP.

Wild Palms. William Faulkner. LC 84-4613. 339p. 1984. 20.00 (*0-394-60513-6*, V262, Vin) Random.

Wild Palms. William Faulkner. LC 84-4613. 1984. 8.95 (*0-318-37465-X*, Modern Lib) Random.

Wild Palms: Nineteen Thirty-Nine. William Faulkner. Ed. by Thomas McHaney. (William Faulkner Manuscripts). 356p. 1986. text ed. 50.00 (*0-8240-6818-1*) Garland.

Wild Palms: The Screenplay. Bruce Wagner. 336p. (Orig.). 1994. pap. 13.95 (*0-312-10616-5*, Thomas Dunne Bks) St Martin.

Wild Palms Reader. Ed. by Roger Trilling. LC 92-36317. 1993. pap. 14.95 (*0-312-09083-8*) St Martin.

Wild Palms (Typescript) William Faulkner. Ed. by Thomas McHaney. (William Faulkner Manuscripts). 408p. 1986. text ed. 60.00 (*0-8240-6819-X*) Garland.

Wild Parrots & the King of La Brea. Gerald Lange. (Illus.). 29p. 1997. pap. write for info. (*0-931460-31-X*) Bieler.

W

An Asterisk (*) at the beginning of an entry indicates that the title is appearing in BIP for the first time.

Wild Party: The Lost Classic. Joseph M. March. LC 94-11682. (Illus.). 1994. 22.00 (0-679-42450-4) Pantheon.
Wild Patience Has Taken Me This Far: Poems 1978-1981. Adrienne Rich. 1981. 12.95 (0-393-01494-0) Norton.
Wild Patience Has Taken Me This Far: Poems 1978-1981. Adrienne Rich. 72p. 1993. pap. 8.95 (0-393-31037-X) Norton.
***Wild Peavines.** Robert Morgan. 32p. (Orig.). 1996. pap. 10.00 (0-917788-63-X) Gnomon Pr.
***Wild Peavines.** limited ed. Robert Morgan. 32p. (Orig.). 1996. pap. 35.00 (0-917788-65-6) Gnomon Pr.
Wild People: Travels with Borneo's Head Hunters. Andro Linklater. LC 91-9047. 216p. 1992. pap. 10.95 (0-87113-477-2, Atlntc Mnthly) Grove-Atltic.
Wild Pigs: The Mountain Bike Adventure Guide to the Pacific Coast. John Zilly. LC 94-78208. 208p. 1995. pap. 12.95 (1-881583-05-8) Advent Pr WA.
Wild Pigs in the United States: Their History, Comparative Morphology, & Current Status. John J. Mayer & I. Lehr Brisbin, Jr. LC 90-10945. (Illus.). 336p. 1991. 50.00 (0-8203-1239-8) U of Ga Pr.
Wild Pill Hickok & Other Old West Riddles. David A. Adler. LC 88-6480. (Illus.). 64p. (J). (gr. 1-4). 1988. lib. bdg. 13.95 (0-8234-0718-7) Holiday.
Wild Places. Bobbie Hoiaday. (Illus.). 136p. (Orig.). 1985. pap. 8.00 (0-8187-0063-7) Harlo Press.
Wild Places. William Neill. 200p. 1989. pap. 35.00 (0-946487-11-1, Pub. by Luath Pr UK) St Mut.
Wild Places. A. Wilkes. (Explainers Ser.). (J). (gr. 4-6). 1980. pap. 12.95 (0-7460-0798-1, Usborne) EDC.
Wild Places: 20 Journeys into the North American Outdoors. Tim Cahill et al. LC 96-45105. 350p. (Orig.). 1996. pap. 15.95 (0-935701-41-9) Foghorn Pr.
Wild Planet! One Thousand & One Extraordinary Events for the Inspired Traveler. Tom Clynes. (Illus.). 669p. 1995. 18.95 (0-7876-0203-5) Visible Ink Pr.
Wild Planet! 1,001 Extraordinary Events for the Inspired Traveler. 625p. 1995. 35.00 (0-7876-0373-2, 109269) Gale.
Wild Plant Companion: A Fresh Understanding of Herbal Food & Medicine. Kathryn G. March & Andrew L. March. (Illus.). 200p. (Orig.). 1986. pap. 11.95 (0-940206-03-X) Meridian Hill.
Wild Plant Conservation & the Law. Cyrille De Klemm. (IUCN Environmental Policy & Law Occasional Paper: No. 24). (Illus.). 224p. (Orig.). 1990. pap. 27.00 (2-8317-0001-9, Pub. by IUCN SZ) Island Pr.
***Wild Plants & Native Peoples of the Four Corners.** William W. Dunmire & Gail D. Tierney. LC 97-2372. (Illus.). 300p. 1997. pap. 22.50 (0-89013-319-0) Museum NM Pr.
Wild Plants in Flower: Eastern Deciduous Forest. T. Korling & R. O. Petty. (Illus.). 95p. Date not set. 10.00 (0-930404-01-7) IN Acad Sci.
Wild Plants of the Pueblo Province: Exploring Ancient & Enduring Uses. William W. Dunmire & Gail D. Tierney. (Illus.). 304p. 1995. pap. 22.50 (0-89013-272-0) Museum NM Pr.
Wild Plants of the Pueblo Province: Exploring Ancient & Enduring Uses. William W. Dunmire & Gail D. Tierney. (Illus.). 1995. 29.95 (0-89013-282-8) Museum NM Pr.
Wild Plants of the San Juan Islands. 2nd ed. Scott Atkinson & Fred Sharpe. LC 93-10809. (Orig.). 1993. pap. 12.95 (0-89886-356-2) Mountaineers.
Wild Plum at Night. Jamie Wheelas. LC 96-3596. 192p. (Orig.). 1996. pap. 18.95 (0-86534-049-8) Sunstone Pr.
Wild Ponies of Assategue Island see Books for Young Explorers
***Wild Ponies of the Outer Banks.** Jean Day & Robert Day. (Illus.). 96p. (Orig.). 1996. pap. 6.00 (1-890238-40-6) Golden Age Pr.
Wild Pony. Jeanne Betancourt. (Pony Pals Ser.: No. 09). (J). 1996. pap. 2.99 (0-590-62974-3) Scholastic Inc.
Wild Puppies. Photos by Peggy Bauer & Erwin A. Bauer. (Illus.). 80p. 1995. pap. 10.95 (0-8118-1039-9) Chronicle Bks.
***Wild Ram of the Mountain: The Story of Lyman Wight.** Jermy B. Wight. (Illus.). 521p. (Orig.). 1996. pap. 19.50 (0-9651163-7-9) Harkness Pubng.
***Wild, Rank Place: One Year on Cape Cod.** David Gessner. LC 96-35908. (Illus.). 149p. 1997. 19.95 (0-87451-802-4) U Pr of New Eng.
Wild Rapture. Cassie Edwards. 352p. (Orig.). 1992. pap. 5.99 (0-451-40330-4, Onyx) NAL-Dutton.
***Wild Raspberries.** Suzie Frankfort & Andy Warhol. LC 97-1193. 1997. 19.95 (0-8212-2340-2) Bulfinch Pr.
Wild Reindeer. E. E. Syroechkovskii. Ed. by David R. Klein. Tr. by P. M. Rao from RUS. (Illus.). 304p. (C). 1995. text ed. 90.00 (1-886106-39-8) Science Pubs.
Wild Rice & the Ojibway People. Thomas Vennum, Jr. LC 87-38333. (Illus.). x, 358p. 1988. 29.95 (0-87351-225-1); pap. 14.95 (0-87351-226-X) Minn Hist.
Wild Rice for all Season Cook Book. Beth Anderson. 179p. 1984. 9.95 (0-9610030-0-6) B Anderson Assocs.
Wild Rice in Canada. S. B. Aiken et al. (Illus.). 176p. (Orig.). pap. 18.95 (1-55021-027-0, Pub. by NC Press CN) U of Toronto Pr.
Wild Ride. Ann Auerbach. 1995. pap. 14.95 (0-8050-4242-3) H Holt & Co.
Wild Ride: Earthquakes, Sneezes, & Other Thrills. Bia Lowe. 192p. 1996. pap. 11.00 (0-06-092695-3) HarpC.
Wild River Massacre. Jack Curtis. Ed. by Doug Grad. 224p. (Orig.). 1993. mass mkt. 3.99 (0-671-79320-9) PB.
Wild River, Timeless Canyons: Balduin Mollhausen's Watercolors of the Colorado. Ben W. Huseman. LC 95-35223. (Illus.). 232p. 1995. 70.00 (0-88360-084-6) Amon Carter.
Wild Rivers. Photos by Peter Dombrovskis. 128p. (C). 1983. 80.00 (0-9597530-4-4, Pub. by West Wind Pr AT) St Mut.
Wild Rivers & Mountains Trails. Don I. Smith. LC 85-60310. (Illus.). 126p. 1985. reprint ed. pap. 7.99 (0-932773-01-X) High Country Bks.
***Wild Rivers, Wild Lands.** Ken Madsen. 1996. pap. text ed. 24.95 (1-896758-01-0, Pub. by Stoddart Pubng CN) Genl Dist Srvs.
Wild Roots: A Forager's Guide to the Edible & Medicinal Roots, Tubers, Corms, & Rhizomes of North America. Doug Elliott. (Illus.). 124p. 1995. pap. 14.95 (0-89281-538-8) Inner Tradit.
***Wild Rose.** Cheryl-Lynn Braun. 1996. mass mkt. 3.99 (1-55197-488-6, Pub. by Comnwlth Pub CN) Partners Pubs Grp.
Wild Rose. Doris Mortman. 848p. 1992. mass mkt. 6.99 (0-553-29761-9) Bantam.
Wild Rose: Meg's Tale. Daisy Vivian. 192p. 1986. 15.95 (0-8027-0876-5) Walker & Co.
Wild Rose - a Folk History of a Cross Timbers Settlement: Keller, Texas. Joyce G. Roach. LC 96-15953. 1996. write for info. (0-89865-972-8, Starblaze) Donning Co.
Wild Rose Inn, No. 3. Jennifer Armstrong. (Wild Rose Inn Ser.). 192p. (YA). (gr. 7 up). 1994. mass mkt. 3.99 (0-553-29909-3) Bantam.
***Wild Rose of Ruby Canyon.** John D. Nesbitt. LC 96-51010. 179p. 1997. 20.95 (0-8027-4159-2) Walker & Co.
Wild Rose Pass. Kent Conwell. 1994. 17.95 (0-8034-9039-9) Bouregy.
***Wild Roses.** Hannah Howell. 352p. 1997. mass mkt. 5.99 (0-8217-5677-X, Zebra Kensgtn) Kensgtn Pub Corp.
Wild Roses. Miriam Minger. 368p. (Orig.). 1996. mass mkt. 5.99 (0-380-78302-9) Avon.
Wild Rue. Bess A. Donaldson. LC 73-6277. (Middle East Ser.). 1977. reprint ed. 19.95 (0-405-05332-0) Ayer.
Wild Rumors. Ann L. Williamson. Ed. by Carol Spelius & Wayne Spelius. 65p. (Orig.). 1993. pap. 7.95 (0-941363-31-7) Lake Shore Pub.
Wild Safari in 3-D! Rick Sammon & Susan Sammon. (3-D Children's Ser.). (Illus.). 28p. (J). (gr. k up). 1996. 9.95 (1-57359-007-X, Starhill Pr) Black Belt Comm.
Wild Sage. Peggy Hanchar. (Orig.). 1994. mass mkt. 4.99 (0-449-14771-1, GM) Fawcett.
Wild Scenes in the Forest & Prairie. Charles F. Hoffman. LC 76-104485. 284p. reprint ed. lib. bdg. 46.00 (0-8398-0784-8) Irvington.
Wild Season. Allan W. Eckert. LC 67-14449. (Illus.). 256p. 1981. reprint ed. pap. 10.00 (0-913428-31-0) Landfall Pr.
Wild Seasons: Gathering & Cooking Wild Plants of the Great Plains. Kay Young. LC 92-39105. (Illus.). xxiv, 320p. 1993. text ed. 45.00 (0-8032-4906-3) U of Nebr Pr.
Wild Seasons: Gathering & Cooking Wild Plants of the Great Plains. Kay Young. LC 92-39105. (Illus.). xxiv, 320p. 1993. pap. 15.00 (0-8032-9904-4, Bison Books) U of Nebr Pr.
Wild Season's Day Book: Aleta Karstad's Canadian Sketches. Aleta Karstad. 1995. 9.95 (0-7737-2254-8) Genl Dist Srvs.
Wild Seasons Daybook. Aleta Karstad. 106p. 1989. 12.95 (0-458-99290-9) Longman.
Wild Seed. Octavia E. Butler. 288p. 1988. mass mkt. 5.99 (0-445-20537-7) Warner Bks.
***Wild Serenade.** Lisa Bingham. 1997. mass mkt. 5.99 (0-671-52810-6, Pocket Books) PB.
Wild Sex: Way Beyond the Birds & the Bees. Susan Windybank. (Illus.). 288p. (Orig.). 1992. pap. 10.95 (0-312-08336-X) St Martin.
Wild Sheep. John Muir. Ed. by William R. Jones. (Illus.). 32p. 1977. reprint ed. pap. 2.95 (0-89646-017-7) Vistabooks.
Wild Sheep Chase. Haruki Murakami. Tr. by Alfred Birnbaum. 304p. 1990. pap. 12.95 (0-452-26516-9, Plume) NAL-Dutton.
Wild Sheep Country. Valerius Geist. LC 93-17235. (Wildlife Country Ser.). (Illus.). 1993. 39.00 (1-55971-212-0) NorthWord.
Wild Shore. Kim S. Robinson. 384p. 1995. pap. 13.95 (0-312-89036-2) Tor Bks.
Wild Shores: Exploring the Wilderness Areas of Eastern North Carolina. Walter Taylor. Ed. by Jerry Bledsoe. LC 93-71244. (Illus.). 159p. (Orig.). 1993. pap. 13.95 (1-878086-19-7) Down Home NC.
***Wild Shores of Australia.** Ron Fisher et al. LC 96-41560. 1996. write for info. (0-7922-2946-0); write for info. (0-7922-2976-2) Natl Geog.
Wild Shots: A New Look at Photographing the Wildlife. Chris Packham. (Illus.). 160p. 1994. 39.95 (1-85585-189-X) Trafalgar.
Wild Side. Scott Shalaway. 140p. 1990. pap. 7.95 (1-882955-00-5) Saddle Ridge.
Wild Side: Philatelic Mischief, Murder & Intrigue. Stephen R. Datz. 164p. 1990. pap. 9.95 (0-88219-024-5) General Trade.
***Wild Side of Maryland: An Outdoor Guide.** Ed. by Molly Dunham. (Illus.). 276p. (Orig.). 1997. pap. 14.95 (0-9649819-4-7) Baltimore Sun.
Wild Side of the Adirondacks, Winter-Spring: An Adirondack Park Centennial Edition. Kip Taylor. Ed. by Sharon B. Taylor. LC 91-91379. (Illus.). 136p. 1992. 45.00 (0-9623422-1-1) K Taylor.
Wild Sierra Rogue. Martha Hix. 448p. 1993. mass mkt. 4.50 (0-8217-4256-6, Zebra Kensgtn) Kensgtn Pub Corp.
Wild Silk Moths of North America: A Natural History of the Saturniidae of the United States & Canada. Paul M. Tuskes et al. (Comstock Bk.). (Illus.). 264p. 1996. 75.00 (0-8014-3130-1) Cornell U Pr.
***Wild Snow.** Louis W. Dawson, II. (Illus.). 350p. 1997. pap. write for info. (0-930410-64-5) Amer Alpine Club.
***Wild Snow: A Historical Guide to North American Ski Mountaineering.** Louis W. Dawson. 1997. 40.00 (0-930410-68-8) Amer Alpine Club.
Wild Sort of Beauty: Public Places & Private Visions. Robert L. McGrath. Ed. by Alice W. Gilborn. (Illus.). 48p. 1992. pap. 10.00 (0-910020-43-4) Adirondack Mus.
Wild Sounds of Northwoods. Elliot. pap. 11.95 (1-878194-00-3) Nature Sound Studio.
Wild Southern Rose. Caroline Bourne. 1985. mass mkt. 3.75 (0-8217-1603-4, Zebra Kensgtn) Kensgtn Pub Corp.
Wild Southern Scenes. John B. Jones. (Notable American Authors Ser.). 1992. reprint ed. lib. bdg. 90.00 (0-7812-3522-7) Rprt Serv.
Wild Spain. 2nd ed. Frederic V. Grunfeld. LC 93-28700. (Natural Traveler Ser.). (Illus.). 224p. (Orig.). 1994. reprint ed. pap. 16.00 (0-87156-477-7) Sierra.
Wild Spirits: Strong Medicine: African Art & the Wilderness. Martha G. Anderson & Christine M. Kreamer. Ed. by Enid Schildkrout. LC 89-7124. (Illus.). 96p. 1989. pap. text ed. 25.00 (0-945802-03-X) Museum African.
Wild Splendor. Cassie Edwards. 384p. 1993. pap. 4.99 (0-451-40404-1, Topaz) NAL-Dutton.
Wild Splendor. Leta Tegler. 384p. (Orig.). 1988. mass mkt. 3.95 (0-380-75615-3) Avon.
Wild Sports in the Far West: The Narratives of a German Wanderer beyond the Mississippi, 1837-1843. Friedrich Gerstacker. LC 68-16624. 409p. reprint ed. pap. 116.60 (0-317-26743-4, 2023381) Bks Demand.
Wild Sports of Southern Africa. W. C. Harris. (Illus.). 359p. 1987. 30.00 (0-940143-53-4) Safari Pr.
Wild Stage: Literary Cabarets of the Weimar Republic. Alan Lareau. LC 94-48349. (Studies in German Literature, Linguistics & Culture). 215p. 1995. 54.95 (1-879751-86-0) Camden Hse.
***Wild Star.** Catherine Coulter. 1986. mass mkt. 6.99 (0-451-40447-5, Onyx) NAL-Dutton.
Wild Star. Catherine Coutler. 1986. pap. 5.99 (0-451-40013-5, Onyx) NAL-Dutton.
Wild Star. Catherine Coulter. 1994. reprint ed. lib. bdg. 22.00 (0-7278-4687-6) Severn Hse.
Wild Steps of Heaven. Victor Villasenor. 320p. 1996. 19.95 (0-385-31566-X) Delacorte.
***Wild Steps of Heaven.** Victor Villasenor. 320p. 1997. pap. 11.95 (0-385-31569-4, Delta) Dell.
Wild Strawberries. Philip French & Kersti French. 80p. 1995. pap. 9.95 (0-85170-481-6, Pub. by British Film Inst UK) Ind U Pr.
Wild Strawberries. Angela M. Thirkell. 1989. pap. 4.95 (0-88184-555-8) Carroll & Graf.
***Wild Strawberries: A Barsetshire Novel.** 2nd ed. Angela M. Thirkell. LC 97-4444. 272p. 1996. pap. 11.95 (0-7867-0438-1) Carroll & Graf.
Wild Strawberries at 3000 Feet. Robert W. Olmsted. LC 86-60424. 64p. (Orig.). 1986. pap. 6.95 (0-89002-244-5) Am Hist Pr.
Wild Strawberries at 3000 Feet. Robert W. Olmsted. LC 86-60424. 64p. (Orig.). 1986. 19.95 (0-89002-245-3) Northwoods Pr.
Wild Streak. Margaret E. Bailey. LC 72-106245. (Short Story Index Reprint Ser.). 1977. 20.95 (0-8369-3281-1) Ayer.
Wild Streak. Kay Thorpe. (Presents Ser.). 1993. pap. 2.89 (0-373-11556-3, 1-11556-7) Harlequin Bks.
Wild Streets. Western Writers of America Staff. LC 73-113693. (Short Story Index Reprint Ser.). 1977. 23.95 (0-8369-3422-9) Ayer.
Wild Summer Rose. Amy E. Saunders. 400p. (Orig.). 1993. mass mkt., pap. text ed. 4.99 (0-505-51902-X, Love Spell) Dorchester Pub Co.
***Wild Swans.** mass mkt. write for info. (0-06-109335-1, Harp PBks) HarpC.
Wild Swans. Hans Christian Andersen. LC 81-65843. (Pied Piper Bks.). (Illus.). 40p. (J). (gr. k up). 1976. pap. 16.95 (0-8037-9381-2) Dial Bks Young.
Wild Swans. Hans Christian Andersen. LC 80-27685. (Illus.). 32p. (J). (gr. k-4). 1981. lib. bdg. 11.89 (0-89375-480-3) Troll Communs.
Wild Swans. Hans Christian Andersen. LC 81-65843. (Pied Piper Bks.). (Illus.). 40p. (J). (gr. k up). 1987. pap. 5.95 (0-8037-0451-8) Dial Bks Young.
Wild Swans. Hans Christian Anderson. 1994. 4.99 (0-517-13520-5) Random Hse Value.
***Wild Swans.** Peg Kerr. 1998. pap. write for info. (0-446-67366-8, Aspect) Warner Bks.
Wild Swans: Three Daughters of China. Jung Chang. LC 92-19078. (Illus.). 528p. reprint ed. pap. 14.95 (0-385-42547-3, Anchor NY) Doubleday.
Wild Swans at Coole: Manuscript Materials. William Butler Yeats. Ed. by Stephen M. Parrish. (Yeats Ser.). (Illus.). 472p. 1995. 62.50 (0-8014-3066-6) Cornell U Pr.
Wild Sweet Flowers: Alvie Skerritt Stories. Marian Eldridge. 1994. pap. 16.95 (0-7022-2622-X, Pub. by Univ Queensland Pr AT) Intl Spec Bk.
Wild Sweet Wilderness. Dorothy Garlock. 400p. 1989. mass mkt. 5.99 (0-445-20678-0) Warner Bks.
Wild Sweet Wilderness. large type ed. Dorothy Garlock. LC 94-47826. 1995. lib. bdg. 21.95 (0-7862-0392-7) Thorndike Pr.
Wild Talents see Complete Books of Charles Fort
Wild Tales. Nikolai Haitov. Tr. by M. Holman from BUL. 239p. 7900. 30.00 (0-7206-0543-1, Pub. by P Owen Ltd UK) Dufour.
Wild Talk. Marilyn Baillie. (Illus.). 32p. (J). (gr. 1-7). 1996. 17.95 (1-895688-54-X, Pub. by Owl Bks CN); pap. 6.95 (1-895688-55-8, Pub. by Owl Bks CN) Firefly Bks Ltd.
Wild Taste: Plant & Mushroom Recipes for the Knowledgeable Cook. Kathryn G. March & Andrew L. March. LC 88-90947. (Illus.). 320p. (Orig.). 1989. pap. 19.95 (0-940206-04-8) Meridian Hill.
Wild Temptation. Elizabeth Duke. (Romance Ser.: No. 200). 1992. pap. 2.89 (0-373-03200-5, 1-03200-2) Harlequin Bks.
Wild Texas Bride. Dana Ransom. 384p. 1995. mass mkt. 4.99 (0-8217-4833-5, Zebra Kensgtn) Kensgtn Pub Corp.
Wild Thailand. Belinda Stewart-Cox & John Hoskin. (Illus.). 208p. (C). 1995. 40.00 (0-262-19364-7) MIT Pr.
Wild Thing. Lynn Patrick. (Temptation Ser.: No. 395). 1992. mass mkt. 2.99 (0-373-25495-4, 1-25495-2) Harlequin Bks.
Wild Thing: The Backstage, on the Road, in the Studio, off the Charts Memoirs of Ian Copeland. Ian Copeland. 368p. 1995. 23.00 (0-684-81508-7, S&S) S&S Trade.
***Wild Things.** S. A. Bartfay. 24p. (Orig.). 1997. pap. 4.00 (0-9656161-1-8) Quale Pr.
Wild Things. Dion Henderson. LC 78-9687. (Illus.). 1979. 7.95 (0-915024-18-7) Wl Tales & Trails.
Wild Things. Karin Kallmaker. 240p. (Orig.). 1996. pap. 10.95 (1-56280-139-2) Naiad Pr.
Wild Things. Michael McIntosh. LC 96-5226. (Illus.). 424p. 1996. 30.00 (0-924357-57-6, 21250-A) Countrysport Pr.
Wild Things: A Guide to the Lower Life Forms. Mike Capuzzo. 288p. (Orig.). 1995. pap. 10.00 (0-449-90895-X) Fawcett.
***Wild Things: A New Species of Desserts.** Janna L. Sheppard. 1996. pap. text ed. 15.95 (0-9646741-3-0) Northstar NV.
Wild Things: Nature, Culture, & Tourism in Ontario, 1790-1914. Patricia Jasen. (Illus.). 216p. 1995. 45.00 (0-8020-0684-1); pap. 18.95 (0-8020-7638-6) U of Toronto Pr.
Wild Things: The Pet Patrol, No. 2. Betsy Duffey. (Illus.). 80p. (J). 1995. pap. 3.99 (0-14-034998-7) Puffin Bks.
Wild Things Happen When I Pray. 2nd rev. ed. Becky Tirabassi. 144p. 1995. pap. 10.99 (0-310-54931-0) Zondervan.
Wild Things in the Yard. Wendy Anderson. 64p. (Orig.). 1986. 9.95 (0-939395-00-2); pap. 5.95 (0-939395-01-0) Thorntree Pr.
Wild Things to Cook. Dale Neutrelle. 1974. pap. 5.00 (0-916552-00-4) Acoma Bks.
Wild Thorns. Sahar Khalifeh. Tr. by Trevor LeGassick & Elizabeth Fernea from ARA. LC 88-21937. 207p. 1989. reprint ed. pap. 9.95 (0-940793-25-3, Olive Branch Pr) Interlink Pub.
Wild Thunder. Cassie Edwards. (Historical Romance Ser.). 384p. 1995. pap. 5.99 (0-451-40586-2, Onyx) NAL-Dutton.
Wild Thyme, Winter Lightning: The Symbolic Novels of L. P. Hartley. Anne Mulkeen. LC 73-18047. 209p. reprint ed. pap. 59.60 (0-318-39794-3, 2033197) Bks Demand.
Wild to the Heart. rev. ed. Rick Bass. (Illus.). 176p. 1997. pap. 12.00 (0-393-31487-1, Norton Paperbks) Norton.
Wild Town. Jim Thompson. LC 92-56367. (Crime - Black Lizard Ser.). 1993. pap. 10.00 (0-679-73312-4, Vin) Random.
Wild Towns of Nebraska. Wayne C. Lee. LC 88-20227. (Illus.). 147p. (Orig.). 1988. pap. 14.95 (0-87004-325-0) Caxton.
***Wild Trails, Wild Tales.** Bernard McKay. (Illus.). 176p. (Orig.). 1996. pap. 12.95 (0-88839-395-4) Hancock House.
Wild Trees of Idaho. Frederic D. Johnson. LC 94-10980. (Northwest Naturalist Bks.). 288p. 1996. pap. 39.95 (0-89301-145-2) U of Idaho Pr.
Wild Trek. Jim Kjelgaard. 256p. (J). 1984. 3.99 (0-553-15687-X) Bantam.
***Wild Tribes of Davao District, Mindanao. The R. F. Cummings Philippine Expedition.** Fay-Cooper Cole. LC 13-24658. (Field Museum of Natural History Anthropological Ser.: Vol. 12, No. 2). (Illus.). 347p. 1913. reprint ed. pap. 98.90 (0-608-02710-3, 2063375) Bks Demand.
Wild Tribes of the Soudan. Frank L. James. LC 73-94481. 280p. 1969. reprint ed. text ed. 38.50 (0-8371-2366-6, JAT&, Greenwood Pr) Greenwood.
Wild Trout. 2nd ed. Walt Franklin. Ed. by Roy Zarucchi & Carolyn Page. (Chapbook Ser.). (Illus.). 32p. (Orig.). 1991. pap. text ed. 5.00 (1-879205-13-0) Nightshade Pr.
***Wild Truth Bible Lessons: 12 Wild Studies for Junior Highers.** Mark Oestreicher. LC 96-22271. 1996. write for info. (0-310-21304-5) Youth Spec.
Wild Truth Journal: Fifty Life Lessons from the Scriptures. Mark Oestreicher. 112p. 1996. spiral bd. 8.99 (0-310-20766-5) Zondervan.
***Wild Turkey.** Gary Clancy & Cy DeCosse Incorporated Staff. LC 96-43709. (Hunting & Fishing Library). (Illus.). 128p. 1996. 19.95 (0-86573-062-8) Cowles Creative.
Wild Turkey: Biology & Management. Ed. by James G. Dickson. LC 92-11214. (Illus.). 496p. 1992. 69.95 (0-8117-1859-X) Stackpole.
Wild Turkey & Its Hunting. Edward A. McIlhenny. (Illus.). 245p. 1984. reprint ed. 24.95 (0-685-62740-3) Real Turkeys Pubs.
Wild Turkey Cookbook. A. D. Livingston. LC 94-20652. 192p. 1995. pap. 12.95 (0-8117-3097-2) Stackpole.
Wild Turkey Country. Lovett E. Williams. LC 90-25087. (Illus.). 1991. 39.00 (1-55971-097-7, 0193) NorthWord.
Wild Turkey Country. Lovett E. Williams. (Illus.). 1993. pap. 19.95 (1-55971-206-6) NorthWord.
Wild Turkey Run. Bob Reese. (Grand Canyon Ser.). (Illus.). (J). (gr. k-6). 1987. 9.95 (0-89868-199-5); pap. 3.95 (0-89868-225-8) ARO Pub.
Wild Turkey, Tame Turkey. Dorothy H. Patent. LC 89-613. (Illus.). 64p. (J). (gr. 3-6). 1989. 14.95 (0-89919-704-3, Clarion Bks) HM.
Wild Type. Jeffrey I. Victoroff. 1990. mass mkt. 4.50 (1-55817-434-6, Pinncle Kensgtn) Kensgtn Pub Corp.
Wild 'Uns. Caroline Andrew. 1985. 15.00 (0-317-89941-4, Pub. by Pentland Pr UK) St Mut.
Wild Vines. large type ed. Helena Leigh. 448p. 1986. 27.99 (0-7089-8340-5) Ulverscroft.

W

An Asterisk (*) at the beginning of an entry indicates that the title is appearing in BIP for the first time.

Wild Water Fun: A Typewriting Simulation. 2nd ed. Jones. (TA - Typing/Keyboarding Ser.). 1987. pap. 13.95 (*0-538-11840-7*) S-W Pub.

***Wild Waters: Canoeing North America's Wilderness Rivers.** Ed. by James Raffan. (Illus.). 168p. (Orig.). 1997. pap. 24.95 (*1-55209-132-5*) Firefly Bks Ltd.

Wild Ways: Zen Poems of Ikkyu. John Stevens. 1995. pap. 11.00 (*1-57062-074-1*) Shambhala Pubns.

Wild Weasel: The SAM Suppression Story. rev. ed. Larry Davis. (Vietnam Studies Group). (Illus.). 72p. 1993. pap. 12.95 (*0-89747-304-3*) Squad Sig Pubns.

Wild Weather. Melvin Berger. Ed. by Natalie Lunis. (Ranger Rick Science Spectacular Ser.). 16p. (J). (gr. 2-4). 1993. pap. 14.95 (*1-56784-203-8*) Newbridge Comms.

Wild Weather: Hurricanes. Lorri H. Egan. LC 92-27946. (Hello Reader! Ser.: Level 4). (Illus.). 48p. (J). (gr. 2-3). 1995. 3.50 (*0-590-46378-0*, Cartwheel) Scholastic Inc.

Wild Weather: Student Book. Melvin Berger. Ed. by Natalie Lunis. (Ranger Rick Science Spectacular Ser.). (Illus.). 16p. (Orig.). (J). (gr. 2-4). 1996. pap. write for info. (*1-56784-228-3*) Newbridge Comms.

***Wild Weather: Theme Pack.** Melvin Berger. Ed. by Natalie Lunis. (Ranger Rick Science Spectacular Ser.). (Illus.). (Orig.). (J). (gr. 2-4). 1996. pap. write for info. (*1-56784-281-X*) Newbridge Comms.

Wild Weather: Tornadoes! Lorraine J. Hopping. LC 92-27947. (Hello Reader! Ser.: Level 4). (Illus.). 48p. (J). (gr. 2-3). 1994. pap. 3.50 (*0-590-46338-1*) Scholastic Inc.

Wild Weather Soup. Caroline Formby. (J). (ps-3). 1995. pap. 6.99 (*0-85953-950-4*) Childs Play.

Wild Weather Soup. Caroline Formby. (Books Published from Other Lands). (Illus.). 24p. (J). (ps-3). 1996. lib. bdg. 12.95 (*1-56674-147-5*, HTS Bks) Forest Hse.

***Wild Web Graphics with Image Composer.** David Karlins. 300p. 1997. 39.99 (*0-7897-1214-8*) Que.

***Wild West.** 1998. pap. 17.99 (*0-670-87528-7*) Viking Penguin.

***Wild West.** Mike Stotter. LC 96-52789. (Illus.). 64p. (J). (gr. 3-7). 1997. 15.95 (*0-7534-5085-2*, Kingfisher LKC) LKC.

Wild West. Tr. by Time-Life Books Editors. 368p. 1993. 49.95 (*0-446-51761-5*) Warner Bks.

Wild West: A Traveler's Guide. Michael McCoy. LC 94-30768. (Discover Historic America Ser.). (Illus.). 384p. 1994. pap. 16.95 (*1-56440-521-4*) Globe Pequot.

***Wild West: A Traveler's Guide.** 2nd rev. ed. Michael McCoy. (Discover Historic America Ser.). (Illus.). 384p. 1998. pap. 16.95 (*0-7627-0115-3*) Globe Pequot.

Wild West: Companion Book to the Acclaimed Television Mini-Series. Time-Life Books Editors. Ed. by Roberta Conlan. LC 92-39521. (Illus.). 368p. 1993. pap. write for info. (*0-8094-7441-7*); lib. bdg. write for info. (*0-8094-7439-5*) Time-Life.

Wild West: Photographs by David Levinthal. Ed. by Constance Sullivan. (Photographers at Work Ser.). (Illus.). 60p. (Orig.). 1993. pap. 15.95 (*1-56098-291-8*) Smithsonian.

Wild West Bears, Bk. 24. (J). (ps-1). write for info. (*0-931363-22-5*) Celia Totus Enter.

Wild West Characters. Dale Pierce. LC 91-2039. (Illus.). 144p. (Orig.). 1991. pap. 6.95 (*0-914846-53-1*) Golden West Pub.

Wild West Country Dancing. Mika Nurminen. LC 95-3836. (Illus.). 128p. 1995. pap. 20.00 (*0-88734-652-9*) Players Pr.

Wild West Frontier Town: A Walking Guide to Historic Downtown San Antonio. Tom Woodley. (Illus.). 112p. (Orig.). 1992. 5.75 (*0-9628295-1-X*) Blue Hse NY.

Wild West in American History, 14 bks. Rita D'Apice et al. (Illus.). 448p. (J). (gr. 3-8). 1990. Set. lib. bdg. 252.00 (*0-86625-367-X*); Set. lib. bdg. 189.00 (*0-685-36328-7*) Rourke Corp.

***Wild West Shows: Rough Riders & Sure Shots.** Judy Alter. LC 96-41099. (First Bks.). (J). 1997. lib. bdg. 21.00 (*0-531-20274-7*) Watts.

***Wild West Shows: Rough Riders & Sure Shots.** Judy Alter. 1997. pap. text ed. 6.95 (*0-531-15875-6*) Watts.

Wild West Shows & the Images of American Indians, 1883-1933. L. G. Moses. LC 95-32450. (Illus.). 384p. (C). 1996. 39.95 (*0-8263-1685-9*) U of NM Pr.

Wild West Wife. Jayne Addison. 1995. mass mkt. 2.99 (*0-373-19117-0*, 1-19117-0) Silhouette.

Wild Western Scenes. John B. Jones. (Notable American Authors Ser.). 1992. reprint ed. lib. bdg. 90.00 (*0-7812-3512-X*) Rprt Serv.

Wild Western Scenes: A Narrative in the Western Wilderness. John B. Jones. LC 71-104501. (Illus.). 263p. reprint ed. lib. bdg. 28.00 (*0-8398-0958-1*) Irvington.

Wild Western Scenes: A Narrative in the Western Wilderness. John B. Jones. (Illus.). 263p. 1986. reprint ed. pap. text ed. 6.95 (*0-8290-1954-5*) Irvington.

Wild Westerns. Ed. by Bill Pronzini. 192p. 1986. 14.95 (*0-8027-4066-9*) Walker & Co.

***Wild, Wet & Windy.** Claire Llewellyn. LC 96-44371. (Supersmarts Ser.). 1997. 11.99 (*0-7636-0304-X*) Candlewick Pr.

***Wild Wheats: A Monograph of Aegilops L. & Amblyopyrum (Jaub. & Spach) Eig (Poaceae)** M. W. Van Slageren. (Wageningen Agricultural University Papers: No. 94-7). (Illus.). 514p. 1994. pap. 165.00 (*90-6754-377-2*, Pub. by Backhuys Pubs NE) Balogh.

Wild Wheels. Harrod Blank. LC 92-62865. (Illus.). 112p. 1994. pap. 18.95 (*1-56640-981-0*) Pomegranate Calif.

Wild Wheels. Franklin W. Dixon. (Hardy Boys Casefiles Ser.: No. 104). (J). (gr. 6 up). 1995. mass mkt. 3.99 (*0-671-88215-5*, Archway) PB.

Wild Wheels Three-D Coloring Book. Illus. by G. Brunswick. 32p. (Orig.). (J). (gr. 4-7). 1988. pap. 3.95 (*0-942025-60-1*) Kidsbks.

Wild Whispers. Cassie Edwards. 1996. pap. 5.99 (*0-451-40679-6*, Topaz) NAL-Dutton.

Wild, White Goose, Vol. I. Roshi P. Jiyu-Kennett. 1977. pap. 8.00 (*0-930066-02-2*) Shasta Abbey.

Wild, White Goose, Vol. II. Roshi P. Jiyu-Kennett. 1978. pap. 9.00 (*0-930066-03-0*) Shasta Abbey.

Wild White Shepherd. Conway Robinson. (Orig.). (J). (gr. 6-9). 1994. pap. 5.00 (*0-88092-091-2*) Royal Fireworks.

***Wild Wicklow.** Richard Nairn. 1997. 29.95 (*1-86059-048-9*) R Rinehart.

Wild Widow of Wolf Creek. large type ed. Marshall Grover. (Linford Western Library). 288p. 1995. pap. 15.99 (*0-7089-7702-2*, Linford) Ulverscroft.

Wild, Wild Cookbook see Acorn Pancakes, Dandelion Salad & 38 Other Wild Recipes

Wild, Wild East: Unusual Tales of Maine History. William Lemke. 188p. 1994. reprint ed. pap. 10.95 (*1-56626-116-3*) Country Rds.

Wild, Wild Hair. Nikki Grimes. (Hello Reader! Ser.). (Illus.). (J). 1997. 3.50 (*0-590-25690-4*, Cartwheel) Scholastic Inc.

Wild, Wild Hair. Nikki Grimes. LC 95-21898. (Hello Reader! Ser.: Level 3). (Illus.). (J). 1997. 3.50 (*0-590-26590-3*) Scholastic Inc.

Wild Wild Sunflower Child Anna. Nancy W. Carlstrom. LC 86-18226. (Illus.). 32p. (J). (ps-1). 1987. lib. bdg. 14.95 (*0-02-717360-7*, Mac Bks Young Read) S&S Childrens.

Wild Wild Sunflower Child Anna. Nancy W. Carlstrom. LC 90-40679. (Illus.). 32p. (J). (ps-1). 1991. reprint ed. pap. 5.99 (*0-689-71445-9*, Aladdin Paperbacks) S&S Childrens.

Wild, Wild West. Richard Wormser. 17.95 (*0-8488-0685-9*) Amereon Ltd.

Wild Wild West: Wildlife Habitats of Western North America. Conatance Perenyi. LC 92-46995. (Illus.). 32p. (J). (gr. 1 up). 1993. text ed. 14.95 (*0-912365-82-X*) Sasquatch Bks.

Wild Wild West: Wildlife Habitats of Western North America. Constance Perenyi. LC 92-46995. (Illus.). 32p. (J). (gr. 1 up). 1993. pap. 8.95 (*0-912365-90-0*) Sasquatch Bks.

***Wild, Wild West Cowboy Cookies.** Tuda Libby Crews. LC 96-50416. (Illus.). 48p. 1997. 12.95 (*0-87905-808-0*) Gibbs Smith Pub.

Wild, Wild Wolves. Joyce Milton. LC 90-8807. (Step into Reading Bks.). (Illus.). 48p. (Orig.). (J). (gr. 1-3). 1992. pap. 3.99 (*0-679-81052-8*); lib. bdg. 11.99 (*0-679-91052-2*) Random Bks Yng Read.

Wild Wildflowers of the West. 4th rev. ed. Edith S. Kinucan & Penney R. Brons. LC 91-90431. (Illus.). 135p. 1991. pap. 9.95 (*0-9615444-1-4*) Kinucan & Brons.

Wild Will. Ingrid Schubert & Dieter Schubert. LC 93-2484. (J). (ps-3). 1993. lib. bdg. 14.96 (*0-87614-816-X*, Carolrhoda) Lerner Group.

Wild Willie. Joosse. (J). Date not set. 13.95 (*0-06-020593-8*, HarpT) HarpC.

Wild Willie & King Kyle Detectives. Barbara Joosse. 80p. (J). (gr. 2-5). 1996. pap. 3.50 (*0-440-41107-6*, YB BDD) BDD Bks Young Read.

Wild Willie & King Kyle Detectives. Barbara M. Joosse. LC 92-9816. (Illus.). 80p. (J). (gr. 2-5). 1993. 12.95 (*0-395-64338-4*, Clarion Bks) HM.

Wild Wind. Marjorie Sinclair. 250p. 1987. reprint ed. mass mkt. 4.95 (*0-935180-30-3*) Mutual Pub HI.

***Wild Winds.** Janelle Taylor. 384p. 1997. 21.95 (*1-57566-190-X*, Knsington) Kensgtn Pub Corp.

Wild Wines, Colas, & Whiskeys. Phil King. LC 85-91054. 40p. (Orig.). 1986. pap. 5.00 (*0-9601900-6-6*) Phil King.

Wild Wings. Michael W. Runtz. (Illus.). 120p. 1996. 32.00 (*1-55046-184-2*, Pub. by Boston Mills Pr CN) Genl Dist Srvs.

Wild Wings: An Introduction to Bird Watching. 2nd ed. Tim Fitzharris. Ed. by Greg Linder. (Illus.). reprint ed. 29.95 (*1-55971-178-7*) NorthWord.

Wild Wings, Wild Heart. Elizabeth Lane. (Special Edition Ser.). 1995. pap. 3.50 (*0-373-09936-3*, 1-09936-5) Silhouette.

Wild Wisconsin. Brent Haglund. 128p. 1991. 24.95 (*1-55971-115-9*, 0131) NorthWord.

Wild Wisconsin. Brent Haglund. (Wild State Ser.). (Illus.). 144p. 1994. pap. 14.95 (*1-55971-413-1*) NorthWord.

Wild with All Regret. Natalie L. Petesch. LC 86-60697. (Illus.). 140p. (Orig.). 1987. 15.95 (*0-930501-06-3*) Livingston U Pr.

Wild with All Regret. 2nd ed. Natalie L. Petesch. LC 86-60697. (Illus.). 140p. (Orig.). 1987. reprint ed. pap. 10.95 (*0-930501-07-1*) Swallows Tale Pr.

***Wild Wives.** Charles Willeford. 108p. (Orig.). 1995. pap. 10.99 (*0-9650469-9-0*) V Search.

Wild Woman: An Inquiry into the Anthropology of an Idea. Kathleen Adams & Sharon Tiffany. 160p. 1985. 18.95 (*0-87073-213-7*); pap. 13.95 (*0-87073-243-9*) Schenkman Bks Inc.

Wild Woman & Other Plays. Felix Mitterer. Tr. by Todd C. Hanlin & Heidi L. Hutchinson. LC 94-43185. (Studies in Austrian Literature, Culture, & Thought). 1995. pap. 28.00 (*1-57241-002-7*) Ariadne CA.

***Wild Women.** Ed. by Melissa M. Hall. LC 97-9874. (Illus.). 384p. 1997. 23.00 (*0-7867-0415-2*) Carroll & Graf.

Wild Women: Contemporary Short Stories for Women Who Run with the Wolves. Intro. by Sue Thomas. 336p. 1994. pap. 14.95 (*0-87951-514-7*) Overlook Pr.

Wild Women: Crusaders, Curmudgeons & Completely Corsetless Ladies in the Otherwise Virtuous Victorian Era. Autumn Stephens. (Illus.). 250p. (Orig.). 1992. pap. 12.95 (*0-943233-36-4*) Conari Press.

Wild Women: Crusaders, Curmudgeons & Completely Corsetless Ladies in the Otherwise Virtuous Victorian Era. Autumn Stephens. (Illus.). 250p. (Orig.). (C). 1993. reprint ed. lib. bdg. 35.00 (*0-8095-5868-8*) Borgo Pr.

Wild Women Don't Wear No Blues: Black Women Writers on Love, Men, & Sex. Ed. & Intro. by Marita Golden. LC 92-21188. 256p. 1994. pap. 12.95 (*0-385-42401-9*, Anchor NY) Doubleday.

Wild Women in the Kitchen: 101 Rambunctious Recipes & 99 Tasty Tales. Ed. by Wild Women Association Staff. (Illus.). 256p. 1996. pap. 12.95 (*1-57324-030-3*) Conari Press.

Wild Women in the Kitchen: 101 Rambunctious Recipes & 99 Tasty Tales. Wild Women Association Staff. 256p. 1996. 33.00 (*0-8095-6060-7*) Borgo Pr.

Wild Women in the Whirlwind: Afra-American Culture & the Contemporary Literary Renaissance. Ed. by Joanne Braxton & Andree Nicola-McLaughlin. LC 89-30380. 419p. (C). 1990. 50.00 (*0-8135-1441-X*); pap. 17.95 (*0-8135-1442-8*) Rutgers U Pr.

***Wild Women in the White House: The Formidable Females Behind the Throne, on the Phone, & (Sometimes) under the Bed.** Autumn Stephens. LC 96-38730. (Illus.). 224p. (Orig.). 1997. pap. 14.95 (*1-57324-069-9*) Conari Press.

***Wild Women of the American West.** Bill Yenne. 1997. 19.98 (*1-57145-133-1*) Advan Mktg Servs.

Wild, Wonderful Winners: Great Football Coaches of W. Va. Fred R. Toothman. (Illus.). 274p. (Orig.). 1991. pap. 9.95 (*0-9617545-4-0*) F R Toothman.

Wild Woods. Simon James. LC 92-54582. (Illus.). 32p. (J). (ps up). 1993. 13.95 (*1-56402-219-6*) Candlewick Pr.

Wild Woods. Simon James. LC 92-54582. (Illus.). (J). (ps up). 1996. pap. 5.99 (*1-56402-637-X*) Candlewick Pr.

Wild Words & How to Tame Them. Sandy Asher. (Illus.). 96p. (J). (gr. 5 up). 1989. 13.95 (*0-8027-6887-3*); lib. bdg. 14.85 (*0-8027-6888-1*) Walker & Co.

Wild Words from Wild Women: An Unbridled. Autumn Stephens. 288p. (Orig.). 1996. lib. bdg. 27.00 (*0-8095-5887-4*) Borgo Pr.

Wild Words from Wild Women: An Unbridled Collection of Candid Observations & Extremely Opinionated Bon Mots. 2nd rev. ed. Ed. by Autumn Stephens. (Illus.). 280p. (Orig.). 1996. reprint ed. pap. 9.95 (*1-57324-038-9*) Conari Press.

Wild Work. Mary E. Bryan. (Works of Mary (Edwards) Bryan). 1989. reprint ed. lib. bdg. 90.00 (*0-7812-2122-6*) Rprt Serv.

Wild Works: The Authorized & Only English Translation of The Major Trilogy. Ramon Del Valle-Inclan. 1997. 39.95 (*1-886449-23-6*) Barrytown Ltd.

Wild Works: Three Plays: Angel Faces, The Sign of the Eagle, Ballad of Wolves. Ramon Del Valle-Inclan. 1997. pap. text ed. 24.95 (*1-886449-21-X*) Barrytown Ltd.

Wild Worlds. Allen H. Benton. (Illus.). viii, 222p. (Orig.). 1988. pap. 8.95 (*0-942788-16-8*) Iris Visual.

Wild Yam: Birth Control without Fear. Willa Shaffer. 8p. pap. 2.95 (*0-913923-10-9*) Woodland UT.

Wild Yearning. Penelope Williamson. 1990. mass mkt. 3.95 (*0-380-75880-6*) Avon.

Wild Yearning. Penelope Williamson. 448p. 1994. mass mkt. 5.99 (*0-440-21731-8*) Dell.

Wildavsky National Budgeting. 1993. pap. text ed. write for info. (*0-7923-2590-7*) Kluwer Ac.

Wildbienen Baden-Wuerttembergs, 2 vols. 2nd ed. Paul Westrich. (Illus.). 972p. (GER.). 1990. Set. lib. bdg. 65.00 (*3-8001-3317-2*, Pub. by Ulmer Verlog GW) Lubrecht & Cramer.

Wildbienen Baden-Wuerttembergs, 2 vols., Vol. 1, Allgemeiner Teil: Lebens Raeume, Verhalten. 2nd ed. Paul Westrich. (Illus.). 972p. (GER.). 1990. Vol. 1: Allgemeiner Teil: Lebens Raeume, Verhalten, Oekologie & Schutz. write for info. (*0-318-68859-X*) Lubrecht & Cramer.

Wildbienen Baden-Wuerttembergs, 2 vols., Vol. 2, Die Gattungen & Arten. 2nd ed. Paul Westrich. (Illus.). 972p. (GER.). 1990. Vol. 2: Die Gattungen & Arten. write for info. (*0-318-68860-3*) Lubrecht & Cramer.

Wildcat. (Vocal Score Ser.). 1982. pap. 35.00 (*0-88188-055-8*, 00385140) H Leonard.

Wildcat. Wayne Barton. 1995. mass mkt. 4.99 (*0-671-74579-4*) PB.

Wildcat. Rebecca Brandewyne. 1995. mass mkt. 3.25 (*0-373-05955-8*, 1-05955-9) Silhouette.

Wildcat: ABC of Bosses. Donald Rooum. (Illus.). 48p. (Orig.). 1991. pap. 3.50 (*0-900384-60-3*) Left Bank.

Wildcat: Anarchist Comics. rev. ed. Donald Rooum. (Illus.). 47p. 1987. pap. 3.50 (*0-900384-30-1*) Left Bank.

Wildcat: The F4F in WWII. 2nd ed. Barrett Tillman. LC 90-5461. (Illus.). 288p. 1990. 29.95 (*0-87021-789-5*) Naval Inst Pr.

Wildcat: Vocal Selections. (Illus.). 1982. 7.95 (*0-88188-122-8*, 00385141) H Leonard.

***Wildcat: Vocal Selections.** Ed. by Sy Feldman. 24p. (Orig.). (C). 1995. pap. text ed. 10.95 (*0-89724-624-1*, MF9529) Warner Brothers.

Wildcat Aces of the Pacific, Vol. No.3. Barrett Tillman. (Aircraft of the Aces Ser.). (Illus.). 96p. 1995. pap. 15.95 (*1-85532-486-5*, Pub. by Osprey Pubng Ltd UK) Motorbooks Intl.

Wildcat Cartridges, I. 16.95 (*1-879356-08-2*) Wolfe Pub Co.

Wildcat Cartridges, II. 34.50 (*1-879356-18-X*) Wolfe Pub Co.

***Wildcat Falling.** Mudrooroo. 160p. pap. 10.00 (*0-207-19056-9*) HarperColl Wrld.

Wildcat Gorge Cave. fac. ed. J. C. Bard et al. (Basin Research Associates Occasional Papers: No. 4). (Illus.). 258p. 1981. reprint ed. pap. text ed. 23.05 (*1-55567-565-4*) Coyote Press.

Wildcat Haven. large type ed. Mike Tomkies. (Non-Fiction Ser.). 496p. 1992. 25.99 (*0-7089-2670-3*) Ulverscroft.

Wildcat Strikes Again. Donald Rooum. (Illus.). 48p. (Orig.). 1989. pap. 3.50 (*0-900384-47-6*) Left Bank.

Wildcat Wedding. Patricia Thayer. (Romance Ser.). 1995. mass mkt. 2.99 (*0-373-19086-7*, 1-19086-7) Silhouette.

Wildcats. Jenny Markert. (Nature Bks.). 32p. (J). (gr. 2-6). 1991. lib. bdg. 22.79 (*0-89565-704-X*) Childs World.

Wildcats. Mike Tomkies. (Illus.). 120p. text ed. 19.95 (*0-905483-86-3*, Pub. by Whittet Bks UK) Diamond Farm Bk.

Wildcats, a History of St. Ignatius High School Football Vol. 1: The Earliest Years, to 1945. Timothy L. Hudak. (Illus.). 83p. (Orig.). 1996. pap. 20.00 (*0-9652659-0-0*) T L Hudak.

***Wildcats of the World.** Alderton. 27.95 (*0-614-30007-X*) Serpents Tale.

Wildcats to Tomcats. Walter M. Schirra et al. LC 94-69497. (Tailhook Navy Ser.). (Illus.). 232p. (C). 1995. 24.95 (*1-883809-07-X*) Phalanx Pub.

***Wilde.** Stefan Rudnicki. 1997. pap. 12.95 (*0-7871-1265-8*, Dove Bks) Dove Audio.

***Wilde: A Novel Inspired by Julian Mitchell's Screenplay.** Stefan Rudnicki. 1997. pap. 24.95 (*0-7871-1410-3*, Dove Bks) Dove Audio.

Wilde: Salome. William Tydeman et al. (Plays in Production Ser.). (Illus.). 180p. (C). 1996. pap. text ed. 17.95 (*0-521-56545-6*) Cambridge U Pr.

Wilde: Salome. William Tydeman & Steven Price. (Plays in Productions Ser.). (Illus.). 180p. (C). 1996. text ed. 54.95 (*0-521-45423-9*) Cambridge U Pr.

Wilde: The Complete Plays. Oscar Wilde. (Methuen World Dramatists Ser.). 606p. (C). 1988. pap. 11.95 (*0-413-18760-8*, A0319, Pub. by Methuen UK) Heinemann.

***Wilde: The Original Screenplay.** Julian Mitchell. 1997. pap. 10.95 (*0-7871-1411-1*, Dove Bks) Dove Audio.

Wilde Bunch. Barbara Boswell. (Desire Ser.). 1995. mass mkt. 3.25 (*0-373-05943-4*, 1-05943-5) Silhouette.

Wilde Century: Effeminacy, Oscar Wilde & the Queer Moment. Alan Sinfield. (Between Men - Between Women Ser.). 216p. 1994. 40.00 (*0-231-10166-X*); pap. 15.00 (*0-231-10167-8*) Col U Pr.

Wilde Heart. Daphne Clair. (Weddings by DeWilde Ser.). 1996. mass mkt. 4.50 (*0-373-82540-4*, 1-82540-5) Harlequin Bks.

Wilde Man. Daphne Clair. (Weddings by DeWilde Ser.). 1997. mass mkt. 4.50 (*0-373-82546-3*, 1-82546-2) Silhouette.

Wilde, Oscar, Five Major Plays: Lady Windermere's Fan, Importance of Being Earnest, Salome, Woman of No Importance, Ideal Husband. Oscar Wilde. (Airmont Classics Ser.). (YA). (gr. 10 up). 1970. mass mkt. 2.75 (*0-8049-0208-9*) Airmont.

Wilde West. Charles Marowitz. 1988. pap. 5.25 (*0-8222-1256-0*) Dramatists Play.

***Wilde Wit.** Francis K. Denuit. 1997. pap. 9.95 (*0-7871-1412-X*, Dove Bks) Dove Audio.

Wildebeest. Franz Berliner. Tr. by Gyldendal. LC 90-82449. (Illus.). 32p. (J). (ps-3). 1991. 13.95 (*0-8249-8488-9*, Ideals Child) Hambleton-Hill.

Wildebeest of Carmine Street. Edmund Pennant. LC 90-31457. 72p. (Orig.). 1990. pap. 10.00 (*0-914061-17-8*) Orchises Pr.

Wildebeest's Great Migration. Lynn M. Stone. LC 90-38384. (Animal Odysseys Ser.). (Illus.). 48p. (J). (gr. 4-6). 1991. lib. bdg. 16.67 (*0-86593-103-8*); lib. bdg. 12.50 (*0-685-59354-1*) Rourke Corp.

Wildeland: Prose. David Wilde. (Sun Also Sets Ser.). (Illus.). (Orig.). 1992. pap. 12.95 (*0-9625472-5-5*) Wilde Pub.

Wilder. Nina Bernstein. 1997. write for info. (*0-679-43979-X*) Pantheon.

***Wilder.** Nina Bernstein. 1998. pap. write for info. (*0-679-75834-8*, Vin) Random.

Wilder Family Advice. Wilder Family Staff. 1995. 19.95 (*0-615-00906-9*) Lifecraft.

Wilder in the West: Eliza Jane's Story of a Lady Homesteader. William T. Anderson. (Laura Ingalls Wilder Family Ser.). (Illus.). 44p. 1985. pap. 3.95 (*0-9610088-4-9*) Anderson-Wade.

Wilder Life: Essays from Home. Ken Wright. 176p. (C). 1995. 23.95 (*1-882308-15-8*) Kivaki Pr.

Wilder Shore. large type ed. Daphne Clair. (Linford Romance Library). 336p. 1985. pap. 15.99 (*0-7089-6049-9*) Ulverscroft.

Wilder Shores: Women's Travel Stories of Australia & Beyond. Ed. by Robin Lucas & Clare Forster. (Orig.). 1992. pap. 15.95 (*0-7022-2477-4*, Pub. by Univ Queensland Pr AT) Intl Spec Bk.

Wilder Shores of Love. Lesley Blanch. 1996. pap. 12.95 (*0-7867-0260-5*) Carroll & Graf.

Wilder Side of Providence: And Other True & False Tales. Margaret Reinhart. 80p. 1992. 11.00 (*0-8233-0479-5*) Golden Quill.

Wilder than Ever. Marie Dillon. 180p. 1997. pap. text ed. 10.95 (*1-57532-087-8*) Press-Tige Pub.

Wilder Times: The Life & Times of Billy Wilder. Kevin Lally. LC 95-33668. (Illus.). 496p. 1996. 30.00 (*0-8050-3119-7*); pap. 14.95 (*0-8050-3120-0*) H Holt & Co.

***Wilderness.** (Bloodshadows Ser.). 18.00 (*0-87431-384-8*, 33003) West End Games.

***Wilderness.** Asante. 1995. 22.50 (*0-684-19608-5*) S&S Trade.

Wilderness. Tony Dawson. 350p. 1987. 19.95 (*0-943698-05-7*) Papyrus Letterbox.

Wilderness. Houghton Mifflin Company Staff. (Literature Experience 1991 Ser.). (J). (gr. 7). 1990. pap. 9.84 (*0-395-55177-3*) HM.

Wilderness. Robert B. Parker, Jr. 256p. 1980. mass mkt. 6.50 (*0-440-19328-1*) Dell.

Wilderness. Yu Ts-ao. Tr. by Joseph S. Lau & Christopher C. Rand. 256p. (C). 1980. pap. text ed. 22.00 (*962-209-018-4*, Pub. by Hong Kong U Pr HK) St Mut.

W

Wilderness. Ts'ao Yu. Tr. by Joseph S. Lau & Christopher C. Rand. 256p. (C). 1980. text ed. 27.00 (*962-209-017-6*, Pub. by Hong Kong U Pr HK) St Mut.

Wilderness. Roger Zelazny & Gerald Hausman. 320p. 1994. pap. 4.99 (*0-8125-3534-0*) Forge NYC.

Wilderness. Dennis Danvers. Ed. by Julie Rubenstein. 320p. 1992. reprint ed. mass mkt. 5.99 (*0-671-72828-8*, Pocket Star Bks) PB.

***Wilderness, Vol. 8.** 96p. 1999. write for info. (*1-55513-351-7*, Victor Bks) Chariot Victor.

Wilderness: A Journal of Quiet Adventure in Alaska. Rockwell Kent. (Illus.). 260p. (C). 1983. reprint ed. pap. 8.95 (*0-918172-12-8*) Leetes Isl.

Wilderness: A Journal of Quiet Adventure in Alaska. Rockwell Kent. LC 95-45450. (Illus.). 240p. (C). 1996. reprint ed. pap. 12.95 (*0-8195-5293-3*, Wesleyan Univ Pr) U Pr of New Eng.

Wilderness: A New Mexico Legacy. Corry McDonald. LC 84-26691. (Illus.). 128p. (Orig.). 1985. pap. 15.95 (*0-86534-056-0*) Sunstone Pr.

Wilderness: The Lost Writings of Jim Morrison, Vol. 1. Jim Morrison. 1989. pap. 11.00 (*0-679-72622-5*, Vin) Random.

Wilderness: The True Story of Simon Girty. Timothy Truman. (J). 1992. pap. 19.95 (*1-56060-167-1*) Eclipse Bks.

Wilderness - Just Bounce. Nigel Wells. LC 88-51315. (Illus.). 64p. (Orig.). 8800. pap. 10.95 (*1-85224-044-X*, Pub. by Bloodaxe Bks UK) Dufour.

Wilderness above the Sound: The Story of Mount Rainier National Park. 2nd ed. Arthur D. Martinson. 96p. 1994. pap. 11.95 (*1-879373-76-9*) R Rinehart.

Wilderness & Gardens: An American Lady's Prospect. Margaret L. Been. Ed. by John E. Westburg. (Illus.). 1974. pap. 6.00 (*0-87423-011-X*) Westburg.

Wilderness & Natural Areas in the Eastern United States: A Management Challenge. Ed. by David L. Kulhavy & Richard N. Conner. 272p. 1986. 25.00 (*0-938361-00-7*) Austin Univ Forestry.

Wilderness, & Other Poems. Louis O. Coxe. LC 58-59912. 74p. reprint ed. pap. 25.00 (*0-317-27943-2*, 2055852) Bks Demand.

Wilderness & People: The Future of the Adirondack Park. Illus. by David S. Utterback. 116p. 1993. 9.95 (*0-9624535-1-X*) Assn Protect Adirondacks.

Wilderness & Rural Life Support Guidelines. Ed. by Robert J. Koester. LC 90-85412. (Illus.). 60p. (Orig.). 1991. pap. 10.00 (*1-879471-02-7*) DBS Prodns.

Wilderness & Soul. Larry Gates. 1991. 27.50 (*0-938434-96-9*); pap. 16.95 (*0-938434-95-0*) Sigo Pr.

Wilderness & Spotsylvania. Gordon C. Rhea. (Civil War Ser.). (Illus.). 56p. (Orig.). 1995. pap. 4.95 (*0-915992-88-4*) Eastern Acorn.

Wilderness & the American Mind. 3rd rev. ed. Roderick Nash. LC 82-4874. 380p. 1982. pap. 16.00 (*0-300-02910-1*, Y-440) Yale U Pr.

Wilderness & the Changing American West. Gundars Rudzitis. LC 96-15426. 220p. 1996. pap. text ed. 34.95 (*0-471-13396-5*, Wiley-Liss) Wiley.

Wilderness & the City: American Classical Philosophy As a Moral Quest. Michael A. Weinstein. LC 82-4769. 176p. 1982. lib. bdg. 25.00 (*0-87023-375-0*) U of Mass Pr.

Wilderness & the War-Path. James A. Hall. 1972. reprint ed. lib. bdg. 24.00 (*0-8422-8069-3*) Irvington.

Wilderness Areas of the Colorado Plateau. Stewart Aitchison. 32p. 1989. pap. 6.95 (*0-89734-098-1*, PL60-4) Mus Northern Ariz.

Wilderness At Dawn: The Settling of the North American Continent. Ted Morgan. 560p. 1994. pap. 15.00 (*0-671-88237-6*, Touchstone Bks) S&S Trade.

Wilderness Basics: The Care & Enjoyment of the Western Wilderness. Ed. by Jerry Schad. (Illus.). 208p. 1991. pap. 12.95 (*0-9628677-0-5*) SD Chap Sierra.

Wilderness Basics: The Complete Handbook for Hikers & Backpackers. 2nd ed. Sierra Club, San Diego Chapter Staff. 1992. pap. 14.95 (*0-89886-348-1*) Mountaineers.

***Wilderness by Design: Landscape Architecture & the National Park Service.** Ethan Carr. LC 97-22127. 1998. write for info. (*0-8032-1491-X*) U of Nebr Pr.

Wilderness Byways see California

Wilderness Called Grand. Random House Value Publishing Staff. 1997. 14.99 (*0-517-18260-2*) Random Hse Value.

Wilderness Called Grand Canyon. Stewart Aitchison. LC 90-25373. (Voyageur Wilderness Ser.). (Illus.). 128p. 1991. 29.95 (*0-89658-149-7*) Voyageur Pr.

Wilderness Called Grand Canyon. Stewart Aitchison. LC 90-25373. (Illus.). 128p. 1993. pap. 19.95 (*0-89658-227-2*) Voyageur Pr.

Wilderness Calling: The Hardeman Family in the American Westward Movement, 1750-1900. Nicholas P. Hardeman. (Illus.). 372p. reprint ed. pap. 106.10 (*0-7837-5390-X*, 2045154) Bks Demand.

***Wilderness Campaign.** Gary W. Gallagher. LC 96-35006. (Military Campaigns of the Civil War Ser.). 320p. (C). (gr. 13). 1997. 29.95 (*0-8078-2334-1*) U of NC Pr.

Wilderness Campaign. Edward Steere. 522p. 1987. reprint ed. 30.00 (*0-942211-29-4*) Olde Soldier Bks.

Wilderness Campaign: March-May 1864. John Cannan. (Great Campaigns Ser.). (Illus.). 240p. 1993. 19.95 (*0-938289-16-0*) Combined Pub.

Wilderness Campaign: The Meeting of Grant & Lee. Edward Steere. LC 93-26944. (Illus.). 544p. 1994. 19.95 (*0-8117-1890-5*) Stackpole.

***Wilderness Canada.** Karl Teuschl. 1997. 27.95 (*1-55868-315-1*) Gr Arts Ctr Pub.

Wilderness Cat. Natalie Kinsey-Warnock. LC 90-24250. (Illus.). 32p. (J). (ps-3). 1992. pap. 14.99 (*0-525-65068-7*, Cobblehill Bks) Dutton Child Bks.

Wilderness Challenge. LC 79-3241. (Books for World Explorers Series 2: No. 1). (Illus.). 104p. (J). (gr. 3-8). 1980. 8.95 (*0-87044-333-X*) Natl Geog.

Wilderness Christmas. Madeline Baker et al. 448p. 1995. reprint ed. mass mkt., pap. text ed. 5.99 (*0-8439-3919-2*) Dorchester Pub Co.

Wilderness Companion. David Backes. Ed. by Greg Linder. 96p. (Orig.). 1992. pap. 6.95 (*1-55971-185-X*) NorthWord.

Wilderness Condition: Essays on Environment & Civilization. Ed. by Max Oelschlaeger. LC 92-52649. 343p. 1992. reprint ed. pap. 16.00 (*1-55963-190-2*) Island Pr.

Wilderness Cuisine: How to Prepare & Enjoy Fine Food on the Trail & in Camp. Carole Latimer. LC 91-9288. 240p. (Orig.). 1990. pap. 12.95 (*0-89997-114-8*) Wilderness Pr.

Wilderness Dawning. Peter Pickford. 160p. (C). 1988. 170.00 (*1-85368-001-X*, Pub. by New Holland Pubs UK) St Mut.

Wilderness Empire Seventeen Fifty-Five. Allan W. Eckert. 768p. 1985. mass mkt. 6.99 (*0-553-26488-5*) Bantam.

Wilderness Encounters, Bk. 1. Michael A. Stackpole. (Illus.). 74p. 1991. pap. 9.95 (*0-940244-85-3*) Flying Buffalo.

Wilderness Ethics: Preserving the Spirit of Wildness. Laura Waterman & Guy Waterman. 240p. (Orig.). 1993. pap. 14.00 (*0-88150-256-1*) Countryman.

***Wilderness First Aid.** National Safety Council Staff & Wilderness Medical Society Staff. 100p. 1998. pap. 15.00 (*0-7637-0407-5*) Jones & Bartlett.

***Wilderness First Aid.** Gilbert Preston. LC 97-11567. 1997. pap. write for info. (*1-56044-579-3*) Falcon Pr MT.

***Wilderness First Aid: For When You Can't Call 911.** Gilbert Preston. (Illus.). 128p. (Orig.). 1997. pap. 6.95 (*1-56044-580-7*) Falcon Pr MT.

***Wilderness First Aid Guide.** Wayne Merry. 1997. pap. text ed. 14.95 (*0-7710-8250-9*) McCland & Stewart.

Wilderness Gourmet. Herschel L. Scott, Jr. & Herschel L. Scott, III. LC 83-61503. (Western Backpacking Ser.). (Illus.). 60p. 1983. pap. 3.95 (*0-88083-006-9*) Poverty Hill Pr.

Wilderness Handbook. rev. ed. Paul Petzoldt. (Illus.). 1984. pap. 11.95 (*0-393-30171-0*) Norton.

Wilderness Homestead. Art Davidson. (Alaska Christmas Ser.: No. I). (Illus.). 16p. 1991. 55.00 (*0-9630863-3-2*); pap. 20.00 (*0-9630863-2-4*) Limner Pr.

Wilderness Hunter: An Account of the Big Game of the United States & its Chase with Horse Hound & Rifle. Theodore Roosevelt. 279p. reprint ed. write for info. (*0-8290-1955-3*) Irvington.

Wilderness Hunting & Wildcraft. Townsend Whelen. (Library Classics Ser.). (Illus.). 368p. 1987. reprint ed. 39.00 (*0-935632-46-8*) Wolfe Pub Co.

Wilderness Lost: The Religious Origins of the American Mind. David R. Williams. LC 85-43475. 296p. 1987. 42.50 (*0-941664-21-X*) Susquehanna U Pr.

Wilderness Management. (Resource Policy Ser.). 85p. (Orig.). 1989. pap. 11.00 (*0-939970-51-1*) Soc Am Foresters.

Wilderness Management. 2nd rev. ed. John C. Hendee et al. LC 90-47810. (Illus.). 546p. (C). 1990. pap. 50.00 (*1-55591-900-6*) Fulcrum Pub.

Wilderness Medical Society Practice Guidelines. Ed. by William W. Forgey. LC 94-41746. 72p. (Orig.). 1994. pap. 12.95 (*1-57034-011-0*) ICS Bks.

Wilderness Medicine: Beyond First Aid. 4th ed. William W. Forgey. LC 94-2004. (Illus.). 256p. (Orig.). 1994. pap. 14.99 (*0-934802-93-9*) ICS Bks.

Wilderness Medicine: Management of Wilderness & Environment Emergencies. 3rd ed. Ed. by Paul S. Auerbach. (Illus.). 1506p. (C). (gr. 13). 1994. text ed. 179.00 (*0-8016-7044-6*) Mosby Yr Bk.

Wilderness Mother: The Chronicle of a Modern Pioneer. Deanna Kawatski. (Illus.). 256p. 1994. 22.95 (*1-55821-201-9*) Lyons & Burford.

Wilderness Movement & the National Forests. 2nd rev. ed. Dennis M. Roth. (Illus.). 106p. (C). 1995. pap. 14.95 (*0-944091-05-9*) Intaglio Pr.

Wilderness North. Dan D. Gapen, Sr. (Illus.). 321p. 1988. text ed. 24.95 (*0-932985-00-9*) Whitewater Pubns.

***Wilderness Novice Survival Skills.** Donald F. Grantham. (Orig.). 1997. mass mkt. 5.99 (*1-55237-094-1*, Pub. by Comnwlth Pub CN) Partners Pubs Grp.

Wilderness of Dreams: Exploring the Religious Meanings of Dreams in Modern Western Culture. Kelly Bulkeley. LC 93-9484. (SUNY Series in Dream Studies). 309p. (C). 1994. pap. 19.95 (*0-7914-1746-8*); text ed. 59.50 (*0-7914-1745-X*) State U NY Pr.

Wilderness of Faith & Love: Contemporary Fiction Ser. Richard Lyons. LC 87-73429. 130p. (Orig.). 1988. pap. 7.95 (*0-935306-42-0*) Barnwood Pr.

Wilderness of Four, No. 2: The Plains of the Sea. Niel Hancock. 288p. 1983. pap. 2.95 (*0-446-31215-0*) Warner Bks.

Wilderness of Four, No. 4: The Road to the Middle Islands. Niel Hancock. 288p. (Orig.). 1983. pap. 2.95 (*0-446-31211-8*) Warner Bks.

***Wilderness of God.** Andrew Louth. 1997. pap. text ed. 14.95 (*0-687-05770-1*) Abingdon.

***Wilderness of Ice.** Jules Verne. lib. bdg. 22.95 (*0-8488-2047-9*) Amereon Ltd.

***Wilderness of Ice & Snow.** Stephen Thomas. Date not set. write for info. (*0-688-09362-0*) Morrow.

Wilderness of Ladies. Eleanor R. Taylor. 1960. 10.95 (*0-8392-1133-3*) Astor-Honor.

Wilderness of Mirrors. Linda Davies. LC 95-35726. 355p. 1996. 23.00 (*0-385-48038-5*) Doubleday.

Wilderness of Mirrors. Linda Davies. 416p. 1996. mass mkt. 6.99 (*0-440-22295-8*, Island Bks) Dell.

Wilderness of Mirrors. large type ed. Linda Davies. 621p. 1996. lib. bdg. 25.95 (*0-7862-0612-8*) Thorndike Pr.

Wilderness of Miseries: War & Warriors in Early America. John E. Ferling. LC 79-8951. (Contributions in Military History Ser.: No. 22). (Illus.). xiv, 227p. 1980. text ed. 49.95 (*0-313-22093-X*, FWW/, Greenwood Pr) Greenwood.

Wilderness of the Gila. Elizabeth F. McFarland. LC 74-78494. (Illus.). 74p. 1974. pap. 2.50 (*0-9615359-2-X*) Crest Pr Inc.

Wilderness of the Southwest: Charles Sheldon's Quest for Desert Bighorn Sheep & Adventures with the Havasupai & Seri Indians. Ed. by Neil B. Carmony & David E. Brown. LC 93-4421. (Illus.). 224p. (Orig.). (C). 1993. pap. 14.95 (*0-87480-417-5*) U of Utah Pr.

Wilderness of Vision: On the Poetry of John Haines. Kevin Walzer & Kevin Bezner. 256p. (Orig.). 1996. pap. 15.95 (*1-885266-22-7*) Story Line.

***Wilderness of Words: Closure & Disclosure in Conrad's Short Fiction.** Ted Billy. LC 97-24388. 320p. 1997. 37.50 (*0-89672-389-5*) Tex Tech Univ Pr.

Wilderness Original: The Life of Bob Marshall. James M. Glover. LC 86-18050. (Illus.). 376p. 1987. 17.95 (*0-89886-121-7*) Mountaineers.

Wilderness Passover. Kathleen Cook-Waldron. (Illus.). 32p. (J). (gr. 4-7). 1994. 13.95 (*0-88995-112-8*, Pub. by Red Deer CN) Orca Bk Pubs.

Wilderness Peril. Thomas J. Dygard. 238p. (J). (gr. 5 up). 1991. pap. 4.99 (*0-14-034785-2*, Puffin) Puffin Bks.

Wilderness Plots: Tales about the Settlement of the American Land. Scott R. Sanders. 128p. 1988. reprint ed. pap. 13.50 (*0-8142-0472-4*) Ohio St U Pr.

Wilderness Politics & Indian Gifts. Wilbur R. Jacobs. (Illus.). 1990. 11.25 (*0-8446-2306-7*) Peter Smith.

Wilderness Preservation. Nancy Matthews. (Earth at Risk Ser.). (Illus.). 112p. (YA). (gr. 5 up). 1991. lib. bdg. 19.95 (*0-7910-1580-7*) Chelsea Hse.

Wilderness Preservation: A Guide to Wilderness Selection on the Public Lands. Haugrud. 124p. 1986. 12.00 (*0-318-04413-7*) Stanford Enviro.

Wilderness Preservation: A Reference Handbook. Kenneth A. Rosenberg. LC 94-19336. (Contemporary World Issues Ser.). 292p. 1994. lib. bdg. 39.50 (*0-87436-731-X*) ABC-CLIO.

Wilderness Preservation & the Sagebrush Rebellions. William L. Graf. (Illus.). 348p. (C). 1990. 52.00 (*0-8476-7420-7*, R 7420) Rowman.

Wilderness Ranger Cookbook. Valerie Brunell & Ralph Swain. (Illus.). 112p. 1990. reprint ed. pap. 7.95 (*1-56044-038-4*) Falcon Pr MT.

Wilderness Reader. Frank Bergon. (Orig.). 1980. pap. 4.95 (*0-451-62589-7*, Ment) NAL-Dutton.

Wilderness Reader. Frank Bergon. LC 94-31862. 384p. 1994. pap. 14.95 (*0-87417-250-0*) U of Nev Pr.

Wilderness Reflections: An Intimate Look at Wild Places in America. Ed. & Illus. by Tim Ernst. LC 96-96103. 156p. 1996. 50.00 (*1-882906-33-0*) Wilderness Visions.

Wilderness Remembered. Karen Kane. LC 94-49440. (Illus.). 160p. 1995. 35.00 (*1-55971-466-2*) NorthWord.

Wilderness Road. James Reasoner. 320p. 1996. mass mkt. 4.99 (*0-06-100957-1*) HarpC.

***Wilderness Road: A Romance of St. Clair's Defeat & Wayne's Victory.** Joseph A. Altsheler. Date not set. lib. bdg. 39.95 (*0-8488-1862-8*, 206) Amereon Ltd.

Wilderness Road Cemeteries in Kentucky, Tennessee, & Virginia. 300p. 25.00 (*0-318-23392-4*); pap. 20.00 (*0-318-32462-8*) West Cent KY Family Re Assoc.

Wilderness Seasons: Life & Adventure in Canada's North. Ian Wilson & Sally Wilson. (Illus.). 208p. (Orig.). 1988. pap. 16.95 (*0-919574-34-3*) Gordon Soules Bk.

Wilderness Skiing & Winter Camping. Chris Townsend. (Illus.). 230p. 1993. pap. text ed. 17.95 (*0-87742-397-0*) Intl Marine.

Wilderness Skiing & Winter Camping. Chris Townsend. 1993. pap. text ed. 17.95 (*0-07-065253-8*) McGraw.

Wilderness Still the Cradle of Nature: Frontier Georgia. Ed. by Edward J. Cashin. (Documentary History Ser.). 204p. 1994. 35.00 (*0-88322-015-6*) Beehive GA.

Wilderness Survival. (Illus.). 48p. (J). (gr. 6-12). 1984. pap. 2.40 (*0-8395-3265-2*, 33265) BSA.

***Wilderness Survival.** 226p. Date not set. 5.95 (*0-89259-154-4*) Am Trust Pubns.

***Wilderness Survival.** Gregory J. Davenport. LC 97-24515. 1998. pap. write for info. (*0-8117-2985-0*) Stackpole.

Wilderness Survival. rev. ed. Bernard Shanks. (Illus.). 224p. 1987. text ed. 19.95 (*0-87663-655-5*) Universe.

Wilderness Survival. 3rd ed. Stanley R. Hamper. LC 66-249. 1975. reprint ed. 1.79 (*0-9601048-1-X*) S Hamper.

Wilderness Survival Handbook, Vol. 1. 2nd ed. Alan Fry. 304p. 1996. pap. 14.95 (*0-312-14763-5*) St Martin.

Wilderness Survival Handbook: A Practical, All-Season Guide to Short Trip Preparation & Survival Techniques for Hikers, Skiers, Backpackers, Canoeists, Travelers in Light Aircraft & Anyone Stranded in the Bush. Alan Fry. (Illus.). 304p. 1982. pap. 10.95 (*0-312-87952-0*) St Martin.

Wilderness Tabernacle. Henry Griffin. 127p. (Orig.). 1989. pap. text ed. 5.95 (*0-934942-79-X*, 1294) White Wing Pub.

Wilderness Tails: A Book to Color, Poetry to Share. Myra Dec & Sam Dec. 32p. (J). (ps-3). 1993. pap. 3.50 (*0-9638192-0-8*) Quinn Pubng.

Wilderness Tapestry: An Eclectic Approach to Preservation. Ed. by Samuel I. Zeveloff et al. LC 92-19508. 320p. (C). 1992. text ed. 33.95 (*0-87417-200-4*) U of Nev Pr.

Wilderness Therapy: Foundations, Theory, & Research. Dene S. Berman & Jennifer Davis-Berman. 288p. 1994. per., pap. text ed. 26.00 (*0-8403-9060-2*) Kendall-Hunt.

Wilderness Therapy for Women: The Power of Adventure. Ed. by Ellen Cole et al. LC 94-17240. 262p. 1994. 39.95 (*1-56024-682-0*) Haworth Pr.

Wilderness Therapy for Women: The Power of Adventure. Ed. by Ellen Cole et al. LC 94-17240. 1994. pap. 12.95 (*1-56023-058-4*) Haworth Pr.

Wilderness Time. Emilie Griffin. LC 97-615. 1997. pap. 13.00 (*0-06-063361-1*) Harper SF.

Wilderness Tips. Margaret Atwood. 256p. 1992. mass mkt. 5.99 (*0-7704-2524-0*) Bantam.

Wilderness Tips. Margaret Atwood. 320p. 1993. mass mkt. 6.99 (*0-553-56046-8*) Bantam.

Wilderness Tips. Margaret Atwood. LC 95-22459. 240p. 1996. pap. 10.95 (*0-553-37793-0*, Bantam Trade Bks) Bantam.

Wilderness to Washington. Eleanor R. Long. LC 81-51895. 166p. 1981. reprint ed. pap. 7.95 (*0-89917-324-1*) Guild Pr IN.

Wilderness Trail, 2 vols. Charles A. Hanna. LC 77-149659. (Illus.). reprint ed. Set. 135.00 (*0-404-03097-1*) AMS Pr.

Wilderness Trail, 2 vols. Charles A. Hanna. 1993. reprint ed. Set. lib. bdg. 150.00 (*0-7812-5463-9*) Rprt Serv.

***Wilderness Trail or the Ventures & Adventures of the Pennsylvania Traders on the Allegheny Path Vol. 1: With Some New Annals of the Old West, & the Records of Some Strong Men & Some Bad Ones.** LC 95-75966. (Great Pennsylvania Frontier Ser.: Vol. 3). (Illus.). 480p. 1995. reprint ed. 39.95 (*1-889037-02-8*, 3) Wennawoods.

***Wilderness Trail or the Ventures & Adventures of the Pennsylvania Traders on the Allegheny Path Vol. 2: With Some New Annals of the Old West, & the Records of Some Strong Men & Some Bad Ones.** LC 95-75966. (Great Pennsylvania Frontier Ser.: Vol. 4). (Illus.). 504p. 1995. reprint ed. 39.95 (*1-889037-03-6*, 4) Wennawoods.

Wilderness Trails of Tennessee's Cherokee National Forest. Sierra Club, Tennessee Chapter, Harvey Broome Group Staff. Ed. by William H. Skelton. LC 92-18726. (Outdoor Tennessee Ser.). (Illus.). 352p. (Orig.). (C). 1992. 32.00 (*0-87049-771-5*); pap. 17.95 (*0-87049-772-3*) U of Tenn Pr.

Wilderness Trek. Zane Grey. 416p. 1991. mass mkt. 3.99 (*0-06-100260-7*, Harp PBks) HarpC.

Wilderness Trek. Dorothy Tell. 160p. 1990. pap. 8.95 (*0-941483-60-6*) Naiad Pr.

Wilderness Treks by Foot, Canoe, & Adobe Rocket, & Father's Far-Flung Fables. William L. Neely. Ed. by Allan Shields. LC 94-80241. (Illus.). xvi, 122p. (Orig.). 1995. pap. 7.95 (*1-882803-10-8*) Jerseydale Ranch.

Wilderness U: Opportunities for Outdoor Education in the U. S. & Abroad. Bill McMillion. LC 92-19616. (Illus.). 288p. 1992. pap. 12.95 (*1-55652-158-8*) Chicago Review.

Wilderness Underground: Caves of the Ozark Plateau. H. Dwight Weaver. (Illus.). 128p. (C). 1992. 29.95 (*0-8262-0811-8*) U of Mo Pr.

Wilderness Virginia: A Guide to Hiking Virginia's National Forest Wilderness Area. Steven Carroll & Mark Miller. LC 95-68417. (Illus.). (Orig.). 1995. pap. 12.95 (*0-9646692-1-8*) Old Forge Prodns.

Wilderness Visionaries. rev. ed. Jim D. Vickery. 280p. 1994. pap. 10.95 (*1-55971-435-2*) NorthWord.

Wilderness Visions: The Western Theme in Science Fiction Literature. 2nd ed. David Mogen. LC 92-46389. (I. O. Evans Studies in the Philosophy & Criticism of Literature: No. 1). 128p. 1993. pap. 19.00 (*0-89370-400-8*); lib. bdg. 29.00 (*0-89370-300-1*) Borgo Pr.

Wilderness Walk. large type ed. Sheila Bishop. 1990. 25.99 (*0-7089-2275-9*) Ulverscroft.

Wilderness Walkers: Naturalists in Early Texas. Betsy Warren. LC 55-7501. (Illus.). 112p. (J). (gr. 4-8). 1987. lib. bdg. 12.95 (*0-937460-26-5*) Hendrick-Long.

Wilderness Wanderings: A Lenten Pilgrimage. Marilyn B. Oden. 144p. (Orig.). 1996. pap. text ed. 9.95 (*0-8358-0743-6*) Upper Room Bks.

***Wilderness Wanderings: Probing 20th-Century Theology.** Stanley M. Hauerwas. LC 97-13025. (Radical Traditions Ser.). 1997. text ed. 28.00 (*0-8133-3349-0*) Westview.

Wilderness Wanton. Dirk Fletcher. (Spur Giant Special Edition Ser.). 368p. (Orig.). 1994. pap. 4.99 (*0-8439-3624-X*) Dorchester Pub Co.

Wilderness War. Allan W. Eckert. (Narratives of America Ser.: No. 4). 608p. 1985. mass mkt. 7.50 (*0-553-26368-4*) Bantam.

Wilderness Waterways: A Guide to Information Sources. Ronald M. Ziegler. LC 78-10410. (Sports, Games, & Pastimes Information Guide Ser.: Vol. 1). 328p. 1979. 68.00 (*0-8103-1434-7*) Gale.

Wilderness Waterways: The Whole Water Reference for Paddlers. Ronald M. Ziegler. 1992. pap. 19.95 (*0-9631595-1-8*) Canoe Am Assocs.

Wilderness Wayfinding: How to Survive in the Wilderness As You Travel. Bob Newman. (Illus.). 160p. 1994. pap. 15.00 (*0-87364-760-2*) Paladin Pr.

Wilderness Wisdom: Tips & Tales from the North Woods. Snow & Nealley Staff. (Illus.). 70p. (Orig.). 1995. pap. 14.95 (*0-9646832-0-2*) Snow & Nealley Co.

Wilderness Within: Journeys in Self-Discovery. Daniel L. Dustin. 152p. 1993. pap. 6.95 (*1-882708-52-0*) Inst Leisure.

***Wilderness Within: The Life of Sigurd F. Olson.** David Backes. LC 97-10891. 1997. write for info. (*0-8166-2842-4*) U of Minn Pr.

Wilderness World of Anne Labastille. Anne LaBastille. (Illus.). 120p. 1992. pap. 14.95 (*0-9632846-0-6*) W Wind Pubns.

Wilderness World of John Muir. Edwin W. Teale. 1975. pap. 13.95 (*0-395-24083-2*); pap. 8.95 (*0-685-26860-8*) HM.

Wilderness World of John Muir. Edwin W. Teale. 1996. 22.75 (*0-8446-6847-8*) Peter Smith.

W

Wilder's Collector Car Review: Spring, 1989 Edition. rev. ed. Henry F. Wilder. (Illus.). 152p. 1988. 29.95 (*0-9621870-0-3*) Car Collector.

Wilder's Wilderness. Macgregor. 1994. pap. 2.99 (*0-373-17172-2*) Harlequin Bks.

***Wilde's Intentions: The Artist in His Criticism.** Lawrence Danson. 208p. 1997. text ed. 49.95 (*0-19-818375-5*) OUP.

Wilde's Use of Irish Celtic Elements in The Picture of Dorian Gray. David A. Upchurch. LC 91-28466. (American University Studies: English Language & Literature: Ser. IV, Vol. 140). 104p. 1993. 32.95 (*0-8204-1756-4*) P Lang Pubng.

Wildest Africa. Paul Tingay. 240p. 1996. 45.00 (*0-312-14479-2*) St Martin.

***Wildest Colts Make the Best Horses.** John Breeding. 210p. (Orig.). 1996. pap. text ed. 16.95 (*1-880092-39-5*) Bright Bks TX.

Wildest Dreams. Alan Ayckbourn. 96p. (Orig.). 1994. pap. 8.95 (*0-571-17304-7*) Faber & Faber.

Wildest Dreams. F. Rosanne Bittner. 608p. 1994. mass mkt. 5.99 (*0-553-56472-2*) Bantam.

Wildest Dreams. J. Blake. Date not set. pap. 8.95 (*0-449-91264-7*) Fawcett.

Wildest Dreams. Jennifer Blake. 1994. mass mkt. 5.99 (*0-449-14739-8*, GM) Fawcett.

***Wildest Dreams.** Carole Mortimer. (Presents Ser.: No. 1894). 1997. mass mkt. 3.50 (*0-373-11894-5*, 1-11894-2) Harlequin Bks.

Wildest Dreams. large type ed. Jennifer Blake. 652p. 1992. reprint ed. lib. bdg. 17.95 (*1-56054-578-X*) Thorndike Pr.

Wildest Dreams: The Sourcebook of Nightmare. Robin D. Laws et al. (Over the Edge Ser.). 64p. 1993. pap. 10.95 (*1-887801-11-1*, Atlas Games) Trident MN.

Wildest Heart. Rosemary Rogers. 608p. 1976. mass mkt. 5.99 (*0-380-00137-3*) Avon.

Wildest Hearts. Jayne Ann Krentz. 400p. (Orig.). 1993. mass mkt. 6.50 (*0-671-72857-1*) PB.

Wildest Hearts. large type ed. Jayne Ann Krentz. LC 92-42498. (General Ser.). (Orig.). 1993. 23.95 (*0-8161-5704-9*, GK Hall) Thorndike Pr.

Wildest of the Wild West: True Tales of a Frontier Town on the Santa Fe Trail. Howard Bryan. LC 88-72480. (Illus.). 288p. 1991. reprint ed. pap. 12.95 (*0-940666-13-8*) Clear Light.

Wildest of the Wild West: True Tales of New Mexico on the Old Santa Fe Trail. Howard Bryan. LC 91-71799. 1988. 19.95 (*0-940666-08-1*) Clear Light.

***Wildest One: The Life of Wild Bill Davison.** Hal Willard. LC 96-86624. (Illus.). 477p. 1996. 26.75 (*0-9654587-0-9*) Avondale Press.

Wildfire. pap. 60.00 (*0-590-08794-0*) Scholastic Inc.

Wildfire. Jo Clayton. (Wild Magic Ser.: No. 2). 400p. (Orig.). 1992. 4.99 (*0-88677-514-0*) DAW Bks.

Wildfire. Patrick Cone. LC 95-40847. (Nature in Action Ser.). (J). 1996. 7.95 (*0-87614-936-0*, Carolrhoda) Lerner Group.

Wildfire. Patrick Cone. 1996. pap. text ed. 7.95 (*1-57505-027-7*, Carolrhoda) Lerner Group.

Wildfire. Lynn Erickson. (Superromance Ser.). 1993. mass mkt. 3.50 (*0-373-70564-6*, 1-70564-9) Harlequin Bks.

Wildfire. Sandra Field. (Presents Ser.). 1994. mass mkt. 2.99 (*0-373-11709-4*, 1-11709-2) Harlequin Bks.

Wildfire. Ken Goddard. 480p. 1995. mass mkt. 5.99 (*0-8125-2302-4*) Forge NYC.

Wildfire. Billie Green. (Loveswept Ser.: No. 618). 1993. pap. 3.50 (*0-553-44247-3*, Loveswept) Bantam.

Wildfire. Zane Grey. 320p. 1990. mass mkt. 3.99 (*0-06-100081-7*, Harp PBks) HarpC.

Wildfire. Zane Grey. 1995. mass mkt. 4.99 (*0-671-52631-6*) PB.

Wildfire. Norah Hess. 352p. 1994. mass mkt., pap. text ed. 4.99 (*0-505-51988-7*, Love Spell) Dorchester Pub Co.

Wildfire. Donna Stephens. 400p. (Orig.). 1995. mass mkt. 4.99 (*0-380-77579-4*) Avon.

Wildfire. large type ed. Cathie Linz. 243p. 1996. lib. bdg. 22.95 (*0-7838-1652-9*) Thorndike Pr.

Wildfire: Grassroots Revolts in Israel in the Post-Socialist Era. Sam Lehman-Wilzig. LC 90-26930. (SUNY Series in Israeli Studies). 198p. (C). 1992. text ed. 57.50 (*0-7914-0871-X*); pap. text ed. 18.95 (*0-7914-0872-8*) State U NY Pr.

Wildfire: Igniting the She-Volution. Sonia Johnson. LC 89-9076. 294p. (Orig.). 1989. pap. 10.95 (*1-877617-00-8*) WildFire Bks.

Wildfire -Fighting Caravans. Zane Grey. 672p. 1995. mass mkt. 4.99 (*0-06-100918-0*, Harp PBks) HarpC.

***Wildfire Loose: The Week Maine Burned.** 3rd ed. Joyce Butler. (Illus.). 304p. 1997. reprint ed. pap. 15.95 (*0-89272-409-9*) Down East.

Wildfire Love. large type ed. Kate Ivory. (Linford Romance Library). 256p. 1992. pap. 15.99 (*0-7089-7281-0*, Linford) Ulverscroft.

Wildfire Pony. Anne E. Crompton. (J). (gr. 3-7). 1996. pap. 3.50 (*0-614-15699-8*, Minstrel Bks) PB.

Wildfire Survival Guide. Maureen Gilmer. LC 95-24497. (Illus.). 176p. 1995. pap. 10.95 (*0-87833-901-9*) Taylor Pub.

***Wildfire Survival Guide.** Maureen Gilmer. 150p. 1995. pap. 10.95 (*0-614-30376-1*, H14) Terrene Inst.

Wildfires. Ann Armbruster. LC 96-13551. (First Books-Science). 64p. (J). 1996. lib. bdg. 21.00 (*0-531-20250-X*) Watts.

Wildfires. Seymour Simon. (J). (gr. 3-5). 1996. 15.00 (*0-688-13935-3*, Morrow Junior) Morrow.

Wildfires. Seymour Simon. (J). (gr. 3-5). 1996. lib. bdg. 14.93 (*0-688-13936-1*, Morrow Junior) Morrow.

Wildfires: Prevention & Control. Harry P. Gaylor. LC 74-14269. (Illus.). 1974. pap. 21.95 (*0-87618-131-0*) P-H.

***Wildflora of the Northeast.** Anita Barbour & Spider Barbour. (Illus.). 200p. 1991. pap. 19.95 (*0-614-26444-8*) Purple Mnt Pr.

Wildflower. Bette W. Castro. (Illus.). 48p. 1996. 17.95 incl. audio (*0-912347-97-X*) Fulcrum Pub.

Wildflower. Helen Hayes et al. (Illus.). 48p. 1991. 11.95 (*0-912347-79-1*) Fulcrum Pub.

Wildflower. Sharon J. McCollum. 1997. pap. text ed. 10.95 (*1-57532-067-3*) Press-Tige Pub.

Wildflower. Mackenzie Munro. 183p. (C). 1990. 90.00 (*0-86439-149-8*, Pub. by Boolarong Pubns AT) St Mut.

Wildflower. Rachel Pomerantz. (Illus.). 442p. (C). 1989. 18.95 (*1-56062-020-X*, Bristol Rhein) CIS Comm.

Wildflower ABC. Diana Pomeroy. LC 96-19748. (J). 1997. 15.00 (*0-15-201041-6*) HarBrace.

Wildflower & the Big Voice in the Sky. Patrick Haley. LC 82-82990. (Illus.). 44p. (J). (gr. 3-4). 1982. 9.00 (*0-9605738-1-X*) East Eagle.

Wildflower Book: An Easy Guide to Growing & Identifying Wildflowers, Eastern Edition. Donald W. Stokes & Lillian Q. Stokes. LC 92-12903. 1992. 12.95 (*0-316-81786-4*) Little.

Wildflower Book: From the Rockies West: An Easy Guide to Growing & Identifying Wildflowers. Donald W. Stokes & Lillian Q. Stokes. LC 92-35840. 1993. 10.95 (*0-316-81801-1*) Little.

Wildflower Designs & Motifs for Artists & Craftspeople. Charlene Tarbox. LC 93-2336. (Pictorial Archive Ser.). (Orig.). 1993. pap. write for info. (*0-486-27700-3*) Dover.

Wildflower Embroidery. Annette Rich. (Illus.). 104p. 1995. pap. 14.95 (*1-86351-141-5*, Pub. by S Milner AT) Sterling.

Wildflower Field Guide & Press for Kids. Carol A. Campbell. LC 91-50963. (J). 1993. pap. 13.95 (*1-56305-242-3*, 3242) Workman Pub.

Wildflower Gardener's Guide: California, Desert Southwest, & Northern Mexico Edition. Henry W. Art. Ed. by Deborah Burns. LC 89-45741. (Wildflower Gardener's Guide Ser.: No. 2). (Illus.). 192p. (Orig.). 1990. pap. 14.95 (*0-88266-565-0*, Garden Way Pub) Storey Comm Inc.

Wildflower Gardener's Guide: Midwest, Great Plains & Canadian Prairies Edition. Henry W. Art. Ed. by Deborah Burns. LC 90-55865. (Illus.). 200p. 1991. pap. 14.95 (*0-88266-668-1*) Storey Comm Inc.

Wildflower Gardener's Guide: Northeast, Mid-Atlantic, Lake States, & Eastern Canada Edition. Henry W. Art. LC 86-45713. (Illus.). 192p. 1987. pap. 18.95 (*0-88266-439-5*, Garden Way Pub) Storey Comm Inc.

Wildflower Gardener's Guide: Pacific Northwest, Rocky Mountain, & Western Canada Edition. Henry W. Art. Ed. by Deborah Burns. LC 89-46017. (Wildflower Gardener's Guide Ser.: No. 3). (Illus.). 192p. 1990. pap. 14.95 (*0-88266-584-7*, Garden Way Pub) Storey Comm Inc.

Wildflower Girl. Marita Conlon-McKenna. LC 92-52711. (Illus.). 176p. (J). (gr. 5-9). 1992. 14.95 (*0-8234-0988-0*) Holiday.

Wildflower Girl. Marita Conlon-McKenna. 176p. (J). (gr. 5 up). 1994. pap. 3.99 (*0-14-036292-4*) Puffin Bks.

Wildflower Handbook: The National Wildflower Research Center. National Wildflower Research Center Staff. (Illus.). 346p. 1992. reprint ed. pap. 12.95 (*0-89658-201-9*) Voyageur Pr.

Wildflower Perennials for Your Garden: A Detailed Guide to Years of Bloom from America's Native Heritage. Bebe Miles. (American Garden Classics Ser.). (Illus.). 320p. 1996. pap. 18.95 (*0-8117-2660-6*) Stackpole.

Wildflower Pony. Anne E. Crompton. (J). (gr. 3-6). 1996. pap. 3.99 (*0-671-51120-3*, Minstrel Bks) PB.

Wildflower Walks in the Santa Monica Mountains, Vol. 1. Milt McAuley. LC 87-72856. (Illus.). 128p. (Orig.). 1988. pap. 5.95 (*0-942568-16-8*) Canyon Pub Co.

Wildflowers. Ed. by Janet Cave. LC 95-24057. (Time Life Complete Gardener Ser.). (Illus.). 160p. 1995. write for info. (*0-7835-4104-X*) Time-Life.

Wildflowers. Juliet A. Hubbard. LC 94-5194. (Burpee American Gardening Ser.). 1995. pap. 9.00 (*0-671-85042-3*, P-H Gardening) P-H Gen Ref & Trav.

Wildflowers. Juliet A. Hubbard & Burpee Staff. (Burpee American Gardening Ser.). 96p. 1995. 9.00 (*0-02-860036-3*, P-H Gardening) P-H Gen Ref & Trav.

Wildflowers. Richard Parker. LC 81-51068. (Illus.). 128p. (Orig.). 1986. pap. 7.95 (*0-89317-034-8*) Windward Pub.

Wildflowers: A Garden Primer. Anne Velghe. (J). 1994. 15.00 (*0-374-38430-4*) FS&G.

***Wildflowers: A Postcard Book.** Illus. by Carl Schreier. 50p. (Orig.). 1997. pap. 8.95 (*0-943972-59-0*) Homestead WY.

Wildflowers: Legends, Poems, & Paintings. Nancy R. Ranson. Ed. by Harold E. Laughlin. LC 89-80596. (Louise Lindsey Merrick Natural Environment Ser.: No. 24). (Illus.). 102p. (C). 1996. 16.95 (*0-89096-702-4*) Tex A&M Univ Pr.

***Wildflowers: Legends, Poems, & Paintings.** Nancy R. Ranson. Ed. by Harold E. Laughlin. LC 89-80596. (Louise Lindsey Merrick Natural Environment Ser.: No. 24). (Illus.). 102p. (C). 1996. 16.95 (*0-89096-740-7*) Tex A&M Univ Pr.

Wildflowers: Seasonal Splendors of the North American West. Graham Osborne. 112p. 1996. pap. 18.95 (*0-8118-0919-6*) Chronicle Bks.

Wildflowers Across America. Lady Bird Johnson & Carlton B. Lees. (Illus.). 288p. 1994. 19.98 (*0-89660-049-1*, Artabras) Abbeville Pr.

Wildflowers Across the Prairie see Wildflowers of the Northern Great Plains

Wildflowers along the Alaska Highway: From Dawson Creek, BC - to Delta Jct., AK & on to Fairbanks, AK. Verna E. Pratt. Ed. by Frank G. Pratt. LC 91-77654. (Illus.). 224p. (Orig.). 1991. pap. 19.95 (*0-9623192-1-X*) Alaskakrafts Pub.

Wildflowers & Weeds of Kansas. Janet E. Bare. LC 78-16862. (Illus.). xii, 512p. 1979. 29.95 (*0-7006-0176-7*) U Pr of KS.

***Wildflowers & Weeds of the Pacific Northwest.** Martha Pedersen. 64p. 1993. pap. 9.95 (*0-9639462-0-X*) Portland Garden.

***Wildflowers & Winter Weeds.** Lauren Brown. Date not set. pap. 12.95 (*0-393-31678-5*) Norton.

Wildflowers Around the World. Elaine Landau. LC 90-13090. (First Bks.). (Illus.). 64p. (J). (gr. 3-5). 1991. lib. bdg. 21.00 (*0-531-20005-1*) Watts.

Wildflowers Around the World. Elaine Landau. (First Bks.). 64p. (J). (gr. 5-8). 1992. pap. 6.95 (*0-531-15649-4*) Watts.

Wildflowers at Babi Yar. Lester G. Paldy. LC 94-67429. 40p. (Orig.). 1994. pap. 6.95 (*0-9632277-1-8*) Night Heron.

***Wildflowers, Blooms & Blossoms.** Diane L. Burns. LC 97-7754. (Take-Along Guide Ser.). (Illus.). 48p. (Orig.). (J). (gr. 3-7). 1997. pap. write for info. (*1-55971-642-8*) NorthWord.

Wildflowers Grasses & Other Plants of the Northern Plains & Black Hills. Theodore Van Bruggen. LC 83-71125. 1983. pap. 6.00 (*0-912410-05-1*) Badlands Natl Hist.

Wildflowers in Candlewicking. Jan Potter. (Illus.). 56p. 1996. pap. 14.95 (*1-86351-174-1*, Pub. by S Milner AT) Sterling.

Wildflowers in Cross Stitch: Twenty-Three Creative Embroidery Designs. Jane Iles. (Illus.). 144p. 1990. 24.95 (*0-87701-755-7*) Chronicle Bks.

Wildflowers in the Carolinas. Wade T. Batson. LC 86-30785. 172p. 1987. pap. 14.95 (*0-87249-505-1*); text ed. 29.95 (*0-87249-504-3*) U of SC Pr.

Wildflowers of Alabama & Adjoining States. Blanche Dean et al. LC 73-10585. (Illus.). 256p. 1983. pap. 19.95 (*0-8173-0147-X*) U of Ala Pr.

Wildflowers of America. Frank Shaw. 1989. 19.99 (*0-517-68242-7*) Random Hse Value.

Wildflowers of Arkansas. Carl G. Hunter. LC 84-60609. (Illus.). viii, 296p. (Orig.). (C). 1984. 32.95 (*0-917659-01-5*) Ozark Soc Bks.

Wildflowers of California. Larry Ulrich. LC 94-71868. (Illus.). 136p. 1994. 34.95 (*0-944197-33-7*); pap. 18.95 (*0-944197-31-0*) Companion CA.

Wildflowers of California: Twenty Postcards. Larry Ulrich. (Illus.). 48p. (Orig.). 1995. pap. 8.95 (*0-944197-35-3*) Companion CA.

Wildflowers of Denali National Park. Verna E. Pratt. Ed. by Frank G. Pratt. LC 92-75672. (Illus.). 176p. (Orig.). 1993. pap. 16.95 (*0-9623192-2-8*) Alaskakrafts Pub.

***Wildflowers of Houston & Southeast Texas.** 2nd ed. John L. Tveten & Gloria A. Tveten. LC 97-3255. (Illus.). 320p. 1997. reprint ed. pap. 21.95 (*0-292-78151-2*) U of Tex Pr.

Wildflowers of Illinois Woodlands. Sylvan T. Runkel & Alvin F. Bull. LC 93-48533. (Illus.). 272p. (C). 1994. pap. 24.95 (*0-8138-1990-3*) Iowa St U Pr.

Wildflowers of Indiana. Maryrose Wampler. LC 88-45102. (Illus.). 198p. 1988. 45.00 (*0-253-36573-2*) Ind U Pr.

Wildflowers of Indiana Woodlands. Sylvan T. Runkel & Alvin F. Bull. LC 93-46821. (Illus.). 272p. (C). 1994. pap. 22.95 (*0-8138-1969-5*) Iowa St U Pr.

Wildflowers of Isle Royale. 2nd rev. ed. Robert A. Janke. 96p. 1996. reprint ed. pap. 5.95 (*0-935289-08-9*) Isle Royale Hist.

Wildflowers of Kuwait. Linda Shuaib. (Illus.). 128p. 1995. boxed 49.95 (*0-905743-81-4*, Pub. by Stacey Intl UK) Intl Bk Ctr.

***Wildflowers of Mammoth Cave National Park.** Randy Seymour. LC 96-18727. 1997. pap. 17.95 (*0-8131-0898-5*) U Pr of Ky.

Wildflowers of Mississippi. S. Lee Timme. LC 89-5691. (Illus.). 278p. 1990. 40.00 (*0-87805-395-6*); pap. 22.95 (*0-87805-484-7*) U Pr of Miss.

Wildflowers of North America. Frank D. Venning. (Golden Field Guide Ser.). (Illus.). 340p. 1984. pap. 11.95 (*0-307-13664-7*, 13668) Western Pub.

Wildflowers of North Dakota. Paul B. Kannowski. (Illus.). 126p. (Orig.). 1989. pap. 12.95 (*0-9608700-3-2*) U NDak Pres.

Wildflowers of Point Reyes National Seashore. Point Reyes National Seashore Association Staff & California Native Plant Society, Marin Chapter Staff. Ed. by Katherine H. Holbrook & Elisabeth Ptak. 24p. (Orig.). 1996. pap. 5.00 (*0-911235-06-X*) Pt Reyes Natl.

***Wildflowers of Prince Edward Island.** Katherine Clough. (Island Pathways Ser.). (Illus.). 152p. 1992. spiral bd. 14.95 (*0-921556-27-6*, Pub. by Gynergy-Ragweed CN) LPC InBook.

Wildflowers of Southwest Utah: Field Guide to Bryce Canyon Cedar Breaks. Hayle Buchanan. LC 92-70128. (Illus.). 119p. 1992. pap. 6.95 (*1-56044-074-0*) Falcon Pr MT.

Wildflowers of Texas. Geyata Ajilvsgi. (Illus.). 414p. 1984. 19.95 (*0-940672-15-4*); pap. 12.95 (*0-940672-46-4*) Shearer Pub.

Wildflowers of Texas: A Nature Picture Book. Aline Speer & Betsy Warren. (Illus.). 32p. 1992. pap. 3.50 (*0-9618660-0-4*) Ranch Gate Bks.

Wildflowers of the Adirondacks. 3rd ed. Anne McGrath. (Illus.). 128p. 1981. pap. 14.95 (*0-932052-27-4*) North Country.

Wildflowers of the Berkshire & Taconic Hills: Taconic Hills. Joseph Strauch. (Berkshire Outdoors Ser.). 1995. pap. 12.95 (*0-936399-66-X*) Berkshire Hse.

***Wildflowers of the Blue Ridge Parkway.** J. Anthony Alderman. LC 96-47698. (Illus.). 136p. (C). 1997. pap. 12.95 (*0-8078-4651-1*) U of NC Pr.

Wildflowers of the Carolina Lowcountry & Lower Pee Dee. Richard D. Porcher. LC 94-18769. (Illus.). 318p. (Orig.). 1995. pap. 24.95 (*1-57003-027-8*) U of SC Pr.

Wildflowers of the Central South. Thomas E. Hemmerly. LC 90-38197. (Illus.). 132p. (Orig.). 1990. pap. 13.95 (*0-8265-1240-2*) Vanderbilt U Pr.

Wildflowers of the Columbia Gorge: A Comprehensive Guide. Russ Jolley. (Jack Murdock Ser.). (Illus.). 344p. (Orig.). 1988. pap. 19.95 (*0-87595-188-0*) Oregon Hist.

***Wildflowers of the Great Lakes Region.** Roberta L. Simonds & Henrietta H. Tweedie. (Illus.). 144p. (Orig.). 1997. pap. text ed. 13.95 (*0-87563-721-3*) Stipes.

Wildflowers of the Iowa Woodlands. Sylvan T. Runkel & Alvin F. Bull. LC 86-27589. (Illus.). 272p. 1987. reprint ed. pap. 22.95 (*0-8138-1929-6*) Iowa St U Pr.

Wildflowers of the Land Between the Lakes Region, Kentucky & Tennessee. Edward W. Chester & William H. Ellis. LC 95-74974. (Illus.). 180p. (Orig.). (C). 1995. pap. text ed. 10.00 (*1-880617-04-8*) APSU Ctr Fld Bio.

Wildflowers of the Llano Estacado. Frances L. Rose. 1990. 12.95 (*0-9617102-0-9*) Rose-Strandtmann.

Wildflowers of the Northeast in the Audubon Fairchild Garden. Patricia Dalton. LC 79-20296. (Illus.). 1979. pap. 6.95 (*0-914016-63-6*) Phoenix Pub.

Wildflowers of the Northern Great Plains. rev. ed. F. R. Vance et al. LC 84-5060. Orig. Title: Wildflowers Across the Prairie. (Illus.). 336p. (C). 1984. pap. 15.95 (*0-8166-1351-6*) U of Minn Pr.

Wildflowers of the Olympics & Cascades. 2nd rev. ed. Charles Stewart. LC 94-92120. (Illus.). 128p. 1994. pap. 11.95 (*0-9621104-2-6*) Nature Educ.

Wildflowers of the Outer Banks: Kitty Hawk to Hatteras. Dunes of Dare Garden Club Staff. LC 79-18927. (Illus.). 183p. reprint ed. pap. 52.20 (*0-7837-6856-7*, 2046685) Bks Demand.

Wildflowers of the Ozarks. Henderson Leake & Dorothy Leake. LC 81-50400. (Illus.). vi, 170p. (Orig.). 1989. pap. 9.95 (*0-912456-04-3*) Ozark Soc Bks.

Wildflowers of the Plateau & Canyon Country. Susan Lamb. (Illus.). 136p. 1996. 34.95 (*0-944197-42-6*); pap. 18.95 (*0-944197-41-8*) Companion CA.

Wildflowers of the Plateau & Canyon Country: Twenty Postcards. Susan Lamb. (Illus.). 24p. 1996. pap. 8.95 (*0-944197-43-4*) Companion CA.

Wildflowers of the Potomac Appalachians: A Hiker's Guide. Molly T. Denton. LC 63-85307. 58p. 1979. 2.50 (*0-915746-11-5*) Potomac Appalach.

Wildflowers of the Santa Monica Mountains. 2nd ed. Milt McAuley. LC 84-73487. (Illus.). 576p. 1996. pap. 19.95 (*0-942568-27-3*) Canyon Pub Co.

Wildflowers of the Shenandoah Valley & Blue Ridge Mountains. Oscar W. Gupton & Fred C. Swope. LC 78-21296. (Illus.). 208p. 1979. 14.95 (*0-8139-0814-0*) U Pr of Va.

Wildflowers of the Smokies. Peter White et al. Ed. by Don DeFoe & Steve Kemp. (Natural History Handbook Ser.). (Illus.). 208p. (Orig.). 1996. pap. 11.50 (*0-937207-20-9*) GSMNH.

Wildflowers of the South to Color & Identify. Wilhelmina F. Greene. (Stemmer House Floralibrary Ser.). (Illus.). 48p. 1986. pap. 5.95 (*0-88045-080-0*) Stemmer Hse.

Wildflowers of the Southern Appalachians: How to Photograph & Identify Them. Kevin Adams & Martha Casstevens. LC 95-51144. (Illus.). 1996. pap. 26.95 (*0-89587-143-2*) Blair.

***Wildflowers of the Tahoe Sierra.** Laird Blackwell. (Illus.). 144p. (Orig.). 1997. pap. write for info. (*1-55105-085-4*) Lone Pine.

Wildflowers of the Tallgrass Prairie: The Upper Midwest. Sylvan T. Runkel & Dean M. Roosa. (Illus.). 292p. (Orig.). 1988. pap. 24.95 (*0-8138-1979-2*) Iowa St U Pr.

Wildflowers of the United States Vol. 6: Central Mountain & Plain States. Harold W. Rickett. LC 66-17920. (Illus.). 784p. 1973. text ed. 70.00 (*0-89327-287-6*) NY Botanical.

Wildflowers of the Wallum. Elizabeth McDonald. 71p. (C). 1990. 33.00 (*0-908175-16-7*, Pub. by Boolarong Pubns AT) St Mut.

Wildflowers of the West. Mabel Crittenden & Dorothy Telfer. 206p. 1992. pap. 14.95 (*0-88839-270-2*) Hancock House.

Wildflowers of the Western Cascades. Robert A. Ross et al. LC 87-29648. (Illus.). 204p. (Orig.). 1988. pap. 19.95 (*0-88192-078-9*) Timber.

Wildflowers of the Western Plains: A Field Guide. Zoe M. Kirkpatrick. LC 91-32320. (Corrie Herring Hooks Ser.: No. 20). (Illus.). 262p. (Orig.). 1992. 35.00 (*0-292-79061-9*); pap. 16.95 (*0-292-79062-7*) U of Tex Pr.

Wildflowers of Tidewater Virginia. Oscar W. Gupton & Fred C. Swope. LC 81-16247. (Illus.). 207p. 1982. 14.95 (*0-8139-0922-8*) U Pr of Va.

***Wildflowers of Washington.** C. P. Lyons. (Illus.). 176p. (Orig.). 1997. pap. write for info. (*1-55105-092-7*) Lone Pine.

Wildflowers of Yellowstone & Grand Teton National Parks. (Nature & Scenic Bks.). 1991. pap. 6.95 (*0-937512-05-2*) Wheelwright UT.

Wildflowers of Yosemite. 3rd ed. Jim Wilson & Lynn Wilson. Ed. by Ardeth Huntington. (Illus.). 144p. (Orig.). 1992. pap. 9.95 (*0-939365-02-2*) Sierra Pr CA.

Wildflowers of Zion National Park. Lee Riddell & Stanley L. Welsh. (Illus.). 136p. pap. 9.95 (*0-915630-27-3*) Zion.

Wildflowers South Florida Natives: Indentification & Habitat of Indigenous Tropical Flora. 2nd ed. Arlene A. Schuyler. Ed. by Charlotte Hall & Richard Oppenheimer. LC 82-90756. (Illus.). 112p. (Orig.). 1982. pap. 5.95 (*0-910991-00-6*) Facts FL.

W

Wildflowers Three, the Sierra Nevada. Elizabeth L. Horn. (Illus.). 1976. pap. 12.95 (0-911518-40-1) Touchstone Oregon.

Wildflowers Through the Season. Mary Ferguson & Richard M. Saunders. (Illus.). 160p. (Orig.). 1996. pap. 19.95 (1-55209-025-6) Firefly Bks Ltd.

Wildflowers Through the Seasons. Mary Ferguson. 1989. 14.98 (0-88486-021-3) Arrowood Pr.

Wildflowers, Trees, & Shrubs of Texas. Delena Tull & George Miller. (Texas Monthly Field Guides Ser.). 352p. 1991. pap. 21.95 (0-87719-195-6) Gulf Pub.

Wildfowl: A World Guide. Eric Soothill & Peter Whitehead. (Illus.). 306p. 1996. pap. 19.95 (0-7137-2622-9, Pub. by Blandford Pr UK) Sterling.

Wildfowl Art: Carvings from the Ward World Championship. Laurel Aziz. (Illus.). 120p. 1996. 40.00 (1-55209-043-4) Firefly Bks Ltd.

Wildfowl Carving Vol. 1: Essential Techniques for Carving, Texturing & Painting Wildfowl. Jim Pearce. (Illus.). 160p. 1995. pap. 16.95 (0-946819-53-X, Pub. by Guild Mstr Craftsman UK) Sterling.

Wildfowl Carving Vol. 2: Power Tools & Painting Techniques, Vol. 2. Jim Pearce. (Illus.). 192p. 1996. pap. 16.95 (1-86108-008-5, Pub. by Guild Mstr Craftsman UK) Sterling.

Wildfowler's Season: Modern Methods for a Classic Sport. Chris Dorsey. (Illus.). 240p. 1995. 37.95 (1-55821-292-2) Lyons & Burford.

Wildhaunts: Reflections on Central Oregon Enchantments. Barbara Butler. (Illus.). 50p. (Orig.). 1989. spiral bd. 8.95 (0-9614105-1-5) B Butler.

Wilding, Money, Murder & the American Dream. Derber. 1995. pap. text ed. 9.00 (0-312-13290-5) St Martin.

Wilding of America: How Greed & Violence Are Eroding Our Nation's Character. Charles Derber. LC 95-36301. (Contemporary Social Issues Ser.). 192p. 1995. 22.95 (0-312-14069-X) St Martin.

***Wildland Firefighting: Fire Behavior, Tactics & Command.** 2nd rev. ed. Donald G. Perry. Ed. by Carol C. Brooks. (Illus.). 412p. 1990. pap. text ed. 29.95 (0-941943-02-X, 35390) Fire Pubns.

Wildland Fires & the Law: Legal Aspects of Forest Fires Worldwide. Ed. by Jacques Bourrinet. LC 92-31200. 1992. lib. bdg. 88.50 (0-7923-1974-5) Kluwer Ac.

Wildland Plants: Physiological Ecology & Developmental Morphology. 710p. (C). 1995. pap. text ed. write for info. (1-884930-02-6) Soc Range Mgmt.

Wildland Recreation: Ecology & Management. William E. Hammitt & David N. Cole. LC 86-23403. 341p. 1987. text ed. 75.00 (0-471-87291-1) Wiley.

Wildland Recreation Policy: An Introduction. J. Douglas Wellman. LC 92-27963. 296p. (C). 1992. reprint ed. lib. bdg. 39.50 (0-89464-791-1) Krieger.

Wildland Water Quality Sampling & Analysis. John D. Stednick. 217p. 1990. pap. text ed. 59.00 (0-12-664100-5) Acad Pr.

Wildland Watershed Management. 2nd ed. Donald R. Satterlund & Paul W. Adams. LC 91-34849. 448p. 1992. text ed. 79.95 (0-471-81154-8) Wiley.

Wildlands & Human Needs: Reports from the Field. Roger D. Stone. LC 91-41567. (Illus.). 159p. (Orig.). (C). 1991. pap. 16.00 (0-942635-17-5) World Wildlife Fund.

Wildlands & Woodlots: The Story of New England's Forests. Lloyd C. Irland. LC 81-69943. (Futures of New England Bks.). 232p. reprint ed. pap. 66.20 (0-7837-2615-5, 2042950) Bks Demand.

Wildland/Urban Interface Fire Protection. 140p. 1995. wbk. ed., text ed. 30.00 incl. vhs (0-614-09696-0, AVA17767VNB1CDL) Natl Tech Info.

Wildlife. (Illus.). 32p. (Orig.). (J). (gr. 1-3). 1994. pap. 4.95 (1-56458-550-6) DK Pub Inc.

Wildlife. Richard Ford. 1996. pap. 11.00 (0-676-51109-0, Vin) Random.

Wildlife. Richard C. Ford. LC 90-55683. 192p. 1991. pap. 11.00 (0-679-73447-3, Vin) Random.

Wildlife. James P. Kelly. 304p. 1995. 4.99 (0-8125-3415-8) Tor Bks.

Wildlife. Molly Perham & Julian Rowe. LC 95-18170. (MapWorlds Ser.). (J). 1997. lib. bdg. 18.60 (0-531-14388-0) Watts.

Wildlife. Joyce Robbins. 1995. 7.98 (0-7858-0416-1) Bk Sales Inc.

Wildlife. Reesey Shaw & Jeff Kelly. LC 94-71072. (Orig.). 1994. pap. text ed. write for info. (1-885088-00-0) CA Ctr Arts.

Wildlife: Making a Comeback. Ed. by Donald J. Crump. (Books for World Explorers Series 9: No. 1). 104p. (J). (gr. 3-8). 1987. 8.95 (0-87044-656-8); lib. bdg. 12.50 (0-87044-661-4) Natl Geog.

Wildlife: The Artist's View. Intro. by Kathy K. Foley. (Illus.). 92p. (Orig.). 1996. pap. 12.50 (0-945529-03-1) Le Yawkey.

***Wildlife: The Artist's View.** Intro. by Robert Kret. (Illus.). 92p. (Orig.). 1996. pap. 12.50 (0-945529-10-4) Le Yawkey.

Wildlife: The Nature Paintings of Carl Brenders. Carl Brenders. LC 94-6382. (Mill Pond Bk.). (Illus.). 1994. 29.95 (0-8109-3977-0) Abrams.

***Wildlife ABC.** Jan Thornhill. (Illus.). 32p. (J). (ps up). 1996. 16.95 (0-920775-29-2, Pub. by Greey dePencier CN); pap. 5.95 (1-895688-13-2, Pub. by Greey dePencier CN) Firefly Bks Ltd.

Wildlife Alert. Gene S. Stuart. LC 79-1792. (Books for World Explorers: No. 3). (Illus.). 104p. (J). (gr. 3-8). 1980. 8.95 (0-87044-318-6); lib. bdg. 12.50 (0-87044-323-2) Natl Geog.

Wildlife & Countryside Act, 1981. Barry Denyer-Green. 265p. (C). 1983. text ed. 110.00 (0-85406-187-8, Pub. by Surveyors Pubns) St Mut.

Wildlife & Fisheries: Career Opportunities. Ed. by Bert Kempers. (Illus.). 146p. 1986. pap. 30.00 (0-935969-00-4) Media Design.

Wildlife & Fisheries Research Needs. 83p. 1979. 1.50 (0-318-16866-9) Wildlife Mgmt.

Wildlife & Forests. Ed. by David Ehrenfeld. LC 94-46716. (Readings from Conservation Biology Ser.). 248p. 1995. 24.95 (0-86542-454-3) Blackwell Sci.

Wildlife & Habitats in Managed Landscapes. Jon E. Rodiek & Eric G. Bolen. LC 90-41593. (Illus.). 217p. 1991. 45.00 (1-55963-053-1); pap. 24.95 (1-55963-052-3) Island Pr.

***Wildlife & Landscape Ecology: Effects of Pattern & Scale.** John A. Bissonette & Wildlife Society Staff. LC 97-7739. 1997. write for info. (0-387-94789-2) Spr-Verlag.

Wildlife & Man in Texas: Environmental Change & Conservation. Robin W. Doughty. LC 83-45103. (Illus.). 268p. 1989. pap. 16.95 (0-89096-416-5) Tex A&M Univ Pr.

Wildlife & Natural Resource Management. Deal. LC 96-20959. (Agriculture Ser.). 336p. 1997. text ed. 26.95 (0-8273-6422-9) Delmar.

Wildlife & Natural Resource Management. Deal. (Agriculture Ser.). 1996. teacher ed., pap. 13.95 (0-8273-6423-7) Delmar.

Wildlife & Natural Resource Management. Deal. (Agriculture Ser.). 1996. teacher ed., pap. 14.95 (0-8273-6424-5) Delmar.

***Wildlife & Natural Resource Management.** Deal. 32p. 1997. teacher ed., wbk. ed., pap. text ed. 12.75 (0-8273-8227-8) Delmar.

Wildlife & Oil Spills: Response, Research, & Contingency Planning. Ed. by Lynne Frink et al. 182p. 1995. pap. 20.00 (1-56268-050-1) Spencer Library.

Wildlife & People: The Human Dimensions of Wildlife Ecology. Gary G. Gray. LC 92-32828. (Environment & the Human Condition Ser.). (Illus.). 320p. (C). 1993. 39.95 (0-252-01947-4) U of Ill Pr.

Wildlife & People: The Human Dimensions of Wildlife Ecology. Gary G. Gray. (Illus.). 272p. (C). 1995. pap. text ed. 14.95 (0-252-06316-3) U of Ill Pr.

Wildlife & Recreationists: Coexistence Through Management & Research. Ed. by Richard L. Knight & Kevin J. Gutzwiller. LC 94-30142. (Illus.). 384p. (C). 1995. text ed. 49.95 (1-55963-257-7); pap. text ed. 27.50 (1-55963-258-5) Island Pr.

Wildlife & the Public Interest: Nonprofit Organizations & Federal Wildlife Policy. James A. Tober. LC 88-19045. (Illus.). 240p. 1989. text ed. 55.00 (0-275-92581-1, C2581, Praeger Pubs) Greenwood.

***Wildlife & Timber from Private Lands: A Landowner's Guide to Planning.** 2nd rev. ed. D. J. Decker et al. (Information Bulletin Ser.). (Illus.). 56p. (Orig.). 1990. pap. 5.50 (1-57753-031-4, 1471B193) Corn Coop Ext.

***Wildlife & Trees in British Columbia.** Stewart Guy. 1997. pap. 15.95 (1-55105-071-4) Lone Pine.

Wildlife & Wilderness: A History of Adirondack Mammals. Philip G. Terrie. LC 93-4311. (Illus.). 175p. 1993. pap. 14.50 (0-935796-39-8) Purple Mnt Pr.

***Wildlife & Woodchips.** David Lindenmayer. (Illus.). 168p. 1996. pap. 29.95 (0-86840-231-1, Pub. by New South Wales Univ Pr AT) Intl Spec Bk.

Wildlife Art in America: February 26 - May 15, 1994. Intro. by Donald T. Luce. (Illus.). 104p. (Orig.). 1994. pap. 15.00 (1-884879-00-4) UMN J F B Mus.

Wildlife at Risk: A Nature & Craft Book, 2 bks. Elizabeth Sides. (Illus.). 32p. (Orig.). (J). (gr. 1-5). 1991. Set. pap. 6.95 (0-685-54745-0) Dufour.

Wildlife at Risk: A Nature & Craft Book, 2 bks., Bk. 1. Elizabeth Sides. (Illus.). 32p. (Orig.). (J). (gr. 1-5). 1991. pap. 6.95 (0-86278-252-X) Dufour.

Wildlife at Risk: A Nature & Craft Book, 2 bks., Bk. 2. Elizabeth Sides. (Illus.). 32p. (Orig.). (J). (gr. 1-5). 1991. pap. 6.95 (0-86278-253-8) Dufour.

Wildlife at Work: Team Kit. Christel M. Cothran & Dan Hendey. 1995. suppl. ed. write for info. (0-9646852-7-2) Wildlife Habitat.

***Wildlife Atlas.** Robin Kerrod & John Stidworthy. LC 97-15967. (Atlas Ser.). (Illus.). 80p. (J). 1997. 18.95 (0-8160-3714-0) Facts on File.

Wildlife Biology. 2nd ed. Raymond F. Dasmann. LC 80-19006. 212p. (C). 1981. text ed. 43.50 (0-471-08042-X) Wiley.

Wildlife Biotelemetry. Ed. by H. P. Kimmich. (Journal: Biotelemetry & Patient Monitoring: Vol. 7, No. 3-4). (Illus.). 116p. 1981. pap. 26.50 (3-8055-2093-X) S Karger.

Wildlife California. Intro. by Judd Howell. (Junior Nature Ser.). (Illus.). 64p. (J). (gr. 3-7). 9.95 (0-87701-886-3) Chronicle Bks.

Wildlife Cameraman. Jim Kjelgaard. 1993. reprint ed. lib. bdg. 21.95 (1-56849-110-7) Buccaneer Bks.

***Wildlife Care for Birds & Mammals: Basic Wildlife Rehabilitation Manuals, 7 vols. in 1.** 3rd ed. Dale Carlson & Irene Ruth. LC 96-79851. (Illus.). 288p. 1997. per. 59.70 (1-884158-16-1) Bick Pub Hse.

Wildlife Carving with Dale Power, Vol. 1. Dale L. Power & Margo Power. (Illus.). 54p. (Orig.). Date not set. pap. 14.95 (1-886199-00-0) Madison Pubng.

Wildlife Carving with Dale Power, Vol. 2. Dale L. Power & Margo Power. (Illus.). 74p. (Orig.). Date not set. pap. 14.95 (1-886199-01-9) Madison Pubng.

Wildlife Chef. 2nd rev. ed. Michigan United Conservation Clubs Staff. 1986. pap. 5.95 (0-933112-02-5) Mich United Conserv.

Wildlife Conference: Proceedings of the 7th Annual Wildlife Conference, 1983, San Francisco, California. San Francisco Zoological Gardens Staff & California Academy of Sciences Staff. Ed. by Nancy Venizelos & Celeste Grijalava. LC 85-1879. 1983. write for info. (0-933155-00-X) SF Zoological.

***Wildlife Conservation.** Hilary D. Claggett. LC 97-14000. (Reference Shelf Ser.). 1997. write for info. (0-8242-0915-X) Wilson.

Wildlife Conservation & Public Policy. Ed. by William R. Mangun. (Orig.). 1991. pap. 15.00 (0-944285-22-8) Pol Studies.

***Wildlife Conservation in Managed Woodlands & Forests.** 2nd ed. Esmond Harris & Jeanette Harris. pap. text ed. 50.00 (0-471-96932-X) Wiley.

***Wildlife Conservation in Metropolitan Environments: Proceedings of a National Symposium on Urban Wildlife.** Ed. by Lowell W. Adams & Daniel L. Leedy. LC 91-60099. (Illus.). 264p. (Orig.). 1991. pap. 26.95 (0-942015-03-7) Urban Wildlife.

Wildlife Conservation Policy. Ed. by Valerius Geist & Ian McTaggart-Cowan. 320p. (Orig.). 1995. pap. text ed. 23.95 (1-55059-114-2, Pub. by Detselig CN) Temeron Bks.

Wildlife Conservation Principles & Practices. rev. ed. Ed. by Richard D. Teague & Eugene Decker. LC 79-2960. (Illus.). 280p. (C). 1979. pap. 11.00 (0-933564-06-6) Wildlife Soc.

Wildlife Dot-to-Dot. Monica Russo. (Illus.). 80p. (J). 1994. pap. 5.95 (0-8069-0638-3) Sterling.

Wildlife Ecology: A Guide to the Ecological Approach of Studying the Wildlife of the Central United States. 4th ed. Gary Twesten. Ed. by Urban Baum. (Illus.). 710p. 1988. 50.00 (0-9602428-8-0) G Twesten.

Wildlife Ecology & Management. Graeme Caughley & A. R. Sinclair. LC 93-41589. 1994. pap. 45.00 (0-86542-144-7) Blackwell Sci.

Wildlife Ecology & Management. 2nd ed. William L. Robinson & Eric G. Bolen. 592p. (C). 1988. text ed. 72.00 (0-02-402251-9, Macmillan Coll) P-H.

Wildlife Ecology & Management. 3rd ed. Eric G. Bolen & William L. Robinson. LC 94-13137. 648p. 1995. text ed. 73.00 (0-02-311951-9, Macmillan Coll) P-H.

Wildlife Extinction. Charles Cadieux. LC 90-71599. (Illus.). 272p. 1991. 24.95 (0-913276-59-6) Stone Wall Pr.

Wildlife Fact-File. (Illus.). 1990. write for info. (1-886614-03-2) Intl Masters Pub.

Wildlife Feeding & Nutrition. 2nd ed. Charles T. Robbins. (Animal Feeding & Nutrition Ser.). (Illus.). 352p. 1992. reprint ed. text ed. 65.00 (0-12-589382-5) Acad Pr.

Wildlife Feeding & Nutrition. 2nd ed. Charles T. Robbins. (Animal Feeding & Nutrition Ser.). (Illus.). 347p. 1994. pap. text ed. 59.95 (0-12-589383-3) Acad Pr.

Wildlife Field Research & Conservation Training Manual. Alan Rabinowitz. (Illus.). 282p. (Orig.). 1993. pap. text ed. 25.00 (0-9642787-0-7) Paul-Art Pr.

Wildlife Folklore. Laura C. Martin. (Folklore Ser.). (Illus.). 200p. 1996. reprint ed. pap. 16.95 (1-56440-974-0) Globe Pequot.

Wildlife, Forests & Forestry: Principles of Managing Forests for Biological Diversity. Malcolm L. Hunter. 400p. 1989. text ed. 83.00 (0-13-959479-5) P-H.

Wildlife Garden: Planning Backyard Habitats. Charlotte Seidenberg. (Illus.). 295p. 1995. pap. 15.95 (0-87805-835-4); text ed. 30.00 (0-87805-808-7) U Pr of Miss.

Wildlife Garden Month-by-Month. Jackie Bennett. (Illus.). 144p. 1994. 24.95 (0-7153-0033-4, Pub. by D & C Pub UK) Sterling.

***Wildlife Garden Month-by-Month.** Jackie Bennett. 1997. pap. text ed. 14.95 (0-7153-0573-5) Sterling.

Wildlife Habitat Conservation Teacher's Pac Series: An Environmental Education Teaching Aid, 10 vols. National Institute for Urban Wildlife Staff. write for info. (0-318-04278-9) Urban Wildlife.

Wildlife-Habitat Relationships: Concepts & Applications. Michael L. Morrison et al. LC 91-37591. (Illus.). 364p. (C). 1992. text ed. 26.95 (0-299-13200-5) U of Wis Pr.

***Wildlife-Habitat Relationships: Concepts & Applications.** 2nd ed. Michael A. Morrison et al. LC 97-9445. (Illus.). 416p. 1998. 34.95 (0-299-15640-0) U of Wis Pr.

Wildlife Habitat Relationships in Forested Ecosystems. David R. Patton. LC 91-14076. (Illus.). 350p. 1992. 45.00 (0-88192-202-1) Timber.

Wildlife Habitat Relationships in Forested Ecosystems. 2nd rev. ed. David R. Patton. LC 96-9410. (Illus.). 442p. 1997. 54.95 (0-88192-371-0) Timber.

Wildlife Homes. Neil Morris. LC 94-66822. (Nature Search Ser.). (Illus.). 32p. (J). 1994. 14.00 (0-89577-645-6) RD Assn.

Wildlife Hospital. Sybil Ferguson. 1991. pap. 12.95 (1-55971-131-0) NorthWord.

Wildlife Identification Pocket Guide. (Illus.). 1995. pap. 1.95 (0-916682-49-8) Outdoor Empire.

Wildlife Images. J. Wooters & J. Smith. 180p. 1981. 17.95 (0-940143-33-X); pap. 12.95 (0-940143-34-8) Safari Pr.

Wildlife Images: A Complete Guide to Outdoor Photography. John Wootters & Jerry T. Smith. LC 81-82706. (Illus.). 200p. 1981. 17.95 (0-8227-3020-0) Petersen Pub.

Wildlife in America. Peter Matthiessen. 1996. 22.25 (0-8446-6893-1) Peter Smith.

Wildlife in America. Peter Matthiessen. 336p. 1978. pap. 12.95 (0-14-004793-X, Penguin Bks) Viking Penguin.

Wildlife in North Carolina. Ed. by Jim Dean & Lawrence S. Earley. LC 87-5858. (Illus.). xiii, 201p. 1987. 29.95 (0-8078-1751-1) U of NC Pr.

Wildlife in the Marketplace. Ed. by Terry L. Anderson & Peter J. Hill. 208p. (C). 1995. lib. bdg. 57.50 (0-8476-8024-X) Rowman.

Wildlife in the Marketplace. Ed. by Terry L. Anderson & Peter J. Hill. 208p. (C). 1995. pap. text ed. 22.95 (0-8476-8025-8) Rowman.

***Wildlife in Today's Landscapes: Experience 4-H Natural Resources.** Marianne E. Krasny. (Illus.). 96p. (J). (gr. 6-8). 1991. pap. 13.25 (1-57753-037-3, 147L520) Corn Coop Ext.

***Wildlife Issues in a Changing World.** Michael Moulton & James Sanderson. (Illus.). 350p. (Orig.). (C). 1996. pap. text ed. 34.95 (1-57444-068-3) St Lucie Pr.

Wildlife Law. David S. Favre. 444p. (C). 1991. ring bd. 46.50 (1-879581-03-5) Lupus Pubns.

Wildlife Law & the Environment. Kate Cook. (Environmental Law Ser.). 220p. 1995. 125.00 (1-874698-01-5, Pub. by Cameron May UK); pap. 45.00 (0-614-07690-0, Pub. by Cameron May UK) Gaunt.

Wildlife Law Enforcement. 4th ed. William F. Sigler. 368p. (C). 1994. per. write for info. (0-697-20269-0) Wm C Brown Pubs.

Wildlife Laws of Oklahoma: Oklahoma Statutes, Title 29, Game & Fish , & Title 22, Double Section Symbol 1111 Through 1113 As Amended Through Laws of the 1986 Regular Session of the Legislature. write for info. (0-318-62392-7) West Pub.

Wildlife Laws of Oklahoma: Oklahoma Statutes: Title 29, Game & Fish, & Title 22, Double Section Symbol 1111 Through 1113 As Amended Through Laws of the 1984 Regular Session of the Legislature. Oklahoma West Publishing Company Staff. 1984. write for info. (0-318-59005-0) West Pub.

Wildlife Mammals As Research Models: In the Laboratory & Field. Ed. by Kathryn A. Bayne & Michael D. Kreger. LC 95-68719. 60p. 1995. pap. 20.00 (0-614-06556-9) Scientists Ctr.

Wildlife Management. S. N. Dhyani. (C). 1995. 32.00 (81-7033-242-7, Pub. by Rawat II) S Asia.

Wildlife Management: Crocodiles & Alligators. Ed. by G. Webb et al. 552p. (C). 1987. text ed. 195.00 (0-949324-09-4, Pub. by Surrey Beatty & Sons AT) St Mut.

Wildlife Management & Subsistence Hunting in Alaska. Henry P. Huntington. LC 92-14143. 172p. 1992. 50.00 (0-295-97224-6) U of Wash Pr.

***Wildlife Management & Subsistence Hunting in Alaska.** Henry P. Huntington. 172p. 1992. pap. 50.00 (0-295-97218-1) U of Wash Pr.

Wildlife Management in Wilderness. Clay Schoenfeld & John C. Hendee. 1978. pap. 4.95 (0-910286-60-4) Boxwood.

***Wildlife Notebook: Sketches of Selected Wildlife in New York State.** Daniel J. Decker. (Information Bulletin Ser.). (Illus.). 80p. (Orig.). 1988. pap. 5.50 (1-57753-030-6, 1471B210) Corn Coop Ext.

Wildlife Observer's Eyes: Optical Equipment for Observing Nature. Galen Geer. (Illus.). 160p. (Orig.). 1990. pap. 8.95 (0-89732-091-3) Menasha Ridge.

Wildlife of Alaska. Lynn M. Stone. LC 93-42649. (North to Alaska Ser.). (J). 1994. write for info. (1-55916-026-8) Rourke Bk Co.

Wildlife of Cactus & Canyon Country. Marj Dunmire. 48p. (J). (gr. 2-8). 1988. pap. 4.95 (0-942559-05-3) Pegasus Graphics.

Wildlife of Canada. Lynn M. Stone. LC 94-47361. (North of the Border Ser.). 24p. (J). (gr. 2-6). 1995. lib. bdg. 13.27 (1-55916-104-3) Rourke Bk Co.

Wildlife of Maine: A Coloring-Learning Book. John Crowder. (Adventures in Maine Ser.). (Illus.). 32p. (Orig.). (J). (ps-3). 1995. pap. 2.95 (1-887487-00-X) Escapade Games.

Wildlife of Mexico. Mel Higginson. LC 94-14999. (South of the Border Ser.). (J). 1994. write for info. (1-55916-055-1) Rourke Bk Co.

Wildlife of Northwest New Jersey: An Introductory Guide to the Birds, Mammals, Reptiles, & Amphibians of the Skylands. Daniela Gioseffi. (Illus.). 140p. (Orig.). 1995. pap. 5.00 (1-886841-00-4) Ladybug Publ.

Wildlife of Saudi Arabia & It's Neighbors. Wilhelm Buttiker. (Illus.). 96p. 1995. 49.95 (0-86685-547-5, Pub. by Stacey Intl UK) Intl Bk Ctr.

Wildlife of the Colorado Plateau. Steven W. Carothers. 50p. 1993. pap. 6.95 (0-89734-063-9) Mus Northern Ariz.

Wildlife of the Florida Keys: A Natural History. James D. Lazell, Jr. LC 89-1780. (Illus.). 250p. (Orig.). 1989. 19.95 (0-933280-98-X); pap. 19.95 (0-933280-97-1) Island Pr.

Wildlife of the Intermountain West. Vinson Brown et al. (Illus.). 144p. 1968. pap. 7.95 (0-911010-14-9) Naturegraph.

Wildlife of the North. Debbie Christ. (Illus.). 36p. (Orig.). 1995. pap. 13.95 (0-935133-55-0) CKE Pubns.

Wildlife of the North American Deserts. 2nd ed. Jim Cornett. (Illus.). 214p. 1987. pap. 8.95 (0-937794-06-6) Nature Trails.

Wildlife of the Prairie. Wilford L. Miller. 1976. 8.95 (0-686-18906-X); pap. 5.95 (0-686-18907-8) Assoc Print.

Wildlife of the Rockies. Ed. by Jeff Nicholas. (Wish You Were Here Postcard Bks.). 32p. 1994. pap. 4.95 (0-939365-35-9) Sierra Pr CA.

Wildlife of the Rockies. David Hancock. 1982. reprint ed. pap. 3.50 (0-919654-33-9) Hancock House.

***Wildlife of the San Juan Islands: A Checklist.** Susan Vernon. (Illus.). 10p. (Orig.). 1996. pap. 1.98 (0-9653185-0-8) Archipelago WA.

Wildlife of the South: The Photographs of Paul T. Brown. Paul T. Brown. 1995. 39.95 (0-9642595-0-8) High Standards.

Wildlife of the Western Mountains. Jim Cornett. (Illus.). 244p. (Orig.). 1982. pap. 8.95 (0-937794-03-1) Nature Trails.

Wildlife of the World, 1. Marshall Cavendish. LC 93-3581. (J). (gr. 5 up). 1993. lib. bdg. write for info. (1-85435-593-7) Marshall Cavendish.

Wildlife of the World, Set. Marshall Cavendish. LC 93-3581. 800p. (J). (gr. 5 up). 1993. lib. bdg. 299.95 (1-85435-592-9) Marshall Cavendish.

***Wildlife of Tibetan Steppes.** Schaller. 1997. 55.00 (0-226-73652-0) U Ch Pr.

An Asterisk (*) at the beginning of an entry indicates that the title is appearing in BIP for the first time.

***Wildlife of Western Canada.** Dennis Schmidt. Date not set. 24.95 (*1-55153-084-8*) Consort Bk Sales.

Wildlife of Yellowstone & Grand Teton National Parks. (Nature & Scenic Bks.). 1988. pap. 5.95 (*0-937512-06-0*) Wheelwright UT.

Wildlife on the Farm. Miriam Druist. (J). (gr. 2 up). 1977. 6.55 (*0-686-23334-4*) Rod & Staff.

Wildlife on the Great Plains. Tony Elliott. (This Is America Ser.). (Illus.). 64p. (J). (gr. 4-7). 1992. pap. 3.95 (*0-914565-41-9*, 41-9, Timbertrails) Capstan Pubns.

Wildlife Painting: Techniques of Modern Masters. Susan Rayfield. (Illus.). 144p. 1990. pap. 18.95 (*0-8230-5748-8*, Watsn-Guptill) Watsn-Guptill.

Wildlife Painting Step by Step. Patrick Seslar. LC 95-1799. (Illus.). 144p. 1995. 28.99 (*0-89134-584-1*, North Lght Bks) F & W Pubns Inc.

***Wildlife Patterns.** Patrick Spielman. 1995. write for info. (*0-8069-3818-8*) Sterling.

Wildlife Pest Control Around Gardens & Homes. Terrell P. Salmon & Robert E. Lickliter. LC 84-50732. (Illus.). 96p. 1984. pap. 8.00 (*0-931876-66-4*, 21385) ANR Pubns CA.

Wildlife Photographer of the Year. Hove Foto Books Staff. 1993. 39.95 (*0-663-43306-1*) Silver.

Wildlife Photographer of the Year: Portfolio Five. BBC Wildlife Magazine Staff. Tr. & Frwd. by David Bellamy. (Wildlife Photographer of the Year Ser.). (Illus.). 160p. 1996. 34.95 (*0-86343-396-0*, Pub. by Fountain Pr UK) Fisher Bks.

Wildlife Photographer of the Year: Portfolio Four. BBC Wildlife Magazine Staff. (Wildlife Photographer of the Year Ser.). (Illus.). 160p. 1995. 29.95 (*0-86343-371-5*, Pub. by Fountain Pr UK) Fisher Bks.

***Wildlife Photographer of the Year: Portfolio Six.** Virginia McKenna. (Illus.). 160p. 1997. 39.95 (*0-86343-327-8*, Pub. by Fountain Pr UK) Fisher Bks.

Wildlife Photographer's Field Manual. Joseph McDonald. (Illus.). 200p. 1991. pap. 14.95 (*0-936262-07-9*) Amherst Media.

Wildlife Photography. 16th ed. Compiled by Rotovision S. A. Staff. (Illus.). 350p. 1996. 69.00 (*0-8230-6417-4*, Rotovision) Watsn-Guptill.

Wildlife Photography: Getting Started in the Field. B. Moose Peterson. (Illus.). 176p. (C). 1997. pap. 29.95 (*1-883403-27-8*, H 702, Silver Pixel Pr) Saunders Photo.

Wildlife Poaching. Laura O. Greene. (Venture Bks.). (Illus.). 128p. (YA). (gr. 9-12). 1994. lib. bdg. 22.00 (*0-531-13007-X*) Watts.

Wildlife Policies in the U. S. National Parks. William F. Porter et al. LC 94-47917. 300p. (C). 1995. pap. text ed. 26.00 (*1-55963-405-7*) Island Pr.

Wildlife Policies in the U. S. National Parks. William F. Porter et al. LC 94-47917. 300p. (C). 1995. text ed. 49.00 (*1-55963-404-9*) Island Pr.

***Wildlife Portraits of Southern Africa.** Donald Heywood. 1997. 50.00 (*0-7981-3645-6*) Human & Rousseau.

Wildlife Preservation Trust Special Scientific Report, No. 3: Conservation Biology of the Black-footed Ferret. Tim W. Clark. LC 89-22739. (Illus.). 192p. (Orig.). (C). 1989. pap. text ed. 15.00 (*0-9624368-0-1*) WPTI.

Wildlife Preserves: A Far Side Collection. Gary Larson. (Illus.). 104p. (Orig.). 1989. pap. 7.95 (*0-8362-1842-6*) Andrews & McMeel.

Wildlife Production Systems: Economic Utilisation of Wild Ungulates. Ed. by R. J. Hudson et al. (Cambridge Studies in Applied Ecology & Resource Management). (Illus.). 400p. 1989. text ed. 110.00 (*0-521-34099-3*) Cambridge U Pr.

Wildlife Protection: Fish & Wildlife Service's Inspection Program Needs Strengthening. (Illus.). 80p. (Orig.). (C). 1995. pap. text ed. 20.00 (*0-7881-1333-X*) DIANE Pub.

Wildlife Protectors Handbook. Donald S. Heintzelman. 160p. 1992. reprint ed. lib. bdg. 29.00 (*0-8095-4092-4*) Borgo Pr.

Wildlife Radio Tagging: Equipment, Field Techniques & Data Analysis. R. E. Kenward. (Biological Techniques Ser.). 1987. text ed. 42.00 (*0-12-404240-6*) Acad Pr.

***Wildlife Rehabilitation: A Coloring & Activity Book.** Rehabilitators of Wildlife Rescue of New Mexico Staff. (Illus.). 32p. (Orig.). (J). (gr. 2-6). 1996. pap. 7.95 (*0-913945-55-2*) Horizon Comms.

Wildlife Requiem. James Balog. (C). 1984. 30.00 (*0-933642-06-7*); pap. 20.00 (*0-933642-07-5*) Intl Ctr Photo.

Wildlife Rescue: The Work of Dr. Kathleen Ramsay. Jennifer Dewey. LC 93-71478. (Illus.). 64p. (J). (gr. 3 up). 1994. 19.95 (*1-56397-045-7*) Boyds Mills Pr.

Wildlife Research & Management in the National Parks. R. Gerald Wright. (Illus.). 240p. 1992. text ed. 32.50 (*0-252-01824-9*) U of Ill Pr.

***Wildlife Reserves & Corridors in the Urban Environment: A Guide to Ecological Landscape Planning & Resource Conservation.** Lowell W. Adams & Louise E. Dove. LC 88-61762. (Illus.). 91p. 1989. pap. 6.95 (*0-942015-02-9*) Urban Wildlife.

Wildlife Resources: The Economic Use. Ed. by Harald H. Roth & Unther G. Merz. LC 96-23063. 416p. 1996. 139.50 (*3-540-61357-9*) Spr-Verlag.

Wildlife Resources & Economic Development. S. K. Eltringham. 340p. 1988. 180.00 (*81-7089-094-2*, Pub. by Intl Bk Distr II) St Mut.

Wildlife Restraint Series. Richard K. Clark et al. 250p. (C). 1992. lib. bdg. 74.00 (*0-9634984-1-X*); student ed. 74.00 (*0-9634984-0-1*) Int Wildlife.

Wildlife Safari. Steve Pollock. (Illus.). 48p. (J). (gr. 7-9). 1992. pap. 7.95 (*0-563-34162-9*, BBC-Parkwest) Parkwest Pubns.

Wildlife Southwest. Jill Skramstad. (Junior Nature Ser.). (Illus.). 64p. (J). (gr. 3-7). 10.95 (*0-8118-0126-8*) Chronicle Bks.

Wildlife Special Agent. Edward R. Ricciuti. Ed. & Photos by Bruce Glassman. LC 95-48143. (Risky Business Ser.). (Illus.). 32p. (J). (gr. 2-5). 1996. lib. bdg. 14.95 (*1-56711-160-2*) Blackbirch.

Wildlife Specialist. Jack Rudman. (Career Examination Ser.: C-896). 1994. pap. 27.95 (*0-8373-0896-8*) Nat Learn.

Wildlife Survivors: The Flora & Fauna of Tomorrow. John R. Quinn. 1993. 21.95 (*0-8306-4346-X*); pap. 12.95 (*0-8306-4345-1*) McGraw-Hill Prof.

Wildlife Telemetry: Remote Monitoring & Tracking Animals. Imants G. Priede & Susan M. Swift. LC 92-20704. (Ellis Horwood Series in Environmental Management, Science & Technology). 500p. 1992. text ed. 162.00 (*0-13-957994-X*, Pub. by Tavistock-E Horwood UK) Routledge Chapman & Hall.

***Wildlife Tourism.** Myra L. Shackley. LC 96-38884. 1997. write for info. (*0-415-11539-6*) Routledge.

Wildlife Toxicology. Tony J. Peterle. 384p. 1991. text ed. 72.95 (*0-442-00462-1*) Van Nos Reinhold.

Wildlife Toxicology - Population Modeling. 592p. 1993. 99.95 (*0-87371-591-8*, L591) Lewis Pubs.

Wildlife Trusts Nature Photographer's Handbook. Ian Beames. (Illus.). 160p. 1996. 27.95 (*0-7153-9826-1*, Pub. by D & C Pub UK) Sterling.

***Wildlife Walks.** Jim Arnosky. (J). Date not set. write for info. (*0-688-05449-8*); lib. bdg. write for info. (*0-688-05450-1*) Lothrop.

Wildlife Walks in the North Cotswolds. O. Ottewell. (C). 1988. pap. 29.00 (*0-946328-00-5*, Pub. by Thornhill Pr UK) St Mut.

***Wildlife Watcher.** Jim Arnosky. Date not set. pap. write for info. (*0-688-10442-8*, Beech Tree Bks) Morrow.

Wildlife Watching with Charles Eastman. Michael E. Ross. LC 96-11470. (Naturalist's Apprentice Ser.). (Illus.). (J). 1996. lib. bdg. write for info. (*1-57505-004-8*, Carolrhoda) Lerner Group.

Wildlife, Wild Death: Land Use & Survival in Eastern Africa. Ed. by Rodger Yeager & Norman N. Miller. LC 86-5791. (SUNY Series in Environmental Public Policy). 173p. 1986. text ed. 64.50 (*0-88706-168-0*); pap. text ed. 21.95 (*0-88706-169-9*) State U NY Pr.

Wildlife Woodcraft. Lois B. Phillips. LC 78-5267. (Illus.). 64p. 1978. pap. 5.95 (*0-87961-066-2*) Naturegraph.

Wildlife 1-2-3: A Nature Counting Book. Jan Thornhill. LC 89-5970. (Illus.). (J). (ps-2). 1989. pap. 16.00 (*0-671-67926-0*, S&S Bks Young Read) S&S Childrens.

***Wildlife 123.** Jan Thornhill. (Illus.). 32p. (J). (ps up). 1996. 16.95 (*0-920775-39-X*, Pub. by Greey dePencier CN); pap. 5.95 (*1-895688-14-0*, Pub. by Greey dePencier CN) Firefly Bks Ltd.

Wildlife 2000: Modeling Habitat Relationships of Terrestrial Vertebrates: Based on an International Symposium Held at Stanford Sierra Camp, Fallen Leaf Lake, CA, 7-11 October 1984. Jared Verner et al. LC 85-40769. (Illus.). 496p. 1986. reprint ed. pap. 141.40 (*0-7837-9798-2*, 2060527) Bks Demand.

Wildlings. Mary Leister. LC 76-2063. (Illus.). 192p. 1976. 14.95 (*0-916144-06-2*) Stemmer Hse.

Wildly FoxTrot: A Fox Trot Treasury. Bill Amend. (Illus.). 256p. 1995. pap. 12.95 (*0-8362-0416-6*) Andrews & McMeel.

Wildly Gross Jokes. Julius Alvin. 144p. 1996. mass mkt. 4.99 (*0-8217-5350-9*, Zebra Kensgtn) Kensgtn Pub Corp.

Wildman's Son. R. L. Coberly. LC 91-77135. (Illus.). 52p. (Orig.). 1991. pap. 6.95 (*1-878149-10-5*) Counterpoint Pub.

Wildmen, Warriors, & Kings: Masculine Spirituality & the Bible. Patrick M. Arnold. 240p. 1992. pap. 13.95 (*0-8245-1252-9*) Crossroad NY.

Wildmen, Wobblies & Whistle Punks: Stewart Holbrook's Lowbrow Northwest. Stewart H. Holbrook. (Northwest Reprints Ser.). (Illus.). 320p. 1994. reprint ed. pap. 15.95 (*0-87071-383-3*) Oreg St U Pr.

Wildness of Worship. William E. Mabry. 1994. pap. 4.95 (*1-55673-826-9*, 7997) CSS OH.

Wildrick: John Wildrick of New Jersey, 1707-1793; Genealogy of the Descendants of His Son George Wildrick. W. C. Armstrong. (Illus.). 67p. 1993. reprint ed. pap. 14.00 (*0-8328-3432-7*); reprint ed. lib. bdg. 24.00 (*0-8328-3431-9*) Higginson Bk Co.

Wildside. Steven Gould. 320p. 1996. 22.95 (*0-312-85473-0*) Tor Bks.

***Wildside.** Steven Gould. 1997. mass mkt. 5.99 (*0-8125-2398-9*) Tor Bks.

Wildside. Benjamin Wright & Mike Roter. (Cyberpunk Ser.). (Illus.). 96p. (Orig.). 1993. pap. 12.00 (*0-937279-42-0*, CP3271) R Talsorian.

Wildsong. Catherine Creel. 1996. mass mkt. 5.99 (*0-449-18320-3*) Fawcett.

Wildspace. Michael Andrews. (Endless Quest Ser.). 192p. (Orig.). 1994. 3.95 (*1-56076-928-9*) TSR Inc.

Wildstar. Nicole Jordan. 384p. (Orig.). 1992. mass mkt. 4.50 (*0-380-76622-1*) Avon.

Wildstar. Linda Ladd. 272p. 1984. mass mkt. 3.95 (*0-380-87171-8*) Avon.

Wildstorm Rising TPB. (Illus.). 272p. (Orig.). (YA). 1996. pap. text ed. 19.95 (*1-887279-23-7*) Image Comics.

Wildtrack. large type ed. Bernard Cornwell. 460p. 1989. lib. bdg. 19.95 (*0-8161-4716-7*, GK Hall) Thorndike Pr.

Wildwater: The Sierra Club Guide to Kayaking & Whitewater Boating. Lito Tejada-Flores. LC 77-28189. (Outdoor Activities Guides Ser.). (Illus.). 334p. 1982. pap. 12.00 (*0-87156-209-X*) Sierra.

Wildwater West Virginia. Paul Davidson. 336p. 1995. pap. 14.95 (*0-89732-156-1*) Menasha Ridge.

Wildwind. large type ed. Vic J. Hanson. (Dales Large Print Ser.). 190p. 1996. pap. 17.99 (*1-85389-596-2*, Dales) Ulverscroft.

***Wildwood.** Lynna Banning. (Historical Ser.: No. 374). 1997. pap. 4.99 (*0-373-28974-X*, 1-28974-3) Harlequin Bks.

Wildwood. John Farris. 448p. (Orig.). 1986. mass mkt. 4.50 (*0-8125-8270-5*) Tor Bks.

Wildwood. Katharine Kincaid. 416p. 1996. mass mkt. 4.99 (*0-8217-5460-2*, Zebra Kensgtn) Kensgtn Pub Corp.

Wildwood Flower: Poems. Kathryn S. Byer. LC 92-2519. 64p. 1992. pap. 8.95 (*0-8071-1771-4*); text ed. 15.95 (*0-8071-1770-6*) La State U Pr.

Wildwood Flowers. Julia Watts. 224p. 1996. pap. 10.95 (*1-56280-127-9*) Naiad Pr.

Wildwoods Dad. Don Oakland. (Illus.). 220p. (Orig.). (YA). (gr. 5 up). 1987. pap. 6.95 (*0-9615242-1-9*) Oak Pr.

Wiles of Destiny: Memoirs by Itzhak Kotkonski. Itzhak Kotkonski. 248p. (Orig.). 1995. pap. write for info. (*0-9649883-0-5*) I Kotkowski.

Wiles of Girlhood. Joanne Arnott. 1991. pap. 9.50 (*0-88974-034-8*, Pub. by Press Gang CN) LPC InBook.

Wiles of Men & Other Stories. Salwa Bakr. Tr. by Denys Johnson-Daview from ARA. LC 93-4648. 190p. (C). 1993. reprint ed. pap. 14.95 (*0-292-70800-9*) U of Tex Pr.

Wiles of War. Tr. by Sun Haichen from CHI. 343p. (C). 1991. pap. 12.95 (*0-8351-2795-8*) China Bks.

Wiles of Women - The Wiles of Men: Joseph & Potiphar's Wife in Ancient Near Eastern, Jewish, & Islamic Folklore. Shalom Goldman. LC 95-17220. 189p. 1995. pap. text ed. 16.95 (*0-7914-2684-X*) State U NY Pr.

Wiles of Women - The Wiles of Men: Joseph & Potiphar's Wife in Ancient Near Eastern, Jewish, & Islamic Folklore. Shalom Goldman. LC 95-17220. 189p. 1995. text ed. 49.50 (*0-7914-2683-1*) State U NY Pr.

***Wiles of Women/Wiles of Men: Joseph & Potiphar's Wife in Ancient Near Eastern, Jewish & Islamic Folklore.** Shalom Goldman. 189p. 1996. pap. 16.95 (*0-614-21564-1*, 1487) Kazi Pubns.

Wiley: One Hundred Seventy-Five Years of Publishing. Wiley Publication Staff. 279p. 1982. text ed. 35.95 (*0-471-86082-4*) Wiley.

***Wiley & Hairy Man.** Judy Sierra. Date not set. pap. write for info. (*0-14-055983-3*) Viking Penguin.

Wiley & the Hairy Man. Molly G. Bang. 1996. pap. 3.99 (*0-689-81142-X*) S&S Childrens.

Wiley & the Hairy Man. Molly G. Bang. (J). 1996. 14.00 (*0-689-81141-1*) S&S Childrens.

Wiley & the Hairy Man. Illus. by Brian Pinkney. LC 94-24512. 32p. (J). (gr. k-3). 1996. pap. 15.99 (*0-525-67477-2*, Lodestar Bks) Dutton Child Bks.

Wiley & the Hairy-Man. Suzan L. Zeder. (J). (gr. k up). 1978. 5.00 (*0-87602-219-0*) Anchorage.

***Wiley Cobol Syntex Reference Guide.** Robert A. Stern & Nancy B. Stern. 1994. pap. text ed. write for info. (*0-471-00370-0*) Wiley.

Wiley CPA Exam Review 1997, 4 vols., Vol. 4. 19th ed. Patrick R. Delaney. 1997. 132.00 (*0-471-16255-8*) Wiley.

Wiley CPA Examination Review, 2 vol., Vol. 2. 23th ed. Patrick R. Delaney. 1996. pap. text ed. 90.00 (*0-471-15334-6*) Wiley.

***Wiley CPA Examination Review for Windows: Accounting & Reporting:Taxation.** Patrick Delaney. Date not set. write for info. (*0-471-13096-6*) Wiley.

***Wiley CPA Examination Review for Windows: Auditing.** Patrick Delaney. Date not set. write for info. (*0-471-15333-8*) Wiley.

***Wiley CPA Examination Review for Windows: Business Law & Professionals.** Patrick Delaney. Date not set. write for info. (*0-471-13093-1*) Wiley.

***Wiley CPA Examination Review for Windows: Complete Exam.** Patrick Delaney. Date not set. write for info. (*0-471-13094-X*) Wiley.

***Wiley CPA Examination Review for Windows: Financial Accounting & Reporting.** Patrick Delaney. Date not set. write for info. (*0-471-15332-X*) Wiley.

Wiley CPA Examination Review, 1996-1997, Vol. 1. 23th ed. Patrick R. Delany. 1430p. 1996. pap. text ed. 45.00 (*0-471-15335-4*) Wiley.

Wiley CPA Examination Review, 1996-1997, Vol. 2. 23th ed. Patrick R. Delaney. 1193p. 1996. pap. text ed. 45.00 (*0-471-15336-2*) Wiley.

Wiley CPA Examination Review, 1997: Accounting & Reporting, Vol. 3. 19th ed. Patrick R. Delaney. 1997. pap. text ed. 32.00 (*0-471-16258-2*) Wiley.

Wiley CPA Examination Review, 1997: Auditing, Vol. 2. 19th ed. Patrick R. Delaney. 1997. pap. text ed. 32.00 (*0-471-16257-4*) Wiley.

Wiley CPA Examination Review, 1997: Business Law & Professional Responsibilities, Vol. 3. 19th ed. Patrick R. Delaney. 1997. pap. text ed. 32.00 (*0-471-16256-6*) Wiley.

Wiley CPA Examination Review, 1997: Financial Accounting & Reporting, Vol. 4. 19th ed. Patrick R. Delaney. 1997. pap. text ed. 36.00 (*0-471-16259-0*) Wiley.

***Wiley CPA Examination Review, 1997-1998.** 24th ed. Patrick Delaney. 1997. pap. text ed. 46.00 (*0-471-17873-X*) Wiley.

***Wiley CPA Examination Review, 1997-1998.** 24th ed. Patrick R. Delaney. 1997. pap. text ed. 92.00 (*0-471-17875-6*) Wiley.

***Wiley CPA Examination Review, 1997-1998, Vol. 2.** 24th ed. Patrick R. Delaney. 1997. pap. text ed. 46.00 (*0-471-17874-8*) Wiley.

***Wiley Dictionary of Civil Engineering & Construction.** Len Webster. LC 97-1237. 1997. pap. text ed. 49.95 (*0-471-18115-3*) Wiley.

Wiley Encyclopedia of Energy & the Environment, 2 vols. Attilio Bisio & Sharon Boots. LC 96-2734. 1562p. 1996. text ed. 195.00 (*0-471-14827-X*) Wiley.

Wiley Encyclopedia of Packaging Technology. Marilyn Bakker. LC 86-4041. 746p. 1986. text ed. 195.00 (*0-471-80940-3*) Wiley.

***Wiley Encyclopedia of Packaging Technology.** 2nd ed. Aaron L. Brody & Kenneth S. Marsh. LC 96-44725. 1040p. 1997. 225.00 (*0-471-06397-5*) Wiley.

Wiley Engineer's Desk Reference: A Guide for the Professional Engineer. Sanford I. Heisler. LC 83-21690. 567p. 1984. text ed. 79.95 (*0-471-86632-6*) Wiley.

Wiley Getting Started: With DOS 6.0, Vol. 2. Babette Kronstadt & David Sachs. 148p. 1995. pap. text ed. 19.95 (*0-471-13552-6*) Wiley.

***Wiley Getting Started: With DOS 6.0, Vol. 2.** Babette Kronstadt & David Sachs. (Getting Started Ser.). 1995. pap. text ed. write for info. (*0-471-13549-6*) Wiley.

Wiley Getting Started: With Microsoft Applications, Vol. 4. Babette Kronstadt et al. 208p. 1995. pap. text ed. 25.95 (*0-471-13810-X*) Wiley.

***Wiley Getting Started: With Microsoft Applications, Vol. 4.** Babette Kronstadt & David Sachs. (Getting Started Ser.). 1995. pap. text ed. write for info. (*0-471-14058-9*) Wiley.

Wiley Getting Started: With Microsoft Office, Vol. 3. Babette Kronstadt & David Sachs. 112p. 1995. pap. text ed. 19.95 (*0-471-13553-4*) Wiley.

***Wiley Getting Started: With Microsoft Office, Vol. 3.** Babette Kronstadt & David Sachs. (Getting Started Ser.). 1995. pap. text ed. write for info. (*0-471-13554-2*) Wiley.

Wiley Getting Started: With Powerpoint, Vol. 5. Babette Kronstadt & David Sachs. 195p. 1995. pap. text ed. 19.95 (*0-471-14059-7*) Wiley.

***Wiley Getting Started: With Powerpoint, Vol. 5.** Babette Kronstadt & David Sachs. (Getting Started Ser.). 1995. pap. text ed. write for info. (*0-471-14057-0*) Wiley.

Wiley Getting Started: With WordPerfect 6.1. Babette Kronstadt & David Sachs. 1995. pap. text ed. 11.95 (*0-471-13550-X*) Wiley.

***Wiley Getting Started with Wordperfect 6.1, Vol. 1.** Babette Kronstadt & David Sachs. (Getting Started Ser.). 1995. pap. text ed. write for info. (*0-471-13551-8*) Wiley.

***Wiley Law Special Report on the 1994 Bankruptcy Reform Act.** Edward J. Jepson, Jr. & David W. Marcouiller. 24p. 1994. pap. 10.00 (*0-86602-311-9*, Sage Prdcls Pr) Sage.

Wiley Law Special Report on the 1994 Bankruptcy Reform Act. Mark A. Shaiken & Irvin C. Ness. LC 95-1252. 1995. write for info. (*0-471-12340-4*) Wiley.

Wiley Medical Research Directory Thesaurus to the Online Database. Wiley Medical Publication Staff. LC 85-10795. 128p. reprint ed. pap. 36.50 (*0-8357-7552-6*, 2036275) Bks Demand.

Wiley NBS Registry of Mass Spectral Data. 2nd ed. Fred W. McLafferty & Douglas B. Stauffer. LC 87-31645. 7875p. 1989. text ed. 995.00 (*0-471-62886-7*) Wiley.

Wiley Office Handbook: Reference Guide, Word Finder, Word Processing Guide. 2nd ed. Rita C. Kutie & Virginia Huffman. LC 83-16707. (Word Processing Ser.). 465p. 1984. pap. text ed. 20.95 (*0-471-87055-2*) P-H.

***Wiley Polymer Networks Review.** K. T. Nijenhuis & W. J. Mijs. LC 97-24361. (Wiley Polymer Networks Group Review Ser.). 1998. write for info. (*0-471-97344-0*) Wiley.

Wiley Project Engineers' Desk Reference: Project Engineering, Operations, & Management. Sanford I. Heisler. LC 93-14694. 503p. 1994. text ed. 79.95 (*0-471-54677-1*) Wiley.

Wiley Static Sims Library. Contrib. by John C. Vickerman et al. 1995. write for info. (*0-471-93818-1*) Wiley.

Wiley's English-German, German-English Business Dictionary. Christa Britt & Lilith E. Schutte. LC 95-37977. 304p. (ENG & GER.). 1995. text ed. 44.95 (*0-471-13401-5*) Wiley.

Wiley's English-German, German-English Business Dictionary. Christa Britt & Lilith E. Schutte. LC 95-37977. 304p. (ENG & GER.). 1995. pap. text ed. 19.95 (*0-471-12140-1*) Wiley.

Wiley's English-Spanish Dictionary of Psychology & Psychiatry. Steven M. Kaplan. LC 95-1653. 575p. 1995. text ed. 52.50 (*0-471-01460-5*) Wiley.

Wiley's English-Spanish, Spanish-English Business Dictionary. Steven M. Kaplan. LC 96-3493. 704p. (ENG & SPA.). 1996. text ed. 44.95 (*0-471-12664-0*) Wiley.

Wiley's English-Spanish, Spanish-English Business Dictionary. Steven M. Kaplan. LC 96-3493. 704p. 1996. pap. text ed. 19.95 (*0-471-12665-9*) Wiley.

Wiley's English-Spanish, Spanish-English Dictionary of Electrical & Computer Engineering: Diccionario de Ingenieria Electrica y de Computadoras Ingles-Espanol, Espanol-Ingles Wiley. Contrib. by Steven M. Kaplan. LC 95-42946. 800p. (SPA.). 1996. text ed. 59.95 (*0-471-01037-5*) Wiley.

Wilford: Mars. 1992. 61.50 (*0-8176-2643-3*) Birkhauser.

Wilfred Bion: His Life & Works 1897-1979. Gerard Bleandonu. Tr. by Claire Pajaczkowska. LC 94-670. 301p. 1994. 40.00 (*0-89862-185-2*, 2185) Guilford Pr.

Wilfred Grenfell, His Life & Work. James L. Kerr. LC 73-21177. 272p. 1977. text ed. 59.75 (*0-8371-6068-5*, KEWG, Greenwood Pr) Greenwood.

Wilfred Owen. Wilfred Owen. Ed. by Jennifer Breen. (English Texts Ser.). 244p. (Orig.). (C). 1988. pap. text ed. 12.95 (*0-415-00733-X*) Routledge.

Wilfred Owen. Jon Stallworthy. (Illus.). 352p. 1993. pap. 19.95 (*0-19-282211-X*) OUP.

Wilfred Owen: The Complete Poems & Fragments, 2 vols. Ed. by Jon Stallworthy. 1984. Slipcased. 65.00 (*0-393-01830-X*) Norton.

W

Wilfred Owen's Voices: Language & Community. Douglas Kerr. 320p. (C). 1993. 58.00 (0-19-812370-1, 4288) OUP.

Wilfredo Lam & His Contemporaries 1938-1952. Studio Museum in Harlem Staff et al. LC 92-62642. (Illus.). 176p. (Orig.). (C). 1992. pap. text ed. 34.95 (0-942949-08-0) Studio Mus Harlem.

Wilfrid: 634-709 AD. Anne Warin. (C). 1988. 40.00 (1-85072-108-4, Pub. by W Sessions UK) St Mut.

Wilfrid Cumbermede. George MacDonald. (George MacDonald Original Works: Series VIII). 540p. 1997. 20.00 (1-881084-52-3) Johannesen.

Wilfrid Gordon McDonald Partridge. Mem Fox. LC 85-14720. (Illus.). 32p. (J). (gr. k-5). 1985. 13.95 (0-916291-04-9) Kane-Miller Bk.

Wilfrid Gordon McDonald Partridge. Mem Fox. (Illus.). 32p. (J). (gr. k-4). 1989. pap. 7.95 (0-916291-26-X) Kane-Miller Bk.

Wilfrid Gordon McDonald Partridge: Big Book. Mem Fox. (Illus.). 32p. (J). (gr. k-4). 1995. 19.95 (0-916291-56-1) Kane-Miller Bk.

Wilhelm Conrad Rontgen & the Early History of the Roentgen Rays. Otto Glasser. (Illus.). 494p. 1993. reprint ed. 125.00 (0-930405-22-6) Norman SF.

Wilhelm Dilthey: A Hermeneutic Approach to the Study of History & Culture. Ilse N. Bulhof. (Martinus Nijhoff Philosophy Library: No. 2). 244p. 1980. lib. bdg. 93.00 (90-247-2360-4, Pub. by M Nijhoff NE) Kluwer Ac.

Wilhelm Dilthey: Introduction to the Human Sciences. Ed. by Rudolf A. Makkreel. (Selected Works of Wilhelm Dilthey: Vol. 1). 528p. 1989. text ed. 69.50 (0-691-07307-4); pap. text ed. 24.95 (0-691-02074-4) Princeton U Pr.

***Wilhelm Dilthey's Selected Works: Poetry & Experience, Vol. 5.** Rudolf A. Makreel. 416p. 1985. pap. text ed. 24.95 (0-691-02928-8) Princeton U Pr.

Wilhelm Friedemann Bach. Martin Falck. iv, 201p. 1977. reprint ed. write for info. (3-487-06267-4) G Olms Pubs.

Wilhelm Hohenzollern: The Last of the Kaisers. Emil Ludwig. LC 74-100815. (Illus.). reprint ed. 31.25 (0-404-04067-5) AMS Pr.

Wilhelm II: Prince & Emperor, 1859-1900. Lamar Cecil. LC 88-27798. (Illus.). xxii, 464p. (C). 1989. 45.00 (0-8078-1828-3) U of NC Pr.

Wilhelm II Vol. 2: Emperor & Exile, 1900-1941. Lamar Cecil. 448p. (C). 1996. 39.95 (0-8078-2283-3) U of NC Pr.

Wilhelm Jordaens's "Avellana" A Fourteenth Century Virtue-Vice Debate. Lawrence J. Johnson. LC 84-62215. (Speculum Anniversary Monographs: No. 9). xi, 101p. (Orig.). 1985. 20.00 (0-910956-89-8); pap. 12.00 (0-910956-90-1) Medieval Acad.

Wilhelm Lehmann Vol. 1: A Critical Biography, Pt. I. David Scrase. (GERM Ser.). (Illus.). xvi, 192p. 1984. 35.00 (0-938100-15-7) Camden Hse.

***Wilhelm Lehmbruck & Joseph Beuys: Of Songs & Silence.** Pamela Kort. (Illus.). 50p. 1997. 25.00 (1-885013-13-2) Dist Art Pubs.

***Wilhelm Leibl - Briefe.** Boris Rohrl. (Illus.). x, 372p. (GER.). 1996. write for info. (3-487-10164-5) G Olms Pubs.

Wilhelm Liebknecht: Letters to the Chicago Workingmen's Advocate (1870-1871) Ed. by Philip S. Foner. LC 81-7042. 190p. 1983. 35.00 (0-8419-0743-9) Holmes & Meier.

Wilhelm Liebknecht & German Social Collections: A Documentary History. William Pelz. Tr. by Erich Hahn. LC 93-31636. (Documentary Reference Collections). 480p. 1994. text ed. 95.00 (0-313-28200-5, Greenwood Pr) Greenwood.

Wilhelm Liebknecht & the Founding of the German Social Democratic Party. Raymond H. Dominick. LC 81-16329. 565p. reprint ed. pap. 161.10 (0-7837-2466-7, 2042619) Bks Demand.

Wilhelm Meister & His English Kinsmen. Susanne Howe. LC 30-1541. reprint ed. 20.00 (0-404-03367-9) AMS Pr.

Wilhelm Meister, Vol. II: The Years of Travel Complete. Johann Wolfgang Von Goethe. Tr. by H. M. Waidson from GER. (Orig.). 1998. pap. 19.95 (0-7145-4218-0) Riverrun NY.

Wilhelm Meister's Apprenticeship: Johann Wolfgang von Goethe. Ed. by Eric A. Blackall & Victor Lange. Tr. by Victor Lange. LC 94-39893. 396p. (ENG & GER.). 1994. pap. text ed. 17.95 (0-691-04344-2) Princeton U Pr.

Wilhelm Meister's Theatrical Calling. Johann W. Von Goethe. Tr. & Intro. by John Russell. LC 94-43843. (Studies in German Literature, Linguistics, & Culture). xvi, 250p. (ENG & GER.). 1995. 54.95 (1-57113-018-7) Camden Hse.

Wilhelm Meister's Travels: Translation of the First Edition by Thomas Carlyle. Johann W. Von Goethe. Tr. by Thomas Carlyle. (GERM Ser.: Vol. 56). xviii, 352p. 1991. 58.00 (0-938100-88-2) Camden Hse.

Wilhelm Raabe: The Fiction of the Alternative Community. Ed. by Jeffrey L. Sammons. 435p. 1987. text ed. 65.00 (0-691-06709-0) Princeton U Pr.

***Wilhelm Raabe's "Der Hungerpastor" & Charles Dickens's "David Copperfield" Intertextuality of Two Bildungsromane.** Peter O. Arnds. (North American Studies in Nineteenth-Century German Literature: Vol. 20). 208p. (C). 1997. 44.95 (0-8204-3321-7) P Lang Pubng.

Wilhelm Reich: The Man Who Dreamed of Tomorrow. W. Edward Mann & Edward Mottman. 295p. (Orig.). (C). Date not set. reprint ed. pap. 14.95 (0-9637902-4-2) Four Worlds.

Wilhelm Reich in Hell. 3rd ed. Robert A. Wilson. LC 87-81290. 165p. (Orig.). 1987. pap. 12.95 (1-56184-108-0) New Falcon Pubns.

Wilhelm Schmidt. Susanne A. Kohl. (Illus.). 83p. (Orig.). 1995. pap. text ed. 11.00 (0-7884-0170-X) Heritage Bk.

Wilhelm Second & the Germans: A Study in Leadership. Thomas A. Kohut. (Illus.). 352p. 1991. 45.00 (0-19-506172-1) OUP.

Wilhelm Tell. Friedrich Von Schiller. Tr. by Gilbert Jordan. LC 63-12200. (Orig.). 1964. pap. 4.90 (0-672-60416-7, Bobbs) Macmillan.

Wilhelm Tell. Friedrich Von Schiller. Ed. by Kenneth J. Northcott. Tr. by William F. Mainland from GER. LC 70-187835. (German Literary Classics in Translation Ser.). 190p. (C). 1973. pap. text ed. 11.50 (0-226-73801-9) U Ch Pr.

***Wilhelm von Humboldt: A Biography, Vol. 1.** Paul R. Sweet. LC 77-26654. 323p. 1978. reprint ed. pap. 92.10 (0-608-04449-0, 2064981) Bks Demand.

***Wilhelm von Humboldt: A Biography, Vol. 2.** Paul R. Sweet. LC 77-26654. 584p. 1978. reprint ed. pap. 166.50 (0-608-04450-4, 2064981) Bks Demand.

Wilhelm Von Humboldt's Conception of Linguistic Relativity. Roger L. Brown. LC 67-30542. (Janua Linguarum, Ser. Minor: No. 65). (Orig.). 1967. pap. text ed. 36.95 (90-279-0593-2) Mouton.

***Wilhelm Von Polenz.** M. Salyamosy. 1985. pap. 75.00 (963-05-3836-9, Pub. by Akad Kiado HU) St Mut.

Wilhelm Waiblinger in Italy. Lawrence S. Thompson. (North Carolina. University. Studies in the Germanic Languages & Literatures: No. 9). reprint ed. 27.00 (0-404-50909-6) AMS Pr.

Wilhelmi: The Clay's the Thing. Ben Holland. (Illus.). 50p. (Orig.). 1996. pap. 10.00 (1-888581-00-X) Art Museum So TX.

Wilhelmi Malmesbiriensis Monachi de Gestis Pontificum Anglorum Libri Quinque: From William of Malmsbury's Autograph. N. E. Hamilton. (Rolls Ser.: No. 52). 1974. reprint ed. 70.00 (0-8115-1111-1) Periodicals Srv.

Wilhelmina Guide to Modeling. Natasha Esch & Christine Walker. (Illus.). 208p. 1996. pap. 14.00 (0-684-81491-9, Fireside) S&S Trade.

Wilhelmina's Model-Actor's Dictionary: Hundreds of Entries on Modeling & Acting Terms from AFTRA to Zed Card. 160p. (Orig.). 1994. pap. 8.95 (1-56414-140-3) Career Pr Inc.

Wilhelmina's World of Child Modeling. Natasha Esch. (Illus.). 168p. (Orig.). 1994. pap. 14.95 (1-56414-141-1) Career Pr Inc.

***Wilhelmine & the Life & Opinions of Sebaldus Nothanker: Masterworks of the German Rococo & Enlightenment, 2 vols. in 1.** Mortiz A. Von Thummel & Friedrich Nicolai. Tr. & Intro. by John R. Russell. (GERM Ser.). 1997. 55.00 (1-57113-145-0) Camden Hse.

***Wiliam Carlos Williams.** Ed. by Crane Doyle. (Critical Heritage Ser.). 483p. (C). 1997. text ed. 35.00 (0-415-15944-X) Routledge.

Wiliam Wordsworth: A Poetic Life. John L. Mahoney. LC 96-39355. (Illus.). 375p. 1996. 32.00 (0-8232-1715-9); pap. 17.00 (0-8232-1716-7) Fordham.

Wilkes-Barre, PA. S. Flood. (Images of America Ser.). 1997. pap. 16.99 (0-7524-0461-X, Arcdia) Chalford.

***Wilkes-Barre (the "Diamond City"), Luzerne County: Its History, Its Natural Resources, Its Industries, 1769-1906.** 160p. 1997. reprint ed. pap. 20.00 (0-8328-6462-5) Higginson Bk Co.

Wilkes-Barre Variation, Two Knights Defense. Yakov B. Estrin. (Illus.). 114p. 1978. pap. 5.00 (0-931462-00-2) Chess Ent.

***Wilkes County, Georgia Early Marriages 1792-1832.** Robbie F. Sutlive. 53p. 1996. pap. text ed. 14.00 (1-57088-041-7) J&W Ent.

Wilkes County, North Carolina Marriage Bonds & Certificates, 1779-1868. Francis T. Ingmire. 202p. 1994. pap. 23.00 (0-8095-8712-2); lib. bdg. 53.00 (0-8095-8374-7) Borgo Pr.

Wilkes County Papers, Seventeen Seventy-Seven to Eighteen Thirty-Three. Robert S. Davis, Jr. 338p. 1979. pap. 25.00 (0-89308-410-7) Southern Hist Pr.

Wilkes Expedition: The First United States Exploring Expedition, 1838-1842. David B. Tyler. LC 68-25931. (American Philosophical Society, Memoirs Ser.: Vol. 73). 453p. reprint ed. pap. 129.20 (0-317-28297-2, 2019713) Bks Demand.

Wilkie Collins. R. Ashley. LC 75-30887. (Studies in Fiction: No. 34). 1975. lib. bdg. 75.00 (0-8383-2095-3) M S G Haskell Hse.

Wilkie Collins. Nayder. LC 97-21447. 1997. 23.95 (0-8057-7059-3, Twayne) Scribnrs Ref.

Wilkie Collins: The Critical Heritage. Ed. by Norman Page. (Critical Heritage Ser.). 1974. 69.50 (0-7100-7843-9, RKP) Routledge.

Wilkie Collins: Women, Property & Propriety. Philip O'Neill. 1988. 50.00 (0-389-20771-3) Rowman.

Wilkie Collins see Later 19th Century Novelists: Critical Heritage

Wilkie Collins, a Critical & Biographical Study. limited ed. Dorothy L. Sayers. Ed. by E. R. Gregory. LC 76-53108. (Illus.). 1977. pap. 12.50 (0-918160-01-4) Friends Univ Toledo.

Wilkie Collins & His Victorian Readers: A Study in the Rhetoric of Authorship. Sue Lonoff. LC 79-8835. (Studies in the Nineteenth Century: No. 2). (Illus.). 1982. 34.50 (0-404-18044-2) AMS Pr.

Wilkie Collins & Other Sensation Novelists: Walking the Moral Hospital. Nicholas Rance. LC 90-48390. 1991. 36.50 (0-8386-3444-3) Fairleigh Dickinson.

Wilkie Collins, le Fanu, & Others. Stewart M. Ellis. LC 68-29203. (Essay Index Reprint Ser.). 1977. reprint ed. 21.95 (0-8369-0413-3) Ayer.

Wilkie Collins, Le Fanu & Others. Stewart M. Ellis. (BCL1-PR English Literature Ser.). 343p. 1992. reprint ed. lib. bdg. 89.00 (0-7812-7049-9) Rprt Serv.

Wilkie Collins to the Forefront: Some Reassessments. Ed. by Nelson Smith & R. C. Terry. LC 91-58772. (Studies in Nineteenth-Century Literature & Culture: No. 1). 1995. 55.00 (0-404-64351-5) AMS Pr.

Wilkin: Robert Wilkin (1766-1835) & Mary (Hyde) Wilkin, Their Parents & Descendants. F. McIntyre & L. M. Wilkin. (Illus.). 802p. 1995. reprint ed. pap. 115.00 (0-8328-4948-0); reprint ed. lib. bdg. 125.00 (0-8328-4947-2) Higginson Bk Co.

Wilkins the Diagnosis & Treatment of Endocrine Disorders in Childhood & Adolescence. 4th ed. Ed. by Michael S. Kappy et al. LC 93-20671. (Illus.). 1270p. (C). 1994. text ed. 149.95 (0-398-05879-2) C C Thomas.

Wilkinson: Genealogy of Wilkinson & Kindred Families, Southern Branch. M. M. Wilkinson. (Illus.). 546p. 1991. reprint ed. pap. 82.50 (0-8328-1842-9); reprint ed. lib. bdg. 92.50 (0-8328-1841-0) Higginson Bk Co.

Wilkinson: The Scottish Law of Evidence. 2nd ed. A. B. Wilkinson. 1993. pap. 62.00 (0-406-01357-8, UK) MICHIE.

Wilkinson Book: Being the Ancestry & Descendants of Major General James Wilkinson of Calvert Co., MD et ux, Ann Biddle of Philadelphia, PA. Patricia W. Balletta. (Illus.). 530p. 1994. text ed. 85.00 (0-9640893-2-7) P W W Balletta.

Will. Kelly Jamison. (Desire Ser.). 1993. mass mkt. 2.99 (0-373-05798-9, 5-05798-9) Silhouette.

Will. G. Gordon Liddy. 1991. mass mkt. 6.99 (0-312-92412-7) St Martin.

Will. G. Gordon Liddy. 1995. mass mkt. 5.99 (0-312-95617-7) Tor Bks.

Will. Dwight A. Osborne. 93p. (Orig.). 1996. pap. 5.95 (0-9632817-9-8) Osborne Bks.

Will: A Modern Day Treasure Hunt. Tod Normot. 62p. 1982. 6.95 (0-686-35968-2) Tricore Assoc.

Will: A Portrait of William Douglas Home. David Fraser. (Illus.). 256p. 1996. 40.00 (0-233-98915-3, Pub. by A Deutsch UK) Trafalgar.

Will: The Autobiography of G. Gordon Liddy. G. Gordon Liddy. 1996. 26.95 (0-312-11915-1) St Martin.

Will: The Potent Force of the Universe. Lester Sumrall. 64p. (Orig.). 1985. pap. text ed. 1.95 (0-937580-85-6) LeSEA Pub Co.

Will a Clownfish Make You Giggle? Answers to Some Very Fishy Questions. Kay Dokken. LC 95-34727. (Illus.). 32p. (J). (ps-2). 1995. boxed 14.95 (1-881652-07-6) Aqua Quest.

Will a Man Rob God? C. Phillip Johnson. 1981. pap. 3.00 (0-933184-29-8) Flame Intl.

Will, a Modern Day Treasure Hunt. 2nd ed. Ronald Franks et al. 1981. pap. text ed. 6.95 (0-9607132-0-4) Tricore Assoc.

Will Abstracts of Brooke County, (West) Virginia 1797-1850. K. T. McFarland. 88p. per. 9.50 (0-933227-26-4) Closson Pr.

Will America Accept Love at Halftime? or How to Survive Pro-Football Sunday. Jim Klobuchar. 1972. pap. 2.95 (0-87018-066-5) Ross.

Will America Go Neo-Tech. Mark Hamilton. (Illus.). 448p. 1995. pap. 49.95 (0-911752-75-7) Neo-Tech Pub.

Will America Grow up Before It Grows Old? How the Coming Social Security Crisis Threatens You, Your Family & Your Country. Pete Peterson. 96p. 1996. 21.00 (0-679-45256-7) McKay.

Will America Surrender? Slobodan Draskovich. 480p. 1972. 12.95 (0-8159-7211-3) Devin.

Will America Surrender? Slobodan Draskovich. 1976. pap. 9.95 (0-8159-7217-2) Devin.

Will & a Way: What the United States Can Learn from Canada about Caring for the Elderly. Robert L. Kane & Rosalie S. Kane. LC 85-16616. (Studies of Social Gerontology & Aging). 275p. 1988. pap. text ed. 17.50 (0-231-06137-4) Col U Pr.

***Will & a Wedding.** Lois Richer. 1997. mass mkt. 4.50 (0-373-87009-4, 1-87009-6) Harlequin Bks.

Will & a Wedding. Judith Yates. 1996. mass mkt. 3.99 (0-373-24026-0) Silhouette.

Will & Circumstance: Montesquieu, Rousseau, & the French Revolution. Norman Hampson. LC 82-40455. 294p. 1983. 19.95 (0-8061-1843-1) U of Okla Pr.

Will & Estate Records in the Virginia State Library: A Researcher's Guide. John Vogt & T. William Kethley, Jr. LC 89-7109. 186p. (Orig.). (C). 1987. reprint ed. lib. bdg. 29.00 (0-8095-8202-3) Borgo Pr.

Will & No Will: or A Bone for the Lawyers: And the New Play Criticized: or the Plague of Envy. Charles Macklin. LC 92-23648. (Augustan Reprints Ser.: Nos. 127-128). 1967. reprint ed. 21.50 (0-404-70127-2, PR3543) AMS Pr.

***Will & Orv.** Walter A. Schulz. (Illus.). (J). (gr. 3). 1995. 7.92 (0-395-73236-0) HM.

Will & Orv. Walter A. Schulz. (On My Own Ser.). (Illus.). 48p. (J). (gr. k-3). 1991. lib. bdg. 13.13 (0-87614-669-8, Carolrhoda) Lerner Group.

Will & Orv. Walter A. Schulz. (J). (gr. k-3). 1992. pap. 5.95 (0-87614-568-3, First Ave Edns) Lerner Group.

***Will & Orv.** large type ed. Walter A. Schulz. (Illus.). 62p. (J). (gr. 3). 15.50 (0-614-20629-4, L-38219-00 APHB) Am Printing Hse.

Will & Political Legitimacy: A Critical Exposition of Social Contract Theory in Hobbes, Locke, Rousseau, Kant, & Hegel. Patrick Riley. 294p. 1982. 37.00 (0-674-95316-9) HUP.

Will & Representation: The Philosophical Foundations of Melville's Theatrum Mundi. Bernhard Radloff. (Studies on Themes & Motifs in Literature: Vol. 17). 368p. (C). 1996. text ed. 62.95 (0-8204-2717-9) P Lang Pubng.

Will & Spirit. Gerald G. May. LC 82-47751. (Illus.). 368p. 1987. pap. 21.00 (0-06-250582-3) Harper SF.

Will & the Grace. Diane Westlake. (Illus.). 80p. (Orig.). (YA). (gr. 10-12). 1984. pap. 9.00 (0-9614438-0-4) Fen Winnie.

Will & the Way. Paul R. Williams & Karen E. Hudson. LC 93-39986. 64p. (J). 1994. 14.95 (0-8478-1780-6) Rizzoli Intl.

***Will & the Way: A History of College Foundation & the Insured Student Loan Program in North Carolina.** T. Harry Gatton. 1989. pap. write for info. (0-9624196-1-3) Coll Fndtn Inc.

Will & Trust Drafting & Estate Planning. Randy Spiro. 363p. (Orig.). 1985. pap. text ed. 41.50 (0-89074-074-7) Lega Bks.

Will & Trust Drafting Software. 1994. pap. text ed. 156.45 incl. disk (0-944490-79-4) Mass CLE.

Will & World: Metaphysics. N. M. Nathan. 192p. 1992. 60.00 (0-19-823954-8) OUP.

Will Anyone Who Saw the Accident. large type ed. Jeffrey Ashford. 384p. 1992. pap. 15.99 (0-7089-7215-2, Trailtree Bookshop) Ulverscroft.

Will Appalachia Finally Overcome Poverty? Anthony J. Salatino. LC 95-79614. (Illus.). 272p. 1995. pap. 16.95 (0-913383-37-6) McClanahan Pub.

***Will Arab Workers Prosper or Be Left Out in the Twenty-First Century?** 44p. (ARA.). 1996. 6.95 (0-8213-3530-8, 13530) World Bank.

Will Barnet. Robert M. Doty. LC 84-396. (Illus.). 172p. 1984. 49.50 (0-8109-0731-3) Abrams.

Will Barnet: Paintings & Prints, 1932-1982. Howard E. Wooden. LC 82-63132. (Illus.). 24p. 1983. pap. 5.00 (0-939324-08-3) Wichita Art Mus.

Will Barnet Drawings 1930-1990. Townsend Wolfe. 96p. 1992. pap. 20.00 (0-9612750-9-X) Arkansas Art Ctr.

Will Bill? Easy Phonics Reader. Carratello. (Illus.). 16p. (J). (ps-1). 1996. pap. 2.49 (1-57690-018-5) Tchr Create Mat.

Will Black Holes Devour the Universe? And 100 Other Questions & Answers about Astronomy. Melanie Melton. 1994. pap. 14.95 (0-913135-20-8, 18541) Kalmbach.

Will Book One, Halifax County, Virginia 1773-1783. Marian D. Chiarito. 136p. 1984. 18.00 (0-945503-04-0) Clarkton Pr.

Will Book Two, Halifax County, Virginia, 1783-1792. Marian D. Chiarito & James H. Prendergast. 136p. 1989. 22.00 (0-945503-17-2) Clarkton Pr.

Will Book Zero, Halifax County, Virginia 1752-1773. Marian D. Chiarito. 88p. 1982. 15.00 (0-945503-02-4) Clarkton Pr.

Will Bradley: His Graphic Art. Will Bradley. Ed. by Clarence P. Hornung & Roberta W. Wong. (Illus.). pap. 10.95 (0-486-20701-3) Dover.

Will Christians Go Through the Great Tribulation? Gordon Lindsay. 1971. 2.95 (0-89985-065-0) Christ for the Nations.

***Will Clark: Boy Adventurer.** Katharine E. Wilkie. LC 97-9861. (Illus.). (J). 1997. pap. 25.00 (0-689-81751-7, Aladdin Paperbacks) S&S Childrens.

Will Clayton: A Short Biography. Ellen C. Garwood. LC 73-157335. (Select Bibliographies Reprint Ser.). 1977. reprint ed. 19.95 (0-8369-5795-4) Ayer.

Will Computer Communication End Geography?, Vol. P-95-4. unabridged ed. Vincent Mosco. (Illus.). 42p. (Orig.). 1995. pap. text ed. write for info. (1-879716-30-5) Ctr Info Policy.

Will Contests. Thomas J. Reed & Eunice L. Ross. LC 92-72560. 1992. ring bd. 135.00 (0-685-59866-7) Clark Boardman Callaghan.

Will Creates Way. Willie Richey. 112p. 1995. per., pap. text ed. 19.95 (0-7872-1371-3) Kendall-Hunt.

Will Dad Ever Move Back Home? Paula Z. Hogan. LC 79-24058. (Life & Living from a Child's Point of View Ser.). (Illus.). 32p. (J). (gr. k-6). 1980. lib. bdg. 21.40 (0-8172-1356-2) Raintree Steck-V.

Will Dad Ever Move Back Home? Paula Z. Hogan. (Life & Living from a Child's Point of View Ser.). (J). (ps-3). 1993. pap. 4.95 (0-8114-7160-8) Raintree Steck-V.

Will Drafting. Dana Shilling. LC 86-30265. 160p. 1987. 27.50 (0-13-959727-1) P-H.

Will Drafting & Probate Practice Handbook, 1993. rev. ed. Wake Forest University School of Law Continuing Legal Education Staff. 715p. 1993. pap. 65.00 (0-685-66748-0) Wake Forest Law.

Will Earns His Mark: And Other Stories from Long Ago. Highlights Staff. LC 94-72489. 96p. (J). (gr. 2-4). 1996. pap. 3.95 (1-56397-448-7) Boyds Mills Pr.

Will Eisner Reader: Seven Graphic Stories by a Comics Master. Will Eisner. Ed. by Dave Schreiner. LC 90-22621. (Illus.). 88p. 1991. 19.95 (0-87816-128-7); pap. 9.95 (0-87816-129-5) Kitchen Sink.

Will Eisner Sketchbook. Will Eisner. LC 95-40776. (Illus.). 1995. 24.95 (0-87816-400-6); pap. 17.95 (0-87816-399-9) Kitchen Sink.

Will Eisner Sketchbook. Will Eisner. 1996. 24.95 (0-87816-464-2) Kitchen Sink.

Will, Estate, Trusts For Legal Assistants. 2nd ed. Gingrich. (Paralegal Ser.). 80p. 1996. teacher ed., text ed. 12.00 (0-8273-7477-1) Delmar.

Will Europe Fight for Oil: Energy Relations in the Atlantic Area. Ed. by Robert J. Lieber. 240p. 1983. 38.50 (0-275-91035-0, C1035, Praeger Pubs) Greenwood.

Will for Peace: Peace Action in the United Methodist Church: A History. Herman Will, Jr. 300p. 9.95 (0-9613222-0-9, CS1007) General Board.

Will Gets a Haircut. Olof Landstrom & Lena Landstrom. LC 93-660. (Illus.). (J). 1993. reprint ed. 13.00 (91-29-62075-9, Pub. by R & S Bks) FS&G.

***Will God Enjoy Your Videotape???** Larry Pico. LC 95-92556. 92p. (Orig.). 1995. pap. 7.95 (0-7880-0642-8) CSS OH.

W

An Asterisk (*) at the beginning of an entry indicates that the title is appearing in BIP for the first time.

***Will God Heal Me? Faith in the Midst of Suffering.** Ron Dunn. 240p. 1997. pap. 18.99 (1-57673-100-6, Multnomah Bks) Multnomah Pubs.

Will Goes to the Beach. Lena Landstrom. Tr. by Carla Wiberg. (Illus.). 32p. (J). (ps). 13.00 (91-29-62914-4) FS&G.

Will Goes to the Post Office. Olof Landstrom & Lena Landstrom. (Illus.). 32p. (J). (ps-k). 1994. 13.00 (91-29-62950-0) FS&G.

Will H. Bradley: A Reference Guide. Compiled by Anthony Bambace. LC 94-43788. 1995. 75.00 (1-884718-08-6) Oak Knoll.

Will H. Bradley: A Reference Guide. deluxe ed. Compiled by Anthony Bambace. LC 94-43788. 1995. 450.00 (1-884718-09-4) Oak Knoll.

***Will Harris Murders.** Bob Terrell. LC 96-61826. (Illus.). 160p. (Orig.). 1996. pap. 9.95 (1-56664-107-1) WorldComm.

Will He Love Me Forever? Sustaining Love Through the Years. Julian D. Ford & Judith G. Ford. 228p. 1992. pap. 12.95 (0-929923-76-6) Lowell Hse.

Will Henry-Clay Fisher. Robert L. Gale. LC 82-71032. (Western Writers Ser.: No. 52). (Illus.). 54p. (Orig.). 1982. pap. 4.95 (0-88430-026-9) Boise St U W Writ Ser.

Will Henry Stevens: From the Mountains to the Sea. Estill C. Pennington. (Illus.). 32p. (Orig.). 1994. pap. 8.00 (0-9641350-0-0) Blue Spiral.

Will Henry Stevens 1881-1949: An Eye Transformed, a Hand Transforming. Estill C. Pennington. LC 93-22164. 1993. 10.95 (0-9618270-7-6) Morris Comms.

Will Henry's West. Dale L. Walker. LC 83-51163. (Illus.). 240p. 1984. 10.00 (0-87404-077-9) Tex Western.

Will Herberg: A Bio-Bibliography. Harry J. Ausmus. LC 85-21955. (Bio-Bibliographies in Law & Political Science Ser.: No. 2). 120p. 1986. text ed. 47.95 (0-313-25067-7, AWH/, Greenwood Pr) Greenwood.

Will Herberg: From Right to Right. Harry J. Ausmus. LC 86-19357. (Studies in Religion). xx, 276p. 1987. 39.95 (0-8078-1724-4) U of NC Pr.

Will Hinds: Artist of the Deep South. Norton, R. W., Art Gallery Staff. LC 79-187911. (Contemporary Realists Ser.). (Illus.). 1972. pap. 2.00 (0-9600182-6-3) Norton Art.

Will I Be Next? Bea Gorman's Life Story - The Terror of Living with Familial Alzheimer's Disease. Lois Bristow. 260p. (Orig.). 1995. pap. 12.00 (0-9648885-0-5) HopeWarren Pr.

Will I Be the Hero of My Own Life? Swami Chetanananda. Ed. by Linda L. Barnes. 250p. 1995. pap. 14.95 (0-915801-38-8) Rudra Pr.

Will I Ever Be Older? Eva Grant. LC 80-24782. (Life & Living from a Child's Point of View Ser.). (Illus.). (J). (gr. k-6). 1981. lib. bdg. 21.40 (0-8172-1363-5) Raintree Steck-V.

Will I Ever Be Older? Eva Grant. (Life & Living from a Child's Point of View Ser.). (J). (ps-3). 1993. pap. 4.95 (0-8114-5206-9) Raintree Steck-V.

Will I Get Breast Cancer? Questions & Answers for Teenage Girls. Carole G. Vogel. LC 94-21979. (Illus.). 128p. (YA). 1995. lib. bdg. 14.95 (0-671-88046-2, Julian Messner) Silver Burdett Pr.

Will I Get Breast Cancer? Questions & Answers for Teenage Girls. Carole G. Vogel. LC 94-21979. (Illus.). 128p. (YA). (gr. 6 up). 1995. pap. 7.95 (0-671-88047-0, Julian Messner) Silver Burdett Pr.

Will I Have a Friend? Miriam Cohen. LC 67-10127. (Illus.). 32p. (J). (ps-1). 1967. lib. bdg. 15.00 (0-02-722790-1, Mac Bks Young Read) S&S Childrens.

Will I Have a Friend? 2nd ed. Miriam Cohen. LC 89-31340. (Illus.). 32p. (J). (ps-1). 1989. reprint ed. pap. 3.95 (0-689-71333-9, Aladdin Paperbacks) S&S Childrens.

Will I Live Another Day Before I Die? Thoughts on Suicide & Life. Ed. by Gallagher. LC 88-72230. (Reflections of Art Ser.). 95p. 1989. pap. 8.95 (0-930194-44-6) Ctr Thanatology.

Will I Still Have to Make My Bed in the Morning? Barry Rudner. (Illus.). 30p. (Orig.). (J). (gr. k-6). 1992. pap. 5.95 (0-925928-10-0) Tiny Thought.

Will, Imagination, & Reason. Claes G. Ryn. LC 86-6588. 392p. (Orig.). 1986. 15.00 (0-89526-579-6); pap. 7.95 (0-89526-807-8) Regnery Pub.

Will, Imagination, & Reason: Babbitt, Croce, & the Problem of Reality. Claes G. Ryn. LC 96-38939. 240p. (Orig.). 1996. pap. text ed. 19.95 (1-56000-918-7) Transaction Pubs.

Will Inflation Destroy America? Arthur Milton. 1977. 7.95 (0-8065-0608-3, Citadel Pr) Carol Pub Group.

Will Insley: The Opaque Civilization. Guggenheim, Solomon R., Foundation Staff. (Illus.). 88p. (Orig.). 1984. pap. 12.00 (0-89207-047-1) S R Guggenheim.

Will Is Not Enough: A Helpful Guide for Your Family. Paul A. Melchert & John Roebke. (Illus.). 24p. (Orig.). 1993. write for info. (0-9638509-0-3) Waconia Pubng.

Will It Ever Be My Birthday? Dorothy Corey. Ed. by Ann Fay. LC 86-1565. (Illus.). 32p. (J). (ps-3). 1986. lib. bdg. 14.95 (0-8075-9106-8) A Whitman.

***Will It Ever Close?** Mari Mahoney et al. 200p. (Orig.). 1995. pap. 6.95 (0-9649346-0-4) BWB Ent.

Will It Liberate? Questions about Liberation Theology. Michael Novak. 330p. (C). 1991. reprint ed. pap. 17.95 (0-8191-8060-2) Madison Bks UPA.

Will It Make a Theatre? Find, Renovate, & Finance the Non-Traditional Performance Space. rev. ed. Eldon Elder. LC 92-36871. (Illus.). 284p. (Orig.). (C). 1993. pap. 26.95 (1-879903-02-4, ACA Bks) Am Council Arts.

Will James: The Last Cowboy Legend. Anthony Amaral. LC 92-30235. (Vintage West Ser.). (Illus.). 192p. (C). 1992. reprint ed. pap. 11.95 (0-87417-190-3) U of Nev Pr.

Will Kit. John Ventura. 224p. 1996. pap. 17.95 (0-7931-1684-8, 56802701) Dearborn Finan.

Will Kit, Do It Yourself: Valid in All 50 States. Timothy J. Smith. 1991. 9.95 (0-9625456-0-0) SJT Enterprises.

Will Lithuania Comstock Please Come to the Courtesy Phone? Marcia Savin. LC 93-28441. (Illus.). 160p. (J). (gr. 5-9). 1996. pap. 13.95 (0-8167-3324-4) BrdgeWater.

Will Man Fly? And Other Strange & Wonderful Predictions from the 1890's. Compiled by Dave Walter. 128p. 1993. pap. 2.95 (1-56037-027-0) Am Wrld Geog.

***Will Melvin's Last Roundup of Special Poems.** Will Melvin. (Orig.). 1996. pap. write for info. (1-57553-391-X) Watermrk Pr.

Will Men Be Like Gods: Humanitarianism or Human Happiness? Owen F. Dudley. 83p. 1979. 2.49 (0-8199-0766-9, Frncscn Herld) Franciscan Pr.

***Will Mentor: Food & Ornament.** Deborah Leveton & I. Michael Danoff. (Illus.). 55p. 1996. pap. 12.00 (1-879003-14-7) Edmundson.

Will My Child Grow Up Okay? Thomas Wright. 176p. (Orig.). 1995. mass mkt. 4.99 (0-425-14948-X) Berkley Pub.

Will My Children Go to Heaven? Hope & Help for Believing Parents. Edward N. Gross. 184p. (Orig.). 1995. pap. 8.99 (0-87552-246-7, Pub. by Evangelical Pr) Presby & Reformed.

***Will My Doggie Go to Heaven.** Austin Ridenour. 50p. (Orig.). (J). 1996. pap. 3.25 (1-57502-293-1, P1004) Morris Pubng.

***Will My Name Be Shouted Out.** O'Connor. 1997. pap. 14.00 (0-684-83210-0, Touchstone Bks) S&S Trade.

Will My Name Be Shouted Out? Reaching Inner City Students Through the Power of Writing. Stephen O'Conner. 382p. 1996. 23.50 (0-684-81186-3) S&S Trade.

Will O' the Mill & Markheim. Robert Louis Stevenson. 1991. lib. bdg. 69.00 (0-8490-4209-7) Gordon Pr.

Will-O'-the Wisp: Mr. Bowen's Days along the Ashley. Thelma Gillam. 70p. (Orig.). 1995. pap. write for info. (1-57502-054-8) Morris Pubng.

Will of a Nation: Awakening the Canadian Spirit. George Radwanski & Julia Luttrell. 208p. 1992. 22.95 (0-7737-2637-3) Genl Dist Srvs.

Will of God. Betty Miller. (Overcoming Life Ser.). 50p. 1994. pap. 5.00 (1-57149-004-3) Christ Unltd.

Will of God. Paul J. Walkowski. 300p. 1988. 19.95 (0-8283-1917-0) Branden Pub Co.

Will of God. Leslie D. Weatherhead. (C). 1990. pap. text ed. 24.00 (0-85305-278-6, Pub. by J Arthur Ltd UK) St Mut.

Will of God. large type ed. Leslie D. Weatherhead. 1986. pap. 6.95 (0-8027-2537-6) Walker & Co.

Will of God. Leslie D. Weatherhead. (Festival Bks.). 1987. reprint ed. pap. 3.95 (0-687-45601-0) Abingdon.

Will of God & the Cross: John Calvin & the Doctrine of Limited Redemption. Jonathan H. Rainbow. LC 90-30695. (Princeton Theological Monographs: No. 22). 217p. (Orig.). 1990. pap. 24.00 (1-55635-005-8) Pickwick.

***Will of God Is Increase of His Kingdom on Earth.** Ron Gartner. 80p. (Orig.). 1997. pap. 6.95 (0-944551-21-1, SunDance Press) Rainbow Tree Pubns.

Will of God Workbook. Betty Miller. (Overcoming Life Ser.). 1995. pap. 10.00 (1-57149-005-1) Christ Unltd.

***Will of Her Own: Sarah Towles Reed & the Pursuit of Democracy in Southern Public Education.** Leslie G. Parr. 248p. 1998. text ed. 40.00 (0-8203-1932-5) U of Ga Pr.

Will of Iron: A Champion's Journey; a Strategy for Fitness. Peter Nielsen. LC 92-27532. (Illus.). 227p. (Orig.). 1992. pap. 14.95 (1-879094-19-3) Momentum Bks.

Will of the People: A Program for Revitalizing America's Economic, Social & Political Systems. Donald R. Totten & D. Ray Stapleton. LC 93-73228. 141p. 1993. pap. write for info. (0-9638598-0-3) GLO Pubng.

Will of the People: Original Democracy in Non-Western Societies. Raul S. Manglapus. LC 86-29594. (Studies in Freedom: No. 4). 200p. 1987. text ed. 49.95 (0-313-25837-6, MWG/, Greenwood Pr) Greenwood.

Will of the Tribe. Arthur Upfield. 20.95 (0-8488-1213-1) Amereon Ltd.

Will of the Wanderer, Bk. 1. Margaret Weis & Tracy Hickman. (Illus.). 384p. 1989. mass mkt. 6.50 (0-553-27638-7, Spectra) Bantam.

Will Our President Die in Office? Gordon Lindsay. 1962. per. 2.25 (0-89985-984-4) Christ for the Nations.

Will Our Tears Never Dry? Japanese Outcastes. John R. Terry. 200p. 1988. pap. 9.95 (0-933704-72-0) Dawn Pr.

Will (Playscript) James M. Barrie. LC 93-17547. 1993. pap. 5.00 (0-88734-329-5) Players Pr.

Will Pop Eat Itself? Pop Music in the Soundbite Era. Jeremy J. Beadle. 288p. 1993. pap. 12.95 (0-571-16241-X) Faber & Faber.

***Will Power: A Biography of Will Smith.** Jan Berenson. (J). 1997. mass mkt. 3.99 (0-671-88784-X, Archway) PB.

Will Power: Essays on Shakespearean Authority. Richard Wilson. 302p. 1993. pap. 16.95 (0-8143-2492-4); text ed. 45.00 (0-8143-2491-6) Wayne St U Pr.

Will-Power: New Works by Papo Colo, Jimmie Durham, David Hammons, Hachivi Edgar Heap of Bird. 1994. pap. 24.50 (1-881390-03-9) OSU Wexner Ctr.

Will Power: Using Shakespeare's Insights to Transform Your Life. George Weinberg. LC 96-8517. 256p. 1996. 22.95 (0-312-14764-3) St Martin.

Will Power & Its Development. 1.00 (0-614-17326-4) Vedanta Pr.

Will Precedents & Inheritance Tax. 4th ed. David T. Davies. 320p. 1991. boxed 94.00 (0-406-11783-7, UK) MICHIE.

Will Requirements of Various States. George G. Coughlin. 40p. 1984. write for info. (0-318-59084-0) Am Coll Trust & Est.

Will Rogers. Betty Rogers. LC 79-4743. (Illus.). 312p. 1982. pap. 15.95 (0-8061-1600-5) U of Okla Pr.

Will Rogers. Jane A. Schott. LC 95-43434. (Illus.). (J). (gr. k-3). 1996. 13.13 (0-87614-983-2, Carolrhoda) Lerner Group.

Will Rogers. Jane A. Schott. 1996. pap. text ed. 5.95 (1-57505-030-7, Carolrhoda) Lerner Group.

Will Rogers: A Bio-Bibliography. Peter C. Rollins. LC 83-10696. (Popular Culture Bio-Bibliographies Ser.). xiii, 282p. 1984. text ed. 42.95 (0-313-22633-4, RWR/, Greenwood Pr) Greenwood.

Will Rogers: A Biography. Ben Yagoda. LC 94-6021. 432p. 1994. pap. 16.00 (0-06-258555-X) HarpC West.

Will Rogers: Ambassador of Good Will. P. J. O'Brien. 1976. 23.95 (0-8488-1114-3) Amereon Ltd.

Will Rogers: An American Life. Ben Yagoda. LC 92-40177. 1993. 27.50 (0-394-58512-7) Knopf.

Will Rogers: An Appreciation. David R. Milsten. 1976. lib. bdg. 59.95 (0-8490-2826-4) Gordon Pr.

Will Rogers: Courtship & Correspondence 1900-1915. Ed. by Reba Collins. (Illus.). 224p. 1992. 24.95 (0-9632882-0-2) Neigh & Quaid.

Will Rogers: Cowboy Philosopher. Mary Malone. LC 95-32149. (People to Know Ser.). (Illus.). 128p. (YA). (gr. 6 up). 1996. lib. bdg. 18.95 (0-89490-695-X) Enslow Pubs.

Will Rogers: Quotable Cowboy. Cathereen L. Bennett. LC 95-10259. (Illus.). 96p. (J). (gr. 4-6). 1995. lib. bdg. 18.95 (0-8225-3155-0, Runestone Pr) Lerner Group.

Will Rogers: Reflections & Observations. Ed. by Frances N. Sterling. (Illus.). 288p. 1993. pap. 10.00 (0-517-88021-0, C P Pubs) Crown Pub Group.

Will Rogers: Reflections & Observations. large type ed. Ed. by Frances N. Sterling. LC 93-15496. 1993. lib. bdg. 20.95 (1-56054-751-0) Thorndike Pr.

Will Rogers, a Boy's Life: An Indian Territory Childhood. rev. ed. Harold Keith. LC 91-62354. 271p. (J). (gr. 3 up). 1992. reprint ed. 17.00 (0-927562-08-1); reprint ed. pap. 11.00 (0-927562-09-X) Levite Apache.

Will Rogers at the Ziegfeld Follies. Will Rogers. Ed. by Arthur F. Wertheim. LC 92-54137. (Illus.). 288p. 1992. 24.95 (0-8061-2357-5) U of Okla Pr.

Will Rogers Book. Paula M. Love. 1972. 11.95 (0-87244-030-3) Texian.

Will Rogers: Cherokee Entertainer see North American Indians of Achievement

Will Rogers: Cherokee Entertainer see North Americans Indians of Achievement

Will Rogers' Daily Telegrams: The Hoover Years, 1929-1931, Vol. 2. Will Rogers. Ed. by James M. Smallwood & Steven K. Gragert. LC 78-70066. (Writings of Will Rogers Ser.: Ser. III, Vol. 2). (Illus.). 390p. 1978. 18.00 (0-914956-11-6) Okla State Univ Pr.

Will Rogers' Daily Telegrams: The Hoover Years, 1931-1933, Vol. 3. Will Rogers. Ed. by James M. Smallwood & Steven K. Gragert. LC 78-78290. (Writings of Will Rogers Ser.: Ser. III, Vol. 3). (Illus.). 389p. 1979. 18.00 (0-914956-12-4) Okla State Univ Pr.

Will Rogers' Daily Telegrams: The Roosevelt Years, 1933-1935, Vol. 4. Will Rogers. Ed. by James M. Smallwood & Steven K. Gragert. LC 77-91791. (Writings of Will Rogers Ser.: Ser. III, Vol. 4). (Illus.). 457p. 1979. 18.00 (0-914956-13-2) Okla State Univ Pr.

Will Rogers Follies. 1993. pap. 16.95 (1-57007-010-5, XW1631) Astor Bks.

Will Rogers Follies: Vocal Selections. Ed. by Sy Feldman. 80p. (Orig.). 1994. pap. 17.95 (0-89724-179-7, VF1755) Warner Brothers.

***Will Rogers Memorial Birthplace: Souvenir Pictorial Guidebook.** (Orig.). Date not set. pap. text ed. write for info. (1-56944-116-2) Terrell Missouri.

Will Rogers Says. Ed. by Reba Collins. (Illus.). 86p. 1993. 11.95 (0-9632882-1-0) Neigh & Quaid.

Will Rogers Speaks: Over 1000 Timeless Quotations for Public Speakers (& Writers... Bryan B. Sterling & Frances N. Sterling. (Illus.). 336p. 1995. 18.95 (0-87131-771-0) M Evans.

Will Rogers Speaks: Over 1000 Timeless Quotations for Public Speakers (& Writers... Bryan B. Sterling & Frances N. Sterling. LC 95-46300. (Illus.). 336p. 1995. pap. 12.95 (0-87131-795-8) M Evans.

Will Rogers Treasury. 1986. 6.98 (0-685-16815-8, 62544X) Random Hse Value.

Will Rogers Treasury: Reflections & Observations. Will Rogers. 1987. 7.99 (0-517-62544-X) Random Hse Value.

Will Rogers' Weekly Articles: The Coolidge Years, 1925-1927, Vol. 2. Will Rogers. Ed. by James M. Smallwood & Steven K. Gragert. LC 79-57650. (Writings of Will Rogers Ser.: Ser. IV, Vol. 2). (Illus.). 368p. 1980. 18.00 (0-914956-16-7) Okla State Univ Pr.

Will Rogers' Weekly Articles: The Coolidge Years, 1927-1929, Vol. 3. Will Rogers. Ed. by James M. Smallwood & Steven K. Gragert. LC 79-57650. (Writings of Will Rogers Ser.: Ser. IV, Vol. 3). (Illus.). 304p. 1981. 18.00 (0-914956-17-5) Okla State Univ Pr.

Will Rogers' Weekly Articles: The Harding-Coolidge Years, 1922-1925, Vol. 1. Will Rogers. Ed. by James M. Smallwood & Steven K. Gragert. LC 79-57650. (Writings of Will Rogers Ser.: Ser. IV, Vol. 1). (Illus.). 431p. 1980. 18.00 (0-914956-15-9) Okla State Univ Pr.

Will Rogers' Weekly Articles: The Hoover Years: 1929-1931, Vol. 4. Will Rogers. Ed. by Steven K. Gragert. LC 79-57650. (Writings of Will Rogers Ser.: Ser. IV, Vol. 4). (Illus.). 278p. 1981. 18.00 (0-914956-18-3) Okla State Univ Pr.

Will Roger's Weekly Articles: The Hoover Years 1931-1933, Vol. 5. Will Rogers. Ed. by Steven K. Gragert. LC 79-57650. (Writings of Will Rogers Ser.: Ser. IV, Vol. 5). (Illus.). 280p. 1982. 18.00 (0-914956-19-1) Okla State Univ Pr.

Will Rogers' Weekly Articles: The Roosevelt Years: 1933-1935, Vol. 6. Will Rogers. Ed. by Steven K. Gragert. LC 79-57650. (Writings of Will Rogers Ser.: Ser. IV, Vol. 6). (Illus.). 309p. 1982. 18.00 (0-914956-21-3) Okla State Univ Pr.

Will Rogers' World: America's Foremost Political Humorist Comments on the '20s & '30s - & '80s & '90s. Bryan B. Sterling & Frances N. Sterling. LC 89-1129. (Illus.). 270p. 1989. 17.95 (0-87131-564-5) M Evans.

Will Rogers' World: America's Foremost Political Humorist Comments on the '20s & '30s - & '80s & '90s. Bryan B. Sterling & Frances N. Sterling. (Illus.). 270p. 1993. pap. 9.95 (0-87131-735-4) M Evans.

Will Roosevelt Succeed? A Study of Fascist Tendencies in America. Archibald F. Brockway. LC 75-180392. reprint ed. 37.50 (0-404-56108-X) AMS Pr.

Will Santa Come? Jan Wahl. 49p. (J). 1993. lib. bdg. 9.95 (0-940696-38-X) Monroe County Lib.

***Will Santa Ever Ride Again?** Sally Bowman. (Illus.). 7p. 1997. pap. 2.50 (0-88680-440-X) I E Clark.

Will Shakespeare: A Factotum & Agent. Alden Brooks. LC 77-39536. reprint ed. 41.50 (0-404-01117-9) AMS Pr.

Will Shakespeare Save Us! Will Shakespeare Save the King! Paul Nimmo. LC 96-28290. 58p. (Orig.). (J). (gr. k-8). 1996. pap. 12.00 (0-88734-658-8) Players Pr.

Will She Understand? New Short Stories. Fielding Dawson. LC 88-2450. (Illus.). 158p. (Orig.). 1988. 20.00 (0-87685-730-6); pap. 10.00 (0-87685-729-2) Black Sparrow.

Will She Understand? New Short Stories, signed ed. deluxe ed. Fielding Dawson. LC 88-2450. (Illus.). 158p. (Orig.). 1988. 30.00 (0-87685-731-4) Black Sparrow.

***Will Shortz's Tournament Crosswords, Vol. 1.** Will Shortz. 1997. pap. 11.00 (0-8129-2934-9, Times Bks) Random.

***Will Smith: Prince of Hollywood.** Frank Sanello. 1997. mass mkt. 5.99 (1-57297-288-2) Blvd Books.

Will Somebody Hold This Thing a Minute? Statue of Liberty Silly Trivia Book. Carole Marsh. (Quantum Leap Ser.). (Illus.). 60p. (Orig.). (J). (gr. 3-12). 1994. 29.95 (1-55609-192-3); pap. 19.95 (0-935326-75-8) Gallopade Pub Group.

Will Spring Be Early or Will Spring Be Late? Crockett Johnson. LC 59-9424. (Trophy Picture Bk.). (Illus.). 48p. (J). (gr. k-3). 1990. pap. 3.95 (0-06-443224-6, Trophy) HarpC Child Bks.

Will Spring Ever Come to Gobbler's Knob? A Punxsutawney Phil Adventure Story. Julia S. Moutran. (Illus.). 64p. (J). (ps-5). 1992. audio 10.95 (0-685-48131-X) Lit Pubns.

Will Spring Ever Come to Gobbler's Knob? A Punxsutawney Phil Adventure Story, Incl. Phil's Field Guide to Woodland Animals. Julia S. Moutran. (Illus.). 64p. (J). (ps-5). 1992. pap. 9.95 (0-9617819-4-7) Lit Pubns.

Will Spring Ever Come to Gobbler's Knob? A Punxsutawney Phil Adventure Story, Incl. Phil's Field to Woodland Animals. Julia S. Moutran. (Illus.). 64p. (J). (ps-5). 1992. Incl. Phil's Field Guide to Woodland Animals. 15.95 (0-9617819-5-5) Lit Pubns.

Will Steger. Bob Italia. Ed. by Rosemary Walner. LC 90-82624. (Explorers of the Past & Present Ser.). (Illus.). 32p. (J). (gr. 4). 1990. lib. bdg. 11.96 (0-939179-97-0) Abdo & Dghtrs.

***Will Teach for Food: Academic Labor in Crisis.** Ed. by Cary Nelson. LC 96-51992. (Cultural Politics Ser.: Vol. 12). (Illus.). 248p. (C). 1997. pap. text ed. 19.95 (0-8166-3034-8) U of Minn Pr.

***Will Teach for Food: Academic Labor in Crisis.** Ed. by Cary Nelson. LC 96-51992. (Cultural Politics Ser.: Vol. 12). (Illus.). 248p. (C). 1997. text ed. 49.95 (0-8166-3033-X) U of Minn Pr.

Will the Antichrist Come Out of Russia? Gordon Lindsay. 1966. 1.95 (0-89985-066-9) Christ for the Nations.

***Will the Bolsheviks Maintain Power?** Lenin. 128p. 1997. 6.95 (0-7509-1677-X, Pub. by Sutton Pubng UK) Bks Intl VA.

Will the Chain Break? Differential Pricing As Part of a New Pricing Structure for Research Literature & Its Consequences for the Future of Scholarly Communication. Ed. by Ulrich Montag. (IFLA Publication Ser.: Vol. 61). 95p. 1992. lib. bdg. 45.00 (3-598-21789-7) K G Saur.

***Will the Cycle Be Unbroken? - Churches of Christ Face the 21st Century.** Douglas A. Foster. 1994. pap. 10.95 (0-89112-158-7) Abilene Christ U.

Will the Dollars Stretch? Teen Parents Living on Their Own: Virtual Reality Through Stories & Check-Writing Practice. Sudie Pollock. Ed. by Jeanne W. Lindsay. (Illus.). 96p. (Orig.). (YA). (gr. 7-12). 1996. pap. text ed. 6.95 (1-885356-12-9, 56129) Morning Glory.

Will the East Wind Blow? Hansi Reports on the Middle East. Maria A. Hirschmann. LC 78-71319. (Illus.). 160p. (Orig.). 1979. pap. text ed. 2.50 (0-932878-04-0, HB-04) Hansi.

Will the Elves Come Tonight? Ed. by Eli A. Cantillon. (Illus.). 12p. (J). (ps). 1993. 12.95 (1-881445-21-6) Sandvik Pub.

Will the Faculty Please Come to Order. John E. Longhurst. 68p. 1969. pap. 5.00 (0-87291-003-2) Coronado Pr.

Will the Jewish People Survive? Susser. 1997. 22.50 (0-02-874092-0) Free Pr.

Will the Jewish People Survive? Susser. 1998. 22.50 (0-684-82749-2) Free Pr.

Will the Last Person to Leave the Planet... Mike Resnick. 368p. 1994. pap. 12.95 (0-312-89010-9) Orb NYC.

W

Will the New Budget Package Create a Recession? Gary Robbins & Aldona Robbins. 1990. pap. 5.00 (0-943802-87-3, BG108) Natl Ctr Pol.

Will the Non-Russians Rebel? State, Ethnicity, & Stability in the U. S. S. R. Alexander J. Motyl. LC 86-24386. (Cornell Studies in Soviet History & Science). 224p. (C). 1987. 32.50 (0-8014-1947-6) Cornell U Pr.

Will the Real Albert Ellis Please Stand Up: Anecdotes by His Colleagues, Students & Friends in Honor of His 75th Birthday. Ed. by Dominic Dimattia & Leonor Lega. (Illus.). 144p. (Orig.). 1990. pap. 5.00 (0-917476-19-0) A Ellis Institute.

Will the REAL American Author Please Stand Up? Gail S. Hennessey. 51p. (J). (gr. 5-9). 1994. 12.95 (1-877673-24-2, AA) Cottonwood Pr.

Will the Real American Company Please Stand Up: Brother's Antidumping Counterattack on Smith Corona. Michael Ryan et al. (Pew Case Studies in International Affairs). 50p. (C). 1995. pap. text ed. 3.50 (1-56927-717-6, GU Schl Foreign) Geo U Inst Dplmcy.

Will the Real Becka Morgan Please Stand Up? Marilyn Kaye. (Three of a Kind Ser.: No. 3). 144p. (J). (gr. 4-7). 1994. mass mkt. 3.50 (0-06-106041-0, PL) HarpC.

Will the Real God Please Stand up. Carolyn Thomas. 96p. 1991. pap. 4.95 (0-8091-3208-7) Paulist Pr.

Will the Real Guru Please Stand up? Mariel Strauss. LC 78-61589. 1980. 7.95 (0-87212-111-9) Libra.

Will the Real Heretics Please Stand Up: A New Look at Today's Evangelical Church in the Light of Early Christianity. David W. Bercot. 192p. (Orig.). 1989. pap. 7.95 (0-924722-00-2) Scroll Pub.

Will the Real Jesus Christ Please Stand Up? Malcolm Marmorstein. 1965. pap. 3.25 (0-8222-1259-5) Dramatists Play.

Will the Real Jesus Please Stand? Keith A. Fournier. 22p. 1988. pap. 1.95 (0-940535-17-3, UP 115) Franciscan U Pr.

Will the Real Jesus Please Stand Up? John Blanchard. 1989. pap. 7.99 (0-85234-258-6, Pub. by Evangelical Pr) Presby & Reformed.

Will the Real Me Please Stand Up! Lee Ezell. 1995. 10.99 (0-7852-8220-3) Nelson.

Will the Real Me Please Stand Up? Elizabeth Van Steenwyk. 160p. (J). (gr. 5-8). 1994. pap. 2.99 (0-87406-667-0) Willowisp Pr.

Will the Real Me Please Stand Up? Twenty-Five Guidelines for Good Communication. Powell. 1990. pap. text ed. 9.95 (0-88347-316-X) Res Christian Liv.

Will the Real Men... Please Stand Up! Ella M. Patterson. Ed. by Sejon Alle. (Illus.). 400p. Date not set. write for info. (0-614-08485-7) Knowledge Concepts.

Will the Real Men Please Stand Up. Ella M. Patterson. (Illus.). 400p. 19.95 (1-884331-11-4) Knowledge Concepts.

Will the Real Men...Please Stand Up! Ella M. Patterson. Ed. by Sejon Alle. (Illus.). 400p. write for info. (0-614-08493-8) Knowledge Concepts.

Will the REAL Notable Woman Please Stand Up? Gail S. Hennessey. 52p. (J). (gr. 5-9). 1994. 12.95 (1-877673-23-4, NW) Cottonwood Pr.

Will the Real Teacher Please Stand Up? Teaching Stories in More Effective Education. R. Hawk Starkey. LC 93-80684. (Illus.). 144p. (Orig.). 1994. pap. 12.95 (0-9639447-4-6) Inreach Pubng.

Will the Real Women Please Stand Up. Ella M. Patterson. Ed. by Lucille Ennix & Marvin Whaley. LC 94-75061. (Illus.). 280p. (Orig.). (C). 1994. 14.95 (1-884331-01-7) Knowledge Concepts.

***Will the Real Women... Please Stand Up! Uncommon Sense about Sex, Sensuality & Self-Discovery.** Ella Patterson. 1997. pap. 12.00 (0-684-83151-1, Fireside) S&S Trade.

Will the Real Women...Please Stand Up! Ella M. Patterson. 240p. 1996. 21.00 (0-684-83018-3, S&S) S&S Trade.

Will the World Break Your Heart? Dimensions & Consequences of Irish-American Assimilation. John D. Ibson. LC 90-3671. (European Immigrants & American Society Ser.). 280p. 1990. reprint ed. text ed. 20.00 (0-8240-0252-0) Garland.

Will There Be a Lap for Me? Dorothy Corey. Ed. by Abby Levine. LC 91-20324. (Illus.). 24p. (J). (ps-1). 1992. pap. 4.95 (0-8075-9110-6); lib. bdg. 12.95 (0-8075-9109-2) A Whitman.

Will There Be Polar Bears for Christmas? Julia Jarman. LC 94-5143. (Illus.). 32p. (J). 1994. 13.95 (0-307-17515-4) Western Pub.

Will They Ever Finish Bruckner Boulevard. Ada L. Huxtable. (C). 1988. pap. 14.00 (0-520-06205-1) U CA Pr.

Will to Arise: Women, Tradition & the Church in Africa. Ed. by Mercy A. Oduyoye & Musimbi R. Kanyoro. LC 91-45847. 1992. 17.00 (0-88344-782-7) Orbis Bks.

Will to Be Well. Charles B. Patterson. 255p. 1997. pap. 20.00 (0-89540-275-0, SB-275) Sun Pub.

Will to Be Well: The Real Alternative Medicine. Neville Hodgkinson. LC 85-26472. 196p. 1986. pap. 9.95 (0-87728-659-0) Weiser.

Will to Believe. William James. LC 78-5315. (Works of William James). 528p. 1979. 39.95 (0-674-95281-2) HUP.

Will to Believe: And Other Writings from William James. William James. 160p. 1995. pap. 6.00 (0-385-48046-6, Image Bks) Doubleday.

Will to Believe & Human Immortality. William James. pap. 7.95 (0-486-20291-7) Dover.

Will to Believe, & Other Essays in Popular Philosophy. William James. (Notable American Authors Ser.). 1992. reprint ed. lib. bdg. 75.00 (0-7812-3474-3) Rprt Serv.

Will to Believe & Other Essays in Popular Philosophy & Human Immortality. William James. 1990. 21.75 (0-8446-2313-X) Peter Smith.

Will to Bondage (Discours de la Servitude Volontaire) Etienne de la Boetie. LC 74-27714. (Libertarian Broadsides Ser.: No. 6). (Illus.). (ENG & FRE.). 1974. pap. 3.25 (0-87926-018-1) R Myles.

Will to Change: Options for Achieving Success Throughout Life. J. T. Sullivan. 144p. 1996. pap. text ed. 9.95 (1-898823-25-1, Pub. by Global Bks UK) Talman.

Will to Change: Poems. Adrienne Rich. LC 78-146842. 1971. pap. 7.95 (0-393-04361-4) Norton.

Will to Civilization: An Inquiry into the Principles of Historic Change. John Katz. LC 74-25761. (European Sociology Ser.). 358p. 1975. reprint ed. 29.95 (0-405-06515-9) Ayer.

Will to Go On. Bernard Brodsky. 64p. (Orig.). 1981. pap. 6.95 (0-931896-01-0) Cove View.

Will to Kill. large type ed. John Penn. (Mystery Ser.). 272p. 1988. 25.99 (0-7089-1764-X) Ulverscroft.

Will to Lead: Managing with Courage & Conviction in the Age of Uncertainty. Neil H. Snyder. LC 96-43763. 240p. 1996. text ed. 24.95 (0-7863-1014-6) Irwin Prof Pubng.

***Will to Lead: Running a Business with a Network of Leaders.** Marvin Bower. LC 96-45357. 208p. 1997. 27.95 (0-87584-758-7) Harvard Busn.

***Will to Lead: Running a Business with a Network of Leaders.** Harvard Business School Press Staff. 1997. text ed. 27.95 (0-07-103866-3) McGraw.

***Will to Live.** Jane Cowles. Date not set. write for info. (0-688-03203-6) Morrow.

Will to Live: One Family's Story of Surviving the Holocaust. Adam Starkopf. LC 95-33065. 242p. (C). 1995. pap. 14.95 (0-7914-2620-3) State U NY Pr.

Will to Live: One Family's Story of Surviving the Holocaust. Adam Starkopf. LC 95-33065. 242p. (C). 1995. text ed. 44.50 (0-7914-2619-X) State U NY Pr.

Will to Live: The Battle of a Young Boy Against Muscular Dystrophy. A. J. Mills. 100p. 1992. pap. 7.95 (0-9633921-0-7) Humor Bks.

Will to Live: 2 Brothers in Auschwitz. Leon Arditti. (Illus.). 111p. 1996. 18.95 (0-88400-286-1) Shengold.

Will to Meaning. Viktor E. Frank. 1988. pap. 12.95 (0-452-01034-9, Mer) NAL-Dutton.

Will to Meaning. Viktor E. Frankl. 204p. 1988. pap. 7.95 (0-452-00946-4, Z5472, Plume) NAL-Dutton.

Will to Murder. Walter Sorrells. 304p. (Orig.). 1996. mass mkt. 5.50 (0-380-78020-8) Avon.

***Will to Orthodoxy: A Critical Genealogy of Northern Chan Buddhism.** Bernard Faure. LC 97-9658. 1997. write for info. (0-8047-2865-8); pap. write for info. (0-8047-2866-6) Stanford U Pr.

Will to Power. Friedrich Wilhelm Nietzsche. 1976. 72.95 (0-8488-1112-7) Amereon Ltd.

Will to Power. Friedrich Wilhelm Nietzsche. Tr. by Walter Kaufmann. 1969. pap. 15.00 (0-394-70437-1, Vin) Random.

Will to Power, 2 vols., Set. Friedrich Wilhelm Nietzsche. 1974. lib. bdg. 600.00 (0-87968-209-4) Gordon Pr.

Will to Resist. J. J. Schreurs. LC 88-50689. (Illus.). 144p. 1988. pap. 12.50 (0-936029-09-9) Western Bk Journ.

Will to Survive: A Historical Novel. Simon Dolin. 1995. 18.95 (0-533-11502-7) Vantage.

Will to Survive: A Private's View As a P.O.W. Douglas McLaggan. (Illus.). 240p. (Orig.). 1995. pap. 17.95 (0-86417-706-2, Pub. by Kangaroo Pr AT) Seven Hills Bk.

Will to Violence: The Politics of Personal Behavior. Susanne Kappeler. (Athene Ser.). 300p. (C). 1995. text ed. 38.00 (0-8077-6281-4); pap. text ed. 18.95 (0-8077-6280-6) Tchrs Coll.

Will to Win. Wolff. (J). 1997. 14.00 (0-689-31901-0, Atheneum Bks Young) S&S Childrens.

Will to Win: The Biography of Ferdinand Eberstadt. Robert C. Perez & Edward F. Willett. LC 89-1898. (Contributions in Economics & Economic History Ser.: No. 96). 181p. 1989. text ed. 45.00 (0-313-26738-3, PWB, Greenwood Pr) Greenwood.

Will Ungodly Perish. Robert Whitelaw. pap. 1.49 (0-87377-119-2) GAM Pubns.

Will Wai Kula & the Three Mongooses. Carol Jossem & Donivee M. Laird. LC 83-8805. (J). (gr. k-3). 1983. 8.95 (0-940350-24-6) Barnaby Bks.

Will Warburton: A Romance of Real Life. George Gissing. LC 71-98635. reprint ed. 35.00 (0-404-02817-9) AMS Pr.

Will We Be Smart Enough? A Cognitive Analysis of the Coming Workforce. Earl Hunt. (Illus.). 416p. 1995. 42.50 (0-87154-392-3) Russell Sage.

Will We Have Jewish Grandchildren? Jewish Continuity & How to Achieve It. Jonathan Sacks. LC 94-10416. 1994. 12.50 (0-85303-282-3, Pub. by Vallentine Mitchell UK) Intl Spec Bk.

Will We Meet Each Other's Needs? James R. Hine. 1979. pap. text ed. 8.95 (0-8134-2052-0, 2052) Interstate.

Will We Miss Them? Alexandra Wright. LC 91-73359. (Illus.). 32p. (J). (ps-8). 1991. 14.95 (0-88106-489-0); pap. 6.95 (0-88106-488-2); lib. bdg. 15.88 (0-88106-675-3) Charlesbridge Pub.

Will We See Tomorrow? A German Cavalryman at War, 1939-1942. Max Kuhnert. (Illus.). 181p. (C). 1993. 37.50 (0-85052-290-0, Pub. by L Cooper Bks UK) Trans-Atl Phila.

Will Weng Crossword Puzzle Omnibus, Vol. 1. Ed. by Will Weng. 240p. 1985. pap. 11.00 (0-8129-1300-0, Times Bks) Random.

Will Weng Crossword Puzzle Omnibus, Vol. 3. Will Weng. 256p. 1991. pap. 11.00 (0-8129-1935-1, Times Bks) Random.

Will Weng Crossword Puzzle, Vol. 15. Will Weng. 1986. pap. 5.95 (0-8129-1611-5, Times Bks) Random.

Will Weng's Crossword Puzzle Omnibus, Vol. 2. Will Weng. 1987. pap. 12.00 (0-8129-1645-X, Times Bks) Random.

Will Weng's Crossword Puzzles, Vol. 2. Ed. by Will Weng. 1977. pap. 5.95 (0-8129-0720-5, Times Bks) Random.

Will Weng's Crossword Puzzles, Vol. 5. Ed. by Will Weng. 64p. 1979. pap. 5.95 (0-8129-0812-0, Times Bks) Random.

Will Weng's Crossword Puzzles, Vol. 6. Ed. by Will Weng. 64p. 1980. pap. 4.95 (0-8129-0874-0, Times Bks) Random.

Will Weng's Crossword Puzzles, Vol. 8. Ed. by Will Weng. 64p. 1982. pap. 5.95 (0-8129-1002-8, Times Bks) Random.

Will Weng's Crossword Puzzles, Vol. 12. Ed. by Will Weng. 64p. 1984. pap. 5.95 (0-8129-1103-2, Times Bks) Random.

Will Weng's Crossword Puzzles, Vol. 13. Ed. by Will Weng. 64p. 1985. pap. 5.95 (0-8129-1138-5, Times Bks) Random.

Will Weng's Crossword Puzzles, Vol. 15. Ed. by Will Weng. 64p. 1985. pap. 5.95 (0-8129-1137-7, Times Bks) Random.

Will Weng's Crossword Puzzles, Vol. 20. Will Weng. 1989. pap. 7.00 (0-8129-1804-5, Times Bks) Random.

Will Weng's Crossword Puzzles, Vol. 21. Will Weng. 1989. pap. 8.50 (0-8129-1813-4, Times Bks) Random.

Will Weng's Crossword Puzzles: Fifty Original Sunday-Sized Crossword Puzzles, Vol. 7. Will Weng. 64p. (Orig.). 1981. pap. 5.95 (0-8129-0933-X, Times Bks) Random.

Will Weng's Crossword Puzzles, Vol. 17. Will Weng. 1987. pap. 7.50 (0-8129-1644-1, Times Bks) Random.

Will Weng's Literary Crossword Puzzles, Vol. 1. Will Weng. 1990. pap. 8.50 (0-8129-1842-8, Times Bks) Random.

Will Weng's Sports Crosswords. Will Weng. 1990. pap. 6.95 (0-8129-1841-X, Times Bks) Random.

Will West. 2nd ed. Paul Metcalf. 76p. 1973. reprint ed. pap. 10.00 (0-912846-03-8) Bookstore Pr.

Will Windward. Mary Tookey. Ed. by Patricia Schultz. LC 89-14569. (Lewiston Poetry Ser.: Vol. 10). (Illus.). 64p. 1989. lib. bdg. 24.95 (0-88946-899-0) E Mellen.

Will Ye Let the Mummers In? Alden Nowlan. 164p. 1984. 14.95 (0-7720-1451-5); 8.95 (0-7720-1407-8) Genl Dist Srvs.

Will You Always Love Me? Joyce C. Oates. 1997. pap. 12.95 (0-452-27413-3, Plume) NAL-Dutton.

Will You Always Love Me? Joyce Carol Oates. 28p. 100.00 (0-9640454-2-7) J Cahill Pubng.

Will You Always Love Me? And Other Stories. Joyce Carol Oates. LC 94-43865. 326p. 1996. pap. 23.95 (0-525-93972-5, Dutton) NAL-Dutton.

Will You Be Mother? Women Who Choose to Say No. Jane Bartlett. 233p. (C). 1995. 42.50 (0-8147-1244-4); pap. 16.50 (0-8147-1245-2) NYU Pr.

Will You Be My Brussels Sprout? Lucy Frank. LC 95-34385. 160p. (YA). (gr. 7 up). 1996. 15.95 (0-8234-1220-2) Holiday.

Will You Be My Friend? James Kavanaugh. LC 84-48223. 96p. 1985. pap. 6.95 (0-06-250443-6) Harper SF.

Will You Be My Friend? Irmtraut Korth-Sander. 1995. 4.98 (0-8317-5362-5) Smithmark.

***Will You Be the Next Victim? How to Avoid Becoming a Violent Crime Statistic.** Herbert Crawford. LC 97-65059. (Orig.). 1997. pap. 9.95 (0-9656026-4-8) Sucess Ventures.

***Will You Be There Plus 13 Contemporary Movie Themes: Theme from Free Willy.** 76p. (YA). 1993. pap. 10.95 (0-89724-096-0) Warner Brothers.

Will You Come Back for Me? Ann Tompert. Ed. by Kathleen Tucker. LC 87-37258. (Illus.). 32p. (J). (ps). 1988. pap. 5.95 (0-8075-9113-0); lib. bdg. 14.95 (0-8075-9112-2) A Whitman.

Will You Do Me a Favor? Barbara L. McCombs & Linda Brannan. (Skills for Job Success Ser.). (Illus.). 32p. (Orig.). 1990. student ed., pap. 4.95 (1-56119-015-2) Educ Pr MD.

Will You Do Me a Favor? Barbara L. McCombs & Linda Brannan. (Skills for Job Success Ser.). (Illus.). 32p. (Orig.). (YA). (gr. 7-12). 1990. teacher ed. 1.95 (1-56119-016-0); disk 39.95 (1-56119-108-6) Educ Pr MD.

Will You Do Me a Favor?, Set. Barbara L. McCombs & Linda Brannan. (Skills for Job Success Ser.). (Illus.). 32p. (Orig.). (YA). (gr. 7-12). 1990. teacher ed., wbk. ed. 44.95 (1-56119-066-7) Educ Pr MD.

Will You Give Me a Dream? Joan L. Nixon. LC 91-19581. (Illus.). 32p. (J). (ps-1). 1994. lib. bdg. 14.95 (0-02-768211-0, Four Winds Pr) S&S Childrens.

Will You Help Me Save America? John A. Lampe. 116p. Date not set. 12.95 (0-9627376-0-7) J A Lampe.

***Will You Hold Me?** Christopher Kenworthy. 182p. 9700. pap. 13.95 (1-899344-11-X) Dufour.

Will You Hold Me? Devotional Thoughts for Parents. Dan Seaborn. 112p. (Orig.). 1996. pap. 6.95 (0-89827-149-5, BK907) Wesleyan Pub Hse.

Will You Make a Wise Marriage Choice? James R. Hine. 1978. 8.95 (0-8134-2002-4, 2002) Interstate.

Will You Marry Me? The World's Most Romantic Proposals. Cynthia C. Muchnick. 128p. 1995. pap. 6.95 (0-02-861048-2) Macmillan.

***Will You Mind the Baby, Davy?** Brigitte Weninger. LC 96-45383. (Illus.). 32p. (J). (gr. k-3). 1997. 15.95 (1-55858-731-4); lib. bdg. 15.88 (1-55858-732-2) North-South Bks NYC.

Will You Play with Us? Margaret Y. Phinney. LC 95-17747. (Illus.). 8p. (J). (ps-1). 1995. pap. 2.95 (1-57255-036-8) Mondo Pubng.

Will You Please Be Quiet, Please. Raymond Carver. 1992. pap. 11.00 (0-679-73569-0) McKay.

***Will You Sign Here, John Hancock?** Jean Fritz. (Illus.). 48p. (J). (gr. 2-6). 1997. pap. 5.95 (0-698-11440-X, Paperstar) Putnam Pub Group.

Will You Still Love Me? Rick Walton. LC 92-341. (Illus.). 32p. (J). (ps). 1992. 11.95 (0-87579-582-X) Deseret Bk.

Will You Still Need Me, Will You Still Feed Me, When I'm 84? Doris Francis. LC 82-49351. (Illus.). 272p. 1984. 27.50 (0-253-36545-7) Ind U Pr.

***Will You Take Care of Me?** Margaret P. Bridges. (J). Date not set. write for info. (0-688-15194-9, Morrow Junior); lib. bdg. write for info. (0-688-15195-7, Morrow Junior) Morrow.

***Will Your Family Survive the Twenty-First Century.** Nellie Stark. 164p. 1996. pap. 16.00 (0-8059-4031-6) Dorrance.

Willa: The Life of Willa Cather. Phyllis C. Robinson. LC 84-632. (Illus.). 352p. 1984. pap. 8.95 (0-03-071931-3, Owl) H Holt & Co.

Willa Cather. Willa Cather. 1994. 11.99 (0-517-10031-2) Random Hse Value.

Willa Cather. Ed. by Philip L. Gerber. LC 75-2287. (Twayne's United States Authors Ser.). 187p. (C). 1975. pap. text ed. write for info. (0-672-61508-8, Bobbs) Macmillan.

Willa Cather. Ann T. Keene. LC 93-45743. (Classic American Writers Ser.). (J). 1994. lib. bdg. 14.95 (0-671-86760-1, Julian Messner) Silver Burdett Pr.

Willa Cather. Janine Steinbauer. LC 93-10628. (Notebooks Ser.). (YA). (gr. 6 up). 1997. 16.95 (0-88682-622-5) Creative Ed.

Willa Cather. Susie Thomas. 192p. (C). 1989. pap. 16.50 (0-389-20883-3); text ed. 40.00 (0-389-20882-5) B&N Imports.

Willa Cather. deluxe ed. Date not set. write for info. (0-517-20031-7) Random Hse Value.

Willa Cather. rev. ed. Philip Gerber. LC 94-45354. (United States Authors Ser.: No. 258). 1995. 22.95 (0-8057-4035-X, Twayne) Scribnrs Ref.

Willa Cather: A Bibliography. Joan St. Crane. LC 81-23134. 440p. 1982. reprint ed. pap. 125.40 (0-7837-8860-6, 2049570) Bks Demand.

Willa Cather: A Checklist of Her Published Writing. JoAnna Lathrop. LC 74-82561. 132p. reprint ed. pap. 37.70 (0-7837-6031-0, 2045843) Bks Demand.

Willa Cather: A Critical Introduction. David Daiches. LC 71-136061. 193p. 1971. reprint ed. text ed. 35.00 (0-8371-5211-9, DAWC, Greenwood Pr) Greenwood.

Willa Cather: A Literary Life. James Woodress. LC 86-30894. (Illus.). xx, 625p. 1987. pap. text ed. 21.00 (0-8032-9708-4, Bison Books) U of Nebr Pr.

Willa Cather: A Memoir. Elizabeth S. Sergeant. LC 91-13075. 300p. 1992. reprint ed. pap. 16.95 (0-8214-1009-1) Ohio U Pr.

Willa Cather: A Pictorial Memoir. Lucia Woods & Bernice Slote. LC 72-91511. (Illus.). x, 134p. 1973. reprint ed. 35.00 (0-8032-0828-6) U of Nebr Pr.

Willa Cather: A Reference Guide. Marilyn Arnold. (Reference Guides to Literature Ser.). 490p. (C). 1986. 45.00 (0-8161-8654-5, Hall Reference) Macmillan.

Willa Cather: Double Lives. Hermione Lee. LC 91-50018. (Illus.). 432p. 1991. pap. 15.00 (0-679-73649-2, Vin) Random.

***Willa Cather: Great American Short Stories I.** Illus. by James Balkovek. LC 94-75018. (Classic Short Stories Ser.). 80p. 1994. pap. 5.95 (0-7854-0620-4, 40007) Am Guidance.

Willa Cather: Her Life & Art. James L. Woodress. LC 82-7041. 288p. reprint ed. pap. 82.10 (0-8357-7774-X, 2036134) Bks Demand.

Willa Cather: Landscape & Exile. Laura Winters. LC 92-51002. 1994. Alk. paper. 27.50 (0-945636-56-3) Susquehanna U Pr.

Willa Cather: The Emerging Voice. Sharon O'Brien. (Illus.). 576p. 1986. 35.00 (0-19-504132-1) OUP.

***Willa Cather: The Emerging Voice.** Sharon Obrien. 1996. pap. text ed. 17.95 (0-674-95322-3) HUP.

Willa Cather: Three Complete Novels. Willa Cather. 1992. 11.99 (0-517-06493-6) Random Hse Value.

Willa Cather: Writing at the Frontier. Jamie Ambrose. LC 87-29969. (Women's Ser.). 188p. 1989. 24.95 (0-85496-152-6) Berg Pubs.

Willa Cather: Writing at the Frontier. Jamie Ambrose. (Women's Ser.). 188p. 1992. pap. 17.50 (0-85496-668-4) Berg Pubs.

Willa Cather see Notable Biographies

Willa Cather see Modern Critical Views Series

Willa Cather & Classical Myth: The Search for a New Parnassus. Mary R. Ryder. LC 90-34815. (Studies in American Literature: Vol. 11). 312p. 1990. lib. bdg. 99.95 (0-88946-113-9) E Mellen.

Willa Cather & European Cultural Influences. Ed. by Helen M. Dennis. LC 95-43271. (Studies in American Literature: Vol. 16). 1996. write for info. (0-7734-8858-8) E Mellen.

Willa Cather & France: In Search of the Lost Language. Robert J. Nelson. LC 87-24484. 192p. (C). 1988. text ed. 24.95 (0-252-01502-9) U of Ill Pr.

Willa Cather & Six Writers from the Great War. James J. Kirschke. 102p. (C). 1990. pap. text ed. 18.00 (0-8191-7918-3); lib. bdg. 34.50 (0-8191-7917-5) U Pr of Amer.

Willa Cather & the Art of Conflict: Re-visioning Her Creative Imagination. Patrick W. Shaw. LC 91-75024. 200p. 1992. 23.50 (0-87875-423-7) Whitston Pub.

Willa Cather & the Fairy Tale. Marilyn B. Callander. Ed. by A. Walton Litz. LC 88-27775. (Studies in Modern Literature: No. 97). 108p. reprint ed. 30.50 (0-8357-1929-4, 2070702) Bks Demand.

An Asterisk (*) at the beginning of an entry indicates that the title is appearing in BIP for the first time.

Willa Cather & the Myth of American Migration. Joseph R. Urgo. LC 95-5730. 224p. 1995. text ed. 39.95 (*0-252-02187-8*); pap. text ed. 14.95 (*0-252-06481-X*) U of Ill Pr.

Willa Cather in Context: Progress, Race, Empire. Guy Reynolds. LC 95-53265. 216p. 1996. pap. 18.95 (*0-312-16071-2*) St Martin.

Willa Cather in Europe: Her Own Story of the First Journey. Willa Cather. LC 88-1125. xiv, 178p. 1988. pap. 9.00 (*0-8032-6333-3*, Bison Books) U of Nebr Pr.

Willa Cather in Person: Interviews, Speeches, & Letters. Willa Cather. Ed. by L. Brent Bohlke. LC 86-19161. (Illus.). xxxii, 202p. 1986. reprint ed. pap. 10.00 (*0-8032-6326-0*, Bison Books); reprint ed. text ed. 30.00 (*0-8032-1184-8*) U of Nebr Pr.

Willa Cather on Writing: Critical Studies on Writing As an Art. Willa Cather. LC 87-30078. xxvi, 126p. 1988. pap. 10.00 (*0-8032-6332-5*, Bison Books) U of Nebr Pr.

***Willa Cather Reader: My Antonia/Sculptor's Funeral/ Paul's Case/The Garden Lodge.** Willa Cather. (Giant Literary Classics Ser.). 488p. 1997. 8.98 (*0-7624-0175-3*) Courage Bks.

Willa Cather's Collected Short Fiction, 1892-1912. rev. ed. Willa Cather. Ed. by Virginia Faulkner. LC 73-126046. xlii, 601p. 1970. text ed. 45.00 (*0-8032-0770-0*) U of Nebr Pr.

Willa Cather's Imagination. David Stouck. LC 74-81363. 263p. reprint ed. pap. 75.00 (*0-7837-0273-6*, 2040582) Bks Demand.

Willa Cather's Modernism: A Study of Style & Technique. Jo A. Middleton. LC 89-45407. 1990. 36.50 (*0-8386-3385-4*) Fairleigh Dickinson.

Willa Cather's My Antonia see Modern Critical Interpretations

Willa Cather's Red Cloud. Gabriel N. Seymour. (Illus.). 1980. 295.00 (*0-915998-07-6*) Lime Rock Pr.

Willa Cather's Transforming Vision: New France & the American Northeast. Gary Brienzo. LC 94-17434. 1995. 28.50 (*0-945636-66-0*) Susquehanna U Pr.

Willa Mae Johnson & the Fayette County Market. Marshall. (J). 1998. 16.00 (*0-689-80855-0*, S&S Bks Young Read) S&S Childrens.

***Willaim H. Gass/Manuel Puig.** (Review of Contemporary Fiction Ser.: Vol. 11, No. 3). 1991. pap. 8.00 (*1-56478-118-6*) Dalkey Arch.

Willamette University - Then & Now: 150th Anniversary. Photos by Gary Brash. (First Edition Ser.). (Illus.). 112p. 1992. 39.95 (*0-916509-95-8*) Harmony Hse Pub.

Willamette Valley Business Directory 1996-97. rev. ed. American Sales Leads Staff. 1440p. 1996. boxed 295.00 (*1-56105-895-5*) Am Busn Direct.

***Willamette Valley Business Directory 1997-1998.** rev. ed. American Business Directories Staff. 1376p. 1997. boxed 295.00 (*1-56105-982-X*) Am Busn Direct.

Willamette Valley, Oregon Obituaries, Vol. 1. 115p. write for info. (*0-939509-45-8*) L Benton Geneal.

Willamette Valley, Oregon Obituaries: Complete Series. pap. 12.00 (*0-317-58917-2*) L Benton Geneal.

Willamette Valley, Oregon Obituaries: Complete Series, Set. write for info. (*0-939509-44-X*) L Benton Geneal.

Willapa Bay. James Petit. (Illus.). 22p. (Orig.). 1992. 37.50 (*0-9630863-4-0*); pap. 20.00 (*0-9630863-5-9*) Limner Pr.

Willapa Bay. deluxe ed. James Petit. (Illus.). 22p. (Orig.). 1992. 50.00 (*0-9630863-6-7*) Limner Pr.

Willard & His Bowling Trophies. Richard Brautigan. 18.95 (*0-8488-0790-1*) Amereon Ltd.

***Willard & Spackman's Occupational Therapy.** 9th ed. Maureen E. Neistadt & Elizabeth Blesedell Crepeau. 976p. 1997. text ed. write for info. (*0-397-55192-4*) Lppncott-Raven.

Willard, Colorado, a Special Place in Time. Gail H. Woerner. Ed. by Robert K. Holz. LC 87-60378. (C). 1987. 19.95 (*0-9618385-0-7*) Paisano Pr.

Willard, Colorado, a Special Place in Time. limited ed. Gail H. Woerner. Ed. by Robert K. Holz. LC 87-60378. (C). 1987. 39.95 (*0-9618385-1-5*) Paisano Pr.

Willard Gibbs. Muriel Rukeyser. LC 87-12394. (Illus.). xiv, 465p. 1988. reprint ed. 35.00 (*0-918024-57-9*); reprint ed. pap. 17.95 (*0-918024-56-0*) Ox Bow.

Willard L. Sperry: A Theological Mind of Second Thought, 1914-1939. William L. Fox. LC 90-21612. (American University Studies: Theology & Religion: Ser. VII, Vol. 90). 240p. (C). 1991. text ed. 40.95 (*0-8204-1429-8*) P Lang Pubng.

***Willard Leroy Metcalf: An American Impressionist.** Richard J. Boyle. (Illus.). 5p. 1995. pap. write for info. (*0-945936-11-7*) Spanierman Gallery.

Willard Memoir: Or, The Life & Times of Major Simon Willard with Notices of Three Generations of His Descendants, & Two Collateral Branches in the U. S. J. Willard. (Illus.). 484p. 1989. reprint ed. pap. 72.50 (*0-8328-1273-0*); reprint ed. lib. bdg. 80.50 (*0-8328-1272-2*) Higginson Bk Co.

***Willard Nash, an American Cezanne.** Photos by Dan Morse. (Illus.). 88p. (Orig.). 1997. pap. 25.00 (*0-935037-92-6*) G Peters Gallery.

Willard Scott's Down Home Stories. Willard Scott. LC 84-11054. 197p. 1984. write for info. (*0-672-52768-5*) Macmillan.

Willard Stone: Sculptor & Philosopher. Margaret W. Hamilton & Sophie I. Stone. Ed. by Jimmy Peacock. LC 93-86428. (Illus.). 220p. (Orig.). 1993. pap. 19.95 (*0-9639183-0-3*) Persimmon Pubns.

Willard Straight. Herbert D. Croly. 1977. 48.95 (*0-8369-7107-8*, 7941) Ayer.

Willard W. Waller on the Family, Education, & War: Selected Papers. Willard W. Waller. Ed. by William J. Goode et al. LC 70-132287. (Heritage of Sociology Ser.). 376p. 1970. lib. bdg. 36.00 (*0-226-87152-5*) U Ch Pr.

Willard Z. Park's Ethnographic Notes on the Northern Paiute of Western Nevada, 1933-1940. Ed. by Catherine S. Fowler. (Anthropological Papers: No. 114). (Illus.). 160p. 1990. pap. text ed. 27.50 (*0-87480-316-0*) U of Utah Pr.

WillBall. Charles C. Wehrenberg. 204p. (Orig.). 1995. pap. 11.00 (*1-886163-02-2*) SoloZone.

Willcox: Willcox & Allied Families. J. Willcox. (Illus.). 139p. 1991. reprint ed. pap. 23.00 (*0-8328-2198-5*) Higginson Bk Co.

Wille & Millin's Mercantile Law of South Africa. 18th ed. J. F. Coaker et al. 952p. 1984. write for info. (*0-7021-7347-9*, Pub. by Juta SA); suppl. ed. write for info. (*0-7021-8173-0*, Pub. by Juta SA) Gaunt.

Wille Wacka Land. Jean-Paul Larocque. (Illus.). 12p. (J). (gr. 1-3). 1992. pap. 6.95 (*1-895583-04-7*) MAYA Pubs.

Willeford. Don Herron. 225p. 1997. 30.00 (*0-939767-26-0*) D McMillan.

Willehalm. 6th ed. Wolfram Von Eschenbach. Ed. by Karl Lachmann & Dieter Kartschoke. (GER.). (C). 1968. 32.35 (*3-11-000314-7*) De Gruyter.

Willelmi Malmesbiriensis Monachi de Gestis Regum Anglorum Libri Quinque: Historiae Novellae Libri Tres., 2 vols., Set. Ed. by William Stubbs. (Rolls Ser.: No. 90). 1974. reprint ed. 140.00 (*0-8115-1166-9*) Periodicals Srv.

Willem De Kooning. Harry F. Gaugh. LC 83-2787. (Modern Masters Ser.). (Illus.). 128p. 1986. 32.95 (*0-89659-332-0*); pap. 22.95 (*1-55859-248-2*) Abbeville Pr.

Willem de Kooning. Klaus Kertess. (Illus.). 58p. 1994. pap. 20.00 (*0-933793-31-6*) Guild Hall.

Willem de Kooning. Diane Waldman. (Library of American Art). (Illus.). 160p. 1988. 45.00 (*0-8109-1134-5*) Abrams.

Willem de Kooning. Sally Yard. LC 94-49682. (Illus.). 128p. 1997. 27.50 (*0-8478-1884-5*) Rizzoli Intl.

Willem de Kooning: Paintings. David Sylvester et al. (Illus.). 240p. 1994. 60.00 (*0-300-06011-4*) Yale U Pr.

Willem De Kooning: The Late Paintings. Gary Garrels & Robert Storr. (Illus.). 1995. 50.00 (*0-935640-49-5*); pap. 29.95 (*0-935640-47-9*) Walker Art Ctr.

***Willem de Looper: A Retrospective Exhibition 1966-1996.** Ed. & Intro. by Terry Gips. 84p. (Orig.). 1996. pap. 20.00 (*0-937123-33-1*) Art Gal U MD.

Willem Einthoven (1860-1927) Father of Electrocardiography: Life & Work, Ancestors & Contemporaries. H. A. Snellen. LC 94-43112. 144p. (C). 1995. pap. text ed. 42.50 (*0-7923-3274-1*) Kluwer Ac.

Willem Marinus Dudok, a Dutch Modernist: A Bio-Bibliography. Donald Langmead. LC 95-46113. (Bio-Bibliographies in Art & Architecture Ser.: No. 4). 1996. text ed. 79.50 (*0-313-29425-9*, Greenwood Pr) Greenwood.

Willer & the Piney Woods Doctor. Maurine W. Liles. LC 95-30740. (Illus.). 108p. (J). (gr. 4-7). 1995. 14.95 (*1-57168-058-6*, Eakin Pr) Sunbelt Media.

Wille's Mortgage & Pledge in South Africa. 3rd ed. G. Wille et al. 283p. 1987. 55.00 (*0-7021-1896-6*, Pub. by Juta SA) Gaunt.

Wille's Principles of South African Law. 8th ed. D. B. Hutchison et al. 1991. 110.00 (*0-7021-2643-8*, Pub. by Juta SA); pap. 89.00 (*0-7021-2642-X*, Pub. by Juta SA) Gaunt.

Willful Injustice: A Post - O. J. Look at Rodney King, American Justice, & Trial by Race. Robert Dietz. 275p. 1996. 24.95 (*0-89526-457-9*) Regnery Pub.

Willful Liberalism: Voluntarism & Individuality in Political Theory & Practice. Richard E. Flathman. LC 91-55559. 256p. 1992. 39.95 (*0-8014-2661-8*); pap. 14.95 (*0-8014-9955-0*) Cornell U Pr.

Willful Marriage. Peggy Moreland. (Desire Ser.). 1996. mass mkt. 3.50 (*0-373-76024-8*, 1-76024-8) Silhouette.

Willful Widow. Valerie King. 320p. 1991. mass mkt. 3.95 (*0-8217-3323-0*, Zebra Kensgtn) Kensgtn Pub Corp.

Willfully Wed. Toni Collins. (Romance Ser.). 1996. pap. 3.25 (*0-373-19159-6*, 1-19159-2) Silhouette.

Willi Baumeister: Drawings, Gouaches & Collages. (Illus.). 276p. 1989. 65.00 (*3-89322-130-1*, Pub. by Edition Cantz GW) Dist Art Pubs.

Willi Baumeister: Paintings. (Illus.). 256p. 1989. 65.00 (*3-89322-136-0*, Pub. by Edition Cantz GW) Dist Art Pubs.

Willi Baumeister: Serigraphs. (Illus.). 164p. 1989. 50.00 (*3-89322-131-X*, Pub. by Edition Cantz GW) Dist Art Pubs.

Willi Baumeister: Typography & Advertising - Design. (Illus.). 352p. 1989. pap. 60.00 (*3-89322-145-X*, Pub. by Edition Cantz GW) Dist Art Pubs.

Willi Warstat on the Aesthetics of Art Photography, Two Selections: Original Anthology. Ed. by Peter C. Bunnell & Robert A. Sobieszek. LC 76-24679. (Sources of Modern Photography Ser.). (Illus.). (GER.). 1979. lib. bdg. 15.95 (*0-405-09659-3*) Ayer.

William A. Albaugh, 1908-1983: His Life & Writings. Compiled & Pref. by Bruce Kusrow. (William Albaugh Collection Ser.: Vol. 3). (Illus.). 196p. 1994. 30.00 (*1-56837-269-8*) Broadfoot.

***William A. Gissberg: An Oral History.** Contrib. by Sharon Boswell. (Illus.). xii, 130p. (Orig.). 1996. pap. write for info. (*1-889320-03-X*) WA St Oral Hist.

William A. Smith: A Retrospective. Contrib. by Alexander Eilot et al. (Illus.). 16p. 1996. pap. 10.50 (*1-879636-06-9*) J A Michener.

William Adam: Architectural Heritage, Vol. 1. Ed. by Deborah Howard. 128p. 1995. pap. 19.50 (*0-7486-0232-1*, Pub. by Edinburgh U Pr UK) Col U Pr.

***William Adams of Ipswich, Massachusetts & Some of His Descendants, 1594-1661.** rev. ed. Kenneth L. Bosworth. (Illus.). 208p. 1996. pap. write for info. (*0-7884-0528-4*) Heritage Bk.

William Adams of Ipswich, Massachusetts, 1594-1661: And Some of His Descendants. Kenneth L. Bosworth. (Illus.). 179p. (Orig.). 1992. pap. 27.50 (*1-55613-650-1*) Heritage Bk.

William Addison Dwiggins. Dorothy Abbe. 1974. 1.00 (*0-89073-018-0*) Boston Public Lib.

William Alanson White: The Autobiography of a Purpose. William A. White. Ed. by Gerald N. Grob. LC 78-22596. (Historical Issues in Mental Health Ser.). 1980. reprint ed. lib. bdg. 25.95 (*0-405-11946-1*) Ayer.

William Albaugh Collection, 11 bks. William Albaugh. Ed. by Bruce Kusrow. (Illus.). 1994. reprint ed. Set. 250.00 (*1-56837-253-1*) Broadfoot.

***William Alexander, Lord Stirling.** Paul D. Nelson. LC 85-16473. (Illus.). 258p. pap. 73.60 (*0-608-05143-8*, 2065704) Bks Demand.

William Allen White. Diane D. Quantic. LC 93-70137. (Western Writers Ser.: No. 109). (Illus.). 52p. 1993. pap. 4.95 (*0-88430-108-7*) Boise St U W Writ Ser.

William Allen White: Maverick on Main Street. John McKee. LC 74-5991. (Contributions in American Studies: No. 17). (Illus.). 264p. 1975. text ed. 55.00 (*0-8371-7533-X*, MAW/, Greenwood Pr) Greenwood.

William Allen White of Emporia. Frank C. Clough. LC 73-100149. 265p. 1970. reprint ed. text ed. 67.50 (*0-8371-3910-4*, CLWA, Greenwood Pr) Greenwood.

William Allingham. Alan Warner. (Irish Writers Ser.). 90p. 1975. 8.50 (*0-8387-7899-2*); pap. 1.95 (*0-8387-7990-5*) Bucknell U Pr.

William Alsop: Buildings & Projects. Ed. by Mel Gooding. (Illus.). 120p. (Orig.). 1992. pap. 14.95 (*1-878271-74-1*) Princeton Arch.

William Alsop & Jan Stoermer. Michael Spens et al. (Architectural Monographs: No. 33). (Illus.). 144p. 1993. 55.00 (*1-85490-263-6*) Academy Ed UK.

William Alsop & Jan Stoermer. Michael Spens et al. (Architectural Monographs: No. 33). (Illus.). 144p. 1994. pap. 38.00 (*1-85490-264-4*) Academy Ed UK.

William & Boomer. Lindsay B. George. LC 86-9789. (Illus.). 24p. (J). (ps-1). 1987. 16.00 (*0-688-06640-2*); lib. bdg. 15.93 (*0-688-06641-0*) Greenwillow.

William & Caroline Herschel. Blair. (J). 1995. text ed. write for info. (*0-7167-6596-9*); pap. text ed. write for info. (*0-7167-6597-7*) W H Freeman.

William & Henry James: Selected Letters. Henry James et al. Ed. by Ignas K. Skrupskelis & Elizabeth M. Berkeley. LC 96-25921. 608p. 1997. 39.95 (*0-8139-1694-1*) U Pr of Va.

William & Mary Cookbook: A Treasury of Recipes & Memories of Good Eating at the College of William & Mary in Virginia Collected by Alumni & Friends. Ed. by Jackie Legg. 276p. 1993. pap. 16.93 (*0-9615670-5-8*) Soc Alu Wm.

***William & the Ex-Prime Minister.** Carol A. Duffy. Date not set. pap. 14.95 (*0-85646-253-5*, Pub. by Anvil Press UK); pap. 7.95 (*0-85646-254-3*, Pub. by Anvil Press UK) Dufour.

William & the Good Old Days. Eloise Greenfield. LC 91-47030. (Illus.). 32p. (J). (gr. k-3). 1993. lib. bdg. 14.89 (*0-06-021094-X*) HarpC Child Bks.

William Appleman Williams: The Tragedy of Empire. Paul Buhle & Edward Rice-Maximin. (American Radicals Ser.). 318p. (C). 1995. pap. 18.95 (*0-415-91131-1*, B4907, Routledge NY) Routledge.

William Appleman Williams: The Tragedy of Empire. Paul Buhle & Edward Rice-Maximin. LC 95-19420. (American Radicals Ser.). 318p. (C). (gr. 13). 1995. text ed. 74.95 (*0-415-91130-3*, B4903, Routledge NY) Routledge.

William Appleman Williams Reader: Selections from His Major Historical Writings. Ed. by Henry W. Berger. LC 92-17013. 416p. 1992. text ed. 35.00 (*1-56663-008-8*) I R Dee.

William Appleman Williams Reader: Selections from His Major Historical Writings. Ed. by Henry W. Berger. LC 92-17013. 416p. (Orig.). 1992. pap. text ed. 16.95 (*1-56663-002-9*) I R Dee.

William Appleton Coolidge Collection. Peter C. Sutton. (Illus.). 200p. 1995. 40.00 (*0-87846-453-0*, Pub. by Arsenale Editrice IT) Antique Collect.

William Archer: A Life. Peter Whitebrook. 400p. 1994. 35.00 (*0-413-65520-2*, A0685, Pub. by Methuen UK) Heinemann.

William Archer on Ibsen: The Major Essays, 1889-1919. Ed. by Thomas Postlewait. LC 84-15744. (Contributions in Drama & Theatre Studies: No. 13). (Illus.). 323p. 1984. text ed. 59.95 (*0-313-24499-5*, PWA/, Greenwood Pr) Greenwood.

William Arthur Deacon: A Canadian Literary Life. Clara Thomas & John Lennox. 320p. 1982. 32.50 (*0-8020-5593-1*) U of Toronto Pr.

William Augustus: Duke of Cumberland. A Life. Rex Whitworth. (Illus.). 265p. (C). 1992. 52.50 (*0-85052-354-0*, Pub. by L Cooper Bks UK) Trans-Atl Phila.

William B. Ide the President of California. George Kirov. (Illus.). 65p. 1995. 13.95 (*1-885852-01-0*) J D Stevenson.

William Bailey. Mark Strand. (Illus.). 80p. 1987. pap. 17.95 (*0-8109-2360-2*) Abrams.

William Bailey: Painting & Drawings. University Art Galleries, Wright State University. Ed. by Barry A. Rosenberg. LC 86-51581. (Illus.). 18p. (Orig.). 1987. pap. 5.00 (*0-932706-12-6*) WSU Art Gallrs.

William Barclay: A Personal Memoir. James Martin. 1985. pap. 3.75 (*0-7152-0579-X*) Outlook.

William Barclay: A Spiritual Autobiography. William Barclay. LC 73-76528. 127p. reprint ed. pap. 36.20 (*0-7837-0511-5*, 2040835) Bks Demand.

***William Barnes (1801-1886) Selected Poems.** Ed. by Robert Nye. pap. write for info. (*0-85635-032-X*, Pub. by Carcanet Pr UK) Paul & Co Pubs.

William Barret Travis. Jean Flynn. (J). (gr. 4-7). 1982. 12.95 (*0-89015-348-5*) Sunbelt Media.

William Barrett Travis: A Biography. Archie P. McDonald. Ed. by Edwin M. Eakin. (Illus.). 216p. 1989. 18.95 (*0-89015-656-5*, Eakin Pr) Sunbelt Media.

William Bartram on the Southeastern Indians. William Bartram. Ed. by Gregory A. Waselkov & Kathryn E. Braund. LC 94-29756. (Indians of the Southeast Ser.). (Illus.). xvi, 343p. 1995. text ed. 50.00 (*0-8032-4772-9*) U of Nebr Pr.

William Bathe, S. J., 1564-1614: A Pioneer in Linguistics. Sean P. O'Mathuna. LC 86-11791. (Studies in the History of Language Sciences: Vol. 37). (Illus.). iv, 211p. 1986. 55.00 (*90-272-4520-7*) Benjamins North Am.

William Baziotes: A Commemorative Exhibition. David S. Rubin. Ed. by Louise S. Bross & Lys Martin. LC 87-80348. (Illus.). 24p. (Orig.). 1987. pap. text ed. 9.00 (*0-941972-05-4*) Freedman.

William Beaumont-Frontier Doctor. 2nd rev. ed. Virginia Law Burns. LC 78-72566. (Illus.). 166p. 1989. reprint ed. lib. bdg. 17.50 (*0-9604726-4-9*) Enterprise Pr.

William Beaumont's Formative Years. William Beaumont. (American Autobiography Ser.). 87p. 1995. reprint ed. lib. bdg. 69.00 (*0-7812-8454-6*) Rprt Serv.

William Beckford. Robert J. Gemmett. LC 76-43256. (Twayne's English Authors Ser.). 189p. (C). 1977. lib. bdg. 17.95 (*0-8057-6674-X*) Irvington.

William Beckford: An English Fidalgo. Malcolm R. Jack. LC 91-12379. (Studies in the Eighteenth Century: No. 20). 1991. 42.50 (*0-404-63520-2*) AMS Pr.

William Bellows of Gloucester 1837-1942. Grace Bellows. (C). 1988. 78.00 (*0-900657-71-5*, Pub. by W Sessions UK) St Mut.

***William Beveridge: A Biography.** 2nd ed. Jose Harris. (Illus.). 360p. 1997. 50.00 (*0-19-820685-2*) OUP.

William "Bill" W. Brown Legend of Oregon's High Deserts Including a History of the Wagontirg Mountain Range Feud. 1993. 25.00 (*0-614-15797-8*) E Gray.

William Billings: Data & Documents. Hans Nathan. LC 75-33593. (Bibliographies in American Music Ser.: No. 2). 69p. 1976. 10.00 (*0-911772-67-7*) Info Coord.

***William Billings of Boston: Eighteenth-Century Composer.** David P. McKay & Richard Crawford. LC 74-19035. (Illus.). 314p. 1975. reprint ed. pap. 89.50 (*0-608-02501-1*, 2063145) Bks Demand.

William Billings's Anthem for Easter: The Persistence of an Early American Hit. Karl Kroger. (Illus.). 19p. 1987. pap. 4.50 (*0-944026-00-1*) Am Antiquarian.

William Blackstone: Sage of the Wilderness. Louise Lind. (Illus.). 108p. (Orig.). 1993. pap. text ed. 11.00 (*1-55613-910-1*) Heritage Bk.

William Blackstone Collection in the Yale Law Library: A Bibliographical Catalogue. Catherine S. Eller. 134p. 1993. reprint ed. 40.00 (*0-9630106-5-4*, 308270) Lawbk Exchange.

William Blake. William Blake. Ed. by Michael Mason. (Oxford Authors Ser.). (Illus.). 628p. 1988. pap. 22.00 (*0-19-282001-X*) OUP.

William Blake. O. Burdett. LC 74-1127. (Studies in Blake: No. 3). 1974. lib. bdg. 42.95 (*0-8383-2021-X*) M S G Haskell Hse.

William Blake. Intro. by Peter Porter & Geoffrey Moore. (Great Poets Ser.). (Illus.). 1988. 10.00 (*0-517-56291-X*, Crown) Crown Pub Group.

William Blake. Punter. 1996. text ed. 39.95 (*0-312-16032-1*) St Martin.

William Blake. Kathleen Raine. (World of Art Ser.). (Illus.). 216p. 1985. pap. 14.95 (*0-500-20107-2*) Thames Hudson.

William Blake. rev. ed. Victor N. Paananen. 1996. 24.95 (*0-8057-7053-4*, Twayne) Scribnrs Ref.

William Blake. Basil De Selincourt. LC 70-173850. (Studies in Blake: No. 3). (Illus.). 1971. reprint ed. lib. bdg. 75.00 (*0-8383-1357-4*) M S G Haskell Hse.

William Blake. Charles Gardner. LC 76-118001. (Studies in Blake: No. 3). 1970. reprint ed. lib. bdg. 59.95 (*0-8383-1056-7*) M S G Haskell Hse.

William Blake. John M. Murry. LC 71-173845. (Studies in Blake: No. 3). 1971. reprint ed. lib. bdg. 75.00 (*0-8383-1344-2*) M S G Haskell Hse.

William Blake. Alfred Story. LC 77-115183. (Studies in Blake: No. 3). (C). 1970. reprint ed. lib. bdg. 49.95 (*0-8383-1009-5*) M S G Haskell Hse.

William Blake. Algernon C. Swinburne. LC 67-12468. (Illus.). 1980. reprint ed. 21.95 (*0-405-09018-8*) Ayer.

William Blake. Arthur Symons. (BCL1-PR English Literature Ser.). 433p. 1992. reprint ed. lib. bdg. 99.00 (*0-7812-7445-1*) Rprt Serv.

William Blake: A Critical Essay. Algernon C. Swinburne. Ed. by Hugh J. Luke. LC 70-81397. 343p. reprint ed. pap. 97.80 (*0-7837-4663-6*, 2044389) Bks Demand.

William Blake: A Man Without a Mask. Jacob Bronowski. 1976. lib. bdg. 250.00 (*0-8490-1300-3*) Gordon Pr.

William Blake: A Man Without a Mask. J. Bronowski. LC 67-30809. (Studies in Blake: No. 3). 1969. reprint ed. lib. bdg. 75.00 (*0-8383-0709-4*) M S G Haskell Hse.

William Blake: A New Kind of Man. Michael Davis. LC 77-71059. (Illus.). 1977. pap. 13.00 (*0-520-03456-2*) U CA Pr.

William Blake: Creative Will & the Poetic Image. Jack Lindsay. LC 70-118005. (Studies in Blake: No. 3). 1970. reprint ed. lib. bdg. 59.95 (*0-8383-1061-3*) M S G Haskell Hse.

W

*William Blake: Images & Texts. Henry E. Huntington Library & Art Gallery Staff. LC 97-1401. 1997. write for info. (0-87328-168-3) Huntington Lib.
William Blake: Painter & Poet. Richard Garnett. LC 77-115857. (Studies in Blake: No. 3). 1970. reprint ed. lib. bdg. 75.00 (0-8383-1074-5) M S G Haskell Hse.
William Blake: Poet & Mystic. P. Berger. LC 67-31287. (Studies in Blake: No. 3). 1969. reprint ed. lib. bdg. 75.00 (0-8383-0778-7) M S G Haskell Hse.
William Blake: Prophet of Universal Brotherhood. Bernard Nesfield-Cookson. 480p. (Orig.). (C). 1989. lib. bdg. 35.00 (0-8095-7102-1) Borgo Pr.
William Blake: Selected Poetry & Prose. Ed. by David Punter. (English Texts Ser.). 256p. (C). 1988. pap. 9.95 (0-415-00666-X) Routledge.
William Blake: The Critical Heritage. Ed. by Gerald E. Bentley, Jr. (Critical Heritage Ser.). (Illus.). 320p. 1975. 69.50 (0-7100-8234-7, RKP) Routledge.
William Blake: The Man. Charles Gardner. LC 79-153324. reprint ed. 27.50 (0-404-07906-7) AMS Pr.
William Blake: The Politics of Vision. Mark Schorer. 1990. 14.50 (0-8446-2886-7) Peter Smith.
William Blake: The Power of the Imagination. James Thorpe. (Illus.). 24p. 1979. pap. 2.00 (0-87328-132-2) Huntington Lib.
William Blake see Romantics: Critical Heritage
William Blake see Modern Critical Views Series
William Blake & His Circle: A Complete Catalogue. Martin Butlin et al. LC 85-10689. (Illus.). 204p. 1989. pap. 12.95 (0-87328-084-9) Huntington Lib.
William Blake & His Contempories & Followers: Selected Works from the Collection of Robert N. Essick. Robert N. Essick. LC 87-29349. (Illus.). 78p. 1987. 3.95 (0-87328-093-8) Huntington Lib.
*William Blake & the Critics. Jeffrey D. Parker. (LCENG Ser.). Date not set. 55.95 (1-57113-045-4) Camden Hse.
*William Blake & the Daughters of Albion. Helen P. Bruder. LC 97-7119. 1997. text ed. write for info. (0-312-17481-0) St Martin.
William Blake & the Moderns. Ed. by Robert J. Bertholf & Annette S. Levitt. LC 82-656. 294p. 1983. text ed. 64.50 (0-87395-615-X); pap. text ed. 24.95 (0-87395-616-8) State U NY Pr.
William Blake at the Huntington: An Introduction to the William Blake Collection in the Henry E. Huntington Library & Art Gallery. Robert N. Essick. (Illus.). 160p. 1994. pap. 29.95 (0-8109-2589-3) Abrams.
William Blake in This World. Harold L. Bruce. 1977. 18.95 (0-8369-6924-3, 7805) Ayer.
William Blake in This World. Harold L. Bruce. LC 73-18085. (Studies in Blake: No. 3). 1974. reprint ed. lib. bdg. 75.00 (0-8383-1732-4) M S G Haskell Hse.
William Blake on the Lord's Prayer: 1757-1827. John H. Clarke. LC 70-95421. (Studies in Blake: No. 3). 1971. reprint ed. lib. bdg. 75.00 (0-8383-0967-4) M S G Haskell Hse.
William Blake, Printmaker. Robert N. Essick. LC 79-3205. (Illus.). 455p. reprint ed. pap. 129.70 (0-8357-3587-7, 2034655) Bks Demand.
William Blake Tarot: The Tarot of the Creative Imagination. Ed Buryn. (Illus.). 160p. 1995. pap. 32.00 (0-06-251316-8) Harper SF.
William Blake Tarot Triumphs. Ed Buryn. (Illus.). 16p. (Orig.). 1991. pap. 19.95 (0-916804-04-6) Ed Buryn Pub.
William Blake (1907) Arthur Symons. 453p. 1996. reprint ed. pap. 35.00 (1-56459-561-7) Kessinger Pub.
William Blake's Circle of Destiny. Milton O. Percival. 340p. 1993. pap. text ed. 21.00 (1-56459-315-0) Kessinger Pub.
William Blake's Epic: Imagination Unbound. Joanne Witke. LC 85-30326. (Illus.). 235p. 1986. text ed. 32.50 (0-312-88024-3) St Martin.
William Blake's Jerusalem. Minna Doskow. LC 81-65463. (Illus.). 388p. 1983. 50.00 (0-8386-3090-1) Fairleigh Dickinson.
William Blake's Poetical Sketches. John W. Ehrstine. LC 67-4010. 118p. reprint ed. pap. 33.70 (0-685-24158-0, 2033032) Bks Demand.
William Blake's The Marriage of Heaven & Hell see Modern Critical Interpretations
William Blake's Works in Conventional Typography. William Blake. LC 82-10815. 1984. 75.00 (0-8201-1388-3) Schol Facsimiles.
William Blount. William H. Masterson. LC 79-88904. 378p. 1970. reprint ed. text ed. 59.75 (0-8371-2308-9, MABL, Greenwood Pr) Greenwood.
*William Bolcom: Piano Rags. Leonard, Hal, Corporation Staff. pap. 12.95 (0-7935-0662-X) H Leonard.
William Bollaert's Texas. William Bollaert. Ed. by W. Eugene Hollon. LC 56-11228. (American Exploration & Travel Ser.: Vol. 21). (Illus.). 456p. 1989. pap. 16.95 (0-8061-2175-0) U of Okla Pr.
William Booth. David Bennett. (Men of Faith Ser.). 192p. 1994. mass mkt. 4.99 (1-55661-307-5) Bethany Hse.
William Booth. Minnie L. Carpenter. 1986. pap. 6.99 (0-88019-185-6) Schmul Pub Co.
William Bostwick: Connecticut Yankee in Antebellum Georgia. Marilyn A. Lavin. LC 77-14787. (Dissertations in American Economic History Ser.). 1978. 37.95 (0-405-11044-8) Ayer.
William Brewster - the Father of New England. Harold Kirk-Smith. (C). 1989. text ed. 160.00 (0-902662-93-7, Pub. by R K Pubns UK) St Mut.
William Brewster - the Father of New England. deluxe ed. Harold Kirk-Smith. (C). 1989. ring bd. 725.00 (0-902662-94-5, Pub. by R K Pubns UK) St Mut.
William Brice: Notations Nineteen Eighty-Two. (Illus.). 120p. 1984. 45.00 (0-942642-06-6) Twelvetrees Pr.
William Brice: Works on Paper, 1982-1992. Ed. by Cynthia Burlingham. LC 93-16424. 1993. 25.00 (0-9628162-1-3) Grunwald Arts.
William Brice Vol. 1: A Selection of Painting & Drawing 1947-1986. Ed. by Ann Goldstein et al. LC 86-80091. (Illus.). 105p. (Orig.). 1986. pap. 20.00 (0-911291-12-1) Fellows Cont Art.
William Bronk. Kimmelman. 1997. text ed. 22.95 (0-8057-4509-2) Macmillan.
William Bronk. Kimmelman. 1997. 23.95 (0-8057-4526-2) Macmillan.
William Buchanan & the Nineteenth Century Art Trade: 100 Letters to His Agents in London & Italy. Hugh Brigstocke. 525p. 1982. 25.00 (0-685-38945-6) Yale Ctr Brit Art.
William Burke & Francisco de Miranda: The Word & Deed in Spanish America's Emancipation. Mario Rodriguez. LC 94-4182. 600p. (C). 1994. lib. bdg. 64.50 (0-8191-9485-9) U Pr of Amer.
William Burroughs: El Hombre Invisible. Barry Miles. LC 92-38285. (Illus.). 272p. 1994. pap. 12.95 (0-7868-8018-X) Hyperion.
William Burroughs Birthday Book. (Illus.). 44p. (Orig.). 1994. pap. 5.00 (1-871744-90-3, Pub. by Temple Pr UK) AK Pr Dist.
*William Burroughs, Brion Gysin, Throbbing Gristle. Ed. by V. Vale. (RE-Search Ser.: Vols. 4 & 5). (Illus.). 100p. (Orig.). 1982. pap. 15.99 (0-9650469-1-5) V Search.
William Butler Yeats. J. M. Hone. LC 72-3620. (English Literature Ser.: No. 33). 1972. lib. bdg. 75.00 (0-8383-1577-1) M S G Haskell Hse.
William Butler Yeats. W. H. Pollock. LC 75-22355. (W. B. Yeats Ser.: No. 72). 1975. lib. bdg. 39.95 (0-8383-2104-6) M S G Haskell Hse.
William Butler Yeats. Peter Porter. (Great Poets Ser.). 1990. 10.00 (0-517-57379-2, Crown) Crown Pub Group.
William Butler Yeats. Denis Donoghue. 176p. 1989. reprint ed. pap. 8.95 (0-88001-208-0) Ecco Pr.
William Butler Yeats see Modern Critical Views Series
*William Butler Yeats Encyclopedia. Sam McCready. LC 96-50288. 496p. 1997. text ed. 95.00 (0-313-28371-0, Greenwood Pr) Greenwood.
William Byrd. Frank S. Howes. LC 77-27081. (Illus.). 267p. 1978. reprint ed. text ed. 55.00 (0-313-20182-X, HOWI, Greenwood Pr) Greenwood.
William Byrd. Frank S. Howes. 267p. 1990. reprint ed. lib. bdg. 69.00 (0-7812-9055-4) Rprt Serv.
*William Byrd: Gentleman of the Chapel Royal. John Harley. LC 96-37221. 480p. 1997. text ed. 76.95 (1-85928-165-6, Pub. by Scolar Pr UK) Ashgate Pub Co.
William Byrd II & His Lost History: Engravings of the Americas. Margaret B. Pritchard & Virginia L. Sites. LC 92-31382. (Illus.). 224p. 1993. 26.99 (0-87935-088-1) Colonial Williamsburg.
William Byrd of Westover. 2nd ed. Richmond C. Beatty. xxxix, 243p. 1970. reprint ed. lib. bdg. 32.50 (0-208-00944-2, Archon Bks) Shoe String.
William Byrd of Westover, 1674-1744. Pierre Marambaud. LC 70-151251. 307p. reprint ed. pap. 87.50 (0-685-15935-3, 2027069) Bks Demand.
William Byrd's Histories of the Dividing Line Betwixt Virginia & North Carolina. William Byrd. (Illus.). xi, 340p. 1987. reprint ed. pap. 9.95 (0-486-25553-0) Dover.
William C. Whitney, Modern Warwick. Mark D. Hirsch. LC 69-19214. (Illus.). xiii, 622p. (C). 1969. reprint ed. lib. bdg. 52.50 (0-208-00722-9, Archon Bks) Shoe String.
William Card Seventeen Ten to Seventeen Eighty-Five with Ancestors & Some Descendants. Grayce H. Alsterda. LC 86-174208. (Illus.). 66p. 1986. pap. text ed. 11.00 (0-9617035-0-4) G H Alsterda.
William Carey. Basil Miller. LC 85-71476. (Men of Faith Ser.). 160p. 1985. reprint ed. mass mkt. 4.99 (0-87123-850-0) Bethany Hse.
*William Carey: Father of Missions. Bargain Books Staff. (Heroes of the Faith Ser.). 208p. (Orig.). 1997. pap. 3.97 (1-57748-106-2) Barbour & Co.
William Carey-Missionary Pioneer. Kellsye M. Finnie. 1987. pap. 4.95 (0-87508-187-8) Chr Lit.
William Carlos Williams. Emily M. Wallace et al. Ed. by Charles Angoff. LC 73-10757. (Leverton Lectures: No. 1). (Illus.). 46p. 1974. 11.50 (0-8386-1441-8) Fairleigh Dickinson.
William Carlos Williams. John M. Brinnin. LC 63-62710. (University of Minnesota Pamphlets on American Writers Ser.: No. 24). 48p. (Orig.). reprint ed. pap. 25.00 (0-7837-2897-2, 2057558) Bks Demand.
William Carlos Williams: A New World Naked. Paul J. Mariani. 1990. pap. 14.95 (0-393-30672-0) Norton.
William Carlos Williams: A Poet in the American Theatre. David A. Fedo. LC 83-1132. (Studies in Modern Literature: No. 7). 213p. reprint ed. pap. 60.80 (0-8357-1410-1, 2070543) Bks Demand.
William Carlos Williams: Man & Poet. Ed. by Carroll F. Terrell. LC 83-61211. (Man & Poet Ser.). 620p. 1983. 45.00 (0-915032-57-0); pap. 15.95 (0-915032-58-9) Natl Poet Foun.
William Carlos Williams: The Critical Heritage. Charles Doyle. (Critical Heritage Ser.). 1980. 69.50 (0-7100-8987-2, RKP) Routledge.
William Carlos Williams: The Knack of Survival in America. Robert Coles. LC 75-6560. (Mason Welch Gross Lectureship Ser.). 207p. 1975. reprint ed. pap. 59.00 (0-7837-5664-X, 2059090) Bks Demand.
William Carlos Williams: The Poet & His Critics. Paul L. Mariani. LC 75-8645. 285p. reprint ed. pap. 81.30 (0-317-27974-2, 2025611) Bks Demand.
William Carlos Williams & Alterity: The Early Poetry. Barry Ahearn. (Cambridge Studies in American Literature & Culture: No. 75). 208p. (C). 1994. text ed. 59.95 (0-521-45200-7) Cambridge U Pr.
William Carlos Williams & Autobiography: The Woods of His Own Nature. Ann W. Fisher-Wirth. LC 88-19620. 232p. 1989. lib. bdg. 30.00 (0-271-00653-6) Pa St U Pr.
William Carlos Williams & Romantic Idealism. Carol Rapp. LC 83-40561. 175p. 1984. reprint ed. pap. 49.90 (0-608-02294-2, 2062935) Bks Demand.
William Carlos Williams & the Diagnostics of Culture. Brian Bremen. 256p. 1993. 49.95 (0-19-507226-X) OUP.
William Carlos Williams & the Ethics of Painting. Terence Diggory. (Illus.). 175p. 1991. text ed. 32.50 (0-691-06852-6) Princeton U Pr.
*William Carlos Williams & the Ethics of Painting. Terence Diggory. LC 90-8995. (Illus.). 181p. 1991. reprint ed. pap. 51.60 (0-608-02562-3, 2063207) Bks Demand.
William Carlos Williams & the Maternal Muse. Kerry Driscoll. LC 87-13855. (Studies in Modern Literature: No. 72). 212p. reprint ed. pap. 60.80 (0-8357-2068-3, 2070170) Bks Demand.
William Carlos William's Paterson: A Critical Appraisal. Margaret G. Lloyd. LC 77-89775. (Illus.). 305p. 1979. 35.00 (0-8386-2152-X) Fairleigh Dickinson.
William Carlos Williams Reader. William C. Williams. LC 66-17817. 1969. reprint ed. pap. 12.95 (0-8112-0239-9, NDP282) New Directions.
William Carlos Williams, the Arts, & Literary Tradition. Peter Schmidt. LC 87-32483. (Illus.). 268p. 1988. text ed. 37.50 (0-8071-1406-5) La State U Pr.
William Carlos Williams's A Dream of Love. Steven R. Loevy. LC 83-4909. (Studies in Modern Literature: No. 22). 94p. reprint ed. pap. 26.80 (0-8357-1450-0, 2070559) Bks Demand.
*William Cavendish: Dramatic Works. William Cavendish. Ed. by Lynn Hulse. (Malone Society Reprints Ser.: No. 158). 176p. 1997. text ed. 45.00 (0-19-729034-5) OUP.
William Caxton. N. F. Blake. Ed. by M. C. Seymour. (Authors of the Middle Ages Ser.). 64p. Date not set. pap. 17.95 (0-86078-418-5, Pub. by Variorum UK) Ashgate Pub Co.
William Caxton: First English Printer, 1844-1989. Charles Knight. 244p. 1992. pap. 25.00 (0-87556-365-1) Saifer.
William Caxton & English Literary Culture. N. F. Blake. 320p. 1991. boxed 55.00 (1-85285-051-5) Hambledon Press.
William Cecil. Alan G. Smith. LC 73-155113. (English Biography Ser.: No. 31). 1971. reprint ed. lib. bdg. 75.00 (0-8383-1286-1) M S G Haskell Hse.
William Chalmers Burns & Robert Murray McCheyne. James A. Stewart. 1964. pap. 3.99 (1-56632-083-6) Revival Lit.
William Christenberry: The Early Works, 1954-1968. J. Richard Gruber. 96p. 1996. 39.95 (0-9638753-4-5) Morris Mus Art.
William Clayton's Journal: A Daily Record of the Journey of the Original Company of Mormon Pioneers from Nauveo, Illinois, to the Valley of the Great Salt Lake. William Clayton. LC 72-9435. (Far Western Frontier Ser.). 380p. 1978. reprint ed. 29.95 (0-405-04965-X) Ayer.
*William Clutz: New Pastels, Duluth & Minneapolis. Steven Klindt. (Illus.). 26p. (Orig.). 1986. pap. 5.00 (1-889523-02-X) Tweed Mus.
William Coaldwell, Caldwell or Coldwell; & a Record of His Descendants. C. T. Coldwell. (Illus.). 82p. 1989. reprint ed. pap. 16.00 (0-8328-1299-4); reprint ed. lib. bdg. 24.00 (0-8328-1298-6) Higginson Bk Co.
William Cobbett. E. I. Carlyle. 1972. 59.95 (0-8490-1301-1) Gordon Pr.
William Cobbett: A Bibliographical Account of His Life & Times. Morris L. Pearl. LC 78-136079. 266p. 1971. reprint ed. text ed. 59.75 (0-8371-5229-1, PEWC, Greenwood Pr) Greenwood.
William Cobbett: His Thoughts & His Times. John W. Osborne. LC 81-13231. (Illus.). x, 272p. 1982. reprint ed. text ed. 52.50 (0-313-23222-9, OSWC, Greenwood Pr) Greenwood.
William Cobbett: The Politics of Style. Leonora Nattrass. (Cambridge Studies in Romanticism: No. 11). 263p. (C). 1995. text ed. 59.95 (0-521-46036-0) Cambridge U Pr.
William Cobbett & Rural Popular Culture. Ian Dyck. (Illus.). 336p. (C). 1992. text ed. 59.95 (0-521-41394-X) Cambridge U Pr.
William Cobbett & the United States, 1792-1835: A Bibliography with Notes & Extracts. Pierce W. Gaines. LC 79-168901. 270p. 1971. 27.50 (0-912296-00-3, 12382) Am Antiquarian.
William Collins. Oliver F. Sigworth. LC 65-18226. (Twayne's English Authors Ser.). 192p. 1965. lib. bdg. 15.95 (0-8290-1729-1) Irvington.
William Collins & Eighteenth-Century English Poetry. Richard Wendorf. LC 81-14674. 243p. reprint ed. pap. 69.30 (0-7837-2906-5, 2057548) Bks Demand.
William Conant Church & the Army & Navy Journal. Donald N. Bigelow. LC 68-59264. (Columbia University. Studies in the Social Sciences: No. 576). reprint ed. 27.50 (0-404-51576-2) AMS Pr.
William Congdon. Peter H. Selz et al. (Illus.). 358p. 1996. 75.00 (0-8028-3818-9) Eerdmans.
William Congreve. Novak. 1971. 13.50 (0-8057-1116-3, Twayne) Scribnrs Ref.
William Congreve. David Thomas. LC 92-5537. (English Dramatists Ser.). 1992. text ed. 35.00 (0-312-08420-X) St Martin.
William Congreve: An Annotated Bibliography 1978-1994. annot. ed. Laurence Bartlett. LC 96-11672. (Author Bibliographies Ser.: No. 97). 1996. 29.00 (0-8108-3166-X) Scarecrow.
William Congreve see Restoration & the Augustans
William Conlon: Paintings 1969-1981. Gene Baro. LC 81-18705. (Illus.). 16p. 1981. pap. text ed. 6.00 (0-88039-001-8) Mus Art Carnegie.
William Conrad. Pierre Boulle. 284p. 1972. pap. 3.95 (0-686-54119-7) Fr & Eur.
William Cooke's U. S. Revenue Cutter Diligence, 1792-1798. Florence Kern. 1979. 3.95 (0-913377-07-4) Alised.
William Cookworthy 1705-1780. (Illus.). 1972. 12.50 (0-686-44225-3) Ars Ceramica.
William Cooper's Town: Power & Persuasion on the Frontier of the Early American Republic. Alan Taylor. (Illus.). 549p. 1995. 35.00 (0-394-58054-0) Knopf.
William Cooper's Town: Power & Persuasion on the Frontier of the Early American Republic. Alan Taylor. 560p. 1996. pap. 17.00 (0-679-77300-2, Vin) Random.
*William Cooper's Town: Signed Edition. Alan Taylor. 1997. 35.00 (0-676-51868-0) Random.
William Cornwall & His Descendants; a Genealogical History of the Family of William Cornwall, Who Came to America in 1633 & Died in Middleton, Connecticut in 1678. E. Cornwall. 185p. 1993. reprint ed. pap. 28.00 (0-8328-1381-8); reprint ed. lib. bdg. 38.00 (0-8328-1380-X) Higginson Bk Co.
William Cowper. Hugh I. Fausset. (BCL1-PR English Literature Ser.). 319p. 1992. reprint ed. lib. bdg. 89.00 (0-7812-7339-0) Rprt Serv.
William Cowper: A Biography. James King. LC 85-25352. (Illus.). xiii, 340p. 1986. text ed. 39.50 (0-8223-0513-5) Duke.
William Cowper: A Critical Life. Maurice J. Quinlan. LC 79-106670. 251p. 1970. reprint ed. text ed. 55.00 (0-8371-3425-0, QUWC, Greenwood Pr) Greenwood.
William Cowper: Poet of Paradise. George M. Ella. 1993. 49.99 (0-85234-306-X, Pub. by Evangelical Pr) Presby & Reformed.
*William Cowper (1731-1800) Selected Poems. Ed. by Nicholas Rhodes. pap. write for info. (0-85635-414-7, Pub. by Carcanet Pr UK) Paul & Co Pubs.
William Crolly, Archbishop of Armagh, 1835-1849. Ambrose Macaulay. 496p. 1994. 35.00 (1-85182-147-3, Pub. by Four Cts Pr IE) Intl Spec Bk.
William Cullen & the 18th Century Medical World. Ed. by Reginald Passmore et al. (Illus.). 256p. 1993. text ed. 49.00 (0-7486-0302-6, Pub. by Edinburgh U Pr UK) Col U Pr.
William Cullen Bryant. Albert F. McLean, Jr. (Twayne's United States Authors Ser.). 1964. pap. 13.95 (0-8084-0323-0, T59) NCUP.
William Cullen Bryant. Samuel Sillen. 16.95 (0-8488-1167-4) Amereon Ltd.
William Cullen Bryant. John Bigelow. LC 70-125678. (American Journalists Ser.). 1978. reprint ed. 25.95 (0-405-01653-0) Ayer.
William Cullen Bryant. Harriot Curtis. (Works of Harriot Curtis Ser.). 1990. reprint ed. lib. bdg. 90.00 (0-7812-2468-3) Rprt Serv.
William Cullen Bryant, 2 vols. Parke Godwin. 1993. reprint ed. Set. lib. bdg. 150.00 (0-7812-5271-7) Rprt Serv.
William Cullen Bryant & His Critics, 1808-1872: A Bibliography. Compiled by Judith T. Phair. LC 74-18203. v, 188p. 1974. 12.50 (0-87875-064-9) Whitston Pub.
William Cullen Bryant & Isaac Henderson: New Evidence on a Strange Partnership. Theodore Hornberger. LC 72-6771. (American Biography Ser.: No. 32). 1972. reprint ed. lib. bdg. 39.95 (0-8383-1645-X) M S G Haskell Hse.
William Cullen Bryant in Roslyn. Diane T. Bennett & Linda Tarleton. LC 78-67782. 164p. 1978. pap. 7.95 (0-9602242-1-1) Bryant Library.
William D. Berry, 1954-1956, Alaskan Field Sketches. Illus. by William D. Berry. LC 89-4927. xvii, 304p. 1989. 39.95 (0-912006-34-X); pap. 19.95 (0-912006-36-6) U of Alaska Pr.
William D. Howells. William M. Gibson. LC 67-26663. (University of Minnesota Pamphlets on American Writers Ser.: No. 63). 48p. (Orig.). 1967. reprint ed. pap. 25.00 (0-7837-2885-9, 2057570) Bks Demand.
William D. Wittliff & the Encino Press: A Bibliography. limited ed. Gould Whaley, Jr. LC 89-4563. (Illus.). 160p. 1989. 15.00 (0-933841-06-X) Still Point TX.
William Daley: Ceramic Works & Drawings. Matthew J. Drutt. LC 93-79842. (Illus.). 36p. (Orig.). 1993. pap. 21.00 (0-8122-1541-9) U of Pa Pr.
William Dawson LeSueur (1840-1917), a Canadian Man of Letters: The Sage of Ottawa. Clifford G. Holland. LC 93-18840. (Illus.). 336p. 1993. text ed. 79.95 (0-7734-2220-X, Mellen Univ Pr) E Mellen.
William de la Pole, Merchant & King's Banker (d1366) E. B. Fryde. 250p. (C). 1988. text ed. 55.00 (0-907628-35-4) Hambledon Press.
William De Morgan Tiles. Jon Catleugh. (Illus.). 134p. pap. 20.00 (0-903685-27-2, Pub. by R Dennis UK) Antique Collect.
William Dean Howells. Rudolf Kirk & Clara M. Kirk. (Twayne's United States Authors Ser.). 1962. pap. 13.95 (0-8084-0324-9, T16) NCUP.
William Dean Howells. A. Harvey. LC 72-697. (American Literature Ser.: No. 49). 267p. 1972. reprint ed. lib. bdg. 42.95 (0-8383-1379-5) M S G Haskell Hse.
William Dean Howells: A Critical Study. Delmar G. Cooke. (BCL1-PS American Literature Ser.). 279p. 1992. reprint ed. lib. bdg. 79.00 (0-7812-6746-3) Rprt Serv.
William Desmond Taylor: A Dossier. Bruce Long. LC 91-32607. (Filmmakers Ser.: No. 28). (Illus.). 471p. 1991. 47.50 (0-8108-2490-6) Scarecrow.
William Diller Matthew, Paleontologist: The Splendid Drama Observed. Edwin H. Colbert. LC 92-14027. (Illus.). 272p. 1992. text ed. 47.50 (0-231-07964-8) Col U Pr.
William Dorsey's Philadelphia & Ours: On the Past & Future of the Black City in America. Roger Lane. (Illus.). 512p. 1991. 42.00 (0-19-506566-2, 11827) OUP.

W

An Asterisk (*) at the beginning of an entry indicates that the title is appearing in BIP for the first time.

William Douglas O'Connor: Walt Whitman's Chosen Knight. Florence B. Freedman. LC 84-25451. (Illus.). 450p. 1985. text ed. 35.00 (*0-8214-0767-8*) Ohio U Pr.

William Duane, Radical Journalist in the Age of Jefferson. Kim T. Phillips. (Outstanding Studies in Early American History). 681p. 1989. reprint ed. 35.00 (*0-8240-6193-4*) Garland.

***William Dunbar.** Priscilla Bawcutt. (C). 1996. pap. text ed. 29.50 (*0-582-06187-3*) Addison-Wesley.

William Dunbar. William H. Smeaton. reprint ed. 29.50 (*0-404-08604-7*) AMS Pr.

William Dunbar: A Biographical Study. John W. Baxter. LC 71-148872. (Select Bibliographies Reprint Ser.). 1977. reprint ed. 23.95 (*0-8369-5672-9*) Ayer.

William Dunbar Poems. William Dunbar. LC 74-161966. 159p. 1958. reprint ed. 29.00 (*0-403-01339-9*) Scholarly.

William E. Barry's "Sketch of an Old River" William E. Barry & Joyce Butler. LC 93-24163. (Illus.). 88p. 1993. 25.00 (*0-914659-64-2*) Phoenix Pub.

William Eastlake: High Desert Interlocutor. W. C. Bamberger. LC 92-24444. (Milford Series: Popular Writers of Today: Popular Writers of Today: Vol. 65). 136p. 1993. pap. 19.00 (*0-89370-296-X*); lib. bdg. 29.00 (*0-89370-196-3*) Borgo Pr.

***William Eastlake/Aidan Higgins.** (Review of Contemporary Fiction Ser.: Vol. 3, No. 1). 1983. pap. 8.00 (*1-56478-102-X*) Dalkey Arch.

***William Edward Dodd: The South's Yeoman Scholar.** Fred A. Bailey. LC 96-47667. (Minds of the New South Ser.). 320p. 1997. text ed. 42.50 (*0-8139-1708-5*) U Pr of Va.

William Elder, Ancestors & Descendants. Mary L. Donnelly. LC 86-180069. (Illus.). 640p. 1986. 45.00 (*0-939142-10-4*) M L Donnelly.

William Ellery Channing. Arthur W. Brown. (Twayne's United States Authors Ser.). 1961. pap. 13.95 (*0-8084-0325-7*, T7) NCUP.

William Ellery Channing: An Essay on the Liberal Spirit in America. Andrew Delbanco. LC 80-19304. 223p. (C). 1981. 28.50 (*0-674-95335-5*) HUP.

William Ellery Channing: Selected Writings. Ed. by David Robinson. LC 84-62567. (Sources of American Spirituality Ser.: Vol. 2). 320p. 1985. 12.95 (*0-8091-0359-1*) Paulist Pr.

William Ellery Channing & l'Academie des Sciences Morales et Politiques, 1870: "L'Etude sur Channing" & the "Lost" Prize Essay. Hester Hastings. LC 59-10107. 67p. reprint ed. 25.00 (*0-685-15662-1*, 2027507) Bks Demand.

William Elliott Shoots a Bear: Essays on the Southern Literary Imagination. fac. ed. Louis D. Rubin. LC 75-5352. 295p. 1975. reprint ed. pap. 84.10 (*0-7837-7820-1*, 2047576) Bks Demand.

William Elphinstone & the Kingdom of Scotland 1431-1514: The Struggle for Order. Leslie J. MacFarlane. (Illus.). 540p. 1985. text ed. 60.00 (*0-08-030408-7*, Pub. by Aberdeen U Pr) Macmillan.

William Empson: Prophet Against Sacrifice. Paul H. Fry. (Critics of the Twentieth Century Ser.). 224p. (C). (gr. 13). 1991. text ed. 65.00 (*0-415-02482-X*, A6176) Routledge.

William Empson: Shakespeare's Shrew Essays, Memoirs & Reviews, & the Inaugural Lecture. Ed. by John Haffenden. (Sheffield Academic Press Ser.). 125p. 1995. 49.00 (*1-85075-608-2*, Pub. by Sheffield Acad UK) CUP Services.

William Empson: The Critical Achievement. Ed. by Christopher Norris & Nigel Mapp. 330p. (C). 1993. text ed. 59.95 (*0-521-35386-6*) Cambridge U Pr.

William Empson & the Philosophy of Literary Criticism. C. C. Norris. 222p. (C). 1978. text ed. 36.50 (*0-485-11175-6*, Pub. by Athlone Pr UK) Humanities.

William Ernest Henley. L. C. Cornford. 1972. 59.95 (*0-8490-1302-X*) Gordon Pr.

William Ernest Henley. Joseph M. Flora. LC 72-120015. (Twayne's English Authors Ser.). 1970. pap. text ed. 4.95 (*0-89197-994-8*); lib. bdg. 17.95 (*0-89197-977-8*) Irvington.

William Ernest Henley. John H. Robertson. 1972. 59.95 (*0-8490-1303-8*) Gordon Pr.

William Ernest Henley. L. C. Cornford. LC 72-3679. (English Biography Ser.: No. 31). 1972. reprint ed. lib. bdg. 45.95 (*0-8383-1580-1*) M S G Haskell Hse.

William Everson. Lee Bartlett. LC 85-70127. (Western Writers Ser.: No. 67). (Illus.). 50p. (Orig.). 1985. pap. 4.95 (*0-88430-041-2*) Boise St U W Writ Ser.

William Everson: A Descriptive Bibliography, 1934-1976. Lee Bartlett & Allan Campo. LC 77-5397. (Author Bibliographies Ser.: No. 33). 119p. 1977. 20.00 (*0-8108-1037-9*) Scarecrow.

William Everson: Poet from the San Joaquin. Campo et al. 1978. pap. 5.00 (*0-912950-44-7*) Blue Oak.

William Everson: The Life of Brother Antoninus. Lee Bartlett. LC 87-11034. (Illus.). 288p. 1988. 25.95 (*0-8112-1060-X*) New Directions.

William Everson: The Light the Shadow Casts. Ed. by Clifton Ross. 1995. write for info. (*1-873012-95-0*, Pub. by Stride Publns UK) New Earth Pr.

William Everson: The Light the Shadow Casts. Clifton Ross. 120p. (Orig.). 1996. pap. 11.95 (*0-915117-05-3*) New Earth Pubns.

William Everson - On Writing the Waterbirds & Other Presentations: Collected Forewords & Afterwords 1935-1981. Ed. by Lee Bartlett. LC 83-3123. 288p. 1983. 22.50 (*0-8108-1617-2*) Scarecrow.

William Ewart Gladstone: Faith & Politics in Victorian Britain. David W. Bebbington. (Library of Religious Biography). 287p. (C). 1993. pap. 15.00 (*0-8028-0152-8*) Eerdmans.

William F. Harrah: My Recollections of the Hotel-Casino Industry & As an Auto Collecting Enthusiast. Ed. by Mary E. Glass. 793p. 1980. Set. lib. bdg. 98.50 (*1-56475-191-0*); Set. fiche write for info. (*1-56475-194-5*) U NV Oral Hist.

William F. Reese. Mary N. Balcomb. LC 83-72443. (Illus.). 176p. 1984. 70.00 (*0-916029-00-X*) Blue Raven Pub Co.

William F. Reese. limited ed. Mary N. Balcomb. LC 83-72443. (Illus.). 176p. 1984. 600.00 (*0-916029-01-8*) Blue Raven Pub Co.

William F. Sauer: Memoirs of a Pioneer Livestock Rancher of Washoe Valley, Nevada. Intro. by Mary E. Glass. 55p. 1969. lib. bdg. 25.50 (*1-56475-071-X*); fiche write for info. (*1-56475-072-8*) U NV Oral Hist.

William Farel & the Story of the Swiss Reform. William M. Blackburn. reprint ed. 44.50 (*0-404-19870-8*) AMS Pr.

***William Faulkner.** Ed. by John E. Bassett. (Critical Heritage Ser.). 438p. (C). 1997. text ed. 35.00 (*0-415-15933-4*) Routledge.

William Faulkner. David Dowling. (Modern Novelists Ser.). 195p. 1992. pap. 12.95 (*0-333-42856-0*) St Martin.

William Faulkner. Michael Gidley. (Modern Fiction Ser.). 128p. 1992. pap. 10.95 (*0-7131-6579-0*, A9461, Pub. by E Arnold UK) Routledge Chapman & Hall.

William Faulkner. William V. O'Connor. LC 59-63269. (University of Minnesota Pamphlets on American Writers Ser.: No. 3). 47p. reprint ed. pap. 25.00 (*0-317-29465-2*, 2055928) Bks Demand.

William Faulkner: A Bibliography of Secondary Works. Compiled by Beatrice Ricks. LC 80-15251. (Author Bibliographies Ser.: No. 49). 684p. 1981. lib. bdg. 57.00 (*0-8108-1323-8*) Scarecrow.

William Faulkner: A Critical Study. 4th ed. Irving Howe. 324p. 1991. pap. text ed. 13.95 (*0-929587-69-3*, Elephant Paperbacks) I R Dee.

William Faulkner: An Interpretation. Irving Malin. LC 76-165664. 109p. 1972. reprint ed. 35.00 (*0-87752-154-9*) Gordian.

William Faulkner: Art in Theological Tension. John W. Hunt. LC 72-6942. (Studies in Fiction: No. 34). 1972. reprint ed. lib. bdg. 75.00 (*0-8383-1658-1*) M S G Haskell Hse.

William Faulkner: Critical Collection...A Guide to Critical Studies with Statements by Faulkner & Evaluative Essays on His Works. Leland H. Cox. (Gale Author Handbook Ser.: Vol. 2). 536p. 1982. 75.00 (*0-8103-1118-6*) Gale.

William Faulkner: First Encounters. Cleanth Brooks. LC 83-3634. 224p. 1985. reprint ed. pap. 15.00 (*0-300-03399-0*, Y-523) Yale U Pr.

William Faulkner: His Life & Work. David Minter. LC 80-13089. 344p. 1982. pap. 15.95 (*0-8018-2463-X*) Johns Hopkins.

***William Faulkner: His Life & Work.** David Minter. 1997. pap. text ed. 15.95 (*0-8018-5747-3*) Johns Hopkins.

William Faulkner: His Tippah County Heritage. limited ed. Jane I. Haynes. 1985. 29.50 (*0-935239-03-0*) Seajay Society.

William Faulkner: Letters & Fictions. James G. Watson. 232p. 1987. reprint ed. pap. 9.95 (*0-292-79044-9*) U of Tex Pr.

William Faulkner: The Abstract & the Actual. Panthea R. Broughton. LC 74-77324. 240p. 1974. pap. 68.40 (*0-7837-8460-0*, 2049265) Bks Demand.

William Faulkner: The Art of Stylization. Lothar Honnighausen. (Cambridge Studies in American Literature & Culture: No. 24). 240p. 1987. 74.95 (*0-521-33280-X*) Cambridge U Pr.

William Faulkner: The Contemporary Reviews. Ed. by M. Thomas Inge. LC 93-45790. (American Critical Archives Ser.: No. 5). 512p. (C). 1995. text ed. 110.00 (*0-521-38377-3*) Cambridge U Pr.

***William Faulkner: The Making of a Modernist.** Daniel J. Singal. LC 96-51459. (Fred W. Morrison Series in Southern Studies). 368p. (C). (gr. 13). 1997. 29.95 (*0-8078-2355-4*) U of NC Pr.

William Faulkner: The Man & the Artist. Stephen B. Oates. (Illus.). 363p. 1991. 6.99 (*0-517-05345-4*) Random Hse Value.

William Faulkner: The Yoknapatawpha Country. Cleanth Brooks. LC 63-17023. 500p. 1990. pap. 18.95 (*0-8071-1601-7*) La State U Pr.

William Faulkner: The Yoknapatawpha Fiction. Ed. by A. Robert Lee. (Critical Studies of Key Texts). 224p. 1990. text ed. 39.95 (*0-312-03571-3*) St Martin.

William Faulkner: Toward Yoknapatawpha & Beyond. Cleanth Brooks. LC 89-13317. 445p. 1990. pap. 18.95 (*0-8071-1602-5*) La State U Pr.

William Faulkner see Modern Critical Views Series

William Faulkner and Southern History. Joel Williamson. (Illus.). 544p. 1995. pap. 17.95 (*0-19-510129-4*) OUP.

William Faulkner & the Rites of Passage. Christopher A. LaLonde. 208p. (C). 1995. text ed. 25.00 (*0-86554-482-4*, MUP/H378) Mercer Univ Pr.

William Faulkner & the Tangible Past: The Architecture of Yoknapatawpha. Thomas S. Hines. LC 95-52565. (Illus.). 164p. 1996. 35.00 (*0-520-20293-7*) U CA Pr.

William Faulkner, Biographical & Reference Guide: A Guide to His Life & Career. Leland H. Cox. (Gale Author Handbook Ser.: Vol. 1). 304p. 1982. 75.00 (*0-8103-1117-8*) Gale.

William Faulkner, Life Glimpses. Louis D. Brodsky. (Illus.). 224p. 1990. 27.50 (*0-292-79048-1*) U of Tex Pr.

William Faulkner, "Man Working," 1919-1962: A Catalogue of the William Faulkner Collections at the University of Virginia. University of Virginia Library Staff & Linton R. Massey. LC 68-19477. 268p. reprint ed. pap. 76.40 (*0-317-30465-8*, 2024829) Bks Demand.

William Faulkner of Oxford. Ed. by James W. Webb & A. Wigfall Green. LC 65-23763. (Illus.). 264p. reprint ed. 75.30 (*0-8357-9395-8*, 2051671) Bks Demand.

William Faulkner, the William B. Wisdom Collection: A Descriptive Catalog. Thomas Bonner, Jr. & Guillermo N. Falcon. LC 79-26556. (Illus.). 1980. pap. 13.00 (*0-9603212-2-5*) Tulane Univ.

William Faulkner's "Absalom, Absalom!" A Critical Study. David P. Ragan. Ed. by A. Walton Litz. LC 87-23300. (Studies in Modern Literature: No. 85). 244p. reprint ed. 66.70 (*0-8357-1840-9*, 2070755) Bks Demand.

William Faulkner's Craft of Revision: The Snopes Trilogy, The Unvanquished, & Go Down, Moses. Joanne V. Creighton. LC 76-51441. 183p. reprint ed. pap. 52.20 (*0-685-20908-3*, 2032040) Bks Demand.

William Faulkner's First Book: The Marble Faun Fifty Years Later. William Boozer. LC 75-6916. (Illus.). 1975. 7.50 (*0-686-12125-2*) Pigeon Roost Pr.

William Faulkner's Old Verities: It's Planting Time in America. Jack Valenti. (Louis Nizer Lecture Ser.). (Illus.). 19p. 1995. pap. write for info. (*0-87641-150-2*) Carnegie Ethics & Intl Affairs.

William Faulkner's Short Stories. James B. Carothers. LC 85-8523. (Studies in Modern Literature: No. 34). 183p. reprint ed. pap. 52.20 (*0-8357-1500-0*, 2070630) Bks Demand.

William Faulkner's Soldier's Pay: A Bibliographical Study. Ed. by Francis J. Bosha. LC 80-54205. 539p. 1982. 42.50 (*0-87875-211-0*) Whitston Pub.

***William Faulkner's The Sound & the Fury.** Harold Bloom. (Bloom's Notes Ser.). (YA). 1997. text ed. 16.95 (*0-7910-4519-6*) Chelsea Hse.

William Faulkner's The Sound & the Fury see Modern Critical Interpretations

William Faulkner's Women Characters: An Annotated Bibliography of Criticism, 1930-1983. Patricia E. Sweeney. LC 84-24572. 497p. 1984. lib. bdg. 61.95 (*0-87436-411-6*) ABC-CLIO.

William Faulkner's Yoknapatawpha: A Kind of Keystone in the Universe. rev. ed. Elizabeth M. Kerr. LC 82-83490. 447p. reprint ed. pap. 127.40 (*0-7837-5606-2*, 2045512) Bks Demand.

William Flete, O. S. A., & Catherine of Siena: Masters of Fourteenth Century Spirituality. Benedict Hackett. Ed. by John E. Rotelle. LC 92-34094. (Augustinian Ser.: Vol. 15). (Illus.). 232p. 1993. 21.00 (*0-941491-52-8*); pap. 13.00 (*0-941491-53-6*) Augustinian Pr.

William Fortune: A Hoosier Biography. Charles Latham. (Illus.). 150p. 1994. 18.95 (*1-878208-37-3*) Guild Pr IN.

William Foxwell Albright: A 20th Century Genius. Leona G. Running & David N. Freedman. LC 75-11180. 466p. (C). 1991. pap. 14.99 (*0-8467-0071-9*) Andrews Univ Pr.

William Frederick Foster, A.N.A. Portrait of a Painter. Phyllis S. Barton. (Illus.). 472p. (C). 1988. 155.00 (*0-9619161-0-9*) Richlaine Pub.

William Freeman Vilas: Doctrinaire Democrat. Horace S. Merrill. 310p. 1992. reprint ed. text ed. 15.00 (*0-87020-269-3*) State Hist Soc Wis.

William Friday: Power, Purpose, & American Higher Education. William A. Link. LC 94-5723. (Illus.). 512p. 1995. 29.95 (*0-8078-2167-5*) U of NC Pr.

***William Friday: Power, Purpose & American Higher Education.** William A. Link. 512p. (C). 1995. pap. 16.95 (*0-8078-4680-5*) U of NC Pr.

William Friedkin: Films of Aberration, Obsession & Reality. Thomas D. Clagett. LC 89-43693. (Illus.). 316p. 1990. lib. bdg. 38.50 (*0-89950-262-8*) McFarland & Co.

William Fryer Harvey 1885-1937. Charles Fryer. (C). 1988. 30.00 (*0-900657-61-8*, Pub. by W Sessions UK) St Mut.

William Fulbright & the Vietnam War: The Dissent of a Political Realist. William C. Berman. LC 87-22600. 247p. 1988. 24.00 (*0-87338-351-6*) Kent St U Pr.

William G. Brownlow: Fighting Parson of the Southern Highlands. E. Merton Coulter. LC 71-136309. (Tennesseana Editions Ser.). (Illus.). 458p. reprint ed. pap. 130.60 (*0-8357-9767-8*, 2016173) Bks Demand.

William Gager: The Complete Works. William Gager. Ed. by Dana F. Sutton. LC 93-38853. (Renaissance Imagination Ser.). 400p. 1994. text ed. 87.00 (*0-8153-1692-5*) Garland.

William Gager: The Complete Works, the Shrovetide Plays. William Gager. Tr. & Comment by Dana F. Sutton. LC 93-38853. (Renaissance Imagination Ser.: Vol. 2). 272p. 1994. text ed. 69.00 (*0-8153-1693-3*) Garland.

William Gager Vol. IV: The Complete Works: Juvenilia, Pyramis, Collected Prose. Dana F. Sutton. LC 93-38853. (Renaissance Imagination Ser.). 320p. 1994. text ed. 78.00 (*0-8153-1695-X*) Garland.

William Gager, the Complete Works, Vol. 3: Poems. William Gager. LC 93-38853. (Renaissance Imagination Ser.). 464p. 1994. text ed. 103.00 (*0-8153-1694-1*) Garland.

William Gager's Pyramis. Charles F. Brooke. (Connecticut Academy of Arts & Sciences Ser., Trans.: Vol. 32). 1936. pap. 49.50 (*0-685-22918-1*) Elliots Bks.

William Garnett, Aerial Photographs. Photos by William Garnett. LC 93-48733. 1994. 45.00 (*0-520-08445-4*) U CA Pr.

William Garnett, Aerial Photographs. William Garnett. LC 92-41827. (Illus.). 159p. (C). 1996. pap. 29.95 (*0-520-08348-2*) U CA Pr.

William Gass. Watson L. Holloway. (Twayne's United States Authors Ser.: No. 564). 160p. (C). 1990. 22.95 (*0-8057-7605-2*, Twayne) Scribnrs Ref.

William George Ward & the Catholic Revival. Wilfrid P. Ward. LC 75-29626. reprint ed. 57.50 (*0-404-14042-4*) AMS Pr.

William George Ward & the Oxford Movement. Wilfrid P. Ward. LC 75-29625. reprint ed. 57.50 (*0-404-14043-2*) AMS Pr.

William Gerhardie: A Biography. Dido Davies. (Illus.). 432p. 1990. 70.00 (*0-19-211794-7*) OUP.

William Gibson. Lance Olsen. LC 93-201910. (Starmont Reader's Guide Ser.: Vol. 58). vii, 131p. 1992. pap. 19.00 (*1-55742-198-6*); lib. bdg. 29.00 (*1-55742-199-4*) Borgo Pr.

William Gilmore Simms. Joseph V. Ridgely. (Twayne's United States Authors Ser.). 1962. pap. 13.95 (*0-8084-0327-3*, T28) NCUP.

William Gilmore Simms. William P. Trent. LC 68-24944. (American Biography Ser.: No. 32). 1969. reprint ed. lib. bdg. 75.00 (*0-8383-0249-1*) M S G Haskell Hse.

William Gilmore Simms. William P. Trent. (BCL1-PS American Literature Ser.). 351p. 1992. reprint ed. lib. bdg. 89.00 (*0-7812-6861-3*) Rprt Serv.

William Gilmore Simms & the American Frontier. John C. Guilds & Caroline Collins. LC 96-24254. 1997. 55.00 (*0-8203-1887-6*) U of Ga Pr.

William Gilpin, Western Nationalist. Thomas L. Karnes. LC 77-105398. 399p. reprint ed. pap. 113.80 (*0-7837-1012-7*, 2041323) Bks Demand.

William Glackens. William H. Gerdts & Jorge H. Santis. LC 95-38383. (Illus.). 288p. 1996. 85.00 (*1-55859-868-5*) Abbeville Pr.

William Glackens & the Eight: The Artists Who Freed American Art. Ira Glackens. (Illus.). 268p. 1991. pap. 12.95 (*0-86316-076-X*) Writers & Readers.

William Godwin. D. Fleisher. 1974. 69.95 (*0-87968-276-0*) Gordon Pr.

William Godwin: A Biographical Study. George Woodcock. 266p. (C). 1989. reprint ed. 36.95 (*0-921689-49-7*, Pub. by Black Rose Bks CN); reprint ed. pap. 16.95 (*0-921689-48-9*, Pub. by Black Rose Bks CN) Consort Bk Sales.

William Godwin: A Chronology. V. Munoz. Tr. by W. Scott Johnson. (Libertarian & Anarchist Chronology Ser.). 1979. lib. bdg. 59.95 (*0-8490-3026-9*) Gordon Pr.

William Godwin: His Friends & Contemporaries, 2 Vols, Set. C. Kegan Paul. LC 73-115359. reprint ed. write for info. (*0-404-04941-9*) AMS Pr.

William Godwin: Philosopher, Novelist, Revolutionary. Peter H. Marshall. LC 83-19823. (Illus.). 498p. 1984. text ed. 55.00 (*0-300-03175-0*) Yale U Pr.

William Godwin & Mary Wollstonecraft. Victor Robinson. 1972. 250.00 (*0-8490-1304-6*) Gordon Pr.

William Goebel: The Politics of Wrath. James C. Klotter. LC 77-76335. (Kentucky Bicentennial Bookshelf Ser.). (Illus.). 152p. 1978. 12.95 (*0-8131-0240-5*) U Pr of Ky.

William Golding. Kulkarni. (C). 1994. 22.00 (*81-7156-391-0*, Pub. by Atlantic Pubs II) S Asia.

William Golding. Kevin McCarron. 1990. 60.00 (*0-7463-0730-6*, Pub. by Northcote House UK) St Mut.

William Golding. Kevin McCarron. (Writers & Their Work Ser.). 95p. 1996. pap. text ed. 15.00 (*0-7463-0735-7*, Pub. by Nrthcote House UK) U Pr of Miss.

William Golding: A Critical Study. V. V. Subbarao. LC 87-80664. 1987. text ed. 22.50 (*0-938719-21-1*, Envoy Pr) Apt Bks.

William Golding: A Structural Reading of His Fiction. Philip Redpath. LC 86-10710. 224p. 1986. 58.50 (*0-389-20647-4*, N8204) B&N Imports.

William Golding: Some Critical Considerations. Ed. by Jack I. Biles & Robert O. Evans. LC 77-73705. 295p. reprint ed. pap. 84.10 (*0-317-26707-8*, 2024357) Bks Demand.

William Golding's Lord of the Flies see Bloom's Notes

William Goldman: Five Screenplays. William Goldman. 580p. 1996. 25.95 (*1-55783-266-8*) Applause Theatre Bk Pubs.

William Goldman: Four Screenplays. William Goldman. 492p. 1995. 25.95 (*1-55783-198-X*) Applause Theatre Bk Pubs.

William Goldman: Four Screenplays. William Goldman. 492p. 1996. pap. 18.95 (*1-55783-265-X*) Applause Theatre Bk Pubs.

William Goyen: A Descriptive Bibliography, 1938-1985. Stuart Wright. 181p. 1986. text ed. 49.95 (*0-313-27710-9*) Greenwood.

William Goyen: Selected Letters from a Writer's Life. William Goyen. Ed. by Robert Phillips. (Illus.). 471p. 1995. 34.95 (*0-292-72773-9*) U of Tex Pr.

William Grant Still: A Bio-Bibliography. Judith A. Still et al. LC 96-21946. (Bio-Bibliographies in Music Ser.: No. 61). 352p. 1996. text ed. 85.00 (*0-313-25255-6*, Greenwood Pr) Greenwood.

William Grant Still & the Fusion of Cultures in American Music. 2nd ed. Ed. by Judith A. Still et al. LC 96-77407. (Illus.). 360p. 1995. reprint ed. lib. bdg. 47.50 (*1-877873-01-2*) Master-Player Lib.

William Grant Still & the Fusion of Cultures in American Music. 2nd ed. Ed. by Judith A. Still et al. LC 96-77407. (Illus.). 360p. 1995. reprint ed. pap. 29.95 (*1-877873-05-5*) Master-Player Lib.

William Greatbatch. David Barker. (Illus.). 288p. 1991. 95.00 (*0-9512140-3-9*, Pub. by J Horne UK) Antique Collect.

William Green: Biography of a Labor Leader. Craig Phelan. LC 88-12356. (SUNY Series in American Labor History). 223p. (Orig.). (C). 1988. pap. text ed. 21.95 (*0-88706-871-5*) State U NY Pr.

William Green: Biography of a Labor Leader. Craig Phelan. LC 88-12356. (SUNY Series in American Labor History). 223p. (Orig.). (C). 1989. text ed. 64.50 (*0-88706-870-7*) State U NY Pr.

William Gropper. Louis Lozowick. (Illus.). 200p. 1983. 40.00 (*0-87982-033-0*) Art Alliance.

William Gropper. Louis Lozowick. LC 80-67118. (Illus.). 240p. 1983. 40.00 (*0-8453-4730-6*, Cornwall Bks) Assoc Univ Prs.

William H. Ashley: Enterprise & Politics in the Trans-Mississippi West. Richard M. Clokey. LC 78-21396. (Illus.). 320p. 1990. reprint ed. pap. 14.95 (0-8061-2216-1) U of Okla Pr.

William H. Crawford, Seventeen Seventy-Two to Eighteen Thirty-Four. Chase Mooney. LC 70-190534. 386p. reprint ed. pap. 110.10 (0-317-26727-2, 2024361) Bks Demand.

William H. Gates: From Whiz Kid to Software King. Ralph Zickgraf. Ed. by Richard G. Young. LC 91-32056. (Wizards of Business Ser.). (Illus.). 64p. (J). (gr. 4-8). 1992. lib. bdg. 17.26 (1-56074-016-7) Garrett Ed Corp.

William H. Gray: Journal of His Journey East, 1836-1837. William H. Gray. Ed. by Donald R. Johnson. 88p. 1980. 12.00 (0-87770-241-1) Ye Galleon.

William H. Taft: Twenty-Seventh President of the United States. Lucille Falkof. Ed. by Richard G. Young. LC 89-39947. (Presidents of the United States Ser.). (Illus.). 128p. (J). (gr. 5-9). 1990. lib. bdg. 17.26 (0-944483-56-9) Garrett Ed Corp.

William H. Webb: Shipbuilder. Edwin L. Dunbaugh & William D. Thomas. LC 89-50473. (Illus.). xiv, 240p. 1989. 35.00 (0-9622631-0-9) Webb Inst Naval Arch.

***William H. Welch & the Rise of Modern Medicine.** Donald Fleming. Ed. by Oscar Handlin. LC 86-46273. 240p. 1987. reprint ed. pap. 68.40 (0-608-03684-6, 2064510) Bks Demand.

William H. Willimon's Last Laugh. Compiled by William H. Willimon. LC 90-49556. 160p. 1991. 14.95 (0-687-45598-7) Abingdon.

William Hale White (Mark Rutherford) A Critical Study. Irvin Stock. LC 72-126260. (Select Bibliographies Reprint Ser.). 1977. 21.95 (0-8369-5487-4) Ayer.

William Harvey: Discoverer of How Blood Circulates. Lisa Yount. LC 94-14254. (Great Minds of Science Ser.). (Illus.). 128p. (J). (gr. 4-10). 1994. lib. bdg. 18.95 (0-89490-481-7) Enslow Pubs.

William Harvey's Natural Philosophy. Roger French. LC 93-36181. (Illus.). 368p. (C). 1994. text ed. 69.95 (0-521-45535-9) Cambridge U Pr.

William Hawkins. F. Ricco & R. Maresea. 1997. 45.00 (0-679-45075-0) McKay.

William Hayes, Eighteen Seventy-One to Nineteen Forty: York Photographic Artist. Terry Buchanan. 82p. 1986. 43.00 (0-907033-39-3) St Mut.

William Hazlitt. A. Ireland. 1972. lib. bdg. 69.95 (0-8490-1305-4) Gordon Pr.

William Hazlitt. J. B. Priestley & R. L. Brett. (Writers & Their Work Ser.). 95p. (Orig.). 1996. pap. text ed. 15.00 (0-7463-0745-4, Pub. by Nrthcote House UK) U Pr of Miss.

William Hazlitt. Augustine Birrell. (BCL1-PR English Literature Ser.). 244p. 1992. reprint ed. lib. bdg. 79.00 (0-7812-7557-1) Rprt Serv.

William Hazlitt: (J. B. Priestley) Michael Foot. 1990. 40.00 (0-7463-0740-3, Pub. by Northcote UK); pap. 21.00 (0-685-67960-8, Pub. by Northcote UK) St Mut.

William Hazlitt, Critic of Power. John Kinnaird. (Illus.). 429p. 1978. text ed. 60.00 (0-231-04600-6) Col U Pr.

William Heath of Roxbury, Massachusetts & Some of His Descendants. Valerie D. Giorgi. LC 93-80090. (Illus.). 441p. 1993. 35.00 (0-9614222-2-X) Giorgi.

William Heighton: Pioneer Labor Leader of Jacksonian Philadelphia. Philip S. Foner. LC 91-29482. 1991. pap. 7.50 (0-7178-0689-8) Intl Pubs Co.

William Heinesen. W. Glyn Jones. LC 73-16402. (Twayne's World Authors Ser.). 201p. (C). 1974. lib. bdg. 17.95 (0-8057-2418-4) Irvington.

William Henry Bartlett: Artist, Author, & Traveller (Containing a Reprint of Dr. William Beattie's Brief Memoir of the Late William Henry Bartlett. Alexander M. Ross. (Illus.). 176p. reprint ed. pap. 50.20 (0-317-10533-7, 2020518) Bks Demand.

William Henry Belk: Merchant of the South. LeGette Blythe. LC 58-14574. xvi, 271p. 1950. 24.95 (0-8078-0729-X) U of NC Pr.

William Henry Bragg & William Lawrence Bragg: A Bibliography of Their Non-Technical Writings. Compiled by Henry Lowood. LC 77-94209. (Berkeley Papers in History of Science: No. 2). 109p. 1978. pap. 5.00 (0-918102-01-4) U Cal Hist Sci Tech.

William Henry Emerson: And the Scientific Discipline at Georgia Tech. Robert C. McMath, Jr. 130p. 1993. write for info. (0-9639968-9-4) C L Emerson.

William Henry Harrison. Christine M. Fitz-Gerald. LC 87-16842. (Encyclopedia of Presidents Ser.). (Illus.). 100p. (J). (gr. 3 up). 1987. lib. bdg. 22.00 (0-516-01392-0) Childrens.

William Henry Harrison: Ninth President of the United States. Rebecca Stefoff. Ed. by Richard G. Young. LC 89-25652. (Presidents of the United States Ser.). (Illus.). 128p. (J). (gr. 5-9). 1990. lib. bdg. 17.26 (0-944483-54-2) Garrett Ed Corp.

William Henry Hudson. John T. Frederick. 150p. 1972. 49.50 (0-685-63205-9) Elliots Bks.

William Henry Jackson: An Annotated Bibliography (1862 to 1995) annot. unabridged ed. Thomas H. Harrell. LC 95-78478. (Illus.). 64p. (Orig.). 1995. pap. 19.95 (1-887694-02-1, Folk Image Pub) C Mautz Pubng.

William Henry Jackson & the Transformation of the American Landscape. Peter B. Hales. (Illus.). 368p. (C). 1996. pap. 24.95 (1-56639-463-5) Temple U Pr.

William Henry Jackson's Colorado. William C. Jones & Elizabeth B. Jones. LC 75-33046. (Illus.). 208p. 1992. 39.95 (0-918654-47-5) CO RR Mus.

***William Henry Pyne & His Microcosm.** Harris Myers. (Illus.). 288p. 1996. 53.95 (0-7509-1232-4, Pub. by Sutton Pubng UK) Bks Intl VA.

William Henry Seward. Thorton K. Lothrop. Ed. by John T. Morse, Jr. LC 77-128959. (American Statesmen Ser.: No. 27). reprint ed. 45.00 (0-404-50877-4) AMS Pr.

William Henry Seward: Lincoln's Right Hand. John M. Taylor. (Illus.). 352p. 1996. pap. 21.95 (1-57488-119-1) Brasseys Inc.

William Henry Welch & the Heroic Age of American Medicine. Simon Flexner & James T. Flexner. LC 92-13529. (Illus.). 572p. 1993. reprint ed. 45.00 (0-8018-4501-7) Johns Hopkins.

***William Henry Wordsworth: The Eternal Romantic.** Chelsea House Publishing Staff. (Illustrated Poetry Anthology Ser.). (Illus.). 1997. 17.95 (1-86019-281-5) Chelsea Hse.

William Hickling Prescott. Harry T. Peck. LC 69-14033. 186p. 1969. reprint ed. text ed. 49.75 (0-8371-0614-1, PEWP, Greenwood Pr) Greenwood.

William Hickling Prescott. Harry T. Peck. (BCL1-PS American Literature Ser.). 186p. 1992. reprint ed. lib. bdg. 69.00 (0-7812-6838-9) Rprt Serv.

William Hickling Prescott: A Biography. Clinton H. Gardiner. LC 72-96223. 388p. reprint ed. pap. 110.60 (0-685-44051-6, 2030548) Bks Demand.

William Hickling Prescott: A Memorial. Ed. by Howard F. Cline et al. LC 59-16153. 189p. reprint ed. pap. 53.90 (0-317-42233-2, 2026192) Bks Demand.

William Hickling Prescott, 1796-1859. (Picture Bks.). 1958. pap. 4.00 (0-934909-54-7) Mass Hist Soc.

William Holman Hunt: The True Pre-Raphaelite. Anne C. Amor. (Illus.). 301p. 1995. reprint ed. pap. 29.50 (0-09-474370-3, Pub. by Constable Pubs UK) Trans-Atl Phila.

William Holmes McGuffey: Schoolmaster to the Nation. Dolores P. Sullivan. LC 92-55120. 1994. 39.50 (0-8386-3526-1) Fairleigh Dickinson.

William Hone: His Life & Times. Frederick W. Hackwood. LC 71-114025. (Illus.). 373p. 1970. reprint ed. lib. bdg. 49.50 (0-678-00640-7) Kelley.

William Howard Russell's Civil War: Private Diary & Letters, 1861-1862. William H. Russell. Ed. by Martin Crawford. LC 91-14194. (Illus.). 336p. 1992. 45.00 (0-8203-1369-6) U of Ga Pr.

William Howard Taft. Jane C. Casey. LC 88-8675. (Encyclopedia of Presidents Ser.). (Illus.). 100p. (J). (gr. 3 up). 1989. lib. bdg. 22.00 (0-516-01366-1) Childrens.

William Howard Taft: A Bibliography. Paolo E. Coletta. LC 89-3388. (Bibliographies of the Presidents of the United States Ser.: No. 26). 312p. 1989. text ed. 69.50 (0-313-28184-X, AP26, Greenwood Pr) Greenwood.

William Howard Taft: Chief Justice. Alpheus T. Mason. LC 83-6461. 354p. (C). 1983. reprint ed. pap. text ed. 34.50 (0-8191-3091-5) U Pr of Amer.

William Howard Taft: Collected Editorials, 1917-1921. Ed. by James Vivian. LC 89-16204. 656p. 1990. text ed. 89.50 (0-275-93199-4, C3199, Praeger Pubs) Greenwood.

William Howard Taft: In the Public Service. David H. Burton. LC 84-27778. 160p. (C). 1985. pap. text ed. 11.50 (0-89874-829-1) Krieger.

William Howard Taft & United States Foreign Policy: The Apprenticeship Years, 1900-1908. Ralph E. Minger. LC 75-6691. 253p. reprint ed. pap. 72.20 (0-317-29034-7, 2020228) Bks Demand.

William Humphrey. Mark R. Winchell. LC 92-52530. (Western Writers Ser.: No. 105). (Illus.). 52p. (Orig.). 1992. pap. 4.95 (0-88430-104-4) Boise St U W Writ Ser.

William Hunter & the Eighteenth Century Medical World. Ed. by William F. Bynum & Roy Porter. 450p. 1985. 95.00 (0-521-26806-0) Cambridge U Pr.

William Huskisson & Liberal Reform. 2nd ed. Alexander Brady. 177p. 1967. 35.00 (0-7146-1456-4, Pub. by F Cass Pubs UK) Intl Spec Bk.

William Hutt: Masks & Faces. Ed. by Keith Garebian. (Illus.). 180p. 1995. lib. bdg. 43.00 (0-8095-4889-5) Borgo Pr.

William Hutt: Masks & Faces. Ed. by Keith Garebian. (Illus.). 180p. 1995. pap. 16.95 (0-88962-583-2) Mosaic.

William I. Myers & the Modernization of American Agriculture. Douglas Slaybaugh. LC 96-10903. (Henry A. Wallace Series on Agricultural History & Rural Studies). 302p. 1996. text ed. 42.95 (0-8138-2038-3) Iowa St U Pr.

William III & the Godly Revolution. Tony Claydon. (Studies in Early Modern British History). (Illus.). 288p. (C). 1996. text ed. 59.95 (0-521-47329-2) Cambridge U Pr.

William III & the Revolution of 1688 & Gustavus Adolphus II Elected King of Sweden of the Goths & Vandals. Marjorie Bowen. 143p. (Orig.). 1988. pap. 7.95 (0-921100-06-X) Inhtce Pubns.

William Inge: A Research & Production Sourcebook. Richard M. Leeson. LC 93-46360. (Modern Dramatists Research & Production Sourcebooks Ser.: Vol. 5). 240p. 1994. text ed. 65.00 (0-313-27407-X, Greenwood Pr) Greenwood.

William Is My Brother. Jane T. Schnitter. LC 90-21364. (Illus.). 32p. (J). (ps-3). 1991. 12.00 (0-944934-03-X) Perspect Indiana.

William Ivey: Three Decades of Painting. Chris Bruce & Robert Sarkis. LC 89-15649. (Illus.). 60p. 1989. pap. 20.00 (0-935558-26-8) Henry Art.

William J. Fellner: A Bio-Bibliography. James N. Marshall. LC 92-15462. (Bio-Bibliographies in Economics Ser.: No. 1). 192p. 1992. text ed. 55.00 (0-313-25856-2, MWF, Greenwood Pr) Greenwood.

William J. Gedney's Central Tai Dialects: Glossaries, Texts, & Translations. Thomas J. Hudak. (Michigan Papers on South & Southeast Asia: No. 43). 75.00 (0-89148-075-7) Ctr S&SE Asian.

William J. Gedney's Southwestern Tai Dialects: Glossaries, Texts, & Translations. Ed. by Thomas J. Hudak. (Michigan Papers on South & Southeast Asia: 42). 1118p. 1995. 75.00 (0-89148-074-9) Ctr S&SE Asian.

William J. Gedney's "The Saek Language: Glossary, Texts, & Translations" Ed. by Thomas J. Hudak. LC 90-86277. (Michigan Papers on South & Southeast Asia: No. 41). (Illus.). 1060p. 1992. 75.00 (0-89148-073-0) Ctr S&SE Asian.

William J. Gedney's "The Tai Dialect of Lungming" Glossary, Texts, & Translations. Ed. by Thomas J. Hudak. LC 91-73886. (Michigan Papers on South & Southeast Asia: No. 39). (Illus.). 1232p. 1992. 75.00 (0-89148-067-6) Ctr S&SE Asian.

William J. Gedney's "The Yay Language" Glossary, Texts, & Translations. Ed. by Thomas J. Hudak. LC 90-86277. (Michigan Papers on South & Southeast Asia: No. 38). (Illus.). 794p. 1991. 65.00 (0-89148-066-8) Ctr S&SE Asian.

William J. Rhees on James Smithson: An Original Anthology, 2 Vols. William J. Rhees. Ed. by I. Bernard Cohen. LC 79-7996. (Three Centuries of Science in America Ser.). (Illus.). 1980. lib. bdg. 25.95 (0-405-12581-X) Ayer.

William Jaffe's Essays on Walras. Ed. by Donald A. Walker. 432p. 1983. text ed. 89.95 (0-521-25142-7) Cambridge U Pr.

William James. Graham Bird. LC 86-6569. 221p. 1987. 39.95 (0-7100-9602-X, RKP) Routledge.

William James. Bernard P. Brennan. (Twayne's United States Authors Ser.). 1968. pap. 13.95 (0-8084-0005-3, T131) NCUP.

William James. Gay W. Allen. LC 79-629874. (University of Minnesota Pamphlets on American Writers Ser.: No. 88). 48p. (Orig.). reprint ed. pap. 25.00 (0-7837-2902-2, 2057553) Bks Demand.

William James: A Biography. Reed. text ed. write for info. (0-7167-2942-3) W H Freeman.

William James: Selected Unpublished Correspondence, 1885-1910. Ed. by Frederick J. Scott. LC 86-720. 603p. 1986. 65.00 (0-8142-0379-5) Ohio St U Pr.

William James: Selected Writings. Intro. by Ron Yezzi. (Guides to Philosophy Ser.). 220p. (Orig.). (C). 1991. pap. text ed. 9.50 (0-9619368-2-7) G Bruno.

***William James: The Center of His Vision.** Daniel W. Bjork. LC 97-25815. 1997. write for info. (1-55798-454-9) Am Psychol.

William James: The Center of His Vision. Daniel W. Bjork. (Illus.). 338p. 1988. text ed. 52.50 (0-231-05674-5) Col U Pr.

William James: The Essential Writings. Ed. by Bruce Wilshire. LC 84-8848. 369p. 1984. text ed. 44.50 (0-87395-935-3); pap. text ed. 14.95 (0-87395-934-5) State U NY Pr.

William James & Henri Bergson: A Study in Contrasting Theories of Life. Horace M. Kallen. LC 75-3213. (Philosophy in America Ser.). reprint ed. 42.50 (0-404-59209-0) AMS Pr.

William James & John Dewey. Gordon H. Clark. Ed. & Intro. by John W. Robbins. 141p. 1995. pap. 8.95 (0-940931-43-5) Trinity Found.

William James & Phenomenology. James M. Edie. LC 86-45894. (Studies in Phenomenology & Existential Philosophy). 128p. 1987. 27.50 (0-253-36570-8) Ind U Pr.

***William James & Phenomenology.** James M. Edie. LC 86-45894. (Studies in Phenomenology & Existential Philosophy). 124p. pap. 35.40 (0-608-05016-4, 2059677) Bks Demand.

William James & Phenomenology: A Study of "The Principles of Psychology" Bruce Wilshire. LC 76-6601. reprint ed. 42.50 (0-404-15226-0) AMS Pr.

William James & the Affirmation of God. George P. Graham. LC 91-4082. (American University Studies: Theology & Religion: Ser. VII, Vol. 110). 321p. 1992. text ed. 39.95 (0-8204-1609-6) P Lang Pubng.

William James & the Reinstatement of the Vague. William J. Gavin. 240p. (C). 1992. 47.95 (0-87722-946-5) Temple U Pr.

William James Bennett: Master of the Aquatint View. Gloria G. Deak. LC 88-25268. (Illus.). (Orig.). 1988. pap. 17.95 (0-87104-411-0) NY Pub Lib.

William James Durant: An Intellectual Biography. Raymond Frey. LC 90-26398. (Studies in the History of Philosophy: Vol. 18). 204p. 1991. lib. bdg. 89.95 (0-88946-596-7) E Mellen.

William James on Consciousness Beyond the Margin. Eugene Taylor. LC 96-898. 232p. 1996. text ed. 35.00 (0-691-01136-2) Princeton U Pr.

William James on Psychical Research. William James. Ed. by Robert O. Ballou. LC 79-122078. viii, 339p. 1973. reprint ed. 39.50 (0-678-03164-9) Kelley.

William James on the Courage to Believe. Robert J. O'Connell. LC 83-83319. xiv, 141p. 1984. 30.00 (0-8232-1108-8) Fordham.

***William James on the Courage to Believe.** 2nd rev. ed. Robert O'Connell. LC 97-12135. (C). 1997. 30.00 (0-8232-1727-2) Fordham.

***William James on the Courage to Believe.** 2nd rev. ed. Robert O'Connell. LC 97-12135. (C). 1997. pap. 15.00 (0-8232-1728-0) Fordham.

William James "Pragmatism" in Focus. Ed. by Doris Olin. LC 91-35744. (Philosophers in Focus Ser.). 256p. (C). 1992. pap. 18.95 (0-415-04057-4, A7479) Routledge.

William James "Pragmatism" in Focus. Ed. by Doris Olin. LC 91-35744. (Philosophers in Focus Ser.). 256p. (C). (gr. 13). 1992. text ed. 89.95 (0-415-04056-6, A7475) Routledge.

William James, Public Philosopher. George Cotkin. LC 89-33036. (New Studies in American Intellectual & Cultural History). 272p. 1989. text ed. 38.00 (0-8018-3878-9) Johns Hopkins.

William James, Public Philosopher. George Cotkin. LC 93-36078. 232p. 1994. pap. text ed. 17.95 (0-252-06392-9) U of Ill Pr.

William James Remembered. Ed. by Linda Simon. LC 95-34521. xxxiii, 277p. 1996. text ed. 30.00 (0-8032-4248-4) U of Nebr Pr.

William James's Radical Reconstruction of Philosophy. Charlene H. Seigfried. LC 89-48392. 433p. (C). 1990. text ed. 64.50 (0-7914-0401-3); pap. text ed. 21.95 (0-7914-0402-1) State U NY Pr.

William Jay: And the Constitutional Movement for the Abolition of Slavery. Bayard Tuckerman. LC 75-108351. 208p. reprint ed. 17.50 (0-8337-3573-X) Ayer.

William Jay: Churchman, Public Servant & Reformer. Robert A. Trendel. 1981. 35.95 (0-405-14110-6) Ayer.

William Jay & the Constitutional Movement for the Abolition of Slavery. Bayard Tuckerman. LC 69-19000. (Illus.). 185p. 1969. reprint ed. text ed. 52.50 (0-8371-4592-9, TUJ&, Greenwood Pr) Greenwood.

William Jefferson Clinton. rev. ed. Zachary Kent. (Encyclopedia of Presidents Ser.). (Illus.). 100p. (J). (gr. 3 up). 1994. lib. bdg. 22.00 (0-516-01344-0) Childrens.

William Jefferson Clinton: 42nd President of the United States. David R. Collins. Ed. by Rebecca Stefoff. LC 95-852. (Presidents of the United States Ser.). (Illus.). 128p. (YA). (gr. 5-9). 1995. lib. bdg. 17.26 (1-56074-056-6) Garrett Ed Corp.

William Jennings Bryan. Robert Allen. (Sower Ser.). (J). (gr. 3-6). 1992. pap. 7.99 (0-88062-160-5) Mott Media.

William Jennings Bryan: Orator of Small-Town America. Donald K. Springen. LC 90-43382. (Great American Orators: Critical Studies, Speeches & Sources: No. 11). 208p. 1991. text ed. 47.95 (0-313-25977-1, SWQ/, Greenwood Pr) Greenwood.

William Jennings Bryan, Missionary Isolationist. Kendrick A. Clements. LC 82-8342. (Illus.). 232p. reprint ed. pap. 66.20 (0-8357-8603-X, 2034999) Bks Demand.

William Jessop, Engineer. Charles Hadfield & S. Skempton. 315p. (C). 1989. 60.00 (0-7153-7603-9, Pub. by S A Baldwin UK) St Mut.

***William John Leech: An Irish Painter Abroad.** Denise Ferran. (Illus.). 300p. 1997. 50.00 (1-85894-034-6, Pub. by Merrell Holberton Pubs UK) U of Wash Pr.

William Johnson's Natchez: The Ante-Bellum Diary of a Free Negro. Ed. by William R. Hogan & Edwin A. Davis. LC 68-25203. (Illus.). 812p. (C). 1993. pap. 19.95 (0-8071-1855-9) La State U Pr.

William Keith: The Saint Mary's College Collection. Alfred C. Harrison, Jr. et al. (Illus.). 158p. 1994. reprint ed. 39.95 (1-886091-06-4); reprint ed. pap. 26.95 (1-886091-07-2) Hearst Art Gal.

William Keith As Prophet Painter. Emily P. Hay. 1983. reprint ed. pap. 15.00 (0-318-00402-X) K Starosciak.

William Kendall Contra Mundum. Willmoore Kendall. Ed. by Nellie D. Kendall. LC 93-6686. 658p. (C). reprint ed. pap. text ed. 30.00 (0-8191-9067-5) U Pr of Amer.

William Kent: Landscape Garden Designer. John D. Hunt. Ed. by Peter Willis. LC 87-61181. (Architects in Perspective Ser.). (Illus.). 176p. 1988. 60.00 (0-302-00600-1, Pub. by Zwemmer Bks UK) Sothebys Pubns.

***William Kienbusch: A Retrospective Exhibition, 1946-1979.** Susan C. Larson et al. (Illus.). 80p. 1996. pap. 7.95 (0-918749-05-0) W A Farnsworth.

William Kirby & His Works. Margot Northey. (Canadian Author Studies). 26p. (C). 1989. pap. text ed. 9.95 (1-55022-048-9, Pub. by ECW Press CN) Genl Dist Srvs.

William Klein: New York 1954-1955. William Klein. (Illus.). 256p. 75.00 (1-899235-25-6, 610151, Pub. by Dewi Lewis UK) Dist Art Pubs.

William Knox: The Life & Thought of an Eighteenth-Century Imperialist. Leland J. Bellot. LC 76-44006. 276p. pap. 78.70 (0-8357-7725-1, 2036082) Bks Demand.

William Kurelek's Huronia Mission Paintings. Michael Pomedli. LC 91-20048. (Canadian Studies: Vol. 14). (Illus.). 196p. 1991. lib. bdg. 79.95 (0-7734-9731-5) E Mellen.

William L. Sonntag, Artist of the Ideal. Nancy D. Moure. (Illus.). 157p. 1980. 35.00 (0-318-01276-6) Goldfld Pub.

William L. Wilson & Tariff Reform: A Biography. Festus P. Summers. LC 74-3627. (Illus.). 288p. 1974. reprint ed. text ed. 79.50 (0-8371-7447-3, SUWW, Greenwood Pr) Greenwood.

William Lambarde & Local Government: His "Ephemeris" & Twenty-Nine Charges to Juries & Commissions. William Lambarde. Ed. by Conyers Read. (Documents Ser.). 1978. 29.50 (0-918016-36-3) Folger Bks.

William Langland. Ralph Hanna, III. Ed. by M. C. Seymour. (Authors of the Middle Ages Ser.: Vol. 3). 65p. 1993. pap. 15.00 (0-86078-382-0, Pub. by Variorum UK) Ashgate Pub Co.

William Langland: The Vision of Piers Plowman, Vol. II. Ed. by Walter W. Skeat. (EETS Original Ser.: Vol. 54). 1963. reprint ed. 30.00 (0-19-722038-X, Pub. by EETS UK) Boydell & Brewer.

William Langland: The Vision of Piers Plowman, Vol. III. Ed. by Walter W. Skeat. (EETS Original Ser.: Vol. 54). 1963. reprint ed. 30.00 (0-19-722054-1, Pub. by EETS UK) Boydell & Brewer.

William Langland Revisited. Wittig. LC 97-9385. 1996. 22.95 (0-8057-7038-0, Twayne) Scribnrs Ref.

William Langland's "Piers Plowman" The C Version. Tr. by George Economou. LC 96-31987. (Middle Ages Ser.). 272p. 1996. pap. text ed. 17.95 (0-8122-1561-3) U of Pa Pr.

William Langland's "Piers Plowman" The C Version. Tr. by George Economou. LC 96-31987. (Middle Ages Ser.). 272p. 1996. text ed. 46.50 (0-8122-3323-9) U of Pa Pr.

William Langshawe, the Cotton Lord. Elizabeth Stone. LC 79-8204. reprint ed. 44.50 (0-404-62130-9) AMS Pr.

W

An Asterisk (*) at the beginning of an entry indicates that the title is appearing in BIP for the first time.

William Larson. (Contemporary Art Ser.: No. 6). (Illus.). 19p. 1995. pap. write for info. (*1-883015-12-X*) Krannert Art.

William Lauder: Arc Conpendious & Breue Fractate Concenyng Ye Office & Dewtie of Kyngis. Ed. by F. Hall. (EETS Original Ser.: Vol. 3). 1965. reprint ed. 20.00 (*0-19-722003-7*, Pub. by EETS UK) Boydell & Brewer.

William Law: A Serious Call to a Devout & Holy Life & the Spirit of Love. Ed. by Paul Stanwood & Austin Warren. LC 78-61418. (Classics of Western Spirituality Ser.). 542p. 1978. pap. 9.95 (*0-8091-2144-1*) Paulist Pr.

William Law: Nauvoo, Dissenter. Lyndon Cook. 164p. (C). 1994. 16.95 (*0-910523-01-0*) Grandin Bk Co.

William Law: Selections on the Interior Life. William Law. Ed. by Mary C. Morrison. LC 62-15272. (Orig.). 1962. pap. 3.00 (*0-87574-120-7*) Pendle Hill.

William Law & Eighteenth-Century Quakerism. William Law. Ed. by Stephen Hobhouse. LC 77-175870. (Illus.). 1972. reprint ed. 26.95 (*0-405-08736-5*) Ayer.

***William Law (1686-1761) Selected Writings.** Ed. by Janet Louth. pap. write for info. (*0-85635-862-2*, Pub. by Carcanet Pr UK) Paul & Co Pubs.

William Le Baron Jenney: A Pioneer of Modern Architecture. Theodore Turak. LC 86-4337. (Architecture & Urban Design Ser.: No. 17). (Illus.). 390p. reprint ed. pap. 111.20 (*0-8357-1734-8*, 2070524) Bks Demand.

William Leech. Denise Ferran. (Lives of Irish Artists Ser.). (Illus.). 36p. 1995. 7.95 (*0-948524-35-9*, Pub. by Town Hse IE) R Rinehart.

William Lescaze, Architect. Lorraine W. Lanmon. LC 83-45295. 216p. 1987. 55.00 (*0-87982-506-5*) Art Alliance.

William Lesch: Expansions. RAM Staff. Ed. by K. Kawaii. (Illus.). 102p. (ENG & JPN.). 1992. 29.95 (*4-8457-0667-9*) RAM Publications.

***William Lindsay White, 1900-1973: In the Shadow of His Father.** E. Jay Jernigan. LC 96-32782. (Illus.). 368p. 1997. 29.95 (*0-8061-2902-6*) U of Okla Pr.

William Lloyd Garrinson. Cain. 1997. pap. 12.95 (*0-312-14991-3*) St Martin.

William Lloyd Garrison. Ed. by George Fredrickson. (Great Lives Observed Ser.). 1968. 8.95 (*0-13-346858-5*, Spectrum IN); pap. 1.95 (*0-13-346841-0*, Spectrum IN) Macmillan Gen Ref.

William Lloyd Garrison. John J. Chapman. (American Newspapermen 1790-1933 Ser.). 1974. reprint ed. 29.95 (*0-8464-0027-8*) Beekman Pubs.

William Lloyd Garrison: Selections from the Liberator & the Fight Against Slavery. William E. Cain. 224p. 1994. pap. text ed. 7.50 (*0-312-10386-7*) St Martin.

William Lloyd Garrison & His Times. Oliver Johnson. 15.00 (*1-56675-017-2*, N310P) Mnemosyne.

William Lloyd Garrison & the Challenge of Emancipation. James B. Stewart. Ed. by Alan M. Kraut & Jon L. Wakelyn. (American Biographical History Ser.). 230p. 1992. pap. text ed. write for info. (*0-88295-885-2*) Harlan Davidson.

William Lloyd Garrison & the Fight Against Slavery: Selections from The Liberator. Ed. by William E. Cain. (Bedford Series in History & Culture). 206p. 1995. text ed. 39.95 (*0-312-12245-4*) St Martin.

William Lloyd Garrison, Eighteen Hundred Five to Eighteen Seventy-Nine, 4 Vols., Set. Wendell P. Garrison & Francis J. Garrison. LC 71-82191. (Anti-Slavery Crusade in America Ser.). 1970. reprint ed. 81.95 (*0-405-00629-2*) Ayer.

William Lloyd Garrison, Eighteen Hundred Five to Eighteen Seventy-Nine, 4 Vols., Vol. 1. Wendell P. Garrison & Francis J. Garrison. LC 71-82191. (Anti-Slavery Crusade in America Ser.). 1970. reprint ed. 24.95 (*0-405-00671-3*) Ayer.

William Lloyd Garrison, Eighteen Hundred Five to Eighteen Seventy-Nine, 4 Vols., Vol. 2. Wendell P. Garrison & Francis J. Garrison. LC 71-82191. (Anti-Slavery Crusade in America Ser.). 1970. reprint ed. 24.95 (*0-405-00672-1*) Ayer.

William Lloyd Garrison, Eighteen Hundred Five to Eighteen Seventy-Nine, 4 Vols., Vol. 3. Wendell P. Garrison & Francis J. Garrison. LC 71-82191. (Anti-Slavery Crusade in America Ser.). 1970. reprint ed. 24.95 (*0-405-00673-X*) Ayer.

William Lloyd Garrison, Eighteen Hundred Five to Eighteen Seventy-Nine, 4 Vols., Vol. 4. Wendell P. Garrison & Francis J. Garrison. LC 71-82191. (Anti-Slavery Crusade in America Ser.). 1970. reprint ed. 24.95 (*0-405-00674-8*) Ayer.

William Lloyd Garrison on Non-Resistance. William L. Garrison. LC 73-10286. (American History & Americana Ser.: No. 47). 1973. reprint ed. lib. bdg. 75.00 (*0-8383-1717-0*) M S G Haskell Hse.

William Lloyd Garrison on Nonresistance Together with a Personal Sketch by His Daughter and a Tribute by Leo Tolstoi. Ed. by Fanny G. Villard. LC 74-137556. (Peace Movement in America Ser.). xii, 79p. 1972. reprint ed. lib. bdg. 21.95 (*0-89198-087-3*) Ozer.

William Lloyd Garrison, the Abolitionist. Archibald H. Grimke. LC 73-168207. reprint ed. 29.50 (*0-404-00057-6*) AMS Pr.

William Lloyd's Life of Pythagoras, with a New Thesis on the Origin of the New Testament. Arthur F. Hallam. 84p. (Orig.). 1982. pap. 8.50 (*0-938770-01-2*) Capitalist Pr OH.

William, Lord Herbert of Pembroke (1507-1570) Politique & Patriot. Narasingha P. Sil. LC 87-11121. (Studies in British History: Vol. 6). 206p. 1988. lib. bdg. 89.95 (*0-88946-458-8*) E Mellen.

William Loring Andrews on Bookbinding History, Vol. 13. Ed. by William L. Andrews. (History of Bookbinding & Design Ser.). (Illus.). 210p. 1990. text ed. 30.00 (*0-8240-4040-6*) Garland.

William Louis Sonntag: Artist of the Ideal. Nancy D. Moure. (Illus.). 157p. 1980. text ed. 35.00 (*0-686-35887-2*) Goldfld Pub.

William Louis Sonntag: Artist of the Ideal. deluxe limited ed. Nancy D. Moure. (Illus.). 157p. 1980. 65.00 (*0-686-37195-X*) Goldfld Pub.

William Lowndes & the Transition of Southern Politics, 1782-1822. Carl J. Vipperman. LC 88-17246. (Fred W. Morrison Series in Southern Studies). xxii, 326p. (C). 1989. 45.00 (*0-8078-1826-7*) U of NC Pr.

William Lowndes & the Transition of Southern Politics, 1782-1822. Carl J. Vipperman. LC 88-17246. (Fred W. Morrison Series in Southern Studies). 348p. 1989. reprint ed. pap. 99.20 (*0-608-02068-0*, 2062721) Bks Demand.

William Lumpkins: Works on Paper 1930-1986. Malin Wilson. (Illus.). 23p. (C). 1987. pap. 10.00 (*0-944282-01-6*) UNM Art Mus.

William Lyon MacKenzie King: The Lonely Heights. H. Blair Neatby. LC 79-9143. (Scholarly Reprint Ser.: Vol. 2: 1924-1932). 464p. reprint ed. pap. 132.30 (*0-317-27005-2*, 2023656) Bks Demand.

William Lyon Mackenzie King Vol. 2: A Political Biography: 1924-1932: The Lonely Heights. H. Blair Neatby. LC 59-347. (Illus.). 474p. reprint ed. pap. 135.10 (*0-8357-8375-8*, 2034057) Bks Demand.

William Lyon Mackenzie King, Vol. II: The Lonely Heights, 1924-1932. H. Blair Neatby. 366p. 1963. text ed. 100.00 (*0-8020-1261-2*) U of Toronto Pr.

William M. Harnett. unabridged ed. Doreen Bolger et al. LC 91-26675. (Illus.). 352p. 1992. pap. 10.00 (*0-88360-069-2*) Amon Carter.

William Makepeace Thackeray, 6 vols., Set. Ed. by Pearson. 2179p. (C). 1996. boxed, text ed. 770.00 (*0-415-13742-X*) Routledge.

William Makepeace Thackeray: A Biography, 2 vols., Set. Lewis S. Benjamin. (BCL1-PR English Literature Ser.). 1992. reprint ed. lib. bdg. 150.00 (*0-7812-7702-7*) Rprt Serv.

William Makepeace Thackeray: A Biography Including Hitherto Uncollected Letters & Speeches & a Bibliography of 1300 Items, 2 vols., Set. Lewis S. Benjamin. LC 15-5841. 1968. reprint ed. 59.00 (*0-403-00112-9*) Scholarly.

William Makepeace Thackeray: An Annotated Bibliography, 1976-1987. Sheldon Goldfarb. LC 89-1482. 100p. 1989. text ed. 34.00 (*0-8240-1212-7*, H857) Garland.

William Manning: A Ten Year Retrospective, 1984-1994. Intro. by Chris Crossman. (Illus.). 24p. (Orig.). 1995. pap. 5.95 (*0-918749-04-2*) W A Farnsworth.

William Manson Seabron: A Triumph in Time. Nathaniel A. Dickens. Ed. by Deborah S. Dickens. (Illus.). 1995. 10.00 (*0-916191-07-9*) Dickens Pubns.

William March: An Annotated Checklist. Roy S. Simmonds. LC 86-30786. 216p. 1988. text ed. 24.95 (*0-8173-0361-8*) U of Ala Pr.

William Marshal: The Flower of Chivalry. Georges Duby. Tr. by Richard Howard from FRE. LC 85-42837. 136p. 1987. pap. 12.00 (*0-394-75154-X*) Pantheon.

William Marshall: Court, Career & Chicalry in the Angevin Empire, 1147-1219. David Crouch. (C). 1994. pap. text ed. 20.50 (*0-582-03786-7*, Pub. by Longman UK) Longman.

William Marshall: Knight-Errant, Baron, & Regent of England. Sidney Painter. (Medieval Academy Reprints for Teaching Ser.). 318p. 1982. pap. 14.95 (*0-8020-6498-1*) U of Toronto Pr.

***William Marshall: The Flower of Chivalry.** Georges Duby. 1987. pap. text ed. write for info. (*0-07-541642-5*) McGraw.

William Mason (1829-1908) An Annotated Bibliography & Catalog of Works. Kenneth Graber. LC 89-11107. (Bibliographies in American Music Ser.: No. 13). 351p. 1989. 50.00 (*0-89990-046-1*) Info Coord.

William Mastrosimone: Collected Plays. William Mastrosimone. (Contemporary Playwrights Ser.). 360p. 1993. pap. 14.95 (*1-880399-32-6*) Smith & Kraus.

William Mathias: A Bio-Bibliography. Stewart R. Craggs. LC 95-21758. (Bio-Bibliographies in Music Ser.: Vol. 58). 264p. 1995. text ed. 65.00 (*0-313-27865-2*, Greenwood Pr) Greenwood.

William Matthews: Cowboys & Images. Illus. by William Matthews. LC 93-14073. 1993. 34.95 (*0-87905-569-3*, Peregrine Smith) Gibbs Smith Pub.

William Maxwell. Thompson. 1997. 22.95 (*0-8057-4582-3*, Twayne) Scribnrs Ref.

William McKinley. Zachary Kent. LC 88-10881. (Encyclopedia of Presidents Ser.). (Illus.). 100p. (J). (gr. 3 up). 1988. lib. bdg. 22.00 (*0-516-01361-0*) Childrens.

William McKinley: A Bibliography. Lewis L. Gould & Craig H. Roell. LC 88-15531. (Bibliographies of the Presidents of the United States Ser.: No. 24). 248p. 1988. text ed. 59.95 (*0-313-28182-3*, AP24, Greenwood Pr) Greenwood.

William McKinley: Twenty-Fifth President of the United States. David R. Collins. Ed. by Richard G. Young. LC 89-39954. (Presidents of the United States Ser.). (Illus.). 128p. (J). (gr. 5-9). 1990. lib. bdg. 17.26 (*0-944483-55-0*) Garrett Ed Corp.

William McKinley & His America. Howard W. Morgan. LC 63-19723. 623p. reprint ed. pap. 177.60 (*0-317-29726-0*, 2022207) Bks Demand.

William McKinley & Our America: A Pictorial History. Richard L. McElroy. (Illus.). 232p. 1996. 35.00 (*0-9634712-0-1*); pap. 19.95 (*0-9634712-1-X*) Stark Cnty Hist.

William Meritt Chase. Barbara D. Gallati. LC 94-3487. 1995. 45.00 (*0-8109-4029-9*) Abrams.

***William Merritt Chase: Master of American Impressionism.** Ronald G. Pisano. (Illus.). 5p. 1994. pap. write for info. (*0-945936-10-9*) Spanierman Gallery.

William Merritt Chase, A Genteel Bohemian. Keith L. Bryant, Jr. (Illus.). 344p. 1991. text ed. 35.00 (*0-8262-0759-6*) U of Mo Pr.

William Merritt Chase in the Company of Friends. Ronald G. Pisano. LC 79-87491. (Illus.). 70p. 1979. 4.00 (*0-943526-06-X*) Parrish Art.

William Merritt Chase (1849-1916) Ronald G. Pisano. (Illus.). 25p. (Orig.). (C). 1976. pap. 5.00 (*0-943526-43-4*) Parrish Art.

William Meyerowitz: The Artist Speaks. Theresa B. Meyerowitz. LC 84-45010. (Illus.). 192p. 1986. 40.00 (*0-87982-513-8*) Art Alliance.

William Meyerowitz: The Artist Speaks. Theresa B. Meyerowitz. LC 84-45010. (Illus.). 192p. 1986. 40.00 (*0-8453-4768-3*, Cornwall Bks) Assoc Univ Prs.

William Miller & the Advent Crisis: 1831 - 1844. Everett N. Dick. Ed. by Gary Land. LC 94-72521. (Illus.). 250p. 1994. pap. 16.99 (*1-883925-02-9*) Andrews Univ Pr.

William Miller: Selected Works see Millennium in America: From the Puritan Migration to the Civil War

William Morris. (Library of Design). (Illus.). 88p. 1991. pap. 7.99 (*0-517-66116-0*) Random Hse Value.

William Morris. Ed. by Linda Parry. LC 95-51845. (Illus.). 394p. 1996. 60.00 (*0-8109-4282-8*) Abrams.

William Morris. Holbrook Jackson. LC 79-110848. 160p. 1971. reprint ed. text ed. 49.75 (*0-8371-4515-5*, JAWM, Greenwood Pr) Greenwood.

William Morris. Alfred Noyes. LC 70-173176. 164p. 1972. reprint ed. 17.95 (*0-405-08822-1*, Pub. by Blom Pubns UK) Ayer.

William Morris. Alfred Noyes. LC 72-39201. (Select Bibliographies Reprint Ser.). 1977. reprint ed. 15.95 (*0-8369-6803-4*) Ayer.

William Morris: A Life for Our Time. Fiona MacCarthy. (Illus.). 780p. 1995. 45.00 (*0-394-58531-3*) Knopf.

William Morris: Art & Kelmscott. Ed. by Linda Parry. (Occasional Papers: Vol. 18). (Illus.). 164p. 1996. pap. 30.00 (*0-85115-670-3*, Boydell Pr) Boydell & Brewer.

William Morris: Artifacts/Glass. Gary Blonston. (Illus.). 128p. 1996. 40.00 (*0-7892-0167-4*) Abbeville Pr.

William Morris: Decor & Design. Elizabeth Wilhide. 1991. 45.00 (*0-8109-3623-2*) Abrams.

William Morris: Designs & Motifs. Norah Gillow. Ed. by Stephen Calloway. (Illus.). 64p. 1996. pap. 9.95 (*1-55921-151-2*) Moyer Bell.

William Morris: His Life & Work. Coote. 1995. 12.98 (*0-8317-1858-7*) Smithmark.

***William Morris: Master of Many Crafts, 1900 Edition.** James Leatham. Ed. by Peter Faulkner. (William Morris Library). 150p. 1996. reprint ed. write for info. (*1-85506-257-7*) Bks Intl VA.

William Morris: Romantic to Revolutionary. 2nd ed. E. P. Thompson. LC 88-60490. 831p. 1988. reprint ed. pap. 24.95 (*0-8047-1509-2*) Stanford U Pr.

William Morris: The Critical Heritage. Ed. by Peter Faulkner. (Critical Heritage Ser.). 480p. 1973. 69.50 (*0-7100-7520-0*, RKP) Routledge.

William Morris see Victorian Thinkers

William Morris, a Critical Study. John Drinkwater. (BCL1-PR English Literature Ser.). 201p. 1992. reprint ed. lib. bdg. 79.00 (*0-7812-7609-8*) Rprt Serv.

William Morris & His Circle. John W. Mackail. LC 79-117585. (English Literature Ser.: No. 33). 1970. reprint ed. lib. bdg. 50.95 (*0-8383-1018-4*) M S G Haskell Hse.

William Morris & Kelmscott. Design Council Staff. 192p. 1987. pap. 50.00 (*0-85072-121-0*) St Mut.

William Morris & News from Nowhere: A Vision for Our Time. Ed. by Stephen Coleman & Paddy O'Sullivan. 224p. (Orig.). 1996. pap. 16.95 (*1-870098-37-4*, Pub. by Green Bks UK) Coun Oak Bks.

William Morris & the Arts & Crafts. Holbrook Jackson. 1972. 59.95 (*0-8490-1306-2*) Gordon Pr.

***William Morris & the Early Days of the Socialist Movement: 1921 Edition.** John B. Glasier. Ed. & Intro. by Peter Faulkner. (William Morris Library). 244p. 1996. reprint ed. write for info. (*1-85506-258-5*) Bks Intl VA.

William Morris As Designer. Ray Witkinson. (Illus.). 148p. 1980. 22.50 (*0-289-70673-4*) Eastview.

***William Morris at Home.** David Rodgers. 1996. 17.98 (*0-7651-9619-0*) Smithmark.

***William Morris Chronology.** Nicholas Salmon & Derek Baker. 290p. 1996. 48.00 (*1-85506-504-5*); pap. 19.75 (*1-85506-505-3*) Thoemmes Pr.

William Morris Full-Color Patterns & Design. William Morris. (Illus.). 48p. 1988. reprint ed. pap. 7.95 (*0-486-25645-6*) Dover.

William Morris Hunt. Sally Webster. (Monographs on American Artists). (Illus.). 256p. (C). 1991. text ed. 110.00 (*0-521-34583-9*) Cambridge U Pr.

***William Morris Library: Second Series, 6 vols.** Incl. Journalism: Contributions to Commonweal 1885-90. Ed. by Nicholas Salmon & Peter Faulkner. 540p. 1996. pap. 29.75 (*1-85506-459-6*); The Glittering Plain & Child Christopher. Ed. by Peter Faulkner. 245p. 1996. pap. 24.75 (*1-85506-461-8*); The Hollow Land & Other Contributions to the Oxford & Cambridge Magazine (The Golden Type Edition). Ed. by Peter Faulkner. 335p. 1996. pap. 26.75 (*1-85506-463-4*); Three Northern Love Stories & Other Tales. Ed. by Peter Faulkner. 172p. 1996. pap. 19.75 (*1-85506-465-0*); Reform & Revolution: Three Early Socialists on the Way Ahead. Ed. by Stephen Coleman & Peter Faulkner. 120p. 1996. pap. 14.75 (*1-85506-467-7*); Arts & Crafts Essays. Arts & Crafts Exhibition Society Staff. Ed. by William Morris & Peter Faulkner. 420p. 1996. pap. 28.75 (*1-85506-469-3*); write for info. (*1-85506-456-1*) Bks Intl VA.

William Morris Lieserson: A Biography. Michael J. Eisner. LC 67-13557. 154p. reprint ed. pap. 43.90 (*0-317-39679-X*, 2023717) Bks Demand.

William Morris Needlepoint. Beth Russell. 1995. 30.00 (*0-517-70166-9*) Crown Pub Group.

William Morris on Architecture. Ed. by Chris Miele. (SAP Literature Ser.). 100p. 1996. pap. 9.95 (*1-85075-612-0*, Pub. by Sheffield Acad UK) CUP Services.

William Morris on Art & Design. Ed. by Christine Poulson. (SAP Literature Ser.). 100p. 1996. pap. 9.95 (*1-85075-611-2*, Pub. by Sheffield Acad UK) CUP Services.

William Morris on History. Ed. by Nicholas Salmon. (SAP Literature Ser.). 100p. 1996. pap. 9.95 (*1-85075-606-6*, Pub. by Sheffield Acad UK) CUP Services.

William Morris, the Man & the Myth. Robert P. Arnot. LC 76-107. 131p. 1976. reprint ed. text ed. 57.50 (*0-8371-8652-8*, ARWM, Greenwood Pr) Greenwood.

William Morris Tiles. Richard Myers. (Illus.). 152p. 1996. 80.00 (*0-903685-43-4*, Pub. by R Dennis UK) Antique Collect.

***William Morris (1834-1896) Selected Poems.** Ed. by Peter Faulkner. pap. write for info. (*0-85635-926-2*, Pub. by Carcanet Pr UK) Paul & Co Pubs.

William Morris's "The Tables Turned": or Nupkins Awakened" Ed. by Pamela B. Wiens. 112p. (C). 1994. text ed. 29.95 (*0-8214-1076-8*) Ohio U Pr.

William Morton Wheeler, Biologist. Mary A. Evans & Howard E. Evans. LC 76-129117. (Illus.). 377p. 1970. 36.50 (*0-674-95330-4*) HUP.

William Nassington: Canon, Mystic, & Poet of the Speculum Vitae. Ingrid J. Peterson. (American University Studies: Theology & Religion: Ser. VII, Vol. 19). 199p. 1987. text ed. 34.00 (*0-8204-0322-9*) P Lang Pubng.

William Newburgh: History of English Affairs II, No. II. Ed. by Walsh. write for info. (*0-85668-473-2*, Pub. by Aris & Phillips UK) David Brown.

William Newby: A Civil War Soldier's Return. G. J. George. (Illus.). 240p. reprint ed. write for info. (*0-9638836-0-7*); reprint ed. pap. write for info. (*0-9638836-1-5*) W Kennann Bks.

William Notman's Studio: The Canadian Picture. Stanley Triggs. (Illus.). 64p. 1992. pap. 22.95 (*0-7735-0967-4*, Pub. by McGill CN) U of Toronto Pr.

William O'Brien & the Course of Irish Politics, 1881-1918. Joseph V. O'Brien. LC 74-22970. (Illus.). 287p. reprint ed. pap. 81.80 (*0-685-23978-0*, 2031542) Bks Demand.

William O'Brien & the Irish Land War. Sally Warwick-Haller. (Illus.). 356p. 1990. 14.95 (*0-7165-2458-9*, Pub. by Irish Acad Pr IE) Intl Spec Bk.

William Ockham, 2 vols. Marilyn McCord Adams. LC 86-40337. (Mediaeval Studies: No. 26). 1216p. 1989. text ed. 103.50 (*0-268-01940-1*); pap. text ed. 49.50 (*0-268-01945-2*) U of Notre Dame Pr.

William of Aurergne De Trinitate: The Trinity, or the First Principle. Roland J. Teske. LC 77-63254. (Medieval Philosophical Texts in Translation Ser.: No. 28). 286p. 1989. pap. text ed. 20.00 (*0-87462-231-X*) Marquette.

William of Auvergne: The Immortality of the Soul. Tr. by Roland J. Teske. LC 91-75282. (Medieval Philosophical Texts in Translation Ser.: No. 30). 1991. 10.00 (*0-87462-233-6*) Marquette.

William of Auvergne & Robert Grosseteste: New Ideas of Truth in the Early Thirteenth Century. Steven P. Marrone. LC 82-61375. 1983. reprint ed. pap. 94.40 (*0-7837-9381-2*, 2060125) Bks Demand.

William of Cavendish, Memoranda. P. D. Brown. (Camden Fourth Ser.: No. 27). 27.00 (*0-86193-097-5*) David Brown.

William of Malmesbury. Rodney Thomson. 252p. 1987. 71.00 (*0-85115-451-4*) Boydell & Brewer.

William of Malmesbury: Gesta Regum Anglorum, Atque Historia Novella, 2 vols. Ed. by T. D. Hardy. (English Historical Society Publications Ser.: Vol. 14). 1974. reprint ed. 110.00 (*0-8115-1544-3*) Periodicals Srv.

William of Malmesbury - Polyhistor: A Critical Edition. Ed. by Helen T. Ouellette. LC 81-18918. (Medieval & Renaissance Texts & Studies: Vol. 10). 176p. 1982. 30.00 (*0-86698-017-2*, MR10) MRTS.

William of Newburgh: Historia Rerum Anglicarum Willelmi Parvi, Ordinis Sancti Augustini Canonici Regularis in Coenobio Beatae Mariae de Newburgh in Argo Eboracensi, 2 vols. in 1. Ed. by H. C. Hamilton. (English Historical Society Publications Ser.: Vol. 15). 1974. reprint ed. 65.00 (*0-8115-1547-8*) Periodicals Srv.

William of Newburgh: History of English Affairs I. Ed. by Walsh. (Classical Texts Ser.). 1988. 49.95 (*0-85668-304-3*, Pub. by Aris & Phillips UK); pap. 24.95 (*0-85668-305-1*, Pub. by Aris & Phillips UK) David Brown.

William of Newburgh: History of English Affairs II, No. II. Ed. by Walsh. pap. write for info. (*0-85668-474-0*, Pub. by Aris & Phillips UK) David Brown.

William of Newburgh, Historia Rerum Anglicarum see Chronicles of the Reigns of Stephen, Henry II & Richard I

***William of Ockham: A Short Discourse on Tyranical Government.** 251p. 1992. pap. text ed. 19.95 (*0-521-35803-5*) Cambridge U Pr.

William of Orange: The Silent Prince. W. G. Vandehulst, Jr. Tr. by Alice Veenendaal from DUT. (Illus.). 142p. (Orig.). 1992. pap. 7.90 (*0-921100-15-9*) Inhtce Pubns.

William of Orange & the English Opposition, 1672-4. K. H. Haley. LC 74-30846. 231p. 1975. reprint ed. lib. bdg. 22.50 (*0-8371-7934-3*, HAWO, Greenwood Pr) Greenwood.

William of Palerne: An Alliterative Romance. G. H. Bunt. xii, 488p. 1985. 89.50 (*90-6088-094-3*, Pub. by Boumas Boekhuis NE) Benjamins North Am.

W

William of Sherwood's Introduction to Logic. William Shirwood. LC 66-16468. 200p. reprint ed. pap. 57.00 (*0-317-08266-3*, 2000830) Bks Demand.

William of St. Thierry: On Contemplating God, Prayer, Meditations. Tr. by Penelope. (Cistercian Fathers Ser.: No. 3). 1970. pap. 7.95 (*0-87907-903-7*) Cistercian Pubns.

William of St. Thierry: The Enigma of Faith, Vol. 3. LC 74-4465. (Cistercian Fathers Ser.: No. 9). 1974. 9.95 (*0-87907-309-8*) Cistercian Pubns.

William of St. Thierry, Golden Epistle. LC 72-152482. (Cistercian Fathers Ser.: No. 12). 1971. pap. 7.00 (*0-87907-712-3*) Cistercian Pubns.

William of Tyre: Historian of the Latin East. Peter W. Edbury & John G. Rowe. (Studies in Medieval Life & Thought, Fourth Ser.: No. 8). (Illus.). 200p. (C). 1991. pap. text ed. 18.95 (*0-521-40728-1*) Cambridge U Pr.

William P. Letchworth: A Man for Others. Irene A. Beale. LC 01-90673. 214p. (Orig.). 1982. pap. 9.00 (*0-9608132-0-9*) Chestnut Hill Pr.

William Paca: A Biography. Gregory A. Stiverson & Phebe R. Jacobsen. LC 76-17519. (Illus.). 1976. pap. 9.95 (*0-938420-44-5*) MD Hist.

William Palmer: A Retrospective. Howard D. Spencer. LC 86-50124. (Illus.). 20p. 1986. pap. 3.00 (*0-939324-24-5*) Wichita Art Mus.

William Parker: Rebel Without Rights. John M. Rosenburg. (Illus.). 144p. (J). (gr. 5-8). 1996. lib. bdg. 16.40 (*1-56294-139-9*) Millbrook Pr.

William Partridge Burpee: American Marine Impressionist. D. Roger Howlett. (Illus.). 96p. 1991. text ed. 29.95 (*0-9628143-0-X*) Copley Sq Pr.

William Paterson, Lawyer & Statesman, 1745-1806. John E. O'Connor. LC 79-15966. 367p. 1979. reprint ed. pap. 104.60 (*0-7837-5679-8*, 2059107) Bks Demand.

William Penhallow Henderson: Master Colorist of Santa Fe. David Bell et al. LC 84-61888. (Illus.). 108p. (Orig.). 1984. pap. 13.00 (*0-910407-12-6*) Phoenix Art.

William Penn. William I. Hull. LC 78-179525. (Select Bibliographies Reprint Ser.). 1977. reprint ed. 35.95 (*0-8369-6654-6*) Ayer.

William Penn: Mystic. Elizabeth G. Vining. LC 74-95891. (Orig.). 1969. pap. 3.00 (*0-87574-167-3*) Pendle Hill.

William Penn: 17th Century Founding Father. Edwin B. Bronner. LC 75-32728. (Illus.). 36p. (Orig.). 1975. pap. 3.00 (*0-87574-204-1*) Pendle Hill.

William Penn & Our Liberties. William W. Comfort. (Illus.). 146p. (C). 1976. reprint ed. pap. 5.00 (*0-941308-02-2*) Phila Yrly Mtg RSOF.

***William Penn & the Dutch Quaker Migration to Pennsylvania.** William I. Hull. (Illus.). 460p. 1990. reprint ed. text ed. 30.00 (*0-614-23562-6*, 2940) Clearfield Co.

William Penn, Architect of a Nation. John B. Trussell, Jr. LC 81-622575. (Illus.). 77p. (Orig.). 1980. pap. 4.95 (*0-89271-008-X*) Pa Hist & Mus.

William Penn on Religion & Ethics: The Emergence of Liberal Quakerism, 2 vols., 1. Ed. by Hugh S. Barbour. LC 90-29146. (Studies in American Religion: Vol. 53). (Illus.). 704p. 1991. lib. bdg. 139.95 (*0-88946-687-4*) E Mellen.

William Penn's Holy Experiment: The Founding of Pennsylvia, 1681-1701. Edwin B. Bronner. LC 78-5882. (Illus.). 306p. 1978. reprint ed. text ed. 89.50 (*0-313-20432-2*, BRWP) Ayer.

***William Penn's Legacy: Politics & Social Structure in Provincial Pennsylvania, 1726-1755.** Alan Tully. LC 77-4548. (Johns Hopkins University Studies in Historical & Political Science: 95th Series, No. 2). 272p. 1977. reprint ed. pap. 77.60 (*0-608-03662-5*, 2064488) Bks Demand.

William Penn's Own Account of Lenni Lenape or Delaware Indians. Ed. by Albert C. Myers. (Illus.). 96p. (YA). (gr. 7 up). 1986. pap. 7.95 (*0-912608-13-7*) Mid Atlantic.

William Perkins 1558-1602, English Puritanist--His Pioneer Works on Casuistry: Discourse on Conscience & the Whole Treatise of Cases of Conscience. Thomas F. Merrill. xx, 242p. 1966. text ed. 67.50 (*90-6004-115-1*, Pub. by B De Graaf NE) Coronet Bks.

William Pitt. Walford D. Green. LC 73-14445. (Heroes of the Nations Ser.). reprint ed. 55.00 (*0-404-58263-X*) AMS Pr.

W

***William Pitt & the French Revolution, 1785-1795.** Jennifer Mori. LC 97-10963. 1997. text ed. 55.00 (*0-312-17308-3*) St Martin.

William Pitt & the Great War. John H. Rose. LC 71-110862. (Illus.). xiv, 596p. 1971. reprint ed. text ed. 65.00 (*0-8371-4533-3*, ROWP, Greenwood Pr) Greenwood.

William Pitt, Earl of Chatham, 1708-1778: A Bibliography. Karl W. Schweizer. LC 93-13010. (Bibliographies of British Statesmen Ser.: No. 14). 176p. 1993. text ed. 75.00 (*0-313-28293-5*, SOQ, Greenwood Pr) Greenwood.

William Pitt the Younger, 1759-1806: A Bibliography. A. D. Harvey. LC 89-2791. (Bibliographies of British Statesmen Ser.: No. 1). 88p. 1988. text ed. 55.00 (*0-313-28096-7*, Greenwood Pr) Greenwood.

William Plumer of New Hampshire, 1759-1850. Lynn W. Turner. LC 62-4988. (Illus.). 382p. reprint ed. pap. 108.90 (*0-685-35418-0*, 2036648) Bks Demand.

William Poel & the Elizabethan Stage Society. Marion O'Connor. (Theatre in Focus Ser.). 120p. 1987. pap. 105.00 (*0-85964-164-3*) Chadwyck-Healey.

William Poel's Hamlets: The Director as Critic. Rinda F. Lundstrom. LC 84-22. (Theater & Dramatic Studies: No. 20). (Illus.). 204p. reprint ed. pap. 58.20 (*0-8357-1547-7*, 2070489) Bks Demand.

William Porcher DuBose: Selected Writings. Ed. by Jon Alexander. (Sources of American Spirituality Ser.). 336p. 1988. 19.95 (*0-8091-0402-4*) Paulist Pr.

William Powell & Myrna Loy Murder Case. George Baxt. LC 95-33657. 208p. 1996. 20.95 (*0-312-14071-1*) St Martin.

William Preston & the Allegheny Patriots. Patricia G. Johnson. LC 76-9446. (Illus.). 1976. 20.00 (*0-9614765-5-9*) Walpa Pub.

William Problem. Barbara Baker. LC 93-32598. (Illus.). (J). 1994. pap. 13.99 (*0-525-45235-4*) Dutton Child Bks.

William Problem. Barbara Baker. (Illus.). (J). 1997. pap. 3.99 (*0-14-037699-2*, Viking) Viking Penguin.

William Randolph Hearst, American. Fremont Older. LC 72-7195. (Select Bibliographies Reprint Ser.). 1977. reprint ed. 42.95 (*0-8369-6951-0*) Ayer.

William Reckitt: An Eighteenth Century Quaker Traveller in America, France & West Indies from 1756. Basil N. Reckitt. (C). 1989. pap. 35.00 (*1-85072-057-6*, Pub. by W Sessions UK) St Mut.

William Richard Lethaby. Rebens. 370p. 1986. 57.95 (*0-85139-350-0*) Buttrwrth-Heinemann.

William Rimmer: A Yankee Michelangelo. Comment by Jeffrey Weidman et al. LC 85-70907. (Illus.). 135p. 1985. pap. 20.00 (*0-934358-14-1*) Fuller Mus Art.

***William Robertson & the Expansion of Empire.** Ed. by Stewart J. Brown. (Ideas in Context Ser.: No. 45). 304p. (C). 1997. text ed. 59.95 (*0-521-57083-2*) Cambridge U Pr.

William Robertson Smith: Essays in Reassessment. Ed. by William Johnstone. (Journal for the Study of the Old Testament Supplement Ser.: Vol. 189). 408p. 65.50 (*1-85075-523-X*, Pub. by Sheffield Acad UK) CUP Services.

William Robinson. Lynn Fern. 216p. 1995. 80.00 (*976-8097-66-3*) IPG Chicago.

William Rothenstein: The Portrait of an Artist in His Time. Robert Speaight. LC 79-8080. reprint ed. 39.50 (*0-404-18389-1*) AMS Pr.

***William Rush: American Sculptor.** (Illus.). 212p. (Orig.). 1982. pap. 25.00 (*0-943836-00-X*) Penn Acad Art.

William S. Burroughs: A Reference Guide. Michael B. Goodman. LC 89-26026. 288p. 1990. text ed. 45.00 (*0-8240-8642-2*) Garland.

William S. Burroughs at the Front: Critical Reception, 1959-1989. Ed. by Jennie Skerl & Robin Lydenberg. LC 90-9403. 256p. (C). 1991. pap. 16.95 (*0-8093-1586-6*) S Ill U Pr.

William S. Burroughs, Nineteen Fifty-Three to Nineteen Seventy-Three: A Bibliography. Ed. by Joe Maynard & Barry Miles. LC 77-2663. (Illus.). 243p. 1978. text ed. 27.50 (*0-8139-0710-1*) U Pr of Va.

William S. Gray, Teacher, Scholar, Leader. Ed. by Jennifer A. Stevenson. LC 85-2465. 80p. reprint ed. pap. 25.00 (*0-8357-2636-3*, 2040124) Bks Demand.

William S. Paley Collection. William S. Rubin & Matthew Armstrong. (Illus.). 192p. 1992. 45.00 (*0-87070-170-3*); pap. 27.50 (*0-87070-193-2*) Mus of Modern Art.

William Said. Arnold Falleder. (Chapbook Ser.). (Orig.). 1994. pap. 6.00 (*0-945112-19-X*) Generator Pr.

William Saroyan. Edward H. Foster. LC 84-70249. (Western Writers Ser.: No. 61). 51p. (Orig.). 1984. pap. 4.95 (*0-88430-035-8*) Boise St U W Writ Ser.

William Saroyan: A Reference Guide. Elisabeth C. Foard. 1988. 45.00 (*0-8161-8943-9*, Hall Reference) Macmillan.

William Saroyan: A Research & Production Sourcebook. LC 94-34224. (Modern Dramatists Research & Production Sourcebook). 288p. 1994. text ed. 69.50 (*0-313-29250-7*) Greenwood.

William Saroyan: The Man & the Writer Remembered. Ed. by Leo Hamalian. LC 86-45936. (Illus.). 264p. 1988. 38.50 (*0-8386-3308-0*) Fairleigh Dickinson.

William Saroyan: Warsaw Visitor & Tales from the Vienna Streets (Two Unpublished Plays) Ed. by Dickran Kouymjian. (Illus.). 200p. (Orig.). 1990. 23.95 (*0-912201-18-5*); pap. 13.95 (*0-912201-19-3*) CSU Pr Fresno.

William Saroyan, My Real Work Is Being. David S. Calonne. LC 83-1184. 200p. reprint ed. pap. 57.00 (*0-8357-3908-2*, 2036642) Bks Demand.

William Saroyan Reader. William Saroyan. LC 94-25439. 498p. 1994. pap. 15.95 (*1-56980-019-7*) Barricade Bks.

William Scharf: Essay. Brian O'Doherty. (Illus.). 12p. 1993. pap. 3.00 (*0-685-72255-4*) Michigan Mus.

William Shakespeare. 1993. pap. 5.25 (*0-19-422704-9*) OUP.

***William Shakespeare, 7 bks.** (Major Literary Characters Ser.). 239.65 (*0-7910-3567-0*) Chelsea Hse.

***William Shakespeare, 10 bks.** (Modern Critical Interpretations Ser.). 334.50 (*0-7910-3571-9*) Chelsea Hse.

William Shakespeare. Terry Eagleton. 110p. 1987. pap. 17.95 (*0-631-14554-0*) Blackwell Pubs.

William Shakespeare. Ed. by Levi Fox. (Shakespeare Travel Ser.). (Illus.). 20p. 1994. pap. 2.50 (*0-7117-0256-X*) Seven Hills Bk.

William Shakespeare. Ibi Lepscky. (Famous People Ser.). (Illus.). 28p. (J). (gr. k-3). 1989. 7.95 (*0-8120-6106-3*) Barron.

William Shakespeare. Georg M. Brandes. (BCL1-PR English Literature Ser.). 721p. 1992. reprint ed. lib. bdg. 169.00 (*0-7812-7279-3*) Rprt Serv.

William Shakespeare. David W. Clarke. LC 70-179330. (Illus.). reprint ed. 49.50 (*0-404-01568-9*) AMS Pr.

William Shakespeare. Victor Hugo. Tr. by M. B. Anderson. LC 70-169455. reprint ed. 42.50 (*0-404-03382-2*) AMS Pr.

William Shakespeare. Victor Hugo. Tr. by Melville B. Anderson. LC 77-128888. (Select Bibliographies Reprint Ser.). 1977. reprint ed. 25.95 (*0-8369-5508-0*) Ayer.

William Shakespeare, Vol. 1. Andrews. 1986. 95.00 (*0-684-18773-6*) Mac Lib Ref.

William Shakespeare, Vol. 2. Andrews. 1986. 95.00 (*0-684-18774-4*) Mac Lib Ref.

William Shakespeare, Vol. 3. Andrews. 1986. 95.00 (*0-684-18775-2*) Mac Lib Ref.

William Shakespeare: A Biography. Frederick J. Pohl. Ed. by Stephen Butterfield & Bruce A. Burton. 256p. 1983. 16.75 (*0-9611422-1-9*) Security Dupont.

William Shakespeare: A Compact Documentary Life. rev. ed. Samuel Schoenbaum. (Illus.). 405p. 1987. pap. 16.95 (*0-19-505161-0*) OUP.

William Shakespeare: A Complete & Systematic Concordance to the Works of Shakespeare, 9 vols. Ed. by Marvin Spevack. 1980. Set. write for info. (*0-318-71990-8*) G Olms Pubs.

William Shakespeare: A Literary Biography. Karl Elze. LC 73-166028. reprint ed. 87.50 (*0-404-02328-2*) AMS Pr.

William Shakespeare: A Study in Elizabethan Literature. Barrett Wendell. LC 72-159972. (Studies in Shakespeare: No. 24). 1971. reprint ed. lib. bdg. 59.95 (*0-8383-1254-3*) M S G Haskell Hse.

William Shakespeare: His Family & Friends. Charles I. Elton. Ed. by A. Hamilton Thompson. LC 72-166025. reprint ed. 57.50 (*0-404-02324-X*) AMS Pr.

William Shakespeare: His Life & Times. Dennis Kay. (English Authors Ser.: No. 513). 208p. 1994. 23.95 (*0-8057-7063-1*, Twayne) Scribnrs Ref.

William Shakespeare: His World, His Work, His Influence, 3 vols., Vol. 3. Ed. by John F. Andrews. LC 85-8305. 1008p. 1985. 285.00 (*0-684-17851-6*) S&S Trade.

***William Shakespeare: Love Sonnets.** Chelsea House Publishing Staff. (Illustrated Poetry Anthology Ser.). (Illus.). 1997. 17.95 (*1-86019-296-3*) Chelsea Hse.

William Shakespeare: Problem Plays. Richard W. Hillman. (Twayne's English Authors Ser.). 180p. 1993. 24.95 (*0-8057-7035-6*) Macmillan.

William Shakespeare: Shakespeare l'Ancien. Victor Hugo. (Illus.). 580p. (FRE.). 1973. pap. write for info. (*0-7859-4762-0*) Fr & Eur.

William Shakespeare: The Complete Works. William Shakespeare. Ed. by Stanley Wells et al. (Oxford Shakespeare Ser.). (Illus.). 1348p. 1988. 35.00 (*0-19-811747-7*) OUP.

William Shakespeare: The Complete Works. William Shakespeare. 1993. 15.99 (*0-517-09294-8*) Random Hse Value.

William Shakespeare: The Critical Heritage, 6 vols. Ed. by Vikers. Incl. Vol. 1. 1623-1692. 460p. (C). 1996. text ed. 130.00 (*0-415-13404-8*); Vol. 2. 1693-1733. 561p. (C). 1996. text ed. 150.00 (*0-415-13405-6*); Vol. 3. 1733-1752. 499p. (C). 1996. text ed. 130.00 (*0-415-13406-4*); Vol. 4. 1753-1765. 597p. (C). 1996. text ed. 150.00 (*0-415-13407-2*); Vol. 5. 1765-1774. 585p. (C). 1996. text ed. 150.00 (*0-415-13408-0*); Vol. 6. 1774-1801. 664p. (C). 1996. text ed. 150.00 (*0-415-13409-9*); 3366p. (C). 1996. Set text ed. 659.00 (*0-415-13403-X*) Routledge.

William Shakespeare: Welt-Werk-Wirkung. Gerhard Mueller-Schwefe. (Sammlung Goeschen Ser.: Vol. 2208). (C). 1978. 15.85 (*3-11-007545-8*) De Gruyter.

William Shakespeare: Writing for Performance. John R. Brown. LC 95-35816. 184p. 1996. text ed. 45.00 (*0-312-15867-X*); text ed. 18.95 (*0-312-15868-8*) St Martin.

William Shakespeare Vol. 1: A Literary Life. William Dutton. 1994. text ed. 18.95 (*0-312-12357-4*) St Martin.

***William Shakespeare - His Life & Times.** Annette Francis. pap. 3.95 (*1-889086-00-2*, WS-103) Pan Mass.

***William Shakespeare, a Textual Companion.** Ed. by Stanley Wells et al. (Illus.). 671p. (C). 1997. pap. 45.00 (*0-393-31667-X*) Norton.

William Shakespeare & Alleged Spanish Prototypes. Albert R. Frey. LC 70-169262. (Shakespeare Society of New York. Publications: No. 3). reprint ed. 27.50 (*0-404-54203-4*) AMS Pr.

William Shakespeare & Robert Greene: The Evidence. W. Chapman. LC 73-18209. (Studies in Shakespeare: No. 24). 1974. lib. bdg. 75.00 (*0-8383-1731-6*) M S G Haskell Hse.

William Shakespeare & "The Birth of Merlin" 2nd rev. ed. Mark Dominik. LC 90-1188. 290p. (C). 1991. reprint ed. 25.00 (*0-945088-03-5*) Alioth Pr.

William Shakespeare: Comedies see Modern Critical Views Series

William Shakespeare, Eighteen Sixty-Four. Victor Hugo. Ed. by B. Levillot. 18.95 (*0-686-54050-6*) Fr & Eur.

William Shakespeare Encyclopaedia, 8 vols. Prints India Staff. (C). 1988. Set. 1,000.00 (*0-7855-0044-8*, Pub. by Print Hse II) St Mut.

William Shakespeare: Histories & Poems see Modern Critical Views Series

William Shakespeare, Player, Playmaker & Poet. Henry C. Beeching. LC 77-168571. (Illus.). reprint ed. 29.50 (*0-404-00724-4*) AMS Pr.

***William Shakespeare Romances.** Intro. by Tony Tanner. 656p. 1997. 20.00 (*0-679-45487-X*) Knopf.

William Shakespeare: Tragedies see Modern Critical Views Series

William Shakespeare's A Midsummer Night's Dream. Illus. by Dennis Nolan. LC 94-12600. 48p. (J). (gr. 2 up). 1996. pap. 16.99 (*0-8037-1784-9*); pap. 16.89 (*0-8037-1785-7*) Dial Bks Young.

William Shakespeare's A Midsummer Night's Dream see Bloom's Notes

William Shakespeare's A Midsummer Night's Dream see Modern Critical Interpretations

William Shakespeare's A Midsummer Night's Dream see Bloom's Notes

William Shakespeare's Antony & Cleopatra see Modern Critical Interpretations

William Shakespeare's Coriolanus see Modern Critical Interpretations

William Shakespeare's Hamlet see Bloom's Notes

William Shakespeare's Hamlet see Modern Critical Interpretations

William Shakespeare's Hamlet see Bloom's Notes

William Shakespeare's Henry IV see Bloom's Notes

William Shakespeare's Julius Caesar see Bloom's Notes

William Shakespeare's Julius Caesar see Modern Critical Interpretations

William Shakespeare's Julius Caesar see Bloom's Notes

William Shakespeare's King Lear see Bloom's Notes

William Shakespeare's King Lear see Modern Critical Interpretations

William Shakespeare's King Lear see Bloom's Notes

***William Shakespeare's Macbeth.** Bruce Coville & William Shakespeare. LC 97-7582. (Illus.). (YA). 1997. pap. 16.99 (*0-8037-1899-3*) Dial Bks Young.

***William Shakespeare's MacBeth.** Bruce Coville & William Shakespeare. LC 97-7582. (Illus.). (YA). 1997. pap. 16.89 (*0-8037-1900-0*) Dial Bks Young.

William Shakespeare's Macbeth see Bloom's Notes

William Shakespeare's Macbeth see Modern Critical Interpretations

William Shakespeare's Macbeth see Bloom's Notes

William Shakespeare's Othello see Bloom's Notes

William Shakespeare's Othello see Modern Critical Interpretations

William Shakespeare's Othello see Bloom's Notes

William Shakespeare's Romeo & Juliet see Bloom's Notes

William Shakespeare's The Sonnets see Modern Critical Interpretations

William Shakespeare's The Tempest see Modern Critical Interpretations

William Shakespeare's The Tragedy of Hamlet: Translated into Modern English Verse. Tr. by Frank P. Zeidler. 1979. pap. 5.00 (*0-87423-025-X*) Westburg.

William Shakspere: A Biography. Charles Knight. LC 73-168057. reprint ed. 49.50 (*0-404-03734-8*) AMS Pr.

William Shakspere: A Study in Elizabethan Literature. Barrett Wendell. LC 79-127906. reprint ed. 24.50 (*0-404-06905-3*) AMS Pr.

William Shatner: A Bio-Bibliography. Dennis W. Hauck. LC 93-45320. (Bio-Bibliographies in the Performing Arts Ser.: No. 51). 1994. text ed. 55.00 (*0-313-28579-9*, Greenwood Pr) Greenwood.

William Shenstone: An Eighteenth-Century Portrait. Arthur R. Humphreys. LC 75-41146. reprint ed. 27.50 (*0-404-14673-2*) AMS Pr.

William Sheppard: Cromwell's Law Reformer. Nancy L. Matthews. (Studies in English Legal History). 320p. 1985. 69.95 (*0-521-26483-9*) Cambridge U Pr.

William Shipley: Founder of the Royal Society of Arts. A Biography with Documents. D. G. Allan. 240p. 1968. 69.50 (*0-09-085700-3*) Elliots Bks.

William Shirley, Governor of Massachusetts, 1741-1756. George A. Wood. LC 72-78001. (Columbia University. Studies in the Social Sciences: No. 209). reprint ed. 21.50 (*0-404-51209-7*) AMS Pr.

William Sidney Mount: Annotated Bibliography & Listings of Archival Holdings of the Museums at Stony Brook. David Cassedy et al. (Illus.). (Orig.). 1983. pap. 3.00 (*0-943924-05-7*) Mus Stony Brook.

William Sidney Mount: Painter of Rural America. Nancy S. Howard. LC 93-72834. (Closer Look Ser.). (Illus.). 48p. (J). 1994. 16.95 (*0-87192-275-4*) Davis Mass.

William Sidney Mount: Works in the Collection of the Museums at Stony Brook. David Cassedy et al. LC 83-23646. (Illus.). 96p. (Orig.). 1983. pap. 8.00 (*0-943924-06-5*) Mus Stony Brook.

***William Somerset Maugham Encyclopedia.** Samuel J. Rogal. LC 96-35025. 376p. 1997. text ed. 79.50 (*0-313-29916-1*, Greenwood Pr) Greenwood.

William Stafford. David A. Carpenter. LC 86-70651. (Western Writers Ser.: No. 72). 51p. (Orig.). 1986. pap. 4.95 (*0-88430-046-3*) Boise St U W Writ Ser.

William Stafford: You Must Revise Your Life. William Stafford. 1986. pap. 13.95 (*0-472-06371-5*) U of Mich Pr.

William Stanley Jevons: Critical Assessments, 3 vols., Set. Ed. by John C. Wood. (Critical Assessments of Leading Economists Ser.). 912p. (C). 1988. boxed, text ed. 495.00 (*0-415-00387-3*) Routledge.

William Steinitz, Chess Champion: A Biography of the Bohemian Caesar. Kurt Landsberger. LC 92-50376. (Illus.). 539p. 1993. lib. bdg. 55.00 (*0-89950-758-1*) McFarland & Co.

William Sterndale Bennett: A Descriptive Thematic Catalogue. Rosemary Williamson. (Illus.). 608p. 1996. text ed. 165.00 (*0-19-816438-6*) OUP.

William Stewart Halsted, Surgeon. William G. MacCallum. LC 30-31890. 263p. reprint ed. pap. 75.00 (*0-317-28138-0*, 2055744) Bks Demand.

William Styron. Melvin J. Friedman. LC 74-16889. 82p. 1974. pap. 3.50 (*0-87972-071-9*) Bowling Green Univ Popular Press.

William Styron. Richard Pearce. LC 74-635458. (University of Minnesota Pamphlets on American Writers Ser.: No. 98). 47p. (Orig.). reprint ed. pap. 25.00 (*0-7837-2868-9*, 2057587) Bks Demand.

William Styron's Lie Down in Darkness: A Screenplay. Richard Yates. LC 85-60434. 208p. (C). 1985. 15.95 (*0-933277-00-8*); pap. 8.95 (*0-933277-01-6*) Ploughshares.

William Styron's Nat Turner: Ten Black Writers Respond. Ed. by John H. Clarke. LC 87-8695. 128p. 1987. reprint ed. text ed. 55.00 (*0-313-25957-7*, CLNT, Greenwood Pr) Greenwood.

William Styron's Sophie's Choice: Crime & Self-Punishment. Rhoda Sirlin & William Styron. LC 89-20458. 144p. 1991. 39.00 (*0-8357-2043-8*) Univ Rochester Pr.

William Swift of Sandwich & Some of His Descendants, 1637-1899. G. H. Swift. 165p. 1993. reprint ed. pap. 29.00 (*0-8328-3789-X*); reprint ed. lib. bdg. 39.00 (*0-8328-3788-1*) Higginson Bk Co.

William T. Porter & the Spirit of the Times: Study of the Bear School of Humor. Norris W. Yates. Ed. by Richard M. Dorson. LC 77-70630. (International Folklore Ser.). 1977. reprint ed. lib. bdg. 21.95 (*0-405-10134-1*) Ayer.

William T. Wiley. Contrib. by Jerry Saltz. LC 94-75644. (Illus.). 44p. (Orig.). 1994. pap. 20.00 (*1-879173-17-4*) Locks Gallery.

William T. Wiley: One Man's Moon... Contrib. by Rosetta Brooks. (Illus.). 24p. (Orig.). 1992. pap. 15.00 (*1-879173-09-3*) Locks Gallery.

William T. Wiley: Watching the World. 32p. 1995. pap. 20.00 (*1-879173-24-7*) Locks Gallery.

William T. Wiley What Is Not Dr. William Wiley. 1989. pap. 20.00 (*0-932499-30-9*) Lapis Pr.

William Tanner, Senior, of South Kingstown, Rhode Island & His Descendants. G. C. Tanner. (Illus.). 516p. 1989. reprint ed. pap. 77.00 (*0-8328-1157-2*); reprint ed. lib. bdg. 85.00 (*0-8328-1156-4*) Higginson Bk Co.

***William Taylor Memorial Lectures 3: Global Risk Management.** Ulrich Cartellieri & Alan Greenspan. 42p. (Orig.). 1996. pap. 10.00 (*1-56708-098-7*) Grp of Thirty.

William Tecumseh Sherman: Defender & Destroyer. Nancy Whitelaw. (Notable Americans Ser.). (J). (gr. 7-10). 1996. lib. bdg. 18.95 (*1-883846-12-9*) M Reynolds.

William Tecumseh Sherman & the Settlement of the West. Robert G. Athearn. LC 95-11480. (Illus.). 400p. 1995. 17.95 (*0-8061-2769-4*) U of Okla Pr.

William Tell. (Stories Ser.). (Illus.). 32p. (J). (gr. 2-5). 1989. lib. bdg. 19.97 (*0-8172-2630-3*) Raintree Steck-V.

William Tell. Illus. & Retold by Margaret Early. 32p. (J). 1991. 17.95 (*0-8109-3854-5*) Abrams.

William Tell. Leonard E. Fisher. LC 95-13861. (Illus.). 32p. (J). (gr. k-3). 1996. 16.00 (*0-374-38436-3*) FS&G.

William Tell 1984. John Deur. 72p. 1986. pap. 11.95 (*0-918805-33-3*) Pac Aero Pr.

William Temple. John Kent. (British Lives Ser.). 212p. (C). 1992. text ed. 44.95 (*0-521-37484-7*); pap. text ed. 14.95 (*0-521-37630-0*) Cambridge U Pr.

William Temple: An Archbishop for All Seasons. Charles W. Lowry. LC 81-43869. 170p. (Orig.). 1982. pap. text ed. 17.00 (*0-8191-2356-0*) U Pr of Amer.

William Temple & Christian Social Ethics Today. Alan M. Suggate. 304p. 1994. pap. text ed. 24.95 (*0-567-29140-5*, Pub. by T & T Clark UK) Bks Intl VA.

William Tenn High Klass Talent: A Working Bibliography. Gordon Benson, Jr. & Phil Stephensen-Payne. (Galactic Central Bibliographies Ser.: No. 7). ix, 22p. (C). 1993. lib. bdg. 25.00 (*0-8095-4706-6*) Borgo Pr.

William Thackeray see 19th Century Novelists: Critical Heritage

William the Baptist. James M. Chaney. 140p. (C). 1994. reprint ed. pap. text ed. 8.95 (*1-884416-04-7*) A Press.

William the Conqueror. Hilaire Belloc. LC 92-60959. 76p. 1992. pap. 7.00 (*0-89555-468-2*) TAN Bks Pubs.

William the Conqueror. E. A. Freeman. 1972. 59.95 (*0-8490-1307-0*) Gordon Pr.

***William the Conqueror.** Robert Green. LC 97-10985. (First Book Ser.). (J). 1998. write for info. (*0-531-20353-0*) Watts.

William the Conqueror: The Norman Impact upon England. David C. Douglas. (English Monarchs Ser.: No. 1). 1964. pap. 15.00 (*0-520-00350-0*) U CA Pr.

***William the Curious: Knight of the Water Lilies.** Charles Santore. LC 97-4981. (J). 1997. 18.00 (*0-679-88742-3*) Random Bks Yng Read.

***William the Curious: Knight of the Water Lilies.** Charles Santore. LC 97-4981. (J). 1997. lib. bdg. 19.99 (*0-679-98742-8*) Random.

William the Last. Giorda. (I Love to Read Collection). (Illus.). 48p. (J). (ps-1). 1992. lib. bdg. 12.79 (*0-89565-884-4*) Childs World.

William the Silent. Ruth Putnam. LC 73-14466. (Heroes of the Nations Ser.). reprint ed. 30.00 (*0-404-58284-2*) AMS Pr.

***William the Third.** H. D. Thrall. (European History Ser.: Vol. 13). 95p. 1997. 9.95 (*1-58057-015-1*, WIII001B) Digital Antiq.

***William the Wonder Kid.** Dennis Silk. LC 96-45952. 251p. (Orig.). 1997. pap. 13.95 (*1-878818-50-3*) Sheep Meadow.

William Third & the Defense of European Liberty, 1650-1702. Stephen B. Baxter. LC 75-8476. (Illus.). 462p. 1976. reprint ed. text ed. 35.00 (*0-8371-8161-5*, BAWI, Greenwood Pr) Greenwood.

William Thomas McKinley: A Bio-bibliography. Jeffrey S. Sposato. LC 95-14503. (Bio-bibliographies in Music Ser.: No. 56). 328p. 1995. text ed. 69.50 (*0-313-28923-9*, Greenwood Pr) Greenwood.

William Thon, Painter. Pat D. Reef. (Maine Artists for Young Readers Ser.: No. 3). (Illus.). 56p. (J). (gr. 4-7). 1991. pap. 12.95 (*0-933858-28-0*) Kennebec River.

William Thornton: Small Star of the American Enlightenment. Beatrice S. Jenkins. Ed. & Pref. by Starr Jenkins. (Illus.). 173p. (Orig.). 1982. pap. 14.95 (*1-886659-00-1*) M Starr Bks.

William Towers. Thomas B. Aldrich. (Works of Thomas Bailey Aldrich). 1989. reprint ed. lib. bdg. 79.00 (*0-685-27374-1*) Rprt Serv.

William Tryon & the Course of Empire: A Life in British Imperial Service. Paul D. Nelson. LC 90-11998. (Illus.). xiii, 250p. (C). 1990. 29.95 (*0-8078-1917-4*) U of NC Pr.

William Turnbull, Jr. A Regional Perspective. Daniel Gregory et al. (Illus.). 82p. (Orig.). 1992. pap. 25.00 (*0-917562-60-7*) Contemp Arts.

William Turner: Tudor Naturalist, Physician & Divine. Whitney R. Jones. 240p. (C). 1988. text ed. 42.50 (*0-415-00359-8*) Routledge.

William Tyndale. Day. 1997. 24.95 (*0-8057-7037-2*, Twayne) Scribnrs Ref.

William Tyndale: A Biography. David Daniell. LC 94-17509. 1994. 32.50 (*0-300-06132-3*) Yale U Pr.

William Tyndale & the Law. Ed. by John A. Dick & Anne Richardson. (Sixteenth Century Essays & Studies: Vol. 26). 240p. 1993. 40.00 (*0-940474-26-3*) Sixteenth Cent.

William Vans Murray, Federalist Diplomat: The Shaping of Peace with France, 1797-1801. Peter P. Hill. LC 71-150347. 1971. 45.00 (*0-8156-0078-X*) Syracuse U Pr.

William Vaughn Moody. Martin Halpern. (Twayne's United States Authors Ser.). 1964. pap. 13.95 (*0-8084-0330-3*, T64) NCUP.

William W. Holden: North Carolina's Political Enigma. Horace W. Raper. LC 84-2353. (James Sprunt Studies in History & Political Science: Vol. 59). xvi, 376p. 1985. 37.50 (*0-8078-5060-8*) U of NC Pr.

William Wake's Gallican Correspondence & Related Documents, 1716-1731, Vol. 3. Ed. by Leonard Adams. (American University Studies: Theology & Religion: Ser. VII, Vol. 55). 402p. (C). 1989. text ed. 51.50 (*0-8204-1053-5*) P Lang Pubng.

William Wake's Gallican Correspondence & Related Documents, 1716-1731, Vol. 4. Ed. by Leonard Adams. LC 87-21382. (American University Studies: Theology & Religion: Ser. VII, Vol. 56). 422p. 1990. text ed. 60.50 (*0-8204-1054-3*) P Lang Pubng.

William Wake's Gallican Correspondence & Related Documents, 1716-1731, Vol. 5. Ed. by Leonard Adams. LC 87-21382. (American University Studies: Vol. 57). 390p. (C). 1991. text ed. 54.95 (*0-8204-1055-1*) P Lang Pubng.

William Wake's Gallican Correspondence & Related Documents, 1716-1731, Vol. 7. Ed. by Leonard Adams. LC 87-21382. (American University Studies: Theology & Religion: Ser. VII, Vol. 134). 310p. (C). 1993. text ed. 57.95 (*0-8204-1882-X*) P Lang Pubng.

William Wake's Gallican Correspondence, 1716-1731, Vol. 6. Ed. by Leonard Adams. LC 87-21382. (American University Studies: Theology & Religion: Ser. VII, Vol. 58). 439p. (C). 1992. text ed. 62.95 (*0-8204-1056-X*) P Lang Pubng.

William Walker: El Predestinado. Alejandro Bolanos-Geyer. LC 92-93040. (Illus.). xx, 444p. (SPA.). (C). 1992. vinyl bd. 40.00 (*1-877926-06-X*) A Bolanos-Geyer.

William Walker: The Gray-Eyed Man of Destiny. Alejandro Bolanos-Geyer. LC 88-92071. (Crescent City Ser.: Bk. 1). (Illus.). xiv, 304p. 1988. pap. 17.50 (*0-9620858-2-0*); lib. bdg. 29.50 (*0-9620858-1-2*) A Bolanos-Geyer.

William Walker: The Gray-Eyed Man of Destiny, 5 vols., Vol. 2. Alejandro Bolanos-Geyer. LC 88-92071. (Crescent City Ser.: Bk. 2). (Illus.). xii, 410p. 1989. lib. bdg. 34.50 (*0-9620858-4-7*) A Bolanos-Geyer.

William Walker Bk. 1: La Ciudad Medialuna. Alejandro Bolanos-Geyer. LC 89-91113. (Illus.). xvi, 328p. (SPA.). 1989. lib. bdg. 34.50 (*0-9620858-8-X*) A Bolanos-Geyer.

William Walker Bk. 3: Nicaragua. Alejandro Bolanos-Geyer. LC 88-92071. (Illus.). xiv, 452p. 1990. lib. bdg. 34.50 (*0-9620858-9-8*) A Bolanos-Geyer.

William Walker Bk. 4: War of Liberation. Alejandro Bolanos-Geyer. LC 90-93235. (Illus.). xiv, 334p. (C). 1990. lib. bdg. 34.50 (*1-877926-00-0*) A Bolanos-Geyer.

William Walker Vol. 5: El Predestinado de los Ojos Grises, 5 vols., Set. Alejandro Bolanos-Geyer. (Illus.). 2020p. (SPA.). 1994. 217.00 (*1-877926-12-4*) A Bolanos-Geyer.

William Walker Vol. 5: El Predestinado de los Ojos Grises, Vol. 1. 2nd ed. Alejandro Bolanos-Geyer. (Illus.). 502p. (SPA.). 1995. 75.00 (*1-877926-16-7*) A Bolanos-Geyer.

William Walker Vol. 5: El Predestinado de los Ojos Grises, Vol. 3: Nicaragua. unabridged ed. Alejandro Bolanos-Geyer. LC 93-73352. (Illus.). xvi, 428p. (SPA.). 1993. 45.00 (*1-877926-09-4*) A Bolanos-Geyer.

William Walker Vol. 5: El Predestinado de los Ojos Grises, Vol. 4: La Guerra Nacional. unabridged ed. Alejandro Bolanos-Geyer. LC 93-74558. (Illus.). xvi, 340p. (SPA.). 1994. 45.00 (*1-877926-10-8*) A Bolanos-Geyer.

William Walker Vol. 5: El Predestinado de los Ojos Grises, Vol. 5: Trujillo. unabridged ed. Alejandro Bolanos-Geyer. (Illus.). xvi, 476p. (SPA.). 1994. 47.50 (*1-877926-11-6*) A Bolanos-Geyer.

William Wallace. Andrew Fisher. 156p. 1996. pap. 35.00 (*0-85976-154-1*, Pub. by J Donald UK) St Mut.

William Wallace: Brave Heart. James MacKay. 288p. 1996. pap. 16.95 (*1-85158-823-X*, Pub. by Mnstream UK) Trafalgar.

William Wallace a Scots Life. Glen Telfer. Ed. by Stuart McHardy. 96p. (Orig.). 1995. pap. 35.00 (*1-874640-46-7*, Pub. by Argyll Pubng UK) St Mut.

William Wallace & Christina Galbraith. Hilary W. Forrester. (C). 1989. pap. 25.00 (*1-85072-045-2*, Pub. by W Sessions UK) St Mut.

William Wallace & Nancie Hancox. Hilary Wallace. (C). 1989. pap. 35.00 (*1-85072-076-2*, Pub. by W Sessions UK) St Mut.

William Wallace Gilchrist, Eighteen Forty-Six to Nineteen Sixteen: A Moving Force in the Musical Life of Philadelphia. Martha F. Schleifer. LC 84-27717. (Composers of North America Ser.: No. 1). 203p. 1985. 22.50 (*0-8108-1784-5*) Scarecrow.

***William Wallace, the Guardian of Scotland.** James Fergusson. (Illus.). 152p. (Orig.). 1995. pap. 8.00 (*0-9634992-3-8*) R Clifton.

William Walton: A Bio-Bibliography. Carolyn J. Smith. LC 88-24644. (Bio-Bibliographies in Music Ser.). 264p. 1988. text ed. 59.95 (*0-313-25391-9*, SMH, Greenwood Pr) Greenwood.

William Walton: A Source Book. Stewart R. Craggs. 300p. 1993. 73.95 (*0-85967-934-9*, Pub. by Scolar Pr UK) Ashgate Pub Co.

William Wanders Off. Illus. by Ed King. LC 90-27677. (Gus Is Gone Ser.). 24p. (J). 1991. pap. 3.95 (*1-56288-011-X*) Checkerboard.

William Ward Watkin & the Rice Institute. Patrick J. Nicholson. 364p. 1991. 24.95 (*0-88415-012-7*) Gulf Pub.

William Wayne Justice: A Judicial Biography. Frank R. Kemerer. LC 91-11743. (Illus.). 503p. 1991. 29.95 (*0-292-79066-X*) U of Tex Pr.

William Waynflete: Bishop & Educationalist. Virginia Davis. (Studies in the History of Medieval Religion: Vol. VI). (Illus.). 205p. (C). 1994. 63.00 (*0-85115-349-6*, Boydell Pr) Boydell & Brewer.

William Wegman: Paintings, Drawings, Photographs, Videotapes. Martin Kunz. 1994. pap. 24.95 (*0-8109-2463-3*) Abrams.

William Wegman: Photographic Works 1969-1976. William Wegman & Frederic Paul. (Illus.). 222p. 1992. pap. 50.00 (*2-908257-05-X*, Pub. by F R A C FR) Dist Art Pubs.

William Wegman's Farm Days. William Wegman. LC 96-35922. (Illus.). 40p. (J). 1997. 16.95 (*0-7868-0216-2*) Hyprn Child.

William Wegman's Mother Goose. William Wegman. (Illus.). 40p. (J). (ps-2). 1996. 17.95 (*0-7868-0218-9*); lib. bdg. 17.89 (*0-7868-2231-7*) Hyprn Child.

***William Wegman's Puppies.** William Wegman. (J). 1997. write for info. (*0-614-29240-9*) Hyprn Child.

William Wells & Maconaquah, White Rose of the Miamis. Julia M. Gilman. LC 85-60341. 317p. (Orig.). 1985. pap. 16.95 (*0-9614890-2-2*) Jewel Pub Co.

William Wells of Southold & His Descendants, 1638-1878. C. W. Hayes. (Illus.). 300p. 1989. reprint ed. pap. 45.00 (*0-8328-1237-4*); reprint ed. lib. bdg. 53.00 (*0-8328-1236-6*) Higginson Bk Co.

William Wetmore Story & His Friends, 2 vols. in one. Henry James. LC 69-18460. (Library of American Art). 1969. reprint ed. lib. bdg. 85.00 (*0-306-71249-0*) Da Capo.

William Whewell 1794-1866, Dionysius Lardner 1793-1859, Charles Babbage 1792-1871. Ed. by Mark Blaug. (Pioneers in Economics Ser.: No. 19). 288p. 1991. text ed. 110.00 (*1-85278-481-4*) E Elgar.

William Whiston. Ed. by Maureen Farrell & I. Bernard Cohen. LC 80-2088. (Development of Science Ser.). (Illus.). 1981. lib. bdg. 35.95 (*0-405-13854-7*) Ayer.

William Whiston: Honest Newtonian. James E. Force. (Illus.). 240p. 1985. text ed. 59.95 (*0-521-26590-8*) Cambridge U Pr.

William Wilberforce, 1759-1833: A Bibliography. Leonard W. Cowie. LC 92-5351. (Bibliographies of British Statesmen Ser.: No. 17). 160p. 1992. text ed. 55.00 (*0-313-28283-8*, CWW, Greenwood Pr) Greenwood.

William Wilfred Campbell & His Works. George Wicken. (Canadian Author Studies). 50p. (C). 1989. pap. text ed. 9.95 (*0-920763-47-2*, Pub. by ECW Press CN) Genl Dist Srvs.

William Wilkins, Seventeen Seventy-Eight to Eighteen Thirty-Nine. Rhodri W. Liscombe. LC 78-73247. 320p. 1980. 95.00 (*0-521-22528-0*) Cambridge U Pr.

William Willya & the Birthday Cake. Skip Masland. (Misadventures of William Willya Ser.). (Illus.). 44p. (J). (gr. k-5). 1995. 9.95 (*1-883016-04-5*) Moonglow.

William Willya & the Washing Machine. Skip Masland. (Misadventures of William Willya Ser.). (Illus.). 44p. (J). (gr. k-5). 1993. 9.95 (*1-883016-01-0*) Moonglow.

William Winchester, 1711-1790. Emma Shelton. LC 93-78773. (Illus.). 104p. (Orig.). 1993. pap. 15.00 (*0-9614125-9-3*) Hist Soc Carroll.

William Windom: Apostle of Positive Government. Robert S. Salisbury. LC 92-32606. (C). 1993. pap. text ed. 39.50 (*0-8191-8922-7*); lib. bdg. 59.50 (*0-8191-8921-9*) U Pr of Amer.

William Winston Seaton on the National Intelligencer. Josephine Seaton. LC 70-125714. (American Journalists Ser.). 1971. reprint ed. 24.95 (*0-405-01695-6*) Ayer.

William Withering & the Foxglove. R. D. Mann et al. 1986. lib. bdg. 273.50 (*0-85200-950-X*) Kluwer Ac.

William Wolk Paintings. William Wolk. (Illus.). 48p. 1994. 39.95 (*1-880396-37-8*, JP0396-37-8) Jalmar Pr.

William Woods Holden, Firebrand of North Carolina Politics. William C. Harris. LC 87-2699. (Southern Biography Ser.). 328p. 1987. text ed. 40.00 (*0-8071-1325-5*) La State U Pr.

William Wordsworth. Ed. by Stephen Gill. LC 83-17278. 784p. 1984. pap. 22.00 (*0-19-281333-1*) OUP.

William Wordsworth. John O. Hayden. (English Authors Ser.: No. 118). 184p. (C). 1991. lib. bdg. 21.95 (*0-685-38165-X*, Twayne) Scribnrs Ref.

William Wordsworth. Elizabeth Wordsworth. LC 74-16289. (Studies in Wordsworth: No. 29). 1974. lib. bdg. 59.95 (*0-8383-1800-2*) M S G Haskell Hse.

William Wordsworth. William Wordsworth. (Poets Ser.). 146p. 1993. 5.95 (*0-7117-0438-4*, Pub. by Jarrold Pub UK) Seven Hills Bk.

William Wordsworth: A Literary Life. John Williams. (Literary Lives Ser.). 203p. 1996. text ed. 35.00 (*0-312-15864-5*) St Martin.

William Wordsworth: Intensity & Achievement. Thomas McFarland. 185p. 1992. 49.95 (*0-19-811253-X*) OUP.

William Wordsworth: Selected Poetry. Intro. by Nicholas Roe. 366p. 1993. pap. 9.95 (*0-14-058661-X*, Penguin Bks) Viking Penguin.

***William Wordsworth: The Only Full Length Popular Biography.** Hunter Davies. (Illus.). 384p. 1997. pap. 17.95 (*0-7509-1482-3*, Pub. by Sutton Pubng UK) Bks Intl VA.

William Wordsworth: The Poems, 2 vols., Vol. 1. William Wordsworth. Ed. by John O. Hayden. LC 81-2994. (English Poets Ser.: Nos. 7-8). 1072p. 1981. reprint ed. pap. 180.00 (*0-7837-3543-X*, 2057717) Bks Demand.

William Wordsworth: The Poems, 2 vols., Vol. 2. William Wordsworth. Ed. by John O. Hayden. LC 81-2994. (English Poets Ser.: Nos. 7-8). 1104p. 1981. reprint ed. pap. 180.00 (*0-7837-3544-8*, 2057717) Bks Demand.

William Wordsworth see Modern Critical Views Series

William Wordsworth & Annette Vallon. rev. ed. Emile Legouis. Ed. by Pierre Legouis. LC 67-16448. xviii, 176p. 1967. lib. bdg. 30.00 (*0-208-00603-6*, Archon Bks) Shoe String.

William Wordsworth & Annette Vallon. Emile H. Legowis. (BCL1-PR English Literature Ser.). 146p. 1992. reprint ed. lib. bdg. 69.00 (*0-7812-7680-2*) Rprt Serv.

William Wordsworth & the Age of English Romanticism. Jonathan Wordsworth et al. (Illus.). 285p. 1987. pap. 29.95 (*0-8135-1274-3*) Rutgers U Pr.

William Wordsworth & the Age of English Romanticism. William Wordsworth et al. (Illus.). 285p. 1987. text ed. 65.00 (*0-8135-1273-5*) Rutgers U Pr.

William Wordsworth & the Hermeneutics of Incarnation. David P. Haney. LC 92-29464. (Literature & Philosophy Ser.). 256p. 1993. 35.00 (*0-271-00911-X*) Pa St U Pr.

William Wordsworth & the Mind of Man: The Poet As Thinker. John O. Hayden. 1993. 24.95 (*0-942104-04-8*) Bibli O Phile Pub Co.

William Wordsworth, His Doctrine & Art in Their Historical Relations. 2nd ed. Arthur Beatty. LC 75-28992. reprint ed. 41.50 (*0-404-14003-3*) AMS Pr.

William Wordsworth of Rydal Mount. Frederika Beatty. LC 74-161730. (Illus.). reprint ed. 32.50 (*0-404-07927-X*) AMS Pr.

William Wright, Candidate: A Wordperfect Simulation. Ambrose. (TA - Typing/Keyboarding Ser.). 1993. pap. 12.95 (*0-538-61368-8*) S-W Pub.

William Wrigley Jr. Company: A Report on the Company's Environmental Policies & Practices. (Illus.). 20p. (C). 1994. reprint ed. pap. text ed. 250.00 (*0-7881-0949-9*, Coun on Econ) DIANE Pub.

William Wyles Collection: Author-Title Catalog; Subject Catalog, 5 vols., Set. Donald C. Davidson. LC 70-19247. 1970. text ed. 1,125.00 (*0-8371-3268-1*, WWA/, Greenwood Pr) Greenwood.

Williams: Descendants of John Williams. Cornelia B. Williams & Anna P. Williams. 179p. 1991. reprint ed. pap. 29.00 (*0-8328-2190-X*); reprint ed. lib. bdg. 39.00 (*0-8328-2189-6*) Higginson Bk Co.

Williams: Roger Williams of Providence, R. I. Bertha W. Anthony & Harriett W. Weeden. (Illus.). 220p. 1991. reprint ed. pap. 34.00 (*0-8328-2192-6*); reprint ed. lib. bdg. 44.00 (*0-8328-2191-8*) Higginson Bk Co.

Williams: Taxation of Employee Share Schemes. 3rd ed. David F. Williams. 1991. 160.00 (*0-406-51250-7*) MICHIE.

Williams: The Families of Joshua Williams of Chester County, Pa., & John McKeehan of Cumberland County, Pa., with Some Allied Families. B. P. Douglas. (Illus.). 504p. 1992. reprint ed. pap. 76.00 (*0-8328-2765-7*); reprint ed. lib. bdg. 86.00 (*0-8328-2764-9*) Higginson Bk Co.

Williams: Triumph Out of Tragedy. Alan Henry. (Illus.). 192p. 1996. 29.95 (*1-85260-510-3*, Pub. by J H Haynes & Co UK) Motorbooks Intl.

Williams Vol. II: Roger Williams of Providence, R. I. Bertha W. Anthony. (Illus.). 213p. 1991. reprint ed. pap. 31.00 (*0-8328-2194-2*); reprint ed. lib. bdg. 41.00 (*0-8328-2193-4*) Higginson Bk Co.

***Williams & Lissner's Biomechanics of Human Motion.** 3rd ed. Barney F. LeVeau. (Illus.). 340p. 1992. pap. write for info. (*0-7216-5743-5*) Saunders.

Williams & Murphy: Records & Related Families of Virginia, North Carolina, Etc. R. M. Williams. 369p. 1992. reprint ed. pap. 57.00 (*0-8328-2763-0*); reprint ed. lib. bdg. 67.00 (*0-8328-2762-2*) Higginson Bk Co.

Williams Collection of Far Eastern Ceramics: Tonnancour Section. Kamer Aga-Oglu. (Special Publications). (Illus.). 1975. pap. 4.00 (*0-932206-75-1*) U Mich Mus Anthro.

Williams Collection of Far Eastern Ceramics, Chinese, Siamese, & Annamese Ceramic Wares: Selected from the Collection of Justice & Mrs. G. M. Williams in the U. of Mich. Museum of Anthropology. Kamer Aga-Oglu. (Special Publications). (Illus.). 1972. pap. 2.00 (*0-932206-74-3*) U Mich Mus Anthro.

Williams College. Photos by Bob Krist. (First Edition Ser.). (Illus.). 112p. 1992. 39.95 (*0-916509-94-X*) Harmony Hse Pub.

***William's Dog.** Richard Chevat. (Look-Look Bks.). (Illus.). (J). (ps-3). 1997. pap. 2.99 (*0-614-28791-X*, Golden Books) Western Pub.

William's Doll. Charlotte Zolotow. LC 70-183173. (Charlotte Zolotow Bk.). (Illus.). 32p. (J). (ps-3). 1972. 14.95 (*0-06-027047-0*); lib. bdg. 14.89 (*0-06-027048-9*) HarpC Child Bks.

William's Doll. Charlotte Zolotow. LC 70-183173. (Trophy Picture Bk.). (Illus.). 32p. (J). (ps-3). 1985. reprint ed. pap. 4.95 (*0-06-443067-7*, Trophy) HarpC Child Bks.

Williams Electronics. Date not set. student ed. write for info. (*0-314-05523-1*); teacher ed., pap. text ed. write for info. (*0-314-05522-3*) West Pub.

Williams Family History. Ruby L. Helmick. (Illus.). (Orig.). 1989. pap. text ed. 15.00 (*0-9613513-2-2*) B R Phillips.

***Williams Gambit.** William L. Williams. (Illus.). 64p. (Orig.). 1997. pap. 10.00 (*0-939433-50-8*) Caissa Edit.

W

Williams, Genealogy of Williams Families: William Williams of New London County, Groton & Ledyard, CT, & Emanuel Williams of Taunton, MA. J. O. Williams. 215p. 1993. reprint ed. pap. 34.00 (0-8328-3759-8); reprint ed. lib. bdg. 44.00 (0-8328-3758-X) Higginson Bk Co.

William's Gift. Jennifer C. Weil. (Illus.). 40p. (J). (gr. k-4). 1994. 14.95 (1-56844-007-3) Enchante Pub.

William's Gift. 2nd rev. ed. Jennifer C. Weil. Ed. by Gudrun Hoy & Bobi Martin. (Emotional Literacy Ser.). (Illus.). 40p. (J). (gr. k-5). 1995. 14.95 (1-56844-106-1) Enchante Pub.

Williams Hematology. 5th ed. Ed. by Ernest Beutler et al. (Illus.). 1920p. 1994. text ed. 145.00 (0-07-070386-8) McGraw-Hill HPD.

Williams Hematology: Companion Handbook. 5th ed. Ed. by William J. Williams. (Illus.). 480p. 1995. pap. text ed. 29.50 (0-07-070394-9) McGraw-Hill HPD.

Williams' Introduction to the Profession of Medical Technology. 4th ed. Margaret R. Williams. Ed. by David S. Lindberg et al. LC 84-912. 124p. reprint ed. pap. 35.40 (0-7837-1489-0, 2057184) Bks Demand.

Williams. Life, Ancestors & Descendants of Robert Williams of Roxbury, Mass., 1607-1693, with Biographical Sketches. H. Williams. 216p. 1991. reprint ed. pap. 33.00 (0-8328-1968-9); reprint ed. lib. bdg. 43.00 (0-8328-1967-0) Higginson Bk Co.

Williams Manuscript of George Herbert's Poems. George Herbert. Ed. by Amy M. Charles. LC 76-54153. 1977. 50.00 (0-8201-1286-0) Schol Facsimiles.

Williams Obstetrics. Gilstrap. 1996. student ed., pap. text ed. 55.00 (0-8385-9641-X) Appleton & Lange.

Williams Obstetrics. 20th ed. Cunningham. 1996. text ed. 115.00 (0-8385-9638-X) Appleton & Lange.

Williams on Wills, 2 vols., Set. 7th ed. C. H. Sherrin et al. 1995. write for info. (0-406-01033-1) MICHIE.

Williams Permanent Alliance. 1977. lib. bdg. 99.50 (90-286-0466-9) Kluwer Ac.

Williams Shakespeare. Intro. by Peter Porter. (Great Poets Ser.). (Illus.). 64p. 1987. 10.00 (0-517-56708-3, Crown) Crown Pub Group.

Williams-Siegel Documentary: Including Williams' Poetry Talked About by Eli Siegel & William Carlos Williams Present & Talking: 1952. Eli Siegel. Ed. by Martha Baird & Ellen Reiss. LC 70-100610. 208p. (Orig.). 1970. 9.50 (0-910492-12-3); pap. 7.95 (0-910492-25-5) Definition.

Williams-Sonoma Cookbook & Guide to Kitchenware. Chuck Williams. LC 85-18366. (Illus.). 304p. 1986. 19.95 (0-394-54411-0) Random.

Williams-Sonoma Wedding Planner. Ed. by Chuck Williams. (Illus.). 1996. write for info. (1-875137-11-4) Weldon Owen.

***Williams-Sonoma's Celebrating the Pleasures of Cooking: Chuck Williams Commemorates 40 Years of Cooking in America.** Chuck Williams. Ed. by Norman Kolpas. LC 97-5712. (Illus.). 176p. 1997. write for info. (0-7835-4934-2) Time-Life.

Williams Spanish English Dictionary. Williams. 1987. pap. 14.95 (0-684-13294-X) S&S Trade.

William's Story. Debra Duel. (Illus.). 48p. (Orig.). (J). (gr. k-8). 1992. pap. 9.95 (1-880812-02-9) S Ink WA.

Williams Textbook of Endocrinology. 8th ed. Wilson. 1991. text ed. 150.00 (0-7216-9514-0) HarBrace.

***Williams Textbook of Endocrinology.** 9th ed. Robert H. Williams & Jean D. Wilson. LC 96-41440. 1998. text ed. 140.00 (0-7216-6152-1) Saunders.

***Williams. The Families of Joshua Williams of Chester Co. Pa. & John McKeehan of Cumberland Co. Pa., with Some Allied Families.** Bessie P. Douglas. (Illus.). 504p. 1996. reprint ed. pap. 76.00 (0-8328-5428-X); reprint ed. lib. bdg. 86.00 (0-8328-5427-1) Higginson Bk Co.

William's Vision of Piers the Plowman: Text A. Ed. by Walter W. Skeat. (EETS, OS Ser.: Vol. 28). 1974. reprint ed. 40.00 (0-8115-3348-4) Periodicals Srv.

William's Vision of Piers the Plowman: Text B, Pt. II. Ed. by Walter W. Skeat. (EETS, OS Ser.: Vol. 38). 1974. reprint ed. 30.00 (0-8115-3349-2) Periodicals Srv.

William's Wife. Jean Plaidy. 1995. mass mkt. 5.99 (0-449-22284-5, Crest) Fawcett.

William's Wife. large type ed. Delia Foster. (Linford Romance Library). 1990. pap. 15.99 (0-7089-6816-3) Ulverscroft.

William's Window: An Introduction to Shakespeare's Plays for Young People. Marina C. Stockdale. 36p. (J). (gr. 3-8). 1983. pap. 3.50 (0-88680-209-1) I E Clark.

***William's Wish Wellingtons: William's Dog.** Illus. by Atholl McDonald. (Big Bag Bks.). 24p. (J). (ps-3). 1997. pap. 2.99 (0-307-12929-2, 12929, Golden Books) Western Pub.

***Williams, 300 Years of Leadership in America Vol. 1: A History of the Descendants of John Williams of Llangollen, Wales.** Lewis J. Williams et al. (Illus.). 1997. write for info. (0-9658376-0-2) Panther Creek.

Williamsburg. 1995. pap. 18.00 (0-7893-0029-X) Universe.

***Williamsburg.** Bill Harris. 1997. 9.95 (1-85833-698-8) BHB Intl.

Williamsburg. Bill Harris. (Picture Memory Ser.). 1992. 8.99 (0-517-07274-2) Random Hse Value.

Williamsburg. Zachary Kent. LC 91-35055. (Cornerstones of Freedom Ser.). (Illus.). 32p. (J). (gr. 3-6). 1992. lib. bdg. 18.00 (0-516-04854-6) Childrens.

Williamsburg. Zachary Kent. LC 91-35055. (Cornerstones of Freedom Ser.). (Illus.). 32p. (J). (gr. 3-6). 1992. pap. 4.95 (0-516-44854-4) Childrens.

***Williamsburg: A Seasonal Sampler.** David M. Doody et al. LC 96-32103. 1996. write for info. (0-87935-165-9); write for info. (0-87935-168-3) Colonial Williamsburg.

Williamsburg: An Artist's Sketchbook. John C. Roach. (Illus.). 50p. 1994. pap. 9.50 (1-884824-05-6) Tryon Pubng.

Williamsburg: Cradle of the Revolution. Ron Goor & Nancy Goor. LC 94-9370. 90p. (J). 1994. text ed. 15.95 (0-689-31795-6, Atheneum S&S) S&S Trade.

Williamsburg Art of Cookery. Helen Bullock. LC 43-6700. (Illus.). 276p. (Orig.). 1966. 12.95 (0-910412-30-8) Colonial Williamsburg.

Williamsburg Before & After: The Rebirth of Virginia's Colonial Capital. George H. Yetter. LC 88-5001. (Illus.). 198p. 1988. 26.95 (0-87935-077-6) Colonial Williamsburg.

Williamsburg Collection of Antique Furnishings. Colonial Williamsburg Foundation Staff. LC 73-86811. (Decorative Arts Ser.). (Illus.). 120p. (Orig.). 1973. pap. 5.95 (0-87935-017-2) Colonial Williamsburg.

Williamsburg Cookbook. enl. rev. ed. Letha Booth & Joan P. Dutton. LC 75-2328. (Illus.). 174p. (Orig.). 1975. 14.95 (0-910412-91-X) Colonial Williamsburg.

Williamsburg Household. Joan W. Anderson. LC 87-33803. (J). (gr. 4-7). 1990. pap. 5.95 (0-395-54791-1, Clarion Bks) HM.

Williamsburg Memories. Gershon Kranzler. (C). 1988. 14.95 (0-935063-58-7) CIS Comm.

Williamsburg Songbook. John A. Edmunds. LC 64-20095. (Colonial Williamsburg Ser.). (Illus.). 152p. reprint ed. pap. 43.40 (0-8357-9820-8, 2016516) Bks Demand.

Williamsburg Trilogy. Daniel Fuchs. 1976. mass mkt. 4.95 (0-380-01468-8) Avon.

Williamsburg's Glorious Gardens. Photos by Roger Foley. LC 95-40938. 1996. write for info. (0-87935-160-8) Colonial Williamsburg.

***Williamson: Alden Williamson Genealogy: Genealogical Record of Alden Williamson's Family in Pike, Martin, Floyd, Johnson, Lawrence & Boyd Counties in Ky., & Mingo, Wayne, Logan, Lincoln, Cabell & Wyoming Cos. in W.V.** Joseph W. Alley. (Illus.). 254p. 1996. reprint ed. pap. 39.00 (0-8328-5595-2); reprint ed. lib. bdg. 49.00 (0-8328-5594-4) Higginson Bk Co.

Williamson Amplifier. D. T. Williamson. LC 90-83998. (Illus.). 40p. 1990. pap. text ed. 4.95 (0-9624191-8-4) Audio Amateur.

Williamson Co., TN: County Court Minutes, July 1812 - Oct. 1815. Carol Wells. 162p. (Orig.). 1994. pap. text ed. 15.00 (0-7884-0112-2) Heritage Bk.

Williamson Co., TN: County Court Minutes, May 1806-April 1812. Carol Wells. 227p. (Orig.). 1994. pap. text ed. 20.00 (0-7884-0072-X) Heritage Bk.

***Williamson Effect.** Zelazny. Date not set. pap. 14.95 (0-312-86395-0) St Martin.

Williamson Effect. Ed. by Roger Zelazny. 352p. 1996. 23.95 (0-312-85748-9) Tor Bks.

Williamsport: Frontier Village to Regional Center. 2nd rev. ed. Robert H. Larson et al. (Illus.). 176p. 1996. 34.95 (0-89781-483-5) Am Historical Pr.

Williamstown: The First Two Hundred Years, 1753-1953. Ed. by R. R. Brooks et al. (Illus.). 458p. 1996. reprint ed. lib. bdg. 48.00 (0-8328-5039-X) Higginson Bk Co.

***Willie.** Ann Colin. 1998. pap. 22.95 (0-14-024908-7) Viking Penguin.

***Willie: Raising & Loving a Child with Attention Deficit Disorder.** Ann Colin. 1996. 22.95 (0-614-19892-5) Viking Penguin.

***Willie: Raising & Loving a Child with Attention Deficit Disorder.** Ann Herbst. 1997. 22.95 (0-614-19867-4) Viking Child Bks.

Willie: The Life of W. Somerset Maugham. Robert Calder. (Illus.). 432p. 1992. pap. 14.95 (0-312-08337-8) St Martin.

Willie, a Girl from a Town Called Dallas. Willie N. Lewis. LC 83-18081. (Illus.). 150p. 1984. 18.95 (0-89096-175-1) Tex A&M Univ Pr.

Willie & the Number Three Door & Other Adventures. Adrienne E. Reeves. (Illus.). 120p. (Orig.). (J). (gr. 1-3). 1991. pap. 5.50 (0-87743-703-3) Bahai.

***Willie & the Rattlesnake King.** Clara G. Clark. LC 96-80400. (Illus.). 180p. (YA). (gr. 7 up). 1997. 14.95 (1-56397-654-4) Boyds Mills Pr.

Willie Bea & the Time the Martians Landed. Virginia Hamilton. LC 83-1659. 224p. (J). (gr. 5-9). 1983. 16.00 (0-688-02390-8) Greenwillow.

Willie Bear & the Wish Fish. Debi Gliori. (Illus.). (J). (ps-3). 1995. 16.00 (0-02-736021-0, Mac Bks Young Read) S&S Childrens.

Willie Boy: A Desert Manhunt. Harry W. Lawton. 1995. 22.00 (0-939046-27-X); pap. 16.00 (0-939046-28-8) Malki Mus Pr.

Willie Brown: Style, Power, & a Passion for Politics. James Richardson. LC 96-16800. (Illus.). 576p. (C). 1996. 29.95 (0-520-20456-5) U CA Pr.

Willie Carson: An Illustrated Biography. Michael Seely. (Illus.). 176p. 1992. 34.95 (0-7472-0431-4, Pub. by Headline UK) Trafalgar.

Willie Dixon - Master Blues Composer: With Notes & Tablature. Willie Dixon. 288p. 1992. otabind 24.95 (0-7935-0305-1, 00660178) H Leonard.

Willie Doherty. Dan Cameron. LC 93-79935. (Illus.). 64p. 1994. 20.00 (0-934349-11-8) Grey Art Gallery Study Ctr.

Willie Goes to Town. Matthew V. Smith. (Illus.). 15p. (J). (gr. k-3). 1994. pap. 9.95 (1-895583-65-9) MAYA Pubs.

***Willie Hogg.** Robin Jenkins. 1993. pap. 12.00 (0-7486-6152-2, Pub. by Polygon UK) Subterranean Co.

Willie Jerome. Alice F. Duncan. LC 94-10444. (J). 1995. text ed. 15.00 (0-02-733208-X, Mac Bks Young Read) S&S Childrens.

Willie Mae. Elizabeth Kytle. LC 92-28227. (Brown Thrasher Bks.). 272p. 1993. reprint ed. pap. 14.95 (0-8203-1518-4) U of Ga Pr.

Willie Masters' Lonesome Wife. William H. Gass. LC 89-11724. (Illus.). 64p. 1989. reprint ed. pap. 9.95 (0-916583-46-5) Dalkey Arch.

Willie Mays. John Grabowski. (Baseball Legends Ser.). (Illus.). 64p. (J). (gr. 3 up). 1990. lib. bdg. 15.95 (0-7910-1183-6) Chelsea Hse.

Willie Mays: Baseball Legend. Mitch Burkhardt. (Black American Ser.). (Illus.). 192p. (YA). 1992. mass mkt. 3.95 (0-87067-587-7, Melrose Sq) Holloway.

Willie Mays: Classical Sports Shots. Bruce Weber. 48p. (J). (gr. 4-6). 1993. pap. 1.25 (0-590-47020-5) Scholastic Inc.

Willie Mays, Young Superstar. Louis Sabin. LC 89-33979. (Illus.). 48p. (J). (gr. 4-6). 1990. lib. bdg. 12.95 (0-8167-1775-3) Troll Communs.

Willie Mays, Young Superstar. Louis Sabin. LC 89-33979. (Illus.). 48p. (J). (gr. 4-6). 1996. pap. 3.95 (0-8167-1776-1) Troll Communs.

Willie Mosconi on Pocket Billiards. Willie Mosconi. (Illus.). 1948. pap. 7.00 (0-517-50779-X, Crown) Crown Pub Group.

Willie Mosconi on Pocket Billiards. Willie Mosconi. 1995. pap. 9.00 (0-517-88428-3) Random.

Willie Nelson: Just Plain Willie. 120p. 1984. per. 12.95 (0-7935-1487-8, 00356382) H Leonard.

Willie Nelson "Cooked Goose" Cookbook & IRS Financial Advisor. Kent Wildman. LC 91-77190. (Illus.). 80p. 1992. pap. 5.95 (1-56352-034-6) Longstreet Pr Inc.

Willie Nelson Guitar Songbook. rev. ed. Ed. by Carol Cuellar & Aaron Stang. 56p. (YA). 1995. pap. text ed. 16.95 (0-89724-533-4, P0896GTA) Warner Brothers.

Willie Nelson Lyrics, 1957-1994. Willie Nelson. 1995. 16.95 (0-312-11917-8) St Martin.

***Willie Randolph: Brooklyn, the Bronx, Baseball & Beyond.** Willie Randolph. LC 92-54757. 288p. 1997. 20.00 (0-06-016946-X) HarpC.

Willie Roy Dewberrys Panther. Ben Douglas. 1995. pap. 7.95 (1-885483-01-5) Sontag Pr.

Willie Stargell. Mike Shannon. (Baseball Legends Ser.). (Illus.). 64p. (J). (gr. 3 up). 1992. lib. bdg. 15.95 (0-7910-1192-5) Chelsea Hse.

Willie Takes a Hike. Gloria Rand. LC 95-13698. (Illus.). (J). (ps-3). 1996. 15.00 (0-15-200272-3) HarBrace.

Willie, the Frog Prince. C. S. Adler. LC 92-44113. (J). 1994. 15.00 (0-395-65615-X, Clarion Bks) HM.

Willie the Groundhog. Grandpa Blair. 6p. (YA). (gr. 10 up). 1991. pap. 4.75 (0-930366-63-8) Northcountry Pub.

Willie the Slowpoke. Rose Greydanus. (Illus.). 32p. (J). (gr. k-2). 1980. audio 8.95 (0-685-04954-X) Troll Communs.

Willie the Slowpoke. Rose Greydanus. (Illus.). 32p. (J). (gr. k-2). 1996. pap. 2.50 (0-89375-294-0) Troll Communs.

Willie the Squowse. Ted Allan. (Illus.). (J). (gr. 2 up). 1991. reprint ed. 9.95 (0-8038-9341-8) Hastings.

Willie the Weenie Whiner. George C. Anderheggen. (Illus.). 20p. (Orig.). (J). (gr. 5 up). 1983. 3.95 (0-910717-01-X) Bookling Pubs.

***Willie Wants a Star.** Doris Regan. (Illus.). 64p. (Orig.). (J). (gr. 1-6). 1997. pap. 6.95 (1-56002-662-6, Univ Edtns) Aegina Pr.

Willie Was Different. Norman Rockwell. LC 94-8785. (J). 1994. 16.95 (0-936399-61-9) Berkshire Hse.

Willie Was Different. Norman Rockwell. (J). 1997. pap. 5.99 (0-679-88262-6) McKay.

***Willie Was Different.** Norman Rockwell. (J). (ps-3). 1997. reprint ed. pap. 5.99 (0-614-28952-1) Random Bks Yng Read.

Willie's Not the Hugging Kind. Joyce D. Barrett. LC 89-1868. (Illus.). 32p. (J). (gr. k-3). 1989. 16.00 (0-06-020416-8); lib. bdg. 15.89 (0-06-020417-6) HarpC Child Bks.

Willie's Not the Hugging Kind. Joyce D. Barrett. LC 89-1868. (Trophy Picture Bk.). (Illus.). 32p. (J). (gr. k-3). 1991. pap. 4.95 (0-06-443264-5, Trophy) HarpC Child Bks.

Willie's Wonderful Pet. Mel Cebulash. (Hello Reader! Ser.). (Illus.). 32p. (J). (ps-1). 1993. pap. 3.50 (0-590-45787-X) Scholastic Inc.

Willimantic Industry & Community: The Rise & Decline of a Connecticut Textile City. Thomas R. Beardsley. (Illus.). 264p. (Orig.). 1993. pap. 15.95 (0-9634524-0-1) Windham Textile.

Willing Captive. large type unabridged ed. (Harlequin Ser.). 1994. lib. bdg. 19.95 (0-263-13590-X, Pub. by Mills & Boon UK) Thorndike Pr.

Willing Dead. Patricia A. Stewart & Edna H. Maples. (Murder Mystery Parties Ser.). (Illus.). 52p. 1984. 8.00 (0-317-31549-8) Univ Games.

Willing Evolution. David L. Laing. (Illus.). 50p. (Orig.). 1995. pap. write for info. (0-9646264-0-3) Elohim Art & Bks.

Willing Heart. (Heartsong ser.). 176p. 1994. pap. text ed. 4.95 (1-55748-465-1) Barbour & Co.

Willing Heart. Lucile Farmer. 246p. (Orig.). (YA). pap. 7.95 (1-877917-10-9) Alpha Bible Pubns.

Willing Hostage. Marlys Millhiser. 256p. 1994. pap. 4.95 (0-7867-0110-2) Carroll & Graf.

***Willing Migrants: Soninke Labor Diasporas, 1848-1960.** Francois Manchuelle. 340p. 1997. text ed. 44.95 (0-8214-1201-9) Ohio U Pr.

***Willing Migrants: Soninke Labor Diasporas, 1848-1960.** Francois Manchuelle. 340p. 1997. pap. text ed. 24.95 (0-8214-1202-7) Ohio U Pr.

Willing Slaves? British Workers under Human Resource Management. Andrew Scott. LC 93-23461. (Studies in Management: Vol. 21). (Illus.). 176p. (C). 1994. text ed. 65.00 (0-521-41257-9); pap. text ed. 22.95 (0-521-46719-5) Cambridge U Pr.

***Willing Spirit.** Piers Anthony & Alfred Tella. LC 96-29211. 1996. 22.95 (0-312-86266-0) Tor Bks.

***Willing Spirit.** Earle P. Barron. 118p. (Orig.). 1997. mass mkt. 4.99 (1-55237-267-7, Pub. by Comnwlth Pub CN) Partners Pubs Grp.

Willing Spirit. Deb Stover. 352p. 1996. mass mkt. 4.99 (0-7860-0334-0, Pinncle Kensgtn) Kensgtn Pub Corp.

***Willing Spirits.** Phyllis Schieber. Date not set. write for info. (0-688-15535-9) Morrow.

***Willing to Believe: Evangelicals & Free Will.** R. C. Sproul. 224p. 1997. 15.99 (0-8010-1152-3) Baker Bks.

Willing to Die, 3 Vols., Set. Joseph S. Le Fanu. Ed. by Devendra P. Varma. LC 76-5280. (Collected Works). 1977. reprint ed. 87.95 (0-405-09242-3) Ayer.

Willing to Die, 3 Vols., Vol. 1. Joseph S. Le Fanu. Ed. by Devendra P. Varma. LC 76-5280. (Collected Works). 1977. reprint ed. 29.95 (0-405-09243-1) Ayer.

Willing to Die, 3 Vols., Vol. 2. Joseph S. Le Fanu. Ed. by Devendra P. Varma. LC 76-5280. (Collected Works). 1977. reprint ed. 29.95 (0-405-09244-X) Ayer.

Willing to Die, 3 Vols., Vol. 3. Joseph S. Le Fanu. Ed. by Devendra P. Varma. LC 76-5280. (Collected Works). 1977. reprint ed. 29.95 (0-405-09245-8) Ayer.

Willing to Grow. Anita Higman. (Illus.). 45p. (YA). (gr. 9-12). 1988. pap. 4.95 (0-945362-01-3) Best Sllrs TX.

Willing to Try Again: Steps Toward Blending a Family. Dick Dunn. LC 92-33555. 128p. 1993. pap. 11.00 (0-8170-1185-4) Judson.

Willing Victims. John Nold. 64p. 1987. 9.95 (0-920806-89-9, Pub. by Penumbra Pr CN) U of Toronto Pr.

Willing Workers: The Work Ethics in Japan, England, & the United States. Tamotsu Sengoku. Tr. by Koichi Ezaki & Yuko Ezaki. LC 85-9552. (Illus.). xv, 152p. 1985. text ed. 45.00 (0-89930-137-1, SWK/, Quorum Bks) Greenwood.

Willingly to School. Margaret M. Phillips. (C). 1989. text ed. 35.00 (0-948929-23-5) St Mut.

Willingness to Pay for Medical Care: Evidence from Two Developing Countries. Paul J. Gertler & Jacques Van der Gaag. LC 90-41549. 144p. 1991. text ed. 22.95 (0-8018-4146-1) Johns Hopkins.

Willis Faber & Dumas Building: Ipswich 1974 Foster Associates. Gabriele Bramante. (Architecture in Detail Ser.). (Illus.). 60p. (C). 1993. pap. 29.95 (0-7148-2772-X, Pub. by Phaidon Press UK) Chronicle Bks.

Willis Haviland Carrier, Father of Air-Conditioning. Margaret Ingels. LC 72-5056. (Technology & Society Ser.). (Illus.). 178p. 1972. reprint ed. 18.95 (0-405-04708-8) Ayer.

Willis O'Brien: Special Effects Genius. Steve Archer. LC 92-50950. (Illus.). 239p. 1993. lib. bdg. 32.50 (0-89950-833-2) McFarland & Co.

Willis R. Whitney, General Electric, & the Origins of U. S. Industrial Research. George Wise. LC 84-27484. (Illus.). 389p. reprint ed. pap. 110.90 (0-8357-4579-1, 2037488) Bks Demand.

***Willis the Frog.** Jean-Paul Larocque. (Illus.). 23p. (J). (gr. k-4). 1997. pap. 14.95 (1-895583-81-0) MAYA Pubs.

Williston on Contracts, 28 vols., Vol. 1. 4th ed. Richard A. Lord. LC 90-63284. 1990. 507.00 (0-686-14488-0) Lawyers Cooperative.

Williston on Sales, 3 vols. 5th ed. Deborah L. Nelson & Jennifer L. Howicz. LC 94-46505. 1994. 265.00 (0-615-00522-5) Clark Boardman Callaghan.

Willits Scrapbook: The Way it Was 1958-1974. Lois Mahan. LC 78-108189. 1975. 3.00 (0-932820-00-X) M P Pubs.

***Williwaw.** Gore Vidal. (Illus.). 136p. 1996. 250.00 (0-614-24921-X) Arion Pr.

Williwaw. Gore Vidal. 176p. 1986. mass mkt. 4.99 (0-345-33233-4) Ballantine.

Williwaw. Gore Vidal. LC 83-45855. reprint ed. 32.50 (0-404-20276-4, PS3543) AMS Pr.

Williwaw War: The Arkansas National Guard in the Aleutians in World War II. Donald M. Goldstein & Katherine V. Dillon. LC 91-42730. (Illus.). 352p. 1992. 30.00 (1-55728-242-0) U of Ark Pr.

Willkommen in Washington. rev. ed. Eugenia M. Horstman. (Illus.). 36p. (Orig.). (GER.). 1991. pap. 6.95 (0-936478-15-2) Interpretive Pubns.

***Willkommenin der Familie Gottes.** Kenneth Copeland. 30p. (GER.). 1970. pap. 0.75 (0-88114-801-6) K Copeland Pubns.

Willmaker 6.0 Macintosh. 6th ed. Legisoft, Inc. Staff. 1996. pap. 69.95 incl. mac hd (0-87337-315-4) Nolo Pr.

Willmaker 6.0 Windows. 6th ed. Barbara K. Repa et al. 1996. pap. 69.95 (0-87337-314-6) Nolo Pr.

Willmar Area Fishing Map Guide. James F. Billig. 1995. spiral bd. 12.95 (1-885010-12-5) Sptsmans Connect.

***Willmington's Bible Handbook.** H. L. Willmington. LC 97-17459. 1997. write for info. (0-8423-8174-0) Tyndale.

Willmington's Complete Guide to Bible Knowledge: Introduction to Theology. Harold L. Willmington. 688p. 1993. text ed. 24.99 (0-8423-8166-X, 60-8166-X, Tyndale Christian) Tyndale.

Willmington's Complete Guide to Bible Knowledge: Old Testament Survey. Harold L. Willmington. 560p. 1992. 24.99 (0-8423-8165-1) Tyndale.

Willmington's Complete Guide to Bible Knowledge, Vol. 1: Old Testament People. Harold L. Willmington. 385p. 1990. 24.99 (0-8423-8161-9) Tyndale.

Willmington's Complete Guide to Bible Knowledge, Vol. 3: Life of Christ. 320p. 1991. 24.99 (0-8423-8163-5) Tyndale.

Willmington's Guide to the Bible. Harold L. Willmington. 1302p. 1981. 39.99 (0-8423-8804-4) Tyndale.

Willo Mancifoot (and the Mugga Killa Whomps) Valerie H. Damon. Ed. by Dave Damon. LC 83-50739. (Illus.). (J). (gr. 2-6). 1985. 14.95 (0-932356-07-9) Star Pubns MO.

Willo Mancifoot (and the Mugga Killa Whomps) limited ed. Valerie H. Damon. Ed. by Dave Damon. LC 83-50739. (Illus.). (J). (gr. 2-6). 1985. 100.00 (0-932356-08-7) Star Pubns MO.

Willoughby Lake: Legends & Legacies. Harriet F. Fisher. Ed. by James Hayford. (Illus.). 114p. (Orig.). 1988. pap. 12.50 (0-9610860-3-3) Orleans.

W

An Asterisk (*) at the beginning of an entry indicates that the title is appearing in BIP for the first time.

Willow. Duffy et al. 64p. 1988. 6.95 (*0-87135-367-9*) Marvel Entmnt.

Willow. Linda L. Miller. Ed. by Linda Marrow. 320p. (Orig.). 1991. mass mkt. 5.99 (*0-671-73773-2*) PB.

Willow Alone. (Illus.). 32p. (J). 1995. 17.95 (*0-85236-297-8*, Pub. by Farming Pr UK) Diamond Farm Bk.

Willow Alone. (Illus.). 32p. (J). 1995. pap. 9.95 (*0-85236-304-4*, Pub. by Farming Pr UK) Diamond Farm Bk.

Willow & I: Manuscript Edition. John Patrick. 1943. pap. 13.00 (*0-8222-1258-7*) Dramatists Play.

Willow Bark & Rosehips: An Introduction to Common Edible & Useful Wild Plants of North... Fritz Springmeyer. LC 96-15794. 80p. 1996. pap. 9.95 (*1-56044-412-6*) Falcon Pr MT.

Willow Basketry. Bernard Verdet-Fierz & Regula Verdet-Fierz. Ed. by Deborah Cannarella. (Illus.). 368p. 1993. reprint ed. 21.95 (*0-934026-88-2*) Interweave.

Willow Basketry of the Amana Colonies: History of Folk Art, Six Willow Basket Patterns. Joanna E. Schanz. Ed. by John Zug & Scott Elledge. LC 86-61010. 105p. (Orig.). 1986. pap. 8.95 (*0-941016-36-6*) Penfield.

Willow Chair: How to Build Your Very Own. rev. ed. Joseph S. Stone. (Illus.). 96p. 1993. pap. 19.95 (*0-9631998-0-3*) Gnsis Pubns CA.

***Willow Chase, Kansas Territory, 1847.** LC 96-35021. (American Diaries Ser.). (J). 1997. pap. 3.99 (*0-689-81355-4*, Aladdin Paperbacks) S&S Childrens.

Willow Creek Home. Janice J. Shefelman. (Stories for Young Americans Ser.). (Illus.). 128p. (J). (gr. 5-7). 1985. 12.95 (*0-89015-535-6*) Sunbelt Media.

Willow Creek Seeker Services: Evaluating a New Way of Doing Church. G. A. Pritchard. LC 95-21487. 336p. (Orig.). (C). 1995. pap. 16.99 (*0-8010-5274-2*) Baker Bks.

Willow File. Lori Herter. (Shadows Ser.). 1994. mass mkt. 3.50 (*0-373-27028-3*, 5-27028-5) Silhouette.

Willow Grove. Laurie Sheck. 80p. 1996. 21.00 (*0-679-44714-8*) Knopf.

***Willow Grove.** Laurie Sheck. 1998. pap. 13.00 (*0-679-76603-0*) Knopf.

***Willow Grove: Signed Edition.** Laurie Sheck. 1996. 21.00 (*0-676-51746-3*) Random.

Willow Harvest. large type ed. Rowena Summers. 520p. 1995. 25.99 (*0-7505-0760-8*, Pub. by Magna Print Bks UK) Ulverscroft.

Willow in Autumn: Ryutei Tanehiko, 1783-1842. Andrew L. Markus. (Harvard-Yenching Institute Monographs: No. 35). 290p. (C). 1993. 28.00 (*0-674-95351-7*) HUP.

Willow in the Tempest. Robert Norton. 324p. (Orig.). 1990. pap. 15.00 (*0-918980-13-5*) St Alban Pr.

***Willow King.** Chris Platt. (J). 1998. 15.00 (*0-679-88655-9*); pap. 4.99 (*0-679-88656-7*) Random Bks Yng Read.

Willow, Oak & Rye: Basket Traditions in Pennsylvania. Jeannette Lasansky. LC 79-2709. (Illus.). 1979. pap. 12.50 (*0-271-00229-8*, Keystone Bks) Pa St U Pr.

Willow Pattern: A Judge Dee Mystery. Robert H. Van Gulik. (Illus.). viii, 192p. 1993. pap. 5.95 (*0-226-84875-2*) U Ch Pr.

Willow Pattern China. Veryl M. Worth & Louise M. Loehr. 12.50 (*0-685-56580-7*) H S Worth.

Willow Pattern China: Collectors Guide. rev. ed. Veryl M. Worth & Louise M. Loehr. Ed. & Illus. by Randel Westley. 120p. (Orig.). 1986. pap. 11.95 (*0-685-17353-4*) H S Worth.

Willow Pattern China: Price Guide. 3rd rev. ed. Veryl M. Worth & Louise M. Loehr. 20p. (Orig.). 1986. pap. 3.50 (*0-685-17358-5*) H S Worth.

Willow Pattern China Price Guide. Louise M. Loehr. 4.00 (*0-685-56581-5*) H S Worth.

Willow Pattern Story. Allan Drummond. LC 91-56239. (Illus.). (J). (gr. k-3). Date not set. pap. 5.95 (*1-55858-413-7*) North-South Bks NYC.

Willow Pattern Story. Allan Drummond. LC 91-46239. (Illus.). 32p. (J). (gr. k-3). Date not set. 14.95 (*1-55858-171-5*) North-South Bks NYC.

Willow Run. Glendon F. Swarthout. LC 74-26210. 248p. 1983. reprint ed. 45.00 (*0-404-58478-0*) AMS Pr.

Willow Run: Colossus of American Industry. Warren B. Kidder. (Illus.). 350p. 1995. lib. bdg. 39.95 (*0-9647205-3-1*) KFT MI.

Willow Run: Study of Industrialization & Cultural Inadequacy. Carl L. Julliard & Edson Stermer. Ed. by Leon Stein. LC 77-70486. (Illus.). 1977. reprint ed. lib. bdg. 30.95 (*0-405-10158-9*) Ayer.

Willow Study. Jocasta Innes & Stewart Watton. (Paintability Ser.). (Illus.). 12p. 1995. pap. 12.95 (*1-85410-136-6*, Pub. by Aurum Pr UK) London Brdge.

Willow Tree's Daughter. Pamela Freeman. (Illus.). 112p. (Orig.). (J). (gr. 3-7). 1996. pap. 6.95 (*1-86373-691-3*, Pub. by Allen & Unwin Aust Pty AT) IPG Chicago.

Willow Umbrella. Christine Widman. LC 91-10989. (Illus.). 32p. (J). (gr. k-3). 1993. lib. bdg. 14.95 (*0-02-792760-1*, Mac Bks Young Read) S&S Childrens.

***Willow Umbrella.** Christine Widman. (Illus.). 32p. (J). 4.98 (*0-7651-0038-X*) Smithmark.

Willow Ware: Ceramics in the Chinese Tradition: With Price Guide. Leslie Bockol. LC 94-42662. (Illus.). 160p. (Orig.). 1995. pap. 29.95 (*0-88740-720-X*) Schiffer.

Willow Water. Erika Mumford. 120p. (Orig.). 1988. pap. 7.95 (*0-9619960-1-3*) Every Other Thursday.

***Willow Weep for Me.** Meri Danquah. LC 97-20515. 1998. 21.95 (*0-393-04567-6*) Norton.

Willow Weep For Me. Iyov Ha-Giben. Tr. by Yonatan Kuperberg from YID. LC 91-29893. 200p. 1992. 17.95 (*0-8197-0596-9*) Bloch.

Willow Whip. Irene B. Brown. (Sunflower Editions Ser.). 208p. (Orig.). (J). (gr. 5 up). reprint ed. pap. 8.95 (*0-936085-23-1*) Blue Heron OR.

***Willowby Mansion Mystery.** Kimberly Sullivan. 100p. (Orig.). (YA). (gr. 4-9). 1998. mass mkt. 6.99 (*1-58006-016-1*, Sherlock Pr) Sovereign.

Willowby's World of Fluffits. Christine W. Vrooman. (Willowby's World Ser.). (Illus.). 56p. (Orig.). (J). (gr. 2-6). 1984. pap. 8.95 (*0-910349-02-9*) Cloud Ten.

Willowby's World of Unicorns. Christine W. Vrooman. Ed. by Sandy Kane & Peggy Ogden. (Willowby's World Ser.). (Illus.). 56p. (J). (gr. 2-6). 1982. pap. 8.95 (*0-910349-01-0*) Cloud Ten.

Willowby's World of Unicorns "Activity Book" Greg Gibbs. (Willowby's World Ser.). 14p. (Orig.). (J). (gr. 2-6). 1984. pap. 4.00 (*0-910349-03-7*) Cloud Ten.

Willowdale Handcar. Edward Gorey. LC 62-17515. (Illus.). 64p. 1986. reprint ed. 11.95 (*0-926637-11-8*) P Weed Bks.

Willowhole Cemetery Madison County Texas. Allie M. Whitley & Mary Collie-Cooper. (Illus.). 61p. (Orig.). 1981. spiral bd. 6.50 (*0-943553-00-8*) Collie-Cooper Ent.

Willowisp Book of Jewish Holidays. Karla Dougherty. (Illus.). 32p. (J). (gr. 3 up). 1992. pap. 3.50 (*0-87406-639-5*) Willowisp Pr.

Willowisp Christmas Book. (Illus.). 40p. (Orig.). 1989. pap. 3.99 (*0-87406-408-2*) Willowisp Pr.

Willowisp Christmas Songbook. Margaret Holland. (Illus.). 24p. (J). (gr. k-8). 1987. 3.50 incl. audio (*0-87406-253-5*) Willowisp Pr.

***Willowood: Further Adventures in Buttonhole Stitch Applique.** Jean Wells. Ed. by Elizabeth Aneloski & Michelle Webber. LC 96-48838. (Illus.). 96p. (Orig.). 1997. pap. 10.50 (*1-57120-026-6*, 10149) C & T Pub.

Willows: The Genus Salix. Christopher Newsholme. (Illus.). 224p. 1992. 34.95 (*0-88192-261-7*) Timber.

Willows in Winter. William Horwood. (Illus.). 304p. 1994. 18.95 (*0-312-11354-4*, Thomas Dunne Bks) St Martin.

Willows in Winter. William Horwood. LC 96-20048. 304p. 1996. pap. 10.95 (*0-312-14825-9*) St Martin.

Willowswood Match. Gayle Buck. 224p. 1989. pap. 3.99 (*0-451-16001-0*, Sig) NAL-Dutton.

Willpower: How to Gain It & Maintain It--A Simple Building Block Approach. Sandy S. Anderson & Robert G. Anderson. LC 87-70328. (Illus.). 96p. (Orig.). 1987. pap. 7.95 (*0-9617964-0-5*, 964A) Calif Dream Pubns.

Willpower Is Not Enough: Why We Don't Succeed at Change. A. Dean Byrd & Mark D. Chamberlain. LC 94-23989. x, 181p. (Orig.). 1995. pap. 11.95 (*0-87579-871-3*) Deseret Bk.

Willpower to Go. Laura Terroux. 175p. 1992. pap. 12.95 (*0-9633327-1-6*) Applewood Pr.

Willpower's Not Enough: Understanding & Recovering From Addictions of Every Kind. Arnold M. Washton & Donna Boundy. LC 88-45069. 288p. 1990. reprint ed. pap. 13.00 (*0-06-091969-8*, PL) HarpC.

Wills. Lawrence P. Keller. LC 91-7831. 1992. ring bd. 135.00 (*0-614-07300-6*); disk 75.00 (*0-685-59865-9*) Clark Boardman Callaghan.

Wills. 2nd ed. David A. Chatterton. (Practice Notes Ser.). 90p. 1990. pap. write for info. (*0-85121-697-8*, Pub. by Cavendish UK) Gaunt.

***Wills.** 3rd ed. David A. Chatterton. (Cavendish Practice Notes Ser.). 1996. pap. 32.00 (*1-85941-296-3*, Pub. by Cavendish UK) Gaunt.

Wills: A Do-It-Yourself Guide. Jean Dimeo & Theresa M. Rudy. (Orig.). 1992. pap. write for info. (*0-910073-16-3*) HALT DC.

Wills: Adaptable to Courses Utilizing Mechem & Atkinson's Casebook on Wills & Administration. Casenotes Publishing Co., Inc. Staff. Ed. by Norman S. Goldenberg et al. (Legal Briefs Ser.). 1980. pap. write for info. (*0-87457-144-8*, 1220) Casenotes Pub.

Wills: Structure, Design & Settlement under New York State Law. Jean Hegler & Leo C. Loughrey. 220p. 1997. ring bd. 24.95 (*0-930137-60-4*) Looseleaf Law.

Wills: To Have or Have Not. John J. DeMarines. 1990. 9.95 (*0-533-08542-X*) Vantage.

Wills: Why You Should Have One & the Lawyer's Role in its Preparation. 1988. pap. write for info. (*0-318-66096-2*, 543-0039-01) Amer Bar Assn.

Wills - Trusts: Adaptable to Courses Utilizing Waggoner, Wellman, Alexander & Fellows's Casebook on Family Property Law (Trusts) Ed. by Norman S. Goldenberg et al. (Legal Briefs Ser.). 1991. pap. write for info. (*0-87457-141-3*, 1231) Casenotes Pub.

Wills & Administration. 5th ed. Floyd R. Mechem. 1961. text ed. 29.00 (*0-88277-392-5*) Foundation Pr.

Wills & Administrations of Accomack County, Virginia, 1663-1800. Ed. by Stratton Nottingham. 563p. 1991. reprint ed. pap. 32.50 (*1-55613-405-3*) Heritage Bk.

Wills & Administrations of Elizabeth City County, Virginia 1688-1800: With Other Genealogical & Historical Items. Blanche Adams-Chapman. 198p. 1995. reprint ed. pap. 20.00 (*0-614-10040-2*, 953) Clearfield Co.

***Wills & Administrations of Isle of Wight County, Virginia, 1647-1800.** Blanche A. Chapman. 370p. 1996. reprint ed. pap. 32.00 (*0-614-23489-1*, 955) Clearfield Co.

***Wills & Administrations of Surry County, Virginia 1671-1750.** Eliza T. Davis. 184p. 1996. reprint ed. pap. 20.00 (*0-614-23571-5*, 1380) Clearfield Co.

Wills & Estate Planning for Oregon. 4th ed. Rees Johnson. (Oregon Legal Ser.). (Illus.). 192p. 1990. pap. 6.95 (*0-88908-829-2*) Self-Counsel Pr.

***Wills & Estate Planning Handbook for Oregon.** 5th ed. Rees C. Johnson. 192p. 1995. pap. 6.95 (*1-55180-054-3*) Self-Counsel Pr.

Wills & Estate Records of McMinn Co. Tennessee, 1820-1870. Reba B. Boyer. 202p. 1983. reprint ed. pap. 25.00 (*0-89308-328-3*) Southern Hist Pr.

Wills & Estates. John Cook. 80p. pap. 7.50 (*0-685-23171-2*, 41,575W) NCLS Inc.

***Wills & Estates Law.** Lawchek, Ltd. Staff. (Lawchek Personal Legal Sourcebooks Ser.). 160p. 1996. pap. 24.95 incl. disk (*0-02-861403-8*) Macmillan.

Wills & Intestacy in Australia & New Zealand. 2nd ed. H. A. Ford et al. xlvi, 561p. 1989. 94.00 (*0-455-20896-4*, Pub. by Law Bk Co AT); pap. 69.00 (*0-455-20897-2*, Pub. by Law Bk Co AT) Gaunt.

Wills & Inventories, from the Register of the Commissary of Bury St. Edmund's & the Archdeacon of Sudbury. Bury St. Edmund's Commissary Court Staff. Ed. by Samuel Tymms. (Camden Society, London. Publications, First Ser.: No. 49). reprint ed. 72.50 (*0-404-50149-4*) AMS Pr.

Wills & Succession. 3rd ed. (Sum & Substance Ser.). 1989. 15.95 (*0-940366-41-X*) Sum & Substance.

Wills & Trusts. Larry Burkett. (Burkett Financial Booklets Ser.). 1992. pap. text ed. 4.99 (*0-8024-2610-7*) Moody.

Wills & Trusts. Elizabeth Moody et al. (Smith's Review Ser.). 180p. 1993. pap. text ed. 15.95 (*1-56542-181-7*) E Pub Corp.

Wills & Trusts. 5th ed. Jesse Dukeminier. 1995. 55.00 (*0-316-19522-7*) Little.

Wills & Trusts: Adaptable to Courses Utilizing Dukeminier & Johanson's Casebook on Family Wealth Transactions: Wills, Trusts, Future Interests & Estate Planning. Casenotes Publishing Co., Inc. Staff. Ed. by Norman S. Goldenberg et al. (Legal Briefs Ser.). 1995. pap. write for info. (*0-87457-068-9*, 1223) Casenotes Pub.

Wills & Trusts Attorney's Record. 32p. 1983. 1.85 (*0-685-07394-7*, 95966-8) P-H.

Wills & Trusts in a Nutshell. 2nd ed. Robert L. Mennell. (Nutshell Ser.). 367p. 1994. pap. 16.00 (*0-314-04025-0*) West Pub.

Wills & Wealth in Medieval Genoa, 1150-1250. Steven Epstein. (Historical Studies: No. 103). (Illus.). 288p. 1985. 25.00 (*0-674-95356-8*) HUP.

Wills Before Eighteen Fifty-Eight. (C). 1987. 60.00 (*0-317-89823-X*, Pub. by Birmingham Midland Soc UK) St Mut.

Wills' Biochemical Basis of Medicine. 2nd ed. Hywel J. Thomas. 590p. 1989. pap. text ed. 65.00 (*0-7506-0849-8*) Buttrwrth-Heinemann.

Wills' Biochemical Basis of Medicine. 3rd ed. Brian Gillham et al. LC 96-24866. 1996. write for info. (*0-7506-2013-7*) Buttrwrth-Heinemann.

Wills, Estates & Trusts. Gingrich. (C). 1996. text ed. 39.95 (*0-8273-7978-1*) Delmar.

Wills, Estates & Trusts for Legal Assistants. 2nd ed. Jay Gingrich. LC 95-21323. (Paralegal Ser.). 624p. 1996. text ed. 46.95 (*0-8273-6560-8*) Delmar.

Wills, Executorship & Tax Planning. John Barlow & Lesley King. (C). 1991. text ed. 18.00 (*1-85431-126-3*, Pub. by Blackstone Pr UK) Gaunt.

Wills, Executorship & Tax Planning. David A. Chatterton. (C). 1990. 150.00 (*1-85431-085-2*, Pub. by Blackstone Pr UK) St Mut.

Wills Eye Hospital Atlas of Clinical Ophthalmology. Ed. by William S. Tasman & Edward A. Jaeger. 435p. 1995. text ed. 165.00 (*0-397-51350-X*) Lppncott-Raven.

Wills Eye Manual: Office & Emergency Room Diagnosis & Treatment of Eye Disease. 2nd ed. Wills Eye Hospital Staff. LC 93-39666. 512p. 1993. spiral bd. 49.95 (*0-397-51380-1*) Lppncott-Raven.

***Wills for Alberta: How to Make Your Own Will - Canadian Edition.** 11th ed. Cheryl Gottselig. (Legal Ser.). 136p. 1997. pap. 7.95 (*1-55180-105-1*) Self-Counsel Pr.

Wills for British Columbia: How to Make Your Own Will - Canadian Edition. 17th ed. Steven G. Wong. (Legal Ser.). 112p. 1995. pap. 6.95 (*1-55180-016-0*) Self-Counsel Pr.

Wills for Florida: How to Make Your Own Will. Suzan Herskowitz. (Legal Ser.). 144p. (Orig.). 1992. pap. 9.95 (*0-88908-777-6*) Self-Counsel Pr.

Wills for Ontario: How to Make Your Own Will. 13th ed. David I. Botnick. (Legal Ser.). 112p. 1993. pap. 6.95 (*0-88908-481-5*) Self-Counsel Pr.

Wills for Washington. 5th rev. ed. D. Van Fredenberg. (Legal Ser.). 96p. (C). 1992. pap. 6.95 (*0-88908-752-0*) Self-Counsel Pr.

***Wills for Washington: How to Make Your Own Will.** 6th ed. Fred Hopkins. 96p. 1996. pap. text ed. 6.95 (*1-55180-021-7*) Self-Counsel Pr.

Wills from Doctors' Commons. Ed. by John G. Nichols & John Bruce. (Camden Society, London. Publications, First Ser.: No. 83). reprint ed. 42.50 (*0-404-50183-4*) AMS Pr.

***Wills Guide for Manitoba & Saskatchewan.** 6th ed. Ronald J. Kruzeniski & Martin Hak. (Canadian Edition Ser.). 96p. 1996. pap. 7.95 (*1-55180-083-7*) Self-Counsel Pr.

Wills, Inheritance & the Family. Janet Finch et al. (Oxford Socio-Legal Studies). 208p. 1996. 49.95 (*0-19-825834-8*) OUP.

Wills, Intestacy & Inheritance. Michael Sladen. 250p. 1993. 54.00 (*1-85431-261-8*, Pub. by Blackstone Pr UK) Gaunt.

Will's Mammoth. Rafe Martin. (Illus.). 32p. (J). (ps-3). 1989. 15.95 (*0-399-21627-8*, Putnam) Putnam Pub Group.

***Will's Mammoth.** Rafe Martin. (Illus.). 32p. (J). (ps-1). 1997. pap. 5.95 (*0-698-11578-3*, Paperstar) Putnam Pub Group.

Will's New Cap. Olof Landstrom & Lena Landstrom. Tr. by Richard E. Fisher. 32p. (J). (ps-2). 1992. 13.00 (*91-29-62062-7*, Pub. by R & S Bks) FS&G.

Wills of the Archdeaconry of Sudbury, 1630-35. Ed. by Nesta Evans. (Suffolk Records Society Ser.: No. 29). 574p. 1988. 39.00 (*0-85115-492-1*) Boydell & Brewer.

Wills of the Archdeaconry of Sudbury, 1636-1638. Ed. by Nesta Evans. (Suffolk Records Society Ser.: Vol. 35). 360p. (C). 1993. 35.00 (*0-85115-345-3*, Boydell Pr) Boydell & Brewer.

Wills of the Archdeaconry of Suffolk, 1620-24. Ed. by Marion Allen. (Suffolk Records Society Ser.: No. 31). 1990. 39.00 (*0-85115-530-8*) Boydell & Brewer.

Wills of the Archdeaconry of Suffolk, 1625-6. Ed. by Marion E. Allen. (Suffolk Records Society Ser.: Vol. 37). (Illus.). 298p. (C). 1995. 35.00 (*0-85115-644-4*) Boydell & Brewer.

Wills of the County of Essex, England, 1558-1565, Vol. 1. F. G. Emmison. LC 82-80974. (Illus.). 369p. lib. bdg. 43.75 (*0-915156-51-2*) Natl Genealogical.

Wills of the Rich & Famous. Herbert E. Nass. 1991. pap. 9.95 (*0-446-39218-9*) Warner Bks.

Wills of Westmoreland County, Virginia, 1654-1800. Augusta B. Fothergill. 229p. (Orig.). 1990. reprint ed. 17.50 (*0-685-60497-7*, 1995) Clearfield Co.

Wills of Westmoreland County, Virginia, 1654-1800. Augusta B. Fothergill. 238p. (Orig.). 1982. reprint ed. pap. 25.00 (*0-89308-323-2*) Southern Hist Pr.

Wills, Probate & Administration. Alison Baxter. 200p. (C). 1990. pap. 60.00 (*1-85352-898-6*, Pub. by HLT Pubns UK) St Mut.

Wills, Probate & Administration. George Miles. 200p. 1993. 34.00 (*1-85431-295-2*, Pub. by Blackstone Pr UK) Gaunt.

Wills, Probate & Administration, Vol. 1. George Miles & Paulene Denyer. 352p. 1994. pap. text ed. 34.00 (*1-85431-370-3*, Blckstone AT) Gaunt.

Wills, Probate & Administration. George Miles & Paulene Denyer. (Legal Practice Course Guides Ser.). 384p. 1996. pap. 34.00 (*1-85431-420-3*, Blckstone AT) Gaunt.

Wills, Probate & Administration. Catherine Rendell. (London Guildhall-Cavendish Legal Practice Course Companion Ser.). 360p. 1994. pap. 26.00 (*1-874241-99-6*, Pub. by Cavendish UK) Gaunt.

Wills, Probate & Administration. Linda S. Spedding. 280p. (C). 1990. pap. 70.00 (*1-85352-522-7*, Pub. by HLT Pubns UK) St Mut.

***Wills, Probate & Administration 1996/97.** 4th ed. George Miles & Paulene Denyer. (Legal Practice Course Guides Ser.). 367p. 1996. pap. 36.00 (*1-85431-546-3*, Pub. by Blackstone Pr UK) Gaunt.

Wills, Probate & Administrative Law in New South Wales. 3rd ed. Charles Rowland et al. 1200p. 1996. 169.00 (*0-455-21364-X*, Pub. by Law Bk Co AT); pap. 135.00 (*0-455-21365-8*, Pub. by Law Bk Co AT) Gaunt.

Wills, Probate & the Administration of the Estates of Deceased Persons in Victoria. 2nd ed. L. McCredie. 280p. 1989. 76.00 (*0-409-49474-7*, AT); pap. 60.00 (*0-409-49475-5*, AT) MICHIE.

Wills Roll of Honour & War Service: Roll, 1914-1918. (C). 1987. 40.00 (*0-685-39336-4*, Pub. by Picton UK) St Mut.

Will's Shoot. Will Garfit. (Illus.). 128p. 1994. 34.95 (*0-948253-64-9*, Pub. by Sportmans Pr UK) Trafalgar.

Wills Styles for Scotland. Alan R. Barr. 1994. text ed. write for info. (*0-406-17940-9*, UK) MICHIE.

Wills, Trust & Estate Administration for the Paralegal. 3rd ed. Dennis R. Hower. Ed. by Hannan. 903p. (C). 1990. text ed. 62.00 (*0-314-66789-X*) West Pub.

Wills, Trusts & Estate Administration for the Paralegal. 4th ed. Dennis R. Hower. LC 95-32140. 750p. (C). 1996. text ed. 62.50 (*0-314-06114-2*); pap. text ed. 50.75 (*0-314-06482-6*) West Pub.

Wills, Trusts & Estate Planning - Law & Taxation, Cases & Materials. Joseph M. Dodge. (American Casebook Ser.). 665p. 1988. text ed. 46.00 (*0-314-37038-2*) West Pub.

Wills, Trusts & Estate Planning Handbook, 1994. John H. Williamson. 348p. 1994. pap. 27.95 (*1-880730-07-3*); pap. text ed. 22.00 (*0-685-71513-2*) Argyle Pub.

***Wills, Trusts & Estates.** Brown. 96p. 1997. pap. text ed. 16.95 (*0-8273-8283-9*) Delmar.

Wills, Trusts, & Estates. Butterworth Staff. (Florida Paralegals Ser.). 250p. 1991. ring bd. 60.00 (*0-409-26086-X*) MICHIE.

Wills, Trusts & Estates. Butterworth Staff. (Florida Paralegals Ser.). 250p. 1993. suppl. ed. 50.00 (*0-250-42172-0*) MICHIE.

Wills, Trusts & Estates. William M. McGovern, Jr. (Law Outlines Ser.). 210p. (Orig.). 1995. pap. text ed. write for info. (*0-87457-183-9*, 5220) Casenotes Pub.

Wills, Trusts, & Estates. Reutlinge. 1993. 23.95 (*0-316-74112-4*) Little.

Wills, Trusts & Estates. 3rd ed. Jesse Dukeminier & Stanley M. Johanson. LC 83-82694. 1140p. (C). 1984. 38.95 (*0-316-19514-6*) Little.

Wills, Trusts, & Gifts. 2nd ed. Charles A. DeGrandpre. LC 92-32062. (New Hampshire Practice Ser.: Vol. 7). 1993. suppl. ed. 30.00 (*0-685-70868-3*) MICHIE.

Wills, Trusts, & Gifts. 2nd ed. Charles A. DeGrandpre. LC 92-32062. (New Hampshire Practice Ser.: Vol. 7). 620p. 1994. 70.00 (*1-56257-339-X*) MICHIE.

Wills, Trusts & Life Insurance Settlement Options. John W. Cochrun. LC 94-93976. 80p. (Orig.). 1995. pap. 5.95 (*0-9601050-1-8*) J W Cochrun.

Wills, Trusts & Probate Administration for the Texas Paralegal. Stonewall Van Wie, III. 540p. (C). 1995. pap. text ed. 45.25 (*0-314-04555-4*) West Pub.

Will's Wonder Book see Louisa's Wonder Book: An Unknown Alcott Juvenile

Willy, a Story of Water. J. Spar. LC 68-56819. (Illus.). 32p. (J). (gr. 2-3). 1968. lib. bdg. 9.95 (*0-87783-051-7*) Oddo.

Willy, a Story of Water. deluxe ed. J. Spar. LC 68-56819. (Illus.). 32p. (J). (gr. 2-3). 1968. pap. 3.94 (*0-87783-117-3*) Oddo.

Willy & Alvirah. Mary Higgins Clark. 1994. pap. 24.95 (*0-7871-0189-3*, Dove Bks) Dove Audio.

W

***Willy & Giraffe.** Robert Williams. (Illus.). 186p. (Orig.). 1996. pap. 15.00 (1-57502-376-8, P01188) Morris Pubng.

Willy & Hugh. Anthony Browne. LC 90-4938. (Illus.). 32p. (J). (ps-3). 1991. 13.00 (0-679-81446-9) Knopf Bks Yng Read.

Willy & Hugh. Anthony Browne. 32p. (J). (gr. k-4). 1996. pap. 6.99 (0-679-87654-5) Random.

Willy & May. Judith B. Schachner. LC 94-43785. (Illus.). (J). 1995. pap. 14.99 (0-525-45347-4) Dutton Child Bks.

Willy & the Carboard Boxes. Lizi Boyd. 1999. pap. 3.95 (0-14-054342-2) NAL-Dutton.

Willy Brandt. Tom Viola. (World Leaders - Past & Present Ser.). (Illus.). 112p. (J). (gr. 5 up). 1988. lib. bdg. 19.95 (0-87754-512-X) Chelsea Hse.

***Willy Brandt: A Political Biography.** Barbara Marshall. LC 96-28750. (St. Antony's Ser.). 1997. text ed. 35.00 (0-312-16438-6) St Martin.

Willy Can Count. Anne Rockwell. (Illus.). 32p. (J). (ps). 1989. lib. bdg. 13.95 (1-55970-013-0) Arcade Pub Inc.

Willy Loman see Major Literary Characters

Willy on Wheels. Sherry Howell. (Illus.). 63p. (Orig.). (J). (gr. k-4). 1986. pap. 2.95 (0-931563-05-4) Wishing Rm.

Willy Slater's Lane. Mitch Wieland. LC 96-30606. 176p. 1996. 22.50 (0-87074-408-9); pap. 12.95 (0-87074-409-7) SMU Press.

Willy the Champ. Anthony Browne. (J). 1995. pap. 6.99 (0-679-87391-0) Random.

***Willy the Champion Ant.** Patricia M. Quinlan. (Illus.). 24p. (J). (ps up). 1996. pap. 4.95 (0-88753-240-3, Pub. by Black Moss Pr CN) Firefly Bks Ltd.

***Willy the Dreamer.** Anthony Browne. LC 97-2135. (J). 1997. write for info. (0-7636-0378-3) Candlewick Pr.

Willy the Hit Man. Barry Chambers. 1992. vhs 18.95 (1-880384-09-4) Coldwater Pr.

Willy the Hit Man. Barry Chambers. 94p. (J). (gr. 4-8). 1992. pap. 4.25 (1-880384-01-9) Coldwater Pr.

Willy the Wimp. Anthony Browne. LC 84-14320. (Illus.). 32p. (J). (ps-2). 1989. reprint ed. 5.99 (0-394-82610-8) Knopf Bks Yng Read.

Willy the Wizard. Anthony Browne. 1996. lib. bdg. 16.99 (0-679-97644-2) Knopf.

Willy the Wizard. Anthony Browne. LC 95-137. (J). 1996. 15.00 (0-679-87644-8) Knopf.

Willy Velvet, Homocide Detective. Robert L. Wimberly. 1956. 3.00 (0-87129-525-3, W34) Dramatic Pub.

Willy Whacker: Hiawatha's Hot Wheel. Glen W. Gonder. Ed. by Sharon J. Gonder. (Illus.). 149p. (J). (ps-2). 1996. lib. bdg. 8.00 (0-614-97211-6) Osage Bend Pub.

Willy Whitefeather's Outdoor Survival Handbook for Kids. Willy Whitefeather. LC 89-26929. (Illus.). 104p. (Orig.). (J). (gr. 3 up). 1990. pap. 10.95 (0-943173-47-7, Harbinger CO) R Rinehart.

Willy Whitefeather's River Book for Kids. Willy Whitefeather. LC 93-38686. (Illus.). 128p. (Orig.). (J). (gr. 1-8). 1994. pap. 11.95 (0-943173-94-9, Harbinger CO) R Rinehart.

Willy Wonka & the Chocolate Factory: Easy Piano. Bricusse. (Easy Play Ser.). 32p. 1991. pap. 6.95 (0-7935-0649-2, 00222530) H Leonard.

Willy's Boot. Martha Alexander. LC 92-53007. (Illus.). 14p. (J). (ps). 1993. 4.95 (1-56402-162-9) Candlewick Pr.

Willy's Hats. Josie Stewart & Lynn Salem. 8p. (Orig.). (J). (gr. k-1). 1995. pap. 3.50 (1-880612-32-1) Seedling Pubns.

Willys Maintenance Manual (Jeep) TM-10-1513. Willys-Overland Motors, Inc. Staff. (U. S. Army Technical Manual, Jeep Ser.). (Illus.). 158p. 1989. reprint ed. pap. 20.00 (0-910667-16-0) USM.

Willys-Overland Jeep Master Parts List: TM-10-1186. Willys-Overland Motors, Inc. Staff. (U. S. Army Technical Manual Ser.). (Illus.). 198p. 1989. pap. 20.00 (0-910667-11-X) USM.

***Willy's Silly Grandma.** Cynthia Defelice. LC 96-42287. (Illus.). 32p. (J). (ps-2). 1997. 15.95 (0-531-30012-9); lib. bdg. 16.99 (0-531-33012-5) Orchard Bks Watts.

Wilma Mankiller. Gini Holland. LC 96-2618. (First Biographies Ser.). (Illus.). (J). 1997. lib. bdg. 21.40 (0-8172-4457-3) Raintree Steck-V.

Wilma Mankiller. Caroline Lazo. LC 94-1229. (Peacemakers Ser.). (J). (gr. 4 up). 1994. pap. 7.95 (0-382-24716-7, Dillon Silver Burdett) Silver Burdett Pr.

Wilma Mankiller. Linda Lowery. LC 95-12203. (On My Own Bks.). (Illus.). (J). 1996. lib. bdg. 13.13 (0-87614-880-1, Carolrhoda) Lerner Group.

Wilma Mankiller. Linda Lowery. (J). (gr. k-3). 1996. pap. text ed. 5.95 (0-87614-953-0) Lerner Group.

Wilma Mankiller. Jacki T. Rand. LC 92-12813. (American Indian Stories Ser.). (Illus.). 32p. (J). (gr. 4-5). 1992. pap. 4.95 (0-8114-4097-4); lib. bdg. 21.40 (0-8114-6576-4) Raintree Steck-V.

Wilma Mankiller: Chief of the Cherokee Nation. Bruce Glassman. LC 91-28249. (Library of Famous Women). (Illus.). 64p. (J). (gr. 3-7). 1992. lib. bdg. 15.95 (1-56711-032-0) Blackbirch.

Wilma Mankiller: Leader of the Cherokee Nation. Della A. Yannuzzi. LC 93-44866. (People to Know Ser.). (Illus.). 104p. (YA). (gr. 6 up). 1994. lib. bdg. 18.95 (0-89490-498-1) Enslow Pubs.

Wilma Mankiller, Principal Chief of the Cherokee Nation. Darryl B. Wilson. (Illus.). (J). (gr. 1-4). 1995. pap. 31.80 (0-8136-5943-4); lib. bdg. 63.60 (0-8136-5931-0) Modern Curr.

Wilma Mankiller: Principal Chief of the Cherokees see North American Indians of Achievement

Wilma Rudolph: Champion Athlete. Tom Biracree. (Black American Ser.). (Illus.). 192p. (YA). 1991. mass mkt. 3.95 (0-87067-565-6, Melrose Sq) Holloway.

Wilma Rudolph: Champion Athlete. Victoria Sherrow. LC 94-21204. (Junior Black Americans of Achievement Ser.). (Illus.). 80p. (J). (gr. 3-6). 1995. pap. 4.95 (0-7910-2293-5); lib. bdg. 15.95 (0-7910-2290-0) Chelsea Hse.

Wilma Rudolph: Champion Athlete see American Women of Achievement

Wilma the Elephant. Erwin Moser. Tr. by Joel Agee. LC 86-1145. (J). (gr. 3-8). 1986. 9.95 (0-915361-45-0) Hemed Bks.

Wilma Unlimited: How Wilma Rudolph Became the World's Fastest Woman. Kathleen Krull. LC 95-32105. (Illus.). 40p. (J). (gr. k-5). 1996. 16.00 (0-15-201267-2) HarBrace.

Wilma's Revenge. Monica L. Ross. (J). 1989. Playscript. 5.00 (0-87602-288-3) Anchorage.

Wilmer Atkinson: An Autobiography. Wilmer Atkinson. (American Newspapermen 1790-1933 Ser.). (Illus.). 375p. 1974. reprint ed. 29.95 (0-8464-0032-4) Beekman Pubs.

Wilmer, Cutler & Pickering's Emergency Babysitting Facility. (National Report on Work & Family Ser.: No. 1). 32p. 1988. 35.00 (0-87179-957-X) BNA Plus.

Wilmer Institute Residents Handbook. Rohit Varma. LC 96-17976. (Illus.). 300p. 1997. text ed. 45.00 (0-397-51317-8) Lppncott-Raven.

Wilmington: Cape Fear Adventure. Diane C. Cashman. 1989. 22.95 (0-89781-057-0) Am Historical Pr.

Wilmington: Port of North Carolina. Alan D. Watson. Ed. by William N. Still. (Studies in Maritime History). (Illus.). 220p. 1992. text ed. 29.95 (0-87249-778-X) U of SC Pr.

Wilmington: Treasure on the Atlantic. Carol Deakin. (Illus.). 1996. 35.00 (1-885352-33-6) Community Comm.

***Wilmington Campaign: "The Last Rays of Departing Hope"** Chris Fonvielle, Jr. (Illus.). 500p. 1996. 32.95 (1-882810-09-0) Savas Woodbury.

Wilmington 1876. Hagley Museum Staff. (Illus.). 32p. 1976. pap. 1.00 (0-614-16880-5) Hagley Museum.

Wilms Tumor: Clinical & Molecular Characterization. Max J. Coppes. Ed. by Christine E. Campbell & Bryan Williams. LC 95-14340. (Molecular Biology Intelligence Unit Ser.). 145p. 1995. 69.00 (1-57059-258-6) R G Landes.

Wilms' Tumor (Nephroblastoma) & Related Renal Neoplasms of Childhood. Ed. by Frank Gonzalez-Crussi. 304p. 1983. 171.00 (0-8493-5670-9, RC280, CRC Reprint) Franklin.

Wilner's Radiology of Bone Tumors. 2nd ed. Daniel Wilner. 1997. text ed. write for info. (0-7216-5274-3) Saunders.

Wilsford Site 22-Co-516, Coahoma County Mississippi. John M. Connaway. LC 84-620008. (Mississippi Department of Archives & History Archaeological Reports: No. 14). 222p. (Orig.). 1984. pap. 15.00 (0-938896-40-7) Mississippi Archives.

Wilson: Genealogy of the Family of Nathaniel Wilson of Kittery, Maine, Born 1760, Died 1841. F. A. Wilson. 25p. 1994. reprint ed. pap. 5.50 (0-8328-4118-8) Higginson Bk Co.

Wilson: Genealogy of the Wilson-Thompson Families, Being an Account of Descendants of John Wilson of County Antrim, Ireland, Whose Sons John & William Founded Homes in Bucks County, & of Elizabeth McGraudy Thompson, Who with Her Four Sons Came from Ireland & Settled in Bucks County about 1740. Ed. by W. S. Ely. (Illus.). 383p. 1992. reprint ed. pap. 57.50 (0-8328-2767-3); reprint ed. lib. bdg. 67.50 (0-8328-2766-5) Higginson Bk Co.

Wilson: Metaphorical Objects. Ellen H. Johnson et al. (Illus.). 12p. (Orig.). 1986. pap. 3.00 (0-940665-01-8) Akron Art Mus.

Wilson Administration & the Shipbuilding Crisis of 1917: Steel Ships & Wooden Steamers. William J. Williams. LC 92-4334. 232p. 1992. 89.95 (0-7734-9492-8) E Mellen.

Wilson & Gisvold's Textbook of Organic Medicinal & Pharmaceutical Chemistry. 9th ed. Jaime N. Delgado & William A. Remers. LC 65-10424. (Illus.). 860p. 1991. text ed. 69.50 (0-397-50877-8, Lippnctt) Lppncott-Raven.

Wilson & Jernigan. Bill Shunas. LC 92-91127. 328p. (Orig.). 1994. pap. 13.95 (1-56002-254-X, Univ Edtns) Aegina Pr.

Wilson & Poland: Four Essays Commemorating the Woodrow Wilson Centennial 1856-1956. 45p. 1.00 (0-940962-45-4) Polish Inst Art & Sci.

Wilson & Revolutions: 1913-1921. Lloyd C. Gardner. LC 82-45089. 160p. (Orig.). 1982. reprint ed. pap. text ed. 22.50 (0-8191-2416-8) U Pr of Amer.

Wilson & the Kid. Leon C. Metz. LC 90-34762. (Illus.). 171p. 1990. 21.95 (0-932702-49-X) Creative Texas.

Wilson & the League of Nations: Why America's Rejection? Ed. by Ralph A. Stone. LC 78-8323. (American Problem Studies). 128p. 1978. reprint ed. pap. 10.50 (0-88275-679-6) Krieger.

Wilson & Wilson's Comprehensive Analytical Chemistry: Thermal Analysis, Part B - Biochemical & Clinical Applications of Thermometric & Thermal Analysis, Vol. 12B. Ed. by N. D. Jespersen et al. 254p. 1982. 196.50 (0-444-42062-2) Elsevier.

Wilson & Wilson's Comprehensive Analytical Chemistry, Vol. XXII: Titrimetric Analysis in Organic Solvents. L. Safarik & Z. Stransky. Ed. by Gyula I. Svehla. 532p. 1987. 374.25 (0-444-98984-6) Elsevier.

Wilson "Bob" Tucker Wild Talent: A Working Bibliography. Gordon Benson, Jr. & Phil Stephensen-Payne. (Galactic Central Bibliographies Ser.: No. 8). ix, 29p. (C). 1994. lib. bdg. 25.00 (0-8095-4707-4) Borgo Pr.

***Wilson Chronology of Ideas.** George Ochoa et al. LC 97-17591. 1997. write for info. (0-8242-0935-4) Wilson.

***Wilson Chronology of Science.** George Ochoa & Melinda Corey. LC 97-22060. 1997. write for info. (0-8242-0933-8) Wilson.

***Wilson Chronology of the Arts.** George Ochoa et al. LC 97-23541. 1997. write for info. (0-8242-0934-6) Wilson.

Wilson County, Tennessee, Circuit Court Records, 1810-1855. Thomas E. Partlow. 144p. 1988. pap. 24.50 (0-89308-635-5, TN 109) Southern Hist Pr.

Wilson County, Tennessee, Deed Books C-M, 1793-1829. Thomas E. Partlow. 248p. 1984. 25.00 (0-89308-540-5) Southern Hist Pr.

Wilson County, Tennessee, Deed Books N-Z, 1829-1853. Thomas E. Partlow. 464p. 1984. 35.00 (0-89308-541-3) Southern Hist Pr.

Wilson County, Tennessee, Deeds, Marriages & Wills, 1800-1902. Thomas E. Partlow. 244p. 1987. pap. 32.50 (0-89308-605-3, TN 101) Southern Hist Pr.

Wilson County, Tennessee, Miscellaneous Records, 1800-1875. Thomas E. Partlow. 270p. 1982. 25.00 (0-89308-283-X, TN 60) Southern Hist Pr.

Wilson Creek & the Big Bend Country, 1902-1907: An Index of the Big Bend Chief Newspaper. Stuart McIntyre. (Illus.). 225p. (C). 1991. 25.00 (0-9622654-1-1) Chief Rsch.

Wilson Era: Essays in Honor of Arthur S. Link. Ed. by John M. Cooper, Jr. & Charles E. Neu. 380p. (C). 1991. text ed. write for info. (0-88295-877-1); pap. text ed. write for info. (0-88295-872-0) Harlan Davidson.

Wilson Era: The Years of War & After, 1917-1923. Josephus Daniels. (History - United States Ser.). 654p. 1993. reprint ed. lib. bdg. 109.00 (0-7812-4924-4) Rprt Serv.

Wilson Farm Country Cookbook: Recipes from New England's Favorite Farm Stand. Lynne C. Wilson. LC 84-24408. (Illus.). 256p. 1985. write for info. (0-201-09676-5); pap. 9.95 (0-201-09677-3) Addison-Wesley.

Wilson Governments, 1964-1970. Ed. by R. Coopey et al. LC 92-42167. 288p. 1993. text ed. 59.00 (0-86187-188-X) St Martin.

Wilson Governments, 1964-1970. Ed. by Richard Coopey et al. 226p. 1995. pap. 19.95 (1-85567-343-6, Pub. by Pntr Pubs UK) Bks Intl VA.

Wilson Harris & the Modern Tradition: A New Architecture of the World. Sandra E. Drake. LC 85-9874. (Contributions in Afro-American & African Studies: No. 93). (Illus.). 240p. 1986. text ed. 55.00 (0-313-24783-8, DWI/, Greenwood Pr) Greenwood.

***Wilson Harris/Alan Burns.** Ed. by John O'Brien. (Review of Contemporary Fiction Ser.: Vol. 17, No. 2). 220p. (Orig.). 1997. pap. 8.00 (1-56478-161-5) Dalkey Arch.

Wilson Hurley: A Retrospective Exhibition. Intro. by Peter H. Hassrick. LC 85-45017. (Illus.). 88p. 1985. 25.00 (0-913504-99-8) Lowell Pr.

Wilson on Children & the Law. Jeffery Wilson. 858p. 1994. ring bd. 225.00 (0-409-91476-2) MICHIE.

Wilson Phillips. (Easy Piano Ser.). (Illus.). 80p. 1990. pap. 12.95 (0-7935-0349-3, 00490523) H Leonard.

Wilson Phillips: Shadows & Light. 88p. 1992. otabind 14.95 (0-7935-1720-6, 00308147) H Leonard.

Wilson Popenoe: Agricultural Explorer, Educator, & Friend of Latin America. Frederic Rosengarten, Jr. 182p. 1993. text ed. 23.00 (0-935868-53-4) Allen Pr.

Wilson Popenoe, Explorador Agricola, Educador y Amigo de America Latina. F. Posengarten, Jr. Tr. by P. Crespo de Paz. (Illus.). 302p. (ENG & SPA.). 1995. pap. 30.00 (1-885995-26-1) Escuela Agricola.

Wilson Reading System: Complete Set. Barbara A. Wilson. 1988. 196.00 (1-56778-000-8) Wilson Lang Trning.

Wilson RV: An In-Basket Simulation. B. Reece & G. Manning. (C). 1977. text ed. 13.40 (0-07-051485-2) McGraw.

Wilson Sat Alone. Debra Hess. LC 93-17616. (J). 1994. pap. 14.00 (0-671-87046-7, S&S Bks Young Read) S&S Childrens.

Wilson Sisters: A Biographical Study of Upper Middle-Class Victorian Life. Martha Westwater. LC 83-8173. (Illus.). xii, 250p. 1984. 29.95 (0-8214-0727-9) Ohio U Pr.

Wilsonian Diplomacy. Edward B. Parsons. LC 77-80967. 1978. text ed. 12.95 (0-88273-006-1) Forum Pr IL.

Wilsonian Idealism in America. David Steigerwald. LC 94-11847. 312p. 1994. 37.50 (0-8014-2936-6) Cornell U Pr.

Wilsonian Impulse: U.S. Foreign Policy, the Alliance, & German Unification. Mary N. Hampton. LC 95-45418. 192p. 1996. text ed. 55.00 (0-275-95505-2, Praeger Pubs) Greenwood.

Wilsonian Statecraft: Theory & Practice of Liberal Internationalism During World War One. Lloyd E. Ambrosius. LC 91-4766. (America in the Modern World Ser.). 170p. (C). 1991. 35.00 (0-8420-2393-3) Scholarly Res Inc.

Wilsons, a House-Painting Team. Alice K. Flanagan. (Our Neighborhood Ser.). (Illus.). 32p. (J). 1996. lib. bdg. 18.00 (0-516-20216-2) Childrens.

***Wilsons, a House-Painting Team.** Alice K. Flanagan. (Our Neighborhood Ser.). 32p. (J). 1997. pap. 5.95 (0-516-26063-4) Childrens.

Wilson's American Ornithology with Additions Including the Birds Described by Audubon, Bonaparte, Nutall, & Richardson. Alexander Wilson. LC 78-125767. (American Environmental Studies). 1977. reprint ed. 51.95 (0-405-02693-5) Ayer.

Wilson's & Wilson's Comprehensive Analytical Chemistry: Volume XXI - New Developments in Conductimetric & Oscillometric Analysis. Ed. by Gyula I. Svehla et al. 330p. 1988. 252.00 (0-444-42637-X) Elsevier.

***Wilson's Disease.** Tjaard U. Hoogenraad. (Major Problems in Neurology Ser.: Vol. 30). (Illus.). 219p. 1996. write for info. (0-7020-1842-2, Pub. by W B Saunders UK) Saunders.

Wilson's Disease. Charles A. Owen, Jr. LC 81-16805. (Copper in Biology & Medicine Ser.). 215p. 1982. 28.00 (0-8155-0879-4) Noyes.

Wilson's Foreign Policy in Perspective. Edward Buehrig. 1990. 14.50 (0-8446-0521-2) Peter Smith.

Wilson's Old Testament Word Studies. William Wilson. 582p. 1984. reprint ed. 19.95 (0-917006-27-5) Hendrickson MA.

Wilson's Photographics. Edward L. Wilson. LC 72-9247. (Literature of Photography Ser.). 1973. reprint ed. 25.95 (0-405-04951-X) Ayer.

Wilsons Promontory: Marine & National Park Victoria. Geoff Westcott. (Illus.). 208p. 1995. pap. 24.95 (0-86840-222-2, Pub. by New South Wales Univ Pr AT) Intl Spec Bk.

Wilson's Revenge. Giles Tippette. 192p. 1994. mass mkt. 4.50 (0-515-11214-3) Jove Pubns.

Wilson's Syndrome: The Miracle of Feeling Well. E. Denis Wilson. 346p. 1991. pap. 21.95 (0-9629875-0-6) Cornerstn FL.

Wilson's Topley Principles of Bacteriology, Virology & Immunity, Vol. 2. 7th ed. 576p. 1984. lib. bdg. 98.00 (0-683-09065-8) Williams & Wilkins.

***Wilson's World.** Edith T. Hurd. (Illus.). (J). (gr. k-3). 1971. 15.89 (0-06-022749-4, 474280) HarpC.

Wilt Chamberlain. Ron Frankl. LC 94-5775. (Basketball Legends Ser.). (Illus.). 64p. (J). (gr. 3 up). 1994. lib. bdg. 15.95 (0-7910-2428-8) Chelsea Hse.

Wilt Thou Be Made Whole? David Rosier & Vernette Rosier. 126p. (Orig.). 1996. pap. 8.99 (1-56043-267-5) Destiny Image.

Wilt Thou Go on My Errand? Three 18th Century Journals of Quaker Women Ministers. Ed. by Margaret H. Bacon. LC 94-21187. (Illus.). 406p. 1995. pap. 16.00 (0-87574-921-6) Pendle Hill.

Wilt Thou Go on My Errand? Three 18th Century Journals of Quaker Women Ministers. Ed. by Margaret H. Bacon. (Illus.). 406p. 1995. 26.00 (0-87574-956-9) Pendle Hill.

Wilt Thou Torchy. Sewell Ford. LC 77-122703. (Short Story Index Reprint Ser.). (Illus.). 1977. 20.95 (0-8369-3536-5) Ayer.

Wilton. Chris Rousell. (Towns & Villages of England Ser.). (Illus.). (Orig.). 1993. pap. write for info. (0-7509-0464-X, Pub. by Sutton Pubng UK) Bks Intl VA.

***Wilton Bridal Cakes.** (Illus.). 96p. (Orig.). 1995. pap. 7.99 (0-912696-80-X) Wilton.

***Wilton Cake Decorating.** (Illus.). 34p. (Orig.). (ITA.). Date not set. pap. 1.99 (0-614-23659-2) Wilton.

***Wilton Cake Decorating: Easy As 1, 2, 3.** (Illus.). 34p. (Orig.). 1987. pap. 1.99 (0-614-23658-4) Wilton.

***Wilton Cake Decorating! 1997 Yearbook.** (Illus.). 192p. (Orig.). 1996. pap. 6.99 (0-912696-96-6) Wilton.

***Wilton Mini Treats: From Appetizers to Desserts...Recipes & Ideas for Delicious Personal-Size Treats.** (Illus.). 50p. (Orig.). 1996. pap. 3.99 (0-912696-94-X) Wilton.

***Wilton Register, 1903-4 (Town History & Directory)** Mitchell & Remick. 98p. 1997. reprint ed. pap. 19.00 (0-8328-5927-3) Higginson Bk Co.

***Wilton the Uses of the Most Popular Decorating Tips.** (Illus.). 48p. (Orig.). 1986. pap. 7.99 (0-614-23656-8) Wilton.

Wilton Way of Cake Decorating, Vol. 1. Ed. by Eugene T. Sullivan & Marilynn C. Sullivan. LC 74-13330. 1974. 29.99 (0-912696-04-4) Wilton.

Wilton Way of Cake Decorating, Vol. 2. Ed. by Eugene T. Sullivan & Marilynn C. Sullivan. LC 74-13330. 1977. 29.99 (0-912696-11-7) Wilton.

Wilton Way of Cake Decorating: Vol. 3, Uses of Tubes. Ed. by Marilynn C. Sullivan & Eugene T. Sullivan. LC 74-13330. 1979. 29.99 (0-912696-16-8) Wilton.

***Wilton Weddings: (Pull-Out Supplement - The Wilton Wedding Planning Guide)** 136p. (Orig.). 1996. pap. 14.99 (0-614-23657-6) Wilton.

Wiltonians: A Centennial History of the Wilton Area. Ed. by Michael J. Goc. (Illus.). 152p. (Orig.). 1990. pap. 21.95 (0-938627-09-0) New Past Pr.

Wilton's Music Hall. Jacqueline S. Bratton. (Theatre in Focus Ser.). (Illus.). 44p. (Orig.). 1980. pap. text ed. 105.00 incl. sl. (0-85964-061-2) Chadwyck-Healey.

Wiltshire Christmas. John Chandler. (Illus.). 176p. 1991. pap. 15.00 (0-86299-929-4, Pub. by Sutton Pubng UK) Bks Intl VA.

Wiltshire Churches: An Illustrated History. Derek Parker & John Chandler. LC 93-5449. 196p. 1993. pap. 30.00 (0-7509-0152-7, Pub. by Sutton Pubng UK) Bks Intl VA.

Wiltshire Essays. Maurice H. Hewlett. LC 78-99702. (Essay Index Reprint Ser.). 1977. 20.95 (0-8369-1355-8) Ayer.

Wiltshire Farm Buildings, 1500-1900. Pamela M. Slocombe. (Illus.). 80p. 1993. pap. text ed. 10.00 (0-9509099-6-3, Pub. by Sutton Pubng UK) Bks Intl VA.

Wiltshire Farmhouses & Cottages, 1500-1850. Pamela M. Slocombe. (Illus.). 72p. 1993. pap. text ed. 10.00 (0-9509099-5-5, Pub. by Sutton Pubng UK) Bks Intl VA.

Wiltshire Landscape: Scenes from the Countryside 1920-40. 96p. 1987. 30.00 (0-905392-36-1) St Mut.

Wiltshire of One Hundred Years Ago. David Buxton. (Illus.). 128p. 1991. 35.00 (0-7509-0031-8, Pub. by Sutton Pubng UK) Bks Intl VA.

Wiltshire Rambles. Roger Jones. 72p. 1987. 30.00 (0-905392-17-5) St Mut.

Wiltshire Village Cookbook. Ed. by Edna M. Knudsen & Raymond B. Knudsen. (Illus.). 72p. 1992. pap. text ed. 5.00 (0-9618108-2-3) Counselor Assn.

Wiltshire Way. Laurence Main. (C). 1988. pap. 40.00 (0-904110-85-0, Pub. by Thornhill Pr UK) St Mut.

W

An Asterisk (*) at the beginning of an entry indicates that the title is appearing in BIP for the first time.

Wiltshire Woollen Industry in the Sixteenth & Seventeenth Centuries. 2nd rev. ed. G. D. Ramsay. 165p. 1965. reprint ed. 35.00 (0-7146-1355-X, Pub. by F Cass Pubs UK) Intl Spec Bk.
Wiltshire Words, From "Britton's Beauties of Wiltshire," 1825, Compared with "Akermans Glossary," 1842 see English Dialect Society Publications, No. 23: Glossaries XVIII-XXII
Wily Beguiled. LC 75-133769. (Tudor Facsimile Texts. Old English Plays Ser.: No. 115). reprint ed. 49.50 (0-404-53415-5) AMS Pr.
***Wily Modesty: Argentine Women Writers, 1860-1910.** Bonnie Frederick. (Special Studies: Vol. 30). (Illus.). (Orig.). (C). 1997. pap. write for info. (0-87918-086-2) ASU Lat Am St.
Wim Crouwel: Art & Design. (Illus.). 96p. 1992. pap. 29.50 (3-89322-231-6, Pub. by Edition Cantz GW) Dist Art Pubs.
Wim Wenders. Jan Dawson & Wim Wenders. (Illus.). (Orig.). 1977. pap. 8.95 (0-918432-04-9) Baseline Bks.
Wimberley, Texas: Historic Belle of the Blanco. Dorothy W. Kerbow. LC 94-1042. 1994. 19.95 (0-89015-964-5) Sunbelt Media.
Wimbledon. Nancy Gilbert. (Great Moments in Sports Ser.). 32p. (J). (gr. 4). 1990. lib. bdg. 14.95 (0-88682-319-6) Creative Ed.
Wimmin Times One Plus Two Equals: Past, Present, Future, & Future Perfect - Birthrite, Liferite, Deathrite, & Rebirthrite. Maria Epes. LC 92-96855. 144p. 1992. pap. 18.95 (0-9634350-0-0) Poythress Pr.
Wimp. Kathy Caple. LC 94-7121. (J). 1994. 14.95 (0-395-63115-7) HM.
Wimp Buster: For a Strong & Drug Free America. Vida C. Baron. 149p. 1990. pap. 9.95 (0-9624701-1-2) Barez Pub.
Wimp of the World. Alison Herzig & Jane L. Mali. 130p. (J). (gr. 2-6). 1994. pap. 13.99 (0-670-85208-2) Viking Child Bks.
***Wimp of the World.** Alison Herzig. Date not set. pap. 3.99 (0-14-036652-0) Penguin.
Wimpole Hall. National Trust Staff. (Illus.). 96p. 1991. pap. 11.95 (0-7078-0139-7, Pub. by Natl Trust UK) Trafalgar.
Win! H. J. Ariston. LC 83-80422. 80p. (Orig.). 1983. pap. 5.95 (0-935344-02-0) Jupiter Bks.
Win: Lotto & Daily Numbers Playing Techniques. Steve Player. LC 88-81912. (LOMAP Ser.: Vol. 7). (Illus.). 108p. 1988. pap. 9.95 (0-936181-17-6) Intergalactic NJ.
Win - Lose - Draw: Three Related Short Plays. Mary Gallagher & Ara Watson. 1983. pap. 5.25 (0-8222-1262-5) Dramatists Play.
Win & Win Again! Techniques for Playing Consistently Great Golf. Curtis Strange. (Illus.). 256p. 1991. reprint ed. pap. 17.95 (0-8092-4000-9) Contemp Bks.
Win at Any Cost: The Sell Out of College Athletics. Francis X. Dealy. 1990. 18.95 (1-55972-052-2, Birch Ln Pr) Carol Pub Group.
Win at Backgammon. Millard Hopper. LC 72-86224. Orig. Title: Backgammon. (Illus.). 111p. 1972. reprint ed. pap. 2.95 (0-486-22894-0) Dover.
Win at Bridge in Thirty Days. David Bird. 128p. 1990. pap. 9.95 (0-571-14241-9) Faber & Faber.
Win at Cards with ESP: Develop Your ESP & Win at Cards. Donald Fair. LC 88-70978. (Illus.). 176p. (Orig.). 1989. 14.95 (0-945060-14-9); pap. 10.95 (0-945060-15-7) Bounty Pub.
Win at Checkers. Millard Hopper. xi, 109p. 1956. pap. 3.95 (0-486-20363-8) Dover.
Win at Chess. Fred Reinfeld. 1945. pap. 3.95 (0-486-20438-3) Dover.
Win at Chess: A Comprehensive Guide to Winning Chess for the Intermediate Player. Ronald H. Curry. Ed. by Robert B. Long. (Illus.). 270p. (Orig.). 1995. pap. 18.95 (0-938650-64-5) Thinkers Pr.
Win at Jai-Alai. Constantine Medici. 64p. 1995. pap. 5.95 (0-9646951-0-3) CCM Prods.
Win at Poker. Jeff Rubens. 218p. 1984. reprint ed. pap. 5.95 (0-486-24626-4) Dover.
Win at the Casino. Dennis R. Harrison. 1984. mass mkt. 5.99 (0-345-31207-4) Ballantine.
***Win at the Casino.** Dennis R. Harrison. 1996. pap. 9.00 (0-345-41062-9) Ballantine.
Win at the Casino: Play the Odds, Play It Smart. rev. ed. Dennis R. Harrison. 224p. 1996. pap. 12.95 (0-8119-0837-2) LIFETIME.
Win at Video Poker. Bob Crovo. (Illus.). 105p. (Orig.). 1994. pap. 12.95 (0-9644003-0-8) B Crovo.
Win at Video Poker: The Guide to Beating the Poker Machines. Roger Fleming. LC 94-45524. (Illus.). 192p. 1995. pap. 9.95 (0-8065-1605-4, Citadel Pr) Carol Pub Group.
Win at Work & at Home. Gunther Gross. 1991. pap. 19.95 (0-13-960436-7) P-H.
Win Big Think Small. Ted Allrich. Date not set. pap. 22.95 (0-525-93975-X) Viking Penguin.
Win G Bible: For Games & Multimedia Programmers. Ori Gurewich & Nathan Gurewich. LC 95-69362. 800p. 1995. 39.99 (0-7821-1727-9) Sybex.
Win Knowlton: New Sculpture. Ed. by Rochelle Barth. (Illus.). 24p. 1990. pap. 15.00 (0-924008-07-5) Blum Helman.
Win Lose & Drew. Litton. 1987. pap. 7.95 (0-914807-06-4) Denver Pub Co.
***Win, Lose & Drew: Greatest Hits.** Drew Litton. 1997. pap. text ed. 9.00 (0-914807-15-3) Denver Pub Co.
Win, Lose or Die. Diane Hoh. (Nightmare Hall Ser.: No. 18). 176p. (YA). (gr. 7-9). 1994. pap. 3.50 (0-590-48649-7) Scholastic Inc.
***Win, Lose or Die.** Cynthia Manson. (A Dead Letter Mystery Ser.). 1997. mass mkt. 5.99 (0-312-96092-1) St Martin.
Win, Lose or Die: Stories from Ellery Queen's Mystery Magazine & Alfred Hitchcock Mystery Magazine. Ed. by Cynthia Manson & Constance Scarborough. 272p. 1996. 23.00 (0-7867-0317-2) Carroll & Graf.
Win, Lose, or Draw: Domestic Politics & the Crucible of War. Allan C. Stam, 3rd. LC 96-10152. (C). 1996. 44. 50 (0-472-10682-1) U of Mich Pr.
Win Millions Playing the Lottery: How to Form a Lottery Club & Win Your Share of Millions. Michael P. Burke. (Illus.). 92p. 1993. pap. 9.95 (0-9637329-1-9) Kennesaw Mount.
Win New Clients. Home Office Staff. 1995. 24.95 (0-679-44338-X) Fodors Travel.
Win New Clients & Grow. Home. 224p. 1996. pap. 20.00 (0-679-76088-1) Random.
***Win NT Internet E-Mail Administrator's Bible.** Lawrence E. Hughes. 1997. pap. 49.99 (0-7645-3096-8) IDG Bks.
Win on Writing: Practice in Con. Laurie G. Kirszner. 1995. pap. text ed. 28.00 (0-312-14224-2) St Martin.
Win One for Sandra. Francine Pascal. (Team Sweet Valley Ser.: No. 2). 144p. (J). (gr. 3-7). 1996. pap. 3.50 (0-553-57026-9, Sweet Valley) BDD Bks Young Read.
Win or Loss. large type ed. Kay Thorpe. (Magna Large Print Ser.). 1994. 25.99 (0-7505-0666-0, Pub. by Magna Print Bks UK) Ulverscroft.
Win, Place or Die. Carolyn Keene. (Nancy Drew Files Ser.: No. 46). 160p. (J). (gr. 6 up). pap. 3.99 (0-671-67498-6, Archway) PB.
Win Some, Lose Some: G. Mennen Williams & the New Democrats. Helen W. Berthelot. LC 94-21329. (Illus.). 334p. (Orig.). 1995. 34.95 (0-8143-2345-6, Great Lks Bks); pap. text ed. 19.95 (0-8143-2476-2, Great Lks Bks) Wayne St U Pr.
Win Some, Lose Some: My Forty Years in Corporate America. John V. Titsworth. LC 91-76795. (Illus.). 220p. 1992. 14.95 (0-9620413-3-5) Info Econ Pr.
Win the Battle Against Back Pain: An Integrated Mind-Body Approach. Michael S. Sinel et al. 352p. 1996. pap. 13.95 (0-440-50705-7, Dell Trade Pbks) Dell.
Win the Battle for Your Mind. Richard L. Strauss. 132p. 1986. reprint ed. pap. 7.99 (0-87213-835-6) Loizeaux.
Win the Job Search Battle: A Tactical Guide for the Executive Job Hunter. 3rd ed. LC 95-92236. 320p. 1995. pap. 16.95 (0-9623305-2-3) Somar Pr.
***Win the Prize: Game Plan for Life.** Mark S. Markuly & Michael Oslance. 12.99 (0-570-09888-2) Concordia.
Win the Value Revolution. Robert Tucker. 256p. 1995. 21. 99 (1-56414-174-8) Career Pr Inc.
Win the War on Drugs Without Firing a Shot. Matthew M. Quinones. 112p. (YA). 1995. pap. 12.95 (1-56167-214-9) Am Literary Pr.
Win the Whining War & Other Skirmishes: A Family Peace Plan. Cynthia Whitham. LC 91-61008. (Illus.). 224p. (Orig.). 1991. pap. 13.95 (0-9622036-3-7) Prspctive Pub.
Win Them Now! Kenneth D. Barney. LC 90-86362. (Radiant Life Ser.). 128p. 1991. pap. 4.50 (0-88243-882-4, 02-0882); teacher ed., pap. 6.95 (0-88243-203-6, 32-0203) Gospel Pub.
***Win 32 Systems Programming for Unix Developers.** Johnson M. Hart. LC 97-23535. 1997. 38.68 (0-201-63465-1) Addison-Wesley.
Win Trots & Flats. E. L. Digirolamo. 2.00 (0-931138-00-0) Maiden Bks.
Win-Win. 5.00 (0-614-05198-3, WW12792M) ASFE.
***Win Win: Student Book.** Ed. by James A. Burke, II. (Illus.). 65p. (Orig.). (YA). (gr. 9-12). Date not set. pap. text ed. 4.59 (1-878227-39-4) Peace Educ.
Win-Win Administration. Stephen K. Blumberg. 1983. pap. text ed. 12.95 (0-913878-26-X) T Horton & Dghts.
Win-Win Day. Carol Cummings. (Learn with Me Ser.). (Illus.). 24p. (Orig.). (J). (ps-3). 1991. pap. 4.99 (0-9614574-6-5) Teaching WA.
Win-Win, Inc. The First Family of Sports. John L. Krause. LC 94-65598. (Illus.). 32p. (Orig.). 1994. pap. 4.95 (1-57087-035-7) Prof Pr NC.
Win-Win Negotiating: A Professional's Playbook. Russ Tirella & Gary D. Bates. LC 92-46659. 112p. 1993. 20. 00 (0-87262-884-1) Am Soc Civil Eng.
Win-Win Negotiating: Turning Conflict into Agreement. Fred E. Jandt. (Sound Business Cassette Bks.). 300p. 1987. pap. text ed. 19.95 (0-471-85877-3) Wiley.
Win-Win Negotiations for Couples. Charlotte Whitney. Ed. by Camilla Ayers & Emily McKeigue. LC 85-72095. (Illus.). 208p. 1986. pap. 12.95 (0-914918-66-4, Whitford Pr) Schiffer.
Win-Win Negotiator. Ross R. Reck. 1989. pap. 10.00 (0-671-67698-9) PB.
Win-Win Partnerships: Be on the Leading Edge with Synergistic Coaching. Steven J. Stowell & Matt M. Starcevich. (Illus.). 230p. 1997. 24.95 (0-9652729-0-7) Ctr Mgmt Org.
Win-Win Relationships: 9 Strategies for Settling Personal Conflicts Without Waging War. H. Newton Malony. LC 94-34802. 192p. 1995. 15.99 (0-8054-1095-3, 4210-95) Broadman.
***Win Win Teacher's Guide.** Ed. by James A. Burke, II & Alice F. Moffat. (Illus.). 46p. (Orig.). Date not set. pap. text ed. 49.95 (1-878227-20-3) Peace Educ.
Win Win Win. R. E. McMaster, Jr. 1989. pap. 2.25 (0-9605316-6-1) Reaper Pub.
Win with Numerology. Myrtle K. Bradley. LC 82-70776. (Illus.). 96p. (Orig.). 1982. pap. 5.95 (0-87516-482-X) DeVorss.
Win with the Djin. Eric Schiller. 86p. (Orig.). 1994. pap. 7.95 (0-945470-40-1) Chess Ent.
Win Your Child Custody War: Child Custody Help Sourcebook. rev. ed. C. Hardwick. 1994. per., spiral bd. 79.95 (0-9640227-0-2) Pale Horse Pubng.
Win Your Personal Tax Revolt. Bill Greene. (Illus.). 444p. 1981. 24.95 (0-936602-10-4) J C Print.
***WinAmos 3.6.** Arbuckle. 1996. 465.00 incl. disk (1-56321-196-3) L Erlbaum Assocs.
Winans: All Out. Ed. by Jeannette DeLisa. 64p. (Orig.). (YA). 1994. pap. text ed. 14.95 (0-89898-784-9, P1044SMX) Warner Brothers.
***Winans: Heart & Soul.** Ed. by Jeannette DeLisa. 88p. (Orig.). (YA). 1996. pap. text ed. 18.95 (1-57623-435-5, PF9614) Warner Brothers.
Winawer! A Mainline French Variation. Jon Edwards & Ron Henley. (ChessBase University Power Play! Ser.). (Illus.). 64p. (Orig.). pap. 10.95 (1-883358-10-8) R&D Pub NJ.
***Winawer Gambit: (D10)** Jerzy Konikowski. Ed. by S. L. Edritrice. (Illus.). 1996. pap. 16.50 (88-86127-56-1) Thinkers Pr.
Winborne Trilogy: A Cross-Generation Curriculum Containing Call My Name...Take My Hand, Linking Links, & the Linker, Set. Wingborne Diaconal Productions Staff. 1993. 25.00 (0-9629755-4-0) Wingborne-Diaconal.
Winch & Cable Systems. Ivar Samset. LC 85-15239. (Forestry Sciences Ser.). 1985. lib. bdg. 178.50 (90-247-3205-0) Kluwer Ac.
Winchcombe Sacramentary: Orleans, Bibliotheque Municipale, 127 (105) Ed. by Anselme Davril. (Henry Bradshaw Society Ser.: No. 109). (Illus.). 461p. (C). 1995. 45.00 (1-870252-07-1, Henry Bradshaw Soc) Boydell & Brewer.
Winchell. Neal Gabler. 1995. pap. 16.00 (0-679-76439-9) Random.
Winchell: Gossip, Power, & the Culture of Celebrity. Neal Gabler. LC 93-44259. 1994. 30.00 (0-679-41751-6) Knopf.
***Winchendon, MA.** G. Wheeler. (Images of America Ser.). 1997. pap. 16.99 (0-7524-0552-7, Arcdia) Chalford.
Winchester. Colin Badcock & Ernest Frank. (C). 1987. text ed. 50.00 (0-907115-51-9, Pub. by Pevensey UK) St Mut.
Winchester: America Legend. Date not set. pap. write for info. (0-87637-066-0, House of Collect) Ballantine.
Winchester: An American Legend. R. L. Wilson. 1991. 65. 00 (0-394-58536-4) Random.
Winchester Affadavit. large type ed. Boyer. Date not set. 20.00 (0-7862-0762-0, Thorndike Lrg Prnt) Thorndike Pr.
***Winchester Affidavit.** G. G. Boyer. 1997. 17.95 (0-614-27914-3, Five Star) Mac Lib Ref.
Winchester Affidavit. large type ed. G. G. Boyer. LC 96-53880. 338p. Date not set. 17.95 (0-7862-0739-6, Thorndike Lrg Prnt) Thorndike Pr.
Winchester Anthology: A Facsimile of British Library Additional Manuscript 60577. Intro. by Edward Wilson. 518p. (C). 1970. 240.00 (0-85991-083-0) Boydell & Brewer.
Winchester Bible. Claire Donovan. (Illus.). 64p. 1993. pap. 24.95 (0-8020-6991-6) U of Toronto Pr.
Winchester Book. 3rd ed. George Madis. LC 79-8991. (Illus.). 1979. 49.50 (0-910156-03-4) Art & Ref.
Winchester Company 1924. Doug Althoff. (Illus.). 112p. 1995. text ed. write for info. (1-886094-05-5) Chicago Spectrum.
Winchester Dates of Manufacture. George Madis. 1984. 6.00 (0-910156-05-0) Art & Ref.
Winchester Eighteen Ninety-Four Carbine: A Ninety Year History of the Variations of the Winchester Carbine from 1894-1984. Gary Twesten. (Illus.). xiv, 75p. 1984. 25.00 (0-9602428-3-X) G Twesten.
Winchester Encyclopedia, 1849-1965, Vol. 2. Bill West. LC 64-66442. (Winchester for over a Century Ser.). (Illus.). 1966. 52.00 (0-911614-02-8) B West.
***Winchester Engraving.** R. L. Wilson. 1975. 115.00 (1-877704-29-6) Pioneer Pr.
Winchester Era. George Madis. (Illus.). 1985. 19.95 (0-910156-08-5) Art & Ref.
Winchester-Frederick County Historical Society Journal, No. I. 69p. 1986. pap. write for info. (0-318-64335-9) Winchester-Frederick Cty Hist Soc.
Winchester-Frederick County Historical Society Journal, No. II. 176p. 1987. pap. write for info. (0-318-64336-7) Winchester-Frederick Cty Hist Soc.
Winchester-Frederick County Historical Society Journal, No. III. 1988. pap. write for info. (0-318-64337-5) Winchester-Frederick Cty Hist Soc.
Winchester Handbook. George Madis. (Illus.). 320p. (YA). 1981. 24.95 (0-910156-04-2) Art & Ref.
Winchester Handbook Vol. 1: All Early Winchester Arms, 1849-1919, All Varieties, 2 vols. LC 81-50260. (West Arms Library - Classic Bks.). (Illus.). 1981. 52.00 (0-911614-15-X) B West.
Winchester Handbook Vol. 2: All Winchester Arms, 1920-1982, All Varieties, 2 vols. LC 81-50260. (West Arms Library - Classic Bks.). (Illus.). 1981. 52.00 (0-911614-16-8) B West.
Winchester Highly Finished Arms Catalog c.1912. (Illus.). 24p. 1995. pap. 15.00 (1-884849-16-4) R&R Bks.
Winchester in the Civil War. Roger U. Delauter, Jr. (Virginia Civil War Battles & Leaders Ser.). (Illus.). 174p. 1992. 19.95 (1-56190-033-8) H E Howard.
Winchester Lever Action Repeating Rifles Vol. 2: The Models of 1886 & 1892. Arthur Pirkle. (For Collectors Only Ser.). (Illus.). 125p. (Orig.). 1996. pap. 19.95 (1-882391-13-6) N Cape Pubns.
Winchester Lever Action Repeating Rifles Vol. I: The Models of 1866, 1873, & 1876. Arthur Pirkle. (For Collectors Only Ser.). (Illus.). 202p. 1995. pap. 19.95 (1-882391-05-5) N Cape Pubns.
Winchester, MA. Frank Sleeper. 1995. pap. 16.99 (0-7524-0215-3, Arcdia) Chalford.
Winchester Model 12. George Madis. (Illus.). 1982. 24.95 (0-910156-06-9) Art & Ref.
Winchester Model 1892 Carbine. Gary Twesten. 1985. pap. 10.00 (0-9602428-4-8) G Twesten.
Winchester Model 42. Ned Schwing. LC 89-63406. (Illus.). 160p. 1990. 34.95 (0-87341-134-X, WG01) Krause Pubns.
***Winchester Model 52: Perfection in Design.** Herbert G. Houze. (Illus.). 192p. 1997. 34.95 (0-87341-487-X, WIN) Krause Pubns.
Winchester Model 94. Robert C. Renneberg. LC 90-63918. (Illus.). 208p. 1991. 34.95 (0-87341-161-7, WN01) Krause Pubns.
Winchester Notes. Fanny W. Hotchkiss. 367p. 1912. 200.00 (0-317-63279-5) Elliots Bks.
Winchester Notes. F. Winchester. (Illus.). 375p. 1989. reprint ed. pap. 56.00 (0-8328-1281-1); reprint ed. lib. bdg. 64.00 (0-8328-1280-3) Higginson Bk Co.
Winchester Reader. Donald McQuade & Robert Atwan. LC 89-63916. 1000p. (Orig.). (C). 1991. pap. text ed. 23.50 (0-312-04880-7, Bedford Bks) St Martin.
***Winchester Run, Vol. 1.** Compton. 1997. pap. write for info. (0-312-96320-3) St Martin.
Winchester Shotguns & Shotshells. Ronald W. Stadt. LC 94-74171. (Illus.). 288p. 1995. 34.95 (0-87341-339-3, WSS01) Krause Pubns.
Winchester Shotshell Catalog 1897: New Haven, Conn. (Illus.). pap. 1.50 (0-686-20761-0) Sand Pond.
Winchester Single-Shot: A History & Analysis. John Campbell. LC 94-73342. (Illus.). 272p. 1996. 55.00 (0-917218-68-X) A Mowbray.
Winchester Single Shot, the Model 1885, 1879-1920, Vol. 3. Bill West. LC 64-66442. (Winchester for over a Century Ser.). (Illus.). 1965. 52.00 (0-911614-03-6) B West.
Winchester Slide Action Rifles, Vol. I: Model 1890 & Model 1906. Ned Schwing. LC 92-71450. (Winchester Firearms Ser.). (Illus.). 352p. 1992. 39.95 (0-87341-209-5, WS01) Krause Pubns.
Winchester Slide Action Rifles, Vol. II: Model 61 & Model 62. Ned Schwing. LC 92-71450. (Illus.). 256p. 1993. 34. 95 (0-87341-234-6, WM01) Krause Pubns.
Winchester Troper, from MSS. of the Xth & XIth Centuries, with Other Documents Illustrating the Tropes in England & France. Ed. by Walter H. Frere. LC 70-178507. reprint ed. 59.50 (0-404-56530-1) AMS Pr.
Winchester, Virginia & Its Beginnings. Katherine G. Greene. 441p. 1993. reprint ed. lib. bdg. 47.50 (0-8328-2944-7) Higginson Bk Co.
Winchester, Virginia, Register of Deaths, 1871-1891. Dola S. Tylor. vi, 204p. (Orig.). 1991. pap. 25.00 (1-55613-390-1) Heritage Bk.
Winchester 94 - America's Rifle. rev. ed. Sam Fadala. 1993. 35.00 (1-879356-29-5) Wolfe Pub Co.
Winchesters. James L. Collier. 176p. (J). (gr. 4). 1989. mass mkt. 2.95 (0-380-70808-6, Flare) Avon.
Winchesters, Cartridges, & History, 1850-1969, Vol. 4. Bill West. LC 64-66442. (Winchester for over a Century Ser.). (Illus.). 1969. 52.00 (0-911614-04-4) B West.
Winchester's Finest: The Model 21. Ned Schwing. LC 90-62406. (Illus.). 360p. 1991. 49.95 (0-87341-157-9, WT01) Krause Pubns.
Winckelmann & the Notion of Aesthetic Education. Jeffrey Morrison. LC 95-46832. (Modern Languages & Literature Monographs). 288p. (C). 1996. 90.00 (0-19-815912-9, Clarendon Pr) OUP.
Wincomm Pro: The Visual Learning Guide. Grace J. Beatty. 1995. pap. text ed. 19.95 (0-7615-0090-1) Prima Pub.
Wind. Bacon. (J). 1989. pap. 19.95 (0-590-72703-6) Scholastic Inc.
Wind. Patricia Barone. 1987. pap. 7.95 (0-89823-085-3) New Rivers Pr.
Wind. Jason Cooper. LC 92-8811. (Science Secrets Ser.). (J). 1992. 12.67 (0-86593-171-2); 9.50 (0-685-59297-9) Rourke Corp.
Wind. Kay Davies & Wendy Oldfield. LC 95-6008. (See for Yourself Ser.). (Illus.). (J). 1995. lib. bdg. 19.97 (0-8172-4041-1) Raintree Steck-V.
Wind. Monique Felix. LC 91-277. (Illus.). 32p. (J). (ps-1). 1995. 7.95 (0-15-200940-X) HarBrace.
Wind. Monique Felix. (J). (ps up). 1993. 7.95 (1-56846-073-2) Creative Ed.
Wind. Jean Holkner. LC 92-21450. (Voyages Ser.). (Illus.). (J). 1993. 3.75 (0-383-03668-2) SRA McGraw.
Wind. Joy A. Palmer. LC 92-38439. (What About...? Ser.). (Illus.). 32p. (J). (gr. 2-3). 1992. lib. bdg. 21.40 (0-8114-3415-X) Raintree Steck-V.
Wind. Dorothy Scarborough. 1993. reprint ed. lib. bdg. 75. 00 (0-7812-5949-5) Rprt Serv.
Wind. Claude Simon. Tr. by Richard Howard from FRE. LC 59-8028. 254p. 1986. reprint ed. 14.95 (0-8076-1157-3); reprint ed. pap. 8.95 (0-8076-1155-7) Braziller.
Wind: What Can It Do? Janet McDonnell. LC 89-24011. (Discovery World Ser.). (Illus.). 32p. (J). (ps-2). 1990. lib. bdg. 21.36 (0-89565-555-1) Childs World.
Wind - Driven Reed & Other Poems. Fouzi El-Asmar. LC 78-13850. 1979. 12.00 (0-89410-034-3, Three Contnts) Lynne Rienner.
Wind Across Kylarmi. Layle Giusto. 416p. 1993. pap. 5.95 (0-963851-2-7) Iami Bks.
Wind Across Texas. Donna Stephens. 400p. (Orig.). 1993. mass mkt. 4.50 (0-380-77273-6) Avon.
Wind After Time. Chris Bunch. 1996. mass mkt. 5.99 (0-345-38735-X, Del Rey) Ballantine.
Wind Against the Mountain: The Crisis of Politics & Culture in Thirteenth-Century China. Richard L. Davis. LC 96-25667. (Harvard-Yenching Institute Monographs: No. 42). 335p. 1996. 40.00 (0-674-95357-6) HUP.
Wind among the Reeds. William Butler Yeats. LC 93-46499. (Decadents, Symbolists, Anti-Decadents Ser.). 1994. 43.00 (1-85477-162-0, Pub. by Woodstock Bks UK) Cassell.

W

Wind among the Reeds: Manuscript Materials. William Butler Yeats. Ed. by Carolyn Holdsworth. (Cornell Yeats Ser.). (Illus.). 256p. 1993. 45.00 (*0-8014-2819-X*) Cornell U Pr.

Wind & Birds & Human Voices & Other Stories. Ellen Wilbur. LC 84-50185. 113p. 1984. 15.00 (*0-913773-11-5*) S Wright.

Wind & Fire: Spreading the Message of Jesus. John Drane. LC 95-22280. (Bible World Ser.). (J). 1995. 9.99 (*0-7852-7905-9*) Nelson.

Wind & Lies. Richard Parrish. Date not set. pap. 22.95 (*0-525-93871-0*) NAL-Dutton.

Wind & Lies. Richard Parrish. 1997. pap. 5.99 (*0-451-40539-0*, Onyx) NAL-Dutton.

Wind & Rain. Claire Llewellyn & Anthony Lewis. LC 94-39686. (Why Do We Have? Ser.). (Illus.). (J). 1995. pap. 4.95 (*0-8120-9279-1*) Barron.

Wind & Rain. Claire Llewellyn. LC 94-39686. (Why Do We Have? Ser.). (Illus.). (J). 1995. 9.95 (*0-8120-6508-5*) Barron.

Wind & Sand: The Story of the Wright Brothers at Kitty Hawk. 2nd ed. Lynanne Wescott & Paula Degen. (Illus.). 56p. 1996. pap. 8.95 (*0-915992-97-3*) Eastern Acorn.

Wind & Seismic Effects, 2 vols., Set. 1994. lib. bdg. 636.75 (*0-8490-6439-2*) Gordon Pr.

Wind & Stone: A Novel. Masaaki Tachihara. Tr. by Stephen W. Kohl from JPN. LC 92-12031. (Rock Spring Collection). (Illus.). 160p. (Orig.). 1992. pap. 10.95 (*0-9628137-7-X*) Stone Bridge Pr.

Wind & the Built Environment: U. S. Needs in Wind Engineering & Hazard Mitigation. Panel on the Assessment of Wind Engineering Issues in the United States Staff et al. 144p. (Orig.). (C). 1993. pap. text ed. 35.00 (*0-309-04449-9*) Natl Acad Pr.

***Wind & the Moon.** MacDonald. 1996. pap. 15.95 (*0-8050-4127-3*) St Martin.

Wind & the Rain. Ed. by Joan Hollander & Harold Bloom. LC 72-8285. (Granger Index Reprint Ser.). 1977. reprint ed. 20.95 (*0-8369-6388-1*) Ayer.

Wind & the Sukkah. Aydel Lebovics. (Illus.). 32p. (J). 1982. reprint ed. 10.00 (*0-8266-0361-0*, Merkos LInyonei Chinuch) Kehot Pubn Soc.

Wind & the Sun. Aesop. 1995. 4.98 (*0-8317-5363-3*) Smithmark.

Wind & the Sun. Tomie De Paola. LC 94-20301. (Illus.). 24p. (J). 1995. pap. 3.95 (*0-382-24657-8*, Silver Pr NJ) Silver Burdett Pr.

Wind & the Waves: Four Modern Korean Poets. Tr. & Intro. by Sung-Il Lee. LC 88-83534. (Illus.). 197p. 1989. reprint ed. pap. 56.20 (*0-608-01776-0*, 2062434) Bks Demand.

Wind & The Wizard, 2 vols., Vol. 1. Richard Roberts. (Illus.). 256p. 1990. pap. 15.95 (*0-942380-07-X*) Vernal Equinox.

Wind & the Wizard, Vol. 2. Richard Roberts. (Illus.). 177p. 1990. pap. 15.95 (*0-942380-09-6*) Vernal Equinox.

Wind & Trees. Ed. by M. P. Coutts & J. Grace. (Illus.). 528p. (C). 1995. text ed. 99.95 (*0-521-46037-9*) Cambridge U Pr.

***Wind & Water.** Audra T. Hendrickson. (Illus.). xvi, 39p. (Orig.). 1996. pap. 9.95 (*1-890068-00-4*) Windflower Press.

Wind & Weather. Gakken Co. Ltd. Editors. Tr. by Time-Life Books Editors. (Child's First Library of Learning). (Illus.). 90p. (J). (gr. k-3). 1989. lib. bdg. 21.27 (*0-8094-4830-0*) Time-Life.

Wind & Weather. Gakken Co. Ltd. Editors. Tr. by Time-Life Books Editors. (Child's First Library of Learning). (Illus.). 88p. (J). (gr. 1-4). 1989. 14.95 (*0-8094-4829-7*) Time-Life.

Wind & Weather: Climates, Clouds, Snow, Tornadoes & How Weather Is Predicted. Scholastic, Inc. Staff. (Voyages of Discovery Ser.). (Illus.). 48p. (YA). (gr. 3 up). 1995. 19.95 (*0-590-47646-7*, Scholastic Voy Discov) Scholastic Inc.

Wind As Messenger. Jack Nims. LC 88-71117. 163p. (Orig.). 1989. pap. 8.00 (*0-916383-71-7*) Aegina Pr.

Wind at Midnight. Georgia W. Pangborn. 1989. lib. bdg. 25.00 (*0-910489-19-X*) Scream Pr.

Wind at My Back: Memoirs of an Irish Immigrant. John McLean. Ed. by Dorothy B. McLean. LC 95-94525. 215p. (Orig.). 1995. pap. 15.00 (*0-9646923-0-9*) Malcolm Pubns.

Wind at Winter's End. Deborah Lewis. (Orig.). 1979. mass mkt. 1.95 (*0-89083-540-3*, Zebra Kensgtn) Kensgtn Pub Corp.

Wind at Work: An Activity Guide to Windmills. Gretchen Woelfle. LC 96-24560. (Illus.). 144p. (J). (gr. 3-8). 1997. pap. 14.95 (*1-55652-308-4*) Chicago Review.

Wind Band, Its Literature & Technique. Richard F. Goldman. LC 73-16627. (Illus.). 286p. 1974. reprint ed. text ed. 35.00 (*0-8371-7200-4*, GOWB, Greenwood Pr) Greenwood.

Wind Bands & Brass Bands in Schools & Music Centres. Kevin Thompson. (Resources of Music Ser.). (Illus.). 128p. 1985. text ed. 30.95 (*0-521-25892-8*); pap. text ed. 19.95 (*0-521-27750-7*) Cambridge U Pr.

Wind Before It Blows. Cynthia D. Devore. LC 93-7723. (Children of Courage Ser.). (Illus.). (J). 1993. lib. bdg. 14.98 (*1-56239-247-6*) Abdo & Dghtrs.

Wind Beneath My Wings: And More Great Popular Hits. Ed. by Carol Cuellar. 96p. (Orig.). (YA). 1996. pap. text ed. 12.95 (*1-57623-259-X*, PF0637A) Warner Brothers.

***Wind Beneath My Wings & 50 Adult Contemporary Classics.** rev. ed. Ed. by Sy Feldman. 240p. (YA). 1997. pap. 18.95 (*0-7692-0047-8*) Warner Brothers.

Wind Beneath My Wings Plus More Top of the Charts: Alto Sax. Ed. by Jeannette Delisa. 24p. (Orig.). 1994. pap. 8.95 (*0-89724-188-6*, IF0428) Warner Brothers.

Wind Between the Houses. Maurice Hill. 1969. pap. 10.00 (*0-8222-1260-9*) Dramatists Play.

Wind Between the Worlds. Robert Ford. LC 87-16519. (Illus.). 352p. 1987. reprint ed. 19.95 (*0-9617066-9-4*); reprint ed. pap. 12.95 (*0-9617066-8-6*) Snow Lion-SLG Bks.

Wind Beyond the Wall. 2nd ed. Joan McBreen. 64p. (Orig.). (C). 1990. pap. 8.95 (*0-934257-33-7*) Story Line.

Wind Birds: Shorebirds of North America. Kevin J. Zimmer. LC 93-48005. (Curious Naturalist Ser.). (Illus.). 168p. 1994. reprint ed. pap. 12.95 (*1-881527-37-9*) Chapters Pub.

Wind Blew. Pat Hutchins. LC 92-44903. (Illus.). 32p. (J). (ps-1). 1993. reprint ed. pap. 5.99 (*0-689-71744-X*, Aladdin Paperbacks) S&S Childrens.

Wind Blew West. Edwin Lanham. 1993. reprint ed. lib. bdg. 75.00 (*0-7812-5968-1*) Rprt Serv.

***Wind Blown Sediments in the Quaternary Record.** Ed. by Edward Derbyshire. (Quaternary Proceedings Ser.). 104p. 1995. pap. text ed. 57.00 (*0-471-95860-3*, ES00) Wiley.

Wind Blows Backward. Mary D. Hahn. LC 92-12245. 272p. (YA). (gr. 9 up). 1993. 13.95 (*0-395-62975-6*, Clarion Bks) HM.

Wind Blows Backwards. Mary D. Hahn. 256p. (YA). 1994. mass mkt. 4.50 (*0-380-77530-1*, Flare) Avon.

Wind Blows Backwards. large type ed. Mary D. Hahn. LC 93-31870. (Teen Scene Ser.). (YA). (gr. 9-12). 1993. pap. 15.95 (*0-7862-0064-2*) Thorndike Pr.

Wind Blows Cold. Kathleen Young. 138p. (C). 1989. text ed. 60.00 (*1-872795-57-9*, Pub. by Pentland Pr UK) St Mut.

Wind Blows Over. Walter J. De La Mare. LC 71-113655. (Short Story Index Reprint Ser.). 1977. 23.95 (*0-8369-3384-2*) Ayer.

Wind Boy. Ethel C. Eliot. LC 96-67921. (Illus.). 240p. (J). (gr. 2-6). 1996. reprint ed. 24.00 (*0-614-28617-4*); reprint ed. pap. 14.00 (*0-9615961-4-7*) Raven Rocks Pr.

Wind Burial: Selected Poems of Hwang Tong-gyu. Hwang Tong-gyu. Tr. by Grace E. Gibson from KOR. 75p. (Orig.). 1990. pap. 9.95 (*0-932662-88-9*) St Andrews NC.

Wind Caller's Children. Amanda Cockrell. (Deer Dancers Ser.: No. 2). 1996. mass mkt. 5.99 (*0-380-77649-9*) Avon.

Wind Cannot Read. large type ed. Richard Mason. 1976. 25.99 (*0-85456-435-7*) Ulverscroft.

Wind Chamber Music: Winds with Piano & Woodwind Quintets: An Annotated Guide. Barbera Secrist-Schmedes. LC 95-49844. 200p. 1996. 27.50 (*0-8108-3111-2*) Scarecrow.

Wind Child. Harness. 1995. 4.98 (*0-8317-5667-5*) Smithmark.

Wind Child. Shirley R. Murphy. LC 94-13861. (J). 1995. 15.00 (*0-06-024903-X*); lib. bdg. 14.89 (*0-06-024904-8*) HarpC.

Wind Chill Factor. Thomas Gifford. 464p. 1992. mass mkt. 6.50 (*0-553-29752-X*) Bantam.

***Wind Chime Tales.** Larry Incollingo. 1997. pap. 10.50 (*0-9619795-7-7*) Reunion Bks.

Wind Chimes. Sallie Chesham. 1983. 7.95 (*0-86544-021-2*) Salv Army Suppl South.

Wind Chimes: The Story of a Family. Jayne R. Murdock. LC 93-33526. (Illus.). 256p. (Orig.). 1993. pap. 14.95 (*0-932916-17-1*) May-Murdock.

Wind Climate in Cities: Proceedings of the NATO Advanced Study Institute, Waldbronn, Germany, July 5-16, 1993. Ed. by Jack E. Cermak. (NATO Advanced Science Institutes: Series E). 800p. (C). 1994. lib. bdg. 348.50 (*0-7923-3202-4*) Kluwer Ac.

Wind Commentary to the Uniform Building Code, 1994 Edition. SEAW Lateral Forces Committee Wind Group Staff. (Illus.). 267p. (C). 1995. 35.00 (*1-886982-01-5*) SEAW.

Wind Cried: An American Discovery of the World of Flamenco. Paul Hecht. (Bold Strummer Flamenco Ser.). (Illus.). 186p. 1993. reprint ed. 23.95 (*0-933224-73-7*) Bold Strummer Ltd.

Wind Crystal. Diana L. Paxson. 1990. pap. 3.95 (*0-8125-0040-7*) Tor Bks.

Wind Dancer. Iris Johansen. 400p. 1991. pap. 5.99 (*0-553-28855-5*) Bantam.

Wind-Diesel Systems: A Guide to the Technology & Its Implementation. Ed. by Ray Hunter & George Elliot. (Illus.). 272p. (C). 1994. text ed. 64.95 (*0-521-43440-8*) Cambridge U Pr.

Wind Eagle: Big Book. Joyce McGreevy. (Wonders! Ser.: Level 2). (Illus.). 16p. (Orig.). (J). (gr. 2-4). 1992. pap. text ed. 29.95 (*1-56334-178-6*) Hampton-Brown.

Wind Eagle: Small Book. Joyce McGreevy. (Wonders! Ser.: Level 2). (Illus.). 16p. (Orig.). (J). (gr. 2-4). 1992. pap. text ed. 6.00 (*1-56334-179-4*) Hampton-Brown.

Wind Eagle & Other Abenaki Folk Stories. Joseph Bruchac. (Bowman Bks.). (Illus.). 48p. (Orig.). 1985. pap. 5.95 (*0-912678-64-X*, Greenfld Rev Pr) Greenfld Rev Lit.

Wind Effects on Buildings & Structures: Proceedings of the International Conference, 4th, Heathrow, London, 1975. 4th ed. International Conference on Wind Effects on Buildings & Structures. Ed. by Keith J. Eaton. LC 75-2730. 859p. reprint ed. pap. 180.00 (*0-685-17868-4*, 2029217) Bks Demand.

Wind Effects on Buildings & Structures: Proceedings of the International Research Seminar, Ottawa, Canada, 11-15, September, 1967, 2 vols., 1. International Research Seminar on Wind Effects on Buildings & Structures Staff. LC 76-358270. reprint ed. pap. 160.00 (*0-317-10749-6*, 2019449) Bks Demand.

Wind Effects on Buildings & Structures: Proceedings of the International Research Seminar, Ottawa, Canada, 11-15, September, 1967, 2 vols., 2. International Research Seminar on Wind Effects on Buildings & Structures Staff. LC 76-358270. reprint ed. pap. 117.30 (*0-317-10750-X*) Bks Demand.

Wind Effects on Compliant Offshore Structures. Ed. by Charles E. Smith & Emil Simiu. (Sessions Proceedings Ser.). 73p. 1986. 17.00 (*0-87262-555-9*) Am Soc Civil Eng.

Wind Effects on Structures: Fundamentals & Design Applications. 3rd ed. Emil Simiu & Robert H. Scanlan. LC 96-5238. 688p. 1996. text ed. 89.95 (*0-471-12157-6*) Wiley.

Wind Energy. Ed. by Susan M. Hock. LC 82-82946. 213p. 1993. pap. 45.00 (*0-7918-0950-1*, H00782) ASME.

Wind Energy. Graham Rickard. (Alternative Energy Ser.). (Illus.). 32p. (J). (gr. 4-6). 1991. lib. bdg. 18.60 (*0-8368-0711-1*) Gareth Stevens Inc.

***Wind Energy, 2 vols.** F. J. Van Hulle et al. xlvi, 1142p. 1991. 362.00 (*0-444-89117-X*) Elsevier.

***Wind Energy.** J. F. Walker & N. Jenkins. LC 96-40504. (UNESCO Energy Engineering Ser.). 1997. write for info. (*0-471-96044-6*) Wiley.

Wind Energy: Potential of Wind Energy in the European Community. Ed. by H. Selzer. 1986. lib. bdg. 78.00 (*90-277-2205-6*) Kluwer Ac.

Wind Energy No. 1: Proceedings of the First Contractors' Meeting, Brussels, Belgium, 1986. E. Van Der Voort & G. Grassi. 268p. 1988. text ed. 150.00 (*3-7186-0470-1*) Gordon & Breach.

Wind Energy No. 2: Proceedings of the Second Contractor's Meeting, Brussels, November 23-24, 1987. B. Rasmussen & G. Caratti. 420p. 1988. text ed. 180.00 (*3-7186-4843-1*) Gordon & Breach.

Wind Energy see Energy Week '96: Conference Proceedings

Wind Energy Abstracts, 1986. Ed. by Farrell S. Seiler. 96p. 1986. 195.00 (*0-88016-071-3*) WindBks.

Wind Energy Abstracts, 1994, Pt. I. Ed. by Farrell S. Seiler. 196p. 1995. pap. 195.00 (*0-88016-070-5*) WindBks.

Wind Energy Comes of Age. Paul Gipe. LC 94-36564. 536p. 1995. text ed. 64.95 (*0-471-10924-X*) Wiley.

Wind Energy Conversion, 1983: Proceedings of the Fifth BWEA Wind Energy Conference. Ed. by Peter J. Musgrove. LC 83-20878. 384p. 1984. 89.95 (*0-521-26250-X*) Cambridge U Pr.

Wind Energy for Developing Countries. LC 88-50452. 110p. (Orig.). 1988. pap. 95.00 (*0-88016-073-X*) WindBks.

Wind Energy for Water Pumping. U. K. Srivastava & G. Sharan. 84p. (C). 1987. 11.00 (*81-204-0251-0*, Pub. by Oxford IBH II) S Asia.

Wind Energy in America: A History. Robert W. Righter. LC 95-24686. (Illus.). 384p. 1996. 34.95 (*0-8061-2812-7*) U of Okla Pr.

***Wind Energy Information Sources Vol. 9: A Guide to Print & Electronic Information about Windpower & Windmills.** F. S. Seiler. (Illus.). 96p. (Orig.). 1997. pap. 39.95 (*0-88016-097-7*) WindBks.

Wind Energy Nineteen Seventy-Five to Nineteen Eighty-Five: A Bibliography. P. R. Farmer. 190p. 1986. 95.00 (*0-387-16103-1*) Spr-Verlag.

Wind Energy Resource Atlas of the United States. 2nd ed. D. L. Elliot et al. (Illus.). 327p. 1992. pap. 60.00 (*0-88016-069-1*) WindBks.

Wind Energy Resource Survey for India. Anna Mani. (C). 1990. text ed. 34.00 (*81-7023-297-X*, Pub. by Allied II) S Asia.

Wind Energy Systems: Export Market Potential. S. K. Griffith et al. LC 83-51687. 308p. (Orig.). 1984. pap. 125.00 (*0-88016-011-X*) WindBks.

Wind Energy Technical Information Guide. (Alternative Energy Ser.). 1991. lib. bdg. 250.00 (*0-8490-4376-X*) Gordon Pr.

Wind Energy Technical Information Guide. F. S. Seiler. 100p. 1997. pap. 39.95 (*0-88016-067-5*) WindBks.

Wind Energy 1987: Wind Turbine Shipments & Applications. Thomas F. Jaras. 314p. 1988. 300.00 (*0-944038-00-X*) T F Jaras.

Wind Energy, 1988: Wind Turbine Markets, Shipments & Applications. Thomas F. Jaras. 121p. 1989. pap. text ed. 300.00 (*0-944038-01-8*) T F Jaras.

Wind Energy 1994, Vol. 15. Ed. by Walter Musial et al. 288p. 1994. pap. 52.50 (*0-7918-1187-5*) ASME.

Wind Energy, 1995: Proceedings: The Energy & Environmental EXPO '95 - the Energy-Sources Technology Conference & Exhibition (1995: Houston, TX) Ed. by Walter D. Musial et al. LC 82-82946. (SED Ser.: Vol. 16). 291p. 1995. pap. 105.00 (*0-7918-1294-4*, H00926) ASME.

Wind Engineering. Ed. by N. J. Cook. 342p. 1993. 115.00 (*0-7277-1972-6*, 1972-6) Am Soc Civil Eng.

Wind Engineering: A Handbook for Structural Engineering. Henry Liu. 224p. 1990. text ed. 46.20 (*0-13-960279-8*) P-H.

Wind Engineering: Proceedings of the 5th International Conference, Colorado State University, July 8-14, 1979, 2 vols. Ed. by J. E. Cermak. LC 80-40753. (Illus.). 1400p. 1980. Set. 639.00 (*0-08-024745-8*, Pub. by Pergamon Repr UK) Franklin.

Wind Engineering: Retrospect & Prospect, Vol. 2. International Association Wind Engineering Staff. 1994. write for info. (*81-224-0715-3*, Pub. by Wiley Estrn II) Franklin.

Wind Engineering: Retrospect & Prospect, Vol. 3. International Association Wind Engineering Staff. 1994. write for info. (*81-224-0716-1*, Pub. by Wiley Estrn II) Franklin.

Wind Engineering: Retrospect & Prospect, Vol. 4. International Association Wind Engineering Staff. 1994. write for info. (*81-224-0717-X*, Pub. by Wiley Estrn II) Franklin.

Wind Engineering Vol. 1: Retrospect & Prospect. International Association Wind Engineering Staff. 1994. write for info. (*81-224-0714-5*, Pub. by Wiley Estrn II) Franklin.

***Wind Ensemble: And Its Repertoire.** Ed. by Frank J. Cipolla & Donald Hunsberger. 324p. (C). Date not set. pap. text ed. 29.95 (*1-57623-983-7*, DHBK01) Warner Brothers.

Wind Ensemble & Its Repertoire: Essays on the 40th Anniversary of the Eastman Wind Ensemble. Ed. by Frank J. Cipolla & Donald R. Hunsberger. LC 94-29156. (Illus.). 320p. (C). 1995. 39.50 (*1-878822-46-2*) Univ Rochester Pr.

Wind Ensemble Sourcebook & Biographical Guide. Marshall L. Stoneham et al. LC 96-22021. (Music Reference Collection: No. 55). 416p. 1997. text ed. 89.50 (*0-313-29858-0*, Greenwood Pr) Greenwood.

Wind Erosion in Niger: Implications & Control Measures in a Millet-Based Farming System. Ed. by B. Buerkert et al. 280p. (ENG & FRE.). (C). 1996. lib. bdg. 91.00 (*0-7923-3885-5*) Kluwer Ac.

Wind-Excited Vibrations of Structures. H. Sockel. (CISM International Centre for Mechanical Sciences Ser.: No. 335). 363p. 1994. 87.95 (*0-387-82516-9*) Spr-Verlag.

***Wind Eyes: A Women's Reader & Writing Source.** Ed. by Susan Bright & Margo LaGattuta. (New Voices Ser.). Date not set. 16.95 (*0-911051-90-2*) Plain View.

Wind Five-Folded. Ed. by Jane Reichhold & Werner Reichhold. 230p. 1994. 12.00 (*0-944676-21-9*) AHA Bks.

Wind from a Burning Woman. Greg Bear. LC 82-16395. (Illus.). 270p. 1983. 13.95 (*0-87054-094-7*) Arkham.

Wind from a Foreign Sky. Katya Reimann. (Tielmaran Chronicles Ser.: Bk. 1). 384p. 1996. 23.95 (*0-312-86007-2*) Tor Bks.

***Wind from a Foreign Sky.** Katya Reimann. (Tielmaran Chronicles Ser.). 1997. mass mkt. 6.99 (*0-8125-4933-3*) Tor Bks.

Wind from an Enemy Sky. D'Arcy McNickle. LC 87-17575. 268p. 1988. reprint ed. pap. 12.95 (*0-8263-1100-8*) U of NM Pr.

Wind from Hastings. Morgan Llywelyn. 1995. reprint ed. lib. bdg. 19.95 (*1-56849-613-3*) Buccaneer Bks.

Wind from Nowhere. Oscar Micheaux. LC 72-4810. (Black Heritage Library Collection). 1977. reprint ed. 35.95 (*0-8369-9109-5*) Ayer.

Wind from the Carolinas. Robert Wilder. 567p. 1995. reprint ed. pap. 13.95 (*1-877838-09-8*) Bluewater Bks.

Wind from the Carolinas. Robert Wilder. 574p. 1991. reprint ed. lib. bdg. 39.95 (*0-89966-881-X*) Buccaneer Bks.

***Wind from the Midwest: A Hillbilly Journalist Out of Bounds.** Jim Sawyer. Ed. by Reta J. Stewart. 1997. pap. 14.95 (*0-9638648-2-3*) Barnabs Pub.

***Wind from the Sea.** John Bierhorst. (J). Date not set. write for info. (*0-688-15585-5*, Morrow Junior) Morrow.

***Wind from the Sea.** John Bierhorst. (J). Date not set. lib. bdg. write for info. (*0-688-15586-3*, Morrow Junior) Morrow.

Wind from the Sea. large type ed. Cynthia S. Roberts. (Romance Suspense Ser.). 1991. 25.99 (*0-7089-2351-8*) Ulverscroft.

Wind from the Stars: Through the Year with George MacDonald. Gordon Reid. 380p. 1992. text ed. 16.95 (*0-00-599320-2*, Pub. by T & T Clark UK) Bks Intl VA.

Wind from the Sun: Stories of the Space Age. Arthur C. Clarke. 176p. 1973. pap. 1.95 (*0-451-11475-2*, AJ1475, Sig) NAL-Dutton.

Wind Garden. Angela McAllister. LC 93-37435. (Illus.). 32p. (J). (gr. k up). 1995. 15.00 (*0-688-13280-4*) Lothrop.

Wind-Generated Electricity. George Burmeister & Eric Sikkema. (State Legislative Reports: Vol. 18, No. 7). 7p. 1993. 5.00 (*1-55516-099-9*, 7302-1807) Natl Conf State Legis.

Wind Gourd of La'amaomao. Tr. by Esther T. Mookini & Sarah Nakoa from HAW. LC 89-64411. 144p. (Orig.). 1990. pap. text ed. 7.95 (*0-9623102-0-4*) Kalamaku Pr.

Wind Harp & Other Angel Tales. Ethel Pochocki. (Illus.). 136p. 1995. pap. 7.95 (*0-86716-255-4*) St Anthony Mess Pr.

***Wind-Honed Islands Rise: Selected Poems.** Reuben Tam. LC 96-45132. (Illus.). 102p. 1997. pap. 12.95 (*1-56279-109-5*) Mercury Hse Inc.

***Wind-Honed Islands Rise: Selected Poems of Reuben Tam.** Reuben Tam. LC 96-45132. 1997. pap. text ed. 12.95 (*0-8248-1932-2*) UH Pr.

Wind in Africa. Pascal J. Imperato. LC 73-24001. (Illus.). 363p. 1975. 10.60 (*0-87527-139-1*) Green.

Wind in Both Ears. 2nd ed. Angus MacLean. 1987. pap. 6.00 (*0-933840-30-6*, Skinner Hse Bks) Unitarian Univ.

Wind in My Fist. Arden Tice. (Illus.). 39p. (Orig.). 1990. pap. 5.95 (*0-9624431-2-3*) Dumont Pr.

Wind in the Ash Tree. Jeanine McMullen. (Illus.). 1989. pap. 8.95 (*0-393-30627-5*) Norton.

***Wind in the Ashes.** William W. Johnstone. 1998. mass mkt. 5.99 (*0-7860-0478-9*, Pinncle Kensgtn) Kensgtn Pub Corp.

***Wind in the Cane.** Kathryn Pippin. 280p. (Orig.). 1998. pap. write for info. (*0-9654213-1-7*) Circle Pr DE.

Wind in the Door. Madeleine L'Engle. 224p. (J). (gr. 5-9). 1974. pap. 4.99 (*0-440-48761-7*, YB BDD) BDD Bks Young Read.

Wind in the Door. Madeleine L'Engle. 224p. (YA). (gr. 5-9). 1976. mass mkt. 4.50 (*0-440-98761-X*, LLL BDD) BDD Bks Young Read.

An Asterisk (*) at the beginning of an entry indicates that the title is appearing in BIP for the first time.

Wind in the Door. Madeleine L'Engle. LC 73-75176. 224p. (J). (gr. 7 up). 1973. 17.00 (*0-374-38443-6*) FS&G.

Wind in the Door. large type ed. Madeleine L'Engle. 270p. (J). 1993. reprint ed. lib. bdg. 15.95 (*1-56054-615-8*) Thorndike Pr.

Wind in the Forest. Inglis Fletcher. 1976. 28.95 (*0-89244-011-2*, Queens House) Amereon Ltd.

Wind in the Pines: Classic Writings of the Way of Tea As a Buddhist Path. Tr. by Dennis Hirota from JPN. LC 95-14057. (Illus.). 352p. (C). 1995. text ed. 60.00 (*0-87573-073-6*) Jain Pub Co.

Wind in the Rock. Ann Zwinger. LC 85-28962. 258p. 1986. reprint ed. pap. 14.95 (*0-8165-0985-9*) U of Ariz Pr.

Wind in the Rose-bush: And Other Stories of the Supernatural. Mary E. Wilkins Freeman. (Illus.). 255p. 1986. reprint ed. pap. 7.00 (*0-89733-232-6*) Academy Chi Pubs.

Wind in the Rose Bush & Other Stories of the Supernatural. Mary E. Wilkins Freeman. 1972. reprint ed. lib. bdg. 29.00 (*0-8422-8053-7*) Irvington.

Wind in the Wheat. Reed Arvin. LC 94-9961. 1994. 12.99 (*0-7852-8146-0*) Nelson.

Wind in the Wheat. Reed Arvin. 1996. mass mkt. 5.99 (*0-7852-7360-3*) Nelson.

Wind in the Willow Coloring Book. Kenneth Grahame. (Illus.). (J). (gr. k-3). 1978. pap. 2.95 (*0-486-23292-1*) Dover.

Wind in the Willows. (Classics Ser.). (J). (gr. 4 up). 1988. pap. 6.50 (*0-318-32663-9*, 74252) Longman.

Wind in the Willows. Humphrey Carpenter. (J). write for info. (*0-318-59416-1*) HM.

***Wind in the Willows.** Peter Glassman. (J). Date not set. write for info. (*0-688-12422-4*, Morrow Junior) Morrow.

Wind in the Willows. Moses Goldberg. (J). (gr. 1-7). 1974. 5.00 (*0-87602-220-4*) Anchorage.

***Wind in the Willows.** Kenneth Graham. Ed. by Joshua Hanft. (Great Illustrated Classics Ser.: Vol. 39). (Illus.). 240p. (J). (gr. 3-6). 9.95 (*0-86611-990-6*) Playmore Inc.

Wind in the Willows. Kenneth W. Graham, Jr. 224p. (J). 1989. pap. 2.50 (*0-8125-0510-7*) Tor Bks.

Wind in the Willows. Kenneth Grahame. (Airmont Classics Ser.). (J). (gr. 4 up). 1966. mass mkt. 2.75 (*0-8049-0105-8*, CL-105) Airmont.

Wind in the Willows. Kenneth Grahame. (Literary Classics Ser.). (J). 1994. 5.98 (*1-56138-455-0*) Courage Bks.

Wind in the Willows. Kenneth Grahame. 256p. (J). 1990. pap. 3.99 (*0-440-40385-5*) Dell.

Wind in the Willows. Kenneth Grahame. (Illus.). 224p. (J). (gr. 4). 1989. pap. 2.95 (*0-451-52164-1*, Sig Classics) NAL-Dutton.

Wind in the Willows. Kenneth Grahame. (Illus.). 56p. (J). (gr. 2-4). 1996. pap. 2.99 (*0-7214-5608-1*, Ladybrd) Penguin.

Wind in the Willows. Kenneth Grahame. (J). 1988. 7.99 (*0-517-49284-9*) Random Hse Value.

Wind in the Willows. Kenneth Grahame. LC 87-15818. (Children's Classics Ser.). (J). 1988. 12.99 (*0-517-63230-6*) Random Hse Value.

Wind in the Willows. Kenneth Grahame. 208p. (J). 1987. pap. 4.50 (*0-590-44774-2*) Scholastic Inc.

Wind in the Willows. Kenneth Grahame. (YA). 1987. 3.98 (*0-671-08895-5*) S&S Trade.

Wind in the Willows. Kenneth Grahame. 1991. pap. 9.95 (*0-8045-1033-4*) Spoken Arts.

Wind in the Willows. Kenneth Grahame. (Deluxe Watermill Classic Ser.). 256p. (YA). 1992. 10.89 (*0-8167-2562-4*) Troll Communs.

Wind in the Willows. Kenneth Grahame. (Deluxe Watermill Classic Ser.). 256p. (YA). 1997. pap. 4.95 (*0-8167-2563-2*) Troll Communs.

Wind in the Willows. Kenneth Grahame. (YA). (gr. 5 up). 1993. 13.95 (*0-679-41802-4*, Everymans Lib) Knopf.

Wind in the Willows. Kenneth Grahame. (Illus.). 256p. (J). 1983. mass mkt. 3.95 (*0-553-21368-7*, Bantam Classics) Bantam.

Wind in the Willows. Kenneth Grahame. LC 93-70550. (Children's Illustrated Classics Ser.). (Illus.). 56p. (J). (gr. 2 up). 1993. 9.98 (*1-56138-276-0*) Courage Bks.

Wind in the Willows. Kenneth Grahame. LC 85-13538. (Illus.). 224p. (J). (gr. 2 up). 1985. 12.95 (*0-915361-32-9*, Watts) Hemed Bks.

Wind in the Willows. Kenneth Grahame. Ed. by Peter Green. (World's Classics Ser.). 224p. (YA). (gr. 5 up). 1983. pap. 4.95 (*0-19-281640-3*) OUP.

Wind in the Willows. Kenneth Grahame. (Classics Ser.). (Illus.). 52p. (J). 1994. 3.50 (*0-7214-1653-5*, Ladybrd) Penguin.

Wind in the Willows. Kenneth Grahame. LC 90-64091. (Illus.). 264p. (YA). (gr. 8 up). 1991. lib. bdg. 25.00 (*0-684-19345-0*, C Scribner Sons Young) S&S Childrens.

Wind in the Willows. Kenneth Grahame. (Illus.). 185p. (J). (gr. 3-5). 1996. pap. 15.95 (*0-575-06209-6*, Pub. by V Gollancz UK) Trafalgar.

Wind in the Willows. Kenneth Grahame. LC 92-13203. (Illustrated Classics Ser.). (Illus.). 48p. (J). (gr. 3-6). 1992. lib. bdg. 14.95 (*0-8167-2870-4*) Troll Communs.

Wind in the Willows. Kenneth Grahame. LC 92-13203. (Illustrated Classics Ser.). (Illus.). 48p. (J). (gr. 3-6). 1997. pap. 5.95 (*0-8167-2871-2*) Troll Communs.

Wind in the Willows. Kenneth Grahame. (Illus.). 240p. (J). (gr. 1 up). 1983. 15.75 (*0-670-77120-1*) Viking Child Bks.

Wind in the Willows. Kenneth Grahame. (Illus.). 240p. (J). (gr. 4-6). 1984. pap. 2.95 (*0-14-031544-6*) Viking Child Bks.

Wind in the Willows. Kenneth Grahame. (Illus.). 216p. 1994. 15.95 (*1-56865-115-5*, GuildAmerica) Dblday Direct.

Wind in the Willows. Kenneth Grahame. (Puffin Classics Ser.). 220p. (YA). (gr. 5 up). 1995. pap. 3.99 (*0-14-036685-7*) Puffin Bks.

Wind in the Willows. Kenneth Grahame. (Signet Classics Ser.). (YA). 1969. mass mkt. 3.95 (*0-451-52462-4*, Sig Classics) NAL-Dutton.

Wind in the Willows. Kenneth Grahame. (Illus.). 1995. 18.95 (*0-312-13624-2*) St Martin.

Wind in the Willows. Kenneth Grahame. 1996. audio 16.99 (*0-553-47654-8*) Bantam.

***Wind in the Willows.** Illus. by Gill Guile. (Classics for Children 8 & Younger Ser.). 48p. (J). (gr. k-3). 1997. 6.98 (*1-85854-601-X*) Brimax Bks.

Wind in the Willows. M. Hague. LC 80-12509. 216p. (J). (gr. 4-6). 1980. 19.95 (*0-8050-0213-8*, Bks Young Read) H Holt & Co.

Wind in the Willows. Random House Value Publishing Staff. (J). 1996. 9.99 (*0-517-16023-4*) Random Hse Value.

Wind in the Willows. abr. ed. Kenneth Grahame. LC 95-6186. (Children's Thrift Classics Ser.). (Illus.). 96p. (J). 1995. pap. text ed. 1.00 (*0-486-28600-2*) Dover.

Wind in the Willows. large type ed. Kenneth Grahame. LC 96-24243. 248p. 1996. lib. bdg. 21.95 (*0-7838-1874-2*, GK Hall) Thorndike Pr.

***Wind in the Willows.** large type ed. Kenneth Grahame. 284p. 1997. reprint ed. lib. bdg. 22.00 (*0-939495-18-X*) North Bks.

Wind in the Willows. 75th anniversary ed. Kenneth Grahame. LC 83-11573. (Illus.). 256p. (J). (gr. 3 up). 1983. lib. bdg. 19.00 (*0-684-17957-1*, C Scribner Sons Young) S&S Childrens.

Wind in the Willows. Kenneth Grahame. 234p. (J). 1981. reprint ed. lib. bdg. 17.95 (*0-89966-305-2*) Buccaneer Bks.

Wind in the Willows. Kenneth Grahame. LC 88-8046. (Illus.). 272p. (J). (ps up). 1989. reprint ed. pap. 4.95 (*0-689-71310-X*, Aladdin Paperbacks) S&S Childrens.

***Wind in the Willows, Vol. 1.** K. Grahame. (J). 1980. write for info. (*0-03-056294-5*) H Holt & Co.

Wind in the Willows, Vol. 1. Kenneth Grahame. 272p. (YA). (gr. 8 up). 1972. lib. bdg. 16.00 (*0-684-12819-5*, C Scribner Sons Young) S&S Childrens.

Wind in the Willows: (El Viento en los Sauces I, II), I. Kenneth Grahame. (SPA.). (J). 9.50 (*84-372-1882-9*) Santillana.

Wind in the Willows: (El Viento en los Sauces I, II), II. Kenneth Grahame. (SPA.). (J). 9.50 (*84-372-1883-7*) Santillana.

Wind in the Willows: A Study Guide. Gloria Levine. (Novel-Ties Ser.). 1989. teacher ed., wbk. ed., pap. text ed. 15.95 (*0-88122-058-2*) Lrn Links.

Wind in the Willows: An Ambiguous Classic. Peter Hunt. (Twayne's Masterwork Studies: 141). 125p. 1994. 23.95 (*0-8057-8816-6*, Twayne) Scribnrs Ref.

Wind in the Willows: An Ambiguous Classic. Peter Hunt. (Twayne's Masterwork Studies: No. 141). 125p. 1994. pap. 13.95 (*0-8057-8817-4*, Twayne) Scribnrs Ref.

Wind in the Willows: Musical. Douglas Post. 87p. 1987. pap. 5.50 (*0-87129-172-X*, W05) Dramatic Pub.

Wind in the Willows - Str. Joseph Baldwin. 118p. 1966. pap. 5.00 (*0-87129-160-6*, W35) Dramatic Pub.

Wind in the Willows Drawings. Grahame. 1986. pap. 1.00 (*0-416-39370-5*) Routledge Chapman & Hall.

Wind in the Willows (Playscript) (A Musical) Liz Peterson. (Orig.). (J). 1993. pap. 5.00 (*0-87602-325-1*) Anchorage.

Wind in the Willows Wordbook. Grahame. 1989. 2.99 (*0-517-68365-2*) Random Hse Value.

Wind in the Wires. Duncan Grinnell-Milne et al. Ed. by Stanley M. Ulanoff & James B. Gilbert. LC 79-7264. (Flight: Its First Seventy-Five Years Ser.). (Illus.). 1980. reprint ed. lib. bdg. 28.95 (*0-405-12174-1*) Ayer.

Wind in the Wires: A Golden Era of Flight 1909-1939. Mike Vines. (Illus.). 128p. 1995. 29.95 (*0-7603-0190-5*) Motorbooks Intl.

Wind Is My Mother: The Life & Teachings of a Native American Shaman. Molly Larkin & Bear Heart. 272p. 1996. 24.00 (*0-517-70283-5*) Random.

***Wind Is My Mother: The Life & Teachings of American Shaman.** Bear Heart & Molly Larkin. 272p. 1998. pap. write for info. (*0-425-16160-9*, Berkley Trade) Berkley Pub.

***Wind Is My Witness: A Wyoming Album.** Mark Junge. (Illus.). 300p. 1997. 39.95 (*1-57098-149-3*) R Rinehart.

Wind Is Not a River. Arnold A. Griese. LC 95-78288. (Illus.). 80p. (J). (gr. 2-4). 1995. pap. 7.95 (*1-56397-564-5*) Boyds Mills Pr.

Wind Is Rising. Viola Wendt. LC 79-53723. 1979. pap. 4.50 (*0-916120-05-8*) Carroll Coll.

Wind Leaves No Shadow. Ruth Laughlin. LC 48-10425. 1951. pap. 8.95 (*0-87004-083-9*) Caxton.

Wind Load on Structures. C. D. Dyrbye. 1996. text ed. 77.95 (*0-471-95651-1*) Wiley.

Wind Loading & Wind-Induced Structural Response. 216p. 1987. 22.00 (*0-87262-625-3*) Am Soc Civil Eng.

Wind Loading Handbook: Guide to the Use of BS 6399, Pt. 2. T. V. Lawson. LC 95-37496. 1996. 56.95 (*0-7506-1094-8*) Buttrwrth-Heinemann.

***Wind Loads & Anchor Bolt Design for Petrochemical Facilities.** American Society of Civil Engineers Staff. LC 97-20890. 1997. write for info. (*0-7844-0262-0*) Am Soc Civil Eng.

Wind Loads on Structures: Proceedings of an International Symposium, New Delhi, 5-7. Dept. of Civil Engineering University of Roorkee, India Staff. (Illus.). 325p. (C). 1991. text ed. 105.00 (*90-6191-178-8*, Pub. by A A Balkema NE) Ashgate Pub Co.

Wind Masters: The Lives of North American Birds of Prey. Pete Dunne. LC 95-18314. (Illus.). 288p. 1995. 22.95 (*0-395-65235-9*) HM.

Wind Mountain: Poems. Fred Chappell. LC 79-12332. 45p. 1979. pap. 6.95 (*0-8071-0567-8*); text ed. 13.95 (*0-8071-0566-X*) La State U Pr.

Wind of a Thousand Tales: Folk Tales from Faraway Places. John Glore. (Illus.). 48p. (Orig.). 1991. pap. 4.50 (*0-88680-350-0*) I E Clark.

Wind of a Thousand Tales: Folk Tales from Faraway Places - Piano Score. John Glore. (Illus.). 48p. (Orig.). 1991. 15.00 (*0-88680-351-9*) I E Clark.

Wind of Chance. Rene Guillot. Tr. by Norman Dale. (Illus.). (J). (gr. 6-9). 1958. 24.95 (*0-87599-048-7*) S G Phillips.

Wind of Chance. Bruce Nicol. 178p. (C). 1989. text ed. 40.00 (*0-946270-98-8*, Pub. by Pentland Pr UK) St Mut.

***Wind of Change.** Julie Soskin. 1997. pap. text ed. 10.95 (*1-85398-075-7*, Pub. by Ashgrove UK) Words Distrib.

***Wind of Change.** large type ed. Helen McCabe. (Linford Romance Library). 192p. 1996. pap. 15.99 (*0-7089-7927-0*) Ulverscroft.

Wind of Change: Cardinal Lavigerie, 1825-1892. Joseph Perrier. 142p. 1993. 29.00 (*0-85439-435-4*, Pub. by St Paul Pubns UK) St Mut.

Wind-of-Fire: The Story of an Untouchable. Joan B. Clair. LC 95-90409. 152p. (Orig.). 1995. pap. 13.95 (*0-9635834-0-9*) Wind-of-Fire.

Wind of Our Going. Patricia Goedicke. LC 84-73336. 120p. (Orig.). 1985. pap. 8.00 (*0-914742-84-1*) Copper Canyon.

Wind of Promise. Dorothy Garlock. 384p. 1987. mass mkt. 5.99 (*0-445-20368-4*) Warner Bks.

Wind of the Spirit. rev. ed. G. De Purucker. Ed. by W. Emmett Small & Helen Todd. 282p. 1971. reprint ed. pap. 9.00 (*0-913004-00-6*) Point Loma Pub.

Wind of the Spirit. rev. ed. G. De Purucker. LC 84-50118. 328p. 1984. reprint ed. pap. 9.00 (*0-911500-68-5*) Theos U Pr.

Wind of the Spirit. 2nd rev. ed. G. De Purucker. LC 84-50118. 328p. 1984. reprint ed. 15.00 (*0-911500-67-7*) Theos U Pr.

Wind of the White Dresses. Mekeel McBride. LC 94-70465. (Poetry Ser.). 80p. 1995. 20.95 (*0-88748-184-1*); pap. 11.95 (*0-88748-185-X*) Carnegie-Mellon.

Wind of Time: A Romantic Mystery Novel with a Touch of the Occult. John Dandola. LC 95-4104. (Illus.). 200p. (Orig.). 1995. pap. 9.95 (*1-878452-22-3*, Rune-Tales) Tory Corner Editions.

Wind off the Island. large type ed. Ernie Bradford. 400p. 1992. 25.99 (*0-7089-2672-X*) Ulverscroft.

Wind on the Buffalo Grass: Native American Artist-Historians. Leslie Tillet. (Quality Paperbacks Ser.). (Illus.). 176p. 1989. pap. 18.95 (*0-306-80357-7*) Da Capo.

Wind on the Heath. large type ed. Thomas Gallagher. 563p. 1988. 25.99 (*0-7089-1877-8*) Ulverscroft.

Wind on the Heath: Sunday Evening Sermons from a Glasgow Pulpit. George H. Morrison. LC 93-37826. 176p. 1993. pap. 9.99 (*0-8254-3289-8*) Kregel.

Wind on the Water. Jim Rearden. 280p. 1990. pap. 19.95 (*0-937708-19-4*) Great Northwest.

Wind on the Waves. Kim R. Stafford. (Illus.). 144p. 1992. 29.50 (*1-55868-090-X*) Gr Arts Ctr Pub.

Wind on Your Cheek. William J. Schaldach. (Illus.). 160p. 1973. 17.50 (*0-88395-015-4*); boxed 75.00 (*0-685-32727-2*) Freshet Pr.

***Wind over Rimfire.** large type ed. Wayne C. Lee. LC 96-42252. 1996. lib. bdg. 17.95 (*1-57490-046-3*, Sagebrush LP West) T T Beeler.

Wind over Sand: The Diplomacy of Franklin Roosevelt. Frederick W. Marks, III. LC 86-24976. (Illus.). 472p. 1990. pap. 24.00 (*0-8203-1270-3*) U of Ga Pr.

Wind Power. Richard K. Miller & Marcia E. Rupnow. LC 90-83925. (Survey on Technology & Markets Ser.: No. 124). 50p. 1991. pap. text ed. 200.00 (*1-55865-147-0*) Future Tech Surveys.

***Wind Power.** Richard K. Miller & Christy H. Gunter. (Market Research Survey Ser.: No. 336). 50p. 1997. pap. 200.00 (*1-55865-355-4*) Future Tech Surveys.

Win[illegible] Source Guide. 1991. lib. bdg. 76.00 (*[illegible]909-1*) Gordon Pr.

Wind Po[illegible]r: A Turning Point. Christopher Flavin. 1981. pap. write for info. (*0-916468-44-5*) Worldwatch Inst.

Wind Power & Other Energy Options. David R. Inglis. LC 78-9102. (Illus.). 1978. pap. 22.50 (*0-472-06303-0*) U of Mich Pr.

Wind Power Equipment. D. F. Warne. (Illus.). 220p. 1982. 57.50 (*0-419-11410-6*, NO. 6684, E & FN Spon) Routledge Chapman & Hall.

Wind Power for Home & Business. Paul Gipe. (Illus.). 432p. 1996. pap. 45.00 incl. disk (*0-930031-90-3*); disk 15.00 (*0-930031-88-1*) Chelsea Green Pub.

Wind Power for Home & Business: Renewable Energy for the 1990s & Beyond. Paul Gipe. (Real Goods Independent Living Bks.). (Illus.). 432p. (Orig.). 1996. pap. 35.00 (*0-930031-64-4*) Chelsea Green Pub.

Wind Prayer. Netan Yonetan. Ed. by Stanley H. Barkan et al. (Review Israeli Writers Chapbook Ser.: No. 1). 48p. (ENG & HEB.). 1991. 15.00 (*0-89304-375-3*); pap. 5.00 (*0-89304-376-1*) Cross-Cultrl NY.

Wind Prayer: Mini Book. Netan Yonetan. Ed. by Stanley H. Barkan et al. (Review Israeli Writers Chapbook Ser.: No. 1). 48p. (ENG & HEB.). 1991. 15.00 (*0-89304-377-X*); pap. 5.00 (*0-89304-378-8*) Cross-Cultrl NY.

Wind Rain & Stars & the Grass Growing. Greg Kuzma. LC 93-18479. 112p. (Orig.). 1993. 21.95 (*0-914061-38-0*); pap. 12.95 (*0-914061-39-9*) Orchises Pr.

Wind Rider. Connie Mason. 448p. 1995. mass mkt. 5.99 (*0-8439-4040-9*, Leisure Bks) Dorchester Pub Co.

***Wind Riders.** Sharon H. Dye. 40p. (Orig.). 1996. pap. 7.95 (*0-533-11655-4*) Vantage.

Wind River. Richard S. Wheeler. 352p. (Orig.). 1993. mass mkt. 3.99 (*0-8125-2142-0*) Tor Bks.

Wind River No. 5: Dark Trail. James Reasoner. 272p. 1995. mass mkt. 3.99 (*0-06-100775-7*) HarpC.

Wind River Kid. large type ed. Will Cook. (Linford Western Library). 368p. 1995. pap. 15.99 (*0-7089-7696-4*, Linford) Ulverscroft.

Wind River Kid. large type ed. Max Stern. 256p. 1992. pap. 15.99 (*0-7089-7168-7*, Trailtree Bookshop) Ulverscroft.

Wind River Kill. Robert Kammen. 1987. mass mkt. 2.50 (*0-8217-2213-1*, Zebra Kensgtn) Kensgtn Pub Corp.

Wind River Kill. Robert Kammen. 1987. pap. 2.95 (*0-8217-3164-5*) NAL-Dutton.

***Wind River Ranch.** Jackie Merritt. (Desire Ser.: No. 1085). 1997. mass mkt. 3.50 (*0-373-76085-X*, 1-76085-9) Silhouette.

Wind River Shoshone Ethnogeography. fac. ed. D. B. Shimkin. Ed. by Robert H. Lowie et al. (University of California Publications: No. 5:4). (Illus.). 46p. (C). 1947. reprint ed. pap. 4.35 (*1-55567-085-7*) Coyote Press.

Wind River Trails. Finis Mitchell. Ed. by Mel Davis. (Illus.). 144p. 1975. pap. 5.00 (*0-915272-03-2*) Wasatch Pubs.

Wind River Winter. Virginia S. Owens. 221p. (C). 1995. reprint ed. spiral bd. 19.95 (*1-57383-051-8*) Regent College.

Wind Rose. Krista Janssen. Ed. by Denise Silvestro. 304p. (Orig.). 1994. mass mkt. 5.50 (*0-671-74499-2*) PB.

Wind, Sand & Silence: Travels with Africa's Last Nomads. Victor Englebert. (Illus.). 192p. 1992. 35.00 (*0-8118-0010-5*) Chronicle Bks.

Wind, Sand & Stars. Antoine de Saint-Exupery. LC 65-35872. 243p. 1967. pap. 9.00 (*0-15-697090-2*, Harvest Bks) HarBrace.

Wind, Sand & Stars. Antoine de Saint-Exupery. 1992. 15.95 (*0-15-197087-4*) HarBrace.

Wind, Sand & Stars. Antoine De Saint-Exupery. 1992. reprint ed. lib. bdg. 26.95 (*0-89968-298-7*, Lghtyr Pr) Buccaneer Bks.

Wind Says Good Night. Katy Rydell. (J). (ps). 1994. 14.95 (*0-395-60474-5*) HM.

Wind Scales. deluxe ed. Keith Waldrop. (Treacle Story Ser.: No. 4). (Illus.). 36p. 1976. 12.50 (*0-914232-13-4*) McPherson & Co.

Wind Song. Margaret Brownley. 384p. (Orig.). 1994. pap. 4.99 (*0-451-40526-9*, Topaz) NAL-Dutton.

Wind Spinners. Deborah Potter. 31p. (Orig.). 1996. pap. 6.95 (*1-888289-18-X*) Mythspinner.

Wind Spins Me Around in the Fall, Vol. 3. Charlotte Agell. (Illus.). 40p. (J). (ps up). 1994. 4.95 (*0-88448-114-X*) Tilbury Hse.

Wind Strategy. 2nd ed. David Houghton. 96p. (C). 1990. text ed. 59.00 (*0-906754-79-8*, Pub. by Fernhurst Bks UK) St Mut.

Wind Surfing. Amanda Wray. (Action Sports Ser.). 48p. (J). (gr. 3-4). 1991. lib. bdg. 17.80 (*1-56065-055-9*) Capstone Pr.

Wind That Shakes the Barley. James Barke. 384p. 9300. pap. 12.95 (*0-85640-488-8*) Dufour.

Wind That Swept Mexico: The History of the Mexican Revolution of 1910-1942. Anita Brenner & George R. Leighton. LC 77-149021. (Texas Pan American Ser.). (Illus.). 320p. (C). 1971. pap. 19.95 (*0-292-79024-4*) U of Tex Pr.

Wind That Tramps the World: Splashes of Chinese Color, Vol. 1. Frank F. Owen. LC 72-4426. (Short Story Index Reprint Ser.). 1977. reprint ed. 18.95 (*0-8369-4186-1*) Ayer.

Wind Trails Vol. 1: Thoughts to Ponder. Constance H. Dembrowsky. 1991. spiral bd. 10.00 (*0-924609-12-5*) Inst Affect Skill.

Wind Tunnel Model Studies of Buildings & Structures. Ed. by Nicholas Isyumov. (ASCE Manual & Report on Engineering Practice Ser.: No. 67). 48p. 1987. 10.00 (*0-87262-620-2*) Am Soc Civil Eng.

Wind Tunnel Modeling for Civil Engineering Applications: Proceedings of the International Workshop on Wind Tunnel Modeling Criteria & Techniques in Civil Engineering Applications, Gaithersburg, Maryland, April, 1982. International Workshop on Wind Tunnel Modeling Criteria & Techniques in Civil Engineering Applications (1982: Gaithersburg, MD). Ed. by Timothy A. Reinhold. LC 82-14594. 702p. reprint ed. pap. 180.00 (*0-685-16104-8*, 2027249) Bks Demand.

Wind Turbine-Diesel System for Irrigation in Remote Applications SP-EN. European Commission Staff. 153p. 1994. pap. 25.00 (*92-826-7077-5*, CS-NA-15073-2SC, Pub. by Europ Com UK) Bernan Associates.

Wind Turbine Engineering Design. David M. Eggleston. Ed. by Forrest S. Stoddard. LC 86-23331. 420p. (gr. 13). 1987. text ed. 92.95 (*0-442-22195-9*) Chapman & Hall.

Wind Turbine Noise. S. J. Wagner et al. LC 96-17661. 1996. write for info. (*0-387-60592-4*) Spr-Verlag.

***Wind Turbine Noise.** S. J. Wagner et al. 205p. 1996. 99.50 (*3-540-60592-4*) Spr-Verlag.

Wind Turbine Technology: Fundamental Concepts of Wind Turbine Engineering. Ed. by David A. Spera. LC 94-11137. 656p. 1994. 80.00 (*0-7918-1205-7*) ASME.

Wind Turbine Worldwide Catalog, 1988-89. Ed. by Thomas F. Jaras. 1989. pap. text ed. 50.00 (*0-944038-02-6*) T F Jaras.

***Wind-Up Bird Chronicles.** Haruki Murakami. 1997. 26.95 (*0-679-44669-9*) Knopf.

***Wind-up Bird Chronicles.** Haruki Murakami. 1998. pap. write for info. (*0-679-77543-9*, Vin) Random.

Wind up the Willow. Alan Brown. 1989. pap. 8.95 (*0-7145-3734-9*) Riverrun NY.

Wind-Ups. Chris Ollerenshaw & Pat Triggs. LC 94-4885. (Toy Box Science Ser.). (Illus.). 32p. (J). (gr. 3 up). 1994. lib. bdg. 18.60 (*0-8368-1122-4*) Gareth Stevens Inc.

Wind Wagon. Celia B. Lottridge. LC 94-39398. (Illus.). (J). (gr. 4-6). 1994. 10.95 (*0-382-24928-3*); pap. 4.95 (*0-382-24929-1*); lib. bdg. 12.95 (*0-382-24927-5*) Silver Burdett Pr.

W

An Asterisk (*) at the beginning of an entry indicates that the title is appearing in BIP for the first time.

***Wind Warrior.** Munn. Date not set. write for info. (0-312-86446-9) St Martin.

***Wind Water.** Jeanne Williams. LC 96-31039. 1997. 23.95 (0-312-14765-1) St Martin.

Wind-Water Wheel: A Feng Shui Tool for Transforming Your Life. Angi Ma Wong. (Illus.). 6p. 1996. 19.95 (0-9635906-7-7) Pacific Herit.

***Wind, Waves, & Sunburn: A Brief History of Marathon Swimmers.** Conrad Wennerberg. 352p. 1997. pap. 16.95 (1-55821-615-4) Lyons & Burford.

Wind, Waves & Weather. Ed. by Vivian Carmona-Agosto. Tr. by Marcela Rossman. (Rotary Drilling Ser.: Univ V, Lesson 1). (Illus.). 49p. (Orig.). (SPA.). 1982. pap. text ed. 14.00 (0-88698-046-1, 2.50112) PETEX.

Wind, Waves & Weather. 2nd rev. ed. Ed. by Nora Sheppard. (Rotary Drilling Ser.: Unit V, Lesson 1). (Illus.). 70p. 1984. pap. text ed. 14.00 (0-88698-069-0, 2. 50120) PETEX.

Wind Whispers, Shadow Shouts. Sharon Green. 336p. (Orig.). 1995. mass mkt. 4.99 (0-380-77724-X, AvoNova) Avon.

Wind Will Not Forget. Carolyn Muentner. 68p. 1983. 8.95 (0-9606240-3-1) Pearl-Win.

Wind Witch. Susan Dexter. 1994. mass mkt. 5.99 (0-345-38770-8, Del Rey) Ballantine.

Wind Without Rain see Krause Trio

Wind Won't Know Me: A History of the Navajo-Hopi Land Dispute. Emily Benedek. 1993. pap. 16.00 (0-679-74386-3, Vin) Random.

Wind Workshop Six: Sixth Biennial Wind Energy Conference & Workshop. Ed. by Barbara Glenn. 1983. Set. pap. text ed. 60.00 (0-89553-125-9) Am Solar Energy.

Windberg Oil Painting Technique. rev. ed. Dalhart Windberg. (Illus.). 50p. 1989. 19.95 (0-9621946-0-3) Windberg Enter.

Windbreak: A Woman Rancher on the Northern Plains. Linda Hasselstrom. LC 87-11428. (Illus.). 256p. (Orig.). 1987. pap. 12.95 (0-9609626-3-8) Barn Owl Bks.

Windbreak Technology: Proc. of an Internat. Symp., Lincoln, NE, 23-27 June, 1986. Ed. by J. R. Brandle et al. 600p. 1988. 333.75 (0-444-43019-9) Elsevier.

***Windburnt Plains of Wonder.** Richie Prosch & Gina Prosch. (Illus.). 170p. (Orig.). 1996. pap. 11.95 (1-57502-343-1, PO1137) Morris Pubng.

Windcatcher. Avi. 128p. (J). 1992. pap. 4.50 (0-380-71805-7, Camelot) Avon.

Windcatcher. Avi. LC 90-40574. 128p. (J). (gr. 3-7). 1991. lib. bdg. 14.00 (0-02-707761-6, Bradbury S&S) S&S Childrens.

Windchaser. Scott Ciencin. 1995. pap. 3.99 (0-679-86981-6) Random.

***Windchimes, Weathervanes & Welcomes, Vol. 1.** Vicki Higley. (Illus.). 70p. (Orig.). 1997. pap. 9.50 (1-56770-387-9) S Scheewe Pubns.

Winders of America. R. Winder Johnson. (Illus.). 112p. reprint ed. pap. 19.50 (0-8328-1669-8); reprint ed. lib. bdg. 29.50 (0-8328-1668-X) Higginson Bk Co.

Windex see Juta's Index to the Government & Provincial Gazettes 1910-1989

***Windfall.** Emily Carmichael. 416p. 1997. mass mkt. 5.99 (0-446-60298-1) Warner Bks.

Windfall. Deborah Potter. 31p. (Orig.). 1996. pap. 6.95 (1-888289-15-5) Mythspinner.

Windfall: A Collection of Modern Poetry. Ed. by Louisa Persing. 1975. 5.95 (0-686-10961-9) Palomar.

WindFall: The End of the Affair. William F. Buckley, Jr. LC 92-54848. (Illus.). 304p. 1993. pap. 14.00 (0-06-097551-2, PL) HarpC.

Windfall & Other Stories. Winifred M. Sanford & Emerett S. Miles. LC 87-43105. (Southwest Life & Letters Ser.). 204p. 1988. reprint ed. pap. 10.95 (0-87074-268-X) SMU Press.

Windfall & Other Stories. Winifred M. Sanford. LC 87-43105. (Southwest Life & Letters Ser.). 204p. 1988. reprint ed. 17.95 (0-87074-267-1) SMU Press.

Windfall Apples. Roma Greth. 1984. pap. 5.95 (0-88145-018-9) Broadway Play.

Windfalls. Alfred G. Gardiner. LC 70-105014. (Essay Index Reprint Ser.). 1977. 21.95 (0-8369-1467-8) Ayer.

Windfalls for Wipeouts: Land Value Capture & Compensation. Ed. by Donald G. Hagman & Dean J. Misczynski. LC 77-82573. 704p. (Orig.). (C). 1978. pap. 25.95 (0-918286-11-5) Planners Pr.

***Windflower.** Gabrielle Roy. 1996. pap. text ed. 5.95 (0-7710-9879-0) McCland & Stewart.

Windham. Richard C. Wiles. 20p. 1987. reprint ed. pap. 3.50 (0-910746-26-5, W01) Hope Farm.

***Windham Company: A Managerial Practice Set, 6 Vols.** 2nd ed. Henry R. Anderson. (C). 1990. teacher ed., text ed. 11.96 (0-395-52978-6) HM.

Windham in the Past. Samuel T. Dole. Ed. by Frederick H. Dole. (Illus.). 611p. 1992. reprint ed. lib. bdg. 62.00 (0-8328-2502-6) Higginson Bk Co.

Windham in the Past. Samuel T. Dole. Ed. by Frederick H. Dole. 611p. 1995. reprint ed. lib. bdg. 62.50 (0-8328-4664-3) Higginson Bk Co.

***Windham in the Past: With Genealogical Sketches.** Samuel T. Dole. Ed. by Frederick H. Dole. (Illus.). 611p. 1997. reprint ed. lib. bdg. 64.00 (0-8328-5928-1) Higginson Bk Co.

Windham, ME. E. Bell. (Images of America Ser.). 1996. pap. 16.99 (0-7524-0445-8, Arcdia) Chalford.

***Windham Register, 1904 (Town History & Directory)** Compiled by Mitchell & Russell. 110p. 1997. reprint ed. pap. 17.00 (0-8328-5929-X) Higginson Bk Co.

Windhaven. George R. Martin & Lisa Tuttle. 1980. 25.00 (0-671-25277-1) Ultramarine Pub.

Windhorse Woman. Lynn V. Andrews. 224p. 1990. pap. 13. 99 (0-446-39172-7) Warner Bks.

Windhover. Brown. LC 96-48759. 1997. write for info. (0-15-201187-0) HarBrace.

Windigo Psychosis: American Ethnological Society Proceedings, 1960. Morton I. Teicher. Ed. by Verne F. Ray. LC 84-45547. 1988. reprint ed. pap. 45.00 (0-404-62654-8) AMS Pr.

Windigo's Return: A North Woods Story. Douglas Wood. LC 95-14832. (Illus.). (J). (ps-3). 1996. 16.00 (0-689-80065-7, S&S Bks Young Read) S&S Childrens.

Winding. Ken Frye. 132p. 1990. 71.00 (0-89852-465-2, 0101R165) TAPPI.

Winding. Kenneth G. Frye. LC 90-11324. 127p. pap. 34.30 (0-8357-3001-8, 2039270) Bks Demand.

Winding Alternating Current Machines: A Book for Winders, Repairmen, & Designers of Electric Machines. Michael Liwschitz-Garik & Celso Gentilini. 772p. 1950. 93.00 (0-911740-03-1) Datarule.

Winding Down a Psychiatric Private Practice. Joseph Deacon. LC 85-7341. (Private Practice Monograph Ser.). 105p. reprint ed. pap. 30.00 (0-8357-7845-2, 2036220) Bks Demand.

Winding Engine Calculations for the Mining. P. K. Chatterjee & P. J. Wetherall. 1982. 39.95 (0-419-12650-3, NO. 6693, E & FN Spon) Routledge Chapman & Hall.

Winding Passage: Sociological Essays & Journeys. Daniel Bell. 371p. (C). 1991. pap. 24.95 (0-88738-899-X) Transaction Pubs.

Winding Path. Carrie Bender. LC 93-44864. (Miriam's Journal Ser.: No. 2). 160p. (Orig.). 1996. pap. 7.99 (0-8361-3656-X) Herald Pr.

***Winding Path to America.** Theodore Archibald. LC 95-83307. 148p. (Orig.). 1996. pap. 7.95 (0-7880-0654-1) CSS OH.

***Winding Road: A History of Cedarville, West Virginia.** Ron Gregory & Betty Gregory. (Illus.). 148p. (Orig.). 1995. pap. 9.50 (1-885935-05-6) Appalchn Log.

Winding Road to West Egg: The Artistic Development of F. Scott Fitzgerald. Robert Roulston & Helen H. Roulston. LC 94-20157. 1995. 37.50 (0-8387-5280-2) Bucknell U Pr.

Winding Stair. Jane A. Hodge. 1980. pap. 2.25 (0-449-23590-4, Crest) Fawcett.

Winding Stair (1929) Manuscript Materials. William Butler Yeats. Ed. by David R. Clark. (Yeats Ser.). (Illus.). 312p. 1995. 49.95 (0-8014-3124-7) Cornell U Pr.

Winding Trail: The Alabama-Coushatta Indians. Vivian Fox. (Illus.). 1983. pap. 6.95 (0-89015-397-3) Sunbelt Media.

Windings of the Labyrinth: Quest & Structure in the Major Novels of Wilkie Collins. Peter Thoms. LC 92-13159. 250p. (C). 1992. text ed. 35.00 (0-8214-1039-3) Ohio U Pr.

Windingsheets of Vineleaf. William S. Church. 128p. 1992. pap. text ed. 9.95 (1-881579-03-4) Theophilus Pr.

Windjammer Cooking. rev. ed. Dee Carstarphen. Orig. Title: Windjammer World. (Illus.). 158p. 1989. pap. 11. 95 (0-9607544-3-1) Pen & Ink.

Windjammer Watching on the Coast of Maine: A Guide to the Famous Windjammer Fleet & Other Traditional Sailing Vessels. 2nd ed. Virginia L. Thorndike. LC 96-83595. (Illus.). 112p. 1996. pap. 11.95 (0-89272-389-0) Down East.

Windjammer World see Windjammer Cooking

Windjammers. Thornton J. Hains. LC 76-103516. (Short Story Index Reprint Ser.). 1977. 20.95 (0-8369-3258-7) Ayer.

Windjammers of the Pacific Rim. Jim Gibbs. LC 86-63762. 232p. 1987. pap. 19.95 (0-88740-086-8) Schiffer.

Windleaf. Josepha Sherman. LC 93-615. 128p. (YA). (gr. 7 up). 1993. 14.95 (0-8027-8259-0) Walker & Co.

Windmaster's Bane. Tom Deitz. 288p. (Orig.). 1986. mass mkt. 4.99 (0-380-75029-5) Avon.

***Windmill.** unabridged ed. Mario Edlosi. LC 96-60780. (Valley of Many Winds Ser.: Pt. III). (Orig.). 1996. pap. 6.95 (1-877649-26-0) Tesseract SD.

***Windmill: Essays from Four Mile Ranch.** David Romtvedt. LC 96-29729. (Illus.). 1997. pap. 14.95 (1-878610-62-7) Red Crane Bks.

Windmill Construction & Generating Power. F. E. Powell. (Illus.). 80p. 1991. reprint ed. pap. 10.00 (1-877767-51-4) Univ Publng Hse.

Windmill Hill. Hope Slaughter. (Illus.). 64p. (J). (gr. 2-5). 1993. 14.95 (0-945912-21-8) Pippin Pr.

Windmill Years. large type ed. Vicky Martin. 590p. 1980. 25.99 (0-7089-0465-3) Ulverscroft.

Windmills & Pumps of the Southwest. Dick Hays & Bill Allen. (Illus.). 120p. 1983. pap. 12.95 (0-89015-394-9) Sunbelt Media.

Windmills & Wind Motors. F. E. Powell. 1985. reprint ed. pap. 6.95 (0-917914-27-9) Lindsay Pubns.

Windmills, Drouths & Cottonseed Cake: A Biased Biography of a West Texas Rancher. John A. Haley. LC 94-30504. (Illus.). 108p. 1995. 19.95 (0-87565-141-0) Tex Christian.

***Windmills of My Mind.** Aline Williams. (Orig.). 1996. pap. write for info. (1-57553-316-2) Watermrk Pr.

Windmills of the Gods. Sidney Sheldon. (Sheldon Continuity Ser.). 288p. 1993. 12.95 (1-56865-028-0, GuildAmerica) Dblday Direct.

Windmills of the Gods. Sidney Sheldon. 448p. 1987. mass mkt. 6.99 (0-446-35010-9) Warner Bks.

Windmills of the Gods. Sidney Sheldon. LC 86-23553. 1987. 22.95 (0-688-06570-8) Morrow.

Windmill's Song & Other Memories of a Country Child. Mary N. Gilhooly. 1995. 13.95 (0-533-11379-2) Vantage.

Windmills Walk the Night. Marilyn Dorf. (Illus.). 48p. (Orig.). 1992. pap. 6.95 (0-9616211-1-7) Marilyn Dorf.

Windmore Writers Anthology. Padgett et al. 1993. pap. 8.50 (0-9636786-0-4) Blue Rdge Mntns.

***Windo Watchman Vol. I: Millions Prayed, God Responded, Witness the Impact.** Ed. by Michael Ebert & Beverly Pegues. LC 94-74935. (Illus.). 240p. (Orig.). 1994. pap. 10.00 (0-9644880-0-0) Christian Info.

***Windo Watchman Vol. I: Millions Prayed, God Responded, Witness the Impact.** Ed. by Michael Ebert & Beverly Pegues. LC 94-74935. (Illus.). 240p. (Orig.). 1994. write for info. (0-9644880-2-7) Christian Info.

***Windo Watchman Vol. II: Millions Prayed, God Responded, Witness the Impact.** Dale Agthe. Ed. by Beverly Pegues & Deborah Strong. (Illus.). 375p. (Orig.). 1997. pap. 14.99 (0-9644880-1-9) Christian Info.

***Windo Watchman Vol. II: Millions Prayed, God Responded, Witness the Impact.** Dale Agthe. Ed. by Beverly Pegues & Deborah Strong. (Illus.). 375p. (Orig.). 1997. write for info. (0-9644880-3-5) Christian Info.

Windover. large type ed. Jane A. Hodge. LC 92-29408. 458p. 1993. reprint ed. lib. bdg. 17.95 (1-56054-553-4) Thorndike Pr.

Window. Jeannie Baker. LC 90-3922. (Illus.). 32p. (J). (ps up). 1991. 16.00 (0-688-08917-8); lib. bdg. 15.93 (0-688-08918-6) Greenwillow.

Window. Jeannie Baker. (Illus.). 32p. (J). (ps-3). 1993. pap. 4.99 (0-14-054830-0) Puffin Bks.

Window. Robert Creeley. (Illus.). 22p. (Orig.). (C). 1988. pap. text ed. 40.00 (0-685-44373-6) SUNYB Poetry Rare Bks.

***Window.** Michael Dorris. (Illus.). 128p. (YA). (gr. 5 up). 1997. pap. 16.95 (0-7868-0301-0); lib. bdg. 16.89 (0-7868-2240-6) Hyprn Child.

Window. Carol Ellis. 176p. (YA). (gr. 7-9). 1992. pap. 3.25 (0-590-44916-8, Point) Scholastic Inc.

Window. Jeanette Ingold. 1996. 12.00 (0-15-201265-6); pap. 5.00 (0-15-201264-8) HarBrace.

Window: New & Selected Poems. Dahlia Ravikovitch. Tr. by Chana Bloch & Ariel Bloch from HEB. LC 88-34896. 117p. (Orig.). 1989. 15.95 (0-935296-81-6); pap. 10.95 (0-935296-82-4) Sheep Meadow.

***Window & Dome Technologies & Materials V.** Ed. by Randal W. Tustison. 34p. 1997. pap. 69.00 (0-8194-2475-7) SPIE.

Window & the Garden: The Modernist Fictions of Ramon Perez de Ayala. John J. Macklin. LC 87-62378. 206p. 1988. pap. 30.00 (0-89295-053-6) Society Sp & Sp-Am.

Window At the White Cat. Mary R. Rinehart. 1990. mass mkt. 3.99 (0-8217-4246-9, Zebra Kensgtn) Kensgtn Pub Corp.

Window at the White Cat. Mary R. Rinehart. 24.95 (0-8488-0316-7) Amereon Ltd.

Window at the White Cat. Mary R. Rinehart. 1992. reprint ed. lib. bdg. 19.95 (0-89968-274-X, Lghtyr Pr) Buccaneer Bks.

***Window at the White House.** Mary R. Rinehart. 1997. mass mkt. 5.99 (0-8217-5794-6) Kensgtn Pub Corp.

Window Back: Photography in a Whaling Port. 2nd ed. Nicholas Whitman. Ed. by Joseph D. Thomas. LC 93-86989. (Illus.). 176p. 1997. reprint ed. 49.95 (0-932027-16-4); reprint ed. pap. 29.95 (0-932027-18-0) Spinner Pubns.

Window Base Primer. Claire Arias & Herald Sawdy. (Trainers' Signature Ser.). 399p. 1992. pap. 29.95 (1-880663-39-2) Ellipsys Intl.

Window Book. Lesley Diamond. 1996. 7.99 (0-517-15957-0) Random Hse Value.

***Window Box Book.** Karen Fausch. (Illus.). 96p. (Orig.). (J). (gr. k-8). 1997. pap. 16.95 (0-9641262-3-0) Little Bkrm.

Window Box Book. Anne M. Halpin. (Illus.). 96p. 1989. 16. 00 (0-671-67965-1) S&S Trade.

***Window Boxes.** (Taylor's Weekend Gardening Guide Ser.). 1997. write for info. (0-614-27235-1) HM.

***Window Boxes.** Stephanie Donaldson. (Illus.). 96p. 1997. 16.95 (1-85967-339-2, Lorenz Bks) Anness Pub.

Window Boxes. Carol Spier. 72p. 1996. pap. text ed. 12.95 (1-56799-269-2, Friedman-Fairfax) M Friedman Pub Grp Inc.

Window Cleaner. Jack Rudman. (Career Examination Ser.: C-893). 1994. pap. 19.95 (0-8373-0893-3) Nat Learn.

Window Clerk (USPS) Jack Rudman. (Career Examination Ser.: C-3314). 1994. pap. 23.95 (0-8373-3314-8) Nat Learn.

Window Covering Basic Training Manual. Carolyn L. Defever. 1992. pap. 12.95 (0-9626117-4-3) Paisley TX.

***Window Covering Basics: A Complete Guide to Creative Window Decorating.** 6th ed. Carolyn L. DeFever. LC 97-67580. (Illus.). 112p. 1998. pap. 14.00 (1-890788-00-7) Paisley TX.

Window Covering Basics: How to Achieve Custom Looks with Ready-Made Products. Carolyn L. DeFever. LC 94-69226. (Illus.). 96p. (Orig.). 1996. pap. text ed. 9.95 (0-9626117-8-6) Paisley TX.

Window Covering Basics: How to Achieve Custom Looks with Ready-Made Products. 3rd ed. Carolyn L. DeFever. LC 91-90553. (Illus.). 80p. (Orig.). 1992. pap. 9.95 (0-9626117-3-5) Paisley TX.

Window Covering Basics: How to Achieve Custom Looks with Ready-Made Products. 4th ed. Carolyn L. DeFever. LC 92-85371. (Illus.). 80p. (Orig.). 1994. pap. 9.95 (0-9626117-5-1) Paisley TX.

Window Displays in Milan. (Illus.). 260p. 1996. 59.95 (88-7685-074-0, Pub. by LArchivoto IT) Bks Nippan.

Window Dressing: New Outlooks on Life - 25 Stylish No-Sew Ideas. Stewart Walton & Sally Walton. (Interior Focus Ser.). (Illus.). 96p. 1996. 12.95 (1-85967-113-6, Lorenz Bks) Anness Pub.

Window for New York. Paul Ramsey. 1968. pap. 10.00 (0-912136-01-4) Twowindows Pr.

***Window Garden.** Patricia Wittmann. (J). Date not set. 14. 95 (0-399-22328-2) Putnam Pub Group.

Window in Air. Ralph J. Mills, Jr. 88p. (Orig.). 1993. pap. 9.95 (1-55921-073-7, Asphodel Pr) Moyer Bell.

Window in Art. Carla Gottlieb. LC 77-86219. 512p. 1981. 60.00 (0-913870-40-4) Abaris Bks.

Window in the Bosom: The Letters of Alexander Pope. James A. Winn. LC 76-58361. 247p. (C). 1977. lib. bdg. 35.00 (0-208-01646-5, Archon Bks) Shoe String.

Window in the Rock. Eugene P. Petersen. LC 93-7109. 1993. 22.50 (0-87770-515-1); pap. 14.95 (0-87770-522-4) Ye Galleon.

***Window in the Sky.** unabridged ed. J. Glenn Evans. Ed. by Kay Stewart. LC 96-92360. (Illus.). 200p. (Orig.). 1996. pap. 11.95 (1-877882-20-8) SCW Pubns.

Window in Thrums. James M. Barrie. 1896. 59.00 (0-403-00118-8) Scholarly.

Window in Thrums. James M. Barrie. (BCL1-PR English Literature Ser.). 272p. 1992. reprint ed. lib. bdg. 79.00 (0-7812-7431-1) Rprt Serv.

Window in Time. Carolyn Lampman. 416p. 1995. mass mkt. 4.50 (0-06-108171-X, Harp PBks) HarpC.

Window in Time. Tom White. LC 91-14479. 5.00 (0-88264-301-0) Living Sacrifice Bks.

Window into History: Family Memory in Children's Literature. Eleanor K. MacDonald. LC 95-40621. 248p. 1995. pap. 27.50 (0-89774-879-4) Oryx Pr.

Window into Yesterday. Irene Keesee. LC 94-72132. (Illus.). 250p. (Orig.). 1994. pap. 14.95 (0-938041-22-3) Arc Pr AR.

Window Magic. Donna Schulze & Suzanne Cooper. (Illus.). 48p. (Orig.). 1986. pap. 7.50 (0-940353-04-0, VA 260-571) Papillon Texas.

Window of Eternity. Edgar Biamonte. LC 83-9944. 145p. 1984. 21.95 (0-87949-230-9) Ashley Bks.

Window of Memory: The Literary Career of Thomas Wolfe. Richard S. Kennedy. LC 62-16110. 477p. 1962. reprint ed. pap. 136.00 (0-7837-9893-8, 2060619) Bks Demand.

Window of Opportunity: Interviewing by the Perinatal Nurse. Mary L. Moore & Susan R. Givens. Ed. by Karla Damus & Margaret C. Freda. LC 94-39542. 1994. write for info. (0-86525-063-4) March of Dimes.

Window of Opportunity in the U. S. A. The Story of My Life. Alex Barazandeh. 230p. 1994. 20.00 (0-9640364-0-1) A Barazandeh.

***Window of Sky.** large type ed. Geoffrey Morgan. (Dales Large Print Ser.). 208p. 1996. pap. 17.99 (1-85389-635-7, Dales) Ulverscroft.

Window of the Soul - Chinese Edition. Moody Institute of Science Staff. Tr. by CRM Staff. 15p. (CHI.). 1983. 0.40 (1-56582-058-4) Christ Renew Min.

Window of Time. Audrey O. Leighton. (Illus.). 32p. (J). 1995. 15.95 (0-9636335-1-1) Nadja Pub.

Window of Time. Karen Weinburg. LC 90-20856. (WM Kids Ser.). (Illus.). 166p. (J). (gr. 2-4). 1991. pap. 9.95 (0-942597-18-4) White Mane Pub.

Window on a Catholic Parish: Granard, County Longford 1933-1968 (The Pastorate of Reverend Denis O'Kane) Frank Kelly. 64p. 1996. pap. 9.95 (0-7165-2594-1, Pub. by Irish Acad Pr IE) Intl Spec Bk.

Window on Eternity: The Life & Poetry of Jane Hess Merchant. Sarah Oftedal. LC 82-16276. (Abingdon Classics Ser.). 336p. 1992. pap. 5.95 (0-687-45602-9) Abingdon.

Window on Goa. Maurice Hall. 1995. pap. text ed. 39.95 (1-870948-98-X, Pub. by Quiller Pr UK) St Mut.

Window on Goa: A History & Guide. Maurice Hall. 1992. 29.95 (1-870948-71-8, Pub. by Quiller Pr UK) St Mut.

Window on Main Street: Life above the Corner Drug. Virgil Lagomarcino. (Illus.). 136p. 1994. pap. 10.95 (0-8138-2949-6) Iowa St U Pr.

Window on My World. Robert E. Conner. 1995. 8.95 (0-533-11462-4) Vantage.

Window on Our World: Plimpton Papers. Ed. by Pauline A. Plimpton. (Illus.). 314p. 1989. 17.95 (0-9621510-0-9) British Amer Pub.

Window on Poland. Ed. by R. Gibbons. 128p. 1983. pap. 3.95 (0-317-36708-0) Kosciuszko.

Window on the Atlantic: The Rise & Fall of Santa Elena South Carolina's Spanish City. Lawrence S. Rowland. Ed. by Judith M. Brimelow. (Illus.). 32p. 1990. pap. 5.00 (1-880067-03-X) SC Dept of Arch & Hist.

Window on the Black Sea: Bulgarian Poetry in Translation. 2nd ed. Ed. by Richard Harteis & William Meredith. Tr. by Stanley Kunitz et al. from BUL. (Poetry Ser.). 184p. 1992. pap. 14.95 (0-88748-141-8) Carnegie-Mellon.

Window on the Prairie: An Artist's Perspective. Georgia Tyler. LC 81-204579. (Illus.). 80p. 1981. 27.95 (0-9607960-0-2) Feather Pr.

Window on the Square. Phyllis A. Whitney. 23.95 (0-8488-0085-0) Amereon Ltd.

Window on the Square. Phyllis A. Whitney. 352p. 1994. mass mkt. 4.99 (0-06-100270-4, Harp PBks) HarpC.

Window on the West: The Collectors' El Palacio. Illus. by Christopher Beisel. 200p. (Orig.). 1989. pap. 19.95 (0-9623304-0-X) MNMF.

Window on the Word. Andrew Kuyvenhoven. (How to Read the Bible Ser.). 1995. student ed. 3.45 (1-56212-096-4) CRC Pubns.

Window on the World: Faces, Places & Plain Talk from 32 Countries. Allen H. Neuharth. (Illus.). 256p. 1988. write for info. (0-944347-16-9) USA Today Bks.

Window on Today. Joan Hohl. 192p. 1994. reprint ed. mass mkt., pap. text ed. 3.99 (0-8439-3653-3) Dorchester Pub Co.

Window on Tomorrow. L. Goligher. 6.99 (1-85792-080-5, Pub. by Christian Focus UK) Spring Arbor Dist.

Window on Tomorrow. Joan Hohl. 192p. 1994. reprint ed. mass mkt., pap. text ed. 3.99 (0-8439-3677-0) Dorchester Pub Co.

An Asterisk (*) at the beginning of an entry indicates that the title is appearing in BIP for the first time.

Window on Williamsburg. John J. Walklet, Jr. et al. LC 82-23596. (Illus.). 80p. (FRE.). 1983. pap. 12.95 (0-87935-073-3); pap. 12.95 (0-87935-101-2); pap. 12.95 (0-87935-074-1); pap. 12.95 (0-87935-100-4) Colonial Williamsburg.

***Window on Williamsburg.** John J. Walklet, Jr. et al. (Illus.). 80p. (ITA.). Date not set. pap. 10.95 (0-87935-170-5) Colonial Williamsburg.

***Window on Williamsburg.** John J. Walklet, Jr. et al. (Illus.). 80p. (RUS.). Date not set. pap. 10.95 (0-87935-171-3) Colonial Williamsburg.

Window on Williamsburg. rev. ed. John J. Walklet, Jr. et al. LC 66-23534. (Illus.). 80p. 1983. pap. 12.95 (0-87935-071-7) Colonial Williamsburg.

Window on Williamsburg. 2nd rev. ed. John J. Walklet, Jr. et al. LC 66-23534. (Illus.). 80p. 1983. 14.95 (0-87935-072-5) Colonial Williamsburg.

Window on Yesterday. Joan Hohl. 192p. 1994. reprint ed. mass mkt., pap. text ed. 3.99 (0-8439-3620-7) Dorchester Pub Co.

Window onto Annapurna. large type ed. Joy Stephens. (Illus.). 336p. 1992. 27.99 (0-7089-8633-1, Trail West Pubs) Ulverscroft.

Window Seat: An Aerial Perspective of America's Forests with General Enlightenment for Civic Leaders. Frank H. Armstrong & Marguerite Oates. LC 92-138582. 163p. (Orig.). 1992. pap. 7.00 (0-9632448-0-9) Bull Run VT.

Window Seat Politics. Mary F. White. 280p. (Orig.). 1992. pap. 7.95 (0-922510-08-3) Lucky Bks.

Window Shopping: Cinema & the Postmodern. Anne Friedberg. LC 92-30917. 1993. 28.00 (0-520-07916-7) U CA Pr.

Window Shopping: Cinema & the Postmodern. Anne Friedberg. 1994. pap. 14.00 (0-520-08924-3) U CA Pr.

***Window Sources Microsoft Excel 97 for Windows Superguide.** Bruce Halberg. 1997. pap. 39.99 (0-614-28488-0, Ziff-Davis Pr) Que.

Window System: A User's Guide. 2nd ed. Niall Mansfield. (C). 1995. pap. text ed. 10.00 (0-201-54438-5) Addison-Wesley.

Window System Programming with OSF-Motif. 2nd ed. Douglas A. Young. 656p. 1994. pap. text ed. 51.00 (0-13-123803-5) P-H.

Window Systems: Programming & Applications with Xt. Douglas A. Young. 528p. 1989. 29.95 (0-13-972167-3) P-H.

Window to Australia. Ed. by Fraeme K. Smith. (Illus.). (C). 1987. 35.00 (0-7300-0498-8, Pub. by Deakin Univ AT) St Mut.

Window to Criticism: Shakespeare's Sonnets & Modern Poetics. Murray Krieger. LC 63-18645. 236p. reprint ed. pap. 67.30 (0-317-27580-1, 2014873) Bks Demand.

Window to Memory, Vol. I. Mary L. Friesz. (Illus.). (Orig.). 1996. per., pap. 9.95 (0-9650788-4-1) Mustard Seed CA.

Window to My Heart. Joy Hawkins. 123p. 1991. mass mkt. 3.95 (0-8423-7977-0) Tyndale.

Window to My Soul. Mike Bowen. (C). 1990. 40.00 (0-7316-0491-1, Pub. by Pascoe Pub AT) St Mut.

Window to My Soul, Vol. I. Christene Bolte-Luthey. LC 89-90753. (Illus.). 120p. 1989. lib. bdg. 12.95 (0-317-93861-4) Luthey Assocs.

***Window to the Divine: A Study of Christian Creation Theology.** Zachary Hayes. LC 97-6526. 1997. write for info. (0-8199-0979-3) Franciscan Pr.

Window to the East. Abdur R. Tabassum. 88p. (C). 1986. 50.00 (81-7002-007-7, Pub. by Himalayan Bks II) St Mut.

Window to the Past. Arthur C. Butt. 1994. 16.95 (0-533-11025-4) Vantage.

Window to the Past: A Photographic Panorama of Early Church History & Doctrine & Covenants. Richard N. Holzapfel & T. Jeffery Cottle. 1993. 15.95 (0-88494-866-8) Bookcraft Inc.

Window to the Past: The Washington State Historical Society's First Century. John McClelland, Jr. LC 92-13738. 1993. pap. 19.00 (0-917048-69-5) Wash St Hist Soc.

***Window Treatments.** Cy DeCosse Incorporated Staff. LC 96-41124. (Singer Sewing Reference Library). (Illus.). 128p. 1996. 18.95 (0-86573-407-0) Cowles Creative.

***Window Treatments.** Cy DeCosse Incorporated Staff. LC 96-41124. (Singer Sewing Reference Library). (Illus.). 128p. 1996. pap. 16.95 (0-86573-408-9) Cowles Creative.

Window Treatments. Karla J. Nielson. (Illus.). 368p. 1989. text ed. 62.95 (0-442-26809-2) Van Nos Reinhold.

Window Units. James H. Doolin. 39p. 1982. pap. 15.00 (0-914626-07-8) Doolco Inc.

Window Washer. Jack Rudman. (Career Examination Ser.: C-1535). 1994. pap. 19.95 (0-8373-1535-2) Nat Learn.

Window Washer: At Work above the Clouds. Keith Greenberg. Ed. by Bruce Glassman. LC 94-41701. (Risky Business Ser.). (Illus.). 32p. (J). (gr. 2-5). 1995. lib. bdg. 14.95 (1-56711-154-8) Blackbirch.

Window Zips: Zippered Vinyl Pockets in Memory Pillows. Marilyn Robinson. Ed. by Sharon Holmes. (Illus.). 28p. 1992. pap. 8.95 (0-9622477-9-0) Pssblts Denver.

Window 95 Step-by-Step. Bill Holtsnider. LC 97-23802. (Illus.). 160p. (Orig.). 1997. pap. text ed. 17.95 (1-57426-008-1) Computer Lit Pr.

Windowbox Gardening. David Joyce. LC 93-4721. (Illus.). 96p. 1993. 22.95 (1-56440-292-4) Globe Pequot.

Windowlight. Ann Nietzke. LC 95-50724. 200p. 1996. 12.00 (1-56947-060-X) Soho Press.

Windows. H. Terry Braunstein. 32p. 1982. 25.00 (0-942868-01-3) W Blake Pr.

Windows. Don Cassel. (Source 1 Ser.). pap. write for info. (0-13-834334-9) P-H.

Windows. Robert Creeley. LC 89-13345. 160p. 1990. 19.95 (0-8112-1122-3); pap. 10.95 (0-8112-1123-1, NDP687) New Directions.

Windows. Jennifer James. LC 87-24881. 144p. 1991. pap. 10.00 (1-55704-004-4) Newmarket.

Windows. Junior League of Rhode Island Staff. 1995. 19.95 (0-9648450-0-8) Jr Leag Rhode Isld.

Windows. Joseph A. Labadie. (Men & Movements in the History & Philosophy of Anarchism Ser.). 1979. lib. bdg. 250.00 (0-87700-312-2) Revisionist Pr.

Windows. Jay Meek. LC 93-73472. (Poetry Ser.). 80p. (Orig.). 1994. pap. 11.95 (0-88748-171-X) Carnegie-Mellon.

Windows. Joseph Murphy. 1985. pap. 23.95 (0-8384-1302-1) Heinle & Heinle.

Windows. Ian Murray-Clark. 1989. 1.98 (0-945603-05-3) Dinnerman Bks.

Windows. Robert L. Whitworth. LC 88-62245. 144p. 1988. pap. 6.95 (0-89221-164-4) New Leaf.

Windows: A Prayer Journal. Andrew M. Greeley. 228p. 1995. pap. 14.95 (0-8245-1517-X) Crossroad NY.

Windows: Advanced Programming & Design. Peter Morris. (Illus.). 900p. 1993. pap. 49.95 (0-7506-0636-3) Buttrwrth-Heinemann.

Windows: Exploring Human Values Through Reading & Writing. Jeff Rackham & Olivia Bertagnolli. LC 92-11049. (C). 1993. 30.50 (0-06-043808-8) Addson-Wesley Educ.

Windows: Healing & Helping Through Loss. Michael H. Popkin & Mary J. Hannaford. (Illus.). 144p. 1992. pap. text ed. 11.95 (0-9618020-9-X) Active Parenting.

Windows: Healing & Helping Through Loss: Leader's Guide. Michael H. Popkin & Mary J. Hannaford. (Illus.). 96p. 1992. spiral bd. 18.95 (1-880283-00-X) Active Parenting.

Windows: Healing & Helping Through Loss: When You Have Lost. Michael H. Popkin & Mary J. Hannaford. 16p. (Orig.). 1992. pap. text ed. 1.50 (1-880283-01-8) Active Parenting.

Windows: Healing & Helping Through Loss: When You Want to Help. Michael H. Popkin & Mary J. Hannaford. 16p. (Orig.). 1992. pap. text ed. 1.50 (1-880283-02-6) Active Parenting.

Windows: Reflections of Taste. Brenau College Alumnae Association Staff. Ed. & Illus. by Brenau College Staff. 352p. 1992. text ed. 18.95 (0-9631804-0-1) Brenau Coll Alum.

Windows: Research & Evaluation on a Distance Education Course. Herbert Altrichter et al. 177p. (C). 1991. pap. 68.00 (0-7300-1347-2, IDE806, Pub. by Deakin Univ AT) St Mut.

Windows: The Introductory Program. LC 93-11446. 1994. write for info. (0-02-802512-1) Glencoe.

Windows++ Writing Reusable Windows Code in C++ Paul DiLascia. LC 92-15872. 608p. 1992. pap. 32.95 (0-201-60891-X) Addison-Wesley.

Windows - Walls - Yard - Ways. Larry Eigner. Ed. by Robert Grenier. LC 93-46410. 196p. (Orig.). 1994. 25.00 (0-87685-921-X); pap. 13.00 (0-87685-920-1) Black Sparrow.

Windows - Walls - Yard - Ways, signed ed. deluxe ed. Larry Eigner. Ed. by Robert Grenier. LC 93-46410. 196p. (Orig.). 1994. 30.00 (0-87685-922-8) Black Sparrow.

Windows & Doors. (Fix-It-Yourself Ser.). (Illus.). 144p. 1987. 17.27 (0-8094-6216-8); lib. bdg. 23.27 (0-8094-6217-6) Time-Life.

Windows & Doors. Time-Life Books Editors. (Home Repair & Improvement Ser.). (Illus.). 128p. 1996. write for info. (0-7835-3902-9) Time-Life.

Windows & DOS File Formats. Tom Campbell. 1993. pap. write for info. (0-201-62241-6) Addison-Wesley.

***Windows & Errors Massages.** Ed. by Ron Petrusha. (Orig.). pap. write for info. (1-56592-356-1) OReilly & Assocs.

Windows & Mirrors. Al Montesi. LC 77-89821. 1977. 3.95 (0-918476-00-3) Cornerstone Pr.

Windows & MS-DOS, Windows 3.1 & 95: MS-DOS 5 & 6. J. Muir. 200p. 1995. pap. 59.95 (1-85805-124-X, Pub. by DP Publns UK) St Mut.

Windows & OS/2 Bitmapped Graphics. 2nd ed. Steve W. Rimmer. LC 96-19103. (Illus.). 512p. 1996. pap. text ed., pap. 38.95 incl. disk (0-07-911903-4) McGraw.

Windows & OS/2 Bitmapped Graphics. 2nd ed. Steve W. Rimmer. LC 96-19103. (Illus.). 512p. 1996. text ed. 49.95 incl. cd-rom (0-07-911902-6) McGraw.

Windows & PCs: A Complete Introduction. Glyn Moody. 320p. 1993. pap. 31.95 (0-7506-0956-7) Buttrwrth-Heinemann.

***Windows & Skylights.** FHB Editors. (Builder's Library). (Illus.). 112p. 1997. 24.95 (1-56158-208-5, 070336) Taunton.

Windows & Skylights: The Best of Fine Homebulding. Taunton Press Staff. LC 95-47082. (Best of Fine Homebuilding Ser.). (Illus.). 112p. (Orig.). 1996. pap. 14.95 (1-56158-127-5, 070265) Taunton.

Windows & Stones: Selected Poems. Tomas Transtromer. Tr. by May Swenson & Leif Sjoberg. LC 71-181400. (Pitt Poetry Ser.). 112p. reprint ed. pap. 32.00 (0-7837-2475-6, 2042629) Bks Demand.

Windows Animation Programming with C++ Michael J. Young. (Illus.). 350p. 1994. pap. text ed., pap. 39.95 incl. 3.5 hd (0-12-773750-2, AP Prof) Acad Pr.

Windows Animation Programming with C++ Michael J. Young. 1995. pap. text ed. 20.00 (0-12-784842-8) Acad Pr.

***Windows Annoyances.** David Karp. 1997. pap. text ed. 29.95 (1-56592-266-2) OReilly & Assocs.

Windows API Bible: The Definitive Programmer's Reference. James L. Conger. (Illus.). 1000p. (Orig.). 1992. pap. 39.95 (1-878739-15-8, Waite Grp Pr) Sams.

Windows Applications Design with Ole 2.0: For Windows & Windows Nt. Marshall Brain. 1995. pap. 50.00 (0-13-097817-5) P-H.

***Windows Architecture.** Bruce T. Prendergast. (MCSD Certification Ser.). 1997. 74.99 (0-7645-3123-9) IDG Bks.

Windows Are Portholes of Life. Lee Hollis. (Orig.). 1996. pap. write for info. (1-57553-139-9) Watermrk Pr.

***Windows Assembly Language & Systems Programming: 16-& 32-Bit Low Level Programming for Windows.** Barry Kauler. (Illus.). 400p. (Orig.). 1997. pap. 44.95 incl. disk (0-87930-474-X) R & D Books.

Windows Batch File Programming. Namir C. Shammas. 384p. 1992. pap. 32.95 (0-8306-4149-1, 4238, Windcrest) TAB Bks.

Windows Batch File Programming. 2nd ed. Namir C. Shammas. 1995. pap. text ed. 39.95 incl. disk (0-07-912048-2) McGraw.

Windows Bible Combo. Fred Davis. 1154p. 1994. 49.95 incl. cd-rom (1-56609-158-6) Peachpit Pr.

Windows Bit-Mapped Graphics. Steve W. Rimmer. 1993. text ed. 38.95 (0-07-052995-7) McGraw.

Windows Bitmapped Graphics. Steve W. Rimmer. (Illus.). 448p. 1992. 38.95 (0-8306-4207-2, 4265, Windcrest); pap. 26.95 (0-8306-4206-4, 4265, Windcrest) TAB Bks.

Windows Black Pentecostalism in Britain: Origins, Functions & Theology. Iain McRobert. 352p. 1993. pap. 40.00 (0-86153-154-X, Pub. by St Andrew UK) St Mut.

Windows by PicTorial. Dennis P. Curtin. LC 93-23110. (PicTorial Ser.). 320p. (C). 1993. pap. text ed. 36.80 (0-13-026551-9) P-H.

***Windows CE Companion.** Chris Deherrara. 1997. 29.99 (0-7897-1306-3) Macmillan.

***Windows CE Developers Handbook.** Ben Ezzell. 1997. pap. text ed. 49.99 incl. cd-rom (0-7821-2054-7) Sybex.

***Windows CE for Dummies.** Jinjer Simon. 1997. pap. 19.99 (0-7645-0260-3) IDG Bks.

***Windows CE Programming: Developing Applications for the HPC.** Jeff Baker. 400p. 1997. 44.99 (1-57870-005-1) Mac Comp Pub.

***Windows CE Programming for Dummies.** 1997. pap. 29.99 (0-7645-0304-9) IDG Bks.

Windows Church in Black & White. John Wilkinson. 272p. 1993. pap. 36.00 (0-86153-155-8, Pub. by St Andrew UK) St Mut.

Windows Configuration Handbook. John Woram. 1122p. 1993. pap. 34.00 (0-679-79113-2) Random.

Windows Desktop Sourcebook. Joseph Kasmer. 1993. pap. 29.95 (1-55828-260-2) MIS Press.

Windows Desktop Utilities. Jeff Prosise. (Techniques & Utilities Ser.). 480p. 1994. pap. 34.95 incl. disk (1-56276-098-X, Ziff-Davis Pr) Que.

Windows Development on Netware. Lori Gauthier. 1994. pap. 34.95 incl. disk (0-8306-4559-4, Windcrest) TAB Bks.

Windows Facing East. Caroline Finkelstein. LC 85-27580. 64p. 1986. 14.00 (0-937872-30-X); pap. 7.00 (0-937872-31-8) Dragon Gate.

Windows Flew Open. Marjorie Welish. (Burning Deck Poetry Ser.). 80p. (Orig.). 1991. pap. 8.00 (0-930901-74-6) Burning Deck.

Windows Flew Open. limited ed. Marjorie Welish. (Burning Deck Poetry Ser.). 80p. (Orig.). 1991. Signed. pap. 15.00 (0-930901-75-4) Burning Deck.

Windows for Beginners. Richard Dungworth. (Computer Guides Ser.). (Illus.). 48p. (YA). (gr. 4 up). 1996. pap. 7.95 (0-7460-2335-9, Usborne) EDC.

Windows for Beginners. Richard Dungworth. (Computer Guides Ser.). (Illus.). 48p. (YA). (gr. 4 up). 1996. lib. bdg. 15.95 (0-88110-852-9, Usborne) EDC.

***Windows for Busy People.** Ron Mansfield. (Illus.). 384p. (Orig.). 1998. pap. 24.99 (0-07-882398-6, Oracle Press) Osborne-McGraw.

Windows for Dummies. Andy Rathbone. (Illus.). 352p. 1993. pap. 16.95 (1-878058-61-4) IDG Bks.

Windows for Teens. Brittanney Trebnik. 1993. pap. 14.95 (1-55958-413-0) Prima Pub.

Windows for the Crown Prince: Akihito of Japan. Elizabeth G. Vining. (Illus.). 320p. 1990. pap. 14.95 (0-8048-1604-2) C E Tuttle.

Windows for Winners: The Tips & Tricks You Need to Get the Power & Performance You Want. Michael Scanlon. Ed. by Kelly Scanlon. (Byte*Wise Ser.). (Illus.). 192p. (Orig.). 1995. spiral bd., pap. 19.95 (1-57294-000-X) SkillPath Pubns.

Windows for Workgroups. 1993. 29.95 (1-56877-095-2) Catapult WA.

Windows for Workgroups. 1993. teacher ed. 49.95 (1-56877-096-0) Catapult WA.

Windows for Workgroups. Karl Schwartz. 1993. pap. 12.00 (1-56243-113-7, WG-18) DDC Pub.

Windows from My Past. Marie R. Herrera. (Orig.). 1996. pap. write for info. (1-57553-228-X) Watermrk Pr.

Windows Game Sdk. Developers Guide. Martyn Deobald. 1996. pap. text ed. 39.99 incl. cd-rom (1-883577-84-5) Coriolis Grp.

Windows Games Adventure Set. Doe Entertainment Staff. 1995. pap. 39.99 (1-883577-43-8) Coriolis Grp.

Windows Gizmos. Brian Livingston & Galen Gruman. (Illus.). 624p. 1992. pap. 39.95 incl. 5.25 hd (1-878058-66-5) IDG Bks.

Windows Graphics & Prepass. Steve W. Rimmer. 1993. pap. write for info. (0-201-62205-X) Addison-Wesley.

Windows Graphics Programming with Borland C Plus Plus. 2nd ed. Loren Heiny. 560p. 1994. pap. text ed. 32.95 (0-471-30930-3) Wiley.

Windows Handbook. Faith M. Ozluturk. (Illus.). 125p. (Orig.). Date not set. pap. 9.95 (1-55852-182-8) Natl Pr Pubns.

Windows Hothouse: Creating Artificial Life with Visual C. Mark Clarkson. LC 93-40077. 1994. pap. 34.95 (0-201-62669-1) Addison-Wesley.

Windows Hothouse: Creative Artificial Life with Visual C Plus Plus. Mark Clarkson. 1994. write for info. (0-318-72316-6) Addison-Wesley.

Windows in a Day. Weber Knox. (C). 1993. pap. 29.95 (0-929704-24-X) Weber Systems.

Windows in a Hurry. Dawn Groves. LC 94-41155. 160p. 1994. student ed., spiral bd. 12.95 (0-938661-82-5) Franklin Beedle.

Windows Interactive Graphics Programming. Lee Adams. 1994. pap. 39.95 incl. disk (0-8306-3820-2, Windcrest) TAB Bks.

Windows Internals: The Design & Implementation of the Windows Operating System. Matt Pietrek. LC 92-46133. 1993. pap. 34.95 (0-201-62217-3) Addison-Wesley.

Windows Internet Tour Guide: Cruising the Internet the Easy Way. 2nd ed. Michael Fraase & Phil James. (Illus.). 424p. 1995. 29.95 (1-56604-174-0) Ventana Communs.

Windows into China. John Parker. 1978. 3.00 (0-89073-050-4) Boston Public Lib.

Windows into Literacy: Assessing Learners K-Eight. Lynn K. Rhodes & Nancy Shanklin. LC 92-25297. 456p. (J). 1993. pap. text ed. 32.50 (0-435-08757-6, 08757) Heinemann.

***Windows into the A. D. D. Mind: Understanding & Treating Attention Deficit Disorder.** Daniel G. Amen. 1996. 39.95 (1-886544-00-X) ISMCHMA.

Windows into the A.D.D. Mind: Understanding & Treating Attention Deficit Disorders, Childhood Through Adulthood. Daniel G. Amen. 238p. 1996. 39.95 (1-886554-00-5) MindWrks.

***Windows into the Add Mind: Understanding & Treating Attention Deficit Disorders in the Everyday Lives of Children, Adolescents & Teenagers.** rev. ed. Daniel G. Amen. (Illus.). 238p. 1997. pap. 29.95 (1-886554-08-0) MindWrks.

***Windows into the Infinite: A Guide to the Hindu Scriptures.** Barbara Powell. 488p. (Orig.). 1997. pap. 19.95 (0-87573-072-8) Jain Pub Co.

Windows into the Infinite: A Guide to the Hindu Scriptures. Barbara J. Powell. (Illus.). 432p. (Orig.). (C). 1996. text ed. 30.00 (0-87573-071-X) Jain Pub Co.

Windows into the Lectionary: Seasonal Anecdotes for Preaching & Teaching. Donald L. Deffner. LC 96-42166. 160p. (Orig.). 1996. pap. 14.95 (0-89390-393-0) Resource Pubns.

Windows Module: Windows Operating System. G. V. Krishnan. (CAD/CAM Ser.). 1997. pap. 15.00 (0-8273-7051-2) Delmar.

Windows Multi-DBMS Programming: Using C Plus Plus, Visual BASIC, ODBC & Tools for DBMS Projects. Ken North. LC 92-27650. 512p. 1995. pap. text ed. 49.95 incl. disk (0-471-01675-6); Incl. CD-ROM. pap. text ed. 59.95 incl. cd-rom (0-471-01676-4) Wiley.

Windows Net X Server Secrets. Valda Hilley. 1996. pap. 49.99 (1-56884-717-3) IDG Bks.

Windows Networking & Connectivity Guide: How to Survive in a World of Windows, Netware, & DOS. Stephen R. Davis. LC 92-28198. 1992. pap. 32.95 (0-201-58133-7) Addison-Wesley.

Windows 95 Client/Server Developer's Guide. Douglas Reilly. 560p. 1996. pap. 39.95 incl. disk (0-201-40762-0) Addison-Wesley.

***Windows 95 at Work.** Ron Person. 700p. 1997. 29.99 (0-7897-1190-7) Que.

***Windows 95 in a Nutshell.** Gookin. Ed. by Tim O'Reilly. (Nutshell Ser.). (Illus.). 300p. (Orig.). 1997. pap. text ed. write for info. (1-56592-316-2) OReilly & Assocs.

Windows 95 Pocket Book. Ian R. Sinclair. 400p. 1995. 26.95 (0-7506-2126-5, Focal) Buttrwrth-Heinemann.

***Windows NT.** Alan R. Carter. (MCSE Certification Ser.). 1997. 99.99 (0-7645-3087-9) IDG Bks.

Windows NT. Karl Schwartz. 1993. pap. 12.00 (1-56243-114-5, NT-18) DDC Pub.

Windows NT: A Developer's Guide. Kevin Goodman. 1994. pap. 39.95 incl. disk (1-55851-306-X, M&T Books) H Holt & Co.

Windows NT: A Practical Guide. Arthur Tennick. (Illus.). 248p. 1994. pap. 31.95 (0-7506-0852-8) Buttrwrth-Heinemann.

Windows NT: Making the Move. Jim Forney. (Illus.). 464p. 1993. pap. 24.95 (0-8306-4391-5, Windcrest) TAB Bks.

Windows NT Administration: Single Systems to Heterogeneous Networks. Marshall Brain. 304p. 1994. pap. text ed. 47.00 (0-13-176694-5) P-H.

***Windows NT Administrators Handbook.** Mark Graham & Becky Campbell. 1997. 24.99 (1-56205-802-9) Macmillan.

Windows NT Advanced Server: Lan Manager for NT. Kenneth L. Spencer. 448p. 1995. pap. text ed. 48.95 (0-13-107046-0) P-H.

***Windows NT & HP-UX System Administrator's "How To" Book.** Marty Poniatowski. 1997. pap. 33.00 (0-614-28520-8) P-H.

***Windows NT & HP-UX System Administrator's How to Book.** Marty Poniatowski. 576p. (C). 1997. pap. text ed. 44.95 (0-13-861709-0) P-H.

***Windows NT & UNIX Integration Guide.** David Gunter et al. (Windows NT Professional Library). (Illus.). 560p. (Orig.). 1997. pap. 49.99 (0-07-882395-1, Oracle Press) Osborne-McGraw.

***Windows NT & Web Site Resource Library, 6 bks., 3 CDs.** 3500p. 1997. pap. 129.99 incl. cd-rom (0-614-28484-8, Sams Sftwre) MCP SW Interactive.

***Windows NT Anti Virus User's Guide, Vol. 1.** Baruch Shapira. (Illus.). 58p. (Orig.). (C). 1996. 169.95 (1-877858-63-3, NTAV) Amer Focus Pub.

W

***Windows NT Backup & Recovery Guide.** John R. McMains. (Windows NT Professional Library). (Illus.). 540p. (Orig.). 1997. pap. 39.99 (*0-07-882363-3*, Oracle Press) Osborne-McGraw.

Windows NT Basics. Technical East Corporation Staff. 1994. pap. 19.95 (*0-13-176579-5*) P-H.

Windows NT Configuration & Troubleshooting. Eric Schall et al. 1600p. 1997. 59.99 (*0-672-30941-6*) Mac Comp Pub.

***Windows NT Database Developer's Guide.** Michael Otey & Paul Conte. (Windows NT Professional Library). (Illus.). 656p. (Orig.). 1997. pap. 44.99 (*0-07-882384-6*, Oracle Press) Osborne-McGraw.

***Windows NT Developers Handbook.** Ben Ezzell. 1997. pap. text ed. 54.99 incl. cd-rom (*0-7821-1945-X*) Sybex.

Windows NT Device Driver Book: A Guide for Programmers. Art Baker. LC 96-22449. 1996. pap. 44. 95 incl. disk (*0-13-184474-1*) P-H.

***Windows NT File System Internals.** Rajeev Nagar. (Illus.). (Orig.). 1997. pap. 34.95 (*1-56592-249-2*) OReilly & Assocs.

Windows NT for Busy People. Stephen Nelson. 1996. pap. text ed. 22.95 (*0-07-882254-8*) Osborne-McGraw.

Windows NT for Dummies. Andy Rathbone. 1996. pap. 19. 99 (*1-56884-613-4*) IDG Bks.

Windows NT for OpenVMS Professionals. David W. Solomon. 250p. 1996. pap. 39.95 (*1-55558-122-6*, Digital DEC) Buttrwrth-Heinemann.

Windows NT for the Technical Professional. Louis Columbus & Nik Simpson. (Illus.). 400p. 1995. pap. 39. 95 (*1-56690-064-6*, 1700, OnWord Pr) High Mtn.

***Windows NT 4.0 Quick Reference.** Que Development Group Staff. 1997. pap. text ed. 19.99 (*0-7897-1299-7*) Que.

***Windows NT 4 Answers! Certified Tech Support.** Barrie Sosinsky. (Illus.). 448p. (Orig.). 1997. pap. 24.99 (*0-07-882381-1*, Oracle Press) Osborne-McGraw.

Windows NT Guide to the Web Vol. VI: Covering Browsers, Servers, & Related Software. Richard Raucci. (Illus.). 130p. 1997. pap. 24.95 (*0-387-94792-2*) Spr-Verlag.

***Windows NT Installation Configuration & Customizing.** 1997. 39.99 (*0-672-30989-0*) Macmillan.

***Windows NT Internals Revealed.** Mark Russinovich & Bryce H. Cogswell. 512p. (Orig.). 1997. pap. write for info. (*0-614-26346-8*) IDG Bks.

***Windows NT Internals Revealed.** Mark Russinovich. 1997. pap. 49.99 (*0-7645-8032-9*) IDG Bks.

***Windows NT Internet & Intranet Development.** 1997. 39. 99 (*0-672-30990-4*) Macmillan.

***Windows NT Internet E-Mail Administrator's Bible.** Lawrence E. Hughes. 800p. (Orig.). 1997. pap. write for info. (*0-614-26358-1*) IDG Bks.

***Windows NT Internet Server.** Kevin Reichard. 1996. 39. 95 (*0-614-20300-7*, M&T Books) H Holt & Co.

Windows NT Internet Server. Kevin Reichard. LC 96-44635. 512p. 1996. pap. 39.95 incl. cd-rom (*1-55851-472-4*, M&T Books) H Holt & Co.

***Windows NT Mojo.** Ventana Publishing Staff. 1997. pap. text ed. 49.99 (*1-56604-669-6*) Ventana Communs.

***Windows NT Netware for Administrators.** R. B. Thompson. Ed. by Robert Denn. (Orig.). 1997. pap. write for info. (*1-56592-280-8*) OReilly & Assocs.

Windows NT Network Programming: How to Survive in a 32-Bit Networking World. Ralph Davis. 576p. 1994. pap. 39.95 incl. disk (*0-201-62278-5*) Addison-Wesley.

Windows NT Networking for Dummies. 1996. pap. 24.99 (*0-7645-0015-5*) IDG Bks.

Windows NT Power User's Toolkit. Mark Riordan. (Illus.). 448p. 1996. text ed., pap. text ed., pap. 49.95 incl. cd-rom (*0-07-912301-5*) McGraw.

Windows NT Programming: An Introduction Using C Plus Plus. Marshall Brain & Kelly Campbell. LC 93-5000. 592p. (C). 1993. pap. text ed. 59.00 (*0-13-097833-7*) P-H.

***Windows NT Programming from the Ground Up.** Herbert Schildt. 1997. pap. text ed. 34.99 (*0-07-882298-X*) Osborne-McGraw.

***Windows NT Programming in Practice: Practical Techniques from Master Programmers.** Ed. by Windows Developer's Journal Staff. (Illus.). 560p. (Orig.). 1997. pap. 49.95 incl. disk (*0-87930-472-3*) R & D Books.

Windows NT Registry Guide. Weiying Chen. LC 96-29753. (C). 1997. pap. text ed. 34.95 (*0-201-69473-5*) Addison-Wesley.

***Windows NT Registry Troubleshooting.** Rob Tidrow. LC 96-45467. 416p. 1996. 40.00 (*1-56205-660-3*) Mac Comp Pub.

Windows NT SECRETS. Brian Livingston. pap. 39.95 (*1-878058-71-1*) IDG Bks.

***Windows NT Security.** Robert Kane. 1997. 44.95 (*1-57870-006-X*) Sams.

***Windows NT Security.** Stephen A. Sutton. LC 96-47632. (C). 1997. pap. text ed. 29.95 (*0-201-41969-6*) Addison-Wesley.

***Windows NT Security.** 2nd ed. Tom Sheldon. (Windows NT Professional Library). (Illus.). 679p. 1997. pap. 44.99 (*0-07-882418-4*, Oracle Press) Osborne-McGraw.

***Windows NT Security: A Practical Guide to Securing Windows NT Servers & Workstations.** Charles B. Rutstein. (Illus.). 320p. 1997. pap. text ed. 34.95 (*0-07-057833-8*) McGraw.

***Windows NT Security: Programming Easy-to-Use Security Options.** Nik Okuntseff. (Illus.). 300p. (Orig.). 1997. pap. 39.95 incl. disk (*0-87930-473-1*) R & D Books.

Windows NT Security Handbook: A Strategic Blueprint for Protecting Your Network. Tom Sheldon. 512p. 1996. pap. text ed. 34.99 (*0-07-882240-8*) Osborne-McGraw.

***Windows NT Security Unleashed.** Robert Crisp. 700p. 1997. 49.99 (*0-672-31088-0*) Sams.

***Windows NT Server Concise.** Jerry Dixon & J. Scott Reeves. 400p. Date not set. pap. 19.99 (*1-56205-691-3*) New Riders Pub.

Windows NT Server Developer's Reference. Sams Development Team Staff. 800p. Date not set. 55.00 (*0-672-30980-7*) Mac Comp Pub.

Windows NT Server 4 Administrator's Guide. 848p. 1996. boxed 50.00 (*0-7615-0751-5*) Prima Pub.

Windows NT Server Professional Reference. Karanjit Siyan. 757p. 1995. pap. text ed. 55.00 incl. cd-rom (*1-56205-481-3*) New Riders Pub.

***Windows NT Server Professional Reference, 1.** 2nd ed. Karanjit Siyan. 1997. 64.99 (*1-56205-805-3*) New Riders Pub.

***Windows NT Server Professional Reference, 2.** Karanjit Siyan. 1997. 64.99 (*1-56205-804-5*) New Riders Pub.

Windows NT Server Resource Library. New Riders Development Group Staff. 450p. 1995. pap. 109.00 (*1-56205-551-8*) New Riders Pub.

***Windows NT Server Security Handbook.** Que Development Group Staff. 400p. 1997. 39.99 (*0-7897-1213-X*) Que.

Windows NT Server Survival Guide. 2nd ed. Rick Santangelo. 800p. 1997. 55.00 (*0-672-30971-8*) Mac Comp Pub.

***Windows NT Server Training Guide.** T. Foley. (Training Guide Ser.). (Illus.). 256p. 1997. pap. 54.95 incl. cd-rom (*0-12-261910-2*, AP Prof) Acad Pr.

***Windows NT Server 4.** Joel Millican. 1997. 64.99 (*1-56205-735-9*) New Riders Pub.

***Windows NT Server 4: No Experience Required.** Robert Cowart. 1997. pap. 29.99 (*0-614-28533-X*) Sybex.

***Windows NT Server 4: Security, Troubleshooting, Optimization.** Chris Goggans. 720p. 1996. pap. text ed. 49.99 (*1-56205-601-8*) New Riders Pub.

Windows NT Server 4 Professional Reference. 2nd ed. Karanjit Siyan. 1500p. 1996. 64.99 (*1-56205-659-X*) Mac Comp Pub.

***Windows NT Server 4 Resource Library.** New Riders Development Group Staff. 1996. 119.99 (*1-56205-694-8*) Mac Comp Pub.

***Windows NT Server 4 Unleashed: MCSE Edition.** Jason Garms. 1997. 65.00 (*0-672-31186-0*) Mac Comp Pub.

***Windows NT Server 4.0 Administrator's Desk Reference.** Que Development Group Staff. 1997. 75.00 (*0-7897-1271-7*) Que.

Windows NT Server 4.0 Administrators Guide. Robert Cowart. 1996. pap. 49.99 (*0-7645-8009-4*) IDG Bks.

***Windows Nt Server 4.0 Advanced Technical Reference.** John Enck. 1100p. 1997. 59.99 (*0-7897-1167-2*) Que.

***Windows NT Server 4.0 Exam Guide.** Jim Blakely. 700p. 1997. 99.99 (*0-7897-0990-2*) Mac Comp Pub.

***Windows NT Server 5: The System Administrator's Guide.** Joe Rudich. 1997. pap. text ed., pap. 49.95 incl. cd-rom (*0-07-913285-5*) McGraw.

***Windows NT SNMP.** James Murray. Ed. by Debby Russell. (Orig.). 1997. pap. write for info. (*1-56592-338-3*) OReilly & Assocs.

***Windows NT System in a Nutshell.** Eric Pearce. Ed. by Robert J. Denn. (Nutshell Handbook Ser.). (Illus.). (Orig.). 1997. pap. 19.95 (*1-56592-251-4*) OReilly & Assocs.

***Windows NT Technical Reference.** Ted Malone. 1200p. 1997. boxed 60.00 (*0-7615-1048-6*) Prima Pub.

***Windows NT Textbook: Extended Edition.** Stewart Venit. 612p. (Orig.). (C). Date not set. pap. text ed. 37.00 (*1-57676-003-0*) Scott Jones Pubng.

***Windows NT Training Guide.** James Turley. LC 96-47583. (Illus.). 330p. 1996. pap. 49.95 (*0-12-703855-8*) Acad Pr.

***Windows NT Training Guide.** James L. Turley. LC 96-47583. 1996. 1.95 (*0-12-703856-6*) Acad Pr.

***Windows NT User Administration.** Ashley Meggitt & Timothy D. Ritchey. Ed. by Robert J. Denn. (Illus.). 350p. (Orig.). 1997. pap. write for info. (*1-56592-301-4*) OReilly & Assocs.

***Windows NT, Version 4, Quick Reference.** Karl Schwartz. (Quick Reference Guides Ser.). (Illus.). (Orig.). 1996. pap. 12.00 (*1-56243-429-2*, G-16) DDC Pub.

Windows NT Versus NetWare: An In-Depth Analysis & Comparison. Computer Technology Research Corporation Staff. (Illus.). 210p. (Orig.). 1996. 285.00 (*1-56607-968-3*) Comput Tech Res.

Windows NT Web Server Book. Larry Budnick. (Illus.). 700p. 1996. cd-rom 49.95 (*1-56604-342-5*) Ventana Communs.

Windows NT Web Server Handbook: Your Guide to Microsoft's Internet Information Server. Tom Sheldon. 640p. 1996. pap. text ed. 32.95 (*0-07-882221-1*) Osborne-McGraw.

Windows NT Web Server Secrets. Programmers Press Staff. 1996. pap. 44.99 incl. cd-rom (*1-56884-807-2*) IDG Bks.

***Windows NT Workstation Professional Reference.** Kathy Ivens. 1056p. 1996. pap. text ed. 59.99 incl. cd-rom (*1-56205-692-1*) New Riders Pub.

***Windows NT Workstation 4 Unleashed: MCSE.** Sean Mathias. 1997. 65.00 (*0-672-31188-7*) Mac Comp Pub.

***Windows NT Workstation 4.0 Administrator's Bible.** Jonathan J. Chau. 1997. pap. 49.99 (*0-7645-3102-6*) IDG Bks.

***Windows NT Workstation 4.0 Administrator's Bible.** Jonathan J. Chaw. 1008p. (Orig.). 1997. pap. write for info. (*0-614-26357-3*) IDG Bks.

***Windows NT Workstation 4.0 Secrets.** Allen L. Wyatt. 1996. pap. 49.99 (*0-7645-8011-6*) IDG Bks.

Windows NT 3.1 Graphics Programming. Ben Ezzell. (Programming Ser.). 480p. 1993. pap. 34.95 incl. disk (*1-56276-113-7*, Ziff-Davis Pr) Que.

Windows NT 3.1 Programming. Ben Ezzell. (Programming Ser.). 640p. 1993. pap. 34.95 incl. disk (*1-56276-112-9*, Ziff-Davis Pr) Que.

Windows NT 3.51 Server Survival Guide. Rick Sant'Angelo & Nadeem Chagtai. (Illus.). 996p. (Orig.). 1996. 55.00 (*0-672-30860-6*) Sams.

Windows NT 3.51 Unleashed. 3rd ed. Robert Cowart et al. (Illus.). 1031p. 1996. pap. 55.00 incl. cd-rom (*0-672-30902-5*) Sams.

Windows NT 4: The Complete Reference. Griffith W. Kadnier. 816p. 1997. pap. text ed. 39.99 (*0-07-882181-9*) McGraw.

***Windows NT 4 Administrator's Black Book.** Paul Taylor. 1997. 39.99 (*1-57610-114-2*) Coriolis Grp.

***Windows NT 4 Adminstrator's Survival Guide.** Rick Sant'Angelo. 900p. 1997. 55.00 (*0-672-31008-2*) Mac Comp Pub.

***Windows NT 4 Advanced Programming.** Raj Rajagopal. (Windows NT Professional Library). (Illus.). 848p. (Orig.). 1997. pap. 49.99 (*0-07-882357-9*, Oracle Press) Osborne-McGraw.

***Windows NT 4 & Web Site Resource Library.** Sams Development Group Staff. 3200p. 1997. pap. 149.99 (*0-672-30995-5*) Sams.

***Windows NT 4 Electronic Resource Kit.** Sams Development Staff. 1996. pap. text ed. 89.99 incl. cd-rom (*0-672-31032-5*) Sams.

Windows NT 4 for Dummies Quick Reference. Valda Hilley. (Illus.). 240p. (Orig.). 1996. pap. 12.99 (*1-56884-992-3*) IDG Bks.

***Windows NT 4 Registry Unleashed.** Bobby Seder et al. 1200p. 1997. 49.99 (*0-672-30985-8*) Mac Comp Pub.

Windows NT 4 Server Book. Peter Hipson. 760p. 1996. pap. text ed. 49.99 (*1-56604-495-2*) Ventana Communs.

***Windows NT 4 Systems Programming.** Jeffry Dwight. 1997. pap. text ed. 39.99 incl. cd-rom (*1-57610-118-5*) Coriolis Grp.

Windows NT 4 Web Development. Sanjaya Hettihewa. 744p. 1996. 59.99 (*1-57521-089-4*) Mac Comp Pub.

***Windows NT 4 Win32 Programming API Bible.** Richard J. Simon. LC 97-6052. 1400p. 1997. 59.99 (*1-57169-089-1*, Waite Grp Pr) Mac Comp Pub.

***Windows NT 4 Workstation Unleashed.** Paul Cassell et al. 1200p. 1997. 59.99 (*0-672-31081-3*) Sams.

Windows NT 4 Workstation Unleashed. Sean Mathias et al. 800p. 1996. 39.99 (*0-672-30972-6*) Mac Comp Pub.

***Windows NT 4.0: Microsoft's Server & Operating System Strategy for the Future.** Computer Technology Research Corp. Staff & Paul Korzeniowski. LC 96-47952. (Illus.). 200p. (Orig.). 1997. pap. 290.00 (*1-56607-987-X*) Comput Tech Res.

***Windows NT 4.0 Server Unleashed.** Jason Garms et al. 1500p. 1997. 65.00 (*0-672-31002-3*) Mac Comp Pub.

Windows NT 4.0 Server Unleashed. Jason Garms. 1152p. 1996. pap. text ed. 55.00 incl. cd-rom (*0-672-30933-5*) Sams.

***Windows NT 4.0 Visual Desk Reference.** Gardner Group Staff. 408p. 1997. 24.99 (*0-7897-1106-0*) Mac Comp Pub.

Windows NT 4.0 Workstation Advanced Technical Reference. Jim Boyce et al. 888p. 1996. 59.99 (*0-7897-0863-9*) Mac Comp Pub.

***Windows NT 4.0 Workstation Exam Guide.** Steve Kaczmarek & Productivity Point International Staff. 832p. 1997. 99.99 (*0-7897-0989-9*) Mac Comp Pub.

Windows NT 4.0 Workstation Installation & Configuration Handbook. Windows Magazine Staff. 840p. 1996. pap. text ed. 44.99 incl. cd-rom (*0-7897-0818-3*) Que.

Windows NT 4.0 Workstation Internet & Networking Handbook. Robert B. Thompson. 936p. 1996. 44.99 (*0-7897-0817-5*) Mac Comp Pub.

***Windows NT 5 Internet Developer's Guide.** Mohammed Kabir. 1998. 49.99 (*1-57169-099-9*) Sams.

***Windows NT 95 for Unix Professionals.** Donald Merusi. LC 97-7962. 1997. write for info. (*1-55558-181-1*, Digital DEC) Buttrwrth-Heinemann.

Windows of a Heart. M. James Uhing. Ed. by Alphonse M. Lauer. (Illus.). 72p. (YA). 1993. pap. 5.00 (*1-56788-013-4*, 20-002) BMH Pubns.

Windows of Christ Church Cathedral, Canterbury. Madeline H. Caviness. (Corpus Vitrearum Medii Aevi, Great Britain: Vol. II). (Illus.). 1981. 175.00 (*0-19-725995-2*) David Brown.

Windows of Confederate Finance: CSA Bearer Bonds. Jule N. Dews. LC 89-62057. (Illus.). 58p. 1989. pap. 16.00 (*0-937300-02-0*) Stoneridge Inst.

***Windows of Faith: Prayers of the Holy Hildegard.** LC 97-13970. 88p. 1997. pap. 13.95 (*0-8146-2448-0*) Liturgical Pr.

Windows of Life. 1997. write for info. (*0-925589-33-0*) JPM Pubs.

Windows of Life. Esther Jensen. (Orig.). 1995. pap. write for info. (*1-57553-072-4*) Watermrk Pr.

Windows of Light: A Bibliography of the Serials Literature Within the Gernsheim & Photography Collections of the Harry Ransom Humanities Research Center. Roy Flukinger. (Illus.). 411p. 1994. pap. 25.00 (*0-87959-132-3*) U of Tex H Ransom Ctr.

Windows of Light: A Journey into the Greatness of Being. Prakasho Thayne. LC 94-76317. 153p. (Orig.). 1994. pap. 12.95 (*0-9641171-0-X*) Gratitude NV.

Windows of Misopportunity: Keeping Your Money. Ronald A. Vejrostek. LC 95-74803. 82p. (Orig.). 1995. pap. 12. 95 (*1-887705-00-7*) CQG.

Windows of My World, Vol. 2. Jackie Claflin. 100p. 1987. pap. text ed. 9.50 (*1-56770-181-7*) S Scheewe Pubns.

***Windows of My World, Vol. 4.** Jackie Claflin. 63p. 1996. pap. 63.00 (*1-56770-359-3*) S Scheewe Pubns.

***Windows of My World 3.** Jackie Claflin. 84p. 1994. pap. 9.50 (*1-56770-303-8*) S Scheewe Pubns.

Windows of Nature: A Story-Coloring Book. Michael Stillwater. 40p. (Orig.). (J). (ps-3). 1987. reprint ed. pap. 6.95 (*0-87516-580-X*) DeVorss.

Windows of Opportunity: Improving Middle Grades Teacher Preparation. Peter C. Scales. 185p. 1992. reprint ed. pap. 15.00 (*1-57482-710-3*) Search Inst.

Windows of Opportunity: Mathematics for Students with Special Needs. Ed. by Carol A. Thornton & Nancy S. Bley. LC 94-140. (Illus.). 466p. 1994. 42.50 (*0-87353-374-7*) NCTM.

Windows of Perception. Anthony O. Constantino. 64p. 1993. pap. 4.95 (*1-57087-177-9*) Prof Pr NC.

Windows of Snow. Elizabeth Revere. LC 85-8722. 78p. 1985. pap. 5.95 (*0-918606-08-X*) Heidelberg Graph.

Windows of Soul. Robert Kugelmann. LC 81-70032. 220p. 1983. 32.50 (*0-8387-5035-4*) Bucknell U Pr.

Windows of the Bible. Vera S. Kelly. 120p. 1993. 12.00 (*0-8233-0489-2*) Golden Quill.

Windows of the Heart. Dorothy Skinner. 24p. (Orig.). 1992. pap. text ed. 2.95 (*0-87227-177-3*, RBP5211) Reg Baptist.

Windows of the Mind: Consciousness Beyond the Body. G. M. Glaskin. 208p. pap. write for info. (*0-907061-81-8*, Pub. by Prism Pr UK) Assoc Pubs Grp.

Windows of the Past: The Ruins of the Colorado Plateau. Florence Lister & Lynn Wilson. Ed. by Nicky Leach. (Wish You Were Here Postcard Bks.). (Illus.). 96p. (Orig.). 1993. 24.95 (*0-939365-22-7*); pap. 14.95 (*0-939365-21-9*) Sierra Pr CA.

Windows of the Soul. Paul Meier & Robert Wise. 288p. 1995. 19.99 (*0-7852-7866-4*, J Thoma Bks) Nelson.

Windows of the Soul. Ed. by Cynthia Stevens. 1996. 69.95 (*1-57553-002-3*) Watermrk Pr.

Windows of the Soul: Experiencing God in New Ways. Ken Gire. 208p. 1996. 14.99 (*0-310-20397-X*) Zondervan.

***Windows of the Soul: Poems of Praise & Sentiment.** Mildred E. Garner. (Illus.). 120p. (Orig.). Date not set. pap. 8.95 (*0-9653436-0-X*) M E Garner.

Windows of Truth. Peter Jeffrey. 58p. 1992. pap. 3.99 (*0-85151-636-X*) Banner of Truth.

Windows of Westminster. Harold Begbie. LC 77-104993. (Essay Index Reprint Ser.). 1977. 21.95 (*0-8369-1447-3*) Ayer.

Windows of Wonderment: Twentieth Century Teachings of Kabir. Sue Schwartz. Ed. by Steve Schwartz. 109p. (Orig.). 1988. pap. 6.95 (*0-317-90483-3*) Steve & Sue Schwartz.

***Windows Office Toolbox: Microsoft Office for Windows 97.** Tim Duffy. 832p. (C). 1997. pap. text ed. 51.95 (*0-8053-2760-6*) Benjamin-Cummings.

Windows on a Lost World. V. E. Mitchell. Ed. by Dave Stern. (Star Trek Ser.: No. 65). 288p. (Orig.). 1993. mass mkt. 5.99 (*0-671-79512-0*) PB.

Windows on a New World: The Third Industrial Revolution. Ed. by Joseph Finkelstein. LC 88-25094. (Contributions in Economics & Economic History Ser.: No. 88). 261p. 1989. text ed. 55.00 (*0-313-26321-3*, FWD/, Greenwood Pr) Greenwood.

Windows on Bilingualism: PL110. Ed. by Eugene Casad. LC 92-81102. xii, 216p. (Orig.). 1992. fiche 16.00 (*0-88312-712-1*) Summer Instit Ling.

Windows on Creativity & Invention. Ed. by Jacques G. Richardson. LC 86-83428. 344p. 1988. 34.75 (*0-912338-57-1*); fiche 15.75 (*0-912338-58-X*) Lomond.

Windows on Day Care. LC 72-76736. 1972. pap. 2.25 (*0-686-81721-4*) NCJW.

Windows on Galaxies. Ed. by Giuseppina Fabbiano et al. (C). 1990. lib. bdg. 151.00 (*0-7923-0663-5*) Kluwer Ac.

Windows on Japanese Education. Ed. by Edward R. Beauchamp. LC 90-45329. (Contributions to the Study of Education Ser.: No. 43). 344p. 1991. text ed. 59.95 (*0-313-26243-8*, BUE, Greenwood Pr) Greenwood.

Windows on Latin America: Understanding Society Through Photographs. Ed. by Robert M. Levine. (Illus.). 154p. 1987. pap. 21.95 (*0-935501-06-1*, WL001) U Miami N-S Ctr.

Windows on Life. Carl H. Kopf. LC 70-76908. (Essay Index Reprint Ser.). 1977. 20.95 (*0-8369-1041-9*) Ayer.

Windows on Manhattan. Gladys Merrifield. (Living Poets' Library). 1986. pap. 5.00 (*0-934218-33-1*) Dragons Teeth.

Windows on Mathematical Meanings: Learning Cultures & Computers. Richard Noss & Celia Hoyles. LC 96-17822. (Mathematics & Its Applications, Soviet Ser.: Vol. 17). 275p. (C). 1996. lib. bdg. 130.00 (*0-7923-4073-6*) Kluwer Ac.

***Windows on Mathematical Meanings: Learning Cultures & Computers.** Richard Noss & Meli. (Mathematics Education Library). 288p. (C). 1996. pap. text ed. 49.00 (*0-7923-4074-4*) Kluwer Ac.

Windows on Modernism: Selected Letters of Dorothy Richardson. Dorothy Richardson. Ed. by Gloria G. Fromm. LC 94-4170. (Illus.). 696p. 1995. 65.00 (*0-8203-1659-8*) U of Ga Pr.

Windows on Music: Learning with Practica Musica. Jeffrey Evans. LC 88-71355. 190p. 1989. pap. text ed. 29.95 (*0-929444-03-5*) Ars Nova SW.

Windows on the Cross. Tom Smail. 120p. (Orig.). 1995. pap. 9.95 (*1-56101-123-1*) Cowley Pubns.

Windows on the Holy Land. J. C. Pedlow. (Illus.). 150p. 1980. pap. 12.50 (*0-227-67839-7*) Attic Pr.

***Windows on the House of Islam: Muslim Sources on Spirituality & Religious Life.** John Renard. LC 97-9853. 1998. write for info. (*0-520-20976-1*); pap. write for info. (*0-520-21086-7*) U CA Pr.

Windows on the Internet: The Complete Toolchest on CD-ROM. John P. Morphet. 1995. pap. text ed. 34.95 (*0-07-912173-X*) McGraw.

Windows on the Japanese Past. Ed. by Richard J. Pearson et al. Tr. by Kazue Pearson & Masao Nishimura. LC 85-16639. (Illus.). xx, 629p. 1986. pap. 29.95 (*0-939512-24-6*) U MI Japan.

***Windows on the Kingdom: Mission Illustrations for Pastors.** 64p. Date not set. 6.50 (0-8341-1587-5) Nazarene.

Windows on the Parables. rev. ed. Warren W. Wiersbe. 160p. 1989. pap. 8.99 (0-89693-682-1, Victor Bks) Chariot Victor.

Windows on the Parables Leaders Guide. Warren W. Wiersbe. 1989. pap. 6.50 (0-89693-683-X, 6-1683, Victor Bks) Chariot Victor.

Windows on the Passion. Donald English. LC 88-62508. 72p. (Orig.). 1988. pap. 5.95 (0-88177-066-3, DR066) Discipleship Res.

Windows on the Passion. Charles C. Wise, Jr. LC 67-11007. 143p. 1974. reprint ed. pap. 2.95 (0-917023-00-5) Magian Pr.

Windows on the Past: Portraits at the Essex Institute. Andrew Oliver & Bryant F. Tolles, Jr. LC 80-70017. (E.I. Museum Booklet Ser.). (Illus.). 64p. (Orig.). 1981. pap. 5.95 (0-88389-079-8, Essx Institute) Peabody Essex Mus.

***Windows on the White House: The Story of Presidential Libraries.** Curt Smith. (Illus.). 245p. 1997. 29.95 (1-888698-10-1) Diamond Communications.

Windows on the Word. Andrew Kuyvenhoven. (How to Read the Bible Ser.). 1995. teacher ed. 7.35 (1-56212-097-2) CRC Pubns.

Windows on the Workplace: Computers, Jobs, & the Organization of Office Work in the Late Twentieth Century. Joan Greenbaum. (Cornerstone Ser.). 144p. 1995. text ed. 26.00 (0-614-00336-9) Monthly Rev.

Windows on the Workplace: Computers, Jobs, & the Organization of Office Work in the Late Twentieth Century. Joan Greenbaum. (Cornerstone Ser.). (Illus.). 160p. (J). (ps-12). 1995. pap. text ed. 13.00 (0-85345-901-0) Monthly Rev.

Windows on the World: Essays on American Social Fiction. C. Hugh Holman. LC 78-13241. 224p. 1979. 29.00 (0-87049-264-0) U of Tenn Pr.

Windows on the World: Multicultural Festivals for Schools & Libraries. Alan Heath. LC 94-10032. 406p. 1995. 49.50 (0-8108-2880-4) Scarecrow.

Windows on the World: Plays & Activities Adapted from Folk Tales from Different Lands. Sylvia Sikundar & Diane Williams. 128p. (Orig.). 1995. pap. 14.95 (0-88865-089-2, Pub. by Pacific Educ Pr CN) Orca Bk Pubs.

Windows on the World: Public Exhibits in the Museum of Natural Science at Louisiana State University. Peter A. Soderbergh. 194p. (Orig.). 1986. pap. 6.00 (0-9617661-0-7) LSU Mus Nat Sci.

Windows on the World: World News Reporting 1900 - 1920. Robert W. Desmond. LC 80-19397. (World News Reporting Ser.: Vol. 2). 626p. 1981. text ed. 75.00 (0-87745-104-4) U of Iowa Pr.

Windows on the World Complete Wine Course. Kevin Zraly. 190p. 19.95 (0-8069-6894-X, 212) Am Bartenders.

Windows on the World Complete Wine Course. Kevin Zraly. 192p. 1989. pap. 14.95 (0-440-59611-4, Dell Trade Pbks) Dell.

Windows on the World Complete Wine Course. Kevin Zraly. 192p. 1996. 23.95 (0-8069-9501-7) Sterling.

***Windows on the World Complete Wine Course.** Kevin Zraly. 1997. 24.95 (0-8069-0345-7) Sterling.

Windows on the World Complete Wine Course: 1997 Edition. Kevin Zraly. LC 84-26851. (Illus.). 192p. 1996. 23.95 (0-8069-8493-7) Sterling.

Windows on the World of Jesus: Time Travel to Ancient Judea. Bruce J. Malina. LC 93-10360. 208p. (Orig.). 1993. pap. 15.00 (0-664-25457-8) Westminster John Knox.

Windows on the World Series, 5 vols. Incl. On the Horn of Africa: Let's Travel to Somalia Together. Jeannette P. Windham. (Illus.). 64p. (Orig.). (J). (gr. 3-10). 1995. pap. 5.95 (1-887176-02-0); Giant Isn't Sleeping Anymore: Let's Travel to China Together. (Illus.). 70p. (Orig.). (J). (gr. 3-10). 1995. pap. 5.95 (1-887176-03-9); At the Top of the World: Let's Travel to Nepal Together. Jeannette P. Windham. (Illus.). 80p. (Orig.). (J). (gr. 3-10). 1995. pap. 5.95 (1-887176-04-7); Reefs, Lagoons & Atolls: Let's Travel to the Maldives Together. Jeannette P. Windham. (Illus.). 60p. (Orig.). (J). (gr. 3-10). 1995. pap. 5.95 (1-887176-06-3); Volcanoes, Betjaks, & Dragons: Let's Travel to Indonesia Together. Jeannette P. Windham. (Illus.). 82p. (Orig.). (J). (gr. 3-8). 1995. pap. text ed. 5.95 (1-887176-05-5); 1995. Set per., pap. write for info. (1-887176-08-X) Globl Age Pub.

Windows on Wisdom. Mary I. Farr. 1993. pap. 12.95 (0-9634700-0-0) Wordwise.

Windows on Writing. Laurie G. Kirszner. 1995. pap. text ed. 26.00 (0-312-07834-X) St Martin.

Windows on Writing. Kirszner. 1995. teacher ed., pap. text ed. 6.04 (0-312-13673-0) St Martin.

Windows pour Workgroups au Quotidien. Cobb Group Staff. 176p. 1993. pap. 75.00 (0-7859-5650-6, 2840820080) Fr & Eur.

Windows Programming for Mere Mortals. Woody Leonhard. (C). 1992. pap. text ed., pap. 36.95 incl. disk (0-201-60832-4) Addison-Wesley.

Windows Programming Power with Custom Controls. Paul Cilwa & Jeff Duntemann. (Software Components Ser.). 492p. (Orig.). 1994. pap. 39.95 incl. disk (1-883577-00-4) Coriolis Grp.

Windows Programming Puzzle Book. Kim Crouse. 464p. 1993. pap. text ed. 49.95 incl. disk (0-471-59713-9); pap. text ed. 29.95 (0-471-59714-7) Wiley.

Windows Programming Puzzle Book. Kim Crouse. 1993. disk 20.00 (0-471-30655-X) Wiley.

***Windows Programming, under the Hood of MFC: A Quick Tour of Visual C++ Tools.** Draxler. 1997. pap. write for info. (0-13-488975-4) P-H.

Windows Programming with Borland C++ Jeff Mackay. 1994. pap. text ed. 34.95 (0-07-044596-6) McGraw.

Windows Programming with Borland C Plus Plus. Jeff Mackay. LC 92-40040. 1993. pap. 34.95 (0-8306-4319-2, Windcrest) TAB Bks.

Windows Programming with Shareware. Victor R. Volkman. 450p. (C). 1996. pap. text ed. 40.00 (0-13-485228-1) P-H.

Windows Programming with Shareware Tools. Victor R. Volkman. 1996. pap. text ed. 44.95 incl. cd-rom (0-87930-434-0) R & D Books.

Windows QuickStart, 3.11 Edition. Ron Person & Laura Acklen. LC 95-129969. 301p. 1994. 29.99 (1-56529-866-7) Que.

Windows Registry: A Troubleshooting Guide. John Woram. 1996. pap. 34.95 (1-55828-494-X) MIS Press.

Windows Registry Troubleshooting: Windows 95 & Windows NT. New Riders Development Group Staff. 350p. 1996. pap. 40.00 (1-56205-556-9) New Riders Pub.

***Windows Revealed.** Lenny Bailes. (Illus.). 912p. (Orig.). 1998. pap. 34.99 (0-07-882400-1, Oracle Press) Osborne-McGraw.

Windows Scanning Book. Luisa Simone. LC 96-14121. 320p. 1996. pap. text ed. 29.95 (0-471-11582-7) Wiley.

Windows Shoppers Guide. Mike Jones. 1993. pap. 24.95 (1-881017-02-8) WhiteFox Comm.

Windows Shopper's Guide, Vol. 4, No. 1. Ed. by John Schmitt. 384p. 1992. pap. 24.95 (1-881017-00-1) WhiteFox Comm.

Windows Socket Programming. Shah. 1996. pap. 39.95 (0-13-433004-8) P-H.

Inside Windows Sockets. Jason Coombs et al. 1996. pap. text ed. 34.95 incl. cd-rom (1-57231-346-3) Microsoft.

Windows Sockets Network Programming. Bob Quinn & David K. Shute. (Advanced Windows Ser.). 576p. 1995. pap. text ed. write for info. (0-201-92457-9) Addison-Wesley.

***Windows Sockets Network Programming.** 2nd ed. Bob Quinn. (C). 1998. text ed. write for info. (0-201-18394-3) Addison-Wesley.

***Windows Sources Microsoft Office 97 for Windows SuperGuide.** Bruce Hallberg. 829p. 1996. 39.99 (1-56276-503-5) Mac Comp Pub.

***Windows Telephony.** Jeffrey R. Shapiro. 300p. 1996. 24.95 (0-936648-94-5, P50010) Flatiron Pubng.

***Windows Telephony Programming: A Developer's Guide to TAPI.** Chris Sells. (Advanced Windows Ser.). 1997. 36.53 (0-201-63450-3) Addison-Wesley.

Windows Textbook. Stewart M. Venit. 426p. (Orig.). (C). 1993. pap. text ed. 26.50 (1-881991-31-8) Scott Jones Pubng.

Windows Textbook: Extended Edition. Stewart M. Venit. 700p. (Orig.). (C). 1997. pap. text ed. 35.00 (1-57676-000-6) Scott Jones Pubng.

Windows That Open Inward: Images of Chile. Pablo Neruda. Tr. by Reid et al. from SPA. (Illus.). 1984. 50.00 (0-934834-51-2) White Pine.

Windows to God: Worship with Young Children. Elizabeth Aylin & Marjorie Bounds. (J). (ps-3). 1986. 23.00 (1-881678-34-2) CRIS.

Windows to His World: The Story of Trevor Kincaid. Muriel L. Guberlet. LC 73-91594. (Illus.). 1975. 18.95 (0-87015-210-6) Pacific Bks.

Windows to My Soul: Reflections of an "Inner" Traveler. Carol L. MacAllister. (Illus.). 100p. (Orig.). 1990. pap. 6.95 (0-9624856-0-8) Handsome Bks.

Windows to Our Children: A Gestalt Therapy Approach to Children & Adolescents. Violet Oaklander. (Illus.). 352p. 1989. reprint ed. pap. 20.00 (0-939266-06-7) Gestalt Journal.

Windows to the Heart. Thea M. Kellogg. 65p. 1995. pap. text ed. write for info. (0-9645035-1-4) WynnHart Pr.

Windows to the Heart of God. Angela Ramage. LC 95-13224. 144p. 1996. 10.99 (0-7852-7912-1) Nelson.

Windows to the Heart of God: Words of Hope from Heaven. Richard Lee. 250p. (Orig.). 1996. pap. 9.99 (1-56507-501-3) Harvest Hse.

Windows to the Past. 1996. write for info. (0-614-96925-5) Abrams.

Windows to the Past: How Psychic Time Travel Reveals the Secrets of History. Hans Holzer. LC 92-38088. (Illus.). 1993. 9.95 (0-8065-1408-6, Citadel Pr) Carol Pub Group.

***Windows to the Soul.** J. M. Barlog. LC 96-94981. 268p. (Orig.). 1996. pap. 7.99 (0-9654716-6-7) BAK Books.

Windows to the Soul. Anita K. Nobles. 384p. 1992. pap. 7.95 (1-882626-10-9) Impress Ink.

***Windows to the Spiritual World: Spirit Realism & the Art of Puskar.** Matthew Goldman & Robert Masla. LC 95-61914. 1997. 4.50 (0-9655784-0-2) Transcndtal Art.

***Windows to the West: The New China & the Church.** LC 97-2477. 1997. write for info. (0-87788-888-4) Shaw Pubs.

Windows to the World. Nancy Everix. (Illus.). 128p. (J). (gr. 2-8). 1984. student ed. 12.99 (0-86653-173-4, GA 527) Good Apple.

Windows to the World: Inside Look at Food, Wine & Travel. Members of the International Food, Wine & Travel Writers Association Staff. Ed. by Ray KaSaker & D. K. Jackson. (Illus.). 254p. 1989. 7.98 (0-9621891-1-1) D & A Pub CA.

Windows to the World: Insider Favorites on Dining, Traveling & Lodging. International Food, Wine & Travel Writers Association Members. Ed. by Ray Kabaker. (Illus.). 250p. (Orig.). 1989. pap. 7.95 (0-317-93271-3) IFW & TWA.

Windows to the World: Themes for Teaching Cross Cultural Understanding. John Kepler et al. 1996. pap. 14.95 (0-673-36153-5, GoodYrBooks) Addson-Wesley Educ.

***Windows Undocumented File Formats: Working Inside Windows 3.X & Windows '95.** Pete Davis. 350p. (Orig.). 1997. pap. 39.95 incl. disk (0-87930-437-5) R & D Books.

Windows VisiRef. Que Development Group Staff. 157p. 1994. 12.99 (1-56529-805-5) Que.

Windows Visualization Programming with C - C Plus Plus: Three-D Visualization, Simulation & Virtual Reality. Lee Adams. 1994. pap. text ed. 39.95 (0-07-000399-8) McGraw-Hill Prof.

Windows Visualization Programming with C-C Plus Plus: 3D Visualization, Simulation, & Virtual Reality. Lee Adams. LC 93-32093. 1993. pap. text ed. 39.95 (0-8306-3812-1, Windcrest) TAB Bks.

***Windows with Style: Do-It-Yourself Window Treatments.** LC 97-15643. (Illus.). 224p. 1997. write for info. (0-86573-349-X) Cowles Creative.

Windows Workshop: Access for Windows, Version 2.0. James E. Shuman. (Management Information Systems Ser.). 160p. 1995. pap. 18.95 (0-534-30558-X) Course Tech.

Windows Workshop: Access 1.1 for Windows. James E. Shuman. 134p. 1994. pap. 18.95 (0-534-30526-1) Course Tech.

Windows Workshop: Excel 4.0 for Windows. James E. Shuman. 142p. 1994. pap. 18.95 (0-534-30520-2) Course Tech.

Windows Workshop: Excel 5.0 for Windows. James E. Shuman. 144p. 1995. pap. 18.95 (0-534-30554-7) Course Tech.

Windows Workshop: Lotus 1-2-3 for Windows (Release 4) James E. Shuman. 150p. 1994. pap. 18.95 (0-534-30516-4) Course Tech.

Windows Workshop: Microsoft Works for Windows 95. Schuman. (Management Information Systems Ser.). 1996. pap. 18.95 (0-7895-0649-1) Course Tech.

Windows Workshop: MS Office 1995 Professional Edition. James E. Shuman. (Management Information Systems Ser.). 1996. pap. 18.95 (0-7895-0646-7) S-W Pub.

Windows Workshop: Paradox for Windows. James E. Shuman. 126p. 1994. pap. 18.95 (0-534-30522-9) Course Tech.

Windows Workshop: Quattro Pro for Windows. James E. Shuman. 140p. 1994. pap. 18.95 (0-534-30518-0) Course Tech.

Windows Workshop: Quattro Pro for Windows, Version 5.0. James E. Shuman. 1995. pap. 18.95 (0-534-30556-3) Course Tech.

Windows Workshop: Windows 3.1. James E. Shuman. 182p. (C). 1994. pap. 18.95 (0-534-30510-5) Course Tech.

Windows Workshop: Word for Windows. James E. Shuman. 178p. 1994. pap. 18.95 (0-534-30514-8) Course Tech.

Windows Workshop: Word for Windows, Version 6.0. James E. Shuman. 1995. pap. 18.95 (0-534-30553-9) Course Tech.

Windows Workshop: WordPerfect 6.0 for Windows. James E. Shuman. 164p. 1995. pap. 18.95 (0-534-30512-1) Course Tech.

***Windows World Wide Web Primer.** Rex Alfes & Robert Sparre. 1997. pap. 26.95 (0-13-454968-6) P-H.

***Windows X for Dummies.** Andy Rathbone. 1997. pap. 19.99 (0-7645-0261-1) IDG Bks.

***Windows X Programming for Dummies.** 2nd ed. 1997. pap. 24.99 (0-7645-0262-X) IDG Bks.

***Windows X Quick & Easy.** Robert Cowart. (Illus.). 272p. 1996. 24.99 (0-7821-1954-9) Sybex.

Windows X.0 Power Tools. 3rd ed. Martin S. Matthews. (Power Tools Ser.). 672p. 1995. pap. 40.00 (0-679-75587-X) Random.

Windows X.0 Slick Tricks. Jack Nimersheim. (Slick Tricks Ser.). 1994. pap. 16.00 (0-679-79178-7) Random.

Windows 3 Pocket Reference: Concise Explanations of All Windows 3 Commands, Illustrated with Examples. S. Roberts. (Info Compact Ser.). (Illus.). 100p. (C). 1991. pap. 5.00 (0-911827-06-4) Elcomp.

Windows 3 Shareware Utilities. PC-SIG, Inc. Staff. 216p. 1992. pap. 29.95 (0-8306-2485-6, Windcrest) TAB Bks.

Windows 3.0. Timothy J. O'Leary et al. 1992. pap. text ed. write for info. (0-07-048854-1) McGraw.

Windows 3.0: Answer Manual - Transparency Masters. Steven G. Forsythe. Ed. by Connie Laser. (Illus.). 160p. (C). 1991. teacher ed. write for info. (0-924491-08-6) Brookside CA.

Windows 3.0: Beginners. 1993. 29.95 (1-56877-053-7) Catapult WA.

Windows 3.0: Beginners. 1993. teacher ed. 49.95 (1-56877-054-5) Catapult WA.

Windows 3.0: Intermediate. 1993. teacher ed. 49.95 (1-56877-110-X) Catapult WA.

Windows 3.0: Intermediate. 1993. 29.95 (1-56877-111-8) Catapult WA.

Windows 3.0: The Supplement. Forsythe. (DF - Computer Applications Ser.). 1992. pap. 22.95 (0-87709-078-5) Course Tech.

Windows 3.0: The Supplement. Steven G. Forsythe. Ed. by Connie Laser. (Illus.). 168p. (C). 1991. teacher ed. write for info. (0-318-68712-7); pap. text ed. 10.95 (0-924491-06-X) Brookside CA.

Windows 3.0 Companion. Charles Bermant. 240p. 1991. pap. 26.00 (1-55623-413-9) Irwin Prof Pubng.

Windows 3.0 for BASIC Programmers with Disk. Mark Hyman. 1990. pap. 29.95 (0-201-57031-9) Addison-Wesley.

Windows 3.0 Programming Primer. Alan Southerton. 1990. pap. 34.95 (0-201-55078-4) Addison-Wesley.

Windows 3.0 Quick Start. Marly K. Bergerud. 1993. pap. 19.95 (0-538-70849-2) S-W Pub.

Windows 3.1. 1993. teacher ed. 49.95 (1-56761-238-5, Alpha Ref) Macmillan Gen Ref.

Windows 3.1. 1993. teacher ed. 49.95 (1-56877-003-0) Catapult WA.

Windows 3.1. Glen Coulthard et al. (C). 1994. 22.50 (0-256-18653-7) Irwin.

Windows 3.1. Jack Nimersheim. LC 93-60164. (In Plain English Ser.). (Illus.). (Orig.). 1993. pap. 9.95 (1-56664-007-5) WorldComm.

Windows 3.1. Timothy J. O'Leary et al. 1993. pap. text ed. write for info. (0-07-048880-0) McGraw.

Windows 3.1. Stacey C. Sawyer et al. 200p. (C). 1993. per. 25.00 (0-256-13521-5) Irwin.

Windows 3.1. Rick Sullivan. (Computer Training Ser.). 1996. text ed. 18.95 (0-538-63429-4) S-W Pub.

Windows 3.1. Rick Sullivan. (Computer Training Ser.). 180p. 1996. pap. text ed. 21.95 (0-538-64127-4) S-W Pub.

Windows 3.1: A Brief Guide. Steven G. Forsythe. LC 93-45262. 1994. pap. 14.95 (0-87709-615-5) Course Tech.

Windows 3.1: A Tutorial to Accompany Peter Norton's Introduction to Computers. Heather Duggan. LC 93-45355. 1994. write for info. (0-02-801329-8) Glencoe.

Windows 3.1: Accessories. Douglas M. Finney et al. 1994. spiral bd. 29.95 incl. 3.5 ld (1-56435-031-2) Finney Lrng Systs.

Windows 3.1: Acumen Series. Boyd & Fraser Staff. (DF - Computer Applications Ser.). 1996. pap. 20.95 (0-87709-965-0) Course Tech.

Windows 3.1: Basics. Douglas M. Finney et al. 1994. spiral bd. 29.95 incl. 3.5 hd (1-56435-024-X) Finney Lrng Systs.

Windows 3.1: Quick Start. Marly K. Bergerud & Don Busche. LC 92-46644. (Quick Start Ser.). 1994. pap. 19.95 (0-538-71086-1) S-W Pub.

Windows 3.1: Smartstart. 1995. teacher ed. 39.99 (0-7897-0002-6) Mac Pub USA.

Windows 3.1: Star Series. Boyd & Fraser Staff. (DF - Computer Applications Ser.). 1995. pap. 12.95 (0-87709-947-2) Course Tech.

Windows 3.1: The Visual Learning Guide. David C. Gardner & Grace J. Beatty. (Illus.). 288p. 1992. pap. 19.95 (1-55958-182-4) Prima Pub.

Windows 3.1 Al Instante, Windows 3.1 Simplified. Richard Maran. 1994. pap. 12.95 (0-13-123316-5) P-H.

***Windows 3.1 & Windows 95 for Beginners.** Philipa Wingate. (Computer Guides Ser.). (Illus.). 144p. (J). (gr. 4 up). 1997. 19.95 (0-7460-2692-7, Usborne) EDC.

Windows 3.1 at Work. Mary Campbell. 1992. pap. 24.95 (0-201-58138-8) Addison-Wesley.

Windows 3.1 au Quotidien. Cobb Group Staff. 528p. 1993. pap. 145.00 (0-7859-5648-4, 2840820005) Fr & Eur.

Windows 3.1 Basics. Que Education & Training Staff. 1995. 16.99 (1-57576-282-X) Que Educ & Trng.

Windows 3.1 Beginning: Beginning. 1992. 29.95 (1-56877-015-4) Catapult WA.

Windows 3.1 Bible CD-ROM. Fred Davis. (Illus.). (C). 1994. pap. 34.95 incl. cd-rom (1-56609-078-4) Peachpit Pr.

Windows 3.1 Cheet Sheet. Joe Kraynak. (Illus.). 381p. (Orig.). 1994. 19.99 (1-56761-491-4, Alpha Ref) Macmillan Gen Ref.

Windows 3.1 Companion. Carolyn Z. Gillay. LC 94-10105. (Illus.). 448p. 1994. pap. 28.95 (0-938661-75-2) Franklin Beedle.

Windows 3.1 Demystified: Tips, Tricks, & Techniques. James S. Forney. (Illus.). 376p. 1992. pap. 24.95 (0-8306-4036-3, 4180, Windcrest) TAB Bks.

Windows 3.1, Easy Reference Guide. Bergerud. (DF - Computer Applications Ser.). 1995. text ed. 7.95 (0-538-63384-0) S-W Pub.

Windows 3.1 Essentials. 1995. 22.99 (0-7897-0133-2) Mac Pub USA.

Windows 3.1 Essentials: Star Series. Boyd & Fraser Staff. (DF - Computer Applications Ser.). 1996. pap. 7.95 (0-7895-0024-8) Course Tech.

Windows 3.1 Exposed! How to Get the Most from Microsoft Windows 3.1! Brian C. Elwood. (Illus.). 200p. 1996. spiral bd. 16.95 (1-881432-13-0) BCS Pub.

Windows 3.1 Font Book. David F. Angell & Brent D. Heslop. (Illus.). 184p. (Orig.). 1992. pap. 12.95 (1-56609-005-9) Peachpit Pr.

Windows 3.1 for Beginners. Bethany Norman. (Quicksteps to Learning Ser.). (Illus.). 198p. 1992. spiral bd. 22.95 (1-56951-000-8) Sftware Trng.

Windows 3.1 for Dummies. 2nd ed. Andy Rathbone. 1994. pap. 16.95 (1-56884-182-5) IDG Bks.

Windows 3.1 Fundamentals. Carolyn Z. Gillay. LC 93-16989. 704p. 1993. pap. 37.95 (0-938661-61-2) Franklin Beedle.

Windows 3.1 Insider. Keith Weiskamp. 592p. 1992. pap. text ed. 26.95 (0-471-57984-X) Wiley.

Windows 3.1 Instant Reference. 2nd ed. Marshall L. Moseley. LC 91-67705. 262p. 1992. pap. 9.95 (0-89588-844-0) Sybex.

Windows 3.1 Intermediate: Intermediate. 1992. teacher ed. 49.95 (1-56877-004-9) Catapult WA.

Windows 3.1 Made Easy, Second Edition. Thomas Sheldon. 512p. 1992. pap. text ed. 27.95 (0-07-881725-0) Osborne-McGraw.

Windows 3.1 Memopoche. Alan Simpson. 360p. 1993. pap. 32.95 (0-7859-5644-1, 2736111273) Fr & Eur.

Windows 3.1 Module 1994: Production Software Guide. Edward G. Martin. 128p. (C). 1994. pap. text ed. 7.25 (0-03-098230-8) HB Coll Pubs.

Windows 3.1 NOW! A Simple Guide to Learning Windows Quickly & Easily! 2nd ed. Robert Medved. Ed. by Katharine Murray. LC 95-60174. (Illus.). 216p. 1995. pap. 17.99 (0-9643450-0-5) Easel Pubng.

Windows 3.1 Pocket Reference for IBM-PC & Compatible: Concise Explanations of Windows 3.1 Commands, Functions & Menus. Winfried Hofacker. (Info Compact Ser.). (Illus.). 102p. 1992. pap. 5.00 (0-911827-16-1) Elcomp.

W

Windows 3.1 pour les Nuls. Andy Rathbone. 350p. (FRE.). 1995. 49.95 (*0-7859-9855-1*) Fr & Eur.

Windows 3.1 Quick. Carolyn Z. Gillay & Patricia L. Sullivan. LC 93-20525. 144p. 1993. pap. 15.95 (*0-938661-50-7*) Franklin Beedle.

Windows 3.1 Quick Course. Rinehart. (Management Information Systems Ser.). 1996. student ed., pap. 18.95 (*0-538-65988-2*) S-W Pub.

Windows 3.1 Quick Reference Guide. 1993. pap. 14.95 (*1-56351-148-7*) Microref Educ Systs.

Windows 3.1 Secrets. 2nd ed. Brian Livingston. LC 92-70931. (InfoWorld Technical Bks.). 980p. 1992. pap. 39.95 (*1-878058-43-6*) IDG Bks.

***Windows 3.1 Simplificado.** Maran Graphics Staff. (SPA.). 1996. pap. 24.99 (*0-7645-6015-8*) IDG Bks.

Windows 3.1 Simplified. Ruth Maran & Richard Maran. 144p. (C). 1993. pap. text ed. 21.60 (*0-13-064627-X*) P-H.

Windows 3.1 Simplified. Southworth. (DF - Computer Applications Ser.). 1996. pap. 17.95 (*0-87709-783-6*) Course Tech.

Windows 3.1 Simplified: Education Edition. Maran Graphics Staff & Ruth Maran. 1995. pap. 14.99 (*1-56884-652-5*) IDG Bks.

Windows 3.1 Simplified & Expanded. expanded ed. Maran Graphics Staff & Ruth Maran. 240p. 1994. pap. 19.99 (*1-56884-654-1*) IDG Bks.

Windows 3.1 Smartstart. 1993. teacher ed. 39.99 (*1-56529-220-0*) Que.

Windows 3.1 SmartStart. M. Hirachi. (SmartStart Ser.). (Illus.). 300p. (Orig.). 1993. 25.99 (*1-56529-203-0*) Que.

Windows 3.1 Smartstart. 2nd ed. 1994. pap. text ed. 29.99 (*0-7897-0010-7*) Que Educ & Trng.

Windows 3.1 Survival Guide. Rinehart. (Management Information Systems Ser.). 1996. pap. 38.95 (*0-534-20706-5*) S-W Pub.

Windows 3.1 Visual Pocket Guide. Maran Graphics Staff & Ruth Maran. 256p. 1994. pap. 14.99 (*1-56884-650-9*) IDG Bks.

Windows 3.1 Walkabout: Training Software & Manual. Webster & Associates Staff. (Illus.). 80p. 1993. pap. 30.00 incl. disk (*1-56609-085-7*) Peachpit Pr.

Windows 3.11 for Dummies. 3rd ed. Andy Rathbone. 384p. 1995. pap. 16.95 (*1-56884-370-4*) IDG Bks.

Windows 3.11 QuickStart. Que Development Group Staff. (Illus.). 246p. (Orig.). 1994. pap. 19.99 (*0-614-06067-2*) Que.

Windows 3.11 Virtual Tutor. Que Education & Training Staff. Date not set. 49.99 incl. cd-rom (*1-57576-087-8*) Que Educ & Trng.

Windows 4.0 Solutions. Brian Underdahl. 608p. pap. text ed. 24.95 (*0-471-02021-4*) Wiley.

***Windows 9X: The Complete Reference.** John Levine & Margaret L. Young. 1997. pap. text ed. 39.99 (*0-07-882343-9*) Osborne-McGraw.

***Windows 9X Programming from the Ground Up.** Herbert Schildt. 1997. pap. text ed. 34.99 (*0-07-882306-4*) Osborne-McGraw.

***Windows 9X Quick Reference.** Que Development Group Staff. 1997. 16.99 (*0-7897-1105-2*) Que.

Windows 95. Cassel. 1996. pap. text ed. 7.67 (*0-13-456377-8*) P-H.

***Windows 95.** Tim Duffy. (C). 1997. pap. text ed. 17.50 (*0-201-31517-3*) Addison-Wesley.

***Windows 95.** Godin, Seth, Productions Staff. (Cader Flip Ser.). 1997. pap. text ed. 3.95 (*0-8362-2574-0*, Cader Bks) Andrews & McMeel.

Windows 95. Marangraphics Development Group Staff. LC 96-23736. (Glencoe Visual Ser.). 1996. write for info. (*0-02-803960-2*); write for info. (*0-02-814046-X*) Glencoe.

***Windows 95.** Timothy J. O'Leary & Linda I. O'Leary. 1996. pap. text ed. write for info. (*0-07-049054-6*) McGraw.

Windows 95. Andy Rathbone. 1996. pap. 24.99 (*1-56884-928-1*) IDG Bks.

***Windows 95.** Brian Underdahl. (New Tutorial Ser.). 1997. pap. 29.99 (*0-7645-3149-2*) IDG Bks.

***Windows 95.** Tapani Vihijarvi. LC 96-27083. (Visual Ser.). 1996. write for info. (*0-7638-0012-0*) Paradigm MN.

***Windows 95.** 2nd ed. Alan Stevens. (Teach Yourself). 1996. pap. text ed. 21.95 (*1-55828-510-5*) MIS Press.

Windows 95: A Developer's Guide. Jonathan Locke & Jeffrey M. Richter. 1995. pap. 39.95 incl. cd-rom (*1-55851-418-X*, M&T Books) H Holt & Co.

Windows '95: Acumen Series. Penrod. (DF - Computer Applications Ser.). 1996. pap. 20.95 (*0-7895-0349-2*) Course Tech.

Windows 95: Clear & Simple. Peter McBride. (Clear & Simple Ser.). 160p. 1996. pap. 10.95 (*0-7506-9800-4*, Digital DEC) Buttrwrth-Heinemann.

Windows 95: Double Diamond. Gary B. Shelly. 1996. pap. 18.00 (*0-7895-0324-7*) Course Tech.

Windows 95: Easy Installation Guide. Andy Reese. 1995. pap. text ed. 12.95 (*0-7615-0241-6*) Prima Pub.

Windows 95: Explanations You Can Understand & Use!... Jack Nimersheim. LC 95-49327. (In Plain English Ser.). Date not set. write for info. (*1-57090-031-0*) Alexander Bks.

Windows 95: Introduction Concepts & Technology. Gary B. Shelly. 1996. pap. 5.00 (*0-7895-1283-1*) Course Tech.

Windows 95: Star Series. Boyd & Fraser Staff. (DF - Computer Applications Ser.). 1996. pap. 12.95 (*0-7895-0180-5*) Course Tech.

Windows 95: The Visual Learning Guide. Grace J. Beatty. 1995. pap. text ed. 19.95 (*1-55958-738-5*) Prima Pub.

Windows 95: Windows Workshop. James E. Shuman. (DF - Computer Applications Ser.). 1996. pap. 39.95 (*0-7895-1220-3*) Course Tech.

Windows 95 - A to Z: The Essential Reference for Every Window's User. Sandra Schnyder. 1995. pap. text ed. 34.95 (*0-7615-0208-4*) Prima Pub.

***Windows 95 - 97.** Kenneth Laudon. LC 97-5548. 1997. pap. text ed. write for info. (*0-07-038441-X*) McGraw.

Windows 95 & NT Networking: A Guide for Professionals. Wayne Robertson & Edward C. Koop. LC 96-30569. (Illus.). 416p. 1996. pap. text ed., pap. 49.95 incl. cd-rom (*0-07-912983-8*) McGraw.

Windows 95 & NT Programming with the Microsoft Foundation Class Library. Ed. by William H. Murray & Chris H. Pappas. (Illus.). 519p. 1996. pap. 34.95 incl. cd-rom (*0-12-511890-2*, AP Prof) Acad Pr.

Windows 95 & NT Programming with the Microsoft Foundation Class Library. William H. Murray & Chris H. Pappas. LC 96-1380. 519p. 1996. pap. 34.95 incl. disk (*0-12-511891-0*, AP Prof) Acad Pr.

Windows 95 & NT, Win 32 from Scratch: A Programmer's Workbook. David Platt. 233p. 1996. Incl. disk. 36.95 incl. disk (*0-13-121484-5*) P-H.

Windows 95 Answers: Certified Tech Support. Martin S. Matthews & Carole B. Matthews. (Certified Tech Support Ser.). 384p. 1995. pap. text ed. 19.95 (*0-07-882128-2*) McGraw.

***Windows 95 Answers! Certified Tech Support.** 2nd ed. Martin S. Matthews & Carole B. Matthews. (Illus.). 448p. 1997. pap. 24.99 (*0-07-882399-4*, Oracle Press) Osborne-McGraw.

Windows 95 API How To. Matthew Telles & Andrew Cooke. 792p. 1996. pap. text ed. 44.99 incl. cd-rom (*1-57169-060-3*, Waite Grp Pr) Sams.

Windows 95 Basics. Que Education & Training Staff. 1996. 16.99 (*1-57576-280-3*) Que Educ & Trng.

Windows 95 Beginning. Joni Racicot. (Quicksteps to Learning Ser.). 1995. spiral bd. 22.95 (*1-56951-029-6*) Sftware Trng.

Windows 95 Bible. 2nd ed. Frederick Davis. (Illus.). 680p. (C). 1995. pap. text ed. 29.95 (*0-201-88388-0*) Peachpit Pr.

***Windows 95 Bible: Explorer Edition.** Alan Simpson. 1997. pap. 49.99 (*0-614-28455-4*) IDG Bks.

***Windows 95 Bible: Explorer Edition.** 2nd ed. Alan Simpson. 1100p. 1997. pap. 49.99 (*0-7645-3069-0*) IDG Bks.

***Windows 95 Bible Explorer Edition.** Alan Simpson. 1100p. (Orig.). 1997. pap. write for info. (*0-614-26283-6*) IDG Bks.

Windows 95 Book: The Definitive Desktop Reference for Windows 95. Richard Mansfield & Charles Brannon. (Illus.). 1232p. 1995. pap. 39.95 incl. cd-rom (*1-56604-154-6*) Ventana Communs.

Windows 95 Booklet: Windows 95 for Dummies Special CompUSA Ed. Review Book. 1995. pap. text ed. 0.49 (*1-56884-612-6*) IDG Bks.

Windows 95 by PAL: Program-Assisted Learning. Dennis P. Curtin et al. 86p. 1996. pap. 33.33 incl. cd-rom (*0-13-456385-9*) P-H.

Windows 95 by Pictorial. Dennis P. Curtin. 1995. pap. text ed. 30.80 (*0-13-456674-2*) P-H.

Windows 95 Cheat Sheet. Joe Kraynak. (Illus.). 461p. (Orig.). 1995. 24.99 (*0-7897-0371-8*, Alpha Ref) Macmillan Gen Ref.

Windows 95 Common Controls & Messages API Bible. Richard J. Simon. (Illus.). 984p. 1996. pap. 54.99 (*1-57169-010-7*, Waite Grp Pr) Sams.

Windows 95 Communication & Online Secrets. David Boles. 1996. pap. 19.99 (*1-56884-837-4*) IDG Bks.

Windows 95 Communications Handbook. Jim Boyce. (Illus.). 662p. (Orig.). 1996. pap. 39.99 incl. cd-rom (*0-7897-0675-X*) Que.

***Windows 95 Complete: Includes Mastering Windows 95 & Expert Guide To Windows 95.** Sybex Press Staff. 1996. pap. text ed. 49.99 incl. cd-rom (*0-7821-2025-3*) Sybex.

Windows 95 Complete Course. Bergerud. (Computer Applications Ser.). 1997. pap. 41.95 (*0-538-71377-1*) S-W Pub.

Windows 95 Concepts & Examples. Carolyn Z. Gillay. (Illus.). 672p. (Orig.). (C). 1996. pap. text ed. 37.95 (*1-887902-00-7*) Franklin Beedle.

Windows 95 Configuration Secrets. 2nd ed. Andy Reese. 1996. pap. 49.99 incl. cd-rom (*1-56884-836-6*) IDG Bks.

Windows 95 Essentials. Laura Acklen. 1995. pap. text ed. 22.99 (*1-57576-012-6*) Que Educ & Trng.

Windows 95 Essentials. Jeff Nelson-Folkerson. 1996. teacher ed., ring bd. 49.99 (*1-57576-250-1*) Que Educ & Trng.

***Windows 95 Essentials.** 2nd ed. Laura Acklen. 1996. spiral bd. 22.99 (*1-57576-632-9*) Macmillan.

Windows 95 Essentials, Level 2. Ellen Colombo. 1996. pap. text ed. 22.99 (*1-57576-255-2*) Que Educ & Trng.

Windows 95 Essentials, IM, Level 2. Jeff Nelson-Fulkersen. 1996. teacher ed., pap. text ed. 49.99 (*1-57576-273-0*) Que Educ & Trng.

Windows 95 Exam Guide. Jim Blakely. 888p. 1996. 99.99 (*0-7897-0744-6*) Mac Comp Pub.

Windows 95 Explorer. Bidgoli. (DF - Computer Applications Ser.). 1996. pap. 40.95 (*0-7895-0659-9*) Course Tech.

Windows 95 Exposed! How to Get the Most from Microsoft Windows 3.1! Brian C. Elwood. (Illus.). 200p. 1997. spiral bd. 16.95 (*1-881432-14-9*) BCS Pub.

***Windows 95 for Beginners.** Philipa Wingate. (Computer Guides Ser.). (Illus.). 48p. (J). (gr. 4 up). 1997. pap. 7.95 (*0-7460-2687-0*, Usborne); lib. bdg. 15.95 (*0-88110-887-1*, Usborne) EDC.

***Windows 95 for Busy People.** (Illus.). 304p. pap. 22.95 (*0-614-19653-1*, OP205195WE) AMA.

***Windows 95 for Busy People.** 2nd ed. Ron Mansfield. 1997. pap. text ed. 24.99 (*0-07-882287-4*) Osborne-McGraw.

***Windows 95 for Dummies.** Andy Rathbone. 1996. pap. 19.99 (*1-56884-240-6*) IDG Bks.

***Windows 95 for Dummies.** 2nd ed. Andy Rathbone. (Illus.). 384p. (Orig.). 1997. pap. 19.99 (*0-7645-0180-1*) IDG Bks.

Windows 95 for Dummies Quick Reference. 2nd ed. Greg Harvey. 1995. pap. 12.99 (*1-56884-981-8*) IDG Bks.

***Windows 95 for Dummies Quick Reference.** 3rd ed. Greg Harvey. (Illus.). 240p. (Orig.). 1997. pap. 12.99 (*0-7645-0183-6*) IDG Bks.

***Windows 95 for Kids & Parents.** 1997. pap. 24.99 (*0-7645-0277-8*) IDG Bks.

Windows 95 for Network Administrators. Kevin Stoltz. (Illus.). 600p. (Orig.). 1995. pap. 40.00 (*1-56205-380-9*) New Riders Pub.

Windows 95 for Teachers. Michelle Robinette. 1996. pap. 19.99 (*1-56884-636-3*) IDG Bks.

***Windows 95 for Teachers.** Michelle Robinette & Dummies Tech Press Staff. (Illus.). 384p. (Orig.). 1997. pap. 24.99 (*0-7645-0081-3*) IDG Bks.

Windows 95 Game Developer's Guide Using the Game SDK. Michael Morrison & Randy Weems. (Illus.). 624p. (Orig.). 1995. 49.99 (*0-672-30661-1*) Sams.

Windows 95 Game S. D. K. Strategy Guide. Clayton Walnum. (Illus.). 580p. (Orig.). 1995. pap. 49.99 incl. cd-rom (*0-7897-0661-X*) Que.

Windows 95 Games Programming. Alan Stevens & Stan Trujillo. 1996. pap. 39.95 incl. cd-rom (*1-55851-448-1*, M&T Books) H Holt & Co.

Windows 95 Installation & Configuration Handbook. Rob Tidrow & Jonathan Maitzkin. (Illus.). 864p. (Orig.). 1997. 39.99 (*0-7897-0580-X*) Que.

***Windows 95 Installation & Configuration Handbook.** 2nd ed. Rob Tidrow. 800p. 1997. 39.99 (*0-7897-1119-2*) Mac Comp Pub.

Windows 95 Instant Reference. Carole B. Matthews & Martin S. Mattews. LC 95-69859. 352p. 1995. 14.99 (*0-7821-1489-X*) Sybex.

Windows 95 Internals: The Implementation of the Windows 95 Operating Environment. 2nd ed. Michael Podanoffsky. 544p. (C). 1996. pap. text ed., pap. 39.95 incl. disk (*0-201-48947-3*) Addison-Wesley.

Windows 95 Internet Server Kit. Peter Harrison. 336p. 1996. pap. 29.99 incl. cd-rom (*0-7821-1815-1*, Strategies & Secrets) Sybex.

Windows 95 is Driving Me Crazy! Kay Y. Nelson. (Illus.). 400p. (C). 1996. pap. text ed. 24.95 (*0-201-88626-X*) Peachpit Pr.

Windows 95 Liferaft. Ronny Richardson. LC 96-15536. 1996. pap. 14.95 (*0-13-492042-2*) P-H.

Windows 95 Made Easy: The Basics & Beyond! Tom Sheldon. (Made Easy Ser.). 656p. 1995. pap. text ed. 27.95 (*0-07-882090-1*) Osborne-McGraw.

Windows 95 Manager's Handbook. Boland. 1995. pap. text ed. 29.95 (*1-56276-267-2*, Ziff-Davis Pr) Que.

Windows 95 Migration Strategies. Computer Technology Research Corp. Staff. (Illus.). 180p. 1995. 285.00 (*1-56607-957-8*) Comput Tech Res.

Windows 95 Multimedia & ODBC API Bible. Richard J. Simon. (Illus.). 1100p. 1996. pap. 54.99 (*1-57169-011-5*, Waite Grp Pr) Sams.

Windows 95 Network Programming with MFC. Ralph Davis. (C). 1996. pap. text ed., pap. 44.95 incl. disk (*0-201-48930-9*) Addison-Wesley.

Windows 95 Networking: A Guide for the Small Office. Corey Sandler. 1996. pap. 24.95 (*1-55828-488-5*) MIS Press.

Windows 95 Networking Secrets. Kevin Stoltz. 1996. pap. 39.99 (*1-56884-815-3*) IDG Bks.

Windows '95 NOW! A Simple Guide to Learning Windows '95 Quickly & Easily! Robert Medved. LC 95-60747. (Illus.). 240p. (Orig.). 1996. pap. 19.99 (*0-9643450-3-X*) Easel Pubng.

Windows 95 on the Job Essentials. Laura Acklen. 1995. pap. text ed. 22.99 (*1-57576-249-8*) Que Educ & Trng.

Windows 95 par Etapes. Catapult, Inc., Staff. 336p. (FRE.). 1995. 95.00 incl. cd-rom (*0-7859-9849-7*) Fr & Eur.

Windows 95 pour les Nuls. Andy Rathbone. 332p. (FRE.). 1995. 49.95 (*0-7859-9853-5*) Fr & Eur.

Windows '95 Power Program Technical Guide. Peter Norton & Paul Yoa. 1995. 34.00 (*0-679-76188-8*) Random.

Windows 95 Power Toolkit: Cutting-Edge Tools & Techniques for Programmers. Richard Mansfield & Evangelos Petroutsos. 800p. 1996. pap. 49.95 incl. cd-rom (*1-56604-319-0*) Ventana Communs.

Windows '95 Power Tools. Martin S. Matthews. 1995. write for info. (*0-679-76902-1*) Random.

***Windows 95 Power Tools.** 3rd ed. Martin Matthews. Date not set. pap. 9.99 (*0-517-19221-7*) Random Hse Value.

Windows 95 Programming Bug Collection: Fixes & Work-Arounds of Pesky Problems When Running Windows 95. Bruce Brown et al. LC 95-38809. 1996. pap. 14.95 (*0-201-48995-3*) Addison-Wesley.

Windows 95 Programming for Dummies. Stephen R. Davis & Randy Davis. 400p. 1995. pap. 19.99 (*1-56884-327-5*) IDG Bks.

Windows 95 Programming for Mere Mortals. Kathleen Krueger. 1995. pap. 39.95 incl. disk (*0-201-48393-9*) Addison-Wesley.

Windows 95 Programming Internals. Kris Jamsa. pap. 49.95 (*1-884133-18-5*) Jamsa Pr.

Windows 95 Programming Nuts & Bolts: For Experienced Programmers. Herbert Schildt. 256p. 1995. pap. text ed. 24.95 (*0-07-882147-9*) McGraw.

Windows 95 Programming with Custom Controls, with CD-ROM. Paul Cilwa. 1996. pap. 39.99 incl. cd-rom (*1-883577-73-X*) Coriolis Grp.

Windows 95 Quick & Easy. 2nd ed. Robert Cowart. LC 95-69863. 248p. 1995. 22.99 (*0-7821-1511-X*) Sybex.

Windows 95 Quick by Example. Carolyn Z. Gillay. LC 97-4124. (Illus.). 320p. (Orig.). (C). 1997. pap. text ed. 22.95 (*1-887902-01-5*) Franklin Beedle.

Windows 95 Quick Course. Bergerud. (DF - Computer Applications Ser.). 1997. pap. 18.95 (*0-538-64113-4*) S-W Pub.

Windows 95 Registry Tuning. Que Development Group Staff. 430p. 1996. 49.99 (*0-7897-0725-X*) Que.

***Windows 95 Revealed.** Jack Nimersheim. Date not set. pap. 4.99 (*0-517-17697-1*) Random Hse Value.

Windows 95 RX. R. Kober & F. Buechel. 1996. 34.95 incl. cd-rom (*1-55755-297-5*) Abacus MI.

***Windows 95 Secrets.** Brian Livingston. 1997. pap. 49.99 (*0-7645-3070-4*) IDG Bks.

Windows 95 Secrets. 3rd ed. Brian Livingston. 800p. 1995. pap. 39.99 (*1-56884-453-0*) IDG Bks.

***Windows 95 Secrets.** 4th ed. Brian Livingston. 1997. 69.99 (*0-7645-3124-7*) IDG Bks.

***Windows 95 Secrets.** 4th ed. Brian Livingston. 1997. pap. 29.99 (*0-7645-3122-0*) IDG Bks.

Windows 95 Secrets Gold. Brian Livingston & Davis Straub. 1996. pap. text ed. 69.99 incl. cd-rom (*0-7645-3005-4*) IDG Bks.

***Windows 95 SECRETS Gold Internet Edition.** deluxe ed. Brian Livingston & Davis Straub. 1008p. (Orig.). 1997. pap. 49.99 incl. cd-rom (*0-614-26278-X*) IDG Bks.

***Windows 95 Simplificado.** (SPA.). 1996. pap. 24.99 (*0-7645-6016-6*) IDG Bks.

Windows 95 Simplified & Expanded. Maran Graphics Staff & Ruth Maran. 240p. 1995. pap. 19.99 (*1-56884-662-2*) IDG Bks.

Windows 95 System Programming Secrets. Matt Pietrek. 1995. pap. 49.99 (*1-56884-318-6*) IDG Bks.

Windows 95 Textbook Standard Edition. Stewart M. Venit. 520p. (Orig.). (C). Date not set. pap. text ed. 38.00 (*1-881991-45-8*) Scott Jones Pubng.

***Windows 95 Training Guide.** James Turley. (Training Guide Ser.). (Illus.). 350p. 1997. pap. text ed. 49.95 (*0-12-703867-1*, AP Prof) Acad Pr.

***Windows 95 Troubleshooting & Configuration.** Eric Schall et al. 1000p. 1997. 49.99 (*0-672-30951-3*) Mac Comp Pub.

Windows 95 Uncut. Alan Simpson & Devra Hall. 1000p. 1995. pap. 39.99 (*1-56884-074-8*) IDG Bks.

Windows 95 Unleashed. Ed Tiley. (Illus.). 1072p. (Orig.). 1995. pap. text ed. 39.99 (*0-672-30474-0*) Sams.

***Windows 95 Unleashed: MCSE Edition.** Paul McFedries. 1997. 65.00 (*0-672-31187-9*) Mac Comp Pub.

Windows 95 Upgrade. Joni Racicot. (Quicksteps to Learning Ser.). 1995. spiral bd. 22.95 (*1-56951-030-X*) Sftware Trng.

Windows 95 Virtual Tutor. Que Education & Training Staff. 1996. pap. text ed. 35.00 incl. cd-rom (*1-57576-083-5*) Que Educ & Trng.

Windows 95 Visual Pocket Guide. Maran Graphics Staff. 256p. 1995. pap. 14.99 (*1-56884-661-4*) IDG Bks.

Windows 95 Visual Quick Reference. Michael Watson. (Illus.). 160p. (Orig.). 1995. pap. 12.99 (*0-614-07849-0*) Que.

Windows 95 Win32 Programming API Bible. Richard J. Simon et al. 1400p. 1996. pap. 54.95 (*1-57169-009-3*, Waite Grp Pr) Sams.

***Windows 97: The Visual Learning Guide.** 288p. 1997. per. 16.99 (*0-7615-1006-0*) Prima Pub.

***Windows 97 Complete.** Sean C. Feeney & Douglas M. Finney. (Illus.). (Orig.). 1997. spiral bd., pap. 39.95 incl. disk (*1-56435-133-5*) Finney Lrng Systs.

***Windows 97 Professional Reference.** Joe Casad. Date not set. 59.99 (*1-56205-786-3*) New Riders Pub.

***Windows 97 Simplified.** Maran Graphics Staff. 1997. pap. 24.99 (*0-7645-6030-1*) IDG Bks.

Windowsill Gardening Book & Kit. (Illus.). 1994. 19.95 (*0-8069-0903-X*) Sterling.

Windowsill Science Centers. Lynn Kepler. 1996. pap. text ed. 10.95 (*0-590-74395-3*) Scholastic Inc.

Windpumps: A Guide for Development Workers. Peter Frankel et al. (Illus.). 144p. (Orig.). 1993. pap. 28.95 (*1-85339-126-3*, Pub. by Intermed Tech UK) Women Ink.

Windrhythm. Ray Buttigieg. 1983. pap. 5.50 (*0-932436-06-4*) Cykx.

Windrider. Pamela Freeman. (Illus.). 112p. (Orig.). (J). (gr. 3-7). 1996. pap. 6.95 (*1-86373-928-9*, Pub. by Allen & Unwin Aust Pty AT) IPG Chicago.

***Windrow & Greene's Militaria Directory & Sourcebook 1997/1998.** Windrow & Greene Staff. 1997. 24.95 (*1-85915-068-3*, Pub. by Windrow & Green UK) Motorbooks Intl.

Winds. Mark Dunster. 26p. (Orig.). (YA). (gr. 9-12). 1996. 5.00 (*0-89642-321-2*) Linden Pubs.

Winds Across Texas. Susan Tanner. 384p. (Orig.). 1994. mass mkt., pap. text ed. 4.99 (*0-8439-3582-0*) Dorchester Pub Co.

Winds in the Cornfields of Early Pueblo County: Ghost Towns & Settlements, 1787-1872. 2nd ed. Arla Aschermann. (Illus.). 72p. 1988. pap. 5.00 (*0-915617-15-3*) Pueblo Co Hist Soc.

Winds of Allegiance. Linda L. Chaikin. LC 95-45788. (Great Northwest Ser.: Vol. 2). 304p. (Orig.). 1996. pap. 9.99 (*1-55661-442-X*) Bethany Hse.

Winds of Altair. Ben Bova. 1988. pap. 3.95 (*0-8125-3227-9*) Tor Bks.

Winds of April. I. D. Baharav. LC 65-17184. 1965. 10.00 (*0-911184-04-X*) Primary.

Winds of Autumn. Rupert Hickman. 1995. 8.95 (*0-533-11281-8*) Vantage.

Winds of Autumn. Janette Oke. LC 86-34299. (Seasons of Heart Ser.: No. 2). 224p. 1987. pap. 8.99 (*0-87123-946-9*) Bethany Hse.

W

***Winds of Autumn.** Dwaine Starr. Ed. by Dave Richey & Sharon Starr. (Illus.). 112p. (Orig.). 1996. pap. 12.95 (*0-9650943-1-6*) Starr Ent.
Winds of Autumn. large type ed. Janette Oke. (Seasons of Heart Ser.: No. 2). 1987. pap. 10.99 (*0-87123-982-5*) Bethany Hse.
Winds of Catawba. Laurie Stahl. LC 94-37439. 240p. 1995. pap. 9.99 (*0-8407-5081-1*) Nelson.
Winds of Change. Mercedes Lackey. (Mage Winds Ser.: Bk. 2). 448p. (Orig.). 1992. 20.00 (*0-88677-534-5*) DAW Bks.
Winds of Change. Mercedes Lcakey. (Mage Winds Ser.: Bk. 2). 480p. 1993. mass mkt. 6.99 (*0-88677-563-9*) DAW Bks.
Winds of Change. Donald Rumble. 54p. 1986. reprint ed. pap. 3.50 (*0-914903-12-8*) Destiny Image.
Winds of Change: A Colloquium in Music Education with Charles Fowler & David J. Elliott. Ed. by Marie McCarthy. LC 94-6524. (State-of-the-Arts Ser.). 1994. write for info. (*1-879903-19-9*) Am Council Arts.
***Winds of Change: Air Transport since Deregulation.** 399p. 1991. pap. 30.00 (*0-309-05104-5*, SR230) Natl Acad Pr.
Winds of Change: And Other Stories. Marie Nowinson. 1984. mass mkt. 4.95 (*0-345-31188-4*) Ballantine.
Winds of Change: Buddhism & the Early Maritime Links of South Asia. Himanshu P. Ray. (Illus.). 240p. 1995. 29.95 (*0-19-563551-5*) OUP.
***Winds of Change: Challenges Confronting Journalism Education.** Betty Medsger. 185p. (Orig.). 1996. pap. write for info. (*0-9655091-0-9*) Freedm Forum.
Winds of Change: Government & Higher Education Relationships over Three Continents: A Report to the World Bank. Ed. by Guy Neave & Frans A. Van Vught. LC 93-23566. (Issues in Higher Education Ser.). 334p. 1994. text ed. 86.50 (*0-08-042391-4*) Elsevier.

Winds of Change: Korean Women in America. Diana Yu. Ed. by Daisy B. Fields. LC 91-65430. 424p. (Orig.). 1991. reprint ed. pap. 11.95 (*0-9629619-0-6*) D Y T Bks.
WINDS OF CHANGE: KOREAN WOMEN IN AMERICA, by Diana Yu, is the first volume to comprehensively & critically address the difficult issue of assimilation into American life that many Korean women experience ... This book makes credible the issues confronting women immigrants to America as well as elaborating the struggle which is present in contemporary Korean life ... Explicit detail & comprehensive examination of individual lives through the use of interviews bring a realistic aspect to the analysis ... A significant & unique contribution to the literature on Women's Studies. A vivid account of the transformation of Korean women when their traditional roles impact with American social values. Written in an engaging narrative style, it depicts the evolution of Korean women from serf-hood to self-hood. The author dramatically reveals the impact of two radically diverse cultures on Korean-American women who cling to traditional roles under male dominance. The author's account combines tireless research with a skillful presentation that challenges the reader by the facts without losing interest. To order: Make check payable to DYT Books for $14.95 ($11.95 plus $3.00 shipping & handling) & mail to DYT Books, 7498 E. Sand Hills Road, Scottsdale, AZ 85255. Phone: 602-585-2996. FAX 602-585-5556. For bookstores call toll free 1-800-999-4650 for Bookpeople or 1-800-243-0138 for Inland Book Company. ***Publisher Provided Annotation.***

Winds of Change: Macmillan to Heath, 1957-1975. John Ramsden. (History of the Conservative Party Ser.). 528p. (C). 1995. text ed. 92.50 (*0-582-27570-9*) Longman.
Winds of Change: The New Economic Challenges, India. D. N. Patodia. 150p. 1987. 21.00 (*0-8364-2060-8*, Pub. by Allied II) S Asia.
Winds of Change: Women in Northwest Commercial Fishing. Charlene J. Allison et al. LC 89-16422. (Illus.). 232p. 1989. 25.00 (*0-295-96840-0*) U of Wash Pr.
***Winds of Change: 1960-1970.** (This Fabulous Century Ser.). (Illus.). 288p. 24.95 (*0-8094-8208-8*) Time-Life.
***Winds of Change in Agricultural Research.** 121p. pap. 33.00 (*0-614-24231-2*) Agri Research Inst.
Winds of Change in Central & Eastern Europe. Daniel Gros & Alfred Steinherr. (Economics of Transition Ser.). 400p. (C). 1995. pap. text ed. 72.95 (*0-582-10271-5*, 76765, Pub. by Longman UK); pap. text ed. 37.50 (*0-582-10270-7*, 76764, Pub. by Longman UK) Longman.
Winds of Change in China. Lesley Francis. 1985. pap. 1.25 (*9971-972-30-1*) OMF Bks.
Winds of Creativity: Finding Fulfillment Through Creative Act. Richard S. Kimball. LC 96-14390. (Illus.). (Orig.). 1996. pap. 18.95 (*0-944443-07-9*) Green Timber.
***Winds of Darkover.** Marion Z. Bradley. (Darkover Ser.). 192p. 1996. 22.00 (*0-7278-5191-8*) Severn Hse.
Winds of Dawn. Deborah Potter. LC 96-94134. (Maran Chronicles Ser.: Bk. 1). 376p. (Orig.). 1996. pap. 12.95 (*1-888289-09-0*, 289090) Mythspinner.
Winds of Death: Iraq's Use of Poison Gas Against Its Kurdish Population. Physicians for Human Rights Staff. 39p. 1989. pap. 6.00 (*0-614-14420-5*) Phy Human Rights.
Winds of Destiny. 1996. pap. 2.99 (*0-8217-5481-5*) Kensgtn Pub Corp.
Winds of Destiny. Laurel Pace. 1994. mass mkt. 3.99 (*0-373-28842-5*, 1-28842-5) Harlequin Bks.
Winds of Destiny. large type ed. Pat Dalton. 255p. 1995. pap. 17.95 (*0-7838-1455-0*, GK Hall) Thorndike Pr.
Winds of Destiny: An Immigrant Girl's Odyssey. Serpoohi C. Jafferian. (Illus.). 288p. (Orig.). 1993. pap. 14.95 (*0-935411-10-0*) Natl Assn Arm.
Winds of Destruction: Cross of Deception. A. R. Tureaud & M. L. Tureaud. 64p. 1995. per., pap. 7.00 (*0-8059-3665-3*) Dorrance.
Winds of Doctrines: The Origin & Development of Southern Baptist Theology. W. Wiley Richards. 244p. 1991. 54.00 (*0-8191-8254-0*) U Pr of Amer.
Winds of Fate. Mercedes Lackey. (Mage Winds Ser.: Bk. 1). (Illus.). 416p. 1991. 18.95 (*0-88677-489-6*) DAW Bks.
Winds of Fate. Mercedes Lackey. (Mage Winds Ser.: Bk. 1). 464p. 1992. mass mkt. 6.99 (*0-88677-516-7*) DAW Bks.
Winds of Fire. Vyankatesh Madgulkar. Tr. by Pramod Kale from MAR. 113p. 1975. pap. 2.50 (*0-88253-693-1*) Ind-US Inc.
Winds of Freedom: The Story of the Navajo Code Talkers of World War II. Margaret T. Bixler. 202p. 1966. pap. text ed. 16.95 (*1-881907-01-5*) Two Bytes Pub.
Winds of Freedom: The Story of the Navajo Code Talkers of World War II. Margaret T. Bixler. 189p. 1994. text ed. 23.95 (*1-881907-00-7*) Two Bytes Pub.
Winds of Fury. Mercedes Lackey. (Mage Winds Ser.). 464p. 1993. 20.00 (*0-88677-562-0*) DAW Bks.
Winds of Fury. Mercedes Lackey. (Mage Winds Ser.: Bk. 3). 448p. 1994. reprint ed. mass mkt. 5.99 (*0-88677-612-0*) DAW Bks.
***Winds of Fury, Circles of Grace: Life after the Palm Sunday Tornadoes.** Dale Clem. 160p. 1997. pap. text ed. 10.95 (*0-687-01795-5*) Abingdon.
***Winds of Fury, Circles of Grace: Life after the Palm Sunday Tornadoes.** Dale Clems. 1997. pap. 10.95 (*0-614-27484-2*) Abingdon.
Winds of Glory. Susan Wiggs. 400p. 1988. pap. 3.95 (*0-380-75482-7*) Avon.
Winds of Glory. Susan Wiggs. 384p. 1995. mass mkt. 4.99 (*0-06-108180-9*, Harp PBks) HarpC.
Winds of God. Norvel Hayes. 90p. (Orig.). 1985. pap. 5.99 (*0-89274-375-1*) Harrison Hse.
Winds of God. Gilbert Morris. LC 94-28712. (Wakefield Dynasty Ser.: No. 2). 422p. 1994. pap. 11.99 (*0-8423-7953-3*) Tyndale.
Winds of God. 2nd ed. Ethel E. Goss. (Illus.). 288p. 1958. pap. 7.99 (*0-912315-26-1*) Word Aflame.
Winds of Grace, Ways of Faith: Expanding the Horizons of Christian Spirituality. William K. McElvaney. 144p. (Orig.). 1992. pap. 12.00 (*0-664-25120-X*) Westminster John Knox.
Winds of Graystone Manor. B. J. Hoff. LC 95-20761. (St. Clare Trilogy Ser.). 1995. audio 14.99 (*1-55661-827-1*) Bethany Hse.
Winds of Graystone Manor. B. J. Hoff. LC 95-20761. (St. Clare Trilogy Ser.: No. 1). 1556615337p. (YA). (gr. 7-10). 1995. pap. 9.99 (*1-55661-435-7*) Bethany Hse.
Winds of Graystone Manor. large type ed. B. J. Hoff. 504p. 1996. 22.95 (*0-7838-1703-7*, GK Hall) Thorndike Pr.
Winds of Hope for a World Out of Breath: A Study of the 23rd Psalm. Robert G. Tuttle. LC 92-31682. 1992. pap. 8.50 (*1-55673-508-1*, 9300) CSS OH.
Winds of Imagination. Petie W. Baldwin. LC 76-17537. 1976. pap. 5.00 (*0-917166-01-9*) Creative Vent.
Winds of Injustice: American Indians & the U. S. Government. Laurence A. French. LC 93-29355. (Library of Sociology: Vol. 7). 288p. 1994. text ed. 48.00 (*0-8153-0886-8*, HH847) Garland.
Winds of Ixtepeji: World View & Society in a Zapotec Town. Michael Kearney. (Illus.). 140p. 1986. reprint ed. pap. text ed. 9.95 (*0-88133-210-0*) Waveland Pr.
Winds of Love. Agnes S. Turnbull. 1978. pap. 1.75 (*0-449-23575-0*, Crest) Fawcett.
Winds of Mars. H. M. Hoover. LC 94-32095. 176p. (J). 1995. pap. 14.99 (*0-525-45359-8*) Dutton Child Bks.
***Winds of Mars.** H. M. Hoover. Date not set. pap. 4.99 (*0-14-038039-6*) Viking Penguin.
Winds of Morning. Harold L. Davis. LC 77-138586. 344p. 1972. reprint ed. text ed. 38.50 (*0-8371-5785-4*, DAWM, Greenwood Pr) Greenwood.
Winds of My Mind. Louise F. Underhill. (Illus.). 60p. (Orig.). 1986. pap. 5.00 (*0-936204-55-9*) Underhill Ent.
Winds of Passion. Barbara A. Cooper. 1981. mass mkt. 2.75 (*0-89083-778-3*, Zebra Kensgtn) Kensgtn Pub Corp.
Winds of Promise. Shirlee Evans. LC 89-11181. 224p. (Orig.). 1990. pap. 7.99 (*0-8361-3506-7*) Herald Pr.
Winds of Renewal. Time-Life Books Editors. LC 95-37240. (American Indians Ser.: Vol. 22). (Illus.). 176p. 1996. 19.95 (*0-8094-9579-1*) Time-Life.
Winds of Revolution: Time Frame: AD 1700-1800. Time-Life Books Editors. (Time Frame Ser.). (Illus.). 176p. 1990. lib. bdg. write for info. (*0-8094-6459-4*) Time-Life.
Winds of Rome. Leigh McAllister. LC 87-42908. 200p. 1988. 9.95 (*1-55523-119-5*) Winston-Derek.
Winds of September. Raymond Borders. (Illus.). 405p. 1994. pap. 5.95 (*0-9648528-0-2*) Bastion Bks.
Winds of the Spirit: A Constructive Christian Theology. Peter C. Hodgson. LC 93-46593. 416p. (Orig.). 1994. pap. 29.00 (*0-664-25443-8*) Westminster John Knox.
Winds of the World & the Many Cloud Forms. Palmer W. Roberts. 1995. 10.95 (*0-533-11198-6*) Vantage.
Winds of the World as Seen in Satellite Imagery. National Environmental Satellite, Data & Information Service Staff & Satellite Applications Lab Staff. (NWA Publication: No. 1-90). 21p. 1990. pap. text ed. 84.00 incl. sl. (*1-883563-07-0*) Natl Weather.
Winds of Time. Jean Duling. LC 94-68579. 1995. 12.95 incl. audio (*0-8158-0508-X*) Chris Mass.
Winds of Time. Jeanne Sanders. LC 86-70863. (Illus.). 50p. (Orig.). 1986. pap. 8.95 (*0-9617109-2-6*) Armagh Press.
Winds of Time. Sy Varlen. 1993. 12.95 (*0-533-10464-5*) Vantage.
***Winds of Time: The VerNooy Family in the New World.** Raymond L. Penoyer. LC 96-77525. (Illus.). xiv, 454p. 1996. 40.00 (*0-9653363-4-4*) Grandview Pr.
Winds of Tomorrow. Donald C. Wilson. 402p. 1995. 25.95 (*0-9648805-0-4*) DCW Pubng.
Winds of War. Herman Wouk. 1971. 35.00 (*0-316-95500-0*) Little.
Winds of War. Herman Wouk. 1056p. 1992. mass mkt. 6.99 (*0-316-95516-7*) Little.
Winds of Wisdom. Luther M. Taylor. 1996. 8.95 (*0-533-11150-1*) Vantage.
Winds over Saddle Creek. Lois Bogue. Ed. by Janet Leih. LC 94-60966. (Illus.). 56p. (Orig.). 1994. pap. 6.00 (*1-877649-23-6*) Tesseract SD.
***Winds Twelve Quarters.** Ursula K. Le Guin. 1995. mass mkt. 4.99 (*0-06-105605-7*) HarpC.
Wind's Will. Gerald W. Brace. 1964. 4.50 (*0-393-08435-3*) Norton.
Wind's Will. Arnold Perrin. 24p. 1993. pap. 4.00 (*0-939736-05-5*) Wings ME.
WINDSHAW LEGACY. Jonathan Coe. LC 94-12842. 1995. 24.00 (*0-679-43385-6*) Knopf.
Windshear. Ed Beamish. 1995. 21.95 (*0-533-11392-X*) Vantage.
Windship Race. large type ed. John Wingate. 400p. 1988. 25.99 (*0-7089-1923-5*) Ulverscroft.
Windships of Warren, Maine, Seventeen Seventy to Eighteen Sixty-Seven. Leland Overlock. LC 88-90850. (Illus.). 306p. 1988. pap. 12.50 (*0-941216-41-1*); lib. bdg. 20.00 (*0-941216-42-X*) Cay-Bel.
***Windshook.** Mary Gallagher. 1997. pap. 5.25 (*0-8222-1596-9*) Dramatists Play.
Windshopping Maui: A Serious Sailor's Guide to the Valley Isle. Arleone Dibben-Young. (Illus.). 176p. (Orig.). 1987. pap. 12.95 (*0-9617864-0-X*) A Dibben-Young.
Windsingers. Ed. by Charlotte M. Babcock et al. 125p. (Orig.). 1984. pap. text ed. write for info. (*0-917557-01-8*) Wyo Writers.
Windsocks & Lyrica. Peter Lawlor. LC 94-90586. 55p. 1994. pap. write for info. (*0-9644104-0-0*) Full Moon CA.
***Windsong.** 317p. 1997. pap. 11.95 (*0-9656811-2-2*) Four Seasons.
Windsong. Judith E. French. 368p. (Orig.). 1988. mass mkt. 3.95 (*0-380-75551-3*) Avon.
Windsong. Lynn Hall. LC 91-46075. 80p. (J). (gr. 6-8). 1992. lib. bdg. 12.95 (*0-684-19439-2*, C Scribner Sons Young) S&S Childrens.
Windsong. Valerie Sherwood. 1986. pap. 4.50 (*0-317-41571-9*) PB.
Windsong: Texas Cherokee Princess. Raven Hail. LC 86-90672. (Illus.). 141p. (Orig.). 1986. pap. 8.95 (*0-9617696-1-0*) Raven Hail Bks.
Windsong Summer. (J). Date not set. pap. 1.50 (*0-590-72048-1*) Scholastic Inc.
Windsongs. Timothy R. Botts. 288p. 1989. 19.99 (*0-8423-8252-6*) Tyndale.
Windsongs & Rainbows. Burton Albert. LC 92-12012. (J). (ps-2). 1993. pap. 14.00 (*0-671-76004-1*, S&S Bks Young Read) S&S Childrens.
Windsor. Mark Girouard. Date not set. write for info. (*0-393-03628-6*) Norton.
Windsor Handbook. Wallace Nutting. LC 73-77579. (Illus.). 256p. 1973. pap. 14.95 (*0-8048-1105-9*) C E Tuttle.
Windsor Knot. Sharyn McCrumb. 1992. mass mkt. 5.99 (*0-345-36427-9*) Ballantine.
***Windsor Locks Historical Sketches.** Jabez H. Hayden. (Illus.). 132p. 1997. reprint ed. pap. 16.50 (*0-8328-5702-5*) Higginson Bk Co.
Windsor Red. Jennie Melville. 1990. mass mkt. 3.50 (*0-373-26051-2*) Harlequin Bks.
***Windsor Style in America, 2 vols.** Charles Santore. (Illus.). 296p. 1997. 39.98 (*0-7624-0190-7*) Courage Bks.
Windsor, the Birth of a City. Gabriel A. Fraire. LC 91-61538. (Illus.). 256p. (C). 1991. 21.95 (*1-877810-91-6*) Rayve Prodns.
Windsor vs. Windsor. Nigel Blundell. 1996. mass mkt. 6.99 (*1-85782-115-7*, Pub. by Blake Publng UK) Seven Hills Bk.
***Windstorm.** Connie Bennett. 1998. mass mkt. 4.50 (*0-373-81016-4*, 1-81016-7) Harlequin Bks.
Windstorm. Katherine Sutcliffe. (Avon Romance Ser.). 368p. 1987. mass mkt. 4.99 (*0-380-75264-6*) Avon.
Windstorm: Women Who Dare. Connie Bennett. (Superromance Ser.). 1993. mass mkt. 3.50 (*0-373-70562-X*, 1-70562-3) Harlequin Bks.
Windsurfing. (Take up Sports! Ser.). (Illus.). 64p. pap. 4.95 (*1-56757-058-5*) Appleton Comms.
Windsurfing. J. Cook & P. Way. (Practical Guides Ser.). (Illus.). (J). (gr. 6 up). 1988. pap. 8.95 (*0-7460-0195-9*) EDC.
Windsurfing. Jeremy Evans. LC 91-7886. (Adventurers Ser.). (Illus.). 48p. (J). (gr. 5-6). 1992. lib. bdg. 13.95 (*0-89686-680-7*, Crstwood Hse) Silver Burdett Pr.
Windsurfing. Ann Gadd. (C). 1989. 45.00 (*1-85368-045-1*, Pub. by New Holland Pubs UK) St Mut.
Windsurfing. Ken Winner. LC 94-25210. (Outdoor Pursuits Ser.). (Illus.). 136p. (Orig.). 1995. pap. 13.95 (*0-87322-760-3*, PWIN0760) Human Kinetics.
Windsurfing: Step by Step to Success. Robert Reichenfeld. (Illus.). 176p. 1993. pap. 24.95 (*1-85223-746-5*, Pub. by Crowood Pr UK) Trafalgar.
Windsurfing: Technique, Tactics, Training. Penny Way. (Illus.). 127p. 1992. pap. 22.95 (*1-85223-481-4*, Pub. by Crowood Pr UK) Trafalgar.
Windsurfing: The Skills of the Game. Ben Oakley. (Illus.). 128p. 1994. pap. 19.95 (*1-85223-830-5*, Pub. by Crowood Pr UK) Trafalgar.
Windsurfing in the Caribbean: Your Guide to the Best Windsurfing Spots in the Caribbean. Florence Chatzigianis. (Illus.). 128p. 1996. pap. 16.95 (*1-888847-26-3*) Poly Media.
Windsurfing (Wind Surf Ing) to Boardsail. Frank Fox. (Illus.). 96p. (Orig.). 1987. pap. 6.95 (*0-934965-03-X*) Amber Co Pr.
Windswept. Deborah Martin. (Historical Romance Ser.). 384p. 1996. pap. 5.50 (*0-451-40676-1*, Onyx) NAL-Dutton.
Windswept. Magdalena Zschokke. LC 95-26696. 192p. (Orig.). 1996. pap. 10.95 (*0-934678-73-1*) New Victoria Pubs.
Windswept House: A Vatican Novel. Malachi Martin. 640p. 1996. 24.95 (*0-385-48408-9*) Doubleday.
Windwalker: A Happening in the Smokies. Anne Long. 192p. (Orig.). 1991. pap. 7.95 (*0-925591-19-X*) Covenant Hse Bks.
Windwalker Speaks. Nadia Giordana. 109p. 1994. pap. 9.99 (*1-886352-02-X*) Crow Feather.
Windward Islands Visitor's Guide. (Visitor's Guides Ser.). (Illus.). 224p. (Orig.). 1996. pap. 15.95 (*0-86190-559-8*) Hunter NJ.
Windward Road: Adventures of a Naturalist on Remote Caribbean Shores. Archie Carr. LC 79-23624. (Illus.). xl, 266p. 1979. reprint ed. pap. 16.95 (*0-8130-0639-2*) U Press Fla.
Windy City. Hugh Holton. 320p. 1996. mass mkt. 5.99 (*0-8125-6714-5*); mass mkt. 5.99 (*0-8125-3695-9*) Forge NYC.
Windy City. Hugh Holton. 352p. 1995. 22.95 (*0-312-85711-X*) Tor Bks.
Windy City Blues. Sara Paretsky. 1995. pap. 24.95 (*0-7871-0478-7*, Dove Bks) Dove Audio.
Windy City Blues. large type ed. Sara Paretsky. LC 95-36362. 336p. 1996. 24.95 (*0-7838-1561-1*, GK Hall) Thorndike Pr.
Windy City Blues. large type ed. Sara Paretsky. LC 95-36362. 1996. pap. 22.95 (*0-7838-1562-X*, GK Hall) Thorndike Pr.
Windy City Blues: V.I. Warshawski Stories. Sara Paretsky. LC 95-8302. 258p. 1995. 19.95 (*0-385-31502-3*) Delacorte.
Windy City Blues: V.I. Warshawski Stories. Paretsky Sara. 352p. 1996. mass mkt. 6.99 (*0-440-21873-X*) Dell.
***Windy City Wars: Labor, Leisure, & Sport in the Making of Chicago.** Gerald R. Gems. LC 97-12133. (American Sports History Ser.). 1997. write for info. (*0-8108-3305-0*) Scarecrow.
Windy Day. Halina Below. (Illus.). 32p. (J). (gr. 1-3). 1995. 14.95 (*1-895555-74-4*, Pub. by Stoddart Pubng CN) Genl Dist Srvs.
Windy Day. Janet Craig. LC 87-10909. (Illus.). 32p. (J). (gr. k-2). 1988. lib. bdg. 9.79 (*0-8167-0982-3*) Troll Communs.
Windy Day. Janet Craig. LC 87-10909. (Illus.). 32p. (J). (gr. k-2). 1997. pap. 2.50 (*0-8167-0983-1*) Troll Communs.
***Windy Day.** G. Brian Karas. LC 97-25427. (J). 1998. write for info. (*0-689-81449-6*) S&S Childrens.
Windy Day. Laura Pegram. (J). (ps). 1994. 5.95 (*0-86316-218-5*) Writers & Readers.
Windy McPherson's Son. Sherwood Anderson. LC 93-11209. (Prairie State Bks.). 392p. 1993. 13.95 (*0-252-06357-0*) U of Ill Pr.
Windy Passage from Nostalgia. Richard Grossinger. 256p. (Orig.). 1974. pap. 5.00 (*0-913028-30-4*) North Atlantic.
Windy Times: Poems & Prose. Gunter Kunert. Tr. by Agnes Stein. (Illus.). 227p. 1984. 14.95 (*0-87376-042-5*) Red Dust.
Windy Woods: Bartholomew & the Fabulous Bumbly-Flop. Michael P. Waite. 32p. (J). 1996. mass mkt. 4.99 (*0-7814-0279-4*) Chariot Victor.
Windy Woods: Treasures of Willowbye Woods. Michael P. Waite. 32p. (J). 1996. mass mkt. 4.99 (*0-7814-0280-8*) Chariot Victor.
***Wine.** LC 96-6591. (101 Essential Tips Ser.: Vol. 30). 72p. 1997. pap. 6.95 (*0-7894-1464-3*) DK Pub Inc.
Wine. rev. ed. Hugh Johnson. 272p. 1987. pap. 18.95 (*0-671-63834-3*, Fireside) S&S Trade.
Wine: A Curse or a Blessing. Muriel Van Loh. (Alcohol in the Bible Ser.: Bk. 1). (Illus.). 1992. write for info. (*0-9629731-0-6*) Promise Hse.
Wine: A Practical Guide. Juan C. Elizalde. (Illus.). 157p. (Orig.). 1983. pap. 7.00 (*0-9608162-0-8*) Ideas CA.
Wine: A Primer. (Illus.). 80p. 1992. 4.95 (*0-8362-3013-2*) Andrews & McMeel.
Wine: A Record Keeping Journal. Illus. by Yan Nascimbene. 160p. 1996. spiral bd. 17.95 (*1-55670-515-8*) Stewart Tabori & Chang.
Wine: An Introduction. rev. ed. Maynard A. Amerine & Vernon L. Singleton. LC 75-46031. 1978. pap. 15.00 (*0-520-03202-0*) U CA Pr.
***Wine: Nutritional & Therapeutic Benefits, Vol. 661.** American Chemical Society Staff. Ed. by Tom R. Watkins. LC 96-52456. (Symposium Ser.: No. 661). (Illus.). 296p. 1997. 89.95 (*0-8412-3497-3*) Am Chemical.
Wine Album. Illus. by Charles Martin. 160p. 1993. 20.00 (*0-517-59212-6*, Crown) Crown Pub Group.
Wine Analysis. Bruce W. Zoecklein. 1989. text ed. 75.00 (*0-442-23463-5*) Chapman & Hall.
Wine Analysis & Production. Bruce W. Zoecklein et al. LC 94-17776. 1994. write for info. (*0-412-98921-2*) Chapman & Hall.
Wine Analysis & Production. Bruce W. Zoecklein. 640p. (gr. 13). 1995. text ed. 79.95 (*0-412-98241-2*) Chapman & Hall.

W

Wine & Bitters. Isabelle K. Savelle. LC 75-18954. (Illus.). 1975. pap. 1.95 (*0-911183-06-X*) Rockland County Hist.

Wine & Conversation. Adrienne Lehrer. LC 82-48538. 256p. 1983. 35.00 (*0-253-36550-3*); pap. 18.95 (*0-253-20308-2*, MB-308) Ind U Pr.

Wine & Dine: California Fine Wines Matched with Gourmet Recipes. Ron Breitstein & Hendrik Van Leuven. LC 96-32400. (Illus.). 266p. (Orig.). 1996. pap. 15.95 (*0-88496-410-8*) Capra Pr.

Wine & Food Guide to the Loire, France's Royal River. Jacqueline Friedrich. (Illus.). 384p. 1996. 27.50 (*0-8050-4390-X*) H Holt & Co.

Wine & Food Handbook: Aide-Memoire du Sommelier. Conrad Tuor. 1993. pap. text ed. 9.95 (*0-614-00701-1*) Wiley.

Wine & Gastronomy: A New Short-Title Bibliography Guide Based on the Andre L. Simon Bibliothecas Vinaria, Gastronomica, & Bacchica. Gail G. Unzelman. LC 90-91676. (Illus.). 345p. 1990. 85.00 (*0-9626543-0-2*) Nomis Pr.

***Wine & Price 1997: International Auction Results Wine & Spirits.** Ed. by Harry Blattel & Frank Stainless. 1700p. 1997. 64.00 (*3-928263-21-8*, Pub. by Arts & Antiques GW) Seven Hills Bk.

Wine & the Vine. Tim Unwin. 448p. 1996. pap. 22.95 (*0-415-14416-7*) Routledge.

Wine & the Will: Rabelais's Bacchic Christianity. Florence M. Weinberg. LC 78-181450. 189p. reprint ed. 53.90 (*0-685-16200-1*, 2027593) Bks Demand.

Wine & Thorns in Tokay Valley: Jewish Life in Hungary: The History of Abaujszanto. Zahava S. Stessel. LC 92-55129. (Illus.). 344p. 1995. 49.50 (*0-8386-3545-8*) Fairleigh Dickinson.

Wine & Wine Offering in the Religion of Ancient Egypt. Mu-chou Poo. LC 95-6571. (Studies in Egyptology). 1995. write for info. (*0-7103-0501-X*) Routledge Chapman & Hall.

Wine & Your Well Being. Salvatore P. Lucia. 160p. 1980. reprint ed. 9.95 (*0-932664-08-3*) Wine Appreciation.

Wine Appreciation. Richard P. Vine. LC 96-8971. 1997. text ed. 59.95 (*0-471-15396-6*) Wiley.

Wine Atlas of Australia & New Zealand. James Halliday. 368p. 1992. 50.00 (*0-207-16476-2*, Pub. by Angus & Robertson AT) HarpC.

***Wine Atlas of California.** 45.00 (*1-85732-162-6*, Pub. by M Beazley Pubs Ltd UK) Antique Collect.

Wine Atlas of California. James Halliday. (Illus.). 368p. 1993. pap. 50.00 (*0-670-84950-2*, Viking) Viking Penguin.

Wine Atlas of California, with Oregon & Washington: A Traveler's Guide to the Vineyards. Bob Thompson. LC 92-42938. 1993. 45.00 (*0-671-79663-1*) S&S Trade.

***Wine Atlas of France.** 45.00 (*1-85732-336-X*, Pub. by M Beazley Pubs Ltd UK) Antique Collect.

Wine Atlas of France: And Traveller's Guide to the Vineyards. Hugh Johnson & Hubrecht Duijker. (Illus.). 280p. 1994. 40.00 (*0-85533-593-9*, Pub. by Reed Illust Books UK) Antique Collect.

Wine Atlas of Germany: And Traveller's Guide to the Vineyards. Stuart Pigott. (Illus.). 232p. 40.00 (*1-85732-625-3*, Pub. by Reed Illust Books UK) Antique Collect.

***Wine Atlas of Italy: And Traveller's Guide to the Vineyards.** Burton Anderson & Stuart Pigott. 40.00 (*0-85533-793-1*, Pub. by M Beazley Pubs Ltd UK) Antique Collect.

Wine Basics: A Quick & Easy Guide. Dewey Markham, Jr. LC 92-27315. 208p. 1993. pap. text ed. 14.95 (*0-471-58258-1*) Wiley.

***Wine, Beer & Spirits: The Concise Guide.** Thomas Owen. LC 96-85517. (Illus.). 152p. (Orig.). 1997. pap. 5.95 (*0-9653295-1-8*) Copacetic Publns.

Wine Behind the Veil. Barbara J. Glenn. LC 94-72420. 1995. 10.95 (*0-8158-0505-5*) Chris Mass.

***Wine Book: How to Choose & Enjoy the World's Best Wines.** Robert Joseph. (Illus.). 272p. 1996. 29.98 (*0-7651-9784-7*) Smithmark.

***Wine Buyer's Companion for Dummies.** Ed McCarthy. 1997. pap. 14.99 (*0-7645-5043-8*) IDG Bks.

***Wine Buyers Guide.** Alexis Bespaloff. Date not set. pap. write for info. (*0-688-03985-5*, Quill) Morrow.

Wine Buyer's Guide see Parker's Wine Buyer's Guide: Third Edition

Wine Cellar Record. Maurice T. Sullivan. (Illus.). 1979. 32.50 (*0-932664-06-7*) Wine Appreciation.

Wine Chemistry: Current Concepts. Ed. by Yair Margalit & James Crum. (Illus.). 446p. (C). 1997. 79.95 (*0-932664-91-1*, 6924) Wine Appreciation.

***Wine Collector's Handbook.** Linda Johnson. LC 97-12779. (Illus.). 224p. 1997. 25.00 (*1-55821-460-7*, 14607) Lyons & Burford.

Wine Cookbook of Dinner Menus. Emily Chase. (Illus.). 1978. 6.95 (*0-932664-04-0*) Wine Appreciation.

Wine Cookbook of Dinner Menus. Wine Advisory Board Staff. LC 70-156348. 1971. 5.95 (*0-87832-038-5*, WAB-6) Piper.

Wine Cooler Market. Ed. by Peter Allen. 200p. 1985. pap. text ed. 295.00 (*0-931634-18-0*) FIND-SVP.

***Wine Country Bike Rides: The Best Tours in Sonoma, Napa, & Mendocino Counties.** Lena Emmery. LC 96-32452. 1997. pap. 10.95 (*0-8118-1355-X*) Chronicle Bks.

***Wine Country France.** 2nd ed. Access Guides Staff. (Access Travel Guides Ser.). 256p. 1997. pap. 18.50 (*0-06-277193-0*, Access NY) HarpC.

Wine Country France Access. (Access Travel Guides Ser.). 176p. 1995. pap. 18.50 (*0-06-277151-5*, Harper Ref) HarpC.

Wine Country Recipes: A Collection of Favorite Wine Country Recipes for Steppin-out Magazine. rev. ed. Jeanne Francis. (Illus.). 160p. 1993. pap. 7.95 (*1-886048-02-9*) Francis Pubns.

***Wine-Dark Opal.** Virginia Coffman. (Romance-Hall Ser.). 407p. 1997. 24.95 (*0-7838-8105-3*, GK Hall) Thorndike Pr.

***Wine-Dark Opal, Vol. 2.** Virginia Coffman. (Jewels Ser.). 320p. 1996. 24.00 (*0-7278-5139-X*) Severn Hse.

Wine-Dark Sea. Patrick O'Brian. LC 93-1521. 1993. 22.50 (*0-393-03558-1*) Norton.

Wine-Dark Sea. Patrick O'Brian. 272p. 1994. pap. 12.95 (*0-393-31244-5*) Norton.

Wine Dictionary: English, French, German. Maria Ibald. (ENG, FRE & GER.). 1994. 295.00 (*0-7859-9993-0*) Fr & Eur.

Wine Dossier. Shawn M. Preston. (Illus.). 160p. 1995. 29.95 (*0-9647874-0-7*) Mako Pubng.

Wine East of the Rockies. Hudson Cattell & Lee Miller. LC 82-90971. (Illus.). 160p. 1982. 17.50 (*0-911301-00-3*) L&H Photojrnl.

Wine Family in America, Section 3. Jacob D. Wine & J. Floyd Wine. LC 53-4352. (Illus.). 1971. 20.00 (*0-9604350-0-X*) J F Wine.

Wine, Food & the Good Life. Arlene Mueller & Dorothy Indelicato. (Wine Cookbook Ser.). (Illus.). 144p. (Orig.). 1985. pap. 9.95 (*0-932664-47-4*) Wine Appreciation.

Wine for Dummies. Mary E. Mulligan. 400p. 1995. pap. 16.99 (*1-56884-390-9*) IDG Bks.

Wine from Two Glasses (Poetry & Politics: Trust & Mistrust in Language) Anthony Rudolf. 1991. pap. 9.00 (*1-870921-03-8*) SPD-Small Pr Dist.

***Wine Growers Guide: How to Grow Wine Grapes.** rev. ed. Philip Wagner. (Illus.). 240p. 1997. pap. 19.95 (*0-932664-92-X*, 546) Wine Appreciation.

***Wine Guide.** Godin, Seth, Productions Staff. (Cader Flip Ser.). 1997. pap. text ed. 3.95 (*0-8362-2559-7*, Cader Bks) Andrews & McMeel.

***Wine in Context: Nutrition, Physiology, Policy: Proceedings of the Symposium on Wine & Health, 1996.** Ed. by Joanne M. Rantz & Andrew L. Waterhouse. 89p. 1996. 40.00 (*0-9630711-3-0*) Am Soc Enology.

Wine in Everyday Cooking: Cooking with Wine for Family & Friends. Patricia Ballard. 128p. pap. 8.95 (*0-932664-45-8*) Wine Appreciation.

Wine in the Wilderness. Alice Childress. 1969. pap. 3.25 (*0-8222-1261-7*) Dramatists Play.

Wine Industry: Market Segment Specialization Program-Audit Technique Guide. 110p. 1995. pap. 38.00 (*1-57402-117-6*) Athena Info Mgt.

Wine into Words: A History & Bibliography of Wine Books in the English Language. James M. Gabler. LC 84-70446. (Illus.). 403p. 1985. 19.00 (*0-9613525-0-7*) Bacchus Pr Ltd.

Wine Inventory Book. Duncan L. LaVigne. 90p. 1990. 59.95 (*0-9625723-0-6*) Wine Bk Co.

Wine Investors' Guide. Gillette. Date not set. write for info. (*0-395-33125-0*) HM.

Wine Journal. Gerald Asher. (Illus.). 128p. 1996. 17.95 (*0-00-225150-7*) Harper SF.

Wine Journal. Larry Springer. 96p. (Orig.). 1996. pap. 8.95 (*0-8362-2142-7*) Andrews & McMeel.

Wine Journal: Wine Recording System. Red Deer College Pr. Staff. 128p. 1993. 14.95 (*0-88995-107-1*, Pub. by Red Deer CN) Orca Bk Pubs.

Wine Log. Irene J. Kleinsinger. (Illus.). 96p. 1982. 24.95 (*0-9605146-4-3*) IJK Intl.

Wine Lover's Companion. Ron Herbert. 1995. pap. 11.95 (*0-8120-1479-0*) Barron.

Wine Lover's Cookbook. Malcolm Herbert & Brian St. Pierre. (Wine Cookbook Ser.). (Illus.). 128p. (Orig.). 1983. pap. 9.95 (*0-932664-82-2*) Wine Appreciation.

***Wine Lover's Gift Set: The Wine Lover's Guide & The Wine Lover's Record Book, 2 bks.** Jane Huges. (Illus.). 128p. 1997. 14.95 (*1-85967-458-5*, Lorenz Bks) Anness Pub.

Wine Microbiology. Kenneth C. Fygelsang. 384p. (gr. 13). 1996. text ed. 79.95 (*0-412-06611-4*) Chapman & Hall.

Wine Microbiology & Biotechnology. Ed. by Graham H. Fleet. LC 92-14987. 1993. pap. write for info. (*3-7186-5293-5*); text ed. 132.00 (*3-7186-5132-7*) Gordon & Breach.

Wine Navigator: How to Pick the Right Wine Every Time. Doug Hexter. 1995. pap. 9.95 (*0-684-80066-7*, Fireside) S&S Trade.

Wine of Astonishment. Rachel Mackenzie. LC 96-83495. 160p. (Orig.). 1997. pap. 13.95 (*1-885983-17-4*) Turtle Point Pr.

***Wine of Astonishment.** Mary Overton. LC 97-65055. 200p. (Orig.). 1997. pap. 12.00 (*0-9644348-1-4*) La Questa Pr.

Wine of Astonishment. William Sears. 192p. 1963. pap. 6.50 (*0-85398-009-8*) G Ronald Pub.

Wine of Astonishment. Earl Lovelace & Marjorie Thorpe. (Caribbean Writers Ser.). 146p. (C). 1986. reprint ed. pap. 9.95 (*0-435-98880-8*, 98880) Heinemann.

Wine of Astonishment see Point of No Return

Wine of Endless Life: Taoists Drinking Songs. Tr. by Jerome Seaton. 1991. pap. 9.00 (*0-934834-59-8*) White Pine.

Wine of Life: And Other Essays on Societies, Energy & Living Things. Harold J. Morowitz. LC 79-16404. 1979. 18.95 (*0-312-88227-0*) Ox Bow.

Wine of Morning. Bob Jones. 252p. 1976. reprint ed. pap. 6.50 (*0-89084-056-3*, 001784) Bob Jones Univ Pr.

Wine of Nishapur. Illus. by Shahrokh Golestan. 120p. 1989. 44.00 (*2-87658-040-3*) Iran Bks.

Wine of the Mystic: A Spiritual Interpretation of the Rubaiyat of Omar Khayyam. Paramahansa Yogananda. LC 94-66217. (Illus.). 248p. 1994. 25.00 (*0-87612-225-X*) Self Realization.

Wine of the Mystic: A Spiritual Interpretation of the Rubaiyat of Omar Khayyam. Paramahansa Yogananda. LC 94-66217. (Illus.). 248p. 1996. pap. 17.50 (*0-87612-226-8*) Self Realization.

Wine of the Spirit: Prayer. Lilian P. Long. LC 87-91322. 208p. (Orig.). 1988. pap. 9.95 (*0-9619722-1-1*) L P Long Pub.

Wine of Youth: Selected Stories of John Fante. John Fante. LC 84-20454. 269p. 1997. reprint ed. 25.00 (*0-87685-583-4*); reprint ed. pap. 14.00 (*0-87685-582-6*) Black Sparrow.

Wine Production Technology in the United States. Ed. by Maynard A. Amerine. LC 80-28041. (Symposium Ser.: No. 145). 1981. 29.95 (*0-8412-0596-5*); pap. 21.95 (*0-8412-0602-3*) Am Chemical.

***Wine Production Technology in the United States.** Ed. by Maynard A. Amerine. LC 80-28041. (ACS Symposium Ser.: No. 145). (Illus.). 240p. 1981. reprint ed. pap. 68.40 (*0-608-03231-X*, 2063750) Bks Demand.

Wine Project: Washington State's Winemaking History. Ronald A. Irvine & Walter J. Clore. Ed. by Miriam Bulmer. 450p. (Orig.). 1996. 49.95 (*0-9650834-6-2*) Sketch Pubns.

Wine Project: Washington State's Winemaking History. Ronald A. Irvine & Walter J. Clore. Ed. by Miriam Bulmer & Kris Fulsaas. LC 96-92401. 450p. (Orig.). 1997. pap. 29.95 (*0-9650834-9-7*) Sketch Pubns.

Wine Quotations. Ed. by Helen Exley. (Quotations Bks.). (Illus.). 60p. 1994. 8.00 (*1-85015-434-1*) Exley Giftbooks.

Wine Regions of America: Geographical Reflections & Appraisals. John J. Baxevanis. LC 92-60540. (Illus.). 400p. (Orig.). (C). 1992. pap. 55.00 (*0-922983-51-8*) Vinifera Wine.

Wine Regions of the World. 2nd ed. Burroughs et al. 1988. pap. 38.95 (*0-7506-0631-2*) Buttrwrth-Heinemann.

Wine Revolution in France: The Twentieth Century. Leo A. Loubere. (Illus.). 331p. (C). 1990. text ed. 47.50 (*0-691-05592-0*) Princeton U Pr.

Wine Roads of Italy. Marc Millon & Kim Millon. (Illus.). 529p. 1993. pap. 22.00 (*0-246-13737-1*, Pub. by HarpC UK) HarpC.

***Wine Routes of Argentina: The Wines, Grapes & Winemakers.** Alan Young. (Illus.). 176p. 1997. 29.95 (*0-932664-99-7*, 6975) Wine Appreciation.

Wine Savvy: The Simple Guide to Buying & Enjoying Wine Anytime, Anywhere. rev. ed. Heidi Yorkshire. (Illus.). 111p. (Orig.). 1995. pap. 12.95 (*1-883970-16-4*) Duplex Media.

***Wine Savvy International: A Global Guide to Wine.** Heidi Yorkshire. (Illus.). 111p. (Orig.). 1997. pap. 12.95 (*1-883970-25-3*) Duplex Media.

Wine Scandal. Fritz Hallgarten. 184p. 1986. 18.95 (*0-932664-52-0*) Wine Appreciation.

Wine Science: Principles & Applications. Ron S. Jackson. (Food Science & Technology Ser.). (Illus.). 475p. 1994. text ed. 79.95 (*0-12-379060-3*) Acad Pr.

Wine-Sip & Other Delicious Poems. Sharon Smith-Knight. 1991. 7.00 (*0-940713-06-3*) Broadside Pr.

***Wine-Song in Classical Arabic Poetry: Abu Nuwas & the Literary Tradition.** Philip F. Kennedy. (Oxford Oriental Monographs). 250p. 1997. 65.00 (*0-19-826392-9*) OUP.

Wine Spectator Magazine's: Ultimate Guide to Buying Wine. James Laube. 992p. 1996. pap. text ed. 24.95 (*1-881659-34-8*) M Shanken Comm.

Wine Spectator Magazine's Guide to Great Wine Values $10 & Under, 1997 Edition. Wine Spectator Press Staff. 264p. 1996. pap. text ed. 9.95 (*1-881659-35-6*) M Shanken Comm.

***Wine Spectator Magazine's Guide to the Wines of Bordeaux 1998 Edition.** Ed. by Wine Spectator Magazine Staff. 256p. 1997. 9.95 (*1-881659-42-9*) M Shanken Comm.

***Wine Spectator Magazine's Guide to White Wines from California & Other U. S. Regions 1998 Edition.** Ed. by Wine Spectator Magazine Staff. 256p. 1997. 9.95 (*1-881659-44-5*) M Shanken Comm.

***Wine Spectator's Guide to Red Wines of California & Other U. S. Regions, 1997.** Wine Spectator Press Staff. 1997. pap. 9.95 (*1-881659-40-2*) M Shanken Comm.

***Wine Spectator's Guide to White Wines of California & Other U. S. Regions 1997 Edition.** 256p. 1996. pap. 9.95 (*1-881659-39-9*, Wine Spectator) M Shanken Comm.

***Wine Spectators Magazine's Guide to Great Wine Values $10 & under 1998 Edition.** Ed. by Wine Spectator Magazine Staff. 256p. 1997. 9.95 (*1-881659-41-0*) M Shanken Comm.

***Wine Spectator's Wine Country Guide to California.** (Illus.). 144p. 1996. pap. 6.95 (*1-881659-33-X*) M Shanken Comm.

Wine Talk. Frank Prial. LC 78-58165. 1978. write for info. (*0-8129-0793-0*, Times Bks) Random.

***Wine Talk: A Vintage Collection of Facts & Legends for Wine Lovers.** Andrew Jones. (Illus.). 144p. (Orig.). 1997. pap. 8.95 (*0-7499-1697-4*, Pub. by Piatkus Bks UK) London Brdge.

Wine-Tasting Course. Judy Ridgway. 1996. 40.00 (*0-517-70559-1*) Random.

Wine Tasting Handbook. Paul Gillette. (Illus.). 1988. pap. 7.95 (*0-913290-88-2*) Camaro Pub.

Wine Tasting in California. LC 73-85632. (Illus.). 1985. 4.95 (*0-913290-05-X*) Camaro Pub.

Wine Tour of Italy: Traveler's Journal. (Illus.). 160p. 1992. pap. 12.95 (*0-8478-5595-8*) Rizzoli Intl.

Wine Trails of the Northeast - 96: From Maine to Maryland. 16p. 1996. pap. 3.95 (*0-918734-46-0*) Reymont.

***Wine Vintages.** 14.95 (*1-85732-762-4*, Pub. by M Beazley Pubs Ltd UK) Antique Collect.

Wine Vintages of the West Coast. 2nd ed. Robin Bradley. (Illus.). 114p. 1986. pap. 12.95 (*0-9590183-1-X*) Aris Bks.

Wine Widow. large type ed. Tessa Barclay. 1993. 39.95 (*0-7066-1012-1*, Pub. by Remploy Pr CN) St Mut.

***Wine with Food.** Simon. 1997. 25.00 (*0-684-83522-3*) S&S Trade.

Wine, Women & Death: Medieval Hebrew Poems on the Good Life. Raymond P. Scheindlin. (Illus.). 204p. 1986. 24.50 (*0-8276-0266-9*) JPS Phila.

Wine, Women, & Song. Ed. & Tr. by John A. Symonds. LC 74-112944. reprint ed. 27.50 (*0-404-06319-5*) AMS Pr.

Wine, Women & Words. Billy Rose. (American Autobiography Ser.). 295p. 1995. reprint ed. lib. bdg. 79.00 (*0-7812-8631-X*) Rprt Serv.

Wine, Women, Warren, & Skis. Warren A. Miller. 1993. pap. 10.95 (*0-9636144-0-1*) W Miller Prods.

Winecoff Fire: The True Story of America's Deadliest Hotel Fire. Sam Heys & Allen Goodwin. LC 92-84011. (Illus.). 276p. 1993. 19.95 (*1-56352-069-9*) Longstreet Pr Inc.

***Winecon Workbook: Interactive Economics.** Jean Soper & Phil Hobbs. LC 96-29123. Date not set. pap. write for info. (*0-631-19795-8*) Blackwell Pubs.

Winegrowers of France & the Government Since 1875. Charles K. Warner. LC 74-14029. 303p. 1975. reprint ed. text ed. 55.00 (*0-8371-7779-0*, WAWF, Greenwood Pr) Greenwood.

Winegrowing in Eastern America: An Illustrated Guide to Viniculture East of the Rockies. Lucie T. Morton. LC 85-47696. (Illus.). 208p. (C). 1985. 32.50 (*0-8014-1290-0*) Cornell U Pr.

Winemaker's Cook Book. Ed. by Ken Parry. 125p. 1993. pap. text ed. 9.95 (*1-886026-01-7*) Wine Grape.

***Winemaker's Record Book.** 96p. (YA). 1997. pap. 6.95 (*1-55192-116-2*, Pub. by Raincoast Bks CN) Orca Bk Pubs.

Winemaking. Stanley F. Anderson & Dorothy Anderson. (Illus.). 224p. 1989. pap. 21.00 (*0-15-697095-3*) HarBrace.

***Winemaking: From Grape Growing to Marketplace.** Richard P. Vine. LC 96-41930. (Enology Library). 1997. write for info. (*0-412-12221-9*) Chapman & Hall.

Winemaking & the Winemaker. Phil King. LC 88-91282. 1989. pap. 5.00 (*0-9601900-5-8*) Phil King.

Winemaking Basics. Cornelius S. Ough. LC 91-2253. (Illus.). 340p. 1992. pap. 29.95 (*1-56022-006-6*); lib. bdg. 59.95 (*1-56022-005-8*) Haworth Pr.

Winemaking Month by Month. 3rd rev. ed. Brian Leverett. (Illus.). 36p. 1995. pap. text ed. 7.95 (*1-85327-096-2*, Pub. by Prism Pr UK) Assoc Pubs Grp.

Winemaking with Concentrates. Peter Duncan. (Illus.). 96p. (Orig.). 1995. pap. 14.95 (*1-85486-118-2*, Pub. by Nexus Special Interests UK) Trans-Atl Phila.

Winequest: The Wine Dictionary. Ted Grudzinski. 1976. 29.95 (*0-8499-0278-9*) Amereon Ltd.

Wineries of British Columbia. John Schreiner. (Illus.). 244p. (Orig.). 1994. pap. 14.95 (*1-55143-024-X*) Orca Bk Pubs.

Wineries of the Eastern States. Marguerite Thomas. (Great Destinations Ser.). (Illus.). 320p. 1996. pap. 17.95 (*0-936399-77-5*) Berkshire Hse.

***Wineries of the Eastern States.** 2nd ed. Marguerite Thomas. LC 97-24979. (Great Destinations Ser.). 1997. write for info. (*0-936399-89-9*) Berkshire Hse.

Wineries of the Great Lakes: A Guidebook. 1995. pap. 15.00 (*1-881892-03-4*) Spradlin & Assocs.

Wineries of the Mid-Atlantic. Jon Palmer. 220p. (Orig.). (C). 1988. pap. 12.95 (*0-8135-1351-0*); text ed. 35.00 (*0-8135-1346-4*) Rutgers U Pr.

Winery, Defenses, & Soundings at Gibeon. James B. Pritchard. (University Museum Monographs: No. 26). (Illus.). viii, 85p. 1964. pap. 15.00 (*0-934718-18-0*) U PA Mus Pubns.

Winery Tours. rev. ed. Nadja Djekich. Ed. by Kristine Miller. 144p. 1996. pap. 5.95 (*1-56413-241-2*) Auto Club.

Winery Utilities. D. Storm. 1992. text ed. write for info. (*0-442-00811-2*) Chapman & Hall.

***Winery Utilities: Planning, Design, & Operation.** David R. Storm. LC 96-2752. (Enology Library). (Illus.). 550p. (C). (gr. 13). 1996. 99.95 (*0-412-06601-7*) Chapman & Hall.

Wines & Beers of Old New England: A How-to-Do-It History. Sanborn C. Brown. LC 77-72519. 185p. reprint ed. pap. 52.80 (*0-7837-2994-4*, 2042947) Bks Demand.

Wines & Grapes of California. rev. ed. John D. Sarles. LC 88-51394. (Illus.). 112p. 1988. pap. 10.95 (*0-9604488-1-0*) Wine Bks.

Wines & Vines of California. Gary L. Peters. (Illus.). 200p. (Orig.). 1989. pap. 16.95 (*0-89863-136-X*) Star Pub CA.

Wines & Vines of Napa County: Coles' Insider's Guide. Ed. by Austin P. Moss. (Insiders Guide Ser.). (Illus.). 280p. (Orig.). 1991. pap. 11.95 (*0-929635-06-X*) Cole Pub Co Inc.

Wines & Vines of Sonoma County. Ed. by Austin P. Moss. LC 90-1763. (Insiders Guide Ser.). 280p. (Orig.). 1990. pap. 9.95 (*0-929635-01-9*) Cole Pub Co Inc.

***Wines & Vineyards: Inside California's Wine Regions.** Gary L. Peters. (Illus.). 270p. 1998. pap. write for info. (*0-89863-203-X*) Star Pub CA.

Wines & Vineyards of Spain. Miguel Torres. 200p. 1982. 19.95 (*0-932664-27-X*) Wine Appreciation.

Wines & Wine Gardens of Austria. S. F. Hallgarten & F. L. Hargaten. (Illus.). 340p. 1979. 15.95 (*0-932664-26-1*) Wine Appreciation.

Wines & Winelands of France: Geological Journeys. Ed. by Charles Pomerol. (Illus.). 370p. 1990. text ed. 45.00 (*1-85365-108-7*, Pub. by McCarta UK) Seven Hills Bk.

Wines Brewing Distillation. Gerald F. Steinlage. LC 72-189987. 91p. 1972. pap. 3.95 (*0-914754-01-7*) Steinlage.

W

An Asterisk (*) at the beginning of an entry indicates that the title is appearing in BIP for the first time.

Wines from a Small Garden: From Planting to Bottling. James Page-Roberts. (Illus.). 128p. 1995. 24.95 (0-7892-0076-7) Abbeville Pr.

Wines from the Wilds. Steven A. Krause. LC 95-26536. (Illus.). 192p. 1996. pap. 14.95 (0-8117-2986-9) Stackpole.

Wines in the Wilderness: Plays by African American Women from the Harlem Renaissance to the Present. Compiled by Elizabeth Brown-Guillory. LC 89-25857. (Contributions in Afro-American & African Studies: No. 135). 272p. 1990. text ed. 59.95 (0-313-26509-7); pap. text ed. 14.95 (0-275-93567-1, B3537) Greenwood.

Wines of Alsace. Tom Stevenson. Ed. by Julian Jeffs. (Books on Wine). (Illus.). 480p. 1993. pap. 22.95 (0-571-14953-7) Faber & Faber.

Wines of Australia: New Edition. Oliver Mayo. (Books on Wine). 246p. 1991. 14.95 (0-571-16396-3) Faber & Faber.

Wines of Bordeaux. Edmund Penning-Roswell. 704p. (Orig.). 1983. pap. 12.95 (0-932664-51-2) Wine Appreciation.

Wines of Bordeaux & Western France. John J. Baxevanis. 288p. 1987. 50.50 (0-8476-7490-8, R7490) Rowman.

Wines of Burgundy. Robert H. Parker. 1990. 45.00 (0-671-63378-3) S&S Trade.

Wines of Burgundy. Serena Sutcliffe. (Illus.). 248p. 15.95 (1-85732-675-X, Pub. by Reed Illust Books UK) Antique Collect.

Wines of Champagne, Burgundy, & Eastern & Southern France. John J. Baxevanis. 296p. 1987. 50.50 (0-8476-7534-3, R7534) Rowman.

Wines of Greece. Miles Lambert-Gocs. (Books on Wine). (Illus.). 336p. 1990. 24.95 (0-571-15387-9); pap. 13.95 (0-571-15388-7) Faber & Faber.

Wines of Italy. Charles G. Bode. Date not set. 8.75 (0-8446-5007-2) Peter Smith.

Wines of Italy. Charles G. Bode. (Illus.). 135p. 1974. reprint ed. pap. 3.95 (0-486-23003-1) Dover.

Wines of New England: A Travel Guide & Tasting Diary. Ed. by Ricia Gordon. 1990. pap. 12.95 (0-9621439-2-8) Whetstone Pub.

Wines of New Zealand. Rosemary George. 298p. 1996. 29.95 (0-571-17419-1) Faber & Faber.

***Wines of New Zealand.** Rosemary George. 298p. 1996. pap. 15.95 (0-571-17420-5) Faber & Faber.

Wines of Portugal. 2nd ed. Jan Read. (Books on Wine). (Illus.). 220p. (Orig.). 1988. pap. 11.95 (0-571-15003-9) Faber & Faber.

***Wines of South Africa.** James Seely. (Illus.). 1997. 29.95 (0-571-17644-5); pap. 16.95 (0-571-17645-3) Faber & Faber.

Wines of South-West France. Paul Strang. (Illus.). 355p. 1995. 35.00 (1-85626-155-7, C Kyle) Trafalgar.

Wines of South-West France. Paul Strang. (Illus.). 288p. 1996. pap. 17.95 (1-85626-222-7, C Kyle) Trafalgar.

Wines of Spain. 2nd ed. Jan Read. (Books on Wine). 272p. (Orig.). 1986. pap. 13.95 (0-571-14621-X) Faber & Faber.

Wines of Texas: A Guide & a History. rev. ed. Sarah J. English. (Illus.). 160p. 1995. 16.95 (1-57168-054-3) Sunbelt Media.

Wines of the Loire. Roger Voss. Ed. by Julian Jeffs. (Books on Wine). 256p. 1995. 29.95 (0-571-16485-4); pap. 14.95 (0-571-16486-2) Faber & Faber.

Wines of the Loire, Alsace & the Rhone: And Other French Regional Wines. Roger Voss. (Illus.). 240p. 1995. 15.95 (1-85732-674-1, Pub. by Reed Illust Books UK) Antique Collect.

Wines of the Rhone. 3rd ed. John Livingstone-Learmonth. (Faber Books on Wine). (Illus.). 384p. 1992. 39.95 (0-571-15111-6) Faber & Faber.

***Wines of the Rhone Valley.** 2nd rev. ed. Parker. LC 97-5507. 1997. 40.00 (0-684-80013-6) S&S Trade.

Winesburg by the Sea: Poems. Harold Witt. 1979. pap. 5.00 (0-914476-71-8) Thorp Springs.

Winesburg, Ohio. Sherwood Anderson. 1988. 22.95 (0-8488-0417-1) Amereon Ltd.

Winesburg, Ohio. Sherwood Anderson. 272p. 1993. pap. 5.95 (0-451-52569-8, Sig Classics) NAL-Dutton.

***Winesburg, Ohio.** Sherwood Anderson. Ed. by Glen A. Love. (The World's Classics Ser.). 256p. 1997. pap. 7.95 (0-19-282405-8) OUP.

Winesburg, Ohio. Sherwood Anderson. 1987. mass mkt. 4.95 (0-14-039059-6, Penguin Classics) Viking Penguin.

Winesburg, Ohio. Sherwood Anderson. 256p. 1988. pap. 3.95 (0-14-043304-X, Penguin Bks) Viking Penguin.

Winesburg, Ohio. Sherwood Anderson. 256p. 1992. pap. 8.95 (0-14-018655-7, Penguin Classics) Viking Penguin.

Winesburg, Ohio. Sherwood Anderson. LC 94-23229. 252p. 1995. 13.50 (0-679-60146-5, Modern Lib) Random.

Winesburg, Ohio. Sherwood Anderson. 256p. 1995. mass mkt. 4.95 (0-553-21439-X) Bantam.

Winesburg, Ohio. large type ed. Sherwood Anderson. (Large Print Ser.). 330p. 1993. reprint ed. lib. bdg. 24.00 (0-939495-45-7) North Bks.

Winesburg, Ohio. unabridged ed. Sherwood Anderson. 96p. 1995. pap. text ed. 2.00 (0-486-28269-4) Dover.

Winesburg, Ohio. Sherwood Anderson. 1993. reprint ed. lib. bdg. 89.00 (0-7812-5336-5) Rprt Serv.

Winesburg, Ohio: An Authoritative Text, Backgrounds & Contexts, Criticism. Ed. by Charles E. Modlin & W. W. Norton. LC 95-10378. (Critical Editions Ser.). 224p. (C). 1995. pap. text ed. 6.95 (0-393-96795-6) Norton.

Winesburg, Ohio: Text & Criticism. Sherwood Anderson. Ed. by John H. Feres. LC 95-52436. 512p. 1996. pap. 14.95 (0-14-024779-3, Penguin Bks) Viking Penguin.

Winesburg, Ohio Notes. Ann R. Morris. 61p. (Orig.). (C). 1974. pap. text ed. 3.75 (0-8220-1382-7) Cliffs.

Winetaster's Secrets: A Step-by-Step Guide to the Art of Wine Tasting. Andrew Sharp. 148p. (Orig.). 1994. pap. 14.95 (1-895629-36-5, Pub. by Warwick Pub CN) Firefly Bks Ltd.

Winfax Pro 4 Visual Learning Guide. David Gardner. 1994. pap. 19.95 (1-55958-470-X) Prima Pub.

WinFax Pro 7 for Windows: The Visual Learning Guide. Grace J. Beatty. 1996. pap. 19.95 (0-7615-0380-3) Prima Pub.

Winfield: A Player's Life. Dave Winfield & Tom Parker. 320p. 1989. mass mkt. 4.50 (0-380-70709-8) Avon.

Winfield Scott: The Soldier & the Man. Charles W. Elliot. Ed. by Richard H. Kohn. LC 78-22379. (American Military Experience Ser.). (Illus.). 1980. reprint ed. lib. bdg. 63.95 (0-405-11856-2) Ayer.

Winfield Scott Hancock: A Soldier's Life. David M. Jordan. LC 87-46091. (Illus.). 416p. 1988. 31.50 (0-253-36580-5) Ind U Pr.

Winfield Scott Hancock: A Soldier's Life. David M. Jordan. (Illus.). 416p. 1995. pap. 14.95 (0-253-21058-5) Ind U Pr.

***Winfield Scott Hancock: Gettysburg Hero.** Perry Jamieson. (Civil War Campaigns & Commanders Ser.). (Illus.). 132p. (Orig.). 1997. pap. 12.95 (1-886661-22-7, 61227) Ryan Place Pub.

Wing. limited ed. Kathleen Fraser. (Illus.). (Orig.). 1995. pap. 75.00 (0-9632085-8-6) Em Pr.

Wing & a Prayer. Harry Crosby. 416p. 1994. mass mkt. 7.99 (0-06-100812-5, Harp PBks) HarpC.

Wing & a Prayer. Paul Hostetler. LC 92-75502. (Illus.). 159p. (Orig.). (YA). 1993. pap. 7.95 (0-916035-58-1) Evangel Indiana.

Wing & a Prayer. Guy Kingston. 192p. 1986. 15.95 (0-8027-0887-0) Walker & Co.

Wing & Shot. Robert G. Wehle. 1964. 25.00 (0-913174-10-6) Country Pr NY.

Wing & Wing. James Fenimore Cooper. (Works of James Fenimore Cooper Ser.). 1990. reprint ed. lib. bdg. 79.00 (0-7812-2389-X) Rprt Serv.

Wing Beat: A Collection of Eagle Woodcuts. G. E. Pogony. Tr. by Douglas J. Graham from HUN. LC 76-22176. (Illus.). 1976. 15.00 (0-933652-10-0) Domjan Studio.

***Wing Beat 1996-97: The Sportsmen's Directory Devoted to Upland Game Bird Hunting & Related Business.** Scott Palmer. (Illus.). 28p. (Orig.). 1996. pap. 5.95 (0-9654342-0-6) Palmer Mktg.

Wing Chun - Jeet Kune Do, Vol. 1. William Cheung & Ted Wong. Ed. by Mike Lee. LC 90-63463. (Illus.). 192p. (Orig.). 1990. pap. 14.95 (0-89750-124-1, 464) Ohara Pubns.

Wing Chun Bil Jee: The Deadly Art of Thrusting Fingers. William Cheung. LC 83-50021. (Illus.). 160p. (Orig.). 1983. pap. 10.95 (0-86568-045-0, 214) Unique Pubns.

Wing Chun Kung-Fu. J. Yimm Lee. LC 72-87863. (Chinese Arts Ser.). (Illus.). 1972. pap. 12.95 (0-89750-037-7, 309, Wehman) Ohara Pubns.

***Wing Chun Kung Fu.** Yip. Date not set. pap. 12.95 (0-312-15695-2) St Martin.

Wing Chun Kung-Fu, Vol. 1: Basic Forms & Principles. Joseph Smith. 1992. pap. 12.95 (0-8048-1718-9) C E Tuttle.

Wing Chun Martial Arts: Principles & Techniques. Yip Chun & Danny Connor. LC 93-9998. 189p. (Orig.). 1993. pap. 12.95 (0-87728-796-1) Weiser.

Wing Chun, the Deceptive Hands. Douglas Wong. 1977. 7.95 (0-685-83178-7) Wehman.

***Wing Commander: Prophecy.** Prima Publishing Staff. 1997. pap. 19.99 (0-7615-1207-1) Prima Pub.

Wing Commander Armada Playtesters' Guide. Chris McCubbin. (Illus.). 96p. (Orig.). 1994. pap. 14.95 (0-929373-23-5) Origin Syst.

Wing Commander I & II: The Ultimate Strategy Guide. Mike Harrison. (Secrets of the Games Ser.). (Illus.). 304p. (Orig.). 1991. pap. 19.95 (1-55958-129-8) Prima Pub.

Wing Commander III: The Unauthorized Strategy Guide. Steven Kent. 1995. pap. text ed. 19.95 (1-55958-607-9) Prima Pub.

Wing Commander IV: Unofficial Secrets & Solutions. Bart Farkas. 1996. pap. text ed. 14.99 (0-7615-0400-1) Prima Pub.

Wing Commander IV Authorized Strategy Guide. BradyGAMES Staff. (Illus.). 300p. (Orig.). 1996. 19.99 (1-56686-414-3) Brady Pub.

Wing Developer's Guide. 1998. 45.00 (0-672-30798-7) Sams.

Wing It: Riddles about Birds. Scott K. Peterson. (J). (gr. 1-4). 1991. pap. 3.95 (0-8225-9591-5, First Ave Edns) Lerner Group.

***Wing It! The Best Boomerang Book Ever.** Steve Tomecek. (Books & Stuff). (Illus.). 24p. (Orig.). (J). (gr. 1 up). 1997. pap. 7.95 (0-448-41570-4, G&D) Putnam Pub Group.

Wing of Madness: The Life & Work of R. D. Laing. Daniel Burston. 304p. 1996. 35.00 (0-674-95358-4) HUP.

Wing of Scarlet. James Banks. (American Autobiography Ser.). 144p. 1995. reprint ed. lib. bdg. 69.00 (0-7812-8449-X) Rprt Serv.

Wing of the Falcon. Jo Franklin. (Illus.). 544p. 1995. 24.95 (0-9645459-0-X) Atlntis Pr.

Wing Shop. Elvira Woodruff. LC 90-55094. (Illus.). 32p. (J). (ps-3). 1991. lib. bdg. 15.95 (0-8234-0825-6) Holiday.

Wing Shop. Elvira Woodruff. (Illus.). (J). (ps-3). 1996. pap. 6.95 (0-8234-1260-1) Holiday.

Wing-Smiths of Japan: A Story of Japan's World War II Aircraft. Jule N. Dews. LC 93-85597. 61p. 1993. pap. 16.00 (0-937300-03-9) Stoneridge Inst.

Wing Span: Poems. Cheryl Fish. Ed. by Patricia Schultz. LC 91-28209. (Lewiston Poetry Ser.: Vol. 17). (Illus.). 72p. 1992. pap. 12.95 (0-7734-9667-X) E Mellen.

Wing Theory. Robert T. Jones. (Illus.). 224p. 1990. text ed. 45.00 (0-691-08536-6) Princeton U Pr.

Wing Theory. Abraham Robinson & J. A. Laurmann. LC 57-601. (Cambridge Aeronautical Ser.: No. 2). 579p. reprint ed. pap. 165.10 (0-317-10805-0, 2051692) Bks Demand.

Wing Theory in Supersonic Flow. E. Carafoli. 1969. 271.00 (0-08-012330-9, Pub. by Pergamon Repr UK) Franklin.

Wing Walker: From Wisconsin to Norway: A Story of Early Flight. Bernice L. Krippene. 256p. (Orig.). pap. 15.00 (0-938627-29-5) New Past Pr.

Wing Walking: A Totally Different Approach to the Job Market. Sam Wein. 168p. (Orig.). 1994. reprint ed. pap. 11.50 (1-879858-04-5) Behaviordyne.

Wing Yi Nei Gung: The Study of Form-Mind Boxing. Sun L. Tang. Tr. by Albert Z. Liu from CHI. (Illus.). 312p. (Orig.). 1993. pap. 19.95 (1-883175-03-8) High View Pubns.

Wingate: His Relevance to Contemporary Warfare. Prithvi Nath. 1990. text ed. 15.95 (81-207-1165-3, Pub. by Sterling Pubs II) Apt Bks.

Wingate Anaerobic Test. Omri Inbar et al. LC 96-12409. (Illus.). 112p. (Orig.). 1996. pap. text ed. 19.00 (0-87322-946-0, BINB0946) Human Kinetics.

Wingate & Thimayya: A Biographical Analysis. Ed. by R. K. Bhonsle. 150p. (C). 1989. pap. 25.00 (81-7002-053-0, Pub. by Himalayan Bks II) St Mut.

Wingate of the Sudan. Ronald Wingate. LC 74-22507. (Illus.). 274p. 1975. reprint ed. text ed. 59.75 (0-8371-7862-2, WIWS, Greenwood Pr) Greenwood.

***Wingbones: Poems.** Tom Chandler. LC 96-53131. 1997. write for info. (0-930095-08-1) Signal Bks.

Wingdom. Bill Keith. 28p. (Orig.). 1993. pap. 5.00 (0-926935-91-7) Runaway Spoon.

Winged. George Held. (Illus.). 32p. pap. text ed. 5.00 (1-878173-42-1) Birnham Wood.

Winged Beetle. Aleister Crowley. LC 92-21980. 256p. 1992. 29.95 (0-933429-06-1) Teitan Pr.

Winged Bull. Dion Fortune. LC 73-27457. 328p. (Orig.). 1980. pap. 9.95 (0-87728-501-2) Weiser.

Winged Cat. Deborah N. Lattimore. LC 90-38441. (Trophy Picture Bk.). (Illus.). 40p. (J). (gr. 2-5). 1995. pap. 5.95 (0-06-443424-9, Trophy) HarpC Child Bks.

Winged Colt of Casa Mia. Betsy C. Byars. (Illus.). 132p. (J). (gr. 3-7). 1981. pap. 2.95 (0-380-00201-9, Camelot) Avon.

Winged Dancer. Camarin Grae. 288p. (Orig.). 1986. reprint ed. pap. 8.95 (0-930044-88-6) Naiad Pr.

Winged Darkness & Other Stories by William Heinesen. William Heinesen. Ed. by Hedin Bronner. Tr. by William Heinesen & Hedin Bronner from FAR. 200p. (C). 1983. reprint ed. 26.50 (0-8290-0990-6) Irvington.

Winged Darkness & Other Stories by William Heinesen. William Heinesen. Ed. by Hedin Bronner. 200p. 1985. reprint ed. pap. 14.95 (0-685-43110-X) Irvington.

Winged Defense: The Development & Possibilities of Modern Air Power - Economic & Military. William Mitchell. 320p. 1988. pap. 9.95 (0-486-25771-1) Dover.

Winged Gospel: America's Romance with Aviation, Nineteen Hundred to Nineteen Fifty. Joseph J. Corn. 177p. 1987. pap. 18.95 (0-19-504158-5) OUP.

Winged Horse: The Story of the Poets & Their Poetry. J. Auslander & F. E. Hill. LC 68-24959. (Studies in Poetry: No. 38). (C). 1968. reprint ed. lib. bdg. 75.00 (0-8383-0328-5) M S G Haskell Hse.

Winged Life. Hannah Hurnard. 173p. 1975. mass mkt. 5.99 (0-8423-8225-9) Tyndale.

Winged Magic. Mary H. Herbert. 1996. pap. 5.99 (0-7869-0484-4) TSR Inc.

Winged Magic. large type ed. Barbara Cartland. (Magna Romance Ser.). 229p. 1992. 25.99 (0-7505-0366-1) Ulverscroft.

Winged Man. Moyra Caldecott. 384p. 1994. pap. 13.95 (0-7472-3930-4, Pub. by Headline UK) Trafalgar.

Winged Monkeys of Oz. Dennis Anfuso. (Oz Ser.). 220p. (YA). 1995. pap. 24.95 (1-57433-000-4) Interset Pr.

Winged Monkeys of Oz. Dennis Anfuso. (Oz Ser.). 152p. 1996. 24.95 (1-57433-039-X) Interset Pr.

Winged Pharaoh. Joan M. Grant. 1980. 33.95 (0-405-11794-9) Ayer.

Winged Pharaoh. Joan Grant. 324p. 1985. reprint ed. pap. 11.95 (0-89804-140-6) Ariel GA.

Winged Prophet from Hermes to Quetzalcoatl: An Introduction to the Mesoamerican Deities Through the Tarot. Carol Miller & Guadalupe Rivera. LC 94-18281. (Illus.). 196p. (Orig.). 1994. pap. 17.95 (0-87728-799-6) Weiser.

Winged Raiders of the Desert. Gilbert Morris. (Seven Sleepers Ser.: No. 5). 1995. pap. 5.99 (0-8024-3685-4) Moody.

Winged Seed. Li-Young Lee. 1995. 20.00 (0-671-70708-6) S&S Trade.

Winged Serpent: American Indian Prose & Poetry. Ed. by Margot Astrov. LC 92-13743. 1992. pap. 16.00 (0-8070-8105-1) Beacon Pr.

Winged Tenacity: The Polish Air Force 1918-1944. Rosme Curtis. (World War II Historical Society Monograph Ser.). 34p. 1995. pap. 5.00 (1-57638-020-3) Merriam Pr.

Winged Tiger's World Peace Party Puzzle Book, Vol. 1. Phil Yeh. Ed. by Kevin Sullivan. (Illus.). 32p. 1995. 11.95 (0-964149-1-0) Hawaya.

***Winged Victory.** (Echoes of War Military History Ser.). 1996. pap. 10.95 (0-907675-45-X, Pub. by Ashland Buchan & Enright UK) Cimino Pub Grp.

***Winged Victory.** Geoffrey Perret. 1997. pap. 15.00 (0-375-75047-9) Random.

***Winged Victory: Altered Images; Transcending Breast Cancer.** Art Myers. LC 96-68207. (Illus.). 56p. (Orig.). 1996. pap. 24.95 (1-889169-00-5) Photo Gallery.

Winged Victory: The Army Air Forces in World War Two. Geoffrey Perret. LC 92-56838. 1993. 30.00 (0-679-40464-3) Random.

Winged Warfare. William A. Bishop. (Illus.). 280p. 1975. 24.95 (0-8464-1439-2) Beekman Pubs.

Winged Watchman. Hilda Van Stockum. LC 95-78064. (Living History Library). (Illus.). 204p. (YA). (gr. 5 up). 1995. reprint ed. pap. 11.95 (1-883937-07-8, 07-8) Bethlehem ND.

Wing'ed Whale from Woefully. Jonathan Woe. Ed. by R. Constantine. (Illus.). 32p. (J). 1992. 16.95 (0-9627946-3-5) Hawk FL.

***Winged Wheel: Peter H. Wood.** Peter H. Wood. (Illus.). 180p. 1995. 24.00 (1-896032-27-3) Battered Silicon.

Winged Word: A Study in the Technique of Ancient Greek Oral Composition As Seen Principally Through Hesiod's Work & Days. Berkeley Peabody. LC 75-4842. 562p. 1975. text ed. 32.50 (0-87395-059-3) State U NY Pr.

Winged Words: American Indian Writers Speak. Laura Coltelli. LC 89-39323. (American Indian Lives Ser.). (Illus.). x, 211p. 1990. reprint ed. pap. 9.95 (0-8032-6351-1, Bison Books) U of Nebr Pr.

Winged Words: Victorian Women's Poetry & Verse. Compiled by Catherine Reilly. 174p. 9500. pap. 19.95 (1-870612-24-8) Dufour.

Winger. K. Winger. 104p. 1991. otabind 19.95 (0-7935-0873-8, 00694786) H Leonard.

Winger: In the. 96p. 1992. 14.95 (0-7935-0794-4, 06621749) H Leonard.

Winger: In the Heart of the Young. K. Winger. 128p. 1991. otabind 16.95 (0-7935-0417-1, 00694766) H Leonard.

Winger: Pull with Notes & Tablature. 104p. 1994. 19.95 (0-7935-2747-3, 00694900) H Leonard.

Winger: The Heart of the Young. 80p. 1991. otabind 19.95 (0-7935-0762-6, 00694782) H Leonard.

Wingfield: It's Church, Castle & College. S. W. Aldwell. (Illus.). 128p. 1995. 40.00 (0-937543-06-3) Wingfield Family Soc.

Wingfields Migrate West to Arizona & Colorado. 50p. 1995. 7.50 (0-937543-08-X) Sacrum Pr.

Wingfoot. large type ed. A. R. Lloyd. 1994. 25.99 (0-7089-3188-X) Ulverscroft.

Winging It... Gyeorgos C. Hatonn. (Phoenix Journals). 201p. 1994. pap. 6.00 (1-56935-044-2) Phoenix Source.

Winging It. Jahnna N. Malcolm & Laura Young. (Rebel Angels Ser.: No. 2). 176p. (Orig.). (J). 1996. mass mkt. 4.50 (0-06-106438-6, Harp PBks) HarpC.

Winging It. Susan Schnidt. 1994. pap. 12.99 (1-85242-229-7) Serpents Tail.

Winging It: A Tale of Turning Thirty. Elizabeth Tippens. LC 95-25421. 224p. 1996. pap. 10.00 (1-57322-528-2, Riverhd Trade) Berkley Pub.

Winging It! Pioneer Alaskan Aviator Jack Jefford. 2nd ed. Carmen J. Fisher & Jack Jefford. Ed. by Cliff Carnick & Mark Fisher. LC 90-414. (Illus.). 320p. 1990. reprint ed. pap. 12.95 (0-88240-371-0) Alaska Northwest.

Winging It! - in Europe: An Empty Nester's Plan for Travel. Linda Stringer & Jim Stringer. LC 92-35520. (Illus.). 444p. (Orig.). 1992. pap. 16.95 (1-882410-00-9) SunCity Pubs.

Winging Through America: A Motorcyclist's Solo Journey Through the 48 States. Gary S. Shumway. LC 91-71882. (Illus.). 176p. (Orig.). 1991. pap. 10.95 (0-9629410-1-8) Ernest Hill.

Wingless. Sid Campbell & Diana Taylor-Christopher. 118p. (Orig.). 1990. write for info. (0-318-68026-2) Gong Prods.

Wingless Bird. large type ed. Catherine Cookson. LC 91-18382. 601p. 1991. reprint ed. lib. bdg. 21.95 (1-56054-211-X) Thorndike Pr.

Wingless Crow: Essays about Science, Country Life, & the Natural World. Charles Fergus. 192p. 1993. pap. 14.95 (1-55821-233-7) Lyons & Burford.

Wingless Crow: Essays from the "Thornapples" Column of the Game News Magazine. Charles Fergus. 1984. write for info. (0-9630088-0-3) PA Game Comm.

***Wingless Flights: Appalachian Women in Fiction.** Danny L. Miller. (Illus.). 187p. 1996. 35.95 (0-87972-717-9); pap. 21.95 (0-87972-718-7) Bowling Green Univ Popular Press.

Wingless Pegasus: A Handbook for Critics. George Boas. 1979. 16.95 (0-405-10584-3) Ayer.

Wingless Victory: A Biography of Gabriele d'Annunzio & Eleonore Duse. Frances Winwar. LC 74-10363. 374p. 1974. reprint ed. text ed. 59.75 (0-8371-7671-9, WIWV, Greenwood Pr) Greenwood.

Wingman. Mark Maloney. 464p. 1987. mass mkt. 3.95 (0-8217-2015-5, Zebra Kensgtn) Kensgtn Pub Corp.

Wingman, No. 1. Mack Maloney. 464p. 1996. mass mkt. 4.99 (0-7860-0310-3, Pinncle Kensgtn) Kensgtn Pub Corp.

Wingman No. 2: The Circle War. Mack Maloney. 416p. 1996. mass mkt. 4.99 (0-7860-0346-4, Pinncle Kensgtn) Kensgtn Pub Corp.

Wingman No. 13: The Death Orbit. Mack Maloney. 416p. 1997. mass mkt. 4.99 (0-7860-0357-X, Pinncle Kensgtn) Kensgtn Pub Corp.

Wingman, No. 2: The Circle War. 1987. mass mkt. 3.95 (0-8217-2120-8, Zebra Kensgtn) Kensgtn Pub Corp.

Wingman, No. 6: The Final Storm. 1989. mass mkt. 3.95 (0-8217-2655-2, Zebra Kensgtn) Kensgtn Pub Corp.

Wingman on Ice. Matt Christopher. (J). (gr. 4-7). 1993. mass mkt. 3.95 (0-316-14269-7) Little.

Wingmen Warriors. Jonathan Bliss. LC 93-39507. (Hockey Heroes Ser.). (J). 1994. write for info. (1-55916-013-6) Rourke Bk Co.

Wings. Bill Brittain. LC 90-19785. 128p. (J). (gr. 4-7). 1991. lib. bdg. 14.89 (0-06-020649-7) HarpC Child Bks.

Wings. Bill Brittain. LC 90-19785. (Trophy Bk.). 144p. (J). (gr. 4-7). 1995. pap. 4.50 (*0-06-440612-1*, Trophy) HarpC Child Bks.

Wings. Mark Meyer. LC 83-51813. (Illus.). 144p. 1984. 19.98 (*0-934738-05-X*); pap. 12.98 (*0-934738-62-9*) Lickle Pubng.

Wings. Gene S. Porter. 39.95 (*0-8488-0883-5*) Amereon Ltd.

Wings. Terry Pratchett. 176p. 1992. mass mkt. 4.50 (*0-552-52649-5*) Bantam.

Wings. Gale T. Richardson. (YA). (gr. 9-12). 1989. write for info. (*0-9614337-4-4*) Poetry Unltd.

Wings. Danielle Steel. LC 93-51253. 408p. 1994. 23.95 (*0-385-30605-9*) Delacorte.

Wings. Danielle Steel. 464p. 1995. mass mkt. 6.99 (*0-440-21751-2*) Dell.

***Wings.** Jane Yolen. (J). 1997. pap. write for info. (*0-15-201567-1*, HB Juv Bks) HarBrace.

Wings. limited ed. Danielle Steel. 408p. 1994. 200.00 (*0-385-31381-0*) Delacorte.

Wings. Gene S. Porter. 1986. reprint ed. lib. bdg. 16.95 (*0-89966-531-4*) Buccaneer Bks.

Wings, 4 vols., Set. Patricia Lantier-Sampon. (Illus.). 24p. (J). (ps-2). 1994. lib. bdg. 69.08 (*0-8368-0755-3*) Gareth Stevens Inc.

Wings: A Tale of Two Chickens. James Marshall. (J). (ps up). 1988. pap. 4.99 (*0-14-050579-2*, Puffin) Puffin Bks.

Wings: Alto Saxophone Solo Unaccompanied. J. Tower. 12p. 1993. per. 9.50 (*0-7935-3007-5*) H Leonard.

Wings: Pocket Poetry. Eydith I. Johnson & Marie Jacobs. 54p. 1996. 10.99 (*1-888188-52-9*); 5.99 (*1-888188-53-7*) E Johnsn.

Wings: Solo Clarinet or Bass Clarinet. J. Tower. 8p. 1986. pap. text ed. 9.50 (*0-7935-3710-X*) H Leonard.

Wings: Student Essays from the Freshman Composition Program at California State University, Northridge, 1995-96. 2nd ed. Patricia Murray. 88p. (C). 1996. per., pap. text ed. 9.39 (*0-7872-2060-4*) Kendall-Hunt.

Wings above the Flames. Rachel Pomerantz. 400p. (C). 1991. 17.95 (*1-56062-066-8*) CIS Comm.

Wings Across the Pacific: The Courageous Aviators Who Challenged & Conquered the Greatest Ocean. Terry Gwynn-Jones. LC 90-31673. (Illus.). 256p. 1995. 35.00 (*0-88740-743-9*) Schiffer.

Wings along the Waterway. Mary B. Brown. LC 91-18559. (Illus.). 80p. (J). (gr. 3-6). 1992. 18.95 (*0-531-05981-2*) Orchard Bks Watts.

***Wings & Hidden Springs.** Monty Martin. (Illus.). (J). (gr. 5-8). Date not set. pap. write for info. (*0-9655669-2-7*, MM-01) Watersedge Muse.

Wings & Roots. Susan Terris. LC 82-2553. 186p. (gr. 7 up). 1982. 14.00 (*0-374-38451-7*) FS&G.

Wings & Tails: Wings & Tails. Jack B. Kochan. (Birds Ser.). (Illus.). 96p. 1996. pap. 12.95 (*0-8117-2503-0*) Stackpole.

***Wings & the Navy 1947-1953.** Colin Jones. (Illus.). 176p. 1998. pap. 16.95 (*0-86417-836-0*, Pub. by Kangaroo Pr AT) Seven Hills Bk.

Wings & Things. Marc Brown. LC 81-12095. (Bright & Early Bks.: No. 26). (Illus.). 36p. (J). (ps-1). 1982. 7.99 (*0-394-85130-7*, XBYR); lib. bdg. 11.99 (*0-394-95130-1*) Random Bks Yng Read.

***Wings & Things.** 2nd ed. Teri Shelton. 60p. 1997. pap. text ed. write for info. (*1-57377-015-9*) Easl Pubns.

Wings & Things: Origami That Flies. Stephen Weiss. (Illus.). 128p. 1984. pap. 10.95 (*0-312-88228-9*) St Martin.

***Wings & Warriors: My Life As a Naval Aviator.** Donald D. Engen. Ed. by Von Hardesty. LC 97-17445. (Smithsonian History of Aviation Ser.). (Illus.). 272p. 1997. 29.95 (*1-56098-795-2*) Smithsonian.

Wings Around the Steeple: Award Winning Poetry on the Church. Ed. by Jackson Wilcox. 32p. 1991. 3.50 (*0-944231-11-X*) Slvr Wings CA.

Wings around the World: The American World Flight of 1924. K. C. Tessendorf. LC 90-977. (Illus.). 112p. (J). (gr. 4 up). 1991. lib. bdg. 14.95 (*0-689-31550-3*, Atheneum Bks Young) S&S Childrens.

Wings at the Ready: 75 Years of the Naval Air Reserve. Richard Shipman. LC 91-20039. (Illus.). 320p. 1991. 39.95 (*1-55750-750-3*) Naval Inst Pr.

Wings at the Window. Theresa Arsenault. (Illus.). 112p. (Orig.). 1992. pap. 10.00 (*0-9633836-0-4*) Brass Oaks Pubns.

W

Wings at War Series, 6 Vols., Vol. 1. U. S. Air Force Staff. Ed. by James B. Gilbert. LC 79-7301. (Flight: Its First Seventy-Five Years Ser.). (Illus.). 1980. reprint ed. lib. bdg. 37.95 (*0-405-12207-1*) Ayer.

Wings Beyond. C. David Hay. LC 95-94991. 1995. 10.00 (*0-9634527-1-1*) C D Hay.

Wings for the Heart: Montana's Upland Birds & Waterfowl. Jerry A. Lewis. 352p. 1992. pap. write for info. (*0-9632227-0-8*) W River Pr.

Wings for the Navy: A History of the Naval Aircraft Factory, 1917-1956. William F. Trimble. LC 90-41959. (Illus.). 360p. 1990. 39.95 (*0-87021-663-5*) Naval Inst Pr.

***Wings for Victory: The Remarkable Story of the British Commonwealth Air Training Plan in Canada.** Spencer Dunmore. 1996. pap. text ed. 19.99 (*0-7710-2918-7*) McCland & Stewart.

Wings for Warriors: A Photographic History of the Australian Flying Corps & the Royal Australian Air Force. unabridged ed. RAAF Public Relations Section Staff. LC 94-30385. (Illus.). 80p. 1995. 39.95 (*0-644-42702-7*, 9430385, Pub. by AGPS Pr AT) Intl Spec Bk.

Wings from Above. Anne Frost. (Illus.). 72p. (Orig.). 1987. pap. 9.95 (*0-9614624-4-2*) Frost Pub.

Wings from Afar: An Ecoregional Approach to Conservation of Neotropical Migratory Birds in South America. Leslie Adkins et al. Ed. by Norah D. Davis. LC 96-68384. (America Verde Publications). (Illus.). 75p. (Orig.). 1996. pap. text ed. write for info. (*0-686-96668-6*) Nature VA.

Wings from Afar: An Ecoregional Approach to Conservation of Neotropical Migratory Birds in South America. Roberto Roca et al. Ed. by Norah D. Davis. LC 96-68384. (America Verde Ser.). (Illus.). 75p. (Orig.). (C). 1996. pap. text ed. 19.95 (*1-886765-03-0*) Nature VA.

Wings from Burma to the Himalayas. Gordon. 1992. 22.50 (*1-879356-10-4*) Wolfe Pub Co.

Wings from Cover: The Upland Images of Robert Abbett & Ed Gray. Illus. by Robert Abbett. 128p. 1996. 35.00 (*1-57223-043-6*, 0436) Idyll Arbor.

Wings in the Night. Willis S. Fitch. (Great War Ser.: No. 1). (Illus.). 302p. 1989. reprint ed. 29.95 (*0-89839-141-5*) Battery Pr.

Wings in the Sea: The Humpback Whale. Lois K. Winn & Howard E. Winn. LC 84-40598. (Illus.). 163p. 1985. pap. 13.95 (*0-87451-336-7*) U Pr of New Eng.

Wings in the Wilderness: More Stories about God's Mysterious Ways from Guideposts. Arthur Gordon et al. 128p. (Orig.). 1995. pap. 8.00 (*0-687-00249-4*) Abingdon.

Wings Moist from the Other World. Peggy Shumaker. (Poetry Ser.). 120p. (C). 1993. text ed. 19.95 (*0-8229-3774-3*); pap. text ed. 10.95 (*0-8229-5518-0*) U of Pittsburgh Pr.

Wings of a Bird see Basic Truths

***Wings of a Dove.** Henry James. 1997. 20.00 (*0-679-45512-4*, Everymans Lib) Knopf.

Wings of a Falcon. Cynthia Voigt. LC 92-41946. 480p. (J). (gr. 7-9). 1993. 15.95 (*0-590-46712-3*) Scholastic Inc.

Wings of a Falcon. Cynthia Voigt. 480p. (J). (gr. 7-9). 1995. mass mkt. 4.50 (*0-590-46713-1*, Point) Scholastic Inc.

Wings of an Angel. Sigmund Brouwer. (Winds of Light Ser.: No. 1). 132p. (J). (gr. 5-8). 1992. pap. 5.99 (*0-89693-115-3*, 6-1115, Victor Bks) Chariot Victor.

Wings of Cessna: Model 120 to Citation. Edward H. Philips. LC 86-72359. (Illus.). 95p. (Orig.). pap. 19.95 (*0-911139-05-2*) Flying Bks.

Wings of Courage. Robert L. Gray. LC 84-61223. 154p. (Orig.). pap. 4.95 (*0-685-09957-1*) Omenana.

Wings of Dawn: A True Story of Tragedy & Triumph. Ida M. Kempel. 100p. (Orig.). 1990. pap. 6.95 (*0-9628132-0-6*) Nascent Pr.

Wings of Democracy: The Influence of Air Power on the Roosevelt Administration, 1933-1941. Jeffery S. Underwood. LC 91-15653. (Military History Ser.: No. 22). (Illus.). 248p. 1991. 41.95 (*0-89096-388-6*) Tex A&M Univ Pr.

Wings of Desire. Elizabeth Lambert. 384p. (Orig.). 1989. mass mkt. 3.95 (*0-380-75599-8*) Avon.

Wings of Destiny. large type ed. Barbara Best. (Linford Romance Library). 272p. 1995. pap. 15.99 (*0-7089-7737-5*, Linford) Ulverscroft.

Wings of Dust. Jamal Mahjoub. (African Writers Ser.). 224p. 1994. pap. 9.95 (*0-435-90984-3*, 90984) Heinemann.

***Wings of Duty.** large type ed. Meredith Webber. (Mills & Boon Large Print Ser.). 288p. 1997. 22.50 (*0-263-15080-1*, Pub. by M & B UK) Ulverscroft.

Wings of Encouragement. Helen Steiner Rice. LC 94-46001. (Illus.). 96p. (gr. 10). 1995. 15.99 (*0-8007-1704-X*) Revell.

Wings of Ethiopia: Studies in African-American Life & Letters. Wilson J. Moses. LC 90-4020. 303p. 1990. reprint ed. pap. 86.40 (*0-608-00135-X*, 2060916) Bks Demand.

Wings of Fire. Charles Ghigna. (Illus.). 62p. (Orig.). 1992. pap. 10.00 (*0-945301-08-1*) Druid Pr.

Wings of Fire: One Hundred Hours - Desert Shield, Desert Storm, Desert Calm. Mattie S. Johnson. LC 93-84609. (Illus.). 168p. (Orig.). 1993. pap. 14.95 (*0-9620115-4-1*) Post Oak Pubns.

Wings of Flight. Margaret Good. (Orig.). 1996. pap. write for info. (*1-57553-172-0*) Watermrk Pr.

Wings of Freedom: Award Winning Poems on Freedom. Ed. by Jackson Wilcox. (Illus.). 32p. 1992. 3.50 (*0-944231-15-2*) Slvr Wings CA.

***Wings of Fury.** 1997. 22.00 (*0-7869-0722-3*) TSR Inc.

***Wings of Fury: From Vietnam to the Gulf War-the Astonishing Stories of America's Elite Fighter Pilots.** Robert K. Wilcox. LC 96-42256. 1997. 24.00 (*0-671-74793-2*) PB.

Wings of Gauze: Women of Color & the Experience of Health & Illness. Ed. by Barbara Bair & Susan E. Cayleff. LC 92-46308. 394p. 1993. pap. text ed. 19.95 (*0-8143-2302-2*) Wayne St U Pr.

Wings of Glory Playtesters' Guide. Melissa Mead. (Illus.). 64p. (Orig.). pap. 9.95 (*0-929373-20-0*) Origin Syst.

***Wings of Gold.** J. P. Matthews. LC 96-96769. 192p. 1996. 17.95 (*0-8034-9217-0*, Avalon Bks) Bouregy.

***Wings of Gold.** Lance Patterson. LC 97-6856. (Illus.). 144p. (Orig.). (J). 1997. pap. 6.49 (*0-89084-933-1*, 106245) Bob Jones Univ Pr.

Wings of Gold: An Account of Naval Aviation Training in World War II,... Ed. by Wesley P. Newton & Robert R. Rea. LC 86-7013. 352p. 1987. 35.95 (*0-8173-0319-7*) U of Ala Pr.

Wings of History: The Air Museums of Europe. Louis Divone. LC 88-5158. (Illus.). 312p. (Orig.). 1989. pap. 19.95 (*0-939047-21-7*) Oakton Hills Pubns.

Wings of Honor: American Airmen in WWI. James J. Sloan, Jr. (Illus.). 460p. 1994. 45.00 (*0-88740-577-0*) Schiffer.

***Wings of Hope.** James R. Jacobson. 1996. pap. 4.95 (*1-55673-992-3*) CSS OH.

Wings of Hope: A Father's Story. Henry Plett. LC 90-82600. 152p. (Orig.). 1990. pap. 8.99 (*0-8361-3527-X*) Herald Pr.

Wings of Hope & Daring: Selected Poems. Eira Stenberg. Tr. by Herbert Lomas from FIN. 64p. 9300. pap. 12.95 (*1-85224-237-X*, Pub. by Bloodaxe Bks UK) Dufour.

***Wings of Icarus, Vol. 1.** Robert L. Allen. Ed. by Robert S. Fifield. v, 121p. (Orig.). 1996. pap. 12.95 (*0-9655100-0-X*) R L Allen.

Wings of Illusions: The Origin, Nature, & Future of Paranormal Belief. John F. Schumaker. 183p. (C). 1990. 27.95 (*0-87975-624-1*) Prometheus Bks.

Wings of Joy. Sri Chinmoy. 1997. pap. 10.00 (*0-684-82242-3*) S&S Trade.

Wings of Judgment: American Bombing in World War II. Ronald Schaffer. 288p. 1988. pap. 16.95 (*0-19-505640-X*) OUP.

Wings of Love. Bernet. (J). 1998. 11.95 (*0-671-75203-0*, S&S Bks Young Read) S&S Childrens.

Wings of Love. Bernet. (J). 1998. pap. 8.00 (*0-671-76959-6*, S&S Bks Young Read) S&S Childrens.

Wings of Love. Teresa George. 384p. 1996. mass mkt. 4.99 (*0-8217-5515-3*, Zebra Kensgtn) Kensgtn Pub Corp.

Wings of Love & Time. Clive X. Williams. LC 90-8158. 35p. (Orig.). 1990. pap. 6.95 (*0-932831-03-6*) Eastern Caribbean Inst.

Wings of Madness: A Novel of Charles Baudelaire. Geoffrey Wagner. LC 78-1039. 224p. 1978. pap. 23.00 (*0-89370-220-X*); lib. bdg. 33.00 (*0-89370-120-3*) Borgo Pr.

Wings of Morning. Thomas Childers. 288p. 1996. pap. 12.00 (*0-201-40722-1*) Addison-Wesley.

Wings of Morning. Karen Harper. 416p. 1994. pap. 5.99 (*0-451-18065-8*, Sig) NAL-Dutton.

Wings of Morning. Danny Peters. 160p. (Orig.). 1996. pap. 9.95 (*1-57502-140-4*) Morris Pubng.

Wings of Morning. large type ed. Karen Harper. LC 93-25728. 1993. lib. bdg. 18.95 (*0-7862-0020-0*) Thorndike Pr.

Wings of Morning. large type ed. Karen Harper. 1993. 100.95 (*0-7862-9995-9*, GK Hall) Thorndike Pr.

Wings of Morning: A Collection of Poetry & Prose. Latayne C. Stanfill. (Illus.). 90p. 1995. per. 8.95 (*1-880799-02-2*) Heirloom CA.

Wings of Morning: The Story of the Last B-24 Shot Down over Germany in World War II. Thomas Childers. 288p. (J). 1995. 23.00 (*0-201-48310-6*) Addison-Wesley.

Wings of Oppression. Leslie P. Hill. LC 76-152921. (Black Heritage Library Collection). 1977. 21.95 (*0-8369-8765-9*) Ayer.

Wings of Paradise: The Great Saturniid Moths. Illus. & Text by John Cody. LC 95-47138. 186p. (C). 1996. 60.00 (*0-8078-2286-8*) U of NC Pr.

***Wings of Passion.** large type ed. Meredith Webber. (Mills & Boon Large Print Ser.). 288p. 1997. 22.50 (*0-263-15100-X*) Ulverscroft.

Wings of Peace: Poetry on Peace. Ed. by Jackson Wilcox. (Illus.). 36p. 1990. 3.50 (*0-944231-08-X*) Slvr Wings CA.

Wings of Pegasus. Brigadier G. Chatterton. (Airborne Ser.: No. 14). (Illus.). 282p. 1982. reprint ed. 29.95 (*0-89839-060-5*) Battery Pr.

Wings of Salvation. Gabriela Klonek. LC 93-85307. 170p. 1994. pap. 9.95 (*1-55523-645-6*) Winston-Derek.

Wings of Silver. Illus. by Gordon Brown. LC 67-21924. 1968. 9.95 (*0-8378-1773-0*) Gibson.

Wings of Silver. large type ed. Jo Petty. 128p. 1986. 9.95 (*0-8027-2546-5*) Walker & Co.

Wings of Song. LC 84-50224. 544p. 1984. 12.95 (*0-87159-176-6*) Unity Bks.

Wings of Song. Phyllis Sparta. LC 83-90430. (Illus.). 84p. 1983. 6.50 (*0-8233-0375-6*) Golden Quill.

Wings of Steel: A Climber's Perspective of the Christian Life & the Story of a World Record--39 Continuous Days & Nights on the Side of El Capitan. Richard Jensen. LC 93-11923. 1993. pap. 8.99 (*0-8280-0739-X*) Review & Herald.

Wings of Stone. Linda Ty-Casper. (Readers International Ser.). 170p. (Orig.). (C). 1986. pap. 10.95 (*0-930523-27-X*) Readers Intl.

Wings of the Canadian Armed Forces 1913-1992. rev. ed. Roy J. Thompson. (Aviation Ser.). (Illus.). 200p. (YA). 1992. pap. text ed. 17.95 (*1-878973-04-5*) Hse History.

***Wings of the Dove.** Andre Hodier. Date not set. lib. bdg. 21.95 (*0-8488-1053-8*) Amereon Ltd.

Wings of the Dove. Henry James. Ed. by Peter Brooks. (World's Classics Ser.). 576p. 1985. pap. 6.95 (*0-19-281631-4*) OUP.

Wings of the Dove. Henry James. LC 93-15338. 712p. 1993. 19.00 (*0-679-60067-1*) Random.

Wings of the Dove. Henry James. Ed. & Intro. by John Bayley. (Classics Ser.). 520p. 1986. pap. 9.95 (*0-14-043263-9*, Penguin Classics) Viking Penguin.

Wings of the Dove. Henry James. Ed. by J. Donald Crowley & Richard A. Hocks. (Critical Editions Ser.). (C). 1978. pap. text ed. 12.95 (*0-393-09088-4*) Norton.

***Wings of the Dove.** Henry James. 1997. pap. 5.95 (*0-460-87617-1*, Everyman's Classic Lib) C E Tuttle.

Wings of the Dove. Henry James. (BCL1-PS American Literature Ser.). 329p. 1993. reprint ed. lib. bdg. 89.00 (*0-7812-6978-4*) Rprt Serv.

Wings of the Dove. Henry James, Jr. (Notable American Authors Ser.). 1992. reprint ed. lib. bdg. 75.00 (*0-7812-3429-8*) Rprt Serv.

Wings of the Dove, Vol. 1. Henry James. LC 79-158798. (Novels & Tales of Henry James Ser.: Vol. 19). xxii, 301p. 1977. reprint ed. lib. bdg. 37.50 (*0-678-02819-2*) Kelley.

Wings of the Dove, Vol. 2. Henry James. LC 79-158798. (Novels & Tales of Henry James Ser.: Vol. 20). 404p. 1977. reprint ed. lib. bdg. 37.50 (*0-678-02820-6*) Kelley.

Wings of the Eagle. William T. Grant. 1994. mass mkt. 5.99 (*0-8041-1062-X*) Ivy Books.

Wings of the Falcon. Barbara Michaels. 1988. mass mkt. 6.99 (*0-425-11045-1*, Berkley Trade) Berkley Pub.

Wings of the Falcon. Barbara Michaels. 1978. pap. 1.95 (*0-449-23750-8*, Crest) Fawcett.

Wings of the Falcon. Barbara Michaels. 230p. 1995. reprint ed. 20.00 (*0-7278-4722-8*) Severn Hse.

Wings of the Hawk. Leigh F. James. 346p. 1991. reprint ed. lib. bdg. 27.95 (*0-89966-879-8*) Buccaneer Bks.

Wings of the Morning. Ron Benjamin & Suzi Benjamin. 164p. (Orig.). 1993. pap. 7.99 (*0-89228-083-2*) Impact Christian.

Wings of the Morning. George H. Morrison. 192p. 1994. pap. 9.99 (*0-8254-3288-X*) Kregel.

Wings of the Morning. Lori Wick. LC 93-23531. (Kensington Chronicles Ser.). 1994. pap. 9.99 (*1-56507-177-8*) Harvest Hse.

Wings of the Morning: An Autobiography of Eldred Echols. Eldred Echols. 286p. 1989. 9.95 (*0-940999-83-8*, C2189); 21.95 (*0-940999-84-6*, C2189L) Star Bible.

Wings of the Morning Vol. 1. Orestes Lorenzo. 1995. mass mkt. 5.99 (*0-312-95317-8*) St Martin.

Wings of the Nationalist Chinese Armed Forces. Roy Thompson. (Illus.). 48p. (Orig.). 1990. pap. 8.00 (*1-878973-02-9*) Hse History.

Wings of the Navy: Flying Allied Carrier Aircraft of World War II. Eric Brown. LC 86-62670. (Illus.). 176p. 1987. 28.95 (*0-87021-995-2*) Naval Inst Pr.

Wings of the North. Dick Turner. (Illus.). 288p. pap. 14.95 (*0-88839-060-2*) Hancock House.

Wings of the Soul: Poems of Akha, the Spiritual Poet of India/Krishnaditya. Akha. LC 92-28949. 110p. 1993. reprint ed. pap. 31.40 (*0-608-01770-1*, 2062428) Bks Demand.

***Wings of the Sun: Traditional Jewish Healing in Theory & Practice.** Avraham Greenbaum. 467p. 1995. pap. 20.00 (*0-930213-53-X*) Breslov Res Inst.

Wings of the Weird & Wonderful. Eric Brown. (Illus.). 160p. 1987. 19.95 (*0-8306-9404-8*, 2404) McGraw-Hill Prof.

Wings of the Whirlwind: (A Tribute to Marcus M. Garvey) rev. ed. Daniel R. Queen. 86p. 1992. pap. 10.00 (*1-881328-00-7*) Queens Palace.

***Wings of the Wind.** Al Lacy & Lew A. Lacy. LC 96-46777. (Battles of Destiny Ser.: No. 7). 260p. (Orig.). 1997. pap. 9.99 (*1-57673-032-8*, Multnomah Bks) Multnomah Pubs.

Wings of Time. Carol D. Perry. (Superromance Ser.). 1993. mass mkt. 3.39 (*0-373-70537-9*, 1-70537-5) Harlequin Bks.

Wings of War: Fighting World War II in the Air. Jeffrey L. Ethell. LC 93-20957. (Illus.). 136p. 1994. 39.95 (*1-55750-249-8*) Naval Inst Pr.

Wings of Winter. LC 90-41016. 1991. pap. 14.95 (*0-87949-319-4*) Ashley Bks.

Wings on My Tennis Shoes. Pauline Addie. (American Autobiography Ser.). 198p. 1995. reprint ed. lib. bdg. 69.00 (*0-7812-8440-6*) Rprt Serv.

Wings over France. Harold E. Hartney. (American Autobiography Ser.). 360p. 1995. reprint ed. lib. bdg. 89.00 (*0-7812-8553-4*) Rprt Serv.

Wings over Idaho: An Aviation History. Arthur A. Hart. LC 91-93140. 176p. 1991. 29.95 (*0-9631258-1-8*); pap. 22.95 (*0-9631258-0-X*) Historic Idaho.

***Wings over New Zealand: A Pictorial Chronicle of New Zealand Aviation.** John King. 80p. (Orig.). 1997. pap. 17.95 (*0-908697-69-4*) Seven Hills Bk.

Wings over Shangri La. E. Janet Steiger. Ed. by Jean G. Hazlatt. 255p. (Orig.). 1995. pap. 14.95 (*0-9648127-0-3*) E J Steiger Pub.

***Wings over Suez: The First Authoritative Account of the Anglo-French Involvement in the Sinai.** Brian Cull. 1997. 49.95 (*1-898697-48-5*, Pub. by Grub St Pubns UK) Seven Hills Bk.

Wings over the Mexican Border: Pioneer Military Aviation in the Big Bend. Kenneth B. Ragsdale. (Illus.). 294p. 1984. 24.50 (*0-292-79025-2*) U of Tex Pr.

***Wings over the Mexican Border: Pioneer Military Aviation in the Big Bend.** Kenneth B. Ragsdale. (Illus.). 294p. 1997. pap. 16.95 (*0-292-77081-2*) U of Tex Pr.

Wings over Wisconsin: A Commemorative History of the Wisconsin Air National Guard. Wisconsin Air National Guard Historical Book Committee Staff. Ed. by Robert E. Fritsch & Roger D. Hendrickson. LC 91-72013. 304p. 1991. 35.00 (*0-9629757-0-2*) Wis Air Nat.

Wing's Poems. Wing Watson. Ed. by Paula Trachtman. 64p. 1990. 10.00 (*0-943959-02-0*) Amagansett Pr.

Wings, Seventy-Eight. (Wings Anthologies Ser.). 1978. pap. 2.00 (*0-939736-02-0*) Wings ME.

Wings, Seventy-Seven. (Wings Anthologies Ser.). 1977. pap. 2.00 (*0-939736-01-2*) Wings ME.

Wings, Seventy-Six. (Wings Anthologies Ser.). 1976. pap. 2.00 (*0-939736-00-4*) Wings ME.

Wings, Stings & Wriggly Things. Martin Jenkins. LC 95-53680. (SuperSmarts Ser.). 24p. (J). (gr. 2-5). 1996. 11.99 (*0-7636-0036-9*) Candlewick Pr.

Wings, the Vines. Katharyn M. Aal et al. LC 82-24978. 96p. 1983. pap. 6.50 (*0-935526-07-2*) McBooks Pr.

***Wings to Fly.** Celia B. Lottridge. 1997. 15.95 (*0-88899-293-9*, Pub. by Groundwood-Douglas & McIntyre CN) Firefly Bks Ltd.

Wings to Fly: Bringing Theatre Arts to Students with Special Needs. Sally Bailey. LC 93-19228. (Illus.). 352p. (Orig.). (C). 1993. pap. text ed. 17.95 (*0-933149-58-1*) Woodbine House.

Wings to My Breath. Eva McGinnis. 112p. (Orig.). (C). 1992. pap. 9.95 (*1-878555-03-0*) Oakbridge Univ Pr.

Wings to the Orient: Pan American Clipper Planes 1935-1945. Stan B. Cohen. LC 85-60319. (Illus.). 214p. 1985. pap. 14.95 (*0-933126-61-1*) Pictorial Hist.

Wings Unfolding. Wesley LaViolette. LC 70-140225. 1971. 5.95 (0-87516-040-9) DeVorss.

Wings, Wheels & Sails. Bobbie Kalman. (Crabapple Ser.). (Illus.). 32p. (J). (ps-3). 1995. lib. bdg. 18.08 (0-86505-608-0) Crabtree Pub Co.

Wings, Wheels & Sails. Bobbie Kalman. (Crabapple Ser.). (Illus.). 32p. (J). (ps-3). 1995. pap. 5.95 (0-86505-708-7) Crabtree Pub Co.

Wings, Wheels & Water. Karen E. Little & A. Thomas. (Explainers Ser.). (Illus.). 72p. (J). (gr. 2-4). 1988. 12.95 (0-7460-0106-1) EDC.

Wings Will Not Be Broken. Darryl Holmes. (Orig.). 1990. pap. 8.00 (0-88378-137-9) Third World.

Wingshooters Autumn. 226p. 1991. 39.00 (1-55971-090-X, 1502) NorthWord.

Wingshooter's Guide to Arizona. William W. Parton. LC 96-60842. (Illus.). 320p. (Orig.). 1996. pap. 26.95 (1-885106-41-6) Wild Adven Pr.

Wingshooter's Guide to Idaho. Ken Retallic & Rocky Barker. (Illus.). 320p. 1997. pap. 26.95 (1-885106-27-0) Wild Adven Pr.

***Wingshooter's Guide to Iowa.** Larry Brown. (Illus.). (Orig.). 1998. pap. 26.95 (1-885106-45-9) Wild Adven Pr.

Wingshooter's Guide to Kansas. William W. Parton. (Illus.). 320p. 1998. pap. 26.95 (1-885106-26-2) Wild Adven Pr.

***Wingshooter's Guide to Michigan: Upland Birds & Waterfowl.** Tom Pink. (Illus.). 300p. (Orig.). 1999. pap. 26.95 (1-885106-57-2) Wild Adven Pr.

Wingshooter's Guide to Montana: Upland Birds & Waterfowl. Chuck Johnson & Ben O. Williams. LC 95-60557. (Illus.). 288p. 1995. pap. 26.00 (1-885106-13-0) Wild Adven Pr.

Wingshooter's Guide to Nebraska. Chuck Johnson & Ben O. Williams. (Illus.). 320p. 1998. pap. 26.95 (1-885106-25-4) Wild Adven Pr.

Wingshooter's Guide to North Dakota: Upland Birds & Waterfowl. Chuck Johnson. LC 97-60641. (Illus.). 320p. (Orig.). 1997. pap. 26.95 (1-885106-23-8) Wild Adven Pr.

***Wingshooter's Guide to Oregon.** Chuck Johnson & Ben O. Williams. (Illus.). (Orig.). 1998. pap. 26.95 (1-885106-46-7) Wild Adven Pr.

Wingshooter's Guide to South Dakota: Upland Birds & Waterfowl. Ben O. Williams & Chuck Johnson. LC 96-60290. (Illus.). 288p. (Orig.). 1996. pap. 26.95 (1-885106-22-X) Wild Adven Pr.

Wingspan Inside the Men's Movement. Christopher S. Harding. (Illus.). 256p. 1992. pap. 16.95 (0-312-07886-2) St Martin.

Wingspread. Aiden W. Tozer. 143p. 1988. pap. 8.99 (0-87509-218-7) Chr Pubns.

***Wingwalker.** Wells. Date not set. 14.95 (0-7868-0397-5); 14.89 (0-7868-2347-X) Hyperion.

Wingz. Donald H. Beil. (Illus.). 612p. (C). 1990. teacher ed. write for info. (1-878748-12-2); pap. text ed. 35.25 incl. disk (1-878748-05-X); disk 50.00 (1-878748-04-1) Course Tech.

Wining & Dining in France. Robin Neillands. 1995. pap. text ed. 30.00 (1-85253-313-7, Pub. by Quiller Pr UK) St Mut.

Wining Ways to Make Quilts. Connie Hester. 96p. 19.95 (1-881588-01-7) EZ Quilting.

Wink. Mark Dunster. 40p. (Orig.). 1994. pap. 5.00 (0-89642-231-3) Linden Pubs.

Wink a Hopeful Eye. Denise Danks. 224p. 1994. 19.95 (0-312-11355-2, Thomas Dunne Bks) St Martin.

Wink at Success, Flirt with Serenity: An Affirmative Guide to Personal Peace. Dennis Alcorn. LC 92-73377. 112p. (Orig.). 1992. pap. 9.95 (0-9633857-0-4) Blue Canoe.

***Wink at the Sphinx.** Judith Prior. LC 96-51654. 55p. (Orig.). 1996. pap. 10.00 (0-88734-020-2) Players Pr.

***Wink of Faith: Living As Expressions of God Without Denying Our Humanity.** 2nd rev. ed. William W. Volkman. 282p. 1983. pap. 8.00 (1-889870-07-2) Union Life.

***Winka Dubbeldam, Architect.** Princeton Architectural Press Staff. 1996. pap. 35.00 (1-56898-102-3) Princeton Arch.

Winker, Buttercup & Blue. Arlene Williams. LC 94-60071. (Illus.). 128p. (J). (gr. 3-5). 1994. pap. 9.95 (0-9605444-3-7); lib. bdg. 15.95 (0-9605444-2-9) Waking Light Pr.

Winkie, the Cross-Eyed Witch. Bridget Fitzgerald. LC 71-189878. (Story & Its Verse Ser.). (Illus.). (J). (gr. 1-2). 1973. 2.50 (0-87884-020-6) Unicorn Ent.

Winking Owl: Art in the People's Republic of China. Ellen J. Laing. 250p. 1988. 65.00 (0-520-06097-0) U CA Pr.

Winkler: Berlin, Nineteen Twenty-Three. Daniel Vian. (Orig.). 1989. mass mkt. 4.50 (0-929654-11-0, 48) Blue Moon Bks.

Winklerowie: Historia Jednego Indygenatu. Wojciech Winkler. (Illus.). 82p. (Orig.). (POL.). 1989. pap. text ed. write for info. (0-9624695-0-5) W Winkler.

Winky Cherry System of Teaching Young Children to Sew: How to Teach - A Script for Classes - How to Start a Teaching Business. Winky Cherry. Ed. & Intro. by Pati Palmer. (My First Sewing Book Ser.). 112p. (Orig.). 1994. pap. 24.95 (0-935278-34-6) Palmer-Pletsch.

Winn L. Rosch Hardware Bible. 3rd ed. Winn L. Rosch. 1248p. (Orig.). 1994. 35.00 (1-56686-127-6) Sams.

***Winn L. Rosch Hardware Bible.** 4th ed. Winn L. Rosch. 1400p. (Orig.). 1997. 59.00 (0-672-30954-8) Mac Comp Pub.

Winn L. Rosch's Printer Bible. Winn L. Rosch. 1995. pap. 34.95 incl. cd-rom (1-55828-436-2) MIS Press.

Winn Rosch Hardware Bible. Winn L. Rosch. 1989. pap. 29.95 (0-13-160979-3) Brady Pub.

Winn Rosch Troubleshooter's Bible. Winn L. Rosch. 1990. pap. 29.95 (0-13-962655-7) P-H.

Winnable War: A Community Guide to Eradicating Street Drug Markets. Roger Conner & Patrick Burns. (Illus.). 105p. (Orig.). 1991. pap. 12.50 (0-9633620-0-3) Am Alliance R & R.

Winnataska Remembered. Katherine P. Garmon & Virginia P. Brown. (Illus.). 144p. (Orig.). 1992. pap. 18.95 (0-912221-04-6) Beechwood.

Winnebago Mysteries. Moira Crone. LC 81-71642. 128p. 1982. 15.95 (0-914590-68-5); pap. 6.95 (0-914590-69-3) Fiction Coll.

Winnebago Oratory: Great Moments in the Recorded Speech of the Hochungra, 1742-1887. Mark Diedrich. (Illus.). 105p. (Orig.). 1991. pap. 16.95 (0-9616901-6-X) Coyote Bks MN.

Winnebago Songs & Stories: A Resource Guide. Jocelyn Riley. 114p. 1995. 20.00 (1-877933-19-8) Her Own Words.

Winnebago Tribe. Paul A. Radin. LC 64-63594. (Illus.). xvi, 573p. 1990. reprint ed. pap. 24.00 (0-8032-5710-4, Bison Books) U of Nebr Pr.

Winneconne, History's Crossing Place. Michael J. Goc. Ed. by Geraldine Driscoll & Monty Giffin. (Illus.). 152p. 1987. 19.95 (0-938627-01-5) New Past Pr.

***Winner.** David Baldacci. 1998. 25.00 (0-446-52259-7) Warner Bks.

Winner. Peg Kehret. (YA). (gr. 7-12). 1988. pap. 4.25 (0-89872-302-7) Turman Pub.

Winner. Elmer Rice. 1954. pap. 5.25 (0-8222-1263-3) Dramatists Play.

Winner & Losers: How Sectors Shape the Developmental Prospects of States. D. Michael Shafer. LC 94-10383. (Cornell Studies in Political Economy). 288p. 1994. 39.95 (0-8014-3000-3); pap. 14.95 (0-8014-8188-0) Cornell U Pr.

***Winner in Every Way.** Jewel C. Allen. LC 96-90247. 1996. 16.95 (0-533-11968-5) Vantage.

Winner Names the Age: A Collection of Writings. Lillian Smith. Ed. by Michelle Cliff. 224p. 1982. pap. 4.95 (0-393-30044-7) Norton.

Winner of the Slow Bicycle Race: The Satirical Writings of Paul Krassner. Paul Krassner. 352p. 1996. 22.00 (1-888363-04-5) Seven Stories.

***Winner of the Slow Bicycle Race: The Satirical Writings of Paul Krassner.** Paul Krassner. 352p. 1997. pap. 11.95 (1-888363-44-4) Seven Stories.

Winner Take All. Sean Flannery. 352p. 1995. 5.99 (0-8125-2288-5) Forge NYC.

Winner Take All. John Gollehon. 256p. 1993. pap. 6.99 (0-914839-18-7) Gollehon Pr.

Winner Take All. Terri Herrington. 368p. 1995. mass mkt. 4.99 (0-06-108267-8, Harp PBks) HarpC.

Winner Take All. Fred Jevons. (C). 1979. 26.00 (0-86828-376-2, Pub. by Deakin Univ AT) St Mut.

***Winner Take All: A Brutally Honest & Irreverent Look at the Motivations & Methods of the Top Traders.** William R. Gallacher. 1997. pap. text ed. 21.95 (0-7863-1191-6) Irwin Prof Pubng.

Winner Take All: A History of the Trans-Canada Canoe Trail. David Lavender. LC 77-4864. 385p. (Orig.). 1985. pap. 15.95 (0-89301-104-5) U of Idaho Pr.

Winner Take All: Inside the Mind of a Top Commodity Trader. rev. ed. William R. Gallacher. 1993. text ed. 32.50 (1-55738-533-5) Irwin Prof Pubng.

Winner Take All: Report of the Twentieth Century Fund Task Force on Reform of the Presidential Election Process. Ed. by William R. Keech. LC 78-9666. 82p. 1978. pap. 14.00 (0-8419-0400-6) Holmes & Meier.

Winner-Take-All Society. Robert H. Frank & Philip J. Cook. LC 95-13340. 272p. 1995. 25.00 (0-02-874034-3) Free Pr.

Winner-Take-All Society: Why the Few at the Top Get So Much More Than the Rest of Us. Robert H. Frank & Philip J. Cook. 288p. 1996. pap. 12.95 (0-14-025995-3, Penguin Bks) Viking Penguin.

***Winner-Take-All Society: Why the Few at the Top Get So Much More Than the Rest of Us.** Robert H. Frank & Philip J. Cook. 1996. pap. 12.95 (0-614-20718-5) Viking Penguin.

Winner Take Nothing. Ernest Hemingway. 162p. 1987. pap. 8.00 (0-02-051820-X) Macmillan.

Winner Takes All. Franklin W. Dixon. Ed. by Ruth Ashby. (Hardy Boys Casefiles Ser.: No. 85). 160p. (Orig.). (YA). (gr. 6 up). 1994. mass mkt. 3.99 (0-671-79469-8, Archway) PB.

Winner Takes All. Vanessa Drucker. 1990. 18.95 (0-517-57469-1, Crown) Crown Pub Group.

Winner Takes All. Sharon Mayne. (Temptation Ser.). 1993. mass mkt. 2.99 (0-373-25535-7, 1-25535-5) Harlequin Bks.

Winner Within. Pat Riley. 272p. 1994. pap. 12.00 (0-425-14175-6, Berkley Trade) Berkley Pub.

Winner Within. Pat Riley. Date not set. 5.98 (0-8317-6520-8) Smithmark.

Winner Within: A Life Plan for Team Players. Pat Riley. 224p. 1993. 22.95 (0-399-13839-0, Putnam) Putnam Pub Group.

Winner Within: Habits of the Happy, Healthy, Wealthy, & Wise. Larry L. Larsen. Ed. by Florence E. French. LC 92-97556. (Illus.). 212p. (Orig.). 1993. pap. 18.00 (0-9634716-0-0) Achieve Bk.

Winners: A Who's Who of Motor Racing Champions. Ed. by Brian Laban. (Illus.). 192p. 1983. 14.95 (0-85613-042-7) Beaufort Bks NY.

Winners! Producing Effective Electronic Media. Eugene Marlow & Janice Sileo. LC 94-30435. 158p. 1995. pap. 32.95 (0-534-24090-9) Wadsworth Pub.

Winners: The Aboriginal & Torres Strait Islander Sports Hall of Fame. Colin Tatz & Paul Tatz. (Illus.). 140p. 1995. pap. 14.95 (0-86840-159-5, Pub. by New South Wales Univ Pr AT) Intl Spec Bk.

Winners: Winning Recipes from the Junior League of Indianapolis. Illus. by Dick Listenberger. 336p. 1985. 14.95 (0-9614447-0-3) Jr League Indianapolis.

Winners All: A Call for Inclusive Schools. 44p. 1992. 10.00 (0-317-05331-0) NASBE.

Winners Also Cry. Jack McCarthy. LC 95-90881. (Orig.). 1996. pap. 12.50 (0-533-11746-1) Vantage.

Winners & Losers. Stephen Hoffius. LC 92-42394. 123p. (YA). (gr. 6 up). 1993. pap. 15.00 (0-671-79194-X, S&S Bks Young Read) S&S Childrens.

Winners & Losers. Stephen Hoffius. (J). 1996. pap. 3.99 (0-689-80165-3, Aladdin Paperbacks) S&S Childrens.

Winners & Losers. McColley. (J). 1998. 16.00 (0-689-80270-6, Aladdin Paperbacks) S&S Childrens.

Winners & Losers. rev. ed. Sydney J. Harris. Ed. by Leslie Britt. LC 73-78534. (Illus.). 119p. 1968. pap. 5.95 (0-913592-21-8) Tabor Pub.

Winners & Losers: Battles, Retreats, Gains, Losses, & Ruins from the Vietnam War. Gloria Emerson. 448p. 1992. pap. 12.95 (0-393-30925-8) Norton.

Winners & Losers: Ethnic Minorities in Sport & Recreation. Gajendra K. Verma & Douglas S. Darby. LC 94-28209. 184p. 1994. 75.00 (0-7507-0342-3, Falmer Pr); pap. 24.95 (0-7507-0343-1, Falmer Pr) Taylor & Francis.

Winners & Losers: Quiet Times Between Teens & God. Stephen Bly & Janet Bly. 167p. (YA). 1993. pap. 8.99 (0-8024-2223-3) Moody.

Winners & Losers: Social & Political Polarities in America. Irving L. Horowitz. LC 83-25353. (Duke Press Policy Studies). xv, 329p. (C). 1984. text ed. 48.00 (0-8223-0495-3); pap. text ed. 22.95 (0-8223-0602-6) Duke.

Winners & Losers at the Bridge Table. Bobby Goldman. 103p. 1979. pap. 3.95 (0-939460-05-X) Devyn Pr.

Winners & Losers in Colombia's Economic Growth of the 1970's. Miguel Urrutia. (World Bank Publication). 152p. 1985. 19.95 (0-19-520468-9) OUP.

Winners & Losers in East-West Trade: A Behavioral Analysis of U. S.; Soviet Detente, 1970-1983. Ronald E. Hoyt. LC 82-18613. 256p. 1983. text ed. 55.00 (0-275-91011-3, C1011, Praeger Pubs) Greenwood.

Winners Are Not Those Who Never Fail, But Those Who Never Quit. Edwin L. Cole. 160p. Date not set. pap. 9.99 (1-56292-110-X, HB-110) Honor Bks OK.

Winners Bible. 1993. write for info. (1-883325-00-5) Res Assocs TX.

Winner's Circle. Allison Estes. (Short Stirrup Club Ser.: No. 4). (J). (gr. 3-7). 1996. mass mkt. 3.99 (0-671-00098-5) PB.

Winner's Circle. Lauraine Snelling. (Golden Filly Ser.: Bk. 10). 192p. (YA). 1995. pap. 5.99 (1-55661-533-7) Bethany Hse.

Winner's Circle: How Ten Stock Brokers Became the Best in the Business. Robert L. Shook. 1992. 22.95 (0-13-587577-3, Busn) P-H.

Winners Circle: Ten Years of Award-Winning Homebrew Recipes. Compiled by American Homebrewers Association Staff. (Illus.). 199p. 1989. pap. 11.95 (0-937381-14-4) Brewers Pubns.

Winner's Circle - Yes, I Can! Self-Esteem Lessons for the Secondary Classroom. Clare La Meres. (Illus.). 272p. 1990. teacher ed., pap. 29.95 (0-9644261-3-7) LaMeres Lifestyles.

Winner's Curse: Paradoxes & Anomalies of Economic Life. Richard H. Thaler. 230p. 1991. 29.95 (0-02-932465-3, Free Press) Free Pr.

Winner's Curse: Paradoxes & Anomalies of Economic Life. Richard H. Thaler. LC 93-27713. 240p. 1994. pap. text ed. 14.95 (0-691-01934-7) Princeton U Pr.

Winner's Cut. Preston Pairo. 256p. 1988. pap. 3.95 (0-373-97069-2) Harlequin Bks.

Winner's Daily Word: Mini Book. Mike Murdoch. (Orig.). 0.98 (1-56292-419-2) Honor Bks OK.

Winner's Edge. Ben Gay, III. 280p. 1987. pap. 19.95 (0-942645-04-9) Hampton Hse Pub.

Winner's Edge. Denis E. Waitley. 192p. 1986. mass mkt. 5.50 (0-425-10000-6) Berkley Pub.

Winner's Edge: The Inside Guide to Betting Pro Football. Richard Raihall. (Guides to Sports Betting Ser.). 180p. (Orig.). 1984. write for info. (0-915643-09-X) Santa Barb Pr.

Winners for Life: A Success Guide for Teenagers Using the Proven Power of Goal Setting. Donny Anderson & Linkie S. Cohn. (Illus.). 100p. (YA). 1996. pap. 9.25 (0-9650545-0-0) Winners for Life.

***Winners for Life Vol. 2: A Refresher Course for Adults Using the Proven Power of Goal Setting.** 2nd ed. Linkie S. Cohn & Donny Anderson. (Illus.). 100p. 1997. pap. 9.25 (0-614-29735-4) Winners for Life.

Winner's Guide on Retail Selling. Peter R. Bol. LC 84-72669. 128p. (Orig.). 1985. pap. text ed. 6.95 (0-9613917-0-7) Dynamic Comm.

Winner's Guide to Casino Gambling. Edwin Silberstang. 368p. 1985. pap. 4.95 (0-451-14844-4, Sig) NAL-Dutton.

Winner's Guide to Casino Gambling. rev. ed. Edwin Silberstang. 432p. 1985. pap. 5.99 (0-451-16553-5, Sig) NAL-Dutton.

Winner's Guide to Casino Gambling. rev. ed. Edwin Silberstang. (Illus.). 368p. 1989. pap. 14.95 (0-452-26326-3, Dutton) NAL-Dutton.

***Winner's Guide to Casino Gambling.** 3rd rev. ed. Edwin Silberstang. LC 96-41984. 1997. pap. 14.95 (0-452-27698-5, Plume) NAL-Dutton.

Winner's Guide to Greyhound Racing. Jones. LC 92-74839. 96p. (Orig.). 1993. 7.95 (0-940685-36-1) Cardoza Pub.

***Winner's Guide to Greyhound Racing.** 2nd ed. Jones. LC 96-71757. 128p. 1997. pap. text ed. 9.95 (0-940685-76-0) Cardoza Pub.

***Winner's Guide to Optimist Sailing: The Essential Manual for Parents, Coaches, & All Kids 8-15.** Gary Jobson. 1997. pap. 15.00 (0-684-83189-9, Fireside) S&S Trade.

Winners Guide to Texas Hold 'Em Poker. 2nd ed. Ken Warren. LC 95-68283. (Illus.). 224p. 1995. pap. 14.95 (0-940685-59-0) Cardoza Pub.

Winner's Guide to the Texas Lottery. Turk Pipkin. (Illus.). 128p. (Orig.). 1992. pap. 4.95 (1-881484-03-3) Softshoe Pub.

Winners in Peace: MacArthur, Yoshida, & Postwar Japan. Richard B. Finn. LC 90-11275. 432p. (C). 1992. 40.00 (0-520-06909-9) U CA Pr.

Winners in Peace: MacArthur, Yoshida, & Postwar Japan. Richard B. Finn. LC 90-11275. 434p. 1995. pap. 16.95 (0-520-20213-9) U CA Pr.

Winners, Losers, & Wannabees. David Willingham. LC 93-10693. (Devotions for Today Ser.). 1993. 7.50 (1-56212-037-9) CRC Pubns.

Winner's Magic. Jenny Robson. (Junior African Writers Ser.). (Illus.). (J). (gr. 3-4). 1992. pap. 3.88 (0-7910-2906-9) Chelsea Hse.

Winners of the Heisman Trophy. 2nd ed. John Devaney. (Illus.). (J). (gr. 5 up). 1990. 14.95 (0-8027-6906-3); lib. bdg. 15.85 (0-8027-6907-1) Walker & Co.

Winners of the West: A Campaign Paper Published in the Interests of the Veterans of All Indian Wars, Their Widows & Orphan Children. 2040p. 1944. 202.00 (0-317-28524-6, J M C & Co) Amereon Ltd.

Winners Playbook. 2nd ed. Avery Cardoza. LC 94-68041. (Illus.). 128p. 1994. pap. 5.95 (0-940685-53-1) Cardoza Pub.

***Winner's Way: Revised Owners & Trainers Manual.** Nancy Marks. Ed. by Donald Currier. (Illus.). 112p. 1997. 24.95 (1-890030-06-6) Las Vegas Insider.

Winners Without Losers: Structures & Strategies for Increasing Student Motivation to Learn. James P. Raffini. 1994. pap. text ed. 43.50 (0-205-16707-1) Allyn.

Winnetka Architecture: Where Past Is Present: A Guide to Timeless Styles. Cynthia G. Fuller. Ed. by Susan S. Benjamin. LC 90-70408. (Illus.). 48p. (Orig.). 1990. pap. 14.95 (0-9625937-0-2) Winnetka Hist Soc.

Winni Allfours. Babette Cole. LC 93-28447. (Illus.). (J). (gr. k-4). 1996. pap. 13.95 (0-8167-3308-2) BrdgeWater.

Winni Allfours. Babette Cole. LC 93-28447. (Illus.). (J). (gr. k-4). 1997. pap. 3.95 (0-8167-3307-4, Troll Medallion) Troll Communs.

Winnibella the Winsome Witch. Bette Rogers. (Illus.). 17p. (J). (gr. k-3). 1996. pap. 16.00 (0-8059-3963-6) Dorrance.

***Winnicot Studies, Vol. 9.** 1995. 17.95 (1-85575-081-3) Brunner-Mazel.

Winnicott. Adam Phillips. LC 88-28390. 192p. 1989. reprint ed. 29.95 (0-674-95360-6); reprint ed. pap. 13.95 (0-674-95361-4) HUP.

Winnicott & Paradox: From Birth to Creation. Anne Clancier & Jeannine Kalmanovitch. (Illus.). 208p. (C). 1987. pap. text ed. 22.00 (0-422-60380-5, Pub. by Tavistock UK) Routledge Chapman & Hall.

Winnicott Studies, Vol. 11. Ed. by Squiggle Foundation Staff. 96p. 1996. pap. text ed. 17.95 (1-85575-131-3, Pub. by Karnac Bks UK) Brunner-Mazel.

Winnicott Studies: The Journal of the Squiggle Foundation, Vol. 2, 1987. Ed. by Squiggle Foundation Staff. 108p. 1990. reprint ed. pap. text ed. 17.95 (0-9510174-1-1, Pub. by Karnac Bks UK) Brunner-Mazel.

Winnicott Studies: The Journal of the Squiggle Foundation, Vol. 3, 1988. Ed. by Squiggle Foundation Staff. 80p. 1990. reprint ed. pap. text ed. 17.95 (0-9510174-2-X, Pub. by Karnac Bks UK) Brunner-Mazel.

Winnicott Studies: The Journal of the Squiggle Foundation, Vol. 4, 1989. Ed. by Squiggle Foundation Staff. 108p. 1990. reprint ed. pap. text ed. 17.95 (0-9510175-3-5, Pub. by Karnac Bks UK) Brunner-Mazel.

Winnicott Studies: The Journal of the Squiggle Foundation, Vol. 5, 1990. Ed. by Squiggle Foundation Staff. 100p. 1991. reprint ed. pap. text ed. 17.95 (0-946439-99-0, Pub. by Karnac Bks UK) Brunner-Mazel.

Winnicott Studies: The Journal of the Squiggle Foundation, Vol. 6, 1991. Squiggle Foundation Staff. 96p. 1992. pap. text ed. 17.95 (1-85575-024-4, Pub. by Karnac Bks UK) Brunner-Mazel.

Winnicott Studies Vol. 10: The Journal of Squiggle Foundation, Vol. 10. Ed. by Laurence Spurling. (Karnac Bks.). 63p. 1995. pap. text ed. 17.95 (1-85575-109-7, Pub. by Karnac Bks UK) Brunner-Mazel.

Winnicott Studies, 1993, Vol. 7: The Journal of the Squiggle Foundation. Squiggle Foundation Staff. 100p. 1993. pap. text ed. 17.95 (1-85575-048-1, Pub. by Karnac Bks UK) Brunner-Mazel.

Winnie. Gwendolyn Brooks. 1991. 4.00 (0-88378-050-X) Third World.

Winnie Ille Pu. A. A. Milne. Tr. by Alexander Lenard. (Illus.). 160p. (LAT.). 1991. pap. 10.95 (0-14-015339-X, Penguin Bks) Viking Penguin.

Winnie-Ille-Pu: A Latin Version of A. A. Milne's Winnie-the-Pooh. A. A. Milne. (Illus.). 120p. (LAT.). 1984. 10.00 (0-525-24267-8, 0971-290, Dutton) NAL-Dutton.

***Winnie in Winter.** Korky Paul. (Illus.). 32p. 1997. 16.95 (0-19-279004-8) OUP.

Winnie l'Ourson. A. A. Milne. (Illus.). (FRE.). (J). (gr. 3-8). 9.95 (0-685-23402-9) Fr & Eur.

Winnie Mandela. Nancy Harrison. LC 85-29134. (Illus.). 183p. 1986. 14.95 (0-8076-1149-2) Braziller.

Winnie Mandela. Nancy Harrison. LC 85-29134. (Illus.). 184p. (C). 1987. reprint ed. pap. 5.95 (0-8076-1173-5) Braziller.

Winnie Mandela: The Soul of South Africa. Milton Meltzer. (Women of Our Time Ser.). (Illus.). (J). (gr. 2-6). 1987. reprint ed. pap. 4.50 (0-14-032181-0, Puffin) Puffin Bks.

W

Winnie-The-Pooh. (Classics Ser.). 96p. (J). 1994. 7.98 (*1-57082-053-8*) Mouse Works.

Winnie-The-Pooh. (Disney Animated Ser.). (Illus.). 48p. (J). (ps-6). 1989. 5.99 (*0-517-67005-4*) Random Hse Value.

Winnie-the-Pooh. (Deluxe Golden Sound Story Bks.). (Illus.). 24p. (J). (ps-2). 1991. 9.95 (*0-307-74019-6*, Golden Pr) Western Pub.

Winnie the Pooh. (J). pap. 1.59 (*0-307-04040-2*) Western Pub.

Winnie-The-Pooh. A. A. Milne. (Illus.). 176p. (J). Date not set. pap. 7.95 (*0-452-27764-7*, Plume) NAL-Dutton.

Winnie-the-Pooh. A. A. Milne. (Illus.). 176p. (J). (ps up). 1988. pap. 10.99 (*0-525-44443-2*) Dutton Child Bks.

Winnie-the-Pooh. A. A. Milne. (Illus.). (J). (gr. 1-5). 1961. 9.95 (*0-525-43035-0*, Dutton) NAL-Dutton.

Winnie-the-Pooh. A. A. Milne. (Illus.). 176p. (J). 1992. pap. 3.99 (*0-14-036121-9*, Puffin) Puffin Bks.

Winnie the Pooh. Walt Disney Company Staff. 96p. (FRE.). (J). (gr. k-5). pap. 9.95 (*0-7859-8848-3*) Fr & Eur.

Winnie-the-Pooh. deluxe ed. A. A. Milne. LC 91-26203. (Illus.). 176p. (J). (ps up). 1991. Full-color Gift Edition. pap. 22.50 (*0-525-44776-8*) Dutton Child Bks.

Winnie the Pooh, 4 vols., Set. A. A. Milne. (J). 1992. pap. 85.00 (*0-525-45004-1*) Dutton Child Bks.

Winnie-the-Pooh: (Small Cast Musical) Le Clanche Du Rand. 1992. pap. 5.00 (*0-87129-182-7*, W72) Dramatic Pub.

Winnie-the-Pooh: (Straight Version) rev. ed. Kristen Sergel. 1992. pap. 5.25 (*0-87129-194-0*, W37) Dramatic Pub.

***Winnie the Pooh: Sleepytime Set, Incl. plush Pooh.** Walt Disney Staff. (Illus.). 32p. (J). 1996. 19.95 (*0-7868-4121-4*) Hyprn Child.

Winnie the Pooh: The Merry Christmas Mystery. Betty Birney. (J). (ps-3). 1993. pap. 2.25 (*0-307-12774-5*, Golden Pr) Western Pub.

Winnie-the-Pooh see Treasury of Winnie-the-Pooh

***Winnie the Pooh - Easter: Super Coloring Books.** (J). 2.29 (*0-307-08300-4*, 08300, Golden Books) Western Pub.

Winnie the Pooh & a Day for Eeyore. Teddy Slater. LC 94-70810. (Illus.). 48p. (J). (ps-4). 1994. 12.95 (*1-56282-657-3*) Disney Pr.

Winnie the Pooh & Eeyore Be Happy. (Disney Collection). 24p. (J). (ps-2). bds. 1.59 (*0-307-00645-X*, Golden Books) Western Pub.

Winnie the Pooh & Some Bees. A. A. Milne. (Pooh Jewelry Bks.). (Illus.). 32p. (J). 1993. pap. 14.99 (*0-525-45044-0*) Dutton Child Bks.

Winnie the Pooh & Some Bees Storybooks. A. A. Milne. 128p. (J). (ps-2). 1993. pap. 4.99 (*0-525-45033-5*) Dutton Child Bks.

Winnie the Pooh & the Blustery Day. Teddy Slater. LC 92-55130. (Many Adventures of Winnie the Pooh Ser.). (Illus.). 48p. (J). (ps-3). 1993. 12.95 (*1-56282-488-0*) Disney Pr.

Winnie the Pooh & the Bumblebee Chase: A Turn-the-Wheel Storybook. Bruce Talkington. LC 94-72231. (Illus.). 14p. (J). (ps-k). 1995. 11.95 (*0-7868-3022-0*) Disney Pr.

Winnie the Pooh & the Grand & Wonderful Day. Mary Packard. (Disney Collection). (Illus.). 24p. (J). bds. 1.49 (*0-307-30263-6*, Golden Pr) Western Pub.

Winnie the Pooh and the Honey Tree. (Little Golden Books Disney Collection). (Illus.). 24p. (J). (ps-2). 1995. bds. 1.49 (*0-307-30201-6*, Golden Pr) Western Pub.

Winnie the Pooh & the Honey Tree. Illus. by John Kurtz. LC 92-53442. (Many Adventures of Winnie the Pooh Ser.). 48p. (J). (ps-4). 1993. 12.95 (*1-56282-379-5*) Disney Pr.

Winnie-the-Pooh & the House at Pooh Corner: Recovering Arcadia. Paula T. Connolly. LC 94-26329. (Twayne's Masterwork Studies). 160p. 1994. 23.95 (*0-8057-8810-7*, Twayne); pap. 13.95 (*0-8057-8811-5*, Twayne) Scribnrs Ref.

Winnie the Pooh & the Little Lost Bird: A Big Golden Book. Betty Birney. (J). (ps-3). 1993. 3.95 (*0-307-12369-3*, Golden Pr) Western Pub.

Winnie the Pooh & the Missing Pots. Betty Birney. (Big Golden Bks.). (Illus.). 24p. (J). (ps-2). 1992. write for info. (*0-307-12337-5*, 12337) Western Pub.

Winnie the Pooh & the Perfect Christmas Tree: A Pop-up Book. Bruce Talkington. LC 93-74714. (Illus.). 12p. (J). (ps-1). 1994. 11.95 (*1-56282-649-2*) Disney Pr.

Winnie the Pooh & the Toy Airplane. (Illus.). (J). 4.50 (*0-614-13221-5*, 21-37078) EAA Aviation.

Winnie the Pooh & Tigger. (Disney Learn to Draw Ser.). (Illus.). 28p. (J). 1991. pap. 6.95 (*1-56010-090-7*, DS05) W Foster Pub.

Winnie the Pooh & Tigger Too. Stephanie Calmenson. LC 93-73813. (Many Adventures of Winnie the Pooh Ser.). (Illus.). 48p. (J). (ps-4). 1994. 12.95 (*1-56282-630-1*) Disney Pr.

Winnie-the-Pooh Christmas Tail: Christmas Musical. James W. Rodgers. 1994. pap. 5.00 (*0-87129-225-4*, W03) Dramatic Pub.

Winnie-the-Pooh (Full-Musical) A. A. Milne. 1964. 5.50 (*0-87129-364-1*, W01) Dramatic Pub.

Winnie the Pooh Helping Hands. (Golden Look Look Bks.). (Illus.). (J). (ps-3). 1995. pap. 2.25 (*0-307-16207-9*, Golden Pr) Western Pub.

Winnie-the-Pooh Lift-the-Flap Rebus Book. A. A. Milne. (Illus.). 16p. (J). (ps-3). 1992. pap. 12.99 (*0-525-44987-6*) Dutton Child Bks.

Winnie the Pooh Mask Book. Petra Craig. LC 94-71798. (Illus.). 26p. (J). (ps-3). 1995. pap. 12.95 (*0-7868-4033-1*) Disney Pr.

Winnie-the-Pooh on Management: In Which a Very Important Bear & His Friends Are Introduced to a Very Important Subject. Roger E. Allen. (Illus.). 224p. 1994. pap. 18.95 (*0-525-93898-2*, Dutton) NAL-Dutton.

Winnie-the Pooh on Problem Solving. Roger E. Allen. 1995. pap. 18.95 (*0-525-94063-4*) NAL-Dutton.

Winnie-the-Pooh on Problem Solving: In Which Pooh, Piglet, & Friends Explore How to Solve Problems So You Can Too. Roger E. Allen & Stephen D. Allen. LC 95-17641. 1995. write for info. (*0-614-07806-7*) NAL-Dutton.

Winnie-the-Pooh Tells Time. A. A. Milne. (J). 1997. pap. 9.99 (*0-525-45535-3*) NAL-Dutton.

Winnie the Pooh, Whose Egg Are You? (Motion Picture Book). 12p. (J). (ps-3). 1995. pap. 7.98 (*1-57082-127-5*) Mouse Works.

Winnie the Pooh's A to Zzzz: Miniature Edition. Don Ferguson. LC 91-73812. (Illus.). 32p. (J). (ps-k). 1992. lib. bdg. 12.95 (*1-56282-015-X*) Disney Pr.

Winnie the Pooh's A to Zzzz: Miniature Edition. Don Ferguson. LC 91-73812. (Illus.). 32p. (J). (ps-k). 1994. 5.95 (*0-7868-3009-3*) Disney Pr.

Winnie-the-Pooh's ABC. Illus. by Ernest H. Shepard. (Winnie-the-Pooh Collection). 32p. (J). 1995. pap. 9.99 (*0-525-45365-2*) Dutton Child Bks.

Winnie-the-Pooh's Baby Book. A. A. Milne. (Illus.). 32p. (J). (gr. k up). 1994. pap. 14.99 (*0-525-45298-2*) Dutton Child Bks.

Winnie the Pooh's Bedtime Stories. Bruce Talkington. LC 93-74308. (Illus.). 96p. (J). (ps-3). 1994. 14.95 (*1-56282-646-8*) Disney Pr.

Winnie-the-Pooh's Birthday Book. Ernest H. Shepard. (Illus.). 128p. (J). 1993. pap. 11.99 (*0-525-45061-0*) Dutton Child Bks.

Winnie-the-Pooh's Book & Toy Box. (Illus.). 32p. (J). (gr. k up). 1994. pap. 24.99 (*0-525-45342-3*) Dutton Child Bks.

Winnie-the-Pooh's Calendar Book 1987. A. A. Milne. (J). (ps up). 1986. 4.95 (*0-525-44235-9*, Dutton) NAL-Dutton.

Winnie-the-Pooh's Calendar Book 1988. A. A. Milne. (J). (ps up). 1987. spiral bd. 4.95 (*0-525-44311-8*, Dutton) NAL-Dutton.

Winnie-the-Pooh's Calendar Book 1989. A. A. Milne. (Illus.). 32p. (J). (ps up). 1988. spiral bd. 5.95 (*0-525-44398-3*, Dutton) NAL-Dutton.

Winnie-the-Pooh's Colors. A. A. Milne. (Illus.). 32p. (J). (ps up). 1995. pap. 9.99 (*0-525-45428-4*) Dutton Child Bks.

Winnie-the-Pooh's Cookie Baking Set. Illus. by Ernest H. Shepard. 64p. (J). (ps up). 1996. pap. 15.99 (*0-525-45601-5*) NAL-Dutton.

Winnie-the-Pooh's Cookie Book. A. A. Milne. (J). 1996. pap. 8.99 (*0-525-45688-0*) Viking Penguin.

Winnie the Pooh's Easter. Bruce Talkington. LC 92-53441. (Illus.). 32p. (J). (ps-4). 1993. 12.95 (*1-56282-377-9*) Disney Pr.

Winnie the Pooh's Easter. Bruce Talkington. LC 92-53441. (Illus.). 32p. (J). (gr. k-4). 1996. pap. 5.95 (*0-7868-4065-X*) Disney Pr.

***Winnie the Pooh's Enchanted Place.** A. A. Milne. (Illus.). 1997. pap. 18.95 (*0-525-45832-8*) NAL-Dutton.

Winnie-the-Pooh's Friendship Book. A. A. Milne. (Illus.). 48p. (J). (gr. 4-7). 1994. pap. 8.99 (*0-525-45204-4*) Dutton Child Bks.

***Winnie the Pooh's Giant Lift the Flap Book.** A. A. Milne. (Illus.). (J). 1997. pap. 9.99 (*0-525-45841-7*) NAL-Dutton.

Winnie-the-Pooh's Hundred Acre Wood: A Press-Out Model Book. A. A. Milne. (Illus.). 40p. (J). (gr. k up). 1994. pap. 9.99 (*0-525-45341-5*) Dutton Child Bks.

***Winnie the Pooh's Most Grand Adventure, Vol. 1.** Bruce Talkington. (J). 1997. 12.95 (*0-7868-3135-9*) Disney Pr.

Winnie the Pooh's Nightmare: A Pop-up Book. Bruce Talkington. LC 94-68043. (Illus.). 12p. (J). (ps-3). 1995. 12.95 (*0-7868-3019-0*) Disney Pr.

Winnie-the-Pooh's Opposites. A. A. Milne. (Illus.). 32p. (J). (ps up). 1995. pap. 9.99 (*0-525-45429-2*) Dutton Child Bks.

Winnie-the-Pooh's Picnic Cookbook. A. A. Milne. LC 96-47814. (J). 1997. pap. 8.99 (*0-525-45533-7*) NAL-Dutton.

***Winnie-the-Pooh's Picnic Cookbook.** Illus. by Ernest H. Shepard. 1997. 8.99 (*0-614-28723-5*) NAL-Dutton.

Winnie the Pooh's Pop-up Theater Book. A. A. Milne. (Illus.). 12p. (J). 1993. pap. 15.99 (*0-525-44990-6*) Dutton Child Bks.

Winnie-the-Pooh's Revolving Picture Book. A. A. Milne. (Illus.). 12p. (J). (ps up). 1990. pap. 13.99 (*0-525-44645-1*) Dutton Child Bks.

Winnie the Pooh's Silly Day. Bruce Talkington. LC 94-69507. 12p. (J). (gr. k-4). 1996. 11.95 (*0-7868-3069-7*) Disney Pr.

Winnie the Pooh's Stories for Christmas. Bruce Talkington. LC 95-73125. (Illus.). 80p. (J). (ps-3). 1996. 14.95 (*0-7868-3107-3*) Disney Pr.

Winnie-the-Pooh's Story Box, 10 bks., Set. A. A. Milne. (Illus.). (J). 1993. pap. 49.90 (*0-525-45168-4*) Dutton Child Bks.

Winnie-the-Pooh's Teatime Cookbook. A. A. Milne. LC 92-35650. (Illus.). 64p. (J). 1993. pap. 8.99 (*0-525-45135-8*) Dutton Child Bks.

Winnie the Pooh's Thanksgiving. Bruce Talkington. LC 94-67862. (Illus.). 32p. (J). 1995. 11.95 (*0-7868-3053-0*) Disney Pr.

Winnie-The-Pooh's Trivia Quiz Book. A. A. Milne. LC 93-39969. (Illus.). 48p. (J). 1994. pap. 8.99 (*0-525-45265-6*) Dutton Child Bks.

Winnie the Pooh's Valentine. Bruce Talkington. LC 94-70525. (Illus.). 32p. (J). (ps-4). 1995. 11.95 (*0-7868-3017-4*) Disney Pr.

Winnie the Pooh's Valentine. Bruce Talkington. (Illus.). 32p. 1997. pap. text ed. 4.95 (*0-7868-4111-7*) Disney Pr.

Winnie-the-Pooh's Visitors Book. A. A. Milne. (Illus.). 128p. (J). 1994. pap. 13.99 (*0-525-45217-6*) Dutton Child Bks.

Winnie-the-Pooh's 1-2-3. A. A. Milne. (Illus.). 32p. (J). 1996. pap. 9.99 (*0-525-45534-5*) NAL-Dutton.

Winnie the Witch. Valerie Thomas. (Illus.). 32p. (J). (ps-3). 1987. 13.95 (*0-916291-13-8*) Kane-Miller Bk.

Winnie the Witch. Valerie Thomas. (Illus.). 32p. (J). (ps-3). 1990. reprint ed. pap. 6.95 (*0-916291-32-4*) Kane-Miller Bk.

Winnie Two-Shadows. Jack Wooldridge. (Potawatomi Fables Ser.). 24p. (J). (gr. 1). 1995. pap. 7.50 (*1-887963-00-6*) Pota Pr.

Winnie's Day Off. Matthew V. Smith. (Illus.). 21p. (J). (gr. k-3). 1995. pap. 11.95 (*1-56606-031-1*) Bradley Mann.

***Winnie's Wisdom: Great Tennis Truths from an 'Old' Pro.** Winifred C. Gilliford. Ed. by Jerry Kinkead. (Illus.). 120p. 1997. pap. 12.50 (*0-9656627-0-5*) Crawford Pr PA.

Winning. Walter E. Adams. 128p. (Orig.). 1985. pap. 4.95 (*0-937408-35-2*) GMI Pubns Inc.

Winning. David Viscott. 1987. mass mkt. 5.50 (*0-671-67935-X*) PB.

Winning. Robin F. Brancato. LC 77-5632. 224p. (YA). (gr. 7 up). 1988. reprint ed. pap. 4.99 (*0-394-80751-0*) Knopf Bks Yng Read.

Winning: A Race Driver's Handbook. George A. Anderson. (Illus.). 192p. 1993. pap. 19.95 (*0-87938-776-9*) Motorbooks Intl.

Winning: A Training & Showing Guide for Hunter Seat Riders. Anna J. White-Mullin. (Illus.). 216p. 1992. 24.95 (*0-943955-51-3*, Trafalgar Sq Pub) Trafalgar.

Winning: Continuous Improvement Theory in High Performance Organizations. Krysztof Obloj et al. LC 94-39616. (SUNY Series in International Management). 205p. (C). 1995. text ed. 49.50 (*0-7914-2521-5*); pap. text ed. 16.95 (*0-7914-2522-3*) State U NY Pr.

Winning: Direct Marketing for Insurance Agents & Brokers. Don Jackson & Irwin Lowen. LC 92-8784. 378p. 1992. boxed 49.95 (*0-942061-22-5*, Financial Sourcebks) Sourcebks.

Winning! Great Coaches & Athletes Share Their Secrets of Success. Compiled by Michael Lynberg. LC 92-40069. 160p. 1993. pap. 6.99 (*0-385-47017-7*) Doubleday.

***Winning: How Teens (& Other Humans) Can Beat Anger & Depression.** Lew Hamburger. LC 96-90796. (Orig.). (YA). (gr. 7 up). 1997. pap. 12.95 (*0-533-12180-9*) Vantage.

Winning! The Awesome & Amazing Insiders' Book of Windows Game Tips, Traps, & Sneaky Tricks. John V. Hedtke. 232p. 1991. 14.95 (*0-938151-77-0*) Peachpit Pr.

Winning: The Psychology of Competition. Stuart H. Walker. 1986. pap. 10.95 (*0-393-30267-9*) Norton.

***Winning! Using Lawyers' Courtroom Techniques to Get Your Way in Everyday Situations.** Noelle C. Nelson. LC 97-2433. 1997. 22.95 (*0-13-287129-7*) P-H.

Winning a Sports Scholarship: Your Game Plan for Getting into College by Playing the Sport You Love. Chris Tenkin. LC 95-50950. 304p. (Orig.). 1996. pap. 12.00 (*1-56980-078-2*) Barricade Bks.

Winning a Tax Assessment Reduction in New York State. (Real Estate Law & Practice Course Handbook Ser.). 220p. 1992. pap. 70.00 (*0-685-69514-X*) PLI.

Winning a Wife, & Other Stories. Peter Neagoe. LC 78-152951. (Short Story Index Reprint Ser.). 1977. reprint ed. 20.95 (*0-8369-3866-6*) Ayer.

Winning Administrator. Robert W. Haacker & Clint Maun. 154p. (Orig.). 1992. per. 169.00 (*0-929442-11-3*) Publicare Pr.

Winning Against the Odds. Sam Robinson. LC 92-29120. (Illus.). 256p. 1993. 17.50 (*0-912526-58-0*) Lib Res.

Winning America: Ideas & Leadership for the 1990s. Ed. by Chester Hartman & Marcus G. Raskin. LC 88-42556. 414p. (Orig.). 1988. 40.00 (*0-89608-344-6*); pap. 16.00 (*0-89608-343-8*) South End Pr.

Winning an Appeal: A Step-by-Step Explanation of How to Prepare & Present your Case Efficiently & with Maximum Effectiveness, with a Sample Brief. rev. ed. Myron Moskovitz. 172p. 1985. 15.00 (*0-87215-878-0*) MICHIE.

Winning an Athletic Scholarship. Dennis K. Reischl. 121p. (Orig.). (YA). (gr. 9-12). 1994. pap. text ed. 19.95 (*0-936295-53-8*) FPMI Comns.

Winning & Keeping Industrial Customers: The Dynamics of Customer Relationships. Barbara B. Jackson. LC 84-48376. 195p. 22.95 (*0-669-11146-5*, Lexington) Jossey-Bass.

Winning & Losing: Australian National Elections. Scott Bennett. 160p. 1996. pap. 24.95 (*0-522-84506-1*, Pub. by Melbourne Univ Pr AT) Paul & Co Pubs.

Winning & Losing in the Civil War: Essays & Stories. Albert Castel. LC 95-40947. 220p. 1996. 29.95 (*1-57003-074-X*) U of SC Pr.

Winning Appeals: Persuasive Argument & the Appellate Process. Josephine R. Potuto. 120p. 1992. pap. 22.95 (*1-55681-291-4*) Natl Inst Trial Ad.

Winning Approach to Taking Charge of Your Future. 37p. write for info. incl. audio (*0-9647962-3-6*) Spence Ewing & Assocs.

***Winning Arbitration Advocacy.** Marvin Hill et al. 1997. 75.00 (*1-57018-061-X*, 1061) BNA Books.

Winning at Blackjack: Simple, Easy to Learn Tips, Techniques & Strategies for Winning at Blackjack. Jeff Harpring. LC 95-70402. 68p. (Orig.). 1995. pap. 5.95 (*0-9645728-0-X*) Premiere One Pub.

Winning at Casino Gambling. Terence Reese. 1979. pap. 3.95 (*0-451-15937-3*, AE3110, Sig); pap. 4.99 (*0-451-16777-5*, ROC) NAL-Dutton.

Winning at Casino Gambling. Lyle Stuart. LC 94-25585. (Illus.). 320p. 1994. pap. 18.00 (*1-56980-012-X*) Barricade Bks.

Winning at Chess. A. J. Gillam. (Better Chess Ser.). 96p. (Orig.). 1994. pap. 6.00 (*0-945470-31-2*) Chess Ent.

Winning at Craps. Lloyd T. Commins. 1965. pap. 5.00 (*0-87980-345-2*) Wilshire.

Winning at Craps: A New Look at an Old Game. Richard F. Schulte. Ed. by Daniel R. Mead. LC 92-62646. (Gambling - How to Win Ser.). (Illus.). 138p. (Orig.). 1993. pap. 9.95 (*0-934422-06-0*, BKS-160560) Mead Pub Corp.

Winning at FDA: A Strategic Guide. 2nd ed. Solomon Goody. Ed. by Jeffrey Yohn & David Swit. LC 89-63272. 48p. 1992. pap. 149.00 (*0-914176-36-6*) Wash Busn Info.

Winning at Flower Shows. Jack Kramer. LC 94-37914. (Illus.). 200p. 1995. pap. 17.95 (*1-55591-155-2*) Fulcrum Pub.

Winning at Gin. Chester Wander & Cy Rice. 1965. pap. 3.00 (*0-87980-351-7*) Wilshire.

Winning at Golf. David W. Smith. 192p. 1995. pap. 9.95 (*0-914984-46-2*) Starburst.

Winning at Losing: Lasting Weight Control from Someone Who's Living It. Jerry B. Jenkins. 1993. pap. 10.99 (*0-8024-1737-X*) Moody.

Winning at Math: Your Guide to Learning Mathematics the Quick & Easy Way. Paul D. Nolting. 208p. (Orig.). 1988. pap. 12.95 (*0-940287-08-0*) Acad Success Pr.

Winning at Math: Your Guide to Learning Mathematics Through Successful Study Skills. Paul D. Nolting. (Illus.). 240p. (C). 1991. pap. 14.95 (*0-940287-19-6*) Acad Success Pr.

***Winning at Math: Your Guide to Learning Mathematics Through Successful Study Skills.** 3rd expanded rev. ed. Paul D. Nolting. 356p. (C). Date not set. pap. text ed. 16.95 (*0-940287-26-9*) Acad Success Pr.

Winning at New Products: Strategy & Process. 2nd ed. Robert G. Cooper. 1993. pap. 20.00 (*0-201-56381-9*) Addison-Wesley.

Winning at Poker: An Expert's Guide. John Archer. 1978. 10.00 (*0-87980-362-2*) Wilshire.

Winning at Public Affairs. Bruce N. Hahn. (Orig.). (C). 1991. pap. text ed. 25.00 (*0-9630335-0-6*) Natl Assoc Mfrs.

Winning at Slot Machines: A Guide to Making Money at the Most Popular of All Casino Games. Jim Regan. 196p. 1995. pap. 5.95 (*0-8065-0973-2*, Citadel Pr) Carol Pub Group.

***Winning at the Frontline.** Brian Dennis. 168p. (Orig.). 1996. pap. 15.95 (*1-886094-37-3*) Chicago Spectrum.

Winning at the Horse Races. 1992. lib. bdg. 354.95 (*0-8490-8882-8*) Gordon Pr.

Winning at the NLRB. Matthew M. Franciewicz. 1995. text ed. 145.00 (*0-87179-884-0*) BNA Books.

***Winning at the NLRB: 1997 Supplement.** Mathew M. Franckiewicz. (Orig.). 1997. pap. write for info. (*1-57018-073-3*, 1073) BNA Books.

Winning at the Track. David L. Christopher. LC 83-81134. (Illus.). 160p. 1991. pap. 9.95 (*0-89709-195-7*) Liberty Pub.

Winning at the Track. David L. Christopher. LC 83-81134. (Illus.). 160p. 1997. disk 59.95 (*0-89709-215-5*) Liberty Pub.

***Winning at the Track.** 4th ed. David L. Christopher. 158p. 1994. pap. 9.95 (*0-89709-211-2*) Liberty Pub.

Winning at Twenty-One. John Archer. 1977. reprint ed. pap. 10.00 (*0-87980-328-2*) Wilshire.

Winning at Work. Michael Podolinsky. (Smart Tapes Ser.). (Orig.). (C). 1995. pap. 19.95 incl. audio (*1-55678-057-5*) Learn Inc.

Winning at Work: How to Be a Great Employee. Walt Mulvey. LC 95-76235. 100p. 1995. pap. 10.00 (*1-883697-45-X*) Hara Pub.

Winning at Work: The Road to Career Success. Kenneth E. Norris. 126p. (Orig.). 1987. pap. 14.95 (*0-8306-3077-5*, 30077, Liberty Hse) TAB Bks.

Winning at Work Without Losing at Love. Stephen F. Arterburn. LC 94-33977. 1995. 18.99 (*0-8407-9703-6*) Nelson.

***Winning at Your Interview.** Michael Stevens. (Personal Development Ser.). 1990. pap. 14.95 (*1-85091-818-X*) Kogan Page Ltd.

***Winning Athlete's Scholarships: The Student's Guide to Winning & Staying Eligible for College Sports.** Joseph Spoonholz. 1997. 18.00 (*0-679-77879-9*) Princeton.

Winning Attitude. Kenneth Copeland. 18p. 1987. pap. 1.00 (*0-88114-791-5*) K Copeland Pubns.

Winning Attitude. John C. Maxwell. 288p. 1996. mass mkt. 5.99 (*0-7852-7535-5*) Nelson.

Winning Attitude: How to Develop Your Most Important Asset! Michelle F. Poley. (Illus.). x, 80p. 1992. pap. 10.95 (*1-878542-28-1*, 12-0009) SkillPath Pubns.

Winning Attitudes, Vol. 1. G & R Publishing Company. 368p. (Orig.). 1995. pap. 7.50 (*1-56383-047-7*, 5020) G & R Pub.

Winning Attorneys' Fees from the U. S. Government. Joel P. Bennett. LC 84-4363. 500p. 1984. ring bd. 90.00 (*0-317-00826-9*) NY Law Pub.

Winning ATV Cases, 2 vols. Joseph W. Moch & Melvin M. Belli. 1986. ring bd. 149.00 (*0-934547-03-3*) CRI-Comm Res.

Winning Baccarat Strategies. Henry J. Tamburin & Dick Rahm. LC 83-60194. (Illus.). 87p. (Orig.). 1983. 19.95 (*0-912177-00-4*) Res Serv Unltd.

Winning Banks. 156p. 1991. text ed. 45.00 (*1-55520-102-4*, 126) Irwin Prof Pubng.

Winning Basketball: Techniques & Drills for Playing Better Basketball. Ralph L. Pim. (Illus.). 192p. 1994. pap. 10.95 (*0-8092-3553-6*) Contemp Bks.

Winning Basketball for Girls. Faye Y. Miller & Wayne Coffey. (Illus.). 160p. 1992. 19.95 (*0-8160-2769-2*); pap. 11.95 (*0-8160-2776-5*) Facts on File.

Winning Bedtime Battles: How to Help Your Child Develop Good Sleep Habits. Charles E. Schaefer & Theresa F. DiGeronimo. 176p. 1992. pap. 9.95 (*0-8065-1318-7*, Citadel Pr) Carol Pub Group.

An Asterisk (*) at the beginning of an entry indicates that the title is appearing in BIP for the first time.

An Asterisk (*) at the beginning of an entry indicates that the title is appearing in BIP for the first time.

Winning Lottery Combinations, Vol. 1: Guaranteed Number Sets for All Pick 5, 6 & 7 Games. Stephen B. Richter & Scott J. Fields. 137p. (Orig.). 1990. pap. 19.95 (0-9625318-0-4) Over Horizon.
Winning Lotto Analysis Secrets: With Lotto Software Reviews & Source Directory. A. L. De Armond. 124p. 1992. per. 12.95 (0-9630841-0-0) Castor-Pollux.
Winning Lotto-Lottery for Everyday Players. 2nd ed. Jones. LC 94-68756. 144p. 1995. 9.95 (0-940685-54-X) Cardoza Pub.
Winning Low Limit Hold'em. Lee F. Jones. LC 94-69515. (Illus.). 176p. 1994. pap. 19.95 (1-886070-04-0) ConJelCo.
Winning Management: 6 Fail-Safe Strategies for Building High Performance Organizations. Wolf J. Rinke. LC 95-83088. 300p. 1997. 24.95 (0-9627913-7-7) Achvmnt Pubs.
*__Winning Manager.__ Julius E. Eitington. LC 96-48028. 1997. pap. 49.95 (0-88415-902-7) Gulf Pub.
Winning Manufacturing: The How-To-Book of Successful Manufacturing. James A. Tompkins. 223p. 1989. pap. 27.00 (0-89806-103-2) Eng Mgmt Pr.
Winning Manufacturing: The How-to-Book of Successful Manufacturing. James A. Tompkins. 1991. text ed. 48.00 (0-07-065044-6) McGraw.
Winning Market Systems. Gerald Appel. 1989. 49.95 (0-930233-33-6) Windsor.
Winning Market Systems: Eighty Three Ways to Beat the Market. Gerald Appel. 232p. 1986. reprint ed. 39.95 (0-934380-12-0, 175) Traders Pr.
Winning Marketing Strategies: Highlights from FIMA's Financial Marketing Awards Competitions. Jill Shtulman. 1993. text ed. 149.00 (1-55738-721-4) Irwin Prof Pubng.
Winning Marketing Techniques: An Introduction to Marketing for Information Professionals. Sharon Dean. 1990. student ed. 75.00 (0-87111-390-2) SLA.
Winning Medical Negligence Cases: A Guide for the Plaintiffs' Lawyer. William A. Trine & Paul N. Luvera. LC 93-2351. 1993. 45.00 (0-941916-53-7) ATLA Pr.
Winning Mind: Steve Backley's Guide to Achieving Success & Overcoming Failure. Steve Backley & Ian Stafford. (Illus.). 256p. 1996. 19.95 (1-85410-404-7, Pub. by Aurum Pr UK) London Brdge.
*__Winning Money for College.__ 4th ed. Alan Deutschman. (Peterson's Guides Ser.). 1997. pap. text ed. 12.95 (1-56079-876-9) Petersons.
Winning Money for College: The High School Student's Guide to Scholarship Contests. 3rd ed. Alan Deutschman. LC 92-21967. 207p. (Orig.). (YA). (gr. 10-12). 1992. pap. 10.95 (1-56079-059-8) Petersons.
Winning Monologs for Young Actors: 65 Honest-to-Life Characterizations to Delight Young Actors & Audiences of All Ages. Peg Kehret. Ed. by Arthur L. Zapel & Kathy Pijanowski. LC 86-61109. 160p. (Orig.). (YA). (gr. 6-12). 1986. pap. text ed. 14.95 (0-916260-38-0, B127) Meriwether Pub.
Winning More Bids. R. Dodge Woodson. 164p. 1995. 74.95 (1-56842-056-0) Marshall & Swift.
Winning Motor Vehicle Accident Cases. Joseph W. Moch. 1986. text ed. 75.00 (0-934547-01-7, 5080) CRI-Comm Res.
Winning Moves of Today for Tomorrow. Lindon C. Flemister. 252p. (Orig.). 1991. pap. 21.95 (1-56485-735-2) Stone Pubns.
Winning My Way: The Glory Years of Marshall Football. Jim Donnan & Lou Sahadi. 256p. 1994. pap. 19.95 (0-9642530-0-3) Tiger Palisades NY.
Winning My Wings: A Woman Airforce Service Pilot in World War II. Marion S. Hodgson. LC 96-12643. (Illus.). 304p. 1996. 29.95 (1-55750-364-8) Naval Inst Pr.
Winning Negotiation Strategies for Bankers. Linda Richardson. 150p. 1987. text ed. 45.00 (0-87094-990-X) Irwin Prof Pubng.
Winning Negotiations in Federal Contracting. Terrence M. O'Connor. 291p. 1992. 139.00 (1-56726-004-7) Holbrook & Kellogg.
*__Winning New Accounts.__ Dartnell Corp. Staff. (Illus.). 80p. (Orig.). 1997. wbk. ed., pap. 12.95 (0-85013-288-6) Dartnell Corp.
Winning Nine Ball: As Taught by the Game's Greatest Players. Illus. & Pref. by Eddie Robin. (Pocket Billiards Ser.). 320p. 1997. 42.00 (0-936362-06-5) Billiard Wld.
Winning NLRB Elections: Management's Strategy & Preventive Programs. 3rd ed. Jackson, Lewis, Schnitzler & Krupman Staff. 217p. 1994. text ed. 47.50 (0-471-11287-9) Wiley.
Winning Numbers: How to Use Business Facts & Figures to Make Your Point & Get Ahead. Michael Thomsett. LC 89-81029. 272p. 1990. 22.95 (0-8144-5958-7) AMACOM.
Winning of Andromache. Richard M. Byers. LC 87-80719. (Illus.). 183p. 1987. 10.00 (0-9602048-2-2) Fairfield Hse.
Winning of Animal Health: 100 Years of Veterinary Medicine. Ole H. Stalheim. LC 94-1629. (Illus.). 268p. 1994. text ed. 44.95 (0-8138-2429-X) Iowa St U Pr.
Winning of Barbara Worth. Harold B. Wright. 1975. lib. bdg. 20.60 (0-89966-208-0) Buccaneer Bks.
Winning of Barbara Worth. Harold B. Wright. (Illus.). 512p. 1987. reprint ed. 24.95 (0-9618473-0-1) Quellen.
Winning of Freedom. William Wood. 1927. 89.50 (0-686-83858-0) Elliots Bks.
Winning of Freedom. William C. Wood. (BCL1 - U. S. History Ser.). 366p. 1991. reprint ed. lib. bdg. 89.00 (0-7812-6040-X) Rprt Serv.
Winning of Independence. Marshall Smelser. LC 73-3104. 415p. (C). 1973. reprint ed. pap. text ed. 6.95 (0-531-06490-5) Wiener Pubs Inc.
*__Winning of the Best.__ Ralph W. Trine. 100p. 1997. pap. 8.00 (0-89540-348-X) Sun Pub.
Winning of the West. Theodore Roosevelt. Ed. & Intro. by Harvey Wish. 1990. 14.00 (0-8446-2827-1) Peter Smith.
Winning of the West, 4 vols. Theodore Roosevelt. 1992. reprint ed. 295.00 (0-403-04339-5) Somerset Pub.
Winning of the West Vol. 1: From the Alleghanies to the Mississippi, 1769-1776. Theodore Roosevelt. LC 94-46645. (Illus.). xl, 352p. 1995. pap. 15.00 (0-8032-8954-5, Bison Books) U of Nebr Pr.
Winning of the West Vol. 2: From the Alleghanies to the Mississippi, 1777-1783. Theodore Roosevelt. LC 94-46645. (Illus.). xvii, 427p. 1995. pap. 15.00 (0-8032-8955-3, Bison Books) U of Nebr Pr.
Winning of the West Vol. 3: The Founding of the Trans-Alleghany Commonwealths, 1784-1790. Theodore Roosevelt. LC 94-46645. (Illus.). xx, 339p. 1995. pap. 15.00 (0-8032-8956-1, Bison Books) U of Nebr Pr.
Winning of the West Vol. 4: Louisiana & the Northwest, 1791-1807. Theodore Roosevelt. LC 94-46645. (Illus.). xx, 363p. 1995. pap. 15.00 (0-8032-8957-X, Bison Books) U of Nebr Pr.
Winning of the White House, 1988. Time Magazine Staff. 272p. 1988. 14.95 (0-451-82209-9, Sig) NAL-Dutton.
Winning Office Politics: Dubrin's New Guide for the 90's. Andrew J. Dubrin. 360p. 1990. pap. text ed. 14.95 (0-13-964958-1) P-H.
Winning on Appeal: Better Briefs & Oral Argument. Ruggero J. Aldisert. LC 92-25687. 1992. 49.95 (0-87632-851-6) Clark Boardman Callaghan.
Winning on the Stock Market: Low Risk & High-Profit Strategies for Investors. Brian J. Millard. LC 00-93. 205p. (Orig.). 1994. pap. text ed. 45.00 (0-471-93881-5) Wiley.
Winning on the Telephone. Donald H. Weiss. LC 88-47700. (Successful Office Skills Ser.). 64p. 1988. pap. 4.00 (0-8144-7699-6) AMACOM.
*__Winning on the Wheel: An Unofficial Guide to Getting on & Winning at Wheel of Fortune.__ rev. ed. Kris Petersen & Brian Matthew. LC 96-80010. vi, 159p. 1997. pap. 19.95 (0-9653049-1-4) BK Enterprises.
Winning on Wall Street. Martin E. Zweig. 304p. 1990. 12.95 (0-446-38684-7) Warner Bks.
Winning 101, 101. Van Crouch. Date not set. pap. 5.99 (1-56292-083-9, HB-083) Honor Bks OK.
*__Winning One-Pocket: As Taught by the Game's Greatest Players.__ 2nd deluxe ed. Eddie Robin et al. Ed. by James W. Haake & Lloyd F. Welcome. (Pocket Billiards Ser.). (Illus.). 328p. 1996. bond lthr. 59.00 (0-936362-15-4) Billiard Wld.
*__Winning One-Pocket: As Taught by the Game's Greatest Players.__ 2nd ed. Eddie Robin et al. Ed. by James W. Haake & Lloyd F. Welcome. (Pocket Billiards Ser.). (Illus.). 328p. 1996. 42.00 (0-936362-14-6) Billiard Wld.
*__Winning Oral Presentations: A Management & Sales Approach.__ Tim Whalen. 250p. pap. 97.00 (1-56726-035-7) Holbrook & Kellogg.
Winning over Asthma. 2nd ed. Eileen Dolan. LC 96-22124. (Illus.). 40p. (J). (ps-5). 1996. pap. 7.00 (0-914625-17-9) Pedipress.
Winning Over Pain, Fear & Worry. John Haggai. 1991. 9.98 (0-88486-041-8, Inspiratnl Pub) Arrowood Pr.
Winning over Stroke. Dean Whiteman. (Orig.). 1996. pap. 25.00 (0-9615226-6-6) Giddings Studio Pub.
Winning Over Temptation. Joseph Seaborn. (Illus.). 110p. (Orig.). 1993. teacher ed., wbk. ed., spiral bd. 14.95 (0-89827-098-7, BKP95) Wesleyan Pub Hse.
Winning Over Temptation. Joseph Seaborn. 120p. 1992. pap. 9.95 (0-614-99277-X) Wesleyan Pub Hse.
Winning Over Weight. Marilyn Hickey. (Mini-Bks.). 32p. 1982. pap. 0.99 (0-89274-248-8, HH-248) Harrison Hse.
Winning Pachinko: The Game of Japanese Pinball. Eric C. Sedensky. (Illus.). 162p. (Orig.). 1991. pap. 9.95 (0-8048-1695-6) C E Tuttle.
Winning Pachinko: The Game of Japanese Pinball. Eric C. Sedensky. LC 91-65056. 1994. pap. text ed. 9.95 (4-900737-28-3, Pub. by Yen Bks JA) C E Tuttle.
Winning Passion. Laurance L. Priddy. LC 93-13982. 288p. (Orig.). 1994. pap. 14.95 (0-86534-200-8) Sunstone Pr.
Winning Peace: Strategies & Ethics for a Nuclear-Free World. Dietrich Fischer et al. (Illus.). 270p. (C). 1989. 52.00 (0-8448-1574-8, Crane Russak); pap. 31.00 (0-8448-1575-6, Crane Russak) Taylor & Francis.
Winning People Over: 14 Days to Power & Confidence with People. Burton Kaplana. 288p. 1996. text ed. 27.95 (0-13-315359-2) P-H.
Winning Photo Contests. Jeanne Stallman. (Illus.). 128p. 1990. 29.95 (0-929667-06-9); pap. 14.95 (0-929667-04-2) Images NY.
Winning Photography Handbook: Simple, Basic Photography for Kids...& Other Beginners. Johnny Weston, pseud. 1994. pap. write for info. (0-9642361-0-9) West n Wilderness.
Winning Pictures: 101 Ideas for Outstanding Photographs. rev. ed. Jeff Wignall. LC 94-62124. (Illus.). 116p. (YA). (gr. 9-12). 1995. pap. 15.95 (0-87985-761-7, AC-200, Kodak) Saunders Photo.
Winning Pitch. Jon Burnham. 154p. (Orig.). 1995. pap. 7.95 (1-883928-10-9) Longwood.
Winning Pitcher: Baseball's Top Pitchers Demonstrate What It Takes to Be an Ace. Tom House. (Illus.). 144p. (Orig.). 1988. pap. 12.95 (0-8092-4878-6) Contemp Bks.
Winning Pocket Billiards. Willie Mosconi. (Illus.). 1965. 7.95 (0-517-50454-5, Crown) Crown Pub Group.
Winning Pocket Billiards. Willie Mosconi. 1995. pap. 9.00 (0-517-88427-5) Random.
Winning Poker for the Serious Player. Edwin Silberstang. LC 92-72608. (Illus.). 224p. (Orig.). 1992. pap. 12.95 (0-940685-32-9) Cardoza Pub.
Winning Poker Strategy. Edwin Silberstang. 1980. pap. 15.00 (0-679-14650-4) McKay.
Winning Poker Systems. Norman Zadeh. reprint ed. 10.00 (0-87980-332-0) Wilshire.
Winning PR Tactics: Effective Techniques to Boost Your Sales. Peter Sheldon-Green. (Institute of Management Foundation Ser.). 184p. (Orig.). 1994. pap. 42.50 (0-273-60552-6, Pub. by Pitman Pub Ltd UK) Trans-Atl Phila.
Winning Proposals: A Step-by-Step Guide to the Proposal Process. Kaye Vivian. LC 92-42620. 1992. 34.50 (0-87051-128-9) Am Inst CPA.
Winning Proposals: How to Write Them & Get Results. Hans Tammemagi. (Business Ser.). 104p. (Orig.). 1995. pap. 13.95 (0-88908-943-4) Self-Counsel Pr.
Winning Proposals in the Nineties: 546 Tips for Winning Extra Point Score & Saving Proposal Dollars. Dick Close. (Illus.). 230p. 1991. 89.00 (0-9628371-0-5) R N Close.
Winning Publicity. 51p. 1991. 50.00 (0-685-69766-5) Sav & Comm Bank.
Winning Pulitzers: The Stories Behind Some of the Best News Coverage of Our Time. Karen Rothmyer. 256p. 1991. text ed. 30.50 (0-231-07028-4) Col U Pr.
Winning Quickly with Black. Iakov Neishtadt. 144p. 1996. pap. 19.95 (1-85744-039-0, Pub. by Cadogan Books UK) Macmillan.
Winning Quickly with White. Iakov Neishtadt. 144p. 1996. pap. 19.95 (1-85744-038-2, Pub. by Cadogan Books UK) Macmillan.
Winning Races: All You Need to Know to Improve Your Yacht's Performance. John Heyes. (Illus.). 144p. 1995. pap. 19.95 (1-57409-001-1) Sheridan.
Winning Racquetball. Larry E. Liles & Robert A. Neimeyer. 192p. (C). 1993. per. write for info. (0-697-13151-3) Brown & Benchmark.
Winning Raquetball: Skills, Drills, & Strategies. Ed Turner & Woody Clouse. LC 95-13029. Orig. Title: Skills & Strategies for Winning Racquetball. (Illus.). 304p. (Orig.). 1995. pap. 16.95 (0-87322-721-2, PTUR0721) Human Kinetics.
Winning Recipes: Better Than Bouillon Cookbook. Superior Quality Foods, Inc. Staff. Ed. by Rebecca Coleman & Jennifer Trzma. 168p. 14.95 (0-9645827-0-8) Inland Ad News.
*__Winning Recipes: Wisconsin State Fair.__ Date not set. pap. 10.95 (0-923944-26-5) Pub Partners.
Winning Recipes from Minnesota with Love. 163p. spiral bd. 13.95 (0-913703-15-X) Strawberry Pt.
Winning Recipes from South Dakota with Love. 153p. spiral bd. 13.95 (0-913703-16-8) Strawberry Pt.
Winning Recipes from Wisconsin with Love. 193p. spiral bd. 13.95 (0-913703-14-1) Strawberry Pt.
Winning Research Skills. Woxland et al. 1993. write for info. (0-314-02777-7) West Pub.
Winning Resumes for Computer Personnel. Anne DeSola Cardoza. LC 93-23142. 1994. pap. 11.95 (0-8120-1758-7) Barron.
Winning Resumes for the Nineties. Matthew Greene. LC 93-21291. 1994. pap. 13.95 (0-452-27136-3, Plume) NAL-Dutton.
*__Winning Roller Hockey.__ Dave Easter & Vern K. Stenlund. LC 96-46412. (Illus.). 224p. (Orig.). 1997. pap. 14.95 (0-88011-657-9, PEAS0657) Human Kinetics.
Winning Running: Successful 800m & 1500m Racing & Training. Peter Coe. 1996. pap. 29.95 (1-85223-997-2, Pub. by Crowood Pr UK) Trafalgar.
Winning Sales Letters: A Handbook of Model Sales & Marketing Letters. Diana D. Booher. 331p. 49.95 (0-669-20876-0, Lexington) Jossey-Bass.
Winning Sales Presentations. Sheila Kessler. LC 90-85527. (Illus.). 112p. (Orig.). 1990. pap. 8.95 (1-879404-11-7) Cmpetitive Edge.
Winning Sales Strategies: Field Tested. Ed. by Kenneth Hanford. (Illus.). 368p. (C). 1989. student ed. 29.50 (0-685-23256-5) Sales Focus.
Winning Scholarships: A Student's Guide to Entrance Awards at Canadian Universities & Colleges. Michael J. Howell. 350p. (C). 1994. pap. 25.95 (0-8020-7481-2) U of Toronto Pr.
Winning Scholarships: A Student's Guide to Entrance Awards at Ontario Universities & Colleges. Michael J. Howell. 288p. 1992. pap. 19.95 (0-8020-7720-X) U of Toronto Pr.
Winning Scholarships: Entrance Awards at Eastern Canadian Universities & Colleges. Michael J. Howell. 350p. 1996. student ed., pap. 24.95 (0-8020-7143-0) U of Toronto Pr.
Winning Scholarships for College: An Insider's Guide. Marianne Ragins. 1994. pap. 10.95 (0-8050-3072-7) H Holt & Co.
Winning Season for the Braves. Nathan Aaseng. LC 82-72711. 128p. (J). (gr. 3-7). 1988. pap. 4.99 (1-55513-950-7, Chariot Bks) Chariot Victor.
Winning Secrets of a Master Sports Bettor - Baseball. Charlie McGee. 32p. 1992. pap. 7.95 (0-934650-21-7) Sunnyside.
Winning Secrets of a Master Sports Bettor - Basketball. Harold Hegan. 32p. 1992. pap. 7.95 (0-934650-20-9) Sunnyside.
Winning Secrets of a Master Sports Bettor - Football. Leo Melanson. 32p. (Orig.). 1991. pap. 7.95 (0-934650-19-5) Sunnyside.
Winning Secrets of a Poker Master. J. D. McEvoy. 32p. 1986. pap. 7.95 (0-934650-11-X) Sunnyside.
*__Winning Secrets of the B. A. S. S. Pros: How the Pros Find Bass & Make Them Strike.__ (Illus.). 160p. (Orig.). Date not set. mass mkt. 4.95 (1-890280-07-0) B A S S.
*__Winning Shoping Center Designs.__ Retail Reporting Staff. 1996. 35.00 (0-688-14809-3) Morrow.
Winning Shopping Center Design. 2nd ed. International Council of Shopping Centers Staff. 1996. text ed. 59.95 (0-07-054272-4) McGraw.
Winning Shopping Center Design No. 3. 3rd ed. International Council of Shopping Centers Staff. (Illus.). 136p. 1996. text ed. 59.95 (0-07-032888-9) McGraw.
*__Winning Shopping Center Designs.__ Retail Reporting Staff. Date not set. 35.00 (0-688-15377-1) Morrow.
*__Winning Shopping Center Designs.__ Retail Reporting Staff. 1994. 32.50 (0-688-14053-X) Morrow.
*__Winning Shopping Center Designs.__ 2nd ed. Retail Reporting Staff. 1995. 32.50 (0-688-14260-5) Morrow.
Winning Shopping Center Designs, No. 3. Ed. by International Council of Shopping Centers Staff. (Illus.). 136p. 1996. 59.95 (0-934590-82-6) Retail Report.
Winning Shopping Center Designs 1: The International Design & Development Awards Winners. International Council of Shopping Centers Staff. 136p. 1994. 64.95 (0-934590-69-9) Retail Report.
Winning Slots Jackpots: Help You See the Light to Win Money in Slots Jackpots. M. Callahan. 52p. 1996. pap. 50.00 (0-915453-04-5) Dollars Info Bks.
Winning Snooker. W. G. Clifford. 64p. 1995. pap. 4.95 (0-572-01148-2, Pub. by Foulsham UK) Assoc Pubs Grp.
Winning Soccer. Jerry Yeagley. (Illus.). 224p. (Orig.). 1994. pap. 14.95 (0-940279-96-7, Spalding Sports) Masters Pr IN.
Winning Soccer Drills. James P. McGettigan. LC 80-15783. 1983. pap. 5.95 (0-13-961086-3, Reward) P-H.
*__Winning Soccer for Girls.__ Deborah Crisfield. 1997. pap. text ed. 12.95 (0-8160-3272-6) Facts on File.
Winning Soccer for Girls. Deborah W. Crisfield. 1996. write for info. (0-8160-3271-8) Facts on File.
Winning Solos: Early Intermediate Piano Solos. S. Covello. 24p. 1991. pap. 4.95 (0-7935-0632-8) H Leonard.
Winning Solos: Late Elementary Piano. S. Covello. 24p. 1991. pap. 4.95 (0-7935-0631-X) H Leonard.
Winning Solos: Late Intermediate. S. Covello. 28p. 1992. pap. 4.95 (0-7935-1846-6) H Leonard.
Winning Solutions. E. Lozansky & C. Rousseau. (Problem Books in Mathematics). 256p. 1996. pap. 34.95 (0-387-94743-4) Spr-Verlag.
Winning Souls the Bible Way. William MacDonald. 1988. pap. 6.00 (0-937396-56-7) Walterick Pubs.
Winning Spirit. Melissa Lowell. (Silver Blades Ser.: Vol. 12). 128p. (J). (gr. 4-7). 1995. pap. 3.50 (0-553-48321-8, Skylark BDD) BDD Bks Young Read.
Winning Spirit. Bill Pennington. 1991. pap. 5.95 (1-55748-247-0) Barbour & Co.
Winning Spirit. Bill Pennington. 1992. pap. 1.99 (1-55748-359-0) Barbour & Co.
Winning Spirit: Achieving Olympic Level Performance in Business & Personal Advancements. Robert B. Sommer. 1996. pap. text ed. 16.95 (1-882180-58-5) Griffin CA.
*__Winning Spirit: Life Lessons Learned in Last Place.__ Zoe Koplowitz & Mike Celizic. LC 97-21799. 208p. 1996. 21.95 (0-385-48987-0, Anchor NY) Doubleday.
*__Winning Spiritual Victories: Preparing for Battles with the Enemy.__ Mark Bubeck. (Christian Life Focus System Ser.). 48p. 1997. rig bd. 5.99 (0-8024-2682-4) Moody.
Winning Spiritual Warfare. Neil T. Anderson. (Harvest Pocket Bks.). 48p. (Orig.). 1991. mass mkt. 2.99 (0-89081-868-1) Harvest Hse.
Winning Spiritual Warfare in the Family. Earl Paulk. 21p. 1987. mass mkt. 1.50 (0-917595-20-3) Kingdom Pubs.
Winning Straight Pool: As Taught by the Game's Greatest Players. Eddie Robin et al. Ed. by Lloyd F. Welcome & George Fels. (Pocket Billiards Ser.). (Illus.). 320p. 1997. 42.00 (0-936362-07-3) Billiard Wld.
*__Winning Straight Pool: As Taught by the Game's Greatest Players.__ deluxe ed. Eddie Robin et al. Ed. by Lloyd F. Welcome & George Fels. (Pocket Billiards Ser.). (Illus.). 320p. 1997. 59.00 (0-936362-31-6) Billiard Wld.
Winning Strategies & Techniques for Civil Litigators. Ed. by James E. Lyons. 339p. 1992. 95.00 (0-685-69515-8, H3-3004) PLI.
Winning Strategies for Capital Formation: Secrets of Funding Start-Ups & Emerging Growth... Linda Chandler. 216p. 1996. per. 32.50 (0-7863-0892-3) Irwin Prof Pubng.
Winning Strategies for Capturing Defense Contracts. Robert M. Hansen & Kim A. Hansen. 232p. (Orig.). 1992. pap. 59.95 (0-9632779-0-1) Gloria Magnus.
Winning Strategies for Lotteries & Sports Pools. A. D. Sacher. 96p. 1990. 3.99 (1-56171-014-8) Sure Seller.
Winning Strategies for Negotiating Claims. Kevin M. Quinley. 256p. (Orig.). 1995. pap. 29.95 (1-56842-045-5) Marshall & Swift.
Winning Strategies for Nursing Managers. Joan O'Leary et al. (Illus.). 165p. 1986. text ed. 16.95 (0-397-54541-X, Lippnctt) Lppncott-Raven.
Winning Strategies for the Nineties - 1990 Tax Act & Beyond. Bertil Westlin. 56p. 1991. pap. 10.00 (0-318-33163-2, 4967) Commerce.
Winning Strategies for Video Poker. Lenny Frome. LC 93-70369. 120p. (Orig.). (C). 1993. pap. 15.95 (0-9623766-3-9) Compu-Flyers.
Winning Strategies in Challenging Times for Advancing Small Colleges. Ed. by Wesley K. Willmer. 1993. pap. 41.50 (0-89964-303-5, 25003) Coun Adv & Supp Ed.
Winning Strategies in Selling. Jack Kinder, Jr. et al. LC 81-10518. 258p. 1983. 18.95 (0-13-961128-2, Busn); 5.95 (0-685-03915-3, Busn) P-H.
*__Winning Strategy: For Provincial Sports Lotteries.__ Al J's Sports Connections Ltd. Staff. 220p. pap. 15.95 (0-7737-5841-0, Pub. by Stoddart Pubng CN) Genl Dist Srvs.
Winning Streak. Olwyn Green. (Orig.). 1993. pap. 11.95 (0-7022-2500-2, Pub. by Univ Queensland Pr AT) Intl Spec Bk.
Winning Streak. Dean Hughes. (Angel Park All-Stars Ser.: No. 3). (Illus.). 96p. (J). (gr. 2-4). 1990. pap. 2.95 (0-679-80428-5) Knopf Bks Yng Read.

W

An Asterisk (*) at the beginning of an entry indicates that the title is appearing in BIP for the first time.

*Winning Streak. J. R. Roberts. (Gunsmith Ser.: No. 182). 192p. 1997. mass mkt. 4.99 (0-515-12017-0) Jove Pubns.

Winning Streak: A Marketing Decision Simulation. 2nd ed. Simon. (SB - Marketing Education Ser.). 1992. pap. 21.95 (0-538-60162-0) S-W Pub.

Winning Streak: Marketing Decision Making. 2nd ed. Simon. (SB - Marketing Education Ser.). 1992. 122.95 (0-538-60163-9) S-W Pub.

Winning Stroke. Matt Christipher. (Illus.). 176p. (J). (gr. 3-7). 1996. pap. 3.95 (0-316-14128-3) Little.

Winning Stroke. Matt Christopher. LC 93-40257. (J). 1994. 15.95 (0-316-14266-2) Little.

Winning Stroke. Sharon D. Wyeth. (American Gold Swimmers Ser.: No. 1). 144p. (J). (gr. 3-7). 1996. mass mkt. 3.50 (0-553-48394-3, Skylark BDD) BDD Bks Young Read.

*Winning Supervisory Techniques for the New Workplace. George Fuller. 352p. 1996. 39.95 (0-13-460106-8); pap. 14.95 (0-13-460098-3) P-H.

Winning Swiss Team Tactics. rev. ed. Harold Feldheim. 272p. reprint ed. pap. 10.95 (0-9637080-4-X) Lorold Pubns.

Winning System. F. Oppel. 1993. 12.98 (1-55521-966-7) Bk Sales Inc.

Winning Table Tennis: Skills, Drills, & Strategies. Dan Seemiller & Mark Holowchak. LC 96-8102. 184p. 1996. pap. 16.95 (0-88011-520-3, PSEE0520) Human Kinetics.

Winning Team. (Girl Talk Ser.). (YA). 1991. write for info. (0-307-22013-3, Golden Pr) Western Pub.

*Winning Team. Abbs & Freebairn. 1993. wbk. ed., pap. text ed. write for info. (0-582-21834-9, Pub. by Longman UK) Longman.

*Winning Telephone Tips: 30 Fast & Profitable Tips for Making the Best Use of Your Phone. Paul R. Timm. LC 97-7899. (30-Minute Solutions Ser.). 96p. (Orig.). 1997. pap. 7.99 (1-56414-299-X) Career Pr Inc.

Winning Tennis. Chuck Kriese. (Spalding Sports Library). (Illus.). 160p. (Orig.). 1993. pap. 14.95 (0-940279-61-4) Masters Pr IN.

Winning Tennis: Complete Guide for Coaches & Advanced Players. Steve Schuyler. LC 92-34251. 1993. pap. 29.95 (0-13-075102-2, Parker Publishing Co) P-H.

Winning Tennis Drills: A Complete Guide for Today's Coach. Gary Sailes. 144p. (C). 1990. per. write for info. (0-697-10744-2) Brown & Benchmark.

Winning Tennis My Way. Jimmy Connors & Robert J. LaMarche. write for info. (0-318-60257-1) S&S Trade.

Winning the Battle Against Drugs: Rehabilitation Programs. Daniel McMillan. LC 91-16344. (Non-Fiction Ser.). (Illus.). 160p. (YA). (gr. 9-12). 1991. lib. bdg. 22.70 (0-531-11063-X) Watts.

Winning the Battle for Sex Education. Irving R. Dickman. LC 82-61000. 64p. (Orig.). 1982. pap. 6.00 (0-9609212-0-6) SIECUS.

*Winning the Battle in Your Own Mind. T. D. Jakes. (Orig.). 1997. pap. write for info. (1-890521-11-6) Jakes Ent.

Winning the Battle to Lose the War: Brazilian Electronics Policy Under U. S. Threat of Sanction. Maria-Ines Bastos. LC 94-3384. 198p. (C). 1994. pap. 35.00 (0-7146-4111-1, Pub. by F Cass Pubs UK) Intl Spec Bk.

Winning the Bid: A Manager's Guide to Competitive Bidding. Neil Tweedley. (Financial Times Management Ser.). 224p. 1995. 67.50 (0-273-60971-8, Pub. by Pitman Pub Ltd UK) Trans-Atl Phila.

Winning the Brain Race: A Bold Plan to Make Our Schools Competitive. rev. ed. David T. Kearns & Denis Doyle. 1991. pap. 14.95 (1-55815-166-4) ICS Pr.

Winning the Career Game: Handbook for Federal Managers. Carl J. Sebastian. LC 89-91660. 1989. pap. 9.95 (0-925997-01-3) CSP Assocs Inc.

Winning the Chain Restaurant Game: Eight Key Strategies. Charles Bernstein & Ronald N. Paul. 285p. 1994. text ed. 39.95 (0-471-30545-6) Wiley.

Winning the Chemo Battle. Joyce S. Mitchell. 1991. pap. 11.00 (0-393-30713-1) Norton.

Winning the Chores Wars: How to Get Your Child to Do Household Chores. Lee Canter & Marlene Canter. (Lee Canter Effective Parenting Bks.). (Illus.). 48p. (Orig.). 1996. pap. 5.95 (0-939007-74-6) Lee Canter & Assocs.

Winning the City. Theodore Weesner. 208p. 1991. pap. 9.00 (0-380-71554-6) Avon.

Winning the Cold War: Preventing & Curing the Common Cold & Flu. Eric A. Mein. (Natural Remedies for Common Ailments & Conditions Ser.). 68p. (Orig.). 1990. pap. 4.95 (0-87604-261-2, 352) ARE Pr.

*Winning the Custody War: Without Casualties. A. Jayne Major & Ronald M. Supancic. (Illus.). 168p. 1996. 98.95 (0-9655939-0-8) MSR Pub.

Winning the Drug War: A National Strategy - A Twentieth Century Fund Paper. Mathea Falco. 87p. 1989. 18.95 (0-87078-263-0); pap. 8.95 (0-87078-262-2) TCFP-PPP.

Winning the Entrepreneurial Game: How to Start, Operate & Be Successful in a New or Growing Business. David E. Rye. LC 94-8712. (Business Advisors Ser.). 1994. pap. 10.95 (1-55850-345-5) Adams Media.

Winning the Entrepreneurial Game: How to Start, Operate & Be Successful in a New or Growing Business. David E. Rye. LC 94-8712. (Business Advisors Ser.). 1994. 29.95 (1-55850-346-3) Adams Media.

*Winning the Fight Against Arthritis: A Natural Healing Program. S. J. Farley. (Illus.). 104p. (Orig.). 1997. pap. text ed. 29.95 (1-889623-03-2) Alternat Med Pub.

Winning the Fight Against Drugs: Resources to Fight Illegal Drugs in Public Housing Communities. Frwd. by Jack Kemp. (Illus.). 71p. (Orig.). (C). 1994. pap. text ed. 25.00 (0-7881-0272-9) DIANE Pub.

Winning the Fight Between You & Your Desk: Use Your Computer to Get Organized, Become More Productive, & Make More Money. Jeffrey J. Mayer. LC 93-48256. (Illus.). 272p. 1995. pap. 10.00 (0-88730-718-3) Harper Busn.

Winning the Fire Service Leadership Game. H. Caulfield. Ed. by Diana Benzaia. LC 85-70551. 292p. 1985. 16.00 (0-912212-09-8) Fire Eng.

Winning the Future (From Bhakra to Narmada, Tehri, Rajasthan Canal) B. G. Verghese. (C). 1995. 30.00 (81-220-0357-5, Pub. by Konark Pubs II) S Asia.

Winning the Games People Play: How to Master the Art of Changing People's Behavior. Nathan B. Miron. LC 76-52149. (Illus.). 1977. 12.95 (0-918418-01-1); pap. 7.95 (0-918418-02-X) Mission Pr CA.

Winning the Games Scientists Play. Carl J. Sindermann. LC 82-12225. (Illus.). 304p. 1982. 19.95 (0-306-41075-3, Plenum Pr) Plenum.

Winning the Girl of the Sea. Brenda Silsbe. (Illus.). 32p. (J). (gr. k-2). 1994. pap. 5.95 (1-55037-312-9, Pub. by Annick CN); lib. bdg. 15.95 (1-55037-313-7, Pub. by Annick CN) Firefly Bks Ltd.

Winning the Global Television News Game. Carla B. Johnston. LC 95-12540. 331p. 1995. pap. 47.95 (0-240-80211-X, Focal) Buttrwrth-Heinemann.

Winning the Grand Award: Successful Strategies for ISEF Competition. Maxine H. Iritz. 1992. pap. text ed. 9.95 (0-07-032392-5) McGraw.

Winning the Grand Award: Successful Strategies for ISEF Competition. Maxine H. Iritz. 152p. 1992. 16.95 (0-8306-3971-3, 4155); pap. 9.95 (0-8306-3972-1, 4155) McGraw-Hill Prof.

Winning the Greatest Game of All. Randy J. Ward. LC 84-72262. (Illus.). 160p. (Orig.). 1984. pap. 12.95 (0-9613958-1-8) Prosperity OK.

*Winning the Heart of Your Stepchild. Robert G. Barnes. LC 97-3341. 1997. pap. write for info. (0-310-21804-7) Zondervan.

Winning the High Technology Sales Game. James T. Healy. (C). 1985. 33.95 (0-8359-8700-0, Reston) P-H.

Winning the Hiring Game: Smart Interviewing & Effective Reference Checking are Vital to Survival in the 90's. Edward C. Andler. LC 91-66848. 174p. (Orig.). 1992. pap. 15.95 (0-9623414-2-8) Smith Collins.

Winning the Image Game see Creating a Million Dollar Image for Your Business: Smart Strategies for Building an Image That Works

Winning the Invisible War. E. M. Bounds. 160p. 1984. mass mkt. 3.99 (0-88368-145-5) Whitaker Hse.

Winning the IRS Game: Secrets of a Tax Attorney. Fred W. Daily. 256p. 1990. 19.95 (0-913257-08-7, Publishers Group) Dropzone Pr.

Winning the Jackpot: Creating Wealth & Abundance. Tolly Burkan. 1996. pap. text ed. 12.95 (1-885223-44-7) Beyond Words Pub.

Winning the Job Interview Game: New Strategies for Getting Hired. Bruce R. Hammond. 1990. pap. 7.95 (0-8306-3505-X) McGraw-Hill Prof.

Winning the Job Interview Game: Tips for the High-Tech Era. Jo Danna. LC 85-61451. (Illus.). 223p. (Orig.). 1986. pap. 10.95 (0-9610036-2-6) Palomino Pr.

Winning the Land Use Game: A Guide for Developers & Citizen Protesters. Carolyn J. Logan. LC 81-15710. 208p. 1982. text ed. 49.95 (0-275-90849-6, C0849, Praeger Pubs) Greenwood.

Winning the Lottery. Ben E. Johnson. 144p. 1993. mass mkt. 3.99 (0-425-13625-6) Berkley Pub.

*Winning the Lottery. Ben E. Johnson. 1993. 3.99 (0-425-13755-4) Berkley Pub.

Winning the Marketing War: A Field Manual for Business Leaders. Gerald A. Michaelson. 272p. 1995. pap. 12.95 (1-883999-04-9) Pressmark Intl.

Winning the Million Dollar Lawsuit. Pat Maloney, Sr. & Jack Pasqual. LC 82-21175. 258p. 1982. text ed. 99.50 (0-87624-848-2, Inst Busn Plan) P-H.

Winning the Mind Game. Paul Lisnek. LC 96-77198. 300p. 1996. pap. 19.95 (0-916990-39-7) META Pubns.

Winning the New Civil War: Recapturing America's Values. Roger Dugan. 226p. (Orig.). 1991. pap. 8.99 (0-88070-408-X, Multnomah Bks) Multnomah Pubs.

Winning the New Product Development Battle. rev. ed. Thomas L. Floyd et al. LC 92-105. (IEEE Engineers Guide to Business Ser.: Vol. 4). 1993. 19.95 (0-7803-0361-X, EG104) Inst Electrical.

Winning the Next War: Innovation & the Modern Military. Stephen P. Rosen. LC 91-55235. (Cornell Studies in Security Affairs). 288p. 1991. 33.95 (0-8014-2556-5) Cornell U Pr.

Winning the Next War: Innovation & the Modern Military. Stephen P. Rosen. (Cornell Studies in Security Affairs). 288p. 1994. pap. 14.95 (0-8014-8196-1) Cornell U Pr.

Winning the Paper Wars: An Executive's Guide to Crystal Clear Communications. Don M. Ricks. 225p. 1990. text ed. 25.00 (1-55623-373-6) Irwin Prof Pubng.

Winning the Parent-Teenager Conflict Game. Peter H. Buntman. 180p. (Orig.). 1990. pap. 14.95 (0-685-28061-6) Ctr FLE Inc.

Winning the Peace: America & World Order in the New Era. John G. Ruggie. LC 96-7385. (Illus.). 288p. 1996. 27.95 (0-231-10426-X) Col U Pr.

Winning the Peace: The Strategic Implication of Military Civic Action. Ed. by John W. De Pauw & George A. Luz. LC 91-18914. (Illus.). 256p. 1991. text ed. 59.95 (0-275-93770-4, C3770, Praeger Pubs) Greenwood.

Winning the Peace: With Creative Capitalism. Kenton S. White. LC 92-17065. 1992. 12.95 (0-9632702-1-4) Lightning.

Winning the Polygraph Test Game: How to Beat the Lie Detector. 1992. lib. bdg. 160.00 (0-8490-5247-5) Gordon Pr.

*Winning the Publications Game: How to Get Published Without Neglecting Your Patients. Tim Albert. LC 96-36426. 1996. write for info. (1-85775-183-3, Radcliffe Med Pr) Scovill Paterson.

Winning the Race for Value: Strategies to Create Competitive Advantage in the Emerging "Age of Abundance" Barry Sheehy et al. Ed. by Adrienne Hickey. 256p. 1996. 24.95 (0-8144-0354-9) AMACOM.

Winning the Rat Race Without Becoming a Rat: The Psychology of Winning in Business. Kevin Leman. LC 96-14886. 256p. 1996. 19.99 (0-8407-3491-3, J Thoma Bks) Nelson.

Winning the Real Estate Game. Harvey Sherman & Patricia J. Sherman. (Illus.). 1977. pap. 4.95 (0-686-20328-3) Sherman.

Winning the Real War: Overcoming the Powers of Darkness. James Robison. LC 91-70018. 150p. (C). pap. text ed. 14.95 (0-88419-287-3) Omega Pubns OR.

Winning the Right to Know: A Handbook for Toxics Activists. Caron Chess. 100p. 1983. 8.95 (0-89788-073-0) CPA Washington.

Winning the School War: Defeating Educationism in America. Edward L. Tottle. LC 92-70455. (Illus.). 224p. 1997. per. 25.00 (0-937117-14-5) Educ Materials.

Winning the Second Battle: Canadian Veterans & the Return to Civilian Life, 1915-1930. Desmond Morton & Glenn Wright. 328p. 1987. 45.00 (0-8020-5705-5); pap. 18.95 (0-8020-6634-8) U of Toronto Pr.

Winning the Service Game. Benjamin Schneider & David E. Bowen. LC 94-34590. 320p. 1995. 24.95 (0-87584-570-3) Harvard Busn.

Winning the Service Game. Benjamin Schneider & David E. Bowen. 1995. text ed. 24.95 (0-07-103613-X) McGraw.

Winning the Slip & Fall Case 1993. (Litigation & Administrative Practice Course Handbook, 1983-84 Ser.: Vol. 462). 296p. 1993. 70.00 (0-685-69733-9, H4-5151) PLI.

Winning the Values War in a Changing Culture: Thirteen Distinct Values That Mark a Follower. Leith Anderson. LC 94-38361. 210p. 1994. 14.99 (1-55661-340-7) Bethany Hse.

Winning the War: How to Pray Prayers That God Answers. Sherry Cook. 250p. (Orig.). 1996. pap. 8.00 (1-57502-246-X, P0923) Morris Pubng.

*Winning the War Against Asthma & Allergies: A Drug-Free Alternative Treatment Plan for Asthma Sufferers & Their Families. Ellen Cutler. LC 97-9404. 1997. write for info. (0-7668-0060-1) Delmar.

*Winning the War Against Asthma & Allergies: A Drug Free Alternative Treatment Plan for Asthma Sufferers & Their Families. Ellen W. Cutler. LC 97-9404. 1996. pap. 17.95 (0-8273-8622-2) Delmar.

Winning the War Against Life-Threatening Diseases. Steven Pradell. LC 94-66759. 256p. 1994. pap. 13.95 (0-88282-125-3) New Horizon NJ.

Winning the War on Drugs: The Role of Workplace Testing. G. John Tysse & Garen E. Dodge. 198p. 1989. 65.00 (0-916559-19-X, 2016-MO-4035) EPF.

Winning the War on Drugs: The Role of Workplace Testing. abr. ed. 29p. 1989. 5.00 (0-916559-22-X, 2016E-MO-4035) EPF.

Winning the War on Drugs: The Role of Workplace Testing, Appendix. 580p. 1989. 65.00 (0-916559-20-3, 2016A-MO-4035) EPF.

Winning the War on Waste: Changing the Way We Work. William E. Conway. (Illus.). 239p. 1996. text ed. 26.95 (0-9631464-2-4) Conway Qual.

*Winning the War on Waste: Changing the Way We Work. 2nd ed. William E. Conway. 250p. 1996. 6.95 (0-9631464-4-0) Conway Qual.

Winning the War Within. Charles Stanley. 192p. 1988. 15.99 (0-8407-9036-8) Nelson.

Winning the War Within: How to Stop Doing What You Don't Want to Do. Peter Wilkes. LC 94-45404. 192p. (Orig.). 1995. pap. text ed. 9.99 (0-8308-1605-4, 1605) InterVarsity.

*Winning the Wealth Game: Strategies of the Rich & Famous. Andrew Westhem. 302p. 1997. 26.95 (0-9637899-6-1) Elliott & James Pubs.

Winning the Weight & Wellness Game. Julie W. Kembel. LC 93-83140. (Illus.). 324p. 1993. pap. 17.95 (0-931836-50-6) Northwest Learn.

Winning the Weight & Wellness Game: Instructor Guide. Julie W. Kembel. (Illus.). 296p. 1993. pap. 39.95 (0-931836-51-4) Northwest Learn.

Winning the West for Christ: Sheldon Jackson & Presbyterianism on the Rocky Mountain Frontier, 1869-1880. Norman J. Bender. 288p. 1996. 40.00 (0-8263-1670-0) U of NM Pr.

Winning the World: Becoming the Bold Soul Winner. Mac Hammond. 45p. 1994. pap. 2.95 (0-88114-958-6) K Copeland Pubns.

Winning the Worry War. 2nd ed. Don Baker. 120p. 1993. pap. 7.99 (1-56476-057-X, 63057, Victor Bks) Chariot Victor.

*Winning Their Spurs: The Tottenham Hotspur Dream Team. Jeremy Novick. (Illus.). 192p. 1997. 34.95 (1-85158-873-6, Pub. by Mnstream UK) Trafalgar.

Winning Thoroughbred Strategy. Dick Mitchell. (Illus.). 118p. (Orig.). 1985. pap. 29.95 (0-9614168-0-7) Cynthia Pub Co.

Winning Thoughts: A Very Special Gift Book. Carl Mays. LC 94-78067. 96p. (Orig.). 1994. pap. 5.95 (1-879111-23-3) Lincoln-Bradley.

Winning Through a Positive Spiritual Attitude. J. J. Turner. 1983. pap. 5.95 (0-89137-318-7) Quality Pubns.

Winning Through Enlightenment. 6th ed. Ron Smothermon. 226p. 1980. 29.90 (0-932654-00-2); pap. 15.00 (0-932654-01-0) Context Pubns.

Winning Through Grooming. Ed. by Bill Weikel. 1971. pap. 4.95 (0-87505-383-1) Borden.

Winning Through Innovation: A Practical Guide to Leading Organizational Change & Renewal. Michael L. Tushman & Charles A. O'Reilly. LC 96-2805. 304p. 1996. 24.95 (0-87584-579-7) Harvard Busn.

*Winning Through Innovation: A Practical Guide to Leading Organizational Change & Renewal. Michael L. Tushman & Charles A. O'Reilly, 3rd. 1996. text ed. 24.95 (0-07-103856-6) McGraw.

Winning Through Integrity. Cliff Jones. 1991. pap. 5.95 (0-687-45605-3) Abingdon.

Winning Through Intimidation. Robert J. Ringer. 304p. 1984. mass mkt. 5.99 (0-449-20786-2, Crest) Fawcett.

Winning Through Participation. I.C.A. Staff. 208p. 1996. per. 29.95 (0-8403-6196-3) Kendall-Hunt.

Winning Ticket! Judy Delton. (Lottery Luck Ser.: Bk. 1). (Illus.). 96p. (J). (gr. 2-5). 1995. pap. 3.95 (0-7868-1018-1) Hyprn Child.

*Winning Ticket: What Your Grandparents Learned about Personal Finances the Hard Way & Why You Need to Know More Than They Did. Stephen C. Johnson. LC 96-90342. (Orig.). 1996. pap. 12.95 (0-533-12008-X) Vantage.

Winning Tips for Casino Games. Consumer Guide Editors. 128p. 1995. pap. 4.99 (0-451-18576-5, Sig) NAL-Dutton.

Winning Tips for Nintendo. 1990. pap. 6.99 (0-517-05653-4) Random Hse Value.

Winning to the Court: How to Argue & Win Non-Jury Cases. Robert L. Simmons. 1972. 64.50 (0-13-961375-7) Exec Reports.

Winning Together: How Small Business Employees Can Help Themselves & Their Companies Succeed. Jim Schell. 96p. 1994. pap. 8.95 (0-9642445-0-0) Brass Tacks.

Winning Tournament Karate. Chuck Norris. Ed. by John Cocoran. LC 75-5497. (Japanese Arts Ser.). (Illus.). 1975. pap. text ed. 14.95 (0-89750-016-4, 121) Ohara Pubns.

Winning Tradition: A History of Kentucky Wildcat Basketball. Bert Nelli. LC 84-7306. (Illus.). 176p. 1984. 20.00 (0-8131-1519-1) U Pr of Ky.

Winning Trainer: Winning Ways to Involve People in Learning. 3rd ed. Julius E. Eitington. LC 96-8382. (Illus.). 496p. 1996. pap. 49.95 (0-88415-900-0, 5900) Gulf Pub.

Winning Trial Advocacy: How to Avoid Mistakes Made by Master Trial Lawyers. Julius B. Levine. 330p. 1989. text ed. 49.95 (0-13-961319-6) P-H.

*Winning Trial Techniques: A Roadmap for Effective Advocacy. William A. Barton. 167p. 1992. pap. 30.00 (0-614-30693-0) PEG MN.

Winning Ugly: Mental Warfare in Tennis - Lessons from a Master. Brad Gilbert & Steve Jamison. LC 93-37993. 224p. 1994. pap. 11.00 (0-671-88400-X, Fireside) S&S Trade.

Winning Vocabulary. Margaret M. Bynum. (Smart Tapes Ser.). 28p. 1994. pap. text ed. 19.95 incl. audio (1-55678-050-8) Learn Inc.

Winning Volleyball. 4th ed. Allen E. Scates. 368p. (C). 1993. per. write for info. (0-697-10966-6) Brown & Benchmark.

Winning Volleyball For Girls. Deborah W. Crisfield. LC 94-27344. (Illus.). 160p. 1995. 22.95 (0-8160-3033-2) Facts on File.

Winning Volleyball For Girls. Deborah W. Crisfield. LC 94-27344. 1996. pap. 12.95 (0-8160-3034-0) Facts on File.

*Winning Wars Without Heroes, Vol. 1. Tom Adams. LC 96-69098. (Illus.). 236p. (Orig.). 1996. pap. 11.95 (1-882792-28-9) Proctor Pubns.

*Winning Ways. Barbara Boswell. 384p. 1996. mass mkt. 5.99 (0-380-72743-9) Avon.

Winning Ways, Vol. 2. Elwyn R. Berlekamp et al. LC 81-66678. 1982. Vol.2. text ed. 111.00 (0-12-091152-3) Acad Pr.

Winning Ways: A Photohistory of American Women in Sports. Sue Lacy. (Illus.). 160p. (J). (gr. 5-9). 1996. 15.95 (0-8050-4147-8) H Holt & Co.

*Winning Ways: Best Practices in Work-Based Learning. Ed. by Albert J. Pautler & Deborah M. Buffamanti. 240p. 1997. pap. text ed. 18.95 (0-911168-94-X) Prakken.

Winning Ways: For Your Mathematical Plays, 2 vols., Vol. 2, Games in Particular. Elwyn R. Berlekamp et al. LC 81-66678. 1982. Vol. 2: For Your Mathematical Plays: Games In Particular. pap. text ed. 56.00 (0-12-091102-7) Acad Pr.

Winning Ways: How to Get to the Top & Stay There. Gayle Carson. Ed. by Charles Flowers. 156p. (Orig.). (C). 1988. text ed. 15.00 (0-9621370-0-6); pap. text ed. 10.00 (0-9621370-1-4) Lane Pub.

Winning Ways: Lessons for Juniors from the Top Trainers. Margaret J. Cannell. LC 93-38198. (Illus.). 224p. 1994. 27.00 (0-87605-960-4) Howell Bk.

Winning Ways Vol. 1: To Raise Your Infant to Successful Adulthood. Sherry K. Stevens. (Illus.). 86p. (Orig.). 1995. pap. 9.95 (0-9644446-1-5) Firelight Pr.

Winning Ways on the Autoharp, 2 vols., Vol. 1. Stevie Beck et al. Ed. by Becky Blackley. (Illus.). 52p. 1985. pap. 8.95 (0-912827-05-X) I A D Pubns.

Winning Ways on the Autoharp, 2 vols., Vol. 2. Stevie Beck et al. Ed. by Becky Blackley. (Illus.). 52p. 1985. pap. 8.95 (0-912827-06-8) I A D Pubns.

Winning Ways to Succeed with People. 2nd rev. ed. Helen H. Clinard. (Illus.). 318p. 1990. text ed. 20.00 (0-9623553-0-5) Effect Trg Consult.

Winning Weapon: The Atomic Bomb in the Cold War, 1945-1950. Gregg Herken. 452p. 1988. pap. text ed. 19.95 (0-691-02286-0) Princeton U Pr.

W

***Winning Web Sites: Plan & Design Your Own.** Bob Whitcroft. 160p. (Orig.). 1997. pap. 15.95 (1-55180-123-X) Self-Counsel Pr.

Winning Weekend Tennis. Charles R. Young. 112p. 1980. pap. 3.95 (0-8187-0044-0) Harlo Press.

Winning Welcome: Helping the Newcomer Feel at Home in Your Church. Sharon Bushey. (Illus.). 84p. 1989. pap. 5.99 (0-8341-1325-2) Beacon Hill.

***Winning with Arthritis.** Harris H. McIlwain et al. pap. text ed. 5.99 (0-471-17691-5) Wiley.

Winning with Arthritis. Harris H. McIlwain et al. LC 90-28903. (Science Editions Ser.). 228p. 1991. pap. text ed. 15.95 (0-471-52847-1) Wiley.

Winning with Astrology. Evelyn M. Nagle. 18p. 1988. 4.00 (0-86690-358-5, N2834-014) Am Fed Astrologers.

Winning with Back Pain. Harris H. McIlwain et al. 202p. 1994. pap. text ed. 12.95 (0-471-30328-3) Wiley.

***Winning with Back Pain: How to Beat Back Pain & Take Control of Your Life.** Harris H. McIlwain. 208p. 1997. pap. text ed. 5.99 (0-471-17694-X) Wiley.

Winning with CASE: Managing Modern Software Development. Robert L. Dixon. 480p. 1991. 39.95 (0-8306-2558-5) McGraw-Hill Prof.

Winning with Chess Psychology. Paul Benko. 1991. pap. 15.00 (0-8129-1866-5) Random.

Winning with Chronic Pain: A Complete Program for Health & Well-Being. Harris H. McIlwain et al. 222p. (C). 1994. 27.95 (0-87975-900-3); pap. 16.95 (0-87975-878-3) Prometheus Bks.

***Winning with Difficult People.** 2nd ed. Arthur H. Bell. LC 97-10353. 1997. pap. text ed. 6.95 (0-8120-9894-3) Barron.

Winning with Diversity: A Practical Handbook for Creating Inclusive Meetings Events, & Organizations. Donald M. Norris & Marie C. Lofton. LC 94-43566. 157p. 1994. 22.95 (0-88034-093-2) Am Soc Assn Execs.

Winning with Frank Chapot. Frank Chapot. (Illus.). 180p. 1992. 27.95 (0-914327-45-3) Breakthrgh NY.

Winning with Grammar: Basic Workbook I. 2nd ed. Bonnie E. Paull. 224p. (C). 1993. per. 24.09 (0-8403-8554-4) Kendall-Hunt.

Winning with Grammar: Basic Workbook II. 2nd ed. Bonnie E. Paull. 240p. (C). 1993. per. 25.14 (0-8403-8705-9) Kendall-Hunt.

Winning with Heart Attack: A Complete Program for Health & Well-Being. Joel C. Silverfield et al. (Illus.). 189p. (C). 1994. 27.95 (0-87975-914-3) Prometheus Bks.

Winning with Heart Attack: A Complete Program for Health & Well-Being. Joel C. Silverfield et al. (Illus.). 189p. (C). 1994. pap. 16.95 (0-87975-915-1) Prometheus Bks.

Winning with Hunter Ponies. John Thorne & Susan Thorne. 192p. (C). 1990. 65.00 (0-85131-473-2, Pub. by J A Allen & Co UK) St Mut.

***Winning with Index Mutual Funds: How to Beat Wall Street at Its Own Game.** Jerry Tweddell & Jack Pierce. 224p. 1997. 24.95 (0-8144-0358-1) AMACOM.

Winning with Managed Futures: How to Select a Top Performing Commodity Trading Advisor. Thomas A. McCafferty. 1994. text ed. 47.50 (1-55738-587-4) Irwin Prof Pubng.

Winning with Osteoporosis. 2nd ed. Harris H. McIlwain et al. LC 93-7530. 150p. 1993. pap. text ed. 15.95 (0-471-30489-1) Wiley.

Winning with People. Michael G. Zey. 224p. (Orig.). 1995. mass mkt. 4.99 (0-425-14512-3) Berkley Pub.

Winning with Promotion Power: 100 Best of the Best Promotions. Promotion Marketing Assn of America Staff. 248p. 1994. 59.95 (0-85013-230-4, TE7609) Dartnell Corp.

Winning with Pure Bred Dogs: Success by Design. Alvin Grossman & Beverly Grossman. Ed. by Luana Luther. LC 91-70230. (Illus.). 280p. 1992. 26.50 (0-944875-17-3); pap. 23.50 (0-944875-27-0) Doral Pub.

Winning With Quality. John W. Wesner. LC 94-17265. 320p. 1995. pap. 31.95 (0-201-63347-7) Addison-Wesley.

Winning with Quality: The FPL Story. John J. Hudiburg. 232p. 1991. text ed. 19.95 (0-527-91646-3, 916463) Qual Resc.

Winning with Small Business. Bill FitzPatrick. 346p. (Orig.). 1994. pap. 29.95 (1-884864-01-5); pap. 57.00 incl. vhs (1-884864-02-3) Am Success Inst.

Winning with Statistics: A Painless First Look at Numbers, Ratios, Percentages, Means & Inference. Richard P. Runyon. (Statistics Ser.). 1977. pap. text ed. write for info. (0-201-06654-8) Addison-Wesley.

Winning with Teamwork. Ed. by Mac Anderson. 77p. (Orig.). 1992. pap. text ed. 7.95 (1-880461-23-4) Celebrat Excell.

Winning with the American Quarter Horse. Don Burt. LC 95-45235. (Equestrian Library). (Illus.). 256p. 1996. 30.00 (0-385-46813-X) Doubleday.

Winning with the Caro Kann: 1.e4 c6. Eric Tangborn. Ed. by Eric Woro. 112p. (Orig.). 1994. pap. 14.95 (1-879479-23-0) ICE WA.

Winning with the Insiders. Earl Hadady et al. Ed. by Martin D. Weiss. 100p. 1987. pap. text ed. 19.50 (0-9613048-8-X) M D Weiss Pub.

Winning with the News Media: A Self-Defense Manual When You're the Story. Clarence Jones. (Illus.). 376p. 1996. pap. 19.95 (0-9619603-3-7) Video Consult.

Winning with the Thoroughbreds: "A Race Fans' Guide to Handicapping & History" Joseph Militello. LC 94-6141. (Illus.). 283p. (Orig.). 1995. pap. 14.95 (0-9641634-0-3) J Militello.

Winning with Water: Soil-Moisture Monitoring for Efficient Irrigation. Gail Richardson & Peter Mueller-Beilschmidt. LC 88-8846. 192p. 1988. pap. 24.95 (0-918780-42-X) INFORM NY.

Winning with Words: An Introduction to the Dictionary. Bonnie E. Paull. 128p. (C). 1993. per. 22.57 (0-8403-8706-7) Kendall-Hunt.

Winning with Words: Secrets of the Job Interview. 2nd ed. J. Brent Pichard. 77p. (C). 1983. pap. 4.95 (0-9612312-1-1) Magister Inc.

***Winning with Your Voice.** Morton Cooper. 1996. pap. 10.00 (0-87980-442-4) Wilshire.

Winning Without Selling: Practice Building Handbook for Accountants. 3rd ed. Galen D. Loven. 96p. 1993. 34.50 (1-883480-01-9) Brkthgh Pubns.

Winning Without Steroids. Gayle Olinekova. (Sports & Fitness Library). (Illus.). 40p. (Orig.). (C). 1988. pap. 2.95 (0-87983-480-3) Keats.

Winning Women. Mitchell & Dyer. Date not set. pap. write for info. (0-14-008091-0, Penguin Bks) Viking Penguin.

Winning Women into Mathematics. Ed. by Patricia C. Kenschaft. 88p. 1991. pap. 16.50 (0-88385-453-8, WIW) Math Assn.

Winning Womens Softball. Karen Linde. 1990. pap. 12.95 (0-13-356148-8) P-H.

Winning Words. Berman. (C). 1994. pap. text ed. 13.00 (0-15-599701-7) HB Coll Pubs.

Winning Words for Daily Living: Reaching New Heights for a Satisfying Life. Charles U. Wagner. LC 89-11120. 416p. 1989. 18.99 (0-8254-3975-2) Kregel.

Winning Words of Champions. Compiled by Larry Bielat. LC 95-13212. Orig. Title: Words of Champions. 1995. 10.99 (0-517-14673-8) Random.

Winning Works. Intro. by Sandy Whelchel. 100p. 1993. pap. 9.95 (0-88100-079-5) Natl Writ Pr.

Winning Worldwide: Strategies for Dominating Global Markets. Douglas Lamont. 336p. 1990. text ed. 30.00 (1-55623-419-8) Irwin Prof Pubng.

Winning Wrestling Moves. Mark Mysnyk et al. LC 93-42161. (Illus.). 208p. 1994. pap. 19.95 (0-87322-482-5, PMYS0482) Human Kinetics.

Winning Writer: Studies in Art of Self Expression. Robin White. (Philosophy Ser.). 134p. (C). Date not set. pap. text ed. 16.25 (0-86720-511-3) Jones & Bartlett.

Winning Year One: A Survival Manual for First Year Teachers. Carol L. Fuery. 118p. 1986. 9.95 (0-944295-01-0) Sanibel Sanddollar Pubns.

Winning Your Audit: Sound Preparation & Attitude: Keys to Proving Deductions. 2nd rev. ed. Holmes F. Crouch. Ed. by Irma J. Crouch. LC 96-84929. (Series 500 Tax Guides: Vol. 502). (Illus.). 224p. 1996. pap. 18.95 (0-944817-31-9, T/G 502) Allyear Tax.

Winning Your Biggest Battles. Mark Finley. LC 94-31511. 1994. pap. 1.49 (0-8163-1232-X) Pacific Pr Pub Assn.

Winning Your Divorce: A Man's Survival Guide. Timothy J. Horgan. 208p. 1995. pap. 11.95 (0-452-27373-0, Plume) NAL-Dutton.

Winning Your Kids Back from the Media. Quentin J. Schultze. Date not set. pap. 49.99 incl. vhs (0-8308-7349-X, 7349) InterVarsity.

***Winning Your Personal Injury Claim.** Evan K. Aidman. LC 97-16712. (Legal Survival Guides Ser.). 180p. (Orig.). 1997. pap. 14.95 (1-57071-165-8) Sourcebks.

***Winning 42: Strategy & Lore of the National Game of Texas.** Dennis Roberson. LC 97-8291. (Illus.). 192p. (Orig.). 1997. pap. 12.95 (0-89672-384-4) Tex Tech Univ Pr.

Winning's Only Part of the Game: Lessons of Life & Football. Bobby Bowden & Ben Brown. LC 96-5540. 256p. 1996. 18.95 (0-446-52050-0) Warner Bks.

Winnington Letters: John Ruskin's Correspondence with Margaret Alexis Bell & the Children at Winnington Hall. John Ruskin. Ed. by Van A. Burd. LC 68-28692. (Illus.). 736p. 1969. 58.00 (0-674-95365-7) Belknap Pr.

Winnipeg: A Social History of Urban Growth, 1874-1914. A. F. Artibise. (Illus.). 400p. 1975. 44.95 (0-7735-0202-5, Pub. by McGill CN) U of Toronto Pr.

Winnipeg General Strike. Donald C. Masters. LC 51-5058. (Canadian University Paperbooks Ser.: No. 136). (Illus.). 179p. reprint ed. pap. 51.10 (0-8357-4160-5, 2036934) Bks Demand.

Winnipeg Jets. Jess Myers. LC 93-48451. (NHL Today Ser.). 32p. (J). 1995. lib. bdg. 15.95 (0-88682-692-6) Creative Ed.

Winnowing Winds. large type ed. Ann Marlowe. 1981. 25.99 (0-7089-0580-3) Ulverscroft.

Winny de Puh. A. A. Milne. (SPA.). (J). 7.50 (0-685-31015-9) Santillana.

Winny De Puh. A. A. Milne. (Illus.). 176p. (SPA.). (J). (ps-3). Date not set. pap. 11.00 (0-525-44986-8) Dutton Child Bks.

Winny De Puh. A. A. Milne. 1995. pap. text ed. 9.95 (84-372-1885-3) Santillana.

Winogrand: Figments from the Real World. John Szarkowski. (Illus.). 260p. 1988. pap. 19.95 (0-87070-641-1, 0-8109-6088-5) Mus of Modern Art.

Winona & the King Philip Locations. (Copper Country Local History Ser.: Vol. 44). (Illus.). 132p. 1993. 3.00 (0-942363-43-4) C J Monette.

***Winona Ryder.** Dave Thompson. LC 96-48841. (Illus.). 216p. (Orig.). 1997. pap. 12.95 (0-87833-926-4) Taylor Pub.

***Winona Ryder.** U. S. Magazine Editors. 1997. 24.95 (0-316-89359-5) Little.

***Winona Ryder Scrapbook.** Ed. by Scott Siegel & Barbara Siegel. LC 97-8681. 208p. 1997. pap. 16.95 (0-8065-1883-9, Citadel Pr) Carol Pub Group.

Winona's Pony Cart. Maud H. Lovelace. 1976. 18.95 (0-8488-1420-7) Amereon Ltd.

Winona's Pony Cart. Maud H. Lovelace. 120p. 1986. reprint ed. lib. bdg. 17.95 (0-89966-566-7) Buccaneer Bks.

Winona's Web. Priscilla Cogan. LC 96-25810. 280p. 1996. 21.00 (1-883953-15-4, Face to Face) Midwest Trad.

***Winona's Web: A Novel of Discovery.** Priscilla Cogan. 224p. 1996. pap. 12.00 (0-385-49048-8, Main St Bks) Doubleday.

Wins, Places & Pro's. Tex Sheanan. (Illus.). (Orig.). 1984. pap. text ed. 6.95 (0-89746-008-1) Gambling Times.

Winshaw Legacy: Or, What a Carve Up! Jonathan Coe. 512p. 1996. pap. 14.00 (0-679-75405-9) Random.

Winship Family. Michael McCarthy. 464p. 1995. mass mkt. 6.99 (1-896329-25-X, Pub. by Comnwlth Pub CN) Partners Pubs Grp.

***Winslow Boy.** Rattigan. 1991. pap. text ed. write for info. (0-582-06019-2, Pub. by Longman UK) Longman.

Winslow Boy. Terence Rattigan. 1950. pap. 5.25 (0-8222-1264-1) Dramatists Play.

Winslow Boy. Terence Rattigan. 96p. 1995. pap. 13.95 (1-85459-296-3, Pub. by N Hern Bks UK) Theatre Comm.

Winslow Homer. Nicolai Cikovsky, Jr. et al. (Illus.). 464p. 1995. 60.00 (0-300-06555-8) Yale U Pr.

Winslow Homer. Nicolai Cikovsky, Jr. (Library of American Art). 1990. 45.00 (0-8109-1193-0) Abrams.

Winslow Homer. Nicolai Cikovsky, Jr. LC 92-15583. (Rizzoli Art Ser.). (Illus.). 24p. 1992. pap. 7.95 (0-8478-1583-8) Rizzoli Intl.

Winslow Homer. Nicolai Cikovsky, Jr & Franklin Kelly. LC 95-19025. 1995. write for info. (0-89468-217-2) Natl Gallery Art.

Winslow Homer. Mary A. Judge. (Crown Art Library). (Illus.). 96p. 1986. 18.00 (0-517-55725-8, Crown) Crown Pub Group.

Winslow Homer: An Annotated Bibliography of Periodical Literature. Melinda D. Davis. LC 75-29243. 138p. 1975. 20.00 (0-8108-0876-5) Scarecrow.

Winslow Homer: Paintings of the Civil War. Marc Simpson et al. LC 88-80734. (Illus.). 280p. (C). 1988. 39.95 (0-318-37565-6); pap. 24.95 (0-88401-060-0) Fine Arts Mus.

Winslow Homer: Prints from Harper's Weekly. David Tatham. (Illus.). 14p. 1979. 10.00 (0-685-70726-1) Gal Assn NY.

Winslow Homer: The Croquet Game. David P. Curry. LC 84-50421. (Illus.). 40p. (Orig.). 1984. pap. 4.00 (0-89467-031-X) Yale Art Gallery.

Winslow Homer & the Illustrated Book. David Tatham. LC 91-13534. (Illus.). 366p. 1992. 45.00 (0-8156-2550-2) Syracuse U Pr.

Winslow Homer & the New England Poets. David Tatham. (Illus.). 1980. pap. 3.00 (0-912296-45-3) Am Antiquarian.

Winslow Homer & the Sea. Carl Little. LC 95-31391. (Illus.). 80p. 1995. pap. 19.95 (0-87654-479-0) Pomegranate Calif.

Winslow Homer at the Addison. Susan Faxon & Paul Metcalf. (Illus.). 96p. (Orig.). 1990. pap. 15.00 (1-879886-27-8) Addison Gallery.

Winslow Homer Illustrations: Forty-Four Wood Engravings after Drawings by the Artist. Winslow Homer. (Illus.). 48p. (Orig.). 1983. pap. 3.95 (0-486-24392-3) Dover.

Winslow Homer in the Adirondacks. David Tatham. (Illus.). (C). 1996. text ed. 45.00 (0-8156-0343-6, TAWI) Syracuse U Pr.

Winslow Homer in the Clark Collection. Alexandra R. Murphy. LC 86-61315. (Illus.). 76p. (Orig.). 1986. pap. 14.95 (0-931102-19-7) S & F Clark Art.

Winslow Homer in the Eighteen Eighties: Watercolors, Drawings, & Etchings. David Tatham. LC 83-81777. 1983. pap. 5.00 (0-914407-01-5) Everson Mus.

Winslow Homer in the Eighteen Seventies: Selections from the Valentine-Pulsifer Collection. John Wilmerding et al. Ed. by Jill Guthrie & Barbara Anderman. LC 89-81414. 77p. (Orig.). 1990. 40.00 (0-943012-13-9); pap. 17.95 (0-943012-12-0) Prince U Art.

Winslow Homer Journal. Universe, Editors. 1995. 10.95 (1-55550-689-5) Universe.

Winslow Homer Journal Old Sett. Universe. 1995. 10.95 (1-55550-690-9) St Martin.

Winslow Homer Watercolors. Philip C. Beam. LC 83-70339. (Illus.). 1983. pap. 9.50 (0-916606-05-8) Bowdoin Coll.

Winslow Homer Watercolors. Donelson F. Hoopes. (Great Artists Ser.). (Illus.). 88p. 1984. pap. 16.95 (0-8230-2326-5, Watsn-Guptill) Watsn-Guptill.

Winslow Homer Watercolors. Helen A. Cooper. (Illus.). 260p. 1987. reprint ed. pap. 27.50 (0-300-03997-2, Y-687) Yale U Pr.

Winslow Homer's Images of Blacks: The Civil War & Reconstruction Years. Peter H. Wood & Karen C. Dalton. (Illus.). 144p. 1989. pap. 22.95 (0-292-79047-3) U of Tex Pr.

Winslow Memorial: Family Records of the Winslows & Their Descendants in America with English Ancestry As Far As Known, 2 vols. in 1. D. P. Holton & F. K. Holton. (Illus.). 1270p. 1989. reprint ed. pap. 175.00 (0-8328-1285-4); reprint ed. lib. bdg. 183.00 (0-8328-1284-6) Higginson Bk Co.

***Winslow Register, 1904 (Town History & Directory)** Mitchell & Davis. 103p. 1997. reprint ed. pap. 17.50 (0-8328-5930-3) Higginson Bk Co.

Winslow's Comprehensive Tamil-English Dictionary. M. Winslow. 974p. (ENG & TAM.). 1984. reprint ed. 95.00 (0-8288-1725-1, M 14408) Fr & Eur.

Winslow's English & Tamil Dictionary. M. Winslow. 1510p. (ENG & TAM.). 1984. reprint ed. 95.00 (0-8288-1726-X, M 14115) Fr & Eur.

Winslows of Careswell in Marshfield. Cynthia H. Krusell. (Illus.). 75p. 1992. pap. 12.95 (0-9627871-1-6) Hist Res Assocs.

***Winsock 2.0.** Lewis Napper. 1997. pap. 39.99 (0-7645-8049-3) IDG Bks.

Winsome Widow. Teresa DesJardien. 256p. 1994. mass mkt. 3.99 (0-8217-4724-X, Zebra Kensgtn) Kensgtn Pub Corp.

Winsome Winnie, & Other New Nonsense Novels. Stephen B. Leacock. LC 74-140333. (Short Story Index Reprint Ser.). 1977. 16.95 (0-8369-3725-2) Ayer.

Winsor McCay: His Life & Art. John Canemaker. LC 86-28792. (Illus.). 224p. 1987. 65.00 (0-89659-687-7) Abbeville Pr.

Winstanley the Digger: A Literary Analysis of Radical Ideas in the English Revolution. Thomas W. Hayes. LC 79-695. (Illus.). 270p. reprint ed. pap. 77.00 (0-7837-4465-X, 2044173) Bks Demand.

Winsted, A.K.A. Winsted: The Promise of a Small Town. Tom Wathen. 365p. (Orig.). 1989. pap. write for info. (0-318-65763-5) Public ISG.

Winster - A Visitor's Guide. John N. Merrill. 20p. 1987. 45.00 (0-907496-21-0, Pub. by JNM Pubns UK) St Mut.

***Winston Churchill.** Robert Blake. (Get a Life...Pocket Biographies Ser.). (Illus.). 128p. Date not set. pap. 10.95 (0-7509-1507-2, Pub. by Sutton Pubng UK) Bks Intl VA.

Winston Churchill. R. G. Grant & Victoria Lloyd-Davies. 224p. 1994. 17.98 (0-8317-9458-5) Smithmark.

Winston Churchill. Bob Italia. Ed. by Rosemary Walner. LC 90-82615. (World War Two Leaders Ser.). (Illus.). 32p. (J). (gr. 4). 1990. lib. bdg. 11.96 (0-939179-78-4) Abdo & Dghtrs.

Winston Churchill. William W. Lace. (Importance of...Ser.). (Illus.). 112p. (J). (gr. 5-9). 1995. lib. bdg. 17.96 (1-56006-067-0, 0670) Lucent Bks.

Winston Churchill. Judith Rodgers. (World Leaders - Past & Present Ser.). (Illus.). 112p. (YA). (gr. 5 up). 1986. lib. bdg. 19.95 (0-87754-563-4) Chelsea Hse.

Winston Churchill. Warren I. Titus. LC 63-17371. (Twayne's United States Authors Ser.). 1963. pap. text ed. 4.50 (0-8290-0015-1); lib. bdg. 17.95 (0-89197-978-6) Irvington.

Winston Churchill. Warren I. Titus. (Twayne's United States Authors Ser.). 1963. pap. 13.95 (0-8084-0331-1, T43) NCUP.

Winston Churchill: An Intimate. Violet B. Carter. 1994. 12.98 (0-8317-5868-6) Smithmark.

Winston Churchill: An Unbreakable Spirit. J. E. Driemen. LC 89-26029. (People in Focus Ser.). (Illus.). 128p. (YA). (gr. 5 up). 1990. lib. bdg. 13.95 (0-87518-434-0, Dillon Silver Burdett) Silver Burdett Pr.

Winston Churchill: Mini-Play & Activities. Lawrence Stevens. (World History Ser.). (YA). (gr. 7 up). 1981. 6.50 (0-89550-346-8) Stevens & Shea.

Winston Churchill: Resolution, Defiance, Magnanimity, Good Will. Ed. by R. Crosby Kemper, 3rd. (Illus.). 264p. (C). 1995. 24.95 (0-8262-1036-8) U of Mo Pr.

Winston Churchill: Soldier, Statesman, Artist. John B. Severance. LC 94-25129. 144p. (YA). (gr. 5 up). 1996. 17.95 (0-395-69853-7, Clarion Bks) HM.

Winston Churchill: Studies in Statesmanship. Ed. & Pref. by Alastair Parker. (Illus.). 282p. (C). 1995. 24.95 (1-85753-151-5, Pub. by Brasseys UK) Brasseys Inc.

Winston Churchill Vol. VIII: Road to Victory, 1941-1945. Martin Gilbert. (Illus.). 1320p. 40.00 (0-317-53569-2) HM.

Winston Churchill - Architect of Peace: A Study of Statesmanship & the Origins of the Cold War. Steven J. Lambakis. LC 92-42674. (Contributions in Political Science Ser.: No. 322). 208p. 1993. text ed. 49.95 (0-313-28823-2, GM8823, Greenwood Pr) Greenwood.

***Winston Churchill & Emery Reves: Correspondence, 1937-1965.** Winston Churchill et al. Ed. & Intro. by Martin Gilbert. LC 97-14310. (Illus.). 432p. 1997. 39.95 (0-292-71201-4) U of Tex Pr.

Winston Churchill & the Dardanelles: A Dialogue in Ends & Means. Trumbull Higgins. LC 77-11017. (Illus.). 308p. 1977. reprint ed. text ed. 59.75 (0-8371-9804-6, HIWCH, Greenwood Pr) Greenwood.

***Winston Churchill As I Knew Him.** Violet B. Carter. 495p. 1996. pap. 24.95 (0-297-81588-1, Weidenfeld) Trafalgar.

Winston Churchill on Empire. Kirk Emmert. LC 88-71080. 174p. 1989. lib. bdg. 24.95 (0-89089-281-4) Carolina Acad Pr.

Winston Churchill on Jewish Problems. Oscar K. Rabinowicz. LC 74-43. 231p. (C). 1974. reprint ed. text ed. 59.75 (0-8371-7357-4, RAWC, Greenwood Pr) Greenwood.

Winston Churchill's Last Campaign: Britain & the Cold War 1951-1955. John Young. (Illus.). 368p. (C). 1996. 75.00 (0-19-820367-5) OUP.

Winston Churchill's World View: Statesmanship & Power. Kenneth W. Thompson. LC 87-2818. viii, 364p. 1987. pap. text ed. 11.95 (0-8071-1419-7) La State U Pr.

Winston-Derek's Traditional Fairy Tales, Vol. II. Fred Crump, Jr. (Illus.). 224p. (J). (gr. k-3). 1992. 39.95 (1-55523-490-9) Winston-Derek.

***Winston-Derek's Traditional Fairy Tales, Vol. II.** Fred Crump, Jr. (Illus.). 224p. (J). (gr. k-3). 1992. write for info. (1-55523-491-7) Winston-Derek.

Winston Estes. Bob J. Frye. LC 92-52528. (Western Writers Ser.: No. 103). (Illus.). 52p. (Orig.). 1992. pap. 4.95 (0-88430-102-8) Boise St U W Writ Ser.

***Winston Grammar Program - Advanced.** Paul R. Erwin. 91p. (Orig.). 1982. reprint ed. teacher ed., pap. text ed. 17.50 (1-889673-08-0) Precious Memories.

***Winston Grammar Program - Advanced: Complete Set, 4 vols.** Paul Erwin. (Orig.). (YA). (gr. 7-12). 1982. student ed., teacher ed., pap. text ed. 35.00 (1-889673-06-4) Precious Memories.

***Winston Grammar Program - Advanced: Parts of Speech Cards.** Paul R. Erwin. (Orig.). 1982. reprint ed. pap. text ed. 7.50 (1-889673-11-0) Precious Memories.

W

An Asterisk (*) at the beginning of an entry indicates that the title is appearing in BIP for the first time.

***Winston Grammar Program - Advanced: Student Package, 2 vols.** Paul R. Erwin. (Orig.). (YA). (gr. 7-12). 1982. reprint ed. student ed., wbk. ed., pap. text ed. 12.50 (*1-889673-07-2*) Precious Memories.

***Winston Grammar Program - Advanced: Student Workbook.** Paul R. Erwin. 88p. (Orig.). (YA). (gr. 7-12). 1982. reprint ed. student ed., wbk. ed., pap. text ed. 10.00 (*1-889673-09-9*) Precious Memories.

***Winston Grammar Program - Advanced: Test Key.** Paul R. Erwin. 1p. (Orig.). 1982. reprint ed. pap. text ed. 5.00 (*1-889673-10-2*) Precious Memories.

***Winston Grammar Program - Basic.** 2nd rev. ed. Paul R. Erwin. 82p. (Orig.). (J). (gr. 3-8). 1992. teacher ed., pap. text ed. 17.50 (*1-889673-02-1*) Precious Memories.

***Winston Grammar Program - Basic: Complete Set, 4 vols.** 2nd rev. ed. Paul R. Erwin. (Orig.). (J). (gr. 3-8). 1992. student ed., teacher ed., pap. text ed. 40.00 (*1-889673-00-5*) Precious Memories.

***Winston Grammar Program - Basic: Parts of Speech Cards.** 2nd rev. ed. Paul R. Erwin. (Orig.). (J). (gr. 3-8). 1992. pap. text ed. 7.50 (*1-889673-05-6*) Precious Memories.

***Winston Grammar Program - Basic: Student Package, 2 vols.** 2nd rev. ed. Paul R. Erwin. (Orig.). (J). (gr. 3-8). 1992. student ed., wbk. ed., pap. text ed. 12.50 (*1-889673-01-3*) Precious Memories.

***Winston Grammar Program - Basic: Student Workbook.** 2nd rev. ed. Paul R. Erwin. 30p. (Orig.). (J). (gr. 3-8). 1992. student ed., wbk. ed., pap. text ed. 10.00 (*1-889673-03-X*) Precious Memories.

***Winston Grammar Program - Basic: Tests & Quizzes.** 2nd rev. ed. Paul R. Erwin. 12p. (Orig.). (J). (gr. 3-8). 1992. pap. text ed. 5.00 (*1-889673-04-8*) Precious Memories.

Winston Reader. Bonnie Carter & Craig Skates. 672p. (C). 1991. pap. text ed. 21.50 (*0-03-026597-5*) HB Coll Pubs.

Winston Roeth. Contrib. by Jan Avgikos. (Illus.). 32p. (Orig.). 1993. 20.00 (*0-9638945-0-1*) Stark Gallery.

Winston S. Churchill: Philosopher & Statesman. Michael R. Fowler. LC 84-29122. (Credibility of Institutions, Policies & Leadership Ser.: Vol. 19). 92p. (Orig.). 1985. lib. bdg. 35.50 (*0-8191-4416-9*) U Pr of Amer.

Winston S. Churchill - War Correspondent 1895-1900. Frederick Woods. (Illus.). 355p. 1992. 29.95 (*0-08-041331-5*, Pub. by Brasseys UK) Brasseys Inc.

Winston-Salem: A Cooperative Spirit. James E. Turner. LC 94-30184. 128p. 1994. 35.00 (*1-885352-06-9*) Community Comm.

Winston-Salem: A History. Frank V. Tursi. LC 94-14333. (Illus.). 310p. 1994. pap. 34.95 (*0-89587-115-7*) Blair.

Winston-Salem Journal: The First One Hundred Years. Frank V. Tursi. LC 96-9652. (Illus.). 1996. 28.95 (*0-89587-156-4*) Blair.

Winter. 1995. 3.98 (*0-7858-0300-9*) Bk Sales Inc.

Winter. Claudia Allen. 54p. 1996. pap. 5.25 (*0-87129-634-9*, W77) Dramatic Pub.

Winter. Richard L. Allington & Kathleen Krull. LC 80-25115. (Beginning to Learn about Ser.). (Illus.). 32p. (J). (gr. k-3). 1985. pap. 3.95 (*0-8114-8243-X*) Raintree Steck-V.

Winter. Auburn University Staff. (Nursing Texts Ser.). (C). (gr. 13). 1996. 165.95 (*0-8151-4499-7*) Mosby Yr Bk.

Winter. Nicola Baxter. LC 95-50049. (Toppers Ser.). 24p. (J). 1996. lib. bdg. 15.00 (*0-516-09277-4*) Childrens.

***Winter.** Nicola Baxter. (Toppers Ser.). 24p. (J). 1997. pap. 4.95 (*0-516-26088-X*) Childrens.

Winter. Pierre Berton. 1994. 50.00 (*0-7737-2505-9*) Genl Dist Srvs.

***Winter.** Pierre Berton. 1996. 40.00 (*0-7737-2805-8*, Pub. by Stoddart Pubng CN) Genl Dist Srvs.

***Winter.** Karen Bryant-Mole. (Picture This! Ser.). (J). 1997. lib. bdg. write for info. (*1-57572-058-2*) Rigby Interact Libr.

Winter. Nancy M. Davis et al. (Davis Teaching Units Ser.: Vol. 1, No. 5). (Illus.). 29p. (J). (ps-2). 1986. pap. 4.95 (*0-937103-05-5*) DaNa Pubns.

Winter. Len Deighton. 1989. mass mkt. 5.95 (*0-345-35931-3*) Ballantine.

***Winter.** Len Deighton. 1997. pap. 14.00 (*0-345-42018-7*) Ballantine.

Winter. Len Deighton. 1988. write for info. (*0-318-62991-7*) Random.

Winter. Chris Demarest. 16p. (J). (ps). 1996. pap. 4.95 (*0-15-201027-0*) HarBrace.

Winter. Mark Dunster. (Rin Ser.: Pt. 36). 47p. (Orig.). 1985. pap. 5.00 (*0-89642-125-2*) Linden Pubs.

Winter. Donald Hall & Clifton C. Olds. LC 85-15767. (Illus.). 152p. 1986. pap. 25.00 (*0-87451-355-3*) U Pr of New Eng.

Winter. Ron Hirschi. LC 89-23935. (Illus.). (J). (ps-3). 1990. pap. 14.99 (*0-525-65026-1*, Cobblehill Bks) Dutton Child Bks.

Winter. Ron Hirschi. (Illus.). 32p. (J). (ps-3). 1996. pap. 4.99 (*0-14-055785-7*) Puffin Bks.

***Winter.** Patrick Lane. 8.95 (*1-55050-002-3*, Pub. by Coteau CN) Genl Dist Srvs.

Winter. Louis Santrey. LC 82-19353. (Discovering the Seasons Ser.). (Illus.). 32p. (J). (gr. 4-7). 1983. lib. bdg. 11.50 (*0-89375-907-4*) Troll Communs.

Winter. Lynn M. Stone. LC 93-39059. (As the World Turns Ser.). (J). 1994. write for info. (*1-55916-021-7*) Rourke Bk Co.

Winter. Ruth Thomson. LC 94-12307. (Get Set...Go! Ser.). (Illus.). 24p. (J). (ps-3). 1994. pap. 4.95 (*0-516-47997-0*); lib. bdg. 15.40 (*0-516-07997-2*) Childrens.

Winter. David Webster. Ed. by Jane Steltenpohl. (Exploring Nature Around the Year Ser.). (Illus.). 48p. (J). (gr. 2-4). 1989. pap. 4.95 (*0-671-65986-3*, Julian Messner) Silver Burdett Pr.

Winter. rev. ed. Marlene J. McCracken & Robert A. McCracken. (Themes Ser.). (Illus.). 72p. (J). (gr. k-4). 1987. pap. 12.00 (*0-920541-10-0*) Peguis Pubs Ltd.

Winter. Don Coyhis. LC 95-79100. (Meditations with Native American Elders Ser.). 112p. 1995. reprint ed. pap. 9.95 (*1-887874-03-8*) Moh-He-Con-Nuck.

Winter: An Ecological Handbook. James Halfpenny & Roy Ozanne. LC 88-81618. (Illus.). 288p. (Orig.). 1989. pap. 16.95 (*1-55566-036-3*) Johnson Bks.

Winter: Celebrating the Seaason in a Christian Home. Peter Mazar. (Illus.). 48p. (Orig.). 1996. pap. 15.00 (*1-56854-134-1*, WINTER) Liturgy Tr Pubns.

Winter: Notes from Montana. Rick Bass. 1992. pap. 14.00 (*0-395-61150-4*) HM.

***Winter: Recipes Inspired by Nature's Bounty.** Joanne Weir. LC 96-34195. (Williams-Sonoma Seasonal Celebration Ser.). 1997. write for info. (*0-7835-4609-2*) Time-Life.

***Winter: Recipes Inspired by Nature's Bounty.** Joanne Weir. LC 96-34195. (Williams-Sonoma Seasonal Celebration Ser.). 1997. write for info. (*1-887451-11-0*) Wldon Owen Ref.

Winter: Tracks in the Snow. Janet McDonnell. LC 93-20172. (Four Season Ser.). (Illus.). 32p. (J). (ps-2). 1993. lib. bdg. 17.40 (*0-516-00679-7*) Childrens.

Winter see Growing Strong in the Seasons of Life: A Season of Reverance

Winter Across America. Seymour Simon. LC 93-45933. (Illus.). 32p. (J). (gr. k-5). 1994. 14.95 (*0-7868-0019-4*) Hyprn Child.

Winter Adventure: A Complete Guide. Peter Stark & Steven M. Krauzer. (Trailside Series Guide). (Illus.). 192p. 1995. pap. 17.95 (*0-393-31400-6*, Norton Paperbks) Norton.

Winter & Summer Dance Series in Zuni in 1918. fac. ed. Elsie C. Parsons. (University of California Publications in American Archaeology & Ethnology: Vol. 17: 3). 45p. (C). 1922. reprint ed. pap. text ed. 4.05 (*1-55567-229-9*) Coyote Press.

Winter & Wild Roses: Seven Haiku. Nina Wicker. Ed. by MaryBelle Campbell. 32p. 1992. reprint ed. pap. 5.00 (*1-879009-11-0*) S P-Persephone Pr.

Winter at Morristown Seventeen Seventy-Nine to Seventeen Eighty: The Darkest Hour. Samuel S. Smith. LC 79-52313. (Revolutionary War Bicentennial Ser.). (Illus.). 1979. pap. 9.95 (*0-685-01784-2*) Freneau.

Winter at Noon. M. B. Thornton. LC 77-86610. (Illus.). 1977. pap. 4.95 (*0-930830-02-4*) Great Basin.

Winter at Valley Forge, Survival & Victory. James E. Knight. LC 81-23151. (Illus.). 32p. (J). (gr. 5-9). 1982. pap. text ed. 3.50 (*0-89375-739-X*) Troll Communs.

Winter at Whitecliffs. large type ed. Miriam MacGregor. (Magna Romance Ser.). 301p. 1992. 25.99 (*0-7505-0411-0*) Ulverscroft.

Winter at Winslade. large type ed. Janis Coles. 256p. 1994. 25.99 (*0-7089-3130-8*) Ulverscroft.

Winter Away from Home: William Barents & the North-East Passage. Rayner Unwin. (Illus.). 263p. 1995. 24.95 (*0-924486-85-6*) Sheridan.

Winter Barn. Dorothy Ripley. LC 93-32420. (Pictureback Ser.). (Illus.). 32p. (Orig.). (J). (ps-1). 1995. pap. 3.25 (*0-679-84472-4*) Random Bks Yng Read.

Winter Beach. Terese Ramin. (Intimate Moments Ser.). 1993. mass mkt. 3.39 (*0-373-07477-8*, 5-07477-8) Silhouette.

Winter Bells: Sheet Music. Sylvia Woods. 4p. 1989. Sheet music. 3.95 (*0-936661-05-4*) Woods Mus Bks.

Winter Birds. Jim Grimsley. LC 94-10349. 224p. 1994. 18.95 (*1-56512-075-2*) Algonquin Bks.

Winter Birds. Jim Grimsley. 1997. pap. 11.00 (*0-684-82991-6*) S&S Trade.

Winter Blues: Seasonal Affective Disorder: What It Is & How to Overcome It. Norman E. Rosenthal. LC 93-30354. 325p. (Orig.). 1993. pap. 14.95 (*0-89862-149-6*) Guilford Pr.

Winter Book, Vol. 8. limited ed. Thomas Rose. (Illus.). 48p. 1995. 300.00 (*1-879832-10-0*) MN Ctr Book Arts.

Winter Book, Vol. 8. limited ed. Thomas Rose. (Illus.). 48p. 1995. pap. 90.00 (*1-879832-11-9*) MN Ctr Book Arts.

Winter Book, Vol. 8. limited ed. Thomas Rose. (Illus.). 48p. 1995. 900.00 (*1-879832-12-7*) MN Ctr Book Arts.

Winter Book of Switzerland. Ed. by Dore Ogrizek. (Illus.). 383p. 1957. 5.00 (*0-686-75372-0*) Bookfinger.

Winter Botany: An Identification Guide to Native & Cultivated Trees & Shrubs. William Trelease. (Illus.). 396p. 1967. pap. 9.95 (*0-486-21800-7*) Dover.

Winter Bride. Carola Salisbury. 1979. pap. 1.95 (*0-449-23838-5*, Crest) Fawcett.

***Winter Bride.** Teresa Southwick. 304p. mass mkt. 3.99 (*0-06-108527-8*) HarpC.

Winter Brothers: A Season at the Edge of America. Ivan Doig. LC 80-7933. (Illus.). 246p. 1982. pap. 10.00 (*0-15-697215-8*, Harvest Bks) HarBrace.

Winter Bulletin Boards. Imogene Forte. (Easy-To-Make-&-Use Ser.). (Illus.). 64p. (J). (gr. k-6). 1987. pap. text ed. 7.95 (*0-86530-168-9*, IP 112-9) Incentive Pubns.

Winter by Degrees. John Smolens. 224p. 1990. pap. 3.50 (*0-380-70943-0*) Avon.

Winter Camp. Kirkpatrick Hill. LC 92-41200. (Illus.). 192p. (J). (gr. 3-7). 1993. lib. bdg. 15.00 (*0-689-50588-4*, McElderry) S&S Childrens.

Winter Camp. Kirkpatrick Hill. LC 94-30014. 192p. (J). 1995. pap. 3.99 (*0-14-037076-5*) Puffin Bks.

Winter Camping. Bob Cary. LC 78-58680. (Environmental Sport Bk.). 1979. 10.95 (*0-8289-0339-5*) Viking Penguin.

Winter Channels. James Schevill. 56p. (Orig.). 1994. pap. 8.00 (*0-912449-49-7*) Floating Island.

Winter Chickens & Other Poems. Wendy Barker. LC 90-61425. (Poets Ser.). 55p. (Orig.). 1990. pap. 6.95 (*0-931722-84-5*) Corona Pub.

Winter Chill. large type ed. Jon Cleary. LC 96-16367. 1996. 24.95 (*1-56895-331-3*, Compass) Wheeler Pub.

Winter Chill: A Scobie Malone Mystery. Jon Cleary. 1996. 23.00 (*0-688-14311-3*) Morrow.

Winter Clip Art a la Carte. Compiled & Concept by Imogene Forte. (Illus.). 80p. (Orig.). 1990. pap. text ed. 8.95 (*0-86530-201-4*, IP 191-4) Incentive Pubns.

Winter College on Fundamental Nuclear Physics: Proceedings of the Winter College on Fundamental Nuclear Physics, Trieste, Italy, March 1984, 3 vols., Set. Ed. by K. Dietrich et al. 2008p. 1985. 293.00 (*9971-978-25-3*) World Scientific Pub.

***Winter Concert.** Yuko Taoka. LC 97-1425. (Illus.). 32p. (J). (gr. k-3). 1997. 13.90 (*0-7613-0301-4*) Millbrook Pr.

Winter Constellations. 3rd ed. Richard Blessing. Ed. by Dale Boyer. LC 77-72388. (Ahsahta Press Modern & Contemporary Poets of the West Ser.). 52p. 1977. pap. 6.95 (*0-916272-05-2*) Ahsahta Pr.

Winter Cooking with Herbs. Margaret Roberts. LC 94-9077. (Illus.). 96p. 1994. pap. 10.95 (*0-8117-3096-4*) Stackpole.

***Winter Count.** Barry Lopez. 1998. pap. write for info. (*0-679-78141-2*, Vin) Random.

Winter Count. Barry H. Lopez. 128p. 1982. mass mkt. 4.95 (*0-380-58107-8*, Bard) Avon.

Winter Count. Barry H. Lopez. 128p. 1993. pap. 8.00 (*0-380-71937-1*) Avon.

Winter Count. deluxe limited ed. Frederick Manfred. 1966. 100.00 (*0-911506-05-5*) Thueson.

Winter Count II Bk. I. Frederick Manfred. 1987. 40.00 (*0-911506-20-9*) Thueson.

***Winter Danger.** William O. Steele. (Illus.). 32p. (J). (ps-3). 1990. pap. 3.95 (*0-15-298037-7*) HarBrace.

Winter Danger. William O. Steele. LC 54-5157. (Illus.). 192p. (J). (gr. 3-7). 1990. reprint ed. pap. 3.95 (*0-685-51103-0*, HB Juv Bks) HarBrace.

Winter Day. Douglas Florian. LC 86-33524. (Illus.). 24p. (J). (ps-1). 1987. 16.00 (*0-688-07351-4*); lib. bdg. 15.93 (*0-688-07352-2*) Greenwillow.

Winter Day in Yosemite. Carl J. Sharsmith. (Illus.). 39p. 1981. pap. 2.95 (*0-939666-20-0*) Yosemite Assn.

Winter Days in the Big Woods. Laura Ingalls Wilder. LC 92-45883. (My First Little House Bks.). (Illus.). 40p. (J). (ps-3). 1994. 12.00 (*0-06-023014-2*); lib. bdg. 11.89 (*0-06-023022-3*) HarpC Child Bks.

Winter Days in the Big Woods. Laura Ingalls Wilder. LC 92-45883. (My First Little House Bks.). (Illus.). 32p. (J). (ps-3). 1995. pap. 4.95 (*0-06-443373-0*, Trophy) HarpC Child Bks.

Winter Days in the Big Woods. Laura Ingalls Wilder. (My First Little House Bks.). (Illus.). 32p. (J). (ps-3). 1996. pap. 3.25 (*0-694-00876-1*, Festival) HarpC Child Bks.

Winter Destiny. Grace Green. (Presents Ser.). 1993. pap. 2.89 (*0-373-11539-3*, 1-11539-3) Harlequin Bks.

***Winter Dialogue.** Tomas Venclova. LC 97-2613. 1997. 22.50 (*0-8101-1491-7*) Northwestern U Pr.

***Winter Dialogue.** Tomas Venclova. 1997. 22.00 (*0-614-28249-7*) Northwestern U Pr.

***Winter Diary: The Poetry of Bari Karoly.** Karoly Bari et al. LC 96-52221. 1997. write for info. (*1-56279-091-9*) Mercury Hse Inc.

Winter Doves: A Love Story. David Cook. LC 84-22678. 225p. 1983. 15.95 (*0-87951-994-0*) Overlook Pr.

Winter Doves: A Love Story. David Cook. LC 84-22678. 225p. 1985. pap. 8.95 (*0-87951-225-3*) Overlook Pr.

Winter Dreams. H. R. Coursen. Ed. by Napoleon St. Cyr. LC 82-4152. (Illus.). (Orig.). 1982. pap. 4.00 (*0-910380-04-X*) Cider Mill.

***Winter Dreams.** Trana M. Simmons. 288p. 1997. mass mkt. 5.99 (*0-515-12164-9*) Jove Pubns.

Winter Dreams & Other Such Friendly Dragons. Joseph J. Juknialis. LC 79-64821. (Illus.). 1979. pap. 7.95 (*0-89390-010-9*) Resource Pubns.

Winter Dreams, Christmas Love. Mary F. Shura. (J). 1993. pap. 3.50 (*0-685-66037-0*) Scholastic Inc.

Winter Dreams, Summer Balms. Joseph Opperman. (Illus.). 160p. 1995. pap. 15.95 (*1-879418-98-3*) Audenreed Pr.

Winter Ecology of Small Mammals. Ed. by Joseph F. Merritt. LC 84-72213. (Special Publications: No. 10). (Illus.). 390p. 1984. 47.50 (*0-935868-10-0*) Carnegie Mus.

Winter Eel. Norman Hindley. 1984. pap. 6.00 (*0-932136-06-0*) Petronium HI.

Winter Evening. Krishna B. Vaid. 100p. 1975. 4.80 (*0-88253-673-7*) Ind-US Inc.

Winter Eyes. Lev Raphael. 256p. 1993. pap. 8.95 (*0-312-10576-2*, Stonewall Inn) St Martin.

Winter Festivals. Nigel Wells. 80p. 8000. pap. 12.95 (*0-906427-18-5*, Pub. by Bloodaxe Bks UK) Dufour.

Winter Fire. Elizabeth Lowell. 400p. 1996. 20.00 (*0-380-97316-2*) Avon.

***Winter Fire.** Elizabeth Lowell. 1997. mass mkt. 6.99 (*0-380-77583-2*) Avon.

Winter Fire. William R. Trotter. 464p. 1994. 4.99 (*0-451-17718-5*, Sig) NAL-Dutton.

***Winter Fire.** large type ed. Elizabeth Lowell. LC 96-46334. (Americana Ser.). 622p. 1997. lib. bdg. 27.95 (*0-7862-0946-1*) Thorndike Pr.

***Winter, Fire & Snow: A Charleston Christmas Storybook.** Bruce Smith. (Illus.). 120p. (Orig.). (J). (gr. 2 up). 1997. pap. 12.95 (*0-9642620-3-7*) Marsh Wind Pr.

Winter Five Seasonal Cookbook. John W. Garvy, Jr. Ed. by Jeremiah Liebermann. (Five Phase Cookbook Ser.: No. 1). (Illus.). 1985. pap. 6.00 (*0-943450-19-5*) Wellbeing Bks.

Winter Friends: Women Growing Old in the New Republic, 1785-1835. Terri L. Premo. LC 89-4980. (Women in American History Ser.). (Illus.). 216p. 1990. text ed. 24.95 (*0-252-01656-4*) U of Ill Pr.

Winter Frolic. 72p. (Orig.). 1994. pap. 9.95 (*0-89724-312-9*, VF2141) Warner Brothers.

Winter Fruit: English Drama, 1642-1660. Dale B. Randall. LC 95-7634. (Illus.). 472p. 1995. 39.95 (*0-8131-1925-1*) U Pr of Ky.

Winter Fun. Rita Schlachter. LC 85-14008. (Illus.). 48p. (Orig.). (J). (gr. 1-3). 1997. pap. 3.50 (*0-8167-0585-2*) Troll Communs.

Winter Fun: A Book Full of Things to Do in Cold Weather. Owl Magazine Editors. (Illus.). 128p. (J). (gr. 3 up). 1992. pap. 9.95 (*0-919872-86-7*, Pub. by Greey dePencier CN) Firefly Bks Ltd.

***Winter Fun in Northern California & Nevada: A Guide to All the Major Trailheads in Northern California & Nevada for Snowshoeing, Nordic Skiing, Snowmobiling & Alpine Skiing, Snowboarding, Skating, Sledding & Play.** Bern Kreissman. LC 96-86489. (Bear Klaw Press Environmental Guide Ser.: No. 3). (Illus.). 176p. (Orig.). 1997. pap. 14.95 (*0-9627489-7-8*) Bear Klaw Pr.

Winter Games. Roger Pare. (Illus.). 24p. (J). 1991. pap. 4.95 (*1-55037-184-3*, Pub. by Annick CN); lib. bdg. 14.95 (*1-55037-187-8*, Pub. by Annick CN) Firefly Bks Ltd.

Winter Games: A Mystery. John Feinstein. 288p. 1995. 21.95 (*0-316-27721-5*) Little.

Winter Garden. Ed. by Erica Glasener. (Plants & Gardens Ser.). (Illus.). 1991. per. 7.95 (*0-945352-69-7*) Bklyn Botanic.

Winter Garden. Bro Halff. 146p. 1992. pap. 12.95 (*1-885238-08-8*) Simpler Gifts.

Winter Garden. Bro Halff. 146p. 1992. 24.95 (*1-885238-09-6*) Simpler Gifts.

***Winter Garden.** Peter H. Loewer. (Illus.). 224p. 1997. pap. 39.95 (*0-8117-2987-7*) Stackpole.

Winter Garden. Pablo Neruda. Tr. by William O'Daly from SPA. LC 86-71837. 80p. (Orig.). 1986. 15.00 (*0-914742-99-X*); pap. 9.00 (*0-914742-93-0*) Copper Canyon.

***Winter Garden.** Price. 1996. 16.98 (*0-8317-6266-7*) Smithmark.

***Winter Garden: Planning & Planting for the Southeast.** Peter H. Loewer & Larry Mellichamp. LC 97-8311. 1997. write for info. (*0-8117-1925-1*) Stackpole.

Winter Garden Glory. Adrian Bloom. 144p. 1994. 25.00 (*0-00-412892-3*, Pub. by HarpC UK) HarpC.

Winter Garden Mystery. large type ed. Carola Dunn. 326p. 1995. 23.95 (*0-7838-1487-9*, GK Hall) Thorndike Pr.

Winter Gardening in the Maritime Northwest: Cool Season Crops for the Year-Round Gardener. 2nd rev. ed. Binda Colebrook. (Illus.). 170p. (Orig.). 1984. pap. 10.95 (*0-916239-00-4*) Maritime Pubns.

Winter Gardening in the Maritime Northwest: Cool-Season Crops for the Year-Round Gardener. 3rd ed. Binda Colebrook. LC 89-6046. (Illus.). 176p. 1989. pap. 10.95 (*0-912365-21-8*) Sasquatch Bks.

***Winter Gardens.** (Taylor's Weekend Gardening Guide Ser.). 1997. pap. 12.95 (*0-614-27240-8*) HM.

***Winter Gifts.** Rylant. (Cobble Street Cousins Ser.). (J). Date not set. mass mkt. 4.50 (*0-689-81715-0*) S&S Childrens.

***Winter Grace: Spirituality & Aging.** Kathleen R. Fischer. LC 97-26908. 1998. write for info. (*0-8358-0850-5*) Upper Room Bks.

Winter Grief, Summer Grace: Returning to Life after a Loved One Dies. James E. Miller. LC 95-22489. 64p. 1995. pap. 14.99 (*0-8066-2833-2*) Augsburg Fortress.

Winter Habitat Relationships of Merriam's Turkeys along the Mogollon Rim, Arizona. B. F. Wakeling & T. D. Rogers. (Arizona Game & Fish Department Technical Report Ser.: No. 16). (Illus.). 41p. (Orig.). 1995. pap. 5.00 (*0-917563-22-0*) AZ Game & Fish.

***Winter Hare.** Freeman. (J). 1998. pap. 4.95 (*0-7868-1242-7*) Hyprn Child.

Winter Hare. Joan E. Goodman. (Illus.). 240p. (J). (gr. 5-9). 1996. 15.95 (*0-395-78569-3*) HM.

Winter Harvest. Rosemary Gill. (Rainbow Romances Ser.). 160p. 1993. 14.95 (*0-7090-4952-8*, Hale-Parkwest) Parkwest Pubns.

Winter Harvest. large type ed. Rosemary Gill. (Dales Large Print Ser.). 199p. 1995. pap. 17.99 (*1-85389-546-6*, Dales) Ulverscroft.

Winter Harvest. large type ed. Joanna Logan. 1991. pap. 15.99 (*0-7089-6980-1*) Ulverscroft.

Winter Harvest: A Retrospective Verses. John Steadman. LC 96-3095. 48p. 1997. pap. 12.95 (*0-7734-2698-1*, Mellen Poetry Pr) E Mellen.

Winter Hawk. Craig Thomas. 1988. mass mkt. 4.95 (*0-380-70389-0*) Avon.

Winter Heart. Jane Bonander. 303p. 1996. mass mkt. 5.99 (*0-671-52982-X*, PB Trade Paper) PB.

***Winter Hearts.** Maureen McKade. 1997. mass mkt. 5.50 (*0-380-78871-3*) Avon.

***Winter Helen Dropped By.** Ed. by W. P. Kinsella. Date not set. write for info. (*0-00-648118-3*, Pub. by HarpC CN) HarpC.

Winter Hero. James L. Collier & Christopher Collier. 132p. (YA). (gr. 9 up). 1985. pap. 3.50 (*0-590-42604-4*) Scholastic Inc.

Winter Holding Spring. Crescent Dragonwagon. LC 88-13747. (Illus.). 32p. (J). (gr. 2-5). 1990. lib. bdg. 14.00 (*0-02-733122-9*, Mac Bks Young Read) S&S Childrens.

Winter Holiday. Arthur Ransome. LC 86-46286. (Swallows & Amazons Ser.: Vol. 4). (Illus.). 352p. (J). (gr. 5-8). 1996. reprint ed. pap. 14.95 (*0-87923-661-2*) Godine.

Winter House: Poems. Robert Gibb. LC 83-16841. (Breakthrough Ser.: No. 43). 80p. 1984. pap. 12.95 (*0-8262-0437-6*) U of Mo Pr.

Winter Hunger. Ann Tracy. 165p. 1990. pap. 10.95 (*0-86492-126-8*, Pub. by Goose Ln Edits CN) Genl Dist Srvs.

Winter Hunt. Henry Tall Bull & Tom Weist. (Indian Culture Ser.). 32p. (J). (gr. 3-9). 1971. pap. 4.95 (*0-89992-006-3*) Coun India Ed.

Winter Idea Book: A Creative Idea Book for the Elementary Teacher, Ps-6. Karen Sevaly & Margaret Bolz. (Illus.). 112p. (Orig.). 1990. pap. 9.95 (*0-943263-15-8*, TF 1602) Teachers Friend Pubns.

W

Winter in Arabia. Freya Stark. LC 86-31222. 336p. 1987. 18.95 (*0-87951-278-4*) Overlook Pr.

***Winter in Eden: Poems by Robert Schultz.** Robert Schultz. 53p. 1997. 22.00 (*0-931209-67-6*, Loess Hills Bks) Mid-Prairie Bks.

***Winter in Eden: Poems by Robert Schultz.** Robert Schultz. 53p. 1997. pap. 12.00 (*0-931209-68-4*, Loess Hills Bks) Mid-Prairie Bks.

Winter in Florida. Edward Falco. LC 89-49206. 300p. 1990. 18.95 (*0-939149-40-0*) Soho Press.

Winter in His Garden: Essays of Faith & Family. Alene A. Roy. LC 94-69070. (In His Gardens Ser.: Bk. 2). (Illus.). 116p. (Orig.). 1995. pap. 7.95 (*0-9635069-1-9*) Closer Walk.

Winter in July. large type ed. Essie Summers. 1991. 25.99 (*0-7089-2561-8*) Ulverscroft.

Winter in July: Visits with Children's Authors Down Under. Janet C. Barley. LC 94-33216. 227p. (YA). 1995. 29.50 (*0-8108-2945-2*) Scarecrow.

Winter in Majorca. George Sand, pseud. Tr. by Robert Graves from FRE. (Illus.). 200p. 1992. reprint ed. pap. 11.00 (*0-915864-68-1*) Academy Chi Pubs.

Winter in Moscow. Thomas M. Muggeridge. LC 87-9170. 270p. reprint ed. pap. 77.00 (*0-7837-3170-1*, 2042808) Bks Demand.

***Winter in Paradise Square.** A. R. Davey. 601p. 1997. pap. 10.95 (*0-340-66602-1*, Pub. by H & S UK) Trafalgar.

Winter in Russia. Theophile Gautier. Tr. by M. M. Ripley. 1977. lib. bdg. 59.95 (*0-8490-2827-2*) Gordon Pr.

Winter in Taos. Mabel D. Luhan. (Illus.). 264p. 1983. reprint ed. 18.95 (*0-911695-50-8*) Las Palomas.

Winter in the Blood. James Welch. (Contemporary American Fiction Ser.). 192p. 1986. pap. 11.95 (*0-14-008644-7*, Penguin Bks) Viking Penguin.

Winter in the Heart. David C. Poyer. Date not set. 4.98 (*0-8317-4649-1*) Smithmark.

Winter in the Heart. David C. Poyer. 416p. 1994. mass mkt. 5.99 (*0-8125-2298-2*) Tor Bks.

Winter in the Morning: A Young Girl's Life in the Warsaw Ghetto, 1939-1945. Janina Bauman. 256p. 1986. 27.95 (*0-02-902530-3*, Free Press) Free Pr.

Winter in the Sun. Bill Robinson. (Illus.). 180p. 1995. pap. 17.95 (*0-924486-69-4*) Sheridan.

Winter in the West. Charles F. Hoffman. (Notable American Authors Ser.). 1992. reprint ed. lib. bdg. 150.00 (*0-7812-3131-0*) Rprt Serv.

Winter in the West, 2 vols., Set. Charles F. Hoffman. LC 70-108493. 1970. reprint ed. 49.00 (*0-403-00215-X*) Scholarly.

Winter in the West, 2 vols., Set. Charles F. Hoffman. (BCL1 - United States Local History Ser.). 1991. reprint ed. lib. bdg. 150.00 (*0-7812-6316-6*) Rprt Serv.

Winter in the West Indies, Described in Familiar Letters to Henry Clay, of Kentucky. 2nd ed. Joseph J. Gurney. LC 69-19356. (Illus.). 282p. 1969. reprint ed. text ed. 35.00 (*0-8371-1022-X*, GUW&, Greenwood Pr) Greenwood.

Winter in the Wood. Janet Fitzgerald. (Science Through the Seasons Ser.). (Illus.). 32p. (J). (gr. 1-3). 1991. 15.95 (*0-237-60215-6*, Pub. by Evans Bros Ltd UK) Trafalgar.

Winter in the Woods. W. S. Doxey. (Illus.). pap. 3.00 (*0-686-12232-1*) Doxey.

Winter in the Woods. W. S. Doxey. 1975. 4.00 (*0-685-67936-5*) Windless Orchard.

Winter in Thrush Green. Read. (J). 21.95 (*0-8488-1456-8*) Amereon Ltd.

Winter in Thrush Green. Miss Read. 1982. reprint ed. lib. bdg. 21.95 (*0-89966-436-9*) Buccaneer Bks.

Winter Insomnia. Joseph Powell. 1993. 19.95 (*0-934847-15-0*); pap. 9.95 (*0-934847-16-9*) Arrowood Bks.

Winter Into Summer: Lapland Diary, 1945-46. Naomi J. Groves. 144p. 1989. pap. 14.95 (*0-920806-93-7*, Pub. by Penumbra Pr CN) U of Toronto Pr.

Winter Is Not Forever. large type ed. Janette Oke. LC 88-2882. (Seasons of Heart Ser.: No. 3). 224p. 1988. pap. 8.99 (*1-55661-002-5*) Bethany Hse.

Winter Is Not Forever. large type ed. Janette Oke. LC 88-2882. (Seasons of Heart Ser.: No. 3). 224p. 1988. pap. 10.99 (*1-55661-008-4*) Bethany Hse.

Winter Is Past: A True Love Story Which Burst the Bounds of the Cloister. Helen Weston. 160p. 1995. pap. 7.95 (*0-687-85003-7*, Pub. by Society Promot Chrst Know UK) Abingdon.

Winter Is Wonderful. Lisa Blau. (Reader's Theatre Resource Bks.). 88p. 1994. teacher ed. 10.95 (*0-9640333-2-1*) One Heart Educ.

Winter Jasmine. large type ed. Doris Howe. 1991. 25.99 (*0-7089-2366-6*) Ulverscroft.

Winter Journey. T. Alan Broughton. 320p. 1981. pap. 2.95 (*0-449-24369-9*, Crest) Fawcett.

Winter Journey. Ronald Frame. 176p. 1986. 13.95 (*0-317-39741-9*) Beaufort Bks NY.

Winter Journey. Georges Perec. Tr. & Pref. by John Sturrock. (Syrens Ser.). 32p. 1996. pap. 3.95 (*0-14-038912-1*) Penguin.

Winter Journeys. John Greening. (C). 1988. 35.00 (*0-904524-52-3*, Pub. by Rivelin Grapheme Pr) St Mut.

Winter Keys to Woody Plants of Maine. rev. ed. Christopher S. Campbell & Fay Hyland. LC 74-30438. (Illus.). 1978. pap. 14.95 (*0-89101-034-3*) U Maine Pr.

Winter Kill. James A. Janke. 1994. 17.95 (*0-8034-9038-0*) Bouregy.

***Winter Kill.** Dodge Tyler. (Dan'l Boone Ser.: No. 4). 320p. (Orig.). 1996. mass mkt. 4.99 (*0-8439-4087-5*, Leisure Bks) Dorchester Pub Co.

Winter Kills. large type ed. Richard Condon. 419p. 1982. 27.99 (*0-7089-8030-9*) Ulverscroft.

***Winter King.** Cornwell. 1997. pap. 14.95 (*0-312-15696-0*) St Martin.

Winter King. large type ed. Bernard Cornwell. 664p. 1996. 26.95 (*0-7862-0729-9*, Thorndike Lrg Prnt) Thorndike Pr.

Winter Kiss. Collum & Linton. 352p. 1997. mass mkt. 4.99 (*0-8217-5546-3*, Zebra Kensgtn) Kensgtn Pub Corp.

Winter Lady. Janet Joyce. (Men Made in America Ser.). 1994. mass mkt. 3.59 (*0-373-45173-3*, 1-45173-1) Harlequin Bks.

Winter Landscapes. Mannie Gonsalves. (How to Draw & Paint Ser.). (Illus.). 32p. (Orig.). 1989. pap. 6.95 (*1-56010-040-0*, HT126) W Foster Pub.

Winter Legacy. Vella Munn. 320p. 1992. mass mkt. 3.99 (*0-8217-3841-0*, Zebra Kensgtn) Kensgtn Pub Corp.

Winter Light. Maria M. Gillan. LC 85-22364. 72p. (Orig.). 1985. pap. 5.95 (*0-941608-05-0*) Chantry Pr.

Winter Light. Snyder Kirtland. (Illus.). 44p. (Orig.). 1987. pap. 14.75 (*0-911623-05-1*) I Klang.

Winter Light: Poems by a Single Publication. Virginia D. Harding. 46p. (Orig.). 1993. pap. 6.95 (*0-9636938-3-2*) Tall Tree Pr.

Winter Lights. Jan McDaniel. LC 95-96215. 192p. 1996. 17.95 (*0-8034-9162-X*, Avalon Bks) Bouregy.

Winter Longing. Christina Cordaire. 288p. (Orig.). 1996. mass mkt. 5.50 (*0-515-11811-7*) Jove Pubns.

Winter Love. Norah Hess. 448p. (Orig.). 1995. mass mkt., pap. text ed. 5.99 (*0-8439-3864-1*) Dorchester Pub Co.

Winter Love Story. Jane C. Miner. 256p. (YA). (gr. 7-9). 1993. pap. 3.50 (*0-590-47610-6*) Scholastic Inc.

Winter Love, Winter Wishes. Jane C. Miner. 352p. (YA). (gr. 7-9). 1994. pap. 3.95 (*0-590-48152-5*) Scholastic Inc.

***Winter Magic.** large type ed. Jennifer Hyde. (Dales Library). 240p. 1996. pap. 17.99 (*1-85389-591-1*, Dales) Ulverscroft.

Winter Maintenance, Roadside Management, & Rating Routine Maintenance Activities. (Transportation Research Record Ser.: No. 1246). 64p. 1989. 12.00 (*0-309-05003-0*) Transport Res Bd.

Winter Man. Denise Vitola. 336p. (Orig.). 1995. mass mkt. 5.50 (*0-425-15055-0*) Berkley Pub.

Winter Mittens. Tim Arnold. LC 88-2736. (Illus.). 32p. (J). (gr. 3-6). 1988. lib. bdg. 13.95 (*0-689-50449-7*, McElderry) S&S Childrens.

***Winter Money: Stories by Andy Plattner.** Andy Plattner. LC 97-12248. (Flannery O'Connor Award for Short Fiction Ser.). 184p. 1997. 22.95 (*0-8203-1958-9*) U of Ga Pr.

***Winter Moon.** Dean R. Koontz. (Orig.). 1997. pap. write for info. (*0-345-41949-9*) Ballantine.

Winter Moon. Dean R. Koontz. 1994. mass mkt. 6.99 (*0-345-38610-8*) Ballantine.

Winter Moon. large type ed. LC 94-14521. (Orig.). 1995. lib. bdg. 18.95 (*0-7862-0251-3*) Thorndike Pr.

Winter Moon. large type ed. Dean R. Koontz. LC 94-14521. 552p. (Orig.). 1994. lib. bdg. 23.95 (*0-7862-0250-5*) Thorndike Pr.

***Winter Morning with Crow.** Clare Rossini. LC 97-15080. (Akron Series in Poetry). 1997. write for info. (*1-884836-30-5*); pap. write for info. (*1-884836-31-3*) U Akron Pr.

Winter Murder Case: A Philo Vance Story. S. S. Van Dine. 196p. 1993. pap. 6.95 (*1-883402-08-5*) S&S Trade.

***Winter Music.** Sarah Kirsch & Margitt Lehbert. 112p. 1994. pap. 17.95 (*0-85646-234-9*, Pub. by Anvil Press UK) Dufour.

Winter Music: A Life of Jessica Powers. Dolores Leckey. LC 92-27486. 180p. (Orig.). 1992. pap. 12.95 (*1-55612-559-3*, LL1559) Sheed & Ward MO.

Winter Myths. fac. ed. Cora Dubois & Dorothy Demetracopoulou. (University of California Publications in American Archaeology & Ethnology: Vol. 28: 5). 127p. (C). 1931. reprint ed. pap. text ed. 11.25 (*1-55567-278-7*) Coyote Press.

Winter Nest: A Poetry Anthology of Midwestern Women Poets of Color. Ed. by Angela Lobo-Cobb. (Poetics of Colors Ser.). 110p. (Orig.). 1987. pap. text ed. 5.00 (*0-916783-05-7*) Blue Reed.

***Winter Night: Selected Poems of Attila Jozsef.** Tr. by John Batki. LC 97-66615. (Field Translation Ser.: Vol. 23). 150p. (Orig.). 1997. pap. 14.95 (*0-932440-78-9*) Oberlin Coll Pr.

Winter Nights Entertainments see Easy-to-Do Entertainments & Diversions with Cards, String, Coins, Paper & Matches

Winter '93-'94 Child Class Schedule. 1994. pap. write for info. (*0-517-11301-5*) Random.

***Winter Notes on Summer Impressions.** Fyodor Dostoesvky. LC 97-15114. 1997. pap. text ed. 14.95 (*0-8101-1518-2*) Northwestern U Pr.

Winter Notes on Summer Impressions. Fyodor Dostoyevsky. Tr. by David Patterson. 78p. 1988. 24.95 (*0-8101-0813-5*); pap. 10.95 (*0-8101-0814-3*) Northwestern U Pr.

Winter Numbers: Poems. Marilyn Hacker. LC 94-18615. 1994. 17.95 (*0-393-03674-X*) Norton.

Winter Numbers: Poems. Marilyn Hacker. 96p. 1995. pap. 10.00 (*0-393-31373-5*, Norton Paperbks) Norton.

Winter of Artifice. Anais Nin. LC 61-17530. 175p. (Orig.). 1961. pap. 8.95 (*0-8040-0322-X*) Swallow.

Winter of Discontent: The Nuclear Freeze & American Politics. David S. Meyer. LC 89-26588. 320p. 1990. text ed. 59.95 (*0-275-93305-9*, C3305, Praeger Pubs); pap. text ed. 18.95 (*0-275-93306-7*, B3306, Praeger Pubs) Greenwood.

Winter of Dreams. large type ed. Susan Napier. 1993. reprint ed. lib. bdg. 18.95 (*0-263-13199-8*, Pub. by Mills & Boon UK) Thorndike Pr.

Winter of Entrapment: A New Look at the Donner Party. Joseph A. King. (Illus.). 278p. 1992. 22.95 (*0-88835-030-9*); pap. 14.95 (*0-88835-032-5*) P D Meany.

Winter of Entrapment: A New Look at the Donner Party. 2nd rev. ed. Joeseph A. King. (Illus.). 265p. 1995. pap. 13.95 (*0-9608500-4-X*) K & K Pubns.

Winter of Entrapment: A New Look at the Donner Party. 2nd rev. ed. Joseph A. King. (Illus.). 265p. 1995. 19.95 (*0-9608500-6-6*) K & K Pubns.

Winter of Frozen Dreams. Karl Harter. (Illus.). 352p. 1992. reprint ed. mass mkt. 4.99 (*1-55817-646-2*, Pinncle Kensgtn) Kensgtn Pub Corp.

Winter of Our Discontent. John Steinbeck. 320p. 1982. pap. 6.95 (*0-14-006221-1*, Penguin Bks) Viking Penguin.

Winter of Our Discontent. John Steinbeck. 288p. 1996. pap. 9.95 (*0-14-018753-7*, Penguin Classics) Viking Penguin.

Winter of Our Discount Tent: A Humorous Look at Flora, Fauna, & Foolishness Outdoors. Jim Mize. LC 94-18752. (Illus.). 140p. 1995. 19.95 (*1-57003-049-9*) U of SC Pr.

Winter of Red Snow: The Revolutionary War Diary of Abigail Jane Stewart, Valley Forge, Pennsylvania, 1777. Kristiana Gregory. LC 95-44052. (Dear America Ser.: Vol. 2). 176p. (J). (gr. 4-9). 1996. 9.95 (*0-590-22653-3*) Scholastic Inc.

Winter of the Blue Snow. Robert Kammen. 288p. 1988. mass mkt. 3.50 (*0-8217-2432-0*, Zebra Kensgtn) Kensgtn Pub Corp.

Winter of the Holy Iron. Joseph Marshall, III. (Illus.). 304p. 1994. 19.95 (*1-878610-44-9*) Red Crane Bks.

Winter of the Raven. Janice K. Johnson. 384p. 1995. 22.95 (*0-312-85491-9*) Tor Bks.

Winter of the Soul: Gay Vampire Fiction. Gary Bowen. 32p. 1995. pap. 5.00 (*1-887666-06-0*) Obelesk Bks.

Winter of the Wildcat. large type ed. Bill Gaston. 1990. 25.99 (*0-7089-2136-1*) Ulverscroft.

Winter of the Wolf. Jory Sherman. 160p. 1989. mass mkt. 3.99 (*0-8125-8871-1*) Tor Bks.

Winter of the Wolf. Jory Sherman. 1987. 15.95 (*0-8027-4071-5*) Walker & Co.

Winter of the World. Poul Anderson. 256p. 1995. mass mkt. 4.99 (*0-8125-2311-3*) Tor Bks.

Winter of 1917. David Campton. 31p. 1990. pap. 3.00 (*0-87129-028-6*, W69) Dramatic Pub.

Winter Offering: Selected Poems, 1934-53. D. S. Savage. 60p. (C). 1989. 50.00 (*0-907839-51-7*, Pub. by Brynmill Pr Ltd UK) St Mut.

***Winter Olympic Made Simple: A Guide for Spectators & Television Viewers.** 2nd rev. ed. Dan Bartges. (Illus.). 160p. 1997. pap. 9.95 (*1-57028-141-6*) Masters Pr IN.

***Winter Olympics.** Larry D. Brimner. LC 97-2272. (True Book Ser.). (J). 1997. write for info. (*0-516-20456-4*) Childrens.

Winter Olympics. Jack C. Harris. (Great Moments in Sports Ser.). 32p. (J). (gr. 4). 1990. lib. bdg. 14.95 (*0-88682-317-X*) Creative Ed.

Winter on Fire Island. Arthur Hawkins. (Illus.). 64p. (Orig.). 1994. pap. 14.95 (*0-9628881-2-5*) KYX Pr.

Winter on Spain's Costa del Sol: A Traveler's Preview. Kit Lane & Art Lane. LC 90-62946. (Illus.). (Orig.). 1990. pap. 5.95 (*1-877703-12-5*) Pavilion Pr.

Winter on the Farm. Janet Fitzgerald. (Science Through the Seasons Ser.). (Illus.). 32p. (J). (gr. 1-3). 1991. 15.95 (*0-237-60219-9*, Pub. by Evans Bros Ltd UK) Trafalgar.

***Winter on the Farm.** Laura I. Wilder. LC 95-35722. (My First Little House Bks.). (Illus.). 32p. (J). (ps-3). 1997. 3.25 (*0-694-00950-4*, Festival) HarpC Child Bks.

Winter on the Farm. Laura Ingalls Wilder. LC 95-35722. (My First Little House Bks.). (Illus.). 40p. (J). (ps-3). 1996. 11.95 (*0-06-027169-8*); lib. bdg. 11.89 (*0-06-027170-1*) HarpC Child Bks.

***Winter on the Farm.** Laura Ingalls Wilder. (My First Little House Bks.). (J). 1997. pap. 4.95 (*0-06-440692-X*) HarpC Child Bks.

Winter Ornamentals. Dan Hinkley. (Cascadia Gardening Ser.). (Illus.). 96p. (Orig.). 1993. pap. 9.95 (*0-912365-87-0*) Sasquatch Bks.

Winter Palace. T. Davis Bunn. (Priceless Collection: No. 3). 352p. (Orig.). 1993. pap. 9.99 (*1-55661-324-5*) Bethany Hse.

Winter Palace. Dennis Jones. 352p. 1988. 17.95 (*0-316-47295-6*) Little.

***Winter Park.** Tracy Salcedo. (Twelve Short Hikes Ser.). (Illus.). 32p. 1997. pap. 4.95 (*1-57540-104-5*) Chockstone Pr.

Winter Park - Central City - Rollins Pass, CO. rev. ed. Ed. by Trails Illustrated Staff. (Illus.). 1993. 8.99 (*0-925873-24-1*) Trails Illustrated.

Winter Park - Grand Lake Mountain Bike Map, CO. rev. ed. Ed. by Trails Illustrated Staff. (Illus.). 1994. 6.99 (*0-925873-89-6*) Trails Illustrated.

Winter Pascha. Thomas Hopko. LC 84-27622. 183p. 1983. pap. text ed. 9.95 (*0-88141-025-X*) St Vladimirs.

Winter People. Gilbert Phelps. 1993. reprint ed. lib. bdg. 18.95 (*0-89968-410-6*, Lghtyr Pr) Buccaneer Bks.

Winter Photographs: A Postcard Folio Book. Ansel Adams. (Illus.). 64p. 1994. 9.95 (*0-8212-2135-3*) Bulfinch Pr.

Winter Pick-a-Project. Linda Milliken. (Illus.). 52p. (J). (gr. 1-5). 1989. student ed., pap. 5.95 (*1-56472-031-4*) Edupress.

Winter Place. Genny Lim. 1989. pap. 8.00 (*0-9609630-4-9*) Kearny St Wkshop.

***Winter Playgrounds: Skiing As a Way of Life.** Eric Hanson. LC 96-53180. 1997. write for info. (*0-8212-2268-6*) Little.

***Winter Pleasures: Preserving & Cooking Herbs.** Noel Richardson. (Illus.). 144p. 9.95 (*1-895099-25-0*) Gr Arts Ctr Pub.

Winter Poems. Illus. by Trina S. Hyman. 40p. (J). (gr. 2 up). 1994. 15.95 (*0-590-42872-1*, Scholastic Hardcover) Scholastic Inc.

Winter Pollen. Ted Hughes. 1996. pap. 18.00 (*0-312-14766-X*) St Martin.

Winter Pollen: Occasional Prose. Ted Hughes. 1995. 27.50 (*0-312-13625-0*, Picador USA) St Martin.

Winter Pollen: Occasional Prose. Ted Hughes. Ed. by William Scammell. 1996. 27.50 (*0-614-12884-6*, Picador USA) St Martin.

Winter Prairie Woman. 2nd ed. Meridel Le Sueur. LC 91-60707. (Illus.). 31p. 1990. reprint ed. pap. 6.00 (*0-935697-05-5*) Midwest Villages.

Winter Prey. 5.98 (*0-8317-5336-6*) Smithmark.

Winter Prey. John Sandford. 352p. 1994. mass mkt. 6.99 (*0-425-14123-3*) Berkley Pub.

Winter Prey. large type ed. John Sandford. LC 93-8649. 1993. lib. bdg. 24.95 (*0-8161-5832-0*, GK Hall) Thorndike Pr.

Winter Prey. large type ed. John Sandford. LC 93-8649. 1994. lib. bdg. 18.95 (*0-8161-5833-9*, GK Hall) Thorndike Pr.

Winter Prince. Elizabeth Wein. LC 91-39129. 208p. (YA). (gr. 7 up). 1993. lib. bdg. 14.95 (*0-689-31747-6*, Atheneum Bks Young) S&S Childrens.

Winter Prince. Elizabeth Wein. 216p. 1994. reprint ed. mass mkt. 4.99 (*0-671-87621-X*) Baen Bks.

Winter Quarters: A Novel of Argentina. Osvaldo Soriano. Tr. by Nick Caistor from SPA. LC 89-61873. (Readers International Ser.). 192p. (Orig.). 1989. 17.95 (*0-930523-69-5*); pap. 9.95 (*0-930523-70-9*) Readers Intl.

Winter Quarters: The 1846-1848 Life Writings of Mary Haskin Parker Richards. Ed. by Maurine C. Ward. (Life Writings of Frontier Women: Vol. 1). (Illus.). 352p. 1996. 29.95 (*0-87421-207-3*) Utah St U Pr.

Winter Rabbit. Patrick Yee. (Illus.). 32p. (J). (ps-1). 1996. pap. 5.99 (*0-14-055535-8*) Puffin Bks.

Winter Rain. Terry C. Johnston. 560p. 1994. mass mkt. 6.50 (*0-553-56770-5*) Bantam.

Winter Reckoning. Noel-Anne Brennan. (Illus.). 1986. 30.00 (*0-937986-85-2*) D M Grant.

***Winter Rescue.** Paul Hutchens. (Sugar Creek Gang Ser.: No. 3). 112p. (J). 1997. mass mkt. 4.99 (*0-8024-7007-6*) Moody.

Winter Rescue. W. D. Valgardson. LC 94-48339. (Illus.). (J). (gr. 2-4). 1995. 15.00 (*0-689-80094-0*, McElderry) S&S Childrens.

Winter Return: A Novel. John Espey. LC 91-47953. 176p. 1992. 18.95 (*0-936784-97-0*) J Daniel.

Winter Return: A Novel. John Espey. 176p. 1993. pap. 10.00 (*1-880284-03-0*) J Daniel.

Winter Rider. Berry Fleming. LC 89-62521. 173p. 1990. reprint ed. 22.00 (*0-933256-76-0*) Second Chance.

Winter Roads, Summer Fields. Marjorie Dorner. LC 91-13673. 208p. 1992. pap. 11.95 (*0-915943-86-7*) Milkweed Ed.

Winter Room. Gary Paulsen. 112p. (J). (gr. 4-7). 1997. pap. 4.50 (*0-440-40454-1*) BDD Bks Young Read.

Winter Room. Gary Paulsen. LC 89-42541. 128p. (J). (gr. 6-9). 1989. 15.95 (*0-531-05839-5*); lib. bdg. 16.99 (*0-531-08439-6*) Orchard Bks Watts.

Winter Rooms. Danny L. Rendleman. LC 75-315873. 65p. 1975. 3.50 (*0-87886-061-4*, Greenfld Rev Pr) Greenfld Rev Lit.

Winter Rose. Patricia A. McKillip. LC 95-39317. 272p. 1996. 19.95 (*0-441-00334-6*) Ace Bks.

***Winter Rose.** Patricia A. McKillip. 272p. 1997. mass mkt. 5.99 (*0-441-00438-5*) Ace Bks.

Winter Rose. Mark A. Webb. (Book of Carolyn Ser.: Vol. 1). 216p. 1993. pap. 8.95 (*1-883471-01-X*) Brandenburg.

***Winter Rose.** Linda Windsor. 384p. 1997. mass mkt. 4.99 (*0-8217-5808-X*, Zebra Kensgtn) Kensgtn Pub Corp.

Winter Roses. Danielle Trent, pseud. 384p. 1996. reprint ed. mass mkt. 4.99 (*0-505-52075-3*) Dorchester Pub Co.

***Winter Rules: A Commonplace Book.** George G. Herrick. LC 97-10567. 142p. 1997. pap. 24.95 (*1-57309-167-7*) Intl Scholars.

***Winter Rules: A Commonplace Book.** George G. Herrick. LC 97-10567. 142p. 1997. 49.95 (*1-57309-168-5*) Intl Scholars.

Winter Safety Handbook. Ed. by Nord World Staff. 1975. pap. 2.95 (*0-02-499880-X*, Macmillan Coll) P-H.

Winter Science Projects. John Williams. LC 96-17638. (Seasonal Science Projects Ser.). (J). 1996. pap. 5.95 (*0-382-39706-1*, Julian Messner); lib. bdg. 11.95 (*0-382-39705-3*, Julian Messner) Silver Burdett Pr.

***Winter Seasons.** Sylvie F. Sommerfield. 400p. (Orig.). 1996. mass mkt. 5.99 (*0-8439-4242-8*) Dorchester Pub Co.

Winter Simulation Conference Proceedings: Washington, DC, 1989. Ed. by Edward A. MacNair et al. 1140p. 1989. 130.00 (*0-911801-58-8*, WSC-89) Soc Computer Sim.

Winter Simulation Conference Proceedings, 1994. IEEE (Computer Society, Systems, Man & Cybernetics Society) Staff. Ed. by IEEE (Institute of Electrical & Electronics Engineers, Inc.) Staff. LC 87-654182. 1994. pap. text ed. write for info. (*0-7803-2108-1*) Inst Electrical.

Winter Sisters. large type ed. Suzanne Goodwin. 430p. 1982. 25.99 (*0-7089-0778-4*) Ulverscroft.

Winter Sky. Chongju So. Tr. by McCann. (QRL Poetry Bks.: Vol. XXII). (KOR.). 1981. 20.00 (*0-614-06394-9*) Quarterly Rev.

Winter Sleep. Goli Taraqqi. Tr. by Francine T. Mahak from PER. (Persian Fiction in Translation Ser.: No. 2). 118p. (Orig.). 1992. pap. 7.95 (*0-685-59541-2*) Mazda Pubs.

Winter Soldier: An Oral History of the Vietnam Veterans Against the War. Stacewicz. 1997. 22.95 (*0-8057-4579-3*, Twayne) Scribnrs Ref.

Winter Soldier: An Oral History of the Vietnam Veterans Against the War. Stacewicz. 1997. 14.95 (*0-8057-4580-7*, Twayne) Scribnrs Ref.

W

An Asterisk (*) at the beginning of an entry indicates that the title is appearing in BIP for the first time.

Winter Solstice. Gerald W. Brace. 1960. 3.95 (*0-393-08488-4*) Norton.

Winter Solstice. Ellen Jackson. LC 92-45065. (Illus.). 32p. (J). (gr. 2-4). 1994. lib. bdg. 17.40 (*1-56294-400-2*) Millbrook Pr.

***Winter Solstice.** Ellen Jackson. 32p. (J). (gr. 2-4). 1997. pap. 7.95 (*0-7613-0297-2*) Millbrook Pr.

***Winter Solstice.** Paul Schmidt. LC 96-3454. 33p. (Orig.). 1996. pap. 10.00 (*0-9651558-2-X*) Painted Leaf.

Winter Solstice Celebrations Through the Ages: A Coloring Book for All Ages. Terri B. Hawthorne & Diane B. Brown. (Illus.). 32p. (J). 1990. pap. 5.99 (*0-929404-01-7*) Tara Educ Servs.

***Winter Song.** Gloria Gaffney. 90p. 1993. pap. 9.50 (*1-56770-271-6*) S Scheewe Pubns.

Winter Song. Karen Lockwood. 1993. mass mkt. 4.99 (*1-55773-958-7*) Diamond.

Winter Song. Vladimir A. Shopov. Ed. by Stanley H. Barkan. (Macedonian Writers Pamphlet Ser.: No. 1). (Illus.). 48p. 1988. pap. 5.00 (*0-89304-975-1*) Cross-Cultrl NY.

Winter Song: An Anthology of Poems on Old Age. Ed. by Georgina Battiscombe. 213p. 1992. 37.50 (*0-09-470990-4*, Pub. by Constable Pubs UK) Trans-Atl Phila.

Winter Songs & Final Dreams: Memoirs of a Wayward Cherub. Paul E. Pross. 120p. 1995. write for info. (*0-9630307-1-X*) Vertex Pr.

Winter Sports. Isidro Sanchez & Carme Peris. (World of Sports Ser.). (Illus.). 32p. (J). (ps-1). 1992. pap. 5.95 (*0-8120-4868-7*) Barron.

Winter Sports Medicine. Ed. by Casey et al. LC 89-11682. (Contemporary Exercise & Sports Medicine Ser.: Vol. 3). 425p. 1990. 75.00 (*0-8036-1683-X*) Davis Co.

Winter Spring. large type ed. Suzanne Goodwin. 468p. 1982. 25.99 (*0-7089-0736-9*) Ulverscroft.

Winter Stars. Larry Levis. LC 84-21957. (Poetry Ser.). 104p. 1985. 19.95 (*0-8229-3511-2*); pap. 10.95 (*0-8229-5368-4*) U of Pittsburgh Pr.

Winter Storm: War in Northern Alsace, November 1944-March 1945. Turner Publishing Company Staff. LC 91-66593. 416p. 1991. 25.00 (*1-56311-056-3*) Turner Pub KY.

Winter Storytime. Rita Kohn. LC 94-38379. (Woodland Adventures Ser.). (Illus.). 32p. (J). (ps-2). 1995. lib. bdg. 19.30 (*0-516-05204-7*) Childrens.

Winter Stripes. Michael J. Rosen. LC 96-23862. (J). 1997. write for info. (*0-15-201535-3*) HarBrace.

Winter Student Exhibition, 1992. Ed. by John Gordon & Clifford La Franboise. (Illus.). 30p. (Orig.). (C). 1992. pap. 8.00 (*1-881396-06-1*) IOA Indian Arts.

***Winter Studies & Summer Rambles in Canada.** Anna B. Jameson. 1996. pap. text ed. 8.95 (*0-7710-9962-2*) McCland & Stewart.

Winter Sunshine. John Burroughs. (Works of John Burroughs). 1989. reprint ed. lib. bdg. 79.00 (*0-7812-2179-X*) Rprt Serv.

Winter Swallows: A Novel. Leonidas Brecoulakis. 1993. 17.95 (*0-533-10597-8*) Vantage.

Winter Tales. George M. Brown. 247p. 1996. 25.95 (*0-7195-5435-7*, Pub. by John Murray UK) Trafalgar.

Winter Tales of the Snowbabies. Carolyn M. Johnson. (Illus.). 72p. (J). (gr. 1-3). 1995. 18.95 (*0-9622603-4-7*) Dept Fifty Six.

Winter Tariff. large type ed. Muriel Howe. 1989. 25.99 (*0-7089-2088-8*) Ulverscroft.

Winter Thunder. Mari Sandoz. LC 85-20977. 61p. 1986. reprint ed. pap. 5.50 (*0-8032-9161-2*, Bison Books) U of Nebr Pr.

***Winter Tides.** James P. Blaylock. LC 96-6548. 352p. 1997. 21.95 (*0-441-00444-X*) Ace Bks.

Winter Toys. Katherine Soniat. Ed. by Craig Goad & William Trowbridge. 44p. (Orig.). 1989. pap. 4.00 (*0-9616467-3-X*) GreenTower Pr.

Winter Tree Finder: A Manual for Identifying Deciduous Trees in Winter East of Rockies. May T. Watts & Tom Watts. (Illus.). 62p. 1970. pap. 3.00 (*0-912550-03-1*) Nature Study.

Winter Verses. Elmo Howell. 153p. (Orig.). 1989. pap. 6.95 (*0-9622026-1-4*) E Howell.

Winter Vision. Geoff Page. 200p. (Orig.). 1989. pap. 14.95 (*0-7022-2239-9*, Pub. by Univ Queensland Pr AT) Intl Spec Bk.

***Winter Visitors.** Elizabeth L. O'Donnell. LC 96-38689. (Illus.). (J). Date not set. 16.00 (*0-688-13063-1*, Morrow Junior); lib. bdg. 15.93 (*0-688-13064-X*, Morrow Junior) Morrow.

Winter War: Antony, Part 2. Mark Dunster. 42p. 1985. pap. 5.00 (*0-89642-124-4*) Linden Pubs.

Winter War: Finland Against Russia, 1939-1940. Vaino A. Tanner. x, 276p. 1957. 39.50 (*0-8047-0482-1*) Stanford U Pr.

Winter War: The Soviet Attack of Finland, 1939-1940. Eloise Engle & Lauri Paananen. 1992. 22.50 (*0-8446-6640-8*) Peter Smith.

Winter War: The Soviet Attack on Finland, 1939-1940. Eloise Engle & Lauri Paananen. LC 91-32208. (Illus.). 208p. 1992. reprint ed. pap. 14.95 (*0-8117-2433-6*) Stackpole.

***Winter Warfare: Red Army Orders & Experiences.** Richard N. Armstrong & Joseph G. Welsh. Ed. by David M. Glantz. LC 96-29933. (Soviet Study of War Ser.: No. 8). (Illus.). 192p. (C). 1997. 42.50 (*0-7146-4699-7*, Pub. by F Cass Pubs UK); pap. 19.50 (*0-7146-4237-1*, Pub. by F Cass Pubs UK) Intl Spec Bk.

Winter Watch. James Ramsey. (Illus.). 154p. (Orig.). (YA). (gr. 10). 1989. pap. 9.95 (*0-88240-329-X*) Alaska Northwest.

Winter Watch of the Leaves. Joan LaBombard. Ed. by Kathleen Iddings. LC 92-60839. (American Bk.). 98p. (Orig.). 1993. per. 10.00 (*0-931289-10-6*) San Diego Poet Pr.

***Winter Wedding.** Carola Dunn et al. 256p. 1998. mass mkt. 4.99 (*0-8217-5828-4*, Zebra Kensgtn) Kensgtn Pub Corp.

Winter Weed Finder: A Guide to Dry Plants in Winter. Dorcas S. Miller. (Illus.). 62p. 1989. pap. 3.00 (*0-912550-17-1*) Nature Study.

Winter Weeds: Poems. Harry Humes. LC 82-11008. (Breakthrough Bks.: No. 41). 56p. (Orig.). 1983. pap. 12.95 (*0-8262-0387-6*) U of Mo Pr.

Winter Whale. Joanne Ryder. LC 90-19174. (Just for a Day Book). (Illus.). 32p. (J). (gr. k up). 1991. lib. bdg. 13.88 (*0-688-07177-5*, Morrow Junior) Morrow.

Winter Whale. Joanne Ryder. Ed. by Amy Cohn. LC 90-19174. (Illus.). 32p. (J). (gr. k up). 1994. reprint ed. pap. 4.95 (*0-688-13110-7*, Morrow Junior) Morrow.

Winter Wheat. Brenda Z. Guiberson. (Illus.). 32p. (J). (gr. 1-3). 1995. 15.95 (*0-8050-1582-5*) H Holt & Co.

Winter Wheat. David Lockwood. 61p. (C). 1986. pap. 20.00 (*0-86383-229-6*, Pub. by Gomer Pr UK) St Mut.

Winter Wheat. Mildred Walker. LC 92-17231. xiv, 306p. 1992. reprint ed. pap. 9.95 (*0-8032-9741-6*, Bison Books) U of Nebr Pr.

Winter White. Joanne Ryder. LC 95-35387. (J). Date not set. 16.00 (*0-688-12992-7*, Morrow Junior); lib. bdg. 15.93 (*0-688-12993-5*, Morrow Junior) Morrow.

Winter Wife. Claire Tomalin. 44p. 1991. pap. 11.95 (*1-85459-104-5*, Pub. by N Hern Bks UK) Theatre Comm.

Winter Winners: To Perk up Primary Programs. Imogene Forte. Ed. by Deborah Gallaway & Jan Keeling. (Illus.). 80p. (Orig.). 1993. teacher ed. 8.95 (*0-86530-245-6*) Incentive Pubns.

Winter Wish. H. P. Lovecraft. Ed. & Intro. by Tom Collins. LC 76-58618. (Illus.). 1977. 15.00 (*0-918372-00-3*) Whispers.

Winter Wolf: Wyatt Earp in Alaska. Richard Parry. LC 96-18269. 384p. 1996. 24.95 (*0-312-86017-X*) St Martin.

Winter Woman. F. M. Parker. 304p. 1996. mass mkt. 4.99 (*0-7860-0347-2*, Pinncle Kensgtn) Kensgtn Pub Corp.

Winter Women Murders. David A. Kaufelt. 1995. mass mkt. 5.50 (*0-671-76095-5*, Pocket Books) PB.

Winter Wonderland. Dick King-Smith & Felix Bernard. (Illus.). 32p. (J). (ps-1). 1993. pap. 2.99 (*0-590-46657-7*, Cartwheel) Scholastic Inc.

Winter Wonderland. Elizabeth Mansfield. 1993. mass mkt. 3.99 (*0-515-11234-8*) Jove Pubns.

Winter Wonders. Toni Bauman & June Zinkgraf. 240p. (J). (gr. k-6). 1978. 13.99 (*0-916456-29-3*, GA89) Good Apple.

Winter Woods. John R. Quinn. LC 76-18486. (Illus.). 1976. 9.95 (*0-85699-138-4*) Chatham Pr.

***Winter Work.** Peter Fallon. 48p. 8300. 18.95 (*0-904011-35-6*) Dufour.

Winter Worm Business. Patricia R. Giff. (Illus.). 144p. (J). (gr. k-6). 1983. pap. 3.50 (*0-440-49259-9*, YB BDD) BDD Bks Young Read.

Winter Wren. Brock Cole. LC 84-1583. (Illus.). 32p. (J). (gr. 2 up). 1984. 15.00 (*0-374-38454-1*, Sunburst Bks) FS&G.

Winter Wren. Brock Cole. LC 84-1583. (Illus.). 32p. (J). (gr. 2 up). 1988. pap. 4.95 (*0-374-48408-2*) FS&G.

Winterburning. Patricia Monaghan. (New Alaskan Poets Ser.). 78p. (Orig.). 1991. pap. 7.95 (*0-914221-10-8*) Fireweed Pr AK.

Winterburn's Rose. Kate Moore. 352p. (Orig.). 1996. mass mkt. 5.50 (*0-380-78457-2*) Avon.

Winterchill. Ernest J. Finney. 240p. 1991. pap. 8.95 (*0-380-71101-X*) Avon.

Winterchill: A Novel. Ernest J. Finney. LC 94-41986. (Western Literature Ser.). 240p. 1995. pap. 14.00 (*0-87417-258-6*) U of Nev Pr.

Winterdance: The Fine Madness of Running the Iditarod. Gary Paulsen. (YA). (gr. 9 up). 1994. 21.95 (*0-15-126227-6*) HarBrace.

Winterdance: The Fine Madness of Running the Iditarod. Gary Paulsen. 264p. (YA). (gr. 9 up). 1995. pap. 12.00 (*0-15-600145-4*, Harvest Bks) HarBrace.

WinterGames/SummerGames. Lawrence D. Moon. 600p. (Orig.). 1996. pap. 13.95 (*0-9651996-0-6*) Edit von Rapp.

Wintergreen: Listening to the Land's Heart. Robert M. Pyle. 303p. 1988. pap. 12.95 (*0-395-46559-1*) HM.

***Wintergreen: Listening to the Land's Heart.** Robert M. Pyle. Date not set. 23.25 (*0-8446-6918-0*) Peter Smith.

Winterhawk Star. Sigmund Brouwer. (Lightning on Ice Ser.: Bk. 4). 128p. (J). (gr. 5-9). 1996. pap. 5.99 (*0-8499-3640-3*) Word Pub.

***Wintering.** Joan Williams. LC 97-19103. (Voices of the South Ser.). 384p. 1997. pap. 14.95 (*0-8071-2227-0*) La State U Pr.

***Wintering Over.** Joan Finnigan. 176p. 1992. pap. 15.95 (*1-55082-049-4*, Pub. by Quarry Pr CN) LPC InBook.

Wintering with the Light: A Bilingual Edition. Paal-Helge Haugen. Tr. by Roger Greenwald from NOR. (Classics Ser.: No. 107). 96p. (Orig.). (ENG & NOR.). 1997. pap. 10.95 (*1-55713-273-9*) Sun & Moon CA.

Winterkill. Nicole Davidson. 192p. (Orig.). (YA). 1991. mass mkt. 3.99 (*0-380-75965-9*, Flare) Avon.

Winterkill. Xavier Jefferson. Ed. by Billie Young. LC 77-77269. 1979. 21.95 (*0-87949-087-X*) Ashley Bks.

***Winterkill.** Lesley. LC 96-48912. 1996. pap. 14.00 (*0-312-15244-2*) St Martin.

Winterkill. Craig Lesley. 336p. 1990. pap. 11.95 (*0-385-31180-X*, Delta) Dell.

Winterkill. David Thompson. (Wilderness Ser.: No. 15). 176p. (Orig.). 1993. mass mkt., pap. text ed. 3.50 (*0-8439-3487-5*) Dorchester Pub Co.

***Winterlong.** Elizabeth Hand. 1997. mass mkt. 5.99 (*0-06-105730-4*, HarperPrism) HarpC.

***Winter's Child.** Mary K. Whittington. (Illus.). 28p. (J). 4.98 (*0-7651-0040-1*) Smithmark.

Winter's Child. Dea T. Morch. Tr. by Joan Tate from DAN. LC 85-24512. (Modern Scandinavian Literature in Translation Ser.). (Illus.). vi, 271p. 1986. reprint ed. pap. 9.95 (*0-8032-8133-1*, Bison Books) U of Nebr Pr.

Winter's Daughter. large type ed. Juliet Dymoke. 752p. 1995. 25.99 (*0-7089-3293-2*) Ulverscroft.

Winter's Edge. Anne Stuart. (Intrigue Ser.). 1995. mass mkt. 3.50 (*0-373-22329-3*, 1-22329-6) Harlequin Bks.

Winter's Edge. Valerie Miner. LC 96-14181. 216p. 1997. reprint ed. pap. 10.95 (*1-55861-150-9*) Feminist Pr.

***Winter's Exile: Poems for My Father.** Isabel Zuber & Sally Logan. Ed. by Mary B. Campbell. (Scots Plaid Press Fine Poetry Ser.: No. 1). 40p. (Orig.). 1997. pap. 12.00 (*1-879009-27-7*) S P-Persephone Pr.

Winter's Fire. Janice Miller. (The Elk Head Creek Saga Ser.: 1). 1995. pap. 10.99 (*0-8024-7921-9*) Moody.

Winter's Flame. Maria Greene. 352p. (Orig.). 1990. mass mkt. 3.95 (*0-380-75774-5*) Avon.

Winters Flower. William A. Raabe & Ranae Johnson. 261p. 1992. pap. 12.95 (*0-9631506-0-X*) Raintree.

Winter's Gold. William Heffernan. 1997. pap. 6.50 (*0-451-18865-9*, Sig) NAL-Dutton.

Winter's Heat. Denise Domning. 348p. (Orig.). 1994. pap. 4.99 (*0-451-40438-6*, Topaz) NAL-Dutton.

Winter's Hero: A Novel. Vassily Aksyonov. LC 95-24409. 496p. 1996. 27.50 (*0-679-43274-4*) Random.

Winter's Journey (Tatar) from Constantinople to Tehran, 2 Vols. James B. Fraser. LC 73-6281. (Middle East Ser.). 1973. reprint ed. 63.95 (*0-405-05339-8*) Ayer.

Winter's Knight. Lianne Racioppo. (Orig.). (YA). 1995. pap. 5.00 (*0-88092-289-3*) Royal Fireworks.

Winter's Light: Reflections of a Yankee Queer. John Preston. Ed. & Intro. by Michael Lowenthal. LC 94-48734. 199p. 1995. text ed. 29.95 (*0-87451-674-9*) U Pr of New Eng.

***Winter's Light: Reflections of a Yankee Queer.** John Preston. Ed. & Intro. by Michael Lowenthal. LC 94-48734. 199p. 1995. pap. 14.95 (*0-87451-781-8*) U Pr of New Eng.

***Winter's Love.** Madeleine L'Engle. LC 96-37645. 1997. 19.99 (*0-87788-889-2*) Shaw Pubs.

Winters of Content, & Other Discussions on Mediterranean Art & Travel. Osbert Sitwell. LC 75-35029. (Illus.). 362p. 1978. reprint ed. text ed. 59.75 (*0-8371-8570-X*, SIWOC, Greenwood Pr) Greenwood.

Winters of that Country: Tales of the Man-Made Seasons. John Sanford. LC 84-4276. (Illus.). 355p. (Orig.). 1984. 20.00 (*0-87685-615-6*); pap. 12.50 (*0-87685-614-8*) Black Sparrow.

Winters of that Country: Tales of the Man-Made Seasons, signed ed. deluxe ed. John Sanford. LC 84-4276. (Illus.). 355p. (Orig.). 1984. 30.00 (*0-87685-616-4*) Black Sparrow.

Winter's Orphans: The Search for a Family of Mountain Lion Cubs, a True Story. Robert Farentinos. (Illus.). 64p. (J). (gr. 4-6). 1993. pap. 13.95 (*1-879373-53-X*) R Rinehart.

Winter's Promise. (Southern Exposure Ser.). 96p. 1980. pap. 3.00 (*0-943810-34-5*) Inst Southern Studies.

Winter's Rose. Erica Spindler. (Special Edition Ser.). 1993. mass mkt. 3.50 (*0-373-09817-0*, 5-09817-3) Silhouette.

Winter's Silent Song. Kay D. Rizzo. LC 94-7118. 1994. pap. 11.99 (*0-8163-1220-6*) Pacific Pr Pub Assn.

Winter's Song: A Liturgy of Healing for Women Suffering from Childhood Sexual Abuse. Jane A. Keene. LC 91-8927. 48p. 1991. pap. 4.95 (*0-8298-0906-6*) Pilgrim OH.

Winter's Tale. Casssie Brown. 304p. 1988. pap. 12.00 (*0-385-25181-5*) Doubleday.

Winter's Tale. Mark Helprin. LC 83-273. 688p. 1983. 26.95 (*0-15-197203-6*) HarBrace.

Winter's Tale. Mark Helprin. 1995. pap. 16.00 (*0-15-600194-2*) HarBrace.

Winter's Tale. Judy McGorray. 19p. (Orig.). 1995. pap. text ed. write for info. (*1-888200-06-5*) JayMac Commun.

***Winter's Tale.** Steven Schnur. (J). Date not set. write for info. (*0-688-13323-1*, Morrow Junior) Morrow.

Winter's Tale. William Shakespeare. Ed. by Frank Kermode. 1974. pap. 2.95 (*0-451-52146-3*, Sig Classics) NAL-Dutton.

Winter's Tale. William Shakespeare. (BBC Television Plays Ser.). 1981. pap. 4.95 (*0-563-17855-8*, Pub. by BBC UK) Parkwest Pubns.

Winter's Tale. William Shakespeare. Ed. by Louis B. Wright & Virginia A. La Mar. (Folger Library). 304p. mass mkt. 3.99 (*0-671-66917-6*, WSP) PB.

Winter's Tale. William Shakespeare. Ed. by Baldwin Maxwell. (Pelican Shakespeare Ser.). 140p. 1956. pap. 4.95 (*0-14-071404-9*, Pelican Bks) Viking Penguin.

Winter's Tale. William Shakespeare. Ed. by Ernest Schanzer. (New Penguin Shakespeare Ser.). 256p. 1981. pap. 5.50 (*0-14-070716-6*, Penguin Classics) Viking Penguin.

Winter's Tale. William Shakespeare. Date not set. write for info. (*0-517-15130-8*) Random Hse Value.

Winter's Tale. William Shakespeare. Ed. by Stephen Orgel. (Oxford Shakespeare Ser.). 304p. (C). 1996. 72.00 (*0-19-812949-1*); pap. 6.95 (*0-19-281956-9*) OUP.

***Winters Tale.** William Shakespeare. Date not set. pap. text ed. write for info. (*0-312-16704-0*) St Martin.

***Winters Tale.** William Shakespeare & Neil Freeman. LC 97-9498. (Applause Shakespeare Library). 1997. pap. write for info. (*1-55783-296-X*) Applause Theatre Bk Pubs.

***Winter's Tale.** William Shakespeare. (English Ser.). (C). Date not set. pap. 9.95 (*0-17-443540-1*) Wadsworth Pub.

***Winter's Tale.** William Shakespeare. (English Ser.). (C). Date not set. text ed. 45.00 (*0-17-443573-8*) Wadsworth Pub.

***Winter's Tale.** Ian Wallace. 1997. 15.95 (*0-88899-286-6*, Pub. by Groundwood-Douglas & McIntyre CN) Firefly Bks Ltd.

Winter's Tale. Jonathan Winters. 1988. write for info. (*0-318-63005-2*) Random.

Winter's Tale. large type ed. William Shakespeare. (Charnwood Large Print Ser.). 1991. pap. 24.95 (*0-7089-4533-3*, Charnwood) Ulverscroft.

Winter's Tale. rev. ed. William Shakespeare. 240p. 1963. pap. 3.95 (*0-451-52260-5*, Sig Classics) NAL-Dutton.

Winter's Tale. rev. ed. William Shakespeare. Ed. by John Andrews. (Everyman Paperback Classics Ser.). (C). 1995. pap. 3.95 (*0-460-87519-1*, Everyman's Classic Lib) C E Tuttle.

***Winter's Tale.** 4th ed. William Shakespeare. (English Text Ser.). 1963. pap. 9.95 (*0-415-02710-1*) Routledge.

Winter's Tale. 4th ed. William Shakespeare. Ed. by J. H. Pafford. (Arden Shakespeare Ser.). 1962. reprint ed. pap. 8.95 (*0-416-47670-8*, NO. 2501) Routledge Chapman & Hall.

Winter's Tale. Mark Helprin. Ed. by Jane Rosenman. 704p. 1990. reprint ed. pap. 14.00 (*0-671-72707-9*, WSP) PB.

Winter's Tale. William Shakespeare. Ed. by Kenneth Muir. (Casebook Ser.). (C). 1970. reprint ed. pap. text ed. 2.50 (*0-87695-054-3*, Pub. by BBC UK) Parkwest Pubns.

Winter's Tale: Critical Essays. Ed. by Maurice Hunt. LC 95-13858. (Shakespeare Criticism Ser.: Vol. 14). (Illus.). 448p. 1995. text ed. 80.00 (*0-8153-1704-2*, H1846) Garland.

Winter's Tale: The Winter's Tale. William Shakespeare. Ed. by Roma Gill. (Oxford School Shakespeare Ser.). (Illus.). 172p. (J). 1996. pap. 7.50 (*0-19-831989-4*) OUP.

Winter's Tale Notes. Evelyn McLellan. (Cliffs Notes Ser.). 66p. (Orig.). (C). 1984. pap. text ed. 3.95 (*0-8220-0096-2*) Cliffs.

Winter's Tales. Isak Dinesen. LC 92-50615. 1993. pap. 13.00 (*0-679-74334-0*, Vin) Random.

Winter's Tales. Isak Dinesen. LC 70-169542. (Short Story Index Reprint Ser.). 1977. reprint ed. 19.95 (*0-8369-4003-2*) Ayer.

Winter's Tales: Stories & Observations for the Unusual. Jonathan Winters. 1988. pap. 5.95 (*0-394-75978-8*, Vin) Random.

Winters Without Snow. Colleen McElroy. LC 79-92501. 81p. 1980. pap. 5.95 (*0-918408-17-2*) Reed & Cannon.

Winter's Yarn. Kathleen C. Waldron & Deborah Turney-Zagwyn. (Illus.). 40p. (J). 1986. pap. 5.95 (*0-88995-048-2*, Pub. by Red Deer CN) Orca Bk Pubs.

Wintersbride. large type ed. Sara Seale. 1974. 12.00 (*0-85456-278-8*) Ulverscroft.

Winterset. Maxwell Anderson. 1946. pap. 5.25 (*0-8222-1266-8*) Dramatists Play.

Winterset: Acting Edition see Six Modern American Plays

Wintershine: A Book of Maps, Pictures, Laments, Celebrations, Praise. Eve Caram. 100p. 1994. pap. 11.95 (*0-911051-74-0*) Plain View.

Wintersigns in the Snow. Gerald Cox. (Illus.). 80p. pap. 5.95 (*0-935576-11-8*) Kesend Pub Ltd.

Wintersong. Madeleine L'Engle & Luci Shaw. LC 96-28370. 144p. 1996. 19.99 (*0-87788-855-8*) Shaw Pubs.

Winterspelt: A Novel about the Last Days of World War II. Alfred Andersch. 480p. 1980. 30.00 (*0-7206-0550-4*) Dufour.

Winterthur. Jay E. Cantor. LC 97-4303. (Illus.). 240p. 1985. 60.00 (*0-8109-1785-6*) Abrams.

Winterthur: A Portrait. J. Cantor. (Illus.). 64p. 1991. pap. text ed. 7.95 (*0-912724-21-8*) Winterthur.

Winterthur Bk., No. 7. Ed. by Ian M. Quimby. (Winterthur Bk.). (Illus.). 256p. 1978. lib. bdg. 24.00 (*0-226-92133-6*) U Ch Pr.

Winterthur Garden: Henry Francis du Pont's Romance with the Land. Denise Magnani. LC 94-14976. (Illus.). 192p. 1995. 39.95 (*0-8109-3779-4*) Abrams.

Winterthur in Bloom: Winter, Spring, Summer, Autumn. Harold Bruce. LC 68-15483. (Illus.). 1986. reprint ed. pap. 16.95 (*0-912724-01-3*) Winterthur.

Winterthur Museum Libraries Collection of Printed Books & Periodicals, 9 vols., Set. LC 73-88753. 1974. lib. bdg. 725.00 (*0-8420-1725-9*) Scholarly Res Inc.

Winterthur Portfolio, No. 3. Ed. by Milo M. Naeve. (Winterthur Bk.). (Illus.). 232p. 1978. lib. bdg. 24.00 (*0-226-92127-1*) U Ch Pr.

Winterthur Portfolio, No. 4. Ed. by Richard K. Doud. (Winterthur Bk.). (Illus.). 232p. 1978. lib. bdg. 24.00 (*0-226-92129-8*) U Ch Pr.

Winterthur Portfolio, No. 5. Richard K. Doud. 202p. 1978. lib. bdg. 24.00 (*0-226-92130-1*) U Ch Pr.

Winterthur Portfolio, No. 6. Richard K. Doud & Ian M. Quimby. (Winterthur Bk.). (Illus.). 232p. 1978. lib. bdg. 24.00 (*0-226-92132-8*) U Ch Pr.

Winterthur Portfolio, No. 9. (Winterthur Bk.). (Illus.). 248p. 1978. lib. bdg. 24.00 (*0-226-92135-2*) U Ch Pr.

Winterthur Portfolio, No. 11. Ed. by Ian M. Quimby. (Winterthur Bk.). (Illus.). 256p. 1978. lib. bdg. 24.00 (*0-226-92137-9*) U Ch Pr.

Winterthur Portfolio, No. 12. Ed. by Ian M. Quimby. (Winterthur Bk.). (Illus.). 248p. 1978. lib. bdg. 24.00 (*0-226-92138-7*) U Ch Pr.

Winterthur Portfolio, No. 8: Thematic Issue on Religion in America. Ed. by Ian M. Quimby. (Winterthur Bk.). (Illus.). 256p. 1978. lib. bdg. 24.00 (*0-226-92134-4*) U Ch Pr.

Winterthur's Culinary Collection. LC 83-50805. (Illus.). 1983. pap. 14.95 (*0-912724-14-5*) Winterthur.

Winterthur's Twelve Months of Flowers. Ed. by Lisa MacDonald. (Illus.). 32p. 1985. 12.95 (*0-939456-11-7*) Galison.

W

An Asterisk (*) at the beginning of an entry indicates that the title is appearing in BIP for the first time.

Wintertime. Ann Schweninger. LC 93-16685. (Let's Look at the Seasons Ser.). 32p. (J). (ps-3). 1993. pap. 4.50 (*0-14-054286-8*, Puffin) Puffin Bks.

Wintertime Cat. rev. ed. Era Zistel. (Illus.). 64p. (J). 1988. reprint ed. pap. 5.95 (*0-9617426-4-X*) J N Townsend.

Winterville: Late Prehistoric Culture Contact in the Lower Mississippi Valley. Jeffrey P. Brain. (Mississippi Department of Archives & History Archaeological Reports: No. 23). (Illus.). 201p. 1989. pap. 15.00 (*0-938896-58-X*) Mississippi Archives.

Winterwise: A Backpacker's Guide. 2nd rev. ed. John M. Dunn. LC 95-15220. (Illus.). 194p. (Orig.). 1997. pap. 12.95 (*0-935272-80-1*) ADK Mtn Club.

Winthrop - Babcock: Ancestors of Henry Rogers Winthrop & His Wife Alice Woodward Babcock. Josephine C. Frost. 595p. 1993. reprint ed. pap. 89.50 (*0-8328-3434-3*); reprint ed. lib. bdg. 99.50 (*0-8328-3433-5*) Higginson Bk Co.

Winthrop Fleet of 1630: An Account of the Vessels, the Voyage, the Passengers & Their English Homes, from Original Authorities. Charles E. Banks. LC 68-57951. (Illus.). 119p. 1994. reprint ed. 15.00 (*0-8063-0020-5*, 306) Genealog Pub.

Winthrop Papers: 1631-1654, Vols. 3-6. LC 29-18409. 1992. 65.00 (*0-685-73386-6*) Mass Hist Soc.

***Winthrop Register, 1903-4 (Town History & Directory)** Mitchell & Remick. 99p. 1997. reprint ed. pap. 18.00 (*0-8328-5931-1*) Higginson Bk Co.

Winthrop's Journal, "History of New England", 1630-1649: Edited by James Kendall Hosmer, 2 vols., Set. John Winthrop. (BCL1 - United States Local History Ser.). 1991. reprint ed. text ed. 150.00 (*0-7812-6268-2*) Rprt Serv.

Wintrobe's Clinical Hematology. 9th ed. G. Richard Lee et al. LC 90-6194. (Illus.). 2320p. 1992. 175.00 (*0-8121-1188-5*) Williams & Wilkins.

***Wintrobe's Clinical Hematology.** 10th ed. Maxwell M. Wintrobe & G. Richard Lee. LC 96-52799. 1997. write for info. (*0-683-18242-0*) Williams & Wilkins.

Wintu Dictionary. Harvey Pitkin. (University of California Publications in Entomology: No. 95). 943p. 1985. pap. 180.00 (*0-7837-7499-0*, 2049221) Bks Demand.

Wintu Ethnography. fac. ed. Cora DuBois. (University of California Publications in American Archaeology & Ethnology: Vol. 36: 1). (Illus.). 154p. (C). 1935. reprint ed. pap. text ed. 13.70 (*1-55567-304-X*) Coyote Press.

Wintu Grammar. Harvey Pitkin. LC 84-16268. (University of California Publications in Entomology: No. 94). 326p. 1984. pap. 93.00 (*0-7837-7498-2*, 2049220) Bks Demand.

Wintu Texts. Alice Shepherd. LC 89-5158. (University of California Publications in Linguistics: No. 117). 509p. 1989. pap. 145.10 (*0-7837-8427-9*, 2049229) Bks Demand.

Wintun Hesi Ceremony. fac. ed. S. A. Barrett. (University of California Publications in American Archaeology & Ethnology: Vol. 14: 4). 54p. (C). 1919. reprint ed. pap. text ed. 4.95 (*1-55567-219-1*) Coyote Press.

Wintun Indians of California & Their Neighbors. Peter M Knudtson. LC 76-5635. (American Indian Map Book: Vol. 3). (Illus.). 96p. (C). 1977. pap. 8.95 (*0-87961-062-X*) Naturegraph.

Win/Win or Else: Collective Bargaining in an Age of Public Discontent. William G. Keane. LC 95-42476. (Illus.). 80p. 1996. 28.95 (*0-8039-6424-2*); pap. 12.95 (*0-8039-6319-X*) Corwin Pr.

***Win/Win Solutions: Resolving Conflict on the Job.** Thomas J. Stevinin. 1997. pap. 12.99 (*1-881273-70-9*) Moody.

Winword 2. 1992. 56.95 (*0-387-55663-X*) Spr-Verlag.

Winzig, Germany, 1933-1946: The History of a Town under the Third Reich. Rita S. Botwinick. LC 91-35255. 176p. 1992. text ed. 49.95 (*0-275-94185-X*, C4185, Praeger Pubs) Greenwood.

***Win32 Programming Secrets.** 1997. pap. 49.99 (*0-7645-3059-3*) IDG Bks.

Win95 Game Programming. Matthias Rasch. 1995. 44.95 incl. cd-rom (*1-55755-294-0*) Abacus MI.

***Wipe Your Feet, Santa Claus!** Konrad Richter. 1997. pap. text ed. 6.96 (*1-55858-775-6*) North-South Bks NYC.

***Wipeout.** Dixon. (Hardy Boys Ser.: No. 96). (J). 1989. mass mkt. 3.50 (*0-671-89513-3*, Pocket Books) PB.

Wipeout. Franklin W. Dixon. Ed. by Ruth Ashby. (Hardy Boys Ser.: No. 90). 160p. (Orig.). (YA). (gr. 3-6). pap. 3.99 (*0-671-66306-2*, Minstrel Bks) PB.

Wipeouts & Their Mitigation: The Changing Context for Land Use & Environmental Law. fac. ed. Joseph F. DiMento. LC 90-46451. (Illus.). 125p. 1990. reprint ed. pap. 35.70 (*0-7837-7828-7*, 2047584) Bks Demand.

Wiper (Uniformed) Jack Rudman. (Career Examination Ser.: C-1632). 1994. pap. 27.95 (*0-8373-1632-4*) Nat Learn.

***Wiping Out Head Lice.** Nicholas Bakalar. 1997. pap. 5.99 (*0-451-19167-6*, Sig) NAL-Dutton.

Wir, das Volk. 2nd ed. Lonnelle Aikman. Tr. by Paul Vidal. (Illus.). 144p. (GER.). 1983. pap. 2.50 (*0-916200-02-7*) US Capitol Hist.

Wir Die Jugend 1990. Created by Harcourt Brace Staff. (GER.). 1990. wbk. ed., pap. 13.00 (*0-15-383552-4*) HR&W Schl Div.

Wir Die Jugend 1990. Created by Harcourt Brace Staff. (GER.). 1990. wbk. ed., pap. text ed. 13.00 (*0-15-383553-2*) HR&W Schl Div.

Wir Die Jugend 1990. Created by Harcourt Brace Staff. (GER.). 1990. teacher ed., wbk. ed., pap. text ed. 17.25 (*0-15-383554-0*) HR&W Schl Div.

Wir Die Jugend 1990. Created by Harcourt Brace Staff. (GER.). 1990. teacher ed., wbk. ed., pap. text ed. 16.00 (*0-15-383555-9*) HR&W Schl Div.

Wir Die Jugend 1990. Created by Harcourt Brace Staff. (GER.). 1990. teacher ed., pap. text ed. 14.50 (*0-15-383557-5*) HR&W Schl Div.

Wir Die Jugend 1990: Testbook. Created by Harcourt Brace Staff. (GER.). 1990. student ed., pap. text ed. 14.50 (*0-15-383556-7*) HR&W Schl Div.

Wir Lernen Deutsch Durch Handeln. Bertha E. Segal-Cook. Tr. by Jeff Corrigan et al. from ENG. 106p. (GER.). 1986. reprint ed. teacher ed., spiral bd. 17.99 (*0-938395-30-0*) B Segal.

Wir Spielen und Uben: Beobachten und Denken. 24p. (GER.). 7.95 (*3-580-63156-X*) Langenscheidt.

Wir Spielen und Uben: Erste Worter Lernen. 24p. (GER.). 1993. 7.95 (*3-580-63166-7*) Langenscheidt.

Wir Spielen und Uben: Lesen Lernen. 24p. (GER.). 1993. 7.95 (*3-580-63167-5*) Langenscheidt.

Wir Spielen und Uben: Richtig Lesen. 24p. (GER.). 1993. 7.95 (*3-580-63169-1*) Langenscheidt.

Wir Spielen und Uben: Spass Beim Rechtschreiben. 24p. (GER.). 1993. 7.95 (*3-580-63172-1*) Langenscheidt.

Wir Spielen und Uben: Spass Mit der Grammatik. 24p. (GER.). 1993. 7.95 (*3-580-63178-0*) Langenscheidt.

Wir Spielen und Uben: Worter Richtig Schreiben. 24p. (GER.). 1993. 7.95 (*3-580-63171-3*) Langenscheidt.

Wir Spielen und Ubenl: Lustige Lesepiele. 24p. (GER.). 7.95 (*3-580-63168-3*) Langenscheidt.

Wir Wollen Deutsche Bleiben. George J. Walters. LC 82-80798. 425p. 1993. pap. 20.00 (*0-911311-41-6*) Acres USA.

Wira Textile Data Book. 2nd ed. Ed. by Rae Wira & Bruce Wira. 1983. 90.00 (*0-317-43606-6*) St Mut.

***Wiradturi Spirit Man: HJ Wedge.** Pref. by Paul Coe. (Illus.). 120p. 1997. 22.50 (*976-641-019-4*, Pub. by Craftsman Hse VB) IPG Chicago.

Wirds An' Wark E' Seasons Roon: On an Aberdeenshire Farm. Alexander Fenton. (Illus.). 96p. 1987. pap. text ed. 10.00 (*0-08-035074-7*, Pub. by Aberdeen U Pr) Macmillan.

Wire. Suzanne Slesin et al. LC 94-11054. (Illus.). 148p. 1994. 29.95 (*1-55859-792-1*) Abbeville Pr.

Wire & Cable for Electronics: A User's Handbook. Neil J. Sclater. 1991. text ed. 29.95 (*0-07-055916-3*) McGraw.

Wire & Cable for Electronics: A User's Handbook. Neil J. Sclater. (Illus.). 256p. 1991. 29.95 (*0-8306-7787-9*, 3787, TAB/TPR) TAB Bks.

***Wire & Cable Reel Sizes.** 20.00 (*0-614-18706-0*, A-9-428) Insulated Cable.

Wire & Cable Technical Information Handbook. rev. ed. Ed. by W. D. Wilkens. (Illus.). 338p. 1996. 80.00 (*0-9638139-0-0*); pap. 50.00 (*0-9638139-1-9*) Anixter Inc.

Wire Association International: Proceedings, 54th Annual Conference. 50.00 (*0-318-04236-3*) Wire Assn Intl.

Wire Association International Proceedings. Incl. 50th Annual Meeting. 50.00 (*0-685-73660-1*, 7680); 51st Annual Meeting. 50.00 (*0-685-73661-X*, 7681); 52nd Annual Meeting. 50.00 (*0-685-73662-8*, 7682); 53rd Annual Meeting. 50.00 (*0-685-73663-6*, 7683); write for info. (*0-318-58150-7*) Wire Assn Intl.

Wire Bonding in Microtechnology. 2nd ed. Hwang. 1997. text ed. 65.00 (*0-07-032619-3*) McGraw.

Wire, Cable, & Fiber Optics. Business Communications Co., Inc. Staff. 131p. 1991. pap. 2,450.00 (*0-89336-514-9*, G-070N) BCC.

***Wire, Cable, & Fiber Optics for Video & Audio Engineers.** Stephen H. Lampen. LC 97-16148. (Video/Audio Engineering Ser.). (Illus.). 350p. 1997. text ed. 55.00 (*0-07-037148-2*); pap. text ed. 34.95 (*0-07-038134-8*) McGraw.

***Wire-Cut EDM: From Purchase to Profit.** Randy J. Bormann. LC 96-42199. 1997. write for info. (*1-56990-219-4*) Hanser-Gardner.

***Wire Cutters.** Mollie E. Moore Davis. 384p. 1997. pap. 16.95 (*0-89096-796-2*) Tex A&M Univ Pr.

Wire 'Em & Win: Turning Thoroughbred Selections into Race Betting Profits, Handicapping Edition. rev. ed. Denny L. Border. LC 95-90734. 1995. pap. 12.95 (*0-9642669-1-1*) Winrose Pubng.

Wire Fence. Henry A. Craig. 160p. 1995. mass mkt. 4.99 (*1-896329-18-7*, Pub. by Comnwlth Pub CN) Partners Pubs Grp.

Wire Flow Photography As a Papermaking Diagnostic Tool. C. W. Howe et al. (Pulp & Paper Technology Ser.: No. 3). 34p. reprint ed. pap. 25.00 (*0-318-34850-0*, 2031007) Bks Demand.

Wire Harness Markets. 70p. 1993. 1,950.00 (*0-945235-70-4*) Lead Edge Reports.

Wire Index. 150.00 (*0-318-03229-5*, 8540) Wire Assn Intl.

Wire Index: A Compendium of the Wire Association's Technical Literature from 1926 to 1981. 2nd ed. Ed. by Rochelle P. Kramer. 374p. 1983. 100.00 (*0-685-26884-5*) Wire Assn Intl.

Wire Rod Defects. (Illus.). 46p. (FRE & GER.). 1973. pap. 78.00 (*3-514-00134-0*, Pub. by Woodhead Pubng UK) Am Educ Systs.

Wire Splicing. R. S. Skirving. (C). 1987. 60.00 (*0-85174-154-1*, Pub. by Brwn Son Ferg) St Mut.

Wire Tappers. Arthur Stringer. 1976. lib. bdg. 15.30 (*0-89968-121-2*, Lghtyr Pr) Buccaneer Bks.

Wire Taps & Surveillance, Bk. 1. abr. ed. Michael P. Jones. (Illus.). 84p. 1984. pap. text ed. 12.00 (*0-89904-078-0*) Crumb Elbow Pub.

Wire Taps & Surveillance, Bk. 2. abr. ed. Michael P. Jones. (Illus.). 31p. 1984. pap. text ed. 6.00 (*0-89904-079-9*) Crumb Elbow Pub.

Wire That Fenced the West. Henry D. McCallum & Frances T. McCallum. LC 65-11234. (Illus.). 1985. pap. 17.95 (*0-8061-1559-9*) U of Okla Pr.

Wire Transfer: The International Guide to the Laws & Regulations Governing Electronic Funds Transfer. Federal Reserve Bank of New York Staff et al. 325p. 1993. text ed. 75.00 (*1-55738-354-5*) Irwin Prof Pubng.

***Wirebending Book: Techniques for Beadlovers.** Wendy S. Conner. (Beading Books Ser.: Vol. 11). (Illus.). 52p. 1997. pap. 11.95 (*0-9645957-9-6*) Interstell Pub.

Wired. Bob Woodward. 1986. mass mkt. 5.99 (*0-671-64077-1*) PB.

Wired, 3 vols., 2. Ed. by Mark V. Ziesing. 1990. 10.00 (*0-929480-24-4*) Mark Ziesing.

Wired, 3 vols., 3. Ed. by Mark V. Ziesing. 1990. 15.00 (*0-929480-56-2*) Mark Ziesing.

Wired: A Novel. Martha R. Carr. 313p. 1993. pap. 14.95 (*0-9638639-0-8*) Nimrod Hse.

***Wired Cat Unlined.** Paperblank Books Staff. (Hnizdovsky's Wired Animals Ser.). 1997. pap. text ed. 9.95 (*1-55156-060-7*, Pub. by Paperblank Bk CN) Consort Bk Sales.

Wired Cities: Shaping the Future of Communications. Ed. by Jay G. Blumier & Kenneth L. Kraemer. (Professional Librarian Ser.). 492p. 1987. 50.00 (*0-8161-1851-5*, Hall Reference); 29.95 (*0-8161-1853-1*, Hall Reference) Macmillan.

Wired for Business: Insider's Guide to Doing Business on the Internet. Anthony Rutkowski. 1995. pap. 29.95 (*0-13-301797-4*) P-H.

***Wired for Learning: Harnessing the Power of the Internet for Education.** Jan Lasarenko. 304p. 1997. 24.99 (*0-7897-1045-5*) Mac Comp Pub.

Wired for Sound: An Advanced Student Workbook on Hearing & Hearing Aids. Carole Bugosh Simko. (Illus.). 156p. (YA). (gr. 8-12). 1986. student ed., pap. text ed. 7.95 (*0-930323-16-5*, Pub. by K Green Pubns) Gallaudet Univ Pr.

Wired for Success: Auto Electrical Made Easy. Randy Rundle. LC 95-77302. (Illus.). 224p. 1995. pap. text ed. 19.95 (*0-87341-402-0*, AEM01) Krause Pubns.

Wired Hard: Erotica for a Gay Universe. Ed. by Cecilia Tan. 90p. (Orig.). 1994. pap. 7.95 (*0-9633970-8-7*) Circlet Pr.

Wired Hard 2: More Erotica for a Gay Universe. Ed. by Cecilia Tan. (Orig.). 1997. pap. 12.95 (*1-885865-11-2*) Circlet Pr.

***Wired Ibex Unlined.** Paperblank Books Staff. (Hnizdovsky's Wired Animals Ser.). 1997. pap. text ed. 9.95 (*1-55156-061-5*, Pub. by Paperblank Bk CN) Consort Bk Sales.

***Wired Museum: Emerging Technology & Changing Paradigms.** Ed. by Katherine Jones-Garmil. LC 97-11054. 250p. 1996. pap. 35.00 (*0-931201-36-5*) Am Assn Mus.

***Wired Nation Continent: The Communication Revolution & Federating Australia.** 2nd ed. Kevin Livingston. (Illus.). 232p. 1997. text ed. 75.00 (*0-19-553633-9*) OUP.

Wired Neighborhood. Stephen Doheny-Farina. LC 96-12241. 240p. 1996. 25.00 (*0-300-06765-8*) Yale U Pr.

***Wired Sheep Unlined.** Paperblank Books Staff. (Hnizdovsky's Wired Animals Ser.). 1997. pap. text ed. 9.95 (*1-55156-062-3*, Pub. by Paperblank Bk CN) Consort Bk Sales.

***Wired Society.** Powell. (C). 1998. teacher ed., pap. text ed. 26.75 (*0-15-508352-X*); pap. text ed. write for info. (*0-15-508353-8*) HB Coll Pubs.

Wired Style: Principles of English Usage in the Digital Age. Constance Hale. 144p. 1996. spiral bd. 15.95 (*1-888869-01-1*) HardWired.

***Wired to Death.** Pamela Mitchell. 218p. 1997. 20.95 (*1-885173-36-9*) Write Way.

Wired to the Net. Butler Eddings. 1994. pap. 39.95 (*1-56276-249-4*, Ziff-Davis Pr) Que.

***Wired Together Vol. 1: The Online Classroom in K-12: Perspectives & Instructional Design.** Ed. by Zane Berge & Mauri L. Collins. LC 97-22976. (Illus.). 272p. (C). 1997. text ed. 52.50 (*1-57273-086-2*) Hampton Pr NJ.

***Wired Together Vol. 1: The Online Classroom in K-12: Perspectives & Instructional Design.** Ed. by Zane Berge & Mauri L. Collins. LC 97-22976. (Illus.). 272p. (C). 1997. pap. text ed. 22.95 (*1-57273-087-0*) Hampton Pr NJ.

***Wired Together Vol. 2: The Online Classroom in K-12: Case Studies.** Ed. by Zane Berge & Mauri L. Collins. LC 97-22976. (Illus.). 240p. (C). 1997. text ed. 45.00 (*1-57273-088-9*) Hampton Pr NJ.

***Wired Together Vol. 2: The Online Classroom in K-12: Case Studies.** Ed. by Zane Berge & Mauri L. Collins. LC 97-22976. (Illus.). 240p. (C). 1997. pap. text ed. 21.95 (*1-57273-089-7*) Hampton Pr NJ.

***Wired Together Vol. 3: The Online Classroom in K-12: Teacher Education & Professional Development.** Ed. by Zane Berge & Mauri L. Collins. LC 97-22976. 224p. (C). 1997. text ed. 45.00 (*1-57273-090-0*) Hampton Pr NJ.

***Wired Together Vol. 3: The Online Classroom in K-12: Teacher Education & Professional Development.** Ed. by Zane Berge & Mauri L. Collins. 224p. (C). 1997. pap. text ed. 21.95 (*1-57273-091-9*) Hampton Pr NJ.

***Wired Together Vol. 4: The Online Classroom in K-12: Writing, Reading & Language Acquisition.** Ed. by Zane Berge & Mauri L. Collins. 272p. (C). 1997. text ed. 52.50 (*1-57273-092-7*) Hampton Pr NJ.

***Wired Together Vol. 4: The Online Classroom in K-12: Writing, Reading & Language Acquisition.** Ed. by Zane Berge & Mauri L. Collins. 272p. (C). 1997. pap. text ed. 22.95 (*1-57273-093-5*) Hampton Pr NJ.

Wired Women: Gender & New Realities in Cyberspace. Ed. by Elizabeth R. Weise & Lynn Cherny. LC 95-51742. 304p. (Orig.). 1996. pap. 16.00 (*1-878067-73-7*) Seal Pr WA.

***Wired Zebra Unlined.** Paperblank Books Staff. (Hnizdovsky's Wired Animals Ser.). 1997. pap. text ed. 9.95 (*1-55156-063-1*, Pub. by Paperblank Bk CN) Consort Bk Sales.

Wiregrass Country. Jerrilyn McGregory. LC 96-32423. (Folklife in the South Ser.). (Illus.). 224p. 1997. 45.00 (*0-87805-925-3*); pap. 18.00 (*0-87805-926-1*) U Pr of Miss.

Wiregrass Reader: Newspaper Abstracts from the Late Nineteenth Century, Featuring Montgomery, Laurens, Telfair, Dodge, Candler & Johnson Counties. Ed. by James E. Dorsey. 209p. 1991. pap. 20.00 (*0-916369-17-X*) Magnolia Pr.

Wireless. Jack O'Connell. 416p. 1993. 19.95 (*0-89296-546-0*) Mysterious Pr.

Wireless. Jack O'Connell. 416p. 1995. mass mkt. 5.99 (*0-446-40356-3*, Mysterious Paperbk) Warner Bks.

***Wireless: Strategically Liberalizing the Telecommunications Market.** Brian Regli. LC 97-5611. (Telecommunications Ser.). 344p. 1997. pap. write for info. (*0-8058-2582-7*); text ed. write for info. (*0-8058-2581-9*) L Erlbaum Assocs.

Wireless: The Revolution in Personal Telecommunications. Ira Brodsky. LC 95-6097. (Artech House Mobile Communications Ser.). 275p. 1995. 50.00 (*0-89006-717-1*) Artech Hse.

Wireless Access & the Local Telephone Network. George Calhoun. (Telecommunications Library). 595p. 1992. text ed. 79.00 (*0-89006-394-X*) Artech Hse.

***Wireless & Cable Voice Services: Forecasts & Competitive Impacts.** Lawrence K. Vanston & Curt Rogers. 75p. 1996. pap. 495.00 (*1-884154-04-2*) Tech Futures.

Wireless & Mobile Communications. Ed. by Jack M. Holtzman & David J. Goodman. LC 94-1237. (International Series in Engineering & Computer Science, VLSI, Computer Architecture, & Digital Screen Processing: Vol. 277). 304p. (C). 1994. lib. bdg. 92.00 (*0-7923-9464-X*) Kluwer Ac.

***Wireless & Personal Communications Systems: Fundamentals & Applications.** V. K. Garg & J. E. Wilkes. (Handbook Ser.). 464p. 1996. 65.00 (*0-13-493735-X*, PC5673) P-H.

Wireless & Personal Communications Systems (PCS) Vijay K. Garg & Joseph E. Wilkes. LC 95-38584. (Feher/Prentice Hall Digital & Wireless Communication Ser.). 1995. boxed, text ed. 68.00 (*0-13-234626-5*) P-H.

Wireless & Satellite Telecommunications: The Technology, the Market, & the Regulations. 2nd ed. Joseph N. Pelton. LC 95-7049. (Digital & Wireless Communication Ser.). (C). 1995. text ed. 60.00 (*0-13-140493-8*) P-H.

Wireless at Sea: The First Fifty Years. Harry E. Hancock. LC 74-7683. (Telecommunications Ser.). (Illus.). 233p. 1974. reprint ed. 28.95 (*0-405-06048-3*) Ayer.

***Wireless ATM & Ad-Hoc Networks: Protocols & Architectures.** C. K. Toh. LC 96-44341. 313p. (C). 1996. lib. bdg. 125.00 (*0-7923-9822-X*) Kluwer Ac.

***Wireless Basics.** 2nd expanded rev. ed. Harry E. Young. (Illus.). 151p. (Orig.). 1996. pap. 29.95 (*0-87288-633-6*) Intertec IL.

***Wireless Business Communications.** 54p. 1993. 995.00 (*0-614-18369-3*, IGIC-66) Info Gatekeepers.

Wireless Cable & SMATV. Frank Baylin & Steve Borkoff. (Illus.). 386p. 1992. 50.00 (*0-917893-17-4*) Baylin Pubns.

***Wireless Cable, 1997.** Michael Percival. Ed. by Mike DeMuro & Rob Agee. (Illus.). 197p. 1996. write for info. (*0-88709-142-3*) Simba Info Inc.

***Wireless Cable, 1997: Review, Trends & Forecast.** 1996. 895.00 (*0-614-25706-9*) Simba Info.

***Wireless Communication.** Wornell & Poor. 1997. text ed. 60.00 (*0-13-620345-0*) P-H.

Wireless Communication: A Market Study. 1995. 1,885.00 (*1-877750-45-X*) ICE Corp.

Wireless Communication in the United States: The Early Development of American Radio Operating Companies. Thorn L. Mayes. Ed. by Arthur C. Goodnow et al. (Illus.). 248p. 1989. pap. text ed. 29.95 (*0-9625170-0-3*) NE Wireless & Steam Mus.

Wireless Communication 1996: A Market Study. Ed. by Hal Becker & Bill McClean. 1996. ring bd. 2,325.00 (*1-877750-50-6*) ICE Corp.

Wireless Communications. Theodore S. Rappaport. 1995. text ed. 71.00 (*0-13-375536-3*) P-H.

Wireless Communications, No. G-131. Business Communications Co., Inc. Staff. 245p. 1993. 2,250.00 (*0-89336-782-6*) BCC.

Wireless Communications: A Management Guide for Implementation. Computer Technology Research Corp. Staff. (Illus.). 222p. (Orig.). 1996. pap. 275.00 (*1-56607-964-0*) Comput Tech Res.

Wireless Communications: Future Directions. Ed. by Jack M. Holtzman & David J. Goodman. LC 92-43366. (International Series in Engineering & Computer Science, VLSI, Computer Architecture, & Digital Screen Processing). 352p. (C). 1993. lib. bdg. 105.00 (*0-7923-9316-3*) Kluwer Ac.

***Wireless Communications: Principles & Practice.** Theodore Rappaport. 656p. 1995. 71.00 (*0-7803-1167-1*, PC5641) Inst Electrical.

Wireless Communications-Addendum, No. G-131R. 245p. 1993. 2,250.00 (*0-89336-971-3*) BCC.

Wireless Communications for Intelligent Transportation Systems. Scott D. Elliott & Daniel J. Dailey. LC 95-33934. 405p. 1995. 77.00 (*0-89006-821-6*) Artech Hse.

Wireless Communications in Developing Countries: Cellular & Satellite Systems. Rachel Schwartz. LC 96-15595. 1996. 67.00 (*0-89006-874-7*) Artech Hse.

***Wireless Communicaton IC's: Design Principles, Technologies, & Applications.** Fazal Ali et al. (C). 1997. text ed. 52.50 (*0-13-487100-6*) P-H.

An Asterisk (*) at the beginning of an entry indicates that the title is appearing in BIP for the first time.

Wireless Computing: A Manager's Guide to Wireless Networking. Ira Brodsky. LC 97-14572. (Communications Ser.). 300p. 1997. text ed. 34.95 (*0-442-01912-2*) Van Nos Reinhold.

Wireless Computing Primer. Veronica Williams. 1995. pap. 27.95 (*1-55851-553-4*, M&T Books) H Holt & Co.

Wireless Data Communications. Alexa A. Dell'Acqua & John F. Mazzaferro. 106p. 1995. pap. 100.00 (*0-9648176-0-8*) TRIAD Svcs.

Wireless Data Handbook. James F. DeRose. LC 94-397. 372p. 1994. 79.00 (*0-930633-19-9*) Quantum Pub.

Wireless Data Modems: Theory & Implementation. Cheah Jonathon. (C). 1998. text ed. write for info. (*0-201-63393-0*) Addison-Wesley.

Wireless Data Networking. Nathan J. Muller. LC 94-23116. 1994. 69.00 (*0-89006-753-8*) Artech Hse.

Wireless Data Networks: A Guide to Mobile Computing. 3rd rev. ed. Patrick Sweeney & David Chamberlain. (Illus.). 97p. (Orig.). 1996. pap. 30.00 (*1-888619-01-5*, 4000) Bishop Co.

***Wireless Data Networks: A Guide to Mobile Computing.** 4th rev. ed. Patrick Sweeney & David Chamberlain. Ed. by Diane Kempen. (Illus.). 100p. (Orig.). 1997. pap. 30.00 (*1-888619-02-3*, 4300) Bishop Co.

***Wireless Digital Communications: Design & Theory.** Tom McDermott. 336p. 1997. pap. 39.99 incl. disk (*0-9644707-2-1*, TK5103) Tucson Amat Pack Rad.

Wireless Digital Communications: Modulation & Spread Spectrum Applications. Kamilo Feher. LC 95-6902. (Digital & Wireless Communication Ser.). 1995. text ed. 73.00 (*0-13-098617-8*) P-H.

Wireless Imagination: Sound, Radio, & the Avant-Garde. Ed. by Douglas Kahn & Gregory Whitehead. (Illus.). 466p. 1994. 17.95 (*0-262-61104-X*) MIT Pr.

Wireless Imagination: Sound, Radio & the Avant-Garde. Ed. by Douglas A. Kahn & Gregory Whitehead. (Illus.). 476p. 1992. 42.00 (*0-262-11168-3*) MIT Pr.

***Wireless In-Building Business Communications Market Opportunities.** 250p. 1991. 2,995.00 (*0-614-18370-7*, IGIC-77) Info Gatekeepers.

Wireless Information Networks. Kaveh Pahlavan & Allen H. Levesque. LC 94-22900. (Telecommunications & Signal Processing Ser.). 592p. 1995. text ed. 79.95 (*0-471-10607-0*) Wiley.

Wireless Information Networks: Architecture, Resource Management & Mobile Data. Ed. by Jack M. Holtzman. (International Engineering & Computer Science Robotic Ser.: Vol. 351). 416p. (C). 1996. lib. bdg. 95.00 (*0-7923-9694-4*) Kluwer Ac.

Wireless Infrared Communications. John R. Barry. LC 94-19272. (International Series in Engineering & Computer Science). 192p. (C). 1994. lib. bdg. 84.50 (*0-7923-9476-3*) Kluwer Ac.

Wireless LAN Systems. A. Santamaria & F. J. Lopez-Hernandez. LC 93-31145. 1993. 75.00 (*0-89006-609-4*) Artech Hse.

Wireless LANS. Raymond P. Wenig. (Illus.). 288p. 1995. pap. text ed. 29.95 (*0-12-744015-1*) Acad Pr.

***Wireless Local Area Networks.** 1994. 895.00 (*0-614-18371-5*, IGIC-67) Info Gatekeepers.

***Wireless Local Area Networks.** K. C. Chen. 300p. (C). 1997. text ed. 21.00 (*0-13-173494-6*) P-H.

Wireless Local Area Networks: Technology, Issues & Strategies. Peter T. Davis & Craig R. McGriffin. LC 94-34083. 1995. text ed. 40.00 (*0-07-015839-8*) McGraw.

Wireless Networked Communications Concepts, Technology & Implementation. Bud Bates. 1994. text ed. 55.00 (*0-07-004674-3*) McGraw.

Wireless Networking Handbook. Jim Geier. 432p. 1996. 39.99 (*1-56205-631-X*) Mac Comp Pub.

Wireless Networks: Catching the Mobile Future, 4 vols., Set. J. H. Weber et al. LC 94-78817. (Proceedings of Two Combined Conferences Held in The Hague, The Netherlands, Sep 18-23, 1994: The Fifth Ser.). 1453p. (gr. 12). 1994. pap. 200.00 (*90-5199-193-2*) IOS Press.

Wireless Office: LAN, PBX Users, Cut Cables, Eye Integration. 287p. 1992. 1,695.00 (*1-56753-008-7*) Frost & Sullivan.

Wireless One Headend Plans: Drawing No. 94138TXA. Robert Garner et al. Ed. by Ronald E. Mohar. (Illus.). 7p. 1995. pap. 49.95 (*1-888552-00-X*, B-012) Elect Pr.

Wireless Personal Communications. Ed. by Martin J. Feuerstein & Theodore S. Rappaport. LC 92-29797. (International Series in Engineering & Computer Science, VLSI, Computer Architecture, & Digital Screen Processing). 336p. (C). 1992. lib. bdg. 115.50 (*0-7923-9280-9*) Kluwer Ac.

***Wireless Personal Communications: A Systems Approach.** David J. Goodman. LC 97-23431. 1997. 51.59 (*0-201-63470-8*) Addison-Wesley.

***Wireless Personal Communications: Advances in Coverage & Capacity.** Ed. by Jeffrey H. Reed et al. LC 96-43020. (Kluwer International Series in Engineering & Computer Science). 240p. (C). 1996. lib. bdg. 89.95 (*0-7923-9788-6*) Kluwer Ac.

Wireless Personal Communications: Research Developments. Ed. by Brian D. Woerner et al. LC 95-3075. (Kluwer International Series in Engineering & Computer Science: Vol. SECS 309). 312p. (C). 1995. lib. bdg. 85.00 (*0-7923-9555-7*) Kluwer Ac.

Wireless Personal Communications: The Evolution of Personal Communications Systems. Ed. by Theodore S. Rappaport et al. (International Series in Engineering & Computer Science, Natural Language Processing & Machine Translation: Vol. 349). 232p. (C). 1995. lib. bdg. 88.50 (*0-7923-9676-6*) Kluwer Ac.

Wireless Personal Communications: Trends & Challenges. Ed. by Theodore S. Rappaport et al. LC 93-50913. (International Series in Engineering & Computer Science, VLSI, Computer Architecture, & Digital Screen Processing: Vol. 262). 280p. (C). 1994. lib. bdg. 110.50 (*0-7923-9430-5*) Kluwer Ac.

Wireless Personal Communications Services. Rajan Kuruppillai. LC 96-34731. (Illus.). 424p. 1996. pap. text ed. 55.00 (*0-07-036077-4*) McGraw.

Wireless Primer: A Basic Description of MMDS Television Systems. Emily Bostick et al. (Illus.). 76p. (Orig.). 1995. pap. 29.95 (*1-888552-02-6*) Elect Pr.

Wireless 'Proofing' Surveys: A Handbook for Wireless & LPTV Survey Technicians. Robert M. Garner et al. LC 95-83079. (Illus.). 99p. (Orig.). 1996. pap. 39.95 (*1-888552-06-9*, B-013) Elect Pr.

Wireless Radio: A History. Lewis Coe. LC 96-25734. (Illus.). 204p. 1996. lib. bdg. 27.50 (*0-7864-0259-8*) McFarland & Co.

Wireless Technologies & the National Information Infrastructure. (Illus.). 290p. (Orig.). (C). 1995. pap. text ed. 50.00 (*0-7881-2496-X*) DIANE Pub.

***Wireless Technologies & the National Information Infrastructure, 2 vols.** 298p. 1995. pap. text ed. 75.00 (*1-57979-137-9*) BPI Info Servs.

***Wireless Technologies & the National Information Infrastructure.** 1997. lib. bdg. 250.99 (*0-8490-7732-X*) Gordon Pr.

Wireless Transport: A Technological Overview. Andrew Novobilski. (C). 1996. pap. text ed. write for info. (*0-201-48405-6*) Addison-Wesley.

Wireline Carrier Billing Systems in Telecommunications: Worldwide Survey & Analysis Report on Service Provider Requirements & Supplier Opportunities in the Telecom Billing Systems Market. Daniel Baker & Stanley Klein. 1996. 4,990.00 (*1-879764-06-7*) Tech Res Inst.

Wireline Logging Tool Catalog. 2nd ed. Ed. by M. Verdier. (Illus.). 424p. 1986. 79.00 (*0-87201-916-0*, 1916) Gulf Pub.

Wireline Logging Tool Catalog: BPB, Dresser Atlas, Gearhart, Geoservices, Micro Log, Prakla Seismos Schmumberger. BPB Instrument Ltd. Staff & M. Verdier. (French Oil & Gas Industry Association Publications). (Illus.). 424p. (C). 1986. 575.00 (*2-7108-0503-0*, Pub. by Edits Technip FR) St Mut.

Wireline Operations. Nancy Gore. LC 83-62077. (Oil & Gas Production Ser.). (Illus.). 80p. (Orig.). 1984. pap. text ed. 15.00 (*0-88698-043-7*, 3.31010) PETEX.

***Wireman.** Billie S. Mosiman. 272p. 1997. reprint ed. mass mkt. 4.50 (*0-8439-4338-6*, Leisure Bks) Dorchester Pub Co.

***Wirespeak: Codes & Jargon of the News Business.** LC 97-91822. 176p. (Orig.). 1997. pap. 14.95 (*0-9657410-5-2*) Unipress Hist.

Wiretapping & Eavesdropping. Clifford S. Fishman. LC 78-18629. 1978. 120.00 (*0-685-59856-X*) Clark Boardman Callaghan.

Wiretapping & Electronic Eavesdropping, the Law & Its Implications: A Comparative Study. Juris Cederbaums. (New York University Criminal Law Education & Research Center Monograph: No. 2). 77p. (Orig.). 1969. pap. text ed. 8.50 (*0-8377-0402-2*) Rothman.

Wiretapping & Electronic Surveillance. 1986. lib. bdg. 150.00 (*0-8490-3530-9*) Gordon Pr.

Wiretapping & Electronic Surveillance. Studies Commission. (Illus.). 1983. reprint ed. pap. 12.95 (*1-55950-005-0*) Loompanics.

Wiretapping in New York City. Ed. by Robert M. Fogelson. LC 74-3843. (Criminal Justice in America Ser.). 1974. reprint ed. 15.95 (*0-405-06180-3*) Ayer.

***Wiring.** John Loew... Ed. by David W. Toht. (Easy-Step Ser.). (Illus.). 64p. (Orig.). 1997. pap. 6.95 (*0-614-18308-1*) Ortho Info.

Wiring. 2nd rev. ed. LC 96-84212. (Quick Guide Ser.). (Illus.). 80p. 1996. pap. 7.95 (*1-880029-83-9*) Creative Homeowner.

Wiring: Basic Repairs & Advanced Projects. Mort Schultz. Ed. by Gail Kummings. LC 81-67293. (Illus.). 160p. 1980. pap. 9.95 (*0-932944-38-8*) Creative Homeowner.

Wiring a Continent: The History of the Telegraph Industry in the United States, 1832-1866. Robert L. Thompson. LC 72-5078. (Technology & Society Ser.). (Illus.). 590p. 1972. reprint ed. 37.95 (*0-405-04727-4*) Ayer.

Wiring a House. Rex Cauldwell. (Illus.). 248p. 1996. 34.95 (*1-56158-113-5*, 070248) Taunton.

Wiring & Cable Designer's Handbook. Barnard S. Matisoff. 1987. 36.95 (*0-07-156237-0*) McGraw.

Wiring & Cable Designer's Handbook. Bernard S. Matisoff. (Illus.). 448p. 1986. 36.95 (*0-8306-2720-0*, NO. 2720, TAB/TPR) TAB Bks.

***Wiring Essentials.** (Black & Decker Quick Steps Ser.). (Illus.). 80p. (Orig.). 1996. pap. 9.95 (*0-86573-650-2*) Cowles Creative.

Wiring Practices for Hazardous Classified Locations Instrumentation Pt. 1: Intrinsic Safety. 1995. pap. 55.00 (*1-55617-545-0*, RP12.6) ISA.

***Wiring Regulations: Inspection, Testing & Certification.** 16th ed. B. Scaddan. (UK Wiring Standards Ser.). (Illus.). 144p. 1997. pap. 18.95 (*0-7506-2857-X*, Newnes) Buttrwrth-Heinemann.

Wiring Simplified: Based on 1996 National Electrical Code. 38th rev. ed. W. C. Schwan & Herbert P. Richter. LC 95-20531. 184p. 1995. pap. 6.95 (*0-9603294-6-3*) Park Pub.

Wiring Systems & Fault Finding for the Installation Electrician. Brian Scaddan. 112p. 1991. pap. 27.95 (*0-7506-0072-1*) Buttrwrth-Heinemann.

Wiring the Ivory Tower: A Round Table on Technology in Higher Education. Donald R. McNeil. 36p. 1990. pap. 7.00 (*0-685-59937-X*) Acad Educ Dev.

Wiring the Workgroup: E-mail & Beyond. Richard H. Baker. (Illus.). 352p. 1996. pap. text ed. 39.95 (*0-07-005725-7*) McGraw.

Wiring Twelve Volts for Ample Power. rev. ed. David Smead & Ruth Ishihara. LC 89-92666. (Illus.). 259p. (Orig.). 1995. pap. text ed. 20.00 (*0-945415-03-6*, RPC-002) Rides Pub.

Wiring up the Workplace: A Practical Guide for Management. Roger Camrass & Ken Smith. (Illus.). 167p. (Orig.). 1987. pap. 59.00 (*0-941723-00-3*) BCR Enterprises.

Wirking des Weizen-und Roggengenoms auf die Mitochondriale Genexpression Bei Titricale. Beate Laser. (Dissertationes Botanicae Ser.: 218). (Illus.). 102p. (GER.). 1994. pap. 59.50 (*3-443-64132-6*) Lubrecht & Cramer.

***Wirklichkeit des Films.** Eva Hohenberger. (Studien Zur Filmgeschichte Ser.: Vol. 5). 387p. (GER.). 1988. write for info. (*3-487-09049-X*) G Olms Pubs.

Wirklungen von Blei und Cadmium auf Wachstum und Mineralstoffhaushalt von Jungbuchen (Fagus Sylvatica L.) in Sandkultur. Henning Kahle. (Dissertationes Botanicae Ser.: Band 127). (Illus.). 226p. (GER.). 1988. spiral bd. 78.00 (*3-443-64039-7*) Lubrecht & Cramer.

Wirkung der Dosierten Distraktion auf das Ellenbogengelenk des Kaninchens. M. H. Hackenbroch. (Journal: Acta Anatomica: Vol. 96, Suppl. 63-1). (Illus.). 1977. 33.00 (*3-8055-2643-1*) S Karger.

Wirkung und Nebenwirkungen Von Bleomycin. Ed. by D. K. Hossfeld & P. Engel. (Beitraege zur Onkologie, Contributions to Oncology Ser.: Vol. 12). x, 220p. 1982. pap. 43.25 (*3-8055-3504-X*) S Karger.

Wirkungsstrukturen in Ausgewahlten Texten T. S. Eliots und Virginia Woolfs. Verena Olejniczak. (Anglistische und Amerikanistische Texte und Studien Ser.: No. 3). 385p. 1987. write for info. (*3-487-07885-6*) G Olms Pubs.

Wirrimanu: Aboriginal Art from the Balgo Hills. James Cowan. 180p. 1994. text ed. 60.00 (*976-8097-75-2*) Gordon & Breach.

Wirtschaft - Auf Deutsch: Glossar Amerikanisch-Englisch. Koeppel et al. 125p. (GER.). (C). 1994. pap. text ed. 18.00 (*3-12-675223-3*) Intl Bk Import.

Wirtschaft - Auf Deutsch: Lehr-/Arbeitsbuch. G. Nicolas et al. 326p. (GER.). (C). 1991. pap. text ed. 38.00 (*3-12-675215-2*, Pub. by Klett Edition GW) Intl Bk Import.

Wirtschaft - Auf Deutsch: Lehrerhandbuch. G. Nicolas et al. 168p. (GER.). (C). 1992. pap. text ed. 25.50 (*3-12-675216-0*, Pub. by Klett Edition GW) Intl Bk Import.

Wirtschaft aus der Zeitung: Lehr-/Arbeitsbuch. W. Schmitz & I. Martelly. 128p. (GER.). (C). 1993. pap. text ed. 22.00 (*3-12-675231-4*, Pub. by Klett Edition GW) Intl Bk Import.

Wirtschaft im Ohr Level 1: Lehrerheft. S. Dondoux-Liberge et al. 48p. (GER.). (C). 1990. pap. text ed. 14.50 (*3-12-675201-2*, Pub. by Klett Edition GW) Intl Bk Import.

Wirtschaft im Ohr Level 1: Uebungsbuch. S. Dondoux-Liberge et al. 48p. (GER.). (C). 1990. pap. text ed. 14.50 (*3-12-675200-4*, Pub. by Klett Edition GW); audio 45.00 (*3-12-675202-0*, Pub. by Klett Edition GW) Intl Bk Import.

Wirtschaft im Ohr Level 2: Lehrerheft. S. Dondoux-Liberge et al. 32p. (GER.). (C). 1990. pap. text ed. 14.50 (*3-12-675204-7*, Pub. by Klett Edition GW) Intl Bk Import.

Wirtschaft im Ohr Level 2: Uebungsbuch. S. Dondoux-Liberge et al. 48p. (GER.). (C). 1990. pap. text ed. 14.50 (*3-12-675203-9*, Pub. by Klett Edition GW); audio 27.00 (*3-12-675205-5*, Pub. by Klett Edition GW) Intl Bk Import.

Wirtschaft Steuerung des Umweltschutzes: Uberlegungen aus finnischer Sicht. Jaako Honko. (Akademie der Wissenschaften zu Berlin, Akademie-Vortrage Ser.: No. 2). xii, 32p. (GER.). (C). 1991. pap. text ed. 12.15 (*3-11-012839-X*) De Gruyter.

***Wirtschaft und Gesellschaft im Wandel: Argentinien.** Antonio Sommavilla. (Hispano-Americana Ser.: Bd. 15). 344p. (GER.). 1996. pap. 57.95 (*3-631-30883-3*) P Lang Pubng.

Wirtschaft und Umwelt Cortaillod -und Horgenzeitlicher Seeufersiedlungen in Zuerich (Schweiz) Ergebnisse Samenanalytischer Unter-Suchungen aus der Praehistorischen Station "Mozartstrasse" M. Dick. (Dissertationes Botanicae Ser.: Vol. 132). (Illus.). 114p. (ENG & GER.). 1989. pap. 48.00 (*3-443-64044-3*, Pub. by Cramer GW) Lubrecht & Cramer.

Wirtschaftende Mensch in der Geschichte. Lujo Brentano. xii, 498p. 1967. reprint ed. 95.00 (*0-318-70729-2*) G Olms Pubs.

Wirtschaftenglisch - Worterbuch. T. Bernem. 350p. (ENG & GER.). 1990. lib. bdg. 95.00 (*0-8288-3848-8*) Fr & Eur.

Wirtschaftinformaik-Lexikon. 4th ed. Lutz Heinrich. 737p. (GER.). 1992. 125.00 (*0-7859-8400-3*, 3486223275) Fr & Eur.

Wirtschaftliche Schwankungen der zeit von Alexander bis Augustus. Fritz M. Heichelheim. Ed. by Moses Finley. LC 79-4981. (Ancient Economic History Ser.). (Illus.). (GER.). 1979. reprint ed. lib. bdg. 18.95 (*0-405-12367-1*) Ayer.

***Wirtschaftliche Verflechtungen Deutscher Mittelstandischer Unternehmen mit der Republik Sudafrika Vol. XVIII: Betrachtungen vor dem Hintergrund Einer Theorie der Internationalen Produktion.** Michael Blank. (Europaische Hochshulschriften: Reihe 5: Bd. 2014). 330p. (GER.). 1996. pap. 57.95 (*3-631-31107-9*) P Lang Pubng.

Wirtschaftliche Zusammenbruch Osterreich-Ungarns: Die Tragodie der Erschopfung. Gustav Gratz & Richard Schuller. (Wirtschafts-Und Sozialgeschichte des Weltkrieges (Osterreichische Und Ungarische Serie)). (GER.). 1930. 100.00 (*0-317-27658-1*) Elliots Bks.

Wirtschafts-Woerterbuch. 2nd ed. Reinhart V. Eichborn & A. Fuentes. 2174p. (GER & SPA.). 250.00 (*3-430-12388-7*) Fr & Eur.

Wirtschafts-Woerterbuch. 4th ed. Reinhart V. Eichborn. 2169p. (ENG & GER.). write for info. (*0-318-52322-1*) Fr & Eur.

Wirtschafts Woerterbuch: Wirtschaft, Handel und Recht. Celestino Sanchez. (GER & SPA.). 1993. cd-rom 295.00 (*0-7859-6886-5*); cd-rom 295.00 (*0-7859-7095-9*) Fr & Eur.

Wirtschafts Woerterbuch: Wirtschaft, Handel und Recht, Vol. 1 German-Spanish. Celestino Sanchez. 519p. (GER & SPA.). 1990. 150.00 (*0-7859-6888-1*) Fr & Eur.

Wirtschafts Woerterbuch: Wirtschaft, Handel und Recht, Vol. 2 Spanish-German. Celestino Sanchez. 368p. (GER & SPA.). 1993. 150.00 (*0-7859-6889-X*) Fr & Eur.

Wirtschaftsdeutsch fuer Anfaenger: Lehr- und Arbeitsbuch. D. Macaire & G. Nicolas. 225p. (GER.). (C). 1995. pap. text ed. 27.00 (*3-12-675128-8*, Pub. by Klett Edition GW); audio 40.50 (*3-12-675130-X*, Pub. by Klett Edition GW) Intl Bk Import.

Wirtschaftsdeutsch in den U. S. A. Zielsetzungen und Programmbeschreibungen. Intro. by Bettina Cothran. 150p. (Orig.). (C). 1993. pap. text ed. 17.95 (*0-942017-12-9*) Amer Assn Teach German.

Wirtschaftsdeutsch Von A-Z: Kommunication und Fachwortschatz In der Wirtschaft. Rosemarie Buhlmann et al. 184p. (GER.). 1996. 24.50 (*3-468-49849-7*) Langenscheidt.

Wirtschaftsinformatik: Worterbuch. 2nd rev. ed. L. Heinrich. 203p. (ENG & GER.). 1990. lib. bdg. 85.00 (*0-8288-3885-2*, F49900) Fr & Eur.

Wirtschaftskonzeptionen und Wirtschaftspolitik der Sozialdemokratie in Bayern, 1945-1949. Hildegard Kronawitter. Ed. by Georg-von-Vollmar-Akademie Staff. (Illus.). 300p. (GER.). 1988. lib. bdg. 27.00 (*3-598-22020-0*) K G Saur.

Wirtschaftsleben der Antiken Welt. Lujo Brentano. vii, 242p. 1970. reprint ed. 40.00 (*0-318-70730-6*) G Olms Pubs.

Wirtschaftssprache Franzoesisch-Deutsch. G. Haensch & Rudiger Renner. 540p. (FRE & GER.). 1975. 105.00 (*0-8288-5958-2*, M7683) Fr & Eur.

Wirtschaftssprache Franzoesisch-Deutsch-Franzoesisch: French-German, German-French Economic Terms. 6th ed. Gunther Haensch & R. Rudiger. 539p. (FRE & GER.). 1980. 85.00 (*0-8288-0811-2*, M15086) Fr & Eur.

Wirtschaftswoerterbuch, Vol. 2. Wilhelm Schafer. 721p. (ENG & GER.). 1983. 135.00 (*0-8288-0103-7*, M 15196) Fr & Eur.

Wirtschaftswoerterbuch Spanisch-Deutsch: Spanish - German Economics Dictionary. Reinhart V. Eichborn & A. Fuentes. (GER & SPA.). 1974. 250.00 (*0-8288-6221-4*, M-7685) Fr & Eur.

Wirtschaftsworterbuch, Vol. 1. Clara-Erika Dietl. 409p. (ENG & GER.). 1989. lib. bdg. 125.00 (*0-8288-3849-6*, M6940) Fr & Eur.

Wirtschaftsworterbuch, Vol. 1. 2nd ed. Jurgen Boelcke. 440p. (FRE & GER.). 1990. lib. bdg. 135.00 (*0-8288-3895-X*, F131470) Fr & Eur.

Wirtschaftsworterbuch, Vol. 2. Jurgen Boelcke. 381p. (FRE & GER.). 1990. lib. bdg. 135.00 (*0-8288-3896-8*, F131190) Fr & Eur.

Wirtschaftsworterbuch, Vol. 2: 1990. Clara-Erika Dietl. 404p. (ENG & GER.). 1990. lib. bdg. 125.00 (*0-8288-3875-5*, M6939) Fr & Eur.

Wirtshaftswachstum und Bevolke Rungsentwicklung in Preussen 1816 Bis 1914: Zur Frage demo-Okonomischer Entwicklungszusammenhange. Gerd Hohorst. Ed. by Stuart Bruchey. LC 77-77193. (Dissertations in European Economic History Ser.). (Illus.). (GER.). 1978. lib. bdg. 47.95 (*0-405-10805-2*) Ayer.

Wirtshaus Im Spessart. unabridged ed. Hauff. (World Classic Literature Ser.). (GER.). pap. 5.95 (*3-89507-016-5*, Pub. by Bookking Intl FR) Distribks Inc.

WISC-III & WPPSI-R Supplement to Assessment of Children. abr. ed. Jerome M. Sattler. 200p. (C). 1992. pap. 17.50 (*0-9618209-3-4*) J M Sattler.

WISC-III Companion. Steve Truch. LC 92-40400. (C). 1993. spiral bd. 34.00 (*0-89079-585-1*, 6600) PRO-ED.

WISC-III Prescriptions. Norma Banas. LC 78-12881. 96p. 1992. pap. 12.00 (*0-87879-206-6*) Acad Therapy.

WISC-R Companion: A Desk Reference for the Wechsler Scales. Steve Truch. LC 88-35570. 272p. (C). 1989. text ed. 44.00 (*0-87562-100-7*, 3665) PRO-ED.

WISC 2 - The History of Wisconsin Through Integrated Student Creations. David Baers et al. 96p. (J). (gr. 3-10). 1996. pap. text ed. 29.95 incl. audio (*1-886790-02-7*) WISC Publ.

Wiscasset in Pownalborough: A History of the Shire Town & Salent Historical Features of the Territory Between the Sheepscot & Kennebee Rivers. Fannie S. Chase. (Illus.). 640p. 1990. reprint ed. lib. bdg. 64.50 (*0-8328-1643-4*) Higginson Bk Co.

Wiscasset, ME. Jim Harnedy. (Images of America Ser.). 128p. 1996. pap. 16.99 (*0-7524-0272-2*, Arcdia) Chalford.

***Wisconsin.** LC 96-46846. (One Nation Ser.). (J). 1997. write for info. (*1-56065-504-6*) Capstone Pr.

Wisconsin. Gretchen Bratvold. (Hello U. S. A. Ser.). (Illus.). 72p. (J). (gr. 3-6). 1995. lib. bdg. 18.95 (*0-8225-2700-6*, Lerner Publctns) Lerner Group.

W

*Wisconsin. Gretchen Bratvold. (Hello U. S. A. Ser.). (J). 1997. pap. text ed. 5.95 (0-8225-9761-6) Lerner Group.

*Wisconsin. Mark Lefebvre. (Illus.). 144p. (Orig.). 1993. 39.95 (1-55868-362-3) Gr Arts Ctr Pub.

Wisconsin. R. Conrad Stein. LC 87-9376. (America the Beautiful Ser.). (Illus.). 144p. (J). (gr. 4 up). 1987. lib. bdg. 28.30 (0-516-00495-6) Childrens.

*Wisconsin. Charlotte Wilcox. (One Nation Ser.). (Illus.). (J). 1997. 18.40 (0-516-20534-X) Childrens.

*Wisconsin. Karen Zeinert. LC 96-49381. (Celebrate the States Ser.). (Illus.). 144p. (YA). (gr. 4 up). 1997. lib. bdg. 22.95 (0-7614-0209-8, Benchmark NY) Marshall Cavendish.

Wisconsin. rev. ed. Kathleen Thompson. LC 95-25728. (Portrait of America Library). 48p. (YA). (gr. 3 up). 1996. lib. bdg. 22.83 (0-8114-7396-1) Raintree Steck-V.

Wisconsin. rev. ed. Kathleen Thompson. LC 95-25728. (Portrait of America Library). 48p. (YA). (gr. 3 up). 1996. pap. 5.95 (0-8114-7477-1) Raintree Steck-V.

*Wisconsin. 2nd ed. Charles Calhoun. (Compass American Guide Ser.). 1997. pap. 18.95 (1-878867-49-0) Fodors Travel.

Wisconsin: A Guide to the Badger State. Federal Writers' Project Staff & Writers Program-WPA Staff. (American Guide Ser.). 1989. reprint ed. lib. bdg. 89.00 (0-7812-1048-8, 1048) Rprt Serv.

Wisconsin: A History. 2nd rev. ed. Robert C. Nesbit. (Illus.). 600p. (C). 1990. 25.00 (0-299-10800-7) U of Wis Pr.

Wisconsin: A Picture Memory. Outlet Book Co. Staff. (Illus.). 1991. 8.99 (0-517-06026-4) Random Hse Value.

Wisconsin: A State Guide. Federal Writers' Project. 89.00 (0-403-02198-7) Somerset Pub.

Wisconsin: Family Adventure Guide: Great Things to See & Do for the Entire Family. Martin Hintz & Dan Hintz. LC 95-13044. (Family Adventure Guide Ser.). (Illus.). 160p. (Orig.). 1995. pap. 9.95 (1-56440-615-6) Globe Pequot.

Wisconsin: Its Geography & Topography, History, Geology & Mineralogy. Increase A. Lapham. LC 74-107. (Mid-American Frontier Ser.). 1975. reprint ed. 21.95 (0-405-06874-3) Ayer.

Wisconsin: Off the Beaten Path: A Guide to Unique Places. 3rd ed. Dan Hintz & Martin Hintz. LC 95-19280. (Off the Beaten Path Ser.). (Illus.). 160p. 1995. pap. 10.95 (1-56440-730-6) Globe Pequot.

Wisconsin: Pathways to Prosperity. Shiela Reaves. (Illus.). 336p. (YA). (gr. 7 up). 1988. 32.95 (0-89781-236-0) Am Historical Pr.

Wisconsin: River of a Thousand Isles. August Derleth. LC 85-40367. 368p. 1985. reprint ed. pap. 12.95 (0-299-10374-9) U of Wis Pr.

Wisconsin: The Americanization of a French Settlement. Reuben G. Thwaites. LC 72-3747. (American Commonwealths Ser.: No. 20). reprint ed. 49.50 (0-404-57220-0) AMS Pr.

Wisconsin: The Story of the Badger State. Norman K. Risjord. LC 95-61444. (Illus.). 240p. 1995. pap. 16.95 (0-915024-49-7) WI Tales & Trails.

Wisconsin: The Way We Were. Mary A. Shafer. LC 92-42347. 1993. 19.95 (1-55971-156-6) NorthWord.

Wisconsin see Atlas of Historical County Boundaries

Wisconsin - Collected Works of Federal Writers Project. Federal Writers' Project Staff. 1991. reprint ed. lib. bdg. 98.00 (0-7812-5812-X) Rprt Serv.

Wisconsin - From Sea to Shining Sea. Dennis B. Fradin. LC 92-8135. (From Sea to Shining Sea Ser.). (Illus.). 64p. (J). (gr. 3-5). 1992. pap. 5.95 (0-516-43849-2); lib. bdg. 24.00 (0-516-03849-4) Childrens.

Wisconsin Almanac. Ed. by Jerry Minnich. 272p. (Orig.). 1989. pap. 9.95 (0-944133-06-1) Nrth Cntry Pr.

Wisconsin & Minnesota Trout Streams: A Fly-Angler's Guide. Jim Humphrey & Bill Shogren. (Illus.). 272p. (Orig.). 1995. pap. 17.00 (0-88150-307-X, Backcountry) Countryman.

Wisconsin & Other State Greats (Biographies) Carole Marsh. (Carole Marsh Wisconsin Bks.). (Illus.). (J). 1994. pap. 19.95 (0-7933-2289-8); lib. bdg. 29.95 (0-7933-2288-X); disk 29.95 (0-7933-2290-1) Gallopade Pub Group.

Wisconsin & the Mentally Ill. Dale W. Robison. Ed. by Gerald N. Grob. LC 78-22588. (Historical Issues in Mental Health Ser.). 1980. lib. bdg. 28.95 (0-405-11939-9) Ayer.

Wisconsin Atlas & Gazetteer. 4th ed. DeLorme Mapping Company Staff. (Illus.). 104p. (Orig.). 1995. pap. 16.95 (0-89933-251-X, 5503) DeLorme Map.

Wisconsin Attorney's - Secretary's Handbook, 1993-94. J. Olker. 1993. 59.00 (1-880919-04-4) Namar Comms.

Wisconsin Attorney's - Secretary's Handbook, 1994-95. J. Olker. 1994. 59.00 (1-880919-07-9) Namar Comms.

*Wisconsin Attorney's Desk Reference, 2 vols. 600p. 1992. ring bd. 115.00 (0-945574-01-0) State Bar WI CLE Bk Div.

Wisconsin Automotive Directory. Ed. by T. L. Spelman. 1985. 24.95 (1-55527-034-4) Auto Contact Inc.

Wisconsin Badgers Facts & Trivia. Jeff Everson & Linda Everson. (Illus.). 80p. (Orig.). 1994. pap. 4.99 (0-938313-07-X) E B Houchin.

Wisconsin Bandits, Bushwackers, Outlaws, Crooks, Devils, Ghosts, Desperadoes & Other Assorted & Sundry Characters! Carole Marsh. (Carole Marsh Wisconsin Bks.). (Illus.). (J). 1994. pap. 19.95 (0-7933-1225-6); lib. bdg. 29.95 (0-7933-1226-4); disk 29.95 (0-7933-1227-2) Gallopade Pub Group.

Wisconsin Biking Guide. Barbara McCaig. Ed. by Cary Vanderboom. (Illus.). 100p. (Orig.). 1989. pap. text ed. 5.95 (0-935201-77-7) Affordable Adven.

Wisconsin Birdlife: Population & Distribution Past & Present. Samuel D. Robbins, Jr. LC 90-50095. 720p. 1991. 75.00 (0-299-10260-2) U of Wis Pr.

Wisconsin Birds: A Seasonal & Geographic Guide. Stanley A. Temple. LC 86-40487. 280p. 1987. text ed. 27.50 (0-299-11430-9) U of Wis Pr.

*Wisconsin Birds: A Seasonal & Geographic Guide. 2nd ed. Stanley A. Temple et al. (North Coast Bks.). (Illus.). 366p. 1997. 29.95 (0-299-15220-0) U of Wis Pr.

*Wisconsin Birds: A Seasonal & Geographic Guide. 2nd ed. Stanley A. Temple et al. (North Coast Bks.). (Illus.). 366p. 1997. pap. 14.95 (0-299-15224-3) U of Wis Pr.

Wisconsin Bookstore Book: A Surprising Guide to Our State's Bookstores & Their Specialties for Students, Teachers, Writers & Publishers. Carole Marsh. (Wisconsin Bks.). (Illus.). 1994. pap. 19.95 (0-7933-3003-3); lib. bdg. 29.95 (0-7933-3002-5); disk 29.95 (0-7933-3004-1) Gallopade Pub Group.

Wisconsin Boy in Dixie: Civil War Letters of James K. Newton. Ed. by Stephen E. Ambrose. LC 94-24104. (Illus.). 214p. 1995. pap. 11.95 (0-299-02484-9) U of Wis Pr.

Wisconsin Business Corporation Law. Ed. by Christopher S Berry et al. LC 92-44987. 980p. 1992. 125.00 (0-945574-52-5) State Bar WI CLE Bk Div.

Wisconsin Business Directory, 1997. rev. ed. 2064p. 1996. boxed 445.00 (1-56105-800-9) Am Busn Direct.

*Wisconsin Business Directory 1997. rev. ed. American Business Directories Staff. 2064p. 1996. boxed 445.00 (1-56105-883-1) Am Busn Direct.

*Wisconsin Business Directory 1998. rev. ed. American Business Directories Staff. 2112p. 1997. boxed 445.00 (1-56105-970-6) Am Busn Direct.

Wisconsin Capitol: Fascinating Facts. Diana Cook. LC 91-7976. 1991. pap. 7.95 (1-879483-02-5) Prairie Oak Pr.

Wisconsin Census Index 1836. Ronald V. Jackson. LC 77-86057. (Illus.). 1976. lib. bdg. 49.00 (0-89593-152-4) Accelerated Index.

Wisconsin Census Index, 1846. Ronald V. Jackson. 1978. 75.00 (0-685-52206-7) Accelerated Index.

Wisconsin Census Index 1850 Mortality Schedule. (Illus.). lib. bdg. 60.00 (0-89593-536-8) Accelerated Index.

Wisconsin Center for Education Research: Twenty-Five Years of Knowledge Generation & Educational Improvement. Klausmeier, Herbert J., & Associates Staff. (Illus.). xviii, 254p. (Orig.). (C). 1990. pap. write for info. (0-9627393-0-8) WI Ctr Educ Rsch.

Wisconsin Central: Railroad Success Story. Photos by Otto P. Dobnick & Steve Glischinski. (Illus.). 160p. 1997. 49.95 (0-89024-562-2, 01069, Kalmbach Books) Kalmbach.

*Wisconsin Central Limited Photo Archive. Frank Jordon. LC 97-70619. (Photo Archive Ser.). (Illus.). 128p. (Orig.). 1997. pap. 29.95 (1-882256-75-1) Iconografix.

*Wisconsin Children's Code & Juvenile Justice Code. 140p. 1997. pap. 25.00 (0-945574-93-2) State Bar WI CLE Bk Div.

Wisconsin Chippewa Myths & Tales & Their Relation to Chippewa Life. Victor Barnouw. LC 76-53647. 304p. (C). 1993. reprint ed. pap. 14.95 (0-299-07314-9) U of Wis Pr.

Wisconsin Christmas Anthology. 2nd ed. Ed. by Theresa R. Engels. (State Anthologies Ser.: No. 2). (Illus.). 1990. pap. 10.95 (0-9621085-1-0) Partridge Pr.

*Wisconsin Citizenship Initiative - Program Guide. Joseph Quick. 74p. (Orig.). 1997. pap. text ed. 15.00 (1-57337-039-8, 7178) WI Dept Pub Instruct.

Wisconsin Civil Litigation Forms Manual. Ed. by Angela B. Bartell et al. LC 95-44419. 600p. 1995. ring bd. 179.00 incl. disk (0-945574-77-0) State Bar WI CLE Bk Div.

Wisconsin Civil Procedure Before Trial. Jean W. Di Motto. LC 96-386. 800p. 1996. ring bd. 125.00 (0-945574-79-7) State Bar WI CLE Bk Div.

Wisconsin Civil War Census, 1885. 1990. 150.00 (0-89593-606-2) Accelerated Index.

Wisconsin Civil War Tokens. Rich Hartzog. (Illus.). 108p. 1991. pap. 15.00 (0-912317-15-9) World Exo.

Wisconsin Classic Christmas Trivia: Stories, Recipes, Activities, Legends, Lore & More. Carole Marsh. (Carole Marsh Wisconsin Bks.). (Illus.). (J). 1994. pap. 19.95 (0-7933-1228-0); lib. bdg. 29.95 (0-7933-1229-9); disk 29.95 (0-7933-1230-2) Gallopade Pub Group.

Wisconsin Coastales. Carole Marsh. (Carole Marsh Wisconsin Bks.). (Illus.). (J). 1994. 29.95 (0-7933-2282-0); pap. 19.95 (0-7933-2283-9); disk 29.95 (0-7933-2284-7) Gallopade Pub Group.

Wisconsin Coastales! Carole Marsh. (Wisconsin Bks.). (J). 1994. lib. bdg. 29.95 (0-7933-7314-X) Gallopade Pub Group.

Wisconsin Collection Law. Robert A. Pasch. LC 79-91165. 1993. 125.00 (0-317-05728-6) Lawyers Cooperative.

Wisconsin Condominium Law Handbook. 2nd ed. Joseph W. Boucher et al. LC 93-48243. 1994. ring bd. 90.00 (0-945574-59-2) State Bar WI CLE Bk Div.

*Wisconsin Construction Lien Law Handbook. 2nd ed. Steven W. Martin. 130p. 1993. ring bd. 55.00 (0-945574-46-0) State Bar WI CLE Bk Div.

Wisconsin Cookin' B. Carlson. (Illus.). 160p. 1994. spiral bd. 5.95 (1-57166-004-6) Hearts N Tummies.

*Wisconsin Corporations. 2nd ed. John M. Olson et al. LC 96-137930. 700p. 1995. text ed. write for info. (0-7620-0035-X) Lawyers Cooperative.

Wisconsin Corporations: Practice Systems Library Manual. Jack A. Postlewaite. LC 79-91166. ring bd. 120.00 (0-317-00430-1) Lawyers Cooperative.

Wisconsin Corporations: Practice Systems Library Manual. Jack A. Postlewaite. LC 79-91166. 1991. suppl. ed. 67.50 (0-317-03171-6) Lawyers Cooperative.

Wisconsin County Maps: A Guide to Fun in Wisconsin. Bruce Taugner. (Illus.). 128p. 1994. pap. text ed. 12.95 (1-878223-00-3) Clarkson Map.

*Wisconsin Cranberry Grower's Favorite Recipes. 2nd rev. ed. Peggy Anderson. 138p. 1991. pap. 12.00 (0-9656821-0-2) Peggy Anderson.

Wisconsin Crime Perspective 1996. Ed. by Kathleen O. Morgan et al. 24p. 1996. pap. 19.00 (1-56692-548-7) Morgan Quitno Corp.

*Wisconsin Crime Perspective 1997. Ed. by Kathleen O. Morgan & Scott E. Morgan. 24p. 1997. pap. 19.00 (1-56692-798-6) Morgan Quitno Corp.

*Wisconsin Criminal Code & Selected Traffic Statutes. 390p. 1997. pap. write for info. (1-57862-000-7) State Bar WI CLE Bk Div.

*Wisconsin Criminal Defense Manual. L. Michael Tobin. 740p. 1996. ring bd. 135.00 incl. disk (0-945574-86-X) State Bar WI CLE Bk Div.

Wisconsin "Crinkum-Crankum" A Funny Word Book about Our State. Carole Marsh. (Wisconsin Bks.). (Illus.). (J). (gr. 3-12). 1994. 29.95 (0-7933-4958-3); pap. 19.95 (0-7933-4959-1); disk 29.95 (0-7933-4960-5) Gallopade Pub Group.

*Wisconsin Damages Awards: 1996 Edition. rev. ed. Ed. by Timothy M. Hall. LC 94-76229. 600p. 1996. pap. text ed. write for info. (0-7620-0086-4) Lawyers Cooperative.

Wisconsin Death Trip. Michael Lesy. 264p. 1991. pap. 19.95 (0-385-41215-0, Anchor NY) Doubleday.

*Wisconsin Developmental Guidance Model: A Resource & Planning Guide for School-Community Teams. rev. ed. Deborah Bilzing-Ernst. 110p. (C). 1997. pap. text ed. 24.00 (1-57337-047-9) WI Dept Pub Instruct.

Wisconsin Dingbats! Bk. 1: A Fun Book of Games, Stories, Activities & More about Our State That's All in Code! for You to Decipher. Carole Marsh. (Wisconsin Bks.). (Illus.). (J). (gr. 3-12). 1994. pap. 19.95 (0-7933-3921-9); lib. bdg. 29.95 (0-7933-3920-0); disk 29.95 (0-7933-3922-7) Gallopade Pub Group.

Wisconsin Directory of International Institutions. Karen L. Niesen & Christine Y. Onaga. 261p. 1994. pap. 25.00 (0-299-97079-5) U of Wis Pr.

*Wisconsin Discovery Law & Practice. Richard L. Bolton et al. 400p. 1990. ring bd. 95.00 (0-945574-39-8) State Bar WI CLE Bk Div.

*Wisconsin Discovery Law & Practice. 2nd ed. Richard L. Bolton. LC 97-11700. 1997. write for info. (0-945574-99-1) State Bar WI CLE Bk Div.

*Wisconsin Educational Technology Plan PK-12. Neah J. Lohr. 130p. (Orig.). (J). (gr. k-12). 1996. pap. text ed. 21.00 (1-57337-038-X) WI Dept Pub Instruct.

Wisconsin Employment Law, 3 vols. Bradden C. Backer et al. LC 94-1855. 1500p. 1994. ring bd. 195.00 (0-945574-62-2) State Bar WI CLE Bk Div.

Wisconsin Environmental Law Handbook. 3rd ed. DeWitt et al. 424p. 1995. pap. text ed. 89.00 (0-86587-457-3) Gov Insts.

*Wisconsin Environmental Regulatory Directory. Ed. by Chesley P. Erwin, Jr. et al. (Illus.). 100p. 1997. spiral bd. 34.99 (1-890332-00-3) Environ Info Servs.

*Wisconsin Ethics Opinions. 600p. 1990. ring bd. 60.00 (0-945574-37-1) State Bar WI CLE Bk Div.

Wisconsin Facts & Factivities. Carole Marsh. (Carole Marsh State Bks.). (Illus.). 1996. 29.95 (0-614-11563-9, C Marsh); teacher ed., pap. 19.95 (0-7933-7945-8, C Marsh) Gallopade Pub Group.

Wisconsin Fair Dealership Law. 2nd ed. Michael A. Bowen & Brian E. Butler. LC 95-136. 400p. 1995. ring bd. 125.00 (0-945574-73-8) State Bar WI CLE Bk Div.

Wisconsin: Family Adventure Guide see Fun with the Family in Wisconsin

*Wisconsin Family Code & Related Statutes. 190p. 1997. pap. 30.00 (0-945574-92-4) State Bar WI CLE Bk Div.

Wisconsin Father's Guide to Divorce & Custody. James Novak. 160p. (Orig.). 1996. pap. 18.95 (1-879483-31-9) Prairie Oak Pr.

Wisconsin Federal Census Index, 1820. 1984. 30.00 (0-89593-600-3) Accelerated Index.

Wisconsin Federal Census Index, 1830. Ronald V. Jackson. (Illus.). 1984. lib. bdg. 48.00 (0-89593-535-X) Accelerated Index.

Wisconsin Federal Census Index, 1840. Ronald V. Jackson. LC 77-86058. (Illus.). 1978. lib. bdg. 58.00 (0-89593-153-2) Accelerated Index.

Wisconsin Federal Census Index, 1850. Ronald V. Jackson. LC 77-86059. (Illus.). 1978. lib. bdg. 88.00 (0-89593-154-0) Accelerated Index.

Wisconsin Federal Census Index, 1860 (Milwaukee & Winnebago Counties) (Includes Cities of Milwaukee & Oshkosh) (Illus.). lib. bdg. 100.00 (0-89593-537-6) Accelerated Index.

Wisconsin Federal Census Index, 1870. (Illus.). lib. bdg. write for info. (0-89593-538-4) Accelerated Index.

Wisconsin Federal Census Index, 1880. (Illus.). lib. bdg. write for info. (0-89593-539-2) Accelerated Index.

Wisconsin Festival Fun for Kids! Includes Reproducible Activities for Kids! Carole Marsh. (Wisconsin Bks.). (Illus.). (J). (gr. 3-12). 1994. pap. 19.95 (0-7933-4074-8); lib. bdg. 29.95 (0-7933-4073-X); disk 29.95 (0-7933-4075-6) Gallopade Pub Group.

Wisconsin Focuses on Career Guidance: Parents, Students, Guidance Counselors & School Administrators Talk about Career Counseling & the School-to-Work Transition Initiative. 46p. 1993. pap. 5.00 (1-887410-72-4) Jobs for Future.

Wisconsin Folklore. Walker B. Wyman. (Illus.). 1981. pap. 4.95 (0-686-27304-4) U Wisc-River Falls Pr.

Wisconsin Food Festivals: Good Food, Good Folks & Good Fun at Community Celebrations. Terese Allen. LC 95-17345. (Illus.). 196p. (Orig.). 1995. pap. 15.95 (0-942495-45-4) Amherst Pr.

Wisconsin from the Sky. Photos by Larry Mayer. (Illus.). 120p. (Orig.). 1994. 29.95 (1-56037-057-2) Am Wrld Geog.

Wisconsin Funeral Service: A Consumer's Guide. 3rd ed. pap. 2.95 (0-318-23655-9) UWIM CCA.

Wisconsin Garden Guide. 3rd ed. Jerry Minnich. LC 95-2342. 1995. pap. 18.95 (1-879483-24-6) Prairie Oak Pr.

*Wisconsin Government! The Cornerstone of Everyday Life in Our State! Carole Marsh. (Carole Marsh Wisconsin Bks.). (Illus.). (J). (gr. 3-12). 1996. pap. 19.95 (0-7933-6329-2); lib. bdg. 19.95 (0-7933-6328-4); disk 29.95 (0-7933-6330-6) Gallopade Pub Group.

Wisconsin Governments Performance Standards, 1990. Ed. by Greg Michels. (Governments Performance Standards Ser.). (Illus.). 150p. 1990. text ed. 125.00 (1-55507-507-X) Municipal Analysis.

*Wisconsin Guide to Citation. 18p. 1997. 6.00 (0-614-24812-4) State Bar WI CLE Bk Div.

*Wisconsin Handbook. Thomas Huhti. 1997. pap. text ed. 16.95 (1-56691-092-7) Moon Trvl Hdbks.

Wisconsin Health Care Perspective 1996. Ed. by Kathleen O. Morgan et al. 24p. 1996. pap. 19.00 (1-56692-648-3) Morgan Quitno Corp.

*Wisconsin Health Care Perspective 1997. Ed. by Kathleen O. Morgan & Scott E. Morgan. 24p. 1997. pap. 19.00 (1-56692-748-X) Morgan Quitno Corp.

Wisconsin Herb Cookbook. Suzanne Breckenridge & Marjorie Snyder. (Illus.). 180p. (Orig.). 1996. pap. 18.95 (1-879483-32-7) Prairie Oak Pr.

Wisconsin Heroes. Marv Balousek. Ed. by J. Allen Kirsch. (Illus.). 200p. (Orig.). 1995. pap. 12.95 (1-878569-28-7) Badger Bks Inc.

Wisconsin Historical & Biographical Index, Vol. 1. Ronald V. Jackson. LC 78-53723. (Illus.). 1984. lib. bdg. 30.00 (0-89593-205-9) Accelerated Index.

*Wisconsin History! Surprising Secrets about Our State's Founding Mothers, Fathers & Kids! Carole Marsh. (Carole Marsh Wisconsin Bks.). (Illus.). (J). (gr. 3-12). 1996. pap. 19.95 (0-7933-6176-1); lib. bdg. 29.95 (0-7933-6175-3); disk 29.95 (0-7933-6177-X) Gallopade Pub Group.

Wisconsin Hot Air Balloon Mystery. Carole Marsh. (Carole Marsh Wisconsin Bks.). (Illus.). (J). (gr. 2-9). 1994. 29.95 (0-7933-2759-8); pap. 19.95 (0-7933-2760-1); disk 29.95 (0-7933-2761-X) Gallopade Pub Group.

Wisconsin Hunting: A Comprehensive Guide to Wisconsin's Public Hunting Lands. Ed. by Brian Lovett. LC 93-77542. (Illus.). 208p. (Orig.). 1993. pap. 16.95 (0-87341-249-4, HW02) Krause Pubns.

Wisconsin Hunting Encyclopedia. 1976. pap. 2.95 (0-932558-06-2) Wisconsin Sptmn.

Wisconsin Ice Trade. Lee E. Lawrence. (Wisconsin Stories Ser.). 12p. pap. 1.25 (0-87020-197-2) State Hist Soc Wis.

Wisconsin in Perspective 1996. Ed. by Kathleen O. Morgan et al. 26p. 1996. pap. 19.00 (1-56692-598-3) Morgan Quitno Corp.

*Wisconsin in Perspective 1997. Ed. by Kathleen O. Morgan & Scott E. Morgan. 26p. 1997. pap. 19.00 (1-56692-698-X) Morgan Quitno Corp.

Wisconsin in the Civil War: The Home Front & the Battle Front, 1861-1865. Frank L. Klement. LC 96-6259. (Illus.). 1996. write for info. (0-87020-286-3) State Hist Soc Wis.

Wisconsin Indian Dictionary for Kids! Carole Marsh. (Carole Marsh State Bks.). (J). (gr. 2-9). 1996. 29.95 (0-7933-7791-9, C Marsh); pap. 19.95 (0-7933-7792-7, C Marsh) Gallopade Pub Group.

Wisconsin Indians. Nancy O. Lurie. (Illus.). 66p. 1987. 3.00 (0-87020-252-9) State Hist Soc Wis.

Wisconsin Insurance Law. 3rd ed. A. P. Anderson. 117p. 1994. suppl. ed. 57.00 (0-471-00644-1) Wiley.

Wisconsin Insurance Law. 3rd ed. Arnold P. Anderson. LC 91-22192. (Business Practice Library). 498p. 1991. text ed. 135.00 (0-471-55307-7) Wiley.

*Wisconsin Insurance Law - 1997 Cumulative Supplement. 3rd ed. Arnold P. Anderson. 1996. pap. text ed. 72.00 (0-471-17255-3) Wiley.

Wisconsin Jeopardy! Answers & Questions about Our State! Carole Marsh. (Wisconsin Bks.). (Illus.). (J). (gr. 3-12). 1994. pap. 19.95 (0-7933-4227-9); lib. bdg. 29.95 (0-7933-4226-0); disk 29.95 (0-7933-4228-7) Gallopade Pub Group.

*Wisconsin Jobbank. Adams Media Staff. 1997. pap. text ed. 16.95 (1-55850-739-6) Adams Media.

Wisconsin "Jography" A Fun Run Thru Our State! Carole Marsh. (Carole Marsh Wisconsin Bks.). (Illus.). (J). 1994. pap. 19.95 (0-7933-2266-9); lib. bdg. 29.95 (0-7933-2265-0); disk 29.95 (0-7933-2267-7) Gallopade Pub Group.

Wisconsin Judicare: A Preliminary Appraisal. Samuel J. Brakel. LC 72-95564. 122p. Date not set. pap. 20.00 (0-910058-56-3, 305080) W S Hein.

*Wisconsin Judicial Benchbooks Vol. I: Criminal & Traffic. 500p. 1982. ring bd. 75.00 (0-945574-17-7) State Bar WI CLE Bk Div.

*Wisconsin Judicial Benchbooks Vol. II: Civil. 460p. 1982. ring bd. 75.00 (0-945574-18-5) State Bar WI CLE Bk Div.

*Wisconsin Judicial Benchbooks Vol. III: Family. 280p. 1982. ring bd. 75.00 (0-945574-19-3) State Bar WI CLE Bk Div.

*Wisconsin Judicial Benchbooks Vol. IV: Juvenile. 430p. 1982. ring bd. 75.00 (0-945574-20-7) State Bar WI CLE Bk Div.

*Wisconsin Judicial Benchbooks Vol. V: Probate, Guardianship, & Mental Health. 310p. 1982. ring bd. 75.00 (0-945574-66-5) State Bar WI CLE Bk Div.

Wisconsin Juvenile Court Practice & Procedure in Protection of Children. 2nd ed. Henry J. Plum & Frank J. Crisafi. LC 93-25982. 425p. 1993. spiral bd. 95.00 (0-250-40708-6) MICHIE.

*Wisconsin Juvenile Law Handbook. Virginia A. Pomeroy & Gina M. Pruski. LC 96-34341. 660p. 1996. ring bd. 115.00 incl. disk (0-945574-88-6) State Bar WI CLE Bk Div.

An Asterisk (*) at the beginning of an entry indicates that the title is appearing in BIP for the first time.

Wisconsin Kid's Cookbook: Recipes, How-To, History, Lore & More! Carole Marsh. (Carole Marsh Wisconsin Bks.). (Illus.). (J). 1994. pap. 19.95 (*0-7933-1237-X*); lib. bdg. 29.95 (*0-7933-1238-8*); disk 29.95 (*0-7933-1239-6*) Gallopade Pub Group.

***Wisconsin Land & Life.** Ed. by Robert C. Ostergren & Thomas R. Vale. LC 96-36447. (North Coast Bks.). 626p. 1997. 69.95 (*0-299-15350-9*); pap. 27.95 (*0-299-15354-1*) U of Wis Pr.

Wisconsin Land Surveying Law: Questions & Answers. John E. Keen. 33p. (C). 1995. pap. text ed. 20.00 (*1-56569-044-3*) Land Survey.

Wisconsin Library Book: A Surprising Guide to the Unusual Special Collections in Libraries Across Our State for Students, Teachers, Writers & Publishers. Carole Marsh. (Wisconsin Bks.). (Illus.). 1994. pap. 19.95 (*0-7933-3153-6*); lib. bdg. 29.95 (*0-7933-3152-8*); disk 29.95 (*0-7933-3154-4*) Gallopade Pub Group.

Wisconsin Library Media Skills Guide. rev. ed. Wisconsin Association of School Librarians, WLA Staff. 142p. 1992. 18.00 (*0-318-23791-1*) Wisc Lib Assn.

***Wisconsin Limited Liability Company Forms & Practice Manual.** Michael Lappin et al. 512p. 1997. ring bd. 149.95 (*1-57400-028-4*) Data Trace Pubng.

Wisconsin Limited Liability Company Handbook. Joseph W. Boucher. LC 94-43138. 450p. 1994. ring bd. 165.00 incl. disk (*0-945574-64-9*) State Bar WI CLE Bk Div.

Wisconsin Magazine of History, Cumulative Index: Vols. 26-35. 1955. pap. 3.00 (*0-87020-025-9*) State Hist Soc Wis.

Wisconsin Magazine of History, Cumulative Index: Vols. 36-45. 1962. pap. 3.00 (*0-87020-026-7*) State Hist Soc Wis.

Wisconsin Magazine of History, Cumulative Index: Vols. 46-55. pap. 9.50 (*0-87020-139-5*) State Hist Soc Wis.

Wisconsin Magazine of History, Cumulative Index: Vols. 56-65. 30.00 (*0-87020-242-1*) State Hist Soc Wis.

Wisconsin Media Book: A Surprising Guide to the Amazing Print, Broadcast & Online Media of Our State for Students, Teachers, Writers & Publishers - Includes Reproducible Mailing Labels Plus Activities for Young People! Carole Marsh. (Wisconsin Bks.). (Illus.). 1994. pap. 19.95 (*0-7933-3309-1*); lib. bdg. 29.95 (*0-7933-3308-3*); disk 29.95 (*0-7933-3310-5*) Gallopade Pub Group.

Wisconsin Medical Directory: April 1995. rev. ed. Ed. by Jola Publications Staff. 182p. 1995. pap. 15.00 (*1-878373-09-9*) Jola Pubns.

Wisconsin Medical Directory: October, 1991. rev. ed. Ed. by Jola Publications Staff. 136p. 1991. pap. 12.00 (*1-878373-01-3*) Jola Pubns.

Wisconsin Medicine: Historical Perspectives. Ronald L. Numbers & Judith W. Leavitt. LC 80-52297. (Illus.). 224p. 1981. 19.95 (*0-299-08430-2*) U of Wis Pr.

Wisconsin Model for Sex Equity in Career & Vocational Education. Barbara A. Bitters & Susan Foxwell. 296p. (C). 1993. pap. text ed. 33.00 (*1-57337-025-8*) WI Dept Pub Instruct.

Wisconsin Municipal Records Manual. Micheal Fox & Kathleen McDonough. 102p. pap. 5.00 (*0-87020-208-1*) State Hist Soc Wis.

Wisconsin My Home. Erna O. Xan. (Illus.). 240p. 1950. reprint ed. 17.50 (*0-299-00711-1*) U of Wis Pr.

Wisconsin My Home. Erna O. Xan. (Illus.). 240p. 1975. reprint ed. pap. 9.95 (*0-299-00714-6*) U of Wis Pr.

Wisconsin Mystery Van Takes Off! Book 1: Handicapped Wisconsin Kids Sneak Off on a Big Adventure. Carole Marsh. (Wisconsin Bks.). (Illus.). (J). (gr. 3-12). 1994. 29.95 (*0-7933-5111-1*); pap. 19.95 (*0-7933-5112-X*); disk 29.95 (*0-7933-5113-8*) Gallopade Pub Group.

Wisconsin, Outagamie Co. Marriage Index, 1861-1907. Ronald V. Jackson. (Illus.). lib. bdg. 75.00 (*0-89593-555-4*) Accelerated Index.

Wisconsin Outdoor Recreation & Camping for Northern Wisconsin: Your Four Season Guide to Wisconsin's Outdoor Fun. 3rd rev. ed. Gary F. Kulibert. (Outdoor Recreation & Camping Ser.). (Illus.). 160p. 1994. pap. 10.95 (*1-879432-00-5*) Explorers Guide Pub.

Wisconsin Outdoor Recreation & Camping Guide for East Central Wisconsin. 3rd rev. ed. Gary F. Kulibert. LC 95-90714. (Illus.). 160p. 1995. pap. 11.95 (*1-879432-12-9*) Explorers Guide Pub.

Wisconsin Outdoor Recreation & Camping Guide for Northwest Wisconsin. 2nd ed. Gary F. Kulibert. LC 96-84668. (Outdoor Recreation & Camping Ser.). (Illus.). 160p. 1996. pap. 11.95 (*1-879432-13-7*) Explorers Guide Pub.

Wisconsin Outdoor Recreation & Camping Guide for Southeast Wisconsin. Gary F. Kulibert. 160p. (Orig.). pap. 11.95 (*1-879432-03-X*) Explorers Guide Pub.

***Wisconsin Outdoor Recreation & Camping Guides: Southwest Wisconsin.** Gary F. Kulibert. 1996. pap. 10.95 (*1-879432-01-3*) Explorers Guide Pub.

***Wisconsin Outdoor Recreation Guide & Topographic Atlas: North Central Edition.** unabridged ed. Robert W. Stenson. (Illus.). 148p. 1997. spiral bd., pap. write for info. (*1-890706-51-5*) BackCntry Enterprises.

***Wisconsin Outdoor Recreation Guide & Topographic Atlas: Northeast Edition.** unabridged ed. Robert W. Stenson. (Illus.). 148p. 1997. spiral bd., pap. write for info. (*1-890706-50-7*) BackCntry Enterprises.

Wisconsin PACE: Program for Athletic Coaches' Education. Ed. by Vern Seefeldt. (Illus.). 425p. (C). 1995. pap. text ed., spiral bd. 30.00 (*1-884125-48-4*) Cooper Pubng.

Wisconsin Place Names: Reprinted from the WSGS Newsletter. 94p. (Orig.). 1985. pap. 10.00 (*0-910255-46-6*) Wisconsin Gen.

Wisconsin Poets at the Elvehjem Museum. LC 95-22022. (Illus.). 1995. pap. 24.95 (*0-932900-38-0*) Elvejhem Mus.

***Wisconsin Poets' Calendar: 1998.** Ed. by Cristine Prucha. (Illus.). 163p. (Orig.). 1997. pap. 9.95 (*0-9618384-0-X*) Wisconsin Fellowship of Poets.

Wisconsin Practice. West Publishing Company Editorial Staff. write for info. (*0-318-62393-5*) West Pub.

Wisconsin Practice Vol. 3B: Civil Rules Handbook, 1996 Edition. Jay Grenig & Daniel D. Blinka. 725p. 1996. pap. text ed. write for info. (*0-314-09769-4*) West Pub.

***Wisconsin Practice Vol. 3B: Civil Rules Handbook, 1997.** Jay Grenig & Daniel D. Blinka. 750p. 1997. pap. text ed. write for info. (*0-314-22621-4*) West Pub.

***Wisconsin Probate & Estate Planning Statutes.** 290p. 1997. pap. 30.00 (*0-945574-96-7*) State Bar WI CLE Bk Div.

Wisconsin Probate System: Forms & Procedures Handbook. 5th ed. William F. Mundt & Michael R. Smith. 1996. ring bd. 135.00 (*0-945574-76-2*) State Bar WI CLE Bk Div.

Wisconsin Progressives: The Charles McCarthy Papers: Guide to a Microfilm Edition. Ed. by Harold L. Miller. 38p. 1986. pap. 25.00 (*0-87020-235-9*) Chadwyck-Healey.

Wisconsin Progressives: The Charles R. Van Hise Papers: Guide to a Microfilm Edition. Ed. by Stephen A. Masar. 70p. 1986. pap. 25.00 (*0-87020-237-5*) Chadwyck-Healey.

Wisconsin Progressives: The Edward A. Ross Papers: Guide to a Microfilm Edition. Ed. by Harold L. Miller & Lynn B. Aber. 51p. 1986. pap. 25.00 (*0-87020-234-0*) Chadwyck-Healey.

Wisconsin Progressives: The John R. Commons Papers: Guide to a Microfilm Edition. Ed. by Harold L. Miller. 48p. 1986. pap. 25.00 (*0-87020-236-7*) Chadwyck-Healey.

Wisconsin Progressives: The Richard T. Ely Papers: Guide to a Microfilm Edition. Ed. by Harold L. Miller. 78p. 1986. pap. 25.00 (*0-87020-233-2*) Chadwyck-Healey.

Wisconsin Public Library Standards. 2nd ed. 60p. (C). 1994. pap. text ed. 18.00 (*1-57337-007-X*) WI Dept Pub Instruct.

Wisconsin Public Library Youth Services Guidelines, 1995. WLA, Youth Services Section Staff. 1995. 13.00 (*0-614-04666-1*) Wisc Lib Assn.

Wisconsin Quiz Bowl Crash Course! Carole Marsh. (Carole Marsh Wisconsin Bks.). (Illus.). (J). 1994. pap. 19.95 (*0-7933-2280-4*); lib. bdg. 29.95 (*0-7933-2279-0*); disk 29.95 (*0-7933-2281-2*) Gallopade Pub Group.

***Wisconsin Real Estate Practice.** 9th ed. Lawrence Sager. 128p. 1998. pap. text ed. 16.95 (*0-7931-2681-9*, 1510-3609) Dearborn Finan.

Wisconsin River Images. Wisconsin University Extension Staff. 128p. 1993. per. 9.95 (*0-8403-8163-8*) Kendall-Hunt.

Wisconsin Rollercoasters! Carole Marsh. (Wisconsin Bks.). (Illus.). (YA). (gr. 3-12). 1994. pap. 19.95 (*0-7933-5372-6*); lib. bdg. 29.95 (*0-7933-5371-8*); disk 29.95 (*0-7933-5373-4*) Gallopade Pub Group.

***Wisconsin Rules & Procedures for Civil Actions.** 265p. 1997. pap. 25.00 (*0-945574-94-0*) State Bar WI CLE Bk Div.

***Wisconsin Rules of Evidence: A Courtroom Handbook.** rev. ed. Thomas H. Barland & Thomas D. Bell. 300p. 75.00 (*0-614-24830-2*) State Bar WI CLE Bk Div.

Wisconsin School Trivia: An Amazing & Fascinating Look at Our State's Teachers, Schools & Students! Carole Marsh. (Carole Marsh Wisconsin Bks.). (Illus.). (J). 1994. pap. 19.95 (*0-7933-1234-5*); lib. bdg. 29.95 (*0-7933-1235-3*); disk 29.95 (*0-7933-1236-1*) Gallopade Pub Group.

Wisconsin Services Directory, 1997. 6th ed. Ed. by Marie A. Lange & Jinger Mandt. 1000p. 1994. 140.00 (*0-942198-19-0*) WMC Serv.

Wisconsin Silly Basketball Sportsmysteries, Vol. 1. Carole Marsh. (Carole Marsh Wisconsin Bks.). (Illus.). (J). 1994. pap. 19.95 (*0-7933-1231-0*); lib. bdg. 29.95 (*0-7933-1232-9*); disk 29.95 (*0-7933-1233-7*) Gallopade Pub Group.

Wisconsin Silly Basketball Sportsmysteries, Vol. 2. Carole Marsh. (Carole Marsh Wisconsin Bks.). (Illus.). (J). 1994. pap. 19.95 (*0-7933-2292-8*); lib. bdg. 29.95 (*0-7933-2291-X*); disk 29.95 (*0-7933-2293-6*) Gallopade Pub Group.

Wisconsin Silly Football Sportsmysteries, Vol. 1. Carole Marsh. (Carole Marsh Wisconsin Bks.). (Illus.). (J). 1994. pap. 19.95 (*0-7933-2271-5*); lib. bdg. 29.95 (*0-7933-2270-7*); disk 29.95 (*0-7933-2272-3*) Gallopade Pub Group.

Wisconsin Silly Football Sportsmysteries, Vol. 2. Carole Marsh. (Carole Marsh Wisconsin Bks.). (Illus.). (J). 1994. pap. 19.95 (*0-7933-2274-X*); lib. bdg. 29.95 (*0-7933-2273-1*); disk 29.95 (*0-7933-2275-8*) Gallopade Pub Group.

Wisconsin Silly Trivia! Carole Marsh. (Carole Marsh Wisconsin Bks.). (Illus.). (J). 1994. pap. 19.95 (*0-7933-2263-4*); lib. bdg. 29.95 (*0-7933-2262-6*); disk 29.95 (*0-7933-2264-2*) Gallopade Pub Group.

Wisconsin State Census Index, 1837. Ronald V. Jackson. lib. bdg. 48.00 (*0-89593-801-4*) Accelerated Index.

Wisconsin State Census Index, 1838. Ronald V. Jackson. (Illus.). lib. bdg. 48.00 (*0-89593-802-2*) Accelerated Index.

Wisconsin State Census Index, 1842. Ronald V. Jackson. (Illus.). lib. bdg. 65.00 (*0-89593-803-0*) Accelerated Index.

Wisconsin State Census Index, 1847. Ronald V. Jackson. 1991. 95.00 (*0-89593-826-X*) Accelerated Index.

Wisconsin State Census Index, 1855. Ronald V. Jackson. (Illus.). lib. bdg. 128.00 (*0-89593-804-9*) Accelerated Index.

Wisconsin State Census Index, 1885. (Illus.). lib. bdg. 115.00 (*0-89593-540-6*) Accelerated Index.

Wisconsin State Census, 1842. 1983. 60.00 (*0-89593-604-6*) Accelerated Index.

***Wisconsin State Constitution: A Reference Guide.** Jack Stark. LC 96-47434. (Reference Guides to the State Constitutions of the United States: Vol. 28). 296p. 1997. text ed. 79.50 (*0-313-30255-3*, Greenwood Pr) Greenwood.

Wisconsin State Parks. Barbara McCaig & Boyce. (Illus.). 100p. (Orig.). 1989. pap. text ed. 5.95 (*0-935201-69-6*) Affordable Adven.

***Wisconsin State Parks: A Complete Recreation Guide.** Bill Bailey. (Illus.). 400p. 1998. pap. 15.95 (*1-881139-21-2*) Glovebox Guidebks.

Wisconsin State Rules of Evidence with Objections. Anthony J. Bocchino et al. 247p. 1995. pap. 16.95 (*1-55681-460-7*) Natl Inst Trial Ad.

Wisconsin State Studies: Activity Manual. rev. ed. Jeffrey Blaga. (Graphic Learning Integrated Social Studies Ser.). (Illus.). 94p. (J). (gr. 4). 1992. 95.00 (*0-87746-159-7*); teacher ed. 10.00 (*0-87746-160-0*) Graphic Learning.

Wisconsin Story. Sharon C. Calhoun & Billy J. English. 202p. (J). (gr. 4). 1987. 59.95 (*0-9619484-1-8*) Apple Corps Pubs.

Wisconsin Story. Sharon C. Calhoun & Billy J. English. 202p. (J). (gr. 4). 1992. 18.95 (*0-9619484-0-X*, TXU-299476) Apple Corps Pubs.

Wisconsin Study Book, No. II. 2nd ed. Jean Shafer. (Illus.). 48p. 1995. reprint ed. teacher ed., ring bd. 17.95 (*0-938682-11-3*) River Rd Pubns.

Wisconsin Survival. rev. ed. Betty L. Hall. 160p. (YA). (gr. 10-12). 1986. pap. text ed. 5.84 (*0-936159-01-4*) Westwood Pr.

Wisconsin Synod Lutherans: A History of the Single Synod, Federation & Merger. Edward C. Fredrich, II. LC 91-68217. 304p. 1992. pap. 23.99 (*0-8100-0423-2*, 15N0541) Northwest Pub.

Wisconsin Tailgating. Illus. by Dorothy Wells. 128p. 1995. pap. 8.95 (*1-885623-10-0*) Owl Bay Pubs.

Wisconsin Timeline: A Chronology of Wisconsin History, Mystery, Trivia, Legend, Lore & More. Carole Marsh. (Wisconsin Bks.). (Illus.). (J). (gr. 3-12). 1994. pap. 19.95 (*0-7933-6023-4*); lib. bdg. 29.95 (*0-7933-6022-6*); disk 29.95 (*0-7933-6024-2*) Gallopade Pub Group.

Wisconsin Town & Country Christmas. Larry Lynch & Renee Lynch. LC 87-83382. (Illus.). 80p. (Orig.). 1987. pap. 5.95 (*0-945309-00-7*) Hedgerow Pr.

Wisconsin Trails Great Weekend Adventures: Favorite Getaways, Festivals & Events from the Editors of Wisconsin Trails. Ed. by Elizabeth McBride. LC 96-60291. 184p. 1996. pap. 14.95 (*0-915024-50-0*) WI Tales & Trails.

***Wisconsin Traveler's Companion Vol. 1: A Guide to Country Sights.** Jerry Apps. Ed. by Elizabeth McBride. (Illus.). 208p. (Orig.). 1997. pap. 16.95 (*0-915024-56-X*) WI Tales & Trails.

Wisconsin Triennial. Rene P. Barilleaux & Stanley I. Grand. (Illus.). 76p. 1987. pap. 5.00 (*0-913883-15-8*) Madison Art.

Wisconsin Triennial. Rene P. Barilleaux et al. (Illus.). 64p. 1990. pap. 10.00 (*0-913883-18-2*) Madison Art.

***Wisconsin Triennial: 1996.** Sheri Castelnuovo et al. (Illus.). 64p. (Orig.). 1996. pap. 15.00 (*0-913883-23-9*) Madison Art.

Wisconsin Triennial, 1993. Intro. by Sheri Castelnuovo et al. (Illus.). (Orig.). (C). 1993. pap. 10.00 (*0-913883-20-4*) Madison Art.

Wisconsin Trivia. Kristin Visser. LC 94-20370. 1994. pap. 6.95 (*1-55853-297-8*) Rutledge Hill Pr.

Wisconsin Unemployment Compensation Law: A Handbook for Employers. rev. ed. 130p. 1989. ring bd. 15.00 (*0-942198-13-1*) WMC Serv.

Wisconsin Wedding. Carla Neggers. (Tyler Ser.: No. 503). 1992. mass mkt. 3.99 (*0-373-82503-X*, 1-82503-3) Harlequin Bks.

Wisconsin Wildlife Viewing Guide. Mary Judd. LC 94-41259. (Watchable Wildlife Ser.). (Illus.). 96p. (Orig.). 1995. pap. text ed. 8.95 (*1-56044-208-5*) Falcon Pr MT.

Wisconsin Willow: Adventures of a Basketmaker. Char TerBeest. Ed. by Pat S. Mantsch. LC 85-52083. (Illus.). 54p. 1985. pap. text ed. 6.95 (*0-9614795-0-7*) Wild Willow.

Wisconsin with Kids. 2nd ed. Kristin Visser & Jerry Minnich. LC 91-7975. 1994. pap. 12.95 (*1-879483-19-X*) Prairie Oak Pr.

Wisconsin Workers' Compensation Law: A Handbook for Employers. rev. ed. 130p. 1988. ring bd. 15.00 (*0-942198-12-3*) WMC Serv.

Wisconsinan Stage. Ed. by Robert F. Black et al. LC 72-89466. (Geological Society of America, Memoir Ser.: No. 136). 344p. reprint ed. pap. 98.10 (*0-317-30054-7*, 2025030) Bks Demand.

Wisconsinan Stage of the First Geological District, Eastern New York. Ed. by Donald H. Cadwell. (Bulletin Ser.: No. 455). 192p. (Orig.). 1986. pap. 12.00 (*1-55557-001-1*) NYS Museum.

Wisconsin's County Forests: Conflict over Indian Timber Rights. Michael F. Sohasky. 100p. 1994. 9.00 (*0-938627-22-8*) New Past Pr.

Wisconsin's Door Peninsula: A Natural History. Ed. by John C. Palmquist. (Illus.). 196p. (Orig.). 1989. pap. 10.95 (*0-929682-00-9*) Perin Pr.

Wisconsin's Early Home Remedies. Lora Di Megilo et al. (Illus.). 172p. (Orig.). 1991. pap. text ed. 9.95 (*1-878488-55-4*) Quixote Pr IA.

Wisconsin's Economy in Nineteen Ninety: Our History, Our Present, Our Future. William A. Strang. (Wisconsin Economy Studies: No. 19). (Orig.). 1982. pap. 6.00 (*0-86603-014-X*) Bur Busn Wis.

Wisconsin's Famous & Historic Trees. R. Bruce Allison & Elizabeth Durbin. (Illus.). 120p. 1982. pap. 14.95 (*0-913370-14-2*) Wisconsin Bks.

Wisconsin's (Most Devastating!) Disasters & (Most Calamitous!) Catastrophies! Carole Marsh. (Carole Marsh Wisconsin Bks.). (Illus.). (J). 1994. pap. 19.95 (*0-7933-1222-1*); lib. bdg. 29.95 (*0-7933-1223-X*); disk 29.95 (*0-7933-1224-8*) Gallopade Pub Group.

Wisconsin's Name: A Linguistic Puzzle. Virgil J. Vogel. (Wisconsin Stories Ser.). 8p. pap. 1.00 (*0-87020-196-4*) State Hist Soc Wis.

Wisconsin's Northwoods Fishing Guides. Bob Andersen. 160p. 1993. pap. write for info. (*1-883347-00-9*) Fish Guides.

***Wisconsin's Outdoor Treasures: A Guide to 150 Natural Destinations.** Tim Bewer. LC 97-12643. (Illus.). 288p. 1997. 17.95 (*1-879483-39-4*) Hunter Coll CEP.

Wisconsin's Professional Fishing Guides: South-Central Edition. Bob Andersen. 120p. 1993. pap. write for info. (*1-883347-01-7*) Fish Guides.

Wisconsin's Roadkill Cookbook. Bruce Carlson. (Illus.). 106p. (Orig.). 1991. pap. 7.95 (*1-878488-40-6*) Quixote Pr IA.

Wisconsin's Rustic Roads: A Road Less Travelled. Photos & Intro. by Bob Rashid. LC 95-14187. (Illus.). 1996. 35.00 (*1-883755-02-6*) Lost Riv Pr.

Wisconsin's Unsolved Mysteries (& Their "Solutions") Includes Scientific Information & Other Activities for Students. Carole Marsh. (Wisconsin Bks.). (Illus.). (J). (gr. 3-12). 1994. pap. 19.95 (*0-7933-5870-1*); lib. bdg. 29.95 (*0-7933-5869-8*); disk 29.95 (*0-7933-5871-X*) Gallopade Pub Group.

Wisconsin's Vanishing Outhouse: A Collection of Illustrations & Stories about a Rapidly Vanishing Insitution in Wisconsin, the Little Outhouse Out Back. Bruce Carlson. (Illus.). 168p. (Orig.). 1990. pap. 9.95 (*1-878488-27-9*) Quixote Pr IA.

Wisden Book of Cricket Laws. Don Oslear & Don Mosey. (Illus.). 256p. 1994. 22.95 (*0-09-177345-8*, Pub. by S Paul UK) Trafalgar.

Wisdom. Christopher Bowman. LC 95-18011. 88p. 1995. pap. 4.95 (*0-87178-944-2*) Brethren.

Wisdom. John E. Rybolt. (Collegeville Bible Commentary - Old Testament Ser.). 64p. 1986. pap. 3.95 (*0-8146-1477-9*) Liturgical Pr.

Wisdom. D. Thomas. 1995. 5.99 (*1-871676-21-5*, Pub. by Christian Focus UK) Spring Arbor Dist.

Wisdom. Charron. LC 78-12595. (Illus.). 1979. reprint ed. text ed. 65.00 (*0-313-21064-0*, CHWO, Greenwood Pr) Greenwood.

Wisdom: A 30-Day Devotional. Wiersbe. (Thirty-Day Devotional Ser.). 72p. 1995. pap. 3.50 (*1-56476-404-4*, 6-3404, Victor Bks) Chariot Victor.

Wisdom: Explorations in Adult Competence. St. G. Holliday. Ed. by M. J. Chandler. (Contributions to Human Development Ser.: Vol. 17). (Illus.). x, 102p. 1986. 41.75 (*3-8055-4283-6*) S Karger.

Wisdom: Its Nature, Origins & Development. Robert J. Sternberg. (Illus.). 375p. (C). 1990. pap. text ed. 20.95 (*0-521-36718-2*) Cambridge U Pr.

Wisdom: Its Nature, Origins & Development. Robert J. Sternberg. (Illus.). 375p. (C). 1990. text ed. 59.95 (*0-521-36453-1*) Cambridge U Pr.

Wisdom: One Hundred One of the Wisest Human Perceptions of All Time. Ed. by Rich Monk. 20p. 1992. 1.99 (*1-882342-00-3*) Panther IL.

***Wisdom: The Gift Worth Seeking.** Larry Lea. 1997. pap. text ed. 12.99 (*0-7852-7350-6*) Nelson.

Wisdom see Little Books of Virtue

Wisdom & Age. John-Raphael Staude. 220p. 1982. pap. 9.95 (*0-89496-110-1*) Ross Bks.

Wisdom & Beauty from Conrad. Joseph Conrad. Ed. by Harriett Capes. LC 76-51355. (Studies in Conrad: No. 8). 1977. lib. bdg. 75.00 (*0-8383-2125-9*) M S G Haskell Hse.

Wisdom & Compassion: The Sacred Art of Tibet. expanded ed. Marylin M. Rhie & Robert A. Thurman. LC 95-39484. (Illus.). 488p. 1996. 75.00 (*0-8109-3985-1*) Abrams.

Wisdom & Creation: The Theology of Wisdom Literature. Leo G. Perdue. LC 94-17507. 208p. (Orig.). 1994. pap. 21.95 (*0-687-45626-6*) Abingdon.

***Wisdom & Humanness in Psychology: Prospects for a Christian Approach.** C. Stephen Evans. 161p. 1996. reprint ed. ring bd. 15.95 (*1-57383-065-8*) Regent College.

***Wisdom & Innocence: A Life of G. K. Chesterton.** Joseph Pearce. 1997. 29.95 (*0-89870-629-7*) Ignatius Pr.

Wisdom & Law in the Old Testament: The Ordering of Life in Israel & Early Judaism. 2nd ed. Joseph Blenkinsopp. (Oxford Bible Ser.). 480p. 1995. 49.95 (*0-19-875503-1*); pap. 18.95 (*0-19-875504-X*) OUP.

Wisdom & Law in the Reign of Solomon. Kim I. Parker. LC 92-45201. (Biblical Press Ser.: Vol. 6). 136p. 1993. text ed. 69.95 (*0-7734-2356-7*) E Mellen.

Wisdom & Love in Saint Thomas Aquinas. Etienne Gilson. (Aquinas Lectures). 1951. 15.00 (*0-87462-116-X*) Marquette.

Wisdom & Mankind see Macro Plays

Wisdom & Spirit: An Investigation of 1 Corinthians 1.18-3. 20 Against the Background of Jewish Sapiential. James A. Davis. (Traditions in the Greco-Roman Period Ser.). 270p. (Orig.). 1984. lib. bdg. 52.00 (*0-8191-4210-7*) U Pr of Amer.

Wisdom & the Millers: Proverbs for Children. 2nd ed. Mildred A. Martin. (Miller Family Ser.). (Illus.). 159p. (J). (gr. 2-8). 1993. 9.50 (*0-685-68129-7*); pap. 6.00 (*0-9627643-5-3*) Green Psturs Pr.

Wisdom & the Senses: The Way of Creativity. Joan M. Erikson. (Illus.). 1988. 19.95 (*0-393-02591-8*) Norton.

Wisdom & the Senses, the Way of Creativity. Joan M. Eirkson. 1991. pap. 12.95 (*0-393-30710-7*) Norton.

W

Wisdom & the Way of Astrology. 2nd ed. Goswami Kriyananda. (Illus.). 430p. reprint ed. pap. 11.95 (*0-9613099-4-6*) Temple Kriya Yoga.

Wisdom & Wit of Rabbi Jesus. William E. Phipps. LC 93-19528. 272p. (Orig.). 1993. pap. 20.00 (*0-664-25232-X*) Westminster John Knox.

***Wisdom & Wonderment: Thirty-One Feasts to Nourish Your Soul.** Alla R. Bozarth. 99p. 1996. pap. 9.95 (*1-55612-803-7*) Sheed & Ward MO.

Wisdom & Worship. Robert Davidson. LC 90-39210. 160p. (Orig.). (C). 1990. pap. 12.95 (*0-334-02461-7*) TPI PA.

Wisdom & Your Spiritual Journey: Wisdom in the Biblical & Quaker Traditions. Charles E. Fager. 80p. (Orig.). 1993. pap. 10.95 (*0-945177-07-0*) Kimo Pr.

Wisdom As a Hermeneutical Construct: A Study in the Sapientializing of the Old Testament. Gerald T. Sheppard. (Beiheft zur Zeitschrift fuer die Alttestamentliche Wissenschaft Ser.: No. 151). (C). 1979. 75.40 (*3-11-007504-0*) De Gruyter.

Wisdom As Moderation: A Philosophy of the Middle Way. Charles Hartshorne. LC 86-25657. (SUNY Series in Philosophy). 157p. 1987. text ed. 57.50 (*0-88706-472-8*); pap. text ed. 18.95 (*0-88706-473-6*) State U NY Pr.

Wisdom at Work: Confucian Ideals & Japanese Business Success. Toshio Itoh. LC 92-497. 112p. (Orig.). 1992. pap. 9.95 (*1-56474-023-4*) Fithian Pr.

Wisdom, Authority & Grammar in the Seventh Century: Decoding Virgilius Maro Grammaticus. Vivien Law. 200p. (C). 1995. text ed. 49.95 (*0-521-47113-3*) Cambridge U Pr.

Wisdom Awakening...The Answer is Within: Deborah's Proverbs. Deborah Thornton. 160p. 1995. 15.99 (*0-614-07470-3*) Inspirat Prayer.

Wisdom Beyond the Mind. Manly P. Hall. pap. 4.95 (*0-89314-372-3*) Philos Res.

Wisdom Beyond Words: Sense & Non-Sense in the Buddhist Prajnaparamita Tradition. Sangharakshita. 302p. (Orig.). 1996. pap. 17.95 (*0-904766-61-6*) Windhorse Pubns.

Wisdom, Bliss & Common Sense: Secrets of Self-Transformation. Darshani Deane. LC 88-40485. 251p. (Orig.). 1989. pap. 8.50 (*0-8356-0644-9*, Quest) Theos Pub Hse.

Wisdom Book. Karyn Martin-Kuri. pap. write for info. (*0-345-39523-9*) Ballantine.

Wisdom, Christology, & Law in Matthew's Gospel. M. Jack Suggs. LC 75-95930. 144p. reprint ed. 41.10 (*0-8357-9185-8*, 2017749) Bks Demand.

Wisdom Christology in the Fourth Gospel. Michael E. Willett. LC 92-36835. 212p. 1992. 89.95 (*0-7734-9947-4*, Mellen Univ Pr) E Mellen.

Wisdom Circle. Wade Blevins. (Cherokee Indian Legend Ser.: Vol. 5). (Illus.). 45p. (J). (gr. k-8). 1993. lib. bdg. 12.95 (*1-56763-075-8*) Ozark Pub.

Wisdom Circle. large type ed. Wade Blevins. (Cherokee Indian Legend Ser.: Vol. 5). (Illus.). 45p. (J). (gr. k-8). 1993. pap. 2.95 (*1-56763-076-6*) Ozark Pub.

***Wisdom Circles: A Guide to Self-Discovery & Community Building in Small Groups.** Charles Garfield et al. LC 97-2804. 256p. 1998. 21.95 (*0-7868-6276-9*) Hyperion.

***Wisdom Comes Dancing: Selected Writings of Ruth St. Denis on Dance, Spirituality & the Body.** Ruth St. Denis. Ed. by Kamae A Miller. LC 96-43529. (Illus.). 232p. (Orig.). 1997. 17.95 (*0-915424-14-2*) PeaceWks Intl Ntwrk.

Wisdom Distilled from the Daily: Living the Rule of Saint Benedict Today. Joan Chittister. LC 90-55779. 1991. pap. 12.00 (*0-06-061399-8*) Harper SF.

Wisdom Distilled from the Daily: Living the Rule of St. Benedict Today. Joan Chittister. LC 89-45557. 224p. 1992. reprint ed. pap. 5.00 (*0-06-061396-3*) Harper SF.

Wisdom Energy: Basic Buddhist Teachings. Lama T. Yeshe & Zopa Rinpoche. Ed. by Jonathan Landaw & Alexander Berzin. (Basic Book - Orange Ser.). (Illus.). 152p. (C). 1994. reprint ed. pap. 10.00 (*0-86171-008-8*) Wisdom MA.

Wisdom Energy II. Thubten Yeshe et al. (Basic Book - Orange Ser.). (Illus.). 94p. (Orig.). 1979. pap. 4.95 (*0-86171-001-0*) Wisdom MA.

Wisdom for a Changing World: Wisdom in Old Testament Theology. Ronald E. Clements. Ed. by Duane L. Christensen. LC 89-62248. (Berkeley Lectures: No. 2). 80p. 1990. pap. 7.95 (*0-941037-13-4*) BIBAL Pr.

***Wisdom for a Lifetime: How to Get the Bible off the Shelf & into Your Hands.** Alden Studebaker. 256p. 1998. write for info. (*0-614-30245-5*) Unity Bks.

***Wisdom for a Woman's Heart.** (Message Ser.). 92p. 1997. 9.99 (*1-881830-38-1*, DS18443) Garborgs.

Wisdom for Caregivers. Tova Navarra. LC 95-19269. 176p. 1995. 12.00 (*1-55642-288-1*) SLACK Inc.

Wisdom for Crisis Times. Mike Murdock. Date not set. pap. 7.99 (*1-56292-024-3*, HB-024) Honor Bks OK.

Wisdom for Earthlings: How to Make Better Choices & Take Action in Your Life & in Your Work. John Newman. 208p. 1996. pap. 16.95 (*0-8144-7911-1*) AMACOM.

Wisdom for Grandparents. Gary Wilde. LC 50-6591. 176p. 1995. pap. 6.99 (*0-7814-0146-1*) Chariot Victor.

Wisdom for Men. Bobb Biehl. Ed. by Cathy Davis. 144p. (Orig.). 1994. pap. 6.99 (*0-7814-0183-6*) Chariot Victor.

Wisdom for the Golden Years: A Day by Day Quote Calendar for Senior Citizens. Gayle T. Watts. 372p. (Orig.). 1992. pap. 14.95 (*0-945772-10-6*) Clarkston Pub.

Wisdom for the Graduate. Larry Richards. (For the Graduate Ser.). 128p. 1993. 6.99 (*0-310-39710-3*) Zondervan.

Wisdom for Today. Bob Yandian. 190p. 1996. mass mkt. 4.99 (*0-88368-362-8*) Whitaker Hse.

Wisdom for Winning. Mike Murdock. 300p. (Orig.). Date not set. pap. 8.99 (*1-56292-398-6*, HB-398) Honor Bks OK.

Wisdom from Atlantis. Ruth B. Drown. 153p. 1981. pap. 14.00 (*0-89540-098-7*, SB-098) Sun Pub.

Wisdom from Mount Athos: The Writings of Staretz Silouan, 1866-1938. Archimandrite Sophrony. 127p. 1974. pap. 7.95 (*0-913836-17-6*) St Vladimirs.

Wisdom from Proverbs: Time-Tested Principles for Living. Compiled by Laura L. Mains. (Pocketpac Bks.). 112p. (Orig.). 1993. pap. text ed. 2.99 (*0-87788-845-0*) Shaw Pubs.

Wisdom from the Bible: Daily Thoughts from the Proverbs. Dan R. Dick & Nancy Dick. 368p. 4.97 (*0-916441-92-X*) Barbour & Co.

Wisdom from the Bible: Daily Thoughts from the Proverbs. Dan R. Dick & Nancy Dick. 368p. 1988. 9.97 (*0-916441-76-8*); pap. 4.97 (*0-916441-75-X*) Barbour & Co.

***Wisdom from the Bible: Daily Thoughts from the Proverbs.** Dan R. Dick & Nancy Dick. 368p. 1992. mass mkt. 2.49 (*1-55748-263-2*) Barbour & Co.

Wisdom from the Bible: Graduation Ed. 1991. pap. 4.95 (*0-916441-17-2*) Barbour & Co.

Wisdom from the Greater Community, Vol. 1. 3rd rev. ed. Marshall V. Summers. LC 90-61254. 448p. 1996. pap. 25.00 (*1-884238-11-4*) New Knowl Lib.

Wisdom from the Greater Community, Vol. 2. Marshall V. Summers. LC 90-61254. 448p. 1996. pap. 25.00 (*1-884238-12-2*) New Knowl Lib.

***Wisdom from the Proverbs.** Bargain Books Staff. 384p. 1997. lthr. 9.97 (*1-57748-097-X*) Barbour & Co.

***Wisdom from the Proverbs: A Daily Devotional.** Barbour Bargain Books Staff. 1997. 7.97 (*1-57748-015-5*) Barbour & Co.

***Wisdom from the Psalms.** Bargain Books Staff. 384p. 1997. lthr. 9.97 (*1-57748-098-8*) Barbour & Co.

***Wisdom from the Psalms: A Daily Devotional.** Barbour Bargain Books Staff. 1997. 7.97 (*1-57748-016-3*) Barbour & Co.

Wisdom from the Walls. Kristen Kammerer & Bridget Snyder. 96p. (Orig.). 1995. pap. 8.00 (*1-57297-006-5*) Blvd Books.

***Wisdom from White Eagle.** White Eagle Staff. 100p. 1967. pap. 8.95 (*0-85487-098-9*, Pub. by White Eagle UK) DeVorss.

Wisdom Goddess: Feminine Motifs in Eight Nag Hammadi Documents. Rose H. Arthur. Tr. by Richard L. Arthur. (Illus.). 256p. (Orig.). 1984. lib. bdg. 49.50 (*0-8191-4171-2*) U Pr of Amer.

Wisdom, Golden Nuggets, & Soul Food to Live By: A Treasure of Poems, Essays, & Words of Inspiration. Compiled & Intro. by Marvin L. Smith. LC 90-81709. 120p. (Orig.). 1990. pap. 5.95 (*0-9625115-2-8*) Campbell Rd Pr.

Wisdom Hunter. rev. ed. Randall Arthur. 320p. (Orig.). 1993. pap. 9.99 (*0-88070-580-9*, Multnomah Bks) Multnomah Pubs.

Wisdom in Ancient Israel. Ed. by John Day et al. (Illus.). 325p. (C). 1995. text ed. 59.95 (*0-521-42013-X*) Cambridge U Pr.

Wisdom in Finances. Chris Harvey. 65p. 1994. pap. 7.00 (*1-886357-01-3*) C Harvey Minist.

Wisdom in Israel. Gerhard Von Rad. Orig. Title: Weisheit in Israel. 352p. 1993. reprint ed. pap. 18.00 (*1-56338-071-4*) TPI PA.

***Wisdom in the Christology of Matthew.** Frances T. Gench. LC 97-7454. 1997. write for info. (*0-7618-0743-8*); pap. write for info. (*0-7618-0744-6*) U Pr of Amer.

Wisdom in the Eye of the Frog. Robert Vermeulen. LC 95-68240. 265p. 1995. 22.95 (*0-9643937-6-X*) Rutledge Bks.

Wisdom in the Hebrew Alphabet: The Sacred Letters As a Guide to Jewish Deed & Thought. Michael L. Munk. (ArtScroll Mesorah Ser.). (Illus.). 240p. 1983. 22.99 (*0-89906-193-1*); pap. 19.99 (*0-89906-194-X*) Mesorah Pubns.

Wisdom in the Open Air: The Norwegian Roots of Deep Ecology. Ed. by Peter Reed & David Rothenberg. (Illus.). 288p. (C). 1992. text ed. 44.95 (*0-8166-2150-0*); pap. text ed. 18.95 (*0-8166-2182-9*) U of Minn Pr.

Wisdom in the Q Tradition: The Aphoristic Teaching of Jesus. Ronald A. Piper. (Society for New Testament Studies Monographs: No. 61). 296p. 1989. text ed. 80.00 (*0-521-35293-2*) Cambridge U Pr.

Wisdom in the Workplace: On the Job Training for the Soul. Ellen Raineri. Ed. by Eleanor K. Sommer. LC 96-96975. (Illus.). 215p. (Orig.). 1997. pap. 14.95 (*0-9654035-0-5*) Braino. "Read WISDOM IN THE WORKPLACE & discover what's been missing from the traditional employee manual -- Survival!"--Ken Blanchard, author THE ONE MINUTE MANAGER. In WISDOM IN THE WORKPLACE, you will learn how to escape & surpass the muck & grit of the workplace, see impossible bosses, crabby clients, & back-stabbing co-workers as opportunities, use spiritual tools to conquer competitiveness, office politics, & misuses of power, nurture your soul & kick it into gear. "Ellen's book will wake up your heart & make it sing as you invest time in the workplace. Read it & smile. I did!"--Mark Victor Hansen, CHICKEN SOUP FOR THE SOUL series. WISDOM IN THE WORKPLACE is a marvelously insightful manual for bringing heart to your career. Putting these valuable principles into action will make all the difference in your life & livelihood."--Alan Cohen, author THE DRAGON DOESN'T LIVE HERE ANYMORE. "Insightful nuggets of wisdom, spirit & love in the workplace."--Gerald Jamplosky, author LOVE IS LETTING GO OF FEAR. ISBN 0-9654035-0-5, $14.95, 215 pp. Available from New Leaf (1-800-326-2665), DeVorss (1-800-843-5743), Baker & Taylor (908-722-8000). Autographed copies can be ordered from Braino, Inc., 227 Seminole Ave., Wilkes Barre, PA 18702. 717-825-5601.** ***Publisher Provided Annotation.

Wisdom in Theology. Ronald E. Clements. 188p. 1992. reprint ed. pap. 13.00 (*0-8028-0576-0*) Eerdmans.

Wisdom Inc. 30 Business Virtues That Turn Ordinary People into Extraordinary Leaders. Seth Godin. LC 96-107241. 144p. 1995. pap. 7.95 (*0-88730-758-2*) Harper Busn.

Wisdom, Information & Wonder: What Is Knowledge For? Mary Midgley. 272p. 1989. 27.50 (*0-415-02829-9*) Routledge.

Wisdom, Information & Wonder: What is Knowledge For? Mary Midgley. 272p. (C). 1991. pap. 15.95 (*0-415-02830-2*, A5460) Routledge.

Wisdom, Insight & Counsel: Three Hundred Sixty-Five Daily Meditations. Ed. by Debby Gullery. 384p. 1995. pap. 8.95 (*1-55778-725-5*) Paragon Hse.

***Wisdom Is Where You Find It or Where It Finds You.** James I. Warren. Ed. by Karen F. Williams. LC 97-896. 96p. (Orig.). 1997. pap. 10.95 (*0-8358-0801-7*, UR801) Upper Room Bks.

Wisdom, Jesus & Psychotherapy. David Klimek. 200p. (Orig.). 1991. pap. 13.95 (*0-9630213-0-3*) Winsted Pubns.

***Wisdom, Let Us Attend: Job, the Fathers & the Old Testament.** Ed. & Compiled by Johanna Manley. 920p. 1997. 34.00 (*0-9622536-4-2*) Monastery Bks.

***Wisdom Literature.** (Interpreting Biblical Texts Ser.). 1997. 18.95 (*0-687-00846-8*) Abingdon.

Wisdom Literature. Kathleen O'Connor. (Message of Biblical Spirituality Ser.: Vol. 5). 199p. 1988. pap. 12.95 (*0-8146-5571-8*) Liturgical Pr.

Wisdom Literature: Job, Proverbs, Ecclesiastes. John T. Willis. LC 81-69494. (Way of Life Ser.: No. 145). 1982. pap. 6.95 (*0-89112-145-5*) Abilene Christ U.

Wisdom Literature & the Structure of Proverbs. T. A. Perry. LC 92-33650. 160p. 1993. 29.50 (*0-271-00929-2*) Pa St U Pr.

Wisdom Made in America. Criswell Freeman. 1996. pap. text ed. 5.95 (*1-887655-07-7*) Walnut Gr Pr.

Wisdom of a Religious Commitment. Terrence W. Tilley. LC 94-32280. 192p. 1995. 40.00 (*0-87840-580-1*) Georgetown U Pr.

Wisdom of a Rice Seller. Said Salah. (Dual Language Ser.). 28p. 1995. pap. 12.00 (*1-887584-32-3*) Intl Prom Art.

Wisdom of Accepted Tenderness. Brennan Manning. 1979. pap. 11.95 (*0-87193-110-9*) Dimension Bks.

Wisdom of Adam Smith. Adam Smith. Ed. by John Haggarty & Benjamin A. Rogge. LC 76-43441. 1977. pap. 4.50 (*0-913966-22-3*) Liberty Fund.

Wisdom of Adam Smith. Adam Smith. Ed. by John Haggarty & Benjamin A. Rogge. LC 76-43441. 1977. 9.00 (*0-913966-21-5*) Liberty Fund.

Wisdom of African Mythology. John J. Ollivier. LC 91-35050. (Illus.). 256p. (Orig.). 1997. reprint ed. pap. 17.95 (*1-56087-023-0*) Top Mtn Pub.

Wisdom of American Indian Mythology. John J. Ollivier. LC 95-9356. (Illus.). 272p. 1995. pap. 17.95 (*1-56087-049-4*) Top Mtn Pub.

Wisdom of Ancient Greece. Photos by Jacques Lacarriere. LC 96-17066. (Illus.). 56p. 1996. 8.95 (*0-7892-0243-3*) Abbeville Pr.

Wisdom of Ancient Rome. Benonit Desombres. LC 96-17065. 56p. 1996. 8.95 (*0-7892-0242-5*) Abbeville Pr.

Wisdom of Baltasar Gracian: A Practical Manuel for Good & Perilous Times. Ed. by J. Leonard Kaye & Julie Rubenstein. 272p. 1992. pap. 10.00 (*0-671-79659-3*) PB.

Wisdom of Being Human. Jean Lanier. (Illus.). 151p. (Orig.). 1989. 13.95 (*0-941255-40-9*); pap. 7.95 (*0-941255-39-5*) Integral Pub.

Wisdom of Ben Sira. Patrick W. Sehan & Alexander A. Di Lella. LC 86-8989. (Anchor Bible Ser.: Vol. 39). (Illus.). 648p. 1987. 38.00 (*0-385-13517-3*) Doubleday.

Wisdom of Buddha. Photos by Jean-Louis Nou. LC 96-21499. (Illus.). 56p. 1996. 8.95 (*0-7892-0238-7*) Abbeville Pr.

Wisdom of Buddha: The Samdhinirmocana Sutra. Tr. by John Powers from TIB. LC 94-25023. 397p. 1994. pap. 25.00 (*0-89800-246-X*) Dharma Pub.

Wisdom of Buddha: The Samdhinirmocana Sutra. Tr. by John Powers from TIB. LC 94-25023. 397p. 1994. 40.00 (*0-89800-247-8*) Dharma Pub.

Wisdom of Buddhism. Ed. by Christmas Humphreys. (C). 1987. 44.00 (*81-85002-05-3*, Pub. by Promilla) S Asia.

Wisdom of Buddhism. 2nd ed. Ed. by Christmas Humphreys. 288p. (C). 1987. pap. text ed. 18.00 (*0-7007-0197-4*, Pub. by Curzon Press UK) UH Pr.

Wisdom of Buddhism. 2nd rev. ed. Ed. by Christmas Humphreys. LC 86-22254. 280p. 1987. pap. 17.50 (*0-391-03464-2*) Humanities.

Wisdom of Christendom. Marvin L. Brown, Jr. 131p. 1982. pap. 5.95 (*0-317-00315-1*) Edenwood Hse.

***Wisdom of Christmas.** Dietrich Bonhoeffer. 96p. 1996. 13.95 (*0-8245-1632-X*) Crossroad NY.

Wisdom of Confucius. 1994. 14.50 (*0-679-60123-6*, Modern Lib) Random.

Wisdom of Confucius. Citadel Staff. LC 95-19792. 160p. 1995. pap. 6.95 (*0-8065-1702-6*, Citadel Pr) Carol Pub Group.

Wisdom of Confucius. Confucius. Ed. & Tr. by Lin Yutang. LC 38-27366. 290p. 1977. 13.50 (*0-394-60426-1*, Modern Lib) Random.

Wisdom of Confucius. Ed. by Miles M. Dawson. 1997. pap. 3.95 (*0-8283-1462-4*, 18, Intl Pocket Lib) Branden Pub Co.

***Wisdom of Depression.** Jonathan Zuess. 1998. write for info. (*0-609-60108-3*, Harmony) Crown Pub Group.

Wisdom of Doctor Dodypoll. LC 73-133771. (Tudor Facsimile Texts. Old English Plays Ser.: No. 90). reprint ed. 49.50 (*0-404-53390-6*) AMS Pr.

Wisdom of Dolphins. Twyman L. Towery. 1996. 14.95 (*0-9646872-1-6*) Wessex House.

***Wisdom of Eagles: A History of Maxwell Air Force Base.** Jerome A. Ennels & Wesley P. Newton. LC 97-3003. 1997. pap. write for info. (*1-57966-000-2*, Black Belt) Black Belt Comm.

Wisdom of Egypt & the Old Testament. A. L. Griffith. (African Studies). reprint ed. 20.00 (*0-938818-79-1*) ECA Assoc.

Wisdom of Eve. rev. ed. Mary Orr. 1994. pap. 5.25 (*0-8222-1429-6*) Dramatists Play.

Wisdom of Fairy Tales. Rudolf Meyer. 267p. 1988. 19.95 (*0-88010-192-X*) Anthroposophic.

Wisdom of Faith. Clifford Whitfield. 48p. (Orig.). 1994. pap. 3.95 (*1-56043-811-8*) Destiny Image.

Wisdom of Faith: Essays in Honor of Dr. Sebastian Alexander Matczak. Ed. by Henry O. Thompson. LC 89-31915. (Illus.). 190p. (C). 1989. lib. bdg. 38.00 (*0-8191-7436-X*) U Pr of Amer.

Wisdom of Father Brown. Gilbert K. Chesterton. 21.95 (*0-89190-336-4*) Amereon Ltd.

Wisdom of FDR. Dagobert D. Runes. 1993. pap. 7.95 (*0-8065-1462-0*, Citadel Pr) Carol Pub Group.

Wisdom of Florence Scovel Shinn. Florence S. Shinn. 384p. 1989. pap. 10.95 (*0-671-68228-8*, Fireside) S&S Trade.

Wisdom of Fools. Margaret W. Deland. LC 72-98567. (Short Story Index Reprint Ser.). 1977. 19.95 (*0-8369-3141-6*) Ayer.

Wisdom of God Manifested in the Works of Creation. John Ray. (Anglistica & Americana Ser.: No. 122). 250p. 1974. reprint ed. 50.70 (*3-487-05403-5*) G Olms Pubs.

Wisdom of God Manifested in the Works of the Creation: Heavenly Bodies, Elements, Meteors, Fossils, Vegetables, Animals. John Ray. Ed. by Frank N. Egerton, 3rd. LC 77-74250. (History of Ecology Ser.). 1978. reprint ed. lib. bdg. 44.95 (*0-405-10419-7*) Ayer.

Wisdom of Healing: Mind-Body Practices for Creating Health. Deepak Chopra. 1997. 26.00 (*0-517-70343-2*) Random.

Wisdom of Henry Hazlitt. Ed. by Henry Hazlitt. 358p. (Orig.). 1993. pap. 16.95 (*0-910614-83-0*) Foun Econ Ed.

Wisdom of Hindus. Brian Brown. (C). 1991. 28.50 (*81-7026-171-6*, Pub. by Heritage IA) S Asia.

***Wisdom of His Word.** Betty J. Carr. Ed. by Dahk Knox & Keith Pearson. (Illus.). 170p. 1996. pap. text ed. 14.95 (*1-881116-79-4*, Kinder Bks) Black Forest Pr.

Wisdom of Insecurity. Alan W. Watts. 1968. pap. 8.00 (*0-394-70468-1*, Vin) Random.

Wisdom of Islam. Compiled by Nacer Khemir. LC 96-21419. (Illus.). 56p. 1996. 8.95 (*0-7892-0237-9*) Abbeville Pr.

Wisdom of Islands. Jacqueline Hartwich. 36p. (Orig.). 1994. pap. 3.95 (*0-9642056-0-2*) Hoyt St Pr.

***Wisdom of Jesus.** Compiled by Philip Law. LC 96-47033. (The Wisdom Ser.). (Illus.). 48p. 1996. 8.00 (*0-8028-3832-4*) Eerdmans.

Wisdom of Jesus. Compiled by Jean-Yves Leloup. LC 96-8010. (Illus.). 56p. 1996. 8.95 (*0-7892-0239-5*) Abbeville Pr.

***Wisdom of Jesus: Bible Wisdom for Today.** James Harpur. 1997. pap. text ed. 14.95 (*0-89577-908-0*) RD Assn.

Wisdom of Judaism. Illus. by Marc Chagall. LC 96-16439. 56p. 1996. 8.95 (*0-7892-0236-0*) Abbeville Pr.

***Wisdom of Judaism.** Hyman. 1997. 24.95 (*0-226-36551-4*) U Ch Pr.

***Wisdom of Judaism.** Ed. by Dale Salwak. LC 97-5271. 160p. 1997. 16.00 (*1-57731-001-2*) New Wrld Lib.

***Wisdom of Julian of Norwich.** Compiled & Intro. by Monica Furlong. LC 96-47032. (Wisdom Ser.). (Illus.). 48p. 1996. 8.00 (*0-8028-3834-0*) Eerdmans.

Wisdom of Kahlil Gibran. Ed. by Joseph Sheban. 1971. reprint ed. pap. 3.95 (*0-8065-0249-5*, Citadel Pr) Carol Pub Group.

Wisdom of Life: Being the First Part of Aphorismen Zur Lebensweisheit. Arthur Schopenhauer. Tr. & Pref. by T. Bailey Saunders. LC 72-487. (Essay Index Reprint Ser.). 1977. reprint ed. 15.95 (*0-8369-2821-0*) Ayer.

Wisdom of Life & Counsels & Maxims. Arthur Schopenhauer. Tr. by T. Bailey Saunders. 220p. 1995. pap. 6.95 (*1-57392-033-9*) Prometheus Bks.

***Wisdom of Love.** Alain Finkielkraut. Tr. by Kevin O'Neill & David Suchoff. LC 96-9823. (Texts & Contexts Ser.). xxvi, 153p. 1997. text ed. 25.00 (*0-8032-1991-1*) U of Nebr Pr.

Wisdom of Love. Edward Riccardo. (Illus.). 255p. (Orig.). 1995. pap. 14.00 (*0-911541-06-3*) Gregory Pub.

***Wisdom of Maati: The Path of Spiritual Enlightenment Through Virtuous Living.** unabridged ed. Abhaya A. Muata. (Illus.). 160p. (Orig.). 1997. pap. 14.99 (*1-884564-20-8*) Cruzian Mystic.

Wisdom of Man: Selected Discourses. M. R. Bawa Muhaiyaddeen. LC 80-20541. (Illus.). 168p. 1980. 12.00 (*0-914390-16-3*) Fellowship Pr PA.

***Wisdom of Man: Selected Discourses.** M. R. Bawa Muhaiyaddeen. LC 80-20541. (Illus.). 168p. 1994. pap. 9.00 (*0-914390-45-7*) Fellowship Pr PA.

An Asterisk (*) at the beginning of an entry indicates that the title is appearing in BIP for the first time.

Wisdom of Many: Essays on the Proverb. Ed. by Wolfgang Mieder & Alan Dundes. LC 94-16235. 346p. 1994. reprint ed. 45.00 (*0-299-14360-0*); reprint ed. pap. 19.95 (*0-299-14364-3*) U of Wis Pr.

Wisdom of Many, the Vision of One: The Proverbs of William Blake. Marvin D. Lansverk. LC 93-35971. (American University Studies, IV, English Language & Literature: Vol. 142). 215p. (C). 1994. text ed. 38.95 (*0-8204-1781-5*) P Lang Pubng.

Wisdom of Martin Luther King, Jr. Ed. by Alex Ayers. LC 92-18999. 1993. pap. 10.00 (*0-452-01104-3*, Mer) NAL-Dutton.

Wisdom of Matthew: An Essay in Contemporary French Educational Theory. Celestin Freinet. Tr. by John Sivell from FRE. LC 90-39391. (Studies in Education: Vol. 13). 252p. 1990. lib. bdg. 89.95 (*0-88946-795-1*) E Mellen.

***Wisdom of Memoir: Reading & Writing Lifes Sacred Texts.** Peter Gilmour. Ed. by Carl Koch. (Illus.). 192p. (Orig.). 1997. pap. 15.95 (*0-88489-427-4*) St Marys.

Wisdom of Milton H. Erickson: Human Behavior & Psychotherapy, Vol. 2. Milton H. Erickson. Ed. by Ronald A. Havens. LC 88-31440. 257p. 1989. reprint ed. pap. 16.95 (*0-8290-2414-X*) Irvington.

Wisdom of Milton H. Erickson: Hypnosis & Hypnotherapy, Vol. 1. Milton H. Erickson. Ed. by Ronald A. Havens. LC 88-31440. 297p. 1989. reprint ed. pap. 16.95 (*0-8290-2413-1*) Irvington.

Wisdom of Nature. Dayton D. Foster. (Illus.). 144p. (C). 1993. pap. 8.95 (*0-87961-233-9*) Naturegraph.

***Wisdom of New York.** Criswell Freeman. 1996. pap. text ed. 5.95 (*1-887655-16-6*) Walnut Gr Pr.

Wisdom of No Escape: And the Path of Loving-Kindness. Pema Chodron. LC 90-53585. 128p. (Orig.). 1991. pap. 10.00 (*0-87773-632-4*) Shambhala Pubns.

Wisdom of Nyaaya. K. P. Bahadur. 1989. text ed. 27.50 (*81-207-0332-4*, Pub. by Sterling Pubs II) Apt Bks.

Wisdom of Oat: An American Indian Philosophy. William Moss. 100p. 1993. pap. 10.00 (*0-9637830-3-5*) Triangle Books.

***Wisdom of Old Time Baseball.** Criswell Freeman. 1996. pap. text ed. 5.95 (*1-887655-08-5*) Walnut Gr Pr.

***Wisdom of Old Time Television: Common Sense & Uncommon Genius from the Golden Age Of...** Criswell Freeman. 1996. pap. text ed. 5.95 (*1-887655-64-6*) Walnut Gr Pr.

Wisdom of One: The Ultimate Existentialist Quote Book. Thomas E. Kelly. LC 95-76234. 175p. (Orig.). 1995. pap. 12.95 (*1-883697-42-5*) Hara Pub.

Wisdom of Plain People. Donna Leahy. 1997. pap. 12.95 (*0-670-87180-X*) Viking Penguin.

***Wisdom of Pleasure: Pleasure Experienced Here & Now Is the Basis of Happiness & Health.** Daniel Chabot. Orig. Title: La Sagesse Du Plaisir. 332p. (Orig.). 1997. pap. 14.95 (*1-880396-39-4*, JP9639-4) Jalmar Pr.

Wisdom of Plotinus: A Metaphysical Study. Charles J. Whitby. 131p. 1992. pap. 17.95 (*1-56459-221-9*) Kessinger Pub.

Wisdom of Poetry: Essays in Early English Literature in Honor of Morton W. Bloomfield. Ed. by Larry D. Benson. 1982. pap. 13.95 (*0-918720-16-8*); boxed 22.95 (*0-918720-15-X*) Medieval Inst.

Wisdom of Practice. Peter P. DeBoer. LC 89-34184. (Studies of Teaching in Christian Elementary & Middle Schools). 170p. (Orig.). (C). 1989. pap. text ed. 19.00 (*0-8191-7485-8*); lib. bdg. 42.00 (*0-8191-7484-X*) U Pr of Amer.

Wisdom of Proverbs. Scott Lindsey. LC 94-69839. 128p. (Orig.). 1995. pap. 6.95 (*0-89221-284-5*) New Leaf.

Wisdom of Proverbs, Job & Ecclesiastes. Derek Kidner. LC 85-11826. 176p. (Orig.). 1985. pap. 12.99 (*0-87784-405-4*, 405) InterVarsity.

Wisdom of Ramala. Centre. (Ramala Trilogy Ser.). 191p. 1986. pap. 15.95 (*0-85435-185-X*, Pub. by C W Daniel UK) Natl Bk Netwk.

Wisdom of Ramala. 3rd ed. 352p. pap. 23.95 (*0-8464-4314-7*) Beekman Pubs.

Wisdom of Saankhya. K. P. Bahadur. 1989. text ed. 27.50 (*81-207-0331-6*, Pub. by Sterling Pubs II) Apt Bks.

Wisdom of St. Francis & His Companions. Compiled by Stephen Clissold. LC 78-27504. (Wisdom Bks.). 1979. pap. 8.95 (*0-8112-0721-8*, NDP477) New Directions.

Wisdom of St. John. Bo Yin Ra. Tr. by Bodo A. Reichenbach from GER. LC 74-15272. 112p. 1975. 8.00 (*0-915034-01-8*) Kober Pr.

Wisdom of Science. Robert Hanbury Brown. (Illus.). 200p. 1986. text ed. 64.95 (*0-521-30726-0*); pap. text ed. 24.95 (*0-521-31448-8*) Cambridge U Pr.

Wisdom of Serpents: A Nate Rosen Mystery. Ronald Levitsky. 256p. 1992. text ed. 19.00 (*0-684-19411-2*) S&S Trade.

Wisdom of Sidereal Astrology. KHM9. Andres Takra. (Illus.). 520p. 1983. pap. write for info. (*0-89540-127-4*, SB-127, Sun Bks) Sun Pub.

Wisdom of Silenus & Other Essays. Howard McCord. 136p. 1996. pap. 11.95 (*1-879934-35-3*) St Andrews NC.

Wisdom of Solomon. David Winston. LC 78-18150. (Anchor Bible Ser.: Vol. 43). 384p. 1979. 28.00 (*0-385-01644-1*, Anchor NY) Doubleday.

Wisdom of Solomon Schechter. Bernard Mandelbaum. 1963. pap. 2.50 (*0-8381-3103-4*) USCJE.

Wisdom of Southern California. Lance Jencks. 68p. (Orig.). 1982. pap. 5.95 (*0-9609678-1-8*) Lindenhof Pr.

Wisdom of Southern Football: Common Sense & Uncommon Genius from 101 Gridiron Greats. Criswell Freeman. (Wisdom Ser.). 160p. (Orig.). pap. 5.95 (*0-9640955-7-2*) Walnut Gr Pr.

Wisdom of Statecraft: Sir Herbert Butterfield & the Philosophy of International Politics. Alberto R. Coll. LC 85-1535. xvii, 173p. (C). 1985. 31.95 (*0-8223-0607-7*) Duke.

Wisdom of Stones. Greg Matthews. 480p. 1995. mass mkt. 5.99 (*0-06-109030-1*, Harp PBks) HarpC.

Wisdom of Tao. Compiled by Marc De Smedt. LC 96-21498. (Illus.). 56p. 1996. 8.95 (*0-7892-0241-7*) Abbeville Pr.

Wisdom of Teams: Creating the High-Performance Organization. Jon R. Katzenbach & Douglas K. Smith. LC 92-20395. 304p. (C). 1993. 29.95 (*0-87584-367-0*) Harvard Busn.

Wisdom of Teams: Creating the High-Performance Organization. Jon R. Katzenbach & Douglas K. Smith. 1993. text ed. 29.95 (*0-07-103383-1*) McGraw.

Wisdom of Teams: Creating the High-Performance Organizations. Jon R. Katzenbach & Douglas K. Smith. 336p. 1994. reprint ed. pap. 13.00 (*0-88730-676-4*) Harper Busn.

***Wisdom of Teresa of Avila.** Ed. by Kieran Kavanaugh & Otilio Rodriguez. LC 96-37720. (Spiritual Samplers Ser.). 96p. (Orig.). 1997. pap. 1.95 (*0-8091-3723-2*) Paulist Pr.

Wisdom of the Adepts: Esoteric Science in Human History. Thomas L. Harris. LC 72-2957. reprint ed. 67.50 (*0-404-10721-4*) AMS Pr.

Wisdom of the African World. Ed. by Reginald McKnight. (Classic Wisdom Collection). 128p. 1996. 14.00 (*1-880032-56-2*) New Wrld Lib.

Wisdom of the Ages. Silvia Silk. (Illus.). 28p. (Orig.). (J). (ps-3). 1987. pap. 5.50 (*0-938861-01-8*) Jasmine Texts.

Wisdom of the Ages: The Mystique of the African American Preacher. Robert Johnson-Smith, II. 192p. 1995. pap. 12.00 (*0-8170-1225-7*) Judson.

Wisdom of the Ages: Themes & Essences of Truth, Love, Struggle, & High-Culture in the Works of Ayi Kwei Armah & Kiarri T-H. Cheatwood. Akili Addae & Yaa Oforiwaa. LC 91-68262. 80p. (Orig.). 1995. pap. 12.98 (*1-879289-01-6*) Native Sun Pubs.

Wisdom of the Ancient One: An Inca Initiation. Anton P. De Leon Paiva. LC 94-40696. 121p. 1995. pap. 9.95 (*1-885394-09-8*) Bluestar Commun.

Wisdom of the Ancient Sages: Mundaka Upanishad. Swami Rama. LC 90-48615. 181p. (Orig.). 1990. pap. 12.95 (*0-89389-120-7*) Himalayan Inst.

Wisdom of the Ancient Seers: Mantras of the Rig Veda. David Frawley. 257p. 1993. pap. 14.95 (*1-878423-16-9*) Morson Pub.

Wisdom of the Ancients. Francis Bacon. 96p. 1992. pap. 14.00 (*1-56459-229-4*) Kessinger Pub.

Wisdom of the Ancients. T. Lobsang Rampa. 192p. 1991. reprint ed. lib. bdg. 23.95 (*0-89966-776-7*) Buccaneer Bks.

Wisdom of the Body. Yogi A. Desai. Ed. by Lisa Sarasohn. (Illus.). 40p. (Orig.). 1984. pap. 2.00 (*0-940258-13-7*) Kripalu Pubns.

***Wisdom of the Body.** Sherwin B. Nuland. 1997. 26.95 (*0-679-44407-6*) Knopf.

***Wisdom of the Body.** Sherwin B. Nuland. 1998. pap. write for info. (*0-679-78140-4*, Vin) Random.

***Wisdom of the Body.** Phil Porter & Cynthia Winton-Henry. 125p. 1995. pap. 14.95 (*0-9636755-4-0*) Wing It Pr.

Wisdom of the Body Moving: An Introduction to Body-Mind Centering. Linda Hartley. LC 93-44829. (Illus.). 400p. (Orig.). (C). 1995. pap. 18.95 (*1-55643-174-0*) North Atlantic.

Wisdom of the Bones. Alan Walker & Pat Shipman. 352p. 1996. 26.00 (*0-679-42624-8*) Random.

***Wisdom of the Bones: In Search of Human Origins.** Alan Walker. 1997. pap. 14.00 (*0-679-74783-4*, Vin) Random.

Wisdom of the Buddha. Jean Boisselier. (Discoveries Ser.). (Illus.). 1994. pap. 12.95 (*0-8109-2807-6*) Abrams.

Wisdom of the Celtic Saints. Edward C. Sellner. LC 92-74778. (Illus.). 208p. (Orig.). 1993. pap. 11.95 (*0-87793-492-4*) Ave Maria.

***Wisdom of the Celts.** Compiled & Intro. by David Adam. LC 96-47030. (Wisdom Ser.). (Illus.). 48p. 1996. 8.00 (*0-8028-3833-2*) Eerdmans.

Wisdom of the Chinese: Their Philosophy in Sayings & Proverbs. Brian Brown. 1974. lib. bdg. 250.00 (*0-87968-138-1*) Krishna Pr.

Wisdom of the Desert: Sayings from the Desert Fathers. Thomas Merton. LC 59-15021. 1970. pap. 6.95 (*0-8112-0102-3*, NDP295) New Directions.

Wisdom of the Desert Fathers. 1979. pap. 3.95 (*0-89981-108-6*) Eastern Orthodox.

***Wisdom of the Divine, Vol. 2.** M. R. Muhaiyaddeen. pap. 8.00 (*0-914390-12-0*) Fellowship Pr PA.

***Wisdom of the Divine, Vol. 3.** M. R. Muhaiyaddeen. (Illus.). pap. 8.00 (*0-914390-40-6*) Fellowship Pr PA.

***Wisdom of the Divine, Vol. 4.** M. R. Muhaiyaddeen. (Illus.). pap. 8.00 (*0-914390-41-4*) Fellowship Pr PA.

Wisdom of the Divine, 4 vols., Vols. 1-4. M. R. Muhaiyaddeen. 90p. 1972. pap. 8.00 (*0-914390-00-7*) Fellowship Pr PA.

Wisdom of the Earth: Visions of an Ecological Faith. Ed. & Photos by Gordon Miller. LC 95-77679. (Wisdom of the Earth Ser.: Vol. 1). (Illus.). 176p. (Orig.). 1997. pap. 19.95 (*0-9647007-1-9*) Green Rock.

Wisdom of the Earth: Visions of an Ecological Faith, 2 vols., Set. Ed. & Photos by Gordon Miller. (Wisdom of the Earth Ser.: Vol. 1). (Illus.). (Orig.). pap. write for info. (*0-9647007-0-0*) Green Rock.

***Wisdom of the East, Vol. 1.** Intro. by Nicholas M. Butler. Date not set. write for info. (*0-8369-4792-4*) Ayer.

Wisdom of the Ego: Sources of Resilience in Adult Life. George E. Vaillant. LC 92-37342. 406p. 1993. 27.95 (*0-674-95372-X*) HUP.

Wisdom of the Ego: Sources of Resilience in Adult Life. George E. Vaillant. (Illus.). 394p. (Orig.). (C). 1995. pap. 15.95 (*0-674-95373-8*) HUP.

***Wisdom of the Elders.** Robert Fleming. 1998. pap. 11.00 (*0-345-40975-2*) Ballantine.

Wisdom of the Elders. David Suzuki & Peter Knudtson. 320p. 1993. pap. 13.95 (*0-553-37263-7*) Bantam.

Wisdom of the Elders: An African American Book of Days. Ed. by Robert Fleming. 384p. 1996. 15.00 (*0-345-39432-1*, One World) Ballantine.

Wisdom of the Far East: A Dictionary of Proverbs, Maxims, & Famous Classical Phrases of the Chinese, Japanese, & Korean. Young H. Yoo. LC 70-168691. (Dictionary Ser.: No. 5). 1972. 15.95 (*0-912580-00-3*) Far Eastern Res.

Wisdom of the Gita: First Series. M. P. Pandit. 144p. 1992. pap. 9.95 (*0-941524-72-8*) Lotus Light.

Wisdom of the Gita: Second Series. Sri Aurobindo. 208p. 1992. pap. 10.95 (*0-941524-75-2*) Lotus Light.

Wisdom of the Great Chiefs: The Classic Speeches of Chief Red Jacket, Chief Joseph, & Chief Seattle. Ed. & Intro. by Kent Nerburn. LC 93-47415. (Classic Wisdom Collection). 96p. 1994. 12.95 (*1-880032-40-6*) New Wrld Lib.

Wisdom of the Gurus: A Sigs Developer's Guide. Ed. by Charles Bowman. 448p. (C). 1996. pap. text ed. 39.00 (*0-13-499849-9*) P-H.

Wisdom of the Gurus: A Vision for Object Technology. Ed. by Charles Bowman. LC 96-41922. (Reference Library). 448p. (Orig.). 1996. pap. 39.00 (*1-884842-55-0*) SIGS Bks & Multimedia.

Wisdom of the Heart. Henry Miller. LC 41-28118. 1942. pap. 10.95 (*0-8112-0116-3*, NDP94) New Directions.

Wisdom of the Heart. Benedetta Papasogli. LC 93-78050. 1993. 11.95 (*0-910984-57-3*) Montfort Pubns.

Wisdom of the Heart: A Study of the Works of Mulk Raj Anand. Marlene Fisher. xiv, 207p. 1985. text ed. 27.50 (*0-86590-724-2*, Pub. by Sterling Pubs II) Apt Bks.

Wisdom of the Heart: Katherine Tingley Speaks. Katherine Tingley. Ed. by W. Emmett Small. LC 78-65338. 1978. pap. 8.95 (*0-913004-33-2*) Point Loma Pub.

***Wisdom of the Heart: Working with Women's Dreams.** Karen Signell. (Illus.). 352p. 1997. reprint ed. pap. 15.95 (*0-88064-188-6*) Fromm Intl Pub.

Wisdom of the Hindus. Brian Brown. 320p. 1981. pap. 27.00 (*0-89540-093-6*, SB-093) Sun Pub.

Wisdom of the Hive: The Social Physiology of Honey Bee Colonies. Thomas D. Seeley. LC 95-3645. (Illus.). 384p. (C). 1995. 49.95 (*0-674-95376-2*) HUP.

Wisdom of the Idiots. Idries Shah. 179p. 1989. reprint ed. 25.00 (*0-900860-10-3*, Pub. by Octagon Pr UK); reprint ed. pap. 12.50 (*0-86304-046-2*, Pub. by Octagon Pr UK) ISHK.

Wisdom of the Jewish Sages. Rabbi R. Shapiro. 1996. pap. write for info. (*0-517-88695-2*, Harmony) Crown Pub Group.

Wisdom of the Kabbalah. Alexandre Safran. 1992. 24.95 (*0-87306-582-4*) Feldheim.

Wisdom of the Master: Words of 'Abdu'l-Baha. Compiled by Peggy Caton. (Illus.). 19.95 (*0-933770-81-2*) Kalimat.

Wisdom of the Masters of the Far East: Questions & Answers by Royal Order of Tibet, Vol. 1. G. Adamski. reprint ed. spiral bd. 6.50 (*0-7873-0739-4*) Hlth Research.

***Wisdom of the Midwest.** Criswell Freeman. 1996. pap. text ed. 5.95 (*1-887655-17-4*) Walnut Gr Pr.

Wisdom of the Mystic Masters. John K. Weed. 220p. 1971. reprint ed. pap. text ed. 9.95 (*0-13-961532-6*, Reward) P-H.

Wisdom of the Mystic Masters. John K. Weed. 1986. reprint ed. 10.95 (*0-13-961516-4*, Reward) P-H.

Wisdom of the Mythtellers. Sean Kane. 288p. 1994. pap. 16.95 (*1-55111-041-5*) Broadview Pr.

Wisdom of the Overself. rev. ed. Paul Brunton. LC 83-60833. 196p. (Orig.). 1972. pap. 18.95 (*0-87728-591-8*) Weiser.

***Wisdom of the Plain Folk: Songs & Prayers from the Amish & Mennonites.** 1997. pap. 12.95 (*0-614-27472-9*) Viking Penguin.

Wisdom of the Poor One of Assisi. Eloi Leclerc. Tr. by Marie-Louise Johnson from FRE. LC 91-27207. 118p. 1992. reprint ed. pap. 8.95 (*0-932727-45-X*); reprint ed. lib. bdg. 15.95 (*0-932727-47-6*) Hope Pub Hse.

Wisdom of the Poverello. Eloi Leclerc. Tr. by Marie-Louise Johnson. 126p. 1989. reprint ed. pap. 6.95 (*0-8199-0147-4*, Frncscn Herld) Franciscan Pr.

***Wisdom of the Prophet.** Thomas Cleary. 144p. 1996. pap. 6.00 (*0-614-21097-6*, 1321) Kazi Pubns.

***Wisdom of the Prophets: Fusus Al-Hikam.** Muhyiddin I. Arabi. Tr. by Titus Burckhardt & Angela Culme-Seymour from ARA. 146p. 1975. 12.50 (*0-904975-01-0*, Pub. by Beshara Pubns UK); pap. 9.25 (*0-904975-00-2*, Pub. by Beshara Pubns UK) New Leaf Dist.

***Wisdom of the Psalms.** Compiled by Philip Law. LC 96-47031. (Wisdom Ser.). (Illus.). 48p. 1996. 8.00 (*0-8028-3831-6*) Eerdmans.

Wisdom of the Psyche. Ann B. Ulanov. LC 88-15964. 144p. (Orig.). 1988. pap. 8.95 (*0-936384-61-1*) Cowley Pubns.

Wisdom of the Root Cellar. Taylor Mali. 16p. (Orig.). 1995. pap. 4.50 (*0-9648118-2-0*) Hot Tamale Enter.

Wisdom of the Saints: An Anthology. Jill H. Adels. 256p. 1989. reprint ed. pap. 15.95 (*0-19-505915-8*) OUP.

Wisdom of the Saints: An Anthology of Voices. Jill H. Adels. 288p. 1987. 27.50 (*0-19-504152-6*) OUP.

Wisdom of the Sands. Antoine De Saint-Exupery. 1992. reprint ed. lib. bdg. 26.95 (*0-89968-297-9*, Lghtyr Pr) Buccaneer Bks.

Wisdom of the Sasanian Sages. Tr. by Shaul Shaked. 1979. 55.00 (*0-89158-376-9*) Mazda Pubs.

Wisdom of the Self: Authentic Experience & the Journey to Wholeness. Paul Ferrini. (Illus.). 256p. (Orig.). 1992. pap. 12.00 (*1-879159-14-7*) Heartways Pr.

Wisdom of the Serpent: The Myths of Death, Rebirth & Resurrection. Joseph L. Henderson & Maud Oakes. 298p. (C). 1963. pap. text ed. 15.95 (*0-691-02064-7*) Princeton U Pr.

Wisdom of the Spotted Owl: Policy Lessons for a New Century. Steven L. Yaffee. LC 93-48897. 1994. 45.00 (*1-55963-203-8*); pap. 26.95 (*1-55963-204-6*) Island Pr.

Wisdom of the Stoics: Selections from Seneca, Epictetus & Marcus Aurelius. Ed. by Frances Hazlitt & Henry Hazlitt. LC 84-3493. 186p. (Orig.). (C). 1984. lib. bdg. 45.00 (*0-8191-3870-3*) U Pr of Amer.

Wisdom of the Supreme Court. Ed. by Percival E. Jackson. LC 73-8565. xvi, 526p. 1991. reprint ed. 45.00 (*0-8371-6960-7*, 306790) W S Hein.

Wisdom of the Taoists. D. Howard Smith. LC 80-15629. (Wisdom Bks.). 96p. 1980. pap. 7.95 (*0-8112-0777-3*, NDP509) New Directions.

Wisdom of the Tarot. Elisabeth Haich. 174p. 1983. reprint ed. pap. 12.50 (*0-943358-01-9*) Aurora Press.

Wisdom of the Torah. Ed. by Dagobert D. Runes. 1966. pap. 2.25 (*0-8065-0015-8*, 236, Citadel Pr) Carol Pub Group.

Wisdom of the Upanishads. Sri Aurobindo. LC 88-83078. 134p. (Orig.). 1988. pap. 7.95 (*0-941524-43-4*) Lotus Light.

Wisdom of the Veda. M. P. Pandit. LC 89-84764. 112p. (Orig.). 1990. pap. 7.95 (*0-941524-55-8*) Lotus Light.

Wisdom of the Vedas. Jagadish C. Chatterji. LC 92-50142. 151p. (Orig.). 1992. pap. 10.00 (*0-8356-0684-8*, Quest) Theos Pub Hse.

Wisdom of the West. Bertrand Russell. 1989. 17.99 (*0-517-69041-1*) Random Hse Value.

***Wisdom of the West: Common Sense & Uncommon Genius from 101 Great Westerners.** Criswell Freeman. 168p. 1997. pap. 5.95 (*1-887655-31-X*) Walnut Gr Pr.

Wisdom of the Wildflowers. Nancy S. Taylor. (Illus.). 32p. 1989. write for info. (*0-937745-03-0*) Traditions Pr.

***Wisdom of the Word: Faith - Great African-American Sermons.** Rhinold L. Ponder & Michele L. Tuck. 1996. 17.00 (*0-614-19798-8*) Crown Pub Group.

Wisdom of the Word: Love: Great African-American Sermons, Bk. 1. Rhinold L. Ponder & Michele L. Tuck. LC 96-37529. 1996. 17.00 (*0-517-70591-5*) Random Hse Value.

Wisdom of the Word Love: Great African-American Sermons, Bk. 2. Rhinold L. Ponder & Michele L. Tuck. 1997. 17.00 (*0-517-70592-3*) Random Hse Value.

Wisdom of the Zen Masters. Ed. by Irmgard Schloegl. LC 75-42115. (Wisdom Bks.). 96p. 1976. pap. 7.95 (*0-8112-0610-6*, NDP415) New Directions.

Wisdom of the Zohar: An Anthology of Texts, 3 vols., Set. Ed. by Isaiah Tishby. Tr. by David Goldstein from HEB. (Littman Library of Jewish Civilization). (Illus.). 1700p. 95.00 (*0-19-710076-7*) Bnai Brith Bk.

Wisdom of the Zohar: An Anthology of Texts, 3 vols., Set. Ed. by Isaiah Tishby. Tr. by David Goldstein from HEB. (Littman Library of Jewish Civilization). (Illus.). 1700p. 1989. 198.00 (*0-19-710043-0*) Bnai Brith Bk.

Wisdom of the Zohar: An Anthology of Texts, 3 vols., Set. Ed. by Isaiah Tishby. Tr. by David Goldstein from HEB. (Littman Library of Jewish Civilization). (Illus.). 1700p. 1991. reprint ed. pap. 95.00 (*1-874774-28-5*, Pub. by Littman Lib UK) Intl Spec Bk.

Wisdom of Upanisads. K. P. Bahadur. 400p. 1989. text ed. 40.00 (*81-207-0896-2*, Pub. by Sterling Pubs II) Apt Bks.

Wisdom of Upanishads. Jaikishandas Sadani. (C). 1993. 8.50 (*81-224-0486-3*) S Asia.

Wisdom of Vedanta. K. P. Bahadur. (Wisdom of India Ser.: No. 6). 412p. (C). 1985. text ed. 35.00 (*0-86590-725-0*, Pub. by Sterling Pubs II) Apt Bks.

Wisdom of Vedanta. H. L. Sharma. 140p. 1981. 15.95 (*0-318-37181-2*) Asia Bk Corp.

Wisdom of Vedanta. 2nd rev. ed. S. Abhayananda. 340p. 1994. pap. 14.95 (*0-914557-06-8*) Atma Bks.

***Wisdom of Wolves.** 2nd rev. ed. Twyman L. Toweny. 160p. 1997. 14.95 (*1-57071-206-9*) Sourcebks.

Wisdom of Wolves: Nature's Way to Organizational Success. Twyman L. Towery. 1995. 14.95 (*0-9646872-0-8*) Wessex House.

Wisdom of Women. 116p. 1992. pap. 6.95 (*1-55586-430-9*) US Catholic.

Wisdom of Women. Intro. & Selected by Carol S. LaRusso. LC 92-17602. (Classic Wisdom Collection). 128p. 1992. 12.95 (*1-880032-09-0*) New Wrld Lib.

***Wisdom of Wooden: A Lifetime of Observations & Reflections on & off the Court.** John Wooden & Steve Jamison. 1997. 14.95 (*0-614-28174-1*) Contemp Bks.

Wisdom of Words: Language, Theology, & Literature in the New England Renaissance. Philip F. Gura. LC 80-25041. 213p. reprint ed. pap. 60.80 (*0-7837-0216-7*, 2040524) Bks Demand.

Wisdom of Yoga. K. P. Bahadur. 1989. text ed. 20.00 (*81-207-0330-8*, Pub. by Sterling Pubs II) Apt Bks.

Wisdom of Zen. Compiled by Marc De Smedt. (Illus.). 56p. 1996. 8.95 (*0-7892-0240-9*) Abbeville Pr.

Wisdom, or Mind, Will, & Understanding. LC 70-133770. (Tudor Facsimile Texts. Old English Plays Ser.: No. 2). reprint ed. 49.50 (*0-404-53302-7*) AMS Pr.

Wisdom Power. Kenneth Edlin. 168p. (Orig.). 1994. pap. 7.99 (*1-56043-832-0*) Destiny Image.

Wisdom Practice: Gateway to Enlightenment. G. De Purucker. Ed. by Kenneth Small. 130p. 1997. pap. 10.50 (*0-913004-90-1*) Point Loma Pub.

Wisdom Revisited: Athena Speaks & Other Owl-Songs. Louise Jaffe. LC 87-91517. 48p. (Orig.). 1987. pap. 5.00 (*0-9613681-1-X*) L Jaffe.

***Wisdom Seeker.** William E. Dickinson. 102p. (Orig.). 1997. mass mkt. 4.99 (*1-55197-833-4*, Pub. by Comnwlth Pub CN) Partners Pubs Grp.

Wisdom Seeks Her Way: Liberating the Power of Women's Spirituality. Maria Riley. 86p. (Orig.). 1987. pap. text ed. 5.95 (*0-934255-04-0*) Center Concern.

***Wisdom Series: A Bible Survey Curriculum for Adults.** Celia M. Hastings. (Illus.). 480p. (Orig.). 1997. pap. 49.95 (*0-9656335-1-9*) Sheepfold Pubg.

W

Wisdom Sits in Places: Landscape & Language among the Western Apache. Keith H. Basso. LC 95-39272. 192p. 1996. 40.00 (*0-8263-1723-5*); pap. 14.95 (*0-8263-1724-3*) U of NM Pr.

Wisdom Stories: Meditations on Fairy Tales, Myths & Legends. Robert M. Hoffstein. 212p. (Orig.). (C). 1992. pap. 16.95 (*0-913002-03-8*) Tsimtsum Hse.

Wisdom Symposium: Papers from the Trinity College Medieval Festival. Ed. by Milla C. Riggio. LC 85-48070. (Studies in the Middle Ages: No. 11). (Illus.). 1986. 32.50 (*0-404-61441-8*) AMS Pr.

Wisdom Tales from Around the World. Heather Forest. 160p. 1996. 27.95 (*0-87483-478-3*); pap. text ed. 17.95 (*0-87483-479-1*) August Hse.

***Wisdom Teachings of Archangel Michael.** Lori J. Flory. 1997. mass mkt. 5.99 (*0-451-19099-8*, Sig) NAL-Dutton.

***Wisdom Teachings of the Dalai Lama.** Matthew Bunson. 1997. pap. 9.95 (*0-452-27927-5*, Plume) NAL-Dutton.

Wisdom Texts from Qumran. Daniel J. Harrington. LC 96-354. (Literature of the Dead Sea Scrolls Ser.). 224p. (C). 1996. pap. 16.95 (*0-415-13907-4*); text ed. 55.00 (*0-415-13906-6*) Routledge.

***Wisdom Through the Ages.** 500p. 1997. 21.99 (*1-57673-176-6*, Multnomah Bks) Multnomah Pubs.

Wisdom Through the Ages: Ethics for the Living Experience. Stanley E. Somers. (Illus.). 80p. (Orig.). 1989. pap. 5.00 (*0-9615032-2-X*) World Relations Pr.

Wisdom to Live By. Henry Gariepy. 216p. 1991. pap. 9.99 (*0-89693-037-8*, 6-1037, Victor Bks) Chariot Victor.

***Wisdom to Live By.** George MacDonald. 218p. 1996. 19.95 (*0-940652-39-0*) Sunrise Bks.

Wisdom Tree. Emma Hawkridge. LC 72-128257. (Essay Index Reprint Ser.). 1977. 36.95 (*0-8369-1881-9*) Ayer.

***Wisdom Tree: A Journey to the Heart of God & Man's Religions.** Gary D. Guthrie. LC 97-22264. 1997. write for info. (*0-943734-35-5*) Ocean Tree Bks.

Wisdom Tree: Studies in James for Children. Donna B. Smith. 1988. pap. 2.95 (*0-89137-055-2*) Quality Pubns.

Wisdom, Understanding, & Knowledge: Basic Concepts of Hasidic Thought. Shmuel Boteach. LC 95-6052. 296p. 1996. pap. 24.95 (*0-87668-557-2*) Aronson.

***Wisdom Which Encircles Circles: Papers on Hildegard of Bingen.** Ed. by Audrey E. Davidson. 1996. pap. 16.00 (*1-879288-71-0*) Medieval Inst.

Wisdom Within. Deepak Chopra. 1997. wbk. ed., pap. write for info. (*0-517-88816-5*, Harmony) Crown Pub Group.

Wisdom Without Answers: A Brief Introduction to Philosophy. 3rd ed. Daniel Kolak & Raymond Martin. LC 95-8845. xii, 158p. (C). 1996. pap. 17.95 (*0-534-25974-X*) Wadsworth Pub.

Wisdom Without Answers: A Guide to the Experience of Philosophy. 2nd ed. Daniel Kolak & Raymond Martin. 141p. (C). 1991. pap. 12.00 (*0-534-14598-1*) Wadsworth Pub.

Wisdom Workshop. Darrel A. Trulson. Ed. by James C. Galvin. (LifeGuide Family Bible Studies). (Illus.). 80p. (Orig.). 1995. wbk. ed., pap. 4.99 (*0-8308-1117-6*, 1117) InterVarsity.

Wisdom Wrapped in Experiences & Labeled Problems: Experiences of a Searching Soul. John J. Belmar. 200p. 1992. text ed. 19.95 (*0-9632645-0-8*) Sci of Thought.

***Wisdom, You Are My Sister: Studies in Honor of Roland E. Murphy, O. Carm on the Occasion of His Eightieth Birthday.** Roland Edmund Murphy & Michael L. Barr. LC 97-16060. (Catholic Biblical Quarterly Monographs). 1997. write for info. (*0-915170-28-0*) Catholic Bibl Assn.

Wisdomkeepers: Meetings with Native American Spiritual Elders. Harvey Arden & Steve Wall. LC 90-83550. (Earthsong Collection Ser.). (Illus.). 128p. 1991. 39.95 (*0-941831-55-8*); pap. 22.95 (*0-941831-66-3*) Beyond Words Pub.

Wisdom's Call. Sutton E. Griggs. LC 75-89411. (Black Heritage Library Collection). 1977. 17.95 (*0-8369-8587-7*) Ayer.

Wisdom's Children. J. C. Bassett. 143p. 1993. pap. 4.95 (*0-88172-202-2*) Believers Bkshelf.

Wisdom's Children: Home Education & the Roots of Restored Biblical Culture. rev. ed. Blair Adams & Joel Stein. LC 88-51537. 602p. 1989. pap. 12.95 (*0-916387-11-9*) Truth Forum.

Wisdom's Daughter: The Life & Love Story of She-Who-Must-Be-Obeyed. H. Rider Haggard. Ed. by R. Reginald & Douglas Melville. LC 77-84230. (Lost Race & Adult Fantasy Ser.). 1978. reprint ed. lib. bdg. 36.95 (*0-405-10983-0*) Ayer.

Wisdom's Daughters. Steve Wall. LC 92-54753. 320p. 1994. pap. 16.00 (*0-06-092561-2*) HarpC.

***Wisdom's Daughters: Stories of Women Around Jesus.** Elizabeth G. Watson. LC 97-23171. 144p. (Orig.). 1997. pap. 12.95 (*0-8298-1221-0*) Pilgrim OH.

Wisdom's Feast: Sophia in Study & Celebration. Hal Taussig et al. LC 96-26534. 240p. (Orig.). 1996. pap. 14.95 (*1-55612-856-8*, LL1856) Sheed & Ward MO.

Wisdom's Fool. Eddie Doherty. 1976. pap. 3.95 (*0-910984-09-3*) Montfort Pubns.

Wisdom's Many Faces. R. Charles Hill. LC 95-40741. 144p. (Orig.). 1996. pap. 11.95 (*0-8146-5515-7*, M Glazier) Liturgical Pr.

Wisdom's Maw: The Acid Novel. Todd B. Fahey. LC 96-83734. 208p. (Orig.). 1996. pap. 16.95 (*0-9651839-0-4*) Far Gone.
WISDOM'S MAW factionalizes the CIA's legendary LSD experiments & their influence on the Sixties' counterculture. Web 'zine editor Christopher Hunt, in CIRCUIT TRACES, goes to the essence of this controversial work: "What if the Sixties were the result of a bizarre experiment in mind control & genetic manipulation perpetrated by the CIA? What if outlaw heroes of the counterculture like Jack Kerouac, Neal Cassady, & Timothy Leary were paid government agents seeking to subvert the American consciousness? What if the twisted path from Father Knows Best to Woodstock was carved out by top-level G-men bent on creating a new world order? This is the raw material for Todd Brendan Fahey's incendiary novel WISDOM'S MAW." Acclaimed novelist Ernest Gaines writes: "You [Fahey] have written a very controversial book here, & if it is published & read, you may have to answer some questions to some pretty big boys. I hope you have the backbone for it." Reviews in counterculture magazine nationwide. Order from: Far Gone Books, P.O. Box 43745. Lafayette, LA 70504-3745. (318) 261-1946. E-mail: fargone@popalex.linknet.net; WISDOM'S MAW Web site: http://www2.linknet.net/fahey/Wisdom. ***Publisher Provided Annotation.***

Wisdom's Passing. Steven Porter. xii, 304p. 1989. pap. 18.00 (*0-935016-71-6*, Barclay House) Zinn Pub Grp.

Wisdom's Watch upon the Hours: English Translation of Paul Kunzle & Dominikus Planzer's Critical Latin Edition of Henry Suso's Horologium Sapientiae. Henry Suso. Tr. by Edmund Colledge from LAT. LC 93-23232. (Fathers of the Church: Medieval Continuation Ser.: Vol. 4). 360p. 1994. 39.95 (*0-8132-0792-4*) Cath U Pr.

***Wisdom's Way: 101 Tales of Chinese Wit.** Ed. by Andrew Murray. Tr. by Walton Lee. LC 96-61429. 176p. (Orig.). 1997. pap. 12.95 (*1-886969-36-1*, B027) YMAA Pubn.

Wise: Col. John Wise of England & Virginia, 1617-1695: His Ancestors & Descendants. J. C. Wise. (Illus.). 355p. 1991. reprint ed. pap. 56.00 (*0-8328-1960-3*); reprint ed. lib. bdg. 66.00 (*0-8328-1959-X*) Higginson Bk Co.

Wise & Healthy Living: A Common Sense Approach for Aging Well. Richard D. Underwood & Brenda B. Underwood. (Retirement Ser.). 120p. 1989. pap. 8.95 (*0-88908-686-9*, 9565) Self-Counsel Pr.

Wise & Otherwise. Isabel Alden. (Grace Livingston Hill Ser.: Vol. 7). 1996. mass mkt., pap. 4.99 (*0-8423-3183-2*) Tyndale.

Wise & Otherwise. Jack B. Scott. (Orig.). 1985. teacher ed. 3.95 (*0-934688-23-0*); pap. text ed. 4.95 (*0-934688-21-4*) Great Comm Pubns.

Wise & Otherwise: Fables, Myths, Fairy Tales & Other Jolly Nonsense. Elmer Otte. 72p. 1995. write for info. (*0-9648628-4-0*); pap. write for info. (*0-9648628-1-6*) Folklore Hse.

Wise & Wacky Proverbs: The Truth Behind Everyday Sayings. Jim Anton. (Illus.). 128p. 1996. pap. 6.95 (*0-8069-8485-6*) Sterling.

Wise & Wacky Wit. Vern McLellan. 160p. 1992. mass mkt. 4.99 (*0-8423-8249-6*) Tyndale.

Wise As Serpents, Innocent As Doves: American Mennonites Engage Washington. Keith G. Miller. LC 95-41822. (Illus.). 328p. (C). 1996. text ed. 36.00 (*0-87049-936-X*) U of Tenn Pr.

Wise Blood. Flannery O'Connor. 232p. 1962. pap. 10.00 (*0-374-50584-5*) FS&G.

Wise Child. large type ed. Elizabeth Murphy. (Magna Large Print Ser.). 735p. 1996. 25.99 (*0-7505-0859-0*, Pub. by Magna Print Bks UK) Ulverscroft.

Wise Children. Angela Carter. 232p. 1992. 21.00 (*0-374-29133-0*) FS&G.

Wise Children. Angela Carter. 240p. 1993. pap. 11.95 (*0-14-017530-X*, Penguin Bks) Viking Penguin.

***Wise Choices: Decisions, Games, & Negotiations.** Ed. by Richard J. Zeckhauser & Ralph L. Keeney. 1996. text ed. 45.00 (*0-07-103680-6*) McGraw.

Wise Choices: Games, Decisions, & Negotiations. Ed. by Richard J. Zeckhauser et al. 496p. (C). 1996. 45.00 (*0-87584-677-7*) Harvard Busn.

Wise Choices, Apt Feelings: A Theory of Normative Judgment. Allan Gibbard. 346p. 1990. 45.00 (*0-674-95377-0*) HUP.

Wise Choices, Apt Feelings: A Theory of Normative Judgment. Allan Gibbard. 360p. 1992. pap. 17.95 (*0-674-95378-9*) HUP.

***Wise Choices Beyond Midlife: Women Mapping the Journey Ahead.** Lucy Scott et al. LC 97-11355. 240p. (Orig.). 1997. pap. 13.95 (*1-57601-051-1*) Papier-Mache Press.

Wise Choices for Tough Times: Innovative Resource Reallocation Strategies to Strengthen the University. LC 93-41336. 1993. write for info. (*0-88044-135-6*) AASCU Press.

Wise County, Virginia. Charles A. Johnson. (Illus.). 430p. 1988. reprint ed. 27.95 (*0-932807-29-1*) Overmountain Pr.

Wise Daughters from Foreign Lands: European Women Writers in China. Elisabeth Croll. 252p. 1989. 29.95 (*0-04-440414-X*) Routledge Chapman & Hall.

***Wise Economies: Brevity & Storytelling in American Short Stories.** Kirk Curnutt. LC 96-50297. 1997. text ed. 35.00 (*0-89301-202-5*) U of Idaho Pr.

***Wise Enough to Play the Fool: A Biography of Duncan Macrae.** Priscilla Barlow. 258p. 1996. 45.00 (*0-85976-418-4*, Pub. by J Donald UK) St Mut.

Wise Extravagance: The Founding of the Carnegie International Exhibitions 1895-1901. Kenneth Neal. LC 95-50881. (Illus.). 300p. 1996. pap. 14.95 (*0-8229-5584-9*) U of Pittsburgh Pr.

Wise Extravagance: The Founding of the Carnegie International Exhibitions 1895-1901. Kenneth Neal. LC 95-50881. (Illus.). 300p. (C). 1996. text ed. 29.95 (*0-8229-3925-8*) U of Pittsburgh Pr.

Wise Grandma Duck. Walt Disney Productions Staff. (Walt Disney's Fun-to-Read Library Ser.: Vol. 10). (Illus.). 44p. (J). (gr. 1-6). 1986. reprint ed. 3.49 (*1-885222-22-X*) Advance Pubs.

Wise Guy - Good Fellas. Nicholas Pileggi. 1990. pap. 6.50 (*0-671-72322-7*) PB.

Wise Have Not Spoken. Paul V. Carroll. 1954. pap. 5.25 (*0-8222-1268-4*) Dramatists Play.

Wise Heart. large type ed. Lucile V. Stevens. (Linford Romance Library). 1991. pap. 15.99 (*0-7089-6987-9*, Trailtree Bookshop) Ulverscroft.

Wise Hombre Quizzes for Westerners. Lannon Mintz. LC 88-29437. (Illus.). 48p. (Orig.). 1989. pap. 3.95 (*0-86534-128-1*) Sunstone Pr.

***Wise Investor: Ten Concepts You Need to Know to Achieve Financial Success.** Neil Elmouchi. (Illus.). 160p. (Orig.). 1997. pap. 14.95 (*0-9654215-0-3*) Dunhill & West.

Wise King: Studies in Royal Wisdom As Divine Revelation in the Old Testament & Its Environment. Leonidas Kaluglia. (Coniectanea Biblica. Old Testament Ser.: No. 15). 160p. (Orig.). 1980. pap. 41.00 (*0-317-65799-2*) Coronet Bks.

Wise King Solomon. (Bible Stories Ser.: No. S846-15). (J). 1989. boxed 3.95 (*0-7214-5261-2*, Ladybrd) Penguin.

Wise King Solomon. R. Woodman. Date not set. pap. 2.50 (*1-85792-052-X*, Pub. by Christian Focus UK) Spring Arbor Dist.

Wise Little Burro. Joe Hayes. (Illus.). 48p. (Orig.). (J). (gr. k-6). 1991. pap. 7.95 (*0-939729-20-2*) Trails West Pub.

***Wise Little Judge.** Ed. by David S. Pape. LC 96-76783. (Illus.). 175p. (J). (gr. 3-9). 1996. 13.95 (*0-922613-66-4*) Hachai Pubns.

Wise Man Stories. Friends Anonymous Staff. Ed. by Harold Smith & Alma Smith. (Orig.). 1979. pap. 4.95 (*0-87516-371-8*) DeVorss.

***Wise Man's House.** Melody Carlson. 286p. 1997. pap. 8.99 (*1-57673-070-0*, Palisades OR) Multnomah Pubs.

***Wise Men.** Walter Isaacson. 1997. pap. 18.00 (*0-684-83771-4*, Touchstone Bks) S&S Trade.

Wise Men & Fools. Joan Berutti. (Illus.). 97p. (Orig.). 1990. pap. 12.00 (*0-912950-60-9*) Blue Oak.

***Wise Men & Their Journey.** pap. 2.99 (*0-87162-557-1*) Warner Pr.

Wise Men Fish Here: The Story of Frances Steloff & the Gotham Book Mart. W. G. Rogers. 288p. 1994. reprint ed. pap. 14.95 (*1-879923-08-4*) Booksellers Pub.

Wise Men of Chelm. Sandra F. Asher. 1992. pap. 3.45 (*0-87129-165-7*, W73) Dramatic Pub.

Wise Men of Helm. Solomon Simon. (Illus.). (J). (gr. 3-7). 1942. pap. 9.50 (*0-87441-469-5*) Behrman.

Wise Men Press Out Model. (Little Lamb Mini Activity Bks.). (Illus.). 12p. (J). 1992. 1.49 (*0-87403-944-4*, 01567) Standard Pub.

Wise Moves in Hard Times: Creating & Managing Resilient Colleges & Universities. David W. Leslie & E. K. Fretwell, Jr. LC 95-40653. (Higher & Adult Education Ser.). 320p. 1996. 32.95 (*0-7879-0196-2*) Jossey-Bass.

Wise Old Owl & the Dodo Bird: "The Dangers of a Stranger" Ethel Williams & Janette Smith. (Wise Old Owl Book Collection). 50p. (J). (ps-5). 1994. 15.00 (*1-884644-00-7*); 8.95 (*1-884644-01-5*); student ed. 27.50 incl. audio (*1-884644-02-3*) E&J Pubng.

Wise Old Owl's Canoe Trip Adventure. Ed. & Illus. by Robert Kraus. LC 91-39014. 32p. (J). (ps-3). 1993. text ed. 11.50 (*0-8167-2947-6*) Troll Communs.

Wise Old Owl's Christmas Adventure. Robert Kraus. LC 93-25544. (Adventures of Wise Old Owl Ser.). (Illus.). 32p. (J). (ps-3). 1993. pap. 2.95 (*0-8167-2946-8*); lib. bdg. 11.50 (*0-8167-2945-X*) Troll Communs.

Wise Old Owl's Halloween Adventure. Robert Kraus. LC 93-18686. (Adventures of Wise Old Owl Ser.). (Illus.). 32p. (J). (gr. k-3). 1993. lib. bdg. 11.50 (*0-8167-2949-2*) Troll Communs.

Wise Old Owl's Halloween Adventure. Robert Kraus. LC 93-18686. (Adventures of Wise Old Owl Ser.). (Illus.). 32p. (J). (gr. k-3). 1997. pap. 2.95 (*0-8167-2950-6*) Troll Communs.

Wise Old Woman. Illus. by Martin Springett. LC 92-46048. 32p. (J). 1994. 14.95 (*0-689-50582-5*, McElderry) S&S Childrens.

***Wise Poet.** Khurram Murad. 24p. 1996. pap. 3.50 (*0-614-21044-5*, 1322) Kazi Pubns.

***Wise Poetry: Celebrating Life.** Rita Wise. Ed. by Dion Newton. (Illus.). 40p. 1996. pap. write for info. (*0-9653991-0-9*) Wise Pubng.

Wise Poison. David Rivard. LC 96-75791. 72p. (Orig.). 1996. pap. 12.95 (*1-55597-247-0*) Graywolf.

***Wise Raoul.** Agnes Adachi. (Orig.). (J). (gr. 3-6). 1995. pap. 10.00 (*0-9621930-4-6*) A Adachi.

Wise Saws & Modern Instances. David H. Smith. LC 91-65833. 64p. 1991. 10.00 (*0-8233-0475-2*) Golden Quill.

Wise Sayings for Boys & Girls. Adebisi T. Aromolaran. (Illus.). 100p. (Orig.). (YA). (gr. 7-12). 1994. pap. text ed. 9.95 (*0-9635862-0-3*) Meroe Pub.

Wise Sayings for Boys & Girls. Adebisi T. Aromolaran. (Illus.). 100p. (Orig.). 1994. text ed. 16.95 (*0-9635862-1-1*) Meroe Pub.

Wise Shoemaker of Studena. LC 93-43481. (J). (gr. 5-8). audio 24.95 (*0-8276-0536-6*) JPS Phila.

Wise Shoemaker of Studena. Syd Lieberman. LC 93-43481. (Illus.). 32p. (J). (gr. 5-8). 1994. 15.95 (*0-8276-0509-9*) JPS Phila.

Wise up, Custom Pub. 2nd ed. Palmer. 1993. pap. text ed. write for info. (*0-07-048453-8*) McGraw.

Wise up to Teens: Insights into Marketing & Advertising to Teenagers. Peter Zollo. 311p. 1995. 34.95 (*0-9628092-9-2*) New Strategist.

Wise Use Agenda. Ed. by Alan M. Gottlieb. 164p. (Orig.). 1989. pap. 9.95 (*0-939571-05-6*) Free Enter Pr.

***Wise Utilization of Tropical Rain Forest Lands.** Ed. by C. F. Van Beusekom et al. (Tropenbos Scientific Ser.: No. 1). (Illus.). 154p. 1987. pap. 25.00 (*90-5113-002-3*, Pub. by Backhuys Pubs NE) Balogh.

***Wise Washerman.** large type ed. Deborah Froese. (Illus.). 32p. (J). (gr. k-4). 1996. 14.95 (*1-895340-10-1*, Pub. by Hyperion Pr Ltd CN) Sterling.

Wise Washerman: A Folktale from Burma. Illus. by Wang Kui. 32p. (J). (ps-2). 1996. 14.95 (*0-7868-0291-X*) Hyprn Child.

Wise Washerman: A Folktale from Burma. Illus. by Wang Kui. (J). (ps-2). 1996. lib. bdg. 14.89 (*0-7868-2232-5*) Hyprn Child.

Wise Why's Y's: The Griot's Tale. Baraka. 1995. pap. text ed. 12.00 (*0-88378-047-X*) Third World.

Wise Woman. Philippa Gregory. 1994. mass mkt. 5.99 (*0-671-79275-X*) PB.

Wise Woman. Naomi Strichartz. (Illus.). 43p. (Orig.). (J). (gr. 2-6). 1986. pap. 3.50 (*0-9618182-0-4*) Cranehill Pr.

Wise Woman: Whisperings of the Angels. Judith D. Parr. Ed. by Dorothy Rome. (Illus.). 52p. 1990. write for info. incl. audio (*0-941971-08-2*); pap. 15.95 incl. audio (*0-941971-07-4*) Peacock CO.

Wise Woman - Gutta Percha Willie (A Duplex) George MacDonald. (George MacDonald Original Works: Series III). (Illus.). 354p. 1993. reprint ed. 16.00 (*1-881084-17-5*) Johannesen.

Wise Woman & Her Secret. Eve Merriam. LC 90-42406. (J). 1991. pap. 16.00 (*0-671-72603-X*, S&S Bks Young Read) S&S Childrens.

Wise Woman & Other Fantasy Stories. George MacDonald. Ed. by Glenn G. Sadler. 176p. 1980. pap. 7.00 (*0-8028-1860-9*) Eerdmans.

Wise Woman Builds Her House. Bessie Patterson. 1979. pap. 6.25 (*0-89137-413-2*) Quality Pubns.

Wise Woman Herbal for the Childbearing Year. Susun S. Weed. LC 85-71064. (Wise Woman Herbal Ser.: No. 1). (Illus.). 192p. (Orig.). (C). 1986. pap. 9.95 (*0-9614620-0-0*) Ash Tree.

Wise Woman Knows. Bessie Patterson. 1982. 6.25 (*0-89137-422-1*) Quality Pubns.

***Wise Woman's Guide to Erotic Videos: 300 Sexy Videos for Every Woman--& Her Lover.** Angela Cohen & Sarah G. Fox. LC 96-2754. 304p. 1997. pap. 15.00 (*0-553-06784-2*) Broadway BDD.

Wise Woman's Guide to Spells, Rituals, & Goddess Love. Elizabeth Brooke. 256p. 1995. pap. 12.95 (*0-89594-779-X*) Crossing Pr.

Wise Woman's Sacred Wheel of the Year. Naomi Strichartz. (Illus.). (Orig.). (J). (gr. 2-6). 1988. pap. 3.50 (*0-9618182-1-2*) Cranehill Pr.

***Wise Women.** Susan Cahill. Date not set. pap. 15.00 (*0-393-31679-3*) Norton.

Wise Women: Folk & Fairy Tales from Around the World. Suzanne I. Barchers. (Illus.). xiii, 324p. 1990. lib. bdg. 21.00 (*0-87287-816-3*) Libs Unl.

***Wise Women: Folk & Fairy Tales from Around the World.** Suzanne I. Barchers. (Illus.). 400p. 1997. lib. bdg. 18.00 (*1-56308-592-5*) Libs Unl.

Wise Women: Over 2000 Years of Spiritual Writing by Women. Ed. by Susan Cahill. LC 95-40575. 416p. 1996. 27.50 (*0-393-03946-3*) Norton.

Wise Women Bearing Gifts: Joys & Struggles of Their Faith. Ed. by Suzan D. Johnson. 96p. (Orig.). 1988. pap. 10.00 (*0-8170-1140-4*) Judson.

Wise Women Don't Have Hot Flashes They Have Power Surges! v, 105p. (Orig.). 1996. pap. write for info. (*0-9652823-0-9*) Yz Woman.

Wise Women Don't Worry: Wise Women Don't Get the Blues. Jane Claypool. 263p. 1996. pap. 11.95 (*0-9643948-1-2*) Cornucopia CA.

Wise Women of the Dreamtime: Aboriginal Tales of the Ancestral Powers. Compiled by K. Langloh Parker. (Illus.). 160p. (Orig.). 1993. pap. 12.95 (*0-89281-477-2*) Inner Tradit.

Wise Words: A Guide to Aphorism. Mary E. Snodgrass. (YA). (gr. 6-12). 1990. pap. text ed. 11.97 (*0-937659-43-6*) GCT.

Wise Words: Essays on the Proverb. Compiled by Wolfgang Mieder. LC 94-3960. (Folklore Casebks.: Vol. 6). 608p. 1994. text ed. 79.00 (*0-8153-0942-2*, H1638) Garland.

***Wise Words: Family Stories that Bring the Proverbs to Life.** Peter Leithart. 169p. 1996. 9.99 (*1-880692-23-6*) GCB.

Wise Words & Wives' Tales: The Origins, Meanings & Time-Honored Wisdom of Proverbs & Folk Sayings, Olde & New. Stuart B. Flexner & Doris Flexner. 224p. (Orig.). 1993. pap. 9.00 (*0-380-76238-2*) Avon.

Wise Words for Little People. Kenneth N. Taylor. 64p. (J). (ps-2). 1987. 11.99 (*0-8423-8232-1*) Tyndale.

Wise Words in a Wicked World: Studies in Proverbs. Charles W. Turner. pap. 7.99 (*0-88469-028-8*) BMH Bks.

Wise Words on the Good Life. Helen Nearing. 192p. 1980. 15.00 (*0-686-73458-0*) Good Life Ctr.

***Wise Words on the Good Life.** Helen Nearing. 15.00 (*0-614-30465-2*) Good Life Ctr.

Wise Words to the Graduate. Robert J. Martin. (Contempo Ser.). (YA). 1978. pap. 2.99 (*0-8010-6043-5*) Baker Bks.

W.I.S.E. (Workplace Information Series on Eldercare) Telesis Corp. Staff. 1996. 125.00 (*1-56117-032-1*) Telesis CA.

***Wisecracker.** William Mann. 1998. pap. 27.50 (*0-670-87155-9*) Viking Penguin.

Wisecracks: The Farces of George S. Kaufman. Jeffrey Mason. Ed. by Oscar G. Brockett. LC 88-11076. (Theater & Dramatic Studies: No. 53). 146p. reprint ed. 41.70 (*0-8357-1887-5*, 2070740) Bks Demand.

An Asterisk (*) at the beginning of an entry indicates that the title is appearing in BIP for the first time.

Wisedome of the Ancients. Francis Bacon. Tr. by A. Gorges. LC 68-54614. (English Experince Ser.: No. 1). 176p. 1968. reprint ed. 25.00 (*90-221-0001-4*) Walter J Johnson.

Wiseguys in Love. C. Clark Criscuolo. 288p. 1995. mass mkt. 4.99 (*0-8217-4802-5*, Zebra Kensgtn) Kensgtn Pub Corp.

***Wisely Chosen.** Nellie McCaslin. LC 96-27212. 55p. (Orig.). (J). (gr. k-6). 1996. pap. 5.00 (*0-88734-478-X*) Players Pr.

Wisely Pray the Psalms: A Prayerful Companion to Reading the Psalms. Ambrose Tinsley. 112p. (Orig.). 1993. pap. 7.95 (*1-85607-081-6*, Pub. by Columba Pr IE) Twenty-Third.

Wisely Train the Younger Women. Bessie Patterson. 1973. pap. 6.25 (*0-89137-406-X*) Quality Pubns.

Wiseman Family & Allied Lines, Vol. I. Eugene M. Wiseman. LC 91-76703. 816p. 1991. lib. bdg. 42.50 (*0-9631228-0-0*) E M Wiseman.

Wisemann Originals. Ron Goulart. 1989. 16.95 (*0-8027-5722-7*) Walker & Co.

***Wisemen: Draw Your Way Through the Bible.** Dan Peters. (Picturethis! Ser.: No. 4). 50p. 1997. ring bd. write for info. (*1-890598-12-7*) PictureThis.

Wiser than Despair: The Evolution of Ideas in the Relationship of Music & the Christian Church. Quentin Faulkner. LC 95-35684. (Contributions to the Study of Music & Dance Ser.: No. 40). 272p. 1996. text ed. 59.95 (*0-313-29645-6*, Greenwood Pr) Greenwood.

Wisest Fool: Sermons on Bible Characters. Clarence E. Macartney. 160p. 1996. pap. 9.99 (*0-8254-3284-7*) Kregel.

Wisest Fool in Christendom. William L. McElwee. LC 74-7449. (Illus.). 296p. 1974. reprint ed. text ed. 35.00 (*0-8371-7522-4*, MCWF, Greenwood Pr) Greenwood.

Wisest Man in America. W. D. Wetherell. LC 94-24662. (Hardscrabble Bks.). 236p. 1995. 24.95 (*0-87451-700-1*) U Pr of New Eng.

Wisest Man in America. W. D. Wetherell. LC 94-24662. (Hardscrabble Bks.). 236p. 1995. reprint ed. pap. 12.95 (*0-87451-761-3*) U Pr of New Eng.

Wish. Diane Hoh. (Nightmare Hall Ser.: No. 4). 176p. (J). (gr. 7-9). 1993. pap. 3.50 (*0-590-46013-7*) Scholastic Inc.

Wish. Ed. by Lee Sun-ai & Don Luce. LC 83-18480. (Illus.). 72p. (Orig.). 1984. pap. 6.95 (*0-377-00136-8*) Friendship Pr.

Wish Book. Stacie Chaiken. 1993. 20.00 (*0-517-59429-3*, Crown) Crown Pub Group.

***Wish Box Keepsake.** (Keepsakes! Ser.). (Illus.). (J). (gr. 1-5). 1997. 9.95 (*0-7624-0146-X*) Running Pr.

***Wish Club.** Stella Cameron. 1998. mass mkt. write for info. (*0-446-60431-3*) Warner Bks.

Wish Come True. Ann Gabhart. 160p. (YA). (gr. 7 up). 1988. pap. 2.50 (*0-380-75653-6*, Flare) Avon.

Wish Coupons for Kids: The Book of Yes. John Boston. (Illus.). 128p. 1994. mass mkt. 3.50 (*0-380-77294-9*) Avon.

Wish Factory: How to Make Wishes Come True. Jana L. Shellman. LC 94-62106. (Illus.). 96p. (Orig.). 1995. pap. 12.95 (*0-9644770-0-9*) Threadbare Pub.

***Wish for Christmas.** large type ed. Josie Metcalfe. (Mills & Boon Large Print Ser.). 288p. 1997. 22.50 (*0-263-15079-8*, Pub. by M & B UK) Ulverscroft.

Wish-for Dinosaur. Jane B. Moncure. LC 88-20302. (Magic Castle Readers Ser.). (Illus.). 32p. (J). (ps-2). 1989. lib. bdg. 21.36 (*0-89565-393-1*) Childs World.

Wish for Love. Gina F. Wilkins. (Temptation Ser.). 1996. mass mkt. 3.50 (*0-373-25692-2*, 1-25692-4) Harlequin Bks.

Wish for Power & the Fear of Having It. Althea J. Horner. LC 88-328. 199p. 1988. 27.50 (*0-87668-924-1*) Aronson.

Wish for Power & the Fear of Having It. Althea J. Horner. 1996. pap. 35.00 (*1-56821-759-5*) Aronson.

Wish for Tomorrow.. Kimberly R. Rinehart. Ed. by Georgia M. Rettmer. (Illus.). 1990. pap. 3.95 (*0-942865-09-X*) It Takes Two.

Wish for Wings & Other Things: A Magical Tale for Everyone of Every Age Ever Touched by Illness. Sara D. Glater. LC 95-94674. (Illus.). 52p. (J). (gr. 3 up). 1995. 15.95 (*0-9647799-1-9*) Lemonade Sundays.

Wish for Wings That Work. Berkeley Breathed. 32p. (J). 1995. pap. 4.95 (*0-316-10691-7*) Little.

Wish for Wings That Work: An Opus Christmas Story. Berkeley Breathed. (Illus.). 32p. (J). 1991. 14.95 (*0-316-10758-1*) Little.

Wish for Your Christmas. George C. Anderheggen. (Illus.). 13p. (Orig.). 1982. write for info. (*0-318-56854-3*) Bookling Pubs.

Wish-Fulfilling Jewel: The Practice of Guru Yoga According to the Longchen Nyingthig Tradition. Dilgo Khyentse. 108p. (Orig.). 1994. pap. 10.00 (*1-57062-052-0*) Shambhala Pubns.

Wish Giver. Brittain. (J). 1990. mass mkt. 3.50 (*0-06-107012-2*, Harp PBks) HarpC.

Wish Giver: A Study Guide. Charlene Forsten. Ed. by Joyce Friedland & Rikki Kessler. (Novel-Ties Ser.). 24p. (J). (gr. 3-6). 1990. pap. text ed. 15.95 (*0-88122-401-4*) Lrn Links.

Wish Giver: Three Tales of Coven Tree. Bill Brittain. LC 82-48264. (Illus.). 192p. (J). (gr. 3-7). 1983. lib. bdg. 14.89 (*0-06-020687-X*) HarpC Child Bks.

Wish Giver: Three Tales of Coven Tree. Bill Brittain. LC 82-48264. (Trophy Bk.). (Illus.). 192p. (J). (gr. 3-7). 1986. pap. 3.95 (*0-06-440168-5*, Trophy) HarpC Child Bks.

Wish I Could've Told You: Portraits of Teenagers Almost Dropping Out. Marge T. Zuba. LC 94-30844. 150p. (YA). (gr. 6-12). 1995. pap. 15.95 (*1-879528-11-8*) LEPS Pr.

Wish I May, Wish I Might: Fantastic Thoughts for a Starry Night. Florian Langenscheidt & Gabriele Langenscheidt. (Illus.). 128p. 1993. 8.95 (*1-55859-638-0*) Abbeville Pr.

Wish in One Hand Spit in the Other: A Collection of Plays by Suzan Zeder. Suzan L. Zeder. (Illus.). 510p. 1990. 30.00 (*0-87602-029-5*) Anchorage.

***Wish in the Bottle.** Morna MacLeod. (J). 1997. mass mkt. 3.99 (*0-590-62970-0*) Scholastic Inc.

Wish List. Saxon Bennett. 224p. 1996. pap. 10.95 (*1-56280-125-2*) Naiad Pr.

***Wish List.** Barbara Ann Kipfer. LC 97-15092. 1997. pap. 6.95 (*0-7611-0756-8*) Workman Pub.

Wish List. Fern Michaels. 352p. 1996. mass mkt. 6.99 (*0-8217-5228-6*, Zebra Kensgtn) Kensgtn Pub Corp.

***Wish List.** Fern Michaels. (Five Star Romances Ser.). 1996. lib. bdg. 23.95 (*0-7862-0851-1*, Five Star) Mac Lib Ref.

Wish List. Jeane Renick. 384p. (YA). 1996. mass mkt. 3.99 (*0-06-108281-3*, Harp PBks) HarpC.

Wish List. large type ed. Fern Michaels. LC 96-15056. (Large Print Bks.). 1996. 25.95 (*1-56895-336-4*) Wheeler Pub.

Wish Magic. Elizabeth Koehler-Pentacoff. (Illus.). 96p. (Orig.). (J). (gr. 1-4). 1996. pap. 3.95 (*0-8167-3875-0*, Little Rainbow) Troll Communs.

Wish Me Luck. James Heneghan. LC 96-12303. (J). 1997. write for info. (*0-374-38453-3*) FS&G.

Wish of Distinction: Colonial Gentility & Femininity. Penny Russell. 244p. 1994. pap. 24.95 (*0-522-84552-5*, Pub. by Melbourne Univ Pr AT) Paul & Co Pubs.

Wish on a Star. Leonard. 1988. pap. 2.95 (*0-8167-1491-6*) Troll Communs.

Wish on a Unicorn. Karen Hesse. LC 90-5320. 128p. (J). (gr. 4-6). 1991. 13.95 (*0-8050-1572-8*, Bks Young Read) H Holt & Co.

Wish on a Unicorn. Karen Hesse. LC 92-26792. 112p. (J). (gr. 3-7). 1993. pap. 3.99 (*0-14-034935-9*) Puffin Bks.

Wish on the Moon. Kari Sutherland. (Special Edition Ser.: No. 741). 1992. mass mkt. 3.39 (*0-373-09741-7*, 5-09741-5) Harlequin Bks.

Wish Peddler. Tom McCoy. 22p. 1983. pap. 3.00 (*0-87129-678-0*, W54) Dramatic Pub.

***Wish Pictures.** Stacy Shoeman. 235p. (Orig.). 1997. mass mkt. 4.99 (*1-55197-874-1*, Pub. by Comnwlth Pub CN) Partners Pubs Grp.

Wish Pillow. Harriet Ziefert. (Fundamentals Ser.). (Illus.). 28p. (J). (ps). 1997. 14.95 (*0-7894-0590-3*) DK Pub Inc.

***Wish Ring.** Suzanne Loebl. (Illus.). 32p. (J). (ps-3). 1997. 13.95 (*1-887734-14-7*) Star Brght Bks.

Wish to Be. C. Lewis. 1994. pap. 11.95 (*1-85230-534-7*) Element MA.

***Wish upon a Star.** Patrick W. Walters. LC 96-61784. 394p. 1997. pap. 15.95 (*1-55523-822-X*) Winston-Derek.

Wish upon a Star: A Story for Children with a Parent Who Is Mentally Ill. Pamela L. Laskin & Addie A. Moskowitz. LC 91-211. (Illus.). 32p. (J). (ps-2). 1991. 16.95 (*0-945354-30-4*) Magination Pr.

Wish upon a Star: A Tale of Bedtime Magic. Armand Eisen. (Illus.). 32p. (J). 1993. 12.95 (*0-8362-4937-2*) Andrews & McMeel.

Wish upon a Starr. Nancy Martin. 1994. mass mkt. 2.99 (*0-373-05858-6*) Silhouette.

Wish Upon a VCR. Parachute Press, Inc. Staff. (Full House Stephanie Ser.: No. 16). (J). (gr. 3-6). 1996. pap. 3.99 (*0-671-53549-8*) S&S Trade.

Wish You Christmas. Mary Gross. (Illus.). 24p. 1977. 10.00 (*0-912760-58-3*) Valkyrie Pub Hse.

Wish You Were Here. Rita Mae Brown. 304p. 1991. mass mkt. 5.99 (*0-553-28753-2*) Bantam.

Wish You Were Here. Lesley Grant-Adamson. 176p. 1996. 19.95 (*0-312-14075-4*) St Martin.

***Wish You Were Here.** Richard Ketchum. (Illus.). 44p. (Orig.). 1997. pap. 8.95 (*0-9658484-0-X*) Kirby Hollow.

***Wish You Were Here.** Kathleen Krull. 1997. mass mkt. 19.95 (*0-385-44696-9*) Doubleday.

Wish You Were Here. Naomi McMillan. LC 90-85435. (Minnie 'n Me Ser.). (Illus.). 32p. (J). (gr. k-3). 1991. 5.95 (*1-56282-036-2*) Disney Pr.

Wish You Were Here. Martina Selway. LC 94-31995. (Illus.). 32p. (J). (ps-3). 1995. 12.95 (*1-57102-032-2*, Ideals Child) Hambleton-Hill.

Wish You Were Here. Barbara Shoup. LC 94-9368. 288p. (YA). 1994. lib. bdg. 16.89 (*0-7868-2023-3*) Hyprn Child.

Wish You Were Here. Barbara Shoup. LC 94-9368. 288p. (YA). (gr. 7 up). 1994. 16.95 (*0-7868-0028-3*) Hyprn Child.

Wish You Were Here. Hilmer Wolitzer. 180p. (J). (gr. 5 up). 1986. pap. 3.45 (*0-374-48412-0*, Sunburst Bks) FS&G.

Wish You Were Here. Martina Selway. LC 94-31995. (Illus.). 32p. (J). (ps-3). 1996. reprint ed. pap. 4.95 (*1-57102-040-3*, Ideals Child) Hambleton-Hill.

Wish You Were Here: A Travel Souvenir for Someone Special. Teresa Cookson. LC 93-81150. 24p. 1994. pap. 8.95 (*1-56352-142-3*) Longstreet Pr Inc.

***Wish You Were Here: Arkansas Postcard Past, 1900-1925.** Steven G. Hanley & Ray Hanley. LC 96-42245. 1997. pap. 48.00 (*1-55728-451-2*) U of Ark Pr.

***Wish You Were Here: Emily's Guide to the 50 States.** Kathleen Krull. LC 93-18511. (J). 1997. 19.95 (*0-385-31146-X*) Doubleday.

Wish You Were Here: France. Robin O'Neill. 224p. (YA). 1996. mass mkt. 4.50 (*0-425-14944-7*) Berkley Pub.

Wish You Were Here: Ireland. Robin O'Neill. 224p. (YA). 1996. mass mkt. 4.50 (*0-425-15416-5*) Berkley Pub.

Wish You Were Here! Letters from Bible People. Pat Wynnejones. (Illus.). 24p. (J). 1994. boxed 11.99 (*0-7847-0165-2*, 03606) Standard Pub.

Wish You Were Here: New Orleans. Robin O'Neill. (YA). 1996. mass mkt. 4.50 (*0-425-14984-6*) Berkley Pub.

***Wish You Were Here! Postcard Views of the Minneapolis Lakes District.** William Lundborg. (Illus.). 134p. 1996. spiral bd. 19.95 (*0-9655500-0-1*) West Forty-Fourth.

Wishbone. Marcia Golub. 335p. 1995. 20.00 (*1-880909-26-X*) Baskerville.

Wishbone Galaxy. Kim Roberts. LC 94-4232. 1994. 10.00 (*0-931846-45-5*) Wash Writers Pub.

***Wishbones.** Tom Perrotta. LC 96-27404. 256p. 1997. 21.95 (*0-399-14267-3*, Putnam) Putnam Pub Group.

Wishbones: A Folk Tale from China. Barbara K. Wilson. LC 92-26993. (Illus.). 32p. (J). (ps-2). 1993. lib. bdg. 14.95 (*0-02-793125-0*, Bradbury S&S) S&S Childrens.

***Wishbook Wife.** large type ed. Jerome Gardner. (Linford Western Library). 272p. 1996. pap. 15.99 (*0-7089-7956-4*, Linford) Ulverscroft.

Wishbringer. Craig S. Gardner. (INFOCOM Ser.: No. 2). 256p. 1988. mass mkt. 3.95 (*0-380-75385-5*) Avon.

Wishcraft: How to Get What You Really Want. Barbara Sher & Annie Gottlieb. 404p. 1986. pap. 12.00 (*0-345-34089-2*, Ballantine Trade) Ballantine.

Wishes. Jude Deveraux. 1991. pap. 6.99 (*0-671-74385-6*, Pocket Books) PB.

***Wishes.** Rita C. Estrada. 1997. mass mkt. 3.50 (*0-373-25734-1*, 1-25734-1) Harlequin Bks.

Wishes. Lisa Jackson. 480p. (Orig.). 1995. mass mkt. 5.99 (*0-8217-5160-3*) NAL-Dutton.

Wishes. Kathleen Kane. 320p. (Orig.). 1995. mass mkt. 5.50 (*0-515-11677-7*) Jove Pubns.

Wishes: A Personal Journal of Hopes & Dreams. Running Press Staff. 1996. pap. text ed. 5.95 (*1-56138-701-0*) Running Pr.

Wishes Level 4: HBJ Reading 1987. Early. (J). 1987. student ed., pap. 26.50 (*0-15-330504-5*) HB Schl Dept.

***Wishes & Dreams.** Tulloch & Richard Wyld. (Bananas in Pajamas Storybook). (J). 1996. pap. 5.99 (*0-679-88597-8*, Bullseye Bks) Random Bks Yng Read.

Wishes & Fishes in Bluebird. Deanna Hansen-Doying. 208p. (Orig.). (YA). (gr. 7-12). 1995. pap. 10.95 (*0-9648099-0-7*) Blue Bird Pr MT.

Wishes at the Bottom of the Well. Alex Roka. LC 90-84625. 216p. 1991. 24.00 (*0-9627936-0-4*) Bk Elan.

Wishes Come True. Patti Berg. 384p. (Orig.). 1996. mass mkt. 5.99 (*0-380-78338-X*) Avon.

Wishes Come True. Jim Valley & Donalee Knowlton. (Illus.). (Orig.). (J). 1995. teacher ed., pap. text ed. write for info. (*0-89724-961-5*, BMR06001) Warner Brothers.

Wishes Come True: Preview Kit. Jim Valley & Donalee Knowlton. (Illus.). (Orig.). (J). 1995. pap. text ed. write for info. (*0-89724-962-3*, BMR06001P) Warner Brothers.

Wishes in the Wind. Andrea Kane. 1996. mass mkt. 5.99 (*0-671-53483-1*) PB.

Wishes, Lies, & Dreams: Teaching Children to Write Poetry. Kenneth Koch et al. LC 74-111920. (Illus.). 1980. reprint ed. pap. 7.50 (*0-06-080530-7*, P 530, PL) HarpC.

Wishes That Could Last. Michael Blumenthal. pap. write for info. (*0-14-009449-0*, Penguin Bks) Viking Penguin.

***Wishes, Whispers, Women.** Russell A. Louden. (Illus.). 108p. (Orig.). 1997. pap. 15.95 (*0-9654569-2-7*) Thunder Rain.

Wishfork Wedding. Margaret H. Rector. LC 95-10803. 16p. 1995. pap. 5.00 (*0-88734-327-9*) Players Pr.

Wishful Lying. Rose Blue. LC 79-21806. (Illus.). 32p. (J). (ps-3). 1980. 16.95 (*0-87705-473-8*) Human Sci Pr.

Wishful Thinking. Barbara Helwig & Susan Stewart. (Little Books for Kids). (Illus.). 44p. (J). (gr. 2-5). 1991. spiral bd. 4.95 (*1-881285-02-2*) Arbus Pub.

***Wishful Thinking.** Marsh. Date not set. pap. text ed. write for info. (*0-582-22453-5*, Pub. by Longman UK) Longman.

Wishful Thinking. rev. ed. Barbara Helwig & Susan Stewart. (Little Books for Kids). (Illus.). 90p. (J). (gr. 2-6). 1992. spiral bd. 4.95 (*1-881285-06-5*) Arbus Pub.

Wishful Thinking: A Seeker's ABC. rev. ed. Frederick Buechner. LC 92-54776. 1993. pap. 12.00 (*0-06-061139-1*) Harper SF.

Wishing. Ruth Tiller. (Illus.). 32p. (J). (ps-3). 1996. 14.95 (*1-56145-118-5*) Peachtree Pubs.

Wishing: Shooting Stars, Four-Leaf Clovers, & Other Wonders to Wish Upon. Gloria T. Delamar. (Miniature Editions Ser.). (Illus.). 128p. 1996. 4.95 (*1-56138-717-7*, Running Pr Mini Edtns) Running Pr.

Wishing Chair. Rick Dupre. LC 92-38880. (Illus.). 32p. (J). (ps-3). 1993. lib. bdg. 14.96 (*0-87614-774-0*, Carolrhoda) Lerner Group.

Wishing Fish: A Totline Teaching Tale. Jean Warren. Ed. by Kathleen Cubley. LC 93-12523. (Nature Ser.). (Illus.). 32p. (Orig.). (J). (ps-2). 1994. pap. 12.95 (*0-911019-73-1*, WPH 1904); pap. 5.95 (*0-911019-74-X*, WPH 1903) Warren Pub Hse.

Wishing for the Worst. Linda Portnay. 40p. 1993. pap. 10.00 (*0-942292-12-X*) Warthog Pr.

***Wishing on a Star.** Raynetta Manees. 256p. 1997. mass mkt. 4.99 (*0-7860-0423-1*, Pinncle Kensgtn) Kensgtn Pub Corp.

Wishing on Daruma. Julie Zimmerman & Kimiaki Tokumasu. LC 91-76745. (Illus.). 112p. (Orig.). (J). (gr. 5 up). 1992. pap. 9.95 (*1-879418-05-3*) Biddle Pub.

Wishing on the Moon: The Life & Times of Billie Holiday. Donald Clarke. (Illus.). 480p. 1995. pap. 13.95 (*0-14-024754-8*, Penguin Bks) Viking Penguin.

Wishing Season. Esther Friesner. 352p. 1996. mass mkt. 5.99 (*0-671-87702-X*) Baen Bks.

***Wishing Star.** Diane R. Houghton. LC 97-71679. (Illus.). 24p. (J). (gr. k-2). 1997. 14.95 (*1-890453-01-3*) Little Frnd.

Wishing Star. Marian Wells. LC 85-21469. (Starlight Trilogy Ser.: No. 1). 288p. 1985. pap. 8.99 (*0-87123-817-9*) Bethany Hse.

Wishing Stone. Christopher Pike. (Spooksville Ser.: No. 9). (J). (gr. 4-6). 1996. pap. 3.99 (*0-671-55068-3*, Minstrel Bks) PB.

Wishing Tree. Christopher Isherwood. Ed. by Robert Adjemian. 229p. 1989. pap. 9.95 (*0-06-250402-9*) Vedanta Pr.

Wishing Tree: A Guide to Memorial Trees, Statues, Fountains, Etc. in the Royal Botanical Gardens, Domain & Centennial Park, Sydney. Edwin Wilson. 160p. 1993. 24.95 (*0-86417-437-3*, Pub. by Kangaroo Pr AT) Seven Hills Bk.

Wishing Upon a Star. Lissa H. Johnson. (China Tate Ser.: No. 4). 1995. pap. 5.99 (*1-56179-345-0*) Focus Family.

Wishing Well. Cocoj. (J). 1998. pap. 13.00 (*0-671-88174-4*, Litl Simon S&S) S&S Childrens.

***Wishing Well.** Robbins. Date not set. write for info. (*0-312-85294-0*) St Martin.

Wishing Well: A Basic Guide to Self-Publishing. Frederick W. Gould, Sr. (Illus.). 256p. (Orig.). 1990. pap. 15.95 (*0-9628350-1-3*) Vesper Pub.

***Wishing Well: Empowering Your Hopes & Dreams.** Patricia Telesco. LC 97-25971. 240p. (Orig.). 1997. pap. 14.95 (*0-89594-870-2*) Crossing Pr.

Wishing You Both Every Happiness. Ed. by Helen Exley. (So-Much-More-Than-a-Card Ser.). (Illus.). 28p. (Orig.). 1995. pap. 2.99 (*1-85015-658-1*) Exley Giftbooks.

Wishing You Happiness. Pam Brown. Ed. by Helen Exley. (To Give & to Keep Ser.). (Illus.). 28p. 1992. 6.99 (*1-85015-323-X*) Exley Giftbooks.

Wishram Texts: Together with Wasco Tales & Myths. Ed. by Edward Sapir & Jeremiah Curtin. LC 73-3536. (American Ethnological Society Publications: No. 2). reprint ed. 49.50 (*0-404-58152-8*) AMS Pr.

Wishsong of Shannara. Terry Brooks. (Shannara Ser.: Bk. 3). 512p. 1988. mass mkt. 6.99 (*0-345-35636-5*, Del Rey) Ballantine.

Wishsong of Shannara. Terry Brooks. (Shannara Ser.: Bk. 3). 1996. mass mkt. 5.99 (*0-345-90959-3*, Del Rey) Ballantine.

***Wishsong of Shannara.** Terry Brooks. (Shannara Ser.). 1997. mass mkt. 6.99 (*0-345-91129-6*, Del Rey) Ballantine.

***Wising up the Marks: The Novels of William S. Burroughs.** Timothy S. Murphy. LC 96-53094. 1998. write for info. (*0-520-20950-8*); pap. write for info. (*0-520-20951-6*) U CA Pr.

Wisp of Smoke. large type ed. Roy H. Lewis. 326p. 1992. 25.99 (*0-7505-0355-6*) Ulverscroft.

Wisps of Violence: Producing Public & Private Politics in the Turn-of-the-Century British Novel. Eileen Sypher. 160p. (C). (gr. 13). 1993. 60.00 (*0-86091-436-4*, B2516, Pub. by Vrso UK) Norton.

Wissen Und Vernunft: Die Logik gesellschaftlicher Prozesse. Thomas Sowell. Tr. by S. Hofheinz from ENG. (International Carl Menger Library). 544p. (GER.). (C). 1991. 69.50 (*3-88405-055-9*) Philosophia Pr.

***Wissen vom Menschen & Erzaehlen vom Einzelfall: Untersuchungen zum Anthropologischen Roman der Spaetaufklaerung.** Jutta Heinz. (Quellen & Forschungen zur Literatur- & Kulturgeschichte Ser.: Vol. 6(240)). xvi, 396p. (GER.). (C). 1996. lib. bdg. 146.70 (*3-11-015145-6*) De Gruyter.

Wissenschaft Aus Kunst: Die Entstehung der Modernen Deutschen Geschichtsschreibung 1760-1860. Daniel Fulda. (European Cultures Ser.: Vol. 7). x, 547p. (GER.). (C). 1996. text ed. 146.70 (*3-11-015014-X*) De Gruyter.

Wissenschaft der Bibel, Das Buch Josua und Das Buch der Richter see Joshua, Judges

Wissenschaft und Geschichte in der Phanomelogie Edmund Husserls. A. Pazanin. (Phaenomenologica Ser.: No. 46). 202p. 1972. lib. bdg. 78.00 (*90-247-1194-0*, Pub. by M Nijhoff NE) Kluwer Ac.

Wissenschaft und Methode: Interpreationen Zur aristotelischen Theorie der Naturwissenschaft. Wolfgang Kullmann. (GER.). (C). 1974. 180.80 (*3-11-004481-1*) De Gruyter.

Wissenschaftliche Bibliothekswesen im Nationalsozialismus: Unter Besonderer Berucksichtigung der Universitatsbibliotheken. Hans-Gerd Happel. (Beitrage zur Bibliothekstheorie und Bibliotheksgeschichte Ser.: Vol. 1). 190p. 1989. lib. bdg. write for info. (*3-598-22170-3*) K G Saur.

***Wissenschaftliche Standpunkt der Theologie Isaak August Dorners.** Thomas Koppehl. (Theologische Bibliothek Toepelmann Ser.: Vol. 78). viii, 351p. (GER.). (C). 1997. lib. bdg. 170.00 (*3-11-015203-7*) De Gruyter.

Wissenschaftliche Syntax Im Lateinischen Unterricht. Wilhelm Kroll. Ed. by Heinz Happ. viii, 103p. 1969. write for info. (*3-296-14100-6*) G Olms Pubs.

***Wissenschaftliche Werk Band 7: Aufklarung III. Deutschland und Spanien.** Werner Krauss. Ed. by Martin Fontius. 810p. (GER.). (C). 1996. lib. bdg. 115.60 (*3-11-014547-2*) De Gruyter.

Wissenschaftlichen Vereine und Gesellschaften Deutschlands Im 19 Jahrhundert, 3 vols., Set. Johannes Muller. 1965. reprint ed. write for info. (*0-318-71848-0*) G Olms Pubs.

Wissenschaftliches Handeln: Aspekte und Bestimmungsgrunde der Forschung. Ralf Twenhofel. xi, 303p. (GER.). (C). 1991. lib. bdg. 113.85 (*3-11-012416-5*) De Gruyter.

Wissenschaftslehre see Bernard Bolzano: Theory of Science

Wissenschaftstheoretisches Lexikon. Edmund Braun. (GER.). 1977. 125.00 (*0-8288-5557-9*, M7688) Fr & Eur.

Wissenwertes uber Warrentermingeschafte. Tr. by Jorg Gruhler. 36p. (GER.). pap. 3.00 (*0-915513-71-4*) Ctr Futures Ed.

W

An Asterisk (*) at the beginning of an entry indicates that the title is appearing in BIP for the first time.

Wister Trace: Classic Novels of the American Frontier. Loren D. Estleman. LC 85-24159. (Frontier Library). 144p. 1987. 14.95 (0-915463-32-6) Jameson Bks.

***Wisteria House.** large type ed. Pamela Hulton. (Large Print Ser.). 432p. 1997. 27.50 (0-7089-3702-0) Ulverscroft.

Wisterias: A Comprehensive Guide. Peter Valder. (Illus.). 160p. 1995. 32.95 (0-88192-318-4) Timber.

Wistful Embers. Nancy J. Massey. LC 93-60414. 31p. 1994. pap. 5.95 (1-55523-630-8) Winston-Derek.

Wistfulness & Other Foibles: Poems. Barbara Hantman. LC 95-13081. 60p. 1996. pap. 12.95 (0-7734-2725-2, Mellen Poetry Pr) E Mellen.

Wit: The Best Things Ever Said by Mark Twain, Oscar Wilde, Disraeli, Voltaire, Dorothy Parker, Winston Churchill, Talleyrand, P. G. Wodehouse, George Bernard Shaw... Illus. by Le-Tan Pierre. LC 91-55510. 64p. 1991. 14.00 (0-06-018223-7, E Burlingame Bks) HarpC.

Wit & Humor from Old Cathay. Tr. by Jon Kowallis. 210p. 1995. lib. bdg. 27.00 (0-8095-4521-7) Borgo Pr.

Wit & Humor of Bench & Bar. Marshall Brown. xv, 578p. 1986. reprint ed. lib. bdg. 45.00 (0-8377-1938-0) Rothman.

Wit & Humor of Norman Rockwell. Illus. by Norman Rockwell. 40p. 1993. 6.95 (0-8362-4708-6) Andrews & McMeel.

Wit & Humor of Oscar Wilde. Oscar Wilde. Ed. by Alvin Redman. 258p. 1959. pap. 4.95 (0-486-20602-5) Dover.

***Wit & Humor of Oscar Wilde.** Oscar Wilde. lib. bdg. 22.95 (0-8488-1882-2) Amereon Ltd.

Wit & Humour of Colonial Days. Carl Holliday. 320p. 1975. reprint ed. 26.95 (0-87928-058-1) Corner Hse.

Wit & Its Relation to the Unconscious. Sigmund Freud. Tr. by A. A. Brill from GER. LC 93-9098. 400p. 1993. reprint ed. pap. 9.95 (0-486-27742-9) Dover.

Wit & the Writing of History: The Rhetoric of Historiography in Imperial Rome. Paul Plass. LC 88-40193. 204p. (Orig.). (C). 1988. pap. text ed. 17.50 (0-299-11804-5) U of Wis Pr.

Wit & Whimsy. S. David Leibowitt. (Illus.). 87p. (Orig.). 1989. pap. 5.95 (0-9625362-0-2) S D Leibowitt.

***Wit & Whimsy of Mary Engelbreit.** Mary Engelbreit. (Illus.). 80p. 1997. 12.95 (0-8362-2775-1) Andrews & McMeel.

***Wit & Wisdom: Mercury in Your Chart.** Maritha Pottenger. 32p. (Orig.). 1996. pap. 5.95 (0-935127-57-7) ACS Pubns.

Wit & Wisdom for Women: How to Stay on Track in These Fast Times. Barbara Jenkins. 176p. 1996. 12.99 (0-7852-7416-2) Nelson.

Wit & Wisdom from the Peanut Butter Gang: A Collection of Wise Words from Young Hearts. H. Jackson Brown. LC 94-7991. 150p. 1994. 14.95 (1-55853-276-5) Rutledge Hill Pr.

Wit & Wisdom from West Africa. Ed. by Richard F. Burton. LC 69-18975. 455p. 1969. reprint ed. text ed. 35.00 (0-8371-1378-4, BUW&, Greenwood Pr) Greenwood.

Wit & Wisdom from West Africa: A Book of Proverbial Philosophy, Idioms, Enigmas, & Laconisms. Richard F. Burton. LC 77-79952. 1969. reprint ed. 35.00 (0-8196-0243-4) Biblo.

Wit & Wisdom in Dynamic Psychotherapy. Ed. by Gregory P. Bauer. LC 90-40191. 320p. 1990. 40.00 (0-87668-768-0) Aronson.

Wit & Wisdom in Morocco: A Study of Native Proverbs. Edward A. Westermarck. LC 76-44800. reprint ed. 64.50 (0-404-15980-X) AMS Pr.

Wit & Wisdom of Abraham Lincoln. Compiled by Bill Adler. 1993. pap. 7.95 (0-8065-1456-6, Citadel Pr) Carol Pub Group.

Wit & Wisdom of Abraham Lincoln. Ed. by Alex Ayres. 240p. (Orig.). 1992. pap. 10.95 (0-452-01089-6, Mer) NAL-Dutton.

Wit & Wisdom of Abraham Lincoln. James C. Humes. LC 95-38431. 250p. 1996. 20.00 (0-06-017244-4, HarpT) HarpC.

Wit & Wisdom of American Presidents. 160p. text ed. write for info. (1-880461-30-7) Celebrat Excell.

Wit & Wisdom of Benjamin Franklin. James C. Humes. LC 95-3174. 208p. 1995. 20.00 (0-06-017172-3, HarpT) HarpC.

Wit & Wisdom of Benjamin Franklin: A Treasury of More Than 900 Quotations & Anecdotes. James C. Humes. 256p. 1996. pap. 13.00 (0-06-092697-X) HarpC.

***Wit & Wisdom of Bill Clinton: Lessons Learned in His First 50 Years.** John S. Keating. LC 96-69868. 128p. (Orig.). 1996. pap. 6.95 (1-57197-044-4) Pentland Pr.

***Wit & Wisdom of Bob Dole: His Greatest Ideas & Vision for 21st Century America.** John S. Keating. LC 96-69869. 128p. (Orig.). 1996. pap. 6.95 (1-57197-045-2) Pentland Pr.

Wit & Wisdom of Dean Inge. William R. Inge. Ed. by James Marchant. LC 68-16941. (Essay Index Reprint Ser.). 1977. 17.95 (0-8369-0558-X) Ayer.

Wit & Wisdom of Dick Versace. Dick Versace. Ed. by Jack Mertes. (Illus.). x, 86p. (Orig.). 1981. pap. 4.00 (0-939846-00-4) St George IA.

Wit & Wisdom of Eleanor Roosevelt. Alex Ayres. 256p. 1996. pap. 10.95 (0-452-01138-8, Mer) NAL-Dutton.

Wit & Wisdom of Famous American Women. Ed. by Evelyn L. Beilenson. (Illus.). 64p. 1986. 7.99 (0-88088-157-7, 881577) Peter Pauper.

Wit & Wisdom of Gene Roddenberry. M. J. Barrett. 96p. 1995. mass mkt. 6.99 (0-06-105316-3) HarpC.

Wit & Wisdom of George Steinbrenner. Frank Coffey. 1993. pap. 3.99 (0-451-17837-8, Sig) NAL-Dutton.

Wit & Wisdom of Harry Truman: A Treasury of Quotations, Anecdotes & Observations. Ed. by Ralph Keyes. LC 95-21467. 256p. 1995. 20.00 (0-06-017207-X, HarpT) HarpC.

Wit & Wisdom of Harry Truman: A Treasury of Quotations, Anecdotes & Observations. Ralph Keyes. 224p. 1996. pap. text ed. 12.00 (0-06-092755-0) HarpC.

Wit & Wisdom of Herbert Hoover: A Compilation of His Quotations. Ruth Dennis. 1994. 12.95 (0-533-11039-4) Vantage.

Wit & Wisdom of Idi Amin. Christopher L. Moody. LC 77-88611. (Illus.). 1977. pap. 2.75 (0-930830-01-6) Great Basin.

Wit & Wisdom of Jimmy Houston: Not Necessarily in That Order, & Sometimes Difficult to Tell Apart. Jimmy Houston. Ed. & Illus. by Ken Conlee. 1984. 14.95 (0-945270-23-2) J Houston.

Wit & Wisdom of John Dewey. John Dewey. Ed. by A. H. Johnson. LC 69-13883. 111p. 1969. reprint ed. text ed. 45.00 (0-8371-0380-0, DEWW, Greenwood Pr) Greenwood.

Wit & Wisdom of John F. Kennedy. Alex Ayres. 256p. 1996. pap. 11.95 (0-452-01139-6, Mer) NAL-Dutton.

Wit & Wisdom of John Smith, USA. 1995. write for info. (0-9623556-1-5) Columbia Rvr Bk Co.

Wit & Wisdom of Lou Albano. Lou Albano & Edward R. Ricciuti. (Illus.). 96p. (Orig.). 1986. pap. 5.95 (0-9616263-0-5) WWF Bks.

Wit & Wisdom of Margaret Fuller Ossoli, Vol. I. Ed. by Laurie James. 1988. pap. 8.50 (0-944382-00-2) Golden Heritage Pr.

Wit & Wisdom of Mark Twain. Ed. by Alex Ayres. 288p. 1989. pap. 7.95 (0-452-00982-0, Mer); pap. 11.95 (0-452-01058-6, Mer) NAL-Dutton.

Wit & Wisdom of Mark Twain. Mark Twain. Ed. by Running Press Staff. LC 90-53463. (Miniature Editions Ser.). 96p. 1991. 4.95 (0-89471-984-X) Running Pr.

Wit & Wisdom of Nelson Mandela. Erasmus Mhalnga. 56p. 1996. pap. 8.00 (0-8059-3846-X) Dorrance.

Wit & Wisdom of Oscar Wilde: A Treasury Of Quotations, Anecdotes & Observations. Ralph Keyes. 192p. 1996. 20.00 (0-06-017367-X) HarpC.

Wit & Wisdom of Politics. rev. ed. Chuck Henning. LC 96-33061. (Illus.). 280p. 1996. pap. 14.95 (1-55591-333-4) Fulcrum Pub.

***Wit & Wisdom of Robert E. Lee.** Ed. by Devereaux D. Cannon, Jr. LC 97-23683. (Illus.). 96p. pap. 5.95 (1-56554-275-4) Pelican.

Wit & Wisdom of the Christian Fathers of Egypt: The Syrian Version of the Apophthegmata Patrum. Tr. by Ernest A. Budge. LC 80-2354. reprint ed. 53.50 (0-404-18900-8) AMS Pr.

***Wit & Wisdom of the Founding Fathers.** Ed. by Paul Zall. 192p. 1998. pap. 12.00 (0-88001-553-5) Ecco Pr.

Wit & Wisdom of the Founding Fathers: George Washington/John Adams/Thomas Jefferson/Benjamin Franklin. Ed. by Paul M. Zall. LC 96-16302. 128p. 1996. 18.00 (0-88001-495-4) Ecco Pr.

Wit & Wisdom of the Great Outdoors. Jerry Wilber. LC 92-61321. (Appointment with Nature Ser.). (Illus.). 408p. (Orig.). 1993. pap. 19.95 (0-938586-72-6) Pfeifer-Hamilton.

Wit & Wisdom of the Immortals. Manly P. Hall. 6.95 (0-89314-826-1) Philos Res.

Wit & Wisdom of "The Nanny" Fran's Guide to Love, Life, & Shopping. Compiled by Nan E. Fine. (Illus.). 144p. 1995. pap. 6.00 (0-380-78320-7) Avon.

***Wit & Wisdom of the Reverend Sydney Smith.** Sydney Smith. (Illus.). 458p. 1972. 26.95 (0-8369-7283-X) Ayer.

Wit & Wisdom of the Talmud. Ed. by Madison C. Peters. 169p. 1997. pap. 15.00 (0-89540-290-4, SB-290) Sun Pub.

Wit & Wisdom of the Twentieth Century: A Dictionary of Quotations. Ed. by Frank S. Pepper. LC 87-47755. 420p. 1987. 19.95 (0-87226-165-4) P Bedrick Bks.

***Wit & Wisdom of the 2000 Year Old Man in the Year 2000.** Mel Brooks & Carl Reine. 160p. 1997. 20.00 (0-06-017480-3) HarpC.

Wit & Wisdom of Wally Hickel. 2nd ed. Malcolm B. Roberts. LC 94-93929. (Illus.). 240p. 1995. reprint ed. text ed. 24.95 (0-9644316-1-0); reprint ed. pap. text ed. 14.95 (0-9644316-0-2) Searchers Pr.

Wit & Wisdom of Will Rogers. Ed. by Alex Ayres. LC 93-424. 256p. 1993. pap. 11.95 (0-452-01115-9, Mer) NAL-Dutton.

Wit & Wisdom of William Bacon Evans. Anna C. Brinton. LC 66-24443. (C). 1966. pap. 3.00 (0-87574-146-0) Pendle Hill.

Wit & Wisdom of William Hughes Mulligan. Ed. by William H. Mulligan. 290p. 1996. 25.00 (0-8232-1718-3) Fordham.

Wit & Wisdom of Winston Churchill. James Humes. LC 93-5360. 256p. 1995. pap. 10.00 (0-06-092577-9, HarpT) HarpC.

Wit & Wisdom of Women: Simple Truths & Wicked Barbs. LC 93-83456. (Illus.). 192p. 1993. 12.95 (1-56138-302-3) Running Pr.

Wit & Wisdom of Yogi Berra. 2nd rev. ed. Phil Pepe. 150p. 1988. 16.95 (0-88736-318-0) Mecklermedia.

Wit, Humor & Shakespeare. John Weiss. 1974. 250.00 (0-8490-1308-9) Gordon Pr.

***Wit 'n' Wisdom from the Lilley Pad.** LC 96-95214. (Illus.). 156p. (Orig.). 1997. pap. 12.00 (0-9629488-1-0) Lilley Pub.

Wit of a Woman. LC 77-133770. (Tudor Facsimile Texts. Old English Plays Ser.: No. 103). reprint ed. 49.50 (0-404-53403-1) AMS Pr.

Wit of Oscar Wilde. Oscar Wilde. 1991. pap. 9.95 (0-86278-248-1) Dufour.

Wit of Seventeenth-Century Poetry. Ed. by Claude J. Summers & Ted-Larry Pebworth. 240p. 1995. 39.95 (0-8262-0985-8) U of Mo Pr.

Wit Twisters. Arthur Swan. 16.95 (0-8488-0779-0) Amereon Ltd.

Wit, Wisdom & Eloquence of Robert G. Ingersoll. Ed. by Garry De Young. reprint ed. 25.00 (0-936128-34-8) De Young Pr.

Wit, Wisdom & Foibles of the Great. Charles A. Shriner. 1973. 35.00 (0-8490-1309-7) Gordon Pr.

Wit, Wisdom, Tall Tales & Philosophy of Herbert Doane: A 94-Year-Old Ozark Native. Herbert Doane. 144p. 1994. pap. write for info. (1-884597-00-9) Tinswac Pubng.

Wit Without Money: A Comedy. Francis Beaumont & John Fletcher. LC 73-25968. (English Experience Ser.: No. 264). 66p. 1970. reprint ed. 20.00 (90-221-0264-5) Walter J Johnson.

Witch. Donald E. McQuinn. 1995. mass mkt. 6.99 (0-345-39737-1, Del Rey) Ballantine.

Witch. Barbara Michaels. 1989. mass mkt. 6.99 (0-425-11831-2, Berkley Trade) Berkley Pub.

Witch. Thomas Middleton. Ed. by Elizabeth Schafer. LC 94-25850. (New Mermaid Ser.). (C). 1994. pap. text ed. 7.95 (0-393-90073-8) Norton.

Witch. Christopher Pike. Ed. by Patricia MacDonald. 240p. (Orig.). (YA). (gr. 8 up). pap. 3.99 (0-671-69055-8, Archway) PB.

Witch. Bebe F. Rice. (Doomsday Mall Ser.: Vol. 4). 128p. (J). (gr. 3-7). 1996. pap. 3.50 (0-553-48184-3, Skylark BDD) BDD Bks Young Read.

Witch. August Strindberg. Tr. by Mary Sandbach from SWE. (Illus.). 140p. (C). 1991. 45.00 (0-932499-65-1) Lapis Pr.

Witch Alone: Thirteen Moons to Master Natural Magic. Marian Green. 192p. 1991. pap. 15.00 (1-85538-112-5, Pub. by Aquarian Pr UK) Thorsons SF.

Witch & Other Stories. Anton P. Chekhov. Tr. by Constance Garnett from RUS. (Tales of Chekhov Ser.: Vol. 6). 200p. 1985. reprint ed. pap. 8.50 (0-88001-053-3) Ecco Pr.

Witch & the Cathedral. C. Dale Brittain. 352p. (Orig.). 1995. mass mkt. 5.99 (0-671-87661-9) Baen Bks.

Witch & the Goddess in the Stories of Isak Dinesen: A Feminist Reading. Sara Stambaugh. LC 88-5393. 150p. 1991. 39.00 (0-8357-1884-0) Univ Rochester Pr.

Witch & the Magic Mountain. Contrib. by Renata Allen & Howard Bodall. 65p. 1991. pap. 5.00 (0-87129-061-8, W70) Dramatic Pub.

Witch & the Roo of Wicky Roo. Jan Loudin. (J). (gr. k-4). 1996. pap. 8.95 (1-888345-02-0) Paper Jam.

Witch & the Sunflower Garden. Paul P. Jesep. LC 92-62305. (Illus.). 20p. (Orig.). (J). (gr. 4-5). 1993. pap. 9.95 (0-9634360-3-1) Seacoast Pubns New Eng.

***Witch & Troll of Royal Forest.** Gretchen S. Moreaux. (Illus.). 20p. (Orig.). (J). (gr. 1-4). 1997. mass mkt. 8.99 (1-55237-140-9, Pub. by Comnwlth Pub CN) Partners Pubs Grp.

***Witch & Wizard Eyewitness Book.** Eyewitness Books Staff. (Eyewitness Bks.). (J). 1997. lib. bdg. 20.99 (0-679-98544-1) Knopf.

Witch & Wombat. Carolyn Cushman. 320p. (Orig.). 1994. mass mkt. 5.50 (0-446-60086-5, Aspect) Warner Bks.

***Witch at Batsford Castle.** Terry H. Henry. Date not set. pap. 7.95 (0-947962-63-8) Dufour.

Witch Baby. Francesca L. Block. LC 90-28916. (Charlotte Zolotow Bk.). 112p. (YA). (gr. 7 up). 1991. lib. bdg. 14.89 (0-06-020548-2) HarpC Child Bks.

Witch Baby. Francesca L. Block. LC 90-28916. (Charlotte Zolotow Bk.: A Trophy Keypoint Bk.). 128p. (YA). (gr. 7 up). 1992. pap. 3.95 (0-06-447065-2, Trophy) HarpC Child Bks.

Witch-Children: From Salem Witch-Hunts to Modern Courtrooms. Hans Sebald. 258p. 1995. 24.95 (0-87975-965-8) Prometheus Bks.

Witch-Craft Delusion of 1692. Thomas Hutchinson. (Notable American Authors Ser.). 1992. reprint ed. lib. bdg. 90.00 (0-7812-3301-1) Rprt Serv.

Witch Doctor. Christopher Stasheff. (Wizard in Rhyme Ser.: Bk. III). 1995. mass mkt. 5.99 (0-345-38851-8, Del Rey Discovery) Ballantine.

Witch Doctor. Lester Sumrall. 64p. (Orig.). 1988. pap. text ed. 1.95 (0-937580-12-0) LeSEA Pub Co.

Witch Doctor: Memoirs of a Partisan. Michael Temchin. (Illus.). 192p. (Orig.). 1983. 10.95 (0-89604-044-5, Holocaust Library) US Holocaust.

Witch Doctor of Wall Street: A Noted Financial Expert Guides You Through Today's Voodoo Economics. Robert H. Parks. 454p. 1996. 25.95 (1-57392-018-5) Prometheus Bks.

Witch Doctors: Making Sense of the Management Gurus. John Micklethwait & Adrian Wooldridge. LC 96-6793. 272p. 1996. 25.00 (0-8129-2833-4, Times Bks) Random.

Witch-Doctor's Apprentice: Hunting for Medicinal Plants in the Amazon. Nicole Maxwell. 1990. pap. 12.95 (0-8065-1174-5, Citadel Pr) Carol Pub Group.

Witch Doctor's Cookbook. Peggy Cochrane. LC 84-52022. (Illus.). 173p. (Orig.). 1984. pap. 7.95 (0-9614031-0-1) Sherman Pr.

Witch Doll. Helen Morgan. 144p. (J). (gr. 3-7). 1994. pap. 3.99 (0-14-037146-X) Puffin Bks.

Witch Family. Eleanor Estes. (Illus.). 186p. (J). (gr. 3-7). 1990. pap. 7.00 (0-15-298572-7, Odyssey) HarBrace.

Witch Fantastic. Ed. by Mike Resnick & Martin H. Greenberg. (Illus.). 352p. (Orig.). 1995. 4.99 (0-88677-640-6) DAW Bks.

Witch-Girl. large type ed. Dilys Gater. 336p. 1996. 25.99 (0-7089-3449-8) Ulverscroft.

Witch, Goblin, & Ghost Are Back. Sue Alexander. LC 83-22157. (Illus.). 62p. (J). (gr. 1-4). 1985. lib. bdg. 9.99 (0-394-96296-6) Pantheon.

Witch, Goblin & Ghost in the Haunted Woods. Sue Alexander. LC 80-20863. (I Am Reading Bks.). (Illus.). 72p. (J). (gr. 1-4). 1981. lib. bdg. 7.99 (0-394-94443-7) Pantheon.

Witch Goes to School. Norman Bridwell. LC 92-12091. (Hello Reader! Ser.). (J). (gr. 1-2). 1992. pap. 3.50 (0-590-45831-0) Scholastic Inc.

Witch Has an Itch. Donna Guthrie. (Illus.). 24p. (J). (ps-1). 1990. pap. 2.50 (0-671-70346-3, Litl Simon S&S) S&S Childrens.

Witch Hazel. Alice Schertle. LC 90-39630. (Illus.). 32p. (J). (gr. k-4). 1991. lib. bdg. 14.89 (0-06-025141-7) HarpC Child Bks.

Witch Hazel: Poems of a Lifetime. George C. Homans. 160p. 1987. 29.95 (0-88738-200-2) Transaction Pubs.

Witch Hazel, Four: The Best of Witch Hazel see Witch Hazel's Whackola Adventures

Witch Hazel's Crazy Adventures. Jonathon J. Thompson, Jr. (Illus.). 80p. (J). (gr. 3-6). 1985. 4.50 (0-933479-05-0) Thompson.

Witch Hazel's Whackey Adventures. Jonathon J. Thompson, Jr. (Illus.). 104p. (J). (gr. 3-6). 1985. 5.50 (0-933479-01-8) Thompson.

Witch Hazel's Whackola Adventures. Jonathon J. Thompson, Jr. Orig. Title: Witch Hazel, Four: The Best of Witch Hazel. (Illus.). 143p. (J). (gr. 4-8). 1986. 6.50 (0-933479-03-4) Thompson.

Witch-Herbalist of the Remote Town. Amos Tutuola. 205p. 1982. pap. 8.95 (0-571-11704-X) Faber & Faber.

Witch Herself. Phyllis R. Naylor. 176p. (J). (gr. k-6). 1988. pap. 3.50 (0-440-40044-9) Dell.

Witch Hill. Marion Zimmer Bradley. 1990. pap. 3.95 (0-8125-0006-7) Tor Bks.

Witch Hill. Marion Zimmer Bradley. 256p. 1992. reprint ed. 20.00 (0-7278-4357-5) Severn Hse.

Witch House. Norma T. Johnson. 144p. (Orig.). (J). 1990. pap. 2.95 (0-380-75789-3, Camelot) Avon.

Witch Hunt. Rosemary Edghill. LC 97-11948. 224p. 1996. 20.95 (0-312-85606-7) Forge NYC.

Witch Hunt! Diana G. Gallagher. (Secret World of Alex Mack Ser.: No. 4). (J). (gr. 3-6). 1995. mass mkt. 3.99 (0-671-53301-0) PB.

Witch Hunt. Levack. (C). 1995. pap. text ed. 28.95 (0-582-02357-2) Addison-Wesley.

Witch Hunt: It Happened in Salem Village. Stephen Krensky. LC 88-42865. (Step into Reading Bks.). (Illus.). 48p. (Orig.). (J). (gr. 2-4). 1989. pap. 3.99 (0-394-81923-3); lib. bdg. 7.99 (0-394-91923-8) Random Bks Yng Read.

Witch-Hunt in Early Modern Europe. Brian P. Levack. 267p. (C). 1987. text ed. 23.75 (0-582-49122-3, 73488); pap. text ed. 24.95 (0-582-49123-1, 73488) Longman.

Witch-Hunt in Early Modern Europe. 2nd ed. Brian P. Levack. 320p. (C). 1995. pap. text ed. 24.50 (0-582-08069-X, 76887) Longman.

Witch Hunt in Wise County: The Persecution of Edith Maxwell. Gary D. Best. LC 94-12351. 192p. 1994. text ed. 49.95 (0-275-94892-7, Praeger Pubs) Greenwood.

Witch-Hunt, or the Triumph of Morality. F. G. Bailey. LC 94-3193. 1994. 39.95 (0-8014-3021-6) Cornell U Pr.

Witch-Hunt: or the Triumph of Morality. F. G. Bailey. (Illus.). 232p. 1996. pap. 14.95 (0-8014-8210-0) Cornell U Pr.

Witch-Hunting in Continental Europe: Regional & Local Studies. Ed. by Brian P. Levack. LC 92-22856. (Witchcraft Magic, Demonology Ser.: Vol. 5). 304p. 1992. text ed. 60.00 (0-8153-1027-7) Garland.

Witch-Hunting in Early Modern Europe: General Studies. Ed. by Brian P. Levack. LC 92-21027. (Articles on Witchcraft, Magic, & Demonology Ser.: Vol. 3). 392p. 1992. text ed. 70.00 (0-8153-1025-0) Garland.

Witch-Hunting in Seventeenth-Century New England: A Documentary History, 1638-1692. David D. Hall. 300p. 1990. text ed. 42.50 (1-55553-084-2); pap. text ed. 15.95 (1-55553-085-0) NE U Pr.

Witch Hunting in Southwestern Germany, 1562-1684: The Social & Intellectual Foundations. H. Erik Midelfort. LC 75-183891. 320p. 1972. 42.50 (0-8047-0805-3) Stanford U Pr.

Witch in Cabin Six. Marilyn Kaye. (Camp Sunnyside Friends Ser.: No. 7). 128p. (J). (gr. 3-4). 1990. pap. 2.95 (0-380-75912-8, Camelot) Avon.

***Witch in Every Woman: Reawakening the Magical Nature of the Feminine to Heal, Protect, Create, & Empower.** Laurie Cabot & Jean Mills. LC 97-3175. 1997. write for info. (0-385-31649-6) Doubleday.

Witch in History: Early Modern & Twentieth-Century Representations. Diane Purkiss. LC 96-11316. 304p. 1996. pap. 17.95 (0-415-08762-7) Routledge.

Witch in History: Early Modern & Twentieth-Century Representations. Diane Purkiss. LC 96-11316. 304p. (C). 1996. text ed. 65.00 (0-415-08761-9) Routledge.

Witch in My Heart: A Play Set in Swaziland in the 1930s. Hilda Kuper. LC 78-518794. 102p. reprint ed. pap. 29.10 (0-8357-6960-7, 2039019) Bks Demand.

Witch in My Heart: Short Stories & Poems. Hilda Kuper. LC 93-45273. 1994. 25.00 (0-942615-18-2) U Wis African Stud.

Witch in the Bushes. Rita A. Higgins. 66p. 9300. reprint ed. pap. 9.95 (1-897648-08-1, Pub. by Salmon Poetry IE) Dufour.

***Witch in the Pumpkin Patch.** Francine Pascal. (Sweet Valley Kids Ser.: No. 73). (J). 1997. pap. 3.50 (0-553-48342-0) BDD Bks Young Read.

Witch Lady. Nancy Carlson. LC 85-3756. (Illus.). 32p. (J). (ps-3). 1985. lib. bdg. 13.13 (0-87614-283-8, Carolrhoda) Lerner Group.

Witch-Light. Melanie Tem & Nancy Holder. 1996. mass mkt. 5.50 (0-440-21718-0) Dell.

W

An Asterisk (*) at the beginning of an entry indicates that the title is appearing in BIP for the first time.

Witch Mama. Judith Caseley. LC 95-35847. (Illus.). 32p. (J). (ps up). 1996. 15.00 (*0-688-14457-8*); lib. bdg. 14.93 (*0-688-14458-6*) Greenwillow.
Witch Miss Seeton. Heron Carvic. 192p. 1988. pap. 4.50 (*0-425-10713-2*) Berkley Pub.
Witch Next Door. Norman Bridwell. (Illus.). 32p. (J). (gr. k-3). 1986. pap. 2.99 (*0-590-40433-4*) Scholastic Inc.
Witch Number. Dorothy Porter. (YA). 1993. pap. 11.95 (*0-7022-2460-X*, Pub. by Univ Queensland Pr AT) Intl Spec Bk.
Witch of Atlas Notebook: Bodleian Ms. Shelley Adds, Vol. V, No. E.6. Contrib. by Carlene A. Adamson. LC 97-15043. (Bodleian Shelley Manuscripts). 512p. 1994. 150.00 (*0-8240-6981-1*) Garland.
Witch of Belsen & Other Stories. L. C. Wheeler. 1981. 15.00 (*0-7223-1389-6*, Pub. by A H S Ltd UK) St Mut.
Witch of Blackbird Pond. Elizabeth G. Speare. 256p. (J). (gr. k-6). 1972. mass mkt. 4.99 (*0-440-49596-2*, YB BDD) BDD Bks Young Read.
Witch of Blackbird Pond. Elizabeth G. Speare. (Illus.). 256p. (YA). (gr. 7 up). 1958. 15.00 (*0-395-07114-3*) HM.
***Witch of Blackbird Pond.** Elizabeth G. Speare. 1997. mass mkt. 2.69 (*0-440-22721-6*) Dell.
Witch of Blackbird Pond. Elizabeth G. Speare. 256p. (YA). (gr. 5 up). 1978. mass mkt. 4.99 (*0-440-99577-9*, LLL BDD) BDD Bks Young Read.
Witch of Blackbird Pond: A Literature Unit. Dona Herweck. (Literature Units Ser.). (Illus.). 48p. (Orig.). 1992. student ed., pap. 7.95 (*1-55734-404-3*) Tchr Create Mat.
Witch of Blackbird Pond: A Study Guide. Joyce Friedland & Rikki Kessler. (Novel-Ties Ser.). 1982. teacher ed., wbk. ed., pap. text ed. 15.95 (*0-88122-012-4*) Lrn Links.
Witch of Blackbird Pond: L-I-T Guide. Charlotte Jaffe & Barbara Roberts. (L-I-T Guides: Literature in Teaching Ser.). 1991. Grades 4-8. teacher ed. 8.95 (*0-910857-98-9*) Educ Impress.
Witch of Blackbird Pond see Newbery Library Award
Witch of Burchard Street: Biography of a Witch. John D. Blacke. Ed. by Richard L. Groffe, Jr. 193p. 1991. 22.95 (*0-9630718-0-7*) New Dawn NY.
***Witch of Bute: A Guardian Angel.** J. Emory McCaw. (Illus.). 152p. (Orig.). 1997. pap. 7.95 (*0-9657052-0-X*) Vinco Pubns.
***Witch of Exmoor.** Margaret Drabble. LC 97-10952. 1997. write for info. (*0-15-100363-7*); write for info. (*0-670-87276-8*) HarBrace.
Witch of Fourth Street: A Study Guide. Joyce Friedland & Rikki Kessler. (Novel-Ties Ser.). 1982. teacher ed., wbk. ed., pap. text ed. 15.95 (*0-88122-013-2*) Lrn Links.
Witch of Fourth Street & Other Stories. Myron Levoy. (J). (gr. 3-6). 1991. 18.00 (*0-8446-6450-2*) Peter Smith.
Witch of Fourth Street & Other Stories. Myron Levoy. LC 74-183174. (Illus.). 128p. (J). (gr. 3-7). 1974. pap. 3.95 (*0-06-440059-X*, Trophy) HarpC Child Bks.
Witch of Goingsnake & Other Stories. Robert J. Conley. LC 88-4762. 184p. 1991. pap. 11.95 (*0-8061-2353-2*) U of Okla Pr.
Witch of Hissing Hill. Mary Calhoun. LC 64-15475. (Illus.). (J). (gr. k-3). 1964. lib. bdg. 15.93 (*0-688-31762-6*, Morrow Junior) Morrow.
***Witch of Kodakery: The Photography of Myra Albert Wiggins, 1869-1956.** Carole Glauber. LC 97-16180. (Illus.). 144p. 1997. 42.00 (*0-87422-149-8*) Wash St U Pr.
***Witch of Kodakery: The Photography of Myra Albert Wiggins, 1869-1956.** Carole Glauber. LC 97-16180. (Illus.). 144p. 1997. pap. 28.00 (*0-87422-148-X*) Wash St U Pr.
Witch of Prague. Francis M. Crawford. (Works of Francis Marion Crawford Ser.). 1990. reprint ed. lib. bdg. 79.00 (*0-7812-2539-6*) Rprt Serv.
Witch of Pungo. Louisa V. Kyle. (Illus.). 87p. (J). (gr. 3). 1973. 12.95 (*0-927044-00-5*) Four OClock Farms.
Witch of Sawtooth Mountain. Dorothy Nickerson. LC 94-60453. 315p. 1995. pap. 9.95 (*1-55523-690-1*) Winston-Derek.
Witch of Shakerag Hollow: And Other Sewanee Ghosts. Marcia Hollis. LC 73-80865. (Illus.). 58p. (Orig.). 1973. pap. 5.95 (*0-918769-22-1*) Univ South Pr.
Witch of the Low Tide. John Dickson Carr. 186p. 1990. pap. 3.95 (*0-88184-672-4*) Carroll & Graf.
Witch of the North. Courtway Jones. Ed. by Claire Zion. 352p. 1994. reprint ed. mass mkt. 5.50 (*0-671-73406-7*) PB.
***Witch of the Palo Duro.** Mardi O. Medawar. LC 97-14713. (A Tal-Bodal Mystery Ser.). 1997. 21.95 (*0-312-17065-3*) St Martin.
Witch of Turner's Bald. Edna C. Pierson. (Illus.). 1971. 5.00 (*0-686-05889-5*) Puddingstone.
Witch of Wall Street Hetty Green. Sparkes & Moore. (Illus.). 362p. 1992. reprint ed. lib. bdg. 32.95 (*0-89966-889-5*) Buccaneer Bks.
Witch on a Windy Night. Bernice W. Carlson. (Illus.). 20p. (J). (ps-1). 1994. pap. 4.99 (*0-14-055000-3*) Puffin Bks.
***Witch on Holiday.** large type ed. Margaret S. Barry. (J). 1997. 16.95 (*0-7451-6906-6*, Galaxy Child Lrg Print) Chivers N Amer.
***Witch or Prophet?** Sabbeleu. (Illus.). 100p. (Orig.). 1997. 20.00 (*0-9653990-1-X*) Whispering Willows.
Witch Poems. Ed. by Daisy Wallace. LC 76-9036. (Illus.). 32p. (J). (ps-3). 1976. reprint ed. lib. bdg. 14.95 (*0-8234-0281-9*) Holiday.
Witch Poems. Ed. by Daisy Wallace. LC 76-9036. (Illus.). 32p. (J). (ps-3). 1990. reprint ed. pap. 4.95 (*0-8234-0850-7*) Holiday.
Witch Purge of Eighteen Seventy-Eight: Oral & Documentary History in the Early Navajo Reservation Years. Martha Blue. pap. 4.75 (*0-912586-66-4*) Navajo Coll Pr.
Witch Returns. Phyllis R. Naylor. 192p. (J). (gr. 4-7). 1993. pap. 3.50 (*0-440-40815-6*) Dell.
Witch Stories. Jane Launchbury. (Illus.). 64p. (J). 1991. 0.75 (*0-517-06526-6*) Random Hse Value.
Witch That Switched. Irene Park. 96p. 1992. mass mkt. 3.99 (*0-88368-254-0*) Whitaker Hse.
Witch That Switched see Heaven Rejoices
Witch Tree: A Collaboration. Joanne Hart. LC 91-73629. (Illus.). 120p. (Orig.). 1992. pap. 12.95 (*0-930100-46-8*) Holy Cow.
Witch Tree Symbol. rev. ed. Carolyn Keene. LC 75-1580. (Nancy Drew Ser.: Vol. 33). (Illus.). 196p. (J). (gr. 4-7). 1956. 5.95 (*0-448-09533-5*, G&D) Putnam Pub Group.
***Witch Tricks.** Groves. (J). 1991. pap. text ed. write for info. (*0-582-19368-0*, Pub. by Longman UK) Longman.
Witch, Warlock & Magician. W. H. Adams. 1974. 250.00 (*0-8490-1310-0*) Gordon Pr.
Witch Watch. Betty Higgins. Ed. by Sun Star Publications Staff. (Jellybean Collection: Vol. 1). (Illus.). 24p. (Orig.). (J). (gr. 3-8). 1986. pap. 2.95 (*0-937787-05-1*) Sun Star Pubns.
Witch Water. Phyllis R. Naylor. 192p. (J). (gr. k-6). 1988. pap. 3.50 (*0-440-40038-4*, YB BDD) BDD Bks Young Read.
***Witch Way to the Beach.** Barbara Mariconda. LC 96-34400. (Illus.). (J). 1997. 13.95 (*0-385-32265-8*, YB BDD) BDD Bks Young Read.
***Witch Way to the Beach.** Barbara Mariconda. (J). 1997. mass mkt. 3.99 (*0-440-41268-4*) BDD Bks Young Read.
***Witch Way To the Beach.** David J. Townsend. (J). 1997. pap. 3.99 (*0-440-91194-X*) BDD Bks Young Read.
Witch Way to the Country. Barbara Mariconda. 48p. (J). 1996. 13.95 (*0-385-32179-1*) Doubleday.
Witch Way to the Country. Barbara Mariconda. 48p. (J). 1996. pap. 3.99 (*0-440-41100-9*) Dell.
Witch Weed. Phyllis R. Naylor. (Illus.). 192p. (J). (gr. 4-7). 1992. pap. 3.50 (*0-440-40708-7*, YB BDD) BDD Bks Young Read.
Witch Week. Diana W. Jones. LC 82-6074. 224p. (YA). (gr. 7 up). 1993. 14.00 (*0-688-12374-0*) Greenwillow.
***Witch Week.** Diana W. Jones. (J). Date not set. pap. 4.95 (*0-688-15545-6*, Beech Tree Bks) Morrow.
Witch Who Changed Her Ways Pop-Up. 10p. (J). (ps-3). 1990. pap. 3.95 (*0-8167-2184-X*) Troll Communs.
***Witch Who Couldn't.** Terry H. Henry. Date not set. pap. 7.95 (*0-947962-65-4*) Dufour.
Witch Who Couldn't. Terry H. Henry. (Illus.). 96p. (YA). (gr. 5). 1988. 10.95 (*0-947962-39-5*, Pub. by Anvil Bks Ltd IE) Irish Bks Media.
Witch Who Couldn't Fly. Mary E. Packard. LC 93-2212. (Glow-in-the-Dark Bk.). (Illus.). (J). (gr. k-3). 1996. pap. 2.95 (*0-8167-3256-6*) Troll Communs.
Witch Who Lives down the Hall. Donna Guthrie. LC 85-887. (Illus.). 32p. (J). (ps-3). 1985. 13.00 (*0-15-298610-3*, HB Juv Bks) HarBrace.
Witch Who Went... Margaret Hillert. (Illus.). (J). (ps). 1981. lib. bdg. 7.95 (*0-8136-5105-0*, TK2386) Modern Curr.
Witch Who Went... Margaret Hillert. (Illus.). (J). (ps-k). 1981. pap. 5.10 (*0-8136-5605-2*, TK2387) Modern Curr.
Witch, Witch. Arden Druce. LC 91-29763. (J). 1991. 13.99 (*0-85953-780-3*) Childs Play.
Witch, Witch. Arden Druce. LC 91-29763. (J). 1991. pap. 6.99 (*0-85953-781-1*) Childs Play.
***Witch, Witch.** Arden Druce. (J). 1996. lib. bdg. 15.95 (*0-85953-887-7*) Childs Play.
***Witch, Witch Come to My Party.** Arden Bruce. (GRE.). (J). 1991. pap. 6.99 (*0-85953-822-2*) Childs Play.
***Witch, Witch Come to My Party.** Arden Bruce. (SPA.). (J). 1996. pap. 6.99 (*0-85953-975-X*) Childs Play.
***Witch with the Warts on Her Nose.** Patricia Thomas. (J). Date not set. write for info. (*0-688-05602-4*) Lothrop.
***Witch with the Warts on Her Nose.** Patricia Thomas. (J). Date not set. lib. bdg. write for info. (*0-688-05603-2*) Morrow.
Witch Wood. John Buchan. 289p. 1989. mass mkt. 3.95 (*0-88184-496-9*) Carroll & Graf.
Witch Wood. John Buchan. (World's Classics Ser.). 1993. 4.99 (*0-19-282941-6*) Carroll & Graf.
Witch Wood. John Buchan. (Canongate Classic Ser.). 306p. 1996. pap. 9.95 (*0-86241-202-1*) Interlink Pub.
Witch Words. Ed. by Gavin Frost & Yvonne Frost. 434p. 1993. pap. text ed. 24.95 (*0-9630657-5-0*) Godolphin Hse.
Witch Words: Poems of Magic & Mystery. Ed. by Robert Fisher. (Illus.). 70p. (J). (gr. 2 up). 1991. pap. 4.95 (*0-571-16319-X*) Faber & Faber.
Witchaven Official Strategy Guide. Bradygames Staff. 348p. 1995. 19.99 (*1-56686-412-7*) Brady Pub.
Witchbroom. Lawrence Scott. (Caribbean Writers Ser.). 288p. (C). 1993. pap. 10.95 (*0-435-98933-2*, 98933) Heinemann.
***Witchcraft.** Ilil Arbel. 125p. (Orig.). (YA). (gr. 7-12). 1996. pap. 6.95 (*1-57515-092-1*) PPI Pubng.
Witchcraft. Carol Crook. 20p. (Orig.). 1988. pap. 2.50 (*0-939399-11-3*) Bks of Truth.
Witchcraft. Ed. by Bob Kahan. (Illus.). 136p. 1996. pap. 14.95 (*1-56389-274-X*, Vertigo) DC Comics.
Witchcraft. Jayne Ann Krentz. 1996. mass mkt. 5.99 (*1-55166-158-6*, 1-66158-6, Mira Bks) Harlequin Bks.
***Witchcraft.** Bill Michaels. 288p. 1997. mass mkt. 4.99 (*0-8217-5601-X*, Zebra Kensgtn) Kensgtn Pub Corp.
Witchcraft. Bernard Sleigh. 1972. 250.00 (*0-8490-1311-9*) Gordon Pr.
Witchcraft. 2nd ed. Charles A. Hoyt. LC 89-5987. 200p. (C). 1989. pap. text ed. 19.95 (*0-8093-1544-0*) S Ill U Pr.
Witchcraft: A Beginner's Guide. Teresa Vidgen-Moorey. (Beginners Ser.). (Illus.). 96p. 1996. pap. 11.95 (*0-340-67014-2*, Pub. by H & S UK) Trafalgar.
Witchcraft: A Tradition Renewed. Doreen Valiente & Evan Jones. 203p. 1990. pap. 10.95 (*0-919345-61-1*) Phoenix WA.
Witchcraft: Exploring the World of Wicca. Craig Hawkins. LC 96-21480. 288p. (gr. 10). 1996. pap. 15.99 (*0-8010-5382-X*) Baker Bks.
Witchcraft: The Gay Counterculture. Arthur Evans. 1977. pap. 12.95 (*0-915480-01-8*) Fag Rag.
Witchcraft: The History & Mythology. Richard Marshall. (Illus.). 160p. 1995. 18.99 (*0-517-14083-7*) Random Hse Value.
Witchcraft: The History & Mythology. Richard Marshall. (Illus.). 160p. 1995. write for info. (*1-887354-03-4*) Saraband CT.
Witchcraft: The Old Religion. Leo L. Martello. 1987. pap. 6.95 (*0-8065-1028-5*, Citadel Pr) Carol Pub Group.
Witchcraft & Black Magic. Montague Summers. LC 89-63006. (Illus.). 228p. 1990. reprint ed. lib. bdg. 48.00 (*1-55888-840-3*) Omnigraphics Inc.
Witchcraft & Demonianism. Cecil H. Ewen. LC 79-8631. (Illus.). reprint ed. 48.50 (*0-404-18410-3*) AMS Pr.
Witchcraft & Demonology in Art & Literature. Ed. by Brian P. Levack. LC 92-22872. (Articles on Witchcraft, Magic, & Demonology Ser.: Vol. 12). (Illus.). 360p. 1992. text ed. 70.00 (*0-8153-1035-8*) Garland.
Witchcraft & Hysteria in Elizabethan England. Edward Jorden & Mary G. Case. Ed. by Michael MacDonald. LC 90-8435. (Tavistock Classic Reprints in the History of Psychiatry Ser.). 368p. (C). 1990. text ed. 99.95 (*0-415-01788-2*, A4903) Routledge.
***Witchcraft & Its Transformations, c.1650- c.1750.** Ian Bostridge. (Oxford Historical Monographs). (Illus.). 288p. 1997. 75.00 (*0-19-820653-4*) OUP.
***Witchcraft & Paganism in Australia.** Lyn Hume. (Illus.). 224p. 1997. pap. 29.95 (*0-522-84782-X*, Pub. by Melbourne Univ Pr AT) Paul & Co Pubs.
Witchcraft & Second Sight in the Highlands & Islands of Scotland. John G. Campbell. 1976. reprint ed. 20.00 (*0-85409-978-6*) Charles River Bks.
Witchcraft & Sorcery. Ed. by Max G. Marwick. 494p. 1987. pap. 7.95 (*0-14-022678-8*, Penguin Bks) Viking Penguin.
Witchcraft & Sorcery of the American Native Peoples. 2nd rev. ed. Ed. by Deward E. Walker. LC 89-20493. 336p. 1990. pap. text ed. 29.95 (*0-89301-127-4*) U of Idaho Pr.
Witchcraft & Superstitious Record in the Southwestern District of Scotland. J. Maxwell Wood. (Illus.). 1976. 25.00 (*0-7158-1139-8*) Charles River Bks.
Witchcraft & Witchhunts Past & Present: The Blame Complex in Action. Mark Graubard. LC 89-192486. (Illus.). 387p. (Orig.). (C). 1990. pap. text ed. 34.50 (*0-930329-31-7*) Kabel Pubs.
Witchcraft at Salem. Chadwick Hansen. LC 69-15825. (Illus.). 256p. 1985. 17.95 (*0-8076-0492-5*); pap. 11.95 (*0-8076-1137-9*) Braziller.
Witchcraft Delusion in Colonial Connecticut, 1647-1747. John Taylor. 172p. 1974. 22.95 (*0-87928-053-0*) Corner Hse.
Witchcraft Fact Book. Edmund M. Buczyski. (Illus.). 30p. 1984. pap. 4.00 (*0-939708-04-3*) Magickal Childe.
Witchcraft for Tomorrow. Doreen Valiente. (Illus.). 205p. 1983. pap. 8.95 (*0-919345-83-2*) Phoenix WA.
Witchcraft from the Inside: Origins of the Fastest Growing Religious Movement in America. 3rd ed. Ray Buckland. LC 94-44804. (Illus.). 226p. 1995. pap. 12.95 (*1-56718-101-5*) Llewellyn Pubns.
Witchcraft Grimoire. Robert Blanchard. LC 93-79457. 104p. (C). 1993. text ed. 29.95 (*1-883147-46-8*) Intern Guild ASRS.
Witchcraft in Colonial America. Ed. by Brian P. Levack. LC 92-22874. (Articles on Witchcraft, Magic, & Demonology Ser.: Vol. 8). 416p. 1992. text ed. 72.00 (*0-8153-1030-7*) Garland.
Witchcraft in Early Modern Europe: Studies in Culture & Belief. Ed. by Jonathan Barry et al. LC 95-22865. (Past & Present Publications). 392p. (C). 1996. text ed. 64.95 (*0-521-55224-9*) Cambridge U Pr.
Witchcraft in England. Ed. by Brian P. Levack. LC 92-21032. (Articles on Witchcraft, Magic, & Demonology Ser.: Vol. 6). 344p. 1992. text ed. 62.00 (*0-8153-1028-5*) Garland.
Witchcraft in England, 1558-1618. Ed. by Barbara Rosen. LC 91-18279. (Illus.). 424p. 1991. reprint ed. pap. 19.95 (*0-87023-753-5*) U of Mass Pr.
Witchcraft in Europe & America: Guide to the Microfilm Collection. Ed. by Diane M. Del Cervo. 112p. 1983. 65.00 (*0-89235-074-1*) Primary Srce Media.
Witchcraft in Europe, 1100-1700: A Documentary History. Ed. by Alan C. Kors & Edward Peters. LC 71-170267. (Middle Ages Ser.). (Illus.). 400p. 1972. pap. text ed. 21.95 (*0-8122-1063-8*) U of Pa Pr.
Witchcraft in History. Ronald Holmes. 1977. pap. 5.95 (*0-8065-0575-3*, Citadel Pr) Carol Pub Group.
Witchcraft in Scotland. Ed. by Brian P. Levack. LC 92-21033. (Articles on Witchcraft, Magic, & Demonology Ser.: Vol. 7). 408p. 1992. text ed. 70.00 (*0-8153-1029-3*) Garland.
Witchcraft in the Ancient World & the Middle Ages. Ed. by Brian P. Levack. LC 92-20731. (Articles on Witchcraft, Magic, & Demonology Ser.: Vol. 2). 344p. 1992. text ed. 62.00 (*0-8153-1024-2*) Garland.
Witchcraft in the Middle Ages. Jeffrey B. Russel. (Illus.). 1976. pap. 5.95 (*0-8065-0504-4*, Citadel Pr) Carol Pub Group.
Witchcraft in the Middle Ages. Jeffrey B. Russell. LC 72-37755. 394p. 1984. 42.50 (*0-8014-0697-8*); pap. 15.95 (*0-8014-9289-0*) Cornell U Pr.
Witchcraft in the Old Testament. G. R. Driver. 1994. pap. 3.95 (*1-55818-307-8*, Near Eastern) Holmes Pub.
***Witchcraft in the Pews.** Bloomer. 1997. pap. 7.99 (*1-56229-447-4*) Pneuma Life Pub.
Witchcraft in the Southwest: Spanish & Indian Supernaturalism on the Rio Grande. Marc Simmons. LC 79-18928. (Illus.). xiv, 184p. 1980. pap. 9.00 (*0-8032-9116-7*, Bison Books) U of Nebr Pr.
Witchcraft in Tudor & Stuart England: A Regional & Comparative Study. Alan MacFarlane. (Illus.). 334p. (C). 1991. reprint ed. pap. text ed. 14.95 (*0-88133-532-0*) Waveland Pr.
Witchcraft in Western India. Sohaila Kapur. 176p. 1983. text ed. 15.95 (*0-86131-402-6*, Pub. by Orient Longman Ltd II) Apt Bks.
***Witchcraft, Lycanthropy, Drugs, & Disease: An Anthropological Study of the European Witch-Hunts.** H. Sidky. (American University Studies XI: Vol. 70). 344p. (C). 1997. pap. text ed. 34.95 (*0-8204-3354-3*) P Lang Pubng.
Witchcraft, Magic & Alchemy. Grillot De Givry. 1974. lib. bdg. 250.00 (*0-87968-515-8*) Krishna Pr.
Witchcraft, Magic & Alchemy. Grillot De Givry. (Illus.). 1990. 22.75 (*0-8446-0113-6*) Peter Smith.
Witchcraft, Magic & Alchemy. Givry De Grillot. Tr. by J. Courtney Locke from FRE. (Illus.). 395p. 1971. reprint ed. pap. 9.95 (*0-486-22493-7*) Dover.
Witchcraft, Magic & Demonology: An Anthology of Scholarly Articles, 12 vols., Set. Intro. by Brian P. Levack. 1992. 710.00 (*0-8153-1022-6*) Garland.
Witchcraft, Magic & Occultism. W. B. Crow. 1974. pap. 10.00 (*0-87980-173-5*) Wilshire.
Witchcraft, Magic & Religion in Seventeenth-Century Massachusetts. Richard Weisman. LC 83-15542. 288p. 1985. pap. text ed. 17.95 (*0-87023-494-3*) U of Mass Pr.
Witchcraft Magic 16th & 17th. Geoffrey F. Scarre. 1996. text ed. 10.95 (*0-333-39933-1*, Pub. by Macm UK) St Martin.
Witchcraft of Salem Village. Shirley Jackson. (Landmark Ser.: No. 69). (Illus.). (J). (gr. 4-6). 1963. lib. bdg. 9.99 (*0-394-90369-2*) Random Bks Yng Read.
Witchcraft of Salem Village. Shirley Jackson. 1987. pap. 4.99 (*0-394-89176-7*) Random.
Witchcraft Papers. Peter Haining. 1974. 7.95 (*0-8216-0223-3*, Univ Bks) Carol Pub Group.
***Witchcraft Persecutions in Bavaria: Popular Magic, Religious Zealotry & Reason of State in Early Modern Europe.** Wolfgang Behringer. (Past & Present Publications). (Illus.). 498p. (C). 1997. text ed. 90.00 (*0-521-48258-5*) Cambridge U Pr.
Witchcraft Poems: Salem, Sixteen Ninety-Two. Constance Carrier. (Chapbook Ser.: No. 4). 1988. 30.00 (*0-937035-11-4*) Stone Hse NY.
Witchcraft, Satanism & Occult Crime: Who's Who & What's What, a Reference Manual for the Professional Investigator. 5th ed. Church of All Worlds Staff. (Illus.). 24p. 1994. pap. 4.00 (*0-919345-86-7*) Phoenix WA.
Witchcraft, Sorcery & Superstition. Jules Michelet. Tr. by A. R. Allinson from FRE. LC 95-9367. Orig. Title: Satanism & Witchcraft. 352p. 1995. pap. 12.95 (*0-8065-1686-0*, Citadel Pr) Carol Pub Group.
Witchcraft-the Sixth Sense. Justine Glass. 206p. 1978. pap. 7.00 (*0-87980-174-3*) Wilshire.
Witchcraft Today. Gerald B. Gardener. (Illus.). 172p. 1989. pap. 9.95 (*0-939708-03-5*) Magickal Childe.
Witchcraft Today. Gerald B. Gardner. 1970. pap. 2.45 (*0-8065-0002-6*, Citadel Pr) Carol Pub Group.
Witchcraft Today Bk. 1: The Modern Craft Movement. Ed. by Chas S. Clifton. LC 92-918. 208p. 1992. pap. 9.95 (*0-87542-377-9*) Llewellyn Pubns.
Witchcraft Today Bk. 2: Modern Rites of Passage. Ed. by Chas S. Clifton. LC 93-22967. (Witchcraft Today Ser.). 288p. 1993. pap. 9.95 (*0-87542-378-7*) Llewellyn Pubns.
Witchcraft Today, Bk. 3: Witchcraft & Shamanism. Ed. by Chas S. Clifton. LC 94-6181. 288p. 1994. pap. 9.95 (*1-56718-150-3*) Llewellyn Pubns.
Witchcraft, Women, & Society. Ed. by Brian P. Levack. LC 92-22873. (Articles on Witchcraft, Magic, & Demonology Ser.: Vol. 10). 310p. 1992. text ed. 60.00 (*0-8153-1032-3*) Garland.
Witchcraze: A New History of the European Witch Hunts. Anne L. Barstow. LC 92-56410. 272p. 1995. pap. 13.00 (*0-06-251036-3*) Harper SF.
Witchdance in Bavaria. large type ed. Robert MacLeod. 1977. 25.99 (*0-7089-0010-0*) Ulverscroft.
***Witcher.** Bill Fry. Ed. by Jan O'Mera. 216p. 1996. pap. 11.95 (*0-9653259-0-3*) Fried Publns.
Witchery of Archery. J. Maurice Thompson. LC 84-60900. 1986. reprint ed. pap. 8.95 (*0-932099-03-3*) Fundingsland.
Witchery of Sleep: An Anthology. Willard Moyer et al. 1977. lib. bdg. 59.95 (*0-8490-2828-0*) Gordon Pr.
***Witches.** 1990. 10.00 (*0-923763-24-4*) Mayfair Games.
***Witches.** Ariel Books Staff. 1996. 3.95 (*0-8362-1009-3*, Arie Bks) Andrews & McMeel.
Witches. Ed. by Isaac Asimov et al. (Isaac Asimov's Magical Worlds of Fantasy Ser.: No. 2). 304p. 1984. pap. 3.95 (*0-451-12882-6*, Sig) NAL-Dutton.
Witches. Roald Dahl. LC 83-14195. (Illus.). 208p. (J). (gr. 3-9). 1983. 16.00 (*0-374-38457-6*) FS&G.
Witches. Roald Dahl. (J). 1989. pap. 4.99 (*0-14-034020-3*, Puffin) Puffin Bks.
Witches. Roald Dahl. LC 85-519. (Illus.). 200p. (J). (gr. 3-7). Date not set. pap. 3.95 (*0-14-031730-9*) Viking Child Bks.
Witches. Kathryn M. Griffith. 384p. 1993. mass mkt. 4.50 (*0-8217-4031-8*, Zebra Kensgtn) Kensgtn Pub Corp.
Witches. Illus. by Colin Hawkins. (Scary Pop-Up Bks.). 10p. (J). (ps-3). 1994. 3.99 (*0-89577-589-1*) RD Assn.
***Witches.** Erica Jong. LC 97-8294. 1997. write for info. (*0-8109-3999-1*) Abrams.
***Witches.** Jim Pipe. LC 97-7460. (Illus.). (J). 1997. lib. bdg. write for info. (*0-7613-0607-2*, Copper Beech Bks) Millbrook Pr.

W

Witches. Stewart Ross. LC 95-38885. (Fact or Fiction Ser.). (Illus.). 48p. (YA). (gr. 5 up). 1996. lib. bdg. 18.90 (0-7613-0452-5, Copper Beech Bks) Millbrook Pr.
Witches. Stewart Ross. LC 95-38885. (Fact or Fiction Ser.). (Illus.). 48p. (YA). (gr. 5 up). 1996. pap. 6.95 (0-7613-0467-3, Copper Beech Bks) Millbrook Pr.
Witches. Thomas C. Lethbridge. LC 68-28449. (Illus.). 1969. reprint ed. 5.95 (0-8065-0221-5, Citadel Pr); reprint ed. pap. 2.45 (0-685-08138-9, Citadel Pr) Carol Pub Group.
Witches: Opposing Viewpoints. 2nd ed. Wendy Stein. (Opposing Viewpoints Ser.). (Illus.). 112p. (YA). (gr. 5-12). 1995. lib. bdg. 17.96 (1-56510-240-1, 2401) Greenhaven.
Witches' Advocate: Basque Witchcraft & the Spanish Inquisition, 1609-1614. Gustav Henningsen. LC 79-20340. (Basque Ser.). (Illus.). xxxii, 640p. 1980. 49.95 (0-87417-056-7) U of Nev Pr.
Witches' Almanac: Aries 1992 to Pisces 1993. Elizabeth Pepper & John Wilcock. (Illus.). 96p. 1992. 5.95 (1-881098-00-1) Witches Almanac.
Witches Almanac: Complete Astrological Guide, Spring 1995 to Spring 1996. Elizabeth Pepper & John Wilcock. 1995. pap. text ed. 6.95 (1-881098-06-0) Witches Almanac.
Witches' Almanac: Spring 1993 to Spring 1994. Elizabeth Pepper & John Wilcock. 1992. pap. 5.95 (1-881098-02-8) Witches Almanac.
***Witches' Almanac: The Complete Guide to Lunar Harmony.** Elizabeth Pepper. 1998. pap. text ed. 83.40 (0-88496-427-2) Capra Pr.
***Witches' Almanac (Spr'98-Spr'99) The Complete Guide to Lunar Harmony.** Ed. by Elizabeth Pepper & John Wilcock. (Illus.). 96p. 1998. pap. 6.95 (0-88496-426-4) Capra Pr.
Witches' Almanac, 1997-98: The Complete Guide to Lunar Harmony. Ed. by Elizabeth Pepper & John Wilcock. 1997. pap. 6.95 (0-88496-415-9) Capra Pr.
Witches & Historians: Interpretations of Salem. Marc Mappen. LC 78-2579. (American Problem Studies). 126p. 1980. pap. 10.50 (0-88275-653-2) Krieger.
Witches & Historians: Interpretations of Salem. 2nd ed. Ed. by Marc Mappen. LC 96-7977. 146p. (C). 1996. pap. 11.50 (0-89464-999-X) Krieger.
Witches & Jesuits: Shakespeare's Macbeth. Garry Wills. LC 94-14201. (Illus.). 288p. 1995. 23.00 (0-19-508879-4) OUP.
Witches & Jesuits: Shakespeare's Macbeth. Garry Wills. (Illus.). 240p. 1996. pap. 11.95 (0-19-510290-8) OUP.
***Witches & Magic Makers.** Eyewitness Books Staff. LC 96-42958. (J). 1997. 19.00 (0-679-88544-7) Knopf.
***Witches & Magic Spells.** (Halloween Coloring & Activity Bks.). (Illus.). 32p. (J). (gr. k-2). 1996. pap. write for info. (1-56144-882-6, Honey Bear Bks) Modern Pub NYC.
Witches & Neighbors: A History of European Witchcraft. Robin Briggs. 480p. 1996. pap. 32.95 (0-670-83589-7, Viking) Viking Penguin.
Witches & Other Things. Marjorie Agosin. Ed. by Yvette E. Miller. Tr. by Cola Franzen. LC 84-768. (Discoveries Ser.). 94p. (ENG & SPA.). 1984. pap. 10.50 (0-935480-16-1) Lat Am Lit Rev Pr.
Witches & Sorcerers. Dauraul. pap. 2.95 (0-8065-0286-X, Citadel Pr) Carol Pub Group.
Witches & Warlocks. Phillip W. Sargeant. 1976. 20.00 (0-7158-1028-6) Charles River Bks.
Witches & Warlocks. Philip W. Sergeant. 1972. 26.95 (0-405-08950-3, 1457) Ayer.
Witches & Warlocks. Philip W. Sergeant. LC 72-82208. (Illus.). 1972. reprint ed. 26.95 (0-405-08898-1) Ayer.
Witches & Warlocks: Tales of Black Magic, Old & New. Ed. by Marvin Kaye. 608p. 1989. 9.98 (1-56865-000-0, GuildAmerica) Dblday Direct.
Witches & Whimsies. Karla Margaret, pseud. 100p. (J). 1975. per., pap. write for info. (0-935430-02-4) In Between.
Witches & Witchcraft. Time-Life Books Editors. Ed. by Jim Hicks. (Mysteries of the Unknown Ser.). (Illus.). 144p. 1990. write for info. (0-8094-6392-X); lib. bdg. write for info. (0-8094-6393-8) Time-Life.
Witches Are a Nuisance. Gwenda Vere-Hodge. 58p. (J). 1987. 20.00 (0-7223-2164-3, Pub. by A H S Ltd UK) St Mut.
***Witches at the Foot of the Mountain.** unabridged ed. Slayton Moorhound, pseud. LC 97-70312. 158p. (Orig.). 1997. pap. 13.95 (0-9656507-0-7, 002-00MP, Manypaws Pr) J N H Waring.
Witches' Bane. Susan W. Albert. 272p. 1994. reprint ed. mass mkt. 5.99 (0-425-14406-2, Prime Crime) Berkley Pub.
***Witches Bible Compleat.** Farrar. 19.95 (0-919345-92-1) Phoenix WA.
Witches' Bible-Compleat. Janet Farrar & Stewart Farrar. 356p. 1987. pap. 19.95 (0-939708-09-4) Magickal Childe.
Witches' Book of Names. Ellen C. Reed. (Illus.). 166p. (Orig.). Date not set. pap. 19.95 (1-885569-10-6) Solar Crown.
Witches' Brew. Terry Brooks. 1996. mass mkt. 6.99 (0-345-38702-3) Ballantine.
Witches' Brew. Ed. by Alfred Hitchcock. 1976. 20.95 (0-8488-0533-X) Amereon Ltd.
Witches' Brew. Marcia Leonard. 1996. pap. 2.95 (0-8167-1886-5) Troll Communs.
Witches Broomstick Manual. Yaj Nomolos. (Illus.). 64p. (Orig.). 1984. pap. 3.95 (0-943832-10-1) Intl Imports.
Witches Cauldron. Annie Kubler. (FRE.). (J). (ps-3). 1996. 14.99 (0-85953-599-1) Childs Play.
Witches' Children. Patricia Clapp. (J). (gr. 4-8). 1992. 18.25 (0-8446-6572-X) Peter Smith.
Witches' Companion: The Official Guide to Anne Rice's Lives of the Mayfair Witches. Katherine Ramsland. LC 94-9747. 528p. 1994. 29.95 (0-345-38947-6) Ballantine.
Witches' Companion: The Official Guide to Anne Rice's Lives of the Mayfair Witches. Katherine Ramsland. 544p. 1996. pap. 17.95 (0-345-40624-9) Ballantine Trade.
Witches, Devils, & Doctors in the Renaissance: Johann Weyer, "De Praestigiis Daemonum" Ed. by George Mora et al. Tr. by John Shea. (Medieval & Renaissance Texts & Studies: Vol. 73). 896p. 1991. 55.00 (0-86698-083-0, MR73) MRTS.
Witches Don't Do Back Flips. Debbie Dadey. 96p. (J). (gr. 4-7). 1994. pap. 2.99 (0-590-48112-6) Scholastic Inc.
Witches Four. (Parents Magazine Press Read-Aloud Library). (Illus.). 42p. (J). (ps-3). 1993. lib. bdg. 17.27 (0-8368-0893-2) Gareth Stevens Inc.
Witches Four. Marc Brown. LC 79-5263. (Illus.). 48p. (J). (ps-3). 1980. 5.95 (0-8193-1013-1); lib. bdg. 5.95 (0-8193-1014-X) Parents.
Witches, Ghosts & Goblins. (Look & Find Ser.). (Illus.). 24p. (J). 1993. 7.98 (1-56173-523-X) Pubns Intl Ltd.
Witches, Ghosts & Loups-Garous. Finnigan. (J). Date not set. pap. 10.95 (1-55082-086-9, Pub. by Quarry Pr CN) LPC InBook.
Witches' God: The Masculine Principle of Divinity. Janet Farrar & Stewart Farrar. (Illus.). 288p. 1989. pap. 15.95 (0-919345-47-6) Phoenix WA.
Witches' Goddess: The Feminine Principle of Divinity. Janet Farrar & Stewart Farrar. (Illus.). 322p. 1987. pap. 14.95 (0-919345-91-3) Phoenix WA.
Witches' Hammer. Jane S. Hitchcock. 1995. mass mkt. 5.99 (0-451-18508-0, Sig) NAL-Dutton.
***Witches' Holiday.** Alice Low. (J). 1997. pap. text ed. 2.99 (0-590-46891-X) Scholastic Inc.
Witches, Magic & Spells. Stuart A. Kallen. Ed. by Rosemary Wallner. LC 91-73058. (Ghastly Ghost Stories Ser.). (J). 1991. lib. bdg. 13.98 (1-56239-043-0) Abdo & Dghtrs.
Witches, Midwives, & Nurses: A History of Women Healers. Barbara Ehrenreich & Deirdre English. LC 80-13400. (Illus.). 48p. 1973. pap. 5.95 (0-912670-13-4) Feminist Pr.
Witches Next Door. J. R. Black. (Shadow Zone Ser.). 120p. (Orig.). (J). (gr. 3-7). 1993. pap. 3.50 (0-679-85108-9, Bullseye Bks) Random Bks Yng Read.
Witches of Eastwick. John Updike. LC 83-49048. 336p. 1984. 25.00 (0-394-53760-2) Knopf.
Witches of Eastwick. John Updike. 352p. 1985. mass mkt. 6.99 (0-449-20647-5, Crest) Fawcett.
***Witches of Eastwick.** John Updike. 1996. pap. 12.00 (0-449-91210-8) Fawcett.
Witches of Hopper Street. Linda Gondosch. (Illus.). (J). (gr. 4-6). pap. 2.99 (0-671-72468-1, Archway) PB.
Witches of Karres. James Schmitz. 1993. reprint ed. lib. bdg. 18.95 (0-89968-361-4, Lghtyr Pr) Buccaneer Bks.
Witches of Oz. Matthew Philips & Julia Philips. 1994. pap. 19.95 (1-898307-18-0, Pub. by Capall Bann Pubng UK) Holmes Pub.
Witches of Pendle. 1995. pap. 5.25 (0-19-421673-X) OUP.
Witches of Wacky Street. Sara James. (J). Date not set. pap. 2.95 (0-8167-1842-3) Troll Communs.
Witches of Wenshar. Barbara Hambly. 352p. (Orig.). 1987. mass mkt. 5.99 (0-345-32934-1, Del Rey) Ballantine.
***Witches of Wenshar.** Barbara Hambly. 1997. pap. 12.00 (0-345-42060-8) Ballantine.
Witches of Worm. Zilpha K. Snyder. 192p. (J). (gr. k-6). 1986. pap. 4.50 (0-440-49727-2, YB BDD) BDD Bks Young Read.
Witches of Worm. Zilpha K. Snyder. LC 72-75283. (Illus.). 192p. (J). (gr. 4-8). 1972. lib. bdg. 16.00 (0-689-30066-2, Atheneum Bks Young) S&S Childrens.
Witches' Olympics. James Magorian. LC 83-71262. 44p. (J). (gr. 4-7). 1983. pap. 5.00 (0-930674-10-3) Black Oak.
Witches' Poker Game & Other Stories. Carlos Montaner. Tr. by Robert Robinson from SPA. LC 73-84203. 171p. 1973. pap. 1.95 (0-913480-18-5) Inter Am U Pr.
Witches, Pumpkins & Grinning Ghosts: The Story of the Halloween Symbols. Edna Barth. LC 72-75705. (Illus.). 96p. (J). (gr. 3-6). 1981. pap. 6.95 (0-89919-040-5, Clarion Bks); pap. 4.95 (0-317-03145-7, Clarion Bks) HM.
***Witches Qabala Bk. 1: The Pagan Path & the Tree of Life.** Ellen C. Reed. LC 97-9197. (Illus.). 192p. (Orig.). 1997. pap. 12.95 (0-87728-880-1) Weiser.
Witches Revenge. Christopher Pike. (Spooksville Ser.: No. 6). (J). (gr. 4-6). 1996. pap. 3.99 (0-671-55065-9, Minstrel Bks) PB.
***Witches' Rings.** Kerstin Ekman & Linda Schenck. 372p. 1997. pap. 16.95 (1-870041-36-4, Pub. by Norvik Pr UK) Dufour.
Witches Sabbats: And Other Reflections. Mike Nichols. (Illus.). 110p. Date not set. pap. 14.95 (1-885569-09-2) Solar Crown.
Witches Scary House. Mick Wells. LC 96-22531. 4p. 1996. 19.95 (0-312-14529-2) St Martin.
Witches' Supermarket. Susan Meddaugh. (Illus.). 32p. (J). (gr. k-3). 1991. 13.95 (0-395-57034-4, Sandpiper) HM.
Witches' Supermarket. Susan Meddaugh. (Illus.). (J). 1994. pap. 4.95 (0-395-70092-2) HM.
Witches Tarot see Secrets of Ancient Witchcraft
Witches Tarot, Bk. II: The Witches Qabala. Ellen C. Reed. LC 88-45181. (Modern Witchcraft Ser.). (Illus.). 316p. (Orig.). 1989. pap. 9.95 (0-87542-668-9) Llewellyn Pubns.
Witches Tarot Kit. Ellen C. Reed. (Illus.). 320p. 1996. boxed 34.95 (1-56718-558-4) Llewellyn Pubns.
***Witches Three.** R. H. Crawford. (Illus.). 272p. 1997. 17.95 (0-614-28389-2) DOBO Bks.
***Witches Three.** R. H. Crawford. (Illus.). 272p. 1997. 17.95 (0-9643695-0-8, Green Jaguar) DOBO Bks.
Witches' Way. Janet Farrar & Stewart Farrar. (Illus.). 349p. 1986. reprint ed. 24.95 (0-919345-71-9) Phoenix WA.
Witchhunt Foiled: The FBI vs. NAMBLA. North American Man-Boy Love Association Staff. LC 85-72763. (Illus.). 93p. (Orig.). 1985. pap. 5.95 (0-9615497-0-X) N Am Man-Boy.
Witching. Fritzen Ravenswood. 1989. mass mkt. 3.95 (0-8217-2657-9, Zebra Kensgtn) Kensgtn Pub Corp.
Witching for Water, Oil, Pipes, & Precious Metals. Walker D. Wyman. (Illus.). 1977. text ed. 7.50 (0-686-20515-4); pap. text ed. 5.25 (0-686-20516-2) U Wisc-River Falls Pr.
Witching Hour. Anne O. Rice. 1990. 27.50 (0-394-58786-3) Knopf.
Witching Hour. Anne O. Rice. 976p. 1991. pap. 14.00 (0-345-36789-8) Ballantine.
Witching Hour. Anne O. Rice. 1056p. 1993. mass mkt. 6.99 (0-345-38446-6) Ballantine.
Witching of Elspie: A Book of Stories. Duncan C. Scott. LC 70-37559. (Short Story Index Reprint Ser.). 1977. reprint ed. 20.95 (0-8369-4118-7) Ayer.
Witching Times. John W. De Forest. Ed. by Alfred Appel, Jr. (Masterworks of Literature Ser.). 1967. 19.95 (0-8084-0332-X); pap. 16.95 (0-8084-0333-8) NCUP.
***Witchlight.** Bradley. Date not set. pap. 13.95 (0-312-85831-0) St Martin.
Witchlight. Marion Z. Bradley. LC 96-20703. 304p. 1996. 23.95 (0-312-86104-4) St Martin.
***Witchlight.** Smith. (Night World Ser.: No. 9). (J). 1998. mass mkt. 3.99 (0-671-01477-3) PB.
Witchrock. large type ed. Bill Knox. (Linford Mystery Library). 304p. 1992. pap. 15.99 (0-7089-7271-3, Trailtree Bookshop) Ulverscroft.
Witch's Book of Divination. Callia Underhill. LC 96-27231. (Illus.). 240p. (Orig.). 1996. pap. 14.95 (1-56718-054-X) Llewellyn Pubns.
Witch's Brew. Marie-Francine Hebert. (Illus.). 54p. (Orig.). (J). 1993. pap. 5.95 (0-929005-52-X, Pub. by Second Story Pr CN) LPC InBook.
***Witch's Brew: Secrets of Scents.** Morwyn. LC 95-68972. (Illus.). 256p. (YA). (gr. 10-13). 1993. pap. 19.95 (0-924608-19-6, Whitford) Schiffer.
Witch's Cat. Ruth Chew. 128p. (J). (gr. 4-7). 1994. pap. 2.95 (0-590-48341-2) Scholastic Inc.
***Witch's Children.** Patricia Clapp. (J). Date not set. pap. write for info. (0-688-12948-X) Morrow.
Witch's Christmas. Norman Bridwell. (Illus.). (J). (gr. k-3). 1972. pap. 1.50 (0-590-09216-2) Scholastic Inc.
Witch's Christmas. Norman Bridwell. (Illus.). 32p. (J). (gr. k-3). 1986. pap. 2.50 (0-590-40434-2) Scholastic Inc.
Witch's Circle: Rituals & Craft of the Cosmic Muse. Maria K. Simms. 1996. pap. text ed. 19.95 (1-56718-657-2) Llewellyn Pubns.
Witch's Dozen. Stewart Farrar. 169p. 1996. pap. text ed. 10.95 (0-9630657-7-7) Godolphin Hse.
Witch's Dream. Florinda Donner-Grau. 1997. pap. 11.95 (0-14-019531-9, Penguin Bks) Viking Penguin.
Witch's Eye. Phyllis R. Naylor. 192p. (J). (gr. 4-7). 1991. pap. 3.50 (0-440-40514-9, YB BDD) BDD Bks Young Read.
Witch's Face: A Mexican Tale. Eric A. Kimmel. LC 92-44380. (Illus.). 32p. (J). (ps-3). 1993. lib. bdg. 15.95 (0-8234-1038-2) Holiday.
Witch's Fang. Heather Kellerbals-Stewart. 192p. (Orig.). (YA). (gr. 8-12). 1994. pap. 7.95 (0-919591-88-4, Pub. by Polestar Bk Pubs CN) Orca Bk Pubs.
Witch's Fire. Beverly Butler. LC 93-44. 144p. (J). (gr. 5 up). 1993. pap. 14.99 (0-525-65132-2, Cobblehill Bks) Dutton Child Bks.
Witch's Fire. Beverly Butler. 144p. (J). (gr. 5-9). 1995. pap. 3.99 (0-14-037614-3) Puffin Bks.
Witch's Formulary & Spellbook. Taro Star. 102p. 1985. pap. 6.95 (0-942272-08-0) Original Pubns.
Witch's Gold. Hamlin Garland. (Collected Works of Hamlin Garland). 1988. reprint ed. lib. bdg. 79.00 (0-7812-1235-9) Rprt Serv.
Witch's Gold see Collected Works of Hamlin Garland
Witch's Guide to Faery Folk: Reclaiming Our Working Relationship with Invisible Helpers. Edain McCoy. LC 93-50837. (Illus.). 379p. 1994. pap. 12.95 (0-87542-733-2) Llewellyn Pubns.
Witch's Hand. Peter Utton. (J). (ps up). 1989. 13.95 (0-374-38463-0) FS&G.
***Witch's Hat.** Joanne Barkan. (Trick-or-Treat Bks.). (J). 1997. 3.99 (0-689-81693-6, Litl Simon S&S) S&S Childrens.
Witch's Kitchen. Keith Morgan. (Orig.). 1993. pap. 7.95 (1-872189-21-0, Pub. by Mandrake Pr UK) Holmes Pub.
Witch's Kitchen: Freud, "Faust" & the Transference. Sabine Prokhoris. Tr. by G. M. Goshgarian. 200p. 1995. 39.95 (0-8014-3043-7); pap. 16.95 (0-8014-8315-8) Cornell U Pr.
Witch's Lullaby. Martha King. 1991. pap. 3.45 (0-87129-071-5, W68) Dramatic Pub.
***Witch's Revenge/The Dark Corner/The Little People/The Wishing Star, 4 Vols.** Christopher Pike. (Spooksville Ser.: Vol. 6-9). 1997. mass mkt. 15.96 (0-671-87829-8, Archway) PB.
Witch's Ring. Rachel Dixon. LC 93-34192. (Illus.). 128p. (J). (gr. 3-7). 1994. 14.95 (1-56282-545-3); lib. bdg. 14.89 (1-56282-546-1) Hyprn Child.
Witch's Sister. Phyllis R. Naylor. 160p. (J). (gr. k-6). 1993. pap. 3.50 (0-440-40028-7) Dell.
Witch's Spellcraft. Tarostar. (Illus.). 127p. (Orig.). 1986. pap. 5.95 (0-943832-13-6) Intl Imports.
Witch's Vacation. Norman Bridwell. (Illus.). 32p. (J). (gr. k-3). 1987. pap. 2.50 (0-590-40558-6) Scholastic Inc.
Witch's Wedding: And Other Random Memories. Charlotte M. Simos. Ed. by Front Desk, LLC Staff. (Illus.). 116p. (Orig.). 1994. pap. write for info. (0-9640120-2-2) Front Desk LLC.
Witchwood Cradle. Esther M. Friesner. 256p. 1987. mass mkt. 3.50 (0-380-75100-3) Avon.
***Witchworks.** Anne M. Rehnert. 596p. (Orig.). 1997. mass mkt. 5.99 (1-55197-787-7, Pub. by Comnwlth Pub CN) Partners Pubs Grp.
Witchy Woman. Steve Brewer. LC 95-33672. 208p. 1996. 21.95 (0-312-14076-2) St Martin.
Witcracks: Jokes & Jests from American Folklore. Alvin Schwartz. (Illus.). 128p. (J). (gr. 4 up). 1973. lib. bdg. 14.89 (0-397-31475-2, Lipp Jr Bks) HarpC Child Bks.
Witenagemot in the Reign of Edward the Confessor: A Study in the Constitutional History of Eleventh-Century England. Trygovi J. Oleson. LC 80-2217. 1981. reprint ed. 32.50 (0-404-18769-2) AMS Pr.
With a Black Platoon in Combat: A Year in Korea. Lyle Rishell. LC 92-27918. (Military History Ser.: No. 29). (Illus.). 200p. 1993. 24.50 (0-89096-526-9) Tex A&M Univ Pr.
***With a Cherry on Top: Daily Devotions for Kids.** Carol Reinsma. LC 96-30007. 87p. (J). 1997. pap. 7.25 (1-56212-236-3, 1701-0403) CRC Pubns.
With a Daughter's Eye: A Memoir of Gregory Bateson & Margaret Mead. Mary C. Bateson. LC 93-39851. (Illus.). 288p. 1994. reprint ed. pap. 13.00 (0-06-097573-3, PL) HarpC.
With a Feather on My Nose. Billie Burke. (American Autobiography Ser.). 272p. 1995. reprint ed. lib. bdg. 79.00 (0-7812-8468-6) Rprt Serv.
With a Flash of His Sword: The Civil War Writings of Holman S. Melcher, 20th Maine Infantry. William B. Styple. LC 94-70662. (Illus.). 358p. (C). 1994. 33.00 (1-883926-00-9) Belle Grv Pub.
With a Fly's Eye, Whale's Wit & Woman's Heart: Animals & Women. Ed. by Theresa Corrigan & Stephanie T. Hoppe. 260p. 1989. pap. 9.95 (0-939416-25-5) Cleis Pr.
With a Gun in Good Country. limited ed. Ian Manning. LC 95-61226. (Illus.). 295p. 1995. 85.00 (0-614-13573-7) Trophy Rm Bks.
***With a Hammer for My Heart.** George E. Lyon. 224p. 1997. 21.95 (0-7894-2460-6) DK Pub Inc.
With a Heart Full of Love: Jack London's Inscriptions to the Women in His Life. limited ed. Jack London. Ed. by Sal Noto. (Illus.). 1986. 75.00 (0-614-17633-6) Twowindows Pr.
With a Little Help from My Friends: The Making of Sgt. Pepper. George Martin & William Pearson. LC 95-75251. (Illus.). 176p. 1995. 22.95 (0-316-54783-2) Little.
***With a Little Help from the Soybean.** Julia Elliott. 63p. 1997. 18.00 (0-9658646-1-8) SCB.
***With a Little Luck.** Alexis. 1993. 20.00 (0-671-70756-6, Pocket Books) PB.
With a Little Luck. Kim Alexis. Ed. by Jane Chelius. 336p. (Orig.). 1994. mass mkt. 5.99 (0-671-70757-4, Pocket Star Bks) PB.
With a Little Luck. Janet Dailey. (Americana Ser.). 1993. mass mkt. 3.59 (0-373-89899-1, 1-89899-8) Harlequin Bks.
With a Little Luck: An American Odyssey. limited ed. Helen F. Boehm. (Illus.). 1985. 35.00 (0-89256-291-9) E M Boehm.
With a Little of Both. Linda Marchisio. (Illus.). 19p. (J). (gr. k-5). 1987. audio 8.95 (0-9624224-0-1) Rainbow Bend.
With a Little of Both. Linda Marchisio. (Illus.). 19p. (J). (ps-5). 1987. teacher ed. 15.95 incl. audio (0-9624224-1-X) Rainbow Bend.
With a Long Spoon: An Over the Edge Adventure. Alison Brooks. (Over the Edge Ser.). 48p. 1994. pap. 8.95 (1-887801-10-3, Atlas Games) Trident MN.
With a Moon in Transit. Jacqueline Osherow. LC 96-18201. 96p. 1996. 18.00 (0-8021-1599-3, Grove) Grove-Atltic.
With a Nugget in My Shoe. Hana J. Barton. (Illus.). 184p. (Orig.). 1997. pap. 16.95 (0-9646326-0-8) Jeffry & Spencer Pub.
With a Poet's Eye: A Tate Gallery Anthology. Ed. by Pat Adams. (Illus.). 164p. 1997. pap. 12.95 (0-295-96783-8) U of Wash Pr.
With a Prehistoric People: A Kikuyu of British East Africa. W. S. Routledge & K. Routledge. (Illus.). 392p. 1968. reprint ed. 49.50 (0-7146-1716-4, Pub. by F Cass Pubs UK) Intl Spec Bk.
With a Quiet Heart: An Autobiography. Eva LeGallienne. LC 74-3745. (Illus.). 311p. 1974. reprint ed. text ed. 59.75 (0-8371-7470-8, LEQH, Greenwood Pr) Greenwood.
With a Servant Heart: Perspectives on Women in Leadership. Bobbie Patterson et al. Ed. by Gina Howard. 86p. (Orig.). 1992. pap. text ed. 3.95 (1-56309-048-1) Womans Mission Union.
***With a Shepherd's Heart.** John R. Sittema. 271p. (Orig.). 1996. pap. 10.00 (0-9653981-0-2) Reformed Fellowship.
With a Single Spell. Lawrence Watt-Evans. (Orig.). 1987. mass mkt. 4.95 (0-345-32616-4, Del Rey) Ballantine.
With a Smile upon His Face: An Inspirational Tale from the Heartland. Mike Delaney. LC 95-83062. 256p. 1996. pap. 10.95 (0-9644007-4-X) Filibuster Pr.
With a Southern Accent. Viola G. Liddell. LC 82-10893. (Library of Alabama Classics). 272p. 1982. pap. 14.95 (0-8173-0130-5) U of Ala Pr.
With a Spot of Tea: Edible Necessities. Susan A. McCreary. (Illus.). 160p. (Orig.). 1997. pap. 14.95 (0-9608428-7-X) Straw Patchwork.
With a Tangled Skein. Piers Anthony. (Incarnations of Immortality Ser.: No. 3). 1986. mass mkt. 5.95 (0-345-31885-4, Del Rey) Ballantine.

An Asterisk (*) at the beginning of an entry indicates that the title is appearing in BIP for the first time.

***With a Thankful Heart.** Alda Ellis. (Remembrance of Times Past Ser.). (Illus.). 16p. (Orig.). 1997. 6.99 (*1-56507-714-8*) Harvest Hse.

With a Voice of Singing. Ed. by COMPAS Staff. (Illus.). 60p. (Orig.). 1992. pap. 5.00 (*0-927663-18-X*) COMPAS.

With a Voice of Singing. M. Shaw. 12p. 1986. pap. 1.25 (*0-7935-5471-3*, 50299170) H Leonard.

With Absolute Respect: The Swedenborgian Theology of Charles Carroll Bonney. George F. Dole & Charles C. Bonney. (Swedenborg Studies: No. 3). 58, vp. 1993. pap. text ed. 6.95 (*0-87785-182-4*) Swedenborg.

With Adjectives see Building English Sentences

With Adverbs see Building English Sentences

With Akhmatova at the Black Gates: Variations. Poems. Stephen Berg. LC 80-14469. 86p. 1981. 14.95 (*0-252-00833-2*) U of Ill Pr.

With All & for the Good of All: The Emergence of Popular Nationalism in the Cuban Communities of the United States, 1848-1898. Gerald E. Poyo. LC 88-21129. (Illus.). xvii, 182p. (C). 1989. text ed. 31.95 (*0-8223-0881-9*) Duke.

***With All Dispatch.** Alexander Kent. 272p. 1989. pap. 14. 95 (*0-330-30837-8*) Trans-Atl Phila.

With All Dispatch. Alexander Kent. 1993. reprint ed. lib. bdg. 25.95 (*1-56849-030-5*) Buccaneer Bks.

With All Holiness. Wilbur Hardwirct. 150p. (Orig.). (C). pap. text ed. 9.95 (*1-883866-05-7*) Clarion Pub.

With All My Heart. Margaret C. Barnes. 23.95 (*0-8488-0783-9*) Amereon Ltd.

***With All My Heart: Reflections on Love.** Ariel Books Staff. 128p. 1997. 5.95 (*0-8362-2950-9*, Arie Bks) Andrews & McMeel.

With All My Heart, with All My Soul. B. D. Da'Ehu. 328p. 1993. 21.95 (*1-880880-01-6*) Israeli Trad.

With All My Love. Mariarosa Guerrini. (C). 1991. 35.00 (*0-85439-411-7*, Pub. by St Paul Pubns UK) St Mut.

With All My Might: An Autobiography. Erskine Caldwell. (Illus.). 368p. 1987. 19.95 (*0-934601-11-9*) Peachtree Pubs.

With All My Might: An Autobiography. deluxe limited ed. Erskine Caldwell. (Illus.). 368p. 1987. 175.00 (*0-934601-21-6*) Peachtree Pubs.

With All My Strength: Dynamic Times with God, Devotions for Men. H. Norman Wright. 380p. (Orig.). 1996. 17.99 (*0-89283-968-6*, Vine Bks) Servant.

With All of Love: Selected Poems. James Blish. Ed. by Keith A. Daniels. LC 95-12340. 208p. 1995. 29.95 (*0-9631203-1-X*) Anamnesis Pr.

With All Our Heart & Mind: The Spiritual Works of Mercy in a Psychological Age. Sidney Callahan. LC 87-34574. 176p. (Orig.). 1988. pap. 8.95 (*0-8245-0971-4*) Crossroad NY.

With All Purity: What You Need to Know about Sexual Ethics. rev. ed. Stanley Rickard. LC 89-29357. 30p. 1989. pap. text ed. 1.95 (*0-87227-139-0*, RBP5123) Reg Baptist.

With All Thy Heart: The Sacred Summoning. Irina Starr. 112p. 1991. 10.95 (*0-930596-04-8*) Pilgrims Path.

With All Your Possessions: Jewish Ethics & Economic Life. Meir Tamari. LC 86-22964. 1987. 40.00 (*0-02-932150-6*, Free Press) Free Pr.

With Americans of Past & Present Days. Jean A. Jusserand. LC 73-156669. (Essay Index Reprint Ser.). 1977. reprint ed. 22.95 (*0-8369-2555-6*) Ayer.

With an Air Debonair: Musical Theatre in America, 1785-1815. Susan L. Porter. LC 90-24921. (Illus.). 648p. (C). 1991. text ed. 59.95 (*1-56098-063-X*) Smithsonian.

***With an Everlasting Love: Promise That You'll Love Me...** Kay Arthur. 144p. 1997. 12.99 (*1-56507-633-8*) Harvest Hse.

With an Extreme Burning. Bill Pronzini. 304p. 1994. 19.95 (*0-7867-0139-0*) Carroll & Graf.

With an Extreme Burning. large type ed. Bill Pronzini. LC 95-7489. 536p. 1995. lib. bdg. 22.95 (*0-7862-0460-5*) Thorndike Pr.

***With an Eye on the Future: Development & Mission in the 21st Century.** Ed. by Duane Elmer & Lois McKinney. 272p. 1996. pap. 24.95 (*0-912552-99-9*) MARC.

With & Without. Jeffrey Sweet. 1997. pap. 5.25 (*0-8222-1558-6*) Dramatists Play.

With Angels to the Rear: An Informal Portrait of Early Meadowdale. Delmar H. Caryl. 172p. 1989. pap. 9.95 (*0-87770-475-9*) Ye Galleon.

With Angels to the Rear: An Informal Portrait of Early Meadowdale. Delmar H. Caryl. 172p. 1989. 14.95 (*0-87770-588-7*) Ye Galleon.

With Anger - With Love. Sherman. 1990. pap. 2.50 (*0-913142-05-0*) Mulch Pr.

With Anger, with Love. Susan Sherman. pap. 3.50 (*0-685-03752-5*) Out & Out.

With Anger, with Love - Selections: Poems & Prose (1963-1973) Susan Sherman. LC 74-77761. (Haystack Bks.). 78p. 1974. pap. 3.50 (*0-685-04482-3*) Mulch Pr.

With Auxiliary Verbs see Building English Sentences

With Baby in Mind. Arlene James. (Special Edition Ser.). 1994. mass mkt. 3.50 (*0-373-09869-3*, 5-09869-4) Silhouette.

With Banners Unfurled. William Hull. (Illus.). 53p. (Orig.). 1991. pap. 10.95 (*1-877871-15-X*) Ed Ministries.

With Be see Building English Sentences

With Bible & Spade, II. Walter E. Sabins. (Illus.). (Orig.). 1988. pap. 4.75 (*1-55673-077-2*, 8874) CSS OH.

With Bitter Herbs They Shall Eat It: Chemical Ecology & the Origins of Human Diet & Medicine. Timothy A. Johns. LC 96-20505. (Arizona Studies in Human Ecology). 356p. 1990. 50.00 (*0-8165-1023-7*) U of Ariz Pr.

With Bleeding Footsteps: Mary Baker Eddy's Path to Religious Leadership. Robert D. Thoreau. LC 92-39053. 1994. 27.50 (*0-679-41495-9*) Knopf.

With Bodilie Eyes: Eschatological Themes in Puritan Literature & Gravestone Art. David H. Watters. LC 81-16466. (Studies in the Fine Arts: Iconography: No. 3). (Illus.). 269p. reprint ed. pap. 76.70 (*0-8357-1249-4*, 2070247) Bks Demand.

***With Bold Knife & Fork.** M. F. Fisher. 1996. 10.98 (*0-7651-9830-4*) Smithmark.

***With Bold Strokes: Boyer Gonzales, 1864-1934.** Edward Simmen. LC 96-46066. (Illus.). 200p. (C). 1997. text ed. 34.95 (*0-89096-739-3*) Tex A&M Univ Pr.

With Borges on an Ordinary Evening in Buenos Aires: A Memoir. Willis Barnstone. 208p. (C). 1992. 27.50 (*0-252-01888-5*) U of Ill Pr.

With Both Eyes Shut Everything Looks the Same. Thomas Camp. 300p. 1992. 19.95 (*1-878208-16-0*) Guild Pr IN.

***With British Snipers to the Reich.** C. Shore. LC 97-2561. 1997. write for info. (*1-85367-292-0*) Stackpole.

With Broadax & Firebrand: The Destruction of the Brazilian Atlantic Forest. Warren Dean. LC 94-5681. 1995. 38.00 (*0-520-08775-5*) U CA Pr.

***With Broadax & Firebrand: The Destruction of the Brazilian Atlantic Forest.** Warren Dean. LC 94-5681. (Illus.). 1997. pap. 16.95 (*0-520-20886-2*) U CA Pr.

With Brush & Canvas in Queensland National Parks. Joan Starr. 71p. (C). 1990. 90.00 (*0-86439-090-4*, Pub. by Boolarong Pubns AT) St Mut.

With Burning Hearts: A Meditation on the Eucharistic Life. Henri J. Nouwen. LC 94-14622. 96p. 1994. 16.00 (*0-88344-984-6*) Orbis Bks.

With Byrd at the Bottom of the World: The South Pole Expedition of 1928-1930. Norman D. Vaughan & Cecil B. Murphey. LC 89-26182. (Illus.). 224p. 1990. 22.95 (*0-8117-1904-9*) Stackpole.

With Caesar's Legions. Reuben F. Wells. LC 60-16709. (Illus.). (J). (gr. 7-11). 1951. pap. 19.00 (*0-8196-0110-1*) Biblo.

With Calculator 1988: Grade 4. Fennell. 1998. student ed. 53.75 (*0-03-010917-5*) HB Schl Dept.

With Calculator 1988: Grade 6. Fennell. 1988. student ed. 53.75 (*0-03-010919-1*) HB Schl Dept.

With Calculator 1988: Grades 5. Fennell. 1988. student ed. 53.75 (*0-03-010918-3*) HB Schl Dept.

***With Cat for Comforter.** Ray Bradbury. LC 97-8081. (Illus.). 32p. 1997. 9.95 (*0-87905-752-1*, Peregrine Smith) Gibbs Smith Pub.

***With Charity for All: Lincoln & the Restoration of the Union.** William C. Harris. LC 96-35903. 336p. 1997. text ed. 37.95 (*0-8131-2007-1*) U Pr of Ky.

With Charity for All: Welfare & Society, Ancient Times to the Present. Meritt Ierley. LC 84-11469. 236p. 1984. text ed. 55.00 (*0-275-91194-2*, Praeger Pubs) Greenwood.

With Charity Toward None: A Fond Look at Misanthropy. Florence King. 208p. 1993. pap. 9.95 (*0-312-09414-0*) St Martin.

***With Chatwin: Portrait of a Writer.** Susannah Clapp. 1997. 23.00 (*0-679-41033-3*) Knopf.

***With Chennault in China: A Flying Tiger's Story.** Robert M. Smith. 176p. 1997. 29.95 (*0-7643-0287-6*) Schiffer.

With Child. Illus. by Bernie Kida et al. LC 95-41110. 1995. write for info. (*1-56796-135-5*) Childbirth Graphics.

With Child. Laurie R. King. LC 95-41355. 240p. 1996. 21. 95 (*0-312-14077-0*, Thomas Dunne Bks) St Martin.

***With Child: A Kate Martinelli Mystery.** Laurie R. King. 1997. mass mkt. 5.99 (*0-553-57458-2*) Bantam.

With Child in Mind: Studies of the Personal Encounter with Infertility. Margarete Sandelowski. LC 92-48536. (Studies in Health, Illness, & Caregiving). 328p. (Orig.). (C). 1993. text ed. 44.95 (*0-8122-3197-X*); pap. text ed. 16.95 (*0-8122-1415-3*) U of Pa Pr.

***With Children on the Spiritual Journey.** Catherine Stonehouse. 256p. Date not set. pap. 15.99 (*0-8010-5807-4*) Baker Bks.

With Christ in the School & the Ministry of Praying. Zacharias T. Fomum. 1992. 14.95 (*0-533-09575-1*) Vantage.

With Christ in the School of Prayer. Andrew Murray. 288p. 1981. mass mkt. 5.99 (*0-88368-106-4*) Whitaker Hse.

With Christ in the School of Prayer. large type ed. Andrew Murray. (Large Print Inspirational Ser.). 1987. pap. 9.95 (*0-8027-2600-3*) Walker & Co.

With Christ the Sun Rose in My Life. 3rd ed. Elizabeth Harris-Charity. Ed. by Samuel Tanguma et al. (Illus.). 122p. 1988. reprint ed. pap. 9.95 (*0-9651866-0-1*) Youth Corp.

***With Christmas Joy.** Ed. by Carole Flatau. 28p. (Orig.). (C). 1997. pap. text ed. 5.95 (*0-7692-0173-3*, EL9745) Warner Brothers.

With Churchills to War: 48th Battalion Royal Tank Regiment at War 1939-45. Peter Gudgin. (Illus.). 224p. 1996. 30.95 (*0-7509-1239-1*, Pub. by Sutton Pubng UK) Bks Intl VA.

***With Cloak & Dagger.** H. H. Meyers. 213p. (Orig.). 1995. pap. 9.95 (*0-923309-28-4*) Hartland Pubns.

With Compass & Chain. Joseph W. Ernst. Ed. by Stuart Bruchey. LC 78-56727. (Management of Public Lands in the U. S. Ser.). 1979. lib. bdg. 31.95 (*0-405-11331-5*) Ayer.

With Compassion Toward Some: Homosexuality & Social Work in America. Ed. by Robert Schoenberg et al. LC 85-5838. (Journal of Social Work & Human Sexuality Ser.: Vol. 2, Nos. 2 & 3). 156p. 1985. reprint ed. pap. 14.95 (*0-918393-14-0*) Harrington Pk.

With Courage: The U.S. Army Air Forces in World War II. Bernard C. Nalty et al. Ed. by Alfred M. Beck. LC 94-4716. (General Histories Ser.). 1995. 31.00 (*0-16-036396-9*, 008-070-00663-4) USGPO.

With Courage & Love: A Journal for Birthmother's. Janet Sieff. (Illus.). 12p. 1993. pap. 5.10 (*1-56123-064-2*) Centering Corp.

With Crockett at the Alamo: Poems. M. L. Hester. LC 95-34309. 1995. write for info. (*0-936389-38-9*); pap. write for info. (*0-936389-35-4*) Tudor Pubs.

With Crook at the Rosebud. J. W. Vaughn. 1994. 19.95 (*0-8117-1911-1*) Stackpole.

***With Custer on Little Big Horn.** William O. Taylor. 1997. pap. 14.95 (*0-14-025576-1*) Viking Penguin.

With Custer on the Little Bighorn. William O. Taylor. 1996. 23.95 (*0-614-96816-X*, Viking) Viking Penguin.

With Custer on the Little Bighorn: By One Who Was There Engaged. William O. Taylor. Ed. by Greg Martin. LC 95-52413. 208p. 1996. pap. 27.95 (*0-670-86803-5*, Viking) Viking Penguin.

***With Custer on the Little Bighorn: The First - & Only - Eyewitness Account Ever.** William O. Taylor. 1997. pap. 14.95 (*0-614-27381-1*) Penguin.

With Custer's Cavalry. Katherine G. Fougera. LC 86-4307. (Illus.). 319p. 1986. reprint ed. pap. 10.95 (*0-8032-6860-2*, Bison Books) U of Nebr Pr.

With Dandelions to Tell the Hours. H. J. Adams. LC 92-71977. (Illus.). 160p. 1992. lib. bdg. 12.95 (*0-923687-20-3*) Celo Valley Bks.

With Daring Faith. Rebecca H. Davis. Ed. by Suzette Jordan. (Light Line Ser.). (Illus.). 187p. (Orig.). (J). 1987. pap. 6.49 (*0-89084-414-3*, 033167) Bob Jones Univ Pr.

With Deadly Intent. Louise Hendricksen. 304p. 1993. mass mkt. 3.99 (*0-8217-4408-9*, Zebra Kensgtn) Kensgtn Pub Corp.

With Deepest Sympathy. Ed. by Helen Exley. (So-Much-More-Than-a-Card Ser.). (Illus.). 28p. (Orig.). 1995. pap. 2.99 (*1-85015-677-8*) Exley Giftbooks.

With Difference Eyes: Insights into Teaching Language Minority Students Across the Disciplines. Ed. by Faye Peitzman & George Gadda. LC 93-33727. 1994. 17.95 (*0-8013-1311-2*) Longman.

With Different Eyes: Insights into Teaching Language Minority Students. F. Pertzman & G. Gadder. 137p. 1994. pap. text ed. 21.32 (*0-8013-1282-5*) Longman.

With Dignity: The Search for Medicare & Medicaid. Sheri I. David. LC 84-27941. (Contributions in Political Science Ser.: No. 12). xiv, 194p. 1985. text ed. 49.95 (*0-313-24720-X*, DWD/, Greenwood Pr) Greenwood.

With Domingo Leal in San Antonio, 1734. Marian L. Martinello & Samuel P. Nesmith. Ed. by Institute of Texan Cultures Research Staff. (University of Texas Institute of Texan Culture Young Readers Ser.). (Illus.). 78p. (Orig.). (J). (gr. 5-8). 1980. pap. 3.95 (*0-933164-40-8*) U of Tex Inst Tex Culture.

With Each Caress: Casanova's Master, 2 vols. in 1. Anne Silverlock. 368p. 1992. reprint ed. mass mkt., pap. text ed. 4.50 (*0-8439-3338-0*) Dorchester Pub Co.

With Each Clouded Peak. Friederike Mayrocker. Tr. by Rosmarie Waldrop & Harriett Watts from ENG. (Classics Ser.: No. 116). 86p. (Orig.). 1997. pap. 11.95 (*1-55713-277-1*) Sun & Moon CA.

With Each Passing Moment. Mary Higginbotham. pap. 1.25 (*0-686-12748-X*) Grace Pub Co.

With Each Remembrance: A Selection of Writings on Memories. Flavia M. Weedn. (Illus.). 90p. reprint ed. 10.00 (*0-929632-08-7*) Applause Inc.

With Eagles to Glory: Napoleon & His German Allies in the 1809 Campaign. John H. Gill. LC 92-29541. 576p. 1992. 50.00 (*1-85367-130-4*, 5609) Stackpole.

With Ears Opening Like Morning Glories: Eudora Welty & the Love of Storytelling. Carol S. Manning. LC 85-921. (Contributions in Women's Studies: No. 58). xv, 221p. 1985. text ed. 55.00 (*0-313-24776-5*, MWE/, Greenwood Pr) Greenwood.

With Ears to Hear: Preaching As Self-Persuasion. Robin R. Meyers. LC 92-42040. 176p. (Orig.). 1993. pap. 12.95 (*0-8298-0951-1*) Pilgrim OH.

With Eisenstein in Hollywood. Ivor Montagu. 356p. 1969. pap. 1.95 (*0-7178-0220-5*) Intl Pubs Co.

With Emphasis on Intangibles. Howard E. Seals. 1968. pap. 4.00 (*0-9600232-0-8*) H E Seals.

With Empty Hands: The Message of Therese of Lisieux. Conrad De Meester. 122p. 1994. pap. 21.00 (*0-86012-160-7*, Pub. by Srch Pr UK) St Mut.

***With Every Breath.** Beverly Bird. 448p. 1997. mass mkt. 5.50 (*0-06-101113-4*, Harp PBks) HarpC.

With Every Drop of Blood: A Novel of the Civil War. James L. Collier & Christopher Collier. 256p. (J). 1997. mass mkt. 4.99 (*0-440-21983-3*) Dell.

With Extreme Prejudice. Conor Cregan. 389p. 1996. pap. 10.95 (*0-340-62305-5*, Pub. by H & S UK) Trafalgar.

With Eyes of Faith: An Introduction to Eastern Theology. 104p. (Orig.). 1985. pap. text ed. 7.00 (*1-887158-03-0*) God With Us.

With Eyes to See: A Journey from Religion to Spirituality. Arthur Melville. 384p. 1992. pap. 13.95 (*0-913299-85-5*) Stillpoint.

With Eyes to See: Church & World in the Third Millenium. Walbert Buhlmann. LC 90-35563. 1990. pap. 17.00 (*0-88344-683-9*) Orbis Bks.

With Eyes to See: Church & World in the Third Millennium. Walbert Buhlmann. 176p. (C). 1990. text ed. 49.00 (*0-85439-342-0*, Pub. by St Paul Pubns UK) St Mut.

With Eyes Toward Zion: Scholars Colloquium on America-Holy Land Studies. Ed. by Moshe Davis. LC 77-2493. (America & the Holy Land Ser.). (Illus.). 1977. lib. bdg. 23.95 (*0-405-10312-3*) Ayer.

With Eyes Toward Zion - Two: Themes & Sources in the Archives of the United States, Breat Britain, Turkey & Israel. Ed. by Moshe Davis. LC 85-28288. (Illus.). 434p. 1986. text ed. 55.00 (*0-275-92090-9*, C2090, Praeger Pubs) Greenwood.

With Eyes Toward ZionFour: America & the Holy Land. Moshe Davis. LC 94-28005. 208p. 1995. text ed. 55.00 (*0-275-94621-5*, Praeger Pubs) Greenwood.

With Face to the Wall. Miltos Sahtouris. Tr. by Kimon Friar. 1980. 7.50 (*0-910350-10-8*) Charioteer.

With Faith & Fury. Delos B. McKown. LC 84-43180. 440p. 1985. 28.95 (*0-87975-280-7*) Prometheus Bks.

With Faith & Physic: The Life of a Tudor Gentlewoman - Lady Grace Mildmay, 1552-1620. Grace Mildmay. Ed. by Linda Pollock. 179p. 1994. 55.00 (*1-85585-071-0*) Trafalgar.

With Faith & Physics: The Life of a Tudor Gentlewoman, Lady Grace Mildmay, 1552-1620. Linda Pollock. LC 94-24503. 179p. 1995. text ed. 45.00 (*0-312-12519-4*) St Martin.

With Fiddle & Well-Rosined Bow: Old-Time Fiddling in Alabama. Joyce H. Cauthen. LC 87-38080. (Illus.). 295p. 1989. reprint ed. pap. 84.10 (*0-608-01686-1*, 2062342) Bks Demand.

With Fire. Kyle Carter. LC 94-19067. (J). 1994. write for info. (*1-57103-076-X*) Rourke Pr.

With Fire & Sword. Henryk Sienkiewicz. 1152p. 1993. pap. 20.00 (*0-02-082044-5*) Macmillan.

With Fire & Sword. S. H. Byers. LC 92-60389. (Illus.). 225p. 1992. reprint ed. 20.00 (*0-9628936-2-5*) Pr Camp Pope.

With Fire & Sword: Italian Spectacles on American Screens, 1958-1968. Patrick Luciano. LC 93-43344. 1994. 67.50 (*0-8108-2816-2*) Scarecrow.

With Firmness in the Right: American Diplomatic Action Affecting Jews, 1840-1945. Cyrus Adler & Aaron M. Margalith. Ed. by Moshe Davis. LC 77-70651. (America & the Holy Land Ser.). 1977. reprint ed. lib. bdg. 44.95 (*0-405-10222-4*) Ayer.

With Fortitude: Poems for James Weldon Johnson. Stephen C. Wright. 20p. (Orig.). 1991. pap. 5.00 (*1-879025-04-3*) Christopher-Burghardt.

With Freedom Fired: The Story of Robert Robinson, Cambridge Nonconformist. G. W. Hughes. 123p. 1955. reprint ed. 4.50 (*0-87921-018-4*) Attic Pr.

With Freedom to Singapore. Oswald W. Gilmour. LC 70-79200. reprint ed. 37.50 (*0-404-54829-6*) AMS Pr.

With Friends. Susan Florence. (Illus.). 1992. 6.95 (*0-8378-2461-3*) Gibson.

With Friends Like That. Emily Chase. (Girls of Canby Hall Ser.: No. 11). 192p. (Orig.). (J). (gr. 7 up). 1985. pap. 2.25 (*0-590-40869-0*) Scholastic Inc.

With Friends Like That. Michael Fairley. LC 80-22068. 14. 95 (*0-87949-194-9*) Ashley Bks.

***With Friends Like These.** Coleridge. LC 97-16646. 1997. 24.95 (*0-312-17066-1*) St Martin.

With Friends Like These... Alan Dean Foster. 1984. mass mkt. 5.99 (*0-345-32390-4*, Del Rey) Ballantine.

With Friends Like These... Gillian Roberts & Alan D. Foster. LC 92-97480. 256p. 1994. mass mkt. 4.99 (*0-345-37784-2*) Ballantine.

With Friends Like These: Reagan, Bush, & Saddam, 1982-1990. Bruce W. Jentleson. LC 94-1610. 1994. 23.00 (*0-393-03665-0*) Norton.

With Friends Like These: Regan, Bush, & Saddam, 1982-1990. Bruce W. Jentleson. 220p. (C). 1995. per., pap. text ed. 11.95 (*0-393-96712-3*) Norton.

With Friends Like These: The Jewish Critics of Israel. Edward Alexander. 1991. pap. 12.95 (*1-56171-056-3*) Sure Seller.

With Friends Like These...Marxism & Gay Politics. Simon Edge. 1995. pap. 7.95 (*0-304-33320-4*, Pub. by Cassell Pubng UK) LPC InBook.

With Friends Like You: What Israelis Really Think about American Jews. Matti Golan. Tr. by Hillel Halkin from HEB. LC 92-22615. 1992. 22.95 (*0-02-912064-0*, Free Press) Free Pr.

***With Full Honors.** Donald E. McQuinn. 1997. mass mkt. 5.99 (*0-345-40045-3*, Del Rey) Ballantine.

With Fury Poured Out: The Power of the Powerless During the Holocaust. Bernard Maza. 256p. 1988. 24.95 (*0-944007-23-6*); pap. 12.95 (*0-944007-13-9*) Sure Seller.

With General Chennault: The Story of the Flying Tigers in World War II. Robert Hotz. 1980. reprint ed. 25.95 (*0-89201-095-9*) Zenger Pub.

With Generosity & Silence: Recollections of a Victorian Rebel. Elizabeth Delehanty. (Illus.). 104p. (Orig.). 1993. pap. write for info. (*0-9632687-1-6*) PenRose Pub.

***With Generous Hearts: How to Raise Capital Funds for Your Church, Church School or Charity.** Glenn Holliman. 80p. 1997. pap. 7.95 (*0-8192-1722-0*) Morehouse Pub.

***With Glad & Generous Hearts.** 11.85 (*0-687-61318-3*) Abingdon.

With Glad & Generous Hearts. William H. Willimon. 176p. 1986. pap. 8.95 (*0-8358-0536-0*, ICN 613183) Upper Room Bks.

With Glory & Honor: Catechesis on the Mystery of Crowning. (Illus.). 23p. (Orig.). 1985. pap. text ed. 4.50 (*1-56125-000-7*) Educ Services.

With God All Things Are Possible. Life-Study Fellowship Staff. 304p. 1984. mass mkt. 5.99 (*0-553-26249-1*) Bantam.

With God & with Meni Prayers. Adrienne Von Speyer. LC 95-79356. 134p. (Orig.). 1995. pap. 9.95 (*0-89870-563-0*) Ignatius Pr.

With God for the People: The Autogiography of...As Told to David Porter. Laszlo Tokes. 226p. 1990. pap. 9.95 (*0-340-54152-0*, Pub. by Hodder & Stoughton Ltd UK) Lubrecht & Cramer.

With God in Hell: Judaism in the Ghettos & Deathcamps. Eliezer Berkovits. 1979. 10.95 (*0-88482-937-5*) Hebrew Pub.

***With God in Russia: My 23 Years in Siberian Prison Camps.** Walter Ciszek. 1997. pap. text ed. 14.95 (*0-89870-574-6*) Ignatius Pr.

With God in Solitary Confinement. Richard Wurmbrand. 1979. pap. 7.00 (*0-88264-002-X*) Living Sacrifice Bks.

W

***With God on Our Side.** Robert Kelly. 118p. 1996. pap. text ed. 10.95 (*1-85390-263-2*) Ignatius Pr.

With God on Our Side. Anthony Tuttle. 1978. mass mkt. 2.25 (*0-89083-324-9*, Zebra Kensgtn) Kensgtn Pub Corp.

With God on Our Side: The Rise of the Religious Right in America. William Martin. 352p. 1996. 27.50 (*0-553-06745-1*) Bantam.

***With God on Our Side: The Rise of the Religious Right in America.** William Martin. 432p. 1997. pap. 15.00 (*0-553-06749-4*) Broadway BDD.

With God's Help Flowers Bloom. Elaine Anderson. 1978. pap. 6.25 (*0-89137-411-6*); student ed. 3.50 (*0-89137-412-4*) Quality Pubns.

With God's Oldest Friends: Pastoral Visiting in the Nursing Home. Henry C. Simmons & Mark Peters. 128p. 1996. pap. 8.95 (*0-8091-3636-8*, 3636-8) Paulist Pr.

With Good Heart: Yaqui Beliefs & Ceremonies in Pascua, Village. Muriel T. Painter. Ed. by Edward H. Spicer & Wilma Kaemlein. LC 86-893. (Illus.). 533p. 1986. 50.95 (*0-8165-0875-5*) U of Ariz Pr.

***With Good Intentions: Quaker Work among the Pawnees, Otos, & Omahas in the 1870's.** Clyde A. Milner, II. LC 81-16238. (Illus.). 262p. 1982. reprint ed. pap. 74.70 (*0-608-03992-6*, 2064724) Bks Demand.

With Good Reason. 5th ed. S. Morris Engel. 1994. teacher ed., pap. text ed. 15.00 (*0-312-09547-3*); teacher ed., pap. text ed. 5.00 (*0-312-09552-X*) St Martin.

***With Good Reason.** 6th ed. Engel. Date not set. pap. text ed. write for info. (*0-312-15758-4*) St Martin.

With Good Reason: An Introduction to Informal Fallacies. 5th ed. S. Morris Engel. 288p. 1994. pap. text ed. 16.00 (*0-312-08479-X*) St Martin.

With Grant & Meade from the Wilderness to Appomattox. Theodore Lyman. Ed. & Selected by George R. Agassiz. LC 93-45368. (Illus.). xxiv, 371p. 1994. pap. 13.95 (*0-8032-7935-3*, Bison Books) U of Nebr Pr.

With Hand & Heart: The Courtship Letters of Franklin B. Hough & Mariah Kilham, January-May, 1849. Ed. by Vivian G. Smith. LC 93-21786. 124p. 1993. 19.95 (*0-925168-15-7*); pap. 14.95 (*0-925168-03-3*) North Country.

With Harney on the Blue Water. Fred H. Werner. 1988. pap. 8.95 (*0-933147-09-0*) Werner Pubn.

With Head & Heart: The Story of Howard Thurman. Howard Thurman. LC 79-1848. (Illus.). 296p. 1981. pap. 15.95 (*0-15-697648-X*, Harvest Bks) HarBrace.

With Heart & Hand: A Manual for Women in God's Service. Beneth Jones & Bobbie Yearick. LC 92-24757. 287p. (C). 1992. pap. 10.95 (*0-89084-641-3*, 062265) Bob Jones Univ Pr.

With Heart & Hand: The Black Church Working to Save Black Children. Susan D. Newman. LC 94-39334. 96p. 1995. pap. 9.00 (*0-8170-1223-0*) Judson.

***With Heart & Mind.** Helen R. Neinast. 22.25 (*0-687-61393-0*) Abingdon.

With Heart & Mind: A Personal Synthesis of Scholarship & Devotion. Kenneth L. Pike. LC 96-15101. 1996. pap. write for info. (*1-887493-06-9*) Adult Lrng Systs.

With Heart & Mind & Soul. Helen R. Neinast & Tom Ettinger. 250p. 1994. pap. 14.95 (*0-8358-0695-2*) Upper Room Bks.

With Heart & Soul: Recipes Created by & Designed to be Shared Among Friends. Roxie Kelley. (Illus.). 174p. 1995. 24.95 (*1-884793-04-5*) Cracom.

With Hearts Light as Feathers: The First Reconciliation of Children. Joseph M. Champlin et al. 12p. (Orig.). 1995. pap. 7.95 (*0-8245-1471-8*) Crossroad NY.

***With Her in Ourland: Sequel to Herland.** Ed. by Charlotte Perkins Gilman et al. LC 96-51135. (Contributions in Women's Studies: Vol. 159). 216p. 1997. text ed. 55.00 (*0-313-27614-5*, Greenwood Pr) Greenwood.

***With Her in Ourland: Sequel to Herland.** Michael Hill. Ed. by Charlotte P. Gilman & Mary J. Deegan. LC 96-51135. 216p. 1997. pap. text ed. 15.95 (*0-275-96077-3*, Praeger Pubs) Greenwood.

With Heroic Truth: The Life of Edward R. Murrow. Norman H. Finkelstein. LC 94-25128. (J). 1997. 17.95 (*0-395-67891-9*, Clarion Bks) HM.

With Him in Life's Struggles: A Woman's Study on the Faithfulness of God from Second Samuel. Myrna Alexander. 128p. (Orig.). 1994. pap. 7.99 (*0-929239-92-X*) Discovery Hse Pubs.

With His Pistol in His Hand: A Border Ballad & Its Hero. Americo Paredes. (Illus.). 275p. 1958. pap. 11.95 (*0-292-70128-4*) U of Tex Pr.

***With His Ring.** Jessica Steele. (Romance Ser.: No. 3459). 1997. mass mkt. 3.25 (*0-373-03459-8*, 1-03459-4) Harlequin Bks.

***With His Ring.** Jessica Steele. 1997. 20.95 (*0-263-14888-2*) Thorndike Pr.

With History - Social Science for All: Access for Every Student. California Department of Education Staff. (Illus.). 74p. 1992. pap. 8.00 (*0-8011-1016-5*) Calif Education.

With History Around Me: Spokane Nostalgia. Lois Ryker. 76p. 1979. pap. 9.95 (*0-87770-229-2*) Ye Galleon.

***With Honor & Purpose.** Kerby. Date not set. write for info. (*0-312-18224-4*) St Martin.

With House in Hand: A Step-by-Step Planner for Home or Office. 5th ed. Marcia McAlister. (Illus.). 54p. (Orig.). Date not set. reprint ed. pap. 13.95 (*0-9615587-1-7*) M McAlister Enterps.

With Integrity of Heart: Living Values in Changing Times. fac. ed. Clifford A. Elliott. LC 91-289. 145p. 1991. pap. 41.40 (*0-7837-7708-6*, 2047467) Bks Demand.

With Intent. Laurence Henderson. 187p. 1989. reprint ed. pap. 5.95 (*0-89733-321-7*) Academy Chi Pubs.

***With Intent to Kill.** large type ed. Frances Ferguson. (Ulverscroft Large Print Ser.). 528p. 1997. 27.50 (*0-7089-3772-1*) Ulverscroft.

With Ironside in North Russia. Andrew Soutar. LC 77-115585. (Russia Observed, Series I). 1970. reprint ed. 18.95 (*0-405-03062-2*) Ayer.

With Issa: Poems, 1964-71. Nelson Ball. 120p. (C). 1991. pap. 12.00 (*1-55022-146-9*, Pub. by ECW Press CN) Genl Dist Srvs.

With Jah Rastafari As My Witness: Traitors in Babylon - I'll Never Betray My People. Ricardo A. Scott. (Ras Cardo Speaks on the Issues Ser.). (Illus.). 75p. (Orig.). Date not set. pap. write for info. (*1-883427-58-4*) Crnerstone GA.

***With Jesus Every Day: Daily Devotions Through the Year.** Rudolph F. Norden. LC 97-7999. 1997. write for info. (*0-570-04987-3*) Concordia.

With Jesus in the World: Mission in Modern, Affluent Societies. Wilbert R. Shenk. LC 92-16599. 144p. (Orig.). 1992. pap. 9.99 (*0-8361-3599-7*) Herald Pr.

With Jesus Through Galilee According to the Fifth Gospel. Bargil Pixner. LC 95-50709. (Illus.). 136p. 1996. pap. 24.95 (*0-8146-2427-8*) Liturgical Pr.

***With Jesus to Calvary: Four Bible Studies for Lent.** Hugh McGinley. 24p. (Orig.). 1996. pap. 5.95 (*1-86407-112-5*, Pub. by JBCE AT) Morehouse Pub.

With Joy & Wonder: Ante-Bellum Taste in the Bluegrass. Estill C. Pennington. (Illus.). 24p. 1992. pap. text ed. 3.50 (*1-882007-04-2*) Univ KY Art Mus.

With Joy Our Spirits Sing: The Hymns of Rae E. Whitney. Rae E. Whitney. 125p. 1995. pap. 12.00 (*0-9622553-4-3*, 125-401) Selah Pub Co.

With Joy, Poems for Children. rev. ed. Ed. by Theodore E. Wade, Jr. LC 88-72233. (Illus.). 48p. (J). (gr. k-7). 1988. pap. 2.00 (*0-930192-20-6*) Gazelle Pubns.

With Just Cause: Unionization of the American Journalist. Walter M. Brasch. 511p. (Orig.). (C). 1991. pap. text ed. 34.50 (*0-8191-8361-X*); lib. bdg. 57.50 (*0-8191-8360-1*) U Pr of Amer.

***With Justice for All? The Nature of the American Legal System.** LC 96-49653. 1997. 36.00 (*0-13-618349-2*) P-H.

With Justice for None. Gerry L. Spence. 384p. 1990. pap. 12.95 (*0-14-013325-9*, Penguin Bks) Viking Penguin.

With Justice for None: Destroying an American Myth. Gerry L. Spence. 1990. 9.95 (*0-685-47606-5*) NAL-Dutton.

With Justice for None: Destroying an American Myth. Gerry L. Spence. (Illus.). 320p. 1989. 19.95 (*0-8129-1696-4*, Times Bks) Random.

With Justice for Some: Protecting Victims in Criminal Trials. George P. Fletcher. 288p. 1995. 24.00 (*0-201-62254-8*) Addison-Wesley.

With Justice for Some: Protecting Victims Rights in Criminal Trials. George P. Fletcher. 352p. 1996. pap. 14.00 (*0-201-40822-8*) Addison-Wesley.

With Kindest Regards: The Correspondence of Charles Lang Freer & James McNeill Whistler, 1890-1903. Ed. by Linda Merrill. LC 94-48202. (Illus.). 224p. 1995. text ed. 21.95 (*1-56098-532-1*) Smithsonian.

With Kitchener to Khartoum. G. W. Steevens. 368p. 1990. 135.00 (*1-85077-161-8*, Pub. by Darf Pubs Ltd UK) St Mut.

With Lawrence in Arabia. Lowell Thomas. 27.95 (*0-8488-1205-0*) Amereon Ltd.

***With Lee in Virginia.** rev. ed. G. A. Henty. LC 96-77552. (Illus.). 410p. (J). (gr. 4-7). 1997. pap. text ed. 19.95 (*0-9652735-5-5*) Lost Classics.

***With Lee in Virginia: A Story of the American Civil War.** G. A. Henty. (Illus.). 337p. 1997. 20.00 (*1-887159-09-6*) Preston-Speed.

***With Liberty & Justice for All: Christian Politics Made Simple.** 2nd ed. Joseph Morecroft, III. (C). 1995. pap. 7.95 (*0-925591-37-8*) Covenant Hse Bks.

With Liberty & Justice for Some: A Critique of the Conservative Supreme Court. David Kairys. LC 92-50820. 256p. 1993. 25.00 (*1-56584-071-2*); pap. 12.95 (*1-56584-059-3*) New Press NY.

With Liberty & Justice for Whom? The Recent Evangelical Debate over Capitalism. fac. ed. Craig M. Gay. LC 91-9781. 288p. 1991. reprint ed. pap. 82.10 (*0-7837-7955-0*, 2047711) Bks Demand.

With Life & Laughter: The Life of Father Pro. Gerald Muller. LC 96-2915. 168p. (Orig.). 1996. pap. 9.95 (*0-8198-8281-X*) Pauline Bks.

With Light & with Might. Shalom Dovbaer Schneersohn Obm. Ed. & Tr. by Uri Kaploun. Tr. by Eliyahu Touger. 128p. (Orig.). 1993. 9.00 (*0-8266-0533-8*) Kehot Pubn Soc.

With Literacy & Justice for All: Recovering the Social in Language & Education. Carole Edelsky. Ed. by Allan Luke. (Critical Perspectives on Literacy & Education Ser.). 224p. 1991. 65.00 (*1-85000-664-4*, Falmer Pr); pap. 24.00 (*1-85000-665-2*, Falmer Pr) Taylor & Francis.

With Literacy & Justice for All: Rethinking the Social in Language & Education. Carole Edelsky. LC 96-18054. 272p. 1996. pap. 24.95 (*0-7484-0583-6*, Pub. by Tay Francis Ltd UK) Taylor & Francis.

With Literacy & Justice for All: Rethinking the Social in Language & Education. 2nd ed. Carole Edelsky. LC 96-18054. 272p. 1996. 64.95 (*0-7484-0582-8*, Pub. by Tay Francis Ltd UK) Taylor & Francis.

With Lord Byron in the Sandwich Islands. James Macrae. 90p. 1972. reprint ed. 9.00 (*0-912180-14-5*) Petroglyph.

With Louis & the Duke: The Autobiography of a Jazz Clarinetist. Barney Bigard. Ed. by Barry Martyn. 176p. 1988. pap. 8.95 (*0-19-520637-1*) OUP.

With Love. Lighten-Up Staff. (Small Wonders Ser.). 120p. 1994. spiral bd. 4.99 (*1-879127-49-0*) Lighten Up Enter.

With Love. Michel Design Staff. (Charming Petites Ser.). (Illus.). 80p. 1991. 4.95 (*0-88088-735-4*) Peter Pauper.

***With Love.** Shelly Ritthaler. (American Dreams Ser.). (YA). (gr. 7 up). 1997. pap. 3.99 (*0-614-28633-6*, Flare) Avon.

***With Love: A Compilation of Romantic Verse & Paper Flowers.** Thomas Nelson Publishers Staff. 1996. 12.99 (*0-7852-7336-0*) Nelson.

With Love: Forever Yours, Bk. 4. Marian J. Yoest. 98p. 1988. spiral bd. 6.50 (*0-945105-04-5*) Yoest Expressions.

With Love: Gratefully Yours, Bk. 2. Marian J. Yoest. 86p. 1987. spiral bd. 6.50 (*0-945105-02-9*) Yoest Expressions.

With Love: Sincerely Yours, Bk. 3. Marian J. Yoest. 88p. 1987. spiral bd. 6.50 (*0-317-89526-5*) Yoest Expressions.

***With Love, Amanda.** Shelly Ritthaler. 1997. mass mkt. 3.99 (*0-380-78375-4*) Avon.

With Love & Better Health: Onward Christian Soldiers. Owen H. Robins. LC 91-90518. 160p. 1995. 16.95 (*0-9630319-0-2*) Larksdale.

With Love As Our Weapon. Howard J. McOmber, II. Ed. by Pamela Holt. (Illus.). 104p. (Orig.). (C). 1990. pap. 9.95 (*0-9626734-0-4*) Plowshare Prodns.

With Love, at Christmas. Mem Fox. LC 88-6332. (Illus.). (J). (gr. 2 up). 1988. 12.95 (*0-687-45863-3*) Abingdon.

With Love, Bev: A Courageous Journey of Healing. Beverly Differding. 274p. 1994. pap. 14.95 (*0-9639586-1-5*) Gander Pubng.

With Love Beyond All Telling: A Biblical Approach to Adult Spiritual Formation. Maureen Abbott & Joseph Doyle. 1991. pap. 14.95 (*0-8091-3209-5*) Paulist Pr.

With Love from Darling's Kitchen. Renny Darling. 1982. pap. 14.95 (*0-930440-17-X*) Royal Hse.

With Love from Diana: The Princess of Wales Personal Astrologer Shares Her First-Hand Account of Diana's Turbulent Years. Penny Thorton. Ed. by Linda Marrow. 224p. (Orig.). 1995. mass mkt. 5.99 (*0-671-89186-3*) PB.

With Love from Gran. Dick Gackenbach. (J). (ps-3). 1990. pap. 6.95 (*0-395-54775-X*, Clarion Bks) HM.

With Love from Grandma. Millie Wolff. (Illus.). 84p. (Orig.). 1992. pap. 8.95 (*0-9631448-2-0*) VA Pub Corp.

With Love, from Jo. Jossy Ann Bolivar. Ed. by Josefa V. Bolivar. LC 80-13999. (Illus.). 120p. (Orig.). 1980. pap. 5.95 (*0-914598-01-5*) Padre Prods.

With Love from Karen. Marie Killilea. 1993. reprint ed. lib. bdg. 26.95 (*1-56849-099-2*) Buccaneer Bks.

With Love from My Kitchen. Nancy R. Edwards. 1984. 22.95 (*0-9613287-0-3*) Strawberry GA.

With Love from My Kitchen-Victorian. Nancy R. Edwards. (Illus.). 264p. (Orig.). 1989. 22.95 (*0-9613287-2-X*) Strawberry GA.

With Love on the Birth of Your New Baby. Ed. by Helen Exley. (So-Much-More-Than-a-Card Ser.). (Illus.). 28p. (Orig.). 1996. pap. 2.99 (*1-85015-722-7*) Exley Giftbooks.

With Love on Your Anniversary. Ed. by Helen Exley. (So-Much-More-Than-a-Card Ser.). (Illus.). 28p. (Orig.). 1995. pap. 2.99 (*1-85015-678-6*) Exley Giftbooks.

With Love on Your Wedding Day. Ed. by Helen Exley. (So-Much-More-Than-a-Card Ser.). (Illus.). 28p. (Orig.). 1995. pap. 2.99 (*1-85015-657-3*) Exley Giftbooks.

With Love Series. Marian J. Yoest. 320p. (Orig.). 1989. spiral bd. 16.95 (*0-945105-00-2*) Yoest Expressions.

With Love to a Special Dad. Ed. by Helen Exley. (So-Much-More-Than-a-Card Ser.). (Illus.). 28p. (Orig.). 1995. pap. 2.99 (*1-85015-660-3*) Exley Giftbooks.

With Love to a Special Daughter. Ed. by Helen Exley. (So-Much-More-Than-a-Card Ser.). (Illus.). 24p. (Orig.). 1994. pap. 2.99 (*1-85015-513-5*) Exley Giftbooks.

With Love to a Special Friend. Ed. by Helen Exley. (So-Much-More-Than-a-Card Ser.). (Illus.). 24p. (Orig.). 1994. pap. 2.99 (*1-85015-512-7*) Exley Giftbooks.

With Love to a Special Grandmother. Ed. by Helen Exley. (So-Much-More-Than-a-Card Ser.). (Illus.). 24p. (Orig.). 1994. pap. 2.99 (*1-85015-514-3*) Exley Giftbooks.

With Love to a Special Husband. Ed. by Helen Exley. (So-Much-More-Than-a-Card Ser.). (Illus.). 28p. (Orig.). 1996. pap. 2.99 (*1-85015-721-9*) Exley Giftbooks.

With Love to a Special Mother. Ed. by Helen Exley. (So-Much-More-Than-a-Card Ser.). (Illus.). 24p. (Orig.). 1994. pap. 2.99 (*1-85015-511-9*) Exley Giftbooks.

With Love to a Special Sister. Ed. by Helen Exley. (So-Much-More-Than-a-Card Ser.). (Illus.). 28p. (Orig.). 1996. pap. 2.99 (*1-85015-720-0*) Exley Giftbooks.

With Love to Dad. Ed. by Helen Exley. (Heart Shaped Bks.). (Illus.). 32p. 1992. pap. 3.99 (*1-85015-297-7*) Exley Giftbooks.

With Love to My Survivors. Richard Hawley. (Cleveland Poets Ser.: No. 32). 23p. (Orig.). 1982. pap. 3.50 (*0-914946-31-5*) Cleveland St Univ Poetry Ctr.

With Love to Someone Special on Your Graduation. Ed. by Helen Exley. (So-Much-More-Than-a-Card Ser.). (Illus.). 28p. (Orig.). 1996. pap. 2.99 (*1-85015-723-5*) Exley Giftbooks.

***With Love to Spare.** Lavon B. Carroll. 394p. (Orig.). 1997. mass mkt. 5.99 (*1-55197-836-9*, Pub. by Comnwlth Pub CN) Partners Pubs Grp.

With Love to the Monsters under My Bed. 2nd ed. Corliss Morris. (Illus.). 60p. (Orig.). reprint ed. pap. 7.95 (*1-879331-08-X*) Marciel Pub & Print.

With Luck Lasting. Bernard Spencer. LC 64-21520. 6500. 15.95 (*0-8023-1096-6*) Dufour.

With Lute & Lyre: History of Instruments. Grizelle Steel. 1977. lib. bdg. 34.95 (*0-8490-2829-9*) Gordon Pr.

***With Magee & Me.** Marguerite D. McCleary. Ed. by Jim Ciano. (Illus.). 50p. (Orig.). 1997. pap. 12.95 (*1-888672-17-X*) J Ciano Pubng.

With Malice Toward None: A War Diary by Cecil King. Cecil King. Ed. by William Armstrong. LC 70-175619. 343p. 1971. 35.00 (*0-8386-1067-6*) Fairleigh Dickinson.

With Malice Toward None: The Life of Abraham Lincoln. Stephen B. Oates. (Illus.). 1978. pap. 4.95 (*0-451-62314-2*, ME2314, Ment) NAL-Dutton.

With Malice Toward None: The Life of Abraham Lincoln. Stephen B. Oates. (Illus.). 512p. 1994. reprint ed. pap. 16.00 (*0-06-092471-3*, PL) HarpC.

With Malice Toward Some: How People Make Civil Liberties Judgments. George E. Marcus et al. (Studies in Political Psychology & Public Opinion). (Illus.). 304p. (C). 1995. pap. text ed. 19.95 (*0-521-43997-3*) Cambridge U Pr.

With Malice Toward Some: How People Make Civil Liberties Judgments. George E. Marcus et al. (Cambridge Studies in Political Psychology & Public Opinion). (Illus.). 304p. (C). 1995. text ed. 59.95 (*0-521-43396-7*) Cambridge U Pr.

With Mallets Aforethought: A Winston Wyc Mystery. Brian Johnston. 256p. 1995. 21.00 (*1-883402-44-1*) S&S Trade.

With Mind & Heart. Howard Singer. (J). (gr. 8 up). 3.95 (*0-8381-0203-4*, 10-203) USCJE.

With Mortal Voice: The Creation of Paradise Lost. fac. ed. John T. Shawcross. LC 80-51944. 208p. 1982. pap. 59.30 (*0-7837-7601-2*, 2047354) Bks Demand.

With Murder in Mind. large type ed. Freda Bream. 1990. pap. 15.99 (*0-7089-6892-9*, Trailtree Bookshop) Ulverscroft.

With Murderous Intent. Robert Hemming. 352p. 1991. pap. 4.99 (*0-451-40266-9*, Onyx) NAL-Dutton.

With Musket, Cannon & Sword: Battle Tactics of Napoleon & His Enemies. Brent Nosworthy. LC 96-6161. (Illus.). 528p. 1996. 35.00 (*1-885119-27-5*) Sarpedon.

With Mustard on My Back. John N. Merrill. 76p. (Orig.). 1985. pap. 30.00 (*0-907496-27-X*) St Mut.

With My Friends: Tales Told in Partnership; with an Introductory Essay on the Art & Mystery of Collaboration, Vol. 1. Brander Matthews. LC 72-3372. (Short Story Index Reprint Ser.). 1977. reprint ed. 23.95 (*0-8369-4155-1*) Ayer.

With My Legs. Harry Bornstein. (Signed English Ser.). (Illus.). 16p. (J). (ps). 1975. pap. 3.50 (*0-913580-42-2*, Pub. by K Green Pubns) Gallaudet Univ Pr.

With My Mom - with My Dad. Meribeth Boelts. (Sunshine Ser.). 32p. (J). 1992. pap. 0.97 (*0-8163-1060-2*) Pacific Pr Pub Assn.

With My Own Eyes: The Autobiography of an Historian. Jacob Katz. Tr. by Ann Brenner & Zipora Brody. LC 94-28397. (Tauber Institute Ser.: Vol. 20). 183p. 1995. 29.95 (*0-87451-639-0*) U Pr of New Eng.

With My Own Wings: The Memoirs of Raymond Lister. Raymond G. Lister. (Illus.). 224p. (Orig.). 1994. pap. 23.95 (*0-906672-66-X*) Oleander Pr.

With My Soul Amongst Lions. Gareth Patterson. LC 96-20057. 228p. 1996. 24.95 (*0-312-14768-6*) St Martin.

***With My Soul Amongst Lions.** large type ed. Gareth Patterson. (Ulverscroft Large Print Ser.). 384p. 1997. 27.50 (*0-7089-3740-3*) Ulverscroft.

With My Whole Heart: Knowing God Through Prayer. Sharlande Sledge. Ed. by Karen Gross. 64p. (J). (gr. 4-6). 1993. pap. text ed. 4.95 (*1-56309-078-3*, New Hope) Womans Mission Union.

***With Nails: The Film Diaries of Richard E. Grant.** Richard E. Grant. (Illus.). 310p. 1996. 39.50 (*0-330-34434-X*, Pub. by Picador UK) Trans-Atl Phila.

With Napoleon in Russia: The Memoirs of General De Caulaincourt, Duke of Vicenza. Armand A. Caulaincourt. Ed. by Jean Hanoteau & George Libaire. LC 75-40914. 422p. 1976. reprint ed. text ed. 35.00 (*0-8371-8689-7*, CAWN, Greenwood Pr) Greenwood.

With Nature's Children: Emma B. Freeman, (1880-1928) Peter E. Palmquist. 134p. 1991. reprint ed. lib. bdg. 39.00 (*0-8095-5955-2*) Borgo Pr.

With Naval Wings: The Autobiography of a Fleet Air Arm Pilot in World War II. John Wellham. (Illus.). 208p. 1996. 27.95 (*0-87811-886-7*) Stackpole.

With Needle & Thread: A Book about Quilts. Raymond Bial. LC 95-16416. 48p. (J). (gr. 3-7). 1996. 14.95 (*0-395-73568-8*) HM.

With Nehru in the Foreign Office. Subimal Dutt. 1977. 14.00 (*0-88386-905-5*) S Asia.

With New & Open Eyes. Wayne Brouwer. 160p. 1994. pap. 11.95 (*0-936497-10-6*) Seven Worlds.

With New Eyes: Toward an Asian American Art History in the West. 45p. 1995. lib. bdg. 33.00 (*0-8095-5957-9*) Borgo Pr.

With New Testament Eyes. Henry T. Mahan. 1993. pap. 8.99 (*0-85234-304-3*, Pub. by Evangelical Pr) Presby & Reformed.

With No Little Regrett: An Historical Novel Based on the Journal of Madam Knight. Janet B. Gerba. LC 95-70216. (Illus.). 275p. 1995. pap. 15.00 (*0-9647752-0-4*) Colonial Am Pr.

With No Reservations. large type ed. Leigh Michaels. 1990. lib. bdg. 18.95 (*0-263-12355-3*, Pub. by Mills & Boon UK) Thorndike Pr.

***With Obligation to All.** George R. Ariyoshi. LC 96-39505. (Illus.). 208p. 1997. text ed. 20.00 (*0-8248-1941-1*) Ariyoshi Fnd.

W

An Asterisk (*) at the beginning of an entry indicates that the title is appearing in BIP for the first time.

With One Heart Bowing to the City of Ten Thousand Buddhas, 9 vols. Incl. Vol. IX. . Heng Sure & Heng Chau. 220p. (Orig.). 1983. pap. Not sold separately (0-88139-509-9); Vol. IV. . Heng Sure & Heng Chau. (Illus.). 136p. (Orig.). (C). 1980. pap. Not sold separately (0-917512-90-1); Vol. VI. . Heng Sure & Heng Chau. (Illus.). 200p. (Orig.). (C). 1981. pap. Not sold separately (0-917512-92-8); Vol. I. . Heng Sure & Heng Chau. (Illus.). 180p. (Orig.). 1977. pap. Not sold separately (0-917512-21-9); Vol. II. . Heng Sure & Heng Chau. (Illus.). 322p. (Orig.). (C). 1979. pap. Not sold separately (0-917512-23-5); Vol. VII. . Heng Sure & Heng Chau. (Illus.). 160p. (Orig.). 1982. pap. Not sold separately (0-917512-99-5); Vol. VIII. . Heng Sure & Heng Chau. (Illus.). 232p. (Orig.). (C). 1982. pap. Not sold separately (0-917512-53-7); Vol. III. . Heng Sure & Heng Chau. (Illus.). 154p. (Orig.). (C). 1979. pap. Not sold separately (0-917512-89-8); Vol. V. . Heng Sure & Heng Chau. (Illus.). 127p. (Orig.). (C). 1981. pap. Not sold separately (0-917512-96-0); 63.00 (0-614-16026-X) Buddhist Text.

With One Look. Jennifer Horsman. 416p. (Orig.). 1994. mass mkt. 4.99 (0-380-77596-4) Avon.

With One Verb see Building English Sentences

With One Voice/B'Qol Echad: The Sermon on the Mount & Rabbinic Literature. Dennis Stoutenburg. (ISP Ser.). 163p. 1996. 69.95 (1-57309-051-4); pap. 49.95 (1-57309-050-6) Intl Scholars.

With One White Wing: Puzzles in Poems & Pictures. Ed. by Elizabeth Spires. LC 94-12927. 32p. (J). (gr. 1-5). 1995. text ed. 14.00 (0-689-50622-8, McElderry) S&S Childrens.

With Only the Will to Live: Accounts of Americans in Japanese Prison Camps, 1941-1945. Ed. by Robert S. LaForte et al. LC 93-42419. 320p. 1994. 24.95 (0-8420-2464-6) Scholarly Res Inc.

With Open Arms: Catholics, Divorce, & Remarriage. John Hosie. LC 95-76121. 96p. (Orig.). 1995. pap. 3.95 (0-89243-810-X) Liguori Pubns.

With Open Arms: Cuban Migration to the United States. Felix Masud-Piloto. LC 87-12809. 168p. 1988. 49.50 (0-8476-7566-1, R7566) Rowman.

With Open Arms? The Evolution of Cuban Migration to the U. S., 1959-1995. rev. ed. Felix Masud-Piloto. 200p. (C). 1995. pap. text ed. 19.95 (0-8476-8038-X); lib. bdg. 49.50 (0-8476-8037-1) Rowman.

With Open Hands. Henri J. Nouwen. 1987. mass mkt. 4.99 (0-345-35299-8) Ballantine.

With Open Hands. large type rev. ed. Henri J. Nouwen. LC 94-79358. 96p. 1995. pap. 9.95 (0-8027-2694-1) Walker & Co.

With Open Hands. rev. ed. Henri J.M. Nouwen. LC 94-79358. (Illus.). 136p. 1995. pap. 8.95 (0-87793-545-9) Ave Maria.

With or Without. Charles Dickinson. 160p. 1993. reprint ed. pap. 9.00 (0-380-71951-7) Avon.

With Our Bodies We Write the Name of Light. Russell Thornton. 80p. 1995. lib. bdg. 35.00 (0-8095-4845-3) Borgo Pr.

With Our Bodies We Write the Name of Light. Russell Thornton. 80p. pap. 12.95 (0-88962-568-9) Mosaic.

With Our Heads Bowed: The Dynamics of Gender in a Maya Community. Brenda Rosenbaum. LC 92-76220. (IMS Studies on Culture & Society: No. 5). (Illus.). 239p. (Orig.). (C). 1993. pap. 18.00 (0-942041-14-3) Univ Albany IFMS.

With Our Own Eyes. Don Mosley & Joyce Hollyday. 304p. 1996. pap. 12.99 (0-8361-9050-5) Herald Pr.

With Paper, About Paper. Ed. by Charlotta Kotik. LC 80-69318. (Illus.). 1980. pap. 7.50 (0-914782-35-5) Buffalo Fine-Albrght-Knox.

With Passion & Compassion: Third World Women Doing Theology. Ed. by Virginia Fabella & Mercy A. Oduyoye. Tr. by Phillip Berryman et al. from FRE. LC 88-6908. 282p. 1988. pap. 17.50 (0-88344-628-6) Orbis Bks.

With Pegasus in India: The Story of 153rd Gurkha Parachute Battalion. Eric Neild. (Airborne Ser.: No. 21). (Illus.). 110p. 1990. reprint ed. 29.95 (0-89839-150-4) Battery Pr.

With Pen & Pencil on the Frontier in 1851: The Diary & Sketches of Frank Blackwell Mayer. Frank B. Mayer. LC 75-103. (Mid-American Frontier Ser.). (Illus.). 1975. reprint ed. 15.95 (0-405-06871-9) Ayer.

With Pen & Pencil on the Frontier in 1851: The Diary & Sketches of Frank Blackwell Mayer. Frank B. Mayer. Ed. by Bertha L. Heilbron. LC 86-717. xvii, 256p. 1986. reprint ed. pap. 9.95 (0-87351-195-6, Borealis Book) Minn Hist.

With Pen & Rifle in Kashmir. Otto Rothfeld. (C). 1993. reprint ed. 18.00 (81-7041-823-2, Pub. by Anmol II) S Asia.

With Pen & Saber: The Letters & Diaries of J. E. B. Stuart's Staff Officers. Robert J. Trout. LC 95-1753. (Illus.). 368p. 1995. 24.95 (0-8117-1930-8) Stackpole.

With Pen & Voice: The Rhetoric of Nineteenth-Century African-American Women. Shirley W. Logan. LC 94-11166. 200p. (C). 1995. 24.95 (0-8093-1874-1); pap. 14.95 (0-8093-1875-X) S Ill U Pr.

With Perfect Faith: The Foundations of Jewish Belief. Anno. & Selected by J. David Bleich. 1982. 19.95 (0-87068-891-X) Ktav.

With Perry to Japan: A Memoir by William Heine. William Heine. Tr. & Anno. by Frederic Trautmann. LC 89-20495. (Illus.). 232p. 1990. text ed. 33.00 (0-8248-1258-1) UH Pr.

***With Pious Gravity: Chronicles of the Volunteers from America 1914-1918.** Theodore Erceg. (Illus.). 76p. 1995. write for info. (0-9649072-6-7) St George Mrkt.

***With Pleasure.** Harkess & Wherly. 1991. student ed., pap. text ed. write for info. (0-17-556241-5) Addison-Wesley.

With Pleasure: Thoughts on the Nature of Human Sexuality. Paul R. Abramson & Steven D. Pinkerton. 288p. 1995. 30.00 (0-19-509358-5) OUP.

With Poor Immigrants to America. Stephen Graham. LC 73-13133. (Foreign Travelers in America, 1810-1935 Ser.). 366p. 1974. reprint ed. 29.95 (0-405-05455-6) Ayer.

With Porter in North Missouri: A Chapter in the History of the War Between the States. Joseph A. Mudd. LC 91-66906. (Illus.). 460p. 1992. reprint ed. 35.00 (0-9628936-1-7) Pr Camp Pope.

With Prayer & Psalm: The History of Wilmot, New Hampshire Churches. Florence Langley. LC 81-5116. 80p. 1981. 7.95 (0-914016-77-6) Phoenix Pub.

With Presidents to the Summit. A. Denis Clift. 1993. 23.95 (0-913969-51-6, G Mason Univ Pr) Univ Pub Assocs.

With Pride They Made These: Tribal Styles in Plains Indian Art. Michael H. Logan & Douglas A. Schmittou. (Illus.). 60p. (Orig.). (C). 1995. pap. 18.50 (1-880174-03-0) U TN F H McClung.

With Promise: Redefining Reading & Writing Needs for Special Students. Ed. by Susan Stires. LC 91-6550. (Illus.). 180p. (Orig.). 1991. pap. text ed. 21.00 (0-435-08573-5, 08573) Heinemann.

With Ptarmigan & Tundra Wolves. Cy Hampson. (Illus.). 144p. (Orig.). 1991. pap. 12.95 (0-920501-59-1) Orca Bk Pubs.

With Raoul Wallenberg in Budapest. Per Anger. LC 95-289. (Illus.). 208p. 1996. reprint ed. pap. 14.95 (0-89604-156-5, Holocaust Library) US Holocaust.

With Raoul Wallenberg in Budapest: Memories of the War Years in Hungary. Per Anger et al. Tr. by David M. Paul & Margareta Paul from SWE. (Illus.). 192p. reprint ed. pap. 4.95 (0-686-99464-7) ADL.

With Reagan: The Inside Story. Edwin Meese, III. LC 92-4222. (Illus.). 350p. 1992. 24.95 (0-89526-522-2) Regnery Pub.

With Reference to Reference. Catherine Z. Elgin. LC 82-15488. 208p. (C). 1983. pap. text ed. 12.95 (0-915145-53-7); lib. bdg. 34.95 (0-915145-52-9) Hackett Pub.

With Respect for Others: Activities for a Global Neighborhood. Cynthia M. Manthey. (Illus.). 160p. (Orig.). 1995. lib. bdg. 27.95 (0-89334-247-5, 2475054) Humanics Ltd.

With Respect for Others: Activities for a Global Neighborhood. Cynthia M Manthey. (Illus.). 160p. (Orig.). (J). (gr. 1-6). 1995. pap. 17.95 (0-89334-241-6, 2416054) Humanics Ltd.

With Respect to the Japanese. John C. Condon. LC 81-85730. (InterAct Ser.). 110p. (Orig.). (C). 1984. pap. text ed. 12.95 (0-933662-49-1) Intercult Pr.

With Respect, Vol. 1P: Successful Primary Theme Activities. Cynthia M. Manthey. 100p. (J). (ps-1). 1992. pap. text ed. 11.95 (0-9634651-0-4); audio 9.95 (0-9634651-1-2) Qual Instruct.

With Reverence & Contempt: How Americans Think about Their President. Thomas S. Langston. LC 94-34134. (Interpreting American Politics Ser.). 192p. 1995. 35.00 (0-8018-5016-9) Johns Hopkins.

With Reverence & Contempt: How Americans Think about Their President. Thomas S. Langston. (Interpreting American Politics Ser.). 328p. 1997. reprint ed. pap. text ed. 14.95 (0-8018-5510-1) Johns Hopkins.

With Rod & Line in Colorado Waters. L. B. France. (Illus.). 178p. (Orig.). 1996. reprint ed. pap. 12.95 (0-87108-881-9) Pruett.

With Rommel in the Dessert. Heinz W. Schmidt. (War & Warriors Ser.). (Illus.). 240p. 1991. 15.95 (0-939482-39-8, Noontide Pr) Legion Survival.

With Roots & Wings: Christianity in an Age of Ecology & Dialogue. Jay B. McDaniel. LC 95-500359. (Ecology & Justice Ser.). 280p. (Orig.). 1995. pap. 17.00 (1-57075-001-7) Orbis Bks.

With Ruth in Mind. Anselm Hollo. LC 79-28147. 50p. 1980. pap. 4.45 (0-930794-18-4) Station Hill Pr.

With Sam Choy: Cooking from the Heart. Sam Choy. (Illus.). 224p. 1995. 35.00 (1-56647-098-6) Mutual Pub HI.

With Santa Anna in Texas: A Personal Narrative of the Revolution. expanded ed. Jose E. De La Pena. Ed. & Tr. by Carmen Perry from SPA. LC 75-16269. (Illus.). 248p. (C). 1997. pap. 16.95 (0-89096-527-7) Tex A&M Univ Pr.

With Scorching Heat & Drought? St. Andrew Press Staff. 80p. (C). 1989. pap. 30.00 (0-86153-113-2, Pub. by St Andrew UK) St Mut.

With Sharp Compassion: Norman Dott: Freeman Surgeon of Edinburgh. Christopher Rush & John F. Shaw. (Illus.). 1990. 35.00 (0-08-037975-3, Pub. by Aberdeen U Pr) Macmillan.

With Signs Following. Stanley H. Frodsham. 288p. 1946. pap. 6.95 (0-88243-635-X, 02-0635) Gospel Pub.

With Silence My Companion. Shuntaro Tanikawa. Tr. by William I. Elliott & Kazuo Kawamura. LC 75-21399. 60p. 1973. pap. 5.00 (0-915986-02-7) Prescott St Pr.

With Sleepless Eye: The Daily Cycle of Services of the Orthodox Church. 2nd rev. ed. Bessarion Agioantonodes. 1988. pap. text ed. write for info. (0-936649-18-6) St Anthony Orthodox.

***With Snow on Their Boots.** Cockfield. LC 97-21440. 1997. text ed. 35.00 (0-312-17356-3) St Martin.

With Songs on My Lips. Craig L. Teed. 1995. pap. 7.95 (0-533-11199-4) Vantage.

With Sound & Color: An Intermediate Chinese-English Reader. Florence C. Chang. LC 80-68257. (Chinese Can Be Fun Bks.: Level 4). (Illus.). 71p. (Orig.). (J). (gr. 7-9). 1980. wbk. ed., pap. 7.00 (0-936620-01-3) Ginkgo Hut.

With Special Distinction. 1993. 19.95 (0-9636101-0-4) MS Coll Ckbk.

With Special Distinction: A Collection of Recipes from the Mississippi College Family. Ed. by Janet Lee. LC 93-77090. (Illus.). 384p. 1993. 19.95 (0-685-65593-8) MS Coll Ckbk.

With Special Section: A Sense of the Past & a Sense of Guilt. Ed. by Walter Goldschmidt & Douglas Price-Williams. (Ethos Ser.: Vol. 5, No. 4). 1977. 10.00 (0-317-66361-5) Am Anthro Assn.

With Stalin Against Tito: Cominformist Splits in Yugoslav Communism. Ivo Banac. LC 88-47717. 320p. 1988. 39.95 (0-8014-2186-1) Cornell U Pr.

With Steinbeck in the Sea of Cortez: A Memoir of the Steinbeck - Ricketts Expedition. Audry Lynch. (Illus.). 96p. (Orig.). 1991. pap. 7.95 (0-944627-56-0) Sand River Pr.

With Stethoscope & Scapular. Joseph C. Evers. LC 96-67917. (Orig.). 1996. pap. 7.95 (1-882972-70-8) Queenship Pub.

With Stethoscope in Asia: Korea. Sherwood Hall. LC 77-81765. 1981. reprint ed. 19.95 (0-930696-01-8) MCL Assocs.

With Stonewall Jackson. J. P. Smith. 24.50 (0-8488-1172-0) Amereon Ltd.

With Stonewall Jackson in the Valley of Northern Virginia. James P. Smith. 110p. 1982. reprint ed. 18.50 (0-942211-38-3) Olde Soldier Bks.

With Strings Attached. Vanessa Grant. (Presents Ser.). 1993. pap. 2.89 (0-373-11528-8, 1-11528-6) Harlequin Bks.

With Strings Attached. Leland R. Long. 1993. 16.95 (0-533-10570-6) Vantage.

With Strings Attached. large type ed. Vanessa Grant. 1992. reprint ed. lib. bdg. 18.95 (0-263-12899-7) Thorndike Pr.

With Strings Attached: Reminiscences & Reflections. Joseph Szigeti. LC 79-11318. (Music Reprint Ser.). 1979. reprint ed. lib. bdg. 42.50 (0-306-79567-1) Da Capo.

With Tails We Win. Crowe & Bowen. (Illus.). 1954. pap. 4.00 (0-9600102-5-4) Shields.

With Teeth in the Earth: Selected Poems of Malka Heifetz Tussman. Malka H. Tussman. Tr. & Intro. by Marcia Falk. LC 92-15705. 180p. (C). 1992. pap. 14.95 (0-8143-2344-8) Wayne St U Pr.

With Thanks. Ed. by Mark Water. LC 96-34713. (Words of Joy & Comfort Ser.). (Illus.). 92p. 1996. 4.95 (0-8192-1659-3) Morehouse Pub.

With Thanks: A Book of Gratitude & Friendship. (Main Street Gift Bks.). (Illus.). 40p. 1996. 6.95 (0-8362-1064-6) Andrews & McMeel.

With the Bark On: Popular Humor of the Old South. John Q. Anderson. LC 67-13998. (Illus.). 349p. reprint ed. pap. 99.50 (0-8357-3200-2, 2039471) Bks Demand.

With the Battlecruisers. Filson Young. (Classics of Naval Literature Ser.). 296p. 1986. 32.95 (0-87021-795-X) Naval Inst Pr.

With the Beatles: The Historic Photographs of Dezo Hoffmann. Ed. by Pearce Marchbank. (Illus.). 128p. (Orig.). pap. 19.95 (0-7119-0111-2, OP 41961) Omnibus NY.

With the Best of Intentions: The Child Sexual Abuse Prevention Movement. Jill D. Berrick & Neil Gilbert. LC 91-24680. 210p. 1991. lib. bdg. 27.95 (0-89862-564-5) Guilford Pr.

With the Border Ruffians: Memories of the Far West, 1852-1868. R. H. Williams. Ed. by E. W. Williams. LC 82-8400. (Illus.). xxii, 490p. 1982. reprint ed. pap. 9.95 (0-8032-9704-1, Bison Books) U of Nebr Pr.

With the Boys: Little League Baseball & Preadolescent Culture. Gary A. Fine. LC 86-16056. 304p. (C). 1987. pap. text ed. 13.95 (0-226-24937-9) U Ch Pr.

With the Camel Corps up the Nile. Count Gleichen. (Illus.). 1976. reprint ed. 25.00 (0-7158-1108-8) Charles River Bks.

With the Dutch in the East: An Outline of the Military Operations in Lombock, 1894. Wouter Cool. Tr. by E. J. Taylor from DUT. LC 77-86968. (Illus.). reprint ed. 47.50 (0-404-16702-0) AMS Pr.

With the Eagles. Paul L. Anderson. LC 57-9447. (Illus.). (J). (gr. 7-11). 1929. 21.00 (0-8196-0100-4) Biblo.

With the Eyes of the Heart. Teresa Whitten. LC 93-27044. 1993. 4.95 (0-8198-8214-3) Pauline Bks.

With the Fathers: Studies in the History of the United States. John B. McMaster. LC 75-173113. 1972. reprint ed. 20.95 (0-405-08771-3, Pub. by Blom Pubns UK) Ayer.

With the Five Year Olds. Joan Gallagher. 44p. 1969. pap. 1.95 (0-87825-253-3) Ed Solutions.

With the French Foreign Legion in Syria. John H. Harvey. 288p. 1995. write for info. (1-85367-212-2, Pub. by Greenhill Bks UK) Stackpole.

***With the Grain.** Ellen H. Brown. 22.95 (0-7867-0573-6) Carroll & Graf.

With the Grain. Raymond A. Sokolov. LC 95-14617. (Illus.). 320p. 1996. 25.00 (0-679-42561-6) Knopf.

With the Grain: The Essentially Vegetarian Way. Ellen H. Brown. 360p. 1990. 22.95 (0-88184-573-6) Carroll & Graf.

With the Guns in the Peninsula: The Peninsular Journal of 2nd Captain William Webber. Ed. by Richard H. Wollocombe. 200p. 1991. 35.00 (1-85367-108-8) Stackpole.

With the Hammer of Truth: James Thomson Callender & America's Early National Heroes. Michael Durey. 225p. 1990. text ed. 29.50 (0-8139-1278-4) U Pr of Va.

With the Help of Love I Can Do Anything. Angelo K. Menefee. (Illus.). (J). (gr. 1-4). 1996. 7.95 (0-533-11694-5) Vantage.

With the Hues of Autumn. Dipak B. Datta. (Illus.). 150p. 1989. 14.95 (0-938057-02-2) Floral Pub.

With the Hungarian Independence Movement, 1943-1947: An Eyewitness Account. Istvan Szent-Miklosy. LC 87-2371. 274p. 1988. text ed. 59.95 (0-275-92574-9, C2574, Praeger Pubs) Greenwood.

With the Immortals. Francis M. Crawford. (Works of Francis Marion Crawford Ser.). 1990. reprint ed. lib. bdg. 79.00 (0-7812-2534-5) Rprt Serv.

With the Immortals. Douglas A. Menville. LC 75-46264. (Supernatural & Occult Fiction Ser.). 1976. reprint ed. lib. bdg. 25.95 (0-405-08122-7) Ayer.

With the Indians in the Rockies. James W. Schultz. LC 83-73493. (J. W. Schultz Reprint Ser.). 1984. pap. 7.95 (0-8253-0319-2) Confluence Pr.

With the Irish Against Rommel: A Diary of 1943. Strome Galloway. 176p. (C). 1987. 110.00 (0-317-90384-5, Pub. by Picton UK) St Mut.

With the Nation Watching: Report of the Twentieth Century Fund Task Force on Televised Presidential Debates. 120p. 1979. 12.95 (0-87078-149-9); pap. 5.95 (0-87078-148-0) TCFP-PPP.

With the Nez Perces: Alice Fletcher in the Field, 1889-92. E. Jane Gay. Ed. by Frederick E. Hoxie & Joan T. Mark. LC 80-23045. (Illus.). xxxviii, 228p. 1981. reprint ed. pap. 10.95 (0-8032-7024-0, Bison Books) U of Nebr Pr.

With the Northwest Wind. R. B. Cunningham Graham & Edward Carpenter. 1972. 59.95 (0-8490-1312-7) Gordon Pr.

With the Offal Eaters. Douglas Houston. 8600. pap. 11.95 (0-906427-70-3, Pub. by Bloodaxe Bks UK) Dufour.

With the Old Breed: At Peleiu & Okinawa. Eugene B. Sledge. (Classics of Naval Literature Ser.). (Illus.). 368p. 1996. 32.95 (1-55750-747-3) Naval Inst Pr.

With the Old Breed: At Peleliu & Okinawa. Eugene B. Sledge, Jr. (Illus.). 352p. 1990. pap. 13.95 (0-19-506714-2) OUP.

With the Old Confeds. Samuel D. Buck. 155p. 1984. reprint ed. 24.50 (0-913419-01-X, J M C & Co) Amereon Ltd.

With the One Hundred Second Infantry Division Through Germany. (Divisional Ser.: No. 19). (Illus.). 296p. 1981. reprint ed. 39.95 (0-89839-045-1) Battery Pr.

***With the Passage of Time: The Baltimore Longitudinal Study of Aging.** (Illus.). 55p. 1996. reprint ed. pap. text ed. 25.00 (0-7881-2840-X) DIANE Pub.

With the Pilgrims to Canterbury: And the History of the Hospital of St. Thomas. Stanley G. Wilson. LC 70-178306. reprint ed. 29.50 (0-404-06997-5) AMS Pr.

With the Pilgrims to Mecca: The Great Pilgrimage of A.H. 1319, A.D. 1902. Gazanfar A. Khan & Wilfred Sparroy. LC 77-876447. reprint ed. 24.50 (0-404-16417-X) AMS Pr.

With the Power of Each Breath: A Disabled Women's Anthology. Ed. by Susan E. Browne et al. 360p. 1985. pap. 10.95 (0-939416-06-9) Cleis Pr.

With the Precision of Bats. Atanas Slavov. LC 86-60064. 309p. 1986. 17.95 (0-911050-59-0) Occidental.

With the Procession. Henry B. Fuller. LC 65-17288. (Chicago in Fiction Ser.). 288p. reprint ed. pap. 82.10 (0-685-15699-0, 2026773) Bks Demand.

With the Procession. Henry B. Fuller. (Collected Works of Henry B. Fuller). 1988. reprint ed. lib. bdg. 79.00 (0-7812-1201-4) Rprt Serv.

With the Procession. Henry B. Fuller. 1983. reprint ed. 39.00 (0-403-04585-1) Scholarly.

With the Risen Jesus at Mass. Veritas Publications Staff. 1989. 30.00 (0-86217-297-7, Pub. by Veritas IE); 35.00 (0-685-66583-6, Pub. by Veritas IE); pap. 30.00 (0-685-65150-9, Pub. by Veritas IE) St Mut.

With the Royal Headquarters in Eighteen Seventy to Seventy-One. Julius A. Von Verdy Du Vernois. LC 79-142243. reprint ed. 45.00 (0-404-06757-3) AMS Pr.

With the Russian Army, 1914-1917. Alfred W. Knox. 1977. lib. bdg. 59.95 (0-8490-2830-2) Gordon Pr.

With the Russian Army, 1914-1917: Being Chiefly Extracts from the Diary of a Military Attache - 2 Vols. in 1. Alfred W. Knox. LC 74-115552. (Russia Observed Ser.). (Illus.). 1971. reprint ed. 52.95 (0-405-03084-3) Ayer.

With the Screaming Eagles in Vietnam: A Personal Narrative of a Soldier in the 101st Airborne Division, 1968-1969. Roger Borroel. LC 95-94850. (Illus.). 110p. (Orig.). (J). (ps-12). 1995. reprint ed. pap. text ed. 13.00 (0-9624727-0-0) LaVillita Pubns.

With the Skin: The Poems of Aleksander Wat. Aleksander Wat. Tr. by Czeslaw Milosz & Leonard Nathan from POL. (Modern European Poets Ser.). 144p. 1988. 17.95 (0-88001-183-1) Ecco Pr.

With the Snow Queen. Joanne Greenberg. 336p. 1993. pap. 10.95 (1-55970-192-7) Arcade Pub Inc.

With the Swamis in America & India. Swami Atulananda. Ed. by Pravrajika Brahmaprana. (Illus.). 347p. (Orig.). 1989. pap. 9.95 (0-87481-233-X, Pub. by Advaita Ashrama II) Vedanta Pr.

With the Tongue of Angels. George D. Durrant. 1994. pap. 1.95 (0-88494-945-1) Bookcraft Inc.

With the Ups Comes the Downs. Connie Crawford. (Illus.). 104p. (Orig.). 1986. pap. 2.95 (0-936369-01-9) Son-Rise Pubns.

***With the West in Her Eyes.** Edward W. Nuffield. 152p. (YA). (gr. 3 up). pap. 2.95 (0-920534-44-9, Pub. by Hyperion Pr Ltd CN) Sterling.

With the Western Sharpshooters: Michigan Boys of Company D, 66th Illinois. Lorenzo A. Barker. (Illus.). 192p. 1994. 22.95 (1-885033-02-8) Blue Acorn Pr.

With the Whales. James Darling. (Illus.). 160p. 1990. 39.95 (1-55971-039-X, 0187) NorthWord.

With the Whales. James Darling. (Illus.). 160p. 1994. pap. 19.95 (1-55971-180-9) NorthWord.

***With the Wind.** Liz Damrell. (Illus.). 32p. (J). 4.98 (0-8317-6779-0) Smithmark.

With the Wind: To Sail the World. Nick Ellison. LC 96-94276. (Illus.). viii, 329p. (Orig.). 1996. pap. 16.95 (*0-9651825-0-9*) Kilo Pubng.

With the Wind As a Witness. Patrick L. Tartell. Ed. & Illus. by D. R. Dries. 70p. (Orig.). 1996. pap. 8.95 (*1-57502-172-2*, P0794) Morris Pubng.

With the Wind, Kevin Dolan. Bryce Milligan. LC 86-70018. (Multicultural Texas Ser.). (Illus.). 194p. (YA). (gr. 7 up). 1992. pap. 7.95 (*0-931722-45-4*) Corona Pub.

With the Wits, 1919 see Shelburne Essays

***With Their Bare Hands.** Al-Othman. 1984. pap. text ed. write for info. (*0-582-78375-5*, Pub. by Longman UK) Longman.

With Their Islands Around Them. Kenneth Brower. LC 74-4455. (Illus.). 1974. 8.95 (*0-03-013121-9*) Friends of Earth.

With Their Own Blood: A Saga of Southwestern Pioneers. Virginia C. Roberts. LC 91-15195. (Illus.). 288p. 1991. 24.95 (*0-87565-090-2*) Tex Christian.

With These Wings, I Can Try: A Personal Story of Courage & Triumph. Lisa M. Koontz. 162p. (Orig.). 1996. pap. 10.00 (*1-57502-096-3*) Morris Pubng.

With These Words...I Thee Wed: Contemporary Wedding Vows for Today's Couples. Barbara Eklof. 140p. 1989. pap. 9.95 (*1-55850-980-1*) Adams Media.

With Thine Adversary in the Way: A Quaker Witness for Reconciliation. Margarethe Lachmund. Tr. by Florence Kite. LC 79-91957. (Orig.). 1979. pap. 3.00 (*0-87574-228-9*) Pendle Hill.

With This Body: Caring & Disability in Marriage. Gillian Parker. LC 92-18284. 1993. 90.00 (*0-335-09947-5*, Open Univ Pr); pap. 32.50 (*0-335-09946-7*, Open Univ Pr) Taylor & Francis.

***With This Kiss.** Candice Poarch. 320p. 1998. mass mkt. 4.99 (*0-7860-0474-6*, Pinncle Kensgtn) Kensgtn Pub Corp.

With This Ring. 1991. mass mkt. 4.95 (*0-373-83228-1*) Harlequin Bks.

***With This Ring.** Robin J. Gunn. LC 97-9. (Sierra Jensen Ser.: Bk. 6). (J). 1997. pap. 5.99 (*1-56179-540-2*) Focus Family.

***With This Ring.** Carla Kelly. 1997. pap. 4.99 (*0-451-18685-0*, Sig) NAL-Dutton.

With This Ring. Marian Wells. LC 84-9301. 192p. (Orig.). 1984. pap. 7.99 (*0-87123-615-X*) Bethany Hse.

With This Ring. Marian Wells. 224p. 1995. mass mkt. 5.99 (*1-55661-582-5*) Bethany Hse.

With This Ring. large type ed. Carol Collins. (Linford Romance Library). 304p. 1994. pap. 15.99 (*0-7089-7552-6*) Ulverscroft.

With This Ring. large type ed. Jean Saunders. (Ulverscroft). 304p. 1994. 25.99 (*0-7089-3070-0*) Ulverscroft.

***With this Ring: A Portrait of Marriage.** Mary M. Kalergis. (Illus.). 127p. 1997. 29.95 (*0-940744-67-8*, 00497) Chrysler Museum.

With This Ring: A Practical Guide for Newlyweds. Renee Bartkowski. LC 91-77984. 112p. (Orig.). 1992. pap. text ed. 5.95 (*0-89243-430-9*) Liguori Pubns.

With This Ring: A True Story of Deception. Sofia Katherine. 1994. 22.95 (*0-88282-089-3*) New Horizon NJ.

With This Ring I Journey. Lorie K. Eckert. (Illus.). 32p. 1995. 15.95 (*1-56554-136-7*) Pelican.

With Those Who Grieve. Kay Soder-Alderfer. LC 50-95. 300p. 1994. pap. 10.95 (*0-7459-2624-X*) Lion USA.

With Three Generations of Vegetarian Hygienists. 2nd rev. ed. Stanley S. Bass. Ed. by Chet Day. 24p. 1996. pap. 10.00 (*1-885194-05-6*) Hlth & Beyond.

With Three Prime Ministers: Nehru, Indira & Rajiv. N. K. Seshan. (C). 1993. 14.00 (*81-224-0512-6*) S Asia.

With Tongue in Cheek. C. H. Malesis. Ed. by Marilyn Stablein. (Illus.). 233p. 1990. pap. 11.95 (*0-939116-25-1*) Frontier OR.

With Tongue in Cheek. Sandra Pittman. LC 86-72589. (Illus.). 128p. (Orig.). 1986. pap. 6.95 (*0-940873-86-9*) AKG.

With Tongues of Fire: Profiles in 20th Century Hymn Writing. Paul Westermeyer. 1995. 10.95 (*0-570-01349-6*, 99-1564) Concordia.

With Trees on Either Hand. Muriel Halvorsen. Ed. by J. Allen Kirsch. 256p. (Orig.). 1995. pap. 12.95 (*1-878569-24-4*) Badger Bks Inc.

With Trotsky in Exile: From Prinkipo to Coyoacban. Jean Van Heijenoort. LC 78-935. (Illus.). 176p. 1978. reprint ed. pap. 50.20 (*0-7837-6080-9*, 2059126) Bks Demand.

With Trumpet & Drum. Eugene Field. LC 70-116402. (Granger Index Reprint Ser.). 1977. 15.95 (*0-8369-6143-9*) Ayer.

With Trumpet & Drum. Eugene Field. (Notable American Authors Ser.). 1992. reprint ed. lib. bdg. 90.00 (*0-7812-2643-0*) Rprt Serv.

With Two Verbs see Building English Sentences

With Unveiled Face: Charismatic Christians & Fulfilled Eschatology. Richard Leonard. 44p. 1993. pap. 4.95 (*1-884454-04-6*) Laudemont Pr.

With Verbals see Building English Sentences

With Verbs & Verb Phrases see Building English Sentences

***With Walt Whitman in Camden, 9 vols., Vol. 8.** Horace Traubel. Ed. by Jeanne Chapman & Robert MacIsaac. (Illus.). xii, 624p. (C). 1996. 50.00 (*0-9653415-8-5*, C44-1) W L Bentley.

***With Walt Whitman in Camden, 9 vols., Vol. 9.** Horace Traubel. Ed. by Jeanne Chapman & Robert MacIsaac. (Illus.). xxiv, 652p. (C). 1996. 50.00 (*0-9653415-9-3*, C44-2) W L Bentley.

With Walt Whitman in Camden, Vol. 7: July 7, 1890-February 10, 1891. Horace Traubel. Ed. by Jeanne Chapman & Robert MacIsaac. LC 08-5603. 512p. (C). 1992. 39.95 (*0-8093-1757-5*) S Ill U Pr.

With Wanda: Town & Country Poems. Paul Zimmer. 1980. pap. 8.95 (*0-931848-32-6*) Dryad Pr.

With Warmest Regards. Dayton Hudson Corporation Staff. LC 95-40775. 1995. 4.25 (*0-8092-3214-6*) Contemp Bks.

With Warmest Thanks. Adventure Staff. (Small Wonders Ser.). 120p. 1995. spiral bd. 4.99 (*1-879127-62-8*) Lighten Up Enter.

With Whom Do You Walk? Raz Autry. LC 89-35148. 144p. (Orig.). 1990. pap. 8.95 (*0-931832-36-5*) Fithian Pr.

***With Wilderness at Heart: A Short History of the Adirondack Mountain Club.** Bruce Wadsworth. LC 96-33029. (Illus.). 128p. 1997. pap. 12.95 (*0-935272-84-4*) ADK Mtn Club.

***With Willful Intent: A Theology of Sin.** David L. Smith. 464p. 1994. 19.99 (*0-8010-2130-8*, Bridgept Bks) Baker Bks.

With William Burroughs. Victor Bockris. LC 96-26668. 304p. 1996. pap. 13.95 (*0-312-14767-8*) St Martin.

With Wine & Songs & Strange People Rushing Thru Me. Fred Pietarinen. (Illus.). 40p. (Orig.). 1983. pap. text ed. 2.50 (*1-879594-07-2*) Androgyne Bks.

With Wing Unspent. Catherine B. Hansen. 144p. 1995. 13.95 (*0-8233-0502-3*) Golden Quill.

With Wings: An Anthology of Literature by & about Women with Disabilities. Ed. by Marsha Saxton & Florence Howe. LC 86-31829. 176p. (C). 1987. pap. 14.95 (*0-935312-62-5*) Feminist Pr.

***With Wings As Eagles.** 1989. pap. 1.20 (*0-8341-9088-5*) Lillenas.

With Wings As Eagles. Andrew Murray. 96p. 1993. mass mkt. 3.99 (*0-88368-262-1*) Whitaker Hse.

With Wings As Eagles. William S. Pinkston, Jr. (English Skills for Christian Schools Ser.). (Illus.). 127p. (J). (gr. 2). 1983. pap. 9.17 (*0-89084-231-0*, 020958) Bob Jones Univ Pr.

With Wings As Eagles. Elaine L. Schulte. LC 90-6305. (California Pioneer Ser.). 275p. (J). 1990. pap. 8.99 (*1-55513-989-2*, 39891, LifeJourney) Chariot Victor.

With Wings As Eagles: Discovering the Master Teacher in the Secret School Within. 2nd rev. ed. John R. Price. LC 96-46850. 112p. 1996. pap. 9.95 (*1-56170-359-1*, 840) Hay House.

With Wings As Eagles: Toward Personal Christian Maturity. William B. Oglesby, Jr. LC 87-51654. 194p. (C). 1987. pap. text ed. 14.95 (*1-55605-036-4*) Wyndham Hall.

With Wings, There Are No Barriers: A Woman's Guide to a Life of Magnificent Possibilities. Sue Augustine. 224p. 1996. 18.95 (*1-56554-195-2*) Pelican.

With Winning in Mind: The Mental Management System. Lanny Bassham. LC 96-84757. (Illus.). 144p. 1996. pap. 12.95 (*1-885221-47-9*) BookPartners.

***With WK in the Workshop: William Kurelek.** Brian Dedora. pap. 9.95 (*0-920544-68-1*, Pub. by Mercury Pr CN) LPC InBook.

With Wolves. Day. 1995. pap. 10.99 (*1-57081-880-0*) Day Dream SBCA.

With Women's Eyes, Visitors to the New World, 1775-1918. Marion Tinling. LC 92-40915. (Illus.). xvii, 207p. (C). 1993. lib. bdg. 29.50 (*0-208-02371-2*, Archon Bks) Shoe String.

With Wooden Sword: A Portrait of Francis Sheehy-Skeffington, Militant Pacifist. Leah Levenson. LC 82-22560. (Illus.). 282p. 1983. text ed. 40.00 (*0-930350-42-1*) NE U Pr.

With Words. Connell McGrath. 32p. 1991. pap. 4.00 (*1-879645-04-1*) Garlic MA.

With You Always: Confirmation. Barry et al. 112p. 1991. 9.50 (*0-8215-1603-5*); teacher ed. 12.00 (*0-8215-1613-2*); 4.00 (*0-8215-1634-5*) Sadlier.

With You Always: First Eucharist. Groome et al. 64p. 1991. 7.00 (*0-8215-1602-7*); teacher ed. 12.00 (*0-8215-1612-4*); 12.00 (*0-685-54325-0*) Sadlier.

With You Always: First Reconciliation. Groome et al. 64p. 1991. 7.00 (*0-8215-1601-9*); teacher ed. 12.00 (*0-8215-1611-6*); 12.00 (*0-685-54326-9*) Sadlier.

With You in Mind. Eleanor H. Kirby. LC 91-90664. 114p. 1991. 14.95 (*0-9631396-0-6*) E H Kirby.

***With Your Own Two Hands: Self Discovery Through Music.** Seymour Bernstein. 320p. 1995. pap. text ed. 12.95 (*0-7935-5712-7*) H Leonard.

With Zola in England: A Story of Exile. Ernest A. Vizetelly. 1977. lib. bdg. 59.95 (*0-8490-2831-0*) Gordon Pr.

Withdrawal from Empire: A Military View. William Jackson. LC 86-29855. (Illus.). 289p. 1987. text ed. 35.00 (*0-312-00552-0*) St Martin.

Withdrawal of Human Projection: A Study of Culture & Internalized Objects. M. D. Faber. LC 89-80571. 99p. (Orig.). 1989. pap. 20.00 (*0-915042-21-5*) Lib Soc Sci.

Withdrawing Room. Charlotte MacLeod. 192p. 1982. mass mkt. 3.99 (*0-380-56473-4*) Avon.

Wither the State? Politics & Public Enterprise in Three Countries. Ira Sharkansky. LC 79-18780. (Illus.). 191p. reprint ed. pap. 54.50 (*0-8357-4824-3*, 2037761) Bks Demand.

Wither Turbulence? Turbulence at the Crossroads: Proceedings of a Workshop Held at Cornell University, Ithaca, New York, March 22-24, 1989. Ed. by John L. Lumley et al. (Lecture Notes in Physics Ser.: Vol. 357). iv, 525p. 1990. 82.95 (*0-387-52535-1*) Spr-Verlag.

Witherby's Dictionary of Insurance. Hugh Cockerell. 261p. (C). 1987. 125.00 (*0-948691-21-2*, Pub. by Witherby & Co UK) St Mut.

Witherby's Insurance Dictionary. Hugh Cockerell. 235p. 1980. 125.00 (*0-900886-50-1*, Pub. by Witherby & Co UK) St Mut.

Withered Branch. Derek S. Savage. LC 75-42377. (Studies in Fiction: No. 34). 1974. lib. bdg. 49.95 (*0-8383-1947-5*) M S G Haskell Hse.

Withered Branch: Six Studies in the Modern Novel. Derek S. Savage. LC 78-58270. (Essay Index in Reprint Ser.). 1978. reprint ed. 20.00 (*0-8486-3031-9*) Roth Pub Inc.

Withered Roots: The Remnants of Eastern European Jewry. Stuart F. Tower. LC 94-69189. 136p. 1994. pap. 18.00 (*0-914615-11-4*) I Nathan Pub Co.

Withering Away of the Totalitarian State: And Other Surprises. Jeane J. Kirkpatrick. 320p. 1991. 21.95 (*0-8447-3727-5*) Am Enterprise.

Withering Away of the Totalitarian State...& Other Surprises. Jeane Kirkpatrick. 320p. 1991. pap. 12.95 (*0-8447-3728-3*) Am Enterprise.

Withering Child. John A. Gould. LC 93-12351. 288p. 1993. 24.95 (*0-8203-1560-5*) U of Ga Pr.

Withernsea. John Whitehead. (C). 1989. text ed. 45.00 (*0-948929-13-8*) St Mut.

Withernsea in Verse. Margaret A. Hall. (C). 1989. text ed. 40.00 (*0-948929-19-7*) St Mut.

Wither's Emblemes. George Wither. Bd. with Foundations Unearthed. 1987. Set pap. 37.50 (*0-938760-11-4*) Veritat Found.

***Withertree Circle: The Mystery of Mrs. Withertree.** Donna Hickey. LC 96-34566. (Illus.). (J). 1997. write for info. (*1-56763-289-0*); write for info. (*1-56763-281-5*); pap. write for info. (*1-56763-290-4*); pap. write for info. (*1-56763-282-3*) Ozark Pub.

Withhold Not Correction. Bruce Ray. 1978. pap. 6.99 (*0-87552-400-1*, Pub. by Evangelical Pr) Presby & Reformed.

Withholding Taxes to & from 101 Countries. Lars-Erik Wenehed. 1995. 85.00 (*91-972352-2-9*, Pub. by Comtax SW) Intl Info Srvcs Inc.

Within. Derrick J. Saint-Julien. Ed. by Christine Cowan & Eleanor Howes. LC 94-90650. 45p. (Orig.). 1994. pap. 5.99 (*0-9643718-0-4*) For A Better Commun.

Within a Budding Grove. Marcel Proust. Tr. by C. K. Moncrieff & Terence Kilmartin from FRE. LC 92-25656. (In Search of Lost Time Ser.: Vol. 2). 784p. 1992. 18.50 (*0-679-60006-X*, Modern Lib) Random.

Within a Delirium. M. A. Lanahan. 23p. 1986. pap. 40.00 (*0-7223-2046-9*, Pub. by A H S Ltd UK) St Mut.

Within a Painted Past. Hazel Hutchins. (Illus.). 120p. (J). (gr. 4-6). 1994. pap. 5.95 (*1-55037-989-5*, Pub. by Annick CN); lib. bdg. 15.95 (*1-55037-369-2*, Pub. by Annick CN) Firefly Bks Ltd.

Within a Rainbowed Sea. deluxe ed. Christopher Newbert. 1987. 2,250.00 (*0-941831-04-3*) Beyond Words Pub.

***Within a Rainbowed Sea, Author's Ed.** anniversary ed. Christopher Newbert. (EarthSong Collection). (Illus.). 210p. 95.00 (*0-614-19289-7*) Beyond Words Pub.

Within a Rainbowed Sea: Ten Year Anniversary Edition. 2nd ed. Christopher Newbert. Ed. by Paul Berry. LC 94-21962. (Illus.). 220p. 1994. 75.00 (*0-941831-99-X*); pap. text ed. 39.95 (*1-885223-00-5*) Beyond Words Pub.

Within & Beyond. Jan Renfrow. (Illus.). 34p. (Orig.). 1993. pap. 10.00 (*0-9613072-7-7*) Jan Renfrow.

Within & Without: Anthology of Prison Literature. 1978. pap. 2.00 (*0-931350-04-2*) Moonlight Pubns.

Within Arm's Reach: A Contemplation of Nature in Words & Photographs. Karen A. Baggott. 32p. 1991. pap. 8.95 (*0-9627087-5-5*) Mt Olive Coll Pr.

Within Bounds: A Brief Guide to Securities Compliance. Thomas R. Keyes & David S. Miller. (Illus.). 32p. (Orig.). (C). 1990. pap. text ed. 9.50 (*0-9624115-1-5*) Keyes Pub.

Within Heaven's Gates. Rebecca R. Springer. 128p. 1984. mass mkt. 4.99 (*0-88368-125-0*) Whitaker Hse.

Within His Hands, Without a Fear. Roy Lessin. 96p. 1993. pap. 5.95 (*1-884009-01-8*) DaySpring.

Within Hospital Walls. Kathryn Kornegay. Ed. by Carolyn S. Zagury. LC 95-61473. 150p. (Orig.). 1995. pap. text ed. 14.95 (*1-880254-31-X*) Vista.

Within Human Experience: The Philosophy of William Ernest Hocking. Leroy S. Rouner. LC 71-75433. 395p. 1969. reprint ed. pap. 112.60 (*0-7837-4186-3*, 2059036) Bks Demand.

Within Me, Without Me: Adoption, Open & Shut. Wells. 1995. 49.95 (*1-85727-047-9*, Pub. by Scarlet Pr UK) LPC InBook.

Within Me, Without Me: Adoption, Open & Shut. Sue Wells. 1994. pap. 18.95 (*1-85727-042-8*, Pub. by Scarlet Pr UK) LPC InBook.

Within Me, Without You... Donita Simpson. 1973. pap. 6.50 (*0-685-99410-4*) Peace Ways.

Within Memory. Ed. by James Sheldon. Date not set. pap. 10.00 (*0-89822-108-0*) Visual Studies.

Within My Sacred Lodge. M. Irving Chriswell. (Illus.). vi, 19p. 1981. reprint ed. pap. 2.00 (*0-88053-006-5*, M-012) Macoy Pub.

Within Nietzsche's Labyrinth. Alan White. 192p. (C). 1990. pap. 15.95 (*0-415-90328-9*, A4614, Routledge NY) Routledge.

Within Our Reach. 80p. 1991. 7.95 (*0-87135-866-2*) Marvel Entmnt.

Within Our Reach: Breaking the Cycle of Disadvantage. Lisbeth B. Schorr & Daniel Schorr. 432p. 1989. pap. 12.95 (*0-385-24244-1*, Anchor Bks) Doubleday.

Within Ourselves. Ellen O'Connor. 91p. 1982. 7.95 (*0-9613897-0-2*) Valen Pub.

Within Pandoras' Box. Linda D. Johnston. 90p. (C). 1994. 17.50 (*0-9640092-0-X*) Selene Pubns.

Within Prison Walls: A Week in Auburn Prison. Thomas M. Osborne. 328p. 1991. reprint ed. pap. 9.95 (*0-9625714-3-1*) Spruce Gulch Pr.

Within Prison Walls, Being a Narrative of Personal Experience During a Week of Voluntary Confinement in the State Prison at Auburn, New York. Thomas M. Osborne. LC 69-14940. (Criminology, Law Enforcement, & Social Problems Ser.: No. 72). 1969. reprint ed. 16.00 (*0-87585-072-3*) Patterson Smith.

Within Range. Gil Ott. (Poetry Chapbooks Ser.). 28p. (Orig.). 1986. pap. 4.00 (*0-930901-38-X*) Burning Deck.

Within Reach. Barbara Delinsky. 400p. 1986. mass mkt. 3.95 (*0-373-97018-8*) Harlequin Bks.

Within Reach. Barbara Delinsky. 528p. 1995. mass mkt. 5.50 (*0-06-104174-2*, Harp PBks) HarpC.

***Within Reach.** Barbara Delinsky. LC 96-29251. (Star-Romance Ser.). 386p. 1997. 23.95 (*0-7862-0848-1*, Five Star) Mac Lib Ref.

Within Reach. Robert L. Millet. LC 95-7681. 132p. 1995. 13.95 (*0-87579-968-X*) Deseret Bk.

Within Reach. Marilyn Pappano. (Men Made in America Ser.). 1995. mass mkt. 3.59 (*0-373-45181-4*, 1-45181-4) Silhouette.

***Within Reach.** large type ed. Barbara Delinsky. LC 97-12436. 1997. write for info. (*0-7838-1935-8*) G K Hall.

***Within Reach: A Guide to Successful Writing.** Anna Ingalls & Dan Moody. teacher ed., pap. write for info. (*0-205-26225-2*) Allyn.

Within Reach: Academic Achievement Through Parent-Teacher Communication. Annabelle M. Markoff. LC 92-17388. 1992. 16.50 (*0-87879-955-9*) Acad Therapy.

Within Reach: Ten Stories. Donald R. Gallo. LC 92-29378. 192p. (J). (gr. 5 up). 1993. lib. bdg. 14.89 (*0-06-021441-4*) HarpC Child Bks.

Within Reason: A Guide to Non-Deductive Reasoning. John Burbidge. 192p. 1990. pap. 14.95 (*0-921149-55-7*) Broadview Pr.

***Within Sound of the Bugle.** Lee Priestley. (Illus.). 74p. 1996. pap. write for info. (*1-881325-18-0*) Yucca Tree Pr.

Within the Bounds. Marc Lodge. 336p. 1994. mass mkt. 5.99 (*0-425-14457-7*) Berkley Pub.

Within the Circle: An Anthology of African American Literary Criticism from the Harlem Renaissance to the Present. Ed. by Angelyn Mitchell. LC 94-12711. 544p. 1994. text ed. 49.95 (*0-8223-1536-X*); pap. text ed. 18.95 (*0-8223-1544-0*) Duke.

***Within the Circle: Parents & Children in an Arab Village.** Andrea B. Rugh. LC 96-31447. (History & Society of the Modern Middle East Series). 263p. 1997. 40.00 (*0-231-10678-5*); pap. write for info. (*0-231-10679-3*) Col U Pr.

***Within the Context of No Context.** George W. Trow. LC 96-36582. 119p. 1997. 20.00 (*0-87113-670-8*, Atlntc Mnthly); pap. 11.00 (*0-87113-674-0*, Atlntc Mnthly) Grove-Atltc.

Within the Dramatic Spectrum: The University of Florida, Department of Classics Comparative Drama Conference Papers, Vol. VI. Ed. by Karelisa V. Hartigan. 236p. (Orig.). (C). 1986. pap. text ed. 26.00 (*0-8191-5186-6*) U Pr of Amer.

Within the Four Seas: The Dialogue of East & West. Joseph Needham. 1979. pap. 8.95 (*0-8020-6360-8*) U of Toronto Pr.

Within the Gates. Rebecca R. Springer. Ed. by Lindsay Gordon. 1971. 3.95 (*0-89985-095-2*) Christ for the Nations.

Within the Halls of Pilate. David T. Lusk. 1983. pap. 4.95 (*0-89137-538-4*) Quality Pubns.

Within the Hollow Hills: An Anthology of New Celtic Writing. Intro. by John Matthews. 336p. (Orig.). 1995. pap. 17.95 (*0-940262-70-3*) Lindisfarne Bks.

Within the Holy of Holies: Attitudes of Attainment. rev. ed. Rellimeo. reprint ed. spiral bd. 6.50 (*0-7873-0712-2*) Hlth Research.

Within the Human Realm: The Poetry of Huang Zunxian, 1848-1905. J. D. Schmidt. LC 93-50082. (Studies in Chinese History, Literature & Institutions). 352p. (C). 1994. text ed. 47.95 (*0-521-46271-1*) Cambridge U Pr.

Within the Labyrinth All. Ellen Cooney. LC 91-72921. 104p. (Orig.). 1992. pap. 10.00 (*0-9602912-7-X*) Duir Press.

Within the Law. Laraine McDaniel. (Intrigue Ser.). 1994. mass mkt. 2.99 (*0-373-22272-6*, 1-22272-8) Harlequin Bks.

Within the Light. Cherie Sutherland. 256p. 1995. mass mkt. 5.99 (*0-553-56981-3*) Bantam.

***Within the Lighted City.** Lisa Lenzo. (John Simmons Short Fiction Award Ser.). 122p. 1997. 19.95 (*0-87745-611-9*) U of Iowa Pr.

Within the Pale: The True Story of Anti-Semitic Persecutions in Russia. Michael Davitt. LC 74-27976. (Modern Jewish Experience Ser.). 1975. reprint ed. 28.95 (*0-405-06705-4*) Ayer.

Within the Perfection of Christ: Essays on Peace & the Nature of the Church. Ed. by Terry L. Brensinger & E. Morris Sider. LC 89-82575. 266p. (C). 1990. pap. 14.00 (*0-916035-37-9*) Evangel Indiana.

Within the Plantation Household: Black & White Women of the Old South. Elizabeth Fox-Genovese. LC 88-40139. (Gender & American Culture Ser.). (Illus.). xix, 544p. (C). 1988. 39.95 (*0-8078-1808-9*); pap. 16.95 (*0-8078-4232-X*) U of NC Pr.

***Within the Red Rose.** Nancy H. Ingraham. 131p. (Orig.). 1997. mass mkt. 4.99 (*1-55197-751-6*, Pub. by Comnwlth Pub CN) Partners Pubs Grp.

Within the Rim, & Other Essays, 1914-15. Henry James. LC 68-22102. (Essay Index Reprint Ser.). 1977. 18.95 (*0-8369-0567-9*) Ayer.

Within the Rose. Hunce Voelcker. (Illus.). 60p. 1976. 6.00 (*0-915572-19-2*) Panjandrum.

Within the Shadows. Scott Shallengarger. 1994. 3.00 (*0-87129-450-8*, W76) Dramatic Pub.

Within the Shell of the Old: Essays in Workers' Self Organization. A Tribute to George Rawick. Ed. by David Roediger & Don Fitz. 112p. (Orig.). (C). 1990. pap. 15.00 (*0-88286-170-0*) C H Kerr.

Within the System: My Half Century in Social Security. Robert J. Myers & Richard L. Vernaci. LC 92-26776. (Illus.). 263p. 1992. 19.50 (*0-936031-12-3*) Actex Pubns.

An Asterisk (*) at the beginning of an entry indicates that the title is appearing in BIP for the first time.

Within the Temple of Isis. Belle M. Wagner. 156p. 1997. pap. 13.00 (*0-89540-264-5*, SB-264) Sun Pub.

Within the Tides. Joseph Conrad. 192p. 1993. pap. 9.95 (*0-14-018065-6*, Penguin Classics) Viking Penguin.

Within the U. S. Orbit: Small National Cultures Vis-a-Vis the United States. Ed. by Rob Kroes. 250p. (Orig.). 1992. pap. text ed. 35.00 (*90-5383-017-0*, Pub. by VU Univ Pr NE) Paul & Co Pubs.

Within the Underworld Sky: Mimbres Art in Context. Barbara L. Moulard & Lee A. Wilson. 190p. 1984. 75.00 (*0-942642-11-2*) Twelvetrees Pr.

***Within the Veil: An Adventure in Time.** Ruth Lee. LC 96-94779. Date not set. pap. 14.95 (*1-888988-05-3*, SAN 299-3228) LeeWay.

Within the Veil: Sequel to Journeying Onward. Lillian De Waters. 57p. 1993. reprint ed. spiral bd. 4.50 (*0-7873-0274-0*) Hlth Research.

Within the Walls of Denial: Conquering Addictive Behaviors. Robert J. Kearney. 200p. 1995. 25.00 (*0-393-70210-3*) Norton.

***Within the Whirlwind.** Eugenia S. Ginzburg. 1997. pap. text ed. 19.95 (*0-8101-1487-9*) Northwestern U Pr.

***Within These Walls.** Luis A. Ramos. Tr. by Samuel A. Zimmerman from SPA. LC 97-17340. (Discoveries Ser.). 1997. pap. 15.95 (*0-935480-89-7*) Lat Am Lit Rev Pr.

Within These Walls: A Study of Communication Between Presidents & Their Senior Staffs. Patricia D. Witherspoon. LC 90-7568. (Praeger Series in Political Communication). 272p. 1991. text ed. 59.95 (*0-275-93394-6*, C3394, Praeger Pubs) Greenwood.

Within This Garden. Ed. by Terry A. Neff. (Illus.). (Orig.). (C). 1993. pap. 29.95 (*0-932026-30-3*) Columbia College Chi.

Within This Garden: Photographs by Ruth Thorne-Thomsen. Ed. by Terry A. Neff. (Illus.). (Orig.). 1993. 45.00 (*0-89381-549-7*) Aperture.

Within Tuscany: Reflections on a Time & Place. Matthew Spender. (Illus.). 304p. 1993. pap. 13.95 (*0-14-017838-4*, Penguin Bks) Viking Penguin.

Within You Is the Power. Joseph Murphy. LC 77-86026. 1978. pap. 8.50 (*0-87516-247-9*) DeVorss.

Within Your Reach. William N. Hodges. Ed. by B. Phyllis Naylor. LC 89-84006. 130p. (Orig.). 1989. pap. 4.95 (*0-9622717-0-5*) Great Day Bks.

Withinsight: Visual Territories of Thirty Artists. Chris Bruce & Kathleen Shields. Ed. & Frwd. by Krista Elrick. (Illus.). 94p. (Orig.). 1995. pap. 18.00 (*0-9611710-0-6*) Western States.

Withnail & I: The Screenplay. 10th anniversary ed. Bruce Robinson. 129p. 1996. pap. 12.95 (*0-87951-658-5*) Overlook Pr.

Withof Lace. Trude V. Heyden-Biemans et al. (Illus.). 160p. 1991. 39.95 (*0-7134-6186-1*, Pub. by Batsford UK) Trafalgar.

Without a Doubt. Marcia Clark & Teresa Carpenter. LC 97-16319. 1997. 25.95 (*0-670-87089-7*) Viking Penguin.

***Without a Doubt.** Robin J. Gunn. LC 96-38991. (Sierra Jensen Ser.). (J). 1997. pap. 5.99 (*1-56179-519-4*) Focus Family.

Without a Dowry & Other Plays. Alexander Ostrovsky. Ed. & Tr. by Norman Henley from RUS. 1997. 37.95 (*0-88233-933-8*) Ardis Pubs.

***Without a Franchise Fee...I Became a Book Publisher.** Joseph A. Jiloty. (Illus.). 1996. text ed. 49.95 (*0-9633287-3-5*) Corporate Image.

Without a Gate. Jean Nightingale. 363p. (Orig.). 1990. pap. 6.95 (*9971-972-92-1*) OMF Bks.

Without a Guide: Contemporary Women's Travel Adventures. Ed. & Pref. by Katherine Govier. 234p. (Orig.). 1996. pap. 16.00 (*1-886913-04-8*) Hungry Mind.

Without a Hero: And Other Stories. T. Coraghessan Boyle. 256p. 1995. pap. 10.95 (*0-14-017839-2*, Penguin Bks) Viking Penguin.

Without a Name. Yvonne Vera. 1996. pap. text ed. 11.95 (*0-920661-54-8*, Pub. by TSAR CN) LPC InBook.

***Without a Name.** Yvonne Vera. LC 96-43064. 128p. 1996. 18.00 (*0-86316-247-9*) Writers & Readers.

Without a Past. Judi Lind. (Intrigue Ser.). 1994. mass mkt. 2.99 (*0-373-22260-2*, 1-22260-3) Harlequin Bks.

***Without a Prayer: Ayn Rand & the Close of Her System.** John W. Robbins. (Trinity Papers: Vol. 50). 300p. (Orig.). 1997. pap. 24.95 (*0-940931-50-8*) Trinity Found.

Without a Prayer: Religious Expression in Public Schools. Robert S. Alley. 230p. 1996. 25.95 (*1-57392-097-5*) Prometheus Bks.

***Without a Prayer: Why American Jews Fear Religion - And Why Only Religion Can Save Them.** Elliot Abrams. 1997. 25.00 (*0-614-28211-X*) Free Pr.

Without a Trace. Nora Roberts. 1996. mass mkt. 5.99 (*1-55166-059-8*, 1-66059-6, Mira Bks) Harlequin Bks.

Without a Trace. Patricia H. Rushford. (Jennie McGrady Mysteries Ser.: No. 5). 192p. (YA). (gr. 7-10). 1995. mass mkt. 4.99 (*1-55661-558-2*) Bethany Hse.

Without a Trace: Criminalistic Examination Methods of the Police, Fingerprints, Footprints, Document Examination, Telephone Usage, Tool Striations & How They are Evaded. 1992. lib. bdg. 99.75 (*0-8490-5306-4*) Gordon Pr.

***Without a Woman to Read: Toward the Daughter in Postmodernism.** Daniel Price. LC 96-43399. (SUNY Series in Radical, Social & Political Theory). 383p. (C). 1997. text ed. 65.50 (*0-7914-3459-1*); pap. text ed. 21.95 (*0-7914-3460-5*) State U NY Pr.

Without a Word: Teaching Beyond Women's Silence. Magda G. Lewis. LC 93-2318. 224p. (C). 1993. pap. 16.95 (*0-415-90594-X*, A7286, Routledge NY) Routledge.

Without Agenda: A Sojourn in South Africa. Avis Crowe & Dyck Vermilye. LC 90-62976. 32p. (Orig.). 1990. pap. 3.00 (*0-87574-293-9*) Pendle Hill.

***Without Apology: Andrea Dworkin's Art & Politics.** Cindy Jenefsky. (Polemics Ser.). 1997. text ed. 60.00 (*0-8133-1826-2*) Westview.

***Without Apology: The Heroes, the Heritage, & the Hope of Liberal Quakerism.** Chuck Fager. (Illus.). 188p. (Orig.). 1996. pap. 8.95 (*0-945177-13-5*) Kimo Pr.

***Without Arms.** Alvis S. Denny. LC 96-69568. 112p. (Orig.). 1996. 16.95 (*1-56167-322-6*) Am Literary Pr.

Without Asking. Jane R. Ransom. (Roerich Poetry Prize Winner Ser.). 64p. 1989. pap. 9.95 (*0-934257-29-9*) Story Line.

***Without Authority.** Soren Kierkegaard et al. LC 96-2929. (Kierkegaard's Writings). 1997. write for info. (*0-691-01239-3*) Princeton U Pr.

***Without Benefit of Clergy: A Challenge to Ministers.** Robert G. Davis. LC 96-70898. 64p. (Orig.). 1996. pap. 8.95 (*1-57736-016-8*) Providence Hse.

Without Bias: A Guidebook for Nondiscriminatory Communication. 200p. 1982. 15.95 (*0-685-43368-4*) Intl Assn Busn Comm.

Without Blare of Trumpets: Walter Drew, the National Erectors' Association, & the Open Shop Movement, 1903-57. Sidney Fine. LC 94-35335. 1995. 52.50 (*0-472-10576-0*) U of Mich Pr.

Without Blemish: Today's Problem. Jeanette H. Walworth. LC 72-3104. (Black Heritage Library Collection). 1977. reprint ed. 32.95 (*0-8369-9089-7*) Ayer.

Without Cherry Blossom. Leonide Zarine. LC 78-142275. (Short Story Index Reprint Ser.). 1977. 17.95 (*0-8369-3759-7*) Ayer.

***Without Child.** Laura Lisle. 1997. pap. write for info. (*0-345-40840-3*) Ballantine.

Without Child: Challenging the Stigma of Childlessness. Laurie Lisle. 288p. 1996. 23.00 (*0-345-37327-8*) Ballantine.

Without Child: Experiencing & Resolving Infertility. Ellen S. Glazer & Susan L. Cooper. 226p. pap. 10.95 (*0-669-21363-2*, Lexington) Jossey-Bass.

Without Clothes, We're All Naked: Reflections on Life in the Real Lane. Carla Perez. LC 95-11443. 208p. (Orig.). 1995. pap. 12.95 (*0-915166-87-9*) Impact Pubs CA.

Without Conscience. Robert D. Hare. Ed. by Tom Miller. (Orig.). 1993. 21.00 (*0-614-02671-7*) PB.

Without Conscience: The Disturbing World of the Psychopaths among Us. Robert D. Hare. Ed. by Tom Miller. 256p. 1995. pap. 16.00 (*0-671-52900-5*) PB.

Without Conscience: The Disturbing World of the Psychopaths Among Us. Robert D. Hare. 1995. pap. 14.00 (*0-671-53606-0*) PB.

***Without Consent.** Frances Fyfield. 1997. pap. 21.95 (*0-670-87682-8*) Viking Penguin.

***Without Consent: Confronting Adult Sexual Violence.** Ed. by Patricia W. Easteal. (Australian Institute Conference Proceedings Ser.: Vol. 20). 412p. 1993. pap. 45.00 (*0-642-19390-8*, Pub. by Aust Inst Criminology) Willow Tree NY.

Without Consent: Mass-Elite Linkages in Presidential Politics. Warren E. Miller. LC 88-3217. 200p. 1988. 22.00 (*0-8131-0550-1*) U Pr of Ky.

Without Consent: The Ethics of Disclosing Personal Information in Public Archives. Heather MacNeil. LC 92-16754. (Society of American Archivists Ser.). 230p. 1992. 30.00 (*0-8108-2581-3*) Scarecrow.

Without Consent or Contract: Evidence & Methods. Ed. by Robert W. Fogel et al. (C). 1992. text ed. 39.95 (*0-393-02790-2*) Norton.

Without Consent or Contract: Technical Papers, 2 vols., Vol. I: Markets & Productions. Ed. by Robert W. Fogel & Stanley L. Engerman. (C). 1990. text ed. 39.95 (*0-393-02791-0*) Norton.

Without Consent or Contract: The Rise & Fall of American Slavery. Robert W. Fogel. 544p. 1994. pap. 16.95 (*0-393-31219-4*) Norton.

Without Consent or Contract Vol. 2: Conditions of Slave Life, & the Transition to Freedom. Robert W. Fogel. (Technical Papers). (C). 1992. text ed. 39.95 (*0-393-02792-9*) Norton.

Without Deep Faith & a Sense of Humor You're Wearing Concrete Boots. Jacque Frederic & Kate Winters. 240p. 1995. lib. bdg. write for info. (*1-888069-00-7*) K Winters.

Without Discovery: A Native Response to Columbus. Ed. by Ray Gonzalez. LC 92-72435. (Turning Point Ser.). 244p. (Orig.). 1992. pap. 14.95 (*0-913089-31-1*) Broken Moon.

Without Doubt. Andy Clausen. 72p. (Orig.). 1991. pap. 5.95 (*0-929730-32-1*) Zeitgeist Pr.

Without Due Process. J. A. Jance. (J. P. Beaumont Ser.). 304p. 1993. mass mkt. 5.99 (*0-380-75837-7*) Avon.

Without Due Process. J. A. Jance. 4.98 (*0-8317-8577-2*) Smithmark.

Without Estrogen. Amy Gross & Dee Ito. 1994. 20.00 (*0-517-58825-0*, Crown) Crown Pub Group.

Without Estrogen. Dee Ito. 1995. pap. 12.00 (*0-517-88406-2*) Random.

***Without Estrogen.** Dee Ito. Date not set. 4.99 (*0-517-17639-4*) Random Hse Value.

Without Evidence. Wagner. 1989. pap. 10.95 (*0-9624239-0-4*) J S Wagner.

Without Evidence: The Rape of Justice in Wyoming. Jeane S. Wagner. (Illus.). 200p. (Orig.). 1989. pap. write for info. (*0-318-65822-4*) J S Wagner.

Without Excuse. Elnora Casey. (Illus.). 100p. (YA). pap. text ed. 6.95 (*1-883866-06-5*) Clarion Pub.

Without Falling. Leslie Dick. 160p. (Orig.). 1988. pap. 6.95 (*0-87286-224-0*) City Lights.

***Without Father: Bastard in the Pulpit.** Ed. by William G. Owens & Selena M. Owens. 96p. (Orig.). 1997. pap. write for info. (*0-9658629-0-9*) Prophetic Ser.

Without Fear. large type ed. Michael Judge. (Mystery Library). 352p. 1995. pap. 15.99 (*0-7089-7647-6*, Linford) Ulverscroft.

Without Fear of Being Happy: Lula, the Workers Party & Brazil. Emir Sader & Ken Silverstein. LC 91-25893. 160p. (C). 1991. pap. 19.00 (*0-86091-523-9*, A4974, Pub. by Vrso UK) Norton.

Without Feathers. Woody Allen. 224p. 1986. mass mkt. 5.99 (*0-345-33697-6*) Ballantine.

Without Feathers. Harry Burrus. LC 90-36267. (Illus.). 64p. (Orig.). 1990. pap. 12.50 (*0-941749-16-9*) Black Tie Pr.

***Without Fitting, Filing, or Chipping: An Illustrated History of the Phoenix Bridge Company.** Thomas R. Winpenny. Ed. by Ann Bartholomew. (Illus.). 176p. 1996. pap. write for info. (*0-930973-15-1*) Canal Hist Tech.

***Without Fitting, Filing, or Chipping: An Illustrated History of the Phoenix Bridge Company.** Thomas R. Winpenny. Ed. by Ann Bartholomew. LC 96-32370. (Illus.). 154p. 1996. 34.00 (*0-930973-16-X*) Canal Hist Tech.

Without Force or Lies: Voices from the Revolution of Central Europe in 1989-90. Ed. by William M. Brinton & Alan Rinzler. LC 90-31716. 512p. 1990. 15.95 (*0-916515-78-8*); pap. 10.95 (*0-916515-92-3*) Mercury Hse Inc.

Without Forgetting the Imam: Lebanese Shi'ism in an American Community. Linda S. Walbridge. LC 96-32617. (Illus.). 280p. 1997. 29.95 (*0-8143-2675-7*) Wayne St U Pr.

Without Form & Void: A Study of the Meaning of Genesis 1.2. Arthur C. Custance. 211p. 1970. reprint ed. pap. 9.95 (*0-919857-65-5*, Pub. by Doorway Pubns CN) Doorway USA.

Without Future: The Plight of Syrian Jewry. Saul S. Friedman. LC 89-3769. 157p. 1989. text ed. 45.00 (*0-275-93313-X*, C3313, Praeger Pubs) Greenwood.

Without God or His Doubles: Realism, Relativism, & Rorty. LC 94-17768. (Philosophy of History & Culture Ser.: Vol. 14). 1994. 68.00 (*90-04-10062-8*) E J Brill.

Without God or Reason: The Plays of Thomas Shadwell & Secular Ethics in the Restoration. Christopher J. Wheatley & Bernd Zolitschka. LC 92-54622. 208p. (C). 1993. 36.50 (*0-8387-5243-8*) Bucknell U Pr.

Without God, Without Creed: The Origins of Unbelief in America. James Turner. LC 84-15397. (New Studies in American Intellectual & Cultural History). 336p. 1986. reprint ed. pap. text ed. 15.95 (*0-8018-3407-4*) Johns Hopkins.

Without Good Reason: The Rationality Debate in Philosophy & Cognitive Science. Edward Stein. (Clarendon Library of Logic & Philosophy). (Illus.). 312p. 1996. text ed. 49.95 (*0-19-823574-7*) OUP.

Without Haste. Francine Porad. (Amelia Chapbooks Ser.). 16p. (Orig.). 1990. pap. 4.50 (*0-936545-16-X*) Amelia.

Without Help or Hindrance: Religious Identity in American Culture. 2nd ed. Eldon G. Ernst. 244p. 1987. reprint ed. pap. text ed. 23.00 (*0-8191-5565-9*) U Pr of Amer.

Without Honor. Elizabeth Stuart. 1994. mass mkt. 4.99 (*0-312-95167-1*) St Martin.

Without Honor: The Impeachment of President Nixon & the Crimes of Camelot. J. M. Zeifman. LC 95-62422. 300p. 1996. 24.95 (*1-56025-128-X*) Thunders Mouth.

Without Just Cause: An Employer's Practical & Legal Guide on Wrongful Discharge. LC 88-600466. 1988. 95.00 (*1-55871-028-0*) BNA Plus.

Without Justice for All: The Constitutional Rights of Aliens. Elizabeth Hull. LC 84-19798. (Contributions in Political Science Ser.: No. 129). xiii, 244p. 1985. text ed. 36.95 (*0-313-23670-4*, HAP/, Greenwood Pr) Greenwood.

***Without Keys: My 15 Weeks with the Street People. Patricia A. McDonough. (Illus.). 427p. (Orig.). 1996. pap. 24.00 (*0-9653467-0-6*); lib. bdg. 42.00 (*0-9653467-1-4*) Terra Sancta.**
What will become of the homeless as the nation reorganizes for welfare reform? People who already fall through the "safety net," they lack even the barest physical & emotional necessities of life, though many work & receive financial aid of some kind. Pat McDonough, a professional housing consultant with a college degree, years of graduate work & career achievements in various fields, details her formula for meaningful change in her new book WITHOUT KEYS: MY FIFTEEN WEEKS WITH THE STREET PEOPLE. McDonough's first-hand account is a primer on homelessness. From its individual & government roots to the emotional, physical & spiritual toll it takes on people to practical solutions for helping the most needy, this book tells it all. It is meticulously researched; generously drenched with the latest statistics & regulations. A page-turner, one is compelled to discover how Pat finally survived to write the book. And somewhere between page 1 & page 393, preconceptions about the homeless are lost, replaced by a sensitivity for severely deprived human beings. To order: The Bookmen, Baker & Taylor, Quality Books, Terra Sancta Press, 612-988-6999, FAX: 612-938-5154. ***Publisher Provided Annotation.***

Without Knowing Why. Jessica Steele. (Romance Ser.: No. 173). 1992. pap. 2.79 (*0-373-03173-4*) Harlequin Bks.

Without Lawful Authority. Manning Coles. (Spies & Intrigues Ser.: No. 4). 246p. 1984. pap. 5.95 (*0-918172-16-0*) Leetes Isl.

Without Locks & Bars: The Normative Culture of the Glen Mills Schools. Grant R. Grisson & William L. Dubnov. LC 88-36410. 268p. 1989. text ed. 49.95 (*0-275-93282-6*, C3282, Praeger Pubs) Greenwood.

Without Lying Down: Frances Marion & the Powerful Women of Early Hollywood. Cari Beauchamp. LC 97-641. (Illus.). 475p. 1997. 29.50 (*0-684-80213-9*) S&S Trade.

***Without Lying Down: Francis Marion & the Powerful Women of Early Hollywood.** Cari Beauchamp. 1997. 26.00 (*0-614-28027-3*, Scribners PB Fict) S&S Trade.

Without Mercy. Keith R. Ablow. 1996. mass mkt. 5.99 (*0-312-95923-0*) St Martin.

Without Mercy: Obsession & Murder under the Influence. Gary Provost. Ed. by Claire Zion. 328p. 1990. reprint ed. mass mkt. 5.99 (*0-671-66997-4*) PB.

Without Miracles: Universal Selection Theory & the Second Darwinian Revolution. Gary Cziko. LC 95-943. 385p. 1995. 30.00 (*0-262-03232-5*, Bradford Bks) MIT Pr.

***Without Miracles: Universal Selection Theory & the Second Darwinian Revolution.** Gary Cziko. (Illus.). 400p. 1997. reprint ed. pap. 17.50 (*0-262-53147-X*, Bradford Bks) MIT Pr.

Without Natural Affection: Is Criminal Hardness Replacing Natural Feelings? Ed J. MacWilliams. 1995. pap. 7.95 (*1-878897-02-0*) Blueprint Revival.

Without Nightfall upon the Spirit: Reflections on Aging. Mary C. Morrison. LC 93-85962. 32p. 1993. pap. 3.00 (*0-87574-311-0*) Pendle Hill.

***Without Our Consent: Forcible Inclusion of the James Bay Crees & Cree Territory into an Independent Quebec.** Grand Council of the Crees Staff. 200p. 1997. pap. 21.95 (*1-55022-301-1*, Pub. by ECW Press CN) Genl Dist Srvs.

Without Our Past: A Handbook for the Preservation of Canada's Architectural Heritage. Ann Falkner. (Illus.). 1976. pap. 9.95 (*0-8020-6298-9*) U of Toronto Pr.

Without Passport: The Life & Work of Paul Richard. Michel P. Richard. (American University Studies: History: Ser. IX, Vol. 28). 281p. (C). 1987. text ed. 44.95 (*0-8204-0444-6*) P Lang Pubng.

Without Precedent: The Life & Career of Eleanor Roosevelt. Ed. by Joan Hoff-Wilson & Marjorie Lightman. LC 83-49062. (Illus.). 288p. 1984. 27.50 (*0-253-19100-9*) Ind U Pr.

Without Precedent: The Life & Career of Eleanor Roosevelt. Ed. by Joan Hoff-Wilson & Marjorie Lightman. LC 83-49062. (Illus.). 288p. 1987. pap. 9.95 (*0-253-20327-9*, MB-327) Ind U Pr.

***Without Precedent: The Life & Career of Eleanor Roosevelt.** Ed. by Joan Hoff-Wilson & Marjorie Lightman. LC 83-49062. (Everywoman: Studies in History, Literature, & Culture). (Illus.). 285p. pap. 81.30 (*0-608-05028-8*, 2059689) Bks Demand.

Without Prejudice. Israel Zangwill. LC 72-13302. (Essay Index Reprint Ser.). 1977. reprint ed. 22.95 (*0-8369-8183-9*) Ayer.

Without Proof or Evidence: Essays of O. K. Bouwsma. O. K. Bouwsma. Ed. by Ronald E. Hustwit. LC 83-10269. 177p. reprint ed. pap. 50.50 (*0-7837-4665-2*, 2044392) Bks Demand.

Without Quarter: A Life of Tom Johnston. Russell Galbraith. (Illus.). 256p. 1996. 45.00 (*1-85158-761-6*, Pub. by Mnstream UK) Trafalgar.

Without Quarter: The Wichita Expedition & the Fight on Crooked Creek. William Y. Chalfant. LC 91-50300. (Illus.). 192p. 1991. 22.95 (*0-8061-2367-2*) U of Okla Pr.

Without Reason: A Family Copes with Two Generations of Autism. Charles Hart. LC 89-45042. 292p. 1995. pap. 19.95 (*0-06-016143-4*, HarpT) Fut Horizons.

Without Regard to Good Manners: A Biography of Gilbert Stuart 1743-86. William Zachs. 226p. 1992. 42.50 (*0-7486-0319-0*, Pub. by Edinburgh U Pr UK) Col U Pr.

Without Remorse. Tom Clancy. 640p. 1993. 24.95 (*0-399-13825-0*, Putnam) Putnam Pub Group.

Without Remorse. limited ed. Tom Clancy. 640p. 1993. 150.00 (*0-399-13840-4*, Putnam) Putnam Pub Group.

Without Remorse. Tom Clancy. 768p. 1994. reprint ed. mass mkt. 7.50 (*0-425-14332-5*) Berkley Pub.

Without Reservation: The Arizona Republic Restaurant Critic's Guide to Dining in Phoenix. Penelope Corcoran. Ed. by David Gianelli. (Illus.). 204p. (Orig.). 1994. pap. 10.95 (*0-9636832-1-7*); disk 10.95 (*0-9636832-2-5*) Phoenix News.

Without Reservations: An Uncensored, Unabashed Look at How People Behave in Hotels. Illus. by George Hoch & Frank Cothran. LC 92-64283. 192p. 1992. 14.95 (*0-9633894-3-2*) Sandcastles.

***Without Reservations: From Harlem to the End of the Santa Fe Trail.** Samuel B. Ballen. LC 97-1151. (Legacy Edition Ser.). 1997. write for info. (*0-943734-36-3*) Ocean Tree Bks.

Without Reserve. Robin Hastings. 160p. 1990. 52.00 (*0-85131-455-4*, Pub. by J A Allen & Co UK) St Mut.

Without Right Angles: The Round Barns of Iowa. Lowell Soike. 1991. pap. 14.95 (*0-941016-80-3*) Penfield.

Without Roof. Kinereth Gensler. LC 80-70829. 64p. (C). 1981. pap. 3.95 (*0-914086-32-4*) Alicejamesbooks.

Without Shelter: Homelessness in the 1980s. Peter Rossi. (Twentieth Century Fund Papers). 1989. 18.95 (*0-87078-235-5*); pap. 8.95 (*0-87078-234-7*) TCFP-PPP.

Without Sin: The Life & Death of the Oneida Community. Spencer Klaw. (Illus.). 352p. 1994. reprint ed. pap. 14.95 (*0-14-023930-8*, Penguin Bks) Viking Penguin.

Without Site Investigation Ground is a Hazard: Site Investigation in Construction, 1. (Site Investigation in Construction Ser.). 52p. 1993. text ed. 10.00 (*0-7277-1982-3*) Am Soc Civil Eng.

Without Sorcery. Theodore Sturgeon. 1993. reprint ed. lib. bdg. 18.95 (*0-89968-373-8*, Lghtyr Pr) Buccaneer Bks.

Without Spanking or Spoiling: A Practical Approach to Toddler & Preschool Guidance. Elizabeth Crary. LC 92-83497. (Illus.). 128p. (Orig.). 1993. pap. 14.95 (*0-943990-74-2*) Parenting Pr.

Without Spanking or Spoiling: A Practical Approach to Toddler & Preschool Guidance. 2nd ed. Elizabeth Crary. LC 92-83497. (Illus.). 128p. (Orig.). 1993. lib. bdg. 19.95 (*0-943990-87-4*) Parenting Pr.

Without Spanking or Spoiling: Leader's Guide. Elizabeth Crary. 1996. pap. text ed. 19.95 (*0-943990-86-6*) Parenting Pr.

Without Stopping. Paul Bowles. (Illus.). 400p. (C). 1985. pap. 14.95 (*0-88001-267-6*) Ecco Pr.

Without the Bomb: The Politics of Nuclear Non-Proliferation. Mitchell Reiss. 368p. 1988. text ed. 52.50 (*0-231-06438-1*) Col U Pr.

Without the Bomb: The Politics of Nuclear Nonproliferation. Mitchell Reiss. 337p. 1989. pap. text ed. 17.00 (*0-231-06439-X*) Col U Pr.

Without the Chrysanthemum & the Sword. Jean Stoetzel. LC 76-7582. (Illus.). 334p. 1976. reprint ed. text ed. 35.00 (*0-8371-8856-3*, STWCS, Greenwood Pr) Greenwood.

***Without the Dawn, 6 vols.** Roger Elwood. 1997. boxed 14.89 (*1-57748-099-6*) Barbour & Co.

Without the Law: Administrative Justice & Legal Pluralism in 19th-Century England. H. W. Arthurs. 328p. 1985. 35.00 (*0-8020-5654-7*) U of Toronto Pr.

***Without the Smell of Fire.** Walter C. Lanyon. 228p. 1983. reprint ed. pap. 8.00 (*1-889870-05-6*) Union Life.

Without Thorns, It's Not a Rose. John M. Scott. LC 86-62479. 176p. 1988. pap. 4.95 (*0-87973-502-3*, 502) Our Sunday Visitor.

Without Trace. Katherine John. LC 95-14714. 1995. 24.95 (*0-312-13218-2*) St Martin.

Without Troops & Tanks: Humanitarism Intervention in Ethiopia & Eritrea. Mark Duffield & John Prendergast. 350p. (Orig.). (C). 1994. 49.95 (*1-56902-002-7*); pap. 16.95 (*1-56902-003-5*) Red Sea Pr.

Without Warning. Charlotte DeClue. 24p. (Orig.). 1985. pap. 3.50 (*0-936574-08-9*) Strawberry Pr NY.

Without Warning. Patricia Donegan. 96p. 1990. per. 8.00 (*0-938077-32-5*) Parallax Pr.

Without Warning. Ann Williams. (Intimate Moments Ser.: No. 436). 1992. mass mkt. 3.39 (*0-373-07436-0*, 5-07436-4) Harlequin Bks.

Without Warning: Poems. Elizabeth Goldring. Ed. by Gloria V. Hickok. 64p. (Orig.). 1995. pap. 10.00 (*1-884235-13-1*) Helicon Nine Eds.

Without Whose Aid: Nursing & the Cleveland Clinic. Diane E. Grabowski. (Illus.). xviii, 310p. 1996. 29.95 (*0-9615424-2-X*) Cleveland Clinic.

***Without Wings How Can I Fly?, Vol. 1.** Farber. LC 97-12863. 1995. pap. 14.95 (*0-8050-3380-7*) St Martin.

Without Words. Joanne Ryder. (Illus.). 32p. (J). 1995. 15.95 (*0-87156-580-3*) Sierra Club Childrens.

Without Words: An Introduction to Nonverbal Communication. M. Van Schaack. 1977. 750.00 (*0-13-961417-6*) P-H.

Without Your Love. large type ed. Kathleen Treves. 352p. 1988. 25.99 (*0-7089-1859-X*) Ulverscroft.

Withstanding Hitler. Michael Balfour. 352p. (C). 1988. text ed. 49.95 (*0-415-00617-1*) Routledge.

Withymead: A Jungian Community for the Healing Arts. Anthony Stevens. 1991. pap. 9.95 (*0-904575-32-2*, Coventure Ltd) Sigo Pr.

***Witi Ihimaera: A Changing Vision.** Umelo Ojinmah. 158p. 1996. pap. 24.95 (*0-908569-57-2*, Pub. by U Otago Pr NZ) Intl Spec Bk.

Witkacy: Stanislaw Ignacy Witkiewicz As an Imaginative Writer. Daniel Gerould. LC 79-3872. (Illus.). 380p. 1981. 30.00 (*0-295-95714-X*) U of Wash Pr.

Witkiewicz Reader: The Life & Work of Stanislaw Ignacy Witkiewicz. Stanislaw I. Witkiewicz. Tr. & Intro. by Daniel Gerould. (Illus.). 400p. (Orig.). 1993. 59.95 (*0-8101-0980-8*); pap. 24.95 (*0-8101-0994-8*) Northwestern U Pr.

W

Witlings. Fanny Burney. Ed. by Clayton J. Delery. (Early Women Writers 1650-1800 Ser.: No. 3). 161p. 1995. 29.95 (*0-937191-55-8*) Colleagues Pr Inc.

Witness. Beau Beausoleil. LC 76-39971. (Illus.). 60p. 1976. pap. 6.00 (*0-915572-23-0*) Panjandrum.

Witness. John G. Bennett. 1983. 16.95 (*0-934254-24-9*); pap. 8.95 (*0-685-01116-X*) Claymont Comm.

***Witness.** S. L. Bhyrappa. 255p. (Orig.). 1997. mass mkt. 4.99 (*1-55197-931-4*, Pub. by Comnwlth Pub CN) Partners Pubs Grp.

Witness. Sandra Brown. 1996. pap. 6.99 (*0-614-98109-3*, Warner Vision) Warner Bks.

Witness. Sandra Brown. 448p. 1996. mass mkt. 6.99 (*0-446-60330-9*, Warner Vision) Warner Bks.

Witness. Sandra Brown. 1995. pap. 17.95 (*0-7871-0296-2*, Dove Bks) Dove Audio.

Witness. Whittaker Chambers. 1976. 42.95 (*0-8488-0958-0*) Amereon Ltd.

Witness. Whittaker Chambers & John Fox. (Illus.). 808p. 1978. pap. 14.95 (*0-89526-789-6*) Regnery Pub.

Witness. Thomas Hennell. 7.95 (*0-8216-0006-0*, Univ Bks) Carol Pub Group.

Witness. Judy McGorray. 47p. 1994. pap. text ed. write for info. (*1-888200-03-0*) JayMac Commun.

Witness. Juan J. Saer. Tr. by Margaret J. Costa from SPA. LC 90-60289. 176p. 1991. pap. 13.95 (*1-85242-184-3*) Serpents Tail.

Witness. Charles G. Taylor. (Illus.). 26p. (Orig.). 1978. pap. 3.25 (*0-88680-204-0*) I E Clark.

Witness. Robert Westall. (Illus.). 32p. (J). 1994. pap. 14.99 (*0-525-45331-8*) Dutton Child Bks.

Witness. large type ed. Sandra Brown. LC 95-14159. 1995. 25.95 (*0-7862-0476-1*) Thorndike Pr.

Witness. large type ed. Sandra Brown. LC 95-14159. 1996. pap. 22.95 (*0-7862-0477-X*) Thorndike Pr.

Witness. Grace L. Hill. 1976. reprint ed. lib. bdg. 25.95 (*0-89190-026-8*, Rivercity Pr) Amereon Ltd.

Witness. Grace L. Hill. 1990. reprint ed. lib. bdg. 21.95 (*0-89968-527-7*) Buccaneer Bks.

Witness, No. 75. Grace L. Hill. (Grace Livingston Hill Ser.: Vol. 75). 320p. 1994. pap. 4.99 (*0-8423-8025-6*) Tyndale.

Witness: Empowering the Church Through Worship, Community, & Mission. rev. ed. A. Grace Wenger et al. LC 88-24492. 208p. 1989. pap. 9.99 (*0-8361-3482-6*) Herald Pr.

Witness: Endangered Species of North America. Susan Middleton & David Liittschwager. LC 93-48877. (Illus.). 256p. 1994. 50.00 (*0-8118-0282-5*); pap. 35.00 (*0-8118-0258-2*) Chronicle Bks.

***Witness: Greenpeace: 25 Years on the Environmental Frontline.** Intro. by Dalai Lama. (Illus.). 160p. 1997. 35.00 (*0-233-99024-0*, Pub. by A Deutsch UK) Trafalgar.

Witness: Poems. Jeanie Thompson. LC 95-16348. 96p. 1995. 17.00 (*1-881320-48-0*, Black Belt) Black Belt Comm.

Witness: The Artist's Vision in the Face of AIDS. Barbara S. Brauer. LC 96-26462. (Illus.). 72p. (Orig.). 1996. pap. 24.95 (*0-7649-0018-8*) Pomegranate Calif.

***Witness: The Story of a Search.** John G. Bennett. LC 97-6407. (Bennett Books "Spiritual Classics" Editions). (Illus.). 352p. 1997. reprint ed. pap. 20.00 (*1-881408-02-7*) Bennett Bks.

Witness: The Uses of Adversity: Essays on the Fate of Central Europe. Timothy G. Ash. 335p. 1990. 19.95 (*0-685-32964-X*) Random.

Witness: Writings of Bartolome de las Casas. Ed. by George Sanderlin. LC 91-30348. 1992. pap. 14.50 (*0-88344-790-8*) Orbis Bks.

Witness against the Beast: William Blake & the Moral Law. E. P. Thompson. LC 92-50819. (Illus.). 256p. 1993. 30.00 (*1-56584-058-5*) New Press NY.

Witness Against the Beast: William Blake & the Moral Law. E. P. Thompson. LC 92-47286. 1993. write for info. (*0-521-22515-9*) Cambridge U Pr.

Witness Against the Beast: William Blake & the Moral Law. E. P. Thompson. 256p. 1995. pap. 17.00 (*1-56584-099-2*) New Press NY.

Witness Against War: Pacifism in Canada, 1900-1945. Thomas P. Socknat. 1987. 40.00 (*0-8020-5704-7*); pap. 18.95 (*0-8020-6632-1*) U of Toronto Pr.

Witness among Friends. Timothy Brown. 119p. (Orig.). (C). 1989. teacher ed. 10.60 (*0-930265-62-9*) CRC Pubns.

Witness among Friends. Cliff Christians. 119p. (Orig.). (C). 1989. pap. text ed. 8.70 (*0-930265-61-0*) CRC Pubns.

Witness & a Warning. Ezra T. Benson. LC 88-70533. ix, 86p. 1988. 12.95 (*0-87579-153-0*) Deseret Bk.

Witness & Existence: Essays in Honor of Schubert M. Ogden. Ed. by Philip E. Devenish & George L. Goodwin. LC 89-30283. (Illus.). 256p. 1989. pap. text ed. 24.00 (*0-226-14358-9*); lib. bdg. 54.00 (*0-226-14357-0*) U Ch Pr.

Witness & I. O. Edmund Clubb. LC 74-11385. 314p. 1974. text ed. 49.50 (*0-231-03859-3*) Col U Pr.

Witness & Scholars: Studies in Musical Biography. Hans Lenneberg. (Monographs on Musicology: Vol. 5). 224p. 1988. text ed. 68.00 (*2-88124-210-3*, ML3797.L46) Gordon & Breach.

Witness & Service in North America. Ed. by Cornelius J. Dyck et al. LC 80-10975. (Mennonite Central Committee Story Ser.: Vol. 3). 122p. 1980. reprint ed. pap. 34.80 (*0-608-01759-0*, 2062417) Bks Demand.

Witness, & the Apparitions & Persecutions in the USSR: Autobiography of Josyp Terelya. Josyp Terelya. Tr. by Michael H. Brown. LC 91-61562. (Illus.). 344p. (Orig.). 1991. pap. 11.00 (*1-877678-17-1*) Riehle Found.

Witness & the Other World: Exotic European Travel Writing, 400-1600. Mary B. Campbell. LC 88-47720. (Illus.). 312p. 1988. 42.50 (*0-8014-2137-3*); 15.95 (*0-8014-9933-X*) Cornell U Pr.

Witness & Wait: Thirteen Poets from New England. Every Other Thursday Writing Group. LC 87-83634. 104p. (Orig.). 1988. pap. 7.95 (*0-9619960-0-5*) Every Other Thursday.

Witness Box. Virginia Scott. 44p. (Orig.). 1985. per. 4.95 (*0-934238-07-3*) Motheroot.

***Witness for a Generation.** John J. Baer. (Illus.). 144p. (Orig.). 1997. pap. 10.95 (*1-56474-219-9*) Fithian Pr.

Witness for Change: Quaker Women over Three Centuries. Ed. by Elisabeth P. Brown & Susan M. Stuard. LC 88-27157. 200p. (C). 1989. text ed. 32.00 (*0-8135-1447-9*); pap. text ed. 17.00 (*0-8135-1448-7*) Rutgers U Pr.

Witness for Eleanor Dare. Robert White. (Illus.). 296p. 1991. pap. 14.95 (*0-938530-51-8*) Lexikos.

Witness for Freedom: African-American Voices on Race, Slavery, & Emancipation. Ed. by C. Peter Ripley et al. LC 92-21591. (Illus.). xxvi, 306p. (C). 1993. 32.50 (*0-8078-2072-5*); pap. 11.95 (*0-8078-4404-7*) U of NC Pr.

Witness for the Defense: The Accused, the Eyewitness, & the Expert who puts Memory on Trial. Elizabeth F. Loftus. 1991. 19.95 (*0-312-05537-4*) St Martin.

Witness for the Defense: The Accused, the Eyewitness, & the Expert Who Puts Memory on Trial. Elizabeth F. Loftus & Katherine Ketcham. (Illus.). 304p. 1992. pap. 12.95 (*0-312-08455-2*) St Martin.

Witness for the Prosecution: Annie Besant's Testimony on Behalf of H. P. Blavatsky in the N. Y. Sun - Coves Law Case. Michael Gomes. Ed. & Pref. by James A. Santucci. (Theosophical History Occasional Papers: Vol. I). (Illus.). i, 60p. (Orig.). 1993. pap. text ed. 12.00 (*1-883279-01-1*) J Santucci.

Witness for the Prosecution & Other Stories. Agatha Christie. 240p. 1984. pap. 5.50 (*0-425-06809-9*) Berkley Pub.

Witness for the Prosecution & Other Stories. large type ed. Agatha Christie. (Popular Author Ser.). 375p. 1988. 21.95 (*0-8161-4619-5*, GK Hall) Thorndike Pr.

Witness Forever: Ancient Israel's Perception of Literature & the Resultant Hebrew Bible. Isaac Rabinowitz. Ed. by David I. Owen. (Occasional Publications of the Department of Near Eastern Studies & the Program of Jewish Studies, Cornell U.). 165p. (C). 1994. 20.00 (*1-883053-02-1*) CDL Pr.

Witness from Beyond. Ed. by Ruth M. Taylor. LC 79-52116. 172p. 1980. reprint ed. pap. 5.95 (*0-9602884-0-6*) Chicago Review.

Witness in Philadelphia. Florence Mars & Lynn Eden. LC 76-50660. (Illus.). 296p. 1989. pap. 11.95 (*0-8071-1566-5*) La State U Pr.

Witness Intimidation: The Law's Response. Michael H. Graham. LC 84-11780. xiii, 317p. 1985. text ed. 59.95 (*0-89930-104-5*, GRW/, Quorum Bks) Greenwood.

Witness of Bones. Leonard Tourney. 1993. reprint ed. mass mkt. 4.99 (*0-345-38319-2*) Ballantine.

Witness of Decline - Albert Camus: Moralist of the Absurd. Lev Braun. LC 72-11082. 283p. 1974. 36.50 (*0-8386-1246-6*) Fairleigh Dickinson.

Witness of Poetry. Czeslaw Milosz. (Charles Eliot Norton Lectures). 128p. 1984. pap. text ed. 7.95 (*0-674-95383-5*) HUP.

Witness of Preaching. Thomas G. Long. 216p. (Orig.). 1989. pap. 18.00 (*0-8042-1571-5*) Westminster John Knox.

Witness of Reconciliation. Wallace B. Smith. 100p. (Orig.). 1992. pap. text ed. 7.50 (*0-8309-0614-2*) Herald Hse.

Witness of the Brothers: A History of the Bruderhof. Yaacov Oved. Tr. by Anthony Berris. 350p. (C). 1996. text ed. 44.95 (*1-56000-203-4*) Transaction Pubs.

Witness of the Light: A Photographic Journey in the Footsteps of the American Prophet, Joseph Smith. Scot F. Proctor. LC 91-71335. (Illus.). 208p. 1991. 39.95 (*0-87579-389-4*) Deseret Bk.

Witness of the Stars. Ethelbert W. Bullinger. LC 68-16762. 212p. 1984. pap. 12.99 (*0-8254-2245-0*, Kregel Class) Kregel.

Witness of the Stars. Ethelbert W. Bullinger. 204p. 1969. reprint ed. spiral bd. 12.50 (*0-7873-0132-9*) Hlth Research.

Witness of "The Vulgate," "Peshitta" & "Septuagint" to the Text of "Zephaniah" Sidney Zandstra. LC 72-948. (Columbia University. Contributions to Oriental History & Philology Ser.: No. 4). reprint ed. 24.50 (*0-404-50534-1*) AMS Pr.

Witness of the Worshiping Community: Liturgy & the Practice of Evangelism. Frank C. Senn. LC 92-34033. 192p. 1993. pap. 12.95 (*0-8091-3368-7*) Paulist Pr.

Witness of Times: Manifestations of Ideology in Seventeenth Century England. Ed. by Katherine Z. Keller & Gerald J. Schiffhorst. LC 93-34481. (Duquesne Studies: Language & Literature Ser.: Vol. 15). 318p. (C). 1993. text ed. 44.95 (*0-8207-0252-8*) Duquesne.

Witness Preparation. V. Hale Starr & Mark McCormick. 1989. write for info. (*0-318-63270-5*) Little.

Witness Primer. Erwin J. Kolb. 128p. (Orig.). 1986. pap. 6.99 (*0-570-04441-3*, 12-3043) Concordia.

Witness Psychology. R. Buckhout & M. Greenwald. (Monographs: No. CR-1). 1981. 4.00 (*1-55524-000-3*) Ctr Respon Psych.

Witness the Love: Stories from AIDS Caregivers. Fawn Moran. (Illus.). 240p. 1996. pap. 14.95 (*0-9640878-0-4*) Journey Home.

Witness Through the Imagination: Jewish-American Holocaust Literature. S. Lillian Kremer. LC 88-34562. 394p. (C). 1989. 39.95 (*0-8143-2116-X*); pap. 19.95 (*0-8143-2117-8*) Wayne St U Pr.

Witness to a Generation: Significant Writings from Christianity & Crisis, 1941-1966. Ed. by Wayne H. Cowan. LC 66-29152. (Orig.). 1966. 6.55 (*0-672-50852-4*, Bobbs) Macmillan.

Witness to America's Past: Two Centuries of Collecting by the Massachusetts Historical Society. Massachusetts Historical Society Staff. 208p. 1990. pap. text ed. 25.00 (*0-87846-334-8*) Mus Fine Arts Boston.

Witness to an Era. Mark Katz. Date not set. pap. write for info. (*0-14-012188-9*, Viking) Viking Penguin.

Witness to an Era: The Civil War Western Photographs of Alexander Gardner. 1998. 19.99 (*0-517-18344-7*) Random Hse Value.

Witness to Annihilation: Surviving the Holocaust - A Memoir. Samuel Drix. (World War II Commemorative Ser.). (Illus.). 272p. 1994. 24.95 (*0-02-881087-2*) Brasseys Inc.

Witness to Disintegration: Provincial Life in the Last Year of the U. S. S. R. Walter L. Hixson. LC 92-56904. 192p. 1993. 19.95 (*0-87451-618-8*) U Pr of New Eng.

***Witness to Evil.** Janet Dawson. LC 97-20594. 1997. 21.95 (*0-449-00042-7*) Fawcett.

***Witness to Freedom.** Belinda Rochelle. (J). (gr. 3-7). 1997. pap. 5.99 (*0-614-28897-5*, Puffin) Puffin Bks.

Witness to Freedom: The Letters in Times of Crisis. Thomas Merton. Ed. & Selected by William H. Shannon. LC 95-22488. (Harvest Bks.). 1995. reprint ed. pap. 16.00 (*0-15-600274-4*, Harvest Bks) HarBrace.

Witness to Freedom: The Letters of Thomas Merton in Times of Crisis. Ed. & Selected by William H. Shannon. LC 94-18347. 1994. 25.00 (*0-374-29191-8*) FS&G.

Witness to Gettysburg. Richard Wheeler. 1994. 9.98 (*0-7858-0212-6*) Bk Sales Inc.

Witness to Gettysburg. Richard Wheeler. (Illus.). 288p. 1989. pap. 11.95 (*0-452-00984-7*, Mer) NAL-Dutton.

Witness to Gettysburg. Richard Wheeler. 1995. 21.50 (*0-8446-6823-0*) Peter Smith.

***Witness to History.** Mauno Koivisto. LC 97-8735. 1997. write for info. (*0-8093-2045-2*) S Ill U Pr.

Witness to History: A Refugee from the Third Reich Remembers. Joachim Von Elbe. (Max Kade Institute Studies). (Illus.). 416p. 1989. 18.95 (*0-299-97068-X*) U of Wis Pr.

Witness to History: A Refugee from the Third Reich Remembers. rev. ed. Joachim Von Elbe. (Max Kade Institute Studies). (Illus.). 416p. 1989. 18.95 (*0-924119-00-4*) German-Am Cult Soc.

Witness to History: Charleston's Old Exchange & Provost Dungeon. Ruth M. Miller & Ann T. Andrus. LC 85-22174. (Illus.). (gr. 4 up). 1986. pap. 5.95 (*0-87844-066-6*) Sandlapper Pub Co.

Witness to History: Man & God in Two Worlds. Joseph Rebhun. Ed. by Nathan Kravetz. LC 95-5340. (Studies in Judaica & the Holocaust: No. 16). 1996. pap. write for info. (*0-8095-1403-6*) Borgo Pr.

Witness to History: Man & God in Two Worlds. rev. ed. Ed. by Joseph Rebhun & Nathan Kravetz. LC 95-5340. (Studies in Judaica & the Holocaust: No. 16). 1996. lib. bdg. write for info. (*0-8095-0403-0*) Borgo Pr.

***Witness to History: The Photographs of Yevgeny Khaldei.** Alexander Nakhimovsky & Alice Nakhimovsky. (Illus.). 96p. 1997. 40.00 (*0-89381-738-4*) Aperture.

Witness to Illness: Strategies for Caregiving & Coping. Karen Horowitz & Douglas M. Lanes. (Illus.). 550p. 1992. write for info. (*0-201-63229-2*); pap. 11.95 (*0-201-56796-2*) Addison-Wesley.

Witness to Injustice. David Frost, Jr. Ed. by Louise Westling. 128p. 1995. pap. 12.95 (*0-87805-843-5*); lib. bdg. 27.50 (*0-87805-820-6*) U Pr of Miss.

Witness to my Life: The Letters of Jean-Paul Sartre to Simone de Beauvoir, 1926-1939. Ed. by Simone De Beauvoir. Tr. by Lee Fahnestock & Norman McAfee. LC 93-6527. (ENG & FRE.). 1993. write for info. (*0-02-031581-3*) Macmillan.

Witness to Revolution: Letters from Russia, 1916-1919. Edward T. Heald. Ed. by James B. Gidney. LC 77-161597. 405p. reprint ed. pap. 115.50 (*0-317-20576-5*, 2023200) Bks Demand.

Witness to the Covenant of Circumcision: Bris Milah. Dale Lieberman. LC 96-48368. (Illus.). 104p. 1997. pap. 27.50 (*1-56821-994-6*) Aronson.

***Witness to the Faith: Catholicism & Culture in the Public Square.** Ed. by Thomas P. Melady. 1997. 21.95 (*0-87973-857-X*) Our Sunday Visitor.

Witness to the Fire: Creativity & the Veil of Addiction. Linda S. Leonard. LC 89-42634. 390p. 1990. pap. 20.00 (*0-87773-588-3*) Shambhala Pubns.

Witness to the Future. Klaus Rifbjerg. Tr. by Steven T. Murray from DAN. LC 87-17359. 217p. (Orig.). 1987. 17.95 (*0-940242-21-4*); pap. 8.95 (*0-940242-18-4*) Fjord Pr.

Witness to the Glory & the Power. Catharine Berliner. Ed. by Lucille B. Smeeth. 47p. (Orig.). 1987. pap. 10.00 (*0-9612592-3-X*) StarRays Pubs.

Witness to the Holocaust: An Illustrated Documentary History of the Holocaust as Told in the Words of its Victims, Perpetrators & Bystanders. Ed. by Michael Berenbaum. LC 96-22595. (Illus.). 352p. 1997. 30.00 (*0-06-270108-8*, Harper Ref) HarpC.

Witness to the Light. Robert Griffin. LC 96-90603. 100p. 1997. 20.00 (*1-889314-21-8*); pap. 10.00 (*1-889314-22-6*) Windhover Pub.

Witness to the Sacred: Mystical Tales of Primitive Hasidism. Alan A. Berger. (Illus.). (C). 1977. pap. text ed. 4.00 (*0-914914-10-3*) New Horizons.

Witness to the Truth: The Complicity of Church & Dictatorship in Argentina. Emilio F. Mignone. Tr. by Phillip Berryman from SPA. LC 88-1448. 180p. reprint ed. pap. 51.30 (*0-8357-2686-X*, 2040222) Bks Demand.

Witness to the Word: A Commentary on First John: Lectures at Munster in 1925 & at Bonn in 1933. Karl Barth. Ed. by Walther Furst. Tr. by Geoffrey W. Bromiley. LC 86-4391. 173p. reprint ed. pap. 49.40 (*0-8357-4354-3*, 2037181) Bks Demand.

Witness to the World. John Meyendorff. LC 87-23493. 262p. (Orig.). 1987. pap. 8.95 (*0-88141-069-1*) St Vladimirs.

Witness to the Young Republic: A Yankee's Journal, 1828-1870. Benjamin B. French. Ed. by Donald B. Cole & John J. McDonough. LC 88-39145. (Illus.). 693p. 1989. text ed. 55.00 (*0-87451-467-3*) U Pr of New Eng.

Witness to War: A Biography of Marguerite Higgins. Antoinette May. (Illus.). 288p. 1983. 17.95 (*0-8253-0161-0*) Beaufort Bks NY.

Witness to War: Images from the Persian War. Los Angeles Times Staff. 128p. 1991. pap. 16.95 (*0-9619095-6-0*) LA Times.

Witness to War: Korea. Rod Paschall. LC 94-39653. (Illus.). 256p. 1995. pap. 12.00 (*0-399-51934-3*, Perigee Bks) Berkley Pub.

Witness to War: The Civil War 1861-1865. Harold Holzer. LC 95-25949. 256p. (Orig.). 1996. pap. 12.50 (*0-399-52203-4*, Perigee Bks) Berkley Pub.

Witness to War: Vietnam. Maurice Isserman. LC 95-11408. 224p. 1995. pap. 12.00 (*0-399-52162-3*, Perigee Bks) Berkley Pub.

Witnessed. Budd Hopkins. 352p. 1996. 23.00 (*0-671-56915-5*, PB Hardcover) PB.

***Witnessed.** Budd Hopkins. (Illus.). 1997. mass mkt. 6.99 (*0-671-57031-5*) PB.

Witnesses. Edgar Bowers. 22p. (Orig.). 1981. 20.00 (*0-936576-05-7*) Symposium Pr.

Witnesses: Meditations on the Way of the Cross. Philip Mansel. (Illus.). 1994. pap. 21.00 (*0-86012-231-X*, Pub. by Srch Pr UK) St Mut.
Witnesses for Freedom: Negro Americans in Autobiography. Rebecca C. Barton. LC 76-29575. 1977. pap. 6.50 (*0-917428-02-1*) Dowling.
Witnesses from the Grave: The Stories Bones Tell, Vol. 1. Christopher Joyce & Eric Stover. 1991. 19.95 (*0-316-47399-5*) Little.
Witnesses in Arbitration: Selection, Preparation, & Presentation. Edward Levin & Donald Grody. LC 86-32727. (BNA Books Arbitration Ser.). 258p. 1987. reprint ed. pap. 73.60 (*0-608-00713-7*, 2061486) Bks Demand.
Witnesses in Stone: Landmarks & Lessons from the Living God. Frederic R. Howe. 144p. 1996. pap. 8.99 (*0-8254-2869-6*) Kregel.
Witnesses of a Third Way: A Fresh Look at Evangelism. Ed. by Henry J. Schmidt. LC 85-27981. 158p. reprint ed. pap. 45.10 (*0-7837-5928-2*, 2045727) Bks Demand.
Witnesses of the Light. Washington T. Gladden. LC 77-84307. (Essay Index Reprint Ser.). 1977. 20.95 (*0-8369-1081-8*) Ayer.
Witnesses of the Russian Revolution. Harvey Pitcher. (Illus.). 303p. 1995. 29.95 (*0-7195-5171-4*, Pub. by John Murray UK) Trafalgar.
Witnesses of the Truth. Paul Lindsay. 1994. mass mkt. 5.99 (*0-449-14794-0*, GM) Fawcett.
Witnesses of Time. Carlos Fuentes. 1992. pap. 40.00 (*0-500-27679-X*) Thames Hudson.
Witnesses to a Vanishing America: The Nineteenth-Century Response. Lee C. Mitchell. LC 80-8567. 339p. reprint ed. pap. 96.70 (*0-7837-1430-0*, 2041785) Bks Demand.
Witnesses to All the World. Jim Plueddemann & Carol Plueddemann. (Fisherman Bible Studyguide Ser.). 1996. pap. 4.99 (*0-87788-379-3*) Shaw Pubs.
Witnesses to Cultural Genocide: First-Hand Reports on Rumania's Minority Policies Today. Intro. by George Schopflin. LC 79-54870. 216p. pap. 14.00 (*0-318-13715-1*, Comm Rights Rumania) Hungarian Rights Found.
***Witnesses to Freedom.** Belinda Rochelle. 1997. pap. 5.99 (*0-14-038432-4*) Viking Penguin.
Witnesses to Freedom: Young People Who Fought for Civil Rights. Belinda Rochelle. LC 93-16165. (Illus.). 112p. (J). (gr. 3-7). 1993. pap. 15.99 (*0-525-67377-6*, Lodestar Bks) Dutton Child Bks.
Witnesses to History: The Jewish Poster, 1770-1985. Florence B. Helzel & Eileen Battat. (Illus.). 116p. (Orig.). 1989. pap. 18.95 (*0-943376-39-4*) Magnes Mus.
***Witnesses to Nuremberg.** Stave & Palmer. 1998. 28.95 (*0-8057-1628-9*) Mac Lib Ref.
Witnesses to Political Violence in Guatemala: The Suppression of a Rural Development Movement. Shelton H. Davis & Julie Hodson. Ed. by Laurence R. Simon. (Impact Audit Ser.: No. 2). (Illus.). 54p. (Orig.). (C). 1984. pap. 5.00 (*0-910281-00-9*) Oxfam Am.
Witnesses to the Custer Massacre. Earle R. Forrest & John M. Carroll. (Custer Monograph: No. 9). 62p. 1986. reprint ed. 13.95 (*0-940696-11-8*) Monroe County Lib.
Witnesses to the End of the Cold War. Ed. by William C. Wohlforth. 272p. 1996. text ed. 39.95 (*0-8018-5382-6*) Johns Hopkins.
Witnesses to the Faith: Community, Infallibility , & the Ordinary Magisterium of Bishops. Richard R. Gaillardetz. LC 92-28043. 248p. 1993. pap. 14.95 (*0-8091-3350-4*) Paulist Pr.
Witnesses to the Historicity of Jesus. Arthur Drews. 1972. 69.95 (*0-8490-1313-5*) Gordon Pr.
Witnesses to the Historicity of Jesus. Arthur Drews. Tr. by Joseph McCabe. LC 70-161327. (Atheist Viewpoint Ser.). 332p. 1972. reprint ed. 25.95 (*0-405-03811-9*) Ayer.
Witnesses to the Origins of the Cold War. Ed. by Thomas T. Hammond. LC 81-21810. 328p. 1986. pap. 20.00 (*0-295-96401-4*) U of Wash Pr.
Witnesses to the Russian Revolution. Roger Pethybridge. (Illus.). 1982. pap. 6.95 (*0-8065-0018-2*, C274, Citadel Pr) Carol Pub Group.
***Witnesses to the Struggle: Imaging the 1930s California Labor Movement.** Anne Loftis. 240p. 1997. 29.95 (*0-87417-305-1*) U of Nev Pr.
Witnessing. Carolyn Maisel. LC 78-60979. 59p. 1978. per. 3.75 (*0-934332-07-X*) LEpervier Pr.
Witnessing: How to Give Away Your Faith. Paul E. Little. (Christian Basics Bible Studies). 64p. (Orig.). 1996. wbk. ed., pap. 4.99 (*0-8308-2012-4*, 2012) InterVarsity.
Witnessing America: The Library of Congress Book of First-Hand Accounts of Life in America 1600-1900. Ed. by Noel Rae. 576p. 1996. pap. 29.95 (*0-670-86400-5*) Viking Penguin.
Witnessing an Era: Georgette de Montenay & the Emblemes ou Devises Chrestiennes. Cornell R. Reynolds. LC 87-61487. (Illus.). 137p. 1987. lib. bdg. 19.95 (*0-917786-53-X*) Summa Pubns.
Witnessing Andre Malraux: Visions & Re-Visions: Essays in Honor of Wilbur Merrill Frohock. Ed. by Brian Thompson & Carl A. Viggiani. LC 83-19647. 238p. reprint ed. pap. 67.90 (*0-7837-0222-1*, 2040530) Bks Demand.
***Witnessing As Anglicans in the Third Millenium: The Official Report of the 10th Meeting of the Anglican Consultative Council.** Ed. by James Rosenthal & Nicola Currie. 320p. 1997. pap. 17.95 (*0-8192-1729-8*) Morehouse Pub.
Witnessing for Sociology: Sociologists in Court. Ed. by Pamela J. Jenkins & Steven Kroll-Smith. LC 95-45421. 288p. 1996. text ed. 65.00 (*0-275-94852-8*, Praeger Pubs) Greenwood.
Witnessing History. S. Archer & N. Shepley. (C). 1988. 65.00 (*0-85950-828-5*, Pub. by S Thornes Pubs UK) St Mut.
Witnessing Insanity: Madness & Mad-Doctors in the English Court. Joel P. Eigen. LC 94-31785. 1995. 32.50 (*0-300-06289-3*) Yale U Pr.
Witnessing Justice in Queensland. Adrian Philpott. 154p. (C). 1990. pap. text ed. 48.00 (*0-646-03848-6*, Pub. by Boolarong Pubns AT) St Mut.
Witnessing Made Easy. C. S. Lovett. 1964. pap. 7.95 (*0-938148-01-X*) Prsnl Christianity.
***Witnessing, Nurturing, Protecting: Therapeutic Responses to Sexual Abuse.** Alan Corbett et al. 160p. 1996. pap. 24.95 (*1-85346-338-8*, Pub. by D Fulton UK) Taylor & Francis.
Witnessing Psychoanalysis: From Vienna Back to Vienna via Buchenwald & the U. S. A. Ernst Federn. 368p. 1990. reprint ed. pap. text ed. 38.50 (*0-946439-57-5*, Pub. by Karnac Bks UK) Brunner-Mazel.
Witnessing Slavery: The Development of Ante-Bellum Slave Narratives. Frances S. Foster. LC 93-34490. (Studies in American Autobiography). 1994. pap. 17.95 (*0-299-14214-0*) U of Wis Pr.
Witnessing Slavery: The Development of the Ante-Bellum Slave Narratives. Ed. by Frances S. Foster. LC 78-22137. (Contributions in Afro-American & African Studies: No. 46). 182p. 1979. text ed. 42.95 (*0-313-20821-2*, FWS/, Greenwood Pr) Greenwood.
Witnessing, Telling Others about Jesus. (BMC Teaching Bks.). (Illus.). 15p. (J). (gr. 1-8). 1972. pap. text ed. 4.50 (*0-86508-155-7*) BCM Pubn.
Witnessing Throughout the Twentieth Century: First Presbyterian Church of Sapula, Oklahoma, Celebrates One Hundred Years. Clyde V. McMasters. 256p. 1995. 16.95 (*1-881576-58-2*) Providence Hse.
Witnessing to the Fire: Spiritual Direction & the Development of Directors. Madeline Birmingham & William J. Connolly. LC 93-27071. 256p. (Orig.). 1994. pap. 16.95 (*1-55612-666-2*) Sheed & Ward MO.
Witnessing Without Fear. Bill Bright. LC 87-45. 215p. 1992. pap. 9.99 (*0-8407-4401-3*) Nelson.
Witnessing 101 - A Guide for Students: Sharing Jesus One-on-One. Cindy Holloway. Ed. by Emily Sutherland. 24p. (Orig.). 1995. wbk. ed., pap. 3.25 (*0-89827-140-1*, BKS95) Wesleyan Pub Hse.
Witney As It Was. Hendon Publishing Co., Ltd. Staff. 1986. 65.00 (*0-317-54193-5*) St Mut.
Wits Miserie & the Worlds Madnesse. Thomas Lodge. LC 70-25896. (English Experience Ser.: No. 198). 112p. 1969. reprint ed. 20.00 (*90-221-0198-3*) Walter J Johnson.
Wits Recreation. Colin Gibson. (Verse Miscellanies of the Seventeenth Century Ser.). 500p. 1990. 64.95 (*0-85967-783-4*, Pub. by Scolar Pr UK) Ashgate Pub Co.
Wits Theatre of the World. Robert Allot. LC 70-17131. (English Experience Ser.: No. 359). 560p. 1971. reprint ed. 51.00 (*90-221-0359-5*) Walter J Johnson.
Witt Genealogy. F. W. Balcomb. 40p. 1993. reprint ed. lib. bdg. write for info. (*0-8328-6586-9*) Higginson Bk Co.
Witta: An Irish Pagan Tradition. Edain McCoy. LC 93-26366. (Llewellyn's New World Magic Ser.). (Illus.). 265p. 1993. pap. 12.95 (*0-87542-732-4*) Llewellyn Pubns.
Wittchen, H. U. (Muenchen) Hexal-Ratbeber Depression: Wege Aus der Krankheit. H. U. Wittchen et al. (Illus.). viii, 132p. 1995. pap. 8.50 (*3-8055-6214-4*) S Karger.
Witte Arrives. Elias Tobenkin. LC 68-57553. (Muckrakers Ser.). 322p. 1979. reprint ed. lib. bdg. 29.50 (*0-8398-1961-7*) Irvington.
Witte de With Lectures. (Illus.). 88p. 1992. pap. 19.50 (*90-73362-09-1*, Pub. by Imschoot BE) Dist Art Pubs.
Wittenberg in Clark County. William A. Kinnison. (Annual Monograph Ser.). 80p. (Orig.). 1970. pap. 4.00 (*0-686-28234-5*) Clark County Hist Soc.
***Wittenberg University Library Catalogue of 1536, Vol. 3: Libri Pertinentes.** Ed. by Sachiko Kusukawa. (Medieval & Renaissance Texts & Studies: Vol. 142). (Illus.). 304p. 1995. 30.00 (*0-86698-182-9*, MR142) MRTS.
Wittenwiler's Ring & the Anonymous Scots Poem Colkelbie Sow. Heinrich Wittenweiler. Tr. by George F. Jones. LC 56-58739. (North Carolina. University. Studies in the Germanic Languages & Literatures: No. 18). (Illus.). reprint ed. 27.00 (*0-404-50918-5*) AMS Pr.
Witter's Deutsch-Englische Schreib-Und Lese-Fibel: German-English Primer (1881) viii, 95p. 1987. 4.50 (*0-614-04950-4*) MKGAC & IGHS.
Witter's German-English Primer: Old German Script for Students of German, Genealogists, Decipherers of Old Manuscripts, Letters & Diaries, Church Records, & Entries in Old Family Bibles. W. Witter. 1971. lib. bdg. 79.95 (*0-87700-959-7*) Revisionist Pr.
Wittes Pilgrimage, (by Poeticall Essaies) Through a World of Amorous Sonnets, Etc. John Davies. LC 79-84099. (English Experience Ser.: No. 919). 172p. 1979. reprint ed. lib. bdg. 20.00 (*90-221-0919-4*) Walter J Johnson.
Wittgenstein. Alfred J. Ayer. LC 86-11278. 168p. (C). 1986. pap. 13.95 (*0-226-03337-6*) U Ch Pr.
Wittgenstein. W. W. Bartley, III. LC 85-8962. 218p. (C). 1985. pap. 15.95 (*0-87548-441-7*) Open Court.
Wittgenstein. R. Fogelin. (C). pap. text ed. 21.58 (*0-7870-0007-8*) Digital Print.
Wittgenstein. Robert J. Fogelin. (Arguments of the Philosophers Ser.). 240p. 1986. pap. text ed. 14.95 (*0-7102-0975-4*, 09754, RKP) Routledge.
Wittgenstein. A. C. Grayling. (Past Masters Ser.). 144p. 1988. pap. 8.95 (*0-19-287677-5*) OUP.
Wittgenstein. Frwd. by David Pears. 224p. 1986. pap. 12.95 (*0-674-53951-6*) HUP.
Wittgenstein: A Life: Young Ludwig, 1889-1921. Brian F. McGuinness. 321p. (C). 1988. 30.00 (*0-520-06451-8*) U CA Pr.
Wittgenstein: A Religious Point of View? Norman Malcolm. Ed. by Peter Winch. LC 93-25808. 152p. 1994. 35.00 (*0-8014-2978-1*) Cornell U Pr.
Wittgenstein: A Religious Point of View? Norman Malcolm. Ed. by Peter Winch. 152p. 1995. pap. 11.95 (*0-8014-8266-6*) Cornell U Pr.
Wittgenstein: A Way of Seeing. Judith Genova. 224p. (C). 1995. pap. 16.95 (*0-415-91063-3*, B4488, Routledge NY) Routledge.
Wittgenstein: A Way of Seeing. Judith Genova. 224p. (C). (gr. 13). 1995. text ed. 62.95 (*0-415-91062-5*, B4484, Routledge NY) Routledge.
Wittgenstein: Aesthetics & Transcendental Philosophy. Ed. by Kjell S. Johannessen & Tore Nordenstam. 193p. 1981. pap. 29.50 (*0-686-34398-0*) Kluwer Ac.
Wittgenstein: An Introduction. Joachim Schulte. Tr. by William H. Brenner & John F. Holley from GER. LC 91-23522. 197p. (C). 1992. pap. 14.95 (*0-7914-1082-X*) State U NY Pr.
Wittgenstein: An Introduction. Joachim Schulte. Tr. by William H. Brenner & John F. Holley from GER. LC 91-23522. 197p. (C). 1992. text ed. 42.50 (*0-7914-1081-1*) State U NY Pr.
Wittgenstein: Attention to Particulars: Essays in Honour of Rush Rhees. Ed. by D. Z. Phillips & Peter Winch. LC 89-34718. 256p. 1990. text ed. 45.00 (*0-312-03499-7*) St Martin.
Wittgenstein: Centenary Essays. Ed. by A. Phillips Griffiths. (Royal Institute of Philosophy Supplements Ser.: No. 28). 250p. (C). 1991. pap. 22.95 (*0-521-40947-0*) Cambridge U Pr.
Wittgenstein: Conversations, 1949-1951. O. K. Bouwsma. Ed. by J. L. Craft & Ronald E. Hustwit. LC 85-27222. 112p. (C). 1986. pap. 9.95 (*0-87220-008-6*); lib. bdg. 29.95 (*0-87220-009-4*) Hackett Pub.
Wittgenstein: Language & World. John V. Canfield. LC 81-4522. 240p. 1981. lib. bdg. 30.00 (*0-87023-318-1*) U of Mass Pr.
Wittgenstein: Lectures & Conversations on Aesthetics, Psychology, & Religious Belief. Ludwig Wittgenstein. Ed. by Cyril Barrett. 1967. pap. 10.00 (*0-520-01354-9*) U CA Pr.
Wittgenstein: Meaning & Mind: An Analytical Commentary on the Philosophical Investigation. P. M. Hacker. (Illus.). 600p. 1990. text ed. 99.95 (*0-631-16784-6*) Blackwell Pubs.
Wittgenstein: Mind & Language. Ed. by Rosaria Egidi. LC 94-37362. (Synthese Library: Vol. 245). 304p. (C). 1995. lib. bdg. 127.00 (*0-7923-3171-0*, Pub. by Klwr Acad Pubs NE) Kluwer Ac.
Wittgenstein: Re-Thinking the Inner. Paul Johnston. LC 92-33980. (Illus.). 256p. (C). (gr. 13). 1993. text ed. 69.95 (*0-415-09177-2*, B0542) Routledge.
Wittgenstein: Sources & Perspectives. Ed. by C. G. Luckhardt. (Wittgenstein Studies). 342p. 1996. pap. 28.95 (*1-85506-491-X*) Bks Intl VA.
Wittgenstein: The Man & His Philosophy. Alfred J. Ayer. 1985. 17.95 (*0-394-54347-5*) Random.
Wittgenstein: The Terry Eagleton Script, the Derek Jarman Film. Terry Eagleton & Derek Jarman. (Illus.). 160p. (C). 1993. 45.00 (*0-85170-396-8*, Pub. by British Film Inst UK); pap. 21.95 (*0-85170-397-6*, Pub. by British Film Inst UK) Ind U Pr.
Wittgenstein Vol. 1: Meaning & Mind: Essays. P. M. Hacker. (Analytical Commentary on the Philosophical Investigations Ser.). 240p. 1993. pap. text ed. 27.95 (*0-631-18934-3*) Blackwell Pubs.
Wittgenstein Vol. 2: Meaning & Mind: Exegesis. P. M. Hacker. (Analytical Commentary on the Philosophical Investigations Ser.). 240p. 1993. pap. text ed. 27.95 (*0-631-19064-3*) Blackwell Pubs.
Wittgenstein Vol. 4: Meaning & Will: Of an Analytical Commentary on the Philosophical Investigations. P. M. Hacker. (Illus.). 576p. (C). 1996. 125.00 (*0-631-18739-1*) Blackwell Pubs.
Wittgenstein & Critical Theory: Beyond Postmodernism & Toward Descriptive Investigations. Susan B. Brill. 240p. (C). 1994. text ed. 40.00 (*0-8214-1092-X*); pap. text ed. 16.95 (*0-8214-1093-8*) Ohio U Pr.
Wittgenstein & Derrida. Henry Staten. LC 84-3525. xx, 182p. 1984. reprint ed. pap. text ed. 13.00 (*0-8032-9169-8*, Bison Books) U of Nebr Pr.
Wittgenstein & His Times. Ed. by Brian F. McGuinness. LC 81-52670. 128p. (C). 1982. 18.00 (*0-226-55881-9*) U Ch Pr.
Wittgenstein & Justice: The Significance of Ludwig Wittgenstein for Social & Political Thought. Hanna R. Pitkin. 1972. reprint ed. 42.50 (*0-520-05471-7*); reprint ed. pap. 15.00 (*0-520-02329-3*) U CA Pr.
Wittgenstein & Kierkegaard. Charles L. Creegan. 176p. 1989. 45.00 (*0-415-00066-1*) Routledge.
Wittgenstein & Metaphor. rev. ed. Jerry H. Gill. 192p. (C). 1996. text ed. 45.00 (*0-391-03912-1*) Humanities.
Wittgenstein & Modern Philosophy. 2nd ed. Justus Hartnack. Tr. by Maurice Cranston from DAN. LC 85-40604. 176p. (C). 1985. reprint ed. pap. text ed. 9.50 (*0-268-01937-1*) U of Notre Dame Pr.
Wittgenstein & Modern Philosophy. Justus Hartnack. Tr. by Maurice Cranston. LC 67-17743. 152p. reprint ed. pap. 43.40 (*0-317-09087-9*, 2050334) Bks Demand.
Wittgenstein & Moral Philosophy. Paul Johnston. 272p. 1989. 37.50 (*0-415-00155-2*, A3628) Routledge.
Wittgenstein & Norway. Ed. by Kjell S. Johannessen et al. 1994. 25.00 (*82-560-0936-5*, Pub. by Solum Verlag NO) Intl Spec Bk.
Wittgenstein & Phenomenology: A Comparative Study of the Later Wittgenstein, Husserl, Heidegger, & Merleau-Ponty. Nicholas F. Gier. LC 80-26980. (SUNY Series in Philosophy). 288p. reprint ed. pap. 82.10 (*0-8357-6580-6*, 2035975) Bks Demand.
Wittgenstein & Quine. Ed. by Robert L. Arrington & Hans-Johann Glock. LC 95-25913. 304p. (C). 1996. text ed. 59.95 (*0-415-09676-6*) Routledge.
Wittgenstein & Religion Vol. 1. D. Z. Philips. 1994. text ed. 20.95 (*0-312-12300-0*) St Martin.
Wittgenstein & Social Theory. David Bloor. LC 83-7183. 250p. 1983. text ed. 49.50 (*0-231-05800-4*) Col U Pr.
Wittgenstein & the Grammar of Literary Experience. James Guetti. LC 92-19181. 208p. 1993. 40.00 (*0-8203-1496-X*) U of Ga Pr.
Wittgenstein & the Mystical: Philosophy As an Ascetic Practice. Frederick Sontag. LC 94-30657. (AAR Reflection & Theory in the Study of Religion Ser.: No. 2). 180p. 1995. 34.95 (*1-55540-992-X*, 011002) Scholars Pr GA.
Wittgenstein & the Mystical: Philosophy As an Ascetic Practice. Frederick Sontag. LC 94-30657. (AAR Reflection & Theory in the Study of Religion Ser.: No. 70). 180p. 1995. pap. 22.95 (*1-55540-993-8*) Scholars Pr GA.
Wittgenstein & the Turning Point in the Philosophy of Mathematics. S. G. Shanker. LC 86-23053. 358p. 1987. text ed. 24.50 (*0-88706-482-5*) State U NY Pr.
Wittgenstein Bibliography. Compiled by V. A. Shanker & Stuart G. Shanker. (Critical Assessment & Bibliography Ser.). 1987. 95.00 (*0-7099-4431-4*, Pub. by Croom Helm UK) Routledge Chapman & Hall.
Wittgenstein Dictionary. Hans J. Glock. (Blackwell Philosopher Dictionaries Ser.). 450p. 1996. pap. text ed. 24.95 (*0-631-18537-2*) Blackwell Pubs.
Wittgenstein, Ethics, & Aesthetics: The View from Eternity. B. R. Tilghman. LC 90-38785. (SUNY Series in Ethical Theory). 193p. (C). 1991. text ed. 59.50 (*0-7914-0594-X*); pap. text ed. 19.95 (*0-7914-0595-8*) State U NY Pr.
***Wittgenstein for Beginners.** Donald D. Palmer. (The For Beginners Ser.). 176p. 11.00 (*0-86316-183-9*) Writers & Readers.
Wittgenstein: From Mysticism to Ordinary Language: A Study of Viennese Positivism & the Thought of Ludwig Wittgenstein. Russell Nieli. LC 86-23144. (SUNY Series in Philosophy). 261p. 1987. text ed. 64.50 (*0-88706-397-7*) State U NY Pr.
Wittgenstein in Florida: Proceedings of the Colloquium on the Philosophy of Ludwig Wittgenstein, Florida State University, 7-8 August 1989. Ed. by Jaakko Hintikka. 340p. (C). 1991. lib. bdg. 103.50 (*0-7923-1345-3*, Pub. by Klwr Acad Pubs NE) Kluwer Ac.
Wittgenstein in 90 Minutes. Paul Strathern. (Philosophers in 90 Minutes Ser.). 96p. 1996. pap. 5.95 (*1-56663-131-9*); text ed. 12.95 (*1-56663-130-0*) I R Dee.
Wittgenstein Legacy. Ed. by Peter A. French et al. LC 92-53749. (Midwest Studies in Philosophy: Vol. XVII). (C). 1992. text ed. 46.00 (*0-268-01394-2*); pap. text ed. 23.00 (*0-268-01395-0*) U of Notre Dame Pr.
Wittgenstein, Ludwig: A Symposium. Ed. by Anthony Serafini & Souren Teghrarian. LC 90-35600. 1990. 37.50 (*0-89341-593-6*, Longwood Academic); pap. 18.50 (*0-89341-594-4*, Longwood Academic) Hollowbrook.
Wittgenstein on Language: Meaning, Use & Truth. Bede Rundle. 288p. (C). 1990. text ed. 60.95 (*0-631-17198-3*) Blackwell Pubs.
Wittgenstein on Mind & Language. David G. Stern. LC 93-34800. (Illus.). 272p. 1995. 39.95 (*0-19-508000-9*) OUP.
Wittgenstein on Mind & Language. David G. Stern. (Illus.). 280p. 1996. reprint ed. pap. 16.95 (*0-19-511147-8*) OUP.
***Wittgenstein on Rules & Institutions.** David Bloor. 192p. (C). 1997. text ed. write for info. (*0-415-16147-9*) Routledge.
Wittgenstein on Rules & Private Language. Saul A. Kripke. 160p. 1984. pap. 12.50 (*0-674-95401-7*) HUP.
Wittgenstein on the Foundations of Mathematics. Crispin Wright. (Modern Revivals in Philosophy Ser.). 500p. (C). 1994. text ed. 80.95 (*0-7512-0295-9*, Pub. by Gregg Revivals UK) Ashgate Pub Co.
Wittgenstein on Universals. Robert Fahrnkopf. (American University Studies: Philosophy: Ser. V, Vol. 56). 219p. (C). 1988. text ed. 34.00 (*0-8204-0707-0*) P Lang Pubng.
***Wittgenstein, Politics & Human Rights.** Robin Holt. LC 96-39528. 184p. (C). 1997. text ed. write for info. (*0-415-15438-3*) Routledge.
Wittgenstein Reader. Ed. by Anthony Kenny. (Blackwell Readers). 256p. 1994. 60.95 (*0-631-19361-8*); pap. 26.95 (*0-631-19362-6*) Blackwell Pubs.
***Wittgenstein Reads Freud: The Myth of the Unconscious.** Jacques Bouveresse. 168p. 1995. pap. text ed. 12.95 (*0-691-02904-0*) Princeton U Pr.
Wittgenstein Reads Freud: The Myth of the Unconscious. Jacques Bouveresse. Tr. by Carol Cosman from FRE. LC 94-40607. (New French Thought Ser.). 176p. (ENG & FRE.). 1995. text ed. 29.50 (*0-691-03425-7*) Princeton U Pr.
Wittgenstein Studies: A Collection of 6 Major Works Relating to Wittgenstein, 6 vols., Set. 1996. 395.00 (*1-85506-494-4*) Bks Intl VA.
Wittgenstein 2E. 2nd ed. Fogelin. 264p. (C). 1995. pap. 17.95 (*0-415-11944-8*) Routledge.
Wittgensteinian Themes: Essays 1978-1989. Norman Malcolm. Ed. by George H. Von Wright. 256p. 1995. 37.50 (*0-8014-3042-9*) Cornell U Pr.
Wittgensteinian Themes: Essays 1978-1989. Norman Malcolm. Ed. by George H. Von Wright. 232p. 1996. pap. 14.95 (*0-8014-8381-6*) Cornell U Pr.
Wittgenstein's City. Robert J. Ackermann. LC 87-10895. 288p. (Orig.). (C). 1988. lib. bdg. 32.50 (*0-87023-589-3*) U of Mass Pr.
Wittgenstein's Conception of Philosophy. K. T. Fann. LC 65-24178. 1969. pap. 13.00 (*0-520-01837-0*) U CA Pr.
Wittgenstein's Definition of Meaning As Use. Garth L. Hallett. LC 66-23620. (Orestes Brownson Series on Contemporary Thought & Affairs). 222p. reprint ed. pap. 63.30 (*0-7837-0448-8*, 2040771) Bks Demand.

W

Wittgenstein's Early Philosophy: Three Sides of the Mirror. Donald Peterson. 216p. 1990. 40.00 (*0-8020-2770-9*) U of Toronto Pr.

Wittgenstein's Ladder: Poetic Language & the Strangeness of the Ordinary. Marjorie Perloff. LC 95-47873. (Illus.). 300p. (C). 1996. 27.95 (*0-226-66058-3*) U Ch Pr.

Wittgenstein's Language. T. Binkley. 236p. 1973. pap. text ed. 64.50 (*90-247-1541-5*, Pub. by M Nijhoff NE) Kluwer Ac.

Wittgenstein's Later Philosophy. Oswald Hanfling. LC 88-27979. (SUNY Series in Logic & Language). 193p. (Orig.). 1989. text ed. 24.50 (*0-7914-0070-0*) State U NY Pr.

Wittgenstein's Lectures on Philosophical Psychology, 1946-47: Notes by P. T. Geach, K. J. Shah, & A. C. Jackson. Ludwig Wittgenstein. Ed. by Peter T. Geach. LC 88-27728. 364p. 1989. 47.95 (*0-226-90428-8*) U Ch Pr.

Wittgenstein's Lectures on the Foundations of Mathematics, Cambridge, 1939: From the Notes of R.G. Bosanquet, Norman Malcolm, Rush Rhees, & Yorick Smythies. Ludwig Wittgenstein. Ed. by Cora Diamond. 300p. 1989. reprint ed. pap. text ed. 15.95 (*0-226-90426-1*) U Ch Pr.

***Wittgenstein's Logical Atomism.** James Griffin. (Wittgenstein Studies). 176p. 1997. pap. 14.95 (*1-85506-536-3*) Thoemmes Pr.

Wittgenstein's Metaphysics. John W. Cook. 400p. (C). 1994. text ed. 69.95 (*0-521-46019-0*) Cambridge U Pr.

Wittgenstein's Metaphysics. John W. Cook. LC 93-28603. (C). 1994. write for info. (*0-521-45536-7*) Cambridge U Pr.

Wittgenstein's Mistress. David Markson. LC 87-73068. 1995. pap. 11.95 (*0-916583-50-3*) Dalkey Arch.

Wittgenstein's Nephew: A Friendship. Thomas Bernhard. Tr. by David McLintock. LC 89-27716. (Phoenix Fiction Ser.). vi, 108p. 1990. pap. 9.95 (*0-226-04392-4*) U Ch Pr.

Wittgenstein's Philosophical Investigations. Ed. by Robert Arrington & Hans-Johann Glock. LC 91-17442. 256p. (C). (gr. 13). 1992. text ed. 59.95 (*0-415-07035-X*, A6495) Routledge.

Wittgenstein's Philosophische Grammatik: Entstehung und Perspektiven der Strategie eines Radikalen Aufklarers. M. Lang. 160p. 1972. pap. text ed. 59.00 (*90-247-1204-1*) Kluwer Ac.

Wittgenstein's Philosophy of Mathematics. Pasquale Frascolla. 208p. (C). 1994. text ed. 59.95 (*0-415-02483-8*, B4468) Routledge.

Wittgenstein's Philosophy of Mathematics. Virginia Klenk. 136p. 1976. pap. text ed. 59.00 (*90-247-1842-2*, Pub. by M Nijhoff NE) Kluwer Ac.

Wittgenstein's Philosophy of Psychology. Malcolm Budd. (International Library of Philosophy). 204p. (C). 1991. pap. 16.95 (*0-415-06452-X*, A5713) Routledge.

Wittgenstein's Place in Twentieth-Century Analytic Philosophy. P. M. Hacker. 368p. (C). 1996. 59.95 (*0-631-20098-3*); pap. 24.95 (*0-631-20099-1*) Blackwell Pubs.

***Wittgenstein's Thought in Transition.** Dale Jacquette. LC 97-9813. (Purdue University Press Series in the History of Philosophy). 1997. write for info. (*1-55753-103-X*); pap. write for info. (*1-55753-104-8*) Purdue U Pr.

Wittgenstein's Tractatus: A Critical Exposition of Its Main Lines on Thought. Erik Stenius. LC 81-13222. xi, 241p. 1982. reprint ed. text ed. 35.00 (*0-313-23246-6*, STWI, Greenwood Pr) Greenwood.

Wittgenstein's "Tractatus" A Critical Exposition of the Main Lines of Thought. Erik Stenius. (Wittgenstein Studies). 252p. 1996. pap. 19.95 (*1-85506-493-6*) Bks Intl VA.

Wittgenstein's Tractatus: An Introduction. H. O. Mounce. LC 81-40474. viii, 144p. (C). 1989. reprint ed. pap. text ed. 13.95 (*0-226-54321-8*) U Ch Pr.

Wittgenstein's Trousers. W. R. Elton. 64p. 1991. pap. 12.95 (*0-7734-0020-6*) E Mellen.

Wittgenstein's Vienna. Allan Janik & Stephen Toulmin. LC 96-24766. 324p. 1996. pap. 14.95 (*1-56663-132-7*) I R Dee.

Wittgenstein's Vienna. Allan Janik & Stephen Toulmin. (Illus.). 316p. 1974. pap. 12.00 (*0-671-21725-9*, Touchstone Bks) S&S Trade.

Wittich Connection: Conflict & Priority in Late Sixteenth-Century Cosmology. Owen Gingerich & Robert S. Westman. LC 88-82932. (Transactions Ser.: Vol. 78, Pt. 7). (Illus.). (Orig.). (C). 1988. pap. 20.00 (*0-87169-787-4*, T787-GIO) Am Philos.

Wittrings. Ed. by Manfred Knebusch et al. (Aspects of Mathematics Ser.: Vol. 2). 1982. 20.00 (*3-528-08512-6*, Pub. by Vieweg & Sohn GW) Informatica.

***Wittry, Witry, Vitry: A Family History.** Eugene J. Wittry. (Illus.). viii, 505p. (Orig.). 1996. pap. 34.00 (*0-7884-0602-7*, W377) Heritage Bk.

***Witts End Almost Beaten Off.** Edwin T. Witt. 1997. mass mkt. 4.99 (*1-55197-331-6*, Pub. by Comnwlth Pub CN) Partners Pubs Grp.

Witty & Witless, or a Dialogue on Wit & Folly. John Heywood. LC 74-133679. (Tudor Facsimile Texts. Old English Plays Ser.: No. 9). reprint ed. 59.50 (*0-404-53309-4*) AMS Pr.

Witty Sayings by Witty People. William H. Browne. LC 74-15727. (Popular Culture in America Ser.). 304p. 1975. reprint ed. 28.95 (*0-405-06363-6*) Ayer.

Witty Women: Wise, Wicked & Wonderful Words. Ariel Books Staff. (Illus.). 80p. 1994. 4.95 (*0-8362-3067-1*, Arie Bks) Andrews & McMeel.

Witty Writing. Date not set. pap. write for info. (*0-87162-643-8*) Warner Pr.

Wivenhoe & Brightlingsea Railway. Paul Brown. (Illus.). 128p. (Orig.). 1991. pap. 20.00 (*0-86025-889-0*, Pub. by Ian Henry Pubns UK); pap. 12.00 (*0-86025-456-9*, Pub. by Ian Henry Pubns UK) Empire Pub Srvs.

Wives. Gamaliel Bradford. LC 72-2591. (American Women Ser.: Images & Realities). 328p. 1975. reprint ed. 24.95 (*0-405-04448-8*) Ayer.

Wives. Gamaliel Bradford. (BCL1 - U. S. History Ser.). 298p. 1991. reprint ed. lib. bdg. 79.00 (*0-7812-6031-0*) Rprt Serv.

***Wives & Daughters.** Elizabeth C. Gaskell. 1997. pap. 12.95 (*0-14-043478-X*) Viking Penguin.

Wives & Midwives: Childbirth & Nutrition in Rural Malaysia. Carol Laderman. LC 83-47664. (Comparative Studies of Health Systems & Medical Care: Vol. 7). (Illus.). 267p. (C). 1984. 48.00 (*0-520-04924-1*); pap. 13.00 (*0-520-06036-9*) U CA Pr.

Wives & Mothers in Victorian Industry. Margaret Hewitt. LC 73-11623. (Illus.). 245p. 1975. reprint ed. text ed. 75.00 (*0-8371-7078-8*, HEWM, Greenwood Pr) Greenwood.

Wives & Mothers, School Mistresses & Scullery Maids: Working Women in Upper Canada, 1790- Elizabeth J. Errington. 1995. pap. 22.95 (*0-7735-1310-8*, Pub. by McGill CN) U of Toronto Pr.

***Wives & Mothers, School Mistresses & Scullery Maids: Working Women in Upper Canada, 1790-1840.** Elizabeth J. Errington. 1995. 55.00 (*0-7735-1309-4*, Pub. by McGill CN) U of Toronto Pr.

Wives & Property: Reform of the Married Women's Property Law in Nineteenth-Century England. Lee Holcombe. 368p. 1982. pap. 16.95 (*0-8020-6476-0*) U of Toronto Pr.

Wives & Property: Reform of the Married Women's Property Law in Nineteenth-Century England. Lee Holcombe. LC 83-105215. (Illus.). 319p. reprint ed. pap. 91.00 (*0-8357-8377-4*, 2034048) Bks Demand.

***Wives & Warriors: Women & the Military in the United States & Canada.** Ed. by Laurie Weinstein & Christie White. 272p. 1997. pap. text ed. 22.95 (*0-89789-526-6*, Bergin & Garvey) Greenwood.

***Wives & Warriors: Women & the Military in the United States & Canada.** Laurie L. Weinstein & Christie White. LC 96-30624. 272p. 1997. text ed. 59.95 (*0-89789-491-X*) Greenwood.

Wives at War & Other Stories. Flora Nwapa. 125p. 1992. 24.95 (*0-86543-327-5*); pap. 9.95 (*0-86543-328-3*) Africa World.

Wives Excuse, or, Cuckolds Make Themselves. Thomas Southerne. Ed. by Ralph R. Thornton. (Illus.). 1974. 7.50 (*0-915180-19-7*); pap. 3.50 (*0-915180-20-0*) Harrowood Bks.

***Wives, Friends & Lovers.** Susan Saunders. 406p. 1997. 25.99 (*1-86110-043-4*) Ulverscroft.

Wives, Husbands & Alcohol: A Study of Informal Drinking Control Within the Family. M. Holmila. (Finnish Foundation for Alcohol Studies: Vol. 36). 1988. pap. 20.00 (*951-9192-37-9*) Rutgers Ctr Alcohol.

Wives of Catholic Clergy. Joseph H. Fichter. LC 91-45845. 208p. (Orig.). 1992. pap. 12.95 (*1-55612-474-0*, LL1474) Sheed & Ward MO.

***Wives of Frankie Ferraro.** Marchetta. Date not set. write for info. (*0-312-18226-0*) St Martin.

Wives of Henry VIII. Antonia Fraser. LC 93-11879. 1993. pap. 17.00 (*0-679-73001-X*, Vin) Random.

Wives of the "Canterbury Tales" & the Tradition of the Valiant Woman of Proverbs 31: 10-31. Frances M. Biscoglio. LC 92-23974. (Illus.). 272p. 1992. text ed. 89.95 (*0-7734-9803-6*) E Mellen.

Wives of the Prophet. F. Hussain. 9.50 (*0-933511-94-9*) Kazi Pubns.

***Wives' Room: Life on the Inside of the NFL.** Sally Gardocki. (Illus.). 256p. (Orig.). 1997. pap. 14.95 (*1-57028-158-0*) Masters Pr IN.

Wives, Widows & Concubines. Christine M. Carpenter. (All the Women in the Bible Ser.: Vol. 4). (Illus.). 216p. 1997. pap. 16.95 (*1-887999-60-4*) CMC Pr OR.

Wiyot Grammer & Texts. fac. ed. Gladys A. Reichard. (University of California Publications in American Archaeology & Ethnology: Vol. 22: 1). 215p. (C). 1925. reprint ed. pap. text ed. 19.40 (*1-55567-255-8*) Coyote Press.

Wiz. pap. 14.95 (*1-57007-011-3*, XW1638) Astor Bks.

Wiz. Sally F. Odgers. LC 92-31952. (Voyages Ser.). (Illus.). (J). 1993. 3.75 (*0-383-03608-9*) SRA McGraw.

Wiz: French's Musical Library Adapted from "The Wonderful Wizard of Oz" Smalls. 1979. pap. 6.00 (*0-573-68091-4*) French.

***Wiz: Vocal Selections.** Ed. by Sy Feldman. 84p. (Orig.). (C). 1984. pap. text ed. 16.95 (*0-89724-197-5*, VF1107) Warner Brothers.

***Wiz Biz.** Rick Cook. 624p. 1997. mass mkt. 6.99 (*0-671-87846-8*) Baen Bks.

***Wizard.** Martin. (J). 1997. pap. write for info. (*0-15-201568-X*, HB Juv Bks) HarBrace.

Wizard. John Varley. 384p. 1987. mass mkt. 5.99 (*0-441-90067-4*) Ace Bks.

Wizard. rev. ed. Jack Kent. (Illus.). 32p. (J). (gr. k-3). 1989. reprint ed. pap. 5.95 (*0-927370-00-X*) WW Pr.

Wizard: Life & Times of Nikola Tesla, Biography of a Genius. Marc J. Seifer. (Illus.). 480p. 1996. 29.95 (*1-55972-329-7*, Birch Ln Pr) Carol Pub Group.

Wizard Vol. 1. Steve Zell. (YA). 1994. mass mkt. 4.99 (*0-312-95373-9*) St Martin.

Wizard Abroad. Duane. LC 96-45406. 1997. write for info. (*0-15-201209-5*) HarBrace.

Wizard Abroad. Duane. LC 96-45406. 1998. pap. write for info. (*0-15-201207-9*) HarBrace.

***Wizard & Glass.** Stephen King. LC 97-15995. 1997. pap. 17.95 (*0-452-27917-8*, Plume) NAL-Dutton.

***Wizard & the Glass.** Stephen King. 1997. pap. 49.95 (*0-14-086688-4*) Viking Penguin.

Wizard & the Golden Acorns. Dawn D. Marion. Ed. by Tim Lingard. (Continuing Adventures of Timothy Glean). (Illus.). 36p. (Orig.). (J). (gr. k-3). 1994. pap. write for info. (*1-885986-00-9*) Glean Pubns.

Wizard & the Magic Spell. (J). Date not set. pap. 3.95 (*0-590-24008-0*) Scholastic Inc.

Wizard & Wart. Janice L. Smith. LC 92-41170. (I Can Read Bk.). (Illus.). 64p. (J). (gr. k-3). 1994. 14.00 (*0-06-022960-8*); lib. bdg. 14.89 (*0-06-022961-6*) HarpC Child Bks.

Wizard & Wart. Janice L. Smith. LC 92-41170. (Trophy I Can Read Bk.). (Illus.). 64p. (J). (gr. k-3). 1995. pap. 3.75 (*0-06-444201-2*, Trophy) HarpC Child Bks.

Wizard & Wart at Sea. Janice L. Smith. LC 94-3200. (Trophy I Can Read Bk.). (Illus.). 48p. (J). (gr. k-3). 1996. pap. 3.75 (*0-06-444218-7*, Trophy) HarpC Child Bks.

Wizard & Wart at Sea. Janice L. Smith. LC 94-3200. (I Can Read Bks.). (Illus.). 48p. (J). (gr. k-3). 1995. 13.95 (*0-06-024754-1*); lib. bdg. 13.89 (*0-06-024755-X*) HarpC.

Wizard at Home. Rick Shelley. (Seven Wonders Ser.: Bk. 2). 256p. (Orig.). 1995. 4.99 (*0-451-45422-7*, ROC) NAL-Dutton.

Wizard at Large. Terry Brooks. (Magic Kingdom Ser.). 320p. 1989. mass mkt. 6.99 (*0-345-36227-6*, Del Rey) Ballantine.

Wizard at MECQ. Rick Shelley. 288p. (Orig.). 1994. pap. 4.99 (*0-451-45361-1*, Dragon Ent) NAL-Dutton.

Wizard Comes to Town. Mercer Mayer. (Illus.). 40p. (J). 1991. reprint ed. pap. 5.95 (*1-879920-00-X*) Rain Bird Prods.

Wizard Comic Book Price Guide Annual 1996. annuals Jon R. Warren. 1995. pap. 14.99 (*0-7615-0415-X*) Prima Pub.

Wizard Exposed: Magic Tricks, Interviews & Experiences by & about Houdini & Other Past Masters of Magic. Harry Houdini & Howard Thurston. Ed. by David Meyer. LC 87-90412. (Illus.). 197p. 1987. 24.50 (*0-916638-39-1*) Meyerbooks.

***Wizard Fantastic.** Martin H. Greenberg. 1997. mass mkt. 5.99 (*0-88677-756-9*) DAW Bks.

Wizard for a Day. Sheryl Jordan. (Little Apple Ser.). (J). (gr. 3-7). 1996. pap. 3.50 (*0-590-22283-X*) Scholastic Inc.

***Wizard in a Tree.** Lloyd Alexander. 1998. pap. 3.99 (*0-14-038801-X*) Viking Penguin.

Wizard in Absentia. Christopher Stasheff. 272p. (Orig.). 1993. mass mkt. 4.99 (*0-441-51569-X*) Ace Bks.

Wizard in Bedlam. Christopher Stasheff. 288p. 1995. 4.99 (*0-8125-3647-9*) Tor Bks.

***Wizard in Chaos.** Stasheff. LC 97-23603. 1997. 21.95 (*0-312-86032-3*) St Martin.

Wizard in Mind. Christopher Stasheff. 224p. mass mkt. 4.99 (*0-8125-3648-7*) Tor Bks.

Wizard in Mind. Christopher Stasheff. 224p. 1996. mass mkt. write for info. (*0-614-05515-6*) Tor Bks.

Wizard in Peace. Christopher Stasheff. LC 96-8452. 288p. 1996. 22.95 (*0-312-86031-5*) Tor Bks.

***Wizard in Peace.** Christopher Stasheff. (Rogue Wizard Ser.: No. 4). 1997. mass mkt. 5.99 (*0-8125-6797-8*) Tor Bks.

Wizard in the Woods. Jean Ure. LC 91-58770. (Illus.). 176p. (J). (gr. 3-6). 1992. 14.95 (*1-56402-110-6*) Candlewick Pr.

Wizard in War: The Third Chronicle of the Rogue Wizard. Christopher Stasheff. 224p. 1995. 20.95 (*0-312-85696-2*) Tor Bks.

Wizard in War: The Third Chronicle of the Rogue Wizard. Christopher Stasheff. 1996. mass mkt. 5.99 (*0-8125-3649-5*) Tor Bks.

Wizard in Wonderland. Jean Ure. LC 92-53020. (Illus.). 176p. (J). (gr. 3-6). 1993. 14.95 (*1-56402-138-6*) Candlewick Pr.

Wizard Next Door. Peter Glassman. LC 92-21562. (Illus.). 40p. (J). (gr. k up). 1993. 15.00 (*0-688-10645-5*, Morrow Junior) Morrow.

Wizard of Abermere. J. Calvin Pierce. 1993. mass mkt. 4.99 (*0-441-01959-5*) Ace Bks.

Wizard of Bergen. Robert B. Benson. (Wolfgang Brandt Ser.). 125p. (Orig.). (YA). (gr. 7-12). 1987. pap. 7.50 (*0-9616327-1-2*) Brandt Bks.

***Wizard of Bones.** Robert Charrette. 368p. 1997. mass mkt. 5.50 (*0-06-105603-0*, HarperPrism) HarpC.

Wizard of Earthsea. Ursula K. Le Guin. 192p. (gr. 9-12). 1984. mass mkt. 6.50 (*0-553-26250-5*) Bantam.

Wizard of Earthsea. Ursula K. Le Guin. LC 68-21992. 208p. (J). 1991. lib. bdg. 16.95 (*0-689-31720-4*, Atheneum Bks Young) S&S Childrens.

Wizard of Emerald City & Urfin Jus & His Wooden Soldiers. Alexander Volkov. Tr. by Peter L. Blystone from RUS. LC 90-62416. (Tales of Magic Land Ser.: No. 1). (J). (gr. 4 up). 1991. pap. 11.95 (*1-878941-16-X*) Red Branch Pr.

Wizard of Fourth Street. Simon Hawke. 1988. mass mkt. 4.50 (*0-445-20842-2*) Warner Bks.

Wizard of Is. James Tipton. 21p. 1995. pap. 5.00 (*0-912549-53-X*) Bread & Butter.

Wizard of Is. rev. ed. Thomas Thiss. LC 95-14312. 200p. 1995. 21.95 (*0-925190-48-9*) Fairview Press.

Wizard of La-La Land. Robert Campbell. Ed. by Jane Chelius. 288p. 1995. 20.00 (*0-671-70321-8*) PB.

Wizard of Law. Zulu Sofola. (Evans Africa Plays Ser.). 44p. 1991. pap. 4.50 (*0-237-49951-7*, Pub. by Evans Bros Ltd UK) Trafalgar.

Wizard of Loneliness. John Nichols. 320p. 1994. pap. 8.95 (*0-393-31073-6*) Norton.

Wizard of Menlo Park. Richard Wettereau. 31.95 (*0-8488-0853-3*) Amereon Ltd.

Wizard of Oz. (Play - a - Sound Ser.). (Illus.). 24p. (J). 1993. 12.98 (*0-7853-0129-1*) Pubns Intl Ltd.

Wizard of Oz. (Look & Find Ser.). (Illus.). 24p. (J). 1993. 7.98 (*0-7853-0066-X*) Pubns Intl Ltd.

Wizard of Oz. (Paint with Water Fairy Tales Ser.). (Illus.). 32p. (Orig.). (J). (gr. k-2). 1994. pap. write for info. (*1-56144-489-8*, Honey Bear Bks) Modern Pub NYC.

Wizard of Oz. (Pocket Play Bks.). (Illus.). 24p. (J). (ps-2). 1996. 9.95 (*0-8362-0953-2*) Andrews & McMeel.

Wizard of Oz. Frank L. Baum. (Illus.). 30p. (J). 1995. pap. 7.95 (*1-55859-820-0*) Abbeville Pr.

Wizard of Oz. L. Frank Baum. LC 79-52644. 240p. (J). 1986. mass mkt. 4.99 (*0-345-33590-2*, Del Rey) Ballantine.

***Wizard of Oz.** L. Frank Baum. (Living Classics Ser.). (J). 1997. 14.95 (*0-7641-7046-5*) Barron.

Wizard of Oz. L. Frank Baum. LC 82-1109. (Illus.). 232p. (J). (gr. 4-6). 1982. 25.95 (*0-8050-0221-9*, Bks Young Read) H Holt & Co.

Wizard of Oz. L. Frank Baum. 256p. (YA). 1984. mass mkt. 3.95 (*0-451-51864-0*, Sig Classics) NAL-Dutton.

Wizard of Oz. L. Frank Baum. (Illus.). 103p. (J). (gr. 2-6). Date not set. 19.95 (*1-55858-638-5*) North-South Bks NYC.

Wizard of Oz. L. Frank Baum. LC 79-52644. (Classics Ser.). (J). (gr. 3-7). 1983. pap. 2.99 (*0-14-035001-2*, Puffin) Puffin Bks.

Wizard of Oz. L. Frank Baum. LC 79-52644. (Puffin Classics Ser.). 189p. (J). 1995. pap. 3.99 (*0-14-036693-8*) Puffin Bks.

Wizard of Oz. L. Frank Baum. Ed. by W. W. Denslow. LC 93-50738. (Illustrated Junior Library). (J). 1994. 14.95 (*0-448-40561-X*, G&D) Putnam Pub Group.

Wizard of Oz. L. Frank Baum. LC 79-52644. (Illus.). 96p. (J). 1991. 15.00 (*0-517-69506-5*) Random Hse Value.

Wizard of Oz. L. Frank Baum. 160p. (J). 1989. pap. 3.50 (*0-590-44089-6*) Scholastic Inc.

Wizard of Oz. L. Frank Baum. 196p. 1993. pap. 2.50 (*0-8125-2335-0*) Tor Bks.

Wizard of Oz. L. Frank Baum. LC 95-9772. (Children's Thrift Classics Ser.). (Illus.). 96p. (Orig.). (J). 1995. pap. text ed. 1.00 (*0-486-28585-5*) Dover.

Wizard of Oz. L. Frank Baum. 1963. 4.25 (*0-87129-402-8*, W39) Dramatic Pub.

***Wizard of Oz.** L. Frank Baum. Ed. by Malvina Vogel. (Great Illustrated Classics Ser.: Vol. 8). (Illus.). 240p. (J). (gr. 3-6). 1989. 9.95 (*0-86611-959-0*) Playmore Inc.

Wizard of Oz. Jan Carr. 96p. (J). (ps-3). 1993. pap. 3.25 (*0-590-46993-2*) Scholastic Inc.

***Wizard of Oz.** Illus. by Gill Guile. (Classics for Children 8 & Younger Ser.). 48p. (J). (gr. k-3). 1997. 6.98 (*1-85854-644-3*) Brimax Bks.

Wizard of Oz. Gail Herman. 32p. (J). (ps-3). 1993. pap. 2.95 (*0-590-46994-0*) Scholastic Inc.

Wizard of Oz. R. Eugene Jackson. 72p. 1977. pap. 4.50 (*0-88680-205-9*); 15.00 (*0-88680-400-0*) I E Clark.

***Wizard of Oz.** Ladybird Books Staff. (J). 1997. pap. 3.50 (*0-7214-5796-7*, Ladybrd) Penguin.

***Wizard of Oz.** Michael Lancy. 76p. 1983. pap. 5.00 (*1-890298-42-5*) Centerstage Pr.

***Wizard of Oz.** Rahn. 1998. 23.95 (*0-8057-8623-6*); pap. 13.95 (*0-8057-8644-9*) Mac Lib Ref.

Wizard of Oz. John R. Taylor. 1990. 19.99 (*0-517-03381-X*) Random Hse Value.

Wizard of Oz. Frwd. by John R. Taylor. (Illus.). 178p. 1993. 19.98 (*0-8317-9462-3*) Smithmark.

Wizard of Oz. Adele Thane. (J). (gr. 1-7). 1957. 5.00 (*0-87602-221-2*) Anchorage.

Wizard of Oz. abr. ed. L. Frank Baum. Ed. by John Escott. (Classics for Young Readers Ser.). (Illus.). 64p. (J). (gr. 1-4). 1996. 5.98 (*1-85854-286-3*) Brimax Bks.

Wizard of Oz. abr. large type ed. Illus. by Nancy Bond. (NanaBanana Classics Ser.). 32p. (J). (gr. k up). 1995. pap. 14.95 (*1-886201-04-8*) Nana Banana.

***Wizard of Oz.** limited ed. L. Frank Baum. (Illus.). 105p. 1996. 100.00 (*1-55858-657-1*) North-South Bks NYC.

Wizard of Oz. rev. ed. William-Alan Landes & Marilyn Standish. LC 89-63872. (Wondrawhopper Ser.). (J). (gr. 3-12). 1985. pap. 6.00 (*0-88734-105-5*) Players Pr.

Wizard of Oz, No. 175. 48p. 1982. pap. 5.95 (*0-7935-1637-4*, 00243140) H Leonard.

Wizard of Oz, No. 282. 48p. 1992. pap. 6.95 (*0-7935-1635-8*, 00102256) H Leonard.

Wizard of Oz, 4 vols., Set. Troll Associates Staff. (J). (ps). 1997. Boxed set. pap. 9.95 (*0-8167-2996-4*) Troll Communs.

***Wizard of Oz, Vol. 1.** M. Hague. (J). 1982. write for info. (*0-03-061661-1*) H Holt & Co.

***Wizard of Oz, Vol. 1.** limited ed. M. Hague. (J). 1983. write for info. (*0-03-062426-6*) H Holt & Co.

Wizard of Oz: (El Mago de Oz) L. Frank Baum. (SPA.). (J). 9.95 (*84-204-3509-0*) Santillana.

Wizard of Oz: BFI Film Classics. Salman Rushdie. (Illus.). 72p. 1992. pap. 9.95 (*0-85170-300-3*, Pub. by British Film Inst UK) Ind U Pr.

Wizard of Oz: Collectors Edition. L. Frank Baum. 1992. 6.98 (*0-88365-797-X*) Galahad Bks.

Wizard of Oz: Director's Guide. rev. ed. William-Alan Landes & Marilyn Standish. LC 89-63872. (Wondrawhopper Ser.). (J). (gr. 3-12). 1985. teacher ed., pap. 30.00 (*0-88734-011-3*) Players Pr.

Wizard of Oz: Easy Piano. Ed. by Carol Cuellar. 32p. (YA). 1995. pap. text ed. 9.95 (*0-7692-0095-8*, AF9502) Warner Brothers.

Wizard of Oz: Music & Lyrics. rev. ed. William-Alan Landes & Marilyn Standish. (Wondrawhopper Ser.). (J). (gr. 3-12). 1985. pap. 15.00 (*0-88734-010-5*) Players Pr.

Wizard of Oz & He Who Was. Martin Gardner. 1994. pap. 18.95 (*0-87013-366-7*) Mich St U Pr.

Wizard of Oz Collector's Treasury. Jay Scarfone & William Stillman. LC 92-60633. (Illus.). 244p. 1992. text ed. 59.95 (*0-88740-430-8*) Schiffer.

W

Wizard of Oz-Color Book. L. Frank Baum. (J). 1978. pap. 2.95 (0-486-20452-9) Dover.
Wizard of Oz Cookbook: Breakfast in Kansas Dessert in Oz. Jennifer Brazil et al. (Illus.). 64p. 1993. 7.95 (1-55859-582-1) Abbeville Pr.
Wizard of Oz Game Book: An Electronic Game Book. (Electronic Game Book Ser.). (Illus.). (J). Date not set. 9.99 (0-88705-953-8, Wshng Well Bks) Joshua Morris.
Wizard of Oz Is You. Barbara Hailey. (Illus.). (J). 1994. 24.95 (1-882306-01-5) Planned Mktg.
Wizard of Oz Movie Selections. CPP Belwin Staff. 1993. pap. 12.95 (0-89898-623-0, TSF0038) Warner Brothers.
Wizard of Oz-Pop Up. (J). 1997. pap. 9.95 (0-8167-0897-5) Troll Communs.
Wizard of Oz-Revealed. Samuel Bousky. 64p. pap. 10.00 (0-9641660-3-8) Writers Consort.
Wizard of Oz-Revealed. Samuel Bowsky. 64p. 1995. 20.00 (0-9641660-1-1) Writers Consort.
Wizard of Oz Waddle Book. L. Frank Baum. LC 93-10069. (Illus.). 208p. (J). 1993. reprint ed. 24.95 (1-55709-205-2); reprint ed. 85.00 (1-55709-203-6) Applewood.
Wizard of Seattle. Kay Hooper. 304p. 1993. mass mkt. 5.50 (0-553-28999-3) Bantam.
Wizard of Sound: A Story about Thomas Edison. Barbara Mitchell. (Creative Minds Ser.). (Illus.). 64p. (J). (gr. 3-6). 1991. lib. bdg. 18.95 (0-87614-445-8, Carolrhoda) Lerner Group.
Wizard of Sound: A Story about Thomas Edison. Barbara Mitchell. (J). (gr. 3-6). 1992. pap. 5.95 (0-87614-563-2, Carolrhoda) Lerner Group.
Wizard of the Floating City. Christopher B. Rowley. 1996. pap. 5.99 (0-451-45469-3, ROC) NAL-Dutton.
Wizard of the Magic Road: Its Hard to Lose. 3rd ed. Illus. by Connie Lovett. 32p. (J). (ps-1). 1996. pap. text ed. write for info. (0-9648643-2-0) Magic Road.
Wizard of the Magic Road: The Secret of Friendship. 2nd ed. Chris Deahr & Molly Corbett. (Illus.). 32p. (J). (ps-1). 1996. pap. text ed. write for info. (0-9648643-1-2) Magic Road.
Wizard of the Upper Amazon. F. Bruce Lamb & Manuel Cordova-Rios. 204p. 1987. reprint ed. pap. 12.95 (0-938190-80-6) North Atlantic.
Wizard of the Winds. Allan Cole. LC 96-41577. 416p. 1998. mass mkt. 12.95 (0-345-40176-X) Ballantine.
Wizard of the Winds: The Timura Trilogy, Book. Allan Cole. Date not set. pap. write for info. (0-345-40177-8) Ballantine.
Wizard of Tubingen: The Bizarre Case of Hary the Wise. William Fitzell. 160p. (Orig.). 1996. pap. 9.95 (0-9632920-3-X, Lone Pine Pr) Global Bk Prods.
***Wizard of White.** Dummy Num. 1989. 3.95 (0-445-77055-4) Warner Bks.
Wizard of Whitechapel. Simon Hawke. 224p. (Orig.). 1988. mass mkt. 4.99 (0-445-20304-8) Warner Bks.
Wizard of Work. Richard Gaither. 96p. (Orig.). 1995. pap. 8.95 (0-89815-639-4) Ten Speed Pr.
***Wizard of 4th Street, Vol. 1.** Dummy Num. 1989. 3.95 (0-445-77054-6) Warner Bks.
***Wizard Quizbook.** Wizard Magazine Editorial Staff. 1997. mass mkt. 4.99 (0-06-105363-5, HarperPrism) HarpC.
Wizard, the Fairy, & the Magic Chicken. Helen Lester. (J). (ps-3). 1983. 14.95 (0-395-33885-9) HM.
Wizard, the Fairy, & the Magic Chicken. Helen Lester. LC 82-21302. (Illus.). 32p. (J). (gr. k-3). 1988. pap. 5.95 (0-395-47945-2) HM.
Wizard Within. A. M. Krasner. Ed. by Caroline Miller. (Illus.). (Orig.). (C). 1990. write for info. (0-9624829-1-9) Amer Bd Hypnotherapy.
***Wizard 1997 Yearbook & Comic.** Ed. by Jon R. Warren. 336p. 1997. mass mkt. 15.00 (0-06-105362-7, HarperPrism) HarpC.
Wizardry: The League of the Crimson Crescent. James E. Reagen. 1995. mass mkt. 5.99 (1-55958-671-0) Prima Pub.
Wizardry Compiled. Rick Cook. 320p. 1991. mass mkt. 4.95 (0-671-72078-3) Baen Bks.
Wizardry Consulted. Rick Cook. 1995. mass mkt. 5.99 (0-671-87700-3) Baen Bks.
Wizardry Cursed. Rick Cook. 1991. mass mkt. 4.95 (0-671-72049-X) Baen Bks.
Wizardry Quested. Rick Cook. 288p. 1996. mass mkt. 5.99 (0-671-87708-9) Baen Bks.
***Wizards.** Mayfair Games Staff. 1986. pap. 10.00 (0-912771-07-0) Mayfair Games.
***Wizards & Sorcerers: From Abracadabra to Zoroaster.** Tom Ogden. LC 96-52305. 1997. write for info. (0-8160-3151-7); pap. write for info. (0-8160-3152-5) Facts on File.
Wizards & the Monster. Bill Brittain. LC 93-47077. (Illus.). 88p. (J). (gr. 2-5). 1994. lib. bdg. 11.89 (0-06-024456-9) HarpC Child Bks.
Wizards & the Warriors. Hugh Cook. (Chronicles of an Age of Darkness Ser.). 352p. 8700. 30.00 (0-86140-244-8, Pub. by Colin Smythe Ltd UK) Dufour.
Wizard's Apprentice. S. P. Somtow. LC 93-12384. (Dragonflight - A Byron Preiss Book Ser.: No. 7). (Illus.). 144p. (YA). (gr. 7 up). 1993. lib. bdg. 14.95 (0-689-31576-7, Atheneum Bks Young) S&S Childrens.
Wizards Apprentice. 2nd ed. Nelson H. White. LC 95-62291. (Illus.). 82p. (Orig.). (C). 1995. pap. 35.00 (1-877884-21-9) Tech Group.
Wizard's Bane. Rick Cook. 320p. 1989. mass mkt. 4.99 (0-671-69803-6) Baen Bks.
***Wizards Betrayal Game.** Mayfair Games Staff. Date not set. pap. 7.00 (0-912771-78-X) Mayfair Games.
Wizard's Bible. Louis G. Sikes. (Illus.). 128p. (Orig.). 1987. pap. 5.95 (0-943832-14-4) Intl Imports.
Wizard's Compendium. J. W. Pickens. 1996. 25.00 (0-7869-0436-4) TSR Inc.
Wizard's Daughter. Barbara Michaels. 336p. (Orig.). 1995. pap. text ed. 5.99 (0-425-14642-1, Berkley Trade) Berkley Pub.
***Wizard's Daughter.** large type ed. Barbara Michaels. LC 96-53155. (Americana Ser.). 479p. 1997. lib. bdg. 24.95 (0-7862-1025-7, Thorndike Lrg Prnt) Thorndike Pr.
Wizard's Daughter. Barbara Michaels. 336p. 1996. reprint ed. 24.00 (0-7278-4917-4) Severn Hse.
***Wizard's Dilemma.** Mayfair Games Staff. 1989. pap. 7.00 (0-912771-85-2) Mayfair Games.
Wizards Don't Need Computers. Debbie Dadey. (The Adventures of the Bailey School Kids Ser.: No. 20). (J). (gr. 2-6). 1996. pap. 3.50 (0-590-50962-4) Scholastic Inc.
***Wizards Don't Need Computers.** Debbie Dadey & Marcia T. Jones. (Adventures of the Bailey School Kids (Collection les Mysteres de Ville-Cartier)). (FRE.). (J). pap. 5.99 (0-590-16024-9) Scholastic Inc.
Wizard's Dozen. Ed. by Michael Stearns. LC 93-22150. (YA). 1993. pap. write for info. (0-15-200966-3, J Yolen Bks) HarBrace.
Wizard's Dozen. Ed. by Michael Stearns. LC 93-22150. 192p. (YA). (gr. 5 up). 1993. 17.00 (0-15-200965-5, J Yolen Bks) HarBrace.
Wizard's Dozen: Stories of the Fantastic. Ed. by Michael Stearns. (J). 1996. pap. 3.99 (0-590-86542-0) Scholastic Inc.
Wizard's First Rule. Terry Goodkind. (Sword of Truth Ser.: Bk. 1). 816p. (J). 1995. pap. 5.99 (0-8125-4805-1) Tor Bks.
Wizard's Gate: Picturing Consciousness. Ann B. Ulanov. 214p. 1995. pap. 14.95 (3-85630-539-4, Pub. by Daimon Pubs SZ) Continuum.
Wizard's Hall. Jane Yolen. Ed. by Bonnie V. Ingber. 144p. (J). (gr. 3-7). 1991. 14.00 (0-15-298132-2) HarBrace.
Wizard's Heir. Daniel Hood. 304p. (Orig.). 1995. mass mkt. 4.99 (0-441-00231-5) Ace Bks.
***Wizard's How to Draw Comics.** Wizard Magazine Editorial Staff. (Illus.). 1997. mass mkt. 15.00 (0-06-105365-1, HarperPrism) HarpC.
Wizard's Lab. Cary I. Sneider & Alan Gould. Ed. by Lincoln Bergman & Kay Fairwell. (Great Explorations in Math & Science (GEMS) Ser.). (Illus.). 116p. (Orig.). 1989. teacher ed., pap. 21.00 (0-912511-71-0) Lawrence Science.
Wizards of Armageddon. Fred Kaplan. LC 90-71236. (Nuclear Age Ser.). 460p. 1991. pap. 17.95 (0-8047-1884-9) Stanford U Pr.
Wizards of Bellmore Castle. Judy Stubbs. Ed. by Myrna Kemnitz. (Illus.). 123p. (Orig.). (YA). (gr. 7 up). 1995. pap. 5.00 (0-88092-137-4) Royal Fireworks.
***Wizards of Conscious Creation: Making the Imponderable Practical.** Lynda M. Dahl. 208p. (Orig.). 1997. pap. 13.95 (1-889964-05-0) Woodbridge Grp.
***Wizards of Consciousness: Making the Imponderable Practical.** Lynda M. Dahi. LC 96-49174. 208p. (Orig.). 1997. pap. 13.95 (1-889964-03-4, WBB008) Woodbridge Grp.
***Wizards of Media Oz: Behind the Curtain of Mainstream News.** Norman Solomon & Jeff Cohen. LC 97-9691. 272p. (Orig.). 1997. pap. 15.95 (1-56751-118-X); lib. bdg. 29.95 (1-56751-119-8) Common Courage.
***Wizards of Odd.** Ed. by Peter Haining. 368p. 1997. mass mkt. 6.50 (0-441-00487-3) Ace Bks.
Wizards of Quiz. Steven Feffer. 1994. pap. 5.25 (0-8222-1406-7) Dramatists Play.
Wizard's Promise. Suzanna Marshak. LC 92-36507. (Illus.). (J). 1994. pap. 15.00 (0-671-78431-5, S&S Bks Young Read) S&S Childrens.
Wizard's Quest. Russell Marrone. LC 87-50268. (Illus.). 102p. (J). (gr. 3-5). 1987. 7.95 (1-55523-078-4) Winston-Derek.
***Wizards Revenge Game.** Mayfair Games Staff. 1989. pap. 7.00 (0-912771-32-1) Mayfair Games.
Wizard's Shadow. Susan Dexter. 1993. mass mkt. 4.99 (0-345-38064-9, Del Rey) Ballantine.
***Wizard's Spell Compendium.** TSR Inc. Staff. 1998. 25.00 (0-7869-0791-6) TSR Inc.
***Wizard's Spell Compendium, Vol. 2.** Pickens & Jon Middleton. 1997. 25.00 (0-7869-0664-2) TSR Inc.
***Wizards Tale.** Kurt Busiuk. (Illus.). 125p. (Orig.). (YA). 1997. pap. 19.95 (1-887279-34-2) Image Comics.
Wizard's Tale, Bk. 1. Kurt Busiek. Ed. by Catherine Yronwode & Lynn Adair. (Illus.). 42p. (Orig.). (J). (gr. 1-4). 1993. pap. 4.95 (1-56060-206-6) Eclipse Bks.
Wizard's Tale, Bk. 2. Kurt Busiek. Ed. by Catherine Yronwode & Lynn Adair. (Illus.). 42p. (Orig.). (J). (gr. 1-4). 1993. pap. 4.95 (1-56060-207-4) Eclipse Bks.
Wizard's Tale, Bk. 3. Kurt Busiek. Ed. by Catherine Yronwode & Lynn Adair. (Illus.). 42p. (Orig.). (J). (gr. 1-4). 1994. pap. 4.95 (1-56060-208-2) Eclipse Bks.
Wizard's Tale, Collection, 3 bks. Kurt Busiek. Ed. by Catherine Yronwode & Lynn Adair. (Illus.). 42p. (Orig.). (J). (gr. 1-4). write for info. (1-56060-210-4); pap. write for info. (1-56060-209-0) Eclipse Bks.
Wizards That Peep. Siegbert W. Becker. Ed. by Mentor Kujath. 1978. pap. 7.99 (0-8100-0054-7, 15N0366) Northwest Pub.
Wizard's Tide. large type ed. Frederick Buechner. (General Ser.). 156p. 1991. lib. bdg. 20.95 (0-8161-5142-3, GK Hall) Thorndike Pr.
***Wizards Vale Game.** Mayfair Games Staff. 1987. pap. 7.00 (0-912771-02-X) Mayfair Games.
Wizards' Worlds. Andre Norton. 1990. mass mkt. 4.95 (0-8125-4750-0) Tor Bks.
Wizdom Within: On Daydreams, Realities, & Revelations. Irving Oyle & Susan Jean. LC 92-53162. 228p. 1992. pap. 12.95 (0-915811-42-1) H J Kramer Inc.
Wizzer Rabbit Wants You to Be Drug Free. Sherry Basinger & Missy Basinger. (Illus.). 17p. (Orig.). (J). 1988. pap. write for info. (0-9620945-0-1) S & M Basinger.
***Wizzer's Christmas.** Sue Kassirer. (101 Dalmations Ser.). (J). 1997. 12.95 (0-7868-3140-5) Disney Pr.
***WJBC's History You Can See: Fifty Historic Journeys into McLean County's Past.** Don Munson & G. Koos. (Illus.). 101p. 1991. 5.00 (0-943788-11-0) McLean County.
WKID: Easy Radio Plays. Carol Adorjan & Yuri Rasovsky. LC 88-132. (Illus.). 80p. (J). (gr. 3-8). 1988. lib. bdg. 10.95 (0-8075-9155-6) A Whitman.
WLT: A Radio Romance. deluxe limited ed. Garrison Keillor. LC 91-50160. 288p. 1992. pap. 125.00 (0-670-84265-6, Viking) Viking Penguin.
WLT: A Radio Romance. Garrison Keillor. 416p. 1992. reprint ed. pap. 11.00 (0-14-010380-5, Penguin Bks); reprint ed. audio write for info. (0-318-69297-X, Penguin Bks) Viking Penguin.
WM Color Guide to Freight & Passenger Equipment. Jack Brown. (Illus.). 128p. 1996. 49.95 (1-878887-53-X) Morning NJ.
WMAC MastersTM: Enter the Battle Dome. Charles Hoffman. (J). (gr. 4-7). 1996. pap. 3.99 (0-679-88211-1, Bullseye Bks) Random Bks Yng Read.
WMAC MastersTM: Quest for the Dragon Star. Charles Hoffman. (J). (gr. 4-7). 1996. pap. 3.99 (0-679-88210-3, Bullseye Bks) Random Bks Yng Read.
W.M.L. de Wette, Founder of Modern Biblical Criticism: An Intellectual Biography. John W. Rogerson. (JSOT Supplement Ser.: No. 126). 296p. (C). 1991. 55.00 (1-85075-330-X, Pub. by Sheffield Acad UK) CUP Services.
WMU Guide. Ed. by Debra Hochgraber. 44p. (Orig.). 1995. pap. text ed. 3.95 (1-56309-121-6) Womans Mission Union.
WNW Concise Encyclopedia. 1995. 45.00 (0-02-860722-8) Macmillan.
WNW Secretarial Handbook. 4th ed. In Plain English Editors. 1992. pap. 12.00 (0-671-86471-8) S&S Trade.
WNW Spanish/English Dictionary of Computer Technical Terms. Onyria H. McElrey. 1997. 10.95 (0-02-861046-6) Macmillan.
Wo ist die Jugend, die ich rufe? see I Long for a New Humanity
Wobble the Witch Cat. Mary Calhoun. LC 58-5018. (Illus.). 32p. (J). (gr. k-3). 1958. lib. bdg. 14.93 (0-688-31621-2, Morrow Junior) Morrow.
Wobblies. Stewart Bird & Peter Robilotta. (Orig.). 1980. pap. 3.95 (0-918266-13-0) Smyrna.
Wobblies: The U. S. vs. Wm. D. Haywood, et al. Stewart Bird & Peter T. Robilotta. LC 88-107256. (Illus.). 79p. 1980. reprint ed. pap. 25.00 (0-7837-9093-7, 2049843) Bks Demand.
Wobblies, Pile Butts, & Other Heroes: Laborlore Explorations. Archie Green. LC 92-20168. (Folklore & Society Ser.). (Illus.). 534p. (C). 1993. text ed. 39.95 (0-252-01963-6) U of Ill Pr.
Wobbling. Bruce Andrews. 93p. (Orig.). 1981. pap. 50.00 (0-937804-06-1) Segue NYC.
Wobbly: Rough & Tumble Story of an American Radical: American Autobiography. Ralph Chaplin. 435p. 1995. lib. bdg. 99.00 (0-7812-8476-7) Rprt Serv.
Wobbly War: The Centralia Story. John McClelland, Jr. LC 87-51095. (Illus.). 256p. 1987. 15.00 (0-917048-62-8) Wash St Hist Soc.
Woburn & the Russells. Georgiana Blakiston. (Illus.). 246p. 1982. pap. 26.50 (0-09-464590-6, Pub. by Constable Pubs UK) Trans-Atl Phila.
Wodehouse Bestiary. P. G. Wodehouse. Ed. by D. R. Bensen. 276p. 1985. 15.95 (0-685-42994-6) HM.
Wodehouse Bestiary. P. G. Wodehouse. Ed. by D. R. Bensen. 336p. 1991. pap. 12.95 (0-395-58774-3) HM.
Wodehouse Is the Best Medicine. P. G. Wodehouse. Ed. by D. R. Bensen. 336p. 1995. pap. 12.95 (1-55882-026-4) Intl Polygonics.
Wodehouse Nuggets. P. G. Wodehouse. (Illus.). 231p. 1995. 17.50 (0-87008-073-3) JAS Heineman.
Wodehouse Redeemed. Iain Sproat. 1994. 15.00 (0-87008-147-0) JAS Heineman.
Woden Dog. deluxe ed. Christopher Middleton. (Burning Deck Poetry Ser.). 32p. (Orig.). 1982. pap. 20.00 (0-930901-06-1) Burning Deck.
Wodwo. Ted Hughes. 184p. 1971. pap. 8.95 (0-571-09714-6) Faber & Faber.
Woe Is I: The Grammarphobe's Guide to Better English in Plain English. Patricia T. O'Connor. LC 96-11473. 192p. 1996. 16.95 (0-399-14196-0, Grosset-Putnam) Putnam Pub Group.
Woe to the Women-the Bible Tells Me So. Annie L. Gaylor. 1981. pap. 10.00 (1-877733-02-4) Freedom Rel Found.
Woe unto You, Lawyers! 2nd ed. Fred Rodell & Jerome Frank. 184p. 1987. reprint ed. lib. bdg. 22.50 (0-8377-2536-4) Rothman.
Woe unto You Lawyers: The Fraud of the Law Profession. 1992. lib. bdg. 75.00 (0-8490-8723-6) Gordon Pr.
Woertatlas der Deutschen Umgangssprachen, Vol. 1. J. Eichoff. 106p. (GER.). 1977. 75.00 (0-8288-5558-7, M7689) Fr & Eur.
Woertebuch Des Buches: Dictionary of Books. Helmut Hiller. 354p. (GER.). 1991. pap. 75.00 (0-8288-1570-4, M6937) Fr & Eur.
Woerter-Bilder-Situationen. Theo Scherling & Walter Lohfert. 48p. (GER.). 1983. 16.50 (3-468-49993-0) Langenscheidt.
Woerter zur Wahl. M. Ferenbach & I. Schuessler. 158p. (GER.). (C). 1971. pap. text ed. 25.25 (3-12-558200-8, Pub. by Klett Edition GW) Intl Bk Import.
Woerterbuch Albanisch-Deutsch. 6th ed. O. Bucholz. 739p. (ALB & GER.). 1993. 79.95 (0-7859-7444-X, 3324002508) Fr & Eur.
Woerterbuch Althochdeutschen. Begrmann. 800p. (GER.). 1990. 395.00 (0-7859-7437-7, 3484106638) Fr & Eur.
Woerterbuch Architektur Hochbau Vol. 1: German-English. 2nd ed. Herbert Bucksch. 942p. (ENG & GER.). 1987. 295.00 (0-7859-7445-8, 3762525765) Fr & Eur.
Woerterbuch Bulgarisch-Deutsch. 5th ed. Dietmar Endler. 931p. (BUL & GER.). 1989. 49.95 (0-7859-8299-X, 3324002273) Fr & Eur.
Woerterbuch Chemie und Chemische Technik, Vol. 2. H. W. Gross. (GER.). 68.00 (0-686-56616-5, M-6965) Fr & Eur.
Woerterbuch Datenerfassung-Programmierung. E. Buerger. (ENG, FRE, GER & RUS.). 1976. 95.00 (0-8288-5767-9, M6967) Fr & Eur.
Woerterbuch der Altgermanischen Personen und Voelkernamen. 2nd ed. M. Schoenfeld. 309p. (GER.). 1965. 95.00 (0-8288-6756-9, M-7045) Fr & Eur.
Woerterbuch der Amerikanismen. 3rd ed. Friedrich Koehler. (GER.). 1972. 49.95 (0-8288-6431-4, M-7044) Fr & Eur.
Woerterbuch der Antike. 8th ed. Hans Lamer. (GER.). 1976. 59.95 (0-8288-5768-7, M7042) Fr & Eur.
Woerterbuch der Antike. 9th ed. Paul Kroh. 832p. (GER.). 1989. 59.95 (0-7859-8408-9, 3520096099) Fr & Eur.
Woerterbuch der Arabischen Wirtschaftssprache und Rechtssprache: Arabisch-Deutsch. Eberhard Leicher. 609p. 1992. 225.00 (0-7859-8473-9, 3789027774) Fr & Eur.
Woerterbuch der Aussenwirtschaft. 4th ed. Siegfried Kohls. 696p. (ENG, FRE, GER, RUS & SPA.). 1991. 295.00 (0-8288-6416-0, M-7574) Fr & Eur.
Woerterbuch der Berufs und Wirtschaftspaedagogik. 320p. (GER.). 1973. pap. 14.95 (0-8288-6341-5, M-7038) Fr & Eur.
Woerterbuch der Bibliothekwessens: Russian-German, German-Russian. Gennadi Wasilewitsch. 253p. (GER & RUS.). 1988. 49.95 (0-7859-8303-1, 3324003245) Fr & Eur.
Woerterbuch der Biochemie: Biochemistry Dictionary. K. Thielmann. 724p. (ENG, FRE, GER, RUS & SPA.). 1978. 150.00 (0-8288-5286-3, M7041) Fr & Eur.
Woerterbuch der Biologie. Werner Jacobs. (GER.). 1976. pap. 24.95 (0-8288-5770-9, M7039) Fr & Eur.
Woerterbuch der Biologie: English-German-French-Spanish. Gunther Haensch. 680p. (ENG, FRE & GER.). 1981. 195.00 (0-7859-8330-9, 3405122767) Fr & Eur.
Woerterbuch der Chinesischen Revolution. P. Dittmar. 224p. (GER.). 1975. pap. 5.95 (0-686-56644-0) Fr & Eur.
Woerterbuch der Chinesischen Wortbildung. Helga Beutel. 121p. (CHI & GER.). 1993. 150.00 (0-7859-8263-9, 3050023236) Fr & Eur.
Woerterbuch der DatenKommunikation: English-German, German-English. 2nd ed. Walter Tietz. 297p. (ENG & GER.). 1989. 75.00 (0-7859-7029-0) Fr & Eur.
Woerterbuch der Datentechnik: German-French, French-German. 2nd ed. Doris Linse. 394p. (FRE & GER.). 1993. 125.00 (0-7859-7068-1) Fr & Eur.
Woerterbuch der DDR Paedagogik. Johannes Niermann. (GER.). 1974. pap. 24.95 (0-7859-0839-0, M-7032) Fr & Eur.
Woerterbuch der Deutschen Geschichte, 3 vols. 2nd rev. ed. Rossler. (GER.). 350.00 (0-7859-7233-1, 3907820835) Fr & Eur.
Woerterbuch der Deutschen Kauffmannsspache Uf Geschichtlichen Grundlagen. Alfred Schirmer. 224p. (GER.). 1991. 225.00 (0-7859-8275-2, 3110124726) Fr & Eur.
Woerterbuch der Deutschen Pflanzennamen. Marzell. 59.95 (0-8288-7889-7, M7031) Fr & Eur.
Woerterbuch der Deutschen Pflanzennamen, Nos. 1-22. fac. ed. Marzell. (GER.). 550.00 (0-686-56642-4, M-7031) Fr & Eur.
Woerterbuch der Deutschen und Japanischen Sprache: German & Japanese Dictionary. R. Schinzinger. 1510p. (GER & JPN.). 1980. 125.00 (0-8288-1020-6, M10012) Fr & Eur.
Woerterbuch der Deutschen und Nierderlaendischen Rechtssprache, Vol. 1. Hans Langendorf. 365p. (DUT & GER.). 1991. 85.00 (0-8288-5771-7, M7025) Fr & Eur.
Woerterbuch der Deutschen und Nierderlaendischen Rechtssprache, Vol. 2. Hans Langendorf. 426p. (DUT & GER.). 1989. 125.00 (0-8288-5772-5, M7026) Fr & Eur.
Woerterbuch der Deutschen und Spanischen Sprache, Vol. 1. 8th ed. Rudolf Slaby. (GER & SPA.). 1990. 150.00 (0-8288-5961-2, S36339) Fr & Eur.
Woerterbuch der Druckbehaltertechnik und Rohrleitungstechnik: Dictionary of Pressure Vessel Piping Techniques. Leon Jentgen. 343p. (ENG & GER.). 1987. 525.00 (0-7859-7112-2) Fr & Eur.
Woerterbuch der Duala-Sprache (Kamerun) German-French-English. Johannes Ittmann. 675p. (GER.). 1976. 250.00 (0-7859-8403-8, 3496007028) Fr & Eur.
Woerterbuch der Elektronik. E. Knaeps & D. Zacharias. 104p. (FRE & GER.). 1976. pap. 17.95 (0-8288-5773-3, M7020) Fr & Eur.
Woerterbuch der Elektronik. Leonhard Schneider. (GER & POL.). 1977. pap. 175.00 (0-8288-5560-9, M7021) Fr & Eur.
Woerterbuch der Elektronik: Dictionary of Electronics. 689p. (ENG & GER.). 1980. 195.00 (0-8288-0285-8, M15128) Fr & Eur.
Woerterbuch der Elektronik und Informationsverarbeitung: English-German, German-English. Peter Wennrich. 770p. 1990. 450.00 (0-7859-8446-1, 3598108850) Fr & Eur.
Woerterbuch der Elektrotechnik, Fernmeldetechnik und Elektonik, Vol. 1. 2nd ed. Werner Goedecke. 906p. (ENG, FRE & GER.). 1968. 135.00 (0-8288-6734-8, M-7018) Fr & Eur.

W

Woerterbuch der Elektrotechnik, Fernmeldetechnik und Elektronik, Vol. 2. Werner Goedecke. 1009p. (ENG, FRE & GER.). 1972. 125.00 (*0-8288-6735-6*, M-7019) Fr & Eur.

Woerterbuch der Elektrotechnik und Elektronik: German & Russian Dictionary of Electronics & Electrical Engineering. Tomislav Miladinovic. (GER & RUS.). 1970. 175.00 (*0-8288-6561-2*, M-7016) Fr & Eur.

Woerterbuch der Elektrotechnik und Fernmeldtechnik, Elektronik, Vol. 3 English-German-French. Werner Goedecke. 1252p. (ENG, FRE & GER.). 1974. 150.00 (*0-7859-7063-0*) Fr & Eur.

Woerterbuch der Englischen und Deutschen Sprache, Vol. 1. Weis Schoeffler. write for info. (*0-8288-7986-9*); pap. 45.00 (*3-12-518100-3*, M-7015) Fr & Eur.

Woerterbuch der Englischen und Deutschen Sprache, Vol. 2. Weis Schoeffler. write for info. (*0-8288-7987-7*); pap. 45.00 (*3-12-518200-X*, M-7014) Fr & Eur.

Woerterbuch der Epilepsie. H. Gastaut. (GER.). 1975. pap. 75.00 (*0-8288-5962-0*, M7013) Fr & Eur.

Woerterbuch der Esoterik. Gerhard Wehr. (GER.). 19.95 (*0-7859-8679-0*, 345108600x) Fr & Eur.

Woerterbuch der Ethnologie: DuMont Taschenbucher. Bernhard Streck. (GER.). 39.95 (*0-7859-8691-X*, 377011728x) Fr & Eur.

Woerterbuch der Falschen Freunde: German & Russian. Karl Gottlieb. 158p. (GER & RUS.). 1991. 29.95 (*0-7859-8290-6*, 3190063389) Fr & Eur.

Woerterbuch der Feministischen Theologie. Elisabeth Gossman. 476p. (GER.). 1991. 125.00 (*0-7859-8444-5*, 3579002856) Fr & Eur.

Woerterbuch der Franzoesischen und Deutschen Sprache, Vol. 1. E. Weis & Heinrich Mattutat. (FRE & GER.). 45.00 (*3-215-01824-1*, M-7004) Fr & Eur.

Woerterbuch der Franzoesischen und Deutschen Sprache, Vol. 2. E. Weis & Heinrich Mattutat. (FRE & GER.). 39.95 (*3-215-01825-X*, M-7003) Fr & Eur.

Woerterbuch der Handelssprache, Finanzsprache und Rechtssprache, 3 vols. Robert Herbst. 3360p. (ENG, FRE & GER.). 1990. 850.00 (*0-7859-8511-5*, 3859420062) Fr & Eur.

Woerterbuch der Handelssprache, Finanzsprache und Rechtssprache, Vol. 1. 4th rev. ed. Robert Herbst. 1155p. (ENG, FRE & GER.). 1990. 295.00 (*0-8288-0146-0*, M8531) Fr & Eur.

Woerterbuch der Handelssprache, Finanzsprache und Rechtssprache, Vol. 2. 4th rev. ed. Robert Herbst. 985p. (ENG, FRE & GER.). 1989. 350.00 (*0-8288-0145-2*, M7002) Fr & Eur.

Woerterbuch der Handelssprache, Finanzsprache und Rechtssprache, 3 vols., Vol. III. R. Herbst. (ENG, FRE & GER.). 225.00 (*3-85942-015-1*) Adlers Foreign Bks.

Woerterbuch der Handelssprache, Finanzsprache und Rechtssprache, Vol. 3. 2nd ed. Robert Herbst. 958p. (ENG, FRE & GER.). 1990. 295.00 (*0-8288-0147-9*, M8536) Fr & Eur.

Woerterbuch der Handelssprache, Finanzsprache und Rechtssprache Vol. I: English-German-French. R. Herbst & A. G. Readett. 155p. (ENG, FRE & GER.). 1990. 205.00 (*3-85942-014-3*) IBD Ltd.

Woerterbuch der Handelssprache, Finanzsprache und Rechtssprache Vol. II: German-English-French. Robert Herbst & A. G. Readett. 147p. (ENG, FRE & GER.). 1992. 205.00 (*3-85942-016-X*) IBD Ltd.

Woerterbuch der Handelssprache, Finanzsprache und Rechtssprache Vol. III: French-English-German. R. Herbst & A. G. Readett. 958p. (ENG, FRE & GER.). 1990. Vol. 3: Fre.-Eng.-Ger., 5th, 1990. 205.00 (*3-85942-012-7*) IBD Ltd.

Woerterbuch der Industriellen Technik, Vol. 5. 2nd ed. R. Ernst. (GER & SPA.). 1973. 110.00 (*0-8288-6344-X*, M6997) Fr & Eur.

Woerterbuch der Industriellen Technik, Vol 6 Spanish-German. 2nd ed. Richard Ernst. 1073p. (GER & SPA.). 1982. 175.00 (*0-7859-7065-7*) Fr & Eur.

Woerterbuch der Industriellen Technik, Vol. 7. R. Ernst. (GER & POR.). 1963. 150.00 (*0-7859-0950-8*, M-6995) Fr & Eur.

Woerterbuch der Internationalen Beziehungen und der Politik. 2nd ed. Guenther Haensch. (GER.). 110.00 (*0-8288-7797-1*, M6993); pap. 110.00 (*3-19-006211-0*, M-6993) Fr & Eur.

Woerterbuch der Jaegerei. 5th ed. W. Frevert. 117p. (GER.). 1992. 39.95 (*0-8288-5965-5*, M6990) Fr & Eur.

Woerterbuch der Jager. Anne Kirchoff. (ENG, FRE & GER.). 1976. 75.00 (*0-8288-5774-1*, M6989) Fr & Eur.

Woerterbuch der Kabeltechnik. Christel Richling. (ENG, FRE & GER.). 1976. pap. 95.00 (*0-8288-5775-X*, M6988) Fr & Eur.

Woerterbuch der Kosmetik. 3rd ed. Horst Fey. 302p. (GER.). 1991. 150.00 (*0-7859-8490-9*, 3804711146) Fr & Eur.

Woerterbuch der Kraftubertragungselemente: German, Spanish, French, English, Italian, Dutch, Swedish, Finnish, 5 vols., Set. Eurotans Staff. 1982. 1,095.00 (*0-7859-8420-8*) Fr & Eur.

Woerterbuch der Kraftubertragungselemente Vol. 5: German, Spanish, French, English, Italian, Dutch, Swedish, Finnish, Kupplungen. Eurotans Staff. 268p. 1993. 295.00 (*0-7859-8419-4*, 3540534253) Fr & Eur.

Woerterbuch der Kraftuebertragungselemente. (DUT, ENG, FIN, FRE, GER, ITA, SPA & SWE.). 1976. 32.00 (*0-7859-0583-9*, M-6985) Fr & Eur.

Woerterbuch der Landwirtschaft. 4th ed. Guenther Haensch. (ENG, FRE, GER & SPA.). 1975. pap. 125.00 (*0-685-01776-1*) Fr & Eur.

Woerterbuch der Literaturwissenschaft. 2nd ed. Claus Trager. 714p. (GER.). 1989. 49.95 (*0-7859-8294-9*, 3323000153) Fr & Eur.

Woerterbuch der Medizin. Koch. Neff Oetinger Staff. 872p. (GER.). 1993. 39.95 (*0-7859-8677-4*, 342303355x) Fr & Eur.

Woerterbuch der Medizin. Margaret Minker. 399p. (GER.). 1991. 59.95 (*0-7859-8495-X*, 3806845352) Fr & Eur.

Woerterbuch der Medizin. 15th ed. Maxim Zetkin. 2377p. (GER.). 1992. 75.00 (*0-7859-8518-2*, 3861260700) Fr & Eur.

Woerterbuch der Medizinischer Fachausdrucke. Josef Hammerschmid-Gollwitzer. 680p. (GER.). 1993. 59.95 (*0-7859-8363-5*, 3442305926) Fr & Eur.

Woerterbuch der Medizinisches Informatik. H. J. Seelos. 550p. (GER.). 1990. 225.00 (*0-7859-8269-8*, 3110112248) Fr & Eur.

Woerterbuch der Modernen Technik. Alfred Oppermann. (ENG & GER.). 350.00 (*0-685-01777-X*, M-6982) Fr & Eur.

Woerterbuch der Muenzkunde. 2nd ed. Ed. by Friedrich Von Schroetter. (GER.). (C). 1970. 108.50 (*3-11-001227-8*) De Gruyter.

Woerterbuch der Musik. Herbert Gerigk. 213p. (GER.). 1983. 14.95 (*0-7859-8498-4*, 3811203460) Fr & Eur.

Woerterbuch der Musik. Heinrich Lindlar. 331p. (GER.). 1989. 59.95 (*0-7859-8378-3*, 3458160329) Fr & Eur.

Woerterbuch der Mystik. Peter Dinzelbacher. 530p. (GER.). 1989. 49.95 (*0-7859-8682-0*, 352045601x) Fr & Eur.

Woerterbuch der Mythologie, Vol. 1. Hans Haussig. 601p. (GER.). 1965. 495.00 (*0-8288-6758-5*, M-6980) Fr & Eur.

Woerterbuch der Mythologie: Dictionary of Mythology. Hans V. Haussig. (GER.). 1973. 195.00 (*0-8288-6345-8*, M-6979) Fr & Eur.

Woerterbuch der Mythologie Vol. 2: Gotter und Mythen Im Alten Europa. Hans Haussig. 976p. (GER.). 1973. 750.00 (*0-7859-8280-9*, 3129098208) Fr & Eur.

Woerterbuch der Mythologie Vol. 4: Gotter und Mythen Im Kaukasischen und Iranischen Volker. Hans Haussig. 546p. (GER.). 1986. 450.00 (*0-7859-8281-7*, 3129098402) Fr & Eur.

Woerterbuch der Mythologie Vol. 5: Gotter und Mythen des Indischen Subkontinents. Hans Haussig. 1040p. (GER.). 1984. 795.00 (*0-7859-8671-5*, 312909850x) Fr & Eur.

Woerterbuch der Mythologie Vol. 6: Gotter und Mythen In Ostasien. Hans Haussig. 896p. (GER.). 1989. 795.00 (*0-7859-8282-5*, 3129098607) Fr & Eur.

Woerterbuch der Mythologie Vol. 7: Gotter und Mythen In Zentraleurasien und Nordeurasien. Hans Haussig. (GER.). write for info. (*0-7859-8283-3*, 3129098704) Fr & Eur.

Woerterbuch der Optik und Feinmechanik, Vol. 3. Ernst Schulz. (ENG, FRE & GER.). 1961. pap. 24.95 (*0-8288-6830-1*, M-6977) Fr & Eur.

Woerterbuch der Optik und Feinmechanik: Dictionary of Optics & Mechanical Engineering, Vol. 2. Ernst Schulz. (ENG, FRE & GER.). 1961. pap. 25.00 (*0-8288-6831-X*, M-6978) Fr & Eur.

Woerterbuch der Optik und Feinmechanik: English-French-German Dictionary of Optics & Mechanical Engineering. Ernst Schulz. (ENG, FRE & GER.). 1961. 24.95 (*0-8288-6829-8*, M-90925) Fr & Eur.

Woerterbuch der Paedagogik, 3 vols., Set. (GER.). 1977. pap. 150.00 (*0-8288-5561-7*, M6971) Fr & Eur.

Woerterbuch der Paedagogischen Psychologie. 3rd ed. (GER.). 1976. 14.95 (*0-8288-5777-6*, M6970) Fr & Eur.

Woerterbuch der Parapsychologie. Hermann Schreiber. (GER.). 1974. pap. 12.00 (*0-7859-0946-X*, M-6969) Fr & Eur.

Woerterbuch der Pflanzennamen im Altwestnordischen. Wilhelm Heizmann. (Ergaenzungsbaende Zum Reallexikon der Germanischen Altertumskunde Ser.: Bd 7). xliv, 337p. (GER.). (C). 1993. lib. bdg. 152.35 (*3-11-013790-9*) De Gruyter.

Woerterbuch der Pharmazie Vol. 1: Biologie, Chemie, Technologie. Harry Von Auterhoff. 532p. (GER.). 1981. 105.00 (*0-7859-8486-0*, 3804706568) Fr & Eur.

Woerterbuch der Pharmazie Vol. 2: Pharmakologie. Ernst Mutschler. 536p. (GER.). 1985. 75.00 (*0-7859-8487-9*, 3804706673) Fr & Eur.

Woerterbuch der Pharmazie Vol. 3: Arzneimittelrecht und Apothekenrecht. Karl Feiden. 253p. (GER.). 1985. 75.00 (*3-8047-0670-3*, 3804706703) Fr & Eur.

Woerterbuch der Pharmazie Vol. 3: Arzneimitttelrecht & Apothekenrecht. Karl Feiden. 253p. (GER.). 1985. pap. 75.00 (*0-7859-8488-7*) Fr & Eur.

Woerterbuch der Pharmazie Vol. 4: Geschichte der Pharmazie. Wolfgang Schneider. 302p. (GER.). 1985. 75.00 (*0-7859-8489-5*, 3804706886) Fr & Eur.

Woerterbuch der Philosophischen Begriffe. 2nd ed. Johannes V. Hoffmeister. (GER.). 95.00 (*3-7873-0164-X*, M-6975) Fr & Eur.

Woerterbuch der Philosophischen Begriffe. 2nd ed. Johannes Van Hoffmeister. 687p. (GER.). 1955. 95.00 (*0-8288-8020-4*, M6975) Fr & Eur.

Woerterbuch der Photo, Film und Kinotechnik: Dictionary of Photo, Film & Cinematechniques. Wolfgang Grau. (ENG, FRE & GER.). 1958. pap. 28.00 (*3-8101-0021-8*) Fr & Eur.

Woerterbuch der Physikalisch-Technischen Begriffe der Medizinischen Radiologie: German, French-English-Deutsch. IEC Staff. 143p. (GER.). 1986. 95.00 (*0-7859-8346-5*, 3410123334) Fr & Eur.

Woerterbuch der Psychologie. Guenther Van Clauss. (GER.). 1976. 35.00 (*0-8288-5779-2*, M6963) Fr & Eur.

Woerterbuch der Psychologie: Dictionary of Psychology. 11th ed. Wilhelm Hehlmann. (GER.). 1974. pap. 59.95 (*0-8288-6225-7*, M-6964) Fr & Eur.

Woerterbuch der Rechtssprache und Wirtschaftssprache Vol. 1: German-Russian. Gyula Decsi. 564p. (GER & RUS.). 1990. 225.00 (*0-7859-8331-7*, 3406090222) Fr & Eur.

Woerterbuch der Rechtssprache und Wirtschaftssprache Vol. 1: Portuguese-German. Erik Jayme. (GER & POR.). 1992. 150.00 (*0-7859-8334-1*, 3406339786) Fr & Eur.

Woerterbuch der Rechtssprache und Wirtschaftssprache Vol. 2: German-Portuguese. Erik Jayme. (GER & POR.). 1990. 175.00 (*0-7859-8335-X*, 3406339794) Fr & Eur.

Woerterbuch der Rechtssprache und Wirtschaftssprache Vol. 2: Russian-German. Gyula Decsi. 725p. (GER & RUS.). 1985. 225.00 (*0-7859-8332-5*, 3406090230) Fr & Eur.

Woerterbuch der Reiterei unde des Fahrsports. 3rd ed. Bianca Simon-Schoen. 157p. (ENG & GER.). 1990. lib. bdg. 45.00 (*0-8288-3403-2*, FC729) Fr & Eur.

Woerterbuch der Religionen. Bertholet. 379p. (GER.). 1985. 59.95 (*0-7859-7438-5*, 3520125048) Fr & Eur.

Woerterbuch der Religionspsychologie. Siegfried R. Dunde. 368p. (GER.). 1993. 125.00 (*0-7859-8445-3*, 3579002864) Fr & Eur.

Woerterbuch der Schulpaedagogik. 4th ed. Arnold Schwendtke. (GER.). 1976. pap. 17.95 (*0-8288-5780-6*, M6960) Fr & Eur.

Woerterbuch der Seeschiffahrt: Dictionary of Merchant Shipping, Vol. 1. 2nd ed. Hans Rinke. (ENG & GER.). 1975. 59.95 (*0-8288-5967-1*, M6958) Fr & Eur.

Woerterbuch der Seeschiffahrt: Dictionary of Merchant Shipping, Vol. 2. 2nd ed. Hans Rinke. (ENG & GER.). 59.95 (*3-19-006295-1*, M-6957) Fr & Eur.

Woerterbuch der Sozialarbeit und der Sozialpaedagogik. 3rd ed. Arnold Schwendtke. 371p. (GER.). 1991. pap. 45.00 (*0-8288-5563-3*, M6955) Fr & Eur.

Woerterbuch der Symbolik. 5th ed. Manfred Lurker. 871p. (GER.). 1991. 49.95 (*0-7859-8409-7*, 3520464055) Fr & Eur.

Woerterbuch der Synonyme. Orbis Staff. 352p. (GER.). 1993. 29.95 (*0-7859-8437-2*, 3572006309) Fr & Eur.

Woerterbuch der Synonyme und Antonyme: 18000 Stichwoerter mit 200000 Worterklaerungen. Erich Bulitta & Hildegard Bulitta. 800p. (GER.). 1995. pap. 22.50 (*3-596-10224-3*, Pub. by Fischer Taschbch Verlag GW) Intl Bk Import.

Woerterbuch der Technik, Vol. 2. 5th ed. Karl-Heinz Radde. 812p. (GER & SPA.). 1989. 175.00 (*0-8288-5565-X*, S40501) Fr & Eur.

Woerterbuch der Technik: Dictionary of Technology. Rudolf Walther. (ENG & GER.). 1974. 88.00 (*0-7859-0848-X*, M-6952) Fr & Eur.

Woerterbuch der Technik: English-German. 5th ed. Rudolf Walther. 1127p. 1986. 125.00 (*0-7859-8466-6*, 3773651058) Fr & Eur.

Woerterbuch der Technik: Spanish-German. Karl-Heinz Radde. 716p. 1977. 95.00 (*0-7859-8467-4*, 3773655304) Fr & Eur.

Woerterbuch der Technik Spanisch - Deutsch. 6th ed. Karl-Heinz Radde. 960p. (GER & SPA.). 1992. 195.00 (*0-8288-2116-X*, S39877) Fr & Eur.

Woerterbuch der Textilindustrie: Dictionary of Textile Industry, Vol. 2. Louis De Vries. (GER.). 95.00 (*0-8288-8029-8*, M6948) Fr & Eur.

Woerterbuch der Textilindustrie: Dictionary of Textile Industry, Vol. 2. Louis de Vries. (ENG & GER.). pap. 65.00 (*0-686-56612-2*, M-6948) Fr & Eur.

Woerterbuch der Ubernommen Ideen. Gustave Flaubert. 125p. (GER.). 1987. 29.95 (*0-7859-8291-4*, 3251000993) Fr & Eur.

Woerterbuch der Umwelttechnik. Friedhelm Nickel. 290p. (GER.). 1990. 95.00 (*0-7859-8483-6*, 3802304217) Fr & Eur.

Woerterbuch der Ungarischen Rechts und Verwaltungssprache, Vol. 2. 2nd ed. (GER & HUN.). 1972. 38.00 (*0-8288-6434-9*, M-859) Fr & Eur.

Woerterbuch der Verlagssprache. 2nd ed. Wilhelm Frieling. 128p. (GER.). 1992. 35.00 (*0-7859-8540-9*, 3890093000) Fr & Eur.

Woerterbuch der Veterinarmedizin, 2 vols. 3rd ed. Ekkehard Wiesner. 1662p. (GER.). 1991. 225.00 (*0-7859-8314-7*, 3334003884) Fr & Eur.

Woerterbuch der Vorschulerziehung: Dictionary of Pre-School Education. Herder Staff. (GER.). 1976. pap. 24.95 (*0-8288-5781-4*, M6944) Fr & Eur.

Woerterbuch der Wasserchemie: German-English-French. Vittorio Anastasio. 362p. (ENG, FRE & GER.). 1991. lib. bdg. 175.00 (*0-8288-3840-2*, F124330) Fr & Eur.

Woerterbuch der Werkstoffprufung Vol. 1: German-English-French. Werner Goedecke. 382p. (ENG, FRE & GER.). 1979. 350.00 (*0-614-00412-8*, 3184011593) Fr & Eur.

Woerterbuch der Werkstoffprufung Vol. 2: English-German-French. Werner Goedecke. 486p. (ENG, FRE & GER.). 1980. 350.00 (*0-7859-8672-3*, 318400435x) Fr & Eur.

Woerterbuch der Werkstoffprufung Vol. 3: French-German-English. Werner Goedecke. 458p. (ENG, FRE & GER.). 1980. 175.00 (*0-7859-8285-X*, 3184004368) Fr & Eur.

Woerterbuch der Wirtschaftsenglisch: English-German. Dieter Hamblock & Dieter Wessels. 323p. (ENG & GER.). 1992. 55.00 (*0-7859-6937-3*) Fr & Eur.

Woerterbuch der Wirtschaftsenglisch: German-English. Dieter Hamblock & Dieter Wessels. 336p. (ENG & GER.). 1991. 55.00 (*0-7859-6936-5*) Fr & Eur.

Woerterbuch der Zauberkunst. Hubert Wedler. 253p. (GER.). 1990. 39.95 (*0-7859-8698-7*, 389487127X) Fr & Eur.

Woerterbuch Des Althochdeutschen Sprachschatzes. Gerhard Kobler. 1660p. (GER.). 1993. 595.00 (*0-7859-8405-4*, 3506746618) Fr & Eur.

Woerterbuch des Arbeits und Sozialrechtd. Alexandre Bonnefoi. (FRE & GER.). 1975. 85.00 (*0-8288-5969-8*, M6938) Fr & Eur.

Woerterbuch Des Bibliothekars in 22 Sprachen: Librarian's Practical Dictionary in 22 Languages. 6th rev. ed. Zoltan Pipics. 385p. 1974. 295.00 (*0-8288-6227-3*, M-7540) Fr & Eur.

Woerterbuch des Juedischen Rechts. M. Cohn. (Illus.). xii, 196p. (GER.). 1981. 78.50 (*3-8055-2062-X*) S Karger.

Woerterbuch des Kraftfahrzeugwesens. Otto Vollnhals. (GER & ITA.). 1975. 125.00 (*0-8288-5970-1*, M6936) Fr & Eur.

Woerterbuch des Pantentwesens in 5 Sprachen: Dictionary of Patents in Five Languages. Gyorgy L. Szendy. (ENG, FRE, GER, RUS & SPA.). 1974. 135.00 (*0-7859-0831-5*, M-6935) Fr & Eur.

Woerterbuch des Steuerrechts. Rudolf Roessler. (GER.). 1971. 75.00 (*0-8288-6491-8*, M-6934) Fr & Eur.

Woerterbuch Deutsch-Esperanto. 4th ed. Erich D. Krause. 591p. (ESP & GER.). 1993. 65.00 (*0-8288-1128-8*, F36460) Fr & Eur.

Woerterbuch Deutsch-Esperanto-Deutsch. Butin. 420p. (ESP & GER.). 1989. 95.00 (*0-7859-7446-6*, 3487070820) Fr & Eur.

Woerterbuch Deutsch-Hindi. Margot Gatzlaff-Halsig. 646p. (GER & HIN.). 1994. 125.00 (*0-7859-8306-6*, 3324003679) Fr & Eur.

Woerterbuch Deutsch-Indonesisch. Adolf Heuken. 667p. (GER & IND.). 1994. 135.00 (*0-7859-8313-9*, 3324006090) Fr & Eur.

Woerterbuch Deutsch-Niederorbisch. Klaus-Peter Jannasch. 355p. (GER.). 1990. 19.95 (*0-7859-8452-6*, 3742005618) Fr & Eur.

Woerterbuch Deutsch-Portugiesisch. Johannes Klare. 551p. (GER & POR.). 35.00 (*0-7859-8298-1*, 3324002125) Fr & Eur.

Woerterbuch Deutsch-Sanskrit. 2nd ed. Klaus Mylius. 322p. (GER & SAN.). 1992. 135.00 (*0-7859-8305-8*, 3324003377) Fr & Eur.

Woerterbuch Deutsch-Swahili. Kersten Legere. 267p. (GER & SWA.). 1990. 65.00 (*0-7859-8311-2*, 3324005051) Fr & Eur.

Woerterbuch Deutsches-Russiches. 5th ed. E. Daum. 719p. (GER & RUS.). 1990. 45.00 (*0-7859-7538-1*, 3324001692) Fr & Eur.

Woerterbuch Deutsches-Vietnamesisch. 7th ed. Gia-Huong Ho. 324p. (GER & VIE.). 59.95 (*0-7859-8289-2*, 3190062269) Fr & Eur.

Woerterbuch EDV-Telematik Vol. 2: French-German. Claude Toulouse. 248p. (FRE & GER.). 1994. pap. 79.95 (*0-7859-8700-2*, 392895203X) Fr & Eur.

Woerterbuch Englisch Elektronische Windows Version. Rossipaul. (ENG & GER.). 1994. 49.95 (*0-614-00372-5*, 3876865247) Fr & Eur.

Woerterbuch Englisch fur die Polizei. Norbert Brauner. 282p. (GER.). 1993. 29.95 (*0-7859-8480-1*, 3801102904) Fr & Eur.

Woerterbuch Englisch Macintosh Version. Rossipaul. (ENG & GER.). 1994. 75.00 (*0-614-00377-6*, 3876867622) Fr & Eur.

Woerterbuch Erdoelverarbeitung-Petrolchemie: Dictionary of Petroleum-Processing. Walter Leipnitz. (ENG, FRE, GER & RUS.). 1977. 125.00 (*0-8288-5568-4*, M6925) Fr & Eur.

Woerterbuch Franzoesich - Windows Version. Rossipaul. (FRE & GER.). 1994. 49.95 (*0-614-00373-3*, 3876865255) Fr & Eur.

Woerterbuch Franzoesich Langenscheidt CD-ROM. Langenscheidt Staff. 125p. (FRE & GER.). 1994. write for info. (*0-614-00360-1*, 3468906153) Fr & Eur.

Woerterbuch fuer Aerzte: Dictionary for Physicians. 2nd ed. F. Lejeune & Werner E. Bunjes. (GER.). 1968. pap. 55.00 (*0-685-01779-6*, M-6924) Fr & Eur.

Woerterbuch fuer Architektur: Hochbau und Baustoffe. (FRE & GER.). 1979. 232.00 (*0-7859-0700-9*, M-6923) Fr & Eur.

Woerterbuch fuer Metallurgie, Mineralogie, Geologie, Bergbau und die Oelindustrie: Dictionary of Metallurgy, Mineralogy, Geology, Mining & Oil Industry. (ENG, FRE, GER & ITA.). 1970. 88.00 (*0-685-01780-X*, M-6912) Fr & Eur.

Woerterbuch fuer Strassenbau und Strassenverkehr. Karl Steinig. 978p. (FRE & GER.). 1970. 175.00 (*0-8288-6565-5*, M-6921) Fr & Eur.

Woerterbuch fuer Wirtschaft: Recht und Handel, Vol. 2. 2nd rev. ed. Georges Potonnier. 1678p. (FRE & GER.). 1990. 350.00 (*0-7859-4850-3*) Fr & Eur.

Woerterbuch fur Handel, Finanz und Recht, Vol. 1 English-German. Robert Herbst. 687p. (ENG & GER.). 1975. 250.00 (*0-7859-7049-5*) Fr & Eur.

Woerterbuch fur Handel, Finanz und Recht, Vol. 2 German-English. Robert Herbst. 906p. (ENG & GER.). 1976. 250.00 (*0-7859-7050-9*) Fr & Eur.

Woerterbuch Georgisch-Deutsch, Deutsch-Georgisch. Wolfgang Lange. 161p. (GEO & GER.). 1987. 39.95 (*0-7859-8523-9*, 3871188506) Fr & Eur.

Woerterbuch Hindi-Deutsch. Erika Klemm. 418p. (GER & HIN.). 95.00 (*0-7859-8309-0*, 3324003970) Fr & Eur.

Woerterbuch Italienisch-Deutsch, Deutsch-Italienisch. Vladimiro Macchi. 1114p. (GER & ITA.). 1989. 29.95 (*0-7859-8442-9*, 3572037522) Fr & Eur.

Woerterbuch Jungscher Psychologie. Samuels. (GER.). 29.95 (*0-614-00380-6*, 3423150882) Fr & Eur.

Woerterbuch Jungscher Psychologie. Andrew Samuels. 252p. (GER.). 1989. 59.95 (*0-614-01952-4*, 3466342325) Fr & Eur.

W

Woerterbuch Kerntechnik: English-German-French-Russian. Ralf Sube. 1200p. (ENG, FRE & GER.). 1985. 295.00 (*0-7859-7032-0*) Fr & Eur.

Woerterbuch Klinisches Medizin German-English. Dressler. 878p. (ENG & GER.). 1991. 195.00 (*0-7859-7548-9*, 3527154647) Fr & Eur.

Woerterbuch Korrosion: German-English-French-Russian. Beneke. 700p. (FRE, GER & RUS.). 450.00 (*0-7859-7435-0*, 380272819X) Fr & Eur.

Woerterbuch Kybernetik: Dictionary of Cybernetics. Alfred Oppermann. (ENG & GER.). 1969. pap. 22.50 (*3-7940-3258-6*, M-6915) Fr & Eur.

Woerterbuch Latein-Deutsch. Helmut Werner. 670p. (GER & LAT.). 1992. 29.95 (*0-7859-8688-X*, 357200540x) Fr & Eur.

Woerterbuch Medizinischer Fachausdruecke. 2nd ed. Fachredaktion. (GER.). 1973. 59.95 (*0-8288-6348-2*, M-6913) Fr & Eur.

Woerterbuch Mikroelecktronik: English-German-English. 2nd ed. Attiyate. 594p. (ENG & GER.). 1992. 150.00 (*0-7859-7246-3*, 3184011097) Fr & Eur.

Woerterbuch Mogolisch-Deutsch. Schalanow Zebek. 276p. (GER & MON.). 1984. 39.95 (*0-7859-8308-2*, 3324003865) Fr & Eur.

Woerterbuch Mongolisch-Deutsch. Hans-Peter Vietze. 417p. (GER & MON.). 1988. 145.00 (*0-7859-8304-X*, 3324003369) Fr & Eur.

Woerterbuch Obersorbisch-Deutsch. Ludmila Budarjowa. 319p. 1990. 24.95 (*0-7859-8451-8*, 3742004190) Fr & Eur.

Woerterbuch Paedegogik. 13th ed. Bohm. 646p. (GER.). 1988. 59.95 (*0-7859-7442-3*, 3520094134) Fr & Eur.

Woerterbuch Papier und Druck. Wolfgang Walenski. 360p. (GER.). 1993. 85.00 (*0-7859-8383-X*, 3465026195) Fr & Eur.

Woerterbuch Pferd und Reiter: Dictionary of Horses & Horsemanship. Zdzislaw Baranowski. (ENG, FRE & GER.). 1977. 16.95 (*0-8288-5570-6*, M6910) Fr & Eur.

Woerterbuch Physik: Dictionary of Physics, 3 vols., Set. Rolf Sube & Gunther Eisenreich. (ENG, FRE, GER & RUS.). 1970. 495.00 (*0-685-42124-4*, M-6909) Fr & Eur.

Woerterbuch Portugiesisch-Deutsch. Johannes Klare. 606p. (GER & POR.). 35.00 (*0-7859-8297-3*, 3324001161) Fr & Eur.

Woerterbuch Radioaktivitat, Strahlenwirkung, Strahlenschutz. 2nd ed. Willibald Pschyrembel. 108p. (GER.). 1987. 39.95 (*0-7859-8270-1*, 3110113430) Fr & Eur.

Woerterbuch Recht und Wirtschafts: English-German. 4th ed. G. Conte. 416p. (ENG & GER.). 1993. 150.00 (*0-7859-7537-3*, 3406377289) Fr & Eur.

Woerterbuch Recht Und Wirtschafts Vol. 2: German-French. 5th ed. Doucet. 656p. (FRE & GER.). 1994. 135.00 (*0-7859-7547-0*, 3406359957) Fr & Eur.

Woerterbuch Russisches-Deutsch. 21th ed. E. Daum. 960p. (GER & RUS.). 1990. 45.00 (*0-7859-7539-X*, 3324000904) Fr & Eur.

Woerterbuch Russisch-Deutsch, Deutsch-Russisch. V. J. Kusawzjow. 480p. (GER & RUS.). 1993. 29.95 (*0-7859-8436-4*, 3572005981) Fr & Eur.

Woerterbuch Sanskrit-Deutsch. 4th ed. Klaus Mylius. 583p. (GER & SAN.). 1992. 150.00 (*0-7859-8300-7*, 3324002451) Fr & Eur.

Woerterbuch Soziale Arbeit. 3rd ed. Dieter Kreft. 670p. (GER.). 1988. 75.00 (*0-7859-8337-6*, 3407557280) Fr & Eur.

Woerterbuch Soziale Arbeit: German-French, French-German. Deutsch Verein Staff. 136p. (FRE & GER.). 1988. 39.95 (*0-7859-7094-0*) Fr & Eur.

Woerterbuch Spanisch-Deutsch, Deutsch-Spanisch. Herbert Koch. (GER & SPA.). 29.95 (*0-7859-8439-9*, 3572010837) Fr & Eur.

Woerterbuch Spanische - Windows Version. Rossipaul. (GER & SPA.). 1994. 49.95 (*0-7859-7230-7*, 3876865271) Fr & Eur.

Woerterbuch Swahili-Deutsch. 5th ed. Hildegard Hoeftmann. 416p. (GER & SWA.). 1992. 85.00 (*0-7859-8312-0*, 3324005213) Fr & Eur.

Woerterbuch Technisches Englisch: English-German Electrical Engineering, Electronics Computers. Werner Herrmann. 87p. (ENG & GER.). 1990. 39.95 (*0-7859-7035-5*) Fr & Eur.

Woerterbuch Tibetisch-Deutsch. 3rd ed. Eberhardt Richter. 444p. (GER & TIB.). 1992. 115.00 (*0-7859-8301-5*, 3324002745) Fr & Eur.

Woerterbuch Umweltschultztechnik: English-German-French-Russian. Egon Seidel. 527p. (FRE, GER & RUS.). 1988. 150.00 (*0-7859-8524-7*, 3871449563) Fr & Eur.

Woerterbuch Vertragswesen: Russian-German, German-Russian. Tatjana Fraer. 200p. (GER & RUS.). 1993. 59.95 (*0-7859-8382-1*, 3464494101) Fr & Eur.

Woerterbuch Vietnamesisch-Deutsch. Gia-Huong Ho. 324p. (GER & VIE.). 75.00 (*0-7859-8307-4*, 3324003784) Fr & Eur.

Woerterbuch Werkzeuge und Werkzeugmaschinen. Kurt Stellhorn. (FRE & GER.). 1969. 115.00 (*0-8288-6622-8*, M-6907) Fr & Eur.

Woerterbuch Wirtschaft: German & English Business Dictionary. W. Wolfel. 784p. (ENG & GER.). 1981. 39.95 (*0-8288-0105-3*, M 15100) Fr & Eur.

Woerterbuch Wirtschaft Englisch-Deutsch. 2nd ed. Andreas Schuller. 784p. (ENG & GER.). 1988. 105.00 (*0-7859-7043-6*) Fr & Eur.

Woerterbuch Wirtschaft Englisch-Deutsch: English-German Business-Dictionary. Gunther Haensch. 784p. (ENG & GER.). 1981. 59.95 (*0-8288-0095-2*, M 15085) Fr & Eur.

Woerterbuch Wirtschatsrussisch: German-Russian. Anna Nikiforowa. 496p. (GER & RUS.). 1993. 105.00 (*0-7859-8380-5*, 3464494063) Fr & Eur.

Woerterbuch Wirtschatsrussisch: Russian-German. Anna Nikiforowa. 496p. (GER & RUS.). 1994. 105.00 (*0-7859-8381-3*, 3464494071) Fr & Eur.

Woerterbuch Zum Neuen Testament. Xavier Leon-Dufour. 469p. (GER.). 1977. 39.95 (*0-7859-8384-8*, 3466202191) Fr & Eur.

Woerterbuch zum Religionsunterricht. Herder Staff. (GER.). 1976. 17.95 (*0-8288-5783-0*, M6906) Fr & Eur.

Woerterbuch zur Bibel. Werner Schmidt. 694p. (GER.). 1971. 39.95 (*0-7859-8284-1*, 3170040480) Fr & Eur.

Woerterbuch Zur Biblischen Botschaft. 2nd ed. Xavier Leon-Dufour. 826p. (GER.). 1981. 95.00 (*0-7859-8373-2*, 3451141779) Fr & Eur.

Woerterbuch Zur Geschichte: Dictionary of History. 4th ed. Erich Bayer. (GER.). 1980. pap. 39.95 (*0-8288-1492-9*, M6905) Fr & Eur.

Woerterbuch zur Medizinischen Soziologie. Paul Luth. 408p. (GER.). 1980. 79.95 (*0-8288-2362-6*, M15305) Fr & Eur.

Woerterbuch zur Politik und Wirtschaftpolitik. Hans E. Zahn. 382p. (ENG, FRE & GER.). 1975. 150.00 (*0-8288-5784-9*, M6904) Fr & Eur.

Woerterbuch zur Politischen Oekonomie. 2nd ed. Gert V. Eynern. (GER.). 1977. pap. 35.00 (*0-8288-5571-4*, M6902) Fr & Eur.

Woerterbuch zur Publizistik: Publicity Dictionary. Kathleen Koszyk. (GER.). 1970. 59.95 (*0-8288-6569-8*, M-6901) Fr & Eur.

Woerterbuch zur Sexualpolitik und ihren Grenzgebieten. (GER.). pap. 39.95 (*3-7615-0016-5*, M-6900) Fr & Eur.

Woerterbuche der Rechtssprache & Wirtschaftssprache, Vol. 1: Spanish-German. 3rd ed. Herbert J. Becher. 1142p. (GER & SPA.). 1988. 250.00 (*0-7859-6881-4*, 3406321852) Fr & Eur.

Woerterbuche der Rechtssprache und Wirtschaftssprache, Vol. 2. 3rd ed. Herbert J. Becher. 1019p. (GER & SPA.). 1989. 250.00 (*0-8288-6432-2*, M7022) Fr & Eur.

Woerterbuecher der Biologie, Mikrobiologie: Dictionary of Biology, Microbiology. Gunther Muller. 25p. (GER.). 1980. 35.00 (*0-8288-1221-7*, M15333) Fr & Eur.

Woes of Wit: A Comedy in Four Acts. Griboedov A. Sergeevich. Tr. & Intro. by Alan Shaw. LC 92-19568. 112p. (Orig.). 1992. pap. 10.00 (*1-55779-043-4*) Hermitage.

Woeterbuch Musik: Dictionary of Terms in Music. 3rd ed. Horst Leuchtmann. 560p. (ENG, FRE & GER.). 1981. 125.00 (*0-8288-2174-7*, M6911) Fr & Eur.

Wofford College. Photos by Tommy Thompson. (Illus.). 112p. 1989. 39.00 (*0-916509-64-8*) Harmony Hse Pub.

Woggle & Butter Harsies. George Clarke. 112p. 1990. pap. 35.00 (*0-86138-081-9*, Pub. by T Dalton UK) St Mut.

Woggle-Bug Book. L. Frank Baum. LC 78-6887. (J). (gr. 1-6). 1978. reprint ed. 50.00 (*0-8201-1308-5*) Schol Facsimiles.

Woggle of Witches. Adrienne Adams. LC 87-18703. (Illus.). 32p. (J). (ps-1). 1985. pap. 4.95 (*0-689-71050-X*, Aladdin Paperbacks) S&S Childrens.

Wohascum County Problem Book. George Gilbert et al. (Dolciani Mathematical Expositions Ser.). 244p. 1993. pap. text ed. 24.95 (*0-88385-316-7*, DOL-14) Math Assn.

Wohnen im Alten Orient: Ein Untersuchung zur Verwendung von Raumen in Altorientalischen Wohnausern. Maria Krafeld-Daugherty. (Illus.). x, 401p. (GER.). 1995. 105.00 (*3-927120-16-2*, Pub. by UGARIT GW) Eisenbrauns.

Wohunge of Ure Lauerd & Other Pieces. Ed. by W. Meredith Thompson. (EETS Original Ser.: Vol. 241). 1963. reprint ed. 30.00 (*0-19-722241-2*, Pub. by EETS UK) Boydell & Brewer.

Wojsko Polskie 1939-1945 Barwa I Bron. Stanislaw Komornicki. (Illus.). 232p. (POL.). 1994. 18.00 (*0-614-02647-4*) Szwede Slavic.

Wok. Gary Lee. LC 79-19094. (Illus.). 192p. (Orig.). 1970. pap. 7.95 (*0-911954-06-6*, Nitty Gritty Ckbks) Bristol Pub Ent CA.

***Wok.** Smithmark Staff. (Little Cookbook Ser.). 1996. 6.98 (*0-7651-9820-7*) Smithmark.

Wok & Stir Fry. Jeni Wright. 128p. 1995. write for info. (*1-57215-106-4*) World Pubns.

Wok Appetizers & Light Snacks. Gary Lee. (Illus.). 182p. (Orig.). 1982. pap. 6.95 (*0-911954-67-8*, Nitty Gritty Ckbks) Bristol Pub Ent CA.

Wok Cooking. Judith Ferguson. 64p. 1995. write for info. (*1-57215-016-5*) World Pubns.

Wok Cooking. Bridget Jones. 1995. (*0-7858-0278-9*) Bk Sales Inc.

Wok Cooking Class Cookbook. Consumer Guide Staff. 1989. pap. 6.99 (*0-517-40269-6*) Random Hse Value.

Wok Cuisine. Better Homes & Gardens Editors. (Better Homes & Gardens Ser.). (Illus.). 216p. 1991. 24.95 (*0-696-01950-7*) Meredith Bks.

Wok for All Seasons. Martin Yan. LC 88-20351. (Illus.). 208p. 1988. pap. 16.95 (*0-385-24386-3*) Doubleday.

Wok This Way. Allison Marx. 208p. 1994. mass mkt. 4.99 (*0-425-14187-X*) Berkley Pub.

***Wok This Way.** Allison Marx. 1994. pap. 4.99 (*0-425-14261-2*) Berkley Pub.

Wok Way. Tuan. LC 74-176166. (Illus.). 1974. pap. 2.95 (*0-915942-01-1*) SF Design.

Wok with Yan Television Cookbook. Stephen Yan. (Illus.). 112p. 1988. pap. 9.95 (*0-921053-00-2*) Gordon Soules Bk.

Wokcraft. Charles Schafer & Violet Schafer. LC 73-183774. (Illus.). 1972. pap. 5.95 (*0-394-70788-5*, Random) Taylor & Ng.

Woke Me up This Morning: Black Gospel Singers & the Gospel Life. Alan Young. (American Made Music Ser.). (Illus.). 256p. 1996. 47.50 (*0-87805-943-1*); pap. 18.00 (*0-87805-944-X*) U Pr of Miss.

Wokingham: The Implementation of Strategic Planning Policy in a Growth Area in the South East. Julian Davis & Patsy Healey. (C). 1983. 75.00 (*0-685-30272-5*, Pub. by Oxford Polytechnic UK) St Mut.

Wokking Your Way to Low Fat Cooking. Norma Chang. Ed. & Illus. by Amy Wong. LC 93-60859. 208p. (Orig.). 1994. pap. 12.50 (*0-9618759-1-7*) Travelling Gourmet.

Woks, Steamers & Fire Pots see Great Cook's Guide to Appetizers

Wolcott Genealogy: The Family of Henry Wolcott, One of the First Settlers of Windor, Connecticut. C. Wolcott. (Illus.). 480p. 1989. reprint ed. lib. bdg. 66.50 (*0-8328-6587-7*) Higginson Bk Co.

Wolcott Genealogy: The Family of Henry Wolcott, One of the First Settlers of Windor, Connecticut. C. C. Wolcott. (Illus.). 480p. 1989. reprint ed. pap. 72.00 (*0-8328-1287-0*) Higginson Bk Co.

Woldman's Engineering Alloys, Mat.DB. 1994. disk 369.00 (*0-614-03550-3*, 7440U); disk 369.00 (*0-614-03551-1*, 7429U) ASM Intl.

Woldman's Engineering Alloys. 6th ed. Norman E. Woldman. Ed. by Robert C. Gibbons. LC 79-20379. 1829p. reprint ed. pap. 180.00 (*0-8357-3589-3*, 2034318) Bks Demand.

***Woldman's Engineering Alloys.** 7th ed. Norman E. Woldman. Ed. by John P. Frick. LC 90-84697. (Materials Data Ser.). 1471p. 1990. reprint ed. pap. 180.00 (*0-608-03986-1*, 2064718) Bks Demand.

Woldman's Engineering Alloys. 7th rev. ed. J. Frick. 1300p. 1990. 123.00 (*0-87170-408-0*, 6087) ASM.

***Woldman's Engineering Alloys.** 8th expanded rev. ed. Ed. by J. Frick. 1400p. 1994. 190.00 (*0-87170-544-3*, 6329) ASM.

Wole Soyinka: A Bibliography of Primary & Secondary Sources. James Gibbs et al. LC 85-14671. (Bibliographies & Indexes in Afro-American & African Studies: No. 7). 117p. 1986. text ed. 49.95 (*0-313-23937-1*, GWS/, Greenwood Pr) Greenwood.

Wole Soyinka: An Appraisal. Adewale Maja-Pearce. 160p. 1994. pap. 17.50 (*0-435-91151-1*, 91151) Heinemann.

Wole Soyinka: Critical Perspectives Past & Present. Ed. by Henry Louis Gates, Jr. & K. A. Appiah. (Literary Ser.). 1994. 24.95 (*1-56743-051-1*); pap. 14.95 (*1-56743-057-0*) Amistad Pr.

Wole Soyinka & Modern Tragedy: A Study of Dramatic Theory & Practice. Ketu H. Katrak. LC 85-27153. (Contributions in Afro-American & African Studies: No. 96). (Illus.). 204p. 1986. text ed. 49.95 (*0-313-24074-4*, KMT/, Greenwood Pr) Greenwood.

***Wolf.** LC 96-48683. (Wildlife of North America Ser.). (J). 1997. write for info. (*1-56065-471-6*) Capstone Pr.

Wolf. Barbalet. pap. 5.99 (*0-517-13338-5*) Random.

Wolf. Gillian Cross. LC 90-47040. 144p. (YA). 1991. 13.95 (*0-8234-0870-1*) Holiday.

Wolf. Gillian Cross. 144p. (YA). (gr. 7-9). 1993. pap. 3.25 (*0-590-45608-3*) Scholastic Inc.

***Wolf.** Michael Dahl. (Wildlife of North America Ser.). (Illus.). (J). 1997. 18.40 (*0-516-20544-7*) Childrens.

Wolf. Sara Fanelli. LC 96-2698. 1997. pap. 14.99 (*0-8037-2093-9*) Dial Bks Young.

Wolf. Maureen Greeley. LC 96-4340. 144p. 1996. 19.98 (*1-56799-296-X*, MetroBooks) M Friedman Pub Grp Inc.

Wolf. Madeline Harper. (Temptation Ser.: No. 389). 1992. mass mkt. 2.99 (*0-373-25489-X*, 1-25489-5) Harlequin Bks.

Wolf. Christian Harvard. (Animal Close-Ups Ser.). (J). (ps-3). 1996. 6.95 (*0-614-15567-3*) Candlewick Pr.

Wolf. Roger Rapoport. (Dare to Love Us Ser.). (J). 1995. 12.95 (*1-57143-049-0*) RDR Bks.

Wolf. Andrienne Soutter-Perrot. (My First Nature Bks.). (YA). (gr. 5 up). 1992. lib. bdg. 10.95 (*0-88682-552-0*) Creative Ed.

Wolf. Sami Sweeten. LC 93-34493. 32p. (J). (gr. 1-4). 1994. lib. bdg. 14.95 (*0-8075-9160-2*) A Whitman.

Wolf: A False Memoir. Jim Harrison. 224p. 1981. pap. 12.95 (*0-385-29160-4*, Delta) Dell.

Wolf: Ghost Hunter. Daniel Leboeuf. (Illus.). 144p. 1996. pap. text ed. 19.95 (*1-895565-98-7*) Firefly Bks Ltd.

Wolf: Night Howler. Christian Havard. LC 94-40535. (Animal Close-Ups Ser.). (Illus.). 28p. (Orig.). (J). (ps-4). 1996. pap. 6.95 (*0-88106-436-X*) Charlesbridge Pub.

Wolf: Return to Yellowstone. Michael Milstein. (Illus.). 96p. (Orig.). 1995. pap. 14.95 (*0-9627618-8-5*) Billings Gazette.

***Wolf: Spirit of the Wild.** Diana Landau. 1997. pap. text ed. 22.95 (*0-8118-1960-4*) Chronicle Bks.

Wolf: The Ecology & Behavior of an Endangered Species. L. David Mech. LC 80-27364. (Illus.). 385p. (C). 1981. reprint ed. pap. 16.95 (*0-8166-1026-6*) U of Minn Pr.

Wolf: The World's Wild Dogs. Jeremy Bradshaw. Ed. by Rebecca Stefoff. LC 92-10244. (Wildlife Survival Library). (Illus.). 31p. (J). (gr. 3-6). 1992. lib. bdg. 17.26 (*1-56074-055-8*) Garrett Ed Corp.

***Wolf: U-Boat Commanders in World War II.** Jordan Vause. LC 96-43105. 1997. 28.95 (*1-55750-874-7*) Naval Inst Pr.

***Wolf: Wild Hunter of North America.** Bruce Obee. LC 97-9750. 1997. pap. write for info. (*1-57145-602-3*) Thunder Bay CA.

Wolf Almanac. Robert Busch. (Illus.). 224p. 1995. 27.95 (*1-55821-351-1*) Lyons & Burford.

Wolf & Bear Stories. Walker D. Wyman. 63p. pap. 3.00 (*0-318-03969-9*) U Wisc-River Falls Pr.

Wolf & Coyote Trapping. A. R. Harding. (Illus.). 252p. pap. 4.00 (*0-936622-27-X*) A R Harding Pub.

Wolf & Iron. Gordon R. Dickson. 480p. 1993. mass mkt. 5.99 (*0-8125-3334-8*) Tor Bks.

Wolf & the Angel. Kathleen Creighton. (Intimate Moments Ser.: No. 417). 1992. mass mkt. 3.29 (*0-373-07417-4*, 5-07417-4) Harlequin Bks.

Wolf & the Buffalo. Elmer Kelton. 384p. 1997. mass mkt. 5.50 (*0-553-25740-4*) Bantam.

Wolf & the Buffalo. Elmer Kelton. LC 85-20814. (Texas Tradition Ser.: No. 5). 426p. 1986. reprint ed. 17.95 (*0-87565-058-9*); reprint ed. pap. 12.95 (*0-87565-059-7*) Tex Christian.

***Wolf & the Cougar.** large type ed. Ted Richardson. (Dales Large Print Ser.). (Illus.). 214p. 1996. pap. 17.99 (*1-85389-641-1*) Ulverscroft.

Wolf & the Dove. Linda Turner. (Fortune's Children Ser.). 1996. mass mkt. 4.50 (*0-373-50181-1*, 1-50181-6) Harlequin Bks.

Wolf & the Dove. Kathleen E. Woodiwiss. 1995. 20.00 (*0-688-12504-2*) Morrow.

Wolf & the Dove. Kathleen E. Woodiwiss. 512p. 1976. reprint ed. mass mkt. 6.99 (*0-380-00778-9*) Avon.

Wolf & the Old Woman. Patricia Gray. LC 93-172. (J). 1994. write for info. (*0-383-03728-X*) SRA McGraw.

Wolf & the Raven. Diana L. Paxson. 352p. 1994. mass mkt. 5.99 (*0-380-76526-8*, AvoNova) Avon.

Wolf & the Raven: Totem Poles of Southeastern Alaska. 2nd ed. Viola E. Garfield & Linn A. Forrest. LC 49-8492. (Illus.). 161p. 1961. reprint ed. pap. 13.95 (*0-295-73998-3*) U of Wash Pr.

Wolf & the Seven Kids. Jacob W. Grimm & Wilhelm K. Grimm. LC 78-18076. (Illus.). 32p. (J). (gr. 1-4). 1979. lib. bdg. 11.89 (*0-89375-138-3*) Troll Communs.

Wolf & the Seven Kids. Jacob W. Grimm & Wilhelm K. Grimm. LC 78-18076. (Illus.). 32p. (J). (gr. 1-4). 1996. pap. 3.95 (*0-89375-116-2*) Troll Communs.

Wolf & the Seven Little Kids. Jacob W. Grimm & Wilhelm K. Grimm. Tr. by Anthea Bell from GER. LC 95-2266. (Illus.). 32p. (J). (ps-3). Date not set. lib. bdg. 15.88 (*1-55858-446-3*) North-South Bks NYC.

Wolf & the Sheep. Richard K. Hoskins. 78p. 1995. pap. 5.00 (*1-881867-03-X*) Virginia Pub.

Wolf & the Winds. Frank B. Linderman. LC 86-40075. 224p. 1986. 19.95 (*0-8061-2007-X*) U of Okla Pr.

Wolf at the Door. Barbara Corcoran. LC 92-45108. 192p. (J). (gr. 3-7). 1993. lib. bdg. 16.00 (*0-689-31870-7*, Atheneum Bks Young) S&S Childrens.

Wol'f Bane, No. 1. Tara K. Harper. 1997. mass mkt. 5.99 (*0-345-40634-6*) Ballantine.

Wolf Boy of Agra & Feral Children & Autistic Children. William F. Ogburn & Bruno Bettelheim. (Reprint Series in Social Sciences). (C). 1993. reprint ed. pap. text ed. 1.90 (*0-8290-2709-2*, S-608) Irvington.

Wolf by the Ears. Ann Rinaldi. 272p. (J). (gr. 7-9). 1991. 13.95 (*0-590-43413-6*, Scholastic Hardcover) Scholastic Inc.

Wolf by the Ears. Ann Rinaldi. 272p. (YA). (gr. 7-9). 1993. pap. 4.99 (*0-590-43412-8*) Scholastic Inc.

Wolf by the Ears: Thomas Jefferson & Slavery. John C. Miller. 336p. 1991. reprint ed. pap. text ed. 14.95 (*0-8139-1365-9*) U Pr of Va.

***Wolf Called Motka.** Stanley A. Moore. LC 96-61463. (Illus.). x, 240p. (Orig.). 1996. pap. 11.95 (*0-9655251-0-4*) Fayetteville Floral Pub Co.

Wolf Child. Dennis Nolan. LC 88-35955. (Illus.). 40p. (J). (gr. 1-5). 1989. lib. bdg. 16.00 (*0-02-768141-6*, Mac Bks Young Read) S&S Childrens.

Wolf Clan Sourcebook: A Battletech Sourcebook. FASA Staff. (BattleTech Ser.). (Illus.). 128p. 1991. pap. 15.00 (*1-55560-136-7*, 1642) FASA Corp.

Wolf Country - A Mystery in Progress. Barbara H. Robbins et al. (Illus.). (J). (gr. k-12). 1996. pap. 17.95 (*0-9630060-2-9*) Robbinspring.

Wolf Creek & the Muskingum: Notes on the Settlement of Southeastern Ohio. Richard Walker. (Illus.). 599p. 1996. 50.00 (*0-9647972-1-6*) G R Walker.

Wolf Creek Station: Kansas Gas & Electric Company in the Nuclear Era. Craig Miner. LC 93-14241. (Historical Perspectives on Business Enterprise Ser.). 1993. 45.00 (*0-8142-0614-X*) Ohio St U Pr.

Wolf Cub Scout Action Book. 64p. 1980. pap. 3.00 (*0-8395-3902-9*, 33902) BSA.

Wolf Cub Scout Book. rev. ed. (Illus.). 224p. (J). (gr. 2). 1986. pap. 4.50 (*0-8395-3234-2*, 33234) BSA.

Wolf Dog of the Woodland Indians. Margaret Z. Searcy. LC 90-26215. (Illus.). 112p. (J). (ps-8). 1991. pap. 6.95 (*0-88289-778-0*) Pelican.

Wolf Dream. Carole Stedronsky. Ed. by Richard Brobst & Richard Smyth. 28p. (Orig.). 1991. pap. text ed. 3.50 (*0-9625011-1-5*) Anabiosis Pr.

Wolf-Dreams. Michael D. Weaver. 192p. 1987. mass mkt. 2.95 (*0-380-75198-4*) Avon.

Wolf Driving Sled: Sel Poems 1970-1980. Gary Lawless. 1981. pap. 3.50 (*0-942396-28-6*) Blackberry ME.

Wolf from Scotland: Robert Reid Kalley. William Forsyth. 1988. pap. 11.99 (*0-85234-256-X*, Pub. by Evangelical Pr) Presby & Reformed.

Wolf Girls. Stemple & Jane Yolen. (J). 1998. 16.00 (*0-689-81080-6*, S&S Bks Young Read) S&S Childrens.

Wolf Girls at Vassar: Lesbian & Gay Experiences 1930-1990. Ed. by Anne MacKay. 128p. 1992. pap. 10.95 (*0-9631911-0-1*) Ten Percent.

Wolf Girls at Vassar: Lesbian & Gay Experiences, 1930-1990. Ed. by Anne McKay. LC 92-42022. 1993. pap. 9.95 (*0-312-08923-6*) St Martin.

Wolf-Heidegger's Atlas of Human Anatomy: Wolf-Heideggers Atlas der HumanAnatomie, Vols. I-III. 4th rev. ed. Ed. by H. F. Frick et al. (Illus.). 600p. 1990. 100.00 (*3-8055-4289-5*) S Karger.

***Wolf-Hirschhorn Syndrome: A Guidebook for Families.** G. Bradley Schaefer et al. (Illus.). 48p. (Orig.). 1996. spiral bd. 11.00 (*1-889843-03-2*) Meyer Rehab Inst.

Wolf Hunter: Ten Years with a United States Biological Survey Hunter. Ray Freeman. (Illus.). 48p. (C). 1989. pap. 4.95 (*0-944402-03-8*) Cmmn Man Inst.

Wolf-Hunting in France in the Reign of Louis XV: The Beast of the Gevaudan. Richard H. Thompson. LC 91-39065. 380p. 1992. lib. bdg. 99.95 (0-88946-746-3) E Mellen.

Wolf Hybrid. 2nd rev. ed. Dorothy Prendergast. (Illus.). (Orig.). 1989. pap. 17.00 (0-9623640-0-2) Rudelhaus Enter.

Wolf in Death's Clothing. Elizabeth Quinn. 1995. mass mkt. 5.50 (0-671-74991-9, Pocket Books) PB.

Wolf in Man's Clothing. Mignon G. Eberhart. LC 96-20496. ix, 294p. 1996. pap. 13.00 (0-8032-6732-0, Bison Books) U of Nebr Pr.

Wolf in Man's Clothing. Mignon G. Eberhart. 224p. 1987. mass mkt. 4.99 (0-446-31470-6) Warner Bks.

***Wolf in Shadow.** David Gemmell. 1997. mass mkt. 2.99 (0-345-41685-6, Del Rey) Ballantine.

***Wolf in Shadow Bk. 3: The Stones of Power.** David Gemmell. 1997. mass mkt. 5.99 (0-345-37903-9, Del Rey) Ballantine.

Wolf in Sheep's Clothing: The Search for a Child Killer. Tommy McIntyre. LC 88-5738. (Great Lakes Bks.). 232p. 1988. 34.95 (0-8143-1966-1); pap. 15.95 (0-8143-1989-0) Wayne St U Pr.

Wolf in the Garden: The Land Rights Movement & the Renewal of the American Environmental Movement. Ed. by Philip Brick & R. McGreggor Cawley. LC 96-433. 315p. 1996. pap. text ed. 23.95 (0-8476-8185-8) Rowman.

Wolf in the Garden: The Land Rights Movement & the Renewal of the American Environmental Movement. Ed. by Philip Brick & R. McGreggor Cawley. LC 96-433. 315p. (C). 1996. lib. bdg. 62.50 (0-8476-8184-X) Rowman.

Wolf in the Shadows. Marcia Muller. 368p. 1993. 18.95 (0-89296-525-8) Mysterious Pr.

Wolf in the Shadows. Marcia Muller. 384p. 1994. mass mkt. 5.50 (0-446-40383-0) Warner Bks.

Wolf in the Shadows: A Sharon McCone Mystery. large type ed. Marcia Muller. LC 93-37404. (Cloak & Dagger Ser.). 1993. lib. bdg. 21.95 (0-7862-0087-1) Thorndike Pr.

Wolf in the Southwest: The Making of an Endangered Species. Ed. by David E. Brown. LC 82-17399. 195p. 1983. pap. 14.95 (0-8165-0796-1) U of Ariz Pr.

Wolf in Waiting. Rebecca Flanders. 1995. mass mkt. 3.50 (0-373-27057-7, 1-27057-8) Silhouette.

Wolf Island. Celia Godkin. (Illus.). (J). (ps-3). 1995. text ed. 15.95 (0-7167-6513-6, Sci Am Yng Rdrs) W H Freeman.

Wolf Kahn. Justin Spring. 1996. write for info. (0-8109-1226-0) Abrams.

Wolf Kahn. Justin Spring. (Illus.). 164p. 1996. 49.50 (0-8109-6322-1) Abrams.

Wolf Kahn, New Landscapes. Lawrence Campbell. Ed. by Gayle Maxon & Diana Hancock. LC 88-80230. (Illus.). 44p. 1988. 12.00 (0-935037-19-5) G Peters Gallery.

Wolf Magic for Kids. Tom Wolpert. LC 90-50720. (Animal Magic for Kids Ser.). (Illus.). 48p. (J). (gr. 2-3). 1991. lib. bdg. 18.60 (0-8368-0662-X) Gareth Stevens Inc.

Wolf-Man. Ed. by Muriel Gardiner. 390p. 1991. pap. 15.00 (0-374-52313-4, Noonday) FS&G.

Wolf Man: The Original Shooting Script. Philip Riley. LC 93-32968. 262p. 1995. pap. 19.95 (1-882127-21-8) Magicimage Filmbooks.

Wolf Man's Magic Word: A Cryptonymy. Nicolas Abraham & Maria Torok. Tr. by Nicholas Rand from FRE. LC 86-7030. (Theory & History of Literature Ser.: Vol. 37). (Illus.). 204p. (Orig.). 1987. pap. text ed. 13.95 (0-8166-1422-9) U of Minn Pr.

Wolf Marshall Basic Guitar Method, Bk. 3. Wolf Marshall. 80p. 1993. pap. 7.95 (0-7935-2096-7, 00697245); pap. 14.95 incl. audio (0-7935-2097-5, 00697246) H Leonard.

Wolf Marshall Basic Guitar Method, Bk. 3. Wolf Marshall. 1993. pap. 16.95 incl. audio compact disk (0-7935-2098-3, 00697247) H Leonard.

Wolf Marshall Guitar Method, Bk. 1. Wolf Marshall. 64p. 1993. pap. 5.95 (0-7935-1605-6, 00697219) H Leonard.

Wolf Marshall Guitar Method, Bk. 1. Wolf Marshall. 1993. pap. 12.95 incl. audio (0-7935-1606-4, 00697220); pap. 14.95 incl. audio compact disk (0-7935-1607-2, 00697221) H Leonard.

Wolf Marshall Guitar Method, Bk. 2. Wolf Marshall. 64p. 1993. pap. 5.95 (0-7935-1608-0, 00697222) H Leonard.

Wolf Marshall Guitar Method, Bk. 2. Wolf Marshall. 1993. pap. 12.95 incl. audio (0-7935-1609-9, 00697223); pap. 14.95 incl. audio compact disk (0-7935-1610-2, 00697224) H Leonard.

Wolf Marshall Guitar Method: Advanced Concepts & Techniques Book. Wolf Marshall. pap. 9.95 (0-7935-2152-1, 0069725311); pap. 14.95 incl. audio (0-7935-2153-X, 00697254); pap. 16.95 incl. audio compact disk (0-7935-2154-8, 00697255) H Leonard.

Wolf Marshall Guitar Method Bk. 1: Power Studies. Wolf Marshall. 1994. pap. 12.95 (0-7935-2674-4, 00697256); pap. 17.95 incl. audio compact disk (0-7935-2676-0, 00697258); pap. 12.95 (0-7935-2679-5, 00697259) H Leonard.

Wolf Marshall Guitar Method Bk. 2: Power Studies. Wolf Marshall. 1994. pap. 14.95 incl. audio (0-7935-2675-2, 00697257); pap. 14.95 incl. audio (0-7935-2680-9, 00697261); pap. 17.95 incl. audio compact disk (0-7935-2681-7, 00697261) H Leonard.

Wolf Marshall Guitar Method Bk. 3: Power Studies. Wolf Marshall. 96p. 1994. pap. 12.95 (0-7935-3274-4, 00697262); pap. 14.95 incl. audio (0-7935-3275-2, 00697263); pap. 17.95 incl. audio compact disk (0-7935-3276-0) H Leonard.

Wolf Marshall Guitar Method Primer. pap. 4.95 (0-7935-4472-6, 00698976) H Leonard.

Wolf Marshall Guitar Trax. pap. 16.95 incl. audio (0-89524-702-X) Cherry Lane.

Wolf Marshall's Rock History Guitar School Presents. 64p. 1994. otabind 12.95 (0-7935-1713-3, 00660331) H Leonard.

***Wolf Moon.** 1997. mass mkt. 5.99 (0-553-29198-X, Spectra) Bantam.

Wolf Moon. Jean Pedrick. LC 73-94067. 72p. 1974. pap. 3.95 (0-914086-03-0) Alicejamesbooks.

Wolf Mountain Moon: The Battle of the Butte, 1877. Terry C. Johnston. 496p. 1997. mass mkt. 6.50 (0-553-29977-8) Bantam.

Wolf Nights. Ed. by Fire. (Illus.). (Orig.). 1988. pap. text ed. 9.00 (0-938885-04-9) Shu Pub.

Wolf No Wolf. Peter Bowen. 224p. 1996. 20.95 (0-312-14078-9) St Martin.

***Wolf, No Wolf.** Peter Bowen. 1997. mass mkt. write for info. (0-614-20527-1) St Martin.

***Wolf, No Wolf: A Dead Letter Mystery.** Peter Bowen. 1997. mass mkt. 5.99 (0-312-96103-0) St Martin.

Wolf of Shadows. Whitley Strieber. LC 84-20133. (Illus.). 128p. (YA). (gr. 7-12). 1985. lib. bdg. 9.99 (0-394-97224-4) Knopf Bks Yng Read.

Wolf Pack. Robert N. Charrette. (BattleTech Ser.: No. 4). 272p. 1992. pap. 5.99 (0-451-45150-3, ROC) NAL-Dutton.

Wolf Pack. David Thompson. (Wilderness Ser.: No. 20). 176p. (Orig.). 1995. mass mkt., pap. text ed. 3.99 (0-8439-3729-7) Dorchester Pub Co.

Wolf Pack: Tracking Wolves in the Wild. Sylvia A. Johnson & Alice Aamodt. (Discovery! Ser.). (Illus.). 96p. (YA). (gr. 5 up). 1985. lib. bdg. 23.95 (0-8225-1577-6, Lerner Publctns) Lerner Group.

Wolf Pack: Tracking Wolves in the Wild. Sylvia A. Johnson & Alice Aamodt. (Illus.). 96p. (J). (gr. 5 up). 1987. reprint ed. pap. 6.95 (0-8225-9526-5, Lerner Publctns) Lerner Group.

Wolf Path. Judith Van Gieson. 256p. 1993. mass mkt. 4.50 (0-06-109139-1, Harp PBks) HarpC.

Wolf-Rayet & High Temperature Stars: Proceedings of the International Astronomical Union Symposium, No. 49, Buenos Aires, Argentina, Aug. 1971. International Astronomical Union Staff. Ed. by M. K. Bappu & J. Sahade. LC 72-87470. 263p. 1973. pap. text ed. 82.50 (90-277-0361-2); lib. bdg. 123.50 (90-277-0246-2) Kluwer Ac.

Wolf-Rayet Stars: Observations, Physics, Evolution. Ed. by C. De Lorre & A. Willis. 1982. pap. text ed. 93.00 (90-277-1470-3); lib. bdg. 187.00 (90-277-1469-X) Kluwer Ac.

Wolf-Rayet Stars - Binaries, Colliding Winds, Evolution: Proceedings of the International Astronomical Union (163rd: 1994: La Biodola, Elba, Italia) Peredur M. Williams. (International Astronomical Union Symposia Ser.). 580p. (C). 1995. lib. bdg. 176.00 (0-7923-3183-4) Kluwer Ac.

Wolf-Rayet Stars - Binaries, Colliding Winds, Evolution: Proceedings of the 163rd Symposium of the International Astronomical Union Held in La Biodola, Elba, Italy, May 2-6, 1994. Ed. by Karel A. Van Der Hucht. (International Astronomical Union Symposia Ser.). 600p. (C). 1995. pap. text ed. 89.50 (0-7923-3184-2) Kluwer Ac.

Wolf Reflections. Ken Jenkins. 64p. (Orig.). 1996. pap. 11.95 (1-57034-035-8) ICS Bks.

Wolf Rider: A Tale of Terror. Avi. LC 86-13607. 216p. (YA). (gr. 7 up). 1986. lib. bdg. 17.00 (0-02-707760-8, Bradbury S&S) S&S Childrens.

Wolf Rider: A Tale of Terror. 2nd ed. Avi. 224p. (YA). (gr. 7 up). 1993. reprint ed. pap. 4.50 (0-02-041513-3) Macmillan.

Wolf Road. Raymond M. Palmer. LC 90-71989. 73p. (Orig.). 1992. pap. 4.50 (1-56002-049-0) Aegina Pr.

Wolf Run. Julian J. Savarin. 288p. 1991. 19.95 (0-8027-1148-0) Walker & Co.

Wolf Shadow. James Reasoner. (Wind River Ser.: No. 3). 304p. 1994. mass mkt. 3.50 (0-06-100773-0, Harp PBks) HarpC.

***Wolf Shadows.** Mary Casanova. 192p. (J). (gr. 3-7). 1997. pap. 14.95 (0-7868-0325-8) Hyprn Child.

Wolf Shall Dwell with the Lamb: A Spirituality for Leadership in a Multicultural Community. Eric H. F. Law. LC 93-9205. 152p. (Orig.). 1993. pap. 14.99 (0-8272-4231-X) Chalice Pr.

Wolf Shall Lie with the Lamb: The Messiah in Chasidic Thought. Shmuel Boteach. LC 92-28697. 296p. 1993. 30.00 (0-87668-339-1) Aronson.

Wolf Solent. John Cowper Powys. 614p. text ed. 35.95 (0-912568-09-7) Colgate U Pr.

Wolf Solent: A Novel, 2 vols., Set. John Cowper Powys. 1971. reprint ed. 79.00 (0-403-01159-0) Scholarly.

Wolf Songs: The Classic Collection of Writings about Wolves. Ed. by Robert Busch. LC 94-1470. (Illus.). 189p. 1994. 15.00 (0-87156-411-4) Sierra.

***Wolf Songs: The Classic Collection of Writings about Wolves.** Ed. by Robert Busch. 208p. 1997. pap. 14.00 (0-87156-911-6) Sierra.

Wolf-Spakker. Tamora Pierce. (J). 1997. pap. 4.99 (0-679-88289-8, Bullseye Bks) Random Bks Yng Read.

Wolf-Speaker. Tamora Pierce. LC 93-21909. (Immortals Ser.). 192p. (J). (gr. 4-8). 1994. lib. bdg. 16.00 (0-689-31833-2, Atheneum Bks Young) S&S Childrens.

***Wolf-Speaker.** Tamora Pierce. (Immortals Ser.). (YA). (gr. 7 up). 1997. pap. 4.99 (0-614-28949-1) Random Bks Yng Read.

Wolf Spiders. James E. Gerholdt. LC 95-12657. (J). 1995. lib. bdg. 13.98 (1-56239-510-6) Abdo & Dghtrs.

Wolf Sponsorship Kit. Merryl Lambert. 1993. 19.95 (0-9641742-4-3) Pequot Pubng.

***Wolf Spring Place: Growing up There.** Hubertine Mog. LC 96-72551. (Illus.). 240p. (Orig.). 1997. pap. 14.95 (1-889902-02-0) Prtnrshp Bk Servs.

***Wolf Stalker.** Gloria Skurzynski & Alane Ferguson. LC 97-11125. (National Parks Mystery Ser.). (J). 1997. write for info. (0-7922-7034-7) Natl Geog.

Wolf Stories: Myths & True Life Tales from Around the World. Susan Strauss. Ed. by Julie Livingston. LC 93-18382. (Illus.). 63p. (Orig.). (J). (gr. 1-6). 1993. 11.95 (0-941831-84-1); pap. 7.95 (0-941831-88-4) Beyond Words Pub.

Wolf Story. James B. Huggins. LC 93-10103. 1993. pap. 9.99 (1-56507-126-3) Harvest Hse.

Wolf Story. William McCleery. LC 87-25977. (Illus.). 82p. (J). (gr. 1-6). 1988. reprint ed. lib. bdg. 16.50 (0-208-02191-4, Linnet Bks) Shoe String.

Wolf Strain: A Western Trio. Max Brand. LC 96-6299. 1996. 16.95 (0-7862-0662-4, Five Star) Mac Lib Ref.

Wolf Strain: A Western Trio. large type ed. Brand. Date not set. 20.00 (0-7838-1673-1, GK Hall) Thorndike Pr.

Wolf Tales: Native American Children's Stories. Ed. & Adapted by Mary Powell. LC 92-29690. (Illus.). 40p. (Orig.). (J). (gr. 3 up). 1993. pap. 8.95 (0-941270-73-4) Ancient City Pr.

Wolf That I Am: In Search of the Red Earth People. Fred McTaggart. LC 84-7352. 216p. 1994. reprint ed. pap. 14.95 (0-8061-1905-5) U of Okla Pr.

Wolf That Rode. Nelson Nye. 224p. (Orig.). 1980. mass mkt. 1.95 (0-89083-612-4, Zebra Kensgtn) Kensgtn Pub Corp.

Wolf, the Woman, the Wilderness: A True Story of Returning Home. Teresa T. Martino. LC 96-45468. 284p. 1996. pap. text ed. 14.95 (0-939165-29-5) NewSage Press.

Wolf to the Slaughter. Ruth Rendell. 224p. 1987. mass mkt. 5.99 (0-345-34520-7) Ballantine.

Wolf Tourist: One Summer in the West. Jay R. Elhard. LC 96-10024. 223p. (Orig.). 1996. pap. 16.95 (0-87421-211-1) Utah St U Pr.

Wolf Tracker. Zane Grey. 320p. 1993. 29.00 (1-56723-118-7) Yestermorrow.

***Wolf Trap.** Casanova. (J). 1997. lib. bdg. 14.89 (0-7868-2269-4) Hyprn Child.

Wolf Trilogy: Red, the Pigs & the Wolf; Lone Wolf, Invisible Wolf; Thick As Thieves. Aubrey Hampton. (Illus.). 200p. (Orig.). 1990. pap. 10.95 (0-939157-03-9) Organica Pr.

***Wolf Walking.** Edwin Daniels. LC 96-43284. (Illus.). 96p. 1997. 19.95 (1-55670-551-4) Stewart Tabori & Chang.

Wolf Wars: The Remarkable Inside Story of the Restoration of Wolves to Yellowstone. Hank Fischer. LC 95-60292. 180p. 1995. 19.95 (1-56044-351-0) Falcon Pr MT.

Wolf Wars: The Remarkable Inside Story of the Restoration of Wolves to Yellowstone. Hank Fischer. LC 95-60292. 180p. 1995. pap. text ed. 12.95 (1-56044-352-9) Falcon Pr MT.

Wolf Watch. Winters. (J). 1997. 16.00 (0-689-80218-8, S&S Bks Young Read) S&S Childrens.

Wolf Whistle. Lewis Nordan. 308p. 1995. pap. 9.95 (1-56512-110-4) Algonquin Bks.

Wolf Whistle: A Novel. Lewis Nordan. LC 93-1011. 294p. 1993. 16.95 (1-56512-028-0) Algonquin Bks.

***Wolf Who Wasn't.** Anne De Graaf. (Tiny Triumphs Ser.). (Illus.). 22p. (J). 1997. pap. text ed. 2.95 (0-687-07109-7) Abingdon.

Wolf, Wildlife Library. Anita Townsend. 1984. 1.98 (0-671-07177-7) S&S Trade.

Wolf Willow. Wallace Stegner. 320p. 1990. pap. 12.95 (0-14-013439-5, Penguin Bks) Viking Penguin.

Wolf Winter. Clare Francis. 1989. mass mkt. 4.95 (0-380-70689-X) Avon.

***Wolf Within.** David Alderton. 1998. pap. 19.95 (0-87605-612-5) Howell Bk.

Wolf-Woman. Sherryl Jordan. Orig. Title: Tanith. 176p. (YA). (gr. 7 up). 1996. mass mkt. 3.99 (0-440-21969-8, LLL BDD) BDD Bks Young Read.

Wolf-Woman. Sherryl Jordan. LC 94-7043. Orig. Title: Tanith. (J). 1994. 13.95 (0-395-70932-6) HM.

Wolf Worlds. Allan Cole & Chris Bunch. 304p. 1984. mass mkt. 5.99 (0-345-31229-5, Del Rey) Ballantine.

Wolf Years: The Renaissance of the Library Company of Philadelphia, 1952-1984. Maria E. Korey. LC 88-152011. (Illus.). 30p. (Orig.). 1984. pap. 2.00 (0-914076-62-0) Lib Co Phila.

Wolfe Expedition to Asia Minor. John R. Sterrett. (Illus.). vii, 448p. write for info. (0-318-71036-6) G Olms Pubs.

Wolfe Tone: Prophet of Irish Independence. Marianne Elliott. LC 89-36283. 492p. (C). 1990. 45.00 (0-300-04637-5) Yale U Pr.

Wolfe Tone: Prophet of Irish Independence. Marianne Elliott. 428p. (C). 1992. reprint ed. pap. text ed. 22.00 (0-300-05195-6) Yale U Pr.

Wolfe Understanding Law. Date not set. teacher ed., pap. text ed. write for info. (0-314-05512-6) West Pub.

Wolfe Wager. Jo A. Ferguson. 256p. 1995. mass mkt. 3.99 (0-8217-4945-5, Pinncle Kensgtn) Kensgtn Pub Corp.

Wolfe Wanting. Joan Hohl. 1994. mass mkt. 2.99 (0-373-05884-5, 1-05884-1) Harlequin Bks.

Wolfe Watching. Joan Hohl. (Desire Ser.). 1994. mass mkt. 2.99 (0-373-05865-9, 1-05865-0) Silhouette.

Wolfe Wedding. Joan Hohl. (Desire Ser.). 1996. mass mkt. 3.25 (0-373-05973-6, 1-05973-2) Silhouette.

Wolfecho. Roger Green. 176p. Date not set. pap. write for info. (0-19-271709-X) OUP.

Wolfen. Whitley Strieber. 288p. 1988. mass mkt. 4.50 (0-380-70440-4) Avon.

Wolfenbutteler Bibliographie zur Geschichte des Buchwesens im Deutschen Sprachgebiet, 1840-1980, Band 1, 2, 3, 4, 5. Ed. by Herzog August Bibliothek, Wolfenbuttel Staff. 2600p. (GER.). 1990. lib. bdg. 800.00 (3-598-30323-8) K G Saur.

Wolfer. Mac McKee. LC 94-47095. (Novel of the West Ser.). 192p. 1995. 19.95 (0-87131-778-8) M Evans.

Wolfe's Army. Robin May. (Men-at-Arms Ser.: No. 48). (Illus.). 48p. pap. 11.95 (0-85045-193-0, 9163, Pub. by Osprey UK) Stackpole.

Wolff: A Centennial Memorial of Christian & Anna Maria Woldd, with Brief Records of Their Children & Relatives. G. W. Fahnestock. 112p. 1992. reprint ed. pap. 19.50 (0-8328-2769-X); reprint ed. lib. bdg. 27.50 (0-8328-2768-1) Higginson Bk Co.

Wolff! The Chess Career of Patrick Wolff. Patrick Wolff. Ed. by Don Maddox. (ChessBase University American Grandmaster Ser.). (Illus.). 64p. (Orig.). 1994. pap. 10.95 (1-883358-12-4) R&D Pub NJ.

Wolff & Byrd, Counselors of the Macabre: Supernatural Law. Batton Lash. LC 92-61485. (Wolff & Byrd, Counselors of the Macabre Ser.). (Illus.). 80p. (Orig.). 1992. pap. 7.95 (0-9633954-0-8) Exhibit A Pr.

Wolff & Byrd, Counselors of the Macabre: Fright Court. Batton Lash. (Illus.). 80p. (Orig.). 1995. pap. 9.95 (0-9633954-2-4) Exhibit A Pr.

Wolff & Byrd, Counselors of the Mocabre Vol. 1: Case Files. Batton Lash. (Illus.). 96p. (Orig.). 1995. pap. 8.95 (0-9633954-1-6) Exhibit A Pr.

Wolff & Byrd, Counselors of the Mocabre Vol. 2: Case Files. Batton Lash. 96p. 1996. pap. 9.95 (0-9633954-3-2) Exhibit A Pr.

***Wolff-Parkinson-White Syndrome.** Carlos A. Morillo et al. LC 96-36747. (Clinical Approaches to Tachyarrhythmias Ser.: Vol. 6). (Illus.). 58p. 1996. 24.00 (0-87993-660-6) Futura Pub.

Wolff's Anatomy of the Eye & Orbit: Including the Central Connections, Development &... 8th ed. A. J. Bron. 704p. (gr. 13). 1992. text ed. 186.95 (0-412-41010-9) Chapman & Hall.

Wolff's Guide to the London Metal Exchange. 4th ed. Rudolf Wolff. 269p. 1992. 91.00 (0-947671-50-1) Metal Bulletin.

Wolff's Headache & Other Head Pain. 6th ed. Ed. by Donald J. Dalessio & Stephen D. Silberstein. LC 92-48683. 552p. (C). 1993. 69.50 (0-19-508250-8) OUP.

Wolff's Law & Connective Tissue Regulation: Modern Interdisciplinary Comments on Wolff's Law of Connective Tissue Regulation & Rational Understanding of Common Clinical Problems. Ed. by Gunter Regling. LC 93-20493. 1993. 121.55 (3-11-013909-X) De Gruyter.

Wolff's Telegraphisches Bureau 1849-Bis 1933, Vol. 21. Dieter Basse. (Kommunikation und Politik Ser.). 346p. (GER.). 1991. lib. bdg. 52.00 (3-598-20551-1) K G Saur.

Wolfgang Amade Mozart. Georg Knepler. Tr. by J. Bradford Robinson. LC 92-46591. (Illus.). 375p. (C). 1994. text ed. 54.95 (0-521-41972-7) Cambridge U Pr.

***Wolfgang Amade Mozart.** Georg Knepler et al. (Illus.). 392p. 1997. pap. text ed. 18.95 (0-521-58823-5) Cambridge U Pr.

Wolfgang Amade Mozart: Essays on His Life & Work. Ed. by Stanley Sadie. (Illus.). 528p. 1996. text ed. 95.00 (0-19-816443-2) OUP.

Wolfgang Amadeus Mozart. Roger K. Blakely. LC 92-41357. (Importance of Ser.). (Illus.). 111p. (J). (gr. 5-8). 1993. lib. bdg. 17.96 (1-56006-028-X) Lucent Bks.

Wolfgang Amadeus Mozart. Friedman-Fairfax & Sony Music Staff. (Life, Times & Music Book/CD Ser.). 1995. pap. 16.98 incl. audio compact disk (1-56799-005-3, Friedman-Fairfax) M Friedman Pub Grp Inc.

Wolfgang Amadeus Mozart. Dyneley Hussey. LC 73-94272. (Select Bibliographies Reprint Ser.). 1977. 26.95 (0-8369-5046-1) Ayer.

***Wolfgang Amadeus Mozart.** John Malam. LC 97-9246. (Tell Me about Ser.). (J). 1998. write for info. (1-57505-247-4, Carolrhoda) Lerner Group.

Wolfgang Amadeus Mozart. Mike Venezia. LC 95-13366. (Getting to Know the World's Greatest Composers Ser.). (Illus.). 32p. (J). (ps-4). 1995. lib. bdg. 19.50 (0-516-04541-5) Childrens.

Wolfgang Amadeus Mozart. Karl Barth. 48p. 1986. reprint ed. pap. 5.00 (0-8028-0007-6) Eerdmans.

Wolfgang Amadeus Mozart. Dyneley Hussey. 368p. 1990. reprint ed. lib. bdg. 79.00 (0-7812-9076-7) Rprt Serv.

Wolfgang Amadeus Mozart. Mike Venezia. (Getting to Know the World's Greatest Artists Ser.). (Illus.). 32p. (J). (ps-4). 1996. reprint ed. 6.95 (0-516-44541-3) Childrens.

Wolfgang Amadeus Mozart: Musical Genius. Carol Greene. LC 92-36879. (Rookie Biographies Ser.). (Illus.). 48p. (J). (gr. k-3). 1993. pap. 4.95 (0-516-44256-2); lib. bdg. 18.30 (0-516-04256-4) Childrens.

Wolfgang Amadeus Mozart- Play by Play: Piano Concerto No. 20 in D Minor & Piano Concerto No. 21 in C: Alfred Brendel, Pianist; Academy of St. Martin-in-the-Fields; Sir Neville Marriner, Conductor. Alan Rich. LC 94-48625. (Newport Classic CD-B Presentation Ser.). (Illus.). 160p. 1995. 25.00 (0-06-263548-4) Harper SF.

***Wolfgang Borchert's Germany: Reflections of the Third Reich.** James L. Stark. LC 96-41691. 184p. 1997. pap. text ed. 27.50 (0-7618-0555-9) U Pr of Amer.

***Wolfgang Borchert's Germany: Reflections of the Third Reich.** James L. Stark. LC 96-41691. 184p. 1997. lib. bdg. 49.00 (0-7618-0554-0) U Pr of Amer.

Wolfgang Borchert's Literary Production in Nazi Germany: Wolfgang Borchert's Literary Production in Nazi Germany. Erwin Warkentin. (GERM Ser.). x, 109p. 1996. 48.00 (1-57113-091-8) Camden Hse.

Wolfgang Caspar Printz: Ausgewahlte Werke: Dritter Band: Realien, 3 vols. Ed. by Helmut K. Krausse. (Ausgaben Deutscher Literatur des XV bis XVIII Jahrhunderts Ser.). vi, 357p. (GER.). (C). 1993. lib. bdg. 247.70 (3-11-003861-7) De Gruyter.

Wolfgang Hildesheimer & His Critics. Patricia H. Stanley. LC 93-8417. (LCGERM Ser.). xiv, 140p. 1993. 55.00 (1-879751-45-3) Camden Hse.

An Asterisk (*) at the beginning of an entry indicates that the title is appearing in BIP for the first time.

***Wolfgang Laib: A Journey.** Wolfgang Laib. 1997. pap. text ed. 14.95 (*3-89322-315-0*, Pub. by Edition Cantz GW) Dist Art Pubs.

***Wolfgang Oehme & James van Sweden.** Process Architecture Editorial Staff. (Process Architecture Ser.: No. 130). (Illus.). 153p. 1997. pap. 44.95 (*4-89331-130-1*, Pub. by Process Archit JA) Bks Nippan.

Wolfgang Pauli: Scientific Correspondence with Bohr, Einstein, Heisenberg, Vol. I: 1919-1929. Ed. by A. Hermann & K. V. Meyenn. (Sources in the History of Mathematics & Physical Sciences Ser.: Vol. 2). (Illus.). 1979. 258.95 (*0-387-08962-4*) Spr-Verlag.

Wolfgang Pauli: Scientific Correspondence with Bohr, Einstein, Heisenberg a. o. Part II: 1930-1939. Ed. by K. V. Meyenn. (Sources in the History of Mathematics & Physical Sciences Ser.: Vol. 6). 800p. 1985. 280.00 (*0-387-13609-6*) Spr-Verlag.

Wolfgang Puck Cookbook. Wolfgang Puck. LC 86-10155. (Illus.). 320p. 1986. 23.00 (*0-394-53366-6*) Random.

Wolfgang Puck Cookbook. Wolfgang Puck. 1996. pap. 16.00 (*0-679-76125-X*) Random.

Wolfgang Puck's Modern French Cooking. Wolfgang Puck. 1986. pap. 15.95 (*0-395-41067-3*) HM.

Wolfgang Stechow: In Memoriam. 204p. 1976. lib. bdg. 30.00 (*0-87920-002-2*) Kennedy Gall.

Wolfgang Tillmans. Photos by Wolfgang Tillmans. (Illus.). 160p. 1995. 24.99 (*3-8228-8853-2*) Taschen Amer.

Wolfhart Spangenberg, Saemtliche Werke Vol. 3, Part 2: Tierdichtungen II. Wolfhart Spangenberg. Ed. by Andras Vizkelity. (Ausgaben Deutscher Literatur des XV bis XVIII Jahrhunderts Ser.). (C). 1978. 223.10 (*3-11-007465-6*) De Gruyter.

Wolfhart Spangenberg, Samtliche Werke, Vol. 3, Pt. 1. Wolfhart Spangenberg. Ed. by Andor Tarnai. (Ausgaben Deutscher Literatur des XV bis XVIII Jahrhunderts Ser.). (C). 1977. 200.00 (*3-11-006938-5*) De Gruyter.

Wolfhelm. Richard A. Knaak. 256p. 1990. mass mkt. 4.99 (*0-445-20966-6*, Aspect) Warner Bks.

Wolfhound. Kristine L. Franklin. LC 94-14595. (J). 1996. 16.00 (*0-688-13674-5*); lib. bdg. 15.93 (*0-688-13675-3*) Lothrop.

Wolfking. Bridget Wood. 1994. mass mkt. 5.99 (*0-345-38328-1*, Avery Pub) Ballantine.

Wolfling. Sterling North. (J). (gr. 5-9). 1996. 17.50 (*0-8446-6894-X*) Peter Smith.

Wolfling. Sterling North. (Illus.). 224p. (J). (gr. 5-9). 1992. pap. 4.99 (*0-14-036166-9*, Puffin) Puffin Bks.

Wolfling. Sterling North. 256p. (J). (gr. 4-6). pap. 2.50 (*0-590-41868-8*) Scholastic Inc.

Wolfman Sam. Elizabeth Levy. LC 96-2542. (Trophy Chapter Bk.). (Illus.). 128p. (J). (gr. 2-5). 1996. pap. 3.95 (*0-06-442048-5*, Trophy); lib. bdg. 13.89 (*0-06-024817-3*) HarpC Child Bks.

Wolfpack. Baker et al. 80p. 1987. 7.95 (*0-87135-306-7*) Marvel Entmnt.

Wolfpack. Mark St. George. 210p. (Orig.). (YA). 14.95 (*0-9620541-2-7*); pap. 4.95 (*0-9620541-3-5*) Proteus LA.

***Wolfpack: U-Boats at War, 1939-1945.** Philip Kaplan & Jack Currie. (Illus.). 240p. 1997. 34.95 (*1-55750-855-0*) Naval Inst Pr.

***Wolfpack Handbook: Stories, Stats & Stuff about NC State Basketball.** Douglas Herakovich. (Illus.). 160p. (Orig.). 1996. pap. 9.95 (*1-880652-66-8*) Wichita Eagle.

Wolfpacks. (Third Reich Ser.). (Illus.). 176p. 1990. lib. bdg. 25.93 (*0-8094-6976-6*) Time-Life.

Wolfpen Notebooks: A Record of Appalachian Life. James Still. (Illus.). 192p. 1991. 21.95 (*0-8131-1741-0*) U Pr of Ky.

Wolfpen Poems. James Still. LC 86-70626. 1986. pap. 7.50 (*0-938211-03-X*) Berea College Pr.

Wolfram. 1969. 465.00 (*0-387-93239-9*) Spr-Verlag.

Wolfram von Eschenbach. James F. Poag. LC 73-187627. (Twayne's World Authors Ser.). 136p. (C). 1972. lib. bdg. 17.95 (*0-8290-1750-X*) Irvington.

Wolfram von Eschenbach. M. A. Rachbauer. LC 73-140041. (Catholic University Studies in German: No. 4). reprint ed. 37.50 (*0-404-50224-5*) AMS Pr.

Wolf's Chicken Stew. Keiko Kasza. 32p. (J). (gr. k-3). 1987. 15.95 (*0-399-21400-3*, Putnam) Putnam Pub Group.

Wolf's Chicken Stew. Keiko Kasza. (Illus.). 32p. (J). (ps-3). 1996. pap. 4.95 (*0-698-11374-8*, Paperstar) Putnam Pub Group.

Wolf's Clothing. Rillo. 80p. 1994. pap. 9.00 (*1-880516-12-8*) Left Hand Bks.

Wolf's Complete Book of Terror. abr. ed. Ed. by Leonard Wolf. LC 94-28272. 352p. 1994. pap. 16.00 (*1-55704-214-4*) Newmarket.

***Wolfs Cub.** Parry. Date not set. 23.95 (*0-312-86018-8*) St Martin.

Wolf's Embrace. Gail Link. 448p. 1992. reprint ed. mass mkt., pap. text ed. 4.50 (*0-8439-3358-5*) Dorchester Pub Co.

Wolf's Head. large type ed. John Benteen. (Linford Western Library). 272p. 1994. pap. 15.99 (*0-7089-7573-9*) Ulverscroft.

Wolf's Hour. Robert R. McCammon. (Orig.). 1990. pap. 6.99 (*0-671-73142-4*) PB.

Wolf's Lady. Mary Butler. 400p. (Orig.). 1992. mass mkt., pap. text ed. 4.50 (*0-8439-3227-9*) Dorchester Pub Co.

Wolf's Lair. Roger Elwood. .p. 1995. mass mkt. 5.99 (*0-8499-3884-8*) Word Pub.

Wolf's Last Cry. R. M. Schneider. 64p. 1984. text ed. 3.22 (*0-07-055474-9*) McGraw.

Wolf's Last Cry: Answer Key. R. M. Schneider. 1986. pap. text ed. 1.53 (*0-07-055509-5*) McGraw.

***Wolf's Lunch.** Olivier Douzou. LC 97-6454. (J). 1997. 6.95 (*0-8118-1806-3*) Chronicle Bks.

***Wolf's Promise.** large type ed. Alice Thornton. (Mills & Boon Large Print Ser.). 350p. 1997. 22.50 (*0-263-15014-3*) Ulverscroft.

Wolfsbane. Craig Thomas. 416p. 1996. mass mkt. 3.99 (*0-06-101047-2*, Harp PBks) HarpC.

Wolfsong: A Novel. Louis Owens. LC 94-36435. (American Indian Literature & Critical Studies Ser.: Vol. 17). 252p. 1995. pap. 12.95 (*0-8061-2737-6*) U of Okla Pr.

***WolfStar.** Donna Chimora. (Illus.). Date not set. write for info. (*0-9656422-8-3*) WolfStar Pr.

Wolftracker & Other Animal Tales. Zane Grey. LC 84-50123. (Zane Grey's West Ser.). (Illus.). 176p. (Orig.). 1984. reprint ed. pap. 7.95 (*0-915643-01-4*) Santa Barb Pr.

Wolfville. Alfred H. Lewis. 1972. reprint ed. lib. bdg. 29.00 (*0-8422-8090-1*) Irvington.

Wolfville. Alfred H. Lewis. 1986. reprint ed. pap. text ed. 8.95 (*0-8290-1957-X*) Irvington.

***Wolfville & Grand Pre: Past & Present.** Brian Cuthbertson. (Illus.). 72p. 1997. pap. 16.95 (*0-88780-360-1*) Formac Dist Ltd.

Wolfwalker. Tara K. Harper. 320p. (Orig.). 1990. mass mkt. 5.99 (*0-345-36539-9*, Del Rey) Ballantine.

Wolfwatching. Ted Hughes. 1991. 18.95 (*0-374-29199-3*) FS&G.

Wolfwatching. Ted Hughes. 80p. 1992. pap. 9.00 (*0-374-52325-8*, Noonday) FS&G.

Wolk's College Guide: Quick Reference Summary of Four-Year College Admission Scores. Robert P. Wolk. 116p. (Orig.). 1987. pap. 9.95 (*0-9619937-0-7*) Wolk Pubns.

***Wollaston Journals Vol. 2: 1842-1844.** Ed. by Geoffrey Bolton et al. 45.00 (*1-875560-02-5*, Pub. by Univ of West Aust Pr AT) Intl Spec Bk.

Wollaston-People Resisting Genocide. Ed. by Miles Goldstick. 315p. 1987. 36.95 (*0-920057-94-2*, Pub. by Black Rose Bks CN); pap. 16.95 (*0-920057-95-0*, Pub. by Black Rose Bks CN) Consort Bk Sales.

Wollstonecraft Anthology. Mary Wollstonecraft Shelley. Ed. by Janet M. Todd. (Illus.). 282p. 1990. text ed. 49.50 (*0-231-07250-3*); pap. text ed. 17.50 (*0-231-07251-1*) Col U Pr.

Wollygoggles & Other Creatures: Problems for Developing Thinking Skills. Thomas C. O'Brien. 64p. (J). (gr. 3-12). 1980. pap. text ed. 9.50 (*0-914040-85-5*) Cuisenaire.

Wolof, 14 vols. Tijan M. Sallah. Ed. by George Bond & Gary V. Wyck. LC 95-13328. (Heritage Library of African Peoples: Set 2). (Illus.). 64p. (YA). (gr. 7-12). 1996. lib. bdg. 15.95 (*0-8239-1987-0*) Rosen Group.

Wolof-French Dictionary: Dictionnaire Wolof-Francais. A. Fall et al. 336p. (FRE.). 1990. lib. bdg. 150.00 (*0-8288-4043-1*) Fr & Eur.

Wolof Phonology & Morphology. Ka Omar. LC 93-30604. 160p. (Orig.). (C). 1993. pap. text ed. 29.50 (*0-8191-9288-0*) U Pr of Amer.

Wolseley. Nick Baldwin. 1995. pap. 25.00 (*0-7478-0297-1*, Pub. by Shire UK) St Mut.

Wolsey. Mark Dunster. (Henry the Eighth: Pt. 1). 54p. (Orig.). 1980. pap. 4.00 (*0-89642-069-8*) Linden Pubs.

***Wolte 2 Proceedings of the Second European Workshop on Low Temperature Electronics.** IEEE (Electron Devices Society) Staff. 350p. 1996. pap. text ed. write for info. (*0-614-18667-6*, 96TH8222); fiche write for info. (*0-7803-3621-6*, 96TH8222) Inst Electrical.

Wolter's Dutch-German Dictionary: Neederland-Duits: Wolter's Woorden Boek. W. H. Wallis. 956p. (GER.). 1981. 49.95 (*0-8288-4670-7*, M9744) Fr & Eur.

Woltz Family. Flora L. Woltz. 139p. 1975. reprint ed. 12.50 (*0-685-65093-6*) VA Bk.

Wolve & Rain. Skip Lindemann. 96p. (Orig.). 1995. pap. write for info. (*1-57502-082-3*) Morris Pubng.

Wolverine. Chris Claremont et al. (Spiderman Ser.). (Illus.). 96p. 1987. pap. 9.95 (*0-87135-277-X*) Marvel Entmnt.

Wolverine: Blood Hungry. 64p. 1993. 6.95 (*0-7851-0003-2*) Marvel Entmnt.

Wolverine: Bloodlust. Alan Davis & Paul Neary. 48p. 1990. 5.95 (*0-87135-705-4*) Marvel Entmnt.

Wolverine: Bloody Choices. Tom Defalco & John Buscema. 64p. 1991. 12.95 (*0-87135-791-7*) Marvel Entmnt.

Wolverine: Bloody Choices. 2nd ed. Tom DeFalco. 1993. pap. 7.95 (*0-87135-980-4*) Marvel Entmnt.

Wolverine: Color & Activity Book. (J). 1994. 0.55 (*0-679-86925-5*) Random.

Wolverine: Rahne of Terra. Peter David. (Illus.). 48p. 1991. 5.95 (*0-87135-843-3*) Marvel Entmnt.

Wolverine: Weapon X. Barry Windsor-Smith. (Illus.). 128p. 1993. 14.95 (*0-87135-987-1*) Marvel Entmnt.

Wolverine: Weapon X. Barry Windsor-Smith. 1994. pap. 12.95 (*0-7851-0033-4*) Marvel Entmnt.

Wolverine - Ghost Rider: Acts of Vengeance. 64p. 1993. 6.95 (*0-7851-0022-9*) Marvel Entmnt.

Wolverine - Jungle Adventure. Mike Magnola et al. 48p. 1989. 4.50 (*0-87135-613-9*) Marvel Entmnt.

Wolverine - Nick Fury: Scorpio Connection. Archie Goodwin & Howard Chaykin. 64p. 1990. reprint ed. pap. 12.95 (*0-87135-662-7*) Marvel Entmnt.

Wolverine - Nick Fury Scorpio Connection. Goodwin & Howard Chaykin. 64p. 1989. 16.95 (*0-87135-577-9*) Marvel Entmnt.

Wolverine Creates the World: Labrador Indian Tales. Lawrence W. Millman. LC 92-46340. (Illus.). 160p. (Orig.). 1993. pap. 12.95 (*0-88496-363-2*) Capra Pr.

Wolverine Creates the World: Labrador Indian Tales. Lawrence W. Millman. (Illus.). 160p. (Orig.). (C). 1993. reprint ed. lib. bdg. 35.00 (*0-8095-4115-7*) Borgo Pr.

***Wolverine-Gambit: Victims.** Jeph Loeb. 1997. pap. text ed. 12.95 (*0-7851-0258-2*) Marvel Entmnt.

***Wolverine Inner Fury.** 1997. pap. 5.95 (*0-87135-956-1*) Marvel Entmnt.

Wolverine Is Eating My Leg. Tim Cahill. (Departures Original Ser.). (Orig.). 1989. pap. 13.00 (*0-679-72026-X*, Vin) Random.

Wolverine Myths & Visions: Dene Traditions from Northern Alberta. Ed. by Patrick J. Moore & Angela Wheelock. LC 89-29379. (Studies in the Anthropology of North American Indians). (Illus.). xvi, 259p. 1990. text ed. 30.00 (*0-8032-8161-7*) U of Nebr Pr.

Wolverine-Typhoid Mary: Typhoid's Kiss. Ann Nocenti & Steve Lightle. 64p. 1994. 6.95 (*0-7851-0056-3*) Marvel Entmnt.

Wolverine vs. Spider-Man. Jim Owsley et al. 64p. 1990. 5.95 (*0-87135-645-7*) Marvel Entmnt.

Wolverine vs. the Hulk. Len Wein et al. 48p. 1990. 5.95 (*0-87135-612-0*) Marvel Entmnt.

Wolverine vs. the Punisher: African Saga - Rep., Nos. 6 & 7. Carl Potts et al. 48p. 1990. 5.95 (*0-87135-611-2*) Marvel Entmnt.

***Wolverines Handbook: Stories, Stats & Stuff about Michigan Football.** John Borton & Paul Dodd. (Illus.). 160p. (Orig.). 1996. pap. 9.95 (*1-880652-60-9*) Wichita Eagle.

Wolvertoons. Basil Wolverton. Ed. by Dick Voll. (Illus.). 160p. (Orig.). 1990. 39.95 (*1-56097-023-5*); pap. 19.95 (*1-56097-022-7*) Fantagraph Bks.

Wolves. (J). Date not set. pap. 1.50 (*0-590-72056-2*) Scholastic Inc.

Wolves. Karen Dudley. LC 96-8365. (Untamed World Ser.). (J). 1997. lib. bdg. 25.68 (*0-8172-4564-2*) Raintree Steck-V.

Wolves. Gail Gibbons. LC 94-2108. (Illus.). 32p. (J). (ps-3). 1994. lib. bdg. 15.95 (*0-8234-1127-3*) Holiday.

Wolves. Gail Gibbons. (Illus.). 32p. (J). (gr. k-3). 1995. pap. 6.95 (*0-8234-1202-4*) Holiday.

Wolves. Nancy Gibson. LC 96-106. (WorldLife Library). (Illus.). 72p. (Orig.). 1996. pap. 14.95 (*0-89658-299-X*) Voyageur Pr.

Wolves. Brian J. Heinz. LC 95-32790. (Illus.). 32p. (J). (gr. k-4). 1996. pap. 15.99 (*0-8037-1735-0*) Dial Bks Young.

Wolves. Brian J. Heinz. LC 95-32790. (Illus.). 32p. (J). (gr. k-4). 1996. pap. 15.89 (*0-8037-1736-9*) Dial Bks Young.

Wolves. Casey Horton. (Endangered! Ser.). 32p. (J). (gr. 3-5). 1995. lib. bdg. 14.95 (*0-7614-0213-6*, Benchmark NY) Marshall Cavendish.

***Wolves.** Maria A. Julivert. (Fascinating World Of...Ser.). (Illus.). 32p. (J). (gr. 2-6). 1996. lib. bdg. 14.95 (*1-56674-203-X*) Forest Hse.

Wolves. R. D. Lawrence. (Sierra Club Wildlife Library). 64p. (J). (gr. 3-6). 1990. 17.95 (*0-316-51676-7*) Little.

Wolves. R. D. Lawrence. (Sierra Club Bks.). (Illus.). 64p. (J). (gr. 3-6). 1994. pap. text ed. 8.95 (*0-316-51677-5*) Little.

Wolves. Emilie U. Lepthien. LC 91-3035. (New True Bks.). (Illus.). 48p. (J). (gr. k-4). 1991. pap. 5.50 (*0-516-41129-2*); lib. bdg. 19.00 (*0-516-01129-4*) Childrens.

Wolves. Kim Long. LC 96-26553. (Johnson Nature Ser.). (Illus.). 192p. (Orig.). 1996. pap. 15.95 (*1-55566-158-0*) Johnson Bks.

Wolves. Jenny Markert. (Nature Bks.). 32p. (J). (gr. 2-6). 1991. lib. bdg. 22.79 (*0-89565-711-2*) Childs World.

Wolves. Jo E. Moore & Joy Evans. (Illus.). 48p. (J). (gr. 3-6). 1990. pap. 5.95 (*1-55799-163-4*, EMC 238) Evan-Moor Corp.

Wolves. Susan Ohanian. LC 93-28973. (Voyages Ser.). (Illus.). (J). 1994. 4.25 (*0-383-03742-5*) SRA McGraw.

Wolves. Candace C. Savage. LC 88-18391. 1990. pap. 22.00 (*0-87156-632-X*) Sierra.

Wolves. Seymour Simon. LC 92-25924. (Illus.). 32p. (J). (gr. 2-5). 1993. 16.00 (*0-06-022531-9*); lib. bdg. 16.89 (*0-06-022534-3*) HarpC Child Bks.

Wolves. Seymour Simon. LC 92-25924. (Trophy Nonfiction Bk.). (Illus.). 32p. (J). (gr. 2-5). 1995. pap. 5.95 (*0-06-446176-9*, Trophy) HarpC Child Bks.

Wolves. Lynn M. Stone. (North American Animal Discovery Library). (Illus.). 24p. (J). (gr. k-5). 1990. lib. bdg. 11.94 (*0-86593-044-9*); lib. bdg. 8.95 (*0-685-36342-2*) Rourke Corp.

Wolves. John B. Wexo. (Zoobooks Ser.). 24p. (J). (gr. 4). 1989. lib. bdg. 14.95 (*0-88682-267-X*) Creative Ed.

***Wolves.** John B. Wexo. (Zoobooks). (Illus.). 24p. (J). (gr. 1-7). 1997. 13.95 (*1-888153-33-4*, 267-X) Wildlife Educ.

Wolves. Wildlife Education, Ltd. Staff. (Zoobooks Ser.). (Illus.). 1984. pap. 2.75 (*0-937934-20-8*) Wildlife Educ.

Wolves. Daniel Wood. 1994. 24.95 (*1-55110-198-X*) Gr Arts Ctr Pub.

Wolves: A Collection of Poems. Jim Johnson. LC 92-64072. (Minnesota Voices Project Ser.: Vol. 57). 72p. (Orig.). 1993. pap. 7.95 (*0-89823-144-2*) New Rivers Pr.

Wolves: A Portrait of the Animal World. Leonard L. Rue. 1995. 10.98 (*0-8317-0976-6*) Smithmark.

***Wolves: Nature's Window.** Ed. by Smallwood & Stewart Staff. (Nature's Window Ser.). 48p. 1997. 6.95 (*0-8362-2785-9*) Andrews & McMeel.

***Wolves: The Howl of the Wild.** Andrews & McMeel Staff. (Little Bks.). (J). 1997. 4.95 (*0-8362-3609-2*) Andrews & McMeel.

Wolves - a Thematic Unit. Linda J. Larsen. (Thematic Units Ser.). (Illus.). 80p. (Orig.). (J). (gr. 5-8). 1994. student ed., pap. 9.95 (*1-55734-583-X*) Tchr Create Mat.

Wolves Against the Moon. Altrocchi & Julia Cooley. 1994. pap. 16.95 (*0-912382-32-5*) Black Letter.

***Wolves & Coyotes.** (Eyes on Nature Ser.). (Illus.). 32p. (J). (gr. 1 up). write for info. (*1-56156-424-9*) Kidsbks.

***Wolves & Humans in Conflict: A Pictorial History of Wolves in North America.** Troy R. Mader. (Illus.). (C). text ed. 24.95 (*0-944402-05-4*) Cmmn Man Inst.

***Wolves & Their Relatives.** Erik D. Stoops & Dagmar Fertl. LC 96-35794. (J). 1997. 16.95 (*0-8069-0926-9*) Sterling.

Wolves Aren't White. I. K. Watson. 256p. 1995. pap. 9.95 (*0-7490-0256-5*, Pub. by A & B UK) London Brdge.

Wolves Come down on the Fold: A War Story from the Lebanon. A. H. Gemayel & G. J. Roddey. 428p. (Orig.). pap. write for info. (*1-881272-04-4*) Whitehurst-Wynn.

Wolves' Dream. Abdon Ubidia. Tr. by Mary E. Fieweger from SPA. LC 96-17102. (Discoveries Ser.). (Orig.). (C). 1996. pap. text ed. 15.95 (*0-935480-79-X*) Lat Am Lit Rev Pr.

Wolves for Kids. Tom Wolpert. (Illus.). (J). 1991. 14.95 (*1-55971-087-X*, 1004); pap. 6.95 (*1-55971-123-X*) NorthWord.

Wolves for the Blue Soldiers: Indian Scouts & Auxiliaries with the United States Army, 1860-90. Thomas W. Dunlay. LC 81-16326. (Illus.). xii, 316p. 1982. reprint ed. pap. 10.95 (*0-8032-6573-5*, Bison Books) U of Nebr Pr.

Wolves in Sheeps' Clothing: How to Recognize False Prophets & Protect Your Family from Their Influence. James H. Reeve. (Orig.). 1994. pap. write for info. (*1-884781-00-4*) Quest For Excell.

***Wolves in Yellowstone.** Randy Houk. (Illus.). 32p. (J). (gr. 1-5). 1995. pap. 9.95 incl. audio (*1-882728-50-5*) Benefactory.

Wolves in Yellowstone. Randy Houk. (Illus.). 32p. (J). (gr. 1-5). 1995. 12.95 (*1-882728-25-4*) Benefactory.

***Wolves in Yellowstone, Incl. plush animal.** Randy Houk. (Illus.). 32p. (J). (gr. 1-5). 1995. pap. 19.95 incl. audio (*1-882728-40-8*); pap. 14.95 (*1-882728-45-9*) Benefactory.

Wolves in Yellowstone, Incl. plush animal. Randy Houk. (Illus.). 32p. (J). (gr. 1-5). 1995. 34.95 incl. audio (*1-882728-30-0*) Benefactory.

***Wolves in Yellowstone, Incl. plush animal.** Randy Houk. (Illus.). 32p. (J). (gr. 1-5). 1995. 29.95 (*1-882728-29-7*) Benefactory.

***Wolves Meet.** Franklin. Date not set. pap. 15.95 (*0-8050-4572-4*) St Martin.

Wolves of Heaven: Cheyenne Shamanism, Ceremonies, & Prehistoric Origins. Karl H. Schlesier. LC 86-27252. 1993. pap. 12.95 (*0-8061-2577-2*) U of Okla Pr.

Wolves of Isle Royale: A Broken Balance. Rolf Peterson. (Illus.). 160p. 1995. 29.50 (*1-57223-031-2*) Idyll Arbor.

Wolves of Minong: Isle Royale's Wild Community. Durward L. Allen. LC 93-8192. (Ann Arbor Paperbacks Ser.). 500p. (C). 1993. pap. text ed. 18.95 (*0-472-08237-X*) U of Mich Pr.

Wolves of Mount McKinley. Adolph Murie. LC 84-22017. (Illus.). (Orig.). 1985. reprint ed. pap. 13.95 (*0-295-96203-8*) U of Wash Pr.

Wolves of Savernake. Edward Marston. 1995. mass mkt. 5.99 (*0-449-22310-8*, Crest) Fawcett.

Wolves of Summer. Joseph Nazel. 224p. (Orig.). 1984. mass mkt. 3.50 (*0-87067-339-4*, BH339) Holloway.

Wolves of the Dawn. William Sarabande. 464p. (Orig.). 1992. mass mkt. 5.99 (*0-553-25802-8*) Bantam.

***Wolves of the Gods: Timura Tri.** Allan Cole. 1998. pap. write for info. (*0-345-40179-4*, Del Rey) Ballantine.

Wolves of the High Arctic. International Wolf Center Staff. LC 92-21714. (Illus.). 128p. 1992. 14.95 (*0-89658-213-2*) Voyageur Pr.

Wolves of the High Arctic: An International Wolf Center Book. L. David Mech. LC 92-21714. (Illus.). 128p. 1995. pap. text ed. 9.95 (*0-89658-222-1*) Voyageur Pr.

Wolves of Willoughby Chase. Joan Aiken. 176p. (J). (gr. k-6). 1987. mass mkt. 3.99 (*0-440-49603-9*, YB BDD) BDD Bks Young Read.

Wolves of Yellowstone. Michael K. Phillips & Douglas W. Smith. LC 96-14286. (Illus.). 112p. 1996. 24.95 (*0-89658-330-9*) Voyageur Pr.

Wolves Postcard Collection One. 22p. 1990. pap. 8.95 (*0-89658-125-X*) Voyageur Pr.

Wolves Postcards Collection Two. Photos by International Wolf Center Staff. (Illus.). 22p. 1994. pap. 8.95 (*0-89658-256-6*) Voyageur Pr.

***Wolves Within the Fold: Religious Leadership & Abuses of Power.** Ed. by Anson Shupe. 272p. 1998. 50.00 (*0-8135-2489-X*) Rutgers U Pr.

***Wolves Within the Fold: Religious Leadership & Abuses of Power.** Ed. by Anson Shupe. 272p. 1998. pap. 20.00 (*0-8135-2490-3*) Rutgers U Pr.

Woman. Sibilla Aleramo. Tr. by Rosalind Delmar from ITA. (Illus.). 200p. 1980. 32.00 (*0-520-04108-9*); pap. 12.00 (*0-520-04949-7*) U CA Pr.

Woman. Edward Bond. 148p. 1981. pap. 5.95 (*0-87129-081-2*, W44) Dramatic Pub.

Woman. Peter Hartling. Tr. by Joachim Neugroschel from GER. LC 87-8657. (Modern German Voices Ser.). 288p. 1988. 29.50 (*0-8419-1046-4*) Holmes & Meier.

Woman. Peter Hartling. Tr. by Joachim Neugroschel from GER. (Portico Paperbacks Ser.). 256p. 1991. pap. 12.95 (*0-8419-1047-2*) Holmes & Meier.

Woman. Leo Jung. 239p. 1970. pap. 9.95 (*0-900689-07-2*) Soncino Pr.

***Woman.** Algimantas Kezys. LC 97-71771. (Illus.). 224p. (Orig.). 1997. pap. 25.00 (*1-886060-09-6*) Galerija.

Woman. Ed. by Rose Sayre. (Pig Iron Ser.: No. 7). 1980. pap. 4.95 (*0-917530-15-2*) Pig Iron Pr.

Woman. Charles R. Swindoll. (Swindoll Booklets Ser.). 32p. 1995. pap. 3.99 (*0-310-20095-4*) Zondervan.

Woman. Alexander Walker. 1987. 35.95 (*0-318-37317-3*) Asia Bk Corp.

Woman. 1977. reprint ed. pap. 3.00 (*0-933574-19-3*) Agni Yoga Soc.

Woman: A Treatise on the Normal & Pathological Emotions of Feminine Love. 7th enl. rev. ed. Bernard S. Talmey. LC 72-9684. (Illus.). reprint ed. 34.00 (*0-404-57504-8*) AMS Pr.

Woman: Dependent or Independent Variable? Rhoda K. Unger & Florence L. Denmark. LC 75-765161. 848p. 1975. 39.95 (*0-88437-000-3*) Psych Dimensions.

W

An Asterisk (*) at the beginning of an entry indicates that the title is appearing in BIP for the first time.

Woman: Earth & Spirit. Helen Luke. 112p. 1984. pap. 9.95 (0-8245-0633-2) Crossroad NY.

Woman: Her Position & Influence in Ancient Greece & Rome & Among the Early Christians. James Donaldson. 1973. 300.00 (0-87968-065-2) Gordon Pr.

Woman: Her Rights, Wrongs, Privileges, & Responsibilities. L. P. Brockett. LC 70-114869. (Select Bibliographies Reprint Ser.). 1977. 35.95 (0-8369-5274-X) Ayer.

***Woman: Image of the Holy Spirit.** Joan P. Schaupp. LC 96-31382. 124p. 1996. 39.95 (1-57309-115-4); pap. 14.95 (1-57309-114-6) Intl Scholars.

Woman: One Act Monologues for Women. Susan Pomerance. 64p. 1988. pap. 8.95 (0-940669-07-2, D-4) Dramaline Pubns.

Woman: The Eternal Primitive. W. J. Fielding. 1972. 59.95 (0-8490-1317-8) Gordon Pr.

Woman: The Password Is Action. 160p. 1988. pap. 8.00 (0-614-17322-1) Int Wom Tribune Centre.

Woman: Your Body, Your Health. Josleen Wilson. 1990. 19.95 (0-685-35046-0, Harvest Bks) HarBrace.

Woman - Image - Text: Readings in Pre-Raphaelite Art & Literature. Lynne Pearce. 85.00 (0-8020-5980-5); pap. 24.95 (0-8020-6912-6) U of Toronto Pr.

Woman - Torch of the Future. Torkom Saraydarian. LC 80-67680. 1980. pap. 10.00 (0-911794-00-X) Aqua Educ.

Woman, A Man, & Two Kingdoms: The Story of Madame d'Epinay & the Abbe Galiani. Francis Steegmuller. LC 92-37881. (Illus.). 300p. (C). 1993. pap. text ed. 16.95 (0-691-02489-8) Princeton U Pr.

Woman-A Synopsis: Vol. A; From the Dawn of Time to the Renaissance. Arthur F. Ide. LC 82-6080. (Woman in History Ser.: Vol. A). (Illus.). 160p. (Orig.). 1982. pap. text ed. 10.00 (0-86663-062-7); lib. bdg. 25.00 (0-86663-061-9) Ide Hse.

Woman Aboard. Janet Stevenson. LC 81-14537. (Illus.). 320p. 1981. pap. 7.95 (0-88316-545-7) Chandler & Sharp.

Woman Abuse: Facts Replacing Myths. Lewis Okun. LC 84-26912. 298p. 1985. text ed. 64.50 (0-88706-077-3); pap. text ed. 21.95 (0-88706-079-X) State U NY Pr.

***Woman Abuse on Campus: Results from the Canadian National Survey.** Walter S. Dekeseredy & Martin D. Schwartz. LC 97-21054. (Series on Violence Against Women). 1997. write for info. (0-7619-0567-7); pap. write for info. (0-7619-0566-9) Sage.

Woman Accused. Sandra Marton. (Presents Ser.). 1995. mass mkt. 3.25 (0-373-11736-1, 1-11736-5) Harlequin Bks.

Woman Activist Fund. Virginia General Assembly Voting Record Staff. 1979. pap. 2.00 (0-917560-14-0) Woman Activist.

Woman Activist Guide to Precinct Politics. 3rd ed. Flora Crater. 1995. pap. 5.00 (0-685-38090-4) Woman Activist.

Woman after God's Own Heart. Dianne L. Haneke. LC 83-90334. (Orig.). 1983. pap. text ed. 3.00 (0-9611312-0-9) Haneke Pub.

***Woman after God's Own Heart: Following His Design for Becoming a Woman of Excellence.** Elizabeth George. LC 96-45436. 250p. (Orig.). 1997. pap. 9.99 (1-56507-533-1) Harvest Hse.

Woman Against Her Sex: A Critique of Nawal el-Saadawi. Georges Tarabishi. 248p. 1990. 39.95 (0-86356-143-8, Pub. by Saqi Bks UK); pap. 15.00 (0-86356-082-2, Pub. by Saqi Books UK) Interlink Pub.

Woman Against Women in Victorian England: A Life of Eliza Lynn Linton. Nancy F. Anderson. LC 86-45798. (Illus.). 272p. 1987. 31.50 (0-253-36600-3) Ind U Pr.

Woman Against Women in Victorian England: A Life of Eliza Lynn Linton. Nancy F. Anderson. LC 86-45798. 270p. 1987. reprint ed. pap. 77.00 (0-608-01044-8, 2059352) Bks Demand.

Woman Aging & Ageism. Evelyn Rosenthal. 1990. pap. 14.95 (0-918393-73-6) Harrington Pk.

Woman Alone. Patricia O'Brien. LC 72-94650. 288p. 1974. write for info. (0-8129-0344-7, Times Bks) Random.

Woman Alone: Autobiographical Writings. Bessie Head. Ed. by Craig MacKenzie. (African Writers Ser.). 107p. (C). 1990. pap. 9.95 (0-435-90578-3, 90578) Heinemann.

Woman Alone & Other Plays. Franca Rame & Dario Fo. Ed. by Stuart Hood. Tr. by Gillian Hanna et al. (Methuen Modern Plays Ser.). 206p. (Orig.). (C). 1991. pap. 13.95 (0-413-64030-2, AO562, Pub. by Methuen UK) Heinemann.

W

Woman among Her People. Board of St. Paul Editorial Staff. (C). 1989. 35.00 (0-85439-297-1, Pub. by St Paul Pubns UK) St Mut.

Woman & African Society. Ed. by Man Singh Das & Vijay Kumar Gupta. 209p. 1995. pap. 150.00 (81-85880-54-9, Pub. by Print Hse II) St Mut.

***Woman & Ape.** Peter Hoeg. 1997. pap. 12.95 (0-14-026844-8) Viking Penguin.

Woman & Child: A Paradigm for Rural Development. Jai S. Chandra. (C). 1993. 22.00 (81-7033-210-9, Pub. by Rawat II) S Asia.

Woman & Child: The Legacy of Baby M. Phyllis Chesler. 256p. 16.95 (0-318-37102-2, Times Bks) Random.

Woman & Chinese Modernity: The Politics of Reading Between West & East. Rey Chow. (Theory & History of Literature Ser.: Vol. 75). 224p. 1991. pap. text ed. 16.95 (0-8166-1871-2) U of Minn Pr.

Woman & Family in Indian & Afro-American Literature: A Literary Perspective. Uma Alladi. 192p. 1989. text ed. 15.95 (0-938719-28-9, Envoy Pr) Apt Bks.

Woman & Her Environment. Ed. by Man Singh Das & Vijay Kumar Gupta. 174p. 1995. pap. 125.00 (81-85880-57-3, Pub. by Print Hse II) St Mut.

Woman & Her Home: Rediscovering the Joy of Serving God in the Place Where Life Really Matters. Ella M. Miller. LC 93-84461. 128p. 1993. reprint ed. pap. 6.95 (0-89221-241-1) New Leaf.

Woman & Her Needs see Liberating the Home

Woman & Home Simple Flower Arranging. Carolyn Bailey. (Illus.). 112p. 1994. write for info. (1-57215-024-6) World Pubns.

Woman & Labor. Olive Schreiner. 1972. 250.00 (0-87968-349-X) Gordon Pr.

Woman & Man in Paul: Overcoming a Misunderstanding. Norbert Baumert & Patrick Madigan. (Good News Studies: No. 40). 560p. (Orig.). 1996. pap. 34.95 (0-8146-5055-4, M Glazier) Liturgical Pr.

Woman & Nation in Irish Literature & Society, 1880-1935. C. L. Innes. LC 93-24067. (Illus.). 208p. 1994. pap. 20.00 (0-8203-1598-2) U of Ga Pr.

Woman & Nature: Literary Reconceptualizations. Maureen Devine. LC 92-33985. 251p. 1992. 29.50 (0-8108-2612-7) Scarecrow.

Woman & Nature: The Roaring Inside Her. Susan Griffin. LC 77-11812. 1979. pap. 12.00 (0-06-090744-4, CN 744, PL) HarpC.

Woman & Other Stories. Gangadhar Gadgil. 1989. text ed. 25.00 (81-207-1102-5, Pub. by Sterling Pubs II) Apt Bks.

Woman & Poet in the Eighteenth Century: The Life of Mary Whateley Darwall (1738-1825) Ann Messenger. (Studies in the Eighteenth Century: No. 27). 1993. write for info. (0-404-63527-X) AMS Pr.

Woman & Society. Rudolf Steiner. 24p. 1986. pap. 5.95 (0-85440-444-9, Steinerbks) Anthroposophic.

Woman & Temperance: The Quest for Power & Liberty, 1873-1900. Ruth Bordin. 221p. (C). 1990. reprint ed. pap. text ed. 15.00 (0-8135-1543-2) Rutgers U Pr.

Woman & Temperance: or The Work & Workers of the Woman's Christian Temperance Union. Frances E. Willard. LC 74-38443. (Religion in America, Ser. 2). 654p. 1977. reprint ed. 41.95 (0-405-04093-8) Ayer.

***Woman & the Ape.** Peter Hoeg. 1997. mass mkt. 7.50 (0-7704-2756-1) Bantam.

Woman & the Ape. Peter Hoeg. 1997. 29.95 (0-385-25627-2) Doubleday.

***Woman & the Ape.** large type ed. Peter Hoeg. LC 96-40160. 364p. 1997. 25.95 (0-7838-8068-5, GK Hall) Thorndike Pr.

Woman & the Ape: A Novel. Peter Hoeg. Tr. by Barbara Haveland. 256p. 1996. 23.00 (0-374-29203-5) FS&G.

Woman & the Demon: The Life of a Victorian Myth. Nina Auerbach. (Illus.). 270p. 1982. 32.00 (0-674-95406-8) HUP.

Woman & the Demon: The Life of a Victorian Myth. Nina Auerbach. 270p. 1984. pap. text ed. 15.50 (0-674-95407-6) HUP.

Woman & the History of Philosophy. Nancy Tuana. (Issues in Philosophy Ser.). 140p. 1991. pap. text ed. 16.95 (1-55778-194-X) Paragon Hse.

Woman & the Infinite: Epiphanic Moments in Pedro Salinas's Art. Vialla Hartfield-Mendez. LC 95-17404. 192p. 1996. 34.50 (0-8387-5295-0) Bucknell U Pr.

Woman & the Lyre: Women Writers in Classical Greece & Rome. Jane M. Snyder. LC 88-10114. (Illus.). 208p. (C). 1989. pap. 14.95 (0-8093-1706-0); text ed. 29.95 (0-8093-1455-X) S Ill U Pr.

Woman & the Miser. Claude-Henri Grignon. LC 79-304330. (French Writers of Canada Ser.). 111p. reprint ed. pap. 31.70 (0-8357-6442-7, 2035813) Bks Demand.

Woman & the Myth: Margaret Fuller's Life & Writings. rev. ed. Bell G. Chevigny. 608p. 1993. reprint ed. text ed. 45.00 (1-55553-182-2); reprint ed. pap. text ed. 16.95 (1-55553-181-4) NE U Pr.

Woman & the New Race see Works

Woman & the Salvation of the World: A Christian Anthropology on the Charisms of Women. Paul Evdokimov. Tr. by Anthony P. Gythiel from FRE. LC 93-44819. 1994. 12.95 (0-88141-093-4) St Vladimirs.

Woman & the Sea. Richard Tregaskis. (Illus.). 19.95 (0-910550-17-4) Elysium.

Woman & the Way: A Marian Path to Jesus. George T. Montague. 238p. 1994. pap. 10.99 (0-89283-856-6, Charis) Servant.

Woman & Work. Grazyna Zajdow. 1995. pap. 40.00 (0-949823-51-1, Pub. by Deakin Univ AT) St Mut.

***Woman Angler.** Morrow. Date not set. 24.95 (0-312-15697-9) St Martin.

***Woman Artist & the American West: A Biographical Dictionary.** Phil Kovinick & Marian Yoshiki-Kovinick. LC 97-3160. (American Studies Ser.). 1997. write for info. (0-292-79063-5) U of Tex Pr.

Woman Artists Text & Prints. (Illus.). 18p. 1992. pap. text ed. 52.50 (0-935493-72-7) Modern Learn Pr.

Woman as a Sexual Criminal. Erich Wulffen. (Criminology Ser.). 1992. lib. bdg. 87.95 (0-8490-5305-6) Gordon Pr.

Woman As Bourgeois Ideal: A Study of Sophie von La Roche's Geschichte des Frauleins von Sternheim & Goethe's Werther. Sally A. Winkle. (Studies in Modern German Literature: Vol. 16). 210p. (C). 1988. text ed. 38.95 (0-8204-0491-8) P Lang Pubng.

Woman As Force in History: A Study in Traditions & Realities. Mary R. Beard. 365p. 1987. reprint ed. pap. 12.95 (0-89255-113-5) Persea Bks.

Woman As Good As the Man: Or the Equality of Both Sexes. Francois P. De la Barre. LC 88-10808. 160p. (C). 1988. 28.95 (0-8143-1953-X); pap. 15.95 (0-8143-1954-8) Wayne St U Pr.

Woman As Healer. Jeanne Achterberg. LC 89-43314. 1991. pap. 17.00 (0-87773-616-2) Shambhala Pubns.

Woman As Hero in Old English Literature. Jane Chance. (Illus.). 192p. 1986. pap. text ed. 16.95 (0-8156-2346-1) Syracuse U Pr.

***Woman as Image in Medieval Literature from the Twelfth Century to Dante.** 176p. (C). 1995. pap. 10.99 (0-8010-2042-5, Labyrinth) Baker Bks.

Woman As Image in Medieval Literature from the Twelfth Century to Dante. Joan M. Ferrante. LC 84-29689. 176p. (C). 1985. reprint ed. pap. 8.95 (0-939464-43-8, Labyrinth) Baker Bks.

Woman As Individual in English Renaissance Drama: A Defiance of the Masculine Code. Carol Hansen. LC 92-39168. (American University Studies: English Language & Literature: Ser. IV, Vol. 156). 228p. 1993. pap. 27.95 (0-8204-2009-3) P Lang Pubng.

Woman As Is: Anthology/20th Century Woman's Poetry. Packard. 480p. 1995. mass mkt. 5.99 (0-440-21779-2) Dell.

Woman As Mediatrix: Essays on Nineteenth-Century European Women Writers-Prepared under the Auspices of Hofstra University. Ed. by Avriel H. Goldberger. LC 86-14236. (Contributions in Women's Studies: No. 73). 210p. 1987. text ed. 49.95 (0-313-25515-6, GWX/) Greenwood.

Woman As 'Nobody' & the Novels of Fanny Burney. Joanne Cutting-Gray. 176p. (C). 1992. lib. bdg. 39.95 (0-8130-1106-X) U Press Fla.

Woman As Priest, Bishop & Laity in the Early Catholic Church to 440 A.D. 2nd ed. Arthur F. Ide. LC 81-13464. (Woman in History Ser.: Vol. 9B). (Illus.). viii, 125p. 1983. 35.00 (0-86663-037-6); pap. 15.00 (0-86663-038-4) Ide Hse.

Woman at Belguardo. large type ed. Margaret Erskine. (Linford Mystery Library). 371p. 1989. pap. 15.99 (0-7089-6632-2, Linford) Ulverscroft.

Woman at Otowi Crossing: A Novel. rev. ed. Frank Waters. LC 66-25961. 314p. 1987. pap. 11.95 (0-8040-0893-0) Swallow.

Woman at Point Zero. 2nd ed. Nawal El Saadawi. Tr. by Sherif Hetata. (C). 1983. pap. 8.50 (0-86232-110-7, Pub. by Zed Bks Ltd UK) Humanities.

Woman at the Altar: The Ordination of Women in the Roman Catholic Church. Lavinia Byrne. LC 94-35168. 136p. 1994. pap. 9.95 (0-8146-2350-6) Liturgical Pr.

Woman at the Edge of Two Worlds. Lynn V. Andrews. LC 92-56215. 297p. 1994. pap. 13.00 (0-06-092550-7) HarpC.

Woman at the Keyhole: Feminism & Women's Cinema. Judith Mayne. LC 90-34125. (Illus.). 270p. 1990. 35.00 (0-253-33719-4); pap. 13.95 (0-253-20606-5, MB-606) Ind U Pr.

Woman at the Window. Marian Eldridge. 220p. (Orig.). 1989. pap. 14.95 (0-7022-2200-3, Pub. by Univ Queensland Pr AT) Intl Spec Bk.

Woman at War. Dacia Maraini. Tr. by Mara Benetti & Elspeth Spottiswood from ITA. LC 88-81204. Orig. Title: Donna in Guerra. 282p. (Orig.). 1989. pap. 14.50 (0-934977-12-7) Italica Pr.

Woman at Work. Mary Anderson. LC 73-13451. (Illus.). 266p. 1973. reprint ed. text ed. 55.00 (0-8371-7133-4, ANWW, Greenwood Pr) Greenwood.

Woman Awake: A Celebration of Women's Wisdom. Christina Feldman. 160p. 1990. pap. 9.00 (0-14-019196-8, Penguin Bks) Viking Penguin.

Woman-Battering: Creative Pastoral Care & Counseling Ser. Carol J. Adams. LC 94-9988. (Creative Pastoral Care & Counseling Ser.). 1994. pap. 12.00 (0-8006-2785-7, 1-2785, Fortress Pr) Augsburg Fortress.

Woman Battering: Policy Responses. Ed. by Michael Steinman. LC 90-84733. (ACJS - Anderson Monographs). 264p. (C). 1991. pap. text ed. 17.95 (0-87084-807-0) Anderson Pub Co.

Woman Battering: Policy Responses. Ed. by Michael Steinman. 274p. Date not set. pap. 17.95 (0-614-11321-0) OICJ.

Woman Battering As Marital Act: The Construction of a Violent Marriage. Margareta Hyden. (Scandinavian University Press Publication). 172p. 1994. 37.50 (82-00-21806-6) Scandnvan Univ Pr.

Woman Battering: The Facts see Battered Women: The Facts

Woman Be Free: Biblical Equality for Women. Patricia Gundry. 112p. 1993. pap. 6.95 (1-882169-00-X) Suitcase Bks.

***Woman Behind the Mirror.** Judith Couchman. LC 97-6535. 1997. pap. 10.99 (0-8054-6077-2) Broadman.

Woman Beneath the Skin: A Doctor's Patients in Eighteenth-Century Germany. Barbara Duden. Tr. by Thomas J. Dunlap from GER. 241p. (C). 1991. 28.50 (0-674-95403-3) HUP.

Woman Betrayed. Barbara Delinsky. 480p. 1991. mass mkt. 5.99 (0-06-104034-7, Harp PBks) HarpC.

***Woman Betrayed.** large type ed. Barbara Delinsky. LC 96-24051. (Romance-Hall Ser.). 639p. 1996. 25.95 (0-7838-1934-X, Thorndike Lrg Prnt) Thorndike Pr.

Woman Between Mirrors. Helena Parente Cunha. Tr. by Fred P. Ellison & Naomi Lindstrom from POR. LC 89-14613. (Texas Pan American Ser.). 144p. 1989. pap. 10.95 (0-292-79052-X) U of Tex Pr.

Woman Between the Wind: The Power of Resistence: An Eagle's Viewpoint of a Shaman's Entry Through the First Door. Winged Wolf & Heather Hughes-Calero. (Illus.). 125p. (Orig.). 1990. pap. 9.95 (0-932927-07-6) Higher Consciousness.

Woman Between Two Worlds: Portrait of an Ethiopian Rural Leader. Judith Olmstead. LC 96-10068. 1997. text ed. 39.95 (0-252-02283-1); pap. text ed. 19.95 (0-252-06587-5) U of Ill Pr.

Woman Bowler. annuals 1992. 6.00 (0-686-30134-X) WIBC.

Woman by Design. Frances Kennett. LC 88-42654. 512p. 1988. 18.95 (0-394-56544-4) Random.

Woman by God's Grace: "...Her Candle Goeth Not Out by Night." Prov. 31: 18. Anna M. Byler. 146p. (Orig.). 1992. pap. 6.95 (0-940883-04-X) Calvary Pubns.

Woman by the Bridge: Stories. John Daniel. 144p. (Orig.). 1991. pap. 8.95 (0-940475-62-6) Dolphin-Moon.

***Woman Called Easter: Easter Straker: Broadcasting Pioneer.** Alice L. Link. LC 96-85324. 156p. (Orig.). 1996. pap. 16.50 (0-7880-0695-9) CSS OH.

Woman Called Truth - Full. Sandra F. Asher. 1993. pap. 5.00 (0-87129-305-6, W74) Dramatic Pub.

Woman Called Truth - One Act. Sandra F. Asher. 1981. pap. 3.95 (0-87129-388-9, W63) Dramatic Pub.

Woman CARE - In Their Own Words: Women's Programs & the Ryan White Care Act. 1995. 2.50 (0-614-06756-1) Ctr Women Policy.

Woman-Centered Economy: Ideals, Reality, & the Space in Between. Ed. by Loraine E. Edwalds & Midge Stocker. LC 94-23364. 352p. (Orig.). 1995. 30.95 (1-879427-16-8); pap. 15.95 (1-879427-06-0) Third Side Pr.

***Woman Chaser.** Charles Willeford. 3.95 (0-7867-0556-6) Carroll & Graf.

Woman Chaser. Charles Willeford. 1990. pap. 3.95 (0-88184-556-6) Carroll & Graf.

Woman, Church, & State: A Historical Account of the Status of Woman Through the Christian Ages, with Reminiscences of the Matriarchate. 2nd ed. Matilda J. Gage. LC 72-2602. (American Women Ser.: Images & Realities). 558p. 1978. reprint ed. 42.95 (0-405-04458-5) Ayer.

Woman Citizen: Social Feminism in the 1920s. J. Stanley Lemons. 288p. 1990. reprint ed. pap. text ed. 14.50 (0-8139-1302-0) U Pr of Va.

Woman Client: Providing Human Services in a Changing World. Dianne Burden. 1986. pap. 14.95 (0-422-79780-4, Pub. by Tavistock UK) Routledge Chapman & Hall.

Woman Clothed with the Sun: Eight Great Apparitions of Our Lady. large type ed. Ed. by John J. Delaney. 320p. 1996. pap. 16.95 (0-8027-2699-2) Walker & Co.

Woman Clothed with the Sun, & Other Stories. Frank L. Lucas. LC 71-122731. (Short Story Index Reprint Ser.). 1977. 20.95 (0-8369-3564-0) Ayer.

***Woman Combing.** Miriam Solan. LC 97-3143. (Lingo Bks.). 1997. write for info. (1-889097-11-X) Hard Pr MA.

***Woman Composer: Creativity & the Gendered Politics of Musical Patronage.** Jill Halstead. (Illus.). 300p. 1997. text ed. 76.95 (1-85928-183-4, Pub. by Scolar Pr UK) Ashgate Pub Co.

Woman Composers. Carol Plantamura. (Illus.). 48p. pap. 3.95 (0-88388-110-1) Bellerophon Bks.

Woman, Cult, & Miracle Recital: A Reactional Critical Investigation of Mark 5: 24-34. Marla J. Selvidge. LC 87-46439. 160p. 1990. 32.50 (0-8387-5143-1) Bucknell U Pr.

Woman, Culture & Politics. Angela Y. Davis. 1989. 17.95 (0-318-41492-9) Random.

Woman, Culture, & Society. Ed. by Michelle Z. Rosaldo & Louise Lamphere. LC 73-89861. 360p. 1974. 49.50 (0-8047-0850-9); pap. 15.95 (0-8047-0851-7) Stanford U Pr.

Woman Cyclist: Training & Racing Techniques. Elaine Mariolle & Michael B. Shermer. (Illus.). 400p. (Orig.). 1988. pap. 12.95 (0-8092-4941-3) Contemp Bks.

Woman Defamed & Woman Defended: An Anthology of Medieval Texts. Ed. by Alcuin Blamires. (Illus.). 280p. 1992. pap. 18.95 (0-19-871039-9) OUP.

Woman-Defined Motherhood. Ed. by Jane P. Knowles & Ellen Cole. LC 90-37912. (Woman & Therapy Ser.: Vol. 10, Nos. 1-2). 234p. 1990. pap. text ed. 19.95 (0-918393-87-6) Harrington Pk.

Woman Destroyed. Simone De Beauvoir. Tr. by Patrick O'Brian. LC 84-1846. 256p. 1987. pap. 14.00 (0-394-71103-3) Pantheon.

Woman Detective: Gender & Genre. 2nd ed. Kathleen G. Klein. 296p. 1995. 14.95 (0-252-06463-1); pap. text ed. 21.95 (0-252-06631-6) U of Ill Pr.

Woman Doctor's Civil War: Esther Hill Hawks' Diary. Ed. by Gerald Schwartz. LC 84-11998. (Illus.). 289p. (Orig.). 1985. text ed. 34.95 (0-87249-435-7) U of SC Pr.

Woman Doctor's Civil War: Esther Hill Hawks' Diary. Ed. by Gerald Schwartz. LC 84-11998. (Illus.). 289p. (Orig.). 1989. pap. 14.95 (0-87249-622-8) U of SC Pr.

Woman Doctor's Diet for Women. 1994. 4.99 (0-345-90195-9) Ballantine.

Woman Doctor's Diet for Women. Barbara Edelstein. 288p. 1989. mass mkt. 5.99 (0-345-34601-7) Ballantine.

***Woman Doctor's Guide to Depression: Essential Facts & Up-To-The-Minute Information on Diagnosis, Treatments, & Recovery.** Jane S. Ferber & Suzanne LeVert. (Illus.). 208p. 1997. pap. 9.95 (0-7868-8146-1) Hyperion.

***Woman Doctor's Guide to Hormone Therapy: How to Choose What's Right for You.** Nananda F. Col. LC 97-60743. 175p. 1997. pap. 14.95 (1-886284-04-0, Tatnuck) Databks.

***Woman Doctor's Guide to Hormone Therapy: How to Choose What's Right for You.** Nananda F. Col. LC 97-60743. 175p. 1998. 24.95 (1-886284-03-2, Tatnuck) Databks.

Woman Doctor's Guide to Infertility: Essential Facts & Up-To-The Minute Information on the Techniques & Treatments to Achieve Pregnancy. Susan Treiser & Robin Levinson. (Illus.). 160p. 1994. pap. 9.95 (0-7868-8010-4) Hyperion.

Woman Doctor's Guide to Menopause: Essential Facts & Up-to-the-Minute Information for a Woman's Change of Life. Lois Jovanovic-Peterson. (Illus.). 208p. 1993. pap. 9.95 (1-56282-855-X) Hyperion.

Woman Doctor's Guide to Miscarriage: Essential Facts & Up-To-The-Minute Information on Coping with Pregnancy Loss & Trying Again. Lynn Friedman & Irene Daria. (Woman Doctor's Ser.). (Illus.). 176p. (Orig.). 1996. pap. 9.95 (0-7868-8145-3) Hyperion.

An Asterisk (*) at the beginning of an entry indicates that the title is appearing in BIP for the first time.

Woman Doctor's Guide to Osteoporosis: Essential Facts & Up-to-the-Minute Information on the Prevention, Treatment & Reversal of Bone Loss. Yvonne Sherrer & Robin K. Levinson. (Illus.). 176p. 1995. pap. 9.95 (*0-7868-8045-7*) Hyperion.

Woman Doctor's Guide to PMS: Essential Facts & Up-To-The-Minute Information on Premenstrual Syndrome. Andrea Rapkin & Diana Tonnessen. LC 93-10992. (Illus.). 160p. 1994. pap. 9.95 (*1-56282-810-X*) Hyperion.

Woman Doctor's Guide to Skin Care: Essential Facts & Up-To-The Minute Information on Keeping Skin Healthy at Any Age. Wilma F. Bergfeld & Shelagh R. Masline. LC 95-1576. (Illus.). 224p. 1996. pap. 9.95 (*0-7868-8100-3*) Hyperion.

Woman Entrepreneur. Linda Pinson & Jerry A. Jinnett. LC 91-90096. 244p. (Orig.). 1993. pap. 14.00 (*0-944205-18-6*) Upstart Pub.

Woman Entrepreneur: Starting, Financing, & Managing a Successful Business. Robert D. Hisrich & Candida G. Brush. 216p. pap. 18.95 (*0-669-24412-0*, Lexington) Jossey-Bass.

Woman Evangelist: The Life & Times of Charismatic Evangelist Maria B. Woodworth-Etter. Wayne E. Warner. LC 86-11854. (Studies in Evangelicalism: No. 8). (Illus.). 354p. 1986. 37.50 (*0-8108-1912-0*) Scarecrow.

Woman for All Ages: Dr. Hallie Earle 1880-1963. Jessie L. Janes. 61p. (Orig.). 1988. pap. 10.00 (*1-879667-14-2*) Dove Pr TX.

Woman for All Seasons: Reflections on Mary. Sally Moran. LC 92-60892. 112p. (Orig.). 1993. pap. 7.95 (*0-89622-531-3*) Twenty-Third.

Woman for President, Foundation of the Federation of the Goths, Stretching from Iran to Norway. H. Winky-Lotz. (Historical Novel, Europe about 175 B. C. to 95 B. C. Ser.: Vol. I). (Illus.). 312p. 1980. 14.55 (*0-936112-02-6*); pap. 11.25 (*0-936112-09-3*) Willyshe Pub.

Woman for President, the Roots of "Cinderella" of Our Fairy Tale. H. Winky-Lotz. (Historical Novel, Europe About 95 B. C. to 57 B. C. Ser.: Vol. II). (Illus.). 245p. 1980. 14.55 (*0-936112-08-5*); pap. 11.25 (*0-936112-03-4*) Willyshe Pub.

Woman from Browhead. Audrey Howard. 480p. 1995. pap. 10.95 (*0-340-60704-1*, Pub. by H & S UK) Trafalgar.

Woman from Memphis. 2nd ed. Robert Sargent. LC 78-64527. (Illus.). 1979. per. 8.00 (*0-915380-07-2*) Word Works.

Woman from Spillertown: A Memoir of Agnes Burns Wieck. David T. Wieck. 288p. (C). 1991. 34.95 (*0-8093-1619-6*) S Ill U Pr.

Woman from the Other Side of the World: A Full-Length Play Employing Poetry, Music & Dance. Linda Faigao-Hall. 78p. 1996. pap. 5.25 (*0-87129-653-5*, W78) Dramatic Pub.

Woman Furiously Sweeping: God's Loving Pursuit of Each Person. Martin Burne. 1990. pap. 11.95 (*0-87193-278-4*) Dimension Bks.

Woman God Can Use. Alice Mathews. LC 90-41671. 192p. 1990. pap. 9.99 (*0-929239-30-X*) Discovery Hse Pubs.

***Woman Hater.** Mahoney. Date not set. write for info. (*0-312-18228-7*) St Martin.

Woman Hating: A Radical Look at Sexuality. Andrea Dworkin. 1991. pap. 12.00 (*0-452-26827-3*, Plume) NAL-Dutton.

Woman Heal Thyself: An Ancient Healing System for Contemporary Women. Jeanne E. Blum. LC 94-46764. (Illus.). 192p. 1995. 19.95 (*0-8048-3045-2*) C E Tuttle.

Woman Heal Thyself: An Ancient Healing System for Contemporary Women. rev. ed. Jeanne E. Blum. LC 96-8886. (Illus.). 328p. 1996. pap. text ed. 16.95 (*0-8048-3101-7*) C E Tuttle.

Woman Herself: A Transdisciplinary Perspective on Women's Identity. Robyn Rowland. 240p. 1990. pap. 19.95 (*0-19-554475-7*) OUP.

Woman Hollering Creek & Other Stories. Sandra Cisneros. 1991. 20.50 (*0-394-57654-3*) Random.

Woman Hollering Creek & Other Stories. Sandra Cisneros. 192p. 1992. pap. 11.00 (*0-679-73856-8*, Vin) Random.

Woman I Am. Dorothy Livesay. 96p. 1991. pap. 9.00 (*0-920717-37-3*) SPD-Small Pr Dist.

***Woman I Am: Poems.** Nancy Keesing. 125p. 1996. pap. 29.95 (*0-7305-8924-2*, Pub. by St Lib NSW AT) Intl Spec Bk.

Woman in a Special House: And Other Stories. Geraldine C. Little. 176p. (Orig.). 1997. pap. 10.95 (*1-56474-196-6*) Fithian Pr.

***Woman in a Special House & Other Stories.** Geraldine C. Little. 1997. 10.95 (*0-614-27262-9*) Fithian Pr.

Woman in All Ages & All Nations. Thomas L. Nichols. 1972. 250.00 (*0-8490-1314-3*) Gordon Pr.

Woman in Amber: Healing the Trauma of War & Exile. Agate Nesaule. LC 95-18907. 284p. 1995. 24.00 (*1-56947-046-4*) Soho Press.

Woman in Amber: Healing the Trauma of War & Exile. Agate Nesaule. 1997. pap. 11.95 (*0-14-026190-7*) Viking Penguin.

Woman in America. Ed. by Robert J. Lifton. LC 77-11064. 293p. 1977. reprint ed. lib. bdg. 49.50 (*0-8371-9810-0*, LIWO, Greenwood Pr) Greenwood.

Woman in America: A Guide to Information Sources. Ed. by Virginia R. Terris. LC 73-17564. (American Studies Information Guide: Vol. 7). 544p. 1980. 68.00 (*0-8103-1268-9*) Gale.

Woman in American Society: A Selected Bibliography, Nos. 810-811. 2nd ed. Ed. by Lenwood G. Davis. 1975. 10.00 (*0-686-20355-0*, Sage Prdcls Pr) Sage.

Woman in Ancient Israel under the Torah & Talmud. Arthur F. Ide. LC 82-9184. (Women in History Ser.: Vol. 5B). (Illus.). 86p. (Orig.). 1982. 35.00 (*0-86663-080-5*) Ide Hse.

Woman in Art Nouveau Decoration: One Hundred Forty-One Designs. Julius Klinger. (Pictorial Archive Ser.). 32p. 1985. reprint ed. pap. 6.95 (*0-486-24797-X*) Dover.

Woman in Battle: A Narrative of the Exploits, Adventures, & Travels of Madame Loreta Janeta Valazquez, Otherwise Known As Lieutenant Harry T. Buford, Confederate States Army. Loreta J. Velazquez. Ed. by C. J. Worthington. LC 72-2632. (American Women Ser.: Images & Realities). 680p. 1974. reprint ed. 42.95 (*0-405-04485-2*) Ayer.

Woman in Black. E. C. Bentley. 1976. lib. bdg. 13.95 (*0-89968-166-2*, Lghtyr Pr) Buccaneer Bks.

***Woman in Black.** Hill. Date not set. pap. text ed. write for info. (*0-582-02660-1*) Addison-Wesley.

Woman in Black: A Ghost Story. Susan Hill. LC 85-70145. (Illus.). 160p. 1986. pap. 12.95 (*0-87923-706-6*) Godine.

Woman in Christian Tradition. George H. Tavard. LC 72-12637. 269p. reprint ed. pap. 76.70 (*0-317-26144-4*, 2024373) Bks Demand.

Woman in Greek Civilization before 100 B.C. 2nd ed. Arthur F. Ide. LC 81-13468. (Woman in History Ser.: Vol. 7B). (Illus.). 83p. 1983. lib. bdg. 35.00 (*0-86663-031-7*) Ide Hse.

Woman in History. pap. text ed. write for info. (*0-86663-005-8*); lib. bdg. write for info. (*0-86663-224-7*) Ide Hse.

Woman in History: Eileen Power, 1889-1940. Maxine Berg. (Illus.). 308p. (C). 1996. text ed. 69.95 (*0-521-40278-6*); pap. text ed. 24.95 (*0-521-56852-8*) Cambridge U Pr.

Woman in Irish Legend, Life & Literature. Ed. by S. F. Gallagher. (Irish Literary Studies: Vol. # 14). 158p. 1983. 35.00 (*0-86140-159-X*, Pub. by Colin Smythe Ltd UK) Dufour.

***Woman in Islam: A Comparative Study.** Said A. Al-Hatimy. 160p. 1996. pap. 5.95 (*0-614-21397-5*, 1579) Kazi Pubns.

Woman in Jewish Law & Tradition. Michael Kaufman. LC 93-1230. 368p. 1995. pap. 24.95 (*1-56821-624-6*) Aronson.

Woman in Love...Mother Teresa. Edward Le Joly. LC 92-75249. (Illus.). 192p. (Orig.). 1993. pap. 7.95 (*0-87793-496-7*) Ave Maria.

Woman in Management: Career & Family Issues. Ed. by Jennie Farley. LC 83-2338. 112p. 1983. pap. 9.95 (*0-87546-100-X*, ILR Press) Cornell U Pr.

Woman in Man's World. U. S. Goswami. 130p. (C). 1993. 45.00 (*81-85880-08-5*, Pub. by Print Hse II) St Mut.

Woman in Medicine. Maria Steward. 1977. lib. bdg. 59.95 (*0-8490-2832-9*) Gordon Pr.

Woman in Mind. Alan Ayckbourn. 96p. (Orig.). 1986. pap. 9.95 (*0-571-14520-5*) Faber & Faber.

Woman in Modern Life. Institute of Pastoral Psychology Staff. Ed. by William C. Bier. LC 68-20626. (Pastoral Psychology Ser.: No. 5). 288p. reprint ed. pap. 82.10 (*0-7837-5880-4*, 2045600) Bks Demand.

Woman in Motion. Marlene Adrian. LC 95-50086. (Illus.). 168p. 1995. 18.95 (*1-884724-04-3*); pap. 11.95 (*1-884724-03-5*) Women Diversity.

Woman in Music. Louis Elson. 1976. 250.00 (*0-87968-459-3*) Gordon Pr.

***Woman in Politics.** Ed. by Diana J. Taylor. (Illus.). 224p. 1996. 21.95 (*1-889937-01-0*) Crescent Hill Bks.

Woman in Question. Parveen Adams & Elizabeth Cowie. (October Book Ser.). (Illus.). 400p. 1992. reprint ed. pap. 14.95 (*0-262-51062-6*) MIT Pr.

Woman in Red. Cynthia Hogue. Ed. by Orvis Burmaster. LC 89-80856. (Ahsahta Press Modern & Contemporary Poets of the West Ser.). 60p. (Orig.). 1989. pap. 6.95 (*0-916272-38-9*) Ahsahta Pr.

Woman in Residence. Michelle Harrison. 1993. mass mkt. 5.99 (*0-449-22238-1*) Fawcett.

Woman in Sacred History. Harriet Beecher Stowe. 1990. 2.00 (*0-517-01511-0*) Random Hse Value.

Woman in Science. H. J. Mozans. LC 90-50964. (C). 1991. reprint ed. pap. text ed. 17.50 (*0-268-01946-0*) U of Notre Dame Pr.

Woman in the Ancient Near East. 2nd rev. ed. Arthur F. Ide. LC 81-24195. (Woman in History Ser.). (Illus.). 100p. 1982. lib. bdg. 25.00 (*0-86663-069-4*) Ide Hse.

Woman in the Bible. Mary J. Evans. LC 84-4641. 160p. (Orig.). 1984. pap. 12.99 (*0-87784-978-1*, 978) InterVarsity.

***Woman in the Body.** Emily Martin. 288p. 1989. pap. 13.99 (*0-335-09909-2*, Open Univ Pr) Taylor & Francis.

Woman in the Body: A Cultural Analysis of Reproduction. Emily Martin. LC 92-7293. (Illus.). 304p. 1992. pap. 16.00 (*0-8070-4619-1*) Beacon Pr.

Woman in the Cloak. large type ed. Pamela Hill. (Nightingale Ser.). 182p. 1991. pap. 13.95 (*0-8161-5153-9*, GK Hall) Thorndike Pr.

Woman in the Colonial South. Arthur F. Ide. (Woman in History Ser.: Vol. 30B). (Illus.). 125p. (Orig.). 1983. pap. 12.00 (*0-86663-079-1*); pap. text ed. 10.00 (*0-86663-077-5*); lib. bdg. 35.00 (*0-86663-078-3*) Ide Hse.

Woman in the Dark. Dashiell Hammett. (Crime Ser.). 1989. pap. 8.00 (*0-679-72265-3*, Vin) Random.

***Woman in the Dark.** T. J. Phillips. 1997. reprint ed. mass mkt. write for info. (*0-425-16110-2*, Prime Crime) Berkley Pub.

***Woman in the Dark: A Joe Wilder Mystery.** T. J. Phillips. LC 96-31437. 288p. 1997. 21.95 (*0-425-15312-6*, Prime Crime) Berkley Pub.

Woman in the Dugout. Gary Lovisi & Terry Arnone. 100p. (Orig.). 1992. pap. 9.95 (*0-936071-29-X*) Gryphon Pubns.

Woman in the Dunes. Kobo Abe. LC 90-50625. 256p. 1991. pap. 12.00 (*0-679-73378-7*, Vin) Random.

Woman in the Dust: Drawings & Poems. Patrick Lane. (Illus.). 80p. 1995. lib. bdg. 29.00 (*0-8095-4921-2*) Borgo Pr.

Woman in the Early Middle Ages 400-800 A.D. Charles A. Ide & Arthur F. Ide. LC 81-7007. (Woman in History Ser.: Vol. 11). (Illus.). 54p. (Orig.). 1981. 150.00 (*0-86663-065-1*) Ide Hse.

Woman in the Glass House Speaks. Martha Mihalyi. (Illus.). 40p. (Orig.). (C). 1989. pap. write for info. (*0-318-65553-5*) Stone & Water Pr.

Woman in the Golden Ages. Amelia R. Mason. 1977. lib. bdg. 250.00 (*0-8490-2833-7*) Gordon Pr.

Woman in the Life of Southern California: An Anthology. Ed. by Doyce B. Nunis, Jr. LC 95-81833. (Illus.). 450p. 1996. 50.00 (*0-914421-16-6*) Hist Soc So CA.

Woman in the Military. Croopsey. 1994. 24.95 (*0-02-906708-1*, Free Press) Free Pr.

Woman in the Mirror. Lynn Turner. (Intrigue Ser.). 1994. mass mkt. 2.99 (*0-373-22268-8*, 1-22268-6) Harlequin Bks.

Woman in the Mirror: Analytical Psychology & the Feminine. Claire Douglas. 260p. (Orig.). (C). 1990. 34.95 (*0-938434-58-6*); pap. 17.95 (*0-938434-57-8*) Sigo Pr.

Woman in the Mists: The Story of Dian Fossey & the Mountain Gorillas of Africa. Farley Mowat. LC 87-40166. 400p. 1988. pap. 11.99 (*0-446-38720-7*) Warner Bks.

Woman in the Moon. 2nd ed. S. Diane Bogus. LC 93-14298. (Illus.). 96p. (C). 1996. reprint ed. 20.00 (*0-934172-37-4*) WIM Pubns.

Woman in the Moon: A Story from Hawai'i. Illus. by Carla Golembe. LC 95-21198. 32p. (J). (ps-3). 1996. 15.95 (*0-316-73446-2*) Little.

Woman in the Mountain: Reconstructions of Self & Land by Adirondack Women Writers. Kate H. Winter. LC 88-6960. 208p. 1989. text ed. 59.50 (*0-88706-886-3*); pap. text ed. 19.95 (*0-88706-888-X*) State U NY Pr.

Woman in the Muslim Unconscious. Fatna A. Sabbah. LC 84-11343. (Athene Ser.). 188p. 1984. text ed. 40.00 (*0-08-031626-3*, Pergamon Pr); pap. text ed. 16.95 (*0-08-031625-5*, Pergamon Pr) Elsevier.

***Woman in the Nineteenth Century: An Authoritative Text, Backgrounds, Criticism.** Margaret Fuller & Larry J. Reynolds. (Norton Critical Edition Ser.). (C). 1997. pap. text ed. 9.95 (*0-393-97157-0*) Norton.

Woman in the Nineteenth Century: And Kindred Papers Relating to the Sphere, Condition & Duties, of Woman. Margaret F. Ossoli. Ed. by Arthur B. Fuller. LC 72-312. (Essay Index Reprint Ser.). 1977. reprint ed. 26.95 (*0-8369-2815-6*) Ayer.

Woman in the Nineteenth Century & Kindred Papers. Margaret F. Ossoli. 1972. 59.95 (*0-8490-1315-1*) Gordon Pr.

Woman in the Nineteenth Century & Other Writings. Margaret Fuller. (World's Classics Ser.). 304p. 1994. pap. 10.95 (*0-19-283085-6*) OUP.

Woman in the Oil Field. Tracy Daugherty. LC 96-26734. 192p. 1996. 22.50 (*0-87074-402-X*); pap. 12.95 (*0-87074-403-8*) SMU Press.

Woman in the Past, Present, & Future. August Bebel. LC 72-9616. (International Library of Social Sciences: Vol. 1). reprint ed. 44.50 (*0-404-57409-2*) AMS Pr.

Woman in the Portrait: The Transfiguring Female in James Joyce's Portrait of the Artist as a Young Man. Julienne H. Empric. (Milford Series: Popular Writers of Today: Popular Writers of Today: Vol. 63). 160p. pap. write for info. (*0-89370-293-5*) Borgo Pr.

Woman in the Portrait: The Transfiguring Female in James Joyce's Portrait of the Artist as a Young Man. Julienne H. Empric. (Milford Series: Vol. 59). 160p. lib. bdg. write for info. (*0-89370-193-9*) Borgo Pr.

***Woman in the Priesthood.** Evelyn F. Capel. 64p. 1992. pap. write for info. (*0-904693-42-2*, Pub. by Temple Ldge Pub UK) Anthroposophic.

Woman in the Pulpit. Carol Noren. 176p. (Orig.). 1992. pap. 13.95 (*0-687-45893-5*) Abingdon.

Woman in the Pulpit. Frances E. Willard. LC 75-34240. 1976. reprint ed. 22.50 (*0-89201-014-2*) Zenger Pub.

Woman in the Red Skirt. Robert Novak. 1971. 4.00 (*0-685-67925-X*) Windless Orchard.

Woman in the Sea. large type ed. Shelley Smith. 480p. 1988. 25.99 (*0-7089-1792-5*) Ulverscroft.

Woman in the Wall. Patrice Kindl. LC 96-24567. (J). 1997. 14.95 (*0-395-83014-1*) HM.

Woman in the War: A Bibliography. U. S. Council of National Defense Staff. Ed. by Marion R. Nims. LC 75-33769. 1976. reprint ed. pap. 20.00 (*0-89201-005-3*) Zenger Pub.

Woman in the White House: Remarkable Story of Hillary Rodham Clinton. Norman King. (Illus.). 240p. 1996. 19.95 (*1-55972-349-1*, Birch Ln Pr) Carol Pub Group.

Woman in the Wilderness: Amalie Dietrich. Ray Sumner. 150p. 1993. pap. 22.95 (*0-86840-197-8*, Pub. by New South Wales Univ Pr AT) Intl Spec Bk.

Woman in the Woods. Joy Kogawa. 80p. 1995. lib. bdg. 29.00 (*0-8095-4906-9*) Borgo Pr.

Woman in the Woods: Poetry. Joy Kogawa. pap. 9.95 (*0-88962-294-9*) Mosaic.

Woman in White. 1988. pap. 5.25 (*0-19-581036-8*) OUP.

Woman in White. 1995. pap. 5.25 (*0-19-585467-5*) OUP.

Woman in White. 734p. 1991. 24.95 (*1-85089-470-1*, Pub. by ISIS UK) Transaction Pubs.

Woman in White. Wilkie Collins. 576p. 1985. mass mkt. 5.95 (*0-553-21263-X*, Bantam Classics) Bantam.

Woman in White. Wilkie Collins. Ed. by Julian Symons. (English Library). 654p. 1975. pap. 6.95 (*0-14-043096-2*, Penguin Classics) Viking Penguin.

Woman in White. Wilkie Collins. 608p. 1991. 20.00 (*0-679-40563-1*, Everymans Lib) Knopf.

Woman in White. William W. Collins. 1985. mass mkt. 5.95 (*0-451-52437-3*, Sig Classics) NAL-Dutton.

Woman in White. Jane Toombs. (Shadows Ser.). 1995. mass mkt. 3.50 (*0-373-27050-X*, 1-27050-3) Silhouette.

Woman in White. Wilkie Collins. 1976. reprint ed. lib. bdg. 35.95 (*0-89190-242-2*, Rivercity Pr) Amereon Ltd.

Woman in White. Wilkie Collins. 1990. reprint ed. lib. bdg. 30.95 (*0-89968-499-8*) Buccaneer Bks.

Woman in White: New Edition. Wilkie Collins. Ed. by John Sutherland. (The World's Classics Ser). 736p. (C). 1996. pap. 6.95 (*0-19-282403-1*) OUP.

Woman Inside: From Incest Victim to Survivor. Patty D. Barnes. LC 88-63769. 152p. (Orig.). 1989. pap. 12.95 (*0-941300-13-7*) Mother Courage.

Woman Invisible: A Personal Odyssey in Christian Feminism. Marga Buhrig. 160p. 1994. pap. 35.00 (*0-86012-202-6*, Pub. by Srch Pr UK) St Mut.

Woman Invisible: A Personal Odyssey in Christian Feminism. Marga Buhrig. LC 92-42838. 128p. 1993. pap. 12.95 (*1-56338-056-0*) TPI PA.

Woman Is... (Main Street Gift Bks.). (Illus.). 40p. 1996. 6.95 (*0-8362-1061-1*) Andrews & McMeel.

Woman Is a Worthy Wight: Women in English Society c. 1200-1500. Ed. by P. J. Goldberg. 160p. (C). 1992. 44.00 (*0-86299-864-6*, Pub. by Sutton Pubng UK) Bks Intl VA.

Woman Jesus Can Teach. Alice Mathews. 160p. 1991. pap. 9.99 (*0-929239-44-X*) Discovery Hse Pubs.

***Woman Jesus Loved: Mary Magdalene in the Nag Hammadi Library & Related Documents.** Antti Marjanen. LC 96-26933. (Nag Hammadi & Manichawan Studies). 1996. write for info. (*90-04-10658-8*) E J Brill.

Woman Journeying: Two-Minute Reflections on the Ordinary & the Everyday. Betty Maher. 104p. (Orig.). 1994. pap. 7.95 (*1-85607-095-6*, Pub. by Columba Pr IE) Twenty-Third.

Woman Killed with Kindness. Thomas Heywood. Ed. by Brian Scobie. (New Mermaid Ser.). (Orig.). (C). 1986. pap. text ed. 6.95 (*0-393-90052-5*) Norton.

Woman Kneeling in the Big City. Elizabeth Macklin. 96p. 1994. pap. 8.95 (*0-393-31105-8*) Norton.

Woman, Knowledge & Reality: Explorations in Feminist Philosophy. Ed. by Ann Garry & Marylin U. Pearsall. 368p. (C). 1989. pap. 17.95 (*0-415-90712-8*, Routledge NY) Routledge.

Woman Like That. large type ed. Constance Bartel. 624p. (Orig.). 1987. 27.99 (*0-7089-8426-6*) Ulverscroft.

Woman Like You: The Face of Domestic Violence. Photos by Vera Anderson. LC 90-20603. (New Leaf Ser.). (Illus.). 80p. (Orig.). 1997. pap. 16.00 (*1-878067-07-9*) Seal Pr WA.

Woman Lit by Fireflies. Jim Harrison. 247p. 1990. 19.95 (*0-685-46958-1*, Seymour Lawrence) HM.

Woman Lit by Fireflies. Jim Harrison. Ed. by Jane Rosenman. 256p. reprint ed. pap. 14.00 (*0-671-74452-6*, WSP) PB.

Woman Love Your Body. rev. ed. Louis S. Greenup, Jr. 160p. 1996. pap. 22.95 (*1-885342-07-1*) Creative Ways.

Woman Making History: Mary Ritter Beard Through Her Letters. Ed. by Nancy Cott. 400p. (C). 1991. text ed. 50.00 (*0-300-04825-4*) Yale U Pr.

Woman Making History: Mary Ritter Beard Through Her Letters. Nancy F. Cott. 392p. (C). 1992. reprint ed. pap. text ed. 19.00 (*0-300-05252-9*) Yale U Pr.

***Woman Manager.** Connie Sitterly. (Better Management Skills Ser.). 1994. pap. 12.95 (*0-7494-1354-9*) Kogan Page Ltd.

Woman Manager: Developing Essential Skills for Success. Connie Sitterly. Ed. by Beverly Manber. LC 92-75717. (Fifty-Minute Ser.). 98p. (Orig.). 1993. pap. 10.95 (*1-56052-206-2*) Crisp Pubns.

Woman Managers Troubleshooter. Vickie Montgomery. LC 96-38662. 1996. pap. text ed. 14.95 (*0-13-460072-X*) P-H.

Woman Managers Troubleshooter. Vickie Montgomery. LC 96-38662. 1996. text ed. 39.95 (*0-13-460080-0*) P-H.

Woman Maps. Kate Blackburn. 68p. Date not set. pap. 8.95 (*0-932622-70-4*) St Andrews NC.

Woman Marine: A Memoir of a Woman Who Joined the U. S. Marine Corps in World War II to Free a Marine to Fight. Theresa K. Yianilos. 459p. (Orig.). 1994. pap. 19.95 (*0-9621142-4-3*) La Jolla Bk Pub.

Woman, Marriage & Family. Ed. by Man Singh Das et al. 118p. 1995. pap. 87.50 (*81-85880-78-6*, Pub. by Print Hse II) St Mut.

Woman: Mission, Position, Ministry see Mujer: Su Mision, Posicion y Ministerio

Woman, Mother of All Living. Manly P. Hall. pap. 4.95 (*0-89314-373-1*) Philos Res.

Woman, Muslim Society, & Islam. Llamya Al-Faruqi. Ed. by American Trust Publications. LC 87-51271. 160p. 1987. pap. 1.50 (*0-89259-068-8*) Am Trust Pubns.

Woman Named Anne. Henry Cecil. 261p. 1993. reprint ed. pap. 5.95 (*0-89733-338-1*) Academy Chi Pubs.

Woman Named Anne see Henry Cecil Reprint Series

Woman Named Damaris. Janette Oke. (Women of the West Ser.: No. 4). 224p. (Orig.). 1991. pap. 8.99 (*1-55661-225-7*) Bethany Hse.

***Woman Named Damaris.** Janette Oke. 1997. pap. text ed. 5.99 (*0-7642-2018-7*) Bethany Hse.

Woman Named Damaris. large type ed. Janette Oke. (Women of the West Ser.: No. 4). 224p. (Orig.). 1991. pap. 10.99 (*1-55661-226-5*) Bethany Hse.

Woman Named Jackie. C. D. Heymann. mass mkt. 6.99 (*0-451-18637-0*) NAL-Dutton.

Woman Named Jackie. C. David Heymann. 768p. 1990. pap. 5.95 (*0-451-16567-5*, Sig) NAL-Dutton.

Woman Named Jackie. C. David Heymann. 1991. pap. 5.99 (*0-451-17269-8*, Sig) NAL-Dutton.

W

Woman Named Jackie: An Intimate Biography of Jacqueline Bouvier Kennedy Onassis. C. David Heyman. 1994. 24.95 (*1-55972-266-5*, Birch Ln Pr); pap. 17.95 (*1-55972-276-2*, Birch Ln Pr) Carol Pub Group.

Woman Named Jackie: An Intimate Biography of Jacqueline Bouvier Kennedy Onassis. C. David Heymann. 1989. 21.95 (*0-8184-0472-8*) Carol Pub Group.

Woman, Native, Other: Writing Postcoloniality & Feminism. Trinh T. Minh-ha. LC 88-45455. (Illus.). 184p. 1989. 39.95 (*0-253-36603-8*); pap. 15.95 (*0-253-20503-4*, MB-503) Ind U Pr.

Woman, Nature, & Psyche. Patricia J. Mills. LC 87-10408. 266p. 1987. 35.00 (*0-300-03537-3*) Yale U Pr.

***Woman Nobly Planned: The History & Heritage of Flora MacDonald.** John J. Toffey. LC 97-12376. 1997. write for info. (*0-89089-957-6*) Carolina Acad Pr.

Woman of Africa. Patricia Harding. 270p. 1996. 27.95 (*1-85756-205-4*, Pub. by Janus Pubng UK) Paul & Co Pubs.

Woman of Balance see Women of Character Bible Studies

Woman of Beauty see Women of Character Bible Studies

Woman of Blessing see Women of Character Bible Studies

Woman of Color, Daughter of Privilege: Amanda America Dickson, 1849-1893. Kent A. Leslie. LC 94-17033. (Illus.). 240p. 1995. 29.95 (*0-8203-1688-1*) U of Ga Pr.

***Woman of Color, Daughter of Privilege: Amanda America Dickson, 1849-1893.** Kent A. Leslie. 1996. pap. text ed. 14.95 (*0-8203-1871-X*) U of Ga Pr.

Woman of Confidence see Women of Character Bible Studies

Woman of Creativity see Women of Character Bible Studies

***Woman of Dreams.** Angela Drake. 400p. (Orig.). 1997. mass mkt. 3.99 (*1-85487-714-3*, Pub. by Scarlet Bks UK) London Brdge.

Woman of Eternity. Larry Spruil. 96p. (Orig.). 1995. pap. 6.99 (*1-56043-819-3*) Destiny Image.

Woman of Excellence. Cynthia Heald. 1991. pap. 2.50 (*0-89109-313-3*) NavPress.

Woman of Faith. John E. Rotelle. 72p. (Orig.). 1987. pap. 1.00 (*0-941491-03-X*) Augustinian Pr.

Woman of Family see Women of Character Bible Studies

Woman of Fifty. Rheta C. Dorr. Ed. by Annette K. Baxter. LC 79-8787. (Signal Lives Ser.). 1980. reprint ed. lib. bdg. 50.95 (*0-405-12835-5*) Ayer.

Woman of Flowers. Susan Schwartz. 320p. (Orig.). 1987. pap. 3.50 (*0-445-20358-7*) Warner Bks.

Woman of Genius. Mary Austin. LC 85-7069. 334p. 1985. pap. 9.95 (*0-935312-44-7*) Feminist Pr.

Woman of Genius. Mary H. Austin. LC 76-51663. (Rediscovered Fiction by American Women Ser.). 1977. reprint ed. lib. bdg. 33.95 (*0-405-10043-4*) Ayer.

Woman of Genius: The Intellectual Autobiography of Sor Juana de la Cruz. Tr. by Margaret S. Peden. (Illus.). 192p. (C). 1982. 37.50 (*0-915998-14-9*); pap. 7.95 (*0-915998-15-7*) Lime Rock Pr.

Woman of Grace see Women of Character Bible Studies

Woman of Her Time. Caroline Gray. 320p. 1995. 22.00 (*0-7278-4780-5*) Severn Hse.

Woman of Her Time & Ours: Mary Magdalen Taylor, SMG. Ruth G. Wells & M. St. Pius. LC 88-627. (Illus.). 249p. 1988. 21.00 (*0-9624488-2-6*) Laney-Smith.

Woman of Her Time & Ours: Mary Magdalen Taylor, SMG. Ruth G. Wells & M. St. Pius. LC 88-627. (Illus.). 249p. 1994. reprint ed. pap. 13.00 (*0-9624488-3-4*) Laney-Smith.

Woman of Her Tribe. Margaret A. Robinson. 160p. (YA). 1992. mass mkt. 4.50 (*0-449-70405-X*, Juniper) Fawcett.

Woman of Her Tribe. Margaret A. Robinson. LC 90-31534. 144p. (YA). (gr. 7 up). 1990. lib. bdg. 13.95 (*0-684-19223-3*, C Scribner Sons Young) S&S Childrens.

Woman of Her Word: Hispanic Women Write. 2nd ed. Ed. by Evangelina Vigil. LC 83-72571. 180p. (Orig.). 1987. pap. 13.00 (*0-934770-27-1*) Arte Publico.

Woman of Independent Means. Elizabeth F. Hailey. 1979. mass mkt. 4.50 (*0-380-42390-1*) Avon.

Woman of Independent Means. Elizabeth F. Hailey. 288p. 1990. mass mkt. 5.99 (*0-440-20550-6*, Dell Trade Pbks) Dell.

Woman of Influence: 10 Traits of Those Who Want to Make a Difference. Pam Farrel. LC 95-26745. 187p. (Orig.). 1996. pap. 9.99 (*0-8308-1951-7*, 1951, Saltshaker Bk) InterVarsity.

Woman of Insight. Dee Brestin. (Dee Brestin Ser.). 96p. 1995. pap. 4.99 (*1-56476-456-7*, 6-3456, Victor Bks) Chariot Victor.

Woman of Joy. Dee Brestin. 96p. 1995. pap. 4.99 (*1-56476-454-0*, 6-3454, Victor Bks) Chariot Victor.

Woman of Means. Peter Taylor. (Southern Writers Ser.). 128p. 1986. mass mkt. 3.95 (*0-380-70099-9*) Avon.

Woman of Means. Peter Taylor. LC 83-71687. 140p. 1983. 16.95 (*0-913720-44-5*) Beil.

Woman of Means. Peter Taylor. LC 96-4261. 144p. 1996. pap. 10.00 (*0-312-14448-2*) St Martin.

Woman of My Age. Nina Bawden. 159p. 1976. reprint ed. lib. bdg. 18.95 (*0-88411-125-3*, Queens House) Amereon Ltd.

Woman of Nazareth. rev. ed. Hala D. Jabbour. LC 88-2785. (Emerging Voices: New International Fiction Ser.). 273p. 1989. reprint ed. pap. 9.95 (*0-940793-07-5*) Interlink Pub.

Woman of No Importance. Ian Small. (New Mermaid Ser.). (C). Date not set. pap. text ed. 6.95 (*0-393-90071-1*, Norton Paperbks) Norton.

Woman of No Importance see Selected Plays

Woman of Passion. Anne Mather. 1996. 3.50 (*0-373-11797-3*, 1-11797-7) Harlequin Bks.

Woman of Passion. Anne Mather. (Harlequin Romance Ser.). 1996. 19.95 (*0-263-14481-X*, Pub. by Mills & Boon UK) Thorndike Pr.

Woman of Passion: The Life of E. Nesbit, 1858-1928. Julia Briggs. LC 87-11215. (Illus.). 473p. (C). 1987. 27.95 (*0-941533-03-4*) New Amsterdam Bks.

Woman of Proper. large type ed. Margaret T. Davis. (Magna Large Print Ser.). 1994. 25.99 (*0-7505-0613-X*, Pub. by Magna Print Bks UK) Ulverscroft.

Woman of Rest see Women of Character Bible Studies

Woman of Spirit. Nora Kay. 394p. 1995. pap. 8.95 (*0-340-61336-X*, Pub. by H & S UK) Trafalgar.

Woman of Steel. Vivien Cherry & Keith Wheatley. (Illus.). 192p. 1994. pap. 20.00 (*0-7136-3996-2*) Sheridan.

***Woman of Strength: Reclaim Your Past, Seize Your Present, & Secure Your Future.** Neva Coyle. LC 97-24505. 1997. pap. text ed. 10.99 (*1-56955-036-0*) Servant.

Woman of Substance. Barbara Taylor Bradford. 832p. 1980. mass mkt. 4.50 (*0-380-49163-X*) Avon.

Woman of Substance. Barbara Taylor Bradford. 928p. 1994. mass mkt. 6.99 (*0-06-100807-9*, Harp PBks) HarpC.

Woman of Substance. Jill Briscoe. (Jill Briscoe Inductive Bible Study Ser.). 112p. (Orig.). 1994. pap. 7.99 (*1-56476-267-X*, 6-3267, Victor Bks) Chariot Victor.

***Woman of Texas: The Story of Jane Wilkinson Long.** Neila A. Petrick. Ed. by Thomas W. Petrick. (YA). (gr. 7-12). 1997. student ed. 21.95 incl. vhs (*1-880384-11-6*) Coldwater Pr.

***Woman of Texas: The Story of Jane Wilkinson Long.** Neila A. Petrick. Ed. by Thomas W. Petrick. 40p. (YA). (gr. 7-12). 1997. student ed. 10.95 (*1-880384-13-2*) Coldwater Pr.

Woman of the American Frontier. William W. Fowler. 1972. 59.95 (*0-8490-1316-X*) Gordon Pr.

Woman of the Boundary Waters: Canoeing, Guiding, Mushing & Surviving. Justine Kerfoot. LC 86-4061. (Illus.). 200p. 1986. 14.95 (*0-910259-03-8*) Womens Times.

Woman of the Boundary Waters: Canoeing, Guiding, Mushing, & Surviving. Justine Kerfoot. LC 93-28588. (C). 1994. pap. 14.95 (*0-8166-2443-7*) U of Minn Pr.

Woman of the Century: 1470 Biographies, 2 vols. F. E. Willard. 1974. lib. bdg. 500.00 (*0-87968-183-7*) Gordon Pr.

Woman of the Cloth. Michael Tracey. 1995. pap. 25.00 (*1-886017-01-8*) Town Sq Bks.

Woman of the Eighteenth Century: Her Life, From Birth to Death, Her Love, & Her Philosophy in the Worlds of Salon, Shop, & Street. Edmond L. Goncourt & Jules A. Goncourt. 1977. 22.95 (*0-8369-6937-5*, 7817) Ayer.

***Woman of the Frontier.** Grey. 1998. 20.00 (*0-7862-1156-3*) Thorndike Pr.

Woman of the Inner Sea. Thomas Keneally. LC 93-27531. 1994. pap. 10.95 (*0-452-27177-0*, Plume) NAL-Dutton.

Woman of the Iron People: Changing Women, Pt. 2. Eleanor Arnason. 288p. (Orig.). 1992. mass mkt. 4.99 (*0-380-75638-2*, AvoNova) Avon.

Woman of the Iron People, Pt. 1: In the Light of Sigma Draconis. Eleanor Arnason. 256p. 1992. mass mkt. 4.99 (*0-380-75637-4*, AvoNova) Avon.

Woman of the Mists. Lynn A. McKee. 1991. mass mkt. 5.50 (*1-55773-520-4*) Diamond.

Woman of the Pharisees. Francois Mauriac. Tr. by Gerard M. Hopkins. 284p. 1988. reprint ed. pap. 8.95 (*0-88184-371-7*) Carroll & Graf.

Woman of the Prairie. Barbara Oaks. LC 88-61831. (Illus.). 228p. (Orig.). (C). 1989. pap. 7.95 (*0-9618582-1-4*) Barbara Oaks.

Woman of the River. Claribel Alegria. Tr. by Darwin J. Flakoll from SPA. LC 88-4775. (Poetry Ser.). 112p. (Orig.). 1988. 19.95 (*0-8229-3594-5*); pap. 10.95 (*0-8229-5409-5*) U of Pittsburgh Pr.

***Woman of the River: Georgie White Clark, White Water Pioneer.** Richard E. Westwood. (Illus.). 280p. 1997. pap. 19.95 (*0-87421-234-0*) Utah St U Pr.

Woman of Valor. L. W. Hayhurst. 1971. pap. 4.25 (*0-89137-432-9*) Quality Pubns.

Woman of Valor: Clara Barton & the Civil War. Stephen B. Oates. LC 93-38830. 1994. 27.95 (*0-02-923405-0*, Free Press) Free Pr.

Woman of Valor: Clara Barton & the Civil War. Stephen B. Oates. 1995. pap. 14.00 (*0-02-874012-2*) Free Pr.

Woman of Valor: Eshet Hayil. Adin Steinsaltz. 112p. 1994. text ed. 45.00 (*1-56821-378-6*) Aronson.

Woman of Valor: Margaret Sanger and the Birth Control Movement in America. Ellen Chesler. LC 93-16110. (Illus.). 640p. 1993. pap. 14.95 (*0-385-46980-2*, Anchor NY) Doubleday.

Woman of Value. Dee Brestin. 96p. 1995. pap. 4.99 (*1-56476-455-9*, 6-3455, Victor Bks) Chariot Victor.

Woman of Vision. Donald C. France. 228p. (Orig.). 1996. mass mkt. 4.99 (*1-55197-207-7*, Pub. by Comnwlth Pub CN) Partners Pubs Grp.

Woman of Wisdom: Lessons for Living from the Book of Proverbs. Myrna Alexander. 128p. 1992. pap. 8.99 (*0-929239-56-3*) Discovery Hse Pubs.

Woman of Wyrrd: The Arousal of the Inner Fire. Lynn V. Andrews. LC 90-56420. 270p. 1991. reprint ed. pap. 12.00 (*0-06-097410-9*, PL) HarpC.

Woman Offender: A Bibliographic Sourcebook. Susan Sturgeon & Laurel Rans. vi, 63p. 1975. pap. 5.00 (*0-938876-02-3*) Entropy Ltd.

Woman on the American Frontier. William W. Fowler. 527p. (Orig.). 1976. reprint ed. 32.95 (*0-87928-074-3*) Corner Hse.

Woman on the American Frontier. William W. Fowler. LC 73-12867. 532p. (Orig.). 1980. reprint ed. 56.00 (*0-8103-3702-9*) Gale.

Woman on the American Frontier. William W. Fowler. 527p. (Orig.). reprint ed. 89.00 (*0-932051-33-2*) Rprt Serv.

Woman on the Bridge Over the Chicago River. Allen Grossman. LC 78-26802. 1979. 8.95 (*0-8112-0714-5*); pap. 3.95 (*0-8112-0715-3*, NDP473) New Directions.

Woman on the Edge. JoAnn Sands. 1994. 17.95 (*0-8034-9036-4*) Bouregy.

Woman on the Edge of Time. Marge Piercy. 384p. 1985. mass mkt. 6.99 (*0-449-21082-0*) Fawcett.

***Woman on the Edge of Time.** Marge Piercy. 1997. pap. 12.00 (*0-449-00094-X*) Fawcett.

Woman on the Front Lines. Belkis C. Male. Tr. & Intro. by Pamella Carmell. 88p. 1987. 17.50 (*0-87775-202-8*); pap. 9.95 (*0-87775-203-6*) Unicorn Pr.

Woman on the Goldfields: Emily Skinner's Diary. Ed. by Edward Duyker. 144p. 1996. 39.95 (*0-522-84652-1*, Pub. by Melbourne Univ Pr AT) Paul & Co Pubs.

Woman Packing a Pistol. Darrell Spencer. LC 86-24362. 128p. 1987. 16.00 (*0-937872-36-9*) Dragon Gate.

Woman Patient Vol. 3: Aggressions, Adaptations, & Psychotherapy. Ed. by Malkah T. Notman & Carol C. Nadelson. LC 82-5325. (Women in Context Ser.). 326p. 1982. 45.00 (*0-306-40859-7*, Plenum Pr) Plenum.

Woman Patient Vol. 1: Sexual & Reproductive Aspects of Women's Health Care. Ed. by Malkah T. Notman & Carol C. Nadelson. (Women in Context Ser.). (Illus.). 376p. 1978. 47.50 (*0-306-31151-8*, Plenum Pr) Plenum.

Woman Patient Vol. 2: Concepts of Femininity & the Life Cycle. Ed. by Carol C. Nadelson et al. LC 82-5326. (Women in Context Ser.). 216p. 1982. 45.00 (*0-306-40846-5*, Plenum Pr) Plenum.

Woman Plus Woman. Dolores Klaich. 304p. 1989. reprint ed. pap. 9.95 (*0-941483-28-2*) Naiad Pr.

Woman Poems. Joel Oppenheimer. LC 74-17641. 128p. 1975. 7.95 (*0-672-52025-7*, Bobbs); pap. 4.95 (*0-672-52026-5*, Bobbs) Macmillan.

Woman Poet: The East. Ed. by Elaine Dallman et al. LC 81-69793. (Woman Poet Ser.). (Illus.). 123p. 1982. pap. 12.50 (*0-935634-02-9*); boxed 19.95 (*0-935634-03-7*) Women-in-Lit.

Woman Poet: The Midwest. Ed. by Elaine Dallman et al. LC 81-69793. (Woman Poet Ser.). (Illus.). 115p. 1985. pap. 12.50 (*0-935634-04-5*); boxed 19.95 (*0-935634-05-3*) Women-in-Lit.

Woman, Poet, Scientist: Essays in New World Anthropology Honoring Dr. Emma Louise Davis. Ed. by Great Basin Foundation Staff. LC 85-6075. (Anthropological Papers: No. 29). (Illus.). 256p. (Orig.). (C). 1985. pap. 15.00 (*0-87919-106-6*) Ballena Pr.

Woman Poet: The West. Ed. by Elaine Dallman et al. LC 79-55988. (Woman Poet Ser.). (Illus.). 100p. (Orig.). 1980. boxed 19.95 (*0-935634-01-0*) Women-in-Lit.

Woman Police Officer in Elevator: Poems. James Lasdun. 72p. 1997. 19.00 (*0-393-04043-7*) Norton.

Woman Power: Status of Women in India. Ashok Kumar. (C). 1991. text ed. 20.00 (*0-685-50084-5*, Pub. by Gian Publng Hse II) S Asia.

***Woman, Power, & Therapy.** Ed. by Marjorie Braude. 340p. 1987. pap. 22.95 (*0-918393-36-1*) Harrington Pk.

Woman Prayer, Woman Song: Resources for Ritual. Miriam T. Winter. pap. 16.95 (*0-8245-1025-9*) Crossroad NY.

Woman Question. 2nd ed. Ed. by Mary Evans. 384p. 1994. 79.95 (*0-8039-8747-1*); pap. 21.95 (*0-8039-8748-X*) Sage.

Woman Question. 2nd ed. Kenneth E. Hagin. 1983. pap. 3.95 (*0-89276-405-8*) Hagin Ministries.

Woman Question Vol. 1: Society & Literature in Britain & America, 1837-1883: Defining Voices. Elizabeth K. Helsinger et al. LC 88-27796. (Illus.). xviii, 169p. 1989. pap. text ed. 11.95 (*0-226-32666-7*) U Ch Pr.

Woman Question see Thoughts on Women & Society

Woman Question in Classical Sociological Theory. Terry R. Kandal. LC 87-18616. 363p. (Orig.). 1988. pap. text ed. 22.95 (*0-8130-0796-8*) U Press Fla.

Woman Questions. Lise Vogel. 224p. (C). (gr. 13 up). 1995. text ed. 59.95 (*0-415-91485-X*, Routledge NY) Routledge.

Woman Questions. Lise Vogel. 224p. 1995. pap. 17.95 (*0-415-91486-8*, Routledge NY) Routledge.

***Woman Questions: Essays for a Materialist Feminism.** Lise Vogel. 224p. (C). 1995. pap. 17.95 (*0-415-91580-5*, Routledge NY); text ed. 62.95 (*0-415-91579-1*, Routledge NY) Routledge.

Woman Reader: Learning & Teaching Women's Writing. Jean Milloy & Rebecca O'Rourke. 176p. (C). (gr. 13). 1991. text ed. 79.95 (*0-415-00983-9*, A5698) Routledge.

Woman Reader, 1837-1914. Kate Flint. LC 93-18195. (Illus.). 384p. 1993. 55.00 (*0-19-811719-1*, Old Oregon Bk Store) OUP.

Woman Reader 1837-1914. Kate Flint. (Illus.). 384p. 1995. pap. 19.95 (*0-19-812185-7*) OUP.

Woman Reads the Gospel of Luke. Loretta C. Dornisch. 232p. (Orig.). 1996. pap. 19.95 (*0-8146-2307-7*, Liturg Pr Bks) Liturgical Pr.

Woman Rebel. Ed. by Margaret Sanger & Alex Baskin. LC 75-3728. 1976. 34.95 (*0-914924-02-8*) Archives Soc Hist.

Woman Rice Planter. Patience Pennington. (Illus.). 496p. (C). 1991. reprint ed. write for info. (*0-318-68580-9*) Seajay Society.

Woman Rice Planter. Patience Pennington, pseud. Ed. by John G. Sproat. LC 91-35167. (Southern Classics Ser.). (Illus.). 501p. 1992. reprint ed. pap. 16.95 (*0-87249-826-3*) U of SC Pr.

Woman Rides the Beast. Dave Hunt. (Orig.). 1994. pap. 12.99 (*1-56507-199-9*) Harvest Hse.

Woman Run Mad. John L'Heureux. Date not set. pap. write for info. (*0-14-010194-2*, Viking) Viking Penguin.

Woman Run Mad. John L'Heureux. 240p. 1989. reprint ed. mass mkt. 4.99 (*0-380-70686-5*) Avon.

Woman Scientist: Meeting the Challenges for a Successful Career. C. M. Yentsch & Carl J. Sindermann. (Illus.). 270p. 1992. 24.95 (*0-306-44131-4*, Plenum Pr) Plenum.

***Woman Scorned.** large type ed. M. R. O'Donnell. (Charnwood Large Print Ser.). 720p. 1996. 27.99 (*0-7089-8919-5*) Ulverscroft.

***Woman Scorned: Acquaintance Rape on Trial.** Peggu R. Sanday. LC 97-12262. 1997. pap. write for info. (*0-520-21092-1*) U CA Pr.

Woman Scorned: Aquaintance Rape on Trial. Peggy R. Sandy. LC 95-22774. 336p. Date not set. 23.95 (*0-385-47791-0*) Doubleday.

Woman Seeking God. Dorothy K. Patterson. 1992. pap. 8.99 (*0-8054-5351-2*, 4253-51) Broadman.

Woman Shall Conquer. Don Sharkey. 268p. 1986. 4.95 (*0-911988-71-8*, 38484) AMI Pr.

Woman Shall Conquer. rev. ed. Don Sharkey. 258p. 1976. reprint ed. pap. 4.95 (*0-913382-01-9*, 101-1) Marytown Pr.

Woman Sitting at the Machine, Thinking: Poems. Karen Brodine. LC 87-83121. 100p. (Orig.). 1990. pap. 8.95 (*0-932323-01-4*) Red Letter Pr.

Woman Song II. Ed. by Stephanie Schmidts et al. (Illus.). 115p. (Orig.). 1987. text ed. 7.95 (*0-934821-02-X*) NRVC.

Woman Songs. Ruth De Menezes. (Illus.). 94p. 1982. pap. 6.00 (*0-941358-02-X*) Claremont CA.

Woman Space: Future & Fantasy Stories by Women. Ed. by Claudia M. Lamperti. LC 80-83471. 96p. (Orig.). 1981. pap. 4.95 (*0-934678-04-9*) New Victoria Pubs.

Woman Speaking Inside Film Noir. Gillian Conoley. LC 84-14317. 26p. 1984. 4.50 (*0-89924-043-7*) Lynx Hse.

Woman Speaks: The Lectures, Seminars, & Interviews of Anais Nin. Ed. by Evelyn Hinz. LC 75-15111. 270p. 1975. 24.95 (*0-8040-0693-8*); pap. 14.95 (*0-8040-0694-6*) Swallow.

Woman Students Handbook. F. Fletcher. 1990. pap. 21.00 (*0-7463-0347-5*, Pub. by Northcote UK) St Mut.

Woman Suffrage & the Origins of Liberal Feminism in the United States, 1820-1920. Suzanne M. Marilley. (Illus.). 304p. 1996. 39.95 (*0-674-95465-3*) HUP.

Woman Suffrage in Australia: A Gift or a Struggle? Audrey Oldfield. (Studies in Australian History). (Illus.). 272p. (C). 1993. text ed. 65.00 (*0-521-40380-4*); pap. text ed. 22.95 (*0-521-43611-7*) Cambridge U Pr.

Woman Suffrage in Mexico. Ward M. Morton. LC 62-20735. (Illus.). 174p. reprint ed. pap. 49.60 (*0-8357-6721-3*, 2035356) Bks Demand.

Woman Suffrage Movement in Canada: The Start of Liberation. Catherine L. Cleverdon. LC 73-82587. (Social History of Canada Ser.). 1974. pap. 12.95 (*0-8020-6218-0*) U of Toronto Pr.

Woman Suffrage, Vol. 19, Pt. I see History of Women in the United States: Topically Arranged Articles on the Evolution of Women's History in the United States

Woman Suffrage, Vol. 19, Pt. II see History of Women in the United States: Topically Arranged Articles on the Evolution of Women's History in the United States

***Woman That I Am.** D. Soyini Madison. 1997. pap. 19.95 (*0-312-15296-5*) St Martin.

Woman That I Am: The Literature & Culture of Women of Color. Ed. by D. Soyini Madison. 720p. 1993. 35.00 (*0-312-10012-4*) St Martin.

Woman That Never Evolved. Sarah B. Hrdy. 265p. 1983. pap. text ed. 10.95 (*0-674-95541-2*) HUP.

Woman the Gatherer. Ed. by Frances Dahlberg. LC 80-25262. 1983. reprint ed. pap. 15.00 (*0-300-02989-6*, Y-476) Yale U Pr.

***Woman the Hunter.** Mary Z. Stange. LC 96-39045. 1997. 25.00 (*0-8070-4638-8*) Beacon Pr.

Woman, the Second Coming. Rose B. Green. 5.95 (*0-8453-2173-0*, Cornwall Bks) Assoc Univ Prs.

Woman, the Writer & Caribbean Society. Ed. by Helen Pyne-Timothy. (CAAS Special Publication Ser.). (Orig.). Date not set. pap. text ed. 22.95 (*0-934934-44-4*) CAAS Pubns.

***Woman, the Writer & Caribbean Society: Critical Analyses of the Writings of Caribbean Women: Proceedings of the Second International Conference.** Helen Pyne-Timothy. LC 97-15896. (CAAS Special Publication Ser.). 1997. write for info. (*0-09-349344-4*) Vipassana Res.

Woman, Thou Art Loosed. T. D. Jakes. 196p. (Orig.). 1993. pap. 8.95 (*1-56043-100-8*) Destiny Image.

Woman, Thou Art Loosed. T. D. Jakes. 48p. (Orig.). 1994. wbk. ed., pap. 5.95 (*1-56043-810-X*) Destiny Image.

***Woman, Thou Art Loosed: Devotional.** T. D. Jakes. 240p. 1997. pap. 11.99 (*1-57778-020-5*) Albury Pub.

Woman to Remember. Miranda Lee. (Harlequin Romance Ser.). 1996. 19.95 (*0-263-14667-7*) Thorndike Pr.

Woman to Remember. Miranda Lee. 1997. mass mkt. 3.50 (*0-373-11861-9*, 1-11861-1) Silhouette.

Woman to the Rescue. Timothy S. Arthur. (Works of Timothy Shay Arthur). 1989. reprint ed. lib. bdg. 79.00 (*0-7812-1806-3*) Rprt Serv.

***Woman to Wed?** Penny Jordan. (Bride's Bouquet Ser.). 1997. mass mkt. 3.50 (*0-373-11883-X*, 1-11883-5) Harlequin Bks.

***Woman to Wed.** Penny Jordan. 1997. 20.95 (*0-263-14821-1*, Pub. by Mills & Boon UK) Thorndike Pr.

***Woman to Woman.** Maria Bakkum. 71p. 1994. per. 5.00 (*0-614-24752-7*) Tesseract SD.

Woman to Woman. Great Quotations Staff. 64p. 1995. 6.50 (*1-56245-194-4*) Great Quotations.

Woman to Woman. Eugenia Price. 256p. 1994. mass mkt. 5.50 (*0-06-104310-9*) Zondervan.

Woman to Woman. Jean Ward-Jones. 368p. 1991. pap. 7.95 (*1-882626-02-8*) Impress Ink.

An Asterisk (*) at the beginning of an entry indicates that the title is appearing in BIP for the first time.

Woman to Woman. large type ed. Eugenia Price. (Large Print Inspirational Ser.). 396p. 1986. pap. 16.95 (*0-8027-2562-7*) Walker & Co.

***Woman to Woman: A Leading Gynecologist Tells You All You Need to Know About Your Body and Your Health.** Yvonne S. Thornton. LC 97-23547. 1997. pap. 24.95 (*0-525-94297-1*) NAL-Dutton.

Woman to Woman: An Anthology of Women's Spiritualities. Phillis Zagano. 127p. (Orig.). 1993. pap. text ed. 8.95 (*0-8146-5025-2*, M Glazier) Liturgical Pr.

Woman to Woman: Entrepreneurial Advice for All Week Long from Ash to Zunkel. Ed. by Sara S. Rau. (Illus.). 55p. (Orig.). 1992. pap. 8.95 (*0-9633089-0-4*) Phillippe-Fenton.

Woman to Woman: From Sabotage to Support. Judith Briles. 1989. 21.95 (*0-88282-032-X*); pap. 15.95 (*0-88282-058-3*) New Horizon NJ.

Woman to Woman: Street Smarts for Women Entrepreneurs. Geraldine A. Larkin. LC 93-4260. 1993. 14.95 (*0-13-706658-9*) P-H.

Woman to Woman Golf Instructions. Candy L. Adams. (Illus.). 168p. (Orig.). 1991. 24.95 (*0-937408-93-X*) GMI Pubns Inc.

Woman Trap. Enki Bilal. Ed. by Bernd Metz. Tr. by Tom Leighton from FRE. (Illus.). 64p. (Orig.). 1988. pap. 12. 95 (*0-87416-050-2*) Catalan Communs.

Woman Traveler: How to Get over the Economic Hurdles along the Way. Blanche Fitzpatrick. LC 90-91894. (Illus.). 103p. (Orig.). 1990. 23.95 (*0-9627397-0-7*); pap. 9.95 (*0-9627397-1-5*) Pemberton Pubs.

***Woman Turning in the Flame.** unabridged ed. Janice De Ruiter. 30p. (Orig.). 1996. pap. 6.95 (*1-889272-01-9*, JDR-086) Navarro Publns.

Woman Unafraid: The Achievements of Frances Perkins. Penny Colman. LC 92-46524. (Illus.). 128p. (J). (gr. 5-9). 1993. lib. bdg. 14.95 (*0-689-31853-7*, Atheneum Bks Young) S&S Childrens.

Woman under Monasticism. Lina Eckenstein. 1972. 59.95 (*0-8490-1318-6*) Gordon Pr.

Woman under the English Law: From the Landing of the Saxons to the Present Time. Arthur R. Cleveland. (Illus.). xvi, 315p. 1987. reprint ed. lib. bdg. 32.50 (*0-8377-2012-5*) Rothman.

Woman under the Surface: Poems & Prose Poems. Alicia S. Ostriker. LC 81-47938. (Contemporary Poets Ser.). 77p. 1982. pap. 10.95 (*0-691-01390-X*) Princeton U Pr.

Woman Ventures. David G. Phillips. LC 78-104543. (Illus.). 337p. reprint ed. lib. bdg. 27.50 (*0-8398-1569-7*) Irvington.

Woman Ventures. David G. Phillips. (Illus.). 337p. (C). 1986. reprint ed. pap. text ed. 6.95 (*0-8290-1958-8*) Irvington.

Woman Ventures. David G. Phillips. (American Author Ser.). 1981. reprint ed. lib. bdg. 49.00 (*0-686-71947-6*) Scholarly.

Woman Version: Theoretical Approaches to West Indian Fiction by Women. Ed. by Evelyn O'Callaghan. LC 93-14204. (Warwick University Caribbean Studies). 1993. text ed. 49.95 (*0-312-10218-6*) St Martin.

Woman, Violence, & the Bible. Marla J. Selvidge. LC 96-23247. (Studies in Women & Religion: Vol. 37). 156p. 1996. text ed. 69.95 (*0-7734-8766-2*) E Mellen.

Woman Wanders Through Life & Science. Irena Koprowska. LC 96-18625. (SUNY Series in the Voices of Immigrant Women). 306p. 1997. 27.50 (*0-7914-3177-0*) State U NY Pr.

Woman Wanders Through Life & Science. Irena Koprowska. LC 96-18625. (SUNY Series in the Voices of Immigrant Women). 306p. 1998. pap. text ed. 19.95 (*0-7914-3178-9*) State U NY Pr.

Woman Warrior. Maxine H. Kingston. 1976. 24.95 (*0-394-40067-4*) Knopf.

Woman Warrior. Maxine H. Kingston. (International Ser.). 224p. 1989. pap. 11.00 (*0-679-72188-6*, Vin) Random.

Woman Who Changed & Other Stories. Pearl S. Buck. 19. 95 (*0-8488-0436-8*) Amereon Ltd.

Woman Who Couldn't Be Stopped. S. Delphine Wedmore. LC 86-61680. (Illus.). 515p. (Orig.). 1986. pap. 7.00 (*0-9616887-0-X*) Sisters Christ Charity.

Woman Who Did. Grant Allen. Ed. by Sarah Wintle & David Trotter. (Oxford Popular Fiction Ser.). 160p. 1995. pap. 8.95 (*0-19-282312-4*) OUP.

***Woman Who Died in Her Sleep.** Gregerson. 1997. pap. 13.00 (*0-395-82289-0*) HM.

Woman Who Died in Her Sleep. Linda Gregerson. 72p. 1996. 19.95 (*0-395-82290-4*) HM.

Woman Who Disappeared see Heinemann Guided Readers

Woman Who Drinks Too Much. Jean Kirkpatrick. 9p. 1976. pap. 2.00 (*0-318-19528-3*) WFS.

Woman Who Fell from Grace. large type ed. David Handler. LC 92-14132. (General Ser.). 1992. pap. 17.95 (*0-8161-5512-7*, GK Hall) Thorndike Pr.

Woman Who Fell from the Sky. Joy Harjo. LC 96-23014. 88p. 1996. pap. 10.00 (*0-393-31362-X*, Norton Paperbks) Norton.

Woman Who Fell from the Sky. Barbara Riefe. 384p. 1995. 5.99 (*0-8125-2377-6*) Forge NYC.

Woman Who Fell from the Sky: Poems. Joy Harjo. LC 96-23014. 1994. 21.00 (*0-393-03715-0*) Norton.

Woman Who Fell from the Sky: The Iroquois Story of Creation. Illus. by Robert A. Parker. LC 92-5591. 32p. (J). (gr. k up). 1993. 15.00 (*0-688-10680-3*, Morrow Junior); lib. bdg. 14.93 (*0-688-10681-1*, Morrow Junior) Morrow.

Woman Who Flummoxed the Fairies. Heather Forest. (Illus.). 32p. (J). (ps-3). 1990. 15.00 (*0-15-299150-6*) HarBrace.

Woman Who Flummoxed the Fairies. Heather Forest. LC 88-28448. (Illus.). 32p. (J). (ps-3). 1996. pap. 5.00 (*0-15-201275-3*) HarBrace.

Woman Who Found Her Voice: A Tale of Transforming. Susan Delattre & Susan O'Halloran. LC 95-48125. 160p. 1997. pap. 12.95 (*1-880913-18-6*) Innisfree Pr.

***Woman Who Gave Birth to Her Mother.** Kim Chernin. 224p. Date not set. 22.00 (*0-06-017196-0*) HarpC.

Woman Who Had Everything. Davidyne S. Mayleas. 1987. mass mkt. 4.50 (*0-380-75327-8*) Avon.

Woman Who Had Imagination & Other Stories. Herbert E. Bates. LC 77-103239. (Short Story Index Reprint Ser.). 1977. 20.95 (*0-8369-3276-5*) Ayer.

Woman Who Has Sprouted Wings: Poems by Contemporary Latin American Women Poets. 2nd ed. Ed. by Mary Crow. LC 88-2695. (Discoveries Ser.). 208p. (ENG & SPA.). 1988. pap. 13.95 (*0-935480-35-8*) Lat Am Lit Rev Pr.

Woman Who Knocked out Sugar Ray. Ralph Dranow. Ed. by Sandy Darlington & Julie Reynolds. LC 81-70081. (Illus.). 192p. (Orig.). (C). 1982. pap. 4.95 (*0-9604152-5-4*) Arrowhead Pr.

Woman Who Laughed. Mildred Cable & Francesca French. 1984. pap. 4.95 (*0-7208-0568-6*) OMF Bks.

Woman Who Lives in the Earth. Swain Wolfe. LC 95-36013. 192p. 1996. 18.00 (*0-06-017411-0*, HarpT) HarpC.

***Woman Who Lives in the Earth: A Novel.** Swain Wolfe. 192p. 1997. pap. 10.00 (*0-06-092792-5*, PL) HarpC.

Woman Who Lost Her Heart: A Tale of Reawakening. rev. ed. Susan O'Halloran & Susan Delattre. LC 92-8661. 160p. (Orig.). 1997. pap. 12.95 (*1-880913-27-5*) Innisfree Pr.

Woman Who Loved Airports: Stories & Narratives. Marusya Bociurkiw. 1994. pap. 12.95 (*0-88974-035-6*, Pub. by Press Gang CN) LPC InBook.

Woman Who Loved Worms & Other Poems. 2nd ed. Colette Inez. (Classic Contemporaries Ser.). 1992. reprint ed. pap. 12.95 (*0-88748-142-6*) Carnegie-Mellon.

Woman Who Married a Bear. John Straley. 240p. 1994. pap. 4.99 (*0-451-40421-1*, Sig) NAL-Dutton.

Woman Who Married a Bear: An Alaskan Mystery. John Straley. LC 91-46609. 240p. 1992. 19.95 (*0-939149-64-8*) Soho Press.

Woman Who Outshone the Sun. Cruz. (J). (gr. 4-7). 1994. pap. 6.95 (*0-89239-126-X*) Childrens Book Pr.

Woman Who Outshone the Sun: The Legend of Lucia Zenteno. Alejandro C. Martinez. LC 91-16646. (Illus.). 32p. (J). (gr. k-5). 14.95 (*0-89239-101-4*) Childrens Book Pr.

Woman Who Owned the Shadows. Paula G. Allen. LC 94-5839. 214p. (Orig.). 1983. pap. 10.95 (*1-879960-18-4*) Aunt Lute Bks.

Woman Who Ran for President: The Many Lives of Victoria Woodhull. Lois B. Underhill. LC 94-49519. (Illus.). 347p. 1995. 23.50 (*1-882593-10-3*) Bridge Wrks.

Woman Who Ran for President: The Many Lives of Victoria Woodhull. Lois B. Underhill. Tr. by Gloria Steinem. 368p. 1996. pap. 13.95 (*0-14-025638-5*, Penguin Bks) Viking Penguin.

Woman Who Read Novels & Peacetime. Constance Urdang. LC 90-2468. 177p. (Orig.). 1990. pap. 9.95 (*0-918273-81-1*) Coffee Hse.

***Woman Who Rides Like a Man.** Tamora Pierce. (Song of the Lioness Ser.). (YA). (gr. 5 up). 1997. pap. 4.99 (*0-614-28948-3*) Random Bks Yng Read.

Woman Who Rides Like a Man. Tamora Pierce. LC 85-20054. 256p. (J). (gr. 6 up). 1990. reprint ed. pap. 4.99 (*0-679-80112-X*) Knopf Bks Yng Read.

***Woman Who Rode Away.** D. H. Lawrence. 1997. pap. 12. 95 (*0-14-018806-1*) Viking Penguin.

Woman Who Rode Away & Other Stories. D. H. Lawrence. Ed. by Dieter Mehl & Christa Jansohn. (Cambridge Edition of the Works of D. H. Lawrence). 554p. (C). 1995. text ed. 95.00 (*0-521-22270-2*) Cambridge U Pr.

Woman Who Saved Things. Alexis Krasilovsky. 1995. 4.98 (*0-8317-4349-2*) Smithmark.

***Woman Who Spilled Words All over Herself: How to Write the Zona Rosa Way.** Rosemary Daniell. LC 96-43624. 1997. 24.95 (*0-571-19906-2*) Faber & Faber.

Woman Who Stole Everything & Other Stories. Arnold Bennett. LC 74-17057. (Collected Works of Arnold Bennett: Vol. 89). 1977. reprint ed. 30.95 (*0-518-19170-2*) Ayer.

Woman Who Toils. Bessie Van Vorst. 163p. 1974. reprint ed. 4.00 (*0-89215-000-9*) U Cal LA Indus Rel.

Woman Who Took Back Her Streets. Rita W. Smith & Tony Chapelle. LC 90-53581. 294p. 1990. 19.95 (*0-88282-065-6*) New Horizon NJ.

***Woman Who Tries to Believe.** Barbara Daniels. 29p. (Orig.). 1996. pap. 6.95 (*0-9636545-6-X*) Wind Pubns.

Woman Who Waits. Frances R. Donovan. LC 74-3941. (Women in America Ser.: From Colonial Times to the 20th Century). 228p. 1974. reprint ed. 20.95 (*0-405-06089-0*) Ayer.

Woman Who Walked into Doors. Roddy Doyle. 256p. 1996. pap. 22.95 (*0-670-86775-6*, Viking) Viking Penguin.

***Woman Who Walked into Doors.** Roddy Doyle. 240p. 1997. pap. 11.95 (*0-14-025512-5*) Viking Penguin.

***Woman Who Walked into Doors.** large type ed. Roddy Doyle. LC 96-21104. 1997. pap. 22.95 (*0-7862-0831-7*, Thorndike Lrg Prnt); pap. 22.95 (*0-614-25142-7*, GK Hall) Thorndike Pr.

Woman Who Walked into the Sea. Philip R. Craig. 224p. 1993. reprint ed. mass mkt. 4.99 (*0-380-71536-8*) Avon.

Woman Who Walked on Water. Lily Tuck. 256p. 1996. 21. 00 (*1-57322-021-3*, Riverhead Books) Putnam Pub Group.

***Woman Who Walked on Water.** Lily Tuck. 256p. 1997. reprint ed. pap. 11.00 (*1-57322-583-5*, Riverhd Trade) Berkley Pub.

Woman Who Was Wild: & Other Tales. Karla Andersdatter & C. E. Brookes. LC 94-28084. 161p. (Orig.). 1995. pap. 16.95 (*0-933029-76-4*) Chiron Pubns.

***Woman, Why Are You Weeping? A Lenten Companion for Women.** Therese J. Borchard. 1997. pap. text ed. 9.95 (*0-8245-1721-0*) Crossroad NY.

Woman, Why Do You Weep? Spirituality for Survivors of Childhood Sexual Abuse. Sandra M. Flaherty. LC 92-18229. 176p. 1992. pap. 10.95 (*0-8091-3331-8*) Paulist Pr.

Woman, Wife, Mother. rev. ed. Pat Harrison. 96p. 1991. pap. 5.99 (*0-89274-862-1*, HH-862) Harrison Hse.

Woman Will Overcome the Warrior: A Dialogue with the Christian - Feminist Theology of Rosemary Radford Ruether. Nicholas J. Ansell. 395p. (C). 1994. pap. text ed. 32.50 (*0-8191-9546-4*); lib. bdg. 64.50 (*0-8191-9545-6*) U Pr of Amer.

Woman with a Past. Ella M. Patterson. 500p. write for info. (*1-884331-09-2*) Knowledge Concepts.

Woman with a Purpose: The Diaries of Elizabeth Smith, 1872-1884. Elizabeth Smith. Ed. by Veronica Strong-Boag. LC 81-113766. (Social History of Canada Ser.: No. 32). 344p. reprint ed. pap. 98.10 (*0-7837-4280-0*, 2043972) Bks Demand.

Woman with Guitar: Memphis Minnie's Blues. Paul Garon & Beth Garon. (Illus.). 370p. (Orig.). 1992. pap. 14.95 (*0-306-80460-3*) Da Capo.

Woman with Horns & Other Stories. Cecilia M. Brainard. 92p. (Orig.). (C). 1988. pap. 9.50 (*971-10-0323-6*, Pub. by New Day Pub PH) Cellar.

Woman with Red Hair. Sigrid Brunel. LC 90-24051. 200p. (Orig.). 1991. pap. 8.95 (*0-934678-30-8*) New Victoria Pubs.

Woman with the Alabaster Jar: Mary Magdalen & the Holy Grail. Margaret Starbird. LC 92-39182. (Illus.). 240p. (Orig.). 1993. pap. 16.95 (*1-879181-03-7*) Bear & Co.

Woman with the Artistic Brush: A Life History of Yoruba Batik Artist Nike Davies. Kim M. Vaz. LC 94-22897. (Foremother Legacies: Autobiographies, & Memoirs of Women from Asia, Africa, the Middle East, & Latin America Ser.). (Illus.). 137p. (C). (gr. 13). 1995. 53.95 (*1-56324-506-X*, East Gate Bk) M E Sharpe.

Woman with the Artistic Brush: A Life History of Yoruba Batik Artist Nike Davies. Kim M. Vaz. LC 94-22897. (Foremother Legacies: Autobiographies, & Memoirs of Women from Asia, Africa, the Middle East, & Latin America Ser.). (Illus.). 192p. (C). 1995. pap. 17.95 (*1-56324-507-8*, East Gate Bk) M E Sharpe.

***Woman with the Flying Head & Other Stories.** Yumiko Kurahshi. Ed. & Tr. by Atsuko Sakaki. LC 97-19074. (Japanese Women Writers in Translation Ser.). 122p. (C). (gr. 13). 1997. text ed. 43.95 (*0-7656-0157-5*, East Gate Bk) M E Sharpe.

***Woman with the Flying Head & Other Stories.** Kurahashi Yumiko. Ed. & Tr. by Atsuko Sakaki. LC 97-19074. (Japanese Women Writers in Translation Ser.). 122p. (C). (gr. 13). 1997. pap. text ed. 19.95 (*0-7656-0158-3*) M E Sharpe.

Woman with Two Vaginas. Denise Duhamel. 96p. (Orig.). (C). 1995. pap. 10.00 (*0-9634000-6-1*) Salmon Run.

Woman Within. Ellen Glasgow. Ed. by Pamela R. Matthews. (C). 1994. pap. text ed. 16.95 (*0-8139-1563-5*) U Pr of Va.

Woman Within: Daily Devotions for Women in Recovery. Jan E. Meier et al. (Serenity Meditation Ser.). 372p. (Orig.). 1992. pap. 8.99 (*0-8407-3239-2*) Nelson.

***Woman Within the Web.** Cheryl Dolby. Ed. by Karen Henderson. (Illus.). 202p. (Orig.). 1996. pap. 24.95 incl. audio, audio compact disk (*0-9654898-2-5*) Earthlght Pr.

Woman Without a Man. Corinne Edwards. 160p. (Orig.). 1996. pap. 10.95 (*1-57789-000-0*) Crest Hse.

Woman Without a Name. Romulus Linney. 57p. 1986. pap. 5.25 (*0-8222-1269-2*) Dramatists Play.

Woman Without a Name. Emilie Richards. 1996. pap. 3.99 (*0-373-07751-3*, 1-07751-0) Silhouette.

Woman Without a Past. Phyllis A. Whitney. 1992. mass mkt. 5.99 (*0-449-22071-0*) Fawcett.

Woman Without a Past. large type ed. Phyllis A. Whitney. LC 93-36326. 1994. pap. 19.95 (*0-8161-5801-0*, GK Hall) Thorndike Pr.

Woman Without a Shadow. Karen Haber. 304p. (Orig.). 1995. mass mkt. 4.99 (*0-88677-627-9*) DAW Bks.

Woman Without a Shadow: Die Frau Ohne Schatten. Hugo Von Hofmannsthal. Tr. by Jean Hollander from GER. LC 93-14865. (Studies in the History & Interpretation of Music: Vol. 39). 116p. 1993. text ed. 59.95 (*0-7734-9282-8*) E Mellen.

Woman Without Eden (Mujer Sin Eden) Carmen Conde. Tr. by Jose R. De Armas et al. LC 85-80641. (Coleccion Alacran Azul). 175p. (Orig.). (SPA.). 1986. pap. 12.00 (*0-89729-375-4*) Ediciones.

Woman Without Experiences. Patricia Dienstfrey. Ed. by Denise Lawson & Rena Rosenwasser. LC 95-43687. 144p. (Orig.). (YA). (gr. 11-12). 1995. pap. text ed. 12. 00 (*0-932716-37-7*) Kelsey St Pr.

Woman Without Lies. Elizabeth Lowell. 384p. 1995. mass mkt. 5.99 (*0-380-76764-3*) Avon.

Woman Worth Following: Renewed Hope on the Road to Maturity. Eileen Wallis. 149p. (Orig.). 1991. pap. 6.95 (*0-939159-23-6*) Cityhill Pub.

Woman Wrapped in Silence. John W. Lynch. 288p. 1976. pap. 9.95 (*0-8091-1905-6*) Paulist Pr.

Woman Writer in Late Nineteenth-Century Italy: Gender & the Formation of Literary Identity. Lucienne Kroha. LC 92-12080. 180p. 1992. lib. bdg. 79.95 (*0-7734-9530-4*) E Mellen.

Woman Writes 1993-1994: Anthology of Southeastern Lesbian Writers Conference. Nancy E. Valmus. (Illus.). 230p. (Orig.). 1995. pap. 18.00 (*0-937025-05-4*) Shadowood Pubns.

Woman Writes 1995: Anthology of Southeastern Lesbian Writers Conference. Ed. by Rand Hall & Pamela Morse. (Illus.). 180p. (Orig.). 1996. pap. write for info. (*0-937025-06-2*) Shadowood Pubns.

***Woman Writes 1996: Anthology of Southeastern Lesbian Writer's Conference.** Ed. by Rand Hall. (Illus.). 180p. (Orig.). 1997. pap. 18.00 (*0-937025-07-0*) Shadowood Pubns.

***Woman Your Hour Is Sounding.** Goldberg. Date not set. text ed. write for info. (*0-312-17707-0*) St Martin.

Womancare: A Gynecological Guide to Your Body. Lynda Madaras & Jane Patterson. 960p. 1983. pap. 15.00 (*0-380-87643-4*) Avon.

WomanGifts: Biblical Models for Forming Church. Pamela Smith. LC 93-60404. (Illus.). 144p. (Orig.). 1994. pap. 9.95 (*0-89622-572-0*) Twenty-Third.

Womanguides: Readings Toward a Feminist Theology. Rosemary R. Ruether. 304p. 1996. reprint ed. pap. 15.00 (*0-8070-1235-1*) Beacon Pr.

Womanhealth. Elaine L. Willis. (Orig.). 1989. pap. write for info. (*0-318-64661-7*) Found Wellness.

WomanHood - A Journey Towards Love: Discover How You Can Become a Woman of Greatness in a World Where the Mold Is Broken. Debra Ann, pseud. 208p. (Orig.). 1994. pap. 11.95 (*0-9640854-0-2*) M J Beth.

Womanhood in Radical Protestantism: 1525-1675. Joyce L. Irwin. LC 79-66370. (Studies in Women & Religion: Vol. 1). 264p. 1979. lib. bdg. 89.95 (*0-88946-547-9*) E Mellen.

Womanhood Media Supplement: Additional Current Resources About Women. Helen R. Wheeler. LC 72-7396. 489p. 1975. 35.00 (*0-8108-0858-7*) Scarecrow.

Womanhood the Feminine in Ancient Hellenism Gnosticism Christianity & Islam. Mortley. 1981. 25.00 (*0-85668-912-2*, Pub. by Aris & Phillips UK); pap. 18.50 (*0-85668-913-0*, Pub. by Aris & Phillips UK) David Brown.

Womaning: Overcoming Male Dominance of Executive Row. Dean B. Peskin. Ed. by Sylvia Ashton. LC 80-13060. 1981. 22.95 (*0-87949-165-5*) Ashley Bks.

***Womanism: And African Consciousness.** Mary E. Kolawole. LC 97-3478. 275p. 1996. 69.95 (*0-86543-540-5*); pap. 19.95 (*0-86543-541-3*) Africa World.

Womanist & Feminist Aesthetics: A Comparative Review. Tuzyline J. Allan. 175p. (C). 1995. text ed. 34.95 (*0-8214-1109-8*) Ohio U Pr.

Womanist & Feminist Aesthetics: A Comparative Review. Tuzyline J. Allan. LC 94-45726. 162p. (C). 1996. reprint ed. pap. text ed. 16.95 (*0-8214-1152-7*) Ohio U Pr.

Womanist Justice, Womanist Hope. Emilie M. Townes. LC 92-45204. (American Academy of Religion Academy Ser.: No. 79). 240p. 1993. 29.95 (*1-55540-682-3*, 01 01 79); pap. 19.95 (*1-55540-683-1*, 01 01 79) Scholars Pr GA.

Womanist Rumblings, Vol. 1: A Place to Record Your Story. Linda H. Hollies. 448p. 1991. pap. 19.95 (*1-880299-01-1*) Woman to Woman.

WomanistCare, Vol. 1: How to Tend the Souls of Women. Ed. by Linda H. Hollies. 200p. (C). 1992. text ed. 14.99 (*1-880299-00-3*) Woman to Woman.

***Womanizer.** Fred Beauford. 192p. (Orig.). 1997. mass mkt. 4.99 (*1-55197-695-1*, Pub. by Comnwlth Pub CN) Partners Pubs Grp.

Womanizing Nietzsche: Philosophy's Relation to "the Feminine" Kelly Oliver. 224p. (C). 1994. pap. 17.95 (*0-415-90682-2*, A9545) Routledge.

Womanizing Nietzsche: Philosophy's Relation to "the Feminine" Kelly Oliver. 224p. (C). (gr. 13). 1994. text ed. 62.95 (*0-415-90681-4*, A9541) Routledge.

Womankind. June Stephenson. LC 86-71940. 355p. (Orig.). 1988. pap. 14.00 (*0-941138-05-4*) Diemer-Smith.

Womankind. Caldwell Van Roden. 32p. (Orig.). 1988. spiral bd. 4.00 (*0-940844-63-X*) Wellspring.

Womankind: Beyond the Stereotypes. 2nd ed. Nancy Reeves. LC 81-71348. 199p. 1982. pap. text ed. 22.95 (*0-202-30300-4*); lib. bdg. 43.95 (*0-202-30299-7*) Aldine de Gruyter.

Womankind: The Poetry of Women. Ed. by Carole J. Heffley. 192p. (Orig.). 1995. pap. 16.25 (*1-883331-14-5*) Anderie Poetry.

Womankind in Western Europe. Thomas Wright. LC 87-23497. 1987. 60.00 (*0-8201-1425-1*) Schol Facsimiles.

Womanly Art of Breastfeeding. La Leche League International Staff. 1991. pap. 9.95 (*0-452-26726-9*, Plume) NAL-Dutton.

***Womanly Art of Breastfeeding.** La Leche League International Staff. 1997. pap. 14.95 (*0-452-27908-9*, Plume) NAL-Dutton.

Womanly Art of Breastfeeding. Leche League International Staff. LC 83-61753. (Illus.). 384p. 1983. pap. 8.95 (*0-452-26212-7*, Plume) NAL-Dutton.

Womanly Art of Breastfeeding. 4th rev. ed. La Leche League International Staff. LC 87-15535. (Illus.). 384p. 1983. pap. 8.95 (*0-452-26000-0*, Plume) NAL-Dutton.

Womanly Art of Breastfeeding: Thirty-Fifth Anniversary Edition. La Leche League International Staff. (Illus.). 480p. 1991. reprint ed. pap. 13.95 (*0-452-26623-8*, Plume) NAL-Dutton.

Womanly Art of Breastfeeding: 35th Anniversary Edition. rev. ed. Ed. by Judy Torgus. LC 91-61539. 447p. 1991. pap. 10.95 (*0-912500-25-5*) La Leche.

Womanpower: A Manual for Workshops in Personal Effectiveness. Laura G. Manis. LC 76-54156. 1977. pap. text ed. 6.75 (*0-910328-10-2*) Sulzburger & Graham Pub.

Womanpower: Changing Workplace Demographics. Uma Sekaran. Ed. by Frederick T. Leong. 312p. (C). 1991. 48.00 (*0-8039-4105-6*); pap. 22.95 (*0-8039-4106-4*) Sage.

W

Womanpower: The Arab Debate on Women at Work. Nadia Hijab. (Illus.). 200p. 1988. pap. text ed. 19.95 (*0-521-26992-X*) Cambridge U Pr.

***Womanpower: The Arab Debate on Women at Work.** Nadia Hijab. 176p. 1996. pap. 13.95 (*0-614-21398-3*, 1324) Kazi Pubns.

Womanpriest: A Personal Odyssey. enl. rev. ed. Alla R. Bozarth. LC 88-2755. 217p. 1988. reprint ed. pap. 11.95 (*0-931055-51-2*) Wisdom House.

Womanrise (Anthology) Rashidah Ismaili et al. Ed. by Louis R. Rivera. (Illus.). 128p. (Orig.). 1978. pap. 4.25 (*0-917886-05-4*) Shamal Bks.

Woman's ABCs of Life: From Women Who Learned the Hard Way. Beca L. Allen. 160p. (Orig.). 1994. pap. 6.95 (*0-915009-35-8*) World Leis Corp.

Woman's Best Friend. Barbara Cohen & Louise Taylor. 1996. 15.95 (*0-614-96842-9*); 15.95 (*0-614-96965-4*) Little.

Woman's Best Friend: A Celebration of Dogs & Their Women. Barbara Cohen. 1996. 16.95 (*0-316-15054-1*) Little.

Woman's Best Medicine: Health, Happiness, & Long Life Through Ayur-Veda. Nancy Lonsdorf et al. LC 94-8619. 1995. 14.95 (*0-87477-785-2*, Tarcher Putnam) Putnam Pub Group.

Woman's Bible. Elizabeth C. Stanton. 187p. 1985. pap. 18.95 (*0-904919-96-X*) Dufour.

Woman's Bible, 2 Vols. Elizabeth C. Stanton. LC 72-2626. (American Women Ser.: Images & Realities). 380p. 1979. reprint ed. 47.97 (*0-405-04481-X*) Ayer.

Woman's Bible. Elizabeth C. Stanton. 1974. reprint ed. 12.95 (*0-9603042-1-5*) Coalition Women-Relig.

Woman's Bible. Elizabeth C. Stanton. 416p. 1993. reprint ed. pap. text ed. 15.95 (*1-55553-162-8*) NE U Pr.

Woman's Birthday Wish. Jerry King. 1994. pap. 5.95 (*0-88032-445-7*) Ivory Tower Pub.

Woman's Body. Ed. by Miriam Stoppard. LC 94-6290. (Illus.). 224p. 1994. 29.95 (*1-56458-617-0*) DK Pub Inc.

Woman's Body, Woman's Right: Birth Control in America. Linda Gordon. 1977. pap. 9.95 (*0-14-004683-6*, Penguin Bks) Viking Penguin.

Woman's Body, Woman's Word: Gender & Discourse in Arabo-Islamic Writing. Fedwa Malti-Douglas. 213p. 1992. text ed. 42.50 (*0-691-06856-9*); pap. text ed. 13.95 (*0-691-01488-4*) Princeton U Pr.

Woman's Book of Choices: Abortion, Menstrual Extraction, RU-486. Rebecca Chalker & Carol Downer. LC 92-13956. (Illus.). 192p. (Orig.). 1992. pap. 13.95 (*1-888363-28-2*) Seven Stories.

***Woman's Book of Confidence: Meditations for Strength & Inspiration.** rev. ed. Sue P. Thoele. 288p. 1997. reprint ed. pap. 10.95 (*1-57324-063-X*) Conari Press.

Woman's Book of Confidence: Meditations for Trusting & Accepting Ourselves. Sue P. Thoele. (Illus.). 288p. (Orig.). (C). 1993. reprint ed. lib. bdg. 29.00 (*0-8095-5870-X*) Borgo Pr.

Woman's Book of Courage: Meditations for Empowerment & Peace of Mind. 2nd rev. ed. Sue P. Thoele. 288p. (Orig.). 1996. reprint ed. pap. 9.95 (*1-57324-062-1*) Borgo Pr.

Woman's Book of Courage: Meditations for Empowerment & Peace of Mind. Sue P. Thoele. 288p. (Orig.). 1991. reprint ed. lib. bdg. 29.00 (*0-8095-5857-2*) Borgo Pr.

Woman's Book of Creativity. C. Diane Ealy. LC 94-44137. (Business of Life Ser.). 250p. (Orig.). 1995. pap. 12.95 (*1-885223-06-4*) Beyond Words Pub.

Woman's Book of Days. Thomas Nelson Publishers Staff. 1996. 17.99 (*0-7852-7963-6*) Nelson.

Woman's Book of Days. Beverly Wettenstein. (Illus.). 160p. 1994. 20.00 (*0-517-59700-4*) Crown Pub Group.

***Woman's Book of Faith: 2000 Years of Inspirational Writings by & for Women.** M. Shawn McGarry. 1997. 15.95 (*1-55972-435-8*, Birch Ln Pr) Carol Pub Group.

Woman's Book of Life: The Biology, Psychology & Spirituality of the Feminine Life Cycle. Joan Borysenko. LC 96-38374. 304p. 1996. 24.95 (*1-57322-043-4*, Riverhead Books) Putnam Pub Group.

Woman's Book of Movie Quotes. Compiled by Jeff Bloch. (Illus.). 240p. 1995. pap. 9.95 (*0-8065-1629-1*, Citadel Pr) Carol Pub Group.

***Woman's Book of Power.** Karen Andes. LC 97-23333. 256p. 1998. pap. write for info. (*0-399-52372-3*, Perigee Bks) Berkley Pub.

Woman's Book of Promise, Purpose, & Love. Melanie Crawford-Lloyd. 190p. (Orig.). 1996. pap. write for info. (*0-9652796-0-X*) Crawford-Lloyd.

Woman's Book of Rituals & Celebrations. Barbara Ardinger. LC 91-42162. 240p. 1992. 14.95 (*0-931432-90-1*) New Wrld Lib.

Woman's Book of Rituals & Celebrations. 2nd rev. ed. Barbara Ardinger. LC 91-42162. 240p. 1995. pap. 11.95 (*1-880032-57-0*) New Wrld Lib.

***Woman's Book of Spirit: Meditations for the Thirsty Soul.** Sue P. Thoele. LC 97-3912. 288p. (Orig.). 1997. pap. 10.95 (*1-57324-056-7*) Conari Press.

Woman's Book of Strength. Karen Andes. LC 94-29498. 288p. (Orig.). 1995. pap. 12.00 (*0-399-51899-1*, Perigee Bks) Berkley Pub.

Woman's Book of Yoga: A Journal for Self-Discovery. Louise Taylor. (Illus.). 208p. (Orig.). 1993. pap. 16.95 (*0-8048-1829-0*) C E Tuttle.

***Woman's Book of Zen.** Illus. & Photos by Lesley Ehlers. (Pocket Gift Editions Ser.). 64p. 1997. 4.95 (*0-88088-064-3*) Peter Pauper.

Woman's Cause: The Jewish Woman's Movement in England and the United States, 1881-1933. Linda G. Kuzmack. (Illus.). 300p. 1990. 50.00 (*0-8142-0515-1*); pap. 21.95 (*0-8142-0529-1*) Ohio St U Pr.

Woman's Christmas: Returning to the Gentle Joys ofthe Season. Hearst Books Staff & Arlene H. Stewart. LC 95-7503. 144p. 1995. 18.95 (*0-688-11663-9*) Hearst Bks.

Woman's Civil War: A Diary with Reminiscences of the War, from March 1862. Cornelia P. McDonald. Ed. by Minrose C. Gwin. LC 91-32345. (Studies in American Autobiography). (Illus.). 314p. (Orig.). (C). 1992. pap. 14.95 (*0-299-13264-1*) U of Wis Pr.

Woman's Comfort Book: A Self-Nurturing Guide for Restoring Balance in Your Life. Jennifer Louden. LC 91-55316. 224p. 1992. pap. 16.00 (*0-06-250531-9*) Harper SF.

***Woman's Conversations with God: Finding Majesty in the Mundane.** Loretta Jenkins. (Illus.). 83p. (Orig.). (C). 1996. pap. write for info. (*0-944547-06-0*) Herit Hse Litho.

Woman's Counsel: A Legal Guide for Women. Gayle L. Niles & Douglas H. Snider. LC 84-11161. 240p. (Orig.). 1984. pap. 8.50 (*0-912869-04-6*) Arden Pr.

Woman's Crisis Handbook. Hartman. (C). 1998. pap. 22.00 (*0-395-70739-0*) HM.

Woman's Day Book of Antique Collectibles. Dorothy Jenkins. 240p. 1982. 12.95 (*0-8065-0814-0*, Citadel Pr) Carol Pub Group.

Woman's Day Book of Holiday Crafts: More Than 100 Festive Projects with Step-by-Step... Woman's Day Editors. (Illus.). 240p. 1996. pap. 24.95 (*0-670-86882-5*, Viking) Viking Penguin.

Woman's Day Book of Soft Toys & Dolls. Joan Russell. 1980. pap. 6.95 (*0-686-61050-4*, 25403, Fireside) S&S Trade.

Woman's Day Book of Weddings. Harvey Ardman. LC 82-4236. 1982. write for info. (*0-672-52729-4*) Macmillan.

***Woman's Day-by-Day Engagement Calendar 1998.** (Illus.). 112p. 1997. 14.95 (*0-7624-0063-3*) Running Pr.

Woman's Day Can't-Fail, Eat-All-Day Diet. Woman's Day Editors & Susan Duff. LC 84-2929. 218p. 1985. write for info. (*0-672-52812-6*) Macmillan.

Woman's Day Christmas Cross-Stitch. Lisbeth Perrone. LC 83-60328. (Illus.). 144p. 1983. write for info. (*0-02-496620-7*, Macmillan Coll) P-H.

Womans Day Cookbook. Woman's Day Editors. 1999. pap. 12.95 (*0-14-025154-5*, Arkana) Viking Penguin.

Woman's Day Cookbook: Great Recipes, Bright Ideas, & Healthy Choices for Today's Cook. Woman's Day Editors. Ed. by Kathy Farrell-Kingsley & Jane Chesnutt. (Illus.). 720p. 1995. pap. 24.95 (*0-670-85876-5*, Viking) Viking Penguin.

Woman's Day Crepes Cookbook. S. Schur. mass mkt. 5.95 (*0-449-90002-9*) Fawcett.

Woman's Day Dictionary of Furniture. Dina Von Zweck. 1983. pap. 4.95 (*0-8065-0842-6*, Citadel Pr) Carol Pub Group.

Woman's Day Dictionary of Glass. Dina Von Zweck. 1983. pap. 4.95 (*0-8065-0841-8*, Citadel Pr) Carol Pub Group.

Woman's Day Soft & Cuddly Toys. Robin Tarnoff. LC 85-50564. (Illus.). 168p. 1986. write for info. (*0-02-616170-2*) Macmillan.

Woman's Day Wooden Toys. Hamilton. 1987. 19.95 (*0-02-547650-5*) Macmillan.

Woman's Decision: Breast Care, Treatment, & Reconstruction. 2nd ed. Karen Berger & John Bostwick, III. LC 93-5544. (Illus.). 564p. 1994. pap. 18.50 (*0-942219-04-X*) Quality Med Pub.

***Womans Decision Breast Care.** Berger. Date not set. pap. write for info. (*0-312-18229-5*) St Martin.

Woman's Diary on the Barlow Road; The Final Segment of the Oregon Trail. Nancy Wilson. Ed. by Bert Webber. (Illus.). (Orig.). 1996. pap. 9.95 (*0-936738-05-7*) Webb Research.

Woman's Dictionary of Symbols & Sacred Objects. Barbara G. Walker. LC 88-45158. 576p. 1988. pap. 26.00 (*0-06-250923-3*, PL4296) Harper SF.

Woman's Dictionary of Symbols & Sacred Objects. Barbara G. Walker. 1995. 11.98 (*0-7858-0460-9*) Bk Sales Inc.

Woman's Dilemma. Alice B. Parsons. LC 74-3966. (Women in America Ser.). 320p. 1974. reprint ed. 28.95 (*0-405-06115-3*) Ayer.

Woman's Dilemma: Mercy Otis Warren & the American Revolution. Rosemarie Zagarri. Ed. by Alan M. Kraut & Jon L. Wakelyn. (American Biographical History Ser.). (Illus.). 144p. (C). 1995. pap. text ed. write for info. (*0-88295-924-7*) Harlan Davidson.

Woman's Dress for Success Book. John T. Molloy. (Illus.). 1987. pap. 11.99 (*0-446-38586-7*) Warner Bks.

Woman's Education Begins: The Rise of the Women's Colleges. Louise S. Boas. LC 74-165705. (American Education, Ser. No. 2). 1974. reprint ed. 20.95 (*0-405-03694-9*) Ayer.

Woman's Education in India. S. P. Agrawal & J. C. Aggarwal. (C). 1992. 33.00 (*81-7022-318-0*, Pub. by Concept II) S Asia.

Woman's Encyclopedia of Myths & Secrets. Barbara G. Walker. LC 83-47736. 1136p. (Orig.). 1983. pap. 30.00 (*0-06-250925-X*, CN 4066) Harper SF.

Woman's Encyclopedia of Natural Healing: The New Healing Techniques of over 100 Leading Alternative Practitioners. Gary Null. LC 96-28291. 480p. (Orig.). 1996. pap. 19.95 (*1-888363-35-5*) Seven Stories.

Woman's Evolution: From Matriarchal Clan to Patriarchal Family. Evelyn Reed. LC 74-26236. 491p. 1974. reprint ed. pap. 22.95 (*0-87348-422-3*); reprint ed. lib. bdg. 65.00 (*0-87348-421-5*) Pathfinder NY.

Woman's Experience of Sex: The Facts & Feelings of Female Sexuality at Every Stage of Life. Sheila Kitzinger. (Nonfiction Ser.). 320p. 1985. pap. 17.95 (*0-14-007447-3*, Penguin Bks) Viking Penguin.

Woman's Eye: A Large Print Anthology. large type ed. Intro. by Sara Paretsky. (General Ser.). 569p. 1992. lib. bdg. 21.95 (*0-8161-5457-0*, GK Hall) Thorndike Pr.

Woman's Eye: Twenty-One Stories. Intro. by Sara Paretsky. 464p. 1992. reprint ed. mass mkt. 6.99 (*0-440-21335-5*) Dell.

Woman's Face of Resistance. Marie-Therese Kerschbaumer & Lowell A. Bangerter. Tr. by Lowell A. Bangerter from GER. (Studies in Austrian Literature, Culture, & Thought). Orig. Title: Der Weibliche Name des Widerstands. 260p. (Orig.). 1996. pap. 19.95 (*1-57241-027-2*) Ariadne CA.

Woman's Fiction: A Guide to Novels by & about Women in America, 1820-70. 2nd ed. Nina Baym. LC 92-25929. 360p. (C). 1993. pap. text ed. 15.95 (*0-252-06285-X*) U of Ill Pr.

Woman's Friendship. Ada Cambridge. Ed. by Elizabeth Morrison. (Colonial Text Ser.). 314p. 1989. pap. 31.95 (*0-86840-163-3*, Pub. by New South Wales Univ Pr AT) Intl Spec Bk.

Woman's Gifts: Monuments to Womanhood, Book B. Annette Bradshaw et al. (Monuments to Womanhood Ser.). 48p. (Orig.). 1982. pap. 6.98 (*0-88290-204-0*, 2805) Horizon Utah.

Woman's Golf Game. Shirli Kaskie. (Illus.). 208p. 1983. reprint ed. pap. 12.95 (*0-8092-5756-4*) Contemp Bks.

Woman's Guide to a Simpler Life. Andrea Van Steenhouse. 240p. 1996. 21.00 (*0-517-70698-9*, Harmony) Crown Pub Group.

***Woman's Guide to a Simpler Life.** Andrea Van Steenhouse. LC 97-23755. 1997. pap. 14.00 (*0-609-80145-7*, Harmony) Crown Pub Group.

Woman's Guide to Autos. 2nd ed. Betty Ostrander. (Illus.). 85p. 1993. 59.00 (*1-56216-153-9*); pap. 29.00 (*1-56216-154-7*) Systems Co.

Woman's Guide to Autos: Basics, Operation, Safety & Maintenance. Betty Ostrander. (Illus.). 60p. 1991. 48.00 (*1-56216-015-X*); pap. 25.00 (*1-56216-016-8*) Systems Co.

Woman's Guide to Being a Man's Best Friend. Michael Levin. 96p. (Orig.). 1996. pap. 4.95 (*0-8362-2582-1*) Andrews & McMeel.

Woman's Guide to Better Golf. Peter R. McCleery & Judy Rankin. (Illus.). 208p. 1996. pap. 15.95 (*0-8092-3126-3*) Contemp Bks.

Woman's Guide to Breaking Bondages. Quin Sherrer & Ruthanne Garlock. 254p. 1994. pap. 9.99 (*0-89283-845-0*, Vine Bks) Servant.

Woman's Guide to Business & Social Success. rev. ed. Ruth Tolman. 1990. text ed. 45.95 (*0-87350-182-9*) Milady Pub.

Woman's Guide to Business Survival: Everything You Wanted to Know about the Male Dominated World of Business - but Weren't Allowed to Ask. A. R. Head & Elle Iterate. LC 93-78893. 100p. 1994. pap. 5.95 (*0-9637859-6-6*) Avia.

Woman's Guide to Care-Free Travel Abroad. Joanne Turpin. LC 89-51131. 248p. 1991. 17.95 (*0-913215-48-1*) Riverdale Co.

***Woman's Guide to Casino Gambling: Table Games.** Denise Richards. Ed. by Debby Frerichs. 140p. (Orig.). 1996. per. 19.95 (*1-890244-00-7*) D&D Pubns.

***Womans Guide to Cigar Smoking.** Kasper. Date not set. write for info. (*0-312-18230-9*) St Martin.

***Woman's Guide to Coping with Disability.** 2nd ed. Resources for Rehabilitation Organization. LC 96-51596. 1997. pap. 42.95 (*0-929718-19-4*) Resc Rehab.

Woman's Guide to Cycling. Susan Weaver. 256p. (Orig.). 1991. reprint ed. pap. 19.95 (*0-89815-400-6*) Ten Speed Pr.

***Woman's Guide to Depression: Esssential Facts & Up-to-the-Minute Information on Diagnosis, Treatment, & Recovery.** Jane S. Ferber & Suzanne LeVert. 1997. pap. 13.95 (*0-614-27355-2*) Hyperion.

***Woman's Guide to Divorce: A Practical Guide to Divorce & Domestic Relations Law for Women.** James A. Clark. 256p. (Orig.). 1997. pap. 19.95 (*1-880090-44-9*) Galde Pr.

***Woman's Guide to Finance.** 2nd ed. Ruth Sunderland. (Daily Express Guides Ser.). 1996. pap. 12.95 (*0-7494-2018-9*) Kogan Page Ltd.

Woman's Guide to Financial Peace of Mind. Ron Blue & Judy Blue. 1991. pap. 8.99 (*1-56179-053-2*) Focus Family.

Woman's Guide to Financial Peace of Mind. Ron Blue & Judy Blue. 1991. 13.99 (*1-56179-026-5*) Focus Family.

Woman's Guide to Financial Savvy. rev. ed. Judith Briles. 240p. 1982. pap. 6.95 (*0-312-88651-9*) St Martin.

Woman's Guide to Football - Written by a Woman. Pam Thomas. (Illus.). 35p. (Orig.). 1993. pap. 4.80 (*0-9639526-0-9*) P O Thomas.

Woman's Guide to Hysterectomy: Expectations & Options. Adelaide Haas & Susan L. Puretz. LC 94-30362. (Illus.). 300p. 1995. pap. 14.95 (*0-89087-743-2*) Celestial Arts.

***Woman's Guide to Investing: Straight Talk Guide with the Information & the Inspiration You Need.** Virginia B. Morris. 1997. pap. text ed. 14.95 (*0-9650932-0-4*) Lghtbulb Pr.

Woman's Guide to Keeping Promises: 52 Ways to Choose Happiness & Fulfillment. Judith Rolfs. LC 96-16867. 176p. 1996. pap. 9.99 (*0-8254-3627-3*) Kregel.

Woman's Guide to Making Therapy Work. Joan Shapiro & Margaret Grant. 256p. 1996. 19.95 (*1-55972-340-8*, Birch Ln Pr) Carol Pub Group.

Woman's Guide to Managing Men. Vicky Hibbert & Sue Baker. 144p. 1995. pap. 14.95 (*0-906097-19-3*) LPC InBook.

Woman's Guide to Martial Arts: How to Choose a Discipline & Get Started. Monica McCabe-Cardoza. 1996. 19.95 (*0-87951-670-4*) Overlook Pr.

Woman's Guide to Men & Sex. Andrew Stanway. (Illus.). 1988. 17.95 (*0-88184-440-3*) Carroll & Graf.

Woman's Guide to Men & Sex. Andrew Stanway. (Illus.). 240p. 1991. pap. 11.95 (*0-88184-706-2*) Carroll & Graf.

Woman's Guide to Mental Health. Beryl W. Langley & E. Joyce Stapp. 144p. (Orig.). 1990. pap. 7.95 (*0-929162-23-4*) PIA Pr.

Woman's Guide to Military Service. 2nd ed. Texe W. Marrs & Karen Read. 176p. 1987. pap. 8.95 (*0-89709-152-3*) Liberty Pub.

Woman's Guide to Online Services. Judith Broadhurst. 304p. 1995. pap. text ed. 19.95 (*0-07-024168-6*) McGraw.

***Woman's Guide to Overcoming Sexual Fear & Pain.** Aurelie J. Goodwin & Marc E. Agronin. (Illus.). 176p. (Orig.). 1997. pap. 14.95 (*1-57224-089-X*) New Harbinger.

***Woman's Guide to Peak Performance.** Susan Puretz. 1998. pap. text ed. 19.95 (*0-89087-841-2*) Celestial Arts.

Woman's Guide to Prime Time Dating: For the Woman Who Wasn't Born Yesterday. Gloria B. Goodman. 1990. pap. 9.95 (*0-8184-0531-7*) Carol Pub Group.

***Woman's Guide to Savvy Investing: Everything You Need to Know to Protect Your Future.** Marsha Bertrand. LC 97-21282. 224p. 1997. 24.95 (*0-8144-0381-6*) AMACOM.

Woman's Guide to Self Defense. Vic Shayne. 116p. (Orig.). 1993. pap. 12.95 (*0-9637641-7-9*) Consumer Press.

Woman's Guide to Sexual Health. Sue DeCotiis. 304p. (Orig.). 1989. mass mkt. 5.50 (*0-671-66011-X*) PB.

Woman's Guide to Spirit-Filled Living. Quin Sherrer & Ruthanne Garlock. 245p. (Orig.). 1996. pap. 10.99 (*0-89283-934-1*, Vine Bks) Servant.

Woman's Guide to Spiritual Power: Through Scriptural Prayer. Nancy L. Dorner. 208p. 1992. pap. 9.95 (*0-914984-47-0*) Starburst.

Woman's Guide to Spiritual Renewal. Nelly Kaufer & Carol Osmer-Newhouse. LC 93-37438. 160p. 1994. pap. 17.00 (*0-06-250882-2*) Harper SF.

Woman's Guide to Spiritual Warfare. Ruthanne Garlock & Quin Sherrer. 230p. (Orig.). 1991. pap. 9.99 (*0-89283-714-4*, Vine Bks) Servant.

Woman's Guide to Starting a Business. 3rd ed. Claudia Jessup & Genie Chipps. 1991. pap. 16.00 (*0-8050-1140-4*, Owl) H Holt & Co.

Woman's Guide to Starting Her Own Business: How to Turn Talent into Profit. Cynthia S. Smith. LC 94-20354. 1994. pap. 8.95 (*0-8065-1568-6*, Citadel Pr) Carol Pub Group.

Woman's Guide to Staying Safe. Cheryl Reimold. write for info. (*0-318-58788-2*) S&S Trade.

***Woman's Guide to Tantra Yoga.** 2nd ed. Vimala McClure. LC 96-54836. Orig. Title: Some Still Want the Moon: A Woman's Guide to Tantra Yoga. (Illus.). 240p. 1997. pap. 14.00 (*1-57731-017-9*) New Wrld Lib.

Woman's Guide to the Bible. Lynne Bundesen. LC 93-28579. 192p. 1993. 18.95 (*0-8245-1373-8*) Crossroad NY.

***Woman's Guide to the Catechism of the Catholic Church.** Susan A. Muto & Adrian Van Kaam. LC 97-8595. 1997. pap. 10.99 (*1-56955-004-2*) Servant.

Woman's Guide to the Language of Success: Communicating with Confidence & Power. Ed. by Phyllis Mindell. 1995. text ed. 27.95 (*0-13-157207-5*) P-H.

Woman's Guide to Vitamins & Minerals. Sherry W. Sultenfuss. 288p. 1995. 16.95 (*0-8092-3509-9*) Contemp Bks.

Woman's Guide to War in the Heavenlies & Peace in Your Life. Coral Kennedy. Ed. by Margaret J. Kinney. (Illus.). 176p. (Orig.). 1991. pap. 9.95 (*1-880563-00-2*) FAME Pub.

Woman's Guide to Yeast Infections. Naomi Bumslag & Dia L. Michels. Ed. by Claire Zion. 288p. (Orig.). 1992. mass mkt. 5.99 (*0-671-74699-5*) PB.

Woman's Hand: Gender & Theory in Japanese Women's Writing. Ed. by Paul G. Schalow & Janet A. Walker. LC 96-12897. 1997. write for info. (*0-8047-2722-8*); pap. write for info. (*0-8047-2723-6*) Stanford U Pr.

***Woman's Hands-On Guide to Home Repair.** Lyn Herrick. LC 97-9549. (Illus.). 208p. (Orig.). 1997. pap. 19.95 (*0-88266-973-7*) Storey Comm Inc.

Woman's Healing Song: Prayers of Consolation. Kerrie Hide. LC 92-60759. 88p. (Orig.). 1993. pap. 7.95 (*0-89622-535-6*) Twenty-Third.

***Woman's Heart.** Rosalyn West. 1997. mass mkt. 5.99 (*0-380-78512-9*) Avon.

Woman's Heart Book: The Complete Guide to Keeping Your Heart Healthy & What to Do If Things Go Wrong. Charlotte Libov. (Illus.). 384p. 1994. pap. 11.95 (*0-452-27212-2*) NAL-Dutton.

Woman's Heritage Scrapbook. Susannah Hay. (Illus.). 128p. (Orig.). 1992. pap. 9.95 (*0-9624836-8-0*) Caillech Pr.

Woman's History of the World. Marilyn French. pap. write for info. (*0-679-44728-8*) Random.

Woman's HIV Sourcebook: A Guide to Better Health & Well-Being. Patricia Kloser & Jane M. Craig. 176p. 1994. pap. 12.95 (*0-87833-867-5*) Taylor Pub.

Woman's Hour Book of Humour. Ed. by Sally Feldman. 256p. (Orig.). 1994. pap. 9.95 (*0-563-36355-X*, BBC-Parkwest) Parkwest Pubns.

Woman's Hour Book of Short Stories. Intro. by Pat McLoughlin. 256p. 1991. pap. 7.95 (*0-563-20905-4*, BBC-Parkwest) Parkwest Pubns.

Woman's Hour Book of Short Stories 2. Ed. by Pat McLoughlin. 282p. (Orig.). 1993. pap. 9.95 (*0-563-36389-4*, BBC-Parkwest) Parkwest Pubns.

***Woman's I Ching: A New Version of the Book of Changes.** Diane Stein. LC 97-9450. 256p. 1997. pap. 16.95 (*0-89594-857-5*) Crossing Pr.

Woman's Identity. Ruth T. Barnhouse. LC 93-91042. Orig. Title: Identity. 150p. 1994. reprint ed. pap. 13.95 (*0-9638398-3-7*) Bonne Chance.

Woman's Issue: The Politics of Family Law Reform in England. Dorothy M. Stetson. LC 81-13465. (Contributions in Women's Studies: No. 34). xiii, 278p. 1982. text ed. 55.00 (*0-313-23087-0*, SWI/, Greenwood Pr) Greenwood.

An Asterisk (*) at the beginning of an entry indicates that the title is appearing in BIP for the first time.

Woman's Journal. Sandy L. Clough. (Illus.). 96p. 1994. pap. 14.95 (*0-9613287-5-4*) Strawberry GA.
Woman's Journal. Illus. by Michel Design. LC 90-61141. 96p. 1990. 9.95 (*0-88088-707-9*) Peter Pauper.
Woman's Journal: A Blank Book with Quotes by Women. Running Press Staff. (Illus.). 192p. 1985. 14.95 (*0-89471-406-6*) Running Pr.
Woman's Journey. Marjorie Michael & Virginia Baron. 30p. 1992. pap. 12.95 (*0-9634822-0-3*) MTwo Media.
Woman's Journey. Cindy Ross. Orig. Title: A Woman's Journey on the Appalachian Trail. (Illus.). 128p. 1996. reprint ed. pap. 9.95 (*0-917953-42-8*) Appalachian Trail.
Woman's Journey on the Appalachian Trail see Woman's Journey
***Woman's Journey Toward Holiness: A Daily Guide for Prayer & Godly Living.** Sheila Cragg. LC 97-8087. 272p. 1997. 11.99 (*0-89107-960-2*) Crossway Bks.
Woman's Kingdom & Other Stories. Anton Chekhov. Ed. & Tr. by Ronald Hingley. (World's Classics Ser.). 304p. 1989. pap. 5.95 (*0-19-282209-8*) OUP.
Woman's Legacy: Essays on Race, Sex, & Class in American History. Bettina Aptheker. LC 81-23137. 192p. 1982. pap. 13.95 (*0-87023-365-3*) U of Mass Pr.
Woman's Life. Guy De Maupassant. Tr. by H. N. Sloman. (Classics Ser.). 208p. 1978. pap. 9.95 (*0-14-044161-1*, Penguin Classics) Viking Penguin.
Woman's Life: Poems. Tarnie G. Tarry. Ed. by Vivian W. Owens. LC 92-73184. (Illus.). 120p. (Orig.). 1992. 16.95 (*0-9623839-2-9*) Eschar Pubns.
Woman's Life: The Story of an Ordinary American & Her Extraordinary Generation. Susan Cheever. 1995. pap. 10.00 (*0-688-14348-2*) Hearst Bks.
Woman's Life in Colonial Days. Carl Holliday. 319p. 1968. reprint ed. 26.95 (*0-87928-003-4*) Corner Hse.
Woman's Life in Colonial Days. Carl Holliday. LC 89-62479. 319p. 1990. reprint ed. lib. bdg. 40.00 (*1-55888-832-2*) Omnigraphics Inc.
***Woman's Life in the Court of the Sun King: Letters of Liselotte von der Pfalz.** Elisabeth Charlotte. Tr. by Elborg Forster. (Illus.). 287p. 1997. reprint ed. pap. 16.95 (*0-8018-5635-3*) Johns Hopkins.
Woman's Life in the Court of the Sun King: Letters of Liselotte von der Pfalz, Elisabeth Charlotte, Duchesse d'Orleans, 1652-1722. Charlotte-Elisabeth Orleans. Tr. & Intro. by Elborg Forster. LC 84-5718. 349p. reprint ed. pap. 99.50 (*0-7837-3391-7*, 2043349) Bks Demand.
Woman's Life on a Southern Tobacco Farm: The Story of Sallie Mae Taylor, 1893-1977. Shirley A. Gandy. LC 93-27051. (Mellen Lives Ser.: Vol. 5). (Illus.). 252p. 1993. pap. 89.95 (*0-7734-9337-9*, Mellen Univ Pr) E Mellen.
Woman's Life-Work: Labors & Experiences. Laura S. Haviland. LC 77-89409. (Black Heritage Library Collection). 1977. 21.95 (*0-8369-8590-7*) Ayer.
Woman's Life-Work: Labors & Experiences of Laura S. Haviland. Laura S. Haviland. LC 78-82198. (Anti-Slavery Crusade in America Ser.). 1970. reprint ed. 41.95 (*0-405-00638-1*) Ayer.
Woman's Love. Padraig Standun. 238p. 1994. pap. 10.95 (*1-85371-346-5*, Pub. by Poolbeg Pr IE) Dufour.
Woman's Love: Monuments to Womanhood, Book C. Annette Bradshaw et al. (Monuments to Womanhood Ser.). 48p. (Orig.). 1982. pap. 6.98 (*0-88290-205-9*, 2806) Horizon Utah.
Woman's Love Life Opus 42: High Voice Piano. R. Schumann. 32p. (ENG & GER.). 1986. pap. 7.95 (*0-7935-4869-1*, 50258720) H Leonard.
Woman's Manual of Law. Mary A. Greene. xvi, 284p. 1986. reprint ed. lib. bdg. 27.50 (*0-8377-2208-X*) Rothman.
***Woman's Manual of Self Defense.** Paul Lockwood. Date not set. pap. 15.95 (*1-58006-029-3*, Appaloosa) Sovereign.
***Woman's Midlife Companion: The Essential Resource for Every Woman's Journey.** Naomi Lucks. LC 97-8883. 400p. 1997. per. 18.00 (*0-7615-1025-7*) Prima Pub.
Woman's Ministry: Mary Collson's Search for Reform As a Unitarian Minister, Hull House Social Worker, & a Christian Science Practitioner. Cynthia G. Tucker. (American Civilization Ser.). 222p. 1984. 29.95 (*0-87722-338-6*) Temple U Pr.
Woman's Ministry see Healer in Harm's Way: Mary Collson, a Clergywoman in Christian Science
Woman's Ministry Reconsidered: Insights & Applications. Ruth M. Armstrong. 1994. 13.95 (*0-533-11079-3*) Vantage.
Woman's Mourning Song. Bell Hooks. 160p. (Orig.). (C). 1992. 18.00 (*0-86316-317-3*); pap. 8.00 (*0-86316-318-1*) Writers & Readers.
Woman's Nature: Rationalizations of Inequality. Marian Lowe & Ruth Hubbard. (Athene Ser.). 140p. 1983. text ed. 50.00 (*0-08-030143-6*, Pergamon Pr); pap. text ed. 19.95 (*0-08-030142-8*, Pergamon Pr) Elsevier.
Woman's Nature: Rationalizations of Inequality. Marian Lowe & Ruth Hubbard. LC 83-4066. (Athene Ser.). (Illus.). 169p. 1983. reprint ed. pap. 48.20 (*0-7837-6797-8*, 2046629) Bks Demand.
***Woman's New Selling Game: How to Sell Yourself--& Anything Else.** Carole Hyatt. LC 97-25257. 1997. pap. text ed. 14.95 (*0-07-031828-X*) McGraw.
Woman's Notebook: Being a Blank Book with Quotes by Women. pap. 5.95 (*0-89471-095-8*) Running Pr.
Woman's Odyssey: Journals, 1976-1992. Linda Aaker. LC 94-16038. 293p. 1994. 22.50 (*0-929398-74-2*) UNTX Pr.
Woman's Odyssey into Africa: Tracks Across a Life. Hanny Lightfoot-Klein. LC 91-18809. (Women's Studies). 150p. 1992. pap. 17.95 (*1-56023-007-X*) Haworth Jrnl Co-Edits.
Woman's Odyssey into Africa: Tracks Across a Life. Hanny Lightfoot-Klein. LC 91-18809. (Women's Studies). 150p. 1992. 39.95 (*1-56024-155-1*) Haworth Jrnl Co-Edits.
Woman's Orgasm: A Guide to Sexual Satisfaction. Georgia Kline-Graber & Benjamin Graber. 240p. 1988. mass mkt. 5.99 (*0-446-31503-6*) Warner Bks.
Woman's Overland Journal to California. Mary R. Powers. (Illus.). 75p. 1985. reprint ed. 14.95 (*0-87770-349-3*) Ye Galleon.
Woman's Own Guide to Pregnancy & Childbirth. Teresa Barker. 64p. (Orig.). 1989. pap. 6.95 (*0-9626223-0-3*) Womens Hlthcare Pr.
Woman's Own Remedy Box: Natural Remedies for Self-Healing. Amy Conway. (Illus.). 84p. 1996. boxed 24.95 (*0-8048-3067-3*) C E Tuttle.
Woman's Part: Feminist Criticism of Shakespeare. Ed. by Carolyn R. Lenz et al. LC 79-26896. 360p. 1983. pap. text ed. 13.95 (*0-252-01016-7*) U of Ill Pr.
Woman's Place. Rex D. Borough. Ed. by Kathleen Herbison. 374p. 1992. text ed. 16.95 (*1-880988-00-3*) Amer W Bks.
***Woman's Place.** Barbara Delinsky. 416p. mass mkt. 6.99 (*0-06-109505-2*, Harp PBks) HarpC.
***Woman's Place.** Barbara Delinsky. LC 97-15358. (Wheeler Large Print Book Ser.). 1997. write for info. (*1-56895-446-8*) Wheeler Pub.
Woman's Place. Marita Golden. 240p. 1988. mass mkt. 5.99 (*0-345-34650-5*) Ballantine.
Woman's Place. Linda Grant. LC 93-39191. 1995. mass mkt. 5.50 (*0-8041-1327-0*) Ivy Books.
Woman's Place. Susan M. Mayer & Becky D. Reese. (Illus.). 20p. 1977. pap. 4.95 (*0-935213-05-8*) A M Huntington Art.
Woman's Place. Marjorie M. Mezvinsky. 1995. 3.99 (*0-517-15354-8*) Random Hse Value.
Woman's Place. Emma L. Thayne. (Illus.). 66p. 1977. pap. text ed. 3.00 (*0-9605652-0-5*) N Grey Inc.
Woman's Place. 2nd ed. Marian Sawer & Marian Simms. 52p. (Orig.). 1993. pap. text ed. 22.95 (*1-86373-169-5*, Pub. by Allen Unwin AT) Paul & Co Pubs.
Woman's Place: A Guide to Seattle & King County History. Mildred T. Andrews. LC 93-79116. (Illus.). 344p. (Orig.). 1994. pap. 14.95 (*0-9640239-0-3*) Gemil Pr.
***Woman's Place: A Novel.** Barbara Delinsky. 416p. 1997. 22.00 (*0-06-017506-0*) HarpC.
Woman's Place? Leadership in the Church. C. S. Cowles. 208p. (Orig.). 1993. pap. 11.99 (*0-8341-1464-X*, 65252) Beacon Hill.
Woman's Place: Options & Limits in Professional Careers. Cynthia F. Epstein. LC 75-98139. 1970. pap. 9.00 (*0-520-01870-2*) U CA Pr.
Woman's Place: Quotations about Women. Ed. by Anne Stibbs. 608p. (Orig.). 1993. pap. 12.50 (*0-380-71850-2*) Avon.
Woman's Place: The Life History of a Rural Ohio Grandmother. Rosemary O. Joyce. LC 83-13188. (Illus.). 308p. 1983. 40.00 (*0-8142-0344-2*) Ohio St U Pr.
Woman's Place? Women & Work. Elizabeth Templeton. 192p. 1993. pap. 26.00 (*0-86153-162-0*, Pub. by St Andrew UK) St Mut.
Woman's Place: Yesterday's Women Is Rural America. Norton Juster. (Illus.). 320p. (Orig.). 1996. pap. 20.95 (*1-55591-250-8*) Fulcrum Pub.
Woman's Place in Education: Historical & Sociological Perspectives on Gender & Education. Sara Delamont. (Cardiff Papers in Qualitative Research: Vol. 6). 224p. 1996. 59.95 (*1-85628-583-9*, Pub. by Avebury Pub UK) Ashgate Pub Co.
Woman's Place Is at the Typewriter: Office Work & Office Workers, 1870-1930. Margery W. Davies. (Class & Culture Ser.). 256p. 1984. reprint ed. pap. 18.95 (*0-87722-368-8*) Temple U Pr.
Woman's Place Is Everywhere: Inspirational Profiles of Female Leaders Who Are Shaping & Expanding the Role of Women in American Society Today. Jackie Joyner-Kersee & Lindsey Johnson. 1994. pap. 9.95 (*0-942361-97-0*) MasterMedia Pub.
Woman's Place Is in the House: Campaigning for Congress in the Feminist Era. Barbara C. Burell. (Orig.). 1995. pap. 19.95 (*0-472-08384-8*) U of Mich Pr.
Woman's Place Is on the Water: And How to Beat Men at Their Own Game. Marjorie B. Sandell. LC 92-61615. (Illus.). 256p. (Orig.). 1992. pap. 12.95 (*0-940107-06-6*) Muskie Mem Pr.
Woman's Power, Man's Game: Essays on Classical Antiquity in Honor of Joy K. King. Ed. by Mary DeForest. LC 93-17713. 458p. 1993. pap. 35.00 (*0-86516-258-1*) Bolchazy-Carducci.
***Woman's Prayer: Notes from a Focusing Journal.** Edwin M. McMahon & Peter A. Campbell. 16p. 1996. pap. text ed. 1.50 (*1-55612-512-7*, LL1512) Sheed & Ward MO.
Woman's Prayer Companion. Carmelite Sisters of Indianapolis Staff. 218p. 1993. pap. 13.95 (*1-886873-04-6*) Carmelites IN.
Woman's Quest. Marie E. Zakrzewska. (American Biography Ser.). 514p. 1991. reprint ed. lib. bdg. 99.00 (*0-7812-8436-8*) Rprt Serv.
Woman's Quest: The Life of Marie E. Zakrzewska, M. D. Ed. by Agnes C. Vietor. LC 72-2630. (American Women Ser.: Images & Realities). (Illus.). 522p. 1974. reprint ed. 33.95 (*0-405-04486-0*) Ayer.
Woman's Quest for Science: A Portrait of Anthropologist Elsie Clews Parsons. Peter H. Hare. LC 84-43055. (Illus.). 192p. 1985. 32.95 (*0-87975-274-2*) Prometheus Bks.
Woman's Quest for Self-Fulfillment. Lois K. Holland. 1983. pap. 3.50 (*0-917652-32-0*) Confluence Pr.
Woman's Quest for Spiritual Direction: The Correspondence of Princess Eulogia Choumnaina Palaiologina. Angela Hero. (Archbishop Iakovos Library of Ecclesiastical & Historical Sources: Vol. 11). 166p. 1986. 9.95 (*0-917653-08-4*); pap. 4.95 (*0-917653-09-2*) Hellenic Coll Pr.
Woman's Reason. William Dean Howells. (Notable American Authors Ser.). 1992. reprint ed. lib. bdg. 75.00 (*0-7812-3236-8*) Rprt Serv.
***Woman's Recipe for Life: A Nurturing Approach Throughout Womenhood from Adolescence to Aging.** Katy O. Arrowood. (Illus.). 205p. 1996. 21.95 (*0-9655351-0-X*) Lifetime Books.
***Woman's Recovery from the Trauma of War: Twelve Responses from Feminist Therapists & Activists.** Ed. by Esther D. Rothblum & Ellen Cole. 124p. 1986. 24.95 (*0-86656-561-2*) Haworth Pr.
***Woman's Retreat Book: A Guide to Restoring, Rediscovering & Reawakening Your True Self.** Jennifer Loudne. LC 97-4954. 1997. pap. text ed. 17.00 (*0-06-251466-0*) Harper SF.
Woman's Revenge: The Chronology of Dispossession in Maupassant's Fiction. Mary Donaldson-Evans. LC 86-80314. (French Forum Monographs: No. 64). 156p. 1986. pap. 12.95 (*0-917058-65-8*) French Forum.
***Woman's Right to Pornography.** Wendy McElroy. 1997. pap. 12.95 (*0-614-27687-X*, Griffin) St Martin.
Woman's Right, 1867 - Woman's Wrongs, a Counter-Irritant, 1868. John Todd & Mary A. Dodge. LC 72-2628. (American Women Ser.: Images & Realities). 246p. 1974. 18.95 (*0-405-04455-0*) Ayer.
Woman's Ritual Headwear (Romania) .Cella Neamtu. Tr. by Eugenia Popescu-Judetz from FRE. (Illus.). 110p. (Orig.). 1981. pap. 10.00 (*0-936922-03-6*) Tamburitza.
Woman's Role. R. K. Campbell. 32p. pap. 0.60 (*0-88172-014-3*) Believers Bkshelf.
Woman's Role Economic Development. Ester Boserup. 288p. 1988. 15.95 (*1-85383-040-2*, Pub. by Erthscan Pubns UK) Island Pr.
Woman's Share in Primitive Culture. Otis T. Mason. 1972. 250.00 (*0-87968-460-7*) Gordon Pr.
Woman's Share in Social Culture. Anna G. Spencer. LC 72-2623. (American Women Ser.: Images & Realities). 342p. 1974. reprint ed. 25.95 (*0-405-04479-8*) Ayer.
***Woman's Softball Book.** Connie P. Johnson & Margie Wright. LC 84-47522. (Illus.). 208p. 1984. reprint ed. pap. 59.30 (*0-608-04287-0*, 2065066) Bks Demand.
Woman's Spirit: More Meditations for Women. Hazelden Foundation Staff. LC 93-37647. 400p. 1994. pap. 14.00 (*0-06-255282-1*) Harper SF.
Woman's Spirit: More Meditations for Women by the Author of Each Day a New Beginning. 1994. pap. 11.00 (*0-89486-869-1*, 5433) Hazelden.
Woman's Spiritual Odyssey. Rose Anna, pseud. 144p. (Orig.). 1991. pap. 8.95 (*0-9630561-0-7*) Rose Pub AZ.
Woman's Story. Annie Ernaux. Tr. by Tanya Leslie. LC 91-137. 112p. 1991. 15.95 (*1-888363-29-0*) Seven Stories.
Woman's Story of Pioneer Illinois. Christina H. Tillson. Ed. by Milo M. Quaife. LC 94-33417. 1995. pap. 12.95 (*0-8093-1981-0*) S Ill U Pr.
Woman's Study. Lisa Lockwood. 119p. 1994. spiral bd. 15.00 (*0-9643021-8-7*) Reality Living.
Woman's Study. Lisa Lockwood & Cindy Madden. 128p. (C). 1996. student ed., text ed. 16.50 (*1-888220-00-7*) Reality Living.
Woman's Survival Booklet: Dealing with Men, Women, Children, Finances, Etc. Carmen B. Subryan. 71p. (Orig.). 1989. pap. 6.95 (*0-685-29014-X*) C Subryan.
Woman's Survival Guide. 192p. 1996. 24.95 (*0-7894-1081-8*) DK Pub Inc.
Woman's Theatrical Space. Hanna Scolnicov. LC 93-29417. (Illus.). 168p. (C). 1994. text ed. 52.95 (*0-521-39467-8*) Cambridge U Pr.
***Woman's Touch.** large type ed. Emma Stirling. (Large Print Ser.). 304p. 1997. 27.50 (*0-7089-3676-8*) Ulverscroft.
Woman's Transformations: A Psychological Theology. Jenny Hammett. LC 82-14287. (Symposium Ser.: Vol. 8). 112p. (C). 1982. lib. bdg. 69.95 (*0-88946-918-0*) E Mellen.
Woman's "True" Profession: Voices from the History of Teaching. Ed. by Nancy Hoffman. LC 80-23329. (Women's Lives - Women's Work Ser.). (Illus.). 352p. (Orig.). (YA). (gr. 11 up). 1981. pap. 12.95 (*0-912670-72-X*) Feminist Pr.
Woman's Unconscious Use of Her Body. Dinora Pines. 256p. 1994. 27.50 (*0-300-05960-4*) Yale U Pr.
Woman's Version of the Faust Legend: The Seven Strings of the Lyre. George Sand, pseud. Tr. & Intro. by George A. Kennedy. LC 88-33796. x, 186p. (C). 1989. text ed. 45.00 (*0-8078-1856-9*) U of NC Pr.
Woman's View: How Hollywood Spoke to Women, 1930-1960. Jeanine Basinger. LC 93-268. 1993. 32.50 (*0-394-56351-4*) Knopf.
Woman's View: How Hollywood Spoke to Women, 1930-1960. Jeanine Basinger. LC 95-17136. (Illus.). 542p. (C). 1995. pap. 18.95 (*0-8195-6291-2*, Wesleyan Univ Pr) U Pr of New Eng.
Woman's View of Yesterday's Women As Portrayed in the Bible. Mary K. Holder. (Illus.). 88p. 1995. pap. 9.00 (*0-8059-3664-5*) Dorrance.
Woman's Voice: Conversations with Australian Poets. Jenny Digby. 320p. 1996. pap. 29.95 (*0-7022-2732-3*, Pub. by Univ Queensland Pr AT) Intl Spec Bk.
Woman's Voice in Latin American Literature. Naomi Lindstrom. LC 86-51313. 200p. (Orig.). 1990. 26.00 (*0-89410-295-8*, Three Contnts); pap. 16.00 (*0-89410-296-6*, Three Contnts) Lynne Rienner.
Woman's Wage: Historical Meanings & Social Consequences. Alice Kessler-Harris. LC 89-48812. 184p. (C). 1990. 12.95 (*0-8131-0803-9*) U Pr of Ky.
Woman's Walden. Ruthe T. Spinnanger. LC 84-71120. 176p. 1985. pap. 6.95 (*0-88270-554-7*) Bridge-Logos.
***Woman's Walk.** Sherry Wells. Ed. by Rodney Charles. LC 97-65712. 300p. 1998. pap. 18.95 (*1-887472-20-7*) Sunstar Pubng.
Woman's Walk with God: A Daily Guide for Prayer & Spiritual Growth. Shelia Cragg. LC 95-46385. 256p. (Orig.). 1996. pap. 11.99 (*0-89107-875-4*) Crossway Bks.
Woman's War. Doris Harris. LC 89-36806. 1991. 13.95 (*0-87949-321-6*) Ashley Bks.
***Woman's War: Southern Women, Civil War, & the Confederate Legacy.** Ed. by Edward D. Campbell, Jr. & Kym S. Rice. LC 96-29648. (Illus.). 236p. (Orig.). 1997. pap. 24.95 (*0-8139-1739-5*) U Pr of Va.
Woman's War Too: U. S. Women in the Military in World War II. Ed. by Paula N. Poulos. LC 95-50372. 1996. write for info. (*1-880875-09-8*) National Archives & Recs.
Woman's Wartime Journal: An Account of Sherman's Devastation of a Southern Plantation. Dolly S. Lunt. LC 88-20209. 64p. 1990. reprint ed. pap. 5.95 (*0-87797-149-8*) Cherokee.
Woman's Way. Ed. by Henry Woodhead. LC 94-38432. (American Indians Ser.). (Illus.). 184p. 1995. lib. bdg. 17.99 (*0-8094-9730-1*) Time-Life.
Woman's Way. Ed. by Henry Woodhead. LC 94-43685. (American Indians Ser.: Vol. 17). (Illus.). 192p. 1995. 19.95 (*0-8094-9729-8*) Time-Life.
Woman's Way Through the Twelve Steps. Stephanie S. Covington. (Illus.). 288p. 1994. pap. 10.00 (*0-89486-993-0*) Hazelden.
Woman's Way Through Unknown Labrador: An Account of the Exploration of the Nascaupee & George Rivers. Mina B. Hubbard. (American Biography Ser.). 338p. 1991. reprint ed. lib. bdg. 79.00 (*0-7812-8204-7*) Rprt Serv.
Woman's Weapon: Spirit Possession in the Tale of Genji. Doris G. Bargen. LC 96-25663. 1997. text ed. 50.00 (*0-8248-1801-6*); pap. text ed. 24.95 (*0-8248-1858-X*) UH Pr.
Woman's Work. Peggy Ellsburg. 1996. write for info. (*0-201-40764-7*) Addison-Wesley.
Woman's Work: A Guide to Growth & Self-Discovery. Ed. by Anne Baxter & Nora O. Lozano-Diaz. LC 94-34353. 120p. (Orig.). 1994. pap. 8.99 (*0-8361-3695-0*) Herald Pr.
Woman's Work & Woman's Culture. Josephine Butler. 1972. 69.95 (*0-8490-1319-4*) Gordon Pr.
Woman's Work in America. Ed. by Annie N. Meyer. LC 72-2615. (American Women Ser.: Images & Realities). 462p. 1980. reprint ed. 26.95 (*0-405-04469-0*) Ayer.
Woman's Work in Municipalities. Mary R. Beard. LC 72-2588. (American Women Ser.). 1978. reprint ed. 23.95 (*0-405-04446-1*) Ayer.
Woman's Work in the Church. John M. Ludlow. LC 75-33300. 1976. reprint ed. 30.00 (*0-89201-007-X*) Zenger Pub.
Woman's Work, Man's Work (Mexico) Reading Level 2. (Fitting In Ser.). 1993. 2.95 (*0-88336-998-2*); audio 6.95 (*0-88336-773-4*) New Readers.
Woman's Workshop on Mastering Motherhood. Barbara Bush. (Women's Workshop Ser.). 176p. 1981. pap. 6.99 (*0-310-43031-3*, 12013P) Zondervan.
Woman's Workshop on Proverbs. Diane B. Bloem. 112p. 1978. student ed., pap. 5.99 (*0-310-21361-4*, 10683P) Zondervan.
Woman's Workshop on the Attributes of God: Behold Your God. Myrna Alexander. 124p. 1978. pap. 5.99 (*0-310-37131-7*, 10916P) Zondervan.
Woman's Workshop on the Fruit of the Spirit. Sandi Swanson. 160p. (Orig.). 1989. pap. 6.99 (*0-310-52241-2*) Zondervan.
Woman's World - Woman's Empire: The Woman's Christian Temperance Union in International Perspective, 1880-1930. Ian Tyrrell. LC 90-43246. (Illus.). xviii, 382p. (C). 1991. 55.00 (*0-8078-1950-6*) U of NC Pr.
Woman's Worth. Marianne Williamson. 160p. 1994. pap. 10.00 (*0-345-38657-4*) Ballantine.
Woman's Worth & Worthlessness. Mary A. Dodge. (Notable American Authors Ser.). 1992. reprint ed. lib. bdg. 90.00 (*0-7812-2660-0*) Rprt Serv.
Woman's Wrongs: A Counter-Irritant. Mary A. Dodge. (Notable American Authors Ser.). 1992. reprint ed. lib. bdg. 75.00 (*0-7812-2658-9*) Rprt Serv.
Womans Yellow Pages N West 91. Geha L. Sorger. 1991. pap. 5.95 (*0-925108-03-0*) WYP NW Washington.
Womans Yellow Pages 92. Geha L. Sorger. 1992. pap. 5.95 (*0-925108-04-9*) WYP NW Washington.
WomanSong Collection. Miriam T. Winter. Date not set. 19.95 (*0-8245-3005-5*) Crossroad NY.
Womansong Collection Piano Accompaniment with Vocal Harmonies. Miriam T. Winter. 1995. pap. 11.95 (*0-8245-3007-1*) Crossroad NY.
Womansong Collection Songbook. Miriam T. Winter. 1995. pap. 2.95 (*0-8245-3006-3*) Crossroad NY.
Womansource Catalog: Tools for Connecting the Community of Women. Ed. by Ilene Rosoff. 490p. 1995. pap. 19.95 (*0-89087-768-8*) Ten Speed Pr.
***Womansource Catalog & Review: Tools for Connecting the Community for Women.** Ilene Rosoff. 1997. pap. text ed. 22.95 (*0-89087-831-5*) Celestial Arts.
Womanspirit: Reclaiming the Deep Feminine in Our Human Spirituality. Susan A. Muto & Adrian Van Kaam. 180p. 1993. reprint ed. pap. 10.95 (*0-8245-1212-X*) Crossroad NY.
WomanSpirit Index: A Comprehensive Guide to a Decade of Women's Spirituality, 1974-1984. Ed. by Jean Mountaingrove & Christine Menefee. (Illus.). 120p. (Orig.). 1989. spiral bd. 13.95 (*0-9621035-1-9*) WomanSpirit.
Womanspirit Meditation Tape. Hallie A. Iglehart. 60p. (C). 1985. 10.00 (*0-9621036-0-8*) Women Spiritual Educ.
Womanspirit Rising: A Feminist Reader in Religion. Carol P. Christ & Judith Plaskow. LC 91-58254. 304p. (Orig.). 1992. reprint ed. pap. 14.00 (*0-06-061377-7*) Harper SF.

W

An Asterisk (*) at the beginning of an entry indicates that the title is appearing in BIP for the first time.

Womansport Directory: The Women's Sports Bible. Greg J. Cylkowski & Kathleen Staiffer. (Illus.). 195p. (Orig.). (C). 1995. pap. write for info. (*0-9636449-3-9*) Athletic Achieve.

WomanStory: Biblical Models for Our Time. Pamela Smith. LC 90-71131. 112p. (Orig.). 1992. pap. 7.95 (*0-89622-460-0*) Twenty-Third.

WomanStrength: Modern Church, Modern Women. Joan Chittister. LC 90-61956. 190p. (Orig.). (C). 1996. pap. 9.95 (*1-55612-373-6*, LL1373) Sheed & Ward MO.

Womansword: What Japanese Words Say about Women. Kittredge Cherry. (Illus.). 160p. 1992. pap. 8.00 (*4-7700-1655-7*) Kodansha.

Womantrees How You Are Blooming. Lois Silverstein. 64p. (Orig.). 1989. pap. 6.00 (*0-9603440-1-2*) Red Shoes Pr.

WomanWisdom: A Feminist Lectionary & Psalter Women of the Hebrew Scriptures, Pt. 1. Miriam T. Winter. (Illus.). (Orig.). 1991. pap. 16.95 (*0-8245-1100-X*) Crossroad NY.

WomanWitness: A Feminist Lectionary & Psalter Women of the Hebrew Scriptures, Pt. 2. Miriam T. Winter. (Illus.). 352p. (Orig.). 1991. pap. 16.95 (*0-8245-1141-7*) Crossroad NY.

WomanWord: A Feminist Lectionary & Psalter on Women of the New Testament. Miriam T. Winter. (Illus.). 352p. (Orig.). 1990. pap. 19.95 (*0-8245-1054-2*) Crossroad NY.

Womanwords: A Dictionary of Words about Women. Jane Mills. 291p. 1992. text ed. 24.95 (*0-02-921495-5*, Free Press) Free Pr.

Womanwords: A Journal for Myself. 96p. 1990. pap. 8.00 (*0-89486-713-X*, 8301A) Hazelden.

Womb Becomes a Tomb: Are We Sacrificing to Moloch? American TFP Staff. (Illus.). 90p. (Orig.). 1992. pap. 5.95 (*1-877905-26-7*) Am Soc Defense TFP.

Womb of Insight. Jimmi Whizz. 22p. (Orig.). 1994. pap. 4.00 (*0-944215-12-2*) Ninth St Lab.

Womb of Mind. Renuka Singh. 1990. text ed. 30.00 (*0-7069-4949-8*, Pub. by Vikas II) S Asia.

Womb of Space: The Cross-Cultural Imagination. Wilson Harris. LC 83-1639. (Contributions in Afro-American & African Studies: No. 73). xx, 151p. 1983. text ed. 45.00 (*0-313-23774-3*, HWO/, Greenwood Pr) Greenwood.

Womb Weary. James Ragan. 1990. 14.95 (*1-55972-053-0*, Birch Ln Pr) Carol Pub Group.

Womb with a View. University of Wisconsin-Madison Medial Genetics Staff. 160p. 1995. spiral bd. 14.95 (*0-7872-0552-4*) Kendall-Hunt.

Womb with Views: A Contradictionary of the English Language. Kate Musgrave. LC 88-63760. (Illus.). 182p. 1989. pap. 8.95 (*0-941300-12-9*) Mother Courage.

Wombat. Pauline Reilly. (Picture Roo Bks.). (Illus.). 32p. (Orig.). (J). 1993. pap. 6.95 (*0-86417-148-X*, Pub. by Kangaroo Pr AT) Seven Hills Bk.

Wombat: Common Wombats in Australia. Barbara Triggs. (Illus.). 168p. 1988. pap. 24.95 (*0-86840-043-2*, Pub. by New South Wales Univ Pr AT) Intl Spec Bk.

***Wombat: Common Wombats in Australia.** 2nd rev. ed. Barbara Triggs. (Illus.). 156p. 1996. pap. 27.95 (*0-86840-263-X*, Pub. by New South Wales Univ Pr AT) Intl Spec Bk.

Wombat Divine. Mem Fox. LC 96-5480. (Illus.). 32p. (J). 1996. 15.00 (*0-15-201416-0*, HB Childrens Bks) HarBrace.

***Wombat Divine: Signed Copy.** Fox. 1996. 15.00 (*0-15-201754-2*) HarBrace.

Wombat Duet. Ed. by Ray G. Cook. (Illus.). 22p. (C). 1984. pap. 10.00 (*0-9602002-6-6*) Ray Cook.

Wombat Stew. Marcia K. Vaughan. LC 85-63492. (Illus.). 32p. (J). (ps-3). 1985. 8.95 (*0-382-09211-2*); pap. 4.95 (*0-382-24356-0*) Silver Burdett Pr.

***Wombat Stew.** Marcia K. Vaughan & Pamela Lofts. (Illus.). (J). pap. 4.99 (*0-86896-258-9*, Pub. by Ashton Scholastic NZ) Scholastic Inc.

Wombats. Lynn M. Stone. (Australian Animals Discovery Library). (Illus.). 24p. (J). (gr. k-5). 1990. lib. bdg. 11.94 (*0-86593-059-7*); lib. bdg. 8.95 (*0-685-36374-0*) Rourke Corp.

***Wombers & Innuendoes.** Hunter Lord & Ariel Masters. 224p. 1997. pap. 6.99 (*1-890096-03-2*) Padwolf Pub.

Wombs & Alien Spirits: Women, Men & the Zar Cult in Northern Sudan. Janice Boddy. LC 89-40250. (New Directions in Anthropological Writing Ser.). 384p. 1989. pap. text ed. 23.95 (*0-299-12314-6*) U of Wis Pr.

Women. 146p. 1972. 20.00 (*0-87130-030-3*); pap. 12.50 (*0-87130-031-1*) Eakins.

Women. 1981. pap. 3.00 (*0-913937-07-X*) Rational Isl.

Women. 1995. pap. 3.00 (*1-885357-24-9*) Rational Isl.

Women. 59p. 1986. pap. 4.95 (*0-88867-045-1*) Bahai.

Women. Hilton Als. 200p. 1996. 21.00 (*0-374-29205-1*) FS&G.

***Women.** Hilton Als. 1998. pap. text ed. 11.00 (*0-374-52529-3*, Noonday) FS&G.

Women. Naim Attallah. 1167p. 1993. pap. 14.95 (*0-7043-0080-X*, Pub. by Quartet UK) Interlink Pub.

Women. Ed. by Evelyn L. Beilenson. (Charming Petites Ser.). (Illus.). 80p. 1991. 4.95 (*0-88088-748-6*) Peter Pauper.

Women. Claire Boothe. 1966. pap. 5.25 (*0-8222-1270-6*) Dramatists Play.

Women. Ralph Gibson. 1994. pap. 16.95 (*0-936859-13-X*) Boca Raton Museum.

***Women.** Luis Royo. (Illus.). 80p. 1997. pap. 16.95 (*1-56163-171-X*) NBM.

Women. Phillipe Sollers. Tr. by Barbara Bray from FRE. (Twentieth-Century Continental Fiction Ser.). 560p. 1990. 32.50 (*0-231-06546-9*) Col U Pr.

Women. Phillipe Sollers. Tr. by Barbara Bray from FRE. (Twentieth-Century Continental Fiction Ser.). 560p. 1992. pap. 17.00 (*0-231-06547-7*) Col U Pr.

Women. Charles Bukowski. LC 78-21998. 296p. 1997. reprint ed. 25.00 (*0-87685-391-2*); reprint ed. pap. 14.00 (*0-87685-390-4*) Black Sparrow.

Women. Booth Tarkington. LC 74-178464. (Short Story Index Reprint Ser.). 1977. reprint ed. 23.95 (*0-8369-4064-4*) Ayer.

Women, Vol. 3, incl. 1984-1988 Suppls. Ed. by Eleanor C. Goldstein. (Social Issues Resources Ser.). 1989. Incl. 1984-1988 Supplements. 95.00 (*0-89777-076-5*) Sirs Inc.

Women: A Bibliography of Bibliographies. 2nd ed. Patricia K. Ballou. (Reference Bks. - Women's Studies). 349p. 1986. 40.00 (*0-8161-8729-0*, Hall Reference) Macmillan.

Women: A Celebration. Intervisual Books Staff. (Illus.). 16p. 1995. 4.95 (*0-8362-0055-1*) Andrews & McMeel.

Women: A Feminist Perspective. 5th ed. Ed. by Jo Freeman. LC 94-16032. 688p. (Orig.). (C). 1994. pap. 31.95 (*1-55934-111-4*, 1111) Mayfield Pub.

Women: A PDI Reference Work, Vol. 1. Ed. by Florence L. Denmark et al. LC 75-5161. 626p. 1977. 39.95 (*0-88437-001-1*) Psych Dimensions.

Women: A Pictorial Archive from Nineteenth Century Sources. Ed. by Jim Harter. (Pictorial Archive Ser.). 1978. pap. 6.95 (*0-486-23703-6*) Dover.

Women: A Worldwide View of Their Management Development Needs. Martha G. Burrow. LC 76-10796. 31p. reprint ed. pap. 25.00 (*0-317-09919-1*, 2051525) Bks Demand.

Women: Challenges to the Year 2000. 96p. 1992. pap. 12.95 (*92-1-100458-6*, 91.I.21) UN.

Women: Contemporary Issues & Perspectives. Ed. by N. Jane McCandless & Myrna Cintron. (Studies in Social Sciences). 100p. (Orig.). 1993. pap. text ed. 5.00 (*1-883199-01-8*) W GA College.

Women: Fifty Ways to See Thru Men. Vernon Howard. 1982. pap. 2.00 (*0-911203-13-3*) New Life.

Women: From the Greeks to the French Revolution. Ed. by Susan G. Bell. LC 80-51750. xiv, 313p. 1973. reprint ed. 42.50 (*0-8047-1094-5*); reprint ed. pap. 16.95 (*0-8047-1082-1*) Stanford U Pr.

Women: How to Evaluate Your Symptoms. American Medical Association Staff. LC 85-25768. (Illus.). 144p. 1986. pap. 14.00 (*0-394-74045-9*) Random.

Women: In the Mask & Beyond. Geraldine C. Little. (QRL Poetry Bks.: Vol. XXX). 1991. 20.00 (*0-614-06436-8*); pap. 10.00 (*0-614-06437-6*) Quarterly Rev.

Women: Looking Beyond 2000. 146p. Date not set. pap. 14.95 (*92-1-100592-2*, E.95.I.40) UN.

Women: Menopause & Middle Age. Vidals Clay. 1977. per. 5.00 (*0-912786-37-X*) Know Inc.

Women: Models of Liberation. Marie A. Mayeski. LC 87-62399. 256p. (Orig.). (C). 1989. pap. 12.95 (*1-55612-086-9*) Sheed & Ward MO.

Women: Photographs of the Top Female Bodybuilders. Bill Dobbins. LC 94-19145. (Illus.). 128p. 1994. 27.50 (*1-885183-01-1*) Artisan.

Women: Prodigal Equals. Betty Kloha. LC 88-64146. 80p. (Orig.). 1989. pap. 6.99 (*0-8100-0310-4*, 12N1749) Northwest Pub.

Women: The Fifth World. Elise Boulding. LC 80-65602. (Headline Ser.: No. 248). (Illus.). 64p. (Orig.). 1980. pap. 5.95 (*0-87124-059-9*) Foreign Policy.

***Women: The New Providers.** Families & Work Institute Staff. (Whirlpool Foundation Study Ser.: Pt. 1). 98p. 1995. pap. write for info. (*0-614-22660-0*, W95-02) Families & Work.

Women: The Recruiter's Last Resort. Dina Portnoy. 40p. 1974. pap. 3.00 (*0-686-43095-6*) Recon Pubns.

Women: Their Changing Roles. Ed. by Elizabeth Janeway. LC 72-5020. (Great Contemporary Issues Ser.). (Illus.). 1973. 30.00 (*0-685-41644-5*) Ayer.

Women: Their Changing Roles. Ed. by Elizabeth Janeway. LC 72-5020. (Great Contemporary Issues Ser.). (Illus.). 1973. 27.95 (*0-405-04164-0*) Ayer.

Women: Your Body, Your Health. Josleen Wilson. 1990. pap. 19.95 (*0-15-698150-5*) HarBrace.

Women Vol. 5: Including 1994 Supplement. Ed. by Eleanor C. Goldstein. (Social Issues Resources Ser.). 1995. 57.00 (*0-89777-186-9*) Sirs Inc.

Women - Images & Realities: A Multicultural Anthology. Amy Kesselman et al. LC 94-17291. 488p. (C). 1994. pap. text ed. 31.95 (*1-55934-117-3*, 1117) Mayfield Pub.

Women - Men - Management. Ann Harriman. LC 95-11265. 272p. 1996. pap. text ed. 22.95 (*0-275-94685-1*, Praeger Pubs) Greenwood.

Women - Men - Management. 2nd ed. Ann Harriman. LC 95-11265. 272p. 1996. text ed. 65.00 (*0-275-94684-3*, Praeger Pubs) Greenwood.

Women - Men (Femmes - Hommes) The Erotic Poetry of Paul Verlaine. William Packard & John D. Mitchell. LC 77-23853. (Illus.). 150p. (Orig.). (ENG & FRE.). (C). 1991. reprint ed. pap. 24.95 (*1-882763-01-7*) IASTA.

Women - New Roles in Society. Ed. by Norma H. Jones et al. (Compact Reference Ser.). 84p. (J). (gr. 6-9). 1995. pap. text ed. 12.95 (*1-57302-011-7*) Info Plus TX.

Women - To Preach or Not to Preach: 21 Outstanding Black Preachers Say Yes! Ella P. Mitchell. 145p. 1991. pap. 13.00 (*0-8170-1169-2*) Judson.

Women, Abuse & the Bible: How Scripture Can Be Used to Hurt or to Heal. Ed. by Catherine C. Kroeger & James R. Beck. 256p. (YA). (gr. 10). 1996. pap. 14.99 (*0-8010-5707-8*) Baker Bks.

Women According to Men: The World of Tudor-Stuart Women. Suzanne W. Hull. LC 95-50244. (Illus.). 200p. 1996. 35.00 (*0-7619-9119-0*); pap. 16.95 (*0-7619-9120-4*) AltaMira Pr.

Women Activists: Challenging the Abuse of Power. Anne W. Garland. LC 88-401. 176p. 1988. 35.00 (*0-935312-79-X*); pap. 9.95 (*0-935312-80-3*) Feminist Pr.

Women Administrators in Education. Mariamma A. Varghese. 1990. text ed. 22.50 (*0-685-37406-8*, Pub. by Vikas II) S Asia.

Women Adrift: Independent Wage Earners in Chicago, 1880-1930. Joanne J. Meyerowitz. (Women in Culture & Society Ser.). (Illus.). xxiv, 248p. 1988. 35.95 (*0-226-52197-4*) U Ch Pr.

Women Adrift: Independent Wage Earners in Chicago, 1880-1930. Joanne J. Meyerowitz. LC 87-22449. (Women in Culture & Society Ser.). (Illus.). xxiv, 248p. 1991. pap. text ed. 14.95 (*0-226-52198-2*) U Ch Pr.

Women Advocates of Reproductive Rights: Eleven Who Led the Struggle in the United States & Great Britain. Moira D. Reynolds. LC 93-41201. (Illus.). 179p. 1994. lib. bdg. 32.50 (*0-89950-940-1*) McFarland & Co.

Women after Prison. Mary Eaton. LC 92-14875. 1993. 85.00 (*0-335-19008-1*, Open Univ Pr); pap. 32.50 (*0-335-19007-3*, Open Univ Pr) Taylor & Francis.

Women After Treatment: A Study of Former Mental Patients & Their Normal Neighbors. Shirley S. Angrist et al. LC 68-20043. (C). 1968. 28.00 (*0-89197-471-7*) Irvington.

Women Against Hitler: Misogyny & Emergence in the Third Reich. Theodore N. Thomas. LC 94-8564. 216p. 1995. text ed. 49.95 (*0-275-94619-3*, Praeger Pubs) Greenwood.

***Women Against Hunger: A Sketchbook Journey.** Betty Laduke. LC 97-13313. 1997. write for info. (*0-86543-605-3*); pap. write for info. (*0-86543-606-1*) Africa World.

Women Against Slavery. Claire Midgley. 296p. (C). 1995. pap. 18.95 (*0-415-12708-4*) Routledge.

***Women Against the "Good War" Conscientious Objection & Gender on the American Home Front, 1941-1947.** Rachel W. Goossen. LC 97-9885. (Gender & American Culture Ser.). 240p. (C). (gr. 13). 1997. pap. 15.95 (*0-8078-4672-4*); lib. bdg. 39.95 (*0-8078-2366-X*) U of NC Pr.

Women Against Women: American Anti-Suffragism, 1880-1920. Jane J. Camhi. LC 94-20242. (Scholarship in Women's History Ser.: Vol. 4). 330p. 1994. 60.00 (*0-926019-65-1*) Carlson Pub.

***Women, Age, & Power: The Politics of Age Difference among Women in Papua New Guinea & Australia.** Ed. by Jeanette Dickerson-Putman. (Pacific Studies: Vol. 19, No. 4). 152p. (C). 1997. pap. text ed. 15.00 (*0-939154-62-5*) Inst Polynesian.

Women, Aging & Ageism. Evelyn Rosenthal. LC 90-4644. (Journal of Women & Aging: Vol. 2, No. 2). 161p. 1990. text ed. 29.95 (*0-86656-984-7*) Haworth Pr.

Women, Aid & Development: Essays in Honour of Professor T. Scarlett Epstein. Ed. by Christine M. Cottam. (C). 1993. 28.00 (*81-7075-026-1*, Pub. by Hindustan IA) S Asia.

Women, AIDS, & Activism. ACT-UP - New York Women & AIDS Book Group Staff & New York Women's Handbook Group Staff. 294p. (Orig.). 1990. 25.00 (*0-89608-394-2*); pap. 9.00 (*0-89608-393-4*) South End Pr.

Women, AIDS & Communities: A Guide for Action. Gerry Pearlberg. LC 91-17428. (Illus.). 141p. 1991. 27.50 (*0-8108-2470-1*); pap. 19.50 (*0-8108-2450-7*) Scarecrow.

Women, Alcohol, Tobacco & Other Drugs: A Resource Guide. 1995. lib. bdg. 251.95 (*0-8490-6807-X*) Gordon Pr.

Women Alone: Creating a Joyous & Fulfilling Life. Julie Keene & Ione Jenson. 224p. (Orig.). 1995. pap. 12.00 (*1-56170-119-X*, 167) Hay House.

Women Analyze Women: In France, England, & the United States. Elaine H. Baruch. 424p. (C). 1991. pap. 16.50 (*0-8147-1170-7*) NYU Pr.

Women Analyze Women: In France, England, & the United States. Lucienne J. Serrano. 320p. (C). 1988. text ed. 32.00 (*0-8147-1098-0*) NYU Pr.

Women & a New Academy: Gender & Cultural Contexts. Ed. by Jean F. O'Barr. LC 88-40441. 192p. (Orig.). (C). 1989. text ed. 35.00 (*0-299-11930-0*); pap. text ed. 12.95 (*0-299-11934-3*) U of Wis Pr.

***Women & Access in Rural Areas: What Makes the Difference? What Difference Does It Make?** Ed. by Polly Chapman & Siobhan Lloyd. 108p. 1996. text ed. 51.95 (*1-85972-291-1*, Pub. by Avebury Pub UK) Ashgate Pub Co.

Women & Aging: A Bibliography. Ed. by Joan Nordquist. (Contemporary Social Issues: A Bibliographic Ser.: No. 35). 72p. (C). 1994. pap. 15.00 (*0-937855-68-5*) Ref Rsch Serv.

***Women & Aging: A Guide to the Literature.** Helen R. Wheeler. LC 96-41175. 275p. (J). 1997. lib. bdg. 65.00 (*1-55587-661-7*, 876617) Lynne Rienner.

Women & Aging: A Selected Annotated Bibliography. Compiled by Jean M. Coyle. LC 88-28975. (Bibliographies & Indexes in Gerontology Ser.). 163p. 1989. text ed. 49.95 (*0-313-26021-4*, CWA, Greenwood Pr) Greenwood.

Women & Aging: An Anthology by Women. Calyx Editorial Collective et al. Ed. by Jo Alexander et al. (Illus.). 262p. (Orig.). (C). 1986. 28.95 (*0-934971-07-2*); pap. 15.95 (*0-934971-00-5*) Calyx Bks.

Women & Aging: Celebrating Ourselves. Ruth R. Thone. LC 91-19330. 166p. 1992. pap. 14.95 (*1-56023-005-3*) Harrington Pk.

Women & Aging: Celebrating Ourselves. Ruth R. Thone. LC 91-19331. 166p. 1992. lib. bdg. 39.95 (*1-56024-151-9*) Haworth Pr.

Women & AIDS. Diane Richardson. 160p. 1987. 29.95 (*0-415-90175-8*, A0762, Routledge NY); pap. 11.95 (*0-416-01751-7*, A0766, Routledge NY) Routledge.

Women & AIDS: A Bibliography. Ed. by Joan Nordquist. (Contemporary Social Issues: A Bibliographic Ser.: No. 29). 64p. (Orig.). 1993. pap. 15.00 (*0-937855-56-1*) Ref Rsch Serv.

Women & AIDS: Coping & Care. Ed. by Ann O'Leary & Loretta S. Jemmott. LC 96-3254. (AIDS Prevention & Mental Health Ser.). (Illus.). 240p. (C). 1996. 45.00 (*0-306-45258-8*, Plenum Pr) Plenum.

***Women & AIDS: Negotiating Safer Practices, Care & Representation.** Ed. by Nancy L. Roth & Linda K. Fuller. LC 97-16980. 300p. 1997. 39.95 (*0-7890-6014-0*); pap. 24.95 (*1-56023-882-8*) Haworth Pr.

Women & AIDS: Psychological Perspectives. Ed. by Corinne Squire. (Gender & Psychology Ser.). (Illus.). 208p. 1993. 69.95 (*0-8039-8587-8*); pap. 22.95 (*0-8039-8588-6*) Sage.

Women & AIDS in Rural Africa: Rural Women's Views of AIDS in Zambia. Genevieve Mwale & Philip Burnard. 135p. 1992. 55.95 (*1-85628-396-8*, Pub. by Avebury Pub UK) Ashgate Pub Co.

***Women & Alcohol.** Plant. 1997. 49.50 (*1-85343-363-2*, Pub. by Free Assoc Bks UK); pap. 22.50 (*1-85343-364-0*, Pub. by Free Assoc Bks UK) NYU Pr.

Women & Alcohol: The Journey Back. M. Ellen Stammer. LC 90-3129. 306p. (Orig.). 1991. pap. 17.95 (*0-89876-162-X*) Gardner Pr.

Women & Alcohol Abuse: Prevention Resource Guide. 32p. (Orig.). (C). 1993. pap. text ed. 25.00 (*0-7881-0167-6*) DIANE Pub.

Women & Alcohol in a Highland Maya Town: Water of Hope, Water of Sorrow. Christine Eber. (Illus.). 336p. (Orig.). (C). 1995. pap. 18.95 (*0-292-72090-4*); text ed. 40.00 (*0-292-72089-0*) U of Tex Pr.

Women & Ambition: A Bibliography. Patricia S. Faunce. LC 79-18347. 724p. 1980. lib. bdg. 45.00 (*0-8108-1242-8*) Scarecrow.

Women & American Foreign Policy: Lobbyists, Critics, & Insiders. Ed. by Edward P. Crapol. LC 86-22798. (Contributions in Women's Studies: No. 76). 213p. 1987. text ed. 49.95 (*0-313-24636-X*, CWF/, Greenwood Pr) Greenwood.

Women & American Foreign Policy: Lobbyists, Critics, & Insiders. 2nd rev. ed. Ed. by Edward P. Crapol. LC 91-46045. (America in the Modern World Ser.). 200p. (C). 1992. reprint ed. 35.00 (*0-8420-2431-X*, SR Bks) Scholarly Res Inc.

Women & American Socialism, 1870-1920. Mari J. Buhle. LC 81-719. (Working Class in American History Ser.). (Illus.). 370p. 1981. text ed. 34.95 (*0-252-00873-1*) U of Ill Pr.

Women & American Socialism, 1870-1920. Mari J. Buhle. LC 81-719. (Working Class in American History Ser.). (Illus.). 370p. 1983. pap. text ed. 15.95 (*0-252-01045-0*) U of Ill Pr.

Women & American Socialism, 1870-1920. fac. ed. Mari J. Buhle. LC 81-719. (Working Class in American History Ser.). 371p. 1981. pap. 105.80 (*0-7837-7609-8*, 2047361) Bks Demand.

Women & Angels. Harold Brodkey. (Author's Workshop Ser.). 176p. 1985. boxed 35.00 (*0-8276-0250-2*) JPS Phila.

Women & Anger. Ed. by Sandra P. Thomas et al. LC 92-44878. (Focus on Women Ser.: Vol. 15). 332p. 1993. 39.95 (*0-8261-8100-7*) Springer Pub.

***Women & Anxiety.** rev. ed. Helen A. Derosis. 1997. pap. text ed. 14.95 (*1-886330-99-9*) Hatherleigh.

Women & Appletrees. Moa Martinson. Tr. by Margaret S. Lacy. LC 85-6898. 224p. 1985. pap. 8.95 (*0-935312-38-2*) Feminist Pr.

Women & Art: A History of Women Painters & Sculptors from the Renaissance to the 20th Century. Elsa H. Fine. 242p. (C). 1991. pap. text ed. 27.50 (*0-8133-1401-1*) Westview.

Women & Art: A History of Women Painters & Sculptors from the Renaissance to the 20th Century. Elsa H. Fine. (Illus.). 242p. 1978. pap. 25.00 (*0-8390-0212-2*, Allanheld & Schram) F Schram.

***Women & Art in South Africa.** Arnold. LC 96-38342. 1997. text ed. 39.95 (*0-312-16586-2*) St Martin.

Women & Authority: Re-emerging Mormon Feminism. Ed. by Maxine Hanks. LC 92-9048. xxxiii, 460p. (Orig.). 1992. pap. 19.95 (*1-56085-014-0*) Signature Bks.

Women & Autobiography. Linda Anderson. 1995. pap. 29.00 (*0-13-355034-6*) P-H.

Women & Beauty: The Role of Class & Economics in Shaping Images of Beauty. 1991. lib. bdg. 79.00 (*0-8490-4631-9*) Gordon Pr.

Women & Bisexuality. Sue George. 224p. (Orig.). 1993. 49.95 (*1-85727-066-5*, Pub. by Scarlet Pr UK); pap. 16.95 (*1-85727-071-1*, Pub. by Scarlet Pr UK) LPC InBook.

***Women & Bull Fighting.** Pink. 1997. 45.00 (*1-85973-956-3*, Pub. by Berg Pubs UK); pap. 17.50 (*1-85973-961-X*) NYU Pr.

Women & Business Ownership: A Bibliography. Marcia LaSota. 180p. 1987. lib. bdg. 37.50 (*0-933474-45-8*) Media Mktg Group.

Women & Cancer. Ed. by Steven D. Stellman. LC 86-26942. (Women & Health Ser.: Vol. 11, Nos. 3-4). 277p. 1987. text ed. 49.95 (*0-86656-613-9*) Haworth Pr.

Women & Cancer. Ed. by Steven D. Stellman. LC 86-26943. (Women & Health Ser.: Vol. 11, No. 3-4). 277p. 1987. reprint ed. pap. text ed. 19.95 (*0-918393-31-0*) Harrington Pk.

Women & Cancer: Gynecologic Nursing Perspectives. Giselle Moore. (Nursing Ser.). 612p. (C). 1996. text ed. 64.95 (*0-86720-714-0*) Jones & Bartlett.

Women & Career: Themes & Issues in Advanced Industrial Societies. Ed. by Julia Evetts. LC 93-15577. (Sociology Ser.). (C). 1995. pap. text ed. 25.50 (*0-582-10194-8*) Longman.

An Asterisk (*) at the beginning of an entry indicates that the title is appearing in BIP for the first time.

Women & Careers: Issues, Pressures, & Challenges. Ed. by Carol W. Konek & Sally L. Kitch. (Illus.). 240p. (C). 1993. text ed. 49.95 (0-8039-5262-7); pap. text ed. 23.50 (0-8039-5263-5) Sage.

Women & Careers: Success & Orientations. Millicent E. Poole & Janice Langan-Fox. 224p. 1993. 60.00 (1-85000-849-3, Falmer Pr); pap. 27.50 (1-85000-850-7, Falmer Pr) Taylor & Francis.

Women & Change in Latin America: New Directions in Sex & Class. Ed. by June Nash & Helen I. Safa. LC 85-18563. (Illus.). 384p. 1985. text ed. 47.95 (0-89789-069-8, Bergin & Garvey); pap. text ed. 19.95 (0-89789-070-1, Bergin & Garvey) Greenwood.

Women & Change in the Caribbean. Ed. by Janet H. Momsen. LC 93-422. 320p. 1993. 35.00 (0-253-33897-2); pap. 17.95 (0-253-33896-4) Ind U Pr.

Women & Child Development: Some Contemporary Issues. G. Narayana Reddy. (C). 1987. 22.00 (0-317-68214-8, Pub. by Chugh Pubns II) S Asia.

*__Women & Childbirth in the Twentieth Century: 1928-1993.__ Susan Williams. (Illus.). 352p. 1997. boxed 35.95 (0-7509-1209-X, Pub. by Sutton Pubng UK) Bks Intl VA.

Women & Children First. Ed. by Hilary Marland et al. LC 92-7627. 304p. (C). 1992. text ed. 110.00 (0-415-08090-8, A7517) Routledge.

Women & Children First: Environment, Poverty & Sustainable Development. Ed. by Filomena C. Steady. LC 92-46449. 650p. (C). 1993. text ed. 34.95 (0-87047-064-7); pap. text ed. 24.95 (0-87047-065-5) Schenkman Bks Inc.

*__Women & Children First: Stories.__ Bill Oliver. (First Series). 192p. (Orig.). 1998. pap. 14.00 (0-922811-35-0) Mid-List.

Women & Children First: The Life & Times of Elsie Wilcox of Kaua'i. Judith D. Hughes. LC 95-30294. 1996. pap. 22.95 (0-8248-1621-8) UH Pr.

Women & Children First, How to Avoid Crime. Ken Berry. 1992. pap. 7.95 (1-881222-92-6) Win Win Pubns.

Women & Children in Healthcare: An Unequal Majority. Mahowald. 304p. (C). 1996. pap. 19.95 (0-19-510870-1) OUP.

Women & Children Last: The Plight of Poor Women in Affluent America. Ruth Sidel. 256p. 1987. pap. 8.95 (0-14-010013-X, Penguin Bks) Viking Penguin.

Women & Children Last: The Plight of Poor Women in Affluent America. rev. ed. Ruth Sidel. 288p. 1992. pap. 11.95 (0-14-016766-8, Penguin Bks) Viking Penguin.

Women & Children of the Alamo. Crystal S. Ragsdale. LC 93-41998. (Illus.). 128p. (J). 1994. pap. 14.95 (1-880510-12-X) State House Pr.

*__Women & Children with HIV & AIDS: Legal Protections, Policy & Programs.__ Theodore Stein. (Child Welfare: Child Welfare Practice, Policy & Research Ser.). 256p. 1997. pap. text ed. 19.95 (0-19-510942-2) OUP.

*__Women & Children with HIV & AIDS: Legal Protections, Policy & Programs.__ Theodore Stein. (Child Welfare: Child Welfare Practice, Policy & Research Ser.). 256p. 1997. 45.00 (0-19-510941-4) OUP.

Women & Chinese Patriarchy: Servitude & Escape. Ed. by Maria Jaschok & Suzanne Miers. LC 94-36047. 320p. (C). 1994. pap. 25.00 (1-85649-126-9, Pub. by Zed Bks Ltd UK); text ed. 59.95 (1-85649-125-0, Pub. by Zed Bks Ltd UK) Humanities.

Women & Chinese Patriarchy: Submission, Servitude & Escape. Ed. by Maria Jaschok & Suzanne Miers. 320p. 1994. pap. 52.50 (962-209-361-2, Pub. by Hong Kong Univ Pr HK) Coronet Bks.

Women & Class in Africa. Ed. by Iris Berger & Claire C. Robertson. LC 85-17568. 300p. (C). 1986. 55.00 (0-8419-0979-2) Holmes & Meier.

Women & Class in Africa. Ed. by Claire C. Robertson & Iris Berger. LC 85-17568. 300p. (C). 1986. pap. 19.95 (0-8419-1187-8) Holmes & Meier.

Women & Colonization: Anthropological Perspectives. Ed. by Mona Etienne & Eleanor B. Leacock. (Illus.). 352p. 1980. 39.95 (0-03-052586-1, Bergin & Garvey); pap. 18.95 (0-03-052581-0, Bergin & Garvey) Greenwood.

Women & Comedy: Rewriting the British Theatrical Tradition. Susan Carlson. 256p. 1990. 42.50 (0-472-10187-0) U of Mich Pr.

*__Women & Common Life.__ Christopher Lasch. Date not set. pap. 12.95 (0-393-31697-1) Norton.

Women & Communicative Power: Theory, Research, & Practice. Ed. by Carol A. Valentine & Nancy J. Hoar. LC 88-63211. 160p. (C). 1988. pap. text ed. 11.50 (0-944811-01-9) Speech Commun Assn.

Women & Community in Oman. Christine Eickelman. (Illus.). 240p. (C). 1984. pap. 16.50 (0-8147-2166-4); text ed. 36.00 (0-8147-2165-6) NYU Pr.

*__Women & Computer Based Technologies: A Feminist Perspective.__ Hope Morritt. LC 97-1652. 202p. 1997. 44.50 (0-7618-0711-X); pap. 28.50 (0-7618-0712-8) U Pr of Amer.

Women & Conflict: Gender & Development. Helen O'Connell. (Gender & Development). (Illus.). 64p. (C). 1993. pap. 12.95 (0-85598-222-5, Pub. by Oxfam UK) Humanities.

Women & Counter-Power. Ed. by Yolande Cohen. 244p. 1989. 39.95 (0-921689-11-X, Pub. by Black Rose Bks CN); pap. 19.95 (0-921689-10-1, Pub. by Black Rose Bks CN) Consort Bk Sales.

Women & Crack-Cocaine. James A. Inciardi et al. LC 92-31430. (Illus.). 208p. (Orig.). (C). 1992. pap. text ed. 24.00 (0-02-359440-3, Macmillan Coll) P-H.

Women & Creativity. Dolores Leckey. (Madeleva Lectures, 1991). 1991. pap. 3.95 (0-8091-3259-1) Paulist Pr.

Women & Credit in Pre-Industrial & Developing Societies. William C. Jordan. LC 92-42835. 176p. (C). 1993. text ed. 29.95 (0-8122-3194-5) U of Pa Pr.

Women & Crime. S. K. Ghosh. xvi, 192p. 1992. 19.95 (1-881338-22-3) Nataraj Bks.

Women & Crime. S. K. Ghosh. (C). 1992. 23.50 (81-7024-506-0, Pub. by Ashish II) S Asia.

Women & Crime: The Life of the Female Offender. Frances M. Heidensohn. 240p. (C). 1987. text ed. 32.00 (0-8147-3433-2); pap. text ed. 13.20 (0-8147-3434-0) NYU Pr.

Women & Crime: The Life of the Female Offender. 2nd ed. Frances M. Heidensohn. 248p. (C). 1996. 40.00 (0-8147-3524-X); pap. 16.50 (0-8147-3526-6) NYU Pr.

Women & Crime in India: A Study in Sociocultural Dynamics. Rekha Saxena. (C). 1994. 16.00 (81-210-0323-7, Pub. by Inter-India Pubns) S Asia.

Women & Criminality: The Woman as Victim, Offender & Practitioner. Ronald B. Flowers. LC 86-33646. (Contributions in Criminology & Penology Ser.: No. 18). 234p. 1987. text ed. 55.00 (0-313-25365-X, FWL/, Greenwood Pr) Greenwood.

Women & Culture: Gender & Development. Caroline Sweetman & Oxfam Staff. (Gender & Development). 64p. (C). 1995. pap. 12.95 (0-85598-310-8, Pub. by Oxfam UK) Humanities.

Women & Dance: Sylphs & Sirens. Christy Adair. LC 92-17279. (Illus.). 304p. (C). 1992. 45.00 (0-8147-0621-5); pap. 16.50 (0-8147-0622-3) NYU Pr.

Women & Death: Linkages in Western Thought & Literature. Beth A. Bassein. LC 83-8544. (Contributions in Women's Studies: No. 44). xii, 236p. 1984. text ed. 55.00 (0-313-23924-X, BWD/, Greenwood Pr) Greenwood.

Women & Depressed Caste Population in India. B. B. Mathur. (C). 1994. text ed. 32.00 (81-85613-79-6, Pub. by Chugh Pubns II) S Asia.

Women & Depression: A Lifespan Perspective. Ed. by Ruth Formanek & Anita Gurian. (Focus on Women Ser.). 328p. 1987. 36.95 (0-8261-5140-X) Springer Pub.

Women & Depression: Risk Factors & Treatment Issues. Ed. by Ellen H. McGrath et al. 123p. (Orig.). 1990. pap. text ed. 19.95 (1-55798-104-3) Am Psychol.

*__Women & Depression: Risk Factors & Treatment Issues: Final Report of the American Psychological Association's National Task Force on Women & Depression.__ Ed. by Ellen McGrath et al. LC 90-14448. reprint ed. pap. 39.10 (0-608-04561-6, 2065300) Bks Demand.

Women & Development. R. K. Saptu. (C). 1989. 50.00 (81-7024-238-X, Pub. by Ashish II) S Asia.

Women & Development: The Sexual Division of Labour in Rural Societies. Ed. by Lourdes Beneria. LC 82-606. 288p. 1982. text ed. 42.95 (0-275-90759-7, C0759, Praeger Pubs) Greenwood.

Women & Development: The Sexual Division of Labour in Rural Societies. Ed. by Lourdes Beneria. LC 82-606. 288p. 1985. pap. text ed. 15.95 (0-275-91637-5, B1637, Praeger Pubs) Greenwood.

Women & Development in Africa: Comparative Perspectives. Ed. by Jane L. Parpart. LC 88-36271. (Dalhousie African Studies: No. 7). (Illus.). 354p. (Orig.). (C). 1989. pap. text ed. 35.50 (0-8191-7379-7, Pub. by Dalhousie Univ Pr CN); lib. bdg. 57.00 (0-8191-7378-9, Pub. by Dalhousie Univ Pr CN) U Pr of Amer.

Women & Development in South-East Asia, Vol. 1. Thitsa Khin & Signe Howell. (Centre for Southeast Asian Studies, University of Kent at Canterbury, England, Occasional Paper Ser.: No. 1). i, 81p. (Orig.). 1988. reprint ed. pap. 12.50 (0-318-18415-X, Pub. by CSEAS UK) Cellar.

Women & Development in the Third World. Janet H. Momsen. LC 90-43653. (Illus.). 128p. (C). 1991. pap. 13.95 (0-415-01695-9, A5479) Routledge.

*__Women & Diabetes.__ Laurinda Poirier & Katharine Coburn. LC 97-3159. (Illus.). (Orig.). 1997. pap. 14.95 (0-945448-77-5, CSMWD) Am Diabetes.

Women & Disability. Esther R. Boylan. LC 91-12443. (Women & World Development Ser.). (Illus.). 111p. (C). 1991. pap. 15.95 (0-86232-987-6, Pub. by Zed Bks Ltd UK); text ed. 49.95 (0-86232-986-8, Pub. by Zed Bks Ltd UK) Humanities.

Women & Disability: The Double Handicap. Mary Jo Deegan & Nancy A. Brooks. 180p. 1984. 34.95 (0-87755-017-4) Transaction Pubs.

Women & Disability: The Experience of Physical Disability among Women. Susan Lonsdale. LC 90-31332. 200p. 1990. text ed. 29.95 (0-312-04613-8) St Martin.

Women & Discourse in the Fiction of Marguerite Duras: Love, Legends, Language. Susan D. Cohen. LC 92-13945. 256p. (C). 1993. 37.50 (0-87023-827-2); pap. 17.95 (0-87023-828-0) U of Mass Pr.

Women & Divorce - Men & Divorce: Gender Differences in Separation, Divorce & Remarriage. Ed. by Sandra S. Volgy. LC 90-25067. (Journal of Divorce & Remarriage). 253p. 1991. text ed. 39.95 (1-56024-090-3); pap. text ed. 17.95 (1-56024-114-4) Haworth Pr.

Women & Drug Abuse Treatment: Needs & Services. 1986. lib. bdg. 79.95 (0-8490-3506-6) Gordon Pr.

Women & Drugs. 1986. lib. bdg. 79.95 (0-8490-3507-4) Gordon Pr.

*__Women & Economic Change: Andean Perspectives.__ Ann Miles et al. LC 97-3481. (Society for Latin American Anthropology Publication Ser.). 1997. write for info. (0-913167-80-0) Am Anthro Assn.

Women & Economic Development: A Study of the Different Facets of Their Role in India. Odeyar D. Heggade. 220p. 1986. 9.00 (0-8364-1624-4, Pub. by Somaiya II) S Asia.

Women & Economic Empowerment: Special Issue. Ed. by Dawn-Marie Driscoll. 272p. (Orig.). 1990. pap. 17.95 (0-87023-644-X) U of Mass Pr.

Women & Economic Policy: Gender Development. Barbara Evers. (Illus.). 64p. (C). 1994. pap. 12.95 (0-85598-260-8, Pub. by Oxfam UK) Humanities.

Women & Economics. Charlotte Perkins Gilman. 1975. 300.00 (0-87968-282-5) Gordon Pr.

Women & Economics: A New Zealand Feminist Perspective. Prue Hyman. 256p. 1996. pap. 19.95 (0-908912-61-7) Paul & Co Pubs.

Women & Economics: A Study of the Economic Relation Between Women & Men. Charlotte Perkins Gilman. (Great Minds Ser.). 340p. (C). 1994. pap. 11.95 (0-87975-884-8) Prometheus Bks.

Women & Education. 2nd ed. Ed. by Jane Gaskell & Arlene McLaren. 399p. (C). 1991. pap. text ed. 24.95 (1-55059-038-3) Temeron Bks.

*__Women & Education in Aotearoa 2, No. 2.__ Ed. by Sue Middleton & Alison Jones. 264p. 1997. pap. 27.50 (1-86940-178-6, Pub. by Auckland Univ NZ) Paul & Co Pubs.

Women & Education in China, Hong Kong & Taiwan. China Education Translation Project Staff. (Special Studies in Comparative Education: No. 26). 141p. (Orig.). 1990. pap. 10.00 (0-937033-19-7) SUNY GSE Pubns.

Women & Education in Latin America: Knowledge, Power, & Change. Ed. by Nelly P. Stromquist. LC 91-22989. (Women & Change in the Developing World Ser.). 320p. 1991. lib. bdg. 44.00 (1-55587-286-7) Lynne Rienner.

*__Women & Education in Latin America: Knowledge, Power, & Change.__ Ed. by Nelly P. Stromquist. (Women & Change in Developing World Ser.). 310p. 1996. pap. 22.50 (1-55587-777-X) Lynne Rienner.

Women & Education Process in India. Susheela Kaushik. (C). 1993. 30.00 (0-7069-5959-0, Pub. by Vikas II) S Asia.

*__Women & Elective Office: Past, Present, & Future.__ Ed. by Sue Thomas & Clyde Wilcox. (Illus.). 256p. (C). 1997. pap. text ed. 17.95 (0-19-511231-8) OUP.

Women & Emergencies: Gender & Development. Bridget Walker. (Gender & Development). (Illus.). 64p. (C). 1994. pap. 12.95 (0-85598-266-7, Pub. by Oxfam UK) Humanities.

Women & Employment in India. Sarala Gopalan. (C). 1995. 28.00 (81-241-0358-5, Pub. by Har-Anand Pubns II) S Asia.

Women & Empowerment: Participation & Decision-Making. Marilee Karl. (Women in World Development Ser.). (Illus.). 173p. (C). 1995. pap. 17.50 (1-85649-192-7, Pub. by Zed Bks Ltd UK) Humanities.

Women & Empowerment: Strategies for Increasing Autonomy. C. Margaret Hall. 140p. 1992. 52.95 (1-56032-266-7); pap. 25.95 (1-56032-267-5) Hemisp Pub.

Women & Environment: Gender & Development. Geraldine Reardon. (Gender & Development). (Illus.). 64p. (C). 1993. pap. 12.95 (0-85598-221-7, Pub. by Oxfam UK) Humanities.

Women & Epilepsy. Ed. by Michael R. Trimble. LC 91-84600. 285p. 1991. text ed. 165.00 (0-471-92998-0, Wiley-L) Wiley.

Women & Equal Pay: The Effects of Legislation on Female Employment & Wages in Britain. A. Zabalza & Zafiris Tzannatos. (Illus.). 148p. 1985. text ed. 44.95 (0-521-30188-2) Cambridge U Pr.

Women & Equality: Changing Patterns in American Culture. William H. Chafe. LC 76-42639. 207p. 1978. reprint ed. pap. 10.95 (0-19-502365-X) OUP.

*__Women & European Employment.__ Jill Rubery. LC 97-6093. (Frontiers of Political Economy Ser.). 352p. (C). 1997. text ed. write for info. (0-415-16985-2) Routledge.

Women & European Politics: Contemporary Feminism & Public Policy. Joni Lovenduski. LC 85-16501. 336p. 1986. lib. bdg. 17.95 (0-87023-507-9) U of Mass Pr.

Women & Evangelism: An Evangelistic Lifestyle from a Woman's Perspective. Sharon Beougher & Mary Dorsett. (Illus.). 292p. (Orig.). 1994. pap. 39.95 incl. audio (1-879089-16-5); lab manual ed. 9.95 (1-879089-15-7) B Graham Ctr.

Women & Evil. Nel Noddings. 293p. 1991. pap. 14.00 (0-520-07413-0) U CA Pr.

Women & Exercise: Physiology & Sports Medicine. 2nd ed. Ed. by Mona M. Shangold & Gabe Mirkin. (Illus.). 330p. (C). 1993. text ed. 52.00 (0-8036-7817-7) Davis Co.

Women & Families: An Oral History, 1940-1970. Elizabeth Roberts. (Family, Sexuality & Social Relations in Past Times Ser.). (Illus.). 272p. 1995. 61.95 (0-631-19612-9); pap. 24.95 (0-631-19613-7) Blackwell Pubs.

Women & Families: Feminist Reconstructions. Kristine M. Baber & Katherine R. Allen. LC 92-20561. (Perspectives on Marriage & the Family Ser.). 276p. 1992. pap. text ed. 20.95 (0-89862-083-X); lib. bdg. 42.00 (0-89862-082-1) Guilford Pr.

Women & Family Law Reform in India: Uniform Civil Code & Gender Equality. Archana Parashar. 348p. (C). 1992. 38.00 (0-8039-9423-0) Sage.

Women & Family Life Education in India. Manindra Kapoor. 1986. 22.50 (81-7044-028-9, Pub. by Manohar II) S Asia.

Women & Fatigue. Holly Atkinson. 1987. mass mkt. 6.50 (0-671-69216-X) PB.

Women & Feminism in American History: A Guide to Information Sources. Ed. by Elizabeth Tingley & Donald F. Tingley. LC 80-19793. (American Government & History Information Guide Ser.: Vol. 12). 304p. (C). 1981. 68.00 (0-8103-1477-0) Gale.

Women & Fertility in Bangladesh. Alia Ahmad. 176p. 1991. 27.50 (0-8039-9682-9) Sage.

Women & Fiction: Short Stories by & About Women. Ed. by Susan Cahill. (YA). (gr. 7 up). 1975. pap. 4.50 (0-451-62411-4, ME2263, Ment) NAL-Dutton.

Women & Fiction: Short Stories by & about Women. Ed. by Susan Cahill. 400p. 1975. pap. 5.99 (0-451-62729-6, Ment) NAL-Dutton.

Women & Fiction: The Manuscript Versions of a Room of One's Own. Virginia Woolf. Ed. by S. P. Rosenbaum. (Illus.). 224p. 1992. 44.95 (0-631-18037-0) Blackwell Pubs.

Women & Film. Cora Kaplan. 1987. pap. 13.95 (0-416-31750-2) Routledge Chapman & Hall.

Women & Film. Ed. by Janet Todd. (Women & Literature Ser.: Vol. 4). 320p. (C). 1988. 47.95 (0-8419-0936-9) Holmes & Meier.

Women & Film: A Bibliography. Rosemary R. Kowalski. LC 76-25051. 287p. 1976. 22.00 (0-8108-0974-5) Scarecrow.

Women & Film: A Sight & Sound Reader. Ed. by Pam Cook & Philip Dodd. LC 93-31694. (Culture & the Moving Image Ser.). 320p. 1993. pap. 18.95 (1-56639-143-1) Temple U Pr.

Women & Film: A Sight & Sound Reader. Ed. by Pam Cook & Philip Dodd. LC 93-31694. (Culture & the Moving Image Ser.). 320p. 1994. text ed. 54.95 (1-56639-142-3) Temple U Pr.

Women & Film: Both Sides of the Camera. E. Ann Kaplan. LC 83-8198. (Illus.). 260p. (C). 1983. pap. 15.95 (0-415-02764-0, NO. 3551) Routledge.

Women & Flight: Portraits of Contemporary Women Pilots. Carolyn Russo & Dorothy Cochrane. 1997. 40.00 (0-8212-2168-X); pap. 24.95 (0-8212-2368-2) Little.

Women & Folklore: A Bibliographic Survey. Compiled by Francis A. De Caro. LC 83-12837. xiv, 170p. 1983. text ed. 49.95 (0-313-23821-9, DWF/, Greenwood Pr) Greenwood.

Women & Food Security: The Experience of the SADCC Countries. Ed. by Marilyn Carr. (Orig.). 1991. pap. 20.95 (1-85339-109-3, Pub. by Intermed Tech UK); text ed. 56.95 (1-85339-118-2, Pub. by Intermed Tech UK) Women Ink.

Women, & Four Other Essays. Maurice Maeterlinck. 1991. lib. bdg. 75.00 (0-8490-4190-2) Gordon Pr.

Women & Freedom in Early America. Ed. by Larry Eldridge. 360p. (C). 1997. 55.00 (0-8147-2193-1); pap. 20.00 (0-8147-2198-2) NYU Pr.

Women & Fundamentalism: Islam & Christianity. Shahin Gerami. LC 95-4925. (Women's History & Culture Ser.: Vol. 9). 196p. 1995. text ed. 40.00 (0-8153-0663-6, H1516) Garland.

Women & Gender: A Feminist Psychology. 2nd ed. Mary Crawford & Rhoda K. Unger. 1996. pap. text ed. write for info. (0-07-065942-7) McGraw.

Women & Gender in Early Modern Europe. Merry E. Wiesner. LC 92-45709. (New Approaches to European History Ser.: No. 1). (Illus.). 276p. (C). 1993. text ed. 49.95 (0-521-38459-1); pap. text ed. 15.95 (0-521-38613-6) Cambridge U Pr.

*__Women & Gender in Islam.__ Leila Ahmed. 320p. 1996. 26.00 (0-614-21400-9, 1325); pap. 15.00 (0-614-21399-1, 1325) Kazi Pubns.

Women & Gender in Islam: Historical Roots of a Modern Debate. Leila Ahmed. 304p. (C). 1993. pap. 16.00 (0-300-05583-8) Yale U Pr.

Women & Gender in Southern Africa to 1945. Ed. by Cherryl Walker. 400p. 1991. 35.00 (0-253-36323-3); pap. 15.95 (0-253-20665-0, MB-665) Ind U Pr.

*__Women & Gender Issues.__ Franklin. (Asians in American Life Ser.). 350p. 1997. text ed. 75.00 (0-8153-2692-0) Garland.

Women & Ghosts. Alison Lurie. 192p. 1995. pap. 9.00 (0-380-72501-0) Avon.

Women & Globalisation: Reflections, Options & Strategies. Ed. by Pam Rajput & Hem L. Swarup. xxxiv, 393p. (C). 1994. 49.00 (81-7024-669-5, Pub. by Ashish Pub Hse II) Nataraj Bks.

*__Women & Goddess Traditions: In Antiquity & Today.__ Karen L. King. LC 97-20399. (Studies in Antiquity & Christianity). 1997. pap. 45.00 (0-8006-2919-1, Fortress Pr) Augsburg Fortress.

Women & Government: New Ways to Political Power. Ed. by Mim Kelber. LC 94-1147. 0275948161p. 1994. text ed. 65.00 (0-275-94816-1, Praeger Pubs); pap. text ed. 16.95 (0-275-94817-X, Praeger Pubs) Greenwood.

Women & Grass Roots Democracy in the Americas: Sustaining the Initiative. 2nd ed. Ed. by Dorrit K. Marks. 288p. (Orig.). 1996. pap. text ed. 24.95 (1-57454-017-3, 540173) Lynne Rienner.

Women & Group Psychotherapy: Theory & Practice. Ed. by Betsy BeChant. LC 96-20155. 1996. lib. bdg. 45.00 (1-57230-098-1) Guilford Pr.

*__Women & Health.__ Saltman. 1992. pap. text ed. 32.50 (0-7295-0285-6) Saunders.

Women & Health. Ed. by Patricia Smyke. LC 91-29612. (Women & World Development Ser.). 256p. (C). 1991. pap. 15.95 (0-86232-983-3, Pub. by Zed Bks Ltd UK); text ed. 49.95 (0-86232-982-5, Pub. by Zed Bks Ltd UK) Humanities.

*__Women & Health: An Annotated Bibliography.__ Frances R. Belmonte. LC 97-22482. (Magill Bibliographies Ser.). 208p. 1997. 35.00 (0-8108-3385-9) Scarecrow.

Women & Health: Cross-Cultural Perspectives. Patricia Whelehan. 240p. 1988. text ed. 59.95 (0-89789-138-4, H138, Bergin & Garvey); pap. text ed. 21.95 (0-89789-139-2, G139, Bergin & Garvey) Greenwood.

Women & Health: Feminist Perspectives. Ed. by Sue Wilkinson & Celia Kitzinger. LC 94-24353. (Gender & Society: Feminist Perspectives on the Past & Present Ser.). 208p. 1994. 79.00 (0-7484-0148-2); pap. 24.95 (0-7484-0149-0) Taylor & Francis.

Women & Health: The Politics of Sex in Medicine. Ed. by Elizabeth Fee. (Baywood Policy, Politics, Health, & Medicine Ser.: Vol. 4). 263p. (Orig.). (C). 1983. pap. text ed. 23.00 (0-89503-034-9) Baywood Pub.

W

Women & Health in Africa. Ed. by Meredeth Turshen. LC 90-81473. 325p. (C). 1990. 45.00 (*0-86543-180-9*); pap. 14.95 (*0-86543-181-7*) Africa World.

Women & Health in America. Ed. by Judith W. Leavitt. LC 83-40267. (Wisconsin Publications in the History of Science & Medicine: No. 4). (Illus.). 536p. 1984. pap. 16.95 (*0-299-09644-0*); text ed. 32.50 (*0-299-09640-8*) U of Wis Pr.

Women & Health Psychology, 2 vols. Cheryl B. Travis. (Environment & Health Ser.). 288p. 1988. Vol. 1, Mental Health Issues, 280 pgs. text ed. 45.00 (*0-8058-0253-3*); Vol. 2, Biomedical Issues, 312 pgs. text ed. 45.00 (*0-89859-974-1*) L Erlbaum Assocs.

Women & Health Psychology, 2 vols., Set. Cheryl B. Travis. (Environment & Health Ser.). 1988. text ed. 70.00 (*0-8058-0292-4*) L Erlbaum Assocs.

Women & Health Research Vol. 2: Ethical & Legal Issues of Including Women in Clinical Studies: Workshop & Commissioned Papers. Committee on the Ethical & Legal Issues Relating to the Inclusion of Women in Clinical Studies Staff. Ed. by Anna C. Mastroianni et al. 264p. (Orig.). (C). 1994. pap. text ed. 29.00 (*0-309-05040-5*) Natl Acad Pr.

Women & Health Research, Vol. 1: Ethical & Legal Issues of Including Women in Clinical Studies. Institute of Medicine Staff. LC 93-50549. 288p. (C). 1994. 34.95 (*0-309-04992-X*) Natl Acad Pr.

Women & Healthy Aging: Living Productively in Spite of It All. Ed. by Alice A. Young. LC 93-40755. (Journal of Women & Aging: Vol. 5, Nos.3-4). (Illus.). 241p. 1993. 49.95 (*1-56024-509-3*); pap. 14.95 (*1-56023-049-5*) Haworth Pr.

Women & Heart Disease: What You Can Do to Stop the Number-One Killer of American Women. Edward B. Diethrich & Carol Cohan. 320p. 1994. pap. 10.00 (*0-345-38620-5*, Ballantine Trade) Ballantine.

***Women & History.** Ed. by Valerie Frith. (Illus.). 262p. pap. 15.95 (*0-7725-2398-3*, Pub. by Irwin Pubng CN) Genl Dist Srvs.

Women & HIV Disease: Falling Through the Cracks. (Illus.). 247p. (Orig.). (C). 1993. pap. text ed. 40.00 (*1-56806-430-6*) DIANE Pub.

Women & Honor: Some Notes on Lying. Adrienne Rich. 16p. 1990. 3.95 (*0-939416-44-1*) Cleis Pr.

Women & Hormones: An Essential Guide to Being Female. Alice T. MacMahon. Ed. by James R. MacMahon. LC 90-81214. (Illus.). 208p. (Orig.). 1990. pap. 9.95 (*0-931128-03-X*) Family Pubns.

Women & Horses. Ron Davis. LC 85-16600. (Chapbooks Ser.). (Illus.). (Orig.). 1981. pap. 3.00 (*0-914140-11-6*) Carpenter Pr.

Women & Household Labor. Ed. by Sarah F. Berk. LC 79-23003. (Sage Yearbooks in Women's Policy Studies: No. 5). (Illus.). 295p. reprint ed. pap. 84.10 (*0-8357-8472-X*, 2034740) Bks Demand.

Women & Human Rights. Katarina Tomasevski. LC 93-24674. (Women & World Development Ser.). 144p. (C). 1993. pap. 17.50 (*1-85649-120-X*, Pub. by Zed Bks Ltd UK); text ed. 49.95 (*1-85649-119-6*, Pub. by Zed Bks Ltd UK) Humanities.

Women & Identity: Value Choices in a Changing World. C. Margaret Hall. 275p. 1989. pap. 29.95 (*1-56032-241-1*) Hemisp Pub.

Women & Ideology in the Soviet Union. Mary Buckley. 1990. pap. 16.95 (*0-472-06410-X*) U of Mich Pr.

Women & Indian Nationalism. Ed. by Leela Kasturi & Vina Mazumdar. (C). 1994. 28.00 (*0-7069-7051-9*, Pub. by Vikas II) S Asia.

Women & Indians on the Frontier, 1825-1915. Glenda Riley. LC 84-13235. (Illus.). 352p. 1984. pap. 16.95 (*0-8263-0780-9*) U of NM Pr.

Women & Industrialization in Asia. Ed. by Susan Horton. (Studies in the Growth Economies of Asia). 368p. (C). 1995. text ed. 85.00 (*0-415-12907-9*, Routledge NY) Routledge.

Women & Information Technology. Ed. by Marilyn J. Davidson & Cary L. Cooper. LC 87-10554. (Psychology & Productivity at Work Ser.). 283p. 1987. text ed. 205.00 (*0-471-91603-X*) Wiley.

Women & International Development Annual Vol. 4. Ed. by Rita S. Gallin et al. 256p. (C). 1995. pap. text ed. 47.50 (*0-8133-8798-1*) Westview.

Women & Islam: An Historical & Theological Enquiry. Fatima Mernissi. (C). 1991. 22.50 (*81-85107-71-8*, Pub. by Kali for Women II) S Asia.

Women & Islamic Law in a Non-Muslim State. Aharon Layish. 352p. 1975. boxed 34.95 (*0-87855-170-0*) Transaction Pubs.

Women & Italy: Essays on Gender Culture & History. Ed. by Zygmunt G. Baranski & Shirley W. Vinall. LC 90-47393. 256p. 1991. text ed. 45.00 (*0-312-05611-7*) St Martin.

Women & Japanese Management: Discrimination & Reform. Alice C. Lam. LC 91-48163. 256p. (C). (gr. 13). 1992. 49.95 (*0-415-06335-3*, A7652) Routledge.

Women & Jesus in Mark: A Japanese Feminist Perspective. Hisako Kinukawa. LC 93-50075. (Bible & Liberation Ser.). 160p. (Orig.). 1994. pap. 17.50 (*0-88344-945-5*) Orbis Bks.

Women & Jewish Law: The Essential Texts, Their History, & Their Relevance for Today. Rachel Biale. 312p. 1995. pap. 15.00 (*0-8052-1049-0*) Schocken.

Women & Labour. Ed. by Roger Blanpain. (Bulletin of Comparative Labour Relations Ser.: No. 9). 1978. 26.00 (*90-312-0077-8*) Kluwer Ac.

Women & Land: An Oxfam-Virago Diary. (Illus.). 224p. 1995. pap. 5.99 (*1-86049-021-2*, Pub. by Oxfam UK) Humanities.

Women & Language Debate: A Sourcebook. Ed. by Camille Roman et al. LC 93-7642. 500p. (C). 1993. text ed. 48.00 (*0-8135-2011-8*); pap. text ed. 18.00 (*0-8135-2012-6*) Rutgers U Pr.

Women & Language in Literature & Society. Ed. by Sally McConnell-Ginet et al. LC 80-20816. 358p. 1980. text ed. 75.00 (*0-275-90520-9*, C0520, Praeger Pubs) Greenwood.

Women & Language in Transition. Ed. by Joyce Penfield. LC 86-23113. 208p. 1987. text ed. 74.50 (*0-88706-485-X*); pap. text ed. 24.95 (*0-88706-486-8*) State U NY Pr.

Women & Laughter. Frances Gray. LC 93-23400. (Feminist Issues Ser.). 224p. (C). 1994. pap. 15.50 (*0-8139-1513-9*); text ed. 35.00 (*0-8139-1512-0*) U Pr of Va.

Women & Law: Contemporary Problems. Ed. by Lotika Sarkar & B. Sivaramayya. (C). 1994. text ed. 28.00 (*0-7069-6967-7*, Pub. by Vikas II) S Asia.

Women & Law in America. Frost Knappman. LC 96-43656. 1996. 49.95 (*0-7876-0384-8*) Gale.

Women & Law in Classical Greece. Raphael Sealey. LC 89-16469. xii, 202p. 1990. text ed. 32.50 (*0-8078-1872-0*); pap. text ed. 13.95 (*0-8078-4262-1*) U of NC Pr.

Women & Law in Late Antiquity & the Early Middle Ages. Antti Arjava. LC 95-53235. 320p. 1996. 65.00 (*0-19-815033-4*) OUP.

Women & Lawyers in the Mid-Nineteenth Century English Novel: Uneasy Alliances & Narrative Misrepresentation. Lynne M. DeCicco. LC 96-17583. (Studies in British Literature: Vol. 25). 328p. 1996. text ed. 99.95 (*0-7734-8756-5*) E Mellen.

Women & Leadership: A Contextual Perspective. Karin Klenke. LC 95-40436. (Illus.). 328p. 1996. 38.95 (*0-8261-9220-3*) Springer Pub.

Women & Leadership in Nineteenth-Century England. Lilian L. Shiman. 298p. 1992. text ed. 39.95 (*0-312-07912-5*) St Martin.

Women & Leadership on Canadian Education. Ed. by Cecilia Reynolds & Beth Young. 253p. (Orig.). 1995. pap. text ed. 26.95 (*1-55059-116-9*, Pub. by Detselig CN) Temeron Bks.

Women & Legal Protection. Paras Diwan & Peeyushi Diwan. (C). 1994. 40.00 (*81-7100-659-0*, Pub. by Deep II) S Asia.

Women & Leisure: A Study of Social Waste. Lorine Pruette. LC 72-2620. (American Women Ser.: Images & Realities). 230p. 1974. reprint ed. 17.95 (*0-405-04473-9*) Ayer.

Women & Library Management: Theories, Skills & Values. Ed. by Darlene E. Weingand. LC 82-60743. (Current Issues in Librarianship Ser.: No. 1). 1982. 24.50 (*0-87650-142-0*) Pierian.

Women & Literacy. Compiled by Marcela Ballara. LC 92-28226. (Women & World Development Ser.). (Illus.). 96p. (C). 1992. pap. 15.95 (*0-86232-981-7*, Pub. by Zed Bks Ltd UK); text ed. 49.95 (*0-86232-980-9*, Pub. by Zed Bks Ltd UK) Humanities.

Women & Literature. Lola L. Szladits. (Illus.). 16p. 1986. pap. 2.00 (*0-685-65652-7*) NY Pub Lib.

Women & Literature in Britain, 1150-1500. Ed. by Carol M. Meale. LC 92-11691. (Cambridge Studies in Medieval Literature: Vol. 17). (Illus.). 220p. (C). 1993. text ed. 52.95 (*0-521-40018-X*) Cambridge U Pr.

Women & Literature in Britain, 1150-1500. 2nd ed. Ed. by Carol M. Meale. (Illus.). 233p. 1997. pap. text ed. 18.95 (*0-521-57620-2*) Cambridge U Pr.

Women & Literature in Britain, 1500-1700. Ed. by Helen Wilcox. 330p. (C). 1996. text ed. 54.95 (*0-521-46219-3*); pap. text ed. 18.95 (*0-521-46777-2*) Cambridge U Pr.

Women & Loss. William Finn. 1984. 49.95 (*0-275-91429-1*, C1429, Praeger Pubs) Greenwood.

Women & Love. Shere Hite. 1989. mass mkt. 5.95 (*0-312-91378-8*) St Martin.

***Women & Madness.** 3rd ed. Phyllis Chesler. 400p. 1997. reprint ed. pap. 15.00 (*1-56858-096-7*) FWEW.

Women & Management: An Expanding Role. Ed. by Donald O. Jewell. LC 76-30748. 413p. (C). 1977. pap. 19.95 (*0-88406-185-X*) GA St U Busn Pr.

Women & Market Societies: Crisis & Opportunity. Ed. by Barbara Einhorn & Eileen Yeo. LC 95-15672. 256p. 1995. 70.00 (*1-85898-317-7*) E Elgar.

Women & Marriage in Kpelle Society. Caroline H. Bledsoe. LC 78-66170. (Illus.). 233p. 1980. 35.00 (*0-8047-1019-8*) Stanford U Pr.

***Women & Marriage in Kpelle Society.** Caroline H. Bledsoe. LC 78-66170. 1980. reprint ed. pap. 30.00 (*0-608-03817-2*, 2064672) Bks Demand.

Women & Marriage in Nineteenth Century England. Joan Perkin. LC 89-8066. 342p. (C). 1989. reprint ed. text ed. 49.95 (*0-925065-18-8*); reprint ed. pap. text ed. 23.95 (*0-925065-16-1*) Lyceum IL.

Women & Mass Communications: An International Annotated Bibliography. Compiled by John A. Lent. LC 90-23780. (Bibliographies & Indexes in Women's Studies: No. 11). 512p. 1991. text ed. 89.50 (*0-313-26579-8*, LWM/, Greenwood Pr) Greenwood.

Women & Mathematics: Balancing the Equation. Ed. by Susan F. Chipman et al. 400p. (C). 1985. text ed. 79.95 (*0-89859-369-7*) L Erlbaum Assocs.

Women & Media. Ed. by Helen Baehr. LC 80-41424. (Illus.). 142p. 1980. 19.75 (*0-08-026061-6*, Pergamon Pr) Elsevier.

Women & Media: Content, Careers, & Criticism. Cynthia M. Lont. LC 94-36309. 415p. 1995. pap. 37.95 (*0-534-24732-6*) Wadsworth Pub.

Women & Medicine in the French Enlightenment: The Debate over Maladies Des Femmes. Lindsay Wilson. LC 92-15475. 256p. 1993. text ed. 39.95 (*0-8018-4438-X*) Johns Hopkins.

Women & Men. Joseph McElroy. 1987. 27.50 (*0-394-50344-9*) Knopf.

Women & Men. Jane H. Wheelwright. 1978. pap. 3.00 (*0-317-13547-3*) C G Jung Frisco.

Women & Men. Joseph McElroy. LC 92-29481. 1192p. 1993. reprint ed. pap. 15.95 (*1-56478-023-6*) Dalkey Arch.

Women & Men, Vol. 1. Ed. by Helena Z. Lopata. (Current Research on Occupations & Professions Ser.). 325p. 1980. Women & Men. 73.25 (*0-89232-066-4*) Jai Pr.

Women & Men: An Anthropologist's View. Ernestine Friedl. (Illus.). 148p. 1984. reprint ed. pap. text ed. 9.95 (*0-88133-040-X*) Waveland Pr.

Women and Men: Cultural Constructs of Gender. Nancy Bonvillain. LC 94-3607. 352p. 1994. pap. text ed. 28.80 (*0-13-103482-0*) P-H.

***Women & Men: Cultural Constructs of Gender.** 2nd ed. Nancy Bonvillain. LC 96-49654. 1997. 26.67 (*0-13-651076-0*) P-H.

Women & Men: New Perspectives on Gender Differences. Ed. by Malkah T. Notman & Carol C. Nadelson. LC 90-548. (Issues in Psychiatry Ser.). 144p. 1991. pap. text ed. 22.00 (*0-88048-136-6*, 8136) Am Psychiatric.

Women & Men Vol. 1: A Philosophical Conversation. Francoise Giroud & Bernard-Henry Levy. Tr. by Richard Miller from FRE. 1995. 22.95 (*0-316-31474-9*) Little.

Women & Men As Leaders: Contemporary Images. Trudy Heller. LC 81-17084. 168p. 1981. text ed. 55.00 (*0-275-90643-4*, C0643, Praeger Pubs) Greenwood.

Women & Men As Leaders: In Business, Education & Social Service Organizations. Trudy Heller. 224p. 1982. 29.95 (*0-03-058948-7*, Bergin & Garvey) Greenwood.

Women & Men at Work. Barbara F. Reskin & Irene Padavic. 240p. 1994. pap. 18.95 (*0-8039-9022-7*) Pine Forge.

Women & Men Communicating: Challenges & Changes. Laurie Arliss & Deborah Borisoff. LC 92-71051. 224p. (C). 1993. pap. text ed. 20.00 (*0-03-074656-6*) HB Coll Pubs.

Women & Men Face to Face: How to Communicate More Effectively & Get Better Results on the Job. Karen Howsam. LC 93-85450. 1993. 16.95 (*0-9637619-0-0*) Ryan Pub CO.

***Women & Men Face to Face: How to Communicate More Effectively & Get Better Results on the Job.** Karen Howsam. 119p. 1993. write for info. (*0-614-30225-0*) Ryan Pub CO.

Women & Men in Management. 2nd ed. Gary N. Powell. (Illus.). 304p. (C). 1993. text ed. 52.00 (*0-8039-5223-6*); pap. text ed. 24.00 (*0-8039-5224-4*) Sage.

Women & Men in My Life. Khushwant Singh. (C). 1995. 11.00 (*81-7476-055-5*, Pub. by UBS Pubs Dist II) S Asia.

***Women & Men in the Early Church: The Full Views of St. John Chrysostom.** David Ford. LC 96-29133. 1996. write for info. (*1-878997-55-6*) St Tikhons Pr.

Women & Men in the Late Eighteenth-Century Egypt. Afaf L. Marsot. LC 95-17236. (Modern Middle East Ser.). (Illus.). 198p. 1995. 35.00 (*0-292-75180-X*) U of Tex Pr.

Women & Men Midwives: Medicine, Morality, & Misogyny in Early America. Jane B. Donegan. LC 77-87968. (Contributions in Medical History Ser.: No. 2). (Illus.). 316p. 1978. text ed. 39.95 (*0-8371-9868-2*, DMA/, Greenwood Pr) Greenwood.

Women & Men of the States: Public Administrators & the State Level. Ed. by Mary E. Guy. LC 92-9035. (Bureaucracies, Public Administration & Public Policy Ser.). 294p. (C). (gr. 13). 1992. text ed. 59.95 (*1-56324-051-3*); pap. text ed. 24.95 (*1-56324-052-1*) M E Sharpe.

Women & Men on the Overland Trail. John M. Faragher. LC 78-10290. (Yale Historical Publications, Miscellany: No. 121). 304p. 1980. pap. 16.00 (*0-300-02605-6*) Yale U Pr.

Women & Men Voters: The 1977-80 Experiment. Usha Mehta et al. 120p. 1981. 120.00 (*0-317-61991-8*, Pub. by Archives Pubs II) St Mut.

Women & Men Who Sexually Abuse Children: A Comparative Analysis. Craig M. Allen. LC 92-60133. 80p. 1991. reprint ed. pap. 17.50 (*1-884444-09-1*) Safer Soc.

Women & Mental Health. Jeri A. Sechzer. LC 96-18877. (Annals of the New York Academy of Sciences Ser.). 1996. write for info. (*1-57331-032-8*); pap. 100.00 (*1-57331-033-6*) NY Acad Sci.

Women & Mental Health: New Directions for Change. Ed. by Carol T Mowbray et al. LC 84-22454. (Women & Therapy Ser.: Vol. 3, Nos. 3 & 4). 202p. 1985. pap. text ed. 19.95 (*0-918393-13-2*) Harrington Pk.

Women & Mental Health: New Directions for Change. Ed. by Carol T. Mowbray et al. LC 84-19228. (Women & Therapy Ser.: Vol. 3, Nos. 3-4). 202p. 1985. pap. text ed. 19.95 (*0-86656-437-3*) Haworth Pr.

Women & Mental Health: New Directions for Change. Ed. by Carol T. Mowbray et al. LC 84-19228. (Women & Therapy Ser.: Vol. 3, Nos. 3-4). 202p. 1985. text ed. 49.95 (*0-86656-331-8*) Haworth Pr.

Women & Mental Health Policy. Ed. by Lenore E. Walker. LC 84-9899. (Sage Yearbooks in Women's Policy Studies: No. 9). 311p. 1984. reprint ed. pap. 88.70 (*0-608-01522-9*, 2059566) Bks Demand.

Women & Millenarian Protest in Meiji, Japan: Deguchi Nao & Omotokyo. Emily G. Ooms. (Cornell East Asia Ser.: No. 61). 163p. (Orig.). (C). 1993. pap. 12.00 (*0-939657-61-9*) Cornell East Asia Pgm.

Women & Minorities in American Professions. Ed. by Joyce Tang & Earl Smith. LC 95-49538. (SUNY Series, the New Inequalities). 224p. (C). 1996. text ed. 59.50 (*0-7914-3105-3*); pap. text ed. 19.95 (*0-7914-3106-1*) State U NY Pr.

Women & Minorities in Science & Engineering. (Illus.). 166p. (Orig.). (C). 1993. pap. text ed. 40.00 (*1-56806-689-9*) DIANE Pub.

Women & Minorities in Science & Engineering: An Update. (Illus.). 185p. (Orig.). (C). 1993. pap. text ed. 35.00 (*1-56806-946-4*) DIANE Pub.

Women & Missions: Past & Present, Anthropological & Historical Perceptions. Ed. by Fiona Bowie et al. LC 92-15997. (Cross-Cultural Perspectives on Women Ser.). 224p. 1993. 38.95 (*0-85496-738-9*); pap. 19.95 (*0-85496-872-5*) Berg Pubs.

Women & Modern Occupation in India. Kumud Ranjan. (C). 1993. 42.00 (*81-85613-78-8*, Pub. by Chugh Pubns II) S Asia.

Women & Modernity: The (Life) Styles of Lou Andreas-Salome. Biddy Martin. LC 90-55718. (Reading Women Writing Ser.). (Illus.). 264p. 1991. 39.95 (*0-8014-2591-3*); pap. 14.95 (*0-8014-9907-0*) Cornell U Pr.

Women & Money Common Sense Handbook. Aleta S. Hodge. Ed. by William E. Ehrich. (Illus.). 58p. 1995. wbk. ed. 10.00 (*0-9648316-0-0*) Money Coun.

Women & Moral Identity. Elisabeth Porter. 224p. pap. 22.95 (*0-04-442332-2*, Pub. by Allen & Unwin Aust Pty AT) Paul & Co Pubs.

Women & Moral Theory. Ed. by Eva F. Kittay & Diana T. Meyers. 336p. 1987. 59.50 (*0-8476-7381-2*); pap. 23.95 (*0-8476-7382-0*) Rowman.

Women & Music: A History. Ed. by Karin Pendle. LC 91-8413. (Illus.). 372p. 1991. 29.95 (*0-253-34321-6*) Ind U Pr.

Women & Music: A Selective Annotated Bibliography on Women & Gender Issues in Music, 1987-1992. Margaret Ericson. LC 94-45222. 1996. 95.00 (*0-8161-0580-4*) G K Hall.

Women & Music in Cross-Cultural Perspective. Ed. by Ellen Koskoff. LC 86-33648. (Contributions in Women's Studies: No. 79). 272p. 1987. text ed. 55.00 (*0-313-24314-X*, KOW/, Greenwood Pr) Greenwood.

Women & Music in Cross-Cultural Perspective. Ed. by Ellen Koskoff. LC 88-23578. (Illus.). 4p. 1989. reprint ed. pap. text ed. 12.95 (*0-252-06057-1*) U of Ill Pr.

Women & Mystical Experience in the Middle Ages. Frances Beer. (Illus.). 180p. (C). 1995. reprint ed. 59.95 (*0-85115-302-X*); reprint ed. pap. 23.00 (*0-85115-343-7*) Boydell & Brewer.

Women & National Development: The Complexities of Change. Wellesley Editorial Committee. LC 77-15038. (Illus.). 360p. 1978. pap. text ed. 8.95 (*0-226-89315-4*, P757) U Ch Pr.

Women & New Orleans: A History. 2nd ed. Mary Gehman. (Illus.). 138p. 1996. reprint ed. pap. 10.95 (*0-9616377-1-4*) Margaret Media.

Women & New Reproductive Technologies: Medical, Psychosocial, Legal & Ethical Dilemmas. Judith Rodin. 176p. (C). 1991. text ed. 36.00 (*0-8058-0919-8*) L Erlbaum Assocs.

Women & Numbers: Lives of Women Mathematicians Plus Discovery Activities. 2nd ed. Teri Perl. LC 93-10535. (Illus.). 192p. 1993. pap. 15.95 (*0-933174-87-X*) Wide World-Tetra.

Women & Nutrition in Third World Countries. Deborah Spicer et al. LC 83-25690. 160p. 1984. text ed. 30.95 (*0-275-91185-3*, C1185, Praeger Pubs) Greenwood.

***Women & Occupational Health Risks: Report on a WHO Meeting.** (Euro Reports & Studies Ser.: No. 76). 41p. 1983. pap. text ed. 4.00 (*92-890-1242-0*) World Health.

***Women & Other Aliens.** Nicola Griffith. mass mkt. write for info. (*0-06-105256-6*, HarperPrism) HarpC.

Women & Other Aliens: Essays from the U. S. - Mexico Border. Debbie Nathan. LC 90-85078. 168p. 1991. pap. 10.95 (*0-938317-08-3*) Cinco Puntos.

Women & Other Bodies of Water. Nancy Roberts. 150p. 1987. 14.00 (*0-937872-38-5*) Dragon Gate.

Women & Paid Work: Issues of Equality. Ed. by Audrey Hunt. LC 87-23477. 200p. 1988. text ed. 45.00 (*0-312-01200-4*) St Martin.

Women & Parapsychology: Proceedings, International Conference, Dublin, Ireland, Sept. 21-22, 1991. Ed. by Lisette Coly & Rhea A. White. LC 94-66458. 1994. 20.00 (*0-912328-45-2*) Parapsych Foun.

Women & Participation in Rural Development: A Framework for Project Design & Policy-Oriented Research. Kathleen A. Staudt. (Occasional Paper Ser.: No. 8). 77p. (Orig.). (C). 1979. pap. text ed. 7.15 (*0-86731-021-9*) Cornell CIS RDC.

Women & Party Politics in Peninsular Malaysia. Virginia H. Dancz. (South-East Asian Social Science Monographs). (Illus.). 292p. 1987. 35.00 (*0-19-582689-2*) OUP.

Women & Peace: Feminist Visions of Global Security. Betty A. Reardon. LC 92-9682. (SUNY Series, Global Conflict & Peace Education). 209p. 1993. text ed. 57.50 (*0-7914-1399-3*); pap. text ed. 19.95 (*0-7914-1400-0*) State U NY Pr.

Women & Peace: Theoretical, Historical & Practical Perspectives. Ed. by Ruth R. Pierson et al. LC 87-6778. 249p. 1987. 45.00 (*0-7099-4068-8*, Pub. by Croom Helm UK) Routledge Chapman & Hall.

Women & Pelvic Inflammatory Diseases: Index of Modern Information. Adela I. Dione. LC 88-47953. 150p. 1991. 44.50 (*1-55914-492-0*); pap. 39.50 (*1-55914-493-9*) ABBE Pubs Assn.

W

An Asterisk (*) at the beginning of an entry indicates that the title is appearing in BIP for the first time.

Women & Pensions in Britain & Hungary: A Cross-National & Comparative Case Study of Social Dependency. Tony Maltby. 260p. 1994. 59.95 (*1-85628-630-4*, Pub. by Avebury Pub UK) Ashgate Pub Co.

Women & Philanthropy: A National Agenda. Anne I. Thompson & Andrea Kaminski. (C). 1993. pap. text ed. 20.00 (*0-9639335-0-7*) U Wis Ctr Women & Phil.

Women & Philanthropy in Nineteenth-Century Ireland. Maria Luddy. 272p. (C). 1995. text ed. 65.00 (*0-521-47433-7*); pap. text ed. 27.95 (*0-521-48361-1*) Cambridge U Pr.

Women & Planning: Creating Genedered Realities. Clara H. Greed. LC 93-41715. 272p. (C). 1994. pap. 18.95 (*0-415-07981-0*, B3830, Routledge NY) Routledge.

Women & Planning: Creating Genedered Realities. Clara H. Greed. LC 93-41715. 256p. (C). (gr. 13). 1994. text ed. 62.95 (*0-415-07980-2*, B3826, Routledge NY) Routledge.

***Women & Poetry: Truth, Autobiography, & the Shape of the Self.** Carol Muske. LC 97-6446. (C). 1997. pap. 13.95 (*0-472-06624-2*) U of Mich Pr.

***Women & Poetry: Truth, Autobiography, & the Shape of the Self.** Carol Muske. LC 97-6446. (C). 1997. text ed. 39.50 (*0-472-09624-9*) U of Mich Pr.

Women & Political Conflict: Portraits of Struggle in Times of Crisis. Ed. by Rosemary Ridd & Helen Callaway. 246p. (C). 1987. text ed. 32.00 (*0-8147-7398-2*) NYU Pr.

Women & Political Conflict: Portraits of Struggle in Times of Crisis. Ed. by Rosemary Ridd & Helen Callaway. 246p. (C). 1987. pap. text ed. 14.80 (*0-8147-7399-0*) NYU Pr.

Women & Political Insurgency: France in the Mid-Nineteenth Century. David Barry. 208p. 1996. text ed. 49.95 (*0-312-12947-5*) St Martin.

Women & Political Participation in Northern Ireland. Robert L. Millar et al. 304p. (C). 1996. 59.95 (*1-85628-991-5*, Pub. by Avebury Pub UK) Ashgate Pub Co.

***Women & Political Representation in Canada.** Ed. by Manon Tremblay & Caroline Andrew. 328p. 1997. pap. 29.95 (*0-7766-0451-1*, Pub. by Univ Ottawa Pr CN) Paul & Co Pubs.

Women & Politics. Githens et al. (C). 1994. text ed. 29.95 (*0-06-501306-9*) Addson-Wesley Educ.

Women & Politics. Norris. (Political Pampheleteer Ser.). (C). 1995. text ed. 3.95 (*0-673-99779-0*) Addson-Wesley Educ.

Women & Politics: Activism, Attitudes & Office-Holding, Vol. 2. Ed. by Gwen Moore & J. Allen Whitt. (Research in Politics & Society Ser.). 304p. 1986. 73.25 (*0-89232-556-9*) Jai Pr.

Women & Politics: An International Perspective. Vicky Randall. xii, 362p. 1988. pap. text ed. 15.95 (*0-226-70392-4*) U Ch Pr.

Women & Politics: An International Perspective. 2nd ed. Vicky Randall. xii, 374p. 1988. lib. bdg. 39.00 (*0-226-70391-6*) U Ch Pr.

Women & Politics in Ancient Rome. Richard A. Bauman. LC 91-45088. 240p. (C). (gr. 13). 1992. text ed. 59.95 (*0-415-05777-9*, A7612) Routledge.

Women & Politics in Ancient Rome. Richard A. Bauman. 304p. (C). 1994. pap. 18.95 (*0-415-11522-1*, B4828) Routledge.

***Women & Politics in Contemporary Ireland: From the Margins to the Mainstream.** Yvonne Galligan. LC 97-8652. 1997. write for info. (*1-85567-432-7*, Pub. by Pntr Pubs UK) Bks Intl VA.

***Women & Politics in India.** Bhawana Jharta. (C). 1996. 30.00 (*81-7100-810-0*, Pub. by Deep II) S Asia.

Women & Politics in India. susheela Kaushik. (C). 1993. 30.00 (*0-7069-5960-4*, Pub. by Vikas II) S Asia.

Women & Politics in Islam: the Trial of Benazir Bhutto. Rafig Zakaria. 168p. 1990. 21.50 (*0-945257-24-4*) Apex Pr.

Women & Politics in the Age of the Democratic Revolution. Ed. by Harriet B. Applewhite & Darline G. Levy. LC 90-10738. (Illus.). 304p. (C). 1993. pap. text ed. 18.95 (*0-472-06413-4*) U of Mich Pr.

Women & Politics in the Third World. Ed. by Haleh Afshar. LC 95-34526. (Women in Politics Ser.). 224p. (C). 1996. pap. 17.95 (*0-415-13861-2*); text ed. 65.00 (*0-415-13853-1*) Routledge.

Women & Politics, Vol. 18, Pt. I see History of Women in the United States: Topically Arranged Articles on the Evolution of Women's History in the United States

Women & Politics, Vol. 18, Pt. II see History of Women in the United States: Topically Arranged Articles on the Evolution of Women's History in the United States

Women & Politics Worldwide. Ed. by Barbara J. Nelson & Najma Chowdhury. LC 93-28668. 818p. (C). 1994. pap. 27.50 (*0-300-05408-4*) Yale U Pr.

Women & Polyandry in Rawain-Jaunpur. G. S. Bhatt. (C). 1991. 16.00 (*0-685-59789-X*, Pub. by Rawat II) S Asia.

Women & Population Dynamics: Perspectives from Asia. Ed. by Kuttan Mahadevan. 320p. (C). 1990. text ed. 25.00 (*0-8039-9615-2*) Sage.

Women & Population Growth: Choice Beyond Childbearing. Kathleen Newland. LC 77-91827. (Worldwatch Papers). 1977. pap. 5.00 (*0-916468-15-1*) Worldwatch Inst.

Women & Poverty. Ed. by Barbara C. Gelpi et al. LC 86-6907. 260p. (C). 1986. pap. text ed. 19.50 (*0-226-28727-0*) U Ch Pr.

Women & Poverty in the Third World. Ed. by Mayra Buvinic et al. LC 82-8992. (Johns Hopkins Studies in Development). 343p. reprint ed. pap. 97.80 (*0-8357-6752-3*, 2035408) Bks Demand.

Women & Power. Jan L. Dargatz. LC 95-2564. 1995. pap. 10.99 (*0-7852-8008-1*) Nelson.

Women & Power in American History: A Reader, Vol. II: From 1870. Kathryn K. Sklar. 320p. (C). 1990. pap. text ed. 24.40 (*0-13-962234-9*) P-H.

Women & Power in American History, a Reader, Vol. I: To 1880. Kathryn K. Sklar & Thomas Dublin. 288p. (C). 1990. pap. text ed. 24.20 (*0-13-962218-7*) P-H.

Women & Power in American Politics. Milda K. Hedblom. (Women & American Politics Ser.). 34p. (Orig.). (C). 1988. pap. text ed. 6.50 (*0-915654-78-4*) Am Political.

Women & Power in Contemporary Australia. Ed. by Sneja Gunew et al. 89p. (C). 1983. 44.00 (*0-7300-0056-7*, Pub. by Deakin Univ AT) St Mut.

Women & Power in Native North America. Ed. by Laura F. Klein & Lillian A. Ackerman. LC 95-5903. 304p. 1995. 24.95 (*0-8061-2752-X*) U of Okla Pr.

Women & Power in Parliamentary Democracies: Cabinet Appointments in Western Europe, 1968-1992. Rebecca H. Davis. LC 96-22358. (Women & Politics Ser.). xi, 139p. 1997. text ed. 32.00 (*0-8032-1707-2*) U of Nebr Pr.

Women & Power in the Middle Ages. Ed. by Mary Erler & Maryanne Kowaleski. LC 87-5840. 288p. 1988. pap. 20.00 (*0-8203-0958-3*) U of Ga Pr.

Women & Power in the Nonprofit Sector. Ed. by Michael O'Neill & Teresa J. Odendahl. LC 93-47558. (Nonprofit Sector-Public Administration Ser.). 353p. text ed. 32.95 (*1-55542-650-6*) Jossey-Bass.

Women & Prenatal Testing: Facing the Challlenges of Genetic Technology. Ed. by Karen H. Rothenberg & Elizabeth J. Thomson. (Women & Health Ser.). 256p. 1994. 59.50 (*0-8142-0640-9*); pap. 17.95 (*0-8142-0641-7*) Ohio St U Pr.

Women & Print Culture: Constructing Femininity in the Early Periodical. Kathryn Shevelow. 300p. 1989. 29.95 (*0-415-01222-8*) Routledge.

Women & Property in Colonial New York: The Transition from Dutch to English Law, 1643-1727. Linda B. Biemer. LC 82-23701. (Studies in American History & Culture: No. 38). 169p. reprint ed. pap. 48.20 (*0-685-20821-4*, 2070036) Bks Demand.

Women & Property in Early Modern England. Amy L. Erickson. 320p. (C). 1995. pap. 18.95 (*0-415-13340-8*, Routledge NY) Routledge.

Women & Prostitution: A Social History. Vern Bullough & Bonnie Bullough. 374p. 1987. pap. 22.95 (*0-87975-372-2*) Prometheus Bks.

Women & Psychotherapy: An Assessment of Research & Practice. Ed. by Annette M. Brodsky & Rachel Hare-Mustin. LC 80-14842. 428p. 1986. pap. text ed. 24.95 (*0-89862-909-8*) Guilford Pr.

Women & Public Administration: International Perspectives. Ed. by Jane H. Bayes. LC 91-36589. (Women & Politics Ser.: Vol. 11, No. 4). 165p. 1992. pap. text ed. 5.95 (*1-56023-014-2*) Harrington Pk.

Women & Public Administration: International Perspectives. Ed. by Jane H. Bayes. LC 91-38143. (Women & Politics Ser.: Vol. 11, No. 4). (Illus.). 165p. 1992. text ed. 29.95 (*1-56024-233-7*) Haworth Pr.

Women & Public Policies. expanded rev. ed. Joyce Gelb & Marian L. Palley. LC 85-43375. 258p. 1987. reprint ed. pap. 73.60 (*0-7837-8169-5*, 2047874) Bks Demand.

Women & Public Policies. 2nd rev. ed. Joyce Gelb & Marian L. Polley. 288p. 1996. pap. text ed. 17.50 (*0-8139-1695-X*) U Pr of Va.

Women & Public Policy: A Revolution in Progress. M. Margaret Conway et al. 213p. 1994. 20.95 (*0-87187-923-9*) Congr Quarterly.

Women & Quakerism. Hope E. Luder. LC 74-82914. 36p. (Orig.). 1974. pap. 3.00 (*0-87574-196-7*) Pendle Hill.

Women & Quakerism in the Seventeenth Century. Christine Trevett. (C). 1989. pap. 21.00 (*1-85072-087-8*, Pub. by W Sessions UK) St Mut.

Women & Racial Minority Representation in School Administration, 1993. Xenia Montenegro. 20p. 1993. pap. 11.00 (*0-87652-203-7*, 21-00417) Am Assn Sch Admin.

Women & Rape. Catherine M. Roberts. 224p. (C). 1989. text ed. 32.00 (*0-8147-7411-3*); pap. text ed. 12.00 (*0-8147-7412-1*) NYU Pr.

Women & Reason. Ed. by Elizabeth D. Harvey & Kathleen Okruhlik. (Illus.). 296p. (C). 1992. text ed. 42.50 (*0-472-10220-6*) U of Mich Pr.

Women & Recession. Ed. by Jill Rubery. (International Library of Economics). 288p. 1988. text ed. 55.00 (*0-7102-0701-8*, RKP); pap. text ed. 19.95 (*0-7102-1337-9*, RKP) Routledge.

Women & Reconciliation. Carlo C. Martini. Tr. by Luke Griffin from ITA. (Cathedral Ser.: No. 3). 66p. (Orig.). 1987. pap. 7.95 (*0-86217-239-X*, Pub. by Veritas Publns IE) Ignatius Pr.

Women & Reconciliation. Carlo C. Martini. 66p. (Orig.). 1989. pap. 30.00 (*0-86217-293-4*, Pub. by Veritas IE) St Mut.

Women & Relapse. Suzanne B. Cusack. 36p. (Orig.). 1984. pap. 3.00 (*0-89486-237-5*, 1379B) Hazelden.

***Women & Religion.** Fatmagul Berktay. 1997. 52.99 (*1-55164-103-8*, Pub. by Black Rose Bks CN); pap. text ed. 23.99 (*1-55164-102-X*, Pub. by Black Rose Bks CN) Consort Bk Sales.

Women & Religion. Yvonne M. Vowels. Date not set. lib. bdg. 65.00 (*0-87436-887-1*) ABC-CLIO.

Women & Religion. Judith Plaskow. Ed. by Joan Arnold & Joan A. Romero. LC 74-83126. (American Academy of Religion. Aids for the Study of Religion Ser.). 216p. reprint ed. 61.60 (*0-8357-9581-0*, 2017557) Bks Demand.

Women & Religion: A Bibliographic Guide to Christian Feminist Liberation Theology. Shelley Finson. (Illus.). 256p. 1991. 70.00 (*0-8020-5881-7*) U of Toronto Pr.

Women & Religion: From the Goddesses to the Present. Marianne Ferguson. LC 93-50535. 304p. (C). 1994. pap. text ed. 31.20 (*0-02-337001-7*, Macmillan Coll) P-H.

Women & Religion: Readings in the Western Tradition from Aeschylus to Mary Daly. Ed. by Elizabeth Clark & Herbert W. Richardson. LC 76-9975. 1977. pap. 14.00 (*0-06-061398-X*, RD-178) Harper SF.

Women & Religion: The Original Sourcebook of Women in Christian Thought. expanded rev. ed. Ed. by Herbert W. Richardson et al. 368p. 1996. pap. 18.00 (*0-06-061409-9*) Harper SF.

Women & Religion in Britain & Ireland: An Annotated Bibliography from the Reformation to 1993. Dale A. Johnson. LC 95-33428. (ATLA Bibliography Ser.: No. 39). (Illus.). 302p. 1995. 37.50 (*0-8108-3063-9*) Scarecrow.

***Women & Religion in England: 1500 to 1750.** Patricia Crawford. 280p. (C). 1996. pap. 22.95 (*0-415-01697-5*) Routledge.

Women & Religion in England, 1500-1720. Patricia Crawford. LC 92-24741. (Christianity & Society in the Modern World Ser.). 224p. (C). 1993. text ed. 59.95 (*0-415-01696-7*, A7891) Routledge.

Women & Religion in India: An Annotated Bibliography of Sources in English 1975-92. Nancy A. Falk. 1994. 30.00 (*0-932826-36-9*); pap. 15.00 (*0-932826-37-7*) New Issues MI.

Women & Religion in Medieval & Renaissance Italy. Ed. by Daniel Bornstein & Roberto Rusconi. LC 95-44343. 320p. 1996. pap. text ed. 16.95 (*0-226-06639-8*) U Ch Pr.

Women & Religion in Medieval & Renaissance Italy. Ed. by Daniel Bornstein & Roberto Rusconi. Tr. by Margery J. Schneider from ITA. LC 95-44343. 1996. lib. bdg. 50.00 (*0-226-06637-1*) U Ch Pr.

Women & Religion in the First Christian Centuries. Deborah F. Sawyer. LC 96-2492. (Religion in the First Christian Centuries Ser.: Vol. 1). 208p. (C). 1996. pap. 17.95 (*0-415-10749-0*); text ed. 65.00 (*0-415-10748-2*) Routledge.

***Women & Religious Ritual.** Lesley Northrop. 205p. 1993. pap. 13.95 (*1-56929-008-3*) Pastoral Pr.

***Women & Revolution: A Discussion of the Unhappy Marriage of Marxism & Feminism.** Ed. by Lydia Sargent. 373p. 41.99 (*0-919619-19-3*, Pub. by Black Rose Bks CN); pap. 12.99 (*0-919619-20-7*, Pub. by Black Rose Bks CN) Consort Bk Sales.

Women & Revolution in Africa, Asia, & the New World. Ed. by Mary A. Tetreault. 472p. 1994. text ed. 39.95 (*1-57003-016-2*) U of SC Pr.

Women & Revolution in Nicaragua. Ed. by Helen Collinson. LC 90-38982. (Illus.). 224p. (C). 1990. pap. 15.00 (*0-86232-935-3*, Pub. by Zed Bks Ltd UK); text ed. 49.95 (*0-86232-934-5*, Pub. by Zed Bks Ltd UK) Humanities.

Women & Revolution in Yugoslavia, 1941-1945. Barbara Jancar-Webster. LC 89-32120. (Women & Modern Revolution Ser.). (Illus.). 250p. (Orig.). 1990. 26.50 (*0-912869-09-7*); pap. 16.95 (*0-912869-10-0*) Arden Pr.

Women & Right-Wing Movements: Indian Experiences. Ed. by Tanika Sarkar & Urvashi Butalia. 224p. (C). 1996. text ed. 55.00 (*1-85649-289-3*, Pub. by Zed Bks Ltd UK) Humanities.

Women & Right-Wing Movements: Indian Experiences. Ed. by Tanika Sarkar & Urvashi Butalia. 224p. (C). 1996. pap. 19.95 (*1-85649-290-7*, Pub. by Zed Bks Ltd UK) Humanities.

Women & Rights: Gender & Development. Caroline Sweetman & Oxfam Staff. (Focus on Gender Ser.). (Illus.). 64p. (C). 1995. pap. 12.95 (*0-85598-317-5*, Pub. by Oxfam UK) Humanities.

Women & Romance: The Consolations of Gender in the English Novel. Laurie Langbauer. LC 90-55116. (Reading Women Writing Ser.). 288p. 1990. 42.50 (*0-8014-2421-6*); pap. 14.95 (*0-8014-9692-6*) Cornell U Pr.

Women & Rural Development in China: Production & Reproduction. Elizabeth Croll. (Women, Work & Development Ser.: No. 11). viii, 172p. (Orig.). 1985. pap. 18.00 (*92-2-105217-6*) Intl Labour Office.

Women & Russia: Feminist Writings from the Soviet Union. Ed. by Tatyana Mamonova. Tr. by Rebecca Park & Catherine A. Fitzpatrick. LC 82-73963. 297p. reprint ed. pap. 84.70 (*0-7837-1386-X*, 2041562) Bks Demand.

Women & Sacrifice: Male Narcissism & the Psychology of Religion. William Beers. LC 92-13007. 214p. (C). 1992. 28.95 (*0-8143-2377-4*) Wayne St U Pr.

Women & Sado Masochistic Tension in Film & Prime Time Television Melodrama: An Application of Psychoanalytic Film Theory to Television. Kelly Witham-Levinstein. LC 95-71269. 112p. 1996. 11.95 (*1-887750-06-1*) Rutledge Bks.

Women & Science. Maithreyi Krishnaraj. 1992. 35.00 (*81-7040-281-6*, Pub. by Himalaya II) Apt Bks.

Women & Science: An Annotated Bibliography. Marilyn B. Ogilvie & Kerry L. Meek. LC 96-21199. 556p. 1996. text ed. 90.00 (*0-8153-0929-5*, SS859) Garland.

Women & Seasonal Labour Migration. Loes Schenk-Sandbergen. LC 94-45240. (Indo-Dutch Studies on Development Alternatives: Vol. 16). (Illus.). 324p. 1995. text ed. 28.00 (*0-8039-9219-X*) Sage.

Women & Self-Confidence: How to Take Charge of Your Life. Carol V. Havey. LC 86-63909. (Women & Success Ser.: Vol. 1). (Illus.). 304p. (Orig.). 1987. pap. 9.95 (*0-9617887-0-4*) Positive Pr.

Women & Self-Esteem. Linda T. Sanford & Mary E. Donovan. (Nonfiction Ser.). 480p. 1985. pap. 12.95 (*0-14-008225-5*, Penguin Bks) Viking Penguin.

***Women & Self-Esteem.** 2nd ed. Daisy Osborn. (Illus.). (Orig.). (RUS.). 1995. mass mkt. write for info. (*1-890863-13-0*) Wrld Wide Print.

Women & Self-Help Culture: Reading Between the Lines. Wendy Simonds. LC 91-44545. 267p. (C). 1992. 35.00 (*0-8135-1833-4*); pap. 16.00 (*0-8135-1834-2*) Rutgers U Pr.

Women & Sex Roles: Social Psychological Perspective. Irene H. Frieze et al. (Illus.). (C). 1978. pap. text ed. 19.95 (*0-393-09063-9*) Norton.

Women & Sex Therapy. Ed. by Ellen Cole & Esther D. Rothblum. LC 88-11068. (Women & Therapy Ser.: Vol. 7, Nos. 2-3). (Illus.). 300p. 1989. text ed. 49.95 (*0-86656-808-5*) Haworth Pr.

Women & Sex Therapy. Ed. by Esther D. Rothblum. LC 88-11068. (Women & Therapy Ser.: Vol. 7, No. 2-3). (Illus.). 300p. 1988. pap. text ed. 19.95 (*0-918393-54-X*) Harrington Pk.

Women & Sexual Harassment: A Guide to the Legal Protections of Title VII & the Hostile Environment Claim. Anja A. Chan. LC 92-44322. 110p. 1993. pap. 9.95 (*1-56023-040-1*) Harrington Pk.

Women & Sexual Harassment: A Guide to the Legal Protections of Title VII & the Hostile Environment Claim. Anja A. Chan. LC 92-44322. 110p. 1994. lib. bdg. 19.95 (*1-56024-408-9*) Haworth Pr.

Women & Sexuality in China: 1949 to the Present. Harriet Evans. LC 96-8161. 236p. 1996. 39.50 (*0-8264-0922-9*) Continuum.

Women & Sexuality in the Novels of Thomas Hardy. Rosemarie Morgan. 224p. 1988. text ed. 45.00 (*0-415-00268-0*) Routledge.

Women & Sexuality in the Novels of Thomas Hardy. Rosemarie Morgan. 224p. (C). 1991. pap. text ed. 15.95 (*0-415-05850-3*, A5669) Routledge.

Women & Simple Truths. Detroit T. Flanagan, Jr. LC 94-73249. (Illus.). (Orig.). 1994. pap. 9.95 (*0-9644273-3-8*) ATEA Pubng.

***Women & Slavery in Africa.** LC 97-18960. 1997. pap. 27.50 (*0-435-07417-2*) Heinemann.

***Women & Soap Operas: A Cultural Feminist Perspective.** Dannielle Blumenthal. 1997. text ed. write for info. (*0-275-96039-0*, Praeger Pubs) Greenwood.

***Women & Social Action: Teleclass Study Guide.** Thompson. 224p. (C). 1996. per., pap. text ed. 25.95 (*0-7872-3266-1*) Kendall-Hunt.

Women & Social Action in Victorian & Edwardian England. Jane Lewis. LC 90-71680. 336p. 1991. 45.00 (*0-8047-1905-5*) Stanford U Pr.

***Women & Social Action in Victorian & Edwardian England.** Jane Lewis. 352p. 1991. 80.00 (*1-85278-023-1*) E Elgar.

Women & Social Change: Nonprofits & Social Policy. Ed. by Felice D. Perlmutter. 188p. (Orig.). (C). 1994. lib. bdg. 24.95 (*0-87101-239-1*, 2391) Natl Assn Soc Wkrs.

Women & Social Change: Reader. rev. ed. Deakin University Press Staff. 287p. (C). 1990. 105.00 (*0-7300-0782-0*, Pub. by Deakin Univ AT) St Mut.

Women & Social Change: Study Guide. rev. ed. Deakin University Press Staff. 236p. (C). 1990. 96.00 (*0-7300-0781-2*, Pub. by Deakin Univ AT) St Mut.

Women & Social Change in India. J. M. Everett. 232p. 1979. 15.95 (*0-318-37318-1*) Asia Bk Corp.

Women & Social Change in India. Snehalata Panda. viii, 124p. 1992. 12.95 (*1-881338-14-2*) Nataraj Bks.

Women & Social Change in India. Snehalata Panda. (C). 1991. 17.50 (*81-7024-423-4*, Pub. by Ashish II) S Asia.

Women & Social Change in Latin America. Ed. by Elizabeth Jelin. Tr. by Marilyn Thomson & Anne Zammit. LC 89-48391. 256p. (C). 1990. pap. 15.00 (*0-86232-871-3*, Pub. by Zed Bks Ltd UK) Humanities.

Women & Social Class. Pamela Abbott & Roger Sapsford. 240p. 1988. text ed. 49.95 (*0-422-60990-0*, Pub. by Tavistock UK) Routledge Chapman & Hall.

***Women & Social Movements in Latin America: Power from Below.** Lynn Stephen. LC 96-45788. (Illus.). 352p. 1997. 37.50 (*0-292-77715-9*); pap. 16.95 (*0-292-77716-7*) U of Tex Pr.

Women & Social Policies in Europe: Work, Family & the State. Ed. by Jane Lewis. 264p. 1993. 80.00 (*1-85278-563-2*) E Elgar.

Women & Social Policies in Europe: Work, Family & the State. Ed. by Jane Lewis. 264p. 1994. pap. 25.00 (*1-85278-918-2*) E Elgar.

Women & Social Policy: An Introduction. Ed. by Christine Hallett. LC 95-22968. 224p. 1995. pap. 29.95 (*0-13-353889-3*) P-H.

Women & Social Protest. Ed. by Guida West & Rhoda L. Blumberg. (Illus.). 416p. (C). 1990. pap. text ed. 21.95 (*0-19-506517-4*) OUP.

Women & Social Security: Progress Towards Equality of Treatment. Anne-Marie Brocas et al. v, 116p. (Orig.). 1990. 31.50 (*92-2-106518-9*); pap. 22.50 (*92-2-105559-0*) Intl Labour Office.

Women & Social Welfare: A Feminist Analysis. Dorothy C. Miller. LC 89-16207. 191p. 1990. text ed. 45.00 (*0-275-92973-6*, C2973, Praeger Pubs) Greenwood.

Women & Social Welfare: A Feminist Analysis. Dorothy C. Miller. 192p. 1992. pap. text ed. 14.95 (*0-275-94384-4*, B4384, Praeger Pubs) Greenwood.

Women & Socialization: A Study of Their Status & Role in the Lower Castes of India. Usha S. Kanhere. 177p. (C). 1987. 25.00 (*0-317-89484-6*, Pub. by Mittal II) S Asia.

Women & Society: A Critical Review of the Literature with a Selected Annotated Bibliography. Ed. by Marie B. Rosenberg & Len V. Bergstrom. LC 73-77874. 360p. reprint ed. pap. 102.60 (*0-317-10619-8*, 2021948) Bks Demand.

Women & Society: Northern India in the Eleventh & Twelfth Centuries. Saroj Gulati. 1985. 35.00 (*0-8364-1413-6*, Pub. by Chanakya II) S Asia.

W

Women & Society, Citations 3601 to 6000: An Annotated Bibliography. Ed. by JoAnn D. Een et al. LC 77-18985. 278p. reprint ed. pap. 79.30 (*0-317-10699-6*, 2021890) Bks Demand.

Women & Society in India. Neera Desai & Maithreyi Krishnaraj. 1987. 41.00 (*81-202-0188-4*, Pub. by Ajanta II) S Asia.

Women & Society in Russia & the Soviet Union. Ed. by Linda H. Edmondson. (International Council for Soviet & East European Studies). 228p. (C). 1992. text ed. 59.95 (*0-521-41388-5*) Cambridge U Pr.

Women & Sovereignty: Cosmos 7. Ed. by Louise O. Fradenburg. (Illus.). 344p. 1993. pap. 45.00 (*0-7486-0320-4*, Pub. by Edinburgh U Pr UK) Col U Pr.

Women & Space: Ground Rules & Social Maps. Ed. by Shirley Ardener. 240p. 1993. pap. 19.95 (*0-85496-728-1*) Berg Pubs.

***Women & Spirituality.** Hazelden Staff. 1986. pap. 2.25 (*0-89486-435-1*) Hazelden.

Women & Spirituality. 2nd ed. Carol Ochs. LC 96-29291. (New Feminist Perspectives Ser.: No. 67). 256p. 1996. 57.50 (*0-8476-8329-X*); pap. 22.95 (*0-8476-8330-3*) Rowman.

Women & Spirituality: Voices of Protest & Promise. Ursula King. 288p. (C). 1989. 30.00 (*0-941533-53-0*) New Amsterdam Bks.

Women & Spirituality: Voices of Protest & Promise. 2nd rev. ed. Ursula King. LC 92-45239. 274p. 1993. reprint ed. pap. 15.95 (*0-271-01069-X*) Pa St U Pr.

Women & Sport: From Myth to Reality. Ed. by Carole A. Oglesby. LC 77-19255. (Illus.). 268p. reprint ed. pap. 76.40 (*0-7837-1492-0*, 2057188) Bks Demand.

Women & Sport: Interdisciplinary Perspectives. Ed. by D. Margaret Costa & Sharon R. Guthrie. LC 93-50167. (Illus.). 416p. 1994. text ed. 45.00 (*0-87322-686-0*, BCOS0686) Human Kinetics.

Women & Spouse Abuse: Index of Modern Information. Willard T. Brainard. LC 90-32062. 150p. 1990. 44.50 (*1-55914-180-8*); pap. 39.50 (*1-55914-181-6*) ABBE Pubs Assn.

Women & St. Bernard of Clairvaux. Jean Leclercq. Tr. by Marie-Bernard Said from FRE. (Cistercian Studies: No. 104). 171p. 1990. 34.95 (*0-87907-604-6*); pap. 16.95 (*0-87907-404-3*) Cistercian Pubns.

Women & State Socialism: Sex Inequality in the Soviet Union & Czechoslovakia. Alena Heitlinger. 253p. reprint ed. pap. 72.20 (*0-7837-1042-9*, 2041353) Bks Demand.

Women & Stepfamilies. Ed. by Nan B. Maglin & Nancy Schniedewind. (Illus.). 448p. 1990. pap. 18.95 (*0-87722-782-9*) Temple U Pr.

Women & Stepfamilies: Voices of Anger & Love. Ed. by Nan B. Maglin & Nancy Schniedewind. LC 88-11719. (Women in the Political Economy Ser.). 448p. (C). 1989. 39.95 (*0-87722-586-9*) Temple U Pr.

Women & Stress. Charmaine Saunders. 1996. 8.99 (*0-517-14909-5*) Random Hse Value.

Women & Stress: A Practical Approach to Managing Tension. Jean Lush & Pamela W. Vredevlet. LC 92-11494. 272p. (gr. 10). 1994. 17.99 (*0-8007-1675-2*) Revell.

***Women & Stress: A Practical Approach to Managing Tension.** Jean Lush. 272p. (gr. 10). 1997. pap. 10.99 (*0-8007-5617-7*) Revell.

Women & Substance Abuse. Ed. by Edith S. Gomberg & Ted D. Nirenberg. LC 93-23065. 400p. 1993. pap. 42.50 (*1-56750-066-8*); text ed. 78.50 (*1-56750-065-X*) Ablex Pub.

Women & Substance Use. Elizabeth Ettorre. LC 92-7113. 200p. (C). 1992. 37.00 (*0-8135-1863-6*); pap. 16.00 (*0-8135-1864-4*) Rutgers U Pr.

Women & Success in American Society in the Works of Edna Ferber. Mary R. Shaughnessy. 1975. lib. bdg. 250.00 (*0-87968-454-2*) Gordon Pr.

Women & Suicidal Behavior. Ed. by Silvia S. Canetto & David Lester. LC 94-31918. (Focus on Women Ser.). (Illus.). 320p. 1995. 38.95 (*0-8261-8630-0*) Springer Pub.

Women & Sustainable Development: An International Dimension. Krishna Ahooja-Patel. xvii, 206p. 1995. 20.00 (*81-7024-650-4*, Pub. by Ashish Pub Hse II) Nataraj Bks.

Women & Sustainable Development in Africa. Ed. by Valentine U. James. LC 95-11276. 224p. 1995. text ed. 57.95 (*0-275-95308-4*, Praeger Pubs); pap. text ed. 18.95 (*0-275-95399-8*, Praeger Pubs) Greenwood.

Women & Symbolic Interaction. Ed. by Mary J. Deegan & Michael Hill. 265p. (C). 1987. pap. text ed. 16.95 (*0-04-497006-4*) Routledge Chapman & Hall.

Women & Tampons: Index of New Information with Authors & Subjects. rev. ed. Valerie J. Gibson. LC 94-35173. 147p. 1994. 47.50 (*0-7883-0376-7*); pap. 44.50 (*0-7883-0377-5*) ABBE Pubs Assn.

Women & Technology. Ed. by Urs E. Gattiker. LC 94-15248. (Technological Innovation & Human Resources Ser.: No. 4). viii, 299p. (C). 1994. lib. bdg. 120.00 (*3-11-014307-0*) De Gruyter.

Women & Technology. S. C. Jain. 1985. 21.00 (*0-8364-1427-6*, Pub. by Rawat II) S Asia.

Women & Technology: An Annotated Bibliography. Cynthia G. Bindocci. LC 92-34400. (Women's History & Culture Ser.: Vol. 7). 248p. 1993. text ed. 44.00 (*0-8240-5789-9*, SS517) Garland.

Women & Terrorism. Luisella De Cataldo Neuburger & Tiziana Valentini. Tr. by Leo M. Hughes from ITA. LC 95-13884. 1996. text ed. 45.00 (*0-312-12716-2*) St Martin.

Women & Texas History: An Archival Bibliography. Ed. by Debbie M. Cottrell. 150p. pap. 14.95 (*0-87611-119-3*) Tex St Hist Assn.

Women & the Alphabet: A Series of Essays. Thomas W. Higginson. LC 72-2607. (American Women Ser.: Images & Realities). 374p. 1974. reprint ed. 29.95 (*0-405-04462-3*) Ayer.

***Women & the American Civil War: A Handbook.** Karen R. Mehaffey. (History-Reference Ser.). 350p. Date not set. text ed. 52.00 (*0-8153-2133-3*) Garland.

Women & the American Experience, Vol. 2. 2nd ed. Nancy Woloch. 1993. pap. text ed. write for info. (*0-07-071547-5*) McGraw.

Women & the American Experience: A Concise History. Nancy Woloch. 1996. pap. text ed. write for info. (*0-07-071549-1*) McGraw.

Women & the American Experience Vol. 1. 2nd ed. Nancy Woloch. LC 93-11850. 1993. text ed. write for info. (*0-07-071541-6*) McGraw.

Women & the American Experience Vol. 1, Vol. 3. 2nd ed. Nancy Woloch. 1993. pap. text ed. write for info. (*0-07-071548-3*) McGraw.

Women & the American Labor Movement: From the First Trade Unions to the Present. Philip S. Foner. LC 80-753. (Illus.). 1980. 37.95 (*0-02-910380-0*, Free Press) Free Pr.

Women & the American Legal Order. Ed. & Intro. by Karen Maschke. LC 96-39902. (Gender & American Law Ser.: Vol. 1). (Illus.). 350p. 1997. text ed. 70.00 (*0-8153-2515-0*) Garland.

***Women & the Ancestors: Black Carib Kinship & Ritual.** 2nd ed. Virginia Kerns. LC 97-1770. 1997. pap. text ed. 18.95 (*0-252-06665-0*) U of Ill Pr.

Women & the Ancestors: Black Carib Kinship & Ritual. Virginia Kerns. LC 82-2601. (Illus.). 272p. 1989. reprint ed. pap. text ed. 16.50 (*0-252-06077-6*) U of Ill Pr.

Women & the Arizona Political Process. Soroptimist International Of Phoenix Staff. LC 88-2632. (Illus.). 202p. (Orig.). (C). 1988. pap. text ed. 22.50 (*0-8191-6892-0*); lib. bdg. 47.00 (*0-8191-6891-2*) U Pr of Amer.

Women & the Blues: Passions That Hurt, Passions That Heal. Jennifer James. LC 87-45708. 280p. 1990. pap. 14.00 (*0-06-250412-6*) Harper SF.

***Women & the Book: Assessing the Visual Evidence.** Jane Taylor. 1997. pap. text ed. 29.95 (*0-8020-8069-3*) U of Toronto Pr.

Women & the Bush: Forces of Desire in the Australian Cultural Tradition. Kay Schaffer. 272p. (C). 1991. pap. text ed. 22.95 (*0-521-36816-2*) Cambridge U Pr.

Women & the Business Game: Strategies for Successful Ownership. rev. ed. Charlotte Taylor. 258p. 1983. pap. 11.95 (*0-9611214-0-8*) Venture Con Pr.

***Women & the Canadian State.** Ed. by Caroline Andrew et al. 364p. 1997. pap. 24.95 (*0-7735-1513-5*, Pub. by McGill CN) U of Toronto Pr.

***Women & the Canadian State.** Ed. by Caroline Andrew & Sanda Rodgers. 432p. 1997. 55.00 (*0-7735-1423-6*, Pub. by McGill CN) U of Toronto Pr.

***Women & the CARE Act.** Edna A. Virnell-Fuentes & Leslie R. Wolfe. 36p. (Orig.). 1996. pap. 5.00 (*1-877966-32-0*) Ctr Women Policy.

Women & the Career Game: Play to Win! Ronald E. Petit. (Illus.). 147p. (Orig.). 1982. pap. 7.95 (*0-685-06198-1*) Prof Dev Serv.

Women & the Chinese Poets. T. B. Partington. 1972. 59.95 (*0-8490-1320-8*) Gordon Pr.

Women & the Church: The Feminine Perspective. Ed. by Lourdes E. Morales-Gudmundsson. LC 95-77895. 235p. (C). 1995. pap. 11.99 (*1-883925-08-8*) Andrews Univ Pr.

Women & the Common Life: Love, Marriage, & Feminism. Christopher Lasch. Ed. by Elizabeth Lasch-Quinn. 192p. 1997. 23.00 (*0-393-04018-6*) Norton.

Women & the Constitution. Marjorie W. Bingham. Ed. by Janet Donaldson. 228p. (C). 1990. student ed., pap. text ed. 14.95 (*1-879413-00-0*) Emory U Carter Ctr.

Women & the Constitution: Symposium Papers Collection. Ed. by Joyce Pair. 169p. (C). 1990. pap. text ed. 14.95 (*1-879413-01-9*) Emory U Carter Ctr.

***Women & the Cross.** J. Clontz & I. A. Norman. LC 97-91734. (Illus.). ix, 246p. (Orig.). 1997. pap. 14.95 (*0-9658097-4-9*, 625) PFPA.

Women & the Cuban Revolution: Speeches & Documents by Fidel Castro, Vilma Espin, Others. Ed. by Elizabeth Stone. LC 81-85647. 156p. 1981. reprint ed. pap. 13.95 (*0-87348-608-0*); reprint ed. lib. bdg. 40.00 (*0-87348-607-2*) Pathfinder NY.

Women & the Definition of AIDS. Kathleen D. Stoll. 45p. 1992. 15.00 (*0-614-06755-3*) Ctr Women Policy.

Women & the Dictionary of National Biography: A Bibliography of DNB Volumes 1885-1985 & Missing Persons. Gillian Fenwick. LC 93-48315. 181p. 1994. 74.95 (*0-85967-914-4*, Pub. by Scolar Pr UK) Ashgate Pub Co.

Women & the Economic Miracle: Gender & Work in Postwar Japan. Mary C. Brinton. (California Series on Social Choice & Political Economy: Vol. 21). (C). 1993. 30.00 (*0-520-07563-3*) U CA Pr.

Women & the Economic Miracle: Gender & Work in Postwar Japan. Mary C. Brinton. LC 91-30670. 1994. pap. 15.00 (*0-520-08920-0*) U CA Pr.

Women & the Enlightenment. Ed. by Margaret Hunt et al. LC 84-590. (Women & History Ser.: No. 9). 93p. 1984. text ed. 32.95 (*0-86656-190-0*) Haworth Pr.

Women & the Environment. Ed. by Irwin Altman & A. Churchman. (Human Behavior & Environment Ser.: Vol. 13). (Illus.). 306p. (C). 1994. 49.50 (*0-306-44680-4*, Plenum Pr) Plenum.

Women & the Environment. Annabel Rodda. (Women & World Development Ser.). (Illus.). 192p. (C). 1991. text ed. 49.95 (*0-86232-984-1*, Pub. by Zed Bks Ltd UK) Humanities.

Women & the Environment. 2nd ed. Annabel Rodda. (Women & World Development Ser.). (Illus.). 192p. (C). 1991. pap. 15.95 (*0-86232-985-X*, Pub. by Zed Bks Ltd UK) Humanities.

Women & the Family. Ed. by Helen O'Connell. LC 94-2289. (Women & World Development Ser.). (Illus.). 144p. (C). 1994. pap. 17.50 (*1-85649-106-4*, Pub. by Zed Bks Ltd UK); text ed. 49.95 (*1-85649-105-6*, Pub. by Zed Bks Ltd UK) Humanities.

***Women & the Family.** Ed. by Caroline Sweetman. (Gender & Development Ser.). (Illus.). 112p. 1996. pap. 11.95 (*0-85598-352-3*, Pub. by Oxfam UK) Humanities.

Women & the Family. 2nd ed. Leon Trotsky. Tr. by Max Eastman et al. from RUS. LC 72-92457. 78p. 1973. reprint ed. pap. 9.95 (*0-87348-218-2*) Pathfinder NY.

Women & the Family: Two Decades of Change. Ed. by Beth B. Hess & Marvin B. Sussman. LC 84-12967. (Marriage & Family Review Ser.: Vol. 7, Nos. 3-4). 252p. 1984. text ed. 49.95 (*0-86656-291-5*); pap. text ed. 14.95 (*0-86656-292-3*) Haworth Pr.

Women & the Family in a Slave Society. Ed. by Paul Finkelman. (Articles on American Slavery Ser.). 472p. 1990. reprint ed. text ed. 60.00 (*0-8240-6789-4*) Garland.

Women & the Family in Post-Famine Ireland: Status & Opportunity in a Patriarchal Society. Rita M. Rhodes. LC 92-836. (Modern European History Ser.). 384p. 1992. text ed. 30.00 (*0-8153-0673-3*) Garland.

Women & the Family in Rural Taiwan. Margery Wolf. LC 70-183895. (Illus.). xiv, 236p. 1972. reprint ed. 39.50 (*0-8047-0808-8*); reprint ed. pap. 14.95 (*0-8047-0849-5*) Stanford U Pr.

Women & the Family in the Middle East: New Voices of Change. Ed. by Elizabeth W. Fernea. (Illus.). 368p. 1985. pap. 16.95 (*0-292-75529-5*) U of Tex Pr.

Women & the Genesis of Christianity. Ben Witherington, III. Ed. by Ann Witherington. 288p. (C). 1990. text ed. 59.95 (*0-521-36497-3*); pap. text ed. 17.95 (*0-521-36735-2*) Cambridge U Pr.

Women & the Health Care Industry: An Unhealthy Relationship? Peggy Foster. LC 94-42684. 1995. write for info. (*0-335-09473-2*, Open Univ Pr); pap. write for info. (*0-335-09472-4*, Open Univ Pr) Taylor & Francis.

Women & the Ideal Society: Plato's "Republic" & Modern Myths of Gender. Natalie H. Bluestone. LC 87-6002. 248p. (Orig.). (C). 1987. pap. text ed. 17.95 (*0-87023-581-8*); lib. bdg. 30.00 (*0-87023-580-X*) U of Mass Pr.

Women & the Israeli Occupation: The Politics of Change. Tamar Mayer. LC 94-3886. (International Studies of Women & Places). (Illus.). 240p. (C). (gr. 13). 1994. text ed. 59.95 (*0-415-09545-X*, B0129) Routledge.

Women & the Israeli Occupation: The Politics of Change. Ed. by Tamar Mayer. LC 94-3886. (International Studies of Women & Places). (Illus.). 209p. (C). 1994. pap. 17.95 (*0-415-09546-8*, B0133) Routledge.

Women & the Italian Resistance, 1943-45. Jane Slaughter. LC 97-4937. (Women & Modern Revolution Ser.). (Illus.). 201p. (Orig.). (C). 1997. 32.00 (*0-912869-13-5*); pap. 22.50 (*0-912869-14-3*) Arden Pr.

Women & the Journey: The Female Travel Experience. Ed. by Bonnie Frederick & Susan H. McLeod. LC 93-29498. 238p. 1993. pap. 19.95 (*0-87422-100-5*) Wash St U Pr.

***Women & the Koran: The Status of Women in Islam.** Anwar Helmat. 1997. 32.95 (*1-57392-162-9*) Prometheus Bks.

Women & the Labor Movement. Alice Henry. LC 70-156416. (American Labor Ser., No. 2). 1977. reprint ed. 18.95 (*0-405-02924-1*) Ayer.

Women & the Labour Market. Teresa L. Rees. LC 92-10512. 224p. 1993. pap. write for info. (*0-415-03802-2*) Routledge.

Women & the Labour Movement in Scotland 1850-1914. Eleanor Gordon. 320p. 1991. 75.00 (*0-19-820143-5*) OUP.

Women & the Law. Marcia M. Boumil & Stephen C. Hicks. LC 92-9675. xv, 642p. 1992. 47.50 (*0-8377-0360-3*) Rothman.

Women & the Law. Mary J. Frug. (University Casebook Ser.). 879p. 1992. text ed. 43.95 (*0-88277-977-X*) Foundation Pr.

Women & the Law. Eve Gary & Kathleen W. Peratis. 1992. pap. 12.95 (*0-8442-6005-3*, Natl Textbk) NTC Pub Grp.

Women & the Law. Carol H. Lefcourt. LC 84-11150. (Civil Rights Ser.). 1984. ring bd. 140.00 (*0-87632-441-3*) Clark Boardman Callaghan.

***Women & the Law.** Ed. by Sandra McKillop & P. W. Easteal. (Australian Institute Conference Proceedings Ser.: Vol. 16). 273p. 1993. pap. 30.00 (*0-642-18639-1*, Pub. by Aust Inst Criminology) Willow Tree NY.

Women & the Law. Laura A. Otten. (Contemporary Legal Issues Ser.). Date not set. lib. bdg. 39.50 (*0-87436-878-2*) ABC-CLIO.

Women & the Law: Commentary & Materials. Jocelynne A. Scutt. lii, 596p. 1990. pap. 69.00 (*0-455-20984-7*, Pub. by Law Bk Co AT) Gaunt.

Women & the Law: The Social Historical Perspective. Ed. by D. Kelly Weisberg. 320p. 1982. pap. 18.95 (*0-87073-587-X*); pap. 18.95 (*0-87073-593-4*) Schenkman Bks Inc.

Women & the Law: The Social Historical Perspective, Vol. I: Woman & the Criminal Law. Ed. by D. Kelly Weisberg. 328p. 1982. 22.95 (*0-87073-586-1*) Schenkman Bks Inc.

Women & the Law: The Social Historical Perspective, Vol. II: Property, Family, & the Legal Profession. Ed. by D. Kelly Weisberg. 328p. 1982. 22.95 (*0-87073-592-6*) Schenkman Bks Inc.

Women & the Law: 1994 Supplement. Gerald E. Frug. Ed. by Judith G. Greenberg. (University Casebook Ser.). 89p. 1994. 5.95 (*1-56662-221-2*) Foundation Pr.

Women & the Law in New York State. 2nd rev. ed. Ed. by Paloma Capanna. LC 94-71712. 1994. pap. 14.95 (*0-938588-12-5*) LWV NYS.

Women & the Law, India. T. N. Srivastava. 1985. 22.50 (*0-8364-1419-5*, Pub. by Intellectual II) S Asia.

Women & the Law of Property in Early America. Marylynn Salmon. LC 85-20865. (Studies in Legal History). xviii, 267p. 1986. pap. 16.95 (*0-8078-4244-3*) U of NC Pr.

***Women & the Law 1996.** Gerald E. Frug & Judith G. Greenberg. (University Casebook Ser.). 177p. 1996. suppl. ed., pap. text ed. write for info. (*1-56662-439-8*) Foundation Pr.

Women & the Life Cycle: Transitions & Turning Points. Ed. by Patricia Allatt et al. LC 87-20281. 220p. 1988. text ed. 39.95 (*0-312-01343-4*) St Martin.

Women & the Limits of Citizenship in the French Revolution. Olwen H. Hufton. (Donald G. Creighton Lectures). (Illus.). 232p. 1992. 35.00 (*0-8020-5898-1*); pap. 16.95 (*0-8020-6837-5*) U of Toronto Pr.

Women & the Literature of the Seventeenth Century: An Annotated Bibliography Based on Wing's Short Title Catalogue. Compiled by Hilda Smith & Susan Cardinale. LC 89-28652. (Bibliographies & Indexes in Women's Studies: No. 10). 353p. 1990. text ed. 55.00 (*0-313-22059-X*, SWL/) Greenwood.

Women & the Mass Media: Sourcebook for Research & Action. Ed. by Matilda Butler & William Paisley. LC 79-16271. 432p. 1980. 52.00 (*0-87705-409-6*) Human Sci Pr.

Women & the Mathematical Mystique: Proceedings of the Hyman Blumberg Symposuim on Research in Early Childhood Education, 8th, Johns Hopkins University, 1976. Hyman Blumberg Symposium on Research in Early Childhood Education Staff. Ed. by Lynn H. Fox & Linda Brody. LC 79-3655. 223p. reprint ed. pap. 63.60 (*0-317-20484-X*, 2022997) Bks Demand.

Women & the Men. Nikki Giovanni. LC 75-16237. 1979. pap. 6.95 (*0-688-07947-4*, Quill) Morrow.

Women & the Military. Martin Binkin & Shirley J. Bach. LC 77-24040. (Studies in Defense Policy). 134p. 1977. 26.95 (*0-8157-0966-8*); pap. 9.95 (*0-8157-0965-X*) Brookings.

Women & the Military: A Hundred Notable Contributors, Historic to Contemporary. John P. Dever & Maria Dever. LC 94-30910. 164p. 1994. lib. bdg. 24.95 (*0-89950-976-2*) McFarland & Co.

Women & the Military: An Encyclopedia. Victoria Sherrow. LC 96-33459. 304p. 1996. lib. bdg. 65.00 (*0-87436-812-X*) ABC-CLIO.

Women & the Military System. Ed. by Eva Isaksson. LC 88-15803. 440p. 1988. pap. 14.95 (*0-312-01978-5*); text ed. 49.95 (*0-312-01976-9*) St Martin.

Women & the Ministries of Christ. Ed. by Roberta Hestenes & Lois Curley. 1979. pap. 15.95 (*0-9602638-2-9*) Fuller Seminary.

Women & the New German Cinema. Julia Knight. LC 92-6408. (Questions for Feminism Ser.). (Illus.). 192p. (C). 1992. pap. text ed. 18.00 (*0-86091-568-9*, A6396, Pub. by Vrso UK) Norton.

Women & the New German Cinema. Julia Knight. LC 92-6408. (Questions for Feminism Ser.). (Illus.). 192p. (C). (gr. 13). 1992. text ed. 55.00 (*0-86091-352-X*, A6392, Pub. by Vrso UK) Norton.

Women & the New Law. V. S. Deshpande. 1985. pap. text ed. 9.50 (*0-8364-1368-7*, Pub. by Punjabi U II) S Asia.

Women & the New Testament: An Analysis of Scripture in Light of New Testament Era Culture. Lesly F. Massey. LC 89-42735. 160p. 1989. lib. bdg. 32.50 (*0-89950-438-8*) McFarland & Co.

Women & the New Trade Agenda. Susan Joekes & Ann Weston. 100p. (Orig.). 1995. pap. 7.95 (*0-912917-34-2*) UNIFEM.

Women & the New World Economy: Feminist Perspectives on Alternative Economic Frameworks. Gita Sen. 192p. (C). 1997. pap. 19.95 (*1-85649-364-4*, Pub. by Zed Bks Ltd UK); text ed. 55.00 (*1-85649-363-6*, Pub. by Zed Bks Ltd UK) Humanities.

Women & the Nicaraguan Revolution. Tomas Borge. 30p. 1982. pap. 2.50 (*0-87348-475-4*) Pathfinder NY.

Women & the Ownership of PMS: The Structuring of a Psychiatric Disorder. Anne Figert. (Social Problems & Social Issues Ser.). 208p. 1996. pap. text ed. 20.95 (*0-202-30551-1*); lib. bdg. 41.95 (*0-202-30550-3*) Aldine de Gruyter.

Women & the Political Process. Marilee Karl. (Women in World Development Ser.). (Illus.). 160p. (C). 1995. text ed. 49.95 (*1-85649-191-9*, Pub. by Zed Bks Ltd UK) Humanities.

***Women & the Political Process in Twentieth-Century Iran.** 424p. 1997. pap. text ed. 22.95 (*0-521-59572-X*) Cambridge U Pr.

Women & the Political Process in Twentieth-Century Iran. Parvin Paidar. (Middle East Studies: No. 1). 392p. (C). 1995. 59.95 (*0-521-47340-3*) Cambridge U Pr.

Women & the Politics of Empowerment. Ed. by Ann Bookman & Sandra Morgen. LC 87-6504. 352p. (C). 1988. pap. 18.95 (*0-87722-525-7*) Temple U Pr.

Women & the Popular Imagination in the Twenties: Flappers & Nymphs. Billie Melman. LC 87-4652. 208p. 1988. text ed. 35.00 (*0-312-00744-2*) St Martin.

Women & the Priesthood. Alice Von Hildebrand & Peter Kreeft. 88p. 1994. pap. 4.95 (*0-940535-72-6*, UP172) Franciscan U Pr.

Women & the Priesthood: Essays from the Orthodox Tradition. Kallistos T. Ware et al. Ed. by Thomas Hopko. 190p. 1982. pap. 11.95 (*0-88141-005-5*) St Vladimirs.

W

An Asterisk (*) at the beginning of an entry indicates that the title is appearing in BIP for the first time.

Women & the Public Sphere in the Age of the French Revolution. Joan B. Landes. LC 88-3723. (Illus.). 296p. 1988. 39.95 (*0-8014-2141-1*); pap. 14.95 (*0-8014-9481-8*) Cornell U Pr.

***Women & the Railroads.** Nancy S. Levinson & Shirley Burman. (J). 1997. write for info. (*0-614-29259-X*, Lodestar Bks) Dutton Child Bks.

Women & the Religious Life in Pre-Modern Europe. Patricia Ranft. 159p. 1996. text ed. 39.95 (*0-312-12434-1*) St Martin.

Women & the Revolution. Ethel Mannin. 1976. lib. bdg. 59.95 (*0-8490-2834-5*) Gordon Pr.

Women & the Scientific Professions: Proceedings of the M. I.T. Symposium on American Women in Science & Engineering, 1964. M.I.T. Symposium Staff. Ed. by Jacquelyn Mattfeld & Carol Van Aken. LC 76-2516. 250p. 1976. reprint ed. text ed. 55.00 (*0-8371-8759-1*, MAWSP) Greenwood.

***Women & the Settlement Movement.** Katherine B. Beauman. (Illus.). 224p. 1996. text ed. 39.50 (*1-86064-129-6*, Pub. by I B Tauris UK) St Martin.

***Women & the Slovakian National Movement: Gender & Class As Components of National Efforts in Slovakia 1848 until 1990.** Nora Weber. 326p. 1997. 74.95 (*1-57309-160-X*); pap. 54.95 (*1-57309-159-6*) Intl Scholars.

Women & the Socialist Revolution. Mary-Alice Waters. 30p. 1976. reprint ed. pap. 3.00 (*0-87348-388-X*) Pathfinder NY.

Women & the State. 1990. pap. text ed. 15.95 (*0-04-445672-7*) Routledge Chapman & Hall.

Women & the State. Ed. by Anne S. Sassoon. 311p. 1988. pap. text ed. 19.95 (*0-09-173148-8*) Routledge Chapman & Hall.

Women & the State. Ed. by Anne Showstack-Sasson. 311p. (C). 1989. pap. 19.95 (*0-415-07908-X*, Routledge NY) Routledge.

Women & the State: International Perspectives. Ed. by Shirin M. Rai & Geraldine Lievesley. LC 95-48108. (Gender, Change & Society Ser.: Vol. 2). 208p. 1996. 69.95 (*0-7484-0360-4*); pap. 24.95 (*0-7484-0361-2*) Taylor & Francis.

Women & the State in Africa. Ed. by Jane L. Parpart & Kathleen A. Staudt. LC 88-23974. 225p. 1987. pap. text ed. 16.95 (*1-55587-223-9*) Lynne Rienner.

Women & the Structure of Society: Selected Research from the Fifth Berkshire Conference on the History of Women. Ed. by Barbara J. Harris & JoAnn K. McNamara. LC 84-15990. xi, 305p. (C). 1984. pap. 18.95 (*0-8223-0603-4*); text ed. 48.00 (*0-8223-0558-5*) Duke.

Women & the Sun. Pierre Gascar. Tr. by D. H. Lawrence. LC 76-54791. 255p. 1977. reprint ed. text ed. 67.50 (*0-8371-9360-5*, GAWS, Greenwood Pr) Greenwood.

Women & the Trades. Elizabeth B. Butler. LC 70-89757. (American Labor, from Conspiracy to Collective Bargaining Ser., No. 1). 440p. 1972. reprint ed. 26.95 (*0-405-02108-9*) Ayer.

Women & the Trades. Elizabeth B. Butler. LC 84-5175. (Social & Labor History Ser.). (Illus.). 568p. (C). 1984. reprint ed. pap. 19.95 (*0-8229-5901-1*) U of Pittsburgh Pr.

Women & the United Nations: Reflections & New Horizons. Ed. by Filomina C. Steady & Remie Toure. 208p. (Orig.). 1995. 24.95 (*0-87047-103-1*); pap. 14.95 (*0-87047-104-X*) Schenkman Bks Inc.

Women & the University Curriculum. Ed. by French National Commission for UNESCO. 172p. 1996. pap. text ed. 34.95 (*1-85302-399-X*, Pub. by J Kingsley Pubs UK) Taylor & Francis.

Women & the Values of American Librarianship. Sydney Chambers & Carolynne Myall. LC 93-38311. vi, 86p. 1993. pap. 10.00 (*0-86663-205-0*) Ide Hse.

Women & the War Story. Miriam Cooke. LC 96-11601. (Illus.). 340p. 1997. 50.00 (*0-520-20612-6*); pap. 18.95 (*0-520-20613-4*) U CA Pr.

Women & the Warlords. Hugh Cook. LC 87-73288. (Chronicles of an Age of Darkness Ser.: Vol. 3). 275p. 8800. 30.00 (*0-8023-1286-1*) Dufour.

Women & the Warriors: The U. S. Section of the Women's International League for Peace & Freedom, 1915-1946. Carrie Foster. LC 94-39571. (Studies on Peace & Conflict Resolution). 424p. 1995. text ed. 49.95 (*0-8156-2625-8*); pap. text ed. 17.95 (*0-8156-2662-2*) Syracuse U Pr.

Women & the Welfare State. Elizabeth Wilson. (Tavistock Women's Studies). 208p. (C). 1977. pap. text ed. 11.95 (*0-422-76060-9*, NO. 2590, Pub. by Tavistock UK) Routledge Chapman & Hall.

Women & the West: A Short Social History. William F. Sprague. LC 72-2624. (American Women Ser.: Images & Realities). (Illus.). 304p. 1972. reprint ed. 20.95 (*0-405-04480-1*) Ayer.

Women & the Women's Movement in Britain. Martin Pugh. 249p. (C). 1994. 49.95 (*1-56924-855-9*) Marlowe & Co.

Women & the Word: (1986 Madaleva Lecture), The Gender of God in the New Testament & the Spirituality of Women. Sandra M. Schneiders. 60p. (Orig.). 1986. pap. 4.95 (*0-8091-2802-0*) Paulist Pr.

Women & the Word of God. Susan Foh. 1980. pap. 9.99 (*0-87552-268-8*, Pub. by Evangelical Pr) Presby & Reformed.

Women & the Work of Benevolence: Morality, Politics & Class in the Nineteenth-Century United States. Lori D. Ginzberg. 256p. (C). 1990. text ed. 35.00 (*0-300-04704-5*) Yale U Pr.

Women & the Work of Benevolence: Morality, Politics, & Class in the Nineteenth-Century United States. Lori D. Ginzberg. 248p. (C). 1992. reprint ed. pap. text ed. 14.00 (*0-300-05254-5*) Yale U Pr.

Women & the Workplace: The Implications of Occupational Segregation. Ed. by Martha Blaxall. LC 76-10536. 336p. 1976. pap. text ed. 13.50 (*0-226-05822-0*) U Ch Pr.

Women & the World Economic Crisis. Jeanne Vickers. LC 90-28525. (Women & World Development Ser.). 192p. (C). 1991. pap. 15.95 (*0-86232-975-2*, Pub. by Zed Bks Ltd UK); text ed. 49.95 (*0-86232-974-4*, Pub. by Zed Bks Ltd UK) Humanities.

Women & Their Emotions. expanded rev. ed. Miriam Neff. 1995. pap. 10.99 (*0-8024-9531-1*) Moody.

Women & their Fathers: The Sexual & Romantic Impact of the First Man in Your Life. Victoria Secunda. 512p. 1993. pap. 13.95 (*0-385-31023-4*, Delta) Dell.

Women & Their Life-Styles: Index of New Information. Paul K. Vogel. 150p. 1994. 44.50 (*0-7883-0056-3*); pap. 39.50 (*0-7883-0057-1*) ABBE Pubs Assn.

Women & Their Quilts: A Washington State Centennial Tribute. Nancyann J. Twelker. 1992. pap. 9.95 (*0-486-27202-8*) Dover.

Women & Their Right to a Health Policy. Jose A. Pinotti & A. Faundes. (Illus.). 150p. 1989. 45.00 (*1-85070-225-X*) Prthnon Pub.

Women & Theology: The 1994 Annual Publication of the College Theology Society. Ed. by Mary A. Hinsdale & Phyllis Kaminski. LC 95-32846. 224p. (Orig.). 1995. pap. 19.95 (*1-57075-035-1*) Orbis Bks.

Women & Tobacco. C. Chollat-Traquet et al. (Illus.). 128p. (Orig.). (C). 1994. pap. 30.00 (*0-7881-1342-9*) DIANE Pub.

Women & Tobacco. C. Chollat-Traquet et al. xi, 128p. (Orig.). (CHI, ENG, FRE, RUS & SPA.). 1992. pap. text ed. 26.00 (*92-4-156147-5*, 1150373) World Health.

Women & Training. Ann Wickham. LC 86-5176. (Gender & Education Ser.). 144p. 1986. pap. 29.00 (*0-335-15119-1*, Open Univ Pr) Taylor & Francis.

Women & Unions: Forging a Partnership. Dorothy S. Cobble. 464p. 1993. 52.00 (*0-87546-300-2*, ILR Press) Cornell U Pr.

Women & Unions: Forging a Partnership. Ed. by Dorothy S. Cobble. 464p. 1993. pap. 19.95 (*0-87546-301-0*, ILR Press) Cornell U Pr.

Women & Urban Settlement. Ed. by Caroline Sweetman. (Gender & Development Ser.). (Illus.). 64p. (C). 1996. pap. 11.95 (*0-85598-348-5*, Pub. by Oxfam UK) Humanities.

Women & Urban Society: A Guide to Information Sources. Ed. by Hasia R. Diner. LC 78-13109. (Urban Studies Information Guide Ser.: Vol. 7). 152p. 1979. 68.00 (*0-8103-1425-8*) Gale.

Women & Vagina Research: Index of Modern Information. Judy J. Hallcrest. LC 88-47636. 150p. 1988. 44.50 (*0-88164-810-8*); pap. 39.50 (*0-88164-811-6*) ABBE Pubs Assn.

Women & Values: Readings in Recent Feminist Philosophy. 2nd ed. Marilyn Pearsall. LC 92-13426. 413p. (C). 1993. pap. 37.95 (*0-534-19554-7*) Wadsworth Pub.

***Women & Victorian Theatre.** Kerry Powell. (Illus.). 250p. (C). 1997. text ed. 49.95 (*0-521-47167-2*) Cambridge U Pr.

Women & Violence. Ed. by Niroj Sinha. 1989. text ed. 25.00 (*0-7069-4340-6*, Pub. by Vikas II) S Asia.

Women & Violence: Realities & Responses Worldwide. Miranda E. Davies. 264p. (C). 1994. pap. 22.50 (*1-85649-146-3*, Pub. by Zed Bks Ltd UK); text ed. 55.00 (*1-85649-145-5*, Pub. by Zed Bks Ltd UK) Humanities.

Women & Violence in Literature: An Essay Collection. Katherine A. Ackley. LC 89-36391. 350p. 1990. text ed. 54.00 (*0-8240-0693-3*, 1271) Garland.

***Women & Visual Culture in Early Nineteenth-Century France.** Gen Doy. LC 97-15449. 1997. write for info. (*0-7185-0148-9*, Pub. by Leicester Univ Pr) Bks Intl VA.

Women & Wallace. Jonathan M. Sherman. 1989. pap. 5.25 (*0-8222-1271-4*) Dramatists Play.

Women & War. Ed. by Maria Diedrich & Dorothea Fischer-Hornung. 176p. 1990. 19.95 (*0-85496-648-X*) Berg Pubs.

Women & War. Jean B. Elshtain. LC 95-755. xvi, 302p. 1995. pap. text ed. 14.95 (*0-226-20626-2*) U Ch Pr.

Women & War. Jeanne Vickers. LC 93-15275. 192p. (C). 1993. pap. 17.50 (*1-85649-230-3*, Pub. by Zed Bks Ltd UK); text ed. 49.95 (*1-85649-229-X*, Pub. by Zed Bks Ltd UK) Humanities.

Women & War in South Africa. Jacklyn Cock. LC 93-16270. 264p. (C). 1993. reprint ed. pap. 16.95 (*0-8298-0966-X*) Pilgrim OH.

Women & War, Vol. 15 see History of Women in the United States: Topically Arranged Articles on the Evolution of Women's History in the United States

Women & Wasteland Development. Ed. by Andrea M. Singh & Neera Burra. (Illus.). 336p. (C). 1993. text ed. 38.00 (*0-8039-9123-1*) Sage.

Women & Water. John Guare. 1990. pap. 5.25 (*0-8222-1272-2*) Dramatists Play.

Women & Water Pumps in Bangladesh: The Impact of Participation in Irrigation Groups On Womens Status. Barbara Van Koppen & Simeen Mahmud. 256p. (Orig.). 1995. pap. 18.95 (*1-85339-336-3*, Pub. by Intermed Tech UK) Women Ink.

***Women & Welfare: A Study of Voluntary Agencies.** Usha Kapoor. 1995. 30.00 (*81-7387-032-2*, Pub. by Indus Pub II) S Asia.

Women & Well-Being. Ed. by Vanaja Dhruvarajan. 272p. (ENG & FRE.). (C). 1990. text ed. 55.00 (*0-7735-0734-5*, Pub. by McGill CN); pap. text ed. 24.95 (*0-7735-0762-0*, Pub. by McGill CN) U of Toronto Pr.

Women & Wilderness. Anne LaBastille. LC 80-14369. (Paperback Library). (Illus.). 320p. 1984. reprint ed. pap. 14.00 (*0-87156-828-4*) Sierra.

***Women & Women's Cancers: The Effects of Gynecologic & Breast Cancers on Our Lives.** Kristine Falco. LC 97-16795. (Illus.). 1997. text ed. 27.50 (*0-7657-0099-9*) Aronson.

Women & Women's Issues: A Handbook of Tests & Measures. Carole A. Beere. LC 79-88106. (Jossey-Bass Social & Behavioral Science Ser.). 568p. reprint ed. pap. 161.90 (*0-8357-4815-4*, 2037752) Bks Demand.

Women & Women's Issues see Modern American Protestantism & Its World

Women & Women's Rights: A Medical, Psychological & International Subject Survey with Research Index & Bibliography. American Health Research Institute Staff. Ed. by John C. Bartone. LC 83-70089. 146p. 1984. 37.50 (*0-941864-98-7*); pap. 39.50 (*0-941864-99-5*) ABBE Pubs Assn.

Women & Words in Saudi Arabia: The Politics of Literary Discourse. Saddeka Arebi. 357p. 1994. 49.00 (*0-231-08420-X*); pap. 17.50 (*0-231-08421-8*) Col U Pr.

Women & Work. Susan Bullock. (Women & World Development Ser.). 160p. (C). 1994. pap. 17.50 (*1-85649-118-8*, Pub. by Zed Bks Ltd UK); text ed. 49.95 (*1-85649-117-X*, Pub. by Zed Bks Ltd UK) Humanities.

Women & Work. Ed. by Tom Cox. (Work & Stress Ser.: Vol. 1, No. 3). 122p. 1988. pap. 29.00 (*0-85066-906-5*) Taylor & Francis.

Women & Work. Marjorie B. Turner. 73p. 1964. 5.00 (*0-89215-025-4*) U Cal LA Indus Rel.

Women & Work: A Handbook. Ed. by Paula J. Dubeck et al. LC 95-49853. (Illus.). 592p. 1996. text ed. 75.00 (*0-8240-7647-8*, SS679) Garland.

Women & Work: A Psychological Perspective. Veronica Nieva & Barbara Gutek. LC 81-2713. 190p. 1981. text ed. 47.50 (*0-275-90688-4*, C0688, Praeger Pubs) Greenwood.

***Women & Work: A Reader.** Ed. by Paula J. Dubeck & Kathryn Borman. LC 97-22828. 550p. 1997. pap. 26.00 (*0-8135-2473-3*) Rutgers U Pr.

Women & Work: An Annual Review, Vol. 3. Ed. by Barbara A. Gutek et al. LC 85-642613. 291p. 1988. pap. 83.00 (*0-7837-8963-7*, 2049744) Bks Demand.

Women & Work: An Annual Review, Vol. 3. Ed. by Barbara A. Gutek et al. 320p. (C). 1988. text ed. 55.00 (*0-8039-3252-9*) Sage.

Women & Work: In Their Own Words. 2nd ed. Maureen R. Michelson. 1994. pap. 14.95 (*0-939165-23-6*) NewSage Press.

***Women & Work Vol. 2-1987: An Annual Review.** Ed. by Ann H. Stromberg et al. LC 85-642613. 272p. 1987. reprint ed. pap. 77.60 (*0-608-02797-9*, 2063864) Bks Demand.

***Women & Work Vol. 6: Exploring Race, Ethnicity, & Class.** Ed. by Elizabeth Higginbotham & Mary Romero. 320p. 1997. 55.00 (*0-8039-5058-6*) Sage.

***Women & Work Vol. 6: Exploring Race, Ethnicity, & Class.** Ed. by Elizabeth Higginbotham & Mary Romero. 320p. 1997. pap. 24.95 (*0-8039-5059-4*) Sage.

Women & Work in Developing Countries: An Annotated Bibliopgraphy. Ed. by Parvin Ghorayshi. LC 93-38803. (Bibliographies & Indexes in Women's Studies: No. 20). 248p. 1994. text ed. 59.95 (*0-313-28834-8*, Greenwood Pr) Greenwood.

Women & Work in Developing Societies, Vol. 12. Nadia H. Youssef. LC 76-4537. 137p. 1976. reprint ed. text ed. 22.50 (*0-8371-8836-9*, YOWW, Greenwood Pr) Greenwood.

Women & Work in Eighteenth-Century Edinburgh. Elizabeth C. Sanderson. LC 95-22032. (Studies in Gender History). 260p. 1996. text ed. 55.00 (*0-312-12917-3*) St Martin.

Women & Work in Pre-Industrial Britain. Ed. by Lindsey Charles & Lorna Duffin. LC 85-14950. (Oxford Women's Ser.). 212p. 1986. pap. 15.95 (*0-7099-0856-3*, Pub. by Croom Helm UK) Routledge Chapman & Hall.

Women & Work in Preindustrial Europe. Ed. by Barbara A. Hanawalt. LC 85-42829. (Illus.). 254p. 1986. 35.00 (*0-253-36610-0*); pap. 12.95 (*0-253-20367-8*, MB-367) Ind U Pr.

Women & Work in South Asia: Regional Patterns & Perspectives. Ed. by Saraswati Raju & Deipica Bagchi. LC 93-10554. 272p. (C). (gr. 13). 1994. text ed. 69.95 (*0-415-04249-6*) Routledge.

Women & Work, Paid & Unpaid: A Selected, Annotated Bibliography. Marianne A. Ferber. LC 87-8652. (Reference Library of Social Science: Vol. 315). 424p. 1987. text ed. 44.00 (*0-8240-8690-2*, SS315) Garland.

Women & Working Lives. Ed. by Sara Arber & Nigel Gilbert. LC 91-24428. 208p. 1992. text ed. 49.95 (*0-312-06866-2*) St Martin.

Women & World Development: An Education & Action Guide for Making Global Connections in Your Community. Anita Mermel & Judy Simons. Ed. by OEF International Staff. LC 89-7220. 92p. (Orig.). 1991. student ed., pap. 16.00 (*0-912917-21-0*) UNIFEM.

Women & World Religions. 2nd ed. Denise L. Carmody. 256p. 1988. pap. text ed. 26.80 (*0-13-962424-4*) P-H.

Women & Worship at Phillipi: Diana, Artemis & Other Cults. Valerie A. Abrahamsen. LC 95-5491. (Illus.). 256p. 1995. per. 16.95 (*1-885349-00-9*) Astarte Shell Pr.

Women & Writing. Virginia Woolf. LC 79-3371. 198p. 1980. pap. 11.00 (*0-15-693658-5*, Harvest Bks) HarBrace.

Women & Writing. Virginia Woolf. 1990. 19.25 (*0-8446-6211-9*) Peter Smith.

Women & Writing in Early Europe: A Sourcebook. Carolyne Larrington. LC 94-30485. 272p. (C). 1995. pap. 18.95 (*0-415-10685-0*, B3166) Routledge.

Women & Writing in Russia & the U. S. S. R. A Bibliography of English-Language Sources. Ed. by Diane M. Ignashev & Sarah Krive. LC 92-9246. 341p. 1992. text ed. 55.00 (*0-8240-3647-6*) Garland.

Women, Androgynes, & Other Mythical Beasts. Wendy D. O'Flaherty. LC 79-16128. 408p. 1982. pap. text ed. 22.00 (*0-226-61850-1*) U Ch Pr.

Women, Anger & Depression: Strategies for Self-Empowerment. Lois P. Frankel. 112p. (Orig.). 1991. pap. 8.95 (*1-55874-161-5*) Health Comm.

Women, Animals, & Vegetables. Maxine Kumin. LC 95-42216. 299p. 1996. reprint ed. pap. 12.95 (*0-86538-084-8*) Ontario Rev NJ.

Women Anthropologists: A Biographical Dictionary. Ed. by Ute D. Gacs et al. LC 87-11983. 445p. 1988. text ed. 65.00 (*0-313-24414-6*, GWA/, Greenwood Pr) Greenwood.

Women Anthropologists: Selected Biographies. Ed. by Ute D. Gacs et al. 448p. 1989. reprint ed. pap. text ed. 17.50 (*0-252-06084-9*) U of Ill Pr.

Women Are Bloody Marvellous. large type ed. Betty Burton. 1993. 50.00 (*0-7066-1017-2*, Pub. by Remploy Pr CN) St Mut.

Women Are Called Girls. Michael Basinski. 22p. 1983. 3.00 (*0-938838-10-5*) Textile Bridge.

Women Are Different. Flora Nwapa. 144p. 1992. 24.95 (*0-86543-325-9*); pap. 9.95 (*0-86543-326-7*) Africa World.

***Women Are from Bras Men Are from Penus.** Anna Collins & Elliot Sullivan. (Illus.). 185p. 1997. pap. 9.95 (*1-890410-10-1*, Ship Of Fools Bks) Sullivan & Foster.

***Women Are from Pluto, Men Are from Uranus: The Big Bang & Other Premature Theories of Love.** Mike Nichols. LC 96-35685. (Illus.). 172p. 1996. 9.99 (*1-56530-224-9*) Summit TX.

Women Are Marching: The Second Sex & the Palestinian Revolution. Philippa Strum. LC 91-42410. (Illus.). 364p. 1992. 29.00 (*1-55652-122-7*); pap. 16.95 (*1-55652-123-5*) L Hill Bks.

Women Are Queer. Grace S. Mason. LC 77-37278. (Short Story Index Reprint Ser.). 1977. reprint ed. 23.95 (*0-8369-4089-X*) Ayer.

Women Around Jesus. Elisabeth Moltmann-Wendel. LC 82-72478. 160p. 1982. pap. 13.95 (*0-8245-0535-2*) Crossroad NY.

Women Around the World. Thorsten D. Sellin. LC 68-16155. (Annals of the American Academy of Political & Social Science Ser.: No. 375). (Orig.). 1968. pap. 18.00 (*0-87761-104-1*) Am Acad Pol Soc Sci.

Women, Art, & Power. Linda Nochlin. LC 88-45118. 1989. pap. 16.00 (*0-06-430183-4*, Icon Edns) HarpC.

Women, Art, & Society. rev. ed. Whitney Chadwick. LC 96-60233. (World of Art Ser.). (Illus.). 448p. (Orig.). 1997. pap. 16.95 (*0-500-20293-1*) Thames Hudson.

Women, Art, & Spirituality: The Poor Clares of Early Modern Itlay. Jeryldene M. Wood. LC 95-44522. (Illus.). 304p. (C). 1996. text ed. 70.00 (*0-521-49602-0*) Cambridge U Pr.

***Women Artist Book of Days.** Signorelli. 1989. pap. 10.95 (*0-88363-481-3*) S&S Trade.

Women Artists. (Shorewood Art Programs for Education Ser.). 16p. 1983. teacher ed. 90.50 (*0-88185-071-3*); 100.00 (*0-685-09213-5*) Shorewood Fine Art.

Women Artists. CEDCO Book Collection Staff. 120p. 1991. pap. 19.95 (*1-55912-252-8*) CEDCO Pub.

Women Artists: An Historical, Contemporary, & Feminist Bibliography. 2nd ed. Sherry Piland. LC 93-27248. (Illus.). 497p. 1994. 59.50 (*0-8108-2559-7*) Scarecrow.

Women Artists: An Illustrated History. expanded rev. ed. Nancy G. Heller. LC 87-904. (Illus.). 256p. 1987. pap. 29.95 (*1-55859-211-3*) Abbeville Pr.

***Women Artists: An Illustrated History.** 3rd ed. Nancy Heller. LC 97-10512. (Illus.). 272p. 1997. pap. 37.50 (*0-7892-0345-6*) Abbeville Pr.

Women Artists: Multi-Cultural Visions. Betty LaDuke. LC 91-68511. (Illus.). 205p. 1992. 49.95 (*0-932415-77-6*); pap. 16.95 (*0-932415-78-4*) Red Sea Pr.

Women Artists: The National Museum of Women in the Arts. Susan F. Sterling. (Tiny Folio Ser.). (Illus.). 320p. 1996. pap. 11.95 (*1-55859-890-1*) Abbeville Pr.

***Women Artists: The National Museum of Women in the Arts.** Susan F. Sterling. (Tiny Folios Ser.). 1997. 11.95 (*0-7892-0411-8*) Abbeville Pr.

Women Artists & the Parisian Avant-Garde: Modernism & "Feminine" Art, 1900 to the Late 1920s. Gill Perry. LC 94-42772. 256p. 1996. text ed. 24.95 (*0-7190-4165-1*, Pub. by Manchester Univ Pr UK) St Martin.

Women Artists & the Surrealist Movement. Whitney Chadwick. LC 90-71450. (Illus.). 256p. 1991. reprint ed. pap. 24.95 (*0-500-27622-6*) Thames Hudson.

Women Artists & Writers: Modernist (Im) Positionings. Bridget J. Elliott & Jo-Ann Wallace. LC 93-44533. (Illus.). 248p. (C). (gr. 13). 1994. pap. 18.95 (*0-415-05366-8*, A7951, Routledge NY) Routledge.

Women Artists & Writers: Modernist (Im) Positionings. Bridget J. Elliott & Jo-Ann Wallace. LC 93-44533. (Illus.). 224p. (C). (gr. 13). 1994. text ed. 62.95 (*0-415-05365-X*, A7947, Routledge NY) Routledge.

Women Artists Book of Days. 128p. 1989. pap. 10.95 (*0-88363-089-3*) H L Levin.

***Women Artists Diary 1998.** 1997. pap. 12.95 (*0-7043-4528-5*, Pub. by Womens Press UK) Trafalgar.

***Women Artists Diary 1998.** 1997. pap. 12.95 (*0-7043-4527-7*, Pub. by Womens Press UK) Trafalgar.

Women Artists in History: From Antiquity to the Present. 3rd ed. Wendy Slatkin. LC 95-41184. 1996. pap. text ed. 26.00 (*0-13-432873-6*) P-H.

Women Artists in the Modern Era: A Documentary History. Susan Waller. LC 91-17047. 404p. 1991. 47.50 (*0-8108-2405-1*) Scarecrow.

W

Women Artists in the U. S. Guide on the Fine & Decorative Arts, 1750-1986. Paula Chiarmonte. (Reference Ser.). 1080p. 1990. 70.00 (*0-8161-8917-X*, Hall Reference) Macmillan.

***Women Artists of Italian Futurism: Almost Lost to History.** Bentivoglio & Zoccoli. LC 94-73077. (Illus.). (Orig.). 1997. text ed. 35.00 (*1-877675-26-1*) Midmarch Arts-WAN.

***Women Artists of Italian Futurism: Almost Lost to History.** Bentivoglio & Zoccoli. LC 94-73077. (Illus.). (Orig.). 1997. pap. text ed. 25.00 (*1-877675-18-0*) Midmarch Arts-WAN.

Women Artists of the Americas. 5p. 1994. 30.00 (*1-56290-101-X*, 6042) Crystal.

Women Artists, Women Exiles: "Miss Grief" & Other Stories. Constance F. Woolson. Ed. by Joan M. Weimer. (American Women Writers Ser.). 350p. (Orig.). (C). 1988. text ed. 42.00 (*0-8135-1347-2*); pap. text ed. 15.00 (*0-8135-1348-0*) Rutgers U Pr.

Women as a Minority Group. Helen M. Hacker. (Reprint Series in Social Sciences). (C). 1993. reprint ed. pap. text ed. 1.00 (*0-8290-3852-3*, S-108) Irvington.

Women As Candidates in American Politics. 2nd ed. Susan J. Carroll. LC 93-41856. 256p. 1994. 31.50 (*0-253-31319-8*); pap. 13.95 (*0-253-20877-7*) Ind U Pr.

Women As Christ's Disciples. Kathy McReynolds & A. Boyd Luter. LC 96-32480. 208p. (YA). (gr. 10). 1996. pap. 11.99 (*0-8010-5711-6*) Baker Bks.

***Women As Demons.** Tarwith Lee. pap. 9.95 (*0-7043-4132-8*, Pub. by Womens Press UK) Trafalgar.

Women As Donors, Women As Philanthropists. Ed. by Abbie J. Von Schlegell & Joan M. Fisher. (New Directions for Philanthropic Fundraising Ser.: No. 2). 161p. (Orig.). 1993. pap. 19.95 (*1-55542-713-8*) Jossey-Bass.

Women As Educational Leaders: Opening Windows, Pushing Ceilings. Marie S. Hill & Joyce C. Ragland. LC 94-46410. 144p. 1995. 40.00 (*0-8039-6136-7*); pap. 18.00 (*0-8039-6137-5*) Corwin Pr.

Women As Elders: Images, Visions & Issues. Ed. by Marilyn J. Bell. LC 86-25699. (Women & Politics Ser.: Vol. 6, No. 2). 90p. 1987. text ed. 24.95 (*0-86656-621-X*) Haworth Pr.

Women As Elders: The Feminist Politics of Aging. Ed. by Marilyn J. Bell. LC 86-25696. (Women & Politics Ser.: Vol. 6, No. 2). 90p. 1987. reprint ed. pap. 9.95 (*0-918393-34-5*) Harrington Pk.

Women As Food Producers in Developing Countries. Ed. by Marion Kalb & Jamie Morson. 1985. pap. 16.00 (*0-918456-56-8*) African Studies Assn.

Women As Healers: Cross-Cultural Perspectives. Ed. by Carol S. McClain. LC 88-16896. 272p. (C). 1989. pap. text ed. 16.00 (*0-8135-1370-7*) Rutgers U Pr.

Women As Healers: The History of Women & Medicine. Hilary Bourdillon. (Women in History Ser.). (Illus.). 48p. (C). 1989. pap. text ed. 11.95 (*0-521-31090-3*) Cambridge U Pr.

Women As Interpreters of the Visual Arts, 1820-1979. Ed. by Claire R. Sherman & Adele M. Holcomb. LC 80-785. (Contributions in Women's Studies: No. 18). (Illus.). xxiv, 487p. 1981. text ed. 49.95 (*0-313-22056-5*, SWS/, Greenwood Pr) Greenwood.

Women As Leaders: Accepting the Challenge of Scripture. Katherine Haubert. 101p. 1993. pap. 3.95 (*0-912552-81-6*) MARC.

***Women As Leaders & Managers in Higher Education.** Heather Eggins & Society for Research into Higher Education Staff. LC 96-53332. 1997. write for info. (*0-335-19880-5*, Open Univ Pr); pap. write for info. (*0-335-19879-1*, Open Univ Pr) Taylor & Francis.

Women As Lovers. Theresa Carilli. (Drama Ser.: No. 1). 274p. 1995. 18.00 (*1-55071-007-9*) Guernica Editions.

Women As Lovers. Theresa Carilli. 1996. pap. 15.00 (*0-614-96969-7*) Guernica Editions.

Women As Lovers. Elfriede Jelinek. Tr. by Martin Chalmers from GER. LC 94-67713. (Masks Ser.). 192p. (Orig.). 1995. pap. 14.99 (*1-85242-237-8*) Serpents Tail.

***Women As Millionaires (WAM), Vol. 1.** Bettina R. Flores. Ed. by Lynn Pribus. (Illus.). 230p. (Orig.). 1997. 26.00 (*0-9625777-0-7*) Bettina Enterprises.

Women As Mothers. Sheila Kitzinger. LC 79-4853. 1980. pap. 5.95 (*0-394-74079-3*) Random.

Women As Mythmakers: Poetry & Visual Art by Twentieth-Century Women. Estella Lauter. LC 83-48636. (Illus.). 288p. 1984. 35.00 (*0-253-36606-2*); pap. 8.95 (*0-253-20325-2*, MB-325) Ind U Pr.

Women As National Leaders. Ed. by Michael A. Genovese. LC 92-33064. (Focus Editions Ser.: Vol. 153). (Illus.). 320p. (C). 1993. text ed. 54.00 (*0-8039-4337-7*); pap. text ed. 24.95 (*0-8039-4338-5*) Sage.

Women As Outsiders: Undercurrents of Oppression in Latin American Women's Novels. Maureen E. Shea. LC 93-29598. 128p. 1994. 64.95 (*1-880921-61-8*); pap. 44.95 (*1-880921-60-X*) Austin & Winfield.

Women as Revolutionary Agents of Change: The Hite Reports & Beyond. Shere Hite. LC 93-39168. 544p. (Orig.). 1994. pap. 22.95 (*0-299-14294-9*) U of Wis Pr.

Women As Ritual Experts: The Religious Lives of Elderly Jewish Women in Jerusalem. Susan S. Sered. (Publications of the American Folklore Society, Bibliographical & Special Ser.). 192p. 1992. 45.00 (*0-19-507161-1*) OUP.

Women as Ritual Experts: The Religious Lives of Elderly Jewish Women in Jerusalem. Susan S. Sered. (Publications of the American Folklore Society, New Ser.). 192p. 1996. reprint ed. pap. 14.95 (*0-19-511146-X*) OUP.

Women As Single Parents: Confronting Institutional Barriers in the Courts, the Workplace, & the Housing Market. Ed. by Elizabeth A. Mulroy. LC 88-11920. 228p. 1988. text ed. 49.95 (*0-86569-176-2*, Auburn Hse) Greenwood.

Women As Subjects: South Asian Histories. Ed. by Nita Kumar. 268p. (C). 1994. text ed. 35.00 (*0-8139-1521-X*); pap. text ed. 16.50 (*0-8139-1522-8*) U Pr of Va.

Women As Survivor: The Evolution of the Female Figure in the Works of Heinrich Boll. Adeidine K. Moeller. LC 91-17714. (American University Studies: Germanic Languages & Literature: Ser. I, Vol. 85). 171p. (C). 1992. text ed. 35.95 (*0-8204-1131-0*) P Lang Pubng.

Women As Teachers & Disciples in Traditional & New Religions. Ed. by Elizabeth Puttick & Peter B. Clarke. LC 93-30865. (Studies in Women & Religion: Vol. 32). 152p. 1993. text ed. 69.95 (*0-7734-9346-8*) E Mellen.

Women As Therapists: A Multi-Theoretical Casebook. Ed. by Dorothy W. Cantor. LC 90-35520. 272p. 1990. 33.95 (*0-8261-6910-4*) Springer Pub.

Women As Therapists: A Multitheoretical Casebook. Ed. by Dorothy W. Cantor. LC 92-21975. 264p. 1992. pap. 25.00 (*0-87668-313-8*) Aronson.

Women As They Age: Challenge, Opportunity & Triumph. Ed. by Susan O. Mercer. LC 88-34803. (Journal of Women & Aging: Vol. 1, Nos. 1-3). (Illus.). 415p. 1989. text ed. 59.95 (*0-86656-805-0*); pap. text ed. 19.95 (*0-86656-873-5*) Haworth Pr.

Women as Wombs: Reproductive Technologies & the Battle Over Women's Freedom. Janice G. Raymond. LC 92-56139. 288p. 1994. reprint ed. pap. 12.00 (*0-06-250899-7*) Harper SF.

Women Assemble: Women Workers & the New Industries in Inter-War Britain. Miriam Glucksmann. 336p. (C). 1990. pap. text ed. 18.95 (*0-415-03197-4*, A4578) Routledge.

Women at Cornell: The Myth of Equal Education. Charlotte W. Conable. LC 77-3117. (Illus.). 176p. 1977. pap. 13.95 (*0-8014-9167-3*) Cornell U Pr.

Women at Gettysburg, 1863. Eileen F. Conklin. (Illus.). 430p. (C). 1993. text ed. 29.95 (*0-939631-63-6*) Thomas Publications.

Women at High Risk to Breast Cancer. Ed. by Basil A. Stoll. (Developments in Oncology Ser.). (C). 1989. lib. bdg. 84.00 (*0-89838-416-8*) Kluwer Ac.

***Women at Home in Victorian America: A Social History.** Ellen M. Plante. LC 97-1417. 1997. write for info. (*0-8160-3392-7*) Facts on File.

Women at Play: The Story of Women in Baseball. Barbara Gregorich. LC 93-16223. 1993. pap. 14.95 (*0-15-698297-8*) HarBrace.

Women at Prayer. Mary Collins. (Madeleva Lectures, 1987). 56p. 1988. pap. 3.95 (*0-8091-2949-3*) Paulist Pr.

***Women at Prayer: A Halakhic Analysis of Women's Prayer Groups.** Avraham Weiss. LC 97-12964. 1997. pap. write for info. (*0-7657-9975-8*) Aronson.

Women at Risk. David Hager & Don Joy. 159p. 1993. pap. 9.95 (*0-917851-62-5*) Bristol Hse.

Women at Risk: Domestic Violence & Women's Health. Evan Stark & Anne Flitcraft. 264p. 1996. 48.00 (*0-8039-7040-4*); pap. 22.95 (*0-8039-7041-2*) Sage.

Women at Risk: Issues in the Primary Prevention of AIDS. Ed. by Ann O'Leary & Loretta S. Jemmott. (AIDS Prevention & Mental Health Ser.). 275p. (C). 1995. 49.50 (*0-306-45041-0*) Plenum.

***Women at Risk of Heart Attack: A Personal Experience; a Personal Research.** Mickey Wapner. LC 97-4454. 1997. 20.00 (*0-934710-35-X*) J Simon.

Women at Risk of Unintended Pregnancy, 1990 Estimates: The Need for Family Planning Services, Each State & County. Stanley Henshaw & Jacqueline D. Forrest. 144p. 1993. pap. 10.00 (*0-939253-27-5*) Guttmacher Inst.

Women at the Center: Development Issues & Practices for the 1990s. Ed. by Gay Young et al. LC 93-26045. (Library of Management for Development). 222p. 1993. pap. 16.95 (*1-56549-029-0*) Kumarian Pr.

***Women at the Change: The Intelligent Woman's Guide to Menopause.** Madonna S. Compton. 288p. (Orig.). 1998. pap. 14.95 (*0-614-31058-X*) Llewellyn Pubns.

Women at the Crossroads: A Path Beyond Feminism & Traditionalism. Kari T. Malcolm. LC 82-7228. 215p. (Orig.). 1982. pap. 12.99 (*0-87784-379-1*, 379) InterVarsity.

***Women at the Crossroads: A Prostitute Community's Response to AIDS in Urban Senegal.** Michelle L. Renaud. 144p. 1997. text ed. 60.00 (*90-5699-530-8*); pap. text ed. 21.00 (*90-5699-531-6*) Gordon & Breach.

Women at the Crossroads: A Sri Lankan Perspective. Ed. by Srima Kiribamune & Vidyamali Samarasinghe. xxi, 248p. 1990. text ed. 35.00 (*0-7069-4525-5*, Pub. by Vikas II) S Asia.

***Women at the Front: Their Changing Roles in the Civil War.** Jean F. Blashfield. LC 96-31319. (First Bks.). (J). 1997. lib. bdg. write for info. (*0-531-20275-5*) Watts.

Women at the Helm. Jeannine E. Talley. LC 89-63620. (Illus.). 228p. 1990. 19.95 (*0-941300-16-1*); pap. 11.95 (*0-941300-15-3*) Mother Courage.

Women at the Helm: Pathfinding Presidents at State Colleges & Universities. Ed. by Judith Sturnick et al. 116p. 1991. pap. text ed. 19.50 (*0-88044-129-1*); lib. bdg. 39.50 (*0-88044-128-3*) AASCU Press.

Women at the Pump. Knut Hamsun. Tr. by Oliver Stallybrass & Gunnvor Stallybrass from NOR. (Sun & Moon Classics Ser.: No. 115). 394p. 1996. pap. 14.95 (*1-55713-244-5*) Sun & Moon CA.

Women at the Wall: A Study of Prisoners' Wives Doing Time on the Outside. Laura T. Fishman. LC 88-30110. (SUNY Series in Critical Issues in Criminal Justice). 337p. (Orig.). (C). 1990. pap. text ed. 21.95 (*0-7914-0059-X*) State U NY Pr.

***Women at the Well.** Grace Bauer. LC 97-66182. (Illus.). 104p. (Orig.). (C). 1997. pap. 15.00 (*0-916620-33-6*) Portals Pr.

Women at the Well: Expressions of Faith, Life & Worship Drawn from Our Own Wisdom. Ed. by Betty Jo Buckingham. Tr. by Maria E. Carachei. LC 87-6224. (Orig.). (YA). (gr. 12). 1987. pap. 7.95 (*0-9618243-0-1*) Ch Brethren Womens Caucus.

Women at the Well: Feminist Perspectives on Spiritual Direction. Kathleen Fischer. 224p. 1988. pap. 14.95 (*0-8091-3018-1*) Paulist Pr.

***Women at the Well: Meditations on Healing & Wholeness.** Ed. by Mary L. Mild. 424p. 1996. pap. 16.00 (*0-8170-1245-1*) Judson.

Women at Their Work. Betty L. English. LC 76-42924. (Pied Piper Bks.). 48p. (J). (gr. k-4). 1988. pap. 4.95 (*0-8037-0496-8*) Dial Bks Young.

Women at Thirtysomething: Paradoxes of Attainment. (Illus.). 70p. (Orig.). (C). 1993. pap. text ed. 20.00 (*1-56806-170-6*) DIANE Pub.

Women at War. Ed. by Lois M. Bujold & Roland J. Green. 384p. 1995. 23.95 (*0-312-85792-6*) Tor Bks.

***Women at War.** Lois M. Bujold. 1997. pap. text ed. 10.99 (*0-8125-4458-7*) Tor Bks.

Women at War: The Ethics of Women in Combat. Lucinda J. Peach. Ed. by Victoria J. Cuffel. LC 93-655022. (MacArthur Scholar Series, Occasional Paper: No. 20). 133p. (Orig.). 1993. pap. 4.50 (*1-881157-23-7*) In Ctr Global.

Women at War: The Story of Fifty Military Nurses Who Served in Vietnam. Elizabeth Norman. LC 90-34487. (Studies in Health, Illness, & Caregiving). (Illus.). 238p. (Orig.). (C). 1990. pap. 16.95 (*0-8122-1317-3*) U of Pa Pr.

Women at War with America: Private Lives in a Patriotic Era. D'Ann Campbell. (Illus.). 320p. 1984. 32.00 (*0-674-95475-0*) HUP.

Women at Work. LC 83-169827. (Picture Bks.). (Illus.). 16p. 1983. pap. 4.00 (*0-934909-20-2*) Mass Hist Soc.

Women at Work. William L. O'Neill. LC 72-182506. 384p. 1972. pap. 4.95 (*0-8129-6237-0*, Times Bks) Random.

Women at Work. Charlotte Rose. (Orig.). 1993. mass mkt. 4.95 (*1-56333-088-1*) Masquerade.

Women at Work. Ed. by Rosalind M. Schwartz. LC 88-13247. (Monograph & Research Ser.: No. 48). 210p. (Orig.). (C). 1988. pap. 12.00 (*0-89215-145-5*) U Cal LA Indus Rel.

Women at Work: Annotated Bibliography, II. Mei L. Bickner & Marlene Shaughnessey. 420p. 1977. 12.00 (*0-89215-064-5*) U Cal LA Indus Rel.

Women at Work: One Hundred Fifty Photographs by Lewis Hine. Lewis Hine. (Illus.). 128p. (Orig.). 1981. pap. 8.95 (*0-486-24154-8*) Dover.

Women at Work: Psychological & Organizational Perspectives. Ed. by Jenny Firth-Cozens & Michael West. 192p. 1990. pap. 32.00 (*0-335-09252-7*, Open Univ Pr) Taylor & Francis.

Women at Work: The Essential Guide for the Working Woman. Deborah Clarke. 176p. 1992. pap. 12.95 (*1-85230-109-0*) Element MA.

Women at Work: The Transformation of Work & Community in Lowell, Massachusetts, 1826-1860. Thomas Dublin. LC 79-10701. 360p. 1981. reprint ed. pap. text ed. 18.00 (*0-231-04167-5*) Col U Pr.

Women at Work: Unity in Diversity. Ed. by James A. Walsh. (Nineteen Ninety Ser.). 100p. 1990. 30.00 (*0-9624822-1-8*) Womens World.

Women at Work II. Ed. by Rosalind M. Schwartz. LC 89-20263. (Monograph & Research Ser.: No. 51). 119p. (Orig.). 1989. pap. 9.00 (*0-89215-158-7*) U Cal LA Indus Rel.

Women at Work in Australia: From the Gold Rushes to World War II. Raelene Frances & Bruce Scates. LC 92-14685. (Women in Australian History Ser.). (Illus.). 152p. (C). 1993. pap. text ed. 25.95 (*0-521-38769-8*) Cambridge U Pr.

Women at Work in India: A Bibliography. Ed. by Suchitra Anant et al. 240p. (C). 1987. text ed. 22.50 (*0-8039-9512-1*) Sage.

Women at Work in India Vol. 2: An Annotated Bibliography. S. V. Rao et al. 324p. 1994. 25.00 (*0-8039-9173-8*) Sage.

Women at Work in the Gulf: A Case Study of Bahrain. Munira A. Fakhiro. 300p. 1990. 69.95 (*0-7103-0337-8*, A3921) Routledge Chapman & Hall.

***Women at Work 1850-1930: The Women's Labour.** History Collective Staff. (Illus.). 416p. reprint ed. pap. 10.95 (*0-88961-012-6*, Pub. by Wmns Pr CN) LPC InBook.

Women at Worship: Interpretations of North American Diversity. Ed. by Marjorie Proctor-Smith & Janet R. Walton. 272p. (Orig.). 1993. pap. 19.00 (*0-664-25253-2*) Westminster John Knox.

Women Attached: The Daily Lives of Women with Young Children. Jacqueline Tivers. LC 85-18439. 334p. 1985. text ed. 39.95 (*0-312-88726-4*) St Martin.

Women, Authority & the Bible. Ed. by Alvera Mickelsen. LC 86-7158. 304p. (Orig.). 1986. pap. 16.99 (*0-87784-608-1*, 608) InterVarsity.

Women Authors of Modern Hispanic South America: A Bibliography of Literary Criticism & Interpretation. Sandra M. Cypess et al. LC 89-10889. 168p. 1989. 22.50 (*0-8108-2263-6*) Scarecrow.

Women Aviators. Lisa Yount. (American Profiles Ser.). (Illus.). 158p. 1995. 17.95 (*0-8160-3062-6*) Facts on File.

Women, Babies, & Drugs: Family-Centered Treatment Options. 33p. 1990. 15.00 (*1-55516-640-7*, 6119) Natl Conf State Legis.

Women Before God: Our Own Spirituality. Lavinia Byrne. LC 88-50331. 144p. (Orig.). 1988. pap. 7.95 (*0-89622-365-5*) Twenty-Third.

Women Before the Bar: Gender, Law, & Society in Connecticut, 1639-1789. Cornelia H. Dayton. LC 95-20116. (Published for the Institute of Early American History & Culture Ser.). (Illus.). 400p. (C). 1995. text ed. 49.95 (*0-8078-2244-2*); pap. text ed. 18.95 (*0-8078-4561-2*) U of NC Pr.

Women Behind Bars. Judy Rowse & Raymond Wojda. LC 96-25770. (Illus.). 95p. (Orig.). 1997. pap. 22.95 (*1-56991-049-9*) Am Correctional.

Women Behind Bars. Neera K. Sohoni. 1989. text ed. 35.00 (*0-7069-4347-3*, Pub. by Vikas II) S Asia.

***Women Behind Bars, Vol. 1.** Clarkson. 1997. mass mkt. write for info. (*0-312-96324-6*) St Martin.

Women Behind Bars in Romania. Annie Samuelli. LC 95-23285. Orig. Title: The Wall Between. 250p. (Orig.). 1996. reprint ed. pap. 19.50 (*0-7146-4217-7*, Pub. by F Cass Pubs UK) Intl Spec Bk.

***Women Behind the Men Behind the Badge: Their Stories.** Alicia Williams. xii, 132p. (Orig.). 1997. pap. 3.99 (*1-889316-01-6*) Ecrivez.

***Women Believer.** 2nd ed. Daisy Osborn. (Orig.). (RUS.). 1995. mass mkt. write for info. (*1-890863-12-2*) Wrld Wide Print.

Women Between Cultures: The Lives of Kinnaird College Alumnae in British India. Michelle Maskiell. (Foreign & Comparative Studies Program, South Asian Ser.: No. 9). (Illus.). 1984. pap. text ed. 10.00 (*0-915984-86-5*) Syracuse U Foreign Comp.

Women Between Two Worlds: Midlife Reflections on Work & Family. Myra Dinnerstein. (Women in the Political Economy Ser.). (C). 1992. 44.95 (*0-87722-884-1*); pap. 18.95 (*0-87722-885-X*) Temple U Pr.

***Women Beware Women.** Mulryne. Date not set. pap. 12.95 (*0-7190-4350-6*) St Martin.

Women Beware Women. 2nd ed. William Carroll. (New Mermaid Ser.). (C). Date not set. pap. text ed. 6.95 (*0-393-90069-X*, Norton Paperbks) Norton.

Women Beware Women. Thomas Middleton. Ed. by J. R. Mulryne. (Revels Plays Ser.). 201p. 1988. reprint ed. text ed. 22.95 (*0-7190-1614-2*, Pub. by Manchester Univ Pr UK) St Martin.

Women Beyond Freud: New Concepts of Feminine Psychology. Ed. by Milton M. Berger. 224p. 1993. text ed. 34.95 (*0-87630-709-8*) Brunner-Mazel.

Women Beyond the Wire. large type ed. Lavinia Warner & John Sandilands. 528p. 1983. 27.99 (*0-7089-8161-5*) Ulverscroft.

Women, Biology, & Public Policy. Ed. by Virginia Sapiro. LC 85-1935. (Sage Yearbooks in Women's Policy Studies: No. 10). 272p. 1985. reprint ed. pap. 77.60 (*0-608-01524-5*, 2059568) Bks Demand.

Women, Birth Control & the Law. B. P. Sehgal. (C). 1991. 21.50 (*81-7100-320-6*, Pub. by Deep II) S Asia.

Women, Black, & Hispanic State Elected Leaders: The 1990 Symposium on the State of the States. 1991. 5.23 (*0-685-61058-6*) U VA Ctr Pub Serv.

***Women Bookbinders, 1880-1920.** Marianne Tidcombe. LC 96-31238. 208p. 1996. 58.00 (*1-884718-23-X*) Oak Knoll.

Women, Branch Stories, & Religious Rhetoric in a Tamil Buddhist Text. Paula Richman. LC 87-31551. (Foreign & Comparative Studies Program, South Asian Ser.: No. 12). 288p. (Orig.). (C). 1988. 19.00 (*0-915984-90-3*) Syracuse U Foreign Comp.

Women Breaking Through: Overcoming the Final 10 Obstacles at Work. Deborah J. Swiss. (Pacesetter Bks.). 256p. 1996. text ed. 24.95 (*1-56079-535-2*, Petersons Pacesetter) Petersons.

Women Builders. enl. rev. ed. Sadie L. Daniel. (YA). 1990. 12.95 (*0-87498-084-4*); pap. 10.95 (*0-87498-085-2*) Assoc Pubs DC.

Women Business Leaders. Robert B. Pile. LC 94-46814. (Profiles Ser.). (Illus.). 160p. (J). (gr. 5-12). 1995. lib. bdg. 16.95 (*1-881508-24-2*) Oliver Pr MN.

Women Business Owners: Selling to the Federal Government. (Illus.). 54p. (Orig.). (C). 1993. pap. text ed. 20.00 (*1-56806-192-7*) DIANE Pub.

***Women by Women: The Treatment of Female Characters by Women Writers of Fiction in Quebec since 1980.** Roseanna L. Dufault. LC 96-53873. 1997. write for info. (*0-8386-3719-1*) Fairleigh Dickinson.

Women Camp Followers of the American Revolution. Walter H. Blumenthal. LC 74-3931. (Women in America Ser.). 104p. 1977. reprint ed. 21.95 (*0-405-06077-7*) Ayer.

Women Carpet Weavers in Rural Turkey: Patterns of Employment, Earnings & Status. Gunser Berik. (Women, Work & Development Ser.: No. 15). xiii, 112p. (Orig.). 1987. pap. 18.00 (*92-2-106004-7*) Intl Labour Office.

***Women Carry River Water: Poems.** Nguyen Q. Thieu. Ed. & Tr. by Martha Collins from VIE. LC 96-48658. 136p. 1997. pap. 13.95 (*1-55849-087-6*); text ed. 27.50 (*1-55849-086-8*) U of Mass Pr.

Women Challenging Unions: Feminism, Democracy, & Militancy. Ed. by Linda Briskin & Patricia McDermott. 346p. 1993. 50.00 (*0-8020-2872-1*); pap. 19.95 (*0-8020-7376-X*) U of Toronto Pr.

Women Champions of Human Rights: Eleven U. S. Leaders of the Twentieth Century. Moira D. Reynolds. LC 91-52505. (Illus.). 168p. 1991. lib. bdg. 28.50 (*0-89950-614-3*) McFarland & Co.

Women Changing Science: Voices from a Field in Transition. Mary Morse. 305p. (C). 1995. 27.95 (*0-306-45081-X*, Plenum Pr) Plenum.

Women Changing Therapy: New Assessments, Values, & Strategies in Feminist Therapy. Ed. by Joan H. Robbins & Rachel J. Siegel. LC 83-12643. (Women & Therapy Ser.: Vol. 2, Nos. 2-3). 240p. 1983. text ed. 39.95 (*0-86656-239-7*); pap. text ed. 14.95 (*0-86656-240-0*) Haworth Pr.

W

Women Changing Therapy: New Assessments, Values & Strategies in Feminist Therapy. Ed. by Joan H. Robbins & Rachel J. Siegel. LC 84-19276. 240p. 1985. pap. text ed. 14.95 (*0-918393-07-8*) Harrington Pk.

Women Changing Work. Patricia W. Lunneborg. LC 89-25673. (Contributions in Women's Studies: No. 112). 256p. 1990. text ed. 55.00 (*0-313-26843-6*, LWD/, Bergin & Garvey); pap. text ed. 14.95 (*0-89789-214-3*, G214, Bergin & Garvey) Greenwood.

Women Chefs: A Collection of Portraits & Recipes from California's Culinary Pioneers. Jim Burns & Betty A. Brown. 220p. 1987. pap. 16.95 (*0-943186-37-4*) Aris Bks.

Women, Children & Family Life in the Nevada Interior, 1900-1930s. Intro. by R. T. King. (Illus.). 135p. 1987. lib. bdg. 40.50 (*1-56475-321-2*); fiche write for info. (*1-56475-322-0*) U NV Oral Hist.

Women, Children, & Health Care. Mary B. Mahowald. LC 92-12912. 320p. 1993. 42.50 (*0-19-506346-5*) OUP.

Women, Children, & HIV - AIDS. Ed. by Felissa L. Cohen & Jerry D. Durham. LC 92-48971. 328p. 1993. 39.95 (*0-8261-7880-4*) Springer Pub.

Women Chosen for Public Office. Isobel V. Morin. LC 94-22097. (Profiles Ser.). (Illus.). 160p. (YA). (gr. 5-12). 1995. lib. bdg. 16.95 (*1-881508-20-X*) Oliver Pr MN.

*__Women Churches: Networking & Reflection in the European Context.__ Ed. by Angela Berlis et al. (Yearbook of the European Society of Women in Theological Research Ser.: Vol. 3/95). 215p. 1995. pap. 21.00 (*90-390-0213-4*, Pub. by KOK Pharos NE) Eisenbrauns.

*__Women, Class, & Society in Early Christianity: Models from Luke-Acts.__ James M. Arlandson. LC 96-48298. 272p. (C). 1997. 24.95 (*1-56563-181-1*) Hendrickson MA.

Women, Class, & the Feminist Imagination: A Socialist-Feminist Reader. Ed. by Karen V. Hansen & Ilene J. Philipson. (Women in the Political Economy Ser.). 670p. (C). 1989. 44.95 (*0-87722-630-X*); pap. 22.95 (*0-87722-654-7*) Temple U Pr.

Women Clergy in England: Sexism, Modern Consciousness, & Church Viability. Edward C. Lehman, Jr. LC 86-28547. (Studies in Religion & Society: Vol. 16). 232p. 1987. lib. bdg. 89.95 (*0-88946-858-3*) E Mellen.

Women Climbing: Engagement Calendar, 1994. Ed. by Rachel DaSilva et al. (Illus.). 1993. spiral bd. 12.95 (*0-9630368-8-2*) Women Climbers.

Women Climbing: 1992 Engagement Calendar. Kathy Phibbs et al. (Illus.). 120p. (Orig.). 1991. pap. 12.95 (*0-9630368-7-4*) Women Climbers.

*__Women Come of Age.__ write for info. (*0-340-55261-1*, Pub. by E Arnold UK) Routledge Chapman & Hall.

Women Communicating: Studies of Women's Talk. Ed. by Barbara A. Bate et al. LC 88-1582. (Communication & Information Science Ser.). 336p. 1988. pap. 39.50 (*0-89391-476-2*); text ed. 73.25 (*0-89391-475-4*) Ablex Pub.

Women, Community, & the Hormel Strike of 1985-86. Neala J. Schleuning. LC 93-28037. (Contributions in Women's Studies: No. 137). 256p. 1994. text ed. 59.95 (*0-313-28976-X*, Greenwood Pr) Greenwood.

Women Composers: A Discography. Jane Frasier. LC 83-22563. (Detroit Studies in Music Bibliography: No. 50). viii, 300p. 1983. 25.00 (*0-89990-018-6*) Info Coord.

*__Women Composers: An Historical Anthology, 6.__ Schiefer & Glickman. 1998. 100.00 (*0-7838-8192-4*) Mac Lib Ref.

*__Women Composers: An Historical Anthology, 7.__ Schiefer & Glickman. 1998. 100.00 (*0-7838-8194-0*) Mac Lib Ref.

*__Women Composers: An Historical Anthology, 8.__ Schliefer & Glickman. 1998. 100.00 (*0-7838-8193-2*) Mac Lib Ref.

Women Composers: An Historical Anthology, No. 4. Martha F. Schleifer. 1997. 100.00 (*0-7838-1613-8*) G K Hall.

Women Composers: The Lost Tradition Found. 2nd ed. Diane P. Jezic. LC 94-39300. 272p. (Orig.). (C). 1994. 35.00 (*1-55861-073-1*); pap. 14.95 (*1-55861-074-X*) Feminist Pr.

Women Composers Vol. 1: Music Through the Ages: Composers Born Before 1599. Ed. by Martha F. Schleifer & Sylvia Glickman. 356p. 1996. 100.00 (*0-8161-0926-5*) G K Hall.

Women Composers Vol. 3: An Historical Anthology. Martha F. Schleifer. 1997. 100.00 (*0-7838-1612-X*) G K Hall.

Women Composers Vol. 5: An Historical Anthology. Martha F, Schleifer. 1998. 100.00 (*0-7838-1614-6*) G K Hall.

Women Composers & Songwriters: A Concise Biographical Dictionary. Gene Claghorn. LC 95-51308. 368p. 1996. text ed. 68.00 (*0-8108-3130-9*) Scarecrow.

Women Composer's Anthology of Music by Women Through the Ages Vol. 2: 1600-1699. Martha F. Schleifer. 390p. 1996. 100.00 (*0-8161-0563-4*) Mac Lib Ref.

Women Composers As Authors & Artists: A Sourcebook. Adel Heinrich. LC 95-47365. 1996. text ed. write for info. (*0-313-27847-4*, Greenwood Pr) Greenwood.

Women Composers, Conductors, & Musicians of the Twentieth Century: Seclected Biographies, Vol. III. Jane W. LePage. LC 80-12162. (Illus.). 333p. 1988. 35.00 (*0-8108-2082-X*) Scarecrow.

Women Composers, Conductors & Musicians of the Twentieth Century: Selected Biographies, Vol. I. Jane W. LePage. LC 80-12162. 388p. 1980. 39.50 (*0-8108-1298-3*) Scarecrow.

*__Women Computer Professionals: Controlled Progress in a Male Occupation.__ Rosemary Wright. LC 97-25032. 1997. write for info. (*0-7734-2244-7*) E Mellen.

Women Connecting: Facilitator's Guide. Maria Riley. 40p. 1994. pap. 15.00 (*0-934255-11-3*) Center Concern.

Women Connecting: Participant's Workbooks. Maria Riley. (Illus.). 21p. (Orig.). 1994. pap. 3.50 (*0-934255-12-1*) Center Concern.

Women Construction Workers. G. P. Sinha. (Illus.). 78p. 1975. 5.95 (*0-318-37319-X*) Asia Bk Corp.

Women Creating Lives: Identities, Resilience, & Resistance. Ed. by Carol E. Franz & Abigail J. Stewart. LC 93-48990. (C). 1994. pap. text ed. 24.00 (*0-8133-1873-4*) Westview.

Women Creating Women: Contemporary Irish Women Poets. Patricia B. Haberstroh. (Illus.). 328p. 1995. 39.95 (*0-8156-2671-1*); pap. 16.95 (*0-8156-0357-6*) Syracuse U Pr.

Women, Creation, & the Fall. Mary A. Kassian. LC 89-81256. 192p. 1990. pap. 12.99 (*0-89107-552-6*) Crossway Bks.

Women, Creativity & the Arts. Ed. by Diane Apostolos-Cappadona & Lucinda Ebersole. (Illus.). 240p. 1995. pap. text ed. 18.95 (*0-8264-0831-1*) Continuum.

Women Crime & Criminal Justice. Allison Morris. 256p. (Orig.). (C). 1987. pap. text ed. 28.95 (*0-631-15445-0*) Blackwell Pubs.

Women, Crime, & Criminology: A Feminist Critique. Carol Smart. 1978. reprint ed. pap. 14.95 (*0-7100-8833-7*, RKP) Routledge.

Women Crime & Law. B. K. Nagla. (C). 1991. 14.00 (*0-685-66147-4*, Pub. by Rawat II) S Asia.

Women, Crime & Poverty. Pat Carlen. 224p. 1988. pap. 29.00 (*0-335-15869-2*, Open Univ Pr) Taylor & Francis.

Women, Crime & the Courts in Early Modern England. Ed. by Jenny Kermode & Garthine Walker. LC 94-21127. (Illus.). 216p. 1995. pap. text ed. 17.95 (*0-8078-4500-0*); lib. bdg. 39.95 (*0-8078-2192-6*) U of NC Pr.

Women Critics 1660-1820: An Anthology. Ed. by Folger Collective on Early Women Critics Staff. LC 94-40962. 448p. 1995. 39.95 (*0-253-32872-1*); pap. 18.95 (*0-253-20963-3*) Ind U Pr.

Women Cross-Culturally: Change & Challenge. Ed. by Ruby Rohrlich-Leavitt. (World Anthropology Ser.). (Illus.). xiv, 670p. 1975. 58.50 (*90-279-7649-X*) Mouton.

*__Women, Culture & Community: Religion & Reform in Galveston, 1880-1923.__ Elizabeth H. Turner. LC 97-13014. (Illus.). 384p. 1997. pap. 19.95 (*0-19-511938-X*) OUP.

*__Women, Culture & Community: Religion & Reform in Galveston, 1880-1923.__ Elizabeth H. Turner. LC 97-13014. (Illus.). 384p. 1997. 49.95 (*0-19-508688-0*) OUP.

Women, Culture, & Development: A Study of Human Capabilities. Ed. by Martha Nussbaum & Jonathon Glover. (WIDER Studies in Development Economics). (Illus.). 376p. 1996. 95.00 (*0-19-828917-0*); pap. 19.95 (*0-19-828964-2*) OUP.

Women, Culture, & Politics. Angela Y. Davis. LC 88-42674. (Illus.). 256p. 1989. 17.95 (*0-394-56976-8*) Random.

Women, Culture, & Politics. Angela Y. Davis. 1990. pap. 12.00 (*0-679-72487-7*, Vin) Random.

Women, Culture, & Politics in Latin America: Seminar on Feminism & Culture in Latin America. (C). 1992. pap. 14.00 (*0-520-06553-0*) U CA Pr.

Women, Culture & Society. Barbara Balliet. (C). Date not set. pap. text ed. write for info. (*0-393-96889-8*); teacher ed., pap. text ed. write for info. (*0-393-96890-1*) Norton.

Women, Culture & Society: A Student Workbook. 2nd ed. Mary Fonow. 172p. (C). 1996. spiral bd. 21.00 (*0-7872-2455-3*) Kendall-Hunt.

Women, Decision Making, & the Future. Barbara B. Clowse. LC 85-18091. 167p. 1985. reprint ed. pap. 47.60 (*0-7837-8937-8*, 2049647) Bks Demand.

Women, Development, & Communities for Empowerment in Appalachia. Virginia R. Seitz. LC 94-15704. (SUNY Series in Gender & Society). 288p. 1995. text ed. 57.50 (*0-7914-2377-8*); pap. text ed. 18.95 (*0-7914-2378-6*) State U NY Pr.

Women, Development & Survival in the Third World. Ed. by Haleh Afshar. 304p. (Orig.). (C). 1991. pap. text ed. 28.50 (*0-582-03494-9*, 78816) Longman.

Women Dimension on Television: Policy, Personnel & Programme. Ila Joshi. (C). 1991. 17.50 (*81-7022-360-1*, Pub. by Concept II) S Asia.

Women Directors. Eurofi Staff. 176p. (C). 1988. 220.00 (*0-907304-24-9*, Pub. by Eurofi UK) St Mut.

Women Directors: The Emergence of a New Cinema. Barbara K. Quart. LC 88-1141. 288p. 1988. text ed. 55.00 (*0-275-92962-0*, C2962, Praeger Pubs) Greenwood.

Women Directors: The Emergence of a New Cinema. Barbara K. Quart. LC 88-1141. 288p. 1989. pap. text ed. 19.95 (*0-275-93477-2*, B3477, Praeger Pubs) Greenwood.

*__Women Divided: Gender, Religion, & Politics in Northern Ireland.__ LC 96-48678. (International Studies of Women & Place). 240p. (C). 1997. pap. write for info. (*0-415-13766-7*); text ed. write for info. (*0-415-13765-9*) Routledge.

*__Women Do This Every Day: Selected Poems of Lillian Allen.__ Lillian Allen. (Not a Luxury Poetry Ser.). 144p. pap. 10.95 (*0-88961-192-0*, Pub. by Wmns Pr CN) LPC InBook.

Women Doctors in Gilded-Age Washington: Race, Gender, & Professionalization. Gloria Moldow. LC 86-19251. (Women in American History Ser.). (Illus.). 262p. 1987. text ed. 27.50 (*0-252-01379-4*) U of Ill Pr.

Women Don't Count: The Challenge of Women's Poverty to Christian Ethics. Pamela K. Brubaker. LC 94-2380. (AAR Academy Ser.: Vol. 87). 288p. 1994. 29.95 (*1-55540-957-1*, 010187) Scholars Pr GA.

*__Women Don't Count: The Challenge of Women's Poverty to Christian Ethics.__ Pamela K. Brubaker. 288p. 1994. pap. 19.95 (*1-55540-958-X*, 010187) Scholars Pr GA.

Women Dreaming-into-Art: Archetypal Patterns of Feminine Creativity. Patricia A. Ariadne. 1991. 27.50 (*0-938434-92-6*); pap. 18.95 (*0-938434-91-8*) Sigo Pr.

Women, Drinking & Pregnancy. Moira Plant. 208p. 1985. 45.00 (*0-422-78610-1*, 9483, Pub. by Tavistock UK) Routledge Chapman & Hall.

Women, Drinking, & Pregnancy. Moira Plant. 184p. (C). 1987. pap. text ed. 16.95 (*0-422-61750-4*, Pub. by Tavistock UK) Routledge Chapman & Hall.

Women Drug Users: An Ethnography of a Female Injecting Community. Avril Taylor. 192p. 1993. 39.95 (*0-19-825796-1*) OUP.

Women, Earth, & Creator Spirit. Elizabeth Johnson. LC 92-42018. (Madeleva Lectures, 1993). 88p. 1993. pap. 4.95 (*0-8091-3415-2*) Paulist Pr.

Women Editing Modernism: "Little" Magazines & Literary History. Jayne Marek. LC 95-14890. (Illus.). 264p. (Orig.). (C). 1996. 34.95 (*0-8131-1937-5*); pap. 14.95 (*0-8131-0854-3*) U Pr of Ky.

Women Education: A Research Approach. Mujibul H. Siddiqui. (C). 1993. 27.00 (*81-7024-594-X*, Pub. by Ashish II) S Asia.

Women, Education, & Development in Asia: Cross-National Perspectives. Ed. by Grace C. Mak & Edward R. Beauchamp. LC 96-16773. (Reference Books in International Education: Vol. 33). (Illus.). 275p. 1996. text ed. 50.00 (*0-8153-0795-0*, H825) Garland.

Women, Education, & Employment: A Bibliography of Periodical Citations, Pamphlets, Newspapers, & Government Documents, 1970-1980. Renee Feinberg. LC 82-7816. 274p. (C). 1982. 36.50 (*0-208-01967-7*, Lib Prof Pubns) Shoe String.

Women Education & the Upanishadic System of Education. K. N. Misra. (C). 1993. 30.00 (*81-85613-76-1*, Pub. by Chugh Pubns II) S Asia.

Women, Education, Employment: Family Living (A Study of Emerging Hindu Wives in Urban India) Mondira Devi. 224p. (C). 1987. 32.00 (*81-212-0104-7*, Pub. by Gian Publng Hse II) S Asia.

Women Educators: Employees of Schools in Western World Countries. Ed. by Patricia A. Schmuck. LC 86-14532. 251p. 1987. text ed. 64.50 (*0-88706-442-6*); pap. text ed. 21.95 (*0-88706-443-4*) State U NY Pr.

Women Educators in the United States, 1820-1993: A Bio-Bibliographical Sourcebook. Ed. by Maxine S. Seller. LC 93-28033. 632p. 1994. text ed. 99.50 (*0-313-27937-3*, Greenwood Pr) Greenwood.

Women Elders in the Kirk? Ed. by A. McGowan. 1995. 6.99 (*1-871676-30-4*, Pub. by Christian Focus UK) Spring Arbor Dist.

Women, Elections, & Representation. 2nd rev. ed. R. Darcy et al. LC 93-2301. (Women & Politics Ser.: Vol. 1). (Illus.). xiv, 276p. 1994. pap. text ed. 15.00 (*0-8032-6597-2*, Bison Books) U of Nebr Pr.

Women, Elections, & Representation. 2nd rev. ed. R. Darcy et al. LC 93-2301. (Women & Politics Ser.: Vol. 1). (Illus.). xiv, 276p. 1994. text ed. 35.00 (*0-8032-1696-3*) U of Nebr Pr.

Women Elite of India. Anand Arora. 225p. 1990. text ed. 32.50 (*0-685-31264-X*, Pub. by Radiant Pubs II) S Asia.

Women Employees & Rural Development: Problems of Employed Women in Rural Areas. Anuradha Bhoite. 150p. 1987. write for info. (*81-212-0085-7*, Pub. by Gian Publng Hse II) S Asia.

*__Women, Employment, & Exclusion.__ Ed. by Caroline Sweetman. (Focus on Gender Ser.). 72p. (C). 1997. pap. 12.95 (*0-85598-364-7*, Pub. by Oxfam UK) Humanities.

Women, Employment & Family in the International Division of Labour. Sharon B. Stichter. 288p. 1990. 39.95 (*0-87722-739-X*) Temple U Pr.

*__Women, Employment & Part-Time Work: A Comparative Study of the United States, the United Kingdom, Canada, & Australia.__ Janet Gornick. (Studies in the History of American Labor). 250p. 1997. 50.00 (*0-8153-2765-X*) Garland.

Women En Large: Images of Fat Nudes. Laurie T. Edison & Debbie Notkin. (Illus.). 116p. (Orig.). 1994. pap. 24.95 (*0-685-74828-6*) Books In Focus.

Women Encounter God: Theology Across the Boundaries of Difference. Linda A. Moody. LC 96-31157. 192p. (Orig.). 1996. pap. 16.00 (*1-57075-082-3*) Orbis Bks.

Women Encounter Information Technology: Perspectives on the Third World. Ed. by Mitter Swasti & Sheila Rowbotham. LC 95-7345. (UNU/INTECH Studies in New Technology & Development). 376p. (C). 1995. text ed. 99.95 (*0-415-12687-8*) Routledge.

*__Women Encounter Technology: Changing Patterns of Employment in the Third World.__ Ed. by Mitter Swasti & Sheila Rowbotham. (UNU/Intech Studies in New Technology & Development). 376p. (C). 1997. pap. 24.95 (*0-415-14118-4*, Routledge NY) Routledge.

Women Encouraging Women: Who Will Disciple Me? Lucibel VanAtta. Ed. by Liz Heaney. LC 87-28264. 169p. (Orig.). 1988. pap. 9.99 (*0-88070-214-1*, Multnomah Bks) Multnomah Pubs.

Women Engravers. Patricia Jaffe. 1989. 19.95 (*0-86068-225-0*) Random.

Women Enter the Wilderness: Male Bonding & the American Novel of the 1980s. Donald J. Greiner. 146p. (C). 1991. pap. 9.95 (*0-87249-776-3*) U of SC Pr.

*__Women Entrepreneurs.__ D. Lalitha Rani. (Illus.). xvi, 392p. 1996. 40.00 (*81-7024-773-X*, Pub. by Assoc Pub Hse II) Nataraj Bks.

Women Entrepreneurs. Kamla Singh. (Illus.). xiii, 209p. (C). 1992. 25.00 (*81-7024-501-X*, Pub. by Ashish II) Nataraj Bks.

*__Women Entrepreneurs: Developing Leadership for Success.__ Sandra J. Wells. (Studies in Entrepreneurship). 250p. 1997. 50.00 (*0-8153-2891-5*) Garland.

*__Women Entrepreneurs: Moving Beyond the Glass Ceiling.__ Dorothy P. Moore & E. Holly Buttner. 276p. 1997. text ed. 46.00 (*0-7619-0463-8*) Sage.

*__Women Entrepreneurs: Moving Beyond the Glass Ceiling.__ Dorothy P. Moore & E. Holly Buttner. 276p. 1997. pap. text ed. 19.95 (*0-7619-0464-6*) Sage.

Women Entrepreneurs in India: Socio-Economic Study of Delhi 1975-85. Medha D. Vinze. 238p. (C). 1987. 22.00 (*0-8364-2094-2*, Pub. by Mittal II) S Asia.

Women Entrepreneurs, Networking & Sweet Patato Pie: Creating Capital in the 21st Century. Dolores Ratcliffe. (YA). (gr. 10 up). 1987. pap. 16.95 (*0-933016-03-4*) Corita Comm.

Women Environment - 3rd World: Alliance for the Future. Irene Dankelman & Joan Davidson. (Illus.). 224p. (Orig.). 1987. 15.95 (*1-85383-003-8*, Pub. by Erthscan Pubns UK) Island Pr.

Women, Equality & the French Revolution. Candice E. Proctor. LC 90-2963. (Contributions in Women's Studies: No. 115). 224p. 1990. text ed. 49.95 (*0-313-27245-X*, PWE, Greenwood Pr) Greenwood.

Women, Ethnics, & Exotics: Images of Power in Mid-Nineteenth-Century American Fiction. Kristin Herzog. LC 82-15881. 280p. 1983. text ed. 33.00 (*0-87049-372-8*) U of Tenn Pr.

*__Women Eucharist.__ Sheila D. Dierks. 360p. (Orig.). 1997. pap. 19.95 (*0-9658137-9-7*) Woven Word.

Women Executives: A Sociological Study of Role Effectiveness. Napasri Kraisonswasdi. 1989. 26.50 (*81-7033-081-5*, Pub. by Rawat II) S Asia.

Women Executives: Attitude Towards Women, Motivation, Leadership Style, & Communication Skills. Raman Kumar. (C). 1993. 19.50 (*81-7100-537-3*, Pub. by Deep II) S Asia.

Women Experiencing Church: A Documentation of Alienation. 1991. pap. 15.95 (*0-85244-187-8*, Pub. by Gracewing UK) Morehouse Pub.

*__Women Explorers in Africa.__ LC 96-43334. 1997. write for info. (*1-56065-505-4*) Capstone Pr.

*__Women Explorers in Africa.__ Mcloone Margo. (Capstone Short Biographies Ser.). (J). 1997. 18.40 (*0-516-20497-1*) Childrens.

*__Women Explorers in Asia.__ Margo Mcloone. (Capstone Short Biographies Ser.). (J). 1997. 18.40 (*0-516-20498-X*) Childrens.

*__Women Explorers in Asia: Susie Carson Rijnhart, Alexandra David-Neel, Lucy Atkinson, Freya Stark, Dervla Murphy.__ Margo Mcloone-Basta. LC 96-43333. 1997. write for info. (*1-56065-506-2*) Capstone Pr.

*__Women Explorers in North America And South America.__ Margo Mcloone. (Capstone Short Biographies Ser.). (J). 1997. 18.40 (*0-516-20499-8*) Childrens.

*__Women Explorers in North & South America: Nellie Cashman, Annie Peck, Ynes Mexia, Blair Niles, Violet Cressy Marcks.__ Margo Mcloone-Basta. LC 96-43332. (Capstone Short Biographies). (J). 1997. write for info. (*1-56065-507-0*) Capstone Pr.

*__Women Explorers in Polar Regions.__ Margo Mcloone. (Capstone Short Biographies Ser.). (J). 1997. 18.40 (*0-516-20500-5*) Childrens.

*__Women Explorers in Polar Regions: Louise Arner Boyd, Kate Marsden, Ida Pfeiffer, Helen Thayer, Agnes Deans Cameron.__ LC 96-45689. (Capstone Short Biographies Ser.). (J). 1997. write for info. (*1-56065-508-9*) Capstone Pr.

*__Women Exposed.__ Jonathon Wright. 1997. boxed write for info. (*0-7615-1051-6*) Prima Pub.

Women Facing Loss: Disease, Bereavement & Emotional Response. Ed. by Margot Tallmer et al. (Current Thanatology Ser.). 115p. 1996. pap. 16.95 (*0-930194-40-3*) Ctr Thanatology.

Women Facing Temptation. Cindy Bunch. (Created Male & Female Bible Studies). 64p. (Orig.). 1993. wbk. ed., pap. 4.99 (*0-8308-1138-9*, 1138) InterVarsity.

Women Faculty at Work in the Classroom: or Why It Still Hurts to Be a Woman in Labor. Bernice R. Sandler. 16p. 1993. 5.00 (*1-877966-15-0*) Ctr Women Policy.

Women Faithful for the Future. Maria Riley. (Illus.). 32p. 1987. pap. text ed. 2.95 (*1-55612-103-2*) Sheed & Ward MO.

Women, Families & Communities: Readings in American History, I. Nancy A. Hewitt. (C). 1990. pap. text ed. 29.50 (*0-673-18859-0*) Addson-Wesley Educ.

Women, Families & Communities: Readings in American History, II. Nancy A. Hewitt. (C). 1990. pap. text ed. 27.95 (*0-673-18860-4*) Addson-Wesley Educ.

Women, Families, & Communities Vol. 1: To 1877, Vol. I. Nancy A. Hewitt. (Readings in American History Ser.). 248p. reprint ed. pap. 27.50 (*1-886746-46-X*, 93494) Talman.

Women, Families, & Communities Vol. 2: From 1865, Vol. II. Nancy A. Hewitt. (Readings in American History Ser.). 272p. reprint ed. pap. 26.00 (*1-886746-47-8*, 93495) Talman.

Women, Family, & Community in Colonial America: Two Perspectives. Linda E. Speth & Alison D. Hirsch. LC 82-23326. (Women & History Ser.: No. 4). 79p. 1983. text ed. 19.95 (*0-86656-191-9*) Haworth Pr.

Women, Family, & Ritual in Renaissance Italy. Christiane Klapisch-Zuber. Tr. by Lydia G. Cochrane. LC 84-28061. (Illus.). xvi, 360p. 1987. pap. text ed. 14.95 (*0-226-43926-7*) U Ch Pr.

Women, Family & Society in Medieval Europe: Historical Essays, 1978-1991. David Herlihy. LC 94-39212. 400p. (C). 1995. 59.95 (*1-57181-023-4*) Berghahn Bks.

Women, Family & Society in Medieval Europe: Historical Essays, 1978-1991. David Herlihy. LC 94-39212. 410p. (C). 1995. pap. 17.95 (*1-57181-024-2*) Berghahn Bks.

W

Women, Family, & Utopia: Communal Experiments of the Shakers, the Oneida Community, & the Mormons. Lawrence Foster. LC 91-8496. (Utopianism & Communitarianism Ser.). (Illus.). 432p. (C). 1991. text ed. 39.95 (*0-8156-2534-0*); pap. text ed. 16.95 (*0-8156-2535-9*) Syracuse U Pr.

Women, Family & Work. Deepa Mathur. (C). 1992. 18.00 (*81-7033-147-1*, Pub. by Rawat II) S Asia.

Women, Family Life, & Rural Welfare. L. N. Dash. (Illus.). 202p. 1993. 22.00 (*81-85445-45-1*, Pub. by Manak Pubns Pvt Ltd) Nataraj Bks.

Women Farmers in Africa: Rural Development in Mali & the Sahel. Ed. by Lucy E. Creevey. LC 85-27771. (Illus.). 232p. 1986. text ed. 39.95 (*0-8156-2358-5*); pap. text ed. 16.95 (*0-8156-2359-3*) Syracuse U Pr.

Women Farmers of Malawi: Food Production in the Zomba District. David Hirschmann & Megan Vaughan. LC 84-19264. (Research Ser.: No. 58). (Illus.). x, 143p. 1984. pap. text ed. 8.95 (*0-87725-158-4*) U of Cal IAS.

Women, Feminism & Biology. Lynda Birke. 232p. 1986. text ed. 27.50 (*0-416-01221-3*, 9810); pap. text ed. 12.95 (*0-416-01231-0*, 9828) Routledge Chapman & Hall.

Women, Feminism & Development. Ed. by Huguette Dagenais & Denise Piche. 464p. (C). 1994. 55.00 (*0-7735-1184-9*, Pub. by McGill CN); pap. text ed. 24.95 (*0-7735-1185-7*, Pub. by McGill CN) U of Toronto Pr.

Women, Feminism & Family Therapy. Ed. by Lois Braverman. LC 87-63475. (Journal of Psychotherapy & the Family: Vol. 3, No. 4). 192p. 1988. text ed. 29.95 (*0-86656-696-1*) Haworth Pr.

Women, Feminism, & Social Change in Argentina, Chile, & Uruguay, 1890-1940. Asuncion Lavrin. LC 95-2729. (Engendering Latin America Ser.). (Illus.). x, 490p. 1995. text ed. 60.00 (*0-8032-2897-X*) U of Nebr Pr.

Women, Feminist Identity & Society in the 1980's: Selected Papers. Iris M. Zavala. LC 84-28286. (Critical Theory Ser.: No. 1). v, 138p. 1985. 52.00 (*0-915027-50-X*); pap. 26.00 (*0-915027-51-8*) Benjamins North Am.

Women Fifteen Hundred to Nineteen Hundred: A Joint Exhibition of Books, & Manuscripts, Prints, Photos & Ephemera from the collections of the Historical Society of Pennsylvania & the Library Company of Philadelphia. (Illus.). 27p. (Orig.). 1974. pap. 2.00 (*0-914076-58-2*) Lib Co Phila.

Women Film Directors: An International Bio-Critical Dictionary. Gwendolyn A. Foster. LC 95-7395. 464p. 1995. text ed. 79.50 (*0-313-28972-7*, Greenwood Pr) Greenwood.

***Women Film Makers & Their Films.** 1998. 110.00 (*1-55862-357-4*, 00157205) St James Pr.

***Women Filmmakers of the African & Asian Diaspora: Decolonizing the Gaze, Locating Subjectivity.** Gwendolyn A. Foster. LC 96-27635. (Illus.). 160p. (C). 1997. 39.95 (*0-8093-2119-X*); pap. 19.95 (*0-8093-2120-3*) S Ill U Pr.

Women, Fire & Dangerous Things. George Lakoff. LC 86-19136. xxvi, 642p. 1990. pap. 19.95 (*0-226-46804-6*) U Ch Pr.

Women First: The Female Tradition in English Physical Education, 1880-1980. Sheila Fletcher. LC 84-70367. (Illus.). 194p. (C). 1984. pap. 25.00 (*0-485-12046-1*, Pub. by Athlone Pr UK) Humanities.

Women, Food & Sex in History, Set. Frwd. by Madalyn M. O'Hair. 1201p. (Orig.). 1989. pap. 40.00 (*0-910309-22-1*, 5427) Am Atheist.

Women, Food & Sex in History, Vol. I. Soledad De Montalvo. 277p. (Orig.). 1988. pap. 12.00 (*0-910309-47-7*, 5421) Am Atheist.

Women, Food & Sex in History, Vol. II. Soledad De Montalvo. 298p. (Orig.). 1989. pap. 12.00 (*0-910309-48-5*, 5422) Am Atheist.

Women, Food & Sex in History, Vol. III. Soledad De Montalvo. 319p. (Orig.). 1989. pap. 12.00 (*0-910309-49-3*, 5423) Am Atheist.

Women, Food & Sex in History, Vol. IV. Soledad De Montalvo. 300p. (Orig.). 1990. pap. 12.00 (*0-910309-61-2*, 5425) Am Atheist.

Women for a Change: A Grassroots Guide to Activism & Politics. Thalia Zepatos & Elizabeth Kaufman. LC 94-42402. 288p. 1995. 22.95 (*0-8160-3032-4*) Facts on File.

Women for a Change: A Grassroots Guide to Activism & Politics. Thalia Zepatos & Elizabeth Kaufman. 1996. pap. 14.95 (*0-8160-3492-3*) Facts on File.

Women for All Seasons: Poetry & Prose about the Transitions in Women's Lives. Ed. by Wanda Coleman. 76p. (Orig.). 1988. pap. 8.00 (*0-944587-00-3*) Womans Bldg.

Women for All Seasons: The Story of the Women's International League for Peace & Freedom. Catherine Foster. LC 88-17516. (Illus.). 248p. 1989. pap. 18.00 (*0-8203-1147-2*) U of Ga Pr.

Women for Hire: Prostitution & Sexuality in France after 1850. Alain Corbin. Tr. by Alan Sheridan from FRE. (Illus.). 512p. 1990. 46.00 (*0-674-95543-9*) HUP.

Women for Hire: Prostitution & Sexuality in France after 1850. Alain Corbin. Tr. by Alan Sheridan. (Illus.). 496p. 1996. pap. 16.95 (*0-674-95544-7*) HUP.

***Women for Peace.** Marlene T. Brill. LC 96-28945. (Women Then - Women Now Ser.). 1997. lib. bdg. 22.70 (*0-531-11328-0*) Watts.

Women, Foreign Assistance, & Advocacy Administration. Kathleen A. Staudt. LC 84-15935. 188p. 1985. text ed. 45.00 (*0-275-90168-8*, C0168, Praeger Pubs) Greenwood.

***Women Founders of the Social Sciences.** Lynn McDonald. (Illus.). 287p. (Orig.). 1994. pap. 26.95 (*0-88629-219-0*) Mich St U Pr.

Women, Freedom, & Calvin. Jane D. Douglass. LC 85-8778. 156p. 1985. pap. 15.00 (*0-664-24663-X*, Westminster) Westminster John Knox.

Women Friends, Men Friends. Serena G. Mills. 56p. 1996. pap. 8.00 (*0-8059-3851-6*) Dorrance.

Women! from Mars. Christopher Langley. LC 76-15099. 1976. 15.00 (*0-87832-018-0*) Piper.

Women from Subjection to Liberation. Rekha Pandey. (C). 1989. 34.00 (*81-7099-085-8*, Pub. by Mittal II) S Asia.

***Women Gardeners: A History.** Yvonne Cuthbertson. (Illus.). 220p. 1997. 32.00 (*0-912869-21-6*) Arden Pr.

Women Gay Games III Vancouver Canada: Celebration 90. Cheryl A. Traendly. 96p. 1992. pap. 19.95 (*0-9634389-9-9*) C Traendly Prods.

***Women Gays & Constitution.** Richards. 1998. lib. bdg. 58.00 (*0-226-71206-0*) U Ch Pr.

***Women, Gender, & Community.** Ed. by Jane D. Douglass & James F. Kay. LC 96-40009. 160p. (Orig.). 1997. pap. 15.00 (*0-664-25728-3*) Westminster John Knox.

Women, Gender & Development Reader. Ed. by Nalini Visvanathan et al. LC 96-47238. 384p. (C). 1997. 65.00 (*1-85649-141-2*, Pub. by Zed Bks Ltd UK) Humanities.

Women, Gender & Development Reader. Ed. by Nalini Visvanathan et al. LC 96-47238. 384p. (C). 1997. pap. 25.00 (*1-85649-142-0*, Pub. by Zed Bks Ltd UK) Humanities.

Women, Gender & Social Psychology. Ed. by Virginia O'Leary et al. 400p. (C). 1985. text ed. 79.95 (*0-89859-447-2*) L Erlbaum Assocs.

Women, Gender & World Politics: Perspectives, Policies & Prospects. Ed. by Peter R. Beckman & Francine D'Amico. LC 94-15857. 264p. 1994. text ed. 65.00 (*0-89789-305-0*, Bergin & Garvey); pap. text ed. 19.95 (*0-89789-306-9*, Bergin & Garvey) Greenwood.

***Women Gender Osiris 12.** Kohlstedt. 1997. pap. text ed. 25.00 (*0-226-30754-9*); lib. bdg. 39.00 (*0-226-30753-0*) U Ch Pr.

Women, Girls, & Psychotherapy: Reframing Resistance. Ed. by Annie G. Rogers et al. LC 91-20845. (Women & Therapy Ser.). 243p. 1991. lib. bdg. 39.95 (*1-56024-196-9*) Haworth Pr.

Women, Girls & Psychotherapy: Reframing Resistance. Ed. by Annie G. Rogers et al. LC 91-20845. (Women & Therapy Ser.). 243p. 1991. lib. bdg. 14.95 (*1-56023-012-6*) Haworth Pr.

Women Giving Birth. Saskiavan Rees et al. (Illus.). 160p. (Orig.). 1995. pap. 18.95 (*0-89087-668-1*) Celestial Arts.

Women Golfer: A Beginner's Guide. Mary J. Dillon & Custis N. Proctor. 112p. 1996. pap. write for info. (*0-9650385-0-5*) Severn Grp.

Women Growing Older: Theoretical Perspectives in the Psychology of Aging. Ed. by Barbara F. Turner & Lillian E. Troll. LC 93-35574. (C). 1993. text ed. 52.00 (*0-8039-3986-8*); pap. text ed. 23.95 (*0-8039-3987-6*) Sage.

Women Guarding Men. Lynn E. Zimmer. LC 85-28857. (Studies in Crime & Justice). xiv, 278p. 1986. 30.00 (*0-226-98339-0*) U Ch Pr.

Women, Guerrillas, & Love: Understanding War in Central America. Ileana Rodriguez. LC 96-33834. 232p. (C). 1996. text ed. 49.95 (*0-8166-2626-X*); pap. text ed. 19.95 (*0-8166-2627-8*) U of Minn Pr.

Women Have Always Worked: An Historical Overview. Alice Kessler-Harris. (Women's Lives - Women's Work Ser.). (Illus.). 208p. (Orig.). (YA). (gr. 11 up). 1981. pap. 9.95 (*0-912670-67-3*) Feminist Pr.

***Women Headed Households.** Chant. 1997. text ed. 69.95 (*0-312-17242-7*) St Martin.

Women-Headed Households in Rural India. Ranjana Kumari. 125p. 1988. text ed. 18.95 (*81-7027-129-0*, Pub. by Radiant Pubs II) S Asia.

***Women, Headship, & the Holy Spirit.** 250p. 1996. pap. write for info. (*1-888435-05-4*) Hyatt Intl.

Women Healers: Portraits of Herbalists, Physicians & Midwives. Elisabeth Brooke. 176p. 1995. pap. 12.95 (*0-89281-548-5*, Heal Arts VT) Inner Tradit.

***Women Healers & Physicians: Climbing a Long Hill.** Lilian R. Furst. LC 96-32389. 320p. 1997. text ed. 34.95 (*0-8131-2011-X*) U Pr of Ky.

Women Healers in Medieval Life & Literature. Muriel J. Hughes. LC 68-57322. (Essay Index Reprint Ser.). 1977. 24.95 (*0-8369-0552-0*) Ayer.

Women Healing Earth: Third World Women on Ecology, Feminism & Religion. Ed. by Rosemary R. Ruether. LC 96-528. (Ecology & Justice Ser.). 175p. 1996. pap. 17.00 (*1-57075-057-2*) Orbis Bks.

Women, Health & Culture. Ed. by Phyllis N. Stern & Shirley Chater. (Health Care for Women International Publication). 170p. 1986. text ed. 35.95 (*0-89116-858-3*) Hemisp Pub.

Women, Health & Development: A Report by the Director-General. (WHO Offset Publication Ser.: No. 90). 41p. 1985. pap. text ed. 7.00 (*92-4-170090-4*, 1120090) World Health.

***Women, Health & Development in the Americas: An Annotated Bibliography.** (PAHO Scientific Publication Ser.: No. 464). 114p. 1984. pap. text ed. 14.00 (*92-75-11464-1*) World Health.

Women, Health, & Development in the South-East Asia Region. (SEARO Regional Health Paper Ser.: No. 22). ix, 90p. 1992. pap. text ed. 7.00 (*92-9022-191-7*, 1580022) World Health.

Women, Health & Healing: Toward a New Perspective. Virginia L. Olesen. Ed. by Ellen Lewin. (Contemporary Issues in Health, Medicine & Social Policy Ser.). 300p. (Orig.). (C). 1985. pap. text ed. 12.95 (*0-422-78030-8*, 9264, Pub. by Tavistock UK) Routledge Chapman & Hall.

Women, Health & Medicine. Agnes Miles. 224p. 1991. pap. 29.00 (*0-335-09905-X*, Open Univ Pr) Taylor & Francis.

Women, Health & Medicine in America: A Historical Handbook. Ed. by Rima D. Apple. LC 90-2719. 600p. 1990. text ed. 20.00 (*0-8240-8447-0*, 483) Garland.

Women, Health, & Medicine in America: A Historical Handbook. Ed. by Rima D. Apple. LC 91-20496. (Illus.). 580p. (Orig.). 1992. reprint ed. pap. text ed. 18.95 (*0-8135-1766-4*) Rutgers U Pr.

Women, Health, & Poverty. Cesar A. Perales & Lauren S. Young. LC 87-26274. (Women & Health Ser.: Vol. 12, Nos. 3-4). 259p. 1989. text ed. 49.95 (*0-86656-684-8*) Haworth Pr.

Women, Health, & Reproduction. Helen Roberts. 208p. (Orig.). 1981. pap. 13.95 (*0-7100-0703-5*, RKP) Routledge.

Women Helping Girls with Choices: A Handbook. Mindy Bingham & Sandy Stryker. (Illus.). 132p. 1989. pap. 14.95 (*0-911655-00-X*) Advocacy Pr.

***Women Helping Women: A Biblical Guide to the Top 20 Issues Women Face.** Ed. by Elyse Fitzpatrick & Carol Cornish. LC 97-5437. 350p. (Orig.). 1997. pap. 16.99 (*1-56507-617-6*) Harvest Hse.

Women Heroes: Six Short Plays from the Women's Project. Ed. by Julia Miles. 256p. 1987. pap. 8.95 (*0-936839-22-8*) Applause Theatre Bk Pubs.

Women, History, & Theory: The Essays of Joan Kelly. Joan B. Kelly. LC 84-2558. (Women in Culture & Society Ser.). (Illus.). xxvi, 190p. 1986. pap. text ed. 12.95 (*0-226-43028-6*) U Ch Pr.

Women Hold up Half the Sky: 285 Spirited Women & What They Said about Life, Love, Work, & Men. Ed. by Lee Wilson. 160p. 1994. pap. 7.95 (*0-9639815-0-1*) Pleasant View.

Women Home Alone: Learning to Thrive. Patricia H. Sprinkle. LC 95-42134. 288p. 1996. pap. 12.99 (*0-310-20183-7*) Zondervan.

Women, Households & Change. 258p. 1991. 45.00 (*0-685-52693-3*, 91.III.A.3) UN.

Women, Households & Change. 241p. 1991. 45.00 (*0-685-53676-9*, E.91.III.A.3) UN.

Women, Households, & the Economy. Catharine R. Stimpson. (Douglass Series on Women's Lives & the Meaning of Gender). 272p. 1987. pap. 15.00 (*0-8135-1264-6*) Rutgers U Pr.

Women, Households, & the Economy. Catharine R. Stimpson. Ed. by Lourdes Beneria. LC 87-4840. (Douglass Series on Women's Lives & the Meaning of Gender). (Illus.). 365p. 1987. reprint ed. pap. 104.10 (*0-7837-9212-3*, 2049962) Bks Demand.

Women, Houses & Home: An Anthology of Prose, Poetry & Photography. Ed. by Janice H. Mikesell & Marilyn Richardson. LC 88-177402. (Illus.). 52p. 1988. reprint ed. pap. 8.00 (*0-9621112-3-6*) Hens Teeth.

Women, Housewives, Whores. Carle. 1994. pap. 12.95 (*0-9642208-0-6*) Buckhorn Bks.

Women, Housing & Community. Willem Van Vliet. 230p. 1989. text ed. 55.95 (*0-566-05653-4*, Pub. by Avebury Pub UK) Ashgate Pub Co.

Women, Human Settlements, & Housing. Ed. by Caroline Moser & Linda Peake. 256p. (C). 1988. text ed. 55.00 (*0-422-61860-8*, Pub. by Tavistock UK); pap. text ed. 14.95 (*0-422-61980-9*, Pub. by Tavistock UK) Routledge Chapman & Hall.

Women I Have Known & Been. Carol L. Pearson. 1993. 11.95 (*1-882723-03-1*) Gold Leaf Pr.

Women, Identity & Private Life in Britain, 1900-50. Judy Giles. LC 95-2958. 1995. text ed. 39.95 (*0-312-12624-7*) St Martin.

Women Images. Ed. by Pratibha Jain & Rajan Mahan. (C). 1996. 37.00 (*0-614-95649-8*, Pub. by Har-Anand Pubns II) S Asia.

***Women Imagine Change: Global Anthology of Women's Resistance from 600 B. C. E. to Present.** Ed. by Eugenia C. Delamotte & Natania Meeker. 480p. (C). 1997. text ed. 74.95 (*0-415-91530-9*, Routledge NY) Routledge.

***Women Imagine Change: Global Anthology of Women's Resistance from 600 B.C.E. to Present.** Ed. by Eugenia C. Delamotte & Natania Meeker. 480p. 1997. pap. 29.95 (*0-415-91531-7*, Routledge NY) Routledge.

Women in a Changing Global Economy: World Survey on the Role of Women in Development. 128p. Date not set. pap. 9.95 (*92-1-130163-7*, E.95.IV.1) UN.

Women in a Changing Society. Anjana Maitra-Sinha. xii, 166p. 1993. 15.95 (*1-881338-35-5*) Nataraj Bks.

Women in a Developing Society, India. Usha Rao. 1984. 14.00 (*0-8364-1057-2*, Pub. by Ashish II) S Asia.

Women in a Restructuring Australia: Work & Welfare. Ed. by Anne Edwards & Susan Magarey. 336p. 1996. pap. 29.95 (*1-86373-824-X*, Pub. by Allen & Unwin Aust Pty AT) Paul & Co Pubs.

Women in a River Landscape: A Novel in Dialogues & Soliloquies. Heinrich Boll. Tr. by David McLintock from GER. LC 95-12352. (European Classics Ser.). 208p. 1995. pap. 14.95 (*0-8101-1205-1*) Northwestern U Pr.

Women in a Strange Land: Search for a New Image. Ed. by Clare B. Fischer et al. LC 74-26326. 143p. reprint ed. pap. 40.80 (*0-685-16024-6*, 2026834) Bks Demand.

Women in a Tribal Community: A Study of Arunachal Pradesh. Kiran Mishra. 1991. text ed. 15.95 (*0-7069-5836-5*, Pub. by Vikas II) S Asia.

***Women in AA Vol. 1: Personal Stories of Recovery.** unabridged ed. Ed. by Kathleen W. Fitzgerald. 275p. (Orig.). 1996. pap. 18.95 (*1-882195-03-5*, 5000) Whales Tale Pr.

Women in Academe. Ed. by Resa L. Dudovitz. 118p. 1984. 19.25 (*0-08-030819-8*, 26/13, Pergamon Pr) Elsevier.

Women in Academe: Progress & Prospects. Ed. by Mariam K. Chamberlain. LC 88-37217. 400p. 1989. 45.00 (*0-87154-204-8*) Russell Sage.

Women in Academe: Progress & Prospects. Mariam K. Chamberlain. (Illus.). 448p. 1991. pap. 14.95 (*0-87154-218-8*) Russell Sage.

Women in Accra: Options for Autonomy. Deborah Pellow. Ed. by Cole Kitchen. LC 77-78740. (Illus.). 1977. 19.95 (*0-917256-03-4*) Ref Pubns.

Women in Action: Rebels & Reformers 1920-1980. Elisabeth I. Perry. 60p. 1995. pap. 6.95 (*0-89959-389-5*, 1019) LWVUS.

Women in Administration: Facilitators for Change. L. Nan Restine. Ed. by Jerry J. Herman & Janice L. Herman. LC 93-16917. (Road Maps to Success Ser.). 64p. 1993. pap. 11.95 (*0-8039-6059-X*) Corwin Pr.

Women in Africa: Studies in Social and Economic Change. Ed. by Nancy J. Hafkin & Edna G. Bay. LC 75-44901. 320p. 1976. 45.00 (*0-8047-0906-8*); pap. 15.95 (*0-8047-1011-2*) Stanford U Pr.

Women in Africa & the African Diaspora. Ed. by Rosalyn Terborg-Penn et al. 256p. 1988. 29.95 (*0-88258-171-6*) Howard U Pr.

***Women in Africa & the African Diaspora: A Reader.** 2nd ed. Ed. by Rosalyn Terborg-Penn & Andrea B. Rushing. LC 96-46285. (Illus.). (C). 1996. pap. text ed. 17.95 (*0-88258-194-5*, TEWRP) Howard U Pr.

Women in Africa & the African Diaspora. Ed. by Rosalyn Terborg-Penn et al. 256p. 1989. pap. 14.95 (*0-88258-177-5*) Howard U Pr.

Women in Africa of the Sub-Sahara: Ancient Times to the 20th Century, Vol. I. Marjorie W. Bingham & Susan H. Gross. (Illus.). 143p. 1982. pap. 15.00 (*0-86596-006-2*) UM Womens Hist.

Women in African Literature Today: A Review. Ed. by Eldred D. Jones & Eustace Palmer. LC 87-70491. (African Literature Today Ser.). 162p. 1987. 29.95 (*0-86543-056-X*); pap. 8.95 (*0-86543-057-8*) Africa World.

Women in Agriculture. Faj M. Sethi. (C). 1991. 23.50 (*81-7033-134-X*, Pub. by Rawat II) S Asia.

Women in Agriculture: A Guide to Research. Marie Maman & Thelma H. Tate. LC 95-41230. (Women's History & Culture Ser.: Vol. 11). 308p. 1996. text ed. 56.00 (*0-8153-1354-3*, SS908) Garland.

Women in Agriculture: A Socio-Economic Analysis. Shashi K. Varma. (C). 1992. 21.00 (*81-7022-363-6*, Pub. by Concept II) S Asia.

Women in Agriculture: Perspective, Issues & Experiences. Ed. by R. K. Samanta. 218p. 1995. pap. 150.00 (*81-85880-86-7*, Pub. by Print Hse II) St Mut.

Women in Agriculture. Bibliography: January 1985-July 1992. 71p. (Orig.). (C). 1993. pap. text ed. 25.00 (*1-56806-935-9*) DIANE Pub.

Women in Aikido. Andrea Siegel. LC 93-183. (Illus.). 232p. (Orig.). 1993. pap. 14.95 (*1-55643-161-9*) North Atlantic.

Women in All Ages & All Nations, 10 vols. Pierce Butler et al. 1975. lib. bdg. 3,000.00 (*0-8490-1322-4*) Gordon Pr.

Women in America: A Guide to Books, 1963-1975: with an Appendix on Books Published 1976-1979. fac. ed. Barbara Haber. LC 80-28029. (Illini Bks.). 279p. 1981. pap. 79.60 (*0-7837-7626-8*, 2047378) Bks Demand.

Women in America: From Colonial Times to the 20th Century, 59 vols, Set. Ed. by Leon Stein. 1974. lib. bdg. 1,636.00 (*0-405-06070-X*) Ayer.

Women in American History. Grace Humphrey. LC 68-57323. (Essay Index Reprint Ser.). 1977. 23.95 (*0-8369-0555-5*) Ayer.

Women in American History: A Series, 4 bks. Ed. by Beverly Sanders. 1986. reprint ed. 25.00 (*0-317-46776-X*) Educ Dev Ctr.

Women in American Indian Society see Indians of North America

Women in American Law Vol. 2: The Struggle Toward Equality from the New Deal to the Present. 2nd rev. ed. Judith A. Baer. LC 96-24654. 380p. (C). 1996. 40.00 (*0-8419-1365-X*); pap. text ed. 19.95 (*0-8419-1366-8*) Holmes & Meier.

Women in American Law, Vol. 1: From Colonial Times to the New Deal. Ed. by Marlene S. Wortman et al. LC 82-10954. (Illus.). 450p. 1985. 49.95 (*0-8419-0752-8*); pap. 25.50 (*0-8419-0753-6*) Holmes & Meier.

Women in American Music: A Bibliography. JoAnn Skowronski. LC 77-26611. 191p. 1978. 29.50 (*0-8108-1105-7*) Scarecrow.

Women in American Music: A Bibliography of Music & Literature. Ed. by Adrienne F. Block & Carol Neuls-Bates. LC 79-7722. (Illus.). 302p. 1979. text ed. 55.00 (*0-313-21410-7*, NBW/, Greenwood Pr) Greenwood.

Women in American Politics: A Symposium of the Women's Program Forum. 1994. write for info. (*0-318-72766-8*) Ford Found.

Women in American Society. 3rd ed. Virginia Sapiro. LC 93-27335. 549p. (C). 1994. pap. text ed. 31.95 (*1-55934-225-0*, 1225) Mayfield Pub.

Women in America's Wars. Silvia A. Sheafer. LC 95-15473. (Collective Biographies Ser.). (Illus.). 112p. (YA). (gr. 6 up). 1996. lib. bdg. 18.95 (*0-89490-553-8*) Enslow Pubs.

Women in Ancient Egypt. Gay Robins. 205p. 1993. pap. text ed. 18.95 (*0-674-95469-6*) HUP.

Women in Ancient Egypt. Barbara Watterson. LC 91-30599. (Illus.). 224p. 1992. text ed. 39.95 (*0-312-07538-3*) St Martin.

Women in Ancient Egypt. Gay Robins. LC 92-38221. 205p. 1993. reprint ed. pap. 18.95 (*0-674-95468-8*) HUP.

Women in Ancient Greece. Sue Blundell. LC 93-36217. (Illus.). 288p. 1995. pap. 19.95 (*0-674-95473-4*, BLUWOX) HUP.

Women in Ancient Greece & Rome. Marjorie W. Bingham & Susan H. Gross. LC 83-14016. (Women in World Area Studies). (Illus.). 125p. (Orig.). 1983. pap. 15.00 (*0-914227-00-9*) UM Womens Hist.

Women in Ancient Greece & Rome. Michael Massey. (Illus.). 40p. (C). 1988. pap. text ed. 10.95 (*0-521-31807-6*) Cambridge U Pr.

W

An Asterisk (*) at the beginning of an entry indicates that the title is appearing in BIP for the first time.

Women in Ancient India: Moral & Literary Studies. Clarisse Bader. LC 72-9617. (Human Sexual Behavior Ser.). reprint ed. 45.00 (0-404-57408-4) AMS Pr.

Women in Ancient Indian Tales. Jagdish C. Jain & Margaret Walter. 129p. 1987. 17.50 (0-8364-2084-5, Pub. by Mittal II) S Asia.

Women in Ancient Persia, 559-331 B.C. Maria Brosius. LC 95-30650. (Oxford Classical Monographs). 272p. (C). 1996. 65.00 (0-19-815009-1, Clarendon Pr) OUP.

Women in Ancient Societies: An Illusion of the Night. Ed. by Leonie J. Archer et al. LC 93-31197. 308p. (C). 1994. pap. 18.95 (0-415-90882-5, Routledge NY) Routledge.

Women in Andean Agriculture: Peasant Production & Rural Wage Employment in Colombia & Peru. 2nd ed. Carmen Deere & Magdalena L. De Leal. (Women, Work & Development Ser.: No. 4). xii, 172p. 1985. pap. 18.00 (92-2-103106-3) Intl Labour Office.

Women in Antiquity. Ed. by Peter Walcot & Ian McAuslan. (Greece & Rome Studies). 240p. (C). 1996. pap. 19.95 (0-19-920303-2) OUP.

Women in Antiquity. Ed. by Peter Walcot & Ian McAuslan. (Greece & Rome Studies). (Illus.). 228p. (C). 1996. 65.00 (0-19-920302-4) OUP.

Women in Antiquity: An Annotated Bibliography. Leanna Goodwater. LC 75-23229. 1975. 20.00 (0-8108-0837-4) Scarecrow.

Women in Antiquity: New Assessments. Ed. by Richard Hawley & Barbara Levick. LC 95-3491. 304p. (C). 1995. pap. 18.95 (0-415-11369-5) Routledge.

Women in Antiquity: New Assessments. Ed. by Richard Hawley & Barbara Levick. LC 95-3491. 304p. (C). (gr. 13). 1995. text ed. 59.95 (0-415-11368-7) Routledge.

Women in Archaeology. Ed. by Cheryl Claassen. LC 94-8818. (Illus.). 264p. (Orig.). (C). 1994. text ed. 38.95 (0-8122-3277-1); pap. text ed. 17.95 (0-8122-1509-5) U of Pa Pr.

Women in Aristophanic Comedy. Lauren K. Taaffe. LC 93-18362. 256p. (C). (gr. 13). 1993. text ed. 49.95 (0-415-09514-X) Routledge.

Women in Asia & the Pacific: Towards an East-West Dialogue. Ed. by Madeleine J. Goodman. LC 85-10034. 359p. reprint ed. pap. 102.40 (0-8357-3590-7, 2034634) Bks Demand.

Women in Athenian Law & Life. Roger Just. 328p. (C). 1991. pap. 18.95 (0-415-05841-4, A5648) Routledge.

Women in Baseball: The Forgotten History. Gai I. Berlage. LC 93-25049. 224p. 1994. text ed. 22.50 (0-275-94735-1, C4735, Praeger Pubs) Greenwood.

Women in Beckett: Performance & Critical Perspectives. Ed. by Linda Ben-Zvi. (Illus.). 280p. 1990. text ed. 37.50 (0-252-01658-0) U of Ill Pr.

Women in Beckett: Performance & Critical Perspectives. Ed. by Linda Ben-Zvi. (Illus.). 280p. 1992. pap. text ed. 14.95 (0-252-06256-6) U of Ill Pr.

Women in Between: Female Roles in a Male World: Mount Hagen, New Guinea. Marilyn Strathern. 372p. (C). 1995. text ed. 65.00 (0-8476-7784-2); pap. text ed. 27.95 (0-8476-7785-0) Rowman.

Women in Bihar: A Study of Their Role in Tasar Silk Production. Gautam Vohra. (Illus.). x, 206p. 1989. text ed. 27.95 (0-7069-3942-5, Pub. by Vikas II) S Asia.

Women in Black. large type ed. Madeleine St. John. 1994. 25.99 (0-7089-3211-8) Ulverscroft.

Women in Boxing. Harry McKinzie. 1994. pap. 16.95 (0-86626-012-9) McKinzie Pub.

***Women in Britain.** 2nd ed. Central Office of Info. (Aspects of Britain Ser.). (Illus.). 131p. 1996. pap. 11.95 (0-11-701982-8, HM19828, Pub. by Stationery Ofc UK) Seven Hills Bk.

Women in Britain Today. Ed. by Veronica Beechey & Elizabeth Whitelegg. 256p. 1985. pap. 29.00 (0-335-15137-X, Open Univ Pr) Taylor & Francis.

Women in British Trade Unions 1874-1976. Norbert C. Soldon. (Illus.). 226p. 1978. 38.00 (0-8476-6056-7) Rowman.

Women in Buddhism: Images of the Feminine in the Mahayana Tradition. Diana M. Paul. 1985. pap. 15.00 (0-520-05428-8) U CA Pr.

Women in Business Yellow Pages: Metro Chicago & Springfield. 194p. 1994. pap. 10.00 (0-9619218-7-0) Women in Busn.

***Women in Business Yellow Pages: Metro Chicago & Springfield.** 154p. 1995. pap. 10.00 (1-887382-00-3) Women in Busn.

Women in Business Yellow Pages: Metro Chicago & Springfield, 1993. Ed. by Women In Business, Inc. Staff. 198p. 1993. pap. 10.00 (0-9619218-5-4) Women in Busn.

Women in Business Yellow Pages: Metro Chicago, 1988. Women in Business, Inc. Staff. 114p. 1987. pap. 6.75 (0-9619218-0-3) Women in Busn.

Women in Business Yellow Pages: Metro Chicago, 1989. Women in Business, Inc. Staff. 163p. 1988. pap. 8.00 (0-9619218-1-1) Women in Busn.

Women in Business Yellow Pages: Metro Chicago, 1990. Women in Business, Inc. Staff. 180p. 1989. pap. 8.00 (0-9619218-2-X) Women in Busn.

Women in Business Yellow Pages: Metro Chicago, 1991. Women in Business, Inc. Staff. 194p. 1990. pap. 9.00 (0-9619218-3-8) Women in Busn.

Women in Business Yellow Pages: Metro Chicago, 1992. Ed. by Women In Business, Inc. Staff. 198p. 1992. pap. text ed. 10.00 (0-9619218-4-6) Women in Busn.

Women in Business Yellow Pages: Springfield. 50p. 1994. pap. 3.00 (0-9619218-8-9) Women in Busn.

Women in Business Yellow Pages: Springfield, 1993. 198p. 1993. pap. 10.00 (0-9619218-6-2) Women in Busn.

Women in Canada: Socio-Economic Status & Other Contemporary Issues. Sandra Harder. 24p. (Orig.). 1994. pap. 9.10 (0-660-15470-6, Pub. by Canada Commun Grp CN) Accents Pubns.

Women in Cars: Poems. Martha McFerren. 72p. (Orig.). 1992. pap. 9.95 (0-9627460-6-1) Helicon Nine Eds.

Women in Celtic Law & Culture. Jack G. Thompson. LC 96-23249. (Women's Studies: Vol. 12). 352p. 1996. text ed. 99.95 (0-7734-8760-3) E Mellen.

Women in Celtic Myth: Tales of Extraordinary Women from Ancient Celtic Tradition. Moyra Caldecott. 224p. (Orig.). 1992. pap. 12.95 (0-89281-357-1) Inner Tradit.

Women in Chains: A Sourcebook on the Agunah. Ed. by Jack N. Porter. LC 95-9843. 288p. 1996. pap. 24.95 (1-56821-440-5) Aronson.

Women in Chains: Abandonment in Love Relationships in the Fiction of Selected West African Writers. Rose U. Mezu. 252p. (Orig.). (C). 1994. text ed. 50.00 (0-87831-169-6); pap. text ed. 25.00 (0-87831-170-X) Blck Acad Pr.

Women in Change: The Psychological Development of American Women. Lillian C. Woo. LC 91-75934. 176p. 1992. 19.95 (0-89089-477-9) Carolina Acad Pr.

Women in Changing Society. S. N. Sahai. 1985. 40.00 (0-8364-1475-6, Pub. by Mittal II) S Asia.

Women in Charge: The Experience of Female Entrepreneurs. Robert Coffee & Richard Scase. 180p. 1985. pap. text ed. 15.95 (0-04-301190-X) Routledge Chapman & Hall.

Women in Chemistry & Physics: A Biobibliographic Sourcebook. Ed. by Louise S. Grinstein et al. LC 92-40224. 736p. 1993. text ed. 115.00 (0-313-27382-0, GWH, Greenwood Pr) Greenwood.

Women in China. Katie Curtin. LC 74-14166. 95p. 1975. pap. 9.95 (0-87348-405-3); lib. bdg. 30.00 (0-87348-404-5) Pathfinder NY.

Women in China. Hasna J. Moudud. 94p. 1980. 17.95 (0-7069-1084-2) Asia Bk Corp.

Women in China: A Selected & Annotated Bibliography. Karen T. Wei. LC 84-10863. (Bibliographies & Indexes in Women's Studies: No. 1). xvii, 250p. 1984. text ed. 69.50 (0-313-24234-8, WEW/, Greenwood Pr) Greenwood.

Women in China: Current Directions in Historical Scholarship. Ed. by Richard W. Guisso & Stanley Johannesen. 1981. lib. bdg. 109.95 (0-88946-151-1) E Mellen.

Women in China: Studies in Social Change & Feminism. Ed. by Marilyn B. Young. (Michigan Monographs in Chinese Studies: No. 15). (Illus.). 259p. 1973. pap. text ed. 15.00 (0-89264-015-4) Ctr Chinese Studies.

Women in Chinese Society. Ed. by Margery Wolf & Roxane Witke. LC 75-82782. (Studies in Chinese Society). xii, 316p. 1975. 45.00 (0-8047-0874-6); pap. 13.95 (0-8047-0977-7) Stanford U Pr.

Women in Church History: A Bibliography. Ed. by Carolyn Blevins. LC 95-24835. 200p. (C). 1995. text ed. 30.00 (0-86554-493-X, MUP/H387) Mercer Univ Pr.

Women in Church History: Twenty Stories for 20 Centuries. Joanne Turpin. 175p. 1990. pap. 6.95 (0-86716-096-9) St Anthony Mess Pr.

Women in Cleveland: An Illustrated History. Marian J. Morton. LC 94-48852. (Encyclopedia of Cleveland History Ser.). (Illus.). 224p. 1995. 39.95 (0-253-32896-9); pap. 29.95 (0-253-20972-2) Ind U Pr.

Women in Colonial India: Essays on Survival, Work & the State. Ed. by J. Krishnamurty. 260p. 1991. 28.00 (0-19-562347-9) OUP.

Women in Colonial Spanish American Literature: Literary Images. Julie G. Johnson. LC 83-1500. (Contributions in Women's Studies: No. 43). x, 212p. 1983. text ed. 49.95 (0-313-23681-X, JOW/, Greenwood Pr) Greenwood.

Women in Combat: Report to the President. Presidential Commission on the Assignment of Women in the Armed Forces. (Association of the U. S. Army Book Ser.). 413p. 1994. 38.95 (0-02-881097-X); pap. 20.00 (0-02-881091-0) Brasseys Inc.

Women in Comedy. Linda Martin & Kerry Segrave. (Illus.). 312p. 1986. 19.95 (0-8065-1000-5, Citadel Pr) Carol Pub Group.

Women in Communication: A Biographical Sourcebook. Ed. by Nancy Signorielli. LC 95-52756. 504p. 1996. text ed. 79.50 (0-313-29164-0, Greenwood Pr) Greenwood.

Women in Communications. Alice Fins. (Illus.). 160p. 1980. pap. 8.95 (0-8442-6646-9, VGM Career Bks) NTC Pub Grp.

***Women in Congress, 1917-1990.** (Illus.). 266p. 1997. reprint ed. pap. text ed. 40.00 (0-7881-4256-9) DIANE Pub.

Women in Conservation: Tools for Analysis & a Framework for Action. Dounia Loudiyi & Alison Meares. 153p. (C). 1993. pap. text ed. 20.00 (2-8317-0196-1, Pub. by IUCN SZ) Island Pr.

Women in Construction: A Resource Guide. Jocelyn Riley. 114p. 1995. 20.00 (0-614-05258-0) Her Own Words.

Women in Contemporary Germany: Life, Work, Politics. rev. ed. Eva Kolinsky. Orig. Title: Women in West Germany: Life, Work & Politics. 368p. 1993. 38.95 (0-85496-391-X); pap. 16.95 (0-85496-818-0) Berg Pubs.

Women in Contemporary India & South Asia. Ed. by A. DeSousa. 227p. 1980. 19.95 (0-318-37321-1) Asia Bk Corp.

Women in Contemporary Russia. Vitalina Koval. LC 95-20447. 160p. (C). 1995. 35.00 (1-57181-885-5) Berghahn Bks.

Women in Context: Towards a Feminist Reconstructions of Psychotherapy. Ed. by Marsha P. Mirkin. LC 94-5534. 502p. 1994. lib. bdg. 46.95 (0-89862-095-3, C2095) Guilford Pr.

Women in Control? The Role of Women in Law Enforcement. Frances M. Heidensohn. LC 92-25902. 304p. 1993. 58.00 (0-19-825255-2) OUP.

Women in Control? The Role of Women in Law Enforcement. Frances M. Heidensohn. 304p. 1996. pap. 19.95 (0-19-826043-1) OUP.

***Women in Corporate Management.** Ronald J. Burke. LC 97-23235. 1997. write for info. (0-7923-4664-5) Kluwer Ac.

Women in Corporate Management: Model Programs for Development & Mobility. 1991. 85.00 (0-89584-176-2) Catalyst.

Women in Corporate Management: Results of a Catalyst Survey. 1990. 25.00 (0-89584-175-4) Catalyst.

Women in Crisis. Ed. by Penelope Russianoff. LC 80-29492. (Sponsored by Women in Crisis, Inc. Ser.). 319p. 1981. 43.95 (0-89885-051-7) Human Sci Pr.

Women in Cross-Cultural Perspective. Ed. by Leonore L. Adler. LC 90-7376. 296p. 1991. text ed. 55.00 (0-275-93658-9, C3658, Praeger Pubs) Greenwood.

Women in Cuba-Twenty Years Later. Margaret Randall. LC 80-54055. (Illus.). 182p. (C). 1981. 19.95 (0-918266-15-7); pap. 8.95 (0-918266-14-9) Smyrna.

***Women in Culture: A Women's Studies Anthology.** Ed. by Lucinda Peach. LC 97-24516. 1998. text ed. 64.95 (1-55786-648-1) Blackwell Pubs.

***Women in Culture: A Women's Studies Anthology.** Ed. by Lucinda Peach. LC 97-24516. 1998. pap. text ed. 29.95 (1-55786-649-X) Blackwell Pubs.

***Women in Cycles of Culture.** Anna De Koven. 333p. Date not set. 23.95 (0-8369-2787-7) Ayer.

Women in Dairy Development. Shagufta Jamal. (C). 1994. text ed. 16.00 (81-7022-500-0, Pub. by Concept II) S Asia.

Women in Decision-Making. 60p. 1991. 12.50 (92-1-130146-7, 91.IV.5) UN.

Women in Decision-Making. Ed. by Ranjana Kumari. (C). 1992. 25.00 (0-7069-5954-X, Pub. by Vikas II) S Asia.

Women in Decision-Making: Case-Study on Greece. 28p. 1991. pap. 10.00 (92-1-130147-5, 91.IV.6) UN.

Women in Developing Countries: A Policy Focus. Ed. by Kathleen A. Staudt & Jane S. Jaquette. LC 83-139. (Women & Politics Ser.: Vol. 2, No. 4). 135p. 1983. text ed. 39.95 (0-86656-226-5) Haworth Pr.

Women in Developing Economies: Making Visible the Invisible. Ed. by L. Massiah et al. 320p. 1993. 45.95 (0-85496-345-6); pap. 19.95 (0-85496-346-4) Berg Pubs.

Women in Developing World: Evidence from Turkey. Nermin Abadan-Unat. (World Affairs Ser.: Vol. 22, Bk. 1). (Orig.). 1986. pap. 9.95 (0-87940-080-3) Monograph Series.

Women in Development: A Creative Role Denied? The Case of Tanzania. Marja-Liisa Swantz. LC 85-2120. 177p. 1985. text ed. 18.95 (0-312-88780-9) St Martin.

Women in Development: An Interpretive Essay. Margaret C. Allan. (C). 1990. pap. 30.00 (0-7300-1200-X, SSS338, Pub. by Deakin Univ AT) St Mut.

Women in Development: Status, Issues, Information: APLIC Proceedings of the 23rd Annual Conference. Ed. by Laurie Leadbetter & William Barrows. 86p. (Orig.). 1991. pap. text ed. 20.00 (0-933438-17-6) APLIC Intl.

Women in Development: The Sericulture Experience in India. Ed. by Jayaraj Acharya. (C). 1995. 28.00 (81-7341-009-7, Pub. by Abhinav II) S Asia.

Women in Disguise: Stories. Marjorie Agosin. Tr. by Diane Russell-Pineda from SPA. LC 95-75220. 168p. (Orig.). (C). 1996. pap. 14.95 (1-885214-01-4) Azul Edits.

Women in Divorce. William J. Goode. LC 78-14243. 381p. 1978. reprint ed. text ed. 35.00 (0-313-21026-8, GOWD, Greenwood Pr) Greenwood.

***Women in Dramatic Place & Time: Contemporary Female Characters on Stage.** Geraldine Cousins. 224p. (C). 1996. pap. 19.95 (0-415-06734-0); text ed. 59.95 (0-415-06733-2) Routledge.

Women in Early Christianity. Ed. by Everett Ferguson. LC 93-2813. (Studies in Early Christianity: Vol. 14). (Illus.). 360p. 1993. Alk. paper. text ed. 65.00 (0-8153-1074-9) Garland.

Women in Early Modern Ireland: 1500-1800. Ed. by Margaret MacCurtain & Mary O'Dowd. 1991. text ed. 65.00 (0-7486-0223-2, Pub. by Edinburgh U Pr UK) Col U Pr.

Women in Early Modern Ireland 1500-1800. Ed. by Margaret MacCurtain & Mary O'Dowd. (Illus.). 240p. 1992. pap. 25.00 (0-7486-0241-0, Pub. by Edinburgh U Pr UK) Col U Pr.

Women in Early Texas. Ed. by Evelyn M. Carrington. LC 94-21170. (Fred H. & Ella Mae Moore Texas History Reprint Ser.). (Illus.). 348p. 1994. pap. 19.95 (0-87611-142-8) Tex St Hist Assn.

Women in Eastern Europe & the Soviet Union. Ed. by T. Yedlin. LC 80-16667. 320p. 1980. text ed. 65.00 (0-275-90570-5, C0570, Praeger Pubs) Greenwood.

Women in Educational Administration. Charol Shakeshaft. (Illus.). 244p. 1987. 21.95 (0-8039-3550-1) Sage.

Women in Educational Management. Ed. by Jenny Ozga. LC 92-17389. (Gender & Education Ser.). 1993. 27.00 (0-335-09340-X, Open Univ Pr) Taylor & Francis.

Women in Egyptian Public Life. Earl L. Sullivan. LC 85-26221. (Contemporary Issues in the Middle East Ser.). 248p. 1986. text ed. 39.95 (0-8156-2354-2) Syracuse U Pr.

Women in Eighteenth-Century America: A Study of Opinion & Social Usage. Mary S. Benson. LC 75-41025. (BCL Ser. II). 1976. reprint ed. 39.50 (0-404-51405-7) AMS Pr.

Women in Electoral Politics: Lessons from Norway. Jill M. Bystydzienski. LC 94-42816. 248p. 1995. text ed. 59.95 (0-275-95072-7, Praeger Pubs) Greenwood.

Women in Electoral Politics: Lessons from Norway. Jill M. Bystydzienski. LC 94-42839. 144p. 1995. text ed. 52.95 (0-275-95108-1, Praeger Pubs) Greenwood.

Women in Emergent Morocco: Changes & Continuities. Fatima Mernissi. 1982. 15.00 (0-933184-40-9) Flame Intl.

Women in Engineering. Ruth Carter & Gill Kirkup. 224p. (C). 1990. text ed. 32.00 (0-8147-1434-X) NYU Pr.

Women in Engineering. Alice Posner. 1995. 13.95 (0-8442-6396-6, VGM Career Bks) NTC Pub Grp.

Women in Engineering: An Untapped Resource. 1992. 85.00 (0-89584-178-9) Catalyst.

Women in Engineering: Gender, Power, & Workplace Culture. Judith S. McIlwee & J. Gregg Robinson. LC 91-2050. (SUNY Series in Science, Technology, & Society). (Illus.). 248p. (C). 1992. text ed. 74.50 (0-7914-0869-8); pap. text ed. 24.95 (0-7914-0870-1) State U NY Pr.

Women in England, c. 1275-1525. Ed. & Tr. by P. J. Goldberg. LC 95-1714. (Manchester Medieval Sources Ser.). 204p. 1996. text ed. 75.00 (0-7190-4055-8, Pub. by Manchester Univ Pr UK); text ed. 24.95 (0-7190-4056-6, Pub. by Manchester Univ Pr UK) St Martin.

Women in England, 1500-1760: A Social History. Anne Laurence. LC 94-7197. 1994. text ed. 45.00 (0-312-12207-1) St Martin.

Women in England, 1870-1950: Sexual Divisons & Social Change. Jane Lewis. LC 84-48437. (Illus.). 288p. 1985. 27.50 (0-253-36608-9); pap. 11.95 (0-253-28926-2) Ind U Pr.

Women in English Religion, 1700-1925. Ed. by Dale A. Johnson. LC 83-12124. (Studies in Women & Religion: Vol. 10). 368p. 1984. lib. bdg. 99.95 (0-88946-539-8) E Mellen.

Women in English Social History, Vol. I. Barbara Kanner. LC 82-49189. 1008p. 1990. text ed. 125.00 (0-8240-9201-5, H408) Garland.

Women in English Social History, 1800-1914: Autobiographical Writings. Barbara Kanner. LC 82-49189. (Autobiographical Writings, Reference Library of Social Sciences: Vol. III). 224p. 1988. text ed. 45.00 (0-8240-9168-X) Garland.

Women in English Society. Mary Prior. 304p. (C). 1985. pap. text ed. 16.95 (0-415-07901-2) Routledge.

Women in English Society Fifteen Hundred to Eighteen Hundred. Mary Prior. 304p. 1985. pap. 13.95 (0-416-35710-5, 9177) Routledge Chapman & Hall.

Women in Espionage: A Biographical Dictionary. M. H. Mahoney. LC 93-36559. 253p. 1993. lib. bdg. 65.00 (0-87436-743-3) ABC-CLIO.

Women in Evangelization: Memories of the Past, Visions of the Future. John Zeleznik et al. 158p. (C). 1992. pap. text ed. 9.95 (0-9629051-1-9) Barry Univ.

Women in Exile. Mahnaz Afkhami. 208p. (C). 1994. pap. 12.95 (0-8139-1543-0); text ed. 35.00 (0-8139-1542-2) U Pr of Va.

Women in Exile: Wives of the Decembrists. Anatole G. Mazour. LC 74-22111. (Illus.). 134p. 1975. 15.00 (0-910512-19-1) Diplomatic IN.

Women in Families: A Framework for Family Therapy. Monica McGoldrick. 1991. pap. 19.95 (0-393-30776-X) Norton.

Women in Film Noir. rev. ed. Ed. by E. Ann Kaplan. LC 81-137135. (British Film Institute Bks.). (Illus.). 132p. 1990. pap. 10.95 (0-85170-105-1, Pub. by British Film Inst UK) Ind U Pr.

Women in Finance. Dian G. Smith. 1995. pap. 10.95 (0-8442-6399-0, VGM Career Bks) NTC Pub Grp.

***Women in Fishing Communities: Guidelines, a Special Target Group of Development Projects.** 71p. 1993. 12.00 (92-5-102835-4, Pub. by FAO IT) Bernan Associates.

Women in Foreign Policy: The Insiders. Nancy E. McGlen & Meredith R. Sarkees. LC 92-41704. 368p. (C). 1993. pap. 17.95 (0-415-90512-5, A6488, Routledge NY) Routledge.

Women in Frankish Society: Marriage & the Cloister, 500-900. Suzanne F. Wemple. LC 80-54051. (Middle Ages Ser.). (Illus.). 352p. (C). 1981. reprint ed. pap. text ed. 24.95 (0-8122-1209-6) U of Pa Pr.

Women in French Literature. Ed. by Michel Guggenheim. LC 88-70956. (Stanford French & Italian Studies: Vol. 58). 256p. 1989. pap. 46.50 (0-915838-74-5) Anma Libri.

Women in Futures Research. Ed. by Margrit Eichler & Hilda Scott. (Women's Studies Quarterly: Vol. 4, No. 1). (Illus.). 124p. 1982. 21.00 (0-08-028100-1, Pergamon Pr) Elsevier.

Women in Gainful Occupations, Eighteen Seventy to Nineteen Twenty. U. S. Bureau of the Census Staff. LC 78-12048. (Illus.). 416p. 1979. reprint ed. text ed. 75.00 (0-313-20679-1, DCWG, Greenwood Pr) Greenwood.

Women in Geology: Proceedings of the Northeastern Women's Geoscientists Conference, First. Northeastern Women's Geoscientists Conference Staff. Ed. by S. D. Halsey et al. LC 76-21580. (Illus.). 1976. pap. 2.00 (0-915492-02-4) Ash Lad Pr.

Women in German History: From Bourgeois Emancipation to Sexual Liberation. Ute Frevert. Tr. by Stuart McKinnon-Evans. LC 88-13123. 352p. 1990. pap. 16.95 (0-85496-685-4) Berg Pubs.

Women in German Yearbook, No. VI. Ed. by Jeanette Clausen & Helen Cafferty. 123p. (C). 1991. pap. text ed. 17.50 (0-8191-8127-7); lib. bdg. 36.00 (0-8191-8126-9) U Pr of Amer.

Women in German Yearbook, Vol. 7. Ed. by Jeanette Clausen & Sara Friedrichsmeyer. LC 91-24637. ix, 179p. 1992. text ed. 35.00 (0-8032-4760-5) U of Nebr Pr.

***Women in German Yearbook, Vol. 8.** Ed. by Jeanette Clausen & Sara Friedrichsmeyer. xii, 267p. 1993. pap. text ed. 18.00 (0-8032-9746-7) U of Nebr Pr.

W

Women in German Yearbook, Vol. 9. Ed. by Jeanette Clausen & Sara Friedrichsmeyer. xii, 267p. (C). 1993. pap. text ed. 18.00 (*0-8032-9754-8*) U of Nebr Pr.

Women in German Yearbook, Vol. 10. Ed. by Jeanette Clausen & Sara Friedrichsmeyer. xii, 282p. 1994. pap. text ed. 18.00 (*0-8032-9771-8*) U of Nebr Pr.

Women in German Yearbook, Vol. 11. Ed. by Sara Friedrichsmeyer & Patricia A. Herminghouse. xi, 232p. 1995. text ed. 40.00 (*0-8032-4781-8*) U of Nebr Pr.

Women in German Yearbook, Vol. 11. Ed. by Sara Friedrichsmeyer & Patricia A. Herminghouse. xi, 232p. (C). 1996. pap. text ed. 18.00 (*0-8032-9785-8*) U of Nebr Pr.

***Women in German Yearbook, Vol. 12.** Ed. by Sara Friedrichsmayer & Patricia A. Herminghouse. x, 244p. 1996. pap. text ed. 18.00 (*0-8032-9791-2*) U of Nebr Pr.

***Women in German Yearbook, Vol. 12.** Ed. by Sara Friedrichsmeyer & Patricia A. Herminghouse. (Illus.). x, 244p. (C). 1997. text ed. 40.00 (*0-8032-4783-4*) U of Nebr Pr.

Women in German Yearbook Vol. 10, Vol. 10. Ed. by Jeanette Clausen & Sara Friedrichsmayer. (Women in German Yearbook Ser.). xii, 282p. 1994. text ed. 40.00 (*0-8032-4776-1*) U of Nebr Pr.

Women in German Yearbook Four: Feminist Studies & German Culture. Ed. by Marianne Burkhard & Jeanette Clausen. (Illus.). 234p. (Orig.). (C). 1988. pap. text ed. 22.50 (*0-8191-6704-5*, Coalition of Women in German); lib. bdg. 45.00 (*0-8191-6703-7*, Coalition of Women in German) U Pr of Amer.

Women in German Yearbook, 5: Feminist Studies & German Culture. Ed. by Jeanette Clausen & Helen Cafferty. 150p. 1989. pap. 23.00 (*0-8191-7551-X*); lib. bdg. 46.00 (*0-8191-7550-1*) U Pr of Amer.

***Women in God's Presence: 260 Christian Women Share Lessons Learned in the Life of Faith.** Compiled by Delores Taylor. 1996. 9.99 (*0-87509-631-X*) Chr Pubns.

Women in God's Presence: 260 Christian Women Share Lessons Learned in the Life of Faith. 2nd ed. Compiled by Delores Taylor. LC 87-71311. 365p. 1988. pap. 9.99 (*0-87509-620-4*, 0016204) Chr Pubns.

Women in God's Service. Marlys Taege. 309p. 1991. 7.95 (*0-9614955-2-9*); pap. 5.95 (*0-9614955-7-X*) Lutheran Womens.

Women in Government. Suzanne E. Sheldon & Roger A. Sheldon. (Illus.). 160p. 1991. pap. 10.95 (*0-8442-6284-6*, VGM Career Bks) NTC Pub Grp.

Women in Grassroots Communication: Effecting Global Social Change. Ed. by Pilar Riano. (Communication & Human Values Ser.: Vol. 15). 332p. (C). 1994. text ed. 52.00 (*0-8039-4905-7*); pap. text ed. 24.95 (*0-8039-4906-5*) Sage.

Women in Greek Myth. Mary R. Lefkowitz. LC 86-7146. 160p. 1990. reprint ed. pap. text ed. 13.95 (*0-8018-4108-9*) Johns Hopkins.

Women in Greek Tragedy: An Anthropological Approach. Synnove Des Bouvrie. (Scandinavian University Press Publication: Vol. XXVII). 394p. 1990. 39.50 (*82-00-21125-8*) Scandnvan Univ Pr.

***Women in Hawaii: Sites, Identities, & Voices.** Ed. by Joyce N. Chinen. (Social Process in Hawaii Ser.: Vol. 38). 192p. 1997. pap. text ed. 18.00 (*0-7376-8713-4*) U of HI Sociology.

***Women in Health & Development.** (PAHO Scientific Publication Ser.: No. 448). 102p. 1983. pap. text ed. 14.00 (*92-75-11448-X*) World Health.

Women in Hellenistic Egypt: From Alexander to Cleopatra. Sarah B. Pomeroy. LC 89-24894. (Illus.). 270p. (C). 1990. reprint ed. pap. text ed. 18.95 (*0-8143-2230-1*) Wayne St U Pr.

***Women in Higher Education: A Select International Bibliography.** David H. Kelly. (Special Studies in Comparative Education: Vol. 25). 64p. (C). 1990. pap. 10.00 (*0-937033-15-4*) SUNY GSE Pubns.

Women in Higher Education: Changes & Challenges. Ed. by Lynne B. Welsh. LC 89-29669. 280p. 1990. text ed. 49.95 (*0-275-93208-7*, C3208, Greenwood Pr) Greenwood.

Women in Higher Education: Progress, Constraints, & Promising Initiatives. K. Subbarao et al. LC 94-16695. (World Bank Discussion Papers: Vol. 244). 1994. 7.95 (*0-8213-2859-X*, 12859) World Bank.

Women in Higher Education Administration. Ed. by Adrian Tinsley et al. LC 83-82747. (New Directions for Higher Ser.: No. HE 45). 1984. pap. 19.00 (*0-87589-995-1*) Jossey-Bass.

Women in Hindu Literature. R. P. Sharma. (C). 1995. 40.00 (*81-212-0501-8*, Pub. by Gian Publng Hse II) S Asia.

Women in His Life. Barbara Taylor Bradford. 1991. mass mkt. 6.99 (*0-345-34573-8*) Ballantine.

***Women in His Life.** Barbara Taylor Bradford. 1997. pap. 12.00 (*0-345-41860-3*) Ballantine.

Women in His Life. large type ed. Barbara Taylor Bradford. (General Ser.). 744p. 1991. 16.95 (*0-8161-5244-6*, GK Hall) Thorndike Pr.

Women in Hispanic Literature: Icons & Fallen Idols. Ed. by Beth Miller. LC 81-14663. 480p. 1983. 45.00 (*0-520-04291-3*); pap. 14.00 (*0-520-04367-7*) U CA Pr.

Women in History. Jerry Aten. 144p. (J). (gr. 4 up). 1986. student ed. 13.99 (*0-86653-344-3*, GA 692) Good Apple.

Women in History, Literature & the Arts: A Festschrift for Hilegard Schnuttgen in Honor of Her Thirty Years of Outstanding Service at Youngstown State University. Ed. by Thomas Copeland. 420p. (Orig.). (C). 1989. pap. 19.95 (*0-9623146-1-7*) Youngstown State Univ.

Women in Hong Kong. Ed. by Veronica Pearson & Benjamin K. Leung. (Illus.). 256p. 1995. 32.00 (*0-19-585954-5*) OUP.

***Women in Human Evolution.** Lori D. Hager. LC 96-29128. 248p. (C). 1997. pap. write for info. (*0-415-10834-9*); text ed. write for info. (*0-415-10833-0*) Routledge.

Women in Ichtyology: An Anthology in Honour of ET, Roland & Genie. Ed. by Eugene K. Balon et al. LC 94-31170. (Developments in Environmental Biology of Fishes Ser.: No. 15). 448p. 1995. lib. bdg. 317.00 (*0-7923-3165-6*) Kluwer Ac.

Women in India. Leelamma Devasia. (C). 1990. text ed. 11.00 (*0-685-50086-1*, Pub. by Manohar II) S Asia.

Women in India. Susan H. Gross & Marjorie W. Bingham. (Women in World Area Studies). (Illus.). 111p. 1980. pap. 15.00 (*0-86596-004-6*) UM Womens Hist.

Women in India. S. D. Maurya. (C). 1988. 31.00 (*81-85076-49-9*, Pub. by Chugh Pubns II) S Asia.

Women in India: A Brief Historical Survey. Tripta Desai. (C). 1992. 21.00 (*81-215-0532-1*, Pub. by Munshiram Manoharial II) S Asia.

Women in India: A Statistical Panorama. Prabhash P. Singh. (C). 1991. 64.00 (*81-210-0264-8*, Pub. by Inter-India Pubns) S Asia.

Women in India: Today & Tomorrow. Ed. by Mukta Mittal. (C). 1995. 40.00 (*81-7488-035-6*, Pub. by Anmol II) S Asia.

Women in India: Two Perspectives. Doranne Jacobson & Susan S. Wadley. (C). 1992. 14.00 (*0-945921-21-7*, Pub. by S Asia Pubs II) S Asia.

Women in India & Nepal. Allen & Mukherjee. 1990. 100.00 (*0-7855-0238-6*, Pub. by Ratna Pustak Bhandar) St Mut.

Women in India & Nepal. M. Allen. (C). 1991. text ed. 75.00 (*0-7855-0165-7*, Pub. by Ratna Pustak Bhandar) St Mut.

Women in India & Pakistan: The Struggle for Independence from British Rule. Rozina Visram. (Women in History Ser.). (Illus.). 48p. (C). 1993. pap. text ed. 14.95 (*0-521-38643-8*) Cambridge U Pr.

Women in India Past & Present. Rehka Pandey & Neelam U. Upadnyay. (C). 1991. pap. 11.00 (*0-685-49090-4*, Pub. by Chugh Pubns II) S Asia.

Women in India, Past & Present. Rekha Pendey. (C). 1990. 32.00 (*0-685-49091-2*, Pub. by Chugh Pubns II) S Asia.

Women in Indian Art. G. S. Bhadouria. (C). 1995. 72.00 (*81-7320-024-6*, Pub. by Agam Kala Prakashan) S Asia.

Women in Indian History: A Biographical Dictionary. T. P. Saxena. 114p. 1979. 14.95 (*0-318-37322-X*) Asia Bk Corp.

Women in Indian Industry. A. Ramanamma. 232p. 1987. 27.50 (*0-8364-2085-3*, Pub. by Mittal II) S Asia.

Women in Indian Society: A Reader. Ed. by Rehana Ghadially. 310p. (C). 1988. text ed. 30.00 (*0-8039-9564-4*); pap. text ed. 14.95 (*0-8039-9565-2*) Sage.

Women in India's Freedom Struggle. 2nd ed. Manmohan Kaur. 1992. 35.00 (*81-207-1399-0*, Pub. by Sterling Pubs II) Apt Bks.

Women in Industry. Edith Abbott. 408p. 1993. reprint ed. lib. bdg. 99.00 (*0-7812-5241-5*) Rprt Serv.

Women in Industry. Louis D. Brandeis & Josephine Goldmark. LC 73-89720. (American Labor, from Conspiracy to Collective Bargaining Ser., No. 1). 121p. 1974. reprint ed. 15.95 (*0-405-02106-2*) Ayer.

Women in Industry: A Study in American Economic History. Edith Abbott. LC 70-89714. (American Labor, from Conspiracy to Collective Bargaining Ser., No. 1). 408p. 1979. reprint ed. lib. bdg. 30.95 (*0-405-02101-1*) Ayer.

Women in Industry: Their Health & Efficiency. Anna M. Baetjer. Ed. by Leon Stein. LC 77-70480. (Work Ser.). (Illus.). 1977. reprint ed. lib. bdg. 35.95 (*0-405-10154-6*) Ayer.

Women in Ireland: An Annotated Bibliography. Compiled by Anna Brady. LC 87-25043. (Bibliographies & Indexes in Women's Studies: No. 6). 520p. (C). 1988. text ed. 75.00 (*0-313-24486-3*, BWR/, Greenwood Pr) Greenwood.

Women in Ireland: Voices of Change. Jenny Beale. LC 86-45747. 224p. 1987. 31.50 (*0-253-36461-2*) Ind U Pr.

Women in Ireland, 1800-1918: A Documentary History. Maria Luddy. 1995. 65.00 (*1-85918-037-X*, Pub. by Cork Univ IE); pap. 28.00 (*1-85918-038-8*, Pub. by Cork Univ IE) Intl Spec Bk.

Women in Irish Society: The Historical Dimension. Ed. by Margaret Mac Curtain & Donncha O'Corrain. LC 79-964. (Contributions in Women's Studies: No. 11). 125p. 1979. text ed. 38.50 (*0-313-21254-6*, MWI/, Greenwood Pr) Greenwood.

Women in Islam. Marjorie W. Bingham & Susan H. Gross. (Illus.). 130p. 1980. pap. 15.00 (*0-86596-000-3*) UM Womens Hist.

Women in Islam. Aisha Lemu & Fatima Heeren. 51p. (Orig.). 1978. pap. 3.50 (*0-86037-004-6*, Pub. by Islamic Fnd UK) New Era Publns MI.

***Women in Islam.** B. Aisha Lemu. 51p. 1996. pap. 3.95 (*0-614-21401-7*, 1327) Kazi Pubns.

Women in Islam. M. M. Siddiqui. 14.50 (*0-933511-95-7*) Kazi Pubns.

Women in Islam: From Medieval to Modern Times. Wibke Walther. Tr. by C. S. Salt from GER. (Illus.). 292p. 1993. 39.95 (*1-55876-052-0*); pap. 16.95 (*1-55876-053-9*) Wiener Pubs Inc.

Women in Islam: Role of Women in Modern Islam. Shari Baig. 320p. 1992. pap. 9.95 (*1-881893-01-4*) Universal Unity.

Women in Islamic Biographical Collections: From Ibn Sad to Who's Who. Ruth Roded. LC 93-28276. 158p. 1993. lib. bdg. 37.00 (*1-55587-442-8*) Lynne Rienner.

***Women in Islamic Biographical Collections from Ibn Sa'd to Who's Who.** Ruth Roded. 175p. 1996. 34.00 (*0-614-21402-5*, 1328) Kazi Pubns.

Women in Israel. Ed. by Yael Azmon & Dafna N. Israeli. (Studies of Israeli Society: Vol. VI). 480p. (C). 1993. text ed. 49.95 (*1-56000-024-4*) Transaction Pubs.

Women in Israel. Susan H. Gross & Marjorie W. Bingham. (Women in World Area Studies). (Illus.). 88p. 1980. pap. 15.00 (*0-86596-001-1*) UM Womens Hist.

Women in Japan: from Ancient Times to the Present. Marjorie W. Bingham & Susan H. Gross. Ed. by Janet M. Donaldson. (Women in World Area Studies). (Illus.). 317p. (Orig.). 1987. pap. 18.00 (*0-914227-08-4*) UM Womens Hist.

Women in Japanese Society: An Annotated Bibliography of Selected English Language Materials. Kristina R. Huber. LC 92-15371. (Bibliographies & Indexes in Women's Studies: No. 16). 544p. 1992. text ed. 69.50 (*0-313-25296-3*, HWJ, Greenwood Pr) Greenwood.

Women in Jazz: A Discography of Instrumental Music, Nineteen Thirteen to Nineteen Sixty-eight. Jan Leder. LC 85-17657. (Discographies Ser.: No. 19). xv, 311p. 1985. text ed. 45.00 (*0-313-24790-0*, LMI/, Greenwood Pr) Greenwood.

Women in Joe Sullivan's Life. Marie Ferrarella. (Romance Ser.). 1995. mass mkt. 2.99 (*0-373-19096-4*, 1-19096-6) Silhouette.

Women in Judaic & Islamic Societies. Ed. by Seth Ward. (Illus.). 350p. 1997. 40.00 (*0-8419-1378-1*) Holmes & Meier.

Women in Khaki: The American Enlisted Woman. Michael Rustad. LC 82-9025. 304p. 1982. text ed. 35.00 (*0-275-90892-5*, C0892, Praeger Pubs) Greenwood.

Women in Kuwait: The Politics of Gender. Haya Al-Mughni. 180p. 1993. 50.00 (*0-86356-199-3*, Pub. by Saqi Bks UK) Interlink Pub.

Women in Late Antiquity: Pagan & Christian Lifestyles. Gillian Clark. (Illus.). 188p. 1994. reprint ed. pap. 16.95 (*0-19-872166-8*) OUP.

Women in Latin America: From Pre-Columbian Times to the 20th Century, Vol. I. Marjorie W. Bingham & Susan H. Gross. Ed. by Janet M. Donaldson. LC 84-73429. (Women in World Area Studies). (Illus.). 210p. (Orig.). 1985. pap. 15.00 (*0-914227-04-1*) UM Womens Hist.

Women in Latin America: The 20th Century, Vol. II. Susan H. Gross & Marjorie W. Bingham. Ed. by Janet M. Donaldson. LC 84-73429. (Women in World Area Studies). (Illus.). 176p. (Orig.). 1985. pap. 15.00 (*0-914227-07-6*) UM Womens Hist.

Women in Latin American History. Ed. by June E. Hahner. LC 80-620044. 1994. pap. 9.95 (*0-87903-051-8*) UCLA Lat Am Ctr.

Women in Law. 2nd ed. Cynthia F. Epstein. LC 92-20172. 520p. (C). 1993. pap. text ed. 17.95 (*0-252-06205-1*) U of Ill Pr.

Women in Law: A Bio-Bibliographical Sourcebook. Ed. by Rebecca M. Salokar & Mary L. Volcansek. LC 96-10747. 376p. 1996. text ed. 85.00 (*0-313-29410-0*, Greenwood Pr) Greenwood.

Women in Law Enforcement. 2nd ed. Peter Horne. (Illus.). 288p. 1980. 46.95 (*0-398-04029-X*) C C Thomas.

Women in Librarianship: Melvil's Rib Symposium. Ed. by Margaret Myers & Mayra Scarborough. (Issues in Library & Information Sciences Ser.: No. 2). 1975. pap. text ed. 15.00 (*0-8135-0807-X*) Rutgers U SICLS.

Women in Literature: Criticism of the Seventies. Carol F. Myers. LC 75-35757. 263p. 1976. 19.50 (*0-8108-0885-4*) Scarecrow.

Women in Literature: Life Stages Through Stories, Poems, Plays. S. Eagleton. 7p. 1988. pap. text ed. 42.67 (*0-13-962283-7*) P-H.

Women in Local Politics. Ed. by Debra W. Stewart. LC 80-14526. vi, 232p. 1980. 25.00 (*0-8108-1312-2*) Scarecrow.

Women in Love. Graham Holderness. LC 86-768. 160p. 1986. 75.00 (*0-335-15254-6*, Open Univ Pr); pap. 22.00 (*0-335-15253-8*, Open Univ Pr) Taylor & Francis.

Women in Love. D. H. Lawrence. 1992. 20.00 (*0-679-41326-X*, Everymans Lib); 20.00 (*0-679-40995-5*) Knopf.

Women in Love. D. H. Lawrence. 480p. 1995. 4.95 (*0-451-52591-4*, Sig) NAL-Dutton.

Women in Love. D. H. Lawrence. 1976. mass mkt. 7.95 (*0-14-004260-1*, Penguin Bks) Viking Penguin.

Women in Love. D. H. Lawrence. Ed. by Charles L. Ross. (English Library). 512p. 1982. mass mkt. 4.95 (*0-14-043156-X*, Penguin Classics) Viking Penguin.

Women in Love. D. H. Lawrence. 608p. 1990. pap. 8.95 (*0-14-018221-7*, Penguin Bks) Viking Penguin.

Women in Love. D. H. Lawrence. Ed. by David Farmer et al. 592p. 1995. pap. 9.95 (*0-14-018816-9*, Penguin Classics) Viking Penguin.

Women in Love. large type ed. D. H. Lawrence. 769p. 1982. 27.99 (*0-7089-8049-X*) Ulverscroft.

Women in Love. D. H. Lawrence. 421p. 1984. reprint ed. lib. bdg. 27.95 (*0-89966-496-2*) Buccaneer Bks.

Women in Love. D. H. Lawrence. 336p. 1996. reprint ed. mass mkt. 4.95 (*0-553-21454-3*, Bantam Classics) Bantam.

Women in Management. Ed. by Nancy J. Adler & Dafna N. Izraeli. LC 88-4520. 304p. (C). (gr. 13). 1989. pap. text ed. 26.95 (*0-87332-570-2*) M E Sharpe.

Women in Management. Douglas C. Basil et al. 140p. 1972. 14.50 (*0-8290-1568-X*) Irvington.

Women in Management. Carol S. Greenwald. (Studies in Productivity: Highlights of the Literature Ser.: Vol. 12). 49p. (Orig.). 1980. pap. 55.00 (*0-89361-019-4*) Work in Amer.

Women in Management. Harvey Lieberman. (Simulation Game Ser.). 1975. pap. 26.25 (*0-89401-095-6*) Didactic Syst.

Women in Management. Irene M. Place. (Illus.). 160p. 1986. pap. 10.95 (*0-8442-6650-7*, VGM Career Bks) NTC Pub Grp.

Women in Management, Vol. 12. Carol Greenwald. LC 80-20757. (Work in America Institute Studies in Productivity). (Orig.). 1982. pap. 35.00 (*0-685-05452-7*, Pergamon Pr) Elsevier.

Women in Management: Current Research Issues. Ed. by Marilyn J. Davidson & Ronald J. Burke. 352p. 1994. 75.00 (*1-85396-235-X*, Pub. by Paul Chapman UK) Taylor & Francis.

Women in Management: Current Research Issues. Ed. by Marilyn J. Davidson & Ronald J. Burke. 352p. 1994. pap. 39.95 (*1-85396-289-9*, Pub. by Paul Chapman UK) Taylor & Francis.

Women in Management: Environment & Role. Milton L. Shuch. (ITT Key Issues Lecture Ser.). 93p. 1981. pap. text ed. write for info. (*0-672-97919-5*) Macmillan.

Women in Management: Trends, Issues, & Challenges in Managerial Diversity. Ellen A. Fagenson. (Women & Work Ser.: Vol. 4). (Illus.). 328p. (C). 1993. text ed. 55.00 (*0-8039-4591-4*); pap. text ed. 24.95 (*0-8039-4592-2*) Sage.

Women in Mass Communication. 2nd ed. Ed. by Pamela J. Creedon. LC 93-20782. 1993. 58.00 (*0-8039-5386-0*); pap. 26.50 (*0-8039-5387-9*) Sage.

Women in Mathematics. Lynn M. Osen. 224p. 1975. pap. 13.95 (*0-262-65009-6*) MIT Pr.

***Women in Mathematics: The Addition of Difference.** Claudia Henrion. LC 97-2546. 1997. 39.95 (*0-253-33279-6*); pap. 16.95 (*0-253-21119-0*) Ind U Pr.

Women in Medical Education: An Anthology of Experience. Ed. by Delese Wear. LC 95-49902. 183p. (C). 1996. text ed. 62.50 (*0-7914-3087-1*); pap. text ed. 20.95 (*0-7914-3088-X*) State U NY Pr.

Women in Medicine. Hedda Garza. (Women Then - Women Now Ser.). (Illus.). 112p. (YA). (gr. 9-12). 1994. lib. bdg. 22.70 (*0-531-11204-7*) Watts.

Women in Medicine. Hedda Garza. (Women Then - Women Now Ser.). (Illus.). 176p. (YA). (gr. 9-12). 1996. pap. 9.00 (*0-531-15805-5*) Watts.

***Women in Medicine.** Jacqueline C. Kent. (Profiles Ser.). (Illus.). 160p. (YA). (gr. 5-12). 1997. lib. bdg. 16.95 (*1-881508-46-3*) Oliver Pr MN.

Women in Medicine. Carol Lopate. LC 68-19526. (Josiah Macy Foundation Ser.). (Illus.). 204p. 1968. 32.50 (*0-8018-0391-8*) Johns Hopkins.

Women in Medicine & Management: A Mentoring Guide. Ed. by Deborah M. Shlian. LC 95-77323. 119p. (C). 1995. pap. text ed. 38.00 (*0-924674-35-0*) Am Coll Phys Execs.

Women in Medieval - Renaissance Europe. Susan H. Gross & Marjorie W. Bingham. LC 83-20787. (Women in World Area Studies). 180p. (Orig.). 1984. pap. 18.00 (*0-914227-02-5*) UM Womens Hist.

Women in Medieval England. Helen M. Jewell. LC 95-33401. 208p. (C). 1996. text ed. 59.95 (*0-7190-4016-7*, Pub. by Manchester Univ Pr UK); text ed. 19.95 (*0-7190-4017-5*, Pub. by Manchester Univ Pr UK) St Martin.

***Women in Medieval English Society.** Ed. by P. J. Goldberg. (History Paperbacks Ser.). 256p. (Orig.). 1997. pap. 26.95 (*0-7509-1477-7*, Pub. by Sutton Pubng UK) Bks Intl VA.

Women in Medieval History & Historiography. Ed. by Susan M. Stuard. LC 89-5287. (Middle Ages Ser.). 222p. 1987. pap. 20.95 (*0-8122-1290-8*) U of Pa Pr.

Women in Medieval Society. Ed. by Susan M. Stuard. LC 75-41617. (Middle Ages Ser.). 220p. 1976. pap. text ed. 16.95 (*0-8122-1088-3*) U of Pa Pr.

Women in Meghalaya. Soumen Sen. (C). 1992. 14.00 (*81-7035-108-1*, Pub. by Daya Pub Hse II) S Asia.

Women in Mid-Life: Planning for Tomorrow. Intro. by Christopher L. Hayes. LC 92-23299. (Journal of Women & Aging Ser.: Vol. 4, No. 4). (Illus.). 138p. 1993. 29.95 (*1-56024-392-9*); pap. 14.95 (*1-56023-035-5*) Harrington Pk.

Women in Middle Eastern History: Shifting Boundaries in Sex & Gender. Nikki R. Keddie & Beth Baron. 352p. (C). 1992. text ed. 40.00 (*0-300-05005-4*) Yale U Pr.

Women in Middle Eastern History: Shifting Boundaries in Sex & Gender. Nikki R. Keddie & Beth Baron. 352p. (C). 1993. pap. 18.00 (*0-300-05697-4*) Yale U Pr.

Women in Ministry. Anne A. Jackson & Cleola I. Spears. (Illus.). 350p. (Orig.). pap. write for info. (*0-9605892-3-6*) Dawn Ministries.

Women in Ministry: An Historical & Biblical Look at the Role of Women in Christian Leadership. L. E. Maxwell. 1995. pap. 8.99 (*0-87509-587-9*) Chr Pubns.

Women in Ministry: Four Views. Ed. by Bonnidell Clouse & Robert G. Clouse. LC 89-1773. 252p. (Orig.). 1989. pap. 12.99 (*0-8308-1284-9*, 1284) InterVarsity.

Women in Ministry: Receptivity & Resistance. Edward C. Lehman, Jr. 1995. pap. 11.50 (*0-85819-874-6*, Pub. by JBCE AT) Morehouse Pub.

Women in Modern America: A Brief History. 2nd ed. Lois W. Banner. 294p. (Orig.). (C). 1984. pap. text ed. 20.00 (*0-15-596196-9*) HB Coll Pubs.

***Women in Modern American Politics: A Bibliography, 1900-1995.** Elizabeth M. Cox. LC 96-38898. 414p. 1996. 129.00 (*1-56802-133-X*) Congr Quarterly.

Women in Modern China. Marjorie W. Bingham & Susan H. Gross. (Women in World Area Studies). (Illus.). 107p. 1980. pap. 15.00 (*0-86596-003-8*) UM Womens Hist.

Women in Modern Drama: Freud, Feminism, & European Theater at the Turn of the Century. Gail Finney. LC 88-47924. 248p. 1989. 39.95 (*0-8014-2284-1*) Cornell U Pr.

Women in Modern Drama: Freud, Feminism, & European Theater at the Turn of the Century. Gail Finney. LC 88-47924. 248p. 1991. reprint ed. pap. 14.95 (*0-8014-9925-9*) Cornell U Pr.

An Asterisk (*) at the beginning of an entry indicates that the title is appearing in BIP for the first time.

Women in Modern India. Neera Desai. 334p. 1977. 12.95 (0-318-37323-8) Asia Bk Corp.

Women in Modern India. Geraldine Forbes. (New Cambridge History of India Ser.: No. IV:2). (Illus.). 312p. (C). 1996. text ed. 49.95 (0-521-26812-5) Cambridge U Pr.

Women in Modern Turkish Society. Ed. by Sirin Tekeli. 288p. (C). 1994. pap. 25.00 (1-85649-152-8, Pub. by Zed Bks Ltd UK); text ed. 60.00 (1-85649-151-X, Pub. by Zed Bks Ltd UK) Humanities.

Women in Motion. Alexa L. Foreman. LC 83-72435. 248p. 1983. 20.95 (0-87972-266-5) Bowling Green Univ Popular Press.

Women in Mourning: Stories of Grieving Women. Jean Clayton. LC 96-8230. 1996. 5.95 (1-56123-094-4) Centering Corp.

Women in Movement: Feminism & Social Action. Sheila Rowbotham. LC 92-12239. (Revolutionary Thought - Radical Movements Ser.). 320p. (C). 1992. pap. 17.95 (0-415-90652-0, A7619, Routledge NY) Routledge.

Women in Music: An Anthology of Source Readings from the Middle Ages to the Present. 2nd ed. Ed. by Carol Neuls-Bates. LC 95-17460. 1995. text ed. 42.50 (1-55553-239-X); pap. text ed. 15.95 (1-55553-240-3) NE U Pr.

Women in Music: An Encyclopedia Biobibliography, 2 vols., Set. 2nd ed. Don L. Hixon & Don A. Hennessee. LC 93-34731. 1852p. 1993. 160.00 (0-8108-2769-7) Scarecrow.

Women in Muslim Family Law. John L. Esposito. LC 81-18273. (Contemporary Issues in the Middle East Ser.). 172p. 1982. pap. text ed. 14.95 (0-8156-2278-3) Syracuse U Pr.

Women in Muslim Rural Society. Joseph Ginat. LC 79-66432. 259p. (C). 1981. 39.95 (0-87855-342-8) Transaction Pubs.

Women in Myth. Bettina L. Knapp. LC 96-31315. 270p. 1996. pap. 19.95 (0-7914-3164-9); text ed. 59.50 (0-7914-3163-0) State U NY Pr.

Women in Native American Society see Junior Library of American Indians

Women in Nazi Germany. Katherine T. Thomas. LC 78-63726. (Studies in Fascism: Ideology & Practice). 104p. reprint ed. 32.50 (0-404-16998-8) AMS Pr.

***Women in New Religions.** Puttick. LC 96-46619. Date not set. text ed. 49.95 (0-312-17259-1); text ed. 18.95 (0-312-17260-5) St Martin.

Women in Nigeria: An Annotated Bibliography. Compiled by Uche Azikiwe. LC 95-47167. (African Special Bibliogrpahic Ser.: No. 20). 160p. 1996. text ed. 59.95 (0-313-29960-9, Greenwood Pr) Greenwood.

Women in Nineteenth Century Egypt. Judith E. Tucker. (Cambridge Middle East Library: No. 7). 264p. 1985. 59.95 (0-521-30338-9) Cambridge U Pr.

Women in Nontraditional Careers. 1996. lib. bdg. 625.95 (0-8490-6910-6) Gordon Pr.

Women in Nontraditional Occupations: References & Resources. Carroll W. Wilkinson. (Women's Studies). 137p. (C). 1991. 35.00 (0-8161-8934-X, Hall Reference) Macmillan.

Women in Nordic Politics: Closing the Gap. Ed. by Lauri Karvonen & Per Selle. LC 95-101. 1995. 62.95 (1-85521-533-0, Pub. by Dartmth Pub UK) Ashgate Pub Co.

Women in Office: Getting There & Staying There. Joanne Rajoppi. LC 93-18135. 200p. 1993. text ed. 49.95 (0-89789-343-3, H343, Bergin & Garvey) Greenwood.

Women in Old Norse Society. Jenny Jochens. 328p. 1996. 39.95 (0-8014-3165-4) Cornell U Pr.

Women in Pain: Gender & Morbidity in Mexico. Kaja Finkler. LC 93-32972. 224p. (Orig.). (C). 1994. text ed. 34.95 (0-8122-3243-7); pap. text ed. 15.95 (0-8122-1527-3) U of Pa Pr.

Women in Panchayti Raj Structures. P. Manikyamba. 180p. 1989. 22.50 (81-212-0286-8, Pub. by Gian Publng Hse II) S Asia.

Women in Perspective: A Guide for Cross-Cultural Studies. Sue-Ellen Jacobs. LC 72-93987. 312p. 1974. pap. text ed. 12.95 (0-252-00345-4) U of Ill Pr.

Women in Policing: A Resource Guide. Jocelyn Riley. 114p. 1995. 20.00 (1-877933-53-8) Her Own Words.

Women in Polish Society, No. 344. Ed. by Rudolf Jaworski. 200p. 1992. 42.00 (0-88033-241-7) Col U Pr.

Women in Political Theory: From Misogyny to Contemporary Feminism. 2nd ed. Diana H. Coole. LC 93-11082. 312p. (C). 1993. pap. text ed. 19.95 (1-55587-457-6) Lynne Rienner.

Women in Politics. Sumana Pandey. 1990. 26.50 (81-7033-088-2, Pub. by Rawat II) S Asia.

Women in Politics. Ed. by Jane S. Jaquette. LC 74-1037. 406p. reprint ed. pap. 115.80 (0-317-07771-6, 2021502) Bks Demand.

Women in Politics: A Global Review. Kathleen Newland. 1975. pap. write for info. (0-916468-02-X) Worldwatch Inst.

Women in Politics - Outsiders or Insiders? A Collection of Readings. 2nd ed. Ed. by Lois L. Duke. LC 95-34262. 372p. 1995. pap. text ed. 30.60 (0-13-185240-X) P-H.

Women in Politics & Decision-Making in the Late Twentieth Century. 128p. 1991. 30.00 (92-1-130144-0, E.91.IV.3) UN.

Women in Politics in Canada: An Introductory Text. Heather MacIvor. 360p. (Orig.). (C). 1996. pap. text ed. 19.95 (1-55111-036-9) Broadview Pr.

Women in Popular Culture: A Reference Guide. Katherine Fishburn. LC 81-13421. (American Popular Culture Ser.). ix, 267p. 1982. text ed. 47.95 (0-313-22152-9, FWC/, Greenwood Pr) Greenwood.

Women in Power: The Secrets of Leadership. Dorothy W. Cantor. 1992. pap. 12.95 (0-395-61860-6) HM.

Women in Power in the Early Modern Drama. Theodora A. Jankowski. 256p. 1992. text ed. 34.95 (0-252-01882-6); pap. text ed. 14.95 (0-252-06238-8) U of Ill Pr.

Women in Praise of the Sacred: 43 Centuries of Spiritual Poetry by Women. Ed. by Jane Hirshfield. 288p. 1995. pap. 12.00 (0-06-092576-0, PL) HarpC.

Women in Prehistory. Margaret Ehrenberg. LC 89-40214. (Oklahoma Series in Classical Culture: Vol. 4). (Illus.). 208p. 1990. pap. 18.95 (0-8061-2237-4) U of Okla Pr.

Women in Prehistory: North America & Mesoamerica. Ed. by Cheryl Claassen & Rosemary Joyce. LC 96-3455. (Illus.). 288p. 1996. pap. text ed. 18.50 (0-8122-1602-4) U of Pa Pr.

Women in Prehistory: North America & Mesoamerica. Ed. by Cheryl Craassen & Rosemary Joyce. LC 96-3455. (Illus.). 288p. 1996. text ed. 39.95 (0-8122-3381-6) U of Pa Pr.

Women in Printing: Northern California, 1857-1890. Roger Levenson. (Illus.). 256p. 1995. pap. 12.95 (0-88496-366-7) Capra Pr.

Women in Prison. Edna W. Chandler. LC 72-88765. 7.95 (0-672-51702-7, Bobbs) Macmillan.

Women in Prison: Inside the Concrete Womb. rev. ed. Kathryn Watterson. 1995. pap. text ed. 16.95 (1-55553-238-1) NE U Pr.

Women in Prison: Inside the Concrete Womb. rev. ed. Kathryn Watterson. 1996. text ed. 45.00 (1-55553-237-3) NE U Pr.

Women in Psychology: A Bio-Bibliographic Sourcebook. Ed. by Agnes N. O'Connell & Nancy F. Russo. LC 89-25787. 456p. 1990. text ed. 69.50 (0-313-26091-5, OWP/, Greenwood Pr) Greenwood.

Women in Public: Between Banners & Ballots, 1825-1880. Mary P. Ryan. LC 89-32863. (Symposia in Comparative History Ser.). (Illus.). 208p. 1990. text ed. 35.00 (0-8018-3908-4) Johns Hopkins.

Women in Public: Between Banners & Ballots, 1825-1880. Mary P. Ryan. (Symposia in Comparative History Ser.). 216p. 1992. reprint ed. pap. text ed. 13.95 (0-8018-4401-0) Johns Hopkins.

Women in Public Life. Ed. by Beryl A. Radin & Hoyt H. Purvis. (Symposia Ser.). 56p. 1976. pap. 3.50 (0-89940-404-9) LBJ Sch Pub Aff.

***Women in Racing.** Michael Benson. LC 97-14226. (Race Car Legends Ser.). (Illus.). 64p. (J). (gr. 3 up). 1997. 15.95 (0-7910-4432-7) Chelsea Hse.

Women in Real Estate: Answers to Career Questions You Should Be Asking. David Wilcox. 1989. ring bd. 17.95 (0-9622547-0-3) Real World IN.

Women in Reformation & Counter-Reformation Europe: Private & Public Worlds. Ed. by Sherrin D. Marshall. LC 88-45758. (Illus.). 224p. 1989. 35.00 (0-253-33678-3); pap. 11.95 (0-253-20527-1, MB-527) Ind U Pr.

Women in Religion. Ed. by Jean Holm & John W. Bowker. LC 94-13748. (Themes in Religious Studies). 1994. 45.00 (1-85567-108-5); pap. 16.95 (1-85567-109-3) St Martin.

Women in Renaissance: An Interdisciplinary Forum, MLA 1989. Ed. by A. R. Jones. 128p. 1991. pap. text ed. 24.00 (2-88124-520-X) Gordon & Breach.

Women in Retrospect: A Research Guide to Studies in English & Romance Languages. Hilda U. Stubbings. LC 93-85424. xxiv, 390p. (C). 1994. Alk. paper. 55.00 (1-880622-04-1) Rubena Pr.

Women in Revolutionary Paris, 1789-1795. Ed. by Darline G. Levy et al. 326p. 1980. pap. text ed. 15.95 (0-252-00855-3) U of Ill Pr.

Women in Revolutionary Russia. Cathy Porter. (Women in History Ser.). (Illus.). 48p. (YA). (gr. 7-12). 1987. pap. text ed. 11.95 (0-521-31969-2) Cambridge U Pr.

Women in Rigveda. 3rd ed. B. S. Upadhyaya. 243p. 1974. 14.95 (0-318-37324-6) Asia Bk Corp.

Women in Robbe-Grillet: A Study in Thematics & Diegetics. Lillian D. Roland. LC 91-43247. (American University Studies: Romance Languages & Literature: Ser. II, Vol. 177). 302p. (C). 1993. text ed. 59.95 (0-8204-1643-6) P Lang Pubng.

Women in Roman Law & Society. Jane F. Gardner. LC 86-45173. 288p. (Orig.). 1986. 35.00 (0-253-36609-7) Ind U Pr.

Women in Roman Law & Society. Jane F. Gardner. LC 86-45173. 288p. (Orig.). 1991. pap. 15.95 (0-253-20635-9, MB-635) Ind U Pr.

Women in Romanticism: Mary Wollstonecraft, Dorothy Wordsworth, & Mary Shelley. Meena Alexander. 180p. (C). 1989. pap. 19.00 (0-389-20885-X); text ed. 52.50 (0-389-20884-1) B&N Imports.

Women in Rural Areas. Kondaveeti Papa. (C). 1992. 16.00 (81-85613-60-5, Pub. by Chugh Pubns II) S Asia.

Women in Rural Australia. Ed. by Kerry James. 136p. (Orig.). 1989. pap. text ed. 29.95 (0-7022-2068-X, Pub. by Univ Queensland Pr AT) Intl Spec Bk.

Women in Rural Development. Satnam Kaur. (C). 1987. 28.00 (81-7099-007-6, Pub. by Mittal II) S Asia.

Women in Rural Development: Critical Issues (WEP Study) iii, 51p. 1990. reprint ed. pap. 11.25 (92-2-102388-5) Intl Labour Office.

***Women in Rural Society: A Quest for Development.** Navaneeta Rath. 183p. 1995. pap. 150.00 (81-85880-89-1, Pub. by Print Hse II) St Mut.

Women in Russia. Ed. by Dorothy Atkinson et al. LC 75-39333. xiv, 410p. 1977. reprint ed. 55.00 (0-8047-0910-6); reprint ed. pap. 16.95 (0-8047-0920-3) Stanford U Pr.

Women in Russia: A New Era in Russian Feminism. Ed. by Anastasia Posadskaya. Tr. by Kate Clarke from RUS. LC 94-17273. 203p. (C). 1994. pap. text ed. 20.00 (0-86091-657-X, B3661, Pub. by Vrso UK) Norton.

Women in Russia: A New Era in Russian Feminism. Ed. by Anastasia Posadskaya. Tr. by Kate Clarke from RUS. LC 94-17273. 256p. (C). (gr. 13). 1994. text ed. 65.00 (0-86091-487-9, B3657, Pub. by Vrso UK) Norton.

Women in Russia & the Soviet Union. Ed. by Rochelle G. Ruthchild. 1992. lib. bdg. 40.00 (0-685-59685-0, Hall Reference) Macmillan.

Women in Russia & the Soviet Union: An Annotated Bibliography. Ed. by Rochelle G. Ruthchild. (Reference Ser.). 203p. 1994. 45.00 (0-8161-8989-7) G K Hall.

Women in Russia & Ukraine. Ed. by Rosalind J. Marsh. (Illus.). 472p. (C). 1996. text ed. 69.95 (0-521-49522-9); pap. text ed. 24.95 (0-521-49872-4) Cambridge U Pr.

Women in Russian History: From the Tenth to the Twentieth Century. Natalia Pushkareva. Ed. & Tr. by Eve Levin. LC 96-30667. (The New Russian History Ser.). 300 (est.)p. (ENG & RUS.). (C). (gr. 13). 1997. text ed. 62.95 (1-56324-797-6); pap. text ed. 24.95 (1-56324-798-4) M E Sharpe.

Women in Russian Literature, Seventeen Eighty to Eighteen Sixty-Three. Joe Andrew. LC 87-28502. 240p. 1988. text ed. 45.00 (0-312-01626-3) St Martin.

Women in Russian Theatre: The Actress in the Silver Age. Catherine Schuler. LC 96-3695. (Gender in Performance Ser.). 272p. (C). 1996. pap. 19.95 (0-415-14397-7); text ed. 69.95 (0-415-11105-6) Routledge.

Women in Samuel Beckett's Prose & Drama: Her Own Other. Mary Bryden. LC 92-39389. 256p. (C). 1993. lib. bdg. 54.50 (0-389-21005-6) B&N Imports.

Women in School Leadership: Survival & Advancement Guidebook. Aretha B. Pigford & Sandra Tonnsen. LC 93-60093. 103p. 1993. pap. text ed. 24.95 (1-56676-017-8) Technomic.

Women in Science. Alice Fins. (Illus.). 154p. 1995. pap. 10.95 (0-8442-6648-5, VGM Career Bks) NTC Pub Grp.

Women in Science: A Report from the Field. Ed. by Jane B. Kahle. LC 84-18715. 200p. 1985. pap. 31.00 (1-85000-020-4, Falmer Pr) Taylor & Francis.

Women in Science: The Snark Syndrome. Eileen M. Byrne. 208p. 1993. 85.00 (1-85000-654-7, Falmer Pr); pap. 27.00 (1-85000-655-5, Falmer Pr) Taylor & Francis.

Women in Science: Token Women or Gender Equality? Ed. by Veronica Stolte-Heiskanen et al. LC 90-28894. 269p. 1991. 38.95 (0-85496-742-7) Berg Pubs.

Women in Science - Antiquity Through the Nineteenth Century: A Biographical Dictionary with Annotated Bibliography. Marilyn B. Ogilive. (Illus.). 272p. 1990. reprint ed. pap. 14.95 (0-262-65038-X) MIT Pr.

Women in Science & Engineering: Increasing Their Numbers in the 1990s; a Statement on Policy & Strategy. fac. ed. National Research Council U. S. Staff. LC 91-66811. (Illus.). 164p. 1991. pap. 46.80 (0-7837-7563-6, 2047316) Bks Demand.

Women in Scientific & Engineering Professions. Ed. by Violet B. Haas & Carolyn C. Perrucci. (Women & Culture Ser.). (Illus.). 272p. (C). 1984. pap. text ed. 16.95 (0-472-08042-3) U of Mich Pr.

***Women in Search of Freedoom: A Biblical Look at Feminism.** Lori Lindsey. 21p. pap. 1.75 (0-614-25151-6) Probe Bks.

Women in Search of the Sacred. Anne Bancroft. 1997. pap. 11.95 (0-14-019494-0, Penguin Bks) Viking Penguin.

Women in Shaker Community & Worship: A Feminist Analysis of Religious Symbolism. Marjorie Procter-Smith. LC 85-13776. (Studies in Women & Religion: Vol. 16). 253p. 1985. lib. bdg. 89.95 (0-88946-533-9) E Mellen.

Women in Social Protest: The U. S. Since 1915. Jocelyn H. Cohen et al. (Photographic Postcard Ser.). (Illus.). 22p. (C). 1989. pap. text ed. 8.95 (0-9623911-0-7, WSP-07) Helaine Victoria.

Women in Social Protest: The U. S. since 1915: A Photographic Postcard Series. Ed. by Jocelyn H. Cohen et al. (Illus.). 22p. (Orig.). (C). 1989. pap. text ed. write for info. (0-318-65535-7) Helaine Victoria.

***Women in Society - Group 1, 5 bks.** Incl. Australia. Gisela Kaplan. LC 92-12371. (Illus.). 128p. (YA). (gr. 7 up). 1992. lib. bdg. 19.95 (1-85435-502-3, Benchmark NY); Egypt. Angele B. Samaan. LC 92-12373. (Illus.). 128p. (YA). (gr. 7 up). 1992. lib. bdg. 19.95 (1-85435-505-8, Benchmark NY); Israel. Beth Uval. LC 92-12372. (Illus.). 128p. (YA). (gr. 7 up). 1992. lib. bdg. 19.95 (1-85435-503-1, Benchmark NY); Japan. Elizabeth Kanematsu. LC 92-12376. (Illus.). 128p. (YA). (gr. 7 up). 1992. lib. bdg. 19.95 (1-85435-501-5, Benchmark NY); South Africa. Dee Rissik. LC 92-12374. (Illus.). 128p. (YA). (gr. 7 up). 1992. lib. bdg. 19.95 (1-85435-504-X, Benchmark NY); 1992. Set lib. bdg. 94.76 (1-85435-553-8, Benchmark NY) Marshall Cavendish.

***Women in Society - Group 2, 5 bks.** Incl. Brazil. Jane K. Winter. LC 92-34403. (Illus.). 128p. (YA). (gr. 7 up). 1993. lib. bdg. 19.95 (1-85435-558-9, Benchmark NY); China. Pamela Tan. LC 92-33354. (Illus.). 128p. (YA). (gr. 7 up). 1993. lib. bdg. 19.95 (1-85435-556-2, Benchmark NY); Germany. Agnes Bohnen. LC 92-12375. (Illus.). 128p. (YA). (gr. 7 up). 1992. lib. bdg. 19.95 (1-85435-506-6, Benchmark NY); Great Britan. Patricia M. Levy. LC 92-33353. (Illus.). 128p. (YA). (gr. 7 up). 1993. lib. bdg. 19.95 (1-85435-555-4, Benchmark NY); Mexico. Jill Dubois. LC 92-34402. (Illus.). 128p. (YA). (gr. 7 up). 1993. lib. bdg. 19.95 (1-85435-557-0, Benchmark NY); 1993. Set lib. bdg. 94.76 (1-85435-554-6, Benchmark NY) Marshall Cavendish.

***Women in Society - Group 3, 4 bks.** Incl. Ireland. Patricia M. Levy. LC 93-40414. (Illus.). 128p. (YA). (gr. 7 up). 1994. lib. bdg. 19.95 (1-85435-563-5, Benchmark NY); Russia. Elena Kotlyarskaya. LC 93-49762. (Illus.). 128p. (YA). (gr. 7 up). 1994. lib. bdg. 19.95 (1-85435-561-9, Benchmark NY); United States. Penny Coleman. LC 93-48706. (Illus.). 128p. (YA). (gr. 7 up). 1994. lib. bdg. 19.95 (1-85435-560-0, Benchmark NY); India. V. Ghose. (Illus.). 128p. (YA). (gr. 7 up). 1996. lib. bdg. 19.95 (1-85435-564-3, Benchmark NY); 1994. Set lib. bdg. 75.81 (1-85435-559-7, Benchmark NY) Marshall Cavendish.

Women in Sociology: A Bio-Bibliographical Sourcebook. Ed. by Mary J. Deegan. LC 90-43376. 488p. 1991. text ed. 79.50 (0-313-26085-0, DWY/, Greenwood Pr) Greenwood.

Women in Southern Literature. Patricia E. Sweeney. LC 85-30208. (Bibliographies & Indexes in American Literature Ser.: No. 6). 141p. 1986. text ed. 45.00 (0-313-24972-5, SYW/, Greenwood Pr) Greenwood.

Women in Soviet Fiction, 1917-1964. Xenia Gasiorowska. LC 68-16060. 300p. reprint ed. 85.50 (0-8357-9781-3, 2010194) Bks Demand.

Women in Soviet Society: Equality, Development, & Social Change. Gail W. Lapidus. LC 74-16710. 1978. pap. 12.00 (0-520-03938-6) U CA Pr.

Women in Space: Reaching the Last Frontier. Carole S. Briggs. (Space & Aviation Ser.). (Illus.). 80p. (J). (gr. 5 up). 1988. pap. 5.95 (0-8225-9547-8, Lerner Publctns); lib. bdg. 21.50 (0-8225-1581-4, Lerner Publctns) Lerner Group.

***Women in Spain.** Jones. LC 97-20797. 1998. pap. write for info. (0-7190-4757-9, Pub. by Manchester Univ Pr UK); text ed. write for info. (0-7190-4756-0, Pub. by Manchester Univ Pr UK) St Martin.

Women in Spiritual & Communitarian Societies in the United States. Ed. by Wendy Chmielewski et al. (Utopianism & Communitarianism Ser.). (Illus.). 320p. 1992. text ed. 42.50 (0-8156-2568-5); pap. text ed. 17.95 (0-8156-2569-3) Syracuse U Pr.

Women in Sport: An Annotated Bibliography. Mary L. Remley. 178p. 1991. 40.00 (0-8161-8977-3, Hall Reference) Macmillan.

Women in Sport: Issues & Controversies. Ed. by Greta L. Cohen. (Illus.). 336p. (C). 1993. text ed. 55.00 (0-8039-4979-0); pap. text ed. 27.50 (0-8039-4980-4) Sage.

Women in Sports. (Initiatives Ser.: Vol. 47, No. 2). 1984. 13.00 (0-614-14215-6) Natl Assn Women.

Women in Sports: A Guide to Information Sources. Ed. by Mary L. Remley. LC 80-14773. (Sports, Games, & Pastimes Information Guide Ser.: Vol. 10). 152p. 1980. 68.00 (0-8103-1461-4) Gale.

***Women in Sports: The Complete Book on the World's Greatest Female Athletes.** Joseph Layden. LC 97-6666. 1997. 29.95 (1-57544-064-4) Genl Pub Grp.

***Women in Sports: The Complete Book on the World's Greatest Female Athletes.** Joseph Layden. (Illus.). 1997. 29.95 (0-614-28164-4) Genl Pub Grp.

Women in Taiwan Politics: Overcoming Barriers to Women's Participation in a Modernizing Society. Chou Bih-er et al. LC 90-8605. 212p. 1990. lib. bdg. 40.00 (1-55587-106-2) Lynne Rienner.

Women in Texas: Their Lives, Their Experiences, Their Accomplishments. limited rev. ed. Ann F. Crawford & Crystal S. Ragsdale. LC 91-29391. (Illus.). 445p. 1992. reprint ed. 60.00 (0-938349-74-0) State House Pr.

Women in Texas: Their Lives, Their Experiences, Their Accomplishments. rev. ed. Ann F. Crawford & Crystal S. Ragsdale. LC 91-29391. (Illus.). 445p. 1992. reprint ed. pap. 16.95 (0-938349-73-2) State House Pr.

Women in Texas Study Guide. Ann F. Crawford. 64p. 1993. pap. 6.95 (1-880510-03-0) State House Pr.

Women in the Acts of the Apostles: A Feminist Liberation Perspective. Ivoni R. Reimer. Tr. by Linda M. Maloney. LC 95-23363. 1995. pap. 27.00 (0-8006-2840-3) Augsburg Fortress.

Women in the Administrative Revolution: The Feminization of Clerical Work. Graham S. Lowe. 1987. 37.50 (0-8020-2657-5); pap. 18.95 (0-8020-6686-0) U of Toronto Pr.

Women in the Age of Economic Transformation: Gender Impact of Reforms in Post-Socialist & Developing Countries. Ed. by Nahid Aslanbeigui et al. LC 94-14949. 240p. (C). 1994. pap. 19.95 (0-415-10423-8, B4464) Routledge.

Women in the Age of Economic Transformation: Gender Impact of Reforms in Post-Socialist & Developing Countries. Ed. by Nahid Aslanbeigui et al. LC 94-14949. 224p. (C). (gr. 13). 1994. text ed. 69.95 (0-415-10422-X, B4460) Routledge.

Women in the Age of the American Revolution. Ed. by Ronald Hoffman & Peter J. Albert. LC 88-29370. (U. S. Capitol Historical Society, Perspectives on the American Revolution Ser.). (Illus.). 515p. 1989. text ed. 49.50 (0-8139-1216-4); pap. text ed. 19.50 (0-8139-1240-7) U Pr of Va.

Women in the American Economy: A Documentary History, 1675 to 1929. W. Elliot Brownlee & Mary M. Brownlee. LC 75-18168. (Yale Paperbound Ser.: No. Y-289). 358p. reprint ed. pap. 102.10 (0-8357-8773-7, 2033683) Bks Demand.

Women in the American Revolution. Ed. by Jeanne M. Bracken. (Perspectives on History Ser.: Vol. 30). (Illus.). 64p. (Orig.). 1997. pap. 5.95 (1-878668-73-0) Disc Enter Ltd.

Women in the American Theatre: Actresses & Audiences, 1790-1870. Faye E. Dudden. LC 93-40780. 1994. 35.00 (0-300-05636-2) Yale U Pr.

W

***Women in the American Theatre: Actresses & Audiences, 1790-1870.** Faye E. Dudden. (Illus.). 270p. 1997. pap. 16.00 (*0-300-07058-6*) Yale U Pr.

Women in the American Welfare Trap. Catherine P. Kingfisher. 224p. 1996. text ed. 37.50 (*0-8122-3287-9*); pap. text ed. 17.50 (*0-8122-1515-X*) U of Pa Pr.

Women in the Americas: Participation & Development. Inter-American Development Bank Staff. 200p. (Orig.). 1995. pap. text ed. 14.95 (*0-940602-98-9*) IADB.

Women in the Ancient World. Ed. by John Peradotto & J. P. Sullivan. LC 83-4975. 377p. (C). 1987. pap. text ed. 16.95 (*0-87395-773-3*) State U NY Pr.

Women in the Arab World: An Annotated Bibliography. Ayad Al-Qazzaz. (Bibliography Ser.: No. 2). 39p. (Orig.). 1975. pap. text ed. 2.00 (*0-937694-15-0*) Assn Arab-Amer U Grads.

Women in the Bible: Examples to Live By. Sylvia Charles. 329p. 1988. pap. 16.99 (*1-56322-021-0*) V Hensley.

Women in the Biblical Tradition. Ed. by George J. Brooke. LC 92-40883. (Studies in Women & Religion: Vol. 31). 302p. 1992. text ed. 99.95 (*0-7734-9216-X*) E Mellen.

Women in the Biblical World: A Study Guide, Vol. 1. Mayer I. Gruber. LC 95-35831. (ATLA Bibliography Ser.: No. 38). (Illus.). 296p. 1995. 39.50 (*0-8108-3069-8*) Scarecrow.

***Women in the Biological Sciences: A Biobibliographic Sourcebook.** Rose K. Rose. Ed. by Louise S. Grinstein & Carol A. Biermann. LC 96-43783. 656p. 1997. text ed. 99.50 (*0-313-29180-2*, Greenwood Pr) Greenwood.

Women in the Chartist Movement. Jutta Schwarzkopf. LC 91-9082. 340p. 1991. text ed. 55.00 (*0-312-06213-3*) St Martin.

Women in the Church. Dean Guest. 126p. (Orig.). 1991. pap. 6.95 (*1-879667-02-9*) Dove Pr TX.

Women in the Church. Dennis R. Kuhns. LC 78-53968. (Focal Pamphlet Ser.: Vol. 28). 81p. (Orig.). 1978. reprint ed. pap. 25.00 (*0-608-01747-7*, 2062405) Bks Demand.

Women in the Church: A Biblical Theology of Women in Ministry. Stanley J. Grenz & Denise M. Kjesbo. LC 95-38605. 280p. (Orig.). 1995. pap. 15.99 (*0-8308-1862-6*, 1862) InterVarsity.

Women in the Church: A Fresh Analysis of 1 Timothy 2:9-15. Ed. by Andreas J. Kostenberger et al. LC 95-39701. 336p. (Orig.). (C). 1995. pap. 21.99 (*0-8010-2020-4*) Baker Bks.

Women in the Church I. Ed. by Madonna Kolbenschlag. 249p. 1987. pap. 11.95 (*0-912405-39-2*) Pastoral Pr.

***Women in the Church's Ministry: A Test Case for Biblical Interpretation.** R. T. France. 96p. 1997. pap. 12.00 (*0-8028-4172-4*) Eerdmans.

Women in the City: Housing, Services, & the Urban Environment. OECD Staff. 169p. (Orig.). pap. 37.00 (*92-64-14570-2*, Pub. by Org for Econ FR) OECD.

Women in the City of the Dead. Helen Watson. LC 91-76981. 194p. 1992. 49.95 (*0-86543-280-5*); pap. 14.95 (*0-86543-281-3*) Africa World.

Women in the Civil Rights Movement: Trailblazers & Torchbearers, 1941-1965. Ed. by Vicki L. Crawford et al. LC 90-1393. (Black Women in United States History Ser.: Vol. 16). (Illus.). 336p. 1990. 50.00 (*0-926019-22-8*) Carlson Pub.

Women in the Civil Rights Movement: Trailblazers & Torchbearers, 1941-1965. Ed. by Vicki L. Crawford et al. LC 93-2727. (Blacks in the Diaspora Ser.). (Illus.). 320p. 1993. Alk. paper. 13.95 (*0-253-20832-7*) Ind U Pr.

Women in the Civil War. Mary E. Massey. LC 93-45580. (Illus.). xxix, 401p. 1994. pap. 14.95 (*0-8032-8213-3*, Bison Books) U of Nebr Pr.

Women in the Civil War: Warriors, Patriots, Nurses & Spies. Intro. by Phyllis R. Emert. LC 94-69090. (Perspectives on History Ser.). (Illus.). 68p. (Orig.). (YA). (gr. 5-12). 1994. pap. text ed. 5.95 (*1-878668-45-5*) Disc Enter Ltd.

Women in the Classical World: Image & Text. Elaine Fantham et al. LC 92-47284. 448p. 1994. 39.95 (*0-19-506727-4*) OUP.

Women in the Classical World: Image & Text. H. A. Shapiro et al. (Illus.). 448p. (C). 1995. pap. text ed. 24.95 (*0-19-509862-5*) OUP.

Women in the Covenant of Grace: Talks Selected from the 1993 Women's Conference. Ed. by Dawn H. Anderson & Susette F. Green. LC 93-42368. vii, 280p. 1994. 14.95 (*0-87579-829-2*) Deseret Bk.

Women in the Criminal Justice System. Clarice Feinman. LC 80-12539. 136p. 1980. 24.95 (*0-275-90478-4*, C0478, Praeger Pubs); pap. 11.95 (*0-275-91492-5*, B1492, Praeger Pubs) Greenwood.

Women in the Criminal Justice System. 3rd ed. Clarice Feinman. LC 93-44499. 224p. 1994. text ed. 59.95 (*0-275-94486-7*, Praeger Pubs); pap. text ed. 19.95 (*0-275-94487-5*, Praeger Pubs) Greenwood.

***Women in the Curriculum.** 1997. write for info. (*1-885303-31-9*) Towson St Univ.

Women in the Developing World: Thoughts & Ideas. Hasna Begum. 128p. 1990. text ed. 20.00 (*81-207-1268-4*, Pub. by Sterling Pubs II) Apt Bks.

Women in the Domicile: The Treatment of Women's Work in International Law. A. Yasmine Rassam. LC 93-655022. (MacArthur Scholar Ser.: No. 24). 67p. (Orig.). 1994. pap. 4.50 (*1-881157-26-1*) In Ctr Global.

Women in the Earliest Churches. Ben Witherington, III. (Society for New Testament Studies Monographs: No. 59). 320p. (C). 1991. pap. text ed. 19.95 (*0-521-40789-3*) Cambridge U Pr.

Women in the Early Church. Elizabeth A. Clark. Ed. by Thomas Halton. LC 83-81477. (Message of the Fathers of the Church Ser.: Vol. 13). 250p. 1984. pap. 14.95 (*0-8146-5332-4*) Liturgical Pr.

Women in the Economy of the United States of America. Mary E. Pidgeon. Bd. with Employed Women Under NRA Codes. LC 75-8784. LC 75-8784. (FDR & the Era of the New Deal Ser.). 1975. reprint ed. Set lib. bdg. 29.50 (*0-306-70731-4*) Da Capo.

Women in the Eighteenth Century: Constructions of Femininity. Ed. by Vivien Jones. (World & Word Ser.). 288p. (C). 1990. pap. 18.95 (*0-415-03489-2*, A4170) Routledge.

Women in the European Labour Markets. Ed. by Anneke Van Doorne-Huiskes et al. 272p. 1995. 59.95 (*1-85396-298-8*, Pub. by Paul Chapman UK) Taylor & Francis.

Women in the Face of Change. Ed. by Hilary Pilkington et al. LC 91-44517. 208p. (C). 1992. pap. 17.95 (*0-415-07541-6*, A7462) Routledge.

Women in the Face of Change. Ed. by Hilary Pilkington et al. LC 91-44517. 208p. (C). (gr. 13). 1992. text ed. 85.00 (*0-415-07540-8*, A7458) Routledge.

Women in the Family & the Economy: An International Comparative Survey. Ed. by George Kurian & Ratna Ghosh. LC 80-28293. (Contributions in Family Studies: No. 5). (Illus.). 448p. 1981. text ed. 65.00 (*0-313-22275-4*, KWF/, Greenwood Pr) Greenwood.

Women in the Field: America's Pioneering Women Naturalists. Marcia M. Bonta. LC 90-20729. 320p. 1992. pap. 16.95 (*0-89096-489-0*) Tex A&M Univ Pr.

Women in the Field: America's Pioneering Women Naturalists. Marcia M. Bonta. LC 90-20729. 320p. 1992. 29.50 (*0-89096-467-X*) Tex A&M Univ Pr.

Women in the Field: Anthropological Experiences. 2nd enl. rev. ed. Ed. by Peggy Golde. 1986. pap. 15.00 (*0-520-05422-9*) U CA Pr.

Women in the Fine Arts: A Bibliography & Illustration Guide. Janet A. Anderson. LC 90-53608. 368p. 1991. lib. bdg. 65.00 (*0-89950-541-4*) McFarland & Co.

Women in the Fine Arts: From the Seventh Century B. C. to the Twentieth Century A. D. Clara E. Clement. (Illus.). 395p. 1977. reprint ed. 26.95 (*0-87928-079-4*) Corner Hse.

Women in the First & Second World Wars: A Checklist of the Holdings of the Hoover Institution War, Revolution & Peace. Compiled by Helena Wedborn. (Bibliographical Ser.: No. B72). 73p. (Orig.). (C). 1988. pap. text ed. 12.95 (*0-8179-2722-0*) Hoover Inst Pr.

Women in the First Capitalist Society: Experiences in Seventeenth-Century England. Margaret George. 272p. 1988. text ed. 29.95 (*0-252-01534-7*) U of Ill Pr.

Women in the Global Factory. Annette Fuentes & Barbara Ehrenreich. (Politics & Economics Ser.: No. 2). (Illus.). 64p. (Orig.). 1983. pap. 6.00 (*0-89608-198-2*) South End Pr.

Women in the Gospels. Carlo M. Martini. 136p. (Orig.). 1990. pap. 9.95 (*0-8245-0986-2*) Crossroad NY.

Women in the History of Political Thought: Ancient Greece to Machiavelli. Arlene W. Saxonhouse. LC 85-6369. (Women & Politics Ser.). 224p. 1985. text ed. 55.00 (*0-275-90160-2*, C0160, Praeger Pubs); pap. text ed. 19.95 (*0-275-91655-3*, B1655, Praeger Pubs) Greenwood.

Women in the History of Variable Star Astronomy. Dorrit Hoffleit. (Illus.). 62p. (Orig.). 1993. pap. text ed. 10.00 (*0-614-14289-X*) A & S Pubng.

Women in the Holocaust. Ed. by Jehoshua Eibeshitz et al. Tr. by Anna Eibeshitz. 33.90 (*0-932351-59-X*, Remember); pap. 27.90 (*0-932351-62-X*, Remember) Besad Prodns.

Women in the Holocaust. Ed. by Jehoshua Eibeshitz et al. Tr. by Anna Eibeshitz. 248p. 1993. 16.95 (*0-932351-44-1*, Remember) Besad Prodns.

Women in the Holocaust, Vol 1. Ed. by Jehoshua Eibeshitz et al. Tr. by Anna Eibeshitz. 248p. 1993. pap. 13.95 (*0-932351-45-X*, Remember) Besad Prodns.

Women in the Holocaust, Vol 2. Ed. by Jehoshua Eibeshitz et al. Tr. by Anna Eibeshitz. 228p. 1994. pap. 13.95 (*0-932351-47-6*, Remember) Besad Prodns.

Women in the Holocaust, Vol. II. Ed. by Jehoshua Eibeshitz et al. Tr. by Anna Eibeshitz. 228p. 1994. 16.95 (*0-932351-46-8*, Remember) Besad Prodns.

Women in the House: A Study of Women Members of Parliament. Elizabeth Vallance. 212p. (C). 1979. reprint ed. pap. 18.95 (*0-485-11229-9*, Pub. by Athlone Pr UK) Humanities.

Women in the House of Fiction. Lorna Sage. 250p. (C). 1992. pap. 17.95 (*0-415-90659-8*, A7601, Routledge NY) Routledge.

Women in the Housing Service. Marion Brion. LC 94-7747. 304p. (C). (gr. 13). 1994. text ed. 74.95 (*0-415-08094-0*, B4520) Routledge.

Women in the Indian Parliament (A Critical Study of their Role) J. K. Chopra. (C). 1993. 44.00 (*81-7099-513-2*, Pub. by Mittal II) S Asia.

Women in the Judicial Process. Beverly B. Cook et al. (Women & American Politics Ser.). 54p. (Orig.). (C). 1988. pap. text ed. 6.50 (*0-915654-80-6*) Am Political.

Women in the Labor Market. Ed. by Cynthia B. Lloyd et al. LC 79-15547. 393p. 1979. text ed. 60.00 (*0-231-04638-3*) Col U Pr.

Women in the Labour Force - Comparative Studies on Labour Market & Organization of Work since the 18th Century: Proceedings of the Tenth International Economic History Congress, Leuven, Belgium, August 1990. Ed. by E. Aerts et al. (Studies in Social & Economic History: No. 11). 145p. (Orig.). 1990. pap. 32.50 (*90-6186-383-X*, Pub. by Leuven Univ BE) Coronet Bks.

Women in the Later Years: Health, Social, & Cultural Perspectives. Ed. by Ida Susser. LC 88-34814. (Women & Health Ser.: Vol 14, Nos. 3-4). (Illus.). 272p. 1989. pap. text ed. 19.95 (*0-918393-65-5*) Harrington Pk.

Women in the Later Years: Health, Social, & Cultural Perspectives. Ed. by Ida Susser. LC 88-35826. (Women & Health Ser.: Vol. 14, Nos. 3-4). (Illus.). 272p. 1989. text ed. 49.95 (*0-86656-888-3*) Haworth Pr.

Women in the Latin American Development Process. Ed. by Christine E. Bose & Edna Acosta-Belen. LC 94-27400. 296p. (Orig.). (C). 1995. pap. text ed. 19.95 (*1-56639-293-4*); lib. bdg. 59.95 (*1-56639-292-6*) Temple U Pr.

Women in the Life of Jesus. Jill Briscoe. (Jill Briscoe Inductive Bible Study Ser.). 96p. 1986. pap. 7.99 (*0-89693-254-0*, 6-2254, Victor Bks) Chariot Victor.

Women in the Marines: The Book Camp Challenge. N. R. Rowan. LC 93-9706. (Illus.). (YA). (gr. 5 up). 1993. lib. bdg. 22.95 (*0-8225-1430-3*, Lerner Publctns) Lerner Group.

Women in the Martial Arts. Ed. by Carol A. Wiley. (Illus.). 146p. (Orig.). 1992. pap. 12.95 (*1-55643-136-8*) North Atlantic.

Women in the Material World. Faith D'Aluisio & Peter Menzel. LC 96-15947. 256p. 1996. 35.00 (*0-87156-398-3*) Sierra.

Women in the Maze: Questions & Answers on Biblical Equality. Ruth A. Tucker. LC 91-41728. 267p. (Orig.). 1992. pap. 12.99 (*0-8308-1307-1*, 1307) InterVarsity.

Women in the Medieval English Countryside. Judith M. Bennett. 338p. (C). 1989. reprint ed. pap. text ed. 18.95 (*0-19-504561-0*) OUP.

Women in the Medieval English Countryside: Gender & Household in Brigstock Before the Plague. Judith M. Bennett. 288p. 1987. 55.00 (*0-19-504094-5*) OUP.

Women in the Metropolis: Gender & Modernity in Weimar Culture. Ed. by Katharina Von Ankum. LC 96-3118. (Weimar & Now Ser.: Vol. II). (Illus.). 1997. 45.00 (*0-520-20464-6*); pap. 15.95 (*0-520-20465-4*) U CA Pr.

Women in the Middle: Facing Midlife Challenges with Faith. Margot Hover. LC 94-60480. 88p. (Orig.). 1995. pap. 7.95 (*0-89622-612-3*) Twenty-Third.

Women in the Middle: Their Parent-Care Years. Elaine Brody. LC 90-9400. 304p. 1990. 36.95 (*0-8261-6380-7*) Springer Pub.

Women in the Middle Ages. Frances Gies. pap. 10.95 (*0-685-69048-2*) HarpC.

Women in the Middle Ages. Joseph Gies. 1991. pap. text ed. 12.50 (*0-06-092304-0*) HarpC.

***Women in the Middle Ages.** Nadia Margolis & Katharina Wilson. 1000p. Date not set. text ed. 100.00 (*0-8240-7272-3*) Garland.

Women in the Middle Ages: Between Pit & Pedestal. Anne Echols & Marty Williams. (Illus.). 320p. (C). 1994. pap. 16.95 (*0-910129-34-7*); text ed. 39.95 (*0-910129-33-9*) Wiener Pubs Inc.

Women in the Middle Ages & the Renaissance: Literary & Historical Perspectives. Mary B. Rose. LC 85-22153. 272p. (Orig.). 1986. pap. 16.95 (*0-8156-2352-6*) Syracuse U Pr.

Women in the Middle East. Ed. by Khamsin Collective Staff. (Khamsin Collective Ser.: Vol. 13). 96p. (C). 1987. pap. 9.95 (*0-86232-675-3*, Pub. by Zed Bks Ltd UK) Humanities.

Women in the Middle East: Perceptions, Realities & Struggles for Liberation. Ed. by Haleh Afshar. LC 91-40070. 240p. 1993. text ed. 65.00 (*0-312-07921-4*) St Martin.

Women in the Middle East: Tradition & Change. Ramsay M. Harik & Elsa Marston. LC 96-11619. (Women Then - Women Now Ser.). 176p. (YA). (gr. 8-12). 1996. lib. bdg. 22.70 (*0-531-11304-3*) Watts.

Women in the Military. Ed. by E. A. Blacksmith. LC 92-34712. (Reference Shelf Ser.: Vol. 64, No. 5). 1992. 15.00 (*0-8242-0829-3*) Wilson.

Women in the Military. Ed. by Carol Wekesser & Matthew Polesetsky. LC 91-25056. (Current Controversies Ser.). 192p. (YA). (gr. 10 up). 1991. pap. text ed. 12.96 (*0-89908-585-7*); lib. bdg. 20.96 (*0-89908-579-2*) Greenhaven.

Women in the Military: An Unfinished Revolution. rev. ed. Heanne Holm. LC 92-17981. 560p. 1993. pap. 16.95 (*0-89141-513-0*) Presidio Pr.

Women in the Military: Deployment in the Persian Gulf War. (Illus.). 58p. (Orig.). (C). 1993. pap. text ed. 30.00 (*0-7881-0102-1*) DIANE Pub.

Women in the Mines: Portraits of Life & Work, 1914-1994. Marat Moore. LC 95-45620. (Oral History Ser.: No. 20). 350p. 1996. 32.95 (*0-8057-7834-9*, Twayne) Scribnrs Ref.

Women in the Ministry of Jesus: A Study of Jesus' Attitude to Women & Their Roles As Reflected in His Earthly Life. Ben Witherington, III. LC 83-18957. (Society for New Testament Studies Monographs: No. 51). 210p. 1987. pap. text ed. 19.95 (*0-521-34781-5*) Cambridge U Pr.

Women in the Mirror. Pat Carr. LC 77-24965. (Iowa Short Fiction Award Ser.). 152p. 1977. pap. 12.95 (*0-87745-082-X*) U of Iowa Pr.

Women in the Modern World. Mirra Komarovsky. (Reprint Series in Sociology). 1971. reprint ed. pap. text ed. 14.95 (*0-89197-979-4*); reprint ed. lib. bdg. 39.50 (*0-697-00213-6*) Irvington.

Women in the Modern World: (the Annals of the American Academy of Political & Social Science, Vol. 143, May, 1929) Ed. by Viva B. Boothe. LC 74-3929. (Women in America Ser.). (Illus.). 404p. 1974. reprint ed. 31.95 (*0-405-06078-5*) Ayer.

Women in the Muslim World. Ed. by Lois Beck & Nikki R. Keddie. LC 78-3633. 712p. 1980. pap. 18.95 (*0-674-95481-5*) HUP.

***Women in the Old Testament.** Irene Nowell. (Orig.). 1997. pap. text ed. 7.95 (*0-8146-2411-1*, Liturg Pr Bks) Liturgical Pr.

***Women in the Ottoman Empire: Middle Eastern Women in the Early Modern Era.** Madeline C. Zilfi. LC 97-17134. (Ottoman Empire & Its Heritage Ser.). 1997. write for info. (*90-04-10804-1*) E J Brill.

Women in the Plays of Henrik Ibsen. Clela Allphin. 1974. lib. bdg. 250.00 (*0-87700-211-8*) Revisionist Pr.

Women in the Politics of Post-Communist Eastern Europe. Ed. by Marilyn Rueschemeyer. LC 93-13580. 272p. (gr. 13). 1994. text ed. 65.95 (*1-56324-168-4*) M E Sharpe.

Women in the Politics of Post-Communist Eastern Europe. Ed. by Marilyn Rueschemeyer. LC 93-13580. 253p. (C). (gr. 13). 1994. pap. text ed. 26.95 (*1-56324-169-2*) M E Sharpe.

Women in the Presence: Constructing Community & Seeking Spirituality in Mainline Protestantism. Jody S. Davie. LC 95-14736. 184p. 1995. text ed. 29.95 (*0-8122-3286-0*); pap. text ed. 14.95 (*0-8122-1514-1*) U of Pa Pr.

Women in the Priesthood? A Systematic Analysis in the Light of the Order of Creation & Redemption. Manfred Hauke. Tr. by David Kipp from GER. LC 87-80794. 497p. 1988. pap. 24.95 (*0-89870-165-1*) Ignatius Pr.

Women in the Professions: What's All the Fuss About? Linda S. Fidell & John Delamater. LC 73-89940. (Sage Contemporary Social Science Issues Ser.: No. 8). 144p. reprint ed. pap. 41.10 (*0-317-29680-9*, 2021898) Bks Demand.

Women in the Qur'an, Traditions, & Commentaries. Barbara F. Stowasser. 240p. 1994. 35.00 (*0-19-508480-2*) OUP.

***Women in the Quran, Traditions, & Interpretation.** Barbara F. Stowasser. 206p. 1996. 29.95 (*0-614-21403-3*, 1329) Kazi Pubns.

Women in the Qur'an, Traditions & Interpretation. Barbara F. Stowasser. 216p. 1996. reprint ed. pap. 15.95 (*0-19-511148-6*) OUP.

***Women in the Rabbinate: Voices from Great Britain.** Sybil Sheridan. LC 97-10845. (Studies in Comparative Religion). 1997. write for info. (*1-57003-088-X*) U of SC Pr.

Women in the Resistance. Margaret L. Rossiter. LC 85-16746. (Illus.). 256p. 1985. text ed. 59.95 (*0-275-90222-6*, C0222, Praeger Pubs) Greenwood.

Women in the Resistance & in the Holocaust: The Voices of Eyewitnesses. Ed. by Vera Laska. LC 82-12018. (Contributions in Women's Studies: No. 37). xv, 330p. 1983. text ed. 59.95 (*0-313-23457-4*, LWH/, Greenwood Pr) Greenwood.

Women in the Sanctuary Movement. Robin Lorentzen. 240p. 1991. 44.95 (*0-87722-768-3*) Temple U Pr.

Women in the Sciences: A Source Guide. 1991. lib. bdg. 79.95 (*0-8490-4827-3*) Gordon Pr.

Women in the Sex Industry. 1991. lib. bdg. 79.85 (*0-8490-4658-0*) Gordon Pr.

Women in the Shadows. Ann Bannon. 176p. 1986. pap. 5.95 (*0-930044-85-1*) Naiad Pr.

Women in the Shadows. Ann Dannon. Ed. by Jonathan N. Katz. LC 75-13751. (Homosexuality Ser.). 1975. reprint ed. 11.95 (*0-405-07407-7*) Ayer.

Women in the Soviet Countryside: Women's Role in Rural Development in the U. S. S. R. Susan Bridger. (Cambridge Russian, Soviet & Post-Soviet Studies: No. 56). (Illus.). 256p. 1988. text ed. 69.95 (*0-521-32862-4*) Cambridge U Pr.

Women in the Spanish Revolution. L. Willis. 1984. lib. bdg. 250.00 (*0-87700-643-1*) Revisionist Pr.

Women in the Streets: Essays on Sex & Power in Renaissance Italy. Samuel K. Cohn, Jr. LC 96-11611. (Illus.). 208p. 1996. text ed. 45.00 (*0-8018-5308-7*) Johns Hopkins.

Women in the Streets & Other Essays on the Italian Renaissance. Samuel K. Cohn, Jr. LC 96-11611. 1996. pap. text ed. 15.95 (*0-8018-5309-5*) Johns Hopkins.

Women in the Tebhaga Uprising: Rural Poor Women & Revolutionary Leadership 1946-47. Peter Custers. 247p. (C). 1987. 18.00 (*0-8364-2174-4*, Pub. by Naya Prokash IA) S Asia.

Women in the Texas Populist Movement: Letters to the Southern Mercury. Marion K. Barthelme. 1996. pap. text ed. 14.95 (*0-89263-344-1*) Tex A&M Univ Pr.

***Women in the Texas Populist Movement: Letters to the Southern Mercury.** Ed. by Marion K. Barthelme. LC 96-53089. (Centennial Series of the Association of Former Students: Vol. 67). (Illus.). 256p. (C). 1997. text ed. 39.95 (*0-89096-742-3*) Tex A&M Univ Pr.

***Women in the Texas Populist Movement: Letters to the Southern Mercury.** Ed. by Marion K. Barthelme. LC 96-53089. (Centennial Series of the Association of Former Students: Vol. 67). (Illus.). 256p. (C). 1997. pap. 16.95 (*0-89096-775-X*) Tex A&M Univ Pr.

Women in the Theatre of Galdos: From Realidad (1892) to Voluntad (1895) Lisa P. Conde. LC 90-5916. 432p. 1990. lib. bdg. 109.95 (*0-88946-391-3*) E Mellen.

***Women in the Third World.** Karen L. Kinnear. LC 97-17330. 256p. 1997. 39.50 (*0-87436-922-3*) ABC-CLIO.

***Women in the Third World: An Encyclopedia of Contemporary Issues.** Edith H. Altbach et al. 760p. 1998. text ed. 135.00 (*0-8153-0150-2*) Garland.

Women in the Third World: Gender Issues in Rural & Urban Areas. Lynne Brydon & Sylvia Chant. LC 89-6119. 336p. (C). 1989. text ed. 45.00 (*0-8135-1470-3*); pap. text ed. 17.95 (*0-8135-1471-1*) Rutgers U Pr.

***Women in the Third World: Gender Issues in Rural & Urban Areas.** Lynne Brydon & Sylvia Chant. 336p. 1989. pap. 25.00 (*1-85278-190-4*) E Elgar.

***Women in the Time of AIDS.** Gillian Paterson. LC 96-39779. 124p. (Orig.). 1997. pap. 14.00 (*1-57075-106-4*) Orbis Bks.

W

An Asterisk (*) at the beginning of an entry indicates that the title is appearing in BIP for the first time.

Women in the Trees: U. S. Women's Short Stories about Battering & Resistance, 1839-1994. Ed. by Susan Koppelman. LC 95-45624. 384p. 1996. pap. 16.00 (*0-8070-6777-6*) Beacon Pr.

Women in the Twentieth Century: A Study of Their Political, Social, & Economic Activities. Sophonisba P. Breckinridge. LC 72-2593. (American Women Ser.: Images & Realities). 380p. 1978. reprint ed. 26.95 (*0-405-04450-X*) Ayer.

Women in the U. S. Labor Force. Ed. by Ann F. Cahn. LC 78-22130. (Praeger Special Studies). 346p. 1979. text ed. 65.00 (*0-275-90337-0*, C0337, Praeger Pubs) Greenwood.

Women in the U. S. S. R. Marjorie W. Bingham & Susan H. Gross. (Woman in World Area Studies). (Illus.). 151p. 1980. pap. 15.00 (*0-86596-005-4*) UM Womens Hist.

Women in the United States: Economic Conditions: A Bibliography. Ed. by Joan Nordquist. (Contemporary Social Issues: No. 38). 72p. (Orig.). (C). 1995. pap. 15.00 (*0-937855-74-X*) Ref Rsch Serv.

Women in the United States Military, 1901-1995: A Research Guide & Annotated Bibliography. Vicki L. Friedl. LC 96-5253. (Research Guides in Military Studies: Vol. 9). 288p. 1996. text ed. 69.50 (*0-313-29657-X*, Greenwood Pr) Greenwood.

Women in the University: A Policy Report. Ed. by Brian G. Wilson & Eileen M. Byrne. LC 87-19120. (Illus.). 227p. (Orig.). 1988. pap. text ed. 24.95 (*0-7022-2094-9*, Pub. by Univ Queensland Pr AT) Intl Spec Bk.

Women in the Unorganized Sector. L. M. Chandola. 202p. 1993. 30.00 (*0-685-60067-X*, Pub. by Radiant Pubs II) S Asia.

Women in the Unorganized Sector. L. M. Chandola. (C). 1995. 14.00 (*81-7027-195-9*, Pub. by Radiant Pubs II) S Asia.

Women in the Vanishing Cloister: Organizational Decline in Catholic Religious Order in the United States. Helen R. Ebaugh. LC 92-8035. 200p. (C). 1993. text ed. 35.00 (*0-8135-1865-2*); pap. text ed. 17.00 (*0-8135-1866-0*) Rutgers U Pr.

Women in the Victorian Art World. Ed. by Clarissa C. Orr. (Illus.). 256p. 1995. text ed. 24.95 (*0-7190-4123-6*, Pub. by Manchester Univ Pr UK) St Martin.

Women in the Viking Age. Judith Jesch. (Illus.). 248p. (C). 1994. 39.00 (*0-85115-278-3*) Boydell & Brewer.

Women in the Viking Age. Judith Jesch. 248p. 1995. pap. 23.00 (*0-85115-360-7*) Boydell & Brewer.

Women in the Visual Arts. W. Martin. 135p. 1992. pap. text ed. 22.00 (*2-88124-581-1*) Gordon & Breach.

Women in the Wesleyan & United Methodist Traditions: A Bibliography. Compiled by Susan M. Eltscher. 160p. 1992. pap. text ed. 5.00 (*1-880927-13-6*) Gen Comm Arch.

Women in the West. Conrad. 1996. 40.00 (*0-8161-1822-1*, Hall Library) G K Hall.

Women in the Western Heritage. Helga Harriman. 403p. (C). 1995. per. 22.47 (*1-56134-245-9*) Dushkin Pub.

*__Women in the Wild: True Stories of Life on the Road.__ Ed. by Lucy McCauley. (Travelers' Tales Guides). (Illus.). 350p. (Orig.). 1997. pap. 17.95 (*1-885211-21-X*) Trvlers Tale.

Women in the Word: Examines the Lives of 64 Women of the Bible. S. Charles. LC 84-72958. 250p. 1984. pap. 5.95 (*0-88270-579-2*) Bridge-Logos.

Women in the Work Force. H. John Bernardin. LC 82-13170. 256p. 1982. text ed. 55.00 (*0-275-90761-9*, C0761, Praeger Pubs) Greenwood.

Women in the Workplace. Pamela Roby. 138p. 1981. 18.95 (*0-87073-172-6*); pap. 11.95 (*0-87073-173-4*) Schenkman Bks Inc.

Women in the Workplace. Phyllis A. Wallace. LC 81-12775. 240p. 1982. text ed. 55.00 (*0-86569-069-3*, Auburn Hse) Greenwood.

Women in the Workplace: A Man's Perspective. Lloyd S. Lewan & Ronald G. Billingsley. LC 88-90731. (Illus.). 125p. (Orig.). 1988. pap. 6.95 (*0-9620360-0-5*) Remington Pr.

Women in the Workplace: Effects of Families. Ed. by Kathryn Borman et al. LC 84-2941. (Modern Sociology Ser.). 280p. 1984. text ed. 73.25 (*0-89391-166-6*) Ablex Pub.

Women in the Workplace: Eliminating Sexual Harassment & Improving Cross-Gender Communication. Catherine D. Fyock. 1993. pap. 10.00 (*0-685-67889-X*); per. 75.00 (*0-7863-0161-9*) Irwin Prof Pubng.

Women in the Workplace: Eliminating Sexual Harassment & Improving Cross-Gender Communication Module II: Participant's Workbook. Catherine Fyock. 48p. 1993. per. 10.00 (*1-55623-826-6*) Irwin Prof Pubng.

*__Women in the Workplace: Proposals for Research & Policy Concerning the Conditions of Women in Industrial & Service Jobs.__ Pamela A. Roby. LC 80-24605. 146p. reprint ed. pap. 41.70 (*0-608-05340-6*, 2065045) Bks Demand.

Women in the Workplace & Employee Assistance Programs: Perspectives, Innovations, & Techniques for Helping Professionals. Ed. by Marta Lundy & Beverly Younger. 144p. 1994. 39.95 (*1-56024-674-X*) Haworth Pr.

*__Women in the World: An International Atlas.__ Joni Seager. 1997. pap. 16.95 (*0-14-051374-4*); pap. 29.95 (*0-670-10008-0*) Viking Penguin.

Women in the World: Annotated History Resources for the Secondary Student. Lyn Reese & Jean Wilkinson. LC 87-16436. (Illus.). 228p. 1987. 30.00 (*0-8108-2050-1*) Scarecrow.

Women in the World Economic System: The Impact on Status & Fertility. Kathryn B. Ward. LC 84-8243. 192p. (C). 1984. text ed. 47.95 (*0-275-91287-6*, C1287, Praeger Pubs) Greenwood.

Women in the World Economy: An INSTRAW Study. Susan Joekes. 176p. 1987. reprint ed. 39.00 (*0-19-504947-0*) OUP.

Women in the World Economy: An INSTRAW Study. Susan Joekes. 176p. 1990. reprint ed. pap. 14.95 (*0-19-506315-5*) OUP.

Women in the World of Work: Statistical Analysis & Projections to the Year 2000. Shirley Nuss et al. (Women, Work & Development Ser.: No. 18). x, 132p. (Orig.). 1989. pap. 18.00 (*92-2-106507-3*) Intl Labour Office.

Women in the World's Religions: Past & Present. Ed. by Ursula King. LC 86-21213. (Contemporary Discussion Ser.). 261p. (Orig.). (C). 1987. 22.95 (*0-913757-32-2*, New Era Bks); pap. 12.95 (*0-913757-33-0*, New Era Bks) Paragon Hse.

Women in Theatre, Vol. 2, Part 3. Ed. by Julia Pascal. (Contemporary Theatre Review Ser). 130p. 1995. pap. text ed. 24.00 (*3-7186-5598-5*, Harwood Acad Pubs) Gordon & Breach.

Women in Theatre: Compassion & Hope. Karen Malpede. LC 84-26138. 304p. 1985. 14.95 (*0-87910-035-4*) Limelight Edns.

Women in Their Beds: New & Selected Stories. Gina Berriault. 352p. 1996. 25.00 (*1-887178-10-4*) Counterpt DC.

*__Women in Their Beds: New & Selected Stories.__ Gina Berriault. 1997. pap. text ed. 17.95 (*1-887178-38-4*) Counterpt DC.

Women in Their Speech Communities. Ed. by Jennifer Coates & Deborah Cameron. (Illus.). 208p. (Orig.). (C). 1989. pap. text ed. 21.47 (*0-582-00969-3*, 70408) Longman.

Women in Therapy. Harriet G. Lerner. LC 88-45938. 320p. 1989. reprint ed. pap. 13.00 (*0-06-097228-9*, PL 7228, PL) HarpC.

Women in Therapy. Harriet G. Lerner. LC 87-19326. 320p. 1992. reprint ed. 40.00 (*0-87668-978-0*) Aronson.

Women in Therapy & Counseling. M. Walker. 1990. 85.00 (*0-335-09376-0*, Open Univ Pr); pap. 27.00 (*0-335-09375-2*, Open Univ Pr) Taylor & Francis.

Women in Third World. Man S. Das. 158p. (C). 1989. 60.00 (*81-85453-01-2*, Pub. by Print Hse II) St Mut.

Women in Thirteenth-Century Spain As Portrayed in Alfonso X's Cantigas de Santa Maria. Connie L. Scarborough. LC 93-8098. (Hispanic Literature Ser.: Vol. 19). (Illus.). 196p. 1993. 79.95 (*0-7734-9316-6*) E Mellen.

Women in Today's Church. George Watkins. 56p. 1984. pap. 2.25 (*0-88144-025-6*) Christian Pub.

Women in Tolstoy: The Ideal & the Erotic. Ruth C. Benson. LC 72-92631. 153p. reprint ed. pap. 43.70 (*0-317-09648-6*, 2020225) Bks Demand.

Women in Traditional China. Susan H. Gross. (Illus.). 120p. 1980. pap. 15.00 (*0-86596-002-X*) UM Womens Hist.

Women in Transition: Career, Family, & Life Satisfaction in Three Cohorts. Catherine A. Faver. LC 84-8246. 192p. 1984. text ed. 49.95 (*0-275-91152-7*, C1152, Praeger Pubs) Greenwood.

*__Women in Transition: Social Control in Papua New Guinea.__ Cundi Banks. 171p. 1993. pap. 30.00 (*0-642-18635-9*, Pub. by Aust Inst Criminology) Willow Tree NY.

Women in Travail & Transition: A New Pastoral Care. Ed. by Maxine Glaz & Jeanne S. Moessner. LC 90-26299. 176p. (Orig.). 1990. pap. 14.00 (*0-8006-2420-3*, 1-2420) Augsburg Fortress.

Women in Trollope's Palliser Novels. Deborah D. Morse. LC 87-21497. 174p. 1991. 39.00 (*0-8357-1847-6*) Univ Rochester Pr.

Women in Tune: Five Secrets for Survival in Today's Hectic World. Betty Malz. LC 87-23384. 192p. (gr. 10). 1995. pap. 7.99 (*0-8007-9220-3*) Chosen Bks.

Women in Twentieth-Century Germany, Vol. 1. Eva Kolinsky. 1995. text ed. 19.95 (*0-7190-4175-9*, Pub. by Manchester Univ Pr UK) St Martin.

Women in Twentieth-Century Literature: A Jungian View. Bettina L. Knapp. LC 86-43033. (Illus.). 256p. 1987. 30.00 (*0-271-00493-2*) Pa St U Pr.

Women in U. S. History: An Annotated Bibliography. Common Women Collective Staff. LC 77-350179. (Illus.). 2.60 (*0-9601122-1-9*) Common Women.

Women in Unorganised Sector. Irene Tom. (C). 1989. 17.50 (*81-85059-09-8*, Pub. by Usha II) S Asia.

Women in Utopia: The Ideology of Gender in the American Owenite Communities. Carol A. Kolmerten. LC 89-45416. (Illus.). 219p. 1990. 15.95 (*0-253-33192-7*) Ind U Pr.

Women in Veterinary Medicine: Profiles of Success. Sue Drum & H. Ellen Whitely. LC 91-7050. (Illus.). 286p. 1991. pap. 21.95 (*0-8138-0667-4*) Iowa St U Pr.

Women in Waiting: Life on the Home Frontier. Linda Peavy & Ursula Smith. LC 93-38832. (Illus.). 400p. 1994. 38.95 (*0-8061-2616-7*); pap. 17.95 (*0-8061-2619-1*) U of Okla Pr.

Women in Washington: Advocates for Public Policy. Ed. by Irene Tinker. LC 83-7761. (Sage Yearbooks in Women's Policy Studies: No. 7). 327p. 1983. reprint ed. pap. 93.20 (*0-608-01523-7*, 2059567) Bks Demand.

Women in West Germany: Life, Work & Politics. Eva Kolinsky. LC 89-31933. (Illus.). 320p. 1989. 19.95 (*0-85496-238-7*) Berg Pubs.

Women in West Germany: Life, Work & Politics see Women in Contemporary Germany: Life, Work, Politics

Women in Western Civilization. Elizabeth Walsh. 320p. 1982. 22.95 (*0-87073-386-9*); pap. 15.95 (*0-87073-387-7*) Schenkman Bks Inc.

Women in Western European History: A Select Chronological, Geographical, & Topical Bibliography from Antiquity to the French Revolution. Ed. by Linda Frey et al. LC 81-20300. iv, 760p. 1982. text ed. 105.00 (*0-313-22858-2*, FEW/, Greenwood Pr) Greenwood.

Women in Western European History: A Select Chronological, Geographical, & Topical Bibliography from Antiquity to the French Revolution. Ed. by Linda Frey et al. LC 81-20300. lxvi, 1088p. 1984. text ed. 89.50 (*0-313-22859-0*, FRW/, Greenwood Pr) Greenwood.

Women in Western European History, First Supplement: A Select Chronological, Geographical, & Topical Bibliography. Ed. by Linda Frey et al. LC 86-22777. 764p. 1986. text ed. 105.00 (*0-313-25109-6*, FYS/, Greenwood Pr) Greenwood.

Women in Western Political Philosophy: Kant to Nietzsche. Ed. by Ellen Kennedy & Susan Mendus. LC 86-26066. 224p. 1987. pap. 12.95 (*0-312-00426-5*); text ed. 39.95 (*0-312-00425-7*) St Martin.

Women in Western Political Thought. Susan M. Okin. LC 79-84004. 384p. 1979. pap. text ed. 17.95 (*0-691-02191-0*) Princeton U Pr.

Women in Wilderness: Writings in Photographs. Ed. by Susan Zwinger & Ann Zwinger. LC 95-12538. (Wilderness Experience Ser.). (Illus.). 108p. (Orig.). (YA). 1995. pap. 16.95 (*0-15-600224-8*, Harvest Bks) HarBrace.

Women in World History: Reading from 1500 to the Present, Vol. 2. Ed. by Sarah S. Hughes & Brady Hughes. LC 94-23644. (Sources & Studies in World History). 272p. (C). (gr. 13). 1997. text ed. 60.95 (*1-56324-312-1*); pap. text ed. 22.95 (*1-56324-313-X*) M E Sharpe.

Women in World History Vol. 1: Readings from Prehistory to 1500. Ed. by Sarah S. Hughes & Brady Hughes. LC 94-23644. (Sources & Studies in World History). 270p. (C). (gr. 13). 1995. text ed. 64.95 (*1-56324-310-5*); pap. text ed. 23.95 (*1-56324-311-3*) M E Sharpe.

Women in World Politics: An Introduction. Ed. by Francine D'Amico & Peter R. Beckman. LC 94-21994. 248p. 1995. text ed. 59.95 (*0-89789-410-3*, Bergin & Garvey); pap. text ed. 19.95 (*0-89789-411-1*, Bergin & Garvey) Greenwood.

*__Women in World Religions.__ Ed. by Arvind Sharma. 310p. (Orig.). 1996. pap. 21.95 (*0-614-21689-3*, 1496) Kazi Pubns.

Women in World Religions. Ed. by Arvind Sharma. LC 87-6475. (McGill Studies in the History of Religions). 302p. (Orig.). (C). 1987. pap. text ed. 16.95 (*0-88706-375-6*) State U NY Pr.

*__Women in 19th Century.__ Linda Nochlin. Date not set. 25.00 (*1-56584-375-4*) New Press NY.

Women in 20th Century Germany. Kolinsky. 1995. text ed. 69.95 (*0-7190-4654-8*, Pub. by Manchester Univ Pr UK) St Martin.

Women, Information & the Future: Collecting & Sharing Resources Worldwide. Ed. by Eva S. Moseley. LC 95-8890. 296p. 1995. pap. 20.00 (*0-917846-67-2*) Highsmith Pr.

Women Inside: The Experience of Women Remand Prisoners in Holloway. Silvia Casale. (C). 1988. 39.00 (*0-685-45100-3*, Pub. by NCCL UK) St Mut.

Women Inside: The Experience of Women Remand Prisoners in Holloway. Silvia Casale. 136p. (C). 1989. pap. text ed. 35.00 (*0-900137-30-4*, Pub. by NCCL UK) St Mut.

*__Women Intellectuals, Modernism, & Difference: Transatlantic Culture, 1919-1945.__ Alice Gambrell. (Cultural Margins Ser.: Vol. 4). (Illus.). 271p. (C). 1997. text ed. 59.95 (*0-521-55341-5*) Cambridge U Pr.

*__Women Intellectuals, Modernism, & Difference: Transatlantic Culture, 1919-1945.__ Alice Gambrell. (Cultural Margins Ser.: Vol. 4). (Illus.). 271p. (C). 1997. pap. text ed. 18.95 (*0-521-55688-0*) Cambridge U Pr.

*__Women, International Development, & Politics: The Bureaucratic Mire.__ 2nd expanded ed. Kathleen A. Staudt. LC 97-3227. (Women in the Political Economy Ser.). 312p. (C). 1997. pap. text ed. 24.95 (*1-56639-546-1*) Temple U Pr.

Women into Computing: Selected Papers 1988-1990. Ed. by G. Lovegrove et al. (Workshops in Computing Ser.). (Illus.). 448p. 1991. 59.00 (*0-387-19648-X*) Spr-Verlag.

Women into the Unknown: A Sourcebook on Women Explorers & Travelers. Marion Tinglin. LC 88-18677. 382p. 1989. text ed. 75.00 (*0-313-25328-5*, TWU/, Greenwood Pr) Greenwood.

*__Women Invent: Two Centuries of Discoveries That Have Shaped Our World.__ Susan Casey. LC 97-18870. (Illus.). 144p. (J). (gr. 4-7). 1997. pap. 14.95 (*1-55652-317-3*) Chicago Review.

Women Inventors. Linda J. Altman. LC 96-20460. (American Profiles Ser.). 1997. write for info. (*0-8160-3385-4*) Facts on File.

Women Inventors, Vol. I. Jean F. Blashfield. (Women Inventors Ser.). (Illus.). 48p. (J). (gr. 3-9). 1995. lib. bdg. 17.80 (*1-56065-274-8*) Capstone Pr.

Women Inventors, Vol. II. Jean F. Blashfield. (Women Inventors Ser.). (Illus.). 48p. (J). (gr. 3-9). 1995. lib. bdg. 17.80 (*1-56065-275-6*) Capstone Pr.

Women Inventors, Vol. III. Jean F. Blashfield. (Women Inventors Ser.). (Illus.). 48p. (J). (gr. 3-9). 1995. lib. bdg. 17.80 (*1-56065-276-4*) Capstone Pr.

Women Inventors, Vol. IV. Jean F. Blashfield. (Women Inventors Ser.). (Illus.). 48p. (J). (gr. 3-9). 1995. lib. bdg. 17.80 (*1-56065-277-2*) Capstone Pr.

Women Inventors & Their Discoveries. Ethlie A. Vare & Greg Ptacek. LC 92-38268. (Profiles Ser.). (Illus.). 160p. (YA). (gr. 5-12). 1993. lib. bdg. 16.95 (*1-881508-06-4*) Oliver Pr MN.

Women Inventors 1. Jean F. Blashfield. (Illus.). 48p. (J). (gr. 3-7). 1995. 13.35 (*0-516-35275-X*) Childrens.

Women Inventors 2. Jean F. Blashfield. (Illus.). 48p. (J). (gr. 3-7). 1995. 13.35 (*0-516-35276-8*) Childrens.

Women Inventors 3. Jean F. Blashfield. (Illus.). 48p. 1995. 13.35 (*0-516-35274-1*) Childrens.

Women Inventors 4. Jean F. Blashfield. (Illus.). 48p. (J). (gr. 3-7). 1995. 13.35 (*0-516-35277-6*) Childrens.

Women, Islam & the State. Ed. by Deniz Kandiyoti. 256p. (C). 1991. pap. 19.95 (*0-87722-786-1*) Temple U Pr.

*__Women Islamisms & State.__ Karam. LC 97-7123. 1997. text ed. 69.95 (*0-312-17501-9*) St Martin.

*__Women Italian Renaissance Pain.__ Tinagli. Date not set. text ed. 59.95 (*0-7190-4053-1*) St Martin.

*__Women Italian Renaissance Pain.__ Tinagli. 1997. text ed. 19.95 (*0-7190-4054-X*, Pub. by Manchester Univ Pr UK) St Martin.

Women, It's Your Turn see If You Only Knew...: An Internationally Known Private Investigator Reveals How You Can Take Control of Your Life

*__Women, Jewish Law & Modernity: New Opportunities in a Post-Feminist Age.__ LC 96-29693. 1997. write for info. (*0-88125-574-2*) Ktav.

Women, Jews, & Muslims in the Texts of Reconquest Castile. Louise Mirrer. LC 96-10301. (Studies in Medieval & Early Modern Civilization). (C). 1996. 42.50 (*0-472-10723-2*) U of Mich Pr.

Women, Knowledge, & Reality: Explorations in Feminist Philosophy. Ed. by Ann Garry & Marilyn Pearsall. 384p. 1989. pap. 16.95 (*0-04-445222-5*) Routledge Chapman & Hall.

Women, Knowledge, & Reality: Explorations in Feminist Philosophy. 2nd ed. Ann Garry & Marilyn Pearsall. LC 96-25166. 448p. (C). 1996. pap. 22.95 (*0-415-91797-2*); text ed. 69.95 (*0-415-91796-4*) Routledge.

Women, Labour & Politics in Trinidad & Tobago: A History. Rhoda Reddock. 304p. (C). 1994. pap. 25.00 (*1-85649-154-4*); text ed. 60.00 (*1-85649-153-6*, Pub. by Zed Bks Ltd UK) Humanities.

*__Women, Land, & Authority: Perspectives from South Africa.__ Ed. by Shamim Meer. 160p. 1997. pap. 15.95 (*0-85598-375-2*, Pub. by Oxfam UK) Humanities.

Women, Law & Social Change. Shamsuddin Shams. (C). 1991. text ed. 36.00 (*81-7024-395-5*, Pub. by Ashish II) S Asia.

Women, Law & Social Change in India. Indu P. Singh. 175p. 1989. text ed. 25.00 (*81-7027-135-5*, Pub. by Radiant Pubs II) S Asia.

Women, Law & Social Change in India. Indu P. Singh. (C). 1988. 200.00 (*0-685-36502-6*) St Mut.

Women, Law & Social Control. Alida V. Merlo. 324p. (C). 1994. pap. text ed. 32.00 (*0-02-380567-6*, Macmillan Coll) P-H.

Women Lawyers. Mona Harrington. pap. 24.00 (*0-679-58025-5*) Random.

Women Lawyers: Rewriting the Rules. Mona Harrington. LC 93-18000. 1994. 24.00 (*0-394-58025-7*) Knopf.

Women Lawyers: Rewriting the Rules. Mona Harrington. LC 94-28332. 1995. pap. 11.95 (*0-452-27367-6*, Plume) NAL-Dutton.

Women Lawyers: Supplementary Data to the 1971 Lawyer Statistical Report. Ed. by Martha Grossblat & Bette H. Sikes. LC 52-1123. 104p. reprint ed. pap. 29.70 (*0-317-29201-3*, 2022253) Bks Demand.

Women Lawyers & the Origins of Professional Community in America: The Letters of the Equity Club, 1886-1890. Virginia G. Drachman. 160p. (C). 1992. text ed. 49.50 (*0-472-10305-9*) U of Mich Pr.

Women Lawyers Journal: 1911-1995/96, 82 vols., Set. Bound set. 1,480.00 (*0-8377-9187-1*) Rothman.

Women Leaders in African History. David Sweetman. (African Historical Biographies Ser.). (Illus.). 100p. (Orig.). (C). 1984. pap. 12.95 (*0-435-94480-0*, 94480) Heinemann.

*__Women Leaders in the Ancient Synagogue: Inscriptional Evidence & Background Issues.__ Bernadette J. Brooten. (Brown Judaic Studies). 290p. 1982. pap. 29.95 (*0-89130-670-6*, 140036) Scholars Pr GA.

Women Leaders of Colorado: "A Success Network of Outstanding Leaders" Doug McNair & Wallace Y. McNair. 78p. 1992. 40.00 (*0-9627600-2-1*) Wstrn Images.

Women Leading in Education. Ed. by Diane M. Dunlap & Patricia A. Schmuck. LC 94-7301. 444p. (C). 1994. text ed. 74.50 (*0-7914-2215-1*); pap. text ed. 24.95 (*0-7914-2216-X*) State U NY Pr.

Women Leaving the Workplace: How to Make the Transition from Work to Home. Larry Burkett. 1995. 18.99 (*0-8024-9161-8*) Moody.

Women, Leisure & the Family in Contemporary Society: A Multinational Perspective. Ed. by Nicole Samuel. 320p. 1996. 80.00 (*0-85199-120-3*) CAB Intl.

Women, Letters & the Novel. Ruth Perry. LC 79-8637. (Studies in the Eighteenth Century: No. 4). (Illus.). 1980. 39.50 (*0-404-18025-6*) AMS Pr.

Women Like Meat: The Folklore & Foraging Ideology of the Kalahari Ju - 'hoan. Megan Biesele. LC 93-12414. 247p. 1993. 31.50 (*0-253-31565-4*); pap. 15.95 (*0-253-31566-2*) Ind U Pr.

Women Like Us. Erica Abeel. 401p. 1993. 22.95 (*0-685-71261-3*) Ticknor & Fields.

Women Like Us, Vol. 1. Erica Abeel. 1995. mass mkt. 5.99 (*0-312-95506-5*) Tor Bks.

*__Women Like Us: Lives of Older Lesbians.__ Suzanne Nedd & Rosaland Pearson. pap. 15.95 (*0-7043-4285-5*, Pub. by Womens Press UK) Trafalgar.

Women Like Us: Wisdom for Today's Issues. R. Ruth Barton. (Fisherman Bible Studyguide Ser.). 96p. 1989. pap. text ed. 4.99 (*0-87788-943-0*) Shaw Pubs.

Women, Literature, Criticism. Ed. by Harry R. Garvin. LC 77-95051. (Bucknell Review Ser.: Vol. 24, No. 1). 177p. 1978. 22.00 (*0-8387-2230-X*) Bucknell U Pr.

Women Living Longer & Better: Ideas & Ideals from Swedish Health Care. Ed. by Gunnela Westlander. LC 88-2927. (Women & Health Ser.: Vol. 13, Nos. 3-4). (Illus.). 180p. 1988. pap. text ed. 3.95 (*0-918393-46-9*) Harrington Pk.

Women Living Single: 30 Women Share Their Stories of Navigating Through a Married World. Lee Reilly. 224p. 1996. 23.95 (*0-571-19888-0*) Faber & Faber.

Women, Love, & Power. Elaine H. Baruch. (C). 1991. text ed. 36.00 (*0-8147-1155-3*) NYU Pr.

Women, Love, & Power: Literary & Psychoanalytic Perspectives. Elaine H. Baruch. 288p. (C). 1992. pap. 17.50 (*0-8147-1199-5*) NYU Pr.

Women, Madness, & Medicine. Denise Russell. 1995. 55.95 (*0-7456-1260-1*) Blackwell Pubs.

Women, Madness & Medicine. Denise Russell. 1995. pap. 22.95 (*0-7456-1261-X*) Blackwell Pubs.

Women Make the Best Friends. large type ed. Lois Wyse. 209p. 1996. 21.95 (*0-7862-0580-6*) Thorndike Pr.

Women Make the Best Friends: A Celebration. Lois Wyse. 192p. 1995. 19.95 (*0-684-80188-4*, S&S) S&S Trade.

Women Making History: Conversations with Fifteen New Yorkers. Helen Benedict et al. Ed. by Maxine Gold. LC 85-2976. 160p. (Orig.). 1985. pap. 6.95 (*0-9610688-1-7*) NYC Comm Women.

Women Making Meaning: New Feminist Directions in Communication. Ed. by Lana F. Rakow. 304p. (C). 1992. pap. 16.95 (*0-415-90630-X*, A7425, Routledge NY) Routledge.

Women Making Music: The Western Art Tradition, 1150-1950. Ed. by Jane Bowers & Judith Tick. LC 85-8642. (Illus.). 424p. 1987. pap. text ed. 16.95 (*0-252-01470-7*) U of Ill Pr.

***Women, Male Violence & the Law.** Ed. by Julie Stubbs. (Institute of Criminology Monograph: No. 6). vi, 262p. 1994. pap. 36.00 (*0-86758-918-3*) Gaunt.

Women Managers: Travellers in a Male World. Judi Marshall. 251p. 1984. pap. text ed. 49.50 (*0-471-90419-8*) Wiley.

Women Managers in Human Services. Karen S. Haynes. 120p. 1989. 21.95 (*0-8261-5860-9*) Springer Pub.

Women Marine Association Pictorial. Turner Publishing Company Staff. LC 95-60551. 112p. 1995. 48.00 (*1-56311-208-6*) Turner Pub KY.

Women Marines: The World War II Era. Peter A. Soderbergh. LC 91-47594. 224p. 1992. text ed. 55.00 (*0-275-94131-0*, C4131, Praeger Pubs) Greenwood.

Women Marines Association History Book. Turner Publishing Co. Staff & Erika S. Nau. LC 91-67162. (Illus.). 176p. 1992. 48.00 (*1-56311-033-4*) Turner Pub KY.

Women Marines in the Korean War Era. Peter A. Soderbergh. LC 94-8382. 216p. 1994. text ed. 49.95 (*0-275-94827-7*, Praeger Pubs) Greenwood.

Women, Media, & Consumption in Japan. Ed. by Lise Skov & Brian Moeran. LC 95-19376. (ConsumAsiaN Ser.). 1995. text ed. 39.00 (*0-8248-1775-3*); pap. text ed. 19.95 (*0-8248-1776-1*) UH Pr.

Women, Media & Politics. Ed. by Pippa Norris. 288p. (C). 1996. 47.00 (*0-19-510566-4*); pap. 18.95 (*0-19-510567-2*) OUP.

Women, Media & Sport: Challenging Gender Values. Ed. by Pamela J. Creedon. LC 93-41211. 320p. (C). 1994. text ed. 55.00 (*0-8039-5233-3*); pap. text ed. 26.00 (*0-8039-5234-1*) Sage.

***Women, Medicine & Science 1500-1700: Mothers & Sisters of the Royal Society.** Ed. by Lynette Hunter & Sarah Hutton. (Illus.). 224p. 1997. 72.00 (*0-7509-1334-7*, Pub. by Sutton Pubng UK) Bks Intl VA.

***Women, Medicine & Science 1500-1700: Mothers & Sisters of the Royal Society.** Ed. by Lynette Hunter & Sarah Hutton. (Illus.). 224p. 1997. pap. 22.95 (*0-7509-1343-6*, Pub. by Sutton Pubng UK) Bks Intl VA.

***Women Memoirists.** Ed. by Harold Bloom. (Women Writers of English Ser.: Vol. 1). (Illus.). 200p. (YA). (gr. 9 up). 1997. pap. 16.95 (*0-7910-4501-3*); lib. bdg. 29.95 (*0-7910-4485-8*) Chelsea Hse.

***Women Memoirists.** Ed. by Harold Bloom. (Women Writers of English Ser.: Vol. 2). (YA). (gr. 9 up). 1997. lib. bdg. 29.95 (*0-7910-4654-0*) Chelsea Hse.

***Women Memoirists.** Ed. by Harold Bloom. (Women Writers of English Ser.: Vol. 2). (YA). (gr. 9 up). 1997. pap. 16.95 (*0-7910-4655-9*) Chelsea Hse.

Women, Men & Ethnicity: Essays on the Structure & Thought of American Jewry. William Toll. LC 90-12030. 240p. (C). 1991. pap. text ed. 27.50 (*0-8191-7759-8*); lib. bdg. 48.00 (*0-8191-7758-X*) U Pr of Amer.

***Women, Men & Eunuchs: Gender in Byzantium.** Liz James. LC 96-44590. 288p. (C). 1997. pap. write for info. (*0-415-14686-0*); text ed. write for info. (*0-415-14685-2*) Routledge.

Women, Men, & Gender: Ongoing Debates. Ed. by Mary R. Walsh. LC 96-16540. 448p. 1996. 45.00 (*0-300-06896-4*) Yale U Pr.

Women, Men & Gender: Ongoing Debates. Ed. by Mary R. Walsh. 448p. 1996. pap. 20.00 (*0-300-06938-3*) Yale U Pr.

Women, Men & Language. Jennifer Coates. (Studies in Language & Linguistics). 200p. 1986. pap. text ed. 16.95 (*0-582-29133-X*, 71759) Longman.

Women, Men, & Language: A Sociolinguistic Account of Gender Differences in Language. 2nd ed. Jennifer Coates. LC 92-30487. (Studies in Language & Linguistics). 272p. (C). 1993. pap. text ed. 24.85 (*0-582-07492-4*) Longman.

Women, Men, & Marriage: Talks from the Tavistock Marital Studies Institute. Ed. by Christopher Clulow. LC 96-1115. 176p. 1996. pap. 23.95 (*1-56821-819-2*) Aronson.

Women, Men & Politeness. Janet Holmes. Ed. by Jennifer Coates et al. LC 94-28156. (Real Language Ser.). 264p. (C). 1995. text ed. 44.95 (*0-582-06362-0*) Longman.

Women, Men, & Power. Hilary M. Lips. LC 90-41065. 245p. (C). 1991. pap. text ed. 24.95 (*0-87484-916-0*, 916) Mayfield Pub.

Women, Men & Society. 3rd ed. Claire M. Renzetti & Daniel J. Curran. LC 94-31685. (LSMS Working Paper Ser.). 1994. pap. text ed. 45.00 (*0-205-15619-3*) Allyn.

Women, Men, & Society: The Sociology of Gender. Claire M. Renzetti & Daniel J. Curran. 400p. 1989. pap. text ed. write for info. (*0-205-11898-4*, H18989) Allyn.

Women, Men, & the Great War: An Anthology of Stories. Ed. & Intro. by Trudi Tate. LC 95-11046. 320p. 1996. text ed. 59.95 (*0-7190-4597-5*, Pub. by Manchester Univ Pr UK); text ed. 19.95 (*0-7190-4598-3*, Pub. by Manchester Univ Pr UK) St Martin.

Women, Men, & the International Division of Labor. Ed. by June C. Nash & Maria P. Fernandez-Kelly. LC 82-10447. (SUNY Series in the Anthropology of Work). (Illus.). 463p. (C). 1984. text ed. 49.50 (*0-87395-683-4*); pap. text ed. 16.95 (*0-87395-684-2*) State U NY Pr.

Women, Men, & Time: Gender Difference in Paid Work, Housework, & Leisure. Beth A. Shelton. LC 91-36332. (Contributions in Women's Studies: No. 127). 192p. 1992. text ed. 49.95 (*0-313-26512-7*, SWX/, Greenwood Pr) Greenwood.

Women Men Love - Women Men Leave. Connell Cowan & Melvyn Kinder. 1988. pap. 5.99 (*0-451-16641-8*, Sig) NAL-Dutton.

Women Men Love - Women Men Leave. Connell Cowan & Melvyn Kinder. 320p. 1990. pap. 4.95 (*0-451-15306-5*, Sig) NAL-Dutton.

Women-Men-Management. 2nd ed. Ann Harriman. 1996. write for info. (*0-02-759468-8*, Praeger Pubs) Greenwood.

Women Mentoring Women: Creative Ways to Start, Maintain & Expand a Biblical Women's Ministry. Vickie Kraft. 1992. wbk. ed., pap. 14.99 (*0-8024-9565-6*) Moody.

Women, Microenterprise, & the Politics of Self-Help. rev. ed. Cheryl R. Rodriguez. LC 94-49558. (Garland Studies in Entrepreneurship). 140p. 1995. text ed. 44.00 (*0-8153-1969-X*) Garland.

Women, Migrants & Tribals: Survival Strategies in Asia. Ed. by G. K. Lieten et al. (C). 1989. 22.50 (*81-85054-77-0*, Pub. by Manohar II) S Asia.

Women, Militarism, & War: Essays in History, Politics, & Social Theory. Ed. by Jean B. Elshtain & Sheila Tobias. LC 88-26409. (New Feminist Perspectives Ser.). 284p. (Orig.). (C). 1990. pap. text ed. 23.95 (*0-8476-7470-3*); lib. bdg. 59.50 (*0-8476-7469-X*) Rowman.

Women Ministers: A Quaker Contribution. Robert J. Leach. Ed. by Ruth Blattenberger. LC 79-84922. 1979. pap. 3.00 (*0-87574-227-0*) Pendle Hill.

***Women Ministers According to Scripture.** Judy L. Brown. 348p. (Orig.). 1997. pap. 15.95 (*1-57502-449-7*, PO1042B) Morris Pubng.

Women, Minorities & Unions in the Public Sector. Norma M. Riccucci. LC 89-7481. (Contributions in Labor Studies: No. 28). 200p. 1990. text ed. 49.95 (*0-313-26043-5*, RWM, Quorum Bks) Greenwood.

Women, Minority & Small Business Discrimination. C. Anthony Chimpa & Anthony Chimpa. LC 89-91070. 96p. (Orig.). 1989. pap. 15.95 (*0-922958-07-6*) H W Parker.

***Women Modern America.** 3rd ed. Banner. (C). 1995. pap. write for info. (*0-15-500948-6*) HB Coll Pubs.

Women, Motherhood, & Childrearing. Diane Richardson. LC 92-19905. 1993. text ed. 35.00 (*0-312-08593-1*) St Martin.

Women Murdered by the Men They Loved. Constance A. Bean. LC 91-23994. 196p. 1992. pap. 14.95 (*1-56023-003-7*); lib. bdg. 29.95 (*1-56024-106-3*) Haworth Pr.

Women Music Makers. Janet Nichols. 224p. (YA). (gr. 7 up). 1992. 18.95 (*0-8027-8168-3*); lib. bdg. 19.85 (*0-8027-8169-1*) Walker & Co.

Women Musicians of Venice: Musical Foundations, 1525-1855. rev. ed. Jane J. Baldauf-Berdes. (Oxford Monographs on Music). 336p. 1996. pap. 24.95 (*0-19-816604-4*) OUP.

Women Must Weep & Women Must Work. Mary Orr. 1963. pap. 5.25 (*0-8222-1273-0*) Dramatists Play.

Women My Husband Married: Prose & Verse. Clarine C. Gren Fell. 136p. reprint ed. pap. 8.50 (*0-9612766-2-2*) Gren Fell Read Ctr.

Women Mystics. Louis Bouyer. Tr. by Ann E. Nash from FRE. LC 92-75067. 200p. (Orig.). 1993. pap. 13.95 (*0-89870-434-0*) Ignatius Pr.

***Women Mystics Confront the Modern World: Marie de l'Incarnation (1599-1672) & Madame Guyon (1648-1717)** Marie-Florine Bruneau. LC 97-19144. (Series in Western Esoteric Traditions). 256p. (C). 1998. text ed. 59.50 (*0-7914-3661-6*) State U NY Pr.

***Women Mystics Confront the Modern World: Marie de l'Incarnation (1599-1672) & Madame Guyon (1648-1717)** Marie-Florine Bruneau. LC 97-19144. (Series in Western Esoteric Traditions). 256p. (C). 1998. pap. text ed. 19.95 (*0-7914-3662-4*) State U NY Pr.

Women Mystics in Medieval Europe. Emilie Z. Brunn & Georgette Epiney-Burgard. Tr. by Sheila Hughes. (Illus.). 233p. 1989. 24.95 (*0-913729-16-7*); pap. 12.95 (*1-55778-196-6*) Paragon Hse.

***Women Mystics, Visionaries, Prophets: An Anthology, 2 vols.** Shawn Madigan. Incl. Vol. 2. . Orig. Title: Beyond Inculturation. (Orig.). 1997. pap. 15.95 (*1-56929-055-5*); Vol. 1. . Orig. Title: Beyond Inculturation. 312p. (Orig.). 1997. pap. 15.95 (*1-56929-054-7*); 30.00 (*1-56929-053-9*) Pastoral Pr.

***Women, Myth, & the Feminine Principle.** Bettina L. Knapp. 352p. (C). 1997. text ed. 59.50 (*0-7914-3527-X*); pap. text ed. 19.95 (*0-7914-3528-8*) State U NY Pr.

Women, Nazis, & Universities: Female University Students in the Third Reich, 1933-1945. Jacques R. Pauwels. LC 83-20161. (Contributions in Women's Studies: No. 50). (Illus.). 288p. 1984. text ed. 49.95 (*0-313-24203-8*, PWU/, Greenwood Pr) Greenwood.

***Women, New Technology & Development: Changing Nature of Gender Relations in Rural India.** Debal K. Roy. (C). 1995. 30.00 (*81-7304-102-4*, Pub. by Manohar II) S Asia.

Women Nineteen Fifty-Seven to Nineteen Seventy-Five. Photos by Joan Liffring-Zug. LC 81-80099. (Illus.). 72p. 1981. pap. 12.95 (*0-9603858-4-3*) Penfield.

Women Novelists. Muriel A. Masefield. 1972. 59.95 (*0-8490-1323-2*) Gordon Pr.

Women Novelists. Reginald Johnson. LC 72-3467. (Studies in Fiction: No. 34). 1972. reprint ed. lib. bdg. 75.00 (*0-8383-1496-1*) M S G Haskell Hse.

Women Novelists. Reginald B. Johnson. LC 67-23235. (Essay Index Reprint Ser.). 1977. reprint ed. 20.95 (*0-8369-0576-8*) Ayer.

Women Novelists. Reginald B. Johnson. (BCL1-PR English Literature Ser.). 299p. 1992. reprint ed. lib. bdg. 79.00 (*0-7812-7023-5*) Rprt Serv.

Women Novelists from Fanny Burney to George Eliot. Muriel A. Masefield. LC 67-23244. (Essay Index Reprint Ser.). 1977. 19.95 (*0-8369-0689-6*) Ayer.

Women Novelists of the Eighteenth Century. Comment by Doreen A. Saar & Mary A. Schofield. 1997. 65.00 (*0-8161-9085-2*) G K Hall.

Women Novelists Today: A Survey of English Writers in the Seventies & Eighties. Olga Kenyon. LC 87-35602. 208p. 1988. text ed. 35.00 (*0-312-01344-2*) St Martin.

Women of a Lesser Cost: Female Labour, Foreign Exchange, & Philippine Development. Sylvia Chant et al. LC 94-45270. (C). 69.95 (*0-7453-0946-1*, Pub. by Pluto Pr UK); pap. 21.95 (*0-7453-0945-3*, Pub. by Pluto Pr UK) LPC InBook.

Women of Academe: Outsiders in the Sacred Grove. Nadya Aisenberg & Mona Harrington. LC 87-30067. 224p. 1988. pap. 17.95 (*0-87023-607-5*) U of Mass Pr.

Women of Algiers in Their Apartment. Assia Djebar. Tr. by Marjolijn De Jager from FRE. LC 92-16856. (CARAF Ser.). 224p. (C). 1992. text ed. 19.95 (*0-8139-1402-7*) U Pr of Va.

Women of America. Berkin. (C). 1995. pap. 38.76 (*0-395-74155-6*) HM.

Women of Amran: A Middle Eastern Ethnographic Study. Susan Dorsky. LC 85-26534. (Illus.). 216p. 1986. 22.50 (*0-87480-250-4*) U of Utah Pr.

Women of Aromatherapy: Complete Aromatherapy by the People Who Made It So. Ed. by Jeanne Rose & Susan Earle. (Illus.). 310p. (Orig.). 1996. pap. 17.95 (*1-879687-06-2*) Herb Studies.

***Women of Awakenings: The Historic Contribution of Women to Revival Movements.** Lewis Drummond & Betty Drummond. 432p. 1997. pap. 16.99 (*0-8254-2474-7*) Kregel.

Women of Azua: Work & Family in the Rural Dominican Republic. Barbara Finlay. LC 89-35842. 204p. 1989. text ed. 49.95 (*0-275-93220-6*, C3220, Praeger Pubs) Greenwood.

Women of Babylon. Sylvia Wilde. (Orig.). 1994. mass mkt. 4.95 (*1-56333-171-3*) Masquerade.

Women of Belize: Gender & Change in Central America. Irma McClaurin. LC 95-52269. (Illus.). 240p. (C). 1996. text ed. 48.00 (*0-8135-2307-9*); pap. text ed. 16.95 (*0-8135-2308-7*) Rutgers U Pr.

Women of Ben Jonson's Poetry: Female Representations in the Non-Dramatic Verse. Barbara Smith. 144p. 1995. 49.95 (*1-85928-228-8*, Pub. by Scolar Pr UK) Ashgate Pub Co.

Women of Bengal. M. M. Urquhart. 165p. (C). 1987. reprint ed. 24.50 (*0-8364-2159-0*, Pub. by Gian Publng Hse II) S Asia.

Women of Bloomsbury: Virginia, Vanessa & Carrington. Mary A. Caws. (Illus.). 218p. (C). 1991. pap. 16.95 (*0-415-90398-X*, A5903, Routledge NY) Routledge.

Women of Brewster Place. Gloria R. Naylor. (Contemporary American Fiction Ser.). 208p. 1983. pap. 10.95 (*0-14-006690-X*, Penguin Bks) Viking Penguin.

Women of Brewster Place: A Novel in Seven Stories. Gloria R. Naylor. 1988. pap. 4.50 (*0-318-37688-1*, Penguin Bks) Viking Penguin.

Women of Cairo: Scenes of Life on the Orient, 2 Vols., Set. Gerard De Nerval. LC 77-87652. 720p. reprint ed. 115.00 (*0-404-16420-X*) AMS Pr.

Women of Candelaria. Mary R. Miller. LC 96-26463. (Illus.). 128p. (Orig.). 1996. pap. 31.95 (*0-7649-0005-6*) Pomegranate Calif.

Women of Catawba. Hilda Stahl. LC 93-32557. 240p. 1993. pap. 9.99 (*0-8407-5080-3*) Nelson.

Women of Character: Life-Changing Examples of Godly Women. Debra Evans. 208p. 1996. 14.99 (*0-310-20153-5*) Zondervan.

***Women of Character Bible Studies, 8 vols.** Incl. Bk. 1. Woman of Balance. Juanita Ryan. 64p. 1997. wbk. ed., pap. 4.99 (*0-8308-2041-8*, 2041); Bk. 2. Woman of Creativity. Sandy Larsen. 64p. (Orig.). 1997. wbk. ed., pap. 4.99 (*0-8308-2045-0*, 2045); Bk. 3. Woman of Confidence. Juanita Ryan. 64p. (Orig.). 1997. wbk. ed., pap. 4.99 (*0-8308-2044-2*, 2044); Bk. 4. Woman of Beauty. Juanita Ryan. 64p. (Orig.). 1997. wbk. ed., pap. 4.99 (*0-8308-2042-6*, 2042); Bk. 5. Woman of Grace. Sandy Larsen. 64p. (Orig.). 1997. wbk. ed., pap. 4.99 (*0-8308-2047-7*, 2047); Bk. 6. Woman of Rest. Phyllis J. LePeau. 64p. (Orig.). 1997. wbk. ed., pap. 4.99 (*0-8308-2048-5*, 2048); Bk. 7. Woman of Family. Carolyn Nystrom. 64p. (Orig.). 1997. wbk. ed., pap. 4.99 (*0-8308-2046-9*, 2046); Bk. 8. Woman of Blessing. Juanita Ryan. 64p. (Orig.). 1997. wbk. ed., pap. 4.99 (*0-8308-2043-4*, 2043); Set wbk. ed. 39.92 (*0-8308-2040-X*, 2040) InterVarsity.

***Women of Christ: Be of Good Cheer.** Lucile Johnson. 50p. 1997. pap. 3.95 (*1-57734-098-1*) Covenant Comms.

Women of Classical Mythology: A Biographical Dictionary. Robert E. Bell. LC 91-26649. (Illus.). 300p. 1991. lib. bdg. 60.00 (*0-87436-581-3*) ABC-CLIO.

Women of Classical Mythology: A Biographical Dictionary. Robert E. Bell. LC 92-22754. 480p. (C). 1993. pap. 15.95 (*0-19-507977-9*) OUP.

Women of Coal. Randall Norris. (Illus.). 128p. 1996. 24.95 (*0-8131-1993-6*) U Pr of Ky.

Women of Color. Mathias. 1996. pap. write for info. (*0-345-40625-7*) Ballantine Trade.

Women of Color. Darlene Mathis. 1996. pap. write for info. (*0-345-39775-4*) Ballantine.

Women of Color: A Filmography of Minority & Third World Women. Maryann Oshana. LC 82-49143. 350p. 1984. text ed. 45.00 (*0-8240-9140-X*) Garland.

Women of Color: Integrating Ethnic & Gender Identities in Psychotherapy. Lillian Comas-Diaz & Beverly Greene. LC 94-10840. 630p. 1994. lib. bdg. 46.95 (*0-89862-371-5*, C2371) Guilford Pr.

Women of Color: Mother-Daughter Relationships in Twentieth-Century Literature. Ed. by Elizabeth Brown-Guillory. LC 96-15697. 1997. write for info. (*0-292-70846-7*); pap. write for info. (*0-292-70847-5*) U of Tex Pr.

Women of Color & Southern Women: A Bibliography of Social Science Research 1975-1988. Ed. by Andrea Timberlake et al. LC 88-63010. 264p. (Orig.). (C). 1988. pap. 10.00 (*0-9621327-0-5*) U Memphis-Ctr Res Women.

Women of Color & Southern Women: A Bibliography of Social Science Research 1975-1988. Annual Supplement, 1989. Ed. by Andrea Timberlake et al. LC 89-63010. 175p. (Orig.). (C). 1990. pap. 8.50 (*0-9621327-1-3*) U Memphis-Ctr Res Women.

Women of Color & Southern Women: A Bibliography of Social Science Research 1975-1988. Annual Supplement, 1990. Ed. by Andrea Timberlake et al. LC 90-656447. 142p. (Orig.). (C). 1991. pap. 8.50 (*0-9621327-2-1*) U Memphis-Ctr Res Women.

***Women of Color & Southern Women: A Bibliography of Social Science Research 1975-1988: Annual Supplement, 1991/1992.** Ed. by Lynn Weber et al. LC 90-656447. 180p. (Orig.). 1992. pap. 8.50 (*0-9621327-3-X*) U Memphis-Ctr Res Women.

***Women of Color & Southern Women: A Bibliography of Social Science Research, 1975-1988: Annual Supplement, 1993/1994.** Ed. by Stella A. Warren et al. LC 90-656447. 183p. (Orig.). 1994. pap. 10.00 (*0-9621327-4-8*) U Memphis-Ctr Res Women.

Women of Color & the Multicultural Curriculum: Transforming the College Classroom. Ed. by Mariam Chamberlain & Liza Fiol-Matta. 350p. (C). 1994. 35.00 (*1-55861-082-0*); pap. 18.95 (*1-55861-083-9*) Feminist Pr.

Women of Color in Librarianship: An Oral History. Committee on the Status of Women in Librarianship Staff. LC 92-42391. (Illus.). 1993. write for info. (*0-8389-7639-5*) ALA.

Women of Color in Science, Mathematics, & Engineering: A Review of the Literature. Beatriz C. Clewell & Bernice Anderson. (Educational Equity Policy Studies). 104p. (Orig.). (C). 1991. pap. 17.00 (*1-877966-04-5*) Ctr Women Policy.

Women of Color in United States Society. Ed. by Maxine B. Zinn & Bonnie T. Dill. LC 93-9448. (Women in the Political Economy Ser.). 360p. 1993. 54.95 (*1-56639-105-9*); pap. 19.95 (*1-56639-106-7*) Temple U Pr.

Women of Congress: A Twentieth-Century Odyssey. Marcy Kaptur. LC 96-22556. 256p. 1996. 23.95 (*0-87187-989-1*) Congr Quarterly.

Women of Country. Friedman-Fairfax & Sony Music Staff. 1995. pap. 16.98 incl. audio compact disk (*1-56799-079-7*, Friedman-Fairfax) M Friedman Pub Grp Inc.

Women of Covenant: The Story of Relief Society. Jill M. Derr et al. LC 91-47981. (Illus.). 544p. 1992. 21.00 (*0-87579-593-5*) Deseret Bk.

Women of Crisis: Lives of Struggle & Hope. 2nd ed. Robert Coles. 1990. pap. 9.95 (*0-201-18608-X*) Addison-Wesley.

Women of Crisis II. Robert Coles. 1990. pap. 9.95 (*0-201-51811-2*) Addison-Wesley.

Women of Darkness II. Ed. by Kathryn Ptacek. 1994. pap. write for info. (*0-8125-0837-8*) Tor Bks.

Women of Deh Koh: Lives in an Iranian Village. Erika Friedl. 256p. 1991. reprint ed. pap. 11.95 (*0-14-014993-7*, Penguin Bks) Viking Penguin.

Women of Devotion. 1991. pap. 13.99 (*0-87148-959-7*) Pathway Pr.

W

An Asterisk (*) at the beginning of an entry indicates that the title is appearing in BIP for the first time.

Women of Early Christianity. Alexander Carroll. 1978. 300.00 (*0-87968-268-X*) Gordon Pr.

Women of Eastern & Southern Africa: A Bibliography, 1976-1985. Compiled by Davis A. Bullwinkle. LC 89-2154. 570p. 1989. text ed. 79.50 (*0-313-26606-9*, BWM, Greenwood Pr) Greenwood.

Women of El Salvador: The Price of Freedom. Marilyn Thomson. 184p. (C). 1986. pap. 17.50 (*0-86232-523-4*, Pub. by Zed Bks Ltd UK); text ed. 45.00 (*0-86232-522-6*, Pub. by Zed Bks Ltd UK) Humanities.

Women of Engelthal. Hindsley. Date not set. text ed. 45.00 (*0-312-16251-0*) St Martin.

Women of Europe: Women Members of the European Parliament & Equality Policy. Elizabeth Vallance & Elizabeth Davies. 200p. 1986. 54.95 (*0-521-26562-2*) Cambridge U Pr.

Women of Exile: German-Jewish Autobiographies Since Nineteen Thirty-Three. Ed. by Andreas Lixl-Purcell. LC 87-24952. (Contributions in Women's Studies: No. 91). 241p. 1988. text ed. 49.95 (*0-313-25921-6*, LXP/, Greenwood Pr) Greenwood.

Women of Fair Hope. Paul M. Gaston. (Illus.). 158p. 1993. pap. 12.00 (*1-881320-15-4*, Black Belt Pr) Black Belt Comm.

***Women of Faith.** Esther Clothes. (J). 1992. write for info. (*5-900522-81-4*, Chariot Bks) Chariot Victor.

Women of Faith: Church of Scotland Woman's Guild. Church of Scotland Woman's Guild Staff. 160p. 1993. pap. 21.00 (*0-86153-170-1*, Pub. by St Andrew UK) St Mut.

Women of Faith: Portraits of Twelve Spirit-Filled Women. Grace S. Swenson. LC 91-18687. 216p. 1991. pap. 19.95 (*0-87839-063-4*) North Star.

Women of Faith, Come into the Knowledge of Who You Are! Carrie Johnson. (Orig.). 1996. pap. 8.95 (*0-533-11826-3*) Vantage.

Women of Faith in Dialogue. Virginia R. Mollenkott. 144p. (Orig.). 1987. pap. 9.95 (*0-8245-0823-8*) Crossroad NY.

Women of Fire & Spirit: History, Faith & Gender in Roho Religion in Western Kenya. Cynthia Hoehler-Fatton. (Illus.). 304p. 1996. 45.00 (*0-19-509790-4*); pap. 19.95 (*0-19-509791-2*) OUP.

Women of Florence. Richard C. Trexler. LC 92-44785. (Power & Dependence in Renaissance Florence Ser.: Vol. 2). 104p. 1993. pap. 8.95 (*0-86698-157-8*, P16) Pegasus Pr.

Women of Flowers: A Tribute to Victorian Women Artists. Jack Kramer. LC 96-17747. (Illus.). 224p. Date not set. 35.00 (*1-55670-497-6*) Stewart Tabori & Chang.

Women of Genesis: From Sarah to Potiphar's Wife. Sharon P. Jeansonne. LC 89-78124. 160p. (Orig.). 1990. pap. 15.00 (*0-8006-2419-X*, 1-2419) Augsburg Fortress.

***Women of God.** Frieda Upson. 143p. pap. 5.50 (*0-86687-094-6*) Greek Orthdx Archdcse.

Women of God, Women of the People: Four Biblical Meditations. Ada M. Isasi-Diaz. 64p. (Orig.). 1995. pap. 5.99 (*0-8272-4233-6*) Chalice Pr.

Women of Grace. Betty J. Grams. LC 77-93409. 127p. 1978. pap. 2.50 (*0-88243-751-8*, 02-0751); teacher ed., pap. 3.95 (*0-88243-336-9*, 02-0336) Gospel Pub.

Women of Grace: A Biographical Dictionary of British Women Saints, Martyrs & Reformers. Kathleen Parbury. 224p. 1984. 25.00 (*0-85362-213-2*) Routledge.

Women of Grace: James's Plays & the Comedy of Manners. Susan Carlson. LC 84-23932. (Studies in Modern Literature: No. 48). 199p. reprint ed. pap. 56.80 (*0-8357-1617-1*, 2070536) Bks Demand.

Women of Granite. Jennings. 1992. 21.95 (*0-15-198367-4*) HarBrace.

***Women of Granite.** Dana A. Jennings. 296p. 3.98 (*0-8317-3670-4*) Smithmark.

Women of Great Taste: A Salute to Women for Their Zest for Food. Junior League Members of Wichita Staff. (Illus.). 256p. 1995. 24.95 (*0-9609676-2-1*) Jr League Wichita.

Women of Hawaii. Don Berry. (Illus.). 84p. (Orig.). 1986. pap. 17.95 (*0-916947-04-1*) Winn Bks.

Women of Helfta: Scholars & Mystics. Mary J. Finnegan. LC 90-39089. 192p. 1991. reprint ed. 35.00 (*0-8203-1291-6*) U of Ga Pr.

Women of Honor: God's Incredible Plan for Fulfillment. Jeanne Hendricks. 1995. 17.99 (*1-885305-13-3*) Multnomah Pubs.

***Women of Hope: African Americans Who Made a Difference.** Joyce Hansen & Bread & Roses Staff. LC 96-32117. (J). 1997. write for info. (*0-590-93973-4*) Scholastic Inc.

***Women of Hull House: A Study in Spirituality, Vocation & Friendship.** Eleanor J. Stebner. LC 97-4960. 256p. (C). 1997. pap. text ed. 19.95 (*0-7914-3488-5*) State U NY Pr.

***Women of Hull House: A Study in Spirituality, Vocation & Friendship.** Eleanor J. Stebner. LC 97-4960. 256p. (C). 1997. text ed. 59.50 (*0-7914-3487-7*) State U NY Pr.

***Women of Illusion.** Frega. Date not set. write for info. (*0-312-17718-6*) St Martin.

Women of Impressionism. Nancy M. Mathews. pap. write for info. (*0-679-42582-9*) Random.

***Women of Impressionism.** Nancy M. Mathews. 288p. Date not set. 35.00 (*0-06-017386-6*) HarpC.

Women of Influence. Philip Burnard. 1995. per. 10.95 (*0-919926-82-7*, Pub. by Coteau CN) Genl Dist Srvs.

Women of Influence, Women of Vision: A Cross-Generational Study of Leaders & Social Change. Helen S. Astin & Carole A. Leland. LC 91-10784. (Social & Behavioral Science Ser.). 229p. 31.95 (*1-55542-357-4*) Jossey-Bass.

***Women of Ireland: A Biographic Dictionary.** Kit O. Ceirin & Cyril O. Ceirin. (Illus.). 228p. (Orig.). 1996. pap. 19.95 (*0-937702-16-1*) Irish Bks Media.

Women of Iron & Velvet & the Books They Wrote in France. Margaret Crosland. LC 77-359824. 255p. reprint ed. pap. 72.70 (*0-317-29891-7*, 2019384) Bks Demand.

Women of Japan & Korea: Continuity & Change. Ed. by Joyce Galb & Marian L. Palley. LC 93-46966. (Women in the Political Economy Ser.). 320p. 1994. text ed. 59.95 (*1-56639-223-3*); pap. text ed. 22.95 (*1-56639-224-1*) Temple U Pr.

***Women of Lebanon: Interviews with Champions for Peace.** Nelda LaTeef. LC 97-14088. (Illus.). 396p. 1997. pap. 37.50 (*0-7864-0329-2*) McFarland & Co.

Women of Letters, 2 vols. Gertrude T. Mayer. LC 73-1197. (Essay Index Reprint Ser.). 1977. reprint ed. 53.95 (*0-518-10059-6*) Ayer.

Women of Letters, 96 vols., Set. (AMS Press Reprint Ser.). reprint ed. write for info. (*0-404-56700-2*) AMS Pr.

Women of Lillian Hall. Sandra Sheffield. 35p. (Orig.). 1987. pap. 10.00 (*0-317-93047-8*) Open Bks Pubs.

Women of Lowell: An Original Anthology. Ed. by Leon Stein & Annette K. Baxter. LC 74-3989. (Women in America Ser.). 362p. 1977. reprint ed. 31.95 (*0-405-06127-7*) Ayer.

Women of Manhattan. John P. Shanley. 1987. pap. 5.25 (*0-8222-1274-9*) Dramatists Play.

Women of Mark: A History of the Woman's Club of Richmond, Virginia, 1894-1994. Sandra G. Treadway. LC 95-76549. 176p. 1995. 24.95 (*0-88490-183-1*) Library of VA.

Women of Marrakech. Leonora Peets. Tr. by Rein Taagepera from EST. LC 87-26536. 200p. 1988. text ed. 35.95 (*0-8223-0812-6*) Duke.

Women of Mathematics: A Bibliographic Sourcebook. Ed. by Louise S. Grinstein & Paul J. Campbell. LC 86-25711. 312p. 1987. text ed. 69.50 (*0-313-24849-4*, GWM/, Greenwood Pr) Greenwood.

Women of Medieval France. Pierce Butler. 1978. 300.00 (*0-87968-269-8*) Gordon Pr.

Women of Mexico: The Consecrated & the Commoners. Bobette Gugliotta. (Mujer Latina Ser.). (Illus.). 191p. 1990. pap. 19.95 (*0-915745-16-X*) Floricanto Pr.

Women of Mexico City, 1790-1857. Silvia M. Arrom. xvi, 384p. (C). pap. 17.95 (*0-8047-2095-9*) Stanford U Pr.

Women of Mexico City, 1790-1857. Silvia M. Arrom. LC 83-51324. (Illus.). 400p. 1985. 49.50 (*0-8047-1233-6*) Stanford U Pr.

Women of Modern Science. Edna Yost. LC 84-12981. (Illus.). xiv, 176p. 1984. reprint ed. text ed. 59.75 (*0-313-23115-X*, YOWS, Greenwood Pr) Greenwood.

Women of Mongolia. Martha Avery. (Illus.). 152p. 1996. write for info. (*0-614-15016-7*); 19.95 (*0-937321-05-2*) Avery Pr CO.

Women of Morning. large type ed. Alan Sewart. 253p. 1993. pap. 17.99 (*1-85389-347-1*) Ulverscroft.

Women of Mr. Wesley's Methodism. Earl K. Brown. LC 83-22010. (Studies in Women & Religion: Vol. 11). 273p. 1984. lib. bdg. 89.95 (*0-88946-538-X*) E Mellen.

Women of Muriel Spark. Judith Sproxton. LC 92-4795. 224p. 1992. text ed. 39.95 (*0-312-08116-2*) St Martin.

Women of My Other Worlds. Olivia Casberg. LC 84-27221. 100p. (Orig.). 1985. pap. 5.95 (*0-933380-30-5*) Olive Pr Pubns.

Women of Mystery. Ed. by Cynthia Mansen et al. 336p. (Orig.). 1993. mass mkt. 5.99 (*0-425-13747-3*) Berkley Pub.

Women of Mystery II. Cynthia Manson. 1995. mass mkt. 5.99 (*0-425-15054-2*) Berkley Pub.

Women of Nauvoo. Richard N. Holzapfel & Jeni B. Holzapfel. 1992. 11.95 (*0-88494-835-8*) Bookcraft Inc.

Women of Nauvoo. Richard N. Holzapfel & Jeni B. Holzapfel. 1995. audio 7.95 (*1-57008-097-6*) Bookcraft Inc.

Women of New Mexico: Depression Era Images. Ed. by Marta Weigle. LC 88-72049. (New Deal & Folk Culture Ser.). (Illus.). 144p. 1993. 32.95 (*0-941270-55-6*); pap. 17.95 (*0-941270-54-8*) Ancient City Pr.

Women of New York: The Underworld of the Great City. George Ellington. LC 72-2600. (American Women Ser.: Images & Realities). 770p. 1974. reprint ed. 44.95 (*0-405-04456-9*) Ayer.

Women of Northern, Western, & Central Africa: A Bibliography, 1976-1985. Compiled by Davis A. Bullwinkle. LC 89-2160. (African Special Bibliographic Ser.: No. 10). 628p. 1989. text ed. 79.50 (*0-313-26609-3*, BWY, Greenwood Pr) Greenwood.

***Women of OJ Simpson.** Linda Marx. Date not set. write for info. (*0-688-14496-9*) Morrow.

***Women of Oklahoma, 1890-1920.** Linda W. Reece. LC 97-7549. (Illus.). 1997. 28.95 (*0-8061-2955-7*) U of Okla Pr.

***Women of Oklahoma, 1890-1920.** Linda W. Reese. LC 97-7549. (Illus.). 384p. 1997. pap. 18.95 (*0-8061-2999-9*) U of Okla Pr.

***Women of Paris & Their French Revolution.** Dominique Godineau. LC 96-31744. (Studies on the History of Society & Culture). 1998. write for info. (*0-520-06718-5*); pap. write for info. (*0-520-06719-3*) U CA Pr.

Women of Peace: Nobel Peace Prize Winners. Anne Schraff. LC 93-37429. (Collective Biographies Ser.). (Illus.). 112p. (YA). (gr. 6 up). 1994. lib. bdg. 18.95 (*0-89490-493-0*) Enslow Pubs.

Women of Phokeng: Consciousness, Life Strategy, & Migrancy in South Africa, 1900-1983. Belinda Bozzoli & Mmantho Nkotsoe. LC 91-9326. (Social History of Africa Ser.). 292p. (C). 1991. pap. 22.95 (*0-435-08056-3*, 08056) Heinemann.

Women of Plums: Poems in the Voice of Slave Women. Dolores Kendrick. 124p. 1990. reprint ed. pap. 11.95 (*0-939618-08-7*) Phillips Exeter.

Women of Power. Laurel King. LC 89-38149. 224p. 1995. pap. 14.95 (*0-89087-580-4*) Celestial Arts.

Women of Power & Grace: Nine Astonishing, Inspiring Luminaries of Our Time. Timothy Conway. (Illus.). 352p. 1995. 22.95 (*1-882978-26-9*) Wake Up Pr.

Women of Power & Grace: Nine Astonishing, Inspiring Luminaries of Our Time. Timothy Conway. (Illus.). 352p. 1995. reprint ed. pap. 16.95 (*1-882978-27-7*) Wake Up Pr.

Women of Power & Presence: The Spiritual Formation of Four Quaker Women Ministers. Maureen Graham. LC 90-62977. 32p. (Orig.). 1990. pap. 3.00 (*0-87574-294-7*) Pendle Hill.

Women of Prague: Ethnic Diversity & Social Change from the 18th Century to the Present. Wilma A. Iggers. LC 95-1636. 400p. (C). 1995. 59.95 (*1-57181-008-0*); pap. 25.00 (*1-57181-009-9*) Berghahn Bks.

Women of Prayer, Released to the Nations. 210p. 1993. pap. 9.95 (*1-56616-004-9*, 531040) Aglow Communs.

Women of Providence. large type ed. Sally Stewart. 540p. 1992. 25.99 (*0-7505-0201-0*) Ulverscroft.

Women of Psychology: Pioneers & Innovators, I. Gwendolyn Stevens & Sheldon Gardner. 273p. 1982. text ed. 22.95 (*0-87073-443-1*); pap. text ed. 18.95 (*0-87073-444-X*) Schenkman Bks Inc.

Women of Psychology: Pioneers & Innovators, II. Gwendolyn Stevens & Sheldon Gardner. 273p. 1982. text ed. 22.95 (*0-87073-445-8*) Schenkman Bks Inc.

Women of Psychology: Pioneers & Innovators, Set. Gwendolyn Stevens & Sheldon Gardner. 273p. 1982. pap. text ed. 18.95 (*0-87073-446-6*) Schenkman Bks Inc.

***Women of Renown: Nineteenth Century Studies.** George B. Smith. 478p. 1972. 23.95 (*0-8369-7288-0*) Ayer.

Women of Rock. (YA). 1996. pap. text ed. write for info. (*0-934551-14-6*) Starlog Pr.

Women of Sand & Myrrh. Hanan Al-Shaykh. Tr. by Catherine Cobham. 288p. 1992. reprint ed. pap. 11.00 (*0-385-42358-6*, Anchor NY) Doubleday.

Women of Science: Righting the Record. Ed. by G. Kass-Simon & Patricia Farnes. LC 88-45463. (Illus.). 416p. 1990. text ed. 39.95 (*0-253-33264-8*) Ind U Pr.

Women of Science: Righting the Record. Ed. by G. Kass-Simon & Patricia Farnes. LC 88-45463. (Illus.). 416p. 1993. pap. 14.95 (*0-253-20813-0*, MB-813) Ind U Pr.

Women of Shakespeare's Plays: Analysis of the Role of the Women in Select Plays with Plot Synopses & Selected One Act Plays. Courtni C. Wright. 220p. (Orig.). (C). 1992. pap. text ed. 26.50 (*0-8191-8826-3*); lib. bdg. 49.50 (*0-8191-8825-5*) U Pr of Amer.

Women of Silence: The Emotional Healing of Breast Cancer. Grace Gawler. 164p. (Orig.). 1995. pap. 16.95 (*0-85572-254-1*, Pub. by Hill Content Pubng AT) Seven Hills Bk.

Women of Skid Row: A Pen & Ink Sketchbook with Commentary. Ann A. Wolken. (Illus.). (Orig.). 1982. pap. 10.00 (*0-943756-00-6*) Shadyside.

Women of Smoke. Marjorie Agosin. Tr. by Naomi Lindstrom. LC 87-36203. (Discoveries Ser.). 112p. (ENG & SPA.). 1988. pap. 10.95 (*0-935480-34-X*) Lat Am Lit Rev Pr.

Women of Smoke: Latin American Women in Literature & Life. Marjorie Agosin. Tr. by Janice Molloy. LC 88-63387. 112p. 1989. 29.95 (*0-932415-42-3*); pap. 8.95 (*0-932415-43-1*) Red Sea Pr.

***Women of Southeast Asia.** rev. ed. Ed. by Penny Van Esterik. (Occasional Papers: No. 17). (Illus.). 229p. (Orig.). (C). 1996. pap. 15.00 (*1-877979-17-1*) SE Asia.

Women of Spirit: Insights & Inspirations from Leading Women. Ed. by Deborah A. Jones et al. (World Voices Collection). 67p. (Orig.). 1995. pap. text ed. 9.95 (*0-9641912-2-9*) Visns Better Wrld.

Women of Steel: Female Blue-Collar Workers in the Basic Steel Industry. Kay Deaux & Joseph C. Ullman. LC 83-2434. 208p. 1983. text ed. 55.00 (*0-275-90969-7*, C0969, Praeger Pubs) Greenwood.

***Women of Steel: Female Bodybuilder.** Lowe. 1997. 45.00 (*0-8147-5093-1*); pap. 17.95 (*0-8147-5094-X*) NYU Pr.

Women of Stone. Alan Haehnel. 28p. (Orig.). (YA). (gr. 8-12). 1994. pap. 3.00 (*1-57514-157-4*, 3027) Encore Perform Pub.

Women of Strength: Biographies of 106 Who Have Excelled in Traditionally Male Fields, 61 A.D. to the Present. Louis Baldwin. LC 96-38693. 254p. 1996. pap. 28.50 (*0-7864-0250-4*) McFarland & Co.

Women of Suye Mura. Robert J. Smith & Ella L. Wiswell. LC 82-2708. (Illus.). 352p. (C). 1982. pap. text ed. 17.95 (*0-226-76345-5*) U Ch Pr.

***Women of Taste: Recipes & Profiles of Famous Women Chefs.** Beverly Russell. LC 97-13168. 200p. 1997. 35.00 (*0-471-17943-4*) Wiley.

***Women of the All-American Girls Professional Baseball League: A Biographical Dictionary.** W. C. Madden. LC 97-9158. (Illus.). 288p. 1997. boxed 35.00 (*0-7864-0304-7*) McFarland & Co.

Women of the American Revolution, 3 vols., Set. Elizabeth F. Ellet. LC 68-31269. (American History & Americana Ser.: No. 47). 1969. lib. bdg. 175.00 (*0-8383-0197-5*) M S G Haskell Hse.

Women of the American Revolution, Vol. I. Elizabeth F. Ellet. 348p. 1980. reprint ed. 29.00 (*0-87928-106-5*) Corner Hse.

Women of the American Revolution, Vol. II. Elizabeth F. Ellet. 312p. 1980. reprint ed. 29.00 (*0-87928-107-3*) Corner Hse.

Women of the American Revolution, Vol. III. Elizabeth F. Ellet. 396p. 1980. reprint ed. 29.00 (*0-87928-108-1*) Corner Hse.

***Women of the American South.** Farnham. 1997. 55.00 (*0-8147-2654-2*); pap. 18.95 (*0-8147-2655-0*) NYU Pr.

Women of the Andes. Susan C. Bourque & Kay B. Warren. (Women & Culture Ser.; Patriarchy & Social Change in Two Peruvian Towns). 320p. 1981. pap. text ed. 16.95 (*0-472-06330-8*) U of Mich Pr.

Women of the Anti-Slavery Movement: The Weston Sisters. Clare Taylor. LC 94-24881. 1995. text ed. 65.00 (*0-312-12319-1*) St Martin.

Women of the Apache Nation: Voices of Truth. H. Henrietta Stockel. LC 90-22003. (Illus.). 226p. 1993. pap. 14.95 (*0-87417-221-7*) U of Nev Pr.

Women of the Beat Generation: The Writers, Artists & Muses at the Heart of a Revolution. Ed. by Brenda Knight. (Illus.). 384p. 1996. 19.95 (*1-57324-061-3*) Conari Press.

Women of the Bible. unabridged ed. Colleen L. Reece. (Value Bks.: Vol. 4). 128p. 1996. mass mkt. 0.99 (*1-55748-817-7*) Barbour & Co.

***Women of the Bible.** 248p. 1997. reprint ed. 21.95 (*0-912141-50-6*) Roman Cath Bks.

Women of the Bible. Frances VanderVelde. LC 83-19894. (Illus.). 260p. 1973. reprint ed. pap. 9.99 (*0-8254-3951-5*) Kregel.

Women of the Bible: Hannah. Lois Erickson. 96p. 1996. pap. text ed. 7.99 (*0-8280-0867-1*) Review & Herald.

Women of the Bible: Huldah. Lois Erickson. 125p. 1996. pap. text ed. 7.99 (*0-8280-0671-7*) Review & Herald.

Women of the Bible: Leah. Lois Erickson. 139p. 1996. pap. text ed. 7.99 (*0-8280-0654-7*) Review & Herald.

Women of the Bible: Sculpture. Edwina Sandys & James P. Morton. Ed. by Thomas E. Piche, Jr. LC 86-83188. (Illus.). 24p. (Orig.). 1986. pap. text ed. write for info. (*0-914407-07-4*) Everson Mus.

***Women of the Bible: Word Search Puzzles.** Rebecca A. Egbert. Ed. by Pat Fittro. 48p. (Orig.). 1997. pap. 3.99 (*0-7847-0640-9*, 14-02688) Standard Pub.

Women of the Bible: Zipporah. Lois Erickson. 1996. pap. text ed. 7.99 (*0-8280-0998-8*) Review & Herald.

Women of the Bible see Mujeres de la Biblia

Women of the Bible Speak to Women of Today. Dorothy Elder. LC 86-70873. (Illus.). 288p. (Orig.). 1986. pap. 14.00 (*0-87516-574-5*) DeVorss.

Women of the Celts. Jean Markale. 315p. 1986. pap. 14.95 (*0-89281-150-1*) Inner Tradit.

Women of the Centre. Adele Pring. 192p. (C). 1990. 51.00 (*0-947087-23-0*, Pub. by Pascoe Pub AT) St Mut.

Women of the Century: Thirty Modern Short Stories. Regina Barreca. LC 92-50040. 376p. (C). 1993. pap. text ed. 12.50 (*0-312-07523-5*) St Martin.

Women of the Commonwealth: Work, Family, & Social Change in Nineteenth-Century Massachusetts. Ed. by Susan L. Porter. LC 95-21715. (Illus.). 248p. (C). 1996. 45.00 (*1-55849-004-3*); pap. 15.95 (*1-55849-005-1*) U of Mass Pr.

Women of the Confederacy. Frances B. Simkins. (History - United States Ser.). 306p. 1993. reprint ed. lib. bdg. 89.00 (*0-7812-4903-1*) Rprt Serv.

Women of the Confederacy. Francis B. Simkins & James W. Patton. LC 70-145300. (Illus.). 1971. reprint ed. 59.00 (*0-403-01212-0*) Scholarly.

Women of the Depression: Caste & Culture in San Antonio, 1929-1939. Julia K. Blackwelder. LC 83-40496. (Southwestern Studies: No. 2). (Illus.). 1984. 15.95 (*0-89096-177-8*) Tex A&M Univ Pr.

Women of the Earth Lodges: Tribal Life on the Plains. Virginia B. Peters. LC 94-9251. (Illus.). xvi, 217p. (C). 1994. lib. bdg. 39.50 (*0-208-02219-8*, Archon Bks) Shoe String.

Women of the English Nobility & Gentry: 1066-1500. Jennifer Ward. 1995. text ed. 24.95 (*0-7190-4115-5*, Pub. by Manchester Univ Pr UK) St Martin.

Women of the English Renaissance & Reformation. Retha M. Warnicke. LC 82-12180. (Contributions in Women's Studies: No. 38). viii, 228p. 1983. text ed. 49.95 (*0-313-23611-9*, WTW/, Greenwood Pr) Greenwood.

Women of the European Union: The Politics of Work & Daily Life. Ed. by Janice Monk & Maria D. Garcia-Ramon. LC 95-44459. (International Studies of Women & Place Ser.). 304p. (C). 1996. pap. 19.95 (*0-415-11880-8*); text ed. 65.00 (*0-415-11879-4*) Routledge.

Women of the Far Right: The Mothers' Movement & World War II. Glen Jeansonne. LC 95-35974. (Illus.). 288p. 1996. 29.95 (*0-226-39587-1*) U Ch Pr.

***Women of the Far Right: The Mothers' Movement & World War II.** Glen Jeansonne. 284p. 1997. pap. 16.95 (*0-226-39589-8*) U Ch Pr.

Women of the Fertile Crescent: An Anthology of Arab Women's Poems. 2nd rev. ed. Ed. & Tr. by Kamal Boullata. LC 77-3834. (Illus.). 260p. 1994. reprint ed. pap. 16.00 (*0-914478-42-7*, Three Contnts) Lynne Rienner.

Women of the Fields: Representations of Rural Women in the Nineteenth Century. Karen Sayer. LC 94-41738. 1995. text ed. 79.95 (*0-7190-4142-2*, Pub. by Manchester Univ Pr UK) St Martin.

Women of the Forest. 2nd ed. Yolanda Murphy & Robert F. Murphy. LC 85-14969. 275p. 1985. text ed. 45.00 (*0-231-06088-2*); pap. text ed. 16.50 (*0-231-06089-0*) Col U Pr.

Women of the Four Winds. Elizabeth F. Olds. (Illus.). 263p. 1985. pap. 13.95 (*0-395-39584-4*) HM.

Women of the Fourteenth Moon: Writings on Menopause. Amber C. Sumrall. 325p. (Orig.). 1991. pap. 14.95 (*0-89594-477-4*) Crossing Pr.

Women of the French Revolution. R. McNair Wilson. 1973. 250.00 (*0-8490-1324-0*) Gordon Pr.

Women of the Future: The Female Main Character in Science Fiction. Betty King. LC 83-21030. 295p. 1984. 25.00 (*0-8108-1664-4*) Scarecrow.

Women of the Golden Dawn: Rebels & Priestesses. Mary K. Greer. LC 94-26269. 512p. 1994. 29.95 (*0-89281-516-7*, Park St Pr) Inner Tradit.

Women of the Golden Dawn: Rebels & Priestesses. Mary K. Greer. (Illus.). 512p. 1996. pap. 24.95 (*0-89281-607-4*, Park St Pr) Inner Tradit.

W

Women of the Gospel: Sharing God's Compassion. Isaias Powers. LC 92-81796. (Illus.). 168p. (Orig.). 1993. pap. 7.95 (*0-89622-521-6*) Twenty-Third.

Women of the Grange: Mutuality & Sisterhood in Rural America, 1866-1920. Donald B. Marti. LC 91-11328. (Contributions in Women's Studies: No. 124). 168p. 1991. text ed. 45.00 (*0-313-25723-X*, MSG/, Greenwood Pr) Greenwood.

Women of the Harlem Renaissance. Cheryl A. Wall. LC 95-3132. (Women of Letters Ser.). 256p. 1995. pap. 14. 95 (*0-253-20980-3*); text ed. 29.95 (*0-253-32908-6*) Ind U Pr.

Women of the Iliad. H. W. Taylor. 66p. 1994. pap. 20.00 (*0-87556-798-3*) Saifer.

Women of the Kalevala. Mary Caraker. LC 96-26021. 128p. 1996. pap. 12.95 (*0-87839-106-1*) North Star.

Women of the Klan: Racism & Gender in the 1920s. Kathleen M. Blee. LC 90-11287. (Illus.). 232p. 1991. 30. 00 (*0-520-07263-4*) U CA Pr.

Women of the Klan: Racism & Gender in the 1920s. Kathleen M. Blee. 1992. pap. 13.00 (*0-520-07876-4*) U CA Pr.

Women of the Klondike. Frances Backhouse. 1995. pap. text ed. 14.95 (*1-55110-375-3*, Pub. by Whitecap Bks CN) Gr Arts Ctr Pub.

Women of the Left Bank: Paris, 1900-1940. Shari Benstock. (Illus.). 566p. (Orig.). (C). 1986. 29.95 (*0-292-79029-5*) U of Tex Pr.

Women of the Left Bank: Paris, 1900-1940. Shari Benstock. (Illus.). 566p. (Orig.). (C). 1986. pap. 14.95 (*0-292-79040-6*) U of Tex Pr.

Women of the Light: The New Sexual Healers. Kenneth R. Stubbs. 256p. (Orig.). 1997. pap. 14.95 (*0-939263-12-2*) Secret Garden.

Women of the Louisiana Legislature. Louise B. Johnson. LC 86-81866. (Illus.). 101p. (Orig.). (C). 1986. 18.50 (*0-9617394-0-1*) Greenbay Pub.

Women of the Mayflower & Women of Plymouth Colony. Ethel J. Noyes. LC 73-12780. 293p. 1980. reprint ed. 36.00 (*0-8103-3668-5*) Gale.

Women of the Mediterranean. Ed. by Monique Gadant. Tr. by A. M. Berrett from FRE. 208p. (C). 1987. pap. 17.50 (*0-86232-528-5*, Pub. by Zed Bks Ltd UK); text ed. 49. 95 (*0-86232-527-7*, Pub. by Zed Bks Ltd UK) Humanities.

Women of the Mexican Countryside, 1850-1990: Creating Spaces, Shaping Transitions. Ed. by Heather Fowler-Salamini & Mary K. Vaughan. LC 94-10179. 253p. (Orig.). 1994. pap. text ed. 16.95 (*0-8165-1431-3*); lib. bdg. 36.00 (*0-8165-1415-1*) U of Ariz Pr.

Women of the Mito Domain: Recollections of Samurai Family Life. Yamakawa Kikue. 210p. 1992. text ed. 39. 50 (*0-86008-477-9*, Pub. by U of Tokyo JA) Col U Pr.

Women of the Native Struggle: Portraits & Testimony of Native American Women. Ed. & Photos by Ronnie Farley. LC 93-14975. (Library of the American Indian). 1993. 25.00 (*0-517-59465-X*, Orion Bks); pap. 22.00 (*0-517-88113-6*, Orion Bks) Crown Pub Group.

Women of the New Mexico Frontier, 1846-1912. Cheryl J. Foote. 1993. pap. 19.95 (*0-87081-298-X*) Univ Pr Colo.

Women of the New Right. Rebecca E. Klatch. (Women in the Political Economy Ser.). 264p. 1988. pap. 18.95 (*0-87722-590-7*) Temple U Pr.

Women of the New Testament. Abraham Kuyper. 111p. 1963. pap. 9.99 (*0-310-36751-4*, 9996P) Zondervan.

Women of the New Testament. Phyllis J. Peau. (Lifeguide Bible Studies). 64p. (Orig.). 1996. wbk. ed., pap. 4.99 (*0-8308-1077-3*, 1077) InterVarsity.

Women of the Night. Ed. by Barbara Hambly & Martin H. Greenberg. 1994. pap. write for info. (*0-446-67035-9*, Aspect) Warner Bks.

Women of the Old Testament. Gladys Hunt. (LifeGuide Bible Studies). 63p. (Orig.). 1990. wbk. ed., pap. 4.99 (*0-8308-1064-1*, 1064) InterVarsity.

Women of the Old Testament. Abraham Kuyper. 178p. 1964. pap. 9.99 (*0-310-36761-1*, 9997P) Zondervan.

Women of the Old West. Judith Alter. LC 88-34549. (First Bks.). (Illus.). 64p. (J). (gr. 3-5). 1989. lib. bdg. 21.00 (*0-531-10756-6*) Watts.

Women of the Orient. Boye L. De Mente. 160p. (Orig.). 1995. pap. 12.95 (*0-8048-1880-0*) C E Tuttle.

Women of the Place: Kastom, Colonialism, & Gender in Vanuatu. Margaret Jolly. LC 93-5291. (Studies in Anthropology & History: Vol. 12). 306, xvip. 1994. text ed. 54.00 (*3-7186-5404-0*) Gordon & Breach.

Women of the Place: Kastom, Colonialism & Gender in Vanuatu. Margaret Jolly. (Studies in Anthropology & History). 1994. text ed. 54.00 (*3-7186-5453-9*, Harwood Acad Pubs) Gordon & Breach.

***Women of the Place: Kastom, Colonialism & Gender in Vanuatu.** Margaret Jolly. (Studies in Anthropology & History Ser.). 1997. pap. text ed. 24.00 (*90-5702-136-6*, Harwood Acad Pubs) Gordon & Breach.

Women of the Plains, Vol. I. Jan Graber & Tracy Archibald. 138p. (Orig.). 1995. pap. 12.00 (*0-9650877-0-0*) Earthly Pubns.

***Women of the Plains, Vol. II.** Jan Graber & Tracy Archibald. 110p. 1996. pap. 12.00 (*0-9650877-1-9*) Earthly Pubns.

***Women of the Plains, Vol. III.** Jan Graber & Tracy Archibald. 1997. pap. 12.00 (*0-9650877-6-X*) Earthly Pubns.

Women of the Pleasure Quarter: Japanese Paintings & Prints of the Floating World. Elizabeth De Sabato Swinton. LC 95-16908. (Illus.). 196p. 1996. 65.00 (*1-55595-115-5*) Hudson Hills.

Women of the Praia: Work & Lives in a Portuguese Coastal Community. Sally Cole. (Illus.). 181p. 1991. text ed. 45. 00 (*0-691-09464-0*); pap. text ed. 15.95 (*0-691-02862-1*) Princeton U Pr.

Women of the Raj. Margaret MacMillan. LC 87-50183. (Illus.). 256p. 1996. pap. 18.95 (*0-500-27898-9*) Thames Hudson.

Women of the Range: Women's Roles in the Texas Beef Cattle Industry. Elizabeth Maret. LC 92-45787. (Illus.). 176p. 1993. 32.00 (*0-89096-532-3*); pap. 12.95 (*0-89096-541-2*) Tex A&M Univ Pr.

Women of the Red Plain: An Anthology of Contemporary Chinese Women's Poetry. Tr. by Julia C. Lin. 208p. 1993. pap. 10.00 (*0-14-058647-4*, Penguin Bks) Viking Penguin.

Women of the Renaissance. Margaret L. King. (Women in Culture & Society Ser.). 350p. 1991. pap. 17.95 (*0-226-43618-7*) U Ch Pr.

Women of the Renaissance: A Study of Feminism. L. De Maulde & R. LaClaviere. 1976. lib. bdg. 69.95 (*0-8490-2835-3*) Gordon Pr.

Women of the Republic: Intellect & Ideology in Revolutionary America. Linda K. Kerber. LC 79-28683. (Institute of Early American History & Culture Ser.). xiv, 304p. 1980. 37.50 (*0-8078-1440-7*) U of NC Pr.

***Women of the Republic: Intellect & Ideology in Revolutionary America.** Linda K. Kerber. LC 79-28683. (Illus.). 318p. (C). 1997. pap. 12.95 (*0-8078-4632-5*) U of NC Pr.

Women of the Roman Aristocracy as Christian Monastics. Anne E. Hickey. LC 86-19242. (Studies in Religion: No. 1). 159p. reprint ed. pap. 45.40 (*0-8357-1757-7*, 2070499) Bks Demand.

Women of the Salons. Evelyn B. Hall. LC 73-90640. (Essay Index Reprint Ser.). 1977. 21.95 (*0-8369-1262-4*) Ayer.

Women of the Shtetl: Through the Eye of Y. L. Peretz. Ruth Adler. LC 78-69895. (Illus.). 152p. 1980. 26.50 (*0-8386-2336-0*) Fairleigh Dickinson.

Women of the Sierra. Anne Seagraves. LC 90-70264. (Illus.). 176p. pap. 11.95 (*0-9619088-1-5*) Wesanne Pubns.

Women of the Silk. Gail Tsukiyama. 304p. 1993. pap. 11.95 (*0-312-09943-6*) St Martin.

Women of the South Distinguished in Literature. Mary Forrest, pseud. 1972. reprint ed. lib. bdg. 28.00 (*0-8422-8047-2*) Irvington.

Women of the Street: Making It in the World's Toughest Business. Sue Herera. LC 96-34284. 1997. text ed. 24. 95 (*0-471-15331-1*) Wiley.

***Women of the Sun.** Hyllus Maris & Sonia Borg. 234p. 1983. 17.95 (*0-86819-081-0*, Pub. by Currency Pr AT) Aubrey Bks.

Women of the Third World. Jeanne Bisilliat et al. Tr. by Enne Amann & Peter Amann. LC 86-46328. 104p. 1987. 26.50 (*0-8386-3311-0*) Fairleigh Dickinson.

Women of the U. S. Congress. rev. ed. Isobel V. Morin. LC 93-26068. (Profiles Ser.). (Illus.). 160p. (YA). (gr. 5-12). 1997. lib. bdg. 16.95 (*1-881508-12-9*) Oliver Pr MN.

Women of the Upper Class. Susan A. Ostrander. LC 83-18214. (Women in the Political Economy Ser.). 256p. 1986. pap. 16.95 (*0-87722-475-7*) Temple U Pr.

Women of the War: Heroines of the War Between the States. Frank Moore. (Illus.). 320p. 1997. reprint ed. pap. 16.95 (*1-888295-00-7*) Elephant Books.

Women of the War: Their Heroism & Self-Sacrifice. Frank Moore. xvi, 596p. reprint ed. 69.00 (*0-932051-34-0*) Rprt Serv.

***Women of the Watermelon Patch.** Ruth James. 120p. (Orig.). 1996. pap. 14.00 (*1-889570-02-8*) ISSA Inc.

Women of the West. A. L. Lake. (Wild West in American History Ser.). (Illus.). 32p. (J). (gr. 3-8). 1990. lib. bdg. 18.00 (*0-86625-373-4*); lib. bdg. 13.50 (*0-685-58656-1*) Rourke Corp.

Women of the West. Cathy Luchetti. LC 92-13653. (Library of the American West). 1992. pap. 24.00 (*0-517-59162-6*, Orion Bks) Crown Pub Group.

Women of the West. Silvia A. Sheafer. (Illus.). 152p. (YA). (gr. 12 up). 1978. 8.95 (*0-201-06670-X*, 920, Journal Publns); pap. 5.95 (*0-201-06671-8*, Journal Publns) Addison-Wesley.

Women of the West. Rick Steber. (Tales of the Wild West Ser.: Vol. 5). (Illus.). 60p. (Orig.). (J). 1988. pap. 4.95 (*0-945134-05-3*); audio 9.95 (*0-945134-55-X*) Bonanza Pub.

***Women of the West.** 2nd ed. Silvia A. Sheafer. (Illus.). 124p. (Orig.). 1997. reprint ed. pap. text ed. 11.95 (*1-889971-04-9*) Journal Pubns.

Women of the West I: Calling of Emily Evans, Julia's Last Hope, Roses for Mama, Woman Named Damaris. Janette Oke. 1991. pap. 35.99 (*1-55661-761-5*) Bethany Hse.

***Women of the West Overland Trail.** Wendi Lee. (Women of the West Ser.). 1997. mass mkt. 5.99 (*0-8125-5528-7*) Tor Bks.

***Women of the Western Frontier in Fact, Fiction & Film.** Ron Lackman. 272p. 1997. boxed 45.00 (*0-7864-0400-0*) McFarland & Co.

Women of the Wild West: Biographies from Many Cultures. Ruth Pelz. LC 94-1031. (Contributions Ser.). (Illus.). 64p. (Orig.). (J). (gr. 4 up). 1994. text ed. 12.95 (*0-940880-49-0*); pap. text ed. 6.95 (*0-940880-50-4*) Open Hand.

Women of the Word. Marilyn Hickey. 32p. (Orig.). pap. 1.00 (*1-56441-169-9*) M Hickey Min.

Women of the Word. Marilyn Hickey. (Mini-Bks.). 32p. 1982. pap. 0.99 (*0-89274-238-0*, HH-238) Harrison Hse.

Women of the Word: Contemporary Sermons by Women Clergy. Jones et al. Ed. by Charles Hackett. LC 84-52656. (Illus.). 144p. (Orig.). 1985. pap. 8.95 (*0-932419-00-3*) Cherokee.

Women of the Word: Jewish Women & Jewish Writing. Ed. by Judith R. Baskin. (Illus.). 382p. 1994. 39.95 (*0-8143-2422-3*); pap. text ed. 18.95 (*0-8143-2423-1*) Wayne St U Pr.

Women of the World. Rebecca Stefoff. (Extraordinary Explorers Ser.). (Illus.). 144p. (J). 1993. lib. bdg. 26.00 (*0-19-507687-7*) OUP.

Women of the World: Illusion & Reality. U. Phadnis & I. Malani. 285p. 1979. 18.95 (*0-7069-0489-3*) Asia Bk Corp.

Women of the World: Women Travelers & Explorers. Rebecca Stefoff. (Extraordinary Explorers Ser.). (Illus.). 152p. (J). (gr. 5 up). 1994. reprint ed. pap. 13.95 (*0-19-507688-5*) OUP.

***Women of the 12th Century.** Duby. LC 97-14198. 1997. pap. 15.95 (*0-226-16780-1*) U Ch Pr.

Women of Theresienstadt: Voices from a Concentration Camp. Ed. by Ruth Schwertferger. 200p. 1989. 29.95 (*0-85496-192-5*) Berg Pubs.

Women of Tijucopapo. Marilene Felinto. Tr. & Afterword by Irene Matthews. LC 93-43538. (Latin American Women Writers Ser.). xii, 136p. (C). 1994. pap. 10.95 (*0-8032-6881-5*, Bison Books); text ed. 30.00 (*0-8032-1988-1*) U of Nebr Pr.

Women of To-Day. Margaret I. Cole. LC 68-16920. (Essay Index Reprint Ser.). 1977. 23.95 (*0-8369-0325-0*) Ayer.

***Women of Trachis.** Sophocles. Tr. by Ezra Pound. 96p. 1985. pap. 6.95 (*0-8112-0948-2*) New Directions.

Women of Trachis. Sophocles. Tr. by C. K. Williams & Gregory W. Dickerson. (Greek Tragedy in New Translations Ser.). 112p. 1991. reprint ed. pap. 6.95 (*0-19-507009-7*) OUP.

Women of Trachis see Sophocles Two

Women of Trachis see Electra & Other Plays

Women of Troy. David Grote. 28p. 1981. pap. 3.00 (*0-87129-162-2*, W50) Dramatic Pub.

Women of Troy see Bacchae & Other Plays

Women of Troy, Hecuba, Helen. Euripides. Tr. by Kenneth McLeish. 208p. 1996. pap. 13.95 (*0-948230-65-7*, Pub. by N Hern Bks UK) Theatre Comm.

Women of Turkey & Their Folk-Lore, 2 vols., Set. Lucy M. Garnett. LC 77-87539. reprint ed. 137.50 (*0-404-16590-7*) AMS Pr.

Women of Valor. Sheila Segal. Ed. by Sarah Feldman. (Illus.). 128p. (J). (gr. 5-7). 1996. text ed. 14.95 (*0-87441-607-8*) Behrman.

***Women of Valor: Stories of Great Jewish Women Who Helped Shape the Twentieth Century.** Sheila F. Segal. LC 96-28372. 1996. write for info. (*0-87441-612-4*) Behrman.

Women of Valor: The Struggle Against the Great Depression As Told in Their Own Life Stories. Ed. by Bernard Sternsher & Judith Sealander. (Illus.). 320p. 1990. text ed. 26.95 (*0-929587-34-0*) I R Dee.

Women of Valour: A Handbook (Hebrew/English) 40p. 1995. text ed. 12.95 (*965-229-136-6*, Pub. by Gefen Pub Hse IS) Gefen Bks.

Women of Value: Feminist Essays on the History of Women in Economics. Ed. by Mary Ann Dimand et al. LC 95-7191. 240p. 1995. 80.00 (*1-85278-959-X*) E Elgar.

Women of Value, Men of Renown: New Perspectives in Trobriand Exchange. Annette B. Weiner. (Sourcebooks in Anthropology: No. 11). (Illus.). 321p. (C). 1987. reprint ed. pap. text ed. 14.95 (*0-292-79019-8*) U of Tex Pr.

Women of Vision, Women of Peace. Nancy D. Potts. 225p. 1994. pap. text ed. 15.95 (*0-9640010-0-4*) Peace Pubng.

Women of Whitechapel & Jack the Ripper. Paul West. LC 92-14925. 420p. 1992. pap. 13.95 (*0-87951-478-7*) Overlook Pr.

Women of Wisdom. Tsultrim Allione. 320p. (Orig.). 1988. pap. 11.95 (*0-14-019072-4*, Penguin Bks) Viking Penguin.

Women of Wonder: The Classic Years: Science Fiction by Women from the 1940s to the 1970s. Ed. by Pamela Sargent. 432p. 1995. pap. 15.00 (*0-15-600031-8*) HarBrace.

Women of Wonder: The Contemporary Years: Science Fiction by Women from the 1970s to the 1990s. Ed. & Intro. by Pamela Sargent. 432p. 1995. pap. 15.00 (*0-15-600033-4*) HarBrace.

Women of Words. Ed. by Janet B. Teacher. (Illus.). 176p. 1996. 14.98 (*1-56138-769-X*) Courage Bks.

***Women on a Wire: A Collection of Poems from the Women's Wire (R) Poetry Room. Ed. by Georgia Jones. LC 96-77239. 136p. (Orig.). 1996. pap. 11. 95 (*1-889409-16-2*) Ladybug Pr CA.**
A collection of poems written by poets collaborating in a workshop setting in electronic medium. All royalties go to the National Coalition Against Domestic Violence. To order contact: Ladybug Press, 751 Laurel St., No. 223, San Carlos, CA 94070. ***Publisher Provided Annotation.***

Women on Campus. Ed. by Elizabeth Janeway. LC 74-32507. 256p. 1975. pap. 19.95 (*0-915390-03-5*) Transaction Pubs.

Women on Campus: The Unfinished Liberation. Ed. by Elizabeth Janeway. LC 74-32507. 256p. 1975. 34.95 (*0-686-95517-X*) Transaction Pubs.

Women on College & University Faculties: A Historical Survey & a Study of Their Present Academic Status. Lucille A. Pollard. Ed. by Walter P. Metzger. LC 76-55186. (Academic Profession Ser.). (Illus.). 1980. reprint ed. lib. bdg. 33.95 (*0-405-10019-1*) Ayer.

Women on Corporate Boards: The Challenge of Change. 66p. 1993. 40.00 (*0-89584-180-0*) Catalyst.

Women on Deadline: A Collection of America's Best. Sherry Ricchiardi & Virginia Young. LC 90-41648. (Illus.). 224p. 1990. pap. 19.95 (*0-8138-1688-2*) Iowa St U Pr.

Women on Deadline: A Collection of America's Best. Sherry Ricchiardi & Virginia Young. LC 90-41648. (Illus.). 224p. 1991. 25.95 (*0-8138-1687-4*) Iowa St U Pr.

Women on Divorce: A Bedside Companion. Ed. by Penny Kaganoff & Susan Spano. LC 95-20287. 256p. 1995. 22. 00 (*0-15-100114-6*) HarBrace.

***Women on Divorce: A Bedside Companion.** Ed. by Penny Kaganoff & Susan Spano. 224p. 1997. pap. 12.00 (*0-15-600462-3*, Harvest Bks) HarBrace.

Women on Film: The Critical Eye. Marsha McCreadie. LC 82-13221. 176p. 1983. text ed. 49.95 (*0-275-91042-3*, C1042, Praeger Pubs) Greenwood.

Women on Heroin. Marsha Rosenbaum. (Crime, Law & Deviance Ser.). 205p. (Orig.). (C). 1981. pap. 15.00 (*0-8135-0946-7*) Rutgers U Pr.

Women on Hunting: Essays, Fiction, & Poetry. Pam Houston. 188p. 1994. 23.00 (*0-88001-332-X*) Ecco Pr.

Women on Hunting: Essays, Fiction, & Poetry. Ed. by Pam Houston. 352p. 1996. pap. 16.00 (*0-88001-443-1*) Ecco Pr.

Women on Ice: Feminist Essays on the Tonya Harding/ Nancy Kerrigan Spectacle. Ed. by Cynthia Baughman. LC 95-24887. (Illus.). 310p. (C). 1995. pap. 16.95 (*0-415-91151-6*, B7157, Routledge NY) Routledge.

Women on Ice: Feminist Essays on the Tonya Harding/ Nancy Kerrigan Spectacle. Ed. by Cynthia Baughman. LC 95-24887. (Illus.). 310p. (C). (gr. 13). 1995. text ed. 74.95 (*0-415-91150-8*, B7153, Routledge NY) Routledge.

Women on Men: Views on the Opposite Sex. Ed. by Lois L. Kaufman. LC 89-63624. (Illus.). 64p. 1990. 7.99 (*0-88088-585-8*) Peter Pauper.

Women on Men, & Other Laughing Matters. Jasmine Birtles. 128p. 1995. 22.50 (*1-85479-729-8*, Pub. by M OMara Books UK) Trans-Atl Phila.

Women on Menopause: A Change for the Better. Anne Dickson & Nikki Henriques. 160p. (Orig.). 1989. pap. 9.95 (*0-89281-237-0*, Heal Arts VT) Inner Tradit.

Women on Mission Guide. Andrea Mullins. Ed. by Susan Hansen. 44p. (Orig.). 1995. pap. text ed. 3.95 (*1-56309-109-7*) Womans Mission Union.

Women on Mission Journal. Ella Robinson. Ed. by Susan Hansen. (Illus.). 64p. (Orig.). 1995. pap. text ed. 3.95 (*1-56309-111-9*) Womans Mission Union.

Women on Sex. Susan Quilliam. LC 94-25589. 256p. 1994. pap. 14.95 (*1-56980-025-1*) Barricade Bks.

***Women on Stamps.** Betty Killingbeck. (Illus.). 82p. (Orig.). Date not set. pap. 7.00 (*0-614-25042-0*) Am Topical Assn.

***Women on Stamps, Vol. 1.** Sophia Webb. (Illus.). 59p. (Orig.). Date not set. pap. 4.00 (*0-614-25047-1*) Am Topical Assn.

Women on Stamps, Vol. III. Helen Cockburn. (Illus.). 176p. 1993. pap. 17.00 (*0-935991-19-0*) Am Topical Assn.

***Women on the Ball: A Guide to Women's Soccer.** Sue Lopez. (Illus.). 210p. 1996. 39.95 (*1-85727-026-6*, Pub. by Scarlet Pr UK) LPC InBook.

***Women on the Ball: A Guide to Women's Soccer.** Sue Lopez. 210p. 1996. pap. text ed. 17.95 (*1-85727-016-9*, Pub. by Scarlet Pr UK) LPC InBook.

Women on the Biblical Road: Ruth, Naomi, & the Female Journey. Mishael M. Caspi & Rachel S. Havrelock. (C). 1996. pap. text ed. 28.00 (*0-7618-0280-0*); lib. bdg. 47. 00 (*0-7618-0279-7*) U Pr of Amer.

Women on the Breadlines. Meridel Le Sueur. LC 78-108080. (Worker Writer Ser.). (Illus.). 1978. pap. text ed. 2.00 (*0-931122-34-1*) West End.

Women on the Brink of Divorce: A Guide to Self-Help Books. Cynthia David. LC 95-15693. 272p. 1995. 29.00 (*0-917846-54-0*) Highsmith Pr.

***Women on the Case.** Sara Paretsky. 1997. mass mkt. 5.99 (*0-440-22325-3*) Dell.

Women on the Case: 26 Original Stories by the Best Women Crime Writers of Our Times. Ed. & Intro. by Sara Paretsky. LC 95-43814. 384p. 1996. 21.95 (*0-385-31401-9*) Delacorte.

Women on the Colonial Frontier: A Study of Frederica & Early Georgia. Lee A. Caldwell. Ed. by Phirizy Spalding. (Illus.). 60p. 1995. pap. 7.95 (*0-930803-02-7*) Fort Frederica.

Women on the Edge. Ed. by Martin H. Greenberg. 384p. 1994. mass mkt. 4.99 (*0-7860-0044-9*, Pinncle Kensgtn) Kensgtn Pub Corp.

Women on the Front Lines: Meeting the Challenge of an Aging America. Ed. by Jessie Allen & Alan Pifer. LC 92-34290. 280p. (Orig.). (C). 1993. lib. bdg. 22.95 (*0-87766-574-5*) Urban Inst.

Women on the Hill: A History of Women in Congress. Jill S. Pollack. LC 96-33831. (Women Then - Women Now Ser.). 128p. (YA). (gr. 9-12). 1996. lib. bdg. 22.70 (*0-531-11306-X*) Watts.

Women on the Hill: Alumnae Reflect on Twenty Years of Coeducation, 1972-1992. Ann J. Cahill. 263p. 1993. pap. text ed. 20.00 (*0-9636118-0-1*) Coll Holy Cross.

Women on the Hill: Culture of Congress. Clara Bingham. LC 96-27801. 1997. 23.00 (*0-8129-6351-2*, Times Bks) Random.

Women on the Inner Journey: Building a Bridge. Noris Binet. LC 93-60850. (Illus.). 72p. 1993. pap. text ed. 24. 95 (*1-55523-646-4*) Winston-Derek.

Women on the Italian Literary Scene: A Panorama. Alba della Fazia Amoia. LC 91-67977. 151p. 1992. 25.00 (*0-87875-428-8*) Whitston Pub.

Women on the Job: The Communist View. Judy Edelman. 56p. 1973. pap. 0.70 (*0-87898-101-2*) New Outlook.

Women on the Land: The Hidden Heart of Rural Australia. Margaret Alston. 1995. pap. 22.95 (*0-86840-382-2*, Pub. by New South Wales Univ Pr AT) Intl Spec Bk.

W

An Asterisk (*) at the beginning of an entry indicates that the title is appearing in BIP for the first time.

Women on the Margins: Three Seventeenth-Century Lives. Natalie Z. Davis. (Illus.). 360p. (C). 1995. 24.95 (*0-674-95520-X*) Belknap Pr.

***Women on the Margins: Three Seventeenth-Century Lives.** Natalie Zemon Davis. 1997. pap. text ed. 14.95 (*0-674-95521-8*) HUP.

Women on the Move: A Christian Perspective on Cross-Cultural Adaptation. Gretchen Janssen. LC 91-43918. 160p. 1989. pap. 15.95 (*1-877864-09-9*) Intercult Pr.

Women on the Move: A Feminist Perspective. Ed. by Jean R. Leppaluoto. 306p. 1972. pap. 6.00 (*0-317-34800-0*, X050) Know Inc.

Women on the Outside Looking In. Linda P. McIllwain. LC 84-90611. 96p. (Orig.). 1985. pap. 5.95 (*0-930555-03-1*, Wings Books) Random.

Women on the Porch. Caroline Gordon. LC 92-62892. (Southern Classics Ser.). 336p. (C). 1993. reprint ed. pap. 10.95 (*1-879941-20-1*) J S Sanders.

Women on the Quilt: Seventeen Women Who Shaped Colorado. Pauli Fry. (Illus.). (Orig.). Date not set. pap. write for info. (*0-86541-032-1*) Filter.

Women on the Road. Rosina Conde. Tr. by Gustavo Segade et al. from SPA. (Baja California Literature in Translation Ser.). 150p. (Orig.). 1994. pap. 12.50 (*1-879691-24-8*) SDSU Press.

Women on the Threshold: Voices of Salvadoran Baptist Women. Kathleen Hayes. 144p. 1996. pap. 13.95 (*1-57312-018-9*, Peake Road) Smyth & Helwys.

Women on the U. S. Mexico Border: Responses to Change. Vicki L. Ruiz & Susan Tiano. LC 86-22305. (Thematic Studies in Latin America). 256p. 1987. text ed. 44.95 (*0-04-497038-2*); pap. text ed. 15.95 (*0-04-497039-0*) Routledge Chapman & Hall.

Women on the Verge. Ed. by Rosette C. Lamont. 1993. pap. 14.95 (*1-55783-148-3*) Applause Theatre Bk Pubs.

***Women on the Verge of a Nervous Breakdown.** Peter Evans. (BFI Modern Classics). (Illus.). 72p. 1996. pap. 9.95 (*0-85170-540-5*, Pub. by British Film Inst UK) Ind U Pr.

Women on the Wall. Wallace Stegner. LC 80-22461. vii, 279p. 1981. reprint ed. pap. 12.00 (*0-8032-9110-8*, Bison Books) U of Nebr Pr.

Women on Top. Nancy Friday. Ed. by Julie Rubenstein. 576p. 1993. reprint ed. pap. 6.99 (*0-671-64845-4*, Pocket Star Bks) PB.

Women on Women, No. 2. Ed. by Naomi Holoch & Joan Nestle. LC 92-35983. 352p. (Orig.). 1993. pap. 12.00 (*0-452-26999-7*, Plume) NAL-Dutton.

Women on Women: An Anthology of American Lesbian Short Fiction. Ed. by Joan Nestle & Naomi Holoch. 1990. pap. 12.95 (*0-452-26388-3*, Plume) NAL-Dutton.

Women on Women 3: A New Anthology of American Lesbian Fiction, Bk. 3. Ed. by Naomi Holoch & Joan Nestle. 352p. 1996. pap. 12.95 (*0-452-27661-6*, Plume) NAL-Dutton.

Women Online: Research in Women's Studies Using Online Databases. Ed. by Steven D. Atkinson & Judith Hudson. LC 90-4430. (Series in Library & Information Sciences). (Illus.). 420p. 1990. text ed. 49.95 (*1-56024-037-7*); pap. text ed. 29.95 (*1-56024-053-9*) Haworth Pr.

Women or Half of Society: A Muslim View. Hujjat Al-Islam Muhammad Taqi Mesbah. Tr. by Islamic Propagation Organization Staff from PER. 24p. (Orig.). 1989. pap. text ed. 1.70 (*1-871031-14-1*) Abjad Bk.

Women, or Pour et Contre, 3 vols. in 2, Set. Charles R. Maturin. LC 79-8173. reprint ed. 84.50 (*0-404-62043-4*) AMS Pr.

***Women Organisation & Power Struggle.** G. Narayana Reddy & Rao D. Ramana. 1995. 18.00 (*81-85613-98-2*, Pub. by Chugh Pubns II) S Asia.

Women Organising. Helen G. Brown. 192p. (C). (gr. 13). 1991. text ed. 85.00 (*0-415-04851-6*, A6519) Routledge.

Women Organizations & Social Networks. Neerja Ahlawat. (C). 1995. 20.00 (*81-7033-269-9*, Pub. by Rawat II) S Asia.

Women Organizing: An Anthology. Bernice Cummings & Victoria Schuck. LC 79-18956. 422p. 1979. 35.00 (*0-8108-1245-2*) Scarecrow.

Women Out of Place. Ed. by Williams. 288p. (C). 1996. pap. 18.95 (*0-415-91497-3*, Routledge NY); text ed. 65.00 (*0-415-91496-5*, Routledge NY) Routledge.

Women Outdoors: The Best One Thousand Nine Hundred Books, Programs & Periodicals. Jennifer Abromowitz. LC 91-142632. (Illus.). 180p. (Orig.). 1990. pap. 28.00 (*0-9630956-0-9*) J Abromowitz.

Women Outside: Meanings & Myths of Homelessness. Stephanie Golden. LC 91-32936. 329p. 1992. 25.00 (*0-520-07158-1*) U CA Pr.

Women Outside: Meanings & Myths of Homelessness. Stephanie Golden. (C). 1993. pap. 14.00 (*0-520-08438-1*) U CA Pr.

Women over Thirty Are Better Because... Herbert I. Kavet. 1992. pap. 5.95 (*0-88032-417-1*) Ivory Tower Pub.

***Women over 50 Are Better Because.** Herbert I. Kavet. (Illus.). 96p. (Orig.). 1996. pap. 5.95 (*1-889647-09-8*) Boston Am.

Women Overseas: A Practical Guide. Nancy J. Piet-Pelon & Barbara Hornby. 168p. (C). 1986. 50.00 (*0-85292-375-9*); pap. 40.00 (*0-685-60719-4*, Pub. by IPM Hse UK) St Mut.

Women-Owned Businesses. Ed. by Oliver Hagan et al. LC 88-13775. 240p. 1989. text ed. 55.00 (*0-275-93177-3*, C3177, Praeger Pubs) Greenwood.

Women Painters East-West. (Illus.). 100p. 1974. pap. 6.50 (*0-685-66768-5*) Pacific Asia.

Women Paraprofessionals in Upper Volta's Rural Development. Ellen Taylor. (Special Series on Paraprofessionals). 56p. (Orig.). (C). 1981. pap. text ed. 6.60 (*0-86731-049-9*) Cornell CIS RDC.

Women Parliamentarians: A Study in the Indian Context. Ranjana Kumari & Anju Dubey. (C). 1995. 16.00 (*81-241-0217-1*, Pub. by Har-Anand Pubns II) S Asia.

Women Participation in Rural Environment. G. P. Swarnkar. (C). 1987. 23.00 (*81-85076-37-5*, Pub. by Chugh Pubns II) S Asia.

Women Pastors. Berkshire Clergywomen & Allison Stokes. 176p. (Orig.). 1995. pap. 14.95 (*0-8245-1465-3*) Crossroad NY.

Women Patriots of the American Revolution: A Biographical Dictionary. Charles E. Claghorn. LC 91-15495. (Illus.). 519p. 1991. 55.00 (*0-8108-2421-3*) Scarecrow.

Women Pay More: And How to Put a Stop to It. Frances C. Whittelsey & Marcia Carroll. 208p. 1995. pap. 9.95 (*1-56584-224-3*) New Press NY.

Women Pay the Price: Structural Adjustment in Africa & the Caribbean. Ed. by Gloria T. Emeagwali. 375p. (Orig.). (C). 1994. 49.95 (*0-86543-428-X*); pap. 16.95 (*0-86543-429-8*) Africa World.

Women Philosophers. Ed. by Mary Warnock. (Everyman Paperback Classics Ser.). 288p. (Orig.). (C). 1996. pap. 8.50 (*0-460-87721-6*, Everyman's Classic Lib) C E Tuttle.

Women Philosophers: A Bibliography of Books Through 1990. Ed. by Else M. Barth. (Philosophical Bibliographies Ser.). 236p. 1992. 39.00 (*0-912632-91-7*) Philos Document.

Women Philosophers: A Bio-Critical Source Book. Ethel M. Kersey. Ed. by Calvin O. Schrag. LC 88-24615. 241p. 1989. text ed. 59.95 (*0-313-25720-5*, Greenwood Pr) Greenwood.

Women Philosophers of the Early Modern Period. Margaret Atherton. LC 94-27004. 176p. (C). 1994. pap. text ed. 6.95 (*0-87220-259-3*); lib. bdg. 29.95 (*0-87220-260-7*) Hackett Pub.

Women Photographers. (Illus.). 30p. 1995. pap. 7.95 (*1-55859-925-8*) Abbeville Pr.

Women Photographers: The Other Observers: 1900 to the Present. Val Williams. 1989. pap. 16.95 (*0-86068-624-8*) Random.

Women Physicians: A Study in Roles & Role-Conflict. Nigar F. Abidi. (Illus.). xvi, 244p. 1993. 24.00 (*81-85445-20-6*, Pub. by Manak Pubns Pvt Ltd) Nataraj Bks.

Women Physicians: Careers, Status & Power. Judith Lorber. 250p. 1985. 25.00 (*0-422-79040-0*, NO. 9071); pap. 12.95 (*0-422-79050-8*, NO. 9103) Routledge Chapman & Hall.

Women Physicians in Leadership Roles. Leah J. Dickstein & Carol C. Nadelson. LC 86-3574. (Issues in Psychiatry Ser.). 333p. 1986. pap. text ed. 24.00 (*0-88048-203-6*, 8203) Am Psychiatric.

***Women Physiologists: An Anniversary Celebration of Their Contribution to British Physiology.** Ed. by L. Bindman et al. (Illus.). 164p. (Orig.). (C). 1993. pap. text ed. 20.00 (*1-85578-049-6*, Pub. by Portland Pr Ltd UK) Ashgate Pub Co.

Women Pilots of World War II. Jean H. Cole. LC 91-29973. (Illus.). 165p. 1995. reprint ed. pap. 12.95 (*0-87480-493-0*) U of Utah Pr.

Women Pilots with the AAF, Nineteen Forty-One - Nineteen Forty-Four. J. Merton England & Joseph Reither. (USAF Historical Studies: No. 55). 122p. 1946. pap. text ed. 27.95 (*0-89126-138-9*) MA-AH Pub.

Women Pioneers. Rebecca Stefoff. LC 95-13552. (American Profiles Ser.). (Illus.). 144p. (YA). (gr. 6 up). 1996. 17.95 (*0-8160-3134-7*) Facts on File.

Women Pioneers in Television: Biographies of Fifteen Industry Leaders. Cary O'Dell. LC 96-46132. (Illus.). 264p. 1997. boxed 42.50 (*0-7864-0167-2*) McFarland & Co.

***Women Pioneers in Texas Medicine.** Elizabeth Silverthorne & Geneva Fulgham. LC 97-18885. (Centennial Series of the Association of Former Students, Texas A&M University: No. 70). (Illus.). 304p. 1997. 24.95 (*0-89096-789-X*) Texas A&M Univ.

Women Pirates & the Politics of the Jolly Roger. Ulrike Klausmann et al. (Illus.). 245p. 1996. 48.99 (*1-55164-059-7*, Pub. by Black Rose Bks CN); pap. 19.99 (*1-55164-058-9*, Pub. by Black Rose Bks CN) Consort Bk Sales.

Women Playwrights: The Best of 1994. Ed. by Marisa Smith. (Contemporary Playwrights Ser.). 368p. 1995. pap. (*1-880399-84-9*) Smith & Kraus.

***Women Playwrights: The Best of 1996.** Ed. by Marisa Smith. 320p. (Orig.). 1997. pap. 19.95 (*1-57525-111-6*) Smith & Kraus.

Women Playwrights: The Best Plays of 1992. Ed. by Robyn Goodman & Marisa Smith. (Contemporary Playwrights Ser.). 242p. 1993. pap. 14.95 (*1-880399-22-9*) Smith & Kraus.

Women Playwrights: The Best Plays of 1993. Ed. by Marisa Smith. (Contemporary Playwrights Ser.). 232p. 1994. pap. 16.95 (*1-880399-45-8*) Smith & Kraus.

Women Playwrights: The Best Plays of 1995. Ed. by Marisa Smith. (Contemporary American Playwrights Ser.). 320p. (Orig.). 1996. 35.00 (*1-57525-036-5*); pap. 19.95 (*1-57525-035-7*) Smith & Kraus.

Women Playwrights in England, Ireland, & Scotland: 1660-1823. Susan G. Mann et al. Ed. by David D. Mann. LC 95-78939. 432p. (C). 1996. text ed. 57.50 (*0-253-33087-4*) Ind U Pr.

***Women Playwrights of Diversity: A Bio-Bibliographical Sourcebook.** Jane T. Peterson & Suzanne Bennett. LC 96-27388. 432p. 1997. text ed. 79.50 (*0-313-29179-9*, Greenwood Pr) Greenwood.

Women Poets & the American Sublime. Joanne F. Diehl. LC 89-45859. (Every Woman Ser.). 224p. 1990. 31.50 (*0-253-31741-X*) Ind U Pr.

Women Poets of China. Tr. by Kenneth Rexroth & Chung Ling from CHI. LC 72-6791. Orig. Title: The Orchid Boat. 160p. 1982. reprint ed. pap. 8.95 (*0-8112-0821-4*, NDP528) New Directions.

Women Poets of Japan. Tr. by Kenneth Rexroth & Ikuko Atsumi from JPN. LC 77-1833. 192p. 1982. reprint ed. pap. 9.95 (*0-8112-0820-6*, NDP527) New Directions.

Women Poets of Spain, 1860-1990: Toward a Gynocentric Vision. John C. Wilcox. LC 96-9948. (Illus.). 400p. 1996. text ed. 49.95 (*0-252-02260-2*); pap. text ed. 19.95 (*0-252-06559-X*) U of Ill Pr.

Women Poets of the Italian Renaissance: Courtly Ladies & Courtesans. Ed. & Tr. by Laura A. Stortoni from ITA. Tr. by Mary P. Lillie from ITA. LC 97-6455. 300p. (Orig.). 1997. pap. 20.00 (*0-934977-43-7*) Italica Pr.

Women Poets of the West: An Anthology, 1850-1950. 4th ed. Ed. by Tom Trusky. LC 77-83227. (Ahsahta Press Modern & Contemporary Poets of the West Ser.). 90p. 1978. pap. 10.95 (*0-916272-08-7*) Ahsahta Pr.

Women Police, a Study of the Development & Status of the Women Police Movement. Chloe Owings. LC 69-14941. (Criminology, Law Enforcement, & Social Problems Ser.: No. 28). 1969. reprint ed. 24.00 (*0-87585-028-6*) Patterson Smith.

Women, Police & Social Change. Shamim Aleem. (C). 1991. text ed. 15.00 (*81-7024-408-0*, Pub. by Ashish II) S Asia.

Women Police Officers: Current Career Profile. Patricia W. Lunneborg. 222p. 1989. pap. 29.95 (*0-398-06251-X*) C C Thomas.

Women Police Officers: Current Career Profile. Patricia W. Lunneborg. 222p. (C). 1989. text ed. 45.95 (*0-398-05623-4*) C C Thomas.

***Women Police Officers, 1900-1946.** Janis Appier. LC 97-9965. (Critical Perspectives on the Past Ser.). 1997. write for info. (*1-56639-559-3*); pap. write for info. (*1-56639-560-7*) Temple U Pr.

Women, Policing & Male Violence: An Internation Perspective. Ed. by Jill Radford et al. 240p. 1988. text ed. 52.50 (*0-415-00692-9*) Routledge.

Women, Policing & Male Violence: An Internation Perspective. Ed. by Jill Radford et al. 240p. (C). 1989. pap. 15.95 (*0-415-00693-7*) Routledge.

Women Political Leaders. Linda R. Healy. (Illus.). 1987. pap. 5.95 (*0-913290-56-4*) Camaro Pub.

Women Politicians & the Media. Maria Braden. (Illus.). 248p. 1996. pap. 14.95 (*0-8131-0869-1*); text ed. 29.95 (*0-8131-1970-7*) U Pr of Ky.

Women, Politics & American Society. Nancy E. McGlen & Karen O'Connor. LC 94-20216. 336p. 1994. pap. text ed. 32.80 (*0-13-962192-X*) P-H.

Women, Politics & Change. Ed. by Louise A. Tilly & Patricia Gurin. LC 90-8381. 688p. 1990. text ed. 49.95 (*0-87154-884-4*) Russell Sage.

Women, Politics, & Change. Ed. by Louise A. Tilly & Patricia Gurin. (Illus.). 670p. 1992. pap. 17.50 (*0-87154-885-2*) Russell Sage.

Women, Politics & Religion. Ed. by Hem L. Swarup. (C). 1991. 34.00 (*81-85489-03-3*, Pub. by Usha II) S Asia.

Women, Politics & Reproduction: The Liberal Legacy. Ingrid Makus. 1996. pap. text ed. 17.75 (*0-8020-7663-7*) U of Toronto Pr.

Women, Politics & the Constitution. Ed. by Naomi B. Lynn. LC 90-37948. (Women & Politics Ser.: Vol. 10, No. 2). 161p. 1990. pap. text ed. 14.95 (*0-918393-75-2*) Harrington Pk.

Women, Politics & the Constitution. Ed. by Naomi B. Lynn. LC 90-37948. (Women & Politics Ser.: Vol. 10, No. 2). 161p. 1990. text ed. 29.95 (*1-56024-029-6*) Haworth Pr.

Women, Politics, & the United Nations. Ed. by Anne Winslow. LC 94-47415. (Contributions in Women's Studies: No. 151). 232p. 1995. text ed. 59.95 (*0-313-29522-0*, Greenwood Pr) Greenwood.

Women, Population & Global Crisis: A Political-Economic Analysis. Asoka Bandarage. LC 96-36915. 288p. (C). 1997. 69.95 (*1-85649-427-6*, Pub. by Zed Bks Ltd UK) Humanities.

Women, Population & Global Crisis: A Political-Economic Analysis. Asoka Bandarage. LC 96-36915. 288p. (C). 1997. pap. 25.00 (*1-85649-428-4*, Pub. by Zed Bks Ltd UK) Humanities.

Women, Poverty & AIDS: Sex, Drugs and Structural Violence. Paul Farmer et al. 350p. (Orig.). 1996. pap. 19.95 (*1-56751-074-4*) Common Courage.

Women, Poverty & AIDS: Sex, Drugs and Structural Violence. Paul Farmer et al. 350p. (Orig.). 1996. lib. bdg. 49.95 (*1-56751-075-2*) Common Courage.

Women, Poverty, & Child Support. Paula Roberts. (Illus.). 166p. (Orig.). 1986. pap. 15.00 (*0-941077-15-2*, 41,980) NCLS Inc.

Women, Poverty & Progress in the Third World. Mayra Buvinic & Sally W. Yudelman. LC 89-84292. (Headline Ser.: No. 289). (Illus.). 64p. (Orig.). 1989. pap. 5.95 (*0-87124-127-7*) Foreign Policy.

Women, Poverty & Resources. Ponna Wignaraja. 242p. (C). 1990. text ed. 26.00 (*0-8039-9624-1*) Sage.

Women, Power, & Change. Ed. by Ann Weick & Susan T. Vandiver. LC 81-83429. 214p. (C). 1981. pap. text ed. 20.95 (*0-87101-092-5*) Natl Assn Soc Wkrs.

Women, Power & Childbirth: A Case Study of a Free-Standing Birth Center. Kathleen Doherty Turkel. LC 95-12839. 184p. 1995. text ed. 52.95 (*0-89789-317-4*, Bergin & Garvey) Greenwood.

Women Power & Consciousness in 19th Century Ireland: Eight Biographical Studies. Ed. by Mary Cullen & Maria Luddy. 304p. 1996. Vol. 1. pap. 32.99 (*1-85594-078-7*, Pub. by Attic Press IE) Intl Spec Bk.

Women, Power, & Economic Change: The Nandi of Kenya. Regina S. Oboler. LC 83-45345. (Illus.). 368p. 1985. 47.50 (*0-8047-1224-7*) Stanford U Pr.

Women, Power & Policy. Ellen Boneparth. (Policy Studies on Social Policy). 300p. 1982. text ed. 72.00 (*0-08-028048-X*, Pergamon Pr); pap. text ed. 20.00 (*0-08-028047-1*, Pergamon Pr) Elsevier.

Women, Power & Policy: Toward the Year 2000. 2nd ed. Ed. by Ellen Boneparth & Emily Stoper. (Government & Politics Ser.). 320p. 1988. text ed. 45.00 (*0-08-034486-0*, Pergamon Pr); pap. text ed. 18.50 (*0-08-034485-2*, Pergamon Pr) Elsevier.

Women, Power & Resistance: An Introduction to Women's Studies. Tess Cosslett et al. LC 96-22705. 301p. 1996. 77.95 (*0-335-19391-9*, Open Univ Pr); pap. 19.95 (*0-335-19390-0*, Open Univ Pr) Taylor & Francis.

Women, Power & Subversion: Social Strategies in British Fiction, 1778-1860. Judith L. Newton. 224p. 1985. pap. text ed. 12.95 (*0-416-41200-9*, 9761) Routledge Chapman & Hall.

Women, Power & Therapy: Issues for Women. Ed. by Marjorie Braude. LC 87-14873. (Women & Therapy Ser.: Vol. 6, Nos. 1-2). 340p. 1987. text ed. 49.95 (*0-86656-653-8*) Haworth Pr.

Women Preaching Revolution: Calling for Connection in a Disconnected Time. Elaine J. Lawless. 232p. 1996. text ed. 36.50 (*0-8122-3198-8*) U of Pa Pr.

Women, Pregnancy & Substance Abuse. Dorothy Roberts. (Law & Pregnancy Ser.). 21p. (Orig.). (C). 1991. pap. 15.00 (*1-877966-09-6*) Ctr Women Policy.

Women Priests: An Emerging Ministry in the Episcopal Church (1960 to 1980) John H. Morgan. 185p. (Orig.). (C). 1985. pap. 14.95 (*0-932269-48-6*) Wyndham Hall.

Women Prime Ministers & Presidents. Olga S. Opfell. LC 92-56675. (Illus.). 237p. (YA). (gr. 9-12). 1993. lib. bdg. 35.00 (*0-89950-790-5*) McFarland & Co.

Women, Prison, & Crime. Joycelyn M. Pollock-Byrne. LC 89-25164. 208p. (C). 1990. pap. 22.95 (*0-534-12888-2*) Wadsworth Pub.

Women Prisoners: A Forgotten Population. Ed. by Beverly R. Fletcher et al. LC 92-38231. 212p. 1993. text ed. 49.95 (*0-275-94220-1*, C4220, Praeger Pubs) Greenwood.

Women, Prisons, & Psychiatry: Mental Disorder Behind Bars. Anthony Maden. LC 95-39178. 224p. 1995. pap. 35.00 (*0-7506-2003-X*) Buttrwrth-Heinemann.

Women, Production, & Patriarchy in Late Medieval Cities. Martha C. Howell & Catherine R. Stimpson. LC 85-31816. (Women in Culture & Society Ser.). xvi, 304p. 1988. pap. text ed. 18.95 (*0-226-35504-7*) U Ch Pr.

Women Professionals in the Agricultural Sector: Cote d'Ivoire Case Study. Nicole Brunet-Perrault & Cheryl R. Doss. Ed. by Denise F. Bryant. (Development Studies Paper). 23p. (Orig.). 1992. pap. 6.00 (*0-933595-14-X*) Winrock Intl.

Women, Property & Islam: Palestinian Experiences, 1920-1990. Annelies Moors. (Middle East Studies: No. 3). 296p. (C). 1996. text ed. 59.95 (*0-521-47497-3*) Cambridge U Pr.

Women, Property & Islam: Palestinian Experiences, 1920-1990. Annelies Moors. (Middle East Studies: No. 3). 296p. (C). 1996. pap. text ed. 19.95 (*0-521-48355-7*) Cambridge U Pr.

Women Prophets. 2nd ed. Marilyn J. Wright. (Illus.). 67p. Date not set. pap. 4.50 (*1-886232-03-2*) Majesty Pubns.

Women Public Speakers in the United States, 1800-1925: A Bio-Critical Sourcebook. Ed. by Karlyn K. Campbell. LC 92-14615. 544p. 1993. text ed. 79.50 (*0-313-27533-5*, CAG, Greenwood Pr) Greenwood.

Women Public Speakers in the United States, 1800-1925: A Bio-Critical Sourcebook. Ed. by Karlyn K. Campbell. 1993. write for info. (*0-318-69324-0*, CAG, Greenwood Pr) Greenwood.

Women Public Speakers in the United States, 1925-1993: A Bio-Critical Sourcebook. Karlyn K. Campbell. LC 93-21145. 520p. 1994. text ed. 79.50 (*0-313-27535-1*, Greenwood Pr) Greenwood.

Women Rabbis: Exploration & Celebration; Papers Delivered at an Academic Conference Honoring Twenty Years of Women in the Rabbinate, 1972-1992. Gary P. Zola. LC 96-25781. 1996. 12.00 (*0-87820-214-5*) Hebrew Union Coll Pr.

Women, Race & Class. Angela Y. Davis. LC 82-40414. 288p. (C). 1983. pap. 11.00 (*0-394-71351-6*, Vin) Random.

Women, 'Race,' & Writing in the Early Modern Period. Ed. by Margo Hendricks & Patricia Parker. LC 93-17049. 392p. (C). (gr. 13). 1993. pap. 18.95 (*0-415-07778-8*, A9825); text ed. 74.95 (*0-415-07777-X*, A9821) Routledge.

Women Readers & the Ideology of Gender in Old French Verse Romance. Roberta L. Krueger. LC 92-36813. (Cambridge Studies in French: No. 43). (Illus.). 336p. (C). 1994. text ed. 69.95 (*0-521-43267-7*) Cambridge U Pr.

Women, Reading, Kroetsch: Telling the Difference. Susan R. Dorscht. 120p. (C). 1991. text ed. 29.95 (*0-88920-205-2*) Wilfrid Laurier.

***Women Reading Shakespeare, 1660-1900: An Anthology of Criticism.** Ann Thompson & Sasha Roberts. LC 96-26247. 1997. text ed. 59.95 (*0-7190-4703-X*, Pub. by Manchester Univ Pr UK); text ed. 19.95 (*0-7190-4704-8*, Pub. by Manchester Univ Pr UK) St Martin.

***Women Reading the World: Policies & Practices of Literacy in Asia.** Carolyn Medel-Anonuevo. 134p. 1996. pap. 20.00 (*92-820-1069-4*, U6940, Pub. by UNESCO-Bangkok TH) Bernan Associates.

Women Reading Women Writing: Self-Invention in Paula Gunn Allen, Gloria Anzaldua, & Andre Lorde. AnaLouise Keating. LC 95-39871. 240p. (C). 1996. 49.95 (*1-56639-419-8*); pap. 18.95 (*1-56639-420-1*) Temple U Pr.

W

An Asterisk (*) at the beginning of an entry indicates that the title is appearing in BIP for the first time.

Women Reformed, Women Empowered: Poor Mothers & the Endangered Promise of Head Start. Lynda J. Ames & Jeanne Ellsworth. LC 96-20537. (Women in the Political Economy Ser.). 224p. (C). 1997. pap. 19.95 (1-56639-493-7); lib. bdg. 54.95 (1-56639-492-9) Temple U Pr.

Women, Relationships & Power: Implications for Counseling. Ellen P. Cook. 296p. (C). 1993. pap. text ed. 29.95 (1-55620-100-1, 72515) Am Coun Assn.

Women, Religion, & Development in the Third World. Theodora C. Foster. LC 83-13670. 288p. 1983. text ed. 59.95 (0-275-90957-3, C0957, Praeger Pubs) Greenwood.

Women, Religion & Sexuality: Studies on the Impact of Religious Teaching on Women. Ed. by Jeanne Becher. LC 91-10003. 278p. (Orig.). (C). 1991. pap. 16.95 (1-56338-013-7) TPI PA.

***Women, Religion, & Social Change.** Ed. by Yvonne Y. Haddad. 510p. 1996. pap. 19.95 (0-614-21404-1, 1331) Kazi Pubns.

Women, Religion, & Social Change. Ed. by Yvonne Y. Haddad & Ellison B. Findlay. LC 85-4747. (Illus.). 508p. 1985. text ed. 64.50 (0-88706-068-4); pap. text ed. 21.95 (0-88706-069-2) State U NY Pr.

***Women, Religion, & Social Change in Brazil's Popular Church.** Carol A. Drogus. Date not set. write for info. (0-268-01951-7) U of Notre Dame Pr.

Women Religious & the Intellectual Life: The North American Achievement. Ed. by Bridget Puzon. 145p. 1995. pap. text ed. 44.95 (1-883255-76-7) Intl Scholars.

Women Religious & the Intellectual Life: The North American Achievement. Ed. by Bridget Puzon. 145p. 1995. text ed. 64.95 (1-883255-77-5) Intl Scholars.

Women Remember the War, 1941-1945. Ed. by Michael E. Stevens & Ellen D. Goldlust. LC 93-23197. 1993. pap. 7.95 (0-87020-272-3) State Hist Soc Wis.

Women Remembered: A Guide to Landmarks of Women's History in the United States. Marion Tinling. LC 85-17639. 810p. 1986. text ed. 85.00 (0-313-23984-3, TWR/, Greenwood Pr) Greenwood.

Women Reshaping Human Rights: How Extraordinary Activists Are Changing the World. Marguerite G. Bouvard. LC 96-5126. (Illus.). 319p. 1996. 50.00 (0-8420-2562-6); pap. 18.95 (0-8420-2563-4) Scholarly Res Inc.

Women Resisting AIDS: Feminist Strategies of Empowerment. Ed. by Beth E. Schneider & Nancy Stoller. LC 94-31407. (Health, Society & Policy Ser.). 368p. (Orig.). (C). 1994. text ed. 59.95 (1-56639-268-3); pap. text ed. 22.95 (1-56639-269-1) Temple U Pr.

Women Resisting Violence: Spirituality for Life. Ed. by Mary J. Mananzan et al. LC 96-22683. 192p. (Orig.). 1996. pap. 16.00 (1-57075-080-7) Orbis Bks.

Women Returner's Network: Returning to Work. 5th ed. Employment Dept. Group Staff. 401p. pap. 39.95 (0-8464-4317-1) Beekman Pubs.

Women Returning to Higher Education. Gillian Pascall & Roger Cox. LC 93-13275. 169p. 1994. 79.00 (0-335-19056-1, Open Univ Pr); pap. 33.00 (0-335-19055-3, Open Univ Pr) Taylor & Francis.

Women Revolutionaries of Bengal, 1905-1939. Tirtha Mandal. (C). 1991. text ed. 14.00 (81-85195-41-2, Pub. by Minerva II) S Asia.

Women, Rites & Sites: Aboriginal Women's Cultural Knowledge. Ed. by Peggy Brock. 208p. (Orig.). 1989. pap. text ed. 14.95 (0-04-370186-8, Pub. by Allen Unwin AT) Paul & Co Pubs.

Women Romantic Poets, 1770-1838: An Anthology. Ed. by Andrew Ashfield. 288p. (C). 1995. text ed. 69.95 (0-7190-3788-3, Pub. by Manchester Univ Pr UK); text ed. 19.95 (0-7190-3789-1, Pub. by Manchester Univ Pr UK) St Martin.

Women Romantic Poets 1785-1832: An Anthology. Intro. & Selected by Jennifer Breen. 240p. 1994. pap. 7.50 (0-460-87456-X, Everyman's Classic Lib) C E Tuttle.

***Women Romantics Writing in Pro.** J. Breen. 1996. 8.50 (0-460-87793-3, 665267Q, Everyman's Classic Lib) C E Tuttle.

Women Saints of East & West. Ed. by Swami Ghanananda & John Stewart-Wallace. LC 79-65731. 292p. 1979. reprint ed. pap. 10.95 (0-87481-036-1) Vedanta Pr.

Women Scientists. Nancy Veglahn. (American Profiles Ser.). (Illus.). 144p. (J). (gr. 6-10). 1992. lib. bdg. 17.95 (0-8160-2482-0) Facts on File.

Women Scientists & Engineers Employed in Industry: Why So Few? National Research Council Committee on Women in Science & Engineering. 144p. (Orig.). (C). 1993. pap. text ed. 29.00 (0-309-04991-1) Natl Acad Pr.

Women Scientists in America: Before Affirmative Action, 1940-1972. Margaret W. Rossiter. 624p. 1995. 35.95 (0-8018-4893-8) Johns Hopkins.

Women Scientists in America: Struggles & Strategies to 1940. Margaret W. Rossiter. LC 81-20902. 1984. reprint ed. pap. 15.95 (0-8018-2509-1) Johns Hopkins.

***Women, Seduction, & Betrayal in Biblical Narrative.** Alice Bach. (Illus.). 352p. (C). 1997. text ed. 59.95 (0-521-47532-5) Cambridge U Pr.

***Women, Seduction, & Betrayal in Biblical Narrative.** Alice Bach. (Illus.). 352p. (C). 1997. pap. text ed. 16.95 (0-521-47560-0) Cambridge U Pr.

Women, Sex, & Addiction: A Search for Love & Power. Charlotte D. Kasl. LC 89-46229. 416p. 1990. reprint ed. pap. 13.00 (0-06-097321-8, PL) HarpC.

Women, Sex & Desire: Exploring Your Sexuality at Every Stage of Life. Elizabeth Davis. LC 95-33256. (Illus.). 224p. 1995. 22.95 (0-89793-195-5); pap. 12.95 (0-89793-194-7) Hunter Hse.

Women, Sex, & Rock 'n' Roll: In Their Own Words. Liz Evans. 1995. pap. 12.00 (0-04-440900-1) Routledge Chapman & Hall.

Women, Sex & the Law. Rosemarie Tong. LC 83-16001. (New Feminist Perspectives Ser.). 224p. (C). 1984. pap. 19.95 (0-8476-7231-X) Rowman.

Women Sex Offenders: Treatment & Dynamics. Adele Mayer. 1991. pap. 16.95 (1-55691-063-0, 630) Learning Pubns.

Women, Sexuality & the Changing Social Order: The Impact of Government Policies on Reproductive Behavior in Kenya. Beth M. Ahlberg. (International Studies in Global Change). viii, 274p. 1991. pap. text ed. 39.00 (2-88124-499-8) Gordon & Breach.

Women Shall Live by the Sweat of Their Brow. Annie Evans, pseud. 170p. (Orig.). 1995. pap. 15.00 (1-57502-044-0) Morris Pubng.

Women Shapeshifters: Transforming the Contemporary Novel. Thelma J. Shinn. LC 95-40027. (Contributions in Women's Studies: Vol. 156). 200p. 1996. text ed. 55.00 (0-313-29676-6, Greenwood Pr) Greenwood.

Women Shaping Art: Profiles in Power. Judy K. Van Wagner. LC 84-4794. 336p. 1984. text ed. 49.95 (0-275-91752-5, C1752, Praeger Pubs) Greenwood.

Women Silversmiths, 1685-1845. Philippa Glanville & Jennifer F. Goldsborough. LC 89-51744. (Illus.). 176p. 1990. 45.00 (0-940979-10-1); pap. 34.95 (0-940979-11-X) Natl Museum Women.

Women Singing in the Snow: A Cultural Analysis of Chicana Literature. Tey D. Rebolledo. 250p. 1995. pap. 17.95 (0-8165-1546-8); lib. bdg. 36.00 (0-8165-1520-4) U of Ariz Pr.

***Women Ski.** 2nd ed. Claudia Carbone. 1996. pap. 14.95 (0-915009-55-2) World Leis Corp.

Women Smokers Can Quit: A Different Approach. Sue F. Delaney. 64p. (Orig.). 1989. pap. 6.95 (0-9626223-1-1) Womens Hlthcare Pr.

Women, Social Science & Public Policy. Ed. by Jacqueline Goodnow & Carole Pateman. 162p. 1985. pap. text ed. 13.95 (0-86861-685-0) Routledge Chapman & Hall.

***Women, Society & Christianity.** Anmol Pub. Staff. (C). 1995. 23.00 (81-7488-088-7, Pub. by Anmol II) S Asia.

Women, Society, the State & Abortion: A Structural Analysis. Patrick J. Sheehan. LC 87-14615. 161p. 1987. text ed. 45.00 (0-275-92744-X, C2744, Praeger Pubs) Greenwood.

Women Soldiers: Images & Realities. Elisabetta Addis et al. Ed. by Valeria E Russo & Lorenza Sebesta. LC 93-39270. 1994. text ed. 49.95 (0-312-12073-7) St Martin.

Women Soldiers Vol. 1: Images & Realities. Elisabetta Addis. 1994. text ed. 20.95 (0-312-12074-5) St Martin.

Women Speak: Of God, Congregations, & Change. Joanna B. Gillespie. LC 94-23531. 256p. 1995. pap. 16.00 (1-56338-104-4) TPI PA.

Women Speak: The Eloquence of Women's Lives. Karen Foss & Sonja Foss. (Illus.). 310p. (Orig.). (C). 1991. pap. text ed. 17.95 (0-88133-547-9) Waveland Pr.

Women Speak & about Time. Candy Klieman. LC 96-23873. 1996. 22.95 (0-914373-40-4) Wieser & Wieser.

Women Speak to God: The Prayers & Poems of Jewish Women. Ed. by Deborah L. Kremsdorf. LC 86-51498. 100p. (Orig.). 1987. pap. 8.95 (0-9608054-6-X) Womans Inst-Cont Jewish Ed.

Women Speaks: Monologues for Actresses from Women Famous, Infamous, & Unknown. Lydia Cosentino. LC 94-49323. 1995. pap. 9.95 (0-940669-30-7, D-36) Dramaline Pubns.

Women, Sport, & Culture. Ed. by Susan Birrell & Cheryl L. Cole. LC 93-38013. 416p. 1994. text ed. 39.00 (0-87322-650-X, BBIR0650) Human Kinetics.

Women, Sports, & the Law: A Comprehensive Research Guide to Sex Discrimination in Sports. Karen Tokarz. LC 86-27039. (Legal Research Guides Ser.: Vol. 3). v, 135p. 1986. lib. bdg. 34.00 (0-89941-528-8, 304650) W S Hein.

Women Stage Directors Speak: Exploring the Influence of Gender on Their Work. Rebecca Daniels. LC 96-28188. 216p. 1996. lib. bdg. 29.50 (0-7864-0235-0) McFarland & Co.

Women, State, & Ideology: Studies from Africa & Asia. Ed. by Haleh Afshar. LC 86-14432. 245p. (C). 1987. text ed. 67.50 (0-88706-393-4); pap. text ed. 24.95 (0-88706-394-2) State U NY Pr.

Women, State, & Party in Eastern Europe. Ed. by Sharon L. Wolchik & Alfred G. Meyer. LC 85-16262. (Duke Press Policy Studies). (Illus.). xiv, 454p. 1985. text ed. 54.95 (0-8223-0660-3); pap. text ed. 24.95 (0-8223-0659-X) Duke.

Women, State, & Revolution: Essays on Power & Gender in Europe Since 1789. Ed. by Sian Reynolds. LC 86-16074. (Illus.). 208p. 1986. lib. bdg. 27.50 (0-87023-552-4) U of Mass Pr.

Women State & Territorial Legislators, 1895-1995: A State-by-State Analysis, with Rosters of 6,000 Women. Elizabeth M. Cox. LC 95-32652. (Illus.). 408p. 1996. lib. bdg. 48.50 (0-7864-0078-1) McFarland & Co.

Women Steadfast in Christ: Talks Selected from the 1991 BYU Women's Conference. Ed. by Dawn H. Anderson & Marie Cornwall. LC 91-47724. 312p. 1992. 13.95 (0-87579-597-8) Deseret Bk.

Women Still Weep: A Sequel to Women Must Weep. Mary Orr. 1980. pap. 5.25 (0-8222-1275-7) Dramatists Play.

***Women, Stress, & Heart Disease.** Ed. by Kristina Orth-Gomer et al. 400p. 1996. write for info. (0-8058-2124-4) L Erlbaum Assocs.

Women Strike for Peace: Traditional Motherhood & Radical Politics in the 1960s. Amy Swerdlow. LC 93-16801. (Women in Culture & Society Ser.). (Illus.). 326p. 1993. pap. 17.95 (0-226-78636-6); lib. bdg. 49.50 (0-226-78635-8) U Ch Pr.

Women Struggling for a New Life: The Role of Religion in the Cultural Passage from Korea to America. Ai R. Kim. LC 95-3470. 233p. (C). 1996. text ed. 59.50 (0-7914-2737-4) State U NY Pr.

Women Struggling for a New Life: The Role of Religion in the Cultural Passage from Korea to America. Ai R. Kim. LC 95-3470. 233p. (C). 1996. pap. text ed. 19.95 (0-7914-2738-2) State U NY Pr.

Women Students in India. S. Sharma. 171p. 1979. 14.95 (0-318-37326-2) Asia Bk Corp.

Women Studies Disc 96B. large type ed. G. K. Hall Staff. 1996. lib. bdg. 495.00 (0-7838-1724-X, GK Hall) Thorndike Pr.

Women Suffrage & the New Democracy. Sara H. Graham. LC 96-18148. 320p. 1996. 27.50 (0-300-06346-6) Yale U Pr.

Women Surviving: Studies in Irish Women's History in 19th-20th Century. Maria Luddy & Cliona Murphy. 224p. 1990. pap. 18.95 (1-85371-064-4, Pub. by Poolbeg Pr IE) Dufour.

***Women Surviving the Holocaust: In Spite of the Horror.** Jutta Bendremer. LC 97-941. (Symposium Ser.). 1997. write for info. (0-7734-8665-8) E Mellen.

***Women Survivors of Childhood Sexual Abuse: Healing Through Group Work: Beyond Survival.** Judy Chew. LC 97-7517. (Illus.). 162p. 1997. pap. text ed. 14.95 (0-7890-0284-1); lib. bdg. 39.95 (0-7890-0110-1) Haworth Pr.

Women Take Charge: Asserting Your Rights in the Marketplace. Nina Easton. 202p. 1983. pap. 6.50 (0-318-04129-4) Ctr Responsive Law.

Women Taken in Adultery: The Poggenpuhl Family. Theodor Fontane. Tr. by Gabriele Annan. 272p. 1996. pap. 10.95 (0-14-043524-7) Penguin.

Women Talk: Conversation Between Women Friends. Jennifer Coates. LC 95-49251. 288p. (C). 1996. 49.95 (0-631-18252-7); pap. 19.95 (0-631-18253-5) Blackwell Pubs.

Women Talk Sex: Autobiographical Writing on Sex, Sexuality & Sexual Identity. Ed. by Pearlie McNeill et al. 233p. 1992. pap. 15.50 (1-85727-000-2) LPC InBook.

Women Talk Sex: Autobiographical Writing on Sex, Sexuality & Sexual Identity. Ed. by Pearlie McNeill et al. 233p. 1993. 45.00 (1-85727-010-X) LPC InBook.

Women Talking. Ed. by Justine Hill. (Illus.). 256p. 1976. 12.95 (0-8184-0235-0) Carol Pub Group.

Women Teachers & Feminist Politics, 1900-1939. Alison Oram. LC 95-36983. 1996. 79.95 (0-7190-2959-7, Pub. by Manchester Univ Pr UK) St Martin.

Women Teachers & Popular Education in Nineteenth Century France: Social Values & Corporate Identity at the Normal School Institution. Anne T. Quartararo. LC 94-45047. (Illus.). 232p. 1995. 38.50 (0-87413-545-1) U Delaware Pr.

Women Teachers in South Asia, Nudity & Discontinuity With Change. Usha Nayar. (C). 1988. 22.50 (81-7001-048-9, Pub. by Chanakya II) S Asia.

Women Teachers on the Frontier. Polly W. Kaufman. LC 83-14699. 272p. 1985. pap. text ed. 15.00 (0-300-03402-4) Yale U Pr.

Women Teachers Working for Equality. Ed. by Hilary De Lyon & Frances W. Migniuolo. 160p. 1989. pap. 27.00 (0-335-15857-9, Open Univ Pr) Taylor & Francis.

Women Teaching for Change: Gender, Class & Power. Kathleen Weiler. LC 87-14604. (Critical Studies in Education). 192p. 1987. text ed. 49.95 (0-89789-127-9, Bergin & Garvey); pap. text ed. 18.95 (0-89789-128-7, Bergin & Garvey) Greenwood.

Women, Texts & Histories 1575-1760. Ed. by Clare Brant & Dianne Purkiss. LC 91-32120. 256p. (C). (gr. 13). 1992. pap. 17.95 (0-415-05370-6, A7145) Routledge.

Women, the Arts, & the 1920's in Paris & New York. Ed. by Kenneth W. Wheeler & Virginia L. Lussier. LC 81-7510. 171p. reprint ed. pap. 48.80 (0-8357-7076-1, 2033586) Bks Demand.

Women, the Book, & the Godly: Selected Proceedings of the St. Hilda's Conference, 1993, Vol. I. Ed. by Jane H. Taylor & Lesley Smith. 205p. (C). 1995. 53.00 (0-85991-420-8) Boydell & Brewer.

Women, the Book, & the Wordly: Selected Proceedings of the St. Hilda's Conference, Oxford, Vol. II. Ed. by Lesley Smith & Jane H. Taylor. (Illus.). 208p. (C). 1995. 53.00 (0-85991-479-8) Boydell & Brewer.

Women, the Courts & Equality. Laura L. Crites & Winifred L. Hepperle. LC 86-15515. (Yearbooks in Women's Policy Studies: Vol. 11). 1987. 44.00 (0-8039-2811-4); pap. 21.95 (0-8039-2812-2) Sage.

Women, the Courts, & Equality. Ed. by Laura L. Crites & Winifred L. Hepperle. LC 86-15515. (Sage Yearbooks in Women's Policy Studies: No. 11). 256p. 1987. reprint ed. pap. 73.00 (0-608-01538-5, 2059582) Bks Demand.

Women, the Earth, the Divine. Eleanor Rae. LC 93-47614. (Ecology & Justice Ser.). 150p. (Orig.). 1994. pap. 15.00 (0-88344-952-8) Orbis Bks.

Women, the Elderly & Social Policy in Finland & in Japan: The Muse or the Working Bee. Ed. by Briitta Koskiaho. 208p. 1995. 55.95 (1-85628-859-5, Pub. by Avebury Pub UK) Ashgate Pub Co.

Women, the Environment & Sustainable Development: Towards a Theoretical Synthesis. Rosi Braidotti et al. LC 94-1964. 240p. (C). 1994. pap. 19.95 (1-85649-184-6, Pub. by Zed Bks Ltd UK); text ed. 55.00 (1-85649-183-8, Pub. by Zed Bks Ltd UK) Humanities.

Women, the Family, & Divorce Laws in Islamic History. Amira El Azhary Sonbol. LC 95-40354. (Contemporary Issues in the Middle East Ser.). (C). 1996. pap. 19.95 (0-8156-0383-5) Syracuse U Pr.

Women, the Family, & Divorce Laws in Islamic History. Ed. by Amira El Azhary Sonbol. LC 95-40354. (Contemporary Issues in the Middle East Ser.). 336p. (C). 1996. text ed. 45.00 (0-8156-2688-6, SOWF) Syracuse U Pr.

Women, the Family, & Freedom: The Debate in Documents, Vol. I, 1750-1880. Ed. by Susan G. Bell & Karen M. Offen. LC 82-61081. xvi, 561p. 1983. 59.50 (0-8047-1170-4); pap. 24.95 (0-8047-1171-2) Stanford U Pr.

Women, the Family, & Freedom: The Debate in Documents, Vol. II, 1880-1950. Ed. by Susan G. Bell & Karen M. Offen. LC 82-61081. xvi, 474p. 1983. 55.00 (0-8047-1172-0); pap. 22.95 (0-8047-1173-9) Stanford U Pr.

Women, the Family & Peasant Revolution in China. Kay A. Johnson. LC 82-24748. x, 296p. 1985. pap. text ed. 15.50 (0-226-40189-8) U Ch Pr.

Women, the Family, & Policy: A Global Perspective. Ed. by Esther N. Chow & Catherine W. Berheide. LC 93-847. (SUNY Series in Gender & Society). 293p. (C). 1994. text ed. 64.50 (0-7914-1785-9); pap. text ed. 21.95 (0-7914-1786-7) State U NY Pr.

Women, the Family & Social Work. Ed. by Eve Brook & Ann Davis. (Tavistock Library of Social Work Practice). 192p. (Orig.). 1985. 27.50 (0-422-77940-7, 9484, Pub. by Tavistock UK); pap. text ed. 13.95 (0-422-77950-4, 9485, Pub. by Tavistock UK) Routledge Chapman & Hall.

Women-The Misunderstood Majority. Gay Hubbard. (Contemporary Christian Counseling Ser.). 1992. 18.99 (0-8499-0834-5) Word Pub.

Women-The Misunderstood Majority. Gay Hubbard. 1992. pap. 14.99 (0-8499-3380-3) Word Pub.

Women, the State, & Development. Ed. by Kathleen A. Staudt et al. LC 88-8531. 248p. (Orig.). 1989. text ed. 74.50 (0-7914-0064-6); pap. text ed. 24.95 (0-7914-0065-4) State U NY Pr.

Women, the State & Revolution: Soviet Family Policy & Social Life, 1917-1936. Wendy Z. Goldman. LC 92-47481. (Cambridge Russian, Soviet & Post-Soviet Studies: No. 90). 275p. (C). 1993. text ed. 64.95 (0-521-37404-9); pap. text ed. 19.95 (0-521-45816-1) Cambridge U Pr.

Women, the State, & Welfare. Ed. by Linda Gordon. LC 90-50089. 328p. (Orig.). (C). 1991. pap. text ed. 14.95 (0-299-12664-1) U of Wis Pr.

Women, the Unions & Work or What Is Not to Be Done. Selma James. 1972. pap. 2.50 (0-912786-33-7) Know Inc.

Women... The World's Greatest Salesmen! Jean R. Nave. 96p. (Orig.). 1984. pap. 6.95 (0-930115-00-7) Windemere Pr.

Women Therapists Working with Women: New Theory & Process of Feminist Therapy. Ed. by Claire Brody. (Focus on Women Ser.: Vol. 7). 192p. 1984. 25.95 (0-8261-4550-7) Springer Pub.

Women Thou Art Loosed. T. D. Jakes. 1996. 14.99 (1-880089-85-8) Albury Pub.

Women Through the Bible: Devotions for Women's Groups. Marlys Taege. 160p. 1987. pap. 8.99 (0-570-04460-X, 12-3064) Concordia.

Women, Time & the Weaving of the Strands of Everyday Life. Karen Davies. (Illus.). 258p. 1990. text ed. 59.95 (0-566-07163-0, Pub. by Avebury Pub UK) Ashgate Pub Co.

Women Times Three: Writers, Detectives, Readers. Ed. by Kathleen G. Klein. LC 95-17734. 1995. 29.95 (0-87972-681-4); pap. 12.95 (0-87972-682-2) Bowling Green Univ Popular Press.

Women to the Glory of God: The Nineteenth Annual Spiritual Sword Lectureship. Ed. by Jim Laws. 475p. 1994. 24.00 (1-886220-00-X) Getwell Church.

Women to Women: Perspectives of Fourteen African-American Christian Women. Ed. by Novella Carter & Matthew Parker. 240p. 1996. pap. 12.99 (0-310-20145-4) Zondervan.

Women Today Series, 8 bks. (J). 1991. 103.60 (0-685-59199-9) Rourke Corp.

Women Today Series, 8 bks., Set. (J). 1991. 138.16 (0-86593-116-X) Rourke Corp.

Women Together, Vol. 16, Organizational Life see History of Women in the United States: Topically Arranged Articles on the Evolution of Women's History in the United States

Women Towards Priesthood: Ministerial Politics & Feminist Praxis. Jacqueline Field-Bibb. 352p. (C). 1991. text ed. 69.95 (0-521-39283-7) Cambridge U Pr.

Women, Tradition & Culture. Malladi Subbamma. 1985. text ed. 22.50 (0-86590-616-5, Pub. by Sterling Pubs II) Apt Bks.

Women Transforming Communications: Global Perspectives. Donna Allen et al. LC 96-4467. 420p. 1996. 58.00 (0-8039-7266-0); pap. 26.95 (0-8039-7267-9) Sage.

***Women Transforming Politics.** Cohen. LC 97-19645. 1997. 65.00 (0-8147-1557-5) NYU Pr.

***Women Transforming Politics: An Alternative Reader.** Cathy Cohen. LC 97-19645. 1997. pap. text ed. 22.95 (0-8147-1558-3) NYU Pr.

Women Transforming Politics: Worldwide Strategies for Empowerment. Ed. by Jill M. Bystydzienski. LC 91-20126. (Illus.). 244p. 1992. text ed. 35.00 (0-253-31294-9); pap. text ed. 13.95 (0-253-20698-7, MB-698) Ind U Pr.

***Women Transforming Politics: Worldwide Strategies for Empowerment.** Ed. by Jill M. Bystydzienski. LC 91-20126. 239p. pap. 68.20 (0-608-05010-5, 2059671) Bks Demand.

Women Travel Writers & the Language of Aesthetics, 1716-1818. Elizabeth A. Bohls. (Studies in Romanticism: No. 13). (Illus.). 320p. (C). 1995. text ed. 54.95 (0-521-47458-2) Cambridge U Pr.

Women Treating Women: Case Material from Women Treated by Female Psychoanalysts. Anne E. Bernstein & Gloria M. Warner. LC 84-8996. xv, 310p. (C). 1985. 45.00 (0-8236-6863-0, 06863) Intl Univs Pr.

W

An Asterisk (*) at the beginning of an entry indicates that the title is appearing in BIP for the first time.

Women Trial Lawyers: How They Succeed in Practice & in the Courtroom. Janine Warsaw. 304p. 1986. 29.95 (*0-13-962374-4*) P-H.

Women Troubadours. Meg Bogin. (Illus.). 192p. 1980. reprint ed. pap. 8.95 (*0-393-00965-3*) Norton.

Women under Apartheid. 119p. 1981. 7.00 (*0-317-36678-5*) Africa Fund.

Women under Assault. Carol Sherman. 24p. pap. text ed. 6.00 (*1-878173-12-X*) Birnham Wood.

Women under Attack: Victories, Backlash & the Fight for Reproductive Freedom. Ed. by Susan E. Davis & Carasa Collective Staff. LC 88-26350. 80p. 1988. pap. 5.00 (*0-89608-356-X*) South End Pr.

***Women under Communism.** Barbara Jancar-Webster. LC 77-16375. 304p. 1978. reprint ed. pap. 86.70 (*0-608-03704-4*, 2064529) Bks Demand.

Women under Communism: Family in Russia & China. Paul Chao. LC 77-89932. 231p. 1977. pap. text ed. 25.95 (*0-930390-00-8*); lib. bdg. 38.95 (*0-930390-01-6*) Gen Hall.

Women under Polygamy. Walter M. Gallichan. LC 72-9639. (Illus.). reprint ed. 55.00 (*0-404-57443-2*) AMS Pr.

Women under Pressure: A Practical Guide for Today's Woman. Ursula Markham. LC 93-16174. (Orig.). 1993. pap. 11.95 (*1-85230-138-4*) Element MA.

Women under Primitive Buddhism: Laywomen & Almswomen. I. B. Horner. 391p. 1990. 24.95 (*81-208-0664-6*) Asia Bk Corp.

Women under the Bo Tree: Buddhist Nuns in Sri Lanka. Tessa J. Bartholomeusz. LC 93-33586. (Studies in Religious Traditions: No. 5). 296p. (C). 1994. text ed. 59.95 (*0-521-46129-4*) Cambridge U Pr.

Women under the Knife. Ann Dally. 289p. (C). 1992. 29.95 (*0-415-90554-0*, A6813, Routledge NY) Routledge.

Women, Unions & the Labour Market: New Perspectives. Joya Sen. 352p. 1993. 39.95 (*0-87411-562-0*) Copley Pub.

Women View Librarianship: Nine Perspectives. Kathryn R. Lundy. LC 80-23611. (ACRL Publications in Librarianship: No. 41). 108p. reprint ed. pap. 30.80 (*0-7837-5951-7*, 2045751) Bks Demand.

Women Viewing Violence. Philip Schlesinger et al. (Illus.). 224p. 1992. 49.95 (*0-85170-330-5*, Pub. by British Film Inst UK); pap. 18.95 (*0-85170-327-5*, Pub. by British Film Inst UK) Ind U Pr.

Women, Violence & Crime Prevention: A West Yorkshire Study. Jalna Hanmer. 383p. 1993. 69.95 (*1-85628-237-6*, Pub. by Avebury Technical UK) Ashgate Pub Co.

Women, Violence & Male Power: Feminist Activism, Research & Practice. Marianne Hester et al. LC 95-15786. 256p. 1995. 24.95 (*0-335-19507-5*, Open Univ Pr); pap. 79.00 (*0-335-19506-7*, Open Univ Pr) Taylor & Francis.

Women, Violence & Social Change. R. Emerson Dobash & Russell P. Dobash. 352p. (C). 1992. pap. 18.95 (*0-415-03610-0*, A6516) Routledge.

Women, Violence & Social Control. Ed. by Jalna Hanmer & Mary Maynard. LC 86-27294. 260p. (C). 1987. pap. 18.50 (*0-391-03515-0*) Humanities.

Women, Vol. 4: (Incl. 1989-1993 Supplements) Ed. by Eleanor C. Goldstein. (Social Issues Resources Ser.). 1994. 95.00 (*0-89777-150-8*) Sirs Inc.

Women, Volunteering, & Health Policy. United Hospital Fund Staff. 81p. 1982. 5.00 (*0-934459-27-4*) United Hosp Fund.

Women vs Men: A Conflict of Navajo Emergence. Berard Haile. Ed. by Karl W. Luckert. LC 81-7433. (American Tribal Religions Ser.: No. 6). 127p. reprint ed. pap. 36.20 (*0-7837-6976-8*, 2046787) Bks Demand.

Women Wage-Earners: Their Past, Their Present, & Their Future. Helen Campbell. LC 72-2594. (American Women Ser.: Images & Realities). 324p. 1978. reprint ed. 23.95 (*0-405-04451-8*) Ayer.

Women, War & Revolution. Ed. by Carol R. Berkin & Clara M. Lovett. LC 79-26450. 310p. (C). 1980. 36.95 (*0-8419-0502-9*); pap. 15.95 (*0-8419-0545-2*) Holmes & Meier.

Women, War, & Work: The Impact of World War I on Women Workers in the United States. Maurine W. Greenwald. LC 89-25288. (Illus.). 352p. 1990. pap. 15.95 (*0-8014-9733-7*) Cornell U Pr.

Women, War, & Work: The Impact of World War I on Women Workers in the United States. Maurine W. Greenwald. LC 80-540. (Contributions in Women's Studies: No. 12). (Illus.). xxvii, 309p. 1980. text ed. 55.00 (*0-313-21355-0*, GWW/, Greenwood Pr) Greenwood.

Women War Correspondents in the Vietnam War, 1961-1975. Virginia Elwood-Akers. LC 87-23313. (Illus.). 294p. 1988. 29.50 (*0-8108-2033-1*) Scarecrow.

Women War Correspondents in World War 2. Lilya Wagner. LC 89-1981. (Contributions in Women's Studies: No. 104). 187p. 1989. text ed. 45.00 (*0-313-26287-X*, WWW, Greenwood Pr) Greenwood.

Women Warriors: A History. David E. Jones. (Illus.). 296p. 1997. 24.95 (*1-57488-106-X*) Brasseys Inc.

Women Warriors of the Plains. Dan Aadland. 192p. 1996. 29.95 (*0-87605-748-2*) Howell Bk.

Women Watching Television: Gender, Class, & Generation in the American Television Experience. Andrea L. Press. LC 90-21274. 258p. (C). 1991. pap. text ed. 17.95 (*0-8122-1286-X*) U of Pa Pr.

Women We Become: Myths, Folktales & Stories about Growing Older. Ann Thomas. 304p. 1996. 23.00 (*0-7615-0654-3*) Prima Pub.

Women Weavers. Indira J. Parikh. (C). 1991. 12.50 (*81-204-0597-8*, Pub. by Oxford IBH II) S Asia.

Women Welfare & Development: A Source Book. D. Paul Chowdhry. (Women in South Asia Ser.: No. W 013). (C). 1992. 32.00 (*81-210-0284-2*, Pub. by Inter-India Pubns) S Asia.

Women, Welfare, & Higher Education: A Selected Annotated Bibliography. Erika Kates. (Economic Opportunities Program Ser.). 25p. (Orig.). (C). 1991. pap. 15.00 (*1-877966-10-X*) Ctr Women Policy.

Women Who Achieved for God. Winnie Christensen. (Fisherman Bible Studyguide Ser.). 80p. 1984. pap. text ed. 4.99 (*0-87788-937-6*) Shaw Pubs.

Women Who Achieved for God - Chinese Edition. Winnie Christensen. Tr. by Jane C. Wu. 90p. (CHI.). 1995. pap. 4.50 (*1-56582-004-5*) Christ Renew Min.

Women Who Achieved Greatness. Cathie Cush. (Twenty Events Ser.). (Illus.). 48p. (J). (gr. 4-8). 1994. lib. bdg. 24.26 (*0-8114-4938-6*) Raintree Steck-V.

Women Who Attract Rich, Powerful & Famous Men, & How They Do It. Cynthia Smith. 1992. pap. 5.50 (*1-56171-180-2*) Sure Seller.

***Women Who Bash/Love Men: How It Hurts Him, Then You!** Ellen Winters et al. 150p. (Orig.). 1997. pap. 14.95 (*0-9657655-9-8*) Parker St.

Women Who Believed God. Winnie Christensen. (Fisherman Bible Studyguide Ser.). 77p. 1983. pap. text ed. 4.99 (*0-87788-936-8*) Shaw Pubs.

***Women Who Can Dish It Out.** Junior League of Springfield, MO Staff. (Illus.). 288p. 1997. 19.95 (*0-9613307-5-9*) Jr League MO.

***Women Who Carry Their Men.** Hattie Hill. (Illus.). 144p. 1996. pap. 18.00 (*1-884363-11-3*) Odenwald Pr.

***Women Who Changed the Heart of the City: The Untold Story of the City Rescue Mission Movement.** Delores Burger. LC 96-32054. 160p. 1997. pap. 9.99 (*0-8254-2146-2*) Kregel.

Women Who Changed Their World. Jill Briscoe. (Jill Briscoe Inductive Bible Study Ser.). 108p. 1991. pap. 7.99 (*0-89693-001-7*, 6-1001, Victor Bks) Chariot Victor.

Women Who Charmed the West. Anne Seagraves. LC 91-65794. (Illus.). 176p. (Orig.). pap. 11.95 (*0-9619088-2-3*) Wesanne Pubns.

***Women Who Dare: Inspiring Stories from the Women Who Lived Them.** Katherine Martin. LC 97-14204. 1997. 18.95 (*1-57036-392-7*) Turner Pub GA.

***Women Who Dared: American Female Test Pilots, Flight Test Engineers, & Astronauts.** Yvonne C. Pateman. (Illus.). 136p. 1996. 29.95 (*0-9654422-0-9*) Norstahr.

Women Who Do & Women Who Don't: Join the Women's Movement. Robyn Rowland. (Illus.). 224p. (Orig.). 1984. pap. 9.95 (*0-7102-0296-2*, RKP) Routledge.

Women Who Do Too Much: Stress & the Myth of the Superwoman. Patricia H. Sprinkle. 176p. 1996. pap. 9.99 (*0-310-53771-1*) Zondervan.

Women Who Embezzle or Defraud: A Study of Convicted Felons. Dorothy Zietz. LC 81-8638. 172p. 1981. text ed. 45.00 (*0-275-90748-1*, C0748, Praeger Pubs) Greenwood.

Women Who Hate Me: Poetry, 1980-1990. Dorothy Allison. LC 91-311. 72p. (Orig.). 1991. pap. 8.95 (*0-932379-98-2*); lib. bdg. 18.95 (*0-932379-99-0*) Firebrand Bks.

Women Who Hurt Themselves: A Book of Hope & Understanding. Dusty Miller. 288p. 1995. pap. 14.00 (*0-465-09219-5*) Basic.

Women Who Joke Too Much. Silver Rose. LC 95-8210. 192p. (Orig.). 1995. pap. 9.00 (*0-399-52154-2*, Perigee Bks) Berkley Pub.

Women Who Kept the Lights: An Illustrated History of Female Lighthouse Keepers. Mary L. Clifford & J. Candace Clifford. LC 93-74066. (Illus.). 192p. (Orig.). 1993. pap. 19.95 (*0-9636412-0-4*) Cypress Communs.

Women Who Kill: With Previously Unpublished Material on the "Battered Women's Syndrome" Ann Jones. 464p. 1996. reprint ed. pap. 15.00 (*0-8070-6775-X*) Beacon Pr.

Women Who Knew Paul. Florence M. Gillman. (Zacchaeus Studies: New Testament). 96p. (Orig.). 1992. pap. 7.95 (*0-8146-5674-9*) Liturgical Pr.

Women Who Knew Too Much. Tania Modleski. 200p. 1987. 35.00 (*0-416-01701-0*, A0412, Routledge NY) Routledge.

Women Who Knew Too Much. Tania Modleski. 200p. 1988. pap. 12.95 (*0-415-90176-6*, Routledge NY) Routledge.

Women Who Knew Too Much. Tania Modleski. 1987. pap. 10.95 (*0-416-01711-8*) Routledge Chapman & Hall.

Women Who Lived, Cities That Died. Geraldine Daesch. (International Poetry Chapbook Ser.). 21p. (Orig.). 1985. write for info. (*0-936600-05-5*) Riverstone Foothills.

Women Who Love Cats Too Much. Allia Zobel. (Illus.). 80p. (Orig.). 1995. pap. 6.95 (*1-55850-541-5*) Adams Media.

Women Who Love Sex. Gina Ogden. Ed. by Denise Silvestro. 288p. 1994. 21.00 (*0-671-86550-1*) PB.

Women Who Love Sex. Gina Ogden. Ed. by Denise Silvestro. 320p. 1995. mass mkt. 5.99 (*0-671-86551-X*) PB.

Women Who Love Sex Addicts: Help for Healing from the Effects of a Relationship with a Sex Addict. Douglass Weiss & Dianne DeBusk. 279p. (Orig.). 1992. pap. 12.95 (*1-881292-78-9*) Discov TX.

Women Who Love Too Much. Robin Norwood. 1990. mass mkt. 6.99 (*0-671-73341-9*) PB.

Women Who Loved Women: An Illustrated Bibliography. Tee A. Corinne. (Illus.). 112p. (Orig.). 1984. pap. write for info. (*0-930143-00-0*) Pearlchild.

***Women Who Made.** S. Glasscock. 1997. pap. 12.95 (*0-590-89645-8*) Scholastic Inc.

Women Who Made a Difference. Carol Crowe-Carraco. LC 89-38085. (Illus.). 64p. 1989. pap. 4.50 (*0-8131-0901-9*) U Pr of Ky.

Women Who Made a Difference in Alabama. 196p. 1996. pap. write for info. (*0-9649012-0-X*) LOWV Alabama.

Women Who Make Our Novels. rev. ed. Grant M. Overton. LC 67-23257. (Essay Index Reprint Ser.). 1977. 23.95 (*0-8369-0758-2*) Ayer.

Women Who Reformed Politics. Isobel V. Morin. LC 93-46336. (Profiles Ser.). (Illus.). 160p. (YA). (gr. 5-12). 1994. lib. bdg. 16.95 (*1-881508-16-1*) Oliver Pr MN.

Women Who Ruled. Guida M. Jackson. LC 89-28282. 190p. 1990. lib. bdg. 55.00 (*0-87436-560-0*) ABC-CLIO.

Women Who Run with the Poodles. Barbara Graham. LC 93-42270. (Illus.). 160p. (Orig.). 1994. pap. 9.00 (*0-380-77632-4*) Avon.

Women Who Run with the Werewolves: Tales of Blood, Lust & Metamorphosis. Ed. by Pam Keesey. 200p. (Orig.). 1996. pap. 12.95 (*1-57344-057-4*) Cleis Pr.

***Women Who Run with the Wolves.** Clarissa P. Estes. 1997. mass mkt. 7.99 (*0-345-40987-6*) Ballantine.

Women Who Run with the Wolves: Myths & Stories of the Wild Woman Archetype. Clarissa P. Estes. LC 91-58630. 448p. 1992. 23.00 (*0-345-37744-3*) Ballantine Trade.

Women Who Run with the Wolves: Myths & Stories of the Wild Women Archetype. Clarissa P. Estes. 576p. 1995. pap. 15.00 (*0-345-39681-2*) Ballantine.

***Women Who Run with Wolves.** Clarissa P. Estes. (SPA.). 1997. pap. write for info. (*0-679-77909-4*, Vin) Random.

***Women Who Sexually Abuse Children: From Research to Clinical Practice.** Jacqui Saradjian & Helga G. Hanks. LC 96-32161. 1996. pap. text ed. 27.95 (*0-471-96072-1*) Wiley.

Women Who Shop Too Much: Overcoming the Urge to Splurge. Carolyn Wesson. 1991. pap. 10.95 (*0-312-06001-7*) St Martin.

Women Who Spied: True Stories of Feminine Espionage. Adolph A. Hoehling. LC 92-14679. (Illus.). 244p. 1992. reprint ed. pap. 14.95 (*0-8191-8486-1*) Madison Bks UPA.

***Women Who Take Care: Choosing to Live with Wisdom, Grace & Power after Fifty-Five.** Lou D. Diekemper. LC 97-1374. 1997. 14.95 (*1-57733-003-X*) B Dolphin Pub.

Women Who Taught: Perspectives on the History of Women & Teaching. Ed. by Alison Prentice & Marjorie R. Theobald. 304p. 1991. 45.00 (*0-8020-2745-8*); pap. 17.95 (*0-8020-6785-9*) U of Toronto Pr.

Women Who Touched My Life: A Memoir. Ruth H. Jacobs. 150p. (Orig.). 1996. pap. 14.95 (*1-879198-22-3*) Knwldg Ideas & Trnds.

Women Who Walk. Stories. Nancy H. Packer. LC 88-28617. x, 184p. 1989. 17.95 (*0-8071-1458-8*) La State U Pr.

Women Who Wear the Breeches see Handsome Heroines: Women as Men in Folklore

Women Who Win. Mary C. Crowley. LC 79-11390. (Illus.). 160p. (gr. 10). 1984. 10.99 (*0-8007-0993-4*) Revell.

Women Who Write: From the Past & the Present to the Future. Lucinda I. Smith. Ed. by Jane Steltenpohl. (Illus.). 160p. (YA). (gr. 7 up). 1989. pap. 9.95 (*0-671-65669-4*, Julian Messner); lib. bdg. 14.95 (*0-671-65668-6*, Julian Messner) Silver Burdett Pr.

Women Who Write II. Lucinda I. Smith. (J). 1994. 16.00 (*0-671-87253-2*) S&S Trade.

Women Who Write the Movies: From Frances Marion to Nora Ephron. Marsha McCreadie. LC 94-18113. (Illus.). 256p. 1995. 19.95 (*1-55972-251-7*, Birch Ln Pr) Carol Pub Group.

Women Whose Lives Are Food, Men Whose Lives Are Money. Poems. Joyce Carol Oates. LC 77-17220. (Illus.). 80p. 1978. 13.95 (*0-8071-0391-8*) La State U Pr.

Women Wielding the Hoe: Lessons from Rural Africa for Feminist Theory & Development Practice. Ed. by Deborah F. Bryceson et al. (Cross-Cultural Perspectives on Women Ser.). 288p. 45.95 (*1-85973-068-X*); pap. 19.95 (*1-85973-073-6*) Berg Pubs.

Women Winning: How to Run for Office. Barbara M. Trafton. LC 83-22875. 160p. 1984. pap. 9.95 (*0-916782-44-1*) Harvard Common Pr.

Women with Alcoholic Husbands: Ambivalence & the Trap of Codependency. Ramona M. Asher. LC 91-27765. xvi, 224p. (C). 1992. pap. 15.95 (*0-8078-4373-3*) U of NC Pr.

Women with & Without. Carol Murray. (American Dust Ser.: No. 14). 200p. 1984. 10.95 (*0-913218-81-2*) Dustbooks.

Women with Attention Deficit Disorder: Embracing Disorganization at Home & in the Workplace. Sari Solden. (Illus.). 288p. (Orig.). 1995. pap. 11.95 (*1-887424-05-9*) Underwood Bks.

Women with Cancer. Ed. by B. L. Andersen. (Contributions to Psychology & Medicine Ser.). (Illus.). 330p. 1986. 122.95 (*0-387-96360-X*) Spr-Verlag.

Women with Disabilities: Essays in Psychology, Policy, & Politics. Ed. by Michelle Fine & Adrienne Asch. (Health, Society, & Policy Ser.). 368p. 1989. pap. 19.95 (*0-87722-669-5*) Temple U Pr.

Women with Disabilities: Found Voices. Ed. by Mary E. Willmuth & Lillian Holcomb. LC 93-30402. (Women & Therapy Ser.: Vol. 14, Nos. 3-4). (Illus.). 209p. 1993. pap. 14.95 (*1-56023-046-0*); lib. bdg. 34.95 (*1-56024-477-1*) Haworth Pr.

Women with Guns: Six New American Plays. B. Dale et al. 299p. (Orig.). 1986. pap. 14.95 (*0-88145-035-9*) Broadway Play.

***Women with Men.** Richard Ford. LC 97-5832. 1997. 22.00 (*0-679-45469-1*) Knopf.

***Women with Men: Three Long Stories.** limited ed. Richard Ford. 1997. write for info. (*0-9631925-8-2*) B E Trice.

Women with Physical Disabilities: Achieving & Maintaining Health & Well-Being. Ed. by Danuta Krotoski. LC 95-50962. 1996. 42.00 (*1-55766-234-7*) P H Brookes.

Women with Vision: The Presentation Sisters of South Dakota, 1880-1985. Susan C. Peterson & Courtney A. Vaughn-Roberson. LC 87-20451. 334p. 1988. text ed. 29.95 (*0-252-01493-6*) U of Ill Pr.

Women with Wings: Female Flyers in Fact & Fiction. Mary Cadogan. (Illus.). 280p. 1993. 25.00 (*0-89733-385-3*) Academy Chi Pubs.

Women without Children: The Reasons, the Rewards, the Regrets. Susan S. Lang. 288p. 1996. pap. 12.00 (*1-55850-597-0*) Adams Media.

Women Without Husbands: An Exploration of the Margins of Marriage. Joan Chandler. LC 90-26212. 200p. 1991. text ed. 35.00 (*0-312-06107-2*) St Martin.

***Women Without Limits.** 2nd ed. Daisy Osborn. (Illus.). (Orig.). (RUS.). 1995. mass mkt. write for info. (*1-890863-14-9*) Wrld Wide Print.

Women Without Men: Female Bonding & the American Novel of the 1980s. Donald J. Greiner. LC 92-39385. 128p. (C). 1993. text ed. 24.95 (*0-87249-884-0*) U of SC Pr.

Women Without Men: Gender & Morality in an Algerian Town. Willy Jansen. (Illus.). xvi, 303p. 1986. pap. 60.25 (*90-04-08345-6*) E J Brill.

***Women Without Superstition: No Gods - No Masters.** Ed. by Annie L. Gaylor. LC 96-90833. (Illus.). 696p. 1997. 25.00 (*1-877733-09-1*) Freedom Rel Found.

Women, Wives, Mothers: Values & Options. Jessie Bernard. LC 74-18210. 286p. 1975. pap. text ed. 26.95 (*0-202-30281-4*) Aldine de Gruyter.

Women, Women Writers & the West. Ed. by Lawrence L. Lee & Merrill E. Lewis. LC 78-69805. 252p. 1978. 15.00 (*0-87875-146-7*) Whitston Pub.

Women Won't Benefit. Hilary Lang & Sue Ward. (C). 1988. 25.00 (*0-685-33954-8*, Pub. by NCCL UK) St Mut.

Women, Work & Achievement: The Endless Revolution. Bernard C. Rosen. LC 88-7802. 256p. 1992. pap. text ed. 18.95 (*0-333-48869-5*) St Martin.

***Women, Work & Computerization.** I. V. Eriksson et al. xii, 438p. 1991. 157.00 (*0-444-89339-3*, North Holland) Elsevier.

Women, Work & Computerization: Breaking Old Boundaries, Building New Forms: Proceedings of the IFIP TC9/WG 9.1 International Conference on Women, Work & Computerization Held in Manchester, U.K., 2-5 July, 1994. Ed. by Alison Adam & International Conference on Women, Work & Computerization Staff. LC 94-37290. (IFIP Transactions A: Computer Science & Technology Ser.: Vol. A-57). 462p. 1994. pap. 152.50 (*0-444-81927-4*) Elsevier.

***Women, Work & Computerization: Spinning a Web from Past to Future.** Ed. by A. F. Grundy et al. 510p. 1997. pap. 74.00 (*3-540-62610-7*) Spr-Verlag.

Women, Work, & Coping: A Multidisciplinary Approach to Workplace Stress. Ed. by Bonita C. Long & Sharon E. Kahn. 368p. 1993. 55.00 (*0-7735-1128-8*, Pub. by McGill CN); pap. 18.95 (*0-7735-1129-6*, Pub. by McGill CN) U of Toronto Pr.

Women, Work, & Divorce. Richard R. Peterson. LC 88-2133. (SUNY Series in the Sociology of Work). 179p. 1989. text ed. 64.50 (*0-88706-858-8*); pap. text ed. 21.95 (*0-88706-859-6*) State U NY Pr.

***Women, Work, & Economic Reform in the Middle East & North Africa.** Valentine Mohgadam. 260p. 1997. 49.95 (*1-55587-785-0*) Lynne Rienner.

Women, Work & Equal Opportunity: A Study of Underachievement in the Civil Service. Barbara Bagilhole. 223p. 1994. 55.95 (*1-85628-525-1*, Pub. by Avebury Pub UK) Ashgate Pub Co.

Women, Work & Family. Louise A. Tilly & Joan W. Scott. 274p. (C). 1987. pap. 12.95 (*0-415-90262-2*, Routledge NY) Routledge.

Women, Work & Family in the British, Canadian & Norwegian Offshore Oilfields. Ed. by Jane Lewis et al. LC 86-31393. 200p. 1988. text ed. 45.00 (*0-312-00528-8*) St Martin.

Women, Work, & Family in the Soviet Union. Ed. by Gail W. Lapidus. LC 81-9281. 358p. reprint ed. pap. 102.10 (*0-8357-2620-7*, 2040108) Bks Demand.

Women, Work, & Fertility 1900-1987. Susan H. Van Horn. (American Social Experience Ser.: No. 8). 256p. (C). 1988. text ed. 45.00 (*0-8147-8759-2*) NYU Pr.

Women, Work, & Fertility 1900-1987. Susan H. Van Horn. (American Social Experience Ser.: No. 8). 256p. (C). 1989. pap. text ed. 12.00 (*0-8147-8760-6*) NYU Pr.

Women, Work, & Gender Relations in Developing Countries: A Global Perspective. Ed. by Parvin Ghorayshi & Claire Belenger. LC 96-10741. (Contributions in Sociology Ser.: Vol. 118). 264p. 1996. text ed. 59.95 (*0-313-29797-5*, Greenwood Pr) Greenwood.

***Women, Work & Gospel Values.** Head & Galligan. 26p. 1996. pap. text ed. 2.95 (*1-55612-199-7*, LL1199) Sheed & Ward MO.

Women, Work, & Health. Ed. by M. Frankenhauser et al. (Stress & Coping Ser.). (Illus.). 300p. 1991. 45.00 (*0-306-43780-5*, Plenum Pr) Plenum.

Women, Work, & Ideology in the Third World. Ed. by Haleh Afshar. 280p. 1985. pap. 15.95 (*0-422-79710-3*, 9607, Pub. by Tavistock UK) Routledge Chapman & Hall.

Women, Work, & Life Cycle in a Medieval Economy: Women in York & Yorkshire c. 1300-1520. P. J. Goldberg. LC 92-12228. (Illus.). 424p. 1992. 79.00 (*0-19-820154-0*, Clarendon Pr) OUP.

Women, Work & Marriage in Urban India: A Study of Dual- & Single-Earner Couples. G. N. Ramu. 200p. (C). 1990. text ed. 24.00 (*0-8039-9626-8*) Sage.

Women, Work, & National Policy: The Kennedy-Johnson Years. Patricia G. Zelman. LC 81-16351. (Studies in American History & Culture: No. 33). 172p. reprint ed. pap. 49.10 (*0-685-20853-2*, 2070095) Bks Demand.

W

Women, Work, & Place. Ed. by Audrey Kobayashi. 264p. 1994. 49.95 (*0-7735-1225-X*, Pub. by McGill CN) U of Toronto Pr.

Women, Work, & Place. Ed. by Audrey Kobayashi. 264p. 1994. pap. 19.95 (*0-7735-1242-X*, Pub. by McGill CN) U of Toronto Pr.

Women, Work & Protest: A Century of U. S. Women's History. Ed. by Ruth Milkman. 320p. (Orig.). 1985. pap. 14.95 (*0-7100-9940-1*, RKP) Routledge.

Women Work & Protest: A Century of U. S. Women's Labor History. Ruth Milkman. 334p. (C). 1985. pap. 16.95 (*0-415-06592-5*) Routledge.

Women, Work & School: Occupational Segregation & the Role of Education. Ed. by Leslie R. Wolfe. LC 90-20997. (Illus.). 237p. 1991. reprint ed. pap. 67.60 (*0-608-00932-6*, 2061726) Bks Demand.

Women, Work, & Sexual Politics in Eighteenth-Century England. Bridget Hill. 273p. 1994. reprint ed. pap. 19.95 (*0-7735-1270-5*, Pub. by McGill CN) U of Toronto Pr.

Women, Work, & Technology: Transformations. Ed. by Barbara D. Wright. (Women & Culture Ser.). 350p. (C). 1988. pap. text ed. 17.95 (*0-472-06373-1*) U of Mich Pr.

Women, Work & Technology in Rural South Asia. Frances Sinha. (ITDG Occasional Paper Ser.). 48p. (Orig.). 1983. pap. write for info. (*0-614-09487-9*, Pub. by Intermed Tech UK) Women Ink.

Women, Work, & the French State: Labour Protection & Social Patriarchy, 1879-1919. Mary L. Stewart. 240p. 1989. 55.00 (*0-7735-0704-3*, Pub. by McGill CN) U of Toronto Pr.

Women, Work, Development, & Ecology. S. Uma Devi. (C). 1994. 14.00 (*81-241-0235-X*, Pub. by Har-Anand Pubns II) S Asia.

***Women Workers: An Annotated Bibliography, 1983-94.** (International Labour Bibliography Ser.: Vol. 14). xii, 290p. 1995. pap. 31.50 (*92-2-109201-1*) Intl Labour Office.

Women Workers & Global Restructuring. Ed. by Kathryn Ward. (International Report: No. 17). 272p. 1990. pap. 15.95 (*0-87546-162-X*, ILR Press) Cornell U Pr.

Women Workers & Technological Change in Europe in the Nineteenth & Twentieth Centuries. Jo Van Every. LC 94-47625. (Gender & Society Series: Feminist Perspectives). 224p. 1995. 75.00 (*0-7484-0283-7*) Taylor & Francis.

Women Workers & Technological Change in Europe in the Nineteenth & Twentieth Centuries. Jo VanEvery. LC 94-47625. (Feminist Perspectives on the Past & Present Ser.). 165p. 1995. pap. 23.00 (*0-7484-0284-5*) Taylor & Francis.

Women Workers & Technological Change in Europe in the Nineteenth & Twentieth Century. Ed. by Gertjan De Groot & Marlou Schrover. 208p. 1995. 75.00 (*0-7484-0260-8*) Taylor & Francis.

Women Workers & Technological Change in Europe in the Nineteenth & Twentieth Century. Ed. by Gertjan De Groot & Marlou Schrover. 208p. 1995. pap. 24.95 (*0-7484-0261-6*) Taylor & Francis.

Women Workers & the Industrial Revolution, 1750-1850. 2nd rev. ed. Ivy Pinchbeck. 342p. 1969. 45.00 (*0-7146-1351-7*, Pub. by F Cass Pubs UK) Intl Spec Bk.

Women Workers at the Grassroot Level: A Sociological Study. Savita S. Joshi. (Illus.). xvi, 178p. 1995. 20.00 (*81-7024-677-6*, Pub. by Ashish Pub Hse II) Nataraj Bks.

Women Workers in India: Studies in Employment & Status. Leela Kasturi. 1990. 24.00 (*81-7001-073-X*, Pub. by Chanakya II) S Asia.

Women Workers in Multinational Enterprises in Developing Countries. xi, 119p. 1988. pap. 13.50 (*92-2-100532-1*) Intl Labour Office.

Women Workers in the Second World War. Penny Summerfield. 214p. 1984. 14.95 (*0-7099-2317-1*, Pub. by Croom Helm UK) Routledge Chapman & Hall.

Women Workers in the Sri Lanka Plantation Sector: An Historical & Contemporary Analysis. Rachel Kurian. (Women, Work & Development Ser.: No. 5). xiv, 138p. 1985. pap. 18.00 (*92-2-102992-1*) Intl Labour Office.

Women Workers of Tea Plantations in India. Mita Bhadra. (C). 1992. 20.00 (*81-7026-172-4*, Pub. by Heritage IA) S Asia.

W

***Women Workers' Rights (Modular Training Package) Equality for Women in Employment: An Interdepartmental Project.** ii, 564p. 1995. 54.00 (*92-2-109741-2*) Intl Labour Office.

***Women Workers: Trends & Issues: 1993 Handbook.** (Illus.). 273p. (C). 1997. reprint ed. pap. text ed. 50.00 (*0-7881-3896-0*) DIANE Pub.

Women Workers View: Their Learning. Jean M. Golaszewski & Joyce L. Kornbluh. (Program on Women & Work Ser.). 82p. 1983. pap. 4.00 (*0-87736-347-1*) U of Mich Inst Labor.

Women Working: An Anthology of Stories & Poems. Ed. by Nancy Hoffman & Florence Howe. LC 78-4636. (Women's Lives - Women's Work Ser.). (Illus.). 304p. 1979. pap. 13.95 (*0-912670-57-6*) Feminist Pr.

Women Working: Comparative Perspectives in Developing Areas. Alma T. Junsay & Tim B. Heaton. LC 88-21335. (Contributions in Women's Studies: No. 99). 140p. 1989. text ed. 45.00 (*0-313-26368-X*, JWK/, Greenwood Pr) Greenwood.

Women Working: Theories & Facts in Perspective. 2nd ed. Ed. by Ann H. Stromberg & Shirley Harkess. LC 87-3215. 431p. (C). 1988. pap. text ed. 31.95 (*0-87484-744-3*, 744) Mayfield Pub.

***Women Working in the Environment.** Carolyn E. Sachs. LC 97-21654. 1997. pap. write for info. (*1-56032-629-8*) Taylor & Francis.

***Women Working Together.** Weeks. Date not set. pap. text ed. write for info. (*0-582-66296-6*, Pub. by Longman UK) Longman.

Women Working Together for Personal, Economic & Community Development. Suzanne Kindervatter. LC 83-61079. (Illus.). 100p. (Orig.). 1983. pap. 13.50 (*0-912917-01-6*) UNIFEM.

Women Working Together for Personal, Economic & Community Development. 2nd ed. Suzanne Kindervatter. LC 87-31276. (Illus.). 105p. (Orig.). 1987. pap. 11.00 (*0-912917-18-0*) UNIFEM.

Women Working Together II: A Collection of Course Outlines on Women in Social Work. Compiled by H. Graber et al. 1995. spiral bd. 12.00 (*0-87293-044-0*) Coun Soc Wk Ed.

***Women World Leaders: Fifteen Great Politicians Tell Their Stories.** Laura A. Liswood. 1997. pap. 16.00 (*0-04-440905-2*) Routledge Chapman & Hall.

Women Worldwalkers: New Dimensions of Science Fiction & Fantasy. Ed. by Jane B. Weedman. (Proceedings of the Comparative Literature Symposium Ser.: Vol. 16). 250p. 1985. 24.95 (*0-89672-133-7*) Tex Tech Univ Pr.

***Women Write for Theatre, Vol. 3.** Aviva Ravel. LC 76-17184. 1997. pap. text ed. 7.95 (*0-88754-050-3*, Pub. by Playwrights CN Pr CN) Theatre Comm.

***Women Writers: There Works a Ways.** Catherine J. Hamilton. (Illus.). 280p. Date not set. 20.95 (*0-8369-2505-X*) Ayer.

Women Writers & Fascism: Reconstructing History. Marie-Luis Gaettens. LC 95-10296. 192p. 1995. 39.95 (*0-8130-1401-8*) U Press Fla.

Women Writers & Poetic Identity: Dorothy Wordsworth, Emily Bronte, & Emily Dickinson. Margaret Homans. LC 80-7527. 271p. reprint ed. pap. 77.30 (*0-8357-7077-X*, 2033375) Bks Demand.

Women Writers & the City: Essays in Feminist Literary Criticism. Ed. by Susan M. Squier. LC 83-17109. 317p. reprint ed. pap. 90.40 (*0-8357-6546-6*, 2035910) Bks Demand.

Women Writers & the Great War, 7. Dorothy Goldman et al. (Twayne's Literature & Society Ser.). 1995. 24.95 (*0-8057-4536-X*) Macmillan.

Women Writers & World War I. Dorothy Goldman. (Literature & Society Ser.). 1995. 26.95 (*0-8057-8858-1*, Twayne) Scribnrs Ref.

Women Writers at Work. Ed. by George Plimpton. 1997. pap. 13.00 (*0-679-77129-8*) Random.

Women Writers, from Page to Screen: A Guide to Literary Sources. Jill R. Fenton et al. LC 89-23479. 512p. 1990. text ed. 72.00 (*0-8240-8529-9*, 687) Garland.

Women Writers from the Caribbean: The Whistling Bird. Ed. by Elaine Campbell & Pierrette Frickey. 208p. (Orig.). 1996. 28.00 (*0-89410-409-8*, Three Contnts); pap. 14.00 (*0-89410-410-1*, Three Contnts) Lynne Rienner.

Women Writers in Black Africa. Lloyd W. Brown. LC 80-1710. (Contributions in Women's Studies: No. 21). vii, 204p. 1981. text ed. 55.00 (*0-313-22540-0*, BRW/, Greenwood Pr) Greenwood.

***Women Writers in German-Speaking Countries: A Bio-Bibliographical Critical Sourcebook.** Ed. by Elke P. Frederiksen & Elizabeth G. Ametsbichler. LC 97-1687. 1997. text ed. write for info. (*0-313-28201-3*, Greenwood Pr) Greenwood.

Women Writers in Pre-Revolutionary France: Strategies of Emancipation. Ed. by Colette H. Winn & Donna Kuizenga. LC 97-11297. (Women Writers of the World Ser.: Vol. 2). 484p. 1997. text ed. 75.00 (*0-8153-2367-0*, H1990) Garland.

Women Writers in Renaissance England. Randall Martin. LC 96-23866. 1997. 26.95 (*0-582-09620-0*, Pub. by Longman UK); 65.95 (*0-582-09621-9*, Pub. by Longman UK) Longman.

Women Writers in Russian Literature. Toby W. Clyman & Diana Greene. LC 93-21143. (Contributions to the Study of World Literature Ser.: No. 53). 312p. 1994. text ed. 69.50 (*0-313-27521-1*, Greenwood Pr) Greenwood.

Women Writers in Russian Literature. Ed. by Toby W. Clyman & Diana Greene. LC 93-21143. 312p. 1994. pap. text ed. 19.95 (*0-275-94941-9*, Praeger Pubs) Greenwood.

***Women Writers in South Indian Languages.** Venugopala Soraba & Hemalatha John. 1995. 14.00 (*81-7018-836-9*, Pub. by BR Pub II) S Asia.

Women Writers in the United States: A Timeline of Literary, Cultural, & Social History. Cynthia J. Davis & West. 504p. (C). 1996. 45.00 (*0-19-509053-5*) OUP.

Women Writers in Twentieth-Century Spain & Spanish America. Ed. by Catherine Davies. LC 92-46176. 224p. 1993. text ed. 89.95 (*0-88946-423-5*) E Mellen.

***Women Writers of Children's Literature.** Ed. by Harold Bloom. (Women Writers & Their Works Ser.). (Illus.). 200p. (C). 1997. 29.95 (*0-7910-4486-6*); pap. 14.95 (*0-7910-4502-1*) Chelsea Hse.

Women Writers of Contemporary Spain. Ed. by Joan L. Brown. LC 89-40296. 1991. 39.50 (*0-87413-386-6*) U Delaware Pr.

Women Writers of Germany, Austria, & Switzerland: An Annotated Bio-Bibliographical Guide. Ed. by Elke Frederiksen. LC 89-7503. (Bibliographies & Indexes in Women's Studies: No. 8). 348p. 1989. text ed. 65.00 (*0-313-24989-X*, FWN, Greenwood Pr) Greenwood.

Women Writers of Great Britain & Europe: An Encyclopedia. Ed. by Katharina M. Wilson et al. LC 97-1409. (Illus.). 612p. 1997. text ed. 95.00 (*0-8153-2343-3*) Garland.

Women Writers of Latin America: Intimate Histories. Magdalena Garcia Pinto. Tr. by Trudy Balch & Magdalena G. Pinto. (Texas Pan American Ser.). (Illus.). 270p. (Orig.). (C). 1991. text ed. 30.00 (*0-292-73862-5*); pap. text ed. 15.95 (*0-292-73866-8*) U of Tex Pr.

Women Writers of Spain: An Annotated Bio-Bibliographical Guide. Ed. by Carolyn L. Galerstein & Kathleen McNerney. LC 86-379. (Bibliographies & Indexes in Women's Studies: No. 2). 410p. 1986. text ed. 79.50 (*0-313-24965-2*, GWO/, Greenwood Pr) Greenwood.

Women Writers of Spanish America: An Annotated Bio-Bibliographical Guide. Ed. by Diane E. Marting. LC 86-33552. (Bibliographies & Indexes in Women's Studies: No. 5). 468p. 1987. text ed. 89.50 (*0-313-24969-5*, MWN/, Greenwood Pr) Greenwood.

Women Writers of the Middle Ages: A Critical Study of Texts from Perpetua (203) to Marguerite Porete (1310) Peter Dronke. LC 83-7456. 348p. 1984. pap. text ed. 19.95 (*0-521-27573-3*) Cambridge U Pr.

Women Writers of the Renaissance & Reformation. Ed. by Katharina M. Wilson. LC 86-3150. 678p. 1987. 40.00 (*0-8203-0865-X*); pap. 20.00 (*0-8203-0866-8*) U of Ga Pr.

Women Writers of the Seventeenth Century. Ed. by Katharina M. Wilson & Frank J. Warnke. LC 88-24994. 568p. 1989. pap. 19.95 (*0-8203-1112-X*) U of Ga Pr.

Women Writers of the West Coast: Speaking of Their Lives & Careers. Ed. by Marilyn Yalom. LC 89-863. 160p. (Orig.). (C). 1988. reprint ed. 29.00 (*0-8095-4053-3*, 19352177) Borgo Pr.

Women Writers of WWI. Margaret Higonnet. Date not set. pap. 24.95 (*0-525-94165-7*) NAL-Dutton.

Women Writers Talk. Ed. by Olga Kenyon. 1990. 18.95 (*0-88184-522-1*) Carroll & Graf.

Women Writers Talk. Olga Kenyon. 224p. 1991. pap. 9.95 (*0-88184-705-4*) Carroll & Graf.

Women Writers Talking. Ed. by Janet Todd. LC 82-3100. 200p. 1983. 37.50 (*0-8419-0756-0*); pap. 16.95 (*0-8419-0757-9*) Holmes & Meier.

Women Writers, Vol. I: Chapbooks 1-5. Ed. by Stanley H. Barkan & Laura Boss. 1991. boxed 75.00 (*0-89304-903-4*); boxed 50.00 (*0-89304-902-6*) Cross-Cultrl NY.

Women Writers, Vol. II: Chapbooks 6-10. Ed. by Stanley H. Barkan & Laura Boss. 1991. boxed 75.00 (*0-89304-905-0*); boxed 50.00 (*0-89304-904-2*) Cross-Cultrl NY.

Women Writing about Money: Women's Fiction in England, 1790-1820. Edward Copeland. (Studies in Romanticism: No. 9). (Illus.). 278p. (C). 1995. text ed. 54.95 (*0-521-45461-1*) Cambridge U Pr.

Women Writing Childbirth: Modern Discourses of Motherhood. Tess Cosslett. LC 93-45572. (Illus.). 204p. 1994. text ed. 65.00 (*0-7190-4323-9*, Pub. by Manchester Univ Pr UK) St Martin.

Women Writing Childbirth: Modern Discourses on Motherhood. Tess Cosslett. LC 93-45572. (Illus.). 204p. 1994. text ed. 24.95 (*0-7190-4324-7*, Pub. by Manchester Univ Pr UK) St Martin.

Women Writing Culture. Ed. by Ruth Behar & Deborah A. Gordon. LC 95-36791. (Illus.). 470p. 1995. 48.00 (*0-520-20207-4*); pap. 16.95 (*0-520-20208-2*) U CA Pr.

Women Writing Culture. Ed. by Gary A. Olson & Elizabeth Hirsh. LC 95-34122. (SUNY Series, Interruptions). 204p. 1995. text ed. 49.50 (*0-7914-2963-6*) State U NY Pr.

Women Writing Culture. Ed. by Gary A. Olson & Elizabeth Hirsh. LC 95-34122. (SUNY Series, Interruptions). 204p. 1995. pap. text ed. 16.95 (*0-7914-2964-4*) State U NY Pr.

Women, Writing, History: 1640-1740. Ed. by Isobel Grundy & Susan Wiseman. LC 91-40025. 224p. 1992. pap. 20.00 (*0-8203-1451-X*) U of Ga Pr.

Women Writing in America: Voices in Collage. Blanche H. Gelfant. LC 84-40298. 290p. 1984. reprint ed. pap. 82.70 (*0-608-02308-6*, 2062949) Bks Demand.

Women Writing in Dutch. Ed. by Kristiaan Aercke. LC 93-37518. (Women Writers of the World Ser.: Vol. 1). 776p. 1994. text ed. 99.00 (*0-8153-0231-2*) Garland.

Women Writing in India, Vol. 1: 600 BC to the Early Twentieth Century. Susie J. Tharu. LC 90-3788. 576p. 1991. 59.95 (*1-55861-026-X*); pap. 29.95 (*1-55861-027-8*) Feminist Pr.

Women Writing in India: 600 B. C. to the Present, Vol. II: The Twentieth Century. Susie J. Tharu. 688p. 1993. 59.95 (*1-55861-028-6*); pap. 29.95 (*1-55861-029-4*) Feminist Pr.

Women Writing the Academy: Audience, Authority, & Transformation. Gesa E. Kirsch. LC 92-41931. (Studies in Writing & Rhetoric). 168p. (Orig.). (C). 1993. pap. 12.95 (*0-8093-1870-9*) S Ill U Pr.

Women Writing Women: An Anthology of Spanish-American Theater of the 1980s. Ed. by Teresa C. Salas & Margarita Vargas. LC 96-22946. (SUNY Series in Latin American & Iberian Thought & Culture). 468p. 1997. pap. 21.95 (*0-7914-3206-8*); text ed. 65.50 (*0-7914-3205-X*) State U NY Pr.

Women...a World Survey 1985. Ruth L. Sivard. (Illus.). 44p. 1987. pap. 6.00 (*0-918281-00-8*) World Prior.

Women...a World Survey 1995. Ruth L. Sivard et al. (Illus.). 48p. 1995. pap. 7.50 (*0-918281-10-5*) World Prior.

Women/Beyond Borders. Lorraine Serena & Suvan Geer. (Illus.). 32p. 1995. pap. text ed. write for info. (*1-880658-10-0*) San Barb CAF.

***Womenfolk: A Novel.** Julie W. Verzuh. 129p. 1997. pap. 14.95 (*0-87839-116-9*) North Star.

Womenfolk & Fairy Tales. Ed. by Rosemary Minard. LC 74-26555. (Illus.). 176p. (J). (gr. 2-5). 1975. 16.95 (*0-395-20276-0*) HM.

***Womenprints: A Detailed Plan of Action for the New Millenium.** Ann Smith et al. 244p. 1997. pap. 17.95 (*0-8192-1697-6*) Morehouse Pub.

Womenpsalms. Ed. by Rosemary Broughton & Carl Koch. (Illus.). 140p. (Orig.). 1992. pap. 6.95 (*0-88489-287-5*) St Marys.

Women's Activism & Social Change: Rochester, New York, 1822-1872. Nancy A. Hewitt. LC 83-45940. 281p. 1984. 39.95 (*0-8014-1616-7*); pap. 15.95 (*0-8014-9509-1*) Cornell U Pr.

***Women's Activism in Contemporary Russia.** Linda Racioppi & Katherine O'Sullivan See. LC 96-36093. 1997. 59.95 (*1-56639-520-8*); pap. 22.95 (*1-56639-521-6*) Temple U Pr.

Women's Acts: Plays by Women Dramatists of Spain's Golden Age. Ed. by Theresa S. Saufas. 360p. (C). 1997. text ed. 45.00 (*0-8131-1977-4*); pap. text ed. 19.95 (*0-8131-0889-6*) U Pr of Ky.

Women's Adornment: What Does the Bible Really Say? Ralph E. Woodrow. LC 76-17711. (Illus.). 1976. pap. 5.00 (*0-916938-01-8*) R Woodrow.

Women's Advantage Diet. Henry Mallek. 1990. mass mkt. 4.95 (*0-671-67676-8*) PB.

Women's Almanac, 3 vols. Linda Schmittroth & Mary R. Mccall. LC 96-25681. 1996. 85.00 (*0-7876-0656-1*, UXL) Gale.

Women's America: Refocusing the Past. Ed. by Linda K. Kerber & Jane S. De Hart. (Illus.). 544p. (C). 1995. pap. 25.00 (*0-19-509147-7*) OUP.

Women's America: Refocusing the Past. 4th ed. Ed. by Linda K. Kerber & Jane S. De Hart. (Illus.). 544p. (C). 1995. 47.00 (*0-19-509146-9*) OUP.

Women's & Children's Fashions of 1917: The Complete Perry, Dame & Co., Catalog. Perry, Dame & Co. Staff. LC 92-12621. Orig. Title: New York Styles - Spring & Summer 1917 Catalog, No. 67. (Illus.). 160p. 1992. reprint ed. pap. 12.95 (*0-486-27128-5*) Dover.

Women's & Childrens Legal Rights. W. Stratton Treadway. LC 94-80058. 200p. (Orig.). 1995. pap. 14.95 (*1-884570-19-4*) Research Triangle.

Women's & Children's Wear & Fashion Accessories Buyers 1996. Ed. by Andrew Grabois et al. 1008p. 1995. pap. 199.95 (*0-87228-081-0*) Salesmans.

Women's & Children's Wear & Fashion Accessories Buyers 1997. Ed. by Elizabeth Onaran et al. 1996. pap. 220.00 (*0-87228-095-0*) Salesmans.

Women's & Children's Wear Buyers Metropolitan New York Directory 1996. Ed. by Edgar Adcock et al. 207p. 1995. pap. 100.00 (*0-87228-079-9*) Salesmans.

Women's & Children's Wear Buyers Metropolitan New York Directory 1997. Ed. by Elizabeth Onaran et al. 1996. pap. 100.00 (*0-87228-097-7*) Salesmans.

Women's & Men's Liberation: Testimonies of Spirit. Ed. by Leonard Grob et al. LC 90-47539. (Contributions in Philosophy Ser.: No. 45). 232p. 1991. text ed. 55.00 (*0-313-25969-0*, GMF/, Greenwood Pr) Greenwood.

Women's & Men's Wars. Ed. by Judith H. Stiehm. 90p. 1983. pap. 18.75 (*0-08-027949-X*, Pergamon Pr) Elsevier.

Women's Annotated Legal Bibliography: 1984-1992, 7 vols., Set. LC 83-15219. 1984. lib. bdg. 295.00 (*0-89941-676-4*, 305230) W S Hein.

Women's Annual: 1984-1985, No. 5. Ed. by Mary D. McFeely. (Reference Publications, Women's Studies Annual). 184p. (C). 1985. 55.00 (*0-8161-8717-7*, Hall Reference); 39.95 (*0-8161-8741-X*, Hall Reference) Macmillan.

Women's Annual, No. 4: 1983-1984. Ed. by Sarah M. Pritchard. 248p. 1984. 39.95 (*0-8161-8725-8*, Hall Reference) Macmillan.

***Women's Armchair Guide to Pro Football.** Betsy Berns. LC 96-97015. (Illus.). 144p. 1996. pap. 12.95 (*0-9653882-0-4*) BVision Sptsmedia.

***Women's Armchoir Guide to Pro Football, 1997-1998 Edition.** 2nd rev. ed. (Illus.). 140p. 1997. pap. 12.95 (*0-9653882-1-2*) BVision Sptsmedia.

Women's Atlas of the United States. rev. ed. Timothy Fast & Cathy C. Fast. LC 94-29084. (Illus.). 256p. 1995. 75.00 (*0-8160-2970-9*) Facts on File.

Women's Atlas of the United States. Anne Gibson & Timothy Fast. LC 86-675059. (Illus.). 256p. reprint ed. pap. 73.00 (*0-7837-5333-0*, 2045073) Bks Demand.

Women's Attitudes Towards Work. Shirley Dex. LC 87-32365. 224p. 1988. text ed. 45.00 (*0-312-01611-5*) St Martin.

Women's Autobiographies. N. A. Walker. 92p. 1991. pap. text ed. 24.00 (*2-88124-521-8*) Gordon & Breach.

Women's Autobiographies in Contemporary Iran. William Hanaway et al. LC 90-81298. (Middle Eastern Monographs: Vol. No. 25). 78p. (Orig.). (C). 1991. pap. 6.95 (*0-932885-05-5*) Harvard CMES.

Women's Autobiographies in Contemporary Iran. Ed. by Afsaneh Najmabadi. (Middle Eastern Monographs: No. 26). 64p. 1991. pap. 9.95 (*0-685-38745-3*, NAJWOM) HUP.

Women's Autobiography: Essays in Criticism. Estelle C. Jelinek. LC 79-2600. 286p. reprint ed. pap. 81.60 (*0-685-20728-5*, AU00356) Bks Demand.

Women's Awakening in Egypt: Culture, Society, & the Press. Beth Baron. LC 93-27067. 264p. 1994. 30.00 (*0-300-05563-3*) Yale U Pr.

***Women's Awakening in Egypt: Culture, Society & the Press.** Beth Baron. 1997. pap. text ed. 17.00 (*0-300-07271-6*) Yale U Pr.

Womens Bar Association of Illinois 75th Anniversary. Turner Publishing Company Staff. LC 91-75256. 88p. 1991. 34.95 (*1-56311-070-9*) Turner Pub KY.

An Asterisk (*) at the beginning of an entry indicates that the title is appearing in BIP for the first time.

*Women's Basketball Drills, 4 vols. Incl. Conditioning Drills. Deborah Ryan. (Orig.). (YA). (gr. 7 up). 1988. pap. Not sold separately (0-932741-58-4); Offensive Drills. Joan Bonvicini. (Orig.). (YA). (gr. 7 up). 1988. pap. Not sold separately (0-932741-57-6); General Drills. Pat Summitt. (Orig.). (YA). (gr. 7 up). 1988. pap. Not sold separately (0-932741-59-2); Defensive Drills. Andy Landers. (Orig.). (YA). (gr. 7 up). 1988. pap. Not sold separately (0-932741-56-8); 1988. pap. 25.95 (1-56404-135-2) Championship Bks & Vid Prodns.

Women's Bible: Study Guide. Coalition on Women & Religion Staff. 1975. 5.95 (0-9603042-2-3) Coalition Women-Relig.

Women's Bible Commentary. Ed. by Carol A. Newsom & Sharon H. Ringe. 384p. 1992. text ed. 29.00 (0-664-21922-5) Westminster John Knox.

Women's Bible Commentary. Ed. by Carol A. Newsom & Sharon H. Ringe. 416p. 1995. reprint ed. pap. 20.00 (0-664-25586-8) Westminster John Knox.

Women's Bibliography of Concerns, Care & Conditions: Index of Modern Information. Zena Y. Webster. LC 89-18646. 150p. 1990. 44.50 (1-55914-124-7); pap. 39.50 (1-55914-125-5) ABBE Pubs Assn.

Women's Bodies: A Social History of Women's Encounter with Health, Ill-Health & Medicine. Edward Shorter. 424p. (C). 1990. pap. 24.95 (0-88738-848-5) Transaction Pubs.

Women's Bodies in Classical Greek Science. Lesley Dean-Jones. (Illus.). 312p. 1996. reprint ed. pap. 19.95 (0-19-815046-6) OUP.

Women's Bodies, Vol. 11, Health & Childbirth see History of Women in the United States: Topically Arranged Articles on the Evolution of Women's History in the United States

Women's Bodies, Women's Wisdom: Creating Physical & Emotional Health & Healing. Christiane Northrup. LC 94-8357. 784p. 1994. 29.95 (0-553-08120-9) Bantam.

Women's Bodies, Women's Wisdom: Creating Physical & Emotional Health & Healing. Christiane Northrup. 784p. 1995. pap. 15.95 (0-553-37466-4) Bantam.

Women's Bodybuilding for Beginners. Mayo. 1984. pap. 2.95 (0-02-499890-7, Macmillan Coll) P-H.

Women's Bodybuilding Photo Book. Fit. (Illus.). 1983. pap. 11.95 (0-02-499900-8, Macmillan Coll) P-H.

Women's Book of Healing. Diane Stein. LC 87-45748. (New Age Ser.). (Illus.). 345p. 1987. pap. 14.95 (0-87542-759-6) Llewellyn Pubns.

Women's Book of Home Remedies. Consumer Guide Editors. 576p. (Orig.). 1994. pap. 6.99 (0-451-18230-8, Sig) NAL-Dutton.

Women's Book of World Records & Achievements. Ed. by Lois D. O'Neill. (Quality Paperbacks Ser.). (Illus.). xiii, 800p. 1983. reprint ed. pap. 14.95 (0-306-80206-6) Da Capo.

Women's Budget. Jane Midgley. (Illus.). 1987. 3.00 (0-9506968-0-3) WILPF.

Women's Bureau: Its History, Activities & Organization. Gustavus A. Weber. LC 72-3030. (No. 22). reprint ed. 37.50 (0-404-57122-0) AMS Pr.

Women's Business Resource Guide: A National Directory. Barbara Littman & Michael Ray. 144p. 1994. pap. 21.95 (1-884565-01-8, Resource Group) Informat Design.

Women's Business Resource Guide: A National Directory of More than 800 Programs, Resources. 2nd ed. Barbara Littman. (Illus.). 224p. 1996. pap. 18.95 (0-8092-3166-2) Contemp Bks.

Women's Cancer Book: A Comprehensive Guide for Patients & Their Families. Thomas W. Montag. (Illus.). 400p. 1996. 24.95 (1-883955-06-8) Penmarin Bks.

Women's Cancers: How to Prevent Them, How to Treat Them, How to Beat Them. Kerry A. McGinn & Pamela J. Haylock. LC 92-41408. (Illus.). 448p. 1993. 26.95 (0-89793-103-3); pap. 16.95 (0-89793-102-5) Hunter Hse.

***Women's Cancers: How to Prevent Them, How to Treat Them, How to Beat Them.** 2nd ed. Kerry A. McGinn. LC 97-20482. 1997. 27.95 (0-89793-224-2); pap. text ed. 17.95 (0-89793-223-4) Hunter Hse.

Women's Career Development. Ed. by Barbara A. Gutek & Laurie Larwood. (Illus.). 240p. 1987. text ed. 38.95 (0-8039-2717-7); pap. text ed. 19.50 (0-8039-3687-7) Sage.

Women's Career Development. Ed. by Barbara A. Gutek & Laurie Larwood. LC 86-6606. (Illus.). 192p. 1987. reprint ed. pap. 54.80 (0-608-01719-1, 2062374) Bks Demand.

Women's Careers: Pathways & Pitfalls. Ed. by Suzanna Rose & Laurie Larwood. LC 88-2344. 234p. 1988. text ed. 55.00 (0-275-92724-5, C2724, Praeger Pubs) Greenwood.

Women's Centers, Pt. 1. (Initiatives Ser.: Vol. 51, No. 2). 1988. 13.00 (0-614-14212-1) Natl Assn Women.

Women's Centers, Pt. 2. (Initiatives Ser.: Vol. 51, No. 3). 1988. 13.00 (0-614-14211-3) Natl Assn Women.

Women's Challenge: Ministry in the Flesh. M. Timothy Prokes. 1969. pap. 4.95 (0-87193-006-4) Dimension Bks.

***Women's Changing Role.** rev. ed. Ed. by Carol D. Foster et al. (Reference Ser.). (Illus.). 180p. 1996. pap. text ed. 23.95 (1-57302-019-2) Info Plus TX.

***Women's Chronology: A History of Women's Achievements.** Timothy L. Gall et al. LC 97-5028. 1997. write for info. (0-7876-0661-8, UXL); pap. write for info. (0-7876-0662-6, UXL) Gale.

***Women's Chronology: A History of Women's Achievements, 2 vol., Set.** Susan B. Gall & Peggy Saari. LC 97-5028. (Women's Reference Library). 288p. 1997. 55.00 (0-7876-0660-X, 00153404, UXL) Gale.

Women's Chronology: A Year-by-Year Record from Prehistory to the Present. James Trager. (Illus.). 802p. 1995. pap. 22.00 (0-8050-4234-2) H Holt & Co.

Women's Collections: Libraries, Archives, & Consciousness. Ed. by Suzanne Hildenbrand. LC 84-22529. (Special Collections: Vol. 3, Nos. 3-4). 194p. 1986. 49.95 (0-86656-273-7) Haworth Pr.

***Womens College Handbook.** Weinberg. (C). 1994. pap. 79.75 (0-8147-9277-4) NYU Pr.

Women's Colleges. Adler. 1994. pap. 17.00 (0-685-71197-8) P-H Gen Ref & Trav.

Women's Colleges. Joe A. Adler & Jennifer A. Friedman. LC 94-4837. 1994. pap. 15.00 (0-671-86706-7) P-H.

Women's Colleges, Pt. 1. (Initiatives Ser.: Vol. 53, No. 3). 1990. 13.00 (0-614-14207-5) Natl Assn Women.

Women's Colleges, Pt. 2. (Initiatives Ser.: Vol. 53, No. 4). 1991. 13.00 (0-614-14206-7) Natl Assn Women.

Women's Comic Visions. Ed. & Intro. by June Sochen. LC 90-21070. (Humor in Life & Letters Ser.). (Illus.). 240p. 1991. 34.95 (0-8143-2307-3); pap. 15.95 (0-8143-2308-1) Wayne St U Pr.

Women's Companion to International Film. Ed. by Annette Kuhn & Susannah Radstone. LC 94-4531. 1994. reprint ed. pap. 15.00 (0-520-08879-4) U CA Pr.

***Women's Companion to Mythology.** Carolyne Larrington. 1997. pap. text ed. 25.00 (0-04-440969-9) Harper SF.

Women's Complete Healthbook. American Medical Women's Association Staff. 720p. 1997. pap. 21.95 (0-440-50723-5, Dell Trade Pbks) Dell.

Women's Complete Healthbook. Ed. by Susan C. Stewart & Roselyn P. Epps. LC 94-36851. 720p. 1995. 39.95 (0-385-31382-9) Delacorte.

***Women's Complete Scholarship Book.** Student Services Inc. Staff. LC 97-23237. (Complete Scholarship Ser.). 288p. (Orig.). 1997. 18.95 (1-57071-150-X) Sourcebks.

Women's Computer Literacy Handbook. Deborah L. Brecher. (Illus.). 1985. pap. 9.95 (0-452-25565-1, Plume) NAL-Dutton.

***Women's Concise Guide to a Healthier Heart.** Karen J. Carlson. LC 97-17310. 1997. 24.95 (0-674-95483-1); pap. text ed. 12.95 (0-674-95484-X) HUP.

***Women's Concise Guide to Emotional Well-Being.** Karen J. Carlson. 1997. 29.95 (0-674-95490-4); pap. text ed. 14.95 (0-674-95491-2) HUP.

Women's Conflicts about Eating & Sexuality: The Relationship Between Food & Sex. Rosalyn M. Meadow. LC 91-19205. 1992. pap. 10.95 (0-918393-98-1) Harrington Pk.

Women's Conflicts about Eating & Sexuality: The Relationship Between Food & Sex. Rosalyn M. Meadow & Lillie Weiss. LC 91-4120. 212p. 1992. lib. bdg. 29.95 (1-56024-131-4) Haworth Pr.

Women's Costume of the Near & Middle East. Jennifer M. Scarce. (Illus.). 192p. 1994. 45.00 (0-7007-0344-6, Pub. by Curzon Pr UK) Paul & Co Pubs.

Women's Culture: American Philanthropy & Art, 1830-1930. Kathleen D. McCarthy. LC 91-16632. (Illus.). xviii, 344p. (C). 1992. pap. text ed. 17.95 (0-226-55584-4) U Ch Pr.

Women's Culture: The Women's Renaissance of the Seventies. Ed. by Gayle Kimball. LC 81-9004. 1981. pap. 15.00 (0-8108-1496-X) Scarecrow.

***Women's Day Desserts: More than 300 Recipes from Brownie Shortbread to Apple Sorbet to Banana Cream Pie.** Ed. by Woman's Day Editors & Kathy Farrell-Kingsley. LC 97-17453. 1997. pap. 24.95 (0-670-87444-2) Viking Penguin.

Women's Decision-Making: Common Themes...Irish Voices. Nancy W. Veeder. LC 92-890. 176p. 1992. text ed. 45.00 (0-275-94354-2, C4354, Praeger Pubs) Greenwood.

Women's Desk Reference. Franck Brownstone. Date not set. pap. 11.95 (0-14-017046-4) Viking Penguin.

***Women's Desk Reference.** Irene Franck & David Brownstone. 840p. 10.98 (0-8317-4473-1) Smithmark.

***Women's Development: Problems & Prospects.** Shamim Aleem. (Illus.). xii, 237p. 1996. 28.00 (81-7024-741-1, Pub. by Assoc Pub Hse II) Nataraj Bks.

Women's Development: Some Critical Issues. Government of India Staff & UNICEF Staff. 92p. 1978. 10.95 (0-318-37328-9) Asia Bk Corp.

Women's Devotional Gift Set. 1994. 40.00 (0-310-96520-9) Zondervan.

Women's Devotional Prayer Journal. 192p. 1995. 16.99 (0-8499-5122-4) Word Pub.

Women's Diaries, Journals, & Letters: An Annotated Bibliography. Cheryl Cline. LC 89-1197. 754p. 1989. text ed. 85.00 (0-8240-6637-5) Garland.

Women's Diaries Miscellany. Jane Begos. 302p. 1989. 30.00 (0-913660-23-X); pap. 22.00 (0-913660-24-8) Magic Cir Pr CT.

Women's Diaries of the Westward Journey. Lillian Schlissel. LC 92-54106. (Illus.). 262p. (Orig.). 1992. pap. 14.00 (0-8052-1004-0) Schocken.

Women's Dionysian Initiation: The Villa of Mysteries in Pompeii. Linda Fierz-David. Tr. by Gladys Phelan from GER. LC 88-4893. (Jungian Classics Ser.: No. 11). (Illus.). 149p. 1988. pap. 15.00 (0-88214-510-X) Spring Pubns.

Women's Earliest Records: From Ancient Egypt & Western Asia. Ed. by Barbara S. Lesko. LC 89-4135. (Brown Judaic Studies). (Illus.). 350p. 1989. 69.95 (1-55540-319-0, 14 01 66) Scholars Pr GA.

Women's Economic Justice Agenda for the States: Issues of the 1990's. Ed. by Linda Tarr-Whelan & Lynne Isensee. 1987. 12.95 (0-89788-098-6) CPA Washington.

Women's Education. Maggie Coats. LC 93-11334. (Cutting Edge Ser.). 173p. 1994. 90.00 (0-335-15735-1, Open Univ Pr); pap. 27.50 (0-335-15734-3, Open Univ Pr) Taylor & Francis.

Women's Education, 2 vols., Set. Betty J. Parker. 1981. text ed. 125.00 (0-313-23205-9, PEV/, Greenwood Pr) Greenwood.

Women's Education, A World View: Annotated Bibliography of Doctoral Dissertations, Vol. 1. Ed. by Betty J. Parker. LC 78-73791. xii, 470p. 1979. text ed. 75.00 (0-313-20891-3, PEW/, Greenwood Pr) Greenwood.

Women's Education, A World View: Vol. 2-Annotated Bibliography of Books & Reports, Vol. 2. Ed. by Franklin Parker & Betty J. Parker. LC 78-73791. xv, 689p. 1981. text ed. 85.00 (0-313-23206-7, PEY/, Greenwood Pr) Greenwood.

Women's Education & Fertility Behaviour: A Case-Study of Rural Maharashtra India. 41p. Date not set. pap. 10.00 (92-1-151257-3, E.93.XIII.12) UN.

Women's Education & Social Development. B. D. Bhatt. (Modern Education Ser.). (C). 1992. 34.00 (81-85475-54-7, Pub. by Kanishka) S Asia.

Women's Education Equity Act: A Review of Program Goals & Strategies Needed. (Illus.). 41p. (Orig.). (C). 1995. pap. text ed. 20.00 (0-7881-2217-7) DIANE Pub.

Women's Education in Developing Countries: Barriers, Benefits, & Policies. Ed. by Elizabeth M. King & M. Anne Hill. 352p. 1993. 34.95 (0-8018-4534-3, 44534) Johns Hopkins.

Women's Education in Developing Countries: Opportunities & Outcomes. Audrey C. Smock. LC 81-8560. 304p. 1981. text ed. 45.00 (0-275-90720-1, C0720, Praeger Pubs) Greenwood.

Women's Education in India, Myth & Reality. Pratima Chaudhury. (C). 1995. 23.00 (81-241-0310-0, Pub. by Har-Anand Pubns II) S Asia.

Women's Education in the Third World: Comparative Perspectives. Ed. by Gail P. Kelly & Carolyn M. Elliott. LC 82-789. 406p. 1983. text ed. 74.50 (0-87395-619-2); pap. text ed. 27.95 (0-87395-620-6) State U NY Pr.

Women's Education in the United States: A Guide to Information Sources. Ed. by Kay S. Wilkins. LC 79-54691. (Education Information Guide Ser.: Vol. 4). 232p. 1979. 68.00 (0-8103-1410-X) Gale.

Women's Employment & Fertility: A Comparative Analysis of World Fertility Survey Results for 38 Developing Countries. 96p. 1986. 15.00 (92-1-151152-6, E.85.XIII.5) UN.

Women's Employment & Pay in Latin America: Overview & Methodology. George Psacharopoulos & Zafiris Tzannatos. LC 92-35611. 264p. 1992. 15.95 (0-8213-2270-2, 12270) World Bank.

Women's Employment & the Capitalist Family: Towards a Political Economy of Gender & Labour Markets. Ben Fine. 240p. (C). (gr. 13). 1992. text ed. 74.95 (0-415-08334-6, A9694) Routledge.

***Women's Encounters of Violence in Australia.** Sandy Cook & Judith Bessant. LC 97-4601. (Sage Series on Violence Against Women). 1997. write for info. (0-7619-0431-X); pap. write for info. (0-7619-0432-8) Sage.

Women's Encyclopedia of Health & Emotional Healing. Denise Foley. 672p. 1995. mass mkt. 6.99 (0-553-56987-2) Bantam.

Women's Encyclopedia of Health & Emotional Healing: Top Women Doctors Share Their Unique Self-Help Advice on Your Body, Your Feelings & Your Life. Prevention Magazine Editors et al. LC 92-23361. 1992. 27.95 (0-87596-151-7, 05-059-0) Rodale Pr Inc.

***Women's Encyclopedia of Myths & Secrets.** B. Walker. 1996. 17.98 (0-7858-0720-9) Bk Sales Inc.

Women's Equality, Demography, & Public Policies: A Comparative Perspective. Alena Heitlinger. LC 93-12. 288p. 1993. text ed. 69.95 (0-312-09638-0) St Martin.

Women's Ethnicities: Journeys Through Psychology. Faye J. Crosby. Ed. by Karen F. Wyche. 208p. (C). 1996. pap. text ed. 19.95 (0-8133-2373-8) Westview.

Women's Experience & Education. Ed. by Sharon L. Rich & Ariel Phillips. LC 84-81321. (Reprint Ser.: No. 17). 312p. (C). 1985. pap. 17.95 (0-916690-19-9) Harvard Educ Rev.

Women's Experience Coloring Book: A Playful Journey in Healing & Hope. Nancy Scheibe. 96p. 1994. student ed., pap. 10.95 (0-9641524-7-9) Creative Jrnys.

Women's Experience of Breastfeeding. Heather Maclean. 208p. 1990. pap. 13.95 (0-8020-6756-5) U of Toronto Pr.

***Women's Experience of Feminist Therapy & Counselling.** Eileen McLeod. 176p. 1994. pap. 11.99 (0-335-19221-1, Open Univ Pr) Taylor & Francis.

Women's Experience of Feminist Therapy & Counselling. Eileen McLeod. LC 93-40802. 1994. pap. write for info. (0-335-19222-X, Open Univ Pr) Taylor & Francis.

***Women's Experiences with HIV/AIDS: An International Perspective.** Lynellen D. Long. Ed. by E. Maxine Ankrah. LC 96-31322. 1997. pap. 17.50 (0-231-10605-X) Col U Pr.

***Women's Experiences with HIV/AIDS: An International Perspective.** Lynellyn D. Long & E. Maxine Ankrah. LC 96-31322. 426p. 1996. 49.50 (0-231-10604-1) Col U Pr.

Women's Fabian Tracts. Sally Alexander. (Women's Source Library). 512p. 1989. 75.00 (0-415-01244-9) Routledge.

Women's Factory Work in World War 1. Gareth Griffiths. (Illus.). 192p. 1991. 34.00 (0-86299-795-X, Pub. by Sutton Pubng UK) Bks Intl VA.

Women's Farming & Present Ethnography: Thoughts on a Nigerian Re-Study. Jane I. Guyer. 1989. 5.00 (0-941934-55-1) Indiana Africa.

Women's Fashions of the Early 1900s: An Unabridged Republication of "New York Fashions, 1909" unabridged ed. National Cloak & Suit Co. Staff. LC 92-21805. (Illus.). 128p. 1992. reprint ed. pap. text ed. 10.95 (0-486-27276-1) Dover.

***Women's Fiction & the Great War.** Ed. by Suzanne Raitt & Trudi Tate. (Illus.). 300p. 1997. 75.00 (0-19-818283-X); pap. 19.95 (0-19-818278-3) OUP.

Women's Fiction from Latin America: Selections from Twelve Contemporary Authors. Ed. & Tr. by Evelyn P. Garfield. LC 88-3670. (Latin American Literature & Culture Ser.). (Illus.). 356p. 1988. 39.95 (0-8143-1858-4); pap. 16.95 (0-8143-1859-2) Wayne St U Pr.

Women's Fiction of the Second World War. Gill Plain. LC 96-26694. 1996. text ed. 49.95 (0-312-16413-0); text ed. 18.95 (0-312-16414-9) St Martin.

***Women's Fictional Responses to the First World War: A Comparative Study of Selected Texts by French & German Writers.** Catherine O'Brien. (Studies in Modern German Literature: No. 82). 216p. (C). 1997. text ed. 44.95 (0-8204-3141-9) P Lang Pubng.

Women's Fight for Liberation. Gail Shaffer. (Topics of Our Times Ser.: No. 11). 32p. lib. bdg. 7.25 (0-87157-812-3) SamHar Pr.

***Women's Figures: The Economic Progress of Women in America.** Diana Furchtgott-Roth & Christine Stolba. 71p. (Orig.). 1996. pap. 7.95 (0-8447-7083-3) Am Enterprise.

Women's Film & Female Experience. Andrea S. Walsh. LC 83-24486. 268p. 1984. text ed. 55.00 (0-275-91753-3, C1753, Praeger Pubs) Greenwood.

Women's Film & Female Experience 1940-1950. Andrea S. Walsh. LC 83-24486. 268p. 1986. pap. text ed. 18.95 (0-275-92599-4, B2599, Praeger Pubs) Greenwood.

Women's Films in Print: An Annotated Guide to Eight Hundred Films Made by Women. Bonnie Dawson. LC 74-80642. 1975. pap. 10.00 (0-912932-02-3) Booklegger Pubng.

***Women's Financial Wisdom: How to Become a Woman of Wealth.** Ivy Gilbert-Vigue. 105p. 1997. 12.95 (0-9629858-1-3) Cnslts Pr.

***Women's First, 2 vol., Set.** 2nd ed. 1997. 55.00 (0-7876-0653-7, 00153397, UXL) Gale.

Women's Firsts. Susan B. Gall. LC 96-9792. (Women's Reference Library). 654p. 1996. 44.95 (0-7876-0151-9, UXL) Gale.

Women's Folklore, Women's Culture. Ed. by Rosan A. Jordan & Susan J. Kalcik. LC 84-12019. (Publications of the American Folklore Society, Bibliographical & Special Ser.). (Illus.). 288p. (Orig.). 1985. pap. text ed. 18.95 (0-8122-1206-1) U of Pa Pr.

Women's Foreign Policy Council Directory: A Guide to Women Foreign Policy Specialists & Listings of Women & Organizations Working on International Affairs. Ed. & Intro. by Mim Kelber. LC 87-10496. 336p. (Orig.). 1987. pap. 35.00 (0-317-58738-2) WFPC.

Women's Foreign Policy Directory. Ed. by Mim Kelber. 318p. 1987. pap. 35.00 (0-9617596-0-7) WFPC.

Women's Friendship. Annette Annechild. 1997. pap. write for info. (0-517-88633-2, Crown) Crown Pub Group.

Women's Friendship in Literature. Janet M. Todd. LC 79-20175. 1980. text ed. 62.50 (0-231-04562-X) Col U Pr.

Women's Friendship in Literature. Janet M. Todd. LC 79-20175. 1983. pap. text ed. 22.00 (0-231-04563-8) Col U Pr.

Women's Friendships: A Collection of Short Stories. Intro. by Susan Koppelman. LC 91-50303. 352p. 1991. 29.95 (0-8061-2376-1); pap. 14.95 (0-8061-2386-9) U of Okla Pr.

Women's Garment Workers. Louis Levine, pseud. LC 72-89752. (American Labor, from Conspiracy to Collective Bargaining Ser., No. 1). 608p. 1976. reprint ed. 23.95 (0-405-02139-9) Ayer.

***Women's Gidayu & the Japanese Theatre Tradition.** Angela K. Coaldrake. LC 96-43188. (Nissan Institute/Routledge Japanese Study Ser.). 288p. (C). 1997. pap. write for info. (0-415-06334-5) Routledge.

Women's Glasnost Vs. Naglost: Stopping Russian Backlash. Contrib. by Tatyana Mamonova & Chandra N. Folsom. LC 93-15181. 208p. 1993. text ed. 55.00 (0-89789-339-5, H339, Bergin & Garvey); pap. text ed. 18.95 (0-89789-340-9, G340, Bergin & Garvey) Greenwood.

Women's Golf Handbook. Cliff Schrock. (Illus.). (Orig.). 1995. pap. 12.95 (1-57028-032-0) Masters Pr IN.

Women's Gothic & Romantic Fiction: A Reference Guide. Kay Mussell. LC 80-28683. (American Popular Culture Ser.). 157p. 1981. text ed. 42.95 (0-313-21402-6, MGF/, Greenwood Pr) Greenwood.

***Women's Great Lakes Reader.** Victoria Brehm. 1997. pap. text ed. 18.95 (0-930100-79-4) Holy Cow.

Women's Growth in Connection: Writings from the Stone Center. Janet L. Surrey et al. LC 91-12093. 310p. 1991. pap. text ed. 19.95 (0-89862-465-7); lib. bdg. 42.00 (0-89862-562-9) Guilford Pr.

***Women's Growth in Diversity: More Writings from the Stone Center.** Ed. by Judith V. Jordan. 342p. 1997. pap. text ed. 18.95 (1-57230-206-2, 0206); lib. bdg. 40.00 (1-57230-205-4, 0205) Guilford Pr.

Women's Guide to Cigar Smoking. Rhona Kasper. (Illus.). 64p. (Orig.). 1996. pap. 6.95 (0-9652959-0-7) Cigar Savvy.

Women's Guide to Credit Fitness: Establishing It, Repairing It, Keeping It. Ken L. Samuel. 160p. (Orig.). 1995. pap. write for info. (1-885591-50-0) Morris Pubng.

Women's Guide to Fighting Back - Don't Be a Victim. Peter M. Wright. Ed. by Christine Bettencourt. (Illus.). 150p. (Orig.). 1988. pap. 12.00 (0-9616742-0-2) Pub Safe Pr-Comet Pub.

Women's Guide to Fighting Heart Disease: A Leading Cardiologist's Breakthrough Program. Richard H. Helfant. LC 94-11088. 224p. 1994. pap. 11.00 (0-399-52141-0) Berkley Pub.

Women's Guide to Financial Self-Defense. June B. Mays. LC 96-20081. 176p. (Orig.). 1997. pap. 12.99 (0-446-67264-5) Warner Bks.

***Womens Guide to Golf.** Kellie Garvin & Hick. 1998. pap. write for info. (1-55611-534-2) D I Fine.

W

Women's Guide to Homeopathy. Andrew Lockie & Nicola Geddes. 352p. (Orig.). 1994. pap. 14.95 (*0-312-09944-4*) St Martin.

Women's Guide to Overseas Living. 2nd rev. ed. Nancy J. Piet-Pelon & Barbara Hornby. LC 92-40422. 210p. 1992. reprint ed. pap. 15.95 (*1-877864-05-6*) Intercult Pr.

***Women's Guide to Surviving Graduate School.** Barbara Rittner & Patricia Trudeau. LC 97-21015. (Surviving Graduate School Ser.). 180p. 1997. 42.00 (*0-7619-0389-5*); pap. 19.95 (*0-7619-0390-9*) Sage.

***Women's Guide to the Wired World.** Shana Penn. LC 97-10031. 1997. pap. 18.95 (*1-55861-167-3*) Feminist Pr.

Women's Gymnastics. Jill Coulton. (EP Sports Ser.). (Illus.). 1977. 7.95 (*0-685-01040-6*) Charles River Bks.

Women's Gymnastics. Elizabeth Danskin. (Hancock House Physical Education Ser.). (Illus.). 120p. (Orig.). (J). (gr. 12). 1983. pap. 14.95 (*0-88839-045-9*) Hancock House.

Women's Gymnastics. Wiley. (Orig.). 1980. pap. 7.95 (*0-02-499910-5*, Macmillan Coll) P-H.

Women's Gymnastics a History Vol. 1: 1966 to 1974. Minot Simons, II. LC 95-90224. (Illus.). xxv, 403p. 1995. 35.00 (*0-9646062-0-8*) Welwyn Pub.

Women's Haggadah. E. M. Broner & Naomi Nimrod. LC 93-21435. (Illus.). 80p. 1994. pap. 10.00 (*0-06-061143-X*) Harper SF.

Women's Hats: Il Cappello da Donna. Adele Campione. Ed. by Jack Jensen. LC 93-47971. (Bella Cosa Ser.). 144p. 1994. pap. 12.95 (*0-8118-0781-9*) Chronicle Bks.

***Women's Hats of the 20th Century for Designers & Collectors.** Maureen Reilly & Mary Beth Detrich. LC 96-38119. (Illus.). 240p. 1997. 49.95 (*0-7643-0204-3*) Schiffer.

***Women's Health.** LC 96-50012. (For Your Information Ser.). 1997. pap. write for info. (*1-56853-034-X*, Signal Hill) New Readers.

Women's Health. Judith A. Lewis & Judith Bernstein. (Nursing Ser.). (C). 1996. text ed. 47.50 (*0-86720-485-0*) Jones & Bartlett.

***Women's Health.** Andrew Weil. 1997. mass mkt. 2.99 (*0-8041-1674-1*) Ivy Books.

***Women's Health.** 4th ed. Ed. by Ann McPherson & Deborah Waller. (Oxford General Practice Ser.). (Illus.). 672p. 1997. pap. 59.50 (*0-19-262750-3*) OUP.

Women's Health: A Primary Care Clinical Guide. Ellis Q. Youngkin. Ed. by Marcia S. Davis. (Illus.). 480p. 1994. pap. text ed. 52.95 (*0-8385-1230-5*, A1230-0) Appleton & Lange.

Women's Health: Across Age & Frontier. vi, 107p. (ENG & FRE.). 1992. pap. text ed. 20.00 (*92-4-156152-1*, 1150379) World Health.

***Women's Health: An Essential Guide for the Modern Woman.** Karen Evennett. (Illus.). 224p. 1997. pap. 17.95 (*0-7063-7459-2*, Pub. by Ward Lock UK) Sterling.

***Women's Health: Complexities & Differences.** Sheryl B. Ruzek et al. LC 96-34047. (Women & Health Ser.). 1997. write for info. (*0-8142-0704-9*); pap. write for info. (*0-8142-0705-7*) Ohio St U Pr.

***Women's Health: Complexities & Differences.** Ed. by Sheryl B. Ruzek et al. 1997. pap. 19.95 (*0-614-27684-5*) Ohio St U Pr.

***Women's Health: Complexities & Differences.** Ed. by Sheryl B. Ruzek et al. 1997. 49.95 (*0-614-27685-3*) Ohio St U Pr.

***Women's Health: Hormones, Emotions & Behavior.** Ed. by Regina C. Casper. (Psychiatry & Medicine Ser.). (Illus.). 325p. (C). 1997. text ed. 85.00 (*0-521-56341-0*) Cambridge U Pr.

***Women's Health: Readings on Social, Economic, & Political Issues.** 2nd ed. Nancy Worcester & Marianne Whately. 432p. (C). 1995. per., pap. text ed. 31.44 (*0-7872-1368-3*) Kendall-Hunt.

Women's Health: The Commonwealth Fund Survey. Ed. by Marilyn M. Falik & Karen S. Collins. 408p. (C). 1996. text ed. 55.00 (*0-8018-5353-2*); pap. text ed. 18.95 (*0-8018-5354-0*) Johns Hopkins.

Women's Health: The Natural Way of Healing. Natural. 320p. 1995. mass mkt. 5.50 (*0-440-21661-3*) Dell.

Women's Health: What Do You Know About It? Baker. 1995. pap. text ed. write for info. (*0-07-003700-0*) McGraw.

Women's Health - Missing from U. S. Medicine. Sue V. Rosser. LC 94-9745. (Race, Gender, & Science Ser.). 224p. 1994. 31.50 (*0-253-34991-5*); pap. 15.95 (*0-253-20924-2*) Ind U Pr.

Women's Health Across the Lifespan: A Comprehensive Perspective. Karen M. Allen. LC 96-22832. (Illus.). 544p. 1996. pap. text ed. 36.95 (*0-397-55216-5*) Lppncott-Raven.

Women's Health Advisor. Alice Feinstein. LC 94-23193. 1995. pap. 14.95 (*0-87596-230-0*) Rodale Pr Inc.

***Women's Health & Aging Study.** 1997. lib. bdg. 259.99 (*0-8490-6221-7*) Gordon Pr.

***Women's Health & Aging Study: Health & Social Characteristics of Older Women with Disability.** 1997. lib. bdg. 253.95 (*0-8490-8204-8*) Gordon Pr.

***Women's Health & Aging Study: Health & Social Characteristics of Older Women with Disability.** Ed. by Jack M. Guralnik et al. 400p. (Orig.). 1996. pap. 45.00 (*0-7881-3122-2*) DIANE Pub.

Women's Health & Development: Global Perspective. Ed. by Beverly J. McElmurry et al. 400p. 1993. 50.00 (*0-86720-799-X*) Jones & Bartlett.

Women's Health & Human Rights: The Promotion & Protection of Women's Health Through International Human Rights Law. R. J. Cook. vii, 62p. (ENG, FRE & SPA.). 1994. pap. text ed. 14.00 (*92-4-156166-1*, 1150412) World Health.

Women's Health & Nutrition: Making a Difference. Anne Tinker. LC 94-28769. (World Bank Discussion Papers: Vol. 256). 1994. 9.95 (*0-8213-2991-X*, 12991) World Bank.

Women's Health & Social Work: Feminist Perspectives. Ed. by Miriam M. Olson. LC 94-3951. (Social Work in Health Care Ser.: Vol. 19, Nos. 3-4). 175p. 1994. 32.95 (*1-56024-683-9*) Haworth Pr.

Women's Health Book. 2nd ed. Loretta H. Kurban. LC 86-91266. 90p. (Orig.). 1990. pap. 8.00 (*0-938863-24-X*) Libra Press Chi.

Women's Health Care: A Comprehensive Handbook. Ed. by Catherine I. Fogel & Nancy F. Woods. 900p. 1994. 95.00 (*0-8039-7022-6*) Sage.

Women's Health Care: A Comprehensive Handbook. Ed. by Catherine I. Fogel & Nancy F. Woods. 900p. 1994. pap. 56.00 (*0-8039-7023-4*) Sage.

Women's Health Care Administration: Forms, Checklists, & Guidelines. Ed. by Sara N. Di Lima et al. Date not set. ring bd. 169.00 (*0-8342-0773-7*) Aspen Pub.

Women's Health Care Handbook. Ed. by Cynda Johnson et al. 700p. (Orig.). 1996. pap. text ed. 49.00 (*1-56053-112-6*) Hanley & Belfus.

Women's Health Care Market. (Market Research Reports: No. 580). 162p. 1995. 995.00 (*0-614-14199-0*) Theta Corp.

Women's Health Care Nurse Practitioner Certification Review Guide. Ed. by Susan Moskosky. LC 95-33625. 500p. (C). 1995. pap. text ed. 47.75 (*1-878028-13-8*) Hlth Lead Assoc.

***Women's Health Care Nurse Practitioner Certification Review Guide.** 2nd ed. Ed. by Susan B. Moskosky. 600p. (C). Date not set. pap. text ed. 47.75 (*1-878028-18-9*) Hlth Lead Assoc.

Women's Health Companion: Self Help Nutrition Guide & Cookbook. Susan M. Lark. 350p. (Orig.). 1995. bds., pap. 26.95 (*0-89087-733-5*) Celestial Arts.

Women's Health Companion: Self Help Nutrition Guide & Cookbook. Susan M. Lark. 384p. 1996. pap. text ed. 18.95 (*0-89087-797-1*) Celestial Arts.

Women's Health Concerns Sourcebook. Ed. by Heather Aldred. LC 97-17093. (Health Reference Ser.). 1997. lib. bdg. 75.00 (*0-7808-0219-5*) Omnigraphics Inc.

Women's Health Counts. Ed. by Helen Roberts. 192p. (C). 1990. pap. text ed. 18.95 (*0-415-04890-7*, A4575) Routledge.

Women's Health Decision Making: A Review of the Literature. Ed. & Intro. by Leslie R. Wolfe. 39p. 1994. 12.00 (*1-877966-19-3*) Ctr Women Policy.

Women's Health Diary: The Essential Health Record for Every Woman Aged 35 to 55. Mary F. Raver. 52p. (Orig.). 1995. pap. 4.95 (*1-886245-00-2*) Adelante CA.

Women's Health Discourses, 4 vols., Set. Jack Tips. 60p. 1996. 19.95 (*0-929167-18-X*) Apple-a-Day.

Women's Health from Womb to Tomb. Penny Kane. 1994. text ed. 18.95 (*0-312-10623-8*) St Martin.

***Women's Health Guide: A Natural Approach to Breast Cancer, Heart Disease, Fibroids, PMS, Balimia, Childbirth, Menopause, & Osteoporosis.** Gale Jack & Wendy Esko. 96p. (Orig.). 1997. pap. 10.95 (*1-882984-25-0*) One Peaceful World.

Women's Health in India: Risk & Vulnerability. Ed. by Chen et al. (Illus.). 332p. 1996. 22.95 (*0-19-563620-1*) OUP.

Women's Health in Menopause: Behaviour, Cancer, Cardiovascular Disease. Ed. by P. G. Crosignani. 272p. (C). 1994. lib. bdg. 102.00 (*0-7923-3068-4*) Kluwer Ac.

Women's Health in Primary Care. Ed. by Jo A. Rosenfeld et al. LC 96-13729. 921p. 1996. 59.95 (*0-683-07366-4*) Williams & Wilkins.

***Women's Health Issues.** Ferrini & Ellingson. 400p. (C). 1997. per. 44.95 (*0-7872-3710-8*) Kendall-Hunt.

Women's Health Issues: HP 570 Course Study Guide. Charlene Allert. 180p. (C). 1992. write for info. (*0-933195-21-4*) CA College Health Sci.

Women's Health Matters. Helen Roberts. 224p. (C). 1991. pap. 19.95 (*0-415-04891-5*, A6525) Routledge.

Women's Health Nursing. Fields. (Nursing Examination Review Ser.: Vol. 2). 1984. pap. 17.75 (*0-8385-9818-8*, A9818-4) Appleton & Lange.

Women's Health Patient Education Resource Manual. Ed. by Kenneth E. Lawrence & Sandra J. Painter. LC 93-33562. ring bd. 189.00 (*0-8342-0547-5*) Aspen Pub.

Women's Health, Politics, & Power: Essays on Sex, Gender, Medicine, & Public Health. Ed. by Elizabeth Fee & Nancy Krieger. LC 94-42. 382p. 1994. text ed. 33.00 (*0-89503-120-5*) Baywood Pub.

Women's Health, Politics, & Power: Essays on Sex, Gender, Medicine, & Public Health. Ed. by Nancy Krieger & Elizabeth Fee. LC 94-42. 382p. 1994. pap. 24.75 (*0-89503-121-3*) Baywood Pub.

Women's Health Products Handbook: Smart Buys for Healthy Bodies. Carol A. Rinzler. 320p. 1996. 25.95 (*0-89793-210-2*); pap. 15.95 (*0-89793-209-9*) Hunter Hse.

***Women's Health Research: A Medical & Policy Primer.** Society for the Advancement of Women's Health Research Staff. Ed. by Florence Haseltine & Beverly Jacobson. LC 96-43828. 386p. 1997. text ed. 42.50 (*0-88048-791-7*, 8791) Am Psychiatric.

Women's Health Services: Index of New Information with Authors & Subjects. American Health Research Institute Staff. LC 92-54209. 150p. 1992. 49.50 (*1-55914-570-6*); pap. 39.50 (*1-55914-571-4*) ABBE Pubs Assn.

Women's Health Today: Perspectives on Current Research & Clinical Practice. Popkin. LC 94-22810. (Illus.). 416p. (C). 1994. text ed. 75.00 (*1-85070-568-2*) Prthnon Pub.

Women's Health Update. 192p. (Orig.). 1994. pap. 14.95 (*1-57327-013-X*, M Pr CA) Busn Concepts.

***Women's Health 98/99.** Maureen Edwards & Nora Howley. (Illus.). 256p. 1998. pap. text ed. 11.75 (*0-07-012568-6*) Dushkin Pub.

Women's Higher Education in Comparative Perspective. Ed. by Gail P. Kelly & Sheila A. Slaughter. (C). 1991. lib. bdg. 154.50 (*0-7923-0800-X*) Kluwer Ac.

Women's History: Britain, 1850-1945: An Introduction. Ed. by June Purvis. (Women's History Ser.). 1995. write for info. (*1-85728-319-8*, Pub. by UCL Pr UK); pap. write for info. (*1-85728-320-1*, Pub. by UCL Pr UK) Taylor & Francis.

Women's History: Britain, 1850-1945, An Introduction. Ed. by June Purvis. 352p. 1996. text ed. 49.95 (*0-312-16023-2*) St Martin.

Women's History & Ancient History. Ed. by Sarah B. Pomeroy. LC 90-24488. (Illus.). xviii, 318p. (C). 1991. 49.95 (*0-8078-1949-2*); pap. 16.95 (*0-8078-4310-5*) U of NC Pr.

Women's History in Minnesota: A Survey of Published Sources & Dissertations. Compiled by Jo Blatti. LC 93-15751. (Illus.). xv, 124p. (Orig.). 1994. pap. 14.95 (*0-87351-291-X*) Minn Hist.

Women's History of Sex. Harriett Gilbert & Christine Roche. 284p. 1988. 29.95 (*0-86358-051-3*); pap. 11.95 (*0-86358-142-0*) Routledge Chapman & Hall.

Women's History of the World. Marilyn French. Date not set. pap. write for info. (*0-345-40522-6*) Ballantine.

Women's History of the World. Rosalind Miles. LC 88-39598. 320p. 1990. reprint ed. pap. 13.00 (*0-06-097317-X*, PL) HarpC.

Women's History, Vol. I: American History. 3rd ed. Intro. by Louise L. Stevenson. (Selected Course Outlines from American College & Universities Ser.). 320p. 1992. pap. text ed. 16.95 (*1-55876-065-2*) Wiener Pubs Inc.

Women's History, Vol. 3: Dramatic Readings on Feminist Issues. Meg Bowman. (Illus.). 210p. (Orig.). (C). 1994. pap. 12.95 (*0-940483-08-4*) Hot Flash Pr.

Women's Home Remedy Health Guide. Consumer Guide Editors. (Illus.). 400p. 1994. 19.98 (*0-7853-0185-2*, 3212100) Pubns Intl Ltd.

Women's Home Remedy Kit: Simple Recipes for Treating Common Health Conditions. Maribeth Riggs. Ed. by Claire Zion. LC 95-14004. (Illus.). 160p. (Orig.). 1995. pap. 12.00 (*0-671-89806-X*, PB Trade Paper) PB.

Women's House. Arlene Stone. LC 78-25662. (Illus.). 1978. pap. 3.00 (*0-931588-05-7*) Allegany Mtn Pr.

Women's Human Rights & Power in Africa. Mohau N. Pheko. LC 94-65531. 210p. (Orig.). write for info. (*1-884921-23-X*) Pheko & Assocs.

***Women's Human Rights Step-by-Step: A Practical Guide to Using International Human Rights Law & Mechanisms to Defend Women's Human Rights.** Women, Law & Devel. Intl. Staff & Human Rights Watch Women's Rights Project Staff. 265p. 1997. pap. 20.00 (*1-890832-00-6*) Women Law & Dev.

Women's Humor in the Age of Gentility: The Life & Works of Frances Miriam Whitcher. Linda A. Morris. (Illus.). 256p. 1992. text ed. 34.95 (*0-8156-2562-6*) Syracuse U Pr.

Women's Images of Men. Sarah Kent & Jacqueline Morreau. (Illus.). (C). 1985. 19.95 (*0-86316-084-0*); pap. 9.95 (*0-86316-081-6*) Writers & Readers.

Women's Images of Men. 2nd ed. Ed. by Sarah Kent & Jacqueline Moreau. (Illus.). 200p. 1989. pap. 17.95 (*0-04-440461-1*) Routledge Chapman & Hall.

***Women's Imaging.** Mendelson. 760p. (C). (gr. 13). 1998. text ed. 160.00 (*0-8151-8468-9*) Mosby Yr Bk.

Women's Information Directory 1992. 1992. 75.00 (*0-8103-8422-1*) Gale.

Women's Insight. Joanne Van Roden. 50p. (Orig.). 1989. spiral bd. 5.00 (*0-940844-69-9*) Wellspring.

Women's Intuition. Elizabeth Davis. LC 89-318870. 1989. pap. 7.95 (*0-89087-572-3*) Celestial Arts.

***Women's Investment Guide: A Practical Approach to Investment Opportunities for Women in the 90's.** J. Michael Ham. (Illus.). 208p. (Orig.). 1996. pap. 16.95 (*0-9654078-1-0*) Intl Legal Pubng.

Women's Issues. Ed. by Robin Brown. LC 93-4940. (Reference Shelf Ser.). 154p. 1993. 15.00 (*0-8242-0844-7*) Wilson.

Women's Issues. Kathleen Rowe. 40p. (Orig.). 1986. pap. 3.00 (*0-89486-361-4*, 5498B) Hazelden.

***Women's Issues: An Annotated Bibliography.** Laura S. Mumford. (Magill Bibliographies Ser.). 163p. 1989. 40.00 (*0-8108-2806-5*) Scarecrow.

Womens' Issues: An Indian Perspective. Lakshmi Misra. (C). 1992. 22.00 (*81-7211-017-0*, Pub. by Northern Bk Ctr II) S Asia.

Women's Issues: Feminism, Classical Liberalism, & the Future. Joan K. Taylor. LC 93-5958. (Essays in Public Policy Ser.: No. 42). 1993. pap. 5.00 (*0-8179-5472-4*) Hoover Inst Pr.

Women's Job Search Handbook: With Issues & Insights Into the Workplace. Gerri Bloomberg & Margaret Holden. LC 90-26614. 264p. 1991. pap. 12.95 (*0-913589-49-7*) Williamson Pub Co.

Women's Journey: Reflections of Life, Love & Happiness. Ariel Books Staff. (Illus.). 368p. 1995. pap. 4.95 (*0-8362-0742-4*) Andrews & McMeel.

***Women's Journey to the Heart of God.** Cynthia Heald. LC 97-17803. 256p. 1997. 18.99 (*0-7852-7239-9*) Nelson.

Women's Journeys Through Crisis. Myrna R. Olson. LC 88-60778. (Illus.). (Orig.). 1988. pap. 10.00 (*0-9620254-0-2*) Nathan Star Pr.

Women's Junior Olympic Program Compulsory Exercises: August, 1992-July, 1996. United States Gymnastics Federation Staff. 197p. 1992. pap. 29.95 (*1-885250-31-2*) USA Gymnastics.

Women's Language Socialization & Self-Image. Ed. by D. Brouwer & D. De Haan. (Women's Studies). ix, 228p. 1986. pap. 50.00 (*90-6765-275-X*) Mouton.

Women's Law: An Introduction to Feminist Jurisprudence. Tove S. Dahl. (Scandinavian University Press Publication). 195p. 1987. 37.50 (*82-00-18490-0*) Scandnvan Univ Pr.

Women's Leadership in Marginal Religions: Explorations Outside the Mainstream. Ed. by Catherine Wessinger. LC 93-7350. 256p. 1993. text ed. 32.50 (*0-252-02025-1*); pap. text ed. 14.95 (*0-252-06332-5*) U of Ill Pr.

Women's Legal Guide. Ed. by Barbara R. Hauser. 528p. 1996. 39.95 (*1-55591-913-8*) Fulcrum Pub.

Women's Legal Guide. Ed. by Barbara R. Hauser. 528p. (Orig.). 1996. pap. 22.95 (*1-55591-303-2*) Fulcrum Pub.

Women's Legal Rights: International Covenants an Alternative to ERA? Malvina Halberstam & Elizabeth Defeis. 250p. 1987. lib. bdg. 46.00 (*0-941320-11-1*) Transnatl Pubs.

Women's Legal Rights in Florida. Gale F. Collins. LC 93-83839. 172p. (Orig.). 1993. pap. 19.95 (*0-913825-73-5*, Leg Surv Guides) Sourcebks.

Women's Legal Rights in the United States: A Selective Bibliography. Joan Ariel et al. LC 85-15733. 64p. reprint ed. pap. 25.00 (*0-7837-6154-6*, 2045876) Bks Demand.

Women's Legal Status in Selected Countries in Asia & the Pacific: Some Reflections on Progress in the Last Decade. 120p. Date not set. pap. 29.95 (*92-1-119686-8*, E.95.II.F.20) UN.

Women's Leisure, What Leisure? Eileen Green et al. 288p. (C). 1990. text ed. 32.00 (*0-8147-3039-6*) NYU Pr.

Women's Liberation: An Anthropological View. Minda Borun et al. 1971. pap. 2.00 (*0-912786-19-1*) Know Inc.

Women's Liberation & the African Freedom Struggle. Thomas Sankara. 36p. 1990. pap. 3.00 (*0-87348-585-8*) Pathfinder NY.

Women's Liberation & the Dialectics of Revolution: Reaching for the Future. Raya Dunayevskaya. LC 96-14153. 308p. 1996. pap. 15.95 (*0-8143-2655-2*) Wayne St U Pr.

Women's Liberation & Voluntary Action. Kalpana Shah. 1985. 20.00 (*0-8364-1301-6*, Pub. by Akhil) S Asia.

Women's Liberation Movement & Pornography. Herb Croner. pap. 3.00 (*0-936128-19-4*) De Young Pr.

Women's Liberation Movement in Russia: Feminism, Nihilism & Bolshevism, 1860-1930. Richard Stites. 512p. 1991. pap. text ed. 21.95 (*0-691-10058-6*) Princeton U Pr.

Women's Life Cycle & Economic Insecurity: Problems & Proposals. Ed. by Martha N. Ozawa. LC 89-7505. (Contributions in Women's Studies: No. 108). 248p. 1989. text ed. 55.00 (*0-313-26753-7*, OWC/, Praeger Pubs); pap. text ed. 19.95 (*0-275-93348-2*, B3348, Praeger Pubs) Greenwood.

Women's Life in Greece & Rome: A Source Book in Translation. rev. ed. Ed. by Mary R. Lefkowitz & Maureen B. Fant. 376p. 1992. pap. text ed. 14.95 (*0-8018-4475-4*) Johns Hopkins.

Women's Life in Greece & Rome: A Source Book in Translation. 2nd rev. ed. Ed. by Mary R. Lefkowitz & Maureen B. Fant. 376p. 1992. text ed. 38.50 (*0-8018-4474-6*) Johns Hopkins.

***Women's Life-Writing: Finding Voice Building Community.** Linda S. Coleman. LC 97-12724. 1997. write for info. (*0-87972-747-0*); pap. write for info. (*0-87972-748-9*) Bowling Green Univ Popular Press.

***Women's Lifeworlds: Women's Ways of Shaping Their Realities.** Edith Sizoo. LC 97-10356. (International Studies of Women & Place). 1997. write for info. (*0-415-17176-8*); pap. write for info. (*0-415-17177-6*) Routledge.

Women's Literature Anthology. Helene L. Keating. (C). 1996. pap. write for info. (*0-02-362181-8*, Macmillan Coll) P-H.

***Women's Little Instruction Book.** Honor Books Staff. 1996. pap. text ed. 5.99 (*1-57757-010-3*) Honor Bks OK.

Women's Lives. Sue Llewelyn. 336p. (C). 1990. pap. text ed. 15.95 (*0-415-01702-5*, A4304) Routledge.

Women's Lives: Themes & Variations in Gender Learning. Bernice Lott. LC 86-26886. 367p. (C). 1987. pap. 27.95 (*0-534-07440-5*) Brooks-Cole.

Women's Lives: Themes & Variations in Gender Learning. 2nd ed. Bernice Lott. 351p. 1994. pap. 37.95 (*0-534-15954-0*) Brooks-Cole.

Women's Lives & Public Policy: The International Experience. Ed. by Meredeth Turshen & Briavel Holcom. LC 92-33331. (Contributions in Women's Studies: No. 132). 248p. 1993. text ed. 65.00 (*0-313-27354-5*, HWI, Greenwood Pr); pap. text ed. 17.95 (*0-275-94523-5*, B4523, Praeger Pubs) Greenwood.

Women's Lives & the Eighteenth-Century English Novel. Elizabeth B. Brophy. 312p. 1991. lib. bdg. 49.95 (*0-8130-1036-5*) U Press Fla.

Women's Lives in Medieval Europe: A Sourcebook. Ed. by Emilie M. Amt. LC 92-12815. 336p. (gr. 13). 1992. pap. 16.95 (*0-415-90628-8*, A7413, Routledge NY) Routledge.

Women's Lives Through Time: Educated American Women of the Twentieth Century. Ed. by Kathleen D. Hulbert & Diane T. Schuster. LC 92-32430. (Social & Behavioral Science & Higher & Adult Education Ser.). 492p. text ed. 49.95 (*1-55542-497-X*) Jossey-Bass.

***Women's Lives/Women's Times: New Essays on Auto/Biography.** Ed. by Trev L. Broughton & Linda Anderson. LC 96-27662. (SUNY Series, Feminist Theory in Education). 291p. 1997. text ed. 59.50 (*0-7914-3397-8*); pap. text ed. 19.95 (*0-7914-3398-6*) State U NY Pr.

Women's Madness: Misogyny or Mental Illness? Jane M. Ussher. LC 91-32410. 352p. (C). 1992. pap. 18.95 (*0-87023-787-X*); lib. bdg. 47.50 (*0-87023-786-1*) U of Mass Pr.

W

An Asterisk (*) at the beginning of an entry indicates that the title is appearing in BIP for the first time.

Womens Magazine from 1940s & 1950s. Walker. Date not set. text ed. 35.00 (0-312-12814-2) St Martin.

Womens Magazines. Walker. Date not set. pap. text ed. 6.50 (0-312-10201-1) St Martin.

Women's Magazines: The First 300 Years. Brian Braithwaite. 192p. 9600. pap. 19.95 (0-7206-0936-4, Pub. by P Owen Ltd UK) Dufour.

Womens Magazines 1940's & 1950's. Walker. Date not set. text ed. 35.00 (0-312-16382-7) St Martin.

Women's Mailing List Directory. 164p. 1990. pap. text ed. 22.00 (1-880547-03-1) Nat Coun Res Wom.

Women's Market Handbook. Ed. by Carol Nelson. 400p. 1993. 64.95 (0-8103-9139-2, 101791) Gale.

***Women's Masonry or Masonry of Adoption.** 1996. pap. 12.95 (1-56459-990-6) Kessinger Pub.

Women's Medicine. Richard E. Blackwell. 644p. 1995. 99. 95 (0-86542-373-3) Blackwell Sci.

Women's Medicine: A Cross Cultural Study of Indigenous Fertility Regulation. Ed. by Lucile F. Newman. (Douglass Ser.). 226p. (C). 1985. text ed. 35.00 (0-8135-1067-8) Rutgers U Pr.

Women's Medicine: A Cross-Cultural Study of Indigenous Fertility Regulation. Lucile F. Newman. 203p. (Orig.). (C). 1995. pap. text ed. 16.00 (0-8135-2257-9) Rutgers U Pr.

Women's Medicine: The Zar-Bori Cult in Africa & Beyond. I. M. Lewis et al. 296p. 1991. text ed. 60.00 (0-7486-0261-5, Pub. by Edinburgh U Pr UK) Col U Pr.

Women's Medicine Ways: Cross-Cultural Rites of Passage. Marcia Starck. 124p. 1993. pap. 12.95 (0-89594-596-7) Crossing Pr.

Women's Mental Health Agenda. American Psychological Association, Women & Health Round Table Staff & Organizations for Professional Women Staff. Ed. by Nancy F. Russo. LC 85-72729. 99p. (Orig.). 1985. pap. 10.00 (0-912704-44-6) Am Psychol.

Women's Mental Health in Africa. Ed. by Esther D. Rothblum & Ellen Cole. (Women & Therapy Ser.). (Illus.). 98p. 1990. text ed. 24.95 (1-56024-043-1); pap. text ed. 9.95 (0-918393-86-8) Haworth Pr.

Womens Minds, Womens Bodies. Joan H. Rollins. 1996. pap. text ed. 46.33 (0-13-720343-8) P-H.

Women's Ministry: A Model for Mobilizing & Equipping Women for Ministry, Set, incl. audiocass. Marvin S. Osborn & James Copeland. 1995. ring bd., vinyl bd. 89. 95 (1-57052-023-2) Chrch Grwth VA.

Women's Ministry Handbook. Carol Porter & Mike Hamel. 272p. 1992. 18.99 (0-89693-885-9, 6-1885, Victor Bks) Chariot Victor.

Women's Monasticism & Medieval Society: Nunneries in France & England, 890-1215. Bruce L. Venarde. LC 96-30260. (Illus.). 264p. 1997. 42.50 (0-8014-3203-0) Cornell U Pr.

Women's Movement. (Social Reform Movements Ser.). (Illus.). 128p. (YA). (gr. 6 up). 1995. 17.95 (0-8160-3042-1) Facts on File.

Women's Movement. Barbara Ryan. 1996. 45.00 (0-8161-7254-4) G K Hall.

Women's Movement: Social & Psychological Perspectives. Ed. by Helen Wortis & Clara Rabinowitz. LC 72-6125. (Studies in Modern Society: Political & Social Issues: No. 2). 1972. 32.50 (0-404-10520-3) AMS Pr.

Women's Movement & Colonial Politics in Bengal: Quest for Political Rights, Education & Social Reform Legislation 1921-1936. Barbara Southard. (C). 1995. 28. 00 (81-7304-059-1, Pub. by Manohar II) S Asia.

***Women's Movement & the Transition to Democracy in Chile.** Annie G. Dandavati. (American University Studies: Series 9, Vol. 172). 192p. (C). 1996. pap. text ed. 24.95 (0-8204-2562-1) P Lang Pubng.

Women's Movement in Latin America: Feminism & the Transition to Democracy. Ed. by Jane S. Jaquette. 224p. 1989. 39.95 (0-04-445186-5); pap. 14.95 (0-04-445185-7) Routledge Chapman & Hall.

Women's Movement in Latin America: Participation & Democracy. 2nd ed. Ed. by Jane S. Jaquette. LC 94-17202. (Thematic Studies in Latin America). (C). 1994. pap. text ed. 21.50 (0-8133-8488-5) Westview.

Women's Movement in the Church of England, 1850-1930. Brian Heeney. 160p. 1988. 55.00 (0-19-822671-3) OUP.

Women's Movements: Organizing for Change. Joyce Gelb & Ethel Klein. (Women & American Politics Ser.). 36p. (Orig.). (C). 1988. pap. text ed. 6.50 (0-915654-76-8) Am Political.

***Women's Movements & Public Policy in Europe, Latin America, & the Caribbean: The Triangle of Empowerment.** Ed. by Lycklamaa G. Nijeholt et al. (Gender, Culture, & Global Politics Ser.: No. 2). 196p. 1997. 38.00 (0-8153-2479-0) Garland.

Women's Movements in America: Their Successes, Disappointments, & Aspirations. Rita J. Simon & Gloria Danziger. LC 91-8619. 184p. 1991. text ed. 55.00 (0-275-93948-0, C3948, Praeger Pubs); pap. text ed. 16. 95 (0-275-93949-9, B3949, Praeger Pubs) Greenwood.

Women's Movements in the United States: Woman Suffrage, Equal Rights & Beyond. Steven M. Buechler. LC 89-49083. 272p. (C). 1990. text ed. 40.00 (0-8135-1558-0); pap. text ed. 17.00 (0-8135-1559-9) Rutgers U Pr.

Women's Movements in the United States & Britain from the 1790s to the 1920s. Christine Bolt. LC 93-1316. 400p. (Orig.). 1993. pap. 17.95 (0-87023-867-1) U of Mass Pr.

Women's Movements of the United States & Western Europe: Consciousness, Political Opportunity & Public Policy. Ed. by Mary F. Katzenstein & Carol M. Mueller. LC 86-30182. (Women in the Political Economy Ser.). 336p. 1992. pap. 22.95 (1-56639-012-5) Temple U Pr.

Women's Mysteries: Toward a Poetics of Gender. Christine Downing. (Illus.). 192p. 1992. 19.95 (0-8245-1197-2) Crossroad NY.

***Women's Mysteries in the Northern Tradition.** Sheena McGrath. (Orig.). 1997. pap. 21.95 (1-86163-004-2, Pub. by Capall Bann Pubng UK) Holmes Pub.

Women's Notes. Ed. by Running Press Staff. (Notes Ser.). (Illus.). 96p. (Orig.). 1994. pap. 3.95 (1-56138-481-X) Running Pr.

Women's Nutrition & Health. Meredith. 1995. write for info. (0-8493-4563-4) CRC Pr.

Women's Occupational Mobility. Shirley Dex. 160p. 1987. text ed. 35.00 (0-312-88789-2) St Martin.

Womens Occupations Through Seven Decades. Janet W. Hooks. LC 75-33403. (U. S. Women's Bureau Bulletin Ser.: No. 218). 1976. reprint ed. 30.00 (0-89201-008-8) Zenger Pub.

Women's Oppression Today: The Marxist-Feminist Encounter. Michele Barrett. 304p. (Orig.). (C). 1988. pap. text ed. 19.00 (0-86091-931-5, Pub. by Vrso UK) Norton.

Women's Organizations: A New York City Directory, 1997. 1997. pap. 12.00 (0-9610688-6-8) NYC Comm Women.

Women's Organizations & Women's Interests. P. M. Mathew. 177p. 1986. 25.00 (81-7024-036-0, Pub. by Ashish II) S Asia.

Women's Orients: English Women & the Middle East, 1718-1918 Sexuality, Religion & Work. Billie Melman. 440p. 1995. pap. text ed. 16.95 (0-472-08279-5) U of Mich Pr.

Women's Orients: Englishwomen & the Middle East, 718-1918 Sexuality, Religion & Work. Billie Melman. LC 91-32433. 440p. (C). 1992. text ed. 42.50 (0-472-10332-6) U of Mich Pr.

Women's Paid & Unpaid Labor: The Work Transfer in Health Care & Retailing. Nona Y. Glazer. (Women in the Political Economy Ser.). 360p. (C). 1993. pap. 19.95 (1-56639-199-7) Temple U Pr.

Women's Participation in the British Antislavery Movement, 1824-1865. Karen I. Halbersleben. LC 93-10512. (Illus.). 256p. 1993. text ed. 89.95 (0-7734-9294-1) E Mellen.

Women's Participation in the Labour Force: A Methods Test in India for Improving Its Measurement. Richard Anker et al. (Women, Work & Development Ser.: No. 16). xiv, 204p. (Orig.). 1988. pap. 24.75 (92-2-106259-7) Intl Labour Office.

Women's Peace Union & the Outlawry of War, 1921-1942. Harriet H. Alonso. LC 89-4923. (Illus.). 248p. 1990. text ed. 31.00 (0-87049-617-4) U of Tenn Pr.

Women's Peace Union & the Outlawry of War, 1921-1942. Harriet H. Alonso. LC 96-33216. (Contemporary Issues in the Middle East Ser.). 224p. 1996. reprint ed. pap. 16. 95 (0-8156-0417-3, ALWPP) Syracuse U Pr.

Women's Perceptions of Transformative Learning Experiences Within Consciousness-Raising. Kathleen A. Loughlin. LC 93-32039. 426p. 1993. text ed. 109.95 (0-7734-2252-8, Mellen Univ Pr) E Mellen.

Women's Periodicals in the United States: Consumer Magazines. Ed. by Kathleen L. Endres & Therese L. Lueck. LC 94-46930. (Historical Guides to the World's Periodicals & Newspapers). 528p. 1995. text ed. 99.50 (0-313-28631-0, Greenwood Pr) Greenwood.

Women's Periodicals in the United States: Social & Political Issues. Ed. by Kathleen L. Endres & Therese L. Lueck. LC 96-7144. (Historical Guides to the World's Periodicals & Newspapers). 576p. 1996. text ed. 110.00 (0-313-28632-9, Greenwood Pr) Greenwood.

Women's Personal Narratives: Essays in Criticism & Pedagogy. Ed. by Leonore Hoffman & Margo Culley. LC 85-329. iv, 244p. 1985. pap. 19.75 (0-87352-343-1, B818P); lib. bdg. 37.50 (0-87352-342-3, B818C) Modern Lang.

Women's Perspectives on the Vietnam War. Marv E. Hass. Ed. by Jerold M. Starr. (Lessons of the Vietnam War Ser.). (Illus.). 32p. (Orig.). (YA). 1993. pap. text ed. 5.00 (0-945919-14-X) Ctr Social Studies.

Women's Pharmacy. Michele Paul. mass mkt. 3.50 (0-318-23489-0, Pinncle Kensgtn) Kensgtn Pub Corp.

Women's Physical Education. Jack Rudman. (National Teacher Examination Ser.: NT-37). 1994. pap. 23.95 (0-8373-8447-8) Nat Learn.

Women's Pictures: Feminism & Cinema. 2nd ed. Annette Kuhn. LC 94-11624. 224p. (Orig.). (C). 1994. pap. text ed. 20.00 (1-85984-010-8, B4692, Pub. by Vrso UK) Norton.

Women's Place. Hortense Odlum. Ed. by Annette K. Baxter. LC 79-8804. (Signal Lives Ser.). 1980. reprint ed. lib. bdg. 33.95 (0-405-12850-9) Ayer.

Women's Place: An Oral History of Working-Class Women 1890-1940. Elizabeth Roberts. 256p. pap. text ed. 24.95 (0-631-14754-3) Blackwell Pubs.

Women's Place in Pope's World. Valerie Rumbold. (Cambridge Studies in Eighteenth-Century English Literature & Thought: No. 2). (Illus.). 336p. (C). 1989. text ed. 65.00 (0-521-36308-X) Cambridge U Pr.

Women's Place in the Academy: Transforming the Liberal Arts Curriculum. Ed. by Marilyn R. Schuster & Susan R. Van Dyne. LC 84-27566. 336p. 1985. pap. 25.00 (0-8476-7408-8) Rowman.

***Women's Poetry in France, 1965-1995: A Bilingual Anthology.** Tr. by Michael Bishop. (French Poetry in Translation Ser.). 175p. (Orig.). (FRE.). 1997. pap. 14.95 (0-916390-79-9) Wake Forest.

Women's Poetry of the First World War. Nosheen Khan. LC 88-17265. 240p. 1988. 26.00 (0-8131-1677-5) U Pr of Ky.

Women's Poetry of the 1930s: A Critical Anthology. Ed. by Jane Dowson. LC 95-14810. 248p. (C). (gr. 13). 1995. pap. 16.95 (0-415-13096-4); text ed. 62.95 (0-415-13095-6) Routledge.

Women's Political Action Guide, 1993: The Women's Political Action Group. Catherine Dee. 1993. pap. 5.95 (1-879682-33-8) Earth Works.

***Women's Political Voice: How Women Are Transforming the Practice & Study of Politics.** Janet A. Flammang. LC 96-35873. (Women in the Political Economy Ser.). 1997. 69.95 (1-56639-533-X) Temple U Pr.

***Women's Political Voice: How Women Are Transforming the Practice & Study of Politics.** Janet A. Flammang. LC 96-35873. (Women in Political Economy Ser.). (C). 1997. pap. text ed. 24.95 (1-56639-534-8) Temple U Pr.

Women's Power & Roles As Portrayed in Visual Images of Women in the Arts & Mass Media. Ed. by Valerie M. Bentz & Philip E. Mayes. LC 93-5817. (Illus.). 240p. 1993. text ed. 89.95 (0-7734-9329-8) E Mellen.

Women's Prayer Groups: A Halakhic Analysis. Avraham Weiss. 1989. pap. 19.95 (0-88125-126-7) Ktav.

***Women's Press Book of New Myth & Magic.** Helen Windrath. pap. 15.95 (0-7043-4347-9, Pub. by Womens Press UK) Trafalgar.

Women's Primary Health Care: Office Practices & Procedures. Ed. by Vicki L. Seltzer & Warren H. Pearse. LC 94-30309. (Illus.). 825p. 1995. text ed. 68.00 (0-07-056225-3) McGraw-Hill HPD.

Women's Primary Health Care: Protocols for Practice. Ed. by Winifred L. Star et al. LC 93-39629. 1995. 95.00 (1-55810-094-6, MS-20) Am Nurses Pub.

Women's Prisms. Roberta Mendel. (Xantippe Ser.). 24p. (Orig.). 1994. pap. 9.00 (0-936424-04-4) Pin Prick.

Women's Problems in General Practice. Ed. by Ann McPherson. LC 92-48910. (Oxford General Practice Ser.: No. 22). 512p. 1993. pap. 37.00 (0-19-262065-7) OUP.

Women's Program Builder, No. 2. Compiled by Paul M. Miller. 1985. 5.50 (0-8341-9250-0, MP-632) Lillenas.

Women's Program Builder, No. 3. Compiled by Paul M. Miller. 1990. 5.50 (0-685-68760-0, MP-665) Lillenas.

Women's Program Rules & Policies 1993-94: Governing Competitions & Competitors. United States Gymnastics Federation Staff. 122p. 1993. pap. 11.50 (1-885250-05-3) USA Gymnastics.

Women's Progress: Promises & Problems. Ed. by J. Spurlock & C. Robinowitz. (Women in Context: Development & Stresses Ser.). (Illus.). 270p. 1990. 47.50 (0-306-43422-9, Plenum Pr) Plenum.

Women's Progress in America. Elizabeth Knappman. LC 94-9355. (Clio Companions Ser.). 401p. 1994. lib. bdg. 55.00 (0-87436-667-4) ABC-CLIO.

Women's Project Two: Five New Plays by Women. Ed. by Julia Miles. LC 84-81624. 1984. 21.95 (0-933826-73-7) PAJ Pubns.

Women's Psyche, Women's Spirit: The Reality of Relationships. Mary L. Randour. LC 86-17180. 240p. 1987. text ed. 45.00 (0-231-06250-8) Col U Pr.

Women's Psychic Lives. 2nd rev. ed. Diane Stein. (New Age Ser.). (Illus.). 384p. 1989. pap. 16.95 (1-56718-692-0) Llewellyn Pubns.

Women's Quest for Economic Equality. Victor R. Fuchs. LC 88-7209. (Illus.). 176p. 1988. 27.50 (0-674-95545-5) HUP.

Women's Quest for Economic Equality. Victor R. Fuchs. (Illus.). 192p. 1990. pap. 11.95 (0-674-95546-3) HUP.

Women's Quest for Power. D. Jain. 271p. 1980. 19.95 (0-7069-1021-4) Asia Bk Corp.

Women's Quotations. Helen Exley. (Best of Quotations Ser.). (Illus.). 60p. 1993. 8.00 (1-85015-308-6) Exley Giftbooks.

Women's Re-Visions of Shakespeare. Marianne Novy. 272p. 1990. pap. text ed. 15.95 (0-252-06114-4) U of Ill Pr.

Women's Realities, Women's Choices: An Introduction to Women's Studies. 2nd ed. (Hunter College Women's Studies Collective Ser.). (Illus.). 704p. (C). 1995. pap. text ed. 37.00 (0-19-505883-6) OUP.

Women's Reality: An Emerging Female System. Anne W. Schaef. LC 90-56446. 1992. reprint ed. pap. 12.00 (0-06-250770-2) Harper SF.

Women's Rebellion & Islamic Memory. Fatima Mernissi. Tr. by Emily Agar. 224p. (C). 1996. pap. 17.50 (1-85649-398-9, Pub. by Zed Bks Ltd UK); text ed. 49. 95 (1-85649-397-0, Pub. by Zed Bks Ltd UK) Humanities.

Women's Recovery Programs: A Directory of Residential Addiction Treatment Centers. Oryx Press Staff. LC 89-23199. 360p. 1989. pap. 55.00 (0-89774-584-1) Oryx Pr.

***Women's Reference Library.** 1995. 339.00 (0-7876-0666-9, UXL) Gale.

Women's Reflections: The Feminist Film Movement. Jan Rosenberg. Ed. by Diane Kirkpatrick. LC 83-1271. (Studies in Cinema: No. 22). 154p. reprint ed. 43.70 (0-8357-1400-4, 2070759) Bks Demand.

Women's Reproductive Health: The Silent Emergency. Jodi L. Jacobson. 70p. (Orig.). 1991. pap. 5.00 (1-878071-03-3) Worldwatch Inst.

Women's Resource & National Development. Ed. by Rajkumari Chandrasekhar. 144p. (C). 1992. 22.50 (81-207-1386-9) Apt Bks.

Women's Resource & National Development: A Perspective. Ed. by Rajkumari Chandrasekar. (C). 1992. 14.00 (81-85006-29-6, Pub. by Gaurav Pub House II) S Asia.

Womens Resource Directory 1995. Ed. by Wendy W. Herumin & C. Dianne Perry. 192p. 1995. 5.95 (0-9637133-2-9) WYP of Prtlnd.

Women's Retirement: Policy Implications of Recent Research. Ed. by Maximiliane Szinovacz. LC 82-16758. (Sage Yearbooks in Women's Policy Studies: No. 6). 271p. reprint ed. pap. 77.30 (0-8357-8394-4, 2034668) Bks Demand.

***Women's Retreat Book: A Guide to Restoring, Rediscovering, & Reawakening Your True Self - in a Moment, an Hour, a Day, or a Week.** Jennifer Louden. 1997. pap. 17.00 (0-614-27682-9) Harper SF.

Women's Rights. Christine A. Lunardini. LC 95-21712. (Social Issues in American History Ser.). (Illus.). 232p. 1995. pap. 29.95 (0-89774-872-7) Oryx Pr.

***Women's Rights.** Wendy Mass. (Overview Ser.). (Illus.). (J). (gr. 4-12). 1997. lib. bdg. 17.96 (1-56006-510-9) Lucent Bks.

***Women's Rights, Vol. 1.** Sklar. Date not set. pap. text ed. write for info. (0-312-10144-9) St Martin.

Women's Rights & Liberation, 13 Vols., Set. Ed. by Jerome S. Ozer. 1969. reprint ed. 321.50 (0-405-00101-0) Ayer.

Women's Rights & the Law. Laura A. Otten. LC 93-20127. 264p. 1993. text ed. 65.00 (0-275-93184-6, C3184, Praeger Pubs); pap. text ed. 18.95 (0-275-93185-4, B3185, Praeger Pubs) Greenwood.

Women's Rights & the Law. John W. Whitehead. (Faith & Freedom Ser.: No. 6). (Orig.). 1996. pap. text ed. 4.99 (0-8024-6690-7) Moody.

Women's Rights & the Law: The Impact of the ERA on State Laws. Barbara A. Brown et al. LC 77-9961. 448p. 1977. text ed. 75.00 (0-275-90257-9, C0257, Praeger Pubs) Greenwood.

Women's Rights & the Rights of Man. A. J. Arnaud & Elizabeth Kingdom. (Enlightenment Rights & Revolution Ser.: No. 5). 1990. pap. text ed. 38.00 (0-08-040923-7, Pub. by Aberdeen U Pr) Macmillan.

Women's Rights & Women's Lives in France, 1944-1968. Claire Duchen. LC 93-30843. 224p. (C). 1994. pap. 18. 95 (0-415-00934-0) Routledge.

Women's Rights & Women's Lives in France, 1944-1968. Claire Duchen. LC 93-30843. 224p. (C). (gr. 13). 1994. text ed. 69.95 (0-415-00933-2) Routledge.

Women's Rights at Work: Campaigns & Policy in Britain & the United States. Elizabeth M. Meehan. LC 84-1597. 253p. 1985. text ed. 35.00 (0-312-88793-0) St Martin.

Women's Rights, Human Rights: International Feminist Perspectives. Ed. by Julie S. Peters & Andrea Wolper. LC 94-15775. 450p. (C). 1994. text ed. 69.95 (0-415-90994-5, B3882, Routledge NY) Routledge.

Women's Rights, Human Rights: International Feminist Perspectives. Ed. by Julie S. Peters & Andrea Wolper. LC 94-15775. 450p. (gr. 13). 1994. pap. 18.95 (0-415-90995-3, B3886, Routledge NY) Routledge.

Women's Rights in America: A Documentary History. Ed. by Winston E. Langley & Vivan C. Fox. LC 94-7429. (Primary Documents in American History & Contemporary Issues Ser.). 400p. 1994. text ed. 49.95 (0-313-28755-4, Greenwood Pr) Greenwood.

Women's Rights in France. Dorothy M. Stetson. LC 86-14988. (Contributions in Women's Studies: No. 74). 255p. 1987. text ed. 55.00 (0-313-25403-6, SWR/, Greenwood Pr) Greenwood.

Women's Rights in International Documents: A Sourcebook with Commentary. Ed. by Winston E. Langley. LC 90-53501. 216p. 1991. lib. bdg. 55.00 (0-89950-548-1) McFarland & Co.

Women's Rights in Islam. Muhammad S. Chaudhry. 204p. 1991. 19.95 (1-56744-419-9) Kazi Pubns.

Women's Rights in Old Testament Times. James R. Baker. LC 92-4953. xii, 186p. 1992. pap. 17.95 (1-56085-029-9) Signature Bks.

Women's Rights in the U. S. A. Policy Debates & Gender Roles. Dorothy M. Stetson. LC 90-44814. 265p. (C). 1991. pap. text ed. write for info. (0-534-14898-0) HarBrace.

***Women's Rights in the U. S. A. Policy Debates & Gender Roles.** 2nd ed. Dorothy M. Stetson. (Social-Psychology Reference Ser.). 408p. 1997. 56.00 (0-8153-2076-0); pap. 22.95 (0-8153-2075-2) Garland.

Women's Rights Movement: Opposing Viewpoints. Ed. by Brenda Stalcup. (American History Ser.). (Illus.). 312p. (YA). (gr. 5-12). 1996. pap. text ed. 12.96 (1-56510-366-1); lib. bdg. 20.96 (1-56510-367-X) Greenhaven.

***Women's Rights Movement Beginning in the Finger Lakes Region.** Emerson Klees. (Illus.). 288p. (YA). (gr. 7-12). 1997. pap. 17.00 (0-9635990-9-7) Frnds Finger Lks.

Women's Rights Movement in Iran: Mutiny, Appeasement, & Repression. Ed. by Eliz Sanasarian. LC 82-7714. 190p. 1982. text ed. 38.50 (0-275-90894-1, C0894, Praeger Pubs) Greenwood.

***Women's Rights on Trial.** Elizabeth Frost-Knappman & Kathryn Cullen-DuPont. 478p. 1996. 49.95 (0-7876-0657-X) Gale.

Women's Rituals: A Sourcebook. Barbara G. Walker. LC 89-45520. 238p. 1990. pap. 16.00 (0-06-250939-X) Harper SF.

Women's Role & First Corinthians 14:33-37. Bill Haberman. 77p. 1993. pap. 4.95 (1-56794-054-4, C-2332) Star Bible.

Women's Role in the Church. Joan Chittister. 20p. 1993. pap. text ed. 2.95 (1-55612-603-4) Sheed & Ward MO.

Women's Roles: A Cross-Cultural Perspective. Eileen Newmark. 128p. 1981. pap. 10.25 (0-08-026073-X, Pergamon Pr) Elsevier.

Women's Roles in Technical Innovation. UNIFEM Staff. 88p. (Orig.). 1995. pap. 15.50 (0-614-09486-0, Pub. by Intermed Tech UK) Women Ink.

Women's Room. Marilyn French. 544p. 1993. pap. 12.00 (0-345-38181-5, Ballantine Trade) Ballantine.

Women's Room. Marilyn French. 512p. 1988. mass mkt. 6.99 (0-345-35361-7) Ballantine.

Women's Room. Marilyn French. 1996. mass mkt. 6.99 (0-345-91021-4) Ballantine.

Women's Roots: Status & Achievements in Western Civilization. 3rd ed. June Stephenson. LC 81-68206. 360p. (Orig.). 1988. pap. 15.00 (0-941138-07-0) Diemer-Smith.

Women's Roots: Status & Achievements in Western Civilization. 4th ed. June Stephenson. 370p. (Orig.). 1993. pap. 20.00 (*0-941138-12-7*) Diemer-Smith.

***Women's Royal Army Corps.** Shelford Bidwell. LC 78-317843. 1997. pap. text ed. 8.95 (*0-85052-099-1*, Pub. by L Cooper Bks UK) Trans-Atl Phila.

Women's Sailing Resource. National Women's Advisory Board on Sailing Staff. 1994. pap. 3.00 (*0-914747-04-5*) Offshore Sail Schl.

Women's Scenes & Monologues. Joyce Devlin. 244p. 1989. pap. text ed. 8.95 (*0-87440-007-4*) Bakers Plays.

Women's Schooling, the Selectivity of Fertility, & Child Mortality in Sub-Saharan Africa. Mark Pitt. (World Bank Living Standards Measurement Series Paper: No. 119). 64p. 1995. lib. bdg. 7.95 (*0-8213-3332-1*, 13332) World Bank.

Women's Seclusion & Men's Honor: Sex Roles in North India, Bangladesh, & Pakistan. David G. Mandelbaum. LC 87-36547. (Illus.). 153p. 1993. reprint ed. pap. text ed. 15.50 (*0-8165-1400-3*) U of Ariz Pr.

Women's Secrets: A Translation of Pseudo-Albertus Magnus' De Secretis Mulierum with Commentaries. Helen R. Lemay. LC 91-30690. (SUNY Series in Medieval Studies). 200p. (C). 1992. text ed. 64.50 (*0-7914-1143-5*); pap. text ed. 21.95 (*0-7914-1144-3*) State U NY Pr.

Women's Seder: Our Spiritual Journey to Freedom. Jill S. Thornton. (Illus.). (Orig.). 1996. pap. 12.00 (*0-9651772-0-3*) New Millenia.

Women's Sexual Experience: Explorations of the Dark Continent. Ed. by Martha Kirkpatrick. LC 82-482. (Women in Context Ser.). 344p. 1982. 55.00 (*0-306-40793-0*, Plenum Pr) Plenum.

Women's Sexual Health. Andrews. 1996. pap. text ed. 45.00 (*0-7020-1898-8*) Saunders.

Women's Sexual Health. Ruth Steinberg & Linda Robinson. (Illus.). 240p. 1995. pap. 12.95 (*1-55611-471-0*, Primus) D I Fine.

Women's Sexuality after Childhood Incest. Elaine Westerlund. 200p. (C). 1992. 27.95 (*0-393-70141-7*) Norton.

Women's Side. Clemence Dane, pseud. LC 70-99629. (Essay Index Reprint Ser.). 1977. 19.95 (*0-8369-1566-6*) Ayer.

Women's Skin. David Stoll. (Illus.). 250p. 1994. pap. 14.95 (*0-8135-2029-0*); text ed. 36.00 (*0-8135-2028-2*) Rutgers U Pr.

Women's Soccer Guide. Tucker. (Orig.). 1981. pap. 5.95 (*0-02-499920-2*, Macmillan Coll) P-H.

Women's Song Still Not Heard: Listen to the Rhythm of the Exiled Drum. Frances L. Drew. LC 91-72233. (Illus.). 120p. (Orig.). 1993. pap. 15.95 (*1-55618-102-7*) Brunswick Pub.

Womens Speaking Justified, Proved & Allowed of by the Scriptures: And Epistle from the Womens-Yearly Meeting at York, 1688 & a Warning to all Friends, Who Profess the Everlasting Truth of God. Margaret Fell et al. LC 92-24042. (Augustan Reprints Ser.: No. 194). 1979. reprint ed. 14.50 (*0-404-70194-9*, BV4527) AMS Pr.

Women's Spiritual Passages: Celebrating Faith after 40. Ed. by Lucinda S. McDowell. LC 95-44698. 240p. 1996. pap. 9.99 (*0-87788-456-0*) Shaw Pubs.

Women's Spirituality: Resources for Christian Development. 2nd ed. Joann W. Conn. LC 96-17621. 352p. (Orig.). 1996. pap. 24.95 (*0-8091-3656-2*) Paulist Pr.

Women's Spirituality Book. Diane Stein. LC 86-45795. (New Age Ser.). (Illus.). 286p. (Orig.). 1986. pap. 12.95 (*0-87542-761-8*) Llewellyn Pubns.

Women's Spirituality, Women's Lives. Ed. by Judith Ochshorn & Ellen Cole. LC 95-11386. 227p. 1995. 29.95 (*1-56024-722-3*); pap. 14.95 (*1-56023-065-7*) Haworth Pr.

Women's Sports: A History. Allen Guttmann. (Illus.). 339p. 1991. 29.95 (*0-231-06956-1*) Col U Pr.

Women's Sports: A History. Allen Guttmann. (Illus.). 339p. 1992. pap. 16.50 (*0-231-06957-X*) Col U Pr.

Women's Sports Encyclopedia. Robert J. Markel. LC 97-8850. 1997. 30.00 (*0-8050-4494-9*) H Holt & Co.

Women's Status & Fertility in Pakistan: Recent Evidence. 29p. Date not set. pap. 10.00 (*92-1-151264-6*, E.94. XIII.6) UN.

***Women's Status in Contemporary China.** Ed. by Sha Jicai & Liu Qiming. 402p. 1996. 64.95 (*7-301-02655-2*) Austin & Winfield.

Women's Status in India: (Policies & Programmes) B. P. Chaurasia. (C). 1992. 36.00 (*81-85613-59-1*, Pub. by Chugh Pubns II) S Asia.

***Women's Struggle for Equality: The First Phase, 1828-1876.** Jean V. Matthews. LC 96-47500. 224p. 1997. 24.95 (*1-56663-145-9*) I R Dee.

Women's Struggle for Higher Education in Russia, 1855-1900. Christine Johanson. 168p. 1987. 49.95 (*0-7735-0565-2*, Pub. by McGill CN) U of Toronto Pr.

***Women's Struggles: A History of the All India Women's Conference 1927-1990.** Aparna Basu & Bharati Ray. (C). 1990. 27.00 (*81-85425-42-6*, Pub. by Manohar II) S Asia.

Women's Studies: A Checklist of Bibliographies. M. Ritchie. 128p. 1980. text ed. 50.00 (*0-7201-0918-3*) Weidner & Sons.

Women's Studies: A Guide to Information Sources. Sarah Carter & Maureen Ritchie. LC 89-39974. 288p. 1990. lib. bdg. 47.50 (*0-89950-534-1*) McFarland & Co.

Women's Studies: A Retrospective: A Report to the Ford Foundation. Beverly Guy-Sheftall & Susan Heath. 1995. write for info. (*0-916584-49-6*) Ford Found.

Women's Studies: An Emerging Discipline. Ed. by A. Suryakumari. (C). 1993. text ed. 15.00 (*81-212-0457-7*, Pub. by Gian Publng Hse II) S Asia.

Women's Studies: An Interdisciplinary Collection. Ed. by Kathleen O. Blumhagen & Walter D. Johnson. LC 77-18110. (Contributions in Women's Studies: No. 2). 142p. 1978. text ed. 35.00 (*0-313-20028-9*, SJW/, Greenwood Pr) Greenwood.

Women's Studies: Essential Readings. Ed. by Stevi Jackson et al. LC 93-17832. 544p. (C). 1993. 60.00 (*0-8147-4214-9*); pap. 19.95 (*0-8147-4215-7*) NYU Pr.

***Women's Studies: Thinking Women.** Joy L. Wetzel. 592p. (C). 1995. per., pap. text ed. 40.89 (*0-7872-0559-1*) Kendall-Hunt.

Women's Studies & Culture: A Feminist Introduction. Ed. by Rosemarie Buikema & Anneke Smelik. LC 95-21716. 256p. (C). 1995. pap. 17.50 (*1-85649-312-1*, Pub. by Zed Bks Ltd UK); text ed. 55.00 (*1-85649-311-3*, Pub. by Zed Bks Ltd UK) Humanities.

Women's Studies Collection Development Policies. Collection Development & Bibliography Committee Staff. 122p. (Orig.). 1992. pap. text ed. 35.95 (*0-8389-7596-8*) ALA.

Women's Studies Encyclopedia, Vol. 1: Views from the Sciences. Ed. by Helen Tierney. LC 88-32806. 433p. 1989. text ed. 59.95 (*0-313-26725-1*) Greenwood.

Women's Studies Encyclopedia, Vol. 1: Views from the Sciences. Ed. by Helen Tierney. LC 88-32806. 433p. 1989. text ed. 184.90 (*0-313-24646-7*, TIW01) Greenwood.

Women's Studies Encyclopedia, Vol. 2: Literature, Arts, & Learning, Vol. 2. Ed. by Helen Tierney. LC 88-32806. 400p. 1990. text ed. 65.00 (*0-313-27357-X*, TIW02, Greenwood Pr) Greenwood.

Women's Studies Encyclopedia, Vol. 3: History, Philosophy & Religion, Vol. 3. Ed. by Helen Tierney. LC 88-32806. 552p. 1991. text ed. 65.00 (*0-313-27358-8*, TIW03, Greenwood Pr) Greenwood.

Women's Studies Graduates: The First Generation. Barbara Luebke & Mary E. Reilly. (Athene Ser.). 224p. (C). 1994. text ed. 44.00 (*0-8077-6275-X*); pap. text ed. 21.95 (*0-8077-6274-1*) Tchrs Coll.

Women's Studies in India: A Directory of Research Institutions. Ed. by S. V. Rao. (Illus.). viii, 123p. 1993. 13.00 (*81-7024-569-9*, Pub. by Ashish Pub Hse II) Nataraj Bks.

Women's Studies in India: Information Sources, Services, & Programmes. Ed. by Sunita Singh. LC 92-16714. 212p. (C). 1992. 28.95 (*0-8039-9438-9*) Sage.

Women's Studies in India: Some Perspectives. Maithreyi K. Raj. 1986. 28.50 (*0-86132-135-9*, Pub. by Popular Prakashan II) S Asia.

Women's Studies in School Education: A New Perspective. Indira K. Noopur. 111p. 1989. text ed. 15.95 (*81-207-1041-X*, Pub. by Sterling Pubs II) Apt Bks.

Women's Studies in the Nineteen Nineties: Doing Things Differently? Ed. by Joanna De Groot & Mary Maynard. LC 92-30627. 244p. 1993. text ed. 39.95 (*0-312-09122-2*) St Martin.

Women's Studies in the United States: A Report to the Ford Foundation. Catherine R. Stimpson & Nina K. Cobb. LC 86-9867. 77p. (Orig.). 1986. pap. text ed. write for info. (*0-916584-26-7*) Ford Found.

Women's Studies Index: 1989. Compiled by G. K. Hall Staff. 600p. 1990. 130.00 (*0-8161-0510-3*) G K Hall.

Women's Studies Index, 1990. annuals Compiled by G. K. Hall Staff. 650p. 1992. 140.00 (*0-8161-0511-1*) G K Hall.

Women's Studies Index 1991. Compiled by G. K. Hall Staff. 650p. 1993. 160.00 (*0-8161-0512-X*) G K Hall.

Womens Studies Index 1993. Hall. 1995. 175.00 (*0-8161-0555-3*) Macmillan.

Womens Studies Index, 1994. G. K. Hall Staff. 1995. 175.00 (*0-7838-2051-8*) Macmillan.

Womens Studies Index 1995. 1996. 175.00 (*0-7838-2109-3*) G K Hall.

Womens Studies Index 1996. 1997. 185.00 (*0-7838-2151-4*) G K Hall.

***Women's Studies Index 1997.** Hall, G. K., Staff. 1998. 185.00 (*0-7838-0077-0*) G K Hall.

Women's Studies International: Nairobi & Beyond. Ed. by Aruna Rao. LC 90-48653. 376p. 1991. 35.00 (*1-55861-031-6*); pap. 15.95 (*1-55861-032-4*) Feminist Pr.

Women's Studies Manuscript Collections from the Schlesinger Library, Radcliffe College: Papers of Mary Ware Dennett... Betsey B. Covel. LC 94-17171. (Research Collections in Women's Studies). 1994. 4,505.00 (*1-55655-510-5*) U Pubns Amer.

Women's Studies of the Christian & Islamic Traditions: Ancient, Medieval & Renaissance Foremothers. Kari E. Borresen. (Diverse Ser.). 368p. (C). 1993. lib. bdg. 137.00 (*0-7923-2206-1*, Pub. by Klwr Acad Pubs NE) Kluwer Ac.

***Women's Studies Quarterly: Teaching African Literatures in a Global Literary Economy.** Tuzyline J. Allan. 1997. pap. text ed. 18.00 (*1-55861-169-X*) Feminist Pr.

***Women's Studies Quarterly: The History & Future of Women's Studies.** Ed. by Elaine Hedges & Dorothy Helly. 1997. pap. text ed. 18.00 (*1-55861-171-1*) Feminist Pr.

Women's Studies Quarterly Vol. 95, Nos. 3-4: Rethinking Women's Peace Studies. Linda Forcey. 1996. pap. text ed. 18.00 (*1-55861-134-7*) Feminist Pr.

Women's Studies Quarterly Vol. 96, Nos. 1-2: Beijing & Beyond: Toward the Twenty-First Century of Women. Ed. by Florence Howe. (Illus.). 420p. 1996. pap. text ed. 22.00 (*1-55861-142-8*) Feminist Pr.

Womens Studies Quarterly, 1996: Curriculum Transformation in Community Colleges, Nos. 3 & 4. Liza Fiol-Matta. 250p. 1996. pap. text ed. 18.00 (*1-55861-161-4*) Feminist Pr.

Women's Studies Quarterly (95:1-2) Teaching Working-Class Studies. Janet Zandy. 1995. pap. 18.00 (*1-55861-121-5*) Feminist Pr.

Womens Studies Index 1992. 1994. 165.00 (*0-8161-0520-0*) G K Hall.

Women's Suffrage. Miriam Sagan. LC 95-1276. (World History Ser.). 112p. (J). (gr. 6-10). 1995. lib. bdg. 17.96 (*1-56006-290-8*) Lucent Bks.

Women's Suffrage: The Reform Against Nature. Horace Bushnell. LC 75-33280. 1976. reprint ed. 23.95 (*0-89201-000-2*) Zenger Pub.

Women's Suffrage & Social Politics in the French Third Republic. Steven C. Hause & Anne R. Kenney. LC 84-42579. 416p. reprint ed. pap. 118.60 (*0-7837-0104-7*, 2040382) Bks Demand.

Women's Suffrage & the Police: Three Senate Documents. U. S. Senate Executive Document Committee. LC 73-154569. (Police in America Ser.). 1971. reprint ed. 59.95 (*0-405-03389-3*) Ayer.

Women's Suffrage in America. Elizabeth Frost & Kathryn Cullen-Dupont. (Eyewitness History Ser.). (Illus.). 452p. 1992. lib. bdg. 45.00 (*0-8160-2309-3*) Facts on File.

***Womens Suffrage Movement.** Joannou. LC 97-21596. 1998. text ed. write for info. (*0-7190-4860-5*, Pub. by Manchester Univ Pr UK) St Martin.

Women's Suffrage Movement & Irish Society in the Early Twentieth Century. Cliona Murphy. LC 89-4705. 240p. (C). 1989. 34.95 (*0-87722-636-9*) Temple U Pr.

Women's Suffrage Movement in Scotland: A Guid Cause. Leah Leneman. (SWSS Ser.). (Illus.). 192p. 1991. pap. text ed. 23.90 (*0-08-041201-7*, Pub. by Aberdeen U Pr) Macmillan.

***Women's Survival Handbook Series, 3 vols., Set.** M. A. Eckels. 1997. write for info. (*0-9647790-9-9*) Exerbian Pr.

Women's Symptoms: A Comprehensive Guide to Common Symptoms & Diseases: Their Causes, & Treatments. Ivan K. Strausz. LC 95-44873. 528p. 1996. pap. 13.95 (*0-440-50642-5*, Dell Trade Pbks) Dell.

Women's Tails: A Book about the Trauma & Subculture of Divorce. Carmelo Inguanti. 1994. 13.95 (*0-533-10965-5*) Vantage.

Women's Talk? A Social History of "Gossip" in Working Class Neighborhoods, 1880-1960. Melanie Tebbutt. LC 94-27195. 1993. 59.95 (*1-85928-026-9*, Pub. by Scolar Pr UK) Ashgate Pub Co.

***Women's Talk? A Social History of "Gossip" in Working-Class Neighborhoods, 1880-1960.** Melanie Tebbutt. 216p. 1997. reprint ed. pap. text ed. 25.95 (*1-85928-435-3*, Pub. by Ashgate UK) Ashgate Pub Co.

Women's Tennis: A Historical Documentary of the Players and Their Game. Angela Lumpkin. LC 79-57328. 203p. 1981. 15.00 (*0-87875-189-0*) Whitston Pub.

Women's Therapy Groups: Paradigms of Feminist Treatment. Claire Brody. (Women's Ser.). 288p. 1987. 35.95 (*0-8261-5570-7*) Springer Pub.

***Women's Thoughts.** Ed. by Helen Exley. (Miniature Square Bks.). (Illus.). 64p. 1996. 6.00 (*1-85015-793-6*) Exley Giftbooks.

Women's Traveler 1995. Damron. 1995. pap. text ed. 10.95 (*0-929435-16-8*) Odysseus Ent.

Women's Traveler 1996. Damron. 1996. pap. text ed. 11.95 (*0-929435-20-6*) Odysseus Ent.

Women's Traveller, Vol. 1. Ed. by Pamela K. Williams. 250p. 1989. pap. 8.00 (*0-929435-03-6*) Damron Co.

Women's Traveller, Vol. 2. Ed. by Pamela K. Williams. 347p. 1991. pap. 10.00 (*0-929435-06-0*) Damron Co.

Women's Two Roles: A Contemporary Dilemma. Phyllis Moen. LC 91-36728. 192p. 1992. text ed. 55.00 (*0-86569-198-3*, T198, Auburn Hse); pap. text ed. 16.95 (*0-86569-199-1*, R199, Auburn Hse) Greenwood.

Women's Utopias in Nineteenth & Twentieth Century Fiction. Nan B. Albinski. 224p. 1988. lib. bdg. 59.50 (*0-415-00330-X*) Routledge.

Women's Ventures: Assistance to the Informal Sector in Latin America. fac. ed. Ed. by Marguerite Berger & Mayra Buvinic. LC 89-39190. (Kumarian Press Library of Management for Development). 288p. 1989. pap. 82.10 (*0-7837-7585-7*, 2047338) Bks Demand.

***Women's Ventures, Women's Visions: 29 Inspiring Stories from Women Who Started Their Own Business.** Shoshana Alexander. LC 97-22531. 232p. (Orig.). 1997. pap. 14.95 (*0-89594-823-0*) Crossing Pr.

Women's Victory Journal. Rosemary Launikonis. 28p. 1994. 15.99 incl. audio (*0-9642143-0-X*) Launikonis & Assocs.

Women's View. Ed. by Natasha Perova & Arch Tait. (Glas Ser.: No. 3). (Illus.). 224p. pap. 14.95 (*0-939010-48-8*) I R Dee.

Women's Views of the Political World of Men. Ed. by Judith H. Stiehm. LC 83-18041. 234p. (C). 1984. lib. bdg. 40.00 (*0-941320-13-8*) Transnatl Pubs.

Women's Voices. Pat C. Hoy et al. 720p. (C). 1990. pap. text ed. write for info. (*0-07-557732-1*) McGraw.

Women's Voices. Lorie J. McElroy. (Women's Reference Library). 320p. 1996. 55.00 (*0-7876-0663-4*, UXL) Gale.

***Women's Voices: A Documentary History of Women in America.** Lorie J. McElroy. LC 96-29247. 1996. write for info. (*0-7876-0664-2*, UXL); write for info. (*0-7876-0665-0*, UXL) Gale.

Women's Voices from Latin America: Interviews with Six Contemporary Authors. Evelyn P. Garfield. LC 87-25354. (Illus.). 190p. (C). 1987. reprint ed. pap. 11.95 (*0-8143-1962-9*) Wayne St U Pr.

Women's Voices from the Oregon Trail: The Times That Tried Women's Souls. 2nd ed. Susan G. Butruille. (Illus.). 253p. (Orig.). 1994. pap. 14.95 (*0-9634839-8-6*) Tamarack Bks.

Women's Voices from the Other Americas: Expanding the Feminist Problematics see **Contemporary Women Writing in Latin America: Expanding the Feminist Problematics**

Women's Voices from the Other Americas: Expanding the Feminist Problematics see **Contemporary Women Writing in the Caribbean**

Women's Voices from the Other Americas: Expanding the Feminist Problematics see **Contemporary Women Writing in Canada & Quebec**

Women's Voices from the Rainforest. Janet G. Townsend. LC 94-12466. (International Studies of Women & Place). (Illus.). 212p. (C). 1995. pap. 17.95 (*0-415-10532-3*, B7049) Routledge.

Women's Voices from the Rainforest. Janet G. Townsend. LC 94-12466. (International Studies of Women & Place). (Illus.). 272p. (C). (gr. 13). 1995. text ed. 62.95 (*0-415-10531-5*, B7045) Routledge.

Womens Voices from the Spanish Civil War. Ed. by Fyrth. (C). 1991. text ed. 49.95 (*0-85315-724-3*, Pub. by Lawrence & Wishart UK) NYU Pr.

Women's Voices from the Western Frontier. Susan G. Butruille. 323p. 1995. pap. 16.95 (*1-886609-00-4*) Tamarack Bks.

Women's Voices in Experiential Education. AEE Staff. Ed. by Karen J. Warren. 336p. 1996. per., pap. text ed. 23.95 (*0-7872-2059-0*) Kendall-Hunt.

Women's Voices in Experiential Education. Ed. by Karen J. Warren. (Illus.). 350p. (Orig.). 1996. 23.95 (*0-614-12913-3*) Assn Exper Ed.

Women's Voices in Our Time: Statements by American Leaders. Ed. by Victoria L. DeFrancisco & Marvin D. Jensen. (Illus.). 281p. (Orig.). (C). 1994. pap. text ed. 15.95 (*0-88133-761-7*) Waveland Pr.

Women's Voices in Russia Today. Ed. by Elina Haavio-Mannila & Anna Rotkirch. LC 95-47698. (Illus.). 304p. 1996. text ed. 62.95 (*1-85521-679-5*, Pub. by Dartmth Pub UK) Ashgate Pub Co.

Women's Voices on Africa. Intro. by Patricia W. Romero. LC 91-36228. (Topics in World History Ser.). (Illus.). 324p. (C). 1992. text ed. 39.95 (*1-55876-047-4*); pap. text ed. 14.95 (*1-55876-048-2*) Wiener Pubs Inc.

Women's Voices on the Pacific: The International Pacific Policy Congress. Ed. by Lenora Foerstel. (Border - Culture Ser.). (Illus.). 160p. 1991. pap. text ed. 13.95 (*0-944624-14-6*); lib. bdg. 26.95 (*0-944624-13-8*) Maisonneuve Pr.

Women's Voting Rights. Miles Harvey. LC 96-5068. (Cornerstones of Freedom Ser.). 32p. (J). 1996. lib. bdg. 18.00 (*0-516-20003-8*) Childrens.

Women's Wages. Emilie J. Hutchinson. LC 68-56661. (Columbia University. Studies in the Social Sciences: No. 202). reprint ed. 37.50 (*0-404-51202-X*) AMS Pr.

Women's Warpath: Iban Ritual Fabrics from Borneo. Traude Gavin. LC 96-17238. (Illus.). 100p. 1996. 40.00 (*0-930741-50-1*); pap. 22.00 (*0-930741-51-X*) UCLA Fowler Mus.

Womens Waterworks: Curing Incontinence. Pauline E. Chiarelli. (Health Bks.). 64p. 1995. pap. 8.95 (*0-9640719-0-8*) Khera Pubns.

Women's Ways of Knowing. 10th anniversary ed. Ed. by Mary F. Belenky. 272p. 1997. pap. 12.00 (*0-465-09099-0*) HarpC.

Women's West. Ed. by Susan Armitage & Elizabeth Jameson. LC 86-14672. (Illus.). 336p. 1987. 32.95 (*0-8061-2043-6*); pap. 16.95 (*0-8061-2067-3*) U of Okla Pr.

***Women's Wheel of Life.** Elizabeth Davis. 1997. pap. 11.95 (*0-14-019505-X*) Viking Penguin.

Women's Wheel of Life: Thirteen Archetypes of Woman at Her Fullest Power. Elizabeth Davis & Carol Leonard. LC 95-39304. 235p. 1996. pap. 22.95 (*0-670-86227-4*, Arkana) Viking Penguin.

Women's Wheels. Intro. by Deb Linc. 38p. (Orig.). 1982. pap. 7.95 (*0-9610084-0-7*) Amelia Pub.

***Women's Wire Web Directory.** Ed. by Women's Wire Staff. 500p. 1997. 29.99 (*0-7897-1068-4*) Mac Comp Pub.

Women's Wisdom. Joanne Van Roden. 50p. (Orig.). 1988. spiral bd. 5.00 (*0-940844-62-1*) Wellspring.

Women's Wisdom Through the Ages. Compiled by Vinita H. Wright & Mary Horner. LC 94-13596. 176p. 1994. pap. 8.99 (*0-87788-900-7*) Shaw Pubs.

Women's Wit & Wisdom. Ed. by Running Press Staff. LC 91-52696. (Miniature Editions Ser.). (Illus.). 128p. 1991. 4.95 (*1-56138-037-7*) Running Pr.

***Women's Words: Essay on French Singularity.** Mona Ozouf. LC 97-2648. 1997. pap. write for info. (*0-226-64334-4*) U Ch Pr.

Women's Words: The Columbia Book of Quotations by Women. Ed. by Mary Biggs. 384p. 1996. 29.95 (*0-231-07986-9*) Col U Pr.

Women's Words: The Feminist Practice of Oral History. Ed. by Sherna B. Gluck & Daphne Patai. 240p. (C). (gr. 13). 1991. pap. 17.95 (*0-415-90372-6*, A5145, Routledge NY) Routledge.

Women's Words from Lona Abbey. Kathy Galloway. 1987. 30.00 (*0-947988-08-4*, Pub. by Wild Goose Pubns UK) St Mut.

Women's Words, Women's Stories: An American Daybook. Lois S. Edgerly. (Illus.). 520p. 1994. 24.95 (*0-88448-143-3*) Tilbury Hse.

Women's Words, Women's Stories: An American Daybook. Lois S. Edgerly. (Illus.). 528p. 1995. pap. 16.95 (*0-88448-144-1*) Tilbury Hse.

Women's Work: Choice, Chance or Socialization? Insights from Psychologists & Other Researchers. Nancy J. Smith & Sylva Leduc. (Illus.). 240p. (Orig.). (C). 1992. pap. text ed. 17.95 (*1-55059-046-4*) Temeron Bks.

Women's Work: Degraded & Devalued. Alice A. Kemp. LC 93-102079. 400p. (C). 1993. pap. text ed. 33.33 (*0-13-203662-2*) P-H.

W

An Asterisk (*) at the beginning of an entry indicates that the title is appearing in BIP for the first time.

Women's Work: Development & the Division of Labor by Gender. Eleanor B. Leacock & Helen I. Safa. LC 85-26674. 320p. 1986. text ed. 59.95 (0-89789-035-3, Bergin & Garvey) Greenwood.

Women's Work: Development & the Division of Labor by Gender. Eleanor B. Leacock & Helen I. Safa. LC 85-26674. 320p. 1988. pap. text ed. 19.95 (0-89789-036-1, Bergin & Garvey) Greenwood.

Women's Work: Essays in Cultural Studies. Shelley Armitage. LC 95-6180. (Locust Hill Literary Studies: No. 15). (Illus.). 311p. (C). 1995. lib. bdg. 32.00 (0-933951-58-2) Locust Hill Pr.

Women's Work: The First 20,000 Years; Women, Cloth, & Society in Early Times. Elizabeth W. Barber. 334p. 1996. 23.00 (0-393-03506-9) Norton.

Women's Work: The First 20,000 Years: Women, Cloth & Society in Early Times. Elizabeth W. Barber. (Illus.). 336p. 1995. pap. 13.00 (0-393-31348-4, Norton Paperbks) Norton.

Women's Work: Vision & Change in Librarianship. Laurel A. Grotzinger et al. (Occasional Papers: Vols. 196-197). 132p. (Orig.). 1994. pap. 15.00 (0-614-10178-6) U of Ill Grad Sch.

Women's Work & Chicano Families: Cannery Workers of the Santa Clara Valley. Patricia Zavella. LC 87-5245. (Anthropology of Contemporary Issues Ser.). 216p. (C). 1987. 39.95 (0-8014-1730-9); pap. 13.95 (0-8014-9410-9) Cornell U Pr.

Women's Work & Family Values, 1920-1940. Winifred D. Wandersee. LC 80-21100. 177p. (C). 1981. 25.95 (0-674-95535-8) HUP.

Women's Work & Wages. Matheson S. Cadbury. 1976. lib. bdg. 59.95 (0-8490-2836-1) Gordon Pr.

***Women's Work & Wages: A Selection of Papers from the 15th Arne Ryde Symposium on Economics of Gender & Family in Honor of Anna Bugge & Knut Wicksell.** Anna Bugge et al. LC 97-20424. 1998. write for info. (0-415-14903-7) Routledge.

Women's Work & Women's Studies 1972. Dicki L. Ellis et al. pap. 6.00 (0-912786-24-8) Know Inc.

Women's Work, Class & the Urban Household. Ursula Sharma. 240p. 1986. text ed. 42.50 (0-422-79320-5, 1003, Pub. by Tavistock UK); pap. text ed. 16.95 (0-422-79330-2, 1012, Pub. by Tavistock UK) Routledge Chapman & Hall.

Women's Work, Collective Bargaining, Comparable Worth-Pay Equity, Job Evaluation...& All That: An Annotated Bibliography. Helene S. Tanimoto & Gail T. Inaba. (Occasional Publications: No. 152). 52p. 1985. 2.00 (0-318-19012-5) U Hawaii.

Women's Work, Collective Bargaining, Comparable Worth-Pay Equity, Job Evaluation...& All That: An Annotated Bibliography. 2nd ed. Helene S. Tanimoto & Gail T. Inaba. (Occasional Publications: No. 159). 76p. 1987. 2.00 (0-318-23504-8) U Hawaii.

Women's Work, Economic Trends & Policy Issues. Heidi Hartmann. 13p. 1988. pap. 5.00 (0-685-29932-5) Inst Womens Policy Rsch.

Women's Work, Families, & Health: The Balancing Act. Ed. by Kristen M. Swanson-Kauffman. LC 66-56847. 98p. 1987. 39.95 (0-89116-755-2) Hemisp Pub.

Women's Work in East & West: The Dual Burden of Employment & Family Life. Norman Stockman et al. LC 95-4969. 246p. (C). 1995. pap. text ed. 21.95 (1-56324-709-7) M E Sharpe.

Women's Work in East & West: The Dual Burden of Employment & Family Life. Norman Stockman et al. LC 95-4969. 232p. (C). (gr. 13). 1995. text ed. 63.95 (1-56324-708-9) M E Sharpe.

***Women's Work in Rural China: Change & Continuity in an Era of Reform.** Tamara Jacka. (Modern China Ser.). (Illus.). 280p. (C). 1997. 64.95 (0-521-56225-2); pap. 19.95 (0-521-59928-8) Cambridge U Pr.

Women's Work in Scotland in the 19th & Early 20th Centuries. Eleanor Gordon & Esther Breitenbach. 192p. 1991. 49.00 (0-7486-0116-3, Pub. by Edinburgh U Pr UK) Col U Pr.

Women's Work in the Third World Agriculture: Concepts & Indicators. Ruth Dixon-Mueller. (Women, Work & Development Ser.: No. 9). xi, 151p. (Orig.). 1994. reprint ed. pap. 22.50 (92-2-105107-2) Intl Labour Office.

Women's Work in the World Economy. Ed. by Nancy Folbre et al. LC 92-31050. (C). 1993. pap. 30.00 (0-8147-2616-X) NYU Pr.

Women's Work, Markets, & Economic Development in Nineteenth-Century Ontario. Marjorie G. Cohen. 286p. 1988. 40.00 (0-8020-2651-6); pap. 19.95 (0-8020-6677-1) U of Toronto Pr.

Women's Work, Men's Work: Sex Segregation on the Job. National Research Council Staff. 186p. (Orig.). (C). 1986. pap. text ed. 29.95 (0-309-03429-9) Natl Acad Pr.

Women's Work, Men's Work: The Ambivalence of Equality. Virginia Novarra. LC 79-67452. (Ideas in Progress Ser.). 160p. 1980. 12.00 (0-7145-2680-0); pap. 6.95 (0-7145-2681-9) M Boyars Pubs.

Women's Work, Men's Work: The Informal Slave Economies of Lowcountry Georgia. Betty Wood. LC 94-5968. 280p. 1995. 45.00 (0-8203-1667-9) U of Ga Pr.

Women's Work, 1840-1940. Elizabeth Roberts. (New Studies in Economic & Social History: No. 6). 86p. (Orig.). (C). 1995. text ed. 34.95 (0-521-55265-6); pap. text ed. 10.95 (0-521-55788-7) Cambridge U Pr.

Women's Working Lives: Patterns & Strategies. Susan Yeandle. 272p. 15.95 (0-422-78960-7, 9277, Pub. by Tavistock UK) Routledge Chapman & Hall.

Women's Works: An Anthology of American Literature. Barbara Perkins et al. LC 93-26558. 1993. pap. text ed. write for info. (0-07-049364-2) McGraw.

Women's Works in Stalin's Time: On Lidiia Chukovskaia & Nadezhda Mandelstam. Beth Holmgren. LC 92-46343. 240p. 1993. 35.00 (0-253-32865-9); pap. 15.95 (0-253-20829-7) Ind U Pr.

Women's World: A Holistic Approach to Dealing with Stress. (Stress in Modern Society Ser.: No. 16). 1987. 32.50 (0-404-63267-X) AMS Pr.

Women's World: Beyond the Headlines. Frwd. by Mary Robinson. 128p. 1996. pap. 12.95 (0-85598-349-3, Pub. by Oxfam UK) Humanities.

Women's World: From the New Scholarship. Ed. by Marilyn Safir et al. LC 84-26327. 336p. 1985. text ed. 59.95 (0-275-90158-0, C0158, Praeger Pubs) Greenwood.

Women's World: Ideas & Procedures for Missions Groups. Dorothy Vander Kaay. LC 89-4001. 154p. 1989. pap. text ed. 5.95 (0-87227-133-1, RBP5036) Reg Baptist.

Womens World Banking: Atlas of Global Trade. Ed. by Women's World Banking Staff. (Orig.). 1989. spiral bd. write for info. (0-318-65967-0) Womens World.

Women's World Banking Atlas of Global Trade, 1989-1990 Edition. Women's World Banking Staff. 352p. (Orig.). pap. 25.00 (0-9624822-0-X) Womens World.

Women's Worlds: Ideology, Femininity, & the Woman's Magazine. Ros Ballaster et al. 196p. (C). 1992. pap. 15.00 (0-333-49236-6) NYU Pr.

Women's Worlds in Shakespeare's Plays. Irene G. Dash. LC 96-2686. (Illus.). 304p. 1997. 45.00 (0-87413-599-0) U Delaware Pr.

Women's Writing: A Challenge to Theory. Ed. by Moira Monteith. LC 86-10056. 192p. 1986. text ed. 35.00 (0-312-88798-1) St Martin.

Women's Writing in Exile. Ed. by Mary L. Broe & Angela Ingram. LC 88-39308. xii, 442p. (C). 1989. 55.00 (0-8078-1849-6); pap. 16.95 (0-8078-4251-6) U of NC Pr.

Women's Writing in Middle English. Ed. by Alexandra Barratt. (Annotated Texts Ser.). (C). 1992. text ed. 45.00 (0-582-06193-8); pap. text ed. 31.95 (0-582-06192-X, 79198) Longman.

***Women's Writing of the Romantic Period, 1789-1836: An Anthology.** Harriet D. Jump. 1997. pap. text ed. 25.00 (0-7486-0915-6, Pub. by Edinburgh U Pr UK) Col U Pr.

Women's Yellow Pages: The Professional Woman's Resource. Intro. by Gehe L. Sorger. (Illus.). 80p. (Orig.). 1989. 5.95 (0-925108-01-4) WYP NW Washington.

Women's Yellow Pages: 1985 Edition. 7th ed. Ed. by Leslie Stone. (Illus.). 192p. 1985. pap. 4.95 (0-9610748-7-6) Womens Yellow Pgs.

Women's Yellow Pages: 1986 Edition. 8th ed. Ed. by Leslie Stone. (Illus.). 192p. 1986. pap. 4.95 (0-9610748-8-4) Womens Yellow Pgs.

Women's Yellow Pages Directory, Inc. of Greater K. C. 3rd ed. 136p. 1991. 8.00 (0-926370-12-X) WYPGKC.

Women's Yellow Pages Directory of Greater K. C. '92. 128p. 1992. 8.00 (0-926370-04-9) WYPGKC.

Women's Yellow Pages of Greater K. C. 136p. 1990. 8.00 (0-926370-00-6) WYPGKC.

Women's Yellow Pages of Greater Kansas City. 136p. 1993. 9.00 (0-926370-06-5) WYPGKC.

Women's Yellow Pages of Greater Philadelphia. 15th ed. Ed. by Ellen T. Fisher. Orig. Title: Greater Phila Women's Yellow Pages. 104p. (Orig.). 1997. pap. 5.95 (1-884018-03-3) Wom Yellw Phila.

Women's Yellow Pages of Greater St. Louis, 1993. Mary D. Selby et al. 1993. pap. 10.00 (0-9637861-0-5) Womens Yel Pgs.

Women's Yellow Pages of Greater St. Louis 1995. Mary D. Selby. 90p. (Orig.). 1994. pap. 10.00 (0-9637861-1-3) Womens Yel Pgs.

***Women's Yellow Pages of Southern California.** (Illus.). 216p. 1997. write for info. (0-937121-13-4) Womens Yellow Pgs.

Women's Yellow Pages, 1987. 9th ed. Ed. & Intro. by Leslie Stone. 192p. (Orig.). 1986. pap. 4.95 (0-9610748-9-2) Womens Yellow Pgs.

Women's Yellow Pages, 1988: Tenth Anniversary Edition. Ed. & Intro. by Leslie Stone. (Illus.). 192p. (Orig.). 1987. pap. 4.95 (0-9610748-0-9) Womens Yellow Pgs.

Women's Yellow Pages, 1989. 11th ed. Ed. & Intro. by Leslie Stone. (Illus.). 192p. 1988. pap. 4.95 (0-9610748-1-7) Womens Yellow Pgs.

Women's Yellow Pages 1991 Edition. (Illus.). 200p. 1991. lib. bdg. 4.95 (0-9610748-2-5) Womens Yellow Pgs.

WomenSki. Claudia Carbone. 308p. (Orig.). 1994. pap. 14.95 (0-915009-32-3) World Leis Corp.

Womenswork. Applause. 1991. 10.95 (0-936830-29-8) Saurian Pr.

Womenswork: Five New Plays from the Women's Project. Ed. by Julia Miles. 356p. (Orig.). 1989. pap. 10.95 (1-55783-029-0) Applause Theatre Bk Pubs.

***Women/Writing/Teaching.** Ed. by Jan Z. Schmidt. 256p. (C). 1998. text ed. 59.50 (0-7914-3591-1) State Univ of New York.

***Women/Writing/Teaching.** Ed. by Jan Z. Schmidt. 256p. (C). 1998. pap. 19.95 (0-7914-3592-X) State Univ of New York.

Womunafu's Bunafu: A Study of Authority in a Nineteenth-Century African Community. David W. Cohen. LC 77-71976. (Illus.). 227p. reprint ed. pap. 64.70 (0-8357-7931-9, 2052331) Bks Demand.

Won Buddhism: A History & Theology of Korea's New Religion. Key R. Chong. 164p. (Orig.). (C). 1995. pap. text ed. 19.95 (0-89341-758-0); lib. bdg. 37.50 (0-89341-757-2) Hollowbrook.

***Won Buddhism (Wonbulgyo) of Sot'Aesan: A Twentieth-Century Religious Movement in Korea.** Kwangsoo Park. 346p. 1997. pap. 54.95 (1-57309-177-4, Cath Scholar Pr) Intl Scholars.

***Won Buddhism (Wonbulgyo) of Sot'Aesan: A Twentieth-Century Religious Movement in Korea.** Kwangsoo Park. 346p. 1997. 74.95 (1-57309-178-2, Cath Scholar Pr) Intl Scholars.

Won-Hyo & Yul-Kok of Tae Kwon Do Hyung. Jhoon Rhee. LC 70-157046. (Korean Arts Ser.). (Illus.). 1971. pap. text ed. 13.95 (0-89750-002-4, 107) Ohara Pubns.

Won More Day. Nels D. Hanson. 1994. pap. 8.95 (1-55673-933-8) CSS OH.

***Won Ton Lust: Adventures in Search of the World's Best Chinese Restaurants.** John Rich. LC 97-25862. 384p. 1997. 24.00 (1-56836-178-5) Kodansha.

Wonder. Rachel Vail. LC 91-10576. 128p. (J). (gr. 6 up). 1991. 15.95 (0-531-05964-2) Orchard Bks Watts.

Wonder. Rachel Vail. 128p. (J). (gr. 5 up). 1993. pap. 3.99 (0-14-036167-7, Puffin) Puffin Bks.

Wonder Album of Filmland. Ed. by C. Winchester. 1976. lib. bdg. 150.00 (0-8490-2837-X) Gordon Pr.

Wonder & Delight: Essays in Science Education in Honour of the Life & Work of Eric Rogers 1902-1990. Ed. by Brenda Jennison & Jon Ogborn. (Illus.). 238p. 1994. 30.00 (0-7503-0315-8) IOP Pub.

Wonder Beasts: Tales & Lore of the Phoenix, the Griffin, the Unicorn, & the Dragon. Joe Nigg. LC 94-46797. (Illus.). xxvi, 160p. (YA). (gr. 7 up). 1995. lib. bdg. 24.50 (1-56308-242-X) Libs Unl.

Wonder Bible. Ed. by Mack Thomas. 603p. (J). (gr. 2-6). 1993. 16.99 (0-945564-59-7, Gold & Honey) Multnomah Pubs.

***Wonder Book.** Martin Handford. (Where's Waldo? Ser.). (Illus.). (J). 1997. 15.99 (0-7636-0312-0) Candlewick Pr.

Wonder Book. Nathaniel Hawthorne. (Airmont Classics Ser.). (J). (gr. 5 up). 1966. mass mkt. 2.25 (0-8049-0118-X, CL-118) Airmont.

Wonder Book & Tanglewood Tales. Nathaniel Hawthorne. Ed. by William Charvat et al. LC 77-150221. (Centenary Edition of the Works of Nathaniel Hawthorne: Vol. 7). (Illus.). 476p. (J). (gr. 5 up). 1972. 60.00 (0-8142-0158-X) Ohio St U Pr.

***Wonder Book for Boys & Girls.** Illus. by Nathaniel Hawthorne. (J). Date not set. 19.95 (0-614-19309-5) OUP.

Wonder Book for Girls & Boys. Nathaniel Hawthorne. LC 94-7352. (Everyman's Library of Children's Classics). (J). (gr. 2 up). 1994. 13.95 (0-679-43643-X) Knopf.

***Wonder Book for Girls & Boys.** Nathaniel Hawthorne. LC 95-26634. (Iona & Peter Opie Library of Children's Literature). (Illus.). 256p. (J). 1996. 21.95 (0-19-510718-7) OUP.

Wonder Book for Girls & Boys. Nathaniel Hawthorne. (Notable American Authors Ser.). (J). 1992. reprint ed. lib. bdg. 75.00 (0-7812-3045-4) Rprt Serv.

Wonder Book of Fun. Graham Rawle. 1994. pap. 11.95 (0-15-600094-6) HarBrace.

Wonder Book of Sex. Glen Baxter. LC 95-44346. 144p. 1996. pap. 12.95 (0-679-76958-7, Villard Bks) Random.

Wonder Book of the Air. Cynthia Shearer. 1997. pap. 12.00 (0-679-75836-4) Random.

Wonder Book of the Air: A Novel. Cynthia Shearer. 352p. 1996. 24.00 (0-679-43982-X) Pantheon.

Wonder Boys. Michael Chabon. 384p. 1995. pap. 13.00 (0-312-14094-0, Picador USA) St Martin.

Wonder Boys. Michael Chabon. LC 94-28921. 1995. 23.00 (0-679-41588-2, Villard Bks) Random.

Wonder Boys. large type ed. Michael Chabon. 1995. 24.95 (1-56895-257-0, Compass) Wheeler Pub.

Wonder Bread & Ecstasy: The Life & Death of Joey Stefano. Charles Isherwood. LC 96-26524. 256p. (Orig.). 1996. pap. 11.95 (1-55583-383-7) Alyson Pubns.

Wonder Child & Other Jewish Fairy Tales. Howard Schwartz & Barbara Rush. LC 94-32542. (Illus.). 80p. (J). (gr. 3 up). 1996. 16.95 (0-06-023517-9); lib. bdg. 16.89 (0-06-023518-7) HarpC Child Bks.

Wonder Circus. E. J. Hall. 64p. 1984. text ed. 2.99 (0-07-025753-1) McGraw.

Wonder City of Oz. John R. Neill. (Illus.). 318p. (J). (gr. 2 up). 1990. 24.95 (0-929605-07-1) Books Wonder.

***Wonder City of Oz.** John R. Neill. (Illus.). 318p. (J). (gr. 3 up). 1996. reprint ed. pap. 12.95 (0-929605-61-6) Books Wonder.

Wonder Clock. Howard Pyle. (Illus.). (J). (gr. 5 up). 1990. 21.25 (0-8446-2767-4) Peter Smith.

Wonder Clock or, Four & Twenty Marvelous Tales, Being One for Each Hour of the Day. Howard Pyle. (Illus.). xiv, 319p. (J). (gr. 3-6). pap. 7.95 (0-486-21446-X) Dover.

Wonder-Full World of Numbers. Stanley Bezuszka & Margaret J. Kenney. (Contemporary Motivated Mathematics Ser.). 97p. (Orig.). (J). (gr. 3-6). 1971. pap. text ed. 2.50 (0-917916-05-0) Boston Coll Math.

Wonder Kid Meets the Evil Lunch Snatcher. Lois Duncan. (J). (gr. 2-4). 1990. pap. 4.50 (0-316-19561-8) Little.

Wonder, Liberty & Love: Huxley's Analogical Uses of Shakespeare. Judith A. Powell. 120p. (C). 1992. text ed. 18.95 (0-9628916-4-9) Vande Vere.

Wonder o' the Wind: A Common Man's Quest for God. W. Phillip Keller. LC 92-23988. 248p. 1993. pap. 11.99 (0-8254-2998-6) Kregel.

***Wonder of a Love.** Brother Roger of Taize. (Illus.). 24p. (Orig.). 1996. pap. 6.00 (0-664-25685-6) Westminster John Knox.

Wonder of Babies. Phyllis Hobe. 64p. 1994. 5.95 (0-8378-7703-2) Gibson.

Wonder of Bald Eagles. Photos by Tom Leeson & Pat Leeson. LC 92-16943. (Animal Wonders Ser.). (Illus.). (J). 1992. lib. bdg. 18.60 (0-8368-0854-1) Gareth Stevens Inc.

Wonder of Barbie. Paris Manos & Susan Manos. (Illus.). 136p. 1995. pap. 9.95 (0-89145-336-9, 1808) Collector Bks.

Wonder of Becoming You: How a Jewish Girl Grows Up. Miriam Grossman. (J). (gr. 6-8). 1988. 11.95 (0-87306-438-0) Feldheim.

Wonder of Being Human. John C. Eccles. 1985. pap. 8.95 (0-394-73521-8) Random.

Wonder of Bison. Rita Ritchie & Todd Wilkinson. LC 96-5004. (Animal Wonders Ser.). (Illus.). (J). 1996. lib. bdg. 18.60 (0-8368-1558-0) Gareth Stevens Inc.

Wonder of Black Bears. Photos by Lynn Rogers. LC 92-16944. (Animal Wonders Ser.). (Illus.). (J). 1992. lib. bdg. 18.60 (0-8368-0855-X) Gareth Stevens Inc.

***Wonder of Boys.** Michael Gurian. Date not set. 17.95 incl. audio (1-57270-020-3) Audio Partners.

Wonder of Boys: What Parents, Mentors & Educators Can Do to Shape Boys into Exceptional Men. Michael Gurian. LC 95-42188. 288p. 1996. 24.95 (0-87477-831-X, Tarcher Putnam) Putnam Pub Group.

***Wonder of Boys: What Parents, Mentors & Educators Can Do to Shape Boys into Exceptional Men.** Michael Gurian. 320p. 1997. 14.95 (0-87477-887-5, Tarcher Putnam) Putnam Pub Group.

Wonder of Childhood - Stepping into Life. Rene Querido. 1991. pap. 5.95 (0-945803-08-7) R Steiner Col Pubns.

***Wonder of Christmas.** 104p. 7.95 (0-8198-8239-9) Pauline Bks.

Wonder of Comfort. large type ed. Phyllis Hobe. (Large Print Inspirational Ser.). 128p. 1986. pap. 7.95 (0-8027-2538-4) Walker & Co.

Wonder of Dad. Phyllis Hobe. 64p. 1994. 5.95 (0-8378-7702-4) Gibson.

Wonder of Dolphins. Rita Ritchie & Patricia Corrigan. LC 96-5005. (Animal Wonders Ser.). (Illus.). (J). 1996. lib. bdg. 18.60 (0-8368-1559-9) Gareth Stevens Inc.

Wonder of Friends. Phyllis Hobe. 64p. 1994. 5.95 (0-8378-7704-0) Gibson.

Wonder of God's Tomorrow. James A. Stewart & Ruth Stewart. 2.99 (1-56632-028-3) Revival Lit.

Wonder of Guadalupe. Francis Johnston. LC 81-53041. 143p. 1993. pap. 7.50 (0-89555-168-3) TAN Bks Pubs.

Wonder of Hawks. Rita Ritchie & Sumner Matteson. LC 96-4999. (Animal Wonders Ser.). (Illus.). (J). 1996. lib. bdg. 18.60 (0-8368-1560-2) Gareth Stevens Inc.

Wonder of It: Exploring How the World Works. rev. ed. Ed. by Bonnie Neugebauer. (Illus.). 88p. (Orig.). (C). 1996. pap. 16.00 (0-942702-05-0) Child Care.

***Wonder of It All.** Julia I. Hardy. (Orig.). 1996. pap. write for info. (1-57553-380-4) Watermrk Pr.

***Wonder of Light: Big Book.** Jan Adkins. Ed. by Donna Schaffer. (Ranger Rick Science Spectacular Ser.). 16p. (J). (gr. 2-5). 1997. pap. text ed. 14.95 (1-56784-450-2) Newbridge Comms.

***Wonder of Light: Student Book.** Jan Adkins. Ed. by Donna Schaffer. (Ranger Rick Science Spectacular Ser.). 16p. (J). (gr. 2-5). 1997. pap. text ed. 19.95 (1-56784-475-8) Newbridge Comms.

Wonder of Little Boys. Phyllis Hobe. 64p. 1994. 5.95 (0-8378-8326-1) Gibson.

Wonder of Little Girls. Phyllis Hobe. 64p. 1994. 5.95 (0-614-01659-2) Gibson.

Wonder of Loons. Adapted by Patricia Lantier-Sampon. LC 92-16945. (Animal Wonders Ser.). (J). 1992. lib. bdg. 18.60 (0-8368-0856-8) Gareth Stevens Inc.

Wonder of Mackinac: A Guide. Phil Porter. (Illus.). 52p. (Orig.). 1984. pap. 7.00 (0-911872-49-3) Mackinac St Hist Pks.

Wonder of Man. Catharine Berliner. 14p. (Orig.). 1981. pap. 7.00 (0-9612592-0-5) StarRays Pubs.

Wonder of Mary. Francis J. Klauder. 1992. 3.95 (1-56036-006-2, 38199) AMI Pr.

***Wonder of Me from A to Z.** Bobbie Kalman. (Alphabasics Ser.). (Illus.). 32p. (J). 1997. lib. bdg. 19.96 (0-86505-375-8) Crabtree Pub Co.

***Wonder of Me from A to Z.** Bobbie Kalman. (Alphabasics Ser.). (Illus.). 32p. (J). 1997. pap. 7.95 (0-86505-405-3) Crabtree Pub Co.

Wonder of Mom. Phyllis Hobe. 64p. 1994. 5.95 (0-8378-7701-6) Gibson.

Wonder of Moose. Rita Ritchie & Jeff Fair. LC 96-5001. (Animal Wonders Ser.). (Illus.). (J). 1996. lib. bdg. 18.60 (0-8368-1561-0) Gareth Stevens Inc.

Wonder of Prayer. large type ed. Ed. by Phyllis Hobe. (Large Print Inspirational Ser.). 1987. pap. 7.95 (0-8027-2585-6) Walker & Co.

Wonder of Raccoons. Rita Ritchie & Jeff Fair. LC 96-5176. (Animal Wonders Ser.). (Illus.). (J). 1996. lib. bdg. 18.60 (0-8368-1562-9) Gareth Stevens Inc.

Wonder of Seeing Double: Poems. Robert B. Shaw. LC 88-1072. 80p. (Orig.). (C). 1988. pap. 9.95 (0-87023-638-5); lib. bdg. 17.50 (0-87023-637-7) U of Mass Pr.

Wonder of Sex, How to Teach Children. J. C. Willke. 1983. pap. 4.95 (0-910728-17-8) Hayes.

***Wonder of Stevie - Stevie Wonder Fakebook.** Ed. by Carol Cuellar. (Orig.). (C). 1989. pap. text ed. 9.95 (0-7692-0833-9, P0846FBX) Warner Brothers.

Wonder of the Word of God. Robert L. Sumner. 1969. pap. 1.95 (0-87398-933-3) Sword of Lord.

Wonder of Whales. Photos by Flip Nicklin. LC 92-16946. (Animal Wonders Ser.). (Illus.). (J). 1992. lib. bdg. 18.60 (0-8368-0857-6) Gareth Stevens Inc.

Wonder of Whitetails. Photos by Daniel J. Cox. LC 92-16947. (Animal Wonders Ser.). (Illus.). (J). 1992. lib. bdg. 18.60 (0-8368-0858-4) Gareth Stevens Inc.

Wonder of Wild Horses. Rita Ritchie & Mark Henckel. LC 96-5177. (Animal Wonders Ser.). (Illus.). (J). 1996. lib. bdg. 18.60 (0-8368-1563-7) Gareth Stevens Inc.

Wonder of Wolves. Photos by Bob Baldwin et al. LC 92-16948. (Animal Wonders Ser.). (Illus.). (J). 1992. lib. bdg. 18.60 (0-8368-0859-2) Gareth Stevens Inc.

***Wonder of Wolves: A Story & Activities.** 2nd ed. Sandra C. Robinson. 1997. pap. text ed. 8.95 (1-57098-123-X) R Rinehart.

W

Wonder of Wolves: A Story & Activity Book. Sandra C. Robinson. (Illus.). (J). (gr. 1-6). 1989. pap. 7.95 (*0-911797-65-3*) R Rinehart.

Wonder of Writing Across the Curriculum. Art Young. Ed. by Lillian Bridwell-Bowles. (Technical Reports: No. 7). 22p. (Orig.). (C). 1994. pap. 3.00 (*0-614-04052-3*) U Minn Ctr Interdis.

Wonder Series No. 1: Observing & Confronting the Enigmas that Surround Us. Norman Weisberg. Ed. by Karen Weisberg & Linda Wicks. (Illus.). 58p. (C). 1991. 5.00 (*1-881100-01-4*) Ziggurat Pr.

Wonder Shoes. Eva Bernatova. 1990. 13.95 (*0-374-38476-2*) FS&G.

Wonder Square. Stanley Bezuszka et al. (Motivated Math Project Activity Booklets). 30p. (Orig.). (YA). (gr. 6-12). 1976. pap. text ed. 1.25 (*0-917916-15-8*) Boston Coll Math.

Wonder Tales: Six French Stories of Enchantment. Ed. & Intro. by Marina Warner. LC 96-14733. (Illus.). 256p. (J). 1996. 22.00 (*0-374-29281-7*) FS&G.

Wonder Tales from Around the World. Illus. by David Boston. (American Storytelling Ser.). 155p. (J). 1995. 26.95 (*0-87483-421-X*) August Hse.

Wonder Tales from Around the World. Illus. by David Boston. (American Storytelling Ser.). 160p. (J). 1995. pap. 16.95 (*0-87483-422-8*) August Hse.

Wonder Tales from Russia. Jeremiah Curtin. (Works of Jeremiah Curtin Ser.). 1990. reprint ed. lib. bdg. 90.00 (*0-7812-2508-6*) Rprt Serv.

Wonder Tales of Alsace-Lorraine. Bernard Henderson & C. Clavert. 1976. lib. bdg. 59.95 (*0-8490-2838-8*) Gordon Pr.

Wonder Tales of Dogs & Cats. Frances Carpenter. 1976. 21.95 (*0-8488-0945-9*) Amereon Ltd.

Wonder Tales of Seas & Ships. Frances Carpenter. 1976. 25.95 (*0-8488-0946-7*) Amereon Ltd.

Wonder Team: The True Story of the Incomparable 1927 New York Yankees. Leo Trachtenberg. LC 95-14665. (Sports & Culture Ser.). 1995. 29.95 (*0-87972-677-6*); pap. 13.95 (*0-87972-678-4*) Bowling Green Univ Popular Press.

Wonder That Was India. A. L. Basham. (C). 1995. reprint ed. 19.00 (*0-8364-2913-3*, Pub. by Rupa II) S Asia.

Wonder That Was India, Vol. I. A. L. Basham. (C). 1992. text ed. 14.00 (*0-8364-2888-9*, Pub. by Rupa II) S Asia.

Wonder That Was India, Vol. II. S. A. Rizvi. (C). 1993. 14.00 (*0-8364-2889-7*, Pub. by Rupa II) S Asia.

Wonder Thing. Libby Hathorn. LC 94-19912. (Illus.). 32p. (J). (ps-2). 1996. 14.95 (*0-395-71541-5*) HM.

***Wonder-Under Book of Christmas Creations.** Leisure Arts Staff. 1997. pap. 14.95 (*1-57486-062-3*) Oxmoor Hse.

Wonder What I Feel Today? A Coloring Book about Feelings. Jeanne Engelmann. (Illus.). 16p. (J). (gr. k-5). 1991. pap. 1.75 (*0-89486-744-X*, 5177B) Hazelden.

Wonder Which Snake Is the Longest & Other Neat Facts about Animal Records. Annabelle Donati. (Illus.). 36p. (J). (ps-3). 1993. pap. 5.50 (*0-307-11326-4*, Golden Pr) Western Pub.

Wonder Window. Dan Witkowski. (J). 1996. write for info. (*0-679-87703-7*) Random Bks Yng Read.

Wonder Within: Warmly Inspiring Reflections on Pregnancy, Childbirth & Motherhood. Jaymie S. Wolfe. LC 95-78702. (Illus.). 192p. (Orig.). 1995. pap. 7.95 (*0-87793-558-0*) Ave Maria.

***Wonder Woman: Amazonia.** William F. Messner-Loebs. (Illus.). 48p. 1997. pap. 4.95 (*1-56389-301-0*) DC Comics.

Wonder Woman: Featuring Over Five Decades of Great Covers. Intro. by Gloria Steinem. LC 94-23837. (Tiny Folios Ser.). (Illus.). 320p. 1995. pap. 11.95 (*0-7892-0012-0*) Abbeville Pr.

***Wonder Woman: Second Genesis.** John Byrne. Ed. by Bob Kahan. (Illus.). 128p. 1997. pap. text ed. 9.95 (*1-56389-318-5*) DC Comics.

Wonder Woman: The Challenge of Artemis. William F. Messner-Loebs. 1996. pap. text ed. 9.95 (*1-56389-264-2*) DC Comics.

Wonder Woman: The Contest. Bill Lords. Ed. by Bob Kahan. (Illus.). 120p. 1995. pap. 9.95 (*1-56389-194-8*) DC Comics.

Wonder Woman Doesn't Live Here Anymore. Carol Schreiner. 76p. 1992. pap. write for info. (*0-9644074-0-X*) C D Communs.

***Wonder Women.** Sydelle Kramer. LC 97-11023. (All Aboard Reading Ser.). (Illus.). (J). 1997. write for info. (*0-448-41589-5*, G&D) Putnam Pub Group.

Wonder Women: Gods & Goddesses - A Novel. John Byrne. 256p. 1997. boxed 20.00 (*0-7615-0483-4*) Prima Pub.

***Wonder Worker.** Susan Howatch. 1997. 25.95 (*0-375-40102-4*) Knopf.

Wonder-Workers! How They Perform the Impossible. Joe Nickell. (Young Readers Ser.). (Illus.). 80p. (Orig.). (YA). 1991. pap. 12.95 (*0-87975-688-8*) Prometheus Bks.

Wonder-Working Lawyers of Talmudic Bablonia: The Theory & Practice of Judaism in Its Formative Age. Jacob Neusner. LC 87-6161. (Studies in Judaism). (Illus.). 372p. (Orig.). (C). 1987. pap. text ed. 29.00 (*0-8191-6288-4*, Studies in Judaism); lib. bdg. 50.50 (*0-8191-6287-6*, Studies in Judaism) U Pr of Amer.

Wonder-Working Power of God. Cornelia Addington. LC 87-70231. 152p. 1987. pap. 5.95 (*0-87516-589-3*) DeVorss.

Wonder-Working Providence of Sion's Saviour in New England. Edward Johnson. (Notable American Authors Ser.). 1992. reprint ed. lib. bdg. 75.00 (*0-7812-3489-1*) Rprt Serv.

Wonder-Working Providence of Sions Saviour in New England (1654) Edward Johnson. LC 74-5118. 256p. 1974. lib. bdg. 50.00 (*0-8201-1130-9*) Schol Facsimiles.

Wonder Worm. Bob Reese. (Ten Word Book Ser.). (Illus.). (J). (gr. k-3). 1994. pap. 3.95 (*0-89868-250-9*, Read Res); lib. bdg. 9.95 (*0-89868-249-5*, Read Res) ARO Pub.

Wonder Worm. Ruth Zakutinsky. (E Z Reader Ser.). (Illus.). 24p. (J). (gr. k-3). 1992. lib. bdg. 6.95 (*0-911643-17-6*) Aura Bklyn.

***Wonder Worm Wars.** Margie Palatini. LC 96-50920. 144p. (J). (gr. 3-7). 1997. pap. 14.95 (*0-7868-0321-5*); lib. bdg. 14.89 (*0-7868-2295-3*) Hyprn Child.

Wonder Years. David Holdgrive et al. 75p. 1989. pap. text ed. 5.95 (*0-685-28073-X*) New Mus Theater Lib.

Wonder Years. Kleinfelder. 1993. 34.95 (*0-671-85020-2*) S&S Trade.

Wonderbook of Fantastic Fold Out. (J). 1989. 7.99 (*0-517-68812-3*) Random Hse Value.

Wonderboy! Sidney Berger & Rob Landes. (J). (gr. 3-9). 1996. pap. 3.50 (*1-57514-160-4*, 0088) Encore Perform Pub.

***Wonderful.** Barnett. 1997. mass mkt. 5.99 (*0-671-00412-3*) S&S Trade.

Wonderful. James Thurber. 1996. pap. 9.95 (*0-7871-0193-1*, Dove Bks) Dove Audio.

Wonderful Adventure of Captain Priest. Samuel A. Hammett. LC 76-166740. 1971. reprint ed. 49.00 (*0-403-01374-7*) Scholarly.

Wonderful Adventures of Mrs. Seacole in Many Lands. Mary Seacole. (Schomburg Library of Nineteenth-Century Black Women Writers). 256p. 1988. 22.00 (*0-19-505249-8*) OUP.

Wonderful Adventures of Mrs. Seacole in Many Lands. Mary Seacole. (Schomburg Library of Nineteenth-Century Black Women Writers). (Illus.). 260p. 1990. reprint ed. pap. 11.95 (*0-19-506672-3*) OUP.

Wonderful Adventures of Nils. Selma O. Lagerlof. Ed. by Velma S. Howard. LC 94-41647. (Illus.). 256p. (J). 1995. pap. text ed. 6.95 (*0-486-28611-8*) Dover.

Wonderful Adventures of Nils. Selma O. Lagerlof. 540p. 1992. reprint ed. lib. bdg. 36.95 (*0-89966-936-0*) Buccaneer Bks.

Wonderful Adventures of Nils, Bk. 1. rev. ed. Velma S. Howard & Selma O. Lagerlof. (Travels of Nils Holgersson Ser.). (Illus.). 254p. (J). (gr. 4-12). 1991. pap. 12.95 (*0-9615394-3-7*) Skandisk.

Wonderful Alexander & the Catwings. Ursula K. Le Guin. LC 93-49397. (Illus.). 48p. (J). (gr. k-3). 1994. 14.95 (*0-531-06851-X*); lib. bdg. 15.99 (*0-531-08701-8*) Orchard Bks Watts.

Wonderful Alexander & the Catwings. Ursula K. Le Guin. (J). 1996. pap. text ed. 2.99 (*0-590-54336-9*) Scholastic Inc.

Wonderful Animals of Australia, Set. Ed. by Donald J. Crump. (Pop-Up Bks.: Set 5). (Illus.). (J). (ps-3). 1990. 21.95 (*0-87044-809-9*) Natl Geog.

Wonderful Art of the Eye. Benvenutus Grassus. Ed. by L. M. Eldredge. (Medieval Texts & Studies: No. 19). 120p. 1995. 24.95 (*0-87013-459-0*) Mich St U Pr.

***Wonderful Cars of the Fifties & Sixties.** Tony Mollica & Bill Northrup. (Coloring the Classics Ser.). (Illus.). 28p. (J). 1994. 3.95 (*1-883029-04-X*) CHP NY.

Wonderful Christ in the Canons of the New Testament. Witness Lee. 270p. per. 10.25 (*0-87083-457-6*, 06015001) Living Stream Ministry.

Wonderful Christmastime. (Piano-Vocal-Guitar Ser.). 64p. 1992. pap. 7.95 (*0-7935-1747-8*, 00311591) H Leonard.

Wonderful Circus Parade. Roy Doty. (J). (ps). 1991. pap. 4.95 (*0-671-72842-3*, Litl Simon S&S) S&S Childrens.

Wonderful Counting Clock. Cooper Edens. LC 93-14404. (Illus.). (J). 1995. 15.00 (*0-671-88334-8*, Green Tiger S&S) S&S Childrens.

Wonderful Discoveries of the Witchcrafts of M. & P. Flower. Margaret Flower. LC 72-5992. (English Experience Ser.: No. 517). 50p. 1972. reprint ed. 15.00 (*90-221-0517-2*) Walter J Johnson.

Wonderful Era of the Great Dance Bands. Leo Walker. (Quality Paperbacks Ser.). (Illus.). 316p. 1990. reprint ed. pap. 18.95 (*0-306-80379-8*) Da Capo.

Wonderful Ethiopians of the Ancient Cushite Empire. Drusilla D. Houston. LC 89-90991. 280p. 1985. reprint ed. 20.00 (*0-933121-00-8*); reprint ed. pap. 14.95 (*0-933121-01-6*) Black Classic.

Wonderful Ethiopians of the Ancient Cushite Empire, Vol. 1. Drusilla D. Houston. Ed. by Al I. Obaba. (Illus.). 126p. (Orig.). 1991. pap. text ed. 10.00 (*0-916157-34-2*) African Islam Miss Pubns.

Wonderful Ethiopians of the Ancient Cushite Empire, Vol. 2. Drusilla D. Houston. Ed. by Al I. Obaba. (Illus.). 148p. (Orig.). 1991. pap. text ed. 10.00 (*0-916157-35-0*) African Islam Miss Pubns.

Wonderful Ethiopians of the Ancient Cushite Empire, Vol. 3. Drusilla D. Houston. Ed. by Al I. Obaba. (Illus.). 122p. (Orig.). 1991. pap. text ed. 10.00 (*0-916157-36-9*) African Islam Miss Pubns.

Wonderful Farm. Marcel Ayme. LC 94-3013. (Trophy Bk.). (Illus.). 192p. (J). (gr. 2-5). 1995. pap. 4.95 (*0-06-440556-7*, Trophy) HarpC Child Bks.

Wonderful Farm. Marcel Ayme. 1995. 18.50 (*0-8446-6811-7*) Peter Smith.

Wonderful Flight to the Mushroom Planet. Eleanor Cameron. (Illus.). (J). (gr. 4-6). 1954. 15.95 (*0-316-12537-7*, Pub. by H K Lewis UK) Little.

Wonderful Flight to the Mushroom Planet. Eleanor Cameron. (Illus.). (J). (gr. 4-6). 1988. mass mkt. 6.95 (*0-316-12540-7*, Joy St Bks) Little.

Wonderful Flying Machines: A History of U. S. Coast Guard Helicopters. Barrett T. Beard. LC 96-25922. (Illus.). 280p. 1996. 32.95 (*1-55750-086-X*) Naval Inst Pr.

Wonderful Focus of You. Joanne Kyger. (Orig.). 1980. pap. 5.00 (*0-915990-22-9*) Z Pr.

Wonderful Fool. Shusaku Endo. Tr. by Francis Mathy from JPN. LC 83-47553. 224p. 1983. 13.95 (*0-06-859853-X*, HarpT) HarpC.

Wonderful Fool. Shusaku Endo. Tr. by Francis Mathy from JPN. 240p. 9500. pap. 28.00 (*0-7206-0979-8*, Pub. by P Owen Ltd UK) Dufour.

Wonderful Good Cooking. Ed. by Johnny Schrock et al. LC 75-1726. 136p. 1975. pap. 8.99 (*0-8361-1765-4*) Herald Pr.

Wonderful Inventions: Motion Pictures, Broadcasting & Recorded Sound. 1991. lib. bdg. 95.00 (*0-8490-4211-9*) Gordon Pr.

Wonderful Jesus! Linda Parry & Alan Parry. (Pop-up & Activity Bk.). (Illus.). 12p. (J). 1993. 15.99 (*0-7847-0045-1*, 03643) Standard Pub.

Wonderful Journey. Gill McBarnet. (Illus.). 32p. (J). (gr. k-2). 1986. 8.95 (*0-9615102-2-6*) Ruwanga Trad.

Wonderful Journey: The Autobiography of Dick Crane. Dick Crane. Ed. by Susan Ryan & Peggy O'Keefe. Tr. by Debbie Johnson & Susan Grant. (Illus.). 188p. 1996. reprint ed. pap. 9.95 (*0-9641092-1-2*) Wrds In Motion.

***Wonderful Journey of Cameron the Cat.** Marjorie Newman. LC 96-48668. (J). 1998. write for info. (*0-7636-0274-4*) Candlewick Pr.

Wonderful Life: The Burgess Shale & the Nature of History. Stephen J. Gould. 1989. 19.95 (*0-393-02705-8*) Norton.

Wonderful Life: The Burgess Shale & the Nature of History. Stephen J. Gould. 1990. pap. 13.95 (*0-393-30700-X*) Norton.

Wonderful Life: The Films & Career of James Stewart. Tony Thomas. (Illus.). 256p. 1988. pap. 15.95 (*0-8065-1081-1*, Citadel Pr) Carol Pub Group.

Wonderful Life: The Films & Career of James Stewart. Tony Thomas. 1992. pap. 24.95 incl. vhs (*0-8065-9982-0*, Citadel Pr) Carol Pub Group.

Wonderful Lips of Thibong Linh. Theodore Roscoe. (Illus.). 1981. 15.00 (*0-937986-36-4*) D M Grant.

Wonderful Little Sex Book. William A. Ross. 288p. (Orig.). 1992. lib. bdg. 29.00 (*0-8095-5865-3*) Borgo Pr.

Wonderful Love. Jack Bemporad & Stephen Bindman. 175p. pap. 9.95 (*0-932385-15-X*) Human Futures.

Wonderful Name. Richard Kingsmore & Christopher Machen. 1996. pap. 4.99 (*0-8341-9456-2*) Nazarene.

Wonderful Name of Jesus. E. W. Kenyon. 79p. (Orig.). (C). 1927. pap. 6.75 (*1-57770-007-4*) Kenyons Gospel.

Wonderful Names of Our Wonderful Lord. Hurlbut Horton. (Christian Library). 276p. 1981. 8.97 (*1-55748-193-8*, Christian Lib) Barbour & Co.

***Wonderful Names of Our Wonderful Lord.** T. C. Horton. 1996. pap. text ed. 3.97 (*1-55748-974-2*) Barbour & Co.

Wonderful Nature, Wonderful You. Karin Ireland. (Illus.). 32p. (J). (gr. 1-7). 1996. 19.95 (*1-883220-48-3*); pap. 11.50 (*1-883220-47-5*) Dawn CA.

***Wonderful Number 1: Amazing Facts about the Number One.** Kitty Higgins. (Birthday Book Ser.). 1998. 6.95 (*0-8362-3217-8*) Andrews & McMeel.

Wonderful Paradoxes of Scripture. L. M. Grant. pap. 0.95 (*0-88172-171-9*) Believers Bkshelf.

Wonderful Pigs of Jillian Jiggs. Phoebe Gilman. 40p. (J). 1989. pap. 2.99 (*0-590-41341-4*) Scholastic Inc.

Wonderful Promise. C. Mackenzie. (Biblewise Ser.). (J). 1995. 2.99 (*1-85792-156-9*, Pub. by Christian Focus UK) Spring Arbor Dist.

Wonderful Pussy Willows. Jerome Wexler. LC 91-32262. (Illus.). 32p. (J). (ps-3). 1992. pap. 14.99 (*0-525-44867-5*) Dutton Child Bks.

Wonderful Revelation to the World: A Conversation of St. Seraphim of Sarov with Nikolai Motovilov. rev. ed. (Illus.). 70p. 1993. pap. 3.00 (*0-913026-42-5*) St Nectarios.

Wonderful Road to Happiness. Joe S. Williams. 86p. 1989. 10.95 (*0-944607-03-9*) J W Comm.

Wonderful Spirit Filled Life. Stanley. Date not set. 25.98 (*0-7852-6910-X*) Nelson.

Wonderful Spirit-Filled Life. Charles Stanley. 256p. 1995. pap. 12.99 (*0-7852-7747-1*) Nelson.

Wonderful Spirit Filled Life. large type ed. Charles Stanley. LC 94-13287. 416p. 1994. 13.95 (*0-8027-2677-1*) Walker & Co.

Wonderful Story of Henry Sugar & Six More. Roald Dahl. LC 77-5354. 32p. (J). (gr. 5 up). 1977. 17.00 (*0-394-83604-9*) Knopf Bks Yng Read.

Wonderful Story of Henry Sugar & Six More. Roald Dahl. 224p. (J). 1988. pap. 4.99 (*0-14-032874-2*, Puffin) Puffin Bks.

Wonderful Story of Henry Sugar & Six More. large type rev. ed. Roald Dahl. 280p. (J). 1989. lib. bdg. 14.95 (*1-85089-984-3*) BDD LT Grp.

Wonderful, Sweet & Wild. 4.95 (*0-89741-024-6*) Gila River.

Wonderful Tang. Beaumont Bruestle. (J). (gr. 1-7). 1952. 5.00 (*0-87602-222-0*) Anchorage.

Wonderful Tennessee. Brian Friel. 96p. (Orig.). 1993. pap. 8.95 (*0-571-17123-0*) Faber & Faber.

Wonderful Things. Daphna Flegal. (Great Big Bk. Ser.). (Illus.). 16p. (J). 1996. pap. 14.95 (*0-687-01449-2*) Abingdon.

***Wonderful Things: Materials & Civilization from the Stone Age to the Age of Silicon.** Stephen Sass. (Illus.). 320p. 1998. 27.95 (*1-55970-371-7*) Arcade Pub Inc.

Wonderful Time. Jonathan M. Sherman. 1997. pap. 5.25 (*0-8222-1541-1*) Dramatists Play.

Wonderful Tonight: Eric Clapton, Les Paul & Queen in Concert. Jim O'Donnell. LC 93-78190. 104p. 1993. 9.95 (*0-9636905-0-7*) Hall Fame Bks.

Wonderful Tower of Humbert. 1990. pap. 5.95 (*0-88145-083-9*) Broadway Play.

Wonderful Towers of Watts. Patricia Zelver. LC 93-20344. (Illus.). 32p. (J). 1994. 15.00 (*0-688-12649-9*, Tambourine Bks); lib. bdg. 14.93 (*0-688-12650-2*, Tambourine Bks) Morrow.

Wonderful Towers of Watts. Patricia Zelver. (J). (ps up). 1996. pap. 4.95 (*0-688-14653-8*, Mulberry) Morrow.

***Wonderful View of the Sea.** Ruth Silcock. 92p. 1996. pap. 15.95 (*0-85646-264-0*, Pub. by Anvil Press UK) Dufour.

Wonderful Visit. H. G. Wells. Ed. by R. Reginald & Douglas Melville. LC 77-84274. (Lost Race & Adult Fantasy Ser.). 1978. reprint ed. lib. bdg. 26.95 (*0-405-11013-8*) Ayer.

Wonderful Washington Events Guide, 1996. rev. ed. Gail Folgedalen. 240p. (Orig.). 1995. pap. 9.95 (*1-881005-13-5*) Gails Guides.

***Wonderful Washington Events Guide, 1997.** 6th ed. Gail Folgedalen. Orig. Title: Old Fashioned Festivals & Community Celebrations in Washington. 254p. (Orig.). 1996. pap. 9.95 (*1-881005-17-8*) Gails Guides.

Wonderful Water. Bobbie Kalman & Janine Schaub. (Primary Ecology Ser.). (Illus.). 32p. (J). (gr. k-8). 1992. pap. 7.95 (*0-86505-579-3*); lib. bdg. 19.16 (*0-86505-553-X*) Crabtree Pub Co.

Wonderful Way That Babies Are Made. Larry Christenson. LC 82-12813. 48p. (Orig.). (J). (ps up). 1982. 12.99 (*0-87123-627-3*) Bethany Hse.

Wonderful Ways to Love a Child. Judy Ford. 160p. (Orig.). 1995. lib. bdg. 29.00 (*0-8095-5891-2*) Borgo Pr.

Wonderful Ways to Love a Child. Judy Ford. LC 94-38252. (Illus.). 190p. (Orig.). 1995. pap. 9.95 (*0-943233-89-5*) Conari Press.

***Wonderful Ways to Love a Child.** Judy Ford. (Orig.). 1997. 6.98 (*1-56731-199-7*, MJF Bks) Fine Comms.

***Wonderful Ways to Love a Grandchild, Vol. 1.** Judy Ford. LC 97-17044. (Wonderful Ways Ser.). 166p. (Orig.). 1997. pap. 11.95 (*1-57324-097-4*) Conari Press.

Wonderful Ways to Love a Teen: Even When It Seems Impossible. Judy Ford. 176p. 1996. 27.00 (*0-8095-6059-3*) Borgo Pr.

Wonderful Ways to Love a Teen...Even When It Seems Impossible. Judy Ford. (Illus.). 176p. 1996. pap. 9.95 (*1-57324-023-0*) Conari Press.

Wonderful Wearables, a Celebration of Creative Clothing. Virginia Avery. 1991. pap. 24.95 (*0-89145-980-4*) Collector Bks.

Wonderful Wedding. George Fitzmaurice & John Guinan. (Lost Play Ser.). 1978. pap. 1.95 (*0-912262-52-4*) Proscenium.

Wonderful Wedding: Dear Barbie. Jean Waricha. (J). (ps-3). 1996. pap. text ed. 3.95 (*0-307-12841-5*, Golden Pr) Western Pub.

Wonderful Wedding Songs. Friedman-Fairfax & Sony Music Staff. (Life, Times & Music Book/CD Ser.). 1995. pap. 16.98 incl. audio compact disk (*1-56799-077-0*, Friedman-Fairfax) M Friedman Pub Grp Inc.

***Wonderful Weekends: San Francisco.** Marilyn Wood. 1997. 15.95 (*0-02-861335-X*) Macmillan.

Wonderful West Maui. Angela K. Kepler. 144p. 1993. pap. 7.95 (*1-56647-013-7*) Mutual Pub HI.

Wonderful Western Hat. Ev Miller. 1985. pap. 3.00 (*0-87129-372-2*, W61) Dramatic Pub.

Wonderful Whistle Stop. Bill Kispert. (Shining Time Station Classics Ser.). (Illus.). 40p. (J). (ps-3). 1994. pap. 5.95 (*1-884336-04-3*) Qual Family.

Wonderful Winks & Weather Wishes. Elaine Weimann & Rita Friedman. (Read to Me Bks.). (Illus.). 30p. (J). (ps-1). 1986. lib. bdg. 12.50 (*0-89796-995-2*) New Dimens Educ.

Wonderful Wisconsin Recipes. Ed. by Juanita Loven. 160p. 1991. spiral bd. 5.95 (*0-941016-79-X*) Penfield.

Wonderful Wisconsin Recipes see License to Cook Wisconsin Style

Wonderful Wizard of Oz. (Fun-to-Read Fairy Tales Series II). (Illus.). 24p. (J). (gr. k-3). 1992. pap. 2.50 (*1-56144-174-0*, Honey Bear Bks) Modern Pub NYC.

***Wonderful Wizard of Oz.** Frank Baum. (J). Date not set. lib. bdg. 99.98 (*0-688-06945-2*, Morrow Junior) Morrow.

Wonderful Wizard of Oz. L. Frank Baum. (Airmont Classics Ser.). (Illus.). (J). (gr. 4 up). 1965. mass mkt. 1.75 (*0-8049-0069-8*, CL-69) Airmont.

Wonderful Wizard of Oz. L. Frank Baum. LC 92-53173. (Everyman's Library of Children's Classics). (Illus.). 192p. (J). 1992. 12.95 (*0-679-41794-X*, Evrymans Lib Childs) Knopf.

***Wonderful Wizard of Oz.** L. Frank Baum. Ed. by Susan Wolstenholme. (The World's Classics Ser.). (Illus.). 336p. 1997. pap. text ed. 9.95 (*0-19-282400-7*) OUP.

Wonderful Wizard of Oz. L. Frank Baum. Ed. by Grace Mabie. LC 92-12704. (Illustrated Classics Ser.). (Illus.). 48p. (J). (gr. 3-6). 1992. pap. 5.95 (*0-8167-2865-8*); lib. bdg. 14.95 (*0-8167-2864-X*) Troll Communs.

Wonderful Wizard of Oz. L. Frank Baum. Ed. by William R. Leach. 188p. (J). 1991. pap. 21.95 (*0-534-14736-4*) Wadsworth Pub.

Wonderful Wizard of Oz. L. Frank Baum. LC 86-62556. (Books of Wonder). (Illus.). 316p. (J). (ps up). 1987. 22.00 (*0-688-06944-4*, Morrow Junior) Morrow.

Wonderful Wizard of Oz. L. Frank Baum. (Illus.). (J). (gr. 4 up). 1990. 20.75 (*0-8446-1610-9*) Peter Smith.

Wonderful Wizard of Oz. L. Frank Baum. (Deluxe Watermill Classic Ser.). 176p. (YA). 1992. 10.89 (*0-8167-2564-0*); pap. 4.95 (*0-8167-2565-9*) Troll Communs.

Wonderful Wizard of Oz. L. Frank Baum. (YA). 1991. pap. 2.95 (*0-89375-991-0*) Troll Communs.

Wonderful Wizard of Oz. Houghton Mifflin Company Staff. (Literature Experience 1993 Ser.). (J). (gr. 4). 1992. pap. 9.16 (*0-395-61804-5*) HM.

Wonderful Wizard of Oz. V. Glasgow Koste. 70p. 1982. pap. 3.45 (*0-87129-009-X*, W67) Dramatic Pub.

Wonderful Wizard of Oz. unabridged ed. L. Frank Baum. LC 95-47924. (Illus.). 128p. 1996. reprint ed. pap. text ed. 1.50 (*0-486-29116-2*) Dover.

W

An Asterisk (*) at the beginning of an entry indicates that the title is appearing in BIP for the first time.

Wonderful Wizard of Oz. L. Frank Baum. 139p. (J). 1981. reprint ed. lib. bdg. 15.95 (*0-89966-347-8*) Buccaneer Bks.

Wonderful Wizard of Oz. L. Frank Baum. 193p. (J). 1981. reprint ed. lib. bdg. 11.95 (*0-89967-021-0*) Harmony Raine.

Wonderful Wizard of Oz. L. Frank Baum. (Illus.). vii, 268p. (J). (gr. k-6). 1960. reprint ed. pap. 7.95 (*0-486-20691-2*) Dover.

Wonderful Wizard of Oz in American Popular Culture: Uneasy in Eden. Neil Earle. LC 93-36485. 248p. 1993. 89.95 (*0-7734-9406-5*) E Mellen.

Wonderful Women by the Sea. Monika Fagerholm. 352p. 1997. 23.00 (*1-56584-338-X*) New Press NY.

Wonderful, Wonderful Times. Elfriede Jelinek & Michael Hulse. LC 90-60292. (Masks Ser.). 256p. (Orig.). 1990. pap. text ed. 13.95 (*1-85242-168-1*) Serpents Tail.

Wonderful Woods. Rose Wyler. (Outdoor Science Ser.). (Illus.). 32p. (J). (gr. k-3). 1990. pap. 4.95 (*0-671-69166-X*, Julian Messner) Silver Burdett Pr.

Wonderful Words: And Inspirational Expressions. (Illus.). 128p. (Orig.). 1993. pap. 9.95 (*0-9624342-7-2*) Carriage Hse Studio Pubns.

Wonderful Words, Silent Truth: Essays on Poetry & a Memoir. Charles Simic. LC 89-49606. (Poets on Poetry Ser.). 136p. 1990. text ed. 39.50 (*0-472-09421-1*); pap. text ed. 13.95 (*0-472-06421-5*) U of Mich Pr.

Wonderful Works of God. Paul E. Eickmann. 88p. (Orig.). 1970. pap. 6.00 (*0-8100-0015-6*, 07N0738) Northwest Pub.

Wonderful World. Lea Rangel-Ribeiro & Victor Rangel-Ribeiro. Ed. by Susan Evento. (Macmillan Early Skills Program - Conversion Ser.). 64p. (J). (ps-2). 1995. pap. 9.95 (*1-56784-514-2*) Newbridge Comms.

***Wonderful World of Christmas Trees.** Henry H. Albers & Ann K. Davis. 110p. (Orig.). 1997. pap. 22.95 (*0-931209-69-2*) Mid-Prairie Bks.

Wonderful World of Cookie Jars. 2nd rev. ed. Mark Supnick & Ellen Supnick. (Illus.). 448p. 1997. 39.95 (*0-89538-032-3*, 1081) L-W Inc.

***Wonderful World of Disney Television: A Complete History.** Bill Cotter. 1997. 24.95 (*0-7868-6359-5*) Hyperion.

***Wonderful World of English, 6 bks.** (J). (gr. 1-5). 1996. 89.95 incl. audio (*0-7166-5300-1*, 6164); 89.95 incl. audio (*0-7166-5302-8*, 6165) World Bk.

Wonderful World of Gift Giving. Linda P. Silbert & Alvin J. Silbert. (Little Twirps Preschool Ser.). (J). (gr. 3-7). 1983. student ed. 4.98 (*0-89544-024-5*) Silbert Bress.

Wonderful World of Honey: The Only Nutrition-Wise Sugarless Cookbook, Beauty Aids & Preventive Medicine. Joe M. Parkhill. 160p. 1994. spiral bd. 7.95 (*0-936744-01-4*) Country Bazaar.

Wonderful World of Horses Coloring Album. Rita Warner. (Color & Story Bks.). (Illus.). 32p. (Orig.). (J). (gr. 1 up). 1988. pap. 5.95 (*0-8431-1709-5*, Troubador) Price Stern Sloan.

Wonderful World of Indian Cookery. Rohini Singh. (Illus.). 160p. 1994. 21.95 (*1-56554-056-5*) Pelican.

Wonderful World of Mathematics: A Critically Annotated List of Children's Books in Mathematics. Ed. by Diane Thiessen & Margaret Matthias. LC 92-36493. (Illus.). 241p. (Orig.). 1992. pap. 17.00 (*0-87353-353-4*) NCTM.

Wonderful World of Memories. Clyde E. Graham. LC 92-74618. (Illus.). 160p. (Orig.). 1992. pap. 10.00 (*1-878149-17-2*) Counterpoint Pub.

Wonderful World of Natural-Food Cookery see Natural Food Cookery

Wonderful World of Netsuke. Raymond Bushell. (Illus.). 72p. (Orig.). 1995. pap. 12.95 (*0-8048-2024-4*) C E Tuttle.

Wonderful World of Netsuke. Raymond Bushell. pap. 12.95 (*0-8048-2022-8*) C E Tuttle.

Wonderful World of Nippon Porcelain, 1891-1921. Kathy Wojciechowski. LC 91-67003. (Illus.). 280p. 1992. pap. 49.95 (*0-88740-377-8*) Schiffer.

Wonderful World of Paper Money. Neil Shafer. (Illus.). 49p. (Orig.). 1993. pap. 2.00 (*0-931960-33-9*) BNR Pr.

Wonderful World of Pizzas, Quiches, & Savory Pies. Anna T. Callen. LC 96-12518. 1996. reprint ed. 9.99 (*0-517-18158-4*, Wings Books) Random.

Wonderful World of Pollen. Joe M. Parkhill. 160p. (Orig.). 1982. pap. text ed. 7.95 (*0-936744-06-5*) Country Bazaar.

***Wonderful World of What.** Scott Sussman. (Illus.). 30p. (Orig.). 1998. pap. write for info. (*1-889691-96-8*) SenSation.

Wonderful World of "Whey Lovers" Christina Dillane & Susan Dusharme. 160p. (Orig.). 1983. pap. text ed. 6.95 (*0-936744-08-1*) Country Bazaar.

Wonderful World of Wigglers: The Mysteries & Magic of the Mighty Earthworm. Julia Hand. 175p. (Orig.). 1995. pap. 14.95 (*1-884430-00-7*) Food Works.

Wonderful World We Live In. Yaffa Ganz. (ArtScroll Youth Ser.). (Illus.). 48p. (J). (gr. k-6). 1989. 11.99 (*0-89906-964-9*); pap. 7.99 (*0-89906-965-7*) Mesorah Pubns.

Wonderful World Within You: Your Inner Nutritional Environment. rev. ed. Roger J. Williams. (Illus.). 278p. 1987. pap. 14.95 (*0-942333-00-4*) Bio-Comns Pr.

Wonderful Worms. Linda Glaser. LC 91-38752. (Illus.). 32p. (J). (gr. k-3). 1992. lib. bdg. 16.40 (*1-56294-062-7*) Millbrook Pr.

Wonderful Worms. Linda Glaser. 32p. (J). (gr. k-3). 1994. pap. 7.95 (*1-56294-730-3*) Millbrook Pr.

Wonderful Wyoming Facts & Foods. 2nd ed. Judy Barbour. 64p. (Orig.). 1989. pap. text ed. 5.95 (*0-9611746-1-7*) J Barbour Bks.

Wonderful Years, Wonderful Year. George V. Higgins. 1989. mass mkt. 4.50 (*0-8217-2779-6*, Zebra Kensgtn) Kensgtn Pub Corp.

Wonderfully! Living Street Ministry Staff. 32p. 2.00 (*0-87083-601-3*, 17010001) Living Stream Ministry.

Wonderfully Made. A. J. White. 1989. pap. 7.99 (*0-85234-262-4*, Pub. by Evangelical Pr) Presby & Reformed.

Wonderguy. Murad Gumen. (Illus.). 40p. (Orig.). per., pap. 6.50 (*0-9631690-0-9*) Take Twelve.

Wondering: Invitations to Think about the Future for Primary Grades. R. E. Myers & E. P. Torrance. (Orig.). 1984. pap. 14.95 (*0-936386-22-3*) Creative Learning.

Wondering at the World: Instructional Manual to Accompany KIO & GUS. Matthew Lipman & Ann M. Sharp. (Philosophy for Children Ser.). 500p. 1986. 45.00 (*0-916834-20-4*) Inst Advncmnt Philos Child.

Wondering of Little Zero. Smart Elephant Peter. (Nursery Math Ser.). (J). 1991. write for info. (*1-879789-76-0*) AdRem.

Wondering Sage. Casca S. MacCrow. (Orig.). 1996. pap. 7.95 (*0-533-11617-1*) Vantage.

Wondering William & the Sandman. John M. Williams. LC 93-61122. (Illus.). 32p. (J). 1993. lib. bdg. 15.95 (*1-883084-01-6*) Wonder Bks.

Wonderings. Kenneth Patchen. LC 79-148535. (Illus.). (Orig.). 1971. pap. 8.95 (*0-8112-0149-X*, NDP320) New Directions.

Wonderland. Joyce Carol Oates. LC 91-41741. 512p. 1992. reprint ed. pap. 12.95 (*0-86538-075-9*) Ontario Rev NJ.

Wonderland Avenue: Tales of Glamour & Excess. Danny Sugerman. 1995. pap. text ed. 13.95 (*0-316-77354-9*) Little.

Wonderland Gambit, No. 3. Jack L. Chalker. 1997. pap. 12.00 (*0-345-38692-2*, Del Rey) Ballantine.

Wonderland Gambit: Book One: The Cybernetic Walrus. Jack L. Chalker. 1996. mass mkt. 5.99 (*0-345-38847-X*) Ballantine.

Wonderland Gambit: The March Hare Network, 2, No. 2. Jack L. Chalker. (The Wonderland Gambit Ser.: 2). 1996. mass mkt. 5.99 (*0-345-38848-8*, Del Rey) Ballantine.

Wonderland Howl-oween. M. C. Varley. LC 93-71351. (J). (gr. 4-7). 1993. pap. 3.95 (*1-56282-515-1*) Disney Pr.

Wonderlijke Problemen Leerzaam Tijoverdrijf Door Puzzle En Spel see Master Book of Mathematical Puzzles & Recreations

Wondermonger. Michael Rothschild. Date not set. pap. 8.00 (*0-14-015266-0*, Viking) Viking Penguin.

Wonderous Drug: Rhubarb. Clifford M. Foust. (Illus.). 376p. 1992. text ed. 47.50 (*0-691-08747-4*) Princeton U Pr.

***Wonderous Weather Dispenser.** (J). 1942. write for info. (*0-89693-971-5*, Chariot Bks) Chariot Victor.

Wonderplay: Interactive & Developmental Games, Crafts, & Creative Activities for Infants, Toddlers, & Preschoolers. Lois A. Mark. (Illus.). 128p. 1995. pap. 12.95 (*1-56138-575-1*) Running Pr.

Wonderpup. Philip Macht. (Illus.). 40p. (J). (gr. 4-6). 1992. 15.00 (*0-930339-03-7*) Maxrom Pr.

Wonders! Dick Hilliard & Beverly Valenti-Hilliard. LC 81-52713. (Center Celebration Ser.). (Illus.). 64p. (Orig.). (J). (gr. 1 up). 1981. pap. text ed. 4.95 (*0-89390-032-X*) Resource Pubns.

Wonders. Ivan Kapetanakos. 56p. 1994. pap. 11.00 (*0-8059-3588-6*) Dorrance.

Wonders! Classroom Set. (Illus.). (Orig.). (J). (gr. 1-3). 1994. student ed., teacher ed., pap. 399.00 (*1-56334-099-2*) Hampton-Brown.

Wonders & Joys of Christmas. Ed. by Mac Anderson. 78p. (Orig.). 1990. pap. 7.95 (*1-56245-002-6*) Great Quotations.

***Wonders & the Order of Nature, 1150-1750.** Lorraine Daston & Katharine Park. LC 96-49411. 1998. write for info. (*0-942299-90-6*) Zone Bks.

Wonders & the Word. James Coggins & Paul Hiebert. 162p. 1989. pap. 7.95 (*0-919797-82-2*) Kindred Prods.

Wonders Big Book Set: Level 2. (Wonders! Ser.). (Illus.). (Orig.). 1992. pap. 232.00 (*1-56334-221-9*) Hampton-Brown.

***Wonder's Champion.** Created by Campbell. 1997. mass mkt. 3.99 (*0-06-106491-2*, Harp PBks) HarpC.

Wonders Classroom Set: Level 2, Set. (Wonders! Ser.). (Illus.). (Orig.). 1992. teacher ed., pap. 399.00 (*1-56334-220-0*) Hampton-Brown.

Wonder's First Race. Joanna Campbell. (Thoroughbred Ser.: No. 3). 192p. (J). (gr. 6-9). 1991. mass mkt. 3.99 (*0-06-106082-8*, Harp PBks) HarpC.

Wonders Hidden see Visionary

Wonders in Numbers. Anthony J. Schneider. (Illus.). 140p. (Orig.). (YA). (gr. 7-12). 1994. pap. 9.75 (*0-9640218-0-3*) Schneider Assocs.

Wonders in Weeds. William Smith. 187p. (C). 1977. pap. 17.95 (*0-8464-1062-1*) Beekman Pubs.

***Wonders in Wood.** 2nd ed. Edwin Wyatt. LC 97-11137. (Illus.). 76p. 1997. reprint ed. pap. 8.95 (*0-941936-40-6*) Linden Pub Fresno.

Wonders of Alaska. Lynn M. Stone. LC 93-42648. (North to Alaska Ser.). (J). 1994. write for info. (*1-55916-028-4*) Rourke Bk Co.

Wonders of America: Reinventing Jewish Culture, 1880-1950. Jenna W. Joselit. 350p. 1996. pap. text ed. 14.00 (*0-8090-1586-2*) Hill & Wang.

Wonders of America Reinventing Jewish Culture, 1880-1950. Weissman J. Joselit. 1995. 23.00 (*0-8090-2757-7*) Hill & Wang.

Wonders of Bible Chronology. Philip Mauro. 1974. pap. 5.99 (*0-87377-060-9*) GAM Pubns.

***Wonders of California & the American Southwest.** Hans-Otto Meissner & Karl Kinne. (Illus.). 144p. 44.95 (*3-921268-35-4*, Pub. by Ziethen-Panorama GW) BookWorld Dist.

Wonders of Canada. Lynda Sorensen. LC 94-48247. (North of the Border Ser.). 24p. (YA). 1995. lib. bdg. 13.27 (*1-55916-103-5*) Rourke Bk Co.

Wonders of Christmas. (Book & Sticker Set Ser.). (Illus.). 16p. (J). 1996. 7.99 (*0-88705-954-6*, Wshng Well Bks) Joshua Morris.

Wonders of Christmas. Sharyn S. Craig. Ed. by Joanne S. Nolt. LC 96-29239. (Illus.). 16p. (Orig.). 1996. pap. 6.95 (*1-885588-12-7*) Chitra Pubns.

Wonders of Creation & the World Hereafter. Elizabeth Walton. 110p. 1986. 30.00 (*0-7212-0746-4*, Pub. by Regency Press UK) St Mut.

Wonders of Energy. David Adler. LC 82-20042. (Question & Answer Bks.). (Illus.). 32p. (J). (gr. 3-6). 1983. lib. bdg. 10.95 (*0-89375-884-1*) Troll Communs.

Wonders of Energy. David Adler. LC 82-20042. (Question & Answer Bks.). (Illus.). 32p. (J). (gr. 3-6). 1997. pap. 3.95 (*0-89375-885-X*) Troll Communs.

Wonders of Engraving. G. Duplessis. 340p. 1989. reprint ed. pap. 35.00 (*0-87556-178-0*) Saifer.

Wonders of God. Paul E. Eickmann. LC 83-61045. 101p. (Orig.). 1983. pap. 6.00 (*0-8100-0170-5*, 07N0746) Northwest Pub.

***Wonders of God.** William MacDonald. 122p. (Orig.). 1996. pap. 7.95 (*1-882701-25-9*) Uplook Min.

Wonders of Inner Space: Mystic Talks. Darshan Singh. LC 88-80368. (Illus.). 208p. 1988. pap. 10.00 (*0-918224-22-5*) S K Pubns.

Wonders of Jesus: My Bible Sticker Storybook. Carolyn Magner. 24p. (J). (ps-3). 1994. pap. 2.99 (*0-7814-0140-2*) Chariot Victor.

Wonders of Light & Shadow. Society for Promoting Christian Knowledge Staff. LC 72-9236. (Literature of Photography Ser.). 1973. reprint ed. 17.95 (*0-405-04941-2*) Ayer.

***Wonders of Little Girls.** Phyllis Hobe. 64p. 1994. 5.95 (*0-8378-8327-X*) Gibson.

Wonders of Magic. John Booth & Doug Henning. LC 86-60002. (Illus.). xiv, 301p. 1986. text ed. 39.50 (*0-943230-03-9*) Ridgeway Pr.

Wonders of Mexico. Laura Conlon. (J). 1994. 15.00 (*1-55916-054-3*) Rourke Bk Co.

Wonders of Nature in South-East Asia. Compiled & Intro. by Earl of Cranbrook. LC 96-25056. (Illus.). 300p. 1997. pap. 35.00 (*967-65-3088-3*) OUP.

Wonders of Nature Take-along Library, 5 vols., Set. (Illus.). 30p. (J). (gr. 2-7). 1991. boxed 5.99 (*0-517-05454-X*) Random Hse Value.

Wonders of Our World, 5 Vols., Set. Neil Morris. (Illus.). (J). (gr. 2-9). 1995. pap. 34.75 (*0-86505-848-2*); lib. bdg. 89.75 (*0-86505-836-9*) Crabtree Pub Co.

Wonders of Plants & Flowers. Laura Damon. LC 89-5003. (Illus.). 32p. (J). (gr. 2-4). 1990. pap. 3.50 (*0-8167-1762-1*); lib. bdg. 12.95 (*0-8167-1761-3*) Troll Communs.

Wonders of Qigong: A Chinese Exercise for Fitness, Health, & Longevity. China Sports Magazine Staff. Ed. by Wayfarer Publications Staff. LC 85-51522. 112p. 1985. pap. 14.95 (*0-935099-07-7*) Wayfarer Pubns.

Wonders of Rivers. Rae Bains. LC 81-7423. (Illus.). 32p. (J). (gr. 2-4). 1982. pap. 3.50 (*0-89375-571-0*); lib. bdg. 12.95 (*0-89375-570-2*) Troll Communs.

Wonders of Salvage: Deep Sea Diving for Sunken Ships & Treasures. David Masters. 1977. lib. bdg. 150.00 (*0-8490-2839-6*) Gordon Pr.

Wonders of Skiing. H. Schneider & A. Fanck. 1976. lib. bdg. 69.95 (*0-8490-2840-X*) Gordon Pr.

Wonders of Solitude: The Classic Wisdom Collection. Ed. by Dale Salwak. LC 94-40474. (Classic Wisdom Collection). 128p. 1995. 12.95 (*1-880032-53-8*) New Wrld Lib.

Wonders of Swamps & Marshes. Stephen Caitlin. LC 89-4967. (Illus.). 32p. (J). (gr. 2-4). 1990. lib. bdg. 12.95 (*0-8167-1765-6*) Troll Communs.

Wonders of Swamps & Marshes. Stephen Caitlin. LC 89-4967. (Illus.). 32p. (J). (gr. 2-4). 1996. pap. 3.50 (*0-8167-1766-4*) Troll Communs.

Wonders of Technology, Level 1. Namestka. (Tech & Industrial Education Ser.). 1992. suppl. ed., pap. 11.95 (*0-8273-4701-4*); teacher ed., pap. 108.95 (*0-8273-4704-9*) Delmar.

Wonders of Technology, Level 2. Namestka. (Tech & Industrial Education Ser.). 1992. suppl. ed., pap. 11.95 (*0-8273-4702-2*); teacher ed., pap. 108.95 (*0-8273-4705-7*) Delmar.

Wonders of Technology, Level 3. Namestka. (Tech & Industrial Education Ser.). 1992. suppl. ed., pap. 11.95 (*0-8273-4703-0*); teacher ed., pap. 108.95 (*0-8273-4706-5*) Delmar.

Wonders of the Ancient World: National Geographic Atlas of Archaeology. National Geographic Society Book Division Staff. LC 94-16650. 1995. 35.00 (*0-87044-982-6*) Natl Geog.

Wonders of the Ancient World: National Geographic Atlas of Archaeology. deluxe ed. National Geographic Society Book Division Staff. LC 94-16650. 1994. pap. 46.95 (*0-87044-983-4*) Natl Geog.

Wonders of the Desert. Louis Sabin. LC 81-7397. (Illus.). 32p. (J). (gr. 2-4). 1982. pap. 3.50 (*0-89375-575-3*); lib. bdg. 12.95 (*0-89375-574-5*) Troll Communs.

Wonders of the Forest. Francene Sabin. LC 81-7401. (Illus.). 32p. (J). (gr. 2-4). 1982. pap. 3.50 (*0-89375-573-7*); lib. bdg. 12.95 (*0-89375-572-9*) Troll Communs.

Wonders of the Himalaya. Francis Younghusband. (C). 1993. 18.50 (*81-206-0875-5*, Pub. by Asian Educ Servs II) S Asia.

Wonders of the Holy Name. Paul O'Sullivan. LC 93-60345. 45p. 1993. pap. 1.50 (*0-89555-490-9*) TAN Bks Pubs.

Wonders of the Mass. Paul O'Sullivan. LC 93-60344. 42p. 1993. pap. 1.25 (*0-89555-491-7*) TAN Bks Pubs.

Wonders of the Natural Mind: The Essence of Dzogchen in the Bon Tradition of Tibet. Tenzin Wangyal. 1993. pap. 14.95 (*0-88268-117-6*) Station Hill Pr.

Wonders of the Oceans: Sharks - Marine Mammals. Barry Levey. (Illus.). 1995. spiral bd. 10.95 (*1-885422-13-X*) Fishermans Tales.

Wonders of the Pond. Francene Sabin. LC 81-7407. (Illus.). 32p. (J). (gr. 2-4). 1982. pap. 3.50 (*0-89375-577-X*); lib. bdg. 12.95 (*0-89375-576-1*); audio 9.95 (*0-685-04956-6*) Troll Communs.

Wonders of the Rain Forest. Janet Craig. LC 89-5001. (Illus.). 32p. (J). (gr. 2-4). 1990. pap. 3.50 (*0-8167-1764-8*); lib. bdg. 12.95 (*0-8167-1763-X*) Troll Communs.

Wonders of the Reef: Diving with a Camera. Photos & Text by Stephen Frink. (Illus.). 160p. 1996. 39.95 (*0-8109-3785-9*) Abrams.

Wonders of the Sea. Louis Sabin. LC 81-3334. (Illus.). 32p. (J). (gr. 2-4). 1982. pap. 3.50 (*0-89375-579-6*); lib. bdg. 12.95 (*0-89375-578-8*) Troll Communs.

Wonders of the Seasons. Keith Brandt. LC 81-7411. (Illus.). 32p. (J). (gr. 2-4). 1982. lib. bdg. 12.95 (*0-89375-580-X*) Troll Communs.

Wonders of the Seasons. Keith Brandt. LC 81-7411. (Illus.). 32p. (J). (gr. 2-4). 1996. pap. 3.50 (*0-89375-581-8*) Troll Communs.

Wonders of the Sky: Observing Rainbows, Comets, Eclipses, the Stars, & Other Phenomena. Fred Schaaf. (Illus.). 224p. (Orig.). 1983. pap. 8.95 (*0-486-24402-4*) Dover.

Wonders of the Weather. unabridged ed. Bob Crowder. LC 94-23494. (Illus.). 280p. (Orig.). 1995. pap. 39.95 (*0-644-35020-2*, 9423494, Pub. by AGPS Pr AT) Intl Spec Bk.

Wonders of the Word: Trails of the Soul & Revelations of the Spirit (1929) Rudolph Steiner. 152p. 1996. pap. 16.95 (*1-56459-780-6*) Kessinger Pub.

Wonders of the World. Giovanni Caselli. LC 92-52798. (See & Explore Library). (Illus.). 64p. (J). (gr. 3 up). 1992. 12.95 (*1-56458-145-4*) DK Pub Inc.

Wonders of the World. Paul Humphrey. LC 94-28181. (Read All about It Ser.). (Illus.). (J). 1995. lib. bdg. 21.40 (*0-8114-5733-8*) Raintree Steck-V.

Wonders of the World: Trials of the Soul & Revelations of the Spirit. Rudolf Steiner. 142p. 1974. reprint ed. spiral bd. 12.00 (*0-7873-1075-1*) Hlth Research.

Wonders of the World, Ordeals of the Soul, Revelations of the Spirit. Rudolf Steiner. Tr. by Dorothy Lenn et al. from GER. 190p. 1983. reprint ed. pap. 14.95 (*0-85440-363-9*, Pub. by Steiner Book Centre CN) Anthroposophic.

Wonders of Water. Jane Dickinson. LC 82-17388. (Question & Answer Bks.). (Illus.). 32p. (J). (gr. 3-6). 1983. lib. bdg. 10.95 (*0-89375-874-4*) Troll Communs.

***Wonders of Water.** Robert E. Rockwell et al. Ed. by Catherine Anderson & Mali Apple. (Discovery Science Ser.). (Illus.). 76p. (Orig.). (J). 1996. pap. text ed. 11.95 (*0-201-49661-5*, 36839) Seymour Pubns.

Wonders of Water. Harold Silvani. (Illus.). 43p. (J). (gr. 4-12). 1988. student ed. 6.95 (*1-878669-29-X*, CTA-6552) Crea Tea Assocs.

Wonders of Would Be Writers. Samuel R. Harvey et al. Ed. by John D. Kasper & Rosemary Ebnet. 105p. (Orig.). Date not set. spiral bd., pap. 10.00 (*0-9633798-1-X*) Harvey Pub MN.

Wonder's Promise. Joanna Campbell. (Thoroughbred Ser.: No. 2). 192p. (J). 1991. mass mkt. 3.99 (*0-06-106085-2*, Harp PBks) HarpC.

Wonders! Series: Big Books. (Illus.). (Orig.). (J). (gr. 1-3). 1991. student ed., teacher ed., pap. 232.00 (*1-56334-101-8*) Hampton-Brown.

Wonder's Sister. Joanna Campbell. (Thoroughbred Ser.: No. 11). 192p. (J). (gr. 4-7). 1994. mass mkt. 3.99 (*0-06-106250-2*) HarpC Child Bks.

Wonders Teacher's Activity Notebook, Level 1. (Wonders! Ser.). (Illus.). 224p. (J). (gr. 1-3). 1991. Grades 1-3. ring bd. 85.00 (*1-56334-058-5*) Hampton-Brown.

Wonders Teacher's Activity Notebook: Level 2. (Wonders! Ser.). (Illus.). 202p. 1992. ring bd. 85.00 (*1-56334-149-2*) Hampton-Brown.

Wonder's Victory. Joanna Campbell. (Thoroughbred Ser.: No. 4). 192p. (J). (gr. 7-9). 1991. mass mkt. 3.99 (*0-06-106083-6*, Harp PBks) HarpC.

Wonders Within Gemstones: The Elusive Beauty of Gemstone Inclusions. Anthony De Goutiere. (Illus.). 135p. 1996. 49.95 (*0-9641733-2-8*) Gemwrld Intl.

Wonder's Yearling. Joanna Campbell. (Thoroughbred Ser.: No. 6). 192p. (J). (gr. 4-7). 1993. mass mkt. 3.99 (*0-06-106747-4*, Harp PBks) HarpC.

Wonderscience: A Developmentally Appropriate Guide to Hands-on Science for Young Children. Wendy Nichols & Kim Nichols. LC 90-60081. 60p. (Orig.). (J). (ps-3). 1990. pap. 14.95 (*0-9625907-0-3*) Learning Expo.

Wonderstruck I. Bob MacDonald & Eric Grace. (Illus.). 96p. 1991. pap. 10.95 (*0-7737-5477-6*) Genl Dist Srvs.

Wonderstruck II. Bob MacDonald & Eric Grace. (Illus.). 96p. 1991. pap. 10.95 (*0-7737-5478-4*) Genl Dist Srvs.

***WonderUnder Book of EZ Applique.** 1997. pap. 14.95 (*0-8487-1572-1*) Oxmoor Hse.

Wonderwoman & Superman: The Ethics of Human Biotechnology. John Harris. (Studies in Bioethics). 288p. 1992. 25.00 (*0-19-217754-0*) OUP.

Wonderworking Kursk-Root Icon of the Mother of God: Discovery & History, Recent Miracles, Liturgical Service, Akathist Hymn. Tr. by Isaac E. Lambertsen from RUS. (Illus.). 64p. (Orig.). 1989. pap. 3.50 (*0-912927-33-X*, X033) St John Kronstadt.

Wonderworks: Science Fiction & Fantasy Art. deluxe ed. Michael Whelan. Ed. by Polly Freas & Kelly Freas. LC 79-12575. (Illus.). 1979. 30.00 (*0-915442-83-3*, Starblaze) Donning Co.

W

An Asterisk (*) at the beginning of an entry indicates that the title is appearing in BIP for the first time.

Wonderworks of Nature, 8 vols., Set. Jenny Wood. (Illus.). 32p. (J). (gr. 3-4). 1991. lib. bdg. 159.44 (*0-8368-0757-X*) Gareth Stevens Inc.

Wondrous Events: Foundations of Religious Belief. James McClenon. LC 94-20228. (Illus.). 296p. (Orig.). (C). 1994. text ed. 41.95 (*0-8122-3074-4*); pap. text ed. 18.95 (*0-8122-1355-6*) U of Pa Pr.

Wondrous in His Saints: Counter-Reformation Propaganda in Bavaria. Philip M. Soregel. LC 92-36732. (Studies on the History of Society & Culture: Vol. 17). 1993. 38.00 (*0-520-08047-5*) U CA Pr.

Wondrous Is God in His Saints. Ed. by Father Benedict. LC 85-63506. (Illus.). 190p. (Orig.). 1985. pap. 6.95 (*0-936649-00-3*) St Anthony Orthodox.

Wondrous Joy of Soul Winning. R. A. Torrey. reprint ed. pap. 4.99 (*0-88019-115-5*) Schmul Pub Co.

***Wondrous Land: The Faery Faith of Ireland.** Kay Mullin. (Orig.). 1997. pap. 23.95 (*1-86163-010-7*, Pub. by Capall Bann Pubng UK) Holmes Pub.

Wondrous Menagerie: Animal Fantasy Stories from American Children's Literature. Ed. by Mark I. West. LC 93-11693. xvi, 139p. (J). (gr. 1 up). 1994. lib. bdg. 27.50 (*0-208-02383-6*, Archon Bks) Shoe String.

Wondrous Realms of the Aegean. Time-Life Books Editors. Ed. by Dale Brown. LC 92-29449. (Lost Civilizations Ser.). (Illus.). 168p. 1993. 19.95 (*0-8094-9875-8*); lib. bdg. 25.93 (*0-8094-9876-6*) Time-Life.

Wondrous Ride: And Other Poems for Children. Sigmund A. Boloz. Ed. by Karen Snow. (Illus.). 32p. (Orig.). (J). (gr. k-6). 1995. pap. 5.00 (*1-886635-01-3*) Wooded Hill AZ.

Wondrous Times on the Frontier. Dee Brown. 320p. 1991. 23.95 (*0-87483-137-7*) August Hse.

Wondrous Times on the Frontier. Dee Brown. LC 92-52623. 320p. 1992. pap. 13.00 (*0-06-097492-3*, PL) HarpC.

Wondrous World of the Mangrove Swamps. Katherine S. Orr. (Illus.). 32p. 1989. pap. 3.95 (*0-9613236-2-0*) Florida Flair Bks.

Wong & Whaley's Clinical Manual of Pediatric Nursing. 4th ed. Donna L. Wong. 000624p. (C). (gr. 13). 1995. spiral bd. 34.95 (*0-8151-9442-0*) Mosby Yr Bk.

***Wong, Dalton College Custom Pub.** Donna L. Wong. (C). (gr. 13). 1996. 81.95 (*0-8151-2709-X*, 31344) Mosby Yr Bk.

Wong Ho Leun: An American Chinatown (Great Basin Foundation), 2 vols., Set. 960p. 1991. reprint ed. lib. bdg. 95.00 (*0-8095-6120-4*) Borgo Pr.

***Wong Kar Wai.** (Illus.). 128p. 1997. pap. 35.00 (*2-906571-67-9*) Dist Art Pubs.

Wonnltatigkeit und Armenpflege Im Vorchristlichen Altertum. Hendrik Bolkestein. Ed. by Gregory Vlastos. LC 78-15858. (Morals & Law in Ancient Greece Ser.). 1979. reprint ed. lib. bdg. 40.95 (*0-405-11531-8*) Ayer.

Wonsook Kim Linton. Frwd. by Sueyun Locks. (Illus.). 6p. 1991. pap. 2.00 (*0-685-62372-6*) Locks Gallery.

Won't Know Till I Get There. Walter D. Myers. LC 87-7340. (J). (gr. 3 up). 1988. pap. 3.99 (*0-14-032612-X*, Puffin) Puffin Bks.

***Won't-Pick-Up-Toys Cure.** Betty B. MacDonald. LC 96-43610. (Mrs. Piggle-Wiggle Adventure Ser.). (Illus.). (J). 1998. lib. bdg. write for info. (*0-06-027629-0*) HarpC Child Bks.

***Won't-Pick-Up-Toys Cure.** Betty B. MacDonald. LC 96-43610. (Mrs. Piggle-Wiggle Adventure Ser.). (Illus.). 40p. (J). (ps-2). 1998. 14.95 (*0-06-027628-2*) HarpC Child Bks.

Won't Somebody Play With Me? Steven Kellogg. 1994. pap. 5.99 (*0-14-054729-0*) NAL-Dutton.

Won't Somebody Play with Me? Steven Kellogg. LC 72-708. (Pied Piper Bks.). (Illus.). (J). (gr. k-3). 1976. reprint ed. pap. 4.95 (*0-8037-9612-9*) Dial Bks Young.

Won't Someone Help Anna? Francine Pascal. (Sweet Valley Twins & Friends Ser.: No. 69). 144p. (J). (gr. 4-7). 1993. pap. 3.50 (*0-553-48056-1*) Bantam.

***Won't-Take-a-Bath-Cure.** Betty B. MacDonald. LC 96-43425. (Mrs. Piggle-Wiggle Adventure Ser.). (Illus.). 40p. (J). (ps-2). 1998. 14.95 (*0-06-027630-4*); lib. bdg. 14.89 (*0-06-027631-2*) HarpC Child Bks.

Won't U Come Home. Grizzard. 1991. 4.95 (*0-446-77582-7*) Warner Bks.

Won't You Be My Husband? Linda Varner. 1996. mass mkt. 3.25 (*0-373-19188-X*, 1-19188-1) Silhouette.

***Won't You Come & Play With Me?** Mary L. Donovan. LC 97-2529. (Illus.). (J). 1998. write for info. (*0-395-84630-7*) HM.

Won't You Ever Listen. Carol Cummings. (Illus.). 24p. (Orig.). (J). (ps-3). 1992. pap. 4.99 (*0-9614574-7-3*) Teaching WA.

Wonted Work: A Guide to the Informal Economy. Graeme Shankland. LC 88-22326. 221p. (Orig.). (C). 1988. pap. 15.50 (*0-942850-09-2*) Bootstrap Pr.

Wood. LC 95-15. (Best of Fine Woodworking Ser.). 1995. pap. 14.95 (*1-56158-099-6*) Taunton.

***Wood.** (FunFax Horror Ser.). (Illus.). 144p. (J). (gr. 3-9). 1996. pap. 2.95 (*0-7894-1158-X*) DK Pub Inc.

Wood. Graham Carrick. (Craft Projects Ser.). (Illus.). 32p. (J). (gr. 2-6). 1990. lib. bdg. 15.94 (*0-86592-484-8*); lib. bdg. 11.95 (*0-685-36306-6*) Rourke Corp.

Wood. Catherine Chambers. LC 95-21400. (J). 1996. lib. bdg. 21.40 (*0-8172-4102-7*) Raintree Steck-V.

Wood. Andy Goldsworthy. (Illus.). 120p. 1996. 49.50 (*0-8109-3992-4*) Abrams.

Wood. Terry J. Jennings. Ed. by Rebecca Stefoff. LC 91-18187. (Threads Ser.). (Illus.). 32p. (J). (gr. 3-5). 1991. lib. bdg. 15.93 (*1-56074-002-7*) Garrett Ed Corp.

Wood: A Manual for Its Use As a Shipbuilding Material. Ed. by U. S. Navy, Bureau of Ships Staff. LC 82-74415. (Illus.). 418p. 1983. reprint ed. 25.00 (*0-9610602-0-4*) Teaparty Bks.

W

Wood: Aircraft Building Techniques. rev. ed. Ed. by Paul H. Poberezny & S. H. Schmid. (EAA How to Ser.). (Illus.). 140p. 1991. pap. 11.95 (*0-940000-44-X*) EAA Aviation.

Wood: An Ancient Fuel with a New Future. Nigel Smith. 1981. pap. write for info. (*0-916468-41-0*) Worldwatch Inst.

Wood: Chemistry, Ultrastructure, Reactions. Dietrich Fengel & Gert Wegener. xii, 600p. (C). 1989. pap. 113.85 (*3-11-012059-3*) De Gruyter.

Wood: Classic Woodworking Woods & How to Use Them. Wood Magazine Editors. (Better Homes & Gardens Ser.). (Illus.). 96p. 1993. 12.95 (*0-696-02469-1*) Meredith Bks.

Wood: Decay, Pests, & Protection. Ra. A. Eaton & M. D. Hale. LC 92-44614. 560p. (gr. 13). 1993. text ed. 138.95 (*0-412-53120-8*) Chapman & Hall.

Wood: Electricity & Magnetism Fundamentals. Robert W. Wood. (Learning Triangle Press FUNdamentals Ser.). (Illus.). 192p. (J). (gr. 3 up). 1996. text ed. 22.95 (*0-07-071808-3*, Lrng Triangle) McGraw-Hill Prof.

Wood: Kids' Projects You Can Make. Wood magazine Editors. (Better Homes & Gardens Ser.). 96p. 1993. 12.95 (*0-696-00031-8*) Meredith Bks.

Wood: Light Fundamentals. Robert W. Wood. LC 96-35967. (Learning Triangle Press NatureScope Ser.). (Illus.). 192p. (YA). (gr. 3 up). 1996. pap. text ed. 14.95 (*0-07-071809-1*, Lrng Triangle) McGraw-Hill Prof.

Wood: Materials & Processes. rev. ed. John L. Feirer. (gr. 7-12). 1980. text ed. 22.20 (*0-02-666240-X*) Glencoe.

Wood: Materials & Processes. rev. ed. John L. Feirer. (YA). (gr. 7-12). 1980. teacher ed. 5.28 (*0-02-666250-7*) Glencoe.

Wood: Nature's Cellular, Polymeric, Fibre Composite. J. M. Dinwoodie. 140p. 1989. pap. text ed. 40.00 (*0-901462-35-7*, Pub. by Inst Materials UK) Ashgate Pub Co.

Wood: The First Hundred Years of Lake County, Indiana, As Lived & Acted by Bartlett Woods & Family & Sam B. Woods & Family. Sam B. Woods. 418p. 1994. reprint ed. pap. 59.50 (*0-8328-4178-1*); reprint ed. lib. bdg. 69.50 (*0-8328-4177-3*) Higginson Bk Co.

Wood: The Internal Optimization of Trees. Hans Kubler & G. Claus Mattheck. (Springer Series in Wood Science). 1995. 108.95 (*3-540-59318-7*) Spr-Verlag.

***Wood: The Internal Optimization of Trees.** Hans Kubler & G. Claus Mattheck. LC 96-49603. 1997. pap. 49.95 (*3-540-62019-2*) Spr-Verlag.

Wood: Yorkshire to Westchester: Chronicle of the Wood Family. H. B. Howe. (Illus.). 290p. 1991. reprint ed. pap. 45.00 (*0-8328-1883-6*); reprint ed. lib. bdg. 55.00 (*0-8328-1882-8*) Higginson Bk Co.

Wood see 1997 Annual Book of ASTM Standards: Construction, Section 4

***Wood Accents for the Home.** Cy DeCosse Incorporated Staff. (Black & Decker Portable Workshop Ser.). (FRE.). 1996. write for info. (*0-86573-686-3*) Cowles Creative.

Wood Accents for the Home. DeCosse, Cy, Incorporated Staff. LC 95-49811. (Portable Workshop Ser.). (Illus.). 96p. 1996. 14.95 (*0-86573-695-2*) Cowles Creative.

Wood Adhesives: Chemistry & Technology, Vol. 2. Antonio Pizzi. 424p. 1989. 195.00 (*0-8247-8052-3*) Dekker.

Wood Adhesives Vol. 1: Chemistry & Technology. Antonio Pizzi. 376p. 1983. 175.00 (*0-8247-1579-9*) Dekker.

Wood Adhesives in Nineteen Eighty-Five: Status & Needs. 328p. 1986. 50.00 (*0-935018-32-8*, 7344) Forest Prod.

Wood Adhesives 1990. 190p. 1990. 50.00 (*0-935018-52-2*, 7354) Forest Prod.

***Wood Adhesives 1995.** 254p. 1996. 55.00 (*0-935018-79-4*, 7296) Forest Prod.

Wood & Agricultural Residue Combustion Systems: Survey of Commercially Available Equipment. Ed. by G. Sarwar et al. 1992. pap. 49.00 (*0-85954-318-8*, Pub. by Nat Res Inst UK) St Mut.

Wood & Canvas Canoe: A Complete Guide to its History, Construction, Restoration & Maintenance. Jerry Stelmok & Rollin Thurlow. LC 87-80698. 296p. (Orig.). 1988. pap. 19.95 (*0-88448-046-1*) Tilbury Hse.

Wood & Canvas Kayak Building. George Putz. (Illus.). 144p. 1990. pap. text ed. 17.95 (*0-87742-258-3*) Intl Marine.

Wood & Canvas Kayak Building. George Putz. 1990. pap. text ed. 17.95 (*0-07-155939-6*) McGraw.

Wood & Cellulosic Chemistry. N. Shiraishi. 1072p. 1990. 275.00 (*0-8247-8304-2*) Dekker.

Wood & Fiber Science, Vol. 28, No. 1. Ed. by Robert Youngs. (Orig.). 1996. pap. text ed. 110.00 (*0-686-40829-2*) Soc Wood.

Wood & Garden. Gertrude Jekyll. 1994. 29.50 (*1-85149-198-8*) Antique Collect.

***Wood & Garden.** Gertude Jekyll. Date not set. write for info. (*0-8434-6216-7*, Pub. by McGrath NH) Ayer.

Wood & Garden. rev. ed. Gertrude Jekyll. LC 82-16364. (Jekyll Garden Bks.). (Illus.). 345p. 1983. reprint ed. 26.95 (*0-88143-004-8*) Ayer.

Wood & Garden. rev. ed. Gertrude Jekyll. LC 82-16364. (Jekyll Garden Bks.). (Illus.). 345p. 1984. reprint ed. pap. 11.95 (*0-88143-058-7*) Ayer.

***Wood & Glory: Muskoka's Classic Launches.** William M. Gray. 1997. 50.00 (*1-55046-177-X*, Pub. by Boston Mills Pr CN) Genl Dist Srvs.

Wood & Technology. Bette Prange & Maureen Kelly. LC 93-28503. (C). 1994. pap. 13.95 (*0-521-43822-5*) Cambridge U Pr.

Wood & Wood Carvings from the Index of American Design. John M. Vlach. (Illus.). 16p. 1988. pap. 2.00 (*0-933793-10-3*) Guild Hall.

Wood & Wood Grains: A Photographic Album for Artists & Designers. Phil Brodatz. 1972. 9.95 (*0-486-22424-4*) Dover.

***Wood & Wood Joints: Building Traditions of Europe & Japan.** Klaus Zwerger. LC 97-12223. 1997. write for info. (*0-8176-5483-6*) Birkhauser.

***Wood & Wood Joints - Building Traditions of Europe & Japan.** Klaus Zwerger. (Illus.). 272p. (GER.). 1997. 64.50 (*3-7643-5482-8*) Birkhauser.

***Wood & Wood Joints - Building Traditions of Europe & Japan: Building Traditions of Europe & Japan.** Klaus Zwerger. LC 97-12223. (Illus.). 272p. 1997. 64.50 (*3-7643-5483-6*) Birkhauser.

Wood & Woodworking Materials: Techniques for Better Woodworking. Nick Engler. (Workshop Companion Ser.). 1995. 19.95 (*0-87596-722-1*) Rodale Pr Inc.

Wood As a Building Material: A Guide for Designers & Builders. 2nd ed. W. Wayne Wilcox et al. LC 91-7815. 232p. 1991. text ed. 69.95 (*0-471-52722-X*) Wiley.

Wood As Fuel: A Source Guide. 1991. lib. bdg. 75.00 (*0-8490-4876-1*) Gordon Pr.

Wood As Fuel: Energy for Developing Countries. Susan V. Bogach. LC 84-26640. 176p. 1985. text ed. 39.95 (*0-275-90062-2*, C0062, Praeger Pubs) Greenwood.

***Wood Ash in the Great Lakes Region: Production, Characteristics & Regulation.** Jagdish Rughani et al. (Illus.). 32p. (C). 1997. reprint ed. pap. text ed. 30.00 (*0-7881-3748-4*) DIANE Pub.

***Wood Beyond.** Reginald Hill. 1997. mass mkt. 5.50 (*0-440-21803-9*) Dell.

Wood Beyond. large type ed. Reginald Hill. 1996. 25.95 (*0-7838-1864-5*, GK Hall) Thorndike Pr.

Wood Beyond: A Dalziel/Pascoe Mystery. Reginald Hill. LC 95-32319. (Dalziel/Pascoe Mystery Ser.). 384p. 1996. 21.95 (*0-385-31271-7*) Delacorte.

Wood Beyond the World. William Morris. 261p. 1972. reprint ed. pap. 8.95 (*0-486-22791-X*) Dover.

Wood, Birds, Water, Stone. Nick Bozanic. 8p. (Orig.). 1983. pap. 2.95 (*0-935306-20-X*) Barnwood Pr.

Wood Block Prints of B. J. O. Nordfeldt: A Catalogue Raisonne. Fiona I. Donovan. Ed. by Susan Brown. LC 90-71792. (Illus.). 72p. (Orig.). 1991. pap. 16.00 (*0-938713-08-6*) Univ MN Art Mus.

***Wood Boxes.** Andrew Crawford. 1998. write for info. (*0-8069-9862-8*) Sterling.

Wood, Brick, & Stone: The North American Settlement Landscape: Vol. 2, Barns & Farm Structures. Allen G. Noble. LC 83-24110. (Illus.). 192p. 1984. pap. 18.95 (*0-87023-518-4*) U of Mass Pr.

***Wood Burcher's Illustrated Manual: Level One.** unabridged ed. John G. Roorda. LC 97-93410. (Illus.). vi, 102p. 1997. spiral bd. 15.95 (*0-9657953-0-6*, WB-100) Able Two.

***Wood Burners.** Daniel Mihalyo. LC 97-976. (Illus.). 112p. (Orig.). 1997. pap. 19.95 (*1-56898-104-X*) Princeton Arch.

Wood Burning with Sue Waters: Rural Scenes. Sue Waters. LC 93-87057. (Illus.). 64p. (Orig.). 1994. pap. text ed. 12.95 (*0-88740-569-X*) Schiffer.

Wood Carbonization Unit: Design & Development of a Prototype with Recovery of Waste Heat. G. R. Breag et al. 1992. pap. 50.00 (*0-85954-306-4*, Pub. by Nat Res Inst UK) St Mut.

Wood Carver of Salem: Samuel McIntire, His Life & Work. Frank Cousins & Phil M. Riley. LC 74-119649. (BCL Ser. II). reprint ed. 39.50 (*0-404-01786-X*) AMS Pr.

Wood-Carver of Salem: Samuel McIntire, His Life & Work. Frank Cousins & Phil M. Riley. (Illus.). 168p. 1989. reprint ed. lib. bdg. 39.00 (*0-8328-1399-0*) Higginson Bk Co.

Wood Carving. (Illus.). 48p. (YA). (gr. 6-12). 1966. pap. 2.40 (*0-8395-3315-2*, 33309) BSA.

Wood Carving. (Art of Woodworking Ser.). (Illus.). 144p. 1996. 19.95 (*0-8094-9544-9*) Time-Life.

Wood Carving: Twenty-Three Traditional Decorative Projects. Alan Bridgewater & Gill Bridgewater. (Illus.). 272p. 1988. 22.95 (*0-8306-0979-2*); pap. 14.95 (*0-8306-2979-3*) McGraw-Hill Prof.

Wood Carvings of Eastern India. Kalyan K. Dasgupta. (C). 1990. text ed. 60.00 (*0-8364-2621-5*, Pub. by Firma KLM II) S Asia.

Wood Chemistry: Fundamentals & Applications. 2nd ed. Eero Sjostrom. LC 92-23493. (Illus.). 293p. 1993. text ed. 59.00 (*0-12-647481-8*) Acad Pr.

***Wood Chips: The Loves of R. T. "Windy" Wood.** 183p. 1996. pap. 14.00 (*0-9658275-0-X*) R T W Wood.

Wood County Historical Church Records Survey. James L. Angel. 56p. 1979. write for info. (*0-932690-01-7*) Ctr for Arch Collects.

Wood Decks: Materials, Construction, & Finishing. Kent A. McDonald et al. (Illus.). 100p. (Orig.). 1996. pap. 19.95 (*0-935018-77-8*, 7298) Forest Prod.

Wood Demon: Leshii. Anton P. Chekhov. Tr. by Nicholas Saunders & Frank Dwyer. LC 93-21865. (Great Translations for Actors Ser.). 128p. 1993. pap. 11.95 (*1-880399-30-X*) Smith & Kraus.

Wood Density Variation in Plantation-Grown Pinus Patula from the Viphya Plateau, Malawi. P. G. Adlard et al. 1978. 45.00 (*0-85074-045-2*) St Mut.

Wood-Detailing for Performance. William Dost & Elmer Botsai. LC 90-80940. (Illus.). 200p. (Orig.). 1990. pap. 42.00 (*0-9614808-7-4*) GRDA Pubns.

Wood Deterioration & Its Prevention by Preservative Treatments. Darrel D. Nicholas. Incl. Vol. 1. Degradation & Protection of Wood. 416p. 1982. pap. text ed. 45.00 (*0-8156-2285-6*); (Wood Science Ser.: No. 5). (Illus.). (C). 1973. Set pap. text ed. 45.00 (*0-8156-2303-8*) Syracuse U Pr.

***Wood Dreaming.** Terry Martin. 208p. 60.00 (*0-207-18723-1*) HarperColl Wrld.

Wood Duck & the Mandarin: The Northern Wood Ducks. Lawton L. Shurtleff & Christopher Savage. (Illus.). 232p. (C). 1996. 34.95 (*0-520-20812-9*) U CA Pr.

Wood Ducks: A Pictorial Study. Tricia Veasey. LC 88-63994. (Illus.). 96p. 1989. pap. 12.95 (*0-88740-155-4*) Schiffer.

Wood Dust & Formaldehyde. (IARC Monographs on the Evaluation of Carcinogenic Risks to Humans: Vol. 62). viii, 405p. (C). 1995. pap. text ed. 80.00 (*92-832-1262-2*, 1720062) World Health.

Wood Effect: Unaccounted Contributor to Error & Confusion in Acoustics & Audio. R. C. Johnsen. (Illus.). 112p. (Orig.). 1988. pap. 7.95 (*0-929383-00-1*) Modern Audio Assn.

Wood Engineering & Construction Handbook. 2nd ed. K. F. Faherty. 1995. text ed. 85.00 (*0-07-019911-6*) McGraw.

Wood Engineering Handbook. U. S. Forest Products Laboratory Staff. LC 82-7610. 1982. 49.95 (*0-13-962449-X*, Busn) P-H.

Wood Engineering Handbook. 2nd ed. Forest Products Laboratory Staff. 480p. 1990. text ed. 87.00 (*0-13-963745-1*) P-H.

Wood Engraving. George E. Mackley. 128p. 1984. 90.00 (*0-905418-84-0*, Pub. by Gresham Bks UK) St Mut.

Wood Engraving. George E. Mackley. 144p. 1985. 45.00 (*0-946095-18-3*, Pub. by Gresham Bks UK) St Mut.

Wood Engravings of Blair Hughes-Stanton. Penelope Hughes-Stanton. 195p. 1991. 90.00 (*0-900002-75-1*, Pub. by Priv Lib Assn UK) Oak Knoll.

Wood-Engravings of Gertude Hermes: Survey & Catalogue. Ed. by Judith Russell. (Illus.). 132p. 1993. 129.95 (*0-85967-888-1*, Pub. by Scolar Pr UK) Ashgate Pub Co.

Wood Engravings of John Farleigh. Monica Poole. (Illus.). 128p. 1985. 125.00 (*0-946095-09-4*, Pub. by Gresham Bks UK); 500.00 (*0-946095-15-9*, Pub. by Gresham Bks UK) St Mut.

Wood Engravings of Lucien Pissarrota: Bibliographical List of Gragny Books. Lois Urbanelli. (Illus.). 140p. (Orig.). (C). 1994. pap. 19.95 (*1-85183-056-1*, 0561X, Pub. by Ashmolean Mus UK) A Schwartz & Co.

Wood Fiber/Polymer Composites: Fundamental Concepts, Processes, & Material Options. 134p. 1993. 52.00 (*0-935018-57-3*, 7341) Forest Prod.

Wood Finisher: How to Finish Everything from Decks to Doors to Floors. Bruce Johnson. 352p. 1993. pap. 12.00 (*0-345-37297-2*, Ballantine Trade) Ballantine.

Wood Finisher's Handbook. Allen. (Sterling Publishing Co. Ser.). 1984. pap. 12.95 (*0-8273-5383-9*) Delmar.

Wood Finisher's Handbook. Sam Allen. LC 84-8557. (Illus.). 160p. (Orig.). 1984. pap. 14.95 (*0-8069-7914-3*) Sterling.

Wood Finishing. LC 92-32892. (Art of Woodworking Ser.). 144p. 1992. 19.95 (*0-8094-9912-6*); lib. bdg. write for info. (*0-8094-9913-4*) Time-Life.

Wood Finishing. J. W. Collier. 1967. 147.00 (*0-08-011242-0*, Pub. by Pergamon Repr UK) Franklin.

Wood Finishing & Refinishing. Creative Homeowner Press Editors. Ed. by Marilyn M. Auer. LC 81-69641. (Illus.). 144p. (Orig.). 1982. pap. 9.95 (*0-932944-54-X*) Creative Homeowner.

Wood Finishing & Refinishing. Alan Hall & James Heard. LC 81-4708. (Illus.). 216p. 1982. pap. 9.95 (*0-03-018861-X*, Owl) H Holt & Co.

Wood Fire in Number Three. Francis H. Smith. LC 76-94743. (Short Story Index Reprint Ser.). 1977. 21.95 (*0-8369-3123-8*) Ayer.

Wood-Fired Stoneware & Porcelain. Jack Troy. 192p. 1995. 34.95 (*0-8019-8484-X*) Chilton.

Wood Frame House Building. 1991. 21.95 (*0-8306-5312-0*) McGraw-Hill Prof.

Wood-Frame House Construction. 1991. lib. bdg. 75.00 (*0-8490-4574-6*) Gordon Pr.

Wood Frame House Construction. National Association of Home Builders NAHB Staff. 280p. 1991. pap. 25.50 (*0-8273-4739-1*) Delmar.

Wood-Frame House Construction. Ed. by William Oberschulte. 336p. (Orig.). 1992. pap. 19.75 (*0-934041-74-1*) Craftsman.

Wood Frame House Construction. Gerald E. Sherwood. 1990. pap. 9.95 (*0-486-26401-7*) Dover.

Wood Frame House Construction. (Illus.). 280p. 1992. reprint ed. pap. 18.00 (*0-86718-377-2*) Home Builder.

Wood Fuel in Kano. 140p. 1990. 30.00 (*92-808-0726-9*, 90.III.A.6) UN.

Wood Furniture: Finishing, Refinishing, Repairing. 3rd ed. James E. Brumbaugh. (Illus.). 384p. 1992. 30.00 (*0-02-517871-7*) Macmillan.

Wood Genealogy & Family Sketches: Memoranda of the Wood Family in England & America. Leland N. Wood. (Illus.). 130p. reprint ed. pap. text ed. 25.00 (*0-8328-1657-4*); reprint ed. lib. bdg. 35.00 (*0-8328-1656-6*) Higginson Bk Co.

Wood Handicraft for Pathfinders: A Basic Youth Enrichment Skill Honor Packet. L. S. Gattis, III. (Illus.). 20p. (Orig.). (J). (gr. 5 up). 1987. teacher ed., pap. 5.00 (*0-936241-28-4*) Cheetah Pub.

Wood Heat. Allan A. Swenson. 1980. pap. 2.95 (*0-449-14248-5*, GM) Fawcett.

Wood Homestead. Barbara M. Hegene. (Illus.). 10p. (YA). (gr. 9-12). 1990. pap. 4.00 (*0-9623847-5-5*) B Hegne.

Wood-Hoopoe Willie. Virginia L. Kroll. LC 92-74501. (Illus.). 32p. (J). (ps-4). 1993. 14.95 (*0-88106-409-2*); lib. bdg. 15.88 (*0-88106-410-6*) Charlesbridge Pub.

Wood-Hoopoe Willie. Virginia L. Kroll. LC 92-74501. 32p. (J). (ps-3). 1995. pap. 6.95 (*0-88106-408-4*) Charlesbridge Pub.

Wood in American Life 1776-2076. Wally G. Youngquist & Herbert O. Fleischer. LC 77-85427. 192p. 1977. 11.00 (*0-935018-00-X*) Forest Prod.

***Wood in Our Future: The Role of Life-Cycle Analysis.** 144p. 1997. pap. 34.00 (*0-309-05745-0*) Natl Acad Pr.

An Asterisk (*) at the beginning of an entry indicates that the title is appearing in BIP for the first time.

***Wood, Ink & Paper.** G. Brender a Brandis. 160p. 1980. pap. 9.95 (0-88984-029-6, Pub. by Porcupines Quill CN) Genl Dist Srvs.

Wood Joiner's Handbook. Sam Allen. LC 89-26189. (Illus.). 288p. (Orig.). 1990. pap. 14.95 (0-8069-6999-7) Sterling.

Wood Joints: Step-by-Step Techniques. Anthony Hontoir. (Illus.). 128p. 1992. 39.95 (1-85223-442-3, Pub. by Crowood Pr UK) Trafalgar.

Wood Joints: Step by Step Techniques. Anthony Hontoir. (Illus.). 128p. 1994. pap. 29.95 (1-85223-758-9, Pub. by Crowood Pr UK) Trafalgar.

Wood Lathe Projects for Fun & Profit. Dick Sing & Alison Levie. LC 94-65857. (Illus.). 64p. (Orig.). 1994. pap. 12.95 (0-88740-675-0) Schiffer.

***Wood, Leather & Some Associated Industries: The Evaluation of Carcinogenic Risks to Humans.** 412p. 1981. text ed. 72.00 (92-832-1225-8) World Health.

***Wood Machines.** Zachary Taylor. 1997. write for info. (0-8069-9704-4) Sterling.

Wood Machining Processes. Peter Koch. LC 64-20120. (Wood Processing Ser.). (Illus.). 542p. reprint ed. pap. 154.50 (0-317-10867-0, 2012599) Bks Demand.

Wood Magic. Richard Jefferies. LC 74-82725. (J). 1974. 20.00 (0-89388-177-5) Okpaku Communications.

Wood Mails Process Nineteen Seventy-Five. Feirer. 1987. pap. 15.96 (0-02-666210-8) Macmillan.

***Wood Material Use in the U. S. Furniture & Cabinet Industries, 1993 & 1995: 1993 & 1995.** Eric Hansen et al. LC 96-36807. 50p. 1997. pap. text ed. 350.00 (0-921577-63-X) AKTRIN.

Wood Microbiology: Decay & Its Prevention. Robert A. Zabel & Jeffrey J. Morrell. (Illus.). 476p. 1992. text ed. 89.00 (0-12-775210-2) Acad Pr.

Wood Motifs in American Domestic Architecture see Ornamental Carpentry of Nineteenth-Century American Houses: One Hundred Sixty-Five Photographs

Wood-Notes Wild: Walking with Thoreau. Henry David Thoreau. Ed. by Mary Kullberg. LC 94-33389. (Illus.). 128p. (C). 1995. 19.95 (0-8093-1988-8) S Ill U Pr.

Wood Nymph & the Cranky Saint. C. Dale Brittain. 320p. 1993. mass mkt. 4.99 (0-671-72156-9) Baen Bks.

Wood of Our Own. Julian Evans. (Illus.). 172p. 1995. 32.50 (0-19-854951-2) OUP.

Wood on Wheels: Making Toys That Rock & Roll, Wiggle & Shake. Kevin McGuire. LC 94-37136. (Illus.). 144p. 1995. pap. 16.95 (0-8069-1286-3) Lark Books.

Wood Ornaments & Creche. U-Bild Enterprises Staff. 24p. 1982. pap. 3.50 (0-910495-01-7) U-Bild.

Wood, Paper, Textiles, Plastics & Photographic Materials, 8 vols., Vol. 6. Intro. by John J. McKetta, Jr. (Illus.). 686p. 1973. 68.50 (0-06-491107-1, 06300) B&N Imports.

Wood Pelletization Source Book: A Sample Business Plan for the Potential Pellet Manufacturer. 125p. (Orig.). 1996. pap. text ed. 35.00 (0-7881-2794-2) DIANE Pub.

Wood Polishing & Finishing Techniques. 1995. 5.98 (0-7858-0400-5) Bk Sales Inc.

Wood Preservation. 2nd ed. Barry A. Richardson. LC 92-30664. 1993. write for info. (0-419-17490-7, E & FN Spon) Routledge Chapman & Hall.

Wood Preservation: Pesticide Application Compendium 3. Patrick J. Marer et al. LC 92-63207. (Illus.). 92p. 1992. pap. 15.00 (1-879906-05-8, 3335) ANR Pubns CA.

Wood Preservation in the '90s & Beyond. 256p. 1995. 55.00 (0-935018-74-3, 7308) Forest Prod.

Wood Preservation Manual. FAO Staff. (FAO Forestry Ser.: No. 76). 152p. 1993. 88.00 (81-7089-194-9, Pub. by Intl Bk Distr II) St Mut.

Wood Preserving Industry: Guides to Pollution Prevention. 48p. (Orig.). 1996. pap. text ed. 30.00 (0-7881-2914-7) DIANE Pub.

Wood Product Demand & the Environment. 288p. 1992. 45.00 (0-935018-54-9, 7366) Forest Prod.

Wood Projects, Bk. 1. Hi Sibley. 96p. 1985. 12.40 (0-87006-545-9) Goodheart.

Wood Projects for the Garden. Ron Hildebrand et al. Ed. by Kate Rider. LC 87-70189. (Illus.). Date not set. 14.95 (0-89721-361-0) Ortho Info.

Wood Projects for the Garden. rev. ed. Ron Hildebrand et al. LC 87-70189. (Illus.). 96p. 1987. pap. 9.95 (0-89721-102-2) Meredith Bks.

Wood Projects for the Home. Ortho Books Staff & Ron Hildebrand. LC 80-66343. (Illus.). 96p. (Orig.). 1980. pap. 9.95 (0-917102-85-1) Meredith Bks.

Wood Protection Techniques & the Use of Treated Wood in Construction. 141p. 1988. 55.00 (0-935018-43-3, 7358) Forest Prod.

Wood Protection with Diffusible Preservatives. 143p. 1990. 50.00 (0-935018-49-2, 7355) Forest Prod.

Wood Quality Factors in Loblolly Pine. Robert A. Megraw. 96p. 1985. 50.00 (0-89852-048-7, 0102B048) TAPPI.

Wood Quay: The Clash over Dublin's Viking Past. Thomas F. Heffernan. (Illus.). 199p. 1988. 19.95 (0-292-79042-2) U of Tex Pr.

Wood Rats of Colorado: Distribution & Ecology. Robert B. Finley, Jr. (Museum Ser.: Vol. 10, No. 6). 340p. 1958. 10.00 (0-686-80280-2) U KS Nat Hist Mus.

Wood Repair, Finishing & Refinishing. Allan E. Fitchett. (Illus.). 144p. (Orig.). 1989. pap. 9.95 (0-910432-00-7) A Constantine & Sons.

Wood Residue As an Energy Source. 118p. 1975. 18.00 (0-935018-10-7) Forest Prod.

Wood Rot: Repair & Prevention. George T. Demaree. (Orig.). pap. 15.95 (0-935831-37-1) Tradesman Pub.

Wood-rotting Aphyllophorales of the Southern Appalachian Spruce-fir Forest. Hack S. Jung. (Bibliotheca Mycologica Ser.: Vol. 119). (Illus.). 260p. 1987. pap. text ed. 85.00 (3-443-59020-9) Lubrecht & Cramer.

***Wood Sanding Book: A Guide to Abrasives, Machines & Methods.** Sandor Nagyszalanczy. LC 97-12591. (Illus.). 224p. 1997. pap. 19.95 (1-56158-175-5, 070302) Taunton.

Wood Science Dictionary: English-German, German-English. Peter Muhle. 460p. (ENG & GER.). 1992. 190.00 (0-7859-7067-3) Fr & Eur.

Wood Shafted Golf Club Value Guide for 1995. deluxe limited ed. Peter Georgiady. (Illus.). 235p. (Orig.). 1995. 50.00 (1-886752-01-X) Airlie Hall Pr.

Wood Shafted Golf Club Value Guide for 1996. 2nd rev. ed. Peter Georgiady. (Illus.). 250p. (Orig.). 1996. pap. 25.00 (1-886752-04-4) Airlie Hall Pr.

***Wood Shafted Golf Club Value Guide for 1997-98.** 3rd rev. ed. Peter Georgiady. (Illus.). 300p. 1997. pap. 25.00 (1-886752-07-9) Airlie Hall Pr.

***Wood Songs: A Folksinger's Social Commentary, Cook Manual & Songbook.** Michael Johnathon. (Illus.). 176p. (Orig.). 1997. pap. 16.95 (0-935680-66-7); pap. 24.95 incl. cd-rom (0-9655154-0-0) PoetMan Rec.

Wood Structure & Composition. Ed. by Menachem Lewin & Irving S. Goldstein. (International Fiber Science & Technology Ser.: Vol. 11). 512p. 1991. 225.00 (0-8247-8233-X) Dekker.

Wood Structure & Identification. 2nd ed. Harold Core et al. (C). 1979. pap. 29.95 (0-8156-5043-4) Syracuse U Pr.

Wood Structures: A Design Guide & Commentary. 426p. 1975. pap. 18.00 (0-87262-109-X) Am Soc Civil Eng.

***Wood Tech & Utility Syll.** Krahmer. pap. 11.75 (0-88246-074-9) Oreg St U Bkstrs.

Wood Technology. Glenn E. Baker & L. Dayle Yeager. LC 72-83817. 1974. write for info. (0-672-97507-6); lab manual ed. write for info. (0-672-97107-0) Macmillan.

Wood Technology: Chemical Aspects. Ed. by Irving S. Goldstein. LC 77-2368. (ACS Symposium Ser.: No. 43). 1977. 38.95 (0-8412-0373-3) Am Chemical.

***Wood Technology, Chemical Aspects.** Ed. by Irving S. Goldstein. LC 77-2368. (ACS Symposium Ser.: Vol. 43). 382p. 1977. reprint ed. pap. 108.90 (0-608-03834-2, 2064281) Bks Demand.

Wood Technology in the Design of Structures. Robert J. Hoyle & Frank E. Woeste. LC 88-27694. (Illus.). 402p. (C). 1989. teacher ed. 9.95 (0-8138-1977-6) Iowa St U Pr.

Wood Technology in the Design of Structures. 5th rev. ed. Robert J. Hoyle & Frank E. Woeste. LC 88-27694. (Illus.). 402p. (C). 1989. text ed. 54.95 (0-8138-1975-X) Iowa St U Pr.

Wood that Sings: The Marimba in Chiapas, Mexico. Laurence D. Kaptain. (Illus.). 160p. (Orig.). 1992. pap. 14.00 (0-9634060-0-0) HoneyRock.

Wood Tidal Dynamics. 1993. lib. bdg. write for info. (0-7923-1909-5) Kluwer Ac.

Wood Turning. LC 94-9598. (Art of Woodworking Ser.). 144p. 1994. 19.95 (0-8094-9516-3) Time-Life.

***Wood Turnings for the Garden with Mike Cripps.** Mike Cripps & Jeffrey B. Snyder. LC 96-70409. (Illus.). 64p. (YA). (gr. 10 up). 1997. pap. 12.95 (0-7643-0032-6) Schiffer.

Wood Type Alphabets. Ed. by Rob R. Kelly. LC 77-78607. (Pictorial Archive Ser.). (Illus.). 1977. pap. 6.95 (0-486-23533-5) Dover.

Wood Type Alphabets: 100 Fonts. Ed. by Rob R. Kelly. 1990. 11.75 (0-8446-5590-2) Peter Smith.

Wood Type & Printing Collectibles. Robert P. Long. (Illus.). 1980. pap. 7.95 (0-9600064-0-0) R P Long.

***Wood Utility & Tech Lab Manual.** Krahmer. pap. 5.00 (0-88246-072-2) Oreg St U Bkstrs.

Wood Variation - Its Causes & Control. Bruce J. Zobel. (Wood Science Ser.). (Illus.). 415p. 1989. 251.95 (0-387-50298-X) Spr-Verlag.

Wood Walkers. William Yno. LC 91-67743. 256p. 1993. pap. 10.00 (1-56002-128-4, Univ Edtns) Aegina Pr.

Wood, Water & Light. Benjamin Mendlowitz. Date not set. 50.00 (0-393-03327-9) Norton.

Wood, Water, & Light: A Celebration of Classic Wooden Boats. Photos by Benjamin Mendlowitz. (Illus.). 1989. 100.00 (0-393-03332-5) Norton.

Wood-Water Relations. C. Skarr. (Wood Science Ser.). (Illus.). 470p. 1988. 177.95 (0-387-19258-1) Spr-Verlag.

Wood Wife. Terri Wildling. 320p. 1996. 22.95 (0-312-85988-0) Tor Bks.

***Wood Wife.** Terri Windling. 1997. mass mkt. 6.99 (0-8125-4929-5) Tor Bks.

***Wood Winds.** Allan D. Goldschmidt. (Illus.). 64p. 1996. pap. 10.00 (0-9658368-2-7) Diamond Hitch.

***Wood Works: The Life & Writings of Charles Erskine Scott Wood.** Charles E. Wood et al. LC 97-25047. 1997. write for info. (0-87071-397-3) Oreg St U Pr.

***Woodall's Campground Directories.** Woodalls Publishing Staff. 1997. pap. text ed. 21.95 (0-7627-0147-1) Globe Pequot.

***Woodall's Campground Directory.** Woodalls Publishing Staff. 1997. pap. text ed. 14.95 (0-7627-0149-8) Globe Pequot.

***Woodall's Campground Directory.** Woodalls Publishing Staffx. 1997. pap. text ed. 15.95 (0-7627-0148-X) Globe Pequot.

Woodall's Campground Directory: Western Edition. 706p. 1989. 8.95 (0-318-40977-1) Woodall.

Woodall's Campground Directory, 1989: Eastern Edition. 1160p. 1989. 8.95 (0-318-40976-3) Woodall.

Woodall's Campground Directory, 1989: North American Edition. 1900p. 1989. 13.95 (0-318-40975-5) Woodall.

Woodall's Camping Guide, 1990: Canada. 211p. 1989. 4.95 (0-318-40986-0) Woodall.

Woodall's Camping Guide, 1990: Far West. 211p. 1989. 4.95 (0-318-40983-6) Woodall.

Woodall's Camping Guide, 1990: Frontier West. 211p. 1989. 4.95 (0-318-40984-4) Woodall.

Woodall's Camping Guide, 1990: Great Lakes. 211p. 1989. 4.95 (0-318-40980-1) Woodall.

Woodall's Camping Guide, 1990: Great Plains & Mountain States. 211p. 1989. 4.95 (0-318-40982-8) Woodall.

Woodall's Camping Guide, 1990: Mid-Atlantic. 211p. 1989. 4.95 (0-318-40979-8) Woodall.

Woodall's Camping Guide, 1990: New York & New England. 211p. 1989. 4.95 (0-318-40978-X) Woodall.

Woodall's Camping Guide, 1990: The South. 211p. 1989. 4.95 (0-318-40985-2) Woodall.

Woodall's Campsite Cookbook. pap. 7.95 (0-685-26586-2) Woodall.

***Woodall's 1997 Camping Guide: Mid-Atlantic, Delaware, District of Columbia, Maryland, New Jersey, Pennsylvania, Virginia, West Virginia.** Globe Pequot Press Staff. 338p. 1996. pap. text ed. 5.99 (0-7627-0026-2, East Woods) Globe Pequot.

***Woodall's Plan It-Pack It-Go: Great Places to Tent, Fun Things to Do!** Woodalls Publishing Staff. 1997. pap. text ed. 12.95 (0-7627-0146-3) Globe Pequot.

***Woodall's, Plan-It, Pack-It, Go..., 1997: Great Places to Tent...Fun Things to Do!** Globe Pequot Press Staff. 890p. 1996. pap. text ed. 12.95 (0-7627-0029-7, East Woods) Globe Pequot.

Woodall's RV Owner's Handbook, Vol. 1. pap. 10.95 (0-671-24614-3) Woodall.

Woodall's RV Owner's Handbook, Vol. 2. pap. 10.95 (0-671-25163-5) Woodall.

Woodall's RV Owner's Handbook, Vol. 3. pap. 10.95 (0-671-30913-7) Woodall.

Woodall's Tenting Directory: Central Edition Nineteen Eighty-Six. Ed. by Woodall Staff. write for info. (0-671-61287-5) S&S Trade.

Woodall's Western Campground Directory: Nineteen Eighty-Six Edition. Ed. by Woodall Staff. write for info. (0-671-61289-1) S&S Trade.

***Woodall's 1997 Campground Directory: Eastern.** Globe Pequot Press Staff. 1308p. 1996. pap. text ed. 13.95 (0-7627-0019-X, East Woods) Globe Pequot.

***Woodall's 1997 Campground Directory: North American.** Globe Pequot Press Staff. 2020p. 1996. pap. text ed. 19.95 (0-7627-0018-1, East Woods) Globe Pequot.

***Woodall's 1997 Campground Directory: Western.** Globe Pequot Press Staff. 928p. 1996. pap. text ed. 12.95 (0-7627-0020-3, East Woods) Globe Pequot.

***Woodall's 1997 Camping Guide: Canada All Provinces.** Glope Pequot Press Staff. 1996. pap. text ed. 5.99 (0-7627-0028-9) Globe Pequot.

***Woodall's 1997 Camping Guide: Frontier West, Arkansas, Kansas, Missouri, New Mexico, Oklahoma.** Globe Pequot Press Staff. 1996. pap. text ed. 5.99 (0-7627-0023-8) Globe Pequot.

***Woodall's 1997 Camping Guide: Frontier West, Far West, Alaska, Arizona, California, Idaho, Nevada, Oregon, Washington, British Columbia, Yukon, Mexico.** Globe Pequot Press Staff. 612p. 1996. pap. text ed. 5.99 (0-7627-0025-4, East Woods) Globe Pequot.

***Woodall's 1997 Camping Guide: Great Lakes, Illinois, Indiana, Iowa, Michigan, Minnesota, Ohio, Wisconsin.** Globe Pequot Press Staff. 432p. 1996. pap. text ed. 5.99 (0-7627-0027-0, East Woods) Globe Pequot.

***Woodall's 1997 Camping Guide: Great Plains & Mountain States, Colorado, Montana, Nebraska, ND, SD, Utah, Wyoming.** Globe Pequot Press Staff. 372p. 1996. pap. text ed. 5.99 (0-7627-0024-6, East Woods) Globe Pequot.

***Woodall's 1997 Camping Guide: New York & New England, Connecticut, Maine, Massachusetts.** Globe Pequot Press. 476p. 1996. pap. text ed. 5.99 (0-7627-0021-1, East Woods) Globe Pequot.

***Woodall's 1997 Camping Guide: The South, Alabama, Florida, Georgia, Kentucky, Louisiana, Mississippi, NC, SC, Tennessee.** Globe Pequot Press Staff. 548p. 1996. pap. text ed. 5.99 (0-7627-0022-X, East Woods) Globe Pequot.

***Woodbending.** Zachary Taylor. 1997. write for info. (0-8069-9702-8) Sterling.

Woodbending Handbook. W. C. Stevens & N. Turner. LC 77-94902. (Illus.). 1979. reprint ed. pap. 11.50 (0-918036-06-2) Woodcraft Supply.

Woodberry Forest School. Photos by Dan Dry. (Illus.). 112p. 1990. 40.00 (0-916509-65-6) Harmony Hse Pub.

Woodblock & the Artist: The Life & Work of Shiko Munakata. Shiko Munakata & Kodansha International Staff. (Illus.). 144p. 1992. 35.00 (4-7700-1612-3) Kodansha.

Woodblock Prints & Watercolored Lithographs 1980. Ed Baynard. (Illus.). 40p. 1980. pap. 8.00 (0-614-13067-0) Tyler Graphics Ltd.

Woodbridge & Vicinity: The Story of a New Jersey Township. Joseph W. Dally. 392p. 1989. reprint ed. lib. bdg. 27.50 (0-912606-34-7) Hunterdon Hse.

Woodburn Glen. Stickney. 4.95 (0-686-14959-9) T E Henderson.

Woodburning Stoves. Norbert Duerichen. (Illus.). 112p. pap. 3.99 (0-88839-133-1) Hancock House.

Woodbury: Annals of the Clan. A. K. Woodbury. 102p. 1991. reprint ed. pap. 19.00 (0-8328-2195-0) Higginson Bk Co.

Woodbury & Page: Photographers Java. Steven Wachlin. (Illus.). 219p. 1994. 65.00 (90-6718-070-X, Pub. by KITLV Pr NE) Cellar.

Woodcarver & Death. Hagar Olsson. Tr. by George C. Schoolfield. (Nordic Translation Ser.). 176p. 1965. 17.50 (0-299-03731-2) U of Wis Pr.

Woodcarver's Workbook: Carving Animals with Mary Duke Guldan. Mary D. Guldan. LC 92-37407. 96p. 1992. pap. 14.95 (1-56523-033-7) Fox Chapel Pub.

Woodcarving. (Americana Bks.). (Illus.). 1976. 3.00 (0-911410-41-4) Applied Arts.

Woodcarving: A Complete Course. Ron Butterfield. (Illus.). 128p. 1992. pap. 14.95 (0-946819-04-1, Pub. by Guild Mstr Craftsman UK) Sterling.

Woodcarving: A Manual of Techniques. Reg Parsons. (Illus.). 192p. 1994. pap. 29.95 (1-85223-770-8, Pub. by Crowood Pr UK) Trafalgar.

Woodcarving: Step-by-Step Techniques. Jeremy Williams. (Illus.). 128p. 1994. pap. 29.95 (1-85223-818-6, Pub. by Crowood Pr UK) Trafalgar.

Woodcarving: The Beginner's Guide. William Wheeler & Charles H. Hayward. LC 74-6469. (Home Craftsman Bks.). (Illus.). 128p. 1992. pap. 10.95 (0-8069-8790-1) Sterling.

Woodcarving: 10 Original Projects. Jeremy Williams. (Illus.). 168p. 1996. 35.00 (1-85223-926-3, Pub. by Crowood Pr UK) Trafalgar.

Woodcarving Adventure Movie Caricatures in Wood: 1-2-3 Step-by-Step Techniques. Jim Maxwell. (Illus.). 128p. 1994. pap. 12.95 (1-56523-051-5) Fox Chapel Pub.

***Woodcarving for Beginners.** Woodcarving Magazine Staff. (Illus.). 1997. 14.95 (1-86108-019-0) Sterling.

Woodcarving Illustrated. Roger Schroeder & Paul McCarthy. LC 82-19626. (Illus.). 304p. 1983. pap. 14.95 (0-8117-2271-6) Stackpole.

Woodcarving Illustrated, Bk. 2: Eight Useful Projects You Can Carve Out of Wood. Paul McCarthy & Roger Schroeder. LC 85-10081. (Illus.). 256p. (Orig.). 1985. pap. 12.95 (0-8117-2285-6) Stackpole.

Woodcarving in the Scandinavian Style. Harley Refsal. LC 92-16979. (Illus.). 132p. 1992. pap. 14.95 (0-8069-8633-6) Sterling.

***Woodcarving Magazine on the Woodcarvers.** Guild of Master Craftsman Staff. 1997. pap. text ed. 17.95 (1-86108-038-7, Pub. by Guild Mstr Craftsman UK) Sterling.

Woodcarving Step by Step with Rick Butz: Woodland Warblers. Rick Butz & Ellen Butz. (Woodcarving Step by Step with Rick Butz Ser.). (Illus.). 128p. 1996. pap. 18.95 (0-8117-2990-7) Stackpole.

Woodcarving the Female Head. Bud LaBranche. (Illus.). 60p. (YA). (gr. 8 up). 1986. pap. 8.95 (0-88625-137-0) Durkin Hayes Pub.

Woodcarving Tools, Materials & Equipment. Chris Pye. (Illus.). 362p. 1995. pap. 24.95 (0-946819-49-1) Sterling.

Woodcarving with Peter Berry. Peter Berry. (Illus.). 96p. 1996. pap. 24.95 (0-7134-7541-2, Pub. by Batsford UK) Trafalgar.

Woodchopper's Ball: The Autobiography of Woody Herman. Woody Herman & Stuart Troup. LC 94-2586. (Illus.). 192p. 1994. reprint ed. pap. 14.95 (0-87910-176-8) Limelight Edns.

Woodchuck at Blackberry Road. C. Drew Lamm. (Smithsonian's Backyard Ser.). (Illus.). 32p. (J). (ps-2). 1994. 19.95 incl. audio (1-56899-091-X); 4.95 (1-56899-088-X); 12.95 (1-56899-090-1); audio write for info. (1-56899-092-8) Soundprints.

Woodchuck at Blackberry Road. C. Drew Lamm. (Smithsonian's Backyard Ser.). (Illus.). 32p. (J). (ps-2). 1994. 15.95 (1-56899-087-1) Soundprints.

Woodchuck at Blackberry Road, Incl. toy. C. Drew Lamm. (Smithsonian's Backyard Ser.). (Illus.). 32p. (J). (ps-2). 1994. 32.95 (1-56899-089-8) Soundprints.

Woodchuck Hunter. Paul C. Estey. (Illus.). 136p. 25.00 (1-884849-12-1) R & R Bks.

Woodchucks. Emilie U. Lepthien. LC 91-35276. (New True Bks.). (Illus.). 48p. (J). (gr. k-4). 1992. pap. 5.50 (0-516-41140-3); lib. bdg. 19.00 (0-516-01140-5) Childrens.

Woodchucks. Lynn M. Stone. LC 94-47385. (Wild Animals of the Woods Ser.). (J). (gr. 2-6). 1995. write for info. (1-57103-093-X) Rourke Pr.

Woodchucks & Woodchuck Rifle. Charles S. Landis. (Library Classics Ser.). 402p. 1988. reprint ed. 42.00 (0-935632-62-X) Wolfe Pub Co.

Woodcock. Colin L. McKelvie. (Illus.). 208p. 1992. 35.95 (1-85310-113-3, Pub. by Swan Hill UK) Voyageur Pr.

Woodcock. John A. Knight. (Illus.). 161p. 1989. reprint ed. 21.95 (0-936075-15-5) Gunnerman Pr.

Woodcock Francis Team Development Toolkit. Mike Woodcock & Dave Francis. 200p. 1996. boxed 450.95 (0-566-07645-4, Pub. by Gower UK) Ashgate Pub Co.

Woodcock-Johnson Psycho-Educational Battery: Recommendations & Reports. rev. ed. Nancy Mather & Lynne E. Jaffe. LC 91-75518. 396p. 1992. pap. text ed. 39.50 (0-88422-115-6) Clinical Psych.

Woodcock-Johnson Psycho-Educational Battery-Revised: Recommendations & Reports. Nancy Mather & Lynne Jaffe. LC 96-20245. 1996. pap. text ed. 39.50 (0-471-16210-8) Wiley.

Woodcock Shooting. Steve Smith. LC 88-6061. (Illus.). 144p. 1988. 16.95 (0-8117-1907-3) Stackpole.

Woodcraft. William G. Simms. Ed. by Charles S. Watson. 1986. pap. 18.95 (0-8084-0423-7) NCUP.

Woodcraft. rev. ed. E. H. Kreps. (Illus.). 126p. 1978. pap. 3.00 (0-936622-28-8) A R Harding Pub.

Woodcraft: Or, Hawks about the Dovecot--a Story of the South at Close of the Revolution. rev. ed. William G. Simms. 518p. 1986. reprint ed. pap. text ed. 9.95 (0-8290-2000-4) Irvington.

Woodcraft & Camping. Nessmuk, pseud. (Illus.). 105p. 1963. pap. 3.95 (0-486-21145-2) Dover.

Woodcraft Gift Projects. Donald P. Ouimet. LC 79-15909. (Illus.). 1979. 12.50 (0-8246-0243-9) Jonathan David.

Woodcraft of the World. Ed. by Leonie A. Draper. LC 95-18367. 1995. 29.95 (1-57145-066-1) Thunder Bay CA.

Woodcraft. Or, Hawks about the Dovecot - a Story of the South at Close of the Revolution. rev. ed. William G. Simms. LC 68-20022. (Americans in Fiction Ser.). 518p. reprint ed. lib. bdg. 20.00 (0-8398-1862-9) Irvington.

An Asterisk (*) at the beginning of an entry indicates that the title is appearing in BIP for the first time.

Woodcrafting Heritage Toys: A Treasury of Classic Projects. H. Leroy Marlow. (Illus.). 192p. 1987. 24.95 (*0-8306-7863-8*, 2863) McGraw-Hill Prof.

Woodcut Art of J. J. Lankes. Welford D. Taylor. LC 95-30823. 120p. 1998. 40.00 (*1-56792-049-7*) Godine.

Woodcut Prints of Nineteenth Century Calcutta. Paul Ashit. 1984. 34.00 (*0-317-05024-9*, Pub. by Seagull Bks II) S Asia.

Woodcuts. Nick Sperakis. 1977. 14.95 (*0-918266-09-2*); pap. 3.95 (*0-918266-03-3*) Smyrna.

Woodcuts & Woodblocks of Albrecht Durer. Walter L. Strauss. LC 75-30428. 1980. 115.00 (*0-913870-09-9*) Abaris Bks.

Woodcuts of Harlan Hubbard: From the Collection of Bill Caddell. Ed. by Bill Caddell. LC 94-13331. (Illus.). 192p. 1994. 27.50 (*0-8131-1879-4*) U Pr of Ky.

Woodcutter. Mark Olson. (Chickadee Ser.: No. 4). 1992. pap. 7.00 (*1-55780-117-7*) Juniper Pr WI.

Woodcutter & Nymph. Edward B. Adams. (Korean Folk Story for Children Ser.). (Illus.). 32p. (J). (gr. 3). 1982. 10.95 (*0-8048-1471-6*, Pub. by Seoul Intl Tourist KO) C E Tuttle.

Woodcutter & the Heavenly Maiden/The Fire Dogs. Ed. by Mark Mueller. (Korean Folk Tales for Children Ser.: Vol. 1.). (Illus.). 45p. (J). (gr. 2-5). 1990. lib. bdg. 10.95 (*0-930878-71-X*) Hollym Intl.

Woodcutters. Thomas Bernhard. Tr. by David McLintock from GER. LC 88-26076. iv, 186p. 1989. pap. 13.95 (*0-226-04396-7*) U Ch Pr.

Woodcutter's Mitten: An Old Ukrainian Tale. Loek Koopmans. LC 90-2545. (Illus.). 32p. (J). (ps-2). 1990. 13.95 (*0-940793-67-9*, Crocodile Bks) Interlink Pub.

Woodcutter's Mitten: An Old Ukrainian Tale. Loek Koopmans. LC 90-2545. (Illus.). 32p. (J). (ps-2). 1994. pap. 6.95 (*1-56656-176-0*, Crocodile Bks) Interlink Pub.

Woodcutter's Wisdom & Other Favorite Stories. Max Lucado. 32p. 1995. pap. 2.99 (*0-8499-5214-X*) Word Pub.

***Wooden: A Lifetime of Observations & Reflections on & off the Court.** Jamison. LC 97-564. 1997. write for info. (*0-8092-3041-0*) Contemp Bks.

Wooden & Brick Buildings with Details. A. J. Bicknell. LC 77-363. (Architecture & Decorative Art Ser.). 1977. reprint ed. 95.00 (*0-306-70832-9*) Da Capo.

Wooden Bench: Inkwells, Slates & Coping Saws. Priscilla Tiller. (Illus.). 442p. (Orig.). 1991. pap. 24.00 (*0-9625151-0-8*) Fernwood Pr.

Wooden Biscuit: A Kwanzaa Tale. Mathis. Date not set. write for info. (*0-15-200095-X*) HarBrace.

Wooden Biscuit: A Kwanzaa Tale. Mathis. 1996. pap. write for info. (*0-15-200097-6*) HarBrace.

***Wooden Boat.** Joseph P. Gribbins. (Illus.). 128p. 1996. 27.50 (*1-56799-371-0*, Friedman-Fairfax) M Friedman Pub Grp Inc.

Wooden Boat Renovation: New Life for Old Boats Using Modern Methods. Jim Trefethen. (Illus.). 302p. 1992. 29.95 (*0-87742-366-0*, 60326) Intl Marine.

Wooden Boat Renovation: New Life for Old Boats Using Modern Methods. Jim Trefethen. 1992. text ed. 29.95 (*0-07-065239-2*) McGraw.

Wooden Boats: From Sculls to Yachts. Joseph Gribbins. LC 91-9799. 128p. 1991. 24.95 (*0-8021-1404-0*, Grove) Grove-Atltic.

***Wooden Boats to Build & Use.** John Gardner. (Illus.). 265p. (Orig.). 1996. pap. 29.95 (*0-913372-78-1*) Mystic Seaport.

Wooden Clock Cases. David Bryant. LC 94-46442. (Illus.). 160p. 1995. pap. 17.95 (*0-8117-2597-9*) Stackpole.

Wooden Crafts for Kids. Ellen J. Hobart & Eva Shaw. LC 93-21213. (Illus.). 1994. pap. 8.00 (*0-517-88175-6*, Crown) Crown Pub Group.

Wooden Dish. Edmund Morris. 1956. pap. 5.25 (*0-8222-1276-5*) Dramatists Play.

Wooden Doll. Susan Bonners. (Illus.). (J). (ps-3). 1991. 13.95 (*0-688-08280-7*); lib. bdg. 13.88 (*0-688-08282-3*) Lothrop.

***Wooden Fences.** George Nash. LC 97-18619. (Illus.). 240p. 1997. 29.95 (*1-56158-151-8*, 070280) Taunton.

Wooden Fish Songs. Ruthanne L. McCunn. 1996. pap. 12.95 (*0-452-27346-3*, Plume) NAL-Dutton.

Wooden Gun. large type ed. Bill Morrison. (Linford Western Library). 1995. pap. 15.99 (*0-7089-7769-3*, Linford) Ulverscroft.

Wooden Heart. LaJoyce Martin. LC 91-11965. 235p. (Orig.). 1991. pap. 7.99 (*0-932581-85-4*) Word Aflame.

Wooden Horse. Homer. LC 83-18061. (Tales from the Odyssey Ser.). (Illus.). 32p. (J). (gr. 4-8). 1984. lib. bdg. 13.95 (*0-8167-0057-5*) Troll Communs.

Wooden Horse. Eric Williams. 263p. 1995. 19.95 (*0-563-36901-9*, BBC-Parkwest) Parkwest Pubns.

***Wooden Horseshoe.** Leonard Sanders. (Texas Tradition Ser.: Vol. 24). 400p. 1997. reprint ed. pap. 14.95 (*0-87565-178-X*) Tex Christian.

***Wooden Houses.** Judith Miller. LC 97-8672. (Illus.). 192p. 1997. 45.00 (*1-55670-610-3*) Stewart Tabori & Chang.

Wooden Indian. John Jacob. (Kestrel Chapbks.). 24p. (Orig.). 1987. pap. 3.00 (*0-914974-45-9*) Holmgangers.

Wooden Leg: A Warrior Who Fought Custer. Tr. by Thomas B. Marquis. LC 31-10067. (Illus.). xii, 389p. 1962. pap. 12.00 (*0-8032-5124-6*, Bison Books) U of Nebr Pr.

Wooden Nickels. Gerald Kaminski. LC 93-26244. (Circumstantial Evidence Ser.: Vol. 4). 55p. 1993. pap. 50.00 (*0-931896-11-8*) Cove View.

Wooden Pear. Gillian Plowman. 1992. pap. 3.00 (*0-87129-131-2*, W71) Dramatic Pub.

Wooden Plane: Its History, Form & Function. John M. Whelan. (Illus.). 513p. 1993. 37.50 (*1-879335-32-8*) Astragal Pr.

Wooden Planes in Nineteenth Century America, Vol. II. Kenneth D. Roberts. (Illus.). 472p. 1983. 40.00 (*0-913602-59-0*) K Roberts.

Wooden Puzzle Toys: Patterns & Instructions for Twenty-Four Easy-to-Do Projects. Ed Sibbett, Jr. (Illus.). pap. 3.95 (*0-486-23713-3*) Dover.

Wooden Ritual Artifacts from Chaco Canyon, New Mexico: The Chetro Ketl Collection. R. Gwinn Vivian et al. LC 78-10684. (Contribution of the Chaco Center, Eleven, Anthropological Papers of the University of Arizona: No. 32). (Illus.). 160p. reprint ed. pap. 45.60 (*0-7837-1915-9*, 2042119) Bks Demand.

***Wooden Road Through the Hollow of God's Hand: Taming the American Sahara.** B. Johnny Rube & Yuma County Historical Society Staff. LC 96-48295. 1996. 18.95 (*1-884172-14-8*) Yuma Cnty Hist.

Wooden Ship: The Art, History, & Revival of Wooden Boatbuilding. Peter H. Spectre & David Larkin. (Illus.). 272p. 1991. 50.00 (*0-395-56692-4*) HM.

Wooden Ship-Building. 2nd ed. Charles Desmond. 224p. 1984. reprint ed. pap. 24.95 (*0-911572-37-6*) Madison Bks UPA.

Wooden Ship Building & the Interpretation of Shipwrecks. J. Richard Steffy. LC 93-30036. (Illus.). 328p. 1994. 78.50 (*0-89096-552-8*) Tex A&M Univ Pr.

Wooden Ships - Iron Men: Four Master Mariners of the Colonial South. J. G. Braddock, Sr. LC 96-90295. (Illus.). 304p. 1996. 20.00 (*0-9652705-0-5*) VJB Pr.

Wooden Shoe People. Lloyd C. Hackl. 198p. 1989. pap. 9.95 (*0-934860-53-X*) Adventure Pubns.

***Wooden Spoon Baking Memoir: Apple-Butter Muffins, Shoofly Pie, & Other Amish-Mennonite Favorites.** Marilyn M. Moore. LC 96-47069. 160p. 1997. 22.00 (*0-87113-700-3*, Atlntc Mnthly) Grove-Atltic.

Wooden Spoon Book of Home-Style Soups, Stews, Chowders, Chilis & Gumbos. Marilyn M. Moore. LC 92-4961. 223p. 1993. pap. 13.00 (*0-87113-555-8*, Atlntc Mnthly) Grove-Atltic.

***Wooden Spoon Book of Old Family Recipes: Meat & Potatoes & Other Comfort Foods.** rev. ed. Marilyn M. Moore. 208p. 1997. reprint ed. pap. 12.00 (*0-87113-694-5*, Atlntc Mnthly) Grove-Atltic.

Wooden Spoon Bread Book: The Secrets of Successful Baking. Marilyn M. Moore. LC 86-32180. 1992. pap. 15.00 (*0-87113-505-1*, Atlntc Mnthly) Grove-Atltic.

Wooden Spoon Cookie Book: Favorite Home-Style Recipes from the Wooden Spoon Kitchen. Marilyn M. Moore. LC 94-1256. 160p. 1994. 15.00 (*0-87113-601-5*, Atlntc Mnthly) Grove-Atltic.

Wooden Spoon Dessert Book: The Best You Ever Ate. Marilyn M. Moore. LC 95-993. 304p. 1995. pap. 12.00 (*0-87113-607-4*, Atlntc Mnthly) Grove-Atltic.

Wooden Sword. Lynn Abbey. 1991. mass mkt. 4.99 (*0-441-90866-7*) Ace Bks.

Wooden Teeth & Jelly Beans: The Tupperman Files. Ray Nelson, Jr. et al. Ed. by Michelle Roehm. LC 95-78729. (Flying Rhinocerous Bks.). (Illus.). 61p. (J). (gr. 1-4). 1996. 12.95 (*1-885223-29-3*) Beyond Words Pub.

Wooden Temples of Japan. Peter Popham. (Travel to Landmarks Ser.). 1992. 24.95 (*1-85043-175-2*, Pub. by I B Tauris UK) St Martin.

Wooden Throne. Carlo Sgorlon. Tr. & Intro. by Jessie Bright. LC 87-82244. Orig. Title: Il Trono di Legno. 320p. (Orig.). 1988. pap. 14.50 (*0-934977-08-9*) Italica Pr.

Wooden Toys. Anthony Hontoir. (Woodwork Projects Ser.). (Illus.). 160p. 1993. 34.95 (*1-85223-449-0*, Pub. by Crowood Pr UK) Trafalgar.

Wooden Toys & Crafts. Time-Life Books Editors. LC 94-24187. (Art of Woodworking Ser.). 144p. 1995. 19.95 (*0-8094-9529-5*) Time-Life.

Wooden Toys, Puzzles & Games. Ralph Dorazio & Mary Dorazio. Ed. by Roundtable Press Staff. LC 85-3839. (Illus.). 160p. (Orig.). 1985. pap. 9.95 (*0-932944-77-9*) Creative Homeowner.

Wooden Walls in Action: The History of Ships from 1340 to 1866. F. C. Bowen. 1977. lib. bdg. 69.95 (*0-8490-2841-8*) Gordon Pr.

Wooden World: An Anatomy of the Georgian Navy. N. A. Rodger. (Illus.). 456p. 1996. pap. 14.95 (*0-393-31469-3*, Norton Paperbks) Norton.

WoodenBoat Index: Issues 1-100. Anne Bray. 115p. 1991. pap. 12.95 (*0-937822-22-1*) WoodenBoat Pubns.

WoodenBoat Index Supplement: Issues 101-126, Issues 101-126. Woodenboat Magazine Editors. 38p. 1995. pap. 6.95 (*0-937822-35-3*) WoodenBoat Pubns.

***Woodfiber-Plastic Composites: Virgin & Recycled Wood Fiber & Polymers for Composites.** 266p. (Orig.). 1996. pap. 55.00 (*0-935018-81-6*, 7293) Forest Prod.

Woodfinishing. Den Hatchard. (Step by Step Techniques Ser.). (Illus.). 128p. 1993. 39.95 (*1-85223-582-9*, Pub. by Crowood Pr UK) Trafalgar.

Woodfinishing: Step-by-Step Techniques. Den Hatchard. (Illus.). 128p. 1995. pap. 29.95 (*1-85223-885-2*, Pub. by Crowood Pr UK) Trafalgar.

Woodfinishing Book. Michael Dresdner. 1993. 29.00 (*0-8446-6721-8*) Peter Smith.

Woodfinishing Book. Michael Dresdner. LC 92-14899. (Illus.). 224p. 1992. pap. 24.95 (*1-56158-037-6*) Taunton.

Woodford County, Kentucky Taxpayers, 1790-1799. T.L.C. Genealogy Staff. 85p. (Orig.). 1990. spiral bd., pap. 7.50 (*1-886633-09-6*) TLC Genealogy.

Woodframe Furniture Restoration. 1995. 5.98 (*0-7858-0407-2*) Bk Sales Inc.

***Woodfrogs in Chaos: A 19th Draft Anthology.** Nineteenth Draft Members. Ed. by Danika Dinsmore. (Illus.). 88p. (Orig.). 1996. pap. 7.00 (*1-890051-00-4*) It Plays in Peoria.

Woodgraining, Marbelizing & Glazing & Related Decorating Techniques. Nat Weinstein. (Illus.). 126p. (Orig.). 1987. pap. write for info. (*0-929405-01-3*) Walnut Pub.

Woodholme: A Black Man's Story of Growing up Alone. DeWayne Wickham. (Maryland Paperback Bookshelf Ser.). 290p. (C). 1996. reprint ed. pap. 14.95 (*0-8018-5402-4*) Johns Hopkins.

Woodholme: Growing up Alone. DeWayne Wickham. LC 94-41244. 240p. 1995. 20.00 (*0-374-29283-3*) FS&G.

Woodhouse Poetry Transcripts at Harvard: A Facsimile of the "W2" Notebook, with Variants & Commentary from the "W1" Notebook. 8,810th ed. Intro. & Notes by Jack Stillinger. (Manuscripts of the Younger Romantics: Vol. VI). 480p. 1988. text ed. 171.00 (*0-8240-7021-6*) Garland.

Woodhull Genealogy: The Woodhull Family in England & America. Mary G. Woodhull & Francis B. Stevens. (Illus.). 366p. 1995. reprint ed. pap. 65.00 (*0-8328-4950-2*); reprint ed. lib. bdg. 75.00 (*0-8328-4949-9*) Higginson Bk Co.

Woodland & Wildlife, Vol. 10. Keith Kirby. (Illus.). 128p. text ed., pap. 34.95 (*0-905483-96-0*, Pub. by Whittet Bks UK) Diamond Farm Bk.

Woodland Carol. Helen E. Simcox. Ed. by Jane Weinberger. LC 96-60478. (Illus.). 40p. (J). (gr. 1-5). 1996. boxed 10.95 (*1-883650-30-5*) Windswept Hse.

Woodland Christmas. Marie Angel. (J). 1991. pap. 12.99 (*0-8037-1088-7*) Dial Bks Young.

Woodland Christmas: Twelve Days of Christmas in the North Woods. Illus. by Frances Tyrrell. 32p. (J). (ps-2). 1996. 15.95 (*0-590-86367-3*) Scholastic Inc.

Woodland Conservation & Management. 2nd ed. George Peterken. LC 94-107989. 374p. (gr. 13). 1993. pap. text ed. 52.95 (*0-412-55730-4*) Chapman & Hall.

Woodland Craftsmen. Ivan G. Sparkes. 1989. pap. 25.00 (*0-85263-381-5*, Pub. by Shire UK) St Mut.

Woodland Creatures. Rick Butz & Ellen Butz. LC 95-3762. (Woodcarving Step by Step with Rick Butz Ser.). (Illus.). 128p. 1995. pap. 14.95 (*0-8117-3064-6*) Stackpole.

Woodland Ecology: Environmental Forestry for the Small Owner. 2nd ed. Leon S. Minckler. (Illus.). 230p. 1980. pap. 16.95 (*0-8156-0154-9*) Syracuse U Pr.

Woodland Gang & the Dark Old House. Irene Schultz. (Woodland Gang Ser.). (Illus.). 128p. (J). (gr. 3 up). 1984. pap. 4.95 (*0-318-40971-2*) Addison-Wesley.

Woodland Gang & the Dinosaur Bones. Irene Schultz. (Woodland Gang Ser.). (Illus.). 128p. (J). (gr. 3 up). 1988. pap. 4.95 (*0-201-50056-6*) Addison-Wesley.

Woodland Gang & the Ghost Cat. Irene Schultz. (Woodland Gang Ser.). (Illus.). 128p. (J). (gr. 3 up). 1988. pap. 4.95 (*0-201-50054-X*) Addison-Wesley.

Woodland Gang & the Hidden Jewels. Irene Schultz. (Woodland Gang Ser.). (Illus.). 128p. (J). (gr. 3 up). 1984. pap. 4.95 (*0-685-25362-7*) Addison-Wesley.

Woodland Gang & the Indian Cave. Irene Schultz. (Woodland Gang Ser.). (Illus.). 128p. (J). (gr. 3 up). 1988. pap. 4.95 (*0-201-50055-8*) Addison-Wesley.

Woodland Gang & the Missing Will. Irene Schultz. (Woodland Gang Ser.). (Illus.). 128p. (J). (gr. 3 up). 1984. pap. 4.95 (*0-201-50073-6*) Addison-Wesley.

Woodland Gang & the Museum Robbery. Irene Schultz. (Woodland Gang Ser.). (Illus.). 128p. (Orig.). (J). (gr. 3 up). 1988. pap. 4.95 (*0-201-50053-1*) Addison-Wesley.

Woodland Gang & the Mystery Quilt. Irene Schultz. (Woodland Gang Ser.). (Illus.). 128p. (J). (gr. 3 up). 1988. pap. 4.95 (*0-201-50051-5*) Addison-Wesley.

Woodland Gang & the Old Gold Coins. Irene Schultz. (Woodland Gang Ser.). (Illus.). 128p. (J). (gr. 3 up). 1984. pap. 4.95 (*0-201-50075-2*) Addison-Wesley.

Woodland Gang & the Secret Spy Code. Irene Schultz. (Woodland Gang Ser.). (Illus.). 128p. (Orig.). (J). (gr. 3 up). 1988. pap. 4.95 (*0-201-50052-3*) Addison-Wesley.

Woodland Gang & the Stolen Animals. Irene Schultz. (Woodland Gang Ser.). (Illus.). 128p. (J). (gr. 3 up). 1984. pap. 4.95 (*0-201-50074-4*) Addison-Wesley.

Woodland Gang & the Two Lost Boys. Irene Schultz. (Woodland Gang Ser.). (Illus.). 128p. (J). (gr. 3 up). 1984. pap. 4.95 (*0-201-50072-8*) Addison-Wesley.

Woodland Garden. Robert Gillmore. LC 95-40155. (Illus.). 208p. 1996. 29.95 (*0-87833-924-8*) Taylor Pub.

Woodland Gardens: Shade Gets Chic. Ed. by C. Colston Burrell & Brooklyn Botanic Garden Staff. (21st-Century Gardening Ser.). (Illus.). 120p. 1995. per., pap. 9.95 (*0-945352-90-5*) Bklyn Botanic.

Woodland Gospels: According to Captain Beaky & His Band. Jeremy Lloyd. LC 83-20790. (Illus.). 63p. (J). (gr. k up). 1984. pap. 4.95 (*0-571-14285-0*) Faber & Faber.

Woodland Indians. C. Keith Wilbur. LC 95-3098. (Illustrated Living History Ser.). (Illus.). 128p. (Orig.). 1995. pap. 16.95 (*1-56440-625-3*) Globe Pequot.

***Woodland Indians.** Keith C. Wilbur. LC 96-41643. (Illustrated Living History Ser.). (Illus.). (J). 1996. 19.95 (*0-7910-4527-7*, Am Art Analog) Chelsea Hse.

Woodland Indians: Ready-to-Use Activities & Materials. Dana Newmann. LC 97-25946. 150p. 1997. pap. 17.95 (*0-87628-610-4*) Ctr Appl Res.

Woodland Indians of the Western Great Lakes. Robert E. Ritzenthaler & Pat Ritzenthaler. (Illus.). 160p. (C). 1991. reprint ed. pap. text ed. 9.95 (*0-88133-548-7*) Waveland Pr.

Woodland Park Zoo Guide. Walt Crowley. (Illus.). 112p. (Orig.). 1995. pap. 11.95 (*0-945973-25-X*) Woodland Pk Zoo Soc.

Woodland Peoples: An Educational Unit. Intro. by Nicholas L. Clark. 32p. (Orig.). 1993. pap. write for info. (*0-9623291-6-9*) Minnetrista.

Woodland Period Occupations of the Napoleon Hollow Site in the Lower Illinois Valley. Ed. by Michael D. Wiant & Charles R. McGimsey. LC 86-29875. (Kampsville Archeological Center Research Ser.: No. 6). (Illus.). 650p. 1987. pap. 13.95 (*0-942118-25-1*) Ctr Amer Arche.

Woodland Sites in Nebraska. Marvin F. Kivett. (Publications in Anthropology: No. 1). 102p. 1970. reprint ed. pap. 2.00 (*0-933307-12-8*) Nebraska Hist.

Woodland Steward. 1985. 14.95 (*0-9615031-0-6*) Am Forests.

Woodland Steward: A Practical Guide to the Management of Small Private Forests. 2nd ed. James R. Fazio. (Illus.). 220p. (Orig.). 1985. pap. 14.95 (*0-9615031-1-4*) Woodland ID.

Woodland Stewardship: A Practical Guide for Midwestern Landowners. Melvin J. Baughman et al. pap. write for info. (*0-9623116-6-9*) MES MN.

Woodland Tales. Ernest T. Seton. (Illus.). 235p. (YA). 1994. pap. 14.95 (*1-885529-10-4*) Stevens Pub.

Woodland Trappers: Hare Indians of Northwestern Canada. Harald B. Broch. (Bergen Studies in Social Anthropology: No. 35). 224p. (Orig.). 1987. pap. text ed. 13.95 (*0-936508-68-X*, Pub. by Bergen Univ Dept Social Anthro NO) Barber Pr.

Woodland Trees. Theresa Greenaway. LC 90-37227. (Green World Ser.). (Illus.). 48p. (J). (gr. 5-9). 1990. lib. bdg. 24.26 (*0-8114-2732-3*) Raintree Steck-V.

Woodland Walk. R. C. Johnson. LC 94-67211. (Magic Window Ser.). (Illus.). 14p. (J). 1994. 9.95 (*0-89577-637-5*) RD Assn.

Woodland Whispers: Reflections of Nature & of Love. Lorraine M. Zdeb. LC 90-80148. (Poetry Ser.). (Illus.). 65p. (Orig.). 1990. pap. text ed. 7.96 (*0-9626576-0-3*) L Zdeb.

Woodland Wildflowers. Mary C. Whiston. 1994. 12.95 (*0-533-11160-9*) Vantage.

Woodlanders. Thomas Hardy. Ed. by Dale Kramer. (World's Classics Ser.). 376p. 1985. pap. 5.95 (*0-19-281600-4*) OUP.

***Woodlanders.** Thomas Hardy. 1997. pap. 23.95 (*0-14-086576-4*) Penguin.

Woodlanders. Thomas Hardy. Ed. by James Gibson. (English Library). 464p. 1981. pap. 7.95 (*0-14-043145-4*, Penguin Classics) Viking Penguin.

***Woodlands.** Marylin Lisowski & Robert A. Williams. LC 96-48487. (Exploring Ecosystems Ser.). (J). 1997. lib. bdg. write for info. (*0-531-11345-0*) Watts.

Woodlands. Lynn M. Stone. LC 95-46285. (J). 1996. write for info. (*0-86593-422-3*) Rourke Corp.

Woodlands: Into the Woods. Richard Payne & Drexl Turner. (Illus.). 98p. 1994. 40.00 (*0-9643743-0-7*); pap. 20.00 (*0-9643743-1-5*) Judson Design.

Woodlands: New Community Development, 1964-1983. George T. Morgan, Jr. & John O. King. LC 86-23081. (Illus.). 176p. 1987. 28.95 (*0-89096-306-1*) Tex A&M Univ Pr.

Woodlands & Waterways: Poems from a Reading. Don Fanning et al. Ed. by Kirk Weiss. (Illus.). 50p. (Orig.). pap. 7.95 (*0-9634299-1-4*) Cumberland Ent.

Woodlawn Plantation Cookbook. rev. ed. Ed. by Joan Smith. (Illus.). 260p. 1984. spiral bd. 9.95 (*0-9608708-0-6*) Woodlawn Plant.

Woodlawn Remembers: Cemetery of American History. Edward F. Bergman. 1988. pap. 24.95 (*0-932052-68-1*) North Country.

***Woodleaf Legacy: The Story of a California Gold Rush Town.** Rosemarie Mossinger. (Illus.). 180p. pap. 22.95 (*0-614-26950-4*) C Mautz Pubng.

Woodleaf Legacy: The Story of California Gold Rush Town. rev. ed. Rosemarie Mossinger. Ed. by Jean Chapman. LC 94-77982. (Illus.). 180p. (J). (gr. 5-8). 1995. 34.95 (*0-9621940-3-4*) C Mautz Pubng.

Woodleaf Legacy: The Story of California Gold Rush Town. rev. ed. Rosemarie Mossinger. Ed. by Jean Chapman. LC 94-77982. (Illus.). 180p. (YA). (gr. 5 up). 1995. pap. 22.95 (*0-9621940-4-2*) C Mautz Pubng.

Woodlore. Cameron Miller & Dominique Falla. LC 94-27987. (Illus.). 32p. (J). (gr. k-4). 1995. 14.95 (*0-395-72034-6*) Ticknor & Flds Bks Yng Read.

***Woodlot Management.** Bruno Wiskel. (Illus.). 134p. (Orig.). 1995. pap. 11.95 (*1-55105-067-6*) Lone Pine.

Woodman & Other Poems. William E. Channing, II. (Works of William Ellery Channing II). 1990. reprint ed. lib. bdg. 79.00 (*0-7812-2263-X*) Rprt Serv.

Woodmont Country Club: A Proud Tradition for the Nation's Capital. Rita R. Mhley. LC 88-50441. (Illus.). 168p. 1988. 30.00 (*0-9620503-0-X*) Woodmont Cntry Club.

Woodner Collection Master Drawings: The Metropolitan Museum of Art. 1990. 70.00 (*0-89835-303-3*) Abaris Bks.

Woodner Collection Master Drawings: The Metropolitan Museum of Art. (Illus.). 1990. pap. 70.00 (*0-89835-318-1*) Abaris Bks.

Woodnotes Wild: Essays on the Poetry & Art of Ian Hamilton Finlay. Ed. by Alex Finlay. 216p. (Orig.). 1995. pap. 20.00 (*0-7486-6185-9*, Pub. by Polygon UK) Subterranean Co.

Woodpecker & the Oak Tree. Patrick Haley. LC 82-82991. (Illus.). 64p. (J). (gr. 3-4). 1982. 9.00 (*0-9605738-2-8*) East Eagle.

Woodpecker in a Red Maserati. Jack Merwin. (Firelight Ser.). 64p. (Orig.). 1996. pap. 5.49 (*1-885962-69-X*) Lincoln Lrning.

Woodpecker Point & Other Stories. Carmel Bird. LC 88-1819. 160p. 1988. 19.95 (*0-8112-1072-3*); pap. 9.95 (*0-8112-1073-1*, NDP662) New Directions.

Woodpeckers. Mary A. McDonald. LC 95-46109. (Nature Bks.). 32p. (J). (gr. 2-6). 1996. lib. bdg. 22.79 (*1-56766-218-8*) Childs World.

W

An Asterisk (*) at the beginning of an entry indicates that the title is appearing in BIP for the first time.

Woodpeckers: A Guide to the Woodpeckers of the World. Hans Winkler et al. LC 94-45570. 1995. 40.00 (*0-395-72043-5*) HM.

Woodpeckers of Eastern North America. Lawrence Kilham. Orig. Title: Life History Studies of Woodpeckers of Eastern North America. (Illus.). 256p. 1992. reprint ed. pap. 7.95 (*0-486-27040-8*) Dover.

Woodpeckers of the World. Lester L. Short. 694p. 1982. 99. 95 (*0-913176-05-2*, Tycooly Pub) Weidner & Sons.

Woodrow: Apostle of Freedom. Fred K. Elder. Ed. by Tait Elder. LC 95-62491. xv, 183p. (Orig.). 1996. pap. 14.95 (*0-9653091-1-8*) Bunchberry Pr.

Woodrow Project: A Sexual Abuse Prevention Curriculum for the Developmentally Disabled. Lynn Dreyer & Beth Haseltine. Ed. by Vicki S. Savageau. 86p. 1986. lab manual ed. 99.95 incl. vhs (*0-914633-11-2*) Rape Abuse Crisis.

Woodrow, the White House Mouse. Peter W. Barnes & Cheryl S. Barnes. (Illus.). 32p. (J). (gr. k-6). 1995. 15.95 (*0-9637688-2-4*) Vacation Spot.

Woodrow Wilson. Perry Leavell. (World Leaders - Past & Present Ser.). (Illus.). 112p. (YA). (gr. 5 up). 1987. lib. bdg. 19.95 (*0-87754-557-X*) Chelsea Hse.

Woodrow Wilson. Alice Osinski. LC 88-8678. (Encyclopedia of Presidents Ser.). (Illus.). 100p. (J). (gr. 3 up). 1989. lib. bdg. 22.00 (*0-516-01367-X*) Childrens.

Woodrow Wilson. Sallie Randolph. (Presidential Biography Ser.). 128p. (J). (gr. 6-9). 1992. 14.95 (*0-8027-8143-8*); lib. bdg. 15.85 (*0-8027-8144-6*) Walker & Co.

***Woodrow Wilson.** Anne E. Schraff. LC 97-4372. (United States Presidents Ser.). 1998. write for info. (*0-89490-936-3*) Enslow Pubs.

Woodrow Wilson. Arthur Walworth. (C). 1979. pap. text ed. 10.95 (*0-393-09012-4*) Norton.

***Woodrow Wilson: A Bibliography.** John M. Mulder et al. (Bibliographies of the Presidents of the United States Ser.: Vol. 27). 1997. text ed. write for info. (*0-313-28185-8*, Greenwood Pr) Greenwood.

Woodrow Wilson: A Bibliography of His Times & Presidency. Peter H. Buckingham. LC 89-10966. (Twentieth-Century Presidential Bibliography Ser.). (Illus.). 370p. 1990. 70.00 (*0-8420-2291-0*) Scholarly Res Inc.

Woodrow Wilson: A Life for World Peace. Jan W. Schulte Nordholt. Tr. by Herbert H. Rowen from DUT. (Illus.). 575p. 1991. 35.00 (*0-520-07444-0*) U CA Pr.

Woodrow Wilson: A Medical & Psychological Biography. Edwin A. Weinstein. LC 81-47162. (Papers of Woodrow Wilson). (Illus.). 402p. 1981. suppl. ed., text ed. 62.50 (*0-691-04683-2*) Princeton U Pr.

Woodrow Wilson: An Intimate Memoir. Cary T. Grayson. LC 60-10998. (Illus.). 154p. 1977. reprint ed. 7.50 (*0-87107-038-3*) Potomac.

Woodrow Wilson: Architect of World War II. Murray L. Eiland, III. LC 91-36796. (American University Studies: History: Ser. IX, Vols. 113). 190p. (C). 1992. text ed. 37. 95 (*0-8204-1603-7*) P Lang Pubng.

Woodrow Wilson: Disciple of Revolution. J. C. Wise. 1972. 59.95 (*0-8490-1325-9*) Gordon Pr.

Woodrow Wilson: Life & Letters, 8 vols., Set. Ray S. Baker. (History - United States Ser.). 1992. reprint ed. lib. bdg. 720.00 (*0-7812-6226-7*) Rprt Serv.

Woodrow Wilson: Mini-Play. (President's Choice Ser.). (YA). (gr. 8 up). 1978. 6.50 (*0-89550-315-8*) Stevens & Shea.

Woodrow Wilson: Race, Community & Politics in Las Vegas, 1940s-1980s. Ed. by Jamie Coughtry. (Illus.). 1989. fiche write for info. (*1-56475-345-X*) U NV Oral Hist.

Woodrow Wilson: Race, Community & Politics in Las Vegas, 1940s-1980s. Ed. by Jamie Coughtry. (Illus.). 160p. 1990. lib. bdg. 37.50 (*1-56475-344-1*) U NV Oral Hist.

Woodrow Wilson: Revolution, War, & Peace. Arthur S. Link. LC 79-50909. 152p. (C). 1979. pap. text ed. write for info. (*0-88295-798-8*) Harlan Davidson.

Woodrow Wilson: Some Princeton Memories - George McLean Harper, Robert K. Root, Edward S. Corwin et al. Ed. by William S. Myers. LC 47-266. 101p. 1946. reprint ed. pap. 28.80 (*0-7837-9399-5*, 2060144) Bks Demand.

Woodrow Wilson: The Academic Years. Henry W. Bragdon. LC 67-27081. (Illus.). 536p. reprint ed. pap. 152.80 (*0-7837-4480-3*, 2044188) Bks Demand.

Woodrow Wilson: The Early Years. George C. Osborn. LC 68-13451. 367p. 1968. pap. 104.60 (*0-7837-8507-0*, 2049315) Bks Demand.

Woodrow Wilson: The Years of Preparation. John M. Mulder. LC 77-72128. (Supplementary Volumes to the Papers of Woodrow Wilson). (Illus.). 334p. reprint ed. pap. 95.20 (*0-8357-6548-2*, 2035912) Bks Demand.

Woodrow Wilson: Twenty-Eighth President of the United States. David R. Collins. Ed. by Richard G. Young. LC 88-24563. (Presidents of the United States Ser.). (J). (gr. 5-9). 1989. lib. bdg. 17.26 (*0-944483-18-6*) Garrett Ed Corp.

***Woodrow Wilson: Visionary for Peace.** James T. Rogers. LC 96-3454. (Makers of America Ser.). (J). 1996. write for info. (*0-8160-3396-X*) Facts on File.

Woodrow Wilson & a Revolutionary World, 1913-1921. fac. ed. Ed. by Arthur S. Link. LC 82-2565. (Supplementary Volumes to The Papers of Woodrow Wilson). 249p. 1982. reprint ed. pap. 71.00 (*0-7837-8053-2*, 2047806) Bks Demand.

Woodrow Wilson & Colonel House: A Personality Study. Alexander L. George & Juliette L. George. 1956. pap. 8.95 (*0-486-21144-4*) Dover.

Woodrow Wilson & His Work. William E. Dodd. 1958. 14. 50 (*0-8446-1156-5*) Peter Smith.

Woodrow Wilson & the American Diplomatic Tradition: The Treaty Fight in Perspective. Lloyd E. Ambrosius. 344p. (C). 1990. pap. text ed. 19.95 (*0-521-38585-7*) Cambridge U Pr.

Woodrow Wilson & the Balance of Power. Edward H. Buehrig. 1990. 14.50 (*0-8446-0522-0*) Peter Smith.

Woodrow Wilson & the Death of John Kennedy. Steven Weston. 240p. 1995. pap. 19.95 (*0-9647892-0-5*) Doaks Commun.

Woodrow Wilson & the Politics of Morality. John M. Blum. (Library of American Biography). (C). 1956. pap. text ed. 16.95 (*0-673-39321-6*) Addson-Wesley Educ.

Woodrow Wilson & the Politics of Morality. John M. Blum. (Library of American Biography). 216p. reprint ed. pap. 15.95 (*1-886746-34-6*, 93481) Talman.

Woodrow Wilson & the World Settlement, 2 vols., Each Volume. R. S. Baker. (Illus.). 1958. 14.50 (*0-8446-1039-9*) Peter Smith.

Woodrow Wilson & the World War. Charles Seymour. (History - United States Ser.). 382p. 1992. reprint ed. lib. bdg. 89.00 (*0-7812-6224-0*) Rprt Serv.

Woodrow Wilson & World Politics: America's Response to War & Revolution. N. Gordon Levin, Jr. LC 68-15893. 352p. 1970. pap. 17.95 (*0-19-500803-0*) OUP.

Woodrow Wilson As I Know Him. Joseph P. Tumulty. LC 71-127912. reprint ed. 45.00 (*0-404-06527-9*) AMS Pr.

Woodrow Wilson As I Know Him. Joseph P. Tumulty. (History - United States Ser.). 553p. 1992. reprint ed. lib. bdg. 129.00 (*0-7812-6228-3*) Rprt Serv.

Woodrow Wilson, Franklin D. Roosevelt, Harry S. Truman. Edmund Lindop. LC 95-19526. (Presidents Who Dared Ser.). 64p. (J). (gr. 5-8). 1995. lib. bdg. 15.98 (*0-8050-3403-X*) TFC Bks NY.

Woodrow Wilson, Revolutionary Germany & Peacemaking, 1918-1919: Missionary Diplomacy & the Realities of Power. Klaus Schwabe. Tr. by Rita Kimber & Robert Kimber from GER. LC 84-13073. (Supplementary Volumes to the Papers of Woodrow Wilson). 575p. reprint ed. pap. 163.90 (*0-8357-4408-6*, 2037228) Bks Demand.

Woodrow Wilson's Fourteen Points after Seventy-Five Years. Gaddis Smith. 27p. 1993. pap. 4.00 (*0-87641-123-5*) Carnegie Ethics & Intl Affairs.

***Woodrow Woodchuck.** Victoria Preminger. (Illus.). (J). 1997. write for info. (*0-614-29214-X*, Dove Kids) Dove Audio.

Woodrow's Trumpet: A Novel. Tim McLaurin. LC 93-71404. 250p. 1993. reprint ed. pap. 11.95 (*1-878086-25-1*) Down Home NC.

Woodruff & Lammers Steam Plant Operation. 6th ed. Everett B. Woodruff et al. LC 92-11706. 1992. text ed. 69.95 (*0-07-036109-6*) McGraw.

Woodruff's Firebase. David Celley. 440p. 1995. mass mkt. 6.99 (*1-896329-16-0*, Pub. by Comnwlth Pub CN) Partners Pubs Grp.

***Woods.** Donald M. Silver. (One Small Square Ser.). 1997. pap. text ed. 10.95 (*0-07-057933-4*, Lrning Triangle) McGraw.

Woods. Shrikrishna Alanahally. Tr. by Rajeeve Taranath from KAN. Orig. Title: Kaadu. 112p. 1979. reprint ed. pap. 2.95 (*0-86578-091-9*) Ind-US Inc.

Woods: Bryan Nash Gill. Patrick McCaughey. LC 63-62002. (Illus.). 8p. Date not set. 3.00 (*0-614-10433-5*) W Benton Mus.

***Woods - McAfee Memorial, Containing an Account of John Woods & James McAfee of Ireland, & Their Descendants in America (with Additional Matter bearing on Virginia & Kentucky History, & Many Related Families)** Neander M. Woods. (Illus.). 503p. 1996. reprint ed. pap. 79.00 (*0-8328-5292-9*) Higginson Bk Co.

***Woods - McAfee Memorial, Containing an Account of John Woods & James McAfee of Ireland, & Their Descendants in America (with Additional Matter Bearing on Virginia & Kentucky History, & Many Related Families)** Neander M. Woods. (Illus.). 503p. 1996. reprint ed. lib. bdg. 89.00 (*0-8328-5291-0*) Higginson Bk Co.

Woods - The Store: Metaphors for Healing Fears of Intimacy & Abandonment. Patricia Sheehan & David Hollinden. 1987. audio 9.95 (*1-55982-024-1*, R108) Grt Lks Training.

***Woods Afire: The Memories of a Georgia Teacher Before & After Desegregation.** Ruth B. Crawford. LC 96-26366. 1996. pap. 15.00 (*0-916147-98-3*) Regent Pr.

Woods & Waters. Michael J. Stula. (Illus.). 512p. 1989. 25. 00 (*0-913337-12-9*) Southfarm Pr.

Woods Dual Power: Manual on Woods Automobile. (Illus.). 24p. reprint ed. pap. 2.95 (*0-8466-6019-9*, U19) Shorey.

Woods Family of Groton, Massachusetts: Extract NEHGR. H. E. Woods. 43p. 1994. reprint ed. pap. 8.50 (*0-8328-4183-8*) Higginson Bk Co.

Woods Hole Cantata: Essays on Science & Society. Gerald Weissmann. 252p. 1985. text ed. 19.50 (*0-88167-181-9*) Lppncott-Raven.

Woods Hole Reflections. Ed. by Mary L. Smith. LC 82-62234. (Illus.). 300p. 1983. 34.95 (*0-9611374-0-1*) Woods Hole Hist.

Woods Home. R. M. Schneider. 64p. 1984. text ed. 3.22 (*0-07-055475-7*) McGraw.

Woods Home: Answer Key. R. M. Schneider. 1986. pap. text ed. 1.53 (*0-07-055507-9*) McGraw.

***Woods' Illustrated English-Russian - Russian-English Dictionary of Exploration Geophysics & Caex Terminologies.** Frwd. by Robert E. Sheriff. (Illus.). 503p. (ENG & RUS.). 1997. 130.00 (*0-9642563-4-7*) Albion Woods.

Woods' Illustrated English-Russian Petroleum Technology Dictionary. Ed. by Leonid M. Serednytsky et al. (ENG & RUS.). 1994. 150.00 (*0-9642563-0-4*) Albion Woods.

Woods' Illustrated Petroleum Technology Dictionary, English-Russian/Russian-English. Ed. by Leonid M. Serednytsky et al. (Illus.). 596p. (ENG & RUS.). 1995. 195.00 (*0-9642563-2-0*) Albion Woods.

Woods' Illustrated Petroleum Technology Dictionary, English-Russian/Russian-English Field Ed. Ed. by Leonid M. Serednytsky et al. (Illus.). 596p. (ENG & RUS.). 1995. 195.00 (*0-9642563-3-9*) Albion Woods.

Woods Injurious to Human Health. Bjorn M. Hausen. (Illus.). 189p. 1981. 53.10 (*3-11-008485-6*) De Gruyter.

Woods, Lakeboat, Edmond. David Mamet. LC 86-33489. 288p. 1987. pap. 10.95 (*0-8021-5109-4*, Grove) Grove-Atltic.

Woods Out Back. R. A. Salvatore. 1993. mass mkt. 5.99 (*0-441-90872-1*) Ace Bks.

Woods, Ponds, & Fields. Ellen Doris. LC 93-61889. (Real Kids - Real Science Ser.). (Illus.). 63p. (J). 1994. 16.95 (*0-500-19006-2*) Thames Hudson.

Woods Walkers. John Hoins. LC 94-90164. 272p. (Orig.). 1995. pap. 11.95 (*1-56002-459-3*, Univ Edtns) Aegina Pr.

Woods We Live With. Herbert F. Schiffer & Nancy N. Schiffer. LC 77-92332. (Illus.). 202p. 1977. 24.95 (*0-916838-10-2*) Schiffer.

***Woods Wisdom-Troop Program Features.** rev. ed. Boy Scouts of America Staff. 530p. 1996. pap. 26.50 (*0-8395-4308-5*, 34308) BSA.

Woodsedge. Barbara Knight. 192p. 1987. 15.95 (*0-8027-0956-7*) Walker & Co.

Woodshed Mystery. Gertrude C. Warner. LC 62-19726. (Boxcar Children Mysteries Ser.: No. 7). (Illus.). 128p. (J). (gr. 2-7). 1962. pap. 3.95 (*0-8075-9207-2*); lib. bdg. 13.95 (*0-8075-9206-4*) A Whitman.

Woodshed on the Moon: Thoreau Poems. Robert M. Chute. Ed. by Roy Zarucchi & Carolyn Page. (Chapbook Ser.). (Illus.). 48p. (Orig.). 1991. pap. 9.95 (*1-879205-10-6*) Nightshade Pr.

Woodshop Accessories You Can Make. Edward A. Baldwin. (Illus.). 224p. 1993. 24.95 (*0-8306-2126-1*, 3767); pap. 14.95 (*0-8306-2124-5*, 3767) McGraw-Hill Prof.

Woodshop Dust Control. Sandor Nagyszalanczy. LC 96-10487. (Illus.). 192p. 1996. 19.95 (*1-56158-116-X*) Taunton.

Woodshop, Jigs & Fixtures. Sandor Nagyszalanczy. Ed. by Helen Albert. (Illus.). 240p. (Orig.). 1994. pap. 22.95 (*1-56158-073-2*) Taunton.

Woodshop Tool Maintenance. rev. ed. Beryl M. Cunningham & Wm. Holtrop. (Illus.). 296p. (C). 1974. pap. text ed. 23.96 (*0-02-666280-9*) Glencoe.

Woodside of Yesterday. Brenda L. Gillie. (Illus.). 142p. 1988. 15.00 (*0-9620624-0-5*); pap. 13.00 (*0-9620624-1-3*) B Gillie.

***Woodside, the North End of Newark: Its History, Legends & Ghost Stories Gathered from the Records & the Older Inhabitants Now Living (1909)** C. G. Hine. (Illus.). 308p. 1997. reprint ed. lib. bdg. 38.00 (*0-8328-6081-6*) Higginson Bk Co.

***Woodsie.** Bruce Brooks. LC 97-2048. (Wolfbay Wings Ser.: No. 1). 144p. (J). 1997. pap. 4.50 (*0-06-440597-4*, Trophy) HarpC Child Bks.

***Woodsie.** Bruce Brooks. (Laura Geringer Book Ser.: No. 1). 144p. (J). (gr. 3-7). 1997. lib. bdg. 13.89 (*0-06-027349-6*) HarpC Child Bks.

Woodsman. Don Wright. 416p. 1986. reprint ed. pap. 3.95 (*0-8125-8989-0*) Tor Bks.

***Woodsman Remembers: The Life & Times of James D. Anderson.** James D. Anderson. (Illus.). 158p. (Orig.). 1996. pap. 9.95 (*0-9655356-0-6*, 1) J D Anderson.

***Woodsmen of the West.** M. Allerdale Grainger. 1997. mass mkt. 7.95 (*0-7710-3461-X*) McCland & Stewart.

Woodsmen of the West. Martin A. Grainger. LC 88-24352. (Western Writers Ser.: No. 2). 216p. 1988. 17.95 (*0-940242-35-4*) Fjord Pr.

Woodsmen: or Thoreau & the Indians: A Novel. Arnold Krupat. LC 94-12134. (American Indian Literature & Critical Studies: Vol. 11). 140p. 1994. reprint ed. pap. 9.95 (*0-8061-2671-X*) U of Okla Pr.

Woodsmith, 4 vols., Set. Donald B. Peschke. (Illus.). 2000p. write for info. (*0-9634375-0-X*) August Home.

Woodsmoke: Collected Writings on Ancient Living Skills. Ed. by Linda Jamison. LC 93-48355. 256p. 1994. 24.95 (*0-89732-151-0*); pap. 15.95 (*0-89732-153-7*) Menasha Ridge.

Woodsmoke & Temple Flowers. Jean Falcomer. 216p. (C). 1989. text ed. 70.00 (*1-872795-68-4*, Pub. by Pentland Pr UK) St Mut.

Woodsong. Gary Paulsen. 144p. (YA). (gr. 7 up). 1991. pap. 4.99 (*0-14-034905-7*, Puffin) Puffin Bks.

Woodsong. Gary Paulsen. LC 89-70835. (Illus.). 160p. (YA). (gr. 7 up). 1990. lib. bdg. 16.00 (*0-02-770221-9*, Bradbury S&S) S&S Childrens.

Woodstock. 48p. 1994. pap. 5.95 (*0-7851-0075-X*) Marvel Entmnt.

Woodstock. 1994. 29.95 (*1-57251-049-8*) TWI.

Woodstock. Ed Baker & Art Williams. (Illus.). 144p. 24.95 (*1-55046-013-7*, Pub. by Boston Mills Pr CN) Genl Dist Srvs.

Woodstock: History of an American Town. Alf Evers. LC 86-16461. (Illus.). 750p. 1987. 39.50 (*0-87951-983-5*) Overlook Pr.

Woodstock: History of an American Town. deluxe ed. Alf Evers. LC 86-16461. (Illus.). 750p. 1987. 125.00 (*0-87951-313-6*) Overlook Pr.

Woodstock & Sycamore Traction Company. William E. Robertson. LC 85-4886. (Illus.). 56p. 1985. pap. 10.00 (*0-933449-00-3*) Transport Trails.

Woodstock Craftsman's Manual. Jean Young. LC 76-185655. (Illus.). 488p. 1973. reprint ed. pap. 24.95 (*0-317-00886-2*) J Young Bks.

Woodstock Festival Remembered. Jean Young & Michael B. Lang. (Illus.). 128p. (Orig.). 1985. reprint ed. pap. 19. 95 (*0-345-28003-2*) J Young Bks.

Woodstock Handmade Houses. Robert Haney & David Ballantine. 96p. (Orig.). 1976. mass mkt. 6.95 (*0-345-25592-5*) Ballantine.

Woodstock Nation. Abbie Hoffman. 1993. reprint ed. lib. bdg. 18.95 (*1-56849-104-2*) Buccaneer Bks.

Woodstock: or The Cavalier, 2 vols., Set. Walter Scott. (BCL1-PR English Literature Ser.). 1992. reprint ed. lib. bdg. 150.00 (*0-7812-7643-8*) Rprt Serv.

Woodstock Originals, Vol. III. Byrdcliffe Writers Group Staff. LC 84-151442. 144p. (Orig.). 1990. pap. 7.95 (*0-9625244-0-9*) Byrdcliffe Writers.

Woodstock Originals: From the Byrdcliffe Writers, Vol. IV. Maria Bauer et al. 142p. (Orig.). 1995. pap. 8.95 (*0-9625244-1-7*) Byrdcliffe Writers.

***Woodstock, Sumner & Buckfield Town Register, 1905 (Town Histories & Directories)** Compiled by Mitchell & Davis. 222p. 1997. reprint ed. pap. 26.50 (*0-8328-5933-8*) Higginson Bk Co.

Woodstock Vision. Elliott Landy. (Illus.). 128p. 1994. 39.50 (*0-8264-0663-7*) Continuum.

Woodstock 1969: The First Festival. Elliott Landy. (Illus.). 1994. 39.95 (*0-916290-75-1*); pap. 24.95 (*0-916290-74-3*) Squarebooks.

Woodstock 94 after the Dawn. Eva. 75p. (YA). 1995. pap. 10.00 (*0-9648429-0-4*) Dragon Pr NJ.

Woodston: The Story of a Kansas Country Town. Leo E. Oliva. (Illus.). viii, 237p. (Orig.). 1985. pap. 15.00 (*0-685-66152-0*) Western Bks.

Woodstove Cookery: At Home on the Range. Jane Cooper. LC 77-10640. (Illus.). 208p. 1977. pap. 12.95 (*0-88266-108-6*, Garden Way Pub) Storey Comm Inc.

Woodswoman. Anne La Bastille. 1991. pap. 11.95 (*0-14-015334-9*, Penguin Bks) Viking Penguin.

Woodswoman. Anne LaBastille. 1978. pap. 8.95 (*0-525-48367-5*, Dutton) NAL-Dutton.

***Woodswoman III: Book Three of the Woodswoman's Adventures.** Anne LaBastille. 256p. (Orig.). 1997. pap. 15.00 (*0-9632846-1-4*) W Wind Pubns.

Woodturner. Stockdale. 1987. 30.00 (*0-02-614830-7*) Macmillan.

Woodturner's Bible. enl. rev. ed. Percy W. Blandford. (Illus.). 1986. pap. 16.95 (*0-8306-1954-2*) McGraw-Hill Prof.

Woodturner's Bible. 3rd ed. Percy W. Blandford. (Illus.). 272p. 1990. 26.95 (*0-8306-8404-2*, 3404); pap. 16.95 (*0-8306-3404-5*) McGraw-Hill Prof.

Woodturner's Companion. Ron Roszkiewicz. LC 84-8557. (Illus.). 256p. (Orig.). 1985. pap. 17.95 (*0-8069-7940-2*) Sterling.

Woodturners Wooden Clock Cases. Tim Ashby & Peter Ashby. LC 92-38120. (Illus.). 32p. (Orig.). 1993. pap. 7.95 (*0-941936-23-6*) Linden Pub Fresno.

Woodturners Workbook: An Inspirational & Practical Guide to Designing & Making. Ray Key. (Illus.). 112p. 1993. 29.95 (*0-7134-6667-7*, Pub. by Batsford UK) Trafalgar.

Woodturning. Klaus Pracht. 1989. pap. 22.95 (*0-486-25887-4*) Dover.

Woodturning: A Foundation Course. Keith Rowley. (Illus.). 151p. 1992. pap. 19.95 (*0-946819-20-3*, Pub. by Guild Mstr Craftsman UK) Sterling.

Woodturning: A Guide to Advanced Techniques. Hugh O'Neill. (Illus.). 192p. 1995. 39.95 (*1-85223-836-4*, Pub. by Crowood UK) Trafalgar.

Woodturning: A Manual of Techniques. Hugh O'Neill. (Illus.). 192p. 1993. pap. 29.95 (*1-85223-723-6*, Pub. by Crowood Pr UK) Trafalgar.

Woodturning: A Source Book of Shapes. John Hunnex. (Illus.). 144p. 1993. pap. 16.95 (*0-946819-45-9*, Pub. by Guild Mstr Craftsman UK) Sterling.

Woodturning: Step-by-Step Techniques. Oliver Plant. (Illus.). 128p. 1994. pap. 29.95 (*1-85223-759-7*, Pub. by Crowood Pr UK) Trafalgar.

Woodturning for Cabinetmakers. Michael Dunbar. LC 90-46055. (Illus.). 192p. (Orig.). 1990. pap. 16.95 (*0-8069-6700-5*) Sterling.

Woodturning Jewellery. Hilary Bowen. (Illus.). 160p. 1995. pap. 14.95 (*0-946819-83-1*, Pub. by Guild Mstr Craftsman UK) Sterling.

Woodturning Masterclass. Tony Boase. 144p. 1996. pap. 17.95 (*0-946819-84-X*, Pub. by Guild Mstr Craftsman UK) Sterling.

Woodturning Techniques: The Very Best from Woodturning Magazine. (Illus.). 128p. 1995. pap. 12.95 (*0-946819-75-0*) Sterling.

Woodturning Traditional Folk Toys. Alan Bridgewater & Gill Bridgewater. LC 94-16756. (Illus.). 128p. 1994. pap. 14.95 (*0-8069-8708-1*) Sterling.

Woodturning Wizardry. David Springett. (Illus.). 248p. 1993. pap. 19.95 (*0-946819-38-6*, Pub. by Guild Mstr Craftsman UK) Sterling.

Woodville Long Ago. Martha Lutz & Arthur Lutz. 68p. (J). (gr. 3-7). 1986. pap. write for info. (*0-318-61400-6*) Vimach Assocs.

Woodville Republican: Woodville's Oldest Existing Newspaper, Vol. 3: January 8, 1848-January 9, 1855. Olevia N. Wiese. 327p. (Orig.). 1992. pap. 25.00 (*1-55613-646-3*) Heritage Bk.

Woodville Republican Vol. 5: Mississippi's Oldest Existing Newspaper January 1, 1881-December 22, 1883. O'Levia N. Wiese. 295p. (Orig.). 1996. pap. 26.00 (*0-7884-0452-0*, W349) Heritage Bk.

Woodville Republican, Vol. 1: Mississippi's Oldest Existing Newspaper, Dec. 18, 1823-Dec. 17, 1839. Compiled by O'Levia N. Wiese. (Illus.). 287p. (Orig.). 1990. pap. 21. 50 (*1-55613-365-0*) Heritage Bk.

***Woodward Martyrs.** Myra Friedman. Date not set. write for info. (*0-688-05920-1*) Morrow.

W

Woodward-Woodard Ancestors of New England. Lindsay S. Reeks. LC 95-77604. (Illus.). 234p. 1995. 30.00 (0-9616950-3-X) L S Reeks.

Woodward's Mill: Its History in Deeds, Stories, Pictures & Memories. 2nd rev. ed. Mary O. Pharr. (Illus.). 79p. 1995. pap. 12.00 (0-614-14824-3) Gwinnett Hist.

Woodward's National Architect see Victorian City & Country Houses: Plans & Designs

Woodward's Postgastrectomy Syndrome. 2nd ed. Hocking. (Illus.). 240p. 1991. text ed. 69.00 (0-7216-2209-7) Saunders.

Woodwind Anthology, 2 vols., Set. (Illus.). 1992. 84.00 (0-686-15891-1) Instrumental.

Woodwind, Brass & Percussion Instruments of the Orchestra: A Bibliographic Guide. Allen B. Skei. LC 83-49079. 240p. 1984. text ed. 20.00 (0-8240-9021-7) Garland.

Woodwind Care & Maintenance. R. G. Pellerin. (Illus.). 107p. (Orig.). 1979. 6.00 (0-317-91154-6) Intro Musicaids.

Woodwind Care & Maintenance. R. G. Pellerin. (Illus.). 107p. (Orig.). (C). 1986. teacher ed. 6.50 (0-685-72228-7); pap. 6.50 (0-685-72226-0); pap. text ed. 6.50 (0-685-72227-9) Intro Musicaids.

Woodwind Concertos: Five Solo Concertos for Woodwind Instruments. Ed. by Ernest Warburton. LC 83-48727. (Johann Christian Bach Ser.: Vol. 36). 272p. 1986. text ed. 90.00 (0-8240-6085-7) Garland.

Woodwind Instruments & Their History. Anthony Baines. (Illus.). 384p. reprint ed. pap. 10.95 (0-486-26885-3) Dover.

***Woodwind Music in Print.** Harry B. Peters. LC 97-25679. (Music-in-Print Ser.). 1997. write for info. (0-88478-045-7) Musicdata.

Woodwind Music of Black Composers. Compiled by Aaron Horne. LC 89-25650. (Music Reference Collection: No. 24). 168p. 1990. text ed. 49.95 (0-313-27265-4, HWM/, Greenwood Pr) Greenwood.

Woodwind Quintet 1948: For Flute-Oboe-Clarinet-French Horn-Bassoon. E. Carter. 1986. pap. 18.95 (0-7935-1573-4) H Leonard.

Woodwind Quintet 1948: Score. E. Carter. 24p. 1988. pap. 15.00 (0-7935-1572-6) H Leonard.

Woodwinds. Alyn Shipton. LC 93-20224. (Exploring Music Ser.). (Illus.). 32p. (J). 1993. lib. bdg. 22.83 (0-8114-2319-0) Raintree Steck-V.

Woodwork. Boy Scouts of America. (Illus.). 48p. (YA). (gr. 6-12). 1970. pap. 2.40 (0-8395-3316-0, 33316) BSA.

Woodwork Designing, Constructions & Workshop Practice. 2nd rev. ed. J. Maynard. Ed. by D. Jones. 166p. (C). 1981. reprint ed. 55.00 (0-7175-0696-7, Pub. by S Thornes Pubs UK) St Mut.

Woodwork for Winemakers. C. J. Dart & D. A. Smith. (Illus.). 136p. 1993. reprint ed. pap. 10.95 (0-9619072-4-X) G W Kent.

Woodwork Now. Jeremy Brown. (Illus.). 160p. 1995. pap. 35.00 (0-7134-7269-3, Pub. by Batsford UK) Trafalgar.

Woodwork of Greek Roofs. A. Trevor Hodge. LC 60-51252. (Cambridge Classical Studies). 190p. reprint ed. pap. 54.20 (0-317-26411-7, 2024467) Bks Demand.

Woodworker's Bible. Percy W. Blandford. 1988. 5.99 (0-517-44862-9) Random Hse Value.

Woodworker's Bible. Alf Martensson. LC 79-7355. (Illus.). 1979. 15.95 (0-672-52607-7, Bobbs) Macmillan.

Woodworker's Bible. Alf Martensson. LC 79-7355. 1982. pap. write for info. (0-672-52717-0) Macmillan.

Woodworkers Bible. Alf Martensson. 288p. 1985. pap. 17.95 (0-02-011940-2) Macmillan.

Woodworker's Book of Wooden Kitchen Utensils see Make Your Own Wooden Kitchen Utensils

Woodworker's Book of Wooden Toys. Vance Studley. Orig. Title: The Woodworker's Book of Wooden Toys: How to Make Toys That Whirr, Bob, & Make Musical Sounds. (Illus.). 112p. reprint ed. pap. 6.95 (0-486-26802-0) Dover.

Woodworker's Book of Wooden Toys: How to Make Toys That Whirr, Bob, & Make Musical Sounds see Woodworker's Book of Wooden Toys

Woodworker's Essential Shop Aids & Jigs. Robert Wearing. LC 91-35985. (Illus.). 160p. 1992. pap. 14.95 (0-8069-8584-4) Sterling.

***Woodworker's Guide to Furniture Design.** Garth Graves. LC 96-29573. (Illus.). 208p. 1997. 27.99 (1-55870-437-X, Betrwy Bks) F & W Pubns Inc.

Woodworker's Guide to Making & Using Jigs, Fixtures, & Setups: How to Get the Most from Every Tool in Your Shop. David Schiff & Kenneth S. Burton, Jr. (Illus.). 450p. 1992. 26.95 (0-87596-137-1, 14-084-0) Rodale Pr Inc.

Woodworker's Guide to Master Craftsman Techniques. Woodworker's Journal Magazine Editors. (Illus.). 288p. 1989. 24.95 (0-8306-9061-1, 3061) McGraw-Hill Prof.

Woodworker's Guide to Pricing Your Work. Dan Ramsey. LC 94-33313. 160p. 1995. pap. 18.99 (1-55870-372-1, Betrwy Bks) F & W Pubns Inc.

Woodworker's Guide to Selecting & Milling Wood. Charles R. Self. (Illus.). 144p. (Orig.). 1994. 22.99 (1-55870-339-X, Betrwy Bks) F & W Pubns Inc.

Woodworker's Guide to Wood. David Johnston. (Illus.). 168p. 1996. pap. 35.00 (0-7134-7514-5, Pub. by Batsford UK) Trafalgar.

Woodworker's Handbook. Roger W. Cliffe. LC 89-22019. (Illus.). 496p. 1990. pap. 24.95 (0-8069-7238-6) Sterling.

Woodworker's Illustrated Benchtop Reference. William P. Spence & L. Duane Griffiths. (Illus.). 368p. (Orig.). 1989. 28.95 (0-8306-0377-8) McGraw-Hill Prof.

Woodworker's Jackpot. John A. Nelson. 1991. 24.95 (0-8306-5316-3) McGraw-Hill Prof.

Woodworker's Jackpot: Forty-Nine Step-by-Step Projects. John A. Nelson. (Illus.). 240p. (Orig.). 1989. 22.95 (0-8306-9154-5); pap. 16.95 (0-8306-3154-2) McGraw-Hill Prof.

Woodworker's Marketing Guide. Martin Edic. LC 94-43972. 151p. 1995. 17.95 (1-56158-091-0) Taunton.

Woodworker's Pattern Library: Borders, Trim & Frames for Scroll Saws. Patrick Spielman & Brian Dahlen. LC 95-6901. (Illus.). 128p. 1995. pap. 10.95 (0-8069-0984-6) Sterling.

***Woodworkers Problem Solver: Over 500 Shop Proven Solutions to Your Most Challenging Woodworking Problems.** Ed. by Tony O'Malley. 320p. 1998. 29.95 (0-87596-773-6) Rodale Pr Inc.

Woodworker's Source Book. 2nd ed. Charles R. Self. (Illus.). 160p. 1995. 19.99 (1-55870-391-8, Betrwy Bks) F & W Pubns Inc.

Woodworker's Thirty Best Projects. Woodworker Magazine Editors. (Illus.). 1988. 23.95 (0-8306-0421-9, 3021); pap. 14.95 (0-8306-9321-1) McGraw-Hill Prof.

Woodworker's Thirty-Nine Sure-Fire Projects. Woodworker Magazine Editors. (Illus.). 224p. 1989. 24.95 (0-8306-9051-4, 3051) McGraw-Hill Prof.

***Woodworker's Tool Guide: Getting the Most from Your Hand Tools, Power Tools & Accessories.** Albert Jackson. 1997. pap. text ed. 14.95 (0-8069-0511-5) Sterling.

Woodworker's Visual Handbook: From Standards to Styles, from Tools to Techniques: the Ultimate Guide to Every Phase of Woodworking. LC 94-27654. 1994. 29.95 (0-87596-652-7) Rodale Pr Inc.

Woodworking. Los Angeles Unified School District Staff. LC 77-73286. 96p. (gr. 7-9). 1978. pap. text ed. 5.32 (0-02-820400-X) Glencoe.

Woodworking. McKnight Staff & Wilbur R. Miller. LC 78-53386. (Basic Industrial Arts Ser.). (Illus.). 1978. pap. 7.72 (0-02-672800-1) Glencoe.

Woodworking: The Right Technique: 3 Step-by-Step Methods for Every Job - & How to Choose the One That's Right for You. Bob Moran & Rodale Woodworking Editors. Date not set. 27.95 (0-87596-712-4) Rodale Pr Inc.

Woodworking: Tools, Fabrication, Design, & Manufacturing. Robert Lento. (Illus.). 1979. student ed. 24.95 (0-685-03911-0) P-H.

Woodworking & Cabinetmaking. F. Richard Boller. 400p. 1986. text ed. 18.95 (0-02-512800-0) Macmillan.

Woodworking & Places Nearby. Carol Cox. 1979. pap. 5.00 (0-914610-13-9) Hanging Loose.

Woodworking Basics: The Essential Benchtop Reference. William P. Spence & L. Duane Griffiths. LC 94-46907. (Illus.). 512p. 1995. pap. 19.95 (0-8069-0941-2) Sterling.

Woodworking Factbook: Basic Information on Wood for Wood Carvers, Home Woodshop Craftsmen, Tradesmen & Instructors. Donald G. Coleman. (Illus.). 22.50 (0-8315-0024-7) Speller.

Woodworking for Beginners. R. J. De Cristoforo. 1992. pap. text ed. 19.95 (0-07-013767-6) McGraw.

Woodworking for Beginners. R. J. De Cristoforo. (Illus.). 304p. 1992. pap. 15.95 (0-8306-3829-6, 4117) McGraw-Hill Prof.

***Woodworking for Fun & Profit.** (Illus.). 350p. 1998. pap. 24.95 (1-56559-934-9) HGI Mrktng.

Woodworking for Industry. 1985. 9.32 (0-02-667530-7) Macmillan.

Woodworking for Industry. John L. Feirer. 1979. teacher ed. 4.60 (0-02-666380-5); text ed. 23.72 (0-02-666350-3); student ed. 7.96 (0-02-666360-0) Glencoe.

Woodworking for Industry. John L. Feirer. 1983. text ed. 27.96 (0-02-666390-2) Glencoe.

Woodworking for Kids: Forty Fabulous, Fun & Useful Things for Kids to Me. Kevin McGuire. (Illus.). 144p. (J). 1994. pap. 14.95 (0-8069-0430-5) Sterling.

Woodworking for the Serious Beginner. Pamela Philpott-Jones & Paul McClure. (Illus.). 185p. (Orig.). 1995. pap. 19.95 (0-9643999-2-X, 9992X) Lyons & Burford.

Woodworking for Wildlife: Homes for Birds & Mammals. Carrol L. Henderson. (Illus.). 112p. (Orig.). (C). 1995. pap. 30.00 (0-7881-2319-X) DIANE Pub.

Woodworking for Young Children. Patsy Skeen et al. LC 84-61512. 87p. 1984. pap. text ed. 5.00 (0-912674-85-7, NAEYC #122) Natl Assn Child Ed.

Woodworking Hand Tools Explained. John Nagle. LC 78-730852. 1979. student ed. 6.00 (0-8064-0263-6, 703); audio, vhs 289.00 (0-8064-0264-4) Bergwall.

Woodworking Machine Operator. William Weiss. LC 76-732033. 1977. student ed. 7.00 (0-8064-0261-X, 702); audio, vhs 369.00 (0-8064-0262-8) Bergwall.

Woodworking Machines: The Art of Woodworking. Time-Life Books Editors. 144p. 1992. pap. 19.95 (0-8094-9900-2) Time-Life.

Woodworking Mistakes & Solutions: Professional Secrets for the Home Craftsman. R. J. DeCristoforo. LC 96-24178. (Illus.). 0943788048p. 1996. pap. 19.95 (0-8069-3886-2) Sterling.

Woodworking Projects. LC 84-22194. (Illus.). 96p. (Orig.). 1984. pap. 8.95 (0-937558-12-5) Shopsmith.

Woodworking Projects for the Garden: 40 Fun & Useful Things for Folks Who Garden. Richard Freudenberger. (Illus.). 144p. 1995. pap. 14.95 (0-8069-0803-3) Sterling.

Woodworking Projects for the Home Workshop. Rosario Capotosto. LC 88-16013. (Popular Science Ser.). (Illus.). 416p. (Orig.). 1988. pap. 17.95 (0-8069-6888-5) Sterling.

Woodworking Projects for the Kitchen: 50 Useful, Easy-to-Make Items. Mark Strom & Lee Rankin. LC 93-17314. (Illus.). 152p. 1993. pap. 16.95 (0-8069-0396-1) Sterling.

***Woodworking Projects with a Few Basic Tools.** Michel Theriault. 1997. pap. text ed. 14.95 (0-8069-9469-X) Sterling.

Woodworking Simplified: Foolproof Carpentry Projects for Beginners. David Stiles & Jeanie Stiles. Ed. by Barry Estabrook. (Weekend Project Book Ser.). (Illus.). 152p. 1996. pap. 18.95 (1-881527-98-0) Chapters Pub.

Woodworking Techniques, Tips & Projects from a Master Craftsman. B. William Bigelow. (Illus.). 224p. 1989. 24.95 (0-8306-9255-X) McGraw-Hill Prof.

Woodworking Together: Projects for Kids & Their Families. Alan Bridgewater & Gill Bridgewater. 1992. pap. text ed. 15.95 (0-07-007773-8) McGraw.

Woodworking Together: Projects for Kids & Their Families. Alan Bridgewater & Gill Bridgewater. (Illus.). 200p. 1992. pap. 15.95 (0-8306-2164-4, 3995) McGraw-Hill Prof.

Woodworking Tools. Philip Waler. 1989. pap. 25.00 (0-85263-501-X, Pub. by Shire UK) St Mut.

Woodworking Tools at Shelburne Museum. Frank H. Wildung. (Museum Pamphlet Ser.: No. 3). (Illus.). (Orig.). 1957. pap. 7.50 (0-939384-00-0) Shelburne.

Woodworking with the Router: Professional Router Techniques & Jigs Any Woodworker Can Use. Bill Hylton & Fred Matlack. 1996. pap. 17.95 (0-87596-751-5) Rodale Pr Inc.

Woodworking with Your Kids. rev. ed. Richard Starr. Ed. by Andrew Schultz. (Illus.). 224p. 1990. pap. text ed. 16.95 (0-942391-61-6) Taunton.

Woodworth, from the Old Colony of New Plymouth to Nebraska, 1620-1920: History & Genealogy of the Family of Mildred Woodworth. Gladys S. Adams & L. H. Hoppe. (Illus.). 123p. 1995. reprint ed. lib. bdg. 27.50 (0-8328-4985-5) Higginson Bk Co.

Woodworth, from the Old Colony of New Plymouth to Nebraska, 1620-1920: History & Genealogy of the Family of Mildred Woodworth. L. H. Hoppe. (Illus.). 248p. 1994. reprint ed. lib. bdg. 47.50 (0-8328-4084-X) Higginson Bk Co.

Woodwright's Apprentice: Twenty Favorite Projects from the Woodwright's Shop. Roy Underhill. (C). 1996. 29.95 (0-8078-2304-X) U of NC Pr.

Woodwright's Apprentice: Twenty Favorite Projects from the Woodwright's Shop. Roy Underhill. (C). 1996. pap. 17.95 (0-8078-4612-0) U of NC Pr.

Woodwright's Companion: Exploring Traditional Woodcraft. Roy Underhill. LC 82-10077. (Illus.). xii, 191p. 1983. pap. 16.95 (0-8078-4095-5) U of NC Pr.

Woodwright's Eclectic Workshop. Roy Underhill. LC 91-50258. (Illus.). viii, 238p. (C). 1991. 29.95 (0-8078-2003-2); pap. 16.95 (0-8078-4347-4) U of NC Pr.

Woodwright's Shop: A Practical Guide to Traditional Woodcraft. Roy Underhill. LC 81-2960. (Illus.). ix, 202p. (Orig.). 1981. pap. 14.95 (0-8078-4082-3) U of NC Pr.

Woodwright's Workbook: Further Explorations in Traditional Woodcraft. Roy Underhill. LC 86-50125. (Illus.). viii, 246p. (Orig.). 1986. pap. 16.95 (0-8078-4157-9) U of NC Pr.

***Woody.** Gerald L. Green. (Illus.). 10p. (Orig.). (J). (gr. 1-2). 1997. pap. 8.99 (1-55197-771-0, Pub. by Comnwlth Pub CN) Partners Pubs Grp.

Woody: Movies from Manhattan. Julian Fox. 285p. 1996. 26.95 (0-87951-692-5) Overlook Pr.

Woody Allen. Eric Lax. 1991. 24.00 (0-394-58349-3) Knopf.

Woody Allen: A Biography. Eric Lax. 1992. pap. 13.00 (0-679-73847-9, Vin) Random.

Woody Allen: His Films & Career. Douglas Brode. 1987. 19.95 (0-8065-0959-7, Citadel Pr); pap. 14.95 (0-8065-1067-6, Citadel Pr) Carol Pub Group.

Woody Allen: His Films & Career. Douglas Brode. 1991. pap. 17.95 (0-8065-1259-8, Citadel Pr) Carol Pub Group.

Woody Allen: New Yorker. Graham McCann. 1991. pap. 19.95 (0-7456-0890-6) Blackwell Pubs.

Woody Allen: Profane & Sacred. Richard A. Blake. LC 95-3312. 250p. (YA). 1995. 45.00 (0-8108-2993-2) Scarecrow.

Woody Allen at Work: The Photographs of Brian Hamill. Charles Champlin. LC 94-48322. (Illus.). 192p. 1995. 39.95 (0-8109-1957-5) Abrams.

Woody Allen on Woody Allen. Ed. by Stig Bjorkman. LC 94-26866. (Illus.). 304p. 1995. pap. 12.00 (0-8021-3425-4, Grove) Grove-Atltic.

Woody Allen's Angst: Philosophical Commentaries on His Serious Films. Sander H. Lee. LC 96-37164. (Illus.). 414p. 1997. lib. bdg. 45.00 (0-7864-0207-5) McFarland & Co.

Woody, Be Good! A First Book of Manners. Margo Lundell. (Illus.). 24p. (J). (ps-2). 1988. 3.95 (0-448-09288-3, G&D) Putnam Pub Group.

Woody Brush Control. Ed. by Edward O. Gangstad. 208p. 1989. 169.00 (0-8493-6251-2, SB611) CRC Pr.

Woody, Cisco, & Me: Seamen Three in the Merchant Marine. Jim Longhi. LC 96-25185. (Music In American Life Ser.). 1997. 24.95 (0-252-02276-9) U of Ill Pr.

Woody Discovers a New Kind of Tree: A Storybook to Color. Leigh A. Arrathoon. Ed. by John Davio. (Storybooks to Color Ser.). (Illus.). 48p. (J). (gr. 4-6). 1996. pap. text ed. 3.95 (0-9648564-1-7) Paint Creek Pr Ltd.

Woody Guthrie: American Balladeer. Janelle Yates. LC 94-61354. (Unsung Americans Ser.). (Illus.). 142p. (YA). (gr. 6 up). 1995. pap. 10.95 (0-9623380-5-2); lib. bdg. 14.95 (0-9623380-0-1) Ward Hill Pr.

Woody Gwyn. Peter Sacks. (Illus.). 210p. 1995. text ed. 49.95 (0-89672-344-5) Tex Tech Univ Pr.

Woody Hayes: The Man & His Dynasty. Ed. by Mike Bynum. LC 91-74093. (Illus.). 245p. 1991. text ed. 19.95 (1-878839-02-0) Gridiron Football.

Woody Herman: A Guide to the Big Band Recordings, 1936-1987. Compiled by Dexter Morrill. LC 90-13989. (Discographies Ser.: No. 40). 144p. 1990. text ed. 39.95 (0-313-27756-7, MGJ/, Greenwood Pr) Greenwood.

Woody Herman: Chronicles of the Herds. William Clancy & Audree C. Kenton. 352p. 1995. 27.50 (0-02-870496-7) Schirmer Bks.

Woody Iridaceae: Nivenia, Klattia, & Witsenia - Systematics, Biology, & Evolution. Peter Goldblatt. LC 92-4731. (Illus.). 128p. 1993. 29.95 (0-88192-233-1) Timber.

Woody Jackson Address & Birthday Book. Woody Jackson. 1993. 19.95 (0-88266-870-6, Garden Way Pub) Storey Comm Inc.

Woody, Mia, & Soon-Yi. David W. Felder. 48p. 1995. pap. text ed. 8.95 (0-910959-90-0, B&G 18A) Wellington Pr.

Woody Ornamentals for Deep South Gardens. David J. Rogers & Constance Rogers. (Illus.). 325p. 1991. pap. 17.95 (0-8130-1021-7); lib. bdg. 34.95 (0-8130-1011-X) U Press Fla.

Woody Ornamentals for the Prairies. rev. ed. Hugh Knowles. 1995. pap. text ed. 29.95 (1-55091-025-6) Lone Pine.

Woody Plant Biotechnology. Ed. by M. R. Ahuja. (NATO ASI Series A, Life Sciences: Vol. 210). (Illus.). 366p. 1991. 115.00 (0-306-44019-9, Plenum Pr) Plenum.

Woody Plants: Evolution & Distribution since the Tertiary. Ed. by F. Ehrendorfer. (Illus.). 329p. 1989. 248.95 (0-387-82124-4) Spr-Verlag.

Woody Plants in Agro-Ecosystems of Semi-Arid Regions: With an Emphasis on the Sahelian Countries. Ed. by H. Bremann & J. J. Kessler. (Advanced Series in Agricultural Sciences: Vol. 23). 330p. 1995. 178.00 (0-387-58354-8) Spr-Verlag.

Woody Plants in Winter. Earl L. Core & Nelle P. Ammons. (Illus.). (Orig.). (YA). (gr. 9 up). 1958. pap. text ed. 12.50 (0-910286-02-7) Boxwood.

Woody Plants of Ohio: Trees, Shrubs, & Woody Climbers Native, Naturalized, & Escaped. E. Lucy Braun. 362p. 1989. pap. 27.50 (0-8142-0497-X) Ohio St U Pr.

Woody Plants of Sphagnous Bogs of Northern New England & Adjacent Canada. Fay Hyland & Barbara Hoisington. LC 80-53996. (Illus.). 110p. 1981. reprint ed. pap. 8.95 (0-89101-045-9) U Maine Pr.

Woody Plants of the Southwest. Samuel H. Lamb. LC 76-357696. (Illus.). 1977. pap. 12.95 (0-913270-50-4) Sunstone Pr.

Woody, the Adventurous Tumbleweed. Jim Heisler. (Illus.). 32p. (J). 1995. pap. 6.00 (0-8059-3599-1) Dorrance.

Woody Watches the Masters: Four Great Artists, Bk. 1. Mary L. Jones. (Illus.). 36p. (J). (gr. 3-7). 1985. 4.95 (0-533-05814-7) Vantage.

Woody Watches the Masters, Bk. 2: Four Artists in France. Mary L. Jones. 1986. 4.95 (0-533-06699-9) Vantage.

Woody Watches the Masters, Bk. 3: Early Western Civilization. Mary L. Jones. 1991. 5.95 (0-533-07901-2) Vantage.

Woody Watches the Masters, Bk. 4: American Artists. Mary L. Jones. 1994. 5.95 (0-533-07900-4) Vantage.

***Woody Woodpecker & Friends: A Coloring Book.** Walter Lantz. (Illus.). (J). 1990. pap. text ed. 1.49 (0-448-09342-1) Putnam Pub Group.

Woodys. David Fetherston. (Illus.). 128p. 1995. pap. 19.95 (0-7603-0014-3) Motorbooks Intl.

Woody's Boys: 20 Famous Buckeyes Talk Amongst Themselves. Alan Natali. (Illus.). 528p. 1995. text ed. 35.00 (1-882203-04-6) Orange Frazer.

Woody's First Dictionary. Deborah Kovacs. (Illus.). 24p. (J). (ps-2). 1988. 3.95 (0-448-09287-5, G&D) Putnam Pub Group.

Woof! Allan Ahlberg. LC 86-40009. (Viking Kestrel Illustrated Bks.). (Illus.). 155p. (J). (gr. 3-7). 1986. pap. 11.95 (0-670-80832-6) Viking Child Bks.

Woof! Matthew Margolis. 1995. pap. 12.00 (0-517-88451-8) Random Hse Value.

Woof! My Twenty-Five Years of Training Dogs. Matthew Margolis & Mordecai Siegal. LC 93-40002. 1994. reprint ed. 20.00 (0-517-59148-0, Crown) Crown Pub Group.

Woof, Woof, Dear Lord. Sotiris Dinitriou. Tr. by Leo Marshall. (Modern Greek Writers Ser.). 112p. pap. 9.95 (960-04-0913-7, Pub. by Kedros Pubs GR) Paul & Co Pubs.

***Woofen Poof.** Linnie Moffitt. (Illus.). 24p. (J). (gr. k-3). 1997. pap. 16.00 (0-8059-4210-6) Dorrance.

Wooing a Harsh Mistress: Glenwood Canyon's Highway Odyssey. John L. Haley. (Illus.). 288p. 1994. 39.95 (0-9641046-0-1) Canyon Commun.

Wooing & Winning Business: The Foolproof Formula for Making Persuasive Business. Spring Asher & Wicke Chambers. LC 96-39234. 1996. text ed. 24.95 (0-471-14192-5) Wiley.

Wooing Customers Back: How to Give Great Service & Increase Your Own Success. Mark Holmes. LC 94-79428. 115p. (Orig.). 1995. pap. text ed. 9.95 (0-9643828-0-6) Adv Mark Pub.

Wooing Customers Back: How to Give Great Service & Increase Your Own Success. rev. ed. Mark Holmes. LC 94-79428. 128p. (Orig.). 1995. pap. text ed. 10.95 (0-9643828-1-4) Adv Mark Pub.

***Wooing Wanda, Vol. 30.** Gwen Pemberton. (Love & Laughter Ser.). 1997. mass mkt. 3.50 (0-373-44030-8) Harlequin Bks.

Wool. Annabelle Dixon. Ed. by Rebecca Stefoff. LC 90-40366. (Threads Ser.). (Illus.). 32p. (J). (gr. 3-5). 1990. lib. bdg. 15.93 (0-944483-73-9) Garrett Ed Corp.

***Wool Embroidery.** Ruth Redhead. (Lothian Craft Ser.). (Illus.). 72p. (Orig.). 1997. pap. 16.95 (0-85091-798-0, Pub. by Lothian Pub AT) Seven Hills Bk.

An Asterisk (*) at the beginning of an entry indicates that the title is appearing in BIP for the first time.

Wool Fibers: Ways to Produce, Select, Process, & Spin Them by Hand. Diane F. Betts. LC 94-94302. (Illus.). 186p. (Orig.). 1995. pap. text ed. 24.90 (*0-9647880-1-2*) D F Betts Enter.

Wool-Gathering. Mary A. Dodge. 1977. text ed. 20.95 (*0-8369-9241-5*, 9095) Ayer.

Wool-Hat Boys: Georgia's Populist Party. Barton C. Shaw. LC 83-19982. xi, 231p. 1984. text ed. 32.50 (*0-8071-1148-1*) La State U Pr.

Wool Man. Jekkers. (J). 1998. 11.95 (*0-671-75221-9*, S&S Bks Young Read) S&S Childrens.

***Wool 'n Magic: Creative Uses of Yarn...Knitting, Crochet, Embroidery.** Jan Messent. Ed. by Pam Dawson. (Illus.). 144p. (YA). Date not set. pap. 22.95 (*0-85532-702-2*, 702-2, Pub. by Search Pr UK) A Schwartz & Co.

***Wool Trade Directory of the World.** 6th ed. 1996. pap. 350.00 (*0-614-20933-1*, Pub. by Textile Inst UK) St Mut.

Wool Trade in English Medieval History. Eileen E. Power. LC 86-29442. 136p. 1987. reprint ed. text ed. 55.00 (*0-313-25656-X*, POWT, Greenwood Pr) Greenwood.

Wool Trade in Tudor & Stuart England. Peter J. Bowden. 242p. 1971. 37.50 (*0-7146-1275-8*, Pub. by F Cass Pubs UK) Intl Spec Bk.

Woolen Industry. rev. ed. S. Brearley & I. Tredale. 154p. 1982. 85.00 (*0-686-87180-4*) St Mut.

Woolens & Tweeds. Harriet Tidball. LC 62-698. (Guild Monographs: No. 4). (Illus.). 46p. 1961. pap. 9.95 (*0-916658-04-X*) Shuttle Craft.

Wooley Meets Horatio: The World's Largest Elephant. Anita Ogden & Walker Ogden. (Illus.). 72p. (J). (gr. k-5). 1995. 17.95 (*0-9647159-0-2*) Stage West.

Woolf. Sue Asbee. (Life & Works: Set II). (Illus.). 112p. (YA). (gr. 7 up). 1990. lib. bdg. 19.94 (*0-86593-019-8*); lib. bdg. 14.95 (*0-685-46453-9*) Rourke Corp.

Woolf & Lessing: Breaking the Mold. Ed. by Ruth Saxton & Jean Tobin. LC 94-15015. 1994. text ed. 45.00 (*0-312-12051-6*) St Martin.

Woolf Studies Annual, Vol. I. Ed. by Mark Hussey. 175p. 1995. 59.50 (*0-944473-20-2*) Pace Univ Pr.

Woolf Studies Annual, Vol. I. Ed. by Mark Hussey. 175p. 1995. pap. 24.50 (*0-944473-21-0*) Pace Univ Pr.

Woolf Studies Annual Vol. 2: 1996. Ed. by Mark Hussey. 224p. (Orig.). 1996. pap. text ed. 24.50 (*0-944473-26-1*) Pace Univ Pr.

Woolf Studies Annual Vol. 2: 1996. Ed. by Mark Hussey. (Orig.). 1996. lib. bdg. 59.50 (*0-944473-25-3*) Pace Univ Pr.

***Woolfolk Tragedy: The Murders, the Trials, the Hanging, & Now Finally, the Truth!** Carolyn DeLoach. LC 96-95336. (Illus.). 384p. (Orig.). 1996. pap. 14.95 (*0-9656027-0-2*, TWT.961) Anneewakee River.

Woolgathered & Fitified: A Native American People's Struggle for Identity. Karen Coronado & Richard Mathis. LC 92-50435. 280p. (Orig.). 1994. pap. 12.95 (*1-879360-23-3*) Noble Pr.

Woolgathering. Patti Smith. (Illus.). 80p. (Orig.). 1992. pap. 5.95 (*0-937815-47-0*) Hanuman Bks.

Woollen Carding. Wira Staff. (C). 1968. 125.00 (*0-900820-06-3*, Pub. by British Textile Tech UK) St Mut.

Woollen Industry. B. Brearley & I. Iredale. (C). 1981. 115. 00 (*0-685-46367-2*, Pub. by British Textile Tech UK) St Mut.

Woollen Industry. 2nd ed. Wira Staff. (C). 1977. 125.00 (*0-900820-10-1*, Pub. by British Textile Tech UK) St Mut.

Woollen Ring Spinning: Assessment of Two Modern Frames. Ed. by Wira Staff. 1986. 40.00 (*0-317-43621-X*) St Mut.

***Woollen Yarn Manufacture.** R. T. Richards & A. B. Sykes. (Manual of Textile Technology Ser.). 1994. pap. 63.00 (*1-870812-18-2*, Pub. by Textile Inst UK) St Mut.

Woolly Bear's Sleeping Bag. Beulah A. Thacker. (J). 1994. 7.95 (*0-533-10853-5*) Vantage.

Woolly Mammoth. Wilson. (Dinosaur Library: Set II). (Illus.). 24p. (J). 1984. lib. bdg. 14.00 (*0-86592-203-9*) Rourke Enter.

Woolly Sheep & Hungry Goats. Allan Fowler. LC 92-36366. (Rookie Read-about Science Ser.). (Illus.). 32p. (J). (ps-2). 1993. pap. 3.95 (*0-516-46014-5*); lib. bdg. 17. 30 (*0-516-06014-7*) Childrens.

Woolly Sheep & Hungry Goats Big Book. Allan Fowler. LC 92-36366. (Rookie Read-about Science Big Bks.). (Illus.). 32p. (J). (ps-2). 1993. pap. 32.40 (*0-516-49645-X*) Childrens.

Woolly the Wolf. Tom LaFleur & Gale Brennan. (Illus.). 16p. (Orig.). (J). (gr. k-6). 1981. pap. 1.25 (*0-685-02459-8*) Brennan Bks.

***Woolly White Where Are You?** A. J. Wood. (Illus.). 16p. (J). (ps). 1997. 13.95 (*0-7613-0291-3*) Millbrook Pr.

***Woolly Wizard.** Anke Van De Waal. (Youth Series: Vol. 7). (Illus.). 78p. (Orig.). (J). (ps-1). Date not set. write for info. incl. audio (*0-614-29702-8*, WW1) Holland Pubng.

Woolly Worms & Wombats: A Sidelong Glance at Flyfishing Down Under. Chris Dawson. LC 94-3132. (Illus.). 176p. (Orig.). 1994. pap. 14.95 (*1-55566-121-1*) Johnson Bks.

Woollybear Good-Bye. Sharon P. Denslow. LC 94-10188. 32p. (J). 1994. text ed. 14.95 (*0-02-728687-8*, S&S Bks Young Read) S&S Childrens.

Woolman & Blake: Prophets of Today. Mildred B. Young. LC 72-170018. (Orig.). 1971. pap. 3.00 (*0-87574-177-0*) Pendle Hill.

Woolsey: Family of George Wood Woolsey & Sarah Nelson Woolsey. Hester W. Brewer. 134p. 1994. reprint ed. pap. 22.00 (*0-8328-4165-X*); reprint ed. lib. bdg. 32.00 (*0-8328-4164-1*) Higginson Bk Co.

Woolu Hat. Alexis De Veaux. 1997. 15.00 (*0-517-70099-9*); lib. bdg. 16.99 (*0-517-70100-6*) Random.

Woolworth Building: An American Cathedral. Gail Fenske. (Illus.). 50.00 (*1-878271-45-8*); pap. 34.95 (*1-878271-46-6*) Princeton Arch.

Woolworth Building Renovation: Precast Concrete Used for Terra Cotta Facade. (PCI Journal Reprints Ser.). 16p. 1983. pap. 12.00 (*0-318-19793-6*, JR280) P-PCI.

Wooly & the Giant Snowzos. Phil Baron. (Teddy Ruxpin Adventure Ser.). (Illus.). 34p. (J). (ps). 1987. 9.95 incl. audio (*0-934323-42-9*) Alchemy Comms.

***Wooly Wizard.** Anke Van De Waal. 78p. Date not set. pap. write for info. (*0-614-30058-4*) Holland Pubng.

Woolygoggles & Other Creatures: Problems for Developing Thinking Skills. Thomas C. Obrien. (J). (gr. 4-7). 1992. pap. 9.50 (*0-201-48018-2*) Addison-Wesley.

Woonsocker, RI. Historical Briefs, Inc. Staff. Ed. by Thomas Antonucci & Michael Antonucci. 176p. 1989. pap. 13.95 (*0-89677-004-4*) Hist Briefs.

***Woonsocket, RI.** R. Bellerose. (Images of America Ser.). 1997. pap. 16.99 (*0-7524-0585-3*, Arcdia) Chalford.

Woodles: Stretching Your Imagination. Perla Fox & Deborah Lieberman. LC 95-60661. (Illus.). 32p. (J). (ps-5). 1996. 15.95 (*0-9645887-5-7*) Full Ct Pr MD.

Woordenboek Duits-Neederland: German-Dutch Dictionary. Icarus Van Gelderen et al. 972p. (DUT & GER.). 1981. 39.95 (*0-8288-0456-7*, M 9745) Fr & Eur.

Woorke of the Excellent Philosopher Lucius Annaeus Seneca. Lucius A. Seneca. LC 74-80233. (English Experience Ser.: No. 694). 240p. 1974. reprint ed. 35.00 (*90-221-0694-2*) Walter J Johnson.

Woosh! I Heard a Sound. Emily Hearn. (Annikin Ser.: No. 4). (Illus.). 24p. (Orig.). (J). (ps-1). 1987. pap. 0.99 (*0-920303-21-8*, Pub. by Annick CN) Firefly Bks Ltd.

Wooster: Edward Wooster of Derby, Connecticut, & Some of His Descendants. Donald L. Jacobus. 21p. 1994. reprint ed. pap. 5.50 (*0-8328-4173-0*) Higginson Bk Co.

Wooster: Genealogy of the Woosters in America, Descended from Edward Wooster, of Connecticut. D. Wooster. (Illus.). 139p. 1993. reprint ed. pap. 22.50 (*0-8328-3436-X*); reprint ed. lib. bdg. 32.50 (*0-8328-3435-1*) Higginson Bk Co.

Wooster Group, 1975-1985: Breaking the Rules. David Savran. LC 86-16145. (Theater & Dramatic Studies: No. 39). (Illus.). 256p. reprint ed. pap. 73.00 (*0-8357-1773-9*, 2070486) Bks Demand.

Wooster of the Middle West. Lucy L. Notestein. 1993. reprint ed. lib. bdg. 89.00 (*0-7812-5394-2*) Rprt Serv.

Wooster Proposes, Jeeves Disposes. Kristin Thompson. (Illus.). 1995. 24.95 (*0-87008-139-X*) JAS Heineman.

Wooten, We All Become Forefathers...Genealogies of the Wooten, Boykin, Whitaker & Broadhurst Families. David R. Wooten. 372p. 1993. pap. 49.50 (*0-8328-3213-8*); lib. bdg. 59.50 (*0-8328-3214-6*) Higginson Bk Co.

WOPPLOT 86 Parallel Processing-Logic, Organization, & Technology. Ed. by J. D. Becker & I. Eisele. (Lecture Notes in Computer Science Ser.: Vol. 253). v, 226p. 1987. 33.00 (*0-387-18022-2*) Spr-Verlag.

Worcester: Heart of the Commonwealth. Margaret A. Erskine. 1986. 19.95 (*0-89781-030-9*) Am Historical Pr.

Worcester Account. limited ed. S. N. Behrman. LC 96-60111. 239p. 1996. reprint ed. 25.00 (*0-9636277-8-3*, Tatnuck); reprint ed. pap. 16.95 (*0-9636277-9-1*, Tatnuck) Databks.

Worcester, Add. 68. Ed. by Luther Dittmer. (Veroffentlichungen Mittelalterlicher Musikhandschriften - Publications of Mediaeval Musical Manuscripts Ser.: Vol. 4). (ENG & GER.). 1961. pap. 24.00 (*0-912024-05-4*) Inst Mediaeval Mus.

Worcester College Library see Printing of Mayne's Plays

Worcester County, Mass. Warnings, 1737-1788. Ed. by Francis E. Blake. LC 91-68586. 128p. 1992. reprint ed. 24.50 (*0-929539-99-0*, 1368) Picton Pr.

Worcester, MA. Historical Briefs, Inc. Staff. Ed. by Thomas Antonucci & Michael Antonucci. 176p. 1992. pap. 14.95 (*0-89677-036-2*) Hist Briefs.

Worcester, MA. L. Yeulenski. (Images of America Ser.). 1994. pap. 14.99 (*0-7524-0076-2*, Arcdia) Chalford.

Worcester Mediaeval Harmony of the 13th & 14th Centuries Transcribed. Don A. Hughes. (Illus.). 148p. 1971. reprint ed. 96.20 (*0-685-66481-3*, 05103297) G Olms Pubs.

Worcester Porcelain: Marshall Collection. Dinah Reynolds. (Illus.). 80p. 1995. pap. 17.95 (*0-907849-75-X*, 75XP, Woodstocker Bks) A Schwartz & Co.

Worcester Porcelain: Marshall Collection. Dinah Reynolds. (Illus.). 80p. 1995. 19.95 (*1-85444-040-3*, 75X, Woodstocker Bks) A Schwartz & Co.

Worcester Porcelain: The Klepser Collection. Simon Spero. (Illus.). 224p. 1984. 75.00 (*0-85331-486-1*) A Wofsy Fine Arts.

Worcester Porcelain: The Zorensky Collection. Simon Spero. 1996. 125.00 (*1-85149-228-3*) Antique Collect.

Worcester Porcelain in the Colonial Williamsburg Collection. Samuel M. Clarke. (Wallace Gallery Decorative Arts Publications). (Illus.). 58p. (Orig.). 1987. pap. 9.95 (*0-87935-124-1*) Colonial Williamsburg.

***Worcestershire.** Barry Freeman. 112p. 1996. pap. 35.00 (*0-7478-0311-0*, Pub. by Shire UK) St Mut.

Worcestershire Anglo-Saxon Charter-Bounds. Della Hooke. (Studies in Anglo-Saxon History: No. II). (Illus.). 453p. 1990. 90.00 (*0-85115-276-7*) Boydell & Brewer.

Worcestershire Christmas. David Green. (Illus.). 160p. 1991. pap. 15.00 (*0-86299-930-8*, Pub. by Sutton Pubng UK) Bks Intl VA.

***Worcestershire Railways.** Mike Hitches & Jim Roberts. (Photographic History of Transport Ser.). (Illus.). 128p. 1997. pap. 19.95 (*0-7509-1367-3*, Pub. by Sutton Pubng UK) Bks Intl VA.

***Word.** Sol Goldberg. LC 96-90137. 1996. 12.95 (*0-533-11905-7*) Vantage.

Word: Jewish Wisdom Through Time- A Spiritual Sourcebook. Compiled by Noah BenShea. LC 95-5649. 401p. 1995. 25.00 (*0-679-42584-5*, Villard Bks) Random.

Word: The Bible from Twenty-Six Translations. Ed. by Curtis Vaughan. 2607p. 1991. reprint ed. 69.95 (*0-935491-00-7*); reprint ed. 89.95 (*0-935491-01-5*) Mathis Pubs.

Word: The Dictionary That Reveals the Hebrew Sources of English. Isaac E. Mozeson. LC 95-17239. 320p. 1995. pap. 30.00 (*1-56821-615-7*) Aronson.

Word: The Greater Mysteries of Welsh Witchcraft. Rhuddlwm Gawr. LC 85-73758. (Illus.). 224p. (Orig.). 1989. 20.95 (*0-931760-48-8*, CP 101277); pap. 16.95 (*0-931760-27-5*) Camelot GA.

Word-A-Day Vocabulary Builder. Bergen Evans. 160p. 1982. mass mkt. 4.99 (*0-345-30610-4*) Ballantine.

Word-a-Holic Quiz Book: Guess the Real Words You Won't Believe. Carolyn Davidson. LC 95-9431. 128p. 1995. pap. 5.95 (*0-8069-0702-9*) Sterling.

Word According to James Joyce: Reconstructing Representation. Cordell D. Yee. LC 96-24032. 176p. 1997. 31.50 (*0-8387-5330-2*) Bucknell U Pr.

Word Aflame Press Sunday School Secretary's Record Book: Fifteen Classes. 96p. (Orig.). 1996. pap. 4.99 (*1-56722-140-8*) Word Aflame.

Word Aflame Press Sunday School Teacher's Class Book, No. 1. Word Aflame Press Staff. (Orig.). pap. 1.25 (*1-56722-030-4*) Word Aflame.

Word Aflame Press Sunday School Teacher's Class Book, No. 2. Word Aflame Press Staff. (Orig.). pap. 1.50 (*1-56722-031-2*) Word Aflame.

Word Agriculture Toward 2000. Nikos Alexandratos. (Illus.). 256p. (C). 1988. text ed. 76.00 (*0-8147-0592-8*) NYU Pr.

***Word Amusements.** Ove Ofteness. Date not set. write for info. (*0-8069-9791-5*) Sterling.

Word & Action: Essays on the Ancient Theater. Bernard Knox. LC 79-11277. 368p. 1986. reprint ed. pap. text ed. 15.95 (*0-8018-3409-0*) Johns Hopkins.

Word & Beyond. Harry Smith et al. LC 81-51491. 400p. 1981. 12.95 (*0-912292-71-7*); pap. 5.95 (*0-912292-67-9*) Smith.

***Word & Concept in Thucydides.** June W. Allison. LC 97-16847. (American Classical Studies). 1997. write for info. (*0-7885-0363-4*) Scholars Pr GA.

Word & Deed: German Studies in Honor of Wolfgang F. Michael. Ed. by Thomas E. Ryan & Denes Monostory. LC 91-28432. 296p. (C). 1992. text ed. 69.95 (*0-8204-1101-9*) P Lang Pubng.

Word & Dictionary Puzzles & Games: Kindergarten-First Grade. Kaye Furlong. (Workshop Workbooks Ser.). (Illus.). 64p. (J). (gr. k-1). 1996. wbk. ed., pap. 4.95 (*1-56565-538-9*) Lowell Hse Juvenile.

Word & Dictionary Workbook: First Grade. Kaye Furlong. (Workshop Workbooks Ser.). (Illus.). 64p. (J). 1996. wbk. ed., pap. 4.95 (*1-56565-530-3*) Lowell Hse Juvenile.

Word & Dictionary Workbook: Kindergarten. Kaye Furlong. (Workshop Workbooks Ser.). (Illus.). 64p. (J). 1996. wbk. ed., pap. 4.95 (*1-56565-528-1*) Lowell Hse Juvenile.

***Word & Dictionary Workbook: Second Grade.** Kaye Furlong. (Wordshop Workbooks Ser.). (J). Date not set. pap. 4.95 (*1-56565-578-8*) Contemp Bks.

Word & Drama in Dante: Essays on the Divina Commedia. Ed. by John Barnes & Jennifer Petrie. (Foundation for Italian Studies at University College Dublin). 208p. (C). 1993. text ed. 39.50 (*0-7165-2488-0*, Pub. by Irish Acad Pr IE) Intl Spec Bk.

Word & Eucharist Handbook. rev. ed. Lawrence J. Johnson. LC 86-60896. 168p. (C). 1993. pap. text ed. 11. 95 (*0-89390-276-4*) Resource Pubns.

Word & Figure: The Language of Nineteenth-Century French Poetry. Carol D. Rifelj. LC 87-1504. 206p. 1987. 47.50 (*0-8142-0422-8*) Ohio St U Pr.

Word & Image: French Painting of the Ancient Regime. Norman Bryson. LC 81-10124. 304p. 1983. pap. text ed. 26.95 (*0-521-27654-3*) Cambridge U Pr.

Word & Image in Arthurian Literature: The Arthurian Yearbook. Ed. by Keith Busby. LC 96-2769. 400p. 1996. text ed. 75.00 (*0-8153-2050-7*) Garland.

Word & Image in Maya Culture: Explorations in Language, Writing, & Representation. Ed. by William F. Hanks & Don S. Rice. LC 89-14817. (Illus.). 384p. (C). 1990. text ed. 45.00 (*0-87480-314-4*) U of Utah Pr.

Word & Information Processing. Betsy Walls & Mary A. Flynn. (C). 1984. pap. text ed. write for info. (*0-8359-8786-8*, Reston) P-H.

Word & Information Processing: Concepts of Office Automation. 3rd ed. Marly Bererud & Jean Gonzalez. 578p. 1987. text ed. 31.95 (*0-471-84504-3*) P-H.

Word & Information Processing on Microcomputers: Systems & Procedures. Dennis P. Curtin. (Illus.). 352p. (C). 1988. pap. text ed. 65.00 (*0-13-964206-4*) P-H.

Word & Language see Selected Writings

Word & Light: Seeing, Hearing, & Religious Discourse. David Chidester. 184p. 1992. text ed. 29.95 (*0-252-01863-X*) U of Ill Pr.

Word & Object. Willard V. Quine. 1964. pap. 16.00 (*0-262-67001-1*) MIT Pr.

Word & Object in Husserl, Frege, & Russell: The Roots of Twentieth-Century Philosophy. Claire O. Hill. LC 91-3291. (Series in Continental Thought: Vol. 17). 232p. (C). 1991. text ed. 34.95 (*0-8214-1002-4*) Ohio U Pr.

Word & Picture: A Study of the Double Talent in Alfred Kubin & Fritz von Herzmanovsky-Orlando. Gabriele Van Zon. LC 91-15731. (Studies in European Thought: Vol. 2). 292p. 1992. 44.95 (*0-8204-1475-1*) P Lang Pubng.

Word & Presence: A Commentary on Deuteronomy. Ian Cairns. (International Theological Commentary Ser.). xii, 310p. (Orig.). 1992. pap. 19.00 (*0-8028-0160-9*) Eerdmans.

Word & Silence: Hans Urs von Balthasar & the Spiritual Encounter Between East & West. Raymond Gawronski. LC 95-25438. 247p. 1996. 35.00 (*0-8028-3810-3*) Eerdmans.

Word & Silence: Reflections on Jesus & Socrates. Paul W. Gooch. LC 96-15792. 1997. write for info. (*0-300-06695-3*) Yale U Pr.

Word & Spirit: A Kierkegaardian Critique of the Modern Age. Ronald L. Hall. LC 92-14596. 244p. (C). 1993. 29. 95 (*0-253-32752-0*) Ind U Pr.

Word & Spirit: Calvin's Doctrine of Biblical Authority. H. Jackson Forstman. viii, 178p. 1962. 29.50 (*0-8047-0070-2*) Stanford U Pr.

Word & Spirit No. 2: In Honor of St. Benedict & Scholastica. 166p. 1980. pap. 6.00 (*0-932506-09-7*) St Bedes Pubns.

Word & Spirit No. 7: St. Bede: A Tribute. 132p. (Orig.). 1985. pap. 7.00 (*0-932506-37-2*) St Bedes Pubns.

Word & Spirit No. 9: St. Augustine. LC 87-9712. (Word & Spirit: A Monastic Review Ser.). 157p. (Orig.). 1987. pap. 7.00 (*0-932506-54-2*) St Bedes Pubns.

Word & Spirit No. 11: Women in Monasticism. (Word & Spirit: A Monastic Review Ser.). 127p. (Orig.). 1989. pap. 8.00 (*0-932506-71-2*) St Bedes Pubns.

Word & Spirit No. 16: The Monastery & the City. Joel Letellier et al. (Word & Spirit Ser.). 160p. (Orig.). 1994. pap. 8.00 (*1-879007-10-X*) St Bedes Pubns.

Word & Spirit at Play: Towards a Charismatic Theology. Jean-Jacques Suurmond. Tr. by John Bowden from DUT. LC 94-46258. 1995. pap. 20.00 (*0-8028-4070-1*) Eerdmans.

Word & Story in C. S. Lewis. Ed. by Peter J. Schakel & Charles A. Huttar. 328p. (C). 1991. text ed. 37.50 (*0-8262-0760-X*) U of Mo Pr.

Word & the Christ: An Essay in Analytic Christology. Richard L. Sturch. 304p. 1991. 85.00 (*0-19-826198-5*) OUP.

Word & the Doctrine. Kenneth E. Geiger. 1989. pap. 18.99 (*0-88019-255-0*) Schmul Pub Co.

Word & the Idea, French-Portuguese-French: Le Mot et l'Idee; Francais-Portugais-Francais. Jacques Fournier. 120p. (FRE & POR.). 1983. pap. 14.95 (*0-8288-1633-6*, M6256) Fr & Eur.

Word & the Law. Milner S. Ball. LC 92-28701. 224p. (C). 1993. 29.95 (*0-226-03625-1*) U Ch Pr.

Word & the Law. Milner S. Ball. viii, 224p. 1995. pap. text ed. 14.95 (*0-226-03627-8*) U Ch Pr.

Word & the Mirror: Critical Essays on the Poetry of Luis Cernuda. Ed. by Salvador Jimenez-Fajardo. LC 87-46418. 248p. 1989. 37.50 (*0-8386-3334-X*) Fairleigh Dickinson.

Word & the World: Explorations in the Form of Sociological Analysis. Michael Mulkay. 240p. (C). 1985. text ed. 49.95 (*0-04-301196-9*); pap. text ed. 19.95 (*0-04-301197-7*) Routledge Chapman & Hall.

***Word & the World: Reformed Theology in America.** James W. Van Hoeven. (Historical Series of the Reformed Church in America: No. 16). 189p. pap. 11.00 (*0-8028-0246-X*) Eerdmans.

Word & Verbal Art: Selected Essays by Jan Mukarovsky. Jan Mukarovsky. Ed. by John Burbank & Peter Steiner. Tr. by Peter Steiner. LC 76-49733. (Yale Russian & East European Studies: No. 13). 256p. reprint ed. pap. 73.00 (*0-8357-8378-2*, 2033837) Bks Demand.

Word & Way of the Cross: Christian Witness among Muslim & Buddhist People. Mark W. Thomsen. 180p. 1993. pap. 5.95 (*0-9636630-0-3*) Evang Luth Church.

Word & Work in the Poetry of Juan Ramon Jimenez. Mervyn Coke-Enguidanos. (Monagrafias A Ser.: Vol. LXXXVIII). 157p. (C). 1982. 45.00 (*0-7293-0139-7*, Pub. by Tamesis Bks Ltd UK) Boydell & Brewer.

Word & World of Discovery. Gerald Garmon et al. 152p. (Orig.). 1994. per., pap. text ed. write for info. (*1-883199-05-0*) W GA College.

***Word & Worship Workbook for Year C: For Ministry in Initiation, Preaching, Religious Education & Formation.** Mary Birmingham. LC 97-22382. 1997. write for info. (*0-8091-3747-X*) Paulist Pr.

***Word & You: A Lectionary-Based Exploration of the Bible.** Ed. by Nan Duerling. LC 97-16314. 248p. (Orig.). 1997. pap. 14.95 (*0-8298-1165-6*) Pilgrim OH.

***Word Annoyances.** Leonhard & Hudspeth. Ed. by Ron Petrusha. (Illus.). (Orig.). 1997. pap. write for info. (*1-56592-308-1*) OReilly & Assocs.

Word As Action: Racine, Rhetoric, & Theatrical Language. Michael Hawcroft. (Oxford Modern Languages & Literature Monographs). 285p. 1992. 69.00 (*0-19-815185-3*) OUP.

Word As Image: The Art of Chinese Seal Engraving. Jason C. Kuo. LC 92-73978. (Illus.). 104p. 1993. pap. 28.00 (*0-295-97253-X*) U of Wash Pr.

***Word As True Myth.** Gary Dorrien. 1997. pap. text ed. 23.00 (*0-664-25745-3*) Westminster John Knox.

***Word Associations of Young Children.** Doris R. Entwisle. LC 66-14374. 613p. 1966. reprint ed. pap. 174.80 (*0-608-04056-8*, 2064792) Bks Demand.

***Word at Hand: With a Selection of Poems.** Lorand Gaspar & Roger Little. 152p. 9500. pap. 15.95 (*1-873790-76-7*) Dufour.

Word at Work from A to Z: A Handbook for Writers & Editors. Marion Van Horne. LC 91-18825. 174p. 1993. pap. 8.95 (*1-55513-532-3*, 44727) Cook Min Intl.

Word at World's End. Francis Brabazon. 88p. 1971. 8.95 (*0-940700-04-2*); pap. 4.95 (*0-940700-03-4*) Meher Baba Info.

W

*__Word Attack Skills (Language)__ Phyllis Edwards. (Reading & Writing Ser.). (Illus.). 32p. (J). (gr. 4-6). 1996. teacher ed., pap. 2.95 (*1-55799-416-1*, 4018) Evan-Moor Corp.

Word Banks, Bulletin Boards & More. Linda Milliken. (Illus.). 112p. 1993. pap. 10.95 (*1-56472-016-0*) Edupress.

Word Basic Example Book. Larry Smith. (Programmer's Example Ser.). 904p. 1996. pap. 39.95 incl. disk (*1-55622-475-3*) Wordware Pub.

Word Became Flesh: A Contemporary Incarnational Christology. Millard J. Erickson. LC 91-24728. 670p. (C). 1996. pap. 24.99 (*0-8010-2063-8*) Baker Bks.

Word Becomes Flesh: Dimensions of Christology. Brian C. McDermott. (New Theology Studies). 302p. (Orig.). 1993. pap. 19.95 (*0-8146-5015-5*, M Glazier) Liturgical Pr.

*__Word Behind Bars & the Paradox of Exile.__ Kofi Anyidoho. LC 97-16003. 1997. write for info. (*0-8101-1392-9*); pap. write for info. (*0-8101-1393-7*) Northwestern U Pr.

Word Bending with Aunt Sarah. Alvin Westcott. LC 68-56821. (Illus.). 48p. (J). (gr. 2-3). 1968. lib. bdg. 9.95 (*0-87783-052-5*) Oddo.

Word Bending with Aunt Sarah. deluxe ed. Alvin Westcott. LC 68-56821. (Illus.). 48p. (J). (gr. 2-3). 1968. pap. 3.94 (*0-87783-118-1*) Oddo.

Word Biblical Commentary: Jude II Peter. Richard J. Bauckham. (Biblical Commentary Ser.: Vol. 50). 1983. 29.99 (*0-8499-0249-5*) Word Pub.

Word Bird & the Whirlies. Jeanne Perrett. (English Language Teaching Ser.). (Illus.). (J). 1994. 7.50 (*0-13-100256-2*) P-H Intl.

Word Bird Asks: What? What? What? Jane B. Moncure. LC 83-15258. (Word Bird Library). (Illus.). 32p. (J). (ps-2). 1983. lib. bdg. 21.36 (*0-89565-258-7*) Childs World.

Word Bird Builds a City. Jane B. Moncure. LC 83-15275. (Word Bird Library). (Illus.). 32p. (J). (ps-2). 1983. lib. bdg. 21.36 (*0-89565-257-9*) Childs World.

Word Bird Makes Words with Cat. Jane B. Moncure. LC 83-23948. (Word Bird Library). (Illus.). 32p. (J). (ps-2). 1984. lib. bdg. 21.36 (*0-89565-259-5*) Childs World.

Word Bird Makes Words with Dog. Jane B. Moncure. LC 83-23946. (Word Bird Library). (Illus.). 32p. (J). (ps-2). 1984. lib. bdg. 21.36 (*0-89565-263-3*) Childs World.

Word Bird Makes Words with Duck. Jane B. Moncure. LC 83-23943. (Word Bird Library). (Illus.). 32p. (J). (ps-2). 1984. lib. bdg. 21.36 (*0-89565-261-7*) Childs World.

Word Bird Makes Words with Hen. Jane B. Moncure. LC 83-23944. (Word Bird Library). (Illus.). 32p. (J). (ps-2). 1984. lib. bdg. 21.36 (*0-89565-260-9*) Childs World.

Word Bird Makes Words with Pig. Jane B. Moncure. LC 83-23945. (Word Bird Library). (Illus.). 32p. (J). (ps-2). 1984. lib. bdg. 21.36 (*0-89565-262-5*) Childs World.

Word Bird's Christmas Words. Jane B. Moncure. LC 86-31666. (Word Bird Library). (Illus.). 32p. (J). (ps-2). 1987. lib. bdg. 21.36 (*0-89565-361-3*) Childs World.

Word Bird's Circus Surprise. Jane B. Moncure. LC 80-29528. (Word Bird Library). (Illus.). 32p. (J). (ps-2). 1981. lib. bdg. 21.36 (*0-89565-162-9*) Childs World.

Word Bird's Dinosaur Day. Jane B. Moncure. (Word Bird Library). (Illus.). 32p. (J). (ps-2). 1990. lib. bdg. 21.36 (*0-89565-617-5*) Childs World.

Word Bird's Easter Words. Jane B. Moncure. (Word Bird Library). (Illus.). 32p. (J). (ps-2). 1987. lib. bdg. 21.36 (*0-89565-363-X*) Childs World.

Word Bird's Fall Words. Jane B. Moncure. LC 85-5935. (Word Bird Library). (Illus.). 32p. (J). (ps-2). 1985. lib. bdg. 21.36 (*0-89565-308-7*) Childs World.

Word Bird's Halloween Words. Jane B. Moncure. LC 86-31024. (Word Bird Library). (Illus.). 32p. (J). (ps-2). 1987. lib. bdg. 21.36 (*0-89565-359-1*) Childs World.

Word Bird's Hats. Jane B. Moncure. LC 81-18065. (Word Bird Library). (Illus.). 32p. (J). (ps-2). 1982. lib. bdg. 21.36 (*0-89565-221-8*) Childs World.

Word Bird's Magic Wand. Jane B. Moncure. LC 90-1645. (Word Bird Library). (Illus.). 32p. (J). (ps-2). 1990. lib. bdg. 21.36 (*0-89565-580-2*) Childs World.

Word Bird's New Friend. Jane B. Moncure. LC 90-37002. (Word Bird Library). (Illus.). 32p. (J). (ps-2). 1990. lib. bdg. 21.36 (*0-89565-616-7*) Childs World.

Word Bird's Rainy-Day Dance. Jane B. Moncure. LC 90-31693. (Word Bird Library). (Illus.). 32p. (J). (ps-2). 1990. lib. bdg. 21.36 (*0-89565-579-9*) Childs World.

Word Bird's School Words. Jane B. Moncure. LC 89-7179. (Word Bird Library). (Illus.). 32p. (J). (ps-2). 1989. lib. bdg. 21.36 (*0-89565-510-1*) Childs World.

Word Bird's Shapes. Jane B. Moncure. LC 83-15255. (Word Bird Library). (Illus.). 32p. (J). (ps-2). 1983. lib. bdg. 21.36 (*0-89565-255-2*) Childs World.

Word Bird's Spring Words. Jane B. Moncure. LC 85-5902. (Word Bird Library). (Illus.). 32p. (J). (ps-2). 1985. lib. bdg. 21.36 (*0-89565-310-9*) Childs World.

Word Bird's Summer Words. Jane B. Moncure. LC 85-5930. (Word Bird Library). (Illus.). 32p. (J). (ps-2). 1985. lib. bdg. 21.36 (*0-89565-311-7*) Childs World.

Word Bird's Thanksgiving Words. Jane B. Moncure. LC 86-32639. (Word Bird Library). (Illus.). 32p. (J). (ps-2). 1987. lib. bdg. 21.36 (*0-89565-360-5*) Childs World.

Word Bird's Valentine Day Words. Jane B. Moncure. (Word Bird Library). (Illus.). 32p. (J). (ps-2). 1987. lib. bdg. 21.36 (*0-89565-362-1*) Childs World.

Word Bird's Winter Words. Jane B. Moncure. LC 85-5942. (Word Bird Library). (Illus.). 32p. (J). (ps-2). 1985. lib. bdg. 21.36 (*0-89565-309-5*) Childs World.

Word Book. Jane Baron & Barbara Jones. 106p. (YA). (gr. 10-12). 1981. pap. text ed. 19.00 (*1-881678-05-9*) CRIS.

WORD Book. David Bolocan. LC 85-2528. (Illus.). 240p. (Orig.). 1985. 24.95 (*0-8306-0958-X*, 1958H); pap. 16.95 (*0-8306-1958-5*, 1958P) McGraw-Hill Prof.

Word Book. Gyles Brandreth. 227p. 1992. pap. 9.95 (*0-86051-670-9*, Robson-Parkwest) Parkwest Pubns.

*__Word Book.__ Claire Henley. (Illus.). 12p. (J). 1996. pap. 13.95 (*1-870956-63-X*) Thunder Bay CA.

Word Book, No. III. rev. ed. American Heritage Dictionary Editors. 372p. 1990. 5.95 (*0-395-53957-9*) HM.

Word Book: For Beginning Writers. Edward Fry. (Illus.). 64p. (Orig.). 1995. pap. 6.95 (*0-87673-034-9*) Laguna Bch Ed.

Word Book II. 2nd ed. Ed. by Houghton Mifflin Company Staff. LC 83-8501. (Word Desk Set II Ser.). 384p. 1983. 3.95 (*0-685-07951-1*) HM.

Word Book in Pathology & Laboratory Medicine. 2nd ed. Sheila B. Sloane & John L. Dusseau. LC 94-30881. 960p. 1995. pap. text ed. 39.00 (*0-7216-4040-0*) Saunders.

Word Book with Huckle Cat & Lowly Worm: Richard Scarry. Richard Scarry. (Look-Look Bks.). (Illus.). 24p. (J). (ps-3). 1993. pap. 1.95 (*0-307-12767-2*, 12767, Golden Pr) Western Pub.

Word, Brother. Will Inman & Chuck Taylor. 40p. (Orig.). 1986. pap. 3.95 (*0-941720-37-3*); lib. bdg. 8.95 (*0-941720-38-1*) Slough Pr TX.

Word Builder. Dennis Graham. Ed. by Livian Perez. (Reading Safari Ser.: Vol. 3). (Illus.). 12p. (Orig.). (J). (gr. 1-3). 1996. pap. 19.95 (*1-56767-156-X*) Educ Insights.

Word Building. Dale McMasters. (Language Arts Ser.). 24p. (gr. 4-7). 1976. student ed. 5.00 (*0-8209-0305-1*, WB-1) ESP.

Word by Microsoft. Robert E. Williams. write for info. (*0-318-58209-0*) P-H.

Word by Word: Teachers Resource Book & Activity Masters. Steven J. Molinsky & Bill Blass. LC 94-231. 1994. pap. text ed. 26.50 (*0-13-124264-4*) P-H.

Word by Word: The Language of Memory. Johnathan Morse. LC 89-23931. (Illus.). 272p. 1990. 37.50 (*0-8014-2383-X*) Cornell U Pr.

Word by Word Basic Picture Dictionary. Steven J. Molinsky & Bill Bliss. LC 95-717. 1995. pap. text ed. 8.50 (*0-13-278565-X*) P-H.

Word by Word Basic Picture Dictionary: Teacher's Resource Book & Activity Masters. Steven J. Molinsky & Bill Bliss. LC 95-47374. 1996. pap. text ed. 26.50 (*0-13-278466-1*) P-H.

Word by Word Beginning Workbook. Steven J. Molinsky. 1995. pap. 7.50 (*0-13-278269-3*) P-H.

Word by Word Intermediate Workbook. Steven J. Molinsky. 1995. pap. 8.00 (*0-13-278458-0*) P-H.

Word by Word Picture Dictionary: English - Haitian Kreyol Edition. Steven J. Molinsky. 1995. pap. text ed. 8.50 (*0-13-278581-1*) P-H.

Word by Word Picture Dictionary: English - Vietnamese Edition. Steven J. Molinsky. 1995. pap. text ed. 8.50 (*0-13-278607-9*) P-H.

Word by Word Songbook. Peter Bliss. 1995. pap. text ed. 16.00 (*0-13-064767-5*) P-H.

Word-by-Word Translations of Songs & Arias, Pt. 1: German & French. Berton Coffin et al. LC 66-13746. 620p. 1966. 49.50 (*0-8108-0149-3*) Scarecrow.

Word-by-Word Translations of Songs & Arias, Pt. 2: Italian. Arthur Schoep & Daniel Harris. LC 66-13746. 575p. 1972. 49.50 (*0-8108-0463-8*) Scarecrow.

Word Cards. Barbara A. Wilson. (Wilson Reading System Ser.). 1988. 10.00 (*1-56778-007-5*) Wilson Lang Trning.

Word-Carrying Giant: The Growth of the American Bible Society. Creighton B. Lacy. LC 77-22655. 311p. 1977. pap. 6.95 (*0-87808-425-8*) William Carey Lib.

Word Check: The Definitive Source for Synonyms You Need. 288p. 1996. 5.95 (*0-395-75693-6*) HM.

Word Child. Iris Murdoch. 392p. 1987. pap. 12.95 (*0-14-008153-4*, Penguin Bks) Viking Penguin.

Word Choice & Narration in Academic Lectures: An Essay on Artistic Language Use. Barbara Strodt-Lopez. LC 92-31937. (Advances in Discourse Processes Ser.). 208p. 1993. pap. 42.50 (*0-89391-988-8*); text ed. 78.50 (*0-89391-834-2*) Ablex Pub.

Word Controlled Humans. John Harland. LC 80-52563. 120p. 1981. 12.00 (*0-914752-13-8*); pap. 7.00 (*0-914752-12-X*) Sovereign Pr.

Word Crazy: Broadway Lyricists from Cohan to Sondheim. Thomas S. Hischak. LC 90-47330. 264p. 1991. text ed. 24.95 (*0-275-93849-2*, C3849, Praeger Pubs) Greenwood.

Word Crimes. Marsh. 1997. 39.00 (*0-226-50690-8*) U Ch Pr.

Word Cultures: Radical Theory & Practice in William S. Burroughs' Fiction. Robin Lydenberg. LC 86-30719. 224p. 1987. text ed. 24.95 (*0-252-01413-8*) U of Ill Pr.

Word Daily Devotional see Spirit Filled Believer's Daily Devotional

Word Dance: The Language of Native American Culture. Carl Waldman. LC 94-10311. (Illus.). 304p. 1994. 27.95 (*0-8160-2834-6*) Facts on File.

Word Dance: The Language of Native American Culture. Carl Waldman. LC 94-10311. (Illus.). 304p. 1996. pap. 15.95 (*0-8160-3494-X*) Facts on File.

*__Word Desire.__ Ducornet. Date not set. pap. 12.95 (*0-8050-5174-0*) H Holt & Co.

*__Word Desire.__ Ducornet. 1997. 22.00 (*0-8050-5173-2*) H Holt & Co.

Word Desk Set II, 3 vols., Set. (Illus.). 1983. pap. 12.95 (*0-685-07052-2*) HM.

Word Diagnostic Imaging Equipment Markets: A Comprehensive Snapshot on Medical Imaging Modalities & Related Products. Market Intelligence Staff. 570p. 1994. 2,895.00 (*1-56753-987-4*) Frost & Sullivan.

Word Dig. Ida Altman. 48p. (J). (gr. 3-7). 1994. pap. text ed. 2.95 (*0-9644604-0-8*) Strother Publ.

Word Division: Supplement to United States Government Printing Office Style Manual. 144p. 1987. pap. 4.25 (*0-16-002864-7*, S/N 021-000-00139-2) USGPO.

Word Division & Spelling. 4th ed. Devern J. Perry. (KM - Office Procedures Ser.). 1994. text ed. 15.95 (*0-538-62750-6*) S-W Pub.

Word Division & Spelling Manual. 4th ed. Devern J. Perry. 1994. text ed. 14.95 (*0-538-61995-3*) S-W Pub.

Word Division Manual. 3rd ed. Devern J. Perry. (KM - Office Procedures Ser.). 1984. text ed. 15.95 (*0-538-11980-2*) S-W Pub.

Word Division Manual. 3rd ed. J. E. Silverthorn & Devern J. Perry. 168p. (C). 1984. text ed. 15.95 (*0-538-11981-0*, K98U) S-W Pub.

Word Encountered: Meditations on the Sunday Scriptures. John F. Kavanaugh. LC 96-13794. 140p. (Orig.). 1996. pap. 12.00 (*1-57075-093-9*) Orbis Bks.

*__Word Engaged: Meditations on the Sunday Readings C-Cycle.__ John F. Kavanaugh. LC 97-6701. 144p. (Orig.). 1997. pap. 12.00 (*1-57075-137-4*) Orbis Bks.

Word Equations & Related Topics: First International Workshop, IWWERT '90 Tubingen, Germany, October 1-3, 1990 Proceedings. Ed. by K. U. Schulz et al. (Lecture Notes in Computer Science Ser.: Vol. 572). vii, 256p. 1992. 46.95 (*0-387-55124-7*) Spr-Verlag.

Word Equations & Related Topics: Second International Workshop, IWWERT '91, Rouen, France, October 7-9, 1991 Proceedings. Ed. by Habib Abdulrab & Jean-Pierre R. Pecuchet. LC 93-29000. (Lecture Notes in Computer Science Ser.: Vol. 677). vii, 213p. 1993. 39.95 (*0-387-56730-5*) Spr-Verlag.

Word Expert Semantics: An Interlingual Knowledge-Based Approach. Bart C. Papegaaij. (Distributed Language Translation Ser.). x, 254p. 1986. 73.85 (*3-11-013331-8*); pap. 65.40 (*90-6765-261-X*) Mouton.

Word Express: The First Twenty-Five Hundred Words of Spoken English. Jerry Stemach & William B. Williams. Ed. by Rick Brownell. 288p. 1988. teacher ed., ring bd. 35.00 (*0-87879-592-8*); 10.00 (*0-87879-614-2*) Acad Therapy.

*__Word Families (Language)__ Jo E. Moore. (Reading & Writing Ser.). (Illus.). 32p. (J). (gr. 2-3). 1996. teacher ed., pap. 2.95 (*1-55799-409-9*, 4011) Evan-Moor Corp.

Word Find Puzzles, No. 4. Linda Doherty. 1988. pap. 1.95 (*0-8125-7881-3*) Tor Bks.

Word Find Puzzles for Kids. Elvira Gamiello. (Illus.). 64p. (Orig.). (J). 1988. pap. 1.95 (*0-942025-38-5*) Kidsbks.

Word Finder: The Phonic Key to the Dictionary. rev. ed. Marvin L. Morrison. LC 86-61846. 408p. 1987. pap. 19.95 (*0-9608376-1-2*) Pilot Light.

Word Finders in English. Anne Civardi. (Word Finders Bks.). 48p. (J). (gr. k-3). 1984. pap. 9.95 (*0-7460-0392-7*) EDC.

Word Finds Three. Linda Doherty. 96p. 1988. pap. 1.95 (*0-8125-7879-1*) Tor Bks.

Word Fitly Spoken: Context, Transmission, & Adoption of the Parables of Jesus. Philip L. Culbertson. LC 94-9989. (SUNY Series in Religious Studies). 390p. (C). 1995. text ed. 74.50 (*0-7914-2311-5*); pap. text ed. 24.95 (*0-7914-2312-3*) State U NY Pr.

Word for Every Day. Jimmy Swaggart. 768p. 1988. 20.00 (*0-935113-09-6*) Swaggart Ministries.

Word for Every Day: Three Hundred & Sixty-Five Devotional Reading. Alvin N. Rogness. LC 81-65650. 376p. 1981. kivar 17.99 (*0-8066-1886-8*, 10-7284, Augsburg) Augsburg Fortress.

Word for Everything. Roger Mitchell. LC 96-22242. 64p. (Orig.). 1996. pap. 10.95 (*1-886157-06-5*) BkMk.

Word for Teaching Is Learning: Essays for James Britton. Ed. by Martin Lightfoot & Nancy Martin. LC 88-5069. 300p. 1988. pap. text ed. 23.50 (*0-86709-237-8*, 0237) Boynton Cook Pubs.

Word for the Day: Reflections for Every Day of the Year. Don Talafous. 376p. (Orig.). 1992. pap. 15.95 (*0-8146-2096-5*) Liturgical Pr.

Word for the Wise: Making Scripture the Heart of Your Counseling Ministry. Henry Brandt & Kerry Skinner. LC 95-15676. 256p. 1995. 17.99 (*0-8054-6276-7*, 4262-76) Broadman.

Word for Us, Gospels of John & Mark, Epistles to the Romans, & the Galations. Joann Haugerud. LC 77-83418. 1977. 7.95 (*0-9603042-3-1*) Coalition Women-Relig.

Word for Windows. Educational Systems Staff. 1992. pap. 19.95 (*1-56351-063-4*) Microref Educ Systs.

Word for Windows: Project Book. Stephen Copestake. 300p. 1995. pap. 31.95 (*0-7506-2084-6*) Buttrwrth-Heinemann.

Word for Windows Essentials, IM, Level 2. Peggy Reising. 1996. teacher ed., ring bd. 49.99 (*1-57576-277-3*) Que Educ & Trng.

Word for Windows Quick & Easy. 2nd ed. Christian Crumlish. LC 93-86870. 184p. 1993. pap. 19.99 (*0-7821-1401-6*) Sybex.

Word for Windows Quick & Easy Reference. Ron Mansfield. LC 93-87028. 150p. 1993. 6.99 (*0-7821-1380-X*) Sybex.

Word for Windows Quick Reference. 2nd ed. Que Development Group Staff & Rich Grace. 224p. 1993. 10.99 (*1-56529-468-8*) Que.

Word for Windows Six Solutions. Elaine J. Marmel. 484p. 1994. pap. text ed. 24.95 (*0-471-30413-1*) Wiley.

Word for Windows Smartstart. 1993. teacher ed. 39.99 (*1-56529-221-9*) Que.

Word for Windows Smartstart. 1993. 25.99 (*1-56529-204-9*) Que.

Word for Windows Two: The Visual Learning Guide. Grace J. Beatty & David C. Gardner. (Illus.). 272p. (Orig.). 1993. pap. 19.95 (*1-55958-240-5*) Prima Pub.

Word for Windows 1.0/1.1: Beginners. 1993. 29.95 (*1-56877-085-5*) Catapult WA.

Word for Windows 1.0/1.1: Beginners. 1993. teacher ed. 49.95 (*1-56877-086-3*) Catapult WA.

Word for Windows 1.0/1.1: Intermediate. 1993. teacher ed. 49.95 (*1-56877-132-0*) Catapult WA.

Word for Windows 1.0/1.1: Intermediate. 1993. 29.95 (*1-56877-133-9*) Catapult WA.

Word for Windows 2 for Dummies. Dan Gookin. 350p. 1993. pap. 16.95 (*1-878058-86-X*) IDG Bks.

Word for Windows 2.0: Advanced. Douglas M. Finney. 1994. student ed., teacher ed., spiral bd. 29.95 incl. disk (*1-56435-019-3*) Finney Lrng Systs.

Word for Windows 2.0: Beginning. 1992. teacher ed. 49.95 (*1-56877-008-1*) Catapult WA.

Word for Windows 2.0: Beginning. 1992. 29.95 (*1-56877-020-0*) Catapult WA.

Word for Windows 2.0: Beginning. Douglas M. Finney. 168p. 1993. spiral bd. 24.95 (*1-56435-018-5*) Finney Lrng Systs.

Word for Windows 2.0: Intermediate. 1992. 29.95 (*1-56877-021-9*) Catapult WA.

Word for Windows 2.0: Intermediate. Douglas M. Finney. (Illus.). 1993. student ed., spiral bd. 29.95 incl. disk (*1-56435-027-4*) Finney Lrng Systs.

Word for Windows 2.0 Print & Presentation Kit. Christine Solomon. 1991. pap. 26.95 (*0-201-58108-6*) Addison-Wesley.

Word for Windows 6. Stephen Guild. (Self-Teaching Guides Ser.). 446p. 1994. pap. text ed. 22.95 (*0-471-30467-0*) Wiley.

Word for Windows 6: The Visual Learning Guide. David C. Gardner & Grace J. Beatty. (Illus.). 270p. (Orig.). 1993. pap. 19.95 (*1-55958-395-9*) Prima Pub.

Word for Windows 6.0. DDC Publishing Staff. 1993. pap. 19.95 incl. disk (*1-56243-170-6*, GR-WDW6); spiral bd. 12.00 (*1-56243-140-4*, OWDW6) DDC Pub.

Word for Windows 6.0 by Pictorial. Dennis Curtis. 1995. pap. text ed. 36.80 (*0-13-121898-0*) P-H.

Word for Windows 95. Keith Brindley. (Clear & Simple Ser.). 160p. 1996. pap. 10.95 (*0-7506-9803-9*, Digital DEC) Buttrwrth-Heinemann.

*__Word for Windows 95: Level III.__ Que Education & Training Staff. LC 96-68610. (Essentials Ser.). 1997. pap. text ed. 22.99 (*1-57576-383-4*) Que Educ & Trng.

Word for Windows 95: The Visual Learning Guide. David C. Gardner. 1995. pap. 19.95 (*1-55958-737-7*) Prima Pub.

Word for Windows 95: Visual QuickStart Guide. David Browne. (Illus.). 200p. (C). 1995. pap. text ed. 15.95 (*0-201-88362-7*) Peachpit Pr.

Word for Windows 95 Bible. Brent Heslop. 1995. pap. 39.99 (*1-56884-496-4*) IDG Bks.

Word for Windows 95 Essentials. Laura Acklen. 1996. pap. text ed. 22.99 (*1-57576-016-9*) Que Educ & Trng.

Word for Windows 95 Essentials: Level 2. Peggy Reising. 1996. pap. text ed. 22.99 (*1-57576-276-5*) Que Educ & Trng.

Word for Windows 95 Essentials, IM. 1996. teacher ed., pap. text ed. 49.99 (*1-57576-275-7*) Que Educ & Trng.

Word for Windows 95 for Busy People, No. 2. Christian Crumlish. (Busy People Bks.). (Illus.). 304p. 1995. pap. text ed. 22.95 (*0-07-882109-6*) McGraw.

Word for Windows 95 for Dummies. Dan Gookin. 1995. pap. 19.99 (*1-56884-932-X*) IDG Bks.

Word for Windows 95 for Dummies Quick Reference. Peter Weverka. 1995. pap. 12.99 (*1-56884-980-X*) IDG Bks.

Word for Windows 95 Instant Reference. 2nd ed. Sheila Dienes. LC 95-69985. 332p. 1995. pap. 12.99 (*0-7821-1766-X*) Sybex.

Word for Windows 95 Quick & Easy. Christian Crumlish. LC 95-71026. 1995. pap. 22.99 (*0-7821-1778-3*) Sybex.

Word for Windows 95 Quick Reference. Catherine Parkerson. (Illus.). 215p. (Orig.). 1995. 12.99 (*0-7897-0080-8*) Que.

Word for Windows 95 Secrets. Doug Lowe. 1995. pap. 39.99 (*1-56884-726-2*) IDG Bks.

Word for Windows 95 Simplified. Maran Graphics Staff. 1995. pap. 19.99 (*1-56884-681-9*) IDG Bks.

Word for Windows 95 Smartstart. Jean S. Insinga. 1996. pap. text ed. 29.99 (*1-57576-044-4*) Que Educ & Trng.

Word for Windows 95 Virtual Tutor. Que Education & Training Staff. 1996. pap. text ed. 49.99 (*1-57576-085-1*) Que Educ & Trng.

Word for Windows 95 Visual Quick Reference. Catherine Parkerson & Ron Holmes. (Illus.). 168p. (Orig.). 1994. 12.99 (*1-56529-740-7*) Que.

Word for Word. Edward C. Pinkerton. LC 77-20391. xxxii, 432p. 1982. 39.95 (*0-930454-06-5*) Verbatim Bks.

*__Word for Word.__ Tribble. Date not set. pap. text ed. write for info. (*0-582-01663-0*, Pub. by Longman UK) Longman.

Word for Word. Ed. by Chris Webster. 160p. (C). 1989. 150.00 (*0-7487-0063-3*, Pub. by S Thornes Pubs UK) St Mut.

Word for Word: Essays on the Arts of Language, Vol.I. Cid Corman. LC 76-48282. 169p. (Orig.). 1977. 14.00 (*0-87685-276-2*); pap. 10.00 (*0-87685-275-4*) Black Sparrow.

*__Word for Yes: New & Selected Stories.__ Tom MacIntyre. 126p. 1991. pap. 14.95 (*1-85235-069-5*) Dufour.

Word for Your Every Need: Hunter Green. 320p. 1993. bond lthr. 14.99 (*0-89274-677-7*, HH-677) Harrison Hse.

Word Force for Science & Social Studies. Nancy M. Allen. (Illus.). 171p. (Orig.). (J). (gr. 2). 1996. pap. 19.95 (*0-913956-90-2*) EBSCO.

Word Force for Science & Social Studies. Nancy M. Allen. (Illus.). 153p. (Orig.). (J). (gr. 3). 1996. pap. 19.95 (*0-913956-91-0*) EBSCO.

Word Force for Science & Social Studies. Nancy M. Allen. (Illus.). 188p. (Orig.). (J). (gr. 4). 1996. pap. 19.95 (*0-913956-92-9*) EBSCO.

Word Force for Science & Social Studies. Nancy M. Allen. (Illus.). 198p. (Orig.). (J). (gr. 5). 1996. pap. 19.95 (*0-913956-93-7*) EBSCO.

Word Force for Science & Social Studies. Nancy M. Allen. (Illus.). 233p. (Orig.). (J). (gr. 6). 1996. pap. 19.95 (*0-913956-94-5*) EBSCO.

Word Formation in the Noun & Adjective. J. K. Norbury. LC 67-10258. (Studies in the Modern Russian Language: No. 13). 135p. reprint ed. pap. 38.50 (*0-317-27313-2*, 2024503) Bks Demand.

Word Formation in the Roman Sermo Plebeius: An Historical Study of the Development of Vocabulary in Vulgar & Late Latin, with Special Reference to the Romance Languages. Frederic T. Cooper. xlvii, 330p. 1975. reprint ed. 80.00 (*3-487-05917-7*) G Olms Pubs.

Word from Below: Essays on Modern Literature & Culture. Robert Langbaum. LC 87-40140. 288p. 1988. text ed. 35.00 (*0-299-11180-6*) U of Wis Pr.

Word from Below: Essays on Modern Literature & Culture. Robert Langbaum. LC 87-40140. 288p. 1987. pap. text ed. 14.95 (*0-299-11184-9*) U of Wis Pr.

Word from the Loki. Maurice Riordan. 64p. (Orig.). 1995. pap. 9.95 (*0-571-17364-0*) Faber & Faber.

Word from the Nerd, Custom Pub. Osborne. 1993. pap. text ed. write for info. (*0-07-047989-5*); teacher ed., pap. text ed. write for info. (*0-07-047990-9*) McGraw.

Word Fun. Dennis Graham. Ed. by Livian Perez. (Reading Safari Ser.: Vol. 5). (Illus.). 12p. (Orig.). (J). (ps-1). 1996. pap. 19.95 (*1-56767-158-6*) Educ Insights.

Word Fun. Walt Disney Productions Staff. (Mickey's Young Readers Library Ser.: Vol. 18). (Illus.). (J). (gr. 1-6). 1990. reprint ed. 3.49 (*1-885222-51-3*) Advance Pubs.

Word fur Windows Lexikon. Manfred Fussinger. (GER.). 1993. 59.95 (*0-7859-8502-6*, 3816910416) Fr & Eur.

Word Games. Rick Detorie. (Magic Answer Bks.). 1989. pap. 1.95 (*0-8125-7323-4*) Tor Bks.

Word Games. Bruce Wetterau. 352p. (YA). (gr. 9-12). 1990. pap. 9.95 (*0-685-31180-5*, Webstrs New) Macmillan Gen Ref.

Word Games to Learn By: Categories. Carlos F. Navarro. Ed. by Judith Navarro. (Start Smart Ser.). (Illus.). 32p. 1989. student ed. 3.50 (*0-685-30103-6*) Start Smart Bks.

Word Games to Learn By: Distinctions. Carlos F. Navarro. Ed. by Judith Navarro. (Start Smart Ser.). 32p. 1989. student ed. 3.50 (*0-685-30105-2*) Start Smart Bks.

Word Games to Learn By: Verbal Correspondences. Carlos F. Navarro. Ed. by Judith Navarro. (Start Smart Ser.). 32p. 1989. student ed. 3.50 (*0-685-30106-0*) Start Smart Bks.

Word Garden: Positive & Inspirational Words of Comfort & Encouragement. Jennifer Whitney. LC 90-72018. 112p. (Orig.). 1991. pap. 12.95 (*1-879493-07-1*) Word Garden Prodns.

Word Goes On. Siegbert Becher. LC 92-61630. 1992. 21.99 (*0-8100-0440-2*, 15N0550) Northwest Pub.

Word Health. Miller. 1978. text ed. 41.25 (*0-03-041931-X*) HR&W Schl Div.

Word Hesed in the Hebrew Bible. G. R. Clark. 70.00 (*1-85075-408-X*, Pub. by Sheffield Acad UK) CUP Services.

Word History: A Guide to Understanding the English Language. Carl B. Smith & Eugene W. Reade. (Illus.). 96p. 1991. pap. 14.95 (*0-927516-12-8*) ERIC-REC.

Word History: A Resource Book for the Teacher. Carl B. Smith & Eugene W. Reade. LC 93-46398. 1994. 12.95 (*0-927516-44-6*) ERIC-REC.

Word-Hoard: An Introduction to Old English Vocabulary. 2nd ed. Stephen A. Barney. LC 76-47003. (Yale Language Ser.). 86p. 1985. pap. 11.00 (*0-300-03506-3*) Yale U Pr.

*__Word Hunt Puzzlers: Giant Print Edition.__ large type ed. Tribune Media Services Staff. (Puzzlers Ser.: Vol. 18). 384p. (Orig.). 1996. pap. write for info. (*1-889372-09-9*) Sweetwtr Pr AL.

Word Identification for Teachers. rev. ed. Marvin E. Oliver. Ed. by Victoria L. Gibson. LC 86-82262. 80p. (C). 1992. pap. text ed. 9.95 (*0-935435-00-X*) High Impact Pr.

Word, Image, Psyche. Bettina L. Knapp. LC 83-17856. (Illus.). 260p. 1985. pap. 74.10 (*0-7837-8387-6*, 2059198) Bks Demand.

Word in & Out of Season: Homilies for the Sundays of Advent & Lent. Richard Viladesau. LC 95-31979. (Word in & Out of Season Ser.: Vol. 4). 144p. (Orig.). 1996. pap. 9.95 (*0-8091-3626-0*) Paulist Pr.

Word in & Out of Season: Homilies for the Sundays of Ordinary Time, Cycle B. Richard Viladesau. 1990. pap. 7.95 (*0-8091-3158-7*) Paulist Pr.

Word in & Out of Season: Homilies for the Sundays of Ordinary Time, Cycle C. Richard Viladesau. 1991. 7.95 (*0-8091-3224-9*) Paulist Pr.

Word In & Out of Season: Homilies for the Sundays of Ordinary Times, Cycle A. Richard Viladesau. LC 92-21093. 144p. 1992. pap. 9.95 (*0-8091-3367-9*) Paulist Pr.

Word in Black & White: Reading "Race" in American Literature 1638-1867. Dana D. Nelson. 189p. 1994. reprint ed. pap. 15.95 (*0-19-508927-8*) OUP.

Word in Black & White: Writing "Race" in American Literature, 1638-1867. Dana Nelson. 208p. 1992. 49.95 (*0-19-506592-1*) OUP.

Word in Desert. Douglas Burton-Christie. 352p. 1993. 26.00 (*0-19-508333-4*) OUP.

Word in Flower: The Visualization of Classical Literature in Seventeenth-Century Japan. Ed. by Carolyn Wheelwright. LC 89-51369. (Illus.). 124p. (Orig.). (J). (ps-3). 1989. lib. bdg. 16.00 (*0-89467-051-4*) Yale Art Gallery.

Word in Season. William F. Maestri. LC 84-11026. 153p. (Orig.). 1983. pap. 6.95 (*0-8189-0459-3*) Alba.

Word in Season. Lesslie Newbigin. Ed. by Eleanor Jackson. 208p. (Orig.). (C). 1994. pap. 15.00 (*0-8028-0730-5*) Eerdmans.

Word in Season. Chet Plimpton. 196p. (Orig.). 1993. pap. 8.95 (*0-9632190-4-9*) Longwood.

Word in Season, 4 vols. Ed. by John E. Rotelle. Tr. by Edith Barnecut. (Orig.). 1987. reprint ed. write for info. (*0-318-62742-6*) Augustinian Pr.

Word in Season, 4 vols., Vol. I: Advent-Christmas. Ed. by John E. Rotelle. Tr. by Edith Barnecut. 230p. (Orig.). 1987. reprint ed. Vol. II, 230p. pap. 12.50 (*0-941491-12-9*) Augustinian Pr.

Word in Season, 4 vols., Vol. II: Lent. Ed. by John E. Rotelle. Tr. by Edith Barnecut. 230p. (Orig.). 1987. reprint ed. Vol. III, 230p. pap. 12.50 (*0-941491-13-7*) Augustinian Pr.

Word in Season, 4 vols., Vol. III. Ed. by John E. Rotelle. Tr. by Edith Barnecut. 230p. (Orig.). 1987. reprint ed. Vol. I, 230p. pap. 12.50 (*0-941491-14-5*) Augustinian Pr.

Word in Season, 4 vols., Vol. IV. Ed. by John E. Rotelle. Tr. by Edith Barnecut. 304p. (Orig.). 1987. reprint ed. 25.00 (*0-941491-45-5*); reprint ed. pap. 15.00 (*0-941491-15-3*) Augustinian Pr.

Word in Season, Vol. V: Ordinary Time, Weeks 1-17. Ed. by John E. Rotelle. Tr. by Edith Barnecut. 264p. 1995. reprint ed. pap. 15.95 (*0-941491-81-1*) Augustinian Pr.

Word in Season, Vol. V: Ordinary Time, Weeks 1-17. Ed. by John E. Rotelle. Tr. by Edith Barnecut. 264p. 1995. reprint ed. 24.95 (*0-941491-82-X*) Augustinian Pr.

Word in Season, Vol. VI: Ordinary Time, Weeks 18-34. Ed. by John E. Rotelle. Tr. by Edith Barnecut. 244p. 1995. reprint ed. pap. 15.95 (*0-941491-83-8*) Augustinian Pr.

Word in Season, Vol. VI: Ordinary TIme, Weeks 18-34. Ed. by John E. Rotelle. Tr. by Edith Barnecut. 244p. 1995. reprint ed. 24.95 (*0-941491-84-6*) Augustinian Pr.

Word in the Hand Bk. 1: An Introduction to Sign Language. Jane Kitterman & S. Harold Collins. (Illus.). 108p. (Orig.). 1984. lib. bdg. 15.00 (*0-931993-68-7*, GP-068); pap. 9.95 (*0-931993-08-3*, GP-008) Garlic Pr OR.

Word in the Hand Bk. 2: An Introduction to Sign Language. Jane Kitterman & S. Harold Collins. (Illus.). 84p. (Orig.). 1991. lib. bdg. 15.00 (*0-931993-69-5*, GP-069); pap. 8.95 (*0-931993-40-7*, GP-040) Garlic Pr OR.

Word in the World: The Cosmological Tale in the Fourth Gospel. Adele Reinhartz. LC 92-38139. 156p. 1992. 39.95 (*1-55540-798-6*, 06 00 45); pap. 25.95 (*1-55540-799-4*) Scholars Pr GA.

Word in Time. rev. ed. Arthur J. Dewey. 234p. (Orig.). 1991. pap. 14.95 (*0-940169-08-8*) Liturgical Pubns.

Word in Worship. Paul M. Miller & Jeff Wyatt. 1992. 9.99 (*0-685-68735-X*, MP-673) Lillenas.

Word-Index of Abhidharmakosa. Shubhangi S. Pradhan. (Bibliotheca Indo-Buddhica Ser.: No. 121). (C). 1993. text ed. 28.00 (*81-7030-369-9*) S Asia.

Word-Index to a Week on the Concord & Merrimack Rivers. James Karabatsos. LC 80-2510. reprint ed. 27.50 (*0-404-19058-8*) AMS Pr.

Word-Index to James Joyce's Dubliners. Ed. by Gary Lane. LC 71-183760. (Reference Ser.: No. 44). 270p. 1972. lib. bdg. 75.00 (*0-8383-1384-1*) M S G Haskell Hse.

Word Index to Poe's Fiction. Ed. by Burton R. Pollin. 512p. (C). 1982. 50.00 (*0-87752-225-1*) Gordian.

Word-Index to the Poems of Walther von der Vogelweide. 2nd ed. Ed. by Roe-Merrill S. Heffner & W. P. Lehmann. 82p. 1950. pap. 11.50 (*0-299-00663-8*) U of Wis Pr.

Word-Index to the Poems of Walther von der Vogelweide. 2nd ed. Roe-Merrill S. Heffner & W. P. Lehmann. LC 50-14330. 82p. reprint ed. pap. 25.00 (*0-7837-7024-3*, 2046839) Bks Demand.

Word Index to the Poetry of C.S. Lewis. Sara P. McLaughlin & Mark O. Webb. LC 88-17562. 232p. (C). 1988. lib. bdg. 7.50 (*0-933951-21-3*) Locust Hill Pr.

Word Index to the Prasastapadabhasya. Johannes Bronkhorst & Yves Ramsaier. (C). 1995. 16.00 (*81-208-1272-7*, Pub. by Motilal Banarsidass II) S Asia.

Word Index to the Texts of Steinmeyer - Die Kleineren Althochdeutschen Sprachdenkmaler. Roe-Merrill S. Heffner. LC 61-11837. 184p. (ENG & GER.). 1961. reprint ed. pap. 52.50 (*0-608-01939-9*, 2062594) Bks Demand.

Word Index to the Vakyapadiya of Bhartrhari: (Together with the Complete Text of the Vakyapadiya) (C). 1992. text ed. 44.00 (*81-85133-54-9*, Pub. by Eastern Bk Linkers II) S Asia.

Word Index to Walden, With Textual Notes. J. Stephen Sherwin. LC 80-2517. (Thoreau Ser.). 176p. 1981. reprint ed. 37.50 (*0-404-19065-0*) AMS Pr.

Word-Information Processing: A Systems Approach. 2nd ed. Mona J. Casady. 544p. (C). 1989. text ed. 49.95 (*0-538-70030-0*, WP40BA) S-W Pub.

Word Information Processing: Administration & Office Automation. 2nd ed. Walter A. Kleinschrod et al. 288p. 1983. teacher ed. write for info. (*0-672-98443-1*); text ed. write for info. (*0-672-98442-3*) Macmillan.

Word-Information Processing: Essentials Concepts. 2nd ed. Marilyn K. Popyk. 240p. 1986. text ed. 22.95 (*0-07-050593-4*) McGraw.

Word-Information Processing Concepts. 3rd ed. Mona J. Casdy. 218p. (C). 1984. pap. text ed. write for info. (*0-538-23611-6*, W62U) S-W Pub.

Word Information Processing Simulations for Text Editors, Information Processors & Personal Computers. Carol A. Wheeler & Marie Dalton. 267p. 1983. pap. text ed. 23.95 (*0-471-08159-0*) P-H.

Word into Silence. John Main. LC 80-84660. 96p. 1981. pap. 6.95 (*0-8091-2369-X*) Paulist Pr.

Word Is a Word. (J). 1993. pap. 7.95 (*0-590-71505-4*) Scholastic Inc.

Word Is Life: An Anthology of Funeral Meditations. LC 93-39596. 64p. 1994. pap. 6.75 (*1-55673-598-7*) CSS OH.

Word Is Movement: Journal Notes from Atlanta to Tulsa to Wounded Knee. Meridel Le Sueur. 74p. 1984. pap. 6.00 (*0-943594-07-3*) Cardinal Pr.

Word is Out: The Bible Reclaimed for Lesbians & Gay Men. Chris Glaser. LC 94-9416. 400p. 1994. pap. 12.00 (*0-06-063134-1*) Harper SF.

Word Is Very Near You: A Guide to Praying with Scripture. Martin L. Smith. LC 89-22144. 214p. 1989. 16.95 (*0-936384-97-2*); pap. 10.95 (*0-936384-81-6*) Cowley Pubns.

*__Word Is Worth a Thousand Pictures: Memories.__ D. A. Boogieman. 28p. 1996. pap. 6.95 (*1-881786-92-7*, OPC Lyrical Tongue Twister) Ohio PC.

WORD Kit: A Program to Build Expressive Vocabulary & Semantic Skills. Rosemary Huisingh et al. 1988. 109.95 (*1-55999-082-1*) LinguiSystems.

Word Kit Adolescent: A Program to Build Expressive Vocabulary & Semantic Skills for Adolescents. Janet R. Lanza & Carolyn C. Wilson. 270p. 1991. student ed. 109.95 (*1-55999-209-3*) LinguiSystems.

Word Like a Bell: John Keats, Music & the Romantic Poet. John A. Minahan. LC 91-29422. 232p. 1992. lib. bdg. 32.00 (*0-87338-453-9*) Kent St U Pr.

Word List from Bucks County, Pennsylvania, 1850-1876. Norman A. Heap. (Publications of the American Dialect Society: No. 70). 59p. 1983. pap. text ed. 6.40 (*0-8173-0202-6*) U of Ala Pr.

Word List from South Carolina, Expressions from Rural Florida, Minorcan Dialect Words in St. Augus-tine, Florida. F. W. Bradley et al. (Publications of the American Dialect Society: No. 14). 81p. 1950. pap. text ed. 8.50 (*0-8173-0614-5*) U of Ala Pr.

Word-List from West Texas; A Word-List from Colorado; A Maine Word-List from David Barker's "My First Courtship"; The Value of Dialect. James N. Tidwell et al. (Publications of the American Dialect Society: No. 11). 68p. 1949. pap. text ed. 7.00 (*0-8173-0611-0*) U of Ala Pr.

Word-List Illustrating the Correspondence of Modern English with Anglo-French Vowel-Sounds. B. M. Skeat. (English Dialect Society Publications: No. 43). 1974. reprint ed. pap. 25.00 (*0-8115-0469-7*) Periodicals Srv.

*__Word-List of the Cuneiform Alphabetic Texts from Ugarit, Ras Ibn Hani & Other Places.__ 2nd enl. ed. Manfried Dietrich & Oswald Loretz. 232p. 1996. 54.00 (*3-927120-40-5*, Pub. by Ugarit-Verlag GW) Eisenbrauns.

Word Lists from the South. Leah H. Dennis et al. (Publications of the American Dialect Society: No. 2). 72p. 1944. pap. text ed. 7.20 (*0-8173-0602-1*) U of Ala Pr.

Word Lovers Dictionary: Unusual Obscure & Preposterous Words. Josefa Heifetz. 264p. 1996. pap. 12.95 (*0-8065-1720-4*, Citadel Pr) Carol Pub Group.

Word Made Clear. James P. McIlhone. 222p. (Orig.). 1992. pap. 16.95 (*0-88347-268-6*, 7268) Res Christian Liv.

*__Word Made Flesh.__ fac. ed. Johanna Drucker. (Illus.). 40p. 1996. 60.00 (*1-887123-09-1*) Granary Bks.

Word Made Flesh: A Christ-Centered Study of the Book of John. A. B. Simpson. (Orig.). 1996. 8.99 (*0-87509-577-1*) Chr Pubns.

Word Made Flesh: An Overview of the Catholic Faith. Anthony J. Marinelli. LC 92-45629. 320p. 1993. pap. 10.95 (*0-8091-3391-1*) Paulist Pr.

Word Made Flesh: Catholicism & Conflict in the Films of Martin Scorsese. Michael Bliss. LC 95-1156. (Filmmakers Ser.: no. 46). 131p. 1995. 29.50 (*0-8108-3019-1*) Scarecrow.

Word Made Flesh Made Word: The Failure & Redemption of Metaphor in Edward Taylor's Christographia. David G. Miller. LC 95-18468. 152p. 1995. 29.50 (*0-945636-85-7*) Susquehanna U Pr.

Word Made Strange: Theology, Language & Culture. John Milbank. LC 96-17201. 300p. (C). 1997. 59.95 (*0-631-20335-4*); pap. 26.95 (*0-631-20336-2*) Blackwell Pubs.

Word Magic: Evaluating & Selecting Word Processing. Michael Scriven. 1985. text ed. 25.00 (*0-317-03932-6*) Edgepress.

Word Magic: Shakespeare's Rhetoric for Gifted Students: Elementary & Secondary Shakespearian Excerpts. 2nd ed. Ellen S. Kester. (Illus.). 194p. (YA). 1989. reprint ed. pap. text ed. 35.00 (*0-685-26279-0*) Pickwick Pubs.

Word Manager: A System for Morphological Dictionaries. Marc Domenig & Pius Ten Hacken. (Informatik und Sprache: Bd. 1). x, 212p. (GER.). 1992. write for info. (*3-487-09677-3*) G Olms Pubs.

Word Mandalas. John M. Feagan. LC 90-71988. 58p. (Orig.). 1992. pap. 6.95 (*1-56002-048-2*, Univ Edtns) Aegina Pr.

Word Mapping for Educational Research Success: A Workbook. Data Notes Publishing Staff. 14p. (YA). (gr. 11-12). 1988. student ed., ring bd. 25.95 (*0-911569-18-9*) Prosperity & Profits.

Word Mapping Reference Handbook. Compiled by Data Notes Publishing Staff. 250p. 1992. student ed., ring bd. 32.95 (*0-911569-01-4*) Prosperity & Profits.

Word Marketing: How to Empower Real Estate Advertising Through the Proper Choice of Words. 2nd rev. ed. Therese F. Kasemodel. Ed. by Laurel A. Kashnn. (Illus.). 120p. 1996. spiral bd. 24.95 (*0-9652256-0-7*, BRSB) Blue Rose Studio.

Word Meaning. Richard A. Hudson. LC 94-32405. (Language Workbooks Ser.). 128p. (YA). (gr. 10 up). 1995. pap. 12.95 (*0-415-08565-9*, C0162) Routledge.

Word Meaning & Belief. S. G. Pulman. LC 83-2622. 192p. 1983. text ed. 73.25 (*0-89391-201-8*) Ablex Pub.

Word Meaning & Montague Grammar. David R. Dowty. (Synthese Language Library: No. 7). 432p. 1979. pap. text ed. 39.00 (*90-277-1009-0*, D Reidel); lib. bdg. 117.50 (*90-277-1008-2*, D Reidel) Kluwer Ac.

Word Meanings in the New Testament. Ralph Earle. 512p. (C). 1988. 34.99 (*0-8010-3434-5*) Baker Bks.

Word Meanings in the New Testament. Ralph Earle. 496p. 1987. 32.99 (*0-8341-1176-4*) Beacon Hill.

*__Word Meanings in the New Testament.__ Ralph Earle. 496p. 1997. reprint ed. 29.95 (*1-56563-298-2*) Hendrickson MA.

*__Word Menu.__ Stephen Glazier. Date not set. write for info. (*0-688-06644-5*) Morrow.

*__Word Menu.__ Stephen Glazier. 1998. pap. 20.00 (*0-375-70083-8*, Random Ref) Random.

Word Menu: With Electronic Version. Stephen Glazier. 1993. Incl. diskette. 35.00 incl. disk (*0-679-42916-6*, Random Ref) Random.

Word Mysteries & Histories. 16.95 (*0-685-54947-X*, H-01033); pap. 9.95 (*0-685-54948-8*, H-01032) HM.

Word Nerd Party: A Book of Word Plays. Barber & Barber Staff. (J). 1996. 17.00 (*0-689-80491-1*) S&S Childrens.

Word NOW! (for Windows '95) A Simple Guide to Learning Word Quickly & Easily. Robert Medved. (Illus.). 224p. (Orig.). 1996. pap. 19.99 (*0-9643450-4-8*) Easel Pubng.

Word of a Prince: A Life of Elizabeth I from Contemporary Documents. Maria Perry. (Illus.). 352p. (C). 1990. 45.00 (*0-85115-261-9*) Boydell & Brewer.

Word of a Prince: A Life of Elizabeth I from Contemporary Documents. Maria Perry. (Illus.). 280p. (C). 1996. pap. 30.00 (*0-85115-633-9*) Boydell & Brewer.

Word of a Woman: Feminist Dispatches 1968-1992. Robin Morgan. 304p. 1994. pap. 10.95 (*0-393-31099-X*) Norton.

Word of a Woman: Selected Prose, 1968-1991. Robin Morgan. 288p. 1992. 19.95 (*0-393-03427-5*) Norton.

*__Word of Cardinal Bernardin.__ Paolo Magagnotti. LC 96-52982. 228p. (Orig.). 1996. pap. 14.95 (*1-57703-000-1*) CMS.

Word of Christ in the Psalms. Bill Freeman. 90p. (Orig.). 1993. pap. 2.00 (*0-914271-48-2*) Mnstry Wrd.

Word of Encouragement to Young Converts. Ernest S. Williams. 24p. 1989. pap. 0.59 (*0-88243-840-9*, 02-0840) Gospel Pub.

Word of God, 4 vols. Marie-Agnes Gaudrat. (What Is God Like? Ser.). (Illus.). 10p. (J). 1992. bds. 4.95 (*0-8146-2136-8*) Liturgical Pr.

Word of God. Ronald D. Tucker. 43p. (Orig.). 1985. pap. 4.00 (*0-933643-26-8*) Grace Ch-St Louis.

Word of God: Essays on Mormon Scripture. Ed. by Dan Vogel. LC 89-27535. (Essays on Mormonism Ser.: No. 2). ix, 271p. 1990. pap. 11.95 (*0-941214-93-1*) Signature Bks.

Word of God across the Ages: Using Christian History in Preaching. enl. ed. 110p. (Orig.). 1991. reprint ed. pap. text ed. 7.95 (*0-9628455-5-8*) Smyth & Helwys.

Word of God & the Languages of Man: Interpreting Nature in Early Modern Science & Medicine. James J. Bono. LC 95-15652. (Science & Literature Ser.). (Illus.). 332p. 1995. 50.00 (*0-299-14790-8*); pap. 22.95 (*0-299-14794-0*) U of Wis Pr.

Word of God & the Mind of Man. Ronald H. Nash. 137p. 1992. reprint ed. pap. 7.99 (*0-87552-354-4*, Pub. by Evangelical Pr) Presby & Reformed.

Word of God & the Word of Man. Karl Barth. Tr. by Douglas Horton. 1958. 19.00 (*0-8446-1599-4*) Peter Smith.

Word of God for All Occasions & Traditional Catholic Prayers. M. Countryman. 334p. 1987. ring bd. 12.95 (*0-937347-13-2*) C & D Intl.

Word of God in the Ethics of Jacques Ellul. David W. Gill. LC 83-20165. (American Theological Library Association Monograph: No. 20). 231p. 1984. 25.00 (*0-8108-1667-9*) Scarecrow.

Word of God in Transition: From Prophet to Exegete in the Second Temple Period. William M. Schniedewind. (Journal for the Study of the Old Testament Supplement Ser.: Vol. 197). 275p. 45.00 (*1-85075-550-7*, Pub. by Sheffield Acad UK) CUP Services.

Word of God, Priceless Treasure. Rachelle Wenger & Renee Wenger. Ed. by Ray M. Wenger. (Nuggets from Christian History Ser.: Vol. 1). (Illus.). 64p. (Orig.). (J). (gr. 3-6). 1993. pap. 5.99 (*0-9634616-1-3*) Plumb Line Pr.

Word of Honor. Nelson DeMille. 752p. 1987. mass mkt. 6.99 (*0-446-30158-2*) Warner Bks.

Word of Honor. T. Elizabeth Renich. (Shadowcreek Chronicles Ser.: Bk. 1). 300p. (Orig.). 1994. pap. 8.99 (*1-883002-10-9*) Emerald WA.

Word of Honor: Interpreting Noble Culture in Sixteenth-Century France. Kristen B. Neushel. LC 88-47916. 256p. 1989. 32.50 (*0-8014-2181-0*) Cornell U Pr.

*__Word of Islam.__ John A. Williams. 272p. 1996. pap. 14.95 (*0-614-21078-X*, 1333) Kazi Pubns.

Word of Islam. Ed. by John Alden A. Williams. LC 93-4676. 272p. (Orig.). 1994. pap. 14.95 (*0-292-79076-7*); text ed. 37.50 (*0-292-79075-9*) U of Tex Pr.

Word of Life: Scripture Selections. Edmund Beaver. (Illus.). 1953. pap. 2.25 (*0-910208-02-6*) Beavers.

*__Word of Life: Using the Bible in Pastoral Care.__ William Challis. 256p. 1997. pap. 13.99 (*0-551-03061-5*, Pub. by Marshall Pickering) Harper SF.

Word of Life Vol. 2: Systematic Theology. Thomas C. Oden. LC 88-46011. 512p. 1992. reprint ed. pap. 25.00 (*0-06-066364-2*) Harper SF.

*__Word of Mouth.__ Ruth Carr & Grainne Tobin. 118p. 9700. pap. 13.95 (*0-85640-584-1*, Pub. by Blackstaff Pr IE) Dufour.

Word of Mouth. Earlcarlin. (College ESL Ser.). 1996. pap. 21.95 (*0-8384-4675-2*) Heinle & Heinle.

W

An Asterisk (*) at the beginning of an entry indicates that the title is appearing in BIP for the first time.

Word of Mouth. Earlcarlin. (College ESL Ser.). 1995. teacher ed., pap. 9.95 (*0-8384-4676-0*) Heinle & Heinle.

Word of Mouth. Ted Greenwald. 240p. (Orig.). 1986. pap. 8.95 (*0-940650-68-1*) Sun & Moon CA.

Word of Mouth: A Collection of Recipes. Friends of Humane Society Knox. 1996. 14.95 (*0-9649385-0-2*) Hum Soc Knox.

Word of Mouth: A Guide to Commercial Voice-over Excellence. Susan Blu & Molly A. Mullin. LC 87-61591. (Illus.). 160p. 1988. audio 9.95 (*0-938817-09-4*) Pomegranate Pr.

Word of Mouth: A Guide to Commercial Voice-over Excellence. 2nd ed. Susan Blu & Molly A. Mullin. LC 87-61591. (Illus.). 176p. 1994. pap. 9.95 (*0-938817-32-9*) Pomegranate Pr.

Word of Mouth: Body Language in Katherine Mansfield & Virginia Woolf. Patricia Moran. LC 96-19760. (Feminist Issues Ser.). 208p. 1996. text ed. 32.50 (*0-8139-1675-5*) U Pr of Va.

Word of Mouth: Triangle Restaurant & Market Guide for 1990. Pat Pons & Elizabeth Goode. (Illus.). (Orig.). 1989. pap. 8.95 (*0-685-29455-2*) Word Mouth NC.

Word of Mouth Marketing. Jerry R. Wilson. 256p. 1994. pap. text ed. 14.95 (*0-471-00858-3*) Wiley.

Word of Now. Marilyn Wilson. 348p. (Orig.). 16.95 (*0-9644086-0-0*) Church of Everlasting.

Word of Now. Marilyn Wilson. 348p. (Orig.). 1994. pap. text ed. 7.95 (*0-9644086-1-9*) Church of Everlasting.

Word of One: Tarot Wisdom of the Ages. rev. ed. John S. Cooke. (Illus.). 70p. 34.95 (*0-9634800-2-2*) Catalyst Ent.

Word of Promise. E. N. Kirk. pap. 5.99 (*0-88019-132-5*) Schmul Pub Co.

Word of the Cross. Watchman Nee. Ed. by Herbert L. Fader. Tr. by Stephen Kaung from CHI. 165p. (Orig.). 1995. pap. 5.00 (*0-935008-80-2*) Christian Fellow Pubs.

Word Of The Cross. Watchman Nee. 34p. 1.25 (*0-87083-606-4*, 07032001) Living Stream Ministry.

Word of the Cross: A Contemporary Theology of Evangelism. Lewis A. Drummond. 1992. 22.99 (*0-8054-6255-4*, 4262-55) Broadman.

Word of the Lord Grows. Martin H. Franzmann. 324p. 1981. pap. 16.99 (*0-570-03848-0*, 12-2952) Concordia.

Word of the Lord Shall Go Forth: Essays in Honor of David Noel Freedman in Celebration of His Sixtieth Birthday. Ed. by Carol L. Meyers & M. O'Connor. LC 83-20589. (American Schools of Oriental Research Special Volume Ser.: No. 1). xviii, 742p. 1983. text ed. 59.50 (*0-931464-19-6*) Eisenbrauns.

Word of the Lord, Year A: Reflections on the Sunday Readings. Philip J. McBride. LC 95-60665. 160p. (Orig.). 1995. pap. 9.95 (*0-89622-659-X*) Twenty-Third.

Word of the Lord, Year B: Reflections to the Sunday Readings. Philip J. McBrien. LC 95-60665. 184p. (Orig.). 1996. pap. 9.95 (*0-89622-700-6*) Twenty-Third.

Word of Truth: A Summary of Christian Doctrine Based on Biblical Revelation. fac. ed. Dale Moody. LC 80-19103. 640p. 1990. reprint ed. pap. 180.00 (*0-7837-7966-6*, 2047722) Bks Demand.

Word of Truth & Disputes about Words. Douglas B. Farrow. LC 87-17656. xiv, 234p. (Orig.). (C). 1988. pap. 18.95 (*0-931464-36-6*, Carpenter Bks) Eisenbrauns.

Word on Finances: Topical Scriptures & Commentary. Larry Burkett. 300p. 1994. pap. 14.99 (*0-8024-9238-X*) Moody.

***Word on the Streets: The Unsanctioned Story of Oasis.** Eugene Masterson. (Illus.). 96p. 1997. pap. 17.95 (*1-85158-890-6*, Pub. by Mnstream UK) Trafalgar.

Word or Two of Advice to William Warburton. Zachary Grey. LC 71-131491. reprint ed. 29.50 (*0-404-02909-4*) AMS Pr.

Word Order & Constituent Structure in German. Hans Uszkoreit. LC 87-70215. (Center for the Study of Language & Information-Lecture Notes Ser.: No. 8). 194p. (Orig.). 1987. 27.50 (*0-937073-09-1*); pap. 14.95 (*0-937073-10-5*) CSLI.

Word-Order Change & Grammaticalization in the History of Chinese. LC 94-26394. 1995. 39.50 (*0-8047-2418-0*) Stanford U Pr.

Word Order in Ancient Greek: A Pragmatic Account of Word Order Variation in Herodotus. Helma Dik. (Amsterdam Studies in Classical Philology: No. 5). xii, 294p. 1995. lib. bdg. 90.00 (*90-5063-457-5*, Pub. by Gieben NE) Benjamins North Am.

W

Word Order in Discourse. Ed. by Pamela Downing & Michael Noonan. LC 94-44088. (Typological Studies in Language: No. 30). x, 595p. 1995. lib. bdg. 135.00 (*1-55619-424-2*) Benjamins North Am.

Word Order in Discourse. Ed. by Pamela Downing & Michael Noonan. LC 94-44088. (Typological Studies in Language: No. 30). x, 595p. 1995. pap. 37.95 (*1-55619-636-9*) Benjamins North Am.

Word-Order in English Verse from Pope to Sassoon. Mats A. Redin. 1977. lib. bdg. 59.95 (*0-8490-2842-6*) Gordon Pr.

Word Order in Sanskrit & Universal Grammar. J. F. Staal. (Foundations of Language Supplementary Ser.: No. 5). 98p. 1967. lib. bdg. 94.50 (*90-277-0549-6*) Kluwer Ac.

***Word-Order of Aelfric.** Graeme Davis. LC 97-2088. (Studies in British Literature: Vol. 28). 320p. 1997. text ed. 99.95 (*0-7734-8649-6*) E Mellen.

Word Order Rules. Anna Siewierska. 250p. 1988. lib. bdg. 65.00 (*0-7099-4484-5*, Pub. by Croom Helm UK) Routledge Chapman & Hall.

Word Order Typology & Comparative Constructions. Paul K. Andersen. (Current Issues in Linguistic Theory Ser.: Vol. 25). xvii, 245p. 1983. 59.00 (*90-272-3517-1*) Benjamins North Am.

Word Order Universals & Their Explanations. John A. Hawkins. (Quantitative Analyses of Linguistic Structure Ser.). 1983. text ed. 60.00 (*0-12-333370-9*) Acad Pr.

Word Origins: The Romance of Language. Cecil Hunt. (Orig.). pap. 3.95 (*0-8065-0685-7*, 105, Citadel Pr) Carol Pub Group.

Word Pal. Robin Q. Buschemeyer. (Professor Elly Fun's Back to Basics Ser.). (Illus.). 40p. (Orig.). (J). (ps-3). 1986. pap. 2.99 (*0-935609-00-8*) Eduplay.

Word Parts Workbook. Sheehan. (C). 1995. teacher ed., pap. text ed. 45.00 (*0-15-502571-6*) HB Coll Pubs.

***Word Perfect.** Harrison. 1992. pap. text ed. write for info. (*0-17-555873-6*) Addison-Wesley.

Word Personalized, Vol. 1: Names of God. Stephen Long. 44p. 1993. pap. 10.97 incl. audio (*0-9629550-2-7*) Word in Action.

Word, Picture & Spectacle. Ed. by Clifford Davidson. (Early Drama, Art & Music Monograph: No. 5). 1984. pap. 10.95 (*0-918720-50-8*); boxed 17.95 (*0-918720-51-6*) Medieval Inst.

Word Picture Puzzles. Fred Justus. (Puzzles Ser.). 24p. (gr. 1). 1980. student ed. 5.00 (*0-8209-0296-9*, PU-10) ESP.

Word Pictures in the New Testament. 160p. 1992. pap. 5.99 (*0-8423-2876-9*, 02-2876-9) Tyndale.

Word Pictures in the New Testament, 6 vols. A. T. Robertson. 1993. 150.00 (*0-8010-7710-9*) Baker Bks.

Word Pictures in the New Testament, 6 vols., Set. Archibald T. Robertson. Incl. Vol. 2. Luke. 1958. 19.99 (*0-8054-1302-2*, 4213-02); Vol. 3. Word Pictures in the New Testament. 1958. 19.99 (*0-8054-1303-0*, 4213-03); Vol. 6. Genesis, Epistles, Revelation & John. 1958. 19.99 (*0-8054-1306-5*, 4213-06); (C). 1958. 110.00 (*0-8054-1307-3*, 4213-07) Broadman.

Word Pictures in the New Testament see Word Pictures in the New Testament

Word Pictures Painted by Paul. Sandy Petro. LC 93-16024. (Women's Inductive Bible Study Ser.). 96p. (Orig.). 1993. pap. 5.99 (*1-56476-034-0*, 6-3034, Victor Bks) Chariot Victor.

***Word Play.** Mary A. Hodge. Ed. by Gayle Bittinger. (101 Tips for Toddler Teachers Ser.). (Illus.). 24p. (Orig.). 1997. pap. 3.95 (*1-57029-157-8*, 4018, Totline Bks) Warren Pub Hse.

Word Play. Hans Holzer. LC 78-3851. (Illus.). 128p. (Orig.). 1978. pap. 4.95 (*0-89407-013-4*) Strawberry Hill.

Word Play: What Happens When People Talk. Peter Farb. LC 92-56361. 1993. pap. 13.00 (*0-679-73408-2*, Publishers Media) Random.

Word Power. pap. 0.67 (*0-590-03068-X*) Scholastic Inc.

Word Power. Birkett. pap. 19.95 (*0-7136-3733-1*, 92916, Pub. by A&C Black UK) Talman.

Word Power! Alana Trisler & Patrice Cardiel. (Illus.). 88p. (Orig.). (J). (gr. 4-6). 1995. wbk. ed., pap. 3.00 (*1-56762-059-0*) Modern Learn Pr.

***Word Power, 7.** Cummings. 1997. pap. 13.00 (*0-7871-1229-1*, Dove Bks) Dove Audio.

***Word Power, 8.** Cummings. 1997. pap. 13.00 (*0-7871-1230-5*, Dove Bks) Dove Audio.

***Word Power, 9.** Cummings. 1997. pap. 13.00 (*0-7871-1231-3*, Dove Bks) Dove Audio.

Word Power: The Words Leaders Use. Charles Ickowicz. Ed. by Robert Cohen & Patricia Godfrey. LC 93-90126. 180p. (Orig.). 1993. pap. 5.95 (*0-9635623-0-4*) Dashir.

Word Power: Vocabulary for Success. Charles Ickowicz. LC 94-71071. 172p. (Orig.). 1994. pap. 7.95 (*0-9635623-1-2*) Dashir.

***Word Power A.** Contemp Bks Staff. 1997. pap. 10.60 (*0-8092-0835-0*) Contemp Bks.

***Word Power B.** Contemp Bks Staff. 1997. pap. 10.60 (*0-8092-0836-9*) Contemp Bks.

***Word Power C.** Contemp Bks Staff. 1997. pap. 10.60 (*0-8092-0837-7*) Contemp Bks.

***Word Power D.** Contemp Bks Staff. 1997. pap. 10.60 (*0-8092-0838-5*) Contemp Bks.

***Word Power E.** Contemp Bks Staff. 1997. pap. 10.60 (*0-8092-0839-3*) Contemp Bks.

Word Power in Twenty-One Days! The Ultimate Challenge for Word Lovers! J. G. Barton. LC 92-60916. (Illus.). 160p. 1992. pap. 5.95 (*0-940685-35-3*) Cardoza Pub.

Word Power Made Easy. Norman Lewis. pap. 5.99 (*0-671-74190-X*) PB.

Word Power Made Easy. Norman Lewis. 1995. 9.98 (*0-88365-925-5*) Galahad Bks.

Word Power Study Guide. James I. Brown. (Illus.). 50p. (C). 1982. reprint ed. pap. text ed. 4.95 (*0-943000-04-1*) Telstar Inc.

Word Prints. Richard Kostelanetz. 1985. 500.00 (*0-932360-33-5*) Archae Edns.

Word Pro for Windows 95 for Dummies. 2nd ed. Jim Meade. 1995. pap. 19.99 (*1-56884-232-5*) IDG Bks.

***Word Problems Bk. 1.** H. S. Lawrence. (Straight Forward Math Ser.). 40p. (Orig.). (J). (gr. 3-6). 1996. wbk. ed., pap. 3.95 (*0-931993-83-0*, GP-083) Garlic Pr OR.

Word Problems for Calculator & Computer. Stanley Bezuszka et al. (Motivated Math Project Activity Booklets). 250p. (Orig.). 1985. pap. text ed. 4.50 (*0-317-39752-4*) Boston Coll Math.

Word Problems for Maxima & Minima. Stanley Bezuszka et al. (Motivated Math Project Activity Booklets). 96p. (Orig.). 1984. pap. text ed. 4.50 (*0-917916-20-4*) Boston Coll Math.

Word Problems Made Easy. J. L. McCabe. Orig. Title: Word Problems Simplified. (Illus.). 127p. 1986. pap. text ed. 14.95 (*0-942465-01-6*) Summertree Bks.

Word Problems Simplified see Word Problems Made Easy

Word Proccessing Today. Flynn. Date not set. wbk. ed., pap. text ed. 21.75 (*0-314-02959-1*) West Pub.

Word Procesing & Desktop Publishing Applications. 2nd ed. Naomi D. Platt. LC 93-8600. 1994. write for info. (*0-02-801021-3*) Glencoe.

Word Processing. Mona J. Casady. LC 94-31574. 1995. pap. 20.95 (*0-538-63095-7*) S-W Pub.

Word Processing: A Guide to Program Planning. Wilma J. Alexander et al. 79p. 1984. 4.95 (*0-318-22248-5*, LT65) Ctr Educ Trng Employ.

Word Processing: Concepts & Applications. Bettie H. Ellis. (Illus.). 48p. 1980. text ed. 17.40 (*0-07-019242-1*) McGraw.

Word Processing: Concepts & Applications. 2nd ed. Bettie H. Ellis. 232p. 1986. pap. text ed. 14.96 (*0-07-019278-2*) McGraw.

Word Processing: Concepts & Careers. 4th ed. Marly K. Bergerud & Jean Gonzales. 336p. 1988. pap. text ed. 30.95 (*0-471-84503-5*) P-H.

Word Processing: Course Code S04-1. Susan Weinman. Ed. by Bonnie Schroeder. (Illus.). 75p. 1989. reprint ed. pap. text ed. 8.00 (*0-917531-52-3*) CES Compu-Tech.

Word Processing: Course Code S04-2. Susan Weinman. Ed. by Bonnie Schroeder. (Illus.). 75p. (J). (gr. 7). 1989. reprint ed. pap. text ed. 8.00 (*0-917531-53-1*) CES Compu-Tech.

Word Processing: Essential Concepts. Marilyn K. Popyk. LC 83-768. (Illus.). 240p. (C). 1983. text ed. 27.95 (*0-07-048472-4*) McGraw.

Word Processing: First Step to the Office of the Future. Kathleen F. Curley. LC 82-18948. 174p. 1983. text ed. 45.00 (*0-275-91717-7*, C1717, Praeger Pubs) Greenwood.

Word Processing: Lab Pack. Yvonne Mullen & Bonnie Schroeder. (Illus.). 1990. teacher ed., wbk. ed. 149.95 incl. disk (*1-56177-135-X*, L404) CES Compu-Tech.

Word Processing: Lab Pack. Susan Weinman et al. (Illus.). 1990. teacher ed., wbk. ed. 199.95 incl. disk (*1-56177-089-2*, L394-1) CES Compu-Tech.

Word Processing: Lab Pack. Susan Weinman & Yvonne Mullen. Ed. by Bonnie Schroeder. (Illus.). 1990. teacher ed., wbk. ed. 149.95 incl. disk (*1-56177-087-6*, L304) CES Compu-Tech.

Word Processing: Lab Pack. Susan Weinman. Ed. by Bonnie Schroeder. (Illus.). 1990. teacher ed., wbk. ed. 149.95 incl. disk (*1-56177-043-4*, L104) CES Compu-Tech.

Word Processing: Lab Pack. Susan Weinman. Ed. by Bonnie Schroeder. 1990. teacher ed., wbk. ed. 199.95 incl. disk (*1-56177-039-6*, L194-1) CES Compu-Tech.

Word Processing: Operations, Applications, & Administration. Walter A. Kleinschrod et al. LC 79-13613. 1980. write for info. (*0-672-97270-0*); teacher ed. write for info. (*0-672-97271-9*) Macmillan.

Word Processing: Progressive Applications. Grismere. (DF - Computer Applications Ser.). 1991. pap. 33.95 (*0-538-70180-3*) S-W Pub.

Word Processing: The Corresponding Secretary. 1977. wbk. ed. 18.95 (*0-87350-326-0*) Milady Pub.

Word Processing: The Corresponding Secretary. 1985. pap. 12.95 (*0-87350-603-0*) Milady Pub.

Word Processing: The Useable Portable Guide. Jon Haber & Herbert R. Haber. (Illus.). 254p. (Orig.). (C). 1988. pap. text ed. 11.95 (*0-945765-00-2*) Useable Portable Pubns.

Word Processing & Information Systems: A Practical Approach to Concepts. Marilyn K. Popyk. LC 82-25902. 352p. 1983. text ed. 34.75 (*0-07-050574-8*) McGraw.

Word Processing & Information Systems: A Practical Approach to Concepts. 2nd ed. Marilyn K. Popyk. 372p. (C). 1986. text ed. 29.50 (*0-07-050594-2*) McGraw.

Word Processing & the Changing Office Environment. Saffer. (KM - Office Procedures Ser.). 1985. pap. 16.95 (*0-538-23800-3*) S-W Pub.

Word Processing Applications & Exercises. 2nd ed. Sandra Muehlman. 256p. (C). 1991. pap. text ed. 36.00 (*0-13-963133-X*) P-H.

Word Processing Applications for Office Professionals. Mckay. 1989. pap. text ed. 13.95 (*0-471-61249-9*) P-H.

Word Processing Applications in Practice. John W. Meroney. (DF - Computer Applications Ser.). 1984. pap. 19.95 (*0-538-23750-3*) S-W Pub.

Word Processing Applications in Practice. 2nd ed. John W. Meroney. (DF - Computer Applications Ser.). 1989. pap. 18.95 (*0-538-23830-5*) S-W Pub.

Word Processing Applications in Practice. 3rd ed. John W. Meroney. LC 93-44960. 1995. pap. 20.95 (*0-538-62529-5*) S-W Pub.

Word Processing Applications in Practice. 3rd ed. John W. Meroney. (DF - Computer Applications Ser.). 1995. 83.95 (*0-538-62757-3*) S-W Pub.

Word Processing Communication Skills. Cheryl M. Luke & Ann J. Swafford. 136p. (C). 1988. pap. text ed. 15.50 (*0-15-596660-X*) Dryden Pr.

Word Processing Cookbook. Glenn Stuart. 1984. 34.00 (*0-13-963398-7*); pap. 19.95 (*0-13-963380-4*) P-H.

Word Processing Exercises: Applications for Word Processing, Advanced Keyboarding, & Electronic Typewriters. Robert R. Zilkowski. LC 92-28894. 1993. pap. 22.95 (*0-87835-804-8*) Course Tech.

Word Processing Experience. Jane Pigoff & R. Atkins-Green. 176p. (C). 1982. 85.00 (*0-85950-386-0*, Pub. by S Thornes Pubs UK) St Mut.

Word Processing Experience - Teacher's Experience: Teacher's Handbook & Solutions. Ed. by J. Pigott. (C). 1982. 75.00 (*0-85950-393-3*, Pub. by S Thornes Pubs UK) St Mut.

Word Processing for Business Publications: How to Produce Proposals, Manuals, Catalogs, Newsletters & More. Herman R. Holtz. (BYTE Book). 256p. 1985. pap. text ed. 9.95 (*0-07-029657-X*) McGraw.

Word Processing for Business Users. Dona Z. Meilach. LC 92-43863. (Barron's Educational Ser.). 1993. pap. 19.95 incl. disk (*0-8120-1466-9*) Barron.

Word Processing for Legal Professionals Using WordPerfect 5.1. Steven L. Mandell et al. LC 95-2009. 633p. (C). 1995. spiral bd. 33.75 (*0-314-05250-X*) West Pub.

Word Processing for Technical Writers. Ed. by Robert Krull. (Technical Communications Ser.: Vol. 3). 172p. (Orig.). (C). 1988. pap. text ed. 25.95 (*0-89503-049-7*) Baywood Pub.

Word Processing Handbook: A Step-by-Step Guide to Automating Your Office. Katherine Aschner. LC 82-3. (Professional Librarian Ser.). (Illus.). 193p. 1986. 25.00 (*0-86729-018-8*, Hall Reference) Macmillan.

Word Processing in Groups. David B. Epstein et al. (Illus.). 352p. (C). 1992. text ed. 49.00 (*0-86720-244-0*) AK Peters.

Word Processing Input. Dorinda Clippinger. 1983. pap. text ed. write for info. (*0-8359-8802-3*, Reston) P-H.

***Word Processing Made Easy.** Wilson. 1990. pap. text ed. write for info. (*0-7299-0176-9*) Addison-Wesley.

Word Processing on Microcomputers: Applications & Exercises. alternate ed. Sandra Muehlman. 256p. (C). 1989. pap. text ed. write for info. (*0-13-964750-3*) P-H.

Word Processing on Microcomputers: Legal Applications & Exercises. Sandra Muehlman. 256p. (C). 1989. pap. text ed. write for info. (*0-318-65463-6*) P-H.

Word Processing on the IBM Personal Computer. Danny Goodman. 1983. pap. write for info. (*0-318-57886-7*) Macmillan.

Word Processing on the Wang Professional Computer. Terry L. Fucci. 158p. (C). 1988. pap. text ed. 28.00 (*0-15-596685-5*) Dryden Pr.

Word Processing Plus: Profiles of Home-Based Success. Marcia Hodson. LC 90-84643. (Orig.). 1991. pap. 15.95 (*0-9627941-3-9*) CountrySide Pubns.

Word Processing Profits at Home: A Complete Business Plan for the Self-Employed Word Crafter. 2nd ed. Peggy Glenn. 210p. 1992. pap. 18.95 (*0-936930-33-0*) Aames-Allen.

Word Processing Simplified for Superscript: TRS 80 Models III IV & IVP. Rosemary K. Bekaert. (Illus.). 208p. (Orig.). 1985. pap. 25.00 (*0-9615582-0-2*) Kelly Ent.

Word Processing Simulations for Electronic Typewriters & Text Editors. Carol A. Wheeler & Marie Dalton. LC 81-11630. (Word Processing Ser.). 224p. 1982. pap. text ed. 23.95 (*0-471-08158-2*) P-H.

Word Processing Six Intermediate Test Papers. D. McFetridge. (C). 1988. 70.00 (*0-85950-829-3*, Pub. by S Thornes Pubs UK) St Mut.

Word Processing Skills & Simulations. Jennie Mason. LC 78-15761. 1979. teacher ed. write for info. (*0-672-97135-6*); pap. write for info. (*0-672-97197-6*) Macmillan.

Word Processing Specialist. 2nd ed. Matthews. (DF - Computer Applications Ser.). 1985. 26.95 (*0-538-23710-4*) S-W Pub.

Word Processing Supervision. Reba B. Davis & John L. Balderson. 320p. (C). 1984. teacher ed. write for info. (*0-672-98449-0*); text ed. write for info. (*0-672-98448-2*) Macmillan.

Word Processing Supervisor. Jack Rudman. (Career Examination Ser.: C-3570). 1994. pap. 27.95 (*0-8373-3570-1*) Nat Learn.

Word Processing Supervisor: User Manual for IBM--Version 1.0. S. E. Warner Software, Inc. Staff. 72p. 1990. pap. text ed. 2.95 (*1-57094-021-5*); 3.5 hd 495.00 (*1-57094-019-3*); 5.25 hd 495.00 (*1-57094-020-7*) S E Warner Sftware.

Word Processing Supervisor: User Manual for IBM--Version 2. S. E. Warner Software, Inc. Staff. 80p. 1994. pap. text ed. 2.95 (*1-57094-024-X*); 3.5 hd 495.00 (*1-57094-022-3*); 5.25 hd 495.00 (*1-57094-023-1*) S E Warner Sftware.

Word Processing, Teacher Edition: Course Code S04-1. Bonnie Schroeder. (Illus.). 82p. 1989. reprint ed. 19.95 (*0-917531-76-0*) CES Compu-Tech.

Word Processing Teacher Edition: Course Code S04-2. Yvonne Mullen. Ed. by Bonnie Schroeder. (Illus.). 80p. 1989. reprint ed. 15.00 (*0-917531-77-9*) CES Compu-Tech.

Word Processing Theory & Practice. J. Stainton-Skinn. (C). 1986. 55.00 (*0-85950-241-4*, Pub. by S Thornes Pubs UK) St Mut.

Word Processing to Desktop Publishing: Exercises & Applications. Alan Blanc. (DF - Computer Applications Ser.). 1994. text ed. 27.95 (*0-538-62352-7*) S-W Pub.

Word Processing Today Using WordPerfect 5.1. Meredith Flyn & Steven L. Mandell. LC 93-19787. 1993. pap. text ed. 38.25 (*0-314-01696-1*) West Pub.

Word Processing Using WANG Systems. Rebecca C. Latif-Pembry. 265p. (C). 1988. pap. text ed. 28.00 (*0-15-596668-5*, WANG) Dryden Pr.

Word Processing with IBM's Displaywrite Series. Judy Crondahl. 256p. 1985. pap. 17.95 (*0-317-37789-2*) S&S Trade.

Word Processing with Superscripsit & the TRS-80: Models III & 4. Lewis M. Elia & Joseph A. Fall. Ed. by Harry R. Moon. (Illus.). 161p. 1985. pap. 34.95 (*0-87350-345-7*) Milady Pub.

Word Processing with Superscripsit & the TRS-80: Models III & 4, Model III. Lewis M. Elia & Joseph A. Fall. Ed. by Harry R. Moon. (Illus.). 161p. 1985. 145.95 (*0-87350-643-X*) Milady Pub.

Word Processing with Word for Windows. (Prisma Be an Expert! Ser.). (Illus.). 192p. (Orig.). (J). 1995. pap. 12.95 (*1-85365-341-1*, Pub. by Spectrum UK) Seven Hills Bk.

Word Processing with Word Perfect 5.1. Bruce J. McLaren. (C). 1991. text ed. 17.00 (*0-06-500531-7*) Addson-Wesley Educ.

An Asterisk (*) at the beginning of an entry indicates that the title is appearing in BIP for the first time.

Word Processing with Wordperfect. (Prisma Be an Expert! Ser.). (Illus.). 192p. (Orig.). (J). 1995. pap. 12.95 (*1-85365-351-9*, Pub. by Spectrum UK) Seven Hills Bk.

Word Processing with WordPerfect 4.2, 5.0, & 5.1. Charles S. Parker. 80p. (C). 1991. pap. text ed. 9.50 (*0-03-072288-8*) Dryden Pr.

Word Processing with WordPerfect 5.1: Productivity Software Guide Module. 4th ed. Charles S. Parker. 72p. (C). 1993. pap. text ed. 12.50 (*0-03-097123-3*) Dryden Pr.

Word Processing with Wordperfect 6.0 for DOS Productivity Software Guide. Edward G. Martin. 84p. (C). 1994. pap. text ed. 12.00 (*0-03-015288-7*) HB Coll Pubs.

Word Processor. Jack Rudman. (Career Examination Ser.: C-3184). 1994. pap. 23.95 (*0-8373-3184-6*) Nat Learn.

Word Processor & Calculator Development System Source. Thomas E. Wempe. (MVP-Forth Bks.: Vol. 10). 220p. (Orig.). 1987. pap. text ed. 25.00 (*0-914699-56-3*) Mntn View Pr.

Word Processor & Calculator Development System MVP-Forth. Thomas E. Wempe. (MVP-Forth Bks.: Vol. 9). 173p. 1987. pap. text ed. 25.00 (*0-914699-32-6*) Mntn View Pr.

***Word Processor Book.** Peter McWilliams. Date not set. 14.95 (*0-698-11200-8*) Putnam Pub Group.

Word Processor to Printed Page: A Guide to Interfacing Word Processors & Phototypesetters. 2nd rev. ed. Michael Card. (Illus.). 224p. 1991. 51.95 (*0-948905-51-4*) Chapman & Hall.

Word Processors & the Writing Process: An Annotated Bibliography. Compiled by Paula R. Nancarrow et al. LC 83-22749. xi, 146p. 1984. text ed. 45.00 (*0-313-23995-9*, NAW/, Greenwood Pr) Greenwood.

Word Processsing: Pearson & Associates. 2nd ed. Lehman & Forde. (DF - Computer Applications Ser.). 1993. pap. 19.95 (*0-538-61332-7*) S-W Pub.

***Word Puzzlers.** Tribune Media Services Staff. (Puzzlers Ser.: Vol. 16). 384p. (Orig.). 1996. pap. write for info. (*1-889372-07-2*) Sweetwtr Pr AL.

***Word Puzzlers.** Tribune Media Services Staff. (Puzzlers Ser.: Vol. 17). 384p. (Orig.). 1996. pap. write for info. (*1-889372-08-0*) Sweetwtr Pr AL.

Word Puzzles. Frank Schaffer Publications, Inc. Staff. (Middle School Bks.). (Illus.). 1996. wbk. ed. 10.95 (*0-7647-0013-8*, FS-10189) Schaffer Pubns.

Word Puzzles. Ken A. Russell. 1994. pap. 7.95 (*0-572-01891-6*, Pub. by W Foulsham UK) Trans-Atl Phila.

Word Recreations: Games & Diversions from Word Ways. A. Ross Eckler. LC 79-51884. (Orig.). 1980. pap. 5.95 (*0-486-23854-7*) Dover.

Word Remains: A Life of Oscar Romero. James R. Brockman. LC 82-3607. 250p. (Orig.). reprint ed. pap. 71.30 (*0-8357-2668-1*, 2040204) Bks Demand.

Word Remains see Romero: A Life

Word Resources. 3rd ed. Thomas E. Walker. (C). 1979. pap. write for info. (*0-318-51128-2*) Macmillan.

Word Resources. 3rd ed. Thomas E. Walker. LC 78-16414. (C). 1979. pap. text ed. 50.00 (*0-02-423840-6*, Macmillan Coll) P-H.

Word Sandwiches. Philomena Marano. 48p. (J). (gr. 1 up). 1994. pap. 1.95 (*0-590-47588-6*) Scholastic Inc.

Word Scan Puzzles. Fred Justus. (Puzzles Ser.). 24p. (gr. 3). 1980. student ed. 5.00 (*0-8209-0297-7*, PU-11) ESP.

***Word Search.** (Home Workbooks Ser.). (Illus.). 64p. (Orig.). (J). (gr. 3). 1997. wbk. ed., pap. 2.49 (*0-88724-377-0*, CD-6874) Carson-Dellos.

***Word Search.** Illus. by Anita Faulkner. (Home Workbooks Ser.). 64p. (Orig.). (J). (gr. 1). 1997. wbk. ed., pap. 2.49 (*0-88724-375-4*, CD-6872) Carson-Dellos.

***Word Search.** Illus. by Pam Thayer. (Home Workbooks Ser.). 64p. (Orig.). (J). (gr. 2). 1997. wbk. ed., pap. 2.49 (*0-88724-376-2*, CD-6873) Carson-Dellos.

Word Search: Favorite Bible Stories from Genesis. John H. Tiner. 1983. pap. 4.50 (*0-89137-615-1*) Quality Pubns.

***Word Search: Having Fun with Medical Terminology.** Cathy A. Bragg. Ed. by Carolyn S. Zagury. LC 96-62089. 280p. (Orig.). 1997. pap. 10.95 (*1-880254-42-5*) Vista.

Word Search Puzzles. T. L. Smith. 34p. (J). (gr. k-6). 1991. 1.69 (*1-880825-02-3*) Tracey Smith.

Word Search Puzzles: Fun with Bible Words & Themes. Edward M. Seagrist. (Quiz & Puzzle Bks.). 80p. 1985. pap. 5.99 (*0-8010-8257-9*) Baker Bks.

Word Searches for Kids. Steve Miller & Becky Miller. (Take Me Through the Bible Ser.). 172p. (J). (gr. 2-7). 1996. pap. 5.99 (*1-56507-461-0*) Harvest Hse.

Word Signals. Sally Strohm. (English Ser.). 24p. (gr. 4-7). 1979. student ed. 5.00 (*0-8209-0185-7*, E-13) ESP.

Word Signs: A First Book of Sign Language. Debby Slier. LC 95-20452. 16p. (J). 1995. 6.95 (*1-56368-048-3*, Pub. by K Green Pubns) Gallaudet Univ Pr.

Word Singers. Ed. by Norman Simms. pap. 12.00 (*0-685-65341-2*, Three Contnts) Lynne Rienner.

Word Skills. Mary F. Pecci. (Super Seatwork Ser.). (Illus.). 238p. 1980. 17.95 (*0-943220-04-1*) Pecci Educ Pubs.

***Word Smart.** Liz Buffa. Date not set. 1.99 (*0-517-17735-8*) Random Hse Value.

Word Smart: Building an Educated Vocabulary. rev. ed. Adam Robinson & Princeton Review Publishing Staff. (Princeton Review Ser.). 1993. pap. 12.00 (*0-679-74589-0*, Villard Bks) Random.

Word Smart - Genius Edition: Erudition at Your Fingertips. Michael Freedman. (Princeton Review Ser.). 1995. pap. 12.00 (*0-679-76457-7*, Villard Bks) Random.

***Word Smart Executive.** 1997. write for info. (*0-609-60041-9*, Living Language) Crown Pub Group.

***Word Smart for Business.** Paul Westbrook. (Princeton Review Ser.). 1997. pap. 12.00 (*0-679-78391-1*) Random.

***Word Smart Genius Edition, Vol. 2.** Princeton Review Publishing Staff. 1997. 25.00 (*0-609-60101-6*, Living Language) Crown Pub Group.

Word Smart II Audio Program. Adam Robinson. 1994. 25.00 (*0-517-59761-6*, Living Language) Crown Pub Group.

***Word Smart, Jr. II.** C. L. Brantley. (Princeton Review Ser.). (J). (gr. 6-8). 1997. pap. 12.00 (*0-375-75030-4*) Random.

Word Smart Junior: How to Build a Straight "A" Vocabulary. C. L. Brantley. (Princeton Review Ser.). (J). (gr. 6-8). 1995. pap. 12.00 (*0-679-75936-0*, Villard Bks) Random.

Word Smart 2: How to Build a More Educated Vocabulary. Adam Robinson & Princeton Review Publishing Staff. 1992. pap. 12.00 (*0-679-73863-0*, Villard Bks) Random.

Word, Sound, Image: The Life of the Text. Saskia Kersenboom. Ed. by John Gledhill et al. (Explorations in Anthropology Ser.). 160p. 1995. 45.95 (*0-85496-424-X*); pap. 19.95 (*1-85973-008-6*) Berg Pubs.

Word Sounds for Alliterates: An Adult Alphabet Book of Alliterative Poetic Commentary for the Child Within You (& Other Selections) Ruth Lewis Fellhauer. (Illus.). 68p. (Orig.). 1996. pap. 9.95 (*0-9652552-0-4*) Hen Tracks.

***Word Speaks to the Faustian Man, Vol. II.** Som R. Gupta. (C). 1995. 48.00 (*81-208-1175-5*, Pub. by Motilal Banarsidass II) S Asia.

Word Stems: A Dictionary. abr. ed. John Kennedy. 297p. 1996. reprint ed. pap. 15.00 (*1-56947-051-0*) Soho Press.

***Word Store Dictionary.** Triggs. 1992. pap. text ed. write for info. (*0-17-556287-3*) Addison-Wesley.

Word Strands 1. Pikebaky. (College ESL Ser.). 1995. pap. 17.95 (*0-8384-6068-2*) Heinle & Heinle.

Word Strands 2. Pikebaky. (College ESL Ser.). 1995. pap. 19.95 (*0-8384-6074-7*) Heinle & Heinle.

Word Strands 3. Christie. (College ESL Ser.). 1996. pap. 12.95 (*0-8384-5882-3*) Heinle & Heinle.

***Word Stretchers.** Flatt. 1991. pap. text ed. write for info. (*1-85503-116-7*) Addison-Wesley.

Word Structure see Universals of Human Language

Word Studies. 8th ed. Devern J. Perry. (C). 1989. text ed. 19.95 (*0-538-05813-7*, E81U) S-W Pub.

Word Studies. 8th ed. Devern J. Perry. (PS - Communication/English Ser.). 1989. text ed. 17.95 (*0-538-05811-0*) S-W Pub.

Word Studies. 9th ed. Devern J. Perry. (PS - Communication/English Ser.). 1996. wbk. ed., pap. 18.95 (*0-538-71274-0*) S-W Pub.

Word-Studies in French & English, 1st Ser. Thomas A. Jenkins. (LM Ser.: No. 14). 1933. pap. 25.00 (*0-527-00818-4*) Periodicals Srv.

Word Studies on the Holy Spirit. Ethelbert W. Bullinger. LC 85-7631. 232p. 1985. pap. 10.99 (*0-8254-2246-9*, Kregel Class) Kregel.

Word Studies, Tests. 9th ed. Devern J. Perry. (PS - Communication/English Ser.). 1996. 5.95 (*0-538-71300-3*) S-W Pub.

Word Sublime & Its Context, 1650-1760. Theodore E. Wood. LC 77-165151. (De Proprietatibus Litterarum, Ser. Major: No. 7). 231p. 1972. text ed. 46.15 (*90-279-2073-7*) Mouton.

Word Surprises. Effie R. Larson. 1995. 12.95 (*0-533-11473-X*) Vantage.

Word Tales. 1994. 19.61 (*1-57251-030-7*) TWI.

Word Teasers. Dympna Hayes. (Mind Benders Ser.). (Illus.). 32p. (J). (gr. 2-6). 1988. pap. 2.95 (*0-88625-148-6*) Durkin Hayes Pub.

Word Test - R, Elementary Test Kit: A Test of Expressive Vocabulary & Semantics. rev. ed. Mark Barrett et al. 80p. (gr. 2-6). 1990. 64.95 (*1-55999-140-2*) LinguiSystems.

Word Test - R, Elementary Test Manual: A Test of Expressive Vocabulary & Semantics. rev. ed. Mark Barrett et al. 80p. (gr. 2-6). 1990. 43.00 (*1-55999-133-X*) LinguiSystems.

Word Test--Adolescent - Complete Kit: A Test of Expressive Vocabulary & Semantics. Mark Barrett et al. (YA). (gr. 7-12). 1989. 64.95 (*1-55999-096-1*) LinguiSystems.

Word Test--Adolescent - Examiner's Manual: A Test of Expressive Vocabulary & Semantics. Mark Barrett et al. (YA). (gr. 7-12). 1989. lab manual ed. 43.00 (*1-55999-097-X*) LinguiSystems.

Word That Will Rouse Them: Reflections on the Ministry of Reader. Aelred R. Rosser. LC 95-11671. 93p. (Orig.). 1995. pap. 9.00 (*1-56854-028-0*, ROUSE) Liturgy Tr Pubns.

Word, the Flesh & Daniel Darling. Edward R. Skane. 258p. 1994. 19.95 (*0-917655-05-2*) Dane Bks.

Word, the Name, the Blood. Joyce Meyer. 139p. 1995. 14.99 (*0-89274-827-3*) Harrison Hse.

Word Thinker Sheets. Becky Daniel. 64p. (J). (gr. 4-8). 1988. student ed. 8.99 (*0-86653-394-X*, GA1034) Good Apple.

Word Three-Point-Zero on the MAC: A Guide to Power & Performance. Tim Knight. (Illus.). 400p. 1988. 19.95 (*0-685-18875-2*) P-H.

Word Thursdays Anthology of Poetry & Fiction. Ed. by Bertha Rogers. 198p. 1995. pap. 12.95 (*0-9646844-1-1*) Bright Hill.

Word Tips & Techniques. Sharon Aker. 1992. pap. write for info. (*0-201-60888-X*) AddVantage Lrn.

Word to the Wise: And Other Proverbs. Illus. by Robert Rayevsky. LC 93-26836. 40p. (J). (ps up). 1994. 15.00 (*0-688-12065-2*, Morrow Junior); lib. bdg. 14.93 (*0-688-12066-0*, Morrow Junior) Morrow.

Word Traces: Readings of Paul Celan. Ed. by Aris Fioretos. LC 92-44195. 432p. (C). 1994. text ed. 65.00 (*0-8018-4525-4*); pap. text ed. 24.95 (*0-8018-4767-2*) Johns Hopkins.

Word Tracking: High Frequency Words - Blackline Masters. B. L. Kaye. 64p. (J). (ps-2). 1989. teacher ed. 12.00 (*0-87879-870-6*, 870-6, Ann Arbor Div) Acad Therapy.

Word Tracking: Limericks. Betty L. Kratoville. 64p. (Orig.). 1990. pap. 12.00 (*0-87879-884-6*, Ann Arbor Div) Acad Therapy.

Word Tracking: Proverbs. Betty L. Kratoville. 64p. 12.00 (*0-87879-869-2*, Ann Arbor Div) Acad Therapy.

Word Up: Hope for Youth Poetry from El Centro de la Raza. Ed. by Zoe Anglesey. (ENG, SPA & TAG.). (YA). 1992. 12.95 (*0-9633275-1-8*) El Centro de la Raza.

Word Warrior: A Book of Poems. Bruce A. Drobot. 128p. 1992. 14.95 (*0-9632706-0-5*) Word Warrior.

Word Was Made Flesh. Ralph Larson. LC 94-60461. 384p. 1995. per. 8.95 (*1-57258-032-1*) Teach Servs.

Word Was Made Flesh: An Introduction to the Theology of the New Testament. John C. Dwyer. LC 88-63858. 160p. (Orig.). (C). 1989. pap. 10.95 (*1-55612-251-9*) Sheed & Ward MO.

Word Watch: The Stories Behind the Words of Our Lives. Anne H. Soukhanov. 448p. 1996. pap. 14.95 (*0-8050-4544-9*, Owl) H Holt & Co.

Word Watcher's Handbook. 3rd ed. Phyllis Martin. 1991. pap. 6.95 (*0-312-05541-2*) St Martin.

Word Watcher's Handbook: A Deletionary of the Most Abused & Misused Words. Phyllis Martin. 144p. 1982. pap. 4.95 (*0-312-88938-0*) St Martin.

Word, Water, Wine, & Bread. William H. Willimon. 1980. pap. 11.00 (*0-8170-0858-6*) Judson.

Word Ways: The Novels of D'Arcy McNickle. John L. Purdy. LC 89-27106. 167p. 1990. 30.95 (*0-8165-1157-8*) U of Ariz Pr.

Word We Celebrate: Commentary on Sunday Lectionary Years A, B & C. Patricia D. Sanchez. LC 89-61926. 404p. (Orig.). (C). 1989. pap. 29.95 (*1-55612-302-7*) Sheed & Ward MO.

Word Wealth: 1978. W. Miller. 1978. teacher ed., pap. text ed. 24.25 (*0-03-041936-0*) HR&W Schl Div.

Word Weaving: A Creative Approach to Teaching & Writing Poetry. David Johnson. (Illus.). 177p. 1990. pap. 12.95 (*0-8141-5822-6*) NCTE.

***Word Wheels.** Claudia Krause. (Orig.). (J). pap. text ed. write for info. (*0-9655689-0-3*) C Krause.

Word Whys from the Would Pile: or, Tom C.'s Short Ease. Tom C. Armstrong. 64p. (Orig.). 1992. pap. 5.99 (*0-9638661-2-5*) AD HOC Bks.

Word Wisdom in the Esoteric Tradition. G. De Purucker. (Study Ser.: No. 2). 1980. 8.00 (*0-913004-35-9*, 913004-35) Point Loma Pub.

***Word-Wise Sourcebook: Laugh-Aloud Rhymes for Learning Language Skills.** Maurice Poe & Barbara Schmidt. (Illus.). (J). (gr. 1-2). 1997. teacher ed., spiral bd. 38.50 (*1-886050-13-9*) Egger Pub Inc.

Word Within. Peter Bowes. Ed. by Andrea Bowes. 184p. (Orig.). 1991. pap. text ed. 9.95 (*0-9628517-0-1*, 399-008) Chariot Pub.

Word Within the Word: An Exploration of the Interior of Language for Academically Motivated Secondary Students, Vol. I. Michael Thompson. 332p. 1994. teacher ed., pap. 15.00 (*0-88092-201-X*) Royal Fireworks.

Word Within the Word: An Exploration of the Interior of Language for Academically Motivated Secondary Students, Vol. I. Michael Thompson. 118p. 1994. student ed., pap. 10.00 (*0-88092-200-1*) Royal Fireworks.

Word Within the Word: An Exploration of the Interior of Language for Academically Motivated Secondary Students, Vol. II. Michael Thompson. 329p. 1994. teacher ed., pap. 15.00 (*0-88092-203-6*) Royal Fireworks.

Word Within the Word: An Exploration of the Interior of Language for Academically Motivated Secondary Students, Vol. II. Michael Thompson. 218p. 1994. student ed., pap. 10.00 (*0-88092-202-8*) Royal Fireworks.

Word Within the Word: An Exploration of the Interior of Language for Academically Motivated Secondary Students, Vol. III. Michael Thompson. 336p. 1995. teacher ed., pap. 15.00 (*0-88092-205-2*) Royal Fireworks.

Word Within the Word: An Exploration of the Interior of Language for Academically Motivated Secondary Students, Vol. III. Michael Thompson. 240p. (YA). (gr. 8-12). 1995. student ed., pap. text ed. 10.00 (*0-88092-204-4*) Royal Fireworks.

***Word Without End: The Old Testament As Abiding Theological Witness.** Christopher R. Seitz. LC 97-23187. 1997. pap. write for info. (*0-8028-4322-0*) Eerdmans.

***Word Wizard.** Cathryn Falwell. LC 97-17710. 1998. write for info. (*0-395-85580-2*, Clarion Bks) HM.

Word Wizard: Medical Term Software Programming, Vol. 1. Johnson. (RT-Medical Terminolgy Ser.). (C). 1993. text ed. 49.95 (*0-8273-5906-3*) Delmar.

Word Wizardry, Level I. Flora Joy. (Illus.). 112p. (J). (gr. 2-8). 1987. pap. 12.99 (*0-86653-403-2*, GA 1016) Good Apple.

Word Wizardry, Level II. Flora Joy. (Illus.). 112p. (J). (gr. 4-12). 1987. pap. 12.99 (*0-86653-404-0*, GA 1017) Good Apple.

Word Wizardry: A Book of Poems. Jan Powers. 64p. 1995. 12.95 (*0-8233-0501-5*) Golden Quill.

Word "Woman" & Other Related Writings. Laura R. Jackson. Ed. by Elizabeth Friedmann & Alan J. Clark. 196p. (Orig.). 1993. 19.95 (*0-89255-184-4*); pap. 9.95 (*0-89255-185-2*) Persea Bks.

Word Works. Shirley Greenslade. 82p. 1997. pap. write for info. (*1-886799-02-4*) Agape Word.

Word Works: Why the Alphabet Is a Kid's Best Friend. Catherine B. Kaye. (Brown Paper School Bks.). (Illus.). 128p. (J). (gr. 4 up). 1985. pap. 10.95 (*0-316-48375-3*) Little.

Word, Worship, World & Wonder: Reflections on Christian Living. Karen Lebacqz. LC 97-13817. 128p. (Orig.). 1997. pap. 14.95 (*0-687-02089-1*) Abingdon.

Word Wounds & Water Flowers. Daniella Gioseffi. (VIA Folios Ser.). 86p. (C). 1995. pap. 8.00 (*1-884419-03-8*) Bordighera.

***Word X for Macs for Dummies.** 1997. pap. 19.99 (*0-7645-0230-1*) IDG Bks.

***Word X Macro & VBA Handbook.** Guy Hart-Davis. 1996. pap. text ed. 44.99 incl. cd-rom (*0-7821-1962-X*) Sybex.

Word 2.0 for Windows. Stacey C. Sawyer. 120p. (C). 1993. per. 12.50 (*0-256-13530-4*) Irwin.

Word 3 for Windows Essentials. 1995. 39.99 (*0-7897-0117-0*) Que.

Word 5 for Macintosh: Print & Presentation Kit: How to Create Brochures, Ads, Flyers, Newsletters, Reports, & Slides. Christine Solomon. LC 92-15140. 1992. write for info. (*0-201-58110-8*) Addison-Wesley.

Word 5 (PC) Advanced. Douglas M. Finney. 197p. 1991. student ed., teacher ed., spiral bd. 29.95 incl. disk (*1-56435-010-X*) Finney Lrng Systs.

Word 5 (PC) Beginning. Douglas M. Finney. 168p. 1991. student ed., teacher ed., spiral bd. 29.95 incl. disk (*1-56435-009-6*) Finney Lrng Systs.

Word 6 Book for Macintosh Users. Tonya Engst. (Illus.). 600p. (Orig.). 1994. pap. 24.95 (*1-56830-110-3*) Hayden.

Word 6 for Macintosh: Visual QuickStart Guide. 2nd ed. David Browne. (Illus.). 208p. (C). 1994. pap. text ed. 13.95 (*1-56609-125-X*) Peachpit Pr.

Word 6 for the Mac: The Visual Learning Guide. David Gardner. 274p. 1995. pap. 19.95 (*1-55958-461-0*) Prima Pub.

Word 6 for the Mac for Dummies. Dan Gookin. 384p. 1994. pap. 19.95 (*1-56884-190-6*) IDG Bks.

Word 6 for Windows: How to Use the Mail Merge Feature. Mike Murach. LC 95-10340. 71p. 1995. pap. 9.95 (*0-911625-88-7*) M Murach & Assoc.

Word 6 for Windows: Instant Reference. Sheila S. Dienes. LC 93-86589. 265p. 1993. 9.99 (*0-7821-1400-8*) Sybex.

Word 6 for Windows: QuickStart Training Software. Webster & Associates Staff. 1994. 19.95 (*1-56609-154-3*) Peachpit Pr.

Word 6 for Windows: Visual QuickStart Guide. Webster & Associates Staff. (Illus.). 368p. (Orig.). 1994. pap. 15.95 (*1-56609-110-1*) Peachpit Pr.

Word 6 for Windows Essentials. Laura Acklen. 1995. 22.99 (*0-7897-0108-1*) Que.

Word 6 for Windows Essentials. Gregory Mandel. (Illus.). 464p. 1994. 29.95 incl. disk (*1-56609-106-3*) Peachpit Pr.

Word 6 for Windows for Dummies. 2nd ed. Dan Gookin. (For Dummies Ser.). (Illus.). 360p. 1994. pap. 16.95 (*1-56884-075-6*) IDG Bks.

Word 6 for Windows Quickstart. 2nd ed. 1994. 29.99 (*1-56529-790-3*) Que.

Word 6 for Windows Simplified. expanded ed. Maran Graphics Staff & Ruth Maran. 256p. 1994. pap. 19.99 (*1-56884-660-6*) IDG Bks.

Word 6 for Windows Simplified: Education Edition. Maran Graphics Staff & Ruth Maran. 1994. pap. 14.99 (*1-56884-659-2*) IDG Bks.

Word 6 for Windows Smartstart. 1995. teacher ed. 39.99 (*1-56529-822-5*) Que.

Word 6 for Windows Smartstart. 1994. 29.99 (*1-56529-796-2*) Que.

Word 6 for Windows Smartstart. 2nd ed. Suzanne Weixel. 1995. 29.99 (*1-57576-339-7*) Mac Pub USA.

Word 6 for Windows Visual Pocket Guide. Maran Graphics Staff & Ruth Maran. 256p. 1994. pap. 14.99 (*1-56884-666-5*) IDG Bks.

Word 6 NOW! (for Windows 3.1) A Simple Guide to Learning Word Quickly & Easily. Robert Medved & Jennifer Ames. LC 95-60569. (Illus.). 208p. (Orig.). 1995. pap. 18.99 (*0-9643450-1-3*) Easel Pubng.

Word 6 Virtual Tutor. Que Education & Training Staff. 1996. pap. text ed. 49.99 incl. cd-rom (*1-57576-089-4*) Que Educ & Trng.

***Word 6 Windows Virtual Tutor.** Que Education & Training Staff. (Essentials Ser.). 1997. pap. text ed. 25.00 (*1-57576-090-8*) Que Educ & Trng.

Word 6/Excel 5/Access 2 Combination Text: Star Series. Boyd & Fraser Staff. (DF - Computer Applications Ser.). 1996. pap. 30.95 (*0-7895-0198-8*) S-W Pub.

Word 6.0 for the Mac Solutions. Elaine J. Marmel. 544p. 1994. pap. text ed. 24.95 (*0-471-00809-5*) Wiley.

Word 6.0 for Windows. (Prisma Computer Courses Ser.). (Illus.). 200p. (Orig.). 1995. pap. 12.95 (*1-85365-395-0*, Pub. by Spectrum UK) Seven Hills Bk.

Word 6.0 for Windows. Steve Eckols. LC 94-19740. (Essential Guide Ser.). (Illus.). 575p. 1994. pap. 25.00 (*0-911625-80-1*) M Murach & Assoc.

Word 6.0 for Windows. Stacey C. Sawyer et al. 208p. (C). 1994. pap. 25.00 (*0-256-17013-4*) Irwin.

Word 6.0 for Windows: A Professional Approach. Deborah A. Hinkle. LC 94-5260. 1995. write for info. (*0-02-803085-0*) Glencoe.

Word 6.0 for Windows: Advanced. Douglas M. Finney & Sean C. Feeney. 1994. spiral bd. 29.95 incl. 3.5 hd (*1-56435-046-0*) Finney Lrng Systs.

Word 6.0 for Windows: Beginning. Douglas M. Finney & Sean C. Feeney. 1994. spiral bd. 24.95 incl. 3.5 ld (*1-56435-044-4*) Finney Lrng Systs.

Word 6.0 for Windows: Intermediate. Douglas M. Finney & Sean C. Feeney. 1993. spiral bd. 29.95 incl. 3.5 hd (*1-56435-045-2*) Finney Lrng Systs.

W

Word 6.0 for Windows: Production Software Guide. 4th ed. Edward G. Martin. 136p. (C). 1994. pap. text ed. 10.75 (*0-03-007248-4*) HarBrace.
Word 6.0 for Windows: QuickStart Training Bundle. Webster & Associates Staff. 368p. 1994. 29.95 (*1-56609-155-1*) Peachpit Pr.
Word 6.0 for Windows in a Hurry. abr. ed. Dawn Groves. LC 94-45614. 168p. 1995. spiral bd. 12.95 (*0-938661-83-3*) Franklin Beedle.
Word 6.0 for Windows Intermediate. Bethany Sunny. (Quicksteps to Learning Ser.). 250p. 1994. spiral bd. 22.95 (*1-56951-046-6*) Sftware Trng.
Word 6.0 for Windows with Style Manual References. John M. Preston & Robert Ferrett. 160p. (C). 1995. spiral bd. 21.75 (*0-697-26016-X*) Bus & Educ Tech.
Word 6.0 For Windows with Style Manuals. John M. Preston & Robert Ferrett. 192p. (C). 1995. per. 15.75 (*0-256-20437-3*) Irwin.
***Word 7.** Esko Valtanen et al. LC 96-21138. (Paradigm Visual Ser.). 1996. write for info. (*0-7638-0010-4*) Paradigm MN.
Word 7 for Windows. spiral bd. 12.00 (*1-56243-248-6*, WDW7) DDC Pub.
Word 7 for Windows 95. (Glencoe Visual Ser.). 1996. write for info. (*0-02-803947-5*) Glencoe.
Word 7 for Windows 95. (Glencoe Visual Ser.). 1996. wbk. ed. write for info. (*0-02-803948-3*) Glencoe.
Word 7 for Windows 95. (Glencoe Visual Ser.). 1996. write for info. (*0-02-803949-1*) Glencoe.
Word 7 for Windows 95. (Glencoe Visual Ser.). 1996. write for info. (*0-02-813941-0*) Glencoe.
***Word 7.0 for Windows, Advanced.** Sean C. Feeney & Douglas M. Finney. 1996. student ed., spiral bd. 29.95 incl. disk (*1-56435-098-3*) Finney Lrng Systs.
***Word 7.0 for Windows, Beginning.** Sean C. Feeney & Douglas M. Finney. 1996. student ed., spiral bd. 29.95 incl. disk (*1-56435-096-7*) Finney Lrng Systs.
***Word 7.0 for Windows, Intermediate.** Sean C. Feeney & Douglas M. Finney. 1996. student ed., spiral bd. 29.95 incl. disk (*1-56435-097-5*) Finney Lrng Systs.
***Word 95 - 97.** Kenneth Laudon. LC 97-2210. 1997. pap. text ed. write for info. (*0-07-038437-1*) McGraw.
Word 95 Essentials. Laura Acklen. 1995. 22.99 (*1-57576-274-9*) Mac Pub USA.
***Word 97.** Tim Duffy. (C). 1997. pap. text ed. 22.95 (*0-201-31505-X*) Addison-Wesley.
***Word 97.** Trudi Reisner. (New Tutorial Ser.). 1997. pap. 29.99 (*0-7645-3129-8*) IDG Bks.
***Word 97: The Visual Learning Guide.** Nancy Stevenson. 384p. 1997. per. 16.99 (*0-7615-1007-9*) Prima Pub.
***Word 97 Bible.** Brent Heslop & David F. Angell. 1008p. 1997. pap. 34.99 (*0-7645-3038-0*) IDG Bks.
***Word 97 Essentials (Academic)** Acklen. 1997. 22.99 (*1-57576-825-9*) Sams.
***Word 97 Essentials (Academic)** Que Education & Training Staff. 1997. 39.99 (*1-57576-872-0*) Que Educ & Trng.
***Word 97 Essentials Level II.** Robert Bringhurst. 1997. 49.99 (*1-57576-806-2*) Que Educ & Trng.
***Word 97 Essentials Level II.** Robert Bringhurst. 1997. 22.99 (*1-57576-801-1*) Sams.
***Word 97 Essentials Level III.** 1997. 22.99 (*1-57576-800-3*) Sams.
***Word 97 for Busy People.** Christian Crumlish. 1997. pap. text ed. 24.99 (*0-07-882282-3*) Osborne-McGraw.
***Word 97 for Windows for Dummies.** Dan Gookin. (For Dummies Ser.). 1996. pap. 19.99 (*0-7645-0052-X*) IDG Bks.
***Word 97 for Windows for Dummies Quick Reference.** Peter Weverka. (For Dummies Quick Reference Ser.). (Illus.). 240p. (Orig.). 1997. pap. 12.99 (*0-7645-0070-8*) IDG Bks.
***Word 97 SECRETS.** Doug Lowe. 752p. (Orig.). 1997. pap. write for info. (*0-614-26296-8*) IDG Bks.
***Word 97 Secrets.** Doug Lowe. 1997. pap. text ed. 39.99 (*0-7645-3045-3*) IDG Bks.
***Word 97 Simplified.** Ruth Macan. (Illus.). 224p. (Orig.). 1997. pap. write for info. (*0-614-26276-3*) IDG Bks.
***Word 97 Simplified.** Maran Graphics Staff. 224p. 1997. pap. 24.99 (*0-7645-6011-5*) IDG Bks.
***Word 97 Simplified.** Ruth Maran. 1997. pap. 24.99 (*0-614-28457-0*) IDG Bks.
***Word 97 Smartstart.** Jerry Horazdovsky. 1997. 29.99 (*1-57576-814-3*) Sams.
Wordbuilders, Vol. 1. 1987. pap. 10.99 (*0-553-45092-1*) Bantam.
WordBuilding. Joan Robinson. (Roots of Language Ser.). (J). (gr. 4-8). 1989. pap. 10.99 (*0-8224-7450-6*) Fearon Teach Aids.
Wordcraft: Concise Dictionary & Thesaurus. 235p. pap. 19.95 (*1-898281-02-5*, Pub. by Anglo-Saxon Bks UK) Paul & Co Pubs.
Wordfinding: A Language Rehabilitation Manual for Aphasic Adults. rev. ed. Daniel F. Carlson. Ed. by Cindy Drolet. LC 87-82069. 155p. 1990. pap. text ed. 65.00 (*0-9609464-4-6*) Imaginart Pr.
***Wordflow: New & Selected Poems.** Michael Heller. LC 97-7529. 128p. 1997. pap. 10.50 (*1-883689-49-X*) Talisman Hse.
***Wordflow: New & Selected Poems.** Michael Heller. LC 97-7529. 128p. 1997. 30.50 (*1-883689-50-3*) Talisman Hse.
Wordforms: Context, Strategies, & Practice, 2 vols., Bk. I. 2nd ed. Helen H. Gordon. 273p. (C). 1991. pap. 31.95 (*0-534-13056-9*) Wadsworth Pub.
Wordforms: Context, Strategies, & Practice, 2 vols., Bk. II. 2nd ed. Helen H. Gordon. 265p. (C). 1991. pap. 31.95 (*0-534-13057-7*) Wadsworth Pub.
Wordful Child. George E. Lyon. LC 96-866. (Meet the Author Ser.). (Illus.). 32p. (J). (gr. 2-5). 1996. 13.95 (*1-57274-016-7*) R Owen Pubs.
Wordgames. 1989. pap. 14.95 (*0-590-76204-4*, Scholastic Hardcover) Scholastic Inc.
Word/Information Processing Concepts. 2nd ed. Casady. (DF - Computer Applications Ser.). 1989. wbk. ed., pap. 20.95 (*0-538-70031-9*) S-W Pub.
Word/Information Processing Concepts. 3rd ed. Casady. (DF - Computer Applications Ser.). 1988. pap. 20.95 (*0-538-23620-5*) S-W Pub.
Wordless Counting Book. Cindy Kosowsky. LC 91-77575. (Illus.). 24p. (J). (ps-k). 1992. 10.95 (*1-880851-00-8*) Greene Bark Pr.
Wordless Rhetoric: Musical Form & the Metaphor of the Oration. Mark E. Bonds. (Studies in the History of Music). 237p. (C). 1991. 45.00 (*0-674-95602-8*) HUP.
Wordless Travel Book. Jonathan Meader. (Illus.). 18p. (Orig.). 1996. pap. 4.95 (*0-89815-809-5*) Ten Speed Pr.
Wordless Workshop. Roy Doty. 1986. pap. 6.95 (*0-312-00061-8*) St Martin.
WordPerfect: A Practical Approach. Mary A. Eisch. (C). 1988. pap. 34.95 (*0-538-80043-7*, WM83ABU) S-W Pub.
WordPerfect: A Practical Approach, 5.0 Version. Mary A. Eisch. (C). 1991. pap. 36.95 (*0-538-70250-8*, WM40ABU) S-W Pub.
WordPerfect: Advanced Features, Version. Sullivan. (Df-Computer Applications Ser.). 1991. pap. 27.95 (*0-538-70465-9*) S-W Pub.
WordPerfect: Advanced Features Version 4.1. Sullivan. (DF - Computer Applications Ser.). 1991. pap. 34.95 (*0-538-70464-0*) S-W Pub.
WordPerfect: Desktop Publishing in Style. 2nd ed. Daniel Will-Harris. 672p. pap. 23.95 (*0-938151-15-0*) Peachpit Pr.
WordPerfect: Hands-On! Jean Knox. (Illus.). 840p. (Orig.). 1990. pap. 26.95 (*0-938862-73-1*) Weber Systems.
WordPerfect: Prospects for Literacy in the Computer Age. Myron C. Tuman. (Series in Composition, Literacy, & Culture). 164p. (C). 1992. text ed. 49.95 (*0-8229-3735-2*); pap. text ed. 19.95 (*0-8229-5489-3*) U of Pittsburgh Pr.
WordPerfect: Quick Start. Sue V. Stacy. (DF - Computer Applications Ser.). 1990. pap. 19.95 (*0-538-70310-5*) S-W Pub.
WordPerfect: Self Teaching Guide. Neil J. Salkind. (Self Teaching Guides Ser.). 400p. 1993. pap. text ed. 19.95 (*0-471-58422-3*) Wiley.
WordPerfect: The Learning Reference & Example Manual 4.2. Marie F. Frasson. 400p. 1988. pap. text ed. 27.20 (*0-13-964495-4*) P-H.
WordPerfect: The Useable Portable Guide. Jon Haber & Herbert R. Haber. (Illus.). 32p. (Orig.). (C). 1988. pap. text ed. 4.95 (*0-945765-01-0*) Useable Portable Pubns.
WordPerfect: Tutorial & Applications. Eisch. (DF - Computer Applications Ser.). 1990. pap. 25.95 (*0-538-60343-7*) S-W Pub.
WordPerfect No. I: Tutorial & Applications. Eisch & Fischer. (DF - Computer Applications Ser.). 1988. pap. 26.95 (*0-538-80042-9*) S-W Pub.
WordPerfect Advanced Applications: Cases & Solutions. Fritz H. Grupe. 208p. (C). 1991. spiral bd. write for info. (*0-697-11723-5*) Bus & Educ Tech.
WordPerfect & Running with Fortran 90. Donald Allock. (C). 1997. pap. text ed. write for info. (*0-201-42783-4*) Addison-Wesley.
WordPerfect Applications. large type ed. 1993. 46.50 (*0-614-09862-9*, L-31426-00) Am Printing Hse.
WordPerfect Book. Assadi. Date not set. 30.00 (*1-56830-259-2*) Mac Pub USA.
WordPerfect Book. Arnold Rosen. 282p. (C). 1988. spiral bd. 20.00 (*0-15-596580-8*) HB Coll Pubs.
WordPerfect Book. Leo J. Scanlon. 1990. 27.95 (*0-8306-7616-3*, Windcrest); pap. 18.95 (*0-8306-3616-1*, Windcrest) TAB Bks.
WordPerfect Book, Version 5.0...to Include Versions 4.0, 4.1, 4.2. Leo J. Scanlon. (Illus.). 224p. 1988. 24.95 (*0-8306-0327-1*, 3127H); pap. 16.95 (*0-8306-3127-5*, 3127) McGraw-Hill Prof.
WordPerfect Certification Success Guide. Brian Ford & Debra Ford. 1995. pap. text ed. 29.95 (*0-07-021519-7*) McGraw.
WordPerfect DOS Certification Curriculum - Essential Skills. WordPerfect Corporation Staff. (NO - Novell/WordPerfect Ser.). 1995. text ed. 30.95 (*0-538-63771-4*) S-W Pub.
WordPerfect DOS Certification for Current Professionals. WordPerfect Corporation Staff. (NO - Novell/WordPerfect Ser.). 1995. text ed. 37.95 (*0-538-63780-3*) S-W Pub.
WordPerfect Easy Instructions. Walter W. Bell. 1994. pap. text ed. 12.95 (*1-880071-29-0*) Simple Sftware.
WordPerfect Essentials: Version 6.0 for DOS. Nita H. Rutkosky. 368p. 1994. pap. text ed. 26.95 (*1-56118-728-3*) Paradigm MN.
WordPerfect Essentials: Version 6.0 for DOS. Nita H. Rutkosky. 368p. 1994. text ed. 26.95 incl. 5.25 hd (*1-56118-750-X*) Paradigm MN.
WordPerfect Essentials: Version 6.0 for DOS. Nita H. Rutkosky. 368p. 1994. pap. text ed. 19.00 (*1-56118-727-5*) Paradigm MN.
WordPerfect Essentials: 6.1 for Windows. Nita H. Rutkosky. LC 95-21963. 1995. pap. text ed. 25.95 (*1-56118-795-X*) Paradigm MN.
WordPerfect Expert 5.0. Neil J. Salkind. 336p. 1989. pap. 25.00 (*1-55623-081-8*) Irwin Prof Pubng.
WordPerfect Express: A Complete Easy-to-Use Book-Disk Tutorial, PC Edition. Philip Casella. 350p. 1992. 40.00 (*1-55623-780-4*) Irwin Prof Pubng.
WordPerfect for Dummies. Dan Gookin. (Illus.). 352p. 1992. pap. 16.95 (*1-878058-52-5*) IDG Bks.
WordPerfect for Kids. Taylor R. Taylor. (LogicNotes Ser.). (Illus.). (Orig.). 1990. pap. text ed. write for info. incl. vhs (*0-929978-54-4*) M-USA Busn Systs.
WordPerfect for Lawyers: How to Easily Automate the Production of Documents in Law Offices. Don Silver. LC 89-15037. 283p. 1989. 149.00 (*0-944708-21-8*) Adams Hall.
WordPerfect for Lawyers: How to Easily Automate the Production of Documents in Law Offices, Version 5.1. Don Silver. 1990. ring bd. 149.00 incl. disk (*0-944708-24-2*) Adams Hall.
WordPerfect for Legal Assistants & Secretaries. Mark Workman. LC 94-70486. (Computer Ser.). 130p. 1994. pap. 11.95 (*1-56052-278-X*) Crisp Pubns.
WordPerfect for the Macintosh: A Practical Approach, Version 2.0. Mary A. Eisch. 1992. pap. 27.95 (*0-538-70456-X*) S-W Pub.
WordPerfect for the Macintosh: Quick Start. Mary S. Stacy. 1992. pap. 19.95 (*0-538-70474-8*) S-W Pub.
WordPerfect for Windows. (Prisma Computer Courses Ser.). (Illus.). 200p. (Orig.). 1995. pap. 12.95 (*1-85365-370-5*, Pub. by Spectrum UK) Seven Hills Bk.
WordPerfect for Windows. Cram. (C). 1995. teacher ed., pap. 11.96 (*0-395-69266-0*) HM.
WordPerfect for Windows. M-USA Video Staff. (LogicNotes Ser.). 1991. write for info. incl. vhs (*0-929978-52-8*) M-USA Busn Systs.
WordPerfect for Windows: Beginners. 1993. teacher ed. 49.95 (*1-56877-142-8*) Catapult WA.
WordPerfect for Windows: Easy Reference Guide. Wynema Anderson & Stacey Golightly. LC 93-4307. 1994. text ed. 7.95 (*0-538-62675-5*) S-W Pub.
WordPerfect for Windows: Level 1. David S. Murphy et al. (Easy Way Ser.). 197p. 1993. pap. 29.95 (*1-57048-100-8*) Trning Express.
WordPerfect for Windows: Quick Course Version 5. Wagoner. (Computer Applications Ser.). 1994. 77.95 (*0-538-71080-2*) S-W Pub.
WordPerfect for Windows: Quick Start. Wagoner. (DF - Computer Applications Ser.). 1994. pap. 19.95 (*0-538-62912-6*) S-W Pub.
WordPerfect for Windows: The Visual Learning Guide. David C. Gardner & Grace J. Beatty. (Illus.). 200p. 1993. pap. 16.95 (*1-55958-181-6*) Prima Pub.
WordPerfect for Windows: Tutorial & Applications. Eisch. (DF - Computer Applications Ser.). 1993. pap. 30.95 (*0-538-62078-1*) S-W Pub.
WordPerfect for Windows: Visual QuickStart Guide with Interactive Training Disk. Webster & Associates Staff. (Illus.). 290p. 1992. pap. 27.95 incl. disk (*0-938151-95-9*) Peachpit Pr.
WordPerfect for Windows Answers: Certified Tech Support. Mary Campbell. (Certified Tech Support Ser.). 336p. 1994. pap. text ed. 16.95 (*0-07-882053-7*) Osborne-McGraw.
WordPerfect for Windows Comprehensive. Katie Layman. (C). 1995. pap. text ed. 58.00 (*0-13-034653-5*) P-H.
WordPerfect for Windows Express: A Complete Easy-to-Use Book Tutorial, PC Edition. Philip Casella. 392p. 1993. per., pap. 40.00 incl. disk (*1-55623-920-3*) Irwin Prof Pubng.
***WordPerfect for Windows for Busy People.** Elden Nelson. 1997. pap. text ed. 24.99 (*0-07-882313-7*) Osborne-McGraw.
WordPerfect for Windows for Dummies. Margaret L. Young. (Illus.). 416p. 1993. pap. 16.95 (*1-56884-032-2*) IDG Bks.
WordPerfect for Windows for Dummies Quick Reference. Greg Harvey. 144p. 1993. pap. 8.95 (*1-56884-039-X*) IDG Bks.
WordPerfect for Windows in Five Days. Chris Kania. LC 91-65116. 300p. 1992. 35.00 (*0-9629003-0-3*) Tech Documentation.
WordPerfect for Windows Made Easy: Covers Version 5.2. Katie Layman. LC 92-46728. 320p. 1993. pap. text ed. 46.00 (*0-13-950981-X*) P-H Gen Ref & Trav.
WordPerfect for Windows Power Macros & Wordperfect for Windows Macros. Jamsa. 912p. 1992. pap. 52.90 (*0-471-57669-7*) Wiley.
WordPerfect for Windows Print & Presentation Kit. Christine Solomon. 1992. pap. 26.95 (*0-201-58109-4*) Addison-Wesley.
WordPerfect for Windows Quick Reference. M. Hobbie. (Quick Reference Ser.). (Illus.). 246p. (Orig.). 1993. 9.99 (*1-56529-139-5*) Que.
WordPerfect for Windows Quick Reference. Micoref Educational Systems Staff. 1992. pap. 19.95 (*1-56351-072-3*) Microref Educ Systs.
WordPerfect for Windows Quick Reference Guide. Marivel Salazar & Cassano. (Illus.). 1992. spiral bd. 12.00 (*1-56243-061-0*, Z-17) DDC Pub.
WordPerfect for Windows Quick Reference Version 5.1 & 5.2. Micoref Educational Systems Staff. 1993. pap. 14.95 (*1-56351-207-6*) Microref Educ Systs.
WordPerfect for Windows Version 5.1 Enhanced: Quick Course. Wagoner. (DF - Computer Applications Ser.). 1994. pap. 18.95 (*0-538-71029-2*) S-W Pub.
WordPerfect for Windows VisiRef. 154p. 1994. 12.99 (*1-56529-742-3*) Que.
WordPerfect for Windows with Style. Daniel Will-Harris. (Illus.). 528p. (Orig.). 1992. pap. 24.95 (*0-938151-61-4*) Peachpit Pr.
WordPerfect for Windows 6.0. DDC Publishing Staff. 1993. pap. 19.95 incl. disk (*1-56243-169-2*, GR-WPW6); spiral bd. 12.00 (*1-56243-139-0*, OWPW6) DDC Pub.
WordPerfect for Windows 6.0a. Rolayne Day. 636p. (Orig.). (C). 1995. pap. text ed. 24.50 (*1-881991-32-6*) Scott Jones Pubng.
WordPerfect for Windows 95. Gary B. Shelly. 1996. pap. 25.00 (*0-7895-1202-5*) Course Tech.
WordPerfect for Windows 95: Double Diamond. Gary B. Shelly. 1996. pap. 15.00 (*0-7895-1205-X*) Course Tech.
WordPerfect for Windows 95 Bible. Stephen E. Harris. 1996. pap. 39.99 (*1-56884-722-X*) IDG Bks.
WordPerfect for Windows 95 Visual Quick Reference. Que Development Group Staff. (Illus.). 224p. (Orig.). 1995. 12.99 (*0-7897-0461-7*) Que.
WordPerfect Guide for Century 21 Keyboard. Eisch. (TA - Typing/Keyboarding Ser.). 1992. text ed. 14.95 (*0-538-61754-3*) S-W Pub.
WordPerfect, Lotus, dbase: Tutorial & Applications. Thompson. (DF - Computer Applications Ser.). 1993. pap. 31.95 (*0-538-62094-3*) S-W Pub.
WordPerfect LSN 121-180, College Keyboard. 14th ed. Susie H. Vanhuss & Duncan. (TE - Keyboarding Ser.). (C). 1998. pap. 40.95 (*0-538-71660-6*) S-W Pub.
WordPerfect LSN 61-120, College Keyboard. 14th ed. Susie H. Vanhuss & Duncan. LC 96-37959. (TE - Keyboarding Ser.). (C). 1998. pap. 40.95 (*0-538-71659-2*) S-W Pub.
WordPerfect Macintosh: The Useable Portable Guide. Jon Haber & Herbert R. Haber. (Illus.). 32p. (Orig.). 1989. pap. 4.95 (*0-945765-07-X*) Useable Portable Pubns.
WordPerfect Macro Expert. Neil J. Salkind. 250p. (Orig.). 1988. pap. 25.00 (*1-55623-080-X*) Irwin Prof Pubng.
WordPerfect Macros: The Windows Version. Robert Bixby et al. 1993. pap. text ed. 29.95 (*0-07-157888-9*) McGraw.
WordPerfect Macros: The Windows Version. Donna M. Mosich et al. 576p. 1992. pap. 29.95 (*0-8306-2501-1*, 3945, Windcrest) TAB Bks.
WordPerfect Macros 5.0. Donna M. Mosich & Pamela Adams-Regan. (Illus.). 304p. (Orig.). 1989. pap. 22.95 (*0-8306-3254-9*, Windcrest) TAB Bks.
WordPerfect Made Perfectly Easy: Complete Course. Sharon A. Fisher-Larson. LC 94-36620. 1995. write for info. (*0-02-802589-X*) Glencoe.
WordPerfect Made Perfectly Easy: Release 6 for DOS. Sharon A. Fisher-Larson. LC 95-17765. 1995. write for info. (*0-02-813861-9*) Glencoe.
WordPerfect on the Macintosh. Eisch & Wood. (DF - Computer Applications Ser.). 1992. pap. 39.95 (*0-538-70453-5*) S-W Pub.
WordPerfect Presentation for Windows: Quick Course. Goldfarb. (DF - Computer Applications Ser.). 1996. pap. 17.95 (*0-538-64909-7*) S-W Pub.
WordPerfect Presentations 3.0 for Windows. Rick Sullivan. (Computer Training Ser.). 140-180p. 1997. spiral bd. 21.95 incl. 3.5 hd (*0-538-65998-X*) S-W Pub.
WordPerfect Print & Presentation Kit. Christine Solomon. 1993. pap. 28.95 (*0-201-62261-0*) Addison-Wesley.
***WordPerfect Quick Reference Guide.** Microref Educational Systems Staff. 1997. pap. text ed. 14.95 (*1-56351-146-0*) Microref Educ Systs.
WordPerfect Rapid Reference. Rick Sullivan. 1991. text ed. 13.95 (*0-538-70616-3*) S-W Pub.
WordPerfect Simplified. Jean Knox. (Orig.). 1989. pap. 19.95 (*0-929704-01-0*) Weber Systems.
WordPerfect Simplified: Including Versions 5.0 & 5.1. Jean Knox. Ed. by Jeff Weber. (Illus.). 370p. (Orig.). 1990. pap. 21.95 (*0-929704-16-9*) Weber Systems.
WordPerfect Simplified: Shortcuts & Macros. Sandra L. Quailes. 1992. pap. 29.95 incl. disk (*0-9629697-8-8*) ASAP Pubns.
WordPerfect Smartstart. 1994. 25.99 (*1-56529-407-6*) Que.
WordPerfect Solutions. Trudi Reisner. 608p. 1993. pap. text ed. 24.95 (*0-471-58935-7*) Wiley.
WordPerfect Sorting Made Easy. Patricia Fordham. LC 93-70780. (Computer Ser.). 84p. 1993. pap. 11.95 (*1-56052-218-6*) Crisp Pubns.
WordPerfect Starter Kit for Macintosh. Hayden Development Group Staff. (Illus.). 500p. (Orig.). 1995. pap. 30.00 (*1-56830-182-0*, Alpha Ref) Macmillan Gen Ref.
***WordPerfect Suite X for Dummies.** Julie A. King. (Illus.). 384p. (Orig.). 1997. pap. 19.99 (*0-7645-0187-9*) IDG Bks.
WordPerfect Suite 7 for Dummies. Julie A. King. 1996. pap. 19.99 (*1-56884-946-X*) IDG Bks.
***WordPerfect Suite 8: The Comprehensive Guide.** Janet Gould. LC 97-9067. 1997. pap. text ed. 39.99 incl. cd-rom (*1-56604-652-1*) Ventana Communs.
***WordPerfect Suite 8 Bible.** Stephen E. Harris & Elizabeth Olson. 912p. (Orig.). 1997. pap. write for info. (*0-614-26291-7*) IDG Bks.
***WordPerfect Suite 8 Bible.** Stephen E. Harris. 1997. pap. 39.99 (*0-7645-3058-5*) IDG Bks.
WordPerfect Version 6 for Windows: The Step-by-Step Approach. Samantha Penrod. 1994. 25.99 (*1-56529-403-3*) Que.
***WordPerfect Web Publishing for Dummies.** David Kay. 384p. 1997. pap. 19.99 (*0-7645-0155-0*, Dummies Tech) IDG Bks.
WordPerfect Windows V. 5.1 Quick Reference Guide. 19.95 (*1-56351-042-1*, G168) Microref Educ Systs.
WordPerfect Workbook. WordPerfect Corporation Staff. (C). 1992. text ed. write for info. (*0-256-11235-5*) Irwin.
WordPerfect Workbook: For IBM Personal Computers & PC Networks (Version 5.1) Eleanor J. Davidson. (Illus.). 160p. (C). 1992. text ed. 41.50 (*0-256-11238-X*, 71-3775-01) Irwin.
WordPerfect Works: Tutorial & Applications. Abbott. (DF - Computer Applications Ser.). 1995. text ed. 28.95 (*0-538-63509-6*) S-W Pub.
WordPerfect Works, Easy Reference Guide. Jim Setcavage. (DF - Computer Applications Ser.). 1995. text ed. 7.95 (*0-538-63387-5*) S-W Pub.
WordPerfect X for Windows for Dummies. 1996. pap. 19.99 (*1-56884-949-4*) IDG Bks.
***WordPerfect X for Windows for Dummies.** Margaret Levine-Young et al. (Illus.). 384p. (Orig.). 1997. pap. 19.99 (*0-7645-0186-0*) IDG Bks.
WordPerfect X for Windows for Dummies Quick Reference. 1995. pap. 12.99 (*1-56884-985-0*) IDG Bks.

W

WordPerfect X for Windows 95 Instant Reference. 3rd ed. Claudia Willen. 304p. 1996. pap. 12.99 (*0-7821-1775-9*) Sybex.

WordPerfect X for Windows 95 Quick & Easy. 2nd ed. Christian Crumlish. 224p. 1996. pap. 22.99 (*0-7821-1777-5*) Sybex.

WordPerfect 3.1 Mac. WordPerfect Corporation Staff. (DF - Computer Applications Ser.). 1995. pap. 20.95 (*0-538-64249-1*) S-W Pub.

WordPerfect 3.1/3.5 Mac: Official Coursework. Novell Staff. (DF - Computer Applications Ser.). 1996. pap. 25.95 (*0-538-66321-9*) S-W Pub.

WordPerfect 3.5 for Macintosh: Visual QuickStart Guide. Rita Lewis. (Illus.). 272p. (C). 1995. pap. text ed. 16.95 (*0-201-88355-4*) Peachpit Pr.

WordPerfect 3.5 for Macs for Dummies. Mark Kellner. 384p. 1995. pap. 19.99 (*1-56884-913-3*) IDG Bks.

WordPerfect 4.2. Don Cassel. 1992. pap. write for info. (*0-13-013681-6*) P-H.

WordPerfect 4.2 Macros. Donna M. Mosich. 1991. 24.95 (*0-8306-6651-6*) McGraw-Hill Prof.

WordPerfect 4.2 Quick Reference Guide. Marivel Salazar & Joyce Yaccarino. (DDC Quick Reference Guides Ser.). 1989. 12.00 (*0-936862-56-4*, W-17) DDC Pub.

WordPerfect 5 Solutions. Richard Mansfield. 126p. (Orig.). 1989. pap. 14.95 (*0-929307-04-6*) GP Pubns.

WordPerfect 5.0: A Ready Reference Manual. Catherine Garrison & Mercedes McGowen. (Illus.). 144p. (C). 1989. pap. text ed. 12.95 (*0-201-19713-8*) Addison-Wesley.

WordPerfect 5.0: Advanced Features with Desktop Publishing. large type ed. Rick Sullivan. 1990. 91.50 (*0-614-09885-8*, L-85819-00) Am Printing Hse.

WordPerfect 5.0: New Features & Advanced Techniques. Donna M. Mosich. (Illus.). 300p. 1988. 29.95 (*0-8306-3084-8*, 3084) McGraw-Hill Prof.

WordPerfect 5.0: Power Word Processing Made Easy. Jennifer De Lasala. (Illus.). 512p. (Orig.). 1989. pap. 24.95 (*0-8306-3249-2*, Windcrest) TAB Bks.

WordPerfect 5.0: The Useable Portable Guide. Jon Haber & Herbert R. Haber. (Illus.). 32p. (Orig.). (C). 1989. pap. text ed. 4.95 (*0-945765-08-8*) Useable Portable Pubns.

WordPerfect 5.0 Macro Expert. Neil J. Salkind. 250p. 1988. pap. 26.00 (*1-55623-176-8*) Irwin Prof Pubng.

WordPerfect 5.0, Quick Reference. 1988. pap. 19.95 (*0-913365-17-3*) Microref Educ Systs.

WordPerfect 5.0 Quick Reference Guide with Template. 1989. pap. 24.95 (*0-913365-55-6*) Microref Educ Systs.

WordPerfect 5.0 Supplement. Lon Ingalsbe et al. (C). 1989. pap. write for info. (*0-675-21276-6*, Merrill Coll) P-H.

WordPerfect 5.0 Workbook & Reference. Lon Ingalsbe & Brent Simonson. (Illus.). 522p. (C). 1989. spiral bd. write for info. (*0-318-69101-9*); IBM-PC version. disk 35.95 (*0-256-08203-0*, 14-3148-01) Irwin.

WordPerfect 5.0-5.1: Easy Reference Guide. Janet Giglia. 1992. text ed. 7.95 (*0-538-61399-8*) S-W Pub.

WordPerfect 5.0/5.1: Tutorial & Applications. Eisch. (DF - Computer Applications Ser.). 1991. pap. 27.95 (*0-538-70253-2*) S-W Pub.

WordPerfect 5.1. (STAR Ser.). 192p. (C). 1992. pap. 12.95 (*0-87835-734-3*) Course Tech.

WordPerfect 5.1. 1993. teacher ed. 49.95 (*1-56761-240-7*, Alpha Ref) Macmillan Gen Ref.

WordPerfect 5.1. Don Cassel. 1992. pap. write for info. (*0-13-013699-9*) P-H.

WordPerfect 5.1. rev. ed. Timothy J. O'Leary & Linda I. O'Leary. 1994. pap. text ed. write for info. (*0-07-048896-7*) McGraw.

WordPerfect 5.1: Advanced. 1993. 29.95 (*1-56877-087-1*) Catapult WA.

WordPerfect 5.1: Advanced. 1993. teacher ed. 49.95 (*1-56877-088-X*) Catapult WA.

WordPerfect 5.1: Advanced. Douglas M. Finney. 170p. 1991. student ed., teacher ed., spiral bd. 29.95 incl. disk (*1-56435-005-3*) Finney Lrng Systs.

WordPerfect 5.1: Advanced Features Applications. Sullivan. (DF - Computer Applications Ser.). 1991. pap. 36.95 (*0-538-70306-7*) S-W Pub.

WordPerfect 5.1: Beginning. 1992. teacher ed. 49.95 (*1-56877-010-3*) Catapult WA.

WordPerfect 5.1: Beginning. 1992. 29.95 (*1-56877-022-7*) Catapult WA.

WordPerfect 5.1: Beginning. Douglas M. Finney. 167p. 1991. student ed., teacher ed., spiral bd. 29.95 incl. disk (*1-56435-004-5*) Finney Lrng Systs.

WordPerfect 5.1: Intermediate. 1992. 29.95 (*1-56877-023-5*) Catapult WA.

WordPerfect 5.1: Level 1. David S. Murphy et al. (Easy Way Ser.). 155p. 1993. pap. 29.95 (*1-57048-040-0*) Trning Express.

WordPerfect 5.1: Power Word Processing Made Easy. 2nd ed. Jennifer De Lasala. 1990. pap. 22.95 (*0-8306-8679-7*, Windcrest) TAB Bks.

WordPerfect 5.1: Quick Course. Mary A. Eisch. 160p. 1992. pap. 17.95 (*0-538-61743-8*) S-W Pub.

WordPerfect 5.1: Quick Course. large type ed. Mary A. Eisch. 1994. 41.50 (*0-614-09871-8*, L-83973-00) Am Printing Hse.

WordPerfect 5.1: Quick Start IBM. Sue V. Stacy. (DF - Computer Applications Ser.). 1993. pap. 19.95 (*0-538-70956-1*) S-W Pub.

WordPerfect 5.1: Special Features. Douglas M. Finney. 173p. 1991. student ed., teacher ed., spiral bd. 29.95 incl. disk (*1-56435-006-1*) Finney Lrng Systs.

WordPerfect 5.1, a Practical Approach: Complete Course. Eisch. (DF - Computer Applications Ser.). 1994. pap. 41.95 (*0-538-62834-0*) S-W Pub.

WordPerfect 5.1 Bible. Susan B. Kelly. 1991. pap. 29.95 (*0-672-22746-0*) MICHIE.

WordPerfect 5.1 Creative Applications. Jack Durish. 1992. pap. 29.95 incl. disk (*0-915391-74-0*) Slawson Comm.

WordPerfect 5.1 Creative Writing. Jacobson et al. 1991. 14.00 (*0-536-58213-0*) Ginn Pr.

WordPerfect 5.1 DOS Advanced. 150p. 1991. 29.95 (*1-57533-009-1*) Comput Confidence.

WordPerfect 5.1 DOS Introduction. 160p. 1991. 29.95 (*1-57533-008-3*) Comput Confidence.

WordPerfect 5.1, DOS Version, Easy Reference Guide. Giglia. (DF - Computer Applications Ser.). 1992. text ed. 7.95 (*0-538-63398-0*) S-W Pub.

WordPerfect 5.1 for Administrative & Office Support. Kathleen Stewart. 720p. (C). 1992. pap. 33.95 (*0-87835-700-9*) Course Tech.

WordPerfect 5.1 for DOS. Stacey C. Sawyer et al. 192p. (C). 1993. per. 12.50 (*0-256-13478-2*) Irwin.

WordPerfect 5.1 For DOS & Windows 3.1. Stacey C. Sawyer et al. (C). 1994. 16.00 (*0-256-19223-5*) Irwin.

WordPerfect 5.1 for DOS Beginners. James Borror. (QuickSteps to Learning Ser.). (Illus.). 163p. 1993. spiral bd. 22.95 (*1-56951-001-6*) Sftware Trng.

WordPerfect 5.1 for DOS Simplified: Educational Edition. Maran Graphics Staff & Ruth Maran. 1995. pap. 14.99 (*1-56884-663-0*) IDG Bks.

WordPerfect 5.1 for DOS Simplified: MaranGraphics Simplified Computer Guide. Ruth Maran & Richard Maran. LC 93-20144. 96p. (C). 1993. pap. text ed. 21.60 (*0-13-106253-0*) Prentice ESL.

WordPerfect 5.1 for Windows. Kathleen L. Mayes. 656p. 1993. pap. 30.95 (*0-87835-966-4*) Course Tech.

WordPerfect 5.1 for Windows: A Practical Approach. Eisch. (DF - Computer Applications Ser.). 1993. pap. 34.95 (*0-538-70908-1*) S-W Pub.

WordPerfect 5.1 for Windows: Beginners. 1993. 29.95 (*1-56877-091-X*) Catapult WA.

WordPerfect 5.1 for Windows: Beginners. 1993. teacher ed. 49.95 (*1-56877-092-8*) Catapult WA.

WordPerfect 5.1 for Windows: Intermediate. 1993. teacher ed. 49.95 (*1-56877-134-7*) Catapult WA.

WordPerfect 5.1 for Windows: Intermediate. 1993. 29.95 (*1-56877-135-5*) Catapult WA.

WordPerfect 5.1 Instant Reference for DOS. Greg Harvey & Kay Y. Nelson. LC 89-90543. 252p. (Orig.). 1990. pap. 9.95 (*0-89588-674-X*) Sybex.

WordPerfect 5.1 Intermediate: Intermediate. 1992. teacher ed. 49.95 (*1-56877-011-1*) Catapult WA.

WordPerfect 5.1 Macro Sourcebook. William Hubbard. LC 93-49584. 1995. text ed. 13.95 (*0-538-62927-4*) S-W Pub.

WordPerfect 5.1 Made Easy. Katie Layman. 320p. (C). 1991. pap. text ed. 44.00 (*0-13-963125-9*) P-H.

WordPerfect 5.1 Plus: Basics & Beyond. M. G. Detienne & J. Marcotte. 105p. 1995. pap. text ed. 29.00 (*1-887580-04-2*) Tec Trek.

WordPerfect 5.1 Project Book. Sanford. 1992. pap. text ed. write for info. (*0-07-054931-1*) McGraw.

WordPerfect 5.1 Quick Reference Guide. 1990. pap. 19.95 (*0-913365-70-X*) Microref Educ Systs.

WordPerfect 5.1 Quick Reference Guide. Marivel Salazar & Angelo Cassano. Ed. by Paul Berube. (Quick Reference Guides Ser.). 238p. (Orig.). 1990. spiral bd. 12.00 (*0-936862-87-4*, W-5.1) DDC Pub.

WordPerfect 5.1 Quick Reference with Template. 1990. pap. 24.95 (*0-913365-74-2*) Microref Educ Systs.

WordPerfect 5.1 Smartstart. 1993. teacher ed. 39.99 (*1-56529-247-2*) Que.

WordPerfect 5.1 SmartStart. Jean S. Insinga. (Illus.). 256p. (Orig.). 1993. 25.99 (*1-56529-246-4*) Que.

WordPerfect 5.1 Step by Step. 2nd ed. Christina Turner. LC 93-72872. (Illus.). 165p. (C). 1993. spiral bd. 17.95 (*1-881432-51-3*) BCS Pub.

WordPerfect 5.1 with Personal, School, Career, & Business Applications. William R. Pasewark. LC 93-37660. 1994. pap. 25.00 (*0-13-097007-7*) P-H.

WordPerfect 5.2 for Windows. Stacey C. Sawyer. 176p. (C). 1993. pap. 12.50 (*0-256-14953-4*) Irwin.

WordPerfect 5.2 for Windows: A Professional Approach: for MS-DOS Computers. Deborah A. Hinkle. LC 92-42253. 1993. write for info. (*0-02-801803-6*) Glencoe.

WordPerfect 5.2 for Windows: Beginners. 1993. student ed. 29.95 (*1-56877-140-1*) Catapult WA.

WordPerfect 5.2 for Windows: Intermediate. 1993. student ed. 29.95 (*1-56877-141-X*) Catapult WA.

WordPerfect 5.2 for Windows: Intermediate. 1993. teacher ed. 49.95 (*1-56877-143-6*) Catapult WA.

WordPerfect 5.2 Windows Introduction. 150p. 1993. 29.95 (*1-57533-007-5*) Comput Confidence.

WordPerfect 5.2 Windows 1995: Production Software Guide. Martin. (C). 1994. pap. text ed. 9.75 (*0-03-098231-6*) HB Coll Pubs.

WordPerfect 6 for DOS: How Do I...? Kristy Clason. (Illus.). 576p. (Orig.). 1994. pap. 24.95 (*1-55958-309-6*) Prima Pub.

WordPerfect 6 for DOS: The Visual Learning Guide. David C. Gardner & Grace J. Beatty. (Illus.). 288p. (Orig.). 1993. pap. 19.95 (*1-55958-310-X*) Prima Pub.

WordPerfect 6 for DOS for Dummies. Dan Gookin. 400p. 1993. pap. 16.95 (*1-878058-77-0*) IDG Bks.

WordPerfect 6 for DOS Simplified. Ruth Maran. 1994. pap. 14.99 (*1-56884-657-6*) IDG Bks.

***WordPerfect 6 for Windows.** Que Staff. (SmartStart Ser.). 1997. pap. text ed. 39.99 (*1-56529-498-X*) Que.

WordPerfect 6 for Windows. 2nd ed. Samantha Pen. 1995. student ed. 29.99 (*0-7897-0008-5*) Que.

WordPerfect 6 for Windows: How Do I...? Kristy Clason. 1994. pap. 24.95 (*1-55958-512-9*) Prima Pub.

WordPerfect 6 for Windows: QuickStart Training Software. Webster & Associates Staff. 1994. 19.95 (*1-56609-156-X*) Peachpit Pr.

WordPerfect 6 for Windows: The Complete Reference. Allen L. Wyatt, Sr. 1993. pap. text ed. 29.95 (*0-07-881926-1*) McGraw.

WordPerfect 6 for Windows: The Visual Learning Guide. David C. Gardner & Grace J. Beatty. (Illus.). 288p. (Orig.). 1993. pap. 19.95 (*1-55958-396-7*) Prima Pub.

WordPerfect 6 for Windows: Visual QuickStart Guide. 2nd ed. Webster & Associates Staff. (Illus.). 272p. (C). 1994. pap. text ed. 14.95 (*1-56609-109-8*) Peachpit Pr.

***WordPerfect 6 for Windows - Illustrated, Incl. instr. resource kit, test bank, transparency.** Brenda L. Nielsen. (Illustrated Ser.). (Illus.). 192p. 1994. text ed. write for info. incl. 3.5 ld (*1-56527-167-X*) Course Tech.

***WordPerfect 6 for Windows - New Perspectives Introductory, Incl. instr. resource kit, test bank, transparency.** S. Scott Zimmerman & Beverly B. Zimmerman. (New Perspectives Ser.). (Illus.). 304p. 1994. text ed. write for info. (*1-56527-082-7*) Course Tech.

WordPerfect 6 for Windows Certification Curriculum Professional Skills. WordPerfect Corporation Staff. (NO - Novell/Wordperfect Ser.). 1995. text ed. 37.95 (*0-538-63726-9*) S-W Pub.

WordPerfect 6 for Windows Certification of Current Esssential Skills. Wordperfect Corporation Staff. (NO - Novell/Wordperfect Ser.). 1995. text ed. 30.95 (*0-538-63704-8*); text ed. 37.95 (*0-538-63753-6*) S-W Pub.

WordPerfect 6 for Windows Insider. Peter Aitken & Scott Jarol. Ed. by Keith Weiskamp. 489p. 1994. pap. text ed. 26.95 (*0-471-04139-4*) Wiley.

WordPerfect 6 for Windows Simplified. Ruth Maran. 1994. pap. 14.99 (*1-56884-656-8*) IDG Bks.

WordPerfect 6 for Windows Solutions. Tom Badgett & Corey Sandler. 374p. 1994. pap. text ed. 24.95 (*0-471-30329-1*) Wiley.

WordPerfect 6 for Windows Tips & Techniques Revealed. David A. Holzgang. 650p. 1994. pap. 39.95 (*1-56884-202-3*) IDG Bks.

WordPerfect 6, Lotus 1-2-3, dBASE for DOS Classpack: Quick Course. Eisch. (DF - Computer Applications Ser.). 1995. wbk. ed., pap. 34.95 (*0-538-65238-1*); pap. 34.95 (*0-538-65239-X*) S-W Pub.

WordPerfect 6 Made Easy. 3rd ed. Mella Mincberg. 1993. pap. text ed. 24.95 (*0-07-881895-8*) Osborne-McGraw.

WordPerfect 6 Quick Reference Guide. 1993. pap. 14.95 (*1-56351-201-7*) Microref Educ Systs.

WordPerfect 6 Secrets. Roger C. Parker & David A. Holzgang. 672p. 1993. pap. 39.95 (*1-56884-040-3*) IDG Bks.

WordPerfect 6 Smartstart. 1994. teacher ed. 39.99 (*1-56529-494-7*) Que.

WordPerfect 6.0. (Prisma Computer Courses Ser.). (Illus.). 200p. (Orig.). 1995. pap. 12.95 (*90-274-4181-2*, Pub. by Spectrum UK) Seven Hills Bk.

WordPerfect 6.0. Alan Boyd & Fraser. (C). 1994. text ed. write for info. (*0-318-70351-3*, BF4152) S-W Pub.

WordPerfect 6.0. Shelly Cashman. (C). 1994. text ed. write for info. (*0-318-70365-3*) S-W Pub.

WordPerfect 6.0. DDC Publishing Staff. 1993. pap. 19.95 incl. disk (*1-56243-168-4*, GR-WP60) DDC Pub.

WordPerfect 6.0. Jim Edwards. (STAR - Software Training & Reference Ser.). 1994. pap. 12.95 (*0-87709-415-2*) Course Tech.

WordPerfect 6.0. Henderson. (C). 1994. text ed. write for info. (*0-318-70353-X*) S-W Pub.

WordPerfect 6.0. Sarah E. Hutchinson et al. LC 94-154353. 179p. (C). 1994. per. 12.50 (*0-256-16197-6*) Irwin Prof Pubng.

WordPerfect 6.0: A Professional Approach, MS-DOS. Deborah A. Hinkle. LC 93-43115. 1994. write for info. (*0-02-801907-5*) Glencoe.

WordPerfect 6.0: A Short Course. Dennis P. Curtin. 200p. 1994. pap. text ed. 29.00 (*0-13-012733-7*) P-H.

WordPerfect 6.0: Advanced. 1993. teacher ed. 49.95 (*1-56877-128-2*) Catapult WA.

WordPerfect 6.0: Advanced. 1993. 29.95 (*1-56877-129-0*) Catapult WA.

WordPerfect 6.0: Beginners. 1993. 29.95 (*1-56877-089-8*) Catapult WA.

WordPerfect 6.0: Beginners. 1993. teacher ed. 49.95 (*1-56877-090-1*) Catapult WA.

WordPerfect 6.0: Intermediate. 1993. teacher ed. 49.95 (*1-56877-130-4*) Catapult WA.

WordPerfect 6.0: Intermediate. 1993. 29.95 (*1-56877-131-2*) Catapult WA.

WordPerfect 6.0: Level 1. David S. Murphy & Margaret E. Goodman. (Easy Way Ser.). 150p. 1993. pap. 29.95 (*1-57048-340-X*) Trning Express.

WordPerfect 6.0: Quick Course. Eisch. (DF - Computer Applications Ser.). 1995. pap. 17.95 (*0-538-63409-X*) S-W Pub.

WordPerfect 6.0 Applications for Reinforcement. Anderson. (DF - Computer Applications Ser.). 1995. pap. 27.95 (*0-538-63444-8*) S-W Pub.

WordPerfect 6.0 Comprehensive Edition. Katie Layman. 550p. (C). 1994. pap. text ed. 58.00 (*0-13-013103-2*) P-H.

Wordperfect 6.0 DOS: Acumen Series. Ewing. (DF - Computer Applications Ser.). 1995. pap. 20.95 (*0-87709-956-1*) Course Tech.

WordPerfect 6.0 (DOS) Advanced. Douglas M. Finney & Sean C. Feeney. 328p. 1994. spiral bd. 29.95 incl. 3.5 ld (*1-56435-038-X*) Finney Lrng Systs.

WordPerfect 6.0 (DOS) Beginning. Douglas M. Finney & Sean C. Feeney. 254p. 1994. spiral bd. 29.95 incl. 3.5 hd (*1-56435-036-3*) Finney Lrng Systs.

WordPerfect 6.0 (DOS) Intermediate. Douglas M. Finney & Sean C. Feeney. 290p. 1994. spiral bd. 29.95 incl. 3.5 hd (*1-56435-037-1*) Finney Lrng Systs.

WordPerfect 6.0 DOS Applications for Reinforcement. large type ed. Wynema Anderson & Stacey Golightly. 1995. 96.50 (*0-614-09617-0*, L-83778-00) Am Printing Hse.

WordPerfect 6.0 DOS Introduction. 160p. 1993. 29.95 (*1-57533-004-0*) Comput Confidence.

WordPerfect 6.0 DOS, Quick Start. Sue V. Stacy. LC 94-7876. 1995. pap. 17.95 (*0-538-71272-4*) S-W Pub.

WordPerfect 6.0 DOS Simplified Tutorial. Jaehne. (DF - Computer Applications Ser.). 1995. text ed. 30.95 (*0-538-63544-4*) S-W Pub.

WordPerfect 6.0, Easy Reference Guide. Sullivan. (DF - Computer Applications Ser.). 1995. text ed. 7.95 (*0-538-63414-6*) S-W Pub.

WordPerfect 6.0 for DOS. Cram. (C). 1994. teacher ed., pap. 4.76 (*0-395-69265-2*) HM.

WordPerfect 6.0 for DOS. Gloria Henderson. LC 93-38630. 1995. 38.95 (*0-87709-311-3*) Course Tech.

WordPerfect 6.0 for DOS. Joel Murach & Tom Murach. LC 94-2216. (Essential Guide Ser.). (Illus.). 498p. 1994. pap. 25.00 (*0-911625-81-X*) M Murach & Assoc.

WordPerfect 6.0 for DOS. Timothy J. O'Leary & Linda I. O'Leary. 1994. pap. text ed. write for info. (*0-07-048998-X*) McGraw.

WordPerfect 6.0 for DOS. Rick Sullivan. (Computer Training Ser.). 144p. 1996. text ed. 17.95 (*0-538-63419-7*) S-W Pub.

WordPerfect 6.0 for DOS. Rick Sullivan. (Computer Training Ser.). 180p. 1996. spiral bd. 21.95 (*0-538-64077-4*) S-W Pub.

WordPerfect 6.0 for DOS Simplified. Ruth Maran. 144p. (C). 1993. pap. text ed. 10.00 (*0-13-064676-8*) P-H.

WordPerfect 6.0 for Windows. E. Leonard. 156p. 1994. pap. 59.95 (*1-85805-097-9*, Pub. by DP Publns UK) St Mut.

WordPerfect 6.0 for Windows. Joel Murach & Tom Murach. LC 94-10557. (Essential Guide Ser.). (Illus.). 600p. 1994. pap. 25.00 (*0-911625-83-6*) M Murach & Assoc.

WordPerfect 6.0 for Windows. Timothy J. O'Leary & Linda I. O'Leary. 1994. pap. text ed. write for info. (*0-07-049000-7*) McGraw.

WordPerfect 6.0 For Windows. Stacey C. Sawyer et al. 192p. (C). 1994. spiral bd. 12.50 (*0-256-17014-2*) Irwin.

WordPerfect 6.0 for Windows. Rick Sullivan. (Computer Training Ser.). 144p. 1996. text ed. 18.95 (*0-538-63433-2*) S-W Pub.

WordPerfect 6.0 for Windows. Rick Sullivan. (Computer Training Ser.). 180p. 1996. spiral bd. 21.95 (*0-538-64137-1*) S-W Pub.

WordPerfect 6.0 for Windows: A Professional Approach. Deborah A. Hinkle. LC 94-22565. 1995. write for info. (*0-02-803087-7*) Glencoe.

WordPerfect 6.0 for Windows: Advanced. Douglas M. Finney & Carlos E. Pereira. 338p. 1994. spiral bd. 29.95 incl. 3.5 hd (*1-56435-042-8*) Finney Lrng Systs.

WordPerfect 6.0 for Windows: Beginning. Douglas M. Finney. 276p. 1994. spiral bd. 29.95 incl. 3.5 hd (*1-56435-040-1*) Finney Lrng Systs.

WordPerfect 6.0 for Windows: Intermediate. Douglas M. Finney & Carlos E. Pereira. 284p. 1994. spiral bd. 29.95 incl. 3.5 hd (*1-56435-041-X*) Finney Lrng Systs.

WordPerfect 6.0 for Windows: Production Software Guide, 1995. Martin. (C). 1995. pap. text ed. 9.75 (*0-03-010817-9*) HarBrace.

WordPerfect 6.0 for Windows: QuickStart Training Bundle. Webster & Associates Staff. 272p. 1994. 29.95 (*1-56609-157-8*) Peachpit Pr.

WordPerfect 6.0 for Windows: Tutorial & Applications. Eisch. (DF - Computer Applications Ser.). 1995. text ed. 33.95 (*0-538-63807-9*) S-W Pub.

WordPerfect 6.0 for Windows Academic Edition. Marangraphics Development Group Staff. 1994. pap. text ed. 10.00 (*0-13-124744-1*) P-H.

WordPerfect 6.0 for Windows at a Glance. Larry W. Smith. LC 93-7805. (At a Glance Ser.). 136p. 1993. pap. 15.95 (*1-55622-350-1*) Wordware Pub.

WordPerfect 6.0 for Windows by Pictorial. Dennis Curtin. 1994. pap. text ed. 36.80 (*0-13-126427-3*) P-H.

WordPerfect 6.0 for Windows Made Easy. Katie Layman & LaVaughn Hart. LC 94-12097. 448p. 1994. pap. text ed. 47.00 (*0-13-142986-8*) P-H.

WordPerfect 6.0 Macros. Robert Bixby & Pamela Adams-Regan. (Illus.). 448p. 1993. pap. text ed. 32.95 (*0-8306-4389-3*, Windcrest) TAB Bks.

WordPerfect 6.0 Made Easy. Katie Layman. 320p. (C). 1993. pap. text ed. 47.00 (*0-13-953829-1*) P-H.

WordPerfect 6.0 Made Perfectly Easy. Sharon A. Fisher-Larson. LC 93-48308. 1994. write for info. (*0-02-802587-3*) Macmillan.

WordPerfect 6.0 MS-DOS: A Tutorial to Accompany Peter Norton's Introduction to Computers. Robert Goldhamer. LC 93-43313. 1994. write for info. (*0-02-801325-5*) Glencoe.

WordPerfect 6.0 Tutorial & Applications: Quick Course. Eisch. (DF - Computer Applications Ser.). 1994. wbk. ed., pap. 30.95 (*0-538-63415-4*) S-W Pub.

WordPerfect 6.0 Windows. 160p. 1994. 29.95 (*1-57533-006-7*) Comput Confidence.

WordPerfect 6.0 Windows Introduction. 160p. 1994. 29.95 (*1-57533-005-9*) Comput Confidence.

WordPerfect 6.0a for Windows, Lotus 1-2-3 Release 5.0, Excel 5.0, dBASE IV, PowerPoint 4.0 for Windows 3.1 & HarvardGraphics for Windows 3.0. Stacey C. Sawyer et al. (C). 1995. text ed. 54.50 (*0-256-20969-3*) Irwin.

WordPerfect 6.0b for DOS: Quick Success. Rosner. (Management Information Systems Ser.). 1995. pap. 8.95 (*0-534-32408-8*) S-W Pub.

WordPerfect 6.0/6.1 for Windows Simplified: Tutorial & Applications. Jaehne. (DF - Computer Applications Ser.). 1996. text ed. 30.95 (*0-538-63802-8*) S-W Pub.

WordPerfect 6.1 For Windows. Sarah E. Hutchinson et al. 208p. (C). 1995. per. 12.50 (*0-256-19433-5*) Irwin.

W

WordPerfect 6.1 for Windows. Timothy J. O'Leary & Linda I. O'Leary. 1995. pap. text ed. write for info. (0-07-047325-0) McGraw.

WordPerfect 6.1 for Windows. Nita H. Rutkosky. LC 95-11473. 1995. 35.95 (1-56118-833-6) Paradigm MN.

WordPerfect 6.1 for Windows. Gary B. Shelly et al. LC 95-35304. (Shelly Cashman Ser.). 1995. write for info. (0-614-08312-5) Course Tech.

WordPerfect 6.1 for Windows. Rick Sullivan. (Computer Training Ser.). 180p. 1996. spiral bd. 21.95 (0-538-65071-0) S-W Pub.

***WordPerfect 6.1 for Windows, Incl. instr. resource kit, test bank, transparency.** Rachel B. Bunin. (Illustrated Ser.). (Illus.). 224p. 1995. text ed. write for info. incl. 3.5 ld (0-7600-3481-8) Course Tech.

WordPerfect 6.1 for Windows: Acumen Series. Boyd & Fraser Staff. (DF - Computer Applications Ser.). 1996. pap. 20.95 (0-87709-953-7) Course Tech.

WordPerfect 6.1 for Windows: Easy Reference Guide. Rick Sullivan. (DF - Computer Applications Ser.). 144-160p. 1997. spiral bd., pap. 7.95 (0-538-71463-8) S-W Pub.

WordPerfect 6.1 for Windows: Instant Reference. Alan Simpson. LC 94-67536. 278p. 1994. pap. 9.99 (0-7821-1628-0) Sybex.

WordPerfect 6.1 for Windows: Quick Course. Wagoner. (DF - Computer Applications Ser.). 1996. pap. 18.95 (0-538-71414-X) S-W Pub.

WordPerfect 6.1 for Windows: Quick Start. Wagoner. (DF - Computer Applications Ser.). 1996. text ed. 19.95 (0-538-71395-X) S-W Pub.

WordPerfect 6.1 for Windows: Star Series. Boyd & Fraser Staff. (DF - Computer Applications Ser.). 1996. pap. 12.95 (0-87709-944-8) Course Tech.

WordPerfect 6.1 for Windows: The Visual Learning Guide. Grace J. Beatty. 1995. pap. text ed. 19.95 (0-7615-0091-X) Prima Pub.

WordPerfect 6.1 for Windows: Tool Kit. Duffy. (Management Information Systems Ser.). 1996. pap. 17.95 (0-7895-0689-0) Course Tech.

WordPerfect 6.1 for Windows: Tutorial & Applications. Eisch. (DF - Computer Applications Ser.). 1996. text ed. 33.95 (0-538-65142-3) S-W Pub.

WordPerfect 6.1 for Windows: Windows Workshop. James E. Shuman. (Management Information Systems Ser.). 1996. pap. 18.95 (0-7895-0643-2) S-W Pub.

***WordPerfect 6.1 for Windows - a Guide to Productivity, Incl. instr. resource kit, test bank, transparency.** Keith Mulbery. (Illus.). 888p. 1995. text ed. write for info. incl. 3.5 ld (1-56527-236-6) Course Tech.

***WordPerfect 6.1 for Windows - New Perspectives Introductory, Incl. instr. resource kit, test bank, transparency.** S. Scott Zimmerman & Beverly B. Zimmerman. (New Perspectives Ser.). (Illus.). 304p. 1995. text ed. write for info. (0-7600-3485-0) Course Tech.

WordPerfect 6.1 for Windows Essentials. 1995. teacher ed. 39.99 (0-7897-0118-9) Que.

WordPerfect 6.1 for Windows Essentials. Que College Staff & Linda Hefferin. 1995. pap. text ed. 22.99 (0-7897-0104-9) Que Educ & Trng.

***WordPerfect 6.1 for Windows, Excel 3.0, & Access 2.0.** Stacey C. Sawyer. (C). 1996. 25.00 (0-256-25175-4) Irwin.

WordPerfect 6.1 for Windows for Dummies. 2nd ed. Margaret L. Young. 384p. 1995. pap. 16.95 (1-56884-243-0) IDG Bks.

WordPerfect 6.1 for Windows Simplified. expanded ed. Maran Graphics Staff & Ruth Maran. 224p. 1995. pap. 19.99 (1-56884-665-7) IDG Bks.

WordPerfect 6.1 for Windows Visual Pocket Guide. Maran Graphics Staff & Ruth Maran. 256p. 1995. pap. 14.99 (1-56884-668-1) IDG Bks.

WordPerfect 6.1 NOW! (for Windows 3.1) A Simple Guide to Learning WordPerfect Quick & Easy! Scott Temple & Robert Medved. (Illus.). 216p. 1996. pap. 18.99 (0-9643450-5-6) Easel Pubng.

***WordPerfect 6.1 Simplificado.** Maran Graphics Staff. (SPA.). 1996. pap. 24.99 (0-7645-6017-4) IDG Bks.

WordPerfect 6.1 Virtual Tutor. Que Education & Training Staff. 1996. text ed. 49.99 incl. cd-rom (1-57576-097-5) Que Educ & Trng.

WordPerfect 7 ESS. 23.00 (0-7897-0434-X) Que.

***Wordperfect 7 for Windows: Level II.** Que Education & Training Staff. LC 96-68612. (Essentials Ser.). 1997. pap. text ed. 22.99 incl. disk (1-57576-389-3) Que Educ & Trng.

WordPerfect 7 for Windows 95 Essentials. Laura Acklen. 1996. pap. text ed. 22.99 (1-57576-018-5) Que Educ & Trng.

***Wordperfect 7.0 for Windows 95 Made Easy: Short Course.** Layman & Lavaughn Hart. (C). 1997. pap. text ed. 47.00 (0-13-456369-7) P-H.

***Wordperfect 8 Visual Learning Guide: Fast & Easy.** Diane Koers. 352p. 1997. per. 16.99 (0-7615-1083-4) Prima Pub.

Wordplay: Origins, Meanings & Uses of the English Language. Robertson Cochrane. 280p. 1996. pap. 18.95 (0-8020-7752-8) U of Toronto Pr.

WordPlay: 600 Words You Need to Know. Paul Allman et al. 1995. pap. 19.95 incl. audio (0-8120-8319-9) Barron.

Wordplay Storybook, Set. 256p. (gr. 2-10). 14.95 (0-318-13725-9) Communacad.

Wordplays, Vol. 1. D. Durband. (C). 1986. 33.00 (0-09-149221-1, Pub. by S Thornes Pubs UK) St Mut.

Wordplays, Vol. 2. Stanley Thornes. (C). 1986. 33.00 (0-09-149241-6, Pub. by S Thornes Pubs UK) St Mut.

Wordplays 5: New American Drama. James Lapine et al. (Wordplays Ser.). 188p. 1986. pap. 15.95 (1-55554-007-4) PAJ Pubns.

Wordpower. Edward De Bono. 1990. 25.00 (0-317-90561-9) Intl Ctr Creat Think.

Wordprocessing Activities to Build Language Arts Skills. Steffe. (DF - Computer Applications Ser.). 1997. pap. 11.95 (0-538-66564-5) S-W Pub.

Wordrows. Bruce Hawkins. 40p. 1975. pap. 5.95 (0-917658-04-3) BPW & P.

Words. Frank Da Cunha. 96p. (Orig.). 1993. pap. 4.95 (1-56167-115-0) Am Literary Pr.

Words. Kenneth E. Hagin. 1979. pap. 0.75 (0-89276-057-5) Hagin Ministries.

Words. Marcia Henry. (C). 1996. pap. text ed. write for info. (0-89079-633-5, 7621) PRO-ED.

Words. Marcia K. Henry. (J). (gr. 3-9). 1990. 14.95 (1-878653-00-8) Lex Pr.

Words. Bill Martin, Jr. (J). (ps-6). 1993. 4.95 (0-671-87174-9, Litl Simon S&S) S&S Childrens.

Words. Jean-Paul Sartre. LC 80-6136. 255p. 1981. pap. 10.00 (0-394-74709-7, V-709, Vin) Random.

Words. Jean-Paul Sartre. 18.95 (0-8488-0846-0) Amereon Ltd.

Words: A Hermeneutical Approach to the Study of Language. Robert Lord. 358p. (C). 1995. lib. bdg. 47.50 (0-7618-0138-3) U Pr of Amer.

Words: A Potpourri of Fascinating Origins. Grant Campbell. (Illus.). 224p. (Orig.). (C). 1992. reprint ed. lib. bdg. 31.00 (0-8095-4099-1) Borgo Pr.

Words! A Vocabulary Power Workbook. Sheehan. (C). 1995. pap. text ed. 34.25 (0-15-502570-8) HB Coll Pubs.

Words: For Robert Burchfield's Sixty-Fifth Birthday. Ed. by E. G. Stanley & Terry F. Hoad. 1988. 79.00 (0-85991-259-0) Boydell & Brewer.

Words: Mediascopie de Vocabulaire Anglais. Florent Gusdorf. 704p. (ENG & FRE.). 1991. pap. 125.00 (0-8288-6981-2, 2729891307) Fr & Eur.

Words: Mediascopie du Vocabulaire Anglais; Classes Preparatoires. Florent Gusdorf. 414p. (ENG & FRE.). 1991. pap. 69.95 (0-8288-6983-9, 2729891676) Fr & Eur.

Words: Mediascopie du Vocabulaire Anglais; Terminales. Florent Gusdorf. 256p. (ENG & FRE.). 1991. pap. 69.96 (0-8288-6982-0, 2829791587) Fr & Eur.

Words: The Words of Jesus. Ed. by Robert L. Cantelon. (Orig.). 1990. 12.95 (0-9626942-0-7); pap. 6.95 (0-9626942-1-5) T Catelon Pub.

Words: Their Use & Abuse. William Matthews. LC 70-37792. (Essay Index Reprint Ser.). 1977. reprint ed. 25.95 (0-8369-2611-0) Ayer.

Words: Thematic Dictionary of Industrial, Technological & Engineering English. Florent Gusdorf. 382p. (ENG & FRE.). 1992. pap. 95.00 (0-8288-6947-2, 272989235-4) Fr & Eur.

***Words: What They Are.** Mary Steele. (J). Date not set. write for info. (0-688-12002-4); lib. bdg. write for info. (0-688-12003-2) Greenwillow.

Words: Writers Talk to Writers. Indiana Chapter, Romance Writers of America Staff. 104p. 1992. pap. text ed. 5.00 (1-881582-00-0) AD-VEN Pr.

Words: Writing, Reading, Spelling Book. Louise Skinner & Dianne Tucker-Laplount. 192p. 1993. pap. text ed. 6.30 (0-13-952466-5) P-H.

Words: Writing, Reading, Spelling Book 2. Louise Skinner & Dianne Tucker-Laplount. 195p. 1993. pap. text ed. 6.30 (0-13-953282-X) P-H.

Words: Writing, Reading, Spelling Book 3. Louise Skinner & Dianne Tucker-Laplount. 204p. pap. write for info. (0-13-953290-0) P-H.

Words: Writing, Reading, Spelling Book 4. Louise Skinner & Dianne Tucker-Laplount. 220p. pap. write for info. (0-13-953308-7) P-H.

Words see Analysis of the Chinese Language: An Etymological Approach

Words about Music: A Treasury of Writings by Celebrated Figures. Ed. by John Amis & Michael Rose. 440p. 1995. pap. 14.95 (1-56924-875-3) Marlowe & Co.

Words about Pictures: The Narrative Art of Children's Picture Books. Perry Nodelman. LC 87-38084. (Illus.). 336p. 1990. pap. 15.00 (0-8203-1271-1) U of Ga Pr.

Words about Wizards: Recollections of Magicians & Their Magic, 1930-1950. Robert Parrish. (Illus.). 72p. 1994. 25.00 (0-916638-79-0) Meyerbooks.

Words about Words about Words: Theory, Criticism, & the Literary Text. Murray Krieger. LC 87-45482. 304p. 1988. text ed. 39.95 (0-8018-3534-8) Johns Hopkins.

Words Across the Strait: A Critique of Beijing's "White Paper" on China's Reunification. John F. Copper. 138p. (Orig.). (C). 1995. pap. text ed. 17.50 (0-8191-9909-5) U Pr of Amer.

Words Across the Strait: A Critique of Beijing's "White Paper" on China's Reunification. John F. Copper. 138p. (Orig.). (C). 1995. lib. bdg. 39.00 (0-8191-9908-7) U Pr of Amer.

Words, Acts & Deeds of H. Khalif Khalifah. H. Khalif Khalifah. 379p. (Orig.). 1993. pap. 14.95 (1-56411-061-3) Untd Bros & Sis.

Words Against the Shifting Seasons: Women Speak of Breast Cancer. Illus. by Hollis Sigler. 125p. 1994. write for info. (0-932026-34-6) Columbia College Chi.

Words & C. John F. Gummere. (Illus.). 128p. 1990. reprint ed. 16.00 (0-86516-239-5) Bolchazy-Carducci.

Words & Deeds: Essays on the Realistic Imagination. Taylor Stoehr. LC 83-45286. (Studies in Modern Literature: No. 8). 185p. 1986. 39.50 (0-404-61578-3) AMS Pr.

Words & Deeds: Language & the Practice of Political Theory. Thomas C. Arnold. LC 92-38025. (Major Concepts in Politics & Political Theory Ser.: Vol. 2). 154p. (C). 1993. text ed. 39.95 (0-8204-1836-6) P Lang Pubng.

Words & Deeds in Foreign Policy. Kenneth W. Thompson. (Fifth Morgenthau Memorial Lectures). 21p. 1986. pap. 4.00 (0-87641-226-6) Carnegie Ethics & Intl Affairs.

Words & Deeds in Renaissance Rome: Trials Before the Papal Magistrates. Thomas V. Cohen & Elizabeth S. Cohen. (Illus.). 304p. 1993. 50.00 (0-8020-2825-X); pap. 19.95 (0-8020-7699-8) U of Toronto Pr.

Words & Ends from E-Z. Jackson MacLow. LC 89-80484. 96p. (Orig.). 1989. pap. 7.50 (0-939691-03-5) Avenue B.

Words & Ends from E-Z. deluxe ed. Jackson MacLow. LC 89-80484. 96p. (Orig.). 1989. 18.00 (0-685-25266-3) Avenue B.

Words & Images: Land Within the Maumee. Philip C. Repp. (Illus.). 83p. (Orig.). 1990. pap. write for info. (0-9623291-1-8) Minnetrista.

***Words & Images on the Page: Improving Children's Writing Through Design.** Paul Johnson. (Manchester Metropolitan University Education Ser.). 112p. 1996. pap. 24.95 (1-85346-443-0, Pub. by D Fulton UK) Taylor & Francis.

Words & Life. Hilary Putnam. Ed. by James Conant. LC 93-39799. 607p. (Orig.). 1994. 47.50 (0-674-95606-0) HUP.

Words & Life. Hilary Putnam. 608p. (Orig.). (C). 1995. pap. text ed. 19.95 (0-674-95607-9) HUP.

***Words & More Words.** (J). (gr. 4-6). Date not set. 14.95 (0-673-36320-1, GoodYrBooks) Addson-Wesley Educ.

Words & Music. David Rees. 220p. 1994. pap. 14.95 (1-873741-11-1, Pub. by Millvres Bks UK) LPC InBook.

Words & Music: Form & Procedure in Theses. Dissertations, Research Papers, Book Reports, Programs, & Theses in Composition. Eugene Helm & Albert T. Luper. 1982. pap. 14.95 (0-913574-00-7, EA00003) Eur-Am Music.

Words & Music in Henry Purcell's First Semi-Opera, Dioclesian: An Approach to Early Music Through Early Theatre. Julia Muller. LC 90-5676. (Studies in History & Interpretation of Music: Vol. 28). 520p. 1990. lib. bdg. 119.95 (0-88946-495-2) E Mellen.

Words & Names. Ernest Weekley. LC 73-164634. (Select Bibliographies Reprint Ser.). 1977. reprint ed. 21.95 (0-8369-5918-3) Ayer.

Words & Notes Coupled Lovingly Together: Thomas Campion, A Critical Study. Christopher Wilson. Ed. by John Caldwell. (British Music Theses Ser.: Vol. 53). 440p. 1989. reprint ed. text ed. 20.00 (0-8240-2048-0) Garland.

Words & Numbers: An Exhibition Organized by the Museum of Contemporary Art at Wright State University Curated by Barry A. Rosenberg with Assistance by Teresa Schalnat. Barry A. Rosenberg & Carol Nathanson. Ed. by Ron Wukeson. 72p. (Orig.). 1991. pap. 15.00 (0-932706-18-5) WSU Art Gallrs.

Words & Occasions: An Anthology of Speeches & Articles from His Papers by the Right Honourable Lester B. Pearson. Lester B. Pearson. LC 70-135191. 310p. 1970. 34.50 (0-674-95611-7) HUP.

Words & Phrases. write for info. (0-318-57490-X) West Pub.

Words & Phrases Legally Defined, 4 vols. 3rd ed. Ed. by John B. Saunders. 1990. 520.00 (0-406-08030-5, U.K.) MICHIE.

Words & Pictures. George Edgar. LC 90-46583. (J). 1989. 14.99 (0-85953-235-6) Childs Play.

Words & Pictures. Arthur Rothstein. (Illus.). 128p. 1983. pap. 15.95 (0-240-51727-X, Focal) Buttrwrth-Heinemann.

Words & Pictures: An Introduction to Photojournalism. Wilson Hicks. LC 72-9209. (Literature of Photography Ser.). reprint ed. pap. 4.95 (0-685-32645-4) Ayer.

Words & Pictures: An Introduction to Photojournalism. Wilson Hicks. LC 72-9209. (Literature of Photography Ser.). 1979. reprint ed. 26.95 (0-405-04917-X) Ayer.

***Words & Pictures: Lessons in Children's Literature & Literacies.** Mikkelsen & Mikke. 1998. pap. text ed. 29.00 (0-697-39357-7) McGraw.

Words & Pictures: On the Literal & the Symbolic in the Illustrations of a Text. 2nd ed. Meyer Schapiro. 1973. pap. text ed. 26.15 (3-11-009815-6) Mouton.

Words & Pictures: Reading with Picture Clues. Siobhan Dodds. LC 91-71817. (Illus.). 32p. (J). (ps up). 1992. 14.95 (1-56402-042-8) Candlewick Pr.

Words & Pictures: Reading with Picture Clues. Siobhan Dodds. LC 91-71817. (Illus.). 32p. (J). (ps up). 1994. pap. 4.99 (1-56402-285-4) Candlewick Pr.

Words & Places. Isaac Taylor. 1972. 250.00 (0-8490-1326-7) Gordon Pr.

Words & Poets. Mark Grover. LC 93-87244. 168p. 1993. pap. 12.95 (0-9640114-0-9) Noble Crown.

Words & Quilts: A Selection of Quilt Poems. Felicia Mitchell. LC 94-38673. 96p. 1995. 18.95 (0-8442-2644-0) Quilt Digest Pr.

***Words & Rhythms of Baseball.** 140p. (Orig.). 1996. pap. 12.95 (0-9653016-1-3) Bennett Publng.

Words & Shadows: Literature on the Screen. Jim Hitt. (Illus.). 256p. 1992. pap. 17.95 (0-8065-1340-3, Citadel Pr) Carol Pub Group.

Words & Sounds, 5 Vols. Belverd E. Needles. (C). 1994. teacher ed., pap. 3.96 (0-395-65625-7) HM.

Words & Testimonies. Thomas H. Silcock. LC 72-80097. (Orig.). 1972. pap. 3.00 (0-87574-186-X) Pendle Hill.

Words & the Grammar of Context. Paul Kay. LC 96-46865. (CSLI Lecture Notes Ser.: No. 40). 1997. 46.95 (1-881526-18-6) CSLI.

Words & the Man in French Renaissance Literature. Barbara C. Bowen. LC 83-80027. (French Forum Monographs: No. 45). 163p. (Orig.). 1983. pap. 12.95 (0-917058-45-3) French Forum.

Words & the Word: Language Poetics, & Biblical Interpretation. Stephen Prickett. 288p. 1986. text ed. 69.95 (0-521-32248-0) Cambridge U Pr.

Words & the Word: Language Poetics, & Biblical Interpretation. Stephen Prickett. 288p. 1988. pap. text ed. 23.95 (0-521-36838-3) Cambridge U Pr.

Words & Their Meaning. Howard Jackson. (Learning about Language Ser.). 320p. (C). 1988. pap. text ed. 20.95 (0-582-29154-2) Longman.

Words & Things. Roger Brown. LC 58-9395. 1968. pap. 13.95 (0-02-904810-9, Free Press) Free Pr.

***Words & Thoughts.** Leon L. Lerner. 60p. (Orig.). 1996. pap. 11.95 (0-9607964-5-2) Galaxy Pr MD.

***Words & Water Ease the Living Dust.** Amelia Haller. 80p. 1996. pap. 15.00 (1-880222-27-2) Red Apple Pub.

Words & What They Do To You. Catherine Minteer. 128p. 1965. 8.00 (0-910780-06-4) Inst Gen Seman.

Words & Works: Writings & Projects. Gerardo Brown-Manrique. 80p. 1989. ring bd. 16.00 (0-9630969-0-7) Interalia Des.

Words & Works of Jesus Christ. J. Dwight Pentecost. 629p. 1981. 24.99 (0-310-30940-9, 17015) Zondervan.

***Words Aptly Spoken.** Bob Moorehead. 198p. 14.99 (0-9639496-6-7) Overlake Press.

Words Are Important: Level A (Blue) Book. E. H. Schuster. (YA). (gr. 5 up). 1985. pap. text ed. 3.99 (0-8437-7985-3) Hammond Inc.

Words Are Important: Level B (Red) Book. E. H. Schuster. (YA). (gr. 6 up). 1985. pap. text ed. 3.99 (0-8437-7991-8) Hammond Inc.

Words Are Important: Level C (Green) Book. E. H. Schuster. (J). (gr. 7). 1985. pap. text ed. 3.99 (0-8437-7980-2) Hammond Inc.

Words Are Important: Level D (Orange) Book. E. H. Schuster. (J). (gr. 8). 1985. pap. text ed. 3.99 (0-8437-7950-0) Hammond Inc.

Words Are Important: Level E (Purple) Book. E. H. Schuster. (YA). (gr. 9). 1985. pap. text ed. 3.99 (0-8437-7955-1) Hammond Inc.

Words Are Important: Level F (Brown) Book. E. H. Schuster. (YA). (gr. 10). 1985. pap. text ed. 3.99 (0-8437-7960-8) Hammond Inc.

Words Are Important: Level G (Pink) Book. E. H. Hammond. (YA). (gr. 11). 1985. pap. text ed. 3.99 (0-8437-7965-9) Hammond Inc.

Words Are Important: Level H (Grey) Book. E. H. Schuster. (YA). (gr. 12). 1985. pap. text ed. 3.99 (0-8437-7970-5) Hammond Inc.

Words Are Important: Primary Level (Tan) Bk. E. H. Schuster. (J). (gr. 4). 1985. pap. text ed. 3.99 (0-8437-7983-7) Hammond Inc.

***Words Are Seeds Containing Your Future.** Michael W. Grant. 48p. 1996. pap. 3.99 (0-9651939-0-X) King Jesus Worship.

Words Are Something Else. David Albahari. Tr. by Ellen Elias-Bursac. (Writings from an Unbound Europe). 200p. 1996. text ed. 49.95 (0-8101-1305-8) Northwestern U Pr.

Words Are Something Else. David Albahari. Tr. by Ellen Elias-Bursac. (Writings from an Unbound Europe). 200p. 1996. pap. 15.95 (0-8101-1306-6) Northwestern U Pr.

Words Are What I've Got: Writings for Learners All Around the World During International Literacy Year. 1995. 19.95 (0-920813-46-1, Pub. by Sister Vision CN) LPC InBook.

Words Are Windows: Word Studies & Illustrations from the Bible. Boyce Mouton. 230p. pap. 5.99 (0-89900-587-X) College Pr Pub.

Words Around the Fire: Reflections on the Scriptures of the Easter Vigil. Gail Ramshaw. (Illus.). 77p. (Orig.). 1990. pap. 6.95 (0-929650-14-X, WORDS) Liturgy Tr Pubns.

Words Around the Font. Gail Ramshaw. LC 94-24022. (Illus.). 110p. (Orig.). 1995. pap. 8.95 (1-56854-063-9, WFONT) Liturgy Tr Pubns.

Words Around the Table. Gail Ramshaw. (Illus.). 122p. (Orig.). 1991. pap. 8.95 (0-929650-28-X, WORDST) Liturgy Tr Pubns.

Words Around the Year. Roy Doty. LC 92-19312. (Illus.). (J). 1994. pap. 11.00 (0-671-77836-6, S&S Bks Young Read) S&S Childrens.

Words Around Us. Tim O'Halloran. (Illus.). 48p. (J). (ps-k). 1985. 10.95 (0-88625-124-9) Durkin Hayes Pub.

Words Around Us in French. Tim O'Halloran. (Illus.). 48p. (FRE.). (J). (ps-k). 1985. 10.95 (0-88625-125-7) Durkin Hayes Pub.

Words As Smoking Guns: What Vocabulary Teaches Us That the Establishment Doesn't Want Us to Know. John Bryant. 75p. (Orig.). 1995. pap. 9.95 (1-886739-24-2) Socratic Pr.

Words As Weapons. Paul Foot. 240p. (gr. 13). 1991. 30.00 (0-86091-325-2, A5367, Pub. by Vrso UK) Norton.

Words at War, Words at Peace: Essays on Language in General & Particular Words. Eric Partridge. LC 76-117911. (Select Bibliographies Reprint Ser.). 1977. reprint ed. 20.95 (0-8369-5364-9) Ayer.

***Words at Work.** Susan Benjamin. LC 97-18551. 1997. pap. 13.00 (0-201-15484-6) Addison-Wesley.

Words at Work. Sobel & Bookman. 1989. pap. 22.95 (0-8384-3327-8) Heinle & Heinle.

Words at Work: The Business Writer's Book of Lists. rev. ed. Maxine B. Segal. LC 94-90038. 200p. 1994. pap. 11.95 (0-9640758-0-6) Write on Queue.

Words Become Worlds: Semantic Studies of Genesis 1-11. Ellen Van Wolde. LC 94-2882. 1994. 48.50 (90-04-09887-9) E J Brill.

Words Before Midnight. Richard Poole. 60p. 8100. pap. 10.95 (0-907476-03-1) Dufour.

***Words Before the Articulate: New & Selected Poems.** Leonard Schwartz. LC 97-10827. 112p. 1997. pap. 10.50 (1-883689-53-8) Talisman Hse.

***Words Before the Articulate: New & Selected Poems.** Leonard Schwartz. LC 97-10827. 112p. 1997. 30.50 (1-883689-54-6) Talisman Hse.

***Word's Body: An Incarnational Aesthetic of Interpretation.** Alla R. Bozarth. LC 96-41457. 192p. 1997. pap. text ed. 22.50 (0-7618-0530-3) U Pr of Amer.

W

Words Book (Roman) Nepali-English Japanese & Japanese-English Nepali. Ed. by Tsutomu Nishimura. (C). 1984. 75.00 (0-89771-086-X, Pub. by Ratna Pustak Bhandar) St Mut.

Words Book, Roman, Nepali English-Japanese & Japanese-English Nepali. Tsutomu Nishimura. (ENG, JPN & NEP.). 1991. 20.00 (0-7855-0292-0, Pub. by Ratna Pustak Bhandar) St Mut.

Words Business: Thematic Dictionary of Economic & Business English. Florent Gusdorf. 299p. (ENG & FRE.). 1992. pap. 69.95 (0-8288-6979-0, 2729892362) Fr & Eur.

Words by Heart. Toni Albert. Ed. by J. Friedland & R. Kessler. (Novel-Ties Ser.). 1992. student ed., pap. text ed. 15.95 (0-88122-724-2) Lrn Links.

***Words by Heart.** Sebestyen Ouida. 144p. (J). 1997. pap. 3.99 (0-440-41346-X, YB BDD) BDD Bks Young Read.

Words by Heart. Ouida Sebestyen. (J). 1996. mass mkt. 4.50 (0-440-22688-0) BDD Bks Young Read.

Words by Heart. Ouida Sebestyen. LC 78-27847. (J). (gr. 5 up). 1979. 15.95 (0-316-77931-8, Joy St Bks) Little.

Words Can Hurt You: Beginning a Program of Anti-Bias Education. Barbara J. Thomson. 1992. pap. 20.00 (0-201-45502-1) Addison-Wesley.

Words Can Kill: The "Certification" Issue. 5.00 (0-614-05242-4, WCK09841M) ASFE.

Words Chiseled from Rock. Eddie B. Pittman, Jr. LC 87-61254. (Illus.). 80p. (Orig.). 1987. pap. 10.00 (0-9618791-0-6) Pub Press.

Words Chiseled into Marble: Artworks in the Prose Narratives of Conrad Ferdinand Meyer. Beth L. Mugge-Meiburg. LC 90-49695. (North American Studies in Nineteenth-Century German Literature: Vol. 9). 236p. (C). 1991. text ed. 41.95 (0-8204-1493-X) P Lang Pubng.

Words Communications: Thematic Dictionary of Publicity, Communications, Tourism & English for the Service Industry. Florent Gusdorf. 236p. (ENG & FRE.). 1992. pap. 59.95 (0-8288-6980-4, 2729892370) Fr & Eur.

Words Every Child Must Hear: Emotional Nourishment for Children of All Ages. Cynthia Good. LC 93-81139. (Illus.). 96p. 1994. 9.95 (1-56352-138-5) Longstreet Pr Inc.

***Words Every Good Reader Knows.** James M. Carroll & Barbara Overton. 56p. (Orig.). (J). (gr. 1-6). 1992. pap. 9.95 (0-89826-032-9) Natl Paperback.

Words, Facts & Phrases. Eliezer E. Edwards. 1973. 59.95 (0-8490-1327-5) Gordon Pr.

Words Fail Me: How Language Develops & What Happens When It Doesn't. Priscilla Vail. (Illus.). 151p. (Orig.). 1996. pap. 10.95 (1-56762-062-0) Modern Learn Pr.

Words Fitly Spoken & Proverbs to Live By. Compiled by Moses Adetumbi. LC 93-90488. (Illus.). 64p. (Orig.). 1996. pap. write for info. (0-9632502-7-2) Adex Bk.

Words for a Deaf Daughter & Gala. Paul West. LC 93-18997. (Illus.). 416p. 1993. reprint ed. pap. 12.95 (1-56478-036-8) Dalkey Arch.

Words for Air Force NCO & Airmen Evaluations: Examples of Commendations & Constructive Suggestions for Thorough Evaluation. Donald R. Wilson. 1993. Set, Vol. 1, 34p., Vol. 2, 41p. lib. bdg. 12.95 (0-939136-17-1) School Admin.

Words for All Seasons. Arthur Lerner. (Illus.). 104p. (Orig.). 1983. pap. 6.95 (0-938292-06-4) Being Bks.

Words for All Seasons. Molly Weir. 1993. 15.00 (0-7152-0627-3, Pub. by St Andrew UK) St Mut.

Words for Army NCO Evaluations: Examples of Commendations & Constructive Suggestions for Thorough Evaluation. Donald R. Wilson. 45p. 1992. lib. bdg. 12.95 (0-939136-08-2) School Admin.

Words for Carla. Barbara B. Robinson. (Illus.). 72p. (Orig.). 1986. pap. 4.95 (0-916630-48-X) Pr Pacifica.

Words for Clothing in the Principal Indo-European Languages. G. S. Lane. (LD Ser.: No. 9). 1931. pap. 25.00 (0-527-00755-2) Periodicals Srv.

Words for Elephant Man. Kenneth Sherman. (Illus.). 85p. 1995. lib. bdg. 31.00 (0-8095-4898-4) Borgo Pr.

Words for Elephant Man. Kenneth Sherman. (Illus.). 85p. 1995. reprint ed. pap. 10.95 (0-88962-199-3) Mosaic.

Words for "Horse" in French & Provencal. Clement M. Woodard. (Language Dissertations Ser.: No. 29). 1939. pap. 25.00 (0-527-00775-7) Periodicals Srv.

Words for Life. Connie Harrison. 1992. pap. 8.95 (1-85230-312-3) Element MA.

***Words for Life: Forty Meditations.** Austin Farrer. 1994. pap. text ed. 10.95 (0-687-86634-0) Abingdon.

Words for Lovers: Snippets, Sonnets & Sensual Sayings. Jim Volz & Evelyn C Case. (Illus.). 120p. 1990. pap. 5.95 (0-929077-18-0) WaterMark Inc.

Words for My Daughter. John Balaban. LC 90-85090. (National Poetry Ser.). 80p. (Orig.). 1991. pap. 10.00 (1-55659-037-7) Copper Canyon.

Words for My Weeping Daughter. Dorothy Farmiloe. 48p. 1980. 5.95 (0-920806-08-2, Pub. by Penumbra Pr CN) U of Toronto Pr.

Words for Myself. Erika Mumford. 48p. (Orig.). 1992. pap. 8.95 (0-9619960-2-1) Every Other Thursday.

Words for Our Feelings: A Concise & Practical Guide to the Names for the Various Moods, Emotions, Sensations, & Feelings. Dan Jones. 58p. 1992. pap. 5.95 (0-9633927-0-0) Mandala B & T.

Words for Our Worship: A Liturgical Dictionary. Ed. by Charles M. Guilbert. 70p. 1988. pap. 9.95 (0-89869-178-8) Church Pub Inc.

Words for Postal Employee Evaluation Reports: Examples of Commendations & Constructive Suggestions for Thorough Evaluation. Donald R. Wilson. 34p. 1993. lib. bdg. 11.95 (0-939136-12-0) School Admin.

Words for Reading: Reading for Words. Elton F. Henly. 1980. pap. text ed. write for info. (0-13-964171-8) P-H.

Words for School Administrators, 2 vols., Set, Vol. 1, 53p, Vol. 2, 41p. rev. ed. Donald R. Wilson. 1992. Set, Vol. 1, 53p., Vol. 2, 41p. lib. bdg. 23.40 (0-939136-15-5) School Admin.

Words for School Administrators, Vol. 1: Examples of Commendations & Constructive Suggestions for Thorough Teacher Evaluation. rev. ed. Donald R. Wilson. 53p. 1992. reprint ed. lib. bdg. 12.95 (0-939136-16-3) School Admin.

Words for School Administrators, Vol. 2: Examples of Commendations & Constructive Suggestions for Thorough Non-Teaching Staff Evaluation. Donald R. Wilson. 41p. 1992. lib. bdg. 12.95 (0-939136-10-4) School Admin.

***Words for Tapes: Examples of Commendations & Constructive Suggestions for Thorough Performance Reports.** Donald R. Wilson. 49p. 1996. lib. bdg. 12.95 (0-939136-28-7) School Admin.

***Words for the Heart.** Linda A. Morgan. LC 96-94558. (Orig.). 1996. pap. 6.95 (0-7880-0903-6) CSS OH.

Words for the Quiet Moments. Reva Mendes. 35p. 1973. reprint ed. pap. 2.00 (0-87516-185-5) DeVorss.

Words for the Soul: Jewish Wisdom for Life's Journey. Ronald H. Isaacs. LC 96-25623. 224p. 1997. pap. 22.50 (1-56821-931-8) Aronson.

Words for the Taking: The Hunt for a Plagiarist. Neal Bowers. 128p. 1997. 17.00 (0-393-04007-0) Norton.

Words for the Wild: The Sierra Club Trailside Reader. Ed. by Ann Ronald. LC 86-22097. (Totebook Ser.). 384p. (Orig.). 1987. pap. 14.00 (0-87156-709-1) Sierra.

Words for the Wind. T. K. Doraiswamy. (Greenbird Ser.). 76p. 1975. pap. 14.00 (0-88253-676-1) Ind-US Inc.

Words for the World. Christine Ege. LC 91-90679. (Illus.). 112p. (J). (gr. k-8). 1992. 38.00 incl. audio (1-884161-00-6) Comprehen Lang.

***Words for United States Army Officer Evaluation Reports (OER's) Examples of Commendations & Constructive Suggestion.** Donald R. Wilson. 50p. 1997. lib. bdg. 12.95 (0-939136-25-2) School Admin.

Words for Women: Promises of Prophets. Shirley W. Thomas & Barbara B. Smith. 1994. 10.95 (0-88494-921-4) Bookcraft Inc.

Words for Worship. Ed. by Arlene M. Mark. LC 95-12504. 240p. (Orig.). 1996. ring bd. 16.99 (0-8361-9037-8) Herald Pr.

Words for Worship. Alan Robinson. 160p. 1994. pap. 35.00 (0-85439-509-1, Pub. by St Paul Pubns UK) St Mut.

Words for You: A Book of Poetry. Michael I. Gangwer. 190p. (Orig.). 1989. pap. write for info. (0-318-65742-2) M I Gangwer.

Words for Your Wedding: The Wedding Service Book. David Glusker & Peter L. Misner. LC 85-45353. 176p. 1986. pap. 12.00 (0-06-063131-7, PL 4126) Harper SF.

Words from a Fearless Heart: A Collection of Wit, Wisdom, & Whimsy. Laura Ingalls Wilder. LC 95-14514. 144p. 1995. 14.99 (0-7852-7723-4) Nelson.

Words from a Litt Universe. Joseph Verrilli. (Illus.). 44p. (Orig.). 1994. 5.95 (1-878116-34-7) JVC Bks.

Words from a Man of No Words. Rajneesh Osho Staff. Ed. by Ma S. Avirbhava. (Compilation Ser.). (Illus.). 132p. 1989. 9.95 (3-89338-024-8, Pub. by Rebel Hse GW) Osho America.

***Words from a Silent Man: Collected Short Writings & Photographs.** Harold Moss. (Illus.). (Orig.). 1997. pap. 11.95 (1-890173-02-9, Pasigram) P Shoemaker.

Words from A to Z. (Illus.). 32p. (J). (gr. k-2). 1991. pap. 4.95 (0-87449-833-3) Modern Pub NYC.

Words from a Wide Land. William D. Barney. LC 93-29508. (Illus.). 194p. 1994. 12.95 (0-929398-64-5) UNTX Pr.

Words from an Old Wife: Tips & Tales from Great Aunt Jane. Jane Birchfield. 192p. (Orig.). 1992. pap. 10.00 (0-9631760-0-5) Possumwood Pr.

Words from an Unchained Mind. Steven Whitehurst. 102p. (Orig.). 1991. pap. 10.00 (1-56411-014-1) Untd Bros & Sis.

***Words from God.** Matthew Kelly. pap. write for info. (0-646-15829-5) Harper SF.

Words from Great Women. Illus. by Darrin Thompson. 78p. (Orig.). 1994. pap. 7.95 (1-56245-101-4) Great Quotations.

Words from Heaven: Mensajes de Nuestra Senora desde Medjugorje. Intro. by St. James Publishing Staff. LC 93-84256. 432p. (Orig.). (SPA.). 1993. pap. 12.00 (1-878909-04-5) St James Pub.

Words from Heaven: Messages of Our Lady from Medjugorje. 3rd ed. Two Friends of Medjugorje Staff. 400p. (Orig.). 1990. pap. 10.00 (1-878909-00-2) St James Pub.

Words from Heaven: Messages of Our Lady from Medjugorje. 4th ed. Two Friends of Medjugorje Staff. 416p. (Orig.). 1991. pap. 12.00 (1-878909-01-0) St James Pub.

Words from Heaven: Messages of Our Lady from Medjugorje. 5th ed. Intro. by St. James Publishing Staff. 416p. 1991. pap. 12.00 (1-878909-02-9) St James Pub.

Words from Heaven: Messages of Our Lady from Medjugorje. 6th ed. Two Friends of Medjogorje Staff. 464p. 1993. pap. 12.00 (1-878909-03-7) St James Pub.

Words from My Father. Sandy Ray. Ed. by Cheryle Sytsma. (Illus.). 192p. (Orig.). 1991. pap. 8.95 (1-879068-03-6) Ray-Ma Natsal.

Words from Paterson: Chamber Orchestra & Baritone. J. Harbison. 72p. 1993. per. 35.00 (0-7935-2074-6) H Leonard.

***Words from Silence: An Invitation to Spiritual Awakening.** Leonard Jacobson. 240p. (Orig.). 1997. pap. 12.95 (1-890580-00-7) Conscious Living.

***Words from the Heart.** Kathaleen Clemons. (Illus.). 42p. 1997. lib. bdg. 6.00 (1-889463-22-1) Golden Apple.

Words from the Heart. Ed. by Nancy Mack. LC 93-85719. 52p. 1993. pap. 4.95 (0-89821-113-1, 12314) Reiman Pubns.

Words from the Heart. J. E. Murdock. 80p. (C). 1991. text ed. 10.95 (1-56394-001-9) Wisdom Intl.

Words from the Heart. Geneva M. Rackley. 35p. 1994. pap. 10.95 (0-9642363-0-3) Joan White.

Words from the Heart. Geneva M. Rackley. pap. 10.95 (0-9623630-3-0) Rainbow Nursery.

Words from the Land. rev. ed. Ed. by Stephen A. Trimble. LC 95-9831. (Illus.). 416p. 1995. pap. 14.95 (0-87417-264-0) U of Nev Pr.

Words from the Masters: A Guide to the God Within. Compiled by William A. Ross. 350p. 1989. pap. 29.95 (0-9619246-3-2) Playful Wisdom.

Words from the Myths. Isaac Asimov. (Illus.). 144p. (J). (gr. 6). 1969. pap. 2.50 (0-451-14097-4, Sig) NAL-Dutton.

Words from the Myths. Isaac Asimov. (Illus.). 144p. (YA). (gr. 9-12). 1969. pap. 3.95 (0-451-16252-8, Sig) NAL-Dutton.

***Words from the Soul.** Beverly Y. Yarborough. (Illus.). 14p. (Orig.). (YA). (gr. 7 up). 1997. pap. 5.50 (0-9656873-0-9) B Yvonne Entrprise.

Words from the Source II. Starr Farish. (Illus.). 300p. 1987. 17.00 (0-9605492-5-0) Touch Heart.

***Words from the War Lord.** David T. Franks. LC 96-90652. 1997. 14.95 (0-533-12120-5) Vantage.

***Words from the Worm: An Unauthorized Trip Through the Mind of Dennis Rodman.** Dave Whitaker. 1997. pap. 6.95 (1-56625-087-0) Bonus Books.

***Words from the (415) Poems & Stories by Youth of San Francisco.** 224p. 1996. 12.95 (1-888048-01-8, WrtrsCorps Bks) SF Art Comm.

***Words Have Wings: Teaching & Learning with Computer Networks.** Kwok-Wing Lai. 1996. 29.95 (0-614-18889-X, Pub. by U Otago Pr NZ) Intl Spec Bk.

***Words Have Wings: Teaching & Learning with Computer Networks.** Ed. by Kwok-Wing Lai. 176p. 1996. pap. 34.95 (1-877133-05-1, Pub. by U Otago Pr NZ) Intl Spec Bk.

Words Hurt. Chris Loftis. LC 94-66754. (Illus.). 40p. (J). (ps-4). 1994. pap. 9.95 (0-88282-132-6) New Horizon NJ.

Words I Have Lived By. Norman Vincent Peale. 1993. Gift boxed. boxed 8.95 (0-8378-5301-X) Gibson.

Words I Know. Debby Slier. (Hello Baby Bks.). 12p. (J). (ps). 1989. 2.95 (1-56288-145-0) Checkerboard.

Words I Know. Cathy Stonehouse. 1994. pap. 12.95 (0-88974-037-2, Pub. by Press Gang CN) LPC InBook.

Words I Never Thought to Speak: Stories of Life in the Wake of Suicide. Victoria G. Alexander. 238p. 22.95 (0-669-20904-X, Lexington) Jossey-Bass.

Words I Use When I Write. Alana Trisler & Patrice H. Cardiel. 36p. (Orig.). (J). (gr. k-3). 1989. pap. text ed. 2.50 (0-935493-33-6) Programs Educ.

Words I Use When I Write Poster Book: Alphabet, Theme & People Support Materials. Alana Trisler & Patrice H. Cardiel. (Illus.). (J). 1992. student ed. 8.95 (0-935493-39-5) Modern Learn Pr.

***Words I Wish I Wrote.** Robert Fulghum. LC 97-18981. 1997. write for info. (0-06-017560-5) HarpC.

Words in a Corner: Studies in Montaigne's Latin Quotations. Mary B. McKinley. LC 80-70810. (French Forum Monographs: No. 26). 129p. (Orig.). 1981. pap. 10.95 (0-917058-25-9) French Forum.

Words in Action: Abstract Expressionism. Janet Ross et al. LC 76-3403. (Illus.). 1976. pap. 4.95 (0-614-02729-2) A M Huntington Art.

Words in Action: Perspectives on Athenian Myths & Institutions. William B. Tyrrell & Frieda S. Brown. 224p. (C). 1991. pap. text ed. 17.95 (0-19-506719-3) OUP.

Words in Ads. Greg Myers. 224p. 1995. text ed. 15.95 (0-340-61444-7, B4707, Pub. by E Arnld UK) St Martin.

Words in Captivity. Emiliano Martin. Ed. by Zulma Gonzalez-Parker. 60p. (Orig.). 1990. pap. write for info. (1-878255-06-1) Heartfelt Pr.

Words in Color. rev. ed. Caleb Gattegno. (Orig.). (J). (gr. k-12). 1977. 15.00 (0-87825-143-X); Word Charts. 100.00 (0-87825-131-6); Phonic Code Charts. 40.00 (0-87825-132-4) Ed Solutions.

Words in Color, Bk. R-0. rev. ed. Caleb Gattegno. (Orig.). (J). (gr. k-12). 1977. Book R-0. 0.25 (0-87825-127-8) Ed Solutions.

Words in Color, Bk. R-1. rev. ed. Caleb Gattegno. (Orig.). (J). (gr. k-12). 1977. Book R-1. 0.65 (0-87825-128-6) Ed Solutions.

Words in Color, Bk. R-2. rev. ed. Caleb Gattegno. (Orig.). (J). (gr. k-12). 1977. Book R-2. 1.50 (0-87825-129-4) Ed Solutions.

Words in Color, Bk. R-3. rev. ed. Caleb Gattegno. (Orig.). (J). (gr. k-12). 1977. Book R-3. 1.50 (0-87825-130-8) Ed Solutions.

Words in Color, Nos. 1-7. Caleb Gattegno. (Orig.). (J). (gr. k-12). 1977. Worksheets 1-7. student ed. 3.65 (0-87825-178-2) Ed Solutions.

Words in Color, Nos. 8-14. Caleb Gattegno. (Orig.). (J). (gr. k-12). 1977. Worksheets 8-14. student ed. 3.65 (0-87825-059-X) Ed Solutions.

Words in Contex. Takao Suzuki. Tr. by Akira Miura. 180p. 1985. pap. 10.00 (0-87011-642-8) Kodansha.

Words in Flight: An Introduction to Poetry. Richard Abcarian. LC 79-181898. 267p. 1972. pap. 16.00 (0-534-00147-5) Krieger.

Words in Indian English: A Readers Guide. S. Muthiah. (C). 1991. text ed. 14.00 (81-7223-000-1, Pub. by Indus Pub II) S Asia.

Words in Motion. 1996. teacher ed. 8.95 (0-19-434459-2) OUP.

Words in My Lovesick Blood: Poems by Haim Gouri. Haim Gouri. Ed. & Tr. by Stanley F. Chyet from HEB. LC 95-21108. 270p. (Orig.). (C). 1996. pap. 19.95 (0-8143-2594-7) Wayne St U Pr.

Words in Our Hands. Ada B. Litchfield. Ed. by Kathleen Tucker. LC 79-28402. (Albert Whitman Concept Bks.: Level 2). (Illus.). (J). (gr. 2-4). 1980. lib. bdg. 14.95 (0-8075-9212-9) A Whitman.

Words in Our Pockets: The Feminist Writers Guild Handbook. Ed. by Celeste West. 368p. 1986. 15.95 (0-913218-02-2) Dustbooks.

Words in Our Pockets: The Feminist Writers' Guild Handbook on How to Get Published & Get Paid. Ed. by Celeste West. LC 81-2106. (Illus.). 368p. 1985. 20.00 (0-912932-09-0); pap. 14.00 (0-912932-10-4) Booklegger Pubng.

Words in Red. Ed. by Michael Pink. 3.99 (0-529-10009-6, WR1) World Publng.

Words in Reverse. Laurie Anderson. 16p. (Orig.). 1979. pap. 3.00 (0-917061-02-0) Top Stories.

Words in Search of Victims: The Achievement of Jerzy Kosinksi. Paul R. Lilly, Jr. LC 88-3021. 212p. 1988. 18.50 (0-87338-366-4) Kent St U Pr.

Words in Season. Ivor J. Brown. LC 74-4839. 159p. 1974. reprint ed. text ed. 49.75 (0-8371-7489-9, BRWS, Greenwood Pr) Greenwood.

Words in the Blood: Contemporary Indian Writers of North & South America. Ed. by Jamake Highwater. LC 84-4905. 416p. 1984. pap. 9.95 (0-452-00680-5, Mer) NAL-Dutton.

Words in the Mind. 2nd ed. Jean Aitchison. (Illus.). 288p. 1994. pap. text ed. 24.95 (0-631-18921-1) Blackwell Pubs.

Words in the Mourning Time: Poems. Robert Hayden. (Orig.). 1970. 7.95 (0-8079-0161-X) October.

Words in the News: A Student's Dictionary of American Government & Politics. Barbara S. Feinberg. LC 93-19373. (America Past & Present Ser.). (Illus.). 160p. (J). 1993. lib. bdg. 22.70 (0-531-11164-4) Watts.

Words in the Wind Bk. 1: An African Fantasy. Demon L. Wood. 413p. 1996. pap. 19.95 (0-9648402-1-9) ProCord Bk.

Words in the Wind Bk. 2: An African Fantasy. Demon L. Wood. 448p. 1996. pap. 19.95 (0-9648402-2-7) ProCord Bk.

Words in Time: New Essays on Eliot's Four Quartets. Ed. by Edward Lobb. 250p. (C). 1993. text ed. 44.50 (0-472-10488-8) U of Mich Pr.

Words into Action: Basic Rights & the Campaign Against World Poverty. Pat Simmons & Oxfam Staff. 112p. (C). 1995. pap. 7.95 (0-85598-331-0, Pub. by Oxfam UK) Humanities.

Words into Type. 3rd ed. M. Skillin & R. Gay. 1974. 39.95 (0-13-964262-5) P-H.

Words into Type. 4th ed. Thomas L. Warren. 608p. (C). 1992. boxed write for info. (0-13-966060-7) P-H.

***Words Just Keep on Coming: Rap Is Poetry but Poetry Ain't All Rap.** Photos by Edward Carley, III. (Illus.). 64p. (Orig.). 1997. pap. 10.00 (1-890138-02-9) Poet Journals.

Words Know the Way. Joel L. Grishaver. (Illus.). 64p. (J). (gr. 3-4). 1990. student ed. 4.95 (0-933873-53-0) Torah Aura.

Words, Languages & Combinatorics: Kyoto, Japan, 28-31 August 1990. Ed. by M. Ito. 500p. (C). 1992. text ed. 130.00 (981-02-0645-3) World Scientific Pub.

Words, Languages & Combinatorics II: Proceedings of the International Conference. M. Ito & H. Jurgensen. 552p. 1994. text ed. 141.00 (981-02-1609-2) World Scientific Pub.

Words Large As Apples: Teaching Poetry in the Secondary School. Mike Hayhoe & Stephen Parker. (Illus.). 192p. (C). 1988. pap. text ed. 16.95 (0-521-33731-3) Cambridge U Pr.

Words Large As Apples: Teaching Poetry in the Secondary School. Mike Hayhoe & Stephen Parker. (Illus.). 192p. (C). 1989. text ed. 34.95 (0-521-33114-5) Cambridge U Pr.

Words Like Arrows: A Collection of Yiddish Folk Sayings. Shirley Kumove. LC 85-171838. (Illus.). 288p. (ENG & YID.). reprint ed. pap. 82.10 (0-8357-6383-8, 2035738) Bks Demand.

Words Like Fate & Pain. Karen Fiser. LC 92-53832. 80p. 1992. pap. 9.95 (0-944072-23-2) Zoland Bks.

Words Like Freedom: Afro-American Books & Manuscripts in the Henry W. & Albert A. Berg Collection of English & American Literature. Richard Newman. (Illus.). 42p. (Orig.). 1989. pap. 10.00 (0-87104-413-7) NY Pub Lib.

Words Like Freedom: Essays on African-American Culture & History. Richard Newman. LC 95-52053. 214p. (C). 1996. lib. bdg. 27.50 (0-933951-67-1) Locust Hill Pr.

Words Like These. Bruce Wetteroth. (Ohio Review Bks.). 72p. 1986. 10.95 (0-942148-07-X); pap. 5.95 (0-942148-06-1) Ohio Review.

Words Made Easy. Visual Education Corporation Staff. LC 83-9816. (Illus.). 296p. (gr. 9 up). 1984. student ed. 13.36 (0-07-039664-7) McGraw.

Words Made Flesh: Scripture, Psychology & Human Communication. Fran Ferder. LC 85-73255. 184p. (Orig.). 1986. pap. 6.95 (0-87793-331-6) Ave Maria.

Words, Meaning & People. Sanford Berman. LC 82-84221. 102p. 1982. pap. text ed. 9.00 (0-918970-31-8) Intl Gen Semantics.

Words More Words, & Ways to Use Them. L. Longheed. (YA). (gr. 7 up). 1993. pap. text ed. 13.00 (0-201-53961-6) Longman.

Words Most Often Misspelled. Ruth G. Gallagner. 1979. mass mkt. 3.95 (0-671-64874-8, PB Trade Paper) PB.

***Words 'n' Action.** E. P. McKnight. Ed. by Lydia Gaveglio. Tr. by Nancy Lomax. 76p. (Orig.). 1997. pap. 10.00 (0-9654807-0-4) E P McKnight.

W

Words, Names & History: Selected Writings of Cecily Clark. Cecily Clark. Ed. by Peter Jackson. (Illus.). 476p. (C). 1996. text ed. 89.00 (*0-85991-402-X*) Boydell & Brewer.

*Words of a Rebel.** Peter Kropotkin. 1996. pap. 19.99 (*1-895431-04-2*, Pub. by Black Rose Bks CN) Consort Bk Sales.

Words of a Rebel. Peter Kropotkin. Tr. & Intro. by George Woodcock. (Collected Works of Peter Kropotkin: Vol. 7). 215p. 1991. reprint ed. text ed. 38.95 (*1-895431-05-0*, Pub. by Black Rose Bks CN) Consort Bk Sales.

Words of Adjustment. Kenneth G. Mills. (Illus.). 130p. (Orig.). 1992. pap. 13.95 (*0-919842-09-7*, KGOB7) Sun-Scape Ent.

Words of Albert Schweitzer. Intro. & Selected by Norman Cousins. LC 84-18890. (Words Ser.). (Illus.). 112p. 1991. reprint ed. 14.95 (*0-937858-41-2*) Newmarket.

Words of Albert Schweitzer. Intro. & Selected by Norman Cousins. 112p. 1996. reprint ed. pap. 10.00 (*1-55704-291-8*) Newmarket.

Words of Certitude. large type ed. Pope John Paul, II. 160p. 1985. reprint ed. pap. 7.95 (*0-8027-2477-9*) Walker & Co.

Words of Champions see Winning Words of Champions

Words of Cheer. Charles H. Spurgeon. 176p. 1994. mass mkt. 4.99 (*0-88368-269-9*) Whitaker Hse.

Words of Cheer for Daily Life. Charles H. Spurgeon. 1973. mass mkt. 6.00 (*1-56186-304-1*) Pilgrim Pubns.

Words of Christ. Ed. & Intro. by Dale Salwak. LC 96-2670. 128p. 1996. 15.00 (*1-880032-84-8*) New Wrld Lib.

Words of Comfort. (Illus.). 72p. 1996. 12.95 (*0-8362-1072-7*) Andrews & McMeel.

Words of Comfort. Ed. by Helen Exley. (Suedel Giftbooks Ser.). (Illus.). 60p. 1996. 9.99 (*1-85015-712-X*) Exley Giftbooks.

Words of Comfort. Ray Comfort. (Illus.). 350p. (Orig.). reprint ed. pap. write for info. (*1-878859-06-4*) Living Wat CA.

*Words of Comfort & Encouragement, Vol. 1.** 60p. (Orig.). 1997. pap. 5.00 (*0-9657373-0-6*) Comfort & Encouragement.

Words of Comfort, Peace, & Hope for Hurting Hearts. Linda M. Christ. 125p. (Orig.). 1989. pap. write for info. (*0-318-65906-9*) Lindys Lifelines.

Words of Conscience: Religious Statements on Conscientious Objection. 220p. 1983. pap. 5.00 (*0-318-15981-3*) NISBCO.

Words of Counsel for Christian Workers. Charles H. Spurgeon. 160p. 1985. mass mkt. 6.00 (*1-56186-345-9*) Pilgrim Pubns.

Words of Delight: A Literary Introduction to the Bible. 2nd ed. Leland Ryken. LC 92-42603. 546p. (gr. 10). 1993. pap. 24.99 (*0-8010-7769-9*) Baker Bks.

Words of Desmond Tutu. Selected by Naomi Tutu. LC 88-34567. (Words Ser.). (Illus.). 112p. 1991. 12.95 (*1-55704-038-9*) Newmarket.

Words of Desmond Tutu. Naomi Tutu. 1996. pap. 10.00 (*1-55704-282-9*) Newmarket.

Words of Desmond Tutu. Naomi Tutu & Desmond Tutu. (Words Ser.). 128p. 1996. reprint ed. pap. 7.95 (*1-55704-215-2*) Newmarket.

*Words of Ecstasy in Sufism.** Carl W. Ernst. 184p. 1996. 20.95 (*0-614-21383-5*, 1334) Kazi Pubns.

Words of Ecstasy in Sufism. Carl W. Ernst. LC 84-113. 184p. 1985. text ed. 59.50 (*0-87395-917-5*); pap. text ed. 19.95 (*0-87395-918-3*) State U NY Pr.

Words of Eternity: Blake & the Poetics of the Sublime. Vincent A. De Luca. (Illus.). 280p. 1991. text ed. 42.50 (*0-691-06874-7*) Princeton U Pr.

*Words of Faith: Prayers by Ostad Elahi.** Bahram Elahi. (Illus.). 52p. 1995. 20.00 (*0-614-31089-X*, Pub. by R Laffont FR) Baker & Taylor.

Words of Farewell: Stories by Korean Women Writers. Kang Sok-kyong et al. Tr. by Bruce Fulton & Ju-Chan Fulton from KOR. LC 89-10860. (Women in Translation Ser.). 274p. (Orig.). 1989. pap. 12.95 (*0-931188-76-8*) Seal Pr WA.

Words of Fire: An Anthology of African-American Feminist Thought. Ed. by Beverly Guy-Sheftall. 608p. (Orig.). 1995. pap. 20.00 (*1-56584-256-1*) New Press NY.

Words of Fire: Essays by Gay Black Writers. Ed. by Charles M. Smith. 216p. 1995. per. 12.00 (*1-880729-10-5*) Vega Pr.

Words of Fire, Deeds of Blood: The Mob, the Monarchy & the French Revolution. Olivier Bernier. (Illus.). 384p. 1989. 21.95 (*0-316-09206-1*) Little.

Words of Friendship: 101 Words to Share With a Friend. Brownlow. (Easelette Miniatures Ser.). (Illus.). 1995. spiral bd. 4.99 (*1-877719-75-7*) Brownlow Pub Co.

Words of Gandhi. Intro. & Selected by Richard Attenborough. LC 82-14403. (Words Ser.). (Illus.). 112p. 1991. reprint ed. 14.95 (*0-937858-14-5*) Newmarket.

Words of Gandhi. Intro. & Selected by Richard Attenborough. 112p. 1996. reprint ed. pap. 10.00 (*1-55704-290-X*) Newmarket.

Words of God. (Walk with Jesus Ser.). 183p. 1991. pap. 25.00 (*1-57277-527-0*) Script Rsch.

Words of God: Australian Edition. large type ed. Baha'u'llah & Abdu'l-Baha. 32p. 1989. pap. 1.00 (*0-909991-44-8*) Bahai.

Words of Grace. Ed. & Selected by James C. Galvin. LC 94-40286. 128p. 1995. 12.99 (*0-8423-7929-0*) Tyndale.

Words of Happiness & Laughter. Joan E. Ratajack. (Words to Live By Ser.). 1992. 4.99 (*0-517-07366-8*) Random Hse Value.

Words of Harry S. Truman. Compiled by Robert J. Donovan. 1996. pap. 9.95 (*0-614-97723-1*) Newmarket.

Words of Harry S. Truman. Robert J. Donovan. (Illus.). 1996. pap. 10.00 (*1-55704-283-7*) Newmarket.

Words of Healing. Monty M. Stanley. LC 89-81407. 200p. 1990. 14.95 (*0-9622667-2-8*) Illini Pubns.

Words of Honor. Dan McKinnon. 309p. 1996. pap. 10.00 (*0-941437-00-0*) House Hits.

Words of Hope. Ed. by Connie Harrison. 128p. 1991. pap. 8.95 (*1-85230-238-0*) Element MA.

Words of Inspiration. Fred Cato, Jr. Ed. by William T. Cato. 150p. (Orig.). 1996. pap. write for info. (*1-57502-204-4*, PO841) Morris Pubng.

Words of Inspiration. Sara Colacurto. (Words to Live By Ser.). 1992. 4.99 (*0-517-07365-X*) Random Hse Value.

Words of Jesus. Allan Fryant. (Illus.). 80p. 1995. 6.95 (*0-87573-055-8*) Jain Pub Co.

Words of Jesus Christ from the Cross. Charles H. Spurgeon. 1978. pap. 6.00 (*1-56186-210-X*) Pilgrim Pubns.

Words of Jesus, with Key Readings from New & Old Testaments. Jose M. De Vinck. 320p. 1977. boxed 35.00 (*0-911726-26-8*, CODE WJL) Alleluia Pr.

Words of Joseph Smith: Nauvoo Contemporary Accounts. Lyndon Cook. 468p. (C). 1993. 24.95 (*0-910523-39-8*) Grandin Bk Co.

Words of Life. Godfried C. Danneels. Tr. by Matthew J. O'Connell from FRE. LC 91-62600. 224p. (Orig.). 1991. pap. 9.95 (*1-55612-313-2*) Sheed & Ward MO.

Words of Light: Theses on the Photography of History. Eduardo Cadava. LC 96-17708. 224p. 1997. text ed. 29.95 (*0-691-03450-8*) Princeton U Pr.

Words of Love. Ed. by Laurie Holz. 144p. (YA). (gr. 8 up). 1992. lib. bdg. 15.00 (*1-56508-001-7*) Seven Wolves.

*Words of Love.** Linfield Krevisky. 1997. 9.99 (*0-517-18870-8*) Random Hse Value.

Words of Love. Joan A. Ratajack. (Words to Live By Ser.). 1992. 4.99 (*0-517-07364-1*) Random Hse Value.

Words of Love. Josefa Menedez et al. LC 84-51596. 95p. (Orig.). 1994. reprint ed. pap. 6.00 (*0-89555-244-2*) TAN Bks Pubs.

*Words of Love: Romantic Quotations from Plato to Madonna.** J. Linfield & J. Krevisky. LC 96-48094. 1997. pap. 18.00 (*0-679-77719-9*, Random Ref) Random.

Words of Martin Luther King, Jr. Intro. by Coretta Scott King. (Pocket Editions Ser.). (Illus.). 128p. 1992. pap. 5.95 (*1-55704-151-2*) Newmarket.

Words of Martin Luther King, Jr. Intro. by Coretta Scott King. LC 83-17306. (Illus.). 128p. 1991. reprint ed. 14.95 (*0-937858-28-5*); reprint ed. pap. 10.00 (*0-937858-79-X*) Newmarket.

Words of Mathematics: An Etymological Dictionary of Mathematical Terms Used in English. Steven Schwartzman. LC 93-80612. (Spectrum Ser.). 262p. 1994. pap. 34.00 (*0-88385-511-9*, WORDS) Math Assn.

*Words of My Mouth: Wrestling with Inclusive Language.** Bruce Hilton. 128p. 1996. pap. 10.95 (*0-687-25091-9*) Abingdon.

Words of My Perfect Teacher: Kunzang Lama'i Shelung. Patrul Rinpoche. Tr. by Association Padmakara Staff from TIB. LC 93-37175. (Sacred Literature Ser.). 1994. 32.00 (*0-06-066449-5*) Harper SF.

Words of Om Raja. Om P. Raja. LC 89-84563. 127p. (Orig.). 1990. pap. 9.95 (*0-9623163-0-X*) FL Pubs.

*Words of 100 Irish Songs & Ballads.** 68p. pap. 6.95 (*0-946005-59-1*, OS 10831, Pub. by Ossian Publns IE) Music Sales.

*Words of 100 Scot Songs & Ballads.** 68p. pap. 6.95 (*0-946005-86-9*, OS 00009, Pub. by Ossian Publns IE) Music Sales.

Words of Our Country: Stories, Place Names & Vocabulary in Yidiny. R. M. Dixon. (C). 1991. pap. 19.95 (*0-7022-2360-3*, Pub. by Univ Queensland Pr AT) Intl Spec Bk.

Words of Paradise: Poetry of Papua New Guinea. Ed. by Ulli Beier. Tr. by Don Laycock & Allan Natachee. LC 72-77912. (Illus.). 112p. 1973. 15.00 (*0-87775-031-9*); pap. 7.50 (*0-87775-081-5*) Unicorn Pr.

Words of Pathology Dictation. 2nd ed. Kaye Atkinson. 288p. 1995. lib. bdg. 29.95 (*1-886117-03-9*, P2115) D & T Prods.

Words of Peace: Selections from the Speeches of the Winners of the Nobel Peace Prize. Ed. by Irwin Abrams. LC 90-5851. (Illus.). 144p. 1991. 14.95 (*1-55704-060-5*) Newmarket.

Words of Peace: Selections from the Speeches of the Winners of the Nobel Peace Prize. rev. ed. Irwin Abrams. LC 95-38763. (Pocket Editions "Words of" Ser.). 1995. pap. 6.95 (*1-55704-250-0*) Newmarket.

Words of Power. James F. McNulty. LC 83-2514. 226p. (Orig.). 1983. pap. 8.95 (*0-8189-0442-9*) Alba.

Words of Power: A Feminist Reading of the History of Logic. Andrea Nye. 256p. (C). 1990. pap. 16.95 (*0-415-90200-2*, A3705, Routledge NY) Routledge.

Words of Power: Voices of Indian America. Ed. by Norbert S. Hill. 64p. 1994. 9.95 (*1-55591-189-7*) Fulcrum Pub.

Words of Praise: Daily Inspiration from Psalms & Proverbs. 325p. 1995. 7.99 (*0-529-10467-9*, GW30) World Publng.

*Words of Promise: Daily Devotions Through the Year.** Compiled by Dianne Krenz. 384p. 1996. per. 13.99 (*0-570-04851-6*, 12-3287) Concordia.

Words of Promise: For Men Only. John L. Mason & Tim Redmond. 1995. 12.99 (*0-88419-392-6*) Creation House.

Words of Promise: For Men Only. John L. Mason & Tim Redmond. 1995. pap. 6.99 (*0-88419-398-5*) Creation House.

Words of Promise & Praise. 1989. Living Bible Text. 14.95 (*0-8423-8307-7*, 20-8308-5) Tyndale.

*Words of Promise for Leaders.** John Mason. 1997. pap. text ed. 5.99 (*1-56292-370-6*) Honor Bks OK.

*Words of Radiology Dictation.** 5th rev. ed. Kaye Atkinson. 1997. pap. 30.95 (*1-886117-04-7*) D & T Prods.

Words of Risk: The Art of Thomas Ingmire. Michael Gullick. Ed. by Karyn L. Gilman & Nancy R. Block. 96p. 1989. 25.00 (*0-9622349-0-7*) CRE Norman.

Words of St. Francis. rev. ed. James Meyer & Lothar Hardick. 434p. 1982. pap. 15.00 (*0-8199-0833-9*, Frncscn Herld) Franciscan Pr.

Words of Still Waters. Peter W. Rigg. 68p. 1980. pap. 4.00 (*0-910477-00-0*) LoonBooks.

Words of Stone. Kevin Henkes. LC 91-28543. (J). (gr. 5-12). 1992. 16.00 (*0-688-11356-7*) Greenwillow.

Words of Stone. large type ed. Kevin Henkes. 1995. 41.50 (*0-614-09618-9*, L-34858-00) Am Printing Hse.

Words of Stone. Kevin Henkes. LC 93-7488. 160p. (J). (gr. 4-7). 1993. reprint ed. pap. 3.99 (*0-14-036601-6*, Puffin) Puffin Bks.

Words of Strength & Courage. Melba Christie. Ed. by Jackie Hooker. (Orig.). 1993. pap. 5.95 (*0-9638434-0-0*) Heavenly Mess.

*Words of the Apostles.** Rudolf E. Stier. 506p. 1987. lib. bdg. 19.99 (*0-8254-5241-4*) Kregel.

Words of the Cosmic Winds. Gerina Dunwich. LC 91-73612. (Illus.). 80p. (Orig.). 1996. pap. 9.95 (*0-9628638-3-1*) Golden Isis Pr.

*Words of the Dragon: Bruce Lee's Interviews with the Press from, 1959-1973.** John Little. (Bruce Lee Library). 1997. pap. text ed. 14.95 (*0-8048-3133-5*) C E Tuttle.

Words of the Father. J. L. Moreno. pap. 6.00 (*0-685-06818-8*) Beacon Hse.

Words of the Heart. Gayle C. Ortiz. (Orig.). 1996. pap. write for info. (*1-57553-264-6*) Watermrk Pr.

Words of the Lagoon: Fishing & Marine Lore in the Palau District of Micronesia. R. E. Johannes. (Illus.). 320p. 1981. 42.50 (*0-520-03929-7*); pap. 15.00 (*0-520-08087-4*) U CA Pr.

Words of the Master. Sri Ramakrishna. Ed. by Swami Brahmananda. 1932. pap. 2.00 (*0-87481-135-X*, Pub. by Advaita Ashrama II) Vedanta Pr.

Words of the Metis Poet. Lyle Lee. 1977. pap. 3.00 (*0-935350-96-9*) Luna Bisonte.

Words of the Mother, Pt. I. pap. 7.00 (*81-7058-130-3*) Aurobindo Assn.

Words of the Mother, Pt. II. 43p. 7.00 (*81-7058-153-2*) Aurobindo Assn.

Words of the Vietnam War: The Slang, Jargon, Abbreviations, Acronyms, Nomenclature, Nicknames, Pseudonyms, Slogans, Specs, Euphemisms, Double-talk, Chants & Names & Places of the Era of United States Involvement in Vietnam. Gregory R. Clark. LC 89-43639. 614p. 1990. lib. bdg. 55.00 (*0-89950-465-5*) McFarland & Co.

Words of the World's Religion. Robert S. Ellwood, Jr. 1977. pap. text ed. 33.00 (*0-13-965004-0*) P-H.

Words of This Life, Vol. 1. Bill Freeman. 175p. (Orig.). Date not set. pap. 5.00 (*0-914271-69-5*) Mnstry Wrd.

Words of This Life, Vol. 2. Bill Freeman. 200p. (Orig.). Date not set. pap. 5.00 (*0-914271-71-7*) Mnstry Wrd.

Words of This Life, Vol. 3. Bill Freeman. 175p. (Orig.). Date not set. pap. 5.00 (*0-914271-72-5*) Mnstry Wrd.

Words of Truth: An Oracle. Diamond Ectasy & Angel Ecstasy. (Illus.). 220p. (C). 1989. text ed. 34.95 (*0-942815-42-4*) MDRE.

Words of Truthful Nature. Wendy J. Jensen. 24p. (Orig.). 1995. pap. write for info. (*1-885206-11-9*, Iliad Pr) Cader Pubng.

Words of Victory. 1992. 7.99 (*0-88419-238-5*) Word Pub.

Words of Wall Street: Two Thousand Investment Terms Defined. Allan H. Pessin & Joseph A. Ross. LC 82-73632. 225p. 1983. pap. 17.00 (*0-87094-417-7*) Irwin Prof Pubng.

Words of War. Ed. by Robert Manning. (Vietnam Experience Ser.). (Illus.). 192p. 1988. 16.30 (*0-201-11943-9*) Addison-Wesley.

Words of Warehousing. Kenneth B. Ackerman. 115p. (Orig.). 1992. pap. text ed. 29.00 (*0-9631776-0-5*) K B Ackerman.

Words of Warning for Daily Life. Charles H. Spurgeon. 1973. mass mkt. 6.00 (*1-56186-303-3*) Pilgrim Pubns.

Words of Welcome. Amy Bolding. 112p. (Orig.). (gr. 10). 1965. pap. 6.99 (*0-8010-0550-7*) Baker Bks.

Words of Welfare: The Poverty of Social Science & the Social Science of Poverty. Sanford F. Schram. LC 94-37312. 1995. pap. text ed. 18.95 (*0-8166-2578-6*) U of Minn Pr.

Words of Wellness: A Treasury of Quotations for Well-Being. Compiled by Joseph Sutton. LC 90-71110. 36p. (Orig.). 1991. pap. 12.00 (*1-56170-005-3*, 130) Hay House.

Words of Wisdom. (Illus.). 80p. 1992. 4.95 (*0-8362-3003-5*) Andrews & McMeel.

Words of Wisdom. Sara Colacurto. (Words to Live By Ser.). 1992. 4.99 (*0-517-07363-3*) Random Hse Value.

Words of Wisdom. William Safire & Leonard Safir. 432p. 1990. pap. 12.00 (*0-671-69587-8*) S&S Trade.

Words of Wisdom. Charles H. Spurgeon. 208p. 1993. mass mkt. 4.99 (*0-88368-368-7*) Whitaker Hse.

Words of Wisdom, Vol. I. Darwin Gross. 80p. 50.00 (*0-931689-22-8*) D Gross.

*Words of Wisdom: A Collection of Powerful, Life-Changing Quotes.** Otis Williams, Jr. 64p. 1997. per. 9.95 (*0-7872-3617-9*) Kendall-Hunt.

*Words of Wisdom: Character Building Family Values for Your Refrigerator Door.** Dan Taddeo. LC 95-61645. 56p. (Orig.). 1995. pap. 5.00 (*1-55673-995-8*) CSS OH.

Words of Wisdom: For Writers, Speakers, & Leaders. Milton Murray. Ed. by Jeff Scoggins & Randy Fox. LC 93-84878. (Illus.). 208p. (Orig.). 1993. pap. 14.95 (*0-9643585-0-6*) Philanthropic Srv.

Words of Wisdom for Daily Life. Charles H. Spurgeon. 1973. mass mkt. 6.00 (*1-56186-302-5*) Pilgrim Pubns.

Words of Wisdom for Our World: The Precautions & Counsels of St. John of the Cross. Susan A. Muto & Adrian Van Kaam. Tr. & Pref. by Kieran Kavanaugh. LC 94-47484. 80p. (Orig.). 1996. pap. 8.95 (*0-935216-52-9*) ICS Pubns.

Words of Wisdom for Parents: Time-Tested Thoughts on How to Raise Kids. Ed. by Charles E. Schaefer. 1995. pap. 20.00 (*1-56821-797-8*) Aronson.

Words of Wisdom from the Masters. 2nd ed. Cylvia Archer Lowe. 120p. 1981. reprint ed. pap. 9.00 (*0-9606080-0-1*) Book Dept.

Words of Wisdom to Live By: An Encyclopedia of Wisdom in Condensed Form. Alfred A. Montapert. LC 86-73036. 280p. 1986. per. 10.00 (*0-9603174-5-7*) Bks of Value.

Words of Wisdom, Words of Wit. S. Himelstein. 1993. 19.99 (*0-89906-923-1*); pap. 16.99 (*0-89906-924-X*) Mesorah Pubns.

Words of Wismer: "But I'm Too Young to Retire" Romaine Wismer. 70p. (Orig.). 1985. pap. 4.95 (*0-9617021-0-9*) R Wismer.

Words of Women: Quotations for Success. Caterina Rando. (Orig.). 1995. spiral bd., pap. 6.95 (*0-9644906-0-9*) PowerDynamics.

Words of Women: Quotations for Success. Compiled by Caterina Rando. (Illus.). 18p. 1996. 19.95 incl. disk (*0-9644906-1-7*) PowerDynamics.

Words of Wonder: Word Studies for Sermon Starters & Group Discussions. Charles Goodwin. 125p. (Orig.). pap. 9.95 incl. audio (*0-9626544-5-0*) Original Word.

Words of Worship: Resources for Sharing the Good News. Glen E. Rainsley. LC 91-17439. 184p. (Orig.). 1991. pap. 12.95 (*0-8298-0899-X*) Pilgrim OH.

Words Old & New. Horatius Bonar. 386p. 1994. pap. 7.99 (*0-85151-643-2*) Banner of Truth.

Words on Aging: A Bibliography of Selected Annotated References Compiled for the Administration on Aging by the Department Library. Ed. by U. S. Department of Health, Education & Welfare, Washington, D. C. Staff. LC 81-2471. vi, 190p. 1981. reprint ed. text ed. 52.50 (*0-313-22860-4*, USWA) Greenwood.

***Words on Cassette 1998. Ed. by Bowker, R. R., Staff. 2400p. 1998. 155.00 (*0-8352-3964-0*) Bowker.**

"...excellent..."--CHOICE. Now, building a strong audiocassette library collection or bookstore has never been easier -- thanks to the enormous help you'll get from WORDS ON CASSETTE. With this tool on hand, you can: * quickly locate tapes, ordering information, prices, & other important details * efficiently build or stock "books-on-tape" sections * track down special requests & field research queries involving even the most obscure recorded materials * provide patrons with a complete guide to the entire words-on-tape field -- covering all genres & subjects. The only complete guide of its kind, WORDS ON CASSETTE provides accurate information on more than 68,000 audiocassettes -- including hard-to-find materials such as lectures, seminars, & old radio programs -- & features more than 7,500 new releases & some 8,000 updated entries! You'll find: * detailed listings in the Title Index that include reader's name, price, running time, number of cassettes, content summary, whether the tape is a "live" or studio recording, publication/release date, abridged or unabridged version, & rental availability * a separate Subject Index that arranges tapes in more than 125 subject categories -- everything from art & architecture to personal growth & language instruction * a unique Authors/Readers/Performers Index * listings for more than 1,750 producers & distributors, complete with names, addresses & telephone numbers in the Producer/Distributor Index. With one-stop convenience like this, WORDS ON CASSETTE 1998 gives you all the information you need to satisfy all your books-on-tape patrons! ***Publisher Provided Annotation.***

Words on Cassette 1996. Ed. by Bowker, R. R., Staff. (Orig.). 1996. pap. 149.95 (*0-8352-3765-6*) Bowker.

*Words on Cassette 1997, Set, 2 vols.** Ed. by Bowker, R. R., Staff. 1997. pap. 149.95 (*0-8352-3914-4*) Bowker.

*Words on Cassette 1997, Vol. 1.** Ed. by Bowker, R. R., Staff. 1997. write for info. (*0-8352-3872-5*) Bowker.

*Words on Cassette 1997, Vol. 2.** Bowker, R. R., Staff. 1997. pap. write for info. (*0-8352-3913-6*) Bowker.

Words on Decroux. Leabhart et al. Ed. by Thomas Leabhart. (Mime Journal Ser.). (Illus.). 229p. (Orig.). 1993. pap. 12.00 (*0-9611066-0-3*) Mime Jour.

Words on Fire: One Woman's Journey into the Sacred. Vanessa Ochs. 1992. pap. 10.95 (*0-15-698363-X*, Harvest Bks) HarBrace.

Words on Fire: The Life & Writing of Elizabeth Gurley Flynn. Baxandall & Rosalyn Fraad. (Douglass Series on Women's Lives & the Meaning of Gender). (Illus.). 320p. 1987. text ed. 45.00 (*0-8135-1240-9*); pap. text ed. 17.95 (*0-8135-1241-7*) Rutgers U Pr.

Words on Mime. Etienne Decroux. Ed. by Thomas Leabhart. Tr. by Mark Piper from FRE. (Mime Journal Ser.). (Illus.). 160p. 1985. pap. 12.00 (*0-9611066-5-4*) Mime Jour.

An Asterisk (*) at the beginning of an entry indicates that the title is appearing in BIP for the first time.

Words on Music. Ed. by Robin Ray. 176p. 1985. 13.95 (*0-8253-0307-9*) Beaufort Bks NY.
Words on Music. Ernst Bacon. LC 73-427. 183p. 1973. reprint ed. text ed. 55.00 (*0-8371-6768-X*, BAWM, Greenwood Pr) Greenwood.
Words on Music: From Addison to Barzun. Ed. by Jack Sullivan. LC 89-72115. 453p. 1990. pap. 19.95 (*0-8214-0959-X*) Ohio U Pr.
Words on Paper. Alvaro Cardona-Hine. 1974. pap. 2.50 (*0-88031-013-8*) Invisible-Red Hill.
***Words on Tape: How to Create & Profit from Spoken Word Audio on Cassettes & CDs.** Judith A. Byers. Ed. by Terri Lonier & Justin Mitchell. (Illus.). 200p. (Orig.). 1997. pap. 27.95 (*0-9655721-4-5*) AudioCP.
Words on Target: For Better Christian Communication. Sue Nichols. LC 63-16410. (Illus.). (Orig.). 1963. pap. 7.00 (*0-8042-1476-X*, John Knox) Westminster John Knox.
Words on the Air: Essays on Language, Manners, Morals, & Laws. John Sparrow. LC 81-3341. 264p. (C). 1981. 18. 00 (*0-226-76851-1*) U Ch Pr.
Words on the Moon. Douglas Gray. (First Poetry Ser.). 112p. (Orig.). 1994. pap. 9.95 (*0-922811-18-0*) Mid-List.
Words on the Wind, Set. Ed. & Illus. by Sam L. Vulgaris. 352p. (Orig.). 1988. pap. 19.95 (*0-9620417-2-6*) SA-DE Pubns.
Words on the Wind, Vol. 1. Sam L. Vulgaris. (Illus.). 152p. (Orig.). 1988. pap. 12.95 (*0-9620417-0-X*) SA-DE Pubns.
Words on the Wind, Vol. 2. Ed. & Illus. by Sam L. Vulgaris. 200p. (Orig.). 1988. pap. 14.95 (*0-9620417-1-8*) SA-DE Pubns.
***Words on Waves: Selected Radio Plays of Earle Birney.** CBC Radio Staff. 320p. 1985. 22.95 (*0-919627-71-4*, Pub. by Quarry Pr CN) LPC InBook.
***Words on Waves: Selected Radio Plays of Earle Birney.** CBC Radio Staff. 320p. 1985. pap. 15.95 (*0-919627-73-0*, Pub. by Quarry Pr CN) LPC InBook.
Words or Power: Essays in Honour of Alison Fairlie, 1917-1993. D. G. Coleman & G. Jondorf. 1993. 65.00 (*0-85261-209-5*, Pub. by Univ of Glasgow UK) St Mut.
Words Our Saviour Gave Us. Daniel Berrigan. 128p. 1978. pap. 7.95 (*0-87243-081-2*) Templegate.
Word's Out: Gay Men's English. William L. Leap. LC 95-35967. 216p. 1996. pap. 17.95 (*0-8166-2253-1*); text ed. 44.95 (*0-8166-2252-3*) U of Minn Pr.
Words People Use. McCallum. 1982. pap. 22.95 (*0-8384-2852-5*) Heinle & Heinle.
Words, Phrases, Clauses. 3rd ed. Edward J. Fox, Jr. & Malcolm T. Moore. 1980. student ed. 12.40 (*0-8013-0106-8*, 76102); teacher ed. 9.28 (*0-685-32858-9*, 75770) Longman.
Words, Phrases, Clauses: Exercises in English Grammar. 3rd ed. Edward J. Fox, Jr. & Malcolm T. Moore. 120p. (gr. 6-12). 1980. pap. text ed. 7.50 (*0-88334-128-X*) Longman.
***Words Problems (Math)** Jo E. Moore. (Mathematics Ser.). (Illus.). 32p. (J). (gr. 1-2). 1996. teacher ed., pap. 2.95 (*1-55799-448-X*, 4050) Evan-Moor Corp.
Words, Science & Learning. Clive Sutton. (Developing Science & Technology Education Ser.). 100p. 1992. 80. 00 (*0-335-09957-2*, Open Univ Pr); pap. 27.00 (*0-335-09956-4*, Open Univ Pr) Taylor & Francis.
Words, Script, & Pictures: Semiotics of Visual Language. Meyer Schapiro. LC 96-18996. (Illus.). 200p. 1996. 30. 00 (*0-8076-1416-5*) Braziller.
Words Spoken, Words Unspoken. Edward J. Byrne. 72p. 1995. pap. write for info. (*0-9627300-1-7*) Chimney Hill.
Words Still Count with Me: A Chronicle of Literary Conversations. Herbert Mitgang. LC 95-5392. 315p. 1995. 25.00 (*0-393-03880-7*) Norton.
Words Take Wing: A Teaching Guide to Creative Writing for Children. Barbara Bennett. LC 82-84013. (Illus.). 194p. 1983. reprint ed. pap. 55.30 (*0-608-00015-9*, 2060781) Bks Demand.
Words, Texts, & Manuscripts: Studies in Anglo-Saxon Cultures: Presented to Helmut Gneuss on the Occasion of His Sixty-Fifth Birthday. Ed. by Michael Korhammer et al. LC 92-23395. (Illus.). 512p. (C). 1992. 79.00 (*0-85991-363-5*, DS Brewer) Boydell & Brewer.
Words That Bind: Judicial Review & the Grounds of Modern Constitutional Theory. John Arthur. LC 94-29699. (C). 1994. pap. text ed. 23.50 (*0-8133-2349-5*) Westview.
Words That Change Minds. Shelle R. Charvet. 208p. 1995. per., pap. text ed. 14.95 (*0-7872-0803-5*) Kendall-Hunt.
***Words That Change Minds: Mastering the Language of Influence.** 2nd ed. Shelle Charvet. 224p. 1997. per. 14. 95 (*0-7872-3479-6*) Kendall-Hunt.
Words That Heal. Douglas Bloch. 128p. (Orig.). 1989. pap. 9.95 (*0-929671-00-7*) Pallas Comns.
Words That Hurt, Words That Heal. Carole Mayhall. LC 86-61136. 108p. 1986. pap. 8.00 (*0-89109-179-3*) NavPress.
Words That Hurt, Words That Heal: Changing Your Life by Changing Your Words. Tim Stafford. 160p. 1995. pap. 10.99 (*0-310-49001-4*) Zondervan.
Words That Hurt, Words That Heal: How to Choose Words Wisely & Well. Joseph Telushkin. LC 95-1116. 192p. 1996. 19.95 (*0-688-12445-3*) Morrow.
Words That Make America Great: An Interpretive Documentary History. Jerome Agel. 1996. 30.00 (*0-679-44959-0*) Random.
Words That Make New Jersey History: A Primary Source Reader. Ed. by Howard L. Green. LC 94-8927. (Illus.). 290p. (C). 1994. text ed. 35.00 (*0-8135-2112-2*); pap. text ed. 14.00 (*0-8135-2113-0*) Rutgers U Pr.
Words That Make Signs Sell. Christopher Moquist. (Illus.). 88p. (Orig.). 1992. pap. 14.95 (*0-9629666-2-2*) Insignia Systs.
Words That Manage. Chris Williams. 1987. pap. 21.95 (*0-87280-131-4*, 3333, Asher-Gallant) Caddylak Systs.
Words That Matter: Linguistic Perception in Renaissance English. Judith H. Anderson. LC 96-3159. 1996. write for info. (*0-8047-2631-0*) Stanford U Pr.
Words That Mean Business: Three Thousand Terms for Access to Business Information. Warner-Eddison Associates Staff. LC 81-16859. 235p. 1981. 54.95 (*0-918212-55-3*) Neal-Schuman.
***Words That Ought to Be Dirty but Aren't.** unabridged ed. Arthur Naiman. 64p. (Orig.). 1997. pap. 4.00 (*1-878825-69-0*) Odonian Pr.
Words That Sell. Richard Bayan. LC 84-71532. (Orig.). 26. 95 (*0-87280-150-0*, 3354, Asher-Gallant) Caddylak Systs.
Words That Sell: The Thesaurus to Help Promote Your Products, Services & Ideas. Richard Bayan. 144p. (Orig.). 1987. pap. 13.95 (*0-8092-4799-2*) Contemp Bks.
Words That Sing. Gail Ramshaw. 167p. (Orig.). 1992. pap. 9.95 (*0-929650-42-5*, WOSING) Liturgy Tr Pubns.
Words That Soar: Wisdom Inspired by the Earth. NorthWord Press, Inc. Staff. LC 96-7873. (Illus.). 96p. (Orig.). 1996. pap. write for info. (*1-55971-592-8*) NorthWord.
Words That Win Children see Palabras Que Se Ganan a los Ninos
Words That Won the War: The Mobilization of Mass Hatred. James R. Mock & Cedric Larson. 1985. lib. bdg. 79.95 (*0-87700-652-0*) Revisionist Pr.
***Words That Work.** Peter Fuller. 1998. 14.95 (*0-02-862158-1*) S&S Trade.
Words That Wound: Critical Race Theory, Assaultive Speech, & the First Amendment. Mari J. Matsuda et al. (New Perspectives on Law, Culture, & Society Ser.). 160p. (C). 1993. pap. text ed. 18.95 (*0-8133-8428-1*) Westview.
***Words They Need: Welcoming Children Who Are Deaf & Hard of Hearing to Literacy.** (Illus.). 290p. (Orig.). (C). 1997. pap. write for info. (*0-912752-44-0*) York Pr.
Words, Thoughts & Gifts of Love: Letters from the Front. 33p. 1996. write for info. (*1-885671-09-1*) Caruso Leader Inst.
Words, Thoughts, & Theories. Alison Gopnik & Andrew N. Meltzoff. (Learning, Development & Conceptual Change Ser.). (Illus.). 350p. 1996. 30.00 (*0-262-07175-4*, Bradford Bks) MIT Pr.
Words to Create a World. Daniel Hoffman. (Poets on Poetry Ser.). 240p. (C). 1992. pap. 13.95 (*0-472-06505-X*); text ed. 39.50 (*0-472-09505-6*) U of Mich Pr.
Words to Know see Child Horizons
Words to Live By. Jim Davis. (Postcard Bks.: No. 2). (Illus.). 64p. 1990. pap. 6.95 (*0-345-36679-4*) Ballantine.
***Words to Live By.** Orley Herron. 80p. 1996. write for info. (*1-886094-47-0*) Chicago Spectrum.

Words to Live By. Orley R. Herron. 79p. 1997. write for info. (*1-889555-02-9*) Stephen Aubry. WORDS TO LIVE BY is a collection of words of wisdom & compassion that are geared to people of all ages. These profound & witty observations are enduring statements that will strengthen one's life as the pressures & challenges seek to undermine it. These words are based on experiences of the author as a University President, businessman, entrepreneur, athlete, husband, father, grandfather, & caring friend. The words are very succinct & will be easily remembered & often quoted. The writings are filled with charm yet bring power & surprise to the inquiring mind. The practicality of the sayings are remarkable & will give the reader a sense of exhilaration, wonderful confidence, & delightful affirmation. The observations truly span all ages & will be lasting thoughts that are timeless & forever enduring.** ***Publisher Provided Annotation.

Words to Live By. Ed. by Jean Van Dyke. LC 90-82144. 68p. 1990. pap. 4.95 (*1-878932-00-4*, 6322) Reiman Pubns.
Words to Live By: A Collection of Original Quotations. Roland T. Satrom. LC 95-92794. 120p. (Orig.). 1996. pap. write for info. (*0-9620837-2-0*) R T Satrom.
Words to Live By: Inspiration for Every Day. 2nd ed. Eknath Easwaran. 400p. 1996. 22.00 (*0-915132-86-9*); pap. 9.95 (*0-915132-85-0*) Nilgiri Pr.
Words to Live By: Selected Writings of Rabbi Sidney Greenberg. Ed. by Arthur Kurzweil. LC 90-40486. 376p. 1990. 30.00 (*0-87668-706-0*) Aronson.
Words to Live By: Thoughts on Living a Happy & Successful Life. Todd L. Mayo. LC 95-70414. 288p. 1995. pap. 9.95 (*0-9647700-0-8*) Pinnacle FL.
Words to Live By: Thoughts on Living a Happy & Successful Life. deluxe rev. ed. Todd L. Mayo. LC 95-70414. 470p. 1996. pap. 15.95 (*0-9647700-2-4*) Pinnacle FL.
***Words to Live By Vol. 2: You Can Do It.** Orley R. Herron. 80p. 1996. write for info. (*1-889555-03-7*) Stephen Aubry.
Words to Live-Die By. Charles Gallagher. (Celebrate Love Ser.). 53p. (Orig.). 1992. pap. text ed. 3.95 (*0-911905-47-2*) Past & Mat Rene Ctr.
Words to Love By. Mother Teresa. LC 82-73373. (Illus.). 80p. (Orig.). 1983. pap. 5.95 (*0-87793-261-1*) Ave Maria.
Words to Love By. large type ed. Mother Teresa. 96p. (Orig.). 1985. reprint ed. pap. 6.95 (*0-8027-2478-7*) Walker & Co.
Words to Make My Dream Children Live: An African-American Book of Quotations. Compiled by Deirdre Mullane. LC 94-32710. 448p. pap. 14.95 (*0-385-42244-X*, Anchor NY) Doubleday.
Words to Rhyme With. Willard Espy. 672p. 1988. pap. 22. 00 (*0-8050-0447-5*, Owl) H Holt & Co.
Words to Rhyme With: A Rhyming Dictionary. Willard Espy. 672p. 1986. 55.00 (*0-8160-1237-7*) Facts on File.
Words to Say It. 9th ed. Marie Cardinal. Ed. & Tr. by Pat Goodheart from FRE. 308p. (Orig.). (ENG.). (C). 1994. pap. 22.95 (*0-941324-09-5*) Van Vactor & Goodheart.
***Words to Strengthen: The Inspirational Writings of Nancy T. Thomas.** Nancy T. Thomas. LC 96-61864. 77p. (Orig.). 1997. pap. 11.00 (*1-887798-06-4*) WriteMore Pubns.
***Words to the Silence.** Schuyler Rhodes. 112p. 1994. pap. 12.95 (*1-877871-74-5*, 3536) Ed Ministries.
Words to the Wise. Manly P. Hall. pap. 12.95 (*0-89314-814-8*) Philos Res.
Words to the Wise: A Wonderful, Witty & Wise Collection of Good Advice on Life. Don Farias. LC 91-50691. 70p. 1992. pap. 6.95 (*0-88247-897-4*, 897) R & E Pubs.
Words to the Wise: A Writer's Guide to Feminist & Lesbian Periodicals & Publishers. Andrea F. Clardy. LC 93-3816. 56p. (Orig.). 1993. pap. 5.95 (*1-56341-032-X*) Firebrand Bks.
Words to Trust. Campbell Gillon. (C). 1991. text ed. 39.50 (*0-389-20948-1*); pap. text ed. 18.50 (*0-389-20949-X*) B&N Imports.
Words to Winners of Souls. Horatius Bonar. 72p. 1995. pap. 3.99 (*0-87552-164-9*, Pub. by Evangelical Pr) Presby & Reformed.
Words Unchained: Language & Revolution in Grenada. Chris Searle. (Latin America Ser.). (Illus.). 284p. (C). 1984. pap. 15.00 (*0-86232-247-2*, Pub. by Zed Bks Ltd UK); text ed. 39.95 (*0-86232-246-4*, Pub. by Zed Bks Ltd UK) Humanities.
Words under Construction. R. L. Cherry. LC 89-4813. 298p. (Orig.). 1989. pap. text ed. 14.95 (*0-8165-1040-7*) U of Ariz Pr.
Words under the Words: Selected Poems. Naomi S. Nye. LC 94-43072. 160p. (Orig.). 1995. pap. 13.95 (*0-933377-29-0*); lib. bdg. 22.95 (*0-933377-32-0*) Eighth Mount Pr.
Words Upon the Window Pane see Eleven Plays of William Butler Yeats
Words upon Words: The Anagrams of Ferdinand de Saussure. Jean Starobinski. Tr. by Olivia Emmet from GER. LC 79-64071. 141p. reprint ed. pap. 40.20 (*0-8357-8379-0*, 2033896) Bks Demand.
Words Used in Herefordshire see English Dialect Society Publications, No. 2: Glossaries VIII-XIV
Words Used in the Isle of Thanet see English Dialect Society Publications, No. 2: Glossaries VIII-XIV
***Words We Live by.** Brian Burrell. LC 96-53537. 1997. 26. 00 (*0-684-83001-9*) S&S Trade.
Words We Use. Marilyn Hayes. (Early Education Ser.). 24p. (gr. 1). 5.00 (*0-8209-0218-7*, K-20) ESP.
Words We Use. Robert Lord. 128p. 1994. 16.95 (*1-871082-44-7*) Paul & Co Pubs.
Words We Use. Diarmaid O. Muirithe. 144p. 1996. pap. 14. 95 (*1-85182-220-8*, Pub. by Four Cts Pr IE) Intl Spec Bk.
Words Were Originally Magic. Steve De Shazer. 320p. (C). 1994. 32.00 (*0-393-70170-0*) Norton.
Words Win Wars. John Hargrave. 1973. 59.95 (*0-8490-1328-3*) Gordon Pr.
Words with Music. Lehman Engel. 300p. 1980. pap. write for info. (*0-318-54252-8*) Macmillan.
Words with Power: Being a Second Study of the Bible & Literature. Northrop Frye. 1992. pap. 10.95 (*0-15-698365-6*, Harvest Bks) HarBrace.
Words with Wrinkled Knees. Barbara J. Esbensen. LC 85-47886. (Illus.). 48p. (J). (gr. 2-7). 1987. lib. bdg. 14.89 (*0-690-04505-0*, Crowell Jr Bks) HarpC Child Bks.
***Words with Wrinkled Knees: Animal Poems.** Barbara J. Esbensen. (J). Date not set. pap. text ed. 8.95 (*1-56397-682-X*) Boyds Mills Pr.
Words Without Pictures. Steve Niles. 1990. 29.95 (*1-56060-031-4*); pap. 8.95 (*1-56060-032-2*) Eclipse Bks.
Words Without Song. Frank Daykin. (Orig.). 1992. pap. text ed. 20.00 (*1-880551-02-0*) Silver Hill.
Words, Wordlessness & the Word: Silence Considered from Literary Point of View. Peter Bien. 32p. 1992. pap. 3.00 (*0-87574-303-X*, PHP303) Pendle Hill.
***Words, Words, Words.** (J). (gr. 1-3). Date not set. 12.95 (*0-673-36319-8*, GoodYrBooks) Addson-Wesley Educ.
Words! Words! Words! 2nd ed. Schachter. (EC - HS Communication/Engl Ser.). 1986. wbk. ed., pap. 16.95 (*0-538-05410-7*) S-W Pub.
Words, Words, Words. 3rd ed. Schachter. (EC - HS Communication/English Ser.). 1992. pap. 15.95 (*0-538-60781-5*) S-W Pub.
Words, Words, Words! Eric Partridge. LC 70-117912. (Select Bibliographies Reprint Ser.). 1977. reprint ed. 23. 95 (*0-8369-5365-7*) Ayer.
Words, Words, Words, Bk 2. Willard D. Sheeler. (Words, Words, Words Ser.). 128p. (gr. 9-12). 1987. pap. text ed. write for info. (*0-13-964289-7*, 18830) Prentice ESL.
Words, Words, Words: A Dictionary for Writers & Others Who Care about Words. John B. Bremner. LC 80-256. 405p. 1980. pap. text ed. 18.00 (*0-231-04493-3*) Col U Pr.
Words, Words, Words: The Translator & the Language Learner. Ed. by Gunilla Anderman & Margaret Rogers. LC 95-43551. (Topics in Translation Ser.: Vol. 7). 120p. 1996. 69.00 (*1-85359-332-X*, Pub. by Multilingual Matters UK); pap. 24.95 (*1-85359-331-1*, Pub. by Multilingual Matters UK) Taylor & Francis.
Word's Worth: A Handbook on Writing & Selling Nonfiction. Terri Brooks. LC 89-10331. 221p. (Orig.). (C). 1989. pap. text ed. 20.25 (*0-312-03581-0*) St Martin.
***Words, Wounds & Wonder.** Nicholas Giosa. (Illus.). 48p. (Orig.). 1996. pap. write for info. (*1-889701-00-9*) N Giosa.
Words You Should Know. David Olsen. 260p. 1991. pap. 6.95 (*1-55850-018-9*) Adams Media.
Words You Should Know How to Spell: The 10,000 Most Commonly Misspelled Words. Michelle Bevilacqua. 144p. (Orig.). 1994. pap. 5.95 (*1-55850-280-7*) Adams Media.
Wordsand. Richard Kostelanetz. LC 78-61088. 1978. pap. 3.00 (*0-932360-25-4*) Archae Edns.
Wordsand. deluxe limited ed. Richard Kostelanetz. LC 78-61088. 1978. 50.00 (*0-932360-24-6*) Archae Edns.
Wordshop. Phillip Stokes. 310p. (C). 1996. per., pap. text ed. 36.69 (*0-7872-2377-8*) Kendall-Hunt.
***Wordsmithery.** 2nd ed. Root. 1997. pap. text ed. 20.00 (*0-205-27024-7*) P-H.
Wordsmithery: A Guide to Working at Writing. Root. 147p. (C). 1993. pap. text ed. 22.00 (*0-02-403541-6*, Macmillan Coll) P-H.
Wordsmithing: A New Approach to Spelling. Ardy Smith & Anne Davies. (Building Connections Ser.: Vol. 4). (Orig.). (J). (gr. 3-8). 1996. teacher ed., pap. 17.00 (*1-895411-85-8*) Peguis Pubs Ltd.
Wordsmiths: Oscar Hammerstein II & Alan Jay Lerner. Stephen Citron. (Great Songwriters Ser.). (Illus.). 448p. 1995. 30.00 (*0-19-508386-5*) OUP.
Wordsongs. Steven Blue. 48p. (Orig.). 1993. pap. 7.95 (*0-9635499-0-1*) Arrowcloud Pr.
***Wordspill.** David R. Swantner. (Illus.). 43p. (Orig.). 1997. pap. 8.95 (*0-9637347-4-1*) C W Pub.
Wordstar: A Practical Approach. Graham. (DF - Computer Applications Ser.). 1991. pap. 34.95 (*0-538-70311-3*) S-W Pub.
Wordstar: The Useable Portable Guide. Jon Haber & Herbert R. Haber. 32p. (Orig.). (C). 1989. pap. text ed. 4.95 (*0-945765-09-6*) Useable Portable Pubns.
WordStar: Tutorial & Applications. Graham. (DF - Computer Applications Ser.). 1991. pap. 23.95 (*0-538-70271-0*) S-W Pub.
Wordstar & CP-M Made Easy. John D. Lee. LC 83-5939. (Illus.). 235p. reprint ed. pap. 67.00 (*0-8357-4600-3*, 2037533) Bks Demand.
Wordstar for the Computer Intimidated. Michael Anderson. 14.95 (*0-13-965054-7*) P-H.
Wordstar Handbook. Dennis P. Curtin. 166p. 1986. pap. 24.95 (*0-938862-84-7*) Weber Systems.
WordStar in English I. Steven Doroff & Larry Doroff. (English I Computer Tutorials Ser.). (Illus.). 184p. reprint ed. pap. 12.95 (*0-915869-01-2*) Eng Comp Tut.
WORDSTAR in Everyday English. Maria H. Goudiss. 157p. 1983. pap. 9.95 (*0-8159-7221-0*) Devin.
WordStar on the IBM PC. Richard Curtis. (BYTE Book). 208p. 1985. pap. text ed. 11.95 (*0-07-014978-X*) McGraw.
WordStar Quick & Dirty. Carol H. Ham. (Illus.). 162p. (Orig.). 1988. pap. 13.95 (*0-935920-43-9*, Ntl Pubs Blck) P-H.
WordStar Release 4 Quick Reference. 1990. pap. 19.95 (*0-913365-61-0*) Microref Educ Systs.
WordStar Simplified for the IBM Personal Computer. Don Cassel. (Illus.). 160p. 1984. pap. 13.50 (*0-13-963612-9*) P-H.
WordStar Simplified with WordStar 3.3: MailMerge, Spellstar & StarIndex. Don Cassel. 176p. (C). 1986. 15.50 (*0-13-963646-3*); text ed. 24.33 (*0-13-963638-2*) P-H.
Wordstar 2000: The Useable Portable Guide. Jon Haber & Herbert R. Haber. 32p. (C). 1989. pap. text ed. 4.95 (*0-945765-15-0*) Useable Portable Pubns.
WordStar 4.0-6.0 Quick Reference Guide. Micoref Educational Systems Staff. 1990. pap. 19.95 (*0-01-336561-4*) Microref Educ Systs.
Wordstar 5 & 5.5 Advanced Course. Graham. 1991. pap. 34.95 (*0-538-70274-5*) S-W Pub.
WordStar 5.0: With Updates for WordStar 5.5. Earl Henry. 576p. 1990. pap. text ed. 36.40 (*0-13-964693-0*) P-H.
WordStar 6.0 Quick Reference Guide. Angelo Cassano & Paul Berube. (DDC Quick Reference Guides Ser.). (Orig.). 1990. spiral bd. 12.00 (*0-936862-98-X*, R-17) DDC Pub.
WordStar 7.0. Alan Boyd & Fraser. (STAR Ser.). 176p. (C). 1994. pap. 12.95 (*0-87835-842-0*, BF8420) S-W Pub.
WordStrength. Joan Robinson. (Roots of Language Ser.). (J). (gr. 4-8). 1989. pap. 10.99 (*0-8224-7451-4*) Fearon Teach Aids.
Wordstruck. Robert MacNeil. 256p. 1990. pap. 11.95 (*0-14-010401-1*, Penguin Bks) Viking Penguin.
Wordstuff Mac Lab Pack. Sanctuary Woods Staff. (Sanctuary Woods CD ROM Ser.). 1994. teacher ed. 200.00 incl. cd-rom (*0-201-87823-2*) Addison-Wesley.
Wordsworth. Peter Burra. LC 72-2096. (Studies in Wordsworth: No. 29). 1972. reprint ed. lib. bdg. 75.00 (*0-8383-1486-4*) M S G Haskell Hse.
Wordsworth. Charles H. Herford. LC 75-28999. reprint ed. 39.50 (*0-404-14010-6*) AMS Pr.
Wordsworth. Walter Raleigh. (BCL1-PR English Literature Ser.). 232p. 1992. reprint ed. lib. bdg. 79.00 (*0-7812-7682-9*) Rprt Serv.
Wordsworth. Walter Raleigh. LC 76-131811. 1970. reprint ed. 29.00 (*0-403-00698-8*) Scholarly.

W

Wordsworth. Herbert E. Read. LC 83-1723. 194p. (C). 1983. reprint ed. text ed. 49.75 (*0-313-23321-7*, REWO, Greenwood Pr) Greenwood.

Wordsworth: "The Prelude" Stephen Gill. (Landmarks of World Literature Ser.). (Illus.). 144p. (C). 1991. text ed. 29.95 (*0-521-36218-0*); pap. text ed. 11.95 (*0-521-36988-6*) Cambridge U Pr.

Wordsworth: A Collection of Critical Essays. Ed. by Meyer H. Abrams. 1972. 12.95 (*0-685-03922-6*, Spectrum IN) Macmillan Gen Ref.

Wordsworth: A Re-Interpretation. Frederick W. Bateson. LC 83-45410. reprint ed. 27.50 (*0-404-20020-6*) AMS Pr.

Wordsworth: Language as Counter-Spirit. Frances Ferguson. LC 76-49932. 281p. reprint ed. pap. 80.10 (*0-8357-8380-4*, 2033722) Bks Demand.

Wordsworth: Poems. William Wordsworth. (Poetry Library). 192p. 1985. mass mkt. 4.95 (*0-14-058506-0*, Penguin Bks) Viking Penguin.

Wordsworth: Selected Poetry & Prose. Ed. by Philip Hobsbaum. (English Texts Ser.). 288p. (C). 1989. pap. text ed. 10.95 (*0-415-01605-3*) Routledge.

Wordsworth: The Chronology of the Early Years, 1770-1799. Mark L. Reed. LC 66-21344. 383p. 1967. reprint ed. pap. 109.20 (*0-7837-4182-0*, 2059031) Bks Demand.

Wordsworth: The Chronology of the Middle Years, 1800-1815. Mark L. Reed. LC 74-77179. 768p. 1975. 46.50 (*0-674-95777-6*) HUP.

Wordsworth: The Sense of History. Alan Liu. (Illus.). 742p. 1989. 67.50 (*0-8047-1373-1*); pap. 24.95 (*0-8047-1893-8*) Stanford U Pr.

Wordsworth: Wordsworth & the Tasty Treat Trick. Todd Strasser. 144p. 1996. mass mkt. 3.50 (*0-06-106327-4*) HarpC.

Wordsworth & Coleridge. Raymond E. Matlak. LC 96-48921. 1997. text ed. write for info. (*0-312-10166-X*) St Martin.

Wordsworth & Coleridge: Lyrical Ballads 1805. R. Roper. 1990. pap. 27.00 (*0-7463-0382-3*, Pub. by Northcote UK) St Mut.

Wordsworth & Coleridge: The Making of the Major Lyrics, 1802-1804. Gene W. Ruoff. LC 88-28292. 320p. (C). 1989. text ed. 45.00 (*0-8135-1398-7*); pap. text ed. 16.95 (*0-8135-1399-5*) Rutgers U Pr.

Wordsworth & Feeling: The Poetry of an Adult Child. G. Kim Blank. LC 94-43068. 272p. 1995. 39.50 (*0-8386-3600-4*) Fairleigh Dickinson.

Wordsworth & His Circle. David W. Rannie. LC 72-3432. (Studies in Wordsworth: No. 29). (Illus.). 1972. reprint ed. lib. bdg. 69.95 (*0-8383-1537-2*) M S G Haskell Hse.

Wordsworth & His Poetry. William H. Hudson. LC 73-120984. (Poetry & Life Ser.). reprint ed. 16.00 (*0-404-52520-2*) AMS Pr.

Wordsworth & Philosophy. Newton P. Stallknecht. (Studies in Wordsworth: No. 29). (C). 1970. reprint ed. lib. bdg. 50.00 (*0-8383-0345-5*) M S G Haskell Hse.

Wordsworth & Tennyson. David G. James. LC 71-39860. (Studies in Comparative Literature: No. 35). 1970. reprint ed. pap. 12.95 (*0-8383-0046-4*) M S G Haskell Hse.

Wordsworth & the Art of Landscape. Russell Noyes. LC 72-6864. (Studies in Wordsworth: No. 29). 1972. reprint ed. lib. bdg. 75.00 (*0-8383-1660-3*) M S G Haskell Hse.

Wordsworth & the Beginnings of Modern Poetry. Robert Rehder. 246p. 1981. 42.00 (*0-389-20209-6*, N6991) B&N Imports.

Wordsworth & the Coldcut Catastrophe. Todd Strasser. (Wordsworth Ser.: No. 1). 128p. 1995. mass mkt. 2.99 (*0-06-106257-X*, Harp PBks) HarpC.

***Wordsworth & the Critics.** John Mahoney. (LCENG Ser.). Date not set. 54.95 (*1-57113-186-8*) Camden Hse.

Wordsworth & the Cultivation of Women. Judith W. Page. LC 93-34121. (C). 1994. 35.00 (*0-520-08493-4*) U CA Pr.

Wordsworth & the Empirical Dilemma. Regina Hewitt. LC 90-5912. (American University Studies: English Language & Literature: Ser. IV, Vol. 120). 250p. (C). 1991. text ed. 50.50 (*0-8204-1358-5*) P Lang Pubng.

Wordsworth & the Enlightenment: Nature, Man, & Society in the Experimental Poetry. Alan J. Bewell. LC 88-20644. 352p. (C). 1989. text ed. 45.00 (*0-300-04393-7*) Yale U Pr.

Wordsworth & the Geologists. John Wyatt. (Studies in Romanticism: No. 16). (Illus.). 285p. (C). 1996. text ed. 54.95 (*0-521-47259-8*) Cambridge U Pr.

Wordsworth & the Kibble Kidnapping. Todd Strasser. (Wordsworth Ser.: No. 2). 128p. (J). 1995. mass mkt. 2.99 (*0-06-106258-8*, Harp PBks) HarpC.

Wordsworth & the Motions of the Mind. Gordon K. Thomas. (American University Studies: English Language & Literature: Ser. IV, Vol. 93). 232p. (C). 1989. text ed. 23.95 (*0-8204-1012-8*) P Lang Pubng.

Wordsworth & the Poetry of Encounter. Frederick Garber. LC 71-157888. 210p. reprint ed. pap. 59.90 (*0-8357-3287-8*, 2039510) Bks Demand.

Wordsworth & the Poetry of Human Suffering. James H. Averill. LC 79-21783. 318p. 1980. 42.50 (*0-8014-1249-8*) Cornell U Pr.

Wordsworth & the Poetry of Sincerity. David D. Perkins. LC 64-10443. 299p. 1964. 25.00 (*0-674-95820-9*) Belknap Pr.

Wordsworth & the Question of "Romantic Religion" Nancy Easterlin. LC 95-42863. 184p. 1996. 33.50 (*0-8387-5309-4*) Bucknell U Pr.

Wordsworth & the Roast Beef Romance. Todd Strasser. (Wordsworth Ser.: No. 3). 128p. 1995. mass mkt. 2.99 (*0-06-106288-X*) HarpC.

Wordsworth & the Sublime. Albert O. Wlecke. LC 79-189218. (Perspectives in Criticism Ser.: No. 23). 175p. reprint ed. pap. 49.90 (*0-685-23680-3*, 2029070) Bks Demand.

Wordsworth & the Zen Mind: The Poetry of Self-Emptying. John G. Rudy. LC 95-19528. 284p. (C). 1996. pap. text ed. 19.95 (*0-7914-2904-0*) State U NY Pr.

Wordsworth & the Zen Mind: The Poetry of Self-Emptying. John G. Rudy. LC 95-19528. 284p. (C). 1996. text ed. 59.50 (*0-7914-2903-2*) State U NY Pr.

Wordsworth Anticlimax. Willard L. Sperry. 228p. (C). 1935. reprint ed. text ed. 75.00 (*0-8383-0627-6*) M S G Haskell Hse.

Wordsworth As Critic. Warwick J. Owen. LC 73-398699. 254p. reprint ed. pap. 72.40 (*0-8357-8381-2*, 2034009) Bks Demand.

Wordsworth Chronology. Frank B. Pinion. 160p. 1988. 40.00 (*0-8161-8950-1*, Hall Reference) Macmillan.

Wordsworth, Dialogics & the Practice of Criticism. Don H. Bialostosky. (Literature, Culture, Theory Ser.: No. 2). 312p. (C). 1992. text ed. 59.95 (*0-521-41249-8*) Cambridge U Pr.

Wordsworth Dictionary of Persons & Places. John R. Tutin. (BCL1-PR English Literature Ser.). 216p. 1992. reprint ed. lib. bdg. 79.00 (*0-7812-7683-7*) Rprt Serv.

Wordsworth, Freud & the Spots of Time: Interpretation in 'The Prelude' David Ellis. 200p. 1985. text ed. 65.00 (*0-521-26555-X*) Cambridge U Pr.

Wordsworth in Context. Ed. by Pauline Fletcher & John Murphy. LC 55-58217. (Bucknell Review Ser.: Vol. XXXVI, No. 1). (Illus.). 192p. 1992. 22.00 (*0-8387-5224-1*) Bucknell U Pr.

Wordsworth, Milton & the Theory of Poetic Relations. Robin Jarvis. LC 90-8820. 195p. 1991. text ed. 45.00 (*0-312-04741-X*) St Martin.

Wordsworth Now & Then: Romanticism & Contemporary Culture. Anthony Easthope. LC 93-14498. 144p. 1993. 69.00 (*0-335-09461-9*, Open Univ Pr); pap. 21.00 (*0-335-09460-0*, Open Univ Pr) Taylor & Francis.

Wordsworth, Shelley, Keats, & Other Essays. David Masson. LC 72-13205. (Essay Index Reprint Ser.). 1977. reprint ed. 21.95 (*0-8369-8168-5*) Ayer.

Wordsworth Treasury. William Wordsworth. (Illus.). 48p. 1978. reprint ed. 7.95 (*0-85683-043-7*) Dufour.

Wordsworth, Turner, & Romantic Landscape: A Study of the Traditions of the Picturesque & Sublime. Matthew C. Brennan. LC 87-70973. (ENGL Ser.: Vol. 5). (Illus.). 166p. 1987. 35.00 (*0-938100-51-3*) Camden Hse.

***Wordsworth Utopian Geographies.** Wiley. Date not set. text ed. 55.00 (*0-312-17655-4*) St Martin.

Wordsworthian Criticism. James V. Logan. LC 74-7025. 304p. 1974. reprint ed. 50.00 (*0-87752-171-9*) Gordian.

Wordsworthian Errancies: The Poetics of Cultural Dismemberment. David Collings. LC 94-6204. 1994. text ed. 39.95 (*0-8018-4848-2*) Johns Hopkins.

Wordsworth's Art of Allusion. Edwin Stein. LC 86-43026. 256p. 1988. 35.00 (*0-271-00483-5*) Pa St U Pr.

***Wordsworth's Counterrevolutionary Turn: Community, Virtue, & Vision in the 1790s.** John Rieder. LC 96-52719. 272p. 1997. 41.50 (*0-87413-610-5*) U Delaware Pr.

Wordsworth's Influence on Shelley: A Study of Poetic Authority. G. Kim Blank. LC 87-13058. 256p. 1988. text ed. 49.95 (*0-312-01179-2*) St Martin.

Wordsworth's Informed Reader: Structures of Experience in His Poetry. Susan E. Meisenhelder. LC 86-28169. 270p. 1989. 27.95 (*0-8265-1218-6*) Vanderbilt U Pr.

Wordsworth's Interest in Painters & Pictures. Martha H. Shackford. LC 75-30013. reprint ed. 31.50 (*0-404-14019-X*) AMS Pr.

Wordsworth's Language of Men. J. P. Ward. LC 84-11076. 256p. 1984. 44.00 (*0-389-20500-1*, N8062) B&N Imports.

Wordsworth's "Natural Methodism" Richard E. Brantley. LC 74-20078. 221p. reprint ed. pap. 63.00 (*0-8357-8774-5*, 2033679) Bks Demand.

Wordsworth's Philosophical Poetry, 1797-1814. John A. Hodgson. LC 79-24921. 238p. 1980. reprint ed. pap. 67.90 (*0-608-02379-5*, 2063021) Bks Demand.

Wordsworth's Poem of the Mind: An Essay on the Prelude. Richard Gaskell. 160p. (C). 1993. pap. 17.00 (*0-7486-0274-7*, Pub. by Edinburgh U Pr UK) Col U Pr.

Wordsworth's Poem of the Mind: An Essay on "The Prelude" William Wordsworth. Ed. by Richard Gaskell. 118p. 1991. text ed. 39.00 (*0-7486-0263-1*, Pub. by Edinburgh U Pr UK) Col U Pr.

Wordsworth's Poetry, 1787-1814 (with the Essay "Retrospect 1971") Geoffrey H. Hartman. LC 64-20920. 444p. reprint ed. pap. 126.60 (*0-8357-8382-0*, 2033747) Bks Demand.

Wordsworth's Pope: A Study in Literary Historiography. Robert J. Griffin. (Studies in Romanticism: No. 17). (Illus.). 202p. (C). 1996. text ed. 49.95 (*0-521-48171-6*) Cambridge U Pr.

***Wordsworth's Profession: Form, Class, & the Logic of Early Romantic Cultural Production.** Thomas Pfau. LC 97-2946. 1997. write for info. (*0-8047-2902-6*); pap. write for info. (*0-8047-3136-5*) Stanford U Pr.

Wordsworth's Reading of Roman Prose. Jane Worthington. LC 74-91194. (Yale Studies in English: No. 102). xi, 81p. (C). 1970. reprint ed. lib. bdg. 26.00 (*0-208-00920-5*, Archon Bks) Shoe String.

Wordsworth's Reading, 1770-1799. Duncan Wu. LC 92-17220. 240p. (C). 1993. text ed. 69.95 (*0-521-41600-0*) Cambridge U Pr.

Wordsworth's Reading 1800-1815. Ed. by Duncan Wu. 339p. (C). 1996. text ed. 59.95 (*0-521-49674-8*) Cambridge U Pr.

Wordsworth's Revisionary Aesthetics. Theresa M. Kelley. (Illus.). 250p. 1988. text ed. 69.95 (*0-521-34398-4*) Cambridge U Pr.

Wordsworth's Second Nature: A Study of the Poetry & Politics. James K. Chandler. LC 84-5979. 326p. 1984. pap. text ed. 17.95 (*0-226-10081-2*) U Ch Pr.

Wordsworth's "Slumber" & the Problematics of Reading. Brian G. Caraher. 288p. 1991. 35.00 (*0-271-00720-6*) Pa St U Pr.

Wordsworth's Style: Figures & Themes in the Lyrical Ballads of 1800. Roger N. Murray. LC 67-13152. 178p. 1967. reprint ed. pap. 50.80 (*0-608-01852-X*, 2062502) Bks Demand.

Wordsworth's Theory of Poetic Diction. Marjorie L. Greenbie. LC 75-28998. reprint ed. 34.50 (*0-404-14009-2*) AMS Pr.

Wordsworth's Vagrant Muse: Poetry, Poverty & Power. Gary Harrison. LC 94-17136. (Illus.). 238p. 1994. text ed. 34.95 (*0-8143-2481-9*) Wayne St U Pr.

Wordtree: A Transitive Cladistic for Solving Physical & Social Problems. Henry G. Burger. LC 84-13007. 380p. 1984. 149.00 (*0-936312-00-9*) Wordtree.

Wordwatcher's Guide to Good Writing & Grammar. Morton S. Freeman. 320p. 1990. pap. 16.99 (*0-89879-436-6*, Wrtrs Digest Bks) F & W Pubns Inc.

Wordweavers. Ed. by Mouat et al. 93p. (Orig.). 1986. pap. write for info. (*0-917557-02-6*) Wyo Writers.

WordWise. Joan Robinson. (Roots of Language Ser.). (J). (gr. 4-8). 1989. pap. 10.99 (*0-8224-7452-2*) Fearon Teach Aids.

Wordwise: A Guide to the Language for Journalists. 2nd rev. ed. Leland B. Ryan & Michael O'Donnell. LC 95-1201. 132p. (Orig.). (C). 1995. pap. text ed. 25.00 (*1-888559-00-4*) Pug Pubng.

Wordworks. Mary C. Southworth. (YA). 1986. pap. text ed. 13.50 (*0-88334-192-1*, 76157) Longman.

Wordworks: Poems Selected & New. Richard Kostelanetz. 212p. 1993. 25.00 (*0-918526-94-9*); pap. 12.50 (*0-918526-95-7*) BOA Edns.

Wordwright. Tom Deitz. 400p. (Orig.). 1993. mass mkt. 4.99 (*0-380-76291-9*, AvoNova) Avon.

Worf's First Adventure. Peter David. (Star Trek: The Next Generation, Starfleet Academy Ser.: No. 1). 128p. (Orig.). (J). (gr. 3-6). mass mkt. 3.99 (*0-671-87084-X*, Minstrel Bks) PB.

***Work.** Ann Morris. Date not set. write for info. (*0-688-14866-2*); lib. bdg. write for info. (*0-688-14867-0*) Lothrop.

Work. Marge Murphy. 9p. (J). (gr. 1). 1988. pap. text ed. 2.50 (*1-882225-08-2*) Tott Pubns.

Work. Ben Patterson. (Christian Basics Bible Studies). 64p. (Orig.). 1994. wbk. ed., pap. 4.99 (*0-8308-2007-8*, 2007) InterVarsity.

Work. Louisa May Alcott. (Works of Louisa May Alcott). 1989. reprint ed. lib. bdg. 79.00 (*0-7812-1632-X*) Rprt Serv.

Work, Vol. 4, incl. 1987-1991 Suppls. Ed. by Eleanor C. Goldstein. (Social Issues Resources Ser.). 1992. Incl. 1987-1991 supplements. 95.00 (*0-89777-129-X*) Sirs Inc.

Work! A Reading Program. Jeffrey E. Stewart. (Illus.). 116p. (Orig.). (YA). 1988. pap. 32.50 (*1-877866-02-4*) J E Stewart.

Work: A Story of Experience. Louisa May Alcott. LC 93-43988. 320p. 1994. pap. 11.95 (*0-14-039091-X*, Penguin Classics) Viking Penguin.

Work: A Story of Experience. Louisa May Alcott. Ed. by Elizabeth Hardwick. LC 76-51662. (Rediscovered Fiction by American Women Ser.). (Illus.). 1977. reprint ed. lib. bdg. 29.95 (*0-405-10042-6*) Ayer.

Work: A Story of Experience. Louisa May Alcott. 1976. reprint ed. 39.00 (*0-403-05873-2*, Regency) Scholarly.

Work: An Investigation into the History of Opus Dei & How It Operates in Ireland Today. Fergal Bowers. LC 89-50988. 176p. (Orig.). 1989. pap. 9.95 (*1-85371-037-7*, Pub. by Poolbeg Pr IE) Dufour.

Work: Canada, No. 61. 200p. 1951. 4.00 (*0-88053-278-5*) Macoy Pub.

Work: Encounters. (Illus.). 84p. 1990. pap. 29.95 (*88-7184-002-X*, Pub. by Domus Acad IT) Dist Art Pubs.

Work: Opposing Viewpoints. Ed. by William Barbour. (Opposing Viewpoints Ser.). (Illus.). 312p. (YA). (gr. 10 up). 1995. pap. text ed. 12.96 (*1-56510-218-5*); lib. bdg. 20.96 (*1-56510-219-3*) Greenhaven.

Work: Pathway to Independence. B. Gooch et al. (Illus.). 450p. 1979. 19.96 (*0-8269-4900-2*) Am Technical.

Work: The Inside Stories. 178p. 1989. 57.00 (*0-909184-23-2*, Pub. by Deakin Univ AT) St Mut.

Work: The Meaning of Your Life. Lester De Koster. 95p. 1982. 4.95 (*0-934874-04-2*) Chr Lib Pr.

Work: What It Has Meant to Men Through the Ages. Adriano Tilgher. Ed. by Leon Stein. Tr. by Dorothy C. Fisher from ITA. LC 77-70538. 1977. reprint ed. lib. bdg. 23.95 (*0-405-10208-9*) Ayer.

Work No. 1: Essay Collection. David Sylvester. LC 97-17125. 1997. 30.00 (*0-8050-4441-8*) H Holt & Co.

Work No. 2: Interviews with Artists. David Sylvester. 1996. 30.00 (*0-8050-4442-6*) H Holt & Co.

Work Vol. 5: (Incl. 1992-94 Supplement) Ed. by Eleanor C. Goldstein. (Social Issues Resources Ser.). 1995. 95.00 (*0-89777-171-0*) Sirs Inc.

Work see IVP Booklets

Work - God's Gift: Life-Changing Choices. Marilyn Kunz & Catherine Schell. 64p. (Orig.). 1993. pap. 4.99 (*1-880266-01-6*) Neighborhood Bible.

Work-a-Day Girl: A Study of Some Present-Day Conditions. Clara E. Laughlin. LC 74-3956. (Women in America Ser.). (Illus.). 320p. 1974. reprint ed. 26.95 (*0-405-06105-6*) Ayer.

Work-a-Day Life of the Pueblos. Ruth M. Underhill. Ed. by Willard W. Beatty. LC 76-43882. (Indian Life & Customs Ser.: No. 4). 1983. reprint ed. 39.50 (*0-404-15735-1*) AMS Pr.

Work a 4-Hour Day. Arthur K. Robertson & William Proctor. 160p. 1996. mass mkt. 4.99 (*0-380-72627-0*) Avon.

Work Abuse: How to Recognize & Survive It. Judith Wyatt & Chauncey Have. LC 96-47856. 224p. 1996. text ed. 29.95 (*0-87047-110-4*); pap. text ed. 19.95 (*0-87047-109-0*) Schenkman Bks Inc.

Work Accidents & the Law. Crystal Eastman. LC 70-89757. (American Labor, from Conspiracy to Collective Bargaining Ser., No. 1). 361p. 1974. reprint ed. 28.95 (*0-405-02118-6*) Ayer.

Work Accidents to Miners in Illinois, Vol. 7. Earl E. Klein. LC 74-1689. (Children & Youth Ser.). 275p. 1974. reprint ed. 25.95 (*0-405-05966-3*) Ayer.

Work Accomplished by the Inter-American Juridical Committee During Its Regular Meeting: Held from August 4-29, 1980. OAS, General Secretariat, Inter-American Commission of Human Rights. (OFA Ser.: No. Q-IV CJI-43). 129p. 1981. pap. text ed. 10.00 (*0-8270-1363-9*) OAS.

Work Activities Interest Checklist: Package of 30. Appalachia Educational Laboratory Staff. (Illus.). 6p. (YA). (gr. 9 up). 1990. pap. text ed. 14.00 (*1-877844-53-5*, 3215) Meridian Educ.

Work Adjustment Intervention Manual. Stephen B. McCarney. 171p. (Orig.). 1992. pap. 16.00 (*1-878372-16-5*) Hawthorne Educ Servs.

Work Alienation: An Integrative Approach. Rabindra N. Kanungo. LC 81-20959. 220p. 1982. text ed. 55.00 (*0-275-90832-1*, C0832, Praeger Pubs) Greenwood.

Work Alternative: Welfare Reform & the Realities of the Job Market. Ed. by Demetra S. Nightingale & Robert H. Haveman. 230p. (C). 1995. 24.95 (*0-87766-623-7*) Urban Inst.

Work Analysis & Pay Structure. T. M. Husband. 1976. 13.80 (*0-07-084462-3*) McGraw.

Work & Aging: A European Prospective. Ed. by Jan Snel & Roel Cremer. 434p. 1994. 99.00 (*0-7484-0164-4*) Taylor & Francis.

Work & Aging: A European Prospective. Ed. by Jan Snel & Roel Cremer. 434p. 1994. pap. 49.50 (*0-7484-0165-2*) Taylor & Francis.

Work & Alcohol Abuse: An Annotated Bibliography. Compiled by John J. Miletich. LC 87-23619. (Bibliographies & Indexes in Sociology Ser.: No. 12). 272p. 1987. text ed. 55.00 (*0-313-25689-6*, MWR/, Greenwood Pr) Greenwood.

Work & Authority in Industry: Ideologies of Management in the Course of Industrialization. Reinhard Bendix. LC 73-78553. 1974. pap. 14.00 (*0-520-02628-4*) U CA Pr.

Work & Change: Labor Market Policies in a Competitive World. (CED Statement on National Policy Ser.). 88p. 1987. pap. 9.50 (*0-87186-083-X*); lib. bdg. 11.50 (*0-87186-783-4*) Comm Econ Dev.

Work & Citizenship in the New Europe. Ed. by Harry Coenen & Peter Leisink. LC 93-9712. 272p. 1993. 80.00 (*1-85278-739-2*) E Elgar.

Work & Community in the Jungle: Chicago's Packinghouse Workers, 1894-1922. James R. Barrett. LC 86-19127. (Working Class in American History Ser.). (Illus.). 328p. 1987. text ed. 29.95 (*0-252-01378-6*); pap. text ed. 11.95 (*0-252-06136-5*) U of Ill Pr.

Work & Compare Arithmetic. 2nd ed. Harry W. Koch. 1975. 6.00 (*0-913164-58-5*) Ken-Bks.

Work & Control in a Peasant Economy: A History of the Lower Tchiri Valley in Malawi, 1859-1960. Elias C. Mandala. LC 90-50093. 480p. (Orig.). (C). 1990. text ed. 49.50 (*0-299-12490-8*); pap. text ed. 22.50 (*0-299-12494-0*) U of Wis Pr.

Work & Democracy in Socialist Cuba. Linda Fuller. (Labor & Social Change Ser.). 400p. (C). 1992. 54.95 (*0-87722-893-0*) Temple U Pr.

Work & Disability: Issues & Strategies in Career Development & Job Placement. Ed. by Edna M. Szymanski & Randall M. Parker. LC 95-42104. 458p. (C). 1996. pap. text ed. 38.00 (*0-89079-640-8*, 7637) PRO-ED.

Work & Employment in Europe: A New Convergence? Ed. by Peter Cressey & Bryn Jones. LC 95-7768. 272p. (C). (gr. 13). 1995. text ed. 74.95 (*0-415-12532-4*) Routledge.

Work & Employment in Liberal Democratic Societies. Ed. by David Marsland. LC 93-46969. (Liberal Democratic Societies Ser.). 240p. (C). 1994. 34.95 (*0-943852-67-6*); pap. text ed. 17.95 (*0-943852-68-4*) Prof World Peace.

Work & Equality in Soviet Society: The Division of Labor by Age, Gender, & Nationality. Michael P. Sacks. LC 82-278. 224p. 1982. text ed. 49.95 (*0-275-90893-3*, C0893, Praeger Pubs) Greenwood.

Work & Family: A Changing Dynamic. (Special Report Ser.). 336p. 1986. 30.00 (*0-87179-901-4*, LDSR37) BNA Plus.

Work & Family: Policies for a Changing Workforce. National Research Council, Panel on Employer Policies & Working Families Staff. Ed. by Marianne A. Ferber & M. Brigid O'Farrell. 268p. 1991. 29.95 (*0-309-04277-1*) Natl Acad Pr.

Work & Family: Program Models & Policies. Karol L. Rose. (Employee Benefits - Human Resources Library). 928p. 1993. ring bd. 130.00 (*0-471-58135-6*) Wiley.

Work & Family: The Complete Resource Guide. LC 91-1353. 1991. ring bd. 195.00 (*1-55871-197-X*, BSP 151) BNA Plus.

Work & Family & Unions: Labor's Agenda for the 1990s. (BNA Special Report Series on Work & Family: No. 20). 32p. 1989. 35.00 (*1-55871-138-4*, BSP161) BNA Plus.

Work & Family in the United States: A Critical Review & Agenda for Research & Policy. Rosabeth M. Kanter. LC 76-46870. (Social Science Frontiers Ser.). 120p. 1977. pap. 9.95 (*0-87154-433-4*) Russell Sage.

An Asterisk (*) at the beginning of an entry indicates that the title is appearing in BIP for the first time.

Work & Family Interface: Toward a Contextual Effects Perspective. Ed. by Gary L. Bowman et al. (Families in Focus Ser.: Vol. 1). 533p. (Orig.). (C). 1995. pap. 36.95 (*0-916174-45-X*, OP9412) Natl Coun Family.

Work & Family Life. Patricia Voydanoff. LC 87-9482. (Family Studies Text: No. 6). 136p. reprint ed. pap. 38. 80 (*0-7837-6723-4*, 2046350) Bks Demand.

Work & Family Life: The Role of the Social Infrastructure in Eastern European Countries. (Illus.). vi, 77p. (Orig.). 1980. pap. 13.50 (*92-2-102167-X*) Intl Labour Office.

Work & Family Manager: Evolution of a New Job. (Special Report Series on Work & Family: No. 45). 32p. 1991. 35.00 (*1-55871-236-4*, BSP223) BNA Plus.

Work & Family Patterns of American Women. (Illus.). 57p. (Orig.). (C). 1994. pap. text ed. 20.00 (*1-56806-167-6*) DIANE Pub.

***Work & Family Program Models & Policies: 1996 Supplement.** Karol L. Rose. LC 93-17361. 1995. suppl. ed., pap. text ed. 53.00 (*0-471-15236-6*, Wiley-Liss) Wiley.

Work & Family Revolution: How Companies Can Keep Employees Happy & Business Profitable. Barbara Vanderkolk & Ardis A. Young. 224p. 1991. 22.95 (*0-8160-2364-6*) Facts on File.

Work & Family Sourcebook. Ed. by Fairlee E. Winfield. LC 88-31312. 526p. 1990. text ed. 89.00 (*0-916592-80-4*) Panel Pubs.

Work & Family Today: One Hundred Key Statistics. (BNA Special Report Series on Work & Family: No. 41). 32p. 1991. 35.00 (*1-55871-222-4*, BSP213) BNA Plus.

***Work & Family Trends.** Dana E. Friedman & Ellen Galinsky. 22p. 1991. 15.00 (*0-614-22668-6*, W91-03) Families & Work.

***Work & Friendship.** Shelagh Canning. (Adventures from the Book of Virtues Ser.). (Illus.). (J). (ps-2). 1997. pap. 3.25 (*0-614-29075-9*, Aladdin Paperbacks) S&S Childrens.

Work & Health: An Introduction to Occupational Health Care. M. Bamford. (Illus.). 208p. 1994. pap. text ed. 35. 00 (*1-56593-199-8*, 0514) Singular Publishing.

Work & Health: Its Your Life, an Action Guide to Job Hazards. Phillip L. Polakoff. LC 84-61087. (Orig.). 1984. pap. 7.95 (*0-918763-00-2*) Pr Assocs.

Work & Health: Strategies for Maintaining a Vital Workforce. LC 89-3103. 300p. 1989. pap. 79.00 (*0-916592-91-X*) Panel Pubs.

Work & Health - Risk Groups & Trends: Scenario Report Commissioned by the Steering Committee on Future Health Scenarios. LC 94-1251. 1994. pap. text ed. 112. 50 (*0-7923-2733-0*) Kluwer Ac.

Work & Human Behavior. 3rd ed. Walter S. Neff. LC 85-1219. (Illus.). 360p. (C). 1985. pap. text ed. 27.95 (*0-202-30320-9*) Aldine de Gruyter.

Work & Identity in the Primary School: A Post-Fordist Analysis. Ian Menter. LC 96-19874. 160p. 1996. 79.95 (*0-335-19724-8*, Open Univ Pr) Taylor & Francis.

Work & Identity in the Primary School: A Post-Fordist Analysis. Ian Menter et al. LC 96-19874. 160p. 1996. pap. 24.95 (*0-335-19723-X*, Open Univ Pr) Taylor & Francis.

Work & Illness: The Cancer Patient. Ed. by Ivan Barofsky. LC 88-25544. 195p. 1989. text ed. 55.00 (*0-275-92390-8*, C2390, Praeger Pubs) Greenwood.

Work & Industry: Structure, Markets, & Processes. Arne L. Kalleberg & Ivar E. Berg, Jr. 230p. 1987. 37.50 (*0-306-42344-8*, Plenum Pr) Plenum.

***Work & Inequality.** Lonsdale. 1985. pap. text ed. write for info. (*0-582-29629-3*, Pub. by Longman UK) Longman.

Work & Inequality. Susan Lonsdale. LC 84-12235. (Social Policy in Modern Britain Ser.). 263p. reprint ed. pap. 75. 00 (*0-7837-1603-6*, 2041895) Bks Demand.

Work & Inequaltiy in Urban China. Yanjie Bian. LC 93-14708. (SUNY Series in the Sociology of Work). 286p. (C). 1994. text ed. 64.50 (*0-7914-1801-4*); pap. text ed. 21.95 (*0-7914-1802-2*) State U NY Pr.

Work & Integrity: The Crisis & Promise of Professionalism in America. William M. Sullivan. LC 94-37870. 352p. 1995. 25.00 (*0-88730-727-2*) Harper Busn.

Work & Islam. Mehdi Bazargan. Tr. by Mohammack Yousefi from PER. 62p. 1979. 6.95 (*0-941722-04-X*) Book Dist Ctr.

Work & Its Inhibitions: Psychoanalytic Essays. Ed. by Charles W. Socarides & Selma Kramer. LC 96-9688. 280p. 1996. 42.50 (*0-8236-6866-5*, BN 06866) Intl Univs Pr.

Work & Labor in Early America. Ed. by Stephen Innes. LC 87-38088. (Institute of Early American History & Culture Ser.). ix, 299p. (C). 1988. 37.50 (*0-8078-1798-8*); pap. 16.95 (*0-8078-4236-2*) U of NC Pr.

Work & Leisure: A Contemporary Social Problem. Ed. by Edwin O. Smigel. (Orig.). 1963. 19.95 (*0-8084-0334-6*) NCUP.

Work & Leisure in the Soviet Union: A Time-Budget Analysis. Jiri Zuzanek. LC 79-67483. 440p. 1980. text ed. 55.00 (*0-275-90573-X*, C0573, Praeger Pubs) Greenwood.

Work & Life of Solon, with a Translation of His Poems. Kathleen Freeman. LC 75-13265. (History of Ideas in Ancient Greece Ser.). 1978. reprint ed. 16.95 (*0-405-07307-1*) Ayer.

Work & Lifecourse in Japan. Ed. by David W. Plath. LC 82-10481. (Illus.). 267p. 1984. pap. text ed. 21.95 (*0-87395-705-9*) State U NY Pr.

Work & Madness: The Rise of Community Psychiatry. Diana Ralph. 206p. 1983. 29.95 (*0-919619-07-X*, Pub. by Black Rose Bks CN); pap. 9.95 (*0-919619-04-5*, Pub. by Black Rose Bks CN) Consort Bk Sales.

Work & Marriage: The Two-Profession Couple. Roslyn Malmaud. LC 84-104. (Research in Clinical Psychology Ser.: No. 10). 299p. reprint ed. pap. 85.30 (*0-8357-1543-4*, 2070403) Bks Demand.

Work & Mental Illness: Transitions to Employment. Bertram J. Black. LC 87-26084. (Contemporary Medicine & Public Health Ser.). 288p. 1988. text ed. 45. 00 (*0-8018-3565-8*) Johns Hopkins.

Work & Motivation. Victor H. Vroom. (Management Ser.). 432p. pap. text ed. 28.00 (*0-7879-0030-3*) Jossey-Bass.

***Work & No Play.** Lindsey Nicoll. (Longman American Business English Skills Ser.). 1994. pap. text ed. 12.00 (*0-582-08421-0*, Pub. by Longman UK) Longman.

Work & Occupation in Modern Turkey. Ed. by Erol Kahveci et al. LC 96-2305. (Employment & Work Relations in Context Ser.). (Illus.). 224p. (C). 1996. text ed. 85.00 (*0-7201-2319-4*, Mansell Pub) Cassell.

Work & Organisational Transformation: The Cadbury Experience. Christopher Smith et al. (Studies in Management: No. 16). (Illus.). 416p. (C). 1991. text ed. 80.00 (*0-521-32304-5*) Cambridge U Pr.

Work & Organizational Psychology. Ed. by A. M. Koopman-Iwema & R. A. Roe. vi, 294p. 1984. pap. 45. 25 (*90-265-0593-0*) Swets.

Work & Pay: Incomes & Differentials. Manfred Davidmann. (C). 1988. text ed. 50.00 (*0-85192-031-4*) St Mut.

Work & Personal Life: Managing the Issues. Renee Y. Magid & Melissa Codkind. Ed. by Andrea Reider. LC 94-68577. (Fifty-Minute Ser.). (Illus.). 74p. (Orig.). 1995. pap. 10.95 (*1-56052-269-0*) Crisp Pubns.

***Work & Personality.** Nicholson. 1996. pap. 49.95 (*0-86377-948-4*) L Erlbaum Assocs.

Work & Personality: An Inquiry into the Impact of Social Stratification. Melvin L. Kohn & Carmi Schooler. LC 82-24485. (Modern Sociology Ser.). 400p. 1983. pap. 39. 50 (*0-89391-199-2*); text ed. 73.25 (*0-89391-121-6*) Ablex Pub.

Work & Play. (YouthTalk Ser.). 32p. (YA). 1994. teacher ed. 4.95 (*0-8066-0272-4*, 15-5227); pap. 5.25 (*0-8066-0271-6*, 15-5226) Augsburg Fortress.

***Work & Play in Early Childhood.** Freya Jaffke. 1997. pap. text ed. 12.95 (*0-88010-442-2*) Anthroposophic.

Work & Play in Grandpa's Day. S. G. Thigpen. (Illus.). 1969. 5.00 (*0-685-20526-6*) Thigpen.

Work & Play of Adrian Wilson. Adrian Wilson. 1983. 600. 00 (*0-935072-05-5*) W T Taylor.

Work & Play of Adrian Wilson. deluxe ed. Joyce L. Wilson. 160p. 1983. 600.00 (*0-614-16153-3*) Oak Knoll.

Work & Play of Winnicott. Simon A. Grolnick. LC 89-18572. 232p. 1990. 30.00 (*0-87668-802-4*) Aronson.

Work & Power in Maale, Ethiopia. Donald L. Donham. 227p. 1994. pap. 16.00 (*0-231-10047-7*) Col U Pr.

Work & Prayer: The Rule of St. Benedict for Lay People. Tr. by Catherine Wybourne. 192p. 1994. pap. 24.00 (*0-86012-196-8*, Pub. by Srch Pr UK) St Mut.

Work & Retirement: A Longitudinal Study of Men. Herbert S. Parnes et al. (Illus.). 320p. 1981. 45.00 (*0-262-16079-X*) MIT Pr.

Work & Revolution in France. William H. Sewell, Jr. LC 80-12103. (Illus.). 336p. 1980. pap. text ed. 19.95 (*0-521-29951-9*) Cambridge U Pr.

Work & Rewards: Redefining Our Work-Life Reality. William F. Roth, Jr. LC 88-25572. 206p. 1989. text ed. 55.00 (*0-275-93166-8*, C3166, Praeger Pubs) Greenwood.

Work & Role Redesign: Tools & Techniques for the Health Care Setting. Ruth Hanson & Betty Sayers. LC 95-1287. 1995. 49.00 (*1-55648-135-7*) AHPI.

Work & Society: An Introduction to Industrial Society. 2nd ed. Curt Tausky. LC 95-72867. (C). 1996. pap. text ed. 20.00 (*0-87581-401-8*) Peacock Pubs.

Work & Society: Labor & Human Resources in East Asia. Ian H. Nish. 244p. (Orig.). 1996. pap. 52.50 (*962-209-391-4*, Pub. by Hong Kong Univ Pr HK) Coronet Bks.

Work & Spirituality: A Comprehensive Directory of Resources to Help Managers Improve Performance by Addressing Workers' Spiritual Concerns. Ed. by Kim D. Shine et al. 100p. 1996. ring bd. 69.00 (*0-9639557-9-9*, Spirit of Hlth) A R K Co.

Work & Stress: A Report on How Work Stress Can Affect the Quality of Life. James J. D'Amato. Ed. by Josephine De Stefano & Maryann Buomaupina. 250p. 1988. 26.95 (*0-9621266-0-8*) IPPD.

Work & Technology in Higher Education: The Social Construction of Academic Computing. Ed. by Mark Shields. (Technology & Education Ser.). 208p. 1994. pap. 19.95 (*0-8058-0357-2*) L Erlbaum Assocs.

Work & Technology in Higher Education: The Social Construction of Academic Computing. Ed. by Mark Shields. (Technology & Education Ser.). 208p. 1995. text ed. 49.95 (*0-8058-0356-4*) L Erlbaum Assocs.

Work & the Enterprise Culture. Ed. by Malcolm Cross & Geoff Payne. 222p. 1991. 65.00 (*1-85000-799-3*, Falmer Pr); pap. 29.00 (*1-85000-800-0*, Falmer Pr) Taylor & Francis.

Work & the Evolving Self: Theoretical & Clinical Considerations. Steven D. Axelrod. 1998. write for info. (*0-88163-207-4*) Analytic Pr.

Work & the Eye. Rachel V. North. LC 92-22606. 240p. 1994. 75.00 (*0-19-262282-X*); pap. 39.95 (*0-19-261885-7*) OUP.

Work & the Family: Career-Friendly Employment Practices. HOST Training & Consultancy Services Staff & IPM National Committees for Equal Opportunities & Pay & Employment Conditions Staff. 76p. (C). 1990. 110.00 (*0-85292-434-8*, Pub. by IPM Hse UK) St Mut.

Work & the Family System: A Naturalistic Study of Working-Class & Lower-Middle-Class Families. Chaya S. Piotrkowski. LC 79-7478. (Illus.). 1979. 19.95 (*0-02-925340-3*, Free Press) Free Pr.

***Work & the Gift of the Holy Spirit.** Oluf L. Pyle. (Orig.). 1997. pap. 8.95 (*0-533-12271-6*) Vantage.

***Work & the Glory: No Unhallowed Hand, Vol. 7.** Gerald N. Lund. 1996. 20.95 (*1-57008-277-4*) Bookcraft Inc.

Work & the Glory Vol. 1: Pillar of Light. Gerald N. Lund. 1990. 15.95 (*0-88494-770-X*) Bookcraft Inc.

Work & the Glory Vol. 3: Truth Will Prevail. Gerald N. Lund. 1992. 15.95 (*0-88494-853-6*) Bookcraft Inc.

Work & the Glory Vol. 5: A Season of Joy. Gerald N. Lund. 1994. 17.95 (*0-88494-960-5*) Bookcraft Inc.

Work & the Glory Vol. 6: Praise to the Man. Gerald N. Lund. 1995. 19.95 (*0-88494-999-0*) Bookcraft Inc.

Work & the Glory, Vol. 2: Like a Fire Is Burning. Gerald N. Lund. 1991. 15.95 (*0-88494-801-3*) Bookcraft Inc.

Work & the Glory, Vol. 4: Thy Gold to Refine. Gerald N. Lund. 1993. 16.95 (*0-88494-893-5*) Bookcraft Inc.

Work & the Health of Women. Vilma R. Hunt. 248p. 1979. 141.00 (*0-8493-5301-7*, RC963, CRC Reprint) Franklin.

Work & the Human Spirit. John Scherer & Larry Shook. 1993. pap. 14.00 (*0-9639348-0-5*) J Scherer & Assocs.

***Work & the Life of the Spirit.** Ed. by Douglas Thorpe. LC 97-20133. (Illus.). 288p. (Orig.). 1997. pap. 16.95 (*1-56279-099-4*) Mercury Hse Inc.

Work & the Work Ethic in American Drama, 1920-1970. Thomas A. Greenfield. LC 82-4909. 200p. 1982. text ed. 27.50 (*0-8262-0374-4*) U of Mo Pr.

Work & Wages: Natural Law, Politics & the Eighteenth-Century French Trades. Michael Sonenscher. (Illus.). 472p. (C). 1989. text ed. 89.95 (*0-521-32984-1*) Cambridge U Pr.

Work & Wealth: A Human Valuation. John A. Hobson. LC 68-30527. (Reprints of Economic Classics Ser.). xv, 367p. 1968. reprint ed. 45.00 (*0-678-00405-6*) Kelley.

Work & Welfare: The Social Costs of Labor in the History of Economic Thought. Donald R. Stabile. LC 95-33972. (Contributions in Economics & Economic History Ser.: No. 169). 224p. 1996. text ed. 59.95 (*0-313-29738-X*) Greenwood.

Work & Welfare in Massachusetts: An Evaluation of the ET Program. June O'Neill. (Pioneer Paper Ser.: No. 3). 114p. (Orig.). 1990. pap. 10.00 (*0-929930-03-7*) Pioneer Inst.

Work & Well-Being: An Agenda for the 1990s. Ed. by Gwendolyn P. Keita & Steven L. Sauter. (Illus.). 228p. (C). 1992. 29.95 (*1-55798-153-1*) Am Psychol.

Work & Well-Being: The Occupational Social Work Advantage. Ed. by Paul A. Kurzman. LC 93-4797. 408p. (C). 1993. 34.95 (*0-87101-228-6*) Natl Assn Soc Wkrs.

Work & Worship among the Shakers. Edward D. Andrews & Faith Andrews. (Illus.). 224p. 1982. pap. 7.95 (*0-486-24382-6*) Dover.

Work Area Hazards. Ed. by Paul N. Cheremisinoff. (Encyclopedia of Environmental Control Technology Ser.: Vol. 8). (Illus.). 804p. 1995. 155.00 (*0-87201-304-9*, 1304) Gulf Pub.

Work As Art: Idaho Logging As an Aesthetic Moment. Charlene James-Duguid. LC 95-48839. (C). 1996. text ed. 29.95 (*0-89301-190-8*) U of Idaho Pr.

Work As Spiritual Practice. Justine Toms & Michael Toms. LC 97-20408. 1997. write for info. (*0-517-70587-7*, Harmony) Crown Pub Group.

Work at Home: The Domestic Division of Labor. Janeen Baxter. pap. 19.95 (*0-7022-2504-5*, Pub. by Univ Queensland Pr AT) Intl Spec Bk.

Work at Home Options. Joanne Cleaver. Ed. by Cathy Davis. LC 50-4007. 160p. (Orig.). 1994. pap. 7.99 (*0-7814-0109-7*) Chariot Victor.

Work-at-Home Sourcebook: How to Find "At-Home" Work That's Right for You. 6th ed. Lynie Arden. (Illus.). 340p. (Orig.). 1996. pap. 19.95 (*0-911781-14-5*) Live Oak Pubns.

Work-Based Learning: The Key to School-to-Work Transition. James L. Hoerner & James B. Wehrley. LC 94-35559. 1994. write for info. (*0-02-801822-2*) Glencoe.

Work-Based Learning: Training America's Workers. (Illus.). 52p. (Orig.). (C). 1993. pap. text ed. 25.00 (*1-56806-608-2*) DIANE Pub.

Work Behavior Analysis of Professional Counselors. National Board for Certified Counselors Staff et al. LC 93-27915. 168p. 1993. 26.95 (*1-55959-053-X*) Accel Devel.

Work Beyond Employment in Advanced Capitalist Countries, Vols. I-II: Classic & Contemporary Perspectives on the Informal Economy, Vol. I: Concepts, Evidence & Measurements. Ed. by Louis A. Ferman et al. LC 92-39614. 436p. 1993. text ed. 109.95 (*0-7734-9222-4*) E Mellen.

Work Beyond Employment in Advanced Capitalist Countries, Vols. I-II: Classic & Contemporary Perspectives on the Informal Economy, Vol. II: Revisions & Criticism. Ed. by Louis A. Ferman et al. LC 92-39614. 408p. 1993. text ed. 109.95 (*0-7734-9224-0*) E Mellen.

***Work, Biography, Ritual: A Muslim Community in North India.** Deepak Mehta. (Illus.). 312p. 1997. 24.95 (*0-19-564021-7*) OUP.

Work Book. Michael Farr. 1987. 12.84 (*0-02-668450-0*); teacher ed. 8.44 (*0-02-676250-1*) Glencoe.

Work Book. Kern & Turner. 316p. pap. 10.00 (*0-686-31217-1*) Owner-Builder.

***Work Book for Advanced Race Car Suspension Development.** Steve Smith. (Illus.). 32p. (Orig.). 1993. pap. text ed. 7.95 (*0-936834-00-5*) S S Autosports.

Work Book in Radiology: With Illustrated Anatomy. Sheila B. Sloane. (Illus.). 544p. 1988. pap. text ed. 39.00 (*0-7216-2100-7*) Saunders.

Work Book of Group-Analytic Interventions. David Kennard et al. LC 92-48526. (International Library of Group Psychotherapy & Group Process). 128p. (C). 1993. pap. 22.95 (*0-415-08784-8*, B0891); text ed. 74.95 (*0-415-08783-X*, B0887) Routledge.

Work by Jail Inmates. Zahir M. Khan. 1990. 26.50 (*81-210-0233-8*, Pub. by Inter-India Pubns) S Asia.

Work, Careers & Social Integration. Harold L. Wilensky. (Reprint Series in Social Sciences). (C). 1993. reprint ed. pap. text ed. 1.90 (*0-8290-3970-8*, S-315) Irvington.

Work Center Management Training Aid. Vincent C. Guess. LC 85-70229. 42p. 1985. 40.00 (*0-935406-63-8*) Am Prod & Inventory.

Work Clothes: Casual Dress for Serious Work. Kim J. Gross & Jeff Stone. LC 96-22654. (Chic Simple Guides Ser.). 176p. 1996. 23.00 (*0-679-44716-4*) Knopf.

Work Commando 311/I: American Paratroopers Become Forced Laborers for the Nazis. Claire E. Swedberg. LC 94-31223. (Illus.). 240p. 1995. 22.95 (*0-8117-1908-1*) Stackpole.

Work, Community & Power: The Experience of Labor in Europe & America, 1900-1925. Ed. by James E. Cronin & Carmen Sirianni. LC 82-19631. 306p. (C). 1983. text ed. 32.95 (*0-87722-308-4*) Temple U Pr.

Work Comp Index 1993 Reform Supplement. James T. Stewart. 32p. 1994. pap. text ed. 19.50 (*0-9635814-2-2*) J T Stewart.

Work Concepts for the Future: Managing Alternative Work Arrangements. Patricia S. Estess. LC 95-71409. 138p. (Orig.). 1996. pap. 13.95 (*1-56052-387-5*) Crisp Pubns.

Work Concerning the Trewnesse of the Christian Religion. Philippe De Mornay. Tr. by Philip Sidney from FRE. LC 75-45384. 680p. 1976. reprint ed. lib. bdg. 90.00 (*0-8201-1166-X*) Schol Facsimiles.

Work Councils: Consultation, Representation, & Cooperation in Industrial Relations. Ed. by Joel Rogers & Wolfgang Streeck. LC 95-13423. (NBER Comparative Labor Markets Ser.). 436p. 1995. 55.00 (*0-226-72376-3*) U Ch Pr.

Work Culture & Identity: Migrant Laborers in Mozambique & South Africa, circa 1860-1910. Patrick Harries. LC 93-26448. (Social History of Africa Ser.). 305p. (C). 1994. text ed. 50.00 (*0-435-08092-X*, 08092) Heinemann.

Work Culture & Identity: Migrant Laborers in Mozambique & South Africa, circa 1860-1910. Patrick Harries. LC 93-26448. (Social History of Africa Ser.). 305p. (C). 1994. pap. 22.95 (*0-435-08094-6*, 08094) Heinemann.

Work, Culture & Society: Issues & Debates in the Sociology of Work. Ed. by Rosemary Deem & Graeme Salaman. LC 85-11542. 256p. 1985. 90.00 (*0-335-15136-1*, Open Univ Pr); pap. 32.00 (*0-335-15135-3*, Open Univ Pr) Taylor & Francis.

Work Culture & Society in Industrializing America: Essays in America's Working Class & Social History. Herbert G. Gutman. 1977. pap. 9.56 (*0-394-72251-5*, Vin) Random.

Work Culture in the Indian Context. Jai B. Sinha. (Illus.). 254p. 1991. 27.50 (*0-8039-9653-5*) Sage.

Work Decisions in the Nineteen Eighties. Eli Ginzberg et al. LC 81-10860. 137p. 1981. text ed. 45.00 (*0-86569-094-4*, Auburn Hse) Greenwood.

Work Design: Industrial Ergonomics. 4th ed. Stephen Konz. 568p. 1995. 67.50 (*0-942280-65-2*) Holcomb Hath.

Work Design see Chemical Engineering Practice

Work Design for Learning & Competence Development. Felix Frei et al. LC 92-34947. 352p. 1993. text ed. 57.95 (*0-89930-589-X*, FDV, Quorum Bks) Greenwood.

Work Design in Practice. Ed. by C. M. Haslegrave et al. 350p. 1990. 105.00 (*0-85066-770-4*) Taylor & Francis.

Work, Education & Leadership: Essays in the Philosophy of Education. V. A. Howard & Israel Scheffler. LC 93-30459. 160p. (C). 1995. pap. text ed. 29.95 (*0-8204-2323-8*) P Lang Pubng.

Work, Employment & Unemployment: Perspectives on Work & Society. Ed. by Kenneth Thompson. 1985. pap. 32.00 (*0-335-10594-7*, Open Univ Pr) Taylor & Francis.

Work, Employment & Unemployment in the Soviet Union. J. L. Porket. LC 88-37127. (Illus.). 304p. 1989. text ed. 59.95 (*0-312-03095-9*) St Martin.

Work Engendered: Toward a New History of American Labor. Ed. by Ava Baron. LC 91-2281. (Illus.). 400p. 1991. 47.50 (*0-8014-2256-6*); pap. 17.95 (*0-8014-9543-1*) Cornell U Pr.

Work Environment: Occupational Health Fundamentals, Vol. I. Ed. by Doan J. Hansen. (Illus.). 480p. 1991. 79. 95 (*0-87371-303-6*, L303) Lewis Pubs.

Work Environment: Occupational Health Fundamentals, Vol. II. Ed. by Doan J. Hansen. (Illus.). 368p. 1992. 75. 95 (*0-87371-392-3*, L392) Lewis Pubs.

Work Environment: Occupational Health Fundamentals, Vol. III. Ed. by Doan J. Hansen. (Illus.). 304p. 1993. 69.95 (*0-87371-393-1*, L393) Lewis Pubs.

Work Ethic. Jay Schleifer. (Values Library). (Illus.). 64p. (YA). (gr. 7-12). 1991. lib. bdg. 15.95 (*0-8239-1227-2*) Rosen Group.

Work Ethic: A Critical Analysis. Ed. by Jack Barbash et al. 15.00 (*0-913447-24-2*) Indus Relations Res.

Work Ethic: Working Values & Values That Work. David J. Cherrington. LC 80-65871. 302p. reprint ed. pap. 86. 10 (*0-317-26705-1*, 2023512) Bks Demand.

Work Ethic Hell. Andy Van't Hul. LC 90-92309. (Illus.). 380p. (Orig.). 1991. pap. 17.95 (*0-9629101-0-4*) Nomad Pub.

Work Ethic in Industrial America: 1850-1920. Daniel T. Rodgers. LC 77-81737. 316p. 1979. pap. text ed. 11.95 (*0-226-72352-6*) U Ch Pr.

W

Work Experience: Labor, Class & Immigrant Enterprise. George E. Pozzetta. LC 90-48320. (Immigration & Ethnicity Ser.: Vol. 6). 528p. 1991. reprint ed. text ed. 77.00 (0-8240-7406-8) Garland.

Work Experience Education: Instructional Guide. California Department of Education Staff. 492p. 1987. pap. 13.50 (0-8011-0670-2) Calif Education.

Work Experience Planner. 2nd ed. Stull. (CA - Career Development Ser.). 1990. pap. 14.95 (0-538-60289-9) S-W Pub.

Work Exploration Checklist. James H. Wolff. LC 75-20074. (YA). (gr. 7 up). 1993. 23.95 (0-912486-67-8) Finney Co.

Work, Families, & Organizations. Ed. by Sheldon Zedeck. LC 91-30661. (Management Ser.). 503p. text ed. 39.95 (1-55542-401-5) Jossey-Bass.

Work, Family, & Personality: Transition to Adulthood. Jeylan Mortimer et al. Ed. by Gerald Platt. LC 85-20951. (Modern Sociology Ser.). 272p. 1986. text ed. 73.25 (0-89391-293-X) Ablex Pub.

Work, Family & Religion in American Society. Ed. by Nancy T. Ammerman & Wade C. Roof. 256p. (C). 1995. pap. 18.95 (0-415-91172-9, C0245, Routledge NY) Routledge.

Work, Family & Religion in American Society. Ed. by Nancy T. Ammerman & Wade C. Roof. 256p. (C). (gr. 13). 1995. text ed. 69.95 (0-415-91171-0, C0242, Routledge NY) Routledge.

Work, Family & the Career: New Frontiers in Theory & Research. Ed. by C. Brooklyn Derr. LC 80-13598. 380p. 1980. text ed. 40.95 (0-275-90469-5, C0469, Praeger Pubs) Greenwood.

Work Family Challenge: Rethinking Employment. Ed. by Suzan Lewis & Jeremy Lewis. 192p. 1996. 65.00 (0-8039-7468-X); pap. 21.50 (0-8039-7469-8) Sage.

Work: Family Conflicts: Private Lives-Public Responses. Bradley K. Googins. LC 90-36656. 344p. 1990. text ed. 55.00 (0-86569-003-0, T003, Auburn Hse); pap. text ed. 17.95 (0-86569-011-1, Auburn Hse) Greenwood.

Work-Family Needs: Leading Corporations Respond. Ed. by Dana E. Friedman & Theresa Brothers. (Report: No. 1017). 54p. (Orig.). 1993. pap. text ed. 100.00 (0-8237-0465-3) Conference Bd.

***Work-Family Research: An Annotated Bibliography.** Teri Ann Lilly et al. (Bibliographies & Indexes in Sociology: Vol. 25). 1997. text ed. write for info. (0-313-30322-3, Greenwood Pr) Greenwood.

Work-Family Role-Choices for Women in Their 20s & 30s: From College Plans to Life Experience. Cherlyn S. Granrose & Eileen E. Kaplan. LC 96-2195. 224p. 1996. text ed. 55.00 (0-275-95525-7, Praeger Pubs) Greenwood.

Work Family Sex Roles Language. Ed. by Mario Barrera. LC 80-53691. 1980. pap. 5.95 (0-89229-007-2) TQS Pubns.

Work for a Dead Man. Simon Ritchie. 1991. mass mkt. 3.50 (0-373-26064-4) Harlequin Bks.

***Work for a Living & Still be Free to Live.** 5th rev. ed. Eileen McDargh. LC 85-1846. 260p. 1997. pap. 14.95 (1-885221-54-1) BookPartners.

Work for All: Full Employment in the Nineties. John Langmore & John Quiggin. 400p. 1994. pap. 24.95 (0-522-84641-6, Pub. by Melbourne Univ Pr AT) Paul & Co Pubs.

Work for All or Mass Unemployment? Computerised Technical Change into the 21st Century. Christopher Freeman & Luc Soete. LC 94-13742. 1994. pap. 18.00 (1-85567-256-1) St Martin.

Work for All or Mass Unemployment? Computerised Technical Change into the 21st Century. Christopher Freeman & Luc Soete. LC 94-13742. 1994. 45.00 (1-85567-255-3) St Martin.

Work for the Night Is Coming. P. B. Carter. 1985. 10.95 (0-02-522090-X) Macmillan.

Work, for the Night Is Coming. 2nd ed. Jared Carter. LC 95-70938. 47p. 1995. reprint ed. pap. 8.00 (1-880834-20-0) Cleveland St Univ Poetry Ctr.

Work for Wages in South Asia. Ed. by Mark Holmstrom. 1990. 29.00 (81-85054-87-8, Pub. by Manohar II) S Asia.

Work Force: Construction Humor. Jack Aragon. LC 92-80790. (Illus.). 94p. 1992. pap. 5.95 (0-9632697-0-4) VJAK Corp.

Work Force Diversity: Corporate Challenges, Corporate Responses. Mary J. Winterle. (Report: No. 1013). (Illus.). 58p. (Orig.). 1992. pap. text ed. 100.00 (0-8237-0461-0) Conference Bd.

***Work Force Management: Life-Changing Roles & Goals for Today's Christian Manager.** Bill McCallister. 1997. pap. text ed. 9.99 (0-88965-133-7) Chr Pubns.

Work (Four Issues) Ed. by John Sinclair & Ron Caplan. Bd. with Whe're (One Issue). (Avant-Garde Magazines Ser.). 716p. 1974. reprint ed. 48.95 (0-405-01754-5) Ayer.

Work-Game Sheets for Magnet Magic Etc. Marie A. Hoyt. (Illus.). 28p. (Orig.). (J). (gr. 2-8). 1984. pap. text ed. 2.50 (0-914911-03-1) Educ Serv Pr.

Work, Gender, & Family in Victorian England. Karl Ittmann. 264p. (C). 1995. 45.00 (0-8147-3756-0) NYU Pr.

***Work Happy Live Healthy: New Solutions for Career Satisfaction Including More Time & Money.** Tom Welch. LC 96-71010. 256p. (Orig.). 1997. pap. 14.95 (0-9649401-6-7) Rhodes & Easton.

Work Hard & You Shall Be Rewarded: Urban Folklore from the Paperwork Empire. Alan Dundes & Carl R. Pagter. LC 92-11158. (Humor in Life & Letters Ser.). (Illus.). 248p. (C). 1992. reprint ed. pap. 15.95 (0-8143-2432-0) Wayne St U Pr.

Work Hardening. Ed. by J. P. Hirth & J. Weertman. LC 67-29669. (Metallurgical Society Conference Ser.: No. 46). 394p. reprint ed. pap. 112.30 (0-317-11258-9, 2001534) Bks Demand.

Work Hardening: A Practical Guide. Linda M. Demers. (Illus.). 160p. 1992. spiral bd. 47.50 (1-56372-022-1) Buttrwrth-Heinemann.

Work Hardening: Helping the Injured Worker Return to Work Through Rehabilitation & Conditioning. Clifford J. Ameduri. 128p. (Orig.). pap. 8.95 (0-929162-56-0) PIA Pr.

Work Hardening: State-of-the-Art. Karen Jacobs & Linda Ogden-Niemeyer. LC 87-43350. 460p. 1989. pap. 35.00 (1-55642-047-1) SLACK Inc.

Work Hardening in Tension & Fatigue: Proceedings of a Symposium, Cincinnati, Ohio, Nov. 11, 1975. Ed. by Anthony W. Thompson. LC 77-76058. 265p. reprint ed. pap. 75.60 (0-317-08184-5, 2015014) Bks Demand.

***Work, Health & Environment: Old Problems, New Solutions.** LC 97-17255. (Democracy & Ecology Ser.). 1997. pap. text ed. 24.95 (1-57230-234-8); lib. bdg. 42.95 (1-57230-233-X, -0233) Guilford Pr.

Work, Health, & Income among the Elderly. Ed. by Gary Burtless. LC 86-26892. (Studies in Social Economics). 276p. 1987. pap. 32.95 (0-8157-1176-X) Brookings.

Work, Health, & Productivity. Ed. by Gareth M. Green & Frank Baker. (Illus.). 328p. 1991. 47.50 (0-19-505778-3) OUP.

Work Horse Handbook. Lynn R. Miller. (Illus.). 224p. 1983. pap. 16.45 (0-9607268-0-2) Small Farmers.

Work, Identity, & Legal Status at Rome: A Study of the Occupational Inscriptions. Sandra R. Joshel. LC 91-34749. (Oklahoma Series in Classical Culture: Vol. 11). (Illus.). 256p. 1992. pap. 14.95 (0-8061-2444-X) U of Okla Pr.

Work in America: Report of a Special Task Force to the U. S. Department of Health, Education, & Welfare. U. S. Department of Health, Education & Welfare Staff. 262p. 1973. pap. 10.95 (0-262-58023-3) MIT Pr.

Work in America: The Decade Ahead. Ed. by Clark Kerr & Jerome M. Rosow. 288p. 1979. 21.95 (0-442-20372-1) Work in Amer.

Work in American Prisons: Private Sector Gets Involved. 100p. (Orig.). (C). 1993. pap. text ed. 30.00 (1-56806-830-1) DIANE Pub.

Work in Ancient & Medieval Thought: Ancient Philosophers, Medieval Monks & Theologians & Their Concept of Work, Occupations & Technology. Birgit Van den Hoven. (Dutch Monographs on Ancient History & Archaeology: Vol. XIV). iv, 295p. 1996. lib. bdg. 84.00 (90-5063-557-1, Pub. by Gieben NE) Benjamins North Am.

Work in France: Representations, Meaning, Organization, & Practice. Ed. by Steven L. Kaplan & Cynthia J. Koepp. LC 85-22352. (Illus.). 576p. 1986. 54.50 (0-8014-1697-3) Cornell U Pr.

Work in Market & Industrial Societies. Ed. by Herbert Applebaum. LC 83-9267. (SUNY Series in the Anthropology of Work). 315p. 1984. text ed. 57.50 (0-87395-810-1); pap. text ed. 18.95 (0-87395-811-X) State U NY Pr.

Work in Mound Exploration of the Bureau of Ethnology. Cyrus Thomas. (Bureau of American Ethnology Bulletins Ser.). 99p. 1995. lib. bdg. 69.00 (0-7812-4004-2) Rprt Serv.

Work in Mound Exploration of the Bureau of Ethnology. Cyrus Thomas. reprint ed. 25.00 (0-403-03727-1) Scholarly.

Work in Organizations. Ed. by Barry M. Staw & Larry L. Cummings. LC 90-4474. (Research in Organizational Behavior Ser.). 296p. 1990. pap. 25.75 (1-55938-216-3) Jai Pr.

Work in Progress. 3rd ed. Ede. 1994. teacher ed., pap. text ed. 0.55 (0-312-10108-2) St Martin.

Work in Progress. 3rd ed. Ede. 1994. teacher ed., pap. text ed. 21.00 (0-312-10109-0) St Martin.

Work in Progress. 3rd ed. Lisa Ede. 336p. 1994. pap. text ed. 22.00 (0-312-10107-4) St Martin.

***Work in Progress.** 4th ed. Date not set. pap. text ed. write for info. (0-312-17944-8) St Martin.

Work in Progress. 4th ed. Ede. Date not set. pap. text ed. 22.00 (0-312-14961-1) St Martin.

***Work in Progress: Building Feminist Culture.** Ed. by Rhea Tregebov. 180p. pap. 10.95 (0-88961-121-1, Pub. by Wmns Pr CN) LPC InBook.

Work in Progress: Christian-to-Christian Satire. Paul McCusker. 1991. 25.00 (0-685-68686-8) Lillenas.

Work in Progress: Christian-to-Christian Satire. Paul McCusker. 1991. 8.99 (0-685-68685-X, MP-669) Lillenas.

***Work in Progress: Essays in New Guinea Highlands Ethnography in Honour of Paula Brown Glick.** Ed. by Hal Levine & Anton Ploeg. 362p. 1996. pap. 61.95 (0-8204-2991-0, GN671) P Lang Pubng.

Work in Progress: Joyce Centenary Essays. Ed. by Richard F. Peterson et al. LC 82-16943. 192p. 1983. 24.95 (0-8093-1094-5) S Ill U Pr.

Work in Progress: Occupational Therapy in Work Programs. Robert Bing et al. (Illus.). 291p. (Orig.). (C). 1989. pap. text ed. 32.00 (0-910317-54-2) Am Occup Therapy.

***Work in Progress: The University of Michigan-Flint.** Robert W. Heywood. 100p. 1996. 15.00 (0-9653426-0-3) Univ Mich-Flint.

Work in Progress: Writing in English As a Second Language. Martha J. McNamara. LC 93-38195. 1994. pap. 26.95 (0-8384-4822-4) Heinle & Heinle.

Work in Progress on Alcoholism, Vol. 273. Ed. by Frank A. Seixas & Suzie Eggleston. (Annals Ser.). 664p. 1976. 43.00 (0-89072-052-5) NY Acad Sci.

Work in Retirement: The Persistence of an American Collective Representation. Fatemeh Givechian. 152p. (Orig.). (C). 1990. pap. text ed. 20.00 (0-8191-7853-5); lib. bdg. 39.00 (0-8191-7852-7) U Pr of Amer.

Work in the Fast Lane: Flexibility, Divisions of Labor, & Inequality in High-Tech Industries. Glenna Colclough & Charles M. Tolbert, II. LC 90-20851. (SUNY Series, the New Inequalities). 160p. (C). 1992. text ed. 67.50 (0-7914-0783-7); pap. text ed. 24.95 (0-7914-0784-5) State U NY Pr.

Work in the Hood: The First Entertaining Organic Chemistry Laboratory Guide. James W. Zubrick. LC 80-69113. (Illus.). 120p. (Orig.). (C). 1980. pap. 4.50 (0-937926-00-0) Scienspot.

Work in the New Economy. 2nd rev. ed. Robert G. Wegmann et al. LC 88-24147. (Careers & Job Seeking into the 21st Century). (Illus.). 303p. 1989. pap. 14.95 (0-942784-19-7, WORK) JIST Works.

Work in the Soviet Union: Attitudes & Issues. Murray Yanowitch. LC 84-27651. 216p. (gr. 13). 1985. text ed. 67.95 (0-87332-307-6) M E Sharpe.

Work in the World: Geographical Practice & the Written Word. Michael R. Curry. LC 96-16478. 256p. (C). 1996. text ed. 49.95 (0-8166-2664-2); pap. text ed. 19.95 (0-8166-2665-0) U of Minn Pr.

Work in Towns. Penelope J. Corfield & Derek J. Keene. 250p. 1990. 45.00 (0-7185-1313-4) St Martin.

Work in Words: A Poetry Chapman's Chapbook. Tom C. Armstrong. 44p. (Orig.). 1993. pap. 3.25 (0-9636452-0-X) AD HOC Bks.

Work, Inc. A Philosophical Inquiry. Edmund F. Byrne. 360p. 1990. 49.95 (0-87722-688-1) Temple U Pr.

Work, Inc. A Philosophical Inquiry. Edmund F. Byrne. 360p. 1992. pap. 22.95 (0-87722-957-0) Temple U Pr.

Work Incentives & Income Guarantees: The New Jersey Negative Income Tax Experiment. Ed. by Joseph A. Pechman & P. Michael Timpane. LC 75-2321. (Studies in Social Experimentation). 232p. 1975. pap. 12.95 (0-8157-6975-X) Brookings.

Work Incentives in the Danish Welfare State: New Empirical Evidence. Ed. by Gunnar V. Mogensen. (Illus.). 280p. (Orig.). (C). 1995. pap. 19.95 (87-7288-480-0, Pub. by Aarhus Univ Pr DK) David Brown.

Work, Income & Inequality. Frances Stewart. LC 81-24065. 304p. 1982. text ed. 39.95 (0-312-88943-7) St Martin.

Work Independence & the Severely Disabled: A Bibliography. Gerardo Bilotto & Veronica Washam. LC 79-91351. 108p. 1980. 7.50 (0-686-38821-6) Human Res Ctr.

Work, Injuries & Compensation: Index of New Information with Authors & Subjects. Science & Life Consultants Association Staff. LC 92-54203. 180p. 1992. 49.50 (1-55914-558-7); pap. 39.50 (1-55914-559-5) ABBE Pubs Assn.

Work Injury: Management & Prevention. Susan J. Isernhagen. LC 88-19334. 392p. (C). 1988. 68.00 (0-87189-788-1) Aspen Pub.

Work Injury & Illness Rates - 1996. rev. ed. NSC Staff. (Illus.). 64p. 1996. pap. 13.95 (0-87912-195-5, 12594-0000) Natl Safety Coun.

Work-ins, Sit-ins & Industrial Democracy: The Implications of Factory Occupations in Great Britain in the Early Seventies. Ken Coates. 175p. 1981. 42.50 (0-85124-278-2, Pub. by Spokesman Bks UK) Coronet Bks.

***Work Is a Contact Sport: A Dilbert Book.** Scott Adams. LC 96-86664. (Illus.). 80p. 1997. 4.95 (0-8362-2878-2) Andrews & McMeel.

Work is Dangerous. Jean Stellman. Date not set. pap. 20.00 (1-56584-065-8) New Press NY.

Work Is Hell: A Cartoon Book. Matt Groening. LC 86-42637. 48p. 1986. pap. 7.95 (0-394-74864-6) Pantheon.

Work Is Not a Four-Letter Word: Improving the Quality of Your Work Life. Stephen Strasser & John Sena. 200p. 1991. text ed. 21.00 (1-55623-398-1) Irwin Prof Pubng.

Work Is Yours. 2nd ed. Luke Salm. (Illus.). 225p. 1996. pap. 15.00 (0-614-11778-X) Christian Brothers.

***Work Is Yours.** 2nd ed. Luke Salm. LC 96-83018. (Illus.). 216p. 1996. pap. 15.00 (1-884904-08-4) Christian Brothers.

Work Issues, 4 bks., Set. (Today's World Ser.). 1994. 12.00 (1-56420-081-7, 2081-7); 11.95 (1-56420-084-1, 2084-1) New Readers.

Work It Out: Clues for Solving People Problems at Work. Sandra K. Hirsh & Jane A. Kise. LC 96-21540. (Illus.). 288p. 1996. pap. 16.95 (0-89106-088-X, 7887) Davies-Black.

Work, Its Rewards & Discontents Series, 65 Vols. Ed. by Leon Stein. (Illus.). 1977. lib. bdg. 1,784.00 (0-405-10150-3) Ayer.

Work, Jobs, & Occupations: A Critical Review of the Dictionary of Occupational Titles. Ed. by Ann R. Miller et al. LC 80-24653. 455p. reprint ed. pap. 129.70 (0-7837-1639-7, 2041932) Bks Demand.

Work, Jobs & Occupations--Distress, Dangers & Diseases: Index of New Information. Arlene L. Lipinski. (Illus.). 150p. 1994. 44.50 (0-7883-0014-8); pap. 39.50 (0-7883-0015-6) ABBE Pubs Assn.

***Work, Learning, & Earnings: Employment & Pay Systems in Japan & the United States.** Clair Brown et al. LC 96-39268. (Illus.). 240p. 1997. 35.00 (0-19-511521-X) OUP.

Work, Learning & the American Future. James O'Toole. LC 76-50726. 256p. reprint ed. pap. 73.00 (0-8357-4956-8, 2037888) Bks Demand.

***Work, Leisure, & Well Being.** John Haworth. 240p. (C). 1997. text ed. 69.95 (0-415-01703-3) Routledge.

***Work Leisure & Well Being.** Ed. by John T. Haworth. 224p. (C). 1997. pap. 19.95 (0-415-14862-6, Routledge NY) Routledge.

Work-Leisure Trade Off: Reduced Work Time for Managers & Professionals. Ann Harriman. LC 81-17782. 200p. 1982. text ed. 55.00 (0-275-90814-3, C0814, Praeger Pubs) Greenwood.

***Work Less & Play More.** rev. ed. Steven Catlin. LC 96-50307. (Illus.). 200p. 1997. pap. 14.00 (0-9654188-0-4) Kimberlite Pub.

Work Life: Based on the Teachings of G. I. Gurdjieff, P. D. Ouspensky & Maurice Nicoll. Beryl Pogson. LC 93-45899. (Illus.). 304p. (Orig.). 1994. pap. 12.95 (0-87728-809-7) Weiser.

Work-Life Book: Managing Is Everybody's Business. Richard Gillespie. Ed. & Illus. by Dan Youra. 186p. (Orig.). 1988. pap. 9.95 (0-940828-21-9) D Youra Studios.

Work-Life Dichotomy: Prospects for Reintegrating People & Jobs. Martin Morf. LC 88-35739. 211p. 1989. text ed. 55.00 (0-89930-421-4, MUP/, Quorum Bks) Greenwood.

Work Lights. David Young. LC 77-75642. (CSU Poetry Ser.: No. IV). 45p. 1977. pap. 4.95 (0-914946-06-4) Cleveland St Univ Poetry Ctr.

Work Like a Pro with Excel for Windows 95. Anne Prince. LC 96-9531. (Illus.). 339p. (Orig.). 1996. pap. 25.00 (0-911625-92-5) M Murach & Assoc.

Work Like a Pro with Excel 5 for Windows. Anne Prince. LC 95-19201. 247p. 1995. pap. 20.00 (0-911625-89-5) M Murach & Assoc.

Work Like a Pro with Word for Windows 95. Mike Murach. LC 96-15269. (Illus.). 369p. (Orig.). 1996. pap. 25.00 (0-911625-91-7) M Murach & Assoc.

Work Like a Pro with Word 6 for Windows. Mike Murach. LC 95-32589. 253p. 1995. pap. 20.00 (0-911625-90-9) M Murach & Assoc.

Work, Love & Marriage: The Impact of Unemployment. I. Mattinson. pap. 37.95 (0-7156-2230-7, Pub. by Duckworth UK) Focus Pub-R Pullins.

Work, Love, Play: Self Repair in the Psychoanalytic Dialogue. Joel Shor. LC 91-36576. 224p. (Orig.). 1992. text ed. 31.95 (0-87630-658-X) Brunner-Mazel.

Work, Love, Play: Self Repair in the Psychoanalytic Dialogue. Joel Shor. LC 89-82165. 222p. (Orig.). 1990. lib. bdg. 20.00 (0-930578-01-5) Double Helix.

Work Manual for Administrative & Personnel Managers. R. Raghunathan. 1994. write for info. (81-224-0649-1, Pub. by Wiley Estrn II) Franklin.

Work Matters. Sara Friedman. Date not set. pap. 10.95 (0-14-015980-0, Viking) Viking Penguin.

Work Matters: Women Talk about Their Jobs & Their Lives. Sara A. Friedman. LC 95-34529. 304p. 1996. pap. 24.95 (0-670-84203-6, Viking) Viking Penguin.

Work Methods & Measurement for Management. Doty. (Mechanical Technology Ser.). 1989. text ed. 52.95 (0-8273-3830-9) Delmar.

Work, Mobility, & Participation: A Comparative Study of American & Japanese Industry. Robert E. Cole. LC 77-80468. 304p. 1979. pap. 14.00 (0-520-04204-2) U CA Pr.

Work Motivation. Ed. by U. Kleinbeck et al. 296p. (C). 1990. text ed. 75.00 (0-8058-0452-8) L Erlbaum Assocs.

Work Motivation: Models for Developing Countries. Ed. by Rabindra N. Kanungo & Manuel Mendonca. LC 93-50135. (OBS for Social Development Ser.: Vol. 1). 1994. 33.50 (0-8039-9157-6) Sage.

Work Motivation Attitudes of Apparel Workers: Methodology Used in the Study. Emma W. Bragg. LC 83-61829. (Illus.). 186p. 1983. pap. 24.75 (0-9611930-0-X) E W Bragg.

Work of a Magistrate. A. J. Maddox. (C). 1980. pap. 58.00 (0-7219-0561-7, Pub. by Scientific UK) St Mut.

Work of Andy Warhol. Ed. by Gary Garrels. LC 89-650815. (Discussions in Contemporary Culture Ser.: No. 3). 208p. (Orig.). (C). 1989. pap. 10.95 (0-941920-11-9) Bay Pr.

Work of Angels: Masterpieces of Celtic Metalwork, 6th - 9th Centuries AD. Ed. by Susan Youngs. 192p. (Orig.). 1990. pap. 29.95 (0-292-79058-9) U of Tex Pr.

Work of Antonio Sant'Elia: Retreat into the Future. Esther da Costa Meyer. LC 94-39125. (Publications in the History of Art). 1995. 45.00 (0-300-04309-0) Yale U Pr.

Work of Art. Arthur Worley. 1994. 15.95 (0-533-10732-6) Vantage.

***Work of Art: Immanence & Transcendence.** Gerard Genette. Tr. by G. M. Goshgarian from FRE. LC 96-46963. (Illus.). 256p. 1996. 42.50 (0-8014-3159-X) Cornell U Pr.

***Work of Art: Immanence & Transcendence.** Gerard Genette. Tr. by G. M. Goshgarian from FRE. LC 96-46963. (Illus.). 256p. 1996. pap. 16.95 (0-8014-8272-0) Cornell U Pr.

Work of Atget: Modern Times, Vol. IV. John Szarkowski. (Illus.). 186p. 1985. 45.00 (0-87070-218-1) Mus of Modern Art.

Work of Betrayal. Mario Brelich. Tr. by Raymond Rosenthal from ITA. LC 88-64144. Orig. Title: L'Opera Del Tradimento. 240p. 1989. 29.95 (0-910395-44-6) Marlboro Pr.

Work of Betrayal. Mario Brelich. 1990. pap. 12.00 (0-910395-45-4) Marlboro Pr.

Work of Boards of Education. Hans C. Olsen. LC 77-177134. (Columbia University. Teachers College. Contributions to Education Ser.: No. 213). reprint ed. 37.50 (0-404-55213-7) AMS Pr.

Work of Brian W. Aldiss: An Annotated Bibliography & Guide. Margaret Aldiss. Ed. by Boden Clarke. LC 87-746. (Bibliographies of Modern Authors Ser.: No. 9). 360p. 1992. lib. bdg. 43.00 (0-89370-388-5) Borgo Pr.

W

Work of Bruce McAllister: An Annotated Bibliography & Guide. rev. ed. David R. Bourquin. Ed. by Boden Clarke. LC 85-22400. (Bibliographies of Modern Authors Ser.: No. 10). 32p. 1986. pap. 13.00 (*0-89370-489-X*); lib. bdg. 23.00 (*0-89370-389-3*) Borgo Pr.

Work of CEDAW: Reports of the Committee on the Elimination of Discrimination Against Women, Vol. I, 1982-1985. 744p. 65.00 (*92-1-130132-7*, E.89.IV.4) UN.

Work of CEDAW: Reports of the Committee on the Elimination of Discrimination Against Women, Vol. II, 1986-87. 1990. 50.00 (*92-1-130140-8*, E 90.IV.4) UN.

Work of Chad Oliver: An Annotated Bibliography & Guide. Hal W. Hall. Ed. by Boden Clarke. LC 86-2288. (Bibliographies of Modern Authors Ser.: No. 12). 88p. 1989. pap. 15.00 (*0-89370-491-1*); lib. bdg. 25.00 (*0-89370-391-5*) Borgo Pr.

***Work of Charles & Ray Eames: A Legacy of Invention.** Donald Albrecht. LC 97-4086. 1997. write for info. (*0-8109-1799-8*); write for info. (*0-8109-2752-7*) Abrams.

Work of Charles Beaumont: An Annotated Bibliography & Guide. 2nd ed. William F. Nolan. Ed. by Boden Clarke. LC 90-15043. (Bibliographies of Modern Authors Ser.: No. 6). 92p. 1990. pap. 17.00 (*0-8095-1517-2*); lib. bdg. 27.00 (*0-8095-0517-7*) Borgo Pr.

Work of Charles Samuel Keene. Simon Houfe. 128p. 1995. 76.95 (*0-85967-986-1*, Pub. by Scolar Pr UK) Ashgate Pub Co.

***Work of Christ.** Peter T. Forsyth. 244p. 1996. pap. 15.00 (*1-57910-004-X*) Wipf & Stock.

Work of Christ see Contours of Christian Theology Series

Work of Colin Wilson: An Annotated Bibliography & Guide. Colin Stanley. Ed. by Boden Clarke. LC 84-11181. (Bibliographies of Modern Authors Ser.: No. 1). 312p. (Orig.). 1989. pap. 29.00 (*0-89370-917-4*); lib. bdg. 39.00 (*0-89370-817-8*) Borgo Pr.

Work of Craft: An Inquiry into the Nature of Crafts & Craftsmanship. Carla Needleman. LC 92-16920. 160p. 1993. reprint ed. pap. 10.00 (*4-7700-1701-4*) Kodansha.

Work of Creation. 1991. pap. 11.95 (*0-904575-33-0*) Sigo Pr.

Work of Culture: Symbolic Transformation in Psychoanalysis & Anthropology. Gananath Obeyesekere. LC 90-10904. (Lewis Henry Morgan Lectures, 1982). 380p. 1990. pap. text ed. 19.95 (*0-226-61599-5*) U Ch Pr.

Work of Culture: Symbolic Transformation in Psychoanalysis & Anthropology. Gananath Obeyesekere. LC 90-10904. (Lewis Henry Morgan Lectures, 1982). 380p. 1990. lib. bdg. 60.00 (*0-226-61598-7*) U Ch Pr.

Work of Dean Ing: An Annotated Bibliography & Guide. Scott A. Burgess. Ed. by Boden Clarke. LC 87-827. (Bibliographies of Modern Authors Ser.: No. 11). 82p. 1990. pap. 15.00 (*0-89370-495-4*); lib. bdg. 25.00 (*0-89370-395-8*) Borgo Pr.

Work of Democracy: Ralph Bunche, Kenneth B. Clark, Lorraine Hansberry, & the Cultural Politics of Race. Ben Keppel. LC 94-20606. (African American Studies). (Illus.). 320p. 1995. text ed. 35.00 (*0-674-95843-8*, KEPWOR) HUP.

Work of Dissimilitude: Essays from the Sixth Citadel Conference on Medieval & Renaissance Literature. Ed. by David G. Allen & Robert A. White. LC 90-51011. (Illus.). 296p. 1992. 42.50 (*0-87413-435-8*) U Delaware Pr.

Work of Elizabeth Chater: An Annotated Bibliography & Guide. Daryl F. Mallett & Annette Y. Mallett. Ed. by Boden Clarke. LC 93-333. (Bibliographies of Modern Authors Ser.: No. 27). 80p. 1994. pap. 13.00 (*0-89370-490-3*); lib. bdg. 23.00 (*0-89370-390-7*) Borgo Pr.

Work of Felix Kaufmann. Harry P. Reeder. (Current Continental Research Ser.: No. 220). 238p. (C). 1991. lib. bdg. 60.00 (*0-8191-7728-8*) U Pr of Amer.

Work of Fire. Maurice Blanchot. Tr. by Charlotte Mandell from FRE. LC 94-32418. Orig. Title: Part de Feu. xi ,p. (ENG.). 1995. 45.00 (*0-8047-2432-6*); pap. 16.95 (*0-8047-2493-8*) Stanford U Pr.

Work of Gary Brandner: An Annotated Bibliography & Guide. Martine Wood. Ed. by Boden Clarke & Daryl F. Mallett. LC 93-2881. (Bibliographies of Modern Authors Ser.: No. 23). 112p. 1995. pap. 17.00 (*0-8095-1519-9*); lib. bdg. 27.00 (*0-8095-0519-3*) Borgo Pr.

***Work of God: A Benedictine Prayer Book.** Ed. by Judith Sutera. LC 96-51704. 248p. 1997. 19.95 (*0-8146-2431-6*) Liturgical Pr.

Work of God at the End-Time. T. A. Sparks. 68p. 1993. pap. text ed. 3.00 (*1-883137-13-6*) Christ Stewards.

Work of Grinling Gibbons. Geoffrey W. Beard. LC 89-20460. (Illus.). 160p. 1990. 47.95 (*0-226-03992-7*) U Ch Pr.

Work of Hanna Segal: A Kleinian Approach to Clinical Practice. Hanna Segal. LC 81-7877. 256p. 1990. reprint ed. 30.00 (*0-87668-422-3*) Aronson.

Work of Hans Loewald: An Introduction & Commentary. Ed. by Gerald Fogel. LC 90-22005. 296p. 1991. 35.00 (*0-87668-615-3*) Aronson.

***Work of Happiness.** Keene. (C). 1998. pap. text ed. 21.00 (*0-15-505421-X*) HB Coll Pubs.

Work of Harry Harrison: An Annotated Bibliography & Guide. Paul Tomlinson. Ed. by Boden Clarke. LC 95-2765. (Bibliographies of Modern Authors Ser.: No. 20). 224p. Date not set. pap. write for info. (*0-8095-1515-6*); lib. bdg. write for info. (*0-8095-0515-0*) Borgo Pr.

Work of Hartford's First Printer. Albert C. Bates. 16p. 1925. pap. 1.00 (*0-940748-47-9*) Conn Hist Soc.

Work of Her Own: A Woman's Guide to Success off the Career Track. Susan W. Albert. LC 93-28850. 272p. 1994. pap. 12.95 (*0-87477-767-4*, Tarcher Putnam) Putnam Pub Group.

Work of Her Own: How Women Create Success & Fulfillment off the Traditional Career Track. Susan W. Albert. 256p. 1994. pap. 12.95 (*0-685-74804-9*, Tarcher Putnam) Putnam Pub Group.

Work of Ian Watson: An Annotated Bibliography & Guide. Douglas A. Mackey. Ed. by Boden Clarke. LC 88-36646. (Bibliographies of Modern Authors Ser.: No. 18). 148p. (C). 1989. pap. 19.00 (*0-8095-1512-1*); lib. bdg. 29.00 (*0-8095-0512-6*) Borgo Pr.

Work of Invisible Helpers. Amber M. Tuttle. 637p. 1996. pap. 39.95 (*1-56459-676-1*) Kessinger Pub.

Work of Invisible Helpers. Amber M. Tuttle. 535p. 1993. reprint ed. spiral bd. 24.50 (*0-7873-0902-8*) Hlth Research.

Work of Jack Vance: An Annotated Bibliography & Guide. Jerry Hewett & Daryl F. Mallett. LC 92-28056. (Bibliographies of Modern Authors Ser.: No. 29). xxii, 293p. 1994. pap. 27.00 (*0-8095-1509-1*); lib. bdg. 37.00 (*0-8095-0509-6*) Borgo Pr.

Work of Jack Vance: An Annotated Bibliography & Guide. Ed. by Jerry Hewett & Daryl F. Mallett. 304p. 1993. 35.00 (*0-88733-165-3*) Underwood Bks.

Work of Jack Williamson: An Annotated Bibliography & Guide. 2nd ed. Richard A. Hauptmann. Ed. by Boden Clarke. LC 95-2763. (Bibliography of Modern Authors Ser.: No. 22). 1997. pap. 19.00 (*0-89370-499-7*); lib. bdg. 29.00 (*0-89370-399-0*) Borgo Pr.

Work of Jacques Le Goff & the Challenges of Medieval History. Ed. by Miri Rubin. LC 96-46634. 272p. 1997. 63.00 (*0-85115-622-3*) Boydell & Brewer.

Work of Jean Dubuffet. Peter H. Selz. 1981. 28.95 (*0-405-12892-4*) Ayer.

Work of Jeffrey M. Elliot: An Annotated Bibliography & Guide. Boden Clarke. LC 84-21745. (Bibliographies of Modern Authors Ser.: No. 2). 50p. 1984. lib. bdg. 23.00 (*0-89370-381-8*) Borgo Pr.

Work of Joseph Payne Brennan: An Annotated Bibliography & Guide. Randall D. Larson. Ed. by Boden Clarke. (Bibliographies of Modern Authors Ser.). 128p. lib. bdg. write for info. (*0-8095-0521-5*) Borgo Pr.

Work of Joseph Payne Brennan: An Annotated Bibliography & Guide. Randall D. Larson. Ed. by Boden Clarke. (Bibliographies of Modern Authors Ser.: No. 26). 128p. pap. write for info. (*0-8095-1521-0*) Borgo Pr.

Work of Julian May: An Annotated Bibliography & Guide. 2nd ed. Thaddeus Dikty & R. Reginald. Ed. by Boden Clarke. (Bibliographies of Modern Authors Ser.: No. 3). 120p. pap. write for info. (*0-8095-1513-X*); lib. bdg. write for info. (*0-8095-0513-4*) Borgo Pr.

Work of Justice: Irish Bishops Pastoral. Veritas Publications Staff. 1989. pap. 22.00 (*0-905092-24-4*, Pub. by Veritas IE) St Mut.

Work of Katherine Kurtz: An Annotated Bibliography & Guide. Boden Clarke & Mary A. Burgess. LC 85-31401. (Bibliographies of Modern Authors Ser.: No. 7). 128p. 1993. pap. 17.00 (*0-89370-486-5*, 13063902); lib. bdg. 27.00 (*0-89370-386-9*, 13063902) Borgo Pr.

Work of Living Art & Man Is the Measure of All Things. Adolpho Appia. 1962. 12.95 (*0-87024-305-5*) U of Miami Pr.

Work of Louis L'Amour: An Annotated Bibliography & Guide. 2nd expanded rev. ed. Hal W. Hall. Ed. by Boden Clarke. LC 95-5113. (Bibliographies of Modern Authors Ser.: No. 15). 268p. 1997. pap. 27.00 (*0-8095-1522-9*); lib. bdg. 37.00 (*0-8095-0522-3*) Borgo Pr.

Work of Many Hands: Card Tables in Federal America, 1790-1820. Benjamin A. Hewitt et al. LC 81-71042. (Illus.). 198p. reprint ed. pap. 56.50 (*0-8357-6410-9*, 2035771) Bks Demand.

Work of Mara Selvini Palazzoli. Ed. by Matteo Selvini. Tr. by Arnold J. Pomerans from ITA. LC 87-12438. 437p. 1988. 50.00 (*0-87668-949-7*) Aronson.

Work of Mary Ellen Rudin. Ed. by Franklin D. Tall. LC 94-696. (Annals Ser.: Vol. 705). 1994. pap. 35.00 (*0-89766-813-8*) NY Acad Sci.

Work of Michael R. Collings: An Annotated Bibliography & Guide. Willard Reuben. Ed. by Boden Clarke. LC 93-340. (Bibliographies of Modern Authors Ser.). 160p. lib. bdg. write for info. (*0-8095-0501-0*) Borgo Pr.

Work of Michael R. Collings: An Annotated Bibliography & Guide. Willard Reuben. Ed. by Boden Clarke. LC 93-340. (Bibliographies of Modern Authors Ser.: No. 22). 160p. pap. write for info. (*0-8095-1501-6*) Borgo Pr.

Work of Music & the Problem of Its Identity. Roman Ingarden. LC 85-24597. 208p. (C). 1986. 42.50 (*0-520-05529-2*) U CA Pr.

Work of Nations: Preparing Ourselves for 21st-Century Capitalism. Robert B. Reich. 1991. 27.50 (*0-394-58352-3*) Knopf.

Work of Nations: Preparing Ourselves for 21st Century Capitalism. Robert B. Reich. 1992. pap. 13.00 (*0-679-73615-8*, Vin) Random.

***Work of Nature: How the Diversity of Life Sustains Us.** Yvonne Baskin. (Illus.). 288p. 1997. 25.00 (*1-55963-519-3*, Shearwater Bks) Island Pr.

***Work of Opera: Genre, Nationhood & Sexual Difference.** Richard Dellamora & Daniel Fischlin. LC 97-19867. 1997. write for info. (*0-231-10944-X*); pap. write for info. (*0-231-10945-8*) Col U Pr.

Work of Orson Scott Card: An Annotated Bibliography & Guide. Michael R. Collings. Ed. by Boden Clarke. LC 95-3909. (Bibliographies of Modern Authors Ser.: No. 19). 200p. 1996. pap. write for info. (*0-8095-1516-4*); lib. bdg. write for info. (*0-8095-0516-9*) Borgo Pr.

Work of Pamela Sargent: An Annotated Bibliography & Literary Guide. 2nd expanded rev. ed. Jeffrey M. Elliot. Ed. by Boden Clarke. LC 96-15693. (Bibliographies of Modern Authors Ser.: No. 13). 144p. 1996. 29.00 (*0-89370-396-6*, 34514643) Borgo Pr.

Work of Pamela Sargent: An Annotated Bibliography & Literary Guide. 2nd expanded rev. ed. Jeffrey M. Elliot. Ed. by Boden Clarke. LC 96-15693. (Bibliographies of Modern Authors Ser.: No. 13). 144p. 1996. pap. 19.00 (*0-89370-496-2*, 34514643) Borgo Pr.

Work of Placement Officers in Teacher Training Institutions. Whit Brogan. LC 79-176593. (Columbia University. Teachers College. Contributions to Education Ser.: No. 434). reprint ed. 37.50 (*0-404-55434-2*) AMS Pr.

***Work of Poetry.** John Hollander. LC 97-10041. 1997. write for info. (*0-231-10896-6*) Col U Pr.

Work of Raymond Z. Gallun: An Annotated Bibliography & Guide. Jeffrey M. Elliot. Ed. by Boden Clarke. LC 93-336. (Bibliographies of Modern Authors Ser.: No. 24). 128p. pap. write for info. (*0-8095-1503-2*); lib. bdg. write for info. (*0-8095-0503-7*) Borgo Pr.

Work of Reconstruction: From Slave to Wage Laborer in South Carolina, 1860-1870. Julie Saville. (Illus.). 240p. (C). 1994. text ed. 54.95 (*0-521-36221-0*) Cambridge U Pr.

Work of Reconstruction: From Slave to Wage Laborer in South Carolina, 1860-1870. Julie Saville. 239p. 1996. pap. text ed. 15.95 (*0-521-56625-8*) Cambridge U Pr.

Work of Reginald Bretnor: An Annotated Bibliography & Guide. Scott A. Burgess. Ed. by Boden Clarke. LC 85-31405. (Bibliographies of Modern Authors Ser.: No. 8). 122p. 1989. pap. 17.00 (*0-89370-487-3*); lib. bdg. 27.00 (*0-89370-387-7*) Borgo Pr.

Work of Restructuring Schools: Building from the Ground Up. Ed. by Ann Lieberman. (The Series on School Reform). 208p. (C). 1995. text ed. 40.00 (*0-8077-3404-7*); pap. text ed. 18.95 (*0-8077-3403-9*) Tchrs Coll.

Work of Richard Sibbes, Vol. 2 of 7. Richard Sibbes. Orig. Title: The Complete Works of Richard Sibbes. 1983. reprint ed. 25.99 (*0-85151-370-0*) Banner of Truth.

Work of Robert A. W. Lowndes: An Annotated Bibliography & Guide. Mike Ashley. Ed. by Boden Clarke. LC 95-3910. (Bibliographies of Modern Authors Ser.). 64p. 1996. pap. write for info. (*0-8095-1504-0*); lib. bdg. write for info. (*0-8095-0504-5*) Borgo Pr.

***Work of Robert K. Merton & Contemporary Sociology.** Robert K. Merton et al. LC 97-16720. 1997. write for info. (*1-56000-318-9*) Transaction Pubs.

Work of Robert Reginald: An Annotated Bibliography & Guide. enl. rev. ed. Michael Burgess. Ed. by Boden Clarke. LC 87-6306. (Bibliographies of Modern Authors Ser.: No. 5). 176p. 1992. pap. 21.00 (*0-8095-1505-9*, 15318070) Borgo Pr.

Work of Robert Reginald: An Annotated Bibliography & Guide. 2nd enl. rev. ed. Michael Burgess. Ed. by Boden Clarke. LC 87-6306. (Bibliographies of Modern Authors Ser.: No. 5). 176p. 1992. lib. bdg. 31.00 (*0-8095-0505-3*, 15318070) Borgo Pr.

Work of Ross Rocklynne: An Annotated Bibliography & Guide. Douglas A. Menville. LC 88-34360. (Bibliographies of Modern Authors Ser.: No. 17). 70p. (C). 1989. pap. 13.00 (*0-8095-1511-3*); lib. bdg. 23.00 (*0-8095-0511-8*) Borgo Pr.

Work of Sartre: Search for Freedom. Istvan Meszaros. (Modern Revivals in Philosophy Ser.). 288p. 1994. 59.95 (*0-7512-0272-X*, Pub. by Gregg Revivals UK) Ashgate Pub Co.

Work of Self-Representation: Lyric Poetry in Colonial New England. Ivy Schweitzer. LC 91-8420. (Gender & American Culture Ser.). xvi, 306p. (C). 1991. pap. text ed. 15.95 (*0-8078-4329-6*) U of NC Pr.

Work of Sir Gilbert Scott. David Cole. (Illus.). 256p. 1980. 60.00 (*0-85139-723-9*) Eastview.

Work of Stephen King: An Annotated Bibliography & Guide. Michael R. Collings. Ed. by Boden Clarke. LC 93-16091. (Bibliographies of Modern Authors Ser.: No. 25). 480p. 1996. 51.00 (*0-8095-0520-7*); pap. 41.00 (*0-8095-1520-2*) Borgo Pr.

Work of Teachers in America: A Social History Through Stories. Ed. by Rosetta M. Cohen & Samuel Scheer. LC 96-43350. 304p. 1997. pap. text ed. 29.95 (*0-8058-2250-X*) L Erlbaum Assocs.

Work of the Afro-American Woman. N. F. Mossell. LC 72-161270. (Black Heritage Library Collection). 1977. reprint ed. 27.95 (*0-8369-8829-9*) Ayer.

Work of the Afro-American Woman. N. F. Mossell. (Schomburg Library of Nineteenth-Century Black Women Writers). 224p. 1988. reprint ed. 26.00 (*0-19-505265-X*) OUP.

Work of the Afro-American Woman. N. F. Mossell. (Schomburg Library of Nineteenth-Century Black Women Writers). 224p. 1990. reprint ed. pap. 9.95 (*0-19-506326-0*) OUP.

Work of the Bond House. Lawrence Chamberlain. LC 75-2626. (Wall Street & the Security Market Ser.). 1975. reprint ed. 20.95 (*0-405-06952-9*) Ayer.

Work of the Bow. Robert H. Long. (CSU Poetry Ser.: Vol. 40). 80p. 1996. pap. 10.00 (*1-880834-23-5*) Cleveland St Univ Poetry Ctr.

Work of the Bow. Robert H. Long. (CSU Poetry Ser.: Vol. L). 80p. 1996. 17.50 (*1-880834-22-7*) Cleveland St Univ Poetry Ctr.

Work of the Chronicler: Its Purpose & Its Date. A. C. Welch. (British Academy, London, Schweich Lectures on Biblical Archaeology Series, 1930). 1974. reprint ed. pap. 25.00 (*0-8115-1280-0*) Periodicals Srv.

Work of the Church: Getting the Job Done in Boards & Committees. David R. Sawyer. 128p. 1987. pap. 9.00 (*0-8170-1116-1*) Judson.

Work of the Church Treasurer. rev. ed. Thomas E. McLeod. LC 92-23564. 64p. 1992. pap. 11.00 (*0-8170-1189-7*) Judson.

Work of the Church Trustee. Orlando L. Tibbetts. 1979. pap. 8.50 (*0-8170-0825-X*) Judson.

***Work of the Clerk.** 2nd rev. ed. M. Ingrid Dvirnak. 64p. (Orig.). 1996. pap. 6.00 (*0-8170-1253-2*) Judson.

Work of the Deacon & Deaconess. Harold Nichols. (Orig.). 1964. pap. 9.00 (*0-8170-0328-2*) Judson.

Work of the Dividend Department. Salvatore Alfano. (Illus.). 208p. 1987. 29.95 (*0-13-965096-2*) NY Inst Finance.

***Work of the Holy Spirit.** Abraham Kuyper. (Bible Study Ser.: Pulpit Legends Collections). 688p. 19.99 (*0-89957-211-1*) AMG Pubs.

Work of the Holy Spirit. Jessie Penn-Lewis. 58p. Date not set. pap. text ed. 3.95 (*0-87508-961-5*) Chr Lit.

Work of the Holy Spirit. Octavius Winslow. 223p. 1991. pap. 7.99 (*0-85151-152-X*) Banner of Truth.

Work of the International Labor Organization. National Industrial Conference Board, Inc. Staff. 1983. reprint ed. lib. bdg. 40.00 (*0-89941-211-4*, 303010) W S Hein.

***Work of the International Law Commission.** 511p. Date not set. pap. 45.00 (*92-1-133485-3*, JX3091) UN.

Work of the International Law Commission. 4th ed. 402p. 1995. 35.00 (*92-1-133303-2*) UN.

Work of the Interstate Commerce Commission. H. T. Newcomb. Ed. by Stuart Bruchey. LC 80-1334. (Railroads Ser.). (Illus.). 1981. reprint ed. lib. bdg. 15.95 (*0-405-13808-3*) Ayer.

Work of the Kabbalist. Z'ev Ben Shimon Halevi. LC 85-51910. (Illus.). 224p. (Orig.). 1985. pap. 12.50 (*0-87728-637-X*) Weiser.

Work of the Pastoral Relations Committee. Emmett V. Johnson. 128p. 1983. pap. 10.00 (*0-8170-0984-1*) Judson.

Work of the Sea, Rivers & Ice. R. Kay Gresswell & G. R. Lawrence. 120p. 1978. pap. 11.95 (*0-7175-0791-2*) Dufour.

Work of the Sea, Rivers & Ice. R. Kay Gresswell. Ed. by G. R. Lawrence. (Illus.). 120p. (C). 1978. 39.00 (*0-685-33834-7*, Pub. by S Thornes Pubs UK) St Mut.

Work of the Soul: Past Life Recall & Spiritual Enlightenment. Pamela Blosser & Paul Blosser. Ed. by Barbara Condron. 208p. (Orig.). 1996. pap. 13.00 (*0-944386-17-2*) SOM Pub.

Work of the Stock Exchange (Revised Edition) James E. Meeker. LC 75-2649. (Wall Street & the Security Market Ser.). (Illus.). 1975. reprint ed. 64.95 (*0-405-06974-X*) Ayer.

Work of the Sunday School Superintendent. rev. ed. Idris W. Jones. LC 94-3591. 1994. pap. 9.00 (*0-8170-1229-X*) Judson.

Work of the Usher. Alvin D. Johnson. (Orig.). 1966. pap. 6.50 (*0-8170-0356-8*) Judson.

Work of the Wrench. Charles E. Eaton. LC 84-45452. 112p. 1985. 13.95 (*0-8453-4794-2*, Cornwall Bks) Assoc Univ Prs.

Work of Their Hands: Mennonite Women's Societies in Canada. Gloria N. Redekop. (Studies in Women & Religion: Vol. 2). xvi, 172p. 1996. pap. 24.95 (*0-88920-270-2*) Wilfrid Laurier.

Work of This Moment. Toni Packer. 128p. (Orig.). 1995. pap. 12.95 (*0-8048-3062-2*) C E Tuttle.

Work of Thomas W. Nason, N. A. (Illus.). 1976. 65.00 (*0-89073-012-1*) Boston Public Lib.

Work of Wall Street: An Account of the Functions, Methods & History of the New York Money & Stock Markets. (Third Edition, Revised & Enlarged) Sereno S. Pratt. LC 75-2661. (Wall Street & the Security Market Ser.). 1975. reprint ed. 41.95 (*0-405-06985-5*) Ayer.

***Work of WHO in the European Region, 1987: Annual Report of the Regional Director.** 1988. pap. text ed. 12.00 (*92-890-1055-X*) World Health.

***Work of WHO in the European Region, 1988: Annual Report of the Regional Director.** 1989. pap. text ed. 12.00 (*92-890-1058-4*) World Health.

Work of WHO Virus Reference Centres & the Services They Provide. 120p. (ENG, FRE & RUS.). 1968. pap. text ed. 12.00 (*92-4-156035-5*, 1150161) World Health.

***Work of WHO 1978-1979: Biennial Report of the Director-General.** WHO Staff. 278p. 1980. 18.00 (*92-4-156063-0*) World Health.

***Work of WHO 1982-1983: Biennial Report of the Director-General.** WHO Staff. 305p. 1984. 25.00 (*92-4-156081-9*) World Health.

Work of WHO, 1984-1985: Biennial Report of the Director-General to the World Health Assembly & to the United Nations. 284p. 1986. pap. text ed. 45.00 (*92-4-156092-4*, 1248485) World Health.

***Work of WHO 1990-1991: Biennial Report of the Director-General to the World Health Assembly & to the United Nations.** WHO Staff. 195p. 1992. 45.00 (*92-4-156149-1*) World Health.

Work of WHO, 1992-1993: Biennial Report of the Director-General to the World Health Assembly & to the United Nations. WHO Staff. 182p. 1994. pap. text ed. 45.00 (*92-4-156165-3*, 1249293) World Health.

Work of William Eastlake: An Annotated Bibliography & Guide. W. C. Bamberger. Ed. by Boden Clarke & Daryl F. Mallett. LC 93-340. (Bibliographies of Modern Authors Ser.: No. 21). 104p. 1994. pap. 17.00 (*0-89370-498-9*); lib. bdg. 27.00 (*0-89370-398-2*) Borgo Pr.

Work of William F. Nolan: An Annotated Bibliography & Guide. 2nd ed. Boden Clarke & James Hopkins. 250p. pap. write for info. (*0-8095-1518-0*) Borgo Pr.

W

Work of William F. Nolan: An Annotated Bibliography & Guide. 2nd ed. Boden Clarke & James Hopkins. LC 95-2762. (Bibliographies of Modern Authors Ser.: No. 14). 250p. 1996. lib. bdg. write for info. (*0-8095-0518-5*) Borgo Pr.

Work of William F. Temple: An Annotated Bibliography & Guide. Mike Ashley. Ed. by Boden Clarke. LC 93-334. (Bibliographies of Modern Authors Ser.: No. 28). 112p. 1994. pap. 17.00 (*0-8095-1507-5*); lib. bdg. 27.00 (*0-8095-0507-X*) Borgo Pr.

Work of William Lawrence Bottomley in Richmond. William B. O'Neal & Christopher Weeks. LC 84-20800. (Illus.). 286p. 1985. reprint ed. pap. 81.60 (*0-7837-9230-1*, 2049981) Bks Demand.

Work of William Morris. Paul Thompson. 7.95 (*0-7043-3118-7*, Pub. by Quartet UK) Charles River Bks.

Work of William Morris. 3rd ed. Paul Thompson. (Illus.). 336p. 1993. reprint ed. pap. 21.00 (*0-19-283149-6*) OUP.

***Work of Women Composers from 1150 to 1995.** Mary Booker. 1995. 59.95 (*0-7223-2975-X*, Pub. by A H S Ltd UK) St Mut.

***Work of Words: The Writing of Susanna Strickland Moodie.** John Thurston. 264p. 1996. 55.00 (*0-7735-1287-X*, Pub. by McGill CN) U of Toronto Pr.

Work of Work: Servitude, Slavery & Labor in Medieval England. Ed. by Allen J. Frantzen & Douglas Moffat. 240p. (C). 1994. 53.00 (*1-873448-03-1*, Pub. by Cruithne Pr UK) Boydell & Brewer.

***Work of Writing: Literature & Social Change in Britain, 1700-1830.** Clifford Siskin. LC 97-20656. 1998. write for info. (*0-8018-5696-5*) Johns Hopkins.

Work on Myth. Hans Blumenberg. (Studies in Contemporary German Social Thought). 304p. 1988. reprint ed. pap. 22.00 (*0-262-52133-4*) MIT Pr.

Work on the Superego. A. H. Almaas. Ed. by Sandra Maitri. 20p. 1992. 4.00 (*0-936713-07-0*) Diamond Bks CA.

Work or Labor: Original Anthology. Ed. by Leon Stein. LC 77-70551. (Illus.). 1977. lib. bdg. 41.95 (*0-405-10205-4*) Ayer.

Work Organisations: A Critical Introduction. Paul Thompson & David McHugh. 416p. (C). 1990. text ed. 44.00 (*0-8147-8192-6*) NYU Pr.

Work Organisations: Resistance & Control. Graeme Salaman. LC 78-40873. 238p. reprint ed. pap. 67.90 (*0-317-27873-8*, 2025260) Bks Demand.

Work Organization: A Study of Manual Work & Mass Production. Ray Wild. LC 74-13085. 234p. reprint ed. pap. 66.70 (*0-685-20669-6*, 2030457) Bks Demand.

Work Organization, High Skills & Public Policy: Report of a Conference. 36p. 1993. pap. 10.00 (*1-887410-56-2*) Jobs for Future.

Work, Organizations & Change. 2nd ed. Stan Aungles & Stan Parker. 240p. 1993. pap. text ed. 22.95 (*1-86373-338-8*, Pub. by Allen Unwin AT) Paul & Co Pubs.

Work, Organizations, & Society: Comparative Convergences. Ed. by Merlin B. Brinkerhoff. LC 84-6676. (Contributions in Sociology Ser.: No. 53). (Illus.). vii, 200p. 1984. text ed. 49.95 (*0-313-23704-2*, BWO/, Greenwood Pr) Greenwood.

Work Orientation & Job Performance: The Cultural Basis of Teaching Rewards & Incentives. Douglas E. Mitchell et al. LC 87-1905. (SUNY Series, Educational Leadership). 245p. 1987. text ed. 64.50 (*0-88706-567-8*); pap. text ed. 21.95 (*0-88706-568-6*) State U NY Pr.

Work Papers - Advanced Accounting. 5th ed. Arnold J. Pahler. (C). 1994. 29.00 (*0-03-003599-6*) HB Coll Pubs.

Work Papers - Intermediate Accounting. 5th ed. Williams et al. 879p. (C). 1995. 29.00 (*0-03-007392-8*) HB Coll Pubs.

Work Paradigm. Paul Ransome. 224p. 1996. 59.95 (*1-85972-183-4*, Pub. by Avebury Pub UK) Ashgate Pub Co.

Work Patterns & Capital Utilization: An International Comparative Study. Ed. by Dominique Anxo et al. LC 94-39862. 1995. lib. bdg. 125.00 (*0-7923-3263-6*) Kluwer Ac.

Work Permit Handbook for California Public Schools. California Department of Education Staff. 78p. 1991. pap. 8.25 (*0-8011-0989-2*) Calif Education.

W

Work-Place: The Social Regulation of Labor Markets. Jamie Peck. (Perspectives on Economic Change Ser.). 320p. 1996. pap. text ed. 17.95 (*1-57230-044-2*); lib. bdg. 42.50 (*1-57230-043-4*) Guilford Pr.

Work Places: Psychology of the Physical Environment in Offices & Factories. Eric Sundstrom. (Environment & Behavior Ser.). 464p. 1986. pap. 29.95 (*0-521-31947-1*) Cambridge U Pr.

Work Plan for the Development of Archeological Overviews & Management Plans for Selected U. S. Department of the Army DARCOM Facilities, No. 1. Ruthann Knudson et al. (Illus.). 108p. 1983. reprint ed. pap. text ed. 9.65 (*1-55567-424-0*) Coyote Press.

Work, Play, & Type: Achieving Balance in Your Life. Judith A. Provost. 128p. 1990. pap. 11.95 (*0-89106-040-5*, 7484) Davies-Black.

Work, Power, & Efficiency. Alois Koller. (Siemens Programmed Instruction Ser.: No. 11). 66p. reprint ed. pap. 25.00 (*0-317-27759-6*, 2052088) Bks Demand.

***Work Practice: International Perspectives.** Joanne Pratt & Karen Jacobs. LC 97-5624. 1997. write for info. (*0-7506-2260-1*) Buttrwrth-Heinemann.

Work Practices Guide for Manual Lifting. 1995. lib. bdg. 251.99 (*0-8490-7525-4*) Gordon Pr.

Work Preparation for the Handicapped. David Hutchinson. (Illus.). 128p. (C). 1982. pap. 19.50 (*0-7099-0283-2*, Pub. by Croom Helm UK) Routledge Chapman & Hall.

Work, Productivity, & Human Performance: Practical Case Studies in Ergonomics, Human Factors, & Human Engineering. T. M. Fraser & P. J. Pityn. LC 94-6168. (Illus.). 194p. 1994. pap. 33.95 (*0-398-06131-9*) C C Thomas.

Work, Productivity, & Human Performance: Practical Case Studies in Ergonomics, Human Factors, & Human Engineering. T. M. Fraser & P. J. Pityn. LC 94-6168. (Illus.). 194p. (C). 1994. text ed. 46.95 (*0-398-05910-1*) C C Thomas.

Work Projects. David P. Weikart et al. (Program Guidebook Ser.). 52p. 1994. pap. 10.95 (*0-929816-85-4*) High-Scope.

Work Psychology: Understanding Human Behaviour in the Workplace. 2nd ed. John Arnold et al. 416p. (Orig.). 1995. pap. 57.50 (*0-273-60324-8*, Pub. by Pitman Pub Ltd UK) Trans-Atl Phila.

Work Psychology & Organizational Behaviour: The Management of the Individual at Work. Wendy Hollway. 240p. (C). 1991. text ed. 55.00 (*0-8039-8353-0*); pap. text ed. 19.95 (*0-8039-8354-9*) Sage.

Work, Recreation, & Culture: Essays in American Labor History. Ed. by Martin H. Blatt & Martha K. Norkunas. LC 95-46207. (Labor in America Ser.: Vol. 02). 288p. 1996. text ed. 50.00 (*0-8153-1650-X*, SS955) Garland.

Work Redesign. J. Richard Hackman & Greg R. Oldham. LC 79-8918. (C). 1980. pap. text ed. 26.95 (*0-201-02779-8*) Addison-Wesley.

Work Redesign Team Handbook: A Step-by-Step Guide to Creating Self-Directed Teams. Darcy Hitchcock. LC 94-8914. 102p. 1994. pap. text ed. 28.00 (*0-527-76243-1*) Qual Resc.

Work-Related Injuries in the U. S. Trucking Industry: A Multi-Billion Dollar Problem. (Illus.). 1994. pap. 175.00 (*0-88711-199-8*) Am Trucking Assns.

Work Related Lung Disease. 1995. lib. bdg. 254.95 (*0-8490-7524-6*) Gordon Pr.

***Work-Related Lung Disease Surveillance Report (1996)** 4th ed. Ed. by Rochelle B. Althouse. (Illus.). 482p. (C). 1997. pap. text ed. 50.00 (*0-7881-3742-5*) DIANE Pub.

***Work-Related Lung Disease Surveillance Report (1994)** Rochelle B. Althouse. (Illus.). 149p. (C). 1997. reprint ed. pap. text ed. 40.00 (*0-7881-3336-5*) DIANE Pub.

Work-Related Musculoskeletal Disorders (WMSDs) A Reference for Prevention. B. Silverstein. 314p. 1994. 85.00 (*0-7484-0131-8*) Taylor & Francis.

Work-Related Musculoskeletal Disorders (WMSDs) A Reference for Prevention. B. Silverstein. 421p. 1994. pap. 37.50 (*0-7484-0132-6*) Taylor & Francis.

Work-Related Programs in Occupational Therapy. Ed. by Florence S. Cromwell. LC 85-17690. (Occupational Therapy in Health Care Ser.: Vol. 2, No. 4). 125p. 1985. 39.95 (*0-86656-487-X*); pap. text ed. 14.95 (*0-86656-519-1*) Haworth Pr.

***Work-Related Upper Limb Disorders: Recognition & Management.** M. A. Hutson. LC 97-5522. 1997. write for info. (*0-7506-2719-0*) Buttrwrth-Heinemann.

Work Relief to Rehabilitation. Harold E. Simmons. (Orig.). 1969. pap. 12.00 (*0-87312-002-7*) Gen Welfare Pubns.

Work, Retirement & Social Policy, Vol. 1. Ed. by Zena S. Blau. (Current Perspectives on Aging & the Life Cycle Ser.). 366p. 1986. 73.25 (*0-89232-296-9*) Jai Pr.

Work Scheduling. (General Aptitude & Abilities Ser.: No. CS-48). 1994. pap. 23.95 (*0-8373-6748-4*) Nat Learn.

Work, Self, & Society: After Industrialism. Catherine Casey. LC 94-44972. 256p. (C). (gr. 13). 1995. text ed. 62.95 (*0-415-11202-8*) Routledge.

Work, Self, & Society: After Industrialism in Asia. Catherine Casey. 256p. (C). 1995. pap. 17.95 (*0-415-11203-6*, Routledge NY) Routledge.

***Work, Self-Discipline, Friendship.** Shelagh Canning. (Illus.). 1997. pap. 3.25 (*0-614-27576-8*) S&S Childrens.

***Work, Sex & Rugby.** Lewis Davies. 174p. 1993. pap. 9.95 (*0-9521558-0-X*) Dufour.

Work Sharing: An Alternative to Layoffs. rev. ed. New Ways to Work Staff & Julie Batz. 24p. (Orig.). 1991. pap. text ed. 12.00 (*0-940173-25-5*) New Ways Work.

Work Sharing: Issues, Policy Options & Prospects. Fred Best. LC 81-7567. 204p. 1981. text ed. 14.00 (*0-911558-79-9*); pap. text ed. 8.00 (*0-911558-80-2*) W E Upjohn.

Work Sharing Case Studies. Maureen E. McCarthy & Gail S. Rosenberg. LC 81-15943. 277p. 1981. pap. 14.00 (*0-911558-88-8*) W E Upjohn.

Work Simplification: An Analyst's Handbook. Pierre Theriault. LC 96-19351. 200p. 1996. 25.00 (*0-89806-163-6*, THERIA) Eng Mgmt Pr.

Work Simplification in Danish Public Libraries: The Report of the Work Simplification Committee of the Danish Library Association. Henning Gimbel. LC 69-15862. (American Library Associaton- Library Technology Program Publication Ser.: No. 15). 289p. reprint ed. pap. 82.40 (*0-317-26345-5*, 2024227) Bks Demand.

Work Simplification in Food Service: Individualized Instruction. Lynne N. Ross. LC 73-171164. 134p. (Orig.). reprint ed. pap. 38.20 (*0-317-27203-9*, 2023865) Bks Demand.

Work, Sister, Work: How Black Women Can Get Ahead in the Workplace. 192p. 1993. 16.95 (*1-55972-147-2*, Birch Ln Pr) Carol Pub Group.

Work, Sister, Work: How Black Women Can Get Ahead in Today's Business Environment. Cydney Shields & Leslie C. Shields. LC 93-20642. 304p. 1994. reprint ed. pap. 10.00 (*0-671-87305-9*, Fireside) S&S Trade.

Work Site Health Programmes: Psychosocial Research & Models for Health Promotion. B. Oldenburg & O. Neville. (Work, Well Being & Stress Ser.). 200p. 1996. text ed. 80.00 (*0-471-95801-8*, SI75) Wiley.

Work Situations Temperaments Checklist: Package of 30. Appalachia Educational Laboratory Staff. (Illus.). 6p. (YA). (gr. 9 up). 1990. pap. text ed. 14.00 (*1-877844-54-3*, 3216) Meridian Educ.

Work Skills, Connections: School & Work Transitions, Set. 1987. 55.00 (*0-317-03923-7*, SP100CX) Ctr Educ Trng Employ.

Work Skills Instructor Guide, Connections: School & Work Transitions. National Center for Research in Vocational Education Staff. 1987. 4.75 (*0-317-03924-5*, SP100CA02) Ctr Educ Trng Employ.

Work Skills Modules, Connections: School & Work Transitions - Work Skills, 13 modules, Set. National Center for Research in Vocational Education Staff. 1987. 39.00 (*0-317-03925-3*, SP100CA03) Ctr Educ Trng Employ.

Work Skills Resource Manual, Connections: School & Work Transitions - Work Skills. National Center for Research in Vocational Education Staff. 1987. 29.95 (*0-317-03926-1*, SP100CA01) Ctr Educ Trng Employ.

Work Smart, Not Hard. George Sullivan. LC 86-24320. 208p. reprint ed. pap. 59.30 (*0-7837-1358-4*, 2041506) Bks Demand.

Work Smarter, Not Harder: The Service That Sells Waitstaff Workbook. Jim Sullivan & Phil Roberts. (Illus.). 120p. (Orig.). 1994. pap. 9.95 (*1-879239-01-9*) Pencom.

Work Smarter, Not Harder, the Service That Sells Workbook for Family Dining Operations. Jim Sullivan & Phil Roberts. (Illus.). 128p. 1995. pap. 9.95 (*1-879239-04-3*) Pencom.

Work, Society & Culture. rev. ed. Yves R. Simon. LC 76-129551. xvi, 192p. 1986. pap. 12.50 (*0-8232-0917-2*) Fordham.

Work, Society & Politics: The Culture of the Factory in Late Victorian England. Patrick Joyce. 382p. 1992. 59.95 (*0-7512-0008-5*, Pub. by Gregg Revivals UK) Ashgate Pub Co.

Work, Society, & Politics: The Culture of the Factory in Later Victorian England. Patrick Joyce. 1980. pap. 16.00 (*0-8135-1083-X*) Rutgers U Pr.

***Work, Society, & Politics: The Culture of the Factory in Later Victorian England.** Patrick Joyce. 1980. pap. 16.00 (*0-8135-0183-0*) Rutgers U Pr.

Work, Society, & Politics: The Culture of the Factory in Later Victorian England. Patrick Joyce. LC 79-93087. 383p. reprint ed. pap. 109.20 (*0-7837-5673-9*, 2059100) Bks Demand.

Work Songs. Compiled by Jerry Silverman. (Traditional Black Music Ser.). (Illus.). 80p. (YA). (gr. 5 up). 1994. lib. bdg. 18.95 (*0-7910-1841-5*) Chelsea Hse.

Work Songs. Compiled by Jerry Silverman. (Traditional Black Music Ser.). (Illus.). 80p. (YA). (gr. 5 up). 1994. pap. 9.95 (*0-7910-1857-1*) Chelsea Hse.

Work Stress: Health Care Systems in the Workplace. Ed. by James C. Quick et al. LC 86-30636. 346p. 1987. text ed. 59.95 (*0-275-92329-0*, C2329, Praeger Pubs) Greenwood.

Work, Stress, Disease & Life Expectancy. Ben Fletcher. LC 91-166. (Series on Studies in Occupational Stress). 255p. 1991. text ed. 130.00 (*0-471-91970-5*) Wiley.

Work, Study, Travel Abroad, 1988-1989. 9th ed. Council on International Educational Exchange Staff. 416p. 1987. pap. 8.95 (*0-312-01539-9*) St Martin.

Work, Study, Travel Abroad, 1990-1991: The Whole World Handbook. 10th ed. Council on International Educational Exchange Staff. (Illus.). 496p. 1990. pap. 10.95 (*0-312-03979-4*) St Martin.

Work, Study, Travel Abroad, 1994-1995: The Whole World Handbook. 12th ed. Council on International Educational Exchange Staff. Ed. by Lazaro Hernandez & Max Terry. (Illus.). 600p. (Orig.). (C). 1994. pap. 13.95 (*0-312-10578-9*) St Martin.

Work Sucks: A Hilarious Guide to Choosing or Changing Your Career. Bob Glickman. Ed. by Cliff Carle. 1992. pap. 5.95 (*0-918259-42-8*) CCC Pubns.

Work Teams & Team Building. Robert H. Guest. (Studies in Productivity: Highlights of the Literature Ser.: Vol. 44). 54p. 1986. pap. 55.00 (*0-08-034240-X*) Work in Amer.

Work Teams That Work: Skills for Managing Across the Organization. Anthony R. Montebello. 1994. 24.95 (*0-9636268-1-7*) Best Sell Pub.

Work, Technology, & Education: Dissenting Essays in the Intellectual Foundations of American Education. Ed. by Walter Feinberg & Henry Rosemont, Jr. LC 75-4854. 222p. 1975. pap. text ed. 12.50 (*0-252-00649-6*) U of Ill Pr.

Work Therapy. Daniel Grippo. LC 95-75533. 80p. 1995. pap. 4.95 (*0-87029-276-5*) Abbey.

***Work This Way: Designing Your Career in the Changing Workplace.** Bruce Tulgan. 256p. 1998. pap. 14.95 (*0-7868-8254-9*) Hyperion.

Work Throughout History Series, 15 vols., Set. Irene M. Franck & David M. Brownstone. 1989. 185.00 (*0-8160-2119-8*) Facts on File.

Work Time: English Departments & the Circulation of Cultural Value. Evan Watkins. LC 89-31002. 304p. 1989. 42.50 (*0-8047-1691-9*); pap. 14.95 (*0-8047-2015-0*) Stanford U Pr.

Work Time-Family Time: Wisconsin's Family & Medical Leave Law. 50p. 1989. 20.00 (*0-932622-31-3*) Ctr Public Rep.

Work to Be Done. Alger E. Pitts. Ed. by Renais J. Hill. LC 92-52943. 90p. (Orig.). 1992. pap. 8.95 (*1-55666-079-0*) Pubs Grp Toluca.

Work Trap: Rediscovering Leisure, Redefining Work. Martin C. Helldorfer. LC 94-61852. 120p. 1995. pap. 9.95 (*0-89622-638-7*) Twenty-Third.

Work Trucks. Patricia Armentrout & David Armentrout. LC 95-3980. (Heavy Equipment Ser.). (J). (gr. 2-6). 1995. write for info. (*1-55916-132-9*) Rourke Bk Co.

Work Trucks. Andy Mayer & Jim Becker. LC 92-61194. (Look & Listen Board Books Ser.). (Illus.). 10p. (J). (ps). 1993. pap. 6.95 (*0-590-46299-7*, Cartwheel) Scholastic Inc.

Work Two Thousand: The Future for Industry, Employment & Safety. John Stanworth & Celia Stanworth. 272p. 1991. 29.95 (*1-85396-106-X*, Pub. by P Chapman Pub UK) Taylor & Francis.

***Work under Capitalism.** Chris Tilly & Charles Tilly. (New Perspectives in Sociology Ser.). (C). 1997. text ed. 60.00 (*0-8133-2278-2*); pap. text ed. 24.00 (*0-8133-2274-X*) Westview.

***Work Values: Organizational Building Blocks.** David Kolb et al. (Illus.). vi, 42p. 1996. wbk. ed., ring bd. write for info. (*1-57740-016-X*, ILW024) Intl LrningWrk.

***Work Values: Organizational Building Blocks.** Barbara Singer. (Illus.). 70p. 1996. pap. write for info. (*1-57740-017-8*, ILW041) Intl LrningWrk.

***Work Values: Organizational Building Blocks - Training Package.** David Kolb et al. (Illus.). 86p. 1996. ring bd. write for info. (*1-57740-015-1*, ILW023) Intl LrningWrk.

Work Values Facilitator Guide. Barbara Singer & Kathleen Von Buren. (Illus.). 108p. 1995. write for info. (*1-57740-008-9*, ILW010) Intl LrningWrk.

Work Values Inventory: MRC Machine-Scorable Test Booklets. Donald E. Super. (C). 56.94 (*0-395-09529-8*); 3.42 (*0-395-09530-1*); 1.62 (*0-395-09531-X*) HM.

Work, Wages, & Poverty: Income Distribution in Post-Industrial Philadelphia. Janice F. Madden & William J. Stull. LC 91-22426. 240p. (Orig.). (C). 1991. pap. text ed. 22.95 (*0-8122-1348-3*) U of Pa Pr.

Work, Wages & Welfare in a Developing Metropolis: Consequences Of Growth in Bogota, Colombia. Rakesh Mohan. (World Bank Publications). 400p. 1987. 29.95 (*0-19-520540-5*) OUP.

Work, Wealth & Happiness of Mankind, 2 Vols, Set. H. G. Wells. LC 69-10170. (Illus.). 1968. reprint ed. text ed. 75.00 (*0-8371-0263-4*, WEHM, Greenwood Pr) Greenwood.

Work, Welfare & Taxation: A Study of Labour Supply Incentives in the U. K. Michael Beenstock. 220p. (C). 1987. text ed. 55.00 (*0-04-331104-0*); pap. text ed. 18.95 (*0-04-331105-9*) Routledge Chapman & Hall.

***Work Well - Live well: Discovering a Biblical View of Work.** David Westcott. 256p. 1997. pap. 13.50 (*0-551-02971-4*, Pub. by Marshall Pickering) Harper SF.

Work-Wise: Learning about the World of Work from Books--Critical Guide to Book Selection & Usage. Diane Gersoni-Edelman. LC 79-11920. (Selection Guide Ser.: No. 3). 258p. 1980. 27.95 (*0-87436-264-4*) Neal-Schuman.

Work Wise: Tactics for Job Success. Edited. 1990. pap. 9.86 (*0-8092-4100-5*) Contemp Bks.

Work with a Dreaming Body. Arnold Mindell. 1989. pap. 10.95 (*0-14-019142-9*, Arkana) Viking Penguin.

Work with Display Units 86: Selected Papers from the International Conference, Stockholm, Sweden, May 12-15, 1986. Ed. by B. Knave & P. G. Wideback. 880p. 1987. 119.25 (*0-444-70171-0*, North Holland) Elsevier.

Work with Display Units 89: Selected Papers from the 2nd International Scientific Conference, Montreal, Quebec, Canada, 11-14 Sept., 1989. Ed. by L. Berlinguet & D. Berthelette. 588p. 1990. 182.50 (*0-444-88710-5*, North Holland) Elsevier.

Work with Display Units '92: Selected Proceedings of the Third International Scientific Conference on Work with Display Units, Berlin, Germany, September 1-4, 1992. Ed. by Holger Luczak et al. LC 93-19702. 566p. 1993. 159.25 (*0-444-89759-3*, North Holland) Elsevier.

Work with Display Units, '94: Selected Papers of the Fourth International Scientific Conference on Work with Display Units, Milan, Italy, 2-5 October, 1994. International Scientific Conference on Work with Display Units Staff. Ed. by Antonio Grieco et al. LC 95-32593. 530p. 1995. 157.50 (*0-444-82145-7*) Elsevier.

Work with Knowledge of Results *see* **Quantitative Aspects of the Evolution of Concepts**

Work with Me! How to Make of Office Support Staff. Betsy Lazary. 1990. pap. 9.95 (*0-942361-23-7*) MasterMedia Pub.

Work with Older People: Challenges & Opportunities. Ed. by Irene A. Gutheil. LC 93-22670. 176p. 1994. pap. 16.95 (*0-8232-1507-5*) Fordham.

Work with Passion: How to Do What You Love for a Living. Nancy Anderson. 224p. 1984. 15.95 (*0-88184-099-8*) Carroll & Graf.

Work with Passion: How to Do What You Love for a Living. Nancy Anderson. 310p. 1986. pap. 9.95 (*0-88184-212-5*) Carroll & Graf.

Work with Passion: How to Do What You Love for a Living. 2nd rev. ed. Nancy Anderson. LC 94-38599. 332p. 1995. pap. 12.95 (*1-880032-54-6*) New Wrld Lib.

***Work with Past, Vol. 1.** Bartholomae. Date not set. pap. text ed. write for info. (*0-312-13816-4*) St Martin.

***Work with Words.** 3rd ed. Brooks. Date not set. wbk. ed., pap. text ed. 28.35 (*0-312-10014-0*) St Martin.

Work Without End. Benjamin K. Hunnicutt. (Illus.). 416p. 1990. pap. 19.95 (*0-87722-763-2*) Temple U Pr.

Work Without End: Abandoning Shorter Hours for the Right to Work. Benjamin K. Hunnicutt. LC 87-13966. (Illus.). 352p. (C). 1988. 39.95 (*0-87722-520-6*) Temple U Pr.

Work Without Hope: Poems. John Burt. (Poetry & Fiction Ser.). 80p. (C). 1996. 16.95 (*0-8018-5371-0*) Johns Hopkins.

An Asterisk (*) at the beginning of an entry indicates that the title is appearing in BIP for the first time.

Work Without Salvation: America's Intellectual & Industrial Alienation, 1880-1910. James B. Gilbert. LC 74-2249. 256p. 1977. 34.00 (0-8018-1954-7) Johns Hopkins.

Work Without Wages: Comparative Studies of Domestic Labor & Self-Employment. Ed. by Jane L. Collins & Martha E. Gimenez. LC 88-37031. (SUNY Series on Women & Work). 264p. 1990. text ed. 65.50 (0-7914-0106-5); pap. text ed. 21.95 (0-7914-0107-3) State U NY Pr.

Work Won't Love You Back: The Dual Career Couple's Survival Guide. Stevan E. Hobfoll. 288p. 1996. text ed. write for info. (0-7167-2598-3); pap. text ed. write for info. (0-7167-2593-2) W H Freeman.

Work Worth Doing: Advances in Brain Injury Rehabilitation. Ed. by Brian T. McMahon & Linda R. Shaw. LC 91-71166. (Illus.). xxx, 412p. 1991. 49.95 (1-878205-19-6) GR Press.

Work Your Way Around the World. 8th rev. ed. 512p. 1997. pap. 17.95 (1-85458-162-7, Pub. by Vacation-Work UK) Petersons.

Work, Youth, & Schooling: Historical Perspectives on Vocationalism in American Education. Ed. by Harvey Kantor & David B. Tyack. LC 81-50788. 384p. 1982. 47.50 (0-8047-1121-6) Stanford U Pr.

Work-Zone Traffic Control & Tests of Delineation Material. (Transportation Research Record Ser.: No. 1230). 76p. 1989. 13.00 (0-309-04961-X) Transport Res Bd.

Workability & Quality Control of Concrete. G. H. Tattersall. (Illus.). 320p. 1991. 44.95 (0-419-14860-4, E & FN Spon) Routledge Chapman & Hall.

Workability of Concrete. G. H. Tattersall. (Illus.). 1976. pap. 30.00 (0-7210-1032-6, Pub. by C & CA UK) Scholium Intl.

Workable Competition in the Radio Broadcasting Industry. Peter O. Steiner. Ed. by Christopher H. Sterling. LC 78-21741. (Dissertations in Broadcasting Ser.). (Illus.). 1980. lib. bdg. 35.95 (0-405-11777-9) Ayer.

Workable Plan for Sensible Government. Frank W. McKay. 116p. (Orig.). 1984. pap. 2.95 (0-930333-00-4) Switz Pr.

Workable Workplace: Excellence at Work for You. Melvin J. LeBaron. LC 87-83597. 200p. (C). 1988. text ed. 18.95 (0-944329-01-2) KOBO Ent.

***Workaholics: The Respectable Addicts.** 2nd ed. Barbara Killinger. (Illus.). 236p. 1997. pap. 14.95 (1-55209-134-1) Firefly Bks Ltd.

Workbased Stress: Prescription Is Not the Cure. Dave Pottage & Mike Evans. 1992. pap. 30.00 (0-902789-79-1, Pub. by Natl Inst Soc Work) St Mut.

Workbased Stress: Prescription Is Not the Cure. Dave Pottage & Mike Evans. (C). 1992. 50.00 (0-7855-0070-7, Pub. by Natl Inst Soc Work) St Mut.

Workbench Book. Scott Landis. LC 86-51321. (Illus.). 256p. 1987. 34.95 (0-918804-76-0) Taunton.

Workbench Guide to Electronic Projects You Can Build in Your Spare Time. Carl G. Grolle & Michael B. Girosky. LC 81-2169. 256p. 1981. 17.95 (0-13-965269-8, Parker Publishing Co) P-H.

Workbench Guide to Electronic Troubleshooting. Robert C. Genn, Jr. 216p. 1977. 17.95 (0-685-05871-9) P-H.

Workbench Treasury of Coffee, Tea & Serving Table Projects. Workbench Magazine Staff. LC 81-80204. (Illus.). 56p. (Orig.). 1981. pap. 4.95 (0-86675-002-9, 29) KC Pub.

Workbench Treasury of Decks, Patios, Gazebos & More. Workbench Magazine Staff. LC 83-17250. (Illus.). 56p. (Orig.). 1984. pap. 4.95 (0-86675-009-6, 96) KC Pub.

Workbench Treasury of Shelves, Racks, & Built-Ins. Workbench Magazine Staff. LC 82-60699. (Illus.). 56p. (Orig.). 1982. pap. 4.95 (0-86675-005-3, 53) KC Pub.

Workbench Treasury of Wooden Toy Projects. Workbench Magazine Staff. LC 81-83667. (Illus.). 56p. 1982. pap. 4.95 (0-86675-003-7, 37) KC Pub.

Workboat Engineer, 2 vols., Bk. 1. rev. ed. Robert J. Ward. Ed. by Richard A. Block. (Illus.). 564p. 1993. pap. 52.00 (1-879778-15-7, BK-107-1) Marine Educ.

Workboat Engineer, Book 2, 2 vols. rev. ed. Robert J. Ward. Ed. by Richard A. Block. (Illus.). 558p. (Orig.). 1993. pap. 52.00 (1-879778-16-5, BK-107) Marine Educ.

Workboat Engineers Tally Book. Glenn L. Pigot & Richard A. Block. 95p. (Orig.). 1985. pap. text ed. 5.00 (0-934114-62-5, BK-496) Marine Educ.

***Workboats of Smith Island.** Paula J. Johnson. LC 96-32866. (Illus.). 112p. 1997. 29.95 (0-8018-5484-9) Johns Hopkins.

Workbook. Michael Farr. 1984. pap. 11.95 (0-02-669610-X) Macmillan.

***Workbook, 4 vols., No. 19.** 1997. 105.00 (1-887528-14-8) Scott & Daughters.

Workbook: A Self-Study Guide for Job-Seekers with Epilepsy. Epilepsy Foundation of America Staff. 64p. 1991. pap. 9.95 (0-916570-00-2) Epilepsy Foundation of America.

Workbook: An Introduction to the Meridians & Points of Acupuncture. Alex Holland & James Blair. (Illus.). 202p. (Orig.). (C). 1988. 20.00 (0-9622665-1-5) A Holland.

***Workbook No. 19, East.** 1997. 28.00 (1-887528-19-9) Scott & Daughters.

***Workbook No. 19, South.** 1997. 28.00 (1-887528-22-9) Scott & Daughters.

***Workbook No. 19: Illustration Portfolio.** 1997. 65.00 (1-887528-16-4) Scott & Daughters.

***Workbook No. 19: Illustration Set.** 1997. 80.00 (1-887528-18-0) Scott & Daughters.

***Workbook No. 19: Photo Portfolio.** 1997. 70.00 (1-887528-15-6) Scott & Daughters.

***Workbook No. 19: Photography Set.** 1997. 85.00 (1-887528-17-2) Scott & Daughters.

***Workbook No. 19: Regional Directories, Midwest.** 1997. 28.00 (1-887528-21-0) Scott & Daughters.

***Workbook No. 19: Regional Directories, West.** 1997. 28.00 (1-887528-20-2) Scott & Daughters.

Workbook - Math 1: Basic Skills, Grade 1-2. Catherine C. Kiaie. (Illus.). 32p. (J). (ps-3). 1984. pap. 2.19 (0-307-23541-6, Golden Pr) Western Pub.

Workbook & Exercises for Introduction to Computer Information Systems. Paul G. Duchow & Spike Meyers. 80p. (C). 1995. per. 15.56 (0-8403-9492-6) Kendall-Hunt.

Workbook & Guide for Commitment: Key to Christian Maturity. Des. by Susan A. Muto et al. 1990. 14.95 (0-8091-3189-7) Paulist Pr.

Workbook & Manual Introduction to Horticulture. 3rd ed. T. Richard Fisher. 1982. pap. text ed. 13.95 (0-89917-366-7) Tichenor Pub.

Workbook & Personal Journal for Parents. Peter H. Buntman & Eleanor M. Saris. 30p. (Orig.). 1990. pap. 9.95 (0-9623986-1-6) Ctr FLE Inc.

Workbook by Kellom Tomlinson: Commonplace Book of an 18th-Century English Dancing Master. fac. ed. Kellom Tomlinson. Ed. by Jennifer Shennan. LC 92-2787. (Dance & Music Ser.: No. 6). 120p. 1992. lib. bdg. 36.00 (0-945193-31-9) Pendragon NY.

Workbook Challenges. Brown. 1993. pap. text ed. 6.95 (0-13-009093-X) P-H.

***Workbook Dyslexia.** Spafford & Grosser. 1997. pap. text ed. 25.95 (0-205-27551-6) P-H.

Workbook English Writing & Skill 1988: Grade 10. Foss. 1988. 19.00 (0-03-014657-7) HR&W Schl Div.

Workbook English Writing & Skills. Carrico. 1988. wbk. ed., text ed. 14.75 (0-03-014648-8) HR&W Schl Div.

Workbook English Writing & Skills: Grade 10. Foss. 1988. text ed. 14.75 (0-03-014654-2) HR&W Schl Div.

Workbook English Writing & Skills 1988. Scholin. 1988. 19.00 (0-03-014642-9) HR&W Schl Div.

Workbook English Writing 1988: Grades 7. Foss. 1988. 19.00 (0-03-014638-0) HR&W Schl Div.

Workbook Exercises in Alphabetic Filing. 3rd rev. ed. R. J. Stewart et al. 48p. 1980. pap. text ed. 7.96 (0-07-061451-2) McGraw.

Workbook for Action Teams. Paul W. Larson. (Illus.). 102p. (Orig.). 1996. pap. text ed. 24.50 (1-888355-08-5) Renaiss Busn.

Workbook for Affective Legal Research. 5th ed. Price. 1979. 9.95 (0-316-71855-6) Little.

Workbook for Airline Pilots. J. Deborah Balter. 195p. 1993. pap. text ed. write for info. (0-941456-20-X) Aviation Lang Sch.

Workbook for Algebra & Trigonometry: A Straightforward Approach. 2nd ed. (Illus.). 573p. 1985. wbk. ed. 19.95 (1-880157-48-9) Ardsley.

Workbook for American Civics 1987. Hartley. 1987. teacher ed., pap. text ed. 23.00 (0-15-371448-4) HR&W Schl Div.

Workbook for Aphasia: Exercises for the Redevelopment of Higher Level Language Functioning. rev. ed. Susan H. Brubaker. LC 85-91276. (William Beaumont Hospital Speech & Language Pathology Ser.). 376p. 1985. reprint ed. spiral bd. 33.00 (0-8143-1803-7) Wayne St U Pr.

Workbook for Archways Level 10: HBJ Reading 1987. Early. (J). 1987. student ed., pap. 14.75 (0-15-330570-3) HB Schl Dept.

Workbook for Archways Level 10: HBJ Reading 1987. Early. (J). 1987. teacher ed., pap. 22.50 (0-15-330585-1) HB Schl Dept.

Workbook for Astronomy. Jerry Waxman. LC 83-7526. 1984. 44.95 (0-521-25312-8) Cambridge U Pr.

Workbook for Career Choices: A Guide for Teens & Young Adults, Who Am I? What Do I Want? How Do I Get It? Mindy Bingham & Sandy Stryker. Ed. by Robert Shafer. (Illus.). 128p. 1990. pap. text ed. 6.95 (1-878787-03-9) Acad Innovat.

Workbook for Clinical Pharmacy & Therapeutics. 5th ed. Linda L. Hart. 296p. 1992. 1.00 (0-683-03936-9) Williams & Wilkins.

Workbook for Clinical Procedures for Medical Assisting. Anne L. Lilly & Mary A. Frew. LC 90-2929. (Illus.). 269p. 1990. Lilly & Frew wkbk. student ed., pap. 13.95 (0-8036-3852-3) Davis Co.

Workbook for Clinical Skills & Assisting Techniques. Sharron M. Zakus. 188p. 1994. pap. 15.95 (0-8016-7183-3) Mosby Yr Bk.

Workbook for Cognitive Skills: Exercises for Thought Processing & Word Retrieval. Susan H. Brubaker. LC 87-7352. (William Beaumont Hospital Speech & Language Pathology Ser.). 292p. 1987. spiral bd. 38.00 (0-8143-1903-3) Wayne St U Pr.

Workbook for Computers & Information Processing. 2nd ed. Clark. (DC -Introduction to Computing Ser.). 1990. wbk. ed., pap. 16.95 (0-538-60132-9) S-W Pub.

Workbook for Creative Problem Solving: The Basic Course. Scott G. Isaksen & Donald J. Treffinger. 28p. (Orig.). 1985. pap. 6.50 (0-943456-11-8) Bearly Ltd.

Workbook for Demotic Greek I: Providing Supplementary Exercises in Writing & Spelling, Complementing the Oral-Aural Emphasis of the Text. Peter Bien et al. (Illus.). 104p. 1973. pap. text ed. 12.00 (0-87451-090-2) U Pr of New Eng.

Workbook for Demotic Greek II: The Flying Telephone Booth. Peter Bien et al. LC 81-51609. (Illus.). 239p. 1983. wbk. ed., pap. text ed. 18.00 (0-87451-209-3) U Pr of New Eng.

Workbook for Elements of English Grammar. Marianne Ratti. 172p. 1991. 18.95 (0-931541-40-9) Mancorp Pub.

Workbook for Emergency Care. 2nd ed. Al Weigel & Nixon. 1983. pap. text ed. 20.00 (0-8359-1677-4, Reston) P-H.

Workbook for Emergency Care in the Streets. 3rd ed. James C. McClintock & Nancy L. Caroline. 1987. 17.50 (0-316-55437-5) Little.

Workbook for Engineering Graphics & Design. Kenneth Stibolt. 240p. (C). 1997. write for info. (0-314-07227-6) West Pub.

Workbook for Essentials of Maternity Nursing. Patricia S. Juneau. (Illus.). 199p. 1985. student ed. 11.95 (0-8036-5157-0) Davis Co.

Workbook for Evaluation: A Systematic Approach. 3rd ed. Gary D. Sandefur et al. LC 85-18413. 92p. reprint ed. pap. 26.30 (0-8357-4852-9, 2037783) Bks Demand.

Workbook for Firefighter's Handbook on Wildland Firefighting. William C. Teie. Ed. by Barbara Hubert. (Illus.). 168p. (Orig.). (C). 1995. pap. text ed. 14.95 (0-9640709-2-8) Deer Valley.

Workbook for General Chemistry. Bassam Z. Shakhashiri & Rodney Schreiner. 503p. (Orig.). 1996. pap. text ed. 26.80 (0-87563-652-7) Stipes.

Workbook for Hair Structure & Chemistry. Jacob J. Yahm. 240p. 1992. pap. 20.25 (0-87350-053-9) Milady Pub.

Workbook for Hair Structure & Chemistry: Teacher's Edition. 240p. 1987. pap. 26.95 (0-87350-136-5) Milady Pub.

Workbook for HBJ General Mathematics 1987. Gerardi. 1987. student ed., pap. 15.75 (0-15-353592-X); teacher ed., pap. 15.75 (0-15-353593-8) HB Schl Dept.

Workbook for HBJ Introduction to Algebra 1 '88. Jacobs. 1988. student ed., pap. text ed. 12.00 (0-15-357855-6) HR&W Schl Div.

Workbook for HBJ Introduction to Algebra 1 '88. Jacobs. 1988. teacher ed., pap. text ed. 17.25 (0-15-357857-2) HR&W Schl Div.

Workbook for HBJ Introduction to Algebra 2 '88. Jacobs. 1988. student ed., pap. text ed. 12.00 (0-15-357856-4) HR&W Schl Div.

Workbook for HBJ Introduction to Algebra '88. Jacobs. 1988. teacher ed., pap. text ed. 17.25 (0-15-357858-0) HR&W Schl Div.

Workbook for HBJ Readers 1987 Level 1-3. Early. (J). 1987. student ed., pap. 16.50 (0-15-330563-0) HB Schl Dept.

Workbook for Holt Essential Math 1987. Wells. (J). 1987. student ed., pap. 12.25 (0-03-006477-5) HB Schl Dept.

Workbook for Human Factors in Engineering & Design. 4th ed. Mark S. Sanders & Ernest J. McCormick. 160p. (C). 1994. spiral bd. 19.89 (0-8403-8226-X) Kendall-Hunt.

Workbook for Information Processing. 2nd ed. Clark. (DC - Introduction to Computing Ser.). 1990. wbk. ed., pap. 16.95 (0-538-60907-9) S-W Pub.

Workbook for Inorganic, Organic, & Biological Chemistry. Thomas Berke. 416p. (C). 1992. spiral bd. 36.69 (0-8403-8070-4) Kendall-Hunt.

***Workbook for Intercultural Encounters.** 4th ed. Donald W. Klopf. 146p. (C). 1997. wbk. ed., pap. text ed. 18.95 (0-89582-407-8) Morton Pub.

Workbook for Kitzur Shulchan Aruch I: Laws of Elul - Yom Kippur. Dovid Kapenstein. Ed. by Yaakov Fruchter. 21p. (Orig.). 1994. pap. text ed. 3.50 (1-878895-10-9, A090) Torah Umesorah.

Workbook for Kitzur Shulchan Aruch II: Laws of Chanuka & Purim. Dovid Kapenstein. Ed. by Yaakov Fruchter. (Orig.). 1994. pap. text ed. 3.50 (1-878895-11-7, A091) Torah Umesorah.

Workbook for Kitzur Shulchan Aruch III: Laws Regarding Meals. Dovid Kapenstein. Ed. by Yaakov Fruchter. (Orig.). 1994. pap. text ed. 3.50 (1-878895-12-5, A092) Torah Umesorah.

Workbook for Land Survey Systems. John G. McEntyre. (Illus.). 186p. 1990. pap. 45.00 (0-910845-41-7) Landmark Ent.

Workbook for Landmark Level 11: HBJ Reading 1987. Early. (J). 1987. student ed., pap. 14.75 (0-15-330571-1) HB Schl Dept.

Workbook for Landmark Level 11: HBJ Reading 1987. Early. (J). 1987. teacher ed., pap. 22.50 (0-15-330586-X) HB Schl Dept.

Workbook for Language Skills: Exercises for Written & Verbal Expression. Susan H. Brubaker. LC 84-11893. (William Beaumont Hospital Speech & Language Pathology Ser.). 288p. 1984. spiral bd. 33.00 (0-8143-1778-2) Wayne St U Pr.

Workbook for Lectors & Gospel Readers 1997. Lawrence E. Mick. 418p. (Orig.). 1996. pap. 12.00 (1-56854-121-X, WL97) Liturgy Tr Pubns.

***Workbook for Lectors & Gospel Readers 1998.** Lawrence Mick. 404p. (Orig.). 1997. pap. 15.00 (1-56854-203-8, WL98) Liturgy Tr Pubns.

***Workbook for Lectors & Gospel Readers 1999.** Lawrence Mick. 404p. (Orig.). 1998. pap. 15.00 (1-56854-221-6, WL99) Liturgy Tr Pubns.

Workbook for Managing Costs in Clinical Laboratories. Eleanor M. Travers. 245p. 1989. student ed., pap. 19.95 (0-07-065162-0) Hlthcare Mgmt Grp.

Workbook for Medical Office Administrative Procedures. 2nd ed. Anne L. Lilly & Mary A. Frew. LC 88-31065. (Illus.). 251p. (C). 1989. teacher ed., pap. 12.95 (0-8036-3863-9) Davis Co.

Workbook for Memory Skills, Vol. 3. Beth M. Kennedy. (Illus.). 320p. 1996. pap. text ed. 39.95 (0-937857-63-7, 1488) Speech Bin.

Workbook for Methods of Macroeconomic Dynamics. Stephen J. Turnovsky & Michael K. Hendrickson. (Illus.). 152p. 1996. pap. 15.00 (0-262-70058-1) MIT Pr.

Workbook for Milady's Hair Structure & Chemistry Simplified. 2nd rev. ed. Milady Publishing Company Staff. 86p. 1993. 21.60 (1-56253-151-4) Milady Pub.

Workbook for Mortim Frog Level 2: HBJ Reading 1987. Early. (J). 1987. teacher ed., pap. 12.50 (0-15-330576-2) HB Schl Dept.

Workbook for Mortim Frog Level 3: HBJ Reading 1987. Early. (J). 1987. student ed., pap. 6.25 (0-15-330561-4) HB Schl Dept.

Workbook for Mr. Fig Level 3: HBJ Reading 1987. Early. (J). 1987. teacher ed., pap. 12.50 (0-15-330577-0) HB Schl Dept.

Workbook for MRI & CT of the Head & Neck. 2nd ed. Anthony A. Mancuso. (Illus.). 236p. 1988. 60.00 (0-683-05478-3) Williams & Wilkins.

Workbook for My Greek Reader. Theodore C. Papaloizos. (Illus.). 88p. (Orig.). (GRE.). 1986. pap. 4.50 (0-932416-47-0) Papaloizos.

Workbook for New Friends Level 1: HBJ Reading 1987. Early. (J). 1987. student ed., pap. 6.25 (0-15-330560-6) HB Schl Dept.

Workbook for New Friends Level 1: HBJ Reading 1987. Early. (J). 1987. teacher ed., pap. 12.50 (0-15-330575-4) HB Schl Dept.

Workbook for Oklahoma: The Story of Its Past & Present. rev. ed. Estelle Faulconer. (Illus.). 105p. 1968. pap. 3.95 (0-8061-0579-8) U of Okla Pr.

Workbook for Our Land Our Time. Conlin. 1987. student ed., pap. text ed. 14.25 (0-15-772003-9) HR&W Schl Div.

Workbook for Our Land Our Time. Conlin. 1987. teacher ed., pap. text ed. 18.75 (0-15-772004-7) HR&W Schl Div.

Workbook for People & Nations: World History 1987. Mazour. 1987. student ed., pap. text ed. 11.00 (0-15-373467-1) HR&W Schl Div.

Workbook for People & Nations: World History 1987. Mazour. 1987. teacher ed., pap. text ed. 17.25 (0-15-373468-X) HR&W Schl Div.

Workbook for Perspectives Level 13: HBJ Reading 1987. Early. (J). 1987. student ed., pap. 15.50 (0-15-330573-8) HB Schl Dept.

Workbook for Perspectives Level 13: HBJ Reading 1987. Early. (J). 1987. teacher ed., pap. 24.25 (0-15-330588-6) HB Schl Dept.

Workbook for Portraits Level 12: HBJ Reading 1987. Early. (J). 1987. student ed., pap. 14.75 (0-15-330572-X) HB Schl Dept.

Workbook for Portraits Level 12: HBJ Reading 1987. Early. (J). 1987. teacher ed., pap. 23.25 (0-15-330587-8) HB Schl Dept.

Workbook for Practical Nurses. 3rd ed. Audrey L. Sutton. 1969. pap. text ed. 23.00 (0-7216-8682-6) Saunders.

Workbook for Professional Barber Styling. Milady Editors. 1984. teacher ed. 26.95 (0-87350-500-X) Milady Pub.

Workbook for Professional Barber Styling. Milady Editors. 1990. pap. 17.95 (0-87350-503-4) Milady Pub.

Workbook for Program Evaluation in the Human Services. Walter E. Riddick & Eva M. Stewart. 196p. (Orig.). 1981. pap. text ed. 23.50 (0-8191-1783-8) U Pr of Amer.

Workbook for Psychological Assessment with the MMPI. Friedman et al. 240p. 1989. pap. 24.50 (0-8058-0311-4) L Erlbaum Assocs.

Workbook for Psycom, Psychology on Computer: Simulations, Experiments, & Projects. Duane Belcher & Stephen Smith. 256p. (C). 1986. per. write for info. (0-697-01198-4) Brown & Benchmark.

Workbook for Public Speaking. 2nd ed. Patricia Comeaux. 400p. (C). 1995. spiral bd. write for info. (0-697-24656-6) Brown & Benchmark.

***Workbook for Public Speaking.** 3rd ed. Comeaux. 1998. pap. text ed. 16.00 (0-697-35505-5) McGraw.

Workbook for Quality Mammography. Carolyn Kimme-Smith. (Illus.). 215p. 1991. 62.00 (0-683-04611-X) Williams & Wilkins.

Workbook for Quality Mammography. 2nd ed. Carolyn Kimme-Smith et al. LC 96-2980. 237p. 1996. pap. 49.00 (0-683-04612-8) Williams & Wilkins.

Workbook for Reading Today & Tomorrow. Beck. (Reading Ser.). (YA). (gr. 12). 1989. teacher ed., pap. 21.50 (0-15-718113-8) HB Schl Dept.

Workbook for Reading Today & Tomorrow Level 2. Beck. (Reading Ser.). (J). (gr. 2). 1989. student ed., pap. 8.50 (0-15-718012-3) HB Schl Dept.

Workbook for Reading Today & Tomorrow Level 2. Beck. (Reading Ser.). (J). (gr. 2). 1989. teacher ed., pap. 13.50 (0-15-718013-1) HB Schl Dept.

Workbook for Reading Today & Tomorrow Level 3. Beck. (Reading Ser.). (J). (gr. 3). 1989. student ed., pap. 8.50 (0-15-718022-0) HB Schl Dept.

Workbook for Reading Today & Tomorrow Level 3. Beck. (Reading Ser.). (J). (gr. 3). 1989. teacher ed., pap. 13.50 (0-15-718023-9) HB Schl Dept.

Workbook for Reading Today & Tomorrow Level 4: Kingdoms. Beck. (Reading Ser.). (J). (gr. 4). 1989. student ed., pap. 8.50 (0-15-718032-8) HB Schl Dept.

Workbook for Reading Today & Tomorrow Level 4: Kingdoms. Beck. (Reading Ser.). (J). (gr. 4). 1989. teacher ed., pap. 13.50 (0-15-718033-6) HB Schl Dept.

Workbook for Reading Today & Tomorrow Level 5. Beck. (Reading Ser.). (J). 1989. student ed., pap. 10.25 (0-15-718042-5) HB Schl Dept.

Workbook for Reading Today & Tomorrow Level 5. Beck. (Reading Ser.). (J). (gr. 5). 1989. teacher ed., pap. 18.50 (0-15-718043-3) HB Schl Dept.

Workbook for Reading Today & Tomorrow Level 6. Beck. (Reading Ser.). (J). (gr. 6). 1989. student ed., pap. 11.00 (0-15-718052-2) HB Schl Dept.

Workbook for Reading Today & Tomorrow Level 6. Beck. (Reading Ser.). (J). (gr. 6). 1989. teacher ed., pap. 19.25 (0-15-718053-0) HB Schl Dept.

Workbook for Reading Today & Tomorrow Level 7. Beck. (Reading Ser.). (J). (gr. 7). 1989. student ed., pap. 13.00 (0-15-718062-X) HB Schl Dept.

Workbook for Reading Today & Tomorrow Level 7. Beck. (Reading Ser.). (J). (gr. 7). 1989. teacher ed., pap. 21.50 (0-15-718063-8) HB Schl Dept.

W

An Asterisk (*) at the beginning of an entry indicates that the title is appearing in BIP for the first time.

Workbook for Reading Today & Tomorrow Level 8. Beck. (Reading Ser.). (J). (gr. 8). 1989. student ed., pap. 13.00 (0-15-718072-7) HB Schl Dept.

Workbook for Reading Today & Tomorrow Level 8. Beck. (Reading Ser.). (J). (gr. 8). 1989. teacher ed., pap. 21.50 (0-15-718073-5) HB Schl Dept.

Workbook for Reading Today & Tomorrow Level 9. Beck. (Reading Ser.). (J). 1989. student ed., pap. 13.00 (0-15-718082-4) HB Schl Dept.

Workbook for Reading Today & Tomorrow Level 9. Beck. (Reading Ser.). (YA). (gr. 9). 1989. teacher ed., pap. 21.50 (0-15-718083-2) HB Schl Dept.

Workbook for Reading Today & Tomorrow Level 10. Beck. (Reading Ser.). (YA). (gr. 10). 1989. student ed., pap. 13.00 (0-15-718092-1) HB Schl Dept.

Workbook for Reading Today & Tomorrow Level 10. Beck. (Reading Ser.). (YA). (gr. 10). 1989. teacher ed., pap. 21.50 (0-15-718093-X) HB Schl Dept.

Workbook for Reading Today & Tomorrow Level 11. Beck. (Reading Ser.). (YA). (gr. 11). 1989. student ed., pap. 13.50 (0-15-718102-2) HB Schl Dept.

Workbook for Reading Today & Tomorrow Level 11. Beck. (Reading Ser.). (YA). 1989. teacher ed., pap. 21.50 (0-15-718103-0) HB Schl Dept.

Workbook for Reading Today & Tomorrow Level 12. Beck. (Reading Ser.). (YA). (gr. 12). 1989. student ed., pap. 13.50 (0-15-718112-X) HB Schl Dept.

Workbook for Reading Today & Tomorrow Level 13. Beck. (Reading Ser.). (YA). 1989. student ed., pap. 13.50 (0-15-718122-7) HB Schl Dept.

Workbook for Reading Today & Tomorrow Level 13. Beck. (Reading Ser.). (J). 1989. teacher ed., pap. 21.50 (0-15-718123-5) HB Schl Dept.

Workbook for Reading Today & Tomorrow Level 14. Beck. (Reading Ser.). (J). 1989. student ed., pap. 14.25 (0-15-718132-4) HB Schl Dept.

Workbook for Reading Today & Tomorrow Level 14. Beck. (Reading Ser.). (J). 1989. teacher ed., pap. 21.50 (0-15-718133-2) HB Schl Dept.

Workbook for Reading Today & Tomorrow Level 15. Beck. (Reading Ser.). (J). 1989. student ed., pap. 14.25 (0-15-718142-1) HB Schl Dept.

Workbook for Reasoning Skills: Exercises for Cognitive Facilitation. Susan H. Brubaker. LC 83-50961. (William Beaumont Hospital Speech & Language Pathology Ser.). 300p. 1983. spiral bd. 33.00 (0-8143-1760-X) Wayne St U Pr.

Workbook for Reflections Level 14: HBJ Reading 1987. Early. (J). 1987. student ed., pap. 15.50 (0-15-330574-6) HB Schl Dept.

Workbook for Reflections Level 14: HBJ Reading 1987. Early. (J). 1987. teacher ed., pap. 24.25 (0-15-330589-4) HB Schl Dept.

Workbook for Respiratory Disease: Principles of Patient Care. 2nd ed. David W. Chang & Fred Corn. (Illus.). 200p. (C). 1998. wbk. ed., pap. text ed. 18.00 (0-8036-0156-5) Davis Co.

Workbook for Salon Management for Cosmetology Students. 4th ed. Edward J. Tezak. 46p. 1992. text ed. 15.95 (1-56253-066-6) Milady Pub.

Workbook for Salon Management for Cosmetology Students Instructor's Guide. 4th ed. Edward J. Tezak. 46p. 1992. text ed. 26.95 (1-56253-067-4) Milady Pub.

Workbook for Science in the Elementary School. Norwood P. Lawfer et al. 100p. (C). 1994. student ed. 15.61 (1-884768-01-6) Charming Forge.

Workbook for Self Image Is the Key, Set. Joyce Duco. LC 89-92547. 26p. (Orig.). (J). (gr. 5-12). 1990. pap. 5.00 (0-9612896-2-7) J Duco.

***Workbook for Self-Mastery: A Course of Study on the Divine Reality.** John R. Price. LC 97-12686. 200p. (Orig.). 1997. pap. 10.95 (1-56170-362-1, 845) Hay House.

Workbook for Smiles Level 5: HBJ Reading 1987. Early. (J). 1987. student ed., pap. 11.00 (0-15-330565-7) HB Schl Dept.

Workbook for Smiles Level 5: HBJ Reading 1987. Early. (J). 1987. teacher ed., pap. 18.50 (0-15-330580-0) HB Schl Dept.

Workbook for Software Entrepreneurs. A. L. Frank. (Illus.). 128p. 1985. text ed. 40.00 (0-13-965302-3) P-H.

Workbook for Spiritual Development of All People. rev. ed. Hua-Ching Ni. LC 92-13036. 240p. 1992. pap. 14.95 (0-937064-54-8) SevenStar Comm.

Workbook for Stairways Level 7: HBJ Reading 1987. Early. (J). 1987. student ed., pap. 13.50 (0-15-330567-3) HB Schl Dept.

Workbook for Stairways Level 7: HBJ Reading 1987. Early. (J). 1987. teacher ed., pap. 21.00 (0-15-330582-7) HB Schl Dept.

Workbook for "Statistical Methods in Education & Psychology" A. K. Kurtz & S. T. Mayo. 1978. 34.95 (0-387-90324-0) Spr-Verlag.

Workbook for Streamers Level 6: HBJ Reading 1987. Early. (J). 1987. student ed., pap. 13.50 (0-15-330566-5) HB Schl Dept.

Workbook for Streamers Level 6: HBJ Reading 1987. Early. (J). 1987. teacher ed., pap. 21.00 (0-15-330581-9) HB Schl Dept.

Workbook for Sunbeams Level 8: HBJ Reading 1987. Early. (J). 1987. student ed., pap. 13.50 (0-15-330568-1) HB Schl Dept.

Workbook for Sunbeams Level 8: HBJ Reading 1987. Early. (J). 1987. teacher ed., pap. 21.00 (0-15-330583-5) HB Schl Dept.

Workbook for Telescope Level 9: HBJ Reading 1987. Early. (J). 1987. student ed., pap. 13.50 (0-15-330569-X) HB Schl Dept.

Workbook for Telescope Level 9: HBJ Reading 1987. Early. (J). 1987. teacher ed., pap. 21.00 (0-15-330584-3) HB Schl Dept.

Workbook for The Art & Science of Manicuring. 96p. 1990. pap. 15.95 (0-87350-424-0) Milady Pub.

Workbook for the First Responder. 3rd ed. Bergeron. 1991. wbk. ed., pap. 16.50 (0-89303-217-4, Medical Exam) Appleton & Lange.

Workbook for the Identification of Phonological Processes. 2nd ed. Robert J. Lowe. Ed. by Jean Blosser. 58p. (C). 1989. pap. text ed. 14.00 (0-89079-646-7, 7805) PRO-ED.

Workbook for the Medical Assistant. 6th ed. Cooper et al. 320p. 1992. pap. 18.95 (0-8016-1011-7) Mosby Yr Bk.

Workbook for the Restoration Ideal. Marshall Leggett. 96p. 1986. student ed., pap. 2.99 (0-87403-068-4, 03176) Standard Pub.

***Workbook for the Six Steps to the Fountain of Youth, by Dennis Kelly, Vol. 1.** large type ed. Ed. by Carol Adler. (Illus.). 150p. (Orig.). 1997. pap. 12.95 (1-890243-04-3) Trineurogenics.

***Workbook for the Study of Rhetoric in Western Thought.** Susan Fillippeli. 158p. (C). 1997. 20.95 (0-7872-3651-9) Kendall-Hunt.

Workbook for the Verbally Apraxic Adult. Karen B. Richards & Maureen O. Fallon. 138p. 1987. student ed. 29.00 (0-88450-986-9, 7367) Commun Skill.

Workbook for United States History. Reich. 1988. student ed., pap. text ed. 13.75 (0-03-014809-X) HR&W Schl Div.

Workbook for Verbal Expression. Beth M. Kennedy. (Illus.). 384p. (YA). (gr. 7 up). 1994. 39.95 (0-937857-48-3, 1435) Speech Bin.

Workbook for Voice & Articulation for the Electronic Media. Gail McGrath. 141p. (C). 1993. student ed. 17.12 (1-56870-070-9) RonJon Pub.

***Workbook For Wheelock's Latin.** 3rd ed. Paul T. Comeau. 1997. pap. text ed. 13.00 (0-06-273471-7, Harper Ref) HarpC.

***Workbook for Wisconsin Estate Planners.** Mark J. Bradley et al. 600p. 1990. ring bd. 185.00 incl. disk (0-614-24847-7) State Bar WI CLE Bk Div.

***Workbook for Wisconsin Estate Planners.** 3rd ed. Mark J. Bradley. LC 97-17079. 1997. write for info. (1-57862-002-3) State Bar WI CLE Bk Div.

Workbook for Wishes Level 4: HBJ Reading 1987. Early. (J). 1987. student ed., pap. 11.00 (0-15-330564-9) HB Schl Dept.

Workbook for Wishes Level 4: HBJ Reading 1987. Early. (J). 1987. teacher ed., pap. 18.50 (0-15-330579-7) HB Schl Dept.

Workbook for Word Retrieval. Beth M. Kennedy. (Illus.). 248p. 1992. 39.95 (0-937857-35-1, 1523) Speech Bin.

Workbook for World History: Story of Progress. Smart. 1987. student ed., pap. text ed. 14.25 (0-03-006083-4) HR&W Schl Div.

Workbook for Writers. Thelma D. Kantorowitz-Shaffer. 112p. (C). 1991. 14.95 (0-940139-22-7) Consortium RI.

Workbook Game Sheets for Kitchen Chemistry & Front Porch Physics. Marie A. Hoyt. (Illus.). 44p. (Orig.). (J). (gr. 3-8). 1983. pap. text ed. 4.00 (0-914911-02-3) Educ Serv Pr.

Workbook Guide to Writing the Romance Novel. Sunday Thompson. 1984. 10.95 (0-932655-00-9) Sunday Edition.

Workbook in Accounting. 3rd ed. F. P. Langley & D. A. Caldicott. 284p. (C). 1981. pap. 24.95 (0-408-10680-8) Buttrwrth-Heinemann.

Workbook in American History, Vol. I. (Illus.). 224p. (Orig.). (C). 1992. Net. wbk. ed., pap. text ed. 12.96 (1-881089-08-8) Brandywine Press.

***Workbook in American History, Vol. I.** rev. ed. (Illus.). 192p. (C). 1996. wbk. ed., pap. text ed. 12.96 (1-881089-80-0) Brandywine Press.

Workbook in American History, Vol. II. (Illus.). 208p. (Orig.). (C). 1992. wbk. ed., pap. text ed. 12.96 (1-881089-09-6) Brandywine Press.

***Workbook in American History, Vol. II.** rev. ed. (Illus.). 208p. (Orig.). (C). 1996. pap. text ed. 12.96 (1-881089-81-9) Brandywine Press.

Workbook in Basic. V. B. Aggarwal & M. P. Goel. 184p. 1989. pap. 50.00 (81-209-0017-0, Pub. by Pitambar Pub II) St Mut.

Workbook in Basic Concepts in Health, Custom Pub. 2nd ed. Olson. 1994. pap. text ed. write for info. (0-07-048024-9) McGraw.

Workbook in Cobol. V. B. Aggarwal & P. C. Bagga. 100p. 1992. 20.00 (81-209-0716-7, Pub. by Pitambar Pub II) St Mut.

Workbook in Drafting for Electronics. 2nd ed. Louis G. Lamit et al. (Illus.). 256p. (C). 1993. pap. text ed. 51.00 (0-02-367345-1, Macmillan Coll) P-H.

Workbook in Ear Training. 2nd ed. Bruce Benward. 256p. (C). 1969. spiral bd. write for info. (0-697-03577-8) Brown & Benchmark.

Workbook in Everyday French, 2 bks. rev. ed. Gerard Charbonneau & Hubert Seguin. 213p. (YA). (gr. 9-11). 1971. teacher ed. 2.95 (0-685-38985-5, 18131) Prentice ESL.

Workbook in Everyday French, 2 bks., Bk. 2. rev. ed. Gerard Charbonneau & Hubert Seguin. 213p. (gr. 9-11). 1971. pap. text ed. 5.45 (0-88345-168-9, 17480) Prentice ESL.

Workbook in Everyday German. Ursula Meyer & Alice Wolfson. (J). (gr. 9-10). 1976. pap. text ed. 4.75 (0-88345-277-4, 18600) Prentice ESL.

***Workbook in Everyday Spanish: Intermediate/Advanced.** 3rd ed. Julio I. Andjar & Robert J. Dixson. 174p. (C). 1996. pap. text ed. 28.80 (0-13-432791-8) P-H.

***Workbook in Everyday Spanish Bk. 1: Elementary/Intermediate.** 3rd ed. Julio I. Andujar & Robert J. Dixson. 208p. (C). 1996. wbk. ed., pap. text ed. 28.80 (0-13-432774-8) P-H.

Workbook in Graphics. Hugh F. Rogers. 1991. pap. text ed. write for info. (0-07-053536-1) McGraw.

Workbook in Introductory Economics. 3rd ed. Ed. by Colin D. Harbury. (Illus.). 176p. 1982. pap. text ed. 9.25 (0-08-027442-0, Pergamon Pr) Elsevier.

Workbook in Introductory Economics. 4th ed. Colin D. Harbury. 193p. 1987. pap. text ed. 18.95 (0-08-034790-8, Prgamon Press) Buttrwrth-Heinemann.

Workbook in Pediatric Echocardiography. Hugh D. Allen et al. LC 76-57460. 291p. reprint ed. pap. 83.00 (0-318-34989-2, 2030837) Bks Demand.

Workbook in Practical Neonatology. 2nd ed. Ed. by Richard A. Polin et al. (Illus.). 496p. 1993. pap. text ed. 52.50 (0-7216-4292-6) Saunders.

Workbook in Program Design for Public Managers. Leonard Ruchelman. LC 85-9936. (SUNY Series in Public Administration). 123p. 1985. pap. text ed. 18.95 (0-88706-025-0) State U NY Pr.

Workbook in Redesigning Public Services. Leonard Ruchelman. LC 88-16022. (SUNY Series in Public Administration). 85p. (C). 1989. pap. text ed. 18.95 (0-88706-943-6) State U NY Pr.

***Workbook in the Structure of English: Linguistic Principles & Language Acquisition.** William Rutherford. 420p. (C). 1998. text ed. 54.95 (0-631-20478-4) Blackwell Pubs.

***Workbook in the Structure of English: Linguistic Principles & Language Acquisition.** William Rutherford. 420p. (C). 1998. pap. text ed. 24.95 (0-631-20479-2) Blackwell Pubs.

Workbook in Tonal Analysis: Questions & Answers. Arthur J. Komar. (Illus.). 160p. (Orig.). (C). 1995. pap. 25.00 (1-886464-02-2) Ovenbird Pr.

Workbook News. Lorenz & Vivian. 1995. pap. text ed. 23.00 (0-205-15849-8) P-H.

Workbook of Accounting Standards. 3rd ed. Alan Sangster. (Illus.). 448p. (Orig.). 1995. pap. 52.50 (0-273-61420-7) Trans-Atl Phila.

Workbook of an Unsuccessful Architect. Harris Stone. LC 73-8052. (Illus.). 192p. 1974. reprint ed. pap. 10.00 (0-85345-332-2) Monthly Rev.

Workbook of Atmospheric Dispersion Estimates: An Introduction to Dispersion Modeling. 2nd ed. D. Bruce Turner. 192p. 1994. 79.95 (1-56670-023-X, L1023) Lewis Pubs.

Workbook of Basic Russian. Mischa Fayer. 1995. pap. 7.95 (0-8442-4201-2) NTC Pub Grp.

Workbook of Clinical Chemistry: Case Presentation & Data Interpretation. Philip Mayne & Andrew P. Day. 224p. 1994. student ed., wbk. ed. 19.95 (0-340-57646-4, Pub. by Ed Arnold UK) OUP.

Workbook of Cuneiform Signs. Daniel C. Snell. (Aids & Research Tools in Ancient Near Eastern Studies: Vol. 3). 140p. 1979. pap. text ed. 17.50 (0-89003-058-8) Undena Pubns.

Workbook of Darkroom Techniques. John Hedgecoe. (John Hedgecoe's Workbook Ser.). (Illus.). 191p. 1994. pap. 14.95 (0-85533-868-7, Focal) Buttrwrth-Heinemann.

Workbook of Donald M. Ayer's English Words from Latin & Greek Elements. Helena Dettmer & Marcia Lindgren. 291p. 1986. student ed. 14.95 (0-8165-0905-0) U of Ariz Pr.

Workbook of Epidemiology. Staffan E. Norell. (Illus.). 352p. 1995. 49.95 (0-19-507490-4); pap. 24.95 (0-19-507491-2) OUP.

Workbook of Intercessory Prayer. Maxie Dunnam. 1989. pap. 8.95 (0-687-61374-4) Abingdon.

Workbook of Intercessory Prayer. Maxie D. Dunnam. LC 78-65617. 1979. pap. 8.95 (0-8358-0382-1) Upper Room Bks.

***Workbook of Living Prayer.** 11.85 (0-687-61378-7) Abingdon.

Workbook of Living Prayer: 20th Anniversary Edition. 20th anniversary ed. Maxie Dunnam. 144p. 1994. pap. 8.95 (0-8358-0718-5) Upper Room Bks.

Workbook of Nudes & Glamour. John Hedgecoe. (John Hedgecoe's Workbook Ser.). (Illus.). 192p. 1994. pap. 14.95 (0-85533-943-8, Focal) Buttrwrth-Heinemann.

Workbook of Photo Techniques. John Hedgecoe. (John Hedgecoe's Workbook Ser.). (Illus.). 191p. 1994. pap. 14.95 (0-85533-867-9, Focal) Buttrwrth-Heinemann.

Workbook of Surgical Anatomy. L. Beaty Pemberton et al. (Pretest Specialty Level Ser.). 320p. 1990. pap. text ed. 39.95 (0-07-049349-9) McGraw-Hill HPD.

Workbook of Words. John W. Coogan. (J). 1987. pap. text ed. 16.20 (0-8013-0116-5, 75780) Longman.

***Workbook Ohio: Its Land & Its People.** James Killoran et al. (Illus.). 124p. (YA). (gr. 4 up). 1995. pap. text ed. 3.95 (1-882422-14-7) Jarrett Pub.

***Workbook Ohio: Its Neighbors, Near & Far.** James Killoran et al. (Illus.). 132p. (YA). (gr. 6 up). 1996. pap. text ed. 3.95 (1-882422-19-8) Jarrett Pub.

Workbook on Becoming Alive in Christ. Maxie Dunnam. 160p. (Orig.). 1986. pap. 8.95 (0-8358-0542-5) Upper Room Bks.

Workbook on Becoming Alive in Christ. Maxie Dunnam. 1986. pap. text ed. 8.95 (0-687-61379-5) Abingdon.

Workbook on Biblical Stewardship. Richard E. Rusbuldt. 128p. 1994. pap. 10.00 (0-8028-0723-2) Eerdmans.

Workbook on Christians under Construction & in Recovery. Maxie Dunnam. 160p. 1993. pap. 8.95 (0-8358-0683-9) Upper Room Bks.

Workbook on Community Accountability in Integrated Delivery. 133p. 1995. pap. 55.00 (0-87125-230-9) Cath Health.

Workbook on Coping As Christians. Maxie Dunnam. 160p. 1988. pap. 8.95 (0-8358-0581-6) Upper Room Bks.

Workbook on Interreligious Affairs. Ed. by CCAR Committee on Interreligious Activities Staff. 24p. 1982. pap. text ed. 1.50 (0-916694-72-0) Central Conf.

Workbook on Introduction to Computer Applications Pt. 2: For Windows. Man M. Sharma & William E. Rogers. 550p. (C). 1995. wbk. ed. 25.00 (1-888469-05-6) EDUCO Intl.

Workbook on Living As a Christian. Maxie Dunnam. 176p. (Orig.). 1994. pap. 7.95 (0-687-00313-X) Abingdon.

Workbook on Long Term Care in Integrated Delivery. 100p. 1995. pap. 55.00 (0-87125-228-7) Cath Health.

***Workbook on Loving Jesus.** Dunnam. 11.85 (0-687-61441-4) Abingdon.

Workbook on Loving the Jesus Way. Maxie Dunnam. 168p. 1995. pap. 8.95 (0-8358-0729-0) Upper Room Bks.

Workbook on Redesigning Care: Becoming the Values-Driven, Low-Cost Provider. 140p. 1995. pap. 55.00 (0-87125-229-5) Cath Health.

Workbook on Spiritual Disciplines. Maxie Dunnam. LC 83-51402. 160p. 1984. pap. text ed. 8.95 (0-8358-0479-8) Upper Room Bks.

***Workbook on the Christ.** Dunnam. 11.85 (0-687-61370-1) Abingdon.

Workbook on the Christian Walk. Maxie Dunnam. 144p. 1992. pap. 8.95 (0-8358-0640-5) Upper Room Bks.

***Workbook on the Seven Deadly Sins.** Maxie Dunnam & Kimberly Dunnam Reisman. 160p. (Orig.). 1997. pap. 9.95 (0-8358-0714-2, UR 714) Upper Room Bks.

Workbook Series. Jack Rudman. 1994. pap. write for info. (0-8373-7900-8) Nat Learn.

Workbook to Accompany: Practical Statistics for Educators. Ruth Ravid. 76p. (Orig.). (C). 1995. pap. text ed. 14.95 (0-7618-0139-1) U Pr of Amer.

***Workbook to Accompany C++ for You++ An Introduction to Programming & Computer Science.** Maria Litvin & Gary Litvin. LC 97-91876. (Illus.). 120p. 1997. wbk. ed., spiral bd. 12.00 (0-9654853-2-3) Skylight Pub.

Workbook to Accompany Cardiopulmonary Anatomy & Physiology Essentials for Respiratory Care. 2nd ed. Terry Des Jardins. 203p. 1993. pap. 14.95 (0-8273-5006-6) Delmar.

Workbook to Accompany "Health Care Law & Ethics" American Association of Medical Assistants Staff. v, 130p. 1995. student ed. 20.00 (0-942732-03-0) Am Med Assts.

Workbook to Accompany Mosby's Paramedic Textbook. Mick J. Sanders. 416p. 1994. pap. 16.95 (0-8016-4314-7) Mosby Yr Bk.

Workbook to Increase Your Meaningful & Purposeful Goals. Robert R. Hutzell & Mary A. Eggert. 156p. (Orig.). 1989. pap. 9.00 (0-917867-10-6) V Frankl Inst.

Workbook to Introduction to Industrial & Systems Engineering. 3rd ed. John W. Nazemetz et al. 1993. pap. text ed. 15.40 (0-13-489485-5) P-H.

Workbook to Russian Root List. Gary L. Browning. 85p. (Orig.). 1985. pap. text ed. 8.95 (0-89357-114-8) Slavica.

Workbook 1 see Orientation in American English

Workbook 1 see Orientation in Business English

Workbook 3 see Orientation in American English

Workbook 3 see Orientation in Business English

Workbook 4 see Orientation in American English

Workbooks for Psychotherapists: Intervening & Validating, Vol. 3. Robert J. Langs. LC 84-62354. (Workbooks for Psychotherapists Ser.). 302p. 1985. pap. text ed. 33.50 (0-931231-03-5) Newconcept Pr.

Workbooks for Psychotherapists: Listening & Formulating, Vol. 2. Robert J. Langs. LC 84-62354. (Workbooks for Psychotherapists Ser.). 304p. 1985. pap. text ed. 36.00 (0-931231-02-7) Newconcept Pr.

Workbooks for Psychotherapists: Understanding Unconscious Communication, Vol. 1. Robert J. Langs. LC 84-62354. (Workbooks for Psychotherapists Ser.). 144p. 1985. pap. text ed. 20.00 (0-931231-01-9) Newconcept Pr.

Workbooks in Immunology One: Antigens & Antibodies. Jules M. Elias. (Illus.). 134p. (Orig.). (C). 1987. student ed. 14.95 (0-936735-00-7) Grove Educ Tech.

Workbooks in Immunology Two: Immunoglobulins, Complement, & the Immune Response. Jules M Elias. (Illus.). 160p. (Orig.). (C). 1987. student ed. 15.95 (0-936735-01-5) Grove Educ Tech.

WorkCare: A Resource Guide for the Working Person. George J. Pfeiffer & Judith A. Webster. Ed. by Sara Piccini. (Illus.). 398p. 1992. pap. text ed. 19.95 (0-9634986-0-6) Workcare Pr.

Workdays, Workhours, & Work Schedules: Evidence for the United States & Germany. Daniel S. Hamermesh. LC 96-11199. (Illus.). 159p. (C). 1996. text ed. 24.00 (0-88099-170-4) W E Upjohn.

Workdays, Workhours, & Work Schedules: Evidence for the United States & Germany. Daniel S. Hamermesh. LC 96-11199. (Illus.). 159p. (C). 1996. pap. text ed. 14.00 (0-88099-169-0) W E Upjohn.

***Worked Examples in Advanced Engineering Mathematics.** L. R. Mustoe. LC 88-2058. (Illus.). 147p. reprint ed. pap. 41.90 (0-608-05295-7, 2065833) Bks Demand.

Worked Examples in Basic Electronics. P. W. Crane. 1967. 128.00 (0-08-012217-5, Pub. by Pergamon Repr UK) Franklin.

Worked Examples in Electrical Machines & Drives. J. Hindmarsh. (Applied Electricity & Electronics Ser.). (Illus.). 150p. 1981. text ed. 28.00 (0-08-026131-0, Pergamon Pr); pap. text ed. 19.25 (0-08-026130-2, Pergamon Pr) Elsevier.

Worked Examples in Essential Organic Chemistry. A. P. Ryles et al. LC 80-42022. 117p. reprint ed. pap. 48.80 (0-8357-6945-3, 2039004) Bks Demand.

Worked Examples in Heat Transfer Fuels & Refractories Fluid Flow in Furnace Technology. D. N. Gwyther. 146p. 1985. pap. text ed. 22.00 (0-901462-25-X, Pub. by Inst Materials UK) Ashgate Pub Co.

W

An Asterisk (*) at the beginning of an entry indicates that the title is appearing in BIP for the first time.

Worked Examples in Kinetics & Thermodynamics of Phase Transformations. E. A. Wilson. 179p. 1983. pap. text ed. 28.00 (*0-901462-17-9*, Pub. by Inst Materials UK) Ashgate Pub Co.

Worked Examples in Metalworking. G. J. Richardson et al. 209p. 1985. pap. text ed. 29.40 (*0-904357-77-5*, Pub. by Inst Materials UK) Ashgate Pub Co.

Worked Examples in Relative Radar Plotting. I. W. Bagshaw. (C). 1987. 50.00 (*0-85174-330-7*, Pub. by Brwn Son Ferg) St Mut.

Worked Examples in X-Ray Analysis. R. Jenkins & J. L. De Vries. LC 72-113623. (Illus.). 1983. 33.00 (*0-387-91068-9*) Spr-Verlag.

Worked Problems in Applied Mathematics. N. N. Lebedev et al. LC 78-67857. 1979. pap. text ed. 11.95 (*0-486-63730-1*) Dover.

Worked Problems in Ophthalmic Lenses. David Jenney & Alan Tunnacliffe. (C). 1989. 100.00 (*0-900099-17-8*, Pub. by Assn Brit Dispen Opticians UK) St Mut.

Worked Problems in Optics. Alan Tunnacliffe. (C). 1989. 115.00 (*0-900099-16-X*, Pub. by Assn Brit Dispen Opticians UK) St Mut.

Worker & His Union: A Study in South India. E. A. Ramaswamy. 1977. 9.00 (*0-88386-991-8*) S Asia.

Worker & the Job: Coping with Change. Ed. by Jerome M. Rosow. LC 74-765. (American Assembly Guides Ser.). 224p. 1974. 6.95 (*0-317-00261-9*) Am Assembly.

Worker at Work. T. M. Fraser. 264p. 1989. 115.00 (*0-85066-476-4*); pap. 57.00 (*0-85066-481-0*) Taylor & Francis.

Worker Benefits: Industrial Welfare in America 1900-1935. Martha J. Soltow & Susan Gravelle. LC 82-25494. 242p. 1983. 22.50 (*0-8108-1614-8*) Scarecrow.

Worker Capitalism: The New Industrial Relations. Keith R. Bradley & Alan Gelb. 192p. (Orig.). 1983. pap. 8.95 (*0-262-52103-2*) MIT Pr.

Worker City, Company Town: Iron & Cotton-Worker Protest in Troy & Cohoes, New York, 1855-84. Daniel J. Walkowitz. LC 78-18305. (Working Class in American History Ser.). (Illus.). 308p. 1978. 11.95 (*0-252-00915-0*); text ed. 29.95 (*0-252-00667-4*) U of Ill Pr.

Worker Cooperatives in America. Ed. by Robert Jackall & Henry M. Levin. LC 84-61. 300p. 1984. pap. 13.00 (*0-520-05741-4*) U CA Pr.

Worker Cooperatives in Theory & Practice. Mary Mellor et al. 192p. 1988. 90.00 (*0-335-15863-3*, Open Univ Pr); pap. 32.00 (*0-335-15862-5*, Open Univ Pr) Taylor & Francis.

***Worker Deaths in Confined Spaces: A Summary of Surveillance Findings & Investigative Case Reports.** Ed. by Thomas R. Bender. (Illus.). 271p. (C). 1996. reprint ed. pap. 35.00 (*0-7881-3183-4*) DIANE Pub.

Worker Dislocation: Case Studies of Causes & Cures. Ed. by Robert F. Cook. LC 87-31717. 219p. 1987. text ed. 23.00 (*0-88099-053-8*); pap. text ed. 13.00 (*0-88099-052-X*) W E Upjohn.

Worker Empowerment: The Struggle for Workplace Democracy. Ed. by Jon D. Wisman. LC 90-43135. (TOES Bks.). 172p. (Orig.). 1990. pap. 14.50 (*0-942850-26-2*) Bootstrap Pr.

Worker Empowerment in a Changing Economy: Jobs, Military Production, & the Environment. Lucinda Wykle et al. LC 90-25834. 84p. (Orig.). 1990. pap. 9.00 (*0-945257-33-3*) Apex Pr.

Worker Flows & the Employment Adjustment of Firms: An Empirical Investigation. W. H. Hassink. 152p. 1996. pap. 25.00 (*90-5170-396-1*, Pub. by Thesis Pubs NE) IBD Ltd.

Worker Grows Old. George S. Rosenberg. LC 78-110628. (Jossey-Bass Behavioral Science Ser.). 222p. reprint ed. pap. 63.30 (*0-317-08640-5*, 2013919) Bks Demand.

***Worker Health & Safety During Nuclear Facility Cleanup.** (Hazardous, Nuclear & Solid Waste Environmental Management Ser.: No. 5). 1996. pap. 10.00 (*1-55516-515-X*, 4662) Natl Conf State Legis.

Worker in Modern Economic Society. Paul H. Douglas et al. LC 70-89730. (American Labor, from Conspiracy to Collective Bargaining Ser., No. 1). 929p. 1970. reprint ed. 46.95 (*0-405-02117-8*) Ayer.

Worker in the Cane: A Puerto Rican Life History. Sidney W. Mintz. (Illus.). 320p. 1974. reprint ed. pap. 12.95 (*0-393-00731-6*) Norton.

Worker Learning & Worktime Flexibility: A Policy Discussion Paper. Gretl S. Meier. LC 83-1348. 64p. (Orig.). 1983. pap. text ed. 4.00 (*0-88099-007-4*) W E Upjohn.

Worker Militancy & Its Consequences: The Changing Climate of Western Industrial Relations. 2nd ed. Ed. by Solomon Barkin. LC 83-9564. 460p. 1983. text ed. 79.50 (*0-275-90943-3*, C0943, Praeger Pubs) Greenwood.

Worker Participation: Productivity & the Quality of Work Life. Bruce Stokes. 1978. pap. write for info. (*0-916468-24-0*) Worldwatch Inst.

Worker Participation: Success & Problems. Ed. by Hem C. Jain. LC 80-57. (Praeger Special Studies). 378p. 1980. text ed. 59.95 (*0-275-90498-9*, C0498, Praeger Pubs) Greenwood.

Worker Participation & American Unions: Threat or Opportunity? Thomas A. Kochan et al. LC 84-13071. 202p. 1984. text ed. 23.00 (*0-88099-021-X*); pap. text ed. 13.00 (*0-88099-022-8*) W E Upjohn.

Worker Participation & Ownership: Cooperative Strategies for Strengthening Local Economies. William F. Whyte et al. LC 82-23413. (ILR Paperback Ser.: No. 19). 164p. (Orig.). 1983. pap. 10.00 (*0-87546-097-6*, ILR Press) Cornell U Pr.

Worker Protection During Hazardous Waste Remediation. 1990. text ed. 67.95 (*0-442-23899-1*) Van Nos Reinhold.

Worker Protection, Japanese Style: Occupational Safety & Health in the Auto Industry. Richard E. Wokutch. (Cornell International Industrial & Labor Relations Reports: No. 21). 280p. 1992. 39.00 (*0-87546-186-7*, ILR Press); pap. 18.95 (*0-87546-187-5*, ILR Press) Cornell U Pr.

Worker Protection Standard for Agricultural Pesticides, How to Comply: What Employers Need to Know. 1994. lib. bdg. 250.00 (*0-8490-5752-3*) Gordon Pr.

***Worker Protection Standard Product Safety Data: Pocket Guide.** Ed. by Earl Tryon. 1916p. (Orig.). 1995. pap. 50.00 (*1-889750-02-6*) Nrth Amer Compendiums.

***Worker Protection Standard Product Safety Data: Pocket Guide.** 2nd ed. 1900p. (Orig.). 1997. pap. 50.00 (*1-889750-06-9*) Nrth Amer Compendiums.

***Worker Protection Standard Product Safety Data Sheets: Desk Reference.** (Orig.). 1997. pap. 85.00 (*1-889750-08-5*) Nrth Amer Compendiums.

Worker Response to Plant Closings: Steelworkers in Johnstown & Youngstown. rev. ed. Scott D. Camp. LC 94-47515. (Garland Studies in the History of American Labor). (Illus.). 324p. 1995. text ed. 83.00 (*0-8153-2017-5*) Garland.

Worker Rights Vol. 1: From Apartheid to Democracy - What Role for Organized Labour? Ebrahim Patel. 203p. 1994. pap. text ed. 28.00 (*0-7021-3076-1*, Pub. by Juta SA) Gaunt.

***Worker Rights & Labor Standards in Asia's Four New Tigers: A Comparative Perspective.** Marvin J. Levine. LC 97-8964. (Illus.). 453p. (C). 69.50 (*0-306-45477-7*, Plenum Pr) Plenum.

Worker Rights under the U. S. Trade Laws. Bruce H. Turnbull & Ethan S. Naftalin. Ed. by Lawyers Committee for Human Rights Staff. (Nineteen Eighty-Eight Project Ser.: No. 2). 77p. (Orig.). 1989. pap. text ed. 5.00 (*0-934143-22-6*) Lawyers Comm Human.

Worker Self-Management in Industry: The West European Experience. Ed. by G. David Garson. LC 77-2774. (Praeger Special Studies). 260p. 1977. text ed. 48.95 (*0-275-90266-8*, C0266, Praeger Pubs) Greenwood.

Worker, Strikes, & Pogroms: The Donbass-Dnepr Bend in Late Imperial Russia, 1870-1905. Charters Wynn. (Illus.). 316p. 1992. text ed. 49.50 (*0-691-03152-5*) Princeton U Pr.

Worker-Student Action Committees: France, May 1968. R. Gregoire & Freddy Perlman. 1969. pap. 2.50 (*0-934868-08-5*) Black & Red.

Worker Takeover in Industry: The Kamani Tubes Experiment. B. Srinivas. LC 93-5206. (Illus.). 224p. (C). 1994. text ed. 28.50 (*0-8039-9125-8*) Sage.

Worker, the Firm, & the Decision to Use Drugs. rev. ed. Gail M. Hoyt. LC 94-47352. (Garland Studies on Industrial Productivity). 272p. 1995. text ed. 62.00 (*0-8153-1963-0*) Garland.

Worker Training: Implications for United States Competitiveness. 1991. lib. bdg. 79.95 (*0-8490-4398-0*) Gordon Pr.

Worker Trait Group Guide. Appalachia Educational Laboratory Staff. 1989. 27.95 (*0-936007-11-7*, 3200) Meridian Educ.

Worker Trait Group Guide. rev. ed. Appalachia Educational Laboratory Staff & David Winefordner. 495p. 1988. 23.95 (*1-55631-119-2*) Chron Guide.

Worker Traits Data Book: Specific Details on the 12,741 Jobs Listed in the Dictionary of Occupational Titles. Compiled by Don Mayall. LC 93-33412. 344p. 1994. pap. 49.95 (*1-56370-110-3*, WTDB) JIST Works.

Worker Views His Union. Joel Seidman et al. LC 58-5686. 312p. reprint ed. 89.00 (*0-8357-9661-2*, 2016975) Bks Demand.

Worker-Writer in America: Jack Conroy & the Tradition of Midwestern Literary Radicalism, 1898-1990. Douglas Wixson. LC 93-3684. (Illus.). 702p. 1994. 34.95 (*0-252-02043-X*) U of Ill Pr.

Workers: An Archaeology of the Industrial Age. Photos & Text by Sebastiao Salgado. (Illus.). 400p. 1993. 100.00 (*0-89381-525-X*) Aperture.

***Workers: An Archaeology of the Industrial Age.** Sebastiao Salgado. 1997. pap. text ed. 85.00 (*0-89381-550-0*) Aperture.

***Workers: An Archeology of the Industrial Age.** Sebastiao Salgado. 1997. pap. text ed. 85.00 (*0-89381-699-X*) Aperture.

***Workers' Access to Education: A Workers' Education Guide.** ix, 97p. 1995. pap. 13.50 (*92-2-108013-7*) Intl Labour Office.

Workers Against Lenin: Labour Protest & the Bolshevik Dictatorship 1920-22. Jonathan Aves. 256p. 1996. text ed. 59.50 (*1-86064-067-2*, Pub. by I B Tauris UK) St Martin.

Workers Against Work: Labor in Paris & Barcelona During the Popular Fronts. Michael Seidman. 384p. 1990. 42.50 (*0-520-06915-3*) U CA Pr.

Workers & Automation: The Impact of New Technology in the Newspaper Industry. Ranabir Samaddar. 268p. 1994. 36.00 (*0-8039-9174-6*) Sage.

Workers & Automation: The Impact of New Technology in the Newspaper Industry. Ranabira Samaddara. 265p. 1994. 36.00 (*81-7036-401-9*) Sage.

Workers & Canadian History. Gregory S. Kealey. (C). 1995. pap. text ed. 27.95 (*0-7735-1355-8*, Pub. by McGill CN) U of Toronto Pr.

Workers & the Right in Spain, 1900-1936. Colin M. Winston. LC 84-42553. (Illus.). 378p. 1985. reprint ed. pap. 107.80 (*0-7837-9487-8*, 2060229) Bks Demand.

***Workers & the State in New Order Indonesia.** Vedi R. Hadiz. LC 97-7098. (Studies in the Growth Economies of Asia). 272p. (C). 1997. text ed. write for info. (*0-415-16980-1*) Routledge.

Workers & Their Wages: Changing Patterns in the United States. Ed. by Marvin H. Kosters. 314p. 1991. pap. 14.95 (*0-8447-3748-8*) Am Enterprise.

Workers & Unions in Bombay, Nineteen Eighteen to Nineteen Twenty-Nine: A Study of Organisation in the Cotton Mills. Richard Newman. 1982. pap. 22.00 (*0-686-91580-1*) S Asia.

Workers & Working Class in the Ottoman Empire & the Turkish Republic, 1839-1950. Ed. by Donald Quataert & Erik J. Zurcher. 224p. 1995. text ed. 59.50 (*1-85043-875-7*) St Martin.

***Workers & Working Classes in the Middle East: Struggles, Histories & Historiographices.** Ed. by Zachary Lockman. 360p. 1996. pap. 19.95 (*0-614-21503-X*, 1359) Kazi Pubns.

Workers & Working Classes in the Middle East: Struggles, Histories, Historiographies. Ed. by Zachary Lockman. LC 92-42701. (SUNY Series in the Social & Economic History of the Middle East). 341p. (C). 1993. pap. text ed. 21.95 (*0-7914-1666-6*) State U NY Pr.

Workers & Working Classes in the Middle East: Struggles, Histories, Historiographies. Ed. by Zachary Lockman. LC 92-42701. (SUNY Series in the Social & Economic History of the Middle East). 341p. (C). 1993. text ed. 64.50 (*0-7914-1665-8*) State U NY Pr.

Workers & Workplace Dynamics in Reconstruction-Era Atlanta: A Case Study. Jonathan W. McLeod. LC 89-963. (Afro-American Culture & Society Monograph Ser.: Vol. 10). (Illus.). 135p. 1989. pap. 15.95 (*0-934934-34-7*) CAAS Pubns.

Workers & Workplace Dynamics in Reconstruction-Era Atlanta: A Case Study. Jonathan W. McLeod. LC 89-963. (Afro-American Culture & Society Ser.). (Illus.). 138p. 1989. pap. 15.00 (*0-89215-155-2*) U Cal LA Indus Rel.

Workers & Workplaces in Revolutionary China. Ed. by Stephen Andors. LC 76-53710. (China Book Project Ser.). 439p. reprint ed. pap. 125.20 (*0-685-23730-3*, 2032771) Bks Demand.

Workers at Risk: The Failed Promise of the Occupational Safety & Health Administration. Thomas O. McGarity & Sidney A. Shapiro. LC 92-1753. 376p. 1993. text ed. 65.00 (*0-275-94281-3*, C4281, Praeger Pubs) Greenwood.

Workers at Risk: Voices from the Workplace. Dorothy Nelkin & Michael S. Brown. LC 83-9319. (Illus.). xviii, 238p. 1984. lib. bdg. 22.50 (*0-226-57127-0*) U Ch Pr.

Workers at Risk: Voices from the Workplace. Dorothy Nelkin & Michael S. Brown. LC 83-9319. (Illus.). xviii, 338p. 1986. pap. text ed. 12.00 (*0-226-57128-9*) U Ch Pr.

Workers at War. Frank J. Warne. LC 74-22762. (Labor Movement in Fiction & Non-Fiction Ser.). reprint ed. 42.50 (*0-404-58515-9*) AMS Pr.

Worker's Bible: The Last Word on Employees' Rights. Joel D. Joseph. 188p. 1991. pap. 12.95 (*0-915765-92-6*) Krantz Co.

Workers, Bosses, & Bureaucrats: A Socialist View of the Labor Movement in the 1930's. Tom Kerry. LC 80-82044. 285p. 1980. pap. 18.95 (*0-87348-603-X*); lib. bdg. 50.00 (*0-87348-604-8*) Pathfinder NY.

Workers' (Communist) Party & American Trade Unions. David M. Schneider. LC 78-64128. (Johns Hopkins University. Studies in the Social Sciences. Thirtieth Ser. 1912: 2). reprint ed. 24.50 (*0-404-61241-5*) AMS Pr.

Workers' Comp Case Management: A "User-Friendly" Approach for Employers. 2nd ed. Charles A. Warnes. 58p. (Orig.). 1994. pap. 17.50 (*0-614-00543-4*) LRP Pubns.

Workers' Comp for Employers: How to Cut Claims, Reduce Premiums, & Stay Out of Trouble. 2nd ed. James Walsh. 334p. 1994. pap. 29.95 (*1-56343-066-5*) Merritt Pub.

***Workers' Comp for Employers: How to Cut Claims, Reduce Premiums & Stay Out of Trouble.** 3rd ed. James Walsh. (Taking Control Ser.). 1997. pap. 29.95 (*1-56343-155-6*) Merritt Pub.

Workers' Compensation. Jack Mandell. (Illus.). 93p. 1992. pap. 35.00 (*0-317-57854-5*) NJ Inst CLE.

Workers' Compensation: Controlling Costs Within a Flawed System. 25.00 (*0-317-05112-1*) Manu All Prod & Innov.

Workers Compensation: Exposures, Coverages, Claims. Dwight E. Levick & Barbara Grzinicic. Ed. by Standard Publishing Corporation Staff. 608p. 1994. 155.00 (*0-923240-12-8*) Stndrd Publishing.

Workers Compensation: Perspective for the Eighties. 133p. 1981. 24.50 (*0-318-16893-6*) Charter Prop Underwriters Soc.

Workers' Compensation: Strategies for Lowering Costs & Reducing Workers' Suffering. Ed. by Edward M. Welch. LC 89-2485. 149p. (Orig.). 1989. pap. 37.50 (*0-934753-33-4*) LRP Pubns.

***Workers Compensation: The Dilemma & Practical Remedies.** Dennis L. DeMey. 22p. 1997. pap. 24.95 (*0-9642774-8-4*) BSP.

Workers' Compensation-ADA Connection: Supervisory Tools for Workers' Compensation Cost Containment That Reduce ADA Liability. Richard Pimentel et al. Ed. by Anita L. Wright. LC 93-12743. 55p. (Orig.). (C). 1993. pap. text ed. 29.50 (*0-942071-24-7*) M Wright & Assocs.

***Workers' Compensation & Disability Insurance: A Survivor's Guide.** Ed. by M. S. Kaye. (Illus.). 360p. (Orig.). 1996. pap. write for info. (*1-57502-275-3*, P0973) Morris Pubng.

Worker's Compensation & Disability Insurance: All-American Holocaust. LC 95-60763. 200p. (Orig.). 1996. pap. 14.50 (*0-9645353-5-1*) Windigo Pr.

Workers' Compensation & Employee Protection Laws in a Nutshell. 2nd ed. Jack B. Hood et al. LC 83-21658. (Nutshell Ser.). 361p. 1990. reprint ed. pap. 16.00 (*0-314-71824-9*) West Pub.

Workers' Compensation & Protection of Employees. 1992. lib. bdg. 250.00 (*0-8490-5289-0*) Gordon Pr.

Workers' Compensation & Work-Related Illnesses & Diseases. Peter S. Barth & H. Allen Hunt. 1980. 52.50 (*0-262-02141-2*) MIT Pr.

Workers' Compensation & Workplace Safety: Some Lessons from Economic Theory. Richard A. Victor et al. LC 83-3145. 1982. pap. 7.50 (*0-8330-0487-5*, R-2918-1CJ) Rand Corp.

Worker's Compensation Benefits: Adequacy, Equity & Efficiency. Ed. by John D. Worrall & David Appel. LC 85-8208. 206p. 1985. reprint ed. pap. 58.80 (*0-608-01690-X*, 2062346) Bks Demand.

Workers' Compensation Claims Desk Book. Gwen Hampton. 367p. (Orig.). (C). 1989. teacher ed. write for info. (*0-318-65065-7*) Wrkrs Compensation.

Workers' Compensation Claims Desk Book 2. Gwen Hampton. LC 93-60762. 475p. (C). 1993. pap. text ed. 82.00 (*0-9622507-3-2*, 793) Wrkrs Compensation.

***Workers Compensation Claims Management.** David Tweedy et al. 528p. 1997. ring bd. 159.00 (*0-923240-19-5*) Stndrd Publishing.

Worker's Compensation Claims Management, 3 vols., Set. CBC Editorial Staff. LC 94-69181. 1994. ring bd. 495.00 (*0-614-07301-4*) Clark Boardman Callaghan.

Workers Compensation Cost Reduction Manual. James R. Whitmer. 210p. (Orig.). 1993. 24.00 (*0-9622252-3-1*) Comfort Hse Pubs.

Workers' Compensation Forms, 1981-1988. Michael P. Cavel. (Nebraska Legal Forms Ser.). 160p. ring bd. 50.00 (*0-86678-023-8*); ring bd. 85.00 incl. disk (*0-685-70859-4*) MICHIE.

Workers' Compensation Forms, 1981-1988. Michael P. Cavel. Ed. by Stephen L. Liebo. (Nebraska Legal Forms Ser.). 16p. 1986. suppl. ed., pap. 95.00 (*0-86678-052-1*) MICHIE.

***Worker's Compensation Fraud Control & Investigation: A Manual Covering the Whole Spectrum of Conducting Worker's Compensation Claims Investigations.** Robert Campbell. 78p. (Orig.). (C). 1997. pap. 35.00 (*0-918487-96-X*) Thomas Pubns TX.

Worker's Compensation Guide. Burgdolf et al. LC 94-60752. 656p. 1994. 149.00 (*0-7913-2020-0*) Warren Gorham & Lamont.

Workers Compensation Guide. 2nd ed. International Risk Management Institute, Inc. Staff. 135p. 1993. pap. 38.50 (*1-886813-08-6*) Intl Risk Mgt.

***Workers' Compensation Guide for Employers: Regulations, Checklists & Forms.** Charles B. Lewis. LC 97-21305. 1997. write for info. (*1-56759-020-9*) Summers Pr.

***Worker's Compensation Handbook.** John D. Neal & Joseph Danas, Jr., Jr. 400p. 1990. ring bd. 90.00 (*0-945574-36-3*) State Bar WI CLE Bk Div.

***Worker's Compensation Handbook.** 4th ed. John D. Neal & Joseph Danas. LC 97-20729. 1997. pap. write for info. (*1-57862-003-1*) State Bar WI CLE Bk Div.

Worker's Compensation Handbook: A Comprehensive Guide to Worker's Compensation in Indiana. Robert A. Fanning. 158p. (Orig.). 1994. 44.00 (*1-883698-06-5*) IN Chamber Comm.

Workers' Compensation Handbook: A Guide to Job-Related Health Problems. Robert D. Power & Frederick Y. Fung. LC 93-79792. (Illus.). 116p. (Orig.). 1994. pap. 10.95 (*0-929894-07-3*) K-W Pubns.

Workers' Compensation Health Care Cost Containment. Ed. by Judith Greenwood & Alfred Taricco. LC 92-17565. 370p. 1992. 59.50 (*0-934753-66-0*) LRP Pubns.

Worker's Compensation in Alabama for On-the-Job Injuries. Grover S. McLeod. 349p. 1990. text ed. 69.00 (*1-884150-30-6*) Manchester AL.

Workers' Compensation in California: Administrative Inventory. Peter S. Barth & Carol A. Telles. LC 92-33150. 1992. 25.00 (*0-935149-38-4*, WC-92-8) Workers Comp Res Inst.

Workers' Compensation in Canada. 2nd ed. Terrence G. Ison. 350p. 1989. boxed 110.00 (*0-409-80516-5*) MICHIE.

***Workers' Compensation in Colorado: Administrative Inventory.** Carol A. Telles & Sharon E. Fox. LC 96-43124. 1996. 29.00 (*0-935149-62-7*, WC-96-8) Workers Comp Res Inst.

Workers' Compensation in Connecticut: Administrative Inventory. Peter S. Barth. LC 87-29445. 1987. 25.00 (*0-935149-08-2*, WC-87-3) Workers Comp Res Inst.

Workers' Compensation in Georgia: Administrative Inventory. Duncan S. Ballantyne & Stacey M. Eccleston. LC 92-20983. 1992. 25.00 (*0-935149-34-1*, WC-92-4) Workers Comp Res Inst.

***Workers' Compensation in Illinois: Administrative Inventory.** Duncan S. Ballantyne & Karen M. Joyce. LC 96-43125. 1996. 29.00 (*0-935149-63-5*, WC-96-9) Workers Comp Res Inst.

Workers' Compensation in Maine: Administrative Inventory. Richard A. Victor et al. LC 90-23368. 1990. 25.00 (*0-935149-26-0*, WC-90-5) Workers Comp Res Inst.

Workers' Compensation in Michigan: Administrative Inventory. H. Allan Hunt & Stacey M. Eccleston. LC 89-25031. 110p. 1990. 25.00 (*0-935149-23-6*, WC-90-1) Workers Comp Res Inst.

Worker's Compensation in Michigan: Law & Practice. rev. ed. Edward M. Welch. LC 84-80266. 748p. 1993. suppl. ed. 40.00 (*0-685-38206-0*, 93-015); suppl. ed., ring bd. 110.00 (*0-685-38205-2*, 91-012) U MI Law CLE.

W

Workers' Compensation in Minnesota: Administrative Inventory. Duncan S. Ballantyne & Carol A. Telles. LC 71-17044. 1991. 25.00 (0-935149-27-9, WC-91-1) Workers Comp Res Inst.

Workers' Compensation in Missouri: Administrative Inventory. Duncan S. Ballantyne & Carol A. Telles. LC 93-7235. 1993. 25.00 (0-935149-40-6, WC-93-1) Workers Comp Res Inst.

Workers' Compensation in New Jersey: Administrative Inventory. Duncan S. Ballantyne & James F. Dunleavy. LC 93-47994. 1994. 25.00 (0-935149-44-9, WC-94-2) Workers Comp Res Inst.

Workers' Compensation in New York: Administrative Inventory. Duncan S. Ballantyne & Carol A. Telles. LC 92-26511. 1992. 25.00 (0-935149-36-8, WC-92-6) Workers Comp Res Inst.

Workers' Compensation in North Carolina: Administrative Inventory. Duncan S. Ballantyne & Stacey Eccleston. LC 93-35600. 1993. 25.00 (0-935149-43-0, WC-93-5) Workers Comp Res Inst.

Workers' Compensation in Ontario. 2nd ed. Garth Dee et al. 600p. 1993. ring bd. 100.00 (0-409-90845-2, Pub. by Buttrwrth Can Acad CN) Buttrwrth-Heinemann.

Workers' Compensation in Oregon: Administrative Inventory. Duncan S. Ballantyne & James F. Dunleavy. LC 95-6284. 1995. 29.00 (0-935149-52-X, WC-95-2) Workers Comp Res Inst.

Workers' Compensation in Pennsylvania: Administrative Inventory. Duncan S. Ballantyne & Carol A. Telles. LC 91-38317. 1991. 25.00 (0-935149-30-9, WC-91-4) Workers Comp Res Inst.

Workers' Compensation in Texas: Administrative Inventory. Peter S. Barth et al. LC 89-5285. 1989. 25.00 (0-935149-18-X, WC-89-1) Workers Comp Res Inst.

Workers' Compensation in Virginia: Administrative Inventory. Carol A. Telles & Duncan S. Ballantyne. LC 93-47994. 1994. 25.00 (0-935149-46-5, WC-94-3) Workers Comp Res Inst.

Workers' Compensation in Washington: Administrative Inventory. Sara R. Pease. LC 89-39120. 1989. 25.00 (0-935149-20-1, WC-89-3) Workers Comp Res Inst.

Workers' Compensation in Wisconsin: Administrative Inventory. Duncan S. Ballantyne & Carol A. Telles. LC 92-33151. 1992. 25.00 (0-935149-37-6, WC-92-7) Workers Comp Res Inst.

Workers' Compensation Insurance: Claim Costs, Prices, & Regulation. Ed. by David Durbin & Philip S. Borba. LC 92-22576. (C). 1992. lib. bdg. 110.00 (0-7923-9170-5) Huebner Foun Insur.

Workers Compensation Insurance: Profiles of the State Systems. 2nd ed. Alliance of American Insurers Staff. 102p. 1995. pap. text ed. 35.00 (1-887271-20-1) Alliance Am Insurers.

***Workers Compensation Insurance: Profiles of the State Systems.** 3rd rev. ed. 102p. 1996. pap. 35.00 (1-887271-26-0) Alliance Am Insurers.

Workers' Compensation Insurance: The Survival Guide for Business. Joseph P. Bacarro. LC 92-19915. 460p. 1994. spiral bd. 80.00 (0-409-25676-5); suppl. ed., ring bd. 45.00 (0-685-74450-7) MICHIE.

Workers Compensation Insurance & Law Practice: The Next Generation. Donald T. De Carlo & Martin Minkowitz. LC 89-12856. 367p. 1989. 55.00 (0-934753-36-9) LRP Pubns.

Workers' Compensation Insurance Pricing. David Appel. (S. S. Huebner International Ser.). 1988. 53.50 (0-89838-268-8) Huebner Foun Insur.

Workers' Compensation Law. Jon L. Gelman. 737p. 1988. write for info. (0-318-69010-1) West Pub.

Workers' Compensation Law. Larson. 1992. write for info. (0-8205-0281-2, 512); teacher ed. write for info. (0-8205-0282-0) Bender.

Workers' Compensation Law of Ohio. 2nd ed. Philip J. Fulton. 500p. 1991. 125.00 (0-87084-660-4) Anderson Pub Co.

Workers' Compensation Law of the State of Alaska: Including Digest & Supplementary Laws. rev. ed. write for info. (0-318-60911-8) Am Ins NY.

Workers' Compensation Law of the State of Arizona: Including Digest & Supplementary Law with Annotations Through January 1981. rev. ed. write for info. (0-318-60913-4) Am Ins NY.

Workers' Compensation Law of the State of Delaware: Including Digest & Laws. rev. ed. write for info. (0-318-60914-2) Am Ins NY.

Workers' Compensation Law of the State of South Dakota: Containing Workers' Compensation Law, Occupational Disease Disability Law, Including Digests & Supplementary Laws. rev. ed. write for info. (0-318-60915-0) Am Ins NY.

Workers' Compensation Law of the State of Utah: Containing the Workers' Compenstion Law, the Occupational Disease Disability Law, Including Digests & Supplementary Laws with Annotations Through July 1979. rev. ed. write for info. (0-318-60918-5) Am Ins NY.

Workers' Compensation Law Review, 1974-93, 15 vols., Vol. 18. William C. Moran. LC 73-93978. 1996. Vols. 1-15. 750.00 (0-930342-54-2, 108550) W S Hein.

Worker's Compensation Laws - 1996. annuals 1996. ring bd. 109.00 (0-614-13247-9) Am Ins NY.

Worker's Compensation Laws - 1996, 52 vols., Set. annuals 1996. ring bd. 1,962.00 (0-614-13246-0) Am Ins NY.

Worker's Compensation Laws of California. Warren L. Hanna. 1985. pap. write for info. (0-8205-1840-9) Bender.

Workers' Compensation Manual: Injury to Persons & Property Section. 1992. ring bd. 55.00 (0-944694-04-7) DC Bar.

Workers' Compensation Manual for Managers & Supervisors: A Guide to Effective Workers' Compensation Management. 2nd ed. 72p. 1996. pap. 19.00 (0-685-67149-6, 4713) Commerce.

***Worker's Compensation Medical Care: Effective Measurement of Outcomes.** Ed. by Kate Kimpan. LC 96-41336. 1996. 50.00 (0-935149-61-9, WC-96-7) Workers Comp Res Inst.

Workers' Compensation Practice: Seminar Materials. New Jersey Institute for Continuing Legal Education Staff. 93p. 1992. 35.00 (0-317-57862-6) NJ Inst CLE.

Worker's Compensation Review Analyst. Jack Rudman. (Career Examination Ser.: C-308). 1994. pap. 29.95 (0-8373-0308-7) Nat Learn.

Workers' Compensation Social Worker I. Jack Rudman. (Career Examination Ser.: C-1319). 1994. pap. 27.95 (0-8373-1319-8) Nat Learn.

Workers' Compensation Social Worker II. Jack Rudman. (Career Examination Ser.: C-1320). 1994. pap. 29.95 (0-8373-1320-1) Nat Learn.

Workers Compensation State Administrative Directory. Alliance of American Insurers. 61p. 1993. ring bd. 35.00 (1-887271-06-6) Alliance Am Insurers.

Workers Compensation State Funds: Disappearing Capital. Roger K. Kenney. 30p. 1992. pap. text ed. 15.00 (1-887271-05-8) Alliance Am Insurers.

Workers' Compensation Success Stories. Ed. by Richard A. Victor. LC 93-24885. 1993. 50.00 (0-935149-67-8, WC-93-3) Workers Comp Res Inst.

Workers' Compensation Supervisor. (Career Examination Ser.: C-3760). pap. 34.95 (0-8373-3760-7) Nat Learn.

Workers' Compensation 1993. rev. ed. Wake Forest University School of Law Continuing Legal Education Staff. 451p. 1993. pap. 65.00 (0-942225-67-8) Wake Forest Law.

Workers' Control in America: Studies in the History of Work, Technology, & Labor Struggles. David Montgomery. 208p. 1980. pap. text ed. 17.95 (0-521-28006-0) Cambridge U Pr.

***Workers' Control in Latin America.** Jonathan C. Brown. LC 97-1880. 392p. (C). (gr. 13). 1997. pap. text ed. 19.95 (0-8078-4666-X); lib. bdg. 49.95 (0-8078-2362-7) U of NC Pr.

Worker's Control under Plan & Market. Comisso. 1979. text ed. 37.50 (0-300-02334-0) Yale U Pr.

Workers' Cooperatives. GMBATU Staff. 1986. pap. text ed. 6.00 (0-08-034050-4, Pergamon Pr) Elsevier.

Workers' Councils in Czechoslovakia. Vladimir C. Fisera. LC 78-25995. 1979. text ed. 29.95 (0-312-88959-3) St Martin.

Workers' Culture in Imperial Germany. Lynn Abrams. 256p. (C). 1992. text ed. 74.95 (0-415-07635-8, Routledge NY) Routledge.

Workers' Culture in Weimar Germany: Between Tradition & Commitment. W. L. Guttsman. LC 89-38853. 356p. 1990. 19.95 (0-907582-59-1) Berg Pubs.

Workers' Detective: A Story about Alice Hamilton. Stephanie S. McPherson. (J). (gr. 3-6). 1992. lib. bdg. 14.21 (0-87614-699-X, Carolrhoda) Lerner Group.

Workers' Dilemmas: Recruitment, Reliability & Repeated Exchange: An Analysis of Urban Social Networks & Labour Circulation. Margaret Grieco. LC 95-26466. 248p. (C). 1996. text ed. 74.95 (0-415-02577-X) Routledge.

Workers' Education in Action: Selected Articles from Labour Education, a Workers' Education Manual. (Illus.). v, 250p. (Orig.). 1991. pap. 18.00 (92-2-107291-6) Intl Labour Office.

Workers' Educational Association: Aims & Achievements 1903-1977. Roger Fieldhouse. (Landmarks & New Horizons Ser.: No. 4). 1977. pap. 3.50 (0-87060-072-9, LHN 4) Syracuse U Cont Ed.

Workers' Emotions in Shop & Home: Study of Individual Workers from the Psychological & Physiological Standpoint. Rexford B. Hersey. Ed. by Leon Stein. LC 77-70503. (Illus.). 1977. reprint ed. lib. bdg. 41.95 (0-405-10175-9) Ayer.

Worker's Enterprise-Alternative in Privatisation. Murat R. Sertel. Date not set. write for info. (0-614-17898-3) Elsevier.

***Workers' Enterprises: Alternative in Privatization.** Murat R. Sertel. LC 96-46549. 222p. 1996. 125.00 (0-444-81550-3) Elsevier.

Workers' Expressions: Beyond Accommodation & Resistance. Ed. by John Calagione et al. LC 90-26178. (SUNY Series in the Anthropology of Work). 233p. 1992. text ed. 74.50 (0-7914-0835-3); pap. text ed. 24.95 (0-7914-0836-1) State U NY Pr.

***Workers' Financial Participation: East-West Experiences.** Daniel V. Whitehead et al. (Labour-Management Relations Ser.: Vol. 80). xv, 240p. 1995. pap. 27.00 (92-2-109186-4) Intl Labour Office.

Workers from the North: Plantations, Bolivian Labor, & the City in Northwest Argentina. Scott Whiteford. (Latin American Monographs: No. 54). 201p. 1981. text ed. 25.00 (0-292-79015-5) U of Tex Pr.

Workers' Health, Workers' Democracy: The Western Miners' Struggle, 1891-1925. Alan Derickson. LC 88-47722. 264p. 1988. 35.00 (0-8014-2060-1) Cornell U Pr.

***Workers' Home Contamination Study: A Report to Congress.** (Illus.). 281p. (C). 1997. reprint ed. pap. text ed. 45.00 (0-7881-3826-X) DIANE Pub.

Workers in American History. 32th ed. James O'Neal. LC 78-156437. (American Labor Ser., No. 2). 1977. reprint ed. 19.95 (0-405-02935-7) Ayer.

Workers in Arms: The Austrian Schutzbund & the Civil War of 1934. Ilona Duczynska. LC 77-70970. 1978. 25.00 (0-85345-410-8) Monthly Rev.

Workers in French Society in the 19th & 20th Centuries. Gerard Noiriel. Tr. by Helen McPhail from FRE. LC 89-35885. 288p. 1990. 19.95 (0-85496-610-2) Berg Pubs.

Workers in Industrial America: Essays on the Twentieth Century Struggle. 2nd ed. David Brody. LC 92-366. 288p. (C). 1993. pap. 16.95 (0-19-504504-1) OUP.

Workers in New Jersey History. Joseph Gowaski. LC 96-19013. (New Jersey History Ser.). 1996. pap. write for info. (0-89743-083-2) NJ Hist Com.

Workers in the Dawn, 3 Vols. in 1. George Gissing. LC 68-59358. reprint ed. 55.00 (0-404-02777-6) AMS Pr.

Workers in the Metropolis: Class, Ethnicity, & Youth in Antebellum New York City. Richard B. Stott. LC 89-42890. (Illus.). 328p. 1990. 39.95 (0-8014-2067-9) Cornell U Pr.

Workers in Third-World Industrialization. Ed. by Inga Brandell. LC 91-11253. (International Political Economy Ser.). (Illus.). 256p. 1991. text ed. 69.95 (0-312-06503-5) St Martin.

Workers, Jobs, & Inflation. Ed. by Martin N. Baily. LC 82-70891. 365p. 1982. 39.95 (0-8157-0764-9); pap. 18.95 (0-8157-0763-0) Brookings.

***Workers League & the Founding of the Socialist Equality Party.** David North. 37p. 1996. 2.00 (0-929087-74-7) Labor Pubns Inc.

Workers' Management in Yugoslavia: Recent Developments & Trends. Ed. by N. Pasic et al. x, 198p. 1982. 31.50 (92-2-103034-2); pap. 22.50 (92-2-103035-0) Intl Labour Office.

Workers, Managers & Technological Change: Emerging Patterns of Labor Relations. Daniel B. Cornfield. (Studies in Work & Industry). 366p. 1987. 52.50 (0-306-42450-9, Plenum Pr) Plenum.

Workers, Managers, & Welfare Capitalism: The Shoeworkers & Tanners of Endicott Johnson, 1890-1950. Gerald Zahavi. LC 87-6035. (Working Class in American History Ser.). 288p. 1988. text ed. 29.95 (0-252-01444-8) U of Ill Pr.

Workers' Movement. Alain Touraine et al. Tr. by Ian J. Patterson. (Illus.). 322p. 1987. 75.00 (0-521-30852-6) Cambridge U Pr.

Workers' Movement in Russia. Simon Clarke et al. LC 95-6826. (Studies of Communism in Transition). 448p. 1995. 80.00 (1-85898-063-1) E Elgar.

Workers Not Wasters: Masculine Respectability, Consumption & Unemployment in Central Scotland. Daniel Wight. (Edinburgh Education & Society Ser.). 240p. 1994. 45.00 (0-7486-0444-8, Pub. by Edinburgh U Pr UK) Col U Pr.

Workers of African Trade. Ed. by Catherine Coquery-Vidrovitch & Paul E. Lovejoy. LC 85-2259. (Sage Series on African Modernization & Development: No. 11). (Illus.). 304p. reprint ed. pap. 86.70 (0-8357-8449-5, 2034713) Bks Demand.

Workers of Closed Textile Mills. B. B. Patel. (C). 1988. 14.50 (81-204-0290-1, Pub. by Oxford IBH II) S Asia.

Workers of Florence. Richard C. Trexler. LC 92-44785. (Power & Dependence in Renaissance Florence Ser.: Vol. 3). 136p. 1993. pap. 8.95 (0-86698-158-6, P17) Pegasus Pr.

Workers of Nations: Industrial Relations in a Global Economy. Ed. by Sanford M. Jacoby. (Illus.). 288p. 1995. 45.00 (0-19-508904-9) OUP.

Workers of the Donbass Speak: Survival & Identity in the New Ukraine, 1989-1992. Lewis H. Siegelbaum & Daniel J. Walkowitz. LC 94-28752. (SUNY Series in Oral & Public History). 226p. (C). 1995. text ed. 57.50 (0-7914-2485-5); pap. text ed. 18.95 (0-7914-2486-3) State U NY Pr.

Workers of the World & Oppressed Peoples Unite! Proceedings & Documents of the Second Congress, 1920, 2 vols. Ed. by John Riddell. LC 91-66263. (Illus.). 1147p. (C). 1991. Set. pap. 65.00 (0-937091-06-5); Set. lib. bdg. 160.00 (0-937091-07-3) Pathfinder NY.

Workers of the World & Oppressed Peoples Unite! Proceedings & Documents of the Second Congress, 1920, 2 vols., 1. Ed. by John Riddell. LC 91-66263. (Illus.). 587p. (C). 1991. pap. 35.95 (0-937091-08-1); lib. bdg. 85.00 (0-937091-09-X) Pathfinder NY.

Workers of the World & Oppressed Peoples Unite! Proceedings & Documents of the Second Congress, 1920, 2 vols., 2. Ed. by John Riddell. LC 91-66263. (Illus.). 560p. (C). 1991. pap. 35.95 (0-937091-10-3); lib. bdg. 85.00 (0-937091-11-1) Pathfinder NY.

Workers of the World Undermined: American Labor's Role in U. S. Foreign Policy. Beth Sims. (Resource Center Bk.). 100p. (Orig.). 1992. 30.00 (0-89608-430-2); pap. 9.00 (0-89608-429-9) South End Pr.

Workers of Tianjin, 1900-1949. Gail Hershatter. LC 86-1270. 328p. 1986. 45.00 (0-8047-1318-9) Stanford U Pr.

Workers of Tianjin, 1900-1949. Gail Hershatter. 325p. (C). 1993. pap. 14.95 (0-8047-2216-1) Stanford U Pr.

Workers on Relief. Grace Adams. LC 74-137154. (Poverty U. S. A. Historical Record Ser.). 1977. reprint ed. 25.95 (0-405-03091-6) Ayer.

Workers on the Edge: Work, Leisure, & Politics in Industrializing Cincinnati, 1788-1890. Steven J. Ross. (History of Urban Life Ser.). 464p. 1985. text ed. 57.50 (0-231-05520-X) Col U Pr.

Workers on the Nile: Nationalism, Communism, Islam, & the Egyptian Working Class, 1882-1954. Joel Beinin & Zachary Lockman. (Illus.). 512p. (C). 1988. pap. text ed. 28.50 (0-691-00845-0) Princeton U Pr.

Workers on the Waterfront: Seamen, Longshoremen, & Unionism in the 1930s. Bruce Nelson. LC 87-28749. 384p. 1990. pap. text ed. 13.95 (0-252-06144-6) U of Ill Pr.

Workers, Owners & Politics in Coal Mining: An International Comparison of Industrial Relations. Ed. by Gerald D. Feldman & Klaus Tenfelde. LC 89-35882. 448p. 1990. 29.95 (0-85496-603-X) Berg Pubs.

***Workers' Participation.** Blanpain. 1992. pap. text ed. 85.00 (90-6544-600-1) Kluwer Ac.

Workers' Participation: A Voice in Decisions, 1981-1985. Ed. by Jacques Monat & Hedva Sarfati. 284p. 1986. pap. 27.00 (92-2-105232-X) Intl Labour Office.

Workers, Participation, & Democracy: Internal Politics in the British Union Movement. Joel D. Wolfe. LC 85-5413. (Contributions in Political Science Ser.: No. 136). (Illus.). xii, 258p. 1985. text ed. 59.95 (0-313-24692-0, WOW/, Greenwood Pr) Greenwood.

Workers' Participation in Decisions Within Undertakings. xi, 224p. (Orig.). 1983. 36.00 (92-2-101987-X); pap. 27.00 (92-2-101988-8) Intl Labour Office.

Workers' Participative Schemes: The Experience of Capitalist & Plan-Based Societies. Helen A. Tsiganou. LC 90-19916. (Contributions in Legal Studies: No. 35). 272p. 1991. text ed. 59.95 (0-313-26479-1, TCN/, Greenwood Pr) Greenwood.

***Workers Party.** Jack Stuart. Ed. by Dan Georgakas. (Labor in America Ser.). 300p. 1997. text ed. 45.00 (0-8153-1882-0) Garland.

Worker's Party & Democratization in Brazil. Margaret E. Keck. 384p. (C). 1992. text ed. 42.50 (0-300-05074-7) Yale U Pr.

Worker's Pockets. Way. (Stickers 'N' Shapes Ser.). (J). 1996. 3.99 (0-689-81105-5) S&S Childrens.

Workers Profit Sharing: The Riddle of History Solved. 2nd ed. Shirley Telford. 32p. (Orig.). (C). 1973. pap. text ed. 4.00 (0-9600202-6-8) William & Rich.

Workers' Revolution in Russia, 1917: The View from Below. Ed. by Daniel H. Kaiser. (Illus.). 176p. 1987. pap. text ed. 13.95 (0-521-34971-0) Cambridge U Pr.

Workers' Revolution in Russia, 1917: The View from Below. Ed. by Daniel H. Kaiser. (Illus.). 176p. 1987. text ed. 54.95 (0-521-34166-3) Cambridge U Pr.

***Worker's Rights.** LC 96-42445. (What Do We Mean By Human Rights? Ser.). (J). 1997. lib. bdg. write for info. (0-531-14434-8) Watts.

Workers Rights, East & West. Adrian Karatnycky et al. 130p. 1980. pap. 24.95 (0-87855-867-5) Transaction Pubs.

Worker's Rights, East, & West. Adrian Karatnycky et al. 150p. 4.95 (0-318-14690-8) League Indus Demo.

Workers' Rights Versus the Secret Police. Larry Seigle. 46p. 1981. pap. 3.00 (0-87348-435-5) Pathfinder NY.

Workers' Self-Management & Organizational Power in Yugoslavia. Ed. by Josip Obradovic & William N. Dunn. LC 78-16307. 464p. reprint ed. pap. 132.30 (0-7837-2145-5, 2042431) Bks Demand.

Workers' Self-Management in Algeria. Ian Clegg. (Illus.). 256p. 1972. 25.00 (0-85345-200-8) Monthly Rev.

Workers' Self-Management in the United States. Christopher E. Gunn. LC 83-45937. 254p. 1986. pap. 15.95 (0-8014-9376-5) Cornell U Pr.

Workers, Society, & the Soviet State: Labor & Life in Moscow, 1918-1929. William J. Chase. LC 85-28823. (Working Class in European History Ser.). 368p. 1987. text ed. 34.95 (0-252-01319-0); pap. text ed. 14.95 (0-252-06129-2) U of Ill Pr.

Workers Speak: Self-Portraits, 1902-1906. Ed. by Leon Stein & Philip Taft. LC 70-156433. (American Labor Ser., No. 2). 1980. 18.95 (0-405-02956-X) Ayer.

Workers' Struggle in Puerto Rico: A Documentary History. Angel Quintero Rivera. Tr. by Cedric Belfrage. LC 76-40343. 236p. 1976. reprint ed. pap. 67.30 (0-7837-9615-3, 2060372) Bks Demand.

Workers Themselves Syndicalism & International Labour: The Origins of the International Working Men's Association, 1913-1923. Wayne Thorpe. (C). 1990. lib. bdg. 129.00 (0-7923-0276-1) Kluwer Ac.

Workers Wanted: Study of Employers' Hiring Policies, Preferences, & Practices in New Haven & Charlotte. William E. Noland & E. Wight Bakke. Ed. by Leon Stein. LC 77-70521. (Illus.). 1977. reprint ed. lib. bdg. 23.95 (0-405-10189-9) Ayer.

Workers Who Built Cleveland. Fred Thompson. 16p. (Orig.). 1987. pap. 3.00 (0-88286-128-X) C H Kerr.

Workers with Multiple Chemical Sensitivities. Ed. by Mark R. Cullen. LC 86-642306. (Occupational Medicine Ser.: Vol. 2, No. 4). 1987. reprint ed. pap. 45.60 (0-608-01985-2, 2062640) Bks Demand.

Workers Without Weapons: The South African Congress of Trade Unions & the Organisation of the African Workers. Edward Feit. LC 75-5738. 230p. (Orig.). (C). 1975. lib. bdg. 32.50 (0-208-01496-9, Archon Bks) Shoe String.

Workers, Women, & Afro-Americans: Images of the United States in German Travel Literature, from 1923 to 1933. Sara Markham. (American University Studies: Germanic Languages & Literature: Ser. I, Vol. 45). 317p. 1986. text ed. 49.90 (0-8204-0266-4) P Lang Pubng.

Workers' World: Kinship, Community & Protest in an Industrial Society, 1900-1940. John Bodnar. LC 82-6626. (Illus.). 256p. 1982. 42.00 (0-8018-2785-X) Johns Hopkins.

Workers' World at Hagley. rev. ed. Glenn Porter. Ed. by Jacqueline Hinsley & Joy Kaufmann. LC 92-53198. 64p. reprint ed. pap. text ed. 9.95 (0-914650-30-0) Hagley Museum.

Workers' World at Hagley. rev. ed. Glenn Porter. (Illus.). 64p. 1982. pap. 9.95 (0-914650-21-1) Hagley Museum.

Workes. Thomas Scott. LC 73-6158. (English Experience Ser.: No. 621). 1265p. 1973. reprint ed. 175.00 (90-221-0621-7) Walter J Johnson.

Workes of Armorie, 3 bks. John Bossewell. LC 72-173. (English Experience Ser.: No. 145). 1969. reprint ed. 50.00 (90-221-0145-2) Walter J Johnson.

Workfare: Does It Work? Is It Fair? Patricia M. Evans et al. Ed. by Adil Sayeed. 145p. 1995. pap. 15.95 (0-88645-165-5, Pub. by Inst Res Pub CN) Ashgate Pub Co.

An Asterisk (*) at the beginning of an entry indicates that the title is appearing in BIP for the first time.

Workfare or Fair Work: Women, Welfare & Government Work Programs. Nancy E. Rose. LC 95-8589. 320p. (C). 1995. text ed. 52.00 (0-8135-2232-3); pap. text ed. 19.95 (0-8135-2233-1) Rutgers U Pr.

***Workflow Handbook, 1997.** Peter Lawrence. 1997. text ed. 80.00 (0-471-96947-8) Wiley.

Workflow Imperative: Building Real World Business Solutions. Thomas M. Koulopoulos. 240p. 1995. text ed. 34.95 (0-442-01975-0) Van Nos Reinhold.

Workflow in Imaging Systems. Marc D'Alleyrand. 1994. pap. 26.00 (0-89258-242-1, C123) Assn Inform & Image Mgmt.

Workflow Management Strategies. James G. Kobielus. 1996. pap. 29.99 (1-56884-993-1) IDG Bks.

***Workflow Management Strategies.** James G. Kobielus. 1997. pap. 39.99 (0-7645-3012-7) IDG Bks.

Workflow Management Systems: Modeling & Architecture. Stefan Jablonski & C. Bussler. 200p. 1996. pap. 39.95 (1-85032-222-8) ITCP.

Workflow Management Systems for Process Organizations, Vol. 1096. T. Schael. LC 96-18724. (Lecture Notes in Computer Science Ser.). 200p. 1996. pap. 43.00 (3-540-61401-X) Spr-Verlag.

Workflow Reengineering. Steve Hannaford. 259p. 1996. 30.00 (1-56830-265-7) Hayden.

***Workflow Strategies.** James G. Kobielus. 400p. (Orig.). 1997. pap. write for info. (0-614-26261-5) IDG Bks.

Workflow-Workspace. Hy Bomberg. 83p. 1986. pap. text ed. 7.50 (0-936658-24-X) H Miller Res.

Workforce America! Managing Employee Diversity As A Vital Resource. Marilyn Loden & Judy B. Rosener. 192p. 1990. text ed. 35.00 (1-55623-386-8) Irwin Prof Pubng.

Workforce Development: Building Statewide Systems. Karin McCarthy & Rebekah Lashman. (Investing in People Ser.). 24p. 15.00 (1-55516-342-4, 3123) Natl Conf State Legis.

Workforce Diversity. William H. Sonnenschein. LC 96-35853. (Practical Executive Ser.). (Illus.). 192p. 1997. pap. 14.95 (0-8442-2981-4, NTC Busn Bks) NTC Pub Grp.

Workforce Diversity in Texas State Government: Texas Natural Resource Conservation Commission. Kenneth W. Tolo. (Policy Research Project Report: No. 110). 238p. 1994. pap. 15.50 (0-89940-718-8) LBJ Sch Pub Aff.

***Workforce Education.** Gray & Herr. 1997. text ed. 40.00 (0-205-19834-1) P-H.

***Workforce Growth Trends: 1996 Edition.** 470p. 1996. pap. text ed. 325.00 (1-878339-51-6) Schonfeld & Assocs.

***Workforce Growth Trends: 1997 Edition.** 470p. 1997. pap. text ed. 345.00 (1-878339-60-5) Schonfeld & Assocs.

***Workforce Keyboarding.** 11th ed. Joyner. (TA - Typing/Keyboarding Ser.). 1997. pap. write for info. (0-314-20568-3) S-W Pub.

Workforce Management: How Today's Companies Are Meeting Business & Employee Needs. Barbara Pope. 225p. 1992. 27.50 (1-55623-537-2) Irwin Prof Pubng.

Workforce Management Module 7: Managing for the Future. Ancona et al. (GI- Organizational Behavior Ser.). 1996. text ed. 7.95 (0-538-85881-8) S-W Pub.

Workforce Management in the Arabian Peninsula: Forces Affecting Development. Ed. by George S. Roukis & Patrick J. Montana. LC 85-24772. (Contributions in Economics & Economic History Ser.: No. 67). 228p. 1986. text ed. 55.00 (0-313-24209-7) Greenwood.

Workforce Policies: State Activity & Innovations. National Association of State Budget Officers Staff. 132p. (Orig.). 1995. pap. text ed. 25.00 (1-887253-00-9) NASBD.

Workforce Policies for the 1990s: A New Labor Market Agenda & The Possibilities of Employment Policy. Ray Marshall & Paul Osterman. LC 89-80284. 1989. 12.00 (0-944826-05-9) Economic Policy Inst.

***Workforce Ratios & Forecasts: 1996 Edition.** 220p. 1996. pap. text ed. 325.00 (1-878339-50-8) Schonfeld & Assocs.

***Workforce Ratios & Forecasts: 1997 Edition.** 220p. 1997. pap. text ed. 345.00 (1-878339-59-1) Schonfeld & Assocs.

***Workforce Readiness: Competence & Assessment.** Ed. by Harold F. O'Neil, Jr. LC 97-13791. 375p. 1997. 79.95 (0-8058-2149-X); pap. 39.95 (0-8058-2150-3) L Erlbaum Assocs.

Workforce Reductions: Downsizing Strategies Used in Selected Organizations. 42p. (Orig.). (C). 1995. pap. text ed. 25.00 (0-7881-2029-8) DIANE Pub.

Workforce Renewal: Increasing the Quality & Quantity of Work. Bernard Petrina. Ed. by Chris Carrigan. LC 93-73205. (Fifty-Minute Ser.). (Illus.). 95p. (Orig.). 1994. pap. 10.95 (1-56052-270-4) Crisp Pubns.

Workforce Two-Thousand: Work & Workers for the 21st Century. William B. Johnston et al. (Illus.). 145p. 1987. pap. 4.25 (0-16-003887-1, S/N 029-014-00240-2) USGPO.

Workforce Two Thousand: Work & Workers in the 21st Century: How to Stimulate World Growth, Improving Productivity, Improving the Dynamism of an Aging Workforce, Integrating Minorities & Improving Workers' Education & Skills. 1991. lib. bdg. 250.00 (0-8490-4392-1) Gordon Pr.

***Workforce 2000 Revisited.** Carol Damico. 1997. pap. text ed. 14.95 (1-55813-061-6) Hudson Instit IN.

***Workforce 2000: The Challenge for Business & Education: Creating Effective Partnerships.** Jo-Ann Vega & Bobbi R. Madry. 123p. (Orig.). 1997. pap. 9.95 (0-9657340-0-5) Rockland Busn.

Workforce 2000: Work & Workers for the Twenty-First Century. William B. Johnston & Arnold E. Packer. 117p. (Orig.). 1987. pap. 10.00 (1-55813-004-7); 5.00 (1-55813-005-5) Hudson Instit IN.

Workforce 2000: Work & Workers for the 21st Century. (Illus.). 117p. (Orig.). (C). 1993. pap. 35.00 (1-56806-590-6) DIANE Pub.

***Workforce 2020: Work & Workers for the 21st Century.** Richard W. Judy & Carol D'Amico. (Illus.). 176p. 1997. pap. text ed. 45.00 (1-57979-207-3) BPI Info Servs.

Workgroup Computing: Messaging, Workflow, & Groupware. Alan R. Simon & William Marion. 1996. pap. write for info. (0-07-056728-X) McGraw.

WorkGroup Computing: Workflow, Groupware, & Messaging. Alan R. Simon. 1996. pap. text ed. 40.00 (0-07-057628-9) McGraw.

***Workguide Modern Topics.** Longman Publishing Staff. Date not set. pap. text ed. write for info. (0-05-003808-7) Addison-Wesley.

Workhealing: The Healing Process for You & Your Job. Charles Mallory. 128p. (Orig.). 1993. pap. 8.95 (0-87516-664-4) DeVorss.

Workholding. Society of Manufacturing Engineers Staff. LC 82-61237. (Productivity Equipment Ser.). (Illus.). 640p. 1982. reprint ed. pap. 180.00 (0-7837-8185-7, 2047890) Bks Demand.

Workholding in the lathe. Tubal Cain. (Workshop Practice Ser.: No. 15). (Illus.). 112p. (Orig.). 1986. pap. 18.50 (0-85242-908-8, Pub. by Nexus Special Interests UK) Trans-Atl Phila.

Workhorse Props. Gerry Manning. (Illus.). 112p. 1995. pap. 21.95 (0-7603-0189-1) Motorbooks Intl.

***Workhouse Children: Infant & Child Paupers under the Worchester Poor Law, 1780-1871.** Frank Crompton. (Illus.). 224p. 1997. 72.00 (0-7509-1281-2, Pub. by Sutton Pubng UK) Bks Intl VA.

***Workhouse Girl.** Jessica Stirling. 1997. 25.95 (0-312-15698-7) St Martin.

Workhouses of Ireland. John O'Connor. (Illus.). 160p. (Orig.). 1995. pap. 19.95 (0-937702-15-3) Irish Bks Media.

***Workin' for Galatti's Lira: An AFS Drivere's Recollections of Cross-Cultural Encounters in World War II.** Willard Walker. (Illus.). 57p. 1996. lib. bdg. 17.50 (1-885752-01-6) Am Fld Srv.

***Workin' It: Women Living Through Drugs & Crime.** Leon E. Pettiway. LC 97-21497. 1997. write for info. (1-56639-579-8); pap. write for info. (1-56639-580-1) Temple U Pr.

Workin' Noon to Five: The Official Workplace Quizbook. Ed. by Shoebox Greetings Staff. (Illus.). 96p. (Orig.). 1993. pap. 6.95 (0-8362-1730-6) Andrews & McMeel.

***Workin on the Railroad.** Vranich. LC 97-13786. 1997. 24.95 (0-312-17182-X) St Martin.

Workin' the Wood. Greg Bohn. (Secrets of a Northwoods Walleye Guide Ser.). (Illus.). 64p. 1989. pap. 6.95 (0-939314-50-9) Fishing Hot.

Working. Helen Oxenbury. (Oxenbury Board Bks.). (Illus.). 7p. (J). (ps up). 1981. bds. 3.95 (0-671-42112-3, Litl Simon S&S) S&S Childrens.

Working. Studs Terkel. 768p. 1985. mass mkt. 6.95 (0-345-32569-9) Ballantine.

Working. Studs Terkel. Date not set. pap. 13.00 (1-56584-342-8) New Press NY.

Working! A Guide for Young Adults. Bryna S. Fraser. 11p. 1992. 2.50 (0-86510-068-3) Natl Inst Work.

Working: Changes & Choices. Ed. by James O'Toole et al. LC 81-6773. 525p. (C). 1981. Reader, 525p. pap. 24.95 (0-89885-111-4); Study guide, 54p. student ed., pap. 18.95 (0-89885-112-2); pap. 18.95 (0-89885-113-0) Human Sci Pr.

Working: Conflict & Change. 3rd ed. George Ritzer & David Walczak. (Illus.). 448p. 1986. text ed. write for info. (0-13-967589-2) P-H.

Working: Learning a Living. Bailey. (CA - Career Development Ser.). 1997. suppl. ed., pap. 6.95 (0-538-66372-3) S-W Pub.

Working: Learning a Living. annot. ed. Bailey. (Career Education Ser.). 1995. 54.00 (0-8273-6563-2) Delmar.

Working: Learning a Living. 2nd ed. Bailey. (Career Education Ser.). 1995. text ed. 38.00 (0-8273-6562-4) Delmar.

Working: Learning a Living. 2nd ed. Bailey. (CA - Career Development Ser.). 1997. wbk. ed., pap. 13.95 (0-538-65097-4) S-W Pub.

Working: Learning a Living. 2nd ed. Bailey. (CA - Career Development Ser.). 1997. pap. 68.95 (0-538-65098-2) S-W Pub.

Working: Learning a Living. 2nd ed. Larry Bailey. (CA - Career Development Ser.). 480p. 1997. pap. 42.95 (0-538-65096-6) S-W Pub.

Working: Skills for a New Age. Bailey. (Career Education Ser.). 1990. student ed., suppl. ed., pap. 22.95 (0-8273-3346-3); teacher ed., pap. 60.95 (0-8273-3349-8); 55.95 (0-8273-3344-7) Delmar.

Working: Skills for a New Age. Bailey. (Career Education Ser.). 1990. teacher ed., pap. 18.95 (0-8273-3345-5); suppl. ed., teacher ed., text ed. 145.95 (0-8273-3323-4) Delmar.

***Working: Sociological Perspectives.** 2nd ed. Robert A. Rothman. LC 97-11883. 1998. write for info. (0-13-621814-8) P-H.

Working a Passage: Or, Life in a Liner. Charles F. Briggs. 1972. reprint ed. lib. bdg. 28.00 (0-8422-8009-X) Irvington.

Working a Passage: or Life on a Liner. Charles F. Briggs. 1986. reprint ed. pap. text ed. 6.95 (0-8290-1947-2) Irvington.

***Working Abroad.** 19th ed. Godfrey Golzen. (Daily Telegraph Guides Ser.). 1996. pap. 15.95 (0-7494-1970-9) Kogan Page Ltd.

Working Actor. Katinka Matson. Date not set. pap. 17.95 (0-670-83594-3) Viking Penguin.

Working Actor: A Guide to the Profession. Katinka Matson. (Handbook Ser.). 1978. mass mkt. 5.95 (0-14-046343-7, Penguin Bks) Viking Penguin.

Working Actor: A Guide to the Profession. rev. ed. Katinka Matson & Judith Katz. LC 93-12324. 192p. 1993. pap. 12.00 (0-14-014433-1, Penguin Bks) Viking Penguin.

Working Actors: The Craft of Television, Film, & Stage Performance. Richard A. Blum. 153p. 1989. pap. 29.95 (0-240-80004-4, Focal) Buttrwrth-Heinemann.

Working after Brain Injury: What Can I Do? Dana S. DeBoskey. (Illus.). 128p. (Orig.). 1995. pap. 12.50 (1-882855-35-3) HDI Pubs.

Working Airedale. Bryan Cummins. LC 94-14298. (Illus.). 192p. 1994. 24.95 (0-940269-07-4) OTR Pubns.

Working Alliance: Theory, Research & Practice. Adam O. Horvath & Leslie S. Greenberg. (Personality Processes Ser.). 304p. 1994. text ed. 62.50 (0-471-54640-2) Wiley.

***Working Alliances & the Politics of Difference: Diversity & Feminist Ethics.** Janet R. Jakobsen. LC 97-22852. 1997. write for info. (0-253-33357-1); pap. write for info. (0-253-21165-4) Ind U Pr.

Working Alone. Murray Felsher. 224p. (Orig.). 1994. pap. 10.00 (0-425-15824-1, Berkley Trade) Berkley Pub.

Working Alone: Making the Most of Self-Employment. Murray Felsher. 224p. (Orig.). 1996. mass mkt. 5.99 (0-425-15264-2) Berkley Pub.

Working Alone: Surviving & Thriving. Diana Lamplugh et al. (Institute of Management Ser.). 208p. (Orig.). 1993. pap. 45.00 (0-273-60196-2, Pub. by Pitman Pubng UK) St Mut.

Working Alongside People with Long-Term Mental Health Problems. R. Perkins & J. Repper. (Illus.). 236p. (Orig.). 1996. pap. 34.95 (1-56593-738-4, 1436) Singular Publishing.

Working & Caring. T. Berry Brazelton. LC 85-11189. 288p. 1985. 16.95 (0-201-10623-X) Addison-Wesley.

Working & Caring. T. Berry Brazelton. (Illus.). 224p. 1992. pap. 13.00 (0-201-63271-3) Addison-Wesley.

Working & Educating for Life: Feminist & International Perspectives on Adult Education. Mechthild U. Hart. 240p. (C). (gr. 13). 1991. text ed. 22.95 (0-415-00558-2, A1513) Routledge.

Working & Education for Life: Feminist & International Perspectives on Adult Education. Mechthild U. Hart. 272p. (C). 1994. pap. 22.95 (0-415-90915-5) Routledge.

Working & Learning Together for Change. Ed. by Colin Biott & Jennifer Nias. (Developing Teachers & Teaching Ser.). 160p. 1992. 90.00 (0-335-09717-0, Open Univ Pr); pap. 32.00 (0-335-09716-2, Open Univ Pr) Taylor & Francis.

Working & Managing in a New Age. Ron Garland. LC 88-31966. 150p. (Orig.). 1989. pap. 12.95 (0-89334-123-1) Humanics Ltd.

Working & Managing in a New Age. Ron Garland. LC 88-31966. (Illus.). 150p. (Orig.). 1989. lib. bdg. 22.95 (0-89334-192-4, 192-4) Humanics Ltd.

Working & Mothering. Linda G. Kuzmack & George Salomon. 28p. 1980. pap. 1.50 (0-87495-030-9) Am Jewish Comm.

Working Around Workers' Injuries: Designing & Implementing Systematic Early Return to Work in the Private & Public Sectors. Ted Taylor. LC 90-92007. 150p. 1990. 96.00 (0-9630175-0-0) Mentor Pub.

Working as if Life Mattered. Margaret A. Lulic. 128p. (Orig.). 1995. pap. 7.95 (0-9638526-1-2) Blue Edge Pub.

***Working As If Life Mattered.** Ed. by Margaret A. Lulic. 120p. (Orig.). 1995. pap. write for info. (0-614-29621-8) Blue Edge Pub.

Working at Archaeological Chronometry: Radiocarbon & Tree-Ring Models & Applications from Black Mesa, Arizona. Francis E. Smiley & Richard V. N. Ahlstrom. LC 93-73672. (Center for Archaeological Investigations Research Paper Ser.: No. 16). (Illus.). 324p. (Orig.). 1997. pap. write for info. (0-88104-080-0) Center Archaeol.

Working at Archaeology. Lewis R. Binford. (Studies in Archaeology). 1983. text ed. 57.00 (0-12-100060-5) Acad Pr.

Working-at-Home Sourcebook. 1992. lib. bdg. 295.95 (0-8490-8894-1) Gordon Pr.

***Working at Home While the Kids Are There, Too.** Loriann H. Oberlin. LC 97-17757. 1997. write for info. (1-56414-305-8) Career Pr Inc.

Working at Human Relations. 2nd ed. Rosemary T. Fruehling & Neild B. Oldham. 196p. (C). 1991. teacher ed. 8.00 (1-56118-071-8); pap. text ed. 16.95 (1-56118-070-X) Paradigm MN.

***Working at Inglis.** David Sobel & Susan Meurer. pap. 24.95 (1-55028-438-X, Pub. by J Lorimer CN) Formac Dist Ltd.

***Working at Inglis.** David Sobel & Susan Meurer. bds. 39.95 (1-55028-439-8, Pub. by J Lorimer CN) Formac Dist Ltd.

Working at Inventing: Thomas Edison & the Menlo Park Experience. Intro. by William S. Pretzer. (Illus.). 144p. 1989. 24.95 (0-933728-33-6, Ford Mus); pap. 12.95 (0-933728-34-4, Ford Mus) Edison Inst.

Working at the Calling: New Directions for the Laborers. John F. Goodman. (Illus.). 224p. 1992. pap. 29.95 (0-9630556-0-7) Laborers Intl.

***Working at the Interface of Culture: Eighteen Lives in Social Science.** Michael H. Bond. LC 97-15834. 248p. (C). 1997. text ed. write for info. (0-415-15846-X) Routledge.

Working at the Stadium: Dodger Players, Fans, & Vendors in a Championship Season. Tom Zimmerman. (Illus.). 120p. (Orig.). 1989. pap. 14.95 (0-962013-0-8) Pac Tides Pr.

Working at Woodworking: How to Organize Your Shop & Your Business. James Tolpin. (Illus.). 160p. 1991. pap. text ed. 21.95 (0-942391-67-5) Taunton.

Working at Writing: Columnists & Critics Composing. Robert L. Root, Jr. LC 90-38873. 264p. (C). 1991. 24.95 (0-8093-1686-2) S Ill U Pr.

***Working Beneath the Surface.** Thomas Riskas. 220p. 1997. 22.95 (1-890009-15-6) Exec Excell.

Working Bibliography of Greek Law. George M. Calhoun et al. (Harvard Series of Legal Bibliographies: Vol. 1). xix, 144p. 1980. reprint ed. lib. bdg. 45.00 (0-89941-132-0, 300120) W S Hein.

Working Bibliography on Behavioral & Emotional Disorders & Assessment Instruments in Mental Retardation. Michael G. Aman. 40p. (Orig.). (C). 1996. pap. text ed. 20.00 (0-7881-2739-X) DIANE Pub.

***Working Border Collie: AKC Rank #83.** Marjorie Quarton & Carole Presberg. (Illus.). 256p. 1998. 35.95 (0-7938-0496-5, TS-287) TFH Pubns.

Working Brain. Aleksandr R. Luria. Tr. by B. Haigh. LC 72-95540. 408p. 1976. pap. 19.00 (0-465-09208-X) Basic.

Working but Poor: America's Contradiction. rev. ed. Sar A. Levitan et al. LC 92-34719. (Illus.). 160p. 1993. text ed. 32.50 (0-8018-4574-2); pap. text ed. 12.95 (0-8018-4575-0) Johns Hopkins.

Working Capital for Small Business: Addressing the Need. Kenneth Poole. Ed. by Jenny Murphy. 32p. (Orig.). 1987. pap. 17.00 (0-317-04818-X) Natl Coun Econ Dev.

Working Capital Management in Small Scale Industries, India. N. M. Khandelwal. 1985. 19.00 (0-317-40620-5, Pub. by Ashish II) S Asia.

Working Carers: International Perspectives on Work & Care of Older People. Ed. by Judith Phillips. 176p. 1996. 59.95 (1-85628-675-4, Pub. by Avebury Pub UK) Ashgate Pub Co.

***Working Chemists with Disabilities: Expanding Opportunities in Science.** Michael Woods & Todd A. Blumenkopf. LC 97-1976. 1997. write for info. (0-8412-3502-3) Am Chemical.

Working Citizen. Safford. (CA - Career Development Ser.). 1983. wbk. ed., pap. 16.95 (0-538-07610-0) S-W Pub.

Working Class. Kenneth Roberts. LC 77-26300. (Aspects of Modern Sociology Ser.). 216p. reprint ed. pap. 61.60 (0-317-27663-8, 2025212) Bks Demand.

Working Class, Chpts. 1-5. Decker. (Computer Science Ser.). 1996. pap. 28.00 (0-534-95288-7) Wadsworth Pub.

Working Class America: Essays on Labor, Community, & American Society. Ed. by Michael H. Frisch & Daniel J. Walkowitz. (Working Class in American History Ser.). 336p. 1983. pap. text ed. 12.95 (0-252-00954-1) U of Ill Pr.

Working-Class Americanism: The Politics of Labor in a Textile City, 1914-1960. Gary Gerstle. (Interdisciplinary Perspectives on Modern History Ser.). (Illus.). 368p. (C). 1989. text ed. 74.95 (0-521-36131-1) Cambridge U Pr.

Working-Class Americanism: The Politics of Labor in a Textile City, 1914-1960. Gary Gerstle. (Interdisciplinary Perspectives on Modern History Ser.). (Illus.). 336p. (C). 1991. pap. 17.95 (0-521-42461-5) Cambridge U Pr.

Working Class & Its Culture. Ed. & Intro. by Neil L. Shumsky. LC 95-36145. (American Cities Ser.: Vol. 5). (Illus.). 416p. 1995. reprint ed. text ed. 75.00 (0-8153-2190-2) Garland.

Working Class & Politics in Europe & America, 1929-1945. Ed. by Stephen Salter & John Stevenson. 384p. (C). 1990. text ed. 48.95 (0-582-05285-8, 78283) Longman.

Working Class & the Natonalist Movement in India: The Critical Years. Rakhahari Chatterji. 1985. 14.50 (0-685-10918-6, Pub. by S Asia Pubs II) S Asia.

Working Class & Welfare: Reflections of the Political Development & the Welfare State in Australia & New Zealand, 1890-1980. Francis G. Castles. 128p. 1985. text ed. 29.95 (0-86861-669-9) Routledge Chapman & Hall.

Working-Class Community in Industrial America: Work, Leisure, & Struggle in Two Industrial Cities, 1880-1930. John T. Cumbler. LC 78-57768. (Contributions in Labor History Ser.: No. 8). 283p. 1979. text ed. 59.95 (0-313-20615-5, CWC/, Greenwood Pr) Greenwood.

Working Class Cultures in Britain, 1890-1960: Gender, Class, & Ethnicity. Joanna Bourke. LC 93-18891. 272p. (C). 1993. pap. 19.95 (0-415-09898-X) Routledge.

Working Class Cultures in Britain, 1890-1960: Gender, Class, & Ethnicity. Joanna Bourke. LC 93-18891. 272p. (C). (gr. 13). 1994. text ed. 69.95 (0-415-09897-1) Routledge.

Working-Class Fiction in Theory & Practice: A Reading of Alan Sillitoe. Peter Hitchcock. LC 89-4747. 144p. 1991. 39.00 (0-8357-1976-6) Univ Rochester Pr.

Working-Class Fight for Peace. Brian Grogan. 143p. 1983. reprint ed. pap. 8.00 (0-87348-637-4) Pathfinder NY.

Working-Class Formation: Nineteenth-Century Patterns in Western European & the United States. Ed. by Ira Katznelson & Aristide R. Zolberg. (Illus.). 464p. 1986. pap. text ed. 22.95 (0-691-10207-4) Princeton U Pr.

Working Class Girls in Nineteenth-Century England: Life, Work, & Schooling. Margaret C. Gomersall. LC 95-51280. 1997. text ed. 55.00 (0-312-12970-X) St Martin.

Working Class Hero: A New Strategy for Labor. Stanley Aronowitz. LC 84-11018. 229p. 1984. reprint ed. pap. 12.95 (0-915361-13-2, Watts) Hemed Bks.

***Working Class Hollywood: Silent Film & the Shaping of Class in America.** Steven J. Ross. LC 97-8462. 1998. write for info. (0-691-03234-3) Princeton U Pr.

***Working-Class Housing in England Between the Wars: The Becontree Estate.** Andrzej Olechnowicz. (Oxford Historical Monographs). (Illus.). 316p. 1997. 85.00 (0-19-820650-X) OUP.

W

Working-Class Images of Society. Martin Bulmer. (Modern Revivals in Sociology Ser.). 296p. (Orig.). (C). 1994. text ed. 59.95 (*0-7512-0288-6*, Pub. by Gregg Revivals UK) Ashgate Pub Co.

Working Class in Bengal: Formative Years. Deepika Basu. (C). 1993. 18.00 (*81-7074-129-7*) S Asia.

Working Class in Britain, 1850-1939. John Benson. (Themes in British Social History Ser.). 240p. (C). 1990. text ed. 39.75 (*0-582-05316-1*, 78286) Longman.

Working Class in Glasgow 1750-1914. R. A. Cage. LC 86-24059. 192p. (C). 1987. 57.50 (*0-7099-3415-7*, Pub. by Croom Helm UK) Routledge Chapman & Hall.

Working Class in Modern Europe. Mary L. McDougall. (Problems in European Civilization Ser.). 176p. (C). 1975. pap. text ed. 16.76 (*0-669-92833-X*) HM College Div.

Working Class in the Making: Belgian Colonial Labor Policy & the African Mineworkerv, 1907-1951. John Higginson. LC 88-40435. 288p. (Orig.). (C). 1990. text ed. 40.00 (*0-299-12070-8*); pap. text ed. 18.75 (*0-299-12074-0*) U of Wis Pr.

Working-Class Life: The "American Standard" in Comparative Perspective, 1899-1913. Peter R. Shergold. LC 81-50921. (Illus.). 323p. 1981. 49.95 (*0-8229-3802-2*) U of Pittsburgh Pr.

Working-Class Mobilization & Political Control: Venezuela & Mexico. Charles L. Davis. LC 88-23314. 224p. 1989. 25.00 (*0-8131-1670-8*) U Pr of Ky.

***Working Class Movement: Study of Jute Mills of Bengal 1937-1947.** Nirban Basu. (C). 1994. 20.00 (*81-7074-148-3*, Pub. by KP Bagchi II) S Asia.

***Working-Class Movement in America.** Eleanor Marx & Edward Aveling. Ed. & Intro. by Paul Le Blanc. 168p. 1998. pap. 15.00 (*0-391-04072-3*) Humanities.

Working Class Movement in America. Edward B. Aveling & Eleanor M. Aveling. LC 78-89716. (American Labor, from Conspiracy to Collective Bargaining Ser., No. 1). 239p. 1971. reprint ed. 17.95 (*0-405-02102-X*) Ayer.

Working Class Movements in India, 1885-1975. Sunil K. Sen. 250p. 1995. 18.95 (*0-19-563396-2*) OUP.

Working Class of India: History of Emergence & Movement, 1930-1970. Sukomal Sen. 1977. 14.00 (*0-8364-0002-X*) S Asia.

Working-Class Organization & the Return to Democracy in Spain. Robert Fishman. LC 89-42887. 352p. 1990. 42.50 (*0-8014-2061-X*) Cornell U Pr.

Working Class Politics in Crisis: Essays on Labour & the State. Leo Panitch. 264p. (C). 1988. text ed. 44.95 (*0-86091-142-X*, A1106, Pub. by Verso UK); pap. text ed. 14.95 (*0-86091-849-1*, A1905, Pub. by Verso UK) Routledge Chapman & Hall.

Working-Class Self-Help in Nineteenth Century England: Responses to Industrialisation. Eric Hopkins. LC 95-17989. 300p. 1995. text ed. 55.00 (*0-312-12874-6*) St Martin.

Working Class U. S. A. The Power & the Movement. Gus Hall. Ed. by Thomas Hopkins. LC 87-3232. 408p. 1987. 14.00 (*0-7178-0660-X*); pap. 6.95 (*0-7178-0659-6*) Intl Pubs Co.

Working Class Unity: The Role of Communists in the Chicago Federation of Labor, 1919-1923. Phil Bart. 1975. pap. 0.40 (*0-87898-114-4*) New Outlook.

Working-Class War: American Combat Soldiers & Vietnam. Christian G. Appy. LC 92-18318. xii, 365p. (C). 1993. 45.00 (*0-8078-2057-1*); pap. 15.95 (*0-8078-4391-1*) U of NC Pr.

Working Class Without Work: High School Students in a De-Industrializing Economy. Lois Weis. (Critical Social Thought Ser.). 256p. (C). 1990. pap. 16.95 (*0-415-90234-7*, A4373, Routledge NY) Routledge.

Working-Class Women & Grass-Roots Politics. Kathleen McCourt. LC 76-26340. 262p. reprint ed. pap. 74.70 (*0-317-09718-0*, 2017628) Bks Demand.

Working-Class Women in the Academy: Laborers in the Knowledge Factory. Ed. by Michelle M. Tokarczyk & Elizabeth A. Fay. LC 92-34935. 344p. 1993. 45.00 (*0-87023-834-5*); pap. 18.95 (*0-87023-835-3*) U of Mass Pr.

***Working Classes.** 2nd ed. Decker. (Computer Science Ser.). (C). Date not set. text ed. 52.95 (*0-534-95091-4*) PWS Pubs.

Working Classes: A Second Course in C++ Programming with Data Structures. Rick Decker & Stuart Hirshfield. LC 94-43941. 495p. 1995. pap. 59.95 (*0-534-94566-X*) PWS Pubs.

Working Classics: Poems on Industrial Life. Ed. by Peter Oresick & Nicholas Coles. 304p. 1990. 13.95 (*0-252-06133-0*); text ed. 34.95 (*0-252-01730-7*) U of Ill Pr.

Working Communally: Patterns & Possibilities. David French & Elena French. LC 74-25854. 288p. 1975. 29.95 (*0-87154-291-9*) Russell Sage.

Working Concepts of Fluid Flow. Robert R. Rothfus. (Illus.). 96p. (Orig.). (C). pap. 3.75 (*0-685-23655-2*) Bek Tech.

***Working Conference on Global Growth of Technology: Is America Prepared?** 1997. lib. bdg. 250.95 (*0-8490-6265-9*) Gordon Pr.

Working Cotton. Sherley Williams. 1997. pap. 6.00 (*0-15-201482-9*) HarBrace.

Working Cotton. Shirley A. Williams. (Illus.). 32p. (J). (ps-3). 1992. 14.95 (*0-15-299624-9*, HB Juv Bks) HarBrace.

Working Countryside: 1862-1945. Robin Hill & Paul Stamper. (Illus.). 176p. 1992. pap. 24.95 (*1-85310-305-5*, Pub. by Swan Hill UK) Voyageur Pr.

Working Cowboy: Recollections of Ray Holmes. Richard W. Slatta et al. LC 94-29445. (Illus.). 288p. 1995. 24.95 (*0-8061-2692-2*) U of Okla Pr.

Working Culture, Bk. 1. David Hemphill et al. 110p. (C). 1989. pap. text ed. 11.70 (*0-13-965187-X*) P-H.

Working Culture, Bk. 2. David Hemphill et al. 110p. (C). 1989. pap. text ed. 11.70 (*0-13-965377-5*) P-H.

Working Daughters of Hong Kong: Filial Piety or Power in the Family? Janet W. Salaff. LC 95-12641. 317p. 1995. pap. 17.50 (*0-231-10225-9*) Col U Pr.

***Working Days: Stories about Teenagers & Work.** Ed. by Anne Mazer. LC 96-50243. 224p. (YA). 1997. 18.95 (*0-89255-223-9*); pap. 7.95 (*0-89255-224-7*) Persea Bks.

Working Days: The Journals of "The Grapes of Wrath" John Steinbeck. Ed. by Robert DeMott. 224p. 1990. reprint ed. pap. 10.95 (*0-14-014457-9*, Penguin Bks) Viking Penguin.

Working Dazed: Why Drugs Pervade the Workplace & What Can Be Done about It. A. Browne Miller. LC 91-7247. (Illus.). 355p. 1991. 26.95 (*0-306-43765-1*, Plenum Insight) Plenum.

Working Decoys of the Jersey Coast & Delaware River Valley. Kenneth L. Gosner. LC 82-70005. (Illus.). 256p. 1985. 45.00 (*0-87982-500-6*) Art Alliance.

Working Decoys of the Jersey Coast & Delaware Valley. Kenneth L. Gosner. LC 83-14312. (Illus.). 184p. 1985. 45.00 (*0-317-19123-3*) Art Alliance.

Working Decoys of the Jersey Coast & Delaware Valley. Kenneth L. Gosner. LC 83-14312. (Illus.). 184p. 1985. 45.00 (*0-8453-4711-X*, Cornwall Bks) Assoc Univ Prs.

Working Detroit. Steve Babson. LC 86-5510. (Illus.). 264p. 1986. reprint ed. pap. 19.95 (*0-8143-1819-3*) Wayne St U Pr.

***Working Document: Quantifying Genocide in the Southern Sudan 1983-1993.** (Issue Papers). 1993. pap. 4.00 (*0-614-25345-4*) US Comm Refugees.

***Working Dogs.** Edward C. Haggerty. LC 97-5974. (Nature's Children Ser.). (J). 1997. write for info. (*0-7172-9123-5*) Grolier Educ.

Working Dogs. Max Marquardt. (Real Readers Ser.: Level Red). (Illus.). 32p. (J). (gr. 1-4). 1989. lib. bdg. 21.40 (*0-8172-3506-X*) Raintree Steck-V.

Working Dogs. Max Marquardt. (Real Reading Ser.). (Illus.). 32p. (J). (gr. 1-4). 1989. pap. 3.95 (*0-8114-6711-2*) Raintree Steck-V.

Working Dogs: Training for Sheep & Cattle. Colin Seis. 144p. 1995. pap. 47.95 (*0-7506-8920-X*) Buttrwrth-Heinemann.

Working Dogs of the World: Exotic & Familiar Breeds. Clifford L. Hubbard. 1992. lib. bdg. 88.99 (*0-8490-5268-8*) Gordon Pr.

Working Drawing Production a Recommended Procedure. J. Webster. 1976. pap. 45.00 (*0-86022-022-2*, Pub. by Build Servs Info Assn UK) St Mut.

Working Drawings: 1895-1938. Ed. by Ian Lowe. (Illus.). 1968. pap. 1.50 (*0-89073-034-2*) Boston Public Lib.

Working Drawings for Residential Interior. A. Dunphy. 1991. pap. write for info. (*0-442-00388-9*) Van Nos Reinhold.

Working Drawings Handbook. 2nd ed. Styles. 1986. pap. 46.95 (*0-7506-0468-9*) Buttrwrth-Heinemann.

Working Drawings Handbook. 3rd ed. Keith Styles. LC 95-23188. (Illus.). 144p. 1995. pap. 34.95 (*0-7506-2494-9*) Buttrwrth-Heinemann.

Working Dress in Colonial & Revolutionary America. Peter F. Copeland. LC 76-15309. (Contributions in American History Ser.: No. 58). (Illus.). 224p. 1977. text ed. 55.00 (*0-8371-9033-9*, COD/, Greenwood Pr) Greenwood.

***Working Drummer.** Modern Drummer Publications Staff. 1997. pap. 14.95 (*0-7935-7358-0*) H Leonard.

Working Easier: A Salute to Black Inventors. rev. ed. Ann C. Howell. Ed. by Evelyn L. Ivery. (Black Inventors Activity Bks.). (Illus.). 24p. (J). (gr. 3-7). 1992. reprint ed. pap. text ed. 1.50 (*1-877804-04-5*) Chandler White.

Working Effectively with Administrative Groups. Ed. by Ronald W. Toseland & Paul H. Ephros. LC 87-23809. (Social Work with Groups Ser.: Vol. 10, No. 2). 117p. 1987. text ed. 29.95 (*0-86656-746-1*) Haworth Pr.

Working Effectively with Trustees: Building Cooperative Campus Leadership. Barbara E. Taylor. Ed. & Frwd. by Jonathan D. Fife. LC 87-71598. (ASHE-ERIC Higher Education Reports: No. 2, 1987). 143p. (Orig.). (C). 1987. pap. text ed. 10.00 (*0-913317-38-1*) GWU Grad Schl E&HD.

Working Emptiness: Toward a Third Reading of Emptiness in Buddhism & Postmodern Thought. Newman R. Glass. (AAR Reflection & Theory in the Study of Religion Ser.: Vol. 1). 180p. 1995. 38.95 (*0-7885-0080-5*); pap. 25.95 (*0-7885-0081-3*, 011001) Scholars Pr GA.

Working Ethics: Strategies for Decision Making & Organizational Responsibility. Marvin T. Brown. LC 90-37973. (Management Ser.). 239p. 31.95 (*1-55542-280-2*) Jossey-Bass.

Working Experience, Bk. 1. 1993. 8.00 (*0-88336-965-6*) New Readers.

Working Experience, Bk. 2. 1993. 8.00 (*0-88336-966-4*) New Readers.

Working Experience, Bk. 3. 1993. 8.00 (*0-88336-967-2*) New Readers.

Working Experience, Bks. 1-3. 1993. teacher ed. 11.95 (*0-88336-968-0*) New Readers.

Working Family's Cookbook. Irena Chalmers. 336p. 1990. ring bd. 24.95 (*0-8120-6147-0*) Barron.

Working Family's Cookbook. Irena Chalmers. (Illus.). 336p. 1993. pap. 12.95 (*0-8120-1566-5*) Barron.

***Working Fathers.** James A. Levine & Todd L. Pittinsky. LC 97-2067. 1997. 23.00 (*0-201-14938-9*) Addison-Wesley.

Working Father's Survival Manual. Peter Schreck. (Illus.). 35p. (Orig.). (YA). (gr. 9-12). 1989. pap. 2.50 (*0-9623787-0-4*) Working Father.

***Working Ferrets: Techniques for Successful Results.** Jackie Drakeford. (Illus.). 128p. 1997. pap. 17.95 (*1-85310-804-9*, Pub. by Swan Hill UK) Voyageur Pr.

Working Firewood for the Night. H. Lloyd Van Brunt. pseud. 112p. 1990. 17.95 (*0-912292-89-X*); pap. 9.95 (*0-912292-88-1*) Smith.

***Working for a Doctorate: Guide for Humanities & Social Sciences.** Ed. by Norman Graves & Ved Varma. 224p. (C). 1997. pap. 19.95 (*0-415-14731-X*, Routledge NY); text ed. 65.00 (*0-415-14730-1*, Routledge NY) Routledge.

Working for a Japanese Company: Insights into the Multicultural Workplace. Robert M. March. 256p. 1996. reprint ed. pap. 10.00 (*4-7700-2085-6*) Kodansha.

Working for a Japanese Company: Managing Relationships in a Multicultural Organization. Robert M. March. 248p. 1992. 19.00 (*4-7700-1533-X*) Kodansha.

Working for America: Employment Opportunities with the Federal Government. James C. Gonyea. 300p. 1992. pap. 12.95 (*0-8120-4963-2*) Barron.

Working for Children. Judith S. Mearing. LC 78-1148. (Jossey-Bass Social & Behavioral Science Ser.). 368p. reprint ed. pap. 104.90 (*0-317-09508-0*, 2021731) Bks Demand.

***Working for Dad.** Claudette C. Mitchell et al. (Visions: African-American Experiences: Vol. 28). (Illus.). 8p. (Orig.). (J). (gr. k-1). 1996. pap. text ed. 3.00 (*1-57518-070-7*) Arborlake.

Working for Democracy: American Workers from the Revolution to the Present. Ed. by Paul Buhle & Alan Dawley. LC 85-5845. (Illus.). 168p. 1985. text ed. 24.95 (*0-252-01220-8*); pap. text ed. 9.95 (*0-252-01221-6*) U of Ill Pr.

Working for Equality in Health. Ed. by Paul Bywaters & Eileen McLeod. LC 95-25987. (State of Welfare Ser.). 240p. (C). 1996. pap. 17.95 (*0-415-12466-2*); text ed. 59.95 (*0-415-12465-4*) Routledge.

***Working for Equity in Heterogeneous Classrooms: Sociological Theory in Practice.** Ed. by Elizabeth G. Cohen & Rachel A. Lotan. LC 97-20465. 516p. (Orig.). 1997. pap. text ed. 19.95 (*0-8077-3643-0*) Tchrs Coll.

***Working for Equity in Heterogeneous Classrooms: Sociological Theory in Practice.** Ed. by Elizabeth G. Cohen & Rachel A. Lotan. LC 97-20465. 516p. 1997. text ed. 68.00 (*0-8077-3644-9*) Tchrs Coll.

Working for Full Employment. Ed. by John Philpott. 256p. (C). 1997. pap. 21.95 (*0-415-14348-9*); text ed. 74.95 (*0-415-14347-0*) Routledge.

Working for God. Andrew Murray. 1980. pap. 4.95 (*0-87508-404-4*) Chr Lit.

Working for Health: The History of COHSE. Carpenter. (C). 1988. pap. 25.00 (*0-85315-682-4*, Pub. by Lawrence & Wishart UK) NYU Pr.

Working for Life: Careers in Biology. 2nd ed. Thomas A. Easton. 127p. 1988. 14.95 (*0-937548-09-X*) Plexus Pub.

Working for Love. large type ed. Tessa Dahl. 190p. 1989. reprint ed. 19.95 (*1-85089-319-5*, Pub. by ISIS UK) Transaction Pubs.

***Working for Myself Basic Set, 10 bks.** Tana Reiff. 1994. pap. 44.95 (*0-7854-1104-6*, 40828) Am Guidance.

***Working for Myself Classroom Library, 30 bks.** Tana Reiff. 1994. pap. 129.95 (*0-7854-1103-8*, 40840) Am Guidance.

***Working for Myself Curriculum Guide.** Tana Reiff. 96p. 1994. pap. 19.50 (*0-7854-1105-4*, 40839) Am Guidance.

Working for Success. Larry Anderson. LC 88-70593. 245p. (Orig.). 1990. pap. 9.95 (*0-9620270-0-6*) Anderson OH.

Working for Teacher Development. Ed. by Peter Woods. 239p. 1990. 90.00 (*1-870167-07-4*, Pub. by P Francis UK) St Mut.

Working for the Best: Can Jump-Start America. Bill Gorden & Johnny Miller. 104p. pap. 5.95 (*0-9643860-2-X*) Wego Bks.

Working for the Chessie System: Olde King Coal's Prime Carrier. Fred R. Toothman. (Illus.). 286p. (Orig.). (C). 1993. 16.95 (*0-9617545-5-9*) F R Toothman.

Working for the Japanese: Inside Mazda's American Auto Plant. Joseph J. Fucini & Suzy Fucini. 258p. 1992. pap. 14.95 (*0-02-910932-9*, Free Press) Free Pr.

Working for the Japanese: The Economic & Social Consequences of Japanese Investment in Wales. Johnathan Morris et al. LC 93-14561. (Illus.). 180p. (C). 1993. text ed. 65.00 (*0-485-11438-0*, Pub. by Athlone Pr UK) Humanities.

Working for the Lord Like the Devil: A Look at Institutionalized Christianity. Frederick M. Archer. 102p. (Orig.). 1990. pap. 7.95 (*0-9625823-0-1*) Archer Pub.

Working for the Poor: NGOs & Rural Poverty Alleviation. Mark Robinson & Roger Riddell. (Illus.). 380p. 1996. 65.00 (*0-19-823330-2*) OUP.

***Working for the Sovereign: Employee Relations in the Federal Government.** Sar A. Levitan & Alexandra B. Noden. LC 82-49064. (Policy Studies in Employment & Welfare: Vol. 39). 165p. 1983. reprint ed. pap. 47.10 (*0-608-03721-4*, 2064546) Bks Demand.

Working for the Union: British Trade Union Officers. John Kelly & Edmund Heery. LC 93-37384. (Studies in Management: Vol. 22). (Illus.). 288p. (C). 1994. text ed. 64.95 (*0-521-38320-X*) Cambridge U Pr.

Working for U. S. in the 1990's. 1994. lib. bdg. 250.00 (*0-8490-8569-1*) Gordon Pr.

Working for Victory? Images of Women in the First World War, 1914-18. Diana Condell & Jean Liddiard. (Illus.). 192p. 1987. 39.50 (*0-7102-0974-6*, A0747, RKP) Routledge.

***Working for Wales.** Dafydd Wigley. 400p. 1996. 29.95 (*1-86057-007-0*, Pub. by Welsh Acad UK) Intl Spec Bk.

Working for Wildlife: The Beginning of Preservation in Canada. Janet Foster. LC 78-315369. 295p. reprint ed. pap. 84.10 (*0-685-15272-3*, 2026455) Bks Demand.

***Working for Women? Gendered Work & Welfare Policies in Twentieth Century Britain.** Celia Briar. (Gender & Society Ser.). 192p. 1997. 74.95 (*0-7484-0552-6*, Pub. by Tay Francis Ltd UK); pap. 24.95 (*0-7484-0553-4*, Pub. by Tay Francis Ltd UK) Taylor & Francis.

Working for You: A Guide to Employing Women in Nontraditional Jobs. rev. ed. 1979. 5.00 (*0-934966-04-4*) Wider Oppor Women.

Working for Your Uncle: Complete Guide to Finding a Job with the Federal Government. Ed. by Federal Jobs Digest Staff. (Illus.). 832p. (Orig.). 1993. pap. 19.95 (*0-914327-27-5*) Breakthrgh NY.

Working for Yourself. Joseph Anthony. 1995. pap. 14.95 (*0-8129-2715-X*) Random.

***Working for Yourself.** 16th ed. Godfrey Golzen. (Daily Telegraph Guides Ser.). 1995. pap. 15.95 (*0-7494-1613-0*) Kogan Page Ltd.

***Working for Yourself.** 17th ed. Godfrey Golzen. (Daily Telegraph Guides Ser.). 1996. pap. 15.95 (*0-7494-2148-7*) Kogan Page Ltd.

Working for Yourself: The Daily Telegraph Guide to Self-Employment. Godfrey Golzen. 320p. 1989. 45.00 (*0-8464-1385-X*); pap. 29.95 (*0-8464-1386-8*) Beekman Pubs.

Working Forces in Japanese Politics, 1867-1920. Uichi Iwasaki. LC 21-7669. (Columbia University. Studies in the Social Sciences: No. 220). reprint ed. 20.00 (*0-404-51220-8*) AMS Pr.

Working Forensics: A Competitor's Guide. 2nd ed. M'Liss S. Hindman. 356p. 1995. spiral bd. 29.34 (*0-8403-8873-X*) Kendall-Hunt.

***Working Free: New Zealand's Employment Contracts Act.** Ellen J. Dannin. 264p. 1997. pap. 27.95 (*1-86940-174-3*, Pub. by Auckland Univ NZ) Paul & Co Pubs.

Working from Home: Everything You Need to Know about Living & Working under the Same Roof. 4th ed. Paul Edwards & Sarah Edwards. 448p. 1994. pap. 15.95 (*0-87477-764-X*, Tarcher Putnam) Putnam Pub Group.

Working from Memory. Lee Passarella. 20p. 1992. pap. 4.00 (*0-9647127-0-9*) Coreopsis Bks.

Working from the Heart: A Guide to Recovering the Soul at Work. Jacqueline McMakin & Sonya Dyer. LC 92-54615. 240p. 1994. pap. 16.00 (*0-06-065381-7*) Harper SF.

Working from the Margins: Voices of Mothers in Poverty. Virginia E. Schein. 184p. 1995. pap. 14.95 (*0-87546-342-8*, ILR Press) Cornell U Pr.

Working from Within: Integrating Rural Health Care. Hospital Research & Educational Trust of the AHA Staff. 150p. (Orig.). 1993. pap. 35.00 (*0-87258-636-7*, 184151) Am Hospital.

Working Girl. Jessica Hart. (Romance Ser.). 1996. mass mkt. 3.25 (*0-373-03429-6*, 1-03429-7) Harlequin Bks.

***Working Girl.** large type ed. Jessica Hart. (Mills & Boon Large Print Ser.). 288p. 1996. 21.50 (*0-263-14749-5*, Pub. by M & B UK) Ulverscroft.

***Working Girl.** large type ed. Jessica Hart. 1996. mass mkt. 3.25 (*0-373-15675-8*) Harlequin Bks.

Working Girl Cooking. B. Carlson. (Illus.). 160p. 1994. spiral bd. 5.95 (*1-57166-010-0*) Hearts N Tummies.

Working Girl in a Man's World. Jan Manette. LC 66-22896. 223p. 1966. 10.00 (*0-915988-01-1*) Reading Gems.

***Working Girls: Prostitute Women, Their Life & Social Control.** R. Perkins. 480p. 1991. pap. 35.00 (*0-642-15876-2*, Pub. by Aust Inst Criminology) Willow Tree NY.

Working Girls of Boston. Carroll D. Wright. LC 73-89711. (American Labor, from Conspiracy to Collective Bargaining Ser., No. 1). 133p. 1972. reprint ed. 16.95 (*0-405-02158-5*) Ayer.

Working Girls of Cincinnati: An Original Anthology. Ed. by Leon Stein & Annette K. Baxter. LC 74-3981. (Women in America Ser.). (Illus.). 182p. 1974. reprint ed. 20.95 (*0-405-06129-3*) Ayer.

***Working Glossary of English-Russian Housing Terms.** Nani Boyce. 110p. 1997. text ed. 49.95 (*1-85972-490-6*, Pub. by Ashgate UK) Ashgate Pub Co.

Working Green Wood with Peg. Patrick Spielman. LC 79-91406. (Illus.). 160p. 1980. pap. 14.95 (*0-8069-8924-6*) Sterling.

Working Guide for Directors of Not-for-Profit Organizations. Charles N. Waldo. LC 85-24396. 160p. 1986. text ed. 49.95 (*0-89930-091-X*, WHD/, Greenwood Pr) Greenwood.

Working Guide to Process Equipment. Norman Lieberman & Elizabeth T. Lieberman. LC 96-30959. (Illus.). 480p. 1996. text ed. 74.95 (*0-07-038075-9*) McGraw.

Working Gundogs: An Introduction to Training & Handling. Martin Deeley. (Illus.). 176p. 1994. 34.95 (*1-85223-764-3*, Pub. by Crowood Pr UK) Trafalgar.

***Working Hard.** Sally Hewitt. LC 97-3550. (It's Science! Ser.). (J). 1997. write for info. (*0-516-20792-X*) Childrens.

Working Hard with the Busy Fire Truck. Jordan Horowitz. 32p. (J). (ps-3). 1993. pap. 2.99 (*0-590-46602-X*) Scholastic Inc.

Working Hard with the Mighty Dump Truck. Justine Korman. 32p. (J). (ps-3). 1993. pap. 2.50 (*0-590-46481-7*) Scholastic Inc.

Working Hard with the Mighty Loader. 32p. (J). 1993. pap. 2.99 (*0-590-47302-6*) Scholastic Inc.

Working Hard with the Mighty Mixer. Justine Korman. 32p. (J). (ps-3). 1993. pap. 2.99 (*0-590-47308-5*) Scholastic Inc.

***Working Hard with the Mighty Tractor Trailer & Bulldozer.** Justine Korman. (Tonka Truck Storybooks Ser.). (Illus.). 32p. (J). (ps-2). 1997. pap. 2.99 (*0-590-13450-7*) Scholastic Inc.

W

An Asterisk (*) at the beginning of an entry indicates that the title is appearing in BIP for the first time.

*Working Hard with the Rescue Helicopter. Cynthia Benjamin. (Tonka Truck Storybooks Ser.). (Illus.). 32p. (J). (ps-2). 1997. pap. 2.99 (0-590-13449-3) Scholastic Inc.

Working High Magick. 3rd ed. Nelson H. White. (Illus.). 75p. (C). 1995. pap. 45.00 (1-877884-17-0) Tech Group.

Working Horse. Geoffrey Patterson. (Illus.). 32p. (Orig.). (J). (gr. 3). 1996. pap. 9.95 (0-85236-320-6, Pub. by Farming Pr UK) Diamond Farm Bk.

*Working Horses. (Sense of History Ser.). Date not set. pap. text ed. write for info. (0-582-04027-2, Pub. by Longman UK) Longman.

Working Horses: Looking Back One Hundred Years to America's Horse-Drawn Days. Charles P. Fox. (Illus.). 250p. 1990. 21.95 (0-9622663-2-9) Heart Prairie Pr.

Working Hours: Assessing the Potential for Reduction. Michael White. ix, 104p. (Orig.). 1987. pap. 18.00 (92-2-106151-5) Intl Labour Office.

Working in a Global Environment. Michael Goodman. (IEEE Engineers Guide to Business Ser.: Vol. 9). 160p. 1995. pap. 19.95 (0-7803-2301-7, EG109) Inst Electrical.

Working in a Very Small Place. Mark L. Shelton. LC 89-40484. 1990. pap. 13.00 (0-679-72815-5, Vin) Random.

*Working in a Windows World. 2nd ed. Michael Perl & Sharon Burton. 216p. (C). 1996. pap. text ed., ring bd. 27.24 (0-7872-2598-3) Kendall-Hunt.

Working in Agricultural Industry. Jasper S. Lee. (Illus.). (J). (gr. 9-10). 1978. text ed. 17.96 (0-07-000831-0) McGraw.

Working in Agricultural Mechanics. Glen C. Shinn & Curtis Weston. Ed. by Max L. Amberson. (Illus.). 1978. text ed. 19.96 (0-07-000843-4) McGraw.

Working in America: A Humanities Reader. Ed. by Robert Sessions & Jack Wortman. LC 91-50579. (C). 1992. text ed. 46.00 (0-268-01947-9); pap. text ed. 23.00 (0-268-01948-7) U of Notre Dame Pr.

*Working in America: Continuity, Conflict, & Change. Amy S. Wharton. LC 97-16790. 1997. write for info. (1-55934-737-6) Mayfield Pub.

Working in Animal Science. Paul Peterson et al. Ed. by Max L. Amberson. (Illus.). (gr. 9-10). 1978. text ed. 19.96 (0-07-000839-6) McGraw.

*Working in Arts, Crafts & Design. 2nd ed. Ed. by David Shacklady. (Careers & Testing Ser.). 1997. pap. 15.95 (0-7494-2138-X) Kogan Page Ltd.

Working in Canada. Ed. by Walter Johnson. 160p. 1983. 29.95 (0-920057-14-4, Pub. by Black Rose Bks CN); pap. 12.95 (0-920057-13-6, Pub. by Black Rose Bks CN) Consort Bk Sales.

*Working in Canada. Ed. by Walter Johnson. 1996. 41.99 (0-919618-64-2, Pub. by Black Rose Bks CN) Consort Bk Sales.

Working in Canvas for Yachtsmen, Cadets & Sea Scouts. Percy W. Blandford. (C). 1987. 36.00 (0-85174-416-8, Pub. by Brwn Son Ferg) St Mut.

Working in Commercials: A Complete Sourcebook for Adult & Child Actors. Elaine K. Beardsley. (Illus.). 194p. 1993. pap. 22.95 (0-240-80160-1, Focal) Buttrwrth-Heinemann.

*Working in Complementary & Alternative Medicine. Loulou Brown. (Careers & Testing Ser.). 1994. pap. 15.95 (0-7494-1223-2) Kogan Page Ltd.

Working in Darkness: A Play about Coal Mining. Sigmund Stoler. (Illus.). 16p. (J). (gr. 5-9). 1996. wbk. ed., pap. 10.00 (1-878668-66-8) Disc Enter Ltd.

Working in English: History, Institution, Resources. Heather Murray. (Theory/Culture Ser.). 253p. 1996. 45.00 (0-8020-2853-5); pap. 16.95 (0-8020-7350-6) U of Toronto Pr.

Working in Film: The Marketplace in the '90s. Paul N. Lazarus, III. LC 93-677. 224p. (Orig.). 1993. pap. 14.95 (0-312-09418-3) St Martin.

Working in Groups. Engleberg. (C). Date not set. pap. 35.96 (0-395-75650-2) HM.

Working in Groups. Engleberg. (C). 1996. teacher ed., pap. 11.96 (0-395-75651-0) HM.

Working in Groups. Engleberg. (C). Date not set. teacher ed., pap. write for info. (0-395-79006-9) HM.

Working in Hawaii: A Labor History. Edward D. Beechert. LC 85-8640. 414p. 1985. 24.95 (0-8248-0890-8) UH Pr.

Working in Health Care: What You Need to Know to Succeed. Michael W. Drafke. LC 94-13881. (Illus.). 213p. 1994. pap. 19.95 (0-8036-2808-0) Davis Co.

Working in Health Care & Wellness. Barbara Lee. LC 95-49876. (Exploring Careers Ser.). (Illus.). (J). (gr. 6-8). 1996. lib. bdg. 16.95 (0-8225-1760-4, Lerner Publctns) Lerner Group.

Working in Higher Education. Robert E. Cuthbert. LC 96-25915. 208p. 1996. 89.00 (0-335-19722-1, Open Univ Pr); pap. 29.95 (0-335-19721-3, Open Univ Pr) Taylor & Francis.

Working in Hollywood. Tom Wright. 1990. 24.95 (0-517-57401-2, Crown) Crown Pub Group.

Working in Hollywood. Alexandra Brower & Thomas L. Wright. 560p. 1991. reprint ed. pap. 14.00 (0-380-71500-7) Avon.

Working in Horticulture. William B. Richardson & Gary Moore. (Career Preparation for Agriculture-Agribusiness Ser.). (Illus.). 1980. text ed. 29.96 (0-07-052285-5) McGraw.

Working in Hot Environments. 1995. lib. bdg. 251.75 (0-8490-7532-7) Gordon Pr.

*Working in Hotels & Catering. Roy C. Wood. 224p. 1992. pap. 17.95 (0-415-04783-8) Routledge.

Working in Hotels & Catering. Roy C. Wood. 208p. (C). 1992. text ed. 85.00 (0-415-04782-X, Routledge NY) Routledge.

*Working in Hotels & Catering. 2nd ed. Roy Wood. 208p. 1997. pap. 19.95 (0-415-13881-7) Inter Thomson.

*Working in Human Service Agencies Practice Field. Allecorliss. (Social Work Ser.). Date not set. pap. 30.95 (0-534-34811-4) Wadsworth Pub.

Working in Jails & Prisons: Becoming Part of the Team. Daniel J. Bayse. LC 95-8358. 87p. 1995. pap. 15.00 (1-56991-021-9, 534) Am Correctional.

Working in Japan: An Insider's Guide for Engineers. Ed. by H. Honda et al. 185p. 1991. 26.95 (0-7918-0025-3) ASME Pr.

Working in Metal Management & Labour in the Metal Industries of Europe & the U. S. A., 1890-1914. Chris McGuffie. (C). 1985. text ed. 29.95 (0-85036-312-8, Pub. by Merlin Pr UK) Humanities.

Working in Microsoft Office. Ron Mansfield. 1008p. 1996. pap. text ed. 34.95 (0-07-882164-9) McGraw.

Working in Music. Barbara Lee. LC 96-4694. (Exploring Careers Ser.). (J). 1996. 16.95 (0-8225-1761-2, Lerner Publctns) Lerner Group.

Working in Orbit & Beyond: The Challenges for Space Medicine. Ed. by David Lorr & Victoria Garshnek. LC 57-43769. (Science & Technology Ser.: Vol. 72). (Illus.). 188p. 1989. pap. text ed. 35.00 (0-87703-296-3); lib. bdg. 45.00 (0-87703-295-5) Univelt Inc.

Working in Organisations. Andrew Kakabadse et al. 400p. 1987. text ed. 50.00 (0-566-02432-2, Pub. by Gower UK) Ashgate Pub Co.

Working in Other Dimensions: Objects & Drawings II. Alan DuBois. 64p. 1994. pap. 20.00 (1-884240-04-6) Arkansas Art Ctr.

Working in Partnership: Clinicians & Careers in the Management of Longstanding Mental Illness. Liz Kuipers & Paul Bebbington. 172p. 1991. pap. 45.00 (0-433-01606-X) Buttrwrth-Heinemann.

Working in Plant Science. Douglas D. Bishop. Ed. by Max L. Amberson et al. (Illus.). (gr. 9-10). 1978. text ed. 19.96 (0-07-000835-3) McGraw.

Working in Plant Science: Activity Guide. Lark P. Carter et al. Ed. by Max Aaberson. (Illus.). (gr. 9-10). 1978. pap. text ed. 12.96 (0-07-000836-1) McGraw.

Working in Precious Metals. Ernest A. Smith. 390p. 1980. 35.00 (0-7198-0032-3, Pub. by NAG Press UK) Antique Collect.

*Working in Ski Resorts: Europe & North America. Victoria Pybus. 304p. (Orig.). 1997. pap. 16.95 (1-85458-109-0, Pub. by Vac Wrk Pubns UK) Seven Hills Bk.

*Working in Ski Resorts: Europe & North America. 4th ed. Victoria Pybus. (Illus.). 320p. 1997. pap. 17.95 (1-85458-176-7, Pub. by Vac Wrk Pubns UK) Seven Hills Bk.

Working in Social Care. D. Evans & J. Kearney. 208p. 1996. pap. 26.95 (1-85742-355-0, Pub. by Arena UK); text ed. 56.95 (1-85742-354-2, Pub. by Arena UK) Ashgate Pub Co.

Working in Social Work: Growing & Thriving in Human Services Practice. Armand Lauffer. LC 86-29700. (Sage Sourcebooks for the Human Services Ser.: No. 6). 320p. reprint ed. pap. 96.70 (0-7837-6582-7, 2046147) Bks Demand.

Working in South Africa. Ed. by Ken Dovey et al. 397p. 1985. pap. 15.95 (0-86975-263-4, Pub. by Ravan Pr ZA) Ohio U Pr.

Working in Sports & Recreation. Barbara Lee. LC 95-46030. (Exploring Careers Ser.). (Illus.). (J). (gr. 6-8). 1996. lib. bdg. 16.95 (0-8225-1762-0, Lerner Publctns) Lerner Group.

*Working in Teams: A Fifty Minute Book. Sandy Pokras. LC 96-86712. 1997. pap. text ed. 10.95 (1-56052-412-X) Crisp Pubns.

*Working in Teams: Interaction & Communication. David J. Pucel & Rosemary T. Fruehling. LC 96-32309. 184p. (C). 1997. pap. 15.95 (1-56118-739-9) Paradigm MN.

*Working in Teams: Interaction & Communication. David J. Pucel & Rosemary T. Fruehling. 68p. (C). 1997. teacher ed., pap. text ed. 8.00 (1-56118-740-2) Paradigm MN.

Working in the Catholic Church: An Attitudinal Survey. National Association of Church Personnel Administrators Staff. LC 93-19042. 184p. (Orig.). 1993. pap. 14.95 (1-55612-568-2) Sheed & Ward MO.

Working in the Dark: Reflections of a Poet of the Barrio. Jimmy S. Baca. LC 91-60328. (Illus.). 182p. (Orig.). 1993. 19.95 (1-878610-08-2) Red Crane Bks.

Working in the Dark: Reflections of a Poet of the Barrio. Jimmy S. Baca. LC 91-60328. (Illus.). 182p. (Orig.). 1994. pap. 11.95 (1-878610-47-3) Red Crane Bks.

*Working in the Environment. Corinna Nelson. LC 97-7394. (Exploring Careers Ser.). (J). 1997. write for info. (0-8225-1763-9, Lerner Publctns) Lerner Group.

Working in the Kitchen. Anthony J. Strianese. (Food & Hospitality Ser.). 1992. 105.00 (0-8273-5219-0) Van Nos Reinhold.

*Working in the Macroeconomy: A Study of the U. S. Labor Market. Martin F. Prachowny. LC 96-33539. (Studies in the Modern World Economy). 240p. (C). 1997. text ed. write for info. (0-415-14927-4) Routledge.

*Working in the Media. 2nd ed. Ed. by Allan Shepherd. (Careers & Testing Ser.). 1997. pap. 15.95 (0-7494-2139-8) Kogan Page Ltd.

Working in the Middle: Strengthening Education & Training for the Mid-Skilled Labor Force. W. Norton Grubb. LC 96-9944. (Higher & Adult Education Ser.). 304p. 1996. 32.95 (0-7879-0258-6) Jossey-Bass.

*Working in the Operating Department. 2nd ed. Bakul Kumar. LC 97-25789. 1997. write for info. (0-443-05573-4) Churchill.

Working in the Operating Theatre. Bakul Kumar & C. Reay. (Illus.). 256p. 1990. pap. text ed. 36.00 (0-443-03908-9) Churchill.

Working in the Persian Gulf - Survival Secrets for Men & Women: The Real Story. Blythe Camenson. LC 91-76802. 160p. 1992. pap. 16.95 (1-880602-00-8) Des Diamond.

Working in the Service Society. Ed. by Cameron Macdonald & Carmen Sirianni. LC 96-23091. (Labor & Social Change Ser.). 352p. (C). 1996. 59.95 (1-56639-479-1); pap. 24.95 (1-56639-480-5) Temple U Pr.

*Working in the Social Services. Sue Balloch. 1995. pap. 56.00 (0-902789-98-8, Pub. by Natl Inst Soc Work) St Mut.

Working in the Vineyards of Genealogy. Willard Heiss. Ed. by Ruth Dorrel. LC 93-37416. 242p. 1993. 25.00 (0-87195-100-2) Ind Hist Soc.

*Working in Tourism: The U. K., Europe & Beyond. Verite R. Collins. 320p. (Orig.). 1997. pap. 17.95 (1-85458-133-3, Pub. by Vac Wrk Pubns UK) Seven Hills Bk.

Working in T.V. News: The Insider's Guide. Carl Filoreto & Lynn Setzer. LC 92-50413. 192p. (Orig.). 1993. pap. 12.95 (0-914457-50-0) Mustang Pub.

Working in Urban Schools. Thomas B. Corcoran et al. 160p. 1988. 12.00 (0-937846-74-0) Inst Educ Lead.

*Working Intersubjectively: Contextualism in Psychoanalytic Practice. Donna M. Orange et al. LC 97-25312. (Psychoanalytic Inquiry Book Ser.). 1997. write for info. (0-88163-229-5) Analytic Pr.

Working Is Learning, Learning Is Working. Lee Droegemueller. (School-to-Work Implementation Ser.). 13p. 1995. pap. write for info. (1-884037-09-7) Coun Chief St Schl Offs.

Working It Out. Ruthy Perlman. LC 90-82185. (YA). (gr. 7 up). 1990. 13.95 (1-56062-033-1); pap. 9.95 (1-56062-035-8) CIS Comm.

Working It Out: A Troubleshooting Guide for Writers. 2nd ed. Barbara F. Clouse. 1996. pap. text ed. write for info. (0-07-011619-9); pap. text ed. 12.00 (0-07-011620-2) McGraw.

Working It Out: A Troubleshooting Guide to the Writing Process. Barbara F. Clouse. 1992. pap. text ed. write for info. (0-07-011416-1) McGraw.

Working It Out: Sanity & Success in the Workplace. Stephen Strasser. 256p. 1988. 25.95 (0-13-965112-8) P-H.

Working it Out: The Domestic Double Standard. Judith K. Sprankle. 224p. 1986. 16.95 (0-8027-0883-8) Walker & Co.

Working It Out Together: A Guide for Dual Career Couples. Jack Loughary & Theresa M. Ripley. 167p. 1987. pap. 12.95 (0-685-19247-4) United Learn.

Working It Through. Elisabeth Kubler-Ross. (Illus.). 167p. 1987. pap. 7.00 (0-02-022000-6) Macmillan.

*Working it Through. Kbler-Ross. 1997. pap. 7.00 (0-684-83942-3, Touchstone Bks) S&S Trade.

Working Knowledge. Douglas A. Harper. LC 92-9882. (C). 1992. 16.00 (0-520-07970-1) U CA Pr.

*Working Knowledge: How Organizations Manage What They Know. Thomas H. Davenport & Lawrence Prusak. LC 97-10781. 232p. 1998. 27.95 (0-87584-655-6, HBS Pr) Harvard Busn.

*Working Knowledge: How Organizations Manage What They Know. Harvard Business School Press. 1997. text ed. 29.95 (0-07-105067-1) McGraw.

Working Knowledge: Skill & Community in a Small Shop. Douglas A. Harper. LC 86-30708. (Illus.). x, 244p. 1987. 35.95 (0-226-31688-2) U Ch Pr.

Working Knowledge: What You Need to Know Before Opening a Business. William A. Walls. LC 92-74766. 200p. 1993. ring bd. 29.95 (0-9634668-0-1) Echelon Pub.

Working Knowledge: What You Need to Know Before Opening a Business. 2nd ed. William A. Walls. LC 93-73758. 200p. 1994. ring bd. 29.95 (0-9634668-1-X) Echelon Pub.

Working Knowledge: What You Need to Know Before Opening a Business. 3rd ed. William A. Walls. LC 94-62063. 200p. 1995. ring bd. 29.95 (0-9634668-2-8) Echelon Pub.

Working Knowledge: What You Need to Know Before Opening a Business. 5th rev. ed. William A. Walls. 200p. 1996. ring bd. 29.95 (0-9634668-5-2) Echelon Pub.

Working Leader: The Triumph of High Performance Over Conventional Management Principles. Leonard R. Sayles. 224p. 1993. 27.95 (0-02-927755-8, Free Press) Free Pr.

Working, Lesson Plans Guide: Learning a Living. 2nd ed. Bailey. (CA - Career Development Ser.). 1997. pap. 5.95 (0-538-65871-1) S-W Pub.

Working Life: A Social Science Contribution to Work Reform. Ed. by Bertil Gardell & Gunn Johansson. LC 80-40289. (Illus.). 361p. reprint ed. pap. 102.90 (0-685-20686-6, 2030476) Bks Demand.

Working Life: Child Labour Through the Nineteenth Century. Alan Bennett. 80p. 1991. pap. 17.95 (0-946184-66-6, Pub. by Waterfront Pubns UK) Maiden Voyage.

Working Life of a Dollar: The Untold Secret of Making Money. Lee Wendelbo & Sam Shannahan. Ed. by Jeanne A. Harris. LC 92-72514. (Illus.). 160p. 1993. pap. text ed. 19.95 (0-9633600-9-4) Calm Pub.

Working Life of Women in the Seventeenth Century. Alice Clark. 368p. 1982. pap. 14.95 (0-7100-9045-5, RKP) Routledge.

Working Life of Women in the Seventeenth Century. Alice Clark. LC 67-31558. (Reprints of Economic Classics Ser.). 328p. 1968. reprint ed. 45.00 (0-678-05039-2) Kelley.

Working Life of Women in the Seventeenth Century. Alice Clark. 328p. 1968. reprint ed. 45.00 (0-7146-1291-X, BHA-01291, Pub. by F Cass Pubs UK) Intl Spec Bk.

Working Life on Severn & Canal: Reminiscences of Working Boatmen. Hugh Conway-Jones. (Illus.). 192p. (Orig.). 1990. pap. 16.00 (0-86299-745-3, Pub. by Sutton Pubng UK) Bks Intl VA.

Working Longshoreman. Ronald E. Magden. (Illus.). 208p. (Orig.). 1991. 10.00 (0-9629616-1-2) Tacoma Lngshore Comm.

Working Machines. John Marshall. LC 95-16003. (Energy & Action Ser.). (J). 1995. write for info. (1-55916-155-8) Rourke Bk Co.

Working Man's Model Family Botanic Guide: Every Man His Own Doctor. William Fox. 310p. 1963. reprint ed. spiral bd. 16.00 (0-7873-0331-3) Hlth Research.

Working Man's Political Economy, Founded upon the Principle of Immutable Justice & the Inalienable Rights of Man: Designed for the Promotion of National Reform. John Pickering. LC 79-156421. (American Labor Ser., No. 2). 1977. reprint ed. 21.95 (0-405-02940-3) Ayer.

Working Manual for Altar Guilds. rev. ed. Dorothy C. Diggs. LC 87-31248. 1988. pap. 6.95 (0-8192-1455-8) Morehouse Pub.

Working Memory. Alan D. Baddeley. (Oxford Psychology Ser.: No. 11). 304p. 1987. pap. 45.00 (0-19-852133-2) OUP.

*Working Memory: A Special Issue of the "Quarterly Journal of Experimental Psychology", Sec. A, Vol. 49A, No. 1, 1996. Hitch & Logie. 1996. 59.95 (0-86377-940-9) L Erlbaum Assocs.

Working Memory & Human Cognition. John T. Richardson et al. (Counterpoints Ser.). 176p. (C). 1996. 45.00 (0-19-510099-9); pap. 19.95 (0-19-510100-6) OUP.

Working Men's College, 1854-1904. Ed. by John L. Davies. LC 75-144594. reprint ed. 32.00 (0-404-01978-1) AMS Pr.

Working Miracles: Women of the English-Speaking Caribbean. Olive Senior. LC 91-4013. (Illus.). 224p. 1992. 35.00 (0-253-35136-7); pap. 15.95 (0-253-28885-1) Ind U Pr.

Working Miracles of Love: A Collection of Teachings. Pref. by Yogi A. Desai. LC 85-50126. (Illus.). 184p. 1985. reprint ed. pap. text ed. 5.95 (0-940258-15-3) Kripalu Pubns.

Working Model Design. Janet K. Allen. (C). 1998. pap. text ed. write for info. (0-201-83265-8) Addison-Wesley.

Working Models of Human Perception. Ed. by Ben Elsendoorn & Herman Bouma. 514p. 1989. text ed. 89.00 (0-12-238050-9) Acad Pr.

Working Mom on the Run Manual: A.K.A. What the Heck Happened to My Life? Debbie Nigro. 220p. 1995. pap. 9.95 (1-57101-011-4) MasterMedia Pub.

Working Moms: A Portrait of Their Lives Series, 7 vols., Set. (Illus.). 40p. (J). (gr. 2-4). 1994. lib. bdg. 111.86 (0-8050-3460-9) TFC Bks NY.

Working Mom's Book of Hints, Tips, & Everyday Wisdom. Louise Lague. LC 95-5094. 192p. (Orig.). 1995. pap. 9.95 (1-56079-461-5, Petersons Pacesetter) Petersons.

Working Mothers: An Evaluative Review of the Consequences for Wife, Husband, & Child. Lois N. Hoffman et al. LC 74-6744. (Jossey-Bass Behavioral Science Ser.). 288p. reprint ed. pap. 82.10 (0-7837-0174-8, 2040471) Bks Demand.

Working Mothers: Understanding Words in Context. Bradley Steffens. LC 89-35434. (Opposing Viewpoints Juniors Ser.). (Illus.). 36p. (J). (gr. 3-6). 1990. lib. bdg. 12.96 (0-89908-644-6) Greenhaven.

Working Mothers & Preschool Children: Getting the Edge on Education. Linda B. Griswold. 1995. pap. 9.95 (0-533-11244-3) Vantage.

Working Mothers & Their Families. Jacqueline V. Lerner. (Family Studies Text Ser.: Vol. 13). (Illus.). 128p. (C). 1993. text ed. 39.95 (0-8039-4209-5); pap. text ed. 17.95 (0-8039-4210-9) Sage.

Working Mother's Guilt Guide: Whatever You're Doing, It Isn't Enough. Mary C. Hickey & Sandra Salmans. (Illus.). 160p. (Orig.). 1992. pap. 9.95 (0-14-016624-6, Penguin Bks) Viking Penguin.

Working Mother's Survival Kit: How to Maintain Sanity While Balancing Career, Home & Family. Mary A. Foley. (Illus.). 110p. (Orig.). 1989. pap. 7.99 (0-685-28941-9) Quailhill Pr.

Working Mothers Survival Kit: How to Maintain Sanity While Balancing Career, Home, & Family. Mary A. Robbe. (Illus.). 110p. (Orig.). 1990. student ed. 9.95 (0-9624357-1-6) Quailhill Pr.

*Working Multi Ethnic. Andre Vries. 1993. pap. text ed. 32.00 (90-6544-620-6) Kluwer Ac.

Working Murder. Eleanor Boylan. 160p. 1989. 16.95 (0-8050-1030-0) H Holt & Co.

Working Murder. Eleanor Boylan. 1992. mass mkt. 5.99 (0-8041-0813-7) Ivy Books.

Working of Miracles. Bill Panko & Margaret Panko. 125p. (Orig.). Date not set. pap. 11.95 (1-885342-15-2) Creative Ways.

Working of State Trading in India. Kulwant R. Gupta. 349p. reprint ed. text ed. 24.00 (0-685-14329-5) Coronet Bks.

*Working on a Miracle. Johnson. 1997. 23.95 (0-553-47824-9) Bantam.

*Working on a Miracle. Mahlon Johnson & Joseph Olshan. 1997. 23.95 (0-553-10519-1) Bantam.

Working on a New Play: A Play Development Handbook for Actors, Directors, Designers & Playwrights. Edward M. Cohen. LC 94-42986. 216p. 1995. pap. 13.95 (0-87910-190-3) Limelight Edns.

*Working on Cruise Ships. Sandra Bow. 1997. pap. 15.95 (1-85458-150-3, Pub. by Vacation-Work UK) Petersons.

W

Working on My Death Chant. Albert Huffstickler. (Illus.). 80p. (Orig.). 1982. pap. 12.00 (*0-9631569-0-X*) Backyard Pr.

Working on the Bomb: An Oral History of World War II. rev. ed. Stephen L. Sanger. Ed. by Craig Wollner. LC 95-69840. Orig. Title: Hanford & the Bomb. (Illus.). 264p. (C). 1995. pap. 17.95 (*0-87678-115-6*) PSU CE Pr.

Working on the Edge. Grant Walker. 1991. 19.95 (*0-312-06002-5*) St Martin.

Working on the Edge. Spike Walker. LC 92-41308. 1993. pap. 11.95 (*0-312-08924-4*) St Martin.

Working on the Land, Vol. 6 see History of Women in the United States: Topically Arranged Articles on the Evolution of Women's History in the United States

Working on the Play & the Role: The Stanislavsky Method for Analyzing the Characters in a Drama. Irina Levin & Igor Levin. 192p. 1992. text ed. 22.50 (*0-929587-94-4*); pap. text ed. 12.95 (*0-929587-93-6*) I R Dee.

Working on the Quality of Working Life. International Council for the Quality of Working Life Staff. (International Series on the Quality of Working Life: Vol. 8). 1979. lib. bdg. 84.00 (*0-89838-001-4*) Kluwer Ac.

Working on Yourself Alone: Inner Dreambody Work. Arnold Mindell. (Illus.). 160p. 1990. pap. 10.95 (*0-14-019201-8*, Arkana) Viking Penguin.

Working Out. Pam Breyer & Jean Bodman. 144p. pap. text ed. write for info. (*0-13-965419-4*) P-H.

Working Out: New Directions for Women's Studies. Ed. by Hilda Hinds et al. LC 92-12797. (Gender & Society Series Feminist Perspectives on the Past & Present). 242p. 1992. 80.00 (*0-7507-0043-2*, Falmer Pr); pap. 27.00 (*0-7507-0044-0*, Falmer Pr) Taylor & Francis.

Working Out in Physical Geograph. Arthur N. Strahler. 614p. 1989. Net. pap. text ed. 23.50 (*0-471-51011-4*) Wiley.

***Working Out Your Child's Design.** LC 89-34232. 1989. pap. write for info. (*1-55513-927-2*, Victor Bks) Chariot Victor.

Working Papers, Chapters 1-15. Charles T. Horngren. 1994. pap. text ed. 30.40 (*0-13-103516-9*) P-H.

Working Papers, Chapters 1-15. Charles T. Horngren & Harrison. 1994. pap. text ed. 30.40 (*0-13-103557-6*) P-H.

Working Papers: Advanced Accounting. 7th ed. Fischer. (AD - Advanced Accounting Ser.). Date not set. text ed. 17.95 (*0-538-86656-X*) S-W Pub.

Working Papers: Astronomy & Astrophysics Panel Reports. National Research Council, Astronomy & Astrophysics Survey Committee Staff. 356p. (C). 1991. pap. text ed. 35.00 (*0-309-04383-2*) Natl Acad Pr.

Working Papers: Reflections on Teachers, Schools, & Communities. Vito Perrone. 256p. (C). 1989. text ed. 35.00 (*0-8077-2945-0*); pap. text ed. 19.95 (*0-8077-2944-2*) Tchrs Coll.

Working Papers - New Perspective on Financial Accounting. Solomon. (AB - Accounting Principles Ser.). Date not set. text ed. 22.95 (*0-538-86485-0*) S-W Pub.

Working Papers in Economics. Ed. by Mary E. Morrison. (Guide to the Microfiche Collection: Ser. 1). v, 110p. 1989. 20.00 (*0-8357-0882-9*) Univ Microfilms.

Working Papers in Economics. Ed. by Mary E. Morrison. (Guide to the Microfiche Collection: Ser. 2). v, 95p. 1989. 20.00 (*0-8357-0890-X*) Univ Microfilms.

Working Papers in Economics: A Guide to the Microfiche Collection - Series III. 66p. (Orig.). 1990. pap. 15.00 (*0-8357-0929-9*); pap. 15.00 (*0-8357-2111-6*) Univ Microfilms.

Working Papers in Economics: A Guide to the Microfiche Collection - Series III. 50p. (Orig.). 1991. pap. 15.00 (*0-8357-2124-8*) Univ Microfilms.

Working Papers in Grammatical Theory & Discourse Structure: Interactions of Morphology, Syntax, & Discourse. Ed. by Masayo Iida et al. LC 86-71108. (CSLI Lecture Notes Ser.: No. 11). 250p. (Orig.). 1987. 44.95 (*0-937073-25-3*); pap. 15.95 (*0-937073-04-0*) CSLI.

Working Papers in Southern African Studies, Vol. 3. Ed. by D. C. Hindson. 190p. 1984. pap. text ed. 19.95 (*0-86975-162-X*, Pub. by Ravan Pr ZA) Ohio U Pr.

Working Papers in the Theory of Action. Talcott Parsons et al. LC 80-24475. 269p. 1981. reprint ed. text ed. 35.00 (*0-313-22468-4*, PAWP, Greenwood Pr) Greenwood.

***Working Papers-Managerial Accounting.** 6th ed. James M. Reeve & Carl S. Warren. (AB - Accounting Principles Ser.). Date not set. pap. 16.95 (*0-538-87359-0*) S-W Pub.

Working Papers of the Twenty-Third Conference. Ed. by D. Christensen & A. Reyes Schramm. 163p. (ENG, FRE & GER.). 1975. 7.00 (*0-318-17461-8*) Intl Coun Trad.

W

Working Parent - Happy Child. Caryl W. Krueger. LC 89-18266. 320p. 1990. pap. 13.95 (*0-687-46191-X*) Abingdon.

Working Parent Dilemma: How to Balance the Responsibilities of Children & Careers. Earl A. Grollman & Gerri L. Sweder. LC 85-47941. 208p. 1988. pap. 9.95 (*0-8070-2703-0*) Beacon Pr.

Working Parents. Linda Ribaudo & Darlyne Walker. LC 94-5504. (Today's World Ser.). 1994. 3.33 (*1-56420-058-2*) New Readers.

Working Parents: Transformations in Gender Roles & Public Policies in Sweden. Phyllis Moen. LC 88-40439. (Life Course Studies). 192p. (Orig.). (C). 1989. pap. text ed. 15.75 (*0-299-12104-6*) U of Wis Pr.

Working Parents' Guide to San Francisco Private Elementary Schools. Susan Vogel. LC 95-92516. (Illus.). 1995. pap. 9.95 (*0-9648757-8-0*, Pince Nez) S Vogel.

***Working Parents' Guide to San Francisco Private Schools (K-8) 1997-98 Academic Year.** 2nd rev. ed. Susan Vogel. (Illus.). 128p. 1996. pap. 15.95 (*0-9648757-5-6*) S Vogel.

Working Parents' Handbook. Katherine Murray. (Illus.). 275p. (Orig.). 1996. pap. 14.95 (*1-57112-075-0*, P0750, Park Avenue) JIST Works.

Working Parents Handbook. June S. Sale et al. 320p. 1996. pap. 13.00 (*0-684-80237-6*, Fireside) S&S Trade.

Working Parents Help Book: Practical Advice for Dealing with the Day-to-Day Challenges of Kids & Careers. Susan C. Price & Tom Price. LC 94-19035. 285p. 1994. pap. 12.95 (*1-56079-333-3*) Petersons.

Working Parents Help Book: Practical Advice for Dealing with the Day-to-Day Challenges of Kids & Careers. 2nd rev. ed. Susan C. Price & Tom Price. 400p. 1996. pap. 16.95 (*1-56079-579-4*) Petersons.

Working Part-Time: Risks & Opportunities. Ed. by Barbara D. Warme et al. LC 91-32680. 384p. 1992. text ed. 69.50 (*0-275-93142-0*, C3142, Praeger Pubs) Greenwood.

Working Partnership: A Collaborative Approach to Care. HMSO Staff. 74p. 1994. pap. 14.00 (*0-11-321716-1*, HM17161, Pub. by Stationery Ofc UK) Bernan Associates.

***Working Parts.** Lucy J. Bledsoe. LC 96-47425. 208p. (Orig.). 1997. pap. 12.00 (*1-878067-94-X*) Seal Pr WA.

Working Party on the Construction of Vehicles: Its Role in the International Perspective. 78p. 1994. 19.00 (*92-1-116617-9*) UN.

Working People & Their Employers. Washington T. Gladden. LC 75-89734. (American Labor, from Conspiracy to Collective Bargaining Ser., No. 1: No. 1). 1972. reprint ed. 18.95 (*0-405-02123-2*) Ayer.

Working People of California. Ed. by Daniel Cornford. LC 94-29274. 503p. 1995. 50.00 (*0-520-08864-6*); pap. 18.00 (*0-520-08865-4*) U CA Pr.

***Working People of Paris, 1817-1914.** Lenard R. Berlanstein. LC 84-47951. (Johns Hopkins University Studies in Historical & Political Science: Vol. 2). 293p. 1984. reprint ed. pap. 83.60 (*0-608-03652-8*, 2064478) Bks Demand.

Working People's Guide to Stress Management. C. Samuel Verghese. (Illus.). 219p. (Orig.). 1989. 29.95 (*0-9622041-0-2*) Pain Stress & Sleep.

Working Person as Caregiver. U. S. Dept. of Health & Human Services Editorial Staff. 74p. 1986. write for info. (*0-318-61582-7*) US HHS.

Working Person's Survival Guide. Steve G. Gabany. 200p. (Orig.). 1990. pap. 11.95 (*0-9624583-0-9*) Hunt & Peck Pub.

Working Person's Survival Guide - Instructor's Guide. Steve G. Gabany. (Illus.). 36p. (YA). (gr. 9-12). 1991. 5.95 (*0-9624583-1-7*) Hunt & Peck Pub.

Working Pit Bull. Dianne Jessup. (Illus.). 320p. 1996. 39.95 (*0-7938-0190-7*, TS235) TFH Pubns.

Working Poor: Farmworkers in the United States. David Griffith & Ed Kissam. LC 94-9120. (Illus.). 368p. (C). 1995. text ed. 59.95 (*1-56639-238-1*); pap. text ed. 19.95 (*1-56639-239-X*) Temple U Pr.

Working Press. Ruth Adler. 1981. 24.95 (*0-405-13783-4*) Ayer.

***Working Press.** Edward V. McCarthy. LC 96-90547. 350p. (Orig.). 1997. pap. 14.95 (*0-533-12094-2*) Vantage.

Working Press of the Nation 1996, 2 vols. Ed. by Bowker, R. R., Staff. 1995. write for info. (*0-8352-3705-2*) Bowker.

Working Press of the Nation 1996, Vol. 1. Ed. by Bowker, R. R., Staff. 1995. write for info. (*0-8352-3700-1*) Bowker.

Working Press of the Nation 1996, Vol. 2. Ed. by Bowker, R. R., Staff. 1995. write for info. (*0-8352-3702-8*) Bowker.

Working Press of the Nation 1997, 3 vols. Ed. by Bowker, R. R., Staff. 1996. 419.95 (*0-8352-3834-2*) Bowker.

Working Press of the Nation 1997: Magazines & Internal Publications Directory, Vol. 2. 1996. 229.00 (*0-8352-3836-9*) Bowker.

Working Press of the Nation 1997: Newspaper Directory, Vol. 1. 1996. 229.00 (*0-8352-3835-0*) Bowker.

Working Press of the Nation 1997: TV & Radio Directory, Vol. 3. 1996. 229.00 (*0-8352-3837-7*) Bowker.

***Working Press Only.** Tracy Dodds. Date not set. write for info. (*0-688-07978-4*) Morrow.

Working Programmers Guide to Serial Protocols. Tim Kientzle. 1995. pap. 39.99 (*1-883577-20-9*) Coriolis Grp.

Working Prototypes: Exhibit Design at the Exploratorium. Exploratorium Staff. (Illus.). 28p. (Orig.). 1986. pap. 5.00 (*0-943451-08-6*) Explorator.

Working Relationship: The Job Development Specialist's Guide to Successful Partnerships with Business. Ellen S. Fabian et al. 160p. 1994. pap. 31.00 (*1-55766-157-X*, 157X) P H Brookes.

Working Relationships: Everyone's Guide to Working with People. Vincent W. Kafka & John H. Schaefer. 210p. (Orig.). 1990. pap. 14.95 (*0-913261-21-1*) Effect Learn Sys.

Working Right: Expressing Your True Colors in Life & Work. Fran W. Abbott & Pam Mackenfuss. (Illus.). 50p. (C). 1990. pap. text ed. write for info. (*0-923400-01-X*) Phantom Pr.

Working River. Fred Powledge. LC 94-33363. 136p. (J). (gr. 4-7). 1995. 15.00 (*0-374-38527-0*) FS&G.

Working Safe: How to Change Behaviors & Attitudes. E. Scott Geller. 1996. pap. 19.95 (*0-8019-8732-6*) Chilton.

Working Safely in Gamma Radiography: A Training Manual for Industrial Radiographers. 1995. lib. bdg. 251.95 (*0-8490-6743-X*) Gordon Pr.

Working Safely in Gamma Radiography: A Training Manual for Industrial Radiographers. (Illus.). 168p. 1989. reprint ed. per. 22.00 (*0-16-006246-2*, S/N052024000021) USGPO.

***Working Safely in Gamma Radiography: A Training Manual for the Industrial Radiographer.** 1997. lib. bdg. 250.95 (*0-8490-7706-0*) Gordon Pr.

***Working Safely in the Auto Shop.** Tony Marchetti. 20p. (YA). (gr. 10 up). 1996. wbk. ed., pap. 7.00 (*0-8064-1327-1*, A40) Bergwall.

Working Safely in the Chemistry Laboratory. Ed. by Harry G. Hajian & Robert L. Pecsok. LC 93-45353. 244p. 1994. pap. 39.95 (*0-8412-2707-1*) Am Chemical.

Working Safely with Asbestos-Cement Pipe. (Illus.). 28p. 1995. pap. 23.00 (*0-89867-795-5*, 20406) Am Water Wks Assn.

Working Safely with Chemicals in the Laboratory. Ed. by Christine E. Gorman. (Illus.). 123p. 1993. pap. 12.00 (*0-931690-52-8*) Genium Pub.

Working Safely with Hazardous Materials in the Workplace: An Employee Handbook. Maureen Gannon et al. Ed. by Christine E. Molluso. (Illus.). 122p. (Orig.). 1993. pap. text ed. 12.00 (*0-931690-58-7*) Genium Pub.

Working Safely with Industrial Robots. Ed. by Peter M. Strubhar. 266p. 1986. 36.50 (*0-317-47605-X*) Robot Inst Am.

Working Safely with Industrial Robots. Ed. by Peter M. Strubhar. 266p. 1986. 42.00 (*0-87263-210-5*) SME.

Working Safely with Nuclear Gauges. 1996. lib. bdg. 250.95 (*0-8490-5958-5*) Gordon Pr.

Working Scared: Achieving Success in Trying Times. Kenneth N. Wexley & Stanley B. Silverman. LC 92-39967. (Management Ser.). 208p. 27.00 (*1-55542-512-7*) Jossey-Bass.

***Working Schemes? Active Labour Market Policy in Ireland.** Philip J. O'Connell & Frances McGinnity. 160p. 1997. text ed. 55.95 (*1-85972-624-0*, Pub. by Ashgate UK) Ashgate Pub Co.

Working Sex: An Odyssey into Our Cultural Underworld. Marianne Macy. LC 96-2943. (Illus.). 320p. 1996. 23.00 (*0-7867-0249-4*) Carroll & Graf.

Working Shadows. David Weitzman. (J). 1996. 15.95 (*0-684-19691-3*, Atheneum Bks Young) S&S Childrens.

Working Sheepdogs: Management & Training. John Templeton & Matt Mundell. (Illus.). 128p. 1992. 34.95 (*1-85223-718-X*, Pub. by Crowood Pr UK) Trafalgar.

Working Sheet Metal. David J. Gingery. (Illus.). 96p. (Orig.). 1993. pap. 8.95 (*1-878087-13-4*) D J Gingery.

***Working, Shirking, & Sabotage: Bureaucratic Responses to a Democratic Public.** John Brehm & Scott Gates. LC 96-43487. (C). 1997. 39.50 (*0-472-10764-X*) U of Mich Pr.

Working Skills in Geometric Dimensioning & Tolerancing. Mike Fitzpatrick. LC 92-18034. 262p. 1991. pap. 29.95 (*0-8273-4900-9*) Delmar.

Working Smart. Madelyn Schulman. (CA - Career Development Ser.). 1994. wbk. ed., pap. 14.95 (*0-538-62415-9*) S-W Pub.

Working Smart: A Union Guide to Participation Programs & Reeingineering. Mike Parker & Jane Slaughter. LC 94-73182. (Illus.). 317p. (Orig.). 1994. pap. 20.00 (*0-914093-08-8*) Labor Notes.

Working Smart: How to Accomplish More in Half the Time. Michael LeBoeuf. 272p. 1988. mass mkt. 5.99 (*0-446-35356-6*) Warner Bks.

Working Smarter from Home: Your Day--Your Way. Nancy Struck. LC 94-68199. (Fifty-Minute Ser.). (Illus.). 111p. (Orig.). 1994. pap. 10.95 (*1-56052-310-7*) Crisp Pubns.

Working Smarter with DOS 5.0. Electronic Learning Facilitators, Inc. Staff. LC 92-73082. 305p. (C). 1993. pap. text ed. 17.50 (*0-03-096376-1*) Dryden Pr.

Working Sober: The Transformation of an Occupational Drinking Culture. William J. Sonnenstuhl. LC 95-43596. (ILR Press Book). 160p. 1996. 35.00 (*0-8014-3267-7*); pap. 14.95 (*0-8014-8348-4*) Cornell U Pr.

Working Solo: The Real Guide to Freedom & Financial Success with Your Own Business. Terri Lonier. LC 93-84901. (Illus.). 400p. (Orig.). 1994. pap. 14.95 (*1-883282-40-3*) Portico Pr.

Working Solo Sourcebook: Essential Resources for Independent Entrepreneurs. Terri Lonier. LC 94-67631. 320p. (Orig.). 1995. 24.95 (*1-883282-50-0*) Portico Pr.

Working Solo Sourcebook: Essential Resources for Independent Entrepreneurs. Terri Lonier. LC 94-67631. (Illus.). 320p. (Orig.). 1995. pap. 14.95 (*1-883282-60-8*) Portico Pr.

Working Space. Frank Stella. (Charles Eliot Norton Lectures). (Illus.). 196p. 1986. pap. text ed. 22.95 (*0-674-95961-2*) HUP.

Working Space: The Milwaukee Repertory Theater Builds a Home. Sara O'Connor & Sherrill M. Myers. LC 91-20250. (Illus.). 144p. (Orig.). 1992. pap. 16.95 (*1-55936-033-X*) Theatre Comm.

Working Stiff. John Richards. LC 96-76624. 224p. 1996. pap. 15.00 (*1-57650-098-5*) Hi Jinx Pr.

Working Stiffs, Union Maids, Reds, & Riffraff: An Organized Guide to Films about Labor. Tom Zaniello. LC 95-47514. (ILR Press Book). (Illus.). 288p. 1996. 39.95 (*0-87546-352-5*); pap. 18.95 (*0-87546-353-3*) Cornell U Pr.

Working the Angles: A Trigonometry for Pastoral Work. Eugene H. Peterson. 200p. (Orig.). 1987. pap. 14.00 (*0-8028-0265-6*) Eerdmans.

Working the Chesapeake: Watermen on the Bay. Mark E. Jacoby. 24.95 (*0-943676-54-1*); pap. 14.95 (*0-943676-53-3*) MD Sea Grant Col.

Working the Countertransference. Lawrence E. Hedges. 1995. 40.00 (*0-87668-509-2*) Aronson.

***Working the Hard Side of the Street: Selected Stories - Poems - Screams.** Kirk Alex. 350p. (Orig.). 1998. pap. 14.95 (*0-939122-25-1*) Tucumcari.

Working the North: Labor & the Northwest Defense Projects, 1942-1946. William R. Morrison & Kenneth A. Coates. LC 93-41687. (Illus.). xiv, 270p. 1994. 30.00 (*0-912006-72-2*); pap. 20.00 (*0-912006-73-0*) U of Alaska Pr.

Working the Organizing Experience: Transforming Psychotic, Schizoid, & Autistic States. Lawrence E. Hedges. LC 94-7821. 336p. 1995. 45.00 (*1-56821-255-0*) Aronson.

Working the Program: The Second & Third Steps for Parents. Judith Strom. 16p. 1990. pap. 1.75 (*0-925190-13-6*, F911023 C) Fairview Press.

Working the Range: Essays on the History of Western Land Management & the Environment. Ed. by John R. Wunder. LC 84-15693. (Contributions in Economics & Economic History Ser.: No. 61). xv, 241p. 1985. text ed. 55.00 (*0-313-24591-6*, WUW/) Greenwood.

Working the Shadow Side: A Guide to Positive Behind-the-Scenes. Gerry Egan. (Management Ser.). 304p. 27.50 (*0-7879-0011-7*) Jossey-Bass.

Working the Soul: Reflections on Jungian Psychology. Charles Ponce. (Illus.). 189p. 1987. pap. 12.95 (*1-55643-033-7*) North Atlantic.

Working the Spirit: Ceremonies of the African Diaspora. Joseph M. Murphy. LC 93-3929. 280p. 1994. pap. 14.00 (*0-8070-1221-1*) Beacon Pr.

Working the Stone. deluxe limited ed. Bryce Milligan. (Illus.). 48p. 1993. pap. 15.00 (*0-930324-30-7*) Wings Pr.

Working the Street: Police Discretion & the Dilemmas of Reform. Michael K. Brown. LC 88-20951. 384p. 1988. pap. 16.95 (*0-87154-191-2*) Russell Sage.

Working the System: Government in Queensland. Peter Coaldrake. 1989. pap. 15.95 (*0-7022-2230-5*, Pub. by Univ Queensland Pr AT) Intl Spec Bk.

Working the Water: The Commercial Fisheries of Maryland's Patuxent River. Ed. by Paula J. Johnson. LC 87-8114. (Illus.). 218p. 1988. pap. 19.95 (*0-8139-1156-7*) Calvert MM Pr.

Working the Water: The Commercial Fisheries of Maryland's Patuxent River. Paula J. Johnson. LC 87-8114. (Illus.). 256p. 1988. text ed. 35.00 (*0-8139-1129-X*) U Pr of Va.

Working the Waterfront: The Ups & Downs of a Rebel Longshoreman. Gilbert Mers. LC 88-2168. (Illus.). 308p. 1988. 19.95 (*0-292-76022-1*) U of Tex Pr.

***Working the Web: A Student's Guide.** Carol L. Clark. 240p. (C). 1996. student ed., pap. text ed. 18.50 (*0-15-504060-X*) HB Coll Pubs.

***Working the 12 Steps.** Hazelden Staff. 1988. pap. 5.50 (*0-89486-563-3*) Hazelden.

Working Theory: Critical Composition Studies for Students & Teachers. Judith Goleman. LC 94-40308. (Series in Language & Ideology). 168p. 1995. text ed. 55.00 (*0-89789-301-8*, Bergin & Garvey); pap. text ed. 14.95 (*0-89789-302-6*) Greenwood.

Working Through Conflict: Strategies for Relationships, Groups, & Organizations. 2nd ed. Marshall S. Poole et al. LC 92-20474. (C). 1992. 30.00 (*0-06-500658-5*) Addson-Wesley Educ.

Working Through Conflict: Strategies for Relationships, Groups, & Organizations. 3rd ed. Joseph P. Folger et al. LC 96-14453. (C). 1997. text ed. 33.95 (*0-673-99766-9*) Addson-Wesley Educ.

Working Through Derrida. Intro. by Gary B. Madison. (Studies in Phenomenology & Existential Philosophy). 294p. (Orig.). 1993. 49.95 (*0-8101-1054-7*); pap. 22.50 (*0-8101-1079-2*) Northwestern U Pr.

***Working Through Embarrassing Revelations: How to Manage the Operational Changes Required & the Enormous Visibility.** James E. Lukaszewski. 8p. 1996. pap. 20.00 (*1-883291-21-6*) Lukaszewski.

Working Time: Essays on Poetry, Culture, & Travel. Jane R. Miller. LC 91-45197. (Poets on Poetry Ser.). 176p. (C). 1992. pap. 13.95 (*0-472-06480-0*); text ed. 39.50 (*0-472-09480-7*) U of Mich Pr.

Working Time & Employment. Robert A. Hart. LC 86-28815. (Illus.). 250p. (C). 1987. text ed. 60.00 (*0-04-331109-1*) Routledge Chapman & Hall.

***Working Time Around the World: Conditions of Work Digest, Vol. 14, 1995.** xi, 398p. 1996. pap. 45.50 (*92-2-109510-X*) Intl Labour Office.

Working Time in Transition: The Political Economy of Working Hours in Industrial Nations. Ed. by Karl Hinrichs et al. (Labor & Social Change Ser.). 352p. 1991. 49.95 (*0-87722-757-8*) Temple U Pr.

***Working to Become an Adult: Diverse Practice, Initiations & Rites.** Richard L. Sartore. 1996. 27.50 (*0-938609-08-4*) Graduate Group.

An Asterisk (*) at the beginning of an entry indicates that the title is appearing in BIP for the first time.

Working Together. Leebov. (gr. 13). 1995. 5.95 (0-8151-5317-1) Mosby Yr Bk.

***Working Together.** 2nd ed. Harrington. (C). 1997. pap. text ed. write for info. (0-15-508164-0) HB Coll Pubs.

Working Together: A Guide for Personal Care Providers & Consumers. 2nd ed. Elaine Baumeister. Ed. by Rita I. McCullough. LC 92-15473. 300p. (Orig.). 1993. pap. write for info. (1-879198-21-5) Knwldg Ideas & Trnds.

Working Together: A How-to-Do-It Manual for Trustees & Librarians. James Swan. (How-to-Do-It Ser.). 225p. 1992. 39.95 (1-55570-096-9) Neal-Schuman.

Working Together: A Manual to Help Groups Work More Effectively. Robert C. Biagi. LC 79-624736. (Illus.). (Orig.). (C). 1978. pap. 7.00 (0-934210-05-5) Devlp Commy.

Working Together: A Personality Centered Approach to Management. Olaf Isachsen & Linda V. Berens. 268p. (Orig.). 1989. pap. 14.95 (0-685-44708-1, Neworld) IMD Inc.

Working Together: A Personality Centered Approach to Management. 2nd ed. Olaf Isachsen & Linda Berens. (Illus.). 349p. (Orig.). 1991. pap. 16.95 (1-877808-00-8) IMD Inc.

Working Together: A Personality Centered Approach to Management. 2nd ed. Olaf Isachsen & Linda Berens. 350p. (Orig.). 1991. 21.95 (1-877808-03-2); pap. 16.95 (1-877808-01-6); spiral bd. 19.95 (1-877808-02-4) IMD Inc.

Working Together: A Personality Centered Approach to Management. 2nd ed. Olaf Isachsen & Linda Berens. 348p. (Orig.). (C). 1991. pap. text ed. 16.95 (0-685-50100-0) IMD Inc.

Working Together: A Study of Cooperation among Producers, Educators, & Researchers to Create Educational Television. James S. Ettema. 220p. (Orig.). 1980. pap. 14.00 (0-87944-251-4) Inst Soc Res.

Working Together: A Study of Cooperation among Producers, Educators, & Researchers to Create Educational Television. James S. Ettema. LC 80-80234. (Institute for Social Research, Research Report Ser.). 222p. (Orig.). reprint ed. pap. 63.30 (0-7837-5251-2, 2044988) Bks Demand.

Working Together: Building Integrated Healthcare Organizations Through Improved Executive-Physician Collaboration. Seth Allcorn. 225p. 1995. text ed. 45.00 (1-55738-614-5) Irwin Prof Pubng.

Working Together: Inter-School Collaboration for Special Needs. Ingrid Lunt et al. 144p. 1994. pap. 18.95 (1-85346-301-9, Pub. by D Fulton UK) Taylor & Francis.

Working Together: Labour-Management Co-operation in Training & in Technological & Other Changes. Ed. by A. Gladstone & Muneto Ozaki. v, 195p. (Orig.). 1991. pap. 33.75 (92-2-106461-1) Intl Labour Office.

***Working Together: Producing Synergy by Honoring Diversity.** Wendy S. Appel et al. Ed. by Angeles Arien. Tr. by Pavel Palazchenko. (Illus.). 272p. 1998. 28.75 (1-886710-02-3) New Leaders.

Working Together: Productive Communication on the Job. Sherod Miller et al. (Illus.). 200p. 1985. teacher ed., text ed. 40.00 (0-917340-14-0); ring bd. 40.00 (0-917340-11-6) Interpersonal Comm.

Working Together: Succeeding in a Multi-Cultural Organization. rev. ed. George Simons & Amy J. Zuckerman. Ed. by Michael Crisp & Francine Lundy-Ruvolo. LC 93-74921. (Illus.). 85p. 1994. pap. 10.95 (1-56052-292-5) Crisp Pubns.

Working Together: The Art of Consulting & Communicating. Anita DeBoer. 246p. 1995. teacher ed., pap. text ed. 22.50 (1-57035-041-8, 71WORK) Sopris.

Working Together: The Collaborative Style of Bargaining. Stuart C. Smith et al. LC 90-80370. xii, 75p. (Orig.). 1990. pap. 7.25 (0-86552-103-4) U of Oreg ERIC.

Working Together: Tools for Collaborative Teaching. Anita DeBoer & Susan Fister. (Working Together Ser.). 142p. 1995. pap. text ed. 19.50 (1-57035-046-9, 70COTEACH) Sopris.

Working Together: What Collaborative Teaching Can Look Like. Susan Fister & Anita DeBoer. 24p. (Orig.). 1996. pap. text ed. 49.00 (1-57035-069-8, 70VIDEO) Sopris.

Working Together: Workplace Culture, Supported Employment, & Persons with Disabilities. David Hagner & Dale DiLeo. 1993. pap. text ed. 27.95 (0-914797-88-3) Brookline Bks.

***Working Together: 55 Team Games.** Lorraine L. Ukens. 1996. pap. text ed. 34.95 (0-7879-0354-X) Jossey-Bass.

Working Together Against AIDS. Barbara H. Draimin. LC 94-15208. (Library of Social Activism). (Illus.). 64p. (YA). 1995. lib. bdg. 15.95 (0-8239-1777-0) Rosen Group.

Working Together Against Crime. Victor Adint. (Library of Social Activism). (Illus.). 64p. (YA). (gr. 7-12). 1996. lib. bdg. 15.95 (0-8239-2264-2) Rosen Group.

Working Together Against Drinking & Driving, 8 vols. Janet Grosshandler-Smith. (Library of Social Activism). (Illus.). 64p. (YA). (gr. 7-12). 1996. lib. bdg. 15.95 (0-8239-2259-6) Rosen Group.

Working Together Against Drug Addiction, 8 vols. Lawrence Clayton. (Library of Social Activism). (Illus.). 64p. (YA). (gr. 7-12). 1996. lib. bdg. 15.95 (0-8239-2263-4) Rosen Group.

Working Together Against Gang Violence, 8 vols. Margi Trapani. (Library of Social Activism). (Illus.). 64p. (YA). (gr. 7-12). 1996. lib. bdg. 15.95 (0-8239-2260-X) Rosen Group.

Working Together Against Gun Violence. Maryann Miller. LC 94-1021. (Library of Social Activism). (Illus.). 64p. (YA). (gr. 7-12). 1994. lib. bdg. 15.95 (0-8239-1779-7) Rosen Group.

Working Together Against Hate Groups. Rose Blue & Corrine J. Naden. LC 94-433. (Library of Social Activism). (Illus.). 64p. (YA). (gr. 7-12). 1994. lib. bdg. 15.95 (0-8239-1776-2) Rosen Group.

Working Together Against Homelessness. Eugene Hurwitz & Sue Hurwitz. LC 94-1022. (Library of Social Activism). (Illus.). 64p. (YA). (gr. 7-12). 1994. lib. bdg. 15.95 (0-8239-1772-X) Rosen Group.

Working Together Against Human Rights Violations. Rodney G. Peck. LC 94-8858. (Library of Social Activism Ser.). (Illus.). 64p. (YA). (gr. 7-12). 1995. lib. bdg. 15.95 (0-8239-1778-9) Rosen Group.

Working Together Against Racism. Ray Milios. LC 94-1023. (Library of Social Activism). (Illus.). 64p. (YA). (gr. 7-12). 1995. lib. bdg. 15.95 (0-8239-1840-8) Rosen Group.

Working Together Against School Violence, 8 vols. Sheila Klee. (Library of Social Activism). (Illus.). 64p. (YA). (gr. 7-12). 1996. lib. bdg. 15.95 (0-8239-2262-6) Rosen Group.

Working Together Against Sexual Harassment, Set. Rhoda McFarland. (Library of Social Activism). (Illus.). 64p. (YA). (gr. 7-12). 1996. lib. bdg. 15.95 (0-8239-1775-4) Rosen Group.

Working Together Against Teen Suicide. Toby Axelrod. (Library of Social Activism). (Illus.). 64p. (YA). (gr. 7-12). 1996. lib. bdg. 15.95 (0-8239-2261-8) Rosen Group.

Working Together Against the Destruction of the Environment: Library of Social Activism. Robert Gartner. LC 94-2278. (Illus.). 64p. (YA). (gr. 7-12). 1994. lib. bdg. 15.95 (0-8239-1774-6) Rosen Group.

Working Together Against Violence Against Women. Aliza Sherman. (Library of Social Activism). (Illus.). 64p. (YA). (gr. 7-12). 1996. lib. bdg. 15.95 (0-8239-2258-8) Rosen Group.

Working Together Against World Hunger. Nancy B. Flood. LC 94-6858. (Library of Social Activism Ser.). (Illus.). 64p. (YA). (gr. 7-12). 1995. lib. bdg. 15.95 (0-8239-1773-8) Rosen Group.

Working Together & Getting Along. Dora C. Fowler. 12p. 1987. pap. text ed. 1.00 (1-57323-030-8) Natl Inst Child Mgmt.

***Working Together for a Better Future.** Marilyn Hays. Ed. by Veronica Zysk. 280p. (Orig.). 1996. pap. 34.95 (1-885477-27-9) Fut Horizons.

Working Together for a Competitive Workforce: A Handbook for State Policy Teams. Barbara A. Puls. (Investing in People Ser.: Vol. 6). 42p. 15.00 (1-55516-330-0, 3127) Natl Conf State Legis.

Working Together for Individual & Community Growth. Debra Kazmerzak. 81p. 1995. wbk. ed., pap. text ed. write for info. (0-9650893-0-4) Outlooks.

Working Together for Optimum Results: Toolbook II. Glen D. Hoffherr & Norm W. Young. Ed. by Mary Conrad. 72p. (Orig.). 1994. pap. text ed. 3.95 (0-9638223-1-4) Markon.

***Working Together for Public Service: Excellence in State & Local Government Through Labor-Management Cooperation.** 1997. lib. bdg. 250.95 (0-8490-7724-9) Gordon Pr.

Working Together for Young Children: Multi-Professionalism in Action. Ed. by Tricia David. LC 93-5900. 224p. (C). 1994. pap. text ed. 17.95 (0-415-09248-5) Routledge.

Working Together for Young Children: Multi-Professionalism in Action. Ed. by Tricia David. LC 93-5900. 224p. (C). (gr. 13). 1994. text ed. 59.95 (0-415-09247-7) Routledge.

Working Together for Youth: A Practical Guide for Individuals & Groups. I. Shelby Andress. 64p. 1993. pap. text ed. 10.00 (1-57482-314-0) Search Inst.

Working Together in Child Protection: An Exploration of the Multi-Disciplinary Task & System. Michael Murphy. 224p. 1995. 59.95 (1-85742-197-3, Pub. by Arena UK); pap. 25.95 (1-85742-198-1, Pub. by Arena UK) Ashgate Pub Co.

Working Together In Child Protection Report of Phase Two, A Survey of Experien. Birchall Elizabeth. 360p. 1995. pap. 75.00 (0-11-321830-3, HM18303, Pub. by Stationery Ofc UK) Bernan Associates.

Working Together in Schools: A Guide for Educators. Gordon A. Donaldson, Jr. & David R. Sanderson. LC 96-10087. (1-Off Ser.). (Illus.). 184p. 1996. 47.95 (0-8039-6377-7); pap. 21.95 (0-8039-6378-5) Corwin Pr.

***Working Together in Troubled Times: Community-Based Therapies.** Jane Piazza. LC 97-1465. 250p. 1997. 49.50 (0-7618-0694-6); pap. 29.50 (0-7618-0695-4) U Pr of Amer.

Working Together on Rudolf Steiner's Mystery Dramas. Hans Pusch. LC 80-67024. (Steiner's Mystery Dramas Ser.). (Illus.). 144p. (Orig.). 1980. 15.95 (0-910142-90-4); pap. 9.95 (0-910142-91-2) Anthroposophic.

Working Together Through Partnerships: A Practical Guide to Labor-Management Partnerships. 82p. (Orig.). 1994. pap. 9.95 (0-936295-50-3) FPMI Comns.

***Working Together to End Domestic Violence.** David A. Wolfe et al. 256p. 1996. 24.95 (0-931541-60-3) Mancorp Pub.

Working Together to Get Things Done: Managing for Organizational Productivity. Dean R. Tjosvold. LC 85-40108. (Issues in Organization & Management Ser.). 224p. 1986. 27.00 (0-669-10834-0) Team Media.

Working Together, Vols. 1 & 2: Gender Analysis in Agriculture, Vol. 2. Ed. by Hilary S. Feldstein & Susan V. Poats. LC 90-4287. (Library of Management for Development). 288p. 1990. pap. 9.95 (0-931816-59-9) Kumarian Pr.

Working Together with Children & Families: Case Studies in Early Intervention. Ed. by P. J. McWilliam & Donald B. Bailey, Jr. LC 92-42852. 288p. 1993. 27.00 (1-55766-123-5) P H Brookes.

Working Too Slowly. Barbara L. McCombs & Linda Brannan. (Skills for Job Success Ser.). (Illus.). 32p. (Orig.). (YA). (gr. 7-12). 1990. teacher ed. 1.95 (1-56119-008-X); disk 39.95 (1-56119-104-3) Educ Pr MD.

Working Toward Enlightenment: The Cultivation of Practice. Nan Huai-Chin. LC 93-13536. 196p. (Orig.). 1993. pap. 14.95 (0-87728-776-7) Weiser.

Working Toward Freedom: Slave Society & Domestic Economy in the American South. Ed. by Larry E. Hudson, Jr. LC 94-31998. (Illus.). 300p. (C). 1995. 45.00 (1-878822-37-3) Univ Rochester Pr.

Working Toward Freedom: Slave Society & Domestic Economy in the American South. Ed. by Larry E. Hudson, Jr. LC 94-31998. (Illus.). 300p. (C). 1995. pap. 24.95 (1-878822-38-1) Univ Rochester Pr.

Working Toward Independence: A Practical Guide to Teaching People with Learning Disabilities. Janet H. Carr & Suzanne Collins. 250p. 1992. pap. 33.00 (1-85302-140-7) Taylor & Francis.

***Working Toward Strategic Change: A Step-by-Step Guide to the Planning Process.** Michael G. Dolence et al. LC 96-35692. (Higher & Adult Education Ser.). 1997. write for info. (0-7879-0796-0) Jossey-Bass.

Working Toward Zion: Principles of the United Order for the Modern World. James W. Lucas & Warner P. Woodworth. 484p. 1996. 19.95 (1-56236-228-3) Aspen Bks.

Working under Different Rules. Ed. by Richard B. Freeman. (Illus.). 224p. 1994. 39.95 (0-87154-276-5); pap. 14.95 (0-87154-277-3) Russell Sage.

***Working under Pressure.** Date not set. pap. 27.95 (0-8464-4430-5) Beekman Pubs.

***Working under the Safety Net: Policy & Practice with the New American Poor.** Stephen Burghardt & Michael Fabricant. LC 86-27970. (Sage Human Services Guide Ser.: No. 13). 180p. 1987. reprint ed. pap. 51.30 (0-608-04302-8, 2065081) Bks Demand.

***Working Vocabulary.** Sid Gold. LC 97-8505. 1997. write for info. (0-931846-49-8) Wash Writers Pub.

***Working Vocabulary.** Sidney Gold. (Poetry Ser.). (Orig.). 1997. pap. text ed. 10.00 (0-614-27189-4) Wash Writers Pub.

Working Wardrobe: Affordable Clothes That Work for You. Janet Wallach. (Illus.). 200p. 1987. pap. 11.95 (0-446-38757-6) Warner Bks.

Working Waterfront: The Story of Tacoma's Ships & Men. Ronald E. Magden & A. D. Martinson. (Illus.). 181p. (Orig.). 1982. pap. 10.00 (0-9629578-2-8) Intl Long WA.

Working Well...? How to Correct the Unhealthy Workplace: The Ergonomic Approach. 2nd rev. ed. Terry McShane. (Illus.). 128p. (Orig.). 1996. pap. 16.95 (0-9636940-1-4) T&M Assocs.

***Working Wheels.** Jan Pienkowski. 1997. pap. 7.99 (0-525-45854-9) Dutton Child Bks.

Working Wheels. Paul Stickland. (Illus.). 14p. (J). (ps). 1993. pap. 3.50 (0-525-67457-8, Lodestar Bks) Dutton Child Bks.

***Working Wife.** Richard Brauer. LC 95-90556. 128p. (Orig.). 1996. pap. 4.99 incl. reel tape (1-56002-593-X, Univ Edtns) Aegina Pr.

Working Windows World. Michael Perl & Sharon Burton. 224p. (C). 1995. pap. text ed. 26.19 (0-7872-1039-0) Kendall-Hunt.

Working Wisdom: Timeless Skills & Vanguard Strategies for Learning Organizations. Robert Aubrey & Paul Cohen. LC 94-47379. (Management Ser.). 224p. 25.00 (0-7879-0058-3) Jossey-Bass.

Working with Acrylics. (Leisure Arts Ser.: No. 25). (Illus.). 32p. pap. 4.95 (0-85532-535-6, 535-6, Pub. by Search Pr UK) A Schwartz & Co.

***Working with Active Server Pages.** Melnick Consulting Group Staff. 552p. 1997. 39.99 (0-7897-1115-X) Mac Comp Pub.

***Working with ADO & OLE DB.** Shelby Gao. LC 97-13131. 350p. 1997. 49.99 (1-56205-739-1) Mac Comp Pub.

Working with Adolescents: Building Effective Communication & Choice-Making Skills. Richard C. Nelson et al. LC 94-70340. 144p. (Orig.). (C). 1994. pap. text ed. 16.95 (0-932796-61-3) Ed Media Corp.

Working with Adult Incest Survivors: The Healing Journey. Sam Kirschner et al. LC 92-33066. (Frontiers in Couples & Family Therapy Ser.: Vol. 6). 240p. 1993. text ed. 30.95 (0-87630-691-1) Brunner-Mazel.

Working with Adult Survivors of Child Sexual Abuse. Elsa Jones. 104p. 1992. pap. text ed. 21.95 (1-85575-017-1, Pub. by Karnac Bks UK) Brunner-Mazel.

Working with Adults in Groups: Integrating Cognitive-Behavioral & Small Group Strategies. Sheldon D. Rose. LC 89-45589. (Social & Behavioral Science Ser.). 382p. 36.95 (1-55542-166-0) Jossey-Bass.

Working with African American Families: A Guide to Resources. Carolyn Ash. 100p. 1994. ring bd. 35.00 (1-885429-08-8) Family Resource.

Working with Aggressive Youth in Open Settings: A Sourcebook for Child-Care Providers. Father Flanagan's Boys' Home Staff. Ed. by Boys Town Writing Division Staff. (Illus.). 100p. (Orig.). (C). 1989. pap. 19.95 (0-938510-16-9) Boys Town Pr.

Working with Americans: A Practical Guide for Asians on How to Succeed with U. S. Managers. Joel Wallach & Gale Metcalf. LC 94-34947. 1995. pap. text ed. 16.95 (0-07-113838-2) McGraw.

***Working with an Interpreter: A Guide for Teaching or Speaking Abroad.** Joseph Scanlon et al. LC 96-3311. 1996. pap. write for info. (0-943089-06-9) U GA CFIMCTR.

Working with Analogical Semantics: Disambiguation Techniques in DLT. Victor Sadler. (Distributed Language Translation Ser.). x, 222p. (Orig.). (C). 1989. 90.80 (90-6765-429-9); pap. 65.40 (90-6765-428-0) Mouton.

Working with & for the Aged. Ed. by Jordan I. Kosberg. LC 79-88366. (Readings in Social Work Ser.). 284p. reprint ed. pap. 81.00 (0-7837-6536-3, 2045673) Bks Demand.

Working with Angels. Robert R. Leichtman & Carl Japikse. 90p. 1992. pap. 7.95 (0-89804-824-9, Enthea Pr) Ariel GA.

Working with Animal Chromosomes. 2nd ed. Herbert C. MacGregor. LC 88-14397. 290p. 1988. pap. text ed. 152.00 (0-471-92028-2) Wiley.

Working with Animals. Schmitt. (J). 1996. 13.95 (0-684-19676-X, Atheneum Bks Young) S&S Childrens.

Working with Anthroposophy. Georg Kuhlewind. Tr. by Michael Lipson & Christopher Bamford from GER. Orig. Title: Vom Umgang mit der Anthroposophie. 96p. (Orig.). 1992. pap. 10.95 (0-88010-361-2) Anthroposophic.

***Working with Appleworks: A Complete Guide.** 11th ed. Mandell. (DF - Computer Applications Ser.). 1988. wbk. ed., pap. 22.95 (0-314-47165-0) S-W Pub.

***Working with Appleworks: A Complete Guide.** 11th ed. Mandell. (DF - Computer Applications Ser.). 1989. text ed. 46.95 (0-314-35874-9) S-W Pub.

Working with Application Software - IBM-PC. Steven L. Mandell. (Illus.). 253p. (C). 1986. text ed. 45.25 (0-314-96495-9) West Pub.

Working with Application Software - TRS-80. Steven L. Mandell. (Illus.). 242p. (C). 1986. text ed. 45.25 (0-314-96493-2) West Pub.

Working with Archival Data. Glen H. Elder, Jr. et al. (Quantitative Applications in the Social Sciences Ser.: Vol. 88). (Illus.). 96p. (C). 1992. pap. 9.95 (0-8039-4262-1) Sage.

Working with Behavioral Disorders, 8 vols. Ed. by Lyndal M. Bullock & Robert B. Rutherford, Jr. (CEC Mini-Library). 1991. Set. pap. text ed. 70.00 (0-685-48113-1, P346) Coun Exc Child.

Working with Bilingual Children: Good Practice in the Primary Classroom. Ed. by Mahendra K. Verma et al. LC 95-6555. (Bilingual Education & Bilingualism Ser.: Vol. 6). 1995. write for info. (1-85359-294-3, Pub. by Multilingual Matters UK); pap. write for info. (1-85359-293-5, Pub. by Multilingual Matters UK) Taylor & Francis.

Working with Bilingual Language Disability. Ed. by Dierdre M. Duncan. (Therapy in Practice Ser.). 230p. 1989. pap. 19.95 (0-412-33940-4) Chapman & Hall.

Working with Birth & Foster Parents. Peg Hess. 187p. 1981. write for info. (0-89695-020-4); 8.00 (0-89695-021-2); 5.75 (0-89695-022-0) U Tenn CSW.

Working with Black Youth: Opportunities for Christian Ministry. Grant S. Shockley. LC 89-7021. 128p. 1989. pap. 10.95 (0-687-46196-0) Abingdon.

Working with Business. Joan Bevelacqua. 116p. 29.95 (0-914951-07-6) LERN.

***Working with Cafeteria Plans.** 208p. 1996. pap. 25.00 (0-614-26856-7, 30595BLS01) Commerce.

Working with Careers: Understanding What We Apply & Applying What We Understand. Michael B. Arthur et al. (C). 1983. text ed. 22.50 (0-914383-00-0); pap. text ed. 19.00 (0-914383-01-9) CU Ctr Career Res.

Working with Carter G. Woodson, the Father of Black History: A Diary, 1928-1930. Lorenzo J. Greene. Ed. & Intro. by Arvarh E. Strickland. LC 88-32588. (Illus.). xli, 464p. 1989. text ed. 55.00 (0-8071-1473-1) La State U Pr.

Working with Child Abuse: Social Work Practice & the Child Abuse System. Brian Corby. 192p. 1987. 90.00 (0-335-15396-8, Open Univ Pr); pap. 32.00 (0-335-15395-X, Open Univ Pr) Taylor & Francis.

Working with Child Sexual Abuse: A Post-Cleveland Guide to Effective Principles & Practice. Kieran O'Hagan. 192p. 1989. 90.00 (0-335-15598-7, Open Univ Pr); pap. 32.00 (0-335-15597-9, Open Univ Pr) Taylor & Francis.

Working with Children. D. Batty. (C). 1989. 50.00 (0-903534-65-7, Pub. by Brit Ag for Adopt & Fost UK) St Mut.

Working with Children. J. Lishman. 1983. 24.50 (1-85302-007-9, Pub. by J Kingsley Pubs UK) Taylor & Francis.

Working with Children. P. Matthews & R. MacLean. 116p. (C). 1986. 50.00 (0-7300-0389-2, Pub. by Deakin Univ AT) St Mut.

Working with Children: Effective Communication Through Self-Awareness. Dana K. Lewis. LC 81-2668. (Sage Human Services Guides Ser.: No. 22). 160p. reprint ed. pap. 45.60 (0-8357-4755-7, 2037677) Bks Demand.

Working with Children & Adolescents in Groups: A Multimethod Approach. Sheldon D. Rose & Jeffrey L. Edleson. LC 86-20181. (Social & Behavioral Science Ser.). 404p. text ed. 35.95 (1-55542-009-5) Jossey-Bass.

Working with Children & Families Affected by Substance Abuse: A Guide for Early Childhood. Kathleen P. Watkins. 224p. 1996. pap. 29.95 (0-87628-935-9) P-H.

Working with Children & Their Families. Martin Herbert. LC 89-2355. 226p. (C). 1989. reprint ed. 22.95 (0-925065-07-2) Lyceum IL.

Working with Children from Violent Homes: Ideas & Techniques. Diane Davis. 37p. 1988. pap. text ed. 7.95 (0-941816-22-2) ETR Assocs.

Working with Children in Art Therapy. Ed. by Caroline Case & Tessa Dalley. 168p. (C). 1990. pap. 17.95 (*0-415-01738-6*, A3879) Routledge.

Working with Children in Grief. Lindsay. 1996. pap. text ed. 25.00 (*0-7020-1960-7*) HarBrace.

Working with Children in Need: Studies in Complexity & Challenge. Ed. by Eric Sainsbury. 250p. 1994. pap. 24.95 (*1-85302-275-6*) Taylor & Francis.

Working with Children with Special Needs: ECE 103 Course. Collins. 250p. (C). 1992. ring bd. write for info. (*0-933195-44-3*) CA College Health Sci.

Working with Clarion. Gary Liming. (Illus.). 304p. 1990. 29.95 (*0-8306-9403-X*, 3403) McGraw-Hill Prof.

Working with Clarion. Gary Liming. (Illus.). 304p. 1990. 19.95 (*0-8306-3403-7*, 3403, Windcrest) TAB Bks.

Working with Claris CAD. Rusel Demaria. (Computer Graphics Technology & Management Ser.). (Illus.). 320p. 1991. pap. 19.95 (*0-8306-3545-9*) McGraw-Hill Prof.

Working with Claris CAD. Rusel DeMaria. (Computer Graphics Technology & Management Ser.). (Illus.). 320p. 1991. 29.95 (*0-8306-7545-0*, 3545) TAB Bks.

Working with Colours: A Beginner's Guide. Pauline Wills. (Beginner's Ser.). (Illus.). 96p. 1997. pap. 11.95 (*0-340-67011-8*, Pub. by Headway UK) Trafalgar.

Working with Computer Applications. Gary G. Bitter. 256p. 1996. text ed. 28.95 (*1-57426-020-0*) Computer Lit Pr.

Working with Computer Applications: ClarisWorks Step-by-Step, Mac Version 3.0, 2 bks., Set. Gary G. Bitter et al. (Illus.). 1996. text ed. 34.95 (*1-57426-022-7*) Computer Lit Pr.

Working with Computer Applications: ClarisWorks Step-by-Step, Mac Version 4.0, 2 bks., Set. Gary G. Bitter et al. (Illus.). 1997. text ed. 34.95 (*1-57426-023-5*) Computer Lit Pr.

Working with Computer Applications: ClarisWorks Step-by-Step, Windows Version 3.0, 2 bks., Set. Gary G. Bitter et al. (Illus.). 1997. text ed. 34.95 (*1-57426-024-3*) Computer Lit Pr.

Working with Computer Applications: Microsoft Office Step-by-Step, Windows 95 Version 4.2, 2 bks., Set. Gary G. Bitter & Bonita Sebastian. (Illus.). 1996. text ed. 34.95 (*1-57426-028-6*) Computer Lit Pr.

Working with Computer Applications: Microsoft Works Step-by-Step, Mac Version 4.0, 2 bks., Set. Gary G. Bitter et al. (Illus.). 1997. text ed. 34.95 (*1-57426-025-1*) Computer Lit Pr.

Working with Computer Applications: Microsoft Works Step-by-Step, Windows Version 3.0, 2 bks., Set. Gary G. Bitter et al. 1997. text ed. 34.95 (*1-57426-026-X*) Computer Lit Pr.

Working with Computer Applications: Microsoft Works Step-by-Step, Windows 95 Version 4.0, 2 bks., Set. Gary G. Bitter et al. 160p. 1996. text ed. 34.95 (*1-57426-027-8*) Computer Lit Pr.

Working With Computer Type: Books, Magazines & Newsletters, 1. Compiled by Rotovision S. A. Staff. 160p. 1995. pap. 29.50 (*0-8230-6478-6*, Rotovision) Watsn-Guptill.

Working With Computer Type: Logo Types, Stationery Systems & Visual Communications, 2. Compiled by Rotovision S. A. Staff. 160p. 1995. pap. 29.50 (*0-8230-6479-4*, Rotovision) Watsn-Guptill.

Working with Computer Type Vol. 3: Color & Type. Rotovision S. A. Staff. 1996. pap. text ed. 35.00 (*0-8230-6500-6*) Watsn-Guptill.

Working with Computers. Blissmer. (C). 1989. teacher ed., pap. 2.76 (*0-395-50505-4*) HM.

Working with Computers. Robert H. Blissmer & Roland Alden. LC 88-81324. 1989. teacher ed. 2.76 (*0-318-36886-2*) HM.

Working with Computers. Robert H. Blissmer & Roland Alden. LC 88-81324. (C). 1989. pap. 59.96 (*0-395-43301-0*) HM.

Working with Computers. Patrick G. McKeown. 350p. (C). 1992. text ed. 32.00 (*0-15-596723-1*) Dryden Pr.

Working with Computers. Keith Wicks. (World of Science Ser.). (Illus.). 64p. (YA). (gr. 4-7). 15.95 (*0-8160-1071-4*) Facts on File.

Working with Computers. 2nd ed. Mckeown. (C). 1994. student ed., pap. text ed. 16.75 (*0-03-098206-5*) HarBrace.

Working with Computers. 2nd ed. Patrick G. McKeown. LC 93-72076. 346p. (C). 1994. pap. text ed. 49.00 (*0-03-098203-0*) Dryden Pr.

Working with Computers. 2nd ed. Patrick G. McKeown. LC 93-72076. 285p. (C). 1994. teacher ed., pap. text ed. 94.00 (*0-03-098205-7*); pap. text ed. 38.00 (*0-03-098207-3*) Dryden Pr.

Working with Computers: Computer Orientation for Foreign Students. Michael Barlow. LC 86-83418. (Illus.). 320p. (Orig.). 1987. 23.95 (*0-940753-07-3*); pap. 15.95 (*0-940753-08-1*) Athelstan Pubns.

***Working with Computers & Windows.** Robert Blissmer & Roland Alden. 144p. (C). 1995. pap. text ed. 20.36 (*0-395-71469-9*) HM.

***Working with Computers & Windows.** Robert Blissmer & Roland Alden. (C). 1995. teacher ed., text ed. 11.96 (*0-395-72112-1*) HM.

Working with Congress: A Practical Guide for Scientists & Engineers. William G. Wells, Jr. 80p. 1993. pap. 12.95 (*0-87168-504-3*, 92-31S) AAAS.

Working with Corel Draw! Aaldrick Koops & Jolanda Dreifkluft. 250p. 1991. boxed 55.00 (*0-13-963729-X*, 220201) P-H.

Working with Couples for Marriage Enrichment. Diana S. Garland. LC 83-48158. (Jossey-Bass Social & Behavioral Science Ser.). 375p. reprint ed. pap. 106.90 (*0-7837-0170-5*, 2040467) Bks Demand.

Working with Culture: Psychotherapeutic Interventions with Ethnic Minority Children & Adolescents. Ed. by Luis A. Vargas & Joan D. Koss-Chioino. LC 92-15281. (Social & Behavioral Science Ser.). 358p. 34.95 (*1-55542-469-4*) Jossey-Bass.

Working with dBASE MAC: A User's Guide & Reference. Rusel DeMaria & George Fontaine. 400p. (Orig.). (C). 1988. pap. 19.95 (*0-685-19366-7*) P-H.

Working with DB2, SQL-DS, SQL & QMF. Tony Fabbri. (Illus.). 256p. 1990. 32.95 (*0-8306-9508-7*) McGraw-Hill Prof.

Working with Deaf People: Accessibility & Accommodation in the Workplace. Susan B. Foster. (Illus.). 250p. 1992. pap. 34.95 (*0-398-06126-2*) C C Thomas.

Working with Deaf People: Accessibility & Accommodation in the Workplace. Susan B. Foster. (Illus.). 250p. (C). 1992. text ed. 49.95 (*0-398-05808-3*) C C Thomas.

***Working with Destiny: The Practice of Karma Research.** Andrew Wolpert. (Golden Blade Ser.: Vol. 49). 1997. pap. text ed. 12.95 (*0-86315-241-4*, Pub. by Floris Books UK) Anthroposophic.

Working with Difficult People. William Lundin & Kathleen Lundin. (WorkSmart Ser.). 128p. (Orig.). 1995. pap. 10.95 (*0-8144-7838-7*) AMACOM.

Working with Difficult People. Muriel Solomon. 288p. pap. 14.00 (*0-13-957390-9*) P-H.

Working with Difficult People. Muriel Solomon. 288p. 1990. text ed. 29.95 (*0-13-957382-8*) P-H.

Working with DisplayWrite Three. Robert Krumm. 320p. 1986. 24.95 (*0-8306-9564-8*, 2664); pap. 17.95 (*0-8306-9664-4*, 2664P) McGraw-Hill Prof.

Working with DNA & Bacteria in Precollege Science Classrooms. 5.00 (*0-614-14064-1*) Natl Assn Bio Tchrs.

Working with DOS & Windows. (Prisma Be an Expert! Ser.). (Illus.). 192p. (Orig.). (J). 1995. pap. 12.95 (*1-85365-302-0*, Pub. by Spectrum UK) Seven Hills Bk.

Working with DOS 5.0. Mark Allen & Jean Gonzalez. 1993. pap. text ed. 37.00 (*0-13-962465-1*) P-H.

Working with DOS 5.0. Mark Allen & Jean Gonzalez. 1992. write for info. (*0-318-69571-5*) Prentice ESL.

Working with Dos 6.0. Mark Allen & Jean Gonzalez. 1994. pap. text ed. 36.80 (*0-13-101460-9*) P-H.

Working with Dr. Schweitzer. Louise Jilek-Aall. 240p. (Orig.). 1990. 16.95 (*0-88839-209-5*) Hancock House.

Working with Dreams in Psychotherapy. Clara Hill. LC 96-14095. (Practicing Professional Ser.). 262p. 1996. lib. bdg. 30.00 (*1-57230-092-2*) Guilford Pr.

Working with Drug Family Support Groups. Paul Lockley. 312p. (C). 1996. 55.00 (*1-85343-336-5*); pap. 20.00 (*1-85343-337-3*) NYU Pr.

Working with Drug Users. Ronno Griffiths & Brian Pearson. (Community Care Practice Handbook Ser.: Vol. 25). 117p. 1988. pap. text ed. 16.50 (*0-7045-0582-7*, Pub. by Gower UK) Ashgate Pub Co.

***Working with Elder Abuse: A Training Manual for Home Care, Residential & Day Care Staff.** Jacki Pritchard. 200p. 1996. pap. 34.95 (*1-85302-418-X*, Pub. by J Kingsley Pubs UK) Taylor & Francis.

Working with Elderly People: Communication Workshops. 2nd ed. Sue Stevens & Kate Swinburn. (Illus.). 1995. ring bd. 190.00 (*1-56593-499-7*, 1156) Singular Publishing.

***Working with Emotions: Changing Core Schemes.** Leslie S. Greenberg & Sandra C. Paivio. LC 97-13521. (Practicing Professional Ser.). 300p. 1997. lib. bdg. 35.00 (*1-57230-243-7*, 0243) Guilford Pr.

Working with Employers & Other Community Partners. National Council of Jewish Women Staff. 1992. 10.00 (*0-614-06655-7*) NCJW.

***Working with English Idioms.** Peaty. Date not set. pap. text ed. write for info. (*0-17-555418-8*) Addison-Wesley.

***Working with English Prepositions.** Hall. 1991. pap. text ed. write for info. (*0-17-555417-X*) Addison-Wesley.

Working with Excel. Blissmer. (C). 1995. pap. 20.36 (*0-395-71471-0*) HM.

Working with Experience: Animating Learning. David Boud & Nod Miller. LC 96-2155. 232p. (C). 1996. pap. write for info. (*0-415-14246-6*); text ed. write for info. (*0-415-14245-8*) Routledge.

Working with Experts & Experts' Reports. Badgery-Parker et al. 70p. 1992. 65.00 (*1-875263-16-0*, Blckstone AT) Gaunt.

Working with Facts & Details see Skillbooster Series Level C

Working with Facts & Details see Skillbooster Series, Level E

Working with Facts & Details see Skillbooster Series, Level F

Working with Faculty in the New Electronic Library. Ed. by Linda Shirato. (Library Orientation Ser.: No. 22). 195p. 1992. pap. 35.00 (*0-87650-291-5*) Pierian.

Working with Families. Richard Carreiro. Ed. by William Schulz. (Options Ser.). 64p. (Orig.). (gr. 1-8). 1989. pap. 8.00 (*0-920541-49-6*) Peguis Pubs Ltd.

Working with Families: An Integrative Model by Level of Functioning. Allie C. Kilpatrick & Thomas P. Holland. LC 94-36532. 1994. pap. text ed. 40.00 (*0-205-15930-3*) Allyn.

***Working with Families & Their Infants at Risk: A Perspective after 20 Years of Experience.** 2nd ed. Rose M. Bromwich. LC 96-9859. 410p. 1997. pap. 34.00 (*0-89079-702-1*, 7957) PRO-ED.

Working with Families in Crisis: School-Based Intervention. William Steele & Melvyn Raider. LC 91-223. (Guilford School Practitioner Ser.). 212p. 1991. pap. text ed. 20.95 (*0-89862-241-7*); lib. bdg. 47.00 (*0-89862-362-6*) Guilford Pr.

Working with Families in Early Intervention. Ed. by James A. Blackman. LC 94-38450. (Infants & Young Children Ser.). 240p. 1995. 31.00 (*0-8342-0646-3*) Aspen Pub.

Working with Families of Children with Special Needs. Naomi Dale. LC 95-13923. 304p. (C). 1995. pap. text ed. 17.95 (*0-415-11411-X*) Routledge.

Working with Families of Children with Special Needs. Naomi Dale. LC 95-13923. 304p. (C). (gr. 13). 1995. text ed. 74.95 (*0-415-11410-1*) Routledge.

Working with Families of the Mentally Ill. Kayla F. Bernheim & Anthony Lehman. LC 85-18754. 1985. 22.95 (*0-393-70009-7*) Norton.

Working with Family Businesses: A Guide for Professionals. David Bork et al. LC 95-36409. (The Jossey-Bass Management Ser.). 252p. Date not set. 29.95 (*0-7879-0172-5*) Jossey-Bass.

Working with Farmers for Better Land Husbandry. Ed. by Norman Hudson et al. LC 92-41100. 1992. 25.50 (*0-935734-29-5*) Soil & Water Conserv.

Working with Fathers: Methods & Perspectives. Minnesota Fathering Aliance Staff. 1992. pap. 21.95 (*0-9633084-0-8*) Nu Ink Unltd.

Working with Feminist Criticism. Mary Eagleton. (Illus.). 256p. (C). 1996. 59.95 (*0-631-19441-X*); pap. 19.95 (*0-631-19442-8*) Blackwell Pubs.

***Working with Financial Advisors.** Barbara Hetzer. (10 Minute Guides). 1997. pap. 10.95 (*0-02-861548-4*) Macmillan.

Working with Foreign Languages & Characters in WordPerfect. Peter Kahrel. LC 92-23678. 1992. 29.95 (*1-55619-482-X*) Benjamins North Am.

Working with French. M. Mitchell. (C). 1986. student ed. 65.00 (*0-85950-604-5*, Pub. by S Thornes Pubs UK); teacher ed. 160.00 (*0-85950-605-3*, Pub. by S Thornes Pubs UK); audio 100.00 (*0-85950-606-1*, Pub. by S Thornes Pubs UK) St Mut.

Working with Full Impact. John L. Campbell. (Illus.). 256p. (Orig.). 1989. pap. 17.95 (*0-8306-2919-X*, Windcrest) TAB Bks.

Working with German, Level 2: Coursebook. Peter Lupson et al. 1990. pap. 35.00 (*0-7487-0148-6*) Dufour.

Working with German, Level 2: Coursebook. Peter Lupson et al. 160p. 9000. pap. 25.00 (*0-7487-0147-8*) Dufour.

***Working with Girls & Young Women in Community Settings.** Janet Batsleer. 240p. 1996. text ed. 56.95 (*1-85742-303-8*, Pub. by Arena UK) Ashgate Pub Co.

Working with God. Gardner Hunting. 1934. 7.95 (*0-87159-174-X*) Unity Bks.

Working with Governors in Schools: Developing a Professional Partnership. Cynthia Beckett et al. 176p. 1991. pap. 32.00 (*0-335-09427-9*, Open Univ Pr) Taylor & Francis.

Working with Graduate Assistants. Jody D. Nyquist & Donald H. Wulff. LC 95-32508. 176p. 1995. 36.00 (*0-8039-5313-5*); pap. 16.95 (*0-8039-5314-3*) Sage.

Working with Groups from Dysfunctional Families. Cheryl Hetherington. 160p. 1994. 24.95 (*1-57025-025-1*) Whole Person.

Working with Groups from Dysfunctional Families: Structured Exercises in Healing. Cheryl Hetherington. 154p. 1992. spiral bd. 24.95 (*0-938586-71-8*) Whole Person.

Working with Groups on Family Issues: Structured Exercises for Exploring Divorce, Balancing Work & Family, Family Problems, Solo-Parenting, Boundaries, Intimacy, Stepfamilies. Sandy S. Christian. LC 96-10142. 1996. pap. write for info. (*1-57025-124-X*) Whole Person.

Working with Groups on Spiritual Themes: Structured Exercises in Healing. Elaine Hopkins et al. 176p. (Orig.). 1995. pap. 24.95 (*1-57025-048-0*) Whole Person.

Working with Groups to Explore Food & Body Connections. Ed. by Sandy S. Christian. LC 95-49465. (Structured Exercises in Healing Ser.). 1996. write for info. (*1-57025-105-3*) Whole Person.

***Working with Groups to Overcome Panic, Anxiety & Phobias.** Shirley Babior & Carol Goldman. LC 95-62472. 192p. (Orig.). 1996. otabind 24.95 (*1-57025-117-7*) Whole Person.

Working with Heat Exchangers. J. P. Gupta. 1989. 54.95 (*1-56032-054-0*) Hemisp Pub.

***Working with Heavy Equipment Coloring Book.** Ed. by Carol A. Vercz. (Illus.). (J). Date not set. pap. 5.95 (*0-910119-50-3*) SOCO Pubns.

Working with History: The Historical Records Survey in Louisiana & the Nation, 1936-1942. Burl Noggle. LC 81-5789. xii, 148p. 1981. text ed. 22.50 (*0-8071-0881-2*) La State U Pr.

Working with Images: Theoretical Bases of Archetypal Psychology. James Hillman et al. Ed. by Benjamin Sells. (Primary Papers in Archetypal Psychology: Vol. 1). 184p. (Orig.). 1997. pap. 18.50 (*0-88214-376-X*) Spring Jrnl.

Working with Insurance & Managed Care Plans: A Guide for Getting Paid. Jan Davison & Maxine Lewis. (Illus.). 470p. (Orig.). 1995. pap. text ed. 39.95 (*0-07-600744-8*, ME117) Practice Mgmt Info.

Working with Interfaith Couples: A Jewish Perspective, a Guide for Facilitators. 220p. 1992. pap. 15.00 (*0-8074-0488-8*, 280059) UAHC.

Working with Ion-Selective Electrodes. Karl Camman. Tr. by A. H. Schroeder from GER. (Chemical Laboratory Practice Ser.). (Illus.). 1979. 59.00 (*0-387-09320-6*) Spr-Verlag.

Working with Jerks. Ron Zemke. 1988. 9.95 (*0-671-65836-0*) S&S Trade.

***Working with Kids Who Hurt: A Program for Working with Students from Dysfunctional Families.** Kathleen Bishop et al. 44p. (Orig.). (J). (gr. 3-8). 1992. pap. 8.95 (*1-884063-99-3*) Mar Co Prods.

Working with Language: A Multidisciplinary Consideration of Language Use in Work Contexts. Ed. by Hywel Coleman. (Contributions to the Sociology of Language Ser.: No. 52). xii, 617p. (C). 1989. lib. bdg. 176.95 (*0-89925-466-7*) Mouton.

***Working with Lesbian, Gay, Bisexual & Transgender College Students: A Handbook for Faculty & Administrators.** Ed. by Ronni L. Sanlo. (Greenwood Educators' Reference Collection Ser.). 1998. text ed. write for info. (*0-313-30227-8*, Greenwood Pr) Greenwood.

Working with Library Boards: A How-to-Do-It Manual for Librarians. Gordon S. Wade. (How-to-Do-It Ser.). 208p. 1991. 39.95 (*1-55570-080-2*) Neal-Schuman.

***Working with Linguistically & Culturally Different Children: Innovative Clinical & Educational Approaches.** Sharon-ann Gopaul-McNicol & Tania Thomas-Presswood. LC 97-23312. (C). 1997. text ed. 45.00 (*0-205-19986-0*) Allyn.

Working with Lotus Agenda. John R. Ottensmann & Jan Neuenschwander. (Illus.). 256p. 1989. pap. 24.95 (*0-8306-3161-5*, 3161) McGraw-Hill Prof.

Working with Lotus Agenda 2.0. John R. Ottensmann & Jan Neuenschwander. (Illus.). 384p. 1991. pap. 24.95 (*0-8306-3703-6*, 3703, Windcrest) TAB Bks.

Working with Lotus HAL: A 1-2-3 User's Guide. Douglas J. Wolf. (Illus.). 176p. 1988. 24.95 (*0-8306-0273-9*, 2973); pap. 15.95 (*0-8306-2973-4*) McGraw-Hill Prof.

Working with Lotus 1-2-3: A Comprehensive Manual: Release 2.2. Hossein Bidgoli. Ed. by Simon. 457p. (C). 1991. pap. text ed. 35.50 (*0-314-77274-X*) West Pub.

Working with Lotus 1-2-3 for Windows. Don Barker et al. 400p. 1993. pap. 28.95 (*0-87835-796-3*) Course Tech.

Working with LUCID. Elna R. Tymes. 1991. 24.95 (*0-8306-6746-6*) McGraw-Hill Prof.

Working with LUCID 3D (3.5) Elna R. Tymes. 1991. 24.95 (*0-8306-7747-X*) McGraw-Hill Prof.

Working with Magellan. Dan Gookin. 1990. pap. 21.95 (*0-8306-3461-4*, Windcrest) TAB Bks.

Working with Manipulative Inmates Correspondence Course, 2 vols., Set. American Correctional Association. (Orig.). 1992. pap. 54.00 (*0-929310-81-0*, 176) Am Correctional.

Working with Men: Feminism & Social Work. Ed. by Kate Cavanagh & Viviene E. Cree. LC 95-16148. (State of Welfare Ser.). 272p. (C). 1995. pap. 17.95 (*0-415-11185-4*) Routledge.

Working with Men: Feminism & Social Work. Ed. by Kate Cavanagh & Viviene E. Cree. LC 95-16148. (State of Welfare Ser.). 272p. (C). (gr. 13). 1995. text ed. 69.95 (*0-415-11184-6*) Routledge.

Working with Men: Women in the Workplace Talk about Sexuality, Success & Their Male Coworkers. Beth Milwid. 288p. (Orig.). 1992. mass mkt. 4.99 (*0-425-13482-2*, Berkley Trade) Berkley Pub.

Working with Men's Groups. Roger Karsk & Bill Thomas. LC 87-50080. 126p. 1979. reprint ed. spiral bd. 14.95 (*0-938586-05-X*) Whole Person.

Working with Men's Groups, Vol. 1. rev. ed. Roger Karsk & Bill Thomas. 192p. 1995. pap. 24.95 (*0-938586-97-1*) Whole Person.

***Working with Merlin.** Geoff Hughes. (Orig.). 1997. pap. 19.95 (*1-86163-001-8*, Pub. by Capall Bann Pubng UK) Holmes Pub.

Working with Metal. rev. ed. (Home Repair & Improvement Ser.). (Illus.). 136p. 1990. 14.60 (*0-8094-7387-9*); lib. bdg. 20.60 (*0-8094-7388-7*) Time-Life.

***Working with Microsoft Backoffice.** John R. Vacca. (Illus.). 500p. pap. text ed. 49.95 (*0-12-710007-5*, AP Prof) Acad Pr.

***Working with Microsoft Office.** Robert Blissmer & Roland Alden. 640p. (C). 1995. pap. text ed. 54.76 (*0-395-72111-3*) HM.

Working with MIDI: For Church Musicians. Robert C. Van Howten. 120p. 1996. 24.95 (*1-888261-00-5*) Laurendale.

Working with Mr. Wright: What It Was Like. Curtis Besinger. (Illus.). 320p. (C). 1995. 60.00 (*0-521-48122-8*) Cambridge U Pr.

***Working with Mr. Wright: What It Was Like.** Curtis Besinger. 355p. 1997. pap. text ed. 19.95 (*0-521-58714-X*) Cambridge U Pr.

Working with MS Access. Blissmer. (C). 1995. pap. 20.36 (*0-395-71472-9*) HM.

Working with MS-DOS V3.2. Weber Systems, Inc. Staff. 300p. 1986. pap. 21.95 (*0-938862-16-2*) Weber Systems.

Working with MS Office. Blissmer. (C). 1995. pap. 50.76 (*0-395-71468-0*) HM.

Working with MS Word. Blissmer. (C). 1995. pap. 20.36 (*0-395-71470-2*) HM.

Working with MS Works 3.0, 2 Vols. Blissmer. (C). 1994. pap. 5.96 (*0-395-65536-6*) HM.

Working with Multiproblem Families. Lisa Kaplan. LC 85-45010. 153p. pap. 18.95 (*0-669-11097-3*, Lexington) Jossey-Bass.

***Working with Netmeeting.** Robert Scoble & Bob Summer. 1997. 29.99 (*0-7897-1275-X*) Macmillan.

Working with Netware: For Network Supervisors & Users. Gilbert Held. 283p. 1994. text ed. 31.95 (*0-442-01783-9*) Van Nos Reinhold.

Working with No Data: Semitic & Egyptian Studies Presented to Thomas O. Lambdin. Ed. by David M. Golomb & Susan T. Hollis. LC 87-30571. (Illus.). xiv, 264p. 1987. text ed. 39.50 (*0-931464-35-8*) Eisenbrauns.

Working with Objects: The OORAM Software Engineering Method. Trygve Reenskaug et al. LC 95-34774. 420p. (C). 1995. text ed. 48.00 (*0-13-452930-8*) P-H.

Working with Offenders. Ed. by Gill McIvor. LC 95-21595. 198p. 1995. pap. 27.95 (*1-85302-249-7*, Pub. by J Kingsley Pubs UK) Taylor & Francis.

W

An Asterisk (*) at the beginning of an entry indicates that the title is appearing in BIP for the first time.

Working with Offenders: Issues, Contexts & Outcomes. Tim May & Antony A. Vass. (New Directions in Social Work Ser.). 256p. 1996. 75.00 (*0-8039-7621-6*); pap. 22.95 (*0-8039-7622-4*) Sage.

***Working With Offenders: Personal Construct, Therapy & Change.** Julia C. Houston. (Offender Rehabilitation Ser.). text ed. 60.00 (*0-471-95415-2*) Wiley.

Working with Offenders: Psychological Practice in Offender Rehabilitation. Ed. by Clive R. Hollin. LC 95-32340. 300p. 1996. text ed. 50.00 (*0-471-95776-3*) Wiley.

Working with Oils. (Leisure Arts Ser.: No. 1). (Illus.). 32p. pap. 4.95 (*0-85532-400-7*, 400-7, Pub. by Search Pr UK) A Schwartz & Co.

Working with Older Adoptees. Ed. by Loren Coleman et al. 1989. reprint ed. pap. write for info. (*0-939561-05-0*) Univ South ME.

Working with Older Adults. J. Stanley Rendahl. LC 84-80708. (Equipping Ser.). (Illus.). 130p. (Orig.). 1984. pap. 5.95 (*0-935797-08-4*) Harvest IL.

Working with Older Adults: A Handbook for Libraries. 3rd ed. Rhea J. Rubin & Gail McGovern. 1990. pap. text ed. 17.50 (*0-929722-37-X*) CA State Library Fndtn.

Working with Older Adults: Group Process. Irene Burnside & Mary G. Schmidt. (Nursing-Health Science Ser.). 550p. (C). 1994. pap. text ed. 42.50 (*0-86720-679-9*) Jones & Bartlett.

***Working with Older People.** Gething. 1989. pap. text ed. 28.95 (*0-7295-0350-X*) Saunders.

Working with Older People. U. S. Department of Health, Education & Welfare, Public Health Service Staff. Ed. by Leon Stein. LC 79-8669. (Growing Old Ser.). 1980. reprint ed. lib. bdg. 17.95 (*0-405-12784-7*) Ayer.

Working with Older Persons: Cognitive & Phenomenological Methods. Edmund Sherman. LC 84-5746. 1984. lib. bdg. 75.00 (*0-89838-144-4*) Kluwer Ac.

Working with Older Workers. (Policy & Practice Publication). 78p. 1993. 10.00 (*0-89215-179-X*) U Cal LA Indus Rel.

Working with ORACLE: An Introduction to Database Management. Jack L. Hursch & Carolyn Hurrsch. (Illus.). 240p. 1987. pap. 19.95 (*0-8306-2916-5*, 2916, TAB/TPR) TAB Bks.

Working with ORACLE Development Tools. Graham H. Seibert. 1991. 14.95 (*0-8306-3551-3*); 14.95 (*0-8306-3552-1*) McGraw-Hill Prof.

Working with ORACLE Development Tools. Graham H. Seibert. (Illus.). 256p. 1991. 34.95 (*0-8306-7714-3*, 3714, Windcrest); pap. 24.95 (*0-8306-3714-1*, Windcrest) TAB Bks.

Working with Organizations & Their People: A Guide to Human Resources Practice. Douglas W. Bray et al. LC 90-20703. (Professional Practice Ser.). 256p. 1991. lib. bdg. 36.95 (*0-89862-475-4*) Guilford Pr.

Working with Others. Los Angeles Unified School District Staff. (Project Get That Job Ser.). (Illus.). 48p. (Orig.). (YA). (gr. 7-12). 1990. Set. teacher ed., wbk. ed. 44.95 (*1-56119-092-6*); student ed. 4.95 (*1-56119-090-X*); teacher ed. 1.95 (*1-56119-091-8*) Educ Pr MD.

Working with Paradox for Windows. Don Barker & John Weingarten. LC 93-8193. (C). 1994. pap. 27.95 (*0-87709-024-6*, BF246) S-W Pub.

Working with Parents. Cliff Cunningham & Hilton Davis. LC 85-13777. (Children with Special Needs Ser.). 160p. 1985. pap. text ed. 32.00 (*0-335-15035-7*, Open Univ Pr) Taylor & Francis.

Working with Parents. Dolores Curran. 1989. teacher ed. 15.95 (*0-88671-271-8*, 6240) Am Guidance.

***Working with Parents: Establishing the Essential Alliance in Child Psychotherapy.** Diana Siskind. LC 96-40017. 1997. 42.50 (*0-7657-0060-3*) Aronson.

Working with Parents & Families of Exceptional Children & Youth: Techniques for Successful Conferencing & Collaboration. 3rd ed. Richard L. Simpson. LC 80-39434. (C). 1996. text ed. 39.00 (*0-89079-638-6*, 7635) PRO-ED.

Working with Parents of Children with Special Needs. Garry Hornby. (Special Needs in Ordinary Schools Ser.). (Illus.). 192p. 1995. 65.00 (*0-304-32859-6*); pap. 19.95 (*0-304-32857-X*) Cassell.

Working with Parents of Handicapped Children. William L. Heward et al. LC 78-61269. (Illus.). 317p. reprint ed. pap. 90.40 (*0-317-58111-2*, AU00347) Bks Demand.

***Working with Parents of SEN Children after the Code of Practice.** Ed. by Sheila Wolfendale. (Home & School - A Working Alliance Ser.). 144p. 1997. pap. 24.95 (*1-85346-429-5*, Pub. by D Fulton UK) Taylor & Francis.

Working with Parents of Young Children with Disabilities. Elizabeth J. Webster & Louise M. Ward. (Early Childhood Intervention Ser.). (Illus.). 124p. (Orig.). (C). 1992. pap. text ed. 29.95 (*1-879105-46-2*, 0359) Singular Publishing.

Working with Pastel. (Leisure Arts Ser.: No. 17). (Illus.). 32p. pap. 4.95 (*0-85532-524-0*, 524-0, Pub. by Search Pr UK) A Schwartz & Co.

Working with People. John L. Beckley. 158p. 1985. 14.95 (*0-910187-03-7*) Economics Pr.

Working with People. 5th ed. Naomi Brill. 300p. (C). 1995. pap. text ed. 35.95 (*0-8013-1259-0*) Longman.

Working with People: The Helping Process. 5th ed. Compiled by Naomi Brill. LC 94-44036. 1995. write for info. (*0-614-03331-4*) Longman.

Working with People: The Helping Process. 5th ed. Naomi Brill. (C). 1995. pap. text ed. write for info. (*0-8013-1555-7*) Addison-Wesley.

***Working with People: The Helping Process.** 6th ed. Naomi I. Brill. LC 97-16304. (C). 1998. pap. text ed. write for info. (*0-8013-1799-1*) Addison-Wesley.

Working with People, Bugs, & Apples: An Old Fashioned Family, L. M. & Grace Smith, Parents of Ten. Malcolm L. Smith. LC 78-73543. (Illus.). 1979. 11.50 (*0-686-28585-9*) M L Smith.

Working with People Called Patients. Milton M. Berger. LC 76-46483. 176p. 1984. pap. text ed. 23.95 (*0-87630-126-X*) Brunner-Mazel.

Working with Phrases on Your Own. Kathryn Kilpatrick & Roberta DePompei. 50p. 1986. student ed. 8.00 (*1-880504-07-3*); student ed. 8.00 (*1-880504-08-1*) Visit Nurse.

Working with Plant Supplies & Services. William Farrington et al. (Illus.). 144p. 1980. text ed. 14.96 (*0-07-019965-5*) McGraw.

Working with Plastic Laminates: A Home Craftsman's Handbook. Roger W. Cliffe & Marc Adams. LC 94-16845. (Illus.). 224p. 1994. pap. 19.95 (*0-8069-0570-0*) Sterling.

Working with Plastics. (Home Repair & Improvement Ser.). (Illus.). 136p. 1982. 14.60 (*0-8094-3506-3*); lib. bdg. 20.60 (*0-8094-3507-1*) Time-Life.

Working with Powerpoint. Blissmer. (C). 1995. pap. 20.36 (*0-395-71473-7*) HM.

Working with Pregnant & Parenting Teenage Clients. Ed. by Neil Cervera & Lynn Videka-Sherman. 256p. 1990. pap. 18.95 (*0-87304-248-4*) Families Intl.

Working with Pregnant & Parenting Teens: Resource Guide: Teenage Pregnancy: A New Beginning. Linda Barr & Catherine P. Monserrat. (Illus.). 175p. 1996. 27.95 (*0-945886-14-4*) New Futures.

Working with Psychology: A Concise Introduction. 2nd ed. Terry F. Pettijohn. (C). 1989. per. write for info. (*0-87967-769-4*) Brown & Benchmark.

Working with Reflex. Walter Stagner. 300p. 1987. pap. 21.95 (*0-938862-75-8*) Weber Systems.

Working with Refugees. Ed. by Peter Rose. LC 85-47916. (CMS Migration & Ethnicity Ser.). 175p. (C). 1986. pap. 12.95 (*0-913256-97-8*) CMS.

Working with Religious Issues in Therapy. Robert J. Lovinger. LC 84-6198. 328p. 1995. reprint ed. pap. 35.00 (*1-56821-236-4*) Aronson.

Working with Resistance. Martha Stark. LC 93-1401. 328p. 1994. 45.00 (*0-87668-037-6*) Aronson.

Working with Roosevelt. Samuel I. Rosenman. LC 75-168391. (FDR & the Era of the New Deal Ser.). (Illus.). 1972. reprint ed. lib. bdg. 55.00 (*0-306-70328-9*) Da Capo.

Working with Rural Youth. Ed. by Loren Coleman & Dan Porter. 250p. (Orig.). (C). 1994. pap. text ed. 15.00 (*0-939561-19-0*) Univ South ME.

Working with Rural Youth. Edmund D. Brunner. LC 74-1669. (Children & Youth Ser.). 132p. 1974. reprint ed. 17.95 (*0-405-05949-3*) Ayer.

Working with Schizophrenia: A Needs Based Approach. Gwen Howe. 200p. 1994. pap. 19.95 (*1-85302-242-X*) Taylor & Francis.

Working with Self-Help. Ed. by Thomas J. Powell. LC 89-14031. 355p. 1990. 28.95 (*0-87101-174-3*) Natl Assn Soc Wkrs.

Working with Sensitizing Concepts: Analytical Field Research. Will C. Van Den Hoonaard. LC 96-25242. (Qualitative Research Methods Ser.: Vol. 41). 96p. 1996. 22.95 (*0-7619-0206-6*) Sage.

Working with Sensitizing Concepts: Analytical Field Research. Will C. Van Den Hoonaard. LC 96-25242. (Qualitative Research Methods Ser.: Vol. 41). 96p. 1996. pap. 9.95 (*0-7619-0207-4*) Sage.

Working with Sex Offenders: Practical Guidelines for Therapist Selection. Michael A. O'Connell et al. 132p. (C). 1990. text ed. 44.00 (*0-8039-3754-7*); pap. text ed. 19.95 (*0-8039-3763-6*) Sage.

Working with Sexuality Today: The Human Perspective. 3rd ed. David H. Dean & Lisa C. Nielsen. LC 92-71361. (Illus.). 286p. (Orig.). (C). 1992. per. 10.95 (*1-56134-112-6*) Dushkin Pub.

Working with Sexually Abused Boys: An Introduction for Practitioners. Jim Christopherson et al. 65p. 1994. pap. 14.95 (*0-902817-51-5*, Pub. by Natl Childrens Bur UK) Paul & Co Pubs.

***Working with Sexually Abusive Adolescents: A Practical Manual.** Ed. by Masud S. Hoghughi et al. (Working with Children & Adolescents Ser.: Vol. 1). 208p. 1997. text ed. 69.95 (*0-8039-7758-1*) Sage.

***Working with Sexually Abusive Adolescents: A Practical Manual.** Ed. by Masud S. Hoghughi et al. (Working with Children & Adolescents Ser.: Vol. 1). 208p. 1997. pap. text ed. 23.95 (*0-8039-7759-X*) Sage.

Working with Shakespeare. Howard Mills. LC 93-13139. 224p. (C). 1993. lib. bdg. 49.50 (*0-389-21009-9*) B&N Imports.

Working with Sidekick. Ronald D. Lee. 150p. (Orig.). 1988. pap. 14.95 (*0-938862-82-0*) Weber Systems.

Working with Soft Furnishings: A Practical Guide to Professional Techniques. Charlotte Dunkerley. (Illus.). 160p. 1996. 29.95 (*0-7063-7408-8*, Pub. by Ward Lock UK) Sterling.

Working with Sources: Case Studies in 20th Century History. W. D. Simpson. (C). 1988. 60.00 (*0-85950-690-8*, Pub. by S Thornes Pubs UK) St Mut.

Working with Spanish, Level 1. T. Kattan-Ibarra Connell. Ed. by J. Kattan-Ibarra. (C). 1984. student ed. 65.00 (*0-685-38652-X*, Pub. by S Thornes Pubs UK); teacher ed. 40.00 (*0-85950-155-8*, Pub. by S Thornes Pubs UK); audio 110.00 (*0-85950-156-6*, Pub. by S Thornes Pubs UK) St Mut.

Working with Spanish, Level 2. T. Kattan-Ibarra Connell & J. Kattan-Ibarra. (C). 1984. student ed. 65.00 (*0-85950-118-3*, Pub. by S Thornes Pubs UK); teacher ed. 60.00 (*0-685-38651-1*, Pub. by S Thornes Pubs UK); audio 110.00 (*0-85950-158-2*, Pub. by S Thornes Pubs UK) St Mut.

Working with Special Needs Offenders Correspondence Course, 3 vols. American Correctional Association. (Orig.). 1992. Set. pap. 65.00 (*0-929310-68-3*, 175) Am Correctional.

Working with Special Students in English-Language Arts. Sharon Sorenson. (Teaching Resources in the ERIC Database (TRIED) Ser.). (Illus.). 71p. 1991. pap. 14.95 (*0-927516-18-7*) ERIC-REC.

Working with Speech: Perspectives on Research into the Lancaster IBM Spoken English Corpus. Gerald Knowles et al. LC 96-25859. 1993. text ed. write for info. (*0-582-04534-7*) Longman.

Working with Street Children. UNESCO Staff. 303p. 1995. pap. 25.00 (*92-3-103096-5*, U3096, Pub. by UNESCO FR) Bernan Associates.

***Working with Student Teachers.** Florence B. Stratemeyer & Margaret Lindsey. LC 58-8555. 512p. 1958. reprint ed. pap. 146.00 (*0-608-02756-1*, 2063819) Bks Demand.

Working with Tax-Sheltered Annuities. 144p. 1993. pap. 15.00 (*0-685-67064-3*, 5423) Commerce.

Working with Teachers Effectively: Communication, Relationship & Problem-Solving Skills for School Principals. Lawrence L. Giandomenico & Lawrence Shulman. (Illus.). 182p. 1991. spiral bd., pap. 27.95 (*0-398-06148-3*) C C Thomas.

Working with Teachers Effectively: Communication, Relationship & Problem-Solving Skills for School Principals. Lawrence L. Giandomenico & Lawrence Shulman. (Illus.). 182p. (C). 1991. text ed. 41.95 (*0-398-05753-2*) C C Thomas.

Working with Teamlinks: Using Digital's Office Client for Microsoft Windows. 2nd ed. Tony Redmond. LC 95-76906. 465p. 1995. pap. 47.95 (*1-55558-140-4*, Digital DEC) Buttrwrth-Heinemann.

Working with Teenagers. Nick Aiken. pap. 11.99 (*0-551-01649-3*) Zondervan.

***Working with Texts: A Core Book for Language Analysis.** Maggie Bowring. LC 96-43097. (Intertext Ser.). 224p. (C). 1997. pap. write for info. (*0-415-14597-X*); text ed. write for info. (*0-415-14596-1*) Routledge.

Working with the Code: A Journeyman Electrician's Exam Preparation Based on 1996 NEC. 5th ed. Michael G. Owen. 133p. 1996. student ed., pap. text ed. 39.95 (*1-888512-03-2*) Elect Trnging.

Working with the Community: A Developer's Guide. Douglas R. Porter et al. LC 85-51835. (Community Builders Handbook Ser.). 185p. 1990. 56.95 (*0-87420-646-4*, W14) Urban Land.

Working with the Courts in Child Protection. Jane N. Feller. 73p. (Orig.). (C). 1995. pap. text ed. 25.00 (*0-7881-1659-2*) DIANE Pub.

Working with the Drama of Democracy. George McKenna. (C). 1990. per. write for info. (*0-87967-564-0*) Brown & Benchmark.

Working with the Drama of Democracy. 2nd ed. George McKenna. (C). 1994. per. write for info. (*1-56134-298-X*) Dushkin Pub.

Working with the Dreaming Body. Arnold Mindell. 1989. pap. 11.95 (*0-14-019275-1*, Arkana) Viking Penguin.

Working with the Elderly: An Introduction. Ed. by Elizabeth Deichman & Regina Kociecki. (Golden Age Books - Perspectives on Aging Ser.). 299p. 1989. 29.95 (*0-87975-520-2*); pap. 19.95 (*0-87975-534-2*) Prometheus Bks.

Working with the Elderly in Their Residence. Dean R. Tjosvold & Mary M. Tjosvold. LC 82-21521. 240p. 1983. text ed. 55.00 (*0-275-91090-3*, C1090, Praeger Pubs) Greenwood.

***Working with the Environment.** Tim Ryder. 272p. (Orig.). 1997. pap. 17.95 (*1-85458-148-1*, Pub. by Vac Wrk Pubns UK) Seven Hills Bk.

Working with the Families of our Children. Rena Shimoni. (C). 1996. pap. text ed. write for info. (*0-201-82906-1*) Addison-Wesley.

Working with the Family in Primary Care: A Systems Approach to Health & Illness. Janet Christie-Seely. LC 83-17772. 576p. 1984. text ed. 65.00 (*0-275-91424-0*, C1424, Praeger Pubs) Greenwood.

Working with the FAR: Course Manual. write for info. (*0-318-61616-5*) Fed Pubns Inc.

Working with the Hands: Being a Sequel to "Up from Slavery"Covering the Author's Experiences in Industrial Training at Tuskegee. Booker T. Washington. LC 76-92241. (American Negro: His History & Literature. Series 3: His History & Literature, Ser. No. 3). 1970. reprint ed. 19.95 (*0-405-01941-6*) Ayer.

Working with the Hands, Being a Sequel to "Up from Slavery" Booker T. Washington. LC 73-77216. (Illus.). 246p. 1969. reprint ed. text ed. 38.50 (*0-8371-1314-8*, WWH&, Greenwood Pr) Greenwood.

Working with the Intermarried: A Practical Guide for Workshop Leaders. Andrew Baker & Lori Goodman. LC 85-71160. 36p. (Orig.). 1985. pap. 4.00 (*0-87495-071-6*) Am Jewish Comm.

Working with the Media. James A. Fox & Jack Levin. (Survival Skills for Scholars Ser.: Vol. 2). (Illus.). 128p. (C). 1993. text ed. 35.00 (*0-8039-5088-8*); pap. text ed. 15.95 (*0-8039-5089-6*) Sage.

Working with the Mentally Disordered Offender in the Community. P. Vaughan & D. Badger. (Illus.). 288p. 1995. pap. text ed. 51.00 (*1-56593-326-5*, 0656) Singular Publishing.

Working with the Music Director: A Handbook for Board Members, Executive Directors, & Music Directors. Ed. by Ellen C. Hirzy. 47p. 1994. pap. 30.00 (*0-614-04617-3*) Am Symphony Orch.

Working with the New Municipal Continuing Disclosure Regulations & Avoiding Issuer Catastrophes - Interactive Workshops. (Corporate Law & Practice Course Handbook, 1985-86 Ser.). 1088p. 1994. pap. 99.00 (*0-614-17191-1*, B4-7119) PLI.

Working with the News Media. Gary Marx & Pat Ordovensky. 32p. 1992. pap. 2.50 (*0-87652-192-8*) Am Assn Sch Admin.

***Working with the Past.** David Bartholomae. Date not set. pap. text ed. write for info. (*0-312-15319-8*) St Martin.

Working with the Person with Schizophrenia: The Treatment Alliance. Michael A. Selzer et al. 432p. (C). 1989. 45.00 (*0-8147-7891-7*) NYU Pr.

Working with the Press: How to Achieve a Competitive Advantage. William R. Deeter. (Illus.). 100p. (Orig.). 1995. pap. 14.95 (*0-945609-17-5*) Keel Pubns.

Working with the Problem Drinker: A Solution-Focused Approach. Insoo K. Berg & Scott D. Miller. 220p. (C). 1992. 27.00 (*0-393-70134-4*) Norton.

***Working with the SAS System.** Erik W. Tilanus. 572p. (C). 1994. pap. 34.95 (*1-55544-645-0*) SAS Inst.

Working with the Sounds of English & Dutch. 3rd enl. rev. ed. Beverley Collins & Inger Mees. (Illus.). 80p. 1994. reprint ed. per., pap. text ed. 21.00 (*90-04-09313-3*) E J Brill.

Working with the Study of Economics. 4th ed. Turley Mings. 336p. (C). 1991. per. write for info. (*0-87967-922-0*) Brown & Benchmark.

Working with the Study of Economics. 5th ed. Turley Mings. 344p. (C). 1995. per. write for info. (*1-56134-383-8*) Dushkin Pub.

Working with the Unions. Colin Pope. 216p. 1993. 75.00 (*0-85292-529-8*, Pub. by IPM Hse UK) St Mut.

Working with the Unions. Colin Pope & Peter Ellis. 216p. 1995. pap. 90.00 (*0-85292-608-1*, Pub. by IPM UK) St Mut.

Working with the 401(a)(4) Nondiscrimination Regulations: A Basic Approach. 72p. 1992. pap. 15.00 (*0-685-67062-7*, 4770) Commerce.

Working with Tile. Ed. by Kimberly Kerrigone. LC 92-74900. 160p. 1993. pap. 12.95 (*1-880029-15-4*) Creative Homeowner.

***Working with Traits: Psychotherapy of Personality Disorders.** Joel Paris. LC 97-18482. 1997. text ed. 40.00 (*0-7657-0096-4*) Aronson.

Working with Traumatized Children: A Handbook for Healing. Kathryn Brohl. LC 96-24093. 105p. (Orig.). 1996. pap. 21.95 (*0-87868-633-9*) Child Welfare.

Working with Troubled Adolescents. John Coleman. 1987. text ed. 66.00 (*0-12-179720-1*) Acad Pr.

Working with Truman: A Personal Memoir of the White House Years. Ken Hechler. Ed. by Robert H. Ferrell. (Give 'Em Hell Harry Ser.). (Illus.). 328p. (C). 1996. pap. 16.95 (*0-8262-1067-8*) U of Mo Pr.

Working with Violent Families. Frank G. Bolton & Susan R. Bolton. 400p. (C). 1987. text ed. 55.00 (*0-8039-2586-7*); pap. text ed. 26.00 (*0-8039-2587-5*) Sage.

Working with Virtual Reality. William Sherman & Alan Craig. 1997. 59.95 (*1-55860-353-0*) Morgan Kaufmann.

Working with Visible Analysis. 6th ed. Kotler. 1995. pap. text ed. 33.60 (*0-13-241878-9*) P-H.

Working with Visual Display Units. (Occupational Safety & Health Ser.: No. 61). vii, 57p. (Orig.). 1990. pap. 11.25 (*92-2-106509-X*) Intl Labour Office.

Working with Visually Impaired Young Students: A Curriculum Guide for Birth-3 Year Olds. Ed. by Ellen Trief. (Illus.). 230p. 1992. text ed. 43.95 (*0-398-05782-6*) C C Thomas.

Working with Visually Impaired Young Students: A Curriculum Guide for Birth-3 Year Olds. Ed. by Ellen Trief. (Illus.). 230p. 1992. pap. 29.95 (*0-398-06466-0*) C C Thomas.

Working with Vulnerable Young Children: Early Intervention. Jean Campion. Ed. by Cedric Cullingford. (Children, Teachers & Learning Ser.). 160p. 1992. text ed. 55.00 (*0-304-32600-3*); pap. text ed. 16.95 (*0-304-32582-1*) Cassell.

Working with Water - Soluble Pencils. Wendy Jelbert. (Leisure Arts Ser.: Vol. 45). 32p. (Orig.). pap. 4.95 (*0-85532-791-X*, 791, Pub. by Search Pr UK) A Schwartz & Co.

Working with Watercolour. (Leisure Arts Ser.: No. 2). (Illus.). 32p. pap. 4.95 (*0-85532-401-5*, 401-5, Pub. by Search Pr UK) A Schwartz & Co.

Working with West Indian Families. Sharon-Ann Gopaul-McNicol. LC 92-31870. 212p. 1993. pap. text ed. 16.95 (*0-89862-024-4*); lib. bdg. 35.00 (*0-89862-229-8*) Guilford Pr.

Working with Windows. Michael A. Henry. 300p. 1992. pap. text ed. 32.00 (*0-13-952748-6*) P-H.

Working with Windows 3.1. Don Barker. 320p. 1993. pap. 28.95 (*0-87709-000-9*) Course Tech.

Working with Windows 3.1. Ian Sinclair. 392p. (Orig.). 1992. pap. 47.50 (*1-85058-318-8*, Pub. by Sigma Press UK) Coronet Bks.

Working with Windows 95. Barker. (DF - Computer Applications Ser.). 1997. pap. 24.95 (*0-7895-0656-4*) Course Tech.

Working with Windows(TM) 3.1. Marshall L. Moseley & Andrew Rathbone. 352p. 1992. pap. 19.95 (*0-8306-7722-4*, 3722, Windcrest) TAB Bks.

Working with Wisdom. Mildred A. Martin. (Miller Family Ser.). (J). (gr. 3-4). 1996. pap. text ed. 4.00 (*1-884377-02-5*) Green Psturs Pr.

Working with Women & AIDS: Medical, Counselling & Social Issues. Ed. by Judy Bury et al. LC 92-9967. (Illus.). 176p. (C). 1992. text ed. 69.95 (*0-415-07658-7*, A9601, Tavistock); pap. text ed. 16.95 (*0-415-07659-5*, A9605, Tavistock) Routledge.

***Working with Women in Poverty: Nine Innovative Approaches Submitted for the ESCAP HRD Award.** 66p. 1996. pap. text ed. 15.00 (*0-614-24925-2*, HV1445) UN.

W

An Asterisk (*) at the beginning of an entry indicates that the title is appearing in BIP for the first time.

Working with Women's Group, Vol. 2. Louise Y. Eberhardt. LC 87-50081. 144p. 1987. reprint ed. spiral bd. 14.95 (*0-938586-11-4*) Whole Person.

Working with Women's Groups, Vol. 1. Louise Y. Eberhardt. 208p. 1994. 24.95 (*0-938586-95-5*) Whole Person.

Working with Women's Groups, Vol. 1. Louise Y. Eberhardt. LC 87-50081. 172p. 1987. reprint ed. spiral bd. 14.95 (*0-938586-10-6*) Whole Person.

Working with Women's Groups, Vol. 2. Louise Y. Eberhardt. 208p. 1994. 24.95 (*0-938586-96-3*) Whole Person.

Working with Wood. (Home Repair & Improvement Ser.). (Illus.). 136p. 1979. 14.60 (*0-8094-2426-6*); lib. bdg. 20.60 (*0-8094-2427-4*) Time-Life.

***Working with Wood.** Time-Life Books Editors. LC 97-16888. (Home Repair & Improvement Ser.). (Illus.). 128p. 1997. write for info. (*0-7835-3911-8*) Time-Life.

Working with Wood: The Basics of Craftsmanship. Peter Korn. (Illus.). 208p. 1993. pap. 24.95 (*1-56158-041-4*) Taunton.

Working with WordPerfect for Windows. Don Barker et al. 272p. 1993. pap. 28.95 (*0-87835-855-2*) Course Tech.

Working with Wordperfect 5.0. Electronic Learning Facilitators, Inc. Staff. 288p. (C). 1990. pap. text ed. 16.00 (*0-15-596717-7*) Dryden Pr.

Working with WordPerfect 5.1. Electronic Learning Facilitators, Inc. Staff. 276p. (C). 1991. pap. text ed. 17.50 (*0-15-596720-7*) Dryden Pr.

Working with Words. Brian S. Brooks. 1996. wbk. ed., pap. text ed. 10.50 (*0-312-13758-3*) St Martin.

Working with Words. Quinlan. (EC - HS Communication/Engl Ser.). 1992. pap. 15.95 (*0-538-61494-3*) S-W Pub.

Working with Words. 3rd ed. Brian S. Brooks. Date not set. pap. text ed. write for info. (*0-312-13759-1*) St Martin.

Working with Words. 3rd ed. Brian S. Brooks. 1996. pap. text ed. 21.00 (*0-312-13760-5*) St Martin.

Working with Words, Vol. 3. Kathryn Kilpatrick. (Illus.). 289p. 1987. student ed. 30.00 (*1-880504-03-0*) Visit Nurse.

Working with Words: Literacy Beyond School. Jane Mace. (Chameleon Education Ser.). 144p. 1981. pap. 4.95 (*0-906495-15-6*) Writers & Readers.

Working with Words & Pictures. Lori Siebert & Mary Cropper. (Graphic Design Basics Ser.). (Illus.). 128p. 1993. 26.99 (*0-89134-437-3*, 30515, North Lght Bks) F & W Pubns Inc.

Working with Words on Your Own. Kathryn Kilpatrick & Roberta DePompei. 50p. 1986. student ed. 8.00 (*1-880504-06-5*) Visit Nurse.

Working with WPS-Plus. Charlotte Temple & Dolores Cordeiro. (VAX Users Ser.). (Illus.). 235p. (Orig.). 1990. 34.95 (*1-55558-043-2*, EY-C198E-DP, Digital DEC) Buttrwrth-Heinemann.

Working with Writing: Exercises in Writing Interpretation & Research. Benjamin Kline. 172p. (C). 1994. pap. text ed. 13.95 (*1-884295-06-1*) Ananta Prnting.

Working with Young Adolescents & Their Families: A National Survey of Family Support Workers. Peter C. Scales. 36p. (Orig.). 1996. spiral bd., pap. 10.00 (*1-57482-344-2*) Search Inst.

Working with Young Children. Judy Herr. LC 93-26391. (Home Economics Ser.). (Illus.). 496p. 1994. text ed. 41.28 (*0-87006-088-0*) Goodheart.

***Working with Young Children.** Judy Herr. LC 97-8351. 550p. 1998. 43.96 (*1-56637-387-5*) Goodheart.

Working with Young Children. Lavisa C. Wilson & Neith Headley. 8p. 1983. pap. 1.95 (*0-87173-101-0*) ACEI.

Working with Young People Leaving Care: A Training & Resource Pack for All. Nick Frost. 178p. 1995. pap. 65.00 (*0-11-321892-3*, HM218923, Pub. by Stationery Ofc UK) Bernan Associates.

***Working with Your Board: Guidelines for CEOs.** John Carver. (Carverguide Ser.: No. 12). 1997. pap. 10.95 (*0-7879-1084-8*) Jossey-Bass.

Working with Your Chakras: A Physical, Emotional, & Spiritual Approach. Ruth White. LC 94-17752. 177p. (Orig.). 1994. pap. 11.00 (*0-87728-813-5*) Weiser.

***Working with Your Foreign Language Assistant.** Robin Page. (Orig.). 1997. pap. 23.50 (*0-7487-3031-1*, Pub. by Stanley Thornes UK) Trans-Atl Phila.

***Working with Your Guides & Angels.** Ruth White. LC 97-22964. 128p. (Orig.). 1997. pap. 9.95 (*1-57863-016-9*) Weiser.

Working with Your Older Patient: A Clinician's Handbook. B. Gastel. (Illus.). 51p. (Orig.). (C). 1995. pap. text ed. 20.00 (*0-7881-1571-5*) DIANE Pub.

Working with Your Shadow: An Imperative on the Spiritual Path. Lazaris. 144p. (Orig.). 1995. pap. 12.95 (*1-55638-289-8*, NPN Pub) Concept Synergy.

Working with Your Woodland: A Landowner's Guide. rev. ed. Mollie Beattie et al. LC 92-56900. (Illus.). 302p. (C). 1993. pap. 21.00 (*0-87451-622-6*) U Pr of New Eng.

***Working with Youth in High-Risk Environments: Experiences in Prevention.** Ed. by Carol E. Marcus & John D. Swisher. (Illus.). 210p. (Orig.). (C). 1996. reprint ed. pap. 30.00 (*0-7881-2972-4*) DIANE Pub.

Working with Zia: Pakistan Power Politics 1977-1988. Khalid M. Arif. (Illus.). 450p. 1995. text ed. 45.00 (*0-19-577570-8*) OUP.

Working with 401(k) Plans under the Final Regulations. 208p. 1991. pap. 25.00 (*0-685-67063-5*, 4851) Commerce.

Working Within the System. Ralph K. Huitt. LC 90-33406. 315p. 1990. pap. text ed. 15.95 (*0-87772-324-9*) UCB IGS.

Working Without a Net: A Study of Egocentric Epistemology. Richard Foley. 256p. 1992. 45.00 (*0-19-507699-0*) OUP.

Working Without a Net: How to Survive & Thrive in Today's High Risk Business World. Morris R. Shechtman. LC 94-29919. 1994. text ed. 22.00 (*0-13-026239-0*) P-H.

Working Without a Net: How to Survive & Thrive Today's High Risk Business World. Morris R. Shechtman. 1995. pap. 14.00 (*0-671-53581-1*) PB.

Working Without a Net: Memoirs of a Small Town Surgeon. Richard Fox. LC 94-71272. (Illus.). 344p. 1996. 24.95 (*0-9641246-0-2*) Agincourt-Galen.

Working Without a Net: The Realities of Going Into Business for Yourself. Daniel J. Fardella. (Illus.). 112p. (Orig.). 1995. pap. 7.95 (*1-886696-12-8*) Worth Pub NY.

Working Without Boal: Digressions & Development in the Theatre of the Oppressed, Vol. 3, Part 1. Ed. by Frances Babbage. (Comtemporary Theatre Review Ser). 128p. 1995. pap. text ed. 23.00 (*3-7186-5600-0*, Harwood Acad Pubs) Gordon & Breach.

Working Without Pain: Eliminate Repetitive Strain Injuries with Alexander Technique. Sherry Berjeron-Oliver & Bruce Oliver. LC 96-68768. (Illus.). 124p. 1996. pap. write for info. (*0-9651047-0-2*) Pac Inst Alexdr.

Working Wives & Dual-Earner Families. Rose M. Rubin & Bobye J. Riney. LC 93-5441. 176p. 1993. text ed. 52.95 (*0-275-94682-7*, Praeger Pubs) Greenwood.

Working Wives & Dual-Earner Families. Rose M. Rubin & Bobye J. Riney. LC 93-5441. 176p. 1995. pap. text ed. 18.95 (*0-275-95338-6*, Praeger Pubs) Greenwood.

Working Wives, Working Husbands. Joseph H. Pleck. LC 85-11974. (New Perspectives on Family Ser.). 167p. 1985. reprint ed. pap. 47.60 (*0-608-01525-3*, 2059569) Bks Demand.

Working Woman: A Male Manager's View. Ray A. Killian. LC 76-138567. 224p. reprint ed. pap. 63.90 (*0-317-09731-8*, 2051532) Bks Demand.

Working Woman's Baby Planner. Marla S. Schwartz. 1993. 18.95 (*0-13-969296-7*) P-H.

Working Woman's Cookbook & Entertainment Guide. Pat McMillen. LC 83-3814. 252p. 1983. write for info. (*0-672-52708-1*) Macmillan.

Working Woman's Guide to Breastfeeding. Anne Price & Nancy B. Dana. 146p. 1987. pap. 7.00 (*0-671-63624-3*) S&S Trade.

Working Woman's Guide to Her Job Rights. (Women's Bureau Leaflet Ser.: No. 55). (Illus.). 68p. 1992. pap. 2.50 (*0-16-003853-7*, 029-002-00081-9) USGPO.

Working Woman's Guide to Her Job Rights. 72p. (C). 1993. pap. text ed. 20.00 (*0-7881-0126-9*) DIANE Pub.

Working Woman's Guide to Her Job Rights. 1992. lib. bdg. 250.00 (*0-8490-8900-X*) Gordon Pr.

Working Woman's Guide to Her Job Rights. 1995. lib. bdg. 253.95 (*0-8490-6735-9*) Gordon Pr.

Working Woman's Guide to Managing Stress. J. Robin Powell & Holly George-Warren. LC 94-11400. 1994. text ed. 27.95 (*0-13-969205-3*) P-H.

Working Woman's Guide to Managing Stress. J. Robin Powell & Holly George-Warren. LC 94-11400. 1994. pap. 14.95 (*0-13-969212-6*) P-H.

Working Woman's Guide to Managing Time: Take Charge of Your Job & Your Life While Taking Care of Yourself. Roberta Roesch. LC 95-37227. 288p. 1996. pap. 14.95 (*0-13-097429-3*) P-H.

Working Woman's Guide to Retirement Planning: Saving & Investing NOW for a Secure Future. Martha P. Patterson. LC 92-42610. 1993. pap. 15.95 (*0-13-952813-X*) P-H.

Working Woman's Husband's Cookbook. Robert Tichane. LC 91-71217. (Illus.). 301p. 1991. 20.00 (*0-914267-07-8*) NYS Inst Glaze.

***Working Woman's Legal Survival Guide: Valuable Tips & Strategies for Women Employees, Executives.** Steven M. Sack. 1997. 24.95 (*0-9636306-8-7*) Legal Strat.

***Working Woman's Organizer.** Darcy Tatsui. 1997. pap. 18.95 (*0-13-655424-5*) P-H.

***Working Woman's Quick Cookbook.** American Business Womens Association Staff. 1996. 15.95 (*0-9652588-0-7*) Am Busn Womens.

Working Woman's Wedding Planner. Susan T. D'Arcy. 160p. 1986. 14.95 (*0-13-966383-5*) P-H.

***Working Woman's World: www.com/help:now.** Lisa Cofield et al. Ed. by Patrick Caton. LC 96-78979. 168p. 1997. pap. 5.95 (*1-56245-277-0*) Great Quotations.

Working Women. Ed. by Karen S. Koziara et al. (IRRA Ser.). 1986. 15.00 (*0-913447-34-X*) Indus Relations Res.

Working Women. Ed. by Tobi Lippin. (Southern Exposure Ser.). (Illus.). 128p. (Orig.). (C). 1981. pap. 4.00 (*0-943810-12-4*) Inst Southern Studies.

***Working Women.** Ed. by Mary E. Williams et al. (Opposing Viewpoints Ser.). (Illus.). (YA). (gr. 5-12). 1997. pap. 12.96 (*1-56510-676-8*) Greenhaven.

***Working Women.** Ed. by Mary E. Williams et al. (Opposing Viewpoints Ser.). (Illus.). (YA). (gr. 5-12). 1997. lib. bdg. 20.96 (*1-56510-677-6*) Greenhaven.

Working Women: A Chartbook. (Illus.). 53p. (Orig.). (C). 1993. pap. text ed. 15.00 (*1-56806-168-4*) DIANE Pub.

***Working Women: An International Survey.** Ed. by Marilyn J. Davidson & Cary L. Cooper. LC 84-3645. (Illus.). 314p. pap. 89.50 (*0-608-05256-6*, 2065794) Bks Demand.

Working Women: And Other Stories. Tricia Bauer. LC 95-14083. 204p. 1995. 19.95 (*1-882593-11-1*) Bridge Wrks.

Working Women: International Perspectives on Labour & Gender Ideology. Ed. by Nanneke Redclift & M. Thea Sinclair. 256p. (C). 1991. pap. 19.95 (*0-415-01843-9*, A5103) Routledge.

Working Women & Infant Care. Shanta K. Chandra & M. Lakshmiswaramma. (C). 1991. 12.50 (*81-7099-303-2*, Pub. by Mittal II) S Asia.

Working Women & Modernization. Sanjay K. Jena. (Illus.). xiv, 216p. 1993. 29.00 (*81-7024-598-2*, Pub. by Ashish Pub Hse II) Nataraj Bks.

Working Women & Popular Movements in Bengal. Sunil K. Sen. 1986. 12.50 (*0-8364-1603-1*, Pub. by KP Bagchi IA) S Asia.

Working Women & Religion. B. Suguna. (C). 1994. text ed. 18.00 (*81-7141-245-9*, Pub. by Discovery Pub Hse II) S Asia.

Working Women & the Aging: Impact on Travel Patterns & Transportation Systems. (Research Record Ser.: No. 1135). 41p. 1987. 7.50 (*0-309-04514-2*) Transport Res Bd.

Working Women & the Law. W. B. Creighton. Ed. by Bob Hepple & Paul O'Higgins. (Studies in Labour & Social Law: Vol. 3). 304p. 1979. 120.00 (*0-7201-0552-8*, Mansell Pub) Cassell.

Working Women & the Law: Equality & Discrimination in Theory & Practice. Anne E. Morris & Susan M. Nott. 272p. (C). 1992. pap. text ed. 17.95 (*0-415-00937-5*, A9855) Routledge.

***Working Women Count!** (Illus.). 52p. 1994. pap. text ed. 30.00 (*1-57979-055-0*) BPI Info Servs.

Working Women Count: A Report to the Nation. (Illus.). 44p. (Orig.). (C). 1995. pap. text ed. 25.00 (*0-7881-1870-6*) DIANE Pub.

Working Women Don't Have Wives: Professional Success in the 1990s. Terri Apter. LC 95-1554. 1995. 13.95 (*0-312-12560-7*) St Martin.

Working Women for Freedom. Angela Terrano et al. (Illus.). 56p. (Orig.). 1976. pap. 1.00 (*0-914441-18-3*) News & Letters.

Working Women in Kashmir. Bashir A. Dabla. (C). 1991. 15.00 (*81-7033-132-3*, Pub. by Rawat II) S Asia.

Working Women in Renaissance Germany. Merry E. Wiesner. (Douglass Series on Women's Lives & the Meaning of Gender). (Illus.). 250p. (C). 1986. text ed. 40.00 (*0-8135-1138-0*) Rutgers U Pr.

Working Women in Russia under the Hunger Tsars: Political Activism & Daily Life. Anne Bobroff-Hajal. LC 94-20199. (Scholarship in Women's History Ser.: Vol. 3). 300p. 1994. 60.00 (*0-926019-64-3*) Carlson Pub.

Working Women in Socialist Countries: The Fertility Connection (WEP Study) Ed. by Valentina Bodrova & Richard Anker. xvi, 234p. (Orig.). 1987. pap. 24.75 (*92-2-103910-2*) Intl Labour Office.

Working Women in South-East Asia: Development, Subordination & Emancipation. Noeleen Heyzer. 192p. 1986. 90.00 (*0-335-15384-4*, Open Univ Pr); pap. 32.00 (*0-335-15383-6*, Open Univ Pr) Taylor & Francis.

Working Women of Collar City: Gender, Class, & Community in Troy, New York, 1864-1886. Carole Turbin. 256p. 1994. pap. text ed. 14.95 (*0-252-06426-7*) U of Ill Pr.

Working Women of Collar City: Gender, Class, & Community in Troy, 1864-86. Carole Turbin. (Working Class in American History Ser.). 256p. (C). 1992. text ed. 39.95 (*0-252-01836-2*) U of Ill Pr.

Working Women of Manila in the 19th Century. M. Luisa Camagay. 208p. 1996. pap. text ed. 18.00 (*971-542-059-1*, Pub. by U of Philippines Pr PH) UH Pr.

Working Women, Workable Lives: Creative Solutions for Managing Home & Career. Karen S. Linamen & Linda Holland. 296p. 1993. reprint ed. pap. 9.99 (*0-87788-851-5*) Shaw Pubs.

Working Women, Working Men: Sao Paulo & the Rise of Brazil's Industrial Working Class, 1900-1955. Joel D. Wolfe. LC 92-40484. (Illus.). 328p. (C). 1993. text ed. 47.95 (*0-8223-1330-8*); pap. text ed. 18.95 (*0-8223-1347-2*) Duke.

Working Womenroots: An Oral History Primer. 2nd ed. Debra Bernhardt et al. 33p. 1980. pap. 5.00 (*0-87736-342-0*) U of Mich Inst Labor.

Working Women's Guide to Managing Stress. J. Robin Powell. 1994. pap. text ed. 14.95 (*0-13-969213-4*) P-H.

Working Wood: A Complete Bench-Top Reference. Jim Tolpin. LC 95-83686. (Illus.). 224p. 1996. pap. 19.95 (*0-87192-301-7*) Davis Mass.

Working Words: The Process of Creative Writing. Wendy Bishop. (C). 1992. teacher ed., pap. write for info. (*1-55934-166-1*, 1166); pap. text ed. 27.95 (*1-55934-076-2*, 1076) Mayfield Pub.

Working World: Language & Culture of the Job Market. Maria M. Baskin & Lois W. Morton. 236p. (C). 1986. pap. text ed. 16.00 (*0-15-596710-X*) HB Coll Pubs.

***Working Wounded: Advice That Adds Insight to Injury.** Bob Rosner. 1998. 14.00 (*0-446-52289-9*) Warner Bks.

Working Writer. Toby Fulwiler. LC 94-23915. 480p. 1994. pap. text ed. 30.80 (*0-13-307372-6*) P-H Gen Ref & Trav.

Working Your Way Through Wordstar. 2nd ed. Graham. (DF - Computer Applications Ser.). 1990. pap. 25.95 (*0-538-60115-9*) S-W Pub.

Working Your Way Through Wordstar, Release 4. 2nd ed. Sally Graham. 560p. (C). 1990. pap. 37.95 (*0-538-60148-5*, WM10BBU) S-W Pub.

Working Your Way to the Nations: A Guide to Effective Tentmaking. Illus. by Jeff Northway & Dona Kacalek. (World Evangelical Fellowship Ser.: No. 1). 208p. (Orig.). 1993. student ed. 12.95 (*0-87808-244-1*, WCL244-1) William Carey Lib.

***Working Your Way to the Nations: A Guide to Effective Tentmaking.** rev. ed. Jonathan Lewis. LC 96-47612. 208p. 1997. pap. 12.99 (*0-8308-1905-3*, 1905) InterVarsity.

Workingclass Giant: The Life of William Z. Foster. Arthur Zipser. LC 81-2503. 228p. (Orig.). (C). 1981. pap. 4.25 (*0-7178-0582-4*) Intl Pubs Co.

Workingman Skiff. William Campbell. 112p. (Orig.). 1995. pap. 9.95 (*0-924771-51-8*, Covered Brdge Pr) D C Press.

Workingman's Wife: Her Personality, World & Life Style. Lee Rainwater et al. Ed. by Lewis A. Coser & Walter W. Powell. LC 79-7014. (Perennial Works in Sociology). 1980. reprint ed. lib. bdg. 21.95 (*0-405-12113-X*) Ayer.

Workingmen in San Francisco, 1880-1901. Jules Tygiel. LC 92-3197. (Modern American History Ser.: Vol. 6). 472p. 1992. reprint ed. text ed. 25.00 (*0-8240-1904-0*) Garland.

Workingmen on Waltham: Mobility in American Urban Industrial Development, 1850-1890. Howard M. Gitelman. LC 74-6822. (Illus.). 208p. reprint ed. pap. 59.30 (*0-8357-8383-9*, 2034139) Bks Demand.

Workingmen's Democracy: The Knights of Labor & American Politics. Leon Fink. LC 82-6902. (Working Class in American History Ser.). 272p. 1985. reprint ed. pap. text ed. 13.95 (*0-252-01256-9*) U of Ill Pr.

Workingmen's Party of the United States: A History of the First Marxist Party in the Americas. Philip S. Foner. LC 83-26553. (Studies in Marxism: Vol. 14). 148p. 1984. 19.95 (*0-930656-35-0*); pap. 6.95 (*0-930656-36-9*) MEP Pubns.

Workings. Robert Watson. 61p. (C). 1979. 25.00 (*0-85088-940-5*, Pub. by Gomer Pr UK); pap. 30.00 (*0-85088-681-3*, Pub. by Gomer Pr UK) St Mut.

Workings of Fiction: Essays. Robert B. Heilman. 400p. 1991. text ed. 39.95 (*0-8262-0787-1*) U of Mo Pr.

Workings of the Brain: Development, Memory & Perception. Rodolfo R. Llinas. 224p. (C). 1995. text ed. 13.95 (*0-7167-2071-X*) W H Freeman.

Workings of the Household: A U. S.-U. K. Comparison. Lydia Morris. (Family Life Ser.). (Illus.). 260p. 1990. pap. text ed. 24.95 (*0-7456-0442-0*) Blackwell Pubs.

Workings of the Household: A U. S.-U. K. Comparison. Lydia Morris. (Family Life Ser.). (Illus.). 260p. 1990. text ed. 60.95 (*0-7456-0441-2*) Blackwell Pubs.

Workings of the Indeterminate-Sentence Law & the Parole System in Illinois. Andrew A. Bruce et al. LC 68-19466. (Criminology, Law Enforcement, & Social Problems Ser.: No. 5). 1968. reprint ed. 26.00 (*0-87585-005-7*) Patterson Smith.

Workings of the Spirit: The Poetics of Afro-American Women's Writing. Houston A. Baker, Jr. LC 90-41980. (Black Literature & Culture Ser.). (Illus.). 256p. 1990. 29.95 (*0-226-03522-0*) U Ch Pr.

Workings of the Spirit: The Poetics of Afro-American Women's Writing. Houston A. Baker, Jr. LC 90-41980. (Black Literature & Culture Ser.). (Illus.). xvi, 256p. 1992. pap. text ed. 13.95 (*0-226-03523-9*) U Ch Pr.

Workings of the Universe. (Voyage Through the Universe Ser.). (Illus.). 144p. 1991. 19.93 (*0-8094-6916-2*); lib. bdg. 25.93 (*0-8094-6917-0*) Time-Life.

Workings of Westminster. Dermot Englefield. 270p. 1991. text ed. 59.95 (*1-85521-184-X*, Pub. by Dartmth Pub UK) Ashgate Pub Co.

Workjobs: Activity-Centered Learning for Early Childhood. Mary Baratta-Lorton. 1972. pap. text ed. 19.95 (*0-201-04311-4*) Addison-Wesley.

Workjobs for Parents: Activity-Centered Learning in the Home. Mary Baratta-Lorton. 1975. pap. text ed. 12.95 (*0-201-04303-3*) Addison-Wesley.

Workjobs II: Number Activities for Early Childhood. Mary B. Lorton. 1978. spiral bd. 17.50 (*0-201-04302-5*) Addison-Wesley.

Workless: An Exploration of the Social Contract Between Society & the Worker. 2nd enl. rev. ed. Dennis Marsden. (Illus.). 275p. 1982. pap. 14.95 (*0-7099-1723-6*, Pub. by Croom Helm UK) Routledge Chapman & Hall.

Workload of the Supreme Court. Gerhard Casper & Richard A. Posner. xiii, 118p. Date not set. 20.00 (*0-910058-78-4*, 305460) W S Hein.

Workload of the Supreme Court. Gerhard Casper & Richard A. Posner. LC 76-49801. 134p. reprint ed. pap. 38.20 (*0-685-15232-4*, 2027140) Bks Demand.

Workload Transition: Implications for Individual & Team Performance. National Research Council Staff. Ed. by Beverly M. Huey & Christopher D. Wickens. 304p. (Orig.). (C). 1993. pap. text ed. 36.00 (*0-309-04796-X*) Natl Acad Pr.

Workloads: Measurement & Management. Joan Orme. 144p. 1995. 55.95 (*1-85628-872-2*, Pub. by Avebury Pub UK) Ashgate Pub Co.

Workman & the Franchise: Chapters from English History on the Representation & Education of the People. Frederick D. Maurice. LC 68-18601. xvi, 244p. 1970. reprint ed. 39.50 (*0-678-00592-3*) Kelley.

Workman's Compensation: Index of Modern Information. Clayton R. Mellows. LC 88-47986. 150p. 1989. 44.50 (*1-55914-064-X*); pap. 39.50 (*1-55914-065-8*) ABBE Pubs Assn.

Workmen of God. William S. Deal. 1975. pap. 0.95 (*0-686-11025-0*) Crusade Pubs.

Workmen's Compensation: Desk Edition, 3 vols., Set. Arthur Larson. 1972. ring bd. write for info. (*0-8205-1347-4*) Bender.

Workmen's Compensation Act, 1923. K. D. Srivastava. (C). 1992. 150.00 (*81-7012-487-5*, Pub. by Eastern Book II) St Mut.

Workmen's Compensation Examiner. Jack Rudman. (Career Examination Ser.: C-1644). 1994. reprint ed. pap. 27.95 (*0-8373-1644-8*) Nat Learn.

Workmen's Compensation in Twentieth Century Britain: Law, History & Social Policy. P. W. Bartrip. 180p. 1987. text ed. 55.95 (*0-566-05485-X*, Pub. by Dartmth Pub UK) Ashgate Pub Co.

Workmen's Compensation Law, 11 vols. Arthur Larson. 1952. write for info. (*0-8205-1340-7*) Bender.

Workout. William G. Ball & Helen B. Ball. 76p. (Orig.). 1992. pap. 7.95 (*1-880322-07-2*) Champions Christ.

***Workout Basics with Free Weights.** Robert Kennedy. Date not set. write for info. (*0-8069-9833-4*) Sterling.

An Asterisk (*) at the beginning of an entry indicates that the title is appearing in BIP for the first time.

Workout C: Learn C Through Exercises. David Himmel. (Illus.). 800p. (Orig.). 1992. pap. 39.95 (*1-878739-14-X*, Waite Grp Pr) Sams.

***Workout Cop-Out: A Daily Avoidance Guide for Fitness Phobics.** Stacey Granger & Dana Mitchell. (Illus.). 144p. (Orig.). 1997. pap. 7.95 (*1-888952-56-3*) Cumberland Hse.

Workout for Seniors. Date not set. pap. write for info. (*0-614-14299-7*) Personal Fitness Pub.

Workout Game: Managing Non-Performing Real Estate Assets. Ed. by Stuart M. Bloch. LC 86-81722. 358p. 1987. 59.95 (*0-317-01444-7*) Land Dev Inst.

***Workout Intermediate.** Radley & Millerchip & Millerchip. Date not set. wbk. ed., pap. text ed. write for info. (*0-17-556462-0*) Addison-Wesley.

***Workout Intermediate.** Radley & Millerchip & Millerchip. 1996. student ed., pap. text ed. write for info. (*0-17-556461-2*) Addison-Wesley.

Workout Manual. Richard Clarke. Ed. by Ned Miller & Joan H. Behr. 64p. 1993. pap. text ed. 50.00 (*0-936742-93-3*, 33211) Robt Morris Assocs.

Workout Master 1: How to Chart Your Fitness Progress. Joel D. Johnson. Ed. by Dave Quison. (Illus.). 16.95 (*0-9637067-9-9*) ABC Pubn.

***Workout Upper Intermediate.** Radley & Millerchip. 1993. student ed., pap. text ed. write for info. (*0-17-556465-5*) Addison-Wesley.

Workouts: A Special Collection from the Journal of Commercial Bank Lending. Intro. by Charlotte Weisman. LC 91-7826. (Illus.). 116p. (Orig.). 1991. pap. text ed. 45.00 (*0-936742-81-X*, 36044) Robt Morris Assocs.

Workouts & Bankruptcy Reorganization Workshop. Michael L. Cook & Wilbur L. Ross. 265p. write for info. (*0-318-61659-9*) HarBrace.

Workouts & Maidens. Vincent M. Reo. 160p. 1994. pap. 11.95 (*1-56625-000-5*) Bonus Books.

Workouts & Turnarounds: The Investor's Guide to Profit Opportunities. Dominic Dinapoli. 816p. 1990. 90.00 (*1-55623-335-3*) Irwin Prof Pubng.

Workouts in Intermediate Microeconomics. 3rd ed. Theodore C. Bergstrom. (C). 1993. pap. text ed. 19.95 (*0-393-96321-7*) Norton.

Workouts in Modern Economics. 3rd ed. Ed. by John Lucock & Robin Peak. LC 94-42567. 1994. pap. text ed. write for info. (*0-582-25938-X*, Pub. by Longman UK) Longman.

Workouts with Weights: Simple Routines You Can Do at Home. Stephenie Karony & Anthony L. Renken. LC 92-36155. 160p. 1993. pap. 12.95 (*0-8069-0325-2*) Sterling.

Workpapers Concerning Waorani Discourse Features. Ed. by Rachel Saint. LC 88-62278. (Language Data, Amerindian Ser.: No. 10). 192p. (Orig.). 1988. fiche 12.00 (*0-88312-721-0*) Summer Instit Ling.

Workpapers 1: Rethinking & Restructuring the Arts Organization. George Thorn et al. Ed. by Keens Company Staff & William Keens. 150p. (Orig.). 1993. 16.95 (*0-9602942-7-9*) ARTS Action.

Workplace. David L. Cohn. (C). 1996. pap. text ed. 30.00 (*0-13-459058-9*) P-H.

Workplace. Zan D. Robinson. 209p. (Orig.). 1992. pap. text ed. 15.00 (*0-9603888-7-7*) Labor Arts.

Workplace: America's Forgotten Environment, a Comparison of Protections under U. S. Workplace Safety & Environmental Laws. (Illus.). 54p. (Orig.). (C). 1995. pap. text ed. 20.00 (*0-7881-2203-7*) DIANE Pub.

Workplace: Questions Women Ask. Judith Briles et al. (Today's Christian Woman Ser.). 180p. 1992. 13.99 (*0-88070-502-7*, Multnomah Bks) Multnomah Pubs.

Workplace Alternatives: How to Make Them Work for Your Institution. Barbara Butterfield et al. 39p. 1993. 20.00 (*1-878240-22-6*) Coll & U Personnel.

Workplace Assessment. IPM Staff. (Assessment of NVQs & SVQs Ser.: No. 3). (C). 1994. 62.25 (*0-08-042118-0*, Pub. by IPM Hse UK) St Mut.

***Workplace Basics, 8 vols.** Multimedia Development Services Staff. Incl. Vol. 8 Ethics in the Workplace. (Illus.). 39p. (Orig.). 1996. pap. text ed. 30.00 (*1-57431-147-6*); Vol. 7 Goal Setting & Planning. (Illus.). 37p. (Orig.). 1996. pap. text ed. 30.00 (*1-57431-145-X*); Vol. 6 Team Building. (Illus.). 31p. (Orig.). 1996. pap. text ed. 30.00 (*1-57431-143-3*); Vol. 5 Workplace Relations. 39p. (Orig.). 1996. pap. text ed. 30.00 (*1-57431-141-7*); Vol. 4 Problem Solving. (Illus.). 31p. (Orig.). 1996. pap. text ed. 30.00 (*1-57431-139-5*); Vol. 3 Communication. (Illus.). 31p. (Orig.). 1996. pap. text ed. 30.00 (*1-57431-137-9*); Vol. 2 Self Esteem & Motivation in the Workplace. (Illus.). 49p. (Orig.). 1996. pap. text ed. 30.00 (*1-57431-135-2*); Vol. 1 Work Force 2000/ Learning to Learn. (Illus.). 23p. (Orig.). 1996. pap. text ed. 30.00 (*1-57431-133-6*); 240.00 (*1-57431-149-2*) Tech Trng Systs.

***Workplace Basics: Teaching the ABC's of the Career World Using Math, Social Studies & Language Arts.** 5th rev. ed. Kevin G. Kuckkan. 58p. Date not set. pap. text ed. 15.95 (*0-9642686-2-0*) Creat Educ Pubng.

Workplace Basics: The Essential Skills Employers Want. Anthony P. Carnevale et al. LC 89-48804. (Management Ser.). 508p. text ed. 41.95 (*1-55542-202-0*) Jossey-Bass.

Workplace Basics Training Manual. Anthony P. Carnevale et al. LC 89-48805. (Management Ser.). 304p. text ed. 41.95 (*1-55542-204-7*) Jossey-Bass.

Workplace Before the Factory: Artisans & Proletarians, 1500-1800. Ed. by Thomas M. Safley & Leonard N. Rosenband. (Illus.). 272p. 1993. 37.50 (*0-8014-2847-5*); pap. 14.95 (*0-8014-8092-2*) Cornell U Pr.

Workplace by Design: Mapping the High-Performance Workscape. Franklin Becker & Fritz Steele. LC 94-32960. (Management Ser.). 246p. 1995. 27.50 (*0-7879-0047-8*) Jossey-Bass.

Workplace Counselling: A Systematic Approach to Employee Care. Michael Carroll. 256p. 1996. 49.95 (*0-7619-5020-6*); pap. 22.95 (*0-7619-5021-4*) Sage.

Workplace Counselling: Developing the Skills in Managers. Dianne Kamp. LC 96-7996. (Training Ser.). 1996. write for info. (*0-07-709152-3*) McGraw.

***Workplace Cultures: a Reality Check: Listening to the Voices of Women of Color.** Jennifer Tucker et al. 16p. (Orig.). 1995. pap. 5.00 (*1-877966-27-4*) Ctr Women Policy.

Workplace Democracy: An Inquiry into Employee Participation in Canadian Work Organizations. Donald V. Nightingale. 336p. 1982. pap. 18.95 (*0-8020-6470-1*) U of Toronto Pr.

Workplace Democracy: The Political Effects of Participation. Edward S. Greenberg. LC 86-47641. 272p. 1986. pap. 16.95 (*0-8014-9530-X*) Cornell U Pr.

Workplace Democracy & Social Change. Ed. by Frank Lindenfeld & Joyce Rothschild-Whitt. LC 82-80137. 456p. (C). 1982. 20.00 (*0-87558-101-3*, Extending Hor Bks); pap. 12.00 (*0-87558-102-1*, Extending Hor Bks) Porter Sargent.

Workplace Discrimination: How to Pursue Your Rights. xiv, 172p. 1993. pap. 11.00 (*0-9640732-0-X*) Srv Fund NOW NYC.

Workplace Discrimination: How to Pursue Your Rights. large type ed. xx, 400p. 1993. 29.00 (*0-9640732-1-8*) Srv Fund NOW NYC.

***Workplace Dispute Resolution: Directions for the Twenty-First Century.** Sandra E. Gleason. LC 97-25092. 1997. write for info. (*0-87013-436-1*) Mich St U Pr.

***Workplace Diversity.** Ed. by Alfrieda Daly. (Orig.). (C). 1997. pap. text ed. write for info. (*0-87101-281-2*, NASW Pr) Natl Assn Soc Wkrs.

Workplace Diversity: A Manager's Guide to Solving Problems & Turning Diversity into a Competitive Advantage. Katharine Esty et al. 228p. (Orig.). 1995. pap. 10.95 (*1-55850-482-6*) Adams Media.

***Workplace Diversity Series, 5 vols.** (Illus.). (Orig.). 1996. pap. 59.95 (*1-883553-73-3*) R Chang Assocs.

Workplace Drug Abuse & AIDS: A Guide to Human Resource Management Policy & Practice. Donald E. Klingner & Nancy G. O'Neill. LC 90-46719. 216p. 1991. text ed. 55.00 (*0-89930-624-1*, KDR/, Quorum Bks) Greenwood.

Workplace Drug Testing: An Employer's Development & Implementation Guide. Mark A. De Bernardo. 107p. 1994. pap. 35.00 (*1-889437-03-4*) Inst Drug-Free Wrkpl.

Workplace Dynamics. 1993. 199.00 (*0-88336-522-7*) New Readers.

***Workplace Eglish Bk. 4.** Contemp Bks Staff. 1996. pap. 11.93 (*0-8092-3356-8*) Contemp Bks.

***Workplace English: Office File Student Book.** Marc Helgesen. 1996. pap. text ed. 12.66 (*0-582-27666-7*, Pub. by Longman UK) Longman.

***Workplace English Bk. 6.** Contemp Bks Staff. 1996. pap. 11.93 (*0-8092-3353-3*) Contemp Bks.

Workplace Environmental Exposure Level Guide Series, 17 sets, Set. AIHA WEEL Committee. (Guide Ser.). 15.00 (*0-685-43791-4*) Am Indus Hygiene.

Workplace Ethics: Winning the Integrity Revolution. Ralph W. Clark & Alice D. Lattal. 176p. (Orig.). (C). 1992. text ed. 50.00 (*0-8476-7789-3*); pap. text ed. 18.95 (*0-8226-3020-6*) Rowman.

Workplace Health Protection. Confer. 560p. 1994. 99.95 (*0-87371-387-7*, L387) Lewis Pubs.

Workplace Industrial Relations & Technical Change. W. W. Daniel. 352p. 1987. 38.00 (*0-86187-917-1*) St Martin.

Workplace Industrial Relations & the Global Challenge. Ed. by Jacque Belanger et al. LC 94-1668. (Cornell International Industrial & Labor Relations Reports: No. 25). 352p. 1994. 58.00 (*0-87546-327-4*, ILR Press); pap. 26.95 (*0-87546-328-2*, ILR Press) Cornell U Pr.

Workplace Industrial Relations in Transition: The ED-ESRC-PSI-ACAS Surveys. Ed. by Mark Stevens et al. 412p. 1992. text ed. 59.95 (*1-85521-321-4*, Pub. by Dartmth Pub UK) Ashgate Pub Co.

***Workplace Investigations: Guidebook for Administrators, Managers & Investigators.** Donald W. Slowik. LC 95-60623. (Unicom Series in Human Resource Development). 334p. 1996. boxed 45.00 (*1-883342-02-3*) Evergrn Pr CO.

Workplace Justice: Employment Obligations in International Perspective. Ed. by Hoyt N. Wheeler et al. LC 92-16829. (Studies in Industrial Relations). (Illus.). 393p. 1992. text ed. 49.95 (*0-87249-781-X*) U of SC Pr.

***Workplace Law.** John Grogan. 278p. 1996. pap. 46.00 (*0-7021-3641-7*, Pub. by Juta SA) Gaunt.

Workplace Learning: Perspectives on Education, Training & Work. Keith Forrester et al. 183p. 1995. text ed. 50.95 (*1-85628-850-1*, Pub. by Avebury Pub UK) Ashgate Pub Co.

Workplace Literacy: A Guide to the Literature & Resources. Susan Imel & Sandra Kerka. 84p. (Orig.). (C). 1994. pap. text ed. 25.00 (*0-7881-0802-6*) DIANE Pub.

***Workplace Literacy: Resharing the American Workplace.** (Illus.). 93p. 1996. reprint ed. pap. 25.00 (*0-7881-3260-1*) DIANE Pub.

Workplace Literacy: The Complete Resource Guide. 1988. 95.00 (*1-55871-024-8*) BNA Plus.

Workplace Literacy Training in Modernizing Manufacturing Environments. Karl O. Haigler & Sondra G. Stein. 52p. (Orig.). 1992. pap. text ed. 15.00 (*1-55877-169-7*) Natl Governor.

***Workplace Mentoring for Youth: Context, Issues, Strategies.** Marc Freedman & Rachel Baker. (Education Reform & School-to-Work Transition Ser.). 21p. 1995. teacher ed., pap. text ed. 12.00 (*0-614-24525-7*) Natl Inst Work.

Workplace Privacy: Employee Testing, Surveillance, Wrongful Discharge, & Other Areas of Vulnerability. 2nd ed. Ira M. Shepard et al. LC 89-22353. (Special Report Ser.). 1989. 70.00 (*1-55871-137-6*, BSP 133) BNA Plus.

Workplace Readiness: Health Occupations. Colbert. (Health Occupations Ser.). 1998. 36.50 (*0-8273-7781-9*); 55.00 (*0-8273-7782-7*) Delmar.

Workplace Readiness: Health Occupations. Colbert. (Health Occupations Ser.). 1998. teacher ed. 13.95 (*0-8273-7783-5*) Delmar.

Workplace Readiness: Health Occupations. Colbert. (Health Occupations Ser.). 1998. 19.95 (*0-8273-7784-3*) Delmar.

Workplace Readiness Business & Industry Edition: Problem Solving Instructor's Guide. Agency for Instructional Technology Staff. 117p. (Orig.). 1995. pap. text ed. write for info. (*0-7842-0786-0*) Agency Instr Tech.

Workplace Readiness Business & Industry Edition: Problem Solving Participant's Guide. Agency for Instructional Technology Staff. 110p. (Orig.). 1995. pap. text ed. write for info. (*0-7842-0787-9*) Agency Instr Tech.

Workplace Readiness Business & Industry Edition: Self-Management Instructor's Guide. Agency for Instructional Technology Staff. 149p. (Orig.). 1995. pap. text ed. write for info. (*0-7842-0784-4*) Agency Instr Tech.

Workplace Readiness Business & Industry Edition: Self-Management Participant's Guide. Agency for Instructional Technology Staff. 145p. (Orig.). 1995. pap. text ed. write for info. (*0-7842-0785-2*) Agency Instr Tech.

Workplace Readiness Business & Industry Edition: Teamwork Instructor's Guide. Agency for Instructional Technology Staff. 136p. (Orig.). 1995. pap. text ed. write for info. (*0-7842-0782-8*) Agency Instr Tech.

Workplace Readiness Business & Industry Edition: Teamwork Participant's Guide. Agency for Instructional Technology Staff. 126p. (Orig.). 1995. pap. text ed. write for info. (*0-7842-0783-6*) Agency Instr Tech.

Workplace Regulation: Information on Selected Employer & Union Experiences, 2 vols., Set. (Illus.). 187p. (Orig.). (C). 1995. pap. text ed. 35.00 (*0-7881-1237-6*) DIANE Pub.

Workplace Resources: Banking Note-Taking for Training Programs & Meeting. Bea Mikulecky. 1990. 12.50 (*0-13-852302-9*) P-H.

Workplace Resources, Building Communication Skills: Strategic Skill Builders. Larry Mikulecky. 1990. 12.50 (*0-13-852310-X*) P-H.

Workplace Safety & Health Guide. LC 95-18705. 1995. write for info. (*0-614-07811-3*) Clark Boardman Callaghan.

Workplace Safety Pocket Guide. rev. ed. Peter A. Roy & Michael Cinquanti. (Illus.). 64p. 1994. pap. text ed. write for info. (*0-931690-37-4*) Genium Pub.

Workplace Sexual Harassment. Anne Levy. LC 96-22254. 256p. (C). 1996. pap. 33.27 (*0-13-450560-3*) P-H.

Workplace Skills: Learning How to Function on-the-Job. Mary J. Haugen. (Life Skills Educational Board Game Ser.: No. 7). 50p. 1991. teacher ed., text ed. 49.95 (*1-884074-06-5*) Program Concepts.

Workplace Skills in Practice: Case Studies of Technical Work. Cathleen Stasz et al. LC 96-19821. 110p. (Orig.). 1996. pap. text ed. 15.00 (*0-8330-2368-3*, MR-722-NCRVEUCB) Rand Corp.

Workplace Smoking: Corporate Practices & Developments. 38p. 1989. pap. 25.00 (*1-55871-159-7*) BNA.

Workplace Stress: Nine One-Hour Workshops. Steven B. Zwickel. LC 94-10230. (Workshop Models for Family Life Education Ser.). 192p. (Orig.). 1994. pap. 19.95 (*0-87304-252-2*) Families Intl.

Workplace Superstars in Resistant Organizations. Seth Allcorn. LC 91-186. 216p. 1991. text ed. 55.00 (*0-89930-657-8*, AWE, Quorum Bks) Greenwood.

Workplace Survival Guide: Tools, Tips, & Techniques for Succeeding on the Job. George Fuller. 1995. text ed. 29.95 (*0-13-341660-7*) P-H.

Workplace Testing: An Employer's Guide to Policies & Practices. Diane Arthur. 272p. 1994. 49.95 (*0-8144-5096-2*) AMACOM.

***Workplace Violence: A Continuum from Threat to Death.** Mittie D. Southerland et al. LC 97-72953. 220p. (C). 1997. pap. text ed. 23.95 (*0-87084-895-X*) Anderson Pub Co.

Workplace Violence: Before, During & After. Sandra L. Heskett. 210p. 1996. 34.95 (*0-7506-9671-0*) Buttrwrth-Heinemann.

***Workplace Violence & Employer Liability.** Philip D. Dickinson. LC 97-20822. 76p. 1997. spiral bd. 47.00 (*0-925773-37-9*) M Lee Smith.

Workplace Wars & How to End Them: Turning Personal Conflicts into Productive Teamwork. Kenneth Kaye. 176p. 1994. 19.95 (*0-8144-0215-1*) AMACOM.

Workplace Wellness. Carol Bayly-Grant. 1992. pap. 42.95 (*0-442-00699-3*) Van Nos Reinhold.

Workplace Within: Psychodynamics of Organizational Life. Larry Hirschhorn. (Organization Studies). 280p. 1990. reprint ed. pap. 16.00 (*0-262-58101-9*) MIT Pr.

Workplace Workbook 2.0: An Illustrated Guide to Workplace Accommodation & Technology. 2nd ed. James Mueller. (Illus.). 148p. 1992. ring bd. 49.95 (*0-87425-200-8*) HRD Press.

Workplace 2000: The Revolution Reshaping American Business. Joseph H. Boyett & Henry P. Conn. 384p. 1992. pap. 14.95 (*0-452-26804-4*, Plume) NAL-Dutton.

***Workplaces & Workspaces: Office Design That Works.** Justin Henderson. (Illus.). 192p. 1997. 39.99 (*1-56496-396-9*) Rockport Pubs.

Workplaces Without Alcohol & Other Drugs: What Works. 66p. (C). 1995. reprint ed. pap. text ed. 20.00 (*0-7881-1998-2*) DIANE Pub.

Workplace/Women's Place: An Anthology. Ed. by Dana Dunn. LC 96-48794. 380p. (C). 1997. pap. text ed. write for info. (*0-935732-81-0*) Roxbury Pub Co.

WorkPlay: Playing to Learn & Learning to Play. 2nd ed. Carmine M. Consalvo. LC 91-67971. 132p. (Orig.). 1996. ring bd. 95.00 (*0-925652-12-1*) Orgn Design & Dev.

WorkPower: A Take Charge Approval & Professional Development. 1992. 80.00 (*1-882361-00-8*) Career Systs.

Workrights. Robert E. Smith. 1983. pap. 16.00 (*0-525-48047-1*) Privacy Journal.

Works, 3 vols. Benjamin De Casseres. 1976. 900.00 (*0-87968-467-4*) Gordon Pr.

Works, 7 vols. Plotinus. No. 440-445, & 468. write for info. (*0-318-53221-2*) HUP.

Works, 2 vols. Prudentius. No. 387, 398. write for info. (*0-318-53222-0*) HUP.

Works, 10 vols. Francis Beaumont & John Fletcher. (BCL1-PR English Literature Ser.). 1992. reprint ed. lib. bdg. 900.00 (*0-7812-7235-1*) Rprt Serv.

Works. Richard Bentley. xxxii, 1378p. 1971. reprint ed. 305.00 (*3-487-04071-9*) G Olms Pubs.

Works, 12 vols. Edmund E. Burke. reprint ed. 895.00 (*0-403-04342-5*) Somerset Pub.

Works, 18 Vols. Charles Darwin. LC 73-147085. reprint ed. 1,485.00 (*0-404-08400-1*) AMS Pr.

Works. William Drummond. (Anglistica & Americana Ser.: No. 60). xlviii, 303p. 1970. reprint ed. 76.70 (*0-685-66461-9*, 05102701) G Olms Pubs.

Works. Stefan George. LC 79-168108. (North Carolina. University. Studies in the Germanic Languages & Literatures: No. 2). reprint ed. 44.50 (*0-404-50902-9*) AMS Pr.

Works. Hugh Kelly. (Anglistica & Americana Ser.: No. 143). xix, 492p. 1973. reprint ed. 109.20 (*3-487-04853-1*) G Olms Pubs.

Works. Gabriel C. Rossetti. (Anglistica & Americana Ser.: No. 135). xxxvii, 684p. 1972. reprint ed. 122.20 (*3-487-04360-2*) G Olms Pubs.

Works, 7 Vols. William Shakespeare. Ed. by Lewis Theobald. LC 68-58620. reprint ed. 350.00 (*0-404-05790-X*) AMS Pr.

Works. William Shakespeare. Ed. by William G. Clark & William A. Wright. LC 69-18315. reprint ed. 95.00 (*0-404-05950-3*) AMS Pr.

Works. Edmund Spenser. (BCL1-PR English Literature Ser.). 562p. 1992. reprint ed. lib. bdg. 99.00 (*0-7812-7222-X*) Rprt Serv.

Works, 9 vols. in 11. Horace Walpole. Ed. by Robert Berry. (Anglistica & Americana Ser.: No. 157). (Illus.). 4900p. 1977. reprint ed. 1,092.00 (*3-487-05815-4*) G Olms Pubs.

Works, 7 vols., 1. Plotinus. (Loeb Classical Library: No. 440-445, & 468). 364p. 1966. text ed. 18.95 (*0-674-99484-1*) HUP.

Works, 2 vols., 1. Prudentius. (Loeb Classical Library: No. 387, 398). 15.50 (*0-674-99426-4*) HUP.

Works, 4 vols., 1. William Temple. LC 68-31006. (Illus.). 1970. reprint ed. lib. bdg. 24.50 (*0-8371-1775-5*, TEWA) Greenwood.

Works, 7 vols., 2. Plotinus. (Loeb Classical Library: No. 440-445, & 468). 312p. 1966. text ed. 18.95 (*0-674-99486-8*) HUP.

Works, 2 vols., 2. Prudentius. (Loeb Classical Library: No. 387, 398). 15.50 (*0-674-99438-8*) HUP.

Works, 4 vols., 2. William Temple. LC 68-31006. (Illus.). 1970. reprint ed. lib. bdg. 24.50 (*0-8371-0851-9*, TEWB) Greenwood.

Works, 7 vols., 3. Plotinus. (Loeb Classical Library: No. 440-445, & 468). 426p. 1967. text ed. 18.95 (*0-674-99487-6*) HUP.

Works, 4 vols., 3. William Temple. LC 68-31006. (Illus.). 1970. reprint ed. lib. bdg. 24.50 (*0-8371-0852-7*, TEWC) Greenwood.

Works, 7 vols., 4. Plotinus. (Loeb Classical Library: No. 440-445, & 468). 452p. 1967. text ed. 18.95 (*0-674-99488-4*) HUP.

Works, 4 vols., 4. William Temple. LC 68-31006. (Illus.). 1970. reprint ed. lib. bdg. 24.50 (*0-8371-0853-5*, TEWD) Greenwood.

Works, 7 vols., 5. Plotinus. (Loeb Classical Library: No. 440-445, & 468). 332p. 1967. text ed. 18.95 (*0-674-99489-2*) HUP.

Works, 7 vols., 6. Plotinus. (Loeb Classical Library: No. 440-445, & 468). 379p. 1988. text ed. 18.95 (*0-674-99490-6*) HUP.

Works, 7 vols., 7. Plotinus. (Loeb Classical Library: No. 440-445, & 468). 352p. 1988. text ed. 18.95 (*0-674-99515-5*) HUP.

Works, Pts. I-IV. David Lindsay. Ed. by J. Small & F. Hall. (EETS, OS Ser.: Nos. 11, 19, 35, 37). 1974. reprint ed. Pts. I-IV. 55.00 (*0-527-00013-2*) Periodicals Srv.

Works, 8 vols., Set. Incl. Vol. 1. Margaret Sanger, an Autobiography. Intro. by A. Guttmacher. 1938. 230.00 (*0-08-018730-7*); Vol. 2. Happiness in Marriage. Margaret Sanger. 1969. 113.00 (*0-08-018731-5*); Vol. 3. Motherhood in Bondage: Motherhood in Bondage. Margaret Sanger. 1956. 205.00 (*0-08-018732-3*); Vol. 4. My Fight for Birth Control. Margaret Sanger. 1959. 168.00 (*0-08-018733-1*); Vol. 5. New Motherhood. Margaret Sanger. 1922. 117.00 (*0-08-018734-X*); Vol. 6. Pivot of Civilization. Margaret Sanger. 1922. 136.00 (*0-08-018735-8*); Vol. 7. What Every Boy & Girl Should Know. Margaret Sanger. 1969. 74.00 (*0-08-018736-6*); Vol. 8. Woman & the New Race. Margaret Sanger. 1940. 114.00 (*0-08-018737-4*); 1976. reprint ed. 1,153.00 (*0-08-020244-6*, Pub. by Pergamon Repr UK) Franklin.

Works, 39 vols., Set. Hubert H. Bancroft. (BCL1 - United States Local History Ser.). 1991. reprint ed. lib. bdg. 3,510.00 (*0-7812-6334-4*) Rprt Serv.

Works, 3 vols, Set. Richard Bentley. Ed. by Alexander Dyce. LC 66-6448. reprint ed. 275.00 (*0-404-00760-0*) AMS Pr.

Works, 6 vols., Set. Thomas Browne. Ed. by Geoffrey L. Keynes. (BCL1-PR English Literature Ser.). 1992. reprint ed. lib. bdg. 540.00 (*0-7812-7323-4*) Rprt Serv.

Works, 12 vols. in 6, Set. Edmund E. Burke. (Anglistica & Americana Ser.: No. 155). 1975. reprint ed. 1,105.00 (*3-487-05619-4*) G Olms Pubs.

Works, 4 vols., Set. John C. Calhoun. (Works of John Calswell Calhoun Ser.). 1990. reprint ed. lib. bdg. 300.00 (*0-7812-2239-7*) Rprt Serv.

Works, 6 vols., Set. Isaac Disraeli. Ed. by Benjamin Disraeli. (Anglistica & Americana Ser.: No. 62). 1969. reprint ed. 323.70 (*0-685-66458-9*, 05102724) G Olms Pubs.

Works, 10 vols, Set. John Galt. Ed. by David S. Meldrum & William Roughead. LC 37-3805. reprint ed. 470.00 (*0-404-02700-8*) AMS Pr.

Works, 8 Vols, Set. Elizabeth C. Gaskell. Ed. by A. W. Ward. LC 70-148782. reprint ed. 540.00 (*0-404-07250-X*) AMS Pr.

Works, 25 vols., Set. Bret Harte. (BCL1-PS American Literature Ser.). 1992. reprint ed. lib. bdg. 2,250.00 (*0-7812-6719-6*) Rprt Serv.

Works, 7 vols., Set. William E. Henley. (BCL1-PR English Literature Ser.). 1992. reprint ed. lib. bdg. 630.00 (*0-7812-7558-X*) Rprt Serv.

Works, 8 vols, Set. Richard Hurd. reprint ed. 632.00 (*0-404-03470-5*) AMS Pr.

Works, 8 vols., Set. Richard Hurd. xciii, 3206p. 1969. reprint ed. write for info. (*3-487-05619-4*) G Olms Pubs.

Works, 14 vols., Set. Washington Irving. 1988. reprint ed. lib. bdg. 998.00 (*0-7812-0425-9*) Rprt Serv.

Works, 7 vols., Set. Vicesimus Knox. (Anglistica & Americana Ser.: No. 86). (Illus.). 1970. reprint ed. 583.70 (*0-685-66486-4*, 05102851) G Olms Pubs.

Works, 7 vols. in 5, Set. William Laud. (Anglistica & Americana Ser.: No. 168). 1977. reprint ed. 518.70 (*3-487-06277-1*) G Olms Pubs.

Works, 9 vols. in 3, Set. William Law. (Anglistica & Americana Ser.: No. 146). 1974. reprint ed. 323.70 (*3-487-05100-1*) G Olms Pubs.

Works, 10 Vols, Set. John Locke. 1963. reprint ed. 800.00 (*3-511-02600-8*) Adlers Foreign Bks.

Works, 14 vols., Set. Henry Wadsworth Longfellow. reprint ed. write for info. (*0-404-04040-3*) AMS Pr.

Works, 29 vols., Set. George Meredith. (BCL1-PR English Literature Ser.). 1992. reprint ed. lib. bdg. 2,610.00 (*0-7812-7593-8*) Rprt Serv.

Works, 8 vols., Set. Thomas Middleton. Ed. by A. H. Bullen. (BCL1-PR English Literature Ser.). 1992. reprint ed. lib. bdg. 720.00 (*0-7812-7264-5*) Rprt Serv.

Works, 20 vols., Set. Francis Parkman. LC 69-19160. (Illus.). reprint ed. 1,395.00 (*0-404-04920-6*) AMS Pr.

Works, 12 vols., Set. Francis Parkman. (BCL1 - History - Canada Ser.). 1991. reprint ed. lib. bdg. 1,060.00 (*0-7812-6353-0*) Rprt Serv.

Works, 10 vols, Set. Thomas L. Peacock. Ed. by H. B. Brett-Smith & C. E. Jones. LC 71-181967. reprint ed. 925.00 (*0-404-04970-2*) AMS Pr.

Works, 10 vols., Set. Thomas L. Peacock. (BCL1-PR English Literature Ser.). 1992. reprint ed. lib. bdg. 900.00 (*0-7812-7616-0*) Rprt Serv.

Works, 22 vols., Set. William H. Prescott. Ed. by Wilfred H. Munro et al. LC 69-16761. reprint ed. 1,250.00 (*0-404-05150-2*) AMS Pr.

Works, 39 vols., Set. John Ruskin. (BCL1-PR English Literature Ser.). 1992. reprint ed. lib. bdg. 3,510.00 (*0-7812-7632-2*) Rprt Serv.

Works, 50 vols., Set. Walter Scott. (BCL1-PR English Literature Ser.). 1992. reprint ed. lib. bdg. 4,500.00 (*0-7812-7639-X*) Rprt Serv.

Works, 9 Vols, Set. William Shakespeare. Ed. by William A. Wright et al. LC 68-59035. reprint ed. 425.00 (*0-404-05940-6*) AMS Pr.

Works, 3 vols, Set. Thomas Shepard. Ed. by John A. Albro. LC 49-1393. reprint ed. 165.00 (*0-404-05990-2*) AMS Pr.

Works, 3 vols., Set. Thomas Shepard. Ed. by John A. Albro. (Anglistica & Americana Ser.: No. 96). 1971. reprint ed. 193.70 (*0-685-66514-3*, 05103054) G Olms Pubs.

Works, 16 vols., Set. Clement K. Shorter. LC 24-5080. reprint ed. 1,224.00 (*0-404-00970-0*) AMS Pr.

Works, 20 vols., Set. William G. Simms. (BCL1-PS American Literature Ser.). 1992. reprint ed. lib. bdg. 1,800.00 (*0-7812-6855-9*) Rprt Serv.

Works, 21 Vols, Set. Herbert Spencer. 1966. reprint ed. 1,990.00 (*3-535-00480-2*) Adlers Foreign Bks.

Works, 26 vols., Set. Robert Louis Stevenson. (BCL1-PR English Literature Ser.). 1992. reprint ed. lib. bdg. 2,340.00 (*0-7812-7664-0*) Rprt Serv.

Works, 4 vols., Set. William Temple. LC 68-31006. (Illus.). 1970. reprint ed. text ed. 195.00 (*0-8371-0679-6*, TEWO) Greenwood.

Works, 7 vols., Set. William Warburton. Ed. by Richard Hurd. (Anglistica & Americana Ser.: No. 182). 1980. reprint ed. 897.00 (*3-487-06516-9*) G Olms Pubs.

Works, 28 vols., Set. H. G. Wells. (BCL1-PR English Literature Ser.). 1992. reprint ed. lib. bdg. 2,520.00 (*0-7812-7542-3*) Rprt Serv.

Works, 15 vols., Set. Oscar Wilde. (BCL1-PR English Literature Ser.). 1992. reprint ed. lib. bdg. 1,350.00 (*0-7812-7599-7*) Rprt Serv.

Works, 14 vols., Set. Israel Zangwill. LC 73-99252. reprint ed. 945.50 (*0-404-07080-9*) AMS Pr.

Works, Vol. I. Cyril of Jerusalem. Tr. by Leo P. McCauley & Anthony A. Stephenson. LC 68-55980. (Fathers of the Church Ser.: Vol. 61). 287p. 1969. 17.95 (*0-8132-0061-X*) Cath U Pr.

Works, Vol. 1. Incl. Hippolytus. (*0-318-53202-6*); Medea. (*0-318-53203-4*); Alcestis. (*0-318-53204-2*); Ion. (*0-318-53205-0*); Madness of Hercules. (*0-318-53206-9*); Children of Hercules. (*0-318-53207-7*); Phoenician Maidens. (*0-318-53208-5*); Suppliants. (*0-318-53209-3*); Bacchanals. (*0-318-53210-7*); Orestes. (*0-318-53211-5*); Iphigeneia in Taurica. (*0-318-53212-3*); Andromache. (*0-318-53213-1*); Cyclops. (*0-318-53214-X*); Electra. (*0-318-53215-8*); Rhesus. (*0-318-53216-6*); Hecuba. (*0-318-53217-4*); Daughters of Troy. (*0-318-53218-2*); Helen. (*0-318-53219-0*); Iphigeneia at Aulis. (*0-318-53220-4*); (Loeb Classical Library: No. 9). 15.50 (*0-674-99010-2*) HUP.

Works, Vol. II. Cyril of Jerusalem. Tr. by Leo P. McCauley & Anthony A. Stephenson. LC 68-55980. (Fathers of the Church Ser.: Vol. 64). 273p. 1970. 16.95 (*0-8132-0064-4*) Cath U Pr.

Works, Vol. 2. Incl. Hippolytus. (*0-318-53202-6*); Medea. (*0-318-53203-4*); Alcestis. (*0-318-53204-2*); Ion. (*0-318-53205-0*); Madness of Hercules. (*0-318-53206-9*); Children of Hercules. (*0-318-53207-7*); Phoenician Maidens. (*0-318-53208-5*); Suppliants. (*0-318-53209-3*); Bacchanals. (*0-318-53210-7*); Orestes. (*0-318-53211-5*); Iphigeneia in Taurica. (*0-318-53212-3*); Andromache. (*0-318-53213-1*); Cyclops. (*0-318-53214-X*); Electra. (*0-318-53215-8*); Rhesus. (*0-318-53216-6*); Hecuba. (*0-318-53217-4*); Daughters of Troy. (*0-318-53218-2*); Helen. (*0-318-53219-0*); Iphigeneia at Aulis. (*0-318-53220-4*); (Loeb Classical Library: No. 10). 15.50 (*0-674-99011-0*) HUP.

Works, Vol. 3. Donald Barthelme. pap. write for info. (*0-679-40984-X*) Random.

Works, Vol. 3. Incl. Hippolytus. (*0-318-53202-6*); Medea. (*0-318-53203-4*); Alcestis. (*0-318-53204-2*); Ion. (*0-318-53205-0*); Madness of Hercules. (*0-318-53206-9*); Children of Hercules. (*0-318-53207-7*); Phoenician Maidens. (*0-318-53208-5*); Suppliants. (*0-318-53209-3*); Bacchanals. (*0-318-53210-7*); Orestes. (*0-318-53211-5*); Iphigeneia in Taurica. (*0-318-53212-3*); Andromache. (*0-318-53213-1*); Cyclops. (*0-318-53214-X*); Electra. (*0-318-53215-8*); Rhesus. (*0-318-53216-6*); Hecuba. (*0-318-53217-4*); Daughters of Troy. (*0-318-53218-2*); Helen. (*0-318-53219-0*); Iphigeneia at Aulis. (*0-318-53220-4*); (Loeb Classical Library: No. 11). 15.50 (*0-674-99012-9*) HUP.

Works, Vol. 4. Incl. Hippolytus. (*0-318-53202-6*); Medea. (*0-318-53203-4*); Alcestis. (*0-318-53204-2*); Ion. (*0-318-53205-0*); Madness of Hercules. (*0-318-53206-9*); Children of Hercules. (*0-318-53207-7*); Phoenician Maidens. (*0-318-53208-5*); Suppliants. (*0-318-53209-3*); Bacchanals. (*0-318-53210-7*); Orestes. (*0-318-53211-5*); Iphigeneia in Taurica. (*0-318-53212-3*); Andromache. (*0-318-53213-1*); Cyclops. (*0-318-53214-X*); Electra. (*0-318-53215-8*); Rhesus. (*0-318-53216-6*); Hecuba. (*0-318-53217-4*); Daughters of Troy. (*0-318-53218-2*); Helen. (*0-318-53219-0*); Iphigeneia at Aulis. (*0-318-53220-4*); (Loeb Classical Library: No. 12). 15.50 (*0-674-99013-7*) HUP.

Works: A Quarterly of Writing, Vol. 1-4, No. 3. reprint ed. ring bd. 87.00 (*0-404-19564-4*) AMS Pr.

Works: And Other Smoky George Stories. Perry Brass. Ed. by Tom Laine. LC 92-71426. 160p. (Orig.). 1992. pap. 9.95 (*0-9627123-2-9*) Belhue Pr.

Works: And Other Smoky George Stories. 2nd expanded ed. Perry Brass. Ed. by Tom Laine. LC 96-83493. 192p. (Orig.). 1996. pap. 9.95 (*0-9627123-6-1*) Belhue Pr.

Works: Centenary Edition, 15 vols., Set. Theodore Parker. LC 75-3307. reprint ed. 595.00 (*0-404-59300-3*) AMS Pr.

Works: Consisting of: The Theory of Painting; Essay on the Art of Criticism, So Far As It Relates to Painting; The Science of a Connoisseur. Jonathan Richardson. (Anglistica & Americana Ser.: No. 37). xix, 346p. 1969. reprint ed. 76.70 (*0-685-66510-0*, 05102433) G Olms Pubs.

Works: Including Hermes, or a Philosophical Inquiry & Philological Inquiries, 3 vols., Set. James Harris. LC 72-147973. reprint ed. 210.00 (*0-404-08240-8*) AMS Pr.

Works: New Edition, 10 vols., Set. Alexander Pope. (BCL1-PR English Literature Ser.). 1992. reprint ed. lib. bdg. 900.00 (*0-7812-7392-7*) Rprt Serv.

Works: Photographs of Enterprise. Martin W. Kane & Christopher T. Baer. LC 91-78297. (Illus.). 95p. 1992. pap. 3.00 (*0-914650-29-7*) Hagley Museum.

Works: Photographs of Enterprise. Photos by Martin W. Kane. LC 91-78297. (Illus.). 96p. 1992. pap. 21.95 (*0-8122-1394-7*) U of Pa Pr.

Works: The Knutsford Edition, 8 vols. in 5, Set. Elizabeth C. Gaskell. (Anglistica & Americana Ser.: No. 147). (Illus.). 4750p. 1974. reprint ed. 648.70 (*3-487-05200-8*) G Olms Pubs.

Works: To Which Is Prefixed an Account of the Life & Writings of the Author, 2 vols., Set. Joshua Reynolds & Edmond Malone. (Anglistica & Americana Ser.: No. 129). 1971. reprint ed. 180.70 (*0-685-66509-7*, 05103014) G Olms Pubs.

Works: With Introductions by George Saintsbury, 18 Vols., Set. Honore De Balzac. LC 78-150468. (Short Story Index Reprint Ser.). reprint ed. 550.00 (*0-8369-3791-0*) Ayer.

Works: With Remarks on Each Play, & an Essay on the Life, Genius, & Writings of the Author, 3 vols. in 2, Set. Samuel Foote. (Anglistica & Americana Ser.: No. 145). 1973. reprint ed. 161.20 (*3-487-04894-9*) G Olms Pubs.

Works: With Some Account of His Life, 2 vols. in 1. George Lillo. (Anglistica & Americana Ser.: No. 140). xlviii, 610p. 1973. reprint ed. 102.70 (*3-487-04677-6*) G Olms Pubs.

Works Vol. 6: Batholomew Fair, The Devil Is an Ass, The Staple of News, The New Inn, The Magnetic Lady. Ben Jonson. Ed. by C. H. Herford. (Illus.). 610p. 1986. 110.00 (*0-19-811357-9*) OUP.

Works Vol. 9: An Historical Survey of the Texts, The Stage History of the Plays, Commentary on the Plays. Ben Jonson. Ed. by C. H. Herford. (Illus.). 748p. 1986. 100.00 (*0-19-811360-9*) OUP.

Works Vols. 1 & 2: Prose & Poetry, 2 vols., Set. Joel Barlow. LC 68-17012. 1970. 150.00 (*0-8201-1062-0*) Schol Facsimiles.

Works - One of Everything: Psychological Type & Temperament Training & Counseling Materials. Murray et al. 124p. 1990. 87.50 (*1-878287-17-6*) Type & Temperament.

Works - the New Shakespeare. William Shakespeare. (BCL1-PR English Literature Ser.). 1992. reprint ed. lib. bdg. 90.00 (*0-7812-7269-6*) Rprt Serv.

Works about John Dewey, 1886-1995. Compiled by Barbara Levine. 536p. (C). 1996. 49.95 (*0-8093-2056-8*); pap. 24.95 (*0-8093-2058-4*) S Ill U Pr.

***Works about John Dewey, 1886-1995.** Compiled by Barbara Levine. 536p. 1996. 79.95 incl. cd-rom (*0-8093-2063-0*) S Ill U Pr.

***Works about John Dewey, 1886-1995.** Compiled by Barbara Levine. 536p. 1996. pap. 59.95 incl. cd-rom (*0-8093-2064-9*) S Ill U Pr.

Works & Correspondence: Index, Vol. 11. David Ricardo. Ed. by P. Sraffa & Maurice H. Dobb. 146p. 1973. text ed. 69.95 (*0-521-20039-3*) Cambridge U Pr.

Works & Correspondence: Principles of Political Economy, Vol. 1. David Ricardo. Ed. by P. Sraffa. 437p. 1981. pap. text ed. 29.95 (*0-521-28505-4*) Cambridge U Pr.

***Works & Correspondence of David Ricardo Vol. 6: Letters, 1810-1815.** 418p. 1952. text ed. 69.95 (*0-521-06071-0*) Cambridge U Pr.

***Works and Correspondence of David Ricardo Vol. 7: Letters, 1816-1818.** 400p. 1952. text ed. 69.95 (*0-521-06072-9*) Cambridge U Pr.

***Works & Correspondence of David Ricardo Vol. 8: etters, 1819-June 1821.** 416p. 1952. text ed. 69.95 (*0-521-06073-7*) Cambridge U Pr.

***Works & Correspondence of David Ricardo Vol. 9: Letters, July 1821-1823.** 414p. 1952. text ed. 69.95 (*0-521-06074-5*) Cambridge U Pr.

***Works & Correspondence of David Ricardo Vol. 10: Biographical Miscellany.** 434p. 1955. text ed. 69.95 (*0-521-06075-3*) Cambridge U Pr.

Works & Criticism of Gerard Manley Hopkins: A Comprehensive Bibliography. Edward H. Cohen. LC 68-31683. reprint ed. pap. 58.50 (*0-685-17859-5*, 2029517) Bks Demand.

Works & Days. Hesiod. Ed. by W. R. Connor. LC 78-18606. (Greek Texts & Commentaries Ser.). 1979. reprint ed. lib. bdg. 24.95 (*0-405-11446-X*) Ayer.

Works & Days. Ed. by T. A. Sinclair. lxvi, 96p. 1985. reprint ed. 25.87 (*3-487-05414-0*) G Olms Pubs.

Works & Days: Theogony & the Shield of Herakles, 2 vols. Hesiod. Ed. by Richard Lattimore. 250p. 1991. pap. 12.95 (*0-472-08161-6*) U of Mich Pr.

Works & Days & Theogony. Hesiod. Tr. by Stanley Lombardo from GRE. LC 93-24370. (Hackett Classics Ser.). 160p. (Orig.) (C). 1993. pap. text ed. 6.95 (*0-87220-179-1*); lib. bdg. 27.95 (*0-87220-180-5*) Hackett Pub.

Works & Life of Christopher Marlowe, 6 Vols, Set. Christopher Marlowe. Ed. by R. H. Case. 1644p. 1966. reprint ed. 300.00 (*0-87752-067-4*) Gordian.

Works & Life of Thomas Browne, 4 Vols, Set. Thomas Browne. Ed. by Simon Wilkin. LC 68-57225. reprint ed. 365.00 (*0-404-01150-0*) AMS Pr.

Works & Lives: The Anthropologist As Author. Clifford Geertz. 167p. 1989. 32.50 (*0-8047-1428-2*); pap. 11.95 (*0-8047-1747-8*) Stanford U Pr.

Works & More. Max Beerbohm. LC 12-30603. 1896. 49.00 (*0-403-00144-7*) Scholarly.

Works & More. Max Beerbohm. 1988. reprint ed. lib. bdg. 79.00 (*0-7812-0152-7*) Rprt Serv.

Works, Annotated, 9 vols., Set. Alfred Tennyson. (BCL1-PR English Literature Ser.). 1992. reprint ed. lib. bdg. 810.00 (*0-7812-7689-6*) Rprt Serv.

Works Babbage, Vol. 1. Babbage. (C). 1989. 150.00 (*0-8147-1114-6*) NYU Pr.

Works Babbage, Vol. 2. Babbage. (C). 1989. 125.00 (*0-8147-1115-4*) NYU Pr.

Works Babbage, Vol. 3. Babbage. (C). 1989. 150.00 (*0-8147-1116-2*) NYU Pr.

Works Babbage, Vol. 4. Babbage. (C). 1989. 150.00 (*0-8147-1117-0*) NYU Pr.

Works Babbage, Vol. 5. Babbage. (C). 1989. 150.00 (*0-8147-1118-9*) NYU Pr.

Works Babbage, Vol. 6. Babbage. (C). 1989. 125.00 (*0-8147-1119-7*) NYU Pr.

Works Babbage, Vol. 7. Babbage. (C). 1989. 125.00 (*0-8147-1120-0*) NYU Pr.

Works Babbage, Vol. 8. Babbage. (C). 1989. 150.00 (*0-8147-1121-9*) NYU Pr.

Works Babbage, Vol. 9. Babbage. (C). 1989. 125.00 (*0-8147-1122-7*) NYU Pr.

Works Babbage, Vol. 10. Babbage. (C). 1989. 125.00 (*0-8147-1123-5*) NYU Pr.

Works Babbage, Vol. 11. Babbage. (C). 1989. 150.00 (*0-8147-1124-3*) NYU Pr.

***Works Big Healeys.** P. Browning. (Illus.). 200p. Date not set. 39.95 (*0-85429-966-1*, Pub. by G T Foulis Ltd) Haynes Pubns.

Works by Arthur B. Davies: From the Collection of Mr. & Mrs. Herbert Brill. John P. Driscoll. (Illus.). 36p. 1979. pap. 3.00 (*0-911209-15-8*) Palmer Mus Art.

Works by Fang Zhaoling. Hong Kong University Press Staff. (Illus.). 172p. (C). 1992. text ed. 150.00 (*962-209-283-7*, Pub. by Hong Kong U Pr HK) St Mut.

Works by Miguel de Cervantes Saavedra in the Library of Congress. Ed. by Georgette M. Dorn. LC 92-34038. 1993. write for info. (*0-8444-0768-2*) Lib Congress.

Works (DOS) Smartstart. 1994. teacher ed. 39.99 (*1-56529-506-4*) Que.

Works (DOS) Smartstart. 1993. 25.99 (*1-56529-396-7*) Que.

Works, Examined, Corrected & Published: By H. Holland. Richard Greenham. LC 72-5999. (English Experience Ser.: No. 524). 496p. 1973. reprint ed. 70.00 (*90-221-0524-5*) Walter J Johnson.

Works for Four Voices with Instruments Part 2. Dieterich Buxtehude. Ed. by Kerala Snyder. (Collected Works Ser.: Vol. 9). 1987. lib. bdg. 200.00 (*0-8450-7509-8*) Broude.

***Works for Library & Media Center Management: DOS & Windows Edition.** Janet N. Naumer & Glenda B. Thurman. LC 97-19924. (Illus.). 200p. (Orig.). 1997. pap. 32.50 (*1-56308-543-7*) Libs Unl.

***Works for Library & Media Center Management: Macintosh Edition.** Glenda B. Thurman & Janet N. Naumer. (Illus.). 200p. (Orig.). 1997. pap. 33.00 (*1-56308-297-7*) Libs Unl.

Works for Munich & Vienna. Ed. by Ernest Warburton. LC 92-33289. (Librettos of Mozart's Operas Ser.: Vol. 2). 424p. 1993. text ed. 95.00 (*0-8153-0109-X*) Garland.

Works for Piano Four Hands & Two Pianos. Wolfgang Amadeus Mozart. 1990. pap. 9.95 (*0-486-26501-3*) Dover.

Works for Salzburg & Milan. Ed. by Ernest Warburton. LC 92-33289. (Librettos of Mozart's Operas Ser.: Vol. 1). (Illus.). 360p. 1993. text ed. 70.00 (*0-8153-0108-1*) Garland.

Works for Violin: The Complete Sonatas & Partitas for Unaccompanied Violin & the Six Sonatas for Violin & Clavier. Johann Sebastian Bach. 1978. pap. 7.95 (*0-486-23683-8*) Dover.

Works for Windows: Smartstart. Jan Lindholm. 1994. 25.99 (*1-56529-394-0*) Que.

Works for Windows: Visual QuickStart Guide with Interactive Training Disk. Webster & Associates Staff. (Illus.). 210p. 1992. pap. 24.95 (*0-938151-83-5*) Peachpit Pr.

Works for Windows for Educators. James H. Wiebe et al. LC 96-1968. (Illus.). 400p. (Orig.). (C). 1995. pap. text ed. 21.95 (*0-938661-74-4*) Franklin Beedle.

Works for Windows Smartstart. 1994. teacher ed. 39.99 (*1-56529-504-8*) Que.

Works for Windows 3.0. DDC Publishing Staff. 1993. spiral bd. 12.00 (*1-56243-141-2*, OWKW3); disk 19.95 (*1-56243-171-4*, GR-WKW3) DDC Pub.

Works for Windows 95 Essentials. Suzanne Weixel. 1996. pap. text ed. 49.99 (*1-57576-020-7*) Que Educ & Trng.

***Works for Windows 95 Essentials.** 2nd ed. Que Education & Training Staff. 1997. teacher ed. 39.99 (*1-57576-876-3*) Que Educ & Trng.

Works for Windows 95 Virtual Tutor. Que Education & Training Staff. 1996. pap. text ed. 49.99 (*1-57576-113-0*) Que Educ & Trng.

Works, Fourteen Sixty to Fourteen Ninety. Peter Schott. Ed. by Murray A. Cowie & Marian L. Cowie. LC 63-63888. (North Carolina. University. Studies in the Germanic Languages & Literatures: No. 41). reprint ed. 39.00 (*0-404-50941-X*) AMS Pr.

Works from the Collection of Dorothy & Herbert Vogel. Bret Waller. (Illus.). 59p. 1977. pap. 3.00 (*0-912303-14-X*) Michigan Mus.

Works in African History: An Index to Reviews, 1978-1982. Ed. by David Henige. (Archival & Bibliographic Ser.). 1984. pap. 10.00 (*0-918456-49-5*) African Studies Assn.

Works in Architecture of John Carr: York Georgian Society. Sessions, William Ltd., Staff. (C). 1988. 30.00 (*0-900657-19-7*, Pub. by W Sessions UK) St Mut.

Works in Architecture of Robert & James Adam. Ed. by Robert Oresko. (Academy Architecture Ser.). (Illus.). 184p. 1982. pap. 19.95 (*0-312-88954-2*) St Martin.

Works in Architecture of Robert & James Adam, 3 vols. in 1. Robert Adam. LC 78-67644. (Scottish Enlightenment Ser.). reprint ed. 245.00 (*0-404-17233-4*) AMS Pr.

Works in Five Volumes. Mykola Khvylovy. Ed. by H. Kostiuk. Incl. Vol. 1. . LC 77-66383. 438p. 15.00 (*0-914834-14-2*); Vol. 2. . LC 77-66383. 409p. 15.00 (*0-914834-19-3*); Vol. 3. . LC 77-66383. 505p. 1982. 20.00 (*0-685-42984-9*); Vol. 4. . LC 77-66383. 662p. 25.00 (*0-914834-21-5*); Vol. 5. . LC 77-66383. 834p. 1985. 30.00 (*0-914834-22-3*); LC 77-66383. write for info. (*0-914834-20-7*) Smoloskyp.

Works in Progress. Alvin Rosenbaum. LC 94-7912. (Illus.). 208p. 1994. 45.00 (*0-87654-069-8*) Pomegranate Calif.

Works in Progress, Vol. 1. Michael P. Jones. (Works in Progress Ser.). (Illus.). 16p. (J). 1984. pap. text ed. 1.60 (*0-89904-075-6*) Crumb Elbow Pub.

W

An Asterisk (*) at the beginning of an entry indicates that the title is appearing in BIP for the first time.

Works in Progress: Student Essays for Developing Writers. Janice Poley Rowan & Eileen Master. 96p. (C). 1996. per. 12.54 (*0-8403-9010-6*) Kendall-Hunt.

Works in Verse & Prose, 2 vols., Set. Nicholas Breton. (BCL1-PR English Literature Ser.). 1992. reprint ed. lib. bdg. 150.00 (*0-7812-7193-2*) Rprt Serv.

Works in Verse & Prose, 3 vols., Set. John Davies. (BCL1-PR English Literature Ser.). 1992. reprint ed. lib. bdg. 270.00 (*0-7812-7197-5*) Rprt Serv.

Works in Verse & Prose Complete, 4 vols., Set. Fulke G. Brooke. (BCL1-PR English Literature Ser.). 1992. reprint ed. lib. bdg. 360.00 (*0-7812-7195-9*) Rprt Serv.

Works in Verse & Prose Complete of Henry Vaughan, Silurist, 4 vols., Set. Henry Vaughan. LC 73-21067. (Fuller Worthies' Library). reprint ed. 306.00 (*0-404-11493-8*) AMS Pr.

Works in Verse & Prose Complete of the Right Honourable Fulke Greville, 4 vols., Set. Fulke G. Brooke. LC 79-181918. (Fuller Worthies' Library). reprint ed. 306.00 (*0-404-02940-X*) AMS Pr.

Works in Verse & Prose of Nicholas Breton see Chertsey Worthies Library

Works in Wrought Iron: From Middle Ages to the Renaissance "Serrurerie" J. H. Hefner. (Illus.). 200p. (FRE.). 1993. reprint ed. pap. 35.00 (*0-87556-815-7*) Saifer.

Works Mac Smartstart. 1994. teacher ed. 39.99 (*1-56529-505-6*) Que.

Works Mac Smartstart. Gregory G. Schultz. 1994. 25.99 (*1-56529-395-9*) Que.

Works Manager to-Day. Sidney Webb. LC 73-148906. (Select Bibliographies Reprint Ser.). 1977. reprint ed. 19.95 (*0-8369-5669-9*) Ayer.

Works Minis: The International History of Competition Minis. Peter Browning. (Illus.). 224p. 1996. 44.95 (*0-85429-967-X*, Pub. by J H Haynes & Co UK) Motorbooks Intl.

Works Of: Charles Dickens. Charles Dickens. 797p. 1995. pap. write for info. (*1-57215-128-5*) World Pubns.

Works Of: D. H. Lawrence. D. H. Lawrence. 800p. 1995. pap. write for info. (*1-57215-127-7*) World Pubns.

Works Of: Jane Austen. Jane Austen. 882p. 1995. pap. write for info. (*1-57215-131-5*) World Pubns.

Works Of: Oscar Wilde. Ed. by Neil Wenborn. 592p. 1995. write for info. (*1-57215-182-X*) World Pubns.

Works Of: Oscar Wilde. Oscar Wilde. 857p. 1995. pap. write for info. (*1-57215-132-3*) World Pubns.

Works Of: The Brontes. Charlotte Bronte & Emily Bronte. 703p. 1995. pap. write for info. (*1-57215-130-7*) World Pubns.

Works Of: Thomas Hardy. Thomas Hardy. 724p. 1995. pap. write for info. (*1-57215-129-3*) World Pubns.

Works of Abigail (Smith) Adams, 1744-1818. Abigail S. Adams. 1989. reprint ed. 600.00 (*0-685-18682-2*) Rprt Serv.

Works of Alan Hovhaness: A Catalog Opus 1-Opus 360. Richard Howard. (General Music Ser.: Ams-1). (Illus.). 28p. (Orig.). 1983. pap. 4.00 (*0-912483-00-8*) Pro-Am Music.

Works of Aleister Crowley, 4 vols., Set. Aleister Crowley. 1986. lib. bdg. 1,500.00 (*0-87968-130-6*) Gordon Pr.

Works of Alexander Agassiz, 1837-1910. Alexander Agassiz. 1987. reprint ed. lib. bdg. 600.00 (*0-685-18567-2*) Rprt Serv.

Works of Alexander Hamilton, 12 Vols. Alexander Hamilton. Ed. by Henry C. Lodge. LC 68-24980. (American History & Americana Ser.: No. 47). 1969. reprint ed. lib. bdg. 450.00 (*0-8383-0160-6*) M S G Haskell Hse.

Works of Alexander Hamilton, 12 vols., Set. Alexander Hamilton. 1987. reprint ed. lib. bdg. 1,080.00 (*0-317-60364-7*) Rprt Serv.

Works of Alexander Pope, 10 Vols, Set. Alexander Pope. Ed. by John W. Croker et al. LC 66-29708. 5462p. 1967. reprint ed. 600.00 (*0-87752-087-9*) Gordian.

Works of Alfred Lord Tennyson: Annotated, 9 Vols, Set. Hallam T. Tennyson. LC 76-120197. reprint ed. 695.00 (*0-404-06370-5*) AMS Pr.

Works of Alfred the Great, 2 vols., Set. Alfred the Great. 1977. lib. bdg. 250.00 (*0-8490-2843-4*) Gordon Pr.

Works of Alice Dunbar-Nelson. Alice Dunbar-Nelson. Ed. by Gloria T. Hull. (Schomburg Library of Nineteenth-Century Black Women Writers). (Illus.). 472p. 1994. reprint ed. pap. 12.95 (*0-19-509055-1*) OUP.

Works of Alice Dunbar-Nelson, Vol. 1. Alice Dunbar-Nelson. Ed. by Gloria T. Hull. (Schomburg Library of Nineteenth-Century Black Women Writers). 480p. 1988. 32.00 (*0-19-505250-1*) OUP.

Works of Alice Dunbar-Nelson, Vol. 2. Alice Dunbar-Nelson. Ed. by Gloria T. Hull. (Schomburg Library of Nineteenth-Century Black Women Writers). 384p. 1988. 32.00 (*0-19-505251-X*) OUP.

Works of Alice Dunbar-Nelson, Vol. 3. Alice Dunbar-Nelson. Ed. by Gloria T. Hull. (Schomburg Library of Nineteenth-Century Black Women Writers). 352p. 1988. 32.00 (*0-19-505252-8*) OUP.

Works of Allen Ginsberg, 1941-1994: A Descriptive Bibliography. Bill Morgan. LC 94-41266. (Bibliographies & Indexes in American Literature Ser.: Vol. 19). 480p. 1995. text ed. 75.00 (*0-313-29389-9*, Greenwood Pr) Greenwood.

Works of Ambrose Gwinett Bierce, Set. Ambrose G. Bierce. 1989. reprint ed. lib. bdg. 79.00 (*0-7812-1969-8*) Rprt Serv.

Works of Anatole France, 40 vols. Anatole France. 1975. 2,700.00 (*0-8490-1329-1*) Gordon Pr.

Works of Andrew Gray. Andrew Gray. 499p. 1992. reprint ed. 27.95 (*1-877611-51-4*) Soli Deo Gloria.

Works of Anne Bradstreet. Anne Bradstreet & Jeannie Hensley. LC 67-17312. (John Harvard Library). 368p. 1981. pap. 16.50 (*0-674-95999-X*) Belknap Pr.

Works of Anne Bradstreet in Prose & Verse. Anne D. Bradstreet. 1976. reprint ed. 69.00 (*0-403-08995-6*, Regency) Scholarly.

Works of Anne Frank. Anne Frank. LC 73-16643. (Illus.). 332p. 1974. reprint ed. text ed. 55.00 (*0-8371-7206-3*, FRWO, Greenwood Pr) Greenwood.

Works of Aphra Behn, 6 vols., 1. Aphra A. Behn. Ed. by Montague Summers. LC 67-22243. 1972. reprint ed. 30.95 (*0-405-08254-1*, Pub. by Blom Pubns UK) Ayer.

Works of Aphra Behn, 6 vols., 2. Aphra A. Behn. Ed. by Montague Summers. LC 67-22243. 1972. reprint ed. 30.95 (*0-405-08255-X*, Pub. by Blom Pubns UK) Ayer.

Works of Aphra Behn, 6 vols., 3. Aphra A. Behn. Ed. by Montague Summers. LC 67-22243. 1972. reprint ed. 30.95 (*0-405-08256-8*, Pub. by Blom Pubns UK) Ayer.

Works of Aphra Behn, 6 vols., 4. Aphra A. Behn. Ed. by Montague Summers. LC 67-22243. 1972. reprint ed. 30.95 (*0-405-08257-6*, Pub. by Blom Pubns UK) Ayer.

Works of Aphra Behn, 6 vols., 5. Aphra A. Behn. Ed. by Montague Summers. LC 67-22243. 1972. reprint ed. 30.95 (*0-405-08258-4*, Pub. by Blom Pubns UK) Ayer.

Works of Aphra Behn, 6 vols., 6. Aphra A. Behn. Ed. by Montague Summers. LC 67-22243. 1972. reprint ed. 30.95 (*0-405-08259-2*, Pub. by Blom Pubns UK) Ayer.

Works of Aphra Behn, 6 vols., Set. Aphra A. Behn. (BCL1-PR English Literature Ser.). 1992. reprint ed. lib. bdg. 450.00 (*0-7812-7319-6*) Rprt Serv.

Works of Aphra Behn, 6 vols., Set. Aphra A. Behn. Ed. by Montague Summers. LC 67-22243. 1967. reprint ed. 179.95 (*0-405-08253-3*, Pub. by Blom Pubns UK) Ayer.

Works of Aphra Behn, 6 vols., Set. Aphra A. Behn. Ed. by Montague Summers. LC 67-24964. 2916p. 1967. reprint ed. 400.00 (*0-87753-004-1*) Phaeton.

Works of Apostolic Fathers, 2 vols. Apostolic Fathers. Incl. Vol. 1. Clement, Ignatius, Polycarp, Didache, Barnabas. 420p. 1912. 18.95 (*0-674-99027-7*); Vol. 2. Shepherd of Hermas, Martyrdom of Polycarp, Epistle to Diognetus. 402p. 1913. 18.95 (*0-674-99028-5*); (Loeb Classical Library: Nos. 24-25). write for info. (*0-318-53223-9*) HUP.

Works of Aristotle: The Famous Philosopher. LC 73-20613. (Sex, Marriage & Society Ser.). (Illus.). 268p. 1974. reprint ed. 23.95 (*0-405-05792-X*) Ayer.

Works of Arminius, 3 vols. 720p. 1986. 75.00 (*0-8341-1126-8*) Beacon Hill.

Works of Arthur B. Davies. Joseph S. Czestochowski. LC 79-11546. (Illus.). 110p. 1980. lib. bdg. 90.00 (*0-226-68946-8*) U Ch Pr.

Works of Asher Benjamin: Boston, 1806-1843, 7 vols. Asher Benjamin. Incl. Country Builder's Assistant: 1797. 84p. 1974. 45.00 (*0-306-71027-7*); American Builder's Companion: 1806. 158p. 1974. 45.00 (*0-306-71026-9*); Rudiments of Architecture: 1814. 162p. 1974. 45.00 (*0-306-71031-5*); Practical House Carpenter: 1830. 248p. 1974. 45.00 (*0-306-71029-3*); Practice of Architecture: 1833. 236p. 1974. 45.00 (*0-306-71030-7*); Builder's Guide: 1839. 174p. 1974. 47.50 (*0-306-70971-6*); Elements of Architecture: 1843. 290p. 1974. 47.50 (*0-306-71028-5*); (Architecture & Decorative Art Ser.). 1974. write for info. (*0-318-51603-9*) Da Capo.

Works of Asher Benjamin: Boston, 1806-1843, 7 vols., Set. Asher Benjamin. Incl. Country Builder's Assistant: 1797. 84p. 1974. 45.00 (*0-306-71027-7*); American Builder's Companion: 1806. 158p. 1974. 45.00 (*0-306-71026-9*); Rudiments of Architecture: 1814. 162p. 1974. 45.00 (*0-306-71031-5*); Practical House Carpenter: 1830. 248p. 1974. 45.00 (*0-306-71029-3*); Practice of Architecture: 1833. 236p. 1974. 45.00 (*0-306-71030-7*); Builder's Guide: 1839. 174p. 1974. 47.50 (*0-306-70971-6*); Elements of Architecture: 1843. 290p. 1974. 47.50 (*0-306-71028-5*); (Architecture & Decorative Art Ser.). 1974. 285.00 (*0-306-71032-3*) Da Capo.

Works of Ausonius. Decimus M. Ausonius. 840p. 1991. 200.00 (*0-19-814463-6*) OUP.

Works of B. Neustadt from 1939-1993. Barbara Neustadt. Ed. by Kay Kipling. LC 95-74960. (Illus.). 160p. 1996. text ed. 45.00 (*0-9616152-1-4*) Pleiades-Studio Graphics.

Works of Beaumont & Fletcher, 11 Vols, Set. Francis Beaumont & John Fletcher. LC 74-119953. (Select Bibliographies Reprint Ser.). 1977. 357.95 (*0-8369-5396-7*) Ayer.

Works of Benedetto & Alessandro Marcello: A Thematic Catalogue. Eleanor Selfridge-Field. (Illus.). 536p. 1990. 140.00 (*0-19-316126-5*) OUP.

Works of Benjamin Disraeli, 20 vols., Set. Benjamin Disraeli. Incl. Vols. 1-2. Vivian Grey: A Romance of Youth. LC 76-148746. 76.00 (*0-404-08801-5*); Vols. 3-4. Young Duke, etc. LC 76-148746. 76.00 (*0-404-08804-X*); Vol. 5. Contarini Fleming: A Psychological Romance, etc. LC 76-148746. 76.00 (*0-404-08805-8*); Vol. 7. Alroy: Or, the Prince of the Captivity. LC 76-148746. 76.00 (*0-404-08807-4*); Vol. 8. Henrietta Temple: A Love Story, etc. LC 76-148746. 76.00 (*0-404-08808-2*); Vols. 10-11. Venetia, etc. LC 76-148746. 76.00 (*0-404-08810-4*); Vol. 12. Coningsby: Or, the New Generation & Selected Speeches. LC 76-148746. 76.00 (*0-404-08812-0*); Vol. 17. Lothair & Letters to His Sister. LC 76-148746. 76.00 (*0-404-08817-1*); Vol. 19. Endymion, Miscellania. LC 76-148746. 76.00 (*0-404-08819-8*); Vol. 14. Sybil: Tancred. LC 76-148746. 76.00 (*0-404-08814-7*); Vol. 9. Henrietta Temple: A Love Story, etc. 76.00 (*0-404-08809-0*); Vol. 13. Coningsby: Or, the New Generation & Selected Speeches. 76.00 (*0-404-08813-9*); Vol. 18. Lothair & Letters to His Sister. 76.00 (*0-404-08818-X*); Vol. 20. Endymion, Miscellania. 76.00 (*0-404-08820-1*); Vol. 15. Sybil: Tancred. 76.00 (*0-404-08815-5*); LC 76-148746. (Illus.). 1904. reprint ed. 1,530.00 (*0-404-08800-7*) AMS Pr.

Works of Benjamin Parke Avery, 1828-1875. Benjamin A. Avery. Bd. with California in Prose & Verse. 1987. reprint ed. 79.00 (*0-685-18610-5*) Rprt Serv.

Works of Bishop Joseph Hall, 10 Vols, Set. Joseph Hall. Ed. by P. Wynter. LC 76-86830. reprint ed. 375.00 (*0-404-03070-X*) AMS Pr.

Works of Brooks Adams, 5 vols., Set. Brooks Adams. (Principle Works of Brooks Adams). 1989. reprint ed. lib. bdg. 79.00 (*0-685-27361-X*) Rprt Serv.

Works of Cadwallader Colden. Cadwallader Colden. 1990. reprint ed. lib. bdg. 79.00 (*0-685-27667-8*) Rprt Serv.

Works of Captain Alexander Radcliffe. Alexander Radcliffe. LC 81-9003. 1981. reprint ed. 50.00 (*0-8201-1365-4*) Schol Facsimiles.

Works of Charles & Mary Lamb, Set. Charles Lamb & Mary Lamb. Ed. by E. V. Lucas. LC 68-59332. (Illus.). reprint ed. write for info. (*0-404-03830-1*) AMS Pr.

Works of Charles & Mary Lamb, 7 vols., Set. Charles Lamb. (BCL1-PR English Literature Ser.). 1992. reprint ed. lib. bdg. 630.00 (*0-7812-7584-9*) Rprt Serv.

Works of Charles & Mary Lamb, 7 vols., Set. Charles Lamb & Mary Lamb. Ed. by E. V. Lucas. LC 70-115252. 1905. reprint ed. 450.00 (*0-403-00366-0*) Scholarly.

Works of Charles Anthon, 1797-1867, Set. Charles Anthon. 1987. reprint ed. lib. bdg. 600.00 (*0-685-18598-2*) Rprt Serv.

Works of Charles Babbage, 11 vols., Set. Charles Babbage. Ed. by Martin Campbell-Kelly. 2160p. (C). 1989. 675.00 (*0-8147-1113-8*) NYU Pr.

Works of Charles Darwin, 29 vols., Set. Charles Darwin. Ed. by Paul H. Barrett & R. B. Freeman. (Illus.). (C). 1990. text ed. 2,595.00 (*0-8147-1830-2*) NYU Pr.

Works of Charles Darwin: Charles Darwin's Diary of the Voyage of H. M. S. Beagle, Vol. I. Ed. by Paul H. Barrett & R. B. Freeman. (Illus.). 464p. (C). 1987. 95.00 (*0-8147-1796-9*) NYU Pr.

Works of Charles Darwin: Geological Observations on South America, Vol. IX. Ed. by Paul H. Barrett & R. B. Freeman. (Illus.). 360p. (C). 1987. 95.00 (*0-8147-1794-2*) NYU Pr.

Works of Charles Darwin: Geological Observations on the Volcanic Island Visited During the Voyage of H. M. S. Beagle (1844), Vol. VIII. Ed. by Paul H. Barrett & R. B. Freeman. (Illus.). 168p. (C). 1987. 95.00 (*0-8147-1793-4*) NYU Pr.

Works of Charles Darwin: Journal of Researches into the Geology & Natural History of the Various Countries Visited by H. M. S. Beagle, Vol. II, Pt. I. Ed. by Paul H. Barrett & R. B. Freeman. (Illus.). 256p. (C). 1987. 95.00 (*0-8147-1787-X*) NYU Pr.

Works of Charles Darwin: Journal of Researches into the Geology & Natural History of the Various Countries Visited by H. M. S. Beagle, Vol. III, Pt. 2. Ed. by Paul H. Barrett & R. B. Freeman. (Illus.). 264p. (C). 1987. 95.00 (*0-8147-1788-8*) NYU Pr.

Works of Charles Darwin: Subset, 10 vols., Set. Charles Darwin. Ed. by Paul H. Barrett & R. B. Freeman. (C). 1987. 895.00 (*0-8147-1799-3*) NYU Pr.

Works of Charles Darwin: Subset, 10 vols., Set. Charles Darwin. Ed. by Paul H. Barrett & R. B. Freeman. (C). 1989. 895.00 (*0-8147-1810-8*) NYU Pr.

Works of Charles Darwin: Subset, 9 vols., Set. Charles Darwin. Ed. by Paul H. Barrett & R. B. Freeman. (C). 1990. 855.00 (*0-8147-1831-0*) NYU Pr.

Works of Charles Darwin: The Foundations of the Origin of the Species, Two Essays Written in 1842 & 1844, Vol. X. Ed. by Frances Darwin et al. 240p. (C). 1987. 95.00 (*0-8147-1795-0*) NYU Pr.

Works of Charles Darwin: The Structure & Distribution of Coral Reefs, Vol. VII. 3rd ed. Ed. by Paul H. Barrett & R. B. Freeman. (Illus.). 256p. (C). 1987. 95.00 (*0-8147-1792-6*) NYU Pr.

Works of Charles Darwin: The Variation of Animals & Plants (Vol. 2), Vol. 20. Ed. by Peter Gautrey. (Illus.). (C). 1989. 95.00 (*0-8147-1809-4*) NYU Pr.

Works of Charles Darwin: The Zoology of the Voyage of H. M. S. Beagle, under the Command of Captain Fitzroy, During the Years 1832-1836, Vol. IV, Pts. I & II. Ed. by Paul H. Barrett & R. B. Freeman. (Illus.). 264p. (C). 1987. 95.00 (*0-8147-1789-6*) NYU Pr.

Works of Charles Darwin: The Zoology of the Voyage of H. M. S. Beagle, under the Command of Captain Fitzroy, During the Years 1832-1836, Vol. V, Pt. III. Ed. by Paul H. Barrett & R. B. Freeman. (Illus.). 264p. (C). 1987. 95.00 (*0-8147-1790-X*) NYU Pr.

Works of Charles Darwin: The Zoology of the Voyage of H. M. S. Beagle, under the Command of Captain Fitzroy, During the Years 1832-1836, Vol. VI, Pt. IV & V. Ed. by Paul H. Barrett & R. B. Freeman. (Illus.). 376p. (C). 1987. 95.00 (*0-8147-1791-8*) NYU Pr.

Works of Charles Darwin Vol. 21: The Descent of Man, & Selection in Relation to Sex, Vol. 1. 2nd ed. Charles Darwin. Ed. by Paul H. Barrett & R. B. Freeman. (C). 1990. 95.00 (*0-8147-1819-1*) NYU Pr.

Works of Charles Darwin Vol. 22: The Descent of Man, & Selection in Relation to Sex, Vol. 2. 2nd ed. Charles Darwin. Ed. by Paul H. Barrett & R. B. Freeman. (C). 1989. 95.00 (*0-8147-1820-5*) NYU Pr.

Works of Charles Darwin Vol. 23: The Expression of the Emotions in Man & Animals. 2nd ed. Charles Darwin. Ed. by Paul H. Barrett & R. B. Freeman. (C). 1990. 95.00 (*0-8147-1821-3*) NYU Pr.

Works of Charles Darwin Vol. 24: Insectivorous Plants. 2nd ed. Ed. by Paul H. Barrett & R. B. Freeman. (C). 1990. 95.00 (*0-8147-1822-1*) NYU Pr.

Works of Charles Darwin Vol. 25: The Effects of Cross & Self Fertilization in the Vegetable Kingdom. 2nd ed. Ed. by Paul H. Barrett & R. B. Freeman. (C). 1990. 95.00 (*0-8147-1823-X*) NYU Pr.

Works of Charles Darwin Vol. 26: The Different Forms of Flowers on Plants of the Same Species. 2nd ed. Ed. by Paul H. Barrett & R. B. Freeman. (C). 1990. 95.00 (*0-8147-1824-8*) NYU Pr.

Works of Charles Darwin Vol. 27: The Power of Movement in Plants. Ed. by Paul H. Barrett & R. B. Freeman. (C). 1990. 95.00 (*0-8147-1825-6*) NYU Pr.

Works of Charles Darwin Vol. 28: The Formation of Vegetable Mould, Through the Action of Worms, with Observations on Their Habits. Ed. by Paul H. Barrett & R. B. Freeman. (C). 1990. 95.00 (*0-8147-1826-4*) NYU Pr.

Works of Charles Darwin Vol. 29: Erasmus Darwin, the Autobiography of Charles Darwin. Ed. by Paul H. Barrett & R. B. Freeman. (C). 1990. 95.00 (*0-8147-1827-2*) NYU Pr.

Works of Charles Darwin Vols. 11-19, 20 vols., 11. Charles Darwin. Ed. by Peter Gautrey. (Illus.). (C). 1989. 95.00 (*0-8147-1800-0*) NYU Pr.

Works of Charles Darwin Vols. 11-19, 20 vols., 12. Ed. by Peter Gautrey. (Illus.). (C). 1989. 95.00 (*0-8147-1801-9*) NYU Pr.

Works of Charles Darwin Vols. 11-19, 20 vols., 13. Ed. by Peter Gautrey. (Illus.). (C). 1989. 95.00 (*0-8147-1802-7*) NYU Pr.

Works of Charles Darwin Vols. 11-19, 20 vols., 14. Ed. by Peter Gautrey. (Illus.). (C). 1989. 95.00 (*0-8147-1803-5*) NYU Pr.

Works of Charles Darwin Vols. 11-19, 20 vols., 15. Ed. by Peter Gautrey. (Illus.). (C). 1989. 95.00 (*0-8147-1804-3*) NYU Pr.

Works of Charles Darwin Vols. 11-19, 20 vols., 16. Ed. by Peter Gautrey. (Illus.). (C). 1989. 95.00 (*0-8147-1805-1*) NYU Pr.

Works of Charles Darwin Vols. 11-19, 20 vols., 17. Ed. by Peter Gautrey. (Illus.). (C). 1989. 95.00 (*0-8147-1806-X*) NYU Pr.

Works of Charles Darwin Vols. 11-19, 20 vols., 18. Ed. by Peter Gautrey. (Illus.). (C). 1989. 95.00 (*0-8147-1807-8*) NYU Pr.

Works of Charles Darwin Vols. 11-19, 20 vols., 19. Ed. by Peter Gautrey. (Illus.). (C). 1989. 95.00 (*0-8147-1808-6*) NYU Pr.

Works of Charles Dickens. Charles Dickens. 1990. 16.99 (*0-517-05360-8*) Random Hse Value.

Works of Charles Follen Adams, 1842-1918, Set. Charles F. Adams. 1989. reprint ed. lib. bdg. 600.00 (*0-685-18559-1*) Rprt Serv.

Works of Charles Francis Adams Jr., 1835-1915, Set. Charles F. Adams, Jr. 1987. reprint ed. lib. bdg. 800.00 (*0-685-18560-5*) Rprt Serv.

Works of Charles Kendall Adams, 1835-1902, Set. Charles K. Adams. 1987. reprint ed. lib. bdg. 800.00 (*0-685-18561-3*) Rprt Serv.

Works of Charles Kingsley, 28 vols., Set. Charles Kingsley. 10200p. 1969. reprint ed. lib. bdg. 1,482.00 (*0-685-13780-5*, 05102156) G Olms Pubs.

Works of Charles Reade, 17 Vols, Set. Charles Reade. LC 73-118070. reprint ed. 1,487.50 (*0-404-05260-6*) AMS Pr.

Works of Charles T. Griffes: A Descriptive Catalogue. Donna K. Anderson. LC 83-4983. (Studies in Musicology: No. 68). (Illus.). 588p. reprint ed. pap. 167.60 (*0-8357-1419-5*, 2070335) Bks Demand.

Works Of Christopher Love, Volume1. Christopher Love. 676p. 1995. 40.00 (*1-57358-007-4*) Soli Deo Gloria.

Works of Colonel John Trumbull: Artist of the American Revolution. rev. ed. Theodore Sizer. LC 67-20337. (Illus.). 381p. reprint ed. pap. 108.60 (*0-317-10479-9*, 2016795) Bks Demand.

Works of Daniel Lagache: Selected Papers, 1938-1964. Daniel Lagache. Tr. by Elisabeth Holder. 446p. 1994. pap. text ed. 54.95 (*0-946439-89-3*, Pub. by Karnac Bks UK) Brunner-Mazel.

Works of Daniel Waterland, 11 Vols, Set. Daniel Waterland. Ed. by William Von Mildert. reprint ed. 215.00 (*0-404-06860-X*) AMS Pr.

Works of David Clarkson, 3 vols., Set, Vol. 1, 544p, Vol. 2, 544p, Vol. 3, 516p. 1988. reprint ed. Set, Vol. 1: 544p., Vol. 2: 544p., Vol. 3: 516p. 79.99 (*0-85151-529-0*) Banner of Truth.

Works of David Everett. David Everett. LC 82-3390. 1983. 75.00 (*0-8201-1378-6*) Schol Facsimiles.

Works of David Mallet, 3 Vols, Set. David Mallet. LC 74-144567. reprint ed. 165.00 (*0-404-08580-6*) AMS Pr.

Works of E. L. Henry: Recollections of a Time Gone by. Norton, R. W., Art Gallery Staff. (Illus.). 56p. 1987. pap. 12.00 (*0-913060-26-7*) Norton Art.

Works of Edgar Allan Poe. Edgar Allan Poe. 1990. 16.99 (*0-517-05358-6*) Random Hse Value.

Works of Edgar Allan Poe, 10 vols, Set. Edgar Allan Poe. Ed. by Edmund C. Stedman & George E. Woodberry. LC 71-169773. (Select Bibliographies Reprint Ser.). reprint ed. 250.00 (*0-8369-5993-0*) Ayer.

Works of Edgar Allan Poe: With a Study of His Life & Writings by Charles Baudelaire. Edgar Allan Poe. Tr. by H. Curwen. LC 77-11472. reprint ed. 42.50 (*0-404-16334-3*) AMS Pr.

Works of Edmund Burke, 12 vols., Set. Edmund E. Burke. 1987. reprint ed. lib. bdg. 895.00 (*0-7812-0439-9*) Rprt Serv.

Works of Edmund Spencer. R. Morris. 1988. reprint ed. lib. bdg. 99.00 (*0-7812-0237-X*) Rprt Serv.

Works of Edmund Spenser, 6 Vols, Set. Edmund Spenser. Ed. by John Hughes. LC 79-175998. reprint ed. 450.00 (*0-404-06200-8*) AMS Pr.

Works of Edmund Spenser: A Variorum Edition, 2 vols., Vol. 1: The Faerie Queene, Bk. 1. Edmund Spenser. Ed. by Edwin Greenlaw et al. LC 66-26133. (Illus.). 568p. reprint ed. pap. 161.90 (*0-7837-3539-1*, 2043355) Bks Demand.

W

Works of Edmund Spenser: A Variorum Edition, 2 vols., Vol. 7. Edmund Spenser. Ed. by Edwin Greenlaw et al. LC 66-26133. (Illus.). 748p. reprint ed. pap. 180.00 (0-7837-3540-5, 2043355) Bks Demand.

Works of Edmund Spenser with the Principal Illustrations of the Various Commentators, 8 Vols, Set. Edmund Spenser. Ed. by H. J. Todd. LC 72-175999. reprint ed. 945.00 (0-404-06210-5) AMS Pr.

Works of Edward Gaylord Bourne. Edward G. Bourne. 1989. reprint ed. lib. bdg. 79.00 (0-685-27338-5) Rprt Serv.

Works of Edward Stillingfleet with a Life by Richard Bentley, 6 Vols, Set. Edward Stillingfleet. LC 78-176444. reprint ed. lib. bdg. 400.00 (0-404-06270-9) AMS Pr.

Works of English Poets, from Chaucer to Cowper, 21 Vols, Set. Alexander Chalmers. 1970. reprint ed. 2,385.00 (3-487-02603-1) G Olms Pubs.

Works of English Poets, From Chaucer to Cowper, 21 vols., Set. Alexander Chalmers. (BCL1-PR English Literature Ser.). 1992. reprint ed. lib. bdg. 1,890.00 (0-7812-7129-0) Rprt Serv.

Works of Ezekiel Hopkins, Vol. 1. Ezekiel Hopkins. Ed. by Charles Quick. 656p. 1995. 40.00 (1-57358-004-X) Soli Deo Gloria.

***Works of Ezekiel Hopkins: Sin, Covenants, Sacraments, Vol. 2.** 2nd ed. Ezekiel Hopkins. Ed. by Charles W. Quick. 708p. 1996. reprint ed. 40.00 (1-57358-053-8) Soli Deo Gloria.

Works of Fisher Ames, 2 vol. set. Fisher Ames. Ed. by Seth Ames & William Allen. LC 83-13568. (C). 1984. 30.00 (0-86597-013-0) Liberty Fund.

Works of Fisher Ames, 2 vol. set, Set. Fisher Ames. Ed. by Seth Ames & William Allen. LC 83-13568. (C). 1984. pap. 15.00 (0-86597-016-5) Liberty Fund.

Works of Flavius Josephus. Tr. by William Whistler. 690p. 1990. reprint ed. lib. bdg. 35.95 (0-89966-752-X) Buccaneer Bks.

Works of Francesco Soriano Vol. 1: Motets for Eight Voices, 1597. Francesco Soriano. Ed. by S. Philip Kniseley. LC 79-25222. 136p. reprint ed. pap. 38.80 (0-7837-4916-3, 2044581) Bks Demand.

Works of Francis Bacon, 15 vols., Set. Francis Bacon. 1995. reprint ed. lib. bdg. 1,200.00 (0-403-00003-3) Scholarly.

Works of Francis Beaumont & John Fletcher, 4 vols., Set. variorum ed. Francis Beaumont. Ed. by A. H. Bullen. LC 75-41306. (BCL Ser. II). 1976. reprint ed. Varorium Edition. 210.00 (0-404-14820-4) AMS Pr.

Works of Francis J. Grimke, 4 vols., Set. Ed. by Carter G. Woodson. 1990. 200.00 (0-685-55181-4) Assoc Pubs DC.

Works of Francis J. Grimke, 4 vols., Vol. I, Addresses. Ed. by Carter G. Woodson. 1990. Vol. I: Addresses. write for info. (0-87498-095-X) Assoc Pubs DC.

Works of Francis J. Grimke, 4 vols., Vol. II, Select Sermons. Ed. by Carter G. Woodson. 1990. Vol. II: Select Sermons. write for info. (0-87498-096-8) Assoc Pubs DC.

Works of Francis J. Grimke, 4 vols., Vol. III, Meditations. Ed. by Carter G. Woodson. 1990. Vol. III: Meditations. write for info. (0-87498-097-6) Assoc Pubs DC.

Works of Francis J. Grimke, 4 vols., Vol. IV, Letters. Ed. by Carter G. Woodson. 1990. Vol. IV: Letters. write for info. (0-87498-098-4) Assoc Pubs DC.

Works of Francis Marion Crawford. Francis M. Crawford. 1990. reprint ed. lib. bdg. 79.00 (0-685-44769-3) Rprt Serv.

Works of Francis Thompson, 3 Vols, Set. Francis Thompson. Ed. by W. Meynell. LC 70-118947. reprint ed. 210.00 (0-404-06460-4) AMS Pr.

Works of Fulke Greville. Morris W. Croll. LC 70-100743. (English Literature Ser.). 1979. pap. 39.95 (0-8383-0019-7) M S G Haskell Hse.

Works of Gabriel Harvey, 3 Vols, Set. Gabriel Harvey. Ed. by Alexander B. Grosart. LC 20-2123. reprint ed. write for info. (0-404-03200-1) AMS Pr.

Works of Geber. Ibn H. Jabir. LC 79-8615. reprint ed. 32.50 (0-404-18479-0) AMS Pr.

Works of Geoffrey Chaucer. Geoffrey Chaucer. Ed. by Alfred W. Pollard. LC 73-399393. (Select Bibliographies Reprint Ser.). 1977. reprint ed. 36.95 (0-8369-9903-7) Ayer.

Works of Geoffrey Chaucer & Others: Being a Reproduction in Facsimile of the First Collected Edition 1532, from the Copy in the British Museum. Geoffrey Chaucer. (BCL1-PR English Literature Ser.). 793p. 1992. reprint ed. lib. bdg. 109.00 (0-7812-7168-1) Rprt Serv.

Works of Geoffrey Chaucer & The Kingis Quair' A Facsimile of Bodlein Library, Oxford, MS Arch. Selden. B. 24. fac. ed. Ed. by Julia Boffey & A. S. Edwards. LC 95-32704. 554p. (C). 1996. 700.00 (0-85991-476-3) Boydell & Brewer.

***Works of George Berkeley: 1901 Edition, 4 vols., Set.** A. C. Fraser. 2070p. 1996. reprint ed. write for info. (1-85506-335-2) Bks Intl VA.

Works of George Berkeley, Bishop of Cloyne, 9 vols., Set. George Berkeley. Ed. by A. A. Luce & Thomas E. Jessop. 1990. reprint ed. pap. 770.00 (0-8115-0322-4) Periodicals Srv.

Works of George Dalgarno of Aberdeen. George Dalgarno. Ed. by Thomas Maitland. LC 74-165338. (Maitland Club, Glasgow. Publications: No. 29). reprint ed. 40.00 (0-404-52987-9) AMS Pr.

Works of George Gissing. Incl. In the Year of the Jubilee. Ed. by P. F. Kropholler. 453p. 1976. 24.50 (0-8386-1886-3); Our Friend the Charlatan. Ed. & Intro. by Pierre Coustillas. 327p. 1976. 24.50 (0-8386-1884-7); Unclassed. Ed. & Intro. by Jacob Korg. 1976. 24.50 (0-685-73243-6); 457p. 1976. write for info. (0-318-51879-1) Fairleigh Dickinson.

Works of George Savile, Marquis of Halifax, Vol. I. George Savile. Ed. by Mark N. Brown. (Oxford English Texts Ser.). (Illus.). 466p. 1989. 110.00 (0-19-812752-9) OUP.

Works of George Savile, Marquis of Halifax, Vol. II. George Savile. Ed. by Mark N. Brown. (Oxford English Texts Ser.). (Illus.). 546p. 1989. 135.00 (0-19-812337-X) OUP.

Works of George Swinnock, 5 vols., Set. 1992. 149.99 (0-85151-642-4) Banner of Truth.

Works of George Tyrrell, 18 titles in 20 vols., Set. George Tyrrell. reprint ed. 265.00 (0-404-07850-8) AMS Pr.

Works of George Washington Cable. George W. Cable. 1990. reprint ed. lib. bdg. 79.00 (0-685-74151-6) Rprt Serv.

Works of Gilbert Crispin, Abbot of Westminster. Anna S. Abulafia & G. Rosemary Evans. (Auctores Britannici Medii Aevi Ser.: Vol. VIII). (Illus.). 288p. 1986. 24.98 (0-19-726035-7) David Brown.

Works of Guy de Maupassant: Short Stories see Necklace & Other Short Stories

Works of Harriot Curtis. Harriot Curtis. 1990. reprint ed. lib. bdg. 79.00 (0-685-44777-4) Rprt Serv.

Works of Heart. Patricia Cudimano. (Great Quotations Ser.). 64p. 1993. 6.50 (1-56245-038-7) Great Quotations.

Works of Heinrich Heine, 20 vols. Heinrich Heine. Tr. by Charles G. Leland. reprint ed. write for info. (0-404-15250-3) AMS Pr.

Works of Henry Adams, 1838-1918, Set. Henry Adams. 1987. reprint ed. lib. bdg. 79.00 (0-685-18563-X) Rprt Serv.

***Works of Henry & Millicent Garrett Fawcett, 8 vols., Set.** 1996. write for info. (1-85506-367-0) Bks Intl VA.

Works of Henry Clay. Henry Clay. 1990. reprint ed. lib. bdg. 79.00 (0-7812-2304-0) Rprt Serv.

Works of Henry Howard & of Sir Thomas Wyatt the Elder, 2 Vols, Set. Henry Howard & Thomas Wyatt. Ed. by George F. Nott. 1816. 97.50 (0-404-04803-X) AMS Pr.

Works of Henry James Jr. Collected Works, 108 vols. Henry James, Jr. Incl. Story of a Year. 1992. reprint ed. lib. bdg. 75.00 (0-7812-3363-1); Watch & Ward. 1992. reprint ed. lib. bdg. 75.00 (0-7812-3364-X); (Notable American Authors Ser.). write for info. (0-7812-3362-3) Rprt Serv.

Works of Henry Mackenzie. Ed. by Manning. 3141p. (C). 1997. text ed. 1,085.00 (0-415-13744-6) Routledge.

Works of Henry Marie Brackenridge. Henry M. Brachenridge. 1989. reprint ed. lib. bdg. 79.00 (0-685-27325-3) Rprt Serv.

Works of Henry Sidgwick, 15 vols., Set. Intro. by John Slater. 6416p. Date not set. 1,350.00 (1-85506-473-1) Bks Intl VA.

***Works of Henry Thomas Buckle: 1872 Edition, 3 vols., Set.** Ed. by Helen Taylor. 2069p. 1996. write for info. (1-85506-415-4) Bks Intl VA.

Works of Henry Ward Beecher, 1813-1887, Set. Henry W. Beecher. 1987. reprint ed. 800.00 (0-685-18614-8) Rprt Serv.

Works of Herbert Baxter Adams, 1850-1901, Set. Herbert B. Adams. 1987. reprint ed. lib. bdg. 800.00 (0-685-18564-8) Rprt Serv.

Works of Herman Melville. Herman Melville. LC 87-14445. 736p. 1987. 9.98 (0-517-65084-3) Random Hse Value.

Works of Herodian, 2 vols. Herodian. No. 454-455. (ENG & GRE.). write for info. (0-318-53224-7) HUP.

Works of Herodian, 2 vols., 1. Herodian. (Loeb Classical Library: No. 454-455). 564p. (ENG & GRE.). 1969. 18.95 (0-674-99500-7) HUP.

Works of Herodian, 2 vols., 2. Herodian. (Loeb Classical Library: No. 454-455). 342p. (ENG & GRE.). 1971. 18.95 (0-674-99501-5) HUP.

Works of Hesiod, 2 vols. in one. Hesiod. Tr. by Thomas Cooke. LC 79-158284. (Augustan Translators Ser.). reprint ed. 64.50 (0-404-54170-4) AMS Pr.

Works of Hew Ainslie, 1792-1878, Set. Hew Ainslie. 1987. reprint ed. lib. bdg. 600.00 (0-685-18570-2) Rprt Serv.

Works of Hezekiah Butterworth. Hezekiah Butterworth. 1989. reprint ed. lib. bdg. 63.00 (0-685-74128-1) Rprt Serv.

Works of Hiram Bingham. Hiram Bingham. 1989. reprint ed. lib. bdg. 63.00 (0-685-27261-3) Rprt Serv.

Works of Horace, 2 vols., Set. Horace. LC 70-179303. (Augustan Translators Ser.). (ENG & LAT.). 1976. reprint ed. 135.00 (0-404-54150-X) AMS Pr.

Works of Horatio Alger Jr., Set. Horatio Alger, Jr. 1989. reprint ed. lib. bdg. 63.00 (0-685-27536-1) Rprt Serv.

Works of Horatio Bridge. Horatio Bridge. 1989. reprint ed. lib. bdg. 63.00 (0-685-27304-0) Rprt Serv.

Works of Hsuntze. Hsun-Tzu. Tr. by Homer H. Dubs from CHI. LC 75-41145. reprint ed. 45.00 (0-404-14753-4) AMS Pr.

Works of Hugh Binning. Hugh Binning. 711p. 1992. reprint ed. 45.00 (1-877611-45-X) Soli Deo Gloria.

Works of Hugh Henry Brackenridge. Hugh H. Brackenridge. 1989. reprint ed. lib. bdg. 63.00 (0-685-27308-3) Rprt Serv.

***Works of Irving Fisher.** Irving Fisher. Ed. by William J. Barber & James Tobin. LC 96-21156. (Pickering Masters Ser.). 6240p. 1997. 1,350.00 (1-85196-225-5, Pub. by Pickering & Chatto UK) Ashgate Pub Co.

Works of Isaac Disraeli, 6 vols., Set. Isaac Disraeli. Ed. by Benjamin Disraeli. 3333p. reprint ed. lib. bdg. 323.70 (0-685-43591-1, 05102724) G Olms Pubs.

Works of Isaac Newton Arnold, 1815-1884, Set. Issac N. Arnold. 1987. reprint ed. lib. bdg. 600.00 (0-685-18603-2) Rprt Serv.

Works of Isaac Watts, 6 Vols, Set. Isaac Watts. Ed. by G. Burder. LC 70-131027. reprint ed. lib. bdg. 1,095.00 (0-404-06890-1) AMS Pr.

Works of J. M. Barrie. Peter Pan Edition, 18 vols. James M. Barrie. Incl. Vol. 1. Auld Licht Idylls etc. LC 79-146660. reprint ed. 57.50 (0-404-08781-7); Vol. 2. My Lady Nicotine, etc. LC 79-146660. reprint ed. 57.50 (0-404-08782-5); Vol. 3. When a Man's Single. LC 79-146660. reprint ed. 57.50 (0-404-08783-3); Vol. 4. Little Minister. LC 79-146660. reprint ed. 57.50 (0-404-08784-1); Vol. 5. Sentimental Tommy. LC 79-146660. reprint ed. 57.50 (0-404-08785-X); Vol. 6. Tommy & Grizel. LC 79-146660. reprint ed. 57.50 (0-404-08786-8); Vol. 7. Little White Bird. LC 79-146660. reprint ed. 57.50 (0-404-08787-6); Vol. 8. Margaret Ogilvy & Others. LC 79-146660. reprint ed. 57.50 (0-404-08788-4); Vol. 9. Courage, etc. LC 79-146660. reprint ed. 57.50 (0-404-08789-2); Vol. 10. Peter Pan & Other Plays. LC 79-146660. reprint ed. 57.50 (0-404-08790-6); Vol. 11. Admirable Crichton etc. LC 79-146660. reprint ed. 57.50 (0-404-08791-4); Vol. 12. What Every Woman Knows & Other Plays. LC 79-146660. reprint ed. 57.50 (0-404-08792-2); Vol. 13. Dear Brutus & Other Plays. LC 79-146660. reprint ed. 57.50 (0-404-08793-0); Vol. 14. Mary Rose & Other Plays. LC 79-146660. reprint ed. 57.50 (0-404-08794-9); Vol. 15. M'Connachie & J. M. B., etc. LC 79-146660. reprint ed. 57.50 (0-404-08795-7); Vol. 16. Greenwood Hat, etc.. LC 79-146660. reprint ed. 57.50 (0-404-08796-5); Vol. 17. Boy David, etc. LC 79-146660. reprint ed. 57.50 (0-404-08797-3); Vol. 18. Professor's Love-Story, etc. LC 79-146660. reprint ed. 57.50 (0-404-08798-1); LC 79-146660. write for info. (0-318-50753-6) AMS Pr.

Works of J. M. Barrie. Peter Pan Edition, 18 vols., Set. James M. Barrie. Incl. Vol. 1. Auld Licht Idylls, etc. LC 79-146660. reprint ed. 57.50 (0-404-08781-7); Vol. 2. My Lady Nicotine, etc. LC 79-146660. reprint ed. 57.50 (0-404-08782-5); Vol. 3. When a Man's Single. LC 79-146660. reprint ed. 57.50 (0-404-08783-3); Vol. 4. Little Minister. LC 79-146660. reprint ed. 57.50 (0-404-08784-1); Vol. 5. Sentimental Tommy. LC 79-146660. reprint ed. 57.50 (0-404-08785-X); Vol. 6. Tommy & Grizel. LC 79-146660. reprint ed. 57.50 (0-404-08786-8); Vol. 7. Little White Bird. LC 79-146660. reprint ed. 57.50 (0-404-08787-6); Vol. 8. Margaret Ogilvy & Others. LC 79-146660. reprint ed. 57.50 (0-404-08788-4); Vol. 9. Courage, etc. LC 79-146660. reprint ed. 57.50 (0-404-08789-2); Vol. 10. Peter Pan & Other Plays. LC 79-146660. reprint ed. 57.50 (0-404-08790-6); Vol. 11. Admirable Crichton etc. LC 79-146660. reprint ed. 57.50 (0-404-08791-4); Vol. 12. What Every Woman Knows & Other Plays. LC 79-146660. reprint ed. 57.50 (0-404-08792-2); Vol. 13. Dear Brutus & Other Plays. LC 79-146660. reprint ed. 57.50 (0-404-08793-0); Vol. 14. Mary Rose & Other Plays. LC 79-146660. reprint ed. 57.50 (0-404-08794-9); Vol. 15. M'Connachie & J. M. B., etc. LC 79-146660. reprint ed. 57.50 (0-404-08795-7); Vol. 16. Greenwood Hat, etc. LC 79-146660. reprint ed. 57.50 (0-404-08796-5); Vol. 17. Boy David, etc. LC 79-146660. reprint ed. 57.50 (0-404-08797-3); Vol. 18. Professor's Love-Story, etc. LC 79-146660. reprint ed. 57.50 (0-404-08798-1); LC 79-146660. 1941. reprint ed. 1,035.00 (0-404-08780-9) AMS Pr.

Works of Jack London. Jack London. 1990. 16.99 (0-517-05359-4) Random Hse Value.

Works of Jacob Abbott, 1803-1879, Set. Jacob Abbott. reprint ed. lib. bdg. 500.00 (0-685-18572-9) Rprt Serv.

Works of Jacques-Auguste de Thou. S. Kinser. (International Archives of the History of Ideas Ser.: No. 18). 366p. 1967. lib. bdg. 70.50 (90-247-0194-5) Kluwer Ac.

Works of Jacques Lacan: An Introduction. Bice Benvenuto & Roger G. Kennedy. LC 86-3847. 237p. 1986. 27.50 (0-685-13555-1); pap. 12.95 (0-685-13556-X) St Martin.

Works of Jakob Boehme, 4 vols. Jakob Boehme. 1974. lib. bdg. 2,900.00 (0-87968-465-8) Gordon Pr.

Works of James Abram Garfield, 2 Vols, Set. James A. Garfield. Ed. by Burke A. Hinsdale. LC 73-117877. (Select Bibliographies Reprint Ser.). 1977. 90.95 (0-8369-5330-4) Ayer.

Works of James Adair, 1709-1783, Set. James Adair. reprint ed. lib. bdg. 500.00 (0-685-18555-9) Rprt Serv.

Works of James Allen, 1849-1925, Set. James L. Allen. 1987. reprint ed. lib. bdg. 500.00 (0-685-18585-0) Rprt Serv.

Works of James Arminius New London Ed: London Edition, 3 vols. James Arminius. Tr. by William Nicoles from DUT. 2280p. (YA). (gr. 10). 1977. reprint ed. 125.00 (0-8010-0206-0) Baker Bks.

***Works of James Beattie, 10 vols.** Intro. by Roger J. Robinson. 4779p. 1996. text ed. 1,315.00 (0-415-13326-2) Routledge.

Works of James Clarence Mangan: With a Biography & Bibliography, 7 vols., Set. Ed. by Augustine Martin. Date not set. write for info. (0-7165-2556-9, Pub. by Irish Acad Pr IE) Intl Spec Bk.

Works of James Fenimore Cooper. James Fenimore Cooper. 1990. reprint ed. lib. bdg. 63.00 (0-685-27629-5) Rprt Serv.

Works of James Gillray. James Gillray. LC 68-21201. (Illus.). 1972. reprint ed. 99.95 (0-405-08562-1, Pub. by Blom Pubns UK) Ayer.

Works of James McNeill Whistler. Elisabeth L. Cary. LC 77-157328. (Select Bibliographies Reprint Ser.). 1977. reprint ed. 26.95 (0-8369-5788-1) Ayer.

Works of James O'Connor, the Deaf Poet, with a Biography Sketch of the Author. James O'Connor. 1972. 59.95 (0-8490-1330-5) Gordon Pr.

Works of James Ussher, 17 Vols, Set. James Ussher. Ed. by C. R. Elrington & J. H. Todd. LC 70-177553. reprint ed. lib. bdg. 67.50 (0-404-06730-1) AMS Pr.

Works of Jane (Goodwin) Austin, 1831-1894, Set. Jane Austin. 1987. reprint ed. lib. bdg. 800.00 (0-685-18608-3) Rprt Serv.

Works of Jeremiah Curtin. Jeremiah Curtin. 1990. reprint ed. lib. bdg. 63.00 (0-685-27759-3) Rprt Serv.

***Works of Jeremy Bentham: Published under the Superintendence of His Executor, John Bowring (1843 Edition), 11 vols., Set.** Intro. by John H. Burton. 6640p. 1996. reprint ed. write for info. (1-85506-414-6) Bks Intl VA.

Works of John Adams, 10 vols, Set. John Adams. LC 78-128978. reprint ed. 745.00 (0-404-00310-9) AMS Pr.

Works of John Adams, Second President of the United States, 10 Vols, Set. John Adams. LC 77-80620. (Select Bibliographies Reprint Ser.). reprint ed. 410.00 (0-8369-5020-8) Ayer.

Works of John Adams, 1704-1740, Set. John Adams. 1987. reprint ed. lib. bdg. 63.00 (0-685-18565-6) Rprt Serv.

Works of John & Charles Wesley. 2nd rev. ed. Richard Green. LC 74-26049. reprint ed. 45.00 (0-404-12924-2) AMS Pr.

Works of John Bartlett. John Bartlett. 1989. reprint ed. lib. bdg. 79.00 (0-685-27839-5) Rprt Serv.

***Works of John Boys: 1854 Edition.** 2nd ed. John Boys. Ed. by Kensey J. Stewart. 789p. 1997. reprint ed. 50.00 (1-57358-054-6) Soli Deo Gloria.

Works of John Bramhall, 5 Vols, Set. John Bramhall. LC 73-39519. reprint ed. 265.00 (0-404-52060-X) AMS Pr.

Works of John Bunyan, 3 Vols, Set. John Bunyan. Ed. by George Offor. LC 78-154136. reprint ed. lib. bdg. 510.00 (0-404-09250-0) AMS Pr.

Works of John Bunyan, 3 vols., Set. John Bunyan. Ed. by George Offor. 2400p. 1992. reprint ed. 116.99 (0-85151-598-3) Banner of Truth.

Works of John Burroughs. John Burroughs. 1989. reprint ed. lib. bdg. 63.00 (0-685-74129-X) Rprt Serv.

Works of John Calswell Calhoun. John C. Calhoun. 1990. reprint ed. lib. bdg. 63.00 (0-685-27708-9) Rprt Serv.

Works of John Cotton. John Cotton. 1990. reprint ed. lib. bdg. 63.00 (0-685-27666-X) Rprt Serv.

Works of John Dryden Vol. I: Poems: 1649-1680. Ed. by Edward N. Hooker & H. T. Swedenberg. 1956. 75.00 (0-520-00358-6) U CA Pr.

Works of John Dryden Vol. II: Poems: 1681-1684. Ed. by H. T. Swedenberg. 1973. 75.00 (0-520-02118-5) U CA Pr.

Works of John Dryden Vol. III: Poems: 1685-1692. Ed. by Earl Miner & Vinton A. Dearing. 1970. 75.00 (0-520-01625-4) U CA Pr.

Works of John Dryden Vol. IV: Poems: 1693-1699. Ed. by A. B. Chambers et al. 1974. 75.00 (0-520-02120-7) U CA Pr.

Works of John Dryden Vol. IX: Plays: The Indian Emperour, Secret Love, Sir Martin Mar-All. Ed. by John Loftis & Vinton A. Dearing. 1966. 75.00 (0-520-00360-8) U CA Pr.

Works of John Dryden Vol. V: Poems: 1697. Ed. by William Frost. 1987. 60.00 (0-520-02121-5) U CA Pr.

Works of John Dryden Vol. VI: Poems: 1697. Ed. by William Frost. 1987. 60.00 (0-520-02122-3) U CA Pr.

Works of John Dryden Vol. VIIII: Plays: The Wild Gallant, The Rival Ladies, The Indian Queen. Ed. by John H. Smith et al. 1962. 60.00 (0-520-00359-4) U CA Pr.

Works of John Dryden Vol. X: Plays: The Tempest, Tyrannick Love, An Evening's Love. Ed. by George R. Guffey & Maxmilliam E. Novak. 1970. 75.00 (0-520-01589-4) U CA Pr.

Works of John Dryden Vol. XI: Plays: The Conquest of Granada, Part I & II, Marriage-a-la Mode, & The Assignation: Or, Love in a Nunnery. Ed. by John Loftis et al. 1978. 60.00 (0-520-02125-8) U CA Pr.

Works of John Dryden Vol. XII: Plays: Amboyna, The State of Innocence, Aureng-Zebe. Ed. by Vinton A. Dearing. 556p. 1995. 75.00 (0-520-08247-8) U CA Pr.

Works of John Dryden Vol. XIII: Plays: All for Love Oedipus, Troilus & Cressida. Ed. by Maxmillian E. Novak. 1984. 60.00 (0-520-02127-4) U CA Pr.

Works of John Dryden Vol. XIV: Plays: The Kind Keeper; The Spanish Fryar; The Duke of Guise; & The Vindication. John Dryden. 646p. (C). 1992. 75.00 (0-520-07561-7) U CA Pr.

Works of John Dryden Vol. XIX: Prose: The Life of St. Francis Xavier. Ed. by Alan Roper & Dearing A. Vinton. 1979. 60.00 (0-520-02132-0) U CA Pr.

Works of John Dryden Vol. XV: Plays: Albion & Albanius, Don Sebastian, Amphitryon. Ed. by Earl Miner. 1976. 60.00 (0-520-02129-0) U CA Pr.

Works of John Dryden Vol. XVII: Prose: 1668-1691, An Essay of Dramatic Poesie & Shorter Works. Ed. by Samuel A. Monk. 1972. 60.00 (0-520-01814-1) U CA Pr.

Works of John Dryden Vol. XVIII: Prose: The History of the League, 1684. Ed. by Alan Roper & Dearing A. Vinton. 1974. 60.00 (0-520-02131-2) U CA Pr.

Works of John Dryden Vol. XX: Prose: 1691-1698, De Arte Graphica & Shorter Works, Vol. XX. Ed. by A. E. Maurer. LC 55-7149. (Illus.). 546p. 1990. 75.00 (0-520-02133-9) U CA Pr.

Works of John Henry Alexander, 1812-1867, Set. John H. Alexander. 1987. reprint ed. lib. bdg. 500.00 (0-685-18580-X) Rprt Serv.

Works of John Howe, 3 vols. John Howe. 1965p. 1991. reprint ed. 80.00 (1-877611-22-0) Soli Deo Gloria.

Works of John Knox, 6 Vols, Set. John Knox. Ed. by David Laing. LC 67-35016. reprint ed. 550.00 (0-404-52880-5) AMS Pr.

Works of John Locke, 2 Vols, 1. John Locke. LC 74-94275. (Select Bibliographies Reprint Ser.). 1977. 30.95 (0-8369-9980-0) Ayer.

W

Works of John Locke, 2 Vols, Set. John Locke. LC 74-94275. (Select Bibliographies Reprint Ser.). 1977. 61.95 (*0-8369-5049-6*) Ayer.

Works of John Locke, 2 Vols, Vol. 2. John Locke. LC 74-94275. (Select Bibliographies Reprint Ser.). 1977. 30.95 (*0-8369-9981-9*) Ayer.

Works of John Locke: A Comprehensive Bibliography from the Seventeenth Century to the Present. John C. Attig. LC 85-14670. (Bibliographies & Indexes in Philosophy Ser.: No. 1). xx, 185p. 1985. text ed. 59.95 (*0-313-24359-X*, AJL/, Greenwood Pr) Greenwood.

Works of John Metham. John Metham. Ed. by H. Craig. (EETS, OS Ser.: No. 132). 1974. 55.00 (*0-527-00129-5*) Periodicals Srv.

Works of John Newton, 6 vols, Set. John Newton. 1985. reprint ed. 169.99 (*0-85151-460-X*) Banner of Truth.

Works of John Owen, 16 vols., Set. John Owen. 1980. 399.99 (*0-85151-392-1*) Banner of Truth.

Works of John Owen, Vol. I. John Owen. 1980. 27.99 (*0-85151-123-6*) Banner of Truth.

Works of John Owen, Vol. II. John Owen. 1980. 27.99 (*0-85151-124-4*) Banner of Truth.

Works of John Owen, Vol. III. John Owen. 1980. 27.99 (*0-85151-125-2*) Banner of Truth.

Works of John Owen, Vol. IV. John Owen. 1980. 27.99 (*0-85151-068-X*) Banner of Truth.

Works of John Owen, Vol. V. John Owen. 1980. 27.99 (*0-85151-067-1*) Banner of Truth.

Works of John Owen, Vol. VI. John Owen. 1980. 27.99 (*0-85151-126-0*) Banner of Truth.

Works of John Owen, Vol. VII. John Owen. 1980. 27.99 (*0-85151-127-9*) Banner of Truth.

Works of John Owen, Vol. VIII. John Owen. 1980. 27.99 (*0-85151-066-3*) Banner of Truth.

Works of John Owen, Vol. IX. John Owen. 1980. 27.99 (*0-85151-065-5*) Banner of Truth.

Works of John Owen, Vol. X. John Owen. 1980. 27.99 (*0-85151-064-7*) Banner of Truth.

Works of John Owen, Vol. XI. John Owen. 1980. 27.99 (*0-85151-128-7*) Banner of Truth.

Works of John Owen, Vol. XII. John Owen. 1980. 27.99 (*0-85151-129-5*) Banner of Truth.

Works of John Owen, Vol. XIII. John Owen. 1980. 27.99 (*0-85151-063-9*) Banner of Truth.

Works of John Owen, Vol. XIV. John Owen. 1980. 27.99 (*0-85151-062-0*) Banner of Truth.

Works of John Owen, Vol. XV. John Owen. 1980. 27.99 (*0-85151-130-9*) Banner of Truth.

Works of John Owen, Vol. XVI. John Owen. 1980. 27.99 (*0-85151-061-2*) Banner of Truth.

Works of John Philip Sousa. Paul E. Bierley. LC 84-80665. 1984. 19.95 (*0-918048-04-4*) Integrity.

Works of John Stevens Cabot Abbott, 1805-1877, Set. John S. Abbott. reprint ed. 500.00 (*0-685-18534-6*) Rprt Serv.

Works of John Webster: An Old-Spelling Critical Edition of The White Devil & The Duchess of Malfi. Ed. by David Gunby et al. (Illus.). 760p. (C). 1995. text ed. 139.95 (*0-521-26059-0*) Cambridge U Pr.

Works of John Wesley, 5 vols. Incl. Vol. 1. Sermons I, 1-33. John Wesley. Ed. by W. Reginald Ward & Richard P. Heitzenrater. 1984. 49.95 (*0-687-46210-X*); Vol. 2. Sermons II, 34-70. John Wesley. Ed. by W. Reginald Ward & Richard P. Heitzenrater. 1985. 49.95 (*0-687-46211-8*); Vol. 3. Sermons III, 71-114. John Wesley. Ed. by W. Reginald Ward & Richard P. Heitzenrater. 1986. 49.95 (*0-687-46212-6*); Vol. 4. Sermons IV, 115-151. John Wesley. Ed. by W. Reginald Ward & Richard P. Heitzenrater. 1987. 49.95 (*0-687-46213-4*); Vol. 18. Journals & Diaries: 1735-1738. John Wesley. Ed. by W. Reginald Ward & Richard P. Heitzenrater. 400p. 1988. 49.95 (*0-687-46221-5*); Vol. 25. Letters: 1721-1739. Frank Baker. 764p. 1987. 49.95 (*0-687-46216-9*); Vol. 26. Letters: 1740-1755. Frank Baker. 684p. 1987. 49.95 (*0-687-46217-7*); Vol. 11. Appeals to Men of Reason & Religion & Certain Related Open Letters. John Wesley. Ed. by Gerald R. Cragg. 594p. 1987. 49.95 (*0-687-46215-0*); Vol. 7. Collection of Hymns for the Use of the People Called Methodists. Ed. by Franz Hildebrandt & Oliver A. Beckerlegge. 848p. 1989. reprint ed. 49.95 (*0-687-46218-5*); Vol. 19. Journals & Diaries Pt. II: 1738-1743. John Wesley. Ed. by Richard W. Heitzenrater & W. Reginald Ward. 684p. 1990. 49.95 (*0-687-46222-3*); Vol. 20. Journals & Diaries Pt. III: 1743-1754. John Wesley. Ed. by Richard W. Heitzenrater & W. Reginald Ward. 476p. 1991. 49.95 (*0-687-46223-1*); Vol. 21. Journals & Letters No. IV: 1755-1765. John Wesley. Ed. by Richard W. Heitzenrater & W. Reginald Ward. 1992. 49.95 (*0-687-46225-8*); Vol. 23. Journals & Diaries No. VI: 1776-1786. John Wesley. Ed. by W. Reginald Ward & Richard W. Heitzenrater. 640p. (Orig.). 1995. 49.95 (*0-687-46227-4*); Vol. 22. Journals & Diaries: 1765-1775. John Wesley. Ed. by Richard W. Heitzenrater & W. Reginald Ward. 469p. 1993. 49.95 (*0-687-46226-6*); Vol. 9. Methodist Societies: History, Nature & Design. John Wesley. Ed. by Rupert E. Davies. 608p. 1989. 49.95 (*0-687-46214-2*); Vol. 24. Journal & Diaries: 1787-1791. Ed. by W. Reginald Ward & Richard P. Heitzenrater. 496p. 1997. 49.95 (*0-687-03349-7*); 1988. write for info. (*0-318-63360-4*) Abingdon.

Works of John Wesley, 7 vols. John Wesley. (Illus.). 7p. (gr. 10). 1996. reprint ed. 300.00 (*0-8010-1111-6*) Baker Bks.

Works of John Woolman, 2 Pts. John Woolman. LC 78-83893. (Black Heritage Library Collection). 1977. 22.95 (*0-8369-8694-6*) Ayer.

Works of Jonathan Edwards, 2 vols., 1. Jonathan Edwards. 1979. 59.99 (*0-85151-216-X*) Banner of Truth.

Works of Jonathan Edwards, 2 vols., 2. Jonathan Edwards. 1979. 59.99 (*0-85151-217-8*) Banner of Truth.

Works of Jonathan Edwards, 2 vols., Set. Jonathan Edwards. 1979. 112.99 (*0-85151-397-2*) Banner of Truth.

Works of Jonathan Edwards: The Typological Writings, Vol. 11. Jonathan Edwards. Ed. by Wallace E. Anderson et al. LC 93-9689. (Illus.). 432p. (C). 1993. 75.00 (*0-300-05352-5*) Yale U Pr.

Works of Jonathan Edwards Vol. 8: Ethical Writings. Jonathan Edwards. Ed. by Paul Ramsey. LC 87-29536. 808p. (C). 1989. text ed. 80.00 (*0-300-04020-2*) Yale U Pr.

Works of Jonathan Edwards Vol. 9: A History of the Work of Redemption from the Sermon Manuscripts of the Redemption Discourse. Jonathan Edwards. Ed. by John F. Wilson. LC 88-14430. 608p. (C). 1989. text ed. 75.00 (*0-300-04155-1*) Yale U Pr.

Works of Jonathan Edwards Vol. 10: Sermons & Discourses, 1720-1723. Jonathan Edwards. Ed. by Wilson E. Kimnach. 688p. (C). 1993. text ed. 75.00 (*0-300-05136-0*) Yale U Pr.

Works of Joseph Alden, 1807-1885, Set. Joseph Alden. 1987. reprint ed. lib. bdg. 500.00 (*0-685-18578-8*) Rprt Serv.

***Works of Joseph Butler, 3 vols.** Ed. by W. E. Gladstone. 1352p. write for info. (*1-85506-377-8*) Bks Intl VA.

Works of Joseph Butler. Joseph Bulter. Ed. by W. E. Gladstone. (C). 1986. reprint ed. lib. bdg. 32.95 (*0-935005-38-2*) Lincoln-Rembrandt.

Works of Joseph Conrad, 22 vols., Set. Conrad. 8450p. (C). 1995. boxed, text ed. 2,010.00 (*0-415-13485-4*) Routledge.

Works of Joseph Henry Allen, 1820-1980, Set. Joseph H. Allen. 1987. reprint ed. lib. bdg. 500.00 (*0-685-18586-9*) Rprt Serv.

Works of Josephus, 10 vols. Incl. Vol. 1. Life: Against Apion. Josephus. Ed. by E. H. Warmington. 448p. 1926. 18.95 (*0-674-99205-9*); Vol. 2, Bks. 1-3. Jewish War. Josephus. Ed. by E. H. Warmington. 764p. 1927. Vol. 2, Bks 1-3. 18.95 (*0-674-99223-7*); Vol. 3, Bks. 4-7, Index to Vols. 2 & 3. Jewish War. Josephus & E. H. Warmington. 693p. 1928. Vol. 3, Bks. 4-7, Index To Vols. 2 & 3. 18.95 (*0-674-99232-6*); Vol. 4, Bks. 1-4. Antiquities. Josephus. Ed. by E. H. Warmington. Vol. 4, Bks 1-4. 14.50 (*0-674-99267-9*); Vol. 5, Bks. 5-8. Antiquities. Josephus. Ed. by E. H. Warmington. Vol. 5, Bks 5-8. 14.50 (*0-674-99310-1*); Vol. 6, Bks. 9-11. Antiquities. Josephus. Ed. by E. H. Warmington. Vol. 6, Bks 9-11. 14.50 (*0-674-99360-8*); Vol. 7, Bks. 12-14. Antiquities. Josephus. Ed. by E. H. Warmington. Vol. 7, Bks 12-14. 14.50 (*0-674-99402-7*); Vol. 8, Bks. 15-17. Antiquities. Josephus. Ed. by E. H. Warmington. Vol. 8, Bks 15-17. 14.50 (*0-674-99451-5*); Vol. 9, Bks. 18-19. Antiquities. Josephus. Ed. by E. H. Warmington. Vol. 9, Bks 18-19. 14.50 (*0-674-99477-9*); Vol. 10, Bk. 20 General Index. Antiquities. Josephus. Ed. by E. H. Warmington. Vol. 10, Bk. 20 general index. 14.50 (*0-674-99502-3*); (Loeb Classical LibraryNos. 186, 203, 210, 242, 281, 326, 365, 410, 433, 456). write for info. (*0-318-53225-5*) HUP.

Works of Josephus. Flavius Josephus. Tr. by William Whiston. 944p. 1987. 24.95 (*0-913573-86-8*) Hendrickson MA.

Works of Josephus. Tr. by William Whiston. 944p. 1995. pap. 14.95 (*1-56563-167-6*) Hendrickson MA.

Works of Julian, 3 vols. Julian. No. 13, 29, 157. write for info. (*0-318-53226-3*) HUP.

Works of Julian, 3 vols., 1. Julian. (Loeb Classical Library: No. 13, 29, 157). 526p. 1913. 18.95 (*0-674-99014-5*) HUP.

Works of Julian, 3 vols., 2. Julian. (Loeb Classical Library: No. 13, 29, 157). 526p. 1913. 18.95 (*0-674-99032-3*) HUP.

Works of Julian, 3 vols., 3. Julian. (Loeb Classical Library: No. 13, 29, 157). 518p. 1932. 18.95 (*0-674-99173-7*) HUP.

Works of Jurek Becker: A Thematic Analysis. Susan M. Johnson. (DDR Studien - East German Studies: Vol. 3). 224p. (C). 1988. text ed. 36.50 (*0-8204-0705-4*) P Lang Pubng.

Works of Kalidasa: Kayva, Vol. II. Ed. by C. R. Devadhar. 1093p. 1984. reprint ed. 46.00 (*81-208-0024-9*, Pub. by Motilal Banarsidass II) S Asia.

Works of Karlheinz Stockhausen. 2nd ed. Robin Maconie. (Illus.). 336p. 1990. 85.00 (*0-19-315477-3*) OUP.

Works of Katherine Davis Chapman Tillman. Katherine D. Tillman. Ed. by Claudia Tate. (Schomburg Library of Nineteenth-Century Black Women Writers). (Illus.). 464p. 1991. 45.00 (*0-19-506200-0*) OUP.

Works of Lady Blessington. Marguerite P. Blessington. LC 71-37681. (Women of Letters Ser.). reprint ed. 64.50 (*0-404-56717-7*) AMS Pr.

Works of Laurence Sterne, 6 Vols, Set. Laurence J. Sterne. Ed. by George Saintsbury. LC 73-129387. reprint ed. 60.00 (*0-404-08080-4*) AMS Pr.

Works of Lord Bolingbroke: With a Life Containing Additional Information Relative to His Personal & Public Character, 4 vols., Set. Henry S. Bolingbroke. LC 67-16351. 1967. reprint ed. 250.00 (*0-678-05028-7*) Kelley.

Works of Lord Byron, 13 vols., Set. George Gordon Byron. (BCL1-PR English Literature Ser.). 1992. reprint ed. lib. bdg. 1,170.00 (*0-7812-7472-9*) Rprt Serv.

Works of Lord Macaulay Complete: The Albany Edition, 12 vols., Set. Thomas B. Macaulay. LC 76-42708. reprint ed. 900.00 (*0-404-59480-8*) AMS Pr.

Works of Louisa May Alcott. Ed. by Claire Booss. (Avenel Readers Library). (Illus.). 800p. 1982. 7.98 (*0-517-37167-7*); 7.98 (*0-517-37146-4*) Random Hse Value.

Works of Louisa May Alcott, 1832-1888, Set. Louisa May Alcott. 1987. reprint ed. lib. bdg. 63.00 (*0-685-18574-5*) Rprt Serv.

Works of Love: Kierkegaard's Writings, Vols. V-XVI. Soren Kierkegaard. Ed. by Howard V. Hong & Edna H. Hong. LC 94-23103. (Kierkegaard's Writings: 16). 576p. 1995. text ed. 67.50 (*0-691-03792-2*) Princeton U Pr.

Works of Love? Reflections on Works of Love. Gene Fendt. 1990. 37.50 (*0-916379-70-1*) Scripta.

Works of Love: Some Christian Reflections in the Form of Discourse. Soren Kierkegaard. 1964. pap. text ed. 14.00 (*0-06-130122-1*, TB122, Torch) HarpC.

Works of Love Are Works of Peace: Mother Teresa & the Missionaraies of Charity. Michael Collopy. 224p. 1996. 34.95 (*0-89870-561-4*) Ignatius Pr.

Works of M. P. Shiel. Incl. Vol. 1. Writings. (Illus.). 426p. 45.00 (*0-934236-00-3*); Vol. 1. Writings. (Illus.). 426p. ring bd. 25.00 (*0-317-39296-4*); Vol. 1. Writings. (Illus.). 426p. pap. 32.50 (*0-317-39297-2*); Vol. II, pg. 1-414. Shielography Updated. 45.00 (*0-317-39299-9*); Vol. II, pg. 1-414. Shielography Updated. ring bd. 37.50 (*0-685-43416-8*); Vol. II, pg. 1-414. Shielography Updated. pap. 32.50 (*0-317-39300-6*); Vol. III, Pt. I. Shielography Updated. 45.00 (*0-317-39301-4*); Vol. III, Pt. I. Shielography Updated. ring bd. 37.50 (*0-317-39302-2*); Vol. III, Pt. I. Shielography Updated. pap. 32.50 (*0-317-39303-0*); Vol. IV. Shiel in Diverse Hands: A Collection of Essays in M. P. Shiel. 501p. 1983. 32.50 (*0-685-11873-8*); Orig. Title: Works of M. P. Shiel, a Study in Bibliography 1948. 1986. write for info. (*0-318-60152-4*) Reynolds Morse.

Works of M. P. Shiel, 2 vols., Vol. 2, Pts. 1 & 2. rev. ed. A. Reynolds Morse. Orig. Title: Works of M. P. Shiel, a Study in Bibliography 1948. (Illus.). 864p. 1980. 90.00 (*0-686-62335-5*); pap. 65.00 (*0-686-62336-3*); 75.00 (*0-685-04347-9*) Reynolds Morse.

Works of M. P. Shiel, a Study in Bibliography 1948 see Works of M. P. Shiel

***Works of Maria Edgeworth, 12 vols.** Ed. by Marilyn Butler et al. LC 96-51468. (Pickering Masters Ser.). 4560p. 1997. 1,100.00 (*1-85196-186-0*, Pub. by Pickering & Chatto UK) Ashgate Pub Co.

***Works of Maria Edgeworth.** Maria Edgeworth. LC 96-51468. 1997. write for info. (*1-85196-175-5*, Pub. by Pickering & Chatto UK); write for info. (*1-85196-176-3*, Pub. by Pickering & Chatto UK); write for info. (*1-85196-178-X*, Pub. by Pickering & Chatto UK); write for info. (*1-85196-179-8*, Pub. by Pickering & Chatto UK); write for info. (*1-85196-180-1*, Pub. by Pickering & Chatto UK); write for info. (*1-85196-181-X*, Pub. by Pickering & Chatto UK); write for info. (*1-85196-182-8*, Pub. by Pickering & Chatto UK); write for info. (*1-85196-183-6*, Pub. by Pickering & Chatto UK); write for info. (*1-85196-184-4*, Pub. by Pickering & Chatto UK); write for info. (*1-85196-185-2*, Pub. by Pickering & Chatto UK); write for info. (*1-85196-187-9*, Pub. by Pickering & Chatto UK); write for info. (*1-85196-177-1*, Pub. by Pickering & Chatto UK) Ashgate Pub Co.

Works of Mark Twain. Mark Twain. 1990. 16.99 (*0-517-05357-8*) Random Hse Value.

Works of Mark Twain, 25 vols., Set. Mark Twain, pseud. 1987. reprint ed. lib. bdg. 1,250.00 (*0-7812-1105-0*) Rprt Serv.

Works of Mary (Edwards) Bryan, Set. Mary E. Bryan. 1989. reprint ed. lib. bdg. 63.00 (*0-685-74125-7*) Rprt Serv.

Works of Mary Wollstonecraft, 7 vols., Set. Mary Wollstonecraft. Ed. by Marilyn Butler & Janet Todd. (C). 1989. 595.00 (*0-8147-9225-1*) NYU Pr.

Works of Mary Wollstonecraft Vol. 1: Mary, Wrongs of Woman, Cave of Fancy. Mary Wollstonecraft. Ed. by Marilyn Butler & Janet Todd. (Gender Studies). (C). 1989. 95.00 (*0-8147-9226-X*) NYU Pr.

Works of Mary Wollstonecraft Vol. 2: Elements of Morality, Young Grandison. Mary Wollstonecraft. Ed. by Marilyn Butler & Janet Todd. (Gender Studies). (C). 1989. 95.00 (*0-8147-9227-8*) NYU Pr.

Works of Mary Wollstonecraft Vol. 3: Religious Opinions. Mary Wollstonecraft. Ed. by Marilyn Butler & Janet Todd. (Gender Studies). (C). 1989. 95.00 (*0-8147-9228-6*) NYU Pr.

Works of Mary Wollstonecraft Vol. 4: Education of Daughters, Female Reader, Original Stories, Management of Infants, Lessons. Mary Wollstonecraft. Ed. by Marilyn Butler & Janet Todd. (Gender Studies). (C). 1989. 95.00 (*0-8147-9229-4*) NYU Pr.

Works of Mary Wollstonecraft Vol. 5: Rights of Men, Rights of Women, Hints. Mary Wollstonecraft. Ed. by Marilyn Butler & Janet Todd. (Gender Studies). (C). 1989. 95.00 (*0-8147-9230-8*) NYU Pr.

Works of Mary Wollstonecraft Vol. 6: French Revolution, Letters. Mary Wollstonecraft. Ed. by Marilyn Butler & Janet Todd. (Gender Studies). (C). 1989. 95.00 (*0-8147-9231-6*) NYU Pr.

Works of Mary Wollstonecraft Vol. 7: On Poetry, Analytical Review, Index. Mary Wollstonecraft. Ed. by Marilyn Butler & Janet Todd. (Gender Studies). (C). 1989. 95.00 (*0-8147-9232-4*) NYU Pr.

Works of Mather Byles. Mather Byles. LC 78-6439. 1978. 75.00 (*0-8201-1309-3*) Schol Facsimiles.

Works of Matthew Arnold, 15 vols. Matthew Arnold. reprint ed. lib. bdg. 900.00 (*0-7812-0170-5*) Rprt Serv.

Works of Matthew Arnold, 15 vols. Matthew Arnold. LC 70-107157. 1970. reprint ed. 40.00 (*0-685-74309-8*) Scholarly.

Works of Matthew Arnold, 15 vols, Set. Matthew Arnold. LC 72-113544. (BCL Ser.: No. 1). reprint ed. 810.00 (*0-404-00450-4*) AMS Pr.

Works of Matthew Arnold, 15 vols., Set. Matthew Arnold. LC 70-107157. 1970. reprint ed. 395.00 (*0-403-00201-X*) Scholarly.

Works of Max Beerbohm. Max Beerbohm. 192p. 1985. reprint ed. lib. bdg. 39.00 (*0-932051-90-1*) Rprt Serv.

Works of Meister Eckhart; Sermons & Collations; Tractates; Sayings; Liber Positionum; In Collationbus; the Book of Benedictus; Bibliography. Franz Pfeiffer. 730p. 1992. reprint ed. pap. 49.95 (*1-56459-274-X*) Kessinger Pub.

Works of Mencius. Mencius. 1990. pap. 11.95 (*0-486-26375-4*) Dover.

***Works of Mercy.** (Saint Joseph Picture Bks.). (Illus.). 1987. pap. 1.25 (*0-89942-305-1*, 305-00) Catholic Bk Pub.

Works of Mercy. Fritz Eichenberg. LC 92-17041. (Illus.). 160p. 1992. 27.50 (*0-88344-828-9*) Orbis Bks.

Works of Michel-Guillaume Jean De Crevecoeur. Michel-Guillaume Jean De Crevecoeur. 1990. reprint ed. lib. bdg. 63.00 (*0-685-27760-7*) Rprt Serv.

Works of Miss Thackeray, 15 vols., Set. Anne I. Ritchie. LC 70-37717. reprint ed. 525.00 (*0-404-56810-6*) AMS Pr.

Works of Moncure Daniel Conway. Moncure D. Conway. 1990. reprint ed. lib. bdg. 63.00 (*0-685-44757-X*) Rprt Serv.

Works of Monsieur Noverre, Translated from the French, 3 vols., Set. Jean G. Noverre. LC 76-43930. reprint ed. 185.00 (*0-404-60110-3*) AMS Pr.

***Works of Mourning: Poetische Trauerarbeit, Selbstreflexion und Kritisches Traditionsbewubtsein in Modernen Englischen Elegien.** Andreas Jager. (Europaische Hochschulschriften, Reihe 14: Bd. 322). 221p. (GER.). 1997. 42.95 (*3-631-30642-3*) P Lang Pubng.

Works of Mr. John Oldham. John Oldham. LC 79-26304. 1980. reprint ed. 90.00 (*0-8201-1337-9*) Schol Facsimiles.

Works of Mr. William Shakespeare, 6 vols, Set. rev. ed. William Shakespeare. Ed. by Thomas Hanmer. LC 69-16818. (Illus.). reprint ed. lib. bdg. 595.00 (*0-404-01970-6*) AMS Pr.

Works of Mr. William Shakespeare, 7 Vols, Set. William Shakespeare. Ed. by Nicholas Rowe. LC 82-74393. reprint ed. 375.00 (*0-404-05770-5*) AMS Pr.

Works of Mrs. Amelia Opie, 3 vols., Set. Amelia A. Opie. LC 70-37706. (Women of Letters Ser.). reprint ed. 270.00 (*0-404-56796-7*) AMS Pr.

***Works of Mrs. Catharine Cockburn: Theological, Moral, Dramatic & Poetical (1751 Edition), 2 vols., Set.** Catharine Cockburn. 1120p. 1996. reprint ed. write for info. (*1-85506-124-4*) Bks Intl VA.

Works of Nathaniel Bowditch. Nathaniel Bowditch. 1989. reprint ed. lib. bdg. 63.00 (*0-685-27332-6*) Rprt Serv.

Works of Nathaniel Hawthorne, 12 vols., Set. Nathaniel Hawthorne. 1987. lib. bdg. 948.00 (*0-7812-1347-9*) Rprt Serv.

Works of Nathaniel Hawthorne, 12 vols., Set. Nathaniel Hawthorne. reprint ed. lib. bdg. 795.00 (*0-403-00022-X*) Scholarly.

Works of Nehemiah Adams, 1806-1878, Set. Nehemiah Adams. 1987. reprint ed. lib. bdg. 500.00 (*0-685-18566-4*) Rprt Serv.

***Works of Nikolai D. Kondratiev.** N. D. Kondratev et al. LC 96-50960. 1997. write for info. (*1-85196-261-1*, Pub. by Pickering & Chatto UK) Ashgate Pub Co.

Works of Orestes A. Brownson, 20 Vols, Set. Orestes A. Brownson. Ed. by Henry F. Brownson. LC 12-30124. reprint ed. 1,530.00 (*0-404-01180-2*) AMS Pr.

Works of Orestes Augustus Brownson. Orestes A. Brownson. 1989. reprint ed. lib. bdg. 63.00 (*0-685-74132-X*) Rprt Serv.

Works of Oscar Wilde, 15 Vols, Set. Oscar Wilde. LC 75-148333. reprint ed. 900.00 (*0-404-59610-X*) AMS Pr.

***Works of Patrick Branwell Bronte: An Edition, Vol. 1.** Ed. by Victor A. Neufeldt. (Literature Reference Ser.). 494p. 1997. text ed. 84.00 (*0-8153-0224-X*, SS1238) Garland.

Works of Paul Allen, 1775-1826, Set. Paul Allen. 1987. reprint ed. lib. bdg. 500.00 (*0-685-18587-7*) Rprt Serv.

Works of Petronius Arbiter, in Prose & Verse. Petronius. LC 73-158324. (Augustan Translators Ser.). reprint ed. 55.00 (*0-404-54129-1*) AMS Pr.

Works of Philo. enl. unabridged ed. Tr. by C. D. Yonge. 944p. 1993. 29.95 (*0-943575-93-1*) Hendrickson MA.

Works of Plato. Plato. Ed. by Irwin Edman. Tr. by Benjamin E. Jowett. 1965. pap. text ed. write for info. (*0-07-553651-X*, T71) McGraw.

Works of Plato, 5 Vols, Set. Plato. LC 78-16080. reprint ed. 380.00 (*0-404-16360-2*) AMS Pr.

Works of Plato Vol. I. Tr. by Thomas Taylor. (Thomas Taylor Ser.: Vol. 9). 1996. 48.00 (*1-898910-08-1*) Minerva CA.

Works of Plato Vol. II. Tr. by Thomas Taylor. (Thomas Taylor Ser.: Vol. 10). 1996. 45.00 (*1-898910-09-X*) Minerva CA.

Works of Plato Vol. III. Tr. by Thomas Taylor. (Thomas Taylor Ser.: Vol. 11). 1996. 45.00 (*1-898910-10-3*) Minerva CA.

Works of Plato Vol. IV. Tr. by Thomas Taylor. (Thomas Taylor Ser.: Vol. 12). 1996. 45.00 (*1-898910-11-1*) Minerva CA.

Works of Plato Vol. V. Tr. by Thomas Taylor. (Thomas Taylor Ser.: Vol. 13). 1996. 45.00 (*1-898910-12-X*) Minerva CA.

Works of Ralph Green. Ralph Green. LC 81-51378. 112p. 1981. reprint ed. 24.95 (*0-932606-02-4*) Ye Olde Print.

Works of Ralph Vaughan Williams. 2nd ed. Michael Kennedy. (Illus.). 464p. 1994. pap. 21.00 (*0-19-816330-4*) OUP.

Works of Reverend G. W., 6 vols., Set. George Whitefield. LC 75-31107. reprint ed. 310.00 (*0-404-13530-7*) AMS Pr.

W

Works of Richard Alsop, 1761-1815, Set. Richard Alsop. 1987. reprint ed. lib. bdg. 500.00 (*0-685-18592-3*) Rprt Serv.

Works of Richard Cobden, 6 vols., Set. 2nd ed. Ed. by Peter Cain. 3185p. (C). (gr. 13 up). 1996. text ed. 660.00 (*0-415-12742-4*, Routledge NY) Routledge.

***Works of Richard Hooker Vol. VII: Index of Names & Works.** Ed. by W. Speed Hill. (Medieval & Renaissance Texts & Studies: Vol. 170). Date not set. 40.00 (*0-86698-211-6*, MR170) MRTS.

Works of Richard Hooker (Folger Library Edition) Vol. 6: Of the Laws of Ecclesiastical Polity, Introductions & Commentary, 2 pts. Ed. by W. Speed Hill et al. LC 92-34130. (Medieval & Renaissance Texts & Studies: Vol. 106). 1296p. 1993. 75.00 (*0-86698-152-7*, MR106) MRTS.

Works of Richard Sibbes, Vol. III. Richard Sibbes. 543p. 1981. 25.99 (*0-85151-329-8*) Banner of Truth.

Works of Richard Sibbes, Vol. IV. Richard Sibbes. 527p. 1983. reprint ed. 25.99 (*0-85151-371-9*) Banner of Truth.

Works of Richard Sibbes, Vol. VI. Richard Sibbes. 560p. 1983. reprint ed. 25.99 (*0-85151-372-7*) Banner of Truth.

Works of Richard Sibbes, Vol. VII. Richard Sibbes. Ed. by Alexander B. Grosart. 604p. 1982. 25.99 (*0-85151-341-7*) Banner of Truth.

Works of Richard Wagner, 10 vols. in 7, Set. Richard Wagner. Ed. by Michael Balling. LC 72-75306. (Music Ser.). 1971. reprint ed. lib. bdg. 550.00 (*0-306-77250-7*) Da Capo.

Works of Robert Boyle, 6 vols., Set. Robert Boyle. Ed. by Thomas Birch. 4769p. 1966. lib. bdg. 1,585.00 (*0-685-13758-9*, 05101127) G Olms Pubs.

Works of Robert Browning, 10 vols., Set. Robert Browning. (BCL1-PR English Literature Ser.). 1992. reprint ed. lib. bdg. 900.00 (*0-7812-7457-5*) Rprt Serv.

Works of Robert Davenport. Robert Davenport. Ed. by Arthur H. Bullen. LC 68-24819. 362p. 1972. 30.95 (*0-405-08436-6*, Pub. by Blom Pubns UK) Ayer.

Works of Robert Fergusson. Robert Fergusson. Ed. by A. B. Grosart. LC 75-144464. reprint ed. 64.50 (*0-404-08555-5*) AMS Pr.

Works of Robert G. Ingersoll, 12 Vols, Set. Robert G. Ingersoll. LC 70-170063. reprint ed. 1,026.50 (*0-404-03490-X*) AMS Pr.

Works of Robert Louis Stevenson, 26 vols., Set. Robert Louis Stevenson. LC 70-143897. reprint ed. 1,980.00 (*0-404-08750-7*) AMS Pr.

Works of Robert Montgomery Bird. Robert M. Bird. 1989. reprint ed. lib. bdg. 63.00 (*0-685-27343-1*) Rprt Serv.

Works of Robert Sanderson, 6 Vols, Set. Robert Sanderson. Ed. by W. Jacobson. LC 76-175433. reprint ed. lib. bdg. 210.00 (*0-404-05570-2*) AMS Pr.

Works of Robert Whytt. Robert Whytt. Bd. with Memoirs on the Nervous System. Marshall Hall. LC 77-72191.; Memoirs. Pierre J. Cabanis. LC 77-72191.; Two Essays. G. S. Hall & E. DuBois-Reymond. LC 77-72191. LC 77-72191. (Contributions to the History of Psychology Ser.: Vol. I, Pt. E, Physiological Psychology). 508p. 1978. reprint ed. Set text ed. 79.50 (*0-313-26949-1*, U6949, Greenwood Pr) Greenwood.

Works of Rufus Choate, 2 vols., Set. Rufus Choate. Ed. by Samuel G. Brown. LC 72-70. reprint ed. 157.50 (*0-404-01526-3*) AMS Pr.

Works of Saint Bonaventure, 6. Bonaventure Staff. Date not set. pap. write for info. (*1-57659-042-9*) Franciscan Inst.

Works of Saint Patrick: Saint Secundius Hymn on St. Patrick. (Ancient Christian Writers Ser.: No. 17). 1953. 11.95 (*0-8091-6254-7*) Paulist Pr.

Works of Samuel Austin Allibone, 1816-1889, Set. Samuel A. Allibone. 1987. reprint ed. lib. bdg. 1,000.00 (*0-685-18590-7*) Rprt Serv.

Works of Samuel Butler, 20 Vols, Set. Samuel Butler. Ed. by Henry F. Jones & A. T. Bartholomew. LC 77-181920. (BCL Ser. II). reprint ed. 800.00 (*0-404-01320-1*) AMS Pr.

Works of Samuel Clemens. Mark Twain, pseud. 1989. reprint ed. lib. bdg. 63.00 (*0-685-74136-2*) Rprt Serv.

Works of Samuel Johnson, 11 Vols, Set. Samuel Johnson. Ed. by Francis P. Walesby. LC 79-126085. reprint ed. 990.00 (*0-404-03610-4*) AMS Pr.

***Work(s) of Samuel Richardson.** Stephanie Fysh. LC 97-3935. 1997. write for info. (*0-87413-626-1*) U Delaware Pr.

W

Works of Shakespeare, 6 Vols, Set. William Shakespeare. Ed. by Alexander Pope. LC 68-55096. reprint ed. lib. bdg. 1,125.00 (*0-404-05780-2*) AMS Pr.

Works of Shakespeare, 8 Vols, Set. William Shakespeare. Ed. by William Warburton. LC 68-55097. reprint ed. lib. bdg. 560.00 (*0-404-05800-0*) AMS Pr.

Works of Sir Francis Bacon, 15 vols., Set. Francis Bacon. 1987. reprint ed. lib. bdg. 1,074.00 (*0-7812-0731-2*) Rprt Serv.

Works of Sir John Suckling in Prose & Verse. John Suckling. (BCL1-PR English Literature Ser.). 424p. 1992. reprint ed. lib. bdg. 99.00 (*0-7812-7411-7*) Rprt Serv.

Works of Sir Thomas Malory, Vol. II. 3rd rev. ed. Thomas Malory. Ed. by Eugene Vinaver. (Oxford English Texts Ser.). 654p. 1990. 150.00 (*0-19-812345-0*) OUP.

Works of Sir Thomas Malory, Vol. III. 3rd rev. ed. Thomas Malory. Ed. by Eugene Vinaver. (Oxford English Texts Ser.). 680p. 1990. 160.00 (*0-19-812346-9*) OUP.

Works of Sir Thomas Urquhart of Cromarty, Knight. Thomas Urquhart. LC 76-165339. (Maitland Club, Glasgow. Publications: No. 30). reprint ed. 67.50 (*0-404-52989-5*) AMS Pr.

Works of Sir William Davenant, 2 vols., Set. William Davenant. LC 67-31454. 1018p. 1972. 60.95 (*0-405-08433-1*, Pub. by Blom Pubns UK) Ayer.

Works of Sir William Davenant, 2 vols., Vol. 1. William Davenant. LC 67-31454. 1972. 30.95 (*0-405-08434-X*, Pub. by Blom Pubns UK) Ayer.

Works of Sir William Davenant, 2 vols., Vol. 2. William Davenant. LC 67-31454. 1972. 30.95 (*0-405-08435-8*, Pub. by Blom Pubns UK) Ayer.

Works of Sir William Jones. William Jones. Ed. by Burton Feldman & Robert D. Richardson. LC 78-60883. (Myth & Romanticism Ser.). 676p. 1984. text ed. 15.00 (*0-8240-3563-1*) Garland.

Works of Solitude. Gyorgy Sebestyen. Tr. & Comment by Michael Mitchell. (Studies in Austrian Literature, Culture, & Thought. Translation Ser.). 1991. 28.50 (*0-929497-21-X*); pap. 22.50 (*0-929497-26-0*) Ariadne CA.

Works of Spinoza, 2 vols., Vol. 1. unabridged ed. Benedict De Spinoza. Tr. by Elwes. Incl. Vol. 2. . 1990. 21.25 (*0-8446-6902-4*); Vol. 1. . 1990. 21.25 (*0-8446-6901-6*); 1990. 42.50 (*0-8446-2986-3*) Peter Smith.

Works of Spiritualism & Healing, 6 vols. Maurice Barbanell. 1973. 800.00 (*0-8490-1331-3*) Gordon Pr.

Works of Splendor & Imagination: The Exhibition Watercolor, 1770-1870. Jane Bayard. LC 81-52432. (Illus.). 83p. (Orig.). 1981. pap. 15.00 (*0-930606-32-9*) Yale Ctr Brit Art.

Works of Stefan George. 2nd ed. Stefan George. Tr. by Olga Marx & Ernst Morwitz. (Studies in the Germanic Languages & Literatures: No. 78). xxvi, 427p. 1974. 35.00 (*0-8078-8078-7*) U of NC Pr.

Works of Stefan George. 2nd enl. rev. ed. Stefan A. George. Tr. by Olga Marx & Ernst Morwitz from GER. LC 73-16133. (University of North Carolina Studies in Comparative Literature: Vol. 78). 459p. 1974. reprint ed. pap. 130.90 (*0-608-02071-0*, 2062724) Bks Demand.

Works of Stephen Crane. Stephen Crane. 1990. reprint ed. lib. bdg. 63.00 (*0-685-27798-4*) Rprt Serv.

***Works of Stephen Crane Vol. 1: Bowery Tales; Maggie & George's Mother.** Stephen Crane. Ed. by Fredson Bowers. LC 68-8536. (Illus.). 184p. (C). 1969. 35.00 (*0-8139-0258-4*) U Pr of Va.

Works of Stephen Crane Vol. 2: The Red Badge of Courage. Stephen Crane. Ed. by Fredson Bowers. LC 68-8536. 420p. 1975. text ed. 35.00 (*0-8139-0514-1*) U Pr of Va.

***Works of Stephen Crane Vol. 3: The Third Violet & the Active Service.** Stephen Crane. Ed. by Fredson Bowers. LC 68-8536. 492p. 1976. 35.00 (*0-8139-0666-0*) U Pr of Va.

Works of Stephen Crane Vol. 4: The O'Ruddy. Stephen Crane. Ed. by Fredson Bowers. LC 68-8536. (Illus.). 362p. 1971. text ed. 35.00 (*0-8139-0341-6*) U Pr of Va.

Works of Stephen Crane Vol. 6: Tales of War. Stephen Crane. Ed. by Fredson Bowers. LC 68-8536. (Illus.). 400p. 1970. text ed. 35.00 (*0-8139-0294-0*) U Pr of Va.

***Works of Stephen Crane Vol. 7: Tales of Whilomville, the Monster, His New Mittens.** Stephen Crane. Ed. by Fredson Bowers. LC 68-8536. (Illus.). 277p. (C). 1969. 35.00 (*0-8139-0259-2*) U Pr of Va.

Works of Stephen Crane Vol. 8: Tales, Sketches, & Reports. Stephen Crane. Ed. by Fredson Bowers. LC 68-8536. (Illus.). 1183p. 1973. text ed. 47.50 (*0-8139-0405-6*) U Pr of Va.

Works of Stephen Crane Vol. 9: Reports of War. Stephen Crane. Ed. by Fredson Bowers. LC 68-8536. (Illus.). 678p. 1971. text ed. 37.50 (*0-8139-0342-4*) U Pr of Va.

Works of Stephen Crane Vol. 10: Poems & Literary Remains. Stephen Crane. Ed. by Fredson Bowers. LC 68-8536. 1975. text ed. 35.00 (*0-8139-0610-5*) U Pr of Va.

Works of Stephen Hawes. Stephen Hawes. LC 75-14304. 400p. 1975. reprint ed. lib. bdg. 50.00 (*0-8201-1148-1*) Schol Facsimiles.

Works of Stephen Pearl Andrews, 1812-1886, Set. Stephen P. Andrews. 1987. reprint ed. lib. bdg. 500.00 (*0-685-18596-6*) Rprt Serv.

Works of Susan Ferrier, 4 vols., Set. Susan Ferrier. LC 74-118948. reprint ed. write for info. (*0-404-02380-0*) AMS Pr.

Works of the English Poets, from Chaucer to Cowper Vol. XX. Ed. by Bernhard Fabian. (Anglistische und Amerikanistische Texte und Studien Ser.: No. 51). 1970. reprint ed. 86.61 (*3-487-04014-X*) G Olms Pubs.

Works of the English Poets, from Chaucer to Cowper Vol. XIX: Homer's Iliad & Odyssey: Translated by Pope; The Works of Virgil: Translated by Dryden; Virgil's Aeneid: Translated by Pitt; Vida's Art of Poetry: Translated by Pitt; The Works of Horace: Translated by Philip Francis. Ed. by Bernhard Fabian. (Anglistica & Americana Ser.: No. 51). 1970. reprint ed. 86.61 (*3-487-04013-1*) G Olms Pubs.

Works of the English Poets, from Chaucer to Cowper Vol. XVI: The Poems of Christopher Smart; William Wilkie; Paul Whitehead; Francis Fawkes; Edward Lovibond; Walter Harte; John Longhorne; Oliver Goldsmith; John Armstrong; Samuel Johnson. Ed. by Bernhard Fabian. (Anglistica & Americana Ser.: No. 51). 1970. reprint ed. 86.61 (*3-487-04011-5*) G Olms Pubs.

Works of the English Poets, from Chaucer to Cowper Vol. XVIII: The Poems of Nathaniel Cotton; John Logan; Thomas Warton; Thomas Blacklock; Richard Owen Cambridge; William Mason; William Jones; James Beattie; William Cowper. Ed. by Bernhard Fabian. (Anglistica & Americana Ser.: No. 51). 1970. reprint ed. 86.61 (*3-487-04012-3*) G Olms Pubs.

Works of the English Poets, from Chaucer to Cowper Vol. XXI: Orlando Furioso: Translated from the Italian of Ludovico Ariosto, with Notes by John Hoole; Jerusalem. Contrib. by Bernhard Fabian. (Anglistica & Americana Ser.: No. 51). 1970. reprint ed. 86.61 (*3-487-04015-8*) G Olms Pubs.

Works of the Ettrick Shepherd, 2 Vols, Set. James Hogg. LC 72-144466. reprint ed. 195.00 (*0-404-08558-X*) AMS Pr.

Works of the Ever Memorable Mr. John Hales of Eaton, 3 vols. in 2. John Hales. Ed. by D. Dalrymple. LC 77-131037. reprint ed. 190.00 (*0-404-03050-5*) AMS Pr.

Works of the Gawain-Poet. Ed. by Charles Moorman. LC 76-40190. (Illus.). 464p. reprint ed. pap. 132.30 (*0-8357-4347-0*, 2037150) Bks Demand.

Works of the Most Reverend Father in God, William Laud, D. D., 9 Pts., Set. William Laud. LC 74-5373. (Library of Anglo-Catholic Theology: No. 11). reprint ed. 805.00 (*0-404-52120-7*) AMS Pr.

Works of the People of Old: Na Hana A Ka Po'e Kahiko. S. M. Kamakau. Ed. by Dorothy B. Barrere. Tr. by Mary K. Pukui. LC 75-21315. (Special Publication Ser.: No. 61). (Illus.). 178p. 1987. 16.50 (*0-910240-18-3*); pap. 15.95 (*0-930897-82-X*) Bishop Mus.

Works of the Right Rev. John England, First Bishop of Charleston. John England & Iqnatius A. Reynolds. 1978. 210.95 (*0-405-10822-2*) Ayer.

Works of Thomas Adams, 3 vols, Set. Thomas Adams. LC 72-158226. reprint ed. 65.00 (*0-404-00350-8*) AMS Pr.

Works of Thomas Bailey Aldrich, 1836-1907, Set. Thomas B. Aldrich. 1987. reprint ed. lib. bdg. 500.00 (*0-685-18584-2*) Rprt Serv.

Works of Thomas Bulfinch. Thomas Bulfinch. 1989. reprint ed. lib. bdg. 63.00 (*0-685-74130-3*) Rprt Serv.

Works of Thomas Carlyle, 30 Vols, Set. Thomas Carlyle. Ed. by H. D. Traill. LC 79-22238. (BCL Ser. II). reprint ed. 2,535.00 (*0-404-09800-2*) AMS Pr.

Works of Thomas Carlyle, 30 vols., Set. Thomas Carlyle. (BCL1-PR English Literature Ser.). 1992. reprint ed. lib. bdg. 2,700.00 (*0-7812-7484-2*) Rprt Serv.

Works of Thomas Chatterton, 3 Vols, Set. Thomas Chatterton. Ed. by Robert Southey & Joseph Cottle. LC 71-80892. 1968. reprint ed. 230.00 (*0-404-01540-9*) AMS Pr.

Works of Thomas Chivers. Thomas H. Chivers. 1990. reprint ed. lib. bdg. 63.00 (*0-685-27674-0*) Rprt Serv.

Works of Thomas Deloney. Thomas Deloney. (BCL1-PR English Literature Ser.). 600p. 1992. reprint ed. lib. bdg. 99.00 (*0-7812-7202-5*) Rprt Serv.

Works of Thomas Gold Appleton, 1812-1884, Set. Thomas G. Appleton. 1987. reprint ed. lib. bdg. 500.00 (*0-685-18599-0*) Rprt Serv.

Works of Thomas Goodwin, 12 vols., Set. 1996. lib. bdg. 399.95 (*0-9651791-0-9*) Tanski Publns.

Works of Thomas Goodwin, 12 Vols, Set. Thomas Goodwin. LC 74-168155. reprint ed. lib. bdg. 450.00 (*0-404-02870-5*) AMS Pr.

Works of Thomas Gray in Verse & Prose, 4 Vols, Set. Thomas Gray. Ed. by Edmund Gosse. LC 76-168185. reprint ed. 210.00 (*0-404-02900-0*) AMS Pr.

Works of Thomas Hardy in Prose: With Prefaces & Notes, 18 vols. Thomas Hardy. LC 83-45547. (Wessex Edition Ser.). 7000p. 1984. reprint ed. 1,485.00 (*0-404-60730-6*) AMS Pr.

Works of Thomas Hardy in Prose & Verse, with Prefaces & Notes, 21 vols., Set. Thomas Hardy. (BCL1-PR English Literature Ser.). 1992. reprint ed. lib. bdg. 1,890.00 (*0-7812-7545-8*) Rprt Serv.

Works of Thomas Hill Green, 3 Vols, Set. 3rd ed. Thomas H. Green. Ed. by R. L. Nettleship. reprint ed. 275.00 (*0-404-02910-8*) AMS Pr.

Works of Thomas Hood, 8 vols, Set. Thomas Hood. LC 70-170044. reprint ed. 612.00 (*0-404-03340-7*) AMS Pr.

Works of Thomas Lovell Beddoes. Thomas L. Beddoes. Ed. by H. W. Donner. LC 75-41023. (BCL Ser. II). 1976. reprint ed. 72.50 (*0-404-14507-8*) AMS Pr.

Works of Thomas Manton, 22 Vols, Set. Thomas Manton. LC 76-172841. reprint ed. 465.00 (*0-404-04200-7*) AMS Pr.

Works of Thomas Manton, 3 vols., Vol. 1. Thomas Manton. 500p. 1993. 25.99 (*0-85151-648-3*) Banner of Truth.

Works of Thomas Manton, 3 vols., Vol. 2. Thomas Manton. 500p. 1993. 25.99 (*0-85151-649-1*) Banner of Truth.

Works of Thomas Manton, 3 vols., Vol. 3. Thomas Manton. 500p. 1993. 25.99 (*0-85151-650-5*) Banner of Truth.

Works of Thomas Middleton, 8 Vols, Set. Thomas Middleton. Ed. by A. H. Bullen. LC 78-181958. reprint ed. write for info. (*0-404-04330-5*) AMS Pr.

Works of Thomas Nabbes, 2 Vols. Thomas Nabbes. Ed. by Arthur H. Bullen. LC 68-24818. 1972. reprint ed. 36.95 (*0-405-08812-4*) Ayer.

***Works of Thomas Reid: 1863 Edition, 2 vols., Set.** Ed. by William Hamilton. 1058p. 1996. reprint ed. write for info. (*1-85506-336-0*) Bks Intl VA.

Works of Thomas Southerne, Vol. II. Thomas Southerne. Ed. by Robert Jordon & Harold Love. (Oxford English Texts Ser.). (Illus.). 512p. 1988. 125.00 (*0-19-812798-7*) OUP.

Works of Thomas Vaughan. Ed. by Arthur E. Waite. 500p. 1992. reprint ed. pap. 33.00 (*1-56459-009-7*) Kessinger Pub.

Works of Thy Hands. Gyla B. Poli & January Taylor. Ed. by Myrna Kemnitz. (Illus.). 186p. (Orig.). (YA). (gr. 9 up). 1996. pap. 7.99 (*0-88092-299-0*, 2990) Royal Fireworks.

Works of Timothy Shay Arthur, 1809-1885, Set. Timothy S. Arthur. 1987. reprint ed. lib. bdg. 500.00 (*0-685-18605-9*) Rprt Serv.

Works of Virgil, 3 vols. Vergilius. Ed. by Henry Nettleship. clxxxii, 1540p. (GER.). 1979. reprint ed. write for info. (*0-318-70514-1*) G Olms Pubs.

Works of Virgil, 3 vols., Set. Vergilius. Ed. by John Conington & Henry Nettleship. clxxxii, 1540p. 1979. reprint ed. 310.70 (*3-487-00545-X*) G Olms Pubs.

Works of Virgil, 3 vols., Vol. I, Eclogues & Georgics. Vergilius. Ed. by Henry Nettleship. clxxxii, 1540p. (GER.). 1979. reprint ed. Vol. I: Eclogues & Georgics. write for info. (*0-318-70515-X*) G Olms Pubs.

Works of Virgil, 3 vols., Vol. II, The First Six Books of the Aeneid. Vergilius. Ed. by Henry Nettleship. clxxxii, 1540p. (GER.). 1979. reprint ed. Vol. II: The First Six Books of the Aeneid. write for info. (*0-318-70516-8*) G Olms Pubs.

Works of Virgil, 3 vols., Vol. III, The Last Six Books of the Aeneid. Vergilius. Ed. by Henry Nettleship. clxxxii, 1540p. (GER.). 1979. reprint ed. Vol. III: The Last Six Books of the Aeneid. write for info. (*0-318-70517-6*) G Olms Pubs.

Works of Voltaire: A Contemporary Version, 2 vols. Voltaire. 1975. lib. bdg. 500.00 (*0-87968-228-0*) Gordon Pr.

Works of Walter Bagehot, 5 vols., Set. Ed. by Forrest Morgan. 2706p. (C). 1995. boxed, text ed. 545.00 (*0-415-13154-5*, Routledge NY) Routledge.

Works of Washington Allston, 1779-1843, Set. Washington Allston. 1987. reprint ed. lib. bdg. 600.00 (*0-685-18591-5*) Rprt Serv.

Works of Washington Irving, 27 vols, Set. Washington Irving. LC 70-170808. reprint ed. 877.50 (*0-404-03510-8*) AMS Pr.

Works of Wilkie Collins, 30 Vols, Set. Wilkie Collins. reprint ed. 2,790.00 (*0-404-01750-9*) AMS Pr.

Works of William Allen, 1784-1868, Set. William Allen. 1987. reprint ed. lib. bdg. 500.00 (*0-685-18589-3*) Rprt Serv.

Works of William Andrus Alcott, 1798-1859, Set. William A. Alcott. 1987. reprint ed. lib. bdg. 500.00 (*0-685-18575-3*) Rprt Serv.

Works of William Apes, Set. William Apes. 1987. reprint ed. lib. bdg. write for info. (*0-318-62095-2*) Rprt Serv.

Works of William Austin 1778-1841. William Austin. reprint ed. lib. bdg. 500.00 (*0-685-18609-1*) Rprt Serv.

Works of William Blake, Poetic, Symbolic, & Critical, 3 Vols, Set. William Blake. LC 79-13496. (Illus.). reprint ed. 145.50 (*0-404-08990-9*) AMS Pr.

Works of William Bradford. William Bradford. 1989. reprint ed. lib. bdg. 63.00 (*0-685-27322-9*) Rprt Serv.

Works of William Bridge, 5 Vols. William Bridge. 2354p. 1989. reprint ed. 120.00 (*1-877611-10-7*) Soli Deo Gloria.

Works of William Byrd. William Byrd. 1989. reprint ed. lib. bdg. 63.00 (*0-685-74127-3*) Rprt Serv.

Works of William Carleton, 2 Vols, Set. William Carleton. LC 77-106257. (Short Story Index Reprint Ser.). 1977. 96.95 (*0-8369-3294-3*) Ayer.

Works of William Chillingworth, 3 Vols, Set. William Chillingworth. reprint ed. lib. bdg. 255.00 (*0-404-01570-0*) AMS Pr.

Works of William Cowper, 15 Vols, Set. William Cowper. Ed. by Robert Southey. LC 71-18097. reprint ed. 1,140.00 (*0-404-01840-8*) AMS Pr.

Works of William Cullen Bryant. William C. Bryant. 1989. reprint ed. lib. bdg. 63.00 (*0-685-74131-1*) Rprt Serv.

Works of William Ellery Channing II. William E. Channing, II. 1990. reprint ed. lib. bdg. 63.00 (*0-685-27685-6*) Rprt Serv.

Works of William Ernest Henley, 7 Vols, Set. William E. Henley. reprint ed. 475.00 (*0-404-03290-7*) AMS Pr.

Works of William Hogarth. deluxe ed. 1978. reprint ed. lib. bdg. 40.00 (*0-932106-03-X*, Pub. by Marathon Press) S J Durst.

Works of William Perkins, 3 Vols, Set. William Perkins. LC 74-144670. reprint ed. lib. bdg. 285.00 (*0-404-05050-6*) AMS Pr.

Works of William Robertson, 12 vols., Set. Ed. by Sher. 5160p. (C). 1996. text ed. 1,545.00 (*0-415-13743-8*) Routledge.

Works of William Shakespeare, 16 Vols, Set. William Shakespeare. Ed. by James O. Halliwell-Phillipps. LC 69-18314. (Illus.). reprint ed. 3,150.00 (*0-404-05920-1*) AMS Pr.

Works of William Wells Brown, 3 vols. in 1. William W. Brown. (B. E. Ser.: No. 73). 1858. Three works in one unit. 45.00 (*0-8115-3024-8*) Periodicals Srv.

Works on Horses & Equitation: A Bibliographical Record of Hippology. F. H. Huth. (Documenta Hippologica Ser.). 439p. 1981. reprint ed. 65.00 (*3-487-08211-X*) G Olms Pubs.

Works on Paper. Eliot Weinberger. LC 86-8763. 160p. 1986. 22.95 (*0-8112-1000-6*); pap. 9.95 (*0-8112-1001-4*, NDP627) New Directions.

Works on Paper 1900-1960 from Southern California Collections. David W. Steadman. LC 77-82659. (Illus.). 132p. 1977. 5.00 (*0-915478-10-2*) Montgomery Gallery.

Works on Subud, 3 vols. J. G. Bennett. 1972. 750.00 (*0-8490-1332-1*) Gordon Pr.

Works on the Foundations of Statistical Physics. Nikolai S. Krylov. Tr. by Ya G. Sinai et al. from RUS. LC 78-70611. (Physics Ser.). 1979. 49.50 (*0-691-08230-8*) Princeton U Pr.

Works on Vision. George Berkeley. Ed. by Colin M. Turbayne. LC 62-11787. (Orig.). 1963. 6.60 (*0-672-51033-2*, Bobbs); pap. 4.35 (*0-672-60267-9*, LLA83, Bobbs) Macmillan.

Works on Vision. George Berkeley. Ed. by Colin M. Turbayne. LC 81-7160. (Library of Liberal Arts: No. 83). lii, 158p. (Orig.). 1981. reprint ed. text ed. 49.75 (*0-313-23186-9*, BEWV, Greenwood Pr) Greenwood.

Works Progress Administration in New York City. J. D. Millett. LC 77-74950. (American Federalism-the Urban Dimension Ser.). 1978. reprint ed. lib. bdg. 23.95 (*0-405-10496-0*) Ayer.

An Asterisk (*) at the beginning of an entry indicates that the title is appearing in BIP for the first time.

Works with English Texts: Vocal & Instrumental Music from Eighteenth-Century Manuscript & Printed Sources. Ed. by Ernest Warburton. LC 83-48727. (Collected Works of Johann Christian Bach: Vol. 25). 448p. 1990. text ed. 150.00 (*0-8240-6074-1*) Garland.

Works Wonders: Rallying & Racing with BMC, Rootes & Chrysler. Marcus Chambers. (Illus.). 320p. 1995. 32.95 (*0-947981-94-2*, Pub. by Motor Racing UK) Motorbooks Intl.

Works Word Processor: Quickstart 2.0. Sue V. Stacy. (DF - Computer Applications Ser.). 1991. pap. 19.95 (*0-538-70459-4*) S-W Pub.

Works, 1850-1851, 14 vols., Set. Washington Irving. 695.00 (*0-403-00384-9*) Scholarly.

Works 3 for Windows: Visual QuickStart Guide. Glen Waller. 224p. pap. 13.95 (*1-56609-132-2*) Peachpit Pr.

Works 3 for Windows Essentials. 1995. 49.99 (*0-7897-0130-8*) Que.

Works (3 Sermons) Charles H. Spurgeon. 1976. pap. 3.00 (*1-56186-407-2*) Pilgrim Pubns.

***Works 3.0 for Windows.** Elf. (C). 1995. 30.95 (*0-03-013907-4*) HB Coll Pubs.

Works 3.0 for Windows: An Innovative Approach. Patricia L. Sullivan. 528p. 1995. pap. 27.95 (*0-938661-86-8*) Franklin Beedle.

***Works 4 For Windows 95 Essentials.** Matherly. 1997. 49.99 (*1-57576-831-3*) Sams.

***Works 4.0 for Windows.** Timothy J. O'Leary. 1996. pap. text ed. write for info. (*0-07-049116-X*) McGraw.

Worksheet & Instructor's Guide to Accompany Your Massachusetts Government. 10th ed. Harold M. Gay. 1985. write for info. (*0-931684-08-0*) Gov Res Pubns.

Worksheet Book: Buiding Skills for 1-2-3 & Symphony. Ed. by Steven E. Miller. (Best of Lotus Magazine Ser.). 400p. 1988. pap. 21.95 (*0-201-15039-5*) Addison-Wesley.

Worksheets for the Abacus, Complete Volume. Joan A. Cotter. (Illus.). 320p. (J). (gr. k-4). 1988. pap. 25.00 (*0-9609636-6-9*) Activities Learning.

Worksheets for Touchpebbles Vol. B. Geoffrey Comber et al. (Touchpebbles Ser.). 32p. (Orig.). (J). (gr. 4-5). 1993. student ed., pap. 1.50 (*1-878461-16-8*) CZM Pr.

Worksheets for Touchpebbles A Vol. A. Geoffrey Comber et al. (Touchpebbles Ser.). 32p. 1994. student ed. 1.95 (*1-878461-28-1*) CZM Pr.

Worksheets for Touchstones Vol. II. Ed. by Geoffrey Comber et al. 30p. (Orig.). (YA). (gr. 9-12). 1988. student ed. 1.50 (*1-878461-30-3*) CZM Pr.

Worksheets for Touchstones for Middle Schools, Vol. A. Geoffrey Comber et al. (Touchstones for Middle Schools Ser.: No. 1). 31p. (Orig.). 1992. student ed. 1.50 (*1-878461-17-6*) CZM Pr.

Worksheets for Touchstones for Middle Schools, Vol. B. Geoffrey Comber et al. (Touchstones for Middle Schools Ser.: No. 2). 32p. (Orig.). 1993. student ed. 1.50 (*1-878461-18-4*) CZM Pr.

Worksheets for Touchstones for Middle Schools en Espanol, Vol. A. Geoffrey Comber et al. 32p. (Orig.). (SPA.). 1994. pap. 1.50 (*1-878461-22-2*) CZM Pr.

***Worship Workbook for Gospel.** CSS Publishing Company, Staff. 1997. pap. text ed. 29.95 (*0-7880-1023-9*) CSS OH.

Workshirts & Silk Suits. Gary Class. 4.00 (*0-318-11914-5*) Great Raven Pr.

Workshop see Parallel Processing, 1996 International Conference

Workshop Appliances of the Nineteenth Century. 1996. lib. bdg. 261.95 (*0-8490-7593-9*) Gordon Pr.

***Workshop Approach: A Framework for Literacy.** Elinor P. Ross. 250p. (J). (gr. k-8). Date not set. pap. 28.95 (*0-926842-52-8*) CG Pubs Inc.

Workshop Book. Scott Landis. (Illus.). 224p. (C). 1991. 34.95 (*0-942391-37-3*) Taunton.

***Workshop Calculus.** Hastings. 27.00 (*0-7637-0248-X*) Jones & Bartlett.

Workshop Calculus: Guided Exploration with Review, Vol. 1. Nancy B. Hastings & Priscilla Laws. LC 95-47550. (Textbooks in Mathematical Sciences Ser.). 264p. 1996. pap. 29.95 (*0-387-94611-X*) Spr-Verlag.

Workshop Companion: Finish Carpentry. Nick Engler. (Illus.). 128p. 1995. 19.95 (*0-87596-138-X*, 14-421-0) Rodale Pr Inc.

Workshop Companion: Making Boxes & Chests. Nick Engler. (Illus.). 128p. 1994. 19.95 (*0-87596-583-0*) Rodale Pr Inc.

Workshop Companion: Making Jigs & Fixtures, Techniques for Better Woodworking. Nick Engler. 128p. 1995. 19.95 (*0-87596-689-6*) Rodale Pr Inc.

Workshop Companion: Making Tables & Chairs. Nick Engler. LC 94-34413. (Workshop Companion Ser.). (Illus.). 128p. 1995. 19.95 (*0-87596-655-1*) Rodale Pr Inc.

Workshop Companion: Using Hand Tools. Nick Engler. (Illus.). 128p. 1995. 19.95 (*0-87596-680-2*) Rodale Pr Inc.

Workshop Companion: Workbenches & Shop Furniture. Nick Engler. LC 92-44580. (Workshop Companion Ser.). 1993. 19.95 (*0-87596-579-2*) Rodale Pr Inc.

***Workshop Construction: Planning, Design & Construction for Workshops up to 3m (10 Ft.) Wide.** Jim Forrest & Peter Jennings. (Workshop Practice Ser.: No. 23). (Illus.). 133p. (Orig.). 1995. pap. 19.95 (*1-85486-131-X*, Pub. by Nexus Special Interests UK) Trans-Atl Phila.

Workshop Drawing. Tubal Cain. (Workshop Practice Ser.: No. 13). (Illus.). 112p. (Orig.). 1987. pap. 18.50 (*0-85242-867-7*, Pub. by Nexus Special Interests UK) Trans-Atl Phila.

Workshop for Managing Diversity in the Workplace. S. Kanu Kogod. 109p. 1991. ring bd. 79.95 (*0-88390-299-0*, Pfffr & Co) Jossey-Bass.

Workshop for Peace: Designing the United Nations Headquarters. George A. Dudley. LC 92-35859. (Architectural History Foundation Ser.). (Illus.). 429p. 1994. 67.50 (*0-262-04137-5*) MIT Pr.

Workshop in Science Photography. Robertson. Date not set. pap. write for info. (*0-240-80093-1*, Focal) Buttrwrth-Heinemann.

Workshop Math. Scharff. 1989. pap. 14.95 (*0-8273-5382-0*) Delmar.

Workshop Math. Robert Scharff. LC 89-33753. 464p. 1989. pap. 16.95 (*0-8069-5802-2*) Sterling.

***Workshop Numeracy.** Ogden. 1986. pap. text ed. write for info. (*0-273-01898-1*) Addison-Wesley.

Workshop of Democracy: The American Experiment, Vol. II. James M. Burns. LC 85-40231. 672p. 1985. 30.00 (*0-394-51275-8*) Knopf.

Workshop of Democracy: The American Experiment from the Emancipation Proclamation to the Eve of the New Deal. James M. Burns. LC 85-40697. 683p. 1986. pap. 25.00 (*0-394-74320-2*, Vin) Random.

Workshop of the Possible: Nurturing Children's Creative Development. Ruth S. Hubbard. (Illus.). 176p. (C). 1996. pap. text ed. 19.50 (*1-57110-007-5*) Stenhse Pubs.

Workshop on Computational Learning Theory: Proceedings of the 1988 Workshop. Ed. by David Haussler & Leonard Pitt. 400p. 1988. 19.95 (*1-55860-019-1*) Morgan Kaufmann.

Workshop on Database for Galactic Structure. Ed. by A. G. Davis Philip et al. 240p. 1993. 33.00 (*0-933485-17-4*) L Davis Pr.

Workshop on Design & Manufacture of Bamboo & Rattan Furniture: Asia Pacific Region, Jakarta, Indonesia. 550p. 1990. 65.00 (*92-1-106250-0*, 90.III.E.13) UN.

Workshop on Disseminated Intravascular Coagulation. Ed. by Berghaus G. Muller. LC 93-41243. 278p. 1993. 204.50 (*0-444-81647-X*) Elsevier.

Workshop on Drug Effects in Animals. Ed. by F. N. Krijzer & W. H. Herrmann. (Journal: Neuropsychobiology: Vol. 28, No. 3, 1993). (Illus.). 64p. 1993. pap. 58.50 (*3-8055-5857-0*) S Karger.

***Workshop on Dynamical Systems: Proceedings of the Conference at the International Centre for Theoretical Physics (ICTP), Trieste, 1988.** Workshop on Dynamical Systems Staff. Ed. by Z. Coelho & E. Shiels. LC 89-14589. (Pitman Research Notes in Mathematics Ser.: Vol. 221). 181p. 1990. reprint ed. pap. 51.60 (*0-608-03606-4*, 2064429) Bks Demand.

Workshop on Federal Programs Involving Supercritical Water Oxidation: Proceedings. Ed. by Gregory J. Rosasco. 303p. (Orig.). (C). 1993. pap. text ed. 65.00 (*0-7881-0042-4*) DIANE Pub.

***Workshop on High Performance Computing & Gigabit Local Area Networks, Vol. 226.** Cooperman, G., IGH Performance Computing & Gigabit Local Area Networks Staff et al. LC 97-19340. (Lecture Notes in Control & Information Sciences Ser.). 1997. pap. write for info. (*3-540-76169-1*) Spr-Verlag.

Workshop on New Directions in Mossbauer Spectroscopy, Argonne National Lab, June 1977. Ed. by Gilbert J. Perlow. LC 77-90635. (AIP Conference Proceedings Ser.: No. 38). (Illus.). 1977. lib. bdg. 15.00 (*0-88318-137-1*) Am Inst Physics.

Workshop on Oxidation Processes, Vol. 55, No. 6. Ed. by Nevill F. Mott. (Philosophical Magazine Ser.). 1987. pap. 34.00 (*0-85066-930-8*) Taylor & Francis.

Workshop on Oxidation Processes II, Vol. 55, No. 6. Ed. by Nevill F. Mott. (Philosophical Magazine Ser.). 1987. pap. 34.00 (*0-85066-917-0*) Taylor & Francis.

Workshop on Perspective in Nuclear Physics at Intermediate Energies, 5th: Short Distance Phenomena, ICTP, Trieste, Italy, May 6-10, 1991. Ed. by S. Boffi et al. LC 92-9940. 700p. (C). 1992. text ed. 143.00 (*981-02-0781-6*) World Scientific Pub.

Workshop on Planetary Boundary Layer 14-18 August 1978 Boulder Colorado. Intro. by J. C. Wyngaard. (Illus.). 322p. 1980. pap. 35.00 (*0-933876-51-3*) Am Meteorological.

Workshop on Polarized 3He Beams & Targets (Princeton, NJ 1984) Ed. by R. W. Dunford & F. P. Calaprice. LC 85-48026. (AIP Conference Proceedings Ser.: No. 131). 224p. 1985. lib. bdg. 39.25 (*0-88318-330-7*) Am Inst Physics.

Workshop on Prepaid Legal Services for Practicing Attorneys. 200p. 1985. 30.00 (*0-317-40256-0*, 2-008) Am Prepaid.

***Workshop on Prevention & Treatment of Childhood Obesity: Research Directions.** (Illus.). 70p. 1996. reprint ed. pap. 30.00 (*0-7881-3302-0*) DIANE Pub.

Workshop on Security Procedures for the Interchange of Electronic Documents: Selected Papers & Results. Ed. by Roy Saltman. (Illus.). 175p. (Orig.). (C). 1994. pap. text ed. 65.00 (*0-7881-0584-1*) DIANE Pub.

Workshop on Self Esteem. Helen M. Johnson. 34p. (Orig.). 1989. teacher ed., pap. text ed. 5.95 (*0-88133-453-7*) Sheffield WI.

Workshop on Small Fatigue Cracks: Proceedings of the Second Engineering Foundation International Conference. Ed. by R. O. Ritchie & J. Lankford. LC 86-19175. (Illus.). 677p. reprint ed. pap. 180.00 (*0-318-39700-5*, 2052268) Bks Demand.

Workshop on Specification of Abstract Data Types. Ed. by Hartmut Ehrig & Fernando Orejas. LC 94-8265. (Lecture Notes in Computer Science Ser.: Vol. 785). 1994. 55.95 (*0-387-57867-6*) Spr-Verlag.

Workshop on Supercomputing in Brain Research: From Tomography to Neural Networks, HLRZ, KFA Julich, Germany, November 21-23, 1994. Ed. by H. J. Herrmann et al. LC 95-13461. 472p. 1995. text ed. 98.00 (*981-02-2250-5*) World Scientific Pub.

Workshop on the Book of James: The Demands of a Practical Faith. Carolyn Nystrom & Margaret Fromer. 122p. (Orig.). 1980. pap. 5.99 (*0-310-41901-8*) Zondervan.

Workshop on the Conservation of the Orangutan. Ed. by Leobert E. De Boer. LC 82-7722. (Illus.). 353p. 1982. lib. bdg. 206.50 (*90-6193-702-7*) Kluwer Ac.

***Workshop on the Earth's Trapped Particle Environment.** Ed. by Geoffrey D. Reeves. (Conference Proceedings Ser.: No. 383). (Illus.). 256p. 1996. 100.00 (*1-56396-540-2*, AIP) Am Inst Physics.

Workshop on the Role of Border Problems in African Peace & Security: A Research Project. 132p. Date not set. pap. 12.00 (*92-1-142202-7*, E.94.IX.4) UN.

Workshop on the Role of Earthworms in the Stabilization of Organic Residues, 2 vols., Set. 1981. 70.00 (*0-939294-09-5*, TD-772-W6-1981) Beech Leaf.

Workshop on the Role of Earthworms in the Stabilization of Organic Residues: Bibliography, Vol. 2. Compiled by Diane D. Worden. LC 81-65289. 490p. (Orig.). 1981. pap. 50.00 (*0-939294-08-7*, TD-772-W6-1981) Beech Leaf.

Workshop on the Role of Earthworms in the Stabilization of Organic Residues: Proceedings, Vol. I. Mary Appelhof. LC 81-65289. 340p. 1981. pap. 25.00 (*0-939294-07-9*, TD-772-W6-1981, Flowerfield Ent) Beech Leaf.

***Workshop on the SPIN Verification System: DIMACS Workshop, August 5, 1996.** Jean-Charles Egoire et al. LC 96-54839. (DIMACS Series in Discrete Mathematics & Theoretical Computer Science: Vol. 32). 1997. 49.00 (*0-8218-0680-7*, DIMACS/32) Am Math.

Workshop on the Use of Race & Ethnicity in Public Health Surveillance. Ed. by Rueben C. Warren. (Illus.). 52p. (Orig.). (C). 1994. pap. text ed. 30.00 (*0-7881-0697-X*) DIANE Pub.

Workshop on Traffic & Granular Flow: HLRZ Forschungszentrum Julich (KFA), Germany, October 9-11, 1995. Ed. by D. E. Wolf et al. LC 96-2180. 392p. 1996. write for info. (*981-02-2635-7*) World Scientific Pub.

Workshop Physics Activity Guide: Set of 4 Modeules, Vol. 4. Priscilla W. Laws. LC 95-37038. 704p. 1996. pap. text ed. 28.00 (*0-471-10957-6*) Wiley.

Workshop Physics Activity Guide Core Volume. Priscilla W. Laws. 1996. pap. text ed. write for info. (*0-471-15593-4*) Wiley.

Workshop Planning. 2nd rev. ed. Ruth S. Smith. LC 78-24240. (Guide Ser.: No. 3). (Illus.). 65p. 1979. pap. 8.00 (*0-915324-15-6*); pap. 8.25 (*0-685-01331-6*) CSLA.

Workshop Proceedings: On Non-Economic Factors in Energy Supply & Demand, Virginia, 1979, Institute for the Future. Electric Power Research Institute Staff. 64p. 1980. 4.00 (*0-318-14428-X*) Inst Future.

Workshop Proceedings NAI National Interpreters, Workshop, 1988: Charting a New Course. Ed. by Debra M. Erickson. (Annual Interpreters Workshop Proceedings Ser.: No. 100). 329p. 1990. pap. 20.00 (*1-879931-01-X*) Natl Assoc Interp.

***Workshop Processes, Practices & Material.** 2nd ed. Black. (Mechanical Engineering Ser.). 1997. pap. 27.95 (*0-340-69252-9*) Van Nos Reinhold.

Workshop Record IEEE Radiation Effects Data Workshop, 1993. IEEE Nuclear & Plasma Sciences Society Staff. Ed. by IEEE Staff. 128p. 1994. pap. write for info. (*0-7803-1906-0*, 93TH0657-7); fiche write for info. (*0-7803-1907-9*, 93TH0657-7) Inst Electrical.

Workshop Record Nineteen Ninety-Four IEEE Radiation Effects Data Workshop. IEEE, Nuclear & Plasma Sciences Society Staff. Ed. by IEEE Staff. LC 94-77158. 144p. 1994. pap. write for info. (*0-7803-2022-0*, 94TH0684-1); fiche write for info. (*0-7803-2023-9*) Inst Electrical.

Workshop Report on EPA Guidelines for Carcinogen Risk Assessment: Use of Human Evidence. (Illus.). 98p. (Orig.). (C). 1994. pap. text ed. 25.00 (*0-7881-0627-9*) DIANE Pub.

Workshop Shortcuts: Tips, Tricks, Jigs & Aids for Woodworkers. Graham McCulloch. LC 93-44539. (Illus.). 1994. pap. 17.95 (*0-8069-0650-2*) Sterling.

***Workshop Statistics: Discovery Through Data & the Graphing Calculator.** Allan J. Rossman & Barr Von Oehsen. LC 97-6178. (TIMS - Texts in Mathematical Science Ser.). (Illus.). 472p. 1997. pap. 29.95 (*0-387-94997-6*) Spr-Verlag.

Workshop Statistics: Discovery with Data. Allan J. Rossman. LC 95-16797. (Texbooks in Mathematical Sciences Ser.). (Illus.). 424p. (C). 1997. 28.95 (*0-387-94497-4*) Spr-Verlag.

***Workshop Statistics: Discovery with Data.** Allan J. Rossman. 452p. 1996. pap. 32.50 (*0-7637-0279-X*) Jones & Bartlett.

Workshop Tips & Techniques. DeCosse, Cy, Incorporated Staff. LC 90-28783. (Black & Decker Home Improvement Library). 128p. 1991. 16.95 (*0-86573-716-9*); pap. 14.95 (*0-86573-717-7*) Cowles Creative.

Workshop to Office: Two Generations of Italian Women in New York City, 1900-1950. Miriam Cohen. LC 92-52746. (Illus.). 256p. 1993. 42.50 (*0-8014-2722-3*); pap. 15.95 (*0-8014-8005-1*) Cornell U Pr.

Workshop Tools & Techniques. Better Homes & Gardens Editors. (Wood Shop Library). (Illus.). 160p. 1996. pap. 14.95 (*0-696-20631-5*, Meredith Pr) Meredith Bks.

Workshop Winners: Developing Creative & Dynamic Workshops. Carol Painter. LC 93-70535. 184p. (Orig.). (C). 1993. pap. text ed. 12.95 (*0-932796-57-5*) Ed Media Corp.

Workshop Wisdom Dollhouse Crafting Tips from Nutshell News. Jim Newman & Kathleen Z. Raymond. Ed. by Andrea L. Kraszewski. (Illus.). 64p. 1992. pap. text ed. 9.95 (*0-89778-289-5*, 10-7745) Kalmbach.

Workshop 1: Writing & Literature. Ed. by Nancie Atwell. (Workshops by & for Teachers Ser.). 133p. (Orig.). (C). 1989. pap. text ed. 17.50 (*0-435-08492-5*, 08492) Heinemann.

Workshop 2: Beyond the Basal. Ed. by Nancie Atwell. (Workshops by & for Teachers Ser.). 135p. (Orig.). 1990. pap. text ed. 17.50 (*0-435-08523-9*, 08523) Heinemann.

Workshop 3: The Politics of Process. Ed. by Nancie Atwell. (Workshops by & for Teachers Ser.). 149p. (Orig.). 1991. pap. text ed. 17.50 (*0-435-08576-X*) Heinemann.

Workshop 4: The Teacher as Researcher. Ed. by Thomas Newkirk. (Workshops by & for Teachers Ser.). 187p. 1992. pap. text ed. 17.50 (*0-435-08728-2*, 08728) Heinemann.

Workshop 5: The Writing Process Revisited. Ed. by Thomas Newkirk. (Workshops by & for Teachers Ser.). 188p. (C). 1993. pap. text ed. 17.50 (*0-435-08798-3*, 08798) Heinemann.

Workshop 6: The Teacher as Writer. Ed. by Maureen Barbieri & Linda Rief. (Workshops by & for Teachers Ser.). 113p. 1994. pap. text ed. 17.50 (*0-435-08816-5*, 08816) Heinemann.

Workshops. David P. Weikart et al. (Program Guidebook Ser.). 109p. 1994. pap. 12.95 (*0-929816-84-6*) High-Scope.

Workshops & Outbuildings. David H. Jacobs, Jr. 1993. pap. 14.95 (*0-8306-4421-0*) McGraw-Hill Prof.

Workshops & Outbuildings. David H. Jacobs. LC 93-38574. 1994. pap. text ed. 14.95 (*0-07-032402-6*) McGraw-Hill Prof.

Workshops & Seminars: Planning, Promoting, Producing, Profiting. Pat R. Materka. 224p. 1986. 15.95 (*0-13-967795-X*) P-H.

Workshops for Active Learning. John F. Parker. (Illus.). 194p. (Orig.). 1990. student ed., pap. 19.95 (*0-9694762-0-5*) JFP Prodns.

Workshops for Jail Library Service: A Planning Manual. Linda Schexnaydre. LC 81-1041. (Illus.). 128p. reprint ed. pap. 36.50 (*0-7837-5955-X*, 2045755) Bks Demand.

Workshops for Legal Assistants 1995: Basic Litigation, Litigation Case Management. (Litigation & Administrative Practice Course Handbook, 1983-84 Ser.). 584p. 1994. pap. 99.00 (*0-614-17262-4*, H4-5218) PLI.

Workshops for Teachers: Becoming Partners for Information Literacy. Lesley S. Farmer. LC 95-1988. (Professional Growth Ser.). 142p. 1995. pap. 21.95 (*0-938865-41-2*) Linworth Pub.

Workshops in Cognitive Processes. 2nd ed. A. Bennett et al. 136p. 1982. pap. 10.95 (*0-7100-0932-1*, RKP) Routledge.

Workshops in Fluid & Electrolyte Disorders. Ed. by Harold M. Szerlip & Stanley Goldfarb. (Illus.). 203p. (Orig.). 1993. 34.95 (*0-443-08791-1*) Churchill.

Workshops in Organizing, 4 manuals. Roger Hayes et al. Ed. by Tim Ledwith. LC 87-146206. (Orig.). 1985. 2.50 (*0-685-73891-4*) Comm Serv Soc NY.

Workshops in Organizing, 4 manuals, Pt. 1: Introduction to Organizing. Roger Hayes et al. Ed. by Tim Ledwith. LC 87-146206. 18p. (Orig.). 1985. 2.50 (*0-88156-056-1*) Comm Serv Soc NY.

Workshops in Organizing, 4 manuals, Pt. 2: Research & Power. Roger Hayes et al. Ed. by Tim Ledwith. LC 87-146206. 18p. (Orig.). 1985. 2.50 (*0-88156-057-X*) Comm Serv Soc NY.

Workshops in Organizing, 4 manuals, Pt. 3: Issues & Strategy. Roger Hayes et al. Ed. by Tim Ledwith. LC 87-146206. 18p. (Orig.). 1985. 2.50 (*0-88156-058-8*) Comm Serv Soc NY.

Workshops in Organizing, 4 manuals, Pt. 4: Leadership. Roger Hayes et al. Ed. by Tim Ledwith. LC 87-146206. 18p. (Orig.). 1985. 2.50 (*0-88156-059-6*) Comm Serv Soc NY.

Workshops in Organizing, 4 manuals, Set. Roger Hayes et al. Ed. by Tim Ledwith. LC 87-146206. (Orig.). 1985. 8.00 (*0-88156-125-8*) Comm Serv Soc NY.

Workshops in Perception. Roderick P. Power et al. 244p. 1981. pap. 9.95 (*0-7100-0931-3*, RKP) Routledge.

Workshops on Workshops. Aurelio M. Montemayor. (Illus.). 106p. (Orig.). 1988. pap. text ed. 16.95 (*1-878550-09-8*) Inter Dev Res Assn.

Workshops That Work: One Hundred Ideas to Make Your Training Events More Effective. Tom Bourner et al. LC 92-46626. (Training Ser.). 1993. pap. text ed. 29.95 (*0-07-707800-4*) McGraw.

Worksite Health Promotion Economics: Consensus & Analysis. Ed. by Robert L. Kaman. LC 94-13975. (Illus.). 248p. 1994. text ed. 32.00 (*0-87322-615-1*, BKAM0615) Human Kinetics.

Worksite Nutrition: A Guide to Planning, Implementation, & Evaluation. 2nd ed. American Dietetic Association Staff & Office of Disease Prevention & Health Promotion Staff. LC 93-6120. 1993. 12.00 (*0-88091-126-3*) Am Dietetic Assn.

Worksite Policy Issues on Alcohol, Tobacco, & Other Drugs. Sally S. Crawford. 57p. 1992. pap. text ed. 12.50 (*1-882802-02-0*) Healthy Life.

Worksite Wellness: A New & Practical Approach to Reducing Health Care Cost. David W. Jensen. (Illus.). 256p. (Orig.). 1987. pap. 25.00 (*0-318-37811-6*, Busn) P-H.

Workskills, Bk. 1. Byrne. 1996. teacher ed., pap. text ed. 5.00 (*0-13-954280-9*) P-H.

Workskills, Bk. 1. Mary L. Byrne et al. 128p. 1993. pap. 11.25 (*0-13-953076-2*) P-H.

W

An Asterisk (*) at the beginning of an entry indicates that the title is appearing in BIP for the first time.

Workskills Book 2. Mary L. Byrne et al. 144p. 1993. pap. 11.25 (*0-13-953084-3*) P-H.

Workskills Book 3. Mary L. Byrne et al. 144p. 1994. pap. text ed. 11.25 (*0-13-953092-4*) P-H.

Worksong. Gary Paulsen. 1997. write for info. (*0-15-200980-9*) HarBrace.

Worksource Nineteen Eighty-Eight. John E. Fogle. 500p. 1987. write for info. (*0-318-62233-5*) Turnbull & Co.

Workspace, Equipment & Tool Design. Anil Mital & Waldemar Karwowski. (Advances in Human Factors-Ergonomics Ser.: Vol. 15). 370p. 1991. 173.50 (*0-444-87441-0*) Elsevier.

Workspace Strategies: Environment As a Tool for Work. Jacqueline C. Vischer. 160p. (C). (gr. 13). 1995. pap. text ed. 39.95 (*0-412-07411-7*) Chapman & Hall.

Workstation Radiation: How to Reduce Electromagnetic Radiation Exposure from Computers, TV Sets, & Other Sources. Lucinda Grant. LC 92-85285. 100p. 1992. pap. 7.95 (*0-9635407-1-8*) Weldon Pub.

Workstation Trends of the 1990s. Richard K. Miller & Terri C. Walker. 212p. 1991. 285.00 (*0-89671-114-5*) SEAI Tech Pubns.

Workstations & Local Area Networks for Librarians. Keith C. Wright. LC 90-489. 156p. (C). 1990. pap. text ed. 15.00 (*0-8389-0538-2*) ALA.

Workstations & Publication Systems. Ed. by R. A. Earnshaw. (Illus.). 230p. 1987. 64.95 (*0-387-96527-0*) Spr-Verlag.

Workstations for Experiments. 1991. 71.95 (*0-387-52898-9*) Spr-Verlag.

WorkStyles Manual: Training Manual, Pre-Employability Skills Training for Limited English Speakers. Spring Institute for International Studies Staff. 255p. 1995. ring bd. write for info. (*0-940723-12-3*) SIIS.

Workteams. (Open Learning for Supervisory Management Ser.). 1986. pap. text ed. 19.50 (*0-08-034161-6*, Pergamon Pr) Elsevier.

Workteams. (Open Learning for Supervisory Management Ser.). 1987. pap. text ed. 19.50 (*0-08-070007-1*, Pergamon Pr) Elsevier.

Workteams. 2nd ed. (Open Learning Super Ser.). 1991. pap. text ed. 26.00 (*0-08-041528-8*, Pergamon Pr) Elsevier.

***Worktext Basic Counseling Responses.** Leibsohn. (Counseling Ser.). 1999. pap. 14.95 (*0-534-35557-9*) Brooks-Cole.

Worktime & Industrialization: An International History. Ed. by Gary Cross. LC 88-12173. (Labor & Social Change Ser.). 256p. (C). 1988. 34.95 (*0-87722-582-6*) Temple U Pr.

Worktowners at Blackpool: Mass-Observation & Popular Leisure in the 1930s. Ed. by Gary Cross. 288p. (C). (gr. 13). 1990. text ed. 85.00 (*0-415-04071-X*, A4656) Routledge.

WORKTypes. Jean Kummerow et al. 272p. (Orig.). 1997. pap. 12.99 (*0-446-67217-3*) Warner Bks.

Workview Office: Student Edition. Viewlogic Systems Staff. LC 96-42298. 192p. (C). 1996. student ed., pap. text ed. 66.67 (*0-13-490327-7*) P-H.

***Workways: Seven Stars to Steer By: Biography Workbook for Building an Enterprising Life.** Kees Locher & Jos Van Der Brug. Tr. by Tony Langham & Plym Peters. (Biography & Self Development Ser.). (Illus.). 352p. 1997. 50.00 (*1-869890-89-2*, Pub. by Hawthorn Press UK) Anthroposophic.

Workwear for Fire & Heat Protection. Shirley Inst. Staff. (C). 1989. 170.00 (*0-685-46369-9*, Pub. by British Textile Tech UK) St Mut.

Workwoman's Guide. Illus. by J. Allen. LC 86-28550. 315p. 1986. reprint ed. pap. 29.95 (*0-904983-02-1*) OPUS Pubns.

Workwoman's Guide. Ed. by Peter H. Tracy. LC 86-28550. (Illus.). 313p. 1987. reprint ed. 29.95 (*0-940983-00-1*, OSV-1) OPUS Pubns.

***WorkWords: The Book on Understanding the Language of the Workplace.** Ronald J. Rakowski. Ed. by John Kovach. iv, 248p. (Orig.). 1996. pap. 18.95 (*0-9654051-0-9*) R J Rakowski.

Workyards: Playgrounds Planned for Adventure. Nancy Rudolph. LC 74-5187. (Illus.). 71p. reprint ed. pap. 25.00 (*0-8357-3033-6*, 2039280) Bks Demand.

***World.** LC 97-3017. (Discovering Geography Ser.). (Illus.). 32p. (YA). (gr. 3 up). 1997. lib. bdg. 14.95 (*0-7614-0543-7*, Benchmark NY) Marshall Cavendish.

World. Dennis Phillips. (New American Poetry Ser.: No. 3). 104p. 1989. pap. 9.95 (*1-55713-072-8*) Sun & Moon CA.

World: A Gateway: Koan Commentaries for Self Study. Albert Low. LC 94-46614. 320p. (Orig.). 1995. pap. 16.95 (*0-8048-3046-0*) C E Tuttle.

World: A General Geography. 19th ed. Dudley Stamp. Ed. by Audrey Clarke. (Illus.). 1978. pap. text ed. 16.95 (*0-582-33055-6*) Longman.

World: A Rainbow of People Learning Center. rev. ed. Irene Handberg. (Multicultural Education Ser.). 68p. 1995. teacher ed. write for info. (*1-56831-111-7*) Lrning Connect.

World: A Rainbow of People Learning Center, Set. rev. ed. Irene Handberg. (Multicultural Education Ser.). 68p. 1995. write for info. (*1-56831-100-1*) Lrning Connect.

World: Lands & People Teacher's Guide. L. Singleton. (Illus.). 247p. 1992. teacher ed. 75.00 (*0-87746-360-3*) Graphic Learning.

World: Lands & Peoples: Copy Masters. Lynn S. Parisi. (Illus.). 236p. 1992. 110.00 (*0-87746-361-1*) Graphic Learning.

***World: People, Politics & International Relations.** Cannon. 1992. pap. text ed. write for info. (*0-05-004484-2*) Addison-Wesley.

World: Social Studies. (J). (gr. 6). 1985. 87.50 (*0-15-373213-X*) HB Schl Dept.

World: Social Studies 1985. Harcourt Brace Staff. 1985. wbk. ed., pap. 11.00 (*0-15-373238-5*) HB Schl Dept.

***World: The 1990s from the Pages of a Real Small-Town Daily Newspaper - A Multi-Level Reader.** Ed. by John N. Miller & Raymond C. Clark. (Illus.). 112p. (Orig.). 1993. pap. text ed. 12.00 (*0-86647-078-6*) Pro Lingua.

World: 2000 A. D. Gordon Lindsay. 1968. 3.95 (*0-89985-064-2*) Christ for the Nations.

***Worldtariff Guidebook on Customs Tariff Schedules of Import Duties for U. S. A. 1996.** 5th ed. Ed. by Worldtariff Staff. (United States of America Naitonal Guidebook Ser.). 500p. 1996. ring bd. 465.00 (*1-56745-122-5*) Wrldtariff.

World - Blank Map Forms. (Illus.). 48p. (J). (gr. 2-6). 1994. pap. text ed. 5.95 (*1-55799-277-0*, EMC 281) Evan-Moor Corp.

World a Department Store: A Story of Life Under a Cooperative System. Bradford Peck. LC 70-154457. (Utopian Literature Ser.). (Illus.). 1979. reprint ed. 23.95 (*0-405-03539-X*) Ayer.

World Ablaze. Con Sellers. Ed. by Paul McCarthy. (Men at Arms Ser.: No. 3). 320p. (Orig.). 1992. mass mkt. 5.99 (*0-671-66767-X*) PB.

World Access. Ross Petras & Kathryn Petras. 720p. 1996. 40.00 (*0-684-81479-X*, Fireside) S&S Trade.

World Access: The Handbook for Citizens of the Earth. Ross Petras & Kathryn Petras. (Illus.). 720p. 1996. pap. 22.00 (*0-684-81016-6*, Fireside) S&S Trade.

***World According to Beaver.** rev. ed. Irwyn Applebaum. (Illus.). 1997. reprint ed. pap. 16.95 (*1-57500-052-0*) TV Bks.

World According to Dave Barry. Dave Barry. LC 94-8402. 1994. 13.99 (*0-517-11870-X*) Random Hse Value.

World According to Denise. Shoebox Greetings Staff. (Illus.). 72p. (Orig.). 1990. pap. 5.95 (*0-87529-635-1*) Hallmark.

World According to Evan Mecham. Mark Siegel. (Illus.). 95p. (Orig.). 1987. pap. 4.95 (*0-945165-00-5*) Blue Sky Pr Inc.

***World According To Garp.** John Irving. 1997. pap. 12.95 (*0-345-41801-8*) Ballantine.

World According to Garp. rev. ed. John Irving. 624p. 1990. mass mkt. 6.99 (*0-345-36676-X*) Ballantine.

World According to Griffin: End of an Era. Brian Meyer. (Illus.). 117p. 1993. pap. 5.95 (*1-879201-11-9*) Meyer Enter.

World According to Hollywood, 1918-1939. Ruth Vasey. LC 96-18042. (Wisconsin Studies in Film). (Illus.). 316p. (Orig.). 1997. 54.00 (*0-299-15190-5*) U of Wis Pr.

World According to Hollywood, 1918-1939. Ruth Vasey. LC 96-18042. (Wisconsin Studies in Film). (Illus.). 316p. (Orig.). 1997. pap. 17.95 (*0-299-15194-8*) U of Wis Pr.

World According to Kids. Harold Dunn. 96p. 1992. pap. 6.95 (*0-930753-11-9*) Spect Ln Pr.

World According to Me. Sandra Wilson. 184p. 1995. pap. 10.99 (*1-56476-487-7*, 6-3487, Victor Bks) Chariot Victor.

World According to Michael: An Old Soul's Guide to the Universe. rev. ed. Joya Pope. (Michael Book Ser.). 160p. (Orig.). (C). 1987. pap. 10.95 (*0-942531-39-6*, Focal) Emerald Wave.

***World According to Mike Leigh.** Michael Coveney. 288p. 1997. 29.00 (*0-00-255518-2*) HarperColl Wrld.

World According to Natasha. Michael G. Michaud. (Illus.). 28p. (Orig.). (C). 1991. pap. 20.00 (*0-9620574-3-6*) MGM Pr.

World According to Nostradamus: A Book of Prophecy. Jack Manuelian. 148p. (ENG & FRE.). 1994. pap. 12.00 (*1-885591-00-4*) Morris Pubng.

***World According to Peter Drucker.** Jack Beatty. 1998. 25.00 (*0-684-83801-X*) Free Pr.

World According to the Heart of God. Tr. by Bertha Gonzalez from SPA. LC 85-73186. 176p. (Orig.). 1986. pap. 5.00 (*0-9607590-1-8*) Action Life Pubns.

World According to Travis McGee. R. A. Ackroyd. 21.95 (*0-8488-0510-0*) Amereon Ltd.

World According to Wally: It's All in How You See It. Lori J. Walter. Ed. by Donald Kehl & Dale Messoner. (Illus.). 30p. (Orig.). (J). (gr. k-8). 1994. Incl. cass. 13.95 incl. audio (*0-9634833-2-3*) Rocking Bridge.

World According to Wavelets: The Story of a Mathematical Technique in the Making. Barbara B. Hubbard. LC 95-26421. 286p. (C). 1996. 38.00 (*1-56881-047-4*) AK Peters.

World Accounting Series, 3 vols. Larry Orsini et al. 1986. Looseleaf updates avail. ring bd. write for info. (*0-8205-1835-2*) Bender.

World Accumulation, Fourteen Ninety-Two to Seventeen Eighty-Nine. Andre G. Frank. LC 77-91746. 303p. reprint ed. pap. 86.40 (*0-8357-3591-5*, 2034344) Bks Demand.

World Administrative Radio Conference, 1992: Issues for U. S. International Spectrum Policy - Background Paper. 134p. (Orig.). (C). 1993. pap. text ed. 45.00 (*1-56806-179-X*) DIANE Pub.

World Aerospace: A Statistical Handbook. Daniel Todd & Ronald Humble. 220p. 1987. 97.50 (*0-7099-4325-3*, Pub. by Croom Helm UK) Routledge Chapman & Hall.

World Aerospace Industry: Competition & Collaboration. K. Hayward. 225p. 59.95 (*0-7156-2602-7*, Pub. by Duckworth UK) Focus Pub-R Pullins.

World Affairs: National & International Viewpoints, 41 bks. Ed. by Ronald Steel. 1972. reprint ed. 1,194.00 (*0-405-04560-3*) Ayer.

World Affairs Don't Have to Be Boring. Harland Cleveland. 1960. 2.50 (*0-87060-085-0*, PUC 11) Syracuse U Cont Ed.

World Affairs Organizations in Northern California: A Guide to the Field. Ed. by Chris Carlisle. 230p. 1995. pap. 11.00 (*0-912018-25-9*) World Without War.

World Affairs, 1992. Ed. by Eleanor C. Goldstein. (Global Perspective & Social Issues Resources Ser.). 1992. 85.00 (*0-89777-857-X*) Sirs Inc.

World Affairs, 1993. Ed. by Eleanor C. Goldstein. (Global Perspectives Ser.). 1993. 85.00 (*0-89777-861-8*) Sirs Inc.

World Affairs 1994. Ed. by Eleanor C. Goldstein. (Global Perspectives Ser.). 1994. 85.00 (*0-89777-865-0*) Sirs Inc.

***World Affairs, 1995.** Ed. by Eleanor C. Goldstein. (Global Perspective & Social Issues Resources Ser.). 1995. 85.00 (*0-89777-869-3*) Sirs Inc.

***World Affairs, 1996.** Ed. by Eleanor C. Goldstein. (Global Perspectives Ser.). 1996. 85.00 (*0-89777-873-1*) Sirs Inc.

World Afganistan to Zimbabwe. Rand McNally Staff. 1995. 49.95 (*0-528-83773-7*) Rand McNally.

World, Afghanistan to Zimbabwe. (Illus.). 1996. 49.95 (*0-614-12855-2*) Rand McNally.

World Aflame. Rick Joyner. 158p. 1995. mass mkt. 4.99 (*0-88368-373-3*) Whitaker Hse.

***World Aflame.** Rick Joyner. 158p. 1996. pap. 6.00 (*1-878327-31-3*, RJI-006) Morning NC.

World Aflame see Mundo en Llamas

World after Nineteen Ninety Two: How Fortress Europe Will Change the Global Power Game. 1991. write for info. (*0-318-65053-3*) S&S Trade.

***World Ages.** Bjorn Hammarskog. LC 97-65968. (Illus.). 288p. (Orig.). 1997. pap. 18.95 (*1-57197-057-6*) Pentland Pr.

***World Agriculture, Vol. 13.** L. Ottenheimer-Maquet. Orig. Title: Our Food. (Illus.). 80p. (YA). (gr. 4 up). 1998. lib. bdg. write for info. (*0-88682-952-6*) Creative Ed.

World Agriculture: Towards 2010: An FAO Study. Ed. by Nikos Alexandratos. LC 94-43232. 488p. 1995. text ed. 150.00 (*0-471-95376-8*) Wiley.

World Agriculture & the GATT. Ed. by William P. Avery. LC 92-28186. (International Political Economy Yearbook Ser.: Vol. 7). 236p. 1993. lib. bdg. 37.00 (*1-55587-309-X*) Lynne Rienner.

World Agriculture in Disarray. 2nd ed. D. Gale Johnson. LC 90-19211. 384p. 1991. text ed. 69.95 (*0-312-05799-7*) St Martin.

World Air Cargo Forecast (1994) David F. Pierce. (Illus.). 74p. (Orig.). (C). 1994. pap. text ed. 65.00 (*0-7881-1198-1*) DIANE Pub.

World Air Cargo Forecast (1995) (Illus.). 75p. (Orig.). (C). 1995. pap. text ed. 40.00 (*0-7881-2484-6*) DIANE Pub.

***World Air Cargo Forecast, 1996-1997.** (Illus.). 62p. (Orig.). (C). 1996. pap. 40.00 (*0-7881-3566-X*) DIANE Pub.

***World Air Cargo Forecast (1996/1997)** (Illus.). 76p. 1996. pap. text ed. 50.00 (*1-57979-103-4*) BPI Info Servs.

World Air Power Journal, Vol. 9. Aerospace Publishing Ltd. Staff. Ed. by David Donald & Jon Lake. (Illus.). 160p. 1992. 24.95 (*1-880588-07-2*) AIRtime Pub.

World Aircraft Industry. Daniel Todd & Jamie Simpson. LC 85-26751. 272p. 1986. text ed. 55.00 (*0-86569-141-X*, Auburn Hse) Greenwood.

***World Airport Ground Equipment Market.** Frost & Sullivan Staff. 402p. 1996. write for info. (*0-7889-0592-9*, 5330) Frost & Sullivan.

World Airports: International Airports & Their Commercial Facilities. Yoishi Arai. (Illus.). 172p. 1996. 69.95 (*4-7858-0039-9*, Pub. by Shotenkenchiku-Sha JA) Bks Nippan.

***World Alive: The Natural Wonders of a New England River Valley.** Lorus J. Milne & Margery Milne. Tr. by Polly Warren. (Illus.). 156p. (Orig.). 1997. reprint ed. pap. 15.00 (*1-880158-14-0*) J N Townsend.

World Almanac & Book of Facts. Ed. by World Almanac & Book of Facts Staff. 1989. pap. write for info. (*0-318-64765-6*) St Martin.

World Almanac & Book of Facts 1995. Ed. by Robert Famighetti. 976p. 1994. pap. 8.95 (*0-88687-766-0*) St Martin.

World Almanac & Book of Facts 1996. Ed. by Robert Famighetti. 1995. pap. 9.95 (*0-88687-780-6*) Wrld Almnc.

World Almanac & Book of Facts 1996. large type ed. 1995. 24.95 (*0-88687-781-4*) Wrld Almnc.

***World Almanac & Book of Facts 1997.** (World Almanac/K-III Reference Ser.). Date not set. pap. 9.95 (*0-614-26589-4*) Wrld Almnc.

***World Almanac & Book of Facts 1997.** Famighetti. 976p. 1996. 27.95 (*0-88687-801-2*) Wrld Almnc.

***World Almanac & Book of Facts 1997.** Ed. by Robert Famighetti. 1996. pap. 9.95 (*0-88687-800-4*) St Martin.

World Almanac & Book of Facts, 1997. World Almanac Book & Book of Facts Staff. 1996. pap. text ed. 19.95 incl. cd-rom (*0-88687-805-5*) Wrld Almnc.

***World Almanac & Book of Facts, 1997: Includes Multimedia World Factbook CD-Rom.** Robert Famighetti. 1996. pap. text ed. 298.50 incl. cd-rom (*0-88687-802-0*) Wrld Almnc.

***World Almanac & Book of Facts, 1998.** Robert Famighetti. 1997. 27.95 (*0-88687-821-7*); pap. text ed. 9.95 (*0-88687-820-9*) Wrld Almnc.

***World Almanac Book for Kids.** Judith Levey. (J). (gr. 3-7). pap. 8.95 (*0-614-19263-3*, World Almanac) Newspaper Ent.

World Almanac Book for Kids 1997. Judith Levey. (J). (gr. 3-7). 16.95 (*0-614-19262-5*, World Almanac) Newspaper Ent.

World Almanac Dictionary of Dates. World Almanac Editors. Ed. by Urdang, Laurence, Inc. Staff. LC 81-71772. 320p. 31.95 (*0-582-28372-8*) Longman.

World Almanac for Kids, 1996. (J). 1995. pap. 7.95 (*0-88687-770-9*) Wrld Almnc.

World Almanac for Kids, 1996. 1995. 16.95 (*0-88687-771-7*) Wrld Almnc.

World Almanac for Kids 1997. 320p. (J). (gr. 4-7). 1996. 16.95 (*0-88687-795-4*, Pharos) FS&G.

World Almanac for Kids 1997. Sylvia Branzei. 320p. (J). (gr. 4-7). 1996. pap. text ed. 8.95 (*0-88687-794-6*, Pharos) Wrld Almnc.

***World Almanac for Kids 1998.** Levy. Date not set. 16.95 (*0-88687-813-6*); pap. 8.95 (*0-88687-812-5*) St Martin.

World Almanac Guide to Good Word Usage. Ed. by Martin H. Manser & Jeffrey McQuain. 288p. 1991. reprint ed. pap. 8.95 (*0-380-71449-3*) Avon.

***World Almanac Job Finder's Guide 1997.** 1997. 89.20 (*0-88687-808-X*) Wrld Almnc.

***World Almanac Job Finder's Guide 1997.** Les Krantz. 1997. 24.95 (*0-88687-807-1*) Wrld Almnc.

***World Almanac Job Finder's Guide 1997.** 9th ed. Les Krantz. 1997. pap. 14.95 (*0-88687-806-3*) Wrld Almnc.

World Almanac of Presidential Campaigns. Eileen Shields-West & MacNelly. 256p. 1992. 21.95 (*0-88687-610-9*); pap. 10.95 (*0-88687-609-5*) Wrld Almnc.

World Almanac of Presidential Quotations. Ed. by Elizabeth Frost. LC 92-39243. 1993. 15.95 (*0-88687-734-2*) Wrld Almnc.

World Almanac of the American Revolution. Intro. by L. Edward Purcell & John A. Garraty. (Illus.). 408p. 1992. 35.00 (*0-88687-574-9*); pap. 16.95 (*0-88687-665-6*) Wrld Almnc.

World Almanac of the U. S. A. Allan Carpenter & Carl Provorse. Ed. by World Almanac Editors. 1996. 19.95 (*0-88687-792-X*); pap. 9.95 (*0-88687-791-1*) Wrld Almnc.

World Almanac of the U. S. A. 1994. World Almanac Editors & Allan Carpenter. (Illus.). 400p. (Orig.). 1993. 18.95 (*0-88687-724-5*); pap. 8.95 (*0-88687-723-7*) Wrld Almnc.

***World Almanac of U. S. Politics: 1997-1999.** World Almanac Editors. Date not set. pap. 29.95 (*0-88687-811-X*) Wrld Almnc.

World Almanac of U. S. Politics, 1995-1997. 1995. pap. 18.95 (*0-88687-773-3*) Wrld Almnc.

World Almanac of U. S. Politics, 1995-1997. 1995. 29.95 (*0-88687-774-1*) Wrld Almnc.

***World Almanac of U. S. Politics, 1997-1999.** World Almanac Editors. 1997. pap. 18.95 (*0-88687-810-1*) K III Ref Corp.

World Almanac of World War II: The Complete & Commprehensive Documentary of World War II. Ed. by Peter Young. (Illus.). 624p. 1992. pap. 18.95 (*0-88687-712-1*) Wrld Almnc.

World Alone. Vicente Alexander. Tr. by Lewis Hyde & David Unger. (Illus.). 76p. 1982. 17.50 (*0-915778-41-6*) Penmaen Pr.

World Alone. deluxe ed. Vicente Alexander. Tr. by Lewis Hyde & David Unger. (Illus.). 76p. 1982. 150.00 (*0-915778-42-4*) Penmaen Pr.

World Aluminium Databook. 2nd ed. Ed. by Richard Serjeantson. 538p. 1990. pap. text ed. 171.60 (*0-947671-38-2*) Metal Bulletin.

World Aluminum Industry in a Changing Era. Ed. by Merton J. Peck. LC 88-4990. 231p. 1988. 30.00 (*0-915707-42-X*) Resources Future.

World Analog & Mix Signal IC Markets. Market Intelligence Staff. 377p. 1993. 1,895.00 (*1-56753-473-2*) Frost & Sullivan.

World & a Very Small Place in Africa. Donald R. Wright. LC 96-44139. 256p. (C). (gr. 13). 1997. 62.95 (*1-56324-959-6*); pap. 19.95 (*1-56324-960-X*) M E Sharpe.

World & Africa: Inquiry into the Part Which Africa Has Played in World History. rev. ed. W. E. B. Du Bois. LC 65-16392. (Illus.). (Orig.). (C). 1965. pap. 7.95 (*0-7178-0221-3*) Intl Pubs Co.

World & Glory. C. A. Evans. 52.50 (*1-85075-448-9*, Pub. by Sheffield Acad UK) CUP Services.

World & Its God. Philip Mauro. 95p. 1981. reprint ed. pap. 4.00 (*0-89084-151-9*, 016527) Bob Jones Univ Pr.

World & Its Streets, Places. Larry Eigner. LC 77-8974. 180p. (Orig.). 1977. pap. 10.00 (*0-87685-268-1*) Black Sparrow.

World & Its Wonders. Peter Lafferty. LC 96-68267. (Child Horizons Ser.). (J). (gr. 4-6). 1996. 22.95 (*0-87392-309-X*) Standard Ed.

World & Language in Wittgenstein's Philosophy. Gordon Hunnings. LC 87-6453. 266p. 1988. text ed. 64.50 (*0-88706-585-6*); pap. text ed. 21.95 (*0-88706-586-4*) State U NY Pr.

World & Life-World: Aspects of the Philosophy of Edmund Husserl. Balazs M. Mezei. LC 95-4145. (European University Studies: Ser. 20, Vol.457). 199p. 1995. pap. 37.95 (*3-631-48394-9*) P Lang Pubng.

World & Literature of the Old Testament. John T. Willis. 1984. 17.95 (*0-915547-39-2*) Abilene Christ U.

World & National Space Programs: Proceedings of the 30th & 31st Goddard Memorial Symposia, Arlington & Alexandria, VA, 1992 & 1993. Ed. by Gayle L. May et al. LC 57-43769. (Science & Technology Ser.: 83). (Illus.). 334p. 1994. pap. text ed. 50.00 (*0-87703-390-0*) Univelt Inc.

World & Other Places. Daniel M. Stokes. 1974. pap. 1.50 (*0-686-18736-9*) Chthon Pr.

***World & People, Vol. 3.** Conolly & Cox. 1991. pap. text ed. write for info. (*0-582-87052-6*, Pub. by Longman UK) Longman.

***World & Regional Supply & Demand Balances for Nitrogen, Phosphate, & Potash, 1993/94-1999/2000.** World Bank Staff & FAO, UNIDO, & the International Fertilizer Working Groups. (World Bank Technical Paper Ser.: No. 309). 56p. 1996. 7.95 (*0-8213-3495-6*, 13495) World Bank.

***World & the Arms, An Hearthly Residence.** Michel Francois. 1997. pap. text ed. 30.00 (*2-908257-21-1*, Pub. by F R A C FR) Dist Art Pubs.

World & the Bo Tree. Helen Bevington. LC 91-7608. 224p. 1991. text ed. 41.95 (*0-8223-1153-4*); pap. text ed. 18.95 (*0-8223-1165-8*) Duke.

World & the Book: A Study of Modern Fiction. Gabriel Josipovici. LC 79-170983. xviii, 318p. 1971. 42.50 (0-8047-0797-9) Stanford U Pr.

World & the Child. LC 74-133774. (Tudor Facsimile Texts. Old English Plays Ser.: No. 6). reprint ed. 49.50 (0-404-53306-X) AMS Pr.

World & the Individual, Vol. 1. Josiah Royce. 1990. Set. 14.50 (0-8446-2842-5) Peter Smith.

World & the Parish: Willa Cather's Articles & Reveiws, 1893-1902, Vol. 2. Willa Cather. Ed. by William M. Curtin. LC 79-21110. 548p. reprint ed. pap. 156.20 (0-7837-8104-0, 2047907) Bks Demand.

World & the Parish: Willa Cather's Articles & Reviews, 1893-1902, Vol. 1. Willa Cather. Ed. by William M. Curtin. LC 79-21110. 524p. 1970. reprint ed. pap. 149.40 (0-7837-8103-2, 2047907) Bks Demand.

World & the Prophets: Mormonism & Early Christianity. Hugh Nibley. LC 87-620. (Collected Works of Hugh Nibley: Vol. 3). xii, 333p. 1987. 17.95 (0-87579-078-X) Deseret Bk.

World & the Word: Between Science & Religion. Michael Heller. Tr. by Adam C. Kisiel from POL. LC 86-61668. (Philosophy in Science Library: Vol. 1). 184p. 1987. pap. 14.95 (0-88126-724-4) Pachart Pub Hse.

World & the Word: Tales & Observations from the Xhosa Oral Tradition. Nongenile M. Zenani. Ed. & Intro. by Harold Scheub. LC 92-50261. (Illus.). 512p. (C). 1992. 39.95 (0-299-13310-9) U of Wis Pr.

World & U. S. Aviation & Space Records. 1995. pap. 13.95 (0-686-20015-2) Natl Aero.

World & West: Readings in Contemporary History. 3rd ed. George J. Lankevich. (Illus.). 218p. 1992. pap. text ed. 10.95 (0-89529-572-5) Avery Pub.

World & William Walker. Walter H. Carr. LC 75-18354. (Illus.). 289p. 1975. reprint ed. text ed. 59.75 (0-8371-8328-6, CAWWW, Greenwood Pr) Greenwood.

World & Yugoslavia's Wars. Ed. by Richard H. Ullman. LC 96-14890. 1996. 18.95 (0-87609-191-5) Coun Foreign.

World Angling Resources & Challenges. Ed. by Richard H. Stroud. 390p. 1985. 25.00 (0-935217-01-0) Intl Game Fish.

World Animal Library, 17 bks. Nadine Saunier et al. (Illus.). 476p. (J). (gr. 2-5). 1983. Set. lib. bdg. 283.39 (0-86592-850-9) Rourke Corp.

World Animal Library, 17 bks., Reading Level 3-4. Nadine Saunier et al. (Illus.). 476p. (J). (gr. 2-5). 1983. lib. bdg. 212.50 (0-685-58814-9) Rourke Corp.

World Anti-Trust. Garrett. 1995. 155.00 (0-316-30480-8) Little.

World Apart. Shawn Slovo. (Illus.). 128p. 1988. pap. 8.95 (0-571-15235-X) Faber & Faber.

World Apart. large type ed. Jean Chapman. (Dales Large Print Ser.). 1995. pap. 17.99 (1-85389-518-0, Dales) Ulverscroft.

World Apart: Imprisonment in a Soviet Labor Camp During World War II. Gustaw Herling-Grudzinski. 256p. 1996. pap. 11.95 (0-14-025184-7, Penguin Bks) Viking Penguin.

World Apart: The Story of the Chasidim in England. Harry Rabinowicz. LC 95-5666. (Illus.). 320p. 1997. 49.50 (0-85303-261-0, Pub. by Vallentine Mitchell UK); pap. 27.50 (0-85303-278-5, Pub. by Vallentine Mitchell UK) Intl Spec Bk.

***World Apparel Fibre Consumption Survey 1989.** 158p. (ENG, FRE & SPA.). 1989. 20.00 (92-5-002844-X, F844X, Pub. by FAO IT) Bernan Associates.

World Apple Market. A. Desmond O'Rourke. LC 93-7919. (Illus.). 238p. 1993. lib. bdg. 59.95 (1-56022-041-4) Haworth Pr.

World Arbitration Reporter, 6 vols., Vols. 1, 2, 2A, 2B, 3, 4, 4A, & 5. Hans Smith & Vratislav Pechota. 5500p. 1991. Set of 6. 760.00 (0-929179-43-9) Juris Pubng.

World Archaeoastronomy. Ed. by Anthony F. Aveni. (Illus.). 450p. (C). 1989. text ed. 150.00 (0-521-34180-9) Cambridge U Pr.

World Architecture Index: A Guide to Illustrations. Compiled by Edward H. Teague. LC 91-7565. (Art Reference Collection: No. 12). 472p. 1991. text ed. 89.50 (0-313-22552-4, TAR, Greenwood Pr) Greenwood.

World Armaments & Disarmament: SIPRI Yearbook, 1985. Taylor & Francis, Ltd. Staff & SIPRI Staff. 1985. 90.00 (0-85066-297-4) Taylor & Francis.

World Armies. 2nd ed. John Keegan. 1984. 80.00 (0-8103-1515-7) Gale.

World Around Me, 21 bks., Set. (Illus.). (Orig.). (J). (ps-2). 1991. pap. 168.00 (1-56334-138-7) Hampton-Brown.

World Around Me: Exploring Home, Friends, Family, Transportation, & Community. Mary B. Minucci. Ed. by Martha A. Hayes. (Creative Concept Ser.). (Illus.). 48p. 1990. pap. 6.95 (1-878727-04-4) First Teacher.

World Around Midnight. Patricia Griffith. Ed. by Jane Rosenman. 256p. 1992. reprint ed. pap. 8.00 (0-671-75950-7, WSP) PB.

World Around the Chinese Artist: Aspects of Realism in Chinese Painting. Richard Edwards. (Illus.). 158p. 1989. text ed. 49.50 (0-472-10130-7) U of Mich Pr.

World Around Us. Sandra Hillstrom-Svercek. LC 84-61985. (Illus.). 151p. (Orig.). (C). 1984. pap. 14.95 (0-932967-00-0) Pacific Shoreline.

World Around Us: A Multicultural Resource, 6 vols., Set. (Illus.). 64 ea.p. (J). (gr. 3-7). 1994. lib. bdg. 159.00 (0-7172-7432-2) Grolier Educ.

World Around Us Theme Set, 6 bks. (Beginners Ser.). 1991. Set. 290.72 (0-8123-7213-1); Newspapers. pap. 10.52 (0-8123-6996-3); Clocks & Watches. pap. 10.52 (0-8123-6981-5); Television. pap. 10.52 (0-8123-6983-1); School. pap. 10.52 (0-8123-6984-X); Clothes. pap. 10.52 (0-8123-6986-6); Money. pap. 10.52 (0-8123-6987-4) McDougal-Littell.

World Art: Themes of Unity in Diversity, Acts of the XXVIth International Congress of the History of Art, 3 vols. Ed. by Irving Lavin. 906p. 1989. 95.00 (0-271-00607-2) Pa St U Pr.

World Arthritis Treatment Products: Rx, OTC & Prosthetics: OTC Changes Dynamics of Rx Markets. Market Intelligence Staff. 280p. 1993. 2,295.00 (1-56753-496-1) Frost & Sullivan.

World Artists, 1950-1980. Claude Marks. LC 84-13152. (Illus.). 928p. 1984. 83.00 (0-8242-0707-6) Wilson.

World Artists, 1980-1990. Ed. by Claude Marks. 432p. 1991. 58.00 (0-8242-0827-7) Wilson.

World As a Company Town: Multinational Corporations & Social Change. Ed. by Ahmed Idris-Soven et al. (World Anthropology Ser.). xii, 456p. 1978. 53.85 (90-279-7610-4) Mouton.

World As a Total System. Kenneth E. Boulding. 1985. 35.00 (0-8039-2443-7) Sage.

World As Creation: Creation in Christ in an Evolutionary World View. Emily Binns. 104p. pap. 7.95 (0-8146-5755-9, M Glazier) Liturgical Pr.

World As Event: The Poetry of Charles Tomlinson. Brian John. 128p. (C). 1989. text ed. 49.95 (0-7735-0720-5, Pub. by McGill CN) U of Toronto Pr.

World As I See It. Albert Einstein. 1979. pap. 5.95 (0-8065-0711-X, Citadel Pr) Carol Pub Group.

World As It Could Be! Herbert Vollmann. 1972. pap. 6.00 (3-87860-052-6) Grail Fndtn-Amer.

World As Lover, World As Self. Joanna Macy. LC 91-681. 280p. (Orig.). 1991. pap. 15.00 (0-938077-27-9) Parallax Pr.

World As Power. John Woodroffe. Bd. with Mahamaya: Power As Consciousness. 1981. 16.00 (0-89744-119-2) Auromere.

World As Teacher. Harold Taylor. LC 74-4130. (Arcturus Books Paperbacks). 400p. 1974. pap. 8.95 (0-8093-0683-2) S Ill U Pr.

World As Will & Idea. Arthur Schopenhauer. Ed. by David Berman & Jill Berman. LC 75-41243. 336p. (Orig.). 1995. pap. 9.50 (0-460-87505-1, Everyman's Classic Lib) C E Tuttle.

World As Will & Idea, 3 vols. Arthur Schopenhauer et al. Tr. by R. B. Haldane & J. Kemp from GER. LC 75-41243. (Orig.). reprint ed. 165.00 (0-404-15060-8) AMS Pr.

World As Will & Representation, 2 Vols. Arthur Schopenhauer. Tr. by E. F. Payne. 1966. pap. text ed. 10.95 (0-685-01503-3) Dover.

World As Will & Representation, 2 vols. Arthur Schopenhauer. Tr. by E. F. Payne. 1990. Set. 45.00 (0-8446-2885-9) Peter Smith.

World As Will & Representation, 2 Vols, 1. Arthur Schopenhauer. Tr. by E. F. Payne. 1966. pap. text ed. write for info. (0-486-21761-2) Dover.

World As Will & Representation, 2 Vols, 2. Arthur Schopenhauer. Tr. by E. F. Payne. 1966. pap. text ed. 10.95 (0-486-21762-0) Dover.

World at Arms: A Global History of World War II. Gerhard L. Weinberg. LC 92-37637. (Illus.). 1200p. (C). 1994. text ed. 39.95 (0-521-44317-2) Cambridge U Pr.

World at Arms: A Global History of World War II. Gerhard L. Weinberg. (Illus.). 1200p. (C). 1995. pap. text ed. 19.95 (0-521-55879-4) Cambridge U Pr.

World at Arms: The Reader's Digest Illustrated History of World War II. Reader's Digest Editors. (Illus.). 512p. 1989. 29.95 (0-89577-333-3, Random) RD Assn.

World at Crossroads. Philip Smith. 1994. pap. 24.95 (1-85383-201-4, Pub. by Erthscan Pubns UK) Island Pr.

World at Eighteen Thousand BP, Vol. 2, Low Latitudes. Ed. by Olga Soffer & C. S. Gamble. (Illus.). 320p. (C). 1989. text ed. 65.00 (0-04-445127-X) Routledge Chapman & Hall.

***World at His Fingertips: A Story about Louis Braille.** Barbara O'Connor. LC 96-49950. (Carolrhoda Creative Minds Bks.). (J). 1997. write for info. (1-57505-052-8, Carolrhoda) Lerner Group.

World at Home. Anne McCormick. LC 70-121486. (Essay Index Reprint Ser.). 1977. 23.95 (0-8369-1985-8) Ayer.

World at Large: New & Selected Poems, 1971-1996. James McMichael. LC 96-15122. (Phoenix Poets Ser.). 232p. (C). 1996. pap. 12.95 (0-226-56105-4); lib. bdg. 29.95 (0-226-56104-6) U Ch Pr.

World at Night. Alan Furst. 320p. 1996. 23.00 (0-679-41313-8) Random.

World at Noon. Eugene Mirabelli. 386p. 1994. pap. 13.00 (1-55071-000-1) Guernica Editions.

***World at Our Table: A Fresh Approach to Cooking from Down Home & around the World.** Woodward Academy Parents Club Staff. 1996. 17.95 (0-9651785-1-X) Woodward Acad.

World at Play in Boccaccio's "Decameron" Giuseppe Mazzotta. LC 85-43299. 310p. 1986. text ed. 45.00 (0-691-06677-9) Princeton U Pr.

World at Risk: Natural Hazards & Climate Change. R. L. Bras & R. G. Prinn. (Conference Proceeding Ser.). 1992. 120.00 (1-56396-066-4) Am Inst Physics.

World at the Crossroads. Boris Brasol. 1973. 75.00 (0-8490-1333-X) Gordon Pr.

World at the Crossroads - New Conflicts, New Solution: Annals of Pugwash 1993. Sven Hellman & Joseph Rotblat. 300p. 1994. text ed. 51.00 (981-02-2036-7) World Scientific Pub.

World at the End of Time. Frederik Pohl. 416p. 1991. mass mkt. 5.95 (0-345-37197-6, Del Rey) Ballantine.

World at the Turning. Charles Piguet & Michel Sentis. Tr. by Ailsa Hamilton from FRE. 132p. 1989. reprint ed. pap. 8.95 (0-901269-63-9) Grosvenor USA.

World at War - The Church at Peace: Studies in Biblical Peacemaking. Jon Bonk. 128p. (Orig.). (C). 1988. pap. 4.95 (0-919797-87-3); student ed. 1.50 (0-919797-89-X) Kindred Prods.

***World at War 50 Years Later Told by Veterans & Civilians from Central New York State.** Sandra Fentiman. 104p. 1997. 34.95 (1-56311-355-4) Turner Pub KY.

***World at Your Door: Reaching International Students in Your Home, Church & School.** Tom Phillips. LC 97-21028. 176p. Date not set. pap. text ed. 9.99 (1-55661-964-2) Bethany Hse.

World at Your Keyboard: An Alternative Guide to Global Computer Networking. Luber. 1993. pap. 15.95 (1-897766-00-9, Pub. by Jon Pubng UK) LPC InBook.

World Atlas. (Giant Step Picture Library). (Illus.). 14p. (J). (gr. 3 up). 1992. 9.95 (0-88679-658-X) Educ Insights.

World Atlas. LC 95-148. (DK Pockets Ser.). (Illus.). 160p. (YA). (gr. 7 up). 1995. pap. 5.95 (0-7894-0215-7, 5-70628) DK Pub Inc.

World Atlas. Hammond, Inc. Staff. LC 82-675036. (Library of Knowledge). (Illus.). 112p. (YA). (gr. 5 up). 1982. lib. bdg. 11.99 (0-394-94663-4) Random Bks Yng Read.

World Atlas. Hammond, Inc. Staff. LC 82-675036. (Library of Knowledge). (Illus.). 112p. (YA). (gr. 5 up). 1982. pap. 14.00 (0-394-84663-X) Random Bks Yng Read.

***World Atlas.** Scoffham. 1992. pap. text ed. write for info. (0-582-06614-X, Pub. by Longman UK) Longman.

***World Atlas.** Universal Map Enterprisese Staff. 1996. pap. text ed. 3.95 (0-7625-0040-9) Universal Map Enterprises Inc.

***World Atlas.** Universal Staff. 1996. pap. 3.95 (0-7625-0337-8) Universal Map Enterprises Inc.

World Atlas. rev. ed. Ed. by B. M. Willett. 1996. pap. 6.99 (0-451-18086-0, Sig) NAL-Dutton.

World Atlas: A Resource for Students. (J). (gr. 5-9). 1990. pap. 3.95 (0-88463-480-9) Nystrom.

World Atlas: The World at Your Fingertips. rev. ed. (Miniature Editions Ser.). (Illus.). 112p. 1995. 4.95 (1-56138-549-2, Running Pr Mini Edtns) Running Pr.

World Atlas of Archaeology. Michael Wood. (Illus.). 1988. 34.99 (0-517-66876-9) Random Hse Value.

World Atlas of Desertification. David S. Thomas & Nicholas J. Middleton. (Illus.). 96p. 1992. 149.50 (0-340-55512-2, A7443, Pub. by E Arnold UK) Routledge Chapman & Hall.

World Atlas of Desertification. United Nations Environment Programme Staff. 69p. 1995. text ed. 149.00 (0-470-24972-2) Halsted Pr.

***World Atlas of Elections.** 1986. 85.00 (0-85058-089-7, 00006939, Gale Res Intl) Gale.

***World Atlas of Holocene Sea-Level Changes.** P. A. Pirazzoli & J. Pluet. (Oceanography Ser.: Vol. 58). 300p. 1991. 155.00 (0-444-89086-6) Elsevier.

World Atlas of Military History 1861-1945. Arthur Banks. (Quality Paperbacks Ser.). (Illus.). 180p. 1988. reprint ed. pap. 12.95 (0-306-80332-1) Da Capo.

World Atlas of Military History 1945-1984. Tom Hartman & John Mitchell. (Quality Paperbacks Ser.). (Illus.). 120p. 1988. reprint ed. pap. 14.95 (0-306-80316-X) Da Capo.

World Atlas of Wine. 4th rev. ed. Hugh Johnson. LC 94-61. 1994. 50.00 (0-671-88674-6) S&S Trade.

World Audiology Product Markets: Competitors Keep Their Ears to the Ground for Hints of Improving Sales. Market Intelligence Staff. 310p. 1994. 1,695.00 (0-7889-0106-0) Frost & Sullivan.

World Audiology Product Markets: Consumer Advertising Overcoming the Stigma. Market Intelligence Staff. 349p. 1992. 1,495.00 (1-56753-390-6) Frost & Sullivan.

World Authors 1900-1950. Ed. by Martin Seymour-Smith & Andrew C. Kimmens. LC 96-16380. (Authors Ser.). (Illus.). 3200p. 1996. lib. bdg. write for info. (0-8242-0899-4) Wilson.

World Authors, 1950-1970: A Companion Volume to Twentieth Century Authors. Ed. by John Wakeman. LC 75-172140. 1593p. 1975. 95.00 (0-8242-0419-0) Wilson.

World Authors, 1970-1975: A Biographical Dictionary. Ed. by Stanley J. Kunitz & John Wakeman. LC 79-21874. (Wilson Authors Ser.). 893p. 1980. 85.00 (0-8242-0641-X) Wilson.

World Authors 1975-1980. Ed. by Vineta Colby. LC 85-10045. 831p. 1985. 85.00 (0-8242-0715-7) Wilson.

World Authors 1980-1985: Authoritative Biographies of 320 Contemporary Writers. Ed. by Vineta Colby. (Wilson Authors Ser.). 938p. 1991. 85.00 (0-8242-0797-1) Wilson.

World Authors, 1985-1990. Ed. by Vineta Colby. (Wilson Authors Ser.). 970p. 1995. 85.00 (0-8242-0875-7) Wilson.

World Automated Plant Lans Markets: An Open Systems Approach. 246p. 1992. 1,695.00 (1-56753-007-9) Frost & Sullivan.

World Automatic Building Control Markets: Recovery in Commercial Building Drives Growth for Systems, Components & Software. 203p. 1992. 1,495.00 (1-56753-003-6) Frost & Sullivan.

World Automotive Electronics OEM Markets. 250p. 1991. 1,950.00 (0-945235-47-X) Lead Edge Reports.

World Awaits: A Comprehensive Guide to Extended Backpack Travel. Paul Otteson. (Illus.). 280p. 1996. pap. 16.95 (1-56261-277-8) John Muir.

World Awakening. Donald Howard. LC 88-62244. 240p. 1988. pap. 7.95 (0-89221-162-8) New Leaf.

World Ballet & Dance: An International Yearbook Vol. 5: 1993-4. Ed. by Bent Schonberg et al. (Illus.). 304p. 1995. 49.95 (0-19-816427-0); pap. 26.00 (0-19-816428-9) OUP.

World Band & Irrigation. William I. Jones. LC 95-2842. (Operations Evaluation Study Ser.). 168p. 1995. 10.95 (0-8213-3249-X, 13249) World Bank.

World Bank: A Critical Analysis. Cheryl Payer. LC 81-84738. 316p. 1982. pap. 17.00 (0-85345-602-X) Monthly Rev.

World Bank: An Annotated Bibliography. Anne C. Salda. LC 94-33739. (International Organizations Ser.: Vol. 9). 306p. 1995. 64.95 (1-56000-198-4) Transaction Pubs.

World Bank: Borrowers Perspective. Y. Venugopal Reddy. 143p. 1986. text ed. 20.00 (81-207-0032-5, Pub. by Sterling Pubs II) Apt Bks.

***World Bank: Its First Half Century.** Ed. by John P. Lewis et al. LC 97-21093. 1000p. 1997. text ed. 74.95 (0-8157-5234-2) Brookings.

***World Bank: Its First Half Century.** John P. Lewis et al. LC 97-21093. 1997. write for info. (0-8157-5230-X); write for info. (0-8157-5236-9) Brookings.

World Bank: Lending on a Global Scale. Ed. by Jo M. Griesgraber & Bernhard G. Gunter. LC 95-53123. (Rethinking Bretton Woods Ser.: Vol. 3). 240p. 1996. write for info. (0-7453-1050-8, Pub. by Pluto Pr UK) LPC InBook.

World Bank: Lending on Global Scale. Jo Marie Griesgraber. 240p. 1996. pap. text ed. 14.95 (0-7453-1049-4, Pub. by Pluto Pr UK) LPC InBook.

***World Bank: U. S. Interests Supported, but Oversight Needed to Help Ensure Improved Performance.** (Illus.). 93p. (Orig.). (C). 1996. pap. 25.00 (0-7881-3577-5) DIANE Pub.

World Bank & Agricultural Development: An Insider's View. Montague Yudelman. 44p. (Orig.). 1985. pap. text ed. 10.00 (0-915825-11-2) World Resources Inst.

***World Bank & the Environment: Environment Matters & the World Bank.** 72p. 1996. 8.95 (0-8213-3579-0, 13579) World Bank.

World Bank & the Environmental Challenge. Philippe Le Prestre. LC 88-42825. 264p. 1989. 40.00 (0-941664-98-8) Susquehanna U Pr.

World Bank & the IMF. Jacques J. Polak. 59p. (C). 1994. pap. 9.95 (0-8157-7149-5) Brookings.

World Bank & the Poor. Aart Van De Laar. (Institute for Social Studies Series on the Development of Societies: Vol. 6). 271p. 1980. lib. bdg. 61.00 (0-89838-042-1) Kluwer Ac.

World Bank & the, Poorest Countries: Support for Development in the 1990s. LC 94-849. 64p. 1994. 6.95 (0-8213-2770-4, 12770) World Bank.

***World Bank Annual Report: 1995 Edition.** 224p. (JPN.). 1995. write for info. (0-8213-2888-3, 12888) World Bank.

***World Bank Annual Report: 1995 Edition.** 224p. (ARA.). 1995. write for info. (0-8213-2890-5, 12890) World Bank.

World Bank Annual Report 1994. World Bank Staff. 254p. (GER.). 1994. write for info. (0-8213-2548-5, 12548) World Bank.

World Bank Approaches to the Environment in Brazil. John Redwood, 3rd. LC 93-14544. (Operations Evaluation Study Ser.). 90p. 1993. 7.95 (0-8213-2511-6, 12511) World Bank.

***World Bank Atlas 1997.** 29th ed. Hess. 48p. (C). 1997. 15.00 (0-8213-3576-6, 13576) World Bank.

World Bank-Financed Projects with Community Participation: Procurement & Disbursement Issues. Gita Gopal & Alexandre Marc. LC 94-32394. (Discussion Papers). 1994. 8.95 (0-8213-3068-3, 13068) World Bank.

World Bank Financing of Education: Lending, Learning & Development. Phillip W. Jones. LC 91-25212. 320p. (C). (gr. 13). 1992. text ed. 62.95 (0-415-06078-8, A6846) Routledge.

World Bank Glossary, 2 vols., Vol. 1, English-French, French-English. rev. ed. 462p. (ENG, FRE & SPA.). 1991. 50.00 (0-8213-1733-4, 11733) World Bank.

World Bank Glossary - Glosario del Banco Mundial: English-Spanish, Spanish-English/Glosario del Banco Mundial: Ingles-Espanol, Espanol-Ingles. LC 96-10217. 434p. (ENG & SPA.). 1996. 50.00 (0-8213-3595-2, 13595) World Bank.

World Bank Governance & Human Rights. 2nd rev. ed. Ed. by George Black & Patricia Armstrong. 126p. 1995. pap. 12.00 (0-934143-78-1) Lawyers Comm Human.

World Bank Group & the SAARC Nations. Vyuptakesh Sharan. (C). 1991. 17.50 (0-685-59776-8, Pub. by Anmol II) S Asia.

World Bank in a Changing World: Selected Essays Compiled & Edited by Franziska Tschofen. Ibrahim F. Shihata. 504p. (C). 1991. lib. bdg. 175.00 (0-7923-1371-2) Kluwer Ac.

World Bank Inspection Panel. Ibrahim F. Shihata. (World Bank Publication). 422p. 1995. 24.95 (0-19-520999-0) OUP.

World Bank Lending for Small Enterprises, 1989-1993. Leila M. Webster et al. LC 95-46679. (Technical Paper Ser.: No. 311). 144p. 1996. 9.95 (0-8213-3518-9, 13518) World Bank.

World Bank Participation Sourcebook. (Environmental Department Papers: Vol. 19). 276p. 1996. 15.95 (0-8213-3558-8, 13558) World Bank.

World Bank Policy on Disclosure of Information. Frwd. by Lewis T. Preston. 24p. 1994. pap. write for info. (0-8213-2807-7, 12807) World Bank.

***World Bank Research Program 1995: Abstracts of Current Studies.** 232p. 1995. 13.95 (0-8213-3288-0, 13288) World Bank.

World Bank Since Bretton Woods. Edward S. Mason & Robert E. Asher. LC 73-1089. 915p. 1973. 44.95 (0-8157-5492-2) Brookings.

World Bank Support for Industrialization in Korea, India, & Indonesia. LC 92-8729. (Operations Evaluation Study Ser.: No. 1011-0984). 1992. 6.95 (0-8213-2109-9, 12109) World Bank.

World Banking & Finance: Cooperation Versus Conflict. George Macesich. LC 84-17908. 192p. 1984. text ed. 42.95 (0-275-91220-5, C1220, Praeger Pubs) Greenwood.

W

An Asterisk (*) at the beginning of an entry indicates that the title is appearing in BIP for the first time.

World Bank's Lending in South Asia. S. Guhan. 81p. (C). 1995. pap. 9.95 (*0-8157-3309-7*) Brookings.
World Bank's Partnership with Nongovernmental Organizations. 44p. 1996. pap. 7.95 (*0-8213-3603-7*) World Bank.
World Bank's Partnership with Nongovernmental Organizations. 44p. (FRE.). 1996. pap. 7.95 (*0-8213-3604-5*) World Bank.
World Bank's Partnership with Nongovernmental Organizations. 44p. (SPA.). 1996. pap. 7.95 (*0-8213-3605-3*) World Bank.
World Bank's Role in Human Resource Development in Sub-Saharan Africa: Education, Training & Technical Assistance. Ronald G. Ridker. LC 94-20212. (Operations Evaluation Study Ser.). 1994. 9.95 (*0-8213-2864-6*, 12864) World Bank.
World Bank's Role in the Electric Power Sector: Policies for Effective Institutional, Regulatory, & Financial Reform. (Policy Paper Ser.). 84p. (SPA.). 1993. 7.95 (*0-8213-2451-9*, 12451) World Bank.
World Bank's Role in the Electric Power Sector: Policies for Effective Institutional, Regulatory & Financial Reform. LC 92-46609. (Policy Paper Ser.). 84p. 1993. 7.95 (*0-8213-2318-0*, 12318) World Bank.
World Bank's Strategy for Reducing Poverty & Hunger. Hans P. Binswanger & Pierre Landell-Mills. LC 95-1366. (Environmentally Sustainable Development Studies & Monographs: No. 4). 68p. 1995. 7.95 (*0-8213-3174-4*, 13174) World Bank.
World Bank's Treatment of Employment & Labor Market Issues. Arvil Van Adams et al. LC 92-20314. (Technical Paper Ser.: No. 177). 73p. 1992. 6.95 (*0-8213-2164-1*, 12164) World Bank.
World Barcode Equipment Markets. Market Intelligence Staff. 410p. 1995. 1,995.00 (*0-7889-0162-1*) Frost & Sullivan.
World Barcode Equipment Markets: Fast Paybacks, Customer Awareness Creates Recession Proof Growth. Market Intelligence Staff. 262p. 1993. 1,895.00 (*1-56753-462-7*) Frost & Sullivan.
World Bayonets 1800 to the Present: An Illustrated Reference Guide for Collectors. expanded rev. ed. Anthony Carter. (Illus.). 96p. 1996. 19.95 (*1-85409-344-4*, Pub. by Arms & Armour UK) Sterling.
World Beat: A Listener's Guide to Contemporary World Music on CD. Peter A. Spencer. LC 91-45607. (Illus.). 168p. 1992. pap. 12.95 (*1-55652-140-5*) A cappella Bks.
World Before. Ruth Montgomery. 1985. mass mkt. 5.95 (*0-449-20923-7*, Crest) Fawcett.
World Before Grace. deluxe limited ed. Herman Sutter. (New Texas Poetry Sampler Ser.). 24p. 1992. 10.00 (*0-930324-18-8*) Wings Pr.
World Before Him. Horatio Alger, Jr. (Works of Horatio Alger Jr.). 1989. reprint ed. lib. bdg. 79.00 (*0-7812-3621-5*) Rprt Serv.
***World Before Man: In Search of the Circle.** Wolf Brinsbury. Ed. & Illus. by William A. Cassady. 256p. (Orig.). 1997. mass mkt. 29.95 (*1-882637-55-0*) SJL Pub.
World Before the Deluge. Louis Figuier. 1977. lib. bdg. 69.95 (*0-8490-2844-2*) Gordon Pr.
World Begins Here: An Anthology of Oregon Short Fiction. Ed. by Glen A. Love. LC 92-43642. (Oregon Literature Ser.: Vol. 1). (Illus.). 320p. (Orig.). (YA). 1993. pap. 21.95 (*0-87071-370-1*); text ed. 35.95 (*0-87071-369-8*) Oreg St U Pr.
World Behind the Scenes. Percy H. Fitzgerald. 1972. 24.95 (*0-405-09133-8*, 1718) Ayer.
World below Five Hundred Kilohertz. Peter Carron, Jr. (Illus.). 64p. (Orig.). 1985. pap. 4.95 (*1-882123-00-X*) Universal Radio Rsch.
***World Beneath a Canopy: Life & Art in the Amazon.** Jennifer Fiore & Stevie Mack. 1997. teacher ed. 89.95 incl. vhs (*0-945666-58-6*) Crizmac.
World Beneath Us. Anita McConnell. LC 84-1654. (World of Science Ser.). (Illus.). 64p. 1985. reprint ed. pap. 25.00 (*0-7837-9921-7*, 2060648) Bks Demand.
World Beneath Your Feet see Books for Young Explorers
World Between the Eyes. Poems. Fred Chappell. LC 73-152706. 60p. 1971. pap. 7.95 (*0-8071-1593-2*) La State U Pr.
World Between the Ox & the Swine: Dada Drawings by Hans Richter. Hans Richter. (Illus.). 56p. 1971. pap. 2.00 (*0-911517-43-X*) Mus of Art RI.
World Between the Wars. Promotional Reprint Company Staff. 1938p. 1995. write for info. (*1-57215-090-4*) World Pubns.
***World Between the Wars, 1919-39: An Economist's View.** Joseph S. Davis. LC 74-6821. 448p. 1975. reprint ed. pap. 127.70 (*0-608-03650-1*, 2064476) Bks Demand.
World Between Waves. Ed. by Frank Stewart. LC 92-14458. 309p. (Orig.). 1992. 24.95 (*1-55963-207-0*); pap. 15.95 (*1-55963-208-9*) Island Pr.
World Between Women. Ed. by Irene Reti et al. (Illus.). 126p. (Orig.). 1987. pap. 7.95 (*0-939821-27-3*) HerBooks.
World Beyond. Ruth Montgomery. 1985. mass mkt. 5.99 (*0-449-20832-X*) Fawcett.
***World Beyond.** Scott Peterson. (Dragon Flyz Ser.). (Illus.). 24p. (J). 1997. 2.50 (*0-694-01018-9*, Festival) HarpC Child Bks.
World Beyond Myself. Rutger Kopland. Tr. & Intro. by James Brockway. 80p. (Orig.). 9100. pap. 16.95 (*1-870612-81-7*, Pub. by Enitha Pr UK) Dufour.
World Beyond the Grave. Athenagoras Cavadas. Tr. by Constantine Andres from GRE. 98p. (Orig.). 1988. pap. 3.95 (*0-917651-52-9*) Holy Cross Orthodox.
World Beyond the Waves: An Environmental Adventure. Kate Kempton & Carol Trehearn. Ed. by David Anderson. (Environmental Adventure Ser.). (Illus.). 164p. (J). (gr. 4-10). 1995. 14.95 (*0-9641330-6-7*) Portunus Pubng.
World Beyond the Waves: An Environmental Adventure. Kate Kempton & Carol Trehearn. Ed. by David Anderson. (Illus.). 164p. (J). (gr. 4-9). 1995. pap. 8.95 (*0-9641330-1-6*) Portunus Pubng.
World Bibliography of Bibliographies, 5 Vols. 4th ed. Theodore Besterman. 1963. Set. 417.50 (*0-87471-294-7*) Rowman.
World Bibliography of Oriental Bibliographies. Theodore Besterman. 339p. 1975. pap. 23.00 (*0-87471-750-7*) Rowman.
World Bibliography of Translations of the Meanings of the Holy Qur'an: Printed Translations 1515-1980. Ed. by Ekmeleddin Ihsanoglu et al. 600p. (C). 1988. lib. bdg. 125.00 (*0-7103-0229-0*) Routledge Chapman & Hall.
World Bibliography on International Documentation, 2 vols. Th. Dimitrov. LC 80-5653. 846p. 1981. Set. 95.00 (*0-89111-010-0*) UNIFO Pubs.
World Biographical Index of Education. 828p. 1996. 450.00 (*3-598-11301-3*) K G Saur.
World Biographical Index of Humanities: Scholars, Philosophers, Historians, Philologists, Art & Music Scholars. 645p. 1995. 450.00 (*3-598-11300-5*) K G Saur.
World Biographical Index of Law & Legal Science. 1322p. 1996. 670.00 (*3-598-11303-X*) K G Saur.
World Biographical Index of Medicine: Physicians, Homeopaths, Veterinarians & Pharmacists. 1300p. 1995. 670.00 (*3-598-11289-0*) K G Saur.
World Biographical Index of Military Affairs. 1322p. 1996. 670.00 (*3-598-11304-8*) K G Saur.
World Biographical Index of Politics, Social Sciences & Economics: Politicians, Sociologists Economists, Political Scientists & Psychologists. 1030p. 1996. 670.00 (*3-598-11302-1*) K G Saur.
World Biographical Index of Religion: Theologians, Preachers, Rabbis & Members of a Religious Order. 2324p. 1996. 115.00 (*3-598-11299-8*) K G Saur.
World Biomedical Sensor Markets. Market Intelligence Staff. 250p. 1994. 1,895.00 (*0-7889-0036-6*) Frost & Sullivan.
World Biomedical Sensor Markets: Cross Contamination & Ease of Use Reshape the Industry. Market Intelligence Staff. 1992. 1,695.00 (*1-56753-416-3*) Frost & Sullivan.
World Biomedical Sensor Markets: Cross Contamination & Ease of Use Reshape the Industry. Market Intelligence Staff. 341p. 1992. 1,695.00 (*1-56753-422-8*) Frost & Sullivan.
World Blindness & Its Prevention, Vol. 3. International Agency for the Prevention of Blindness Staff. Ed. by Carl Kupfer. (Illus.). 200p. 1988. 47.50 (*0-19-261755-9*) OUP.
World Blood Banking: A Plasma Product Markets: Patient & Healthcare Professionals Shape Product Development. Market Intelligence Staff. 340p. 1994. 1,695.00 (*1-56753-931-9*) Frost & Sullivan.
World Book. Steven Cramer. LC 92-6797. 63p. (Orig.). 1992. pap. 9.95 (*0-914278-59-2*) Copper Beech.
World Book: Rush-Presbyterian-St. Luke's Medical Center; Medical Encyclopedia; Your Guide to Good Health. LC 94-61785. 1069p. 1995. 48.10 (*0-7166-4202-6*) World Bk.
***World Book Atlas.** LC 95-62473. (Illus.). 432p. 1996. text ed. 87.00 (*0-7166-2698-5*, 6009) World Bk.
World Book Desk Reference Set: World Book Grammar & Style Guide, 4 vols. Ed. by World Book, Inc. Staff. (Illus.). 936p. 1987. lib. bdg. write for info. (*0-318-62216-5*) World Bk.
World Book Desk Reference Set: World Book of Home Facts, 4 vols. Ed. by World Book, Inc. Staff. (Illus.). 936p. 1987. lib. bdg. write for info. (*0-318-62218-1*) World Bk.
World Book Desk Reference Set: World Book of Instant Facts, 4 vols. Ed. by World Book, Inc. Staff. LC 87-50569. (Illus.). 936p. 1987. lib. bdg. write for info. (*0-318-62215-7*) World Bk.
World Book Desk Reference Set: World Book of Nations, 4 vols. Ed. by World Book, Inc. Staff. (Illus.). 936p. 1987. lib. bdg. write for info. (*0-318-62217-3*) World Bk.
World Book Dictionary. Robert K. Barnhart & World Book Editors. LC 96-25617. 1996. write for info. (*0-7166-0297-0*) World Bk.
World Book Dictionary. World Book Editors. LC 94-60814. (Illus.). 2430p. 1995. lib. bdg. write for info. (*0-7166-0295-4*) World Bk.
***World Book Encyclopedia.** LC 96-602090. (Illus.). (YA). (gr. 3 up). 1996. lib. bdg. write for info. (*0-7166-0097-8*) World Bk.
***World Book Encyclopedia: 1996 Edition.** (Illus.). 1996. 644.00 (*0-7166-0096-X*, 6171) World Bk.
World Book Encyclopedia of People & Places. World Book Editors. LC 94-61377. (Illus.). 1630p. 1994. 160.00 (*0-7166-3794-4*) World Bk.
***World Book Encyclopedia of Science, 8 vols.** LC 95-61672. (Illus.). (YA). (gr. 6 up). 1996. write for info. (*0-7166-3394-9*) World Bk.
World Book Encyclopedia of Science, 8 vols. rev. ed. Ed. by World Book Editors & Verlagsgruppe Bertelsmann International Staff. LC 90-70521. (Illus.). 1200p. (YA). 1994. lib. bdg. write for info. (*0-7166-3393-0*) World Bk.
World Book Encyclopedia, 1995, 22 vols., Set. World Book Editors. LC 94-60689. (Illus.). 14000p. 1994. lib. bdg. 559.00 (*0-7166-0095-1*) World Bk.
***World Book Health & Medical Annual.** LC 87-648075. (Illus.). 352p. (YA). (gr. 4 up). 1996. text ed. write for info. (*0-7166-1197-X*) World Bk.
World Book Health & Medical Annual - 1993. World Book Editors. LC 87-648075. (Illus.). 400p. (YA). (gr. 6 up). 1992. lib. bdg. write for info. (*0-7166-1193-7*) World Bk.
World Book Health & Medical Annual, 1992. World Book Editors. LC 87-648075. (Illus.). 400p. 1991. lib. bdg. write for info. (*0-7166-1192-9*) World Bk.
World Book Health & Medical Annual, 1995. LC 87-648075. 368p. 1995. 28.40 (*0-7166-1195-3*) World Bk.
World Book Health & Medical Annual, 1995. World Book Editors. LC 87-648075. (Illus.). 368p. 1994. text ed. write for info. (*0-7166-1194-5*) World Bk.
***World Book Looks at the American West.** World Book Editors. 1997. 10.95 (*0-7166-1805-2*); pap. 6.95 (*0-7166-1809-5*) World Bk.
***World Book Looks at Wonders of the World.** World Book Editors. 1997. 10.95 (*0-7166-1804-4*); pap. 6.95 (*0-7166-1812-5*) World Bk.
World Book New Illustrated Information Finder: The Interactive Visual CD-ROM Encyclopedia, Windows Version CD-ROM. (Illus.). 1995. 395.00 (*0-7166-8417-9*) World Bk.
World Book of America's Heritage: The Peoples, Traditions, & Aspirations That Shaped North America. World Book Editors. LC 91-65695. (Illus.). 384p. 1991. lib. bdg. write for info. (*0-7166-3239-X*) World Bk.
World Book of America's Presidents. rev. ed. World Book Editors. LC 93-60575. (Illus.). 448p. (YA). (gr. 6 up). 1993. lib. bdg. 39.95 (*0-7166-3694-8*) World Bk.
World Book of Family Surnames. Numa Research Department Staff. 95p. 1994. 40.00 (*1-885808-00-3*); pap. text ed. 30.00 (*1-885808-01-1*) Numa Corp.

***World Book of Generations: A Genealogical History, 6 vols., Vol. 1. Lyman D. Platt. LC 96-70854. (Illus.). 288p. (Orig.). 1996. pap. 29.95 (*1-888106-24-7*) Custom Fmly.**
The first of six volumes THE WORLD BOOK OF GENERATIONS is a monumental work of over thirty years in the making. There has been a great need since genealogy became a popular pastime to have available a reference to which people could turn to find which genealogies or pedigrees are accurate, inaccurate, or incomplete, & which are fraudulent. In Volume 1 critical data has been compiled to show: 1) when Adam & Eve left the Garden of Eden; 2) the birth years of the Patriarchs; 3) when the Flood occurred; 4) the births & histories of Abraham; 5) Joseph; 6) Moses; 7) David; 8) Jesus Christ, & 9) the populating of the Earth after the Flood, documenting which nations came from which races. The Flood in 2345 B.C. & the Tower of Babel in 1996 B.C. are key dates in history. Establishing all these signposts allows for Ancient Nations (volumes 2-3) & Ancient Genealogies (volumes 4 plus), to be developed in their right places in time, thereby creating an encyclopedic work that will become a standard reference for documenting all pre-Christian records. Price: $29.95 + $3.50 s&h. To order send check to The Teguayo Press, 316 West 500 North, St. George, UT 84770. FAX (801) 674-5787. Libraries & bookstores may discount $2.95.
Publisher Provided Annotation.

World Book of Math Power, 2 vols. rev. ed. World Book Editors. LC 90-70044. (Illus.). 800p. (YA). (gr. 6 up). 1992. write for info. (*0-7166-1392-1*) World Bk.
World Book of Math Power Activities: Level 1. Ed. by World Book Editors. LC 93-61407. (Illus.). 64p. (J). (gr. k-2). 1994. lib. bdg. 9.95 (*0-7166-3894-0*) World Bk.
World Book of Math Power Activities 2. World Book Editors. LC 93-61456. (Illus.). 64p. (J). (gr. 3-5). 1994. lib. bdg. write for info. (*0-7166-4895-4*) World Bk.
***World Book of People & Places, 6 vols.** LC 95-61458. (Illus.). 1632p. (J). (gr. 4-12). 1996. write for info. (*0-7166-3795-2*) World Bk.
World Book of Science Power, 2 vols., Set. World Book Editors. LC 93-61591. (Illus.). 480p. 1994. write for info. (*0-7166-2294-7*) World Bk.
World Book of Science Power Activities: Level 1, Bk. 1. World Book Editors. LC 94-61378. (Illus.). 64p. (J). (gr. k-2). 1995. student ed. 9.95 (*0-7166-2295-5*) World Bk.
World Book of Science Power Activities: Level 2, Bk. 2. World Book Editors. LC 93-61378. (Illus.). 64p. (J). (gr. 3-5). 1995. student ed. 9.95 (*0-7166-2296-3*) World Bk.
World Book of Space Exploration: Wonders of the Universe & Space Travel, 2 vols. rev. ed. World Book Editors. (Illus.). 415p. 1990. Set. lib. bdg. write for info. (*0-7166-3229-2*) World Bk.
World Book of Sport Psychology. John H. Salmela. 1981. pap. 15.95 (*0-685-42271-2*); text ed. 22.95 (*0-932392-08-3*) Mouvement Pubns.
World Book of Study Power, 2 vols. Ed. by World Book Editors. LC 93-61400. (Illus.). 592p. (YA). (gr. 7-12). 1994. Set. lib. bdg. 43.10 (*0-7166-3594-1*) World Bk.
World Book of Study Power Activities: Level 1, Bk. 1. World Book Editors. LC 94-61379. (Illus.). 64p. (J). (gr. k-2). 1995. student ed. 9.95 (*0-7166-3595-X*) World Bk.
World Book of Study Power Activities: Level 2, Bk. 2. World Book Editors. LC 94-61379. (Illus.). 64p. (J). (gr. 3-5). 1995. student ed. 9.95 (*0-7166-3596-8*) World Bk.
World Book of Word Power, 2 vols. World Book Editors. LC 90-72119. (Illus.). 726p. (YA). 1991. Set. 43.10 (*0-7166-3238-1*) World Bk.
World Book of Word Power, 2 vols., Vol. 1, Language. World Book Editors. (Illus.). 726p. (YA). 1991. Vol. 1: Language. write for info. (*0-318-68413-6*) World Bk.
World Book of Word Power Vol. 2: Writing & Speaking, 2 vols., Vol. 2, Writing & Speaking. World Book Editors. (Illus.). 726p. (YA). 1991. write for info. (*0-318-68414-4*) World Bk.
World Book of Word Power Activities: Level 1. Ed. by World Book Editors. LC 93-61408. (Illus.). 64p. (J). (gr. k-2). 1994. lib. bdg. 9.95 (*0-7166-3994-7*) World Bk.
World Book of Word Power Activities: Level 2. Ed. by World Book Editors. LC 93-61457. (Illus.). 64p. (J). (gr. 3-5). 1994. lib. bdg. 9.95 (*0-7166-3995-5*) World Bk.
World Book Science Desk Reference. World Book Editors. LC 94-60635. (Illus.). 415p. (J). (gr. 4-6). 1994. write for info. (*0-7166-2504-0*) World Bk.
***World Book Student Dictionary.** LC 95-60190. 944p. (J). (gr. 2-6). 1995. write for info. (*0-7166-1595-9*, 6018) World Bk.
World Book Student Dictionary. rev. ed. World Book Editors. LC 92-64304. (Illus.). 900p. (J). (gr. 3-6). 1993. write for info. (*0-7166-1593-2*) World Bk.
World Book Student Information Finder, 2 vols. World Book Editors. LC 90-71009. (Illus.). 590p. (YA). (gr. 7-12). 1993. Set. lib. bdg. write for info. (*0-7166-3247-0*) World Bk.
World Book Student Information Finder, 2 vols., Vol. 2, Math & Science. World Book Editors. (Illus.). 590p. (YA). (gr. 7-12). 1993. Vol. 2: Math & Science. write for info. (*0-318-69777-7*) World Bk.
***World Book Year Book.** LC 62-4818. 544p. (YA). 1997. text ed. write for info. (*0-7166-0497-3*) World Bk.
World Book Year Book. Ed. by World Book Editors. LC 62-4818. 576p. (YA). (gr. 6-12). 1994. lib. bdg. write for info. (*0-7166-0494-9*) World Bk.
World Book Year Book - 1993. World Book Editors. LC 62-4818. (Illus.). 576p. (YA). (gr. 6-12). 1993. lib. bdg. write for info. (*0-7166-0493-0*) World Bk.
World Book Year Book, 1992. World Book Editors. LC 62-4818. (Illus.). 576p. (YA). (gr. 6-12). 1992. write for info. (*0-7166-0492-2*) World Bk.
World Book Year Book, 1995. World Book Editors. LC 62-4818. (Illus.). 544p. 1995. text ed. write for info. (*0-7166-0495-7*) World Bk.
***World Book 1996 Annual Supplements, 3 vols.** Incl. 1996 Health & Medical Annual. 368p. 1996. 29.40 (*0-7166-1196-1*, 95050); 1996 Year Book Ninety-Six Year Book. 544p. 1996. 29.40 (*0-7166-0496-5*, 92095); 1996 Science Year. LC 65-21776. 368p. 1995. 29.40 (*0-7166-0596-1*, 93091); 80.00 (*0-614-23188-4*) World Bk.
***World Book's Science Desk Reference & Teacher's Resource.** (Illus.). 64p. (YA). (gr. 6-12). 1996. teacher ed., pap. 10.00 (*0-7166-2507-5*, 6037) World Bk.
***World Book's Science Desk Reference & Teacher's Resource: Science Desk Reference.** (Illus.). 416p. (YA). (gr. 6-12). 1996. teacher ed. 38.00 (*0-7166-2506-7*, 6038) World Bk.
***World Book's Young Scientist, 10 vols.** (Illus.). (J). (gr. 3-8). 1997. write for info. (*0-7166-2796-5*) World Bk.
World Book's Young Scientist, 10 vols. rev. ed. Ed. by World Book Editors. LC 93-60294. (Illus.). 1270p. (J). (gr. 3-6). 1993. Set. lib. bdg. write for info. (*0-7166-2794-9*) World Bk.
***World Boundaries & Borderlands, 5 vols., Set.** The International Boundaries Staff. (World Boundaries Ser.). (C). (gr. 13). 1994. text ed. 350.00 (*0-415-08840-2*) Routledge.
World Brain. H. G. Wells. LC 78-128332. (Essay Index Reprint Ser.). 1977. 21.95 (*0-8369-2033-3*) Ayer.
World Brain. H. G. Wells. 1994. lib. bdg. 24.95 (*1-56849-382-7*) Buccaneer Bks.
World Broadcast Advertising: Four Reports. U. S. Bureau of Foreign & Domestic Commerce Staff. LC 84-27466. (History of Broadcasting: Radio to Television Ser.). 1977. 23.95 (*0-405-03586-1*, 11253) Ayer.
***World Broadcasting: A Comparative View.** Ed. by Alan Wells. (Communication, Culture & Information Studies). (Illus.). 300p. 1997. pap. 39.50 (*1-56750-246-6*); text ed. 78.50 (*1-56750-245-8*) Ablex Pub.
World Broadcasting in the Age of the Satellite: Comparative Systems, Policies & Issues in Mass Telecommunication. W. J. Howell, Jr. Ed. by Melvin J. Voigt. LC 86-3380. (Communication & Information Science Ser.). 344p. 1986. pap. 39.50 (*0-89391-390-1*) Ablex Pub.
World Broadcasting in the Age of the Satellite: Comparative Systems, Policies & Issues in Mass Telecommunication. W. J. Howell, Jr. Ed. by Melvin J. Voigt. LC 86-3380. (Communication & Information Science Ser.). 344p. 1986. text ed. 73.25 (*0-89391-340-5*) Ablex Pub.
World Builder's Guide Book. Richard L. Baker. 1996. 20.00 (*0-7869-0434-8*) TSR Inc.
World-Building. Stephen L. Gillett. LC 95-25826. (Science Fiction Writing Ser.). (Illus.). 208p. 1996. 16.99 (*0-89879-707-1*, Wrtrs Digest Bks) F & W Pubns Inc.
World Business & Economic Review 1996. 900p. 1996. 240.00 (*0-7494-1607-6*, Pub. by Kogan Pg UK) Cassell.
World Business Cycles. Ed. by Economist Books, Ltd. Staff. 191p. 1982. 95.00 (*0-85058-057-9*) Gale.
World Business Desk Reference: How to Do Business with 192 Countries by Phone, Fax, & Mail. Alice A. Gelder & Rudy Yuly. LC 93-1677. 448p. 1993. text ed. 75.00 (*1-55623-934-3*) Irwin Prof Pubng.
World Business Directory: Private - Public WW, 2 vols. 3rd ed. Meghan Omeara. 1994. 495.00 (*0-8103-8053-6*) Gale.
***World Business Rankings Annual.** 1997. 189.00 (*0-7876-1880-2*, 00157357) Gale.
World by Itself: The Pastoral Moment in Cooper's Fiction. H. Daniel Peck. LC 76-25868. 227p. reprint ed. pap. 64.70 (*0-8357-3755-1*, 2036481) Bks Demand.
World Came to St. Louis: A Visit to the 1904 World's Fair. Dorothy D. Birk. LC 79-10396. (Illus.). 1979. 9.99 (*0-8272-4213-1*) Chalice Pr.

World Canals: Inland Navigation Past & Present. Charles Hadfield. LC 85-29272. (Illus.). 432p. reprint ed. pap. 123.20 (*0-7837-5334-9*, 2045074) Bks Demand.

World Cancer Therapeutic Markets: Strategic Alliances Globalize the Marketplace. Market Intelligence Staff. 295p. 1993. 2,495.00 (*1-56753-524-0*) Frost & Sullivan.

***World Cancer Therapeutic Markets - a Product Based Analysis.** Frost & Sullivan. 279p. 1997. write for info. (*0-7889-0640-2*, 5224) Frost & Sullivan.

World Cancer Therapeutic Markets by Disease Cite: Accelerated R & D Intensifies Race for Cure. Market Intelligence Staff. 400p. (Orig.). 1994. 2,895.00 (*1-56753-886-X*) Frost & Sullivan.

World Cancer Therapeutic Pharmaceuticals Market: Biotech Becomes Big Business. Market Intelligence Staff. 258p. (Orig.). 1992. 2,295.00 (*1-56753-063-X*) Frost & Sullivan.

World Capital Shortage. Alan Heslop. (Key Issues Lecture Ser.). 1978. write for info. (*0-672-97208-5*); pap. write for info. (*0-672-97170-4*) Macmillan.

World Capitalist Crisis & the Tasks of the Fourth International: Perspectives Resolution of the International Committee of Fourth International. International Committee of the Fourth International Staff. 75p. (Orig.). (SPA.). (C). 1989. pap. 5.95 (*0-929087-35-6*) Labor Pubns Inc.

World Capitalist Crisis & the Tasks of the Fourth International: Perspectives Resolution of the International Committee of Fourth International. International Committee of the Fourth International Staff. 63p. (Orig.). (RUS.). (C). 1989. pap. 4.95 (*0-929087-40-2*) Labor Pubns Inc.

World Capitalist Crisis & the Tasks of the Fourth International: Perspectives Resolution of the International Committee of the Fourth International. 75p. (Orig.). (C). 1988. pap. 5.95 (*0-929087-34-8*) Labor Pubns Inc.

***World Car Forecasts.** 1996. 945.00 (*0-85058-899-5*, R340) Economist Intell.

World Car Forecasts No. R328: The Outlook for Sales, Production & Vehicles in Use to 2000: 1995 Edition. 1995. 825.00 (*0-85058-838-3*) Economist Intell.

***World Car Forecasts 97.** 1997. write for info. (*0-614-25453-1*) Econ Intel.

World Cardiac Diagnostic Imaging Markets. Frost & Sullivan Staff. 346p. 1996. write for info. (*0-7889-0406-X*, 969-50) Frost & Sullivan.

World Cardiovascular Diagnostic & Therapeutic Equipment Markets: Multi-Billion Dollar Battle, Technology Advances vs Cost Constraints. Market Intelligence Staff. 313p. (Orig.). 1992. 1,995.00 (*1-56753-043-5*) Frost & Sullivan.

World Cardiovascular Drug Markets: Primary Prevention Creates Opportunities. Market Intelligence Staff. 430p. (Orig.). 1994. 2,695.00 (*1-56753-925-4*) Frost & Sullivan.

World Cartography. Incl. Vol. 15. . (Illus.). 89p. 1979. pap. 7.00 (*0-685-12669-2*, E.78.1.14); Vol. 16. . 97p. 1980. pap. 9.00 (*0-686-72721-5*, E.80.1.12); Vol. XIX. . 68p. 1987. pap. 9.00 (*92-1-100317-2*, E.87.1.15); write for info. (*0-318-60554-6*) UN.

World Cartography, Vol. XVIII. 67p. 1986. 8.50 (*92-1-100284-2*, E.85.1.23) UN.

World Cartography, Vol. XX. 148p. 19.00 (*92-1-100432-2*) UN.

World Cartography, Vol. XXI. 40p. 1990. pap. 10.00 (*92-1-100436-5*, 90.1.12) UN.

World Cartography, Vol. XXII. 138p. Date not set. 20.00 (*92-1-100508-6*, E.93.1.10) UN.

World Catalog of Shore Files (Diptera: Ephydridae) Wayne N. Mathis & Tadeusz Zatwarnicki. Ed. by Virendra K. Gupta. LC 95-79418. (Memoirs on Entomology, International Ser.: Vol. 4). 430p. 1995. 60.00 (*1-56665-059-3*) Assoc Pubs FL.

World Catalog of the Bethylidae (Hymenoptera: Aculeata) Gordon Gordh & L. Moczar. (Memoir Ser.: No. 46). 374p. 1990. 45.00 (*1-56665-045-3*) Assoc Pubs FL.

***World Catalog of the Family Tethinidae (Diptera)** Wayne N. Mathis & Lorenzo Munari. LC 96-32911. (Smithsonian Contributions to Zoology Ser.: No. 584). (Illus.). 33p. 1996. reprint ed. pap. 25.00 (*0-608-04255-2*, 2065010) Bks Demand.

World Catalogue. Ed. by Marian V. Cooper. 256p. 1990. 16.95 (*0-945332-20-3*) Agora Inc MD.

World Catalogue of Dermaptera. Henrik Steinmann. 933p. (C). 1989. 165.00 (*963-05-4819-4*, Pub. by Akad Kiado HU) St Mut.

World Catalogue of Dermapters. H. Steinmann. (Series Entolologica). (C). 1990. lib. bdg. 440.50 (*0-7923-0096-3*) Kluwer Ac.

World Catholicism in Transition. Gannon. 1988. 35.00 (*0-02-911280-X*) Mac Lib Ref.

World Celebrities in Ninety Photographic Portraits. Fred Stein. 96p. 1989. pap. 9.95 (*0-486-25843-2*) Dover.

World Cell Therapy Markets: Harnessing the Power of the Cell. Market Intelligence Staff. 1995. 2,895.00 (*0-7889-0193-1*, 5033-52) Frost & Sullivan.

World Cellular & PCN Telephone, Pager & Accessories Markets: Changes ... Changes ... Changes. Market Intelligence Staff. 630p. 1992. 1,695.00 (*1-56753-334-5*) Frost & Sullivan.

World Centre for Jewish Music in Palestine, 1936-1940: Jewish Musical Life on the Eve of World War II. Philip V. Bohlman. (Illus.). 320p. 1992. 75.00 (*0-19-816237-5*) OUP.

World Ceramics: An Illustrated History. Ed. by Robert J. Charleston. (Illus.). 1991. 39.95 (*0-517-35149-8*) Random Hse Value.

***World Chamber of Commerce Directory.** 400p. 1997. pap. 35.00 (*0-943581-10-9*) WWCCD.

World Chamber of Commerce Directory. rev. ed. Ed. by Jan Pierce. 400p. (Orig.). 1996. pap. 35.00 (*0-943581-09-5*) WWCCD.

World Champion Atlanta Braves 1871-1995. Bob Klapisch. 1995. pap. 24.95 (*1-57036-344-7*) Turner Pub GA.

***World Champion Atlanta Braves 1871-1995.** Bob Klapisch. 1995. 34.95 (*1-57036-346-3*) Turner Pub GA.

***World Champion Combinations.** Raymond Keene & Eric Schiller. LC 97-65488. (Illus.). 256p. 1997. pap. 16.95 (*0-940685-77-9*) Cardoza Pub.

World Champion on Winning Pool & Trick Shots. 3rd ed. Nick Varner. (Illus.). 141p. 1988. pap. 14.00 (*0-685-20278-X*) Nick Varner.

***World Champion Openings.** Eric Schiller. LC 96-85740. (Illus.). 384p. (Orig.). 1997. pap. 16.95 (*0-940685-69-8*) Cardoza Pub.

World Champions at Work. Purdy. Date not set. pap. write for info. (*0-938650-81-5*) Thinkers Pr.

World Championship Dutch Oven Cookbook. Juanita Kohler et al. (Illus.). 104p. (Orig.). 1989. pap. 8.95 (*0-9623918-0-8*) Kohler Kohler Michaud.

World Chancelleries: Sentiments, Ideas Expressed by Famous Statesmen of the World. Ed. by Edward P. Bell. 1977. lib. bdg. 59.95 (*0-8490-2845-0*) Gordon Pr.

World Changers. (Cross Training Ser.: Vol. 2). 64p. (YA). (gr. 10-12). 1994. pap. 29.95 (*1-57405-017-6*) CharismaLife Pub.

World Changes: Thomas Kuhn & the Nature of Science. Ed. by Paul Horwich. (Illus.). 368p. 1994. pap. 16.95 (*0-262-58138-8*, Bradford Bks) MIT Pr.

World Changes in Divorce Patterns. William J. Goode. LC 92-44530. 360p. 1993. 40.00 (*0-300-05537-4*) Yale U Pr.

***World Checklist & Bibliography of Magnoliaceae.** David Frodin & Rafael Govaerts. vii, 72p. 1996. pap. 30.00 (*1-900347-07-5*, Pub. by Royal Botnic Grdns UK) Balogh.

World Checklist of Birds. Burt L. Monroe, Jr. & Charles G. Sibley. 400p. 1993. 50.00 (*0-300-05547-1*) Yale U Pr.

***World Checklist of Birds.** Burt L. Monroe, Jr. & Charles G. Sibley. 416p. 1997. pap. 20.00 (*0-300-07083-7*) Yale U Pr.

World Chemistry. Melvin D. Joesten. (C). 1990. pap. text ed. 38.25 (*0-03-073166-6*) HB Coll Pubs.

World Chess Champions. E. G. Winter. (Illus.). 185p. 1981. 25.95 (*0-08-024094-1*, Pergamon Pr); pap. 15.95 (*0-08-024117-4*, Pergamon Pr) Elsevier.

World Chess Championship Match - Moscow 1985. Garry Kasparov. Tr. by Kenneth P. Neat. (Russian Chess Ser.). 132p. 1986. 25.90 (*0-08-034044-X*, Pub. by PPL UK) Elsevier.

World Chess Championship 1995. Daniel King. 1995. pap. 12.95 (*1-85744-146-X*) S&S Trade.

World Chess Championships 1993. Daniel King. 1993. pap. 14.95 (*1-85744-066-8*) S&S Trade.

World Christian Encyclopedia, 3 vols. 2nd ed. Ed. by David B. Barrett et al. (Illus.). 2608p. 1998. 395.00 (*0-19-507963-9*) OUP.

World Christian Encyclopedia: A Comparative Survey of Churches & Religions in the Modern World, A. D. 1900 to 2000. Ed. by David Barrett. (Illus.). 1026p. 1982. text ed. 225.00 (*0-19-572435-6*) OUP.

World Christian Starter Kit. rev. ed. Glenn Myers. 126p. reprint ed. pap. text ed. 4.99 (*0-9630908-5-2*) O M Lit.

World Christianity: South Central Africa. Ed. by Marjorie Froise. 182p. 1991. pap. 1.95 (*0-912552-76-X*) MARC.

World Christianity: Southern Africa. Ed. by Marjorie Froise. 125p. 1989. 1.95 (*0-912552-63-8*) MARC.

World Cinema: Diary of a Day. Peter Cowie & Martin Scorsese. LC 94-28116. 1995. 29.95 (*0-87951-573-2*) Overlook Pr.

World Cinema: Hungary. Bryan Burns. LC 96-16839. (Illus.). 240p. (C). 1996. 38.50 (*0-8386-3722-1*) Fairleigh Dickinson.

World Cinema: Israel. Amy Kronish. (Illus.). 272p. 1996. 38.50 (*0-8386-3697-7*) Fairleigh Dickinson.

World Cities in a World-System. Ed. by Paul L. Knox & Peter J. Taylor. 336p. (C). 1995. text ed. 64.95 (*0-521-48165-1*); pap. text ed. 22.95 (*0-521-48470-7*) Cambridge U Pr.

***World Citizenship.** Joseph Rotblat. LC 96-50106. 1997. text ed. 65.00 (*0-312-17359-8*); text ed. 21.95 (*0-312-17361-X*) St Martin.

World Civil Aircraft Since Nineteen Forty-Five. Michael Hardy. (Illus.). 1981. 4.50 (*0-684-16266-0*) S&S Trade.

World Civilization. (National Teacher Examination Ser.: NT-63). pap. 23.95 (*0-8373-8483-4*) Nat Learn.

World Civilization, Vol. 1. 8th ed. Edward Burns. (C). Date not set. student ed., pap. text ed. 19.95 (*0-393-95920-1*) Norton.

World Civilization, Vol. 2. Adler. Date not set. wbk. ed. write for info. (*0-314-09737-6*) West Pub.

World Civilization: A Brief History. 2nd ed. Robin W. Winks. (Illus.). 550p. (C). 1993. pap. text ed. 34.90 (*0-939693-28-3*) Collegiate Pr.

World Civilization Map Exercise Workbook. Adler. Date not set. wbk. ed., pap. text ed. 6.75 (*0-314-09412-1*) West Pub.

World Civilization Readings. Raymond Lockett. 1992. 18.70 (*0-536-58217-3*) Ginn Pr.

World Civilizations. Adler. Date not set. student ed. 17.75 (*0-314-09414-8*) West Pub.

World Civilizations, 2 vols. Phillip J. Adler. Incl. Vol. 1. . LC 95-34878. 350p. (C). 1996. pap. text ed. 45.25 (*0-314-06800-7*); Vol. 2. . LC 95-34878. 350p. (C). 1996. pap. text ed. 45.25 (*0-314-06801-5*); 700p. (C). Date not set. Set text ed. 61.50 (*0-314-06799-X*) West Pub.

World Civilizations. Burgess. (C). 1995. pap. 33.56 (*0-395-72310-8*) HM.

World Civilizations. Mark A. Kishlansky & Patrick J. Geary. 576p. (C). 1995. text ed. 48.95 (*0-06-500351-9*) Addson-Wesley Educ.

World Civilizations, 2 vols. Peter N. Stearns. (C). 1992. Set. text ed. 61.50 (*0-06-046431-3*) Addson-Wesley Educ.

World Civilizations, 2 vols. 2nd ed. F. Roy Willis. LC 85-80720. (C). 1986. Instr.'s guide. teacher ed. 2.66 (*0-669-09361-0*) HM College Div.

World Civilizations. 9th ed. Ralph Philip. (C). Date not set. student ed., pap. text ed. 19.95 (*0-393-96882-0*) Norton.

World Civilizations. 9th ed. Meredith Veldman. (C). Date not set. suppl. ed., teacher ed., pap. text ed. write for info. (*0-393-96884-7*) Norton.

World Civilizations, 1. 8th ed. Edward Burns. (C). Date not set. student ed., pap. text ed. 47.95 (*0-393-96526-0*) Norton.

World Civilizations, 1. 9th ed. Edward Burns. LC 96-23844. (C). 1997. pap. text ed. 47.95 (*0-393-96880-4*, Norton Paperbks) Norton.

World Civilizations, 2 vols., I. Peter N. Stearns. (C). 1992. text ed. 47.50 (*0-06-500260-1*) Addson-Wesley Educ.

World Civilizations, 2 vols., II. Peter N. Stearns. (C). 1992. text ed. 44.00 (*0-06-500261-X*) Addson-Wesley Educ.

World Civilizations, 2 vols., II. Peter N. Stearns. (C). 1992. 20.00 (*0-06-500431-0*) Addson-Wesley Educ.

World Civilizations, III. Edward M. Burns et al. (C). 1986. pap. text ed. 22.95 (*0-393-95521-4*) Norton.

World Civilizations, Vol. 1. 8th ed. Philip L. Ralph. (C). pap. text ed. 47.95 (*0-393-95915-5*, Norton Paperbks) Norton.

World Civilizations, 2 vols., Vol. 1, From Ancient Times Through the 16th Cent. 2nd ed. F. Roy Willis. LC 85-80720. 726p. (C). 1986. Vol. I: From Ancient Times through the Sixteenth Century, 726 p. pap. text ed. 45.56 (*0-669-09359-9*) HM College Div.

World Civilizations, Vol. 2. 8th ed. Edward Burns. (C). Date not set. pap. text ed. 47.95 (*0-393-95916-3*, Norton Paperbks) Norton.

World Civilizations, Vol. 2. 8th ed. Edward Burns. (C). Date not set. student ed., pap. text ed. 19.95 (*0-393-95921-X*) Norton.

World Civilizations, Vol. 2. 8th ed. Edward Burns. (C). Date not set. student ed., pap. text ed. 47.95 (*0-393-96527-9*) Norton.

World Civilizations, Vol. 2. 9th ed. Edward Burns. LC 96-23844. (C). 1997. pap. text ed. 47.95 (*0-393-96881-2*) Norton.

World Civilizations, Vol. 2. 9th ed. Ralph Philip. (C). Date not set. student ed., pap. text ed. 19.95 (*0-393-96883-9*) Norton.

World Civilizations, 2 vols., Vol. II: From the 16th Century to the Contemp. Age. 2nd ed. F. Roy Willis. LC 85-80720. 773p. (C). 1986. Vol. II: From the Sixteenth Century to the Contemporary Age, 773 p. pap. text ed. 45.56 (*0-669-09360-2*) HM College Div.

World Civilizations: Sources, Images, & Interpretations, 2 vols., 1. Ed. by Dennis Sherman & A. Tom Grunfeld. LC 93-34784. 1993. pap. text ed. write for info. (*0-07-056831-6*) McGraw.

World Civilizations: Sources, Images, & Interpretations, 2 vols., Vol. 2. Ed. by Dennis Sherman & A. Tom Grunfeld. LC 93-34784. 1993. pap. text ed. write for info. (*0-07-056833-2*) McGraw.

World Civilizations: The Global Experience. Bischoff. (C). Date not set. write for info. (*0-673-97073-6*) Addson-Wesley Educ.

World Civilizations: The Global Experience. 2nd ed. Stearns et al. (C). 1995. teacher ed. write for info. (*0-673-55569-0*) Addson-Wesley Educ.

World Civilizations: The Global Experience, Vol. 2. 2nd ed. Stearns et al. (C). 1996. student ed., pap. text ed. 18.95 (*0-673-99931-9*) Addson-Wesley Educ.

World Civilizations Vol. 1: The Global Experience, Vol. 1. 2nd ed. Stearns et al. (C). 1996. student ed., pap. text ed. 18.95 (*0-673-99930-0*) Addson-Wesley Educ.

World Civilizations Vol. 1: The Global Experience: To 1750. 2nd ed. Peter Stearns. (Illus.). 560p. 1996. pap. text ed. 45.00 (*1-886746-65-6*) Talman Pub.

World Civilizations Vol. 2: The Global Experience, Vol. 2. 2nd ed. Peter N. Stearns et al. 608p. (C). 1996. text ed. 47.95 (*0-673-99428-7*) Addson-Wesley Educ.

World Civilizations Vol. I: The Global Experience: To 1750. 2nd ed. Michael Adas et al. (Illus.). 560p. 1996. pap. 45.00 (*0-614-14581-3*) Talman Pub.

World Civilizations Vol. II: The Global Experience: From 1450. 2nd ed. Michael Adas et al. (Illus.). 560p. 1996. pap. 45.00 (*1-886746-66-4*) Talman Pub.

***World Civilizations - Races, Tribes & Culture Vol. 1: General Introduction: A Historical Survey of Characteristics, Societies, Customs, Languages, Mythologies, Traditions, Flora, Fauna etc. of Natives of the World.** James C. Prichard. (Illus.). xvi, 380p. 1996. 80.00 (*81-7305-088-0*, Pub. by Aryan Bks Intl II) Nataraj Bks.

***World Civilizations - Races, Tribes & Culture Vol. 2: Africa: A Historical Survey of Characteristics, Societies, Customs, Languages, Mythologies, Traditions, Flora, Fauna etc. Natives of the World.** James C. Prichard. (Illus.). xiv, 373p. 1996. 80.00 (*81-7305-089-9*, Pub. by Aryan Bks Intl II) Nataraj Bks.

***World Civilizations - Races, Tribes & Culture Vol. 3: Europe: A Historical Survey of Characteristics, Societies, Customs, Languages, Mythologies, Traditions, Flora, Fauna etc. of Natives of the World.** James C. Prichard. (Illus.). xvi, 507p. 1996. 80.00 (*81-7305-090-2*, Pub. by Aryan Bks Intl II) Nataraj Bks.

***World Civilizations - Races, Tribes & Culture Vol. 4: Asia: A Historical Survey of Characteristics, Societies, Customs, Languages, Mythologies, Traditions, Flora, Fauna etc. of Natives of the World.** James C. Prichard. (Illus.). xv, 631p. 1996. 80.00 (*81-7305-091-0*, Pub. by Aryan Bks Intl II) Nataraj Bks.

***World Civilizations - Races, Tribes & Culture Vol. 5: Oceanaica & America: A Historical Survey of Characteristics, Societies, Customs, Languages, Mythologies, Traditions, Flora, Fauna etc. of Natives of the World.** James C. Prichard. (Illus.). xv, 570p. 1996. 80.00 (*81-7305-092-9*, Pub. by Aryan Bks Intl II) Nataraj Bks.

***World Civilizations Since the 16th Century.** Ed. by Kishlansky. (C). 1995. text ed. 48.95 (*0-673-67523-8*) Addison-Wesley.

***World Civilizations to the 16th Century.** Ed. by Kishlansky. (C). 1995. text ed. 44.50 (*0-673-67522-X*) Addison-Wesley.

World Class. Rosabeth M. Kanter. 1997. pap. 14.00 (*0-684-82522-8*) S&S Trade.

World Class: A Champion Runner Reveals What Makes Her Run. Grete Waitz & Gloria Averbuch. (Illus.). 224p. 1986. pap. 9.95 (*0-446-38315-5*) Warner Bks.

World Class: Measuring Its Achievement. Peter L. Grieco, Jr. LC 90-7122. 287p. 1990. 39.95 (*0-945456-05-0*) PT Pubns.

World Class! Strategies for Winning with Your Customer. 2nd rev. ed. Tony Manning. (Illus.). 418p. 1991. text ed. 50.30 (*0-7021-2663-2*, Pub. by Juta & Co SA) Intl Spec Bk.

World Class: Thriving Locally in the Global Economy. Rosabeth M. Kanter. 1995. 25.00 (*0-684-81129-4*, S&S) S&S Trade.

World-Class Accounting & Finance. Carol J. McNair. (APICS Ser.). 372p. 1993. text ed. 45.00 (*1-55623-550-X*) Irwin Prof Pubng.

World-Class Accounting for World-Class Manufacturing. Lamont F. Steedle. Ed. by Claire Barth. (Illus.). 180p. 1990. reprint ed. pap. 20.00 (*0-86641-193-3*, 90255) Inst Mgmt Account.

World Class Brands. Chris Macrae. (C). 1991. text ed. 30.25 (*0-201-54407-5*) Addison-Wesley.

World-Class Community Relations, Vol. 2. Joe Williams & Reba Payne. 246p. 1988. 149.00 (*0-944607-01-2*) J W Comm.

***World-Class Contracting.** Gregory A. Garrett. Ed. by Sue Deavors. 250p. (Orig.). Date not set. 50.00 (*0-9626190-6-X*) Educ Servs Inst.

World Class Cuisine: Europen Regional Cooking from Great Inns & Grand Hotel. Gail Greco. LC 94-34068. (Illus.). 224p. 1994. 24.95 (*1-55853-324-9*) Rutledge Hill Pr.

World Class Cuisine Cookbook: Market-Fresh Recipes from Europe's Star Chefs. Arna Vogel. 1993. pap. 16.95 (*0-8128-8555-4*, Scrbrough Hse) Madison Bks UPA.

World Class Cuisine of Italy & France: Great Adventures in European Regional Cooking. Gail Greco. LC 95-42893. 198p. 1995. 24.95 (*1-55853-362-1*) Rutledge Hill Pr.

World Class Customer Satisfaction. Jonathan Barsky. 252p. 1996. text ed. 25.00 (*0-7863-0128-7*) Irwin Prof Pubng.

World-Class Diabetic Cooking. Kay Spicer. LC 96-2756. 224p. 1996. pap. 12.95 (*0-945448-70-8*) Am Diabetes.

***World Class Elementary Activity Book.** Harris. Date not set. pap. text ed. write for info. (*0-582-05325-0*, Pub. by Longman UK) Longman.

***World Class Elementary Schools: An Agenda for Action.** Richard M. Haynes & Donald M. Chalker. LC 96-61848. 330p. 1997. text ed. 44.95 (*1-56676-290-1*) Technomic.

World Class Exporting: A Strategic Guide to Export Market Entry. Terry Patrick. (Financial Times Management Ser.). 320p. 1996. 68.50 (*0-273-60522-4*, Pub. by Pitman Pub Ltd UK) Trans-Atl Phila.

World Class Injection Molding: 1994 RETEC, September 25, 26, 27, 1994. Society of Plastics Engineers Staff. (Illus.). 290p. 1994. reprint ed. pap. 82.70 (*0-7837-9719-2*, 2060450) Bks Demand.

***World Class Intermediate Level 4.** Harris & Mower. 1994. student ed., pap. text ed. write for info. (*0-582-05321-8*, Pub. by Longman UK) Longman.

***World Class Intermediate Activity Book Level 4.** Harris & Mower. 1994. pap. text ed. write for info. (*0-582-05327-7*, Drumbeat) Longman.

World Class Leaders for the 1990s see Demystifying Baldrige

World Class Legs: The Effective Six-Week Program to Shaping Your Legs, Butts, & Thighs. Felix Schmitt & Cynthia Tivers. LC 93-5946. (Illus.). 160p. 1994. pap. 10.95 (*0-671-87025-4*, Fireside) S&S Trade.

World Class Maintenance Management. Terry Wireman. 190p. 1990. 34.95 (*0-8311-3025-3*) Indus Pr.

World Class Manager: Olympic Quality Performance in the New Global Economy. Gerhard J. Plenert. LC 95-3860. 1995. 24.95 (*0-7615-0030-8*) Prima Pub.

World Class Manufacturing. Steven J. Bennett & Thomas F. Wallace. LC 93-60672. 350p. 1994. 81.00 (*0-939246-42-2*) Wiley.

World-Class Manufacturing. Jim Todd. LC 94-17157. 1994. 35.00 (*0-07-707623-0*) McGraw.

World-Class Manufacturing: The Lessons of Simplicity Applied. Richard J. Schonberger. 256p. 1986. 37.50 (*0-02-929270-0*, Free Press) Free Pr.

World Class Manufacturing: The Next Decade: Building Power, Strength, & Value. Richard J. Schonberger. (Illus.). 288p. 1996. 30.00 (*0-684-82303-9*) Free Pr.

World Class Manufacturing Casebook. Schonberge. 1987. teacher ed. 4.95 (*0-02-929370-7*) S&S Trade.

World Class Manufacturing Casebook: Implementing JIT & TQC. Richard J. Schonberger. 288p. 1987. 37.50 (*0-02-929340-5*, Free Press); pap. 27.95 (*0-02-929350-2*, Free Press) Free Pr.

World Class New Product Development: Benchmarking Best Practices of Agile Manufacturers. Dan Dimancescu & Kemp Dwenger. (Illus.). 276p. 1995. 29.95 (*0-8144-0311-5*) AMACOM.

W

***World Class Pre-Intermediate Activity Book.** Harris & Mower. 1993. pap. text ed. write for info. (0-582-05326-9, Pub. by Longman UK) Longman.

World Class Production & Inventory Management. Darryl V. Landvater. LC 92-61829. 280p. 1993. 114.00 (0-939246-19-8, TM7525) Wiley.

World Class Production & Inventory Management. Darryl V. Landvater. 288p. 1995. text ed. 45.00 (0-471-13218-7) Wiley.

***World Class Production & Inventory Management.** 2nd ed. Darryl V. Landvater. LC 97-1493. 1997. 55.00 (0-471-17855-1) Wiley.

World Class Puzzles. Erwin Brecher. LC 96-28212. (Illus.). 96p. 1996. pap. 5.95 (0-8069-9458-4) Sterling.

World Class Quality: Using Design of Experiments to Make It Happen. Keki R. Bhote. 212p. 1991. 24.95 (0-8144-5053-9, 040537) AMACOM.

World Class Schools: New Standards for Education. Richard M. Haynes & Donald M. Chalker. LC 94-60606. 275p. 1994. 39.95 (1-56676-144-1) Technomic.

World Class Selling: The Complete Selling Process. Roy Chitwood. 274p. 1995. 24.95 (0-9636268-3-3) Best Sell Pub.

World Class Ski Tuning: The Manual. Michael Howden. (Illus.). 108p. (Orig.). pap. 16.95 (0-9615712-0-9) World Class Ski.

World Class Tours. Esther Bangsund & Wanda Grimsrud. (Illus.). 96p. (Orig.). 1992. teacher ed., pap. 10.00 (1-895411-39-4) Peguis Pubs Ltd.

World-Class Warehousing. Edward H. Frazelle. LC 95-81975. (Illus.). 274p. 1996. 49.95 (0-9649893-0-1) Logistics Res.

World Clinical Lab Analytical Instrument Markets: Reorientating for the Future. Date not set. write for info. (0-614-11870-0) Frost & Sullivan.

World Clinical Laboratory Instrument Markets: Cost Containment...Consolidation...Point of Care; Report #909-56. Market Intelligence Staff. 306p. 1994. 2,195.00 (1-56753-702-2) Frost & Sullivan.

World Coin Catalog, 1988-89. 6th ed. Gunter Schon. (Illus.). 1633p. 1988. pap. 24.95 (0-944945-00-7) Amos Ohio.

World Coinage Report. 1991. lib. bdg. 79.95 (0-8490-5104-5) Gordon Pr.

World Collectors Annuary, July 1, 1991-June 30, 1992, Vol. 42. Hadewych Van Der Lande. 735p. 1993. 175.00 (90-73165-05-9, Pub. by Wrld Collect Pubs NE) IBD Ltd.

World Collectors Annuary July 1, 1992-June 30, 1993, Vol. 43. Hadewych Van Der Lande. 590p. 1994. 175.00 (90-73165-06-7) IBD Ltd.

World Collectors Annuary, Vol. 41: 1990-1991. Hadewych Van Der Lande. 480p. 1992. 175.00 (90-73165-04-0, Pub. by Wrld Collect Pubs NE) IBD Ltd.

World Collectors Annuary (1988-89), Vol. 39. Ed. by Hadewych Van Der Lande. 489p. 1990. 175.00 (90-73165-02-4) IBD Ltd.

***World Colors: Dress & Dolls - Folk & Ethnic Dolls.** Susan Hedrick & Vilma Matchette. (Illus.). 1997. 75.00 (0-87588-473-3, 5275) Hobby Hse.

World Comes to Iowa: Iowa International Anthology. Ed. by Paul Engle et al. LC 87-3524. (Illus.). 327p. 1987. reprint ed. pap. 93.20 (0-608-00077-9, 2060840) Bks Demand.

World Commercial Avionic Markets: Industry Rebounds As New Technologies & Niche Segments Increase Opportunities. Frost & Sullivan Staff. Date not set. write for info. (0-7889-0429-9, 5331-22) Frost & Sullivan.

World Commercial Vehicle Forecasts No. R327: The Outlook for Sales, Production & Vehicles in Use to 2000. 1995. 775.00 (0-85058-826-X) Economist Intell.

***World Commercial Vehicle Forecasts 1997 Edition.** 1997. 1,095.00 (0-614-25458-2, M955) Econ Intel.

***World Commercial Vehicle Forecasts 97.** 1997. write for info. (0-614-25455-8) Econ Intel.

World Communication: Disempowerment & Self-Empowerment. Cees J. Hamelink. LC 95-40144. 176p. (C). 1996. pap. 17.50 (1-85649-394-6, Pub. by Zed Bks Ltd UK); text ed. 52.50 (1-85649-393-8, Pub. by Zed Bks Ltd UK) Humanities.

World Communication: Threat of Promise?: A Socio-Technical Approach. rev. ed. Colin Cherry. LC 78-3761. 243p. reprint ed. pap. 69.30 (0-317-55718-1, 2029268) Bks Demand.

World Communication & Transportation: A Compendium of Current Information for All Countries of the World. (World Facts & Figures Ser.). 160p. 1989. lib. bdg. 40.00 (0-87436-548-1) ABC-CLIO.

***World Communications Directory & Buyer's Guide, 1996.** 835p. 1996. pap. 349.00 (1-890403-00-8) Counterpart.

***World Communications Directory & Buyer's Guide, 1997.** 2nd ed. 850p. 1997. pap. 349.00 (1-890403-01-6) Counterpart.

World Communism at the Crossroads: Military Ascendancy, Political Economy & Human Welfare. Ed. by Steven Rosefielde. 1980. lib. bdg. 61.00 (0-89838-041-3) Kluwer Ac.

World Communist Movement: Theory, Strategy & Tactics of World Communist Parties. Vadim V. Zagladin et al. 485p. 1975. 25.00 (0-8464-0978-X) Beekman Pubs.

World Comparison of Incomes, Prices & Product - Contributions to Economic Analysis. Ed. by Jorge Salazar-Carrillo & Rao D. Prasado. 173p. 1988. 125.75 (0-444-70459-0, North Holland) Elsevier.

World Comparisons of Real Gross Domestic Product & Purchasing Power, 1985: Phase V of the International Comparison Programme. International Comparison Programme Staff. (United Nations & Commission of the European Communities Ser.). 97p. 1994. 19.95 (92-1-161363-9) UN.

World Computer Integrated Manufacturing, CIM, Hardware Markets: Increasing International Competition Accentuates the Move Towards Implementation of CIM. 216p. 1992. 1,495.00 (1-56753-006-0) Frost & Sullivan.

World Computer Numerical Control Markets: Technological Advancements Contributing to Market Resources. Frost & Sullivan Staff. 332p. 1996. write for info. (0-7889-0453-1, 5356) Frost & Sullivan.

World Computer Numerical Controller Market: Waking up to Japanese Manufacturing Expertise. Market Intelligence Staff. 219p. (Orig.). 1992. 1,495.00 (1-56753-039-7) Frost & Sullivan.

World Computer Numerical Controller Markets: User Interest Sparked by 32-Bit Architecture & Graphics Capabilities. Market Intelligence Staff. 221p. 1993. 1,695.00 (1-56753-612-3) Frost & Sullivan.

World-Conception of the Chinese: Their Astronomical Cosmological & Physico-Philosophical Speculations. Alfred Forke. LC 74-26262. (History, Philosophy & Sociology of Science Ser.). 1979. reprint ed. 26.95 (0-405-06590-6) Ayer.

World Concerns & the United Nations: Model Teaching Units for Primary, Secondary & Teacher Education. 239p. 1986. pap. 12.00 (0-8002-1144-8, UN) Taylor & Francis.

World Concerns & the United Nations: Model Teaching Units for Primary, Secondary & Teacher Education. rev. ed. 12.00 (92-1-100292-3, E.86.I.8) UN.

***World Conference on Computers in Education 6: WCCE '95 Liberating the Learner.** Ed. by D. Tinsley & T. Van Weert. (Illus.). 1168p. 1995. text ed. 174.95 (0-412-62670-5, Chap & Hall NY) Chapman & Hall.

World Conference on Edible Fats & Oils Processing: Basic Principles & Modern Practices. Ed. by David Erickson. 456p. 1990. 130.00 (0-935315-30-6) AOCS Pr.

World Conference on Emerging Technologies in the Fats & Oils Industry: Proceedings. Ed. by A. R. Baldwin. 432p. 1986. 40.00 (0-935315-13-6) AOCS Pr.

World Conference on Natural Disaster Reduction 1994: Scientific & Technical Poster Session Abstracts. 176p. (Orig.) (C). 1995. pap. text ed. 45.00 (0-7881-1603-7) DIANE Pub.

World Conference on Oleochemicals. Ed. by Thomas H. Applewhite. 336p. (C). 1991. 130.00 (0-935315-34-9) AOCS Pr.

World Conflicts. David W. Felder. LC 95-90508. 106p. (Orig.). 24.95 (0-910959-11-0, B&G 11H) Wellington Pr.

World Conflicts. David W. Felder. 98p. (Orig.). 1995. teacher ed. 44.95 (0-910959-31-5, B&G 11T) Wellington Pr.

***World Congress for Microcirculation, 6th Congress, Munich, August 1996: Abstracts.** Ed. by K. Messmer & W. M. Kuebler. (Journal Ser.: Vol. 16, Supplement 1, 1996). (Illus.). x, 308p. 1996. pap. 77.50 (3-8055-6388-4) S Karger.

World Congress of Nonlinear Analysts '92: Proceedings of the First, Tampa, Florida, August 19-26, 1992, 4 vols., Set. Ed. by V. Lakshmikantham. LC 95-44204. xlvi, 3954p. 1995. lib. bdg. 798.95 (3-11-013215-X) De Gruyter.

World Congress of Psychiatry. Allan Beigel et al. 1548p. 1994. text ed. 202.00 (981-02-1500-2) World Scientific Pub.

World Congress on Land Policy, 1980: Proceedings. World Congress on Land Policy Staff. Ed. by Matthew Cullen & Sharon Woolery. LC 81-47762. (Lincoln Institute of Land Policy Bk. Ser.). 455p. reprint ed. pap. 129.70 (0-7837-3263-5, 2043282) Bks Demand.

World Congress on Neural Networks: 1993 International Neural Network Society Annual Meeting. (INNS Series of Texts, Monographs, & Proceedings). 3200p. 1993. pap. 360.00 (0-8058-1497-3) L Erlbaum Assocs.

World Congress on Neural Networks: 1994 International Neural Network Society Annual Meeting. INNS Staff. Ed. by Harold Szu. (INNS Series of Texts, Monographs, & Proceedings). 3580p. 1994. pap. 295.00 (0-8058-1745-X) L Erlbaum Assocs.

***World Congress on Superconductivity.** 2nd ed. 428p. 1992. text ed. 49.00 (981-02-1999-7) World Scientific Pub.

World Congress on Superconductivity: Prog. in Hts, Vol. 8. 704p. 1988. pap. 53.00 (9971-5-0610-6); text ed. 138.00 (9971-5-0609-2) World Scientific Pub.

World Congress, 1984: Proceedings of the IFAC Conference, 9th, Budapest, Hungary, July, 1984. IFAC Congress Staff. 400p. 1985. write for info. (0-318-57882-4, Pergamon Pr) Elsevier.

***World Conquered by the Faithful Christian.** Richard Alleine. 172p. 1997. 20.95 (1-57358-018-X) Soli Deo Gloria.

World Conqueror & World Renouncer. Stanley J. Tambiah. LC 76-8290. (Cambridge Studies in Social & Cultural Anthropology: No. 15). 1977. pap. 39.95 (0-521-29290-5) Cambridge U Pr.

World Constitutions. 2nd enl. rev. ed. Vishnoo Bhagwan & Vidya Bhushan. 590p. (C). 1987. text ed. 50.00 (81-207-0545-9, Pub. by Sterling Pubs II) Apt Bks.

World Consumption of Wood Trends & Prognoses. A. Madas. 130p. (C). 1974. 30.00 (963-05-0183-X, Pub. by Akad Kiado HU) St Mut.

World Contrast Media Markets: New Dynamics in an Evolving Market. Market Intelligence Staff. (Orig.). 1994. 2,295.00 (0-7889-0121-4) Frost & Sullivan.

World Cookbook of Leftovers see Art of Cooking with Leftovers

World Copper Databook. 2nd ed. 508p. 1992. pap. text ed. 191.00 (0-947671-61-7) Metal Bulletin.

World Copper Industry. Raymond F. Mikesell. 1979. pap. 19.95 (0-8018-2270-X) Johns Hopkins.

World Copper Industry: Structure & Economic Analysis. Raymond F. Mikesell. 393p. 1979. pap. 19.95 (0-8018-2210-6) Resources Future.

World Copper Market. Gerhard Wagenhals. (Lecture Notes in Economics & Mathematical Systems Ser.: Vol. 233). xi, 190p. 1984. 35.50 (0-387-13860-9) Spr-Verlag.

World Corporate Identity, No. 1. Ed. by David E. Carter. LC 90-80342. 192p. 1990. text ed. 39.95 (0-88108-073-X) Art Dir.

World Corporate Identity Vol. 3. David E. Carter. LC 93-71473. 192p. 1993. 42.50 (0-88108-120-5) Art Dir.

World Corporate Identity 2. Ed. by David E. Carter. LC 90-80342. (Illus.). 192p. 1992. 39.95 (0-88108-102-7) Art Dir.

World Cosmology Book. Steve Zeitlin. (J). 1996. 15.95 (0-8050-4816-2) H Holt & Co.

***World Cost of Living Survey.** 1997. 235.00 (0-7876-1038-0, 00156129, Gale Res Intl) Gale.

World Cotton Market: Prospects for the Nineties. ICAC Staff & FAO Staff. LC 93-61078. 60p. 1993. pap. text ed. 25.00 (0-9638361-0-2) Intl Cotton Adv.

World Council for Gifted & Talented Children: Journal of the World Council, 4 vols., Vol. I, No. 1. Ed. by Dorothy A. Sisk. 1979. pap. 8.00 (0-317-06552-1) Trillium Pr.

World Council for Gifted & Talented Children: Journal of the World Council, 4 vols., Vol. I, No. 2. Ed. by Dorothy A. Sisk. 1982. pap. 8.00 (0-89824-990-2) Trillium Pr.

World Council for Gifted & Talented Children: Journal of the World Council, 4 vols., Vol. II, No. 1. Ed. by Dorothy A. Sisk. 1983. pap. 8.00 (0-317-06553-X) Trillium Pr.

World Council for Gifted & Talented Children: Journal of the World Council, 4 vols., Vol. II, No. 2. Ed. by Dorothy A. Sisk. 1984. pap. 8.00 (0-685-42712-9) Trillium Pr.

World Council of Churches. David P. Gaines. 1966. 30.00 (0-87233-816-9) Bauhan.

World Council of Churches & Politics: 1975-1986. J. A. Vermaat. LC 88-30956. 136p. 1989. 24.00 (0-932088-30-9); pap. 12.00 (0-932088-29-5) Freedom Hse.

World Council of Churches & the Catholic Church. John J. McDonnell. (Toronto Studies in Theology: Vol. 21). 479p. 1985. lib. bdg. 109.95 (0-88946-765-X) E Mellen.

World Council's Annotated Bibliography of Gifted Education. Ed. by James J. Gallagher & Richard D. Courtright. 124p. 1987. pap. 15.00 (0-89824-165-0) Trillium Pr.

World Countermarks on Medieval & Modern Coins. Ed. by Gregory G. Brunk. LC 75-39496. (Gleanings from the Numismatist Ser.: Vol. 8). (Illus.). 1976. 35.00 (0-88000-074-0) Quarterman.

***World Court.** Rosenne. 1997. student ed., pap. text ed. 20.00 (90-411-0609-X) Kluwer Law Tax Pubs.

World Court. Antonio De Sanchez Bustamante y Sirven. LC 25-23295. xxv, 379p. 1983. reprint ed. lib. bdg. 52.00 (0-89941-272-6, 303060) W S Hein.

World Court: What It Is & How It Works. Date not set. 60.00 (92-1-157071-9, E.94.III.K.ST/1) UN.

World Court: What It Is & How It Works. 5th rev. ed. Shabtai Rosenne. LC 94-15816. (Legal Aspects of International Organizations Ser.: Vol. 16). 1995. lib. bdg. 127.00 (0-7923-2861-2) Kluwer Ac.

World Court & the Contemporary International Law-Making Process. Edward J. McWhinney. 227p. 1979. lib. bdg. 80.50 (90-286-0908-3) Kluwer Ac.

World Court Digest. Rainer Hofmann et al. LC 92-40003. 1992. 64.00 (0-387-56141-2) Spr-Verlag.

***World Court Digest Vol. 2: 1991-1995, Vol. 2.** Ed. by Max Planck Institute for Comparative Public Law & International Law Staff. 453p. 1997. 79.95 (3-540-62083-4) Spr-Verlag.

World Court Enhancements to Advance the Rule of Law. Bryan F. MacPherson. (CURE Monographs: No. 13). 78p. (Orig.). 1994. pap. text ed. 5.00 (1-881520-03-X) Ctr U N Reform Educ.

World Court in the Light of the United States Supreme Court. Thomas W. Balch. 165p. 1983. reprint ed. lib. bdg. 22.50 (0-8377-0340-9) Rothman.

World Court Project on Nuclear Weapons & International Law. Saul H. Mendlovitz. LC 92-10955. 1992. 8.00 (1-880831-00-7) Aletheia Pr.

World Court Project on Nuclear Weapons & International Law. 2nd ed. Saul H. Mendlovitz. LC 93-24199. 1993. 8.00 (1-880831-03-1) Aletheia Pr.

World Court Reports, 1922-1942, 4 vols. 1969. reprint ed. lib. bdg. 220.00 (0-379-00429-1) Oceana.

World Court Reports, 1922-1942, 4 vols., Set. Permanent Court of International Justice Staff. Ed. by Manley O. Hudson. 1969. reprint ed. lib. bdg. 220.00 (0-379-00428-3) Oceana.

World Crafts: An Oxfam Book. Jacqueline Herald. (Illus.). 192p. 1993. 35.00 (0-937274-66-6) Lark Books.

***World Criminal Justice Systems: A Survey.** 3rd ed. Richard J. Terrill. LC 96-85278. 428p. (C). 1996. pap. text ed. 34.95 (0-87084-937-9) Anderson Pub Co.

World Crisis: Its Explanation & Solution. Walter Russell & Lao Russell. (Illus.). 203p. 1984. reprint ed. text ed. 8.00 (1-879605-19-8) U Sci & Philos.

World Crisis & American Responsibility. Reinhold Niebuhr. Ed. by Ernest W. Lefever. LC 74-10643. 128p. 1974. reprint ed. text ed. 35.00 (0-8371-7649-2, NIWC, Greenwood Pr) Greenwood.

World Crisis & British Decline, 1929-1956. Roy Douglas. LC 85-24992. 288p. 1986. text ed. 35.00 (0-312-89115-6) St Martin.

World Crisis by the Professors of the Institute. Graduate Institute of International Studies - Geneva Staff. LC 73-86753. (Essay Index Reprint Ser.). 1977. 21.95 (0-8369-1133-4) Ayer.

World Crisis in Social Security. Ed. by Jean J. Rosa. 245p. (Orig.). 1982. pap. text ed. 24.95 (0-917616-44-8) Transaction Pubs.

World Crop Protection, 1. J. H. Stapley. LC 69-14512. (International Scientific Ser.). (Illus.). reprint ed. pap. 71.00 (0-317-41721-5, 2025728) Bks Demand.

World Crop Protection, 2. J. H. Stapley. LC 69-14512. (International Scientific Ser.). (Illus.). reprint ed. pap. 64.30 (0-317-41722-3) Bks Demand.

World Cruising Guide: Port Facilities Around the World. Jimmy Cornell. (Illus.). 202p. (C). 1995. pap. 39.95 (0-9517486-5-3, Pub. by World Cruising UK) Bluewater Bks.

World Cruising Handbook. Jimmy Cornell. (Illus.). 464p. 1991. 69.95 (0-87742-297-4, 60279) Intl Marine.

World Cruising Handbook. Jimmy Cornell. 1994. pap. text ed. 49.95 (0-07-013324-7) McGraw.

***World Cruising Handbook.** 2nd ed. Jimmy Cornell. 1996. text ed. 69.95 (0-07-013396-4, M-H Bk Intl Group) McGraw.

World Cruising Handbook. 3rd ed. Jimmy Cornell. LC 95-6914. (Illus.). 560p. 1995. text ed. 44.95 (0-07-013344-1) Intl Marine.

World Cuisines. Sunset Magazine & Book Editors. Incl. . 1987. (0-318-61432-4); . 1987. (0-318-61433-2); . 1987. (0-318-61434-0); . 1986. (0-318-61435-9); . 1987. (0-318-61432-4); . 1987. (0-318-61433-2); . 1987. (0-318-61434-0); (Orig.). 1987. 19.95 (0-376-02950-1) Sunset Bks Inc.

World Culture & the Curricular Content of Primary Education. Aaron Benavot et al. 240p. 1992. 75.00 (1-85000-948-1, Falmer Pr); pap. 26.00 (1-85000-949-X, Falmer Pr) Taylor & Francis.

***World Cultures & Geography - Grade 7: Curriculum Unit.** rev. ed. Center for Learning Network Staff. (Social Studies Ser.). 240p. 1996. teacher ed. 34.95 (1-56077-489-4) Ctr Learning.

World Cultures Through Art Activities. Dindy Robinson. 200p. 1996. pap. text ed. 23.00 (1-56308-271-3) Teacher Ideas Pr.

World Cup. Walter Chyzowych. (Illus.). 200p. 1984. 21.95 (0-89651-900-7); pap. 14.95 (0-89651-905-8) Hardwood Pr.

World Cup Action! Bill Gutman. LC 93-41721. (Illus.). 32p. (J). (gr. 2-6). 1997. pap. 3.95 (0-8167-3376-7) Troll Communs.

World Cup Rotterdam, 1989. Fred Van der Vliet et al. (International Chess Data System Ser.). 156p. 1990. pap. text ed. 13.25 (0-917237-09-9) Chess Combi.

World Cup Ski Technique: Learn & Improve. Olle Larsson & James Major. Ed. by Doug Smith. LC 79-90395. (Illus.). (Orig.). 1979. pap. 18.95 (0-935240-00-4) Poudre Pr.

World Cup Ski Technique 2. James Major & Doug Smith. (World Cup Ski Technique Ser.). (Illus.). 384p. (Orig.). 1990. 33.00 (0-935240-08-X) Poudre Pr.

World Cup (Soccer) Michael E. Goodman. (Great Moments in Sports Ser.). 32p. (J). (gr. 4). 1990. lib. bdg. 14.95 (0-88682-320-X) Creative Ed.

World Cup U. S. A. 94: The Official FIFA Book. Peter Arnold. LC 93-51039. 1994. write for info. (0-00-025523-8) Collins SF.

World Cup, 1930-1990. Jack Rollin. (Illus.). 208p. 1990. 24.95 (0-8160-2523-1, Pub. by Guinness Pub UK) Facts on File.

World Cup, 1994: The Official Book. 1994. 10.00 (0-00-255231-0) Collins SF.

World Currency Yearbook. 27th ed. Currency Data & Intelligence Staff. Ed. by Carolyn Edwards et al. (World Currency Yearbook Ser.). (Illus.). 1000p. 1995. 650.00 (0-9648104-0-9) Currency Data & Intell.

World Currency Yearbook. 28th ed. Ed. by Carolyn A. Edwards et al. 1000p. 1996. 520.00 (0-9648104-1-7) Currency Data & Intell.

World Currency Yearbook 1984. International Currency Analysis Staff. Ed. by Philip Cowitt. 1985. 250.00 (0-917645-00-6) Currency Data & Intell.

World Currency Yearbook, 1985. 24th ed. International Currency Analysis Staff. Ed. by Philip Cowitt. 1987. 250.00 (0-917645-01-4) Currency Data & Intell.

World Currency Yearbook, 1986-1987: International Currency Analysis. 25th ed. Ed. by Philip Cowitt. 1984. 250.00 (0-917645-02-2) Currency Data & Intell.

World Currency Yearbook, 1988-1989: International Currency Analysis. 26th ed. Philip P. Cowitt. 900p. 1991. 250.00 (0-917645-03-0) Currency Data & Intell.

World Dancer. Elliot Richman. LC 93-71191. 112p. (Orig.). 1993. pap. 9.95 (1-878580-44-2) Asylum Arts.

***World Dances.** Tracy Maurer. LC 97-8395. (Let's Dance Ser.). (J). 1997. write for info. (1-57103-173-1) Rourke Pr.

World Data Acquisition Boards Software & System Markets: Vendors Focus on Technology to Gain Competitive Edge. 501p. 1995. write for info. (0-7889-0288-1) Frost & Sullivan.

World Data Acquisition Boards, Systems & Software: New Entrants Flood the Market. Market Intelligence Staff. 231p. 1993. 1,895.00 (1-56753-466-X) Frost & Sullivan.

***World Data Business Info Sources 96.** 96th ed. 1996. 1,390.00 (0-86338-672-5, 00156388, Gale Res Intl) Gale.

World Databases in Agriculture. Ed. by C. J. Armstrong. (World Databases Ser.). 1142p. 1995. 250.00 (1-85739-043-1) Bowker-Saur.

World Databases in Biosciences & Pharmacology. C. J. Armstrong. LC 96-42191. 1200p. 1996. 200.00 (1-85739-068-7) Bowker-Saur.

An Asterisk (*) at the beginning of an entry indicates that the title is appearing in BIP for the first time.

World Databases in Chemistry. Ed. by C. J. Armstrong. 1200p. 1995. 235.00 (*1-85739-101-2*) Bowker-Saur.

World Databases in Company Information. C. J. Armstrong. 1700p. 1996. 325.00 (*1-85739-195-0*) Bowker-Saur.

World Databases in Geography & Geology. Ed. by C. J. Armstrong. 1272p. 1995. 200.00 (*1-85739-111-X*) Bowker-Saur.

World Databases in Humanities. Ed. by C. J. Armstrong. (World Databases Ser.). 1200p. 1996. 250.00 (*1-85739-048-2*) Bowker-Saur.

World Databases in Industry. Ed. by C. J. Armstrong. LC 94-43151. (World Databases Ser.). 852p. 1994. 165.00 (*1-85739-185-3*) Bowker-Saur.

World Databases in Management. Ed. by C. J. Armstrong. LC 94-24953. (World Database Ser.: Vol. 3). 1200p. 1995. 165.00 (*1-85739-190-X*) Bowker-Saur.

World Databases in Medicine. 1650p. 1993. 275.00 (*0-86291-613-5*) Bowker-Saur.

World Databases in Patents. Ed. by C. J. Armstrong. 750p. 1995. 165.00 (*1-85739-106-3*) Bowker-Saur.

World Databases in Physics-Mathematics. Ed. by C. J. Armstrong. (World Databases Ser.). 1300p. 1995. 200.00 (*1-85739-038-5*) Bowker-Saur.

World Databases in Social Sciences. C. J. Armstrong. 1200p. 1995. 235.00 (*1-85739-116-0*) Bowker-Saur.

World Debt & Stability. George Macesich. LC 90-37787. 128p. 1991. text ed. 49.95 (*0-275-93669-4*, C3669, Praeger Pubs) Greenwood.

World Debt & the Human Condition: Structural Adjustments & the Right to Development. Ed. by Ved P. Nanda et al. LC 92-9329. (Studies in Human Rights: No. 14). 272p. 1992. text ed. 59.95 (*0-313-28531-4*, NWD, Greenwood Pr) Greenwood.

World Debt Crisis & Its Resolution. 1990. lib. bdg. 250.00 (*0-8490-4043-4*) Gordon Pr.

World Debt Tables see Global Development Finance 1997

World Debt Tables 1996, 2 vols. 810p. 1996. 200.00 (*0-8213-3302-X*) World Bank.

World Debt Tables 1996: External Finance for Developing Countries - Analysis & Summary Tables. 250p. 1996. 24.95 (*0-8213-3300-3*) World Bank.

World Decision. Robert Herrick. (Collected Works of Robert Herrick). 1988. reprint ed. lib. bdg. 79.00 (*0-7812-1277-4*) Rprt Serv.

World Decision see Collected Works of Robert Herrick

World Defense Forces, 1989: A Compendium of Current Military Information for All Countries of the World. (World Facts & Figures Ser.). 137p. 1989. lib. bdg. 40.00 (*0-87436-273-3*) ABC-CLIO.

World Deforestation in the Twentieth Century. Ed. by John F. Richards & Richard P. Tucker. LC 87-31953. (Duke Press Policy Studies). x, 321p. 1989. reprint ed. pap. text ed. 20.95 (*0-8223-1013-9*) Duke.

World Dental Product Markets: Esthetics Expand Globally. Market Intelligence Staff. 313p. 1993. 1,995.00 (*1-56753-528-3*) Frost & Sullivan.

World Dental Products Markets: European Prosthetic Markets Triple North American Growth. 353p. 1992. 1,895.00 (*1-56753-016-8*) Frost & Sullivan.

World Desertification Bibliography. 294p. 1995. 40.00 (*92-1-127017-0*, E.95.III.D.70) UN.

World Destroyed: Hiroshima & the Origins of the Arms Race. Martin J. Sherwin. LC 86-40523. 1987. pap. 15.00 (*0-394-75204-X*, Vin) Random.

World Development Directory. Ed. by Roger East et al. 575p. 1990. 85.00 (*1-55862-067-2*) St James Pr.

***World Development Indicators 1997.** 400p. 1997. 60.00 (*0-8213-3701-7*, 13701) World Bank.

World Development Report Nineteen Eighty-Six. World Bank Staff. (World Bank Publication Ser.). (Illus.). 250p. 1986. pap. text ed. 22.95 (*0-19-520518-9*) World Bank.

World Development Report, 1984. World Bank Staff. (Illus.). 300p. 1984. pap. 19.95 (*0-19-520460-3*) OUP.

World Development Report, 1988. World Bank Staff. (World Bank Publication). (Illus.). 320p. (C). 1988. pap. text ed. 25.95 (*0-19-520650-9*) OUP.

World Development Report, 1989. World Bank Staff. (World Bank Publication). (Illus.). 264p. (C). 1989. pap. text ed. 25.95 (*0-19-520788-2*) OUP.

World Development Report, 1990. World Bank Staff. (World Bank Publication). (Illus.). 272p. (C). 1990. 37.95 (*0-19-520850-1*); pap. text ed. 19.95 (*0-19-520851-X*) OUP.

World Development Report, 1990: Poverty. (World Development Indicators Ser.). 312p. (FRE.). 1990. French, 312p. pap. 25.95 (*0-8213-1504-8*, 11504) World Bank.

World Development Report, 1992. World Bank Staff. (World Bank Publication). (Illus.). 320p. (C). 1992. pap. 19.95 (*0-19-520876-5*, 60876); disk 70.00 (*0-685-59174-3*, 12134) OUP.

World Development Report, 1992: Development & the Environment, World Development Indicators. 320p. 1992. pap. 25.95 (*0-8213-2070-X*, 12070) World Bank.

World Development Report 1993: Investing in Health. (FRE.). 1993. pap. 25.95 (*0-8213-2360-1*, 12360); pap. 25.95 (*0-8213-2361-X*, 12361) World Bank.

World Development Report 1993: Investing in Health. (ARA.). 1993. pap. 25.95 (*0-8213-2365-2*, 12365) World Bank.

World Development Report 1993: Investing in Health. World Bank Staff. (World Bank Publication). (Illus.). 344p. (C). 1993. pap. text ed. 19.95 (*0-19-520890-0*, 60890) OUP.

World Development Report 1994: Infrastructure for Development. (SPA.). 1994. 25.95 (*0-8213-2535-3*, 12535) World Bank.

World Development Report 1994: Infrastructure for Development. (RUS.). 1994. 25.95 (*0-8213-2540-X*, 12540) World Bank.

World Development Report 1994: Infrastructure for Development. (GER.). 1994. 25.95 (*0-8213-2536-1*, 12536) World Bank.

World Development Report 1994: Infrastructure for Development. World Bank Staff. (World Bank Publication). 254p. (C). 1994. pap. 19.95 (*0-19-520992-3*, 60992) OUP.

World Development Report 1994: Infrastructure for Development. World Bank Staff. (World Bank Publication). 224p. (C). 1994. text ed. 37.95 (*0-19-520991-5*, 60991) OUP.

World Development Report 1994: Infrastructure for Development. World Bank Staff. (FRE.). 1994. 25.95 (*0-8213-2534-5*, 12534) World Bank.

World Development Report 1995: Workers in an Integrating World. 292p. (FRE.). 1995. pap. 25.95 (*0-8213-2892-1*, 12892) World Bank.

World Development Report 1995: Workers in an Integrating World. 292p. (SPA.). 1995. pap. 25.95 (*0-8213-2893-X*, 12893) World Bank.

World Development Report 1995: Workers in an Integrating World. (GER.). 1995. pap. 25.95 (*0-8213-2894-8*, 12894) World Bank.

World Development Report 1995: Workers in an Integrating World. (JPN.). 1995. pap. 25.95 (*0-8213-2895-6*, 12895) World Bank.

World Development Report 1995: Workers in an Integrating World. (RUS.). 1995. pap. 25.95 (*0-8213-2898-0*, 12898) World Bank.

World Development Report 1995: Workers in an Integrating World. (POR.). 1995. pap. 25.95 (*0-8213-2899-9*, 12899) World Bank.

World Development Report 1995: Workers in an Integrating World. World Bank Staff. (World Bank Publications). 250p. (C). 1995. text ed. 37.95 (*0-19-521103-0*); pap. text ed. 19.95 (*0-19-521102-2*) OUP.

***World Development Report 1996: From Plan to Market.** (ARA.). 1996. 25.95 (*0-8213-3269-4*, 13269) World Bank.

***World Development Report 1996: From Plan to Market.** (CHI.). 1996. 25.95 (*0-8213-3268-6*, 13268) World Bank.

***World Development Report 1996: From Plan to Market.** (FRE.). 1996. 25.95 (*0-8213-3264-3*, 13264) World Bank.

***World Development Report 1996: From Plan to Market.** (GER.). 1996. 25.95 (*0-8213-3266-X*, 13266) World Bank.

***World Development Report 1996: From Plan to Market.** (JPN.). 1996. 25.95 (*0-8213-3267-8*, 13267) World Bank.

***World Development Report 1996: From Plan to Market.** (POR.). 1996. 25.95 (*0-8213-3271-6*, 13271) World Bank.

***World Development Report 1996: From Plan to Market.** (RUS.). 1996. 25.95 (*0-8213-3270-8*, 13270) World Bank.

***World Development Report 1996: From Plan to Market.** (SPA.). 1996. 25.95 (*0-8213-3265-1*, 13265) World Bank.

World Development Report 1996: From Plan to Market. World Bank Staff. (World Bank Publications). (Illus.). 250p. 1996. pap. 22.95 (*0-19-521107-3*, 61107) OUP.

World Development Report 1996: From Plan to Market. World Bank Staff. (World Bank Publications). (Illus.). 250p. 1996. 45.95 (*0-19-521108-1*, 61108) OUP.

***World Development Report 1997.** 354p. (ENG & SPA.). 1997. pap. 25.95 (*0-8213-3770-X*, 13770) World Bank.

***World Development Report 1997.** 354p. (ENG & FRE.). 1997. pap. 25.95 (*0-8213-3771-8*, 13771) World Bank.

***World Development Report 1997.** 354p. (ENG & GER.). 1997. pap. 25.95 (*0-8213-3772-6*, 13772) World Bank.

***World Development Report 1997.** 354p. (ENG & JPN.). 1997. pap. 25.95 (*0-8213-3773-4*, 13773) World Bank.

***World Development Report 1997.** 354p. (CHI & ENG.). 1997. pap. 25.95 (*0-8213-3774-2*, 13774) World Bank.

***World Development Report 1997.** 354p. (ARA & ENG.). 1997. pap. 25.95 (*0-8213-3775-0*, 13775) World Bank.

***World Development Report 1997.** 354p. (ENG & RUS.). 1997. pap. 25.95 (*0-8213-3776-9*, 13776) World Bank.

***World Development Report 1997.** 354p. (ENG & POR.). 1997. pap. 25.95 (*0-8213-3777-7*, 13777) World Bank.

***World Development Report 1997: The State in a Changing World.** World Bank Staff The. (A World Bank Publication). (Illus.). 250p. (C). 1997. pap. text ed. 25.95 (*0-19-521114-6*, 61114) OUP.

***World Development Report 1997: The State in a Changing World.** World Bank Staff The. (A World Bank Publication). (Illus.). 250p. (C). 1997. text ed. 49.95 (*0-19-521115-4*, 61115) OUP.

World Diagnostic Imaging Company Profiles. Market Intelligence Staff. 478p. (Orig.). 1994. 1,595.00 (*0-7889-0131-1*) Frost & Sullivan.

World Diagnostic Imaging Contrast Media: Manufacturers Vie for Japanese Market. Market Intelligence Staff. 216p. 1993. 1,995.00 (*1-56753-439-2*) Frost & Sullivan.

World Dictionary of Livestock Breeds, Types & Varieties. 4th ed. I. L. Mason. 296p. 1996. 75.00 (*0-85199-102-5*, Pub. by CAB Intntl UK) OUP.

World Digital Signal Processor (DSP) Markets: Increasing Price - Performance Ratio Generates New Applications. Market Intelligence Staff. 250p. (Orig.). 1994. 1,995.00 (*1-56753-894-0*) Frost & Sullivan.

World Diplomacy. Richard Sidy. 192p. 1992. pap. text ed. 8.95 (*0-9633744-0-0*) SNS Pr.

World Direct: The RMI Directory of UK Direct Marketing Suppliers. 187p. (Orig.). (C). 1994. pap. 75.00 (*0-7881-0388-1*) DIANE Pub.

World Directory Business Information Libraries. 1993. 395.00 (*0-86338-461-7*, 073015, Pub. by Euromonitor Pubns UK) Gale.

World Directory Crystal. Maslen. 1991. pap. text ed. 25.00 (*0-7923-1023-3*) Kluwer Ac.

World Directory Multinational ENT, Vol. 3. 2nd ed. Gale. (Education Ser.). 1983. write for info. (*0-8103-0521-6*) Van Nos Reinhold.

World Directory Non Official Statistical Sources. 1996. 390.00 (*0-86338-655-5*) Gale.

World Directory of Advertising Agents. 93th ed. 1993. 500.00 (*0-86338-510-9*, 074001, Pub. by Euromonitor Pubns UK) Gale.

World Directory of Aerospace Vehicle Research & Development. (Foreign Aerospace Investment Ser.: No. 1). (Illus.). 587p. (Orig.). 1991. pap. 75.00 (*0-941375-16-1*) DIANE Pub.

***World Directory of Airliner Crashes.** T. Denham. (Illus.). 320p. 1996. 29.95 (*1-85260-554-5*, Pub. by P Stephens UK) Motorbooks Intl.

World Directory of Awards & Prizes. 500p. 1996. 225.00 (*1-85743-022-0*, Pub. by Eurpa Publns UK) Taylor & Francis.

***World Directory of Business Information.** 96th ed. 1996. 550.00 (*0-86338-547-8*, 00156597, Gale Res Intl) Gale.

World Directory of Criminological Institutes. 1987. 45.00 (*92-9078-002-9*, E.87.III.N.1) UN.

World Directory of Criminological Institutes. 6th ed. Ed. by Carla M. Santoro. 625p. 1995. 50.00 (*92-9078-031-2*) UN.

World Directory of Crimonological Institutes, 1990. 5th ed. 661p. 1990. 54.00 (*92-9078-009-6*, 90.III.N.1) UN.

World Directory of Crystallographers: And of Other Scientists Employing Crystallographic Methods. 9th ed. Ed. by Yves Epelboin. LC 95-11941. 1995. pap. text ed. 27.50 (*0-7923-3180-X*) Kluwer Ac.

World Directory of Crystallographers & of Other Scientists Employing Crystallographic Methods, 1986. 7th ed. Ed. by Allan L. Bednowitz & Armin P. Segmuller. 1986. pap. text ed. 17.50 (*90-277-2094-0*) Kluwer Ac.

World Directory of Defense & Security. Donald Kerr. 550p. 1995. 195.00 (*1-56159-145-9*, Stockton Pr) Groves Dictionaries.

World Directory of Diplomatic Representation. 671p. 1992. 375.00 (*0-946653-78-X*) Intl Pubns Serv.

World Directory of Energy Information, 1. Ed. by Christopher Swain & Andrew Buckley. LC 81-754. pap. 84.00 (*0-685-16007-6*, 2027221) Bks Demand.

World Directory of Energy Information, 2. Ed. by Christopher Swain & Andrew Buckley. LC 81-754. pap. 107.50 (*0-685-16008-4*) Bks Demand.

World Directory of Environmental Organizations. 5th ed. Ed. by Thaddeus C. Trzyna & Roberta Childers. 232p. 1996. pap. write for info. (*1-85383-307-X*, Pub. by Erthscan Pubns UK) Island Pr.

World Directory of Environmental Organizations: A Handbook of National & International Organizations & Programs. 5th ed. Ed. by Thaddeus C. Trzyna. 272p. (Orig.). 1996. pap. 50.00 (*0-912102-97-7*) Cal Inst Public.

World Directory of Environmental Organizations: A Handbook of National & International Organizations & Programs. 5th ed. Ed. by Thaddeus C. Trzyna. (Orig.). 1996. pap. write for info. (*0-614-11900-6*) Cal Inst Public.

World Directory of Environmental Testing, Monitoring & Treatment 1995-96. Ed. by Bruce Cross. (Illus.). 320p. (Orig.). 1995. pap. 75.00 (*1-873936-42-7*, Pub. by J & J Sci Pubs UK) Bks Intl VA.

***World Directory of Environmental Testing, Monitoring & Treatment 1996/7.** Ed. by Bruce Cross. 320p. 1996. pap. text ed. 75.00 (*1-873936-66-4*) Bks Intl VA.

World Directory of Human Rights Research & Training Institutions: World Social Science Information Directories. UNESCO Staff. 306p. 1992. pap. 30.00 (*92-3-002794-4*, U7944, Pub. by UNESCO-Bangkok TH) Bernan Associates.

World Directory of Map Collections. 3rd ed. Ed. by Lorraine Dubreuil. (IFLA Publications: Vol. 63). 310p. 1993. 80.00 (*3-598-21791-9*) K G Saur.

World Directory of Marketing Information Sources. 400p. 1996. 390.00 (*0-86338-543-5*, Pub. by Euromonitor Pubns UK) Gale.

***World Directory of Medical Schools.** 6th ed. WHO Staff. 320p. 1988. 45.00 (*92-4-150009-3*) World Health.

World Directory of Minorities. Minority Rights Group Staff. 427p. 1990. 85.00 (*1-55862-016-8*) St James Pr.

***World Directory of Minorities.** Ed. by Minority Rights Group Staff. (Illus.). 1000p. 1997. 145.00 (*1-873194-36-6*, Pub. by Minority Rts Pubns UK) Paul & Co Pubs.

World Directory of Missionary Training Programmes: A Catalogue of over 500 Missionary Training Programmes from Around the World. Ed. by Raymond Windsor. (World Evangelical Fellowship Ser.: Vol. 5). 344p. (Orig.). 1995. pap. text ed. 12.95 (*0-87808-259-X*, WCL259-X) William Carey Lib.

World Directory of Moving Image & Sound Archives. Compiled by Wolfgang Klaue. (Film-Television-Sound Archives Ser.: Vol. 5). 400p. 1993. 86.00 (*3-598-22594-6*) K G Saur.

World Directory of New Electric Power Plants. Utility Data Institute Staff. Ed. by Chris Bergesen. 400p. 1995. pap. 395.00 (*1-56760-052-2*) Utility Data Inst.

World Directory of Nuclear Utility Management. 1987. 200.00 (*0-89448-510-5*, 250009) Am Nuclear Soc.

World Directory of Old Age Organizations. Ed. by Crosby & Dunn. 200p. 1989. 85.00 (*1-55862-023-0*) St James Pr.

World Directory of Peace Research & Training Institutions, 1988. 6th ed. UNESCO. 287p. 1988. 56.00 (*0-85496-156-9*) Berg Pubs.

World Directory of Pesticide Control Organisations. Ed. by George Ekstrom & Hamish Kidd. 300p. 1989. 99.00 (*0-85186-723-5*) CRC Pr.

World Directory of Pesticide Control Organizations. 2nd ed. Ed. by George Ekstrom. LC 41-50522. 423p. 1994. pap. 70.00 (*0-948404-78-7*) Blackwell Sci.

World Directory of Post-Basic & Post-Graduate Schools of Nursing. 223p. (ENG, FRE & RUS.). 1965. pap. text ed. 18.00 (*92-4-150000-X*, 1150166) World Health.

World Directory of Renewable Energy Suppliers & Services 1995. Ed. by Bruce Cross. (Illus.). 576p. (Orig.). 1995. pap. 120.00 (*1-873936-40-0*, Pub. by J & J Sci Pubs UK) Bks Intl VA.

World Directory of Renewable Energy Suppliers & Services, 1996. Ed. by Bruce Cross. (Illus.). 544p. 1996. pap. text ed. 120.00 (*1-873936-56-7*, Pub. by J & J Sci Pubs UK) Bks Intl VA.

World Directory of Restrictions & Requirements Affecting Textile & Apparel Export Sales. 240p. (Orig.). 1991. pap. 50.00 (*0-941375-29-3*) DIANE Pub.

World Directory of Schools for Animal Health Assistants. 1974. pap. text ed. 24.00 (*92-4-150005-0*, 1150164) World Health.

***World Directory of Schools for Auxiliary Sanitarians 1973: Bilingual English/French.** 81p. 1978. pap. text ed. 16.00 (*92-4-050005-7*) World Health.

***World Directory of Schools for Dental Auxiliaries: Bilingual English/French.** 379p. 1973. text ed. 42.00 (*92-4-050003-0*) World Health.

***World Directory of Schools for Medical Assistants 1973: Bilingual English/French.** 112p. 1976. pap. text ed. 24.00 (*92-4-050002-2*) World Health.

***World Directory of Schools for Medical Laboratory Technicians & Assistants: Bilingual English/French.** 567p. 1973. text ed. 55.00 (*92-4-050004-9*) World Health.

World Directory of Scottish Associations. M. Brander & I. Macleod. 242p. (C). 1986. 100.00 (*0-317-89989-9*) St Mut.

***World Directory of Scottish Associations.** Michael Brander. 240p. 1997. pap. 22.95 (*1-897784-27-9*, Pub. by N Wilson UK) Interlink Pub.

World Directory of Trade & Business Associations. 2nd ed. 350p. 1996. 550.00 (*0-86338-556-7*, Pub. by Euromonitor Pubns UK) Gale.

***World Directory of Trade & Business Journals.** 378p. 1996. 550.00 (*0-86338-629-6*, GML00197-110747, Pub. by Euromonitor Pubns UK) Gale.

World Directory of Trade Fairs & Exhibitions. 500p. 1995. 390.00 (*0-86338-453-6*, Pub. by Euromonitor Pubns UK) Gale.

World Directory of Veterinary Schools: 1971. 1973. pap. text ed. 36.00 (*92-4-150004-2*, 1150169) World Health.

***World Directory to Chambers of Commerce.** 1900. lib. bdg. write for info. (*92-842-0014-8*) Kluwer Ac.

World Disarmament. Ed. by Ron Huzzard & Christopher Meredith. LC 85-71752. 238p. 1985. pap. 13.95 (*0-685-11822-3*, Pub. by Spkesman UK) Dufour.

World Disarmament. Ed. by Ron Huzzard & Christopher Meredith. LC 85-71752. 238p. 8500. pap. 17.95 (*0-85124-413-0*) Dufour.

World Disaster Report, 1993. Compiled by International Federation of Red Cross & Red Crescent Societies Staff. 128p. (C). 1993. pap. text ed. 51.00 (*0-7923-2268-1*) Kluwer Ac.

World Disasters Report: 1994. (Illus.). 176p. (Orig.). (C). 1995. pap. text ed. 50.00 (*0-7881-2261-4*) DIANE Pub.

World Disasters Report, 1994. Compiled by International Federation of Red Cross & Red Crescent Societies Staff. 180p. 1994. pap. text ed. 54.50 (*0-7923-2826-4*, Pub. by M Nijhoff NE) Kluwer Ac.

World Disasters Report 1996. International Federation of Red Cross & Red Crescent Societies Staff. (Illus.). 178p. 1996. pap. 29.95 (*0-19-829079-9*); text ed. 75.00 (*0-19-829080-2*) OUP.

***World Disasters Report 1997.** International Federation of Red Cross & Red Crescent Societies Staff. (Illus.). 208p. 1997. pap. 30.00 (*0-19-829290-2*) OUP.

World Discrete Electronic Active Device Markets: New Opportunities Arise in Telecommunications & Medical Applications. Market Intelligence Staff. 245p. 1993. 1,495.00 (*1-56753-436-8*) Frost & Sullivan.

World Discrete Electronic Passive Device Markets: Century-Old Technology Thrives on Leading-Edge Telecommunication Products. Market Intelligence Staff. 273p. 1992. 1,495.00 (*1-56753-406-6*) Frost & Sullivan.

World Discrete Manufacturing Software Markets: Shop Floor Goes High Tech - 3 Million Dollar Market Doubles. Market Intelligence Staff. 248p. 1993. 1,495.00 (*1-56753-420-1*) Frost & Sullivan.

World Discrete Resistors Markets: Surface Mount Technology Activates Passive Components Market. Frost & Sullivan Staff. 470p. 1996. write for info. (*0-7889-0486-8*, 5258) Frost & Sullivan.

***World Disorders.** 1998. write for info. (*0-8476-8574-8*); pap. write for info. (*0-8476-8575-6*) Rowman.

World Divided: Militarism & Development after the Cold War. Ed. by Geoff Tansey et al. LC 94-28087. 1994. text ed. 49.95 (*0-312-12350-7*) St Martin.

World Does Move. Booth Tarkington. LC 76-8903. 294p. 1976. reprint ed. text ed. 38.50 (*0-8371-8876-8*, TAWD, Greenwood Pr) Greenwood.

World Does Move. Booth Tarkington. (BCL1 - U. S. History Ser.). 294p. 1991. reprint ed. lib. bdg. 79.00 (*0-7812-6377-8*) Rprt Serv.

World Doesn't End: Prose Poems. Charles Simic. 1989. pap. 11.00 (*0-15-698350-8*) HarBrace.

W

An Asterisk (*) at the beginning of an entry indicates that the title is appearing in BIP for the first time.

***World Don't Owe Me Nothing: The Life & Times of Delta Bluesman Honeyboy Edwards.** David H. Edwards. (Illus.). 224p. 1997. 22.00 (*1-55652-275-4*) Chicago Review.

World Drama. Oscar G. Brockett & Mark Pape. 656p. (C). 1984. pap. text ed. 30.75 (*0-03-057668-7*) HB Coll Pubs.

World Drama Vol. 1: Ancient Greece, Rome, India, China, Japan, Medieval Europe, England. Ed. by Barrett H. Clark. pap. 11.95 (*0-486-20057-4*) Dover.

World Drama Vol. 2: Italy, Spain, France, Germany, Denmark, Russia, Norway. Ed. by Barrett H. Clark. 1933. pap. 11.95 (*0-486-20059-0*) Dover.

World Drinks Databook. 295p. 1994. 510.00 (*0-86338-531-1*, Pub. by Euromonitor Pubns UK) Gale.

World Drinks Databook. 2nd ed. 1995. 510.00 (*0-86338-604-0*) Gale.

***World Drug Situation.** WHO Staff. 129p. 1988. 20.00 (*92-4-156114-9*) World Health.

World Dynamics. Jay W. Forrester. 144p. 1994. reprint ed. 35.00 (*1-56327-059-5*) Prod Press.

World Eco-Crisis: International Organizations in Response. Ed. by David A. Kay & Eugene B. Skolnikoff. LC 79-178153. 332p. reprint ed. pap. 94.70 (*0-8357-6787-6*, 2035464) Bks Demand.

***World Economic & Social Survey: Trends & Policies in the World Economy.** 353p. 1996. pap. text ed. 55.00 (*92-1-109131-4*, HC59) UN.

World Economic & Social Survey, 1995: Current Trends & Policies in the World Economy. 345p. 1995. pap. 55.00 (*92-1-109130-6*, UN95 2C 1) UN.

World Economic Collapse: The Last Decade & the Global Depression. Khafra Om-ra-zeti. (Illus.). 278p. (Orig.). 1995. pap. 18.95 (*0-9635645-0-1*) KMT Pubns.

World Economic Crisis & Japanese Capitalism. Makoto Itoh. (Illus.). 264p. 1990. pap. 14.95 (*0-312-03149-1*); text ed. 49.95 (*0-312-03148-3*) St Martin.

World Economic Data. 3rd ed. (World Facts & Figures Ser.). 250p. 1991. lib. bdg. 40.00 (*0-87436-658-5*) ABC-CLIO.

World Economic Environment & Prospects for India. M. Narasimham. 190p. 1988. text ed. 27.50 (*81-207-0769-9*, Pub. by Sterling Pubs II) Apt Bks.

World Economic Factbook. 93th ed. 1993. 290.00 (*0-86338-471-4*, 074000, Pub. by Euromonitor Pubns UK) Gale.

World Economic Factbook 1994. 94th ed. 461p. 1994. 310.00 (*0-86338-565-6*, Pub. by Euromonitor Pubns UK) Gale.

World Economic Factbook 96. 96th ed. 1996. 350.00 (*0-86338-622-9*) Gale.

***World Economic Factbook 97.** 97th ed. 1996. 350.00 (*0-86338-682-2*, 00156609, Gale Res Intl) Gale.

World Economic Growth. Ed. by Arnold C. Harberger. LC 84-19179. 508p. (C). 1985. pap. text ed. 14.95 (*0-917616-62-6*) ICS Pr.

World Economic Order: The Trade Crisis & Its Implications for Australia. Richard A. Higgott. LC 88-116143. 97p. reprint ed. pap. 27.70 (*0-8357-6824-4*, 2035510) Bks Demand.

World Economic Outlook, April 1985: A Survey by the Staff of the International Monetary Fund. ix, 283p. 1985. pap. 12.00 (*0-939934-45-0*) Intl Monetary.

World Economic Outlook, April 1986: A Survey by the Staff of the International Monetary Fund. (World Economic & Financial Surveys Ser.). x, 268p. 1986. 15.00 (*0-939934-66-3*) Intl Monetary.

World Economic Outlook, April 1987: A Survey by the Staff of the International Monetary Fund. (World Economic & Financial Surveys Ser.). iv, 194p. 1987. pap. 15.00 (*0-939934-85-X*) Intl Monetary.

World Economic Outlook, April 1988: A Survey by the Staff of the International Monetary Fund. (World Economic & Financial Surveys Ser.). 189p. 1988. pap. 15.00 (*1-55775-011-4*) Intl Monetary.

World Economic Outlook, April 1989: A Survey by the Staff of the International Monetary Fund. (World Economic & Financial Surveys Ser.). 201p. 1989. pap. 25.00 (*1-55775-112-9*) Intl Monetary.

World Economic Outlook, April 1995. International Monetary Staff. 1995. pap. write for info. (*1-55775-468-3*) Intl Monetary.

World Economic Outlook, May 1990: A Survey. International Monetary Fund Staff. (World Economic & Financial Surveys Ser.). 199p. (ENG, FRE & SPA.). 1990. English. pap. 30.00 (*1-55775-138-2*) Intl Monetary.

World Economic Outlook, May 1991: A Survey. International Monetary Fund Staff. LC 84-640155. (World Economic & Financial Surveys Ser.). 208p. 1991. pap. 30.00 (*1-55775-210-9*) Intl Monetary.

World Economic Outlook, May 1991: A Survey. International Monetary Fund Staff. LC 84-640155. (World Economic & Financial Surveys Ser.). 208p. (FRE.). 1991. French Ed. pap. 30.00 (*1-55775-212-5*); Spanish Ed. pap. 30.00 (*1-55775-211-7*) Intl Monetary.

World Economic Outlook, May, 1992: A Survey by the Staff of the International Monetary Fund. (World Economic & Financial Surveys Ser.). 186p. (ENG, FRE & SPA.). 1992. English. pap. 30.00 (*1-55775-268-0*) Intl Monetary.

World Economic Outlook, May, 1992: A Survey by the Staff of the International Monetary Fund. (World Economic & Financial Surveys Ser.). 186p. (ENG, FRE & SPA.). 1992. French. pap. 30.00 (*1-55775-269-9*); Spanish. pap. 30.00 (*1-55775-270-2*) Intl Monetary.

World Economic Outlook, May 1993: A Survey by the Staff of the International Monetary Fund. (World Economic & Financial Surveys Ser.). 197p. 1993. English ed. pap. 30.00 (*1-55775-286-9*) Intl Monetary.

World Economic Outlook, May 1993: A Survey by the Staff of the International Monetary Fund. (World Economic & Financial Surveys Ser.). 197p. (FRE.). 1993. French ed. write for info. (*1-55775-287-7*); Spanish ed. write for info. (*1-55775-288-5*); Arabic ed. write for info. (*1-55775-289-3*) Intl Monetary.

World Economic Outlook, May 1994: Survey by the Staff of the International Monetary Fund. (World Economic & Financial Surveys Ser.). 1994. pap. 30.00 (*1-55775-381-4*) Intl Monetary.

World Economic Outlook, May 1994: Survey by the Staff of the International Monetary Fund. (World Economic & Financial Surveys Ser.). (FRE.). 1994. pap. 30.00 (*1-55775-383-0*); pap. 30.00 (*1-55775-384-9*); pap. 30.00 (*1-55775-382-2*) Intl Monetary.

World Economic Outlook, October 1985: Revised Projections by the Staff of the International Monetary Fund. 109p. (FRE.). 1985. French. write for info. (*1-55775-145-5*); Spanish. write for info. (*1-55775-144-7*); pap. 10.00 (*0-939934-54-X*) Intl Monetary.

World Economic Outlook, October 1986: Revised Projections by the Staff of the International Monetary Fund. (World Economic & Financial Surveys Ser.). 112p. 1986. pap. 12.00 (*0-939934-78-7*) Intl Monetary.

World Economic Outlook, October 1988: Revised Projections by the Staff of the International Monetary Fund. (World Economic & Financial Surveys Ser.). 137p. 1988. pap. 15.00 (*1-55775-033-5*) Intl Monetary.

World Economic Outlook, October 1989: A Survey by the Staff of the International Monetary Fund. (World Economic & Financial Surveys Ser.). 149p. 1989. pap. 20.00 (*1-55775-131-5*) Intl Monetary.

World Economic Outlook, October 1990: A Survey by the Staff of the International Monetary Fund. International Monetary Fund Research Dept. Staff. (World Economic & Financial Surveys Ser.). 188p. (ENG, FRE & SPA.). 1990. Spanish. pap. 30.00 (*1-55775-152-8*) Intl Monetary.

World Economic Outlook, October 1990: A Survey by the Staff of the International Monetary Fund. International Monetary Fund Staff. (World Economic & Financial Surveys Ser.). 188p. (ENG, FRE & SPA.). 1990. English. pap. 30.00 (*1-55775-150-1*) Intl Monetary.

World Economic Outlook, October 1990: A Survey by the Staff of the International Monetary Fund. International Monetary Staff. (World Economic & Financial Surveys Ser.). 188p. (ENG, FRE & SPA.). 1990. French. pap. 30.00 (*1-55775-151-X*) Intl Monetary.

World Economic Outlook, October 1991: A Survey by the Staff of the International Monetary Fund. ix, 165p. 1991. 30.00 (*1-55775-186-2*) Intl Monetary.

World Economic Outlook, October 1992: A Survey by the Staff of the International Monetary Fund. (World Economic & Financial Surveys Ser.). 179p. (ARA, ENG, FRE & SPA.). 1992. English. pap. 30.00 (*1-55775-313-X*); French. pap. 30.00 (*1-55775-314-8*); Spanish. pap. 30.00 (*1-55775-315-6*); Arabic. pap. 30.00 (*1-55775-316-4*) Intl Monetary.

World Economic Outlook, October 1993: Survey by the Staff of the International Monetary. (World Economic & Financial Surveys Ser.). 1993. English. pap. 30.00 (*1-55775-340-7*); French. pap. 30.00 (*1-55775-341-5*); Spanish. pap. 30.00 (*1-55775-342-3*) Intl Monetary.

World Economic Outlook, October 1994: Survey of the Staff of the International Monetary Fund. (World Economic & Financial Surveys Ser.). 196p. 1994. 34.00 (*1-55775-385-7*) Intl Monetary.

***World Economic Outlook, October 1996.** (World Economic & Financial Surveys Ser.). 256p. 1996. 35.00 (*1-55775-610-4*) Intl Monetary.

***World Economic Outlook, October 1996.** (World Economic & Financial Surveys Ser.). 256p. (FRE.). 1996. 35.00 (*1-55775-611-2*) Intl Monetary.

***World Economic Outlook, October 1996.** (World Economic & Financial Surveys Ser.). 256p. (SPA.). 1996. 35.00 (*1-55775-612-0*) Intl Monetary.

***World Economic Outlook, October 1996.** (World Economic & Financial Surveys Ser.). 256p. (ARA.). 1996. 35.00 (*1-55775-613-9*) Intl Monetary.

World Economic Outlook, September 1984: Revised Projections by the Staff of the International Monetary Fund. (Occasional Papers: No. 32). 73p. 1984. pap. 7.50 (*1-55775-086-6*) Intl Monetary.

World Economic Primacy: 1500-1990. Charles P. Kindleberger. (Illus.). 360p. 1996. 35.00 (*0-19-509902-8*) OUP.

World Economic Prospects. 93th ed. 300p. 1993. 190.00 (*0-86338-512-5*, 074002, Pub. by Euromonitor Pubns UK) Gale.

World Economic Survey. 416p. 1990. 45.00 (*92-1-109119-5*, 90.II.C.1) UN.

World Economic Survey, 1988: Current Trends & Policies in the World Economy. 174p. 1988. 32.00 (*92-1-109114-4*, E.88.II.C.1) UN.

World Economic Survey, 1989. 45.00 (*92-1-109116-0*) UN.

World Economic Survey 1991. UN Staff. 240p. 1991. pap. 55.00 (*92-1-109120-9*, E.91.II.C.1) UN.

World Economic Survey 1992: Current Trends & Policies in the World Economy. United Nations Staff. 232p. (C). 1992. pap. text ed. 55.00 (*92-1-109123-3*) UN.

World Economic Survey 1994. 308p. 1994. 55.00 (*92-1-109128-4*) UN.

World Economic System: Performance & Prospects. Ed. by Jacob A. Frenkel & Michael L. Mussa. LC 84-14554. (ITT Key Issues Lecture). 115p. 1984. pap. 5.95 (*0-86569-103-7*, R103, Auburn Hse) Greenwood.

World Economy. Ed. by Stuart Corbridge. LC 93-6489. 256p. 1993. 45.00 (*0-19-520946-X*) OUP.

World Economy. Ted Walther. LC 96-35526. 440p. 1996. text ed. write for info. (*0-471-13831-2*) Wiley.

World Economy. 4th ed. Beth V. Yarbrough. (C). 1997. teacher ed., pap. text ed. 22.75 (*0-03-017768-5*) HarBrace.

World Economy. David Killingray. Ed. by Malcolm Yapp et al. (World History Program Ser.). (Illus.). 32p. (YA). (gr. 6-11). 1980. reprint ed. pap. text ed. 4.72 (*0-89908-118-5*) Greenhaven.

World Economy: A Textbook in International Economics. rev. ed. John Williamson & Chris Milner. 480p. (C). 1992. 75.00 (*0-8147-9245-6*); pap. 25.00 (*0-8147-9246-4*) NYU Pr.

World Economy: Challenges of Globalization & Regionalization. Ed. by Marjan Svetlicic & H. W. Singer. 256p. 1996. text ed. 69.95 (*0-312-15886-6*) St Martin.

World Economy: Global Trade Policy 1994. Ed. by Sven Arndt & Chris Milner. 200p. (Orig.). (C). 1995. pap. 31.95 (*0-631-19411-8*) Blackwell Pubs.

***World Economy: Global Trade Policy, 1996.** Sven Arndt. 1996. pap. text ed. 29.95 (*0-631-20348-6*) Blackwell Pubs.

World Economy: Patterns of Growth & Change. B. J. McCormick. LC 88-14639. 256p. (Orig.). (C). 1988. pap. text ed. 38.50 (*0-389-20801-9*, N8359); lib. bdg. 75.50 (*0-389-20800-0*, N8358) B&N Imports.

World Economy: Resources, Location, Trade & Development. 2nd ed. Anthony DeSouza & Frederick Stutz. (Illus.). 544p. (C). 1994. text ed. 73.00 (*0-02-328722-5*, Macmillan Coll) P-H.

World Economy: Trade & Finance. Beth V. Yarbrough & Robert M. Yarbrough. LC 93-73042. 830p. (C). 1993. text ed. 55.00 (*0-03-097567-0*) Dryden Pr.

World Economy: Trade & Finance. 2nd rev. ed. Beth V. Yarbrough & Robert M. Yarbrough. (Illus.). 736p. (C). 1991. text ed. 55.00 (*0-03-032824-1*) Dryden Pr.

World Economy: Trade & Finance. 4th ed. Beth V. Yarbrough & Robert M. Yarbrough. 240p. (C). 1997. teacher ed., pap. text ed. 42.00 (*0-03-017767-7*) Dryden Pr.

World Economy: Trade & Finance. 4th ed. Beth V. Yarbrough & Robert M. Yarbrough. 960p. (C). Date not set. text ed. write for info. (*0-03-017764-2*) Dryden Pr.

World Economy & East-West Trade, Vol. 1. Ed. by F. Nemschak. 1977. 39.95 (*0-387-81390-X*) Spr-Verlag.

World Economy & Its Main Developmental Tendencies. Jozsef Nyilas. 1982. lib. bdg. 141.50 (*90-247-2650-6*) Kluwer Ac.

World Economy & National Finance in Historical Perspective. Charles P. Kindleberger. LC 95-11280. (C). 1995. 49.50 (*0-472-10642-2*) U of Mich Pr.

World Economy & the East. 1989. 27.95 (*0-387-82114-7*) Spr-Verlag.

World Economy & the Environment: A New Relationship. (Illus.). 64p. (Orig.). (C). 1994. pap. text ed. 25.00 (*0-7881-0602-3*) DIANE Pub.

World Economy & the Spatial Organisation of Power. Arie Shachar & Sture Oberg. 260p. 1990. text ed. 57.95 (*0-566-05789-1*, Pub. by Avebury Pub UK) Ashgate Pub Co.

World Economy & World Hunger: The Response of the Churches. Robert L. McCan. 119p. (C). 1982. text ed. 45.00 (*0-313-27078-3*, U7078) Greenwood.

World Economy & World Politics, 1924-1931: From Reconstruction to Collapse. Gilbert Ziebura. Tr. by Bruce Little from GER. LC 89-35884. 204p. 1990. 29.95 (*0-85496-646-3*) Berg Pubs.

World Economy in Nineties: A Portfolio Approach. V. K. Bhalla. 260p. 1990. 100.00 (*81-7041-434-2*, Pub. by Scientific Pubs II) St Mut.

World Economy in Perspective: Essays on International Trade & European Integration. Herbert Giersch. (Economists of the Twentieth Century Ser.). 336p. 1991. text ed. 85.00 (*1-85278-457-1*) E Elgar.

World Economy in the Twentieth Century. OECD Staff & Angus Maddison. 146p. (Orig.). 1989. pap. 30.00 (*92-64-13274-0*) OECD.

World Economy in Transition. 2nd ed. Michael Beenstock. 250p. 1984. pap. text ed. 19.95 (*0-04-339035-8*) Routledge Chapman & Hall.

World Economy in Transition: Essays Presented to Surendra Patel on his Sixtieth Birthday. Ed. by K. Ahooja-Patel. 314p. 1986. text ed. 89.00 (*0-08-031285-3*, Pergamon Pr) Elsevier.

World Economy in Transition: What Leading Economists Think. Ed. by Randall W. Hinshaw. LC 95-30782. 208p. 1996. 60.00 (*1-85898-343-6*) E Elgar.

World Economy Macroeconomics. Harland W. Whitmore. LC 96-32419. 374p. (C). (gr. 13). 1996. text ed. 64.95 (*1-56324-897-2*) M E Sharpe.

World Economy Macroeconomics. Harland W. Whitmore. LC 96-32419. 272p. (gr. 13). 1996. pap. text ed. 29.95 (*1-56324-898-0*) M E Sharpe.

World Economy Series, 37 bks. Ed. by Mira Wilkins. 1982. write for info. (*0-318-50915-6*) Ayer.

World Economy since the War: The Politics of Uneven Development. E. A. Brett. 1985. pap. 14.95 (*0-685-46009-6*, B1668, Praeger Pubs); text ed. 65.00 (*0-275-90197-1*, C0197, Praeger Pubs) Greenwood.

World Education Encyclopedia, 3 vols., Set. George T. Kurian. (Illus.). 1800p. 1988. 195.00 (*0-87196-748-0*) Facts on File.

***World Education Encyclopedia, Vol. 1.** Ed. by George T. Kurian. LC 82-18188. 582p. 1988. reprint ed. pap. 165.90 (*0-608-02849-5*, 2063915) Bks Demand.

***World Education Encyclopedia, Vol. 2.** Ed. by George T. Kurian. LC 82-18188. 589p. 1988. reprint ed. pap. 167.60 (*0-608-02850-9*, 2063915) Bks Demand.

***World Education Encyclopedia, Vol. 3.** Ed. by George T. Kurian. LC 82-18188. 583p. 1988. reprint ed. pap. 166.20 (*0-608-02851-7*, 2063915) Bks Demand.

World Education Report, 1993. 172p. 1993. pap. 40.00 (*92-3-102935-5*, U2935, Pub. by UNESCO-Bangkok TH) Bernan Associates.

World Education Report 1995. UNESCO Staff. (Illus.). 176p. 1996. pap. 40.00 (*92-3-103180-5*, U3180, Pub. by UNESCO FR) Bernan Associates.

World Electronic Cleaning Equipment Markets: Spurred by Regulations, North America Leads "Clean" Revolution. Market Intelligence Staff. 231p. (Orig.). 1992. 1,495.00 (*1-56753-397-3*) Frost & Sullivan.

World Electronic Data Interchange Market: Countries Trading Partners Press for Cooperation & Standards. Market Intelligence Staff. 561p. (Orig.). 1992. 1,895.00 (*1-56753-848-7*) Frost & Sullivan.

World Electronic Switch Markets. Market Intelligence Staff. 289p. (Orig.). 1994. 1,995.00 (*0-7889-0093-5*) Frost & Sullivan.

World Electronics Data 1996 Ser. B: US/Japan/Asia Pacific. 1996. text ed. 2,600.00 incl. disk (*1-85617-312-7*) Elsevier.

World Electronics Data Yearbook 1996. 1996. text ed. 3,705.00 incl. disk (*1-85617-313-5*) Elsevier.

World Electronics Industry. Daniel Todd. 352p. (C). 1990. text ed. 74.95 (*0-415-02497-8*, A3698) Routledge.

World Elsewhere. Nirmal Verma. (Readers International Ser.). 238p. 1988. reprint ed. 16.95 (*0-930523-46-6*) Readers Intl.

World Elsewhere: Europe's Encounter with Japan in the Sixteenth & Seventeenth Centuries. Derek Massarella. LC 89-22639. 352p. (C). 1990. text ed. 35.00 (*0-300-04633-2*) Yale U Pr.

World Elsewhere: Life in the American Southwest. Jon M. White. LC 89-4652. (Southwest Landmark Ser.: No. 8). (Illus.). 336p. 1989. reprint ed. pap. 15.95 (*0-89096-385-1*) Tex A&M Univ Pr.

***World Elsewhere: The Life of Bruno Walter.** Ryding & Pechefsky. 1998. 35.00 (*0-02-864848-X*) S&S Trade.

World Elsewhere: The Place of Style in American Literature. Richard Poirier. LC 85-40376. 272p. 1985. reprint ed. pap. 10.95 (*0-299-09934-2*) U of Wis Pr.

World Embassy Director: A Guide to the World's Embassies. Ed. by Chimezia Ezenwa. 460p. 1993. text ed. 125.00 (*0-9637710-2-7*) Dev Info Libs.

World Embedded Controller Markets: Industry Goes Mainstream with 386 & Power PC. Market Intelligence Staff. 370p. 1994. 1,995.00 (*0-7889-0038-2*) Frost & Sullivan.

***World Emerging & Specialized Sensor Markets.** Frost & Sullivan. 333p. 1996. write for info. (*0-7889-0625-9*, 5456) Frost & Sullivan.

World Emerging Sensor Technologies: High Growth Markets Uncovered. Market Intelligence Staff. 317p. 1993. 1,495.00 (*1-56753-456-2*) Frost & Sullivan.

***World Employment 1996/97: National Policies in a Global Context.** 200p. 1996. pap. 29.95 (*92-2-110326-9*) Intl Labour Office.

World Encompassed. Francis Drake. 1992. reprint ed. lib. bdg. 75.00 (*0-7812-5027-7*) Rprt Serv.

World Encompassed by Sir F. Drake, Being His Next Voyage to That to Nombre De Dios. Francis Drake. LC 78-26252. (English Experience Ser.: No. 103). 108p. 1969. reprint ed. 20.00 (*90-221-0103-7*) Walter J Johnson.

World Encyclopedia of Aero Engines. 3rd ed. Bill Gunston. (Illus.). 192p. 1995. 39.95 (*1-85260-509-X*, Pub. by J H Haynes & Co UK) Motorbooks Intl.

World Encyclopedia of Aircraft Manufacturers: From the Pioneers to the Present Day. Bill Gunston. (Illus.). 336p. 1994. 39.95 (*1-55750-939-5*) Naval Inst Pr.

***World Encyclopedia of Beer.** Brian Glover. (Illus.). 256p. 1997. 24.95 (*1-85967-459-3*, Lorenz Bks) Anness Pub.

World Encyclopedia of Black Peoples, Vol. 1. Ed. by Harry Waldman. LC 74-28076. 1981. lib. bdg. 59.00 (*0-403-01796-3*) Scholarly.

World Encyclopedia of Cities, 1. George T. Kurian. 610p. 1993. lib. bdg. 75.00 (*0-87436-650-X*) ABC-CLIO.

World Encyclopedia of Cities, 2. George T. Kurian. 1993. lib. bdg. 165.00 (*0-87436-649-6*) ABC-CLIO.

World Encyclopedia of Cities: North America (United States N-Z & Canada), Vol. 2. George T. Kurian. LC 93-43133. 571p. 1993. 75.00 (*0-87436-651-8*) ABC-CLIO.

***World Encyclopedia of Comics.** 2nd rev. ed. Ed. by Maurice Horn. (Illus.). 1000p. 1997. 59.95 (*0-7910-4856-X*) Chelsea Hse.

***World Encyclopedia of Comics, Vols. 1-7.** 2nd rev. ed. Ed. by Maurice Horn. (Illus.). 1000p. 1997. lib. bdg. 199.95 (*0-7910-4854-3*) Chelsea Hse.

***World Encyclopedia of Contemporary Theatre, Vol. 6.** annot. ed. Date not set. 124.95 (*0-415-05934-8*, B0400) Routledge.

World Encyclopedia of Contemporary Theatre: The Americas, Vol. 2. Ed. by Carlos Solorzano. (Illus.). 576p. (C). 1995. text ed. 125.00 (*0-415-05929-1*, Routledge NY) Routledge.

World Encyclopedia of Contemporary Theatre Vol. 1: Europe. Ed. by Don Rubin. (Illus.). 768p. (C). (gr. 13). 1995. text ed. 150.00 (*0-415-05928-3*, B0376) Routledge.

***World Encyclopedia of Contemporary Theatre Vol. 3: Africa.** Ed. by Ousmane Diakhate et al. (Illus.). 526p. (C). 1997. text ed. 124.95 (*0-415-05931-3*, B0384) Routledge.

***World Encyclopedia of Contemporary Theatre Vol. 4: The Arab World.** Ed. by Ghassan Maleh & Samir Sirhan. (Illus.). 1998. 124.95 (*0-415-05932-1*, B0388) Routledge.

An Asterisk (*) at the beginning of an entry indicates that the title is appearing in BIP for the first time.

***World Encyclopedia of Contemporary Theatre Vol. 5: Asia/Oceania.** Ed. by James Brandon. (Illus.). 1998. 124.95 (*0-415-05933-X*, B0392) Routledge.

World Encyclopedia of Library & Information Services. 3rd ed. Ed. by Robert Wedgeworth. LC 93-25159. (Illus.). 1200p. 1993. lib. bdg. 200.00 (*0-8389-0690-7*) ALA.

World Encyclopedia of Model Soldiers. John F. Garratt. LC 80-84376. (Illus.). 224p. 1981. 85.00 (*0-87951-129-X*) Overlook Pr.

World Encyclopedia of Organized Crime. Jay R. Nash. 1994. 49.95 (*1-56924-898-2*) Marlowe & Co.

World Encyclopedia of Organized Crime. Jay R. Nash. (Illus.). 634p. 1993. reprint ed. pap. 25.00 (*0-306-80535-9*) Da Capo.

World Encyclopedia of Peace, 4 vols. Ed. by Ervin Laszlo & Jong Y. Yoo. LC 86-25520. (Illus.). 1930p. 1986. 615.00 (*0-08-032685-4*, Pergamon Pr) Elsevier.

World Encyclopedia of Peace, 4 vols., Vols. 1-4. Ervin Laszlo. 1986. 250.00 (*0-08-032686-2*, Pergamon Pr) Elsevier.

World Encyclopedia of Police Forces & Penal Systems. George T. Kurian. 592p. 1988. 95.00 (*0-8160-1019-6*) Facts on File.

World Encyclopedia of Soccer. Richard Henshaw & Michael L. Lablanc. (Illus.). 444p. 1993. pap. 14.95 (*0-8103-9442-1*, 089155) Visible Ink Pr.

World Encyclopedia of Soccer. 2nd ed. Richard Henshaw & Michael L. Lablanc. 500p. 1993. 42.00 (*0-8103-8995-9*, 101778) Gale.

World Encyclopedia of the Tank: An International History of the Armoured Fighting Machine. Christopher Chant. (Illus.). 384p. 1994. 49.95 (*1-85260-114-0*, Pub. by J H Haynes & Co UK) Motorbooks Intl.

World Encyclopedia of Water Polo. Jimmy Smith. LC 89-8608. 534p. 1990. 25.00 (*0-933380-05-4*) Olive Pr Pubns.

World Encyclopedia of 20th Century Murder. Jay R. Nash. 1994. 49.95 (*1-56924-872-9*) Marlowe & Co.

World Energy. Euromonitor Staff. 300p. 1986. 250.00 (*0-86338-121-9*, Pub. by Euromonitor Pubns UK) Gale.

World Energy: The Facts & the Future. 2nd ed. Don Hedley. (Illus.). 304p. 1986. 45.00 (*0-8160-1615-1*) Facts on File.

World Energy: Will There Be Enough in 2020? Ed. by William Nesbit. (Decisionmakers Bookshelf Ser.: Vol. 6). (Illus.). 88p. (Orig.). 1979. pap. 2.50 (*0-931032-06-7*) Edison Electric.

World Energy & Nuclear Directory. 450.00p. 1993. 450.00 (*0-582-22965-0*) Longman.

World Energy & Nuclear Directory. 3rd ed. 385p. 1995. 515.00 (*1-56159-180-7*, Stockton Pr) Groves Dictionaries.

World Energy & Nuclear Directory. 5th ed. 1996. write for info. (*0-8103-9724-2*) Longman.

World Energy Conference-Energy Terminology. World Energy Conference Staff. 275p. (ENG, FRE, GER & SPA.). 1982. 125.00 (*0-8288-0720-5*, M 15113) Fr & Eur.

World Energy Directory. 2nd ed. Ed. by J. A. Bauly & C. B. Bauly. 600p. 1985. 230.00 (*0-582-90026-3*, Pub. by Longman Grp UK) Gale.

World Energy Horizons 2000-2020 14th Congress of the World Energy Conference: Conservation & Studies Committee, Montreal, September 1989. J. R. Frisch. (Illus.). 416p. (C). 1989. 465.00 (*2-7108-0570-7*, Pub. by Edits Technip FR) St Mut.

World Energy Outlook to the Twenty-First Century. Cyrus H. Tahmassebi. 28p. 1990. pap. 10.00 (*0-918714-21-4*) Intl Res Ctr Energy.

***World Energy Outlook, 1996.** 352p. 1996. 86.00 (*92-64-14816-7*, 61-96-06-1, Pub. by Org for Econ FR) OECD.

World Energy Supply. Manfred Grathwohl. (Illus.). 450p. 1982. 96.95 (*3-11-008153-9*) De Gruyter.

World Energy Supply & International Security. Herman Franssen et al. LC 82-49243. (Special Report Ser.). 93p. 1983. 11.95 (*0-89549-048-X*) Inst Foreign Policy Anal.

World Energy Survey. Ruth L. Sivard. 1979. 3.50 (*0-918281-02-4*) World Prior.

World Energy Survey 1981. 1981. pap. 5.00 (*0-685-19223-7*) World Prior.

World Engineering Industries & Automation: Performance & Prospects 1992-1994. 372p. 1994. 75.00 (*92-1-116587-3*) UN.

World Engineering Industries & Automation: Performance & Prospects, 1993-1995. 445p. 1995. pap. 75.00 (*92-1-116621-7*, HD9650) UN.

***World Engineering Industries & Automation: Performance & Prospects, 1994-1996.** Economic Commission for Europe Staff. 480p. 1996. pap. 75.00 (*92-1-116641-1*, 68573) UN.

World English 1. Ed. by Peter Jovanovich. (HBJ English Program Ser.). 152p. (C). 1983. pap. text ed. 1.50 (*0-15-597550-1*) HB Coll Pubs.

World English 2. Ed. by Peter Jovanovich & Christopher Morris. (HBJ English Program Ser.). 152p. (C). 1983. pap. text ed. 1.50 (*0-15-597551-X*) HB Coll Pubs.

World English 3. Ed. by Peter Jovanovich & Christopher Morris. (HBJ English Program Ser.). 152p. (C). 1983. pap. text ed. 1.50 (*0-15-597552-8*) HB Coll Pubs.

World English 4. Ed. by Peter Jovanovich & Christopher Morris. (HBJ English Program Ser.). 152p. (C). 1983. pap. text ed. 1.50 (*0-15-597553-6*) HB Coll Pubs.

World English 5. Ed. by Peter Jovanovich & Christopher Morris. (HBJ English Program Ser.). 152p. (C). 1983. pap. text ed. 1.50 (*0-15-597554-4*) HB Coll Pubs.

World English 6. Ed. by Peter Jovanovich & Christopher Morris. (HBJ English Program Ser.). 152p. (C). 1983. pap. text ed. 1.50 (*0-15-597555-2*) HB Coll Pubs.

World Enough & Space-Time: Absolute vs. Relational Theories of Space & Time. John Earman. 250p. 1989. 30.00 (*0-262-05040-4*, Bradford Bks) MIT Pr.

World Enough & Time: Successful Strategies for Resource Management. Robert C. Repetto. LC 85-20180. 160p. 1986. text ed. 25.00 (*0-300-03648-5*) Yale U Pr.

World Environment Law Bibliography: Non-Periodical Literature in Law & the Social Sciences Published Since 1970 in Various Languages with Selected Reviews & Annotations from Periodicals. Virginia E. Templeton & Howard J. Taubenfeld. LC 86-31559. xxi, 502p. 1987. 47.50 (*0-8377-2736-7*) Rothman.

World Environment, 1972-1982: A Report by UNEP, Vol. 8. Ed. by Martin W. Holdgate et al. (Natural Resources & the Environment Ser.). 670p. 1982. pap. 85.00 (*0-907567-14-2*, Tycooly Pub); text ed. 210.00 (*0-907567-13-4*, Tycooly Pub) Weidner & Sons.

World Environment 1972-1992: Two Decades of Challenge. O. A. El-Kholy et al. 608p. 1992. 120.00 (*0-412-46990-1*, A9454); pap. 39.95 (*0-412-47000-4*, A9458) Chapman & Hall.

World Environmental Business Handbook. 300p. 1993. 190.00 (*0-86338-458-7*, 073006, Pub. by Euromonitor Pubns UK) Gale.

World Environmental Equipment & Services Market 1996. Frost & Sullivan Staff. 394p. 1996. write for info. (*0-7889-0451-5*, 2874) Frost & Sullivan.

World Environmental Research Directory. 1993. 125.00 (*1-85802-015-8*, Pub. by PIRA Intl UK) Gale.

World Environmental Research Directory. Gale Research, Inc., Staff. 1993. 125.00 (*0-902799-95-9*) Gale.

World Ephemeris for the 20th Century 1900 to 2000 Noon. Para Research Staff. 622p. pap. 19.95 (*0-914918-61-3*) Whitford Pr.

World Evolution: Our Future in the Twenty-First Century. Margaret McCormick. LC 91-91572. 240p. 1991. pap. 12.95 (*0-9631930-3-1*) Channel CA.

World Explorer. (First Activity Packs Ser.). 24p. (J). (ps-3). 1995. pap. 15.95 (*1-56458-898-X*) DK Pub Inc.

***World Explorers, 3 vols.** Ed. by William H. Goetzmann. (Illus.). 3696p. (YA). (gr. 5 up). 1993. pap. 29.85 (*0-7910-3763-0*) Chelsea Hse.

***World Explorers.** Visual Education Staff. 1998. 100.00 (*0-02-864891-9*); 100.00 (*0-02-864892-7*); 249.00 (*0-02-864893-5*) Mac Lib Ref.

***World Explorers, 1.** Visual Education Staff. 1998. 100.00 (*0-02-864890-0*) Mac Lib Ref.

World Explorers, 30 vols., Set. Ed. by William H. Goetzmann. (Illus.). 3696p. (YA). (gr. 5 up). 1993. lib. bdg. 598.50 (*0-7910-1290-5*) Chelsea Hse.

World Explorers & Discoveries. Visual Education Corporation Staff. 544p. 1992. 100.00 (*0-02-897445-X*) Macmillan.

World Explorers Series. (J). 1994. 75.00 (*0-679-87014-8*) Random.

World Faces Johnny Tripod. John Millet. 80p. 1992. pap. 8.00 (*0-909185-52-2*) Story Line.

World Fact Book. 1995. pap. 29.00 (*0-87511-696-5*) Claitors.

World Factbook: Geographic, Economic & Demographic, Government, Communications, Defense Forces with Maps. (Illus.). 1992. lib. bdg. 295.75 (*0-8490-5576-8*) Gordon Pr.

World Factbook: 1994-95. CIA Staff. 420p. 1994. 32.00 (*0-02-881052-X*) Brasseys Inc.

World Factbook: 1995. (Illus.). 560p. (Orig.). 1995. pap. 65.00 (*0-7881-2605-9*) DIANE Pub.

World Factbook: 1995-96. CIA Staff. 512p. 1995. 32.95 (*0-02-881053-8*) Brasseys Inc.

World Factbook: 1996-97. CIA Staff. 572p. 1996. 32.95 (*1-57488-014-4*) Brasseys Inc.

World Factbook: 1997-98. CIA Staff. (Illus.). 572p. 1997. 32.95 (*1-57488-100-0*) Brasseys Inc.

World Factbook, 1993-94. Central Intelligence Agency Staff. 464p. 1993. 30.00 (*0-02-881044-9*) Brasseys Inc.

***World Factbook 1995.** (Illus.). 602p. 1995. pap. text ed. 70.00 (*1-57979-056-9*) BPI Info Servs.

***World Factbook '95.** Central Intelligence Agency Staff. 1995. pap. 40.00 (*0-614-30823-2*, CWDR95) Claitors.

***World Factbook '96.** Central Intelligence Agency Staff. 1997. pap. 44.00 (*1-57980-009-2*, CWOR96) Claitors.

***World Facts.** Dorling Kindersley Staff. (Funfax Eyewitness Library). (J). 1997. pap. text ed. 1.95 (*0-7894-1834-7*) DK Pub Inc.

World Facts & Figures. 3rd ed. Victor Showers. LC 88-31698. 721p. 1989. text ed. 145.00 (*0-471-85775-0*) Wiley.

***World Facts & Maps, 1997.** Rand McNally Staff. 1996. pap. text ed. 10.95 (*0-528-83881-4*) Rand McNally.

World Faith. Ruth Cranston. LC 68-58782. (Essay Index Reprint Ser.). 1977. 19.95 (*0-8369-0108-8*) Ayer.

World Faiths. 2nd ed. Solomon A. Nigosian. 234p. (Orig.). 1994. text ed. 39.95 (*0-312-10274-7*) St Martin.

World Faiths. 2nd ed. Solomon A. Nigosian. 560p. 1993. pap. text ed. 25.00 (*0-312-08414-5*) St Martin.

World Faiths. 2nd ed. Solomon A. Nigosian. 1993. teacher ed., pap. text ed. 5.00 (*0-312-09598-8*) St Martin.

World Faiths. 3rd ed. Solomon A. Nigosian. Date not set. pap. text ed. write for info. (*0-312-15268-X*) St Martin.

World Families Watch Television. Ed. by James Lull. LC 88-9658. (Communication & Human Values Ser.). (Illus.). 264p. 1988. pap. 75.30 (*0-7837-8965-3*, 2049746) Bks Demand.

World Family Targeted for Death. Lester Sumrall. 73p. (C). 1982. pap. text ed. 10.00 (*0-937580-72-4*) LeSEA Pub Co.

World Famous Crimes. Colin Wilson. 352p. 1995. pap. 10.95 (*0-7867-0217-6*) Carroll & Graf.

World Famous Investors Advice for 1993-2000: The Greatest Investors of All Time & Their Favorite Stocks, Bonds, Mutual Funds, Income & New Strategies for 1993-2000. R. D. Rockefeller & Gerald H. Chen. Ed. by M. Michael Folder. LC 93-77404. 96p. 1993. pap. 12.95 (*0-9632572-2-6*) MDMI Int Pubns.

World Famous Muriel & the Magic Mystery. Sue Alexander. LC 89-22396. (Illus.). 32p. (J). (gr. k-3). 1990. lib. bdg. 12.89 (*0-690-04789-4*) HarpC Child Bks.

***World Famous Music Vol. 1: Children's Songs.** Ed. by Carol Cuellar. 160p. (Orig.). (YA). 1993. pap. text ed. 12.95 (*0-89898-709-1*) Warner Brothers.

***World Famous Music Vol. 2: Nostalgia's Golden Greats.** Ed. by Carol Cuellar. 144p. (YA). 1993. pap. text ed. 12.95 (*0-89898-710-5*) Warner Brothers.

***World Famous Music Vol. 3: Songs of the Gay Nineties.** Ed. by Carol Cuellar. 128p. (Orig.). (YA). 1993. pap. text ed. 12.95 (*0-89898-711-3*) Warner Brothers.

***World Famous Music Vol. 4: Irish Melodies.** Ed. by Carol Cuellar. 128p. (Orig.). (YA). 1993. pap. text ed. 12.95 (*0-89898-712-1*) Warner Brothers.

***World Famous Music Vol. 6: Piano Classics.** Ed. by Carol Cuellar. 160p. (Orig.). (YA). 1993. pap. text ed. 12.95 (*0-89898-721-0*) Warner Brothers.

***World Famous Music Vol. 7: Light Classics.** Ed. by Carol Cuellar. 160p. (Orig.). (YA). 1993. pap. text ed. 12.95 (*0-89898-722-9*) Warner Brothers.

***World Famous Music Vol. 8: Enchanting Songs.** Ed. by Carol Cuellar. 160p. (Orig.). (YA). 1993. pap. text ed. 12.95 (*0-89898-708-3*) Warner Brothers.

***World Famous Music Vol. 10: Piano Selections.** Ed. by Carol Cuellar. 144p. (Orig.). (YA). 1993. pap. text ed. 12.95 (*0-89898-724-5*) Warner Brothers.

***World Famous Music Vol. 11: Classic Piano Solos.** Ed. by Carol Cuellar. 144p. (YA). 1993. pap. text ed. 12.95 (*0-89898-725-3*) Warner Brothers.

***World Famous Music Vol. 12: Barbershop Favorites.** Contrib. by Frank Milone & Odalis Soto. 96p. (Orig.). (YA). 1994. pap. text ed. 12.95 (*0-89898-726-1*) Warner Brothers.

World Famous Piano Pieces, MFM1. Ed. by Hugo Frey. (Illus.). 160p. 1984. pap. 12.95 (*0-8256-4001-6*, AM41419) Music Sales.

World Famous Vidalia Sweet Onion Cookbook. Morris. 1992. pap. 12.95 (*0-9644537-0-3*) Morris Farms.

World Farming. F. Watt. (Understanding Geography Ser.). (Illus.). 48p. (J). (gr. 5-8). 1994. pap. 7.95 (*0-7460-0737-X*, Usborne); lib. bdg. 15.95 (*0-88110-705-0*, Usborne) EDC.

World FDDI, Sonet, & 802.6 Man Equipment Markets: New Fiber Optic Standards Ignite Multi-Billion Dollar Growth. 256p. 1992. 1,695.00 (*1-56753-026-5*) Frost & Sullivan.

World Federalist Reader One: On the Bicentennial of the United States Constitution a Message for Our Times. Barbara M. Walker. (Illus.). 217p. 1987. pap. 5.00 (*1-880533-01-4*) Wrld Federal.

World Federation? A Critical Analysis of Federal World Government. Ronald J. Glossop. LC 92-56647. 272p. 1993. lib. bdg. 33.00 (*0-89950-854-5*) McFarland & Co.

World Fertilizer Economy. Mirko Lamer. xvi, 715p. 1957. 79.50 (*0-8047-0474-0*) Stanford U Pr.

World Fertilizer Progress Into the 1980s. J. Lastigzon. (Technical Bulletin Ser.: No. T-22). (Illus.). 64p. (Orig.). 1981. pap. 4.00 (*0-88090-021-0*) Intl Fertilizer.

World Fertilizer Situation & Outlook 1978-85. G. T. Harris & E. A. Harre. (Technical Bulletin Ser.: No. T-13). (Illus.). 33p. (Orig.). 1979. reprint ed. pap. 4.00 (*0-88090-012-1*) Intl Fertilizer.

World Fetal, Neonatal & Infant Monitor Markets: Manufacturers Push Hi-Tech Products Through One-Stop Shopping. Market Intelligence Staff. 433p. (Orig.). 1992. 1,995.00 (*1-56753-033-8*) Frost & Sullivan.

World Fiber Optic Communication Markets: Cable, Transmitters, Connectors, Couplers, Receivers. Market Intelligence Staff. 244p. 1993. 1,695.00 (*1-56753-463-5*) Frost & Sullivan.

World Fiber Optic Sensor Markets: Phenomenal Growth Across All Segments by Medical Applications. Market Intelligence Staff. 335p. 1993. 1,495.00 (*1-56753-435-X*) Frost & Sullivan.

***World Fibre Crops.** R. K. Maiti. (Illus.). 220p. (C). 1997. 59.50 (*1-886106-91-6*) Science Pubs.

World Film Directors, 2 vols., Vol. I. Ed. by John Wakeman. 1248p. 1987. 90.00 (*0-8242-0757-2*) Wilson.

World Film Directors, 2 vols., Vol. II. 1205p. 1988. 90.00 (*0-8242-0763-7*) Wilson.

World Film Encyclopedia: 1933. Ed. by Clarence Winchester. 1976. 300.00 (*0-87968-462-3*) Gordon Pr.

World Filmography, Vol.1. Peter Cowie. 35.00 (*0-8453-1565-X*, Cornwall Bks) Assoc Univ Prs.

World Filmography, Vol.2. Peter Cowie. 35.00 (*0-8453-1569-2*, Cornwall Bks) Assoc Univ Prs.

World Finance & Adjustment: An Agenda for Reform. Graham Bird. LC 85-2157. 368p. 1985. text ed. 39.95 (*0-312-89125-3*) St Martin.

World Finance, Nineteen Fourteen to Nineteen Thirty-Five. Paul Einzig. Ed. by Mira Wilkins. LC 78-3911. (International Finance Ser.). 1979. reprint ed. lib. bdg. 36.95 (*0-405-11215-7*) Ayer.

World Financial Markets after 1992. Ed. by Hans Genberg & Alexander K. Swoboda. LC 92-13931. (Publication of the Graduate Institute of International Studies, Geneva). 210p. 1993. 89.95 (*0-7103-0453-6*, B0090) Routledge Chapman & Hall.

World Financial Systems. 2nd ed. 1993. 165.00 (*0-582-09652-9*, 070470, Pub. by Longman Grp UK) Gale.

***World Financl System, 1944.** Fraser. 0987. pap. text ed. write for info. (*0-582-90278-9*, Pub. by Longman UK) Longman.

***World Fire: The Culture of Fire on Earth.** Stephen J. Pyne. (Illus.). 408p. 1997. pap. 19.95 (*0-295-97593-8*) U of Wash Pr.

World Fish Farming: Cultivation & Economics. 2nd ed. E. Evan Brown. (Illus.). 1983. text ed. 69.95 (*0-87055-427-1*) AVI.

World Fisheries Resources. James R. Coull. LC 93-7177. (Ocean Management & Policy Ser.). 272p. (C). (gr. 13). 1993. text ed. 69.95 (*0-415-07578-5*) Routledge.

World Fishes Important to North Americans Exclusive of Species from the Continental Waters of the United States & Canada. C. Richard Robins et al. (Special Publication Ser.: No. 21). 243p. 1991. pap. 35.95 (*0-913235-53-9*); text ed. 45.00 (*0-913235-54-7*) Am Fisheries Soc.

World Fit for People: Thinkers from Many Countries Address the Political, Economic, & Social Problems of Our Time. Uner Kirdar & Leonard Silk. LC 93-8945. 481p. (C). 1994. 40.00 (*0-8147-4648-9*) NYU Pr.

World Fitness Guide: European Edition. Frank S. Giordano. 294p. (Orig.). 1992. pap. 11.95 (*0-9633949-0-8*) Stayfit Pubns.

World Flow Sensor Markets: End-User Preferences Force Major Market Shifts. Frost & Sullivan Staff. 466p. 1996. write for info. (*0-7889-0481-7*, 5322) Frost & Sullivan.

World Flow Sensor Markets: Moderate Overall Growth Belies High Growth Opportunities. Market Intelligence Staff. 466p. 1993. 1,695.00 (*1-56753-475-9*) Frost & Sullivan.

World Folk Art: A Multicultural Approach. 46p. 1989. student ed. 185.00 (*0-685-67864-4*, 6013) Crystal.

World Folktales: A Multicultural Approach to Whole Language, Vol. 1. Jerry J. Mallett & Keith Polette. LC 94-21691. 70p. (J). (gr. k-2). 1994. pap. 10.95 (*0-917846-43-5*, Alleyside) Highsmith Pr.

World Folktales: A Multicultural Approach to Whole Language, Vol. 2. Jerry J. Mallett & Keith Polette. LC 94-21691. 70p. (J). (gr. 3-5). 1994. pap. 10.95 (*0-917846-44-3*, Alleyside) Highsmith Pr.

World Folktales: A Multicultural Approach to Whole Language, Vol. 3. Jerry J. Mallett & Keith Polette. LC 94-21691. 70p. (J). (gr. 6-8). 1994. pap. 10.95 (*0-917846-45-1*, Alleyside) Highsmith Pr.

World Folktales: An Anthology of Multicultural Folk Literature. Anita Stern. 160p. 1994. pap. 12.95 (*0-8442-0781-0*, Natl Textbk) NTC Pub Grp.

***World Food.** Sally Morgan & Paule Lalor. LC 97-7255. (Living for the Future Ser.). (J). 1998. write for info. (*0-531-14477-1*) Watts.

World Food Aid. John Shaw et al. LC 93-38251. 244p. 1994. text ed. 45.00 (*0-435-08097-0*, 08097) Heinemann.

World Food & Agriculture: Economic Problems & Issues. Ed. by Sisay Asefa. LC 88-29044. 144p. 1988. text ed. 19.00 (*0-88099-067-8*); pap. text ed. 9.00 (*0-88099-066-X*) W E Upjohn.

World Food & Fiber Crops. A. J. Bockholt. 1975. spiral bd. 14.00 (*0-88252-037-7*) Paladin Hse.

World Food & You. Nan Unklesbay. LC 91-8347. (Illus.). 442p. 1992. pap. 39.95 (*1-56022-011-2*) Haworth Jrnl Co-Edits.

World Food & You. Nan Unklesbay. LC 91-8347. (Illus.). 442p. 1992. lib. bdg. 79.95 (*1-56022-010-4*) Haworth Jrnl Co-Edits.

World Food Conference Proceedings, 1988, Vol. 1. World Food Conference Staff. Ed. by John W. Helmuth et al. LC 89-15634. (Illus.). 285p. 1989. reprint ed. pap. 81.30 (*0-608-00071-X*, 2060837) Bks Demand.

World Food Conference Proceedings, 1988, Vol. 2. World Food Conference Staff. Ed. by John W. Helmuth et al. LC 89-15634. (Illus.). 336p. 1989. reprint ed. pap. 95.80 (*0-608-00072-8*, 2060837) Bks Demand.

World Food Crisis. 2nd ed. Sayed A. Marei. LC 77-14527. (Illus.). 144p. reprint ed. pap. 41.10 (*0-685-20308-5*, 2030346) Bks Demand.

World Food Crisis: An International Directory of Organizations & Information Resources. Thaddeus C. Trzyna & Joan D. Smith. LC 76-4270. (Who's Doing What Ser.: No. 2). 166p. 1977. pap. 20.00 (*0-912102-21-7*) Cal Inst Public.

***World Food Outlook.** Donald O. Mitchell et al. (Trade & Development Ser.). 250p. (C). 1997. text ed. 54.95 (*0-521-58010-2*); pap. text ed. 17.95 (*0-521-58984-3*) Cambridge U Pr.

World Food, Population & Development. Gigi M. Berardi. LC 85-14398. (Illus.). 368p. (C). 1986. pap. 29.00 (*0-8476-7456-8*, R7456) Rowman.

World Food Problem. 2nd ed. David Grigg. LC 93-3274. (Illus.). 320p. 1994. pap. 22.95 (*0-631-17633-0*) Blackwell Pubs.

World Food Problem: Consensus & Conflict. Ed. by Radha Sinha & Gordon Drabek. 1978. pap. 26.00 (*0-08-024318-5*, Pergamon Pr) Elsevier.

World Food Problem: Selective Bibliography of Reviews. Miloslav Rechcigl. LC 74-30748. 352p. 1975. 128.00 (*0-8493-5098-0*) CRC Pr.

World Food Problem: Tackling the Causes of Undernutrition in the Third World. Phillips Foster. LC 91-31493. 372p. (C). 1992. pap. text ed. 22.00 (*1-55587-274-3*); lib. bdg. 48.50 (*1-55587-296-4*) Lynne Rienner.

World Food Problem & U. S. Food Politics & Policies, 1972-1976: A Readings Book. Ross B. Talbot. LC 76-55686. 401p. 1977. reprint ed. pap. 114.30 (*0-608-00553-3*, 2061436) Bks Demand.

World Food Problem & U. S. Food Politics & Policies, 1977: A Readings Book. Ross B. Talbot. LC 78-58157. 207p. 1978. reprint ed. pap. 59.00 (*0-608-00186-4*, 2060968) Bks Demand.

W

World Food Problem & U. S. Food Politics & Policies, 1978: A Readings Book. Ross B. Talbot. LC 79-88297. 220p. 1979. reprint ed. pap. 62.70 (*0-608-00036-1*, 2060802) Bks Demand.

World Food Problem & U. S. Food Politics & Policies, 1979-1980: A Readings Book. Ross B. Talbot. LC 81-80762. 186p. 1981. reprint ed. pap. 53.10 (*0-608-00187-2*, 2060969) Bks Demand.

World Food Problems & Prospects. David G. Johnson. LC 75-13927. (Foreign Affairs Study Ser.: No. 20). 89p. reprint ed. pap. 25.40 (*0-8357-4545-7*, 2037443) Bks Demand.

World Food Production, Demand, & Trade. Leroy L. Blakeslsee et al. LC 72-2785. (Illus.). 423p. 1973. reprint ed. pap. 120.60 (*0-608-00017-5*, 2060783) Bks Demand.

***World Food Programme: Report of the 30th Session of the Committee on Food Aid Policies & Programmes, Rome, December 1990.** 70p. 1991. 9.00 (*92-5-103051-0*, Pub. by FAO IT) Bernan Associates.

***World Food Programme: Report of the 31st Session of the Committee on Food Aid Policies & Programmes, Rome, May 1991.** 93p. 1991. 12.00 (*92-5-103083-9*, Pub. by FAO IT) Bernan Associates.

World Food Prospects & Agriculture Potential. Marilyn Chou et al. LC 76-24346. 336p. 1977. text ed. 59.95 (*0-275-90258-7*, C0258, Praeger Pubs) Greenwood.

World Food Situation: Resource & Environmental Issues in the Developing Countries & the United States. Pierre R. Crosson & Kenneth D. Frederick. LC 77-90817. (RFF Research Paper Ser.: No. R6). 238p. reprint ed. pap. 67.90 (*0-7837-3135-3*, 2042852) Bks Demand.

***World Food Summit: Background Documents, 3 vols.** FAO Staff. 727p. 1997. pap. 85.00 (*92-5-103877-5*, F38775, Pub. by FAO IT) Bernan Associates.

World Food Supply, 33 vols. Ed. by D. Gale Johnson. 1976. 866.00 (*0-405-07766-1*) Ayer.

***World Food Survey 6th 1996.** (Illus.). 75p. 1996. pap. 30.00 (*92-5-103837-6*, F38376, Pub. by FAO IT) Bernan Associates.

World Foods. Duyff. Date not set. text ed. write for info. (*0-314-07143-1*) West Pub.

World Foods. annot. ed. Duyff. Date not set. teacher ed., text ed. write for info. (*0-314-07144-X*) West Pub.

World for a Marketplace: Episodes in the History of European Expansion. John Parker. LC 78-71068. (Illus.). 1978. 15.00 (*0-9601798-0-1*) Assocs James Bell.

World for Julius: A Novel. Alfredo Bryce Echenique. Tr. by Dick Gerdes from SPA. LC 91-45310. (Texas Pan American Ser.). 444p. (Orig.). 1992. pap. 19.95 (*0-292-79071-6*); text ed. 45.00 (*0-292-79046-5*) U of Tex Pr.

World for the Meek: A Fantasy Novel. Harry Willson. LC 86-72835. 192p. (Orig.). 1987. pap. 9.00 (*0-938513-01-X*) Amador Pubs.

World Forest Resources. P. Persson. (C). 1992. 287.50 (*81-7136-034-3*, Pub. by Periodical Expert II) St Mut.

World Forests for the Future: Their Use & Conservation. Ed. by Kilaparti Ramakrshna & George M. Woodwell. LC 92-34492. 208p. (C). 1993. text ed. 25.00 (*0-300-05749-0*) Yale U Pr.

World Frame Relay Markets: Preparing for ATM. Market Intelligence Staff. 305p. 1993. 1,995.00 (*1-56753-542-9*) Frost & Sullivan.

World from Brown's Lounge: An Ethnography of Black Middle-Class Play. Michael J. Bell. LC 82-4732. 208p. 1983. text ed. 24.95 (*0-252-00956-8*) U of Ill Pr.

World from Jackson Square. Ed. by Etolia S. Basso & Hamilton Basso. LC 72-8579. (Essay Index Reprint Ser.). 1977. reprint ed. 24.95 (*0-8369-7306-2*) Ayer.

World from My Window. Sheila W. Samton. LC 90-85732. (Illus.). 28p. (J). (ps-2). 1991. reprint ed. 14.95 (*1-878093-15-0*) Boyds Mills Pr.

World Full of Animals: The Roger Caras Story. Roger Caras. LC 93-31009. (Great Naturalists Ser.). 48p. (J). 1994. 13.95 (*0-8118-0654-5*); pap. 6.95 (*0-8118-0682-0*) Chronicle Bks.

***World Full of Places: And Other Stories.** Michael Carragher. 176p. 1997. pap. 15.95 (*0-85640-595-7*, Pub. by Blackstaff Pr IE) Dufour.

World Full of Strangers. David Alman. LC 74-29040. (Labor Movement in Fiction & Non-Fiction Ser.). reprint ed. 49.50 (*0-404-58521-3*) AMS Pr.

World Full of Women. Martha C. Ward. LC 95-9022. 1995. pap. text ed. 28.00 (*0-205-16992-9*) Allyn.

World Furniture: An Illustrated History. Helena Hayward. 1988. 29.99 (*0-517-35150-1*) Random Hse Value.

World Futures: A Critical Analysis of Alternatives. Barry B. Hughes. LC 84-47964. 256p. (C). 1985. text ed. 38.50 (*0-8018-3236-5*); pap. text ed. 15.95 (*0-8018-3237-3*) Johns Hopkins.

World Futures & Options Directory, 1991-1992. Nick Battley. 1990. 95.00 (*0-07-707343-6*) McGraw.

World Futures & the United Nations: An Annotated Guide to 250 Recent Books & Reports. Michael Marien. LC 95-13952. (Future Survey Guidebooks Ser.: Vol. 1). 1995. pap. 25.00 (*0-930242-49-1*) World Future.

World Game: What It Is: The Rules for Playing. Caryl Browne. (Illus.). 118p. (Orig.). 1994. pap. text ed. 6.50 (*0-9644390-0-X*) Software World.

World Games: The Tradition of Anti-realist Revolt. Christopher Nash. 440p. 1988. text ed. 42.50 (*0-416-34710-X*) Routledge Chapman & Hall.

World Games & Recipes. 56p. 1979. pap. 3.75 (*0-900827-43-2*, 23-105) Girl Scouts USA.

World Gas Industry: English-French. Michel Valais et al. (Illus.). 330p. 1982. 590.00 (*2-7108-0424-7*, Pub. by Edits Technip FR) St Mut.

World Gas Option Symposium March 1980. (Fuel Applications Ser.). 189p. 1980. pap. 25.00 (*0-910091-46-3*) Inst Gas Tech.

World Gastrointestinal Drug Markets: Generic Competition Intensified As Block Buster Drugs Lose Patent Protection. Market Intelligence Staff. 537p. (Orig.). 1992. 2,295.00 (*1-56753-400-7*) Frost & Sullivan.

World Gene Therapy Markets: Gene-Based Services & Products to Provide Numerous Commercial Opportunities. Market Intelligence Staff. (Illus.). 475p. 1994. 2,995.00 (*0-7889-0076-5*) Frost & Sullivan.

***World Geographic Information Systems Market.** Frost & Sullivan. 422p. 1996. write for info. (*0-7889-0601-1*, 5382) Frost & Sullivan.

World Geographic Information Systems Software & Service Markets. Market Intelligence Staff. (Orig.). 1994. 1,995.00 (*0-7889-0134-6*) Frost & Sullivan.

World Geographical Encyclopedia, 5 vols., Set. LC 94-29086. Orig. Title: Enciclopedia Geografica Universale. (Illus.). 1800p. (YA). (gr. 9 up). 1995. text ed. 400.00 (*0-07-911496-2*) McGraw.

World Geographical Scheme for Recording Plant Distributions: World Geographic Scheme for Recording Plant Distributions, No. 2. S. Hollis & R. K. Brummitt. (Illus.). x, 105p. (Orig.). 1992. pap. 25.00 (*0-913196-56-8*, Pub. by Royal Botnic Grdns UK) Balogh.

World Geography. John Carratello & Patty Carratello. (Illus.). 48p. (J). (gr. 3-6). 1989. student ed. 7.95 (*1-55734-161-3*) Tchr Create Mat.

World Geography. Jenny Tyler. (Illus.). 160p. (J). (gr. 3-6). 1986. 22.95 (*0-7460-1848-7*, Usborne) EDC.

World Geography: Activity Worksheets. Bacon. 1989. pap. text ed. 19.75 (*0-15-373532-5*); teacher ed., pap. text ed. 24.25 (*0-15-373533-3*) HR&W Schl Div.

***World Geography: Case Studies.** 160p. 1994. pap. text ed. 19.95 (*0-521-45667-3*) Cambridge U Pr.

World Geography: Earth People 89. Bacon. 1988. 97.75 (*0-15-373531-7*) HR&W Schl Div.

World Geography: Lesson Planner. Harcourt Brace Staff. 1989. pap. 14.00 (*0-15-373554-6*) HR&W Schl Div.

***World Geography: Regional & Global Perspectives.** Ed. by Alwin. (C). Date not set. text ed. write for info. (*0-321-01365-4*) Addson-Wesley Educ.

World Geography Earth People. 1989. text ed. 63.25 (*0-15-373530-9*) HarBrace.

World Geography Lab Manual. Russell Ivy. 60p. (C). 1995. pap. text ed., ring bd. 26.19 (*0-7872-1491-4*) Kendall-Hunt.

World Geography of Human Diseases. Ed. by G. Melvyn Howe. 1978. text ed. 259.00 (*0-12-357150-2*) Acad Pr.

World Geography Study Aid. Herbert O. Kruger et al. (J). 1986. pap. 1.95 (*0-87738-044-9*) Youth Ed.

World Geography Today. 1992. student ed., wbk. ed., pap. text ed. 18.50 (*0-03-073307-3*); teacher ed., wbk. ed., pap. text ed. 23.00 (*0-03-073308-1*) HR&W Schl Div.

World Geography Today. Helgren. 1989. 58.50 (*0-03-016673-X*) HB Schl Dept.

World Geography Today. Helgren. 1989. wbk. ed., pap. text ed. 16.00 (*0-03-016672-1*); teacher ed., wbk. ed., pap. text ed. 23.00 (*0-03-021378-9*); teacher ed., pap. text ed. 89.00 (*0-03-021379-7*) HR&W Schl Div.

World Geography Today: Lecture Notes. 92th ed. 1992. suppl. ed., pap. text ed. 17.25 (*0-03-073309-X*) HR&W Schl Div.

World Geography Today: Testbook. Helgren. 1989. pap. text ed. 21.75 (*0-03-023033-0*) HR&W Schl Div.

World Geography Today: 1995. Sager. 1995. student ed., text ed. 58.50 (*0-03-096795-3*); teacher ed., text ed. 82.50 (*0-03-097673-1*) H Holt & Co.

World Geography Today: 1997. rev. ed. Helgren. 1997. student ed., text ed. 63.25 (*0-03-016802-3*) HR&W Schl Div.

World Geography Today: 1997. 97th ed. 1997. teacher ed., text ed. 281.50 (*0-03-095649-8*) HR&W Schl Div.

World Geography Today 1989: Texas Edition. Holt Staff. 1989. teacher ed., pap. 82.50 (*0-03-030002-9*) H Holt & Co.

World Geography Today 1992. Halgren. 1992. student ed., text ed. 63.25 (*0-03-072903-3*) HR&W Schl Div.

World Geography Today 1992. Helgren. 1992. teacher ed., text ed. 89.00 (*0-03-072904-1*) HR&W Schl Div.

World Geomorphology. Edwin M. Bridges. 288p. (C). 1990. pap. text ed. 32.95 (*0-521-28965-3*) Cambridge U Pr.

World God Made. Donna Cooner. LC 94-3333. (Illus.). (J). 1994. 12.99 (*0-8499-1162-1*) Word Pub.

World God Made: The Story of Creation. Alyce Bergey. (Arch Bks.). (J). (ps-3). 1970. pap. 1.99 (*0-570-06011-7*, 59-1114) Concordia.

World Gold: Mines-Deposits-Discoveries, Vol. I, North, Central, South America. E. A. Elevatorski. LC 88-62688. (Illus.). 1989. 118.20 (*0-942218-25-6*) Minobras.

World Gold: Mines-Deposits-Discoveries, Vol. II, Europe, Africa, Asia, Australia. E. A. Elevatorski. LC 88-62688. 136p. 1989. 146.80 (*0-942218-32-9*) Minobras.

World Gold Coin Value Guide. Lorraine S. Durst & Sanford J. Durst. LC 80-51832. 1981. pap. 9.00 (*0-915262-54-1*) S J Durst.

World Gone Wrong. Russ Hall. LC 96-83355. 443p. 1996. pap. 14.95 (*1-885487-21-5*) Brownell & Carroll.

World Gone Wrong. Russ Hall. LC 95-83660. 1996. pap. 14.95 (*0-614-12680-0*) Brownell & Carroll.

World Government. rev. ed. Peter J. Taylor. (Illustrated Encyclopedia of World Geography Ser.). (Illus.). 256p. 1995. 45.00 (*0-19-521096-4*) OUP.

***World Government by Stealth.** Gug Arnold. LC 97-6554. 1997. write for info. (*0-312-17494-2*) St Martin.

World Grasses. J. W. Bews. (C). 1979. text ed. 115.00 (*0-89771-553-5*, Pub. by Intl Bk Distr II) St Mut.

World Grasses. J. W. Bews. (Illus.). xii, 408p. 1979. reprint ed. 165.00 (*0-685-54012-X*, Pub. by Intl Bk Distr II) St Mut.

World Growing Old: The Coming Health Care Challenges. Ed. by Daniel Callahan et al. LC 95-6447. (Hastings Center Studies in Ethics). 240p. 1995. 42.50 (*0-87840-591-7*) Georgetown U Pr.

***World Growing Old: The Coming Health Care Challenges.** Ed. by Daniel Callahan et al. LC 95-6447. 190p. 1996. pap. 16.95 (*0-87840-632-8*) Georgetown U Pr.

World Growth Factor Markets: Tissue Applications Poised for Commercialization. Market Intelligence Staff. 300p. (Orig.). 1993. 2,495.00 (*1-56753-620-4*) Frost & Sullivan.

***World Guide to Abbreviations.** 6th ed. 1980. 115.00 (*0-8103-2024-X*, 00001843, Gale Res Intl) Gale.

***World Guide to Abbreviations.** 7th ed. 1984. 115.00 (*0-8103-2049-5*, 00001699, Gale Res Intl) Gale.

World Guide to Abbreviations. 9th ed. Buttress. 1991. 140.00 (*0-8103-5544-2*, Pub. by B & Sons UK) Gale.

World Guide to Abbreviations. 10th ed. 1995. write for info. (*0-8103-9740-4*, 070750, Pub. by B & Sons UK) Gale.

World Guide to Abbreviations of Organizations. 8th ed. Ed. by G. A. Buttress & Henry J. Heaney. 777p. 1987. 125.00 (*0-8103-2048-7*, Pub. by B & Sons UK) Gale.

***World Guide to Abbreviations of Organizations.** 11th ed. 1996. 170.00 (*0-7514-0261-3*, GML00197-070848, Pub. by B & Sons UK) Gale.

World Guide to Battery-Powered Road Transportation. Electric Vehicle Council Staff. 393p. 1980. 50.00 (*0-317-34116-2*, 0479202) Edison Electric.

***World Guide to Bottled Mineral Water.** Derek Kingwell. 320p. 1996. pap. 24.95 (*1-897784-18-X*, Pub. by N Wilson UK) Interlink Pub.

***World Guide to Dolls.** Valerie J. Douet. (Illus.). 144p. 1996. 19.98 (*0-614-23817-X*, N4723) Hobby Hse.

World Guide to Dolls. Brenda J. Gilbert. 1993. 19.98 (*1-55521-967-5*) Bk Sales Inc.

World Guide to Environmental Issues & Organizations. Ed. by Peter Braackley. 400p. 1990. write for info. (*0-8103-8353-5*, 079320-M99406) Gale.

World Guide to Environmental Issues & Organizations. Ed. by Peter Brackley. 400p. 1991. 125.00 (*0-582-06270-5*, 079320-M99348) Gale.

World Guide to Expendable Launch Vehicles. Frank Sietzen, Jr. 306p. (C). 1991. pap. 395.00 (*0-935453-39-3*) Pasha Pubns.

***World Guide to Gay, Lesbian & Queer Film.** Australian Catalogue Company Staff. (Illus.). 450p. 1997. pap. write for info. (*1-86452-010-8*) D W Thorpe.

World Guide to Infections: Diseases, Distribution, Diagnosis. Mary E. Wilson. (Illus.). 784p. 1991. 98.00 (*0-19-504385-5*) OUP.

World Guide to Libary & Information Science Education. 2nd ed. Ed. by Josephine Riss-Fang et al. (IFLA: vol. 72/73). 600p. 1995. 130.00 (*3-598-21799-4*) K G Saur.

World Guide to Libraries. 11th ed. 1180p. 1993. 350.00 (*3-598-20720-4*) K G Saur.

World Guide to Libraries, 2 vols. 12th ed. 1300p. 1995. 385.00 (*3-598-20721-2*) K G Saur.

World Guide to Libraries. 13th ed. Ed. by Saur, K. G., Staff. 1997. 450.00 (*3-598-20723-9*) K G Saur.

World Guide to Libraries Plus. 1996. 535.00 (*3-598-40289-9*) K G Saur.

World Guide to Library, Archival, & Information Science Associations. 3rd ed. Alice H. Songe. (IFLA Publication Ser.: Vol. 52/53). 430p. 1990. lib. bdg. 95.00 (*3-598-10814-1*) K G Saur.

World Guide to Nude Beaches & Resorts. Lee Baxandall. (Illus.). 274p. 1995. pap. 28.00 (*0-934106-20-7*) Naturists.

World Guide to Packaging 1997. North American Publishing Company Staff. 800p. 1996. pap. 300.00 (*0-912920-97-1*) North Am Pub Co.

World Guide to Religious & Spiritual Organizations. Ed. by Union of International Associations Staff. 471p. 1996. 375.00 (*3-598-11296-3*) K G Saur.

World Guide to Scientific Association & Learned Societies. 6th ed. 1000p. 1994. 275.00 (*3-598-20580-5*) K G Saur.

World Guide to Social Work Education. 2nd ed. Ed. by Katherine A. Kendall. LC 83-78853. 1984. pap. 5.00 (*0-87293-001-7*) Coun Soc Wk Ed.

World Guide to Special Libraries, 2 Vols. 3rd ed. Ed. by Helmut Opitz & Elisabeth Richter. 1258p. 1994. 325.00 (*3-598-22234-3*) K G Saur.

***World Guide to Television 1997.** Ed. by Donna Witzleben. 1997. pap. 395.00 (*1-888576-13-8*) North Am Pub Co.

World Guide to Trade Associations. 4th ed. Michael Zils. 600p. 1995. 400.00 (*3-598-20722-0*) K G Saur.

World, Guilt & Self-Conflict: The Guilt Chapter. Eli Siegel. 1966. pap. write for info. (*0-911492-15-1*) Aesthetic Realism.

World Ham Net Directory, 1995. 3rd ed. Mike Witkowski. 55p. 1995. 12.95 (*0-936653-27-2*) Tiare Pubns.

World Handbook of Political & Social Indicators. Bruce M. Russett et al. LC 77-13514. (Tools & Methods of Comparative Research Ser.: No. 1). (Illus.). 373p. 1977. reprint ed. text ed. 69.50 (*0-8371-9857-7*, RUWH, Greenwood Pr) Greenwood.

World Handbook of Political & Social Indicators II: Cross-National Aggregate Data, 1950-1965. 2nd ed. Charles Lewis Taylor & Michael C. Hudson. 1973. write for info. (*0-89138-059-0*) ICPSR.

World Handbook of Political & Social Indicators II: Sections 2-5, 1948-1967. 2nd ed. Charles Lewis Taylor & Michael C. Hudson. LC 75-40942. 1975. write for info. (*0-89138-123-6*) ICPSR.

World Handbook of Political & Social Indicators, Vol. 1: Cross-National Attributes & Rates of Change. Charles L. Taylor & David A. Jodice. LC 82-40447. (Illus.). 331p. reprint ed. pap. 94.40 (*0-8357-8384-7*, 2033901) Bks Demand.

World Harvesters. Bill Huxley. (Illus.). 112p. 1995. 29.95 (*0-85236-302-8*, Pub. by Farming Pr UK) Diamond Farm Bk.

World Has Definitely Changed: New Economic Forces & Their Implications for the Next Decade. A. Gary Shilling. (Illus.). 179p. 1987. pap. 10.00 (*0-9618562-1-1*) LESP.

World Has Definitely Changed: New Economic Forces & Their Implications for the Next Decade. A. Gary Shilling. (Illus.). 250p. 1988. reprint ed. text ed. 19.95 (*0-9618562-0-3*) Weiss Grp.

World Health. J. Hampton. (World Issues Ser.). (Illus.). 48p. (J). (gr. 5 up). 1988. lib. bdg. 18.60 (*0-86592-281-0*); lib. bdg. 13.95 (*0-685-58318-X*) Rourke Corp.

World Health & Disease. Alistair Gray & Philip Payne. LC 92-42625. (Health & Disease Ser.: Book 3). 1993. pap. 26.00 (*0-335-19078-2*, Open Univ Pr) Taylor & Francis.

World Health & World Politics: The World Health Organization & the U. N. System. Javed Siddiqi. 286p. 1995. text ed. 34.95 (*1-57003-038-3*) U of SC Pr.

World Health Report 1995: Bridging the Gaps. 120p. (ENG & FRE.). (C). 1995. pap. text ed. 22.00 (*92-4-156178-5*, 1241995) World Health.

***World Health Report 1997: Conquering Suffering, Enriching Humanity.** 172p. 1997. pap. 15.00 (*92-4-156185-8*, 1241997) World Health.

***World Health Statistics Annual 1968.** 1971. pap. 29.60 (*92-4-067681-3*) World Health.

World Health Statistics Annual, 1970, Pt. 2. 1974. Vol. 2. pap. 9.60 (*92-4-067702-X*) World Health.

World Health Statistics Annual, 1970, Pt. 3. 1974. Vol. 3. pap. 12.00 (*92-4-067703-8*) World Health.

World Health Statistics Annual, 1970 see Advances in Behavior Therapy: Proceedings

World Health Statistics Annual, 1971, Pt. 1. 1975. Vol. 1. pap. 40.00 (*92-4-067711-9*) World Health.

World Health Statistics Annual, 1971, Pt. 2. 1975. Vol. 2. pap. 22.40 (*92-4-067712-7*) World Health.

World Health Statistics Annual, 1971, Pt. 3. 1975. Vol. 3. pap. 12.80 (*0-686-16945-X*) World Health.

World Health Statistics Annual, 1971 see Advances in Behavior Therapy: Proceedings

World Health Statistics Annual, 1972, Pt. 1. 1976. Vol. 1. pap. 51.20 (*92-4-067721-6*) World Health.

World Health Statistics Annual, 1972, Pt. 2. 1976. Vol. 2. pap. 12.80 (*92-4-067722-4*) World Health.

World Health Statistics Annual, 1972, Pt. 3. 1976. Vol. 3. pap. 12.80 (*92-4-067723-2*) World Health.

World Health Statistics Annual, 1972 see Biblio (Catalogue-Dictionnaire Des Ouvrages Parus En Francais Dans le Monde)

World Health Statistics Annual 1985: Global Overview, Vital Statistics & Life Tables, Environmental Health, Causes of Death. 531p. 1985. pap. text ed. 76.50 (*92-4-067851-4*, 0178500) World Health.

World Health Statistics Annual 1987: Global Review, Evaluation of the Global Strategy for Health for All Vital Statistics & Life Tables, Causes of Death. 472p. 1986. pap. text ed. 81.00 (*92-4-067861-1*, 0178700) World Health.

***World Health Statistics Annual 1990: Global Overview International Statistics on Causes of Disability Vital Statistics.** 447p. 1990. text ed. 90.00 (*92-4-067905-7*) World Health.

World Health Statistics Annual 1991. WHO Staff. xxii, 349p. 1992. pap. text ed. 100.00 (*92-4-067910-3*, 0179100) World Health.

***World Health Statistics Annual 1992.** 463p. 1993. text ed. 100.00 (*92-4-067920-0*) World Health.

***World Health Statistics Annual 1993.** 555p. 1994. text ed. 100.00 (*92-4-067930-8*) World Health.

World Health Statistics Annual 1994. 600p. (FRE.). (C). 1995. pap. text ed. 100.00 (*92-4-067940-5*, 0179400) World Health.

***World Health Statistics Annual 1995.** (Illus.). 835p. 1995. pap. 150.00 (*92-4-067950-2*, 0179500) World Health.

World Health Statistics, 1969, Pt. 1. 1973. Vol. 2. pap. 9.60 (*92-4-067692-9*) World Health.

World Health Statistics, 1969, Pt. 2. 1973. Vol. 3. pap. 12.00 (*92-4-067693-7*) World Health.

World Health Statistics, 1969 see Advances in Behavior Therapy: Proceedings

World Held Hostage: The War Waged by International Terrorism. Desmond McForan. LC 87-4776. 278p. 1987. text ed. 39.95 (*0-312-00835-X*) St Martin.

World Historians & Their Goals: Twentieth-Century Answers to Modernism. Paul Costello. 307p. 1993. lib. bdg. 30.00 (*0-87580-173-0*) N Ill U Pr.

World Historians & Their Goals: Twentieth-Century Answers to Modernism. Paul Costello. LC 94-15134. 325p. 1995. pap. 18.00 (*0-87580-564-7*) N Ill U Pr.

World Historical Fiction Guide for Young Adults. Lee Gordon & Cheryl Tanaka. LC 95-9689. 301p. 1995. text ed. 30.00 (*0-917846-41-5*, 95627) Highsmith Pr.

World History. (College Board SAT II Subject Test Ser.). 1997. pap. 23.95 (*0-8373-6315-2*, SATII-15) Nat Learn.

***World History.** (Works). 664p. 1996. pap. 6.99 (*1-57215-206-0*, JG1205) World Pubns.

World History. Robert J. Field. 1993. text ed. 17.95 (*0-87594-350-0*); teacher ed., pap. text ed. 9.95 (*0-87594-351-9*); student ed., pap. text ed. 9.95 (*0-87594-352-7*) Book-Lab.

World History. Ken Hills. LC 93-20105. (Visual Factfinders Ser.). (Illus.). 96p. (Orig.). (J). (gr. 5 up). 1993. pap. 9.95 (*1-85697-853-2*, Kingfisher LKC) LKC.

World History. William H. McNeill. (Illus.). 576p. 1979. pap. text ed. 27.95 (*0-19-502555-5*) OUP.

World History. B. V. Rao. 466p. (C). 1984. pap. 15.95 (*0-86590-315-8*, Pub. by Sterling Pubs II); text ed. 30.00 (*0-86590-808-7*, Pub. by Sterling Pubs II) Apt Bks.

W

An Asterisk (*) at the beginning of an entry indicates that the title is appearing in BIP for the first time.

World History. Reich. 1984. teacher ed., pap. text ed. 43.00 (0-15-773001-8) HR&W Schl Div.

*World History. Reich. 1990. text ed. 62.00 (0-03-028898-3) HR&W Schl Div.

*World History. Reich. 1985. teacher ed., wbk. ed., pap. 17.25 (0-15-773005-0) HarBrace.

*World History. Spielvogel. (Social Studies Ser.). 1998. student ed., pap. 28.95 (0-314-22496-3) S-W Pub.

*World History. Spodek. 1997. text ed. 60.00 (0-13-644469-5) P-H.

World History. Jiu-Hwa Upshur. Date not set. teacher ed., pap. text ed. write for info. (0-314-83987-9) West Pub.

*World History. 2nd ed. Duiker. Date not set. write for info. (0-314-22045-3) Wadsworth Pub.

World History. 2nd ed. Jiu-Hwa Upshur et al. LC 94-30769. 958p. (C). 1995. text ed. 62.00 (0-314-04399-3) West Pub.

*World History. 11th ed. Spielvogel. 1998. text ed. 70.95 (0-314-20561-6) Wadsworth Pub.

World History. 90th ed. Billings. 1990. wbk. ed., pap. text ed. 14.25 (0-03-028902-5) HR&W Schl Div.

World History. 90th ed. Billings. 1990. teacher ed., wbk. ed., pap. text ed. 17.25 (0-03-028903-3) HR&W Schl Div.

World History. 90th ed. Reich. 1990. teacher ed., pap. text ed. 43.00 (0-03-028899-1) HR&W Schl Div.

World History, 2 vols., Set. William J. Duiker & Jackson J. Spielvogel. Ed. by Baxter. LC 93-36207. 1050p. (C). 1994. text ed. 63.00 (0-314-02844-7) West Pub.

World History, 2 vols., Vol. I. William J. Duiker & Jackson J. Spielvogel. Ed. by Baxter. LC 93-36207. 756p. (C). 1994. pap. text ed. 46.50 (0-314-02845-5) West Pub.

World History, Vol. 1. Jiu-Hwa Upshur. Date not set. student ed., wbk. ed., pap. text ed. 17.75 (0-314-83988-7) West Pub.

World History, 2 vols., Vol. II. William J. Duiker & Jackson J. Spielvogel. Ed. by Baxter. LC 93-36207. 701p. (C). 1994. pap. text ed. 46.50 (0-314-02846-3) West Pub.

World History, Vol. 2. Jiu-Hwa Upshur et al. Ed. by Baxter. 770p. (C). 1991. pap. text ed. 43.25 (0-314-79267-8) West Pub.

World History, Vol. 2. Jiu-Hwa Upshur. Date not set. student ed., wbk. ed., pap. text ed. 17.75 (0-314-83986-0) West Pub.

World History: A Brief Introduction. Joseph Reither. LC 65-17275. Orig. Title: World History at a Glance. (Illus.). 512p. 1973. reprint ed. pap. text ed. 12.95 (0-07-051875-0) McGraw.

World History: A Dictionary of Important People, Places & Events from Ancient Times to the Present. Bruce Wetterau. 1198p. 1995. pap. 25.00 (0-8050-4241-5) H Holt & Co.

World History: Before 1600: The Development of Great Civilizations, Vol. 1, Chapters 1-9. 2nd ed. Jiu-Hwa Upshur et al. 498p. (C). 1995. pap. text ed. 46.50 (0-314-04585-6) West Pub.

*World History: Comprehensive Edition. 2nd ed. William J. Duiker & Jackson J. Spielvogel. (History Ser.). (C). 1997. text ed. 65.95 (0-534-53121-0) Wadsworth Pub.

World History: Continuity & Change 97. 97th ed. HR&W School Division Staff. 680p. 1997. text ed. 275.25 (0-03-095510-6) HR&W Schl Div.

World History: Patterns of Change & Continuity. 2nd ed. Peter N. Stearns. LC 94-11468. (C). 1995. text ed. 56.95 (0-673-99153-9) Addson-Wesley Educ.

World History: Patterns of Change & Continuity. 2nd ed. Peter N. Stearns. LC 94-11468. 608p. reprint ed. pap. 48.00 (1-886746-11-7, 93375) Talman.

World History: People & Nations. Mazour. 1990. 58.50 (0-15-373458-2) HB Schl Dept.

World History: Selected Course Outlines from Leading American Colleges & Universities. Ed. by Kevin Reilly & Michael Adas. (Orig.). 1997. pap. text ed. 16.95 (1-55876-136-5) Wiener Pubs Inc.

World History: Since 1500: The Age of Global Integration, Vol. 2, Chapters 9-17. 2nd ed. Jiu-Hwa Upshur et al. 573p. (C). 1995. pap. text ed. 46.50 (0-314-04584-8) West Pub.

World History: Skills Activity Book. 90th ed. Billings. 1990. wbk. ed., pap. text ed. 8.75 (0-03-028909-2) HR&W Schl Div.

*World History: Story of Progress. Smart. 1987. text ed. 62.00 (0-03-005228-9); teacher ed., pap. text ed. 72.00 (0-03-005229-7) HR&W Schl Div.

World History: Testbank, Vol. 1. Duiker. Date not set. suppl. ed., pap. text ed. write for info. (0-314-03271-1) West Pub.

World History: Testbank, Vol. 2. Duiker. Date not set. suppl. ed., teacher ed., pap. text ed. write for info. (0-314-03272-X) West Pub.

World History: Testbook. Reich. 1984. pap. text ed. 11.00 (0-15-773003-4) HR&W Schl Div.

World History: Testmasters. 90th ed. Reich. 1990. teacher ed., pap. text ed. 11.00 (0-03-028908-4) HR&W Schl Div.

World History: The Story of Mankind from Prehistory to the Present. rev. ed. Hugh Thomas. 816p. 1996. 35.00 (0-06-017477-3) HarpC.

*World History: To 1500. 2nd ed. William J. Duiker & Jackson J. Spielvogel. (History Ser.). 500p. (C). 1997. pap. text ed. 37.95 (0-534-53120-2) Wadsworth Pub.

*World History Vol. I: To 1800. 2nd ed. Duiker. (History Ser.). 1998. student ed., pap. 17.95 (0-534-53128-8) Wadsworth Pub.

*World History Vol. I: To 1800. 2nd ed. William J. Duiker & Jackson J. Spielvogel. (History Ser.). 724p. (C). 1997. pap. text ed. 46.95 (0-534-53118-0) Wadsworth Pub.

*World History Vol. II: Since 1500. 2nd ed. Duiker. (History Ser.). 1998. student ed., pap. 17.95 (0-534-53129-6) Wadsworth Pub.

*World History Vol. II: Since 1500. 2nd ed. William J. Duiker & Jackson J. Spielvogel. (History Ser.). 1174p. (C). 1997. pap. text ed. 46.95 (0-534-53119-9) Wadsworth Pub.

World History & Comparative Cultures: A Thematic Analysis. Steve Wallech. 288p. (C). 1995. per., pap. text ed. 23.62 (0-8403-8560-9) Kendall-Hunt.

World History at a Glance see World History: A Brief Introduction

World History, Book Of. Anne Millard. (Picture History Ser.). (Illus.). 195p. (J). (gr. 3-9). 1986. 24.95 (0-86020-959-8) EDC.

World History (Combined) Jiu-Hwa Upshur et al. Ed. by Baxter. 770p. (C). 1991. text ed. 57.50 (0-314-79265-1) West Pub.

World History Conflict Simulations. David W. Felder. LC 95-90522. 152p. 1995. 24.95 (0-910959-26-9, B&G 26H); teacher ed. 44.95 (0-910959-46-3, B&G 26T) Wellington Pr.

World History Dates. J. Chisholm. (Illustrated World History Ser.). (Illus.). 128p. (J). (gr. 6 up). 1987. pap. 12.95 (0-86020-954-7); lib. bdg. 20.95 (0-88110-232-6) EDC.

World History in the Twentieth Century. 2nd ed. R. D. Cornwell. (Illus.). 1981. text ed. 24.80 (0-582-33074-2, 72032) Longman.

World History Made in the Present. Ilija Poplasen. (Illus.). 350p. 1986. 20.00 (0-935352-20-1) MIR PA.

World History Made in the Present. Ilija Poplasen. (Illus.). 403p. 1991. 20.00 (0-935352-32-5) MIR PA.

World History of Photography. rev. ed. Naomi Rosenblum. (Illus.). (C). pap. text ed. 40.00 (1-55859-055-2) Abbeville Pr.

World History of Photography. rev. ed. Naomi Rosenblum. (Illus.). 674p. 1989. 65.00 (1-55859-054-4) Abbeville Pr.

*World History of Photography. 3rd ed. Naomi Rosenblum. LC 96-36153. (Illus.). 696p. 1997. 65.00 (0-7892-0028-7); pap. 40.00 (0-7892-0329-4) Abbeville Pr.

World History of the Towing & Recovery Industry. John L. Hawkins, II. (Illus.). 280p. Date not set. 39.95 (0-9625135-0-4) T T Pubns.

World History of the Twentieth Century Vol. 1: Western Dominance, 1900-1945. John A. Grenville. LC 84-40300. 605p. reprint ed. pap. 172.50 (0-7837-2614-7, 2042949) Bks Demand.

World History Simulations. Max W. Fischer. (Illus.). 96p. (J). (gr. 5-8). 1993. student ed. 11.95 (1-55734-481-7) Tchr Create Mat.

World History Study. 2nd ed. Ed. by Elizabeth Burchard. (Exambusters Ser.). 384p. (YA). (gr. 7 up). 1996. pap. 9.95 (1-881374-82-3) Ace Acad.

*World History the Easy Way, Vol. 1. Charles A. Frazee. LC 97-14772. (Easy Way Ser.). 1997. pap. text ed. 12.95 (0-8120-9765-3) Barron.

*World History the Easy Way, Vol. 2. Charles A. Frazee. LC 97-14772. (Easy Way Ser.). 1997. pap. text ed. 12.95 (0-8120-9766-1) Barron.

World History to Fifteen Hundred. William J. Duiker & Jackson J. Spielvogel. Ed. by Baxter. 522p. (C). pap. text ed. 39.00 (0-314-03763-2) West Pub.

World History to 1648. Jay P. Anglin & William J. Hamblin. LC 91-55404. (College Outline Ser.). (Illus.). 400p. (Orig.). 1993. pap. 14.00 (0-06-467123-2, Harper Ref) HarpC.

World History to 1700...the Final Exam. Terry Moss. LC 94-77898. (Final Exam Ser.). 60p. 1994. pap. 4.95 (1-885962-56-8) Lincoln Lrning.

World History 1600 to 1960...the Final Exam. Terry Moss. LC 94-77899. (Final Exam Ser.). 77p. 1994. pap. 5.49 (1-885962-55-X) Lincoln Lrning.

*World History, 1776-1984. Koutsoukis. 1985. pap. text ed. write for info. (0-582-66348-2, Pub. by Longman UK) Longman.

World History 1984. Reich. 1984. text ed. 62.00 (0-15-773000-X) HR&W Schl Div.

World History 1997. 97th ed. Hanes. 1997. teacher ed., text ed. 95.75 (0-03-094989-0) HarBrace.

World Hoax. Ernest F. Elmhurst. 233p. 1976. reprint ed. pap. 8.00 (0-911038-81-7, Noontide Pr) Legion Survival.

World Holiday Book: Celebrations for Every Day of the Year. Anneli Rufus. LC 94-557. 400p. 1994. pap. 15.00 (0-06-250912-8) Harper SF.

*World Holiday, Festival & Calendar Books. annot. ed. Ed. by Tanya Gulevich. 800p. 1997. lib. bdg. 55.00 (0-7808-0073-7) Omnigraphics Inc.

*World Hotel Directory, 1988. Financial Times Staff. Date not set. pap. text ed. write for info. (0-582-00432-2, Pub. by Longman UK) Longman.

*World Hotel Directory '94. 94th ed. 1993. 162.00 (0-582-21895-0, 00107374, Pub. by Longman Grp UK) Gale.

World Hotel Industry. Euromonitor Staff. (C). 1992. 15,800.00 (0-318-67339-8, Pub. by Euromonitor Pubns UK) Gale.

World Human Rights Guide. Charles Humana. LC 85-27584. 368p. reprint ed. pap. 104.90 (0-8357-3491-9, 2039750) Bks Demand.

World Human Vaccine Markets: Over 60 Productions: Which Competitors Are Attacking Viruses? Market Intelligence Staff. 478p. 1993. 2,295.00 (1-56753-460-0) Frost & Sullivan.

World Hunger. Liza N. Burby. (Overview Ser.). (Illus.). 112p. (J). (gr. 5-9). 1995. lib. bdg. 17.96 (1-56006-120-0, 1200) Lucent Bks.

World Hunger. Patricia L. Kutzner. LC 90-25185. (Contemporary World Issues Ser.). 359p. 1991. lib. bdg. 39.50 (0-87436-558-9) ABC-CLIO.

*World Hunger. Liz Young. LC 96-36545. (Routledge Introductions to Development Ser.). 176p. (C). 1997. pap. write for info. (0-415-13773-X) Routledge.

World Hunger: A Challenge to American Policy. Sol M. Linowitz. LC 80-85486. (Headline Ser.: No. 252). (Illus.). 64p. 1980. pap. 5.95 (0-87124-065-3) Foreign Policy.

World Hunger: A Neo-Malthusian Perspective. Mitchell H. Kellman. LC 86-21221. 261p. 1987. text ed. 59.95 (0-275-92247-2, C2247, Praeger Pubs) Greenwood.

World Hunger: An Annotated Bibliography. 1991. lib. bdg. 69.95 (0-8490-5196-7) Gordon Pr.

World Hunger: Twelve Myths. Frances M. Lappe & Joseph Collins. 224p. 1986. pap. 10.95 (0-8021-5041-1, Grove) Grove-Atltic.

World Hunger & Morality. 2nd rev. ed. Ed. by William Aiken & Hugh LaFollette. LC 95-23514. 208p. (C). 1995. pap. text ed. 27.40 (0-13-448284-0) P-H.

World Hunger & the World Economy: And Other Essays in Development Economics. Keith B. Griffin. 525p. (C). 1987. 49.50 (0-8419-1128-2); pap. 19.95 (0-8419-1129-0) Holmes & Meier.

World Hypotheses: A Study in Evidence. Stephen C. Pepper. (C). 1970. pap. 16.00 (0-520-00994-0) U CA Pr.

World I See. Debra W. Alexander. 24p. (J). (gr. k-5). 1992. 3.95 (1-56688-054-8) Bur For At-Risk.

World I Used to Know. Walter Rinder. LC 89-81211. 1990. pap. 7.95 (0-89087-596-0) Celestial Arts.

World Illiteracy at Mid-Century, a Statistical Study. UNESCO Staff. LC 75-88962. 200p. 1970. reprint ed. text ed. 55.00 (0-8371-3405-6, UNWI, Greenwood Pr) Greenwood.

World Image Processing & Enhancement Equipment: Clinical Applications Open Market to New Entrants. Market Intelligence Staff. 287p. 1993. 1,695.00 (1-56753-849-5) Frost & Sullivan.

World Impact of NAFTA. Ed. by Richard L. Bolin. 83p. (Orig.). 1994. pap. text ed. 40.00 (0-945951-10-8) Flagstaff Inst.

World in a Bowl of Tea: Healthy, Simple, Seasonal Foods Inspired by the Japanese Tea Ceremony. Bettina Vitell. LC 96-28146. (Illus.). 256p. 1997. 25.00 (0-06-018740-9, PL) HarpC.

World in a Classroom. Chris Searle. (Education Ser.). 288p. 1980. 16.00 (0-904613-45-3); pap. 4.45 (0-904613-46-1) Writers & Readers.

World in a Classroom: Language in Education in Britain & Canada. Viv Edwards & Angela Redfern. LC 92-15154. 1992. 69.00 (1-85359-159-9, Pub. by Multilingual Matters UK); pap. 24.95 (1-85359-158-0, Pub. by Multilingual Matters UK) Taylor & Francis.

World in a Frame: What We See in Films. Leo Braudy. LC 84-225. XII, 286p. 1984. reprint ed. pap. text ed. 11.95 (0-226-07155-3) U Ch Pr.

World in a Grain of Sand: Twenty-Two Interviews with Northrop Frye. Robert D. Denham & Thomas Willard. LC 90-15518. 359p. (C). 1990. text ed. 59.95 (0-8204-1215-5) P Lang Pubng.

*World in a Supermarket. Rozanne L. Williams. (Social Studies Learn to Read Ser.). (Illus.). 8p. (Orig.). (J). (ps-2). 1996. pap. 1.59 (1-57471-126-1, 3907) Creat Teach Pr.

*World in a Supermarket. Rozanne L. Williams. (Social Studies Big Bks.). (Illus.). 8p. (Orig.). (J). (ps-2). 1997. pap. 7.98 (1-57471-172-5, 3964) Creat Teach Pr.

World in an Olive Leaf. Cynthia Pickard. 48p. (Orig.). 1985. 25.00 (0-931757-26-6); pap. 15.00 (0-931757-27-4) Pterodactyl Pr.

World in Arms: Time Frame A. D. Nineteen Hundred to Nineteen Twenty-Five. Time-Life Books Editors. (Illus.). 176p. 1989. lib. bdg. write for info. (0-8094-6471-3) Time-Life.

*World in Art: Masterworks from the Last Five Centuries of Traditional Chinese Paintings. Ed. by Yang Guanghe et al. (Illus.). 197p. 1994. 69.95 (7-119-01605-9, Pub. by Foreign Lang CH) China Bks.

World in Between: Christian Healing & the Struggle for Spiritual Survival. Emmanuel Milingo. LC 84-191633. 144p. (Orig.). reprint ed. pap. 41.10 (0-7837-5520-1, 2045290) Bks Demand.

World in Conflict: War Annual 7: Contemporary Warfare Described & Analysed. John Laffin. (Illus.). 150p. 1996. 39.95 (1-85753-196-5, Pub. by Brasseys UK) Brasseys Inc.

World in Crisis? Geographical Perspectives. 2nd ed. R. J. Johnston & P. J. Taylor. (Illus.). 320p. 1989. pap. text ed. 25.95 (0-631-16271-2) Blackwell Pubs.

*World in Crisis: Politics of Survival at the End of the Twentieth Century. Medicins Sans Frontieres Staff. 224p. 1996. pap. 15.95 (0-415-15378-6) Routledge.

World in Danger - Too Many People! Jane W. Watson. (Illus.). 80p. (Orig.). (J). (gr. 4-6). 1994. pap. 8.95 (1-56474-099-4) Fithian Pr.

World in Depression, 1929-1939. enl. rev. ed. Charles P. Kindleberger. (History of the World Economy in the Twentieth Century Ser.: Vol. 4). 1986. 55.00 (0-520-05591-8); pap. 15.00 (0-520-05592-6) U CA Pr.

World in Disorder: 1994-1995: An Anthropological & Interdisplinary Approach to Global Issues. Sheldon Smith. 462p. (Orig.). (C). 1995. pap. text ed. 39.50 (0-8191-9720-3); lib. bdg. 64.00 (0-8191-9719-X) U Pr of Amer.

World in Falseface. George J. Nathan. LC 75-120099. 326p. 1975. 29.50 (0-8386-7963-3) Fairleigh Dickinson.

*World in Flames. Kitchen. 1990. text ed. write for info. (0-582-03408-6, Pub. by Longman UK) Longman.

World in Flames: A Short History of the Second World War in Europe & Asia, 1939-1945. Martin Kitchen. 377p. (Orig.). (C). 1990. pap. text ed. 27.50 (0-582-03407-8, 78605) Longman.

World in Flames: Concise History of World War II. Martha B. Hoyle. 1992. 7.98 (0-8317-9604-9) Smithmark.

*World in Fragments: Writings on Politics, Society, Psychoanalysis, & the Imagination. Cornelius Castoriadis. Ed. & Tr. by David A. Curtis from FRE. LC 96-37014. (Deridian Ser.). 1997. write for info. (0-8047-2762-7); pap. write for info. (0-8047-2763-5) Stanford U Pr.

World in Grandfather's Hands. Craig K. Strete. LC 94-26799. (J). (gr. 3-7). 1995. 13.95 (0-395-72102-4, Clarion Bks) HM.

World in Miniature: Container Gardens & Dwellings in Far Eastern Religious Thought. Rolf A. Stein. Tr. by Phyllis Brooks from FRE. (Illus.). 424p. 1990. 47.50 (0-8047-1674-9) Stanford U Pr.

World in My Head: A Collection of Columns from the San Antonio Express-News. Claude Stanush. LC 84-16367. 1984. pap. 10.00 (0-914476-21-1) Thorp Springs.

*World in One Day. Russell Ash. LC 97-16465. 1997. write for info. (0-7894-2028-7) DK Pub Inc.

World in Our Hands: In Honor of the 50th Anniversary of the United Nations. Young People of the World Staff. LC 95-16236. 96p. (YA). (gr. 6 up). 1995. pap. 15.95 (1-883672-31-7) Tricycle Pr.

World in Our Hearts: The Life Story of YWAM Missionaries Alan & Fay Williams. Fay Williams & Meredith P. Hofmann. LC 95-90115. (Illus.). 260p. (Orig.). 1995. pap. 7.95 (0-9645458-0-2) Williams HI.

World in Peril: The Story Behind the Discovery of Imminent Global Change. 2nd rev. ed. Ken White. LC 93-61798. (Illus.). 297p. 1994. 29.95 (1-883218-10-1) Vande Vere.

World in Perspective: A Directory of World Map Projections. Frank Canters & Hugo Decleir. LC 89-14811. 181p. 1989. text ed. 125.00 (0-471-92147-5) Wiley.

*World in Pieces. Bart Midwood. LC 97-23559. 1998. write for info. (1-57962-006-6) Permanent Pr.

World in Review: A Geographic Perspective. Chester E. Zimolzak. (Illus.). 128p. (Orig.). (C). 1992. Update. pap. write for info. (0-02-431745-4, Macmillan Coll) P-H.

World in the Balance: Behind the Scenes of World War II. Gerhard L. Weinberg. LC 81-51606. (Tauber Institute Ser.: No. 1). (Illus.). 185p. (C). 1981. pap. 13.95 (0-87451-217-4) U Pr of New Eng.

World in the Evening. Christopher Isherwood. (Michael di Capua Bks.). 312p. 1988. pap. 8.95 (0-374-52088-7) FS&G.

World in the Postwar Decade: 1945-1955. John H. Jackson. LC 76-124267. (Select Bibliographies Reprint Ser.). 1977. reprint ed. 20.95 (0-8369-5448-3) Ayer.

*World in the Time of Abraham Lincoln. Fiona MacDonald. LC 96-53372. (World in the Time of...Ser.). (J). 1997. pap. write for info. (0-382-39744-4, Dillon Silver Burdett) Silver Burdett Pr.

*World in the Time of Abraham Lincoln. Fiona MacDonald. LC 96-53372. (World in the Time of...Ser.). (J). 1997. lib. bdg. write for info. (0-382-39745-2) Silver Burdett Pr.

*World in the Time of Alexander the Great. Fiona McDonald. LC 96-53371. (World in the Time of...Ser.). (J). 1997. pap. write for info. (0-382-39742-8, Dillon Silver Burdett) Silver Burdett Pr.

*World in the Time of Alexander the Great. Fiona McDonald. LC 96-53371. (World in the Time of...Ser.). (J). 1997. lib. bdg. write for info. (0-382-39743-6, Dillon Silver Burdett) Silver Burdett Pr.

*World in the Time of Leonardo da Vinci. Fiona MacDonald. LC 97-20216. (World in the Time of...Ser.). 1998. pap. write for info. (0-382-39740-1, Dillon Silver Burdett); lib. bdg. write for info. (0-382-39741-X, Dillon Silver Burdett) Silver Burdett Pr.

*World in the Time of Marco Polo. Fiona Macdonald. (World in the Time of...Ser.). (Illus.). 48p. (J). (gr. 4-8). 1997. pap. 9.95 (0-382-39748-7, Dillon Silver Burdett); lib. bdg. 16.95 (0-382-39749-5, Dillon Silver Burdett) Silver Burdett Pr.

*World in the Time of Marie Antoinette. Fiona MacDonald. LC 97-22085. (World in the Time of...Ser.). 1998. pap. write for info. (0-382-39734-7, Dillon Silver Burdett) Silver Burdett Pr.

*World in the Time of Marie Antoinette. Fiona Macdonald. (World in the Time of...Ser.). 1998. lib. bdg. write for info. (0-382-39735-5, Dillon Silver Burdett) Silver Burdett Pr.

*World in the Time of Tutankhamun. Fiona Macdonald. (World in the Time of...Ser.). (Illus.). 48p. (J). (gr. 4-8). 1997. pap. 9.95 (0-382-39746-0, Dillon Silver Burdett); lib. bdg. 16.95 (0-382-39747-9, Dillon Silver Burdett) Silver Burdett Pr.

World in the Twentieth Century. Louis L. Snyder. LC 79-10024. (Anvil Ser.). 192p. 1979. reprint ed. pap. 11.50 (0-88275-909-4) Krieger.

World in the Twentieth Century: The Age of Global War & Revolution. 3rd ed. Daniel R. Brower. LC 95-24118. 366p. 1995. pap. text ed. 32.80 (0-13-190844-8) P-H.

*World in the Year 1000. Kunhardt. Date not set. write for info. (0-688-07935-0) Morrow.

World in Their Minds: Information Processing, Cognition, & Perception in Foreign Policy Decisionmaking. Yaacov Y. Vertzberger. 460p. (C). 1993. pap. 18.95 (0-8047-2245-5) Stanford U Pr.

World in Their Minds: Information Processing, Cognition, & Perception in Foreign Policy Decisionmaking. Yaacov Y. Vertzberger. LC 89-30921. 460p. 1990. 57.50 (0-8047-1688-9) Stanford U Pr.

*World in Transition. Rob Long. Date not set. write for info. (0-688-09437-6) Morrow.

*World in Transition: The Research Challenge, Annual Report 1996. Ed. by German Advisory Council on Global Change. LC 97-20227. (World in Transition Ser.). (Illus.). xx, 194p. 1997. 76.00 (3-540-61832-5) Spr-Verlag.

W

World in Transition: Ways Towards Global Environmental Solutions - Annual Report 1995. German Advisory Council on Global Change. 256p. 1996. 74.95 (*3-540-61016-2*) Spr-Verlag.

World in Tune: Prayers, Poetry, & Prose Selections. Comment by Elizabeth G. Vining. LC 54-9007. 1993. pap. 10.00 (*0-87574-918-6*) Pendle Hill.

World in Turmoil: An Integrated Chronology of the Holocaust & World War II. Hershel Edelheit & Abraham J. Edelheit. LC 91-22265. (Bibliographies & Indexes in World History Ser.: No. 22). 464p. 1991. text ed. 85.00 (*0-313-28218-8*, EDC, Greenwood Pr) Greenwood.

World in 2020: Power, Culture & Prosperity. Hamish McRae. LC 94-24545. 320p. 24.95 (*0-87584-604-1*) Harvard Busn.

World in 2020: Power, Culture & Prosperity. Hamish McRae. 1995. text ed. 24.95 (*0-07-103616-4*) McGraw.

***World in 2020: Power, Culture & Prosperity.** Hamish McRae. 1996. pap. text ed. 14.95 (*0-07-103852-3*) McGraw.

World in Winter. John Christopher. (Alpha Bks.). (Orig.). 1988. pap. text ed. 4.95 (*0-19-424238-2*) OUP.

World in Your Backyard: And Other Stories of Insects & Spiders. (Illus.). 63p. (J). (gr. 3-5). 1989. 10.95 (*0-88309-132-1*) Zaner-Bloser.

World in Your Kitchen. Troth Wells. 176p. 1993. pap. 16.95 (*0-89594-577-0*) Crossing Pr.

World in 1492. Jean Fritz et al. (Illus.). 160p. (J). (gr. 6-9). 1992. 19.95 (*0-8050-1674-0*, Bks Young Read) H Holt & Co.

World in 2020: Power, Culture & Prosperity. Hamish McRae. 320p. 1996. pap. 14.95 (*0-87584-738-2*) Harvard Busn.

World Index of Economic Forecasts. Ed. by George Cyriax. LC 78-56982. (Praeger Special Studies). 395p. 1978. text ed. 295.00 (*0-275-90288-9*, C0288, Praeger Pubs) Greenwood.

World Index of Economic Forecasts. 4th ed. Ed. by Robert Fildes. 672p. (C). 1995. text ed. 199.95 (*0-566-07488-5*, Pub. by Gower UK) Ashgate Pub Co.

World Index of Resources & Population. David Hargreaves et al. LC 93-38638. 432p. 1993. text ed. 149.95 (*1-85521-503-9*, Pub. by Dartmth Pub UK) Ashgate Pub Co.

World Indoor Air Quality Monitoring & Building Control System Markets: Opportunities for Non-Traditional Suppliers. Market Intelligence Staff. 326p. 1994. 1,895.00 (*0-7889-0034-X*) Frost & Sullivan.

World Industrial - Broadcast Solid State Camera & System Markets: Picture This...Revenues Double. Market Intelligence Staff. 322p. 1993. 1,695.00 (*1-56753-438-4*) Frost & Sullivan.

World Industrial & Scientific Laser Systems Markets: Rebounding Global Economy Eases Price Wars. Market Intelligence Staff. 538p. 1993. 1,695.00 (*1-56753-446-5*) Frost & Sullivan.

World Industrial Robot Statistics: 1994. 200p. 1994. 50.00 (*92-1-100686-4*) UN.

***World Industrial Robots 1996: Statistics 1983-1996 & Forecasts to 1999.** United Nations Economic Commission for Europe. 240p. 1996. pap. 120.00 (*92-1-100726-7*, TS191) UN.

World Inequality. Ed. & Tr. by Immanuel Wallerstein from FRE. Tr. by Ferry De Kerckhove from FRE. 170p. 1978. 16.95 (*0-919618-66-9*, Pub. by Black Rose Bks CN); pap. 7.95 (*0-919618-65-0*, Pub. by Black Rose Bks CN) Consort Bk Sales.

World Inflation & the Developing Countries. William R. Cline et al. LC 80-25426. 266p. 1981. 34.95 (*0-8157-1468-8*); pap. 14.95 (*0-8157-1467-X*) Brookings.

***World Information Report: Pt. 1: Information Services Worldwide; Pt. 2: Infrastructures for Information, Pts. 1 & 2.** UNESCO Staff. 450p. 1997. 70.00 (*92-3-103341-7*, U0344, Pub. by UNESCO-Bangkok TH) Bernan Associates.

World Information Technology Manual, 2 vols. Ed. by A. E. Cawkell. 1010p. 1991. Set. 165.00 (*0-685-50930-3*, North Holland) Elsevier.

World Information Technology Manual, 2 vols. A. E. Cawkell. 1991. Set. 258.75 (*0-444-89314-8*) Elsevier.

World Information Technology Manual, 2 vols., Vol. 1, Computers, Telecommunications & Info. Ed. by A. E. Cawkell. 1010p. 1991. Vol. 1: Computers, Telecommunications & Information. 138.25 (*0-444-87488-7*, North Holland) Elsevier.

World Information Technology Manual, 2 vols., Vol. 2: Systems & Services. Ed. by A. E. Cawkell. 1010p. 1991. 138.25 (*0-444-89313-X*, North Holland) Elsevier.

World Insurance Yearbook 1982. Ed. by Financial Times Staff. 500p. 1982. 90.00 (*0-582-90312-2*) Longman.

***World Intellectual Property Guidebooks.** D. S. Chisum & W. R. Cornish. 600p. 90.00 (*0-8205-1899-9*) Juris Pubng.

World Intellectual Property Guidebooks: Canada. D. S. Chisum & W. R. Cornish. 500p. 90.00 (*0-8205-1888-3*) Juris Pubng.

World Intellectual Property Guidebooks: United States. D. S. Chisum & W. R. Cornish. 650p. 90.00 (*0-8205-1886-7*) Juris Pubng.

World Intelligent Materials Handling Markets: Installation of Modular Designs & Integrated Systems on the Rise. Market Intelligence Staff. 576p. 1993. 1,695.00 (*1-56753-459-7*) Frost & Sullivan.

World Interactive Television & Video Transmission Overview. 193p. 1994. write for info. (*0-9626749-8-2*) Primary Research.

***World Internet Address Book: Hollywood Edition.** Illus. by John Findley. 115p. (Orig.). 1996. pap. 6.95 (*1-889778-05-2*) Graphic Visions.

***World Internet Address Book: Home Edition.** Photos by Mark Weiss. (Illus.). 115p. (Orig.). 1996. pap. 6.95 (*1-889778-01-X*) Graphic Visions.

***World Internet Address Book: Internet Address Book.** Photos by Hugh Kretschmer. (Illus.). 115p. (Orig.). 1996. pap. 6.95 (*1-889778-00-1*) Graphic Visions.

***World Internet Address Book: Kids Edition.** Illus. by Giovannia. 115p. (Orig.). 1996. pap. 6.95 (*1-889778-02-8*) Graphic Visions.

***World Internet Address Book: Music Edition.** Photos by Hugh Kretschmer. (Illus.). 115p. (Orig.). 1996. pap. 6.95 (*1-889778-03-6*) Graphic Visions.

***World Internet Address Book: Silicon Valley.** Photos by Everard Williams. (Illus.). 115p. (Orig.). 1996. pap. 6.95 (*1-889778-08-7*) Graphic Visions.

***World Internet Address Book: Sports Edition.** Photos by Masitiko Kono. (Illus.). 115p. (Orig.). 1996. pap. 6.95 (*1-889778-04-4*) Graphic Visions.

***World Internet Address Book: Wall Street Edition.** Photos by Mark Weiss. (Illus.). 115p. (Orig.). 1996. pap. 6.95 (*1-889778-06-0*) Graphic Visions.

***World Internet Address Book: Washington Edition.** Photos by Teisuke Shinoda. (Illus.). 115p. (Orig.). 1996. pap. 6.95 (*1-889778-07-9*) Graphic Visions.

World Inventory of Avian Anatomical Specimens, 1982: Geographic Analysis. Scott Wood & Marion A. Jenkinson. 290p. 1984. ring bd. 25.00 (*0-943610-42-7*) Am Ornithologists.

World Inventory Of Avian Skeletal Specimens, 1982. D. Scott Wood et al. 224p. 1982. ring bd. 25.00 (*0-943610-36-2*) Am Ornithologists.

World Inventory of Avian Spirit Specimens, 1982. D. Scott Wood et al. 181p. 1982. ring bd. 25.00 (*0-943610-37-0*) Am Ornithologists.

World Inventory of Plutonium & Highly Enriched Uranium, 1992. David Albright et al. LC 92-31562. 200p. 1993. 42.00 (*0-19-829153-1*) OUP.

World Investment Directory. 478p. 1994. 65.00 (*92-1-104431-6*, E.94.II.A.10) UN.

World Investment Directory: Asia & the Pacific, Vol. I. 356p. 1992. 65.00 (*92-1-104389-1*, E.92.II.A.11) UN.

World Investment Directory: Central & Eastern Europe. 432p. 1993. 65.00 (*92-1-104402-2*, E.93.II.A.9) UN.

World Investment Directory: Developed Countries. 516p. 1992. 75.00 (*92-1-104411-1*, E.93.II.A.9) UN.

World Investment Report: 1991-1994, Set. 1994. 100.00 (*92-1-104429-4*, E.94.II.A.8) UN.

World Investment Report 1991: The Triad in Foreign Direct Investment. 108p. 1991. 25.00 (*92-1-104370-0*, 91.II.A.12) UN.

World Investment Report 1992: The Triad in Foreign Direct Investment. 108p. 1991. 25.00 (*92-1-104417-0*, E.91.II.A.12) UN.

World Investment Report 1992: Transnational Corporations as Engines of Growth. United Nations Staff. 358p. 1992. 45.00 (*92-1-104396-4*) UN.

World Investment Report 1994: Transnational Corporations, Employment & the Work Place. 446p. 1994. 45.00 (*92-1-104435-9*, E.94.II.A.14) UN.

***World Investment Report 1996: Investment Trade, & International Policy Arrangements.** United Nations Conference on Trade & Development Staff. 332p. 1996. pap. 45.00 (*92-1-104468-5*, HG4538) UN.

World Is a Prayerful Place. Dianne Bergant. 132p. 1987. pap. 8.95 (*0-8146-5583-1*) Liturgical Pr.

World Is a Rainbow. (Songs for Kids Ser.). (Illus.). 80p. (Orig.). (J). 1994. pap. 10.95 (*0-7935-2934-4*, 00815028) H Leonard.

World Is a Room, & Other Stories. Yehuda Amichai. 197p. 1984. 19.95 (*0-8276-0234-0*) JPS Phila.

World Is As You Dream It: Shamanic Teachings from the Amazon & Andes. John Perkins. 140p. (Orig.). 1994. pap. 10.95 (*0-89281-459-4*) Inner Tradit.

***World Is Blue & White.** Garland B. Johnson. 205p. (Orig.). 1997. mass mkt. 4.99 (*1-55197-860-1*, Pub. by Comnwlth Pub CN) Partners Pubs Grp.

World Is Burning: Murder in the Rain Forest. Alex Shoumatoff. 1991. pap. 9.95 (*0-380-71542-2*) Avon.

World Is for the Young: & Other Stories. Blanche M. Girouard. LC 70-167450. (Short Story Index Reprint Ser.). 1977. reprint ed. 20.95 (*0-8369-3976-X*) Ayer.

World Is Full of Babies! How All Sorts of Babies Grow & Develop. Mick Manning & Brita Granstrom. (Illus.). 32p. (J). 1996. 14.95 (*0-385-32258-5*) Doubleday.

World Is Full of Divorced Women. Jackie Collins. 416p. 1991. mass mkt. 6.99 (*0-446-35719-7*) Warner Bks.

World Is Full of Married Men. Jackie Collins. 1993. mass mkt. 5.99 (*0-671-73788-0*) PB.

***World is Full of Married Men.** Jackie Collins. 224p. mass mkt. 5.99 (*0-06-101254-8*, Harp PBks) HarpC.

World Is Getting to Be a Funner Place: How I Applied to CalArts under Four Aliases & Was Accepted or Denied. Burt Payne. LC 92-90633. (Illus.). 90p. (Orig.). 1995. 40.00 (*0-9633321-0-4*) Smart Art Pr.

World Is Growing Smaller. Judy Stoehr. (Illus.). (Orig.). (J). 1995. teacher ed., pap. text ed. write for info. (*0-89724-965-8*, BMR06013P); teacher ed., pap. text ed. write for info. (*0-89724-966-6*, BMR06013) Warner Brothers.

World Is Growing Smaller: Singer's Pack. Judy Stoehr. Ed. by Debbie Cavalier. (Illus.). (J). 1995. pap. text ed. 12.95 (*1-57623-378-2*, BMR06013SP); audio 34.95 (*1-57623-380-4*, BMR06013AT); audio compact disk 34.95 (*1-57623-379-0*, BMR06013CD) Warner Brothers.

World Is Ill Divided: Women's Work in Scotland in the 19th & Early 20th Centuries. Ed. by Eleanor Gordon & Esther Breitenbach. 192p. 1991. pap. text ed. 29.00 (*0-7486-0212-7*, Pub. by Edinburgh U Pr UK) Col U Pr.

World Is Made of Glass. Morris West. 320p. 1984. mass mkt. 3.95 (*0-380-68015-7*) Avon.

World Is My Home. limited ed. James A. Michener. 1992. 125.00 (*0-679-41118-6*) McKay.

***World Is New.** Joel S. Goldsmith. 1997. reprint ed. 17.95 (*1-889051-08-X*, 1 Lvl) Acrpls Bks CO.

***World Is Not Enough.** Zoe Oldenbourg. LC 97-17488. 512p. 1998. pap. 13.95 (*0-7867-0489-6*) Carroll & Graf.

World Is Out There Waiting. Landry & Anna H. Fesmire. 256p. (C). 1994. pap. text ed. 49.00 (*0-13-474735-6*) P-H.

World Is Round. Iva Pekarkova. Tr. by David Powelstock. LC 94-653. (RUS.). 1994. 22.00 (*0-374-29287-6*) FS&G.

World Is Round. Gertrude Stein. LC 65-15900. (Illus.). 59p. (C). 1965. lib. bdg. 75.00 (*0-8383-0629-2*) M S G Haskell Hse.

World Is Round: Contemporary Panoramas. Marcia Clark. LC 87-31092. (Illus.). 64p. (Orig.). 1987. pap. 7.50 (*0-943651-03-4*) Hudson Riv.

World Is Round: Poems. Carol Edelstein. 1994. pap. 12.00 (*0-941895-09-2*) Amherst Wri Art.

World Is So Big & I'm So Small. William Kotzwinkle. (J). (ps). 1996. pap. text ed. 5.95 (*1-56924-793-5*) Marlowe & Co.

World Is Sound - Nada Brahma: Music & the Landscape of Consciousness. Joachim-Ernst Berendt. 240p. 1991. reprint ed. pap. 14.95 (*0-89281-318-0*, Destiny Bks) Inner Tradit.

World Is Split. N. K. Sethi. 8.00 (*0-89253-736-1*) Ind-US Inc.

***World is the Home of Love.** Harold Brodkey. LC 97-16459. 1997. 27.00 (*0-8050-5513-4*) H Holt & Co.

World Is Your Market. John Newlin. LC 93-33154. 1994. 24.95 (*1-55958-439-4*) Prima Pub.

World Is Yours - Enjoy Listening to International Radio. Samuel R. Alcorn. LC 84-82453. 64p. 1984. pap. 2.95 (*0-914542-14-1*) Gilfer.

World Is Yours, Enjoy Listen to International Radio. 2nd ed. Gilfer. 96p. 1988. pap. 5.95 (*0-914542-19-2*) Gilfer.

World Is Yours on Shortwave Radio. 3rd ed. Samuel L. Alcorn. 80p. (Orig.). 1991. pap. 9.95 (*0-685-49826-3*) Gilfer.

World Issues, 2 bks. Tony Reynolds et al. (Illus.). 336p. (YA). (gr. 5 up). 1990. Set. lib. bdg. 126.00 (*0-86592-095-8*); Set. lib. bdg. 94.50 (*0-685-36375-9*) Rourke Corp.

World Jewry & the State of Israel. Ed. by Moshe Davis. LC 77-72730. (Individual Publications). 1976. lib. bdg. 15.95 (*0-405-10305-0*) Ayer.

World Jones Made. Philip K. Dick. LC 92-50644. 1993. pap. 11.00 (*0-679-74219-0*, Vin) Random.

World Keys to Health & Long Life. Bernard Jensen. 1975. reprint ed. pap. 9.95 (*0-932615-04-X*) B Jensen.

World Labour Market: A History of Migration. Lydia Potts. Tr. by Terry Bond from GER. LC 89-25041. (Illus.). 304p. (C). 1990. pap. 17.50 (*0-86232-883-7*, Pub. by Zed Bks Ltd UK); text ed. 55.00 (*0-86232-882-9*, Pub. by Zed Bks Ltd UK) Humanities.

World Labour Report, Vol. 2. viii, 245p. 1985. 40.50 (*92-2-103848-3*) Intl Labour Office.

World Labour Report No. 3: Incomes from Work: Between Equity & Efficiency. vii, 169p. (Orig.). 1987. 36.00 (*92-2-105951-0*) Intl Labour Office.

World Labour Report, 1989: Employment & Labour Incomes - Government & Its Employees Statistical Appendix, Vol. 4. ix, 159p. (Orig.). 1989. pap. 27.00 (*92-2-106444-1*) Intl Labour Office.

World Labour Report 1995 No. 8: Controversies in Labour Statistics; Ageing Societies: Problems & Prospects for Older Workers; Privatization, Employment & Social Protection, Public Authorities & the Other Social Partners: Changing Relationships; Retraining & Returning to Work: an Issue That Concerns Us All; Select Bibliography; Statistical Annex. v, 121p. 1995. pap. 22.50 (*92-2-109447-2*) Intl Labour Office.

World Language. Frank Hill. (Pocket Pac Ser.). 1990. Incl. 10 phrasecards. 4.00 (*0-88699-053-X*) Travel Sci.

World Languages for Business Professionals: Language Survival Kit. Sam L. Slick et al. (Illus.). 212p. 1994. text ed. 70.00 (*0-9649928-0-9*) Command Spanish.

World Law School Directory, 1993. LC 93-13414. 344p. 1993. 97.50 (*0-89941-839-2*, 307640) W S Hein.

***World Leaders, 14 vols.** (Illus.). 11312p. (YA). (gr. 5 up). 1989. pap. 125.30 (*0-7910-3764-9*) Chelsea Hse.

World Leaders: Heads of Government in the Postwar Period. Jean Blondel. LC 79-63826. (Political Executives in Comparative Perspective: A Cross-National Empirical Study: No. 1). (Illus.). 291p. reprint ed. pap. 83.00 (*0-8357-8478-9*, 2034743) Bks Demand.

***World Leaders: Past & Present, 90 vols.** (Illus.). 11312p. (YA). (gr. 5 up). 1989. lib. bdg. 1,795.50 (*0-7910-2576-4*) Chelsea Hse.

World Leaders: People Who Shaped the World. Ed. by Rob Nagel & Anne Commire. LC 94-20544. 1994. Set. 62.00 (*0-8103-9768-4*, UXL) Gale.

World Leaders - Boris Yeltsin. Shlomo Lambroza. LC 92-46479. (Biographies Ser.). (J). 1993. 19.93 (*0-86625-482-X*); 14.95 (*0-685-66417-1*) Rourke Pubns.

World Leadership & International Development. John O'Manique & Michael Lerner. 138p. 1986. mass mkt. 8.00 (*0-86346-011-9*, Tycooly Pub) Weidner & Sons.

World Leadershp & Hegemony. Ed. by David P. Rapkin. (International Political Economy Yearbook Ser.: Vol. 5). 286p. 1990. lib. bdg. 45.00 (*1-55587-189-5*) Lynne Rienner.

World Leasing Yearbook 1996. Ed. by Adrian Hornbrook. 460p. 1996. 195.00 (*0-614-17424-4*, Pub. by Euromoney UK) Am Educ Systs.

World Leisure Participation: Free Time in the Global Village. Jiri Zuzanek. 288p. 1996. 70.00 (*0-85198-975-6*) CAB Intl.

World Librarianship: A Comparative Study. Krzys et al. (Books in Library & Information Science: Vol. 42). 264p. 1983. 99.75 (*0-8247-1731-7*) Dekker.

World Like a Knife. Ellen Akins. LC 91-15802. (Poetry & Fiction Ser.). 144p. 1991. pap. 11.95 (*0-8018-4289-1*); text ed. 30.00 (*0-8018-4288-3*) Johns Hopkins.

World Link. Linda C. Joseph. 143p. 1994. pap. text ed. 9.95 (*1-57074-148-4*) Greyden Pr.

World Link: An Internet Guide for Educators, Parents, & Students. Linda C. Joseph. 275p. (J). 1995. pap. text ed. 24.95 (*1-57074-244-8*) Greyden Pr.

World List of Aquatic Sciences & Fisheries Serial Titles. (Fisheries Technical Papers: No. 147, Suppl. 2). (Illus.). 159p. 1976. pap. 12.00 (*92-5-100341-6*, F880, Pub. by FAO IT) Bernan Associates.

World List of Phomopsis Names with Notes on Nomenclature, Morphology & Biology. F. A. Uecker. (Mycologia Memoirs Ser.: No. 13). 232p. 1988. lib. bdg. 72.00 (*3-443-76003-1*) Lubrecht & Cramer.

World List of Scientific Periodicals Published in the Years 1900-1960, 3 vols., 1. 4th ed. Ed. by Peter Brown & George Stratton. LC 64-9729. reprint ed. pap. 158.80 (*0-317-41919-6*, 2025752) Bks Demand.

World List of Scientific Periodicals Published in the Years 1900-1960, 3 vols., 2. 4th ed. Ed. by Peter Brown & George Stratton. LC 64-9729. reprint ed. pap. 180.00 (*0-317-41920-X*) Bks Demand.

World List of Scientific Periodicals Published in the Years 1900-1960, 3 vols., 3. 4th ed. Ed. by Peter Brown & George Stratton. LC 64-9729. reprint ed. pap. 180.00 (*0-317-41921-8*) Bks Demand.

***World List of Seed Sources.** 4th ed. E. Sgaravatti & J. Beaney. 628p. 1996. pap. 62.00 (*92-5-003782-1*, F37821, Pub. by FAO IT) Bernan Associates.

World List of Serials in Agricultural Biotechnology. Ed. by Robert D. Warmbrodt & Diana Airozo. 471p. (Orig.). (C). 1994. pap. text ed. 65.00 (*0-7881-1224-4*) DIANE Pub.

World List of Universities. 20th ed. Compiled by International Association of Universities Staff. 800p. 1995. 160.00 (*1-56159-109-2*, Stockton Pr) Groves Dictionaries.

World Lit Only by Fire: The Medieval Mind & the Renaissance - Portrait of an Age. William Manchester. 1992. 25.95 (*0-316-54531-7*) Little.

World Lit Only by Fire: The Medieval Mind & the Renaissance - Portrait of an Age. William Manchester. 1993. pap. 14.95 (*0-316-54556-2*) Little.

World Literary Anecdotes. Robert Hendrickson. 320p. 1990. 27.95 (*0-8160-2248-8*) Facts on File.

***World Literary Anecdotes.** Robert Hendrickson. LC 89-34089. 288p. 1990. reprint ed. pap. 82.10 (*0-608-02859-2*, 2063923) Bks Demand.

World Literary Criticism, Vol. 1. James P. Draper. 1992. write for info. (*0-8103-8362-4*) Gale.

World Literary Criticism, Vol. 2. James P. Draper. 1992. write for info. (*0-8103-8363-2*) Gale.

World Literary Criticism, Vol. 3. James P. Draper. 1992. write for info. (*0-8103-8364-0*) Gale.

World Literary Criticism, Vol. 4. James P. Draper. 1992. write for info. (*0-8103-8365-9*) Gale.

World Literary Criticism, Vol. 5. James P. Draper. 1992. write for info. (*0-8103-8366-7*) Gale.

World Literary Criticism, Vol. 6. James P. Draper. 1992. write for info. (*0-8103-8367-5*) Gale.

World Literature. Ed. by Arthur E. Christy & Henry W. Wells. LC 77-149100. (Granger Index Reprint Ser.). 1977. 63.95 (*0-8369-6225-7*) Ayer.

***World Literature.** HR&W School Division Staff. 1993. text ed. 62.50 (*0-03-053608-1*) HR&W Schl Div.

***World Literature.** Plaks. 1993. text ed. 100.25 (*0-03-075204-3*) HR&W Schl Div.

World Literature. Donna Rosenberg. 896p. 1995. pap. 30.60 (*0-8442-5482-7*, Natl Textbk) NTC Pub Grp.

World Literature: A Multicultural Perspective. Robert Turley. 96p. (C). 1995. student ed., per., pap. text ed. 13.12 (*0-8403-8145-X*) Kendall-Hunt.

World Literature: Early Origins to 1800. 2nd ed. Arthur Bell et al. (College Review Ser.). 450p. (C). 1994. pap. 11.95 (*0-8120-1811-7*) Barron.

World Literature: 1800-Present. 2nd ed. Arthur Bell et al. (College Review Ser.). 450p. (C). 1994. pap. 11.95 (*0-8120-1812-5*) Barron.

World Literature Activities Kit: Ready-to-Use Worksheets. Sharon Neumayr. 288p. 1994. pap. 27.95 (*0-87628-948-0*) Ctr Appl Res.

World Literature & Thought Vol. 1: The Ancient Worlds. Donald S. Gochberg et al. 688p. (C). 1997. pap. text ed. write for info. (*0-15-500919-2*) HB Coll Pubs.

***World Literature Criticism, 6 vols.** 2nd ed. 1998. 360.00 (*0-7876-0204-3*, 00108771, Gale Res Intl) Gale.

World Literature Criticism, 1500 to the Present: A Selection of Major Authors from Gale's Literary Criticism, 6 vols. Ed. by James P. Draper. 1992. 360.00 (*0-8103-8361-6*, 101204) Gale.

World Literature On: Prazosin: An Evaluation of Its Clinical Efficacy & Safety in the Treatment of Benign Prostatic Hypertrophy. Ed. by Elizabeth Milroy. (Journal: Urologia Internationalis: Vol. 45, Suppl. 1, 1990). (Illus.). iv, 64p. 1990. pap. 29.75 (*3-8055-5181-9*) S Karger.

***World Literature Readings: World History.** Spielvogel. (Social Studies Ser.). 1998. pap. 13.95 (*0-314-14094-8*) S-W Pub.

World Literature since 1960 on Women & Development: An Index to Articles, Books & Research Papers in the Joint Bank-Fund Library, Washington, D.C. 250p. 1987. 200.00 (*0-8161-0464-6*) G K Hall.

***World Literatures.** Joseph Remenyi & Various. 315p. Date not set. write for info. (*0-8369-1010-9*) Ayer.

W

An Asterisk (*) at the beginning of an entry indicates that the title is appearing in BIP for the first time.

World Lost. Wendell Berry. LC 96-18624. 160p. 1996. 20.00 (*1-887178-22-8*) Counterpt DC.

***World Lost.** Wendell Berry. 1997. pap. 12.50 (*1-887178-54-6*) Counterpt DC.

World Lottery Almanac, 1993. Terri LaFleur & Bruce LaFleur. 394p. 1993. pap. 139.00 (*1-883567-61-0*) TLF Pubns.

***World Machine Condition Monitoring Equipment Markets: Growing Importance of Predictive Maintenance among Commercial Application Areas.** Frost & Sullivan Staff. 512p. Date not set. write for info. (*0-7889-0517-1*, 5442) Frost & Sullivan.

World Machine Tool Cutting Tool Markets: Expansion Driven by Innovation: New Materials, New Coatings, New Geometries. Market Intelligence Staff. 283p. 1992. 1,495.00 (*1-56753-384-1*) Frost & Sullivan.

World Machine Vision System, Component & Software Markets: Innovative, Affordable & Reliable Solutions Lead Way to Billion Dollar Industry. Market Intelligence Staff. 389p. (Orig.). 1992. 1,495.00 (*1-56753-376-0*) Frost & Sullivan.

World Made by Men: Cognition & Society, 400-1200. Charles M. Radding. LC 85-1111. xi, 286p. 1985. text ed. 39.95 (*0-8078-1664-7*) U of NC Pr.

World Made by Men: Cognition & Society, 400-1200. Charles M. Radding. LC 85-1111. (Illus.). 298p. 1985. reprint ed. pap. 85.00 (*0-7837-9036-8*, 2049787) Bks Demand.

World Made New: Frederick Soddy, Science, Politics, & Environment. Linda Merricks. (Illus.). 240p. (C). 1996. 105.00 (*0-19-855934-8*) OUP.

World Made of Fire. Mark Childress. 272p. 1985. mass mkt. 5.99 (*0-345-32466-8*) Ballantine.

***World Made of Fire.** Mark Childress. 1997. pap. 11.00 (*0-345-41904-9*) Ballantine.

***World Magnetic Resonance Imaging Markets.** Frost & Sullivan Staff. 245p. 1996. write for info. (*0-7889-0554-6*, 5494) Frost & Sullivan.

World-making: The Literary Truth-Claim & the Interpretation of Texts. Mario J. Valdes. 192p. 1991. 40.00 (*0-8020-2791-1*); pap. 16.95 (*0-8020-6847-2*) U of Toronto Pr.

World Manual for Group & Incentive Travel. Ed. by Catherine Brashich. 1000p. 1990. 149.00 (*0-9627465-0-9*) Networld.

***World Map.** 1996. 8.95 (*2-06-701901-5*, 901) Michelin.

***World Map Project: A Handbook.** Ed. by Mary Koller & Margaret Legowoski. (Illus.). 74p. (Orig.). (C). 1996. pap. text ed. 25.00 (*0-7881-2688-1*) DIANE Pub.

***World Map Project Handbook.** 1997. lib. bdg. 252.99 (*0-8490-6147-4*) Gordon Pr.

World Mapping Today. R. B. Parry & C. R. Perkins. (Illus.). 608p. 1987. 240.00 (*0-408-02850-5*) Buttrwrth-Heinemann.

***World Mapping Today.** 2nd ed. Ed. by Parry & Perkins. 1997. 250.00 (*1-85739-035-0*) Bowker-Saur.

World Maps: A Dialect Atlas of England. Clive Upton et al. 256p. 1988. text ed. 59.50 (*0-7099-4410-1*, Pub. by Croom Helm UK) Routledge Chapman & Hall.

World Marina '91. LC 91-25770. 736p. 1991. pap. text ed. 68.00 (*0-87262-842-6*) Am Soc Civil Eng.

***World Market for Crystal Oscillators & Quartz Crystals: 1996-2000 Analysis & Forecasts.** Frank Kuzler. 400p. 1996. pap. text ed. 6,900.00 (*1-878218-71-9*) World Info Tech.

World Market for Dairy Products, 1991. GATT Staff. 92p. 1992. pap. 25.00 (*92-870-1065-X*, GATT/1991-3, Pub. by Wrld Trade SZ) Bernan Associates.

World Market for Dairy Products, 1992. GATT Staff. 71p. 1992. pap. 25.00 (*92-870-1079-X*, GATT/1992-3, Pub. by Wrld Trade SZ) Bernan Associates.

World Market for Dairy Products, 1993. GATT Staff. 108p. 1993. pap. 25.00 (*92-870-1095-1*, GATT/1993-3, Pub. by Wrld Trade SZ) Bernan Associates.

***World Market for Dairy Products 1994.** GATT Staff. (World Market for Dairy Products Ser.). 108p. 1994. pap. 14.00 (*92-870-1131-1*, GATT/1994-14A, Pub. by Wrld Trade SZ) Bernan Associates.

World Market for Data Converters: Medical & Business Applications Spur High Performance Monolithic Growth. 201p. 1992. 1,695.00 (*1-56753-017-6*) Frost & Sullivan.

World Market for Electronic Ceramics: Developments Enable Next Generation Products. Market Intelligence Staff. 345p. (Orig.). 1992. 1,695.00 (*1-56753-066-4*) Frost & Sullivan.

World Market for High Technology Industrial Ceramics. Ed. by Peter Allen. 351p. 1985. pap. 295.00 (*0-931634-29-6*) FIND-SVP.

***World Market for Tropical Horticultural Products.** 257p. 1988. 35.00 (*92-5-102783-8*, Pub. by FAO IT) Bernan Associates.

World Market for Voice & Data Premises: Cabling & Apparatus: 1994-2000. Amadee Bender et al. 250p. 1995. pap. text ed. 6,900.00 (*1-878218-62-X*) World Info Tech.

***World Market Share Reporter.** 3rd ed. 1997. 305.00 (*0-7876-0063-6*, 00108712, Gale Res Intl) Gale.

World Market Share Reporter, Vol. 2. 2nd ed. Arsen Darnay. 1996. 305.00 (*0-7876-0062-8*) Gale.

World Market Share Reporter 1: A Compilation of Reported World Market Share Data & Rankings on Companies Products & Services. Ed. by Marlita A. Reddy & Robert S. Lazich. 620p. 1994. 295.00 (*0-8103-9641-6*) Gale.

World Marketing. Virgil D. Collins. Ed. by Henry Assael. LC 78-271. (Century of Marketing Ser.). 1979. reprint ed. lib. bdg. 29.95 (*0-405-11186-X*) Ayer.

World Marketing Congress: Proceedings of the Fifth Bi-Annual International Conference of the Academy of Marketing Science, Copenhagen, Denmark, August 11-14, 1991. fac. ed. Academy of Marketing Science Staff. Ed. by Kristina D. Frankenberger et al. LC 89-110901. (International Conference Ser.: No. 5). 355p. 1991. reprint ed. pap. 101.20 (*0-7837-8122-9*, 2047929) Bks Demand.

World Marketing Congress: Proceedings of the Fourth Bi-Annual International Conference of the Academy of Marketing Science, Singapore, Republic of Singapore, July 16-19, 1989. Academy of Marketing Science Staff. Ed. by William Lazer et al. LC 89-110901. (International Conference Ser.: No. 4). 435p. 1989. reprint ed. pap. 124.00 (*0-7837-8124-5*, 2047931) Bks Demand.

World Marketing Congress Vol. 3-1987: Proceedings of the Third Bi-Annual International Conference of the Academy of Marketing Science, Barcelona, Spain, August 23-26, 1987. fac. ed. Academy of Marketing Science Staff. Ed. by Kenneth D. Bahn & M. Joseph Sirgy. LC 89-110901. (International Conference Ser.: No. 3). 275p. 1987. reprint ed. pap. 78.40 (*0-7837-8123-7*, 2047930) Bks Demand.

World Marketing Congress Vol. 6-1993: Proceedings of the Sixth Bi-Annual International Conference of the Academy of Marketing Science, Istanbul, Turkey, July 15-19, 1993. fac. ed. Academy of Marketing Science Staff. Ed. by M. Joseph Sirgy et al. LC 89-110901. 716p. 1993. reprint ed. pap. 180.00 (*0-7837-8121-0*, 2047928) Bks Demand.

***World Marketing Congress Vol. 7, Pt. 2: Proceedings of the Seventh Bi-Annual World Marketing Congress, Melbourne, Australia, July 6-10, 1995.** Academy of Marketing Science Staff. Ed. by Peter Chandler et al. LC 89-110901. 487p. pap. write for info. (*0-608-05109-8*, 2065699) Bks Demand.

***World Marketing Congress Vol. 7, Pt. 3: Proceedings of the Seventh Bi-Annual World Marketing Congress, Melbourne, Australia, July 6-10, 1995.** Academy of Marketing Science Staff. Ed. by Peter Chandler et al. LC 89-110901. 566p. pap. write for info. (*0-608-05110-1*, 2065669) Bks Demand.

World Markets & International Practice. AIA Press Staff. 1994. pap. 40.00 (*1-879304-45-7*) AIA DC.

***World Markets for Cotton: Forecasts to 2000.** D. Morris & A. Stogdon. 1995. pap. 531.00 (*0-85058-860-X*, Pub. by Textile Inst UK) St Mut.

World Markets for Single-Use Medical Products: Industry Responds Strongly to Infection Control, AIDS Concerns. 264p. 1992. 1,495.00 (*1-56753-018-4*) Frost & Sullivan.

***World Markets for Spun Yarns: Forecasts to 2000.** D. Morris. 1994. pap. 531.00 (*0-614-20917-X*, Pub. by Textile Inst UK) St Mut.

***World Markets for Textured Yarns: Forecasts to 2000.** D. Morris & D. Tunney. 1995. pap. 531.00 (*0-85058-859-6*, Pub. by Textile Inst UK) St Mut.

World Markets for Tire & Rubber. 350p. 1995. 1,995.00 (*0-945235-39-9*) Lead Edge Reports.

World Media Handbook. 504p. 1994. 65.00 (*92-1-100488-8*, E.92.1.21) UN.

World Media Handbook: Selected Country Profiles, 1995 Edition. 50th ed. 348p. 1995. 65.00 (*92-1-100574-4*, P95) UN.

World Media Handbook: 1990 Edition. 299p. 38.00 (*92-1-100426-8*, E.DPI/1021) UN.

***World Medical Diagnostic Ultrasound Imaging Equipment.** Frost & Sullivan Staff. 340p. 1996. write for info. (*0-7889-0594-5*, 5493) Frost & Sullivan.

World Medical Diagnostic Ultrasound Imaging Equipment Markets at the Forefront of Diagnostic. Market Intelligence Staff. 1995. 2,495.00 (*0-7889-0247-4*) Frost & Sullivan.

***World Medical Image Management.** Frost & Sullivan. 356p. 1997. write for info. (*0-7889-0623-2*, 5355) Frost & Sullivan.

World Medical Image Management Markets: Minipacs & Facility-to-Facility Teleradiology Offer Cost Effective Solutions. Market Intelligence Staff. 310p. 1994. 2,495.00 (*0-7889-0082-X*) Frost & Sullivan.

World Medical Imaging & Therapeutic Immunoconjugate Markets: Competitors Refocusing R&D & Marketing Strategies. Market Intelligence Staff. 351p. 1994. 2,695.00 (*1-56753-954-8*) Frost & Sullivan.

World Medical Laser Markets: Manufacturers Focus on Alternate Cites & New Applications. Market Intelligence Staff. 332p. 1993. 1,995.00 (*1-56753-440-6*) Frost & Sullivan.

World Medical Resonance Imaging Markets: Dedicated Imaging Coils Lead Shift to Lower Field Systems. Market Intelligence Staff. 250p. (Orig.). 1994. 2,495.00 (*0-685-71178-1*) Frost & Sullivan.

World Medicine: East West Guide to Healing Your Body. EastWest Natural Health Editors & Tom Monte. LC 92-43052. 352p. 1993. pap. 15.95 (*0-87477-733-X*, Tarcher Putnam) Putnam Pub Group.

World Meetings Vol. 19: Medicine 1996, 4. Macmillan Publishing Co. Staff. 1995. pap. 175.00 (*0-02-864646-0*) Macmillan.

World Meetings Vol. 19 No. 1: Medicine. Macmillan Publishing Co. Staff. 1996. pap. 43.75 (*0-02-864647-9*) Macmillan.

World Meetings Vol. 19 No. 2: Medicine. Macmillan Publishing Co. Staff. 1996. pap. 43.75 (*0-02-864648-7*) Macmillan.

World Meetings Vol. 19 No. 3: Medicine. Macmillan Publishing Co. Staff. 1996. pap. 43.75 (*0-02-864649-5*) Macmillan.

World Meetings Vol. 19 No. 4: Medicine. Macmillan Publishing Co. Staff. 1996. pap. 43.75 (*0-02-864650-9*) Macmillan.

World Meetings Vol. 26: Social & Behavorial Sciences Human Service & Management 1996, 4. Macmillan Publishing Co. Staff. 1995. 180.00 (*0-02-864641-X*) Macmillan.

World Meetings Vol. 26 No. 1: Social & Behavioral Sciences Human Services & Management. Macmillan Publishing Co. Staff. 1996. pap. 45.00 (*0-02-864642-8*) Macmillan.

World Meetings Vol. 26, No. 2: Social & Behavioral Sciences, Human Services & Management. Macmillan Publishing Co. Staff. 1996. pap. 45.00 (*0-02-864643-6*) Macmillan.

World Meetings Vol. 26 No. 4: Social & Behavorial Sciences, Human Service & Mgmt. Macmillan Publishing Co. Staff. 1996. pap. 45.00 (*0-02-864645-2*) Macmillan.

World Meetings Vol. 26 No.3: Social & Behavorial Sciences, Human Services & Management. Macmillan Publishing Co. Staff. 1996. pap. 45.00 (*0-02-864644-4*) Macmillan.

World Meetings Vol. 29: Outside United States & Canada 1996, 4. Macmillan Publishing Co. Staff. 1995. pap. 195.00 (*0-02-864636-3*) Macmillan.

World Meetings Vol. 29 No. 1: Outside United States & Canada. Macmillan Publishing Co. Staff. 1996. pap. 48.75 (*0-02-864637-1*) Macmillan.

World Meetings Vol. 29 No. 2: Outside United States & Canada. Macmillan Publishing Co. Staff. 1996. pap. 48.75 (*0-02-864638-X*) Macmillan.

World Meetings Vol. 29 No. 3: Outside United States & Canada. Macmillan Publishing Co. Staff. 1996. pap. 48.75 (*0-02-864639-8*) Macmillan.

World Meetings Vol. 29 No. 3: Outside United States & Canada. Macmillan Publishing Co. Staff. 1996. pap. 48.75 (*0-02-864640-1*) Macmillan.

World Meetings Vol. 34: United States & Canada 1996, 4. Macmillan Publishing Co. Staff. 1995. pap. 195.00 (*0-02-864631-2*) Macmillan.

World Meetings Vol. 34 No. 1: United States & Canada. Macmillan Publishing Co. Staff. 1996. pap. 48.75 (*0-02-864632-0*) Macmillan.

World Meetings Vol. 34 No. 2: United States & Canada. Macmillan Publishing Co. Staff. 1996. pap. 48.75 (*0-02-864633-9*) Macmillan.

World Meetings Vol. 34 No. 3: United States & Canada. Macmillan Publishing Co. Staff. 1996. pap. 48.75 (*0-02-864634-7*) Macmillan.

World Meetings Vol. 34 No. 4: United States & Canada. Macmillan Publishing Co. Staff. 1996. pap. 48.75 (*0-02-864635-5*) Macmillan.

World Memory IC Markets. Market Intelligence Staff. 386p. 1995. 2,195.00 (*0-7889-0164-8*) Frost & Sullivan.

***World Mental Health: Problems & Priorities in Low-Income Countries.** Ed. by Robert Desjarlais et al. (Illus.). 400p. 1996. reprint ed. pap. 24.95 (*0-19-511311-X*) OUP.

World Mental Health: Problems, Priorities & Responses in Low-Income Countries. Ed. by Robert Desjarlais et al. (Illus.). 432p. 1995. text ed. 42.00 (*0-19-509540-5*) OUP.

World Metal Demand: Trends & Prospects. Ed. by John E. Tilton. LC 90-8953. 341p. 1990. 45.00 (*0-915707-56-X*) Resources Future.

***World Metal Markets: The United States Strategic Stockpile & Global Market Influence.** Patricia E. Perkins. LC 96-47617. 1997. text ed. write for info. (*0-275-94258-9*, Praeger Pubs) Greenwood.

World Meteorological Organization Annual Report, 1989. World Meteorological Organization Staff. (WMO Ser.: No. 734). (Illus.). 56p. 1990. pap. 26.00 (*92-63-10734-3*, Pub. by Wrld Meteorological SZ) Am Meteorological.

World Microdisk Drive & PCMCIA Flash Memory Card Markets: Flash Encroaches on Hard Drives Even as Capacities Increase. Market Intelligence Staff. 250p. 1994. 1,995.00 (*1-56753-958-0*) Frost & Sullivan.

World Micromachine & Microstructure Markets: Technology Qualified: After Sensors, the Real Search for Applications Begins. Market Intelligence Staff. 1992. 1,695.00 (*1-56753-395-7*) Frost & Sullivan.

World Microscope & Spectrometer Markets: Hyphenate Technologies & Software Enhancements Spawn New Breed of Inspection & Testing Equipment. Market Intelligence Staff. 427p. 1992. 1,895.00 (*1-56753-393-0*) Frost & Sullivan.

World Military Aircraft Since Nineteen Forty-Five. Robert Jackson. (Illus.). 1981. 4.50 (*0-684-16265-2*) S&S Trade.

World Military & Social Expenditure 1987-88. 12th ed. Ruth L. Sivard. (Illus.). 56p. 1988. pap. 6.00 (*0-918281-05-9*) World Prior.

World Military & Social Expenditures 1983. Ruth L. Sivard. (World Military & Social Expenditures Ser.: No. 9). (Illus.). 46p. (C). 1983. pap. 5.00 (*0-918281-03-2*) World Prior.

World Military & Social Expenditures, 1985. 10th anniversary ed. Ruth L. Sivard. (Illus.). 52p. 1985. pap. 5.00 (*0-918281-01-6*) World Prior.

World Military & Social Expenditures, 1986. 11th ed. Ruth L. Sivard. (Illus.). 52p. 1986. pap. 5.00 (*0-918281-04-0*) World Prior.

World Military & Social Expenditures 74. Ruth L. Sivard. 30p. pap. 5.00 (*0-614-14097-8*) World Prior.

World Military & Social Expenditures 76. Ruth L. Sivard. 32p. pap. 5.00 (*0-614-14098-6*) World Prior.

World Military & Social Expenditures 77. Ruth L. Sivard. 32p. 1977. pap. 5.00 (*0-614-14099-4*) World Prior.

World Military & Social Expenditures 78. Ruth L. Sivard. 32p. 1978. pap. 5.00 (*0-614-14100-1*) World Prior.

World Military & Social Expenditures 79. Ruth L. Sivard. 36p. 1979. pap. 5.00 (*0-614-14101-X*) World Prior.

World Military & Social Expenditures 80. Ruth L. Sivard. 36p. 1980. pap. 5.00 (*0-614-14102-8*) World Prior.

World Military & Social Expenditures 81. Ruth L. Sivard. 44p. 1981. pap. 5.00 (*0-614-14103-6*) World Prior.

World Military & Social Expenditures 82. Ruth L. Sivard. 44p. 1982. pap. 5.00 (*0-614-14104-4*) World Prior.

World Military & Social Expenditures 89. Ruth L. Sivard. 60p. 1989. pap. 6.50 (*0-918281-06-7*) World Prior.

World Military & Social Expenditures 91. Ruth L. Sivard. 64p. 1991. pap. 6.50 (*0-918281-07-5*) World Prior.

World Military & Social Expenditures 93. Ruth L. Sivard. 56p. 1993. pap. 7.00 (*0-918281-08-3*) World Prior.

World Military & Social Expenditures 96. Ruth L. Sivard. 1996. pap. 7.50 (*0-918281-09-1*) World Prior.

World Military Expenditures & Arms Transfers. 1992. lib. bdg. 300.00 (*0-8490-5257-2*) Gordon Pr.

World Military Leaders: A Collective & Comparative Analysis. Mostafa Rejai & Kay Phillips. LC 95-22011. 192p. 1996. text ed. 55.00 (*0-275-95386-6*, Praeger Pubs) Greenwood.

World Military Microwave Component & Assembly Markets. Market Intelligence Staff. 213p. (Orig.). 1994. 1,895.00 (*0-7889-0110-9*) Frost & Sullivan.

World Military Order. Mary Kaldor & Ashborn Eide. LC 79-878855. 314p. 1979. text ed. 65.00 (*0-275-90372-9*, C0372, Praeger Pubs) Greenwood.

World Military Weapons: An Encyclopedia. 1991. lib. bdg. 95.00 (*0-8490-4986-5*) Gordon Pr.

World, Mind & Ethics: Essays on the Ethical Philosophy of Bernard Williams. Ed. by J. E. Altham & Ross Harrison. 248p. (C). 1995. text ed. 59.95 (*0-521-36024-2*) Cambridge U Pr.

World, Mind & Ethics: Essays on the Ethical Philosophy of Bernard Williams. Ed. by J. E. Altham & Ross Harrison. 248p. (C). 1995. pap. text ed. 18.95 (*0-521-47930-4*) Cambridge U Pr.

World Mineral Exploration: Trends & Economic Issues. Ed. by John E. Tilton et al. LC 87-27527. 464p. 1988. 75.00 (*0-915707-28-4*) Resources Future.

World Mineral Trends & U. S. Supply Problems. Leonard L. Fischman. xxxiv, 535p. 1981. 30.00 (*0-8018-2491-5*) Resources Future.

World Mirrors. Graham Child. (Illus.). 400p. 1990. 95.00 (*0-85667-355-2*, Pub. by P Wilson Pubs) Sothebys Pubns.

World Mission: Canadian Protestantism & the Quest for a New International Order, 1918-1939. Robert Wright. 1991. 49.95 (*0-7735-0873-2*, Pub. by McGill CN) U of Toronto Pr.

World Mission People: The Best of the Missionary Tidings, 1990-95. Ed. by Daniel V. Runyon. 400p. 1995. pap. 15.00 (*1-878559-04-4*) Saltbox Pr.

World Missions: Building Bridges or Barriers. Ed. by Theodore Williams. 101p. (Orig.). 1979. pap. 2.00 (*0-936444-02-9*) World Evang Fellow.

World Missions Syllabus. Lester Sumrall. 81p. 1989. pap. text ed. 12.00 (*0-937580-89-9*) LeSEA Pub Co.

World Missions Today. LC 78-68233. 90p. 1990. teacher ed., ring bd. 19.95 (*0-910566-28-3*) Evang Trg Assn.

World Missions Today. Terry C. Hulbert & Kenneth Mulholland. LC 78-68233. 96p. 1990. pap. text ed. 8.95 (*0-910566-16-X*) Evang Trg Assn.

World Mobile Communication Sourcebook 1995. Frost & Sullivan Staff. 316p. 1995. write for info. (*0-7889-0402-7*, 2877-65) Frost & Sullivan.

World Mobile Data Communications Markets: Market Emerges, Alliances Follow Quickly. Market Intelligence Staff. 400p. 1994. 1,995.00 (*0-7889-0013-7*) Frost & Sullivan.

***World Model Production Forecasts 97.** 1997. write for info. (*0-614-25454-X*) Econ Intel.

World Monetary & Financial System: Issues for Reforms. N. A. Sarma & V. K. Bhalla. (C). 1987. 17.50 (*81-7017-227-6*, Pub. by Abhinav II) S Asia.

World Monetary Equilibrium: International Monetary Theory in an Historical-Institutional Context. John E. Floyd. (Illus.). 224p. 1985. text ed. 44.95 (*0-8122-7983-2*) U of Pa Pr.

World Monetary Reform: Plans & Issues. Ed. by Herbert G. Grubel. x, 446p. 1963. 55.00 (*0-8047-0169-5*) Stanford U Pr.

World Money & National Policies. Henry C. Wallich et al. (Occasional Papers: No. 12). 71p. 1983. pap. write for info. (*1-56708-011-1*) Grp of Thirty.

***World Monuments Fund: The First Thirty Years.** 1996. pap. 25.00 (*0-9627931-6-7*) World Monuments.

***World Monuments Watch - List of 100 Most Endangered Sites 1996.** (Illus.). 64p. 1996. pap. 20.00 (*0-9627931-7-5*) World Monuments.

World More Attractive. Irving Howe. LC 70-134096. (Essay Index Reprint Ser.). 1977. 20.95 (*0-8369-1958-0*) Ayer.

World More Human: A Church More Christian. Ed. by George Devine. 204p. 1984. reprint ed. pap. text ed. 17.00 (*0-8191-3851-7*) U Pr of Amer.

***World, More or Less.** Jean Ronaud. Tr. by Barbara Wright from FRE. 192p. 1998. 22.95 (*1-55970-405-5*) Arcade Pub Inc.

World Motor Vehicle Data Book. 1986. 35.00 (*0-317-05087-7*) Motor Veh Man.

World Motorcycle Endurance Racing. Mark Wernham. (Color Library). (Illus.). 128p. 1994. pap. 15.95 (*1-85532-434-2*, Pub. by Osprey Pubng Ltd UK) Motorbooks Intl.

World Multi-chip Module Markets: From Concept Through Testing Applications Drive the Technology. Market Intelligence Staff. 288p. (Orig.). 1992. 1,695.00 (*1-56753-053-2*) Frost & Sullivan.

W

World Multimedia Application Markets. Market Intelligence Staff. 370p. 1994. 1,995.00 (*0-7889-0049-8*) Frost & Sullivan.

World Multimedia Application Markets: The Complete Market & Sales Targeting Tool. Market Intelligence Staff. 338p. 1993. 2,495.00 (*1-56753-425-2*) Frost & Sullivan.

World Multimedia Hardware & Software Markets. (Quarterly Business Planning Ser.). 541p. 1995. write for info. (*0-7889-0340-3*) Frost & Sullivan.

World Multimedia Hardware & Software Markets. Market Intelligence Staff. (Quarterly Business Planning Ser.). 425p. 1994. 2,995.00 (*0-7889-0020-X*) Frost & Sullivan.

World Multimedia Hardware & Software Markets: Finally a Definition. Market Intelligence Staff. 430p. (Orig.). 1992. 1,495.00 (*1-56753-403-1*) Frost & Sullivan.

World Music in the Music Library. Ed. by Carl Rankonen. 77p. 1994. 24.00 (*0-914954-49-0*) Music Library Assn.

World Music Navigator. Neuman. 1996. 150.00 (*0-02-864518-9*, Hall Reference) Macmillan.

World Musics in Education. Ed. by Malcom Floyd. 288p. (C). 1996. text ed. 49.95 (*1-85928-144-3*, Pub. by Scolar Pr UK) Ashgate Pub Co.

World Must Know: A History of the Holocaust As Told in the United States Holocaust Memorial Museum. Michael Berenbaum. LC 92-32813. 1993. 40.00 (*0-316-09135-9*); pap. 21.95 (*0-316-09134-0*) Little.

World My Church: Learning & Living My Orthodox Faith. 2nd ed. John Chryssavgis & Sophie Chryssavgis. (Illus.). 60p. (J). 1990. reprint ed. text ed. 9.95 (*0-614-96357-5*) Holy Cross Orthodox.

World Mystery. 2nd ed. G. R. Mead. 200p. 1974. reprint ed. spiral bd. 12.00 (*0-7873-0606-1*) Hlth Research.

World Mystery. G. R. Mead. 200p. 1992. reprint ed. pap. 17.95 (*0-922802-91-2*) Kessinger Pub.

World Mythology. Donna Rosenberg. 544p. 1993. pap. 23.95 (*0-8442-5548-3*, Natl Textbk) NTC Pub Grp.

World Mythology. Roy Willis. (Illus.). 320p. 1996. pap. 22.50 (*0-8050-4913-4*) H Holt & Co.

World Mythology. 2nd ed. Donna Rosenberg. 584p. 1995. pap. 19.95 (*0-8442-5767-2*, Natl Textbk) NTC Pub Grp.

World Mythology: An Annotated Guide to Collections & Anthologies. Thomas J. Sienkewicz. LC 96-10156. (Magill Bibliographies Ser.). 480p. 1996. 49.50 (*0-8108-3154-6*) Scarecrow.

World Myths & Tales. Carolyn Swift. (Illus.). 123p. (J). (gr. 4-7). 1994. pap. 8.95 (*1-85371-295-7*, Pub. by Poolbeg Pr IE) Dufour.

World National Parks: Progress & Opportunities. LC 63-62002. 11.95 (*0-614-10444-0*, L110) Natl Parks & Cons.

World Nature Encyclopedia, 24 vols., Set, 128p ea. (Illus.). (YA). (gr. 6 up). 1988. Set of 24 vols., 128 pp. ea. lib. bdg. 570.00 (*0-8172-3325-3*) Raintree Steck-V.

World Needs Monasticism. Father Benedict. (Illus.). 36p. (Orig.). 1993. pap. 4.95 (*1-880364-11-5*) New Sarov.

World Neurological Diagnostic Imaging Equipment Markets: New Technologies & Lower Prices Increase Market Potential. 450p. 1995. write for info. (*0-7889-0346-2*) Frost & Sullivan.

World News & Bible Prophecy. Charles H. Dyer. 303p. 1993. pap. 9.99 (*0-8423-5017-9*) Tyndale.

World News Prism: Changing Media of International Communication. 4th ed. William A. Hachten. LC 95-49494. 236p. 1996. text ed. 24.95 (*0-8138-1571-1*) Iowa St U Pr.

World Newspaper Industry. Peter J. Dunnett. 288p. 1988. text ed. 52.50 (*0-7099-0834-2*, Pub. by Croom Helm UK) Routledge Chapman & Hall.

World Next Door. Brad Ferguson. 1990. pap. 3.95 (*0-8125-3795-5*) Tor Bks.

World Niche & Specialized Sensor Markets: Growth Potential Lies in Exploring New Applications. Market Intelligence Staff. 219p. 1993. 1,295.00 (*1-56753-411-2*) Frost & Sullivan.

World Non-Destructive Test Equipment Markets: Increasing Automation & Integration Represent Wave of the Future. Market Intelligence Staff. 383p. 1992. 1,495.00 (*1-56753-407-4*) Frost & Sullivan.

World Non-Ferrous Metal Production & Prices, 1700-1976. Christopher J. Schmitz. 432p. 1979. 42.00 (*0-7146-3109-4*, Pub. by F Cass Pubs UK) Intl Spec Bk.

World Nuclear Capacity & Fuel Cycle Requirements. 1994. lib. bdg. 255.95 (*0-8490-5782-5*) Gordon Pr.

World Nuclear Capacity & Fuel Cycle Requirements (1993) (Illus.). 176p. (Orig.). (C). 1994. pap. text ed. 4.00 (*0-7881-0494-2*) DIANE Pub.

World Nuclear Directory. 7th ed. C. W. Wilson. 100p. 1985. 220.00 (*0-582-90025-5*, Pub. by Longman Grp UK) Gale.

World Nuclear Directory. 8th ed. 1988. 250.00 (*0-582-01776-9*, Pub. by Longman Grp UK) Gale.

World Nuclear Energy: Toward a Bargain of Confidence. Ed. by Ian Smart. LC 82-179. 416p. (C). 1982. text ed. 59.50 (*0-8018-2652-7*) Johns Hopkins.

World Nuclear Handbook. Euromonitor Staff. 250p. 1988. 240.00 (*0-86338-149-9*, Pub. by Euromonitor Pubns UK) Gale.

World Nuclear Handbook. Alice Freundlich. 320p. 1989. 65.00 (*0-8160-1924-X*) Facts on File.

World Nuclear Medical Imaging Markets: Oncology Applications & Global Opportunities Lead Market. 582p. 1995. write for info. (*0-7889-0322-5*) Frost & Sullivan.

World Nuclear Medical Imaging, NMI, Market: Radiopharmaceutical Applications Drive Double-Digit Growth Despite Cost-Benefit Concerns. Market Intelligence Staff. 323p. (Orig.). 1992. 2,295.00 (*1-56753-074-5*) Frost & Sullivan.

World Nuclear Outlook 1994. 131p. (C). 1995. pap. text ed. 50.00 (*0-7881-2269-X*) DIANE Pub.

World Nuclear Power: A Geographical Appraisal. Peter R. Mounfield. (Illus.). 416p. (C). 1991. text ed. 150.00 (*0-415-00463-2*, A5086) Routledge.

World Nutritional Determinants. Ed. by G. H. Bourne. (World Review of Nutrition & Dietetics Ser.: Vol. 45). (Illus.). x, 226p. 1984. 158.50 (*3-8055-3948-7*) S Karger.

World Observed: Reflections on the Fieldwork Process. Ed. by Bruce Jackson & Edward D. Ives. LC 95-50152. (Folklore & Society Ser.). (C). 1996. text ed. 32.95 (*0-252-02229-7*) U of Ill Pr.

World Observed: Reflections on the Fieldwork Process. Ed. by Bruce Jackson & Edward D. Ives. LC 95-50152. (Folklore & Society Ser.). (C). 1996. pap. text ed. 14.95 (*0-252-06533-6*) U of Ill Pr.

World Observed: The Art of Everett Longley Warner (1877-1963) Helen K. Fusscas. (Illus.). 48p. (Orig.). 1992. pap. 14.00 (*1-880897-10-5*) Lyme Hist.

***World Ocean Atlas.** (Illus.). 1997. lib. bdg. 250.95 (*0-8490-8243-9*) Gordon Pr.

World Ocean Atlas: Arctic Ocean, Vol. 3. Ed. by Sergei G. Gorshkov. LC 78-40616. 218p. 1983. 1,005.00 (*0-08-028735-2*, Pergamon Pr) Elsevier.

World Ocean Atlas Vol. 2: Atlantic & Indian Oceans. Sergei G. Gorshkov. 352p. 1979. 810.00 (*0-08-021953-5*, Pergamon Pr) Elsevier.

***World Ocean Atlas, 1994 Vol. 1: Nutrients.** Margarita E. Conkright et al. (Illus.). 150p. (Orig.). 1996. pap. 50.00 (*0-7881-3076-5*) DIANE Pub.

World Ocean Atlas, 1994 Vol. 2: Oxygen. (Illus.). 202p. (Orig.). (C). 1995. pap. text ed. 50.00 (*0-7881-1631-2*) DIANE Pub.

World Ocean Atlas, 1994 Vol. 3: Salinity. (Illus.). 111p. (Orig.). (C). 1995. pap. text ed. 45.00 (*0-7881-1630-4*) DIANE Pub.

***World Ocean Atlas, 1994 Vol. 4: Temperature.** Sydney Levitus & Timothy P. Boyer. (Illus.). 117p. (Orig.). (C). 1996. pap. 50.00 (*0-7881-3077-3*) DIANE Pub.

***World Ocean Atlas, 1994 Vol. 5: Interannual Variability of Upper Ocean Thermal Structure.** Sydney Levitus et al. (Illus.). 176p. (Orig.). (C). 1996. pap. 50.00 (*0-7881-3078-1*) DIANE Pub.

World Oceans: An Introduction. Alun C. Duxbury & Alison Duxbury. (Illus.). 475p. 1984. write for info. (*0-201-11364-3*); text ed. 31.16 (*0-201-11348-1*) Addison-Wesley.

World Oestridae (Diptera), Mammals & Continental Drift. N. Papavero. (Series Entomologica: No. 14). 1977. lib. bdg. 117.50 (*90-6193-124-X*) Kluwer Ac.

World of a Hasidic Master: Levi Yitzhak of Berditchev. Samuel H. Dresner. LC 94-9916. 228p. 1995. pap. 25.00 (*1-56821-239-9*) Aronson.

World of a Renaissance Jew: The Life & Thought of Abraham Ben Mordecai Farissol. David B. Ruderman. LC 81-2551. (Monographs of the Hebrew Union College: No. 6). 283p. reprint ed. pap. 80.70 (*0-7837-2998-7*, 2042943) Bks Demand.

***World of Aden.** 20.00 (*0-87431-467-4*, 29200) West End Games.

World of African Music, Vol. 2. Ronnie Graham. (Stern's Guide to Contemporary African Music Ser.: Vol. 2). (C). 66.50 (*0-7453-0552-0*, Pub. by Pluto Pr UK) LPC InBook.

World of Alexander Pope. Maynard Mack. (Illus.). 70p. (Orig.). 1988. pap. 5.00 (*0-685-59700-8*) Yale Ctr Brit Art.

World of Amazon Parrots. Dieter Hoppe. (Illus.). 192p. 1992. text ed. 35.95 (*0-86622-928-0*, H-1093) TFH Pubns.

World of Amish Quilts. Kenneth Pellman & Rachel T. Pellman. LC 84-80651. (Illus.). 128p. 1984. 24.95 (*0-934672-48-2*) Good Bks PA.

World of Amish Quilts. deluxe ed. Kenneth Pellman & Rachel T. Pellman. LC 84-80651. (Illus.). 128p. 1984. pap. 19.95 (*0-934672-22-9*) Good Bks PA.

***World of Amish Quilts.** deluxe ed. Rachel Pellman & Kenneth Pellman. LC 84-80651. (Illus.). 128p. 1997. pap. 21.95 (*1-56148-237-4*) Good Bks PA.

World of Ancient Israel: Sociological, Anthropological & Political Perspectives. Ed. by Ronald E. Clements. (Society for Old Testament Studies Monographs). (Illus.). 448p. (C). 1991. pap. text ed. 22.95 (*0-521-42392-9*) Cambridge U Pr.

World of Ancient Times. Carl Roebuck. (Illus.). 758p. (C). 1974. pap. text ed. 54.00 (*0-02-402700-6*, Macmillan Coll) P-H.

World of Ancient Times. Carl Roebuck. 1984. 18.95 (*0-684-13726-7*) S&S Trade.

World of Andrew Wyeth: In the Footsteps of the Artist. Henry David Thoreau. 1991. 19.98 (*0-88365-783-X*) Galahad Bks.

***World of Animals.** Kenneth Lilly. (J). Date not set. lib. bdg. write for info. (*0-688-07697-1*) Lothrop.

World of Animals. Tom Stacy. LC 90-42619. (Tell Me about Bks.). (Illus.). 40p. (J). (gr. 2-5). 1991. pap. 4.99 (*0-679-80864-7*) Random Bks Yng Read.

World of Animals: The San Diego Zoo & the Wild Animal Park. Bill Burns. 1990. 17.99 (*0-517-03561-8*) Random Hse Value.

World of Animals Big Books Set. Melvin Berger. Ed. by Susan Evento. (Macmillan Early Science Big Bks.). (Illus.). (J). (ps-2). 1995. pap. write for info. (*1-56784-170-8*) Newbridge Comms.

World of Animals Set. Melvin Berger. Ed. by Susan Evento. (Macmillan Early Science Big Bks.). (Illus.). (J). (ps-2). 1995. pap. write for info. (*1-56784-169-4*) Newbridge Comms.

World of Ants. Melvin Berger. Ed. by Natalie Lunis. (Early Science Big Bks.). (Illus.). 16p. (J). (ps-2). 1993. pap. 14.95 (*1-56784-008-6*) Newbridge Comms.

World of Ants: Mini Books. Melvin Berger. Ed. by Natalie Lunis. (Early Science Big Bks.). (Illus.). 16p. (J). (ps-2). 1993. pap. 2.95 (*1-56784-033-7*) Newbridge Comms.

World of Ants Theme Pack. Melvin Berger. Ed. by Susan Evento. (Macmillan Early Science Big Bks.). (Illus.). (J). (ps-2). 1995. pap. write for info. (*1-56784-140-6*) Newbridge Comms.

***World of Architectural Wonders.** Mike Corbishley. LC 96-47596. (World of...Ser.). (Illus.). 48p. (YA). (gr. 5 up). 1997. 19.95 (*0-87226-279-0*) P Bedrick Bks.

World of Aromatherapy. Ed. by Jeanne Rose & Susan Earle. LC 95-48253. (Illus.). 350p. (Orig.). 1996. pap. 16.95 (*1-883319-49-8*) Frog Ltd CA.

***World of Art.** Nicola Barber & Mary Mure. LC 97-20487. (J). 1998. pap. write for info. (*0-382-39811-4*) Silver Burdett Pr.

***World of Art.** Nicola Barber & Mary Mure. LC 97-20487. (J). 1998. lib. bdg. write for info. (*0-382-39812-2*) Silver Burdett Pr.

***World of Art.** Vsevolod Petrov. 1997. 55.00 (*1-85995-350-6*) Parkstone Pr.

***World of Art.** 2nd ed. Sayre. 1997. pap. text ed. 17.33 (*0-13-485690-2*) P-H.

World of Art. 2nd ed. Henry M. Sayre. LC 96-26340. 544p. (C). 1996. pap. text ed. 52.00 (*0-13-476011-5*) P-H.

World of Art & Museums. Carl Zigrosser. 309p. 1975. 30.00 (*0-87982-014-4*) Art Alliance.

World of Art Deco. Bevis Hillier. (Illus.). 224p. 1981. pap. 14.50 (*0-525-47680-6*, Dutton) NAL-Dutton.

World of Art Education. Vincent Lanier. 56p. 1991. pap. 15.00 (*0-937652-57-1*) Natl Art Ed.

World of Art Movement in Early Twentieth Century Russia. V. Petrov & A. Kamensky. 332p. (C). 1991. 175.00 (*0-569-09298-1*, Pub. by Collets) St Mut.

***World of Art Movement in Early 20th Century Russia.** Aleksander Kamensky. Ed. by Irina Kharitonova. Tr. by Arthur Shkarovsky-Raffe from RUS. 331p. 1991. 75.00 (*0-8285-5158-8*) Firebird NY.

World of Asia. 2nd rev. ed. Akira Iriye et al. 432p. 1995. pap. text ed. write for info. (*0-88295-921-2*) Harlan Davidson.

World of Asif Currimbhoy. Faubion Bowers. 4.80 (*0-89253-664-0*); 3.00 (*0-89253-665-9*) Ind-US Inc.

World of Athens: An Introduction to Classical Athenian Culture. Joint Association of Classical Teachers Staff. (Illus.). 416p. 1984. pap. text ed. 23.95 (*0-521-27389-7*) Cambridge U Pr.

World of Athens: An Introduction to Classical Athenian Culture. Joint Association of Classical Teachers Staff. (Illus.). 416p. 1984. text ed. 69.95 (*0-521-26789-7*) Cambridge U Pr.

World of Atoms & Quarks. Albert Stwertka. (Scientific American Update Ser.). (Illus.). 96p. (J). (gr. 5-8). 1995. pap. 8.95 (*0-8050-3534-6*) TFC Bks NY.

World of Atoms & Quarks. Albert Stwertka. (Scientific American Sourcebooks Ser.). (Illus.). 96p. (J). (gr. 5-8). 1995. lib. bdg. 18.98 (*0-8050-3533-8*) TFC Bks NY.

World of Baby Names. Teresa Norman. 592p. 1996. pap. 14.95 (*0-399-51948-3*, Perigee Bks) Berkley Pub.

World of Ballet. Judy Tatchell. (Illus.). 64p. (J). (gr. 4 up). 1994. pap. 8.95 (*0-7460-1692-1*, Usborne); lib. bdg. 16.95 (*0-88110-707-7*, Usborne) EDC.

World of Barbara Pym. Janice Rossen. LC 86-24810. 208p. 1987. text ed. 29.95 (*0-312-00090-1*) St Martin.

World of Barbie Dolls. Paris Manos & Susan Manos. (Illus.). 144p. 1994. pap. 9.95 (*0-89145-229-X*) Collector Bks.

World of Baroque & Classical Musical Instruments. Jeremy Montagu. LC 78-65227. (Illus.). 136p. 1979. 39.95 (*0-87951-089-7*) Overlook Pr.

World of Bats. Klaus Richardz & Alfred Limbrunner. (Illus.). 192p. 1993. 35.95 (*0-86622-540-4*, TS192) TFH Pubns.

World of Beads: How to Make Your Own Unique Jewellery. Barbara Case. (Illus.). 128p. 1996. 24.95 (*0-7153-0190-X*, Pub. by D & C Pub UK) Sterling.

World of Beautifully Tattooed Women. Photos by Jan Seeger. 14.95 (*0-9646031-0-1*) de Medici Pr.

World of Bede. Peter H. Blair. (Studies in Anglo-Saxon England). 356p. (C). 1990. text ed. 65.00 (*0-521-39138-5*) Cambridge U Pr.

World of Bede. Peter Hunter Blair. (Studies in Anglo-Saxon England). 356p. (C). 1990. pap. text ed. 24.95 (*0-521-39819-3*) Cambridge U Pr.

***World of Beer Memorabilia.** Herb Haydock & Helen Haydock. 184p. 24.95 (*0-89145-749-6*) Collector Bks.

World of Bells, Vol. 5. Dorothy M. Anthony. (Illus.). 50p. 1984. 8.95 (*0-9607944-3-3*) D M Anthony.

***World of Benjamin Cardozo: Personal Values & the Judicial Process.** Richard Polenberg. LC 97-2053. 1997. write for info. (*0-674-96051-3*) HUP.

World of Benjamin of Tudela: A Medieval Mediterranean Travelogue. Ed. by Sandra Benjamin. LC 94-54882. 1995. 49.50 (*0-8386-3506-7*) Fairleigh Dickinson.

***World of Biology.** Solomon. (C). 1995. pap. write for info. (*0-03-016568-7*) HB Coll Pubs.

World of Biology. 4th ed. Davis. (C). 1990. student ed., suppl. ed., pap. text ed. 34.00 (*0-03-032613-3*) HB Coll Pubs.

World of Biology. 4th ed. William P. Davis et al. 927p. (C). 1990. text ed. 59.00 (*0-03-030253-6*) SCP.

World of Biology. 4th ed. Eldra P. Solomon. (C). 1990. teacher ed., pap. text ed. 30.25 (*0-03-022113-7*) HB Coll Pubs.

World of Biology. 5th ed. Eldra P. Solomon. (C). 1995. teacher ed., pap. text ed. 33.75 (*0-03-005948-8*) HB Coll Pubs.

World of Biology. 5th ed. Eldra P. Solomon. (C). 1995. student ed., pap. text ed. 22.75 (*0-03-005949-6*) HB Coll Pubs.

World of Biology. 5th ed. Eldra P. Solomon. (C). 1995. 235.75 (*0-03-005963-1*) HB Coll Pubs.

World of Biology. 5th ed. Eldra P. Solomon. (C). 1994. text ed. 70.00 (*0-03-094865-7*) HB Coll Pubs.

World of Biology: School Edition. 4th ed. Davis. (C). 1990. text ed. 70.00 (*0-03-053263-9*) HB Coll Pubs.

World of Biology: Test Bank. 5th ed. Eldra P. Solomon. (C). 1995. suppl. ed., teacher ed., pap. text ed. 32.00 (*0-03-005954-2*) HB Coll Pubs.

World of Black Singles: Changing Patterns of Male-Female Relations. Robert Staples. LC 80-1025. (Contributions in Afro-American & African Studies: No. 57). xxi, 259p. 1981. text ed. 38.50 (*0-313-22478-1*, SBS/, Greenwood Pr) Greenwood.

World of Black Singles: Changing Patterns of Male-Female Relations. Robert Staples. LC 80-1025. (Contributions in Afro-American & African Studies: No. 57). (Illus.). xxi, 259p. (C). 1982. pap. 12.95 (*0-313-23609-7*, SBSPB, Greenwood Pr) Greenwood.

***World of Bloodshadows.** (Bloodshadows Ser.). boxed 30.00 (*0-87431-378-3*, 33000) West End Games.

***World of Bloodshadows.** (Bloodshadows Ser.). 20.00 (*0-87431-379-1*, 33001) West End Games.

World of Blues. David Harrison. 1994. 17.98 (*1-55521-935-7*) Bk Sales Inc.

World of Bohr & Dirac: Images of Twentieth Century Physics. N. Mukunda. (C). 1993. reprint ed. 10.00 (*81-224-0483-9*) S Asia.

World of Books. 2nd rev. ed. Dorothy S. Brown. 70p. 1988. pap. 7.50 (*0-939791-32-3*) Tchrs Eng Spkrs.

World of Brendan Behan. Sean McCann. 1976. 20.95 (*0-8488-0572-0*) Amereon Ltd.

World of Buddhism. Ed. by Heinz Bechert & Richard F. Gombrich. LC 91-65147. (Illus.). 308p. 1991. reprint ed. pap. 29.95 (*0-500-27628-5*) Thames Hudson.

World of Buddhist Awakening. Takamaro Shigaraki. LC 82-20677. 96p. 1983. pap. 8.95 (*0-938474-02-2*) Buddhist Study.

***World of Business.** Cotton. 1991. student ed., pap. text ed. write for info. (*0-17-555855-8*) Addison-Wesley.

World of Business. Lawrence J. Gitman & Carl McDaniel, Jr. (C). 1992. text ed. 52.95 (*0-538-81490-X*, GB60AA) S-W Pub.

World of Business. Wichita State University Staff & Gerald H. Graham. 1985. teacher ed. write for info. (*0-201-11441-0*); text ed. write for info. (*0-201-11440-2*, 150A13); Activity guide. student ed. 17.56 (*0-201-11442-9*) Addison-Wesley.

World of Business. 2nd ed. Gitman et al. (GC - Principles of Management Ser.). 1995. student ed., pap. 20.95 (*0-538-83626-1*) S-W Pub.

World of Business. 2nd ed. Lawrence J. Gitman & Carl McDaniel. LC 94-17198. 832p. 1995. text ed. 62.95 (*0-538-83625-3*) S-W Pub.

World of Business. 3rd ed. Gitman. (Miscellaneous/Catalogs Ser.). Date not set. pap. 18.95 (*0-538-86762-0*) S-W Pub.

World of Business: Test File. Dan Steinhoff. 1979. pap. text ed. write for info. (*0-07-061129-7*) McGraw.

World of Business, English-Spanish, Spanish-English Lexicon: El Mundo de los Negocios, Lexico Espanol-Ingles-Espanol. 2nd ed. Ivan De Renty. 333p. 1981. pap. 29.95 (*0-8288-0128-2*, S32370) Fr & Eur.

World of C. A. Stephens: Commemorative Edition. Ronald G. Whitney. LC 76-8714. (Illus.). 201p. 1996. reprint ed. pap. 19.95 (*1-888853-02-6*, CAS02) Frnds C A Stephens.

World of Cacti: How to Select & Care for over 1,000 Species. Danny Schuster. 248p. 1990. 29.95 (*0-8160-2506-1*) Facts on File.

World of Cactus & Succulents. Ed. by Ortho Books Staff. LC 77-89689. (Illus.). 96p. 1977. pap. 9.95 (*0-917102-59-2*) Meredith Bks.

World of Camelot: King Arthur & the Knights of the Round Table. Michael Foss. LC 94-48137. (Illus.). 240p. 1995. 19.95 (*0-8069-1314-2*) Sterling.

World of Carl Larsson. Ed. by Gorel Cavalli-Bjorkman & Bo Lindwall. Tr. by Allan L. Rice. LC 93-23754. (J). 1991. 39.95 (*0-671-75264-2*) S&S Trade.

World of Carnegie Hall. Richard Schickel. LC 73-7674. (Illus.). 438p. 1973. reprint ed. text ed. 35.00 (*0-8371-6946-1*, SCWC, Greenwood Pr) Greenwood.

World of Carpets. Mauizio Cohen. 1996. 24.99 (*0-517-18451-6*) Random Hse Value.

***World of Cars.** Roy Bacon. (Illus.). 192p. 1996. 24.99 (*1-57215-134-X*, PRC003) World Pubns.

World of Cartooning with Mike Peters: How Caricatures Develop. Mike Peters. Ed. by Marilyn Jarvis. (Illus.). 128p. (Orig.). 1985. pap. 12.00 (*0-913428-55-8*) Gifted Psych Pr.

World of Cartooning...a Complete Guide: How to Draw & Sell Cartoons. Bill Barry. (Illus.). 176p. 1989. pap. 19.95 (*0-944099-02-5*) Comic Art.

World of Castles & Forts. Malcolm Day. (World of Ser.). (Illus.). 48p. (YA). (gr. 5 up). 1996. 19.95 (*0-87226-278-2*) P Bedrick Bks.

World of Catfishes. Midori Kobayagawa. Ed. by Warren E. Burgess. Tr. by T.F.H. Publications Staff from JPN. (Illus.). 192p. 1991. lib. bdg. 35.95 (*0-86622-407-6*, TS-161) TFH Pubns.

World of Cats. Joan Moore. 1995. 3.99 (*0-517-14196-5*) Random Hse Value.

World of Cats. Dorothy S. Richards. (Fact Finders Ser.). (Illus.). 64p. (J). 1989. 7.99 (*0-517-69085-3*) Random Hse Value.

World of CB Radio. rev. ed. Mark Long et al. LC 87-70878. (Illus.). 240p. 1987. pap. 12.95 (*0-913990-53-1*) Book Pub Co.

An Asterisk (*) at the beginning of an entry indicates that the title is appearing in BIP for the first time.

W

World of Herbs. 1995. 7.99 (*0-517-12346-0*) Random Hse Value.

World of Herman Kahn. Briggs. 1997. 22.95 (*0-02-904841-9*, Free Press) Free Pr.

World of Herman Kahn. Briggs. 416p. 1996. 30.00 (*0-684-82775-1*) Free Pr.

World of Heroes: Selections from Homer, Herodotus & Sophocles. Joint Association of Classical Teachers Staff. LC 79-10740. (Illus.). 152p. 1979. pap. text ed. 19.95 (*0-521-22462-4*) Cambridge U Pr.

World of Hesiod. Andrew R. Burn. LC 66-29859. 262p. 1972. reprint ed. 18.95 (*0-405-08332-7*, Pub. by Blom Pubns UK) Ayer.

***World of Hi-Tech Sales: Rules & Realities.** Robert Davis. (Illus.). 5p. (Orig.). 1996. pap. 20.00 (*0-9656094-0-5*) Wrld of Hi-Tech Sales.

World of Higher Education: An Annotated Guide to the Major Literature. Paul L. Dressel & Sally R. Pratt. LC 71-158562. (Jossey-Bass Higher Education Ser.). 256p. reprint ed. pap. 73.00 (*0-317-10873-5*, 2013934) Bks Demand.

World of His Own: The Artwork of Warren A. Van Ess. Warren A. Van Ess. LC 74-4372. (Illus.). 69p. reprint ed. pap. 25.00 (*0-317-10400-4*, 2012826) Bks Demand.

World of Holidays! Family Festivities All over the World. Louisa Campbell. LC 93-22591. (Family Ties Ser.). (Illus.). 64p. (J). (ps-4). 1993. lib. bdg. 13.95 (*1-881889-08-4*) Silver Moon.

World of Holly Prickle: For Women Who Have Worked for Men. Mary A. Redd. LC 93-92632. 290p. (Orig.). 1993. pap. 10.00 (*0-9636548-0-2*) Shenandoah Bks.

World of Home Video Entertainment. Mark Long. (Illus.). 202p. (Orig.). 1990. pap. 15.95 (*0-929548-01-9*) MLE Inc.

World of Homer. Andrew Lang. LC 68-54281. reprint ed. 37.50 (*0-404-03870-0*) AMS Pr.

World of Homes: A Beginning Social Studies Big Book. Kari J. Gold. Ed. by Janet Reed. (Early Learning Program Ser.). (Illus.). 16p. (Orig.). (J). (ps-1). 1996. pap. 14.95 (*1-56784-305-0*) Newbridge Comms.

World of Homes: A Beginning Social Studies Mini Book. Kari J. Gold. Ed. by Janet Reed. (Early Learning Program Ser.). (Illus.). 16p. (Orig.). (J). (ps-1). 1996. pap. 2.95 (*1-56784-330-1*) Newbridge Comms.

World of Horses. 1996. 6.99 (*0-517-15938-4*) Random Hse Value.

***World of Horses.** Jane Kidd. LC 97-5068. 1997. write for info. (*0-87605-604-4*) Howell Bk.

World of Horses. Angela S. Rixon. 96p. 1994. 12.98 (*0-8317-9323-6*) Smithmark.

World of Human Sexuality: Behaviors, Customs & Beliefs. Edgar A. Gregersen. (Illus.). 442p. (C). 1994. text ed. 49.95 (*0-8290-2633-9*) Irvington.

World of Humanism, Fourteen Fifty-Three to Fifteen Seventeen. Myron P. Gilmore. LC 83-10718. (Rise of Modern Europe Ser.). (Illus.). xv, 326p. 1983. reprint ed. text ed. 52.50 (*0-313-24081-7*, GIWO, Greenwood Pr) Greenwood.

***World of Hummingbirds.** Esther Tyrell & Robert Tyrell. 1998. pap. write for info. (*0-609-80007-8*) Crown Pub Group.

World of Hunger: A Strategy for Survival. Jonathan Power & Anne-Marie Holenstein. 1977. 24.00 (*0-85117-097-8*) Transatl Arts.

World of Hunting. Meriel Buxton. (Illus.). 128p. 1991. 34.95 (*0-948253-53-3*, Pub. by Sportsmans Pr UK) Trafalgar.

World of Hurt. Bo Hathaway. (Vietnam Ser.). 304p. (Orig.). 1984. mass mkt. 3.50 (*0-380-69567-7*) Avon.

World of Hurt. Richard Rosen. LC 94-11253. 1994. 20.95 (*0-8027-3251-8*) Walker & Co.

World of Ibn Tufayl: Interdisciplinary Studies on Hayy ibn Yaqzan. Ed. by Lawrence L. Conrad. LC 95-6229. (Islamic Philosophy, Theology & Science, Studies & Texts Ser.: No. 24). 270p. write for info. (*90-04-10135-7*) E J Brill.

World of Ideas. 4th ed. Jacobus. 1993. teacher ed., pap. text ed. 5.00 (*0-312-08536-2*) St Martin.

***World of Ideas.** 5th ed. Jacobus. Date not set. pap. text ed. write for info. (*0-312-16705-9*) St Martin.

World of Ideas, Vol. II. Bill Moyers. 304p. 1990. pap. 22.95 (*0-385-41665-2*) Doubleday.

World of Ideas: Conversations with Thoughtful Men & Women about American Life Today & the Ideas Shaping Our Future. Bill Moyers. 528p. 1989. pap. 25.00 (*0-385-26346-5*) Doubleday.

World of Ideas: Essays on the Past & Future. World of Ideas Staff. LC 68-15678. 161p. reprint ed. pap. 45.90 (*0-317-09763-6*, 2005010) Bks Demand.

World of Imagery: Metaphor & Kindred Imagery. Stephen J. Brown. LC 65-26462. 352p. (C). 1965. text ed. 75.00 (*0-8383-0677-2*) M S G Haskell Hse.

World of Images. Laura H. Chapman. (Discover Art Ser.). (Illus.). (J). (gr. 7). 1994. teacher ed., text ed. 51.60 (*0-87192-270-3*) Davis Mass.

World of Images. Laura H. Chapman. (Discover Art Ser.). (Illus.). (J). (gr. 7). 1992. text ed. 35.50 (*0-87192-230-4*) Davis Mass.

***World of Indiana Jones.** (Indiana Jones Roleplaying Game Ser.). boxed 30.00 (*0-87431-425-9*, 45000) West End Games.

***World of Indiana Jones.** (Indiana Jones Roleplaying Game Ser.). 20.00 (*0-87431-426-7*, 45001) West End Games.

World of Indonesian Textiles. Wanda Warming & Michael Gaworski. (Illus.). 200p. 1991. reprint ed. pap. 35.00 (*4-7700-1611-5*) Kodansha.

World of Insects. Susanne S. Whayne. (Illus.). 48p. (J). (gr. 3-7). 1990. pap. 9.95 (*0-671-69018-3*, S&S Bks Young Read) S&S Childrens.

World of Invention. Ed. by Bridget E. Travers. 750p. 1993. 75.00 (*0-8103-8375-6*, 101196) Gale.

World of Irises. Ed. by Bee Warburton. LC 77-73698. (Illus.). 1978. 15.00 (*0-9601242-1-7*) Am Iris.

World of Islam. Xavier De Planhol. 153p. 1959. pap. 12.95 (*0-8014-9830-9*) Cornell U Pr.

World of Islam. Julian C. Hollick. (C). 1985. 40.00 (*1-56709-052-4*) Indep Broadcast.

World of Islam. Ed. by James Kritzeck. LC 79-52558. (Islam Ser.). (Illus.). 1980. reprint ed. lib. bdg. 40.95 (*0-8369-9265-2*) Ayer.

World of Islam. Ed. by Bernard Lewis. LC 91-65146. (Illus.). 360p. 1992. reprint ed. pap. 29.95 (*0-500-27624-2*) Thames Hudson.

World of Islam. John B. Taylor. LC 78-27187. (Illus.). 64p. (Orig.). reprint ed. pap. 25.00 (*0-7837-1960-4*, 2042177) Bks Demand.

***World of Islam of to 1500s.** Fiana Macdonald. 64p. 1996. pap. 12.95 (*0-614-21045-3*, 1335) Kazi Pubns.

World of Israel Weissbrem: "Between the Times" & "The Lottery & the Inheritance" LC 92-22730. (Modern Hebrew Classics Ser.). 171p. (C). 1993. pap. text ed. 22.95 (*0-8133-1631-6*) Westview.

World of Jade. Ed. by Stephen Markel. 1992. 64.00 (*81-85026-20-3*, Pub. by Marg) S Asia.

World of James McNeill Whistler. Horace Gregory. LC 70-80621. (Select Bibliographies Reprint Ser.). 1977. 25.95 (*0-8369-5033-X*) Ayer.

***World of Jane Austen: Her Houses in Fact & Fiction.** Nigel Nicolson. (Illus.). 384p. 1997. pap. 19.95 (*0-7538-0017-9*, Pub. by Orion Bks UK) Trafalgar.

World of Jay Leno: His Humor & His Life. Bill Adler & Bruce Cassiday. (Illus.). 192p. 1992. 15.95 (*1-55972-145-6*, Birch Ln Pr) Carol Pub Group.

***World of Jazz.** R. Dale. 1996. 15.98 (*0-7858-0599-0*) Bk Sales Inc.

World of Jazz. Jim Godbolt. 1990. 17.98 (*1-55521-623-4*) Bk Sales Inc.

World of Jeffrey Vallance: Collected Writings, 1978-1994. Jeffrey Vallance. Ed. by David A. Greene & Gary Kornblau. LC 94-71893. 112p. (Orig.). 1994. pap. 12.95 (*0-9637264-1-2*) Fnd Adv Crit.

World of Jennie G. Elisabeth Ogilvie. LC 94-14449. (Jennie Trilogy Ser.: Bk. 2). 368p. 1994. reprint ed. pap. 13.95 (*0-89272-346-7*) Down East.

World of Jesse Stuart: Selected Poems. Ed. by J. R. LeMaster. 303p. 1975. 40.00 (*0-07-062212-4*) McGraw.

World of Jesus: First-Century Judaism in Crisis. John E. Riches. (Understanding Jesus Today Ser.). 144p. (C). 1990. text ed. 34.95 (*0-521-38505-9*); pap. text ed. 9.95 (*0-521-38676-4*) Cambridge U Pr.

World of Jewish Cooking. Gil Marks. 384p. 1996. 30.00 (*0-684-82491-4*) S&S Trade.

World of Jimmy Carter: U. S. Foreign Policy, 1977-1981. Timothy P. Maga. Ed. by Thomas Katsaros. 200p. (Orig.). 1994. pap. text ed. 10.99 (*0-936285-23-0*) U New Haven Pr.

World of John Taylor the Water-Poet 1578-1653. Bernard Capp. (Illus.). 240p. 1994. 42.00 (*0-19-820375-6*) OUP.

World of Kameda Bosai. Stephen Addiss. LC 84-2004. (Illus.). 127p. 1984. pap. 16.95 (*0-89494-019-8*) New Orleans Mus Art.

World of Kameda Bosai: The Calligraphy, Poetry, Painting & Artistic Circle of a Japanese Literatus. Stephen Addiss. LC 84-2004. (Illus.). 128p. 1984. 35.00 (*0-7006-0251-8*) U Pr of KS.

World of Kate Roberts: Selected Stories, 1925-1981. Tr. by Joseph P. Clancy from WEL. (Border Lines: Works in Translation Ser.). 1991. 54.95 (*0-87722-794-2*); pap. 16.95 (*0-87722-795-0*) Temple U Pr.

World of Killies: Atlas of the Oviparous Cyprinodontiform Fishes of the World, 5 vols., Set, Vols. 1-5. Rudolf H. Wildekamp. text ed. write for info. (*1-883494-00-1*) Am Killifish.

World of Killies: Atlas of the Oviparous Cyprinodontiform Fishes of the World, 5 vols., Set, Vols. 1-5. Rudolf H. Wildekamp. pap. text ed. write for info. (*1-883494-01-X*) Am Killifish.

World of Killies Vol. 1: Atlas of the Oviparous Cyprinodontiform Fishes of the World. Rudolf H. Wildekamp. 311p. 1993. text ed. 80.00 (*1-883494-02-8*); pap. text ed. 65.00 (*1-883494-03-6*) Am Killifish.

World of Killies Vol. 2: Atlas of the Oviparous Cyprinodontiform Fishes of the World. Rudolf H. Wildekamp. 1995. text ed. 80.00 (*1-883494-04-4*) Am Killifish.

World of Killies Vol. 2: Atlas of the Oviparous Cyprinodontiform Fishes of the World. Rudolf H. Wildekamp. 1995. pap. text ed. 65.00 (*1-883494-05-2*) Am Killifish.

World of Killies Vol. 3: Atlas of the Oviparous Cyprinodontiform Fishes of the World. Rudolf H. Wildekamp. 1996. text ed. write for info. (*1-883494-06-0*) Am Killifish.

World of Killies Vol. 3: Atlas of the Oviparous Cyprinodontiform Fishes of the World. Rudolf H. Wildekamp. 1996. pap. text ed. write for info. (*1-883494-07-9*) Am Killifish.

World of Killies Vol. 4: Atlas of the Oviparous Cyprinodontiform Fishes of the World. Rudolf H. Wildekamp. text ed. write for info. (*1-883494-08-7*) Am Killifish.

World of Killies Vol. 4: Atlas of the Oviparous Cyprinodontiform Fishes of the World. Rudolf H. Wildekamp. pap. text ed. write for info. (*1-883494-09-5*) Am Killifish.

World of Killies Vol. 5: Atlas of the Oviparous Cyprinodontiform Fishes of the World. Rudolf H. Wildekamp. text ed. write for info. (*1-883494-10-9*) Am Killifish.

World of Killies Vol. 5: Atlas of the Oviparous Cyprinodontiform Fishes of the World. Rudolf H. Wildekamp. pap. text ed. write for info. (*1-883494-11-7*) Am Killifish.

World of Knowing: A Story about Thomas Hopkins Gallaudet. Alexandria Bowen. LC 95-1900. (Creative Minds Bks.). (Illus.). 64p. (J). (gr. 3-5). 1995. lib. bdg. 14.21 (*0-87614-871-2*, Carolrhoda) Lerner Group.

World of Knowing: A Story about Thomas Hopkins Gallaudet. Andy R. Bowen. (Illus.). 64p. (J). (gr. 3-5). 1995. pap. 5.95 (*0-87614-954-9*) Lerner Group.

World of Knowledge Encyclopedia. (Encyclopedias Ser.). (Illus.). 384p. (J). (gr. 3-7). 1994. 29.95 (*0-7460-1843-6*, Usborne) EDC.

World of K'ung Shang-Jen: A Man of Letters in Early Ch'ing China. Richard E. Strassberg. LC 83-1838. 520p. 1983. text ed. 59.00 (*0-231-05530-7*) Col U Pr.

World of Landscape Architects. World of Environmental Design Staff. 1996. 80.00 (*84-8185-003-9*) Watsn-Guptill.

World of Language: Noah & the Ark. Lenore Paxxton & P. Siadi. (Sing, Color 'n Say Bible Story Ser.). (Illus.). 32p. (J). (ps-4). 1994. reprint ed. pap. 7.95 incl. audio (*1-880449-11-0*) Wrldkids Pr.

World of Late Antiquity. Peter Brown. (Library of World Civilization). (Illus.). 216p. (Orig.). (C). 1989. pap. text ed. 12.95 (*0-393-95803-5*) Norton.

World of Learning, 1989. 89th ed. 1925p. 1989. 255.00 (*0-946653-46-1*, 70553-02604) Gale.

World of Learning 1991. 91th ed. 1991. 310.00 (*0-946653-62-3*) Gale.

World of Learning 1996. 96th ed. 2100p. 1996. 415.00 (*1-85743-016-6*, Pub. by Europa UK) Gale.

***World of Learning 1997.** 47th ed. 2025p. 1997. 445.00 (*1-85743-032-8*, Pub. by Eurpa Publns UK) Taylor & Francis.

World of Lego Toys. Henry Wiencek. (Illus.). 176p. (J). 1987. pap. 19.95 (*0-8109-2362-9*) Abrams.

World of Letters: Learning Center. rev. ed. Irene Handberg. 64p. 1995. teacher ed. write for info. (*1-56831-712-3*) Lrning Connect.

World of Letters: Learning Center, Set. rev. ed. Irene Handberg. 64p. 1995. write for info. (*1-56831-710-7*) Lrning Connect.

World of Light: Portraits & Celebrations. May Sarton. (Illus.). 1988. pap. 4.95 (*0-393-30500-7*) Norton.

World of Literature. Lim. (C). 1993. teacher ed., pap. 3.96 (*0-395-58881-2*) HM.

World of Little House. Christina W. Eriksson & Carolyn S. Collins. LC 94-46569. (Little House Bks.). (Illus.). 160p. (J). (gr. 3 up). 1996. lib. bdg. 24.89 (*0-06-024423-2*) HarpC Child Bks.

World of Logotypes, Vol. 1. Al Cooper. LC 75-29774. 1976. pap. 25.95 (*0-910158-20-7*) Art Dir.

World of Logotypes, Vol. 2. Al Cooper. LC 75-29774. (Illus.). 1978. 32.50 (*0-910158-34-7*) Art Dir.

World of Logotypes, Vol. 3. Al Cooper. LC 75-29774. (Illus.). 356p. 1982. 32.50 (*0-910158-82-7*) Art Dir.

World of Louisa May Alcott. William Anderson. (Illus.). 200p. 1995. lib. bdg. 51.00 (*0-8095-9168-5*) Borgo Pr.

World of Louisa May Alcott. William Anderson. LC 95-24373. 128p. 1995. pap. 22.50 (*0-06-095156-7*, PL) HarpC.

***World of Love.** Maggie Conroy. 256p. 1997. 23.00 (*1-57566-159-4*, Knsington) Kensgtn Pub Corp.

World of Lovebirds. J. Brockmann & W. Lantermann. Tr. by William Charlton from GER. (Illus.). 192p. 1990. 35.95 (*0-86622-927-2*, H-1092) TFH Pubns.

World of Luck. (Library of Curious & Unusual Facts). 1991. 17.95 (*0-8094-7711-4*); lib. bdg. write for info. (*0-8094-7712-2*) Time-Life.

World of M. C. Escher. M. C. Escher & J. C. Locher. pap. 9.95 (*0-451-79961-5*, G9961) NAL-Dutton.

World of Macaws. Dieter Hoppe. Tr. by Arthur Freud & R. Edward Ugarte from GER. (Illus.). 144p. 1985. reprint ed. 39.95 (*0-86622-125-5*, H-1079) TFH Pubns.

World of Magnificent Discovery: A Journey Through Time. Sheldrick Williams. LC 94-96666. (American Classic Ser.). (Illus.). 200p. (Orig.). 1996. pap. 14.95 (*0-9647234-3-3*) Z L Pub Hse.

World of Magnolias. Dorothy J. Callaway. LC 93-2793. (Illus.). 322p. 1994. 49.95 (*0-88192-236-6*) Timber.

World of Maluku: Eastern Indonesia in the Early Modern Period. Leonard Y. Andaya. LC 93-18245. 304p. (C). 1993. text ed. 38.00 (*0-8248-1490-8*) UH Pr.

World of Marcus Garvey: Race & Class in Modern Society. Judith Stein. LC 85-7084. 294p. 1991. pap. text ed. 14.95 (*0-8071-1670-X*) La State U Pr.

***World of Matter: Big Book.** Ron Cole. Ed. by Lauren Weidenman. (Ranger Rick Science Spectacular Ser.). 16p. (J). (gr. 2-4). 1997. pap. text ed. 14.95 (*1-56784-451-0*) Newbridge Comms.

***World of Matter: Mini-Book.** Ron Cole. Ed. by Lauren Weidenman. (Ranger Rick Science Spectacular Ser.). 16p. (J). (gr. 2-4). 1997. pap. text ed. 19.95 (*1-56784-476-6*) Newbridge Comms.

World of Matthew Brady. Roy Meredith. 1988. 9.99 (*0-517-21640-X*) Random Hse Value.

World of Medieval & Renaissance Musical Instruments. Jeremy Montagu. LC 76-5987. (Illus.). 136p. 1976. 39.95 (*0-87951-045-5*) Overlook Pr.

World of Medieval Women. Ed. by Constance H. Berman & Charles W. Connell. 163p. (Orig.). 1985. pap. 18.00 (*0-937058-22-X*) West Va U Pr.

World of Megaliths. Jean-Pierre Mohen. LC 89-16972. (Illus.). 318p. reprint ed. pap. 90.70 (*0-7837-6689-0*, 2046305) Bks Demand.

World of "Mestre" Tamoda: Angolan Stories. Uanhenga Xitu. Tr. by Annella McDermott from POR. 200p. (Orig.). 1988. 16.95 (*0-930523-42-3*); pap. 8.95 (*0-930523-43-1*) Readers Intl.

World of Mirth. Michael G. Michaud. 31p. (Orig.). 1988. pap. 5.95 (*0-9620574-0-1*) MGM Pr.

World of Miss Universe. Ana M. Cumba. LC 75-26269. (Illus.). 270p. 1976. 9.95 (*0-87141-053-2*) Manyland.

World of Missoni. (Illus.). 160p. 1995. 55.00 (*0-7892-0048-1*) Abbeville Pr.

***World of Money from the Earliest Times: A Concise Non-Eurocentric History of the World's Native Currencies.** Allen M. Blair. (Illus.). 158p. (Orig.). 1996. spiral bd., pap. 35.00 (*0-930366-88-3*) Northcountry Pub.

World of Monsieur Vincent. Mary Purcell. 256p. 1989. pap. 22.00 (*1-85390-019-2*, Pub. by Veritas IE) St Mut.

World of Monsieur Vincent: The Life St. Vincent de Paul. Mary Purcell. 250p. 1988. 2.50 (*0-8294-0606-9*); pap. 2.00 (*0-8294-0607-7*) Loyola Pr.

***World of Motorcycling: From Myth & Legend to Nuts & Bolts.** Roland Brown. 1997. 12.98 (*0-7651-9421-X*) Smithmark.

World of Music. Nicola Barber & Mary Mure. LC 95-1394. 94p. (J). (gr. 5-7). 1995. pap. 8.95 (*0-382-39117-9*); lib. bdg. 15.95 (*0-382-39116-0*) Silver Burdett Pr.

World of Music. David Willoughby. (C). 1995. audio write for info. (*0-697-27166-8*) Brown & Benchmark.

World of Music. 2nd ed. David Willoughby. LC 91-78213. 400p. (C). 1992. per. 43.50 (*0-697-12558-0*) Brown & Benchmark.

World of Music. 2nd ed. David Willoughby. LC 91-78213. 385p. (C). 1993. audio write for info. (*0-697-12560-2*); cd-rom write for info. (*0-697-12561-0*) Brown & Benchmark.

World of Music. 3rd ed. David Willoughby. 381p. (C). 1995. per. 40.23 (*0-697-25838-6*) Brown & Benchmark.

World of Music. 3rd ed. David Willoughby. (C). 1995. audio write for info. (*0-697-27165-X*) Brown & Benchmark.

World of Music. 3rd ed. David Willoughby. (C). 1995. audio write for info. (*0-697-27163-3*) Brown & Benchmark.

World of Music. George W. Woodworth. LC 64-13432. 217p. 1964. reprint ed. pap. 61.90 (*0-7837-4202-9*, 2059052) Bks Demand.

World of Music: Black & White Version. 2nd ed. David Willoughby. 400p. (C). 1995. per. write for info. (*0-697-34204-2*) Brown & Benchmark.

World of Musical Comedy. 4th ed. Stanley Green. LC 83-26340. (Quality Paperbacks Ser.). (Illus.). 494p. 1984. reprint ed. pap. 24.50 (*0-306-80207-4*) Da Capo.

World of Musical Instrument Makers: A Guided Tour. William Lasker. (Illus.). 109p. 29.95 (*0-88962-349-X*) Mosaic.

World of Muslim Women in Colonial Bengal: 1876-1939. Sonia Amin. LC 96-8399. (Social, Economic & Political Studies of the Middle East: Vol. 55). 312p. 1996. 97.00 (*90-04-10642-1*) E J Brill.

World of My Own. Anthony Castorini. (Orig.). 1995. pap. write for info. (*1-56167-277-7*) Watermrk Pr.

World of My Own. Robin Knox-Johnston. 240p. 1994. 29.95 (*0-393-02900-X*) Norton.

World of Mystery Fiction. Ed. by Elliot F. Gilbert. LC 78-2272. (Illus.). 441p. 1978. 19.95 (*0-89163-042-2*) Boulevard.

World of Myth: An Anthology. David A. Leeming. (Illus.). 384p. 1991. 27.50 (*0-19-505601-9*) OUP.

World of Myth: An Anthology. David A. Leeming. 384p. 1992. pap. 14.95 (*0-19-507475-0*) OUP.

World of Myths: A Dictionary of Universal Mythology. F. C. Bray. 1972. 75.00 (*0-8490-1335-6*) Gordon Pr.

World of Nagas. Murkot Ramunny. 1993. reprint ed. 30.00 (*81-7211-035-9*, National Bk Ctr) S Asia.

World of Names: A Study in Hungarian Onomatology. B. Kalman. 198p. (C). 1978. 40.00 (*963-05-1399-4*, Pub. by Akad Kiado HU) St Mut.

World of Nat Nakasa. Essop Patel & Nat Nakasa. (Writers Ser.). (Illus.). 206p. (C). 1995. reprint ed. pap. text ed. 12.95 (*0-86975-464-5*, Pub. by Ravan Pr ZA) Ohio U Pr.

World of Nations: Problems of Political Modernization. Dankwart A. Rustow. LC 67-26139. 320p. 1967. reprint ed. pap. 91.20 (*0-608-00491-X*, 2061310) Bks Demand.

***World of Native Americans.** Marion Wood. (World of Ser.). (Illus.). 48p. (YA). (gr. 5 up). 1997. 19.95 (*0-87226-280-4*) P Bedrick Bks.

World of Natural Sciences & Its Phenomenology. 2nd ed. H. Kuhlenbeck. Ed. by J. Gerlach. (Human Brain & Its Universe Ser.: Vol. 1). (Illus.). xiv, 282p. 1981. 132.00 (*3-8055-1817-X*) S Karger.

World of Nature. Margery A. Kranyik. (Creative Concept Ser.). (Illus.). 48p. 1990. pap. 6.95 (*1-878727-03-6*) First Teacher.

World of Nature in the Works of Federico Garcia Lorca. Ed. by Joseph W. Zdenek. (Winthrop College: Studies on Major Modern Writers). 150p. 1980. pap. 8.00 (*0-933040-01-6*) Spanish Lit Pubns.

***World of Necroscope.** boxed 30.00 (*0-87431-475-5*, 25000) West End Games.

***World of Necroscope.** 20.00 (*0-87431-476-3*, 25001) West End Games.

World of Negotiations: Never Being a Loser. Peter L. Grieco, Jr. & Paul G. Hine. LC 90-26684. 242p. 1991. 39.95 (*0-945456-06-9*) PT Pubns.

World of Nematodes: A Fascinating Component of the Animal Kingdom. David R. Viglierchio. 266p. (Orig.). 1991. pap. 24.95 (*0-932857-07-8*) Ag Access.

World of New Testament. F. Freyne. 1989. pap. 21.00 (*0-86217-028-1*, Pub. by Veritas IE) St Mut.

World of Ngugi Wa Thiong'o. Ed. by Charles Cantalupo. 248p. 1995. pap. 16.95 (*0-86543-459-X*) Africa World.

***World of Ngugi Wa Thiong'o.** Ed. by Charles Cantalupo. 248p. 1996. 49.95 (*0-86543-458-1*) Africa World.

World of Night Wind. Geary Gravel. 1992. pap. write for info. (*0-345-37290-5*) Ballantine.

W

An Asterisk (*) at the beginning of an entry indicates that the title is appearing in BIP for the first time.

World of North Koreans In Japan. Sonia Ryang. (Transitions Ser.). (C). 1997. text ed. 64.95 (*0-8133-8952-6*) Westview.

World of Northern Evergreens. E. C. Pielou. (Illus.). 200p. 1988. 39.95 (*0-8014-2116-0*); pap. 14.95 (*0-8014-9424-9*) Cornell U Pr.

World of Nothing. Ronald L. Fair. LC 71-105237. 1970. 25.00 (*0-89366-096-5*) Ultramarine Pub.

World of Nothing: Two Novellas. Ronald L. Fair. 133p. 1970. 11.95 (*0-911860-44-4*) Chatham Bkseller.

World of Nuclear Power? Ed. by Alastair Buchan. LC 66-29073. 1966. 3.95 (*0-317-02972-X*, 95875); pap. 1.95 (*0-317-02973-8*, 96874) Am Assembly.

World of Null-A. A. E. Van Vogt. 1988. pap. 8.95 (*0-89804-153-8*) Ariel GA.

World of Null-A. A. E. Van Vogt. 1993. reprint ed. lib. bdg. 18.95 (*0-89968-382-7*, Lghtyr Pr) Buccaneer Bks.

World of Numbers. Compiled by Susan Lyon. LC 92-36323. (Science in Action Ser.). (J). (gr. 4-9). 1993. lib. bdg. 15.95 (*0-86307-939-3*) Marshall Cavendish.

World of O. Henry - Five One Act Plays. Jesse F. Knight. LC 77-15687. (Lion Theatrical Ser.: No. 1). 1980. pap. 3.50 (*0-930962-03-6*) Villegas Pub.

World of Odysseus. M. I. Finley. 1988. 21.50 (*0-8446-6298-4*) Peter Smith.

World of Odysseus. Neil Grant. (Illus.). 48p. (J). (gr. 7-9). 1992. 13.95 (*0-563-34414-8*, BBC-Parkwest); pap. 7.95 (*0-563-34415-6*, BBC-Parkwest) Parkwest Pubns.

World of Odysseus. rev. ed. Moses I. Finley. 1979. mass mkt. 6.95 (*0-14-020570-5*, Penguin Bks) Viking Penguin.

World of Opera. Robert Lawrence. LC 77-2268. (Illus.). 208p. 1977. reprint ed. text ed. 55.00 (*0-8371-9551-9*, LAWO, Greenwood Pr) Greenwood.

***World of Opera: Puccini.** Timothy Ramsden. (Illus.). 144p. (Orig.). pap. 14.95 (*0-7119-5499-2*, OP 47815) Omnibus NY.

World of Opportunities: Lifestyle & Economic Behavior of Heroine Addicts in Amsterdam. Martin Grapendaal et al. LC 94-815. (SUNY Series in New Social Studies on Alcohol & Drugs). 240p. (C). 1995. text ed. 49.50 (*0-7914-2241-0*); pap. text ed. 16.95 (*0-7914-2242-9*) State U NY Pr.

***World of Opposites.** Claire Henley. (Illus.). 12p. (J). 1996. pap. 13.95 (*1-57145-054-8*) Thunder Bay CA.

World of Options: A Guide to International Educational Exchange, Community Service & Travel. 3rd rev. ed. Christa Bucks & Susan Sygall. 658p. Date not set. pap. 40.00 (*1-880034-24-7*) Mobility Intl.

World of Orderic Vitalis: Norman Monks & Norman Knights. Marjorie Chibnall. LC 96-3456. (Illus.). 264p. 1996. pap. 30.00 (*0-85115-621-5*, Boydell Pr) Boydell & Brewer.

World of Origami. abr. ed. Isao Honda. LC 65-27101. (Illus.). 200p. 1976. pap. 24.00 (*0-87040-383-4*) Japan Pubns USA.

***World of Orthodox Judaism.** Eli W. Schlossberg. LC 96-41189. 128p. 1997. pap. 18.00 (*0-7657-5955-1*) Aronson.

World of Our Fathers. Irving Howe. LC 75-16342. (Illus.). 714p. 1989. 34.95 (*0-15-146353-0*) HarBrace.

World of Our Fathers: The Journey of the East European Jews to America & the Life They Found. Irving Howe. 1994. 9.98 (*0-88365-882-8*) Galahad Bks.

World of Our Fathers: The Journey of the East European Jews to America & the Life They Found & Made. Irving Howe. LC 89-42550. 768p. 1990. pap. 19.00 (*0-8052-0928-X*) Schocken.

World of Our Making: Rules & Rule in Social Theory & International Relations. Nicholas G. Onuf. Ed. by Charles W. Kegley, Jr. & Donald J. Puchala. (Studies in International Relations). 352p. 1989. text ed. 39.95 (*0-87249-626-0*) U of SC Pr.

***World of Our Mothers: The Lives of Jewish Immigrant Women.** Sydney S. Weinberg. LC 87-13233. (Illus.). 351p. 1988. reprint ed. pap. 100.10 (*0-608-03184-4*, 2063637) Bks Demand.

World of Ovid's Metamorphoses. Joseph B. Solodow. LC 87-24159. (Illus.). x, 278p. (C). 1988. text ed. 39.95 (*0-8078-1771-6*) U of NC Pr.

World of Ovid's Metamorphoses. Joseph B. Solodow. LC 87-24159. 1988. reprint ed. pap. 82.10 (*0-608-02065-6*, 2062718) Bks Demand.

World of Owen Gromme. Michael Mentzer. 240p. 1991. pap. 29.95 (*1-55971-130-2*, 0123) NorthWord.

***World of Parmenides: Essays on the Presocratic Enlightenment.** Karl R. Popper et al. LC 97-17466. 1998. write for info. (*0-415-17301-9*) Routledge.

World of Passion: A Cross-Cultural Perspective on Love & Sex. Elaine Hatfield & Richard L. Rapson. LC 95-13436. 1995. pap. 18.95 (*0-205-16103-0*) Allyn.

World of Pasta. Maria L. Scott. 1996. 8.98 (*0-88365-667-1*) Galahad Bks.

World of Pastoralism: Herding Systems in Comparative Perspective. Ed. by John G. Galaty & Douglas L. Johnson. 436p. 1990. lib. bdg. 52.50 (*0-89862-785-0*) Guilford Pr.

World of Patience Gromes: Making & Unmaking a Black Community. Scott C. Davis. LC 88-98. 232p. 1988. 25.00 (*0-8131-1644-9*) U Pr of Ky.

World of Paul Crume. Paul Crume. Ed. by Marion Crume. LC 80-14072. 312p. 1981. reprint ed. 15.00 (*0-87074-176-4*) SMU Press.

World of Peptides: A Brief History of Peptide Chemistry. T. Wieland & M. Bodanszky. (Illus.). xiv, 298p. 1991. 158.95 (*0-387-52830-X*) Spr-Verlag.

***World of Percy French.** Brendan O'Dowda. 192p. 1997. pap. 22.95 (*0-85640-604-X*, Pub. by Blackstaff Pr IE) Dufour.

World of Percy French. 2nd ed. Brendan O'Dowda. (Illus.). 208p. 1992. pap. 21.00 (*0-85640-482-9*, Pub. by Blackstaff Pr IE) Dufour.

***World of Perfume.** Fabienne Pavia. (Illus.). 144p. 1996. 29.95 (*1-57715-004-X*) Knckerbocker.

World of Peter Rabbit & Friends: Bedtime Stories, 2. Beatrix Potter. 1997. pap. 12.99 (*0-7232-4381-6*) Warner Pr.

World of Peter Rabbit & Friends: Posters. (Illus.). (J). 1994. Set. pap. 7.95 (*0-7232-4129-5*) Warne.

World of Peter Rabbit & Friends Bedtime Storybook. Beatrix Potter. (Illus.). 128p. (J). (ps-3). 1995. pap. 12.99 (*0-7232-4182-1*) Warne.

World of Peter Rabbit Postcard Book. Beatrix Potter. (Illus.). (J). 1990. pap. 6.95 (*0-7232-3647-X*) Warne.

World of Peter Rabbit Sticker Book. Beatrix Potter. (Illus.). 32p. (J). (ps-3). 1990. pap. 6.99 (*0-7232-3645-3*) Warne.

World of Petroleum. B. G. Deshpande. (C). 1992. 36.00 (*81-224-0370-0*) S Asia.

World of Philosophy. H. Kuhlenbeck. Ed. by J. Gerlach. (Limited Volume Series: The Human Brain & Its Universe: Vol. 3). xiv, 508p. 1982. 237.75 (*3-8055-3419-1*) S Karger.

World of Phyllis Haylor & Ballroom Dancing. Bryan Allen. (Ballroom Dance Ser.). 1986. lib. bdg. 79.95 (*0-8490-3366-7*) Gordon Pr.

World of Phyllis Haylor & Ballroom Dancing. Ed. by Bryan Allen. (Ballroom Dance Ser.). 1985. lib. bdg. 79.95 (*0-87700-660-1*) Revisionist Pr.

World of Physical Chemistry. Keith J. Laidler. (Illus.). 448p. 1995. pap. 60.00 (*0-19-855919-4*) OUP.

World of Pooh. A. A. Milne. (Illus.). 320p. (J). (ps up). 1988. pap. 19.99 (*0-525-44447-5*) Dutton Child Bks.

World of Pooh. A. A. Milne. (Illus.). (J). (gr. 1-4). 1957. 13.95 (*0-525-43320-1*, 01258-370, Dutton); Incl. "World of Christopher". boxed 29.95 (*0-685-46952-2*, 01258-370, Dutton) NAL-Dutton.

World of Possibilities: Flexibility & Mass Production in Western Industrialization. Ed. by Charles F. Sabel & Jonathan Zeitlin. (Studies in Modern Capitalism). 512p. (C). 1997. text ed. 79.95 (*0-521-49555-5*) Cambridge U Pr.

World of Possibilities: Romantic Irony in Victorian Literature. Clyde D. Ryals. (Studies in Victorian Life & Literature). 163p. 1990. 45.00 (*0-8142-0522-4*) Ohio St U Pr.

World of Potatoes. Wilma G. Van Kersbergen. 109p. 1989. spiral bd. 5.98 (*0-9625100-0-9*) Vans Co.

World of Prayer, 2 vols. Elie Munk. pap. 26.95 (*0-87306-170-5*) Feldheim.

World of Prayer, 2 vols., Set. Elie Munk. 35.95 (*0-87306-080-6*) Feldheim.

World of Pro & Con. Vicki Frye. LC 95-94756. 80p. (Orig.). 1996. pap. 8.00 (*1-56002-579-4*, Univ Edtns) Aegina Pr.

World of Professional Golf, Nineteen Ninety-One. Mark H. McCormack. (Illus.). 596p. 1991. 24.95 (*1-878843-01-X*) Intl Merc OH.

World of Professional Golf 1989: Presented by ICI. Mark H. McCormack. (Illus.). 556p. 1989. 24.95 (*0-9615344-5-1*) Intl Merc OH.

World of Professional Golf, 1990. Mark H. McCormack. (Illus.). 1990. 24.95 (*0-9615344-8-6*) Intl Merc OH.

World of Professional Golf, 1992. Mark H. McCormack. 1992. 24.95 (*0-685-57141-6*) Contemp Bks.

World of Professional Golf, 1994. Mark H. McCormack. (Illus.). 640p. 1994. 29.95 (*1-878843-06-0*) Intl Merc OH.

World of Professional Golf, 1994. Mark H. McCormack. 1993. 29.95 (*0-87884-306-X*) Unicorn Ent.

World of Professional Golf, 1995. Mark H. McCormack. (Illus.). 640p. 1995. 29.95 (*1-878843-12-5*) Intl Merc OH.

World of Professional Golf 1996. Mark H. McCormack. (Illus.). 672p. 1996. 29.95 (*1-878843-15-X*) Intl Merc OH.

***World of Professional Golf 1997.** Mark H. McCormack. (Illus.). 704p. 1997. write for info. (*1-878843-17-6*) Intl Merc OH.

World of Professional Golf '92. Mark H. McCormack. 1992. 24.95 (*0-87884-303-5*) Unicorn Ent.

World of Programming Languages. M. W. Marcotty. (Books on Professional Computing). (Illus.). 385p. 1986. 62.95 (*0-387-96440-1*) Spr-Verlag.

***World of Propensities.** Karl R. Popper. 60p. 1990. pap. write for info. (*1-85506-000-0*) Bks Intl VA.

***World of Prostitutes.** S. K. Ghosh. (Illus.). xxv, vi, 1154p. 1996. 195.00 (*81-7024-793-4*, Pub. by Assoc Pub Hse II) Nataraj Bks.

World of Psychology. Allyn & Bacon Editorial Staff & Washington Post Writers Staff. 1992. pap. text ed. 3.00 (*0-205-14902-2*) Allyn.

World of Psychology. annot. ed. Ellen R. Wood & Samuel E. Wood. LC 92-48992. 1992. teacher ed. write for info. (*0-205-15001-2*) Allyn.

World of Psychology. 2nd ed. Ellen R. Wood & Samuel E. Wood. 1996. student ed., pap. text ed. 18.00 (*0-205-17765-4*) Allyn.

World of Psychology. 2nd ed. Samuel E. Wood & Ellen G. Wood. LC 95-36411. 1995. text ed. 65.00 (*0-205-16302-5*) Allyn.

World of Ptavvs. Larry Niven. 192p. 1986. mass mkt. 4.99 (*0-345-34508-8*, Del Rey) Ballantine.

World of Quality: Business Transformation at Xerox. Xerox Quality Services Staff. Ed. by Richard C. Palermo & Gregory H. Watson. 212p. 1996. pap. 20.00 (*0-614-12581-2*) Irwin Prof Pubng.

World of Quality: Business Transformation at Xerox. Xerox Quality Services Staff. Ed. by Richard C. Palermo. 212p. 1996. per. 19.95 (*0-7863-0803-6*) Irwin Prof Pubng.

World of Quantum Chemistry: Proceedings, First International Congress of Quantum Chemistry, Menton, France, July 4-10, 1973. Ed. by Raymond Daudel & Bernard Pullman. LC 73-91429. 1974. lib. bdg. 146.00 (*90-277-0421-X*) Kluwer Ac.

World of Quino. Quino. LC 85-80182. (Illus.). 128p. 1986. pap. 8.95 (*0-8050-0092-5*, Owl) H Holt & Co.

***World of Qumran from Within: Collected Studies.** Shemaryahu Talon. 324p. 1989. 35.00 (*0-614-25934-7*, Pub. by Magnes Press IS) Eisenbrauns.

***World of Raggedy Ann Collectibles: Identification & Values.** Kim Avery. (Illus.). 240p. 1997. pap. 24.95 (*0-89145-792-5*, 4880) Collector Bks.

World of Rashid Hussein: A Palestinian Poet in Exile. Ed. by Kamal Boullata & Mirene Ghossein. LC 78-62611. (Monographs: No. 12). (Illus.). 208p. (Orig.). (C). 1979. pap. 6.50 (*0-937694-07-X*) Assn Arab-Amer U Grads.

World of Rav Kook's Thought. 498p. 1991. write for info. (*0-9623723-2-3*) AVI CHAI.

World of Reptiles. Darlyne Murawski. (Ranger Rick Science Spectacular Ser.). (Illus.). 16p. (Orig.). (J). (gr. 2-4). 1996. pap. 14.95 (*1-56784-224-0*) Newbridge Comms.

World of Reptiles: Student Book. Darlyne Murawski. (Ranger Rick Science Spectacular Ser.). (Illus.). (Orig.). (J). (gr. 2-4). 1996. pap. write for info. (*1-56784-249-6*) Newbridge Comms.

World of Reptiles Theme Pack. Darlyne Muranski. Ed. by Donna Schaffer. (Ranger Rick Science Spectacular Ser.). (Illus.). 16p. (J). (gr. 2-5). 1996. pap. write for info. (*1-56784-286-0*) Newbridge Comms.

World of Rice. Priti Mehta. 1992. 45.00 (*1-869828-06-2*, Pub. by Moonstone Bks UK) St Mut.

World of Richard Stine. Richard Stine. LC 94-12455. (Illus.). 148p. (Orig.). 1994. 29.95 (*1-55670-375-9*) Stewart Tabori & Chang.

World of Richard Stine. Richard Stine. (Illus.). 144p. (Orig.). 1996. pap. 22.50 (*1-55670-512-3*) Stewart Tabori & Chang.

World of Richard Wright. Michel Fabre. LC 85-6230. (Center for the Study of Southern Culture Ser.). 268p. 1985. 39.50 (*0-87805-258-5*) U Pr of Miss.

World of Risk Management. Bill Kizorek & George Ushiba. LC 96-1549. (Illus.). 1996. write for info. (*1-884230-04-0*) InPhoto Surv.

World of Robert Bateman. Ramsay Derry. LC 84-29837. (Illus.). 180p. 1985. 50.00 (*0-394-54654-7*) Random.

World of Robert Flaherty. Richard Griffith. LC 72-166104. 1972. reprint ed. lib. bdg. 32.50 (*0-306-70296-7*) Da Capo.

***World of Robert Jordan's the Wheel of Time.** Robert Jordan. (Wheel of Time Ser.). 1997. 49.95 (*0-312-86219-9*) Tor Bks.

World of Roman Costume. Ed. by Judith L. Sebesta & Larissa Bonfante. LC 93-12709. (Studies in Classics). (Illus.). 292p. (C). 1994. text ed. 47.50 (*0-299-13850-X*) U of Wis Pr.

World of Romanian Theater. Ruth S. Lamb. (Illus.). 136p. 1976. pap. 8.95 (*0-912434-20-1*) Ocelot Pr.

World of Romantic & Modern Musical Instruments. Jeremy Montagu. LC 80-26106. (Illus.). 136p. 1981. 39.95 (*0-87951-126-5*) Overlook Pr.

World of Rome. Michael Grant. 1987. pap. 14.95 (*0-452-00849-2*, Mer) NAL-Dutton.

***World of Rome: An Introduction to Roman Culture.** Ed. by Peter Jones & Keith Sidwell. (Illus.). 424p. (C). 1997. 59.95 (*0-521-38421-4*); pap. 22.95 (*0-521-38600-4*) Cambridge U Pr.

***World of Rosamunde Pilcher.** Pilcher. Date not set. pap. write for info. (*0-312-18234-1*) St Martin.

World of Rosamunde Pilcher. Rosamunde Pilcher. LC 96-20046. 160p. 1996. 30.00 (*0-312-14771-6*) St Martin.

World of Rosaphrenia: The Sexual Psychology of the Female. Major J. Baisden, Jr. LC 72-178852. 224p. 1971. 6.95 (*0-912984-01-5*) Allied Res Soc.

World of Rottweilers. Anna K. Nicholas. (Illus.). 336p. 1986. 47.95 (*0-86622-124-7*, H-1083) TFH Pubns.

World of Rozome: Wax-Resist Textiles of Japan. Betsey S. Benjamin. (Illus.). 224p. 1995. 107.00 (*4-7700-1774-X*, Pub. by Kodansha Int JA) OUP.

World of Rural Dissenters, 1520-1725. Ed. by Margaret Spufford. (Illus.). 450p. (C). 1995. text ed. 80.00 (*0-521-41061-4*) Cambridge U Pr.

World of Russo. Illus. by Michele Russo. 110p. (Orig.). 1981. pap. 12.95 (*0-938996-00-2*) Bigoni Bks.

World of Salt Shakers. 2nd ed. Mildred Lechner. 1996. 24.95 (*0-89145-467-5*) Collector Bks.

World of Samuel Beckett. Ed. by Joseph H. Smith. LC 90-40273. (Psychiatry & the Humanities Ser.: Vol. 12). (Illus.). 256p. 1991. text ed. 42.50 (*0-8018-4079-1*); pap. text ed. 14.95 (*0-8018-4135-6*) Johns Hopkins.

World of Samuel Beckett, 1906-1946. Lois Gordon. (Illus.). 250p. 1996. 28.50 (*0-300-06409-8*) Yale U Pr.

World of Sapphires. I. A. Mumme. 212p. (C). 1989. pap. text ed. 70.00 (*0-89771-027-4*, Pub. by Bob Mossel AT) St Mut.

World of Satellite TV: International Edition for Asia, the Middle East, & the Pacific Rim. Mark Long & Jeffrey Keating. (Illus.). 220p. (Orig.). 1992. pap. 19.95 (*0-929548-08-6*) MLE Inc.

World of Satellite TV: International Edition for Europe & Africa. Mark Long & Jeffrey Keating. (Illus.). 1993. pap. 24.95 (*0-929548-10-8*) MLE Inc.

World of Satellite TV: North & South America. 6th ed. Mark Long & Jeffrey Keating. LC 92-81289. (Illus.). 308p. (Orig.). (C). 1992. pap. text ed. 24.95 (*0-929548-07-8*) MLE Inc.

World of Satish Gujral: In His Own Words. Satish Gujral. Ed. by Rohini Chopra. (C). 1993. 68.00 (*81-85674-67-1*, Pub. by UBS Pubs Dist II) S Asia.

***World of Satyajit Ray.** Bidyut Sarkar. (C). 1992. reprint ed. 20.00 (*81-85674-04-3*, Pub. by UBS Pubs Dist II) S Asia.

World of Savannas: Economic Driving Force, Ecological Constraints & Policy. Otto T. Solbrig. (Man & the Biosphere Ser.: No. 12). 370p. 1993. pap. 85.00 (*92-3-102750-6*, U2750, Pub. by UNESCO-Bangkok TH) Bernan Associates.

World of Schnauzers: Standard, Giant, Miniature. Johan Gallant. LC 96-25948. (Illus.). 224p. 1996. 34.95 (*0-931866-93-6*) Alpine Pubns.

World of Science. Peter Lafferty. LC 94-20019. (One Hundred One Questions & Answers Ser.). (Illus.). 48p. (J). 1994. 9.95 (*0-8160-3219-X*) Facts on File.

World of Science. Jenny Vaughan. (Can You Believe It Ser.). (Illus.). 36p. (J). (gr. 2-6). 1990. 3.99 (*0-517-69907-9*) Random Hse Value.

World of Science & Technology: A Theme-Based, Study-Skills Approach. Frances Luttikhuizen. 200p. 1994. pap. text ed. 16.95 (*0-472-08269-8*) U of Mich Pr.

World of Science Series, 16 vols. (J). (gr. 4-7). 1985. Set. bds. 225.00 (*0-8160-1563-5*) Facts on File.

World of Scientific Discovery: Scientific Milestones & the People Who Made Them Possible. Ed. by Bridget E. Travers. 1993. 75.00 (*0-8103-8492-2*, 101434) Gale.

World of Serendipity. Marcus Bach. 167p. 1980. reprint ed. pap. 8.95 (*0-87516-398-X*) DeVorss.

***World of Shakespeare.** Anna Claybourne & Rebecca Treays. (Illus.). 64p. (J). (gr. 5 up). 1997. pap. 9.95 (*0-7460-2454-1*, Usborne); lib. bdg. 17.95 (*0-88110-916-9*, Usborne) EDC.

World of Shapes & Colors: Learning Center. Irene Handberg. 90p. 1992. teacher ed. write for info. (*1-56831-212-1*) Lrning Connect.

World of Shapes & Colors: Learning Center, Set. rev. ed. Irene Handberg. 90p. 1995. write for info. (*1-56831-210-5*) Lrning Connect.

World of Sharks, 6 vols. Sarah Palmer. (J). 1990. 7.99 (*0-517-02747-X*) Random Hse Value.

***World of Sharks.** Herbert Zim. Date not set. lib. bdg. write for info. (*0-688-04083-7*, Morrow Junior) Morrow.

***World of Sharks.** Herbert Zim. (J). Date not set. write for info. (*0-688-04081-0*) Morrow.

World of Sholom Aleichem. Arnold Perl. 1955. pap. 5.25 (*0-8222-1277-3*) Dramatists Play.

World of Show Jumping. Neil F. Blake. 1973. reprint ed. 15.95 (*0-912830-29-8*) Printed Horse.

World of Silence. Don Coldsmith. (Spanish Bit Saga Super Ser.: No. 3). 336p. 1992. pap. 4.99 (*0-553-28945-4*) Bantam.

World of Small: Nature Explorations with a Hand Lens. Michael E. Ross. Ed. by Steven P. Medley. (Illus.). 64p. (J). (gr. k-6). 1993. spiral bd. 15.95 (*0-939666-62-6*) Yosemite Assn.

World of Snakes, 12 vols. in 1. (J). 1990. 9.99 (*0-517-03756-4*) Random Hse Value.

World of Snakes. Peter Brazaltis & Myrna E. Wantanabe. (Illus.). 176p. 1994. 26.95 (*1-56465-117-7*, 16091) Tetra Pr.

World of Social Welfare: Social Welfare & Services in an International Context. Doreen Elliott et al. (Illus.). 328p. 1990. pap. 34.95 (*0-398-06105-X*) C C Thomas.

World of Social Welfare: Social Welfare & Services in an International Context. Doreen Elliott et al. (Illus.). 328p. (C). 1990. text ed. 56.95 (*0-398-05710-9*) C C Thomas.

World of Sofia Velasquez: Autobiography of a Bolivian Market Vendor. Hans Buechler & Judith-Maria Buechler. LC 95-50815. (Illus.). 256p. (C). 1996. pap. 17.50 (*0-231-10467-7*) Col U Pr.

World of Somerset Maugham: An Anthology. Ed. by Klaus W. Jonas. LC 73-156196. 200p. 1972. reprint ed. text ed. 38.50 (*0-8371-6147-9*, JOSM, Greenwood Pr) Greenwood.

World of Sorrow: The African Slave Trade to Brazil. fac. ed. Robert E. Conrad. LC 85-23160. 231p. 1986. reprint ed. pap. 65.90 (*0-7837-7727-2*, 2047483) Bks Demand.

***World of Species.** (MasterBook Ser.). 25.00 (*0-87431-364-3*, 29000) West End Games.

World of Spirits & Ancestors: In the Art of Western Sub-Saharan Africa. Elizabeth S. Sasser. (Illus.). 208p. 1995. text ed. 49.95 (*0-89672-346-1*) Tex Tech Univ Pr.

World of Sports Series, 4 bks., Set. Isidro Sanchez & Carme Peris. (Illus.). 32p. (J). (ps-1). 1992. Boxed set. boxed 23.95 (*0-8120-7862-4*) Barron.

World of St. John: The Gospel & the Epistles. E. Earle Ellis. LC 94-30654. 96p. (C). 1994. reprint ed. pap. text ed. 13.50 (*0-8191-9683-5*) U Pr of Amer.

World of States: An Introduction to Explanation & Theory. Charles Reynolds. 256p. 1992. 80.00 (*1-85278-133-5*); pap. 30.00 (*1-85278-134-3*) E Elgar.

***World of States of Affairs.** D. M. Armstrong. (Cambridge Studies in Philosophy). 299p. (C). 1997. text ed. 54.95 (*0-521-58064-1*); pap. text ed. 19.95 (*0-521-58948-7*) Cambridge U Pr.

World of Stereographs. William C. Darrah. LC 77-92123. 246p. 1977. 22.50 (*0-913116-04-1*) W C Darrah.

***World of Stereographs.** 2nd ed. William C. Darrah. (Illus.). 256p. 1997. reprint ed. pap. 21.95 (*0-9650513-1-5*) Land Yacht Pr.

World of Story: Short Fiction of the Twentieth Century. Selected by Clifton Fadiman. 1985. pap. write for info. (*0-318-60288-1*) HM.

World of Storytelling: A Practical Guide to the Origins, Development, & Applications of Storytelling. enl. rev. ed. Anne Pellowski. 322p. 1990. 40.00 (*0-8242-0788-2*) Wilson.

World of Strangers. Nadine Gordimer. 272p. 1984. pap. 11.95 (*0-14-001704-6*, Penguin Bks) Viking Penguin.

W

World of Strangers: Order & Action in Urban Public Space. Lyn H. Lofland. 223p. (C). 1985. reprint ed. pap. text ed. 12.95 (*0-88133-136-8*) Waveland Pr.

World of Suffering in a la Recherche du Temps Perdu. Burgunde H. Winz. LC 89-8197. (American University Studies: Romance Languages & Literature: Ser. II, Vol. 121). 384p. (C). 1989. text ed. 47.50 (*0-8204-0956-1*) P Lang Pubng.

***World of Super Service.** Ken Irons. (C). 1997. pap. text ed. write for info. (*0-201-40384-6*) Addison-Wesley.

World of Suzie Wong. Richard Mason. 25.95 (*0-8488-0052-4*) Amereon Ltd.

World of Suzie Wong. Richard Mason. 1993. reprint ed. lib. bdg. 21.95 (*1-56849-097-6*) Buccaneer Bks.

World of Swing. Stanley Dance. LC 79-15249. (Quality Paperbacks Ser.). (Illus.). 436p. 1979. pap. 14.95 (*0-306-80103-5*) Da Capo.

World of Talk on a Fijian Island: An Ethnography of Law & Communicative Causation. Andrew Arno. Ed. by Brenda Dervin. LC 92-21909. (Communication & Information Science Ser.). 152p. (C). 1993. pap. 39.50 (*0-89391-961-6*); text ed. 73.25 (*0-89391-866-0*) Ablex Pub.

***World of Tank Girl.** (MasterBook Ser.). boxed 30.00 (*0-87431-362-7*, 28001) West End Games.

***World of Tank Girl.** (MasterBook Ser.). 20.00 (*0-87431-363-5*, 28002) West End Games.

World of Tantra. B. Bhattacharya. 1988. 48.50 (*81-215-0080-X*, Pub. by Munshiram Manoharial II) S Asia.

World of Ted Serios: "Thoughtographic" Studies of an Extraordinary Mind. rev. ed. Jule Eisenbud. LC 89-42712. (Illus.). 260p. 1989. lib. bdg. 45.00 (*0-89950-423-X*) McFarland & Co.

World of Telecommunication: Introduction to Broadcasting, Cable & New Technologies. Phillip O. Keirstead & Sonia-Kay Keirstead. (Illus.). 320p. 1989. pap. 39.95 (*0-240-80014-1*, Focal) Buttrwrth-Heinemann.

World of Texas Politics. George Christian. (Symposia Ser.). 170p. 1989. pap. 7.00 (*0-89940-424-3*) LBJ Sch Pub Aff.

***World of Texas Politics.** Elliott. Date not set. pap. text ed. write for info. (*0-312-13897-0*) St Martin.

World of the Aggadah. Avigdor Shinan. 148p. 1990. pap. 12.00 (*965-05-0497-4*, Pub. by Israel Ministry Def IS) Gefen Bks.

***World of the Akita.** Barbara J. Andrews. (Illus.). 416p. 1997. 69.95 (*0-7938-2080-4*, TS-256) TFH Pubns.

World of the American Indian. (Illus.). 400p. 1994. 40.00 (*0-87044-799-8*) Natl Geog.

World of the American Indian. rev. ed. LC 93-23294. 1993. 29.95 (*0-87044-972-9*); 40.00 (*0-87044-973-7*) Natl Geog.

World of the American Pit Bull Terrier. Richard F. Stratton. LC 83-215316. (Illus.). 288p. 1983. 39.95 (*0-87666-851-1*, H-1063) TFH Pubns.

World of the Ancient Maya. John S. Henderson. (Illus.). 271p. 1983. 18.95 (*0-8014-9257-2*) Cornell U Pr.

World of the Ancient Maya. John S. Henderson. 1981. 29.95 (*0-8014-1232-3*) Cornell U Pr.

***World of the Ancient Maya.** 2nd ed. John S. Henderson. LC 97-14353. 352p. 1997. 60.00 (*0-8014-3183-2*); pap. 24.95 (*0-8014-8284-4*) Cornell U Pr.

World of the Arabs. Edward J. Byng. LC 74-869. (Essay Index Reprint Ser.). 1977. reprint ed. 21.95 (*0-518-10144-4*) Ayer.

World of the Arctic Whales: Belugas, Bowheads & Narwhals. Stefani Paine. LC 95-1168. (Illus.). 128p. (YA). 1995. 26.00 (*0-87156-378-9*) Sierra.

***World of the Arctic Whales: Belugas, Bowheads & Narwhals.** Stefani Paine. 128p. 1997. pap. 18.00 (*0-87156-957-4*) Sierra.

World of the Arts. William Reed. LC 95-19642. (Child Horizons Ser.). (J). (gr. 4-6). 1995. 22.95 (*0-87392-307-3*) Standard Ed.

World of the Arts see Child Horizons

World of the Autistic Child: Understanding & Treating Autism Spectrum Disorders. Bryna Siegal. (Illus.). 320p. 1996. 30.00 (*0-19-507667-2*) OUP.

***World of the Autistic Child: Understanding & Treating Autistic Spectrum Disorders.** Bryna Siegel. (Illus.). 368p. 1998. reprint ed. pap. 13.95 (*0-19-511917-7*) OUP.

W

***World of the Bach Cantatas: Early Sacred Cantatas, Vol. 1.** Ed. by Christoph Wolff & Ton Koopman. LC 97-2417. (Illus.). 240p. (YA). 1997. 35.00 (*0-393-04106-9*) Norton.

World of the Bible. Roberta Harris. LC 94-60285. (Illus.). 192p. 1995. 29.95 (*0-500-05073-2*) Thames Hudson.

World of the Bichon Frise, AKC Rank No. 32. Anna K. Nicholas. (Illus.). 288p. 1996. 39.95 (*0-7938-0191-5*, TS245) TFH Pubns.

World of the Bizarre. Stuart A. Kallen. LC 91-73059. (Ghastly Ghost Stories Ser.). 202p. (J). 1991. lib. bdg. 13.98 (*1-56239-042-2*) Abdo & Dghtrs.

***World of the Boxer: AKC Rank #13.** Richard Tomita. (Illus.). 432p. 1997. 89.95 (*0-7938-0465-5*, TS-273) TFH Pubns.

World of the Brontes. Photos by Paul Barker. (Illus.). 144p. 1996. 29.95 (*1-85793-687-6*, Pub. by Pavilion UK) Trafalgar.

World of the Buddha: An Introduction to Buddhist Literature. Ed. by Lucien Stryk. LC 81-48543. 480p. 1987. pap. 14.95 (*0-8021-3095-X*, Grove) Grove-Atltic.

***World of the Castrati: The History of an Extraordinary Operatic Phenomenon.** Patrick Barbier. Tr. by Margaret Copeland. (Illus.). 240p. 1997. 24.95 (*0-285-63309-0*, Pub. by Souvenir UK) IPG Chicago.

World of the Cell. 2nd ed. Becker. (C). 1991. pap. text ed. 25.95 (*0-8053-0871-7*) Addison-Wesley.

World of the Cell. 2nd ed. Wayne M. Becker & David W. Deamer. Ed. by David Rogelberg. (Illus.). 928p. (C). 1991. text ed. 62.50 (*0-8053-0870-9*) Benjamin-Cummings.

World of the Cell. 3rd ed. Wayne M. Becker. (C). 1996. student ed., pap. text ed. 17.95 (*0-8053-0882-2*) Benjamin-Cummings.

World of the Cell. 3rd ed. Jane B. Reece & Wayne F. Poenie. (C). 1996. text ed. 65.95 (*0-8053-0880-6*) Benjamin-Cummings.

***World of the Cell Accompanying: Solutions Manual.** 3rd ed. Wayne M. Becker. (C). 1996. 82.95 (*0-8053-0884-9*) Addison-Wesley.

World of the Celts. Simon James. LC 92-80340. (Illus.). 192p. 1993. 29.95 (*0-500-05067-8*) Thames Hudson.

World of the Child. Owens. 1993. student ed., pap. text ed. 21.00 (*0-675-21337-1*, Merrill Coll) P-H.

World of the Child. Karen B. Owens. 640p. (C). 1987. text ed. 44.00 (*0-03-069853-7*) HB Coll Pubs.

World of the Child. Karen B. Owens. LC 92-9837. 752p. (C). 1992. text ed. 81.00 (*0-675-21336-3*, Merrill Coll) P-H.

World of the Child. Aline D. Wolf. LC 81-83762. (Illus.). 56p. 1982. 11.95 (*0-614-06595-X*); pap. 5.95 (*0-9601016-5-9*) Parent-Child Pr.

World of the Chinese Shar-pei. Anna K. Nicholas. 1992. 89.95 (*0-86622-199-9*, TS-176) TFH Pubns.

World of the Chow Chow. Samuel Draper & Joan M. Brearley. (TS Ser.). (Illus.). 525p. 1992. 89.95 (*0-86622-630-3*, TS-149) TFH Pubns.

World of the Citizen in Republican Rome. Claude Nicolet. LC 77-80474. 1980. pap. 15.00 (*0-520-06342-2*) U CA Pr.

***World of the Coffin Texts: Proceedings of the Symposium Held on the Occasion of the 100th Birthday of Adriaan de Buck, Leiden, 17-19 December 1992.** Ed. by Harco Willems. 210p. 1996. 56.00 (*90-6258-209-5*, Pub. by Netherlands Inst NE) Eisenbrauns.

***World of the Color of Salt.** Noreen Ayres. 302p. 4.98 (*0-8317-8572-1*) Smithmark.

World of the Coyote. Wayne Grady. LC 94-1464. (Illus.). 144p. 1995. pap. 18.00 (*0-87156-376-2*) Sierra.

World of the Crow Indians: As Driftwood Lodges. Rodney Frey. LC 87-40212. 1993. pap. 12.95 (*0-8061-2560-8*) U of Okla Pr.

***World of the Druids.** Miranda Green. Date not set. 29.95 (*0-500-05083-X*) Thames Hudson.

***World of the Early Christians.** Joseph F. Kelly. LC 97-11070. (Fathers of the Church Ser.: Vol. 1). 248p. 1997. 29.95 (*0-8146-5341-3*, M Glazier); pap. 22.95 (*0-8146-5313-8*, M Glazier) Liturgical Pr.

World of the Early Church: A Companion to the New Testament. Priscilla C. Patten & Rebecca Patten. LC 90-44322. 296p. 1991. lib. bdg. 89.95 (*0-88946-598-3*) E Mellen.

World of the Enlightenment: Die Welt der Aufklarung. Ed. by Bruno Coppieters. 128p. 1994. pap. 19.95 (*90-5487-039-7*) Paul & Co Pubs.

***World of the Fish.** William Andris. LC 96-69165. 318p. (Orig.). 1996. pap. 12.00 (*0-9604278-2-1*) St Basil Pr.

World of the Florentine Renaissance Artist: Projects & Patrons, Workshop & Art Market. Martin Wackernagel. Tr. by Alison Luchs. LC 80-39683. 480p. reprint ed. pap. 136.80 (*0-8357-7899-1*, 2036318) Bks Demand.

World of the Founders: New York Communities in the Federal Period. Ed. by Stephen L. Schechter & Wendell Tripp. LC 89-9238. 172p. (Orig.). (C). 1990. pap. text ed. 13.95 (*0-945660-02-2*, NYSC BUSC) Madison Hse.

World of the Fox. Rebecca L. Grambo. LC 95-1167. Orig. Title: The Nature of Foxes. (Illus.). 144p. 1995. 25.00 (*0-87156-377-0*) Sierra.

***World of the Fox.** Rebecca L. Grambo. Orig. Title: The Nature of Foxes. 1997. pap. 18.00 (*0-87156-958-2*) Sierra.

World of the Great White Heron. Marjory B. Sanger. LC 67-18236. (Illus.). 1967. 14.95 (*0-8159-7214-8*) Devin.

World of the Heart. John Island. (Illus.). 48p. (J). (ps-6). text ed. 14.95 (*0-9637712-0-5*) Island Flowers.

World of the Huns: Studies in Their History & Culture. Otto J. Maenchen-Helfen. Ed. by Max Knight. LC 79-94985. (Illus.). 634p. reprint ed. pap. 180.00 (*0-7837-4764-0*, 2044511) Bks Demand.

World of the Imagination: Sum & Substance. Eva T. H. Brann. 992p. (C). 1990. lib. bdg. 80.00 (*0-8476-7650-1*) Rowman.

World of the Incas: A Socialist State of the Past. Otfrid Von Hanstein. 1976. lib. bdg. 59.95 (*0-8490-2846-9*) Gordon Pr.

World of the Incas: A Socialistic State of the Past. Otfrid Von Hanstein. Tr. by Anna Barwell. LC 75-165811. (Select Bibliographies Reprint Ser.). 1977. reprint ed. 19.95 (*0-8369-5968-X*) Ayer.

World of the Indian Field Administrator. Byron T. Mook. 272p. 1983. text ed. 25.00 (*0-7069-1960-2*, Pub. by Vikas II) S Asia.

World of the Industrial Revolution: Comparative & International Aspects of Industrialization. Ed. by Robert Weible. LC 86-31242. (Business & Technology Ser.). (Illus.). 178p. 1986. pap. text ed. 10.00 (*0-937474-08-8*) Am Textile Hist.

World of the Irish Wonder Tale. Elliott B. Gose, Jr. 256p. 1985. pap. 17.95 (*0-8020-6585-6*) U of Toronto Pr.

World of the Irish Wonder Tale: An Introduction to the Study of Fairy Tales. Elliott B. Gose. LC 85-187404. 254p. reprint ed. pap. 72.40 (*0-8357-8385-5*, 2034033) Bks Demand.

World of the Japanese Garden: From Chinese Origins to Modern Landscape Art. Loraine Kuck. LC 68-26951. (Illus.). 416p. 1968. 52.50 (*0-8348-0029-2*) Weatherhill.

World of the Jaredites see Lehi in the Desert

World of the Manager Vol. 11: Food Administration in Berlin During World War I. George Yaney. LC 93-39524. (Studies in Modern European History: Vol. 11). 407p. (C). 1994. text ed. 71.95 (*0-8204-2434-X*) P Lang Pubng.

World of the Medieval Knight. Christopher Gravett. (World of Ser.). (Illus.). 64p. (YA). (gr. 5 up). 1996. 19.95 (*0-87226-277-4*) P Bedrick Bks.

World of the Meiji Print: Impressions of a New Civilization. Julia Meech-Pekarik. (Illus.). 299p. 1986. 60.00 (*0-8348-0209-0*) Weatherhill.

World of the Mexican Worker in Texas. Emilio Zamora. LC 92-24318. (Centennial Series of the Association of Former Students: No. 44). (Illus.). 304p. (Orig.). (C). 1995. 39.50 (*0-89096-514-5*) Tex A&M Univ Pr.

World of the Mexican Worker in Texas. Emilio Zamora. LC 92-24318. (Centennial Series of the Association of Former Students: Vol. 44). (Illus.). 304p. (Orig.). (C). 1995. pap. 15.95 (*0-89096-678-8*) Tex A&M Univ Pr.

World of the Microscope. Corinne Stockley. (Science & Experiments Ser.). (Illus.). 48p. (YA). 1989. pap. 7.95 (*0-7460-0289-0*); lib. bdg. 15.95 (*0-88110-364-0*) EDC.

***World of the Monarch Butterfly.** Eric S. Grace. 1997. 27.50 (*0-87156-981-7*) Sierra.

World of the Mountain Gorillas, 3 vols. (Illus.). (J). (gr. 2-3). 1994. Set. lib. bdg. 55.80 (*0-8368-0441-4*) Gareth Stevens Inc.

World of the New Testament. Abraham J. Malherbe. LC 68-5578. 1984. 12.95 (*0-915547-16-3*) Abilene Christ U.

World of the Old Testament. Ed. by A. S. Van Der Woude. Tr. by Sierd Woudstra. LC 88-21381. (Bible Handbook Ser.: No. 2). 336p. reprint ed. pap. 95.80 (*0-7837-6573-8*, 2046138) Bks Demand.

World of the Oratorio. Kurt Pahlen & Thurston J. Dox. Tr. by Judith Schaeffer from GER. LC 89-17757. (Illus.). 397p. 1990. 39.95 (*0-931340-11-X*, Amadeus Pr) Timber.

World of the Orthodox Jewish Mother. Sarah S. Bunim. 1995. 14.95 (*0-88125-308-1*) Ktav.

World of the Paris Cafe: Sociability among the French Working Class, 1789-1914. W. Scott Haine. LC 95-30624. (Studies in Historical & Political Science, 112th Series (1994): Series 114, No. 2). (Illus.). 368p. (C). 1996. text ed. 39.95 (*0-8018-5104-1*) Johns Hopkins.

World of the Penguin. Jonathan Chester. LC 96-17675. (Illus.). 128p. 1996. 27.50 (*0-87156-900-0*) Sierra.

***World of the Pirate.** Valerie Garwood. (World of Ser.). (Illus.). 48p. (YA). (gr. 5 up). 1997. 19.95 (*0-87226-281-2*) P Bedrick Bks.

World of the Polar Bear. Fred Bruemmer. (Illus.). 160p. 1991. 19.99 (*0-517-05423-X*) Random Hse Value.

World of the Polar Bear. Norbert Rosing. (Illus.). 176p. 1996. 40.00 (*1-55209-068-X*) Firefly Bks Ltd.

World of the Policy Analyst: Rationality, Values, & Politics. Robert A. Heineman et al. LC 90-39484. (Chatham House Studies in Political Thinking). 192p. (Orig.). (C). 1990. pap. text ed. 17.95 (*0-934540-75-6*) Chatham Hse Pubs.

***World of the Policy Analyst: Rationality, Values, & Politics.** 2nd ed. Robert A. Heineman et al. LC 96-46153. (Studies in Political Thinking). (Illus.). (Orig.). (C). 1997. pap. text ed. 19.95 (*1-56643-047-X*) Chatham Hse Pubs.

World of the Polis see Order & History

World of the Relic Hunter. Ed Fedory. 188p. 1995. 14.95 (*1-882279-04-2*) Whites Elect.

World of the Romans. Charles Freeman. Ed. by J. F. Drinkwater & Andrew Drummon. LC 93-16142. 192p. 1993. 39.95 (*0-19-521019-0*) OUP.

World of the Rural Labourer in Colonial India. Gyan Prakash. (Themes in Indian History Ser.). 276p. 1992. 29.95 (*0-19-562832-2*) OUP.

World of the Rural Labourer in Colonial India. Ed. by Gyan Prakash. (Oxford in India Readings: Themes in Indian History, Oxford India Paperbacks Ser.). 320p. 1994. reprint ed. pap. 10.95 (*0-19-563440-3*) OUP.

World of the Scythians. Renate Rolle. 1990. 40.00 (*0-520-06864-5*) U CA Pr.

World of the Sea Otter. Stefani Paine. LC 93-2820. (Illus.). 144p. 1995. pap. 18.00 (*0-87156-375-4*) Sierra.

World of the Senses & the World of the Spirit. Rudolf Steiner. 88p. (GER.). 1979. reprint ed. pap. 6.95 (*0-919924-10-7*, Pub. by Steiner Book Centre CN) Anthroposophic.

World of the Shining Prince: Court Life in Ancient Japan. Ivan Morris. Ed. by Paul De Angelis. 352p. 1994. pap. 15.00 (*1-56836-029-0*) Kodansha.

World of the Shorebirds. Harry Thurston. LC 96-17674. 128p. 1996. 27.50 (*0-87156-901-9*) Sierra.

World of the Short Story. Clifton Fadiman. 1990. 12.99 (*0-517-03400-X*) Random Hse Value.

***World of the Southern Indians.** Virginia P. Brown & Laurella Owens. LC 83-6376. (Illus.). 176p. (YA). (gr. 6-9). 1997. reprint ed. pap. 15.95 (*0-912221-06-2*) Beechwood.

World of the Sufi. Idries Shah. 307p. 1979. 23.00 (*0-900860-66-9*, Pub. by Octagon Pr UK) ISHK.

World of the Swahili: An African Mercantile Civilization. John Middleton. (Illus.). 320p. (C). 1992. text ed. 35.00 (*0-300-05219-7*) Yale U Pr.

World of the Swahili: An African Mercantile Civilization. John Middleton. (Illus.). 266p. 1994. pap. 17.00 (*0-300-06080-7*) Yale U Pr.

World of the Talmud. Morris Adler. 1987. 5.95 (*0-394-20058-6*) Pantheon.

World of the Tarot: The Secret Teachings of the 78 Cards of the Gypsies. Sergius Golowin. LC 87-34100. (Illus.). 196p. 1988. pap. 14.95 (*0-87728-642-6*) Weiser.

World of the Ten Thousand Things: Poems 1980-1990. Charles Wright. 230p. 1991. pap. 13.00 (*0-374-52326-6*, Noonday) FS&G.

World of the Tent-Makers: A Natural History of the Eastern Tent Caterpillar. Vincent G Dethier. LC 80-11361. (Illus.). 160p. 1980. pap. 13.95 (*0-87023-301-7*) U of Mass Pr.

World of the Theatre. 2nd ed. Robert W. Corrigan. 408p. (C). 1991. per. write for info. (*0-697-11289-6*) Brown & Benchmark.

World of the Theatre. 2nd ed. Robert W. Corrigan. 408p. (C). 1992. write for info. (*0-697-16926-X*) Brown & Benchmark.

World of the Thriller. Ralph Harper. LC 69-17681. 152p. 1969. 16.95 (*0-8295-0148-7*) Boulevard.

***World of the Thriller.** Ralph Harper. LC 69-17681. 152p. 1969. reprint ed. pap. 43.40 (*0-608-03693-5*, 2064518) Bks Demand.

World of the Troubadours: Medieval Occitan Society, c. 1100-c. 1300. Linda M. Paterson. (Illus.). 381p. (C). 1995. pap. text ed. 22.95 (*0-521-55832-8*) Cambridge U Pr.

World of the Troubadours: Medieval Occitan Society, c. 1100-c.1300. Linda M. Paterson. LC 92-37723. (Illus.). 352p. (C). 1993. text ed. 69.95 (*0-521-35240-1*) Cambridge U Pr.

World of the Urban Working Class. Marc Fried et al. LC 73-81673. (Illus.). 422p. reprint ed. pap. 120.30 (*0-7837-4146-4*, 2057994) Bks Demand.

World of the Wolf. Candace C. Savage. LC 96-17673. (Illus.). 128p. 1996. 27.50 (*0-87156-899-3*) Sierra.

World of Theater: The History of Actors, Singers, Costumes, Audiences, & Scenery. Scholastic Staff. (Voyages of Discovery Ser.: No. 8). 48p. (J). (gr. 4-6). 1995. bds., spiral bd. 19.95 (*0-590-47642-4*, Blue Sky Press) Scholastic Inc.

World of Their Own: Twentieth-Century American Folk Art. Joseph Jacobs. Ed. by Vajra Kilgour & Rena Zurofsky. (Illus.). 87p. (Orig.). 1995. pap. text ed. 19.95 (*0-932828-31-0*) Newark Mus.

World of their Own Making: Myth, Ritual, & the Quest for Family Values. John Gillis. 256p. 1996. 25.00 (*0-465-05414-5*) Basic.

***World of Their Own Making: Myth, Ritual & the Quest for Family Values.** John R. Gillis. 1997. 16.95 (*0-674-96188-9*) HUP.

World of Things to Do. Margaret McKelway. Ed. by Donald J. Crump. (Books for World Explorers Series 8: No. 2). (Illus.). 104p. (J). 1987. lib. bdg. 12.50 (*0-87044-615-0*) Natl Geog.

World of Things to Do. Margaret McKelway & National Geographic Society Staff. Ed. by Donald J. Crump. (Books for World Explorers Series 8: No. 2). (Illus.). 104p. (J). 1994. 12.50 (*0-87044-610-X*) Natl Geog.

World of Thought in Ancient China. Benjamin I. Schwartz. (Illus.). 456p. 1985. 37.00 (*0-674-96190-0*) Belknap Pr.

World of Thought in Ancient China. Benjamin I. Schwartz. 456p. 1989. reprint ed. pap. 17.95 (*0-674-96191-9*) HUP.

World of Tibetan Buddhism: An Overview of Its Philosophy & Practice. Tenzin Gyatso. Ed. & Tr. by Geshe T. Jinpa from TIB. LC 94-30512. 224p. (Orig.). 1995. pap. 25.00 (*0-86171-097-5*) Wisdom MA.

World of Tibetan Buddhism: An Overview of Its Philosophy & Practice. Dalai Lama. Ed. & Tr. by Geshe T. Jinpa. 224p. (Orig.). 1995. pap. 14.00 (*0-86171-100-9*) Wisdom MA.

World of Tiers. Philip Jose Farmer. LC 96-23840. 1996. pap. 15.95 (*0-312-85761-6*) St Martin.

World of Tiers. Philip Jose Farmer. 1996. 25.95 (*0-312-85762-4*) St Martin.

World of Tiers, Vol. 1. Philip Jose Farmer. 250p. 1993. 7.25 (*1-56865-071-X*, GuildAmerica) Dblday Direct.

***World of Tiers, Vol. 2.** Farmer. Date not set. 25.95 (*0-312-86376-4*) St Martin.

***World of Tiers, Vol. 2.** Farmer. Date not set. pap. 18.95 (*0-312-86377-2*) St Martin.

World of Tiers, Vol. II. Philip Jose Farmer. 250p. 1993. 7.25 (*1-56865-072-8*, GuildAmerica) Dblday Direct.

World of Tikal. Jacques VanKirk et al. Ed. by Hal Bamford. Tr. by Carmen A. Feliciano. LC 85-819891. (Illus.). (Orig.). 1985. pap. 14.95 (*0-8200-9916-3*) Great Outdoors.

World of Touch. Ed. by D. Katz & Lester E. Krueger. 272p. (C). 1989. text ed. 55.00 (*0-8058-0529-X*) L Erlbaum Assocs.

World of Transformations. Gloria Sanok. 1988. teacher ed. 20.00 (*0-9626222-0-6*) WOT.

World of Transformations: World of Transformations & Fractals Supplement. rev. ed. Gloria Sanok. (Illus.). 1992. reprint ed. teacher ed. 25.00 incl. sl. (*0-9626222-1-4*) WOT.

World of Translation. Intro. by Gregory Rabassa. vii, 382p. 1987. 10.95 (*0-934638-06-3*) PEN Am Ctr.

World of Travel Tips. Jean Nieman. (Illus.). 170p. (Orig.). 1982. write for info. (*0-9609388-0-X*) Travel Inter.

World of Treasure. V. Ben Kendrick. LC 82-332. 204p. 1981. pap. 5.95 (*0-87227-081-5*, RBP5099) Reg Baptist.

World of Tropical Flowers. Laurie Perrero. LC 76-12926. (Illus.). 64p. (Orig.). 1976. pap. 4.95 (*0-89317-008-9*) Windward Pub.

***World of Tudors Films.** (Then & There Ser.). Date not set. pap. text ed. write for info. (*0-7056-2067-0*) Addison-Wesley.

World of Turtles. John Lehrer. (Illus.). 160p. 1993. 26.95 (*1-56465-116-9*, 16089) Tetra Pr.

***World of Turtles: A Literary Celebration.** Gregory McNamee & Luis A. Urrea. (Illus.). 176p. 1997. pap. 14.00 (*1-55566-190-4*) Johnson Bks.

An Asterisk (*) at the beginning of an entry indicates that the title is appearing in BIP for the first time.

World of Two Thousand Forty-Four: Technological Development & the Future of Society. Ed. by Charles Sheffield et al. LC 94-3101. 384p. 1994. 29.95 (0-943852-49-8); pap. text ed. 19.95 (0-943852-57-9) Prof World Peace.

World of Unseen Spirits. Bernard N. Schneider. pap. 7.99 (0-88469-024-5) BMH Bks.

World of Venice. rev. ed. James Morris. LC 73-18461. (Illus.). 328p. 1995. reprint ed. pap. 14.00 (0-15-698356-7, Harvest Bks) HarBrace.

World of Victorian Humor. Ed. by Harold Orel. LC 61-8018. (Goldentree Books in English Literature). (Illus.). (Orig.). 1961. pap. text ed. 12.95 (0-89197-474-1) Irvington.

World of Villa-Lobos in Pictures & Documents. Lisa M. Peppercorn. LC 95-44199. (Illus.). 336p. 1997. 59.95 (1-85928-261-X, Pub. by Scolar Pr UK) Ashgate Pub Co.

World of Violence: Corrections in America. Matthew Silberman. 232p. 1995. pap. 26.95 (0-534-24540-4) Wadsworth Pub.

World of Voltaire. Intro. by Paul Spurlin. (Illus.). 74p. 1969. pap. 3.00 (0-317-99610-X) Michigan Mus.

World of W. E. B. Du Bois: A Quotation Sourcebook. Ed. by Meyer Weinberg. LC 92-15481. 296p. 1992. text ed. 69.50 (0-313-28619-1, WWJ, Greenwood Pr) Greenwood.

World of W. Edwards Deming. 2nd rev. ed. Cecelia S. Kilian. (Illus.). 380p. 1992. 28.00 (0-945320-29-9) SPC Pr.

World of Wade, Bk. 2. Ian Warner & Mike Posgay. 252p. 1994. 42.95 (1-57080-001-4) Antique Pubns.

World of Wade: Collectable Porcelain & Pottery, Bk. 1. Ian Warner & Mike Posgay. (Illus.). 190p. 1988. 37.95 (0-915410-51-6) Antique Pubns.

World of Wade: Collectable Porcelain & Pottery, Bk. 2. Ian Warner & Mike Posgay. (Illus.). 252p. 1994. pap. 34.95 (1-57080-000-6) Antique Pubns.

World of Waste. Peg Kocher & Anita Siegenthaler. LC 87-37868. (Illus.). 198p. 1988. 7.50 (0-9619818-0-6) LWV Tri-State.

World of Waste: Dilemmas of Industrial Development. K. A. Gourlay. 256p. (C). 1992. pap. 17.50 (0-86232-989-2, Pub. by Zed Bks Ltd UK) Humanities.

***World of Watches.** J. Lassqussios. 1996. 17.98 (0-7858-0743-8) Bk Sales Inc.

World of Water: Linking Fiction to Nonfiction. Phyllis J. Perry. LC 94-44426. (Literature Bridges to Science Ser.). xvi, 149p. (J). (gr. 5-9). 1995. pap. text ed. 21.50 (1-56308-321-3) Teacher Ideas Pr.

World of Weather. David Adler. LC 82-17398. (Question & Answer Bks.). (Illus.). 32p. (J). (gr. 3-6). 1983. lib. bdg. 10.95 (0-89375-870-1) Troll Communs.

World of Weather. David Adler. LC 82-17398. (Question & Answer Bks.). (Illus.). 32p. (J). (gr. 3-6). 1996. pap. 3.95 (0-89375-871-X) Troll Communs.

***World of Weather.** Brian Cosgrove. (Illus.). 160p. (YA). 1997. 29.95 (1-85310-765-4, Pub. by Swan Hill UK) Voyageur Pr.

World of Weather. Jon Nese et al. 400p. (C). 1996. spiral bd. 52.44 (0-7872-0593-1) Kendall-Hunt.

World of Whales, 6 vols. Sarah Palmer. (J). 1990. 7.99 (0-517-02746-1) Random Hse Value.

World of Whales & Dolphins. Day. 1995. pap. 10.99 (1-57081-881-9) Day Dream SBCA.

World of Widows. Margaret Owen. 240p. (C). 1996. 55.00 (1-85649-419-5, Pub. by Zed Bks Ltd UK) Humanities.

World of Widows. Margaret Owen. 240p. (C). 1996. pap. 19.95 (1-85649-420-9, Pub. by Zed Bks Ltd UK) Humanities.

World of Wilderness: Essays on the Power & Purpose of Wild Country. T. H. Watkins. 288p. 1995. 24.95 (1-57098-017-9); pap. 14.95 (1-57098-016-0) R Rinehart.

World of Willa Cather. Mildred R. Bennett. LC 94-44205. (Illus.). xvi, 304p. 1995. pap. 12.00 (0-8032-5013-4, Bison Books) U of Nebr Pr.

World of William & Mary: Anglo-Dutch Perspectives on the Revolution of 1688-89. Ed. by Dale E. Hoak & Mordechai Feingold. LC 94-36712. xviii, 339p. 1995. 49.50 (0-8047-2406-7) Stanford U Pr.

World of William Clissold, 2 vols. H. G. Wells. (BCL1-PR English Literature Ser.). 1992. reprint ed. Set. lib. bdg. 150.00 (0-7812-7562-8) Rprt Serv.

***World of William Joyce.** Illus. by William Joyce & Philip Gould. (Laura Geringer Book Ser.). 48p. (J). (ps up). 16.95 (0-06-027432-8) HarpC Child Bks.

***World of William Joyce.** Illus. by William Joyce & Philip Gould. (Laura Geringer Book Ser.). 48p. (J). (ps up). lib. bdg. 16.89 (0-06-027433-6) HarpC Child Bks.

World of William Notman. Dodds. 240p. 1993. 75.00 (0-87923-939-5) Godine.

***World of William Saroyan: A Literary Interpretation.** Nona Balakian. LC 97-4379. 1997. write for info. (0-8387-5368-X) Bucknell U Pr.

World of Wings & Things. Alliott Verdon-Roe. Ed. by James B. Gilbert. LC 79-7293. (Flight: Its First Seventy-Five Years Ser.). (Illus.). 1980. reprint ed. lib. bdg. 25.95 (0-405-12200-4) Ayer.

World of Winners. 3rd ed. Gita Siegman. 1998. 80.00 (0-8103-7615-6) Gale.

***World of Winners.** 4th ed. Date not set. 80.00 (0-8103-9074-4, 00000293, Gale Res Intl) Gale.

World of Winners: A Current & Historical Perspective on Awards & Their Winners. Ed. by Gita Siegman. 200p. 1988. 75.00 (0-8103-0474-0) Gale.

World of Winners: A Current & Historical Perspective or Awards & Their Winners. 2nd ed. Intro. by Gita Siegman. 1000p. 1991. 80.00 (0-8103-6981-8, 006287) Gale.

World of Winnie-the-Pooh, 2 bks. A. A. Milne. (Illus.). (J). (ps up). 1988. Set. pap. 39.98 (0-525-44452-1) Dutton Child Bks.

***World of Women.** Janice W. Wetzel. (C). 1992. pap. text ed. 16.00 (0-8147-9255-3) NYU Pr.

World of Women: In Pursuit of Human Rights. Janice W. Wetzel. 260p. (C). 1992. 55.00 (0-8147-9254-5); pap. text ed. 16.00 (0-333-55031-5) NYU Pr.

World of Women's Trade Unionism: Comparative Historical Essays. Ed. by Norbert C. Soldon. LC 84-3800. (Contributions in Women's Studies: No. 52). (Illus.). ix, 256p. 1985. text ed. 59.95 (0-313-22792-6, STU/, Greenwood Pr) Greenwood.

World of Wonders. Robertson Davies. 320p. 1977. pap. 11.95 (0-14-016796-X, Penguin Bks); mass mkt. 6.95 (0-14-004389-6, Penguin Bks) Viking Penguin.

World of Wooden Bobbins. Ed. by Graham Fellowes. (Illus.). 80p. (Orig.). 1995. lib. bdg. 22.00 (0-9646720-0-6, 22) Discov Collection.

World of Words. Margaret A. Richek. 1992. pap. text ed. write for info. (0-318-68492-6) HM.

World of Words, 4 Vols. Margaret A. Richek. (C). 1995. pap. 30.76 (0-395-75051-2) HM.

World of Words, 4 Vols. Margaret A. Richek. (C). 1995. pap. 31.96 (0-395-71984-4) HM.

World of Words. Margaret A. Richek. (C). Date not set. write for info. (0-395-77733-X) HM.

World of Words, 4 Vols. Margaret A. Richek. (C). 1995. 43.96 (0-395-78236-8) HM.

***World of Words.** Thomas-Cochran. 1994. student ed., pap. text ed. write for info. (0-582-80144-3, Pub. by Longman UK) Longman.

World of Words. Tobi Tobias. LC 96-16313. (Illus.). (J). Date not set. write for info. (0-688-12129-2); lib. bdg. write for info. (0-688-12130-6) Lothrop.

World of Words. Paul F. Wells. 491p. (Orig.). 1995. pap. 15.95 (0-9647101-1-0) World of Words.

World of Words. 2nd ed. Margaret A. Richek. 352p. 1988. write for info. (0-318-63333-7); pap. 23.56 (0-685-44112-1) HM.

World of Words, 4 Vols. 4th ed. Margaret A. Richek. (C). 1995. 38.76 (0-395-78235-X) HM.

World of Words: An Introduction to Language in General & to English & American in Particular. 3rd ed. Eric Partridge. LC 73-117913. (Select Bibliographies Reprint Ser.). 1977. reprint ed. 24.95 (0-8369-5366-5) Ayer.

World of Words: Language & Displacement in the Fiction of Edgar Allan Poe. Michael J. Williams. LC 87-30331. xvii, 182p. (C). 1988. text ed. 34.95 (0-8223-0780-4) Duke.

World of Work. Jeri A. Carroll & Tom Foster. (Focus On... Ser.). 112p. 7.99 (0-86653-748-1, GA1463) Good Apple.

***World of Work.** Edmund Flood. 24p. 1996. pap. 1.95 (1-55612-872-X) Sheed & Ward MO.

World of Work. Ruth C. Rosen. (Life Skills Library). (Illus.). 48p. (YA). (gr. 7-12). 1993. lib. bdg. 14.95 (0-8239-1467-4) Rosen Group.

World of Work: Careers & the Future. Ed. by Howard Didsbury. 1983. pap. 14.50 (0-930242-21-1) World Future.

World of Work: Handbook of Contemporary Issues. Paul C. Sartoris. (Illus.). 800p. 1997. text ed. 189.50 (0-8290-2628-2) Irvington.

World of Wrestling Coloring Book. Louis Tate. (Illus.). 48p. 1989. write for info. (0-9622725-0-7) L Tate.

World of Yesterday. Stefan Zweig. LC 43-5821. (Illus.). xxv, 463p. 1964. reprint ed. pap. text ed. 15.00 (0-8032-5224-2, Bison Books) U of Nebr Pr.

World of Yesterday's Humanist Today: Proceedings of the Stefan Zweig Symposium. Ed. by Marion Sonnenfeld. LC 83-541. 357p. 1984. text ed. 29.50 (0-87395-599-4) State U NY Pr.

World of Young Andrew Jackson. Suzanne Hilton. (Young Presidents Ser.). (Illus.). (J). (gr. 5-8). 1988. 12.95 (0-8027-6814-8); lib. bdg. 13.85 (0-8027-6815-6) Walker & Co.

World of Young George Washington. Suzanne Hilton. LC 86-13296. (Illus.). 112p. (J). (gr. 5-9). 1987. 12.95 (0-8027-6657-9); lib. bdg. 12.85 (0-8027-6658-7) Walker & Co.

World of Young Herbert Hoover. Suzanne Hilton. (J). (gr. 5-8). 1987. 12.95 (0-8027-6708-7); lib. bdg. 13.85 (0-8027-6709-5) Walker & Co.

World of Young Tom Jefferson. Suzanne Hilton. (Illus.). 96p. (J). (gr. 3-6). 1986. 12.95 (0-8027-6621-8); lib. bdg. 12.85 (0-8027-6622-6) Walker & Co.

World of Your Dreams. Debbie Friedman. Ed. & Tr. by Randee Friedman. (ENG & HEB.). 1993. audio 10.95 (1-890161-17-9) Sounds Write.

World of Your Dreams. Debbie Friedman. Ed. & Tr. by Randee Friedman. (ENG & HEB.). 1993. audio compact disk 17.95 (1-890161-18-7) Sounds Write.

World of Your Dreams. Debbie Friedman. Ed. & Tr. by Randee Friedman. 33p. (ENG & HEB.). 1993. pap. 12.95 (0-9626286-3-8) Sounds Write.

World of Zen. Ed. by Nancy W. Ross. (Illus.). 1964. pap. 16.00 (0-394-70301-4, Vin) Random.

World Offshore Field Development Guide, 3. Oilfield Publications Limited Staff. (World Offshore Field Development Guide Ser.). (Illus.). 1885p. 1995. pap. 695.00 (1-870945-60-3, Pub. by Oilfld Pubns Ltd UK) Am Educ Systs.

World Offshore Field Development Guide: Africa, Mediterranean, & Middle East, Vol. 1. Oilfield Publications Limited Staff. (Illus.). 750p. 1995. pap. 350.00 (1-870945-69-7, Pub. by Oilfld Pubns Ltd UK) Am Educ Systs.

World Offshore Field Development Guide: Asia, Indian Sub-Continent, Vol. 2. 2nd ed. Oilfield Publications Limited Staff. (World Offshore Field Development Guide Ser.). (Illus.). 385p. 1995. pap. 350.00 (1-870945-70-0, Pub. by Oilfld Pubns Ltd UK) Am Educ Systs.

World Offshore Field Development Guide: North & South America, Vol. 3. Oilfield Publications Limited Staff. (World Offshore Field Development Guide Ser.). (Illus.). 750p. 1993. pap. 350.00 (1-870945-42-5, Pub. by Oilfld Pubns Ltd UK) Am Educ Systs.

World Offshore Field Development Guide Series, Vol. 1: Mediterranean, Middle East & Africa. Oilfield Publications Limited Staff. 750p. (C). 1993. 805.00 (1-870945-22-0, Pub. by Oilfield Pubns UK) St Mut.

World Offshore Field Development Guide Series, Vol. 2: Asia, Indian Sub-Continent, Australasia & Far East. Oilfield Publications Limited Staff. 750p. (C). 1993. 805.00 (1-870945-25-5, Pub. by Oilfield Pubns UK) St Mut.

World Offshore Field Development Guide Series, Vol. 3: North & South America. Oilfield Publications Limited Staff. (C). 1993. 805.00 (1-870945-11-5, Pub. by Oilfield Pubns UK) St Mut.

World Oil: Coping With the Dangers of Success. Christopher Flavin. LC 85-51495. (Worldwatch Papers). 1985. pap. 5.00 (0-916468-66-6) Worldwatch Inst.

World Oil & Gas Atlas 1995-96 Edition. Oilfield Publications Limited Staff. (Illus.). 36p. 1995. pap. 79.00 (1-870945-73-5, Pub. by Oilfld Pubns Ltd UK) Am Educ Systs.

World Oil Co. v. Northeast Shipbuilding, Inc. & Toiler Salvage Co. Defective Designs, Negligence. Thomas F. Geraghty. 230p. 1983. pap. 18.95 (1-55681-099-7) Natl Inst Trial Ad.

World Oil Co. v. Northeast Shipbuilding, Inc. & Toiler Salvage Co. Teaching Notes: Defective Designs, Negligence. Thomas F. Geraghty. 31p. 1984. teacher ed., pap. 8.95 (1-55681-074-1) Natl Inst Trial Ad.

World Oil Prices: Demand, Supply, & Substitutes. Yousuf Hasan Mohammad & Walter J. Mead. LC 89-83487. 120p. 1990. 24.00 (0-918714-16-8) Intl Res Ctr Energy.

World Oil's Cementing Oil & Gas Wells: Including Casing Handling Procedures. George O. Suman & Richard C. Ellis. (World Oil Handbook Ser.: Vol. 3). 74p. reprint ed. pap. 25.00 (0-317-26814-7, 2024313) Bks Demand.

***World Oil's Handbook of Horizontal Drilling & Completion Technology.** World Oil Staff. LC 90-45596. (Illus.). 136p. reprint ed. pap. 38.80 (0-608-04547-0, 2065289) Bks Demand.

World Oilseed Market: Policy Impacts & Market Outlook. OECD Staff. 62p. (Orig.). 1994. pap. 15.00 (92-64-14247-9) OECD.

World Oilseeds: Chemistry, Technology, & Utilization. D. K. Salunkhe et al. (Illus.). 600p. (gr. 13). 1991. text ed. 109.95 (0-442-00112-6) Chapman & Hall.

World on a String. John D. Pollack. LC 96-46478. 1997. pap. 12.95 (0-8050-4842-1) H Holt & Co.

World on Blood. Jonathan Nasaw. 341p. 1996. pap. 22.95 (0-525-94066-9, Dutton) NAL-Dutton.

World on Blood. Jonathan Nasaw. Date not set. pap. 16.95 (0-14-086268-4) Viking Penguin.

World on Blood. Jonathan Nasaw. 1997. pap. 6.99 (0-451-18658-3, Sig) NAL-Dutton.

***World on Display: Photographs from the St. Louis World's Fair, 1904.** Eric Breitbart. 108p. 1997. 34.95 (0-8263-1742-1) U of NM Pr.

World On-Line Transaction Terminal Markets: Communicaiton & Information Technologies Go Retail. Market Intelligence Staff. 550p. 1993. 1,695.00 (1-56753-876-2) Frost & Sullivan.

World on My Doorstep: American Autobiography. Harriet Davis. 274p. 1995. lib. bdg. 79.00 (0-7812-8496-1) Rprt Serv.

World on Paper: A Celebration of the Mapmaker's Art Catalogue of an Exhibition, March 3-June 3, 1994, Rare Book & Manuscript Library. Mead T. Cain. Ed. by Rudolph Ellenbogen & Claudia Funke. (Illus.). 56p. 1994. pap. 20.00 (0-9607862-7-9) Columbia U Libs.

World on Paper: The Conceptual & Cognitive Implications of Writing & Reading. David R. Olson. (Illus.). 304p. (C). 1994. 25.95 (0-521-44311-3) Cambridge U Pr.

World on Paper: The Conceptual & Cognitive Implications of Writing & Reading. David R. Olson. (Illus.). 338p. 1996. pap. text ed. 19.95 (0-521-57558-3) Cambridge U Pr.

World on the Move: The Portuguese in Africa, Asia, & America, 1415-1808. A. J. Russell-Wood. LC 92-35178. 305p. 1993. text ed. 39.95 (0-312-09427-2) St Martin.

World on Time: How Federal Express' 12 Management Principles Delivered Tomorrow's Corporation Today. James C. Wetherbe. 225p. 1996. 22.95 (1-888232-06-4); audio 12.00 (1-888232-07-2) Knowldge Exchange.

World on Wheels: Or, Carriages, with Their Historical Associations from the Earliest to the Present Time. Ezra Stratton. LC 72-83800. (Illus.). 1977. reprint ed. 31.95 (0-405-09006-4) Ayer.

World One. Timothy Cooper. LC 87-73424. 1990. 19.95 (0-9619914-0-2) Americus Pr.

***World Ophthalmic Pharmaceutical Markets: Development of New Products Boosts Market.** Frost Sullivan Staff. Date not set. write for info. (0-7889-0523-6, 5228) Frost & Sullivan.

World Ophthalmic Pharmaceutical Markets: Technology Driven Products for Shifting Global Economies. Market Intelligence Staff. 470p. (Orig.). 1994. 2,395.00 (1-56753-923-8) Frost & Sullivan.

World Optical Disk Drive & Media Markets. Market Intelligence Staff. 1995. 2,995.00 (0-7889-0190-7, 5177-73) Frost & Sullivan.

***World Order.** Goliszek. Date not set. 22.95 (0-312-85908-2) St Martin.

World Order & Local Disorder: The United Nations & Internal Conflicts. Linda B. Miller. LC 67-16953. 245p. reprint ed. pap. 69.90 (0-8357-7078-8, 2033382) Bks Demand.

World Order & Religion. Ed. by Wade C. Roof. LC 90-45447. (SUNY Series in Religion, Culture, & Society). 328p. (C). 1991. pap. text ed. 21.95 (0-7914-0740-3) State U NY Pr.

World Order & Religion. Ed. by Wade C. Roof. LC 90-45447. (SUNY Series in Religion, Culture, & Society). 328p. (C). 1991. text ed. 64.50 (0-7914-0739-X) State U NY Pr.

World Order in History: Russia & the West. Paul Dukes. LC 95-20020. 198p. (C). 1996. text ed. 62.95 (0-415-12936-2) Routledge.

World Orders. B. P. Menon. (Writers Workshop Blackbird Ser.). 32p. 1978. 6.00 (0-86578-056-0) Ind-US Inc.

World Orders: Old & New. Noam Chomsky. 311p. 1996. pap. 15.95 (0-231-10157-0) Col U Pr.

World Orders, Old & New. Noam Chomsky. LC 94-21950. 360p. 1994. 24.95 (0-231-10156-2) Col U Pr.

World Orthopedic & Prosthetic Product Markets: Impact of Lifestyles, Demographics & Biomaterials. Market Intelligence Staff. 627p. 1992. 1,995.00 (1-56753-386-8) Frost & Sullivan.

***World Orthopedic Implants Market.** (Market Research Reports: No. 621). 130p. 1996. 995.00 (0-614-20540-9) Theta Corp.

World OTC Dermatology Pharmaceutical Markets. Market Intelligence Staff. 1995. 2,295.00 (0-7889-0196-6, 960-52) Frost & Sullivan.

World out of Balance: Our Polluted Planet. Jon S. Erickson. 184p. 1992. 22.95 (0-8306-2823-1); pap. 14.95 (0-8306-2804-5) McGraw-Hill Prof.

World Out of Time. Larry Niven. 1986. mass mkt. 5.99 (0-345-33696-8, Del Rey) Ballantine.

World Out There: Becoming Part of the Lesbian & Gay Community. Michael T. Ford. 224p. (Orig.). Date not set. pap. 14.95 (1-56584-234-0) New Press NY.

***World Outlook 1997.** 1996. write for info. (0-614-25459-0, M955) Econ Intel.

World Outside: The Fiction of Paul Bowles. Richard F. Patteson. 167p. 1987. pap. 7.95 (0-292-79035-X) U of Tex Pr.

World Outside the Window: The Selected Essays of Kenneth Rexroth. Kenneth Rexroth. Ed. by Bradford Morrow. LC 86-28610. 352p. 1987. 24.95 (0-8112-1024-3); pap. 12.95 (0-8112-1025-1, NDP639) New Directions.

World Owes Me Lunch. David McCord. 112p. 1993. pap. 6.00 (1-887151-02-8) Andromeda CA.

World PAC. Data Trek Inc. Staff. (Illus.). 60p. 1996. 35.00 (0-929795-40-7) EOS Intl.

World Packaged Holidays Market. Euromonitor Staff. 135p. 1988. 975.00 (0-86338-327-0, Pub. by Euromonitor Pubns UK) Gale.

World Painting Index: First Supplement 1973-1980, 2 vols. Patricia P. Havlice. LC 82-3355. 1233p. 1982. 95.00 (0-8108-1531-1) Scarecrow.

World Painting Index, 1980-1989 Suppl. 2. Patricia P. Havlice. LC 95-2326. 1890p. 1995. suppl. ed. 149.50 (0-8108-3020-5) Scarecrow.

World Palaeontological Collections. R. J. Cleevely. 366p. 1983. text ed. 160.00 (0-7201-1655-4, Mansell Pub) Cassell.

World Paper Money: Collectors Guide & Catalogue. 3rd ed. John Aiello. 312p. pap. 19.95 (0-917515-00-5) Sunrise NJ.

World Partners, 6 bks. Martin Nabhan et al. (Illus.). 384p. (YA). (gr. 7 up). 1990. Set. lib. bdg. 95.58 (0-86593-087-2); Set. lib. bdg. 77.70 (0-685-36361-9) Rourke Corp.

World Passed By: Great Cities in Jewish Diaspora History. Marvin Lowenthal. LC 90-30824. (Illus.). 560p. (C). 1990. reprint ed. 34.50 (0-934710-19-8) J Simon.

World Patent Law & Practice, 3 vols. J. W. Baxter & John P. Sinnott. (Patent Law & Practice Ser.). 1968. Updates. ring bd. write for info. (0-8205-1055-6) Bender.

World Patent Law & Practice, 14 Vols. John P. Sinnot. 1974. ring bd. write for info. (0-8205-1622-8) Bender.

World PBX & Key System Markets. Market Intelligence Staff. 553p. 1994. 2,295.00 (0-7889-0021-8) Frost & Sullivan.

World PC-Based Instrumentation & Software Markets: Invading the Laboratory & Industrial Environments. Market Intelligence Staff. 447p. 1992. 1,895.00 (1-56753-076-1) Frost & Sullivan.

World PC Card Markets: PCMCIA Standard Opens the Flood Gates. Market Intelligence Staff. 250p. 1993. 1,495.00 (1-56753-448-1) Frost & Sullivan.

World PC Card Markets: Peripheral & Flash Cards Byte into Ram Share. Market Intelligence Staff. 320p. 1994. 1,995.00 (0-7889-0089-7) Frost & Sullivan.

World Peace? A Work Based on Interviews with Foreign Diplomats. Anthony J. Donovan. LC 86-71893. 128p. (Orig.). 1986. pap. write for info. (0-9617258-0-X) A J Donovan.

World Peace: A Written Debate Between William Howard Taft & William Jennings Bryan. William H. Taft. LC 73-137553. (Peace Movement in America Ser.). 156p. 1972. reprint ed. lib. bdg. 22.95 (0-89198-083-0) Ozer.

World Peace & the Human Family. Roy Weatherford. LC 92-36242. (Points of Conflict Ser.). 192p. (C). 1993. pap. 14.95 (0-415-06303-5, B0736) Routledge.

World Peace & the Human Family. Roy Weatherford. LC 92-36242. (Points of Conflict Ser.). 192p. (C). (gr. 13). 1993. text ed. 59.95 (0-415-06302-7, B0732) Routledge.

World Peace & World Government: From Vision to Reality: A Baha'i Approach. J. Tyson. 96p. (Orig.). 1986. pap. 4.50 (0-85398-235-X) G Ronald Pub.

W

World Peace Ceremony: Prayers at Holy Places 1989-1994. unabridged ed. Tarthang Tulku. (Prayers for World Peace Ser.: Vol. 3). (Illus.). 150p. (Orig.). 1994. pap. 35.00 (0-89800-270-2) Dharma Pub.

World Peace Ceremony: Prayers at Holy Places, 1995. unabridged ed. Tarthang Tulku. (Prayers for World Peace Ser.: Vol. 4). (Illus.). 123p. (Orig.). 1994. pap. 35.00 (0-89800-276-1) Dharma Pub.

World Peace Ceremony, Bodh Gaya. Tarthang Tulku. (Illus.). 270p. 1993. pap. 35.00 (0-89800-260-5) Dharma Pub.

World Peace Ceremony, Bodh Gaya, 1994. unabridged ed. Tarthang Tulku. (Prayers for World Peace Ser.: Vol. 2). (Illus.). 213p. (Orig.). 1994. pap. 35.00 (0-89800-269-9) Dharma Pub.

World Peace Council & Soviet Active Measures. Herbert Romerstein. 1983. pap. 5.00 (0-935067-01-9) Nathan Hale Inst.

World Peace Gathering. Sino-American Buddist Association Staff. (Illus.). 128p. (Orig.). 1974. pap. 5.00 (0-917512-05-7) Buddhist Text.

World Peace Through World Law. 2nd rev. ed. Grenville Clark & Louis B. Sohn. 388p. 1960. 34.95 (0-87855-358-4) Transaction Pubs.

World Peace Through World Law: Two Alternative Plans. 3rd ed. Grenville Clark. LC 66-21198. 589p. reprint ed. pap. 167.90 (0-317-09601-X, 2003006) Bks Demand.

World-Peacemaker. Joe Lewis. 1983. pap. 2.95 (0-87505-329-7) Borden.

World Pen, Palmtop & Notebook Computer & Peripheral Markets: Solid Profits in Accessories, but Will PDA's Follow? Market Intelligence Staff. 370p. 1993. 1,995.00 (1-56753-608-5) Frost & Sullivan.

World Perspectives: A European Assessment. Jacques Lesourne. Tr. by Sharon L. Romeo. viii, 352p. (FRE.). 1986. text ed. 65.00 (2-88124-179-4) Gordon & Breach.

World Perspectives in the Sociology of the Military. Ed. by George A. Kourvetaris & Betty A. Dobratz. LC 76-45941. 294p. (C). 1977. text ed. 39.95 (0-87855-207-3) Transaction Pubs.

World Petroleum Arrangements, 1993. Gordon H. Barrows. Ed. by D. Jeune & M. Guerra. (Basic Oil Laws & Concession Contracts Ser.). 589p. 1989. 695.00 (0-89069-027-8) Barrows Co.

World Petroleum Industry: The Market for Petroleum & Petroleum Products in the 1980's. Stuart W. Sinclair. LC 84-13558. 367p. reprint ed. pap. 104.60 (0-7837-2672-4, 2043043) Bks Demand.

World Petroleum Market. M. A. Adelman. LC 72-4029. (Resources for the Future Ser.). (Illus.). 456p. (C). 1973. 37.00 (0-8018-1422-7) Johns Hopkins.

World Petroleum Market. Morris A. Adelman. LC 72-4029. 458p. reprint ed. pap. 130.60 (0-7837-2179-X, 2042517) Bks Demand.

World Petroleum Market: Perspectives to the Year 2010. International Energy Analysis Group Staff. (International Energy Ser.). 200p. 1995. pap. text ed. 199.99 (0-9645169-0-X) IEAG.

World Philatelic Programmes: The Official Halley's Comet Collection Postage Stamp Catalog, Vol. 1. (Illus.). 80p. (Orig.). 1989. pap. 9.95 (0-317-93272-1) Interpostal Philatelic.

World Philosophies: An Historical Introduction. David E. Cooper. LC 95-5864. 400p. (C). 1995. pap. 29.95 (0-631-18867-3) Blackwell Pubs.

World Philosophy: A Contemporary Bibliography. John R. Burr. LC 93-18031. (Bibliographies & Indexes in Philosophy Ser.: No. 3). 400p. 1993. text ed. 85.00 (0-313-24032-9, BWP/) Greenwood.

World Philosophy: A Text with Readings. Ed. by Robert C. Solomon & Kathleen M. Higgins. LC 94-31513. 1994. pap. text ed. 11.25 (0-07-059674-3) McGraw.

World Philosophy of Religion. Phillips. (C). 1995. 46.75 (0-15-501753-5) HB Coll Pubs.

*World Place Location Learning System. 8th rev. ed. Richard M. MacKinnon. 104p. (C). 1996. pap. 14.00 (1-57182-410-3) Hayden-McNeil.

World Plant Conservation Bibliography. Compiled by World Conservation Monitoring Centre, Royal Botanic Garden, Threatened Plants Unit Staff. 645p. 1990. pap. 30.00 (0-947643-24-9, Pub. by Royal Botnic Grdns UK) Balogh.

World Plastics: Opportunities. Howard Kibbel. 253p. 1995. 2,750.00 (0-614-10904-3, P-224) BCC.

*World Poetry: An Anthology of Verse from Antiquity to Our Time. Katharine Washburn et al. LC 97-10879. 1997. 45.00 (0-393-04130-1) Norton.

World Point-World Line. Kathleen M. Podolsky. LC 82-15164. (Illus.). 72p. (Orig.). 1982. pap. 14.95 (0-942714-00-8) LIM Press CA.

World Politics. Spiegel. (C). 1995. teacher ed., pap. text ed. 33.75 (0-03-047577-5) HB Coll Pubs.

*World Politics. 2nd ed. Spiegel. (C). 1998. teacher ed., pap. text ed. 42.00 (0-15-505654-9) HB Coll Pubs.

World Politics. 4th ed. Bruce M. Russett. (C). 1995. pap. text ed. write for info. (0-7167-2290-9) W H Freeman.

World Politics. 5th ed. Bruce M. Russett. Date not set. text ed. write for info. (0-7167-2926-1) W H Freeman.

World Politics. 6th ed. Charles W. Kegley. 1996. pap. text ed. 3.33 (0-312-14984-0) St Martin.

World Politics. 6th ed. Charles W. Kegley. 1996. pap. text ed. 10.00 (0-312-14832-1) St Martin.

*World Politics. 7th ed. Charles W. Kegley. Date not set. pap. text ed. write for info. (0-312-16657-5) St Martin.

World Politics: An Interdisciplinary Approach. Saliba Sarsar & Kenneth R. Stunkel. 242p. (Orig.). (C). 1995. pap. text ed. 26.50 (0-7618-0007-7) U Pr of Amer.

*World Politics: An Introduction. Ed. by Morgan. (C). 1992. write for info. (0-673-38951-0) Addison-Wesley.

World Politics: An Introduction to International Relations. 2nd ed. Brian L. Hocking. 1996. pap. text ed. 32.50 (0-13-353922-9) P-H.

*World Politics: Managing Conflict. 6th ed. Charles W. Kegley. 1996. pap. text ed. 49.50 (0-312-15420-8) St Martin.

World Politics: Printed Test Bank. 5th ed. Bruce M. Russett. (C). 1996. suppl. ed. write for info. (0-7167-2939-3) W H Freeman.

World Politics: The Menu for Choice. 5th ed. Bruce M. Russett. (C). 1996. text ed. 47.95 (0-7167-2821-4) W H Freeman.

World Politics: The Menu for Choice. 5th ed. Bruce M. Russett & Harvey Starr. LC 88-28780. (C). 1996. pap. text ed. 39.95 (0-7167-2820-6) W H Freeman.

World Politics: Trend & Transformation. 4th ed. Charles W. Kegley, Jr. & Eugene R. Wittkopf. (Illus.). 614p. (C). 1992. pap. text ed. write for info. (0-318-70019-0) St Martin.

World Politics: 1996-1997. annuals 17th ed. Purkitt. 256p. (C). 1996. per. write for info. (0-697-31682-3) Brown & Benchmark.

World Politics & International Economics. Ed. by C. Fred Bergsten & Lawrence B. Krause. LC 75-15684. 373p. reprint ed. pap. 106.40 (0-317-20637-0, 2024128) Bks Demand.

World Politics & International Law. Francis A. Boyle. LC 85-4374. (Duke Press Policy Studies). xii, 366p. (C). 1985. 45.00 (0-8223-0609-3); pap. text ed. 21.95 (0-8223-0655-7) Duke.

World Politics & the Cause of War Since 1914. Amos Yoder. LC 85-22759. (Illus.). 254p. (Orig.). (C). 1986. pap. text ed. 24.00 (0-8191-5046-0); lib. bdg. 49.50 (0-8191-5045-2) U Pr of Amer.

World Politics & the Evolution of War. John J. Weltman. 248p. 1995. text ed. 38.50 (0-8018-4948-9); pap. text ed. 14.95 (0-8018-4949-7) Johns Hopkins.

World Politics & Western Reason: Universalism, Pluralism, Hegemony. R. J. Walker. 32p. 1982. pap. 12.95 (0-911646-25-6) Transaction Pubs.

World Politics & You. James E. Harf. 224p. (C). 1996. student ed., per. write for info. (0-697-32687-X) Brown & Benchmark.

World Politics & You: International Politics on the World State. 5th ed. James E. Harf & John T. Rourke. 240p. (C). 1995. student ed. write for info. (1-56134-451-6) Brown & Benchmark.

World Politics Debated. 4th ed. Herbert M. Levine. 1992. text ed. write for info. (0-07-037512-7) McGraw.

World Politics in a New. Spiegel. (C). 1995. teacher ed., pap. text ed. 32.00 (0-03-010783-0) HB Coll Pubs.

World Politics in a New Era. Steven L. Spiegel. (Illus.). 756p. (Orig.). (C). 1994. pap. text ed. 43.75 (0-03-047574-0) HB Coll Pubs.

*World Politics in a New Era. 2nd ed. Spiegel. (C). 1998. pap. text ed. 35.25 (0-15-505625-5) HB Coll Pubs.

World Politics in Modern Civilization, 2 vols. Harry E. Barnes. 1973. Set. 600.00 (0-87700-038-7) Revisionist Pr.

World Politics in the General Assembly. Hayward R. Alker & Bruce M. Russett. LC 65-22313. (Yale Studies in Political Science: No. 15). 352p. reprint ed. pap. 100.40 (0-317-09370-3, 2021974) Bks Demand.

World Politics since Nineteen Forty-Five. 6th ed. Peter Calvocoressi. (Illus.). 754p. (C). 1991. pap. text ed. 30.50 (0-582-07379-0, 79013) Longman.

World Politics Since 1945. 5th ed. Peter Calvocoressi. 546p. (C). 1987. pap. text ed. 22.95 (0-582-29713-3, 71838) Longman.

World Politics since 1945. 7th ed. P. Calvocoressi. LC 96-21988. 754p. (C). 1996. pap. text ed. 27.50 (0-582-27796-5) Longman.

*World Population. Nance L. Fyson. LC 97-7787. (Living for the Future Ser.). (J). 1998. write for info. (0-531-14479-8) Watts.

World Population: The Present & Future Crisis. Phyllis T. Piotrow. LC 80-69582. (Headline Ser.: No. 251). (Illus.). 80p. (Orig.). (C). 1980. pap. 5.95 (0-87124-064-5) Foreign Policy.

World Population - Turning the Tide: Three Decades of Progress. Stanley P. Johnson. 387p. (C). 1994. pap. text ed. 41.50 (1-85966-047-9, Pub. by Graham & Trotman UK); lib. bdg. 134.50 (1-85966-046-0, Pub. by Graham & Trotman UK) Kluwer Ac.

World Population & Development: Challenges & Prospects. Ed. by Philip M. Hauser. (Illus.). 708p. (C). 1979. 49.95 (0-8156-2216-3); pap. 18.95 (0-8156-2219-8) Syracuse U Pr.

World Population & U. S. Policy: The Choices Ahead. Ed. by Jane Menken. (American Assembly Book). 255p. 1986. pap. 8.95 (0-393-30399-3) Norton.

World Population & World Food Supplies. Edward J. Russell. LC 76-23307. (Illus.). 513p. 1976. reprint ed. text ed. 35.00 (0-8371-8997-7, RUWP, Greenwood Pr) Greenwood.

World Population at the Turn of the Century. (Population Studies: No. 111). 134p. 1989. pap. 15.50 (92-1-151174-7, E.89.XIII.2) UN.

World Population Control: Rights & Restrictions. Columbia Human Rights Law Review Staff. LC 75-27963. (Symposia of the Columbia Human Rights Law Review Ser.). 575p. reprint ed. pap. 163.90 (0-685-24008-8, 2031594) Bks Demand.

World Population Crisis: Policy Implications & the Role of Law: Proceedings of the American Society of International Law Regional Meeting & the John Bassett Moore Society of International Law Symposium. Ed. by John M. Paxman. LC 80-19753. vi, 179p. 1980. reprint ed. text ed. 52.50 (0-313-22619-9, PAWO) Greenwood.

World Population Growth. George E. Immerwahr. 208p. 1994. pap. 14.95 (0-89716-552-7) P B Pubng.

World Population Growth & Aging: Demographic Trends in the Late Twentieth Century. Nathan Keyfitz & Wilhelm Flieger. LC 90-11015. (Illus.). 608p. 1991. lib. bdg. 78.00 (0-226-43237-8) U Ch Pr.

World Population Growth & Response 1965-1975: A Decade of Global Action. Population Reference Bureau Editors. (Illus.). 271p. (C). 1976. pap. text ed. 4.00 (0-917136-00-4) Population Ref.

World Population Monitoring. (Population Studies: No. 139). 45.00 (92-1-151279-4, E.95.XIII.8) UN.

World Population Monitoring: With Special Emphasis on Age Structure. (Population Studies: No. 126). 242p. 1991. pap. 35.00 (92-1-151240-9, E.92.XIII.2) UN.

World Population Monitoring, 1989: Special Report - The Population Situation in the Least Developed Countries. 260p. 1989. 28.50 (92-1-151186-0, 89.XIII.12) UN.

World Population Policies. Jyoti S. Singh. LC 78-19756. 228p. 1979. text ed. 59.95 (0-275-90424-5, C0424, Praeger Pubs) Greenwood.

World Population Policies: Oman to Zimbabwe, Vol. 3. 270p. 1990. 35.00 (92-1-151188-7, 90.XIII.2) UN.

World Population Policies Vol. 2: Gabon to Norway. (Population Studies: No. 102). 253p. 1989. 28.00 (92-1-151175-5, E.89.XIII.3) UN.

World Population Problems: An Introduction to Population Geography. D. Gordon Bennett. LC 83-62691. 250p. (C). 1984. pap. text ed. 12.95 (0-941226-04-2) Park Pr Co.

World Population Profile. 1995. lib. bdg. 250.00 (0-8490-5850-3) Gordon Pr.

World Population Profile: Demographic Information for 208 Countries of the World. 1991. lib. bdg. 75.00 (0-8490-5059-6) Gordon Pr.

World Population Profile, 1994: With a Special Chapter Focusing on HIV-AIDS. Ellen Jamison & Frank B. Hobbs. (Illus.). 135p. (Orig.). (C). 1994. pap. text ed. 40.00 (0-7881-1417-4) DIANE Pub.

World Population Prospects. rev. ed. 886p. 1995. pap. 95.00 (92-1-151287-5) UN.

World Population Prospects. rev. ed. (Population Studies: No. 135). 677p. 1992. 85.00 (92-1-151253-0, E.93.XIII.7) UN.

World Population Prospects, Nineteen Ninety. (Population Studies: No. 120). 607p. 1991. 85.00 (92-1-151223-9, E.91.XIII.4) UN.

World Population Trends: Signs of Hope, Signs of Stress. Lester R. Brown. 1976. pap. write for info. (0-916468-07-0) Worldwatch Inst.

World Population Trends & Policies, 1987 Monitoring Report: Special Topics: Fertility & Women's Life Cycle & Socio-Economic Differentials in Mortality, No. 103. (Population Studies). 411p. 1988. 47.50 (92-1-151168-2, E.88.XIII.3) UN.

World Population Trends & Their Impact on Economic Development. Ed. by Dominick Salvatore. LC 87-32268. (Contributions in Economics & Economic History Ser.: No. 82). 251p. 1988. text ed. 49.95 (0-313-25765-5, SVE/, Greenwood Pr) Greenwood.

World Population Trends, Population & Development Interrelations & Population Policies: 1983 Monitoring Report, Vol. II. (Population & Development Interrelations & Population Policies Ser.). 279p. 1985. pap. text ed. 29.00 (92-1-151155-0, E.85.XIII.2) UN.

World Populations Prospects. (Population Studies: No. 106). 1988. Incl. chart. 70.00 (92-1-151172-0, 88.XIII.7) UN.

World Portable Computer, Pen Computer, Palmtop, & Peripherals Markets. 315p. Date not set. write for info. (0-7889-0378-0) Frost & Sullivan.

World Poultry Industry. Richard Henry & Graeme Rothwell. (IFC Global Agribusiness Ser.). 82p. 1995. 80.00 (0-8213-3429-8, 13429) World Bank.

World Poverty: Challenge & Response By. Nigel Dower. (C). 1988. 50.00 (0-900657-78-2, Pub. by W Sessions UK) St Mut.

World-Power & Evolution. Ellsworth Huntington. LC 73-14157. (Perspectives in Social Inquiry Ser.). 292p. 1974. reprint ed. 19.95 (0-405-05503-X) Ayer.

World Prefix. Harrison Fisher. 32p. (Orig.). 1989. pap. 4.00 (0-9619097-1-4) Edge Bks.

World Prehistory. 2nd ed. Brian M. Fagan. (C). 1993. 25.00 (0-673-52262-8) Addson-Wesley Educ.

World Prehistory: A Brief Introduction. 3rd ed. Fagan. (Illus.). 320p. (C). 1996. text ed. 26.50 (0-673-52372-1) Addson-Wesley Educ.

World Prehistory in New Perspective. 3rd ed. John G. Clark. LC 76-51318. (Illus.). 554p. 1977. pap. text ed. 35.95 (0-521-29178-X) Cambridge U Pr.

World Premiere Performance of "Gold" Jack London et al. 32p. 1973. pap. 3.00 (0-918466-03-2) Quintessence.

World Premiere Performance of "Scorn of Women" Jack London et al. 1979. pap. 3.00 (0-918466-04-0) Quintessence.

World Prescription Dermatology Markets. Market Intelligence Staff. 380p. 1994. 2,695.00 (0-7889-0043-9) Frost & Sullivan.

World Press Encyclopedia, Vol. 1. Ed. by George T. Kurian. LC 80-25120. 664p. reprint ed. pap. 180.00 (0-7837-1579-X, 2041871) Bks Demand.

World Press Photo 1991. (Illus.). 128p. (Orig.). 1991. pap. 17.95 (0-500-97397-0) Thames Hudson.

World Press Photo 1992. 128p. 1992. pap. 17.95 (0-500-97399-7) Thames Hudson.

World Press Photo 1993. (Illus.). 128p. 1993. pap. 19.95 (0-500-97408-X) Thames Hudson.

World Press Photo 1994. (Illus.). 1994. pap. 19.95 (0-500-97412-8) Thames Hudson.

World Press Photo 1995. World Press Photo Foundation Staff. (Illus.). 128p. 1995. pap. 19.95 (0-500-97418-7) Thames Hudson.

World Press Photo 1996. LC 91-65423. (Illus.). 128p. 1996. pap. 19.95 (0-500-97436-5) Thames Hudson.

*World Press Photo 1997. (Illus.). 132p. (Orig.). 1997. pap. 19.95 (0-500-97449-7) Thames Hudson.

*World Pressure Sensor Markets: A Competitive Industry Forces Niche Applications. Frost & Sullivan Staff. 410p. 1996. write for info. (0-7889-0509-0, 5454) Frost & Sullivan.

World Pressure Sensor Markets: Fiber Optic & Silicon Micromachine Technologies Usher in New Era of Growth. Market Intelligence Staff. 340p. 1994. 1,695.00 (1-56753-982-3) Frost & Sullivan.

World Pressure Sensor Markets: Micromachined Applications Rejuvenate Growth. Market Intelligence Staff. 219p. (Orig.). 1992. 1,495.00 (1-56753-051-6) Frost & Sullivan.

World Priorities. Ed. by Boris Pregel et al. LC 75-29389. 277p. 1977. reprint ed. pap. text ed. 21.95 (0-87855-633-8) Transaction Pubs.

World Problems. Brian Ferris & Peter Toyne. (Illus.). 236p. (C). 1979. 60.00 (0-685-33833-9, Pub. by S Thornes Pubs UK) St Mut.

*World Process Analytical Instrument Markets: Manufacturers Targeting Rapidly Growing Pacific Rim & Rest-of-World Markets. Frost & Sullivan Staff. 439p. Date not set. write for info. (0-7889-0515-5, 5444) Frost & Sullivan.

World Process Controller Markets: PC-Based Technology Offers New Opportunity in a Highly Competitive Environment. Market Intelligence Staff. 320p. 1994. 1,995.00 (0-7889-0098-6) Frost & Sullivan.

World Process Flow Control Markets: Electronics Revolutionizes Values & Accessories, Pumps & Controllers. Market Intelligence Staff. 168p. (Orig.). 1992. 1,495.00 (1-56753-050-8) Frost & Sullivan.

World Product & Income: International Comparisons of Real Gross Product Phase 3. Irving B. Kravis et al. LC 81-15569. (United Nations International Comparison Project: Phase One Ser.). 398p. reprint ed. pap. 113.50 (0-7837-5382-9, 2045146) Bks Demand.

World Programmable Logic Controller & Software Markets: Downsizing, Eroding Brand Loyalty & New Entrants Challenge Leader. Market Intelligence Staff. 300p. 1992. 1,495.00 (1-56753-391-4) Frost & Sullivan.

World Programmable Logic Controller & Software Markets: Software & Service Become Key Industry Issues. Market Intelligence Staff. 298p. 1993. 1,695.00 (1-56753-613-1) Frost & Sullivan.

World Programme of Industrial Statistics, 1983: Principal Indicators & Related Data. 1990. 80.00 (92-1-161315-9, 90.XVII.7) UN.

World Protein Resources: Proceedings of the American Chemical Society Evaluation of World Resources Symposium, Atlantic City, 1965. American Chemical Society Evaluation of World Resources Symposium Staff & Aaron M. Altschul. LC 66-28666. (American Chemical Society Advances in Chemistry Ser.: No. 57). 303p. reprint ed. pap. 86.40 (0-317-09899-3, 2050185) Bks Demand.

World Proximity & Displacement Sensor Markets: Applications Boom with the Advent of Smaller, Smarter & Faster Sensors. Market Intelligence Staff. 340p. 1993. 1,495.00 (1-56753-433-3) Frost & Sullivan.

*World Psychology. 2nd ed. Wood. 1996. pap. text ed. 35.00 (0-205-26718-1) P-H.

World Public Order of the Environment: Towards an International Ecological Law & Organization. Jan Schneider. LC 78-11712. 335p. reprint ed. pap. 95.50 (0-318-34720-2, 2031928) Bks Demand.

World Quality Life Indicators. Timothy S. O'Donnell. (World Facts & Figures Ser.). 1991. lib. bdg. 40.00 (0-87436-657-7) ABC-CLIO.

World Quite Round: Two Stories & Novella. fac. ed. Gordon Weaver. LC 85-23680. 142p. 1986. reprint ed. pap. 40.50 (0-7837-7932-1, 2047688) Bks Demand.

World Racism & Related Inhumanities: A Country-by-Country Bibliography. Compiled by Meyer Weinberg. LC 92-4094. (Bibliographies & Indexes in World History Ser.: No. 26). 1056p. 1992. text ed. 125.00 (0-313-28109-2, WWH/, Greenwood Pr) Greenwood.

World Radio & TV Handbook, 1995. Andrew G. Sennitt. 576p. 1995. pap. 24.95 (0-8230-5926-X, Billboard Bks) Watsn-Guptill.

World Radio TV Handbook 1996. Ed. by Andrew G. Sennitt. 608p. 1996. pap. 24.95 (0-8230-5927-8, RAC Bks) Watsn-Guptill.

*World Radio TV Handbook 1997. Ed. by Andrew G. Sennitt. 608p. 1996. pap. 24.95 (0-8230-7797-7) Watsn-Guptill.

World Railway Systems. Bernard De Fontgalland. Tr. by V. Hoskins. 220p. 1984. 50.00 (0-521-24541-9) Cambridge U Pr.

World Re-Made: The Results of the First World War. Ed. by Josh Brooman. (Twentieth Century History Ser.). (Illus.). 32p. (Orig.). (YA). (gr. 4-12). 1985. pap. text ed. 10.92 (0-582-22370-9, 70923) Longman.

World Reacts to the Holocaust. Ed. by David S. Wyman. LC 96-15395. 944p. 1996. text ed. 65.00 (0-8018-4969-1) Johns Hopkins.

World Recession & Global Interdependence: Effects on Employment, Poverty & Policy Formation in Developing Countries. Ed. by R. Van der Hoeven & P. J. Richards. xi, 139p. 1987. 27.00 (92-2-105609-0); pap. 18.00 (92-2-105608-2) Intl Labour Office.

*World Record Breakers in Track & Field Athletics. Gerald Lawson. LC 96-54043. (Illus.). 480p. (Orig.). 1997. pap. 24.95 (0-88011-679-X, PLAW0679) Human Kinetics.

An Asterisk (*) at the beginning of an entry indicates that the title is appearing in BIP for the first time.

World Record Game Fishes, 1986. IGFA Staff. Ed. by Ray Crawford. (Illus.). 320p. 1986. pap. 12.00 (0-935217-00-2) Intl Game Fish.
World Record Game Fishes, 1987. IGFA Staff. Ed. by Ray Crawford. (Illus.). 320p. 1987. pap. 12.00 (0-935217-02-9) Intl Game Fish.
World Record Game Fishes, 1988. IGFA Staff. Ed. by Ray Crawford. (Illus.). 320p. (C). 1988. pap. 12.00 (0-935217-03-7) Intl Game Fish.
World Record Game Fishes, 1989. IGFA Staff. Ed. by Ray Crawford. (Illus.). 320p. 1989. pap. 12.00 (0-935217-15-0) Intl Game Fish.
World Record Game Fishes, 1990. IGFA Staff. Ed. by Ray Crawford. (Illus.). 340p. 1990. pap. 12.00 (0-935217-16-9) Intl Game Fish.
World Record Game Fishes, 1991. IGFA Staff. Ed. by Ray Crawford & Elwood K. Harry. (Illus.). 340p. 1991. pap. 12.00 (0-935217-17-7) Intl Game Fish.
World Record Game Fishes, 1992. IGFA Staff. Ed. by Ray Crawford. (Illus.). 356p. 1992. pap. 12.00 (0-935217-18-5) Intl Game Fish.
World Record Game Fishes, 1993. IGFA Staff. Ed. by Ray Crawford. (Illus.). 356p. 1993. pap. 12.00 (0-935217-19-3) Intl Game Fish.
World Record Game Fishes, 1994. IGFA Staff. Ed. by Ray Crawford. (Illus.). 352p. 1994. pap. 12.00 (0-935217-20-7) Intl Game Fish.
World Record Game Fishes, 1995. IGFA Staff. Ed. by Ray Crawford. (Illus.). 1995. pap. 12.00 (0-935217-21-5) Intl Game Fish.
***World Record Game Fishes 1997.** 22th rev. ed. Ed. by Ray Crawford. (Illus.). 354p. 1997. pap. write for info. (0-935217-23-1) Intl Game Fish.
World Record Games Fishes, 1996. Ed. by Ray Crawford. (Illus.). 354p. 1996. pap. 11.75 (0-935217-22-3) Intl Game Fish.
World Record of Major Conflict Areas. Ed. by David Munro. 600p. 1990. 85.00 (1-55862-066-4) St James Pr.
World Record Paper Airplane Book. Ken Blackburn & Jeff Lammers. LC 94-7800. (Illus.). 1994. pap. 14.95 (1-56305-631-3, 3631) Workman Pub.
World Record Paper Airplane Kit. Jeff Lammers & Ken Blackburn. 32p. 1992. pap. 9.95 (0-9634845-0-8) Wrld Rec Paper.
World Record Whitetail: The Hanson Buck Story. Milo Hanson. LC 95-77305. (Illus.). 144p. 1995. pap. text ed. 9.95 (0-87341-363-6, WRH01) Krause Pubns.
World Record Wind: Measuring Gusts of 231 Miles an Hour. Alexander A. McKenzie. (Illus.). 36p. (Orig.). 1984. pap. 2.00 (0-9613227-0-5) A A McKenzie.
World Recorder, Datalogger & Indicator Markets: Niche Recorder Segments Counter PC-Based Data Acquisition. Market Intelligence Staff. 297p. (Orig.). 1992. 1,495.00 (1-56753-038-9) Frost & Sullivan.
World Recovery Without Inflation? Ed. by Randall Hinshaw. LC 85-188. 176p. 1985. text ed. 32.00 (0-8018-2764-7) Johns Hopkins.
World Reference Atlas. (Illus.). 734p. 1996. 49.95 (0-7894-1085-0) DK Pub Inc.
***World Refuge Survey.** 19.00 (0-614-25342-X) US Comm Refugees.
World Refugee Survey-1985 in Review. Ed. by Virginia L. Hamilton & James Silk. 72p. 1986. 6.00 (0-936548-06-1) US Comm Refugees.
World Refugee Survey-1986 in Review. Ed. by Virginia Hamilton & William Frelich. 1987. 6.00 (0-317-58044-2) US Comm Refugees.
World Refugee Survey-1988 in Review. Ed. by Hamilton. 1988. pap. 6.00 (0-685-70532-3) US Comm Refugees.
World Refugee Survey-1989 in Review. Ed. by Hamilton. 1989. pap. 8.00 (0-685-70533-1) US Comm Refugees.
World Refugee Survey-1991 in Review. Ed. by Hamilton. 1991. pap. 10.00 (0-685-70534-X) US Comm Refugees.
World Refugee Survey-1993 in Review. U. S. Committee for Refugees Staff. (Illus.). 65p. 1993. pap. 10.00 (0-936548-05-3) US Comm Refugees.
World Refugue Survey-1987 in Review. Ed. by Hamilton. 1987. pap. 8.00 (0-317-52828-9) US Comm Refugees.
***World Regional Geography.** Michael Bradshaw & Richard A. Walasek. 112p. (C). 1997. student ed., spiral bd. write for info. (0-697-21694-2) Wm C Brown Pubs.
World Regional Geography. Kromm. 608p. (C). 1981. text ed. 48.00 (0-03-057781-0) SCP.
World Regional Geography. Robert E. Norris. Ed. by LaMarre. 571p. (C). 1990. text ed. 62.50 (0-314-48133-8) West Pub.
World Regional Geography. Stutz. (C). 1998. teacher ed., pap. text ed. 28.00 (0-03-097624-3) HB Coll Pubs.
World Regional Geography. Stutz. (C). Date not set. pap. text ed. write for info. (0-03-097623-5) HB Coll Pubs.
World Regional Geography. Stutz. (C). 1998. student ed., pap. text ed. 13.25 (0-03-097625-1) HB Coll Pubs.
World Regional Geography. Wheeler. (C). 1990. student ed., pap. text ed. 18.75 (0-03-032632-X) HB Coll Pubs.
World Regional Geography. Jesse H. Wheeler, Jr. & J. Trenton Kostbade. 800p. (C). 1990. text ed. write for info. (0-03-005371-4) SCP.
World Regional Geography. 4th ed. Wheeler. (C). 1990. teacher ed., pap. text ed. 34.00 (0-03-058489-2) HB Coll Pubs.
***World Regional Geography: A Development Approach.** 6th ed. Clawson. LC 97-23645. 1997. text ed. 63.00 (0-13-857400-6) P-H.
World Regional Geography: A Guide to Learning. 2nd ed. Joel B. Splansky. 124p. (C). 1996. 18.37 (0-7872-2451-0) Kendall-Hunt.
World Regional Geography: A Problem Approach. Fred E. Dohrs & Lawrence M. Sommers. LC 76-3748. 700p. reprint ed. pap. 180.00 (0-317-20533-1, 2022841) Bks Demand.
World Regional Geography: A Question of Place. 3rd ed. Paul W. English & James A. Miller. LC 88-27903. 535p. 1989. text ed. 64.95 (0-471-61648-6) Wiley.
World Regional Geography: An Atlas Study Guide. Craig L. Torbenson. 232p. (C). 1994. spiral bd. 35.64 (0-8403-9393-8) Kendall-Hunt.
World Regional Geography: Issues for Today. 3rd ed. Richard H. Jackson & Lloyd E. Hudman. 588p. 1990. Net. text ed. 46.00 (0-471-50633-8) Wiley.
World Regional Geography: Issues for Today. 3rd ed. Richard H. Jackson & Lloyd E. Hudman. 192p. 1990. Net. student ed. 17.00 (0-471-51997-9) Wiley.
World Regional Geography Update. Hepner. Date not set. pap. text ed. write for info. (0-314-06426-5) West Pub.
World Reinsurers Yearbook 1994/1995. (DYP Directory Ser.). 250.00 (1-870255-42-9) LLP.
World Religion: Great Lives. Jacobs. (J). 1995. 22.95 (0-684-19703-0, Atheneum Bks Young) S&S Childrens.
World Religion-World Peace: Unabridges Proceedings. Conference on Religion & Peace 2nd Conference. Ed. by Jack A. Homer. 200p. 1979. 3.95 (0-317-61733-8) World Confer Rel & Peace.
World Religions. 1994. pap. 19.95 (0-7871-0044-7, Dove Bks) Dove Audio.
World Religions. Gabriel Arquilevich et al. (Interdisciplinary Units Ser.). 1995. pap. text ed. 21.95 (1-55734-624-0) Tchr Create Mat.
***World Religions.** John Bowker. LC 96-38277. 200p. 1997. 34.95 (0-7894-1439-2) DK Pub Inc.
World Religions. John T. Catoir. LC 91-45842. 146p. (Orig.). 1992. pap. 7.95 (0-8189-0640-5) Alba.
World Religions. Warren Matthews. Ed. by Baxter. 491p. (C). 1991. pap. text ed. 42.50 (0-314-78261-3) West Pub.
World Religions. Sue Meredith. (Illus.). (J). (gr. 4 up). 1996. pap. 9.95 (0-7460-1750-2, Usborne) EDC.
World Religions. Sue Meredith. (Illus.). 64p. (J). (gr. 4 up). 1996. lib. bdg. 17.95 (0-88110-830-8, Usborne) EDC.
World Religions. Young Oon Young. 1976. pap. 10.00 (0-686-13408-7) Unification Church.
World Religions. 2nd ed. Alfred W. Matthews. LC 94-26811. 528p. (C). 1995. pap. text ed. 46.50 (0-314-04598-8) West Pub.
World Religions: A Sourcebook for Students of Christian Theology. Ed. by Richard Viladesau & Mark Massa. LC 93-43666. 288p. 1994. pap. 13.95 (0-8091-3461-6) Paulist Pr.
World Religions: A Story Approach. Leonard Biallas. LC 91-65738. (Illus.). 336p. (C). 1991. pap. 14.95 (0-89622-493-7) Twenty-Third.
World Religions: An Introduction. Charles E. Monroe. 439p. (C). 1995. pap. 15.95 (0-87975-942-9) Prometheus Bks.
***World Religions: An Introduction for Students.** Jeaneane Fowler et al. 300p. 1997. 65.00 (1-898723-48-6, Pub. by Sussex Acad Pr UK); pap. 24.95 (1-898723-49-4, Pub. by Sussex Acad Pr UK) Intl Spec Bk.
World Religions: Beliefs Behind Today's Headlines. rev. ed. John Catoir. xxiii, 148p. reprint ed. pap. 5.00 (0-317-46551-1) Chrstphrs NY.
World Religions: Eastern Traditions. Ed. by Willard G. Ostoby. 560p. 1996. pap. 27.95 (0-19-540750-4) OUP.
World Religions: From Ancient History to the Present. Ed. by Geoffrey Parrinder. (Illus.). 528p. 1984. 35.00 (0-87196-129-6); pap. 17.95 (0-8160-1289-X) Facts on File.
World Religions: Our Quest for Meaning. David A. Rausch & Carl H. Voss. LC 93-21711. (Pathways Bks.). 232p. (Orig.). 1993. pap. 15.00 (1-56338-069-2) TPI PA.
World Religions: Western Traditions. Ed. by Oxtoby. 608p. 1996. pap. 27.95 (0-19-540751-2) OUP.
World Religions & Educational Practice. Witold Tulasiewicz & Cho-Yee To. 224p. 1993. text ed. 70.00 (0-304-32675-5); pap. text ed. 24.95 (0-304-32269-5) Cassell.
World Religions & Human Liberation. Daniel Cohn-Sherbok. (Faith Meets Faith Ser.). 1992. pap. 17.00 (0-88344-795-9) Orbis Bks.
World Religions & World Community. Robert H. Slater. LC 63-9805. (Lectures on the History of Religions, New Ser.: No. 6). 313p. reprint ed. pap. 89.30 (0-8357-4571-6, 2037481) Bks Demand.
***World Religions in America: An Introduction.** Ed. by Jacob Neusner. 330p. (Orig.). 1996. pap. 12.99 (0-614-21690-7, 1336) Kazi Pubns.
World Religions in America: An Introduction. Ed. by Jacob Neusner. LC 93-32886. 320p. (Orig.). 1994. 24.00 (0-664-22053-3); pap. 15.00 (0-664-25300-8) Westminster John Knox.
World Religions in War & Peace. Henry O. Thompson. LC 88-42516. 259p. 1988. lib. bdg. 35.00 (0-89950-341-1) McFarland & Co.
***World Religions Reader.** Gwilym Beckerlegge. LC 97-25948. 1997. write for info. (0-415-17487-2) Routledge.
***World Religions Reader.** Gwilym Beckerlegge. LC 97-25948. 1997. pap. write for info. (0-415-17488-0) Routledge.
World Religions Reader. Ed. & Intro. by Ian S. Markham. (Illus.). 416p. (C). 1996. 57.95 (0-631-18239-X); pap. 29.95 (0-631-18242-X) Blackwell Pubs.
World Remembered, 1925-1950. Bernard Smith. LC 93-2060. (Historical Memories Ser.). 216p. (C). 1994. pap. 15.00 (0-391-03803-6) Humanities.
World Remembered, 1925-1950. Bernard Smith. LC 93-2060. (Historical Memories Ser.). 216p. (C). 1994. text ed. 49.95 (0-391-03820-6) Humanities.
World Renal & Hemodialysis Equipment & Supplies Market: U. S. Struggles with Cost Constraints While Europe & Japan Expand. Market Intelligence Staff. 309p. 1992. 1,895.00 (1-56753-383-3) Frost & Sullivan.
World Renal & Hemodialysis Equipment & Supply Markets: Cost Containment Pressures Influence World Markets. Market Intelligence Staff. 347p. 1994. 1,995.00 (0-7889-0015-3) Frost & Sullivan.
World Renewal, a Cult System of Native Northwest Calfornia. fac. ed. E. W. Gifford & A. L. Kroeber. Ed. by Robert H. Lowie et al. (University of California Publications: No. 13:1). 160p. (C). 1949. reprint ed. pap. 14.30 (1-55567-132-2) Coyote Press.
***World Report on Money Laundering.** Ed. by Ernesto Savona. 1996. text ed. 128.00 (90-5702-071-8) Gordon & Breach.
World Reshaped. Cobbold. LC 96-16747. 1996. text ed. 59.95 (0-312-16221-9) St Martin.
World Reshaped: Fifty Years After the War in Europe. Ed. by Richard Cobbold. (RUSI Defence Studies). 264p. 1996. text ed. 65.00 (0-312-16020-8) St Martin.
World Resources: Comprehensive Coursework on the Global Environment. Sarah A. Snyder. Ed. by Mary Paden. (Illus.). 180p. (C). 1994. teacher ed., pap. 6.95 (1-56973-003-2) OUP.
World Resources Data Base on Diskette. World Resources Institute Staff. (Illus.). (C). 1992. text ed. 119.95 (0-685-55003-6) OUP.
World Resources-Engineering Solutions: Proceedings of a Joint Conference of ASCE & the Institution of Civil Engineers. 208p. 1976. 36.00 (0-7277-0016-2, Pub. by T Telford UK) Am Soc Civil Eng.
***World Resources 1996-97.** World Resources Institute Staff et al. (C). 1996. text ed. 99.95 incl. disk (1-56973-094-6) World Resources Inst.
World Resources 1992-93. World Resources Institute Staff. (Illus.). 384p. (C). 1992. pap. 19.95 (0-19-506231-0) OUP.
World Resources 1994-1995. World Resources Institute Staff. (Illus.). 400p. (C). 1994. pap. 21.95 (0-19-521045-X) OUP.
World Resources 1994-95 Data Base on Diskette. World Resources Institute Staff. (C). 1994. text ed. 99.95 incl. 3.5 hd, 5.25 hd (1-56973-004-0) OUP.
World Resources, 1996-1997. World Resources Institute Staff. (Illus.). 320p. (C). 1996. pap. 24.95 (0-19-521161-8) OUP.
World Respiratory Therapy Equipment Market: Strongest Growth Centered in Europe. 289p. 1992. 1,995.00 (1-56753-027-3) Frost & Sullivan.
World Restaurant Designs. (Illus.). 188p. 1995. 59.95 (4-7858-0033-X, Pub. by Shotenkenchiku-Sha JA) Bks Nippan.
World Restored: Europe After Napoleon. Henry A. Kissinger. 1990. 18.25 (0-8446-2384-9) Peter Smith.
World Restored: Metternich, Castlereagh & the Problems of Peace, 1812-1822. Henry A. Kissinger. 1973. pap. 14.95 (0-395-17229-2, 79, SenEd) HM.
World Restored Not Destroyed. LC 82-50127. 132p. 1982. 8.95 (0-9608002-0-4) Quest Prods.
World Retail Directory. Ed. by Euromonitor Staff. 500p. 1992. 390.00 (0-86338-435-8, 070444, Pub. by Euromonitor Pubns UK) Gale.
World Retail Directory & Sourcebook. 2nd ed. 1995. 510.00 (0-86338-549-4, Pub. by Euromonitor Pubns UK) Gale.
World Review of Highly Migratory Species & Straddling Stocks. Food & Agriculture Organization Staff. (Fisheries Technical Papers: No. 337). 70p. 1994. pap. 10.00 (92-5-103523-7, F35237, Pub. by FAO IT) Bernan Associates.
World Review of Nutrition & Dietetics, Vol. 12. Ed. by G. H. Bourne. 1970. 153.75 (3-8055-0663-5) S Karger.
World Review of Nutrition & Dietetics, Vol. 13. Ed. by G. H. Bourne. 1971. 78.50 (3-8055-1180-9) S Karger.
World Review of Nutrition & Dietetics, Vol. 14. Ed. by Geoffrey H. Bourne. 1972. 107.25 (3-8055-1282-1) S Karger.
World Review of Nutrition & Dietetics, Vol. 15. Ed. by G. H. Bourne. (Illus.). 300p. 1972. 91.25 (3-8055-1397-6) S Karger.
World Review of Nutrition & Dietetics, Vol. 17. Ed. by G. H. Bourne. (Illus.). 300p. 1973. 115.25 (3-8055-1336-4) S Karger.
World Review of Nutrition & Dietetics, Vol. 18. Ed. by G. H. Bourne. 1973. 132.00 (3-8055-1458-1) S Karger.
World Review of Nutrition & Dietetics, Vol. 19. Ed. by G. H. Bourne. (Illus.). 319p. 1974. 132.00 (3-8055-1589-8) S Karger.
World Review of Nutrition & Dietetics, Vol. 20. Ed. by G. H. Bourne. (Illus.). 350p. 1975. 151.25 (3-8055-1841-2) S Karger.
World Review of Nutrition & Dietetics, Vol. 21. Ed. by G. H. Bourne. (Illus.). x, 327p. 1975. 152.00 (3-8055-2133-2) S Karger.
World Review of Nutrition & Dietetics, Vol. 22. Ed. by G. H. Bourne. (Illus.). 1975. 158.50 (3-8055-2135-9) S Karger.
World Review of Nutrition & Dietetics, Vol. 23. Ed. by G. H. Bourne. (Illus.). xii, 315p. 1975. 142.50 (3-8055-2243-6) S Karger.
World Review of Nutrition & Dietetics, Vol. 24. Ed. by Geoffrey H. Bourne. (Illus.). 250p. 1976. 121.75 (3-8055-2344-0) S Karger.
World Review of Nutrition & Dietetics, Vol. 25. Ed. by G. H. Bourne. (Illus.). 300p. 1976. 137.75 (3-8055-2363-7) S Karger.
World Revolution: The Plot Against Civilization. Nesta H. Webster. 1973. 250.00 (0-8490-1336-4) Gordon Pr.
World Revolution of Westernization: The Twentieth Century in Global Perspective. Theodore H. Von Laue. (Illus.). 418p. 1989. reprint ed. pap. 16.95 (0-19-504907-1) OUP.
World Revolution, 1917-1936: The Rise & Fall of the Communist International. Cyril L. James. (B. E. Ser.: No. 64). 1937. 40.00 (0-8115-3015-9) Periodicals Srv.
World Revolution, 1917-1936: The Rise & Fall of the Communist International. C. L. James. LC 92-36830. (Revolutionary Studies). 464p. (C). 1993. reprint ed. pap. 19.95 (0-391-03790-0) Humanities.
World Revolutionary Elites: Studies in Coercive Ideological Movements. Ed. by Harold D. Lasswell & Daniel Lerner. LC 80-21600. xi, 478p. 1980. reprint ed. text ed. 79.50 (0-313-22572-9, LAWE, Greenwood Pr) Greenwood.
World Revolutionary Propaganda. Harold D. Lasswell & Dorothy Blumenstock. LC 78-114887. (Select Bibliographies Reprint Ser.). 1977. 29.95 (0-8369-5291-X) Ayer.
World Ride: Going the Extra Mile Against Cancer. Richard Drorbaugh. 224p. 1995. pap. 11.95 (1-57101-052-1) MasterMedia Pub.
World Risotto. 256p. 1996. 25.00 (0-02-860357-5) Macmillan.
World Rubber Economy: Structure, Changes, & Prospects. Enzo R. Grilli et al. LC 80-554. (World Bank Staff Occasional Papers: No. 30). 224p. reprint ed. pap. 63.90 (0-7837-4231-2, 2043919) Bks Demand.
World Rule of Law: Prospects & Problems. Ann V. Thomas & A. J. Thomas. LC 74-13554. (SMU Law School Study Ser.). 106p. reprint ed. pap. 30.30 (0-8357-7079-6, 2033439) Bks Demand.
World Ruled by Number: William Stanley Jevons & the Rise of Mathematical Economics. Margaret Schabas. 184p. 1990. text ed. 37.50 (0-691-08543-9) Princeton U Pr.
World Rushed In. J. S. Holliday. 1983. pap. 15.95 (0-671-25538-X, Touchstone Bks) S&S Trade.
World Rushed in: The California Gold Rush Experience; an Eyewitness Account of a Nation Heading West. J. S. Holliday. (Illus.). 559p. 1981. pap. 9.95 (0-685-04458-0) S&S Trade.
World Satellite Almanac, 1985. Mark Long. Ed. by Bruce Kinnaird. (Illus.). 544p. (Orig.). 1985. pap. 39.95 (0-934543-00-3) CommTek Pub.
World Satellite Communications. Ackroyd. 1990. 88.00 (0-8493-7703-X, QA) CRC Pr.
World Satellite Communications Equipment Markets: VSAT 7 Mobile Applications Unleash SatCom. Market Intelligence Staff. 394p. 1993. 1,695.00 (1-56753-437-6) Frost & Sullivan.
World Satellite Communications in Developing Countries (Wordlwide) Market Intelligence Staff. 397p. 1992. 3,700.00 (1-56753-877-0, W1597) Frost & Sullivan.
World Satellite Directory, 1989. 2nd ed. Ed. by Silvano Payne. (Illus.). 225p. 1989. 175.00 (0-936361-10-7) Design Pubs.
World Satellite Directory, 1990. 3rd ed. Ed. by Silvano Payne. (Illus.). 1990. 125.00 (0-936361-11-5) Design Pubs.
World Satellite Ground Segment Equipment Markets. Frost & Sullivan Staff. 747p. 1996. write for info. (0-7889-0446-9, 5176-60) Frost & Sullivan.
World Satellite TV & Scrambling Methods: The Technicians' Handbook. 3rd ed. Frank Baylin et al. (Illus.). 362p. (Orig.). 1993. pap. 40.00 (0-917893-19-0) Baylin Pubns.
World Satellite Yearly, 1993. Frank Baylin. (Illus.). 412p. 1993. 50.00 (0-917893-18-2) Baylin Pubns.
World Satellite Yearly, 1994. Frank Baylin. (Illus.). 780p. 1994. 90.00 (0-917893-20-4) Baylin Pubns.
World Satellite Yearly, 1995. Frank Baylin. (Illus.). 860p. 1995. 90.00 (0-917893-23-9) Baylin Pubns.
World Saving, Prosperity & Growth. Ed. by Mario Baldassarri et al. LC 92-40362. (Central Issues in Contemporary Economic Theory & Policy Ser.). 403p. 1993. text ed. 79.95 (0-312-09582-1) St Martin.
World Savings: An International Survey. Ed. by Arnold Heertje. LC 92-27435. 320p. 1993. 55.95 (0-631-18521-6) Blackwell Pubs.
World Scripture: A Comparative Anthology of Sacred Texts. Ed. by Andrew Wilson. LC 95-8045. 882p. 1994. 39.95 (0-89226-129-3) Paragon Hse.
World Scripture: A Comparative Anthology of Sacred Texts. Ed. by Andrew Wilson. LC 95-8045. 882p. 1995. pap. 19.95 (1-55778-723-9) Paragon Hse.
World Scriptures: An Introduction to Comparative Religion. Kenneth P. Kramer. LC 85-62933. 304p. 1986. pap. 16.95 (0-8091-2781-4) Paulist Pr.
World Security. 3rd ed. Klare. Date not set. pap. text ed. write for info. (0-312-14990-5) St Martin.
***World Security.** 3rd ed. Klare. Date not set. text ed. 45.00 (0-312-17635-X) St Martin.
World Security: Challenges for a New Century. Ed. by Michael T. Klare & Daniel C. Thomas. 448p. 1993. text ed. 45.00 (0-312-10265-8) St Martin.
World Security: Challenges for a New Century. 2nd ed. Michael T. Klare & Daniel C. Thomas. 416p. 1993. pap. text ed. 24.00 (0-312-08584-2) St Martin.
World Security: Trends & Challenges at Century's End. Michael T. Klare & Daniel C. Thomas. LC 89-63910. 441p. (Orig.). 1991. text ed. 49.95 (0-312-06180-3) St Martin.
World Security & Equity. Jan Tinbergen. LC 89-23686. (Illus.). 144p. 1990. text ed. 70.00 (1-85278-187-4) E Elgar.
World, Self, Poem: Essays on Contemporary Poetry from the "Jubilation of Poets" Ed. by Leonard M. Trawick. LC 90-4516. (Illus.). 260p. 1990. 29.50 (0-87338-419-9) Kent St U Pr.
World Semiconductor Production Equipment Markets: Increased Productivity Justifies Higher Prices, Industry Profits. Market Intelligence Staff. 300p. 1994. 1,995.00 (1-56753-948-3) Frost & Sullivan.

W

***World Sensor Technology Assessment: Pressure, Flow, & Level: In-Depth Analysis of over Forty Sensor Types.** 350p. 1996. write for info. (0-7889-0576-7, 5514) Frost & Sullivan.
World Series. Richard M. Cohen & David S. Neft. 448p. 1990. pap. 16.95 (0-685-28832-3) St Martin.
World Series. William McGuire. (Great Moments in Sports Ser.). 32p. (J). (gr. 4). 1990. lib. bdg. 14.95 (0-88682-313-7) Creative Ed.
World Series. John R. Tunis. (Illus.). 248p. (J). (gr. 3-7). 1989. pap. 4.00 (0-15-299646-X, Odyssey) HarBrace.
World Series. John R. Tunis. 248p. (J). (gr. 3-7). 1990. 15.00 (0-15-299647-8) HarBrace.
World Series. John R. Tunis. (J). (gr. 3-7). 1988. 16.25 (0-8446-6354-9) Peter Smith.
World Series, No. 2. Cohen. 1986. pap. 22.50 (0-02-526980-1) Macmillan.
World Series: Great Moments & Dubious Achievements. John S. Snyder. LC 94-45032. 208p. 1995. pap. 6.95 (0-8118-0913-7) Chronicle Bks.
World Series Classics. Dan Gutman. (Illus.). 208p. (J). (gr. 4 up). 1994. pap. 14.99 (0-670-85286-4) Viking Child Bks.
World Series Classics. Dan Gutman. (Illus.). 256p. (J). 1996. pap. 4.99 (0-14-037751-4) Viking Penguin.
World Series Factbook. George Cantor. (Illus.). 600p. 1996. 18.95 (0-7876-0821-1) Visible Ink Pr.
World Series Heroes & Goats: The Men Who Made History in America's October Classics. Joe Gergen. LC 82-611. (Sports Library). (Illus.). 160p. (J). (gr. 5-9). 1982. pap. 1.95 (0-394-85018-1) Random Bks Yng Read.
***World Series Trivia: 75 Quizzes from A to Z.** Allen Leache & J. M. Colbert. 176p. (Orig.). 1997. pap. 14.95 (0-9653182-2-2) Tuff Turtle.
World Series Trivia, 1982. 2nd ed. Bill Borst & Pat Riley. (Suds Ser.). (Illus.). 48p. 1982. pap. text ed. 3.95 (0-686-47437-6) Krank Pr.
World Shapers: A Treasury of Quotes from Great Missionaries. Ed. by Carol Plueddemann. 160p. 1991. pap. 7.99 (0-87788-946-5) Shaw Pubs.
World Shipping Industry. Ernst G. Frankel. 320p. 1987. lib. bdg. 62.50 (0-7099-1087-8, Pub. by Croom Helm UK) Routledge Chapman & Hall.
***World Shops & Fashion Boutiques.** Shotenkenchiku-Sha Editors. (Illus.). 180p. 1997. 69.95 (4-7858-0111-5, Pub. by Shotenkenchiku-Sha JA) Bks Nippan.
World Sign, No. 3. (Illus.). 240p. 1995. 55.00 (4-7661-0793-4, Pub. by Graphic Sha JA) Bks Nippan.
World Sign Design, No. 2: Marks & Logos. (Illus.). 240p. 1994. 55.00 (4-7661-0742-X, Pub. by Graphic Sha JA) Bks Nippan.
World Silver & Monetary History in the 16th & 17th Centuries. Dennis O. Flynn. LC 96-14651. (Collected Studies: No. CS537). 350p. 1996. 89.95 (0-86078-595-5, Pub. by Variorum UK) Ashgate Pub Co.
World Silver Coin Value Guide. Lorraine S. Durst & Sanford J. Durst. LC 80-51831. 1981. pap. 9.00 (0-686-64441-7); lib. bdg. 12.00 (0-915262-46-0) S J Durst.
World Silver Survey, 1992: Statistical Analysis of the World Silver Market. 70p. 1992. pap. 15.00 (1-880936-00-3) Silver Inst.
World since Fifteen Hundred. 4th ed. Leften S. Stavrianos. (Illus.). 528p. (C). 1982. write for info. (0-13-968164-7) P-H.
World Since Nineteen Hundred. Josh Brooman. (J). 1989. pap. text ed. 16.00 (0-582-00989-8, 78443) Longman.
World since 1500. 6th ed. L. S. Stavrianos. 1991. student ed., pap. write for info. (0-13-966011-9) P-H.
World since 1500. 7th ed. Moczar. 1995. pap. text ed. 20.80 (0-13-251175-4) P-H.
World Since 1500: A Global History. 7th ed. L. S. Stavrianos. LC 94-25899. 496p. 1995. pap. text ed. 52.00 (0-13-250912-1) P-H.
World Since 1945. Goff et al. 1994. pap. text ed. write for info. (0-07-024078-7) McGraw.
World since 1945. T. E. Vadney. (Illus.). 592p. pap. 10.95 (0-14-013562-6, Penguin Bks) Viking Penguin.
World since 1945. T. E. Vadney. 560p. 1988. pap. 10.95 (0-14-022723-7, Penguin Bks) Viking Penguin.
World since 1945. T. E. Vadney. 1992. pap. 12.95 (0-14-015221-0, Viking) Viking Penguin.
World since 1945: A History of International Relations. 3rd ed. Wayne C. McWilliams & Harry Piotrowski. LC 93-16357. 558p. (C). 1993. pap. text ed. 19.95 (1-55587-319-7) Lynne Rienner.
***World since 1945: A History of International Relations.** 4th ed. Wayne C. McWilliams & Harry Piotrowski. 550p. 1997. pap. 22.00 (1-55587-621-8) Lynne Rienner.
***World since 1945: A History of International Relations.** 4th ed. Wayne C. McWilliams & Harry Piotrowski. 550p. 1997. 55.00 (1-55587-788-5) Lynne Rienner.
World Sings: Visas to Our Musical World for Voices & Orff Instruments. Memphis Orff Specialists. Ed. by Michael D. Bennett. (Illus.). 1991. audio 8.95 (0-934017-15-8) Memphis Musicraft.
World Situation And God's Move. Witness Lee. 85p. per. 3.25 (0-87083-092-9, 04010001) Living Stream Ministry.
World Situation And The Direction Of The Lord's Move. Witness Lee. 59p. 2.25 (0-87083-586-6, 04017001) Living Stream Ministry.
World Size Records, 1990. Robert J. Wagner & R. T. Abbott. 80p. 1990. pap. 8.50 (0-915826-24-0) Am Malacologists.
***World Ski & Snowboarding Guide 1996-97.** Ed. by Patrick Thorne. (Illus.). 270p. 1996. 59.95 (0-946393-70-2) SF Comns.
World SMT Manufacturing Equipment Markets: End-User Demands Prompt Explosive Growth - Test & Inspection Revenues Double. Market Intelligence Staff. 315p. 1993. 1,695.00 (0-685-66576-3) Frost & Sullivan.
World Social Situation in the 1990s. 319p. Date not set. pap. 19.95 (92-1-130161-0, E.94.IV.4) UN.
World Social Studies Yellow Pages for Students & Teachers. Kathy LaMorte & Sharen Lewis. Ed. by Rebecca Newton. (Illus.). 64p. (Orig.). (J). 1993. pap. text ed. 8.95 (0-86530-268-5) Incentive Pubns.
World Socialism at the Crossroads: An Insider's View. Silviu Brucan. LC 87-11704. 203p. 1987. text ed. 55.00 (0-275-92782-2, C2782, Praeger Pubs) Greenwood.
World Society. Landheer. 1971. pap. text ed. 46.00 (90-247-5088-1, Pub. by M Nijhoff NE) Kluwer Ac.
World Society, 4 Vols. John P. McKay. (C). 1996. suppl. ed., teacher ed., pap. 11.96 (0-395-74080-0) HM.
World Society. John W. Burton. LC 71-176252. 192p. reprint ed. pap. 54.80 (0-685-15562-5, 2026335) Bks Demand.
World Society, 4 Vols., Vol. 1. John P. McKay. (C). 1996. student ed., pap. 19.56 (0-395-74077-0) HM.
World Society, 4 Vols., Vol. 2. John P. McKay. (C). 1996. student ed., pap. 19.56 (0-395-74078-9) HM.
World Society for Stereotactic & Functional Neurosurgery. Ed. by R. R. Tasker et al. (Advances in Stereoencephalotomy Ser.: Vol. 10). (Illus.). xii, 500p. 1986. pap. 158.50 (3-8055-4401-4) S Karger.
World Society for Stereotactic & Functional Neurosurgery, 8th Meeting, & the European Society for Stereotactic & Functional Neurosurgery, 5th Meeting, Zurich, July 1981. World Society for Stereotactic & Functional Neurosurgery Staff & European Society for Stereotactic & Functional Neurosurgery Staff. Ed. by Philip L. Gildenberg et al. (Advances in Stereoencephalotomy Ser.: Vol. 9). (Illus.). viii, 548p. 1982. pap. 124.00 (3-8055-3501-5) S Karger.
World Society for Stereotatic & Functional Neurosurgy, 10th Meeting, Maebashi, Japan, 1989: Journal: Stereotactic & Functional Neurosurgery, Vols. 54 & 55, 1990. Ed. by O. Chihiro et al. (Illus.). xiv, 564p. 1990. pap. 327.00 (3-8055-5337-4) S Karger.
World Society of Stereotactic & Functional Neurosurgery, 8th Meeting, Technical Advances. Ed. by J. Gybels et al. (Journal: Applied Neurophysiology: Vol. 45, No. 4-5). (Illus.). iv, 208p. 1981. pap. 62.50 (3-8055-3499-X) S Karger.
World Sociology, 4 Vols. John P. McKay. (C). Date not set. suppl. ed., teacher ed., pap. 38.76 (0-395-76587-0) HM.
World Soil Erosion & Conservation. Ed. by David Pimental. (Studies in Applied Ecology & Resource Management). (Illus.). 360p. (C). 1993. text ed. 110.00 (0-521-41967-0) Cambridge U Pr.
***World Soil Resources: An Explanatory Note on the FAO World Soil Resources Map at 1:25 000 000 Scale.** rev. ed. (Illus.). 71p. 1993. 40.00 (92-5-103394-3, F33943, Pub. by FAO IT) Bernan Associates.
World Soils. 2nd ed. Edwin M. Bridges. LC 77-90204. (Illus.). 128p. 1979. pap. text ed. 29.95 (0-521-29339-1) Cambridge U Pr.
World Sourdoughs from Antiquity. Ed Wood. 160p. (Orig.). 1996. reprint ed. pap. 16.95 (0-89815-843-5) Ten Speed Pr.
World Special Forces Insignia. Gordon L. Rottman. (Elite Ser.: No. 22). (Illus.). 64p. pap. 12.95 (0-85045-865-X, 9422, Pub. by Osprey UK) Stackpole.
World Sport Psychology Sourcebook. 2nd ed. John H. Salmela. LC 90-49043. (Illus.). 184p. (Orig.). 1992. pap. text ed. 32.00 (0-87322-315-2, BSAL0315) Human Kinetics.
World Sports Cars. Frank Oleski. (Illus.). 468p. 1990. 195.00 (3-907004-02-7, 3-AQ-0060) Auto Quarterly.
World Sports Cars: Series Built from 1945-1980. Hartmut Lehbrink & Frank Oleski. (Illus.). 468p. (C). 1993. reprint ed. 40.00 (3-927258-19-9) Gingko Press.
World Sports Ski Directory Vol. 4, No. 1: Lake Tahoe Issue. Lynne M. Hrabko. (Illus.). 32p. 1991. pap. 1.50 (0-9625106-2-9) World Sports.
World Standard & Special Machine Tool Markets: Competitors Move into New Segments. Market Intelligence Staff. 444p. 1993. 2,395.00 (1-56753-504-6) Frost & Sullivan.
World Statistical Compendium for Raw Hides & Skins, Leather & Leather Footwear, 1972-1990: 1992 Edition & Supplement. 131p. 1992. pap. 35.00 (92-5-103190-8, F31908, Pub. by FAO IT) Bernan Associates.
***World Statistical Compendium for Raw Hides & Skins, Leather & Leather Footwear, 1997-1995.** 182p. 1996. pap. 24.00 (92-5-003833-X, F3833X, Pub. by FAO IT) Bernan Associates.
World Statistics in Brief. 13th ed. 100p. 1990. 7.50 (92-1-161314-0, 90.XVII.5) UN.
World Statistics in Brief, No. 16. 1995. pap. 9.95 (92-1-161376-0, E.95.XVII.7) UN.
World Statistics in Brief: U. N. Statistical Pocket Book. 12th ed. 97p. 5.00 (92-1-161294-2, E. 88. XVII.8) UN.
World Stock Exchange Fact Book: Historical Securities Data for the International Investor. annuals ECI Staff. (Illus.). 509p. (Orig.). 1995. spiral bd. 390.00 incl. disk (0-9648930-0-2) Meridian Securities.
***World Stock Exchange Fact Book: Historical Securities Data for the International Investor.** annuals unabridged ed. ECI Staff. (Illus.). 1997. disk 95.00 (0-9648930-2-9) Meridian Securities.

World Stock Exchange Fact Book: Historical Securities Data for the International Investor. annuals unabridged ed. Institutional Contributor Staff. (Illus.). 509p. 1995. spiral bd. 295.00 (0-9648930-1-0) Meridian Securities. Comprehensive annual reference publication covering over 45 international stock exchanges. Regulatory information & over 20 years of historical data collected directly from the exchanges. Provides an exceptional single-source reference on international stock markets. STOCK EXCHANGE & GOVERNMENT REGULATIONS--Listing & Disclosure Requirements, Investor Protection Codes, Rules of Mergers & Acquisitions, Restrictions on Foreign Investment, Taxation & Repatriation Regulations. STOCK MARKET STATISTICS--Market capitalization, trading value & volume, P/E & P/BV ratios & dividend yields, stock ownership profiles, number of listed companies broken down by sector. STOCK INDEX DATA-Monthly high, low, close & average data on the official exchange indices & other prominent stock indices (Dow Jones, S&P, Nikkei, Hang Seng, Financial Times, etc.). Index calculation methodology & constituent stocks arranged by industry. Optional data disk provides all the statistics, graphs, & charts in the book electronic form. No-risk trial copy sent on request to qualifying institutional customers within the USA. Also see HANDBOOK OF WORLD STOCK INDICES, RANK OF WORLD STOCK MARKETS, & THE GLOBAL STOCKPICKER'S GUIDE. Contact: Meridian Securities Markets, 11900 Stone Hollow Drive, #927, Austin, TX 78758. Phone/FAX: 512-834-1027.** ***Publisher Provided Annotation.

***World Stompers: A Guide to Travel Manifesto.** 3rd rev. ed. Brad Olsen. LC 96-86305. (Illus.). 280p. 1997. pap. 16.95 (1-888729-01-5) Cnsrtm Cllctive Cnscnss.
***World Stroke Congress & European Stroke Conference: 3rd Congress & 5th Conference, Munich, September 1996 - Abstracts.** Ed. by J. Bogousslavsky et al. (Journal: Cerebrovascular Diseases: Vol. 6, Suppl. 2, 1996). (Illus.). ii, 192p. 1996. pap. 59.25 (3-8055-6370-1) S Karger.
World Studies: Education or Indoctrination? Roger Scruton. (C). 1990. 65.00 (0-907967-70-1, Pub. by Inst Euro Def & Strat UK) St Mut.
World Studies: Global Issues & Assessments. Sue A. Kime et al. Ed. by Eugene Fairbanks et al. (Illus.). 500p. (Orig.). (YA). (gr. 8-10). 1994. text ed. 27.95 (0-935487-24-7); pap. text ed. 19.95 (0-935487-62-X) N & N Pub Co.
World Sugar Economy in War. Ed. by Bill Albert & Adrian Graves. 272p. 1988. lib. bdg. 55.00 (0-415-00127-7) Routledge.
***World Summit for Social Development: Position Paper.** International Commission of Jurists. 23p. 1995. reprint ed. pap. 25.00 (0-608-02970-X, 2063438) Bks Demand.
World Survey. Neil Dalgleish. (Illus.). 128p. 1976. pap. 9.95 (0-7175-0750-5) Dufour.
World Survey of Economic Freedom 1995-1996. Ed. by Richard Messick. 220p. (Orig.). 1996. pap. text ed. 29.95 (1-56000-929-2) Transaction Pubs.
World Survey of Geomorphological Hazards, Pt. 1. Ed. by C. Embleton. LC 97-3778. (Developments in Earth Surface Processes Ser.). 534p. 1997. 240.75 (0-444-88824-1) Elsevier.
World Survey of Islamic Manuscripts, Vol. 1. Ed. by Geoffrey Roper. xvi, 569p. 1992. 170.00 (1-873992-01-7) E J Brill.
World Survey of Islamic Manuscripts, Vol. 2: Iraq-Russian Federation. Geoffrey Roper. 724p. 1993. 171.00 (1-873992-02-5, Pub. by Al-Furqan Islamic UK) E J Brill.
World Survey of Major Activities in Controlled Fusion Research, 1991. 563p. 1991. pap. 190.00 (92-0-139091-2, STI/PUB/23/1991, Pub. by IAEA AU) Bernan Associates.
World Survey of Nonferrous Smelters: Proceedings of Symposium on World Survey of Nonferrous Smelters Sponsored by the Pyrometallurgical Committee of TMS, at the TMS-AIME Annual Meeting in Phoenix, January 25-29, 1988. Symposium on World Survey of Nonferrous Smelters Staff. Ed. by John C. Taylor & Heinrich R. Traulsen. LC 87-42883. (Illus.). 409p. reprint ed. pap. 116.60 (0-7837-4080-8, 2052477) Bks Demand.
World Survey on the Role of Women in Development. 238p. 1986. 11.00 (92-1-130109-2, E.86.IV.3) UN.
World Survey on the Role of Women in Development, 1989. 397p. 45.50 (92-1-130130-0, E.89.IV.2) UN.
World Switching Power Supply Markets: European Standards, New Technologies & Increased Defense Cuts Redirect the Markets. Market Intelligence Staff. 349p. 1993. 1,895.00 (1-56753-484-8) Frost & Sullivan.
World Symposium for Quality in Health Care. 50p. 1988. 10.50 (0-86688-132-8) Joint Comm Hlthcare.
World System: Five Hundred or Five Thousand Years? Ed. by Andre G. Frank & Barry Gills. LC 92-45844. 344p. (C). (gr. 13). 1994. text ed. 69.95 (0-415-07678-1, Routledge NY) Routledge.
***World System: Five Hundred Years Or Five Thousand?** Andre G. Frank. 352p. (C). 1996. pap. 24.95 (0-415-15089-2) Routledge.
World System in the Thirteenth Century: Dead-End or Precursor? Janet L. Abu-Lughod. Ed. by Michael Adas. (Essays on Global & Comparative History Ser.). 1994. 6.00 (0-87229-071-9) Am Hist Assn.
World Tables 1976: From the Data Files of the World Bank. World Bank Staff. LC 76-41204. 560p. reprint ed. pap. 159.60 (0-317-29213-7, 2022228) Bks Demand.
World Tables 1989-90: From the Data Files of the World Bank. World Bank Staff. LC 89-647121. 663p. reprint ed. pap. 180.00 (0-7837-4247-9, 2043937) Bks Demand.
World Tables 1994. World Bank Staff. 694p. (Orig.). 1994. 35.95 (0-8018-4789-3, 44789) Johns Hopkins.
World Tales. Compiled by Idries Shah. 410p. 1991. pap. 20.00 (0-86304-036-5, Pub. by Octagon Pr UK) ISHK.
World Tapestry Today. Ed. by Jim Brown. Tr. by Trans-Laangg Co. Staff. LC 88-70295. (Illus.). 80p. (Orig.). (ENG, FRE & GER.). 1988. per. 14.95 (0-945858-01-9) Am Tapestry Alliance.
World Task of Pacifism. A. J. Muste. (C). 1942. pap. 3.00 (0-87574-013-8) Pendle Hill.
World Tax Havens: A Reference Guide. 1992. lib. bdg. 350.00 (0-8490-5383-8) Gordon Pr.
World Tax Reform: A Progress Report. Ed. by Joseph A. Pechman. LC 88-70469. 294p. 1988. pap. 16.95 (0-8157-6999-7) Brookings.
World Tax Reform: Case Studies of Developed & Developing Countries. Ed. by Michael J. Boskin & Charles E. McLure, Jr. LC 89-26902. 335p. 1990. pap. 14.95 (1-55815-077-3) ICS Pr.
World Telecom & Datacom Test Equipment Markets: Fiber, TIMS, & PC-Based Instrumentation Stimulate Growth. Market Intelligence Staff. 432p. (Orig.). 1992. 1,895.00 (1-56753-067-2) Frost & Sullivan.
World Telecom & Datacom Test Equipment Markets: Technology & Integration Pave the Way for Growth. Date not set. write for info. (0-7889-0385-3) Frost & Sullivan.
World Telecom Factbook. 52p. (Orig.). (C). 1992. pap. text ed. 20.00 (1-56806-112-9) DIANE Pub.
World Telecommunications Services Database 1994. Market Intelligence Staff. 1994. 595.00 (1-56753-981-5) Frost & Sullivan.
World Teleconferencing System & Service Markets: Look Who's Talking. Market Intelligence Staff. 410p. 1993. 1,695.00 (1-56753-450-3) Frost & Sullivan.
World Television Industry: An Economic Analysis. Peter J. Dunnett. LC 89-27591. 240p. (C). (gr. 13). 1990. text ed. 74.95 (0-415-00162-5, A4622) Routledge.
World Temple Tour Coloring Book. Brad Teare. (Illus.). 1993. pap. 4.95 (0-87579-746-6) Deseret Bk.
World Tennis Magazine's Guide to the Best Tennis Resorts. Peter M. Coan. 208p. (Orig.). 1991. pap. 10.95 (0-8065-1272-5, Citadel Pr) Carol Pub Group.
World Test & Measurement Equipment Markets: Multiple Trends Converge to Promote Impressive ATE & Time Growth. Market Intelligence Staff. 288p. (Orig.). 1992. 1,895.00 (1-56753-032-X) Frost & Sullivan.
World Test & Measurement Equipment Markets: The Industry Makes a Comeback As Technology Advances & New Markets Emerge. Market Intelligence Staff. 630p. 1994. 1,695.00 (1-56753-947-5) Frost & Sullivan.
World Textile Demand. International Cotton Advisory Committee Staff. 110p. 1994. pap. 250.00 (0-9638361-1-0) Intl Cotton Adv.
***World Textile Demand.** International Cotton Advisory Committee Staff. 125p. 1996. write for info. (0-9638361-3-7) Intl Cotton Adv.
World Textile Demand. 2nd ed. International Cotton Advisory Committee Staff. 1995. pap. text ed. 250.00 (0-9638361-2-9) Intl Cotton Adv.
***World Textile Industry.** John Singleton. LC 96-31745. (Competitive Advantage in World Industry Ser.). 224p. (C). 1997. text ed. write for info. (0-415-10767-9) Routledge.
World Textile Trade: An International Perspective. E. L. Love. 52p. 1978. 39.00 (0-686-63809-3) St Mut.
World That Came in from the Cold. Gabriel Partos. 303p. (C). 1994. pap. 15.95 (0-905031-58-X) Brookings.
World That Crumbled. Malka Moskovits. LC 93-6758. 1993. pap. 13.95 (0-89604-155-7, Holocaust Library) US Holocaust.
World That Perished. John C. Whitcomb. pap. 9.99 (0-88469-059-8) BMH Bks.
World That Perished. 2nd rev. ed. John C. Whitcomb. LC 73-84109. (Illus.). 184p. 1988. pap. 9.99 (0-8010-9690-1) Baker Bks.
World That Perished see Mundo Que Perecio
World That Shaped the New Testament. Calvin J. Roetzel. LC 85-12492. 180p. 1985. pap. 15.00 (0-8042-0455-1, John Knox) Westminster John Knox.
World That Was. Philip G. Young. Ed. by Wayne Brumagin. 121p. (Orig.). (J). (gr. 4 up). 1993. pap. 8.95 (1-880451-03-4) Rainbows End.
World That Was. John G. Bowman. (American Biography Ser.). 83p. 1991. reprint ed. lib. bdg. 59.00 (0-7812-8033-8) Rprt Serv.
World That Will Hold All the People. Suzanne Gardinier. (Poets on Poetry Ser.). (Orig.). 1996. pap. 13.95 (0-472-06642-0); text ed. 39.50 (0-472-09642-7) U of Mich Pr.
***World That Works: Building Blocks for a Just & Sustainable Society.** Ed. by Trent Schroyer. 200p. (Orig.). 1997. pap. 15.00 (0-942850-38-6) Bootstrap Pr.
World That Works for Everybody: Visions of Utopia. Marvin Surowitz. 96p. (C). 1993. 10.44 (0-8403-8357-6) Kendall-Hunt.
World, the Church, & Preaching: The Best of Good News Commentary. Joseph T. Nolan. 142p. (Orig.). 1996. pap. 19.95 (0-940169-13-4) Liturgical Pubns.
World the Cold War Made. Cronin. 256p. (C). 1996. text ed. 65.00 (0-415-90820-5, Routledge NY) Routledge.
World the Cold War Made. James E. Cronin. 256p. (C). 1996. pap. 18.95 (0-415-90821-3, Routledge NY) Routledge.
World the Color of Salt. Noreen Ayres. 304p. 1993. mass mkt. 4.99 (0-380-71571-6) Avon.

W

World the Slaveholders Made: Two Essays in Interpretation. Eugene D. Genovese. LC 87-34504. 304p. 1988. pap. 19.95 (*0-8195-6204-1*, Wesleyan Univ Pr U Pr of New Eng.

World, the Text, & the Critic. Edward W. Said. 336p. 1984. pap. 15.95 (*0-674-96187-0*) HUP.

World the World. Norman Lewis. LC 97-12711. 1997. 25.00 (*0-8050-5112-0*) H Holt & Co.

World, the Worldless. William Bronk. LC 64-16822. 1964. 10.00 (*0-685-79023-1*); 5.00 (*0-685-04480-7*) SPD-Small Pr Dist.

World Their Household: The American Woman's Foreign Mission Movement & Cultural Transformation, 1870-1920. Patricia R. Hill. LC 84-13206. (Women & Culture Ser.). 241p. 1985. reprint ed. pap. 68.70 (*0-7837-5651-8*, 2059076) Bks Demand.

World Theology: The Central Spiritual Reality of Humankind. N. Ross Reat & Edmund F. Perry. 340p. (C). 1991. text ed. 65.00 (*0-521-33159-5*) Cambridge U Pr.

World They Made Together: Black & White Values in Eighteenth Century Virginia. Mechal Sobel. (Illus.). 388p. (C). 1988. text ed. 57.50 (*0-691-04747-2*); pap. text ed. 17.95 (*0-691-00608-3*) Princeton U Pr.

World Thought Police. T. Schuman. 62p. 1985. pap. 5.60 (*0-935090-14-2*) Almanac Pr.

***World Through an Artist's Eye: Collected Paintings of Tai Shuangyuan.** Shuangyuan Tai. Ed. by Haibo Luo. Tr. by Frank Liu. (Contemporary Chinese Artist Ser.). (Illus.). 218p. 1995. 39.95 (*0-9644818-1-2*) Waymont Intl.

World Through Blunted Sight. Patrick Trevor-Roper. LC 87-83463. (Illus.). 260p. 1989. 24.95 (*0-7139-9006-6*) Allen Lane.

World Through Literature. Ed. by Charlton G. Laird. LC 77-99639. (Essay Index Reprint Ser.). 1977. 36.95 (*0-8369-1359-0*) Ayer.

***World Through Their Eyes.** Ruth Fangmeier. 1994. 25.00 (*1-888504-08-0*, P500) Lighthouse NYC.

World Through Their Eyes: A Manual for Nursing Home Staff. Ruth Fangmeier. (Illus.). 56p. (Orig.). 1994. pap. 10.00 (*0-9603444-7-0*) Lighthouse NYC.

World Tin Market: Political Pricing & Economic Competition. William L. Baldwin. LC 83-8888. (Duke Press Policy Studies). xii, 273p. 1983. text ed. 58.95 (*0-8223-0505-4*) Duke.

World to Fifteen Hundred. 3rd ed. Leften S. Stavrianos. (Illus.). 384p. (C). 1982. pap. write for info. (*0-13-968263-5*) P-H.

World to Make: Development in Perspective. Francis X. Sutton. 255p. 1989. pap. 21.95 (*0-88738-813-2*) Transaction Pubs.

World to Win, Heart to Lose. Netta Martin. 416p. (Orig.). 1993. pap. 4.99 (*0-451-17686-3*, Onyx) NAL-Dutton.

World to 1500. 6th ed. Moczar. 1995. pap. text ed. 21.80 (*0-13-251126-6*) P-H.

World to 1500: A Global History. 6th ed. L. S. Stavrianos. LC 94-25898. 1995. pap. text ed. 52.00 (*0-13-250904-0*) P-H.

World to 1500: Global. 5th ed. Bafumo. 1991. student ed., pap. write for info. (*0-13-966029-1*) P-H.

World Today. Keith Lye. (World of Science Ser.). (Illus.). 64p. (YA). 1985. 12.95 (*0-8160-1072-2*) Facts on File.

World Tourism Directory, 3 vols., Set. 3rd ed. Ed. by Saur, K. G., Staff. 1900p. 1995. 325.00 (*3-598-11181-9*) K G Saur.

World Tourism Directory: Africa, Middle East, Asia and Oceania, 3. 3rd ed. 726p. 1995. 140.00 (*3-598-11204-1*) K G Saur.

World Tourism Directory: Europe, 1. 3rd ed. 589p. 1995. 140.00 (*3-598-11202-5*) K G Saur.

World Tourism Directory: The Americas, 2. 3rd ed. 680p. 1995. 140.00 (*3-598-11203-3*) K G Saur.

World Tourism Directory Vol. 1: Europe, 3 Vol. Set. WTO Staff. 1995. pap. 85.00 (*92-844-0100-3*, WTO0099, Pub. by Wrld Tourism Org SP) Bernan Associates.

World Tourism Directory Vol. 2: The Americas, 3 Vol. Set. W. T. O. Staff. 1995. pap. 85.00 (*92-844-0101-1*, WTO0100, Pub. by Wrld Tourism Org SP) Bernan Associates.

World Tourism Directory Vol. 3: Middle East, Asia & Ocenia, 3 Vol. Set. WTO Staff. 1995. pap. 140.00 (*92-844-0102-X*, WTO0101, Pub. by Wrld Tourism Org SP) Bernan Associates.

***World Trade.** Jo Griesgraber. 1997. pap. text ed. 14.95 (*0-7453-1053-2*, Pub. by Pluto Pr UK) LPC InBook.

World Trade: Monetary Order & Latin America. Paola Savona & George Sutija. LC 89-34301. 200p. 1990. text ed. 49.95 (*0-312-03555-1*) St Martin.

***World Trade: Toward a Fair & Free Trade in the Twenty-First Century.** Jo M. Griesgraber & Bernhard G. Gunter. LC 96-34394. (Rethinking Bretton Woods Ser.). 1997. write for info. (*0-7453-1054-0*, Pub. by Pluto Pr UK) LPC InBook.

World Trade after the Uruguay Round: Prospects & Policy Options for the 21st Century. Ed. by Harald Sander & Andras Inotai. LC 95-37225. (Studies in the Modern World Economy Ser.: Vol. 2). 216p. (C). 1996. text ed. 69.95 (*0-415-13736-5*) Routledge.

World Trade & Payments. 6th ed. Caves. (C). 1992. student ed. 21.00 (*0-673-52275-X*) Addson-Wesley Educ.

World Trade & Payments: An Introduction. 6th ed. Richard E. Caves et al. LC 92-24764. (C). 1992. 43.00 (*0-673-52274-1*) Addson-Wesley Educ.

World Trade & Payments: An Introduction. 7th ed. Bishop. (C). 1995. teacher ed. write for info. (*0-673-54316-1*) Addson-Wesley Educ.

World Trade & Payments: An Introduction. 7th ed. Richard E. Caves et al. (Illus.). 784p. (C). 1996. text ed. 71.95 (*0-673-52418-3*) Addson-Wesley Educ.

World Trade & Payments: An Introduction. 7th ed. Evenhouse & Reilly. (C). 1996. student ed., pap. text ed. 21.95 (*0-673-52482-5*) Addson-Wesley Educ.

World Trade & Payments Cycles: The Advance & Retreat of the Postwar Order. Richard M. Cohen. LC 89-3856. 322p. 1989. text ed. 59.95 (*0-275-93251-6*, C3251, Praeger Pubs) Greenwood.

World Trade & Trade Policy: Comprising Three Studies of the "Canada in the Atlantic Economy" Series. Harry E. English. LC 68-106606. (Canada in the Atlantic Economy Ser.: No. 1). 287p. reprint ed. pap. 81.80 (*0-8357-8386-3*, 2034004) Bks Demand.

World Trade Centers Assoc. World Business Directory, 4 vols. 2nd ed. Meghan Omeara. (Business Directory Worldwide Ser.). 1993. 450.00 (*0-8103-8056-0*) Gale.

World Trade Centers Assoc. World Business Directory 2, Vol. 1. 2nd ed. Meghan Omeara. (Business Directory Worldwide Ser.). 1993. write for info. (*0-8103-8057-9*) Gale.

World Trade Centers Assoc. World Business Directory 2, Vol. 2. 2nd ed. Meghan Omeara. (Business Directory Worldwide Ser.). 1993. write for info. (*0-8103-8058-7*) Gale.

World Trade Centers Assoc. World Business Directory 3, Vol. 1. 3rd ed. Meghan Omeara. 1994. write for info. (*0-8103-8054-4*) Gale.

World Trade Centers Assoc. World Business Directory 3, Vol. 2. 3rd ed. Meghan Omeara. 1994. write for info. (*0-8103-8055-2*) Gale.

***World Trade Centers Association, 4 vols.** 1992. 45.00 (*0-8103-9142-2*, 00009555, Gale Res Intl) Gale.

World Trade Centers Association, 4 vols., Set. 4th ed. Ed. by K. Forster & M. Napierkowski. 1995. 520.00 (*0-8103-5677-5*, 030198) Gale.

World Trade Centers Association, 4 vols., Vol. 1. 4th ed. Forster-Napierkowski. 1995. write for info. (*0-8103-5678-3*) Gale.

World Trade Centers Association, 4 vols., Vol. 2. 4th ed. Forster-Napierkowski. 1995. write for info. (*0-8103-5679-1*) Gale.

World Trade Centers Association, 4 vols., Vol. 3. 4th ed. Forster-Napierkowski. 1995. write for info. (*0-8103-5680-5*) Gale.

World Trade Centers Association, 4 vols., Vol. 4. 4th ed. Forster-Napierkowski. 1995. write for info. (*0-8103-5681-3*) Gale.

World Trade Centers Association, Vol. 4. 5th ed. Forster & Napierowski. 1996. 540.00 (*0-8103-6188-4*) Gale.

World Trade Centers Association: World Business Directory 1: Private - Public WW, 4 vols. Ed. by Meghan Omeara & Kimberley Peterson. 1992. Set. 395.00 (*0-8103-7715-2*, 030195) Gale.

World Trade Competition: Western Countries & Third World Markets. Ed. by Center for Strategic & International Studies Staff. LC 81-11930. 464p. 1981. text ed. 75.00 (*0-275-90600-0*, C0600, Praeger Pubs) Greenwood.

World Trade in Forest Products. Ed. by James S. Bethel. LC 83-17012. (George S. Long Publications). 551p. (C). 1983. 40.00 (*0-295-96078-7*) U of Wash Pr.

World Trade in Forest Products, 2: An International Symposium. Ed. by Gerard F. Schreuder. 564p. (C). 1986. 40.00 (*0-295-96337-9*) U of Wash Pr.

World Trade Issues: Regime, Structure & Policy. James M. Lutz & Young W. Kihl. LC 84-15986. 288p. 1985. text ed. 55.00 (*0-275-90127-0*, C0127, Praeger Pubs) Greenwood.

World Trade Issues in the Mid-1980s. Sidney Golt. (British-North American Committee Ser.). 112p. 1982. pap. 7.00 (*0-902594-42-7*, BN32-NPA198) Natl Planning.

World Trade Organization. John H. Jackson. (Chatham House Papers). 128p. (C). 1997. pap. 15.95 (*1-85567-353-3*, Pub. by Pntr Pubs UK); text ed. 39.95 (*1-85567-352-5*, Pub. by Pntr Pubs UK) Bks Intl VA.

World Trade Organization: GATT to WTO, Set. Kenneth R. Simmonds. 30p. 1995. boxed, ring bd. 80.00 incl. disk (*1-898029-13-X*, Pub. by Simmonds & Hill Pubng UK) Gaunt.

***World Trade Organization: Resource Guide.** Jamie Boucher & Joseph F. Dennin. 16p. 1996. pap. text ed. 25.00 (*0-379-21382-6*) Oceana.

World Trade Resources Guide One. Meghan Omeara. 1991. 169.00 (*0-8103-8404-3*) Gale.

World Trade since 1431. Peter J. Hugill. 400p. 1995. pap. text ed. 24.95 (*0-8018-5126-2*) Johns Hopkins.

World Trade since 1431: Geography, Technology, & Capitalism. Peter J. Hugill. (Illus.). 416p. 1993. text ed. 65.00 (*0-8018-4241-7*) Johns Hopkins.

World Trade Systems: Comprehensive Reference Guide. 1992. 165.00 (*0-582-08696-5*, Pub. by Longman Grp UK) Gale.

World Trade War. Jon Woronoff. LC 83-23097. 320p. 1984. text ed. 59.95 (*0-275-91294-9*, C1294, Praeger Pubs) Greenwood.

***World Trade Without Barriers: The World Trade Organization (WTO) & Dispute Resolution, Vol. 1.** Frank W. Swacker et al. 1995. 110.00 (*1-55834-236-2*, 67195) MICHIE.

***World Trade Without Barriers: The World Trade Organization (WTO) & Dispute Resolution, Vol. 1.** Frank W. Swacker et al. 1996. suppl. ed. write for info. (*0-614-25248-2*, 67198) MICHIE.

***World Trade Without Barriers: The World Trade Organization (WTO) & Dispute Resolution, Vol. 2.** Frank W. Swacker et al. Date not set. 110.00 (*1-55834-383-0*, 67199) MICHIE.

World Trademark Law & Practice, 3 vols. Ethan Horwitz. (Illus.). 1982. Updates. ring bd. write for info. (*0-8205-1425-X*) Bender.

***World Trading System, 4 vols.** Ed. by Robert Hosue. LC 97-12820. (Critical Perspectives on the World Economy Ser.). 1800p. (C). 1998. text ed. 660.00 (*0-415-12364-X*) Routledge.

***World Trading System.** Robert Howse. LC 97-12820. (Critical Perspectives on the World Economy Ser.). 1997. write for info. (*0-415-12365-8*) Routledge.

***World Trading System: Challenges Ahead.** Institute for International Economics Staff & Jeffrey J. Schott. LC 96-46212. (Illus.). 200p. 1996. pap. 20.00 (*0-88132-235-0*) Inst Intl Eco.

World Trading System: Law & Policy of International Economic Relations. John Jackson. 400p. 1989. 54.00 (*0-262-10040-1*) MIT Pr.

***World Trading System: Law & Policy of International Economic Relations.** 2nd ed. John H. Jackson. LC 97-15310. (Illus.). 504p. 1997. pap. 25.00 (*0-262-60027-7*) MIT Pr.

***World Trading System: Law & Policy of International Economic Relations.** 2nd ed. John H. Jackson. LC 97-15310. (Illus.). 504p. 1997. 50.00 (*0-262-10061-4*) MIT Pr.

World Trading System: Law & Policy of International Economic Relations. John Jackson. (Illus.). 432p. 1992. reprint ed. pap. 23.00 (*0-262-60021-8*) MIT Pr.

World Trading System at Risk. Jagdish Bhagwati. 144p. 1991. text ed. 27.50 (*0-691-04284-5*) Princeton U Pr.

World Transducer-Sensor Technology Assessment: A Qualitative Analysis of the State of the Art Based on More Than 500 Interviews with Industry Experts. Market Intelligence Staff. 342p. 1992. 1,495.00 (*1-56753-392-2*) Frost & Sullivan.

World Transformed. George W. Bush & Brent Scowcroft. 480p. 1997. 30.00 (*0-679-43248-5*) McKay.

World Transplantation, 3 vols. A. G. Sheil & Felix T. Rapaport. (Illus.). 3216p. 1989. text ed. 325.00 (*0-8385-9773-4*, A9773-1) Appleton & Lange.

***World Transport Research Vol. 1: Travel Behaviour.** 1996. write for info. (*0-08-042778-2*, Pergamon Pr) Elsevier.

***World Transport Research Vol. 2: Modelling Transport Systems.** 1996. write for info. (*0-08-042779-0*, Pergamon Pr) Elsevier.

***World Transport Research Vol. 3: Transport Policy.** 1996. write for info. (*0-08-042780-4*, Pergamon Pr) Elsevier.

***World Transport Research Vol. 4: Transport Management.** 1996. write for info. (*0-08-042781-2*, Pergamon Pr) Elsevier.

World Travel: A Guide to International Ecojourneys. Dwight Holing et al. LC 96-636. (Nature Company Guides Ser.). (Illus.). 228p. 1996. 29.95 (*0-7835-4804-4*) Time-Life.

World Travel & Tourism Report 1995. World Travel & Tourism Co. Staff. 1995. pap. text ed. 411.75 (*0-08-042763-4*, Pergamon Pr) Elsevier.

World Travel & Tourism Review Vol. 2: Indicators, Trends, & Issues, Vol. 2. Ed. by J. R. Ritchie & D. F. Hawkins. 320p. 1992. 175.00 (*0-85198-771-0*) CAB Intl.

World Travel & Tourism Review Vol. 3: Indicators, Trends & Issues, Vol. 3. Ed. by J. R. Ritchie et al. 320p. 1993. 155.00 (*0-85198-853-9*) CAB Intl.

World Travel Atlas 1996-97. 3rd ed. Ed. by Mike Taylor. (Illus.). 160p. 1996. pap. 39.95 (*0-946393-64-8*) SF Comns.

***World Travel Atlas 1997-98.** Ed. by Mike Taylor. (Illus.). 1120p. 1997. 159.00 (*0-946393-79-6*) SF Comns.

World Travel Guide, 1993-94. 12th ed. Ed. by Brian Quinn & Helen Mott. (Illus.). 1400p. 1993. 139.00 (*0-946393-23-0*, Pub. by Columbus Pr Ltd UK) SF Comns.

World Travel Guide 1994-95. 13th ed. Ed. by Brian Quinn & Helen Mott. (Illus.). 1300p. 1994. 159.00 (*0-946393-35-4*, Pub. by Columbus Pr Ltd UK) SF Comns.

World Travel Guide 1995-96. 14th ed. Ed. by Brian Quinn & Helen Mott. (Illus.). 1350p. 1995. 159.00 (*0-946393-47-8*) SF Comns.

World Travel Guide 1996-97. Ed. by Brian Quinn. (Illus.). 1200p. 1996. 159.00 (*0-946393-62-1*) SF Comns.

***World Travel Guide 1997-98.** Ed. by Brian Quinn. (Illus.). 1120p. 1997. 159.00 (*0-946393-81-8*) SF Comns.

***World Travel Health Guide, 1996-97.** Ed. by Michael Hart. (Illus.). 244p. 1996. 69.95 (*0-946393-71-0*) SF Comns.

World Travel Market. Robert Senior. 266p. 1992. 510.00 (*0-686-92044-9*, Pub. by Euromonitor Pubns UK) St Mut.

World Traveler: What's the Climate? What to Wear? E. M. Dickson et al. (Illus.). 230p. 1989. 29.95 (*0-9622780-0-9*) Advantage Quest.

World Travellers' Manual of Homoeopathy. Colin Lessell. 373p. pap. 33.95 (*0-85207-242-2*, Pub. by C W Daniel UK) Natl Bk Netwk.

World Travelogue. Fernando Lozano. (Illus.). 64p. 1991. 32.00 (*1-56721-004-X*) Twenty-Fifth Cent Pr.

World Treasury of Grand Opera: Its Triumphs, Trials & Great Personalities. Ed. by George R. Marek. LC 74-167383. (Essay Index Reprint Ser.). 1977. reprint ed. 35.95 (*0-8369-2463-0*) Ayer.

World Treasury of Great Poems. Ed. by Eddie-Lou Cole. 39.95 (*0-317-29095-9*) World Poetry Pr.

World Treasury of Love Stories. Ed. by Lucy Rosenthal. 768p. 1995. 30.00 (*0-19-509361-5*) OUP.

World Treasury of Physics, Astronomy, & Mathematics. Timothy Ferris. 1993. pap. 22.95 (*0-316-28133-6*) Little.

World Treaty Index, 5 vols., 2. 2nd ed. Peter H. Rohn. LC 83-3872. 4271p. 1983. lib. bdg. 210.00 (*0-87436-160-5*) ABC-CLIO.

World Treaty Index, 5 vols., 3. 2nd ed. Peter H. Rohn. LC 83-3872. 4271p. 1983. lib. bdg. 210.00 (*0-87436-161-3*) ABC-CLIO.

World Treaty Index, 5 vols., 4. 2nd ed. Peter H. Rohn. LC 83-3872. 4271p. 1983. lib. bdg. 210.00 (*0-87436-162-1*) ABC-CLIO.

World Treaty Index, 5 vols., 5. 2nd ed. Peter H. Rohn. LC 83-3872. 4271p. 1983. lib. bdg. 210.00 (*0-87436-163-X*) ABC-CLIO.

World Tree: Selected Poems. Thorkild Bjornvig. Ed. by Sven H. Rossel. Tr. by Paula Hostrup-Jessen from DAN. 66p. (Orig.). (C). 1993. pap. 6.95 (*1-880755-07-6*) Mermaid Pr.

World Trends in Medical Education: Faculty, Students, & Curriculum. Ed. by Elizabeth F. Purcell. LC 79-144335. (Josiah Macy Foundation Ser.). 248p. reprint ed. 70.70 (*0-8357-9292-7*, 2015693) Bks Demand.

World Turned Right Side Up. Godfrey Hodgson. 336p. 1996. 25.00 (*0-465-09253-5*) Basic.

World Turned Rightside. Hodgson. 1996. pap. 13.00 (*0-395-82293-9*) HM.

World Turned Rightside Up. Godfrey Hodgson. 336p. 1996. 27.50 (*0-395-82294-7*) HM.

World Turned Upside Down. Christopher Hill. 1984. pap. 7.95 (*0-14-055147-6*, Penguin Bks) Viking Penguin.

World Turned Upside Down. Christopher Hill. (J). (gr. 4-7). 1984. pap. 13.95 (*0-14-013732-7*) Viking Penguin.

World Turned Upside Down: Children of 1776. Ann D. Jensen. (Illus.). 32p. (Orig.). (J). (gr. 4-5). 1993. pap. 5.95 (*0-9638113-0-4*) Sands Hse.

World Turned Upside Down: Essex County During America's Turbulent Years, 1763-1790. Ronald N. Tagney. LC 89-85400. 512p. (C). 1989. 29.95 (*0-9623792-0-4*) Essex County MA.

World Turned Upside Down: Indian Voices from Early America. Colin G. Calloway. 160p. 1994. text ed. 39.95 (*0-312-10281-X*) St Martin.

World Turned Upside Down: Indian Voices from Early America. Ed. by Colin G. Calloway. 224p. 1994. pap. text ed. 7.50 (*0-312-08350-5*, Bedford Bks) St Martin.

World Turned Upside Down: The American Victory in the War of Independence. Ed. by John E. Ferling. LC 88-15482. (Contributions in Military Studies: No. 79). 260p. 1988. text ed. 55.00 (*0-313-25527-X*, FWT/, Greenwood Pr) Greenwood.

World Turned Upside Down: The Palmers of South Santee, 1818-1881. Louis P. Towles. LC 95-41779. (Illus.). 1100p. 1996. text ed. 39.95 (*1-57003-047-2*) U of SC Pr.

World Two Thousand Ten: A New Order of Nations. Charles W. Taylor. 125p. (Orig.). (C). 1992. pap. text ed. 30.00 (*1-56806-043-2*) DIANE Pub.

World Tyre Industry No. R324: Competitive Challenge to 2000. 1995. 770.00 (*0-85058-619-4*) Economist Intell.

World Ultrasound Imaging Markets: Manufacturers Focus on Developing Niche Applications. Market Intelligence Staff. 365p. 1993. 2,295.00 (*1-56753-618-2*) Frost & Sullivan.

World under God's Law. 5th ed. T. Robert Ingram. LC 62-16216. 1970. pap. text ed. 6.95 (*0-686-05040-1*) St Thomas.

World Under My Fingers: Personal Reflections on Braille. large type ed. Ed. by Barbara Pierce. (Illus.). 150p. (Orig.). (C). 1995. pap. 1.00 (*1-885218-01-X*) Natl Fed Blind.

***World under Sentence: John Richardson & the Interior.** Dennis Duffy. 180p. 1996. pap. 20.00 (*1-55022-250-3*, Pub. by ECW Press CN) Genl Dist Srvs.

***World Uninterruptible Power Supply Markets: A Reliance on Technology to Conduct Business Sparks a Need for Clean, Uninterrupted Power.** Frost & Sullivan Staff. Date not set. write for info. (*0-7889-0528-7*, 5192) Frost & Sullivan.

World Uninterruptible Power Supply Markets: Increased Awareness of Data & Equipment Protection Sustains Growth. Market Intelligence Staff. 336p. 1994. 2,195.00 (*1-56753-972-6*) Frost & Sullivan.

World Uninterruptible Power Supply Markets: Mission Critical Applications & Fierce Competition Characterize Markets. Market Intelligence Staff. 271p. (Orig.). 1992. 1,895.00 (*1-56753-028-1*) Frost & Sullivan.

World Union on the Horizon: The Case for Supernational Federation. James A. Yunker. LC 92-42458. (C). 1993. 64.00 (*0-8191-9037-3*); pap. 34.00 (*0-8191-9038-1*) U Pr of Amer.

World University Insights: With Your Future in Mind. Howard J. Zitko. Orig. Title: New Age Perspectives in Questions & Answers. 208p. 1980. pap. 10.50 (*0-941902-01-3*) World Univ AZ.

World Unsuspected: Portraits of Southern Childhood - Sheila Bosworth, Robb Forman Dew, Barry Hannah, Josephine Humphreys, James Alan McPherson, Bobbie Ann Mason, T. R. Pearson, Padgett Powell, Dave Smith, Ellease Southerland, Al Young. Intro. by Alex Harris. LC 87-5085. (Lyndhurst Series on the South). (Illus.). 259p. reprint ed. pap. 73.90 (*0-7837-7072-3*, 2046884) Bks Demand.

World up Close. Mary Packard. (J). (gr. 4-7). 1994. pap. 6.95 (*0-8167-3524-7*) Troll Communs.

World Upside Down: Cross-Cultural Contact & Conflict in Sixteenth-Century Peru. Susan E. Ramirez. 1996. 45.00 (*0-8047-2416-4*) Stanford U Pr.

***World Upside-Down: English Misericords.** Christa Grossinger. (Illus.). 192p. 1997. text ed. 60.00 (*1-872501-98-2*, Pub. by Harvey Miller UK) Gordon & Breach.

***World Upside-Down: English Misericords.** Christa Grossinger. (Illus.). 192p. 1997. pap. text ed. 29.95 (*1-872501-64-8*, Pub. by Harvey Miller UK) Gordon & Breach.

World Urbanization Prospects. (Population Studies: No. 136). 164p. 1992. pap. 35.00 (*92-1-151256-5*, E.93.XIII. 11) UN.

W

World Urbanization Prospects: The 1994 Revision; Estimates & Projections of Urban & Rural Populations & of Urban Agglomerations. (United Nations Publications, Databases & Software on Population). 178p. 1995. 37.50 (92-1-151283-2) UN.

World Urbanization Prospects, 1990. 223p. 1991. 29.00 (92-1-151232-8) UN.

World Vegetables: Principles, Production & Nutritive Values. Masatoshi Yamaguchi. (Illus.). 1983. text ed. 54.95 (0-87055-433-6) AVI.

World Vegetables: Principles, Production, & Nutritive Values. 2nd ed. Vincent E. Rubatzky & Masatoshi Yamaguchi. LC 96-23732. 704p. (C). (gr. 13). 1996. text ed. 74.95 (0-412-11221-3) Chapman & Hall.

World View. Michael Kearney. Ed. by L. L. Langness & Robert B. Edgerton. LC 83-20945. (Publications in Anthropology & Related Fields). (Illus.). 244p. (Orig.). 1984. pap. text ed. 14.95 (0-88316-550-3) Chandler & Sharp.

World View: Its Importance & Problems. Muhammad T. Misbah. Tr. by Shahyar Saadat from PER. 24p. (Orig.). 1989. pap. text ed. 1.70 (1-871031-21-4) Abjad Bk.

***World View Enviromental Issue.** 3rd ed. Kirkpatric. (C). 1997. pap. text ed. 9.50 (0-03-024393-9) HB Coll Pubs.

World View of Art History: Selected Readings, Vol. I. Virgil Bird. 196p. (C). 1994. ring bd. 41.94 (0-8403-9287-7) Kendall-Hunt.

World View of Art History: Selected Readings, Vol. II. Virgil Bird. 200p. (C). 1994. ring bd. 41.94 (0-8403-9286-9) Kendall-Hunt.

World View of Contemporary Physics: Does It Need a New Metaphysics? Ed. by Richard F. Kitchener. LC 87-24084. 185p. 1988. text ed. 59.50 (0-88706-741-7); pap. text ed. 19.95 (0-88706-742-5) State U NY Pr.

***World View of Environmental.** Kirkpatric. (C). 1995. pap. text ed. 13.75 (0-03-006734-0) HB Coll Pubs.

World View of Paul Cezanne. Jane Roberts. 1994. lib. bdg. 24.95 (1-56849-495-5) Buccaneer Bks.

World Viewed: Reflections on the Ontology of Film. enl. ed. Stanley Cavell. 278p. 1980. pap. 12.95 (0-674-96196-X) HUP.

World Viewed: Reflections on the Ontology of Film. enl. ed. Stanley Cavell. (Harvard Film Studies: No. 151). 278p. 1980. 32.00 (0-674-96197-8) HUP.

World Views & Scientific Discipline Formation: Science Studies in the German Democratic Republic. Ed. by William R. Woodward & Robert S. Cohen. (Boston Studies in the Philosophy of Science: No. 134). 472p. 1991. lib. bdg. 186.00 (0-7923-1286-4) Kluwer Ac.

World Voice Processing Application & End-User Markets: Technologies Merge, Obstacles Recede. Market Intelligence Staff. 460p. 1994. 1,895.00 (1-56753-963-7) Frost & Sullivan.

World Waiting to Be Born: Rediscovering Civility. M. Scott Peck. 384p. 1994. pap. 13.95 (0-553-37317-X) Bantam.

World War I. Peter Bosco. (America at War Ser.). (Illus.). 144p. (YA). (gr. 9-12). 1991. 17.95 (0-8160-2460-X) Facts on File.

***World War I.** Ed. by William Dudley. (Opposing Viewpoints Ser.). (Illus.). (YA). (gr. 5-12). 1997. pap. 12.96 (1-56510-702-0) Greenhaven.

***World War I.** Ed. by William Dudley. (Opposing Viewpoints Ser.). (Illus.). (YA). (gr. 5-12). 1997. lib. bdg. 20.96 (1-56510-703-9) Greenhaven.

World War I. Kathyln Gay & Martin Gay. (Voices from the Past Ser.). (Illus.). 64p. (J). (gr. 5-8). 1996. lib. bdg. 15.98 (0-8050-2848-X) TFC Bks NY.

World War I. Ken Hills. (Wars That Changed the World Ser.). (Illus.). 32p. (J). (gr. 3-9). 1988. lib. bdg. 11.95 (0-86307-931-8) Marshall Cavendish.

World War I. Samuel L. Marshall. LC 85-3968. (American Heritage Library). (Illus.). 384p. (Orig.). 1985. pap. 14.95 (0-8281-0434-4) HM.

World War I. Tom McGowen. LC 92-28329. (First Bks.). (J). 1993. pap. 6.95 (0-531-15660-5); lib. bdg. 21.00 (0-531-20149-X) Watts.

World War I. Gail B. Stewart. LC 91-16729. (America's Wars Ser.). (Illus.). 112p. (J). (gr. 5-8). 1991. lib. bdg. 20.96 (1-56006-406-4) Lucent Bks.

World War I: "The War to End Wars" Zachary Kent. LC 93-46357. (American War Ser.). (Illus.). 128p. (YA). (gr. 5 up). 1994. lib. bdg. 18.95 (0-89490-523-6) Enslow Pubs.

World War I: A Cataloging Reference Guide. Buckley B. Barrett. LC 93-19745. (Cataloging Guide Ser.: No. 4). iv, 380p. 1995. pap. 33.00 (0-89370-924-7); lib. bdg. 43.00 (0-89370-824-0) Borgo Pr.

World War I: A Short History. Michael J. Lyons. LC 93-19794. 401p. (C). 1993. pap. text ed. 31.00 (0-13-953514-4) P-H.

World War I - over the Top. Turner Publishing Company Staff. LC 93-60962. 250p. 1993. 48.00 (1-56311-113-6) Turner Pub KY.

World War I & Its Consequences. Cowper et al. 1990. 90.00 (0-335-09307-8, Open Univ Pr); pap. 32.00 (0-335-09306-X, Open Univ Pr) Taylor & Francis.

World War I & the American Novel. Stanley Cooperman. 264p. 1970. reprint ed. pap. 14.95 (0-8018-1151-1) Johns Hopkins.

World War I & the Origin of Civil Liberties in the United States. Paul L. Murphy. (Essays in American History Ser.). (C). 1979. pap. text ed. 9.95 (0-393-95012-3) Norton.

World War I Aviation Books in English: An Annotated Bibliography. James P. Noffsinger. LC 86-26109. (Illus.). 331p. 1987. 32.50 (0-8108-1951-1) Scarecrow.

***World War I in Photographs.** Smithmark Staff. 1996. 9.98 (0-7651-9601-8) Smithmark.

World War I in Postcards. John Laffin. LC 89-36281. (Illus.). 256p. 1989. 25.00 (0-86299-370-9, Pub. by Sutton Pubng UK); pap. 15.00 (0-86299-612-0, Pub. by Sutton Pubng UK) Bks Intl VA.

World War I in the Air: A Bibliography & Chronology. Myron J. Smith, Jr. LC 76-45461. (Illus.). 291p. 1977. 27.50 (0-8108-0990-7) Scarecrow.

World War I Infantry. Laurent Mirouze. (Europa Militaria Ser.: No. 3). 64p. 1990. pap. 15.95 (1-872004-25-3) Motorbooks Intl.

World War I Letters of Private Milford Manley. Bob N. Manley. Ed. by Elaine M. McKee. LC 95-83258. (Illus.). 144p. (Orig.). 1995. pap. 14.95 (1-886225-06-0) Dageforde Pub.

World War I Soldier at Chateau Thierry. (Soldier Ser.). 48p. (J). (gr. 5-6). 1991. lib. bdg. 17.80 (1-56065-004-4) Capstone Pr.

World War I Songs: A History & Dictionary of Popular American Patriotic Tunes, with over 300 Complete Lyrics. Frederick G. Vogel. LC 95-10420. (Illus.). 542p. 1995. lib. bdg. 85.00 (0-89950-952-5) McFarland & Co.

World War I: The Great War see Perspectives on History Series: Part II

World War II. Ed. by William Dudley. LC 96-44978. (Opposing Viewpoints Ser.). (Illus.). (J). (gr. 5-12). 1997. pap. 12.96 (1-56510-527-3) Greenhaven.

World War II. Ed. by William Dudley. LC 96-44978. (Opposing Viewpoints Ser.). (Illus.). (J). (gr. 5-12). 1997. lib. bdg. 20.96 (1-56510-528-1) Greenhaven.

World War II. Kathyln Gay & Martin Gay. (Voices from the Past Ser.). (Illus.). 64p. (J). (gr. 5-8). 1996. lib. bdg. 15.98 (0-8050-2849-8) TFC Bks NY.

World War II. Maurice Isserman. (America at War Ser.). 192p. (YA). (gr. 7-12). 1991. 17.95 (0-8160-2374-3) Facts on File.

World War II. Tom McGowen. LC 92-28328. (First Bks.). 64p. (J). 1993. 21.00 (0-531-20150-3) Watts.

World War II. Tom McGowen. (First Bks.). (Illus.). 64p. (J). (gr. 5-8). 1993. pap. 6.95 (0-531-15661-3) Watts.

World War II. Stewart Ross. LC 95-7740. (Causes & Consequences Ser.). (J). 1995. lib. bdg. 25.68 (0-8172-4050-0) Raintree Steck-V.

World War II. Ian Slater. 1990. mass mkt. 5.99 (0-449-14562-X) Fawcett.

World War II. C. L. Sulzberger. LC 85-3978. (American Heritage Library). (Illus.). 300p. 1985. pap. 13.95 (0-8281-0331-3) HM.

World War II: A Statistical Survey. John Ellis. LC 93-10627. 315p. 1993. 85.00 (0-8160-2971-7) Facts on File.

World War II: An Account of Its Documents. Ed. by James E. O'Neill & Robert Krauskopf. LC 74-34112. (National Archives Conference Ser.: Vol. 8). (Illus.). 1976. 24.50 (0-88258-053-1) Howard U Pr.

World War II: Crucible of the Contemporary World Commentary & Readings. Ed. by Loyd E. Lee. LC 90-25544. 448p. (C). 1991. pap. text ed. 23.95 (0-87332-732-2) M E Sharpe.

World War II: Crucible of the Contemporary World Commentary & Readings. Ed. by Loyd E. Lee. LC 90-25544. 448p. (C). (gr. 13). 1991. text ed. 69.95 (0-87332-731-4) M E Sharpe.

World War II: It Changed Us Forever: Collection of True Experiences. Bob Barnes et al. Ed. by Margaret G. Bigger. LC 94-70744. 140p. 1994. pap. 12.95 (0-9640606-0-4) A Borough Bks.

World War II: Order of Battle. Shelly L. Stanton. 1991. 24.98 (0-88365-775-9) Galahad Bks.

World War II: Personal Accounts; Pearl Harbor to V-J Day. Gary A. Yarrington. LC 92-9108. (Illus.). 436p. 1992. 25.00 (0-911333-95-9, 200055) National Archives & Recs.

World War II: Some Decisive Episodes. R. Stanhope-Palmer. 152p. (C). 1989. 30.00 (0-7223-1169-9, Pub. by A H S Ltd UK) St Mut.

World War II: South Queensland. Peter Charlton. (C). 1990. pap. 39.00 (0-86439-132-3, Pub. by Boolarong Pubns AT) St Mut.

World War II: The Best of American Heritage. Ed. by Stephen W. Sears. (American Heritage Library). 288p. 1993. pap. 9.95 (0-395-61907-6) HM.

World War II: The War in Europe. John Vail. LC 91-23062. (America's Wars Ser.). (Illus.). 112p. (J). (gr. 5-8). 1991. lib. bdg. 20.96 (1-56006-407-2) Lucent Bks.

World War II: Time-Life Books History of the Second World War. Time-Life Books Editors. 1989. 39.95 (0-685-28476-X) P-H.

***World War II: Total Warfare Around the Globe, Chpts. 21-26.** Robert Doughty et al. 224p. (C). 1996. pap. text ed. 19.16 (0-669-41681-9) HM College Div.

World War II: 4,139 Strange & Fascinating Facts. Donald McCombs & Fred L. Worth. 1994. 12.99 (0-517-42286-7) Crown Pub Group.

World War II see American Story

World War II - a Thematic Unit. Julie R. Strathman. (Thematic Units Ser.). (Illus.). 80p. (Orig.). (J). (gr. 5-8). 1994. student ed., pap. 9.95 (1-55734-581-3) Tchr Create Mat.

World War II - An Ex-Sergeant Remembers. Ernest D. Whitehead, Sr. (Orig.). 1996. pap. 11.95 (1-57502-182-X, P0806) Morris Pubng.

World War II a Fifty Year Perspective on 1939: Selected Papers. Ed. by Robert W. Hoeffner. 141p. 1992. 5.95 (1-882520-01-7) Siena Coll Res.

***World War II Airplanes.** Nancy Robinson-Masters. LC 97-5996. (Wings Ser.). (J). 1998. write for info. (1-56065-531-3) Capstone Pr.

World War II & the American Dream: How Wartime Building Changed a Nation. Peter S. Reed et al. Ed. & Intro. by Donald Albrecht. (Illus.). 328p. 1995. 45.00 (0-262-01145-X) MIT Pr.

World War II & the American Dream: How Wartime Building Changed a Nation. Peter S. Reed et al. Ed. & Intro. by Donald Albrecht. (Illus.). 328p. 1995. pap. 25.00 (0-262-51083-9) MIT Pr.

***World War II & the People & Events of Morgan County, Colorado.** Compiled by Shirley Gilliland. 130p. 1995. 35.00 (0-88107-256-7) Curtis Media.

World War II & the Transformation of Business Systems: Proceedings of the Fuji Conference. Ed. by Jun Sakudo & Takao Shiba. (International Conferences on Business History Ser.: No. 20). 284p. 1994. 59.50 (0-86008-505-8, Pub. by U of Tokyo JA) Col U Pr.

***World War II & the West: Reshaping the Economy.** Gerald D. Nash. LC 89-4935. 326p. 1990. reprint ed. pap. 93.00 (0-608-03474-6, 2064184) Bks Demand.

World War II Armoured Fighting Vehicles. David Fletcher. (Illus.). 208p. 1996. 29.95 (1-85532-582-9, Pub. by Osprey Pubng Ltd UK) Motorbooks Intl.

World War II at Sea: A Bibliography of Sources in English, 1974-1989. Myron J. Smith, Jr. LC 89-28213. 314p. 1990. 32.50 (0-8108-2260-1) Scarecrow.

World War II Bombadiers History Book. Turner Publishing Company Staff. LC 91-67147. 224p. 1992. 45.00 (1-56311-076-8) Turner Pub KY.

***World War II Bombers.** Nancy Robinson-Masters. LC 97-5998. (Wings Ser.). (J). 1997. write for info. (1-56065-532-1) Capstone Pr.

World War II Cavalcade: An Offer I Couldn't Refuse. John L. Munschauer. (Illus.). 200p. 1996. pap. 18.95 (0-89745-194-5) Sunflower U Pr.

World War II Combat Drawings & Memoirs of Benedict I. Goldsmith, 1942-45. Benedict I. Goldsmith & Paul E. Mulrenin. LC 95-81581. (Marauder Memoirs (Trilogy) Ser.). (Illus.). 125p. (Orig.). (C). 1995. pap. 75.00 (0-9619535-1-9) Four Fifty Fifth.

World War II Combat Squadrons of the U. S. Air Force. 1992. 12.98 (0-8317-1501-4) Smithmark.

World War II Diary by Lawrence E. Davies the West Coast Correspondent for the New York Times. Lawrence E. Davies. LC 94-75079. 216p. (Orig.). (C). 1994. pap. 12.95 (0-9634413-3-7) HiSt Ink Bks.

***World War II Fighters.** Nancy Robinson-Masters. LC 97-5999. (Wings Ser.). (J). 1998. write for info. (1-56065-533-X) Capstone Pr.

World War II Fighting Jets. Jeffrey Ethell & Alfred Price. LC 94-65971. (Illus.). 211p. 1994. 32.95 (1-55750-940-9) Naval Inst Pr.

World War II Fighting Ships: Sidelights to Their Fighting Histories. 2nd rev. ed. Compiled by Walter Jacob. (Southfarm Sidelights to History Ser.). (Illus.). 128p. (Orig.). 1996. pap. 14.00 (0-913337-13-7) Southfarm Pr.

World War II Fighting Vehicles Anthology, Vol. 1. Ed. by Ray Merriam. (World War II Historical Society Monograph Ser.). 102p. 1993. pap. 12.50 (1-57638-033-5) Merriam Pr.

World War II, Film, & History. John W. Chambers, 2nd & David Culbert. (Illus.). 192p. 1996. 30.00 (0-19-509966-4); pap. 15.95 (0-19-509967-2) OUP.

World War II for Beginners. Errol Selkirk. LC 91-50559. (Writers & Readers Documentary Comic Bks.). (Illus.). 176p. (Orig.). (C). 1991. pap. 8.95 (0-86316-103-0) Writers & Readers.

***World War II G. I. U. S. Army Uniforms 1941-45 in Colour Photographs.** Richard Windrow. 1997. pap. 24.95 (1-85915-049-7, Pub. by Windrow & Green UK) Motorbooks Intl.

World War II GI: U. S. Army Uniforms 1941-1945 in Color Photographs. Richard Winrow. Ed. by Tim Hawkins. LC 93-27893. (Uniforms in Color Photographs Ser.). (Illus.). 144p. 1993. 39.95 (0-87938-832-3) Motorbooks Intl.

World War II in Alaska. Penny Rennick & L. J. Campbell. (Alaska Geographic Ser.: Vol. 22, No. 4). (Illus.). 96p. (Orig.). 1996. pap. 19.95 (1-56661-028-1) Alaska Geog Soc.

World War II in Europe: "America Goes to War" R. Conrad Stein. LC 93-47396. (American War Ser.). (Illus.). 128p. (YA). (gr. 5 up). 1994. lib. bdg. 18.95 (0-89490-525-2) Enslow Pubs.

World War II in Europe: An Encyclopedia, 2, 6. David T. Zabecki. (Illus.). 1541p. 1997. text ed. 175.00 (0-8240-7029-1) Garland.

World War II in Europe: Causes, Course, & Consequences. L. H. Gann & Peter Duignan. LC 95-33611. (Hoover Essays Ser.: No. 12). 58p. 1995. pap. 5.00 (0-8179-3752-8) Hoover Inst Pr.

***World War II in Europe, Africa & the Americas, with General Sources: A Handbook of Literature & Research.** Ed. by Loyd E. Lee. LC 96-37044. 556p. 1997. text ed. 95.00 (0-313-29325-2, Greenwood Pr) Greenwood.

***World War II in Photographs.** Smithmark Staff. 1996. 9.98 (0-7651-9602-6) Smithmark.

World War II in the Mediterranean, 1942-1945. Carlo D'Este. (Major Battles & Campaigns Ser.: Vol. II). 272p. 1990. 22.95 (0-945575-04-1) Algonquin Bks.

World War II in the North Pacific: Chronology & Fact Book. Kevin D. Hutchison. LC 94-5822. 328p. 1994. text ed. 69.50 (0-313-29130-6, Greenwood Pr) Greenwood.

World War II in the Pacific: "Remember Pearl Harbor" R. Conrad Stein. LC 93-33623. (American War Ser.). (Illus.). 128p. (YA). (gr. 5 up). 1994. lib. bdg. 18.95 (0-89490-524-4) Enslow Pubs.

World War II International Aircraft Recognition Manual. (Illus.). 160p. 1973. pap. 8.25 (0-87994-017-4) Aviat Pub.

World War II Love Letters. Audrey Gettings. LC 95-76646. (Illus.). 132p. (Orig.). 1995. pap. 10.00 (0-938041-60-6) Arc Pr AR.

***World War II... Memories.** Leonard Zerlin. (Illus.). 140p. 1996. pap. 25.00 (0-9653520-0-5) L Zerlin.

World War II Nose Art in Color. Jeffrey L. Ethell. LC 93-13072. (Enthusiast Color Ser.). (Illus.). 96p. 1993. pap. 12.95 (0-87938-819-6) Motorbooks Intl.

***World War II Odyssey - Pennsylvania Dutch Farmboy Becomes 8th Air Force Navigator.** Bill Frankhouser. (Illus.). 234p. 1997. 19.95 (1-883912-03-2) Hamiltons.

World War II Pacific War Eagles: China/Pacific Air War. Jeff Ethell & Warren M. Bodie. 224p. (YA). 1996. 39.95 (0-9629359-3-X) Widewing Pubns.

World War II Quiz & Fact Book. Timothy B. Benford. 1993. 9.98 (0-88365-826-7) Galahad Bks.

World War II Quiz & Fact Book. Timothy B. Benford. 1993. 9.98 (0-88394-086-8) Promntory Pr.

World War II Remembered: History in Your Hands, a Numismatic Study. C. Frederick Schwan & Joseph E. Boling. LC 94-96515. (Illus.). 784p. 1995. 75.00 (0-931960-40-1) BNR Pr.

World War II Reminiscences. 2nd ed. Ed. & Illus. by John H. Roush, Jr. LC 95-92808. 378p. (Orig.). 1996. pap. 20.00 (0-9600830-3-0) J H Roush.

World War II Sites in the United States: A Directory & Tour Guide. Richard E. Osborne. LC 91-68129. (Illus.). (Orig.). 1995. per. 19.95 (0-9628324-1-3) Riebel Roque.

World War II Soldier at Monte Cassino. (Soldier Ser.). 48p. (J). (gr. 5-6). 1991. lib. bdg. 17.80 (1-56065-005-2) Capstone Pr.

World War II: The European Theatre see Perspectives on History Series: Part II

World War II to the New Frontier, 1940-1963. William L. Katz. 1995. pap. text ed. 6.95 (0-8114-2917-2) Raintree Steck-V.

***World War II Trainers.** Nancy Robinson-Masters. LC 97-6000. (Wings Ser.). (J). 1998. write for info. (1-56065-534-8) Capstone Pr.

World War II War Birds: Solid Wood Airplane Modeling. Angelo A. Principe. (Illus.). 200p. 1993. spiral bd. 19.95 (0-9634736-0-3) Hist In Wood.

World War II Warship Anthology, Vol. 1. Ed. by Ray Merriam. (World War II Historical Society Monograph Ser.). 100p. 1993. pap. 12.50 (1-57638-034-3) Merriam Pr.

World War II Wrecks of the Kwajalein & Truk Lagoons. 3rd rev. ed. Dan E. Bailey. Ed. by Bill Remick. LC 82-63006. (Illus.). 224p. 1992. 34.95 (0-911615-05-9) North Valley.

World War II Wrecks of the Truk Lagoon. (Illus.). pap. write for info. (0-911615-06-7) North Valley.

World War III: Dispatches from the Soviet Front. Ed. by S. Krasilshchik. Tr. by Antonina W. Bouis from RUS. LC 85-2371. (Illus.). xv, 372p. (Orig.). 1985. 27.50 (0-943071-11-9) Sphinx Pr.

World War III: Population & the Biosphere at the End of the Millennium. Michael Tobias. 656p. 1994. 29.95 (1-879181-18-5) Bear & Co.

World War III, America's Last Stand. James Silvia. LC 95-91020. (Orig.). 1996. pap. 7.95 (0-533-11820-4) Vantage.

World War III When the Arabs Attack Jerusalem. 2nd ed. Charles R. Taylor. Orig. Title: When the Arabs Attack Jerusalem. (Illus.). 88p. 1991. pap. 5.95 (0-937682-12-8) Today Bible.

World War IV: China's Quest for Power in the 21st Century. Richard Hobbs. 221p. Date not set. spiral bd. 19.95 (0-9647788-7-4) ColDoc Pubng.

***World War I.** Neil M. Heyman. LC 97-1686. (Greenwood Press Reference Guides to Historic Events of the 20th Century). 1997. text ed. write for info. (0-313-29880-7, Greenwood Pr) Greenwood.

World War One: A Chronological Narrative. Philip Warner. (Illus.). 272p. 1995. 27.95 (1-85409-294-4, Pub. by Arms & Armour UK) Sterling.

World War One: A Comprehensive History. John C. Ridpath. (Illus.). 530p. 1992. reprint ed. text ed. 59.95 (1-877767-80-8) Univ Pubng Hse.

World War One: Concise Military Histories of America's Major Wars. Ed. by Maurice Matloff. (Illus.). 1979. 7.95 (0-679-51450-3) McKay.

World War One & the Serving British Soldier. R. H. Haigh & P. W. Turner. (Orig.). 1979. pap. 30.95 (0-89126-070-6) MA-AH Pub.

World War One Army Ancestry. (C). 1987. 30.00 (0-317-89897-3, Pub. by Birmingham Midland Soc UK) St Mut.

World War One at Home: Readings on American Life, 1914-20. Ed. by David E. Trask. LC 70-96958. 224p. (C). reprint ed. 63.90 (0-8357-9002-9, 2012592) Bks Demand.

World War One Aviation: A Bibliography of Books in English, French, German, & Italian, Incl. price list suppl. rev. ed. James P. Noffsinger. LC 95-37995. 576p. (FRE & GER.). 1996. 98.00 (0-8108-3085-X) Scarecrow.

***World War One British Poets: Brooke, Owen, Sassoon, Rosenberg, & Others.** Ed. by Candace Ward. LC 96-51566. (Thrift Editions Ser.). 64p. (Orig.). 1997. pap. text ed. 1.00 (0-486-29568-0) Dover.

***World War One in the Air.** Ken Davies. (Illus.). 160p. 1997. 44.95 (1-86126-080-6, Pub. by Crowood UK) Motorbooks Intl.

World War One Remembered: Paintings by Frank E. Schoonover & Gayle Porter Hoskins. Francis A. Ianni. LC 93-73027. 80p. (Orig.). (YA). (gr. 7-12). 1993. pap. 5.00 (0-924117-05-2) Delaware HP.

World War One Source Book. Philip J. Haythornthwaite. (Illus.). 288p. 1996. pap. 24.95 (1-85409-351-7, Pub. by Arms & Armour UK) Sterling.

World War Three Collection. Ed. by Peter Kuper & Seth Tobocman. 120p. 1989. pap. 12.95 (1-56097-002-2) Fantagraph Bks.

An Asterisk (*) at the beginning of an entry indicates that the title is appearing in BIP for the first time.

World Within the World. John D. Barrow. (Illus.). 416p. 1990. reprint ed. pap. 15.95 (0-19-286108-5) OUP.

World Within Walls. Donald Keene. LC 75-21484. 606p. 1976. 22.95 (0-03-013626-1) H Holt & Co.

World Within Walls. Donald Keene. 1996. pap. 35.00 (0-8050-3569-9) H Holt & Co.

World Within War. Linderman. 1997. 26.00 (0-02-919115-7, Free Press) Free Pr.

World Within War. Linderman. 1997. 26.00 (0-684-82797-2) Free Pr.

World Within World: An Autobiography. Stephen Spender. 568p. 1994. pap. 14.95 (0-312-11358-7) St Martin.

World Without Borders. Mary J. Coreth. Ed. by Mary Caroland. LC 90-83591. 88p. 1991. 6.95 (1-55523-375-9) Winston-Derek.

World Without Cancer: The Story of Vitamin B17. 2nd rev. ed. LC 96-84094. (Illus.). 386p. 1996. pap. 17.50 (0-912986-19-0) Am Media.

World Without End. Molly Cochran & Warren Murphy. 1996. 23.95 (0-312-85597-4) Tor Bks.

***World Without End.** Molly Cochran. 1997. mass mkt. 6.99 (0-8125-3427-1) Tor Bks.

World Without End. N. X. Cruciatus. 1996. pap. 12.95 (0-533-11592-2) Vantage.

World Without End. Edward Gula. 184p. 1996. pap. 13.00 (0-8059-3889-3) Dorrance.

World Without End. Joe W. Haldeman. (Star Trek Ser.). 1993. mass mkt. 4.99 (0-553-24174-5) Bantam.

World Without End. Dan Masterson. LC 90-10890. 81p. 1991. pap. 12.00 (1-55728-178-5) U of Ark Pr.

***World Without End.** Ev Miller & William-Alan Landes. 63p. (Orig.). 1997. pap. 6.00 (0-88734-714-2) Players Pr.

World Without End. Sean Russell. (Moontide & Magic Rise Ser.: No. 1). 608p. (Orig.). 1995. pap. 5.99 (0-88677-624-4) DAW Bks.

***World Without End.** Del Sneller. LC 96-69569. 96p. 1996. pap. 10.95 (1-56167-321-8) Am Literary Pr.

World Without End: Economics, Environment, & Sustainable Development. David W. Pearce & Jeremy J. Warford. LC 92-39551. 456p. 1993. 49.95 (0-19-520881-1, 60881) World Bank.

World Without End: Economics, Environment, & Sustainable Development, a Summary. David W. Pearce. 52p. 1993. 6.95 (0-8213-2502-7, 12502) World Bank.

***World Without End: New Vistas in Biblical Prophecy.** Jim Strickling. 144p. pap. 12.95 (0-614-29719-2) BookMasters.

***World Without Famine.** O'Neill. Date not set. text ed. 79.95 (0-312-21022-1) St Martin.

World Without Heroes: The Brooklyn Novels of Daniel Fuchs. Marcelline Krafchick. LC 86-46339. 120p. 1988. 24.50 (0-8386-3312-9) Fairleigh Dickinson.

World Without Heroes: The Modern Tragedy. George Roche. LC 87-80235. 368p. 1987. pap. 12.95 (0-916308-89-8) Hillsdale Coll Pr.

World Without Homosexuals. Jason Ross. LC 94-66316. (Illus.). 104p. (Orig.). 1994. pap. 10.00 (0-9641408-1-0) Road Kill Pr.

World Without Men. Valerie Taylor. 160p. 1982. pap. 3.95 (0-930044-32-0) Naiad Pr.

World Without Money: An Alternative. A. Wicklow. 53p. 1982. 35.00 (0-7223-1326-8, Pub. by A H S Ltd UK) St Mut.

World Without Tears: The Case of Charles Rothenberg. Harry J. Gaynor et al. LC 89-71193. 152p. 1990. text ed. 29.95 (0-275-93693-7, C3693, Praeger Pubs) Greenwood.

***World Without the Mind Within: An Essay on First Person Authority.** Andre Gallois. (Cambridge Studies in Philosophy). 225p. (C). 1997. text ed. 49.95 (0-521-56093-4) Cambridge U Pr.

***World Without the Rinderpest.** Food & Agriculture Organization Staff. (Animal Production & Health Papers: No. 129). 173p. 1997. pap. 19.00 (92-5-103900-3, F39003, Pub. by FAO IT) Bernan Associates.

World Without Tyranny. Dean Curry. LC 89-81259. (Turning Point Christian Worldview Ser.). 192p. 1990. pap. 12.99 (0-89107-509-7) Crossway Bks.

World Without Violence: Can Gandhi's Vision Become Reality. A. Gandhi. 1994. reprint ed. write for info. (81-224-0674-2, Pub. by Wiley Estrn II) Franklin.

World Without Wages (Money, Poverty & War!) Samuel Leight. 229p. 1981. pap. text ed. 12.95 (0-9613654-1-2) WWW Pubs.

***World Without War: How U. S. Feminists & Pacifists Resisted World War I.** Frances H. Early. LC 97-16767. (Studies on Peace & Conflict Resolution). (Illus.). 288p. 1997. 44.95 (0-8156-2745-9) Syracuse U Pr.

***World Without War: How U. S. Feminists & Pacifists Resisted World War I.** Frances H. Early. 288p. 1997. pap. 22.95 (0-8156-2764-5) Syracuse U Pr.

World Without Women. large type ed. Day Keene. (Linford Mystery Library). 384p. 1993. pap. 15.99 (0-7089-7432-5, Trailtree Bookshop) Ulverscroft.

World Without Women: The Christian Clerical Culture of Western Science. David F. Noble. LC 92-44613. 352p. (C). 1993. pap. 12.95 (0-19-508435-7) OUP.

World Without Wool Shops. Dulan Barber. LC 90-33106. 1990. 19.95 (0-7145-2902-8) M Boyars Pubs.

World Without Words: Social Construction of Children Born Deaf & Blind. David Goode. LC 93-51038. (Health, Society, & Policy Ser.). 272p. (C). 1994. pap. text ed. 19.95 (1-56639-216-0) Temple U Pr.

World Without Work: The Story of the Welsh Miners. Eli Ginzberg. 260p. (C). 1992. 39.95 (0-88738-330-0) Transaction Pubs.

World Woods in Color. William A. Lincoln. LC 90-23574. (Illus.). 320p. 1991. reprint ed. 49.95 (0-941936-20-1) Linden Pub Fresno.

World Workers' Educational Movements, Their Social Significance. Marius Hansome. LC 68-58587. (Columbia University. Studies in the Social Sciences: No. 338). reprint ed. 37.50 (0-404-51338-7) AMS Pr.

World Workshop in Clinical Periodontics - Proceedings. American Academy of Periodontology Staff. 260p. 1989. 65.00 (0-9624699-1-2) Amer Acad Periodontology.

World Workstation Markets: Proven Applications, with New Pentium-Power PC Chips, Attract New Users. Market Intelligence Staff. 306p. 1993. 1,995.00 (1-56753-609-3) Frost & Sullivan.

World, World What Can I Do? Barbara S. Hazen. LC 90-43764. (Illus.). 36p. (J). (ps-3). 1991. 10.95 (0-8192-1537-6) Morehouse Pub.

World Wound Closure Product Markets: Developing Nations Contribute to Markets Rebound. Frost & Sullivan Staff. 1995. write for info. (0-7889-0269-5) Frost & Sullivan.

World Wound Closure Products: Staplers Invade Suture Markets. Market Intelligence Staff. 345p. 1992. 1,695.00 (1-56753-387-6) Frost & Sullivan.

World Wreckers. Marion Zimmer Bradley. 288p. 1994. mass mkt. 4.99 (0-88677-629-5) DAW Bks.

***World X-Ray & Computed Tomography Equipment Markets.** 273p. 1996. write for info. (0-7889-0569-4, 5391) Frost & Sullivan.

World X-Ray & Computed Tomography Equipment Markets: Manufacturers Exploit Niche Opportunities & Polarized Markets. Market Intelligence Staff. 293p. (Orig.). 1992. 1,895.00 (1-56753-041-9) Frost & Sullivan.

World Zoo Conservation Strategy Executive Summary: The Role of the Zoos & Aquaria of the World in Global Conservation. IUDZG - The World Zoo Organization & the Captive Breeding Specialist Group of IUCN-SSC Staff. 12p. 1993. pap. text ed. write for info. (0-913934-21-6) Chicago Zoo.

World 1995/1996: A Third World Guide. Third World Institute Staff. (Information & Reference). (Illus.). 640p. (C). 1995. pap. 39.95 (0-85598-291-8, Pub. by Oxfam UK) Humanities.

***World 1997-1998: A Third World Guide.** Oxfam Staff. (C). 1997. pap. 39.95 (0-85598-360-4, Pub. by Oxfam UK) Humanities.

***World 1997/98: A Third World Guide.** Compiled by Third World Inst. Staff. 624p. 1997. 80.00 (1-869847-42-3, Pub. by Oxfam UK) Humanities.

***World 1997/98: A Third World Guide.** Compiled by Third World Inst. Staff. 624p. 1997. pap. 39.95 (1-869847-43-1, Pub. by Oxfam UK) Humanities.

World 3-D Diagnostic Medical Imaging Equipment & Software Markets: Dramatic Global Expansion Led by Clinical Applications & Ultrasound Technology. Market Intelligence Staff. 250p. 1992. 1,995.00 (1-56753-413-9) Frost & Sullivan.

Worldbeat: Current Readings for ESL Students. Laurie Blass & Meredith P. Baky. 1992. pap. text ed. write for info. (0-07-005866-0) McGraw.

Worldcrafters. Geary Gravel. 1997. mass mkt. write for info. (0-345-38294-3) Ballantine.

Worlde of Wordes. John Florio. (Anglistica & Americana Ser.: No. 114). 462p. 1972. reprint ed. 102.70 (3-487-04227-4) G Olms Pubs.

***Worlding Women: Feminist International Politics.** Jan J. Pettman. 224p. (C). 1996. pap. 17.95 (0-415-15202-X); text ed. 65.00 (0-415-15201-1) Routledge.

Worldling. Elizabeth Spires. LC 95-7885. 72p. 1995. 18.95 (0-393-03855-6) Norton.

***Worldling.** Elizabeth Spires. 80p. 1997. pap. 10.00 (0-393-31628-9) Norton.

Worldly Art: The Dutch Republic, 1585-1718. Mariet Westermann. LC 95-24695. (The Perspectives Ser.). (Illus.). 192p. 1996. 16.95 (0-8109-2741-1) Abrams.

Worldly Christianity. Paul Kuenning. 1995. pap. 10.00 (0-7880-0614-2, 6142) CSS OH.

Worldly Church: A Call for Biblical Renewal. 2nd ed. C. Leonard Allen. LC 87-81827. 116p. 1991. pap. 8.95 (0-89112-150-1) Abilene Christ U.

Worldly Goods: A New History of the Renaissance. Lisa Jardine. (Illus.). 400p. 1996. 32.50 (0-385-47684-1, N A Talese) Doubleday.

Worldly Hopes: Poems. A. R. Ammons. 51p. 1982. pap. 5.95 (0-393-00081-8) Norton.

Worldly Innocent. Joanna Harris. 240p. (Orig.). 1989. mass mkt. 2.95 (0-380-75575-0) Avon.

Worldly Phenomenology: The Continuing Influence of Alfred Schutz on North American Human Science. Ed. by Lester Embree. LC 88-14341. (Current Continental Research Ser.: No. 013). 334p. (Orig.). (C). 1988. pap. text ed. 27.00 (0-8191-7035-6, Ctr Adv Res); lib. bdg. 53.50 (0-8191-7034-8, Ctr Adv Res) U Pr of Amer.

Worldly Philosophers: The Lives, Times & Ideas of the Great Economic Thinkers. 6th ed. Robert L. Heilbroner. 366p. 1987. pap. 14.00 (0-671-63318-X, Touchstone Bks) S&S Trade.

Worldly Philosophers Notes. Joseph M. Leon. 1974. pap. 3.95 (0-8220-1385-1) Cliffs.

Worldly Power: The Making of the Wall Street Journal. Edward E. Scharff. LC 85-26741. (Illus.). 315p. 1985. 18.95 (0-8253-0359-1) Beaufort Bks NY.

Worldly Power: The Making of the Wall Street Journal. Edward E. Scharff. 1987. pap. 9.95 (0-317-56711-X, Plume) NAL-Dutton.

Worldly Saints. Leland Ryken. 272p. 1990. pap. 17.99 (0-310-32501-3) Zondervan.

Worldly Spirituality. W. Robert McClelland. 176p. (Orig.). 1990. pap. 10.99 (0-8272-4227-1) Chalice Pr.

Worldly Years. John English. 1992. pap. 25.50 (0-394-22729-8) Knopf.

Worldmaking. Ed. by William Pencak. (Critic of Institutions Ser.: Vol. 6). 416p. (C). 1996. text ed. 59.95 (0-8204-2804-3) P Lang Pubng.

***Worldmark Chronologies.** Karen Christensen. 2100p. 1997. 249.00 (0-7876-0521-2, 00152859, Gale Res Intl) Gale.

***Worldmark Chronologies Africa, Vol. 1.** 1997. 65.00 (0-7876-0522-0, 00152863, Gale Res Intl) Gale.

***Worldmark Chronologies Americas, Vol. 2.** 1997. 65.00 (0-7876-0523-9, 00152860, Gale Res Intl) Gale.

***Worldmark Chronologies Oceanic.** 3rd ed. 1997. 65.00 (0-7876-0524-7, 00152867, Gale Res Intl) Gale.

***Worldmark Encyclopedia of Culture & Daily Life, 4 vols.** 1997. 299.00 (0-7876-0552-2, 00152949, Gale Res Intl) Gale.

***Worldmark Encyclopedia of Culture & Daily Life in Africa.** LC 97-3278. 1997. 80.00 (0-7876-0553-0, 00152950, Gale Res Intl) Gale.

***Worldmark Encyclopedia of Culture & Daily Life in America.** 1997. 80.00 (0-7876-0554-9, 00152951, Gale Res Intl) Gale.

***Worldmark Encyclopedia of Culture & Daily Life in Asia.** 1997. 80.00 (0-7876-0555-7, 00152952, Gale Res Intl) Gale.

***Worldmark Encyclopedia of Culture & Daily Life in Europe.** 1997. 80.00 (0-7876-0556-5, 00152953, Gale Res Intl) Gale.

Worldmark Encyclopedia of Nations, Vol. 1. 8th ed. Susan. 1994. write for info. (0-8103-9893-1) Gale.

Worldmark Encyclopedia of Nations, Vol. 2. 8th ed. Susan. 1994. write for info. (0-8103-9880-X) Gale.

Worldmark Encyclopedia of Nations, Vol. 3. 8th ed. Susan. 1994. write for info. (0-8103-9881-8) Gale.

Worldmark Encyclopedia of Nations, Vol. 4. 8th ed. Susan. 1994. write for info. (0-8103-9882-6) Gale.

Worldmark Encyclopedia of Nations, Vol. 5. 8th ed. Susan. 1994. write for info. (0-8103-9883-4) Gale.

***Worldmark Encyclopedia of Nations, Vol. 5.** 10th ed. Date not set. 335.00 (0-7876-0511-5, 00152842, Gale Res Intl) Gale.

***Worldmark Encyclopedia of Nations 9, 5 vols.** 9th ed. Eastword Pubns., Inc. Staff. Ed. by Timothy L. Gall & Susan B. Gall. 2000p. 1997. 345.00 (0-7876-0074-1, 00108742, Gale Res Intl) Gale.

Worldmark Encyclopedia of the Nations, 5 vols., Set. 7th ed. Ed. by Moshe Y. Sachs. (Illus.). 1750p. 1988. text ed. 495.00 (0-471-62406-3) Wiley.

***Worldmark Encyclopedia of the Nations & State.** 1995. 299.00 (0-7876-0875-0, 00155811, UXL) Gale.

***Worldmark Encyclopedia of the States.** 4th ed. Eastword Pubns., Inc. Staff. Ed. by Timothy L. Gall & Susan B. Gall. 400p. 1997. 140.00 (0-7876-0080-6, 00108724, Gale Res Intl) Gale.

***Worldmask.** Akiva Tatz. 1995. 17.95 (1-56871-080-1) Targum Pr.

World/Odysseus. M. I. Finley. 192p. 1979. pap. 11.95 (0-14-013686-X) Viking Penguin.

***Worldproofing Your Kids: Helping Moms Prepare Their Kids to Navigate Today's Turbulent Times.** Lael Arrington. LC 97-11017. 304p. (Orig.). 1997. pap. 12.99 (0-89107-956-4) Crossway Bks.

Worlds. Edward Bond. 176p. (C). 1988. pap. 8.95 (0-413-46610-8, A0321) Heinemann.

Worlds. Joseph Soulson. Ed. by Isay Davydov. LC 91-75647. Orig. Title: Miry. (Illus.). 400p. (RUS.). 1991. 20.00 (0-9630594-0-8) Intl Sci Ctr.

Worlds, Bk. 1. Joe W. Haldeman. 240p. 1990. mass mkt. 3.95 (0-380-70823-X, Flare) Avon.

World's a Small Town. Roger Granet. 1993. write for info. (0-942544-20-X) Negative Capability Pr.

World's a Small Town. Roger Granet. 72p. 1993. pap. 8.95 (0-942544-18-8) Negative Capability Pr.

***Worlds Aligned: The Politics of Culture in the Shadow of Capital.** David Lloyd & Lisa Lowe. LC 97-8900. 1997. write for info. (0-8223-2033-9); pap. write for info. (0-8223-2046-0) Duke.

World's All-Time Best Collection of Good Clean Jokes. Bob Phillips. 352p. 1996. 9.98 (0-88365-967-0) Galahad Bks.

Worlds & I. Ella W. Wilcox. Ed. by Annette K. Baxter. LC 79-8823. (Signal Lives Ser.). (Illus.). 1980. reprint ed. lib. bdg. 49.95 (0-405-12867-3) Ayer.

***Worlds & Words.** Daugherty. (C). Date not set. pap. write for info. (0-395-68565-6); teacher ed., pap. write for info. (0-395-68566-4) HM.

***Worlds Apart.** Judy Baer. (Cedar River Daydreams Ser.: No. 26). 1997. pap. 4.99 (1-55661-836-0) Bethany Hse.

Worlds Apart. Marilyn Campbell. 384p. (Orig.). 1994. pap. 4.99 (0-451-40522-6, Topaz) NAL-Dutton.

Worlds Apart. Joe Haldeman. LC 83-47875. 227p. 1983. 25.00 (0-89366-190-2) Ultramarine Pub.

Worlds Apart. Joe W. Haldeman. 240p. 1992. mass mkt. 4.50 (0-380-71682-8, AvoNova) Avon.

Worlds Apart. William MacDonald. 76p. (Orig.). 1993. pap. 4.95 (1-882701-05-4) Uplook Min.

Worlds Apart. Jane Plead. 150p. 1995. 19.95 (0-9646885-0-6) Manoa Valley.

Worlds Apart. Sudy Rosengarten. 214p. 1992. 14.95 (0-944070-81-7); pap. 11.95 (0-944070-82-5) Targum Pr.

***Worlds Apart.** large type ed. Nicola Thorne. LC 97-15346. (Paperback Ser.). 416p. 1997. pap. 21.95 (0-7838-8233-5, GK Hall) Thorndike Pr.

Worlds Apart. Owen Barfield. LC 63-17798. 213p. 1971. reprint ed. pap. 13.95 (0-8195-6017-0, Wesleyan Univ Pr) U Pr of New Eng.

Worlds Apart: A Novel of the Future. Joe W. Haldeman. LC 83-47875. 252p. 1983. 14.95 (0-685-06795-5) Viking Penguin.

Worlds Apart: A Textbook in Planetary Sciences. Guy Consolmagno. 496p. 1994. text ed. 67.00 (0-13-964131-9) P-H.

Worlds Apart: An Anthology of Lesbian & Gay Science Fiction & Fantasy. Ed. by Camilla Decarnin et al. 288p. (Orig.). 1994. reprint ed. pap. 5.95 (1-55583-600-3) Alyson Pubns.

Worlds Apart: Collective Action in Simulated Agrarian & Industrial Societies. Richard L. Dukes. (Theory & Decision Library). 206p. (C). 1990. lib. bdg. 94.50 (0-7923-0620-1) Kluwer Ac.

Worlds Apart: Housing, Race-Ethnicity & Income in New York City, 1978-1987. Phillip Weitzman. LC 90-198040. 130p. 1989. 12.00 (0-88156-103-7) Comm Serv Soc NY.

Worlds Apart? Long-Term Care in Australia & the United States. Ed. by Sandra J. Newman. LC 87-29770. (Home Health Care Services Quarterly Ser.: Vol. 8, No. 3). (Illus.). 113p. 1988. text ed. 32.95 (0-86656-703-8) Haworth Pr.

Worlds Apart: Modernity Through the Prism of the Local. Ed. by Daniel Miller. LC 94-46805. (Uses of Knowledge Ser.). 288p. (C). 1995. pap. 18.95 (0-415-10789-X) Routledge.

Worlds Apart: Modernity Through the Prism of the Local. Ed. by Daniel Miller. LC 94-46805. (Uses of Knowledge Ser.). 288p. (C). (gr. 13). 1995. text ed. 62.95 (0-415-10788-1) Routledge.

Worlds Apart: Narratology of Science Fiction. Carl D. Malmgren. LC 90-25045. 222p. 1991. 9.95 (0-253-33645-7) Ind U Pr.

Worlds Apart: Recent Chinese Writing & Its Audience. Ed. by Howard Goldblatt. LC 90-30354. (Studies on Contemporary China). 264p. (gr. 13). 1990. 62.95 (0-87332-502-8, East Gate Bk) M E Sharpe.

Worlds Apart: Structural Parallels in Poetry of Paul Valery, Saint-John Perse, Benjamin Peret & Rene Char. Elizabeth R. Jackson. (De Proprietatibus Litterarum, Ser. Practica: No. 106). 256p. 1976. pap. text ed. 60.80 (90-279-3394-4) Mouton.

Worlds Apart: Technology & North-South Relations in the Global Economy. Sam Cole & Ian Miles. LC 84-125439. 256p. (C). 1984. 38.50 (0-8476-7374-X) Rowman.

Worlds Apart: The Market & the Theater in Anglo-American Thought, 1550-1750. Jean-Christophe Agnew. 248p. 1986. text ed. 49.95 (0-521-24322-X) Cambridge U Pr.

Worlds Apart: The Market & the Theater in Anglo-American Thought, 1550-1750. Jean-Christophe Agnew. 248p. 1988. pap. text ed. 18.95 (0-521-37910-5) Cambridge U Pr.

Worlds Apart: The North-South Divide & the International System. Nassau A. Adams. LC 92-39550. 256p. (C). 1993. pap. 22.50 (1-85649-166-8, Pub. by Zed Bks Ltd UK); text ed. 59.95 (1-85649-165-X, Pub. by Zed Bks Ltd UK) Humanities.

Worlds Apart: The Unholy War Between Religion & Science. Karl Giberson. 221p. 1993. pap. 21.99 (0-8341-1504-2) Beacon Hill.

World's Apart: Readings for a Sociology of Education see Toward a Sociology of Education

World's Bankers: The Multilateral Financial Institutions in the 1900's. Jerome I. Levinson. LC 94-8560. 1993. pap. 9.95 (0-87078-181-2) TCFP-PPP.

World's Beef Business. James R. Simpson & Donald E. Farris. LC 81-20770. (Illus.). 344p. 1982. reprint ed. pap. 98.10 (0-608-00012-4, 2060778) Bks Demand.

World's Best. 3rd ed. Ed. by Marian V. Cooper. 600p. 1988. 19.95 (0-945332-08-4) Agora Inc MD.

World's Best. 5th enl. rev. ed. Ed. by Kathleen Peddicord. 650p. 1992. pap. 29.00 (0-945332-33-5) Agora Inc MD.

World's Best Anatomical Charts. Anatomical Chart Company Staff. (Illus.). 72p. (Orig.). 1993. pap. 14.95 (0-9603730-5-5) Anatomical Chart.

World's Best & Easiest Photography Book. Jerry Hughes. Orig. Title: The World's Simplest Photography Book. (Illus.). 96p. (Orig.). 1994. pap. 9.95 (0-9634348-2-9) P Lane Pub.

World's Best & Easiest Photography Book. 5th ed. Jerry Hughes. Orig. Title: The World's Simplest Photography Book. (Illus.). 128p. (Orig.). 1996. pap. 12.95 (0-9634348-6-1) P Lane Pub.

World's Best Blonde Jokes. Laura Crenshaw & April Stokes. 56p. 1992. pap. 4.95 (0-9632280-0-5) Peroxide Pr.

World's Best Card Games for One. Sheila A. Barry. (Illus.). 128p. 1993. pap. 4.95 (0-8069-8637-9) Sterling.

World's Best Card Tricks. Bob Longe. LC 90-46641. (Illus.). 128p. (YA). 1992. pap. 4.95 (0-8069-8233-0) Sterling.

World's Best Christmas Stories. LC 93-27249. (Illus.). 80p. (J). (gr. 4-6). 1993. pap. 2.95 (0-8167-3142-X) Troll Communs.

World's Best Coin Tricks. Bob Longe. LC 92-11370. (Illus.). 128p. (J). (gr. 5-10). 1993. pap. 4.95 (0-8069-8661-1) Sterling.

World's Best Colorbook of Dragons. Deborah L. Schoenholz & Terry Lang. (Modern Mythologies Ser.: Vol. 1). (Illus.). 64p. (Orig.). 1988. ring bd. 14.50 (0-317-91171-6) Uptown Bkworks.

World's Best Crossword & Word Puzzle Book, Vol. 37. 128p. Date not set. 5.95 (1-56987-316-X) Landoll.

World's Best Crossword & Word Puzzle Book, Vol. 38. 128p. Date not set. 5.95 (1-56987-317-8) Landoll.

World's Best Crossword & Word Puzzle Book, Vol. 39. 128p. Date not set. 5.95 (1-56987-318-6) Landoll.

World's Best Crossword & Word Puzzle Book, Vol. 40. 128p. Date not set. 5.95 (1-56987-319-4) Landoll.

World's Best Dirty Jokes. Mr. J. 1985. mass mkt. 4.95 (0-345-33106-0) Ballantine.

World's Best Dirty Jokes. Mr. J. (Illus.). 160p. 1976. 7.95 (0-8184-0223-7) Carol Pub Group.

An Asterisk (*) at the beginning of an entry indicates that the title is appearing in BIP for the first time.

World's Best Dirty Jokes. Mr. J. (Illus.). 1979. pap. 4.95 (*0-8065-0702-0*, Citadel Pr) Carol Pub Group.
World's Best Dirty Limericks. David M. (Illus.). 192p. 1982. 8.95 (*0-8184-0324-1*) Carol Pub Group.
World's Best Drama Index. Roth Publishing, Inc. Staff. 159p. 1989. pap. 24.95 (*0-89609-294-1*) Roth Pub Inc.
World's Best Home Study Mail Order Guide. 1987. lib. bdg. 150.00 (*0-317-55330-5*) Gordon Pr.
World's Best Home-Study Mail Order Guide. rev. ed. Robert Hildreth. 40p. 1987. pap. 5.00 (*0-915665-19-0*) Premier Publishers.
World's Best Hope. Francis B. Biddle. (History - United States Ser.). 175p. 1993. reprint ed. lib. bdg. 69.00 (*0-7812-4815-9*) Rprt Serv.
World's Best Jewish Humor. Stanley Kramer. LC 93-45498. 1994. write for info. (*0-8065-1503-1*, Citadel Pr) Carol Pub Group.
World's Best Jinx McGee. Katherine Applegate. 80p. (Orig.). (J). (gr. 2). 1992. pap. 2.99 (*0-380-76728-7*, Camelot Young) Avon.
***World's Best Kept Beauty Secrets: What Really Works in Beauty, Diet & Fashion.** rev. ed. Diane Irons. LC 97-1556. (Illus.). 250p. 1997. pap. 12.95 (*1-57071-142-9*) Sourcebks.
World's Best Kept Secrets - African-American Spiritual Roots of Health & Medicine. 25.00 (*0-685-52661-5*) Holistic Rsch Exch.
World's Best Known Marketing Secret: Building Your Business with Word-of-Mouth Marketing. Ivan R. Misner. (Illus.). 224p. 1994. 24.95 (*1-885167-05-9*); pap. 14.95 (*1-885167-04-0*) Bard Press.
World's Best Loved Christian Poems. Selected by Gordon Lindsay. 1972. 1.95 (*0-89985-251-3*) Christ for the Nations.
World's Best Magic Tricks. Charles B. Townsend. LC 91-41310. (Illus.). 128p. (J). (gr. 3-9). 1993. pap. 4.95 (*0-8069-8583-6*) Sterling.
World's Best Marriage Advice. J. J. Turner. (Orig.). 1989. pap. 3.95 (*0-89315-401-6*) Lambert Bk.
World's Best Music, 6 vols. New York University Society Staff. 1991. reprint ed. Set. lib. bdg. 540.00 (*0-7812-9365-0*) Rprt Serv.
World's Best Optical Illusions. Charles H. Paraquin. Tr. by Paul Kuttner. LC 87-13885. (Illus.). 96p. (Orig.). (YA). (gr. 4-12). 1987. pap. 5.95 (*0-8069-6644-0*) Sterling.
World's Best Optical Illusions. large type ed. Charles H. Paraquin. 1993. 25.50 (*0-614-09863-7*, L-34121-00) Am Printing Hse.
World's Best (or Worst) Firefighter Jokes. James R. Evans. 110p. 1994. pap. text ed. 7.50 (*0-9641530-0-9*) Evans & Assocs.
World's Best Outdoor Games. Glen Vecchione. LC 92-19101. (Illus.). 128p. (J). (gr. 6 up). 1992. 14.95 (*0-8069-8436-8*) Sterling.
World's Best Outdoor Games. Glen Vecchione. (Illus.). 128p. (J). (gr. 3-10). 1993. pap. 5.95 (*0-8069-8437-6*) Sterling.
World's Best Party Games. Sheila A. Barry. LC 86-30038. (Illus.). 128p. (J). (gr. 6-10). 1987. pap. 5.95 (*0-8069-6484-7*) Sterling.
World's Best Piano. Ed. by David C. Olsen. 280p. (Orig.). (YA). 1991. pap. text ed. 19.95 (*0-89898-598-6*, TMF0227) Warner Brothers.
World's Best Poetry, 10 Vols. Ed. by Bliss Carman. LC 81-83524. 4944p. 1982. reprint ed. lib. bdg. 459.99 (*0-89609-300-X*) Roth Pub Inc.
World's Best Poetry, 10 vols, Set. Ed. by Bliss Carman. 1975. lib. bdg. 1,200.00 (*0-87968-323-6*) Gordon Pr.
***World's Best Poetry Suppl. IX: Multicultural Poetry & Major Poetic Schools Examined.** LC 82-84763. 309p. 1997. 49.95 (*0-89609-344-1*) Roth Pub Inc.
World's Best Poetry, Supplement III: Critical Companion, Supplement III. Roth Publishing, Inc. Staff. LC 82-84763. 400p. 1986. 49.95 (*0-89609-242-9*) Roth Pub Inc.
World's Best Poetry, Supplement IV. Ed. by Roth Publishing, Inc. Staff. LC 82-84763. 370p. 1987. 49.95 (*0-89609-265-8*) Roth Pub Inc.
World's Best Poetry, Supplement One: Twentieth Century English & American Verse, 1900-1929, No. I. Granger Book Company Editorial Board. LC 82-84763. 352p. 1983. 49.95 (*0-89609-236-4*) Roth Pub Inc.
World's Best Poetry, Supplement Two: Twentieth Century English & American Verse, 1930-1950. Granger Book Company, Editorial Board Staff. LC 82-84763. 1984. 49.95 (*0-89609-239-9*) Roth Pub Inc.
World's Best Poetry, Supplement V: Tweentieth-Century Women Poets. Ed. by Roth Publishing, Inc. Staff. LC 82-84763. 375p. 1987. 49.95 (*0-89609-270-4*) Roth Pub Inc.
World's Best Poetry, Supplement VI: Twentieth Century African & Latin American Verse. Ed. by Roth Publishing, Inc. Staff. LC 82-84763. 238p. 1989. 49.95 (*0-89609-271-2*, Poetry Index Pr) Roth Pub Inc.
World's Best Poetry, Supplement VII: Twentieth-Century Asian Verse. Ed. by Roth Publishing, Inc. Staff. LC 82-84763. 350p. 1990. 49.95 (*0-89609-289-5*) Roth Pub Inc.
World's Best Poetry, Supplement VIII, Cumulative Index. Roth Publishing, Inc. Staff. LC 82-84763. 257p. 1993. 49.95 (*0-89609-327-1*) Roth Pub Inc.
***World's Best Posters.** Date not set. write for info. (*0-688-09811-8*) Morrow.
World's Best Puzzles. Charles B. Townsend. LC 85-30284. (Illus.). 128p. (Orig.). (J). (gr. 6-10). 1986. pap. 5.95 (*0-8069-4734-9*) Sterling.
***World's Best Recipes.** Hippocrene Editorial Staff. (Illus.). 150p. (Orig.). 1997. pap. 9.95 (*0-7818-0599-6*) Hippocrene Bks.
World's Best Sailboats. Ferenc Mate. 1986. 50.00 (*0-920256-11-2*) Norton.
***World's Best Scary, Spooky Sounds.** (J). 1993. 10.95 incl. audio (*0-8069-0572-7*) Sterling.
World's Best Short Stories, 10 vols. Ed. by Roth Publishing, Inc. Staff. LC 89-60440. 35000p. 1994. Set. 499.50 (*0-89609-400-6*) Roth Pub Inc.
World's Best Short Stories Vol. 1: Short Story Masters, Vol. I. Ed. by Roth Publishing, Inc. Staff. LC 89-60440. 350p. 1989. 49.95 (*0-89609-303-4*) Roth Pub Inc.
World's Best Short Stories Vol. 2: Short Story Masters, Vol. II. Ed. by Roth Publishing, Inc. Staff. LC 89-60440. 378p. 1990. 49.95 (*0-89609-304-2*) Roth Pub Inc.
World's Best Short Stories Vol. 3: Famous Stories. Ed. by Roth Publishing, Inc. Staff. LC 89-60440. 376p. 1990. 49.95 (*0-89609-305-0*) Roth Pub Inc.
World's Best Short Stories Vol. 4: Fables & Tales. Ed. by Roth Publishing, Inc. Staff. LC 89-60440. 389p. 1991. lib. bdg. 49.95 (*0-89609-306-9*) Roth Pub Inc.
World's Best Short Stories Vol. 5: Genres, Mystery & Detection. Ed. by Roth Publishing, Inc. Staff. LC 89-60440. 350p. 1991. 49.95 (*0-89609-307-7*) Roth Pub Inc.
World's Best Short Stories Vol. 6: Genres, Horror & Science Fiction. Ed. by Roth Publishing, Inc. Staff. LC 89-60440. 350p. 1991. 49.95 (*0-89609-312-3*) Roth Pub Inc.
World's Best Short Stories Vol. 7: Characters. Ed. by Roth Publishing, Inc. Staff. LC 89-60440. 350p. 1992. 49.95 (*0-89609-313-1*) Roth Pub Inc.
World's Best Short Stories Vol. 8: Places. Ed. by Roth Publishing, Inc. Staff. LC 89-60440. 350p. 1993. 49.95 (*0-89609-314-X*) Roth Pub Inc.
World's Best Short Stories Vol. 9: Cultures. Ed. by Roth Publishing, Inc. Staff. LC 89-60440. 350p. 1994. 49.95 (*0-89609-315-8*) Roth Pub Inc.
World's Best Short Stories Vol. 10: Research & Reference: Criticism & Indexes. Ed. by Roth Publishing, Inc. Staff. LC 89-60440. 350p. 1996. 49.95 (*0-89609-316-6*) Roth Pub Inc.
World's Best Street & Yard Games. Glen Vecchione. LC 88-38273. (Illus.). 128p. (J). (gr. 2-8). 1990. pap. 5.95 (*0-8069-5762-X*) Sterling.
World's Best Travel Games. Sheila A. Barry. LC 87-7065. (Illus.). 128p. (J). (gr. 5 up). 1988. pap. 4.95 (*0-8069-6776-5*) Sterling.
***World's Best Trout Flies.** Ed. by John Roberts. (Illus.). 184p. 15.98 (*0-8317-7471-1*) Smithmark.
World's Best "True" Ghost Stories. C. B. Colby. LC 88-11703. (Illus.). 128p. (J). (gr. 4 up). 1989. pap. 4.95 (*0-8069-6898-2*) Sterling.
World's Best "True" UFO Stories. Jenny Randles & Peter Hough. LC 94-19807. (Illus.). 96p. 1994. 14.95 (*0-8069-1258-8*) Sterling.
World's Best "True" UFO Stories. Jenny Randles & Peter Hough. (Illus.). 96p. 1995. pap. 4.95 (*0-8069-1259-6*) Sterling.
World's Best Writing Advice. Joan Bolker. 1996. 22.50 (*0-8050-4892-8*) H Holt & Co.
World's Best Writing Advice. Joan Bolker. 1997. pap. 14.95 (*0-8050-4893-6*) H Holt & Co.
World's Best Yiddish Dirty Jokes. Mr. P. (Illus.). 128p. 1984. pap. 4.95 (*0-8065-0887-6*, Citadel Pr) Carol Pub Group.
Worlds Between: Historical Perspectives on Gender & Class. Leonore Davidoff. LC 95-16491. 288p. (C). 1995. pap. 17.95 (*0-415-91488-4*) Routledge.
Worlds Between: Historical Perspectives on Gender & Class. Leonore Davidoff. LC 95-16491. 288p. (C). (gr. 13). 1995. text ed. 62.95 (*0-415-91487-6*) Routledge.
Worlds Between Two Rivers: Perspectives on American Indians in Iowa. Ed. by Gretchen M. Bataille et al. LC 86-27337. (Iowa Heritage Collection Ser.). (Illus.). 148p. 1987. reprint ed. pap. 9.95 (*0-8138-1794-3*) Iowa St U Pr.
Worlds Beyond: The Everlasting Frontier. Ed. by New Dimensions Foundation Staff. LC 78-54345. 320p. 1978. pap. 6.95 (*0-915904-36-5*) And-Or Bks.
Worlds Beyond the Poles. F. Amadeo Giannini. 218p. 1959. reprint ed. spiral bd. 31.00 (*0-7873-0347-X*) Hlth Research.
Worlds Beyond the World: The Fantastic Vision of William Morris. Richard Mathews. LC 78-247. (Milford Series: Popular Writers of Today: Vol. 13). 63p. 1978. pap. 13.00 (*0-89370-218-8*); lib. bdg. 23.00 (*0-89370-118-1*) Borgo Pr.
Worlds Beyond Thought: Conversations on Now-Consciousness. Albert Blackburn. LC 87-82604. 218p. (Orig.). 1988. pap. 12.00 (*0-9613054-3-6*) Idylwild Bks.
World's Bible Dictionary. Don Fleming. 1992. student ed. 14.99 (*0-529-07309-9*, WBD) World Publng.
World's Bible Handbook. Robert T. Boyd. LC 92-22091. 1992. 17.99 (*0-529-07311-0*, WBH) World Publng.
World's Biggest Chicken. Marian Bray. LC 92-7556. 96p. (YA). 1992. pap. 4.99 (*1-55513-929-9*) Chariot Victor.
World's Biggest Tummy. Harry S. Monesson. LC 92-96830. (Illus.). 40p. (Orig.). (J). (gr. k-3). 1992. pap. 4.95 (*0-9633735-0-1*) H S Monesson.
World's Birthday: A Rosh Hashanah Story. Barbara D. Goldin. LC 89-29208. (Illus.). 32p. (J). (ps-3). 1990. 14.00 (*0-15-299648-6*) HarBrace.
World's Birthday: A Rosh Hashanah Story. Barbara D. Goldin. LC 89-29208. (Illus.). 32p. (J). (ps-3). 1995. pap. 5.00 (*0-15-200045-3*, Voyager Bks) HarBrace.
World's Body. fac. ed. John C. Ransom. LC 68-7658. (Louisiana Paperbacks Ser.: No. L-28). 408p. 1968. reprint ed. pap. 116.30 (*0-7837-7931-3*, 2047687) Bks Demand.
World's Championship Matches: 1921 & 1927. Jose R. Capablanca. LC 76-28101. 1977. reprint ed. pap. 4.50 (*0-486-23189-5*) Dover.
Worlds Collide on Vieques: An Intimate Portrait from the Time of Columbus. Elizabeth Langhorne. LC 92-28718. (Illus.). 100p. 1992. 12.95 (*0-944957-36-6*) Rivercross Pub.
***World's Columbian Catholic Congresses & Educational Exhibit.** Date not set. write for info. (*0-405-10871-0*) Ayer.
World's Columbian Exposition, 2 vols. Daniel Burnham. Ed. by Joan E. Draper & Thomas Hines. (Illus.). 8500p. 1989. text ed. 125.00 (*0-8240-3723-5*) Garland.
World's Columbian Exposition: A Centennial Bibliographic Guide. Ed. by Susan M. Neumeister. LC 93-37791. (Bibliographies & Indexes in American History Ser.: No. 26). 448p. 1996. text ed. 85.00 (*0-313-26644-1*, Greenwood Pr) Greenwood.
World's Compact Bible Dictionary & Concordance, Slim. Ed. by Dan Penwell. 96p. 1990. pap. 4.99 (*0-529-06936-9*, WDC) World Publng.
World's Debt to the Irish. J. J. Walsh. 1976. 250.00 (*0-87968-360-0*) Gordon Pr.
World's Design. Salvador De Madariaga. 1938. 20.00 (*0-686-17395-3*) R S Barnes.
World's Desire. H. Rider Haggard. 317p. 1989. reprint ed. pap. 20.00 (*0-87556-758-4*) Saifer.
World's Dirtiest Dirty Jokes. Illus. by Bob Schochet. LC 93-44128. 1994. pap. 7.95 (*0-8065-1478-7*, Citadel Pr) Carol Pub Group.
World's Discoverers: The Story of Bold Voyages by Brave Navigators During a Thousand Years. William H. Johnson. 1977. lib. bdg. 59.95 (*0-8490-2847-7*) Gordon Pr.
***World's Dumbest Criminals.** Daniel Butler et al. (Illus.). 240p. (Orig.). 1997. pap. 7.95 (*1-55853-541-1*) Rutledge Hill Pr.
World's Easiest Guide to Using the APA. Carol J. Amato. Ed. by Claudia Suzanne. (Illus.). 368p. (Orig.). 1995. lib. bdg., per. 19.95 (*0-9643853-5-X*) Stargazer.
World's Easiest Guide to Using the APA, College ed. Carol J. Amato. Ed. by Claudia Suzanne. 368p. (Orig.). (C). 1995. pap. text ed., spiral bd. 19.95 (*0-9643853-4-1*) Stargazer.
World's Easiest Songs. (Easy Play Ser.: Vol. 311). 1990. pap. 4.95 (*0-7935-0172-5*, 00001382) H Leonard.
World's Economic Crisis, & the Way of Escape. Arthur Salter et al. LC 79-152221. (Essay Index Reprints - Halley Stewart Lecture Ser., 1931). 1977. reprint ed. 20.95 (*0-8369-2340-5*) Ayer.
World's Economic Plight & Community Responsibility. Community Service Editors. 1977. pap. 1.00 (*0-910420-24-6*) Comm Serv OH.
World's Edge: An Anthology. Ed. by Sherry Reniker. 1991. pap. 12.00 (*0-87924-077-6*) Membrane Pr.
World's Emerging Markets. 1992. 290.00 (*0-86338-427-7*, 072420, Pub. by Euromonitor Pubns UK) Gale.
World's Emerging Stock Markets: Structure, Development, Regulations & Opportunities. Ed. by Keith K. Park & Antoine W. Van Agtmael. (Guide to World Markets Ser.). 375p. 1992. text ed. 70.00 (*1-55738-240-9*) Irwin Prof Pubng.
World's End. T. Coraghessan Boyle. 480p. 1990. pap. 8.95 (*0-14-009760-0*, Penguin Bks); pap. 12.95 (*0-14-029993-9*, Penguin Bks) Viking Penguin.
World's End. Joan D. Vinge. 288p. 1993. mass mkt. 4.99 (*0-8125-2368-7*) Tor Bks.
World's End. Joan D. Vinge. 230p. 1984. 25.00 (*0-89366-141-4*) Ultramarine Pub.
Worlds Enough & Time. Joe W. Haldeman. 336p. 1993. reprint ed. mass mkt. 4.99 (*0-380-70801-9*, AvoNova) Avon.
Worlds Envisioned: Alighiero e Boetti & Frederic Bruly Bouabre. Lynne Cooke et al. LC 94-62122. (Illus.). 102p. 1995. 40.00 (*0-944521-32-0*) Dia Ctr Arts.
World's Eye. Albert M. Potts. LC 79-4009. (Illus.). 104p. 1982. 22.00 (*0-8131-1387-3*) U Pr of Ky.
World's Fair. E. L. Doctorow. 384p. 1986. mass mkt. 5.95 (*0-449-21237-8*, Crest) Fawcett.
World's Fair. E. L. Doctorow. 384p. 1996. pap. 10.95 (*0-452-27572-5*, Plume) NAL-Dutton.
World's Fair. E. L. Doctorow. 1993. 22.00 (*0-8446-6696-3*) Peter Smith.
***World's Fair for the Global Village.** Carl Malamud. LC 97-11146. (Illus.). 320p. 1997. 45.00 (*0-262-13338-5*) MIT Pr.
World's Fair Fun Trivia Book. Carole Marsh. (Quantum Leap Ser.). (Illus.). (Orig.). (J). (gr. 4 up). 1994. pap. 19.95 (*0-935326-06-5*) Gallopade Pub Group.
Worlds Fair Kit S. P. A. R. K. Carole Marsh. (S. P. A. R. K. Ser.). (Illus.). (Orig.). (J). (gr. 3-12). 1994. pap. 19.95 (*0-935326-85-5*) Gallopade Pub Group.
World's Fair Midways: An Affectionate Account of American Amusement Areas from the Crystal Palace to the Crystal Ball. Edo McCullough. LC 75-22828. (America in Two Centuries Ser.). (Illus.). 1976. reprint ed. 18.95 (*0-405-07700-9*) Ayer.
World's Fair, New Orleans. Joshua M. Pailet. LC 85-81259. (Illus.). 120p. 1987. 39.95 (*0-9615647-0-9*) Gallery Fine.
World's Fair New Orleans. Ed. by Jean W. Stastny. (Illus.). 48p. (C). 1984. write for info. (*0-318-57991-X*) Picayune Pr.
World's Fair Notes: A Woman Journalist Views Chicago's 1893 Columbian Exposition. Marian Shaw. LC 92-50329. (Illus.). 124p. (Orig.). 1992. pap. 12.95 (*1-880654-00-8*) Pogo Pr.
World's Fair Spoons, Vol. I: The World's Columbian Exposition. Chris A. McGlothlin. LC 85-70480. (Illus.). 1985. 35.00 (*0-9614824-0-0*) Fla Rare Coin.
World's Fastest Airplanes. write for info. (*1-882663-03-9*) Plymouth MI.
Worlds Fastest Cars. 1990. 29.99 (*0-517-68756-9*) Random Hse Value.
World's Fastest Cars. Giles Chapman. 1990. 12.98 (*1-55521-670-6*) Bk Sales Inc.
World's Fastest Motorcycles. John Cutts. 1991. 12.98 (*1-55521-708-7*) Bk Sales Inc.
World's Fastest Motorcycles. John Martin. (Wheels Ser.). 48p. (J). (gr. 3-10). 1994. lib. bdg. 17.80 (*1-56065-208-X*) Capstone Pr.
***World's Fastest Motorcycles.** John Martin. (Wheels Ser.). (Illus.). 48p. (J). (gr. 3-6). 1994. 18.40 (*0-516-35208-3*) Childrens.
World's Fastest Motorcycles. Michael Scott. 1988. 9.98 (*1-55521-001-5*) Bk Sales Inc.
Worlds Fighting Shotguns. Thomas F. Swearengen. (World Weapons Ser.: Vol. IV). 1978. 29.95 (*0-686-73789-X*) TBN Ent.
World's Finest. Walter Simonson. 160p. 1992. pap. 19.95 (*1-56389-068-2*) DC Comics.
World's Finest Chicken Dishes. Sonia Slyer. (Illus.). 160p. 1996. 29.95 (*1-55670-452-6*) Stewart Tabori & Chang.
World's Finest Food: 180 Classic Recipes from Around the World. Ann Creber & Elisabeth King. Ed. by Margaret Olds. LC 94-17050. (Illus.). 304p. 45.00 (*1-55670-374-0*) Stewart Tabori & Chang.
World's Finest Pasta & Grain Dishes. Anne Marshall. (Illus.). 160p. 1996. 29.00 (*1-55670-453-4*) Stewart Tabori & Chang.
World's First Jet Bombers - Arado Ar 234 - Junkres Ju 287 - Arado 234 B-2. Franz Kober. LC 89-63357. (Illus.). 48p. 1989. pap. 8.95 (*0-88740-203-8*) Schiffer.
World's First Love: A Moving Portrayal of the Virgin Mary. Fulton J. Sheen. 276p. 1996. pap. text ed. 12.95 (*0-89870-597-5*) Ignatius Pr.
World's Food. Ed. by Clyde L. King. LC 75-26307. (World Food Supply Ser.). (Illus.). 1976. reprint ed. 26.95 (*0-405-07786-6*) Ayer.
World's Food: A Study of the Interrelations of World Populations, National Diets & Food Potentials. M. K. Bennett. LC 75-26295. (World Food Supply Ser.). (Illus.). 1976. reprint ed. 25.95 (*0-405-07768-8*) Ayer.
World's Funniest Clown Skits. Barry DeChant. LC 95-10589. 190p. (Orig.). 1995. pap. 15.00 (*0-941599-31-0*) Piccadilly Bks.
Worlds Futures & Options Markets: A Country by Country Directory of the Exchanges Contracts. Nick Battley. 1993. text ed. 95.00 (*1-55738-513-0*) Irwin Prof Pubng.
World's Game: A History of Soccer. Bill Murray. LC 95-13742. (Illinois History of Sports Ser.). (Illus.). 224p. 1996. 27.95 (*0-252-01748-X*) U of Ill Pr.
World's Goin' to End at Loonchtime: Poems of the Free School Community Members. Free School Community Members. Ed. by Mary M. Leue. (Illus.). 119p. (Orig.). 1993. pap. 10.95 (*1-878115-07-3*) Dwn-To-Erth Bks.
***World's Gonna Listen! Songbook.** Joanne O. Hammil. (J). (gr. k-6). 1997. 10.00 (*0-9626239-3-8*) JHO Music.
World's Grasses: Their Differention, Distribution, Economics. John W. Bews. 1977. lib. bdg. 59.95 (*0-8490-2848-5*) Gordon Pr.
World's Great Adventure Stories. LC 79-163049. (Short Story Index Reprint Ser.). (YA). (gr. 7 up). 1977. reprint ed. 42.95 (*0-8369-3963-8*) Ayer.
World's Great Chess Games. Ed. by Reuben Fine. (Chess Ser.). 397p. 1983. reprint ed. pap. 8.95 (*0-486-24512-8*) Dover.
World's Great Contemporary Poems. Ed. by Eddie-Lou Cole. 39.95 (*0-317-29100-9*) World Poetry Pr.
World's Great Folktales: A Collection of 172 of the Best Stories from World Folklore. James R. Foster. 1994. 11.98 (*0-88365-883-6*) Galahad Bks.
World's Great Interceptor Aircraft. (Illus.). 248p. 1989. 20.98 (*0-8317-9676-6*) Smithmark.
World's Great Marques. (Illus.). 164p. 1992. 17.98 (*0-8317-9302-3*) Smithmark.
World's Great Men of Color, Vol. I. J. Rogers. (Illus.). 448p. 1996. pap. 15.00 (*0-684-81581-8*, Touchstone Bks) S&S Trade.
World's Great Men of Color, Vol. II. J. Rogers. (Illus.). 592p. 1996. pap. 15.00 (*0-684-81582-6*, Touchstone Bks) S&S Trade.
World's Great Operas. John T. Howard. LC 80-2278. reprint ed. 49.50 (*0-404-18848-6*) AMS Pr.
World's Great Speeches. 3rd rev. ed. Ed. by Lewis Copeland & Lawrence Lamm. 1958. pap. 11.95 (*0-486-20468-5*) Dover.
World's Great Year: The Esoteric Time Cycle. Gerald Massey. 1988. reprint ed. pap. 7.95 (*1-55818-116-4*, Sure Fire) Holmes Pub.
***World's Greatest Aircraft.** C. Chant. 1996. 19.98 (*0-7858-0602-4*) Bk Sales Inc.
***World's Greatest Airplanes.** Random House Value Publishing Staff. 1997. 3.99 (*0-517-18645-4*) Random Hse Value.
***World's Greatest Airplanes.** Random Value Publishing Staff. 1997. 3.99 (*0-517-18644-6*) Random Hse Value.
World's Greatest Blackjack Book. rev. ed. Lance Humble & Carl Cooper. LC 86-24387. (Illus.). 432p. 1987. pap. 10.95 (*0-385-15382-1*) Doubleday.
World's Greatest Book of Chicken Jokes & Other Fowl Humor. Sol Morrison. (Illus.). 124p. (Orig.). 1995. pap. 9.95 (*0-940861-57-7*) Poetry Ctr Pr.
World's Greatest Brain Bogglers. 81p. 1996. pap. 14.95 (*1-882664-19-1*) Prufrock Pr.
***World's Greatest Brands.** Nick Kochan & Interbrand (Firm) Staff. LC 96-37320. 1997. 55.00 (*0-8147-4701-9*) NYU Pr.
World's Greatest Brands: An International Review by Interbrand. Interbrand Group Staff. LC 91-42205. 260p. 1992. text ed. 49.95 (*0-471-57283-7*) Wiley.
World's Greatest Business Cartoons. Ed. by Mark Bryant. (World's Greatest Cartoons Ser.). (Illus.). 80p. (Orig.). 1994. pap. 4.99 (*1-85015-507-0*) Exley Giftbooks.
World's Greatest Card Tricks. Bob Longe. LC 95-46815. (Illus.). 128p. 1996. pap. 4.95 (*0-8069-5991-6*) Sterling.
World's Greatest Cat Cartoons. Ed. by Mark Bryant. (World's Greatest Cartoons Ser.). (Illus.). 79p. 1993. pap. 4.99 (*1-85015-440-6*) Exley Giftbooks.

W

World's Greatest Chocolate Chip Cookies. Peter Murray. (Umbrella Bks.). (Illus.). 32p. (J). (gr. 2-6). 1992. lib. bdg. 21.36 (0-89565-892-5) Childs World.
World's Greatest Collection of Clean Jokes. Bob Phillips. 176p. 1985. reprint ed. mass mkt. 3.99 (0-89081-456-2) Harvest Hse.
World's Greatest Collection of Knock Knock Jokes. Bob Phillips. 112p. 1995. mass mkt. 1.99 (1-55748-650-6) Barbour & Co.
World's Greatest Computer Cartoons. Ed. by Mark Bryant. (World's Greatest Cartoons Ser.). (Illus.). 79p. 1993. pap. 4.99 (1-85015-441-4) Exley Giftbooks.
World's Greatest Conspiracy Series, 2 vols. Ray Foster. (Illus.). 800p. (Orig.). 1992. Set. 48.50 (0-9632592-2-9) Integrated CA.
World's Greatest Conspiracy Series, 2 vols., Vol. 1, Change Your Words, Your Life, the World. Ray Foster. (Illus.). 800p. (Orig.). 1992. Vol. 1, Change Your Words, Change Your Life, Change the World. pap. 26.95 (0-9632592-0-2) Integrated CA.
World's Greatest Conspiracy Series, 2 vols., Vol. 2, Have Fun Destroying Evil. Ray Foster. (Illus.). 800p. (Orig.). 1992. pap. 26.95 (0-9632592-1-0) Integrated CA.
World's Greatest Dad Cartoons. Ed. by Mark Bryant. (World's Greatest Cartoons Ser.). (Illus.). 79p. 1993. pap. 4.99 (1-85015-461-9) Exley Giftbooks.
World's Greatest Direct Mail Sales Letters. Herschell G. Lewis & Carol Nelson. 460p. 1995. 79.95 (0-8442-3570-9) NTC Pub Grp.
World's Greatest Disasters. Joyce Robins. 1990. 14.98 (1-55521-566-1) Bk Sales Inc.
World's Greatest Do-It-Yourself Cartoons. Ed. by Mark Bryant. (World's Greatest Cartoons Ser.). (Illus.). 80p. (Orig.). 1994. pap. 4.99 (1-85015-509-7) Exley Giftbooks.
World's Greatest Explorers. William G. Scheller. LC 92-18418. (Profiles Ser.). (Illus.). 160p. (YA). (gr. 5-12). 1992. lib. bdg. 16.95 (1-881508-03-X) Oliver Pr MN.
Worlds Greatest Fake Book. Ed. by Chuck Sher. 484p. 1983. pap. 32.00 (0-9614701-1-9) Sher Music.
***World's Greatest Fake Book.** Warner Brothers Staff. 1996. pap. text ed. 39.95 (1-57623-690-0) Warner Bros.
World's Greatest Fakebook. rev. ed. CPP Belwin Staff. 1996. pap. 39.95 (0-89898-814-4, F3287FBA) Warner Brothers.
World's Greatest Golf Cartoons. Ed. by Mark Bryant. (World's Greatest Cartoons Ser.). (Illus.). 79p. 1993. pap. 4.99 (1-85015-439-2) Exley Giftbooks.
World's Greatest Golf Excuses: All the Good Reasons for Playing So Bad in the 1990's. Mark Oman & Hal Gevertz. LC 89-81851. (Illus.). 112p. (Orig.). 1990. pap. 9.95 (0-917346-03-3) Golfaholics Anon.
World's Greatest Golf Jokes. McDougal. 1983. pap. 4.95 (0-8065-0831-0, Citadel Pr) Carol Pub Group.
World's Greatest Golf Jokes. Stan McDougal. 1990. 4.98 (0-89009-600-7) Bk Sales Inc.
World's Greatest Golf Jokes. Ed. by Stan McDougal. (Illus.). 180p. 1991. pap. 4.95 (0-8216-2502-0, Carol Paperbacks) Carol Pub Group.
Worlds Greatest Golf Lesson. Burleigh J. Withers. 61p. 1995. 20.00 (0-9649324-0-7) W W W Publns.
***World's Greatest Hypnotists.** John C. Hughes & Andrew E. Rothovius. LC 96-33340. 296p. 1996. pap. text ed. 32.00 (0-7618-0504-4); lib. bdg. 52.00 (0-7618-0503-6) U Pr of Amer.
World's Greatest Investor's Reveal Their Most Profitable Investment Strategies. David Kennedy. 96p. 1992. pap. 12.95 (0-9632572-0-X) MDMI Int Pubns.
World's Greatest Keep-Fit Cartoons. Ed. by Mark Bryant. (World's Greatest Cartoons Ser.). (Illus.). 80p. (Orig.). 1994. pap. 4.99 (1-85015-506-2) Exley Giftbooks.
World's Greatest Left-Handers. James T. De Kay & Sandy Huffaker. LC 85-1474. (Illus.). 128p. 1985. pap. 5.95 (0-87131-449-5, 0578-170) M Evans.
***Worlds Greatest Magic Secrets Revealed: A Complete Guide to the Most Famous Tricks.** Herbert L. Becker. 1997. 19.95 (1-56171-970-6) Sure Seller.
World's Greatest Magic Tricks. Charles B. Townsend. (Illus.). 128p. 1996. pap. 4.95 (0-8069-0581-6) Sterling.
World's Greatest Mallets. Eugene L. Huddleston. (Illus.). 56p. (Orig.). 1986. pap. 7.95 (0-939487-08-X) Ches & OH Hist.
World's Greatest Marriage Cartoons. Ed. by Mark Bryant. (World's Greatest Cartoons Ser.). (Illus.). 80p. 1995. pap. 4.99 (1-85015-625-5) Exley Giftbooks.
World's Greatest Middle Age Cartoons. Ed. by Mark Bryant. (World's Greatest Cartoons Ser.). (Illus.). 80p. (Orig.). 1994. pap. 4.99 (1-85015-508-9) Exley Giftbooks.
World's Greatest Music Teacher's Guide. William V. May et al. (Orig.). (C). 1989. teacher ed., pap. 37.50 incl. vhs (0-940796-58-9, 3021) Music Ed Natl.
World's Greatest Name: (H-K) see Names & Titles of Jesus Christ
World's Greatest Paper Airplane & Toy Book. Keith R. Laux. (Illus.). 1987. pap. text ed. 7.95 (0-07-155079-8) McGraw.
World's Greatest Paper Airplane & Toy Book. Keith R. Laux. (Illus.). 120p. 1987. pap. 7.95 (0-8306-2846-0) McGraw-Hill Prof.
World's Greatest Paper Airplanes. Peter Murray. (Umbrella Bks.). (Illus.). 32p. (J). (gr. 2-6). 1992. lib. bdg. 21.36 (0-89565-963-8) Childs World.
***World's Greatest Project Vol. 1: One Project Team on the Path to Quality.** Russell W. Darnall. LC 96-36169. (Illus.). 173p. (Orig.). 1996. pap. 19.95 (1-880410-46-X) Proj Mgmt Inst.
World's Greatest Put Down Lines. Butch Fisco & Pat Hanifin. Ed. by Cliff Carle. 1995. pap. text ed. 5.95 (0-918259-59-2) CCC Pubns.
World's Greatest Puzzles. Charles B. Townsend. LC 92-17484. (Illus.). 128p. 1992. 14.95 (0-8069-8664-6) Sterling.
World's Greatest Puzzles. Charles B. Townsend. LC 92-17484. (Illus.). 128p. (J). (gr. 5-10). 1993. pap. 5.95 (0-8069-8665-4) Sterling.
World's Greatest Riddle Collection: Over 10,000 Smart, Funny, Cute, Sweet, Spicy, Outrageous, & Zany Witticisms. Eliza Gemstone. LC 94-79652. (Illus.). 218p. (Orig.). (J). (gr. 2 up). 1996. vinyl bd. 24.00 (1-886197-00-8) Joy Books.
World's Greatest Sales Meeting Idea Book. Art Fettig. 80p. (Orig.). 1990. pap. 9.95 (0-916927-12-1) Growth Unltd.
World's Greatest Sex Cartoons. Ed. by Mark Bryant. (World's Greatest Cartoons Ser.). (Illus.). 80p. 1995. pap. 4.99 (1-85015-624-7) Exley Giftbooks.
Worlds Greatest Ship: The Story of the S. S. Leviathan, Vol. I. Frank O. Braynard. Ed. by Walter Hamshar. (Illus.). 288p. 1972. 50.00 (0-9606204-0-0) F O Braynard.
World's Greatest Ship: The Story of the S. S. Leviathan, Vol. II. Frank O. Braynard. Ed. by Walter Hamshar. (Illus.). 382p. 1974. 30.00 (0-9606204-1-9) F O Braynard.
World's Greatest Ship: The Story of the S. S. Leviathan, Vol. III. F. O. Braynard. Ed. by Walter Hamshar. (Illus.). 400p. 1976. 30.00 (0-9606204-2-7) F O Braynard.
World's Greatest Ship: The Story of the S. S. Leviathan, Vol. V. Frank O. Braynard. Ed. by Walter Hamshar. (Illus.). 424p. (C). 1980. 45.00 (0-9606204-3-5) F O Braynard.
World's Greatest Ship: The Story of the S. S. Leviathan, Vol. VI. Frank O. Braynard. (Illus.). 448p. (C). 1983. 59.00 (0-9606204-5-1) F O Braynard.
World's Greatest Songbook. Ed. by Sandy Feldstein. 232p. (Orig.). 1987. pap. 24.95 (0-88284-359-1, 900) Alfred Pub.
World's Greatest Stamp Collectors. Stanley Bierman. (Illus.). 288p. (Orig.). 1990. 30.00 (0-940403-26-9); pap. 14.95 (0-940403-25-0) Linns Stamp News.
World's Greatest Stamp Collectors. Stanley M. Bierman. (Orig.). 1990. pap. 15.95 (0-8119-0668-X) LIFETIME.
World's Greatest Stamp Collectors & More of the World's Greatest Stamp Collectors, 2 vols. Stanley M. Bierman. (Illus.). 512p. 1990. boxed 60.00 (0-940403-35-8); boxed 29.95 (0-940403-34-X) Linns Stamp News.
World's Greatest Star Trek Quiz: Commemorating the 30th Anniversary of the Original TV Series. Nan Clark. 221p. (Orig.). 1997. pap. 14.95 (1-878044-33-8) Mayhaven Pub.
World's Greatest Stealth & Reconnaissance Aircraft. (Illus.). 204p. 1991. 19.98 (0-8317-9558-1) Smithmark.
World's Greatest Television Trivia Quiz Book. John C. Biardo. LC 85-70386. 518p. (Orig.). 1985. pap. 12.95 (0-933181-00-0) Elmwood Park Pub.
World's Greatest Tenors. Millicent Jones. 80p. 1995. write for info. (1-57215-056-4) World Pubns.
World's Greatest Toe Show. Nancy Lamb & Muff Singer. LC 93-28440. (Illus.). 64p. (J). (gr. 2-5). 1996. pap. 13.95 (0-8167-3322-8) BrdgeWater.
World's Greatest Toe Show. Nancy Lamb & Muff Singer. LC 93-28440. (Illus.). 64p. (J). (gr. 2-5). 1997. pap. 2.50 (0-8167-3323-6, Little Rainbow) Troll Communs.
World's Greatest Tow Trucks. Earl Johnson. (Illus.). 108p. 1995. pap. 19.95 (0-7603-0271-5) Motorbooks Intl.
***World's Greatest Toy Train Maker: Insiders Remember Lionel.** Roger Carp. (Illus.). 112p. 1997. write for info. (0-89778-439-1, 10-8225, Kalmbach Books) Kalmbach.
World's Greatest Truths. James D. Bramlett. LC 88-70056. 197p. 1988. 12.95 (0-945642-06-7) Creative FL.
World's Greatest Unpublished Short Stories & Poetry: By the Greatest Rejected Writer. Harold L. Hamburg. (Illus.). 200p. 1996. pap. 5.95 (1-57502-146-3) Morris Pubng.
***World's Greatest Working Trucks.** Earl Johnson & Grace Hawkins. 96p. (Orig.). 1997. pap. 19.95 (0-9649645-4-6) Lotus Pubns.
World's Guide to Understanding the Bible. A. T. Pierson. 349p. 1994. 14.99 (0-529-10336-2, WGB) World Publng.
World's Healthiest Food. Anne Marshall. (Illus.). 224p. 1996. 45.00 (1-55670-493-3) Stewart Tabori & Chang.
Worlds in Collision. Immanuel Velikovsky. 28.95 (0-8488-1500-9) Amereon Ltd.
Worlds in Collision. Immanuel Velikovsky. 400p. 1991. reprint ed. lib. bdg. 34.95 (0-89966-785-6) Buccaneer Bks.
Worlds in Collision: Interactive Multicultural Dialogue Toward a Truer American Art History. Ed. by Carlos Villa. LC 94-8433. 324p. 1994. 54.95 (1-883255-47-3); pap. 34.95 (1-883255-46-5) Intl Scholars.
***Worlds in Creation.** Daniel Greenberg. 397p. (Orig.). 1994. pap. 15.00 (1-888947-10-1) Sudbury Valley.
Worlds in Harmony. Dalai Lama. LC 92-16826. 185p. 1992. pap. 12.50 (0-938077-77-5) Parallax Pr.
Worlds in Interaction - Small Bodies & Planets of the Solar System: Proceedings of the Meeting "Small Bodies in the Solar System & Their Interactions with the Planets" Held in Mariehamn, Finland on August 8 - 12, 1994. Ed. by H. Rickman & M. J. Valtonen. LC 95-48428. 528p. (C). 1996. lib. bdg. 224.00 (0-7923-3930-4) Kluwer Ac.
Worlds in Motion. Maurice G. Moore. 46p. (Orig.). 1964. pap. text ed. 7.95 (0-943956-05-6) Trippensee Pub.
Worlds in Our Words. Clark & Kallet. LC 96-25044. 768p. (C). 1996. pap. text ed. 40.00 (0-13-182130-X) P-H.
Worlds in Regression: Some Novels of Vladimir Nabokov. D. Barton Johnson. 258p. 1985. 12.95 (0-88233-908-7) Ardis Pubs.
Worlds in the Sky: Planetary Discovery from Earliest Times Through Voyager & Magellan. William Sheehan. LC 91-39398. (Illus.). 243p. (Orig.). 1992. pap. 19.95 (0-8165-1308-2) U of Ariz Pr.
World's Inhabitants. George T. Bettany. LC 72-5744. (Black Heritage Library Collection). 1977. reprint ed. 90.95 (0-8369-9134-6) Ayer.
Worlds Interpenetrating & Apart: Collected Poems 1959-1995. William I. Thompson. 160p. (Orig.). 1997. pap. 17.95 (0-940262-72-X) Lindisfarne Bks.
World's Largest Elephant in Captivity. Jon Jeck. 48p. (Orig.). 1989. pap. 4.00 (0-944920-02-0) Bellowing Ark Pr.
World's Largest Market: A Business Guide to Europe 1992. Robert Williams et al. 280p. 1991. reprint ed. pap. 19.95 (0-8144-7774-7) AMACOM.
World's Largest Prestressed LPG Floating Vessel. (PCI Journal Reprints Ser.). 24p. 1985. pap. 12.00 (0-318-19759-6, JR183) P-PCI.
World's Largest Record Catalogue: A Guide to Shopping for Compact Discs, Records & Cassettes Via Mail Order. 1992. lib. bdg. 255.95 (0-8490-5335-8) Gordon Pr.
World's Last Bachelor. Pamela Browning. (American Romance Ser.). 1995. pap. 3.50 (0-373-16565-X, 1-16565-3) Harlequin Bks.
***Worlds Last Dictator.** Dwight Kinman. 319p. 1996. pap. 10.99 (0-88368-445-4) Whitaker Hse.
World's Last Dictator. 2nd ed. Dwight L. Kinman. pap. 9.99 (1-879112-27-2) Solid Rock OR.
World's Last Mysteries. Reader's Digest Editors. LC 77-87127. (Illus.). 320p. 1978. 23.97 (0-89577-044-X) RD Assn.
World's Last Night & Other Essays. C. S. Lewis. LC 73-4887. 113p. 1973. reprint ed. pap. 8.00 (0-15-698360-5, Harvest Bks) HarBrace.
World's Leading Poets. Henry W. Boynton. LC 68-8439. (Essay Index Reprint Ser.). 1977. 20.95 (0-8369-0238-6) Ayer.
World's Living Religions. 2nd ed. Archie J. Bahm. LC 92-20681. 384p. (C). 1993. reprint ed. pap. 12.95 (0-87573-000-0) Jain Pub Co.
World's Machine Pistols & Submachine Guns: Developments from 1963-1980, Vol. 2A. Thomas B. Nelson & Daniel D Musgrave. 1980. 29.95 (0-686-15933-0) TBN Ent.
World's Major Companies Directory. 756p. 1994. 550.00 (0-86338-460-9, 070836, Pub. by Euromonitor Pubns UK) Gale.
World's Major Languages. Ed. by Bernard Comrie. (Illus.). 1040p. 1990. reprint ed. pap. 35.00 (0-19-506511-5) OUP.
World's Master Paintings: Catalogue & Location Index, 2 vols., Set. Christopher Wright. (Illus.). 2032p. (C). 1992. text ed. 495.00 (0-415-02240-1) Routledge.
World's Mercy. Mary G. Tuttiett. LC 72-125239. (Short Story Index Reprint Ser.). 1977. 19.95 (0-8369-3606-X) Ayer.
***World's Monetary System.** Jo Griesgraber. 1997. pap. text ed. 14.95 (0-7453-1051-6, Pub. by Pluto Pr UK) LPC InBook.
World's Monetary System: Toward Stability & Sustainability in the Twenty-First Century. Ed. by Jo M. Griesgraber & Bernhard G. Gunter. LC 95-49683. (Rethinking Bretton Woods Ser.: Vol. 4). 1996. write for info. (0-7453-1052-4, Pub. by Pluto Pr UK) LPC InBook.
World's Most Amazing Puzzles. Charles B. Townsend. (Illus.). 128p. 1994. pap. 5.95 (0-8069-8761-8) Sterling.
World's Most Baffling Puzzles. Charles B. Townsend. LC 91-21324. (Illus.). 128p. 1992. pap. 5.95 (0-8069-5833-2) Sterling.
***World's Most Beautiful Dolls.** 2nd ed. Dolls Magazine Editors. 160p. 1995. 17.98 (1-56852-032-8, Konecky & Konecky) W S Konecky Assocs.
World's Most Beautiful Seashells. Pele Carmichael & Leonard Hill. Ed. by Tim Ohr. 240p. 34.95 (1-884942-03-2) Carmichael Pubns.
World's Most Beautiful Seashells. Pele Carmichael & Leonard Hill. Ed. by Tim Ohr. 240p. 1995. pap. 22.95 (1-884942-00-8) Carmichael Pubns.
World's Most Bone-Chilling "True" Ghost Stories. John Macklin. (Illus.). 96p. 1994. pap. 4.95 (0-8069-0391-0) Sterling.
World's Most Challenging Puzzles. Charles B. Townsend. LC 88-19729. (Illus.). 128p. (J). (gr. 3-9). 1989. pap. 5.95 (0-8069-6731-5) Sterling.
World's Most Complete Auto Troubleshooting Guide. Alden G. Zimmer. (Illus.). 84p. 1993. pap. 10.95 (0-533-10343-6) Vantage.
World's Most Complete Guide to Alexandria's Restaurants. Alan Tanenbaum. 112p. (Orig.). 1995. pap. 4.95 (0-9647481-0-X) Wrlds Most Complete.
World's Most Difficult Maze. Dave Phillips. 1981. pap. 3.50 (0-486-23970-5) Dover.
World's Most Exotic Cars. John Martin. (Wheels Ser.). 48p. (J). (gr. 3-10). 1994. lib. bdg. 17.80 (1-56065-209-8) Capstone Pr.
***World's Most Exotic Cars.** John Martin. (Wheels Ser.). (Illus.). 48p. (J). (gr. 3-6). 1994. 18.40 (0-516-35209-1) Childrens.
World's Most Extraordinary Yachts. 4th ed. Jill R. Bobrow. (Illus.). 234p. 1992. reprint ed. 50.00 (0-393-03314-7) Concepts Pub.
World's Most Famous Ghosts. Daniel Cohen. (Illus.). 112p. (J). (gr. 3-6). 1989. pap. 2.99 (0-671-69145-7, Minstrel Bks) PB.
World's Most Famous Math Problem: The Proof of Fermat's Last Theorem & Other Mathematical Mysteries. Marilyn Vos Savant. LC 93-37559. 1993. pap. 7.95 (0-312-10657-2) St Martin.
World's Most Incredible Puzzles. Charles B. Townsend. LC 93-39527. (Illus.). 128p. (J). 1994. 14.95 (0-8069-0504-2) Sterling.
World's Most Incredible Puzzles. Charles B. Townsend. (Illus.). 128p. 1995. pap. 5.95 (0-8069-0505-0) Sterling.
World's Most Incredible Stories: The Best of Fortean Times. Ed. by Adam Sisman. 192p. (Orig.). 1992. pap. 12.00 (0-380-76754-6) Avon.
World's Most Mysterious Plan for Economic Sanity. Kenna. 1984. write for info. (0-318-59095-6) Port Love Intl.
World's Most Mysterious "True" Ghost Stories. Ron Edwards. LC 95-46304. (Illus.). 96p. (J). (gr. 3). 1996. 4.95 (0-8069-3872-2) Sterling.
***World's Most Mystifying "True" Ghost Stories.** Ron Edwards. LC 96-37874. (Illus.). 96p. (J). 1997. pap. 4.95 (0-8069-9677-3) Sterling.
World's Most Ornery Crosswords. Will Shortz. 1992. pap. 14.00 (0-8129-2081-3, Times Bks) Random.
World's Most Perplexing Puzzles. Charles B. Townsend. LC 94-38522. 128p. (J). 1995. 14.95 (0-8069-1266-9) Sterling.
World's Most Perplexing Puzzles. Charles B. Townsend. (Illus.). 128p. 1996. pap. 5.95 (0-8069-1267-7) Sterling.
World's Most Powerful Cars. Graham Robson. 1990. 12.98 (1-55521-563-7) Bk Sales Inc.
World's Most Powerful Rifles & Guns. Rob Adam. 1991. 12.98 (1-55521-712-5) Bk Sales Inc.
World's Most Powerful Rifles & Handguns. Robert Adam. 128p. 1996. write for info. (1-57215-176-5) World Pubns.
World's Most Provocative Questions: Rarely Discussed in Public But on Everyone's Mind. Roger Pierangelo. 1994. pap. 4.99 (1-56171-310-4, S P I Bks) Sure Seller.
World's Most Spectacular Reptiles & Amphibians. Bill Lamar & Bill Love. (World's Most Ser.). (Illus.). 208p. 1997. 29.95 (1-884942-07-5) Carmichael Pubns.
World's Most Spectacular Reptiles & Amphibians. Bill Lamar & Bill Love. Ed. by Tim Ohr. (World's Most Ser.). (Illus.). 208p. 1997. pap. 22.95 (1-884942-06-7) Carmichael Pubns.
World's Most Spine-Tingling True Ghost Stories. Sheila A. Barry. LC 92-19862. (Illus.). 96p. (J). (gr. 3 up). 1993. pap. 4.95 (0-8069-8687-5) Sterling.
World's Most Valuable Investment Strategy: Power Methods to Safely Multiply Your Money. B. Beck Fisher. 1990. 24.95 (0-930233-43-3) Windsor.
World's My University. large type ed. Jim Ingram. 1977. 25.99 (0-7089-0050-X) Ulverscroft.
World's News Media: Comprehensive Reference Guide. 1992. 198.00 (0-582-08554-3, Pub. by Longman Grp UK) Gale.
World's Number One, Flat-Out, All-Time Great, Stock Car Racing Book. rev. ed. Jerry Bledsoe. 335p. 1995. pap. 13.95 (1-878086-36-7) Down Home NC.
Worlds of a Maasai Warrior: An Autobiography. Tedilit Ole Saitoti. 1988. pap. 12.00 (0-520-06325-2) U CA Pr.
Worlds of Alfonso the Learned & James the Conqueror: Intellect & Force in the Middle Ages. Ed. by Robert I. Burns. LC 85-42678. (Center for Medieval & Renaissance Studies, UCLA: Contribution). (Illus.). 276p. 1985. text ed. 45.00 (0-691-05451-7) Princeton U Pr.
Worlds of Andre Maurois. Jack Kolbert. LC 85-40033. (Illus.). 280p. 1985. 42.50 (0-941664-16-3) Susquehanna U Pr.
***Worlds of Art.** 2nd ed. Bersson. 1998. pap. text ed. 31.50 (0-697-25819-X) McGraw.
Worlds of Art: Painters in Victorian Society. Paula Gillett. LC 89-30373. (Illus.). 275p. (C). 1989. text ed. 45.00 (0-8135-1459-2) Rutgers U Pr.
Worlds of Belief: Religion & Spirituality. Lisa Sita. Ed. by Bruce Glassman. LC 94-38278. (Our Human Family Ser.). (Illus.). 80p. (YA). (gr. 5 up). 1995. lib. bdg. 21.95 (1-56711-125-4) Blackbirch.
Worlds of Childhood: The Art & Craft of Writing for Children. Ed. by William Zinsser. 192p. 1990. pap. 13.00 (0-395-51425-8) HM.
Worlds of Children. Center for Equal Education Staff. 1981. 7.50 (0-912008-20-2) Equity & Excel.
Worlds of Christopher Columbus. William D. Phillips, Jr. & Carla R. Phillips. (Illus.). 336p. (C). 1991. text ed. 49.95 (0-521-35097-2) Cambridge U Pr.
Worlds of Christopher Columbus. William D. Phillips, Jr. & Carla R. Phillips. (Illus.). 336p. (C). 1993. pap. text ed. 15.95 (0-521-44652-X) Cambridge U Pr.
Worlds of Clifford Simak. Clifford D. Simak. 1993. reprint ed. lib. bdg. 18.95 (0-89968-368-1, Lghtyr Pr) Buccaneer Bks.
Worlds of Common Sense: Equality, Identity & Two Modes of Impulse Management. Pauline N. Pepinsky. LC 94-7432. (Contributions in Psychology Ser.: No. 26). 232p. 1994. text ed. 59.95 (0-313-28991-3, Greenwood Pr) Greenwood.
***Worlds of Communication, Vol. 1.** Masiello. Date not set. pap. text ed. write for info. (0-312-02529-7) St Martin.
Worlds of Desire, Realms of Power: A Cultural Geography. Pamela Shurmer-Smith & Kevin Hannam. 250p. 1995. pap. text ed. 29.95 (0-470-23517-9) Halsted Pr.
Worlds of Desire, Realms of Power, a Cultural Geography. Pamela Shurmer-Smith & Kevin Hannam. 250p. 1995. pap. 24.95 (0-340-59217-6, Pub. by E Arnold UK) Routledge Chapman & Hall.
***Worlds of Devis Grebu.** Ori Z. Soltes. (Illus.). (Orig.). Date not set. pap. text ed. write for info. (1-881456-27-7) B B K Natl Jew Mus.
Worlds of Difference: Inequality in the Aging Experience. Eleanor P. Stoller & Rose C. Gibson. 300p. 1994. pap. 26.95 (0-8039-9030-8) Pine Forge.

W

An Asterisk (*) at the beginning of an entry indicates that the title is appearing in BIP for the first time.

Worlds of Difference: Inequality in the Aging Experience. 2nd ed. Eleanor P. Stoller & Rose C. Gibson. LC 95-15613. 320p. (C). 1996. pap. 27.95 (*0-8039-9099-5*) Pine Forge.

Worlds of Existentialism: A Critical Reader. Ed. & Intro. by Maurice Friedman. LC 90-45608. (Humanities Paperback Library). 592p. (C). 1991. pap. 19.95 (*0-391-03700-5*) Humanities.

Worlds of Experience: Communities in Colonial Virginia. Rhys Isaac. (Foundations of America Ser.). (Illus.). 58p. (Orig.). 1987. pap. 9.95 (*0-87935-117-9*) Colonial Williamsburg.

Worlds of Fear. Ed. by David G. Hartwell. (Foundations of Fear Ser.: No. 2). 544p. 1994. pap. 4.99 (*0-8125-5002-1*) Tor Bks.

Worlds of Fiction. Roberta Rubenstein & Charles R. Larson. (Illus.). 1472p. (Orig.). (C). 1992. pap. text ed. 43.33 (*0-02-404185-8*, Macmillan Coll) P-H.

Worlds of French Poetry. Ed. by Bradley R. Strahan & Jean-Clarence Lambert. (Visions Anthologies Ser.: No. 2). (Illus.). 52p. 1990. pap. 6.00 (*0-938872-13-3*) Black Buzzard.

Worlds of Friendship. Robert R. Bell. LC 81-13565. (Sociological Observations Ser.: No. 12). 216p. reprint ed. pap. 61.60 (*0-7837-6583-5*, 2046148) Bks Demand.

Worlds of Hume & Kant. rev. ed. Ed. by James B. Wilbur & Harold J. Allen. LC 82-80553. 195p. (C). 1982. reprint ed. pap. 19.95 (*0-87975-163-0*) Prometheus Bks.

Worlds of Hurt: Reading the Literatures of Trauma. Kali Tal. (Studies in American Literature & Culture: No. 95). 320p. (C). 1995. text ed. 59.95 (*0-521-44504-3*); pap. text ed. 18.95 (*0-521-56512-X*) Cambridge U Pr.

Worlds of Illness: Biographical & Cultural Perspectives on Health & Disease. Ed. by Alan Radley. 224p. (C). 1995. pap. 17.95 (*0-415-13152-9*) Routledge.

Worlds of Intizar Husain: Selected Short Stories. Ed. by Intizar Husain. LC 95-49396. (Three Continents Ser.). 240p. 1997. 45.00 (*0-89410-821-2*, Three Contnts); pap. 19.95 (*0-89410-822-0*, Three Contnts) Lynne Rienner.

Worlds of Jewish Prayer: A Festschrift in Honor of Rabbi Zalman M. Schachter-Shalomi. Ed. by Shohama H. Wiener & Jonathan Omer-Man. LC 93-1227. 392p. 1993. 35.00 (*0-87668-582-3*) Aronson.

Worlds of Literacy. Ed. by Mary Hamilton et al. LC 93-13326. (Language & Education Library: Vol. 5). 1993. 69.00 (*1-85359-196-3*, Pub. by Multilingual Matters UK); pap. 24.95 (*1-85359-195-5*, Pub. by Multilingual Matters UK) Taylor & Francis.

Worlds of Lucy Larcom, 1824-1893. Shirley Marchalonis. LC 88-28660. (Illus.). 336p. 1989. 45.00 (*0-8203-1113-8*) U of Ga Pr.

Worlds of Modern Chinese Fiction: Short Stories & Novellas from the People's Republic, Taiwan, & Hong Kong. Ed. by Michael S. Duke. LC 91-2564. 360p. (C). (gr. 13). 1991. 69.95 (*0-87332-757-8*, East Gate Bk); pap. 23.95 (*0-87332-758-6*, East Gate Bk) M E Sharpe.

Worlds of Music. Cecil Smith. LC 73-7312. 328p. 1973. reprint ed. text ed. 65.00 (*0-8371-6925-9*, SMWM, Greenwood Pr) Greenwood.

Worlds of Music: An Introduction to the Music of the World's Peoples. 2nd ed. Jeff T. Titon. 480p. 1992. Demo package. write for info. (*0-02-872604-9*); audio write for info. (*0-02-872603-0*) Schirmer Bks.

Worlds of Music: An Introduction to the Music of the World's Peoples. 3rd ed. Ed. by Jeff T. Titon et al. (C). 1996. 36.00 (*0-02-872612-X*) Schirmer Bks.

Worlds of Never: An Original Anthology. Ed. by R. Reginald & Douglas Melville. LC 77-84278. (Lost Race & Adult Fantasy Ser.). (Illus.). 1978. lib. bdg. 41.95 (*0-405-11016-2*) Ayer.

Worlds of Pain: Life in the Working-Class Family. Lillian B. Rubin. LC 92-52719. 1992. pap. 16.00 (*0-465-09248-9*) Basic.

Worlds of Pain: Life in the Working Class Family. Lillian B. Rubin. 288p. (C). 1990. reprint ed. lib. bdg. 41.00 (*0-8095-9016-6*) Borgo Pr.

Worlds of Petrarch. Giuseppe Mazzotta. LC 93-19793. (Monographs in Medieval & Renaissance Studies: Vol. 14). 248p. 1993. text ed. 37.95 (*0-8223-1363-4*); pap. text ed. 16.95 (*0-8223-1396-0*) Duke.

Worlds of Plato & Aristotle. Ed. by J. B. Wilbur & H. J. Allen. LC 79-3090. 204p. (C). 1979. pap. 19.95 (*0-87975-116-9*) Prometheus Bks.

Worlds of Political Economy: Alternative Approaches to the Study of Contemporary Political Economy. R. J. Jones. 256p. 1992. 49.00 (*0-86187-946-5*) St Martin.

Worlds of P'otsunu: Geronima Cruz Montoya of San Juan Pueblo. Jill Mellick & Jeanne Shutes. LC 95-4412. (Illus.). 256p. 1996. 37.50 (*0-8263-1643-3*) U of NM Pr.

***Worlds of Production: The Action Frameworks of the Economy.** Robert Salais & Michael Storper. LC 96-48228. 1997. write for info. (*0-674-96203-6*) HUP.

Worlds of Sense: Exploring the Senses in History & Across Cultures. Constance Classen. LC 93-9901. 184p. (C). (gr. 13). 1993. pap. 16.95 (*0-415-10126-3*) Routledge.

Worlds of Shadow: Teaching with Shadow Puppetry. David Wisniewski & Donna Wisniewski. LC 96-27720. 200p. 1997. pap. text ed. 24.00 (*1-56308-450-3*) Teacher Ideas Pr.

***Worlds of Talk: The Presentation of Self in Everyday Conversation.** Martin Malone. 224p. 1997. text ed. 54.95 (*0-7456-1433-7*) Blackwell Pubs.

***Worlds of Talk: The Presentation of Self in Everyday Conversation.** Martin Malone. 224p. 1997. pap. text ed. 21.95 (*0-7456-1897-9*) Blackwell Pubs.

Worlds of the Early Greek Philosophers. Ed. by J. B. Wilbur & H. J. Allen. LC 79-3089. 280p. (C). 1979. pap. 19.95 (*0-87975-115-0*) Prometheus Bks.

Worlds of the Federation. Shane Johnson. (Illus.). 1989. pap. 15.00 (*0-671-70813-9*) PB.

Worlds of the Imperium. Keith Laumer. 288p. 1986. 2.95 (*0-8125-4379-3*) Tor Bks.

Worlds of the Mentally Ill: How Deinstitutionalization Works in the City. Dan A. Lewis et al. LC 89-18058. 208p. (C). 1990. text ed. 29.95 (*0-8093-1477-0*) S Ill U Pr.

Worlds of Thomas Jefferson at Monticello. Susan R. Stein. LC 92-27218. (Illus.). 464p. 1993. 65.00 (*0-8109-3967-3*) Abrams.

Worlds of Thrush Green. large type ed. Miss Read. LC 93-16776. 326p. 1993. 22.95 (*0-8161-5507-0*, GK Hall) Thorndike Pr.

Worlds of TSR. Ed. by Marlys Heeszel. (Illus.). 144p. (Orig.). 1995. pap. 18.99 (*0-7869-0337-6*) TSR Inc.

Worlds of Victorian Fiction. Ed. by Jerome H. Buckley. LC 75-5549. (English Studies: No. 6). 439p. 1975. 34.95 (*0-674-96205-2*); pap. 10.95 (*0-674-96207-9*) HUP.

World's of Visions: Poetry from the World's Less Known Languages & Cultures. Ed. by Bradley R. Strahan & Shirley G. Sullivan. (Visions Anthologies Ser.). (Illus.). 60p. (Orig.). 1993. pap. 6.00 (*0-938872-18-4*) Black Buzzard.

Worlds of Welfare: Understanding the Changing Geographies of Social Welfare Provision. Steven Pinch. LC 96-7594. 208p. (C). 1997. pap. 18.95 (*0-415-11189-7*); text ed. 65.00 (*0-415-11188-9*) Routledge.

***Worlds of Women: The Makings of an International Women's Movement.** Leila J. Rupp. LC 97-14449. 1998. write for info. (*0-691-01676-3*); pap. write for info. (*0-691-01675-5*) Princeton U Pr.

Worlds of Wonder, Days of Judgment: Popular Religious Belief in Early New England. David D. Hall. 316p. 1990. pap. 16.50 (*0-674-96216-8*) HUP.

Worlds of Writing. Ed. by Carolyn B. Matalene. 1989. pap. text ed. write for info. (*0-07-557260-5*) McGraw.

World's Oldest Health Plan: Health, Nutrition & Healing from the Bible. Kathleen O. Baldinger. 352p. 1994. pap. 14.95 (*0-914984-57-8*) Starburst.

World's 100 Greatest Mysteries. 1996. pap. 18.95 (*0-7871-0963-0*, Dove Bks) Dove Audio.

World's Own (Play) Julia W. Howe. (Notable American Authors Ser.). 1992. reprint ed. lib. bdg. 90.00 (*0-7812-3214-7*) Rprt Serv.

World's Parliament of Religions: The East-West Encounter, Chicago, 1893. Richard H. Seager. LC 94-5510. (Religion in North America Ser.). 160p. 1995. 35.00 (*0-253-35137-5*) Ind U Pr.

World's Pharmaceutical Industries: An International Perspective on Innovation, Competition & Policy. Robert Ballance et al. 288p. 1992. 85.00 (*1-85278-646-9*) E Elgar.

World's Philosophies: A History of Ideas. Ninian Smart. 512p. write for info. (*0-697-14790-8*) Brown & Benchmark.

World's Postmodern Fiction: A Guide. Christopher Nash. LC 92-39356. (C). 1993. pap. text ed. 34.50 (*0-582-20910-2*, 79761) Longman.

World's Punniest Joke Book. Mike Benny. LC 92-42578. (Illus.). 96p. (J). (gr. 2-8). 1993. pap. 4.95 (*0-8069-8545-3*) Sterling.

Worlds Reborn: The Hero in the Modern Spanish American Novel. William L. Siemens. 249p. (Orig.). 1984. pap. 18.00 (*0-937058-19-X*) West Va U Pr.

World's Regions & Weather: Linking Fiction to Nonfiction. Phyllis J. Perry. (Literature Bridges to Science Ser.). xvi, 157p. 1996. pap. text ed. 22.00 (*1-56308-338-8*) Teacher Ideas Pr.

World's Religions. Ninian Smart. (Illus.). 576p. (C). 1989. text ed. 59.95 (*0-521-34005-5*) Cambridge U Pr.

World's Religions. Ninian Smart. (Illus.). 576p. (C). 1995. pap. text ed. 22.95 (*0-521-42906-4*) Cambridge U Pr.

World's Religions. Huston Smith. 1992. 24.00 (*0-8446-6528-2*) Peter Smith.

World's Religions. Ed. by Steward Sutherland. 800p. 1988. 80.00 (*0-8161-8978-1*, Hall Reference) Macmillan.

World's Religions. rev. ed. Ed. by J. N. Anderson. LC 75-26654. 1954. pap. 15.00 (*0-8028-1636-3*) Eerdmans.

World's Religions: Completely Revised & Updated Edition of The Religions of Man. Huston Smith. 384p. 1991. pap. 13.00 (*0-06-250811-3*) Harper SF.

***World's Religions: The Religions of Man.** rev. ed. Huston Smith. write for info. (*0-06-251463-6*) HarpC.

World's Religions: Worldviews & Contemporary Issues. William A. Young. LC 94-19431. 560p. 1994. text ed. 52.67 (*0-13-032806-5*) P-H.

World's Savannas: Economic Driving Forces, Ecological Constraints & Policy Options for Sustainable Land Use. Otto T. Solbrig. LC 92-41899. (Man & the Biosphere Ser.: Vol. 12). 1993. 68.00 (*1-85070-417-1*) Prthnon Pub.

World's Saviors. Charles H. Vail. (African Heritage Classical Research Studies). 213p. 1990. reprint ed. 25.00 (*0-938818-52-X*) ECA Assoc.

World's Saviors. Charles H. Vail. 213p. 1970. reprint ed. spiral bd. 10.00 (*0-7873-0906-0*) Hlth Research.

Worlds Seen & Imagined: Japanese Screens from the Idemitsu Museum of Arts. Taizo Kuroda et al. LC 95-32833. (Illus.). 168p. 1995. 49.95 (*0-7892-0081-3*) Abbeville Pr.

Worlds Seen & Imagined: Japanese Screens from the Idemitsu Museum of Arts. Taizo Kuroda et al. LC 95-32833. 1995. pap. write for info. (*0-87848-081-1*) Asia Soc.

World's Sex Records. Herbert I. Kavet. 1991. pap. 5.95 (*0-88032-406-6*) Ivory Tower Pub.

***World's Silliest Jokes.** Philip Yates & Matt Rissinger. (Illus.). 96p. (J). 1997. 14.95 (*0-8069-4884-1*) Sterling.

World's Simplest Photography Book. 2nd rev. ed. Jerry Hughes. (Illus.). 144p. 1992. pap. 17.95 (*0-9634348-1-0*) P Lane Pub.

World's Simplest Photography Book see World's Best & Easiest Photography Book

World's Sixteen Crucified Saviors. Kersey Graves. 436p. spiral bd. 16.00 (*0-317-55125-6*) Truth Seeker.

World's Sixteen Crucified Saviors. Kersey Graves. 436p. 1993. reprint ed. spiral bd. 16.50 (*0-7873-0354-2*) Hlth Research.

World's Sixteen Crucified Saviors: or Christianity Before Christ. Kersey Graves. 440p. 1992. pap. text ed. 29.95 (*1-56459-288-X*) Kessinger Pub.

World's Smallest Dogs. Barbara J. Patten. LC 96-19943. (Read All about Dogs Ser.). (J). 1996. write for info. (*0-86593-457-6*) Rourke Corp.

***World's Strangest Aircraft.** Michael Taylor. 1996. 14.98 (*0-7651-9702-2*) Smithmark.

World's Strangest Animal Facts. Jocelyn Little. (Illus.). 96p. (J). (gr. 4 up). 1995. pap. 5.95 (*0-8069-8521-6*) Sterling.

***World's Strangest Automobiles.** Adrienne Kessel. 1996. 14.98 (*0-7651-9701-4*) Smithmark.

World's Strangest Baseball Stories. Bart Rockwell. LC 92-10120. (Illus.). 96p. (J). (gr. 3-7). 1992. pap. 2.95 (*0-8167-2850-X*); lib. bdg. 11.89 (*0-8167-2933-6*) Troll Communs.

World's Strangest Basketball Stories. Bart Rockwell. LC 92-25676. (J). 1992. lib. bdg. 11.89 (*0-8167-2935-2*) Troll Communs.

World's Strangest Basketball Stories. Bart Rockwell. LC 92-25676. (J). 1996. pap. 2.95 (*0-8167-2852-6*) Troll Communs.

World's Strangest Football Stories. Bart Rockwell. LC 92-10121. (Illus.). 96p. (J). (gr. 3-7). 1992. lib. bdg. 11.89 (*0-8167-2934-4*) Troll Communs.

World's Strangest Football Stories. Bart Rockwell. LC 92-10121. (Illus.). 96p. (J). (gr. 3-7). 1996. pap. 2.95 (*0-8167-2851-8*) Troll Communs.

World's Strangest Hockey Stories. Bart Rockwell. LC 92-25992. (Illus.). 96p. (J). (gr. 3-7). 1992. lib. bdg. 11.89 (*0-8167-2936-0*) Troll Communs.

World's Strangest Hockey Stories. Bart Rockwell. LC 92-25992. (Illus.). 96p. (J). (gr. 3-7). 1996. pap. 2.95 (*0-8167-2853-4*) Troll Communs.

World's Strangest Secret: Judgement Day 20th Century Style. Kenna E. Farris. 24.95 (*0-318-03803-X*) Port Love Intl.

World's Strangest "True" Ghost Stories. John Macklin. LC 89-26125. (Illus.). 96p. (J). (gr. 4 up). 1991. pap. 4.95 (*0-8069-5785-9*) Sterling.

***World's Stupidest Criminals: A Comical Collection of Real-Life Bumbling Burglars, Dithering Delinquents, & Other Foolish Felons.** Ed. by Fortean Times Editors. (Illus.). 128p. (Orig.). 1997. pap. 14.95 (*0-8362-3744-7*, Cader Bks) Andrews & McMeel.

World's Stupidest I. Q. Test. Eldon C. Romney. (Illus.). 64p. (Orig.). (C). 1992. pap. 4.95 (*0-9632451-0-4*) Creat Diversions.

World's Submachine Guns: Developments from 1915 to 1963, Vol. I. rev. ed. Thomas B. Nelson & Hans B. Lockhoven. 1985. 29.95 (*0-85368-481-2*) TBN Ent.

***World's Submarine Telephone Cable Systems.** (Fiber Optics User's Manual & Design Ser.: Vol. XII). 415p. 1984. 75.00 (*0-614-18468-1*, 152U12) Info Gatekeepers.

World's Sugar: Progress & Policy. Vladimir P. Timoshenko & Boris C. Swerling. xii, 364p. 1957. 52.50 (*0-8047-0501-1*) Stanford U Pr.

World's Tallest Midget: The Best of Frank Deford. Frank Deford. 1988. pap. 8.95 (*0-316-17946-9*) Little.

Worlds That Passed. Abraham S. Sachs. Tr. by Harold Berman & Judah Joffe from YID. LC 74-29521. (Modern Jewish Experience Ser.). 1975. reprint ed. 26.95 (*0-405-06746-1*) Ayer.

Worlds, Times & Selves. Arthur N. Prior & Kit Fine. LC 76-45042. 176p. 1977. 25.00 (*0-87023-227-4*) U of Mass Pr.

Worlds Together. Patricia A. Richard-Amato & Wendy A. Hansen. 192p. 1995. pap. text ed. 17.86 (*0-201-82386-1*) Addison-Wesley.

Worlds Together Anthology. Amato. (J). 1995. pap. text ed. 86.52 (*0-201-80978-8*) Addison-Wesley.

Worlds Together Anthology. Patricia A. Richard-Amato & Wendy A. Hansen. (Teachers Guide Ser.). 1995. pap. text ed. write for info. (*0-201-82389-6*) Addison-Wesley.

World's Top Retirement Havens. 3rd ed. Ed. by Marian Cooper. 480p. 1991. 15.95 (*0-945332-25-4*) Agora Inc MD.

***World's Toughest Golf Holes.** Tom Hepburn & Selwyn Jacobson. (Illus.). 78p. (Orig.). 1997. pap. 14.95 (*0-908697-65-1*, Pub. by St Pub Ltd NZ) Seven Hills Bk.

World's Toughest Puzzles. Charles B. Townsend. LC 89-49131. 96p. (YA). (gr. 6-12). 1991. pap. 5.95 (*0-8069-6963-6*) Sterling.

***World's Toughest Tongue Twisters.** (Illus.). (J). (gr. 3-7). Date not set. pap. write for info. (*0-8069-4802-7*) Sterling.

World's Toughest Tongue Twisters. Joseph Rosenbloom. LC 86-5983. (Illus.). 128p. (J). (gr. 2-8). 1987. pap. 4.95 (*0-8069-6596-7*) Sterling.

World's Tragedy. rev. ed. Aleister Crowley. LC 85-80865. 160p. 1991. pap. 12.95 (*1-56184-014-9*) New Falcon Pubns.

World's Trickiest Puzzles. Charles B. Townsend. LC 95-17934. (Illus.). 128p. (Orig.). 1995. 14.95 (*0-8069-0964-1*) Sterling.

World's Trickiest Puzzles. Charles B. Townsend. (Illus.). 128p. (Orig.). 1996. pap. 5.95 (*0-8069-0965-X*) Sterling.

***Worlds Unnumbered: The Quest to Discover Other Solar Systems.** Donald Goldsmith. LC 96-51826. (Illus.). 225p. 1997. 28.50 (*0-935702-97-0*) Univ Sci Bks.

***Worlds Unspoken.** J. Nestle & N. Holden. 1998. pap. write for info. (*0-679-75952-2*, Vin) Random.

World's Wackiest Lawsuits. K. R. Hobbie. LC 92-18234. (Illus.). 128p. 1992. pap. 5.95 (*0-8069-8668-9*) Sterling.

World's Wasted Wealth 2: Save Our Wealth, Save Our Environment. J. W. Smith. 460p. (Orig.). 1994. 27.95 (*0-9624423-3-X*); pap. 17.95 (*0-9624423-2-1*) Inst Econ Dem.

***Worlds We Have Lost.** Broadhead. 1996. pap. text ed. write for info. (*0-07-024568-1*) McGraw.

World's Weirdest Bats. M. L. Roberts. LC 96-8323. (Illus.). 32p. (Orig.). (J). (ps-3). 1996. pap. 3.95 (*0-8167-4133-6*, Whistlstop) Troll Communs.

World's Weirdest Birds. M. L. Roberts. LC 95-17781. (Illus.). 32p. (J). (gr. k-3). 1995. lib. bdg. 13.95 (*0-8167-3733-9*, Whistlstop) Troll Communs.

World's Weirdest Birds. M. L. Roberts. LC 95-17781. (Illus.). 32p. (J). (gr. k-3). 1995. pap. 3.95 (*0-8167-3734-7*, Whistlstop) Troll Communs.

World's Weirdest Bugs & Other Creepy Crawlies. M. L. Roberts. LC 94-18027. (Illus.). 32p. (J). (ps-2). 1994. lib. bdg. 13.95 (*0-8167-3536-0*, Whistlstop) Troll Communs.

World's Weirdest Bugs & Other Creepy Crawlies. M. L. Roberts. LC 94-18027. (Illus.). 32p. (J). (ps-2). 1994. pap. 3.95 (*0-8167-3537-9*, Whistlstop) Troll Communs.

World's Weirdest Dinosaurs. M. L. Roberts. LC 95-42215. (World's Weirdest Ser.). (Illus.). 32p. (J). (gr. k-3). 1995. lib. bdg. 13.95 (*0-8167-3864-5*, Whistlstop) Troll Communs.

World's Weirdest Dinosaurs. M. L. Roberts. LC 95-42215. (World's Weirdest Ser.). (Illus.). 32p. (J). (gr. k-3). 1996. pap. 3.95 (*0-8167-3865-3*, Whistlstop) Troll Communs.

***World's Weirdest Dinosaurs.** M. L. Roberts. (Illus.). 32p. (J). (gr. 1-2). 1997. reprint ed. pap. 3.50 (*0-7881-3957-6*) DIANE Pub.

World's Weirdest Reptiles. M. L. Roberts. LC 93-8493. (Illus.). 32p. (J). (gr. 2-9). 1993. lib. bdg. 13.95 (*0-8167-3229-9*) Troll Communs.

World's Weirdest Reptiles. M. L. Roberts. LC 93-8493. (Illus.). 32p. (J). (gr. 2-9). 1994. pap. 3.95 (*0-8167-3221-3*) Troll Communs.

World's Weirdest Sea Creatures. M. L. Roberts. LC 93-21053. (J). 1993. lib. bdg. 13.95 (*0-8167-3230-2*) Troll Communs.

World's Weirdest Sea Creatures. M. L. Roberts. 1995. pap. 3.95 (*0-8167-3689-8*) Troll Communs.

World's Weirdest "True" Ghost Stories. John Beckett. LC 91-15408. (Illus.). 96p. (J). (gr. 4 up). 1992. pap. 4.95 (*0-8069-8411-2*) Sterling.

World's Weirdest Underwater Creatures. M. L. Roberts. LC 93-21053. (J). 1993. pap. 3.95 (*0-8167-3222-1*) Troll Communs.

World's Weirdest Web Pages. Hank Duderstadt. LC 96-32857. 1996. pap. text ed. 12.95 (*1-886411-12-3*) No Starch Pr.

***World's Who Is Who & Does What in Environment & Conservation.** Nicholas Polunin & Lynn M. Curme. LC 97-1651. 1997. text ed. 75.00 (*0-312-17448-9*) St Martin.

***World's Wild Cats.** Fiona Sunquist. 1990. pap. text ed. 14.95 (*0-226-78000-7*); lib. bdg. 34.95 (*0-226-77999-8*) U Ch Pr.

World's Wild Places. Sally Morgan. LC 96-23349. (Remarkable World Ser.). 1997. lib. bdg. 24.26 (*0-8172-4536-7*) Raintree Steck-V.

World's Wild Shores. Ed. by Donald J. Crump. LC 89-13952. (Special Publications Series 24: No. 4). (Illus.). (YA). 1990. 12.95 (*0-87044-716-5*); lib. bdg. 12.95 (*0-87044-721-1*) Natl Geog.

***World's Wisdom.** P. Novak. 1996. 8.98 (*0-7858-0718-7*) Bk Sales Inc.

World's Wisdom: Sacred Texts of the World's Religions. Philip Novak. LC 93-43995. 448p. 1995. pap. 14.00 (*0-06-066342-1*) Harper SF.

Worlds Within: Children's Fantasy from the Middle Ages to Today. Sheila A. Egoff. LC 88-10058. 384p. 1988. text ed. 20.00 (*0-8389-0494-7*) ALA.

Worlds Within Women: Myth & Mythmaking in Fantastic Literature by Women. Thelma J. Shinn. LC 86-7592. (Contributions to the Study of Science Fiction & Fantasy Ser.: No. 22). 229p. 1986. text ed. 49.95 (*0-313-25101-0*, SWN/, Greenwood Pr) Greenwood.

Worlds Within Worlds: The Novels of Ivan Turgenev. Jane T. Costlow. 186p. 1990. text ed. 29.50 (*0-691-06783-X*) Princeton U Pr.

***Worlds Within Worlds: The Richard Rosenblum Collection of Chinese Scholars' Rocks.** Robert D. Mowry et al. LC 97-5214. (Illus.). 317p. (Orig.). 1997. pap. 40.00 (*0-916724-92-1*) Harvard Art Mus.

Worlds Within Worlds: The Story of Nuclear Energy. Isaac Asimov. LC 84-167298. (Illus.). 156p. reprint ed. pap. 44.50 (*0-8357-2922-2*, 2039154) Bks Demand.

Worlds Without Content: Against Formalism. John O'Neill. 176p. (C). 1992. text ed. 59.95 (*0-415-06791-X*, A6515) Routledge.

Worlds Without End. George Myers, Jr. LC 90-80551. 98p. 1990. pap. 8.95 (*0-929968-12-3*) Another Chicago Pr.

Worlds Without End: Shadowrun 18. Caroline Spector. 288p. 1995. pap. 4.99 (*0-451-45371-9*, ROC) NAL-Dutton.

***Worlds Without End: The Art & History of the Soap Opera.** Museum of Television & Radio (New York, N.Y.) Staff. LC 97-307. 1997. write for info. (*0-8109-3997-5*) Abrams.

World's Women 1970-1990: Trends & Statistics. 1991. 19.95 (*92-1-161313-2*) UN.

Worlds Women 1995: Trends & Statistics. 2nd ed. United Nations Staff. 188p. (C). 1995. pap. 15.95 (*92-1-161372-8*, E.95.XVII.2) UN.

World's Wonder & Other Essays. Gabrielle M. Long. (Essay Index Reprint Ser.). 1977. 23.95 (*0-8369-1223-3*) Ayer.

W

An Asterisk (*) at the beginning of an entry indicates that the title is appearing in BIP for the first time.

World's Worst Disasters at Sea. John Protasio. 212p. 1993. reprint ed. pap. 5.50 (*1-56171-196-9*, S P I Bks) Sure Seller.

World's Worst Fairy Godmother. Bruce Coville. (J). (gr. 3-6). 1996. 14.00 (*0-671-00229-5*, PB Hardcover) PB.

World's Worst Fairy Godmother. Bruce Coville. (J). (gr. 3-6). 1996. mass mkt. 3.99 (*0-671-00228-7*) PB.

World's Worst Golf Courses: A Collection of Courses Not up to Par. John Garrity. LC 93-22367. (Illus.). 212p. 1994. pap. 10.00 (*0-02-043235-6*) Macmillan.

World's Worst Golf Jokes. Martin A. Ragaway. 48p. (J). 1973. pap. 2.95 (*0-8431-0200-4*) Putnam Pub Group.

World's Worst Knock Knock Jokes. Kati Stern & Claudia Sloan. (J). 1974. 2.50 (*0-8431-0204-7*) Putnam Pub Group.

World's Worst Poet. William McGonagall. 128p. (Orig.). 1979. pap. 6.95 (*0-87243-088-X*) Templegate.

World's Worst Weed, Its Impact & Utilisation. S. A. Abbasi. 224p. 1993. pap. 225.00 (*0-614-09633-2*, Pub. by Intl Bk Distr II) St Mut.

World's Worst Weeds: Distribution & Biology. LeRoy G. Holm. LC 74-78866. 621p. reprint ed. pap. 177.00 (*0-685-17119-1*, 2027026) Bks Demand.

World's Worst Weeds: Distribution & Biology. LeRoy G. Holm et al. LC 89-15640. (Illus.). 622p. (C). 1991. reprint ed. 89.50 (*0-89464-415-7*) Krieger.

World's Writing Systems. Ed. by Peter T. Daniels & Bright. 968p. 1996. 150.00 (*0-19-507993-0*) OUP.

***World's 18 Top Retirement Havens.** Ed. by International Living Staff. 416p. 1998. pap. 16.95 (*1-56261-377-4*) John Muir.

Worldscapes. 2nd ed. Ed. by T. H. Masterton. 1987. pap. text ed. 13.05 (*0-05-004028-6*, 70094) Longman.

WorldScope. Ed. by Ann H. Hagen. (Illus.). 80p. 1989. 14.95 (*0-9624244-0-4*) WorldScope.

WorldScope, a Desk Reference. Ed. by Ann H. Hagen. 80p. 1989. 14.95 (*0-685-29111-1*) WorldScope.

Worldscope of Company Profiles 1990: Financial & Service Companies, 3 vols. 90th ed. 1990. Set. 245.00 (*0-944703-02-X*, 071150-M99406) Gale.

Worldscope of Company Profiles 1990: Industrial Companies, 5 vols. 90th ed. 1990. Set. 525.00 (*0-944703-01-1*, 071101-M99406) Gale.

Worldscope of Company Profiles 1990: 1990 Edition, 8 vols. 90th ed. 1990. Set. 695.00 (*0-944703-00-3*, 071100-M99406) Gale.

***Worldtariff Guidebook on Customs Tariff Schedules of Import Duties for Argentina: 1997.** Ed. by Worldtariff Staff. (Argentina National Guidebook Ser.). 500p. 1997. ring bd. 490.00 (*1-56745-244-2*); disk 390.00 (*1-56745-245-0*) Wrldtariff.

***Worldtariff Guidebook on Customs Tariff Schedules of Import Duties for Argentina: 1997, Duty & Tax Analyst.** Ed. by Worldtariff Staff. (Argentina National Guidebook Ser.). 500p. 1997. ring bd. 735.00 incl. disk (*1-56745-243-4*) Wrldtariff.

***Worldtariff Guidebook on Customs Tariff Schedules of Import Duties for Australia: 1997.** Ed. by Worldtariff Staff. (National Guidebook Ser.). 500p. 1997. 490.00 (*1-56745-251-5*) Wrldtariff.

***Worldtariff Guidebook on Customs Tariff Schedules of Import Duties for Brazil: 1996.** 3rd ed. Ed. by Worldtariff Staff. (Brazil National Guidebook Ser.). 500p. 1996. ring bd. 465.00 (*1-56745-127-6*); disk 375.00 (*1-56745-128-4*) Wrldtariff.

***Worldtariff Guidebook on Customs Tariff Schedules of Import Duties for Brazil: 1997.** 4th ed. Ed. by Worldtariff Staff. (Brazil National Guidebook Ser.). 500p. 1997. ring bd. 490.00 (*1-56745-188-8*); disk 390.00 (*1-56745-189-6*) Wrldtariff.

***Worldtariff Guidebook on Customs Tariff Schedules of Import Duties for Brazil: 1997, Duty & Tax Analyst.** 4th ed. Ed. by Worldtariff Staff. (Brazil National Guidebook Ser.). 1997. ring bd. 735.00 incl. disk (*1-56745-232-9*) Wrldtariff.

***Worldtariff Guidebook on Customs Tariff Schedules of Import Duties for Bulgaria: 1996.** 3rd ed. Ed. by Worldtariff Staff. (Bulgaria National Guidebook Ser.). 500p. 1996. ring bd. 465.00 (*1-56745-114-4*); disk 375.00 (*1-56745-115-2*) Wrldtariff.

***Worldtariff Guidebook on Customs Tariff Schedules of Import Duties for Bulgaria: 1997.** 4th ed. Ed. by Worldtariff Staff. (Bulgaria National Guidebook Ser.). 500p. 1997. ring bd. 490.00 (*1-56745-175-6*); disk 390.00 (*1-56745-176-4*) Wrldtariff.

***Worldtariff Guidebook on Customs Tariff Schedules of Import Duties for Bulgaria: 1997, Duty & Tax Analyst.** 4th ed. Ed. by Worldtariff Staff. (Bulgaria National Guidebook Ser.). 1997. ring bd. 735.00 incl. disk (*1-56745-226-4*) Wrldtariff.

***Worldtariff Guidebook on Customs Tariff Schedules of Import Duties for Canada: 1996.** 5th ed. Ed. by Worldtariff Staff. (Canada National Guidebook Ser.). 500p. 1996. ring bd. 360.00 (*1-56745-120-9*); disk 285.00 (*1-56745-121-7*) Wrldtariff.

***Worldtariff Guidebook on Customs Tariff Schedules of Import Duties for Canada: 1997.** 6th ed. Ed. by Worldtariff Staff. (Canada National Guidebook Ser.). 500p. 1997. ring bd. write for info. (*1-56745-181-0*); disk 300.00 (*1-56745-182-9*) Wrldtariff.

***Worldtariff Guidebook on Customs Tariff Schedules of Import Duties for Canada: 1997, Duty & Tax Analyst.** 6th ed. Ed. by Worldtariff Staff. (Canada National Guidebook Ser.). 1997. ring bd. 570.00 incl. disk (*1-56745-229-9*) Wrldtariff.

***Worldtariff Guidebook on Customs Tariff Schedules of Import Duties for Chemical/Cosmetic/Pharmaceutical: 1996.** Ed. by Worldtariff Staff. (Chemical/Cosmetic/Pharmaceutical Sector Guidebook Ser.). 750p. 1996. ring bd. 1,000.00 (*1-56745-158-6*); disk 800.00 (*1-56745-159-4*) Wrldtariff.

***Worldtariff Guidebook on Customs Tariff Schedules of Import Duties for Chemical/Cosmetic/Pharmaceutical: 1997.** 2nd ed. Ed. by Worldtariff Staff. (Chemical/Cosmetic/Pharmaceutical Sector Guidebook Ser.). 750p. 1997. ring bd. 1,000.00 (*1-56745-212-4*); disk 800.00 (*1-56745-213-2*) Wrldtariff.

***Worldtariff Guidebook on Customs Tariff Schedules of Import Duties for Chemical/Cosmetic/Pharmaceutical: 1997, Duty & Tax Analyst.** 2nd ed. Ed. by Worldtariff Staff. (Chemical/Cosmetic/Pharmaceutical Sector Guidebook Ser.). 1997. ring bd. 1,500.00 incl. disk (*1-56745-248-5*) Wrldtariff.

***Worldtariff Guidebook on Customs Tariff Schedules of Import Duties for Chile: 1996.** Ed. by Worldtariff Staff. (Chile National Guidebook Ser.). 500p. 1996. ring bd. 360.00 (*1-56745-149-7*); disk 285.00 (*1-56745-150-0*) Wrldtariff.

***Worldtariff Guidebook on Customs Tariff Schedules of Import Duties for Chile: 1997.** 2nd ed. Ed. by Worldtariff Staff. (Chile National Guidebook Ser.). 500p. 1997. ring bd. 380.00 (*1-56745-191-8*); disk 300.00 (*1-56745-192-6*) Wrldtariff.

***Worldtariff Guidebook on Customs Tariff Schedules of Import Duties for Chile: 1997, Duty & Tax Analyst.** 2nd ed. Ed. by Worldtariff Staff. (Chile National Guidebook Ser.). 1997. ring bd. 570.00 incl. disk (*1-56745-233-7*) Wrldtariff.

***Worldtariff Guidebook on Customs Tariff Schedules of Import Duties for Columbia: 1997.** Ed. by Worldtariff Staff. (National Guidebook Ser.). 500p. 1997. 490.00 (*1-56745-258-2*) Wrldtariff.

***Worldtariff Guidebook on Customs Tariff Schedules of Import Duties for Computer/Electronics/Machinery: 1997.** 3rd ed. Ed. by Worldtariff Staff. (Computer/Electronics/Machinery Sector Guidebook Ser.). 750p. 1997. ring bd. 1,000.00 (*1-56745-214-0*); disk 800.00 (*1-56745-215-9*) Wrldtariff.

***Worldtariff Guidebook on Customs Tariff Schedules of Import Duties for Computer/Electronics/Machinery: 1997, Duty & Tax Analyst.** 3rd ed. Ed. by Worldtariff Staff. (Computers/Electronics/Machinery Sector Guidebook Ser.). 1997. ring bd. 1,500.00 incl. disk (*1-56745-249-3*) Wrldtariff.

***Worldtariff Guidebook on Customs Tariff Schedules of Import Duties for Computers/Electronics/Machinery: 1996.** 2nd ed. Ed. by Worldtariff Staff. (Computers/Electronics/Machinery Sector Guidebook Ser.). 750p. 1996. ring bd. 1,000.00 (*1-56745-145-4*); disk 800.00 (*1-56745-146-2*) Wrldtariff.

***Worldtariff Guidebook on Customs Tariff Schedules of Import Duties for Consumer Durables: 1996.** 2nd ed. Ed. by Worldtariff Staff. (Consumer Durables Sector Guidebook Ser.). 750p. 1996. ring bd. 1,000.00 (*1-56745-147-0*); disk 800.00 (*1-56745-148-9*) Wrldtariff.

***Worldtariff Guidebook on Customs Tariff Schedules of Import Duties for Consumer Durables: 1997.** 3rd ed. Ed. by Worldtariff Staff. (Consumer Durables Sector Guidebook Ser.). 750p. 1997. ring bd. 1,000.00 (*1-56745-216-7*); disk 800.00 (*1-56745-217-5*) Wrldtariff.

***Worldtariff Guidebook on Customs Tariff Schedules of Import Duties for Consumer Durables: 1997, Duty & Tax Analyst.** 3rd ed. Ed. by Worldtariff Staff. (Consumer Durables Sector Guidebook Ser.). 1997. ring bd. 1,500.00 incl. disk (*1-56745-250-7*) Wrldtariff.

***Worldtariff Guidebook on Customs Tariff Schedules of Import Duties for Czech Republic: 1996.** 3rd ed. Ed. by Worldtariff Staff. (Czech Republic National Guidebook Ser.). 500p. 1996. ring bd. 360.00 (*1-56745-106-3*); disk 285.00 (*1-56745-107-1*) Wrldtariff.

***Worldtariff Guidebook on Customs Tariff Schedules of Import Duties for Czech Republic: 1997, Duty & Tax Analyst.** 4th ed. Ed. by Worldtariff Staff. (Czech Republic National Guidebook Ser.). 1997. ring bd. 570.00 incl. disk (*1-56745-222-1*) Wrldtariff.

***Worldtariff Guidebook on Customs Tariff Schedules of Import Duties for Egypt: 1997.** Ed. by Worldtariff Staff. (National Guidebook Ser.). 500p. 1997. 490.00 (*1-56745-261-2*) Wrldtariff.

***Worldtariff Guidebook on Customs Tariff Schedules of Import Duties for European Union: 1996, 2 vols.** 36th ed. Ed. by Worldtariff Staff. (European Union-15 Ser.). 500p. 1996. ring bd. 465.00 (*1-56745-098-9*); disk 375.00 (*1-56745-099-7*) Wrldtariff.

***Worldtariff Guidebook on Customs Tariff Schedules of Import Duties for Food/Agriculture: 1996.** 5th ed. Ed. by Worldtariff Staff. (Food/Agriculture Sector Guidebook Ser.). 750p. 1996. ring bd. 1,000.00 (*1-56745-137-3*); disk 800.00 (*1-56745-138-1*) Wrldtariff.

***Worldtariff Guidebook on Customs Tariff Schedules of Import Duties for Food/Agriculture: 1997.** 6th ed. Ed. by Worldtariff Staff. (Food/Agriculture Sector Guidebook Ser.). 750p. 1997. ring bd. 1,000.00 (*1-56745-208-6*); disk 800.00 (*1-56745-209-4*) Wrldtariff.

***Worldtariff Guidebook on Customs Tariff Schedules of Import Duties for Food/Agriculture: 1997, Duty & Tax Analyst.** 6th ed. Ed. by Worldtariff Staff. (Food/Agriculture Sector Guidebook Ser.). 1997. ring bd. 1,500.00 incl. disk (*1-56745-246-9*) Wrldtariff.

***Worldtariff Guidebook on Customs Tariff Schedules of Import Duties for Hungary: 1996.** 3rd ed. Ed. by Worldtariff Staff. (Hungary National Guidebook Ser.). 500p. 1996. ring bd. 360.00 (*1-56745-109-8*); disk 285.00 (*1-56745-110-1*) Wrldtariff.

***Worldtariff Guidebook on Customs Tariff Schedules of Import Duties for Hungary: 1997.** 4th ed. Ed. by Worldtariff Staff. (Hungary National Guidebook Ser.). 500p. 1997. ring bd. 380.00 (*1-56745-170-5*); disk 300.00 (*1-56745-171-3*) Wrldtariff.

***Worldtariff Guidebook on Customs Tariff Schedules of Import Duties for Hungary: 1997, Duty & Tax Analyst.** 4th ed. Ed. by Worldtariff Staff. (Hungary National Guidebook Ser.). 1997. ring bd. 570.00 incl. disk (*1-56745-224-8*) Wrldtariff.

***Worldtariff Guidebook on Customs Tariff Schedules of Import Duties for India: 1996.** 3rd ed. Ed. by Worldtariff Staff. (India National Guidebook Ser.). 500p. 1996. ring bd. 465.00 (*1-56745-135-7*); disk 375.00 (*1-56745-136-5*) Wrldtariff.

***Worldtariff Guidebook on Customs Tariff Schedules of Import Duties for India: 1997.** 4th ed. Ed. by Worldtariff Staff. (India National Guidebook Ser.). 500p. 1997. ring bd. 490.00 (*1-56745-205-1*); disk 390.00 (*1-56745-207-8*) Wrldtariff.

***Worldtariff Guidebook on Customs Tariff Schedules of Import Duties for India: 1997, Duty & Tax Analyst.** 4th ed. Ed. by Worldtariff Staff. (India National Guidebook Ser.). 500p. 1997. ring bd. 735.00 incl. disk (*1-56745-242-6*) Wrldtariff.

***Worldtariff Guidebook on Customs Tariff Schedules of Import Duties for Indonesia: 1997.** Ed. by Worldtariff Staff. (National Guidebook Ser.). 500p. 1997. 490.00 (*1-56745-264-7*) Wrldtariff.

***Worldtariff Guidebook on Customs Tariff Schedules of Import Duties for Israel: 1996.** 3rd ed. Ed. by Worldtariff Staff. (Israel National Guidebook Ser.). 500p. 1996. ring bd. 465.00 (*1-56745-118-7*); disk 375.00 (*1-56745-119-5*) Wrldtariff.

***Worldtariff Guidebook on Customs Tariff Schedules of Import Duties for Israel: 1997.** 4th ed. Ed. by Worldtariff Staff. (Israel National Guidebook Ser.). 500p. 1997. ring bd. 490.00 (*1-56745-179-9*); disk 390.00 (*1-56745-180-2*) Wrldtariff.

***Worldtariff Guidebook on Customs Tariff Schedules of Import Duties for Israel: 1997, Duty & Tax Analyst.** 4th ed. Ed. by Worldtariff Staff. (Israel National Guidebook Ser.). 1997. ring bd. 735.00 incl. disk (*1-56745-228-0*) Wrldtariff.

***Worldtariff Guidebook on Customs Tariff Schedules of Import Duties for Japan: 1996.** 30th ed. Ed. by Worldtariff Staff. (Japan National Guidebook Ser.). 500p. 1996. ring bd. 360.00 (*1-56745-129-2*); disk 285.00 (*1-56745-130-6*) Wrldtariff.

***Worldtariff Guidebook on Customs Tariff Schedules of Import Duties for Japan: 1997.** 31th ed. Ed. by Worldtariff Staff. (Japan National Guidebook Ser.). 500p. 1997. ring bd. 380.00 (*1-56745-193-4*); disk 300.00 (*1-56745-194-2*) Wrldtariff.

***Worldtariff Guidebook on Customs Tariff Schedules of Import Duties for Japan: 1997, Duty & Tax Analyst.** 31th ed. Ed. by Worldtariff Staff. (Japan National Guidebook Ser.). 1997. ring bd. 570.00 incl. disk (*1-56745-234-5*) Wrldtariff.

***Worldtariff Guidebook on Customs Tariff Schedules of Import Duties for Kuwait: 1997.** Ed. by Worldtariff Staff. (National Guidebook Ser.). 500p. 1997. 490.00 (*1-56745-267-1*) Wrldtariff.

***Worldtariff Guidebook on Customs Tariff Schedules of Import Duties for Malaysia: 1996.** Ed. by Worldtariff Staff. (Malaysia National Guidebook Ser.). 500p. 1996. ring bd. 360.00 (*1-56745-155-1*); disk 285.00 (*1-56745-157-8*) Wrldtariff.

***Worldtariff Guidebook on Customs Tariff Schedules of Import Duties for Malaysia: 1997.** 2nd ed. Ed. by Worldtariff Staff. (Malaysia National Guidebook Ser.). 500p. 1997. ring bd. 380.00 (*1-56745-201-9*); disk 300.00 (*1-56745-202-7*) Wrldtariff.

***Worldtariff Guidebook on Customs Tariff Schedules of Import Duties for Malaysia: 1997, Duty & Tax Analyst.** 2nd ed. Ed. by Worldtariff Staff. (Malaysia National Guidebook Ser.). 1997. ring bd. 570.00 incl. disk (*1-56745-239-6*) Wrldtariff.

***Worldtariff Guidebook on Customs Tariff Schedules of Import Duties for Mexico: 1996.** 5th ed. Ed. by Worldtariff Staff. (Mexico National Guidebook Ser.). 500p. 1996. ring bd. 465.00 (*1-56745-124-1*); disk 375.00 (*1-56745-126-8*) Wrldtariff.

***Worldtariff Guidebook on Customs Tariff Schedules of Import Duties for Mexico: 1997.** 6th ed. Ed. by Worldtariff Staff. (Mexico National Guidebook Ser.). 500p. 1997. ring bd. 490.00 (*1-56745-185-3*); disk 390.00 (*1-56745-186-1*) Wrldtariff.

***Worldtariff Guidebook on Customs Tariff Schedules of Import Duties for Mexico: 1997, Duty & Tax Analyst.** 6th ed. Ed. by Worldtariff Staff. (Mexico National Guidebook Ser.). 500p. 1997. ring bd. 735.00 incl. disk (*1-56745-231-0*) Wrldtariff.

***Worldtariff Guidebook on Customs Tariff Schedules of Import Duties for Morocco: 1997.** Ed. by Worldtariff Staff. (National Guidebook Ser.). 500p. 1997. 490.00 (*1-56745-272-8*) Wrldtariff.

***Worldtariff Guidebook on Customs Tariff Schedules of Import Duties for New Zealand: 1997.** Ed. by Worldtariff Staff. (National Guidebook Ser.). 500p. 1997. 490.00 (*1-56745-275-2*) Wrldtariff.

***Worldtariff Guidebook on Customs Tariff Schedules of Import Duties for Norway: 1996.** 33th ed. Ed. by Worldtariff Staff. (Norway National Guidebook Ser.). 500p. 1996. ring bd. 360.00 (*1-56745-102-0*); disk 285.00 (*1-56745-103-9*) Wrldtariff.

***Worldtariff Guidebook on Customs Tariff Schedules of Import Duties for Norway: 1997.** 34th ed. Ed. by Worldtariff Staff. (Norway National Guidebook Ser.). 500p. 1997. ring bd. 380.00 (*1-56745-164-0*); disk 300.00 (*1-56745-165-9*) Wrldtariff.

***Worldtariff Guidebook on Customs Tariff Schedules of Import Duties for Norway: 1997, Duty & Tax Analyst.** 34th ed. Ed. by Worldtariff Staff. (Norway National Guidebook Ser.). 1997. ring bd. 570.00 incl. disk (*1-56745-220-5*) Wrldtariff.

***Worldtariff Guidebook on Customs Tariff Schedules of Import Duties for Pakistan: 1997.** Ed. by Worldtariff Staff. (National Guidebook Ser.). 500p. (Orig.). 1997. 490.00 (*1-56745-278-7*) Wrldtariff.

***Worldtariff Guidebook on Customs Tariff Schedules of Import Duties for Peoples' Republic of China: 1996.** 3rd ed. Ed. by Worldtariff Staff. (Peoples' Republic of China National Guidebook Ser.). 500p. 1996. ring bd. 465.00 (*1-56745-133-0*); disk 375.00 (*1-56745-134-9*) Wrldtariff.

***Worldtariff Guidebook on Customs Tariff Schedules of Import Duties for Peoples' Republic of China: 1997.** 4th ed. Ed. by Worldtariff Staff. (Peoples' Republic of China National Guidebook Ser.). 500p. 1997. ring bd. 490.00 (*1-56745-203-5*); disk 390.00 (*1-56745-204-3*) Wrldtariff.

***Worldtariff Guidebook on Customs Tariff Schedules of Import Duties for Peoples' Republic of China: 1997, Duty & Tax Analyst.** 4th ed. Ed. by Worldtariff Staff. (Peoples' Republic of China Naitonal Guidebook Ser.). 1997. ring bd. 735.00 incl. disk (*1-56745-241-8*) Wrldtariff.

***Worldtariff Guidebook on Customs Tariff Schedules of Import Duties for Philippines: 1997.** Ed. by Worldtariff Staff. (National Guidebook Ser.). 500p. (Orig.). 1997. 490.00 (*1-56745-281-7*) Wrldtariff.

***Worldtariff Guidebook on Customs Tariff Schedules of Import Duties for Poland: 1996.** 3rd ed. Ed. by Worldtariff Staff. (Poland National Guidebook Ser.). 500p. 1996. ring bd. 360.00 (*1-56745-104-7*); disk 285.00 (*1-56745-105-5*) Wrldtariff.

***Worldtariff Guidebook on Customs Tariff Schedules of Import Duties for Poland: 1997.** 4th ed. Ed. by Worldtariff Staff. (Poland National Guidebook Ser.). 500p. 1997. ring bd. 380.00 (*1-56745-166-7*); disk 300.00 (*1-56745-167-5*) Wrldtariff.

***Worldtariff Guidebook on Customs Tariff Schedules of Import Duties for Poland: 1997, Duty & Tax Analyst.** 4th ed. Ed. by Worldtariff Staff. (Poland National Guidebook Ser.). 1997. ring bd. 570.00 incl. disk (*1-56745-221-3*) Wrldtariff.

***Worldtariff Guidebook on Customs Tariff Schedules of Import Duties for Republic of China (Taiwan) 1997.** 2nd ed. Ed. by Worldtariff Staff. (Republic of China (Taiwan) National Guidebook Ser.). 500p. 1997. ring bd. 380.00 (*1-56745-195-0*); disk 300.00 (*1-56745-196-9*) Wrldtariff.

***Worldtariff Guidebook on Customs Tariff Schedules of Import Duties for Republic of China (Taiwan) 1997, Duty & Tax Analyst.** 2nd ed. Ed. by Worldtariff Staff. (Republic of China (Taiwan) National Guidebook Ser.). 1997. ring bd. 570.00 incl. disk (*1-56745-235-3*) Wrldtariff.

***Worldtariff Guidebook on Customs Tariff Schedules of Import Duties for Republic of Korea (South) 1996.** 3rd ed. Ed. by Worldtariff Staff. (Republic of Korea (South) National Guidebook Ser.). 500p. 1996. ring bd. 465.00 (*1-56745-131-4*); disk 375.00 (*1-56745-132-2*) Wrldtariff.

***Worldtariff Guidebook on Customs Tariff Schedules of Import Duties for Republic of Korea (South) 1997.** 4th ed. Ed. by Worldtariff Staff. (Republic of Korea (South) National Guidebook Ser.). 500p. 1997. ring bd. 490.00 (*1-56745-197-7*); disk 390.00 (*1-56745-198-5*) Wrldtariff.

***Worldtariff Guidebook on Customs Tariff Schedules of Import Duties for Republic of Korea (South) 1997, Duty & Tax Analyst.** 4th ed. Ed. by Worldtariff Staff. (Republic of Korea (South) National Guidebook Ser.). 1997. ring bd. 735.00 incl. disk (*1-56745-236-1*) Wrldtariff.

***Worldtariff Guidebook on Customs Tariff Schedules of Import Duties for Romania: 1996.** 3rd ed. Ed. by Worldtariff Staff. (Romania National Guidebook Ser.). 500p. 1996. ring bd. 465.00 (*1-56745-112-8*); disk 375.00 (*1-56745-113-6*) Wrldtariff.

***Worldtariff Guidebook on Customs Tariff Schedules of Import Duties for Romania: 1997.** 4th ed. Ed. by Worldtariff Staff. (Romania National Guidebook Ser.). 500p. 1997. ring bd. 490.00 (*1-56745-172-1*); disk 390.00 (*1-56745-174-8*) Wrldtariff.

***Worldtariff Guidebook on Customs Tariff Schedules of Import Duties for Romania: 1997, Duty & Tax Analyst.** 4th ed. Ed. by Worldtariff Staff. (Romania National Guidebook Ser.). 1997. ring bd. 735.00 incl. disk (*1-56745-225-6*) Wrldtariff.

***Worldtariff Guidebook on Customs Tariff Schedules of Import Duties for Russia: 1997.** Ed. by Worldtariff Staff. (National Guidebook Ser.). 500p. (Orig.). 1997. 490.00 (*1-56745-284-1*) Wrldtariff.

***Worldtariff Guidebook on Customs Tariff Schedules of Import Duties for Saudi Arabia: 1997.** Ed. by Worldtariff Staff. (National Guidebook Ser.). 500p. (Orig.). 1997. 490.00 (*1-56745-288-4*) Wrldtariff.

***Worldtariff Guidebook on Customs Tariff Schedules of Import Duties for Slovakia: 1997.** Ed. by Worldtariff Staff. (National Guidebook Ser.). 500p. (Orig.). 1997. 380.00 (*1-56745-291-4*) Wrldtariff.

***Worldtariff Guidebook on Customs Tariff Schedules of Import Duties for South Africa: 1997.** Ed. by Worldtariff Staff. (National Guidebook Ser.). 500p. (Orig.). 1997. 490.00 (*1-56745-294-9*) Wrldtariff.

***Worldtariff Guidebook on Customs Tariff Schedules of Import Duties for Switzerland: 1996.** 32th ed. Ed. by Worldtariff Staff. (Switzerland National Guidebook Ser.). 500p. 1996. ring bd. 360.00 (*1-56745-100-4*); disk 285.00 (*1-56745-101-2*) Wrldtariff.

***Worldtariff Guidebook on Customs Tariff Schedules of Import Duties for Switzerland: 1997.** 33th ed. Ed. by Worldtariff Staff. 500p. 1997. ring bd. 380.00 (*1-56745-162-4*); disk 300.00 (*1-56745-163-2*) Wrldtariff.

W

An Asterisk (*) at the beginning of an entry indicates that the title is appearing in BIP for the first time.

***Worldtariff Guidebook on Customs Tariff Schedules of Import Duties for Switzerland: 1997, Duty & Tax Analyst.** 33th ed. Ed. by Worldtariff Staff. (Switzerland National Guidebook Ser.). 1997. ring bd. 570.00 incl. disk (*1-56745-219-1*) Wrldtariff.

***Worldtariff Guidebook on Customs Tariff Schedules of Import Duties for Taiwan, Republic of China: 1996.** Ed. by Worldtariff Staff. (Republic of China (Taiwan) National Guidebook Ser.). 500p. 1996. ring bd. 360.00 (*1-56745-151-9*); disk 285.00 (*1-56745-152-7*) Wrldtariff.

***Worldtariff Guidebook on Customs Tariff Schedules of Import Duties for Textile/Apparel: 1996.** 5th ed. Ed. by Worldtariff Staff. (Textiles/Apparel Sector Guidebook Ser.). 750p. 1996. ring bd. 1,000.00 (*1-56745-140-3*); disk 800.00 (*1-56745-141-1*) Wrldtariff.

***Worldtariff Guidebook on Customs Tariff Schedules of Import Duties for Textile/Apparel: 1997, Duty & Tax Analyst.** 6th ed. Ed. by Worldtariff Staff. (Textile/Apparel Sector Guidebook Ser.). 750p. 1997. ring bd. 1,500.00 incl. disk (*1-56745-247-7*) Wrldtariff.

***Worldtariff Guidebook on Customs Tariff Schedules of Import Duties for Textiles/Apparel: 1997.** 6th ed. Ed. by Worldtariff Staff. (Textile/Apparel Sector Guidebook Ser.). 750p. 1997. ring bd. 1,000.00 (*1-56745-210-8*); disk 800.00 (*1-56745-211-6*) Wrldtariff.

***Worldtariff Guidebook on Customs Tariff Schedules of Import Duties for Thailand: 1996.** Ed. by Worldtariff Staff. (Thailand National Guidebook Ser.). 500p. 1996. ring bd. 360.00 (*1-56745-153-5*); disk 285.00 (*1-56745-154-3*) Wrldtariff.

***Worldtariff Guidebook on Customs Tariff Schedules of Import Duties for Thailand: 1997.** 2nd ed. Ed. by Worldtariff Staff. (Thailand National Guidebook Ser.). 500p. 1997. ring bd. 380.00 (*1-56745-199-3*); disk 300.00 (*1-56745-200-0*) Wrldtariff.

***Worldtariff Guidebook on Customs Tariff Schedules of Import Duties for Thailand: 1997, Duty & Tax Analyst.** 2nd ed. Ed. by Worldtariff Staff. (Thailand National Guidebook Ser.). 1997. ring bd. 570.00 incl. disk (*1-56745-238-8*) Wrldtariff.

***Worldtariff Guidebook on Customs Tariff Schedules of Import Duties for the Czech Republic: 1997.** 4th ed. Ed. by Worldtariff Staff. (Czech Republic National Guidebook Ser.). 500p. 1997. ring bd. 380.00 (*1-56745-168-3*); disk 300.00 (*1-56745-169-1*) Wrldtariff.

***Worldtariff Guidebook on Customs Tariff Schedules of Import Duties for the European Union: 1997.** 37th ed. Ed. by Worldtariff Staff. (European Union-15 National Guidebook Ser.). 500p. 1997. ring bd. 490.00 (*1-56745-160-8*); disk 390.00 (*1-56745-161-6*) Wrldtariff.

***Worldtariff Guidebook on Customs Tariff Schedules of Import Duties for the European Union: 1997, Duty & Tax Analyst.** 37th ed. Ed. by Worldtariff Staff. (European Union-15 Ser.). 1997. ring bd. 735.00 incl. disk (*1-56745-218-3*) Wrldtariff.

***Worldtariff Guidebook on Customs Tariff Schedules of Import Duties for Tunisia: 1997.** Ed. by Worldtariff Staff. (National Guidebook Ser.). 500p. (Orig.). 1997. 490.00 (*1-56745-297-3*) Wrldtariff.

***Worldtariff Guidebook on Customs Tariff Schedules of Import Duties for Turkey: 1996.** 3rd ed. Ed. by Worldtariff Staff. (Turkey National Guidebook Ser.). 500p. 1996. ring bd. 465.00 (*1-56745-116-0*); disk 375.00 (*1-56745-117-9*) Wrldtariff.

***Worldtariff Guidebook on Customs Tariff Schedules of Import Duties for Turkey: 1997.** 4th ed. Ed. by Worldtariff Staff. (Turkey National Guidebook Ser.). 500p. 1997. ring bd. 490.00 (*1-56745-177-2*); disk 390.00 (*1-56745-178-0*) Wrldtariff.

***Worldtariff Guidebook on Customs Tariff Schedules of Import Duties for Turkey: 1997, Duty & Tax Analyst.** 4th ed. Ed. by Worldtariff Staff. (Turkey National Guidebook Ser.). 1997. ring bd. 735.00 incl. disk (*1-56745-227-2*) Wrldtariff.

***Worldtariff Guidebook on Customs Tariff Schedules of Import Duties for U. S. A. 1997.** 6th ed. Ed. by Worldtariff Staff. (United States of America National Guidebook Ser.). 500p. 1997. ring bd. 490.00 (*1-56745-183-7*); disk 390.00 (*1-56745-184-5*) Wrldtariff.

***Worldtariff Guidebook on Customs Tariff Schedules of Import Duties for U. S. A. 1997, Duty & Tax Analyst.** 6th ed. Ed. by Worldtariff Staff. (United States of America National Guidebook Ser.). 1997. ring bd. 735.00 incl. disk (*1-56745-230-2*) Wrldtariff.

***Worldtariff Guidebook on Customs Tariff Schedules of Import Duties for Ukraine: 1997.** Ed. by Worldtariff Staff. (National Guidebook Ser.). 500p. (Orig.). 1997. 490.00 (*1-56745-301-5*) Wrldtariff.

***Worldtariff Guidebook on Customs Tariff Schedules of Import Duties for United Arab Emirates: 1997.** Ed. by Worldtariff Staff. (National Guidebook Ser.). 500p. (Orig.). 1997. 380.00 (*1-56745-305-8*) Wrldtariff.

***Worldtariff Guidebook on Customs Tariff Schedules of Import Duties for Vietnam: 1997.** Ed. by Worldtariff Staff. (National Guidebook Ser.). 500p. (Orig.). 1997. 490.00 (*1-56745-308-2*) Wrldtariff.

***Worldtariff Guidebook on Customs Tariff Schedules of Import Duties for 22 Major Customs Areas: 1996, 22 vols.** Ed. by Worldtariff Staff. 1996. ring bd. write for info. (*1-56745-108-X*); disk write for info. (*1-56745-111-X*) Wrldtariff.

***Worldtariff Guidebook on Customs Tariff Schedules of Import Duties for 40 Major Customs Areas: 1997, 40 vols.** Ed. by Worldtariff Staff. 1997. ring bd. write for info. (*1-56745-173-X*); disk write for info. (*1-56745-187-X*) Wrldtariff.

***Worldtariff Guidebook on Customs Tariff Schedules of Import Duties for 40 Major Customs Areas: 1997, Duty & Tax Analyst, 40 vols.** Ed. by Worldtariff Staff. 1997. write for info. (*1-56745-190-X*) Wrldtariff.

Worldviews: Crosscultural Explorations of Human Beliefs. 2nd ed. Ninian Smart. LC 94-28525. 192p. 1994. pap. text ed. 22.00 (*0-02-412031-6*, Macmillan Coll) P-H.

Worldviews: From Fragmentation Towards Integration. Diederik Aerts et al. 80p. 1994. pap. 12.00 (*90-5487-069-9*, Pub. by VUB Univ Pr BE) Paul & Co Pubs.

Worldviews & Decisions: A Course in Ethical Philosophy. Todd Eckerson. 1993. student ed. 16.25 (*1-881678-52-0*) CRIS.

Worldviews & Decisions: A Course in Ethical Philosophy, 3 vols., Set. Todd Eckerson. 1993. 68.00 (*0-614-13448-X*) CRIS.

Worldviews & Decisions: A Course in Ethical Philosophy, Vol. I. Todd Eckerson. 1993. teacher ed. 29.00 (*1-881678-50-4*) CRIS.

Worldviews & Decisions: A Course in Ethical Philosophy, Vol. II. Todd Eckerson. 1993. teacher ed. 29.00 (*1-881678-51-2*) CRIS.

Worldviews & Ecology. 1994. 22.00 (*0-8387-5272-1*) Bucknell U Pr.

Worldviews & Ecology. Ed. by Mary E. Tucker & John A. Grim. LC 55-58217. (Bucknell Reviews: Vol. 37, No. 2). 248p. 1993. 22.00 (*0-685-68125-4*) Bucknell U Pr.

Worldviews & Ecology: Religion, Philosophy, & the Environment. Ed. by Mary E. Tucker & John A. Grim. LC 94-21625. (Ecology & Justice Ser.). 242p. (Orig.). 1994. pap. 18.00 (*0-88344-967-6*) Orbis Bks.

Worldviews & Perceiving God. Joseph Runzo. LC 93-26988. 1993. text ed. 45.00 (*0-312-10379-4*) St Martin.

Worldviews & Warrants: Plurality & Authority in Theology. Intro. by William Schweiker & Per M. Anderson. LC 87-18987. 126p. (Orig.). (C). 1987. pap. text ed. 16.50 (*0-8191-6614-6*) U Pr of Amer.

Worldviews in Conflict: Choosing Christianity in the World of Ideas. Ronald H. Nash. 224p. 1992. pap. 10.99 (*0-310-57771-3*) Zondervan.

***Worldviews on the Air: The Struggle to Create a Pluralist Broadcasting System in the Netherlands.** John L. Hiemstra. LC 96-52484. 182p. 1997. 49.50 (*0-7618-0672-5*); pap. 27.50 (*0-7618-0673-3*) U Pr of Amer.

Worldwalk. Steven M. Newman. 560p. 1990. mass mkt. 5.95 (*0-380-71150-8*) Avon.

WorldWalk: Internet Power. David Hamblin & Ron Speirs. Ed. by Lee R. Phillips. (Advanced Course Ser.). (Illus.). 194p. 1995. pap. 99.95 incl. audio, vdisk (*0-9649424-3-7*); pap. 99.95 incl. audio, disk, vdisk (*0-9649424-2-9*) Info Directions.

Worldwar: Finding the Balance. Harry Turtledove. 1996. write for info. (*0-345-40549-8*) Ballantine.

***Worldwar: In the Balance.** Harry Turtledove. 1997. pap. 12.95 (*0-345-42056-X*) Ballantine.

Worldwar: Striking the Balance. Harry Turtledove. LC 96-22118. 432p. 1996. 23.00 (*0-345-40550-1*, Del Rey) Ballantine.

***Worldwar: Striking the Balance.** Harry Turtledove. 1997. mass mkt. 6.99 (*0-345-41208-7*, Del Rey) Ballantine.

***Worldwar: Striking the Balance.** Harry Turtledove. 1997. mass mkt. 6.99 (*0-345-41230-3*, Del Rey) Ballantine.

***Worldwar: Tilting the Balance.** Harry Turtledove. 1997. pap. 12.95 (*0-345-42057-8*) Ballantine.

Worldwar: Upsetting the Balance. Harry Turtledove. (Worldwar Ser.: No. 3). 1996. mass mkt. 6.99 (*0-345-40240-5*, Del Rey) Ballantine.

***Worldwar: Upsetting the Balance.** Harry Turtledove. 1997. pap. 12.95 (*0-345-42058-6*) Ballantine.

Worldwar: In the Balance: An Alternative History of the Second World War. Harry Turtledove. 576p. 1995. mass mkt. 5.99 (*0-345-38852-6*, Del Rey Discovery) Ballantine.

Worldways: Bringing the World into the Classroom. Pamela Elder. 1987. pap. text ed. 21.95 (*0-201-22126-8*) Addison-Wesley.

Worldwide Advances in Communication Networks. Ed. by B. J. Jabbari. (Illus.). 196p. 1994. 69.50 (*0-306-44818-1*, Plenum Pr) Plenum.

Worldwide Advances in Structural Concrete & Masonry: Proceedings of the CCMS Symposium Held in Conjunction with Structures Congress XIV. Ed. by A. E. Schultz & S. L. McCabe. LC 96-6763. 592p. 1996. pap. 59.00 (*0-7844-0164-0*) Am Soc Civil Eng.

Worldwide Aeronautical Communications Frequency Directory. 2nd ed. Robert E. Evans. (Illus.). 260p. 1994. pap. 19.95 (*1-882123-33-6*) Universal Radio Rsch.

Worldwide Bicycling with Safety. Tim A. Bouquet. (Illus.). 80p. (Orig.). 1991. pap. 30.00 (*1-56216-007-9*); text ed. 50.00 (*1-56216-006-0*) Systems Co.

Worldwide Branch Location of Multinational Co's. David S. Hoopes. 1993. 200.00 (*0-8103-8399-3*, 101241) Gale.

Worldwide Brochures: The Official Travel Brochure Directory, Vol. 4, No. 1. Travel Companions International, Inc. Staff. Ed. by Janet L. Mohr et al. 1066p. 1992. pap. 39.00 (*1-880624-04-4*) Trvl Companions.

Worldwide Chemical Detection Equipment Handbook. Nancy R. Brletich et al. (Illus.). 482p. 1995. pap. text ed. 299.95 (*1-888727-00-4*, HB-95-02) CBIAC.

Worldwide Chronology of Fifty-Three Prehistoric Inventions. John Troeng. (Acta Archaeologica Lundensia Ser.: Vol. 8.0, No. 21). 311p. (Orig.). 1993. pap. 52.50 (*91-22-01569-8*) Coronet Bks.

***Worldwide Competition in Cellular Communications.** 94p. 1994. 995.00 (*0-614-18368-5*, IGIC-18) Info Gatekeepers.

***Worldwide Cost Comparisons.** 1997. write for info. (*0-614-25445-0*) Econ Intel.

Worldwide Crafts, 4 vols., Set. Chris Deshpande & Iain Macleod-Brudenell. (Illus.). 1994. lib. bdg. 85.08 (*0-8368-1150-X*) Gareth Stevens Inc.

Worldwide Creative Ojo Book. Diane Thomas. LC 79-88350. 1979. pap. 2.95 (*0-918126-06-1*) Hunter Ariz.

Worldwide Cruise Ships, & Inland & Coastal Waterways Entertainment Vessels Vol. 4: Foreign & U. S. A. Companies. Compiled by James L. Pelletier. 42p. 1997. 45.00 (*0-9644915-5-9*) Marine Techn.

***Worldwide Cruises & Ports of Call 1998.** Fodors Travel. 1997. pap. 19.50 (*0-679-03547-8*) Fodors Travel.

***Worldwide Cruises & Ports of Call '97.** 1996. pap. 19.50 (*0-614-20480-1*) Fodors Travel.

Worldwide Directory of Securities Lending & Repo 1995/96. 200.00 (*0-614-17841-X*, Pub. by Euromoney UK) Am Educ Systs.

***Worldwide Electric Vehicle Directory.** 8th ed. Philip Terpstra. (Illus.). 60p. 1996. pap. 12.00 (*1-883063-08-6*) Spirit Pub Hl.

Worldwide Electronic Messaging Market Strategies & Issues: Technologies Interact & Complete in a Dynamic World Environment. 305p. 1992. 995.00 (*1-56753-001-X*) Frost & Sullivan.

Worldwide Endoscopy Sourcebook. George Cristino. Ed. by Donna M. Cristino. 400p. (C). 1995. text ed. 245.00 (*1-886974-07-1*) Inst Knowledge.

Worldwide Expert Systems Activities & Trends. Ed. by Jay Liebowitz. LC 94-4690. (Illus.). 178p. (C). 1994. 48.00 (*1-882345-02-9*) Cognizant Comm.

Worldwide Family History. Noel Currer-Briggs. 200p. 1982. 32.50 (*0-7100-0934-8*, RKP) Routledge.

Worldwide Financial Reporting & Audit Requirements: A Peat Marwick Inventory. Peat Marwick International Staff. 258p. write for info. (*0-318-57848-4*) Peat Marwick.

Worldwide Foundation Directory. Ed. by Saur, K. G., Staff. 440p. 1996. 225.00 (*3-598-11315-3*) K G Saur.

Worldwide Franchise Directory. Ed. by Susan B. Martin. 1300p. 1991. 129.50 (*0-8103-7805-1*, 100824-99854); pap. 129.50 (*0-685-50197-3*, 100824-M99348) Gale.

Worldwide Government Directory 1991. 1996. 140.00 (*0-8103-9958-X*) Gale.

Worldwide Government Directory 1991: With International Organizations. 7th ed. Ed. by Jonathan D. Hixon & Candace R. Coombs. LC 83-641103. 950p. (C). 1991. text ed. 325.00 (*0-9629283-0-5*); pap. text ed. 275.00 (*0-9629283-1-3*) Wrldwide Govt.

Worldwide Government Directory 1992. 1996. 140.00 (*0-8103-9978-4*) Gale.

Worldwide Government Directory, 1992. 1000p. 1992. 325.00 (*0-9629283-2-1*, 101178) Wrldwide Govt.

Worldwide Government Directory, 1993. 1993. 347.00 (*0-9629283-5-6*) Wrldwide Govt.

Worldwide Government Directory 1994. 1994. 347.00 (*0-9629283-7-2*) Wrldwide Govt.

Worldwide Government Directory 1995. 95th ed. Ed. by Ken Gause et al. LC 93-641103. 1477p. 1995. 347.00 (*1-886994-00-5*) Gale.

Worldwide Government Directory 1996. 96th ed. 1996. 347.00 (*1-886994-03-X*) Gale.

Worldwide Guide to Accommodations. 1991. 12.95 (*0-945332-29-7*) Agora Inc MD.

Worldwide Guide to Beneficial Animals Used for Pest Control Purposes. W. T. Thomson. 91p. 1992. pap. text ed. 16.50 (*0-913702-55-2*) Thomson Pubns.

Worldwide Guide to Cheap Airfares: How to Travel the World Without Breaking the Bank. 6th rev. ed. Michael W. McColl. LC 94-77556. (Illus.). 250p. 1996. pap. 14.95 (*0-9633512-3-0*) Insider Pubns.

Worldwide Guide to Equivalent Irons & Steels, Mat.DB Database: Version 1.0 or higher (7.5 MB) 3rd ed. 1992. disk 369.00 (*0-614-03598-8*, 7446U) ASM Intl.

Worldwide Guide to Equivalent Irons & Steels, Microsoft Excel Version 4.0. 3rd ed. 1992. disk 369.00 (*0-614-03599-6*, 7467U) ASM Intl.

Worldwide Guide to Equivalent Nonferrous Metals & Alloys. 2nd ed. 466p. 1987. 173.00 (*0-87170-306-8*, 6261) ASM.

Worldwide Guide to Equivalent Nonferrous Metals & Alloys. 3rd rev. ed. Ed. by W. Mack. 500p. 1995. 180.00 (*0-87170-540-0*, 6331) ASM.

Worldwide Guide to Taxation of Financial Instruments. 1996. 350.00 (*0-614-17018-4*, Pub. by IBC Finan Pubng UK) IBC Pubns.

Worldwide Healthcare Directory. 500p. 1994. 510.00 (*0-86338-467-6*, Pub. by Euromonitor Pubns UK) Gale.

Worldwide Inflation: Theory & Recent Experience. Ed. by Lawrence B. Krause & Walter S. Salant. LC 76-51580. 686p. 1976. 39.95 (*0-8157-5030-7*); pap. 18.95 (*0-8157-5029-3*) Brookings.

Worldwide Intelligent Systems: Approaches to Telecommunications & Network Management. David S. Prerau & Janet Liebowitz. LC 94-77523. (Frontiers in Artificial Intelligence & Applications Ser.: Vol. 24). 279p. (gr. 12). 1994. 75.00 (*90-5199-183-5*) IOS Press.

Worldwide Interesting People: 162 History Makers of African Descent. George L. Lee. LC 91-50939. (Illus.). 144p. (J). 1992. lib. bdg. 23.95 (*0-89950-670-4*) McFarland & Co.

Worldwide Investor: Risks, Rewards & Opportunities for the Astute Investor. William J. Corney & Leonard E. Goodall. 250p. 1991. 27.50 (*1-55738-205-0*) Irwin Prof Pubng.

***Worldwide Laws of Life: 200 Eternal Spiritual Principles.** John M. Templeton. LC 96-51495. 400p. 1997. 24.95 (*0-8264-1018-9*) Continuum.

Worldwide Loss of Cropland. Lester R. Brown. 1978. pap. write for info. (*0-318-70406-4*) Worldwatch Inst.

Worldwide Marine: Answers to Combat Questions. W. J. Davis. 167p. 1987. pap. 11.00 (*1-885541-05-8*) Marine Bks.

Worldwide Medical Applications of Shape Memory Alloy Implants & Instrumentation. Yuri N. Zhuk. (Illus.). 56p. (C). 1997. text ed. 625.00 (*1-886974-11-X*) Inst Knowledge.

Worldwide Military Threats: Implications for U. S. Forces. (Illus.). 208p. (Orig.). (C). 1992. pap. text ed. 40.00 (*0-941375-66-8*) DIANE Pub.

Worldwide Mission Stories for Young People. J. Lawrence Driskill. (Illus.). 131p. (J). (gr. 4-9). 1996. pap. 19.95 (*0-932727-85-9*) Hope Pub Hse.

Worldwide NBC Mask Handbook. Nancy R. Brletich et al. (Illus.). 433p. 1992. pap. text ed. 299.95 (*1-888727-01-2*, HB-92-01) CBIAC.

Worldwide Perspective: Understanding God's Purposes in the World from Genesis to Revelation. Ed. by Meg Crossman. LC 95-7841. 1995. ring bd. 24.95 (*0-87808-765-6*) William Carey Lib.

Worldwide Petroleum Economics, 6. David Fox. (Worldwide Petroleum Economics Ser.). (Illus.). 2500p. 1995. 4,300.00 (*1-870945-56-5*, Pub. by Oilfld Pubns Ltd UK) Am Educ Systs.

Worldwide Petroleum Economics: Asia-Pacific, Vol. 6. David Fox. (Worldwide Petroleum Economics Ser.). (Illus.). 416p. 1995. 995.00 (*1-870945-55-7*, Pub. by Oilfld Pubns Ltd UK) Am Educ Systs.

Worldwide Petroleum Economics: Europe, Vol. 1. David Fox. (Worldwide Petroleum Economics Ser.). (Illus.). 416p. 1995. 995.00 (*1-870945-50-6*, Pub. by Oilfld Pubns Ltd UK) Am Educ Systs.

Worldwide Petroleum Economics: North Africa, Vol. 2. David Fox. (Worldwide Petroleum Economics Ser.). (Illus.). 416p. 1995. 1,095.00 (*1-870945-52-2*, Pub. by Oilfld Pubns Ltd UK) Am Educ Systs.

Worldwide Petroleum Economics: South Africa, Vol. 3. David Fox. (Worldwide Petroleum Economics Ser.). (Illus.). 416p. 1995. 850.00 (*1-870945-51-4*, Pub. by Oilfld Pubns Ltd UK) Am Educ Systs.

Worldwide Petroleum Economics: The Americas, Vol. 4. David Fox. (Worldwide Petroleum Economics Ser.). (Illus.). 416p. 1995. 895.00 (*1-870945-53-0*, Pub. by Oilfld Pubns Ltd UK) Am Educ Systs.

Worldwide Petroleum Economics: The Middle East. David Fox. (Worldwide Petroleum Economics Ser.). (Illus.). 416p. 1995. 795.00 (*1-870945-54-9*, Pub. by Oilfld Pubns Ltd UK) Am Educ Systs.

Worldwide Photovoltaics. Business Communications Co., Inc. Staff. 207p. 1988. pap. 1,950.00 (*0-89336-512-2*, E-038R) BCC.

Worldwide Pirate Radio Logbook 1993. Andrew Yoder. 1992. pap. text ed. 10.00 (*0-9635842-0-0*) Snallygaster.

Worldwide Practical Petroleum Reservoir Engineering Methods. 2nd ed. H. C. Slider. LC 83-4067. 848p. 1983. 125.95 (*0-87814-234-7*, P4334) PennWell Bks.

Worldwide Publishing, Inc. A Microcomputer Applications Simulation. Rosemary T. Fruehling & Constance K. Weaver. (C). 1991. teacher ed. 7.10 (*1-56118-098-X*); pap. text ed. 16.95 (*1-56118-099-8*) Paradigm MN.

Worldwide Resort Timesharing Industry: 1992. 56p. 1992. 75.00 (*0-614-04633-5*, 21300) ARDA.

Worldwide Restrictions on Advertising: An Outline of Principles, Problems & Solutions. Robert Bruce et al. 65p. 1986. 70.00 (*0-317-01165-0*) Intl Advertising Assn.

Worldwide Riches Opportunities, 2 vols., Set. 600p. 1996. 65.00 (*0-317-55735-1*) B Klein Pubns.

Worldwide Riches Opportunities, Vol. 1. 8th ed. Tyler G. Hicks. 280p. 1996. pap. 25.00 (*1-56150-160-3*) Intl Wealth.

***Worldwide Riches Opportunities, Vol. 1.** 9th ed. Tyler G. Hicks. 280p. 1998. pap. 25.00 (*1-56150-210-3*) Intl Wealth.

Worldwide Riches Opportunities, Vol. 2. 8th ed. Tyler G. Hicks. 280p. 1996. pap. 25.00 (*1-56150-161-1*) Intl Wealth.

***Worldwide Riches Opportunities, Vol. 2.** 9th ed. Tyler G. Hicks. 280p. 1998. pap. 25.00 (*1-56150-211-1*) Intl Wealth.

***Worldwide Riding Vacations.** 204p. (Orig.). 1996. pap. 14.00 (*0-9653558-0-2*) Compleat Trvllr.

Worldwide Science & Technology Advice to the Highest Levels of Governments. Ed. by William T. Golden. 430p. (C). 1994. pap. 25.95 (*0-08-040407-3*) Transaction Pubs.

Worldwide Secrets for Staying Young. Paavo Airola. 206p. 1984. pap. 6.95 (*0-932090-12-5*) Health Plus.

Worldwide Ship & Boat Repair Facilities Vol. 1: Shipyards, Repair Yards & Dry Docks (Foreign & U. S. A. Companies) Compiled by James L. Pelletier. 230p. 1997. 75.00 (*0-9644915-2-4*) Marine Techn.

Worldwide Sourdoughs from Your Bread Machine. Donna R. German & Ed Wood. (Illus.). 176p. (Orig.). 1994. pap. 8.95 (*1-55867-095-5*, Nitty Gritty Ckbks) Bristol Pub Ent CA.

***Worldwide Space - a Travel Handbook.** (Travel/Military Ser.). 244p. 1996. 16.00 (*1-881341-09-7*) Two-Ten-Four.

Worldwide Space - a Travel Handbook. 7th ed. (Travel Ser.). (Illus.). 248p. 1994. 14.00 (*1-881341-05-4*) Two-Ten-Four.

Worldwide State of the Family: Reports & Observations Prepared for the 6th International Congress of Professors World Peace Academy. Ed. by Gordon L. Anderson. LC 96-18496. 222p. (Orig.). 1995. pap. 19.95 (*1-885118-00-7*) Prof World Peace.

Worldwide Student Guide for Studying in America: How to Get a Degree from An American College or University - No Matter Where You Live in the World. Michael R. Huddleston. LC 94-96831. 150p. (Orig.). (YA). (gr. 9 up). 1995. pap. text ed. 29.95 (*0-9644111-9-9*) Intl Career Cnslts. Students - have you ever thought about going to

W

college or a university in America? Would obtaining a graduate degree & studying in the United States be a life-long dream of yours? Do you know how to choose a major or prepare for a high quality career? What do you want out of life - success, happiness, adventure, money? Difficult questions, right? Important questions no matter whether you are an American student or an aspiring international student. Only when you have answered these questions for yourself will you be able to choose a school or program of study that is right for you. With the help of Dr. Huddleston's THE WORLDWIDE STUDENT GUIDE FOR STUDYING IN AMERICA, your questions regarding the complex task of getting a degree from an American college or university will be answered in twenty chapters of solid, practical advice. You will be surprised how much useful information is packed into this book. Step-by-step ACTIONS are explained in helpful ways relating to college entrances tests, TOEFL, choosing a major, selecting a good career, finding the right college, financing your dream, institutional requirements - even information concerning the Visa/I-20 process if you are an international student (& much, much more). Your future success & fulfillment of personal or family goals for higher education are fully discussed, researched & documented in this book. Also, several chapters are targeted toward career development & job-getting activities. THE WORLDWIDE STUDENT GUIDE FOR STUDYING IN AMERICA is a logical, first step in assisting you in your quest for educational excellence & successful career development. Read this book, future graduate, & you will not be disappointed! Book Orders: Talking Textbooks, Inc., 610 A East Battlefield, #255, Springfield, MO 65807. Phone: 417-887-8847. Discount information: 25% for orders of 5 or more.
Publisher Provided Annotation.

Worldwide Telecom Services Markets: Comprehensive Forecast of Basic, Mobile, Private Line, & Value-Added Services by Five Geographic Regions. Market Intelligence Staff. 305p. (Orig.). 1992. 1,495.00 (*1-56753-068-0*) Frost & Sullivan.
Worldwide Telecommunications Guide for the Business Manager. Walter L. Vignault. LC 87-2002. (Telecommunications Ser.). 417p. 1987. text ed. 132.00 (*0-471-85828-5*) Wiley.
Worldwide Theory Testing. Raoul Naroll et al. LC 76-48559. (HRAF Manuals Ser.). 139p. 1976. pap. 15.00 (*0-87536-662-7*) HRAFP.
Worldwide Threats to National Security: Implications for U. S. Forces. 151p. (Orig.). (C). 1992. pap. text ed. 35.00 (*1-56806-017-3*) DIANE Pub.
Worldwide Tours: A Travel Agents Guide to Selling Tours. Doris S. Davidoff & Philip G. Davidoff. 80p. 1990. pap. text ed. 25.60 (*0-13-964891-7*) P-H.
Worldwide Trade Secrets Law. Ed. by Terrence F. MacLaren. LC 93-27434. (IP Ser.). 1993. ring bd. 425.00 (*0-87632-921-0*) Clark Boardman Callaghan.
Worldwide Trademark Transfers: Law & Practice. annuals United States Trademark Association Staff. Ed. by Richard J. Taylor & Susan B. Montgomery. LC 92-8085. (ENG, FRE, GER & SPA.). 1996. ring bd. 175.00 incl. disk (*0-87632-830-3*) Intl Trademark.
Worldwide Travel Information Contact Book. 2nd ed. Linda Irvin & Burkhard Herbote. 1992. 175.00 (*0-8103-8080-3*) Gale.
Worldwide Travel Information Contact Book: A Country by Country Listing of Approximately 25,000 Sources of Information. Ed. by Burkhard Herbote. (Illus.). 1990. 169.50 (*0-8103-7777-2*) Gale.
Worldwide Trends in Engine Coolants, Cooling System Materials & Testing. 208p. 1990. 19.00 (*1-56091-020-8*, SP811) Soc Auto Engineers.
Worldwide Trends in Youth Sport. Ed. by Paul DeKnop. LC 95-33994. (Illus.). 320p. 1996. text ed. 39.00 (*0-87322-729-8*, BDEK0729) Human Kinetics.
Worldwide Variation in Human Growth. 2nd ed. Phyllis B. Eveleth & James M. Tanner. (Illus.). 360p. (C). 1991. text ed. 150.00 (*0-521-35024-7*); pap. text ed. 52.95 (*0-521-35916-3*) Cambridge U Pr.
Worldwide VAT & Sales Tax: A Guide to Practice & Procedures in Sixty Countries. Ernst & Young Staff. 800p. 1996. text ed. 85.00 (*0-471-95573-6*) Wiley.
Worldwide Wonders. Tina Harris et al. (BrainBooster Ser.). (Illus.). 32p. (J). (gr. 3 up). 1986. 6.95 (*0-88679-461-7*) Educ Insights.
Worldwide Yellow Pages Markets, 1995. Karen Blakely et al. (Illus.). 286p. 1995. 7,000.00 (*0-88709-095-8*) Simba Info Inc.
Worlf Blachs: Self Help & Achievement. James H. Boykin. LC 79-53631. 193p. 1979. pap. 11.99 (*0-9603342-0-3*) Boykin.
Worm Club. Laurie Lawlor. Ed. by Lisa Clancy. 128p. (Orig.). 1994. pap. 2.99 (*0-671-78900-7*, Minstrel Bks) PB.
***Worm Dissection Explained.** Barbara S. Bergman. 22p. (YA). (gr. 10 up). 1988. wbk. ed., pap. 7.00 (*0-8064-1209-7*, B18) Bergwall.
Worm Farm. Charlie Morgan. 1962. pap. 6.00 (*0-914116-00-2*) Shields.
***Worm Gear Contact Temperatures.** G. H. Acker. (Technical Papers). 1944. pap. text ed. 30.00 (*1-55589-423-2*) AGMA.
Worm in the Bud. David W. Chambers. 242p. (C). 1979. 44.00 (*0-86828-296-0*, Pub. by Deakin Univ AT) St Mut.
Worm Ouroboros. E. R. Eddison. 1993. reprint ed. lib. bdg. 18.95 (*0-89968-396-7*, Lghtyr Pr) Buccaneer Bks.
Worm Queen: Memoirs of Santa Ynez Valley. Alicia Landon. LC 91-29351. (Illus.). 112p. (Orig.). 1992. pap. 9.95 (*1-56474-006-4*) Fithian Pr.
Worm That Never Dies. rev. ed. Melvin Mincey. Ed. by Ethel Abrims. Orig. Title: Ward Street. (Illus.). 223p. 1995. pap. 8.95 (*0-9637969-2-5*) Mincey Pub Hse.
Worm Whistle. Jan M. Lowry. (Illus.). (J). (gr. 2). 1994. pap. text ed. 12.95 (*1-881116-36-0*) Black Forest Pr.
Worm Whistle. Jan M. Lowry. (Illus.). 39p. (J). (ps-4). 1995. pap. 12.95 (*0-9646183-0-3*) J M Lowry.
***Worm World: A Somerville House Book.** Shar Levin. Ed. by Somerville House Staff. (Illus.). 64p. (Orig.). 1997. 14.95 (*0-8362-2890-1*) Andrews & McMeel.
***Wormhaven Gardening Book.** Gregory Jackson. LC 96-86580. (Illus.). 155p. (Orig.). (C). 1996. pap. 9.95 (*0-9649354-3-0*) M Chemnitz Pr.
***Wormholes: Essays & Occasional Writings.** John Fowles. 1997. 24.95 (*0-316-29090-4*) Little.
Wormology. Michael E. Ross. LC 94-42435. (Backyard Buddies Ser.). (Illus.). 48p. (J). (gr. 1-4). 1995. 18.95 (*0-87614-937-9*, Carolrhoda) Lerner Group.
Worms. Graham Coleman. (New Creepy Crawly Collection). (Illus.). (J). 1996. lib. bdg. 18.60 (*0-8368-1583-1*) Gareth Stevens Inc.
Worms. Lynn M. Stone. LC 95-16559. (J). 1995. write for info. (*1-55916-160-4*) Rourke Bk Co.
Worms Are Singing. Jerry Bumpus. 1979. 3.00 (*0-912824-22-0*) Vagabond Pr.
Worms, Cocoons, & Butterflies. Alyson E. Mihalenko. 1994. pap. 12.95 (*0-533-10825-X*) Vantage.
Worms Eat My Garbage. Mary Appelhof. LC 82-242012. (Illus.). (Orig.). 1982. pap. 9.95 (*0-942256-03-4*, Flower Pr) Flowerfield Ent.
Worms Eat My Garbage: How to Set up & Maintain a Worm Composting System. 2nd ed. Mary Appelhof. LC 82-242012. (Illus.). 110p. (Orig.). 1996. pap. 10.95 (*0-942256-10-7*) Flowerfield Ent.
Worms Eat Our Garbage: Classroom Activities for a Better Environment. Mary Appelhof et al. (Illus.). 232p. (Orig.). (J). (gr. 4 up). 1993. Wkbk. student ed. 21.95 (*0-942256-05-0*) Flowerfield Ent.
Worm's Eye View: Make Your Own Wildlife Refuge. Kipchak Johnson. (Lighter Look Bk.). (Illus.). 40p. (J). (gr. 2-6). 1991. lib. bdg. 15.40 (*1-878841-30-0*) Millbrook Pr.
Worm's Eye View: Make Your Own Wildlife Refuge. Kipchak Johnson. (Lighter Look Bk.). (Illus.). 40p. (J). (gr. 2-6). 1991. pap. 5.95 (*1-878841-42-4*) Millbrook Pr.
Worms for Winston: The Good News Kids Learn about Love. Dorothy K. Mock. (Good News Kids Ser.). (Illus.). 32p. (Orig.). (J). (ps-2). 1992. pap. 4.99 (*0-570-04716-1*, 56-1675) Concordia.
Worms in My Tea: And Other Mixed Blessings. Becky Freeman & Ruthie Arnold. LC 93-37622. 144p. 1994. pap. 9.99 (*0-8054-6143-4*, 4261-43) Broadman.
Worms to Wasps: An Illustrated Guide to Australia's Terrestrial Invertebrates. Mark S. Harvey & Alan L. Yen. (Illus.). 216p. 1990. pap. 24.95 (*0-19-553081-0*) OUP.
Worms Wiggle. David Pelham. (Illus.). (J). (ps-1). 1989. pap. 9.95 (*0-671-67218-5*, Litl Simon S&S) S&S Childrens.
Worms, Wonderful Worms. Kathie Atkinson. LC 93-28968. (J). 1994. 4.25 (*0-383-03788-3*) SRA McGraw.
Wormwood. Z. Brite. 256p. 1996. mass mkt. 5.50 (*0-440-21798-9*) Dell.
***Wormwood.** Terry Dowling. 253p. (Orig.). pap. 10.00 (*1-875346-02-3*, Pub. by Aphelion AT) Firebird Dist.
Wormwood. Kevin Siembieda & Truman Henry. Ed. by Alex Marciniszyn et al. (Rifts Dimension Bk.: No. 1). (Illus.). 160p. (Orig.). 1993. pap. 15.95 (*0-916211-59-2*, 809) Palladium Bks.
Wormwood. Ken A. Smith. LC 87-73049. 64p. (Orig.). 8800. pap. 12.95 (*1-85224-037-7*, Pub. by Bloodaxe Bks UK) Dufour.
Wormwood Regulars. Marvin Malone. 40p. (Orig.). 1986. pap. 4.00 (*0-935390-11-1*) Wormwood Bks & Mag.
Worn Earth. Paul Engle. LC 72-144738. (Yale Series of Younger Poets: No. 31). reprint ed. 18.00 (*0-404-53831-2*) AMS Pr.
Worn Path. Eudora Welty. (Classic Short Stories Ser.). (J). 1991. lib. bdg. 13.95 (*0-88682-471-0*) Creative Ed.
Woronin. (Phytopathological Classics Ser.). 32p. 1934. 15.00 (*0-89054-005-5*) Am Phytopathol Soc.
Worrell New Testament. rev. ed. A. S. Worrell. 432p. 1980. 12.95 (*0-88243-392-X*, 01-0392) Gospel Pub.
Worried about Crime: Constructive Approaches to Violence. Kit Kuperstock. LC 84-25150. 176p. (Orig.). 1985. pap. 7.99 (*0-8361-3385-4*) Herald Pr.
Worried Little Lamb. Valerie Guidoux. LC 93-27048. (Little Animal Adventures Ser.). (Illus.). 24p. (J). (ps-3). 1994. 6.99 (*0-89577-563-8*) Rdrs Dgst Yng Fam.
Worried Sick: Our Troubled Quest for Wellness. Arthur J. Barsky, III. LC 87-32508. 1988. 17.95 (*0-316-08255-4*) Little.
Worried Widow. large type ed. Gerald Hammond. 384p. 1989. 25.99 (*0-7089-1994-4*) Ulverscroft.
Worry. Concordia Publishing Staff. (Connections Ser.). 1994. pap. 3.99 (*0-570-09373-2*, 20-2470) Concordia.
***Worry, Vol. 5.** Upper Room Books Staff. (In Your Time of Ser.). 1997. pap. text ed. 19.75 (*0-8358-0750-9*) Upper Room Bks.
***Worry: When Life is More Scary Than It Should Be & What You Can Do About It.** Edward M. Hallowell. LC 97-8609. 1997. 26.00 (*0-679-44237-5*); audio 18.00 (*0-679-46058-6*) Pantheon.
Worry Bead Book. Michael Larsen. 1989. pap. 8.95 (*0-312-03455-5*) St Martin.
Worry Beads. Novel. Kay Sloan. LC 90-22655. 197p. 1991. 18.95 (*0-8071-1636-X*) La State U Pr.
Worry-Free RRSPs. Richard Birch. 144p. 1989. pap. 12.95 (*0-7737-5252-8*) Genl Dist Srvs.
Worry Girl: Stories from a Childhood. Andrea F. Loewenstein. LC 92-8021. 160p. (Orig.). 1992. pap. 8.95 (*1-56341-016-8*); lib. bdg. 18.95 (*1-56341-017-6*) Firebrand Bks.
Worry Machine. Rita Friedman & Elaine Weimann. (Fables from the Letter People Ser.). (Illus.). 30p. (J). (ps-1). 1989. lib. bdg. 12.95 (*0-89796-022-X*) New Dimens Educ.
Worry Stone. Marianna Dengler. LC 96-33837. (Illus.). 40p. (J). (gr. 1 up). 1996. lib. bdg. 14.95 (*0-87358-642-5*) Northland AZ.
Worry Warts. Morris Gleitzman. LC 92-22631. 176p. (J). (gr. 3-7). 1993. 12.95 (*0-15-299666-4*) HarBrace.
Worry Warts. Morris Gleitzman. LC 92-22631. 176p. (J). (gr. 3-7). 1995. pap. 5.00 (*0-15-200871-3*) HarBrace.
Worry Week. Anne Lindberg. (J). (gr. 3-7). 1988. pap. 2.95 (*0-380-70394-7*, Camelot) Avon.
Worrying: Perspectives on Theory, Assessment, & Treatment. Ed. by Graham C. Davey & Frank Tallis. LC 93-21368. (Clinical Psychology Ser.). 311p. 1994. text ed. 75.00 (*0-471-94114-X*) Wiley.
Worrying about Race 1985-1995: Reflections During a Troubled Time. Sanford Pinsker. LC 95-62173. viii, 144p. 1996. 18.50 (*0-87875-474-1*) Whitston Pub.
Worrywart's Companion: Twenty-One Ways to Soothe Yourself & Worry Smart. Beverly A. Potter. LC 97-2363. 128p. (Orig.). 1997. pap. 11.95 (*1-885171-15-3*) Wldcat Canyon.
Worse Than Death. large type ed. Thomas Bunn. LC 90-34618. 407p. 1990. reprint ed. lib. bdg. 19.95 (*1-56054-005-2*) Thorndike Pr.
***Worse Than He Says He Is: Or, White Girls Don't Bounce: My Walk on the Wild Side with Dennis Rodman.** Anicka B. Rodman. 1997. pap. 18.95 (*0-7871-1517-7*) Dove Audio.
Worse Than Rotten, Ralph. Jack Gantos. (Illus.). (J). (gr. k-3). 1982. pap. 6.95 (*0-395-32919-1*) HM.
Worse Than Slavery: Parchman Farm & the Ordeal of Jim Crow Justice. David M. Oshinsky. (Illus.). 336p. 1996. 25.00 (*0-684-82298-9*) Free Pr.
***Worse Than Slavery: Parchman Farm & the Ordeal of Jim Crow Justice.** David M. Oshinsky. 1997. pap. 12.00 (*0-684-83095-7*, Fireside) S&S Trade.
Worse Than the Disease: Pitfalls of Medical Progress. Diana B. Dutton. 544p. (C). 1992. pap. text ed. 22.95 (*0-521-39557-7*) Cambridge U Pr.
Worse Than the Worst. James Stevenson. LC 93-239. (Illus.). 32p. (J). (gr. k up). 1994. 14.00 (*0-688-12249-3*); lib. bdg. 13.93 (*0-688-12250-7*) Greenwillow.
Worse Than Willy! James Stevenson. LC 83-14201. (Illus.). 32p. (J). (gr. k-3). 1984. lib. bdg. 11.88 (*0-688-02597-8*) Greenwillow.
Worship. John E. Burkhart. LC 81-23116. 162p. (C). 1982. pap. 11.00 (*0-664-24409-2*, Westminster) Westminster John Knox.
Worship. Ed. by Jean Holm & John Bowker. LC 94-15088. (Themes in Religious Studies). 1994. 45.00 (*1-85567-110-7*); pap. 16.95 (*1-85567-111-5*) St Martin.
Worship. Ben Patterson. (Christian Basics Bible Studies). 64p. (Orig.). 1994. wbk. ed., pap. 4.99 (*0-8308-2008-6*, 2008) InterVarsity.
Worship. Evelyn Underhill. 264p. 1992. pap. 14.99 (*0-86347-047-5*, Pub. by Eagle Bks UK) Shaw Pubs.
Worship. John Woolman. (C). 1950. pap. 3.00 (*0-87574-051-0*) Pendle Hill.
***Worship: Acknowledging God in All of Life.** Navpress Publishing Staff. (Foundations for Christian Living Ser.). 1997. pap. text ed. 6.00 (*1-57683-007-1*) NavPress.
Worship: Adoration & Action. Ed. by D. A. Carson. LC 93-25994. (World Evangelical Fellowship Ser.). 256p. (C). 1993. pap. 14.99 (*0-8010-2584-2*) Baker Bks.
Worship: At the Margins Spirituality & Liturgy. Michael Downey. (Orig.). (C). 1994. pap. text ed. 13.95 (*1-56929-021-0*) Pastoral Pr.
Worship: Beyond Inculturation. Anscar J. Chupungco. (C). 1994. pap. text ed. 11.95 (*1-56929-018-0*) Pastoral Pr.
Worship: City, Church, & Renewal. John F. Baldovin. (Orig.). 1991. pap. 11.95 (*0-912405-78-3*) Pastoral Pr.
Worship: Culture & Theology. David N. Power. 284p. (Orig.). (C). 1991. pap. 11.95 (*0-912405-77-5*) Pastoral Pr.
Worship: Discovering What Scripture Says. Larry Sibley. (Fisherman Bible Studyguide Ser.). 80p. (Orig.). 1993. pap. 4.99 (*0-87788-911-2*) Shaw Pubs.
Worship: Initiation & the Churches. Leonel L. Mitchell. (Orig.). 1991. pap. 12.95 (*0-912405-84-8*) Pastoral Pr.
Worship: Our Gift to God. Cathi Trzeciak. (Concept Books for Children). (Illus.). 24p. (J). (gr. k-4). 1986. pap. 3.99 (*0-570-08531-4*, 56-1558) Concordia.
Worship: Prayers from the East. Bryan D. Spinks. 125p. (Orig.). (C). 1993. pap. text ed. 12.95 (*1-56929-000-8*) Pastoral Pr.
***Worship: Progress & Tradition.** Anscar J. Chupungco. 312p. 1995. pap. text ed. 12.95 (*1-56929-051-2*) Pastoral Pr.
Worship: Rediscovering the Missing Jewel. Ronald B. Allen & Gordon Borror. LC 82-2198. (Critical Concern Ser.). 200p. 1982. pap. 9.99 (*0-88070-140-4*, Multnomah Bks) Multnomah Pubs.
Worship: Reforming Tradition. Thomas J. Talley. 238p. (Orig.). 1990. pap. 11.95 (*0-912405-70-8*) Pastoral Pr.
Worship: Renewal to Practice. Mary Collins. 295p. (Orig.). 1987. 11.95 (*0-912405-32-5*) Pastoral Pr.
Worship: Searching for Language. Gail Ramshaw-Schmitt. 213p. (Orig.). 1988. pap. 11.95 (*0-912405-49-X*) Pastoral Pr.
***Worship: Stewardship of the Mysteries.** Frank C. Senn. 1997. pap. 14.95 (*1-56929-063-6*) Pastoral Pr.
Worship: The Christian's Highest Occupation. A. P. Gibbs. pap. 8.00 (*0-937396-57-5*) Walterick Pubs.
Worship: The Missing Jewel of the Evangelical Church. Aiden W. Tozer. (Heritage Ser.). 30p. 1979. pap. 1.49 (*0-87509-219-5*) Chr Pubns.
***Worship: Touching God.** Virgilio P. Elizondo & Timothy M. Matovina. 1997. 11.95 (*1-56929-050-4*) Pastoral Pr.
Worship: Unleashing the Supernatural Power of God in Your Life. Norvel Hayes. 128p. 1993. pap. 6.99 (*0-89274-628-9*, HH-628) Harrison Hse.
***Worship: Wedding to Marriage.** German Martinez. 177p. 1993. pap. 12.95 (*1-56929-009-1*) Pastoral Pr.
Worship: Wonderful & Sacred Mystery. Kenneth W. Stevenson. 232p. (Orig.). (C). 1992. pap. text ed. 14.95 (*0-912405-90-2*) Pastoral Pr.
Worship & Conflict under Colonial Rule: A South Indian Case. Arjun Appadurai. LC 80-24508. (Cambridge South Asian Studies: No. 27). 276p. reprint ed. pap. 78.70 (*0-318-34755-5*, 2031614) Bks Demand.
Worship & Ethics: Lutherans & Anglicans in Dialogue. Alan M. Suggate. LC 95-42323. (Theologische Bibliothek Toepelmann Ser.: Vol. 70). xv, 295p. (C). 1996. lib. bdg. 152.30 (*3-11-014377-1*) De Gruyter.
Worship & Freedom: A Black American Church in Zambia. Walton R. Johnson. LC 78-317228. 172p. reprint ed. pap. 49.10 (*0-8357-6959-3*, 2039018) Bks Demand.
Worship & Love of God. Emanuel Swedenborg et al. LC 96-25694. 1997. 16.95 (*0-87785-297-9*) Swedenborg.
Worship & Music Ministry. Rick Ryan & Dave Newton. Ed. by Chuck Smith. (Calvary Basics Ser.). 96p. (Orig.). 1995. pap. 3.50 (*0-936728-63-9*) Word for Today.
Worship & Politics. Rafael Avila. LC 81-38356. 144p. (Orig.). reprint ed. pap. 41.10 (*0-8357-2664-9*, 2040200) Bks Demand.
Worship & Program Helps, 1996: Journeying with Christ. Ed. by Peter Judd & Leonard M. Young. 124p. (Orig.). 1996. pap. 16.00 (*0-8309-0709-2*) Herald Hse.
Worship & Reformed Theology: The Liturgical Lessons of Mercersburg. Jack M. Maxwell. LC 75-45492. (Pittsburgh Theological Monographs: No. 10). 1976. pap. 12.00 (*0-915138-12-3*) Pickwick.
Worship & Secular Man: An Essay on the Liturgical Nature of Man. Raimundo Panikkar. LC 72-93339. 119p. reprint ed. pap. 34.00 (*0-317-26670-5*, 2025123) Bks Demand.
***Worship & Spirituality.** 2nd rev. ed. Don E. Saliers. 102p. 1996. pap. 14.95 (*1-878009-27-3*, 273, OSL Pubns) Order St Luke Pubns.
***Worship & Theology in England, Vols. 1-3.** Horton Davies. pap. 150.00 (*0-8028-0890-5*) Eerdmans.
Worship & Theology in England Vol. 1: From Cranmer to Baxter 1534-1690. Horton Davies. 1108p. 1996. pap. 50.00 (*0-8028-0891-3*) Eerdmans.
Worship & Theology in England Vol. 2: From Watts & Wesley to Martineau 1690-1900. Horton Davies. 762p. 1996. pap. 50.00 (*0-8028-0892-1*) Eerdmans.
Worship & Theology in England Vol. 3: The Ecumenical Century, 1900 to the Present. Horton Davies. 799p. 1996. pap. 50.00 (*0-8028-0893-X*) Eerdmans.
Worship & Work. 3rd rev. ed. Colman J. Barry. LC 80-10753. (Illus.). 606p. (Orig.). 1994. pap. 24.95 (*0-8146-1123-0*) Liturgical Pr.
Worship As Body Language: Introduction to Christian Worship: An African Orientation. Elochukwu E. Uzukwu. LC 96-51705. 384p. (Orig.). 1997. pap. 29.95 (*0-8146-6151-3*, Pueblo Bks) Liturgical Pr.
Worship As David Lived It. Judson Cornwall. 196p. 1991. pap. 8.99 (*1-56043-700-6*) Destiny Image.
Worship As Jesus Taught It. Judson Cornwall. 240p. (Orig.). 1987. pap. 7.95 (*0-932081-16-9*) Victory Hse.
Worship As Pastoral Care. rev. ed. William H. Willimon. LC 79-894. 1982. 15.95 (*0-687-46388-2*) Abingdon.
Worship as Theology: Foretaste of Glory Divine. Don E. Saliers. Ed. by Ulrike Guthrie. LC 94-17519. 256p. (Orig.). 1994. pap. 15.95 (*0-687-14693-3*) Abingdon.
Worship Beyond the Usual: An Echo of the Voice of John W. Carlton. Ed. by John Durham. 134p. 1993. text ed. 11.95 (*0-86554-413-1*, MUP-H335) Mercer Univ Pr.
Worship Celebrations for Youth. John Brown. 1980. pap. 6.50 (*0-8170-0866-7*) Judson.
Worship Come to Its Senses. Don E. Saliers. 96p. (Orig.). 1996. pap. 11.95 (*0-687-01458-1*) Abingdon.
***Worship, Community & the Triune God of Grace.** James B. Torrance. LC 97-8456. 128p. 1997. pap. 12.99 (*0-8308-1895-2*, 1895) InterVarsity.
Worship Directory with Radio Callsigns & Frequencies, Vol. 1: U. S., Canada, Great Britain. James T. Pogue. 90p. 1990. 14.95 (*0-936653-24-8*) Tiare Pubns.
***Worship Drama Library.** 89p. 1993. 17.99 (*0-8341-9486-4*) Lillenas.
Worship Drama Library, Vol. 1. Mike Gray & Colleen Gray. 1993. 17.99 (*0-685-72843-9*, MP-689) Lillenas.
***Worship Drama Library, Vol. 2.** 88p. 1993. 17.99 (*0-8341-9487-2*) Lillenas.
Worship Drama Library, Vol. 2. Mike Gray & Colleen Gray. 1993. 17.99 (*0-685-72844-7*, MP-690) Lillenas.
Worship Drama Library, Vol. 3. Kristin Witt. 1993. 17.99 (*0-685-72845-5*, MP-691) Lillenas.
Worship Drama Library, Vol. 4. Brad Kindall. 1993. 17.99 (*0-685-72846-3*, MP-692) Lillenas.
Worship Drama Library, Vol. 5. Jerry Cohagan. 1993. 17.99 (*0-685-72847-1*, MP-693) Lillenas.
Worship Drama Library, Vol. 6. Mike Gray & Colleen Gray. 1994. 17.99 (*0-8341-9055-9*, MP-706) Lillenas.

An Asterisk (*) at the beginning of an entry indicates that the title is appearing in BIP for the first time.

Worship Drama Library, Vol. 8. Mike Gray & Colleen Gray. 1994. 17.99 (*0-8341-9103-2*, MP-708) Lillenas.

Worship Drama Library, Vol. 9. Lawrence G. Enscoe & Annie Enscoe. 1994. 17.99 (*0-8341-9134-2*, MP-709) Lillenas.

***Worship Drama Library, Vol. 12.** 1995. 17.99 (*0-8341-9331-0*) Lillenas.

***Worship Drama Library, Vol. 13.** 1995. 17.99 (*0-8341-9332-9*) Lillenas.

***Worship Drama Library, Vol. 14.** 1995. 17.99 (*0-8341-9333-7*) Lillenas.

***Worship Drama Library, Vol. 15.** 1996. 17.99 (*0-8341-9441-4*) Lillenas.

Worship Drama Library Vol. 7: 13 Sketches for Enhancing Worship, Vol. 7. Jim Custer & Bob Hoose. 1994. 17.99 (*0-8341-9102-4*, MP-707) Lillenas.

Worship Drama Library Vol. 10: 12 Sketches for Enhancing Worship. Mike Gray & Colleen Gray. 1995. 17.99 (*0-8341-9264-0*, MP-710) Lillenas.

Worship Drama Library Vol. 11: 12 Sketches for Enhancing Worship. Jerry Cohagan. 1995. 17.99 (*0-8341-9268-3*, MP-711) Lillenas.

Worship Evangelism: Inviting Unbelievers into the Presence of God. Sally Morgenthaler. 224p. 1995. 19.99 (*0-310-48561-4*) Zondervan.

Worship God. Watchman Nee. Ed. by Stephen Kaung & Herbert L. Fader. 107p. (Orig.). 1990. pap. 4.50 (*0-935008-73-X*) Christian Fellow Pubs.

Worship His Majesty. Ed. by Larry Reftery. 32p. 1981. pap. 0.75 (*0-88144-056-6*) Christian Pub.

Worship Hymnal. LC 74-152488. 671p. 1971. 17.50 (*0-919797-30-X*) Kindred Prods.

***Worship Ideas for Youth Ministry.** Ed. by Amy Simpson. LC 97-7449. 128p. (Orig.). 1997. pap. 14.99 (*0-7644-2002-X*) Group Pub.

Worship in Diverse Cultures. Peter A. Judd. LC 95-7947. (Blue Valley Stake Lectures). 134p. (Orig.). 1995. pap. text ed. 8.50 (*0-8309-0706-8*) Herald Hse.

Worship in Early Christianity. Ed. by Everett Ferguson. LC 92-42826. (Studies in Early Christianity: Vol. 15). 392p. 1993. text ed. 70.00 (*0-8153-1075-7*) Garland.

***Worship in Song.** Jimmy Jurden. 194p. (Orig.). 1987. pap. 8.95 (*0-940999-24-2*, C-2135) Star Bible.

Worship in Song: A Friends Hymnal. 400p. 1996. 20.00 (*1-888305-01-0*) Friends Genl Conf.

Worship in Spirit & Truth. John M. Frame. 180p. 1996. pap. 9.99 (*0-87552-242-4*, Pub. by Evangelical Pr) Presby & Reformed.

Worship in the Early Church. rev. ed. Ralph P. Martin. 144p. 1975. reprint ed. pap. 11.00 (*0-8028-1613-4*) Eerdmans.

Worship in the Lutheran Congregation: The '90s & Beyond. Ed. by Robert Rosin. (Monograph Series - Symposium Papers: No. I). (Orig.). 1992. pap. 5.00 (*0-911770-58-5*) Concordia Seminary.

Worship in the Primary School. Elaine McCreery. (Roehampton Teaching Studies). 144p. 1993. pap. 29.00 (*1-85346-233-0*, Pub. by D Fulton UK) Taylor & Francis.

Worship in Transition: The Liturgical Movement in the Twentieth Century. John R. Fenwick & Bryan D. Spinks. LC 95-8724. 224p. 1995. pap. text ed. 17.95 (*0-8264-0827-3*) Continuum.

Worship Inside Out. Handt Hanson. 1995. pap. 12.95 (*0-933173-65-2*) Chging Church Forum.

Worship is a Verb: Eight Principles for Transforming Worship. 2nd ed. Robert E. Webber. 240p. 1996. reprint ed. pap. 12.95 (*1-56563-242-7*) Hendrickson MA.

***Worship Is...What?!** Tom Kraeuter. 109p. (Orig.). 1996. pap. 8.99 (*1-883002-38-9*) Emerald WA.

***Worship Leader: A Divine Call.** Diane L. Sykes. 80p. (Orig.). 1996. pap. write for info. (*1-889474-00-2*) D L Sykes.

Worship Now, Bk. 2. deluxe ed. Church of Scotland, Committee on Public Worship & Aids to Devotion. 1989. 12.95 (*0-686-75148-5*) Outlook.

Worship Now, Bk. 11. Duncan B. Forrester et al. 248p. 1993. Spiral bdg. spiral bd. 45.00 (*0-7152-0633-8*, Pub. by St Andrew UK) St Mut.

Worship of God: Some Theological, Pastoral & Practical Reflections. Ralph P. Martin. 237p. (Orig.). 1982. pap. 14.00 (*0-8028-1934-6*) Eerdmans.

Worship of Nature. James G. Frazer. 700p. 1996. pap. 49. 95 (*1-56459-532-3*) Kessinger Pub.

Worship of Nature. James G. Frazer. LC 73-21271. (Gifford Lectures: 1924-25). reprint ed. 45.00 (*0-404-11427-X*) AMS Pr.

Worship of Priapus. Richard P. Knight. LC 73-76829. (Illus.). 300p. 1974. reprint ed. 25.00 (*0-8216-0207-1*, Univ Bks) Carol Pub Group.

Worship of the American Puritans, 1629-1730. Horton Davies. LC 90-47784. 304p. (C). 1990. text ed. 49.95 (*0-8204-1222-8*) P Lang Pubng.

Worship of the Frontier. Henry R. Rust. (Worship Through the Centuries Ser.). 1990. pap. 5.95 (*0-940754-82-7*, 3513) Ed Ministries.

Worship of the Heart: A Study of Maimonides' Philosophy of Religion. Ehud Benor. LC 94-39855. (SUNY Series in Jewish Philosophy). 262p. (C). 1995. text ed. 49.50 (*0-7914-2635-1*); pap. text ed. 19.95 (*0-7914-2636-X*) State U NY Pr.

Worship of the Scottish Reformed Church, 1550-1638: The Hastie Lectures in the University of Glasgow, 1930. William McMillan. LC 83-45585. reprint ed. 35.00 (*0-404-19903-8*) AMS Pr.

Worship of the Serpent. John B. Deane. 391p. 1970. reprint ed. spiral bd. 17.50 (*0-7873-0279-1*) Hlth Research.

Worship of the Serpent: Traced Throughout the World & Its Ancient Traditions. John B. Deane. 1991. lib. bdg. 88.95 (*0-8490-4989-X*) Gordon Pr.

Worship of the Serpent Traced Throughout the World & Its Traditions Referred to the Events in Paradise (1830) John B. Deane. 405p. 1996. pap. 29.95 (*1-56459-898-5*) Kessinger Pub.

Worship of the Visible Spectrum. Judith Skillman. LC 87-23275. 80p. 1988. 14.95 (*0-932576-55-9*); pap. 7.95 (*0-932576-56-7*) Breitenbush Bks.

Worship Old & New. rev. ed. Robert E. Webber. 272p. 1994. 18.99 (*0-310-47990-8*) Zondervan.

Worship Planbook. Paul E. Engle. (Orig.). 1981. pap. 3.95 (*0-934688-03-6*) Great Comm Pubns.

Worship Resources for Christian Congregations: A Symphony for the Senses. Don W. Nixon. 320p. (Orig.). 1995. pap. 18.95 (*1-880837-91-9*) Smyth & Helwys.

Worship Resources for Youth. Jerry O. Cok. 133p. (Orig.). 1983. pap. 12.00 (*0-914527-25-8*) C-Four Res.

Worship Resources for Youth. Jerry O. Cook. 132p. 1983. pap. 12.95 (*0-87178-948-5*) Brethren.

Worship Service for Erev Shabbat...in Russian. Task Force of Soviet Jewry of the UAHC Staff. 64p. (RUS.). 1980. pap. 4.00 (*0-8074-0247-8*, 381500) UAHC.

Worship Services for Youth Groups: 12 Complete, Thematic & Seasonal Services. Jim Marian. LC 96-20118. 144p. 1996. pap. 14.99 (*0-310-20782-7*) Youth Spec.

Worship Space Sound Systems: A Guide to Better Sound in Your Parish. George R. Riley. (Orig.). 1994. pap. text ed. 10.95 (*1-56929-017-2*) Pastoral Pr.

***Worship the King.** 1988. pap. 1.20 (*0-8341-9256-X*) Lillenas.

Worship, Theology & Ministry in the Early Church: Essays in Honor of R. P. Martin. Ed. by M. Wilkins & T. Paige. (Journal for the Study of the New Testament, Supplement Ser.: No. 87). 335p. 1992. 75.00 (*1-85075-417-9*, Pub. by Sheffield Acad UK) CUP Services.

Worship Through the Seasons. Mary I. Hock. LC 86-43231. 112p. (Orig.). 1987. pap. 8.95 (*0-89390-104-0*) Resource Pubns.

Worship Time Music: Junior New Testatment. (J). 1995. 10.99 (*1-55513-227-8*) Cook.

Worship Time Music Book: Junior Old Testament. (J). 1995. 10.99 (*1-55513-769-5*) Cook.

***Worship with One Accord: Where Liturgy & Ecumenism Embrace.** Geoffrey Wainwright. LC 96-53170. 288p. 1997. 35.00 (*0-19-511610-0*) OUP.

Worship Wordbook: A Practical Handbook for the Lutheran Book of Worship. Ralph R. Van Loon & S. Anita Stauffer. LC 95-34528. 1995. 20.95 (*0-8066-0548-0*, 3-1610) Augsburg Fortress.

Worship Workbook for the Gospels: Cycle B. Robert D. Ingram. (Illus.). (Orig.). 1996. pap. 29.95 (*0-7880-0809-9*) CSS OH.

Worshipbook: Services. 1970. 10.00 (*0-664-21287-5*, Westminster) Westminster John Knox.

Worshipbook: Services & Hymns. 688p. 1972. 12.95 (*0-664-10108-9*, Westminster) Westminster John Knox.

Worshipful Company of Fletchers: Poems. James Tate. LC 94-9821. 1994. 20.00 (*0-88001-380-X*) Ecco Pr.

Worshipful Company of Fletchers: Poems. James Tate. LC 94-9821. 96p. 1995. pap. 13.00 (*0-88001-431-8*) Ecco Pr.

Worshipful Master's Assistant. 15.00 (*0-685-19506-6*) Powner.

Worshipful Master's Assistant. rev. ed. Robert Macoy. xiv, 253p. 1993. reprint ed. 17.95 (*0-88053-008-1*, M-026) Macoy Pub.

Worshipping Athena: Panathenaia & Parthenon. Ed. by Jenifer Neils. LC 96-8274. (Wisconsin Studies in Classics). (Illus.). 262p. (Orig.). 1996. 55.00 (*0-299-15110-7*) U of Wis Pr.

Worshipping Athena: Panathenaia & Parthenon. Ed. by Jenifer Neils. LC 96-8274. (Wisconsin Studies in Classics). (Illus.). 262p. (Orig.). 1996. pap. 22.95 (*0-299-15114-X*) U of Wis Pr.

Worshipping the Unknown God. Rod Parsley. 31p. 1986. pap. 2.75 (*0-88144-070-1*) Christian Pub.

Worshipping Together. Church of Scotland Panel on Worship. 208p. (C). 1992. pap. 45.00 (*0-86153-128-0*, Pub. by St Andrew UK) St Mut.

Worshipping Well: A Mass Guide for Planners & Participants. Lawrence E. Mick. LC 96-29593. 120p. (Orig.). 1997. pap. text ed. 9.95 (*0-8146-2423-5*, Liturg Pr Bks) Liturgical Pr.

Worshipping with United Methodists: A Guide for Pastors & Leaders. Hoyt L. Hickman. 192p. (Orig.). 1996. pap. 12.95 (*0-687-00782-8*) Abingdon.

Worshipping Women: Re-Forming God's People for Praise. Heather M. Elkins. LC 94-28767. 144p. (Orig.). 1994. pap. 14.95 (*0-687-46402-1*) Abingdon.

Worst Baby Name Book. Bob Glickman. 128p. (Orig.). 1990. pap. 6.95 (*0-8362-1812-4*) Andrews & McMeel.

Worst Baseball Pitchers of All Time: Bad Luck, Bad Arms, Bad Teams & Just Plain Bad. Alan S. Kaufman & James C. Kaufman. LC 92-50894. (Illus.). 232p. 1993. pap. 23.95 (*0-89950-824-3*) McFarland & Co.

Worst Baseball Pitchers of All Time: Bad Luck, Bad Arms, Bad Teams & Just Plain Bad. Alan S. Kaufman & James C. Kaufman. LC 94-48362. 1995. pap. 13.95 (*0-8065-1653-4*, Citadel Pr) Carol Pub Group.

Worst-Case Performance of Scheduling Heuristics. Bo Chen. (Tinbergen Institute Research Ser.). 137p. 1994. pap. 25.00 (*90-5170-282-5*, Pub. by Thesis Pubs NE) IBD Ltd.

***Worst Case Scenario: A Washington, D. C. Mystery.** LC 96-52775. 1997. 23.95 (*0-7838-8072-3*) G K Hall.

Worst Christmas Ever. Connie Remlinger-Trounstine. LC 94-14326. (Illus.). 128p. (J). (gr. 3-6). 1996. pap. 2.95 (*0-8167-3516-6*, Rainbow NJ) Troll Communs.

Worst Day of Your Life. Edward Packard. (Choose Your Own Adventure Ser.: No. 100). 128p. (J). 1990. pap. 3.50 (*0-553-28316-2*) Bantam.

Worst Day of Your Life. large type ed. Edward Packard. (Choose Your Own Adventure Ser.: No. 100). (Illus.). 128p. (J). (gr. 4 up). 1995. lib. bdg. 15.93 (*0-8368-1312-X*) Gareth Stevens Inc.

***Worst Days: A Journal from a Young Cancer Patient for Health-Care Professionals.** Leonaye Bulger & Judy Dierkheising. LC 96-41962. 1996. 4.95 (*1-56123-098-7*) Centering Corp.

Worst Desert on Earth: Crossing the Taklamakan. Charles Blackmore. (Illus.). 224p. 1996. 35.00 (*0-7195-5436-5*, Pub. by John Murray UK) Trafalgar.

Worst Disaster: The Fall of Singapore. Raymond A. Callahan. LC 75-29730. 293p. 1977. 39.50 (*0-87413-112-X*) U Delaware Pr.

Worst Fears. Fay Weldon. 208p. 1996. 21.00 (*0-87113-635-X*, Atlntc Mnthly) Grove-Atltic.

***Worst Fears.** Fay Weldon. 208p. 1997. pap. 12.00 (*0-87113-682-1*, Atlntc Mnthly) Grove-Atltic.

Worst Goes South. James Stevenson. LC 94-25354. (Illus.). 32p. (J). (gr. k up). 1995. 15.00 (*0-688-13059-3*); lib. bdg. 14.93 (*0-688-13060-7*) Greenwillow.

Worst High School Play in the World. William Gleason. 1983. pap. 5.00 (*0-87129-269-6*, W53) Dramatic Pub.

Worst Joke Box in the History of the World...Ever! Clive Brown. (Illus.). 192p. (J). 1995. boxed, pap. 4.50 (*0-14-037243-1*) Puffin Bks.

***Worst Journey in the World.** 2nd ed. Apsley Cherry-Garrard. LC 96-54510. 656p. 1997. pap. 16.95 (*0-7867-0437-3*) Carroll & Graf.

Worst Journey in the World: Antarctic 1910-13. Apsley Cherry-Garrard. 652p. 1989. pap. 13.95 (*0-88184-478-0*) Carroll & Graf.

Worst Journey in the World: Antarctic, 1910-1913. Apsley Cherry-Garrard. (Illus.). 660p. 1994. 34.00 (*0-330-33585-5*, Pub. by Picador UK) Trans-Atl Phila.

Worst Loss. Barbara D. Rosof. 1995. pap. 14.95 (*0-8050-3241-X*) H Holt & Co.

Worst Movies of All Time: or What Were They Thinking? Michael Sauter. (Illus.). 272p. 1995. pap. 14.95 (*0-8065-1577-5*, Citadel Pr) Carol Pub Group.

Worst Noel. Ilene Cooper. (Holiday Five Ser.: No. 2). 128p. (J). (gr. 3-7). 1994. pap. 14.99 (*0-670-85058-6*) Viking Child Bks.

Worst Noel. Ilene Cooper. (Holiday 5 Ser.: Bk. 2). 160p. (J). (gr. 3-7). 1995. pap. 3.99 (*0-14-036518-4*) Puffin Bks.

Worst of Paul Finebaum. Paul Finebaum. 128p. 1994. pap. 9.95 (*1-881548-12-0*) Crane Hill AL.

Worst of Truly Tasteless Jokes. Blanche Knott. 160p. 1986. 9.95 (*0-312-89291-8*) St Martin.

Worst Ordeal: A Photographic Essay. Peter H. Liddle. (Illus.). 232p. 1994. 47.50 (*0-85052-417-2*, Pub. by L Cooper Bks UK) Trans-Atl Phila.

Worst Person in the World. James Stevenson. LC 77-22141. (Illus.). 32p. (J). (gr. k-3). 1978. lib. bdg. 13.93 (*0-688-84127-9*) Greenwillow.

Worst Person in the World. James Stevenson. LC 77-22141. (Illus.). 32p. (J). (ps up). 1995. pap. 4.95 (*0-688-14394-6*, Mulberry) Morrow.

Worst Pills, Best Pills Vol. II: The Older Adult's Guide to Avoiding Drug-Induced Death or Illness. rev. ed. Public Citizen Health Research Group Staff & Sidney M. Wolfe. (Illus.). 690p. (C). 1993. pap. text ed. 15.00 (*0-937188-52-2*) Pub Citizen Inc.

Worst Pills Best Pills News Collection March 1995-April 1996: Recent Articles about Prescription & Over-the-Counter Drugs. Public Citizen Health Research Group Staff. Ed. by Sidney M. Wolfe. 94p. (Orig.). 1996. pap. 10.00 (*0-937188-09-3*) Pub Citizen Inc.

Worst Poverty: A History of Debt & Debtors. Hugh Barty-King. (Illus.). 224p. 1991. 30.00 (*0-86299-868-9*, Pub. by Sutton Pubng UK) Bks Intl VA.

Worst Rock & Roll Records of All Time: A Fan's Guide to the Stuff You Love to Hate. Jimmy Guterman. 1991. pap. 14.95 (*0-8065-1231-8*, Citadel Pr); pap. 14.95 (*0-8065-9965-0*, Citadel Pr) Carol Pub Group.

Worst Show-and-Tell Ever. Rita A. Walsh. LC 93-24844. (Illus.). 32p. (J). (gr. 2-4). 1993. pap. text ed. 2.95 (*0-8167-3177-2*) Troll Communs.

Worst Speller in Jr. High. Caroline Janover. Ed. by Rosemary Wallner. LC 94-26409. 208p. (Orig.). (YA). (gr. 5 up). 1994. pap. 4.95 (*0-915793-76-8*) Free Spirit Pub.

Worst Street in North London: A Social History of Campbell, Bunk, Islington, Between the Wars. Jerry White. (History Workshop Ser.). 228p. (C). 1986. pap. text ed. 19.95 (*0-7102-0700-X*, RKP) Routledge.

Worst Tax? A History of the Property Tax in America. Glenn W. Fisher. LC 95-40704. (Studies in Government & Public Policy). 264p. 1996. 35.00 (*0-7006-0753-6*) U Pr of KS.

Worst Thing I've Ever Done. Ted Rall. (Illus.). 64p. (Orig.). 1996. pap. 8.95 (*1-56163-157-4*) NBM.

Worst Things First? The Debate over Risk-Based National Environmental Priorities. Ed. by Adam M. Finkel & Dominic Golding. 348p. (Orig.). (C). 1995. pap. text ed. 27.95 (*0-915707-76-4*) Resources Future.

Worst Weather on Earth. William Putnam. (Illus.). 266p. 1993. 29.50 (*0-930410-35-1*) Amer Alpine Club.

Worst Witch. Jill Murphy. (Illus.). 80p. (J). (gr. 3-7). 1982. pap. 2.50 (*0-380-60665-8*, Camelot) Avon.

Worst Witch at Sea. Jill Murphy. LC 95-10319. (Illus.). 222p. (J). (gr. 3-6). 1995. 16.95 (*1-56402-421-0*) Candlewick Pr.

***Worst Witch at Sea.** Jill Murphy. LC 95-10319. (Illus.). 224p. (J). (gr. 3-6). 1997. reprint ed. pap. 4.99 (*0-7636-0384-8*) Candlewick Pr.

Worst Witch Strikes Again. Jill Murphy. 80p. (J). (gr. 3-7). 1982. pap. 2.50 (*0-380-60673-9*, Camelot) Avon.

Worst Years of Our Lives: Irreverent Notes from a Decade of Greed. Barbara Ehrenreich. LC 90-55985. 288p. 1991. pap. 12.00 (*0-06-097384-6*, PL) HarpC.

Worsted Industry. rev. ed. S. Brearley & I. Tredale. 198p. 1982. 60.00 (*0-686-87182-0*) St Mut.

Worsted Industry. 2nd ed. Wira Staff. (C). 1980. 125.00 (*0-900820-14-4*, Pub. by British Textile Tech UK) St Mut.

Worsted Spinning. Ed. by Wira Staff. 1988. 30.00 (*0-317-43619-8*) St Mut.

***Wort, Satz und Text: Praktische Ubungen fur Sprachgestorte 2. Korr. und Erg. Auflage.** Berthold Simons. (GER.). 1996. 44.95 (*3-631-30115-4*) P Lang Pubng.

Wort und Antwort: Geschichte und Gestaltung der Konfirmation am Beispiel der Ev.-luth. Landeskirche Hannovers. Michael Meyer-Blanck. (Arbeiten zur Praktischen Theoligie Ser.: Bd. 2). xii, 338p. (GER.). (C). 1992. lib. bdg. 106.15 (*3-11-013258-3*, 248-91) De Gruyter.

Wort und Tat Bei Homer. Christophorus Barck. (Spudasmata Ser.: Bd. XXXIV). 180p. (GER.). 1976. 35. 00 (*3-487-06233-X*) G Olms Pubs.

Wortabet Dictionary. John Wortabet & Porter. 900p. (ARA & ENG.). 1979. 24.95 (*0-86685-120-8*, LDL1208, Pub. by Librairie du Liban FR); pap. 16.95 (*0-86685-121-6*, LDL1216, Pub. by Librairie du Liban FR) Intl Bk Ctr.

Wortakzent in Den Lyrischen Versen Des Horaz. Ernst Zinn. vii, 240p. write for info. (*0-318-71251-2*) G Olms Pubs.

Wortarten & Wortartenwechsel: Zu Konversion & Verwandten Erscheinungen im Deutschen & in Anderen Sprachen. Petra M. Vogel. (Studia Linguistica Germanica: Vol. 39). x, 311p. (GER.). (C). 1995. lib. bdg. 130.80 (*3-11-014823-4*) De Gruyter.

***Wortbedeutung und Termassoziation.** Gerda Ruge. (Sprache und Computer Ser.: Vol. 14). 246p. (GER.). 1995. write for info. (*3-487-09964-0*) G Olms Pubs.

Wortbedeutungen - & Wie Sie im Worterbuch Beschrieben Werden Konnen. Gisela Harras et al. (Schriften des Instituts fur Deutsche Sprache Ser.: Band 3). vi, 292p. (GER.). (C). 1991. lib. bdg. 98.50 (*3-11-012903-5*) De Gruyter.

Wortbildung des Nuernberger Fruehneuhochdeutsch: Verbale Wortbildung um 1500. Mechthild Habermann. (Vol. 2). 601p. (GER.). (C). 1994. lib. bdg. 216.95 (*3-11-013178-1*) De Gruyter.

Wortbildung des Nuernberger Frueneuhochdeutsch, Bd. 1: Substantiv-Derivation in den Schriften Albrecht Duerers. Peter O. Mueller. xx, 532p. (GER.). (C). 1993. lib. bdg. 200.00 (*3-11-012815-2*) De Gruyter.

***Wortbildung und Literatur: Panorama Einer Stilistik des Komplexen Wortes.** Peter Handler. (GER.). 1993. 55. 80 (*3-631-43852-4*) P Lang Pubng.

Wortbildungslehre see Schwedische Sprachgeschichte

***Worte des Dankes: Ein Gruss an Die Naturwelt.** John Stokes. Tr. by Dan Thompson et al. Orig. Title: Thanksgiving Address: Greetings to the Natural World. (Illus.). 40p. (Orig.). (GER.). 1996. pap. write for info. (*0-9643214-1-6*) Six Nations.

Worterbuch Automobil-Industrie. Hans Schnellman. 120p. (GER & ITA.). 1987. 95.00 (*0-8288-0766-3*, F24430) Fr & Eur.

Worterbuch der Abkurzungen. (Duden-Taschenbucher Ser.: No. 11). 288p. 1987. 12.25 (*3-411-02741-X*, Pub. by Bibliogr Inst Brockhaus GW) Langenscheidt.

Worterbuch der Alten Geographie. Paul F. Nitzsch. Ed. by J. G. Hopfner. xxviii, 648p. (GER.). 1983. reprint ed. write for info. (*3-487-06958-X*) G Olms Pubs.

Worterbuch der Computer & Datenverarbeitung. Hans Schnellman. 120p. (GER & ITA.). 1985. 75.00 (*0-8288-0900-3*, F 115855) Fr & Eur.

Worterbuch der Computerai. 9th ed. Gunther Daubach. 121p. (ENG & GER.). 1990. lib. bdg. 75.00 (*0-8288-3599-3*) Fr & Eur.

Worterbuch der Deutschen & Niederlandischen Rechtssprache. M. Scheer. 426p. (DUT & GER.). 1989. lib. bdg. 125.00 (*0-8288-3897-6*, F63830) Fr & Eur.

Worterbuch der Eipo-Sprache: Ipo, German, English. Wolker Heeschen. 249p. (ENG & GER.). 1983. 250.00 (*0-7859-8404-6*, 3496015055) Fr & Eur.

Worterbuch der Ernahrungswissenschaft. C. Leitzmann. 298p. (ENG, FRE, GER, ITA & SPA.). 1988. lib. bdg. 115.00 (*0-8288-3592-6*, F113450) Fr & Eur.

Worterbuch der ICAO-Terminologie: Dictionary of ICAO Terminology. International Civil Aviation Organization Staff. 265p. (ENG & GER.). 1981. 49.95 (*0-8288-0014-6*, M8312) Fr & Eur.

Worterbuch der Mikroelektronik, Dictionary Microelectronics: English-German, German-English. 218p. (ENG & GER.). 1980. pap. 39.95 (*0-7859-0858-7*, M-9219) Fr & Eur.

Worterbuch der Psychologie & Psychiatrie. R. Haas. 453p. (ENG & GER.). 1980. lib. bdg. 175.00 (*0-8288-3410-5*, F79922) Fr & Eur.

Worterbuch der Psychologie & Psychiatrie. R. Haas. 438p. (ENG & GER.). 1988. lib. bdg. 225.00 (*0-8288-3411-3*, F140130) Fr & Eur.

Worterbuch der Technik: Italienisch-Deutsch. Albert Schlegelmich. 630p. (GER & ITA.). 1981. 95.00 (*0-8288-4683-9*, M-122653) Fr & Eur.

Worterbuch des Bibliothekswesens. Eberhardt Sauppe. 428p. (ENG & GER.). 1988. lib. bdg. 250.00 (*0-8288-3394-X*, F88871) Fr & Eur.

Worterbuch fur Alle Sparten der Versicherung, 2 vols., Ea. 12th ed. K. H. Stocks. 634p. (ENG & GER.). 1988. 95. 00 (*0-8288-8001-8*) Fr & Eur.

W

Worterbuch fur Kraftfahrzeugtechnik. 3rd rev. ed. Jean De Coster. (ENG, FRE & GER.). 1990. lib. bdg. 250.00 (*0-8288-3841-0*, M14314) Fr & Eur.

Worterbuch fur Recht Wirtschaft & Politik, Vol. 2. Clara-Erika Dietl. (ENG & GER.). lib. bdg. 375.00 (*0-685-48755-5*, M15095) Fr & Eur.

Worterbuch fur Recht Wirtschaft & Politik, Vol. 1: 1990 Edition. Clara-Erika Dietl. (ENG & GER.). lib. bdg. 300.00 (*0-685-48754-7*, F132140) Fr & Eur.

Worterbuch GeoTechnik Dictionary Vol. 1: Geological Engineering. H. Buckschl. 1000p. (ENG & GER.). 1996. 235.00 (*0-387-58163-4*) Spr-Verlag.

Worterbuch Handel und Finanzen. Hans Schnellman. 120p. (GER & ITA.). 1987. 95.00 (*0-8288-1273-X*, M10375) Fr & Eur.

Worterbuch Khmer-Deutsch, 2 vols. Rudiger Gaudes. 1321p. (CAM & GER.). 1989. 250.00 (*0-7859-8302-3*, 3324002915) Fr & Eur.

Worterbuch Kunstoffprufung. J. Durzok. 200p. (ENG & GER.). 1991. lib. bdg. 125.00 (*0-8288-3600-0*, 3527280359) Fr & Eur.

Worterbuch Lichttechnik. R. Von Zimmerman. 426p. (ENG, FRE, GER & RUS.). 1990. lib. bdg. 125.00 (*0-8288-3847-X*, F112460) Fr & Eur.

Worterbuch Musik. 4th ed. Horst Von Leuchtmann. 411p. (ENG & GER.). 1992. lib. bdg. 225.00 (*0-8288-3407-5*, F81960) Fr & Eur.

Worterbuch Persisch-Deutsch. 7th ed. Heinrich Junker & B. Alavi. 864p. (GER & PER.). 1992. 150.00 (*0-8288-1124-5*, F18540) Fr & Eur.

Worterbuch Robotik. H. Schenk. 210p. (FRE & GER.). 1989. lib. bdg. 95.00 (*0-8288-3834-8*, F124170) Fr & Eur.

Worterbuch Soziale Arbeit, in Zweites Bandes Vol. 1. Deutsche Verein Staff. 120p. (ENG & GER.). 1988. lib. bdg. 45.00 (*0-8288-3406-7*, F106530) Fr & Eur.

Worterbuch Wortschaft: 1990. A. Schuler. (ENG & GER.). 1991. lib. bdg. 95.00 (*0-685-48756-3*, F116470) Fr & Eur.

Worterbuch Zu Arrians Anabasis. August Weise. vi, 246p. 1971. reprint ed. write for info. (*0-318-72085-X*) G Olms Pubs.

Worterbuch zu den Inschriften im Kyprischen Syllabar: Unter Berucksichtigung Einer Arbeit Von Almut Hintze. Markus Egetmeyer. (Kadmos Ser.: Supplement III). xvi, 351p. (GER.). (C). 1992. lib. bdg. 206.15 (*3-11-012270-7*, 108-92) De Gruyter.

Worterbucher - Dictionaries - Dictionnaires: Ein Internationales Handbuch zur Lexikographie - An International Encyclopedia of Lexicography - Encyclopedie Internationale de Lexicographie, 3 vols., Set, Teil 1. Ed. by Franz J. Hausmann et al. lii, 1056p. (C). 1989. lib. bdg. 596.15 (*3-11-009585-8*) De Gruyter.

Worterbucher - Dictionaries - Dictionnaires: Ein Internationales Handbuch zur Lexikographie - An International Encyclopedia of Lexicography - Encyclopedie Internationale de Lexicographie, 3 vols., Teil 3. Ed. by Franz J. Hausmann et al. (HSK Ser.: Vol. 53). xxvi, 1017p. (ENG, FRE & GER.). (C). 1991. lib. bdg. 600.00 (*3-11-012421-1*, 262-91) De Gruyter.

Worth. Mark Dunster. 11p. (Orig.). 1992. pap. 4.00 (*0-89642-206-2*) Linden Pubs.

Worth: The Father of Haute Couture. 2nd ed. Diana De Marly. LC 90-4786. (Fashion Designers Ser.). (Illus.). 253p. (C). 1991. pap. 24.95 (*0-8419-1242-4*) Holmes & Meier.

Worth a Dime. Peggy A. Griffin. 1975. pap. text ed. write for info. (*1-884056-02-4*) Scribes Pubns.

***Worth a Thousand Words: An Annotated Guide to Picture Books for Older Readers.** Bette D. Ammon & Gale W. Sherman. LC 96-31489. 230p. 1996. lib. bdg. 26.50 (*1-56308-390-6*) Libs Unl.

Worth a Thousand Words: Scanning to Communicate. Phillip Moffitt & Rick Smolan. 80p. 1991. pap. 7.95 (*0-9630008-0-2*) Light Source.

Worth Book of Softball: A Celebration of America's True National Pastime. Paul Dickson. LC 93-19312. 288p. 1994. 22.95 (*0-8160-2897-4*) Facts on File.

Worth Dying For. D. L. Carey. (Distress Call 911 Ser.: No. 3). (YA). (gr. 7 up). 1996. mass mkt. 3.99 (*0-671-55308-9*) PB.

Worth Guide to Computerized Investing: Everything You Need to Know to Use Your Home Computer. Jim Jubak. LC 96-10717. (Illus.). 323p. 1996. pap. 17.50 (*0-88730-769-8*) Harper Busn.

Worth It All: My War for Peace. Jim Wright. LC 93-17287. 336p. 1993. 24.95 (*0-02-881075-9*) Brasseys Inc.

Worth Keeping: An Architectural History of Sutter & Yuba Counties, California. Jacqueline Lowe et al. 168p. (Orig.). (C). 1990. pap. 18.00 (*0-9625659-0-3*) Comm Mem Mus Sutter Cnty.

Worth of a Child. Thomas H. Murray. LC 95-46977. 214p. (C). 1996. 29.95 (*0-520-08836-0*) U CA Pr.

Worth of a Man. Dave Dravecky & C. W. Neal. 208p. 1996. 18.99 (*0-310-20560-3*) Zondervan.

Worth of a Soul. Steven Cramer. 127p. 1995. pap. 10.95 (*1-55517-171-0*) CFI Dist.

Worth of a Woman. Iverna M. Tompkins. 168p. pap. text ed. 5.00 (*0-9611260-7-8*) I Tompkins.

Worth of a Woman. David C. Phillips. (Collected Works of David G. Phillips). 1988. reprint ed. lib. bdg. 79.00 (*0-7812-1336-3*) Rprt Serv.

Worth of a Woman see Collected Works of David G. Phillips

Worth of the Game: Being a Final Travel Guide to the England of Sherlock Holmes. David L. Hammer. (Sherlock Holmes Sites Ser.: No. 3). (Illus.). 384p. (Orig.). 1993. per. 18.95 (*0-938501-17-8*) Wessex.

***Worth of Women: Wherein Is Clearly Revealed Their Nobility & Their Superiority to Men.** Moderata Fonte & Virginia Cox. LC 96-52270. (The Other Voice in Early Modern Europe Ser.). 1996. pap. 17.95 (*0-226-25682-0*); lib. bdg. 45.00 (*0-226-25681-2*) U Ch Pr.

Worth of Women's Work: A Qualitative Synthesis. Ed. by Anne Statham et al. LC 87-6472. (SUNY Series on Women & Work). 331p. 1987. text ed. 69.50 (*0-88706-591-0*); pap. text ed. 24.95 (*0-88706-592-9*) State U NY Pr.

Worth Protecting: Women, & Men, & Freedom from Sexual Aggression. Pamela Woll & Terence T. Gorski. LC 95-8001. 301p. (Orig.). 1995. pap. text ed. 15.00 (*0-8309-0702-5*) Herald Hse.

Worth Remembering: Ten Year Family Diary. John Mays & Jeanne Mays. (Illus.). 1994. pap. 20.00 (*1-880994-33-X*) Mt Olive Coll Pr.

Worth Remembering: Ten Year Family Diary. John Mays & Jeanne Mays. (Illus.). 274p. 1994. 20.00 (*1-880994-22-4*) Mt Olive Coll Pr.

Worth the Wait. Risa Kirk. (Superromance Ser.). 1993. mass mkt. 3.39 (*0-373-70542-5*, 1-70542-5) Harlequin Bks.

Worth Their Salt: Notable but Often Unnoted Women of Utah. Ed. by Collen Whitley. (Illus.). 280p. 1996. 37.95 (*0-87421-212-X*); pap. 19.95 (*0-87421-206-5*) Utah St U Pr.

Worth Waiting For. Bay Matthews. (Special Edition Ser.). 1993. mass mkt. 3.50 (*0-373-09825-1*, 5-09825-6) Silhouette.

***Worth Waiting for.** large type ed. Josie Metcalfe. (Mills & Boon Large Print Ser.). 288p. 1997. 22.50 (*0-263-14907-2*) Ulverscroft.

Worth Waiting For: Sexual Abstinence Before Marriage. Brent A. Barlow. LC 94-40476. 1995. 13.95 (*0-87579-920-5*) Deseret Bk.

Worth Your Weight. Barbara A. Bruno. 192p. 1996. pap. 12.95 (*1-887750-32-0*) Rutledge Bks.

Worthing Saga. Orson Scott Card. 480p. 1992. mass mkt. 5.99 (*0-8125-3331-3*) Tor Bks.

Worthington Miner: A Directors Guild of America Oral History. Franklin J. Schaffner. LC 84-22184. 323p. 1985. 29.50 (*0-8108-1757-8*) Scarecrow.

Worthington Whittredge. Anthony F. Janson. (Cambridge Monographs on American Artists). (Illus.). 288p. (C). 1990. 85.00 (*0-521-32432-7*) Cambridge U Pr.

Worthwhile. Emma L. Moffatt. 14p. (Orig.). 1995. pap. write for info. (*1-885206-24-0*, Iliad Pr) Cader Pubng.

Worthwhile Places: The Correspondence of John D. Rockefeller Jr. & Horace M. Albright. John D. Rockefeller, Jr. & Horace M. Albright. Ed. by Joseph W. Ernst. LC 91-70235. 354p. 1991. pap. 19.95 (*0-8232-1330-7*) Fordham.

Worthy Company: Brief Lives of the Framers of the Constitution. M. E. Bradford. 250p. 1982. 10.95 (*0-942516-00-1*); pap. 7.95 (*0-685-04105-0*) Plymouth Rock Found.

Worthy Foes: Differently Abled Heroes. Lela E. Buis et al. Ed. by Gary Bowen. (Orig.). 1996. pap. 6.00 (*1-887666-12-5*) Obelesk Bks.

Worthy Foundation: The Cathedral Church of St. Canice, Kilkenny. Siuban Barry et al. 104p. 1985. pap. 14.95 (*0-85105-435-8*, Pub. by Colin Smythe Ltd UK) Dufour.

***Worthy Is the Child.** Richard Polzin. (Illus.). 132p. (J). (gr. k-6). 1995. 19.95 (*0-9645911-0-3*) Nite Lite Stories.

***Worthy Is the Lamb.** 1988. pap. 1.20 (*0-8341-9199-7*) Lillenas.

Worthy Is the Lamb. Ray Summers. 1951. 16.99 (*0-8054-1314-6*, 4213-14) Broadman.

Worthy is the Lamb see Digno Es el Cordero

Worthy Is the World: The Hindu Philosophy of Sri Aurobindo. Beatrice Bruteau. LC 73-144091. (Illus.). 288p. 1975. 25.00 (*0-8386-7872-6*) Fairleigh Dickinson.

Worthy Man. large type ed. Fiona Bullen. 576p. 1995. 25.99 (*0-7089-3388-2*) Ulverscroft.

Worthy Monuments: Art Museums & the Politics of Culture in Nineteenth-Century France. Daniel J. Sherman. LC 88-7939. (Illus.). 352p. 1989. 40.00 (*0-674-96230-3*) HUP.

Worthy of Love. Karen Casey. (Meditation Ser.). 106p. 1985. 10.00 (*0-89486-339-8*, 5005A) Hazelden.

Worthy Partner: The Papers of Martha Washington. Martha Washington. LC 93-35842. (Contributions in American History Ser.: No. 155). 544p. 1994. text ed. 49.95 (*0-313-28024-X*, Greenwood Pr) Greenwood.

Worthy Tract of Paulus Iovius. Paolo Giovio. Tr. by Samuel Daniel. LC 76-13497. 300p. 1976. reprint ed. lib. bdg. 50.00 (*0-8201-1272-0*) Schol Facsimiles.

Worthy Women of Our First Century. Ed. by Sarah B. Wister & Agnes Irwin. LC 72-13216. (Essay Index Reprint Ser.). 1977. reprint ed. 22.95 (*0-8369-8182-0*) Ayer.

Wortindex zu Georg Buechner, Dichtungen und Uebersetzungen. Ed. by Monika Roessing-Hager. (Deutsche Wortindices Ser.: No. 1). (C). 1970. 132.30 (*3-11-006448-0*) De Gruyter.

Wortindex zu Gottfried Keller. "Der gruene Heinrich" Erste Fassung, 2 vols. Ed. by Edda Schrader. (Deutsche Wortindices Ser.: No. 3). 1255p. (C). 1971. 334.60 (*3-11-003354-2*) De Gruyter.

Wortindex zu Gottfried Keller, Die Leute von Seldwyla, 2 Pts. Ed. by Monika Roessing-Hager & Niels Soerensen. (Deutsche Wortindices Ser.: No. 2). (C). 1971. 280.75 (*3-11-006441-3*) De Gruyter.

Wortparallelismus als ein Stilmittel der 'Nord'ostjakischen Volksdichtung. Brigette Schulze. (Studia Uralo-altaica Ser.: Vol. 29). x, 152p. (Orig.). (C). 1988. pap. 35.00 (*0-318-40021-9*) Benjamins North Am.

Wortschatz der Information und Dokumentation. G. Schmoll. 160p. (GER.). 35.00 (*3-7940-4037-6*, M-7690); 35.00 (*0-8288-7984-2*, M7690) Fr & Eur.

Wortschatz des Hans Sachs, Vol. 2. Walter Tauber. 282p. (GER.). 1983. 75.40 (*3-11-009790-7*) De Gruyter.

Wortschatz in den deutschen Schriften Thomas Murners: Band 1: Untersuchengen - Band 2: Worterbuch. Susanne M. Raabe. (Studia Linguistica Germanica: Band 29). xviii, 358p. (C). 1990. lib. bdg. 275.40 (*3-11-012456-4*) De Gruyter.

Wortschatz und Bedeutungsvermittlung. B. Muller. Ed. by Gerd Neuner. (Fernstudienangebot Ser.). 119p. (GER.). 1996. 11.25 (*3-468-49672-9*) Langenscheidt.

Woses of the Black Wood. Peter C. Fenlon, Jr. & Jeffrey McKeage. (Middle-Earth Read-to-Run Adventure Ser.). 32p. (YA). (gr. 10-12). 1987. pap. 6.00 (*0-915795-99-X*, 8107) Iron Crown Ent Inc.

Woster Brothers' Brand: Episodes Out of a Shared Inheritance. Jim Woster et al. Ed. & Intro. by Mary A. Haug. LC 90-82116. (Illus.). 186p. 1990. pap. 5.95 (*0-944287-07-7*) Ex Machina.

Wotan Missions. Leo Kessler. (SS Wotan Ser.). 224p. 22.00 (*0-7278-4901-8*) Severn Hse.

Wotan, My Enemy: Can Britain Live with the Germans in the European Union? Leo Abse. 274p. 1995. 29.95 (*0-86051-910-4*, Robson-Parkwest) Parkwest Pubns.

Would a Capital Gains Tax Cut Increase or Reduce Government Revenue? John C. Goodman. 1990. pap. 5.00 (*0-943802-82-2*, BG103) Natl Ctr Pol.

Would Be Gentleman see Seventeenth Century French Drama

Would-Be Gentleman see Miser & Other Plays

Would be Witch. Rita Boucher. 1997. pap. 5.50 (*0-451-19078-5*, Sig) NAL-Dutton.

Would-Be Worlds: How the New Science of Simulation Is Breaking the Complexity Barrier. John L. Casti. LC 96-16841. 256p. 1996. text ed. 24.95 (*0-471-12308-0*) Wiley.

Would-Be Writer. 3rd ed. Clinton S. Burhans. LC 74-13349. reprint ed. pap. 36.80 (*0-317-09496-3*, 2012513) Bks Demand.

Would God It Were Night the Ordeal of a Jewish Boy from Cracow - Through Auschwitz, Meuthausen, & Gusen. Zvi Barlev. 1991. 18.95 (*0-533-09150-0*) Vantage.

Would God Leave a Record? Keith G. Barr. (Illus.). 96p. (C). 1989. per. 9.95 (*0-9622727-1-X*) Voice Revival Pubns.

Would God Leave a Record? 3rd rev. ed. Keith G. Barr. Ed. by Christopher Group. (Illus.). 96p. (C). 1995. pap. 7.95 (*0-9622727-0-1*) Voice Revival Pubns.

Would I? Would You? Ed. by Henry Einspruch & Marie Einspruch. 91p. 1970. pap. 3.95 (*1-880226-13-8*) M J Pubs.

Would My Fortune Cookie Lie? Stella Pevsner. LC 95-36720. 186p. (J). 1996. 14.95 (*0-395-73082-1*, Clarion Bks) HM.

Would Somebody Hold My Purse While I Preach: A Collection of Miss Father Cartoons. Mary B. Craft. LC 89-82713. (Miss Father Ser.). (Orig.). 1990. pap. 6.00 (*0-938991-44-2*) Colonial Pr AL.

Would They Love a Lion? Kady M. Denton. LC 94-28576. (Illus.). (J). 1995. 14.95 (*1-85697-546-0*, Kingfisher LKC) LKC.

Would You Believe? Marilyn Kleinhardt. 103p. 1990. pap. 7.95 (*1-884694-00-4*) Wood n Needle.

Would You Believe an Angel? Ed Brainerd et al. Ed. by Helen Johns. LC 92-72130. (Illus.). 56p. (Orig.). 1992. pap. 6.95 (*0-916035-50-6*) Evangel Indiana.

Would You Believe It. Patricia M. St. John. 1995. pap. 9.99 (*0-551-02887-4*) Zondervan.

Would You Climb a Banana? Viki Woodworth. LC 92-40672. (Reading, Rhyme & Riddle Ser.). (Illus.). 24p. (J). (ps-2). 1995. lib. bdg. 18.50 (*1-56766-074-6*) Childs World.

Would You Kill Him? George P. Lathrop. LC 73-104507. 388p. reprint ed. lib. bdg. 29.00 (*0-8398-1151-9*) Irvington.

Would You Kill Him? George P. Lathrop. 388p. (C). 1986. reprint ed. pap. text ed. 6.95 (*0-8290-1959-6*) Irvington.

Would You Like a Parrot? France Barberis. LC 67-28671. (Illus.). 32p. (J). (ps). 8.95 (*0-87592-060-8*) Scroll Pr.

Would You Like to Play Hide & Seek in This Book with Lovable, Furry Old Grover? Jon Stone. LC 76-8120. (Pictureback Ser.). (Illus.). (J). (ps-1). 1976. pap. 3.25 (*0-394-83292-2*) Random Bks Yng Read.

***Would You Love Me?** Andrea W. Von Konigslow. 32p. 1997. pap. 5.95 (*1-55037-430-3*, Pub. by Annick CN) Firefly Bks Ltd.

***Would You Love Me?** Andrea W. Von Konigslow. (Illus.). 32p. (J). (ps). 1997. 15.95 (*1-55037-431-1*, Pub. by Annick CN) Firefly Bks Ltd.

Would You Mail a Hippo? Viki Woodworth. LC 94-45828. (Reading, Rhymes& Riddles Ser.). (Illus.). 24p. (J). (ps-2). 1995. lib. bdg. 18.50 (*1-56766-179-3*) Childs World.

Would You Put That in Writing? rev. ed. Dianna Booher. 176p. 1992. 18.95 (*0-8160-2765-X*) Facts on File.

Would You Rather? Barbara J. Menzel. LC 81-6810. (Illus.). 32p. (J). (ps-3). 1982. 16.95 (*0-89885-076-2*) Human Sci Pr.

***Would You Rather... Over 200 Incerdibly Inane, Utterly Unprofound, Absolutely Absurd Dilemmas to Ponder.** David Gomberg & Justin Heimberg. LC 97-14304. 1997. pap. 8.95 (*0-452-27851-1*, Plume) NAL-Dutton.

Would You Rather...? 465 Provocative Questions to Get Teenagers Talking. Doug Fields. 128p. 1996. pap. 7.99 (*0-310-20943-9*) Zondervan.

***Would You Really Rather Die Than Give a Talk? The Comic Book Guide to Brilliantly Surviving Your Next Business Presentation.** Michael Egan. LC 97-23151. (Illus.). 176p. 1997. pap. 12.95 (*0-8144-7941-3*) AMACOM.

Would You Spread a Turtle on Toast? Viki Woodworth. (Reading, Rhymes & Riddles Ser.). (Illus.). 20p. (J). (ps-2). 1992. lib. bdg. 18.50 (*0-89565-823-2*) Childs World.

Would You Wear a Snake? Viki Woodworth. (Reading, Rhymes & Riddles Ser.). (Illus.). 20p. (J). (ps-2). 1992. lib. bdg. 18.50 (*0-89565-821-6*) Childs World.

Woulda, Coulda, Shoulda: Handicapping Tips for Anyone Who Ever Bet on a Horse Race or Wanted To. Dave Feldman & Frank Sugano. LC 96-18775. 316p. 1996. pap. 12.95 (*1-56625-069-2*) Bonus Books.

Woulda, Coulda, Shoulda: Overcoming Regrets, Mistakes, & Missed Opportunities. Arthur Freeman & Rose DeWolf. LC 89-46500. 288p. 1990. reprint ed. pap. 11.00 (*0-06-097335-8*, PL) HarpC.

Wouldbegoods. Edith Nesbit. (J). (gr. 5-8). 1988. 17.75 (*0-8446-6347-6*) Peter Smith.

Wouldbegoods. Edith Nesbit. 304p. (J). 1996. pap. 3.99 (*0-14-036751-9*) Viking Penguin.

***Wouldn't Change a Thing.** John G. Smith. 256p. 1996. 30.00 (*0-9652932-0-3*); pap. 15.00 (*0-9652932-1-1*) J G Smith.

Wouldn't Take Nothin' for My Journey Now. Jock Lauterer. LC 80-13425. (Illus.). 186p. reprint ed. pap. 53.10 (*0-8357-3888-4*, 2036620) Bks Demand.

Wouldn't Take Nothing for My Journey. large type ed. Maya Angelou. LC 93-47350. 1994. 22.95 (*1-56895-058-6*) Wheeler Pub.

Wouldn't Take Nothing for My Journey Now. Maya Angelou. pap. 15.00 (*0-394-22363-2*) Random.

Wouldn't Take Nothing for My Journey Now. Maya Angelou. 1993. 17.00 (*0-679-42743-0*) Random.

Wouldn't Take Nothing for My Journey Now. Maya Angelou. 160p. 1994. mass mkt. 5.50 (*0-553-56907-4*) Bantam.

***Wouldn't Take Nothing for My Journey Now.** Maya Angelou. 160p. 1994. mass mkt. 5.50 (*0-553-85176-4*) Bantam.

***Wouldn't Take Nothing for My Journey Now.** Maya Angelou. 1997. mass mkt. 10.00 (*0-553-38017-6*) Bantam.

Wouldn't You Rather Be Rich? How to Achieve Financial Independence Soundly & Surely. Alexa M. Selph. LC 88-9188. 320p. 1990. pap. 13.95 (*0-87797-163-3*) Cherokee.

Wound & Burn Management. Jim Wardrope & John A. Smith. LC 92-8609. (Oxford Handbooks in Emergency Medicine Ser.: No. 3). 192p. (C). 1992. 58.95 (*0-19-262238-2*); pap. 26.95 (*0-19-262064-9*) OUP.

***Wound & the Bow: Seven Studies in Literature.** Edmund Wilson. LC 96-51164. 260p. 1997. reprint ed. pap. text ed. 17.95 (*0-8214-1189-6*) Ohio U Pr.

Wound Ballistics. K. G. Selleir & B. P. Kneubuehl. (Illus.). 502p. 1994. pap. 168.75 (*0-444-81511-2*) Elsevier.

Wound Ballistics in World War II & Korea 2 vols., Set. 1995. lib. bdg. 599.95 (*0-8490-6583-6*) Gordon Pr.

Wound Care. Clark. 1998. text ed. write for info. (*0-7216-7104-7*) HarBrace.

Wound Care. William M. Cocke et al. LC 86-21621. 132p. reprint ed. pap. 37.70 (*0-7837-1371-1*, 2041520) Bks Demand.

Wound Care: A Collaborative Practice Manual for Physical Therapists & Nurses. Bates-Jensen & Sussman. 58p. 1996. 58.00 (*0-8342-0748-6*) Aspen Pub.

Wound Care for Health Professionals. G. Bennett & M. Moody. (Illus.). 176p. 1995. pap. 44.75 (*1-56593-348-6*, 0672) Singular Publishing.

***Wound Care Nursing: A Patient-Centered Approach.** Sue Bale & Vanessa Jones. (Illus.). 255p. 1997. write for info. (*0-7020-1870-8*, Pub. by W B Saunders UK) Saunders.

***Wound Care Protocols: Choosing Techniques & Products to Heal Wounds Effectively.** Brynn Doyle. Ed. by John Wolf. 145p. (C). 1996. pap. text ed. 64.95 (*1-878025-85-6*) Western Schls.

Wound Closure Biomaterials & Devices. Ed. by Chih-Chang Chu et al. LC 96-8975. 416p. 1996. 110.00 (*0-8493-4964-8*) CRC Pr.

Wound Closure Systems Markets. (Market Research Reports: No. 271). (Illus.). 46p. 1992. 795.00 (*0-317-05030-3*) Theta Corp.

***Wound-Dresser's Dream.** Pauline Stainer. 80p. 1996. pap. 15.95 (*1-85224-370-8*, Pub. by Bloodaxe Bks UK) Dufour.

Wound for Wound. Janie Bolitho. 224p. 1995. 20.00 (*0-7278-4739-2*) Severn Hse.

***Wound for Wound.** large type ed. Jane Bolitho. (Dales Large Print Ser.). (Illus.). 329p. 1996. pap. 17.99 (*1-85389-632-2*) Ulverscroft.

Wound Healing. Cohen. 1991. text ed. 157.00 (*0-7216-2564-9*) Saunders.

Wound Healing. Ed. by J. Ian Robertson & Herwig Janssen. 232p. 1991. 75.00 (*1-871816-10-6*, Pub. by Wrightson Biomed UK) Taylor & Francis.

Wound Healing: Alternatives in Management. 2nd ed. Ed. by Joseph M. McCulloch et al. LC 94-1175. (Contemporary Perspectives in Rehabilitation Ser.). 442p. 1994. 37.95 (*0-8036-5966-0*) Davis Co.

Wound Healing: Directory of Authors of New Medical & Scientific Reviews with Subject Index. Science & Life Consultants Association Staff. 160p. 1995. 44.50 (*0-7883-0618-9*); pap. 39.95 (*0-7883-0619-7*) ABBE Pubs Assn.

Wound Healing & Skin Physiology. P. Altmeyer et al. LC 94-29175. 1995. 178.00 (*0-387-56124-2*) Spr-Verlag.

W

An Asterisk (*) at the beginning of an entry indicates that the title is appearing in BIP for the first time.

Wound Healing in Cardiovascular Disease. Ed. by Karl T. Weber. LC 95-12157. (Illus.). 336p. 1995. 88.00 (*0-87993-620-7*) Futura Pub.

Wound Healing in Glaucoma Filtering Surgery. Franz Fankhauser. LC 92-49572. 96p. 1992. 34.50 (*90-6299-088-6*) Kugler Pubns.

Wound Healing Products. (Market Research Reports: No. 272). (Illus.). 122p. 1992. 795.00 (*0-317-05028-1*) Theta Corp.

***Wound Management.** Madeleine Flanagan. LC 97-16014. (Access to Clinical Education Ser.). 1997. write for info. (*0-443-05531-9*) Churchill.

Wound Management & Dressings. Thomas. 1991. 59.95 (*0-85369-215-7*, Pub. by Pharmaceutical Pr UK) Rittenhouse.

***Wound Management Pocket Survival Guide.** Thomas M. Masterson et al. (Pocket Survival Guides Ser.). 72p. 1996. pap. 7.50 (*1-883205-30-1*) Intl Med Pub.

Wound Management Products in Europe. Market Intelligence Staff. 300p. 1993. 3,900.00 (*1-56753-500-3*) Frost & Sullivan.

Wound of Knowledge: Christian Spirituality from the New Testament to St. John of the Cross. rev. ed. Rowan Williams. LC 91-32858. 198p. 1991. reprint ed. pap. 12.95 (*1-56101-047-2*) Cowley Pubns.

Wound of the Unloved: Releasing the Life Energy. Peter Schellenbaum. 1993. pap. 14.95 (*1-85230-124-4*) Element MA.

Wound Repair. 3rd ed. Earle E. Peacock. (Illus.). 544p. 1984. text ed. 159.00 (*0-7216-7145-4*) Saunders.

Wound-up Cat & Other Bedtime Stories. Ed. by Elisavietta Ritchie. pap. 4.95 (*1-895450-14-4*) Signal Bks.

Wounded. Betty P. Peebles. 38p. (Orig.). 1992. pap. text ed. 7.00 (*0-918925-42-8*) Jericho Chr Trng.

Wounded: And Other Stories about Sons & Fathers. Ian G. Leask. LC 91-61264. 232p. 1992. pap. 9.95 (*0-89823-139-6*) New Rivers Pr.

Wounded Alphabet. George Hitchcock. 354p. 1984. pap. 9.95 (*0-937310-05-0*) Story Line.

Wounded Body of Christ. 2nd ed. Earl Paulk. 160p. 1985. pap. 4.95 (*0-917595-06-8*) Kingdom Pubs.

Wounded Body of Christ see Cuerpo Herido de Cristo

Wounded Buzzard on Christmas Eve. John R. Erickson. (Hank the Cowdog Ser.: No. 13). (Illus.). 122p. 1989. 11.95 (*0-87719-176-X*, 9176); pap. 6.95 (*0-87719-175-1*, 9175) Gulf Pub.

Wounded by Love: Intimations of an Outpouring Heart. rev. ed. Mark Gruber. Ed. by M. Michele Ransil. (Illus.). xvi, 227p. 1993. pap. 17.95 (*1-886565-01-5*) St Vincent Spirit.

Wounded Healer. John Gagnon. LC 93-44570. (Frontiers in Psychotherapy Ser.). 184p. 1994. pap. 39.50 (*1-56750-063-3*); text ed. 73.25 (*0-89391-973-X*) Ablex Pub.

Wounded Healer: Countertransference from a Jungian Perspective. David Sedgwick. LC 93-40465. 176p. (C). 1994. pap. 16.95 (*0-415-10620-6*, B3211) Routledge.

Wounded Healer: Countertransference from a Jungian Perspective. David Sedgwick. LC 93-40465. 176p. (C). 1994. text ed. 59.95 (*0-415-10619-2*, B3207) Routledge.

Wounded Healer: Ministry in Contemporary Society. Henri J. Nouwen. LC 72-186312. 128p. 1979. pap. 8.95 (*0-385-14803-8*, Image Bks) Doubleday.

Wounded Healers: Creative Illness in the Pioneers of Depth Psychology. Marvin Goldwert. 164p. (Orig.). (C). 1992. lib. bdg. 47.00 (*0-8191-8776-3*) U Pr of Amer.

Wounded Healers: Creative Illness in the Pioneers of Depth Psychology. Marvin Goldwert. 164p. (Orig.). (C). 1992. pap. text ed. 24.00 (*0-8191-8777-1*) U Pr of Amer.

Wounded Healers: Mental Health Workers' Experiences of Depression. Ed. by Vicky Rippere & Ruth Williams. LC 84-29118. 192p. 1987. pap. text ed. 72.00 (*0-471-90592-5*) Wiley.

Wounded Heart. LC 92-71627. 116p. (Orig.). 1992. pap. 9.95 (*1-878149-11-3*) Counterpoint Pub.

Wounded Heart: Hope for Adult Victims of Sexual Abuse. Dan B. Allender. LC 90-61684. 264p. (Orig.). 1990. pap. 15.00 (*0-89109-289-7*) NavPress.

Wounded Heart of God. Andrew S. Park. 224p. (Orig.). 1993. pap. 17.95 (*0-687-38536-9*) Abingdon.

Wounded Heart Workbook: A Companion Workbook for Personal or Group Use. Dan B. Allender. 192p. 1992. wbk. ed., pap. 17.00 (*0-89109-665-5*) NavPress.

Wounded Heroes: The Secrets of Charles Spurgeon, Hudson Taylor, Amy Carmichael, C. S. Lewis, Isobel Kuhn & Others Who Triumphed over Emotional Pain. Elizabeth Skoglund. 232p. 1992. pap. 9.99 (*0-8010-8342-7*, Ravens Ridge) Baker Bks.

***Wounded in Action.** John Sullivan. (Orig.). 1997. pap. 10.95 (*1-57532-027-4*) Press-Tige Pub.

Wounded in the House of a Friend. Sonia Sanchez. 128p. 1995. 15.00 (*0-8070-6826-8*) Beacon Pr.

***Wounded in the House of a Friend.** Sonia Sanchez. 1997. pap. 10.00 (*0-8070-6827-6*) Beacon Pr.

Wounded Innocents: The Real Victims of the War Against Child Abuse. rev. ed. Richard Wexler. 429p. (C). 1995. pap. 16.95 (*0-87975-936-4*) Prometheus Bks.

Wounded Jung: Effects of Jung's Relationships on His Life & Work. Robert C. Smith. (Psychosocial Issues Ser.). 280p. 1996. 30.00 (*0-8101-1270-1*) Northwestern U Pr.

Wounded Knee: An Indian History of the American West. Dee Brown. (Illus.). 224p. (YA). (gr. 7 up). 1993. pap. 9.95 (*0-8050-2700-9*, Bks Young Read) H Holt & Co.

Wounded Knee: Death of a Dream. Laurie A. O'Neill. LC 92-12998. (Spotlight on American History Ser.). (Illus.). 64p. (J). (gr. 4-6). 1993. pap. 5.95 (*1-56294-748-6*); lib. bdg. 16.40 (*1-56294-253-0*) Millbrook Pr.

Wounded Knee: Lest We Forget. Alvin M. Josephy, Jr. et al. LC 90-84774. (Illus.). 64p. 1992. pap. 21.95 (*0-931618-32-0*) U of Wash Pr.

Wounded Knee see Calvalry Bits: Custer & the Seventh Cavalry

Wounded Knee & the Ghost Dance Tragedy. Jack Utter. LC 91-61211. (Illus.). iv, 29p. (Orig.). (YA). (gr. 7-12). 1991. pap. 3.95 (*0-9628075-1-6*) Natl Woodlands Pub.

Wounded Knee II. Rolland Dewing. 230p. 1995. 21.95 (*0-9646780-0-4*); pap. 10.95 (*0-9646780-1-2*) Grt Plains Ntwrk.

Wounded Knee, 1973: A Personal Account. Stanley D. Lyman. Ed. by Floyd A. O'Neil et al. LC 90-12653. (Illus.). xxxx, 196p. 1991. text ed. 35.00 (*0-8032-2889-9*) U of Nebr Pr.

Wounded Knee 1973: A Personal Account. Stanley D. Lyman. Ed. by Floyd A. O'Neil et al. LC 90-12653. (Illus.). xxxx, 196p. 1993. pap. 9.95 (*0-8032-7933-7*, Bison Books) U of Nebr Pr.

***Wounded Land.** Stephen R. Donaldson. 1997. pap. 12.00 (*0-345-41846-8*, Del Rey) Ballantine.

Wounded Land, Bk. 1. Stephen R. Donaldson. 512p. 1987. mass mkt. 6.99 (*0-345-34868-0*, Del Rey) Ballantine.

Wounded Lover: A Book for Women Raising Sons & Men Coming to Terms with Their Fathers. John Lee. Orig. Title: At My Father's Wedding. 195p. 1995. pap. 12.00 (*0-915408-53-8*) Ally Pr.

Wounded Lovers. Marilyn Rickabaugh. Ed. by Dave Eaton & Greg Flessing. 20p. 1988. 34.95 (*0-317-90947-9*); vhs 29.95 (*0-317-90948-7*) Flessing & Flessing.

Wounded Male. Steven Farmer. 208p. 1992. pap. 10.00 (*0-345-37432-0*, Ballantine Trade) Ballantine.

Wounded Mattress. Sotere Torregian. 1970. 5.00 (*0-685-04681-8*); pap. 2.75 (*0-685-04682-6*) Oyez.

Wounded Meeting: Dealing with Difficult Behavior in Meeting for Worship. Ministry & Nurture Committee Staff. 60p. (Orig.). 1993. pap. text ed. 5.00 (*0-9620912-7-8*) Friends Genl Conf.

Wounded Night. Michael Kuciak. Ed. by Lawrence R. Sims. (Illus.). 96p. (Orig.). (YA). 1996. pap. 11.95 (*1-889155-11-X*, ODS911) Optimus Design.

Wounded River: Civil War Letters of John Vance Lauderdale, M.D. Ed. by Peter Josyph. LC 92-56859. (C). 1993. 29.95 (*0-87013-328-4*) Mich St U Pr.

Wounded Sky. Diane Duane. (Star Trek Ser.). 224p. (Orig.). 1991. mass mkt. 5.50 (*0-671-74352-X*) PB.

Wounded Spirit: T. E. Lawrence's "Seven Pillars of Wisdom" 2nd ed. Jeffrey Meyers. 220p. 1989. text ed. 39.95 (*0-312-02721-4*) St Martin.

Wounded Stag: Fifty-Four Poems. Bienvenido N. Santos. 70p. (Orig.). 1992. pap. 7.50 (*971-10-0486-0*, Pub. by New Day Pub PH) Cellar.

***Wounded Storyteller: Body, Illness & Ethics.** Arthur W. Frank. 231p. 1997. pap. 14.95 (*0-226-25993-5*) U Ch Pr.

Wounded Titans: American Presidents & the Perils of Power. Max Lerner. 464p. 1996. 29.95 (*1-55970-339-3*) Arcade Pub Inc.

***Wounded Tree: The Lies & Legacies of Generational Abuse.** Bonnie J. Stanley. 1996. pap. text ed. 12.95 (*1-884213-03-0*) Vision Christ.

***Wounded Underneath: God's Power Shows up Best in the Suffering Person.** James Brooks. 120p. (Orig.). 1996. pap. 10.00 (*1-57502-362-8*, PO1166) Morris Pubng.

Wounded Warriors. R. Loren Sandford. 1987. pap. 7.95 (*0-932081-17-7*) Victory Hse.

Wounded Warriors: A Time for Healing. Doyle Arbogast. 330p. (Orig.). 1995. pap. 22.00 (*0-9645066-0-2*) Little Trtle.

Wounded Woman: Healing the Father-Daughter Relationship. Linda S. Leonard. LC 83-42801. 179p. 1983. pap. 12.00 (*0-394-72183-7*) Shambhala Pubns.

Wounded Woman: Healing the Father-Daughter Relationship. Linda S. Leonard. LC 82-6289. xx, 186p. 1982. 24.95 (*0-8040-0397-1*) Swallow.

Wounded Yankee. Gilbert Morris. (House of Winslow Ser.: Bk. 10). 304p. (Orig.). 1991. pap. 9.99 (*1-55661-116-1*) Bethany Hse.

Wounding Words: A Woman's Journal in Tunisia. Evelyne Accad. Tr. by Cyntha T. Hahn. (African Writers Ser.). 1996. pap. 13.95 (*0-435-90523-6*, 90523) Heinemann.

Wounds & Lacerations: Emergency Care & Closure. 2nd ed. Trott. (Illus.). 352p. (C). (gr. 13). 1990. text ed. 59.00 (*0-8016-5154-9*) Mosby Yr Bk.

Wounds & Lacerations: Emergency Care & Closure. 2nd ed. Trott. LC 97-22239. 380p. (C). (gr. 13). 1997. text ed. 54.95 (*0-8151-8853-6*) Mosby Yr Bk.

Wounds Beneath the Flesh: Anthology of Native American Poetry. Ed. by Maurice Kenny. 1987. pap. 8.00 (*0-934834-10-5*) White Pine.

Wounds Healed by Love Alone: A Charismatic Interview with St. Therese of Lisieux. Daniel Ange. Tr. by Marjorie Flower & Elaine Chariot. (Illus.). 168p. (Orig.). (ENG & FRE.). 1996. pap. 8.95 (*0-9628088-3-0*) Laser Pr Pubs.

Wounds in the Rain. Stephen Crane. LC 72-3294. (Short Story Index Reprint Ser.). 1977. reprint ed. 26.95 (*0-8369-4145-4*) Ayer.

Wounds in the Rain. Stephen Crane. (Works of Stephen Crane Ser.). 1990. reprint ed. lib. bdg. 79.00 (*0-7812-2435-7*) Rprt Serv.

***Wounds of Civil War.** Thomas Lodge. Ed. by Joseph W. Houppert. LC 68-63050. (Regents Renaissance Drama Ser.). 137p. 1969. reprint ed. pap. 39.10 (*0-608-02672-7*, 2063325) Bks Demand.

Wounds of Passion. Bell Hooks. LC 96-7308. 1997. 25.00 (*0-8050-4146-X*) H Holt & Co.

Wounds of Passion. Charlotte Lamb. 1994. mass mkt. 2.99 (*0-373-11687-X*, 1-11687-0) Harlequin Bks.

Wounds of Passion. large type ed. Charlotte Lamb. (Harlequin Ser.). 1994. lib. bdg. 19.95 (*0-263-13777-5*) Thorndike Pr.

Wounds of War & the Process of Healing. rev. ed. Fred A. Wilcox. (Lessons of the Vietnam War Ser.). (Illus.). 32p. (C). 1991. pap. text ed. 5.00 (*0-945919-10-7*) Ctr Social Studies.

Wounds That Heal. Keith Fournier. 220p. (Orig.). 1992. pap. 10.99 (*0-89283-764-0*, Charis) Servant.

Woven & Graphic Art of Anni Albers: Essays by Nicholas Fox Weber, Mary Jane Jacob, & Richard S. Field. Intro. by Lloyd E. Herman. LC 85-600008. (Illus.). 140p. 1985. pap. 29.95 (*0-87474-977-8*, HEAAP) Smithsonian.

Woven & Graphic Art of Anni Albers: Essays by Nicholas Fox Weber, Mary Jane Jacob, & Richard S. Field. Nicholas F. Weber et al. LC 85-600008. (Illus.). 140p. 1985. 48.00 (*0-87474-978-6*, HEAA) Smithsonian.

Woven by the Grandmothers: Nineteenth-Century Navajo Textiles from the National Museum of the American Indian. Ed. by Eulalie H. Bonar. (Illus.). 240p. (Orig.). 1996. pap. 29.95 (*1-56098-728-6*) Smithsonian.

Woven Cloth Construction. S. Robinson & T. Marks. 178p. 1973. 70.00 (*0-686-63810-7*) St Mut.

Woven Fabric Composites. Niranjan Naik. LC 93-60363. 200p. 1993. pap. 89.95 (*0-87762-990-0*) Technomic.

***Woven Figure: Conservatism & America's Fabric.** George F. Will. 1997. 27.50 (*0-684-82562-7*) S&S Trade.

Woven Gods: Female Clowns & Power in Rotuma. Vilsoni Hereniko. LC 94-13120. (Pacific Islands Monographs: No. 12). (Illus.). 216p. (C). 1995. text ed. 32.00 (*0-8248-1655-2*) UH Pr.

***Woven in Sunlight: A Garden Companion.** Illus. by Tracy Porter. 48p. 1997. 6.95 (*0-8362-3179-1*) Andrews & McMeel.

***Woven in Time.** Martha M. Snyder. (Orig.). 1996. pap. write for info. (*1-57553-369-3*) Watermrk Pr.

Woven Jewels: Tibetan Rugs from Southern California Collections. Murray L. Eiland, Jr. et al. (Illus.). 96p. 1992. pap. 38.50 (*0-685-66767-7*) Pacific Asia.

Woven on the Loom of Time: Stories by Enrique Anderson-Imbert. Enrique Anderson-Imbert. Tr. by Carleton Vail from SPA. (Texas Pan American Ser.). 200p. (Orig.). 1990. pap. 14.95 (*0-292-79060-0*); text ed. 32.50 (*0-292-79054-6*) U of Tex Pr.

***Woven Ribbons.** Marilyn Doheny. Ed. & Illus. by Chuck Eng. (Strata Art Ser.). 12p. (Orig.). 1991. pap. 10.95 (*0-945169-10-8*) Doheny Pubns.

Woven Silks of India. Ed. by Jasleen Khamija. (C). 1995. 98.50 (*81-85026-28-9*, Pub. by Marg) S Asia.

Woven Spirit of the Southwest. Don McQuiston & Debra McQuiston. LC 95-7347. (Illus.). 120p. 1995. 35.00 (*0-8118-0864-5*); pap. 19.95 (*0-8118-0880-7*) Chronicle Bks.

***Woven Splendor: Five Centuries of European Tapestry in the Detroit Institute of Arts.** Tracey Albainy et al. (Illus.). 88p. (Orig.). 1996. pap. 14.95 (*0-89558-146-9*) Det Inst Arts.

Woven Stone. Simon J. Ortiz. LC 92-12507. (Sun Tracks Ser.: Vol. 21). 367p. 1992. pap. 21.50 (*0-8165-1330-9*); lib. bdg. 50.00 (*0-8165-1294-9*) U of Ariz Pr.

Woven Structure & Design, Vol. 1. Wira Staff. (C). 1986. 125.00 (*0-900820-17-9*, Pub. by British Textile Tech UK) St Mut.

Woven Structure & Design: Single Cloth Construction by Goerner, Wira, 1986, Pt. 1. Doris Goerner. 1986. 85.00 (*0-317-56739-X*) St Mut.

Woven Structure & Design, Pt. 1: Single Cloth Construction. Doris Goerner. 1986. 110.00 (*0-317-68394-2*) St Mut.

Woven Structure & Design, Pt. 2: Compound Structures. British Textile Tech. Group Staff. 140p. (C). 1989. 145.00 (*0-903669-51-X*, Pub. by British Textile Tech UK) St Mut.

Woven Textiles in Britain from 1750 to 1850. (Victoria & Albert Museum Textile Collection Ser.). (Illus.). 112p. 1994. pap. 24.95 (*1-55859-850-2*) Abbeville Pr.

Woven Textiles in Britain to 1750. (Victoria & Albert Museum Textile Collection Ser.). (Illus.). 128p. 1994. pap. 24.95 (*1-55859-849-9*) Abbeville Pr.

Woven with Love. Ann E. Marshall. (Illus.). 36p. (Orig.). (J). (gr. 2-5). 1988. pap. 4.50 (*0-934351-02-3*) Heard Mus.

Woven with the Ship. Cyrus T. Brady. LC 73-128722. (Short Story Index Reprint Ser.). 1977. 24.95 (*0-8369-3613-2*) Ayer.

***Wovoka & the Ghost Dance.** Michael Hittman. 1997. pap. text ed. 20.00 (*0-8032-7308-8*) U of Nebr Pr.

Wow! Amy Auden. 324p. 1996. pap. 19.95 (*1-85158-694-6*, Pub. by Mnstream UK) Trafalgar.

Wow: Workshop on Workshops. rev. ed. Aurelio M. Montemayor. (Illus.). 134p. 1994. pap. text ed. 25.00 (*1-878550-52-7*) Inter Dev Res Assn.

***Wow! Babies.** Penny Gentieu. LC 97-5344. (J). 1997. 12.00 (*0-517-70963-5*) Crown Bks Yng Read.

WOW Factory: Creating a Customer Focus Revolution in Your Business. Paul Levesque. LC 94-31410. 192p. 1994. text ed. 22.95 (*0-7863-0386-7*) Irwin Prof Pubng.

Wow God. Frances Clare. LC 75-32009. 192p. 1975. pap. 7.95 (*0-89221-131-8*) New Leaf.

Wow! I Got to Go to the North Pole. R. W. Thompson, Jr. (Illus.). 16p. (J). (ps-3). 1994. 8.95 (*0-9636442-0-3*) N Pole Chron.

***Wow, I'm a Big Brother!** Penny Nye. (Illus.). 16p. (Orig.). (J). (ps-4). 1997. pap. 10.00 (*1-890703-02-8*) Penny Laine.

***Wow, I'm a Big Sister!** Penny Nye. (Illus.). 16p. (Orig.). (J). (ps-4). 1997. pap. 10.00 (*1-890703-03-6*) Penny Laine.

***Wow! It's Great Being a Duck.** Rankin. 1998. pap. 16.00 (*0-689-81756-8*) S&S Childrens.

Wow! Nemo, Toss a Lasso to Me Now! Dona Smith. 96p. (J). (gr. 4-6). 1994. pap. 1.95 (*0-590-47710-2*) Scholastic Inc.

Wow, Prompter Did It Again.... Myungkark Park. (Illus.). 100p. (Orig.). 1991. pap. write for info. (*1-877974-15-3*) Prompter Pubns.

***Wow! Resumes for Administrative Careers: How to Put Together a Winning Resume.** Rachel Lefkowitz. LC 96-38146. 1997. pap. text ed. 10.95 (*0-07-037102-4*) McGraw.

***Wow! Resumes for Creative Jobs.** Matthew J. DeLuca & Nanette F. DeLuca. LC 97-9589. 160p. 1997. pap. text ed. 10.95 (*0-07-016381-2*) McGraw.

WOW! The Wonders of Wetlands: An Educator's Guide. Alan S. Kesselheim et al. (Illus.). 331p. (Orig.). 1995. teacher ed. 15.95 (*1-888631-00-7*) Watercourse.

WOW! The Wonders of Wetlands: An Educator's Guide. 2nd rev. ed. Britt E. Slattery. 160p. (J). (gr. k-12). 1992. pap. text ed. write for info. (*1-883226-00-7*) Environ Concern.

WOW! The Wonders of Wetlands: An Educator's Guide. 3rd ed. Britt E. Slattery. (Illus.). 164p. (J). (gr. k-12). 1993. teacher ed. 12.00 (*1-883226-01-5*) Environ Concern.

Wow, What a Week! Big Book. Mark Porter. (Wonders! Ser.). (Illus.). 24p. (Orig.). (J). (gr. 1-3). 1991. pap. text ed. 29.95 (*1-56334-051-8*) Hampton-Brown.

Wow, What a Week! Small Book. Mark Porter. (Wonders! Ser.). (Illus.). 24p. (Orig.). (J). (gr. 1-3). 1991. pap. text ed. 6.00 (*1-56334-057-7*) Hampton-Brown.

Wow! Wool-on-Wool Folk Art Quilts. Janet C. Brandt. 1995. pap. 19.95 (*1-56477-117-2*, B234) That Patchwork.

Wow 18. (J). pap. 1.25 (*0-590-11718-1*) Scholastic Inc.

***WOWBugs: New Life for Life Science.** Robert W. Matthews et al. (Illus.). 320p. 1996. 19.95 (*1-888499-06-0*) Riverview GA.

WOWO, the Radio Dog. Kevin McCloskey. LC 92-44165. (Illus.). (J). (gr. 3 up). Date not set. write for info. (*0-688-12657-X*); lib. bdg. write for info. (*0-688-12658-8*) Lothrop.

WOWW Companion: A Guide to the Communities Surrounding Central & Eastern European Towns. Compiled by Gary Mokotoff. LC 95-1210. (Monographs). 208p. (Orig.). 1995. text ed. 25.95 (*0-9626373-6-X*) Avotaynu.

Woyzeck. Georg Buchner. Tr. by John Mackendrick. 39p. (Orig.). (C). 1988. pap. 9.95 (*0-413-38820-4*, A0322) Heinemann.

***Woyzeck.** Georg Buchner. Tr. by Gregory Motton from GER. (Drama Classics Ser.). 128p. (Orig.). 1997. pap. 6.95 (*1-85459-183-5*, Pub. by N Hern Bks UK) Theatre Comm.

Woyzeck. J. Guthrie. (German Texts Ser.). 120p. 1988. pap. text ed. 16.95 (*1-85399-374-3*, Pub. by Duckworth UK) Focus Pub-R Pullins.

Woyzeck see Leonce & Lena: Lenz; Woyzeck

Woyzeck, Cuchner: Critical Monographs in English. Edward McInnes. 1993. pap. 32.00 (*0-85261-341-5*, Pub. by Univ of Glasgow UK) St Mut.

Woyzeck-Lenz. Georg Buchner. Tr. & Intro. by Hedwig Rappolt. 77p. (Orig.). 1988. pap. text ed. 4.50 (*0-939858-06-1*) T S L Pr.

Woza Afrika! A Collection of South African Plays. Ed. by Duma Ndlovu. LC 86-20762. 272p. 1987. pap. 14.95 (*0-8076-1170-0*) Braziller.

Woza Albert! Percy Mtwa et al. 80p. (C). 1988. pap. 9.95 (*0-413-53000-0*, A0323) Heinemann.

Woza Shakespeare! Sher & Doran. 1996. 34.95 (*0-614-17657-3*, Pub. by Methuen UK) Heinemann.

***Woza Shakespeare.** Sher. Date not set. write for info. (*0-312-17068-8*) St Martin.

Wozu Philosophie? Stellungnahmen eines Arbeitskreises. Ed. by Herrmann Luebbe. (C). 1978. 29.25 (*3-11-007513-X*) De Gruyter.

Wozu Wissenschaftsphilosophie? Positionen und Fragen zur Gegenwartigen Wissenschaftphilosophie. Ed. by Paul Hoyningen-Huene & Gertrude Hirsch. viii, 433p. (GER.). 1988. pap. text ed. 35.40 (*3-11-011472-0*) De Gruyter.

Wozzeck. Alban Berg. Ed. by Nicholas John. Tr. by Eric Blocknel & Vicki Hartfold. LC 90-44450. (English National Opera Guide Series: Bilingual Libretto, Articles: No. 42). (Illus.). (Orig.). 1991. pap. 9.95 (*0-7145-4201-6*) Riverrun NY.

WP for Windows 95 Virtual Tutor. Que Education & Training Staff. 1996. 49.99 incl. cd-rom (*1-57576-109-2*) Que Educ & Trng.

WPA & the Federal Relief Policy. Donald S. Howard. LC 72-2374. (FDR & the Era of the New Deal Ser.). 888p. 1973. reprint ed. lib. bdg. 95.00 (*0-306-70489-7*) Da Capo.

WPA Collection of the Oklahoma City Art Museum. Contrib. & Intro. by Jayne Hazleton. 1996. pap. 10.00 (*0-614-13530-3*) Okla City Art.

WPA Dallas Guide & History. Intro. by Gerald D. Saxon. LC 92-4505. (Illus.). 450p. 1992. 24.95 (*0-929398-31-9*) UNTX Pr.

WPA Guide to Cincinnati. Writers Program of WPA, Ohio Staff. LC 87-72224. (Illus.). 611p. 1988. reprint ed. lib. bdg. 25.00 (*0-318-37560-5*) Cinc Hist Soc.

WPA Guide to Cincinnati. Writers' Program of WPA, Ohio Staff. LC 87-72224. (Illus.). 611p. 1988. reprint ed. text ed. 29.95 (*0-318-37561-3*) Cinc Hist Soc.

WPA Guide to Kentucky. Ed. by Kevin Simon. (Illus.). 608p. 1996. 39.95 (*0-8131-1997-9*) U Pr of Ky.

WPA Guide to Minnesota. Federal Writers' Project. LC 84-29475. xl, 539p. 1985. reprint ed. pap. 9.95 (*0-87351-185-9*, Borealis Book) Minn Hist.

WPA Guide to New York City. Federal Writers' Project Staff. (Illus.). 736p. 1995. pap. 15.95 (*1-56584-321-5*) New Press NY.

W

WPA Guide to Nineteen Thirties Arizona. WPA Staff. LC 88-27652. Orig. Title: Arizona: A State Guide. 530p. 1989. reprint ed. pap. 21.50 (*0-8165-1099-7*) U of Ariz Pr.

WPA Guide to Nineteen Thirties New Jersey. Federal Writers' Project of the Works Progress Administration. 735p. (Orig.). 1989. pap. 19.95 (*0-8135-1465-7*) Rutgers U Pr.

WPA Guide to Nineteen Thirties New Mexico. WPA Staff. LC 88-27891. Orig. Title: New Mexico: A Guide to the Colorful State. 458p. 1989. reprint ed. pap. 19.95 (*0-8165-1102-0*) U of Ariz Pr.

WPA Guide to Tennessee. Federal Writers' Project of the Work Progress Administration. LC 85-31507. Orig. Title: Tennessee: A Guide to the State. (Illus.). 608p. 1986. reprint ed. pap. 16.95 (*0-87049-384-1*); reprint ed. lib. bdg. 32.50 (*0-87049-383-3*) U of Tenn Pr.

WPA Guide to the Arrowhead Country. Workers of the WPA Writers Program Staff. LC 87-34923. (Illus.). xxxv, 235p. 1988. reprint ed. pap. 9.95 (*0-87351-227-8*, Borealis Book) Minn Hist.

WPA Guide to the Monterey Peninsula. Work Projects Administration Staff. LC 89-20183. 247p. 1990. reprint ed. pap. 14.95 (*0-8165-1145-4*) U of Ariz Pr.

WPA Guide to 1930s Arkansas. Federal Writers' Project of the Works Progress Administration. LC 87-81307. (Illus.). lxvi, 512p. 1987. reprint ed. pap. 12.95 (*0-7006-0341-7*) U Pr of KS.

WPA Guide to 1930s Kansas. Federal Writers' Project of the Work Progress Administration. LC 84-51694. Orig. Title: Kansas: A Guide to the Sunflower State. (Illus.). xxxiv, 540p. 1984. reprint ed. pap. 12.95 (*0-7006-0249-6*) U Pr of KS.

WPA Guide to 1930s Montana. WPA Staff. (Illus.). 442p. 1994. reprint ed. pap. 21.50 (*0-8165-1503-4*) U of Ariz Pr.

WPA Guide to 1930s Nevada. LC 90-25810. (Vintage West Ser.). (Illus.). 408p. 1991. pap. 15.95 (*0-87417-170-9*) U of Nev Pr.

WPA Guide to 1930s New Jersey. Federal Writers' Project of the Works Progress Administration. 750p. (C). 1986. 45.00 (*0-8135-1152-6*) Rutgers U Pr.

WPA Guide to 1930s Oklahoma. Federal Writers' Project of the Works Progress Administration. LC 86-50226. (Illus.). xxxviii, 442p. 1986. reprint ed. pap. 12.95 (*0-7006-0294-1*) U Pr of KS.

WPA Museum Extension Quilt Project: So. Langhorne, Pennsylvania. (Illus.). 1990. reprint ed. pap. 24.95 (*0-9618293-1-1*) Variable Star.

WPA Oklahoma Slave Narratives. T. Lindsay Baker & Julie P. Baker. LC 95-16222. (Illus.). 544p. 1996. pap. 24.95 (*0-8061-2859-3*) U of Okla Pr.

WPA Oklahoma Slave Narratives. Ed. by T. Lindsay Baker & Julie P. Baker. LC 95-16222. 1996. 49.95 (*0-8061-2792-9*) U of Okla Pr.

WPA Writers' Program Publications Catalogue: The American Guide Series, The American Life Series: September 1941. 2nd ed. WPA Staff. 54p. 1990. reprint ed. pap. 7.50 (*0-924772-14-X*) CH Bookworks.

WPFW 89.3FM Poetry Anthology: The Poet & the Poem. Ed. by Grace Cavalieri. LC 91-78328. 340p. (Orig.). 1992. pap. 18.00 (*0-938572-03-2*) Bunny Crocodile.

*__WPFW 89.3FM Poetry Anthology: The Poet & the Poem.__ 2nd ed. Ed. by Grace Cavalieri. 340p. (Orig.). Date not set. pap. write for info. (*0-938572-19-9*) Bunny Crocodile.

WPPSS Fraud Perpetrated by Washington State. Norman A. Benson. LC 92-19777. 1992. pap. 4.95 (*0-87770-509-7*) Ye Galleon.

WPS Career Planning Program: Leader's Handbook. Jacqueline N. Buck et al. 53p. (Orig.). 1985. pap. text ed. 19.00 (*0-87424-201-0*, W-200B) Western Psych.

WPS Career Planning Program: Student Handbook. Jacqueline N. Buck et al. 109p. 1986. pap. text ed. 29.50 (*0-87424-200-2*, W-200A) Western Psych.

WRA, a Story of Human Conservation see U. S. War Relocation Authority

Wrack & Rune. Charlotte MacLeod. 208p. 1983. mass mkt. 3.99 (*0-380-61911-3*) Avon.

Wraeththu. Storm Constantine. 800p. 1993. pap. 17.95 (*0-312-89000-1*) Orb NYC.

Wraith: Buried Secrets. 2nd ed. Richard Dansky. (Wraith Ser.). (Illus.). 72p. 1996. pap. 15.00 (*1-56504-603-X*, 6601) White Wolf.

Wraith: The Oblivion. 2nd ed. Richard Dansky. (Illus.). 272p. 1996. 28.00 (*1-56504-600-5*, 6600) White Wolf.

Wraith Players Guide. Mark R. Hagan. (Wraith: the Oblivion Ser.). 96p. 1995. per., pap. 18.00 (*1-56504-601-3*, 6007/4601) White Wolf.

*__Wraiths.__ Larry C. Gillies. 1996. mass mkt. 4.99 (*1-55197-102-X*, Pub. by Comnwlth Pub CN) Partners Pubs Grp.

Wraiths of Time. Andre Norton. 256p. 1992. mass mkt. 3.99 (*0-8125-4752-7*) Tor Bks.

Wraith's Vale. Robert Griffin. LC 96-90683. (Mischka's Tale Ser.: Vol. 4). 120p. 1997. 15.00 (*1-889314-19-6*); pap. 7.00 (*1-889314-20-X*) Windhover Pub.

Wrangell & the Gold of the Cassiar. Clarence L. Andrews. 61p. reprint ed. pap. 4.95 (*0-8466-0267-9*, S267) Shorey.

*__Wrangell-St. Elias National Park & Preserve, Alaska.__ Ed. by Trails Illustrated Staff. (Illus.). 1996. 8.99 (*1-56695-046-5*) Trails Illustrated.

Wrangler. Dorsey Kelley. (Romance Ser.). 1993. pap. 2.69 (*0-373-08938-4*, 5-08938-8) Silhouette.

Wrangler & the Rich Girl. Joan Johnston. (Desire Ser.). 1993. mass mkt. 2.99 (*0-373-05791-1*, 5-05791-4) Silhouette.

*__Wrangler's Bride.__ Justine Davis. 1997. mass mkt. 4.50 (*0-373-50186-2*, 1-50186-5) Harlequin Bks.

Wrangler's Lady. Jackie Merritt. (Desire Ser.). 1994. mass mkt. 2.99 (*0-373-05841-1*, 5-05841-7) Silhouette.

Wrangler's Wedding. Robin Nicholas. (Romance Ser.). 1996. mass mkt. 3.25 (*0-373-19149-9*, 1-19149-3) Silhouette.

Wrap Account Investment Advisor: How to Profit from Wall Street's Hottest New Product. Daniel R. Bott & Larry Chambers. 325p. 1993. text ed. 32.50 (*1-55738-497-5*) Irwin Prof Pubng.

Wrap It Up. Cy DeCosse Incorporated Staff. LC 96-10564. (Great Gifts Ser.). (Illus.). 95p. 1996. 14.95 (*0-86573-986-2*) Cowles Creative.

Wrap It Up: Gift Ideas for Teachers & Parents. Susan Horton. (J). (ps-5). 1989. pap. 12.95 (*1-55691-033-9*, 339) Learning Pubns.

*__Wrap It Up: 100 Fresh, Bold, & Bright Sandwiches with a Twist.__ Amy Cotler. 1998. pap. write for info. (*0-609-80236-4*) Crown Pub Group.

Wrap It up, I'll Take It. Deborah C. Edwards. LC 79-55884. (Illus.). 62p. (Orig.). 1980. pap. 3.95 (*0-9603750-0-7*) Teachers Load.

Wrap Me in My Dreams, Only Today, Country School. Helen I. Beatty. (Illus.). 180p. 1991. pap. 12.00 (*0-685-52572-4*) Fords Landing Pr.

Wrap Myself in a Rainbow. Paul Alexander. 96p. 1995. pap. 13.95 (*0-8245-1520-X*) Crossroad NY.

Wrap Myself in a Rainbow: A Grief Guide & Healing Workbook. Paul Alexander. 1995. pap. write for info. (*0-8245-3000-4*) Crossroad NY.

Wrap Myself in a Rainbow Workbook. Paul Alexander. 100p. 1994. 9.95 (*0-9642083-0-X*) P Alexander.

Wrap-up Guide. 2nd ed. Gary E. Bird. 170p. 1993. pap. 49.95 (*1-886813-09-4*) Intl Risk Mgt.

Wrapped Church. Duncan McNaughton. 32p. (Orig.). 1996. pap. 5.00 (*0-9631462-1-1*) Blue Millennium.

Wrapped in a Ribbon: A Selection of Inspirational Writings. Flavia M. Weedn. (Illus.). 90p. reprint ed. 10.00 (*0-929632-05-2*) Applause Inc.

Wrapped in a Riddle. Sharon E. Heisel. LC 92-26954. (J). 1993. 14.95 (*0-395-65026-7*) HM.

*__Wrapped in Light: Poems by Elizabeth Hazen.__ Elizabeth Hazen. Ed. by R. D. Baker. (Poetry Chapbook Ser.). (Illus.). 28p. (Orig.). 1995. pap. 4.00 (*1-887641-04-1*) Argonne Hotel Pr.

Wrapped in the Colours of the Earth: Cultural Heritage of the First Nations. Moira McCaffrey et al. (Illus.). 128p. 1992. pap. 39.95 (*0-7735-0968-2*, Pub. by McGill CN) U of Toronto Pr.

Wrapped in Wishes. Olga Bicos. 432p. 1996. mass mkt. 5.50 (*0-8217-5370-3*, Zebra Kensgtn) Kensgtn Pub Corp.

Wrapped Reichstag, Berlin, 1971-1995. Christo & Jeanne-Claude. 80p. 1996. pap. 8.99 (*3-8228-8683-1*) Taschen Amer.

Wrapped up in God: A Study of Several Canadian Revivals & Revivalists. George A. Rawlyk. 184p. 1993. pap. 16.95 (*0-7735-1131-8*, Pub. by McGill CN) U of Toronto Pr.

*__Wrapper: Faces Looking for the Future from the Past: 40 Possible City Surfaces for the Museum of Jurassic Technology.__ Robert Mangurian & Mary-Ann Ray. (Illus.). 108p. (Orig.). 1997. pap. write for info. (*1-889629-02-2*) Form Zero.

Wrapper Rockets & Trombone Straws: Science at Every Meal. Edwin J. Sobey. LC 96-42090. (Illus.). 144p. (J). 1996. pap. text ed. 14.95 (*0-07-021745-9*) McGraw.

*__Wrapper Rockets & Trombone Straws: Science at Every Meal.__ Edwin J. Sobey. (Illus.). 144p. (J). (gr. 3 up). 1996. pap. 14.95 (*0-07-044388-2*, Lrng Triangle) McGraw-Hill Prof.

Wrapping Culture: Politeness, Presentation, & Power in Japan & Other Societies. Joy Hendry. LC 92-23254. (Oxford Studies in the Anthropology of Cultural Forms). (Illus.). 240p. (C). 1993. 49.95 (*0-19-827389-4*, Old Oregon Bk Store) OUP.

Wrapping Culture: Politeness, Presentation, & Power in Japan & Other Societies. Joy Hendry. (Oxford Studies in the Anthropology of Cultural Forms). (Illus.). 240p. 1995. pap. 21.00 (*0-19-828028-9*) OUP.

Wrapping Gifts Beautifully. Packo Jansen. LC 91-14172. (Illus.). 80p. 1991. pap. 10.95 (*0-8069-8456-2*) Sterling.

Wrapping in Images: Tattooing in Polynesia. Alfred Gell. (Oxford Studies in the Anthropology of Cultural Forms). (Illus.). 364p. (C). 1993. 55.00 (*0-19-827869-1*, 14144) OUP.

Wrapping in Images: Tattooing in Polynesia. Alfred Gell. (Oxford Studies in Social & Cultural Anthropology). (Illus.). 360p. 1996. pap. 19.95 (*0-19-828090-4*) OUP.

Wrappings. Harmony Hammond. LC 83-50232. (Illus.). 112p. (Orig.). (C). 1983. pap. text ed. 9.50 (*0-939858-05-3*) T S L Pr.

*__Wraps: Easy Recipes for Handheld Meals.__ Mary C. Barber. LC 97-17111. 1998. pap. text ed. 14.95 (*0-8118-1812-8*) Chronicle Bks.

Wrath of Allah. Robert E. Burns. (Illus.). 200p. (Orig.). 1994. pap. 12.95 (*1-880628-01-5*) A Ghosh.

*__Wrath of Almighty God: Jonathan Edwards on God's Judgment Against Sinners.__ Jonathan Edwards. Ed. by Don Kistler. 396p. 1996. 27.95 (*1-57358-060-0*) Soli Deo Gloria.

*__Wrath of Angels.__ Jim Risen & Judy Thomas. 224p. 1998. 24.00 (*0-465-09272-1*) Basic.

Wrath of Asher. Angus Wells. (Book of Kingdoms Ser.: No. 1). 416p. 1990. mass mkt. 5.50 (*0-553-28371-5*, Spectra) Bantam.

Wrath of Athena: Gods & Men in the Odyssey. Jenny S. Clay. (Greek Studies). (C). 1996. pap. text ed. 19.95 (*0-8226-3069-9*) Littlefield.

Wrath of Condo. Vico Confino. 171p. (Orig.). 1985. pap. 7.95 (*0-9615100-0-5*) Maxsell Corp.

*__Wrath of Dionysus: A Novel.__ E. Nagrodskaia & Louise McReynolds. LC 97-445. 1997. write for info. (*0-253-33304-0*); pap. write for info. (*0-253-21132-8*) Ind U Pr.

Wrath of God. (Walk with Jesus Ser.). 179p. 1993. pap. 25.00 (*1-57277-503-3*) Script Rsch.

Wrath of God. Jack Higgins. 1995. pap. 16.95 (*0-7871-0170-2*, Dove Bks) Dove Audio.

*__Wrath of God.__ Jerry Pournelle & Joe Gleason. Date not set. write for info. (*0-688-07056-6*) Morrow.

Wrath of God. large type ed. Jack Higgins. LC 95-45719. 1996. reprint ed. 24.95 (*0-7862-0589-X*) Thorndike Pr.

Wrath of God. Jack Higgins. Ed. by Julie Rubenstein. 256p. 1990. reprint ed. mass mkt. 6.50 (*0-671-72454-1*) PB.

*__Wrath of Grapes: Or the Hangover Companion.__ Andy Toper. 1997. 10.95 (*0-285-63338-4*, Pub. by Souvenir UK) IPG Chicago.

Wrath of Heaven on Earth. Wim Malgo. 9.95 (*0-937422-30-4*); pap. 6.95 (*0-937422-29-0*) Midnight Call.

Wrath of John Steinbeck. Robert Bennett. 1972. 59.95 (*0-8490-1337-2*) Gordon Pr.

Wrath of John Steinbeck. Robert Bennett. LC 74-34402. (Studies in Fiction: No. 34). 1970. reprint ed. lib. bdg. 75.00 (*0-8383-0347-1*) M S G Haskell Hse.

Wrath of Nations. William Pfaff. 256p. 1994. pap. 12.00 (*0-671-89248-7*, Touchstone Bks) S&S Trade.

*__Wrath of Poseidon.__ John G. Betancourt. (Hercules Ser.). 1997. mass mkt. 4.99 (*0-8125-3910-9*) Tor Bks.

*__Wrath of Poseidon.__ John G. Betancourt. (Hercules Ser.). (Orig.). 1997. mass mkt. 4.99 (*0-614-27804-X*) Tor Bks.

Wrath of Sparky. Tom Tomorrow. 112p. 1996. pap. 9.95 (*0-312-13753-2*) St Martin.

Wrath of Squat. Bruce Coville. (Space Brat Ser.: No. 3). (J). (gr. 2-4). 1994. 14.00 (*0-671-89198-7*, Minstrel Bks) PB.

Wrath of the Lion. Jack Higgins. 1995. pap. 16.95 (*0-7871-0169-9*, Dove Bks) Dove Audio.

*__Wrath of the Princes.__ Holly Lisle & Aaron Allston. (Bard's Tale Novel Ser.). 352p. 1997. mass mkt. 5.99 (*0-671-87771-2*) Baen Bks.

*__Wrath of the Prophets, Vol. 20.__ Peter David. (Deep Space Nine Ser.). 1997. mass mkt. 5.99 (*0-671-53817-9*, Star Trek) PB.

Wrath of the Seven Horsemen. Andrew Robinson. Ed. by George MacDonald & S. Coleman Charlton. 32p. (Orig.). (YA). (gr. 10-12). 1987. pap. 6.00 (*0-915795-86-8*, 31) Iron Crown Ent Inc.

Wreadings. G. Huth. 60p. (Orig.). 1987. pap. 3.00 (*0-926935-02-X*) Runaway Spoon.

Wreadings. 2nd rev. ed. G. Huth. 68p. (Orig.). 1995. pap. 3.00 (*1-57141-007-4*) Runaway Spoon.

Wreath at the Foot of the Mountain. Li Cunbao. Tr. by Chen Hanming & James O. Belcher from CHI. LC 90-3019. (Library of World Literature in Translation: Vol. 6). 136p. 1991. text ed. 20.00 (*0-8240-2992-5*) Garland.

Wreath Book: Celebrate the Holidays. Rob Pulleyn. 144p. 1996. pap. 14.95 (*0-8069-6841-9*) Sterling.

Wreath for Jenny's Grave. large type ed. Charlotte Hunt. 496p. 1988. 25.99 (*0-7089-1836-0*) Ulverscroft.

Wreath for Miss Wong. large type ed. Charles Leader. (Linford Mystery Library). 352p. 1996. pap. 15.99 (*0-7089-7869-X*, Linford) Ulverscroft.

Wreath for the Bride. Lillian O'Donnell. 224p. 1991. mass mkt. 4.99 (*0-449-21867-8*, Expression) Fawcett.

Wreath for the Enemy. Pamela Frankau. LC 86-33325. (Recovered Classics Ser.). 320p. 1991. reprint ed. pap. 10.00 (*0-914232-84-3*) McPherson & Co.

Wreath for Udomo. Peter Abrahams. LC 83-45608. reprint ed. 45.00 (*0-404-20001-X*) AMS Pr.

*__Wreath from Bangkok.__ large type ed. Charles Leader. (Linford Mystery Library). 352p. 1996. pap. 15.99 (*0-7089-7907-6*) Ulverscroft.

Wreath Magic: Eighty-Six Magnificent Wreaths, Garlands & Swags to Make. Leslie Dierks. LC 93-25678. (Illus.). 128p. 1994. 27.95 (*0-8069-0578-6*) Sterling.

Wreath Magic: 86 Magnificent Wreaths, Garlands & Swags to Make. Leslie Dierks. (Illus.). 128p. (Orig.). 1996. pap. 14.95 (*0-8069-0579-4*) Sterling.

Wreath Making Basics: More Than Eighty Wreath Ideas. Dawn Cusick. LC 92-41411. (Illus.). 96p. 1993. pap. 9.95 (*0-8069-0279-5*) Sterling.

*__Wreath of Cherry Blossom.__ large type ed. Charles Leader. (Linford Mystery Library). 352p. 1996. pap. 15.99 (*0-7089-7933-5*) Ulverscroft.

Wreath of Honesty. large type ed. Pat Burden. 368p. 1992. 25.99 (*0-7089-2583-9*) Ulverscroft.

Wreath of Poppies. large type ed. Charles Leader. (Linford Mystery Library). 1996. pap. 15.99 (*0-7089-7862-2*, Linford) Ulverscroft.

*__Wreath of Wild Olive: Play, Liminality, & the Study of Literature.__ Mihai I. Spariosu. LC 96-37257. 350p. (C). 1997. pap. text ed. 19.95 (*0-7914-3366-8*) State U NY Pr.

*__Wreath of Wild Olive: Play, Liminality, & the Study of Literature.__ Mihai I. Spariosu. LC 96-37257. 350p. (C). 1997. text ed. 59.50 (*0-7914-3365-X*) State U NY Pr.

Wreath on the Crown. John Cule. 140p. (C). 1967. pap. 20.00 (*0-85088-077-7*, Pub. by Gomer Pr UK) St Mut.

Wreath on the Grave of the New Hieromartyr Vladimir of Kiev. Ed. by Theodore Titov. Tr. by Antonina L. Janda from RUS. (Illus.). 96p. (Orig.). 1987. pap. 6.00 (*0-912927-21-6*, X021) St John Kronstadt.

*__Wreath Products.__ Meldrum. 1995. 86.95 (*0-582-02693-8*, Pub. by Longman UK) Longman.

Wreath Ribbon Quilt. Ruth Moose. 126p. 1988. 14.00 (*0-932662-66-8*); pap. 10.00 (*0-932662-67-6*) St Andrews NC.

Wreaths. Richard Kollath. 1993. 23.00 (*0-8446-6711-0*) Peter Smith.

Wreaths: Creative Ideas for the Year Round. Richard Kolbath. (Illus.). 144p. 1990. pap. 12.95 (*0-395-55414-4*) HM.

Wreaths: Techniques, Materials, Step-by-Step Projects & Creative Ideas for All the Year Round. Richard Kollath. (Illus.). 144p. 1988. 18.95 (*0-8160-1863-4*) Facts on File.

Wreaths & Garlands. Malcolm Hillier. LC 94-6292. (Illus.). 96p. 1994. 22.95 (*1-56458-618-9*) DK Pub Inc.

Wreaths Around the House: More Than 80 Distinctive Wreaths to Make, Enjoy & Give as Gifts. Deborah Morgenthal. LC 93-39715. (Illus.). 144p. 1994. 27.95 (*0-8069-0712-6*) Sterling.

Wreaths Around the House: More Than 80 Distinctive Wreaths to Make, Enjoy & Give As Gifts. Deborah Morgenthal. (Illus.). 144p. (Orig.). 1995. pap. 14.95 (*0-8069-0713-4*) Lark Books.

Wreaths, Arrangements & Basket Decorations: Using Flowers, Foliage, Herbs & Grasses to Make Colorful Crafts. Eleanor S. Platt. (Illus.). 176p. 1994. 24.95 (*0-87596-587-3*) Rodale Pr Inc.

Wreaths from the Garden: Seventy-Five Fresh & Dried Floral Wreaths to Make. Leslie Dierks. LC 93-40711. (Illus.). 128p. 1994. 27.95 (*0-8069-0604-9*) Sterling.

Wreaths from the Garden: Seventy-Five Fresh & Dried Floral Wreaths to Make. Leslie Dierks. (Illus.). 128p. 1995. pap. 14.95 (*0-8069-0605-7*) Sterling.

Wreaths of All Sorts. Bertha Reppert. 40p. 1987. pap. 6.50 (*0-9617210-1-4*) Remembrance.

Wreaths 'Round the Year. Dawn Cusick & Rob Pulleyn. (Illus.). 112p. 1992. pap. 9.95 (*0-8069-7468-0*) Sterling.

*__Wreaths with Ease.__ 1997. pap. 19.95 (*1-57486-060-7*) Oxmoor Hse.

Wreck. Rabindranath Tagore. 414p. 1985. 8.50 (*0-333-90359-5*) Asia Bk Corp.

Wreck Ashore: The United States Life-Saving Service on the Great Lakes. Frederick Stonehouse. Ed. by Paul L. Hayden. LC 94-76420. (Illus.). 240p. (Orig.). 1994. pap. 24.95 (*0-942235-22-3*) LSPC Inc.

Wreck Diver Manual. Karl Shreeves. 60p. (C). 1995. pap. 24.95 (*1-878663-20-8*) PADI.

Wreck Diving: The Diver's Field Guide to Wreck Exploration Procedures. Liam Rooney & Ed Christini. 31p. 1986. pap. text ed. 5.50 (*0-943717-29-9*) Concept Sys.

Wreck Diving Adventures. Gary Gentile. (Illus.). 144p. 1994. pap. 20.00 (*1-883056-00-4*) GGP.

*__Wreck Diving Instructor Manual.__ 42p. 1995. pap. text ed. write for info. (*1-880229-24-2*) Concept Sys.

*__Wreck Diving Manual.__ Daniel Berg. (Specialty Diver Ser.). 88p. 1995. pap. text ed. write for info. (*1-880229-23-4*) Concept Sys.

*__Wreck Diving Manual.__ Lizzie Bird. (Illus.). 160p. 1997. pap. 29.95 (*1-86126-023-7*, Pub. by Crowood Pr UK) Trafalgar.

*__Wreck of the Apollo.__ Paul Davies. 32p. 1994. pap. 5.95 (*1-55022-228-7*, Pub. by ECW Press CN) Genl Dist Srvs.

Wreck of the Barque Stefano off the North West Cape of Australia in 1875. Gustave Rathe. (Illus.). 160p. (YA). 1992. 17.00 (*0-374-38585-8*) FS&G.

*__Wreck of the Edmund Fitzgerald.__ Frederick Stonehouse. (Illus.). 1996. reprint ed. pap. 13.95 (*0-932212-84-0*) Avery Color.

Wreck of the General Arnold: The Mystery of a Revolutionary Privateer in Plymouth Harbor. David W. Bowley. Ed. by Doris M. Johnson. LC 92-70659. (Illus.). 196p. (Orig.). 1992. pap. 15.00 (*0-9628738-3-7*) Jones Riv Pr.

Wreck of the Hippocampus & Other Tales of Saugatuck. Kit Lane. LC 92-80010. (Illus.). 96p. (Orig.). 1992. pap. 5.50 (*1-877703-22-2*) Pavilion Pr.

Wreck of the Isabella. David Miller. LC 95-67721. (Illus.). 272p. 1995. 27.95 (*1-55750-768-6*) Naval Inst Pr.

Wreck of the Isabella: Naval Actions During the Napoleonic Wars. David Miller. (Illus.). 259p. 1995. 42.50 (*0-85052-456-3*, Pub. by L Cooper Bks UK) Trans-Atl Phila.

Wreck of the Mary Deare. Hammond Innes. 296p. 1985. mass mkt. 3.50 (*0-88184-152-8*) Carroll & Graf.

*__Wreck of the Moby Dick.__ Bill Cosby. LC 97-16833. (Little Bill Book Ser.). (J). 1998. write for info. (*0-590-16400-7*); pap. write for info. (*0-590-95620-5*) Scholastic Inc.

*__Wreck of the Parker M. Whitmore.__ rev. ed. M. Edward Burtt. (Illus.). i, 46p. (Orig.). 1996. pap. write for info. (*1-888913-25-8*) M E Burtt.

Wreck of the Santa Clara I: Arsenic Trioxide in the Atlantic. Hearings Before the New Jersey Legislature. (Illus.). 102p. (Orig.). (C). 1994. pap. text ed. 30.00 (*0-7881-0608-2*) DIANE Pub.

Wreck of the SV. Nikolai. Tr. by Alton S. Donnelly from RUS. (North Pacific Studies: No. 8). (Illus.). 128p. 1985. 19.95 (*0-87595-124-4*) Oregon Hist.

Wreck of the Tian: or Futility & Morgan Robertson the Man. Morgan Robertson. 19.95 (*0-8488-1461-4*) Amereon Ltd.

Wreck of the Titan. Morgan Robertson. LC 71-132125. (Short Story Index Reprint Ser.). 1977. 27.95 (*0-8369-3682-5*) Ayer.

Wreck of the Titanic Foretold? Ed. by Martin Gardner. LC 85-46045. 157p. 1986. 28.95 (*0-87975-321-8*) Prometheus Bks.

Wreck of the Zanzibar. Michael Morpurgo. (Illus.). 80p. (J). (gr. 3-5). 1995. pap. 14.99 (*0-670-86360-2*) Viking Child Bks.

Wreck of the Zephyr. Chris Van Allsburg. LC 82-23371. (Illus.). 32p. (J). (ps up). 1983. 17.95 (*0-395-33075-0*) HM.

*__Wreck of Zanzibar.__ Michael Morpurgo. 1999. pap. 5.99 (*0-14-038190-2*) Viking Penguin.

Wreck on the Road to Damascus: Innocence, Guilt & Conversion in Flannery O'Connor. Brian A. Ragen. 230p. 1989. 12.95 (*0-8294-0605-0*) Loyola Pr.

Wreck Shun. Terri Weist. 12p. (Orig.). 1993. pap. 1.50 (*1-884047-53-X*) Mass Extinct.

Wreck Valley, Vol. 2: A Record of Shipwrecks off Long Island's South Shore & New Jersey. 2nd ed. Daniel Berg. (Illus.). 200p. (Orig.). 1990. pap. 18.95 (*0-9616167-3-3*) Aqua Explorers.

***Wrecked, Blessed Body of Shelton Lafleur.** John G. Brown. 272p. 1997. pap. 12.00 (*0-380-72965-2*) Avon.

Wrecked, Blessed Body of Shelton Lafleur. John G. Brown. LC 95-38114. 256p. 1996. 21.95 (*0-395-72988-2*) HM.

Wrecked, Blessed Body of Shelton Lafleur. John G. Brown. 1996. write for info. (*0-614-17410-4*) HM.

***Wrecked, Blessed Body of Shelton Lafleur.** large type ed. John G. Brown. LC 97-9267. 1997. pap. 21.95 (*0-7838-8198-3*) G K Hall.

Wrecked Japanese Junks Adrift in the North Pacific Ocean. Bert Webber. (Illus.). 202p. 1984. pap. 9.00 (*0-87770-309-4*) Ye Galleon.

Wrecked on the Feejees. William S. Cary. 74p. 1987. pap. 9.95 (*0-87770-435-X*) Ye Galleon.

Wrecker. David Skinner. LC 93-46895. 106p. (YA). (gr. 7 up). 1995. lib. bdg. 14.00 (*0-671-79771-9*, S&S Bks Young Read) S&S Childrens.

***Wrecker.** David Skinner. (J). 1997. 3.99 (*0-689-81537-9*, Aladdin Paperbacks) S&S Childrens.

Wreckers. David Edgar. 60p. (C). 1988. pap. 6.95 (*0-413-38510-8*, A0324) Heinemann.

Wreckers & Tow Trucks. Don Wood. (Crestline Ser.). (Illus.). 224p. 1995. pap. 19.95 (*0-87938-981-8*, Crestline Pub) Motorbooks Intl.

Wreckers Must Breathe. large type ed. Hammond Innes. 1968. 25.99 (*0-85456-644-9*) Ulverscroft.

Wrecking Crew: Poems. Larry Levis. LC 78-181398. (Pitt Poetry Ser.). 72p. 1972. reprint ed. pap. 25.00 (*0-608-02057-5*, 2062710) Bks Demand.

Wrecking Crews - Salvage Squads: Media Misinformers & the Misfits Who Oppose Them. Hazel S. Guyol. LC 94-62002. xxii, 294p. (Orig.). 1995. pap. 12.95 (*0-934955-28-X*) Watercress Pr.

Wrecking Yard: And Other Short Stories. Pinckney Benedict. 224p. 1995. pap. 10.95 (*0-452-27435-4*, Plume) NAL-Dutton.

***Wrecking Yard of Games & Activities.** Alanna Jones. (Illus.). 245p. (Orig.). 1996. pap. 24.00 (*1-882883-35-7*, 298) Idyll Arbor.

Wrecks, Accidents & Collisions. James T. Bradley. (Illus.). 96p. (C). 1991. 35.00 (*0-9624633-3-7*) Bradley Enterprises.

Wrecks & Reputations. Don Charlwood. 192p. 1988. pap. 30.00 (*0-614-04020-5*, Pub. by Deakin Univ AT) St Mut.

Wrecks & Rescues of the Great Lakes: A Photographic History. James P. Barry. (Illus.). 1994. reprint ed. pap. 18.95 (*1-882376-01-3*) Thunder Bay Pr.

Wrecks of Scapa Flow. David M. Ferguson. (C). 1986. 50.00 (*0-907618-06-5*, Pub. by Orkney Pr UK) St Mut.

Wrecks of Scapa Flow. Maritime Books Staff. (C). 1986. text ed. 65.00 (*0-685-38773-9*, Pub. by Maritime Bks UK) St Mut.

Wrecks, Rescues & Investigations: Selected Documents of the U. S. Coast Guard & Its Predecessors. Ed. by Bernard C. Nalty et al. LC 78-12312. (Illus.). 473p. 1978. lib. bdg. 65.00 (*0-8420-2130-2*) Scholarly Res Inc.

Wren. Ger Killeen. (Bluestem Poetry Ser.). 62p. 1989. 18.00 (*1-878325-01-9*); pap. 8.50 (*1-878325-00-0*) Bluestem Press.

Wren to the Rescue. Sherwood Smith. 228p. (YA). (gr. 7 up). 1990. 16.00 (*0-15-200975-2*, J Yolen Bks) HarBrace.

Wrench. Patricia Armentrout & David Armentrout. LC 94-45590. (Learning about Tools Ser.). (J). (gr. 2-6). 1995. write for info. (*1-55916-118-3*) Rourke Bk Co.

***Wrens.** Anne V. McGravie. 85p. 1997. pap. 5.50 (*0-87129-772-8*, W82) Dramatic Pub.

Wren's Quest. Sherwood Smith. LC 92-18988. 240p. (YA). (gr. 7 up). 1993. 17.00 (*0-15-200976-0*, J Yolen Bks) HarBrace.

Wren's War. Sherwood Smith. 208p. (YA). (gr. 7 up). 1995. 17.00 (*0-15-200977-9*, J Yolen Bks) HarBrace.

Wrestle the Angel. David Birch. LC 93-60917. (Illus.). 44p. (J). (gr. k-3). 1994. 8.95 (*1-55523-652-9*) Winston-Derek.

Wrestle to Win! Be Smart. Be Ready. Beasey S. Hendrix, III. 208p. 1996. pap. 13.95 (*1-888397-00-4*) High Prfmnce Athltcs.

Wrestlemania. Edward R. Ricciuti. Ed. by Tom Emanuel. (Illus.). 100p. (Orig.). 1986. pap. 5.95 (*0-9616263-2-1*) WWF Bks.

Wrestlers. Bill C. Davis. 1987. pap. 5.25 (*0-8222-1278-1*) Dramatists Play.

Wrestler's Body: Identity & Ideology in North India. Joseph S. Alter. (C). 1992. 45.00 (*0-520-07697-4*) U CA Pr.

Wrestler's Cruel Study. Stephen Dobyns. LC 92-40861. 448p. 1993. 22.95 (*0-393-03511-5*) Norton.

Wrestler's Cruel Study. Stephen Dobyns. 432p. 1995. pap. 11.00 (*0-393-31212-7*) Norton.

Wrestler's Training Diary. Jerry W. Stanley. 120p. (YA). (gr. 7-12). 1988. spiral bd. 7.95 (*0-685-21917-8*) Sports Diary Pub.

Wrestlers with Christ. Karl Pfleger. Tr. by Edward I. Watkin. LC 68-16968. (Essay Index Reprint Ser.). 1977. 23.95 (*0-8369-0785-X*) Ayer.

***Wrestling.** (Composite Guide to...Ser.). (Illus.). 64p. (YA). (gr. 3 up). 1998. lib. bdg. 15.95 (*0-7910-4721-0*) Chelsea Hse.

Wrestling. Doug Marx. LC 93-36544. (Pro-Am Sports Ser.). (J). 1993. write for info. (*0-86593-347-2*) Rourke Corp.

Wrestling: A Commitment to Excellence. Ken Chertow. 156p. 1994. pap. text ed. 9.95 (*0-944183-15-8*) Prof Reports Corp.

Wrestling: A Guide for Parents & Coaches. Cooper Publishing Group Staff. (USOC Sports Education Ser.). (Illus.). 128p. 1997. pap. 18.00 (*1-884125-58-1*) Cooper Pubng.

Wrestling Angels into Song: The Fictions of Ernest J. Gaines & James Alan McPherson. Herman Beavers. (Penn Studies in Contemporary American Fiction). 304p. (C). 1995. text ed. 36.50 (*0-8122-3150-3*) U of Pa Pr.

Wrestling Back: A Family's Trial with Paralyzing Injury. Caren Topliff. LC 96-60109. 240p. 1996. pap. 14.95 (*0-931625-31-9*) DIMI Pr.

Wrestling Basics. Jackson Jay & Jeff Savage. LC 95-44720. (New Action Ser.). 48p. (J). (gr. 3-9). 1996. 17.80 (*1-56065-402-3*) Capstone Pr.

***Wrestling Basics.** Jeff Savage. (New Action Sports Ser.). (Illus.). 48p. (J). (gr. 3-7). 1996. 18.40 (*0-516-20100-X*) Childrens.

Wrestling Coach's Survival Guide: Practical Techniques & Materials for Building an Effective Program & a Winning Team. Keith T. Manos. (Illus.). 256p. 1996. spiral bd. 32.95 (*0-13-458951-3*, Parker Publishing Co) P-H.

***Wrestling Coach's Survival Guide: Practical Techniques & Materials for Building an Effective Program & a Winning Team.** Keith T. Manos. 256p. 1996. pap. 32.50 (*0-13-490392-7*, Parker Publishing Co) P-H.

Wrestling Drill Book. Dennis A. Johnson. LC 90-38916. (Illus.). 248p. (Orig.). 1991. pap. 17.95 (*0-88011-401-0*, PJOH0401) Human Kinetics.

Wrestling for Beginners. Tom Jarman & Reid Hanley. (Illus.). 244p. (Orig.). 1983. pap. 12.95 (*0-8092-5656-8*) Contemp Bks.

Wrestling for Remote Control. Ron G. Darbee. 200p. 1996. pap. 10.99 (*0-8054-6193-0*, 4261-93) Broadman.

Wrestling Match. Buchi Emecheta. LC 82-17750. 74p. (J). (gr. 6-10). 1983. pap. 6.95 (*0-8076-1061-5*) Braziller.

Wrestling on & off the Mat. Wayne Baughman. (Illus.). 300p. 1992. text ed. write for info. (*0-9618446-0-4*) R W Baughman.

Wrestling Physical Conditioning Encyclopedia. John Jesse. LC 74-5197. (C). 1974. pap. 9.95 (*0-87095-043-6*, Athletic) Gldn West Bks.

***Wrestling Sturbridge.** (Reading Group Guides Ser.). (J). 1997. pap. write for info. (*0-676-76017-1*) Knopf Bks Yng Read.

Wrestling Sturbridge. Rich Wallace. LC 95-20468. 144p. (YA). (gr. 7-12). 1996. 16.00 (*0-679-87803-3*) Knopf.

***Wrestling Sturbridge.** Rich Wallace. (J). 1997. pap. 4.99 (*0-679-88555-2*) Knopf.

Wrestling the Light: Ache & Awe in the Human-Divine Struggle. Ted Loder. LC 91-37123. (Illus.). 176p. (Orig.). 1991. pap. 14.95 (*0-931055-79-2*) Innisfree Pr.

***Wrestling Till Dawn.** Blomquist. 13.35 (*0-687-61415-5*) Abingdon.

Wrestling to Rasslin: Ancient Sport to American Spectacle. Gerald W. Morton & George M. O'Brien. LC 85-70425. 169p. 1985. 19.95 (*0-87972-323-8*) Bowling Green Univ Popular Press.

Wrestling with Angels: New & Selected Poems 1960-1995. Doug Beardsley. Ed. by Michael Harris. (Signal Editions Ser.). 176p. (Orig.). 1995. pap. 12.95 (*1-55065-063-7*, Pub. by Vehicule Pr CN) Genl Dist Srvs.

Wrestling with Angels: What Genesis Teaches Us about Our Spiritual Identity, Sexuality, & Personal Relationships. Naomi H. Rosenblatt & Joshua Horwitz. 416p. pap. 12.95 (*0-385-31333-0*, Delta) Dell.

Wrestling with Angels: What the First Family of Genesis Teaches Us about Our Spiritual Identity, Sexuality & Personal Relationships. Naomi H. Rosenblatt & Joshua Horwitz. LC 95-2563. 336p. 1995. 22.95 (*0-385-31330-6*) Delacorte.

Wrestling with Change: The Dilemmas of Teaching Real Mathematics. Lew Romagnano. LC 93-38257. (Illus.). 191p. (J). 1994. pap. text ed. 21.50 (*0-435-08342-2*, 08342) Heinemann.

Wrestling with Day-Break: Searching for Meaning in the Thinking on the Holocaust. Eliezer Schweid. LC 93-39954. (Milken Library of Jewish Public Affairs). 185p. (Orig.). 1994. pap. 51.50 (*0-8191-9358-5*) U Pr of Amer.

Wrestling with Day-Break: Searching for Meaning in the Thinking on the Holocaust. Eliezer Schweid. LC 93-39954. (Milken Library of Jewish Public Affairs). 240p. (Orig.). 1994. pap. text ed. 22.50 (*0-8191-9359-3*) U Pr of Amer.

Wrestling with Depression: A Spiritual Guide to Reclaiming Life. William Hulme & Lucy Hulme. LC 95-22352. 1995. pap. 8.99 (*0-8066-2699-2*) Augsburg Fortress.

Wrestling with God: Religious Life in Search of Its Soul. Barbara Fiand. 1996. pap. text ed. 14.95 (*0-8245-1620-6*) Crossroad NY.

Wrestling with Love: How Men Struggle with Intimacy. Samuel D. Osherson. 496p. 1993. pap. 12.00 (*0-449-90826-7*, Columbine) Fawcett.

Wrestling with Obedience. Joy Gage. 96p. 1991. pap. text ed. 1.20 (*0-89693-147-1*, Victor Bks) Chariot Victor.

Wrestling with Parenthood: Contemporary Dilemmas. Irwin Matus. LC 94-41833. 180p. (Orig.). 1995. pap. 12.95 (*1-880197-12-X*) Gylantic Pub.

Wrestling with Rationality in Paul: Romans 1-8 in a New Perspective. John D. Moores. (Society for New Testament Studies Monographs: No. 82). 235p. (C). 1995. text ed. 59.95 (*0-521-47223-7*) Cambridge U Pr.

Wrestling with Reality. Martin Weber. (Anchor Ser.). 144p. 1993. pap. 0.97 (*0-8163-1153-6*) Pacific Pr Pub Assn.

Wrestling with Special Ed: Recollections by Bill Nunn (Written Without Assistance) of His Trials & His Triumphs As a Learning-Disabled Student. Bill Nunn. Ed. & Illus. by Corinne Sharkey. LC 94-93958. 352p. (Orig.). 1994. 15.00 (*0-9644490-0-5*) Bill Nunn.

Wrestling with the Angel. Lance Lee. 92p. 1990. pap. 9.95 (*0-912292-86-5*) Smith.

Wrestling with the Angel: A Memoir of My Triumph over Illness. Max Lerner. 1990. 18.95 (*0-393-02846-1*) Norton.

Wrestling with the Angel: Faith & Religion in the Lives of Gay Men. Brian Bouldrey. 1996. pap. 14.00 (*1-57322-545-2*, Riverhd Trade) Berkley Pub.

Wrestling with the Angel: Faith & Religion in the Lives of Gay Men. Brian Bouldrey. 1995. 23.95 (*1-57322-003-5*, Riverhead Books) Putnam Pub Group.

Wrestling with the Angel: Jewish Insights on Death & Mourning. Ed. by Jack Riemer. 432p. 1995. 25.00 (*0-8052-4129-9*) Schocken.

Wrestling with the Big Issues. G. Grogan. 8.99 (*1-85792-051-1*, Pub. by Christian Focus UK) Spring Arbor Dist.

Wrestling with the Church. Ed. by Mary Levison. (C). 1992. pap. 24.00 (*0-85305-307-3*, Pub. by J Arthur Ltd UK) St Mut.

Wrestling with the Divine: A Jewish Response to Suffering. Shmuel Boteach. LC 94-1288. 312p. 1995. 30.00 (*1-56821-176-7*) Aronson.

***Wrestling with the Ox: A Theology of Religious Experience.** Paul O. Ingram. LC 97-20365. 1997. pap. write for info. (*0-8264-1040-5*) Continuum.

Wrestling with the Patriarchs: Retrieving Women's Voices in Preaching. Lee McGee & Thomas H. Troeger. (Preacher's Library). 144p. 1996. pap. 13.95 (*0-687-00621-X*) Abingdon.

Wrestling with the Prophets: Essays on Creation Spirituality & Everyday Life. Matthew Fox. LC 94-36434. 334p. 1995. pap. 14.00 (*0-06-062919-3*, PL) HarpC.

Wrestling with the Word. Foster R. McCurley. LC 96-23. 256p. 1996. pap. 20.00 (*1-56338-142-7*) TPI PA.

Wrestling with Time: Problems in Economic Theory. Martin Currie & Ian Steedman. LC 89-35138. 261p. 1990. reprint ed. text ed. 49.50 (*0-472-10152-8*) U of Mich Pr.

Wrestling with Your Angels: A Spiritual Journey to Great Writing. Janet O. Hagberg. 192p. (Orig.). 1995. pap. 9.95 (*1-55850-496-6*) Adams Media.

Wretched Excess: Sensationalism & the New York Press. John D. Stevens. (Illus.). 216p. 1991. text ed. 39.50 (*0-231-07396-8*) Col U Pr.

***Wretched Exotic: Essays on Edith Wharton in Europe.** Ed. by Katherine Joslin & Alan Price. (American University Studies, Series XXIV, American Literature). 432p. (C). 1996. pap. text ed. 29.95 (*0-8204-3698-4*) P Lang Pubng.

Wretched "I" & Its Liberation: Paul in Romans 7 & 8. Jan Lambrecht. (Louvain Theological & Pastoral Monographs). 165p. 1993. pap. 25.00 (*0-8028-0570-1*) Eerdmans.

Wretched of the Earth. Frantz Fanon. Tr. by Constance Farrington from FRE. LC 65-14196. 320p. 1988. pap. 12.00 (*0-8021-5083-7*, Grove) Grove-Atltic.

Wretched Stone. Chris Van Allsburg. (Illus.). 32p. (YA). 1991. 17.95 (*0-395-53307-4*, Sandpiper) HM.

Wright: Descendants of Owen Wright & Letitia Dow Collins Wright, James Wright & Lydia E. Sorrels Wright & Anna L. Davenbrock Wright. Evelyn W. Brown & Opal W. Sikes. (Illus.). 870p. 1994. reprint ed. pap. 89.50 (*0-8328-4044-0*); reprint ed. lib. bdg. 99.50 (*0-8328-4043-2*) Higginson Bk Co.

Wright: Genealogical & Biographical Notices of Descendants of Sir John Wright of Kelvedon Hall, Essex, England, in America, Thomas Wright of Wethersfield, Connecticut, 1610-1670, & Dea. Samuel Wright of Northampton, MA, 1614-1665. Curtis Wright. (Illus.). 321p. 1994. reprint ed. pap. 49.50 (*0-8328-4032-7*); reprint ed. lib. bdg. 59.50 (*0-8328-4031-9*) Higginson Bk Co.

Wright Book: Descendants of Owen & Letitia Dow (Collins) Wright; James & Lydia E. (Sorrels) Wright - Anna L. Dannenbrock Wright. Evelyn W. Brown & Opal W. Sikes. 1000p. 1993. pap. 109.00 (*0-8328-2825-4*); lib. bdg. 99.00 (*0-8328-2824-6*) Higginson Bk Co.

***Wright Brothers.** HarBrace Staff. 1995. pap. 11.00 (*0-15-305611-8*) HarBrace.

Wright Brothers. Richard Haynes. (Pioneers in Change Ser.). (Illus.). 144p. (J). (gr. 5-9). 1992. pap. 6.95 (*0-382-24175-4*); lib. bdg. 13.95 (*0-382-24168-1*) Silver Burdett Pr.

Wright Brothers. Paul Joseph. (Inventors Ser.). (J). 1996. lib. bdg. 13.98 (*1-56239-637-4*) Abdo & Dghtrs.

Wright Brothers. Fred C. Kelly. 1989. pap. 7.95 (*0-486-26056-9*) Dover.

Wright Brothers. Quentin Reynolds. LC 50-11766. (Landmark Bks.). (Illus.). 160p. (J). (gr. 5-9). 1981. pap. 5.99 (*0-394-84700-8*) Random Bks Yng Read.

Wright Brothers. 95th ed. HB Staff. (J). (gr. 6). 1995. text ed., lib. bdg., pap. text ed. 13.25 (*0-15-305230-9*) HB Coll Pubs.

Wright Brothers: A Discovery Book. (Illus.). 32p. (Orig.). (J). (gr. 5-7). 1995. pap. 3.75 (*0-915992-74-4*) Eastern Acorn.

Wright Brothers: Heirs of Prometheus. Ed. by Richard P. Hallion. LC 78-606141. (Illus.). 146p. 1978. 22.50 (*0-87474-504-7*, HAWBP) Smithsonian.

Wright Brothers: How They Invented the Airplane. Russell Freedman. LC 90-48440. (Illus.). 132p. (J). (gr. 4-8). 1991. 19.95 (*0-8234-0875-2*) Holiday.

Wright Brothers: How They Invented the Airplane. Russell Freedman. (Newbery Honor Book Ser.). (J). 1994. pap. 12.95 (*0-8234-1082-X*) Holiday.

Wright Brothers: How They Invented the Airplane. large type ed. Russell Freedman. 1995. 38.00 (*0-614-09619-7*, L-81906-00) Am Printing Hse.

Wright Brothers: They Gave Us Wings. Charles Ludwig. (Sower Ser.). (Illus.). (J). (gr. 3-6). 1985. pap. 6.99 (*0-88062-141-9*) Mott Media.

Wright Brothers' Aeroplane. Orville Wright & Wilbur Wright. Ed. by William R. Jones. (Illus.). 1981. reprint ed. pap. 3.95 (*0-89646-065-7*) Vistabooks.

Wright Brothers & Aviation see Science Discoveries

Wright Brothers at Kitty Hawk. Donald J. Sobol. 128p. (J). (gr. 4-6). 1987. pap. 3.99 (*0-590-42904-3*) Scholastic Inc.

Wright Brothers from Bicycle to Biplane. 3rd ed. Fred Fisk. (Illus.). 128p. 1995. reprint ed. 19.95 (*0-9626975-0-8*) Toddfisk.

Wright County Area Fishing Map Guide. James F. Billig. 1994. spiral bd. 14.95 (*1-885010-03-6*) Sptsmans Connect.

Wright County, Missouri. Turner Publishing Company Staff. LC 92-85252. 500p. 1993. 48.00 (*1-56311-090-3*) Turner Pub KY.

Wright Diet - Food for Humans - The First Lesson in Medicine for Everyone. 2nd unabridged ed. Patrick Wright. Orig. Title: Grains & Greens. (Illus.). 220p. 1997. 14.95 (*0-9628681-2-4*) IRFD.

Wright Family, a Genealogical Record from 1740-1914 of the Descendants of Peter Wright, 1740-1821. Fred P. Wright. 35p. 1994. reprint ed. pap. 7.00 (*0-8328-4115-3*) Higginson Bk Co.

Wright Howes: The Final Edition (of USiana) 757p. 1994. lib. bdg. 97.00 (*0-9640905-0-3*) WHR Bks.

Wright in Arizona: The Early Work of Pedro E. Guerrero. Bernard M. Boyle. (Illus.). 56p. 1996. pap. text ed. 19.95 (*1-884320-14-7*) ASU Herberger Ctr.

Wright in Hollywood: Visions of a New Architecture. Robert L. Sweeney. (AAF Ser.). (Illus.). 256p. 1994. 50.00 (*0-262-19337-X*) MIT Pr.

Wright Like This. Thomas A. Kloskey & Judith A. Lancioni. 96p. 1992. 12.54 (*0-8403-5562-9*) Kendall-Hunt.

Wright Morris. David Madden. (Twayne's United States Authors Ser.). 1964. pap. 13.95 (*0-8084-0336-2*, T71) NCUP.

Wright Morris. Leon Howard. LC 68-64752. (University of Minnesota Pamphlets on American Writers Ser.: No. 69). 48p. (Orig.). reprint ed. pap. 25.00 (*0-7837-2880-8*, 2057575) Bks Demand.

Wright Morris: Memory & Imagination. Roy K. Bird. (American University Studies: English Language & Literature: Ser. IV, Vol. 20). 155p. (C). 1985. text ed. 23.30 (*0-8204-0181-1*) P Lang Pubng.

Wright Morris: Origin of a Species. Wright Morris et al. LC 92-16260. (Illus.). 96p. 1992. pap. 19.95 (*0-918471-24-9*) San Fran MOMA.

Wright Morris Revisited. Madden. 1998. 23.95 (*0-8057-4531-9*, Twayne) Scribnrs Ref.

Wright: Peter Wright & Mary Anderson, a Family Record: Genealogy of Their Descendants & Those of Cecelia Anderson, Who Married Daniel Neall. E. N. Wright. (Illus.). 198p. 1993. reprint ed. pap. 29.50 (*0-8328-2821-1*); reprint ed. lib. bdg. 39.50 (*0-8328-2820-3*) Higginson Bk Co.

Wright Reunion 1977. Laura C. Uhl. 1984. reprint ed. pap. 2.00 (*0-943240-19-0*) UHLs Pub.

Wright Sites: A Guide to Frank Lloyd Wright Public Places. 2nd ed. Ed. by Arlene Sanderson. (Illus.). 128p. 1995. pap. 12.95 (*1-56898-041-8*) Princeton Arch.

Wright Space: Pattern & Meaning in Frank Lloyd Wright's Houses. Grant Hildebrand. LC 90-12154. (Illus.). 192p. (Orig.). 1991. pap. 35.00 (*0-295-97108-8*) U of Wash Pr.

Wright State: Frank Lloyd Wright in Wisconsin. Neil Levine & Jonathan Lipman. LC 92-30063. 1992. pap. 19.95 (*0-944110-27-4*) Milwauk Art Mus.

Wright Studies Vol. 1: Taliesin 1911-1914. Ed. by Narciso G. Menocal. (Illus.). 160p. (C). 1991. 39.95 (*0-8093-1624-2*); pap. 19.95 (*0-8093-1625-0*) S Ill U Pr.

Wright Style: Re-Creating the Spirit of Frank Lloyd Wright. Carla Lind. (Illus.). 224p. 1992. 50.00 (*0-671-74959-5*) S&S Trade.

Wright Vision: The Story of the New England Fellowship. Elizabeth Evans. (Illus.). 160p. 1990. 28.00 (*0-8191-7899-3*, New Eng Fellowship) U Pr of Amer.

***Wright vs. Wrong: The True & Not So True Story of the Airplane.** Gigi Tegge. (Illus.). 32p. (J). (gr. 2). 1997. 16.95 (*1-880851-26-1*) Greene Bark Pr.

Wrightown in Eighteen Hundreds. Esther G. Houghtalen & Laura C. Uhl. 1984. pap. 2.00 (*0-943240-18-2*) UHLs Pub.

Wrights & Privileges: The Mills & Shops in Pelham, Massachusetts 1739-1937. Paul Bigelow. LC 93-79547. (Illus.). 152p. (Orig.). 1993. pap. 11.95 (*0-9626308-6-1*) Haleys.

Wrights & the Wright Reunion. Laura C. Uhl. 1984. pap. 2.00 (*0-943240-17-4*) UHLs Pub.

Wrights & the Wright Reunion, Spencer N.Y. Laura C. Uhl. 1983. pap. text ed. 2.00 (*0-943240-04-2*) UHLs Pub.

Wright's Chaste Wife. Ed. by F. J. Furnivall & William A. Clouston. (EETS, OS Ser.: Nos. 12 & 84). 1976. reprint ed. 45.00 (*0-527-00015-9*) Periodicals Srv.

Wright's Complete Disaster Survival Manual: How to Prepare for Earthquakes, Floods, Tornadoes & Other Natural Disasters. Ted Wright. (Illus.). 288p. (Orig.). 1993. pap. 14.95 (*1-878901-80-X*) Hampton Roads Pub Co.

***Wright's Liver & Biliary Disease: Pathophysiology, Diagnosis & Management, 2 vols.** 3rd ed. Ed. by G. H. Millward-Sadler et al. (Illus.). 1667p. 1992. write for info. (*0-7020-1392-7*, Pub. by W B Saunders UK) Saunders.

Wrightsman Collection: Furniture, Snuffboxes, Silver, Porcelain, Vols. 3 & 4. Carl C. Dautermann & F. J. Watson. LC 66-10181. (Illus.). 860p. 1970. 65.00 (*0-87099-105-1*) Metro Mus Art.

Wrightsman Collection: Paintings, Drawings, Sculpture, Vol. 5. Everett Fahy & Francis Watson. LC 66-1081. (Illus.). 472p. 1973. 40.00 (*0-87099-012-8*) Metro Mus Art.

Wrightstown Township: A Tricentennial History. Jeffrey L. Marshall & Bertha S. Davis. (Illus.). 96p. (Orig.). 1992. pap. 10.00 (*0-9624245-1-X*) Wrightstown Twp Hist Comm.

***Wrigleyville.** Peter Golenbock. 1997. pap. 15.95 (*0-312-15699-5*) St Martin.

Wrigleyville: A Magical History Tour of the Chicago Cubs. Peter Golenbock. 560p. 1996. 24.95 (*0-312-14079-7*) St Martin.

***Wringer.** Jerry Spinelli & Cliff Nielsen. LC 96-37897. (Joanna Cotler Bks.). (Illus.). 192p. (J). (gr. 3-6). 1997. 13.95 (*0-06-024913-7*) HarpC.

***Wringer.** Jerry Spinelli & Cliff Nielsen. LC 96-37897. (Joanna Cotler Bks.). (Illus.). 192p. (J). (gr. 3-7). 1997. lib. bdg. 13.89 (*0-06-024914-5*) HarpC.

Wrinkle-Faced Bat. Pamela J. Gerholdt. LC 95-7350. (J). (gr. k-3). 1995. lib. bdg. 13.98 (*1-56239-504-1*) Abdo & Dghtrs.

Wrinkle In Time. 1997. text ed. 13.32 (*0-395-77154-4*) HM.

***Wrinkle in Time.** Madeleine L'Engle. 1997. mass mkt. 2.69 (*0-440-22715-1*) Dell.

Wrinkle in Time. Madeleine L'Engle. 224p. (J). (gr. 5-9). 1973. pap. 5.50 (*0-440-49805-8*, YB BDD) BDD Bks Young Read.

Wrinkle in Time. Madeleine L'Engle. 224p. (J). (gr. 5-9). 1976. mass mkt. 5.50 (*0-440-99805-0*, LLL BDD) BDD Bks Young Read.

Wrinkle in Time. Madeleine L'Engle. LC 62-7203. 224p. (J). (gr. 7 up). 1962. 17.00 (*0-374-38613-7*) FS&G.

***Wrinkle in Time.** Madeleine L'Engle. 224p. 1996. mass mkt. 2.49 (*0-440-22039-4*) Dell.

***Wrinkle in Time.** Madeline Lengle. (Scholastic Literature Guide Ser.). (J). 1997. pap. text ed. 3.95 (*0-590-37360-9*) Scholastic Inc.

***Wrinkle in Time, 2 vols.** Madeline L'Engle. 20.00 (*0-89064-014-9*) NAVH.

Wrinkle in Time. Kandi Stirling. Ed. by Terry Wallock. (Illus.). (Orig.). 1987. pap. text ed. 9.95 (*0-932045-02-2*) Dace Pub.

Wrinkle in Time: (Una Arruga en el Tiempo) Madeleine L'Engle. (J). (gr. 1-6). 15.95 (*84-204-4074-4*) Santillana.

Wrinkle in Time: A Literature Unit. John Carratello & Patty Carratello. (Illus.). 48p. (Orig.). (gr. 3-5). 1991. student ed., pap. 7.95 (*1-55734-403-5*) Tchr Create Mat.

Wrinkle in Time: L-I-T Guide. Charlotte Jaffe & Barbara Roberts. (L-I-T Guides: Literature in Teaching Ser.). Grades 4-8. teacher ed. 8.95 (*0-910857-84-9*) Educ Impress.

Wrinkle in Time - Study Guide. Joyce Friedland & Rikki Kessler. (Novel-Ties Ser.). (YA). (gr. 6-10). 1993. pap. text ed. 15.95 (*0-88122-014-0*) Lrn Links.

Wrinkled Wrappings: Sermons for Advent & Christmas. John R. Brokhoff. 1995. 7.50 (*0-7880-0700-9*) CSS OH.

Wrinkles. Charles Simmons. LC 78-9269. 182p. 1978. 8.95 (*0-374-29333-3*) FS&G.

Wrinkles. 2nd ed. Gary R. Wallace. (Illus.). 187p. 7.50 (*0-9616463-0-6*) Wrinkles.

***Wrinkles Are God's Makeup.** Rose Rosetree. (Illus.). 272p. (Orig.). 1998. pap. write for info. (*0-9651145-4-6*) Womens Intuition.

Wrinkles in Time. George Smoot & Keay Davidson. 352p. 1994. reprint ed. pap. 13.00 (*0-380-72044-2*) Avon.

Wriothesley's Roses in Shakespeare's Sonnets, Poems & Plays. Martin Green. LC 92-82974. (Illus.). 448p. 1993. 29.95 (*0-937715-03-4*, Clevedon Bks) Green Fields Bks.

Wrist. Cooney et al. LC 97-14867. 1400p. (C). (gr. 13). 1997. text ed. 269.00 (*0-8016-6644-9*) Mosby Yr Bk.

Wrist. Ed. by Richard H. Gelberman. LC 93-26040. (Master Techniques in Orthopaedic Surgery Ser.). 448p. 1994. text ed. 189.00 (*0-7817-0037-X*); sl. 575.00 (*0-7817-0210-0*) Lppncott-Raven.

Wrist. Julio Taleisnik. LC 85-13264. (Illus.). 442p. 1985. text ed. 122.00 (*0-443-08134-4*) Churchill.

Wrist & Its Disorders. David M. Lichtman. (Illus.). 496p. 1988. text ed. 162.00 (*0-03-011842-5*) Saunders.

Wrist & Its Disorders. 2nd ed. David M. Lichtman. 1997. text ed. 195.00 (*0-7216-4774-X*) Saunders.

Wrist & Its Disorders. 2nd ed. David M. Lichtman. 1997. write for info. (*0-7216-6758-9*) Saunders.

Wrist Arthroscopy. import ed. Stanley. 1994. text ed. 69.00 (*0-7216-5310-3*) Saunders.

Wrist Disorders: Current Concepts & Challenges. Ed. by R. Nakamura et al. LC 92-29763. 1993. 221.00 (*0-387-70102-8*) Spr-Verlag.

Wrist Imaging. G. Brunelli & P. Saffar. (Illus.). 220p. 1993. 286.00 (*0-387-59561-9*) Spr-Verlag.

Wrist in Rheumatoid Arthritis. Ed. by B. R. Simmen & N. Gschwend. (Rheumatology, the Interdisciplinary Concept Ser.: Vol. 17). (Illus.). xii, 220p. 1992. 211.50 (*3-8055-5514-8*) S Karger.

Wriston: Walter Wriston, Citibank & the Rise & Fall of American Financial Supremacy. Phillip L. Zweig. 960p. 1996. 40.00 (*0-517-58423-9*, Crown) Crown Pub Group.

Wriston Speaking: A Selection of Addresses. Henry M. Wriston. LC 57-11230. 271p. reprint ed. pap. 77.30 (*0-317-20020-8*, 2023230) Bks Demand.

Wristwatches. Gisbert L. Brunner & Christian Pfeiffer-Belli. LC 93-85223. (Illus.). 166p. 1993. pap. 19.95 (*0-88740-557-6*) Schiffer.

***Wristwatches: A Connoisseur's Guide.** Frank Edwards. 1997. 29.95 (*1-55209-083-3*) Firefly Bks Ltd.

Wristwatches: History of a Century's Development. rev. ed. Helmut Kahlert et al. Tr. by Edward Force from GER. LC 86-61198. (Illus.). 410p. 1991. reprint ed. 79.95 (*0-88740-362-X*) Schiffer.

***Writ in Blood.** Chelsea Q. Yarbo. LC 97-161. 544p. 1997. 26.95 (*0-312-86318-7*) St Martin.

Writ in Sand. Robert B. Cunninghame-Graham. LC 69-17571. (Essay Index Reprint Ser.). 1977. 19.95 (*0-8369-0068-5*) Ayer.

Writ of Habeas Corpus: How & When to Use It, Including Examples. 1991. lib. bdg. 250.00 (*0-8490-5103-7*) Gordon Pr.

Writ of Quo Warranto in Georgia Local Government Law. R. Perry Sentell. LC 86-32559. 163p. 1986. pap. 5.95 (*0-89854-120-4*) U of GA Inst Govt.

Write: A Program for Success in English Composition. Robert Frew. 1978. pap. text ed. 20.95 (*0-917962-45-1*) T H Peek.

Write! Cooperative Learning & the Writing Process. Virginia DeBolt. (Illus.). 208p. 1993. pap. text ed. 20.00 (*1-879097-20-6*) Kagan Cooperative.

Write a Book of Haiku. Patricia Pasda & Mary A. DiEdwardo. (Illus.). 40p. (J). (gr. 2 up). 1994. student ed. write for info. (*0-9641468-1-9*) M DiEdwardo Pubng.

Write a Good Resume. Dorothy L. White. 16p. (Orig.). 1986. pap. 1.99 (*0-915257-04-1*) Wordpower.

***Write a Research Paper in Six Easy Steps.** D. Bryant Morris. Ed. by Margarette Jennings. 69p. (Orig.). 1996. pap. 9.95 (*0-9653791-0-8*) JenPrint Publns.

Write a SUPER Sentence. Jo E. Moore & Joy Evans. (Illus.). 32p. (J). (gr. 1-3). 1984. pap. text ed. 4.95 (*1-55799-059-X*, EMC 205) Evan-Moor Corp.

Write a Tale of Terror. Richard Peck. (Illus.). 32p. (YA). (gr. 5-10). 1987. pap. 4.95 (*0-913839-60-4*) Pieces of Lrning.

Write-a-Thon! Susie Wilde. LC 96-49058. 1995. teacher ed., pap. 13.95 (*0-435-08141-1*) Heinemann.

Write A to Z. Joy Evans & Jo E. Moore. (Illus.). 54p. (J). (gr. k-3). 1979. teacher ed., pap. 5.95 (*1-55799-027-1*, EMC 138) Evan-Moor Corp.

Write About... Cullup et al. 1983. pap. 19.95 (*0-8384-0413-8*) Heinle & Heinle.

Write about It: Activities for Teaching Basic Writing Skills, Beginning Writers see Write about It Series

Write about It: Activities for Teaching Basic Writing Skills, Primary see Write about It Series

Write about It: Activities for Teaching Basic Writing Skills, Middle Grades see Write about It Series

Write about It Series, 3 vols. Incl. Write about It: Activities for Teaching Basic Writing Skills, Beginning Writers. Imogene Forte. Ed. by Mary C. Mahoney. (Illus.). 80p. (Orig.). (J). (gr. k-1). 1983. pap. text ed. 9.95 (*0-86530-044-5*, IP-445); Write about It: Activities for Teaching Basic Writing Skills, Primary. Imogene Forte. Ed. by Mary C. Mahoney & Susan Oglander. (Illus.). 80p. (Orig.). (J). (gr. 2-4). 1983. pap. text ed. 9.95 (*0-86530-045-3*, IP-453); Write about It: Activities for Teaching Basic Writing Skills, Middle Grades. Imogene Forte. Ed. by Mary C. Mahoney & Susan Oglander. (Illus.). 80p. (Orig.). (J). (gr. 4-6). 1983. pap. text ed. 9.95 (*0-86530-046-1*, IP-461); (Illus.). (J). (gr. k-6). 1983. Set pap. text ed. 23.50 (*0-685-06165-5*, IP 43-7) Incentive Pubns.

Write about Math. 1995. pap. 9.95 (*0-590-67476-5*, Scholastic Hardcover) Scholastic Inc.

Write after the Wedding: Wedding Gift Registry & Thank-You Note Guide. Katherine Aertker & Paul Aertker. (Illus.). 144p. (Orig.). 1994. pap. 12.95 (*0-9640166-0-5*) Paint Pr.

Write All about It: Activities for the Writing Process. John Carratello & Patty Carratello. (Illus.). 80p. (Orig.). (J). (gr. 1-3). 1993. student ed., pap. 9.95 (*1-55734-500-7*) Tchr Create Mat.

Write All about It: Activities for the Writing Process. Dona Herweck. (Illus.). 80p. (Orig.). (J). (gr. 6-8). 1993. student ed., pap. 9.95 (*1-55734-503-1*) Tchr Create Mat.

Write All about It: Activities for the Writing Process. Dona Herweck. (Illus.). 80p. (Orig.). (J). (gr. 4-6). 1993. student ed., pap. 8.95 (*1-55734-502-3*) Tchr Create Mat.

Write All about It: Activities for the Writing Process. Mary E. Sterling. (Illus.). 80p. (Orig.). (J). (gr. 3-5). 1993. student ed., pap. 9.95 (*1-55734-501-5*) Tchr Create Mat.

Write All about It: Reading Level 5-7. 1993. 12.00 (*0-88336-375-5*); teacher ed. 9.95 (*0-88336-376-3*) New Readers.

Write All These Down: Essays on Music. Joseph Kerman. LC 93-1876. 1994. 35.00 (*0-520-08355-5*) U CA Pr.

Write & Get Paid for It. Terry Prone. 198p. 1989. pap. 9.95 (*1-85371-030-X*, Pub. by Poolbeg Pr IE) Dufour.

Write & Play Time, Pt. A. Frances Clark & Louise Goss. (Frances Clark Library for Piano Students). 64p. (Orig.). (J). (gr. k-6). 1974. pap. text ed. 9.95 (*0-87487-196-4*) Summy-Birchard.

Write & Playtime, Pt. B. Frances Clark & Louise Goss. (Frances Clark Library for Piano Students). 64p. 1957. pap. text ed. 7.95 (*0-87487-197-2*) Summy-Birchard.

Write & Sell Your Free-Lance Article. Linda B. Allen. LC 91-27068. (Orig.). 1991. pap. 12.00 (*0-87116-164-8*) Writer.

Write & Write Again. Jane Paznik-Bondarin & Milton Baxter. 675p. (C). 1987. pap. write for info. (*0-02-393220-1*, Macmillan Coll) P-H.

Write Approach. Graham Beals. (J). 1995. pap. text ed. 12.95 (*1-871098-13-0*, Kiwi Kids) Parkwest Pubns.

Write Approach, 2 vols., II. Joen Gladich & Paula A. Sassi. 1991. pap. 13.50 (*0-945803-20-6*) R Steiner Col Pubns.

Write Approach, 2 vols., Vol. 1. Joen Gladich & Paula A. Sassi. 1991. Vl. 1. pap. 13.50 (*0-945803-19-2*) R Steiner Col Pubns.

***Write Approach, Vol 1.** Singleton. Date not set. pap. text ed. write for info. (*0-312-13731-1*) St Martin.

Write at the Start: A Guide for Using Writing in Freshman Seminar. Lea Masiello. (Freshman Year Experience Monograph: No. 9). 70p. (Orig.). 1993. pap. 30.00 (*1-889271-07-1*) Nat Res Ctr.

Write Away, Bk. 1. Byrd & Gallingane. 1991. pap. 17.95 (*0-8384-2717-0*) Heinle & Heinle.

Write Away, Bk. 2. Byrd & Gallingane. 1990. pap. 17.95 (*0-8384-2719-7*) Heinle & Heinle.

Write Away, Bk. 2. Byrd & Gallingane. 1990. teacher ed., pap. 7.95 (*0-8384-2720-0*) Heinle & Heinle.

Write Away, Bk. 3. Byrd & Gallingane. 1990. pap. 17.95 (*0-8384-2721-9*); teacher ed., pap. 7.95 (*0-8384-2722-7*) Heinle & Heinle.

Write Away! A Friendly Guide for Teenage Writers. Peter Stillman. 174p. 1995. pap. 14.95 (*0-86709-350-1*, 0350) Boynton Cook Pubs.

***Write Away: A Handbook for Young Writers & Learners.** Dave Kemper et al. (Illus.). 336p. (J). (gr. 2). 1996. text ed. 17.27 (*0-669-44043-4*); pap. text ed. 13.27 (*0-669-44042-6*) Great Source.

Write Better, Speak Better. Reader's Digest Editors. LC 75-183859. 730p. 1972. 24.99 (*0-89577-006-7*) RD Assn.

Write Book for Christian Families. Robert Allen. LC 93-37031. (C). 1993. pap. 9.95 (*0-89084-723-1*, 078014) Bob Jones Univ Pr.

Write Business Letters Right: How to Be Effective & Save Time Too. Jay Jones. 124p. 1986. spiral bd. 9.95 (*0-941135-00-4*) Busn Letters.

Write Business Reference. Communicate, Inc. Staff. LC 94-40700. (C). 1995. pap. text ed. 24.00 (*0-13-036708-7*) P-H.

Write Choices: New Options for Effective Communication. Alan M. Perlman. 82p. 1989. 26.95 (*0-398-05586-6*) C C Thomas.

***Write Connection: Love a Child by Mail.** Melanie Rahn. (Illus.). (Orig.). (J). (gr. k-8). 1989. ring bd., pap. 16.85 (*0-614-30250-1*) Write Connect.

Write Connection: Love a Child by Mail. Write Connection Co. Staff. (Illus.). 104p. 1989. student ed. 16.85 (*0-9621840-0-4*) Write Connect.

Write Connection Program, Military Edition: Love a Child by Mail. Write Connection Co. Staff. (Illus.). 75p. 1989. student ed. 16.85 (*0-9621840-1-2*) Write Connect.

Write 'Em Roughshod: Life n' Such Like. Peggy Godfrey. 70p. 1994. pap. 11.95 (*0-9644375-0-3*) Media Chaos.

Write English!, Bk. 1. Margaret Gall & Barbara Weitz. (Illus.). 64p. (Orig.). 1993. pap. text ed. 7.95 (*0-8325-0505-6*, Natl Textbk) NTC Pub Grp.

Write English, Bk. 3. Thomas Bauder. (Illus.). 72p. (Orig.). (C). 1994. pap. text ed. 7.95 (*0-8325-0513-7*, Natl Textbk) NTC Pub Grp.

Write English!, Book 2. Jane Hershberger & Sherry Royce. (Illus.). 64p. (Orig.). 1993. pap. text ed. 7.95 (*0-8325-0509-9*, Natl Textbk) NTC Pub Grp.

Write English Right. Lawrence Klepinger. 160p. 1993. 24.95 incl. audio (*0-8120-8018-1*) Barron.

Write English Right: An ESL Homonym Workbook. Lawrence Klepinger. 160p. pap. 8.95 (*0-8120-1462-6*) Barron.

Write English Well: A Handbook of Written English for Foreign - Overseas Students. Domino Books Ltd Staff. 400p. (C). 1988. 140.00 (*1-85122-042-9*, Pub. by Domino Bks Ltd UK); pap. 100.00 (*1-85122-053-4*, Pub. by Domino Bks Ltd UK) St Mut.

Write Every Day. Jo E. Moore et al. (Illus.). 48p. (J). (gr. 1-6). 1988. pap. 5.95 (*1-55799-128-6*, EMC 225) Evan-Moor Corp.

Write Every Day: 178 Reproducible Research & Writing Activities. Jane Schall. 184p. 1990. pap. 19.95 (*0-590-49075-3*) Scholastic Inc.

***Write Fiction - the Easy Way! Vol. 1: How to Enjoy Writing Fiction Plus Secrets to Revisions!** Sandra E. Haven. LC 96-96101. (Illus.). 102p. (Orig.). 1996. pap. 12.95 (*0-9651358-0-2*) Bristol Servs.

***Write Fiction to Sell!** 2nd ed. Joyce Brandon. 148p. (Orig.). 1997. pap. 16.95 (*0-913611-08-5*) W E C Plant.

Write for a Reason. Patricia T. Bates. LC 89-63884. 432p. (Orig.). (C). 1991. pap. text ed. 24.00 (*0-312-00397-8*) St Martin.

Write for a Reason. Patricia T. Bates. LC 89-63884. 432p. (Orig.). (C). 1991. pap. text ed. 5.00 (*0-312-00398-6*) St Martin.

Write for Fun & Money: How to Make Money Writing & Selling Simple Information. J. Barnes. 192p. 1995. pap. 15.00 (*0-915665-31-X*) Premier Publishers.

***Write for Life: A Practical Approach to Creative Writing.** Nicki Jackowska. 1997. pap. 13.95 (*1-86204-148-2*) Element MA.

***Write for Success.** Zacharias Rosner. Date not set. write for info. (*0-688-10023-6*) Morrow.

Write for Success: A Guide to Effective Technical & Professional Writing. David H. Klein & Jean H. Klein. 350p. 1996. pert. 14.50 (*0-8403-9110-2*) Kendall-Hunt.

Write for Success: Preparing a Sucessful Professional School Application. Evelyn W. Jackson & Harold R. Bardo. 50p. 1987. pap. 5.00 (*0-911899-02-2*) NAAHP Inc.

Write for the Religion Market. John A. Moore. LC 80-25607. 128p. 1981. 14.95 (*0-88280-084-1*) ETC Pubns.

Write from History: Right from History. Larry J. Martin. 131p. 1994. pap. 12.95 (*1-885339-06-2*) Buttonwillow.

Write from the Beginning. Amy Maid. (Illus.). 94p. (Orig.). (J). (gr. k-5). 1987. pap. 19.95 (*0-8290-0993-0*) Irvington.

Write from the Edge: A Creative Borders Book. Ken Vinton. Ed. by Pamela Espeland. (Free Spirited Classroom Ser.). (Illus.). 120p. (Orig.). 1996. teacher ed., pap. 19.95 (*0-915793-98-9*) Free Spirit Pub.

Write from the Heart: From Idea to Publication of a Non-Fiction Book. Keith Miller. 1993. student ed. 8.95 (*1-55725-071-5*); student ed. 79.95 incl. vhs (*1-55725-072-3*) Paraclete MA.

Write from the Heart: Lesbians Healing from Heartache. rev. ed. Anita L. Pace et al. 256p. 1996. pap. 13.95 (*0-9631666-4-6*) Baby Steps Pr.

Write from the Heart: Unleashing the Power of Your Creativity. Hal Z. Bennett. 176p. (Orig.). 1995. pap. 11.95 (*1-882591-27-5*) Nataraj Pub.

Write from the Heart - Lesbians Healing from Heartache: An Anthology. Anita L. Pace et al. 226p. 1992. pap. 10.95 (*0-9631666-0-3*) Baby Steps Pr.

Write from the Start. rev. ed. Cork Millner. 236p. 1994. pap. 10.95 (*1-56474-120-6*) Fithian Pr.

Write from the Start. 2nd ed. David Blot. (College ESL Ser.). 1994. suppl. ed., pap. 7.95 (*0-8384-4849-6*) Heinle & Heinle.

Write from the Start. 2nd ed. David M. Davidson & David Blot. LC 93-43511. 1994. pap. 21.95 (*0-8384-4848-8*) Heinle & Heinle.

Write from the Start: How to Tap Your Child's Innate Writing Abilities. Donald Graves & Virginia Stuart. 192p. 1985. pap. 11.95 (*0-525-48170-2*, Dutton) NAL-Dutton.

Write from the Start: Process & Practice. Mary A. Peters. 504p. (C). 1992. write for info. (*0-03-025479-5*); pap. text ed. 23.50 (*0-03-025478-7*) HB Coll Pubs.

Write Good Stuff. J. M. Taylor. (Illus.). 23p. (J). (gr. 6-8). 1995. student ed., pap. text ed. 5.95 (*1-879043-01-7*) Taylor Commns.

Write Great Ads: A Step-by-Step Approach. Erica L. Klein. 180p. 1990. text ed. 32.50 (*0-471-52418-2*); pap. text ed. 19.95 (*0-471-50703-2*) Wiley.

Write Here: Ideas, Activities, & Bulletin Boards to Spark Creative Writing. Marianne V. Standley. (Illus.). 80p. (Orig.). (J). (gr. 3-6). 1984. pap. text ed. 9.95 (*0-86530-013-5*, IP-135) Incentive Pubns.

Write His Answer: Encouragement for Christian Writers. Marlene Bagnull. 96p. (Orig.). 1990. pap. 6.95 (*0-939513-41-2*) Joy Pub SJC.

Write Ideas. Connie Shoemaker & Susan Polycarpou. LC 93-27955. 1994. pap. 21.95 (*0-8384-3987-X*) Heinle & Heinle.

Write in Our Midst: An Anthology of South Florida Writers. Ed. by Michael Hettich. 100p. 1993. pap. write for info. (*0-9636824-0-7*) Miami Bk Fair.

Write in the Middle. Connie Shoemaker. 280p. (C). 1989. pap. text ed. 16.00 (*0-03-006508-9*) HB Coll Pubs.

***Write in the Middle.** Connie Shoemaker. (C). 1989. teacher ed., pap. text ed. 3.00 (*0-03-006509-7*) HB Coll Pubs.

Write in Time: Essay Exam Strategies. Jeanne F. Campanelli & Jonathan L. Price. (Illus.). 167p. (C). 1991. pap. text ed. 13.50 (*0-03-032593-5*) HB Coll Pubs.

Write into a Job. (YA). (gr. 9 up). 1989. pap. 7.95 (*0-936007-28-1*, 3315) Meridian Educ.

Write into a Job: Instructor's Guide. 1990. teacher ed., pap. 12.95 (*0-936007-34-6*, 3316) Meridian Educ.

***Write It.** 96p. 1989. pap. text ed. 13.95 (*0-521-31171-3*); pap. text ed. 16.95 (*0-521-31172-1*) Cambridge U Pr.

Write It in French. Christopher Kendris. 1990. pap. 10.95 (*0-8120-4361-8*) Barron.

Write It in Spanish. Christopher Kendris. 160p. 1990. pap. 9.95 (*0-8120-4359-6*) Barron.

Write It Now: A Timesaving Guide to Writing Better. William C. Paxson. 1985. pap. 10.95 (*0-201-16878-2*) Addison-Wesley.

Write It on Your Heart: The Epic World of an Okanagan Story Teller. Ed. by Robinson & Wickwire. 1994. pap. 16.95 (*0-88922-273-8*) Genl Dist Srvs.

Write It Right. Ambrose Bierce et al. LC 86-71638. 73p. 1987. 12.95 (*0-9617270-0-4*) Terripam Pubs.

Write It Right. James W. Graham. 1994. pap. 7.00 (*0-9648399-0-3*) Page Edit Serv.

Write It Right. Robert Maidment. LC 87-2247. 112p. (Orig.). 1987. pap. 6.95 (*0-88289-647-4*) Pelican.

Write It Right. Ambrose G. Bierce. (Principle Works of Ambrose Gwinett Bierce). 1989. reprint ed. lib. bdg. 79.00 (*0-7812-1968-X*) Rprt Serv.

Write It Right! A Guide for Clear & Correct Writing. Richard Andersen & Helene Hinis. (Self-Study Sourcebook Ser.). ix, 158p. 1993. pap. 15.95 (*1-878542-30-3*, 13-0001) SkillPath Pubns.

Write It Right: A Manual for Writing Family History & Genealogies. 2nd ed. Ed. by Donald R. Barnes & Richard S. Lackey. (C). 1988. pap. 7.95 (*0-9620190-0-3*) Lyon Press.

Write It Right: Beginning Handwriting & Composition for Students of ESL. Helen T. Abdulaziz & Ellen Shenkarow. (Illus.). 208p. (C). 1986. pap. text ed. 17.70 (*0-13-969437-4*) P-H.

Write It Up! Participant's Workbook - Leader's Guide. Fran W. Shaw. 96p. (Orig.). 1990. pap. 15.00 (*0-944234-01-1*) Advan Writ Systs.

Write Like a Pro! A Guide for Freelance Writers. Jerry L. McGuire. (Illus.). 224p. (Orig.). (C). 1992. pap. 22.95 (*0-9632004-0-2*) J L McGuire.

Write Me a Letter. David M. Pierce. 272p. 1993. 18.95 (*0-89296-484-7*) Mysterious Pr.

Write Me a Murder. Frederick Knott. 1962. pap. 5.25 (*0-8222-1279-X*) Dramatists Play.

Write Me a Poem: Reading, Writing, & Performing Poetry. Lorraine Wilson. LC 94-13725. 80p. 1994. pap. text ed. 16.00 (*0-435-08823-8*, 08823) Heinemann.

Write Me a Poem, Baby. H. Allen Smith. 16.95 (*0-8488-0149-0*) Amereon Ltd.

Write Me a Poem Daddy. Howe. (J). 1997. 14.00 (*0-689-80185-8*, Atheneum Bks Young) S&S Childrens.

Write More! Eileen Prince. (College ESL Ser.). 1993. suppl. ed., pap. 9.95 (*0-8384-4314-1*) Heinle & Heinle.

An Asterisk (*) at the beginning of an entry indicates that the title is appearing in BIP for the first time.

W

An Asterisk (*) at the beginning of an entry indicates that the title is appearing in BIP for the first time.

Writer in Pennsylvania, 1681-1981. John J. Burke. LC 81-85496. 93p. 1982. pap. 5.95 (0-686-36440-6) St Joseph.

Writer in Philadelphia, 1682-1982. John J. Burke. LC 81-51298. 84p. 1981. pap. 5.95 (0-686-36439-2) St Joseph.

Writer in Politics. Ed. by William H. Gass & Lorin Cuoco. LC 95-45539. (International Writers Center Ser.). 211p. (C). 1996. 24.95 (0-8093-2050-9) S Ill U Pr.

Writer in Residence. Herbert Burkholz. 1992. 24.95 (0-685-53582-7) Permanent CA.

Writer in Residence. Herbert Burkholz. LC 91-29696. 310p. 1992. 24.95 (1-877946-11-7) Permanent Pr.

Writer in the Catastrophe of Our Time. Ernesto Sabato. Tr. by Asa Zatz from SPA. LC 90-80356. (Fiction & Ser.). 216p. 1995. pap. 9.95 (0-933031-24-6) Coun Oak Bks.

Writer in the Jewish Community. Ed. by Richard Siegel & Tamar Sofer. LC 92-58951. 1993. 29.50 (0-8386-3459-1) Fairleigh Dickinson.

Writer in Transition: Roger Mais & the Decolonizing of Caribbean Culture. Evelyn J. Hawthorne. (American University Studies: General Literature: Ser. XIX, Vol. 20). 191p. (C). 1989. text ed. 34.00 (0-8204-0816-6) P Lang Pubng.

Writer in You: A Writing Process Reader. Barbara Lounsberry. (C). 1991. text ed. 27.50 (0-06-044118-6) Addson-Wesley Educ.

***Writer Inc: A Student Handbook for Writing & Learning.** Patrick Sebranek et al. (Illus.). 440p. (YA). (gr. 9-12). 1996. pap. text ed. 15.33 (0-669-38813-0) Great Source.

Writer Is a State of Being: Your Personal Desktop Conference. Susan Henry. LC 87-51002. (Illus.). 144p. (Orig.). 1988. pap. 12.95 (0-943149-05-3) Alpha Bks OR.

***Writer of the Plains: A Story about Willa Cather.** Thomas Streissguth. LC 96-27244. (Creative Minds Bks.). (Illus.). (J). 1997. lib. bdg. 14.21 (1-57505-015-3, Carolrhoda) Lerner Group.

Writer of the Plains: The Biography of B. M. Bower. Orrin A. Engen. (Illus.). 56p. (Orig.). 1973. 6.00 (0-686-05538-1); text ed. 3.60 (0-686-05539-X) Pontine Pr.

Writer of the Purple Rage. Joe R. Lansdale. 320p. 1997. mass mkt. 5.95 (0-7867-0389-X) Carroll & Graf.

Writer on Her Work. Ed. by Janet Sternburg. 228p. 1992. pap. 11.95 (0-393-00071-0) Norton.

Writer on Her Work, Vol. 2: New Essays in New Territory. Ed. by Janet Sternberg. 240p. 1992. pap. 11.95 (0-393-30867-7) Norton.

Writer Publisher. Charles N. Aronson. LC 75-36854. (C). 1976. 10.00 (0-915736-07-1); pap. 7.00 (0-915736-08-X) C N Aronson.

Writer Teaches Writing, 2 Vols. 2nd ed. Donald M. Murray. LC 84-81981. 304p. (C). 1984. pap. 35.16 (0-395-35441-2) HM.

Writer to Writer. Bodie Thoene & Brock Thoene. 176p. (Orig.). 1990. pap. 8.99 (1-55661-042-4) Bethany Hse.

***Writer Within: A Guide to Creative Nonfiction.** Lary Bloom. 216p. 1997. reprint ed. pap. 14.95 (0-939883-01-5) Bibliopola Pr.

***Writer Workplace with Readings.** 3rd ed. Scarry. (C). 1998. pap. text ed. write for info. (0-15-508174-8) HB Coll Pubs.

Writer Writing: Philosophic Acts in Literature. Francis-Noel Thomas. LC 92-14220. (Illus.). 224p. (C). 1993. text ed. 37.50 (0-691-06955-7) Princeton U Pr.

Writer Written: The Artist & Creation in the New Literatures in English. Jean-Pierre Durix. LC 87-7518. (Contributions to the Study of World Literature Ser.: No. 21). 192p. 1987. text ed. 45.00 (0-313-25894-5, DXA/, Greenwood Pr) Greenwood.

***Writers, 8 bks.** (American Women of Achievement Ser.). (YA). (gr. 5 up). 159.60 (0-7910-3504-2) Chelsea Hse.

Writers. Photos by Sally Soames. LC 95-16889. (Illus.). 160p. 1995. 35.00 (0-8118-1234-0) Chronicle Bks.

Writers see International Dictionary of Films & Filmmakers 3

Writer's Advisor. Ed. by Leland G. Alkire, Jr. & Cheryl I. Westerman. LC 84-24715. 478p. 1985. 70.00 (0-8103-2093-2) Gale.

Writers after World War II, 1945-1960 see Concise Dictionary of British Literary Biography

Writer's Almanac & Fact Book. Mary A. De Vries. 1986. pap. 3.95 (0-317-38976-9, Sig) NAL-Dutton.

Writers' & Artists' Yearbook 1996. 89th ed. A & C Black Staff. (Illus.). 680p. 1996. pap. 18.95 (0-7136-4233-5, Pub. by A&C Black UK) Talman.

Writers & Company. E. Wachtel. 1993. pap. 14.00 (0-394-22738-7) Knopf.

Writers & Company. Eleanor Wachtel. 1994. pap. 12.95 (0-15-600112-8) HarBrace.

Writers & Partisans: A History of Literary Radicalism in the United States. James B. Gilbert. LC 92-35427. 313p. (C). 1993. pap. 17.00 (0-231-08255-X, Mrngside); text ed. 45.00 (0-231-08254-1, Mrngside) Col U Pr.

Writers & Performers in Italian Drama, from the Time of Dante to Pirandello: Essays in Honour of G.H. McWilliam. Ed. by Julie R. Dashwood & Jane E. Everson. LC 91-26556. (Studies in Theatre Arts: Vol. 1). (Illus.). 204p. 1991. lib. bdg. 89.95 (0-7734-9717-X) E Mellen.

Writers & Philosophers: A Source Book of Philosophical Influences on Literature. Edmund J. Thomas & Eugene Miller. LC 90-34139. 288p. 1990. text ed. 42.95 (0-313-25684-5, TWS, Greenwood Pr) Greenwood.

Writers & Politics. Ed. by Bill Bourne et al. 96p. 8700. 30.00 (0-85124-483-1) Dufour.

Writers & Politics in Modern Italy. J. A. Gatt-Rutter. LC 78-18829. (Writers & Politics Ser.). 66p. 1978. pap. 10.50 (0-8419-0416-2) Holmes & Meier.

Writers & Politics in Modern Scandinavia. Janet Mawby. LC 78-18931. (Writers & Politics Ser.). 53p. 1978. pap. text ed. 10.50 (0-8419-0417-0) Holmes & Meier.

Writers & Politics in Modern Spain. John Butt. LC 78-18704. (Writers & Politics Ser.). 75p. 1978. pap. 10.50 (0-8419-0415-4) Holmes & Meier.

Writers & Politics in Nigeria. James Booth. LC 80-17670. (Writers & Politics Ser.). 128p. (C). 1981. pap. text ed. 16.50 (0-8419-0651-3, Africana) Holmes & Meier.

Writers & Publishers Guide to Texas Markets, 1997-1999. 4th rev. ed. LC 96-54725. (Practical Guide Ser.: Vol. 3). 291p. (Orig.). 1997. pap. 14.95 (1-57441-019-9) UNTX Pr.

Writers & Readers. George B. Hill. LC 72-8517. (Essay Index Reprint Ser.). 1977. reprint ed. 20.95 (0-8369-7317-8) Ayer.

Writers & Readers in Medieval Italy: Studies in the History of Written Culture. Armando Petrucci. Ed. & Tr. by Charles M. Radding. LC 94-41633. 1995. 30.00 (0-300-06089-0) Yale U Pr.

Writers & the Law. Colin Golvan & Michael McDonald. xix, 262p. 1986. pap. 40.00 (0-455-20711-9, Pub. by Law Bk Co AT) Gaunt.

Writers & Their Craft: Short Stories & Essays on the Narrative. Ed. by Laurence Goldstein & Nicholas Delbanco. LC 90-49018. 456p. (C). 1991. pap. text ed. 24.95 (0-8143-2193-3) Wayne St U Pr.

Writers & Their Houses. Ed. by Kate Marsh. (Illus.). 544p. 1993. pap. 30.00 (0-241-12769-6, H Hamilton) Viking Penguin.

Writer's Arena: An Anthology for Christian Writers. Marian B. Forschler et al. 120p. (Orig.). 1994. pap. 11.95 (0-9624346-3-9) Ready Writer.

Writer's Art. James J. Kilpatrick. (Illus.). 262p. 1985. pap. 9.95 (0-8362-7925-5) Andrews & McMeel.

Writers at Work. Ed. by Dana K. Cassell. 88p. (Orig.). 1989. pap. 4.95 (0-942980-09-3) CNW.

Writers at Work. Linda Flower. (C). 1993. teacher ed., pap. text ed. 33.75 (0-15-500206-6) HB Coll Pubs.

***Writers at Work.** Singleton. Date not set. pap. text ed. write for info. (0-312-13732-X) St Martin.

Writers at Work: Casebook. Linda Flower. (C). 1994. pap. text ed. 14.00 (0-15-501582-6) HB Coll Pubs.

Writers at Work: Strategies for Communicating in Business & Professional Settings. Linda Flower & John Ackerman. LC 93-77899. 382p. 1995. pap. 33.25 (0-15-500007-1) HarBrace.

Writer's Audience: A Reader for Composition. Nancy G. Anderson. 544p. (Orig.). (C). 1991. pap. text ed. 19.50 (0-03-028773-1) HB Coll Pubs.

Writers' Block. Zachary Leader. LC 90-4744. 272p. 1991. 45.00 (0-8018-4032-5) Johns Hopkins.

Writer's Book of Memory: An Interdisciplinary Study for Writing Teachers. Janine Rider. 152p. 1995. pap. 17.50 (0-8058-1981-9); text ed. 34.50 (0-8058-1980-0) L Erlbaum Assocs.

Writer's Book of Synonyms. Evelyn Rothstein. (Illus.). 52p. (Orig.). (J). (gr. 2-8). 1988. pap. text ed. 5.00 (0-9606172-9-9) ERA-CCR.

Writers, Books & Trade: An Eighteenth-Century English Miscellany for William B. Todd. Ed. by O M Brack, Jr. LC 91-53014. (Studies in the Eighteenth Century: No. 19). 1993. 57.50 (0-404-63519-9) AMS Pr.

Writer's Brief Handbook. 2nd ed. Alfred Rosa & Paul Eschholz. LC 95-36515. 1995. pap. text ed. 26.00 (0-205-19655-1) Allyn.

***Writer's Choice.** R. Hills. Date not set. lib. bdg. 29.95 (0-8488-1709-5) Amereon Ltd.

Writer's Choices with Handbook. 2nd ed. Ed. by Leonora Woodman & Thomas P. Adler. (C). 1988. text ed. 41.50 (0-673-18840-X) Addson-Wesley Educ.

Writer's Community. Dale H. Klooster. 1995. teacher ed., pap. text ed. 5.00 (0-312-09556-2) St Martin.

Writer's Community. David J. Klooster & Patricia L. Bloem. 250p. 1995. pap. text ed. 20.50 (0-312-09539-2) St Martin.

Writer's Companion. Marcella Frank. 144p. (C). 1983. pap. text ed. write for info. (0-13-969790-X) P-H.

Writer's Companion. Louis D. Rubin & Jerry L. Mills. LC 95-158. 1088p. (C). 1995. 39.95 (0-8071-1992-X) La State U Pr.

Writer's Companion. 3rd ed. Richard Marius. 1994. pap. text ed. write for info. (0-07-040526-3) McGraw.

***Writer's Companion: A Handy Compendium of Useful But Hard-To-Find Information on History, Literature, Art, Science, Travel, Philosophy, & Much More.** Ed. by Louis D. Rubin & Jerry L. Mills. LC 96-45543. 1056p. 1997. pap. 20.00 (0-06-273472-5, Harper Ref) HarpC.

Writer's Compass. McWhorter. (C). 1994. pap. 35.16 (0-395-66701-1) HM.

***Writer's Compass: A Sentence & Paragraph Text with Readings.** annot. ed. Kathleen T. McWhorter. (C). 1994. teacher ed., text ed. 34.36 (0-395-72141-5) HM.

Writer's Complete Crime Reference Book. rev. ed. Martin Roth. 304p. 1993. 19.99 (0-89879-564-8, Wrtrs Digest Bks) F & W Pubns Inc.

Writer's Complete Guide to Conducting Interviews. Michael Schumacher. 236p. 1993. pap. 14.95 (0-89879-593-1, Wrtrs Digest Bks) F & W Pubns Inc.

Writer's Complete Guide to Firearms: Get Your Facts Straight on Revolvers & Pistols, Shotguns, Machine Guns, Rifles, Silencers, Ammunition... Doug Briggs. (Illus.). 224p. 1993. 14.95 (1-881287-03-3) Beverly Bk.

Writer's Craft: A Process Reader. 3rd ed. Sheena Gillespie et al. LC 92-27987. (C). 1993. text ed. 31.95 (0-673-46650-7) Addson-Wesley Educ.

Writer's Craft: Grade 10. McDougal. Date not set. text ed. write for info. (0-395-73037-6) HM.

Writer's Craft: Grade 11. McDougal. Date not set. text ed. write for info. (0-395-73038-4) HM.

Writer's Craft: Grade 12. McDougal. Date not set. text ed. write for info. (0-395-73039-2) HM.

Writer's Craft: Grade 6. McDougal. Date not set. text ed. write for info. (0-395-73033-3) HM.

Writer's Craft: Grade 7. McDougal. Date not set. text ed. write for info. (0-395-73034-1) HM.

Writer's Craft: Grade 8. McDougal. Date not set. text ed. write for info. (0-395-73035-X) HM.

Writer's Craft: Grade 9. McDougal. Date not set. text ed. write for info. (0-395-73036-8) HM.

Writer's Craft: Hopwood Lectures, 1965-1981. Ed. by Robert A. Martin. 304p. 1982. pap. 15.95 (0-472-06337-5) U of Mich Pr.

Writers Craft, Blue Level. Elbow. 33.25 (0-8123-7004-X) McDougal-Littell.

Writers Craft, Orange Level. Elbow. 33.25 (0-8123-7002-3) McDougal-Littell.

Writers Craft, Purple Level. Elbow. 33.25 (0-8123-7008-2) McDougal-Littell.

Writer's Craft, Teacher's Art: Teaching What We Know. Ed. by Mimi Schwartz. LC 90-37593. 192p. (Orig.). 1990. pap. text ed. 21.50 (0-86709-263-7, 0263) Boynton Cook Pubs.

Writers Craft, Yellow Level. Elbow. 33.25 (0-8123-7006-6) McDougal-Littell.

Writer's Desk. Jill Krementz. 1996. 35.00 (0-679-45014-9) Fodors Travel.

***Writer's Desk.** Jill Krementz. 35.00 (0-614-28300-0) Random.

Writer's Diary, Vol. 2. Fyodor Dostoyevsky. Tr. by Kenneth Lantz from RUS. 900p. (Orig.). 1994. 39.95 (0-8101-1101-2) Northwestern U Pr.

Writer's Diary: Being Extracts from the Diary of Virginia Woolf. Virginia Woolf. Ed. by Leonard Woolf. LC 73-5737. 355p. 1973. reprint ed. pap. 14.00 (0-15-698380-X, Harvest Bks) HarBrace.

***Writer's Diary: 1873-1876, Vol. 1.** Fyodor Dostoevsky. 1997. pap. text ed. 22.50 (0-8101-1516-6) Northwestern U Pr.

Writer's Diary: 1873-76, Vol. 1. Fyodor Dostoyevsky. Tr. by Kenneth Lantz from RUS. 1000p. (Orig.). 1993. 49.95 (0-8101-1094-6) Northwestern U Pr.

***Writer's Diary: 1877-1881, Vol. 2.** Fyodor Dostoevsky. 1997. pap. text ed. 22.50 (0-8101-1517-4) Northwestern U Pr.

Writer's Digest Character Naming Sourcebook. Sherrilyn Kenyon et al. 352p. 1994. 18.99 (0-89879-632-6, Wrtrs Digest Bks) F & W Pubns Inc.

Writer's Digest Dictionary of Concise Writing. Robert H. Fiske. LC 96-6788. Orig. Title: Guide to Concise Writing - Publisher's Info. 352p. 1996. 19.99 (0-89879-755-1, Wrtrs Digest Bks) F & W Pubns Inc.

Writer's Digest Guide to Good Writing. Writer's Digest Editors Staff. 352p. 1994. 18.99 (0-89879-640-7, Wrtrs Digest Bks) F & W Pubns Inc.

***Writer's Digest Guide to Good Writing.** Ed. by Writer's Digest Editors Staff. 352p. 1997. pap. 14.99 (0-89879-807-8, Wrtrs Digest Bks) F & W Pubns Inc.

Writer's Digest Guide to Manuscript Formats. Dian D. Buchman & Seli Groves. 200p. 1988. 19.99 (0-89879-293-2, Wrtrs Digest Bks) F & W Pubns Inc.

Writer's Digest Handbook of Magazine Article Writing. Ed. by Jean M. Fredette. 248p. 1990. pap. 13.99 (0-89879-408-0, Wrtrs Digest Bks) F & W Pubns Inc.

***Writer's Digest Handbook of Making Money Freelance Writing.** Ed. by Writer's Digest Editors Staff. LC 96-43403. 320p. 1997. 19.99 (0-89879-777-2, Wrtrs Digest Bks) F & W Pubns Inc.

Writer's Digest Handbook of Novel Writing. Writer's Digest Editors Staff. 260p. 1992. 18.99 (0-89879-507-9, Wrtrs Digest Bks) F & W Pubns Inc.

Writer's Digest Handbook of Short Story Writing Vol. 1, Vol. I. Ed. by Frank Dickson & Sandra Smythe. 238p. 1981. pap. 13.99 (0-89879-049-2, Wrtrs Digest Bks) F & W Pubns Inc.

Writer's Digest Sourcebook for Building Believable Characters. Marc McCutcheon. 288p. 1996. 17.99 (0-89879-683-0, Wrtrs Digest Bks) F & W Pubns Inc.

Writers Directory, 1986-88. 7th ed. 1986. 85.00 (0-912289-28-7) St James Pr.

Writers Directory, 1988-90. 8th ed. 1042p. 1988. 95.00 (0-912289-87-2) St James Pr.

Writers Directory, 1990-92. 90th ed. 1990. 125.00 (1-55862-032-X) St James Pr.

Writers Directory, 1992-94. 92th ed. 1087p. 1991. 125.00 (1-55862-093-1, 200161) St James Pr.

Writers Directory 1994-96. 94th ed. Ed. by Miranda H. Ferrara & George W. Schmidt. 1404p. 1993. 130.00 (1-55862-317-5) St James Pr.

Writers Directory 1996-98. 96th ed. Ed. by Miranda H. Ferrara. 1836p. 1995. 140.00 (1-55862-328-0) St James Pr.

***Writers Directory 1998-2000.** 1997. 140.00 (1-55862-360-4, 00107999) St James Pr.

Writer's Divided Self in Bulgakov's The Master & Margarita. Riitta H. Pittman. LC 91-2123. 224p. 1991. text ed. 49.95 (0-312-06148-X) St Martin.

Writer's Do's & Don'ts. Carol A. Osley. (Orig.). (C). 1982. pap. 2.00 (0-910119-03-1) SOCO Pubns.

Writer's Drawing Book: The Russians. Ed. by Cathy Porter. (Illus.). 176p. (Orig.). 1995. spiral bd., pap. 16.00 (1-57062-193-4) Shambhala Pubns.

Writers Dreaming: Twenty-Five Writers Talk about Their Dreams & the Creative Process. Naomi Epel. 1994. pap. 12.00 (0-679-74141-0, Vin) Random.

Writer's Electronic Publishing Kit. Colin Haynes. (Paperless Publishing Ser.). (Illus.). 100p. (Orig.). 1994. pap. 49.95 (1-884648-01-0) Nomad Pr Intl.

Writer's Encyclopedia. 3rd ed. Writer's Digest Editors Staff. Orig. Title: Writing A to Z. (Illus.). 560p. 1996. 22.99 (0-89879-749-7, Wrtrs Digest Bks) F & W Pubns Inc.

Writer's Essential Desk Reference: A Companion to Writer's Market. 2nd ed. Writer's Digest Editors Staff. 384p. 1996. 24.99 (0-89879-759-4, Wrtrs Digest Bks) F & W Pubns Inc.

Writers Express. McWhorter. (C). 1992. pap. 34.36 (0-395-59895-8) HM.

Writer's Express, 2 Vols. McWhorter. (C). 1996. pap. 34.36 (0-395-78292-9) HM.

***Writers Express: A Handbook for Young Writers, Thinkers, & Learners.** Dave Kemper et al. (Illus.). 452p. (J). (gr. 4-5). 1995. pap. text ed. 14.60 (0-669-38632-4) Great Source.

***Writers Express: A Handbook for Young Writers, Thinkers & Learners.** Dave Kemper et al. (Illus.). 452p. 1995. text ed. 18.60 (0-669-38633-2) Great Source.

***Writer's Express: A Paragraph & Essay Text with Readings, 2 Vols.** 2nd ed. Kathleen McWhorter. (C). 1997. teacher ed., text ed. 11.96 (0-395-84069-4) HM.

Writer's Eye: Collected Book Reviews. Eudora Welty. Ed. by Pearl A. McHaney. LC 93-33643. 308p. 1994. 27.50 (0-87805-683-1) U Pr of Miss.

Writers for Children. Ed. by Jane M. Bingman. (Illus.). 720p. 1987. 100.00 (0-684-18165-7) S&S Trade.

***Writers for the Nation: American Literary Modernism.** C. Barry Chabot. LC 96-45920. 1997. write for info. (0-8173-0877-6) U of Ala Pr.

***Writers for Young Adults, 3 vols.** Hipple. LC 97-6890. 1997. 195.00 (0-684-80474-3) S&S Trade.

Writers for Young Adults. 3rd ed. Gale Research, Inc., Staff. 1993. 92.00 (0-8103-1833-4) Gale.

Writers for Young Adults. 4th ed. 1999. 92.00 (0-8103-6982-6) Gale.

Writers for Young Adults, Vol. 1. Hipple. LC 97-6890. 1997. 80.00 (0-684-80475-1) Mac Lib Ref.

Writers for Young Adults, Vol. 2. Hipple. LC 97-6890. 1997. 80.00 (0-684-80476-X) Mac Lib Ref.

Writers for Young Adults, Vol. 3. Hipple. LC 97-6890. 1997. 80.00 (0-684-80477-8) Mac Lib Ref.

Writers for Young Adults: Biographies Master Index. 2nd ed. Ed. by Adele Sarkissian. (Biographical Index Ser.: No. 6). 416p. 1984. 92.00 (0-8103-1473-8) Gale.

Writers Forum, No. 7. Ed. by Alex Blackburn. LC 78-649046. 1981. pap. 8.95 (0-9602992-1-1) Writers Forum.

Writers Forum, No. 8. Ed. by Alex Blackburn. LC 78-649046. 1982. pap. 8.95 (0-9602992-2-X) Writers Forum.

Writers Forum, No. 10. Ed. by Alex Blackburn. LC 78-649046. 1984. pap. 8.95 (0-9602992-4-6) Writers Forum.

Writers' Forum, No. 13. Ed. by Alex Blackburn. LC 78-649046. 245p. (Orig.). 1987. pap. 8.95 (0-9602992-7-0) Writers Forum.

Writers' Forum, No. 14. Ed. by Alex Blackburn. LC 78-649046. (Orig.). 1988. pap. 8.95 (0-9602992-8-9) Writers Forum.

Writers' Forum, No. 16. Ed. by Alex Blackburn. LC 78-649046. 200p. (C). 1990. pap. 8.95 (1-878359-00-2) Writers Forum.

Writers' Forum, No. 17. Ed. by Alex Blackburn. LC 78-649046. (Illus.). 220p. (Orig.). 1991. pap. text ed. 8.95 (1-878359-01-0) Writers Forum.

Writers' Forum, No. 18. Ed. by Alex Blackburn. LC 78-649046. (Illus.). 200p. (Orig.). 1992. pap. text ed. 10.00 (1-878359-02-9) Writers Forum.

Writers' Forum, No. 19. Ed. by Alex Blackburn. LC 78-649046. 228p. (Orig.). 1993. pap. text ed. 10.00 (1-878359-03-7) Writers Forum.

Writers' Forum, Vol. 12. Ed. by Alex Blackburn. LC 78-649046. 240p. (Orig.). (C). 1986. pap. text ed. 8.95 (0-9602992-6-2) Writers Forum.

Writers' Forum, September 1994, No. 20. Ed. by Alex Blackburn. LC 78-649046. 245p. 1994. pap. 10.00 (1-878359-04-5) Writers Forum.

Writers' Forum, 1989, No. 15. Ed. by Alex Blackburn. LC 78-649046. 1989. pap. 8.95 (0-9602992-9-7) Writers Forum.

Writers Forum 9, 1983. Ed. by Alex Blackburn. LC 78-649046. 1983. pap. 8.95 (0-9602992-3-8) Writers Forum.

Writers from South Africa: Fourteen Writers on Culture, Politics & Literary Theory & Activity in South Africa. Ed. by Reginald Gibbons. 128p. 1988. 6.50 (0-916384-03-9) TriQuarterly.

Writers from the South Pacific. Norman Simms. (Illus.). 324p. 1991. pap. 14.00 (0-89410-595-7, Three Contnts) Lynne Rienner.

Writer's Guide: Easy Ground Rules for Successful Written English. Jane R. Walpole. 1980. 9.95 (0-13-969782-9, Spectrum IN) Macmillan Gen Ref.

Writer's Guide: The Essential Points. Harold H. Kolb, Jr. 102p. (C). 1980. pap. text ed. 10.75 (0-15-597680-X) HB Coll Pubs.

Writer's Guide to a Children's Book Contract. Mary Flower. LC 88-81247. 62p. (Orig.). 1988. pap. 15.00 (0-9620567-0-7) Fern Hill Bks.

Writer's Guide to Book Editors, Publishers & Literary Agents. Jeff Herman. 864p. 1996. pap. text ed. 25.00 (0-7615-0508-3) Prima Pub.

***Writer's Guide to Book Editors, Publishers, & Literary Agents, 1998-1999: Who They Are! What They Want! & How to Win Them Over!** Jeff Herman. 864p. 1997. per. 25.00 (0-7615-1012-5) Prima Pub.

Writer's Guide to Book Publishing. 3rd rev. ed. Richard Balkin. LC 93-46730. 288p. 1994. pap. 13.95 (0-452-27021-9, Plume) NAL-Dutton.

Writer's Guide to Chicago-Area Publishers & Other Freelance Markets. rev. ed. Jerold L. Kellman & Hilary Richardson Bagnato. LC 93-61808. 336p. 1994. pap. 19.95 (0-936192-01-1, Writers Guide Pubns) Gabriel Hse.

Writer's Guide to College Economics. Thomas Wyrick. 129p. 1995. pap. text ed. 19.50 (0-314-06043-X) West Pub.

Writer's Guide to Copyright. 2nd ed. Poets & Writers, Inc. Staff et al. (Illus.). 64p. 1990. pap. 6.95 (0-913734-21-7) Poets & Writers.

W

An Asterisk (*) at the beginning of an entry indicates that the title is appearing in BIP for the first time.

*Writer's Guide to Corporate Communications. Mary Moreno. 192p. (Orig.). 1997. pap. 18.95 (1-880559-74-9) Allworth Pr.

Writer's Guide to Creating a Science Fiction Universe. George Ochoa & Jeffrey Osier. 336p. 1993. 18.95 (0-89879-536-2, Wrtrs Digest Bks) F & W Pubns Inc.

Writer's Guide to Electronic Publishers, Editors & Agents. Sydney Harriet. 352p. 1996. per. 23.00 (0-7615-0062-6) Prima Pub.

Writer's Guide to Everyday Life: Prohibition to World War II. Marc McCutcheon. 272p. 1995. 18.99 (0-89879-697-0, Wrtrs Digest Bks) F & W Pubns Inc.

Writer's Guide to Everyday Life from Prohibition Through World War II, Vol. 2. Ed. by Jean M. Fredette. (Writer's Guide to Everyday Life Ser.). 252p. (Orig.). 1991. pap. 13.99 (0-89879-463-3, Wrtrs Digest Bks) F & W Pubns Inc.

*Writer's Guide to Everyday Life in Colonial America. Dale Taylor. LC 96-38093. (Writer's Guide to Everyday Life Ser.). (Illus.). 288p. 1997. 18.99 (0-89879-772-1, Wrtrs Digest Bks) F & W Pubns Inc.

Writer's Guide to Everyday Life in Renaissance England. Kathy L. Emerson. LC 96-22416. (Writer's Guide to Everyday Life Ser.). (Illus.). 272p. 1996. 18.99 (0-89879-752-7, Wrtrs Digest Bks) F & W Pubns Inc.

Writer's Guide to Everyday Life in the Middle Ages. Sherrilyn Kenyon. (Writer's Guide to Everyday Life Ser.). (Illus.). 256p. 1995. 17.99 (0-89879-663-6, Wrtrs Digest Bks) F & W Pubns Inc.

Writer's Guide to Everyday Life in the 1800's. Marc McCutcheon. (Writer's Guide to Everyday Life Ser.). (Illus.). 320p. 1993. 18.99 (0-89879-541-9, Wrtrs Digest Bks) F & W Pubns Inc.

Writer's Guide to Hollywood Producers, Directors, & Screenwriters' Agents: Who They Are! What They Want! & How to Win Them Over! Skip Press. LC 96-46996. 416p. 1997. per. 23.00 (0-7615-0399-4) Prima Pub.

Writer's Guide to Magazine Editors & Publishers, 1997-98: Who They Are! What They Want! & How to Win Them Over! Judy Mandell. 416p. 1996. per. 23.00 (0-7615-0409-5) Prima Pub.

Writer's Guide to Software Documentation. Donald G. Steely. 1983. ring bd. 34.50 (0-9612620-0-1) Goode-Steely Assocs.

Writer's Guide to the Internet. Dawn Groves. LC 96-39488. (Orig.). 1996. pap. 18.95 (1-887902-13-9) Franklin Beedle.

*Writer's Guide to the Internet. No Starch Press Staff. 1996. pap. 18.95 (1-886411-17-4) No Starch Pr.

Writer's Guide to the New York Times. Myron Schwartzman. 64p. 1980. pap. text ed. write for info. (0-912853-04-2) NY Times.

Writer's Guide to the Photographic Craft. Mark Baczynsky. (Illus.). 1982. pap. 9.95 (0-89816-004-9) Embee Pr.

Writer's Guide to the Usage of Economic & Business English. 501p. 1985. 125.00 (0-8288-1546-1, F82740) Fr & Eur.

Writer's Guide to Transitional Words & Expressions. 5th rev. ed. Victor C. Pellegrino. LC 83-34726. 48p. 1995. pap. 7.95 (0-945045-02-6) Maui Arthoughts.

Writer's Guide to Typesetting & Book Design. Larry Morton. 16p. (Orig.). 1996. 1.50 (1-888834-02-1, ITD-196, Stonehill Bks) Idyllwild Typeset.

Writer's Guide to Using Eight Methods of Transition. Victor C. Pellegrino. LC 93-77683. 52p. (Orig.). (C). 1993. pap. 5.95 (0-945045-03-4) Maui Arthoughts.

Writer's Guide to Washington. Ed. by Isolde Chapin et al. LC 83-50044. 192p. (Orig.). 1983. pap. 7.95 (0-912521-00-7) Wash In Writers.

*Writers Guidebook. Axelrod. Date not set. pap. text ed. 19.00 (0-312-16755-5) St Martin.

Writer's Guidebook. rev. ed. Robert Frew et al. LC 82-81771. 270p. (Orig.). 1986. pap. text ed. 17.95 (0-917962-85-0) T H Peek.

Writer's Handbook. Jeff Griffith & Donna Ignatavicius. 207p. (Orig.). 1986. pap. text ed. 14.95 (0-932491-37-5) Res Appl Inc.

Writer's Handbook. John McKernan. LC 87-4096. (Illus.). 800p. (C). 1988. pap. text ed. 16.00 (0-03-001582-0) HB Coll Pubs.

Writer's Handbook. McWhorter. (C). Date not set. pap. 20.76 (0-395-72819-3) HM.

Writer's Handbook. Mcwhorter. (C). Date not set. pap. 35.56 (0-395-72820-7) HM.

Writer's Handbook. 2nd ed. John McKernan. 544p. (C). 1991. pap. text ed. 18.75 (0-03-053453-4) HB Coll Pubs.

Writer's Handbook. 2nd ed. John McKernan. (C). 1991. teacher ed., pap. text ed. 34.00 (0-03-054213-8) HB Coll Pubs.

Writer's Handbook. 2nd ed. Elizabeth McMahan & Susan Day. 1988. pap. text ed. write for info. (0-07-045432-9) McGraw.

Writer's Handbook. 3rd ed. John McKernan. (C). 1995. pap. text ed. write for info. (0-15-502426-4) HB Coll Pubs.

Writer's Handbook: A Guide to the Essentials of Good Writing. 256p. 1994. 15.95 (0-8442-5375-8, Natl Textbk); pap. 9.95 (0-8442-5372-3, Natl Textbk) NTC Pub Grp.

Writer's Handbook: Answer Key. Stafford. 1991. pap. 4.00 (0-15-597652-4) HB Coll Pubs.

Writer's Handbook: Style & Grammar. James D. Lester. 512p. (C). 1990. pap. text ed. 20.00 (0-15-597648-6) HB Coll Pubs.

Writer's Handbook: Test Bank. Lester. (C). 1991. suppl. ed., teacher ed., pap. text ed. 9.25 (0-15-597658-3) HB Coll Pubs.

*Writer's Handbook: 1997 Edition. annuals 61th enl. rev. ed. Ed. by Sylvia K. Burack. LC 36-28596. 900p. (C). 1997. 29.95 (0-87116-180-X) Writer.

Writer's Handbook for Editing & Revisions. Rick Wilber. 224p. (C). 1996. pap. text ed. 18.95 (0-8442-5916-0) NTC Pub Grp.

Writer's Handbook from A to Z. Gorrell. 1994. student ed., pap. text ed. 4.00 (0-205-15485-9) P-H.

Writer's Handbook from A to Z. Donna Gorrell. LC 93-32599. 1993. pap. text ed. 26.00 (0-205-13764-4) Allyn.

*Writer's Handbook from A to Z. 2nd ed. Gorrell. 1997. pap. text ed. 25.00 (0-205-27560-5) P-H.

*Writer's Handbook 1997: A Comprehensive Map of the Literary Marketplace. Barry Turner. (Orig.). 1996. pap. 36.50 (0-333-64205-8, Pub. by Sidgwick & Jackson UK) Trans-Atl Phila.

*Writer's Handbook 1998 Edition. annuals 62th enl. rev. ed. Ed. by Sylvia K. Burack. 900p. (C). 1997. 29.95 (0-87116-183-4) Writer.

Writer's Harvest, No. 2. Shore. Ed. by Ethan Canin. 336p. 1996. pap. 12.00 (0-15-600246-9) HarBrace.

*Writers Harvest 2: A Collection of New Fiction. Ed. by Ethan Canin. 1996. pap. 12.00 (0-614-20734-7, Harvest Bks) HarBrace.

Writers Have No Age: Creative Writing with Older Adults. Lenore M. Coberly et al. LC 84-15715. (Activities, Adaptation & Aging Ser.: Vol. 6, No. 2). 128p. 1985. text ed. 29.95 (0-86656-320-2); pap. text ed. 19.95 (0-86656-351-2) Haworth Pr.

*Writer's Helper. Woods. 1993. pap. text ed. write for info. (0-582-91194-X, Pub. by Longman UK) Longman.

*Writer's Helper: Mac 4.0. 3rd ed. Wresch. 1996. teacher ed., pap. text ed. 13.33 (0-13-614703-8) P-H.

Writer's Hotline Handbook: A Guide to Good Usage & Effective Writing. Michael S. Montgomery & John Stratton. 384p. 1981. pap. 4.95 (0-451-62225-1, ME2225, Ment) NAL-Dutton.

Writers' Houses. Francesca Premoli-Droulers. (Illus.). 200p. 1995. 50.00 (0-86565-964-8) Vendome.

Writer's I. Sheena Gillespie & Linda C. Stanley. (C). 1988. pap. text ed. 26.50 (0-673-39722-X) Addson-Wesley Educ.

*Writers in a Landscape. Jeremy Hooker. 175p. 1997. 55.00 (0-7083-1362-0, Pub. by Univ Wales Pr UK) Paul & Co Pubs.

*Writers in a Landscape. Jeremy Hooker. 175p. 1997. pap. 24.95 (0-7083-1391-4, Pub. by Univ Wales Pr UK) Paul & Co Pubs.

Writers in Action: The Writer's Choice Evenings. Ed. by Gerry Turcotte. (C). 1990. 49.00 (0-86819-274-0) Aubrey Bks.

*Writers in Hollywood. Ian Hamilton. 11.95 (0-7867-0710-0) Carroll & Graf.

Writers in Hollywood, 1915-1951. Ian Hamilton. (Illus.). 326p. 1991. pap. 11.95 (0-88184-710-0) Carroll & Graf.

*Writers in Politics. (Studies in African Literature). 1997. 65.00 (0-435-07423-7); pap. 19.95 (0-435-07424-5) Heinemann.

Writers in Prison: The Pen Anthology of Imprisoned Writers. Ed. by Siobhan Dowd. (Global Issues Ser.). 192p. 1996. write for info. (0-304-33304-2); pap. write for info. (0-304-33306-9) Cassell.

Writers in Transition. Ed. by Minni & Ciampolini. 1990. pap. 12.00 (0-920717-26-8) Guernica Editions.

*Writers INC. 2nd ed. Patrick Sebanek et al. (Illus.). 360p. 1993. text ed. 19.33 (0-669-38560-3) Great Source.

*Writers INC. 2nd ed. Patrick Sebranek et al. (Illus.). 360p. 1993. pap. text ed. 15.33 (0-669-38559-X) Great Source.

*Writers Inc: A Student Handbook for Writing & Learning. 2nd ed. Patrick Sebranek et al. (Illus.). 360p. (YA). (gr. 9 up). 1996. 19.33 (0-669-38812-2) Great Source.

*Writers Inc: School to Work: A Student Handbook. Patrick Sebranek et al. (Illus.). 528p. (Orig.). (C). 1996. text ed. 19.33 (0-669-40874-3); pap. text ed. 15.33 (0-669-40873-5) HM College Div.

Writer's Internet Handbook. Timothy K. Maloy. (Illus.). 208p. (Orig.). 1997. pap. 18.95 (1-880559-61-7) Allworth Pr.

*Writer's Internet Sourcebook. Michael Levin. LC 97-8055. 1997. pap. text ed. 16.95 (1-886411-11-5) No Starch Pr.

Writer's Journal: 40 Contemporary Writers & Their Journals. Ed. by Sheila Bender. LC 96-21346. 256p. 1997. pap. 12.95 (0-385-31510-4, Delta) Dell.

Writer's Journey. Geoffrey Platt. LC 90-82233. 258p. (C). 1991. pap. text ed. 33.96 (0-669-20298-3) HM College Div.

*Writer's Journey. 2nd ed. Geoffrey Platt. (C). 1995. teacher ed., text ed. 33.16 (0-669-35143-1) HM College Div.

Writer's Journey. 2nd ed. Geoffrey Platt. 320p. (C). 1995. pap. text ed. 33.96 (0-669-35142-3) HM College Div.

Writer's Journey: Mythic Structure for Storytellers & Screenwriters. Christopher Vogler. LC 93-37885. 200p. 1992. pap. 22.95 (0-941188-13-2) M Wiese Prodns.

*Writer's Journey with "Newsweek" 2nd ed. Geoffrey Platt. (C). 1995. text ed. 39.96 (0-669-39522-6) HM College Div.

Writer's Law Primer. Linda F. Pinkerton. 224p. 1990. pap. 12.95 (1-55821-085-7) Lyons & Burford.

Writer's Lawyer: Essential Legal Advice for Writers & Editors in All Media. Ronald L. Goldfarb & Gail E. Ross. 1989. 19.95 (0-8129-1744-8, Times Bks) Random.

Writer's Legal Companion. Brad Bunnin & Peter Beren. 320p. 1988. pap. 18.00 (0-201-14409-3) Addison-Wesley.

Writer's Legal Guide. rev. ed. Tad Crawford & Tony Lyons. LC 95-83301. 304p. 1996. pap. 19.95 (0-927629-13-5) Allworth Pr.

Writer's Library Vol. 1: Growing up, Growing Old. Josephine K. Tarvers & Judith Olson-Fallon. (C). 1992. text ed. 8.75 (0-06-501123-6) Addson-Wesley Educ.

Writer's Library Vol. 2: Women & Men. Josephine K. Tarvers. (C). 1992. text ed. 8.95 (0-06-501124-4) Addson-Wesley Educ.

Writer's Little Book of Wisdom. John Long. (Little Books of Wisdom: Vol. 8). 160p. (Orig.). 1996. pap. 5.95 (1-57034-037-4) ICS Bks.

*Writer's Manual. Edward B. Fry. LC 96-44848. (Contemporary's Reading & Writing Handbooks). 1996. pap. 8.33 (0-8092-0878-4) Contemp Bks.

Writer's Manual. Porter, Roy E., & Assocs. Staff. LC 75-43588. 1979. 27.95 (0-88280-063-9) ETC Pubns.

Writer's Manual: A Practical Guide to Creative & Vocational Writing. Jeff Lewis. 120p. (C). 1990. 60.00 (0-7316-2314-2, Pub. by Pascoe Pub AT) St Mut.

*Writer's Market, 1998: 4000 Places to Sell What You Write. Mark Garvey. 1997. pap. text ed. 49.99 incl. cd-rom (0-89879-802-7, Wrtrs Digest Bks) F & W Pubns Inc.

*Writer's Market, 1998: 4000 Places to Sell What You Write. Kirsten Holm. 1997. pap. text ed. 27.99 (0-89879-792-6, Wrtrs Digest Bks) F & W Pubns Inc.

Writer's Mind: Crafting Fiction. Richard Cohen. 256p. 1994. 19.95 (0-8442-5819-9, Passport Bks) NTC Pub Grp.

Writer's Mind: Crafting Fiction. Richard Cohen. 288p. 1996. pap. 12.95 (0-8442-5864-4) NTC Pub Grp.

Writers Northwest Handbook. Joleen Colombo. (Illus.). 1995. pap. 19.95 (0-9647212-0-1) Media Weavers.

Writer's Notebook. English. (C). Date not set. pap. write for info. (0-395-58461-2) HM.

Writer's Notebook. Ed. by Howard Junker. 1995. pap. 12.00 (0-06-258618-1) HarpC.

Writer's Notebook. W. Somerset Maugham. 336p. (C). 1984. mass mkt. 6.95 (0-14-002644-4, Penguin Bks) Viking Penguin.

Writer's Notebook: Language Medallion. (J). (gr. 4). 1993. pap. text ed. 8.25 (0-15-301103-3) HB Schl Dept.

Writer's Notebook: Language Medallion Grade 3. 1993. pap. text ed. 8.25 (0-15-301102-5) HB Schl Dept.

Writer's Notebook: Language Medallion Grade 5. 1993. pap. text ed. 8.25 (0-15-301104-1) HB Schl Dept.

Writer's Notebook: Language Medallion Grade 6. 1993. pap. text ed. 8.25 (0-15-301105-X) HB Schl Dept.

Writer's Notebook: Language Medallion Grade 7. 1993. pap. text ed. 8.25 (0-15-301106-8) HB Schl Dept.

Writer's Notebook: Language Medallion Grade 8. 1993. pap. text ed. 8.25 (0-15-301107-6) HB Schl Dept.

Writer's Notebook: Unlocking the Writer Within You. Ralph Fletcher. LC 96-1064. 160p. (Orig.). (J). (gr. 3-7). 1996. pap. 4.99 (0-380-78430-0, Camelot) Avon.

*Writers of English: Lives & Works, 22 bks. Incl. Black American Women Fiction Writers. Intro. by Harold Bloom. LC 94-5887. 1995. 29.95 (0-7910-2208-0); Black American Women Poets & Dramatists. Ed. by Harold Bloom. LC 94-4337. 1995. 29.95 (0-7910-2209-9); Major Black American Writers Through the Harlem Renaissance. Intro. by Harold Bloom. LC 94-5886. 1995. 29.95 (0-7910-2218-8); Major Modern Black American Writers. Ed. by Harold Bloom. LC 94-4336. 1995. 29.95 (0-7910-2219-6); Modern Crime & Suspense Writers. Ed. by Harold Bloom. LC 94-44311. 186p. 1995. 29.95 (0-7910-2222-6); Modern Horror Writers. Ed. by Harold Bloom. 200p. 1995. 29.95 (0-7910-2224-2); Modern Mystery Writers. Intro. by Harold Bloom. LC 94-5888. 1995. 29.95 (0-7910-2375-3); Black American Poets & Dramatists Before the Harlem Renaissance. Ed. by Harold Bloom. LC 93-8433. (Illus.). 1994. 29.95 (0-7910-2205-6); Black American Poets & Dramatists of the Harlem Renaissance. Intro. by Harold Bloom. LC 94-5881. 1995. 29.95 (0-7910-2207-2); Black American Prose Writers Before the Harlem Renaissance. Intro. by Harold Bloom. LC 93-13022. (Illus.). 1994. 29.95 (0-7910-2202-1); Black American Prose Writers of the Harlem Renaissance. Intro. by Harold Bloom. LC 93-17979. (Illus.). 1994. 29.95 (0-7910-2203-X); Classic Crime & Suspense Writers. Ed. by Harold Bloom. LC 93-22607. (Illus.). 1994. 29.95 (0-7910-2206-4); Classic Fantasy Writers. Ed. by Harold Bloom. LC 93-8346. (Illus.). 1994. 29.95 (0-7910-2204-8); Classic Horror Writers. Intro. by Harold Bloom. LC 93-13020. (Illus.). 1994. 29.95 (0-7910-2201-3); Classic Mystery Writers. Intro. by Harold Bloom. LC 94-5882. 1995. 29.95 (0-7910-2210-2); Classic Science Fiction Writers. Intro. by Harold Bloom. LC 94-5901. 29.95 (0-7910-2211-0); Contemporary Black American Fiction Writers. Intro. by Harold Bloom. LC 94-5883. 1995. 29.95 (0-7910-2212-9); Contemporary Black American Poets & Dramatists. Intro. by Harold Bloom. LC 94-5885. 1995. 29.95 (0-7910-2213-7); Modern Black American Fiction Writers. Intro. by Harold Bloom. LC 94-5880. 1995. 29.95 (0-7910-2220-X); Modern Black American Poets & Dramatists. Ed. by Harold Bloom. LC 94-5902. 1995. 29.95 (0-7910-2221-8); Modern Fantasy Writers. Ed. by Harold Bloom. 200p. 1995. 29.95 (0-7910-2223-4); Science Fiction Writers of the Golden Age. Ed. by Harold Bloom. LC 94-4322. 1995. 14.95 (0-7910-2199-8); 658.90 (0-7910-2200-5) Chelsea Hse.

*Writers of English: Lives & Works. Incl. Black American Women Fiction Writers. Intro. by Harold Bloom. LC 94-5887. pap. 14.95 (0-7910-2233-1); Black American Women Poets & Dramatists. Ed. by Harold Bloom. LC 94-4337. 1995. pap. 14.95 (0-7910-2234-X); Major Black American Writers Through the Harlem Renaissance. Intro. by Harold Bloom. LC 94-5886. 1995. pap. 14.95 (0-7910-2243-9); Major Modern Black American Writers. Ed. by Harold Bloom. LC 94-4336. 1995. pap. 14.95 (0-7910-2244-7); Modern Horror Writers. Ed. by Harold Bloom. 200p. 1995. pap. 14.95 (0-7910-2249-8); Modern Mystery Writers. Intro. by Harold Bloom. LC 94-5888. 1995. pap. 14.95 (0-7910-2376-1); Modern Crime & Suspense Writers. Ed. by Harold Bloom. LC 94-44311. 200p. 1995. pap. 14.95 (0-7910-2247-1); Black American Poets & Dramatists Before the Harlem Renaissance. Ed. by Harold Bloom. LC 93-8433. (Illus.). 1994. pap. 14.95 (0-7910-2230-7); Black American Poets & Dramatists of the Harlem Renaissance. Intro. by Harold Bloom. LC 94-5881. pap. 14.95 (0-7910-2232-3); Black American Prose Writers Before the Harlem Renaissance. Intro. by Harold Bloom. LC 93-13022. (Illus.). 1994. pap. 14.95 (0-7910-2227-7); Black American Prose Writers of the Harlem Renaissance. Intro. by Harold Bloom. LC 93-17979. (Illus.). 1994. pap. 14.95 (0-7910-2228-5); Classic Crime & Suspense Writers. Ed. by Harold Bloom. LC 93-22607. (Illus.). 1994. pap. 14.95 (0-7910-2231-5); Classic Fantasy Writers. Ed. by Harold Bloom. LC 93-8346. (Illus.). 1994. pap. 14.95 (0-7910-2229-3); Classic Horror Writers. Intro. by Harold Bloom. LC 93-13020. (Illus.). 1994. pap. 14.95 (0-7910-2226-9); Classic Mystery Writers. Intro. by Harold Bloom. LC 94-5882. 1995. pap. 14.95 (0-7910-2235-8); Classic Science Fiction Writers. Intro. by Harold Bloom. LC 94-5901. pap. 14.95 (0-7910-2236-6); Contemporary Black American Fiction Writers. Intro. by Harold Bloom. LC 94-5883. pap. 14.95 (0-7910-2237-4); Contemporary Black American Poets & Dramatists. Intro. by Harold Bloom. LC 94-5885. 1995. pap. 14.95 (0-7910-2238-2); Modern Black American Fiction Writers. Intro. by Harold Bloom. LC 94-5880. pap. 14.95 (0-7910-2245-5); Modern Black American Poets & Dramatists. Ed. by Harold Bloom. LC 94-5902. 182p. 1995. pap. 14.95 (0-7910-2246-3); Modern Fantasy Writers. Ed. by Harold Bloom. 1995. pap. 14.95 (0-7910-2248-X); 349.65 (0-7910-3779-7) Chelsea Hse.

Writers of Knickerbocker New York. Hamilton W. Mabie. 121p. 1993. reprint ed. lib. bdg. 69.00 (0-7812-5278-4) Rprt Serv.

*Writers of Modern America, Vol. 18. Date not set. write for info. (0-8369-4809-2) Ayer.

Writers of Montreal. Elaine K. Naves. (Illus.). 192p. (Orig.). 1993. pap. 16.00 (1-55065-045-9, Pub. by Vehicule Pr CN) Genl Dist Srvs.

Writers of Multicultural Fiction for Young Adults: A Bio-Critical Sourcebook. Ed. by M. Daphne Kutzer. LC 95-502. 496p. 1996. text ed. 75.00 (0-313-29331-7, Greenwood Pr) Greenwood.

Writers of the Caribbean & Central America: A Bibliography, 2 vols., Set. M. J. Fenwick. LC 91-35701. 1630p. 1992. text ed. 215.00 (0-8240-4010-4, H1244) Garland.

Writers of the Caribbean & Central America: A Bibliography, 2 vols., Vol. 1, 776p. M. J. Fenwick. 1992. write for info. (0-318-68857-3) Garland.

Writers of the Caribbean & Central America: A Bibliography, 2 vols., Vol. 2, 845p. M. J. Fenwick. 1992. write for info. (0-318-68858-1) Garland.

Writers of the Indian Diaspora: A Bio-Bibliographical Critical Sourcebook. Ed. by Emmanuel S. Nelson. LC 92-27898. 504p. 1993. text ed. 89.50 (0-313-27904-7, NWI/, Greenwood Pr) Greenwood.

Writers of the Middle Ages & Renaissance Before 1660 see Concise Dictionary of British Literary Biography

Writers of the Purple Sage. Barbara B. Smith. 304p. 1994. 20.95 (0-312-11352-8, Thomas Dunne Bks) St Martin.

Writers of the Purple Sage. Barbara B. Smith. (Mystery Ser.). 1996. mass mkt. 4.99 (0-373-26214-0, Wrldwide Lib) Harlequin Bks.

Writers of the Restoration & 18th Century see Concise Dictionary of British Literary Biography

Writers of the Romantic Period, 1789-1832 see Concise Dictionary of British Literary Biography

Writers of the Western World. Hibbard. (C). 1995. pap. 41.56 (0-395-73885-7) HM.

Writers on Artists. Daniel Halpern. 1990. pap. 15.95 (0-86547-340-4, North Pt Pr) FS&G.

*Writers on Life. Carol Edgarian & Tom Jenks. LC 96-6949. 1997. pap. 13.00 (0-679-76957-9, Vin) Random.

Writers on Life: Wit & Wisdom from the Intimate Notebooks, Journals & Diaries of More Than 200 of the World's Best Writers. Ed. by Carol Edgarian & Tom Jenks. LC 96-6949. 1997. 22.00 (0-679-44836-5) Random.

Writers on Organizations. 4th ed. D. S. Pugh & D. J. Hickson. 240p. (C). 1989. text ed. 48.00 (0-8039-3507-2); pap. text ed. 22.95 (0-8039-3508-0) Sage.

Writers on Organizations. 5th ed. Derek S. Pugh et al. LC 96-25180. 288p. 1996. pap. 21.95 (0-7619-0476-X) Sage.

Writers on Organizations. 5th ed. Derek S. Pugh et al. LC 96-25180. 288p. 1996. 46.00 (0-7619-0475-1) Sage.

Writers on the Left. Daniel Aaron. LC 92-16360. 496p. 1992. pap. 17.50 (0-231-08039-5, Mrngside); text ed. 49.50 (0-231-08038-7, Mrngside) Col U Pr.

Writers on the Mound: Nonfiction Baseball Prose. Orodenker. 1996. pap. 22.95 (0-8057-3998-X, Hall Reference) Macmillan.

Writers on Writers. Graham Tarrant. 64p. 1995. 9.95 (1-85410-318-0, Pub. by Aurum Pr UK) London Brdge.

W

Writers on Writing. Ed. by Robert Pack & Jay Parini. LC 91-50372. (Bread Loaf Anthology Ser.). 306p. 1991. pap. 19.95 (0-87451-560-2); text ed. 45.00 (0-87451-559-9) U Pr of New Eng.

Writers on Writing: An Anthology. Ed. by Robert Neale. 272p. 1993. pap. 22.00 (0-19-558256-X) OUP.

Writers on Writing for Young Adults: Anthology. Ed. by Patricia E. Feehan & Pamela Barron. 447p. 1991. lib. bdg. 45.00 (1-55888-740-7) Omnigraphics Inc.

Writers Outside the Margin: An Anthology. Ed. & Intro. by Jeffrey H. Weinberg. LC 86-80331. (Illus.). 125p. (Orig.). 1986. pap. 14.98 (0-934953-06-6) Water Row Pr.

***Writer's Partner: For Fiction, Television, & Screen.** 2nd ed. Martin Roth. 360p. (Orig.). 1997. pap. 19.95 (1-56866-148-7) Index Pub Grp.

Writer's Perspective: Voices from American Culture. Compiled by Maria C. Freeman. LC 93-3518. 416p. (C). 1993. pap. text ed. 26.20 (0-13-948308-X) P-H.

Writer's Place: Interviews on the Literary Situation in Contemporary Britain. Ed. by Peter Firchow. LC 74-22835. 375p. reprint ed. pap. 106.90 (0-317-41720-7, 2055864) Bks Demand.

Writer's Plan. Susan S. Webb & William E. Tanner. 422p. (C). 1985. teacher ed. write for info. (0-15-597899-3) HB Coll Pubs.

Writer's Plan: Reproducible Forms to Organize Your Writing for Pleasure & Profit. Carole Marsh. (Lifewrite Ser.). (Orig.). 1994. pap. 19.95 (1-55609-951-7); lib. bdg. 24.95 (1-55609-950-9); ring bd. 39.95 (1-55609-952-5); Apple II 29.95 (1-55609-953-3) Gallopade Pub Group.

Writer's Pocket Almanac. (Illus.). 192p. 1988. pap. text ed. 9.95 (0-931137-08-X) Infobooks.

Writer's Pocket Pal 2. Underwood. 1992. pap. text ed. write for info. (0-07-065764-5) McGraw.

Writer's Portfolios. English. (YA). (gr. 9-12). 1991. student ed., pap. write for info. (0-395-58460-4) HM.

Writers Presence. 2nd ed. Donald McQuade. 1994. pap. text ed. 10.00 (0-312-09433-7) St Martin.

Writers Presence. 2nd ed. Donald McQuade. 1997. pap. text ed. 22.00 (0-312-13632-3) St Martin.

Writer's Presence: A Pool of Essays. Donald McQuade & Robert Atwan. 704p. 1994. pap. text ed. 22.00 (0-312-08480-3) St Martin.

Writer's Reader. Ed. by Donald Hall & D. L. Emblem. LC 96-33814. (C). 1997. teacher ed. write for info. (0-673-52333-0) Addson-Wesley Educ.

Writer's Reader. 7th ed. Ed. by Donald Hall & D. L. Emblen. LC 93-8126. (C). 1993. 18.25 (0-673-52332-2) Addson-Wesley Educ.

Writer's Reader. 7th ed. Donald Hall. 1996. pap. text ed. 28.50 (0-8230-6533-2) Watsn-Guptill.

Writer's Reader. 8th ed. Ed. by Donald Hall & D. L. Emblem. LC 96-33814. (C). 1997. student ed., pap. text ed. 33.50 (0-673-52505-8) Addson-Wesley Educ.

Writers, Readers, & Occasions: Selected Essays on Victorian Literature & Life. Richard D. Altick. (Illus.). 335p. 1989. text ed. 45.00 (0-8142-0459-7) Ohio St U Pr.

Writer's Reality. Mario Vargas Llosa. 192p. 1992. pap. 11.95 (0-395-62234-4) HM.

Writer's Reality. Mario Vargas Llosa. 232p. 1990. 35.00 (0-8156-0253-7) Syracuse U Pr.

Writer's Reference. 2nd ed. Diana Hacker. 288p. (Orig.). (C). 1992. wbk. ed. write for info. (0-318-68817-4) St Martin.

Writers Reference. 3rd ed. Hacker. (C). 1994. suppl. ed., pap. text ed. 3.00 (0-312-11922-4) St Martin.

Writers Reference. 3rd ed. Diana Hacker. 1995. pap. text ed. 19.50 (0-312-13417-7) St Martin.

***Writers Reference.** 4th ed. Hacker. Date not set. pap. text ed. write for info. (0-312-17161-7) St Martin.

Writer's Reference: Answers & Exercises. 3rd ed. Hacker. 1995. pap. text ed. 5.00 (0-312-11512-1) St Martin.

Writer's Reference: Developmental Exercises. 3rd ed. Diana Hacker. 1995. pap. text ed. 3.00 (0-312-10141-4) St Martin.

***Writers Reference Genie.** Hacker. Date not set. pap. text ed. write for info. (0-312-16741-5) St Martin.

Writer's Repertoire. Gwendolyn Gong & Sam Dragga. LC 94-13236. (C). 1995. text ed. 35.95 (0-06-501070-1) Addson-Wesley Educ.

Writer's Resource: Readings for Composition. 4th ed. Ed. by Susan Day & Elizabeth McMahan. LC 93-23204. 1993. pap. text ed. write for info. (0-07-016176-3) McGraw.

***Writer's Resource: The Watson-Guptill Guide to Workshops, Conferences, Artists' Colonies & ACA.** David Emblidge. (Getting Your Act Together Ser.). 1997. pap. text ed. 19.95 (0-8230-7651-2) Watsn-Guptill.

***Writer's Resource Handbook.** Daniel Grant. 272p. (Orig.). 1997. pap. 19.95 (1-880559-79-X) Allworth Pr.

Writer's Resources. Robitaille. (C). pap. text ed. 31.00 (0-15-504148-7) HarBrace.

Writers Revision Handbook: Summary Points for Revising. Blair Adams & Joel Stein. 52p. 1993. pap. 4.95 (0-916387-27-5) Truth Forum.

Writer's Rhetoric. Suzanne Britt. 463p. (C). 1988. teacher ed. write for info. (0-15-597661-3); pap. text ed. 20.00 (0-15-597660-5) HB Coll Pubs.

Writer's Rhetoric & Handbook. 3rd rev. ed. Elizabeth McMahan & Susan Day. 544p. (C). 1988. text ed. write for info. (0-07-045426-4) McGraw.

Writer's Rhyming Dictionary. Langford Reed. LC 61-16086. 1985. pap. 8.95 (0-87116-143-5) Writer.

Writer's Rights. Michael Legat. pap. 15.95 (0-7136-4018-9, 93360, Pub. by A&C Black UK) Talman.

Writer's Roles. Mason. (C). 1994. teacher ed., pap. text ed. 33.75 (0-15-500161-2) HB Coll Pubs.

Writers' Roles: Enactments of the Process. Nondita Mason & George Otte. (Illus.). 768p. (Orig.). (C). 1993. pap. text ed. 24.00 (0-15-500160-4) HB Coll Pubs.

***Writer's Selections: Shaping Our Lives.** Kathleen McWhorter. 288p. (C). 1996. pap. text ed. 25.16 (0-395-72821-5) HM.

Writer's Sense of the Past: Essays on Southeast Asian & Australasian Literature. Ed. by Kirpal Singh. 250p. (Orig.). 1987. pap. 33.50 (9971-69-108-6, Pub. by Sgapore Univ SI) Coronet Bks.

Writers Shelf: Literature Through, Pt. I. Harwayne. (J). 1992. 174.05 (0-06-027097-7, Festival) HarpC Child Bks.

Writers Sourcebook. Laurie G. Kirszner. (C). 1987. teacher ed., pap. text ed. 27.50 (0-03-002594-X) HB Coll Pubs.

***Writer's Sourcebook.** 2nd ed. Rachel F. Ballon. 272p. 1997. reprint ed. pap. 15.00 (1-56565-816-7, Extension Pr) Lowell Hse.

Writer's Sourcebook: From Writing Blocks to Writing Blockbusters. Rachel Ballon. 256p. 1996. 25.00 (1-56565-466-8) Lowell Hse.

Writers Sourcebook: Strategies for Reading & Writing in the Disciplines. Laurie G. Kirszner & Stephen R. Mandell. 608p. (C). 1987. pap. text ed. 21.50 (0-03-002593-1) HB Coll Pubs.

Writer's Story: From Life to Fiction. Marion Dane Bauer. LC 94-48800. (YA). (gr. 5 up). 1995. 14.95 (0-395-72094-X, Clarion Bks); pap. 6.95 (0-395-75053-9, Clarion Bks) HM.

Writer's Survival Guide. George Ehrenhaft. 124p. (Orig.). (YA). (gr. 9-12). 1988. teacher ed. 14.99 (0-87438-048-0); pap. text ed. 14.99 (0-87438-047-2) Media Basics.

***Writer's Survival Guide.** Rachel Simon. LC 96-43433. 224p. 1997. 18.99 (1-884910-23-8, Story Press) F & W Pubns Inc.

Writers Talk to Ralph D. Gardner. Ralph D. Gardner. LC 88-27552. (Illus.). 355p. 1989. 35.00 (0-8108-2143-5) Scarecrow.

***Writer's Tax Guide: Writing & Writing It Off.** Michael A. Jones. LC 96-90847. (Illus.). 216p. (Orig.). 1997. pap. 19.95 (0-9655787-0-4) Veritas Pub.

Writers Thesaurus. 1994. 15.95 (0-673-12379-0, ScottFrsmn) Addson-Wesley Educ.

Writer's Time. Atchity Kenneth. 1994. 22.00 (0-393-03693-6) Norton.

Writer's Time: Making the Time to Write. Kenneth Atchity. LC 94-15014. 1995. pap. 11.95 (0-393-31263-1) Norton.

Writer's Toolbox: A Sentence-Combining Workshop. William Strong. LC 95-8524. 1995. teacher ed. write for info. (0-07-062562-X) McGraw.

Writer's Toolbox: A Sentence-Combining Workshop. William Strong. LC 95-8524. 1995. pap. text ed. write for info. (0-07-062561-1) McGraw.

Writer's Toolkit: Essays, Poems, Stories. Charles Brashear. 288p. (Orig.). 1991. pap. 14.95 (0-933362-13-7) Assoc Creative Writers.

Writer's Tools. Starr. (C). 1991. teacher ed., pap. text ed. 34.00 (0-03-054878-0) HB Coll Pubs.

Writer's Tools: Building Paragraphs & Essays. Alvin J. Starr. 377p. (C). 1991. pap. text ed. 19.50 (0-03-033127-7) HB Coll Pubs.

Writer's Triangle: A Literature-Based Writing Program. Carla Heymsfield & Joan Lewis. (J). (gr. 5 up). 1989. pap. 14.99 (0-8224-7496-4) Fearon Teach Aids.

Writer's Tutor: One Hundred Self-Correcting Lessons. J. N. Hook & William H. Evans. 516p. (C). 1988. pap. text ed. 26.00 (0-15-597670-2) HB Coll Pubs.

Writer's Ultimate Research Guide. Ellen Metter. 336p. 1995. 19.99 (0-89879-668-7, Wrtrs Digest Bks) F & W Pubns Inc.

Writer's Utopia Formula Report. rev. ed. Jerry Buchanan. 1977. 12.00 (0-930668-05-7) Towers Club.

Writer's Way, 3 Vols. Jack P. Rawlins. (C). 1995. pap. 27.56 (0-395-74533-0) HM.

***Writer's Way, 3 Vols.** 3rd ed. Jack P. Rawlins. (C). 1995. teacher ed., text ed. 11.96 (0-395-75384-8) HM.

***Writers' Web: Get Online & Get Published.** Brian Howard. (Illus.). 280p. (Orig.). 1997. pap. 29.95 (1-55755-332-7, B-332) Abacus MI.

Writers Who Cook: A Tasty Assortment of Prose, Poetry & Recipes. Ed. by Jane Boers et al. 83p. (Orig.). 1995. pap. 12.95 (0-9634813-0-4) Herringbone.

Writer's Work: A Guide to Effective Composition. 3rd ed. Frank O'Hare & W. Dean Memering. 592p. (C). 1989. Casebound. text ed. 38.40 (0-13-969635-0) P-H.

Writer's Workbook. Judith Appelbaum & Florence Janovic. 1991. pap. 15.95 (0-916366-69-3) Pushcart Pr.

Writer's Workbook. Susan Day. 1980. text ed. write for info. (0-07-016150-X) McGraw.

Writer's Workbook. Shirley Fondiller. 200p. (C). 1992. pap. text ed. 20.95 (0-88737-548-0, 14-2470) Natl League Nurse.

Writer's Workbook. Sharon Wooten et al. 148p. (C). 1996. ring bd. 27.24 (0-7872-2339-5) Kendall-Hunt.

Writer's Workbook. 3rd ed. Smoke. 1996. teacher ed., pap. text ed. 0.37 (0-312-11509-1) St Martin.

Writers Workbook: An Interactive Writing Text for ESL Students. 3rd ed. Trudy Smoke. 1996. pap. text ed. 18.50 (0-312-11508-3) St Martin.

Writer's Workbook: Style & Grammar. Norman E. Stafford. 320p. (C). 1991. pap. text ed. 27.50 (0-15-597651-6) HB Coll Pubs.

Writer's Workout Book: 113 Stretches Toward Better Prose. Art Peterson. LC 96-7329. 1996. write for info. (1-883920-12-4) Nat Writing Proj.

Writer's Workplace. 2nd ed. John Scarry & Sandra Scarry. (C). 1991. suppl. ed., teacher ed., pap. text ed. 2.75 (0-03-055944-8) HB Coll Pubs.

Writer's Workplace. 4th ed. John Scarry & Sandra Scarry. (C). 1996. pap. text ed. 35.00 (0-15-503725-0) HB Coll Pubs.

***Writer's Workplace.** 4th ed. Sandra Scarry & John Scarry. 496p. (C). 1996. write for info. (0-614-21807-1) HB Coll Pubs.

***Writer's Workplace.** 5th ed. Scarry. (C). 1998. text ed. write for info. (0-15-508136-5) HB Coll Pubs.

Writer's Workplace, Vol. 1. John Scarry & Sandra Scarry. (C). 1996. pap. text ed. 28.00 (0-15-505193-8) HarBrace.

Writer's Workplace, Vol. 13. John Scarry & Sandra Scarry. (C). 1996. pap. text ed. 21.00 (0-15-505276-4) HarBrace.

Writer's Workplace, Vol. B. John Scarry & Sandra Scarry. (C). 1997. pap. text ed. 21.00 (0-15-505195-4) HarBrace.

Writer's Workplace: Building College Writing Skills. 2nd annot. ed. Sandra Scarry & John Scarry. 544p. (C). 1991. teacher ed. write for info. (0-03-055538-8) HB Coll Pubs.

Writer's Workplace: Building College Writing Skills. 2nd ed. Sandra Scarry & John Scarry. 544p. (C). 1987. 27.50 (0-03-012087-X) HB Coll Pubs.

Writer's Workplace: Building College Writing Skills. 2nd ed. Sandra Scarry & John Scarry. 544p. (C). 1991. pap. text ed. 24.00 (0-03-053862-9); disk write for info. (0-318-69140-X) HB Coll Pubs.

***Writer's Workplace: Paragraphs (Answer Key)** Sandra Scarry & John Scarry. 144p. (C). 1996. pap. text ed. 28.00 (0-15-505278-0) HB Coll Pubs.

***Writer's Workplace & Readings: Paragraphs to Essays.** Sandra Scarry & John Scarry. 592p. (C). 1996. pap. text ed. 37.25 (0-15-503830-3) HB Coll Pubs.

Writer's Workplace & Readings: Sentences to Paragraphs, Vol. A. John Scarry & Sandra Scarry. 155p. (C). 1996. pap. text ed. 26.75 (0-15-505196-2) HB Coll Pubs.

***Writer's Workplace with Reading.** John Scarry & Sandra Scarry. (C). 1997. pap. text ed. 35.00 (0-15-503833-8) HB Coll Pubs.

***Writer's Workplace with Reading-Paragraphs.** Sandra Scarry & John Scarry. 480p. (C). 1997. pap. text ed. 35.00 (0-15-503832-X) HB Coll Pubs.

***Writer's Workplace with Readings.** 2nd ed. Scarry. (C). 1997. pap. write for info. (0-15-503474-X) HB Coll Pubs.

***Writer's Workplace with Readings.** 2nd ed. Scarry. (C). 1997. wbk. ed. write for info. (0-15-505279-9) HB Coll Pubs.

***Writer's Workplace with Readings.** 2nd ed. Sandra Scarry & John Scarry. 528p. (C). 1996. write for info. (0-614-21808-X) HB Coll Pubs.

***Writer's Workplace with Readings: Sentences to Paragraphs.** Sandra Scarry & John Scarry. 466p. (C). 1996. pap. text ed. 37.25 (0-15-503829-X) HB Coll Pubs.

***Writer's Workplace with Readings - Essays.** Sandra Scarry & John Scarry. 416p. (C). 1996. pap. text ed. write for info. (0-614-23021-7) HB Coll Pubs.

***Writer's Workplace with Readings - Sentence.** Sandra Scarry & John Scarry. 414p. (C). 1997. pap. text ed. 35.00 (0-15-503831-1) HB Coll Pubs.

***Writer's Workplace, 4e & The Writer's Workplace with Readings, 2e (The Resource Manual)** Sandra Scarry & John Scarry. 168p. (C). 1996. pap. text ed. 28.00 (0-15-505194-6) HB Coll Pubs.

Writer's Workshop: A Self-Paced Program for Composition Mastery. 6th rev. ed. 282p. 1992. pap. text ed. 22.95 (0-917962-24-9) T H Peek.

***Writer's Workshop: Sharing Ideas.** Sandi Fisher. (Reading & Writing Ser.). (Illus.). 101p. 1994. teacher ed., pap. text ed. 12.95 (0-88095-200-8) Gallaudet U Pre Coll.

Writers Workshop Handbook of Assamese Literature, Vol. 1: A-D. P. N. Shastri & P. Lal. (Greybird Ser.). 106p. (C). 1975. text ed. 14.00 (0-88253-702-4); pap. text ed. 8.00 (0-88253-703-2) Ind-US Inc.

Writers Workshop Handbook of Gujarati Literature: Vol. 1, A-F. Ed. by P. N. Shastri & P. Lal. (Writers Workshop Greybird Ser.). 96p. 1981. 14.00 (0-86578-043-9); 8.00 (0-86578-042-0) Ind-US Inc.

***Writer's Workshop to Accompany Lannon: Technical Writing.** 7th ed. Daedalus. (C). 1997. pap. text ed. write for info. (0-321-01710-2) Addison-Wesley.

***Writer's Workshop to Accompany Lannon: Technical Writing, Windows Version.** 7th ed. Daedalus. (C). 1997. pap. text ed. write for info. (0-321-01711-0) Addison-Wesley.

Writer's World: An Essay Anthology. Linda Woodson. 380p. (C). 1986. pap. text ed. 20.00 (0-15-597683-4) HB Coll Pubs.

Writers Worlds. 2nd ed. Smoke. 1995. teacher ed., pap. text ed. 20.50 (0-312-09565-1) St Martin.

Writers Worlds. 2nd ed. Smoke. 1994. teacher ed., pap. text ed. 0.43 (0-312-09566-X) St Martin.

Writer's Worlds. 2nd ed. Trudy Smoke. 592p. 1994. pap. text ed. 22.00 (0-312-09564-3) St Martin.

Writers Writing. Lil Brannon et al. LC 82-14587. 179p. (Orig.). (C). 1982. pap. text ed. 19.50 (0-86709-045-6, 0045) Boynton Cook Pubs.

Writers.Net: Every Writer's Essential Guide. Gary Gach. LC 96-43378. 1997. per., pap. 22.00 (0-7615-0641-1) Prima Pub.

WriteType: Personality & Writing Styles. Stephen D. Gladis. 144p. 1993. pap. 15.00 (0-87425-221-0) HRD Press.

Writing. 1988. 12.95 (0-19-437098-4) OUP.

Writing. (College Board SAT II Subject Test Ser.). 1997. pap. 23.95 (0-8373-6316-0, SATII-16) Nat Learn.

Writing. (Regents Competency Test Ser.). 1997. pap. 23.95 (0-8373-6404-3, RCT-4) Nat Learn.

Writing. Blythe Camenson. (VGM Career Portraits Ser.). 96p. (J). 1995. 13.95 (0-8442-4372-8, VGM Career Bks) NTC Pub Grp.

Writing. David Mellinkoff. Date not set. text ed. 22.00 (0-684-17293-3) West Pub.

Writing. 3rd ed. Elizabeth Cowan-Neeld. (C). 1990. text ed. 41.50 (0-673-38399-7) Addson-Wesley Educ.

Writing: A College Handbook. James W. Heffernan & John E. Lincoln. (C). 1990. Wkbk. student ed., pap. text ed. 16.95 (0-393-95952-X) Norton.

Writing: A College Handbook. James W. Heffernan & John E. Lincoln. (C). 1994. pap. text ed. write for info. (0-393-96502-3); pap. text ed. write for info. (0-393-96506-6) Norton.

Writing: A College Handbook. James W. Heffernan & John E. Lincoln. (C). 1994. Diagnostic Achievement Test. student ed. write for info. (0-393-99825-8); write for info. (0-393-99826-6); pap. text ed. write for info. (0-393-96471-X); pap. text ed. 16.95 (0-393-96472-8); pap. text ed. 16.95 (0-393-96504-X); pap. text ed. 16.95 (0-393-96503-1) Norton.

Writing: A College Handbook. 4th ed. James W. Heffernan & John E. Lincoln. (C). 1994. text ed. 24.95 (0-393-96470-1) Norton.

Writing: A College Rhetoric. 2nd ed. Laurie G. Kirszner & Stephen R. Mandell. (Illus.). 652p. (C). 1988. pap. text ed. 26.75 (0-03-012094-2) HB Coll Pubs.

Writing: A College Rhetoric Brief. 2nd ed. Laurie G. Kirszner & Stephen R. Mandell. LC 87-23673. (Illus.). 496p. (C). 1988. pap. text ed. 23.50 (0-03-012089-6) HB Coll Pubs.

Writing: A Content Approach to ESL Composition. Mark D. Jenkins. (Illus.). 240p. (C). 1986. pap. text ed. 19.25 (0-13-969544-3) P-H.

Writing: A Diagnostic Approach. Eva S. Weiner. 1987. reprint ed. pap. 7.00 (0-13-969858-2) P-H.

Writing: A Fact & Fun Book. Amanda Lewis. 1992. pap. 8.95 (0-201-63236-5) Addison-Wesley.

***Writing: A Fact & Fun Book.** unabridged ed. Amanda Lewis. (Illus.). 96p. (J). (gr. 3-8). 1992. pap. 8.95 (1-55074-052-0, Pub. by Kids Can Pr CN) Genl Dist Srvs.

Writing: A Guide for Business Professionals. C. W. Griffin. 419p. (C). 1987. pap. text ed. 20.00 (0-15-597676-1) HB Coll Pubs.

Writing: A Guide for Therapists. Sally French & Julius Sim. (Illus.). 160p. 1993. pap. 30.00 (0-7506-0580-4) Buttrwrth-Heinemann.

Writing: A Norton Handbook. James A. Heffernan. (C). Date not set. pap. text ed. write for info. (0-393-95843-4) Norton.

Writing: A Window to Our Minds. Nancy Marashio. (Writing Teachers at Work Ser.). 172p. 1982. pap. text ed. 6.50 (1-883920-03-5) Nat Writing Proj.

Writing: A Workshop Approach. LaRene Despain. LC 91-33509. 365p. (C). 1992. pap. text ed. 28.95 (0-87484-988-8, 988); teacher ed., pap. text ed. write for info. (1-55934-024-X, 1024) Mayfield Pub.

Writing: An Unnatural Act. James C. Raymond. (C). 1986. pap. text ed. 29.50 (0-06-045341-9) Addson-Wesley Educ.

Writing: Brief. 3rd ed. Elizabeth Cowan-Neeld & Kathleen E. Kiefer. (C). 1990. pap. text ed. 36.50 (0-673-38383-0) Addson-Wesley Educ.

Writing: College Handbook. 4th ed. James A. Heffernan. (C). Date not set. text ed. 24.95 incl. 3.5 hd (0-393-96740-9); text ed. 24.95 incl. 5.25 hd (0-393-96741-7) Norton.

Writing: Communicative Activities in English. Christina B. Paulston et al. (Illus.). 288p. (C). 1983. pap. text ed. 14.00 (0-13-970277-6) P-H.

Writing: Description. Carol Gladstone. 55p. 1989. student ed. 3.95 (0-910307-09-1) Comp Pr.

Writing: Getting into Print: A Business Guide for Writers. Jo Frohbieter-Mueller. LC 93-79254. (Illus.). 287p. 1994. 21.95 (0-944435-23-8) Glenbridge Pub.

Writing: Invitation & Response. Vincent Ruggiero & Patricia Morgan. LC 92-70919. (Illus.). 560p. (C). 1992. pap. text ed. write for info. (0-03-023089-6) HB Coll Pubs.

Writing: Man's Great Invention. J. Hambleton Ober. (Illus.). 1965. 19.95 (0-8392-1139-2) Astor-Honor.

***Writing: Paul de Sainte Colombe's Simplified Handwriting Style.** Bonnie Kalchev & Rose L. Toomey. (Illus.). 68p. (Orig.). 1993. pap. text ed. 10.00 (0-9654514-1-0) R L Toomey.

Writing: Personal Expression. Carol Gladstone. 55p. 1986. student ed. 3.95 (0-910307-07-5) Comp Pr.

Writing: Personal Narrative. Carol Gladstone. 55p. 1986. student ed. 3.95 (0-910307-08-3) Comp Pr.

Writing: Process & Purpose. Ellen A. Knodt. 415p. (C). 1986. pap. write for info. (0-02-365340-X, Macmillan Coll) P-H.

Writing: Process, Product, & Power. Kenneth W. Davis & Kim B. Lovejoy. 320p. (C). 1992. pap. text ed. 31.40 (0-13-971011-6) P-H.

Writing: Processes & Intentions. Richard C. Gebhardt & Dawn Rodrigues. LC 88-81108. 281p. (C). 1989. pap. text ed. 28.36 (0-669-09132-4) HM College Div.

Writing: Readings & Advice. Enno Klammer. 319p. (C). 1984. pap. text ed. 20.00 (0-15-597997-3) HB Coll Pubs.

Writing: Research, Theory & Applications. Stephen D. Krashen. 56p. (C). 1992. reprint ed. pap. text ed. 7.95 (1-56492-090-9) Laredo.

***Writing: Resources for Conferencing & Collaboration.** Mary S. Koeppel. LC 88-19614. Date not set. write for info. (0-13-969965-1) P-H.

Writing: Skill Enhancement. Gary McLean et al. 1994. teacher ed. 8.00 (0-318-70383-1); text ed. 10.95 (1-56118-232-X) Paradigm MN.

Writing: Strategies for All Disciplines. Barbara F. Walvoord. (Illus.). 480p. (C). 1985. text ed. 15.95 (0-13-147349-2) P-H.

W

An Asterisk (*) at the beginning of an entry indicates that the title is appearing in BIP for the first time.

Writing: Student's Book. Ron White & Don McGovern. LC 94-26133. (English for Academic Study Ser.). 1994. 9.75 (0-13-017880-2) P-H.

Writing: Style & Grammar. James D. Lester, Sr. & James D. Lester, Jr. 400p. (J). (gr. 6-10). 1994. pap. 9.95 (0-673-36093-8, GoodYrBooks); spiral bd. 14.95 (0-673-36128-4, GoodYrBooks) Addson-Wesley Educ.

Writing: Teachers & Children at Work. Donald Graves. LC 82-21177. 326p. (C). 1983. pap. text ed. 22.50 (0-435-08203-5, 08203) Heinemann.

***Writing: Techniques for Survival.** 2nd ed. Mary E. Grasso & James Ledford. 464p. (C). 1996. per., pap. text ed. 44.95 (0-7872-2708-0) Kendall-Hunt.

Writing: The Business Letter. Albert G. Craz & Edward P. Mavragis. 68p. 1988. student ed. 3.95 (0-560-78025-7) Comp Pr.

Writing: The Essay. Edward P. Mavragis. 91p. 1991. student ed. 4.95 (1-56078-025-8) Comp Pr.

Writing: The Process Essay. Carol Gladstone. 55p. 1986. student ed. 3.95 (0-910307-11-3) Comp Pr.

Writing: The Report. Albert G. Craz & Edward P. Mavragis. (Writing Ser.). 66p. 1981. student ed. 3.95 (0-9602800-2-2) Comp Pr.

Writing: The Story of Alphabets & Scripts. Georges Jean. (Discoveries Ser.). (Illus.). 208p. 1992. pap. 12.95 (0-8109-2893-0) Abrams.

Writing: The Translation of Memory. Eve Shelnutt. 806p. (C). 1990. pap. write for info. (0-02-409820-5, Macmillan Coll) P-H.

Writing: To Finish a Story. Carol Gladstone. 54p. 1988. student ed. 3.95 (0-910307-10-5) Comp Pr.

Writing - A Way to Pray. Arnold B. Cheyney. 111p. 1995. pap. 9.95 (0-8294-0813-4, WAWTP) Loyola Pr.

Writing - College Handbook: A Diagnostic Test. 4th ed. James A. Heffernan. (C). Date not set. pap. text ed. write for info. (0-393-96507-4) Norton.

Writing, a Concise Handbook. James A. Heffernan & John E. Lincoln. LC 96-19887. (C). 1996. pap. text ed. 23.95 (0-393-97092-2) Norton.

Writing a Convincing Business Plan. Art DeThomas & Bill Fredenberger. LC 95-7940. (Barron's Business Library Ser.). 249p. 1995. pap. 16.95 (0-8120-9091-8) Barron.

Writing a Country Report. John Carratello & Patty Carratello. (Illus.). 48p. (J). (gr. 3-6). 1989. student ed. 7.95 (1-55734-163-X) Tchr Create Mat.

Writing a Family History. Nancy E. Carlberg. 150p. (Orig.). 1991. pap. 15.00 (0-944878-16-4) Carlberg Pr.

Writing a Life. Mary Rubio & Elixabeth Waterston. 1995. pap. 9.95 (1-55022-220-1) LPC InBook.

***Writing a Life: L. M. Montgomery.** large type ed. Mary Rubio & Elizabeth Waterston. (Illus.). 188p. 1995. pap. 15.95 (1-55022-239-2, Pub. by ECW Press CN) Genl Dist Srvs.

Writing a Living Will: Using a Durable Power-of-Attorney. George J. Alexander. LC 87-15816. 160p. 1987. pap. text ed. 12.95 (0-275-92939-6, B2939, Praeger Pubs) Greenwood.

Writing a Living Will: Using a Durable Power-of-Attorney. George J. Alexander. LC 87-15816. 160p. 1987. text ed. 37.95 (0-275-92801-2, C2801, Praeger Pubs) Greenwood.

***Writing a Musical.** Richard Andrews. 1997. 14.95 (0-7090-5913-2, Hale-Parkwest) Parkwest Pubns.

Writing a National Identity: Political, Economic & Cultural Perspectives on the Written Constitution. Ed. by Vivien Hart & Shannon Stimson. (Fulbright Papers). (Illus.). 288p. (C). 1993. text ed. 79.95 (0-7190-3589-9, Pub. by Manchester Univ Pr UK) St Martin.

Writing a Non-Fiction Book the Easy Way. Nancy E. Carlberg. 150p. (Orig.). 1991. pap. 15.00 (0-944878-17-2) Carlberg Pr.

Writing a Novel. J. Braine. 224p. 1975. pap. text ed. 8.95 (0-07-007112-8) McGraw.

Writing a Novel. Dorothy Bryant. LC 78-69766. 120p. 1978. pap. 9.95 (0-931688-02-7) Ata Bks.

Writing a Novel. Nigel Watts. (Teach Yourself Ser.). 224p. (Orig.). 1996. pap. 10.95 (0-8442-3106-1, Teach Yoursl) NTC Pub Grp.

Writing a Play. 2nd ed. Steve Gooch. 1996. pap. 15.95 (0-7136-4175-4, Pub. by A&C Black UK) Talman.

Writing a Publishable Research Report: In Education, Psychology, & Related Disciplines. Ronald P. Carver. (Illus.). 156p. (C). 1984. pap. text ed., spiral bd. 30.95 (0-398-04986-6) C C Thomas.

Writing a Regional History Book with a Committee. Patricia Torrance. (Illus.). 108p. (Orig.). 1994. pap. text ed. 17.00 (0-7884-0004-5) Heritage Bk.

Writing a Research Paper. Jonatha Ceely et al. 92p. (Orig.). (YA). (gr. 9-12). 1992. pap. text ed. 8.00 (1-877653-44-6, 57) Wayside Pub.

Writing a Research Paper. Lionel Menasche. LC 83-12492. (Pitt Series in English As a Second Language). (Illus.). 144p. 1984. pap. 15.95 (0-472-08119-5) U of Mich Pr.

Writing a Research Paper. rev. ed. Jonatha Ceely et al. (Orig.). (C). 1983. pap. text ed. 5.25 (0-88334-108-5) Longman.

Writing a Research Paper. rev. ed. Lionel Menasche. 1995. pap. text ed. 16.95 (0-472-08369-4) U of Mich Pr.

Writing a Research Paper. 4th ed. Jonatha Ceely et al. 87p. (Orig.). 1992. pap. 10.99 (0-8013-0698-1, 78725) Longman.

Writing a Research Paper American Style: An ESL/EFL Handbook. Sydney L. Langosch. LC 96-17072. 1996. pap. 9.95 (0-8120-9637-1) Barron.

Writing a State Report. John Carratello & Patty Carratello. (Illus.). 48p. (J). (gr. 3-6). 1989. student ed. 7.95 (1-55734-162-1) Tchr Create Mat.

Writing a Striking Cover Letter. Travis Young. (Orig.). 1997. pap. 12.95 (0-9650566-8-6, F-008) Active Edit.

Writing a Successful College Application Essay. 2nd rev. ed. George Ehrenhaft. LC 93-13380. 120p. (YA). (gr. 9 up). 1993. pap. 9.95 (0-8120-1415-4) Barron.

Writing a Successful Grant Application. 2nd rev. ed. Liane Reif-Lehrer. 200p. 1989. pap. 25.00 (0-86720-104-5) Jones & Bartlett.

Writing a Television Play. 2nd rev. ed. Michelle Cousin. xiii, 202p. (Orig.). 1986. pap. 14.95 (0-931642-18-3) Lintel.

Writing a Thesis: Substance & Style. Keith Van Wagenen. 192p. (C). 1990. pap. text ed. 23.00 (0-13-971086-8) P-H.

Writing A to Z see Writer's Encyclopedia

Writing a UNIX 3 Device Driver. 2nd ed. Janet I. Egan & Thomas J. Teixeira. LC 92-8536. 368p. 1992. pap. text ed. 29.95 (0-471-53574-5) Wiley.

Writing a UNIX-3 Device Driver. 2nd ed. Janet I. Egan & Thomas J. Teixeira. LC 92-8536. 368p. 1992. text ed. 45.00 (0-471-53575-3) Wiley.

Writing a Winning College Application Essay: Peterson's Practically Painless Guide. Wilma Davidson & Susan McCloskey. 136p. (Orig.). (YA). (gr. 10-12). 1996. pap. 9.95 (1-56079-601-4) Petersons.

***Writing a Winning Graduate School Application Essay: Exclusive Tips from Admissions Officers at the Nation's Top Law, Business, Medical & Graduate Schools.** 3rd ed. Richard J. Stelzer. Ed. by Karen Hansen. 160p. 1997. pap. 12.95 (1-56079-855-6) Petersons.

Writing a Woman's Life. Carolyn G. Heilbrun. 144p. 1989. pap. 10.00 (0-345-36256-X, Ballantine Trade) Ballantine.

Writing a Woman's Life. Carolyn G. Heilbrun. 1988. 14.95 (0-393-02601-9) Norton.

***Writing about African-American Literature, 97 Vols.** (C). 1997. text ed. write for info. (0-395-83835-5) HM.

Writing about Art. 2nd ed. Henry M. Sayre. LC 94-12960. 144p. 1994. pap. text ed. 17.80 (0-13-124975-4) P-H.

Writing about Biology. Moore. (C). 1992. teacher ed., pap. text ed. 34.00 (0-03-093237-8) HB Coll Pubs.

Writing about Business & Industry. Beverly E. Schneller. (Illus.). 352p. (C). 1995. 41.95 (0-19-507378-9); pap. text ed. 20.95 (0-19-507379-7) OUP.

Writing about Diversity. Clark. (C). 1993. teacher ed., pap. text ed. 33.75 (0-15-500950-8) HB Coll Pubs.

***Writing about Diversity.** 2nd ed. Irene L. Clark. 92p. (C). 1996. teacher ed., pap. text ed. 28.00 (0-15-503564-9) HB Coll Pubs.

Writing about Diversity: An Argument-Reader & Guide. Irene L. Clark. LC 93-11785. 1993. write for info. (0-15-500949-4) HB Coll Pubs.

Writing about Diversity: An Argument Reader & Guide. 2nd ed. Irene L. Clark. 784p. (C). 1996. pap. text ed. 30.25 (0-15-503563-0) HB Coll Pubs.

Writing about Eakins: The Manuscripts in Charles Bregler's Thomas Eakins Collection. Ed. by Kathleen A. Foster & Cheryl Leibold. LC 89-40402. (Illus.). 430p. 1990. text ed. 38.50 (0-8122-8107-1); fiche 176.95 (0-8122-8224-8) U of Pa Pr.

Writing about Food & Families, Fashion & Furnishings. Ann Burkhardt. LC 83-10843. (Illus.). 136p. 1984. pap. text ed. 14.95 (0-8138-1941-5) Iowa St U Pr.

Writing about Imaginative Literature. Edward J. Gordon. 196p. (C). 1973. pap. text ed. 13.50 (0-15-597850-0) HB Coll Pubs.

Writing About Literature. Barberousse. (C). 1993. pap. 3.96 (0-395-67166-3) HM.

***Writing about Literature.** Griffith. (C). 1999. pap. text ed. 27.50 (0-15-505490-2) HB Coll Pubs.

Writing about Literature. 8th ed. Edgar V. Roberts. LC 94-30182. 256p. 1994. pap. text ed. 20.67 (0-13-097593-1) P-H.

Writing about Literature: Aims & Process. Joyce MacAllister. 320p. (C). 1987. pap. write for info. (0-02-373030-7, Macmillan Coll) P-H.

Writing about Literature: An Anthology for Reading & Writing. Lynn Klamkin & Margot Livesey. 964p. (C). 1986. pap. text ed. 28.75 (0-03-001508-1) HB Coll Pubs.

Writing about Music. 2nd ed. Richard Wingell. 1996. pap. text ed. 20.67 (0-13-463332-6) P-H.

Writing about Music: A Guide to Publishing Opportunities for Authors & Reviewers. Ann P. Basart. LC 89-1644. (Reference Books in Music: No. 11). xxiv, 588p. 1989. pap. 39.50 (0-914913-10-7) Fallen Leaf.

Writing about Music: A Style Sheet from the Editors of 19th-Century Music. D. Kern Holoman. 72p. (Orig.). 1988. pap. 10.00 (0-520-06382-1) U CA Pr.

Writing about My Feelings. Charlie Daniel & Becky Daniel. 64p. (J). (gr. 1-4). 1978. 8.99 (0-916456-18-8, GA80) Good Apple.

Writing about Pictures: Using Pictures to Develop Language & Writing Sklls, 6 bks. A. J. Evans & Marilyn Palmer. (gr. 1-3). 1982. teacher ed. 2.95 (0-8077-6036-6) Tchrs Coll.

Writing about Pictures: Using Pictures to Develop Language & Writing Sklls, 6 bks., Bk. 1: Completing Sentences. A. J. Evans & Marilyn Palmer. (gr. 1-3). 1982. pap. text ed. 3.95 (0-8077-5994-5) Tchrs Coll.

Writing about Pictures: Using Pictures to Develop Language & Writing Sklls, 6 bks., Bk. 2: Writing Sentences. A. J. Evans & Marilyn Palmer. (gr. 1-3). 1982. pap. text ed. 3.95 (0-8077-6031-5) Tchrs Coll.

Writing about Pictures: Using Pictures to Develop Language & Writing Sklls, 6 bks., Bk. 3: Getting at the Story. A. J. Evans & Marilyn Palmer. (gr. 1-3). 1982. Bk. 3: Getting At The Story. pap. text ed. 3.95 (0-8077-6032-3) Tchrs Coll.

Writing about Pictures: Using Pictures to Develop Language & Writing Sklls, 6 bks., Bk. 4: Linking Story Ideas. A. J. Evans & Marilyn Palmer. (gr. 1-3). 1982. pap. text ed. 3.95 (0-8077-6033-1) Tchrs Coll.

Writing about Pictures: Using Pictures to Develop Language & Writing Sklls, 6 bks., Bk. 5: Writing Your Story, I. A. J. Evans & Marilyn Palmer. (gr. 1-3). 1982. pap. text ed. 3.95 (0-8077-6034-X) Tchrs Coll.

Writing about Pictures: Using Pictures to Develop Language & Writing Sklls, 6 bks., Bk. 6: Writing Your Story, II. A. J. Evans & Marilyn Palmer. (gr. 1-3). 1982. pap. text ed. 3.95 (0-8077-6035-8) Tchrs Coll.

Writing about Science. 2nd ed. Elizabeth C. Bowen & Beverly E. Schneller. (Illus.). 400p. (C). 1991. pap. text ed. 20.95 (0-19-506274-4) OUP.

Writing about the World. McLeod. (C). 1990. teacher ed., pap. text ed. 34.00 (0-15-597755-5) HB Coll Pubs.

Writing about the World. Susan McLeod et al. 608p. (C). 1990. pap. text ed. 21.50 (0-15-597754-7) HB Coll Pubs.

Writing about the World. 2nd ed. McLeod. (C). 1995. teacher ed., pap. text ed. 33.75 (0-15-502173-7) HB Coll Pubs.

Writing about the World. 2nd ed. Susan McLeod et al. (Illus.). 800p. (C). 1994. pap. text ed. 31.00 (0-15-501314-9) HB Coll Pubs.

Writing about Travel. 2nd ed. Morag Campbell. 112p. 1996. pap. 13.95 (0-7136-4174-6, Pub. by A&C Black UK) Talman.

Writing about Vietnam: A Bibliography of the Literature of the Vietnam Conflict. Sandra M. Wittman. (Reference Guides to Literature Ser.). 400p. 1989. 45.00 (0-8161-9083-6, Hall Reference) Macmillan.

Writing Abstracts. (National Information Standards Ser.). 1979. reprint ed. 12.00 (0-88738-987-2, Z39.14) Transaction Pubs.

Writing Academic English. Oshimal A. Hogue & Alice Oshima. 264p. (Orig.). (C). 1983. pap. text ed. 14.58 (0-201-05479-5) Addison-Wesley.

Writing Achievement of California Eighth Graders: A First Look. California Department of Education Staff. 58p. 1989. pap. 5.50 (0-8011-0814-4) Calif Education.

Writing Achievement of California Eighth Graders: Year Two. California Department of Education Staff. 74p. 1989. pap. 5.50 (0-8011-0832-2) Calif Education.

Writing Across Culture: An Introduction to Study Abroad & the Writing Process. Anthony S. Magistrale & Kenneth Warner. 176p. (C). 1995. pap. text ed. 19.95 (0-8204-1923-0) P Lang Pubng.

Writing Across Cultures: A Handbook on Writing Poetry & Lyrical Prose. Edna Kovacs. 160p. (Orig.). 1994. pap. 11.95 (0-936085-25-8) Blue Heron OR.

Writing across Languages: Analysis of L2 Text. Ulla Connor & Robert Kaplan. (A-W Second Language Professional Library). (C). 1987. pap. text ed. 30.74 (0-201-11184-5) Addison-Wesley.

Writing Across Languages & Cultures: Issues in Contrastive Rhetoric. Ed. by Alan C. Purves. LC 88-80974. (Written Communication Annual Ser.: No. 2). 309p. reprint ed. pap. 88.10 (0-7837-6720-X, 2046347) Bks Demand.

***Writing Across the Curriculum.** Ed. by Behrens. (C). 1996. text ed. 21.50 (0-673-67599-8) Addison-Wesley.

Writing across the Curriculum: A Guide to Developing Programs. Margot K. Soven. (Illus.). 304p. 1992. 52.00 (0-8039-4599-X); pap. 24.95 (0-8039-4600-7) Sage.

Writing Across the Curriculum: An Annotated Bibliography. Ed. by Chris M. Anson et al. LC 93-29897. (Bibliographies & Indexes in Education Ser.: No. 13). 192p. 1993. text ed. 59.95 (0-313-25960-7, Greenwood Pr) Greenwood.

Writing-Across-the-Curriculum & the Academic Library: A Guide for Librarians, Instructors & Writing Program Directors. Ed. by Jean Sheridan. LC 95-10224. 264p. 1995. text ed. 69.50 (0-313-29134-9, Greenwood Pr) Greenwood.

Writing Across the Curriculum in Community Colleges. Linda Stanley & Joanna Ambron. LC 85-644753. (New Directions for Community Colleges Ser.: No. CC 73). 1991. 19.00 (1-55542-785-5) Jossey-Bass.

Writing Across the Curriculum in Middle & High Schools. Rhoda J. Maxwell. LC 95-456. 1995. pap. text ed. 25.00 (0-205-15325-9) Allyn.

Writing across the Disciplines: Research into Practice. Ed. by Art Young & Toby Fulwiler. LC 85-24329. 254p. (Orig.). (gr. 13). 1986. pap. text ed. 23.00 (0-86709-121-2, 0131) Boynton Cook Pubs.

Writing Across the Social Studies Curriculum. Roger Sensenbaugh. LC 89-28757. (Teaching Resources in the ERIC Database (TRIED) Ser.). (Illus.). 1989. pap. 14.95 (0-927516-05-5) ERIC-REC.

Writing Across Worlds: Literature & Migration. Ed. by Russell King et al. LC 95-3573. 312p. (C). 1995. pap. 18.95 (0-415-10530-7) Routledge.

Writing Across Worlds: Literature & Migration. Ed. by Russell King et al. LC 95-3573. 312p. (C). (gr. 13). 1995. text ed. 69.95 (0-415-10529-3) Routledge.

***Writing Activities for Every Month of the School Year: Ready-to-Use Writing Process Activities for Grades 4-8.** Carol H. Behrman. LC 97-7551. 1997. write for info. (0-87628-974-X) Ctr Appl Res.

Writing Activities for Newspaper Readers. 1993. 5.05 (0-88336-920-6) New Readers.

***Writing Activities Resource Manual (WARM)** 2nd ed. Dalton Public Schools Staff. (Illus.). 170p. 1996. ring bd. 27.50 (1-57035-115-5, C12WARM) Sopris.

Writing Activities to Develop Mathematical Thinking. M. A. Dirkes. 116p. 1990. pap. 12.99 (0-89824-049-2) Trillium Pr.

Writing African Women: Gender, Popular Culture & Literature in West Africa. Ed. by Stephanie Newell. LC 96-39523. 192p. (C). 1997. 55.00 (1-85649-449-7, Pub. by Zed Bks Ltd UK) Humanities.

Writing African Women: Gender, Popular Culture & Literature in West Africa. Ed. by Stephanie Newell. LC 96-39523. 192p. (C). 1997. pap. 19.95 (1-85649-450-0, Pub. by Zed Bks Ltd UK) Humanities.

Writing after War: American War Fiction from Realism to Postmodernism. John Limon. 288p. 1994. 48.00 (0-19-508758-5); pap. 18.95 (0-19-508759-3) OUP.

Writing Against God: Language As Message in the Literature of Flannery O'Connor. Joan McMullen. 176p. (C). 1996. text ed. 25.00 (0-86554-488-3, MUP/H383) Mercer Univ Pr.

Writing Against the Family: Gender in Lawrence & Joyce. Cynthia Lewiecki-Wilson. LC 93-7829. (Illus.). 288p. 1994. 34.95 (0-8093-1881-4) S Ill U Pr.

Writing AIDS. Timothy F. Murphy & Suzanne Poirier. 1994. pap. 16.50 (0-231-07865-X) Col U Pr.

Writing AIDS: Gay Literature, Language, & Analysis. Ed. by Timothy F. Murphy & Suzanne Poirier. LC 92-20373. (Between Men - Between Women Ser.). 352p. (C). 1993. 35.00 (0-231-07864-1) Col U Pr.

Writing Air, Written Water. Roberta Gould. 102p. (Orig.). 1980. 7.00 (0-936628-00-6) Waterside.

Writing All the Way. William J. McCleary. 350p. (C). 1988. pap. 33.95 (0-534-08604-7) Wadsworth Pub.

Writing Almanack: The Ben & Zen Now & Then Writing Almanack. Harvey Gotliffe. (Illus.). 60p. (Orig.). (C). 1995. pap. 6.50 (1-882302-99-0) Cogitator Pubns.

Writing American English. Bernard Seward. Ed. by Roger E. Olsen. (Illus.). 90p. (J). (gr. 3-12). 1982. pap. text ed. 5.75 (0-13-971102-3) Alemany Pr.

Writing American History: Essays on Modern Scholarship. John Higham. LC 70-108209. 217p. reprint ed. pap. 61.90 (0-317-27824-X, 2056038) Bks Demand.

Writing an Expression see Language Learning: The Intermediate Phase

Writing Analytically. Rosenwasse. (C). 1996. teacher ed., pap. text ed. 26.75 (0-15-504210-6) HarBrace.

Writing Analytically. David Rosernwasser & Jill Stephen. 272p. (C). 1996. pap. text ed. 18.75 (0-15-501889-2) HB Coll Pubs.

Writing & Acting in French: Nous Tou '86, Vol. II. Jarvis. 1985. pap. text ed. 13.25 (0-03-002253-3) HB Schl Dept.

Writing & Africa. Mpalive-Hangson Msiska & Paul Hyland. LC 96-25811. (C). 1996. text ed. 52.95 (0-582-21419-X); pap. text ed. 21.50 (0-582-21418-1) Longman.

Writing & America. Gavin Cologne-Brookes et al. LC 95-49355. (Crosscurrents Ser.). (C). 1996. pap. text ed. 21.50 (0-582-21417-3, Pub. by Longman UK) Longman.

Writing & America. Neil Sammells et al. Ed. by Gavin Cologne-Brookes. LC 95-49355. (Crosscurrents Ser.). (C). 1996. text ed. 54.50 (0-582-21416-5, Pub. by Longman UK) Longman.

Writing & Analysis in the Law. 2nd ed. Melene S. Shapiro et al. 141p. (C). 1991. pap. text ed. write for info. (0-88277-909-5) Foundation Pr.

Writing & Analysis in the Law. 2nd ed. Helene S. Shapo et al. (University Casebook Ser.). 346p. 1991. pap. text ed. 19.95 (0-88277-874-9) Foundation Pr.

Writing & Analysis in the Law. 3rd ed. Helen S. Shapo et al. 403p. (C). 1995. pap. text ed. 21.95 (1-56662-244-1) Foundation Pr.

Writing & Arithmetic: Ancient Civilizations. Paul Russell. (J). (gr. 4-7). Date not set. 15.95 (0-688-13906-X, Tambourine Bks) Morrow.

Writing & Art Go Hand in Hand. Diane Bonica. 80p. (J). (gr. 2-6). 1988. pap. text ed. 9.95 (0-86530-068-2, IP 13-2) Incentive Pubns.

Writing & Balancing Chemical Equations. Conrad L. Stanitski & H. Anthony Neidig. (Modular Laboratory Program in Chemistry Ser.). 12p. (C). 1996. pap. text ed. 1.35 (0-87540-477-4, MISC 477-4) Chem Educ Res.

Writing & Being. Nadine Gordimer. (Charles Eliot Norton Lectures). 134p. (C). 1995. 18.95 (0-674-96232-X) HUP.

Writing & Being. Nadine Gordimer. (Charles Eliot Norton Lectures). 160p. 1996. pap. 10.95 (0-674-96233-8) HUP.

Writing & Being: Taking Back Our Lives Through the Power of Language. G. Lynn Nelson. LC 94-3776. 160p. (Orig.). 1994. pap. 14.95 (1-880913-11-9) Innisfree Pr.

Writing & Censorship in Britain. Ed. by Paul Hyland & Neil Sammells. LC 91-48118. 272p. (C). 1992. pap. text ed. 24.95 (0-415-08353-2, A7648) Routledge.

Writing & Censorship in Britain. Ed. by Paul Hyland & Neil Sammells. LC 91-48118. 368p. (C). (gr. 13). 1992. text ed. 74.95 (0-415-07332-4, A7644) Routledge.

Writing & Defending a Thesis or Dissertation in Psychology & Education. Roy Martin. 120p. 1980. spiral bd., pap. 24.95 (0-398-03947-X) C C Thomas.

Writing & Designing Manuals: Operator Manuals, Service Manuals, Manuals for International Markets. 2nd ed. Gretchen H. Schoff & Patricia A. Robinson. 200p. 1991. 49.95 (0-87371-421-0, L421) Lewis Pubs.

Writing & Desktop Publishing on the Computer. Lifter. 80p. (J). (gr. 1-3). 1996. wbk. ed., pap. 9.95 (1-55734-922-3) Tchr Create Mat.

Writing & Desktop Publishing on the Computer. Rosengart. 80p. (J). (gr. 5-8). 1996. wbk. ed., pap. 9.95 (1-55734-924-X) Tchr Create Mat.

Writing & Difference. Jacques Derrida. 1994. 24.00 (0-8446-6738-2) Peter Smith.

Writing & Difference. Jacques Derrida. Tr. by Alan Bass from FRE. LC 77-25933. 362p. 1980. pap. text ed. 14.95 (0-226-14329-5, P863) U Ch Pr.

Writing & Editing. Jules H. Masserman. 122p. 1996. 34.95 (0-916147-64-9); pap. 14.95 (0-916147-65-7) Regent Pr.

Writing & Enforcing Parking Rules for Community Associations. rev. ed. (C). 1991. pap. 14.50 (0-941301-16-8) CAI.

Writing & European Thought, 1600-1830. Nicholas Hudson. (Illus.). 240p. (C). 1995. text ed. 54.95 (0-521-45540-5) Cambridge U Pr.

W

An Asterisk (*) at the beginning of an entry indicates that the title is appearing in BIP for the first time.

Writing & Fantasy in Proust - La Place de la Madeleine (La Place de la Madeleine, Ecriture et Fantasme Chez Proust) Serge Doubrovsky. Tr. by Carol M. Bove & Paul A. Bove. LC 85-31823. 183p. 1986. reprint ed. pap. 52.20 (*0-7837-8861-4*, 2049572) Bks Demand.

Writing & Gender: Virginia Woolf's Writing Practice. Sue Roe. LC 90-19424. 214p. 1990. text ed. 45.00 (*0-312-05766-0*) St Martin.

Writing & Getting Published: A Primer for Nurses. Barbara S. Barnum. LC 94-43634. 216p. 1995. 28.95 (*0-8261-8690-4*) Springer Pub.

Writing & Grammar: English 200. Jean Mather & Allan Leavitt. 127p. (C). 1992. pap. text ed. 22.42 (*1-56226-131-2*) CT Pub.

***Writing & Identity: The Discoursal Construction of Identity in Academic Writing.** Roz Ivanic. LC 97-23076. (Studies in Written Language & Literacy). 1997. write for info. (*1-55619-322-X*); pap. write for info. (*1-55619-323-8*) Benjamins North Am.

Writing & Illuminating & Lettering. Johnson. pap. 24.95 (*0-7136-4001-4*, 93187, Pub. by A&C Black UK) Talman.

Writing & Illuminating, & Lettering. Edward Johnston. LC 94-46428. (Illus.). 480p. 1995. pap. text ed. 13.95 (*0-486-28534-0*) Dover.

Writing & Illustrating Children's Books for Publication: Two Perspectives. Berthe Amoss & Eric Suben. LC 95-17164. (Illus.). 128p. 1995. 24.95 (*0-89879-722-5*, Wrtrs Digest Bks) F & W Pubns Inc.

Writing & Implementing a Marketing Plan: A Guide for Small Business Owners. Richard Gerson. Ed. by Nancy Shotwell. LC 90-84077. (Fifty-Minute Ser.). (Illus.). 89p. (Orig.). 1991. pap. 10.95 (*1-56052-083-3*) Crisp Pubns.

Writing & Inscription in Golden Age Drama. Charles Oriel. LC 92-26368. (Studies in Romance Literatures: Vol. 1). 200p. 1992. reprint ed. pap. 18.95 (*1-55753-074-2*) Purdue U Pr.

Writing & Laterality Characteristics of Stuttering Children: A Comparative Study of 70 Grade School Stutterers & 70 Matched Non-Stutterers. Egbert J. Spadino. LC 70-177754. (Columbia University. Teachers College. Contributions to Education Ser.: No. 837). reprint ed. 37.50 (*0-404-55837-2*) AMS Pr.

Writing & Learning About World Art. Henry M. Sayre. 1994. pap. text ed. 7.20 (*0-13-336900-5*) P-H.

Writing & Learning in the Disciplines. Feldman. (Illus.). 640p. (C). 1996. pap. 29.50 (*0-673-46070-3*) Addison-Wesley Educ.

Writing & Learning in the Disciplines. Feldman. Date not set. teacher ed., pap. write for info. (*0-673-97711-0*) Addison-Wesley Educ.

Writing & Life. Michael Lydon. LC 95-13843. 110p. (C). 1995. pap. 9.95 (*0-87451-730-3*) U Pr of New Eng.

Writing & Literacy in Chinese, Korean & Japanese. Insup Taylor. LC 95-43614. (Studies in Written Language & Literacy: Vol. 3). xiii, 412p. 1995. lib. bdg. 68.00 (*1-55619-319-X*) Benjamins North Am.

Writing & Logic. Gerald Levin. 276p. (C). 1982. pap. text ed. 20.00 (*0-15-597788-1*); pap. text ed. 3.00 (*0-15-597789-X*) HB Coll Pubs.

Writing & Madness: (Literature Philosophy Psychoanalysis) Shoshana Felman. Tr. by Martha N. Evans & Brian Massumi from FRE. LC 84-19845. 256p. (C). 1985. 42.50 (*0-8014-1285-4*); pap. 16.95 (*0-8014-9394-3*) Cornell U Pr.

Writing & Managing Winning Technical Proposals. 2nd rev. ed. Timothy Whalen. (Illus.). 1994. write for info. (*1-56726-021-7*) Holbrook & Kellogg.

Writing & Managing Winning Technical Proposals. 3rd rev. ed. Timothy Whalen. 296p. 1996. pap. 68.00 (*1-56726-033-0*, B530A) Holbrook & Kellogg.

Writing & Marketing a Family History in the Mid-1990's. Dwain L. Kitchel. 90p. 1994. pap. 9.50 (*1-882194-03-9*) TN Valley Pub.

Writing & Marketing Shareware. 2nd enl. rev. ed. Steve Hudgik. 304p. 1991. pap. 18.95 (*0-8306-2552-6*, Windcrest) TAB Bks.

Writing & Orality: Nationality, Culture, & Nineteenth-Century Scottish Fiction. Penny Fielding. LC 95-49059. 260p. (C). 1996. 60.00 (*0-19-812180-6*, Clarendon Pr) OUP.

Writing & Personality: Finding Your Voice, Your Style, Your Way. John K. DiTiberio & George H. Jensen. LC 94-24284. 248p. (Orig.). 1995. pap. 14.95 (*0-89106-071-5*, 7192) Davies-Black.

Writing & Politics. Ed. by Harold Jaffe & Larry McCaffery. (Fiction International Ser.: No. 15). (Illus.). 224p. (Orig.). 1984. pap. 5.00 (*0-916304-94-9*) SDSU Press.

Writing & Printing. Steve Harrison & Patricia Harrison. (Fact Finders Ser.). 48p. (Orig.). (J). (gr. 4 up). 1992. pap. 7.95 (*0-563-34787-2*, BBC-Parkwest) Parkwest Pubns.

Writing & Printing. Chris Oxlade. LC 94-37191. (Craft Topics Ser.). 32p. (J). (gr. 4-6). 1995. lib. bdg. 19.10 (*0-531-14371-6*) Watts.

Writing & Printing. Scott Steedman. LC 96-16051. (Worldwise Ser.). (Illus.). 1997. lib. bdg. 22.70 (*0-531-14424-0*) Watts.

Writing & Printing. Scott Steedman. LC 96-16051. (Worldwise Ser.). (Illus.). (J). 1997. pap. write for info. (*0-531-15311-8*) Watts.

Writing & Psychoanalysis: A Reader. Ed. by John Lechte. LC 95-34257. 256p. 1996. text ed. 49.95 (*0-340-64561-X*, Pub. by E Arnld UK) St Martin.

Writing & Psychoanalysis: A Reader. Ed. by John Lechte. LC 95-34257. 256p. 1996. text ed. 18.95 (*0-340-62498-1*, Pub. by E Arnld UK) St Martin.

Writing & Psychology: Understanding Writing & Its Teaching from the Perspective of Composition Studies. Douglas Vipond. LC 93-15815. 160p. 1993. text ed. 55.00 (*0-275-94637-1*, Praeger Pubs) Greenwood.

Writing & Public Information Occupations. Jack Rudman. (Career Examination Ser.: C-3556). 1994. pap. 27.95 (*0-8373-3556-6*) Nat Learn.

Writing & Publishing Books for Children in the 1990s: The Inside Story, from the Editor's Desk. Olga Litowinsky. 144p. (Orig.). 1992. 17.95 (*0-8027-8130-6*); pap. 11.95 (*0-8027-7375-3*) Walker & Co.

Writing & Publishing for Academic Authors. 2nd ed. Ed. by Joseph M. Moxley & Todd Taylor. LC 96-34251. 192p. 1996. pap. 16.95 (*0-8476-8258-7*) Rowman.

***Writing & Race.** John Lucas. LC 97-1412. (Crossconcurrents Ser.). 1997. write for info. (*0-582-27375-7*); pap. write for info. (*0-582-27374-9*) Longman.

Writing & Radicalism. Ed. by John Lucas. (Crosscurrents Ser.). 320p. (C). 1996. text ed. 60.95 (*0-582-21414-9*, Pub. by Longman UK) Longman.

Writing & Radicalism. Ed. by John Lucas. (Crosscurrents Ser.). 320p. (C). 1996. pap. text ed. 27.50 (*0-582-21415-7*, Pub. by Longman UK) Longman.

Writing & Ratification of the U. S. Constitution: A Bibliography. Russell R. Wheeler. 44p. 1986. write for info. (*0-318-62560-1*) Bates Info Serv.

Writing & Reading Across the Curriculum. Ed. & Intro. by Malcolm P. Douglass. (Claremont Reading Conference Yearbook Ser.). 276p. (Orig.). 1985. pap. 15.00 (*0-941742-03-2*) Claremont Grad.

Writing & Reading Across the Curriculum. 5th ed. Laurence Behrens & Leonard J. Rosen. LC 93-22929. (C). 1993. text ed. 28.00 (*0-673-52272-5*) Addison-Wesley Educ.

Writing & Reading Across the Curriculum. 6th ed. Laurence Behrens & Leonard J. Rosen. LC 95-50386. (C). 1997. pap. text ed. 27.95 (*0-673-52475-2*) Addison-Wesley Educ.

Writing & Reading Differently: Deconstruction & the Teaching of Composition & Literature. Ed. by G. Douglas Atkins & Michael L. Johnson. LC 85-13464. x, 222p. (C). 1985. pap. 12.95 (*0-7006-0283-6*) U Pr of KS.

Writing & Reading in a Balanced Curriculum. Ed. by Malcolm P. Douglass. (Claremont Reading Conference Yearbook Ser.). 222p. (Orig.). 1982. pap. 5.00 (*0-941742-00-8*) Claremont Grad.

Writing & Reading in Early Childhood: A Functional Approach. Roy Moxley. LC 81-9686. (Illus.). 290p. 1982. 39.95 (*0-87778-180-X*) Educ Tech Pubns.

Writing & Reading in Henry James. Susanne Kappeler. LC 80-18181. 242p. 1980. text ed. 49.50 (*0-231-05198-0*) Col U Pr.

Writing & Reading Mental Health Records: Issues & Analysis. John F. Reynolds et al. (Illus.). 144p. 1992. 34.00 (*0-8039-4097-1*); pap. 15.95 (*0-8039-4098-X*) Sage.

Writing & Reading Mental Health Records: Issues & Analysis in Professional Writing & Scientific Rhetoric. 2nd ed. John F. Reynolds et al. 120p. 1995. pap. 17.50 (*0-8058-2002-7*) L Erlbaum Assocs.

Writing & Reading Mental Health Records: Issues & Analysis in Professional Writing & Scientific Rhetoric. 2nd ed. John F. Reynolds et al. 120p. 1995. text ed. 29.95 (*0-8058-2001-9*) L Erlbaum Assocs.

Writing & Reading the Essay: A Process Approach. Patricia Cronin. LC 93-27123. (Illus.). 1993. pap. 12.00 (*0-8092-4216-8*) Contemp Bks.

Writing & Reading to Learn. Ed. by Nea Stewart-Dore. 101p. (Orig.). 1987. pap. text ed. 17.50 (*0-909955-65-4*, 00595) Heinemann.

Writing & Reality: A Study of Modern British Diary Fiction. Andrew Hassam. LC 92-25764. (Contributions to the Study of World Literature Ser.: No. 47). 192p. 1992. text ed. 49.95 (*0-313-28540-3*, HWY, Greenwood Pr) Greenwood.

Writing & Rebellion: England in 1381. Steven Justice. LC 93-558. (New Historicism Ser.: Vol. 27). 1994. 40.00 (*0-520-08325-3*) U CA Pr.

Writing & Rebellion: England in 1381. Steven Justice. (New Historicism: Studies in Cultural Poetics: 27). 330p. 1996. pap. 15.95 (*0-520-20697-5*) U CA Pr.

Writing & Reporting News. Rich. (Mass Communication Ser.). 1994. wbk. ed., pap. 16.50 (*0-534-19076-6*) Wadsworth Pub.

***Writing & Reporting News.** 2nd ed. Lanson. (C). 1994. pap. write for info. (*0-03-079177-4*) HB Coll Pubs.

Writing & Reporting News. 2nd ed. Rich. (Mass Communication Ser.). 1997. wbk. ed., pap. 22.95 (*0-534-50880-4*) Wadsworth Pub.

Writing & Reporting News: A Coaching Method. Carole Rich. 590p. (C). 1994. pap. 33.75 (*0-534-19074-X*) Wadsworth Pub.

Writing & Reporting the News. Mitchell Stephens & Gerald Lanson. 448p. (C). 1986. pap. text ed. 30.00 (*0-03-060483-4*) HB Coll Pubs.

Writing & Reporting the News: A Coaching Method. 2nd ed. Carol Rich. (Mass Communication Ser.). (Illus.). 624p. (C). 1997. pap. 46.95 (*0-534-50879-0*) Wadsworth Pub.

Writing & Revising Your Fiction. Mark Wisniewski. LC 94-37234. 120p. (Orig.). 1995. pap. text ed. 8.95 (*0-87116-174-5*) Writer.

Writing & Rewriting the Holocaust: Narrative & the Consequences of Interpretation. James E. Young. LC 87-35791. (Illus.). 256p. (Orig.). 1988. 35.00 (*0-253-36716-6*) Ind U Pr.

Writing & Rewriting the Holocaust: Narrative & the Consequences of Interpretation. James E. Young. LC 87-35791. (Illus.). 256p. (Orig.). 1990. pap. 15.95 (*0-253-20613-8*, MB-613) Ind U Pr.

Writing & Selling a Successful Self-Help Book. Jean M. Stine. LC 96-26886. 208p. (Orig.). 1997. pap. text ed. 14.95 (*0-471-03739-7*) Wiley.

Writing & Selling Magazine Articles. Eva Shaw. 157p. (Orig.). 1995. pap. 9.95 (*1-56924-818-4*) Marlowe & Co.

Writing & Selling Poetry, Fiction, Articles, Plays & Local History. Marcia Muth. LC 85-490. 96p. (Orig.). 1985. pap. 8.95 (*0-86534-048-X*) Sunstone Pr.

Writing & Selling Your Novel. Jack M. Bickham. 208p. 1996. 17.99 (*0-89879-788-8*, Wrtrs Digest Bks) F & W Pubns Inc.

Writing & Speaking for Excellence. Deborah St. James & Howard Spiro. (Health Science Ser.). 234p. 1995. pap. 30.00 (*0-86720-935-6*) Jones & Bartlett.

Writing & Speaking in Business: Chapters 1-8. 10th ed. Gretchen N. Vik et al. (C). 1994. pap. text ed. 21.00 (*0-256-18466-6*) Irwin.

Writing & Speaking in the Technology Professions: A Practical Guide. Ed. by David F. Beer. LC 91-21418. (Illus.). 278p. (C). 1992. pap. text ed. 34.95 (*0-87942-284-X*, PP0278-2) Inst Electrical.

Writing & Synthesis: A Multicultural Approach to Writing. Tracey Baker & Barbara Kennedy. LC 92-26176. (C). 1993. 26.50 (*0-673-38964-2*) Addison-Wesley Educ.

Writing & the English Renaissance. Ed. by William Zunder & Suzanne Trill. LC 95-37771. 360p. (C). 1996. pap. text ed. 29.50 (*0-582-22975-8*, Pub. by Longman UK) Longman.

Writing & the Experience of Limits. Phillipe Sollers. Ed. by David Hayman. Tr. by Phillip Barnard. LC 82-25258. (European Perspectives Ser.). 224p. 1983. text ed. 49.50 (*0-231-05292-8*) Col U Pr.

***Writing & the Graduate Experience.** 2nd rev. ed. Lewis Pyenson et al. (Publications of the Graduate School, University of Southwestern Louisiana: Vol. 3). (Illus.). 40p. (C). 1996. pap. 5.00 (*1-889911-01-1*) U SW LA Grad.

Writing & the Holocaust. Ed. by Berel Lang. LC 88-11249. 301p. 1988. 45.00 (*0-8419-1184-3*); pap. 19.95 (*0-8419-1185-1*) Holmes & Meier.

Writing & the Moral Self. Berel Lang. 160p. (C). 1991. pap. 16.95 (*0-415-90296-7*, A4293, Routledge NY) Routledge.

Writing & the Rise of Finance: Capital Satires of the Early Eighteenth Century. Colin Nicholson. (Cambridge Studies in Eighteenth-Century English Literature & Thought: No. 21). 236p. (C). 1994. text ed. 59.95 (*0-521-45323-2*) Cambridge U Pr.

Writing & the Writer. 2nd ed. Frank Smith. 296p. 1994. pap. 29.95 (*0-8058-1422-1*); text ed. 59.95 (*0-8058-1421-3*) L Erlbaum Assocs.

Writing & Thinking for Young Authors: Blue. Linda Adelman et al. Ed. by Elena D. Wright. (J). (gr. 4). 1995. teacher ed., ring bd. 99.50 (*0-88106-204-9*, W420) Charlesbridge Pub.

Writing & Thinking for Young Authors: Gold. Linda Adelman et al. Ed. by Elena D. Wright. (J). (gr. 6). 1996. teacher ed., ring bd. 99.50 (*0-88106-206-5*, W620) Charlesbridge Pub.

Writing & Thinking for Young Authors: Green. Linda Adelman et al. (J). (gr. 2). 1994. teacher ed., ring bd. 99.50 (*0-88106-202-2*, W220) Charlesbridge Pub.

Writing & Thinking for Young Authors: Orange. Linda Adelman et al. Ed. by Elena D. Wright. (J). (gr. 3). 1994. teacher ed., ring bd. 99.50 (*0-88106-203-0*, W320) Charlesbridge Pub.

Writing & Thinking for Young Authors: Red. Linda Adelman et al. Ed. by Elena D. Wright. (J). (gr. 1). 1994. teacher ed., ring bd. 99.50 (*0-88106-201-4*, W120) Charlesbridge Pub.

Writing & Thinking for Young Authors: Tan. Linda Adelman et al. Ed. by Elena D. Wright. (J). (gr. 5). 1994. teacher ed., ring bd. 99.50 (*0-88106-205-7*, W520) Charlesbridge Pub.

Writing & Thinking in the Social Sciences. Sharon Friedman & Stephen Steinberg. 240p. (C). 1989. pap. text ed. 33.60 (*0-13-970062-5*) P-H.

Writing & Thinking with Computers: A Practical & Progressive Approach. Rick Monroe. (Illus.). 121p. (Orig.). 1993. pap. 16.95 (*0-8141-5893-5*) NCTE.

***Writing & Victorianism.** J. B. Bullen. LC 96-41669. (Crossconcurrents Ser.). 1997. 22.95 (*0-582-28916-5*); 54.95 (*0-582-28917-3*) Longman.

Writing & Vulnerability in the Late Renaissance. Jane Tylus. LC 92-32209. 328p. 1993. 42.50 (*0-8047-2138-6*) Stanford U Pr.

Writing Another's Dream: The Poetry of Wen Tingyun. Paul F. Rouzer. LC 92-33907. 276p. (C). 1993. 39.50 (*0-8047-2165-3*) Stanford U Pr.

Writing Antiques. George Mell. (Album Ser.: No. 54). (Illus.). 32p. 1988. pap. text ed. 5.25 (*0-85263-519-2*, Pub. by Shire Pubns UK) Lubrecht & Cramer.

Writing Applications for Sun Systems, Vol. I. Sun Microsystems Staff. 1990. pap. 22.95 (*0-201-57029-7*) Addison-Wesley.

Writing Applications for Sun Systems, Vol. II: A Guide for Windows Programmers. SunSoft Staff. 1992. pap. 24.95 (*0-201-58147-7*) Addison-Wesley.

Writing Apprehension & Anti-Writing: A Naturalistic Study of Composing Strategies Used by College Freshmen. Linda Bannister. LC 92-9604. 220p. 1992. lib. bdg. 89.95 (*0-7734-9832-X*) E Mellen.

Writing Arabic: A Practical Introduction to Ruq'ah Script. T. F. Mitchell. 164p. 1979. pap. 22.00 (*0-19-815150-0*) OUP.

Writing Architecture: Fantamos Fragments Fictions an Architectural Journey Through the Twentieth Century. Roger Connah. (Illus.). 456p. 1990. 95.00 (*0-262-03164-7*) MIT Pr.

***Writing Argumentative Essays.** Wood. LC 97-25209. 1997. pap. text ed. 26.67 (*0-13-680620-1*) P-H.

***Writing Arguments.** 4th ed. Ramage & Bean. LC 97-18531. 1997. pap. text ed. 31.00 (*0-205-26917-6*) P-H.

Writing Arguments: A Rhetoric with Readings. 3rd abr. ed. John D. Ramage & John C. Bean. 512p. (C). 1994. pap. text ed. 30.00 (*0-02-398141-5*, Macmillan Coll) P-H.

Writing Arguments: A Rhetoric with Readings. 3rd ed. John D. Ramage & John C. Bean. 800p. (C). 1994. pap. text ed. 34.00 (*0-02-398145-8*, Macmillan Coll) P-H.

***Writing Arguments: A Rhetoric with Readings.** 4th ed. John D. Ramage. LC 97-15605. 1997. pap. text ed. 27.00 (*0-205-26918-4*) Appleton & Lange.

Writing Articles from the Heart: How to Write & Sell Your Life Experiences. Marjorie Holmes. 176p. 1993. 16.99 (*0-89879-540-0*, Wrtrs Digest Bks) F & W Pubns Inc.

Writing As a Lifelong Skill. Sanford Kaye. 260p. 1994. pap. 26.95 (*0-534-22218-8*) Wadsworth Pub.

Writing As a Personal Product. Laura D. Latulippe. 2081p. (C). 1992. pap. text ed. 20.10 (*0-13-005869-6*) P-H.

***Writing As a Road to Self-Discovery.** 2nd ed. Barry Lane. Date not set. reprint ed. pap. 17.00 (*0-9656574-2-6*) Discover Writing.

Writing As a Second Language. Barbara Danish. LC 81-5755. 185p. (Orig.). 1981. pap. 15.95 (*0-915924-10-2*) Tchrs & Writers Coll.

Writing As a Thinking Process. Mary S. Lawrence. LC 78-185153. (Illus.). (C). 1972. Net. teacher ed. 2.95 (*0-472-08551-4*) U of Mich Pr.

Writing As a Thinking Process. rev. ed. Mary S. Lawrence. LC 78-185153. 1996. pap. text ed. 18.95 (*0-472-08368-6*) U of Mich Pr.

Writing as a Visual Art. Graziella Tonfoni & James Richardson. (Illus.). 189p. 1995. 29.95 (*1-871516-38-2*, Pub. by Intellect Bks UK) Cromland.

***Writing As a Way of Knowing.** Lois Bridges. LC 97-16320. (Strategies for Teaching & Learning Ser.). Date not set. pap. text ed. write for info. (*1-57110-062-8*) Stenhse Pubs.

Writing As Resistance: Four Women Confronting the Holocaust, Edith Stein, Simone Weil, Anne Frank & Etty Hillesum. Rachel F. Brenner. LC 96-20613. 1997. 26.50 (*0-271-01623-X*) Pa St U Pr.

Writing As Revelation. Marie Ford & Ford. (C). 1992. text ed. 29.50 (*0-06-042165-7*) Addson-Wesley Educ.

Writing As Sculpture. Louwrien Wijers. (Illus.). 272p. 1996. pap. 60.00 (*1-85490-184-2*) Academy Ed UK.

Writing As Social Action. Marilyn M. Cooper & Michael Holzman. LC 88-31483. 243p. (Orig.). 1989. pap. text ed. 24.00 (*0-86709-244-0*, 0244) Boynton Cook Pubs.

Writing as Thinking: Guided Process Approach. Frank. 1989. pap. text ed. 22.20 (*0-13-969619-9*) P-H.

***Writing As Witness: Essay & Talk.** Beth Brant. 126p. pap. 12.95 (*0-88961-200-5*, Pub. by Wmns Pr CN) LPC InBook.

Writing Assessment Handbook Grade 8. California Department of Education Staff. 170p. 1990. pap. 10.00 (*0-8011-0887-X*) Calif Education.

Writing Assessment Handbook, High School. California Department of Education Staff. 224p. 1993. pap. 11.00 (*0-8011-1073-4*) Calif Education.

Writing Assignments for Today's Media. 6th ed. James L. Julian & Byron St. Dizier. 272p. (C). 1992. spiral bd. write for info. (*0-697-14778-9*) Brown & Benchmark.

***Writing at Good Hope: A Study of Negotiated Composition in a Community of Nurses.** Jennie Dautermann. LC 96-38040. (ATTW Studies in Technical Communication). Date not set. pap. 39.50 (*1-56750-317-9*); text ed. 73.25 (*1-56750-316-0*) Ablex Pub.

Writing at Risk: Interviews in Paris with Uncommon Writers. Jason Weiss. LC 91-4787. (Illus.). 232p. 1991. 39.00 (*0-87745-348-9*); pap. 15.95 (*0-87745-349-7*) U of Iowa Pr.

Writing at the Margin: Discourse Between Anthropology & Medicine. Arthur Kleinman. (Illus.). 327p. 1996. 40.00 (*0-520-20099-3*) U CA Pr.

***Writing at the Margin: Discourse Between Anthropology & Medicine.** Arthur Kleinman. 1997. pap. text ed. 16.95 (*0-520-20965-6*) U CA Pr.

Writing at Work. Russell. 1994. pap. text ed. write for info. (*0-07-054956-7*) McGraw.

Writing at Work. rev. ed. Ernst Jacobi. LC 76-13607. 224p. 1985. pap. 7.95 (*0-89815-147-3*) Ten Speed Pr.

Writing at Work: A Text for Insurance Personnel. Michael J. Betz. LC 93-79637. 242p. (C). 1993. pap. text ed. 20.00 (*0-89462-079-7*) IIA.

***Writing at Work: Professional Writing Skills for People on the Job.** Edward L. Smith & Stephen A. Bernhardt. LC 96-46402. 1996. pap. write for info. (*0-8442-5983-7*) NTC Pub Grp.

Writing at Work: The Russell & Associates Papers. J. Stephen Russell. 400p. (C). 1985. pap. text ed. 21.50 (*0-03-070596-7*) HB Coll Pubs.

Writing Audit Reports. 2nd ed. Mary C. Bromage. 1984. text ed. 45.00 (*0-07-008064-X*) McGraw.

Writing Autobiography, Diaries & Letters. Theresa Sullivan. 1992. pap. text ed. 9.32 (*0-582-07878-4*) Longman.

Writing Away: The PEN Canada Travel Anthology. Ed. by Constance Rooke. 304p. 1994. pap. 14.95 (*0-7710-6956-1*) McCland & Stewart.

Writing Baseball. Jerry Klinkowitz. 216p. 1991. 28.95 (*0-252-01820-6*); 11.95 (*0-252-06192-6*) U of Ill Pr.

Writing Basics. rev. ed. Sandra Panman & Richard Panman. Ed. by Linda Gluck. (Illus.). 128p. (YA). (gr. 6-12). 1996. pap. text ed. 8.95 (*0-912813-24-5*) Active Lrn.

Writing Because We Love To: Homeschoolers at Work. Susannah Sheffer. LC 91-46813. 140p. 1992. pap. 12.95 (*0-86709-301-3*, 0301) Boynton Cook Pubs.

Writing Begins at Home: Preparing Children for Writing Before They Go to School. Marie M. Clay. 64p. (Orig.). 1987. pap. 13.50 (*0-435-08452-6*, 08452) Heinemann.

An Asterisk (*) at the beginning of an entry indicates that the title is appearing in BIP for the first time.

Writing Behavioral Contracts: A Case Simulation Practice Manual. William J. DeRisi & George Butz. (Illus.). 94p. (Orig.). (C). 1975. pap. text ed. 9.95 (*0-87822-123-9*, 1239) Res Press.

Writing Below the Belt. Michael Rowe. 1995. 19.95 (*1-56333-363-5*, R Kasak Bks) Masquerade.

*__Writing below the Belt: Conversations with Erotic Authors.__ Michael Rowe. (Orig.). 1997. reprint ed. mass mkt. 7.95 (*1-56333-540-9*, Hard Candy) Masquerade.

*__Writing Bestselling Suspense.__ Tom Byrnes. 304p. 1997. per. 17.00 (*0-7615-1026-5*) Prima Pub.

Writing Better Computer User Documentation from Paper to Hypertext, Version 2.0: The First Quarter Century of Service. R. John Brockmann. LC 90-12133. 384p. 1990. pap. text ed. 39.95 (*0-471-62260-5*) Wiley.

Writing Better Lyrics. Pat Pattison. LC 95-20964. 192p. 1995. 19.99 (*0-89879-682-2*, Wrtrs Digest Bks) F & W Pubns Inc.

Writing Better Technical Articles. Harley Bjelland. 180p. 1990. pap. 12.95 (*0-8306-3439-8*) McGraw-Hill Prof.

Writing Between the Lines: An Anthology on War & Its Social Consequences. Ed. by Kevin Bowen & Bruce Weigl. LC 96-9591. 336p. (C). 1997. pap. 17.95 (*1-55849-054-X*); text ed. 55.00 (*1-55849-053-1*) U of Mass Pr.

Writing Between the Lines: Race & Intertextuality. Aldon L. Nielsen. LC 93-23000. 312p. 1994. 45.00 (*0-8203-1603-2*) U of Ga Pr.

Writing Biology: Texts in the Social Construction of Scientific Knowledge. Greg Myers. LC 89-40263. (Science & Literature Ser.). (Illus.). 320p. (Orig.). (C). 1990. text ed. 37.50 (*0-299-12230-1*); pap. text ed. 15.75 (*0-299-12234-4*) U of Wis Pr.

Writing Book. George Kennedy et al. 160p. (C). 1984. 12.95 (*0-685-07566-4*) P-H.

Writing Book. Ron Padgett. 12p. (gr. 3-6). 1986. teacher ed., pap. 5.95 (*0-915924-70-6*) Tchrs & Writers Coll.

Writing Book. Inky Penguin. (Illus.). 44p. (gr. 3-6). 1986. student ed., pap. 7.95 (*0-915924-66-8*) Tchrs & Writers Coll.

Writing Book: A Workbook for Fiction Writers. Kate Grenville. 208p. (Orig.). 1993. pap. 12.95 (*0-04-442124-9*, Pub. by Allen & Unwin Aust Pty AT) IPG Chicago.

Writing Book: English in Everyday Life. Tina K. Carver et al. 200p. (C). 1982. pap. text ed. 19.95 (*0-13-970129-X*) P-H.

Writing Book Reviews. John E. Drewry. LC 73-17951. 230p. 1974. reprint ed. text ed. 62.50 (*0-8371-7285-3*, DRWB, Greenwood Pr) Greenwood.

Writing Books for Young People. 2nd expanded rev. ed. James C. Giblin. LC 94-39243. 160p. 1995. pap. text ed. 12.95 (*0-87116-175-3*) Writer.

Writing Brainstorms. Becky Daniel. 80p. (J). (gr. 1-4). 1990. 10.99 (*0-86653-569-1*, GA1172) Good Apple.

Writing Broadcast News: Shorter, Sharper, Stronger. Mervin Block. 231p. 1989. pap. 24.95 (*0-933893-20-5*) Bonus Books.

*__Writing Broadcast News: Shorter, Sharper, Stronger.__ Mervin Block. LC 97-6266. 1997. 29.95 (*1-56625-084-6*) Bonus Books.

Writing Bug. Lee B. Hopkins. LC 93-11994. (Meet the Author Ser.). (Illus.). 32p. (J). (gr. 2-5). 1992. 13.95 (*1-878450-38-7*) R Owen Pubs.

Writing Business Letters & Reports. Carmella E. Mansfield & Margaret H. Bahniuk. 1981. teacher ed. write for info. (*0-672-97375-8*); pap. write for info. (*0-672-97374-X*) Macmillan.

Writing Business Letters & Reports. Carmella E. Mansfield. 1986. pap. write for info. (*0-02-682970-3*) Macmillan.

Writing Business Plans That Get Results: A Step-by-Step Guide. Michael O'Donnell. 160p. (Orig.). 1991. pap. 15.95 (*0-8092-4007-6*) Contemp Bks.

Writing Business Proposals & Reports: Key Strategies for Success. Susan L. Brock. Ed. by Beverly Manber. LC 91-76247. (Fifty-Minute Ser.). (Illus.). 85p. (Orig.). 1992. pap. 10.95 (*1-56052-122-8*) Crisp Pubns.

Writing Business Research Reports: A Guide to Scientific Writing. Matthew J. Rehart. 201p. (C). 1993. pap. text ed. 18.95 (*0-9623744-6-6*) Pyrczak Pub.

Writing by Candlelight. E. P. Thompson. (C). 1980. pap. 7.95 (*0-85036-260-1*, Pub. by Merlin Pr UK) Humanities.

Writing by Choice: Intermediate Composition for Students of ESL. Judith Rodby. (Illus.). 144p. (C). 1987. pap. text ed. 12.00 (*0-13-970328-4*) P-H.

Writing by Design: A Handbook for Technical Professionals. Michael Greene & Jonathan G. Ripley. 384p. (C). 1992. pap. text ed. 32.20 (*0-13-969346-7*) P-H.

*__Writing by Doing: Learning to Write Effectively.__ 3rd ed. Elaine Hughes & David A. Sohn. LC 96-30484. (J). 1996. write for info. (*0-8442-5909-8*) NTC Pub Grp.

Writing by Wilbers: Entertaining, Helpful Advice for Everyone Who Writes on the Job. Stephen Wilbers. (Collected Columns Ser.: Vol. 2). 150p. 1995. pap. 9.95 (*0-9635995-1-8*) Good Writing.

Writing Capital & Small Letters. Fred Justus. (Early Education Ser.). 24p. (gr. 1). 1981. student ed. 5.00 (*0-8209-0223-3*, K-25) ESP.

Writing Centers: An Annotated Bibliography. Christina Murphy et al. LC 96-18521. (Bibliographies & Indexes in Education Ser.: Vol. 17). 312p. 1996. text ed. 69.50 (*0-313-29831-9*, Greenwood Pr) Greenwood.

Writing Centers in Context: Twelve Case Studies. Ed. by Joyce A. Kinkead & Jeanette G. Harris. LC 93-8361. (Illus.). 274p. (Orig.). 1993. pap. 24.95 (*0-8141-5868-4*) NCTE.

Writing Challenge. Batchelor & Slaughter. 1991. pap. 22.95 (*0-8384-3377-4*) Heinle & Heinle.

*__Writing Changes Everything.__ Brodie. LC 96-40453. 1997. 18.95 (*0-312-15432-1*) St Martin.

Writing Chemical Equations & Identifying Unknown Solutions Using Microscale Techniques. Marcia L. Gillette & H. Anthony Neidig. (Modular Laboratory Program in Chemistry Ser.). 16p. (C). 1992. pap. text ed. 1.35 (*0-87540-406-5*, REAC 406-5) Chem Educ Res.

Writing Chicago: Modernism, Ethnography, & the Novel. Carla Cappetti. Ed. by Jonathan Arac. LC 92-41092. (Social Foundations of Aesthetic Forms Ser.). 320p. (C). 1993. pap. 18.00 (*0-231-08129-4*); text ed. 49.50 (*0-231-08128-6*) Col U Pr.

Writing Children's Books: Getting Started: A Home Study Course. Wendy Pfeffer. (Home Study Ser.). 62p. Notebook. ring bd. 33.00 (*0-939926-28-8*); audio (*0-939926-27-X*) Fruition Pubns.

*__Writing Chinese with Reference to Its Characteristics.__ K. S. Lee & Y. K. Tse. 112p. (CHI.). 1994. pap. write for info. (*962-209-372-8*, Pub. by Hong Kong Univ Pr HK) Coronet Bks.

Writing Choices. Hoffman. 1996. pap. text ed. write for info. (*0-205-26490-5*) Allyn.

*__Writing Choices.__ Andrew J. Hoffman. LC 96-46886. 400p. 1996. pap. 36.00 (*0-205-19818-X*) Allyn.

Writing Clear Essays. 3rd ed. Robert B. Donald et al. LC 95-35813. 1995. pap. text ed. 32.00 (*0-13-454547-8*) P-H.

Writing Clear Paragraphs. 5th ed. Robert B. Donald. (C). 1995. pap. text ed. 35.00 (*0-13-102054-4*) P-H.

Writing Clear Sentences. E. Donald et al. (Illus.). 320p. (C). 1986. pap. text ed. 42.00 (*0-13-970401-9*) P-H.

Writing Clearly. Lane et al. 1993. pap. 26.95 (*0-8384-3849-0*); teacher ed., pap. 22.95 (*0-8384-4207-2*) Heinle & Heinle.

Writing Clearly: A Home Study Course. David W. Cochran. (Home Study Ser.). 1983. 33.00 (*0-939926-20-2*); audio (*0-939926-19-9*) Fruition Pubns.

Writing Clearly & Effectively. 2nd ed. Michael L. Murdock. 166p. (Orig.). 1981. pap. 7.25 (*0-930124-01-4*) Transemantics.

Writing Clinic: Writing-Grammar-Readings. 4th ed. Ralph E. Loewe. (Illus.). 384p. 1988. pap. text ed. 44.00 (*0-13-970112-5*) P-H.

*__Writing Cogito: Montaigne, Descarte, & the Institution of the Modern Subject.__ Hassan Melehy. LC 97-679. (SUNY Series, The Margins of Literature). 256p. (C). 1997. text ed. 59.50 (*0-7914-3571-7*) State U NY Pr.

*__Writing Cogito: Montaigne, Descarte, & the Institution of the Modern Subject.__ Hassan Melehy. LC 97-679. (SUNY Series, The Margins of Literature). 256p. (C). 1997. pap. text ed. 19.95 (*0-7914-3572-5*) State U NY Pr.

Writing Commitment. 4th ed. Michael E. Adelstein & Jean G. Pival. 602p. (C). 1988. text ed. 28.00 (*0-15-597835-7*) HB Coll Pubs.

Writing Commitment. 5th ed. Michael E. Adelstein & Jean G. Pival. LC 91-78064. (Illus.). 624p. (C). 1993. reprint ed. pap. text ed. write for info. (*0-15-500167-1*); reprint ed. pap. text ed. 4.00 (*0-15-500302-X*) HB Coll Pubs.

Writing Competency Practice. Andrea L. Kane & Barbara Martorana. (YA). (gr. 7-12). 1980. student ed. 5.75 (*0-89525-134-5*) Ed Activities.

Writing Compilers & Interpreters: An Applied Approach. Ronald L. Mak. 516p. 1991. text ed. 52.00 (*0-471-54712-3*); text ed. 59.95 (*0-471-55580-0*) Wiley.

Writing Compilers & Interpreters: An Applied Approach Using C++ 2nd ed. Ronald L. Mak. LC 96-5938. 528p. 1996. pap. text ed. 49.95 (*0-471-11353-0*) Wiley.

Writing Connection. Rebecca B. Carosso & Judith D. Stanford. (Illus.). 448p. 1983. pap. text ed. write for info. (*0-13-970541-4*) P-H.

Writing Contracts: A Distinct Discipline. Peter Siviglia. 102p. 1996. per. 12.75 (*0-89089-933-9*) Carolina Acad Pr.

Writing Contracts in Plain English. Carl Felsenfeld & Alan M. Siegel. LC 81-12972. 290p. 1981. pap. 21.00 (*0-314-60871-0*) West Pub.

*__Writing Cookbooks.__ Judith Comfort. (Writing Ser.). 160p. (Orig.). 1997. pap. 15.95 (*1-55180-115-9*) Self-Counsel Pr.

Writing Course by & for ESL Students. Jacqueline Costello & Amy Tucker. 320p. (C). 1985. pap. text ed. write for info. (*0-07-554586-1*) McGraw.

Writing Creative Nonfiction. rev. ed. Theodore R. Cheney. 224p. 1991. reprint ed. pap. 14.95 (*0-89815-411-1*) Ten Speed Pr.

Writing Creative Nonfiction: The Literature of Reality. Gay Talese & Barbara Lounsberry. LC 95-7544. 352p. (C). 1996. text ed. 27.50 (*0-06-046587-5*) Addson-Wesley Educ.

Writing Creative Nonfiction: The Literature of Reality. Gay Talese & Barbara Lounsberry. 400p. 1995. pap. 24.95 (*0-8230-5013-0*) Watsn-Guptill.

Writing Crime & Suspense Fiction. Lesley Grant-Adamson. (Teach Yourself Ser.). 224p. (Orig.). 1996. pap. 10.95 (*0-8442-3105-3*, Teach Yourslf) NTC Pub Grp.

Writing Crime Fiction. H. R. Keating. 1991. pap. 8.95 (*0-312-05542-0*) St Martin.

Writing Critical Reviews. Frank Schaffer Publications, Inc. Staff. (Middle School Bks.). (Illus.). 1996. wbk. ed. 12.95 (*0-7647-0014-6*, FS-10190) Schaffer Pubns.

*__Writing Cultural History in Colonial & Postcolonial India.__ Henry Schwarz. LC 97-2875. (Critical Histories Ser.). 192p. 1997. text ed. 32.50 (*0-8122-3373-5*) U of Pa Pr.

Writing Culture: The Poetics & Politics of Ethnography. Ed. by James Clifford & George E. Marcus. 345p. 1986. pap. 15.00 (*0-520-05729-5*) U CA Pr.

Writing Cycle. 2nd rev. ed. Clela Allphin-Hoggatt. LC 86-26093. 260p. (C). 1991. pap. text ed. write for info. (*0-935732-27-6*) Roxbury Pub Co.

Writing Dancing in the Age of Postmodernism. Sally Banes. LC 93-8225. (Illus.). 428p. 1994. pap. 19.95 (*0-8195-6268-8*, Wesleyan Univ Pr); text ed. 50.00 (*0-8195-5266-6*, Wesleyan Univ Pr) U Pr of New Eng.

Writing Dangerously: Mary McCarthy & Her World. Carol Brightman. 1994. pap. 18.95 (*0-15-600067-9*) HarBrace.

*__Writing Decisions.__ Rosen. 1997. pap. text ed. 22.00 (*0-205-20020-6*) P-H.

Writing Degree Zero. Roland Barthes. 94p. 1977. pap. 9.95 (*0-374-52139-5*) FS&G.

*__Writing Desire: Ideology & Aesthetics in the Work of Henry Miller.__ Caroline Blinder. (EuroSH Ser.). Date not set. 52.95 (*1-57113-168-X*) Camden Hse.

Writing Development: Magic in the Brain. Roslyn Arnold. (English, Language & Education Ser.). 160p. 1991. pap. 27.00 (*0-335-15195-7*, Open Univ Pr) Taylor & Francis.

Writing Device Drivers: Tutorial & Reference. Tim Burke et al. 1152p. 1995. pap. 73.95 incl. disk (*1-55558-141-2*, Digital DEC) Buttrwrth-Heinemann.

Writing Device Drivers for SCO UNIX: A Practical Approach. Peter Kettle & Stephen Statler. LC 92-36521. (C). 1993. pap. text ed. 37.75 (*0-201-54425-3*) Addison-Wesley.

Writing Device Drivers for Windows 95. Art Baker. (C). 1997. pap. text ed. write for info. (*0-201-40715-9*) Addison-Wesley.

Writing Device Drivers in C for MS-DOS Systems. Philip M. Adams & Clovis L. Tondo. 320p. 1990. pap. 29.95 (*0-13-970864-2*) P-H.

Writing Diaspora: Tactics of Intervention in Contemporary Cultural Studies. Rey Chow. LC 92-23064. (Arts & Politics of the Everyday Ser.). 236p. 1993. 31.50 (*0-253-31366-X*); pap. 11.95 (*0-253-20785-1*, MB-785) Ind U Pr.

Writing Differences: Readings from the Seminar of Helene Cixous. Ed. by Susan Sellers. 170p. 1988. pap. 14.95 (*0-312-02051-1*) St Martin.

*__Writing Differences: Readings from the Seminar of Helene Cixous.__ Ed. by Susan Sellers & Kate Flint. (Gender in Writing Ser.). 200p. 1988. 45.00 (*0-335-09010-9*, Open Univ Pr); pap. 14.99 (*0-335-09009-5*, Open Univ Pr) Taylor & Francis.

Writing Differences: Readings from the Seminar of Helene Cixous. Susan. Sellers. LC 88-4538. 1988. text ed. 35.00 (*0-312-02050-3*) St Martin.

Writing, Directing, & Producing Documentary Films & Videos. rev. ed. Alan Rosenthal. LC 95-17159. (C). 1996. pap. 19.95 (*0-8093-2014-2*) S Ill U Pr.

Writing, Directing, & Producing Documentary Films & Videos. 2nd rev. ed. Alan Rosenthal. LC 95-17159. 320p. (C). 1996. 39.95 (*0-8093-2013-4*) S Ill U Pr.

Writing Disaster Recovery Plans for Telecommunications Networks & LANs. Leo A. Wrobel. LC 93-7163. 1993. text ed. 55.00 (*0-89006-694-9*) Artech Hse.

Writing Docudrama: Dramatizing Reality for Film & TV. Alan Rosenthal. 224p. 1994. pap. 26.95 (*0-240-80195-4*, Focal) Buttrwrth-Heinemann.

Writing Does Make a Difference - Pass It On: Memoirs of the N. C. Women Writers Conference, March 13-15, 1992, in Winston-Salem, N. C. Pepper Worthington. (Illus.). 33p. (Orig.). 1992. pap. 5.00 (*1-880994-03-8*) Mt Olive Coll Pr.

Writing Dos Device Drivers in C. 2nd ed. Phillip Adams & Clovis L. Tondo. 1994. Incl. disk. 39.95 incl. disk (*0-13-108622-7*) P-H.

Writing down the Bones: Freeing the Writer Within. Natalie Goldberg. LC 86-11840. 192p. (Orig.). 1986. pap. 10.00 (*0-87773-375-9*) Shambhala Pubns.

Writing down the Bones: Freeing the Writer Within. Natalie Goldberg. 192p. (Orig.). 1996. 20.00 (*1-57062-258-2*) Shambhala Pubns.

Writing down the Days: 365 Creative Journaling Ideas for Young People. Lorraine Dahlstrom. LC 88-29616. (Illus.). 176p. (YA). (gr. 6 up). 1990. pap. 12.95 (*0-915793-19-9*) Free Spirit Pub.

Writing Down the Light. Jay B. Fowler, Jr. LC 87-10996. 48p. (Orig.). 1987. pap. 5.00 (*0-914061-05-4*) Orchises Pr.

Writing DR DOS Batch Files. Ronny Richardson. 432p. 1992. pap. 32.95 (*0-8306-4244-7*, 4289, Windcrest) TAB Bks.

*__Writing East: The "Travels" of Sir John Mandeville.__ Iain M. Higgins. LC 96-45601. (Middle Ages Ser.). 336p. 1997. text ed. 49.95 (*0-8122-3343-3*) U of Pa Pr.

*__Writing Effective Letters & Memos.__ 2nd rev. ed. Arthur H. Bell. LC 97-6359. (Business Success Ser.). (Orig.). 1997. pap. text ed. 6.95 (*0-8120-9824-2*) Barron.

Writing Effective News Releases: How to Get Free Publicity for Yourself, Your Business, or Your Organization. Catherine V. McIntyre. LC 91-45516. (Illus.). 176p. (Orig.). 1992. pap. 17.00 (*0-941599-19-1*) Piccadilly Bks.

*__Writing Effective Policies & Procedures: A Step-by-Step Resource for Clear Communication.__ Nancy Campbell. 320p. 1997. spiral bd. 60.00 (*0-8144-7960-X*) AMACOM.

Writing Effective Resumes: A Complete Guide. McCabe. (CA - Career Development Ser.). 1993. pap. 11.95 (*0-538-61750-0*) S-W Pub.

Writing Effective Sentences. George Bell. LC 92-22630. 1992. pap. text ed. 30.00 (*0-205-14037-8*) Allyn.

Writing Effective Sentences. Berle Haggblade. LC 93-48318. 1994. pap. 13.95 (*0-538-71054-3*) S-W Pub.

Writing Effective Speeches. Henry Ehrlich. (Orig.). 1994. pap. 8.95 (*1-56924-922-9*) Marlowe & Co.

*__Writing Effectively.__ Fearn & Farnan. LC 97-11949. 1997. pap. text ed. 24.00 (*0-205-26764-5*) P-H.

Writing Effectively for Business & Government. David G. Byrd & Phyllis Fleishel. (Illus.). 1986. pap. 8.00 (*0-917069-04-8*) Univ SC Inst Pub Affairs.

Writing Effectively in Business. Beth S. Neman & Smythe. (C). 1992. text ed. 45.95 (*0-06-044809-1*) Addson-Wesley Educ.

Writing Efficiently: A Step-by-Step Composition Course. Barbara Seale. (Illus.). 1978. pap. text ed. write for info. (*0-13-970160-5*) P-H.

Writing Empirical Research Reports: A Basic Guide for Students of the Social & Behavioral Sciences. Fred Pyrczak & Randall R. Bruce. 128p. (C). 1992. pap. text ed. 16.95 (*0-9623744-3-1*) Pyrczak Pub.

Writing Engineering Specifications: A Guide to Content, Style & Layout. Jeremy M. Haslam. 172p. 1989. 39.95 (*0-419-13750-5*, E & FN Spon) Routledge Chapman & Hall.

Writing English: A User's Manual. Nancy Harrison. LC 84-23144. 232p. 1985. 26.00 (*0-7099-3708-3*, Pub. by Croom Helm UK); pap. 9.95 (*0-7099-3709-1*, Pub. by Croom Helm UK) Routledge Chapman & Hall.

Writing Erotic Fiction. Derek Parker. 115p. (Orig.). 1996. pap. 10.95 (*1-56924-833-8*) Marlowe & Co.

Writing Essays. Carol Pemberton. LC 92-14216. 1992. pap. text ed. 33.00 (*0-205-13986-8*) Allyn.

Writing Essays: A Process Approach. Quentin L. Gehle & Duncan J. Rollo. 400p. (C). 1987. teacher ed. write for info. (*0-318-61583-5*) St Martin.

*__Writing Essays about Literature.__ 5th ed. Griffith. (C). 1997. pap. text ed. 21.00 (*0-15-503708-0*) HB Coll Pubs.

Writing Essays about Literature: A Guide & Style Sheet. 3rd ed. Kelley Griffith, Jr. 269p. (C). 1989. pap. text ed. 18.75 (*0-15-597863-2*) HB Coll Pubs.

Writing Essays about Literature: A Guide & Style Sheet. 4th ed. Kelley Griffith. (Illus.). 275p. (C). pap. text ed. write for info. (*0-15-500157-4*) HB Coll Pubs.

Writing Essays & Dissertations: A Guide to the Preparation of Written Assignments in Colleges & Universities. G. R. Phillips & L. J. Hunt. pap. 6.95 (*0-85564-118-5*, Pub. by Univ of West Aust Pr AT) Intl Spec Bk.

Writing, Ethics, & Group Projects for Accounting. Stuart. (AB - Accounting Principles Ser.). 1997. text ed. 13.95 (*0-538-86286-6*) S-W Pub.

*__Writing Ethnicity: Cross-Cultural Consciousness in Canadian & Quebecois Literature.__ Winfried Siemerling. 234p. 1996. pap. 19.95 (*1-55022-280-5*, Pub. by ECW Press CN) Genl Dist Srvs.

Writing Exchange Business Style Guide: A Concise, Practical Reference for Error-Free Business Correspondence. Joy Van Skiver. LC 95-16049. 233p. (Orig.). 1995. pap. 21.95 (*0-9643824-0-7*) WREXpress.

Writing Exercises for High School Students. Barbara Vultaggio. LC 90-30861. (Teaching Resources in the ERIC Database (TRIED) Ser.). 1990. pap. 14.95 (*0-927516-09-8*) ERIC-REC.

Writing Experience. 3rd ed. Carol Schoen et al. (C). 1989. text ed. 23.50 (*0-673-39910-9*) Addson-Wesley Educ.

Writing Exploratory Essays. Steven M. Strang. LC 94-41376. 806p. (C). 1995. pap. text ed. 28.95 (*1-55934-262-5*, 1262) Mayfield Pub.

Writing Exposition: Writing Strands. Dave Marks. 125p. 1994. pap. text ed. 21.95 (*1-888344-03-2*) National Writing.

Writing Family Histories & Memoirs. Kirk Polking. 272p. 1995. pap. 14.99 (*1-55870-394-2*, Betrwy Bks) F & W Pubns Inc.

Writing Fast Code for the Pentium Processor. Ramech Subramaniam. 352p. 1996. pap. write for info. (*0-201-63437-6*) Addison-Wesley.

Writing Feature Articles: A Practical Guide to Methods & Markets. 2nd ed. Brendan Hennessy. 307p. 1993. pap. 29.95 (*0-7506-0884-6*) Buttrwrth-Heinemann.

Writing Feature Articles: A Pratical Guide to Methods & Markets. 3rd ed. Brendan Hennessy. LC 97-943. (Illus.). 256p. 1996. pap. 32.95 (*0-240-51471-8*, Focal) Buttrwrth-Heinemann.

Writing Fiction. 3rd ed. Janet Burroway. (C). 1991. text ed. 28.00 (*0-673-52119-2*) Addson-Wesley Educ.

Writing Fiction. August W. Derleth. LC 72-141413. 201p. 1971. reprint ed. text ed. 38.50 (*0-8371-4694-1*, DEWF, Greenwood Pr) Greenwood.

Writing Fiction: A Guide to Narrative Craft. 4th ed. Janet Burroway. LC 95-3562. 400p. (C). 1996. pap. text ed. 30.50 (*0-673-52345-4*) Addson-Wesley Educ.

Writing Fiction: A Guide to Narrative Craft. 4th ed. Janet Burroway. 425p. 1995. pap. 30.00 (*0-8230-5012-2*) Watsn-Guptill.

Writing Fiction: Grades Three & Above. Lois S. Roets. 60p. 1989. reprint ed. teacher ed. 12.00 (*0-911943-16-1*) Leadership Pub.

Writing Fiction in a Post-Structural World. Schecter. (C). 1995. pap. text ed. write for info. (*0-15-502032-3*) HB Coll Pubs.

Writing Field Notes. Robert M. Emerson. 272p. 1995. pap. 12.95 (*0-226-20681-5*) U Ch Pr.

Writing Filipino Grammar: Traditions & Trends. Nelly I. Cubar & Ernesto H. Cubar. xvii, 186p. (Orig.). 1994. pap. 12.50 (*971-10-0500-X*) Cellar.

Writing for a Reader. Trudy B. Krisher. LC 94-5834. 336p. 1995. pap. text ed. 36.20 (*0-13-031170-7*) P-H.

*__Writing for a University.__ Phyllis Creme & Mary R. Lea. LC 97-16321. 1997. write for info. (*0-335-19643-8*, Open Univ Pr); pap. write for info. (*0-335-19642-X*, Open Univ Pr) Taylor & Francis.

Writing for Academic Publication: A Guide to Getting Started. Frank Parker & Kathryn Riley. 160p. 1995. pap. text ed. 21.95 (*0-9644636-1-X*) Parlay Enter.

Writing for Accountants. Aletha Hendrickson. (Illus.). 310p. 1993. teacher ed. write for info. (*0-538-81737-2*) S-W Pub.

Writing for Accountants. Aletha Hendrickson. (Illus.). 310p. 1993. pap. 26.95 (*0-538-83040-9*) S-W Pub.

Writing for Antiquity. Glyn Daniel. 1992. 24.95 (*0-500-01532-5*) Thames Hudson.

W

*Writing for Business. Wilson. 1991. pap. text ed. write for info. (0-17-555686-5) Addison-Wesley.

Writing for Business. 2nd ed. Mary C. Bromage. LC 79-25634. 192p. (C). 1980. pap. text ed. 14.95 (0-472-06317-0) U of Mich Pr.

Writing for Business: A Casebook. 3rd ed. John T. Farrell. 128p. 1995. per. 19.89 (0-8403-7169-1) Kendall-Hunt.

Writing for Business: Helpful, Easy-to-Apply Advice for Everyone Who Writes on the Job. Stephen Wilbers. 160p. (Orig.). 1993. pap. 9.95 (0-9635995-0-X) Good Writing.

Writing for Business & Industry: Process & Product. Kevin J. Harty & John Keenan. (Illus.). 512p. (C). 1987. pap. text ed. 53.00 (0-02-351400-0, Macmillan Coll) P-H.

Writing for Business Results. Patricia E. Seraydarian. LC 92-41874. 112p. 1993. per. 10.00 (1-55623-854-1) Irwin Prof Pubng.

Writing for Business Results. Patricia E. Seraydarian. LC 96-84772. (How-To Book Ser.). 96p. 1996. reprint ed. pap. 12.95 (1-884926-48-7, BUSWR) Amer Media.

Writing for Challenger, Bk. 1. 1994. 7.40 (1-56420-010-8, 2010-8) New Readers.

Writing for Challenger, Bk. 2. 1994. 7.40 (1-56420-011-6, 2011-6) New Readers.

Writing for Challenger, Bk. 3. 1994. 7.40 (1-56420-012-4, 2012-4) New Readers.

Writing for Challenger, Bk. 4. 1994. 7.40 (1-56420-013-2, 2013-2) New Readers.

Writing for Challenger, Bks. 1-4. 1994. teacher ed. 7.40 (1-56420-014-0, 2014-0) New Readers.

Writing for Change: A Community Reader. Ann Watters & Marjorie Ford. LC 94-22116. 1994. pap. text ed. write for info. (0-07-068615-7) McGraw.

Writing for Children. Margaret Clark. pap. 19.95 (0-7136-3736-6, 92955, Pub. by A&C Black UK) Talman.

Writing for Children. Catherine Woolley. 208p. 1991. pap. 10.95 (0-452-26600-9) NAL-Dutton.

Writing for Children: How to Apply Writing Basics, Target Children's Needs & Communicate in Fresh Formats. Cook Communications Ministries International Staff. (Interlit Imprint Ser.: Unit 11). 40p. 1995. pap. text ed. 5.95 (1-884752-18-7, 44131) Cook Min Intl.

Writing for Children & Getting Published. Lesley Pollinger. (Teach Yourself Ser.). 192p. (Orig.). (J). 1996. pap. 10.95 (0-8442-3104-5, Teach Yourslf) NTC Pub Grp.

Writing for Children & Teenagers. Lee Wyndham & Arnold Madison. 272p. (Orig.). 1985. pap. 14.99 (0-89879-347-5, Wrtrs Digest Bks) F & W Pubns Inc.

Writing for College. 2nd ed. Robert E. Yarber. (C). 1988. pap. text ed. 33.50 (0-673-38219-2) Addson-Wesley Educ.

Writing for College. 3rd ed. Robert E. Yarber & Hoffman. 464p. (C). 1995. teacher ed., pap. text ed. write for info. (0-673-55183-0) Addson-Wesley Educ.

Writing for College: A Practical Approach. 3rd ed. (C). 1995. teacher ed., pap. write for info. (0-673-99873-8) Addson-Wesley Educ.

Writing for College: A Practical Approach. 3rd ed. Robert E. Yarber & Andrew J. Hoffman. LC 95-12193. 400p. (C). 1996. text ed. 35.95 (0-673-46795-3) Addson-Wesley Educ.

*Writing for Computer Science: The Art of Effective Communication. Justin Zobel. LC 97-13754. 1997. write for info. (981-3083-22-0) Spr-Verlag.

Writing for Corporate Videos. Grant Eustace. 143p. 1990. pap. 42.95 (0-240-51295-2, Focal) Buttrwrth-Heinemann.

Writing for Daytime Drama. Jean Rouverol. 368p. 1992. pap. 42.95 (0-240-80102-4, Focal) Buttrwrth-Heinemann.

Writing for Dollars. Compiled by John C. McCollister. LC 94-43195. 1995. 19.95 (0-8246-0372-9) Jonathan David.

Writing for Dough. William Idelson. LC 89-80414. 321p. (Orig.). (C). 1990. pap. 15.00 (1-55666-036-7) Empire Pub Srvs.

Writing for Employment. McGowan. (YA - Adult Education Ser.). 1993. pap. 5.95 (0-538-70773-9) S-W Pub.

Writing for Excellence: A Four-Stage Approach to Creating Maximum Impact in Business Writing. Michael Doherty. LC 92-17062. 1992. write for info. (0-07-707654-0) McGraw.

Writing for Fishery Journals. J. Hunter. LC 90-81939. 100p. (C). 1990. pap. text ed. 26.00 (0-913235-65-2) Am Fisheries Soc.

*Writing for Fun & Profit. (Illus.). 350p. (Orig.). 1998. pap. 24.95 (1-56559-929-2) HGI Mrktng.

Writing for Growth. Arthur Seamans. Ed. by T. E. Dennison. (Illus.). 60p. (Orig.). (C). 1987. pap. text ed. 8.50 (0-923231-06-4) Mohican Pub.

Writing for Health Professionals: A Manual for Writers. Philip Burnard. LC 92-20116. (Therapy in Practice Ser.: Vol. 32). 1992. 41.50 (1-56593-074-6, 0371) Singular Publishing.

Writing for Health Professionals: A Manual for Writers. 2nd ed. Philip Burnard. (Illus.). 256p. 1996. pap. 38.25 (1-56593-765-1, 1488) Singular Publishing.

Writing for Industry: An Instruction Manual. Anita J. Lehman. 224p. (C). 1984. pap. text ed. 20.00 (0-03-061963-7) HB Coll Pubs.

Writing for Life. Ed. by John Collerson. (Illus.). 122p. (Orig.). 1988. pap. text ed. 16.50 (0-909955-81-6, 00625) Heinemann.

Writing for Life: A Writer's Reader. Marilyn M. Culpepper & Perry E. Gianakos. 625p. (C). 1988. pap. text ed. 40.00 (0-02-341850-8, Macmillan Coll) P-H.

Writing for Love or Money. Saturday Review Staff. Ed. by Norman Cousins. LC 70-107736. (Essay Index Reprint Ser.). 1977. 20.95 (0-8369-1534-8) Ayer.

Writing for Magazines. Jill Dick. pap. 19.95 (0-7136-3850-8, 93178, Pub. by A&C Black UK) Talman.

Writing for Magazines: A Beginner's Guide. Cheryl S. Wray. LC 96-24828. 224p. (C). 1996. pap. 17.95 (0-8442-5961-6) NTC Pub Grp.

Writing for Magazines - Like a Pro! Jerry L. McGuire. (Illus.). 220p. 1995. pap. text ed. 23.95 (0-9632004-1-0) J L McGuire.

*Writing for Magazines & Newspapers. Griffin & Sullivan. 1991. pap. text ed. write for info. (0-582-05944-5, Drumbeat) Longman.

Writing for Many Roles. Mimi Schwartz. LC 84-16817. 230p. (Orig.). (YA). 1984. pap. text ed. 18.50 (0-86709-097-9, 0097) Boynton Cook Pubs.

Writing for Mass Communication. Earl R. Hutchison, Sr. (Illus.). 474p. (C). 1986. pap. text ed. 39.50 (0-582-29033-3, 71732) Longman.

Writing for Me. Roberta Mendel. (Scribbler Ser.). 6p. (Orig.). 1984. pap. 5.00 (0-936424-11-7) Pin Prick.

Writing for Me. rev. ed. Roberta Mendel. (Scribbler Ser.). 7p. (Orig.). 1994. pap. 5.00 (0-936424-15-X) Pin Prick.

Writing for Meaning: A Basic Worktext. Michael Shea. 361p. (C). 1988. pap. text ed. 17.50 (0-15-597870-5); pap. text ed. 3.00 (0-15-597871-3) HB Coll Pubs.

Writing for Money: Dozens of Ways to Boost Your Freelance Writing Income. Loriann H. Oberlin. LC 94-27112. 256p. 1995. 17.99 (0-89879-654-7, Wrtrs Digest Bks) F & W Pubns Inc.

*Writing for Money in Mental Health. Douglas H. Ruben. LC 96-51806. (Illus.). 294p. 1997. pap. text ed. 24.95 (0-7890-0240-X); lib. bdg. 49.95 (0-7890-0101-2) Haworth Pr.

Writing for Multimedia: A Guide & Sourcebook for the Digital Writer. Michael D. Korolenko. (Multimedia Ser.). 400p. (C). 1997. pap. text ed. 36.95 (0-534-51293-3) Wadsworth Pub.

Writing for Multimedia: Entertainment, Education, Training, Advertising, & the World Wide Web. Timothy Garrand. 352p. 1996. pap. 34.95 incl. cd-rom (0-240-80247-0, Focal) Buttrwrth-Heinemann.

*Writing for New Media: The Essential Guide to Writing for Interactive Media, CD-ROMS, & the Web. Andrew Bonime & Ken C. Pohlmann. (Books for Writers Ser.). 240p. 1997. pap. 16.95 (0-471-17030-5) Wiley.

Writing for Our Lives, Vol. 5, No. 1. Ed. by Janet M. McEwan. 80p. (Orig.). 1996. pap. 6.00 (0-9633743-8-9) Running Deer.

*Writing for Our Lives, Vol. 5, No. 2. Ed. by Janet M. McEwan. 92p. (Orig.). 1996. pap. 6.00 (0-9633743-9-7) Running Deer.

*Writing for Our Lives, Vol. 6, No. 1. Ed. by Janet M. McEwan. 80p. (Orig.). 1997. pap. 8.00 (1-890882-00-3) Running Deer.

Writing for Our Lives Vol. 1, No. 1: Creative Expressions in Writing by Women. Ed. by Janet M. McEwan. 64p. 1992. per. 4.00 (0-9633743-0-3) Running Deer.

Writing for Our Lives Vol. 1, No. 2: Creative Expressions in Writing by Women. Ed. by Janet M. McEwan. 80p. 1992. Vol. 1, No. 2. per. 4.00 (0-9633743-1-1) Running Deer.

Writing for Our Lives Vol. 2, No. 1: Creative Expressions in Writing by Women. Ed. by Janet M. McEwan. 80p. 1993. per. 6.00 (0-9633743-2-X) Running Deer.

Writing for Our Lives Vol. 2, No. 2: Creative Expressions in Writing by Women. Ed. by Janet M. McEwan. 80p. 1993. per. 6.00 (0-9633743-3-8) Running Deer.

Writing for Our Lives Vol. 3, No. 1: Creative Expressions in Writing by Women. Ed. by Janet M. McEwan. 80p. 1994. per. 6.00 (0-9633743-4-6) Running Deer.

Writing for Our Lives Vol. 3, No. 2: Creative Expressions in Writing by Women. Ed. by Janet M. McEwan. 80p. 1994. per. 6.00 (0-9633743-5-4) Running Deer.

Writing for Our Lives Vol. 4, No. 1: Creative Expressions in Writing by Women. Ed. by Janet M. McEwan. 80p. 1995. per. 6.00 (0-9633743-6-2) Running Deer.

Writing for Our Lives Vol. 4, No. 2: Creative Expressions in Writing by Women. Ed. by Janet M. McEwan. 80p. 1995. per. 6.00 (0-9633743-7-0) Running Deer.

Writing for Pleasure: How to Achieve Personal Growth Through Self Expression. Susan D. Artof. 120p. (C). 1991. pap. text ed. 10.00 (0-9626888-0-0) Ctr Pr CA.

Writing for Pleasure: Use of Personal Writing for Personal Growth. 224p. 1992. 12.95 (0-9626888-1-9) Ctr Pr CA.

Writing for Pleasure & Profit in Retirement. David A. Phillips. (Self Confidence - Self Competence Ser.). 52p. (Orig.). 1985. pap. 6.95 (0-932123-01-5) Stone Trail Pr.

*Writing for Publication in Reading & Language Arts. Ed. by James F. Baumann & Dale O. Johnson. LC 91-13333. 250p. 1991. reprint ed. pap. 71.30 (0-608-03471-1, 2064181) Bks Demand.

Writing for Radio. John Griffin. 1992. pap. text ed. 9.32 (0-582-07879-2) Longman.

Writing for "Real World" Reasons: A Ten Week Step-by-Step Outline for Writing, Producing & Performing Student's Original Works. Mary A. Duke. LC 93-70816. (Illus.). 100p. (Orig.). 1993. pap. 18.95 (1-883241-06-5) Cognitive Pr.

Writing for Results. Betty M. Dietsch. 512p. (C). 1985. pap. text ed. 24.00 (0-03-064037-7) HB Coll Pubs.

Writing for Results. Jeff Herrington. (Illus.). 122p. 1988. 35.00 (0-944607-02-0) J W Comm.

Writing for Science, Industry, & Technology. Howard H. Hirschhorn. LC 79-63643. 282p. 1982. 26.00 (0-442-21905-9) Van Nos Reinhold.

Writing for Social Scientists: How to Start & Finish Your Thesis, Book, or Article. Howard S. Becker. LC 85-16504. (Chicago Guides to Writing, Editing & Publishing Ser.). xii, 192p. 1986. pap. 8.95 (0-226-04108-5) U Ch Pr.

Writing for Story: Craft Secrets of Dramatic Nonfiction by a Two-Time Pulitzer Prize Winner. Jon Franklin. 288p. 1994. pap. 12.95 (0-452-27295-5, Plume) NAL-Dutton.

Writing for Study Purposes: A Teacher's Guide to Developing Individual Writing Skills. Arthur Brookes & Peter Grundy. 160p. (C). 1991. pap. text ed. 17.95 (0-521-35853-1) Cambridge U Pr.

Writing for Study Purposes: A Teacher's Guide to Developing Individual Writing Skills. Arthur Brookes & Peter Grundy. 160p. (C). 1991. text ed. 44.95 (0-521-35325-4) Cambridge U Pr.

*Writing for Success. Mary T. Brown & Frederick L. Hildebrand. LC 96-75257. 559p. (Orig.). 1996. pap. text ed. 35.95 (0-943202-54-X) H & H Pub.

Writing for Technical & Professional Journals. John H. Mitchell. LC 67-31374. (Wiley Series on Human Communication). (Illus.). 415p. reprint ed. pap. 118.30 (0-317-10698-8, 2016469) Bks Demand.

Writing for Technicians. 3rd ed. Marva T. Barnett. LC 86-19843. 358p. (C). 1987. pap. 25.95 (0-8273-2833-8) Delmar.

Writing for Technicians. 3rd ed. Marva T. Barnett. LC 86-19843. 358p. (C). 1987. teacher ed., pap. 10.00 (0-8273-2834-6) Delmar.

Writing for Television. Gerald Kelsey. pap. 17.95 (0-7136-4032-4, 93322, Pub. by A&C Black UK) Talman.

Writing for Television. Gilbert V. Seldes. LC 68-8743. (Illus.). 254p. 1968. reprint ed. text ed. 59.75 (0-8371-0217-0, SEWT, Greenwood Pr) Greenwood.

Writing for Television & Radio. 5th ed. Robert L. Hilliard. 485p. (C). 1991. pap. 32.25 (0-534-14262-1) Wadsworth Pub.

Writing for Television & Radio. 6th ed. Robert L. Hilliard. LC 96-24437. (Radio/TV/Film Ser.). (Illus.). 496p. (C). 1997. pap. 43.95 (0-534-50750-6) Wadsworth Pub.

Writing for the Business World. Robert Cason. LC 96-35424. 256p. (C). 1996. text ed. 37.27 (0-13-440264-2) P-H.

Writing for the Computer Industry. Kristin R. Woolever & Helen M. Loeb. LC 93-20056. 208p. (C). 1993. pap. text ed. 35.20 (0-13-971227-5) P-H.

Writing for the Computer Screen. Hillary Goodall & Susan S. Reilly. LC 88-22447. 137p. 1988. text ed. 45.00 (0-275-92947-7, C2947, Praeger Pubs) Greenwood.

Writing for the Corporate Market: How to Make Big Money Freelancing for Business. George Sorenson. 204p. 1990. pap. 14.95 (0-922811-07-5) Mid-List.

Writing for the Electronic Media. 2nd ed. Peter Mayeux. 464p. (C). 1993. per. write for info. (0-697-14399-6) Brown & Benchmark.

Writing for the Ethnic Markets. Meera Lester. 272p. (Orig.). 1991. pap. 14.95 (0-9622592-4-1) Writers Connection.

Writing for the Joy of It. Marshall J. Cook. 134p. (Orig.). 1990. pap. 7.95 (0-9625546-0-X) Will Beymer Pr.

Writing for the Mass Media. 3rd ed. James G. Stovall. LC 93-5369. 1993. pap. text ed. 45.00 (0-13-097965-1) P-H.

Writing for the Media. Martin J. Maloney & Paul M. Rubenstein. 1980. text ed. write for info. (0-13-970558-9) P-H.

Writing for the Media: Film, Television, Video & Radio. 2nd ed. Paul M. Rubenstein & Martin J. Maloney. (Illus.). 320p. (C). 1987. pap. text ed. 63.00 (0-13-971508-8) P-H.

Writing for the Medium: Television in Transition. Ed. by Thomas Elsaesser et al. (Orig.). (C). 1995. pap. 24.95 (90-5356-054-8, Pub. by Amsterdam U Pr NE) U of Mich Pr.

Writing for the Orchestra: An Introduction to Orchestration. Merton Shatzkin. 432p. 1993. text ed. 55.00 (0-13-953431-8) P-H.

Writing for the Press. Ed. by A. Aitchison. (C). 1989. 110.00 (0-09-182252-1, Pub. by S Thornes Pubs UK) St Mut.

Writing for the Real World see Writing on the Job

Writing for the Religious Market. Marvin Ceynar. 1986. 2.50 (0-89536-804-8, 6822) CSS OH.

*Writing for the Technical Professions. Ed. by Woolever. (C). 1998. text ed. write for info. (0-321-01122-8) Addison-Wesley Educ.

*Writing for the World Wide Web. Victor J. Vitanza. 154p. 1997. pap. 20.00 (0-205-26693-2) Allyn.

Writing for Their Lives: The Modernist Women, 1910-1940. Gillian Hanscombe & Virginia L. Smyers. (Illus.). 294p. 1988. text ed. 42.50 (1-55553-044-3); pap. text ed. 15.95 (1-55553-045-1) NE U Pr.

*Writing for Video. Gene Bjerke. LC 96-92002. 176p. (Orig.). 1997. pap. 15.95 (0-9631505-3-7) Petrel Pub.

Writing for Women: The Example of Woman As Reader in Elizabethan Romance. Caroline Lucas. (Gender in Writing Ser.). 160p. 1990. 90.00 (0-335-09018-4); pap. 32.00 (0-335-09017-6) Taylor & Francis.

Writing for Workplace Success. Gary McLean & Art Lyons. 299p. (C). 1991. pap. text ed. 17.95 (1-56118-228-1); teacher ed., pap. text ed. 8.00 (1-56118-229-X) Paradigm MN.

Writing for Your Life: A Guide & Companion to the Inner Worlds. Deena Metzger. LC 91-55323. 1992. pap. 14.00 (0-06-250612-9) Harper SF.

Writing for Your Life: Ninety-Two Contemporary Authors Talk about the Art of Writing & the Job of Publishing. Ed. by Sybil S. Steinberg. 1992. 30.00 (0-916366-75-8); pap. 18.50 (0-916366-78-2) Pushcart Pr.

Writing for Your Life No. 2: Fifty Authors Talk about the Art of Writing and the Job of Publishing. Ed. by Sybil S. Steinberg. 316p. 1994. 29.50 (0-916366-94-4) Pushcart Pr.

Writing for Your Life No. 3: 50 Authors Talk about Writing & Publishing. Ed. by Sybil S. Steinberg. 280p. 1997. 29.50 (0-916366-29-4) Pushcart Pr.

*Writing for Your Life No. 3: 50 Authors Talk about Writing & Publishing, No. 3. Ed. by Sybil S. Steinberg. 280p. 1998. pap. 15.00 (1-888889-02-0) Pushcart Pr.

Writing for Your Life, No. 2. 2nd ed. Ed. by Sybil S. Steinberg. 320p. 1995. pap. 15.00 (0-916366-87-1) Pushcart Pr.

Writing for Your Peers: The Primary Journal Paper. Sylvester P. Carter. LC 87-2513. 137p. 1987. pap. text ed. 11.95 (0-275-92229-4, B2229, Praeger Pubs) Greenwood.

Writing for Your Peers: The Primary Journal Paper. Sylvester P. Carter. LC 87-2513. 137p. 1987. text ed. 49.95 (0-275-92630-3, C2630, Praeger Pubs) Greenwood.

Writing for Your Readers: Notes on the Writer's Craft from the Boston Globe. 2nd ed. Donald M. Murray. LC 92-12446. (Illus.). 256p. 1992. pap. text ed. 14.95 (1-56440-051-4) Globe Pequot.

Writing for 100 Days: A Student-Centered Approach to Composition & Creative Writing. Gabriel Arquilevich. 105p. 1995. pap. text ed. write for info. (0-9649042-0-9) G Arquilevich.

Writing Foundations Instructor's Resource Guide. (Foundations TV Ser.). 195p. 1990. ring bd. 180.00 (0-910475-91-1) KET.

Writing Foundations Student's Guide. (Foundations TV Ser.). 142p. 1990. 20.00 (0-910475-89-X) KET.

Writing from A to Z: The Easy-to-Use Reference Handbook. Sally B. Reagan et al. LC 93-39639. 518p. (C). 1994. spiral bd. 22.95 (1-55934-025-8, 1025) Mayfield Pub.

*Writing from A to Z: The Easy-to-Use Referency Handbook. 2nd rev. ed. Sally B. Ebest et al. LC 96-46333. xxvi, 550p. 1997. pap. text ed. 22.95 (1-55934-707-4, 1707) Mayfield Pub.

Writing from Canada. Jim Rice & Mike Hayhoe. LC 93-11687. (Figures in a Landscape Ser.). 1996. pap. 9.95 (0-521-42305-8) Cambridge U Pr.

Writing from Experience. Marcella Frank. 288p. (C). 1982. pap. text ed. 18.75 (0-13-970285-7) P-H.

Writing from Experience. Ed. by Richard A. Condon & Burton O. Kurth. LC 72-8541. (Essay Index Reprint Ser.). 1977. reprint ed. 21.95 (0-8369-7310-0) Ayer.

Writing from History: The Rhetoric of Exemplarity in Renaissance Literature. Timothy Hampton. LC 90-1322. 328p. 1990. pap. 17.95 (0-8014-9709-4) Cornell U Pr.

Writing from Home: A Portfolio of Homeschooled Student Writing. Susan P. Richman. (Illus.). 372p. (Orig.). 1990. 16.95 (0-929446-02-X); pap. 8.95 (0-929446-03-8) PA Homeschoolers.

*Writing from India. Lakshmi Holmstrom & Mike Hayhoe. (Figures in a Landscape Ser.). 1911. write for info. (0-521-42380-5) Cambridge U Pr.

*Writing from Life: Collecting & Connecting. Phyllis Ballata. LC 96-38642. x, 422p. (Orig.). (C). 1997. pap. text ed. 26.95 (1-55934-555-1, 1555) Mayfield Pub.

Writing from Life: Telling Your Soul's Story. Susan W. Albert. LC 96-20142. (Inner Work Book Ser.). 240p. (Orig.). 1997. pap. 16.95 (0-87477-848-4, Tarcher Putnam) Putnam Pub Group.

*Writing from Life Instructor's Manual. Phyllis Ballata. 107p. (Orig.). (C). 1997. pap. text ed. write for info. (1-55934-556-X, 1556) Mayfield Pub.

*Writing from Personal Experience. Nancy D. Kelton. LC 97-282. 208p. 1997. 16.99 (0-89879-789-6, Wrtrs Digest Bks) F & W Pubns Inc.

Writing from Scratch: For Business. Arthur G. Elser. 168p. 1990. 24.95 (0-8476-7632-3) Rowman.

Writing from Scratch: Freelancing. John Calderazzo. 168p. 1990. pap. 10.95 (0-8226-3007-9) Littlefield.

Writing from Scratch: Freelancing. John Calderazzo. 168p. 1990. 24.95 (0-8476-7633-1) Rowman.

Writing from Sources. 4th ed. Brenda Scott. 1995. pap. text ed. 23.50 (0-312-10132-5) St Martin.

Writing from Start to Finish: A Rhetoric with Readings. Jeffrey L. Duncan. 474p. (C). 1985. pap. text ed. 17.50 (0-15-598260-5) HB Coll Pubs.

Writing from Start to Finish: Teacher's Manual. John Schultz. 246p. 1982. teacher ed., pap. text ed. 12.00 (0-86709-103-7, 0103) Boynton Cook Pubs.

Writing from Start to Finish: The "Story Workshop" Basic Forms Rhetoric-Reader. John Schultz. LC 90-40075. 258p. (C). 1990. pap. text ed. 23.00 (0-86709-267-X, 0267) Boynton Cook Pubs.

Writing from the Body. John Lee & Ceci Miller-Kritsberg. 160p. 1994. pap. 9.95 (0-312-11536-9) St Martin.

Writing from the Center. (Indiannual Ser.: No. 5). 147p. 1990. pap. 6.95 (1-880649-24-1) Writ Ctr Pr.

Writing from the Center. Scott R. Sanders. LC 95-7146. 216p. 1995. text ed. 20.00 (0-253-32941-8) Ind U Pr.

Writing from the Exterior Dramatic Perspective: A New Vision for Literature. Laurine Ark. Ed. by Tatiana Stoumen. LC 95-83137. 170p. (Orig.). 1996. pap. 24.95 (0-9648009-1-8) Ft Tryon Pr. Finally, there is a method to teach any writer, regardless of age or level of experience, to create compelling & satisfying written works of art. All the secrets to literary success are revealed in this revolutionary approach to writing. Here, for the first time, author & educator Laurine Ark, guides writers through this extraordinary series of fiction writing techniques. Ms. Ark shows writers how to incorporate these new concepts into any type of writing & immediately begin the rise to excellence. Established writers will find this complete & practical guide brings new depth, insight, energy, & potency to their work.

An Asterisk (*) at the beginning of an entry indicates that the title is appearing in BIP for the first time.

Writing from the Heart: Inspirations & Exercises for Women Who Want to Write. Leslea Newman. 160p. 1993. pap. 12.95 (*0-89594-641-6*) Crossing Pr.

***Writing from the Heart: Tapping the Power of Your Inner Voice.** Nancy S. Aronie. 256p. 1998. pap. 13.95 (*0-7868-8287-5*) Hyperion.

***Writing from the Inner Self.** Elaine Hughes. LC 90-4630. 1991. 14.95 (*0-06-016572-3*) HarpC.

Writing from the Inner Self. Elaine F. Hughes. LC 93-14406. (Orig.). (C). 1993. 18.00 (*0-06-501437-5*) Addson-Wesley Educ.

Writing from the Inner Self. Elaine F. Hughes. LC 93-14406. (Orig.). (C). 1993. 10.00 (*0-06-501890-7*) Addson-Wesley Educ.

Writing from the Inner Self. Elaine F. Hughes. LC 90-4630. 208p. (Orig.). 1992. reprint ed. pap. 12.00 (*0-06-272023-6*, Harper Ref) HarpC.

Writing from the Inside. George Core & Walter Sullivan. (C). 1983. pap. text ed. 22.95 (*0-393-95246-0*) Norton.

Writing from the Inside. George Core & Walter Sullivan. (C). 1983. Instr's. manual. teacher ed., pap. text ed. write for info. (*0-393-95337-8*) Norton.

Writing from the Inside Out. Christopher C. Burnham. 296p. (C). 1988. pap. text ed. 17.00 (*0-15-597865-9*); pap. text ed. 3.00 (*0-15-597866-7*) HB Coll Pubs.

Writing from the Left. Alan M. Wald. 270p. (C). 1994. pap. 19.00 (*1-85984-001-9*, B4769, Pub. by Vrso UK) Norton.

Writing from the Left. Alan M. Wald. 270p. (C). (gr. 13). 1994. text ed. 60.00 (*1-85984-906-7*, B4765, Pub. by Vrso UK) Norton.

Writing from the Margins: Power & Pedagogy for Teachers of Composition. Carolyn E. Hill. 304p. (C). 1990. pap. 21.00 (*0-19-506637-5*) OUP.

Writing from Within: A Step-by-Step Guide to Telling Your Life's Story. 2nd ed. Bernard Selling. 288p. (C). 1990. reprint ed. lib. bdg. 33.00 (*0-8095-6308-8*) Borgo Pr.

Writing from Within: A Unique Guide to Writing Your Life's Stories. 2nd rev. ed. Bernard Selling. Ed. by Jackie Melvin. LC 90-47964. 288p. 1990. pap. 11.95 (*0-89793-079-7*) Hunter Hse.

***Writing from Within: A Unique Guide to Writing Your Life's Stories.** 3rd ed. Bernard Selling. LC 97-15745. 1997. pap. text ed. 13.95 (*0-89793-217-X*) Hunter Hse.

Writing Fun with Phonics. Jeri Carroll & Dennis Kear. (Illus.). 160p. (J). (ps-2). 1992. student ed. 12.99 (*0-86653-686-8*, 1420) Good Apple.

***Writing Fundamentals: Robinson's Resource Guide to Grammar & Writing.** Zan D. Robinson, Sr. 173p. (Orig.). (C). 1997. pap. text ed. 22.50 (*0-9635587-5-7*) E W Connors.

Writing Game: A Biography of Will Irwin. Robert V. Hudson. LC 82-150. (Illus.). 222p. 1982. reprint ed. pap. 63.30 (*0-608-00022-1*, 2060788) Bks Demand.

***Writing Games.** Charles Hadfield & Jill Hadfield. 1989. pap. text ed. write for info. (*0-17-555898-1*) Addison-Wesley.

***Writing GNU Emacs Extensions.** Ed. by Andy Oram. (Illus.). (Orig.). 1997. pap. 29.95 (*1-56592-261-1*) OReilly & Assocs.

Writing Good Prose: A Simple Structural Approach. 4th ed. Alexander E. Jones & Claude W. Faulkner. 269p. 1979. pap. write for info. (*0-02-361290-8*, Macmillan Coll) P-H.

Writing Good Sentences. 3rd ed. Claude W. Faulkner. 320p. (C). 1981. pap. text ed. 44.00 (*0-02-336470-X*, Macmillan Coll) P-H.

Writing Good Sentences. 3rd rev. ed. Faulkner. 1985. 16.95 (*0-684-41242-X*) S&S Trade.

Writing, Grammar, & Usage. Carolyn O'Hearn. 433p. (C). 1988. pap. text ed. 46.00 (*0-02-389130-0*, Macmillan Coll) P-H.

***Writing, Grammar, Usage & Style Quick Review.** Jean Eggenschwiler. 230p. (Orig.). (J). (gr. 10-12). 1997. student ed., pap. text ed. 9.95 (*0-8220-5367-5*) Cliffs.

Writing Grant Proposals That Win. Phale Hale. 1993. spiral bd. 75.00 (*0-937925-96-9*, PTW) Capitol Publns.

Writing Great Characters: The Psychology of Character Development. Michael Halperin. 1996. pap. text ed. 19.95 (*0-943728-79-7*) Lone Eagle Pub.

Writing Great Screenplays for Television & Film. Dona Cooper. 1994. pap. 14.00 (*0-671-84783-X*) P-H Gen Ref & Trav.

Writing Ground Zero: Japanese Literature & the Atomic Bomb. John W. Treat. (Illus.). 508p. 1994. 29.95 (*0-226-81177-8*) U Ch Pr.

Writing Ground Zero: Japanese Literature & the Atomic Bomb. John W. Treat. (Illus.). 488p. (C). 1996. pap. text ed. 16.95 (*0-226-81178-6*) U Ch Pr.

Writing Groups: History, Theory & Implications. Anne R. Gere. LC 86-26137. (Studies in Writing & Rhetoric). 128p. 1987. pap. text ed. 12.95 (*0-8093-1354-5*) S Ill U Pr.

Writing Guide for Air Force Efficiency Reports. Douglas L. Drewry. 389p. (Orig.). 1990. pap. 23.95 (*0-9623673-3-8*) Prof Mgmt Spectrum.

Writing Guide for Army Efficiency Reports. Douglas L. Drewry. 389p. (Orig.). 1990. pap. 23.95 (*0-9623673-2-X*) Prof Mgmt Spectrum.

Writing Guides. 3rd ed. Sandra Panman & Richard Panman. (YA). (gr. 6-12). 1996. pap. text ed. 15.95 (*0-912813-25-3*) Active Lrn.

Writing Habit. David Huddle. LC 93-38327. 219p. (Orig.). (C). 1994. reprint ed. pap. 14.95 (*0-87451-668-4*) U Pr of New Eng.

Writing Handbook. 2nd rev. ed. Ed. by Michael P. Kammer et al. LC 96-1445. 908p. (C). 1996. 29.95 (*0-8294-0910-6*) Loyola Pr.

Writing Health Care Plans, a Handbook for Dietary Managers. 3rd rev. ed. Karen Walton. 162p. (C). 1995. pap. text ed. 16.00 (*1-877735-07-8*, 108) M&H Pub Co TX.

Writing High-Tech Copy That Sells. Janice M. King. 256p. 1995. pap. text ed. 17.95 (*0-471-05846-7*) Wiley.

Writing High-Tech Copy That Sells. Janice M. King. 256p. 1995. text ed. 39.95 (*0-471-04259-5*) Wiley.

Writing Historical Fiction. Rhona Martin. 96p. 1988. 12.95 (*0-312-01848-7*) St Martin.

Writing Historical Fiction. Rhonda Martin. pap. 15.95 (*0-7136-4068-5*, 93321, Pub. by A&C Black UK) Talman.

Writing Histories of Rhetoric. Ed. by Victor J. Vitanza. LC 92-46300. 384p. (C). 1993. 39.95 (*0-8093-1902-0*) S Ill U Pr.

Writing History: Essay on Epistemology. Paul Veyne. Tr. by Mina Moore-Rinvolucri. LC 84-7281. 352p. 1984. reprint ed. pap. 100.40 (*0-608-02295-0*, 2062936) Bks Demand.

Writing History & Making Policy, Vol. VI: The Cold War, Vietnam, & Revisionism. Richard A. Melanson. LC 83-10362. (Exxon Education Foundation Series on Rhetoric & Political Discourse). 260p. (C). 1983. pap. text ed. 21.00 (*0-8191-3353-1*); lib. bdg. 50.50 (*0-8191-3352-3*) U Pr of Amer.

Writing History As a Prophet: Postmodernist Innovations of the Historical Novel. Elisabeth Wesseling. LC 91-23204. (Utrecht Publications in General & Comparative Literature: Vol. 26). ix, 218p. 1991. 65.00 (*1-55619-425-0*) Benjamins North Am.

Writing History Papers: An Introduction. James D. Bennett & Lowell H. Harrison. LC 78-66987. 64p. 1979. pap. text ed. 6.95 (*0-88273-105-X*) Forum Pr IL.

Writing Home. Alan Bennett. LC 95-16075. (Illus.). 417p. 1995. 25.00 (*0-679-44489-0*) Random.

Writing Home. Katharyn Machan Aal & Barbara Crooker. LC 83-1715. (Orig.). 1983. pap. 4.50 (*0-935020-08-X*) Gehry Pr.

***Writing Home: American Women Abroad, 1830-1920.** Mary S. Schriber. LC 96-53086. 1997. 50.00 (*0-8139-1730-1*) U Pr of Va.

***Writing Home: American Women Abroad, 1830-1920.** Mary S. Schriber. Date not set. pap. 18.50 (*0-8139-1779-4*) U Pr of Va.

Writing Home: Immigrants in Brazil & the United States, 1890-1891. Witold Kula et al. (East European Monographs: No. 210). 698p. 1987. text ed. 103.00 (*0-88033-107-0*) East Eur Monographs.

***Writing Horror: A Handbook by the Horror Writers Association.** Mort Castle. LC 97-17493. 1997. pap. text ed. 17.99 (*0-89879-798-5*) F & W Pubns Inc.

Writing Horror & the Body: The Fiction of Stephen King, Clive Barker, & Anne Rice. Linda Badley. LC 95-38665. (Contributions to the Study of Popular Culture Ser.: No. 51). 192p. 1996. text ed. 55.00 (*0-313-29716-9*, Greenwood Pr) Greenwood.

Writing HotJava Applets with CD-ROM. John Rodley. 1996. pap. 39.99 incl. cd-rom (*1-883577-78-0*) Coriolis Grp.

Writing How & Why: Instructional Manual to Accompany Suki. Ed. by Matthew Lipman & Ann M. Sharp. 384p. 1980. teacher ed. 45.00 (*0-916834-14-X*, TX 726-631) Inst Advncmnt Philos Child.

Writing Huck Finn: Mark Twain's Creative Process. Victor A. Doyno. LC 91-25114. (Illus.). 290p. (C). 1992. pap. text ed. 16.95 (*0-8122-1448-X*) U of Pa Pr.

Writing Ideas Ready to Use! Barbara Gruber. (Instant Idea Bks.). (Illus.). 64p. 1983. 7.95 (*0-86734-050-9*, FS-8304) Schaffer Pubns.

Writing Illinois: The Prairie, Lincoln, & Chicago. James Hurt. 168p. 1992. text ed. 29.95 (*0-252-01850-8*) U of Ill Pr.

Writing Implements & Accessories. Whalley. 1975. 28.00 (*0-8103-2017-7*) Gale.

Writing Improvement for Business Communication. Zane K. Quible. 1995. pap. text ed. 24.60 (*0-13-367574-2*) P-H.

Writing in a Bilingual Program: Habia Una Vez. Carole Edelsky. Ed. by Marcia Farr. LC 85-31569. (Writing Research Ser.: Vol. 5). 248p. 1986. pap. 39.50 (*0-89391-381-2*); text ed. 73.25 (*0-89391-304-9*) Ablex Pub.

Writing in a Film Age: Essays by Contemporary Novelists. Ed. by Keith Cohen. 208p. (C). 1991. pap. 17.50 (*0-87081-180-0*); text ed. 29.95 (*0-87081-183-5*) Univ Pr Colo.

Writing in a Milieu of Utility: The Move to Technical Communication in American Engineering Programs 1850-1950. Teresa C. Kynell. (Communication, Culture & Information Studies). 120p. 1996. pap. 20.95 (*1-56750-193-1*); text ed. 73.25 (*1-56750-192-3*) Ablex Pub.

Writing in a Milieu of Utility: The Move to Technical Communication in American Engineering Programs, 1850-1950. Teresa C. Kynell. LC 96-18487. (Communication, Culture & Information Studies). 1996. 36.50 (*1-56750-264-4*); pap. 39.50 (*1-56750-265-2*) Ablex Pub.

Writing in a Modern Temper: Essays on French Literature & Thought, in Honor of Henri Peyre. Ed. by Mary A. Caws. (Stanford French & Italian Studies: Vol. 33). 286p. 1984. pap. 46.50 (*0-915838-04-4*) Anma Libri.

***Writing in a New Convertible with the Top Down: A Unique Guide for Writers.** rev. ed. Sheila Bender & Christi Killien. LC 97-7219. 160p. 1997. reprint ed. pap. 12.95 (*0-936085-38-X*) Blue Heron OR.

Writing in a Second Language: Issues from L1 & L2 Theory. Ed. by Bruce Leeds. LC 95-15296. 1996. pap. text ed. 33.33 (*0-201-82589-9*) Addison-Wesley.

Writing in Academic Disciplines. David A. Jolliffe. (Advances in Writing Research Ser.: Vol. 2). 272p. 1988. text ed. 73.25 (*0-89391-434-7*) Ablex Pub.

Writing in Action. Paul Mills. LC 95-17125. 223p. (C). 1995. pap. 15.95 (*0-415-11989-8*) Routledge.

Writing in Action. Paul Mills. LC 95-17125. 208p. (C). (gr. 13). 1995. text ed. 49.95 (*0-415-11988-X*) Routledge.

Writing in an Alien World: Basic Writing & the Struggle for Equality in Higher Education. Deborah Mutnick. LC 95-44181. (Crosscurrent Ser.). 221p. 1995. pap. text ed. 24.50 (*0-86709-371-4*, 0371) Boynton Cook Pubs.

Writing in Context. Connelly. (C). 1996. pap. text ed. 26.00 (*0-15-503169-4*) HarBrace.

***Writing in Context & Action.** Ed. by Laure. (C). 1983. text ed. write for info. (*0-321-01590-8*) Addison-Wesley Educ.

Writing in Dante's Cult of Truth: From Borges to Boccaccio. Maria R. Menocal. LC 90-45998. 232p. 1991. text ed. 41.00 (*0-8223-1104-6*); pap. text ed. 16.95 (*0-8223-1117-8*) Duke.

Writing in Focus. Ed. by Florian Coulmas & Konrad Ehlich. LC 83-13095. (Trends in Linguistics, Studies & Monographs: No. 24). viii, 405p. 1983. 126.95 (*90-279-3359-6*) Mouton.

Writing in General & the Short Story in Particular. Rust Hills. 1987. pap. 11.95 (*0-395-44268-0*) HM.

Writing in Groups: New Techniques for Good Writing Without Drills. 4th ed. Goran G. Moberg. 200p. 1994. spiral bd. 21.95 (*0-8403-9342-3*) Kendall-Hunt.

Writing in Hope & Fear: Literature As Politics in Postwar Australia. John McLaren. 256p. (C). 1996. text ed. 64.95 (*0-521-56146-9*) Cambridge U Pr.

Writing in Limbo: Modernism & Caribbean Literature. Simon Gikandi. LC 91-23284. 272p. 1992. 42.50 (*0-8014-2575-1*) Cornell U Pr.

***Writing in Maine, New Hampshire & Vermont: Guide to Publishers, Writers Groups, Educational Opportunities & More.** (Writing in...Ser.). 200p. (Orig.). 1997. pap. 18.95 (*0-9631441-5-4*) Writers Wrld.

Writing in Modern Classic Society. Raymond Williams. 271p. (C). 1985. pap. text ed. 19.00 (*0-86091-772-X*, Pub. by Vrso UK) Norton.

***Writing in Multicultural Settings.** Ed. by Carol Severino et al. LC 96-49853. (Research & Scholarship in Composition Ser.: No. 5). xi, 370p. 1997. pap. 19.75 (*0-87352-584-1*, RS05P); lib. bdg. 37.50 (*0-87352-583-3*, RS05C) Modern Lang.

Writing in Multilingual Classrooms. 1995. student ed. 179.00 (*0-7049-0771-2*, Pub. by Multilingual Matters UK); teacher ed., pap. 12.95 (*0-7049-0772-0*, Pub. by Multilingual Matters UK) Taylor & Francis.

Writing in Nonacademic Settings. Ed. by Lee Odell & Dixie Goswami. LC 85-27239. (Guilford Perspectives in Writing Research Ser.). 553p. 1986. pap. text ed. 26.95 (*0-89862-906-3*); lib. bdg. 55.00 (*0-89862-252-2*) Guilford Pr.

Writing in Ohio: Guide to Publishers, Writers' Groups, Educational Opportunities & More... Lavern Hall. LC 91-68414. 208p. 1992. pap. 11.95 (*0-9631441-3-8*) Writers Wrld.

Writing in Ohio: Guide to Publishers, Writer's Groups, Educational Opportunities & More... 2nd ed. Lea L. Oldham. (Writing in...Ser.). 288p. 1995. pap. text ed. 16.95 (*0-9631441-4-6*) Writers Wrld.

Writing in Organizations: Purposes, Strategies & Processes. P. Maki & C. Schilling. 416p. 1987. pap. text ed. write for info. (*0-07-030361-4*) McGraw.

Writing in Parts: Imitation & Exchange in Nineteenth-Century Literature. Kevin McLaughlin. (Illus.). 200p. 1995. 32.50 (*0-8047-2411-3*) Stanford U Pr.

***Writing in Primary Grades.** Wagstaff. 1991. pap. text ed. write for info. (*0-582-06632-8*, Pub. by Longman UK) Longman.

***Writing in Psychoanalysis: A Clinical Synthesis.** Ed. by Emma Piccioli et al. 144p. 1996. pap. 24.95 (*0-88163-239-2*) Analytic Pr.

Writing in Psychology: A Student Guide. 2nd ed. T. Raymond Smith. 214p. 1996. student ed., pap. text ed. 15.95 (*0-471-15341-9*) Wiley.

***Writing in Psychology: A Training Guide.** Szuchman. (Psychology Ser.). (C). Date not set. pap. 17.95 (*0-534-34942-0*) Brooks-Cole.

Writing in Real Time: Modeling Production Processes. Ann Matsuhashi. Ed. by Marcia Farr. LC 86-22214. (Writing Research Ser.: Vol. 16). 320p. (C). 1987. pap. 39.50 (*0-89391-417-7*); text ed. 73.25 (*0-89391-400-2*) Ablex Pub.

Writing in Restaurants. David Mamet. 176p. 1987. pap. 9.95 (*0-14-008981-0*, Penguin Bks) Viking Penguin.

Writing in Schools (ECT418) Deakin University Press Staff. (C). 1989. 71.00 (*0-7300-0633-6*, Pub. by Deakin Univ AT); student ed. 86.00 (*0-7300-0632-8*, Pub. by Deakin Univ AT) St Mut.

Writing in Service-Learning Courses. Linda A. Kassner & Terence Collins. Ed. by Lillian Bridwell-Bowles & Mark Olson. (Technical Reports: No. 9). 10p. (Orig.). (C). 1994. pap. 2.00 (*1-881221-16-4*) U Minn Ctr Interdis.

Writing in Subject-Matter Fields: A Bibliographic Guide, with Annotations & Writing Assignments. Eva M. Burkett. LC 76-30397. 204p. 1977. 20.00 (*0-8108-1012-3*) Scarecrow.

Writing in the Academic Disciplines, 1870-1990: A Curricular History. David R. Russell. 208p. (C). 1991. 24.95 (*0-8093-1596-3*); pap. 16.95 (*0-8093-1597-1*) S Ill U Pr.

Writing in the Center: Teaching in a Writing Center Setting. Irene L. Clark. 180p. (C). 1994. per. 24.09 (*0-8403-7558-1*) Kendall-Hunt.

Writing in the Community. Ed. by David Barton & Roz Ivanic. (Written Communication Annual Ser.: Vol. 6). (Illus.). 320p. 1991. 55.00 (*0-8039-3632-X*); pap. 24.95 (*0-8039-3633-8*) Sage.

Writing in the Design Disciplines. Roger Martin et al. Ed. by Lillian Bridwell-Bowles et al. (Monographs: Vol. 3). (Illus.). 108p. (Orig.). 1992. pap. 6.00 (*1-881221-02-4*) U Minn Ctr Interdis.

Writing in the Disciplines: A Reader for Writers. 3rd ed. Mary L. Kennedy et al. LC 95-17174. 1995. pap. text ed. 31.00 (*0-13-141400-3*) P-H Gen Ref & Trav.

Writing in the Father's House: The Emergence of the Feminine in the Quebec Literary Tradition. Patricia Smart. 304p. 1991. 50.00 (*0-8020-2732-6*); pap. 18.95 (*0-8020-6771-9*) U of Toronto Pr.

Writing in the Feminine: Feminism & Experimental Writing in Quebec. Karen Gould. LC 89-31608. 326p. (C). 1990. text ed. 34.95 (*0-8093-1582-3*) S Ill U Pr.

Writing in the Humanities. (C). 1995. pap. text ed. write for info. (*0-15-503745-5*) HB Coll Pubs.

Writing in the Information Age: A Sales & Marketing Approach. Richard Peres. 224p. (C). 1991. teacher ed. 8.00 (*1-56118-326-1*); pap. text ed. 13.25 (*1-56118-324-5*) Paradigm MN.

Writing in the Liberal Arts Tradition. 2nd ed. James L. Kinneavy et al. 672p. (C). 1990. pap. text ed. 39.50 (*0-06-043663-8*) Addson-Wesley Educ.

Writing in the Margin: Spanish Literature of the Golden Age. Paul J. Smith. 240p. 1988. 65.00 (*0-19-815847-5*) OUP.

Writing in the New Nation: Prose, Print, & Politics in the Early United States. Larzer Ziff. 224p. (C). 1991. text ed. 30.00 (*0-300-05040-2*) Yale U Pr.

***Writing in the Primary School.** O'Brien. 1992. pap. text ed. write for info. (*0-582-87139-5*, Pub. by Longman UK) Longman.

Writing in the Real Classroom. Les Parsons. LC 90-28694. 112p. 1991. pap. text ed. 16.50 (*0-435-08587-5*, 08587) Heinemann.

Writing in the Schools: Improvement Through Effective Leadership. Allan A. Glatthorn. LC 81-210342. (Illus.). 95p. reprint ed. pap. 27.10 (*0-685-23750-8*, 2032791) Bks Demand.

***Writing in the Sciences.** Katz. Date not set. pap. text ed. 26.50 (*0-312-11971-2*) St Martin.

Writing in the Shadow: Newspapers & Books Published by the Resistance Movements of Occupied Europe During the Second World War. Harry Stone. (Illus.). 224p. 1996. 47.50 (*0-7146-3424-7*, Pub. by F Cass Pubs UK) Intl Spec Bk.

Writing in the Shadow: Newspapers & Books Published by the Resistance Movements of Occupied Europe During the Second World War. Harry Stone. (Illus.). 224p. (Orig.). 1996. pap. 25.00 (*0-7146-4257-6*, Pub. by F Cass Pubs UK) Intl Spec Bk.

Writing in the Technical Fields: A Step-by- Step Guide for Engineers, Scientists, & Technicians. Mike Markel. LC 93-26817. (Illus.). 296p. 1994. 34.95 (*0-7803-1059-4*, PC3855); pap. 34.95 (*0-7803-1036-5*, PC3855) Inst Electrical.

Writing in the Workplace: New Research Perspectives. Ed. by Rachel Spilka. LC 92-13211. 320p. (C). 1993. 34.95 (*0-8093-1724-9*) S Ill U Pr.

Writing in Three Dimensions. Linda T. Woodson & Margaret W. Batschelet. LC 95-610. 1995. pap. text ed. 34.00 (*0-205-15795-5*) Allyn.

Writing in Time: A Political Chronicle. Jonathan Schell. LC 96-8516. 416p. 1997. 24.95 (*1-55921-177-6*) Moyer Bell.

Writing Incisively: Do It Yourself Prose Surgery. William Strong. 1991. pap. text ed. write for info. (*0-07-062270-1*) McGraw.

Writing "Independent" History: African Historiography, 1960-1980. Caroline Neale. LC 84-15756. (Contributions in Afro-American & African Studies: No. 85). ix, 208p. 1985. text ed. 49.95 (*0-313-24652-1*, NID/, Greenwood Pr) Greenwood.

Writing India, 1757-1990: The Literature of British India. Ed. by Bart Moore-Gilbert. LC 95-31538. 256p. 1996. text ed. 74.95 (*0-7190-4265-8*, Pub. by Manchester Univ Pr UK); text ed. 24.95 (*0-7190-4266-6*, Pub. by Manchester Univ Pr UK) St Martin.

Writing in/Out of Sequence. Mark Sonnenfeld. 32p. Date not set. pap. 3.00 (*1-887379-03-7*) M Sonnenfeld.

Writing Inside & Out: A Content-Centered Approach to Writing. Michael J. Quinn et al. LC 96-1364. (C). 1997. text ed. 29.50 (*0-673-46988-3*) Addson-Wesley Educ.

***Writing Inside & Out: A Content-Centered Approach to Writing.** Judy Ryan. 1997. pap. text ed. 28.50 (*0-8230-5014-9*) Watsn-Guptill.

Writing Insights: What Professional Writers Know about Structure & Content. Paul Aamot. 89p. 1993. pap. text ed. 4.95 (*0-9637070-0-0*) Arden Pubs.

W

*Writing Inspirations: A Fundex of Individualized Activities for English Language Practice. Arlene Marcus. Ed. by Raymond C. Clark. (Illus.). 96p. (Orig.). 1995. pap. text ed. 20.00 (0-86647-092-1) Pro Lingua.

Writing Instruction for Verbally Talented Youth: The Johns Hopkins Model. rev. ed. Ben Reynolds et al. 204p. (YA). 1994. teacher ed., pap. text ed. 27.00 (1-881622-14-2) JHU IAAY.

Writing Instruction in Nineteenth-Century American Colleges. James A. Berlin. LC 83-20116. (Studies in Writing & Rhetoric). 128p. (Orig.). 1984. pap. 12.95 (0-8093-1166-6) S Ill U Pr.

Writing Instruction in the Intermediate Grades: What Is Said, What Is Done, What Is Understood. Robin Bright. 134p. (Orig.). 1995. pap. 14.95 (0-87207-124-3, 124-3) Intl Reading.

Writing-Intensive Courses: Possible Criteria, National Patterns, & Resources. Lillian Bridwell-Bowles et al. (Technical Reports: No. 11). 25p. (Orig.). (C). 1994. pap. 3.00 (1-881221-18-0) U Minn Ctr Interdis.

Writing Intermediate. 1992. 6.95 (0-19-453405-7) OUP.

Writing Ireland: Colonialism, Nationalism & Culture. David Cairns & Shaun Richards. LC 88-1540. (Cultural Politics Ser.). 192p. 1988. text ed. 24.95 (0-7190-2372-6, Pub. by Manchester Univ Pr UK) St Martin.

Writing Is a Social Disease. Gerald Kaminski. 86p. 1986. pap. 6.95 (0-931896-06-1) Cove View.

Writing Is an Aid to Memory. Lyn Hejinian. (Sun & Moon Classics Ser.: No. 141). 64p. 1996. pap. 9.95 (1-55713-271-2) Sun & Moon CA.

Writing is Child's Play: A Guide for Teaching Young Children to Write. 2nd ed. Donna Connell. (J). (ps-3). 1993. pap. 12.95 (0-201-81884-1) Addison-Wesley.

Writing Is Critical Action. Tilly Warnock. LC 88-30602. (Illus.). 478p. reprint ed. pap. 136.30 (0-7837-4748-9, 2044557) Bks Demand.

Writing is Fighting: Forty-Three Years of Boxing on Paper. Ishmael Reed. 1998. pap. write for info. (0-201-48399-8) Addison-Wesley.

Writing Is Learning: Strategies for Math, Science, Social Studies, & Language Arts. Howard Wills. LC 93-29626. 140p. (Orig.). 1993. pap. 14.95 (1-883790-00-X, EDINFO Pr) Grayson Bernard Pubs.

Writing Is Thinking. Edith T. Sharp. (Illus.). 210p. 1987. pap. text ed. 19.95 (0-9619393-0-3) Saxon Pr.

Writing It Down. 1993. 8.60 (0-88336-381-X) New Readers.

Writing It Down. Vicki Cobb. LC 88-14191. (Illus.). 32p. (J). (gr. k-3). 1989. lib. bdg. 12.89 (0-397-32327-1, Lipp Jr Bks) HarpC Child Bks.

Writing It down for James: Writers on Life & Craft. Ed. by Kurt Brown. 216p. (Orig.). 1995. pap. 12.00 (0-8070-6349-5) Beacon Pr.

*Writing It Out: Self Awareness & Self Help Through Journaling. Lisa M. Schab. (Illus.). xiv, 217p. (Orig.). 1996. pap. 12.95 (0-9653988-0-3) Wainsley Pr.

Writing Jazz. Ed. by David Meltzer. (Illus.). 208p. (Orig.). 1997. pap. 13.95 (1-56279-096-X) Mercury Hse Inc.

Writing Journals: Activities Across the Curriculum. Linda Western. 160p. (J). (gr. 4-6). 1995. pap. 11.95 (0-673-36177-2, GoodYrBooks) Addson-Wesley Educ.

Writing Joyce: A Semiotics of the Joyce System. Lorraine Weir. LC 88-45501. (Advances in Semiotics Ser.). (Illus.). 152p. 1989. 10.95 (0-253-36432-9) Ind U Pr.

Writing Legal Descriptions in Conjunction with Survey Boundary Control. 4th ed. Gurdon H. Wattles. LC 78-68650. 346p. 1979. reprint ed. 30.00 (0-9606962-8-8) Wattles Pubns.

Writing Lesson. Richard Grabman. (Chapbook Series I: No. 4). 16p. 1980. pap. 2.00 (1-880649-04-7) Writ Ctr Pr.

*Writing Letters. Date not set. pap. text ed. write for info. (0-85896-904-1) Addison-Wesley.

Writing Letters & Thank-You Notes. Carson & Dellosa. (Home Workbooks Ser.). (Illus.). 64p. (Orig.). (J). (gr. 2-5). 1995. wbk. ed., pap. 2.49 (0-88724-338-X, CD6835) Carson-Dellos.

Writing Letters & Words. Bearl Brooks. (Handwriting Ser.). 24p. (gr. k-1). 1980. student ed. 5.00 (0-8209-0268-3, W-0) ESP.

Writing Letters, Memos & Reports. Joan Minninger & C. Delos Putz, Jr. (Illus.). 162p. (Orig.). 1981. pap. 11.95 (0-9604042-2-8) Wkshops Innovative Teach.

Writing Letters That Sell: You, Your Ideas, Products & Services. Patrick C. Monaghan. LC 68-19911. 205p. reprint ed. pap. 58.50 (0-317-58163-5, 2029743) Bks Demand.

*Writing Lewis Structures. Roberts. Date not set. 1.20 (0-7167-9191-9) W H Freeman.

Writing Lewis Symbols & Lewis Structures. H. Anthony Neidig & J. N. Spencer. (Modular Laboratory Program in Chemistry Ser.). 8p. (C). 1994. pap. text ed. 1.35 (0-87540-434-0, STRC 434-0) Chem Educ Res.

Writing Life. Neil Baldwin. (Illus.). 128p. 1995. pap. 15.00 (0-679-76983-8) Random.

Writing Life. Annie Dillard. 1990. pap. 8.95 (0-06-092988-X, PL) HarpC.

Writing Life. Annie Dillard. LC 89-45034. 1990. reprint ed. pap. 11.00 (0-06-091988-4, Harp PBks) HarpC.

Writing Like a Woman. Alicia S. Ostriker. (Poets on Poetry Ser.). 200p. 1983. pap. 13.95 (0-472-06347-2) U of Mich Pr.

Writing Like an Enginner: A Rhetorical Education. Dorothy Winsor. (Rhetoric, Knowledge, & Society Ser.). 136p. 1996. 29.95 (0-8058-1957-6); pap. text ed. 14.95 (0-8058-1958-4) L Erlbaum Assocs.

Writing Links. Cozzens. (C). 1998. pap. text ed. 19.00 (0-15-505324-8) HB Coll Pubs.

*Writing Linux Device Drivers. Ed. by Andy Oram. (Orig.). 1997. pap. write for info. (1-56592-292-1) OReilly & Assocs.

Writing Literary Features. Berner. (Communication Textbook-McCombs Sub-Series). 115p. (Orig.). (C). 1988. text ed. 29.95 (0-8058-0278-9); pap. text ed. 14.95 (0-8058-0279-7) L Erlbaum Assocs.

Writing Lives Is the Devil: Essays of a Biographer at Work. Gale E. Christianson. LC 93-22847. xvi, 229p. (C). 1993. lib. bdg. 27.50 (0-208-02382-8, Archon Bks) Shoe String.

*Writing Lives of Children. Dan Madigan & Victoria T. Koivu-Rybicki. LC 96-51055. (Illus.). 128p. (Orig.). (C). 1997. pap. text ed. 16.00 (1-57110-011-3) Stenhse Pubs.

Writing Localizable Software for the Macintosh. Daniel R. Carter. 1991. pap. 26.95 (0-201-57013-0) Addison-Wesley.

Writing Logically, Thinking Critically. 2nd rev. ed. Sheila Cooper & Rosemary Patton. (C). 1997. pap. text ed. 24.95 (0-673-98069-3) Addson-Wesley Educ.

Writing Love: Letters, Women, & the Novel in France, 1605-1776. Katharine A. Jensen. LC 94-9807. (Sandra M. Gilbert's 'Ad Feminam: Women & Literature Ser.). 217p. (C). 1995. 29.95 (0-8093-1849-0) S Ill U Pr.

Writing Management Reports. R. E. Horn. 1979. 375.00 (0-686-83947-1) Info Map Inc.

Writing Mass Communication. 2nd ed. Earl R. Hutchinson. 480p. (C). 1996. pap. text ed. 45.50 (0-8013-1235-3, 79790) Longman.

Writing Math: Project-Based Activities to Integrate Math & Language Arts. Sharon Z. Draznin. 184p. (Orig.). (J). (gr. k-3). 1995. pap. 12.95 (0-673-36127-6, GoodYrBooks) Addson-Wesley Educ.

Writing Mathematics Well. Leonard Gillman. 64p. (Orig.). 1987. pap. 10.00 (0-88385-443-0, WMW) Math Assn.

Writing Matter: From the Hands of the English Renaissance. Jonathan Goldberg. LC 89-36949. (Illus.). 368p. 1990. 45.00 (0-8047-1743-5); pap. 16.95 (0-8047-1958-6) Stanford U Pr.

Writing Matters. Peter G. Beidler. (Illus.). 176p. (Orig.). (C). 1991. pap. text ed. 32.00 (0-02-307865-0, Macmillan Coll) P-H.

Writing Me! A First Writing Course for Adults. 1993. 6.40 (0-88336-385-2) New Readers.

Writing Modern Research Paper. 2nd ed. Dees. 400p. 1996. spiral bd. 19.00 (0-205-26142-6) Allyn.

Writing Montana: Literature under the Big Sky. Rick Newby. LC 96-76992. 348p. 1996. pap. 19.95 (1-56044-417-7) Falcon Pr MT.

Writing Mothers, Writing Daughters: Tracing the Maternal in American Jewish Women's Stories. Janet H. Burstein. LC 95-50191. 224p. (C). 1996. 14.95 (0-252-06555-7); text ed. 34.95 (0-252-02252-1) U of Ill Pr.

Writing MS-DOS Device Drivers. 2nd ed. Robert S. Lai & Waite Group Staff. 576p. 1992. pap. 29.95 (0-201-60837-5) Addison-Wesley.

Writing Music for Hit Songs. 2nd ed. Jai Josefs. 1996. 20.00 (0-02-871191-2) Schirmer Bks.

Writing Music for Hit Songs: Including Songs from the '90s. 2nd ed. Jai Josefs. LC 96-10359. 200p. 1996. 20.00 (0-02-864678-9) Schirmer Bks.

Writing My Life: An Autobiography. Wright Morris. LC 93-13802. 484p. (Orig.). (C). 1993. 25.00 (0-87685-909-0); pap. 15.00 (0-87685-908-2) Black Sparrow.

Writing My Life: An Autobiography, signed ed. deluxe ed. Wright Morris. LC 93-13802. 484p. (Orig.). (C). 1993. 35.00 (0-87685-910-4) Black Sparrow.

Writing Mysteries: A Handbook by the Mystery Writers of America. Sue Grafton. 208p. 1992. 18.99 (0-89879-502-8, Wrtrs Digest Bks) F & W Pubns Inc.

Writing Narrative & Beyond. John Dixon & Leslie Stratta. 88p. 1986. pap. text ed. 16.00 (0-920472-07-9, 0190) Heinemann.

Writing Nation & Writing Region in America. Ed. by Theo D'Haen & Hans Bertens. 300p. 1996. pap. 40.00 (90-5383-422-2, Pub. by VU Univ Pr NE) Paul & Co Pubs.

Writing Natural History: Dialogues with Authors. Ed. by Edward Lueders. LC 89-4764. (Illus.). 144p. 1989. pap. 11.95 (0-87480-323-3) U of Utah Pr.

Writing Nature. Carolyn Ross. 1995. teacher ed., pap. text ed. 0.28 (0-312-10392-1) St Martin.

Writing Nature. Carolyn Ross. 1995. teacher ed., pap. text ed. 23.00 (0-312-10811-7) St Martin.

Writing Nature: An Ecological Reader for Writers. Carolyn Ross. 550p. 1995. pap. text ed. 21.00 (0-312-10391-3) St Martin.

Writing Nature: Henry Thoreau's Journal. Sharon Cameron. LC 88-25163. 186p. 1989. pap. 14.50 (0-226-09228-3) U Ch Pr.

Writing New Identities: Gender, Nation, & Immigration in Contemporary Europe. Ed. by Gisela Brinker-Gabler & Sidonie Smith. 384p. (C). 1996. text ed. 57.95 (0-8166-2460-7); pap. text ed. 22.95 (0-8166-2461-5) U of Minn Pr.

Writing News for Broadcast. 2nd ed. Edward Bliss, Jr. & John M. Patterson. LC 93-29715. 216p. 1978. text ed. 31.00 (0-231-04372-4) Col U Pr.

Writing News for Broadcast. 3rd ed. Edward Bliss, Jr. & James L. Hoyt. LC 93-29715. 161p. 1994. pap. 15.50 (0-231-07973-7) Col U Pr.

*Writing News for Television: Style & Format. Victoria M. Carroll. LC 97-19031. 1997. pap. text ed. 32.95 (0-8138-2533-4) Iowa St U Pr.

Writing North Carolina History. Ed. by Jeffrey J. Crow & Larry E. Tise. LC 79-439. xviii, 249p. 1979. 29.95 (0-8078-1369-9) U of NC Pr.

Writing North Carolina History. Ed. by Jeffrey J. Crow & Larry E. Tise. LC 79-439. 268p. reprint ed. pap. 76.40 (0-8357-3893-0, 2036625) Bks Demand.

Writing Notes with a Personal Touch. Daria P. Bowman & Maureen La Marcha. (Illus.). 72p. 1994. 11.95 (1-56865-078-7, GuildAmerica) Dbldy Direct.

Writing Novels on Your Computer. Mike Flashner. (Illus.). (Orig.). lib. bdg. write for info. (0-9642718-0-X) Flashners Pub Co.

Writing Nursing Diagnoses: A Case Study Approach. Idolia C. Collier. 256p. (C). (gr. 13). 1995. pap. text ed. 25.00 (0-8151-1639-X) Mosby Yr Bk.

Writing of American History. rev. ed. Michael Kraus & Davis D. Joyce. LC 84-40689. 464p. 1990. 37.95 (0-8061-1519-X); pap. 18.95 (0-8061-2234-X) U of Okla Pr.

Writing of Canadian History: Aspects of English-Canadian Historical Writing 1900-1970. 2nd ed. Carl Berger. 376p. 1986. 35.00 (0-8020-2546-3); pap. 20.95 (0-8020-6568-6) U of Toronto Pr.

Writing of Economics. Donald N. McCloskey. 97p. (C). 1986. pap. text ed. 20.00 (0-02-379520-4, Macmillan Coll) P-H.

Writing of Elena Poniatowska: Engaging Dialogues. Beth E. Jorgensen. LC 93-37776. (Texas Pan American Ser.). (Illus.). 192p. (Orig.). (C). 1994. pap. 12.95 (0-292-74033-6); text ed. 27.50 (0-292-74032-8) U of Tex Pr.

Writing of Ezekiel (Es'kia) Mphahlele, South African Writer: Literature, Culture & Politics. Tyohdauah Akosu. LC 95-3003. 332p. 1996. 99.95 (0-7734-2285-4, Mellen Univ Pr) E Mellen.

*Writing of Fiction. Wharton. LC 97-14791. 1997. pap. 10.00 (0-684-84531-8) S&S Trade.

Writing of History. Michel De Certeau. Tr. by Tom Conley from FRE. 368p. (C). 1992. pap. 17.00 (0-231-05575-7) Col U Pr.

*Writing of History & the Study of Law. Donald R. Kelley. LC 97-7874. (Variorum Collected Studies Ser.: Vol. 576). 352p. 1997. text ed. 98.95 (0-86078-639-0, Pub. by Ashgate UK) Ashgate Pub Co.

Writing of Informal Essays. Ed. by Mary E. Chase & Margaret E. Macgregor. LC 79-93326. (Essay Index Reprint Ser.). 1977. 29.95 (0-8369-1556-9) Ayer.

*Writing of John Bunyan. Tamsin Spargo. LC 97-15586. 224p. 1997. text ed. 68.95 (1-85928-449-3, Pub. by Scolar Pr UK) Ashgate Pub Co.

Writing of Melancholy: Modes of Opposition in Early French Modernism. Ross Chambers. Tr. by Mary Trouille. LC 92-27590. 256p. (C). 1993. 32.95 (0-226-10070-7) U Ch Pr.

Writing of Nathanael West. Alistair Wisker. LC 89-24046. 295p. 1990. text ed. 39.95 (0-312-04014-8) St Martin.

Writing of Official History under the T'ang. Denis C. Twitchett. (Studies in Chinese History, Literature & Institutions). 384p. (C). 1992. text ed. 69.95 (0-521-41348-6) Cambridge U Pr.

Writing of Rebecca West. Diana Mosley. 48p. 1986. 35.00 (0-930126-18-1) Typographeum.

Writing of the Disaster. Maurice Blanchot. Tr. by Ann Smock from FRE. LC 85-8562. xvi, 151p. 1986. text ed. 30.00 (0-8032-1186-4) U of Nebr Pr.

Writing of the Disaster. Maurice Blanchot. Tr. by Ann Smock. LC 94-46856. xiii, 153p. (ENG & FRE.). 1995. pap. 12.00 (0-8032-6120-9, Bison Books) U of Nebr Pr.

Writing of the Eighteen Nineties: Stories, Verses & Essays. Ed. by Leon Cantrell. (UQP Australian Authors Ser.). 1978. pap. 14.95 (0-7022-2019-1) Intl Spec Bk.

Writing of the Mayan Indians: Selected Chapters. Yuri V. Knorozov. Tr. by Sophie Coe. (Illus.). (C). 1992. pap. 24.80 (0-89412-182-0) Aegean Park Pr.

Writing of the Walls. Anthony Vidler. LC 86-25402. (Illus.). 320p. 1987. pap. 24.95 (0-910413-75-4) Princeton Arch.

*Writing of Urban Histories in Eighteenth-Century England. Rosemary Sweet. (Oxford Historical Monographs). (Illus.). 310p. 1997. 85.00 (0-19-820669-0) OUP.

Writing of Women: Essays in a Renaissance. rev. ed. Phyllis Rose. LC 84-23446. 187p. 1986. pap. 13.95 (0-8195-6173-8, Wesleyan Univ Pr) U Pr of New Eng.

Writing of Writing. Ed. by Andrew Wilkinson. LC 86-1446. (English, Language & Education Ser.). 192p. 1986. pap. 32.00 (0-335-15233-3, Open Univ Pr) Taylor & Francis.

Writing of Yehuda Amichai: A Thematic Approach. Glenda Abramson. LC 89-4193. (SUNY Series in Modern Jewish Literature & Culture). 254p. 1989. text ed. 67.50 (0-88706-994-0); pap. text ed. 24.95 (0-88706-995-9) State U NY Pr.

Writing off Center. Spear. (C). 1994. teacher ed., pap. text ed. 33.75 (0-15-502174-5) HB Coll Pubs.

Writing off Center. Spear. (C). 1994. pap. text ed. 30.00 (0-15-501415-3) HB Coll Pubs.

Writing OLE Controls: A Practical & Comprehensive Approach. John P. Puopolo. LC 96-2761. 426p. 1996. pap. 39.95 (0-13-254962-X) P-H.

Writing on Both Sides of the Brain: Breakthrough Techniques for People Who Write. Henriette A. Klauser. 176p. (Orig.). 1987. pap. 13.00 (0-06-254490-X) Harper SF.

Writing on Computers in English Composition. 2nd ed. Goran G. Moberg. 160p. 1990. spiral bd. 21.95 (0-8403-5753-2) Kendall-Hunt.

Writing on Line. Dawn Rodriques. LC 95-26680. (C). 1996. pap. text ed. 12.95 (0-393-96933-9) Norton.

Writing on Line. Dawn Rodriques. (C). Date not set. pap. text ed. 9.95 (0-393-96934-7) Norton.

*Writing on the Body: Female Embodiment & Feminist Theory. Katie Conboy et al. LC 96-48177. (Gender & Culture Reader Ser.). 1997. write for info. (0-231-10544-4) Col U Pr.

*Writing on the Body: Female Embodiment & Feminist Theory. 7th ed. Katie Conboy et al. LC 96-48177. (Gender & Culture Reader Ser.). 1997. pap. write for info. (0-231-10545-2) Col U Pr.

*Writing on the Cloud: American Culture Confronts the Atomic Bomb. Ed. by Alison M. Scott & Christopher D. Geist. LC 97-6848. 256p. 1997. 57.50 (0-7618-0745-4); pap. 34.50 (0-7618-0746-2) U Pr of Amer.

*Writing on the Heart. Dawson. 14.80 (0-687-61442-2) Abingdon.

Writing on the Heart: Inviting Scripture to Shape Daily Life. Gerrit S. Dawson. 160p. 1995. pap. 9.95 (0-8358-0713-4) Upper Room Bks.

*Writing on the Internet: Finding. Halio. (C). 1998. pap. text ed. 18.50 (0-15-505503-8) HarBrace.

Writing on the Job. John Breeton. 176p. 1996. 19.95 (0-393-03969-2) Norton.

Writing on the Job. John Brereton. (C). Date not set. pap. text ed. 14.95 (0-393-97089-2) Norton.

Writing on the Job. 2nd ed. Robert E. Mehaffy & Irene Mehaffy. Orig. Title: Writing for the Real World. 380p. (C). 1993. pap. text ed. 23.95 (0-917962-29-X) T H Peek.

Writing on the Job: A Handbook for Business & Government. John Stratton & John Schell. LC 83-24423. 832p. 1984. pap. 9.95 (0-452-25531-7, Plume) NAL-Dutton.

Writing on the Job: Quick, Practical Solutions to All Your Business Writing Problems. Cosmo F. Ferrara. LC 94-28367. 1995. write for info. (0-13-068727-8) P-H.

Writing on the Renaissance Stage: Written Words, Printed Pages, Metaphoric Books. Frederick Kiefer. LC 96-10170. (Illus.). 384p. 1996. 52.50 (0-87413-595-8) U Delaware Pr.

Writing on the Tongue. Ed. by A. L. Becker. LC 88-63411. (Michigan Papers on South & Southeast Asia: No. 33). (Illus.). 321p. 1989. 31.95 (0-89148-047-1); pap. 17.95 (0-89148-048-X) Ctr S&SE Asian.

*Writing on the Wall. Janet Weller. LC 97-280. (Hello Out There Ser.!). (J). 1997. write for info. (0-531-14470-4) Watts.

Writing on the Wall. Hilda G. Howard. LC 73-91563. (Social History of Canada Ser.: No. 20). 181p. reprint ed. pap. 51.60 (0-317-27041-9, 2023623) Bks Demand.

Writing on the Wall: The Architectural Context of Late Assyrian Palace Reliefs. John M. Russell. (Mesopotamian Civilizations Ser.: Vol. 8). text ed. write for info. (0-931464-95-1) Eisenbrauns.

Writing on the Wall: The Commonwealth & the Manchurian Crisis. Eric Andrews. 304p. (C). 1987. text ed. 44.95 (0-04-909027-5) Routledge Chapman & Hall.

Writing on the Wall: Women's Autobiography & the Asylum. Mary E. Wood. LC 93-38401. 192p. 1994. text ed. 36.95 (0-252-02098-7); pap. text ed. 13.95 (0-252-06389-9) U of Ill Pr.

Writing on the Wall & Other Literary Essays. Mary McCarthy. LC 70-100498. Orig. Title: Hanging by a Thread & Other Literary Essays. 221p. 1971. reprint ed. pap. 4.95 (0-15-698390-7, HB207, Harvest Bks) HarBrace.

Writing on the Walls. Elizabeth Berry. (C). 1989. 45.00 (0-9505159-2-2, Pub. by Saltire Soc) St Mut.

Writing on the Water: Chronicles of a Seeker on the Islamic Sufi Path. Muhyiddin Shakoor. 242p. 1993. pap. 15.95 (1-85230-026-4) Element MA.

*Writing on Trial No. 32: Timothy Findley's Famous Last Words. Diana Brydon. (Canadian Fiction Studies). pap. 14.95 (1-55022-181-7, Pub. by ECW Press CN) Genl Dist Srvs.

Writing Online Help. Marion Lindsey. Date not set. 39.99 (0-672-30807-X, Bobbs) Macmillan.

Writing Open VMS Alpha Device Drivers in C: Developer's Guide & Reference Manual. Margie Sherlock. (Illus.). 751p. 1996. pap. 59.95 (1-55558-133-1, Digital DEC) Buttrwrth-Heinemann.

Writing Operating Procedures for Process Plants. Ian S. Dutton. LC 94-29180. 1995. write for info. (0-412-99341-4) Chapman & Hall.

Writing Operating Procedures for Process Plants. Sutton. 176p. (gr. 13). 1995. text ed. 60.50 (0-412-98561-6) Chapman & Hall.

Writing or the Sex? Or Why You Don't Have to Read Women's Writing to Know It's No Good. Dale Spender. 256p. 1989. text ed. 32.50 (0-08-033180-7, Pergamon Pr); pap. text ed. 13.95 (0-08-033179-3, Pergamon Pr) Elsevier.

Writing or the Sex?: Or Why You Don't Have to Read Women's Writing to Know It's No Good. Dale Spender. (Athene Ser.). 256p. (C). 1989. text ed. 32.50 (0-8077-6249-0); pap. text ed. 15.95 (0-8077-6248-2) Tchrs Coll.

Writing Organic Reaction Mechanisms: A Practical Guide. Michael Edenborough. LC 94-20790. 1994. 29.50 (0-7484-0171-7, Pub. by Tay Francis Ltd UK) Taylor & Francis.

*Writing Organic Reaction Mechanisms: A Practical Guide. 2nd ed. Michael Edenborough. 480p. 1997. pap. 34.95 (0-7484-0641-7, Pub. by Tay Francis Ltd UK) Taylor & Francis.

Writing OS-2 Resident Utilities. Ben R. Ezzell. 1989. pap. 24.95 (0-201-51788-4) Addison-Wesley.

Writing OS 2 REXX Programs. Ronny Richardson. LC 94-913. 1994. pap. text ed. 42.95 (0-07-052372-X) McGraw.

Writing OS/2 2.1 Device Drivers in C. 2nd ed. Steven J. Mastrianni. 416p. 1995. 39.95 incl. disk (0-471-13152-0) Wiley.

Writing Our Lives: Autobiographies of American Jews, 1890-1990. Steven J. Rubin. LC 91-3599. 384p. 1991. text ed. 44.95 (0-8276-0393-2) JPS Phila.

Writing Our Lives: Reflections on Dialogue Journal Writing with Adults. Ed. by Joy K. Peyton & Jana Staton. LC 95-36190. (Language in Education Ser.: No. 77). 1995. write for info. (*0-937354-71-6*) Delta Systems.

***Writing Our Lives: Reflections on Dialogue Journal Writing with Adults Learning English.** Joy K. Peyton et al. LC 91-6444. (Language in Education Ser.). Date not set. write for info. (*0-13-969338-6*) P-H.

Writing Our Way. William L. Knox. 96p. (C). 1992. pap. text ed. 16.74 (*0-8403-7858-0*) Kendall-Hunt.

Writing Our Way Out of the Dark: An Anthology by Child Abuse Survivors. Ed. by Elizabeth Claman. LC 95-68828. (Illus.). 308p. (Orig.). 1995. pap. 16.95 (*0-9638992-2-8*) Queen of Swords.

Writing Ourselves into the Story: Unheard Voices from Composition Studies. Ed. by Sheryl I. Fontaine & Susan Hunter. LC 92-10625. 400p. (C). 1993. 34.95 (*0-8093-1826-1*); pap. 16.95 (*0-8093-1827-X*) S Ill U Pr.

Writing Out Loud: Updated for the Electronic Age. Jefferson D. Bates. 1996. pap. text ed. 14.95 (*0-87491-977-0*) Acrpls Bks CO.

Writing Out My Heart: Selections from the Journal of Frances E. Willard, 1855-96. Ed. by Carolyn D. Gifford. LC 94-43878. (Women in American History Ser.). (Illus.). 510p. (C). 1995. 29.95 (*0-252-02139-8*) U of Ill Pr.

***Writing Out Your Life.** Jo Stanley. 1997. pap. 16.95 (*1-85727-073-8*, Pub. by Scarlet Pr UK) LPC InBook.

***Writing Outside the Lines.** LC 97-4945. 1997. pap. text ed. write for info. (*0-86709-422-2*) Heinemann.

Writing Papers: A Handbook for Students at Smith College. 2nd rev. ed. Joan H. Garrett-Goodyear et al. 60p. (YA). (gr. 9-12). 1986. pap. 3.25 (*0-88741-098-7*) Sundance Pub.

***Writing Papers in Psychology.** 4th ed. Mimi Rosnow. LC 97-3844. (Psychology Ser.). 1998. pap. 12.95 (*0-534-34826-2*) Wadsworth Pub.

Writing Papers in Psychology: A Student Guide. 2nd ed. Ralph L. Rosnow & Mimi Rosnow. 105p. (C). 1992. pap. 21.95 (*0-534-16986-4*) Brooks-Cole.

Writing Papers in Psychology: A Student Guide. 3rd ed. Ralph L. Rosnow & Mimi Rosnow. LC 94-9163. 1995. pap. 13.95 (*0-534-24378-9*) Brooks-Cole.

Writing Papers in the Biological Sciences. 2nd ed. Victoria E. McMillan. 176p. (C). 1996. pap. text ed. 13.50 (*0-312-11504-0*) St Martin.

Writing Paragraphs. 3rd ed. Carol Pemberton. 254p. 1996. pap. text ed. 28.00 (*0-205-26079-9*) Allyn.

***Writing Paragraphs.** 3rd ed. Carol Pemberton. teacher ed., pap. write for info. (*0-205-26541-3*) Allyn.

Writing Paragraphs & Essays: Integrating Reading, Writing, & Grammar Skills. Joy Wingersky et al. 425p. (C). 1992. pap. 28.95 (*0-534-15990-7*) Wadsworth Pub.

Writing Paragraphs & Essays: Integrating Reading, Writing, & Grammar Skills. 2nd ed. Joy Wingersky et al. 462p. 1995. pap. text ed., spiral bd., pap. 37.95 (*0-534-21972-1*) Wadsworth Pub.

***Writing Paragraphs (Language)** Jo E. Moore. (Reading & Writing Ser.). (Illus.). 32p. (J). (gr. 2-4). 1996. teacher ed., pap. 2.95 (*1-55799-424-2*, 4026) Evan-Moor Corp.

Writing Past Dark. Bonnie Friedman. LC 92-54732. 160p. 1994. reprint ed. pap. 11.00 (*0-06-092200-1*, PL) HarpC.

Writing Path to Success. Louis Gallo. 272p. (C). 1994. per., pap. text ed. 26.19 (*0-7872-0257-6*) Kendall-Hunt.

Writing Path 1: Poetry & Prose from Writers' Conferences. Ed. by Michael Pettit. 238p. 1995. 32.95 (*0-87745-508-2*) U of Iowa Pr.

Writing Path 1: Poetry & Prose from Writers' Conferences. Ed. by Michael Pettit. 238p. 1995. pap. 14.95 (*0-87745-509-0*) U of Iowa Pr.

Writing Path 2: Poetry & Prose from Writers' Conferences. Ed. by Michael Pettit. 299p. 1996. pap. 14.95 (*0-87745-548-1*); text ed. 32.95 (*0-87745-552-X*) U of Iowa Pr.

Writing Performance Documentation: A Self-Paced Training Program. Janis F. Chan & Diane Lutovich. 95p. 1994. pap. 30.00 (*0-9637455-3-0*) Adv Comm Designs.

Writing Permitted in Designated Areas Only. Linda Brodkey. (Pedagogy & Cultural Practices Ser.: Vol. 4). (C). 1996. pap. 21.95 (*0-8166-2807-6*) U of Minn Pr.

Writing Personal Essays: How to Shape Your Life Experiences for the Page. Sheila Bender. 272p. 1995. 17.99 (*0-89879-665-2*, Wrtrs Digest Bks) F & W Pubns Inc.

Writing Persuasive Briefs. Girvan Peck. LC 84-80192. 246p. 1984. 55.00 (*0-316-69666-8*) Little.

Writing Persuasive Cover Letters. Brian Jud. Ed. by Charles Lipka. 20p. (Orig.). (C). 1995. student ed., pap. 1.45 (*1-880218-20-8*) Mktg Dir Inc.

Writing Philosophy: A Guide to Professional Writing & Publishing. Richard A. Watson. 120p. 1992. pap. 9.95 (*0-8093-1810-5*) S Ill U Pr.

Writing Philosophy Papers. Hugo A. Bedau. 1996. pap. text ed. 12.50 (*0-312-10082-5*) St Martin.

Writing Philosophy Papers. Zachary Seech. 134p. (C). 1993. pap. 10.50 (*0-534-19758-2*) Wadsworth Pub.

Writing Philosophy Papers. 2nd ed. Zachary Seech. LC 96-12011. (Philosophy Ser.). (C). 1997. pap. text ed. 13.95 (*0-534-50652-6*) Wadsworth Pub.

Writing Plan. Irene D. Betts & Carol C. Howell. 288p. (C). 1984. pap. text ed. write for info. (*0-13-971770-6*) P-H.

Writing Poems. Peter Sansom. 128p. 9500. pap. 16.95 (*1-85224-204-3*, Pub. by Bloodaxe Bks UK) Dufour.

Writing Poems. 3rd ed. Wallace. (C). 1990. pap. text ed. 28.50 (*0-673-46214-5*) Addson-Wesley Educ.

Writing Poems. 4th ed. Robert Wallace & Michelle Boisseau. LC 95-3563. 432p. (C). 1996. pap. text ed. 29.50 (*0-673-99013-3*) Addson-Wesley Educ.

Writing Poems. 4th ed. Robert Wallace. 480p. 1995. pap. 27.00 (*0-8230-5010-6*) Watsn-Guptill.

Writing Poetry. Barbara Drake. 312p. (C). 1983. pap. text ed. 21.50 (*0-15-597990-6*) HB Coll Pubs.

Writing Poetry. Elaine Hardt. (Illus.). 32p. (Orig.). (J). (gr. 1-9). 1983. pap. 1.95 (*0-940406-09-8*) Perception Pubns.

Writing Poetry. Shelley Tucker. 160p. (Orig.). (J). (gr. 6-10). 1992. pap. 7.95 (*0-673-36039-3*, GoodYrBooks) Addson-Wesley Educ.

***Writing Poetry.** 2nd ed. Drake. (C). 1994. pap. write for info. (*0-15-500154-X*) HB Coll Pubs.

Writing Poetry: Where Poems Come from & How to Write Them. 2nd rev. ed. David Kirby. LC 88-33811. 120p. (Orig.). 1994. pap. 12.00 (*0-87116-171-0*) Writer.

Writing Poetry with Children. Jo E. Moore & Joy Evans. (Illus.). 64p. (J). (gr. 1-6). 1988. pap. 6.95 (*1-55799-129-4*, EMC 226) Evan-Moor Corp.

Writing Police Reports: A Practical Guide. Alec Ross & David Plant. LC 76-55879. 1977. pap. 5.95 (*0-916070-03-4*, MTI Film & Video) Coronet.

Writing Policy in Action: The Middle Years. Eve Bearne & Cath Farrow. (English, Language & Education Ser.). 160p. 1991. pap. 27.00 (*0-335-09444-9*, Open Univ Pr) Taylor & Francis.

Writing Portfolios: A Bridge from Teaching to Assessment. Sandra Murphy & Mary A. Smith. (Illus.). 96p. 1995. pap. text ed. 14.00 (*0-88751-044-2*, 00707) Heinemann.

Writing Portfolios in the Classroom: Policy & Practice, Promise & Peril. Ed. by Robert C. Calfee & Pamela Perfumo. LC 96-22692. 384p. 1996. text ed. 69.95 (*0-8058-1835-9*); pap. text ed. 29.95 (*0-8058-1836-7*) L Erlbaum Assocs.

***Writing Power Applications with Perl.** Wall & Schwartz. Ed. by Steve Talbot. (Illus.). 700p. (Orig.). 1997. pap. write for info. (*1-56592-220-4*) OReilly & Assocs.

Writing Power Workshop, Level 1. Shirley A. Jackson. 1991. teacher ed. 16.32 (*0-932957-30-7*); 5.95 (*0-932957-31-5*); 4.95 (*0-932957-32-3*); 285.00 (*0-932957-37-4*); write for info. (*0-932957-33-1*) Natl School.

Writing Power Workshop, Level 2. Shirley A. Jackson. 1991. teacher ed. 16.32 (*0-932957-35-8*); 5.95 (*0-932957-36-6*); 4.95 (*0-932957-39-0*); 285.00 (*0-932957-38-2*); write for info. (*0-932957-34-X*) Natl School.

Writing Power Workshop, Level 3. Shirley A. Jackson. 1993. teacher ed. 16.32 (*0-932957-40-4*); 5.95 (*0-932957-41-2*); 4.95 (*0-932957-42-0*); 285.00 (*0-932957-44-7*); write for info. (*0-932957-43-9*) Natl School.

Writing Practical English 1. 2nd ed. Tim Harris & Allan Rowe. 176p. (C). 1986. pap. text ed. 8.00 (*0-15-570915-1*) HB Coll Pubs.

Writing Practical English 2. 2nd ed. Tim Harris & Allan Rowe. 140p. (C). 1987. pap. text ed. 8.00 (*0-15-570923-2*) HB Coll Pubs.

***Writing Process.** 6th ed. Ed. by Lannon. LC 97-14278. (C). 1998. text ed. write for info. (*0-321-01109-0*) Addison-Wesley Educ.

Writing Process: A Concise Rhetoric. 5th ed. 736p. (C). 1995. teacher ed., pap. write for info. (*0-673-52400-0*) Addison-Wesley Educ.

Writing Process: A Concise Rhetoric. 5th ed. John M. Lannon. LC 94-18589. 640p. (C). 1995. pap. text ed. 23.50 (*0-673-52399-3*) Addson-Wesley Educ.

Writing Process: A Guide for ESL Students: A Workbook to Accompany the HarperCollins Concise Handbook for Writers. Amy Tickle. LC 94-26071. (C). 1994. pap. text ed. 17.50 (*0-06-502022-7*) Addson-Wesley Educ.

Writing Process: English 101. Geoffrey Grimes. (C). 1993. student ed. 16.89 (*1-56870-082-2*) RonJon Pub.

Writing Process: One Writer's Approach to Writing with Children. Olivier Dunrea. Ed. by Mary A. Heltshe. (Illus.). 72p. (C). 1990. pap. 11.50 (*0-9627288-0-2*) Stonetrow Studio.

Writing Process: With MLA Update. 5th ed. Lannon. 640p. (C). 1995. text ed. 31.50 (*0-673-52492-2*) Addson-Wesley Educ.

Writing Process Activities Kit. Mary L. Brandvik. 256p. 1990. 24.95 (*0-87628-968-5*) P-H.

***Writing Process & Product.** Heenan. Date not set. pap. text ed. write for info. (*0-582-87724-5*, Pub. by Longman UK) Longman.

Writing Process 2000. Albert Joseph. 1995. pap. text ed. 25.80 (*0-13-441916-2*) P-H.

Writing, Producing & Selling Your Play see Playwriting: Writing, Producing & Selling Your Play

Writing Proficiency Examinations Preparation Guide: For California State Universities Graduation Writing Assessment Requirement. Jerry Bobrow & Peter Z. Orton. (Illus.). (C). 1990. pap. text ed. 8.95 (*0-8220-2043-2*) Cliffs.

Writing Program Viewer's Guide. Contemporary Book Editors. 1986. pap. 9.50 (*0-8092-4933-2*) Contemp Bks.

***Writing Progressions.** Hoy. Date not set. pap. text ed. write for info. (*0-312-15412-7*) St Martin.

Writing Proposals for Contract Training. Shannon McBride. 67p. 39.95 (*0-914951-76-9*) LERN.

Writing Prose: Techniques & Purposes. 6th ed. Ed. by Thomas S. Kane & Leonard J. Peters. 698p. 1986. pap. text ed. 28.00 (*0-19-503678-6*) OUP.

Writing Proxy Voting Guidelines: A Handbook for the Institutional Investor. 244p. 1990. pap. 45.00 (*0-931035-44-9*) IRRC Inc DC.

Writing Psychological Reports: A Guide for Clinicians. Greg J. Wolber & William F. Carne. LC 93-26909. 128p. 1993. pap. 19.70 (*0-943158-93-1*, WPRBP, Prof Resc Pr) Pro Resource.

Writing Pynchon: Strategies in Fictional Analysis. Alec McHoul & David Wills. 256p. 1990. 29.95 (*0-252-01700-5*) U of Ill Pr.

Writing Rackets. Robert L. Byrne. LC 69-17965. 1969. 4.00 (*0-8184-0095-1*) Carol Pub Group.

Writing R&D Proposals. Larry Best & Terry R. Bacon. (Illus.). 166p. 1994. write for info. (*1-57740-007-0*, ILW006) Intl LrningWrk.

Writing Ravenna: The Liber Pontificalis of Andreas Agnellus. Joaquin M. Pizarro. LC 95-8303. (Recentiores Later Latin Texts and Contexts Ser.). 1995. text ed. 39.50 (*0-472-10606-6*) U of Mich Pr.

Writing Re-Creatively: A Spiritual Quest for Women. Gail Collins-Ranadive. 104p. 1994. pap. 10.00 (*1-55896-276-X*, Skinner Hse Bks) Unitarian Univ.

Writing Reaction Mechanisms in Organic Chemistry. Audrey Miller. (Illus.). 488p. 1992. pap. text ed. 48.00 (*0-12-496711-6*) Acad Pr.

Writing Readable Reports. Venkata Iyer. 96p. 1987. text ed. 13.95 (*81-207-0676-5*, Pub. by Sterling Pubs II) Apt Bks.

Writing Reader. Carolyn B. Raphael. 432p. (C). 1986. pap. write for info. (*0-02-398280-2*, Macmillan Coll) P-H.

Writing, Reading & Research. 4th ed. Veit & Gould. LC 96-46885. 560p. 1996. pap. 32.00 (*0-205-20033-8*) Allyn.

***Writing, Reading, & Research.** 4th ed. Richard Veit et al. 560p. pap. write for info. (*0-205-26519-7*) Allyn.

Writing Realism: Howells, James, & Norris in the Mass Market. Daniel H. Borus. LC 89-31157. xii, 260p. (C). 1989. 45.00 (*0-8078-1869-0*) U of NC Pr.

Writing Red: An Anthology of American Women Writers, 1930-1940. Ed. by Charlotte Nekola & Paula Rabinowitz. LC 89-25023. 368p. 1987. pap. text ed. 15.95 (*0-935312-76-5*) Feminist Pr.

Writing Reference: Exercises. 3rd ed. Hacker. 1994. pap. text ed. 3.00 (*0-312-10142-2*) St Martin.

Writing Relationships: What Really Happens in the Composition Class. Lad Tobin. LC 92-40759. 156p. (C). 1993. pap. text ed. 19.50 (*0-86709-322-6*, 0322) Boynton Cook Pubs.

Writing Religiously: A Guide to Writing Nonfiction Religious Books see Christian Writer's Book: A Practical Guide to Writing

Writing Repair Shop. Ascher. 1993. pap. 13.95 (*0-8384-3411-8*) Heinle & Heinle.

***Writing Reports That Work.** rev. ed. 1989. 75.00 (*0-8103-6939-7*, 00002386, Gale Res Intl) Gale.

Writing Reports to Get Results: Guidelines for the Computer Age. Ron S. Blicq. LC 87-16850. 216p. 1987. 27.95 (*0-87942-228-9*, PC0215-4) Inst Electrical.

Writing Reports to Get Results: Quick, Effective Results Using the Pyramid Method. 2nd ed. Ron S. Blicq & Lisa A. Moretto. LC 94-13312. 240p. 1994. pap. 24.95 (*0-7803-1019-5*, PP03673) Inst Electrical.

Writing Research. Veit. 1989. student ed., pap. text ed. 22.00 (*0-02-423040-5*, Macmillan Coll) P-H.

***Writing Research.** 5th ed. Stephen Weidenborner. Date not set. pap. text ed. write for info. (*0-312-15321-X*) St Martin.

Writing Research Papers. 2nd ed. Edward P. Bailey & Philip A. Powell. 240p. (C). 1987. pap. text ed. 14.00 (*0-03-006529-1*) HB Coll Pubs.

***Writing Research Papers.** 2nd ed. Ed. by Andrew Hamack. LC 97-25083. (Opposing Viewpoints Ser.). (YA). (gr. 8-12). 1997. pap. 11.96 (*1-56510-593-1*) Greenhaven.

Writing Research Papers. 4th ed. Melissa Walker. (C). Date not set. pap. text ed. 19.95 (*0-393-97108-2*) Norton.

***Writing Research Papers.** 4th ed. Melissa Walker. (C). Date not set. teacher ed., pap. text ed. write for info. (*0-393-97119-8*) Norton.

Writing Research Papers. 4th ed. Melissa Walker. LC 96-29447. (C). 1996. pap. text ed. write for info. (*0-393-97091-4*) Norton.

Writing Research Papers. 5th ed. Stephen Weidenborner. 1996. pap. text ed. 13.50 (*0-312-13748-6*) St Martin.

Writing Research Papers: A Complete Guide. 7th ed. Ed Lester. (C). 1993. text ed. 13.95 (*0-673-46643-4*) Addison-Wesley Educ.

Writing Research Papers: A Complete Guide. 7th ed. James D. Lester. 1993. write for info. (*0-318-69537-5*, HarpT) HarpC.

Writing Research Papers: A Complete Guide. 8th ed. 400p. (C). 1995. teacher ed., spiral bd. write for info. (*0-673-55870-3*) Addson-Wesley Educ.

Writing Research Papers: A Complete Guide. 8th ed. Lester. 1996. 17.50 incl. audio compact disk (*0-673-98221-1*) Addson-Wesley Educ.

Writing Research Papers: A Complete Guide. 8th ed. James D. Lester. LC 95-17065. 400p. (C). 1996. text ed. 15.95 (*0-673-99449-X*) Addson-Wesley Educ.

Writing Research Papers: A Complete Guide, Tabbed. 8th ed. Lester. 416p. (C). 1996. text ed. 18.95 (*0-673-99450-3*) Addson-Wesley Educ.

Writing Research Papers: A Norton Guide. Melissa Walker. LC 92-14009. (C). 1993. pap. text ed. write for info. (*0-393-95944-9*) Norton.

Writing Research Papers: A Norton Guide. 3rd ed. Melissa Walker. LC 92-14009. (C). 1993. pap. text ed. 7.98 (*0-393-95943-0*) Norton.

Writing Research Papers: A Student Guide for the Use with Opposing Viewpoints. Andrew Harnack. LC 93-4317. 154p. (YA). 1994. 11.96 (*1-56510-099-9*) Greenhaven.

***Writing Research Papers: City University Style Manual.** Lester. (C). 1995. text ed. 17.95 (*0-673-67571-8*) Addison-Wesley.

***Writing Research Papers: Investigating Resources in Cyberspace.** Jeannette A. Woodward. LC 96-43725. 1996. pap. write for info. (*0-8442-5929-2*) NTC Pub Grp.

Writing Research Papers Across the Curriculum. 2nd ed. Susan M. Hubbuch. LC 88-12951. (C). 1989. pap. text ed. 16.50 (*0-03-023737-8*) HB Coll Pubs.

Writing Research Papers Across the Curriculum. 3rd ed. Susan M. Hubbuch. 400p. (C). 1992. pap. text ed. 16.00 (*0-03-054978-7*) HB Coll Pubs.

Writing Research Papers Across the Curriculum. 4th ed. Susan M. Hubbuch. (C). 1995. pap. text ed. 17.00 (*0-15-502655-0*) HB Coll Pubs.

Writing Resource Activities Kit: Ready-to-Use Worksheets & Enrichment Lessons for Grades 4-9. Gary R. Muschla. 272p. 1989. spiral bd. 27.95 (*0-87628-970-7*) Ctr Appl Res.

***Writing Resumes That Work: A How-to-Do-It Manual for Librarians.** Robert R. Newlen. 150p. 1996. pap. 39.95 (*1-55570-263-5*) Neal-Schuman.

Writing Rhino. Beverly Armstrong. 56p. (J). (gr. 1-3). 1995. 5.95 (*0-88160-269-8*, LW108) Learning Wks.

Writing Right & Left: A Comprehensive Resource Guide for Today's Business Writer. Camille Selman. 168p. 1992. write for info. (*0-9637588-5-3*); teacher ed. write for info. (*0-9637588-8-8*); student ed. write for info. (*0-9637588-9-6*); pap. write for info. (*0-9637588-6-1*); pap. text ed. write for info. (*0-9637588-7-X*) Growth & Leadership.

Writing Right!, Bk. 1: Manuscript. Carol R. Pendergrass. 96p. 1994. pap. 4.75 (*0-88323-261-8*, 149) Pendergrass Pub.

Writing Right!, Bk. 2: Cursive. Carol R. Pendergrass. 96p. (J). (gr. 1 up). 1994. pap. text ed. 4.75 (*0-88323-262-6*, 150) Pendergrass Pub.

***Writing Right for Today's Mass Media.** Paul Adams. 400p. (C). 1997. pap. text ed. 32.95 (*0-8304-1456-8*) Nelson-Hall.

Writing Road to Reading: A Modern Method of Phonics for Teaching Children to Read. 2nd ed. Romalda B. Spalding & Walter T. Spalding. LC 82-21428. 272p. 1956. 17.95 (*0-688-15001-2*, Quill) Morrow.

Writing Road to Reading: A Modern Method of Phonics for Teaching Children to Read. 2nd ed. Romalda B. Spalding & Walter T. Spalding. LC 82-21428. 272p. 1972. pap. 13.45 (*0-688-07818-4*, Quill) Morrow.

Writing Road to Reading: A Proven Method of Phonics for Teaching Speech, Writing, & Reading. 4th rev. ed. Romalda B. Spalding & Walter T. Spalding. (Illus.). 288p. 1990. pap. 17.95 (*0-688-10007-4*, Quill) Morrow.

Writing Road to Reading: The Spalding Method of Phonic for Teaching Speech, Writing & Reading. 3rd rev. ed. Romalda B. Spalding & Walter T. Spalding. LC 86-647. 288p. 1986. pap. 15.95 (*0-688-06634-8*, Quill) Morrow.

***Writing Romance.** Vanessa Grant. 160p. (Orig.). 1997. pap. 14.95 (*1-55180-096-9*) Self-Counsel Pr.

***Writing Romances.** Ed. by Rita C. Estrada & Rita Gallagher. LC 96-3192. 224p. 1997. 18.99 (*0-89879-756-X*, Wrtrs Digest Bks) F & W Pubns Inc.

Writing Rome: Textual Approaches to the City. Catharine Edwards. (Roman Literature & Its Contexts Ser.). (Illus.). 144p. (C). 1996. pap. text ed. 16.95 (*0-521-55952-9*) Cambridge U Pr.

Writing Rome: Textual Approaches to the City. Catharine Edwards. (Roman Literature & Its Contexts Ser.). (Illus.). 144p. (C). 1996. text ed. 49.95 (*0-521-55080-7*) Cambridge U Pr.

Writing Room: A Resource Book for Teachers of English. Harvey S. Wiener. 352p. (C). 1981. pap. text ed. 12.95 (*0-19-502826-0*) OUP.

Writing S. O. A. P. Notes. 2nd ed. Ginge Kettenbach. LC 89-25960. (Illus.). 183p. (C). 1995. pap. text ed. 22.95 (*0-8036-0037-2*) Davis Co.

Writing Scholar: Language & Conventions of Academic Disclosure. Ed. by Walter Nash. (Written Communication Annual Ser.: Vol. 3). (Illus.). 320p. (C). 1990. 55.00 (*0-8039-3692-3*) Sage.

Writing School-Master. John Davies. LC 76-57376. (English Experience Ser.: No. 794). 1977. reprint ed. lib. bdg. 20.00 (*90-221-0794-9*) Walter J Johnson.

Writing, Schooling, & Deconstruction. Pamela Gilbert. 208p. 1989. 58.00 (*0-415-00825-5*) Routledge.

Writing Science: Literacy & Discursive Power. M. A. Halliday & J. R. Martin. (Series in Composition, Literacy, & Culture). 300p. (C). 1993. text ed. 49.95 (*0-8229-1180-9*); pap. text ed. 19.95 (*0-8229-6103-2*) U of Pittsburgh Pr.

Writing Science Fiction & Fantasy. Analog & Isaac Asimov's Science Fiction Magazine Editors. LC 92-41283. 1993. pap. 9.95 (*0-312-08926-0*) St Martin.

Writing Science News for the Mass Media. 2nd rev. ed. David W. Burkett. LC 72-84334. 224p. reprint ed. pap. 63.90 (*0-685-23781-8*, 2032863) Bks Demand.

Writing Science Research Papers: An Introductory Step-by-Step Approach to A's. David B. Williams. LC 94-79789. 104p. (Orig.). (YA). (gr. 7 up). 1995. pap. 14.95 (*1-880319-17-9*) Biotech.

Writing Scientific Programs under the OS-2 Presentation Manager. James W. Cooper. 403p. 1990. text ed. 94.95 (*0-471-51928-6*) Wiley.

Writing Screenplays That Sell: The Complete, Step-by-Step Guide for Writing & Selling to the Movies & TV, from Story Concept to Development Deal. Michael Hauge. LC 91-55005. 320p. (Orig.). 1991. pap. 15.00 (*0-06-272500-9*, Harper Ref) HarpC.

Writing Screenplays That Sell: The Complete Step-by-Step Guide for Writing & Selling to the Movies & TV, from Story Concept to Development Deal. Michael Hauge. 352p. 1994. lib. bdg. 37.00 (*0-8095-9150-2*) Borgo Pr.

Writing Scripts for Television, Radio, & Film. 3rd ed. Camille D'Arienzo & Edgar E. Willis. LC 92-53792. (Illus.). 352p. (C). 1992. pap. text ed. 30.75 (*0-03-075011-3*) HB Coll Pubs.

Writing Scripts Hollywood Will Love: An Insider's Guide to Film & Television Scripts That Sell. Katherine A. Herbert. LC 95-72262. 160p. 1994. pap. 12.95 (*1-880559-20-X*) Allworth Pr.

W

Writing Security: United States Foreign Policy & the Politics of Identity. David Campbell. 266p. (C). 1992. text ed. 44.95 (*0-8166-2221-3*); pap. text ed. 19.95 (*0-8166-2222-1*) U of Minn Pr.

Writing Self, Writing Nation. L. H. Kang & Elaine H. Kim. Ed. by Norma Alarcon. LC 94-4916. (Illus.). 176p. (Orig.). 1994. pap. 12.95 (*0-943219-11-6*) Third Woman.

Writing Selves: Contemporary Feminist Autography. Jeanne Perreault. 176p. 1995. text ed. 44.95 (*0-8166-2654-5*); pap. text ed. 17.95 (*0-8166-2655-3*) U of Minn Pr.

Writing Sense: A Handbook of Composition. David R. Pichaske. LC 74-15134. (C). 1975. pap. text ed. 10.95 (*0-02-925170-2*, Free Press) Free Pr.

Writing Series 1: Quarter 1. Rudy Moore & Betty Moore. (J). (gr. 1). 1988. pap. 8.99 (*0-88062-216-4*) Mott Media.

Writing Series 1: Quarter 2. Rudy Moore & Betty Moore. (J). (gr. 1). 1988. pap. 8.99 (*0-88062-217-2*) Mott Media.

Writing Series 1: Quarter 3. Rudy Moore & Betty Moore. (J). (gr. 1). 1989. pap. 8.99 (*0-88062-218-0*) Mott Media.

Writing Series 1: Quarter 4. Rudy Moore & Betty Moore. (J). (gr. 1). 1991. 8.99 (*0-88062-219-9*) Mott Media.

Writing Series 2: Quarter 1. Rudy Moore & Betty Moore. (J). (gr. 2). 1988. pap. 8.99 (*0-88062-220-2*) Mott Media.

Writing Series 2: Quarter 2. Rudy Moore & Betty Moore. (J). (gr. 2). 1988. pap. 8.99 (*0-88062-221-0*) Mott Media.

Writing Series 2: Quarter 3. Rudy Moore & Betty Moore. (J). (gr. 2). 1989. pap. 8.99 (*0-88062-222-9*) Mott Media.

Writing Series 2: Quarter 4. Rudy Moore & Betty Moore. (J). (gr. 2). 1991. 8.99 (*0-88062-223-7*) Mott Media.

Writing Series 3: Quarter 1. Rudy Moore & Betty Moore. (J). (gr. 3). 1988. pap. 8.99 (*0-88062-224-5*) Mott Media.

Writing Series 3: Quarter 2. Rudy Moore & Betty Moore. (J). (gr. 3). 1988. pap. 8.99 (*0-88062-225-3*) Mott Media.

Writing Series 3: Quarter 3. Rudy Moore & Betty Moore. (J). (gr. 3). 1991. 8.99 (*0-88062-226-1*) Mott Media.

Writing Series 3: Quarter 4. Rudy Moore & Betty Moore. (J). (gr. 3). 1991. 8.99 (*0-88062-227-X*) Mott Media.

Writing Series 4: Quarter 1. Rudy Moore & Betty Moore. (J). (gr. 4). 1988. pap. 8.99 (*0-88062-228-8*) Mott Media.

Writing Series 4: Quarter 2. Rudy Moore & Betty Moore. (J). (gr. 4). 1988. pap. 8.99 (*0-88062-229-6*) Mott Media.

Writing Series 4: Quarter 3. Rudy Moore & Betty Moore. (J). (gr. 4). 1989. pap. 8.99 (*0-88062-230-X*) Mott Media.

Writing Series 4: Quarter 4. Rudy Moore & Betty Moore. (J). (gr. 4). 1994. 8.99 (*0-88062-231-8*) Mott Media.

Writing Set, 3 bks., Set. Linda L. Dollard. (J). (gr. k-1). 25.99 (*1-56417-728-9*, FE0004) Fearon Teach Aids.

Writing Short Business Reports. N. Carr-Ruffino. 1980. text ed. 19.50 (*0-07-010155-8*) McGraw.

Writing Short Films: Structure & Content for Screenwriters. Linda Cowgill. LC 97-2155. 256p. (Orig.). 1997. pap. 19.95 (*0-943728-80-0*) Lone Eagle Pub.

Writing Short Scripts. William H. Phillips. LC 89-21961. (Illus.). 240p. (C). 1990. text ed. 35.00 (*0-8156-2485-9*); pap. text ed. 16.95 (*0-8156-2486-7*) Syracuse U Pr.

Writing Sites: A Genealogy of the Postmodern World. Jon Stratton. LC 89-49647. 288p. (C). 1990. reprint ed. text ed. 39.50 (*0-472-10190-0*) U of Mich Pr.

Writing Skills. (Open Learning for Supervisory Management Ser.). 1986. pap. text ed. 19.50 (*0-08-070073-X*, Pergamon Pr) Elsevier.

Writing Skills. Irvin. (C). 1996. pap. text ed. write for info. (*0-15-503237-2*) HarBrace.

Writing Skills. Carol V. Murdock. Ed. by Susan Evento. (Macmillan Early Skills Program - Conversion Ser.). 64p. (J). (ps-2). 1995. pap. 9.95 (*1-56784-511-8*) Newbridge Comms.

Writing Skills. Nebsm Staff. (Open Learning for Supervisory Management). 1985. pap. text ed. 19.50 (*0-08-033963-8*, Pergamon Pr) Elsevier.

Writing Skills. Ed. by NEBSS Staff & NRMC Staff. (Open Learning for Supervisory Management Ser.: 302). (Illus.). 106p. 1986. 25.95 (*0-08-070072-1*, Pub. by PPL UK) Elsevier.

Writing Skills. 2nd ed. (Open Learning Super Ser.). 1991. pap. text ed. 26.00 (*0-08-041608-X*, Pergamon Pr) Elsevier.

***Writing Skills: A Problem-Solving Approach.** 96p. 1983. pap. text ed. 12.95 (*0-521-28142-3*) Cambridge U Pr.

Writing Skills for Bankers. Mildred S. Myers. (Illus.). 1992. student ed. 49.00 (*0-685-62688-1*) Am Bankers.

Writing Skills for Foodservice Managers Skillbook. Educational Foundation of the National Restaurant Association Staff. (Management Skills Program Ser.). 56p. (Orig.). 1992. pap. 10.95 (*0-915452-46-4*) Educ Found.

Writing Skills for Technical Students. Delaware Technical & Community College, English Department Staff. 400p. (C). 1982. pap. text ed. write for info. (*0-13-970665-8*) P-H.

Writing Skills for Technical Students. 3rd ed. Delaware Technical & Community College Staff. 400p. (C). 1992. pap. text ed. 37.80 (*0-13-981986-X*) P-H.

Writing Skills Handbook, 3 Vols. Charles Bazerman. (C). 1992. pap. 4.36 (*0-395-61456-2*) HM.

***Writing Skills Handbook, 3 Vols.** 3rd ed. Charles Bazerman & Harvey S. Wiener. 160p. (C). 1992. pap. text ed. 14.36 (*0-395-61455-4*) HM.

Writing Skills in 20 Minutes a Day. LC 96-17815. 1996. pap. 16.00 (*1-57685-040-4*) LrningExprss.

Writing Skills with Readings. R. Kent Smith et al. 424p. 1995. pap. text ed. 15.00 (*0-944210-71-6*) Townsend NJ.

Writing Smart: Your Guide to Great Writing. Marcia Lerner. (Princeton Review Ser.). 1994. pap. 12.00 (*0-679-75360-5*, Villard Bks) Random.

Writing Smart Junior: An Introduction to the Art of Writing. C. L. Brantley. (J). (gr. 6-8). 1995. pap. 12.00 (*0-679-76131-4*, Villard Bks) Random.

Writing Smarter, Not Harder: The Workbook Way. Colleen L. Reece. Ed. by Penny Lent. (Illus.). 112p. (Orig.). 1995. pap. 13.95 (*1-885371-13-6*) Kldoscope Pr.

Writing Smarter, Not Harder, the Workbook Way. Colleen L. Reece. Ed. by Penny Lent. (Illus.). 80p. (J). (gr. 1-6). 1996. pap. 9.95 (*0-614-14790-5*) Kldoscope Pr.

***Writing Sociology Essays.** M. Morrison. 1985. pap. text ed. write for info. (*0-582-35490-0*, Pub. by Longman UK) Longman.

***Writing Software & Responsive Writer.** Jocelyn Siler. (C). 1996. teacher ed., pap. text ed. write for info. (*0-15-504021-9*) HB Coll Pubs.

***Writing Software Documentation: A Task-Oriented Approach.** Thomas T. Barker. LC 97-22198. 1997. 38.00 (*0-205-19576-8*) Allyn.

Writing Software Manuals: A Practical Guide. Martyn Thirlway. LC 94-14088. (BCS Practioner Ser.). 250p. 1995. pap. text ed. 48.00 (*0-13-138801-0*) P-H.

Writing Solid Code. Steve Maguire. (Code Ser.). 288p. 1993. pap. 24.95 (*1-55615-551-4*) Microsoft.

Writing Solutions: Beginnings, Middles & Endings. Thomas Fensch. (Communication Textbook Ser.). 160p. 1989. 18.50 (*0-8058-0410-2*) L Erlbaum Assocs.

Writing South Carolina's History. Ed. by Archie V. Huff, Jr. LC 89-39788. 216p. 1991. 25.00 (*0-87152-439-2*) Reprint.

Writing Space: The Computer Hypertext, & the History of Writing. J. Bolter. 272p. (C). 1991. pap. 34.50 (*0-8058-0428-5*); text ed. 75.00 (*0-8058-0427-7*); disk 12.95 (*1-56321-067-3*) L Erlbaum Assocs.

Writing Specifications for Construction. Peter Cox. LC 93-12838. 1993. write for info. (*0-07-707803-9*) McGraw.

***Writing Start-Ups.** Mike Artell. (Ten-Minute Ser.). (Illus.). 96p. (Orig.). (J). (gr. 3-6). 1997. pap. 10.95 (*1-57612-002-3*, MM2030) Monday Morning Bks.

Writing Stories: The Nuts & Bolts of Writing Fiction. Ken Lewis. 186p. (Orig.). (YA). 1996. pap. text ed. 18.95 (*1-55059-133-9*, Pub. by Detselig CN) Temeron Bks.

Writing Stories for Little Children. 1972. pap. 1.90 (*0-686-32338-6*) Rod & Staff.

Writing Strands Ser., 2 vols., Set. Dave Marks. 265p. 1992. pap. text ed. write for info. (*1-888344-00-8*) National Writing.

Writing Strategies: Reaching Diverse Audiences. Laurel W. Richardson. (Qualitative Research Methods Ser.: Vol. 21). 88p. (C). 1990. 22.95 (*0-8039-3521-8*); pap. 9.95 (*0-8039-3522-6*) Sage.

Writing Structured COBOL Programs. David L. Johnson. 550p. (C). 1986. teacher ed. write for info. (*0-201-11592-1*); pap. text ed. 25.56 (*0-201-11591-3*); write for info. (*0-201-11594-8*); write for info. (*0-201-11596-4*) Addison-Wesley.

Writing Student Papers. Marvin E. Oliver. LC 94-77264. (Illus.). (Orig.). 1994. pap. 7.95 (*0-935435-10-7*) High Impact Pr.

Writing Students: Composition, Testimonials, & Representations of Students. Marguerite H. Helmers. LC 93-49080. (SUNY Series, Literacy, Culture, & Learning: Theory & Practice). 171p. 1994. pap. text ed. 16.95 (*0-7914-2164-3*) State U NY Pr.

Writing Students: Composition, Testimonials, & Representations of Students. Marguerite H. Helmers. LC 93-49080. (SUNY Series, Literacy, Culture, & Learning: Theory & Practice). 171p. 1994. text ed. 49.50 (*0-7914-2163-5*) State U NY Pr.

***Writing Style.** Sue Young. (YA). (gr. 4 up). 1997. 12.95 (*0-614-29044-9*, Scholastic Ref) Scholastic Inc.

Writing Style Differences in Newspaper, Radio, & Television News. Irving Fang. Ed. by Lillian Bridwell-Bowles & Paul Prior. (Monographs: Vol. 1). 40p. (Orig.). (C). 1991. pap. 4.50 (*1-881221-00-8*) U Minn Ctr Interdis.

***Writing Successful Self-Help & How-To-Books.** Jean Stine. (Orig.). 1997. pap. 14.95 (*0-614-27617-9*) Wiley.

Writing Successfully. Richard Hanson. LC 95-35818. 1995. pap. text ed. 30.00 (*0-205-15277-5*) Allyn.

***Writing Successfully in Science.** Ed. by M. O'Connor. (Illus.). 229p. (Orig.). (C). (gr. 13 up). 1992. pap. text ed. 18.95 (*0-412-44630-8*, Chap & Hall NY) Chapman & Hall.

Writing Successfully in Science. Maeve O'Connor. 200p. (C). 1992. text ed. 49.95 (*0-04-445805-3*, A8245); pap. text ed. 14.95 (*0-04-445806-1*, A8246) Routledge Chapman & Hall.

***Writing Superheroes: Contemporary Childhood, Popular Culture, & Classroom Literacy.** Anne H. Dyson. LC 97-1488. (Language & Literacy Ser.). (Illus.). 264p. 1997. 46.00 (*0-8077-3640-6*); pap. 21.95 (*0-8077-3639-2*) Tchrs Coll.

Writing Survival Skills for the Middle Grades. Imogene Forte & Joy MacKenzie. (Illus.). 80p. 1991. pap. text ed. 9.95 (*0-86530-219-7*, IP 192-0) Incentive Pubns.

Writing System of La Mojarra & Associated Monuments, 2 vols., Set. Lloyd B. Anderson. 212p. 1995. 39.00 (*1-879910-00-4*) Ecological Linguistics.

Writing System of Modern Persian. Herbert H. Paper & Mohammad A. Jazayery. LC 76-40543. 40p. (C). 1976. reprint ed. pap. 5.00 (*0-87950-284-3*) Spoken Lang Serv.

Writing System Workbook: A Step-by-Step Guide for Business & Technical Writers. Judith Graham & Daniel Graham. 210p. 1995. 28.95 (*0-9644495-0-1*) Preview Pr.

Writing Systems: A Linguistic Introduction. Geoffrey Sampson. (Illus.). 235p. 1985. 39.50 (*0-8047-1254-9*); pap. 12.95 (*0-8047-1756-7*) Stanford U Pr.

Writing Systems & Cognition: Perspectives from Psychology, Physiology, Linguistics, & Semiotics. Ed. by W. C. Watt. LC 93-41366. 488p. (C). 1994. lib. bdg. 240.00 (*0-7923-2592-3*) Kluwer Ac.

Writing Systems of the World. Florian Coulmas. (Language Library). 1993. pap. 24.95 (*0-631-18028-1*) Blackwell Pubs.

Writing Systems of the World: Alphabets, Syllabaries, Pictograms. Akira Nakanishi. LC 79-64826. (Illus.). 122p. 1980. 29.95 (*0-8048-1293-4*); pap. 14.95 (*0-8048-1654-9*) C E Tuttle.

***Writing Talk.** Anthony C. Winkler & Jo R. McCuen. LC 96-47493. 528p. (C). 1997. pap. 33.60 (*0-13-434887-7*) P-H.

***Writing Talk: Paragraphs & Short Essays.** Anthony C. Winkler & Jo R. McCuen. LC 96-39352. (Illus.). 496p. (C). 1997. pap. text ed. 30.80 (*0-13-434853-2*, Prentice Hall) P-H.

***Writing Talk: Sentence & Paragraphs.** Anthony C. Wilkler & Jo R. McCuen. LC 96-35020. 1996. pap. 30.80 (*0-13-436023-0*) P-H.

***Writing Talk: Sentences & Paragraphs with Readings.** Anthony C. Winkler & Jo R. McCuen. LC 96-46258. 1996. pap. 33.60 (*0-13-434895-8*) P-H.

Writing Talks. Ed. by Bob Perelman. LC 83-20338. 305p. 1985. pap. 14.95 (*0-8093-1180-1*) S Ill U Pr.

Writing Talks: Views on Teaching Writing from Across the Professions. Ed. by Muffy E. Siegel & Toby Olson. LC 83-11891. 158p. (gr. 13). 1983. pap. text ed. 21.00 (*0-86709-077-4*, 0077) Boynton Cook Pubs.

Writing Tall: New Fables, Myths, & Tall Tales by American Teen Writers. Ed. by Kathryn Kulpa & R. James Stahl. 144p. (YA). (gr. 7-12). 1996. pap. 9.75 (*1-886427-06-2*) Merlyns Pen.

Writing Tasks: An Authentic-Task Approach to Individual Writing Needs. David Jolly. 166p. 1984. pap. text ed. 13.95 (*0-521-22924-3*); pap. text ed. 16.95 (*0-521-28972-6*) Cambridge U Pr.

Writing Teacher As Researcher: Essays in the Theory & Practice of Class-Based Research. Ed. by Donald A. Daiker & Max Morenberg. LC 89-36957. 357p. (Orig.). 1990. pap. text ed. 27.50 (*0-86709-255-6*, 0255) Boynton Cook Pubs.

Writing, Teachers, & Students in Graeco-Roman Egypt. Raffaella Cribiore. LC 96-8012. (American Studies in Papyrology: No. 36). 316p. 1997. 49.95 (*0-7885-0277-8*, 31 00 36) Scholars Pr GA.

Writing Teacher's Book of Lists: With Ready-to-Use Activities & Worksheets. Gary R. Muschla. 256p. 1991. pap. 24.95 (*0-13-971169-4*, 710302) P-H.

Writing Teacher's Companion. Peterson. (C). 1994. suppl. ed., pap. 12.36 (*0-395-35033-6*) HM.

Writing Teacher's Sourcebook. 3rd ed. Gary Tate et al. 384p. (C). 1994. pap. text ed. 22.95 (*0-19-508306-7*) OUP.

Writing, Teaching & Learning: Incorporating Writing Throughout the Curriculum. Laurie Adams. (C). 1994. text ed. 7.50 (*0-06-502185-1*) Addson-Wesley Educ.

Writing, Teaching, & Learning in the Disciplines. Ed. by Anne Herrington & Charles Moran. LC 92-8756. (Research & Scholarship in Composition Ser.: No. 1). xi, 265p. 1992. pap. 19.75 (*0-87352-578-7*, RS01P); lib. bdg. 37.50 (*0-87352-577-9*, RS01C) Modern Lang.

Writing Technical Articles, Speeches, & Manuals. Mark Forbes. LC 91-40431. 220p. (C). 1993. reprint ed. 26.50 (*0-89464-688-5*) Krieger.

Writing Technology: Studies on the Materiality of Literacy. Christina Haas. 280p. 1995. text ed. 59.95 (*0-8058-1306-3*); pap. text ed. 27.50 (*0-8058-1994-0*) L Erlbaum Assocs.

Writing Term Papers. 3rd ed. Alan Heineman & Hulon Willis. 165p. (C). 1988. pap. text ed. 14.75 (*0-15-598284-2*) HB Coll Pubs.

Writing Test Items. Haladyna. LC 96-19255. 224p. 1997. pap. 25.95 (*0-205-17875-8*) P-H.

Writing That Sells. John C. Bancroft. (Illus.). 180p. 1975. pap. 10.95 (*0-686-11023-4*) J C Bancroft.

Writing That Works. Sharon L. Pywell. LC 93-9288. (Business Skills Express Ser.). 96p. 1993. per. 10.00 (*1-55623-856-8*) Irwin Prof Pubng.

Writing That Works. Kenneth Roman. 160p. 1996. mass mkt. 4.99 (*0-06-109381-5*, Harp PBks) HarpC.

Writing that Works. 5th ed. Walter E. Oliu et al. 1995. teacher ed., pap. text ed. 5.00 (*0-312-10377-8*) St Martin.

Writing that Works. 5th ed. Walter E. Oliu et al. 1995. teacher ed., pap. text ed. 35.00 (*0-312-10378-6*) St Martin.

***Writing That Works.** 6th ed. Walter E. Oliu. Date not set. pap. text ed. write for info. (*0-312-15390-2*); pap. text ed. 35.00 (*0-312-15391-0*) St Martin.

Writing That Works: A Practical Guide for Business & Creative People. Richard Andersen. 1989. pap. text ed. 14.95 (*0-07-001693-3*) McGraw.

Writing that Works: Effective Communication in Business. Walter E. Oliu et al. 608p. 1995. pap. text ed. 36.75 (*0-312-10376-X*) St Martin.

Writing the Advanced Short Story. Simone Bibeau. (Illus.). 32p. (J). (gr. 1-12). 1983. pap. text ed. 1.95 (*0-940406-07-1*) Perception Pubns.

Writing the American Classics. James Barbour & Tom Quirk. LC 89-16648. xvi, 288p. (C). 1990. 49.95 (*0-8078-1896-8*); pap. 16.95 (*0-8078-4280-X*) U of NC Pr.

Writing the Apocalypse: Historical Vision in Contemporary U. S. & Latin American Fiction. Lois P. Zamora. 230p. 1989. text ed. 65.00 (*0-521-36223-7*) Cambridge U Pr.

Writing the Apocalypse: Historical Vision in Contemporary U. S. & Latin American Fiction. Lois P. Zamora. 233p. (C). 1993. pap. text ed. 19.95 (*0-521-42691-X*) Cambridge U Pr.

***Writing the Australian Child: Text & Contexts in Fictions for Children.** Ed. by Clare Bradford. 1995. pap. 19.95 (*1-875560-75-0*, Pub. by Univ of West Aust Pr AT) Intl Spec Bk.

Writing the Australian Crawl. William Stafford. Ed. by Donald Hall. LC 77-5711. (Poets on Poetry Ser.). 1978. pap. 13.95 (*0-472-87300-8*) U of Mich Pr.

Writing the Beginning Short Story. Simone Bibeau. (Illus.). 32p. (Orig.). (J). (gr. 1-9). 1983. pap. text ed. 1.95 (*0-940406-06-3*) Perception Pubns.

Writing the Blockbuster Novel. Albert Zuckerman. 224p. 1994. 18.99 (*0-89879-598-2*, Wrtrs Digest Bks) F & W Pubns Inc.

Writing the Book of Esther. Henri Raczymow. Tr. by Dori Katz from FRE. (French Expressions Ser.). 220p. 1995. 24.00 (*0-8419-1335-8*) Holmes & Meier.

Writing the Broadway Musical. Aaron Frankel. LC 76-58925. 192p. 1981. pap. 19.95 (*0-89676-044-8*, Drama Pubs) QSMG Ltd.

Writing the Business Research Paper: A Complete Guide. Thomas J. Farrell & Charlotte Donabedion. LC 91-73930. 224p. 1991. pap. 14.95 (*0-89089-445-0*); lib. bdg. 24.95 (*0-89089-446-9*) Carolina Acad Pr.

Writing the Character-Centered Screenplay. Andrew Horton. LC 93-37307. (C). 1994. 40.00 (*0-520-08455-1*); pap. 13.00 (*0-520-08457-8*) U CA Pr.

Writing the Circle: Native Women of Western Canada, an Anthology. Ed. by Sylvia Vance. LC 91-50857. 1993. pap. 14.95 (*0-8061-2437-7*) U of Okla Pr.

Writing the City: Literature & the Urban Experience. Peter Preston & Paul Simpson-Housley. LC 93-44177. (Illus.). 300p. (C). (gr. 13). 1994. text ed. 79.95 (*0-415-10667-2*, B3896, Routledge NY) Routledge.

Writing the College Essay: A Handbook & Workbook in Composition Research & Grammar. 3rd ed. James D. Zamagias. 464p. (C). 1996. per., pap. text ed. 38.79 (*0-7872-1821-9*) Kendall-Hunt.

Writing the Colonial Adventure: Race, Gender & Nation in Anglo-Australian Popular Fiction 1875-1914. Robert Dixon. (Illus.). 204p. (C). 1996. text ed. 59.95 (*0-521-48190-2*) Cambridge U Pr.

***Writing the Community: Concepts & Models for Service-Learning in Composition.** Ed. by Linda Adler-Kassner et al. (Service-Learning in the Disciplines Ser.). 1997. pap. 28.50 (*1-56377-006-7*) Am Assn Higher Ed.

Writing the Creole: Jean Rhys's Historical Imagination. Veronica M. Gregg. LC 94-32011. 260p. 1995. pap. text ed. 17.95 (*0-8078-4504-3*); lib. bdg. 39.95 (*0-8078-2196-9*) U of NC Pr.

Writing the Doctoral Dissertation. Gordon B. Davis & Clyde A. Parker. LC 78-7598. 1979. pap. 9.95 (*0-8120-0997-5*) Barron.

***Writing the Doctoral Dissertation.** 2nd rev. ed. Gordon B. Davis. 160p. 1997. pap. text ed. 10.95 (*0-8120-9800-5*) Barron.

Writing the Easy Way. 2nd ed. Harriet Diamond. 1991. pap. 11.95 (*0-8120-4615-3*) Barron.

Writing the Economics Paper. Lawrence Morse. 1981. pap. text ed. 6.95 (*0-8120-2113-4*) Barron.

Writing the Environment: Ecocriticism & Literature. Ed. by Richard Kerridge & Neil Sammells. 256p. 1997. 59.95 (*1-85649-429-2*, Pub. by Zed Bks Ltd UK); pap. 22.50 (*1-85649-430-6*, Pub. by Zed Bks Ltd UK) Humanities.

Writing the Family Narrative. Lawrence P. Gouldrup. LC 87-70106. 157p. (Orig.). 1987. pap. 12.95 (*0-916489-27-2*, 141) Ancestry.

Writing the Family Narrative. Lawrence P. Gouldrup. 168p. (Orig.). 1993. wbk. ed., pap. 16.95 (*0-916489-41-8*) Ancestry.

Writing the Fantasy Story. Simone Bibeau. (Illus.). 32p. (Orig.). (J). (gr. 1-9). 1983. pap. text ed. 1.95 (*0-940406-08-X*) Perception Pubns.

Writing the Female Voice: Essays on Epistolary Literature. Ed. by Elizabeth C. Goldsmith. 320p. 1989. text ed. 40.00 (*1-55553-038-9*) NE U Pr.

Writing the Future. Ed. by David Wood. (Warwick Studies in Philosophy & Literature). 224p. (C). (gr. 13). 1990. text ed. 39.95 (*0-415-04423-5*, A4025) Routledge.

Writing the Good Fight: Political Commitment in the International Literature of the Spanish Civil. Peter Monteath. LC 93-21130. (Contributions to the Study of World Literature Ser.: No. 52). 240p. 1994. text ed. 55.00 (*0-313-28766-X*, Greenwood Pr) Greenwood.

Writing the History of the American West. Martin Ridge et al. (Illus.). 110p. 1991. pap. 12.95 (*0-944026-31-1*, 42179) Am Antiquarian.

***Writing the Image after Roland Barthes.** Jean-Michel Rabate. LC 97-9579. (New Cultural Studies). 1997. write for info. (*0-8122-3369-7*); pap. write for info. (*0-8122-1596-6*) U of Pa Pr.

Writing the Incommensurable: Kierkegaard, Rossetti, & Hopkins. Mary E. Finn. (Literature & Philosophy Ser.). 232p. 1993. 29.95 (*0-271-00854-7*) Pa St U Pr.

***Writing the Information Superhighway.** William Condon & Wayne Butler. LC 96-43596. 300p. 1997. pap. 32.00 (*0-205-19575-X*) Allyn.

***Writing the Information Superhighway.** William Condon & Wayne Butler. teacher ed., pap. write for info. (*0-205-26720-3*) Allyn.

Writing the Irish Famine. Christopher Morash. 256p. 1995. 45.00 (*0-19-818279-1*) OUP.

Writing the Laboratory Notebook. H. M. Kanare. 1985. 34.95 (*0-8412-0906-5*); pap. 24.95 (*0-8412-0933-2*) Am Chemical.

Writing the Margins: Edith Wharton, Ellen Glasgow, and the Literary Tradition of the Ruined Woman. Catherine E. Saunders. LC 86-73024. (LeBaron Russell Briggs Prize Honors Essays in English Ser.). 92p. 1987. pap. 5.00 (*0-674-96235-4*) HUP.

Writing the Memoir: From Truth to Art. Judith Barrington. LC 96-43065. 192p. (Orig.). 1997. pap. 12.95 (*0-933377-40-1*); lib. bdg. 22.95 (*0-933377-41-X*) Eighth Mount Pr.

Writing the Modern Mystery. Barbara Norville. 224p. 1992. pap. 14.99 (*0-89879-523-0*, Wrtrs Digest Bks) F & W Pubns Inc.

W

An Asterisk (*) at the beginning of an entry indicates that the title is appearing in BIP for the first time.

Writing the Natural Way: Using Right-Brain Techniques to Release Your Expressive Powers. Gabriele L. Rico. LC 81-126. (Illus.). 288p. 1983. pap. 14.95 (*0-87477-236-2*, Tarcher Putnam) Putnam Pub Group.

Writing the New Testament: A Reader's Approach. Arthur Wormhoudt. 130p. 1994. pap. 6.50 (*0-940307-47-2*) Wormhoudt.

Writing the New World: Imaginary Voyages & Utopias of the Great Southern Land. David Fausett. (Utopianism & Communitarianism Ser.). (Illus.). 360p. 1993. text ed. 49.95 (*0-8156-2585-5*); pap. text ed. 17.95 (*0-8156-2586-3*) Syracuse U Pr.

Writing the News: A Guide for Print Journalists. 2nd ed. Walter Fox. LC 93-8730. 168p. (C). 1993. text ed. 24.95 (*0-8138-2454-0*) Iowa St U Pr.

Writing the Novel: From Plot to Print. Lawrence Block. 218p. 1985. pap. 12.99 (*0-89879-208-8*, Wrtrs Digest Bks) F & W Pubns Inc.

***Writing the Novel - Craft & Style.** Jeremy Crain. 136p. (Orig.). 1997. pap. 13.95 (*0-9657212-7-2*) Trail Rdge.

Writing the Orgy: Power & Parody in Sade. Lucienne Frappier-Mazur. 232p. 1996. text ed. 37.95 (*0-8122-3251-8*); pap. text ed. 18.95 (*0-8122-1590-7*) U of Pa Pr.

Writing the Past, Inscribing the Future: History As Prophecy in Colonial Java. Nancy K. Florida. LC 94-45845. (Illus.). 464p. 1995. text ed. 49.95 (*0-8223-1605-6*); pap. text ed. 18.95 (*0-8223-1622-6*) Duke.

Writing the Politics of Difference. Ed. by Hugh J. Silverman. LC 90-32126. (Selected Studies in Phenomenology & Existential Philosophy: No. 14). 390p. (C). 1991. pap. text ed. 21.95 (*0-7914-0498-6*) State U NY Pr.

Writing the Politics of Difference. Ed. by Hugh J. Silverman. LC 90-32126. (Selected Studies in Phenomenology & Existential Philosophy: No. 14). 390p. (C). 1991. text ed. 64.50 (*0-7914-0497-8*) State U NY Pr.

***Writing the Private Eye Novel: A Handbook by the Private Eye Writers of America.** Robert J. Randisi. LC 97-13699. 1997. pap. text ed. 18.99 (*0-89879-767-5*, Wrtrs Digest Bks) F & W Pubns Inc.

Writing the Qualitative Dissertation: Understanding by Doing. Judith Meloy. 128p. 1994. pap. 14.95 (*0-8058-1417-5*); text ed. 29.95 (*0-8058-1416-7*) L Erlbaum Assocs.

***Writing the Range: Race, Class, & Culture in the Women's West.** Ed. by Elizabeth Jameson & Susan Armitage. LC 96-39163. (Illus.). 672p. 1997. 45.00 (*0-8061-2929-8*); pap. 21.95 (*0-8061-2952-2*) U of Okla Pr.

Writing the Renaissance: Essays on Sixteenth-Century French Literature in Honor of Floyd Gray. Ed. by Raymond C. La Charite. LC 91-73985. (French Forum Monographs: No. 77). 266p. (Orig.). 1992. pap. 17.95 (*0-917058-81-X*) French Forum.

Writing the Research Paper. Lotte Blustein & Rosemary J. Geary. (Illus.). 62p. (gr. 7 up). 1985. pap. text ed. 6.50 (*0-9605248-2-7*) Blustein-Geary.

Writing the Research Paper. Lotte Blustein & Rosemary J. Geary. 70p. (YA). (gr. 9 up). 1992. pap. text ed. 7.50 (*0-9605248-3-5*) Blustein-Geary.

Writing the Research Paper: A Handbook. 3rd ed. Anthony C. Winkler & Jo R. McCuen. 322p. (C). 1989. pap. text ed. 15.50 (*0-15-598292-3*) HB Coll Pubs.

Writing the Research Paper: A Handbook with Both the MLA & APA Documentation Styles. 4th ed. Anthony Winkler & Jo R. McCuen. 352p. (C). 1993. pap. text ed. write for info. (*0-318-69921-4*) HB Coll Pubs.

Writing the Research Paper: A Handbook with Both the MLA & APA Documentation Styles. 4th ed. Anthony C. Winkler. 1993. pap. 16.75 (*0-15-500166-3*) HarBrace.

Writing the River. Luci Shaw. LC 94-10388. 87p. 1994. 12.00 (*0-89109-823-2*) Pinon Press.

Writing the Romance Novel. Leigh Michaels. 190p. (Orig.). 1996. pap. 13.95 (*0-9641275-2-0*) PBL Ltd.

Writing the Scene of Speaking: Theories of Dialogue in the Late Italian Renaissance. Jon R. Snyder. LC 88-34254. 320p. 1989. 42.50 (*0-8047-1459-2*) Stanford U Pr.

Writing the Screenplay: TV & Film. 2nd ed. Alan A. Armer. LC 92-12141. 314p. (C). 1993. pap. 37.95 (*0-534-16668-7*) Wadsworth Pub.

Writing the Script: A Practical Guide for Films & Television. Wells Root. LC 79-1927. 228p. 1980. pap. 11.95 (*0-8050-0237-5*, Owl) H Holt & Co.

Writing the Short Film. Pat Cooper & Ken Dancyger. 220p. 1994. pap. 24.95 (*0-240-80165-2*, Focal) Buttrwrth-Heinemann.

Writing the Short Story: A Hands-On Writing Program. Jack M. Bickham. 224p. 1994. 16.99 (*0-89879-670-9*, Wrtrs Digest Bks) F & W Pubns Inc.

Writing the Social Text: Poetics & Politics in Social Science Discourse. Ed. by Richard H. Brown. (Communication & Social Order Ser.). 240p. 1992. pap. text ed. 25.95 (*0-202-30387-X*); lib. bdg. 47.95 (*0-202-30386-1*) Aldine de Gruyter.

***Writing the South: Ideas of an American Region.** Richard Gray. LC 97-24280. (Illus.). 368p. 1997. pap. text ed. 14.95 (*0-8071-2217-3*) La State U Pr.

Writing the Southwest. Ed. by David K. Dunaway & Sara L. Spurgeon. LC 95-13241. 272p. (Orig.). 1995. pap. 12.95 (*0-452-27394-3*, Plume) NAL-Dutton.

Writing the Speech. William Wiethoff. 200p. 1994. pap. text ed. 13.95 (*0-9616489-5-3*) Educ Vid Grp.

Writing the Subject: Bildung & the African American Text. Gunilla T. Kester. LC 93-37319. (American University Studies: Vol. 54). 192p. (C). 1995. text ed. 52.95 (*0-8204-2332-7*) P Lang Pubng.

***Writing the Subject: Bildung & the African American Text.** Gunilla T. Kester. (American University Studies: Vol. 54). 192p. (C). 1997. reprint ed. pap. 33.95 (*0-8204-3727-1*) P Lang Pubng.

Writing the Western Landscape. Mary Austin & John Muir. LC 94-9139. (Concord Library). (Illus.). 182p. 1994. 17.50 (*0-8070-8526-X*) Beacon Pr.

Writing the Woman Artist: Essays on Poetics, Politics, & Portraiture. Ed. by Suzanne W. Jones. 448p. (C). 1991. text ed. 48.95 (*0-8122-3089-2*); pap. text ed. 19.95 (*0-8122-1343-2*) U of Pa Pr.

Writing the World. Kelly Cherry. 160p. 1995. 22.50 (*0-8262-0992-0*) U of Mo Pr.

Writing the World. William Stafford. (Orig.). (C). 1988. pap. 25.00 (*0-9621666-1-8*) Haw River Bk.

Writing Their Nations: The Tradition of Nineteenth-Century American Jewish Women Writers. Diane Lichtenstein. LC 91-47015. 196p. 1992. 27.50 (*0-253-33346-6*) Ind U Pr.

Writing Themes about Literature: A Guide to Accompany the Norton Introduction to Literature. 3rd ed. Ed. by Carl E. Bain et al. (C). 1983. pap. text ed. 15.95 (*0-393-95350-5*) Norton.

Writing Theory & Critical Theory. Ed. by John Clifford & John Schilb. LC 93-50595. (Research & Scholarship in Composition Ser.: No. 3). ix, 374p. (Orig.). 1994. pap. 19.75 (*0-87352-576-0*, RS03P) Modern Lang.

Writing Theory & Critical Theory. John L. Schilb. LC 93-50595. (Research & Scholarship in Composition Ser.: No. 3). ix, 374p. (Orig.). 1994. lib. bdg. 37.50 (*0-87352-575-2*, RS03C) Modern Lang.

Writing Theory & Practice in the Second Language Classroom: A Selected Annotated Bibliography. Torild Homstad & Helga Thorson. Ed. by Lillian Bridwell-Bowles & Mark Olson. (Technical Reports: No. 10). 24p. (Orig.). (C). 1994. pap. 3.00 (*1-881221-17-2*) U Minn Ctr Interdis.

Writing Thinker Sheets. Becky Daniel. 64p. (J). (gr. 4-8). 1989. 8.99 (*0-86653-490-3*, GA1098) Good Apple.

Writing Through Children's & Young Adult Literature, Grades 4-8: From Authors to Authorship. Mary Strong & Mimi Neamen. (Illus.). 150p. (Orig.). 1993. pap. text ed. 21.00 (*1-56308-038-9*) Teacher Ideas Pr.

Writing Through Literature. Linda Anstendig & David Hicks. LC 95-34512. 1995. pap. text ed. 40.00 (*0-02-303564-1*, Macmillan Coll) P-H.

Writing Through Music. rev. ed. Paul F. Ronnholm. (Illus.). 74p. (J). (gr. k-3). 1989. pap. text ed. 4.00 (*0-941911-09-8*) Two Way Bilingual.

Writing Through Repression: Literature, Censorship, Psychoanalysis. Michael G. Levine. 232p. (C). 1994. text ed. 35.00 (*0-8018-4835-0*) Johns Hopkins.

Writing to Be Published. Gene Boone. 1984. pap. 4.95 (*0-317-11581-2*, Pub. by Exploits Pub Ltd CN) RSVP Press.

Writing to Be Published. 2nd ed. Gene Boone. 40p. 1986. pap. 4.00 (*0-930865-00-6*) RSVP Press.

Writing to Be Read. 3rd rev. ed. Ken Macrorie. LC 84-14922. 287p. (YA). (gr. 9-12). 1986. pap. text ed. 21.50 (*0-86709-133-9*, 0133) Boynton Cook Pubs.

Writing to Create Ourselves: New Approaches for Teachers, Students, & Writers. T. D. Allen. LC 82-1878. 255p. 1982. 22.95 (*0-8061-1768-0*) U of Okla Pr.

Writing to Explain. Kathleen A. Rogers. (J). (gr. 3-6). 1987. pap. 8.99 (*0-8224-7537-5*) Fearon Teach Aids.

***Writing to God's Glory: A Complete Writing Course from Crayon to Quill.** Jill Bond. 300p. Date not set. lib. bdg. 39.99 (*1-888306-15-7*, Home School Pr) GCB.

Writing to Grow: Keeping a Personal-Professional Journal. Mary L. Holly. LC 89-32195. (Illus.). 193p. (Orig.). 1994. pap. text ed. 22.50 (*0-435-08494-1*, 08494) Heinemann.

Writing to Inform. Kathleen A. Rogers. (J). (gr. 3-6). 1987. pap. 8.99 (*0-8224-7536-7*) Fearon Teach Aids.

***Writing-To-Learn.** LC 96-39400. 1996. write for info. (*0-88737-723-8*) Natl League Nurse.

Writing to Learn. James Howard. 53p. (Orig.). (C). 1983. pap. 7.95 (*0-931989-10-8*) Coun Basic Educ.

Writing to Learn. William K. Zinsser. 256p. (C). 1988. pap. text ed. 7.95 (*0-06-047398-3*) Addson-Wesley Educ.

Writing to Learn. William K. Zinsser. 1993. pap. 11.00 (*0-06-272040-6*, PL) HarpC.

Writing to Learn Across the Curriculum. John W. Myers. LC 84-61203. (Fastback Ser.: No. 209). 50p. (Orig.). 1984. pap. 3.00 (*0-87367-209-7*) Phi Delta Kappa.

Writing to Learn Biology. Randy Moore. 352p. (C). 1992. pap. text ed. 17.00 (*0-03-074189-0*) SCP.

Writing to Learn Botany. Randall C. Moore. 112p. (C). 1995. spiral bd. write for info. (*0-697-17455-7*) Wm C Brown Pubs.

Writing to Learn in Mathematics: An Annotated Bibliography. Aparna B. Ganguli & Richard Henry. Ed. by Lillian Bridwell-Bowles & Mark Olson. (Technical Reports: No. 5). 21p. (Orig.). (C). 1994. pap. 2.50 (*1-881221-13-X*) U Minn Ctr Interdis.

Writing to Learn Mathematics. Joan Countryman. LC 91-38215. 101p. 1992. pap. text ed. 16.00 (*0-435-08329-5*, 08329) Heinemann.

Writing to Learn Mathematics: Student Journals & Student Constructed Questions. Ramarkrishnan Menon. 1993. pap. 45.00 (*0-7300-2059-2*, Pub. by Deakin Univ AT) St Mut.

Writing to Learn Mathematics & Science. Ed. by Paul Connolly & Teresa Vilardi. 336p. 1989. text ed. 32.00 (*0-8077-2962-0*) Tchrs Coll.

Writing to Learn Science. Moore. (C). 1995. pap. text ed. 19.75 (*0-03-096488-1*) HB Coll Pubs.

Writing to Learn Science. 2nd ed. Moore. (C). 1995. teacher ed., pap. text ed. 6.75 (*0-03-097927-7*) HB Coll Pubs.

Writing to Others: Reading Level 5. 1993. 9.00 (*0-88336-384-4*); teacher ed. 1.60 (*0-88336-386-0*) New Readers.

Writing to Persuade. Kathleen A. Rogers. (J). (gr. 3-6). 1987. pap. 8.99 (*0-8224-7538-3*) Fearon Teach Aids.

Writing to Read. John H. Martin & Ardy Friedberg. 224p. 1989. reprint ed. pap. 12.95 (*0-446-39051-8*) Warner Bks.

Writing to Richie. Patricia Calvert. LC 94-14458. (J). 1994. text ed. 13.95 (*0-684-19764-2*) S&S Trade.

Writing to Sell. 4th ed. Scott Meredith. LC 95-41413. 240p. 1996. 17.99 (*0-89879-750-0*, Wrtrs Digest Bks) F & W Pubns Inc.

Writing to Survive: The Private Notebooks on Conrad Richter. Harvena Richter. LC 87-34237. 289p. reprint ed. pap. 82.40 (*0-7837-5851-0*, 2045570) Bks Demand.

Writing to the Point. Algis Budrys. 64p. 1994. per., pap. text ed. 10.50 (*1-886211-00-0*) Unifont.

Writing to the Point. 4th ed. William J. Kerrigan & Allen Metcalf. 192p. (C). 1987. pap. text ed. 16.00 (*0-15-598313-X*) HB Coll Pubs.

Writing to Win: A Down-to-Earth Guide to Creating Prize-Winning Short Stories. Jim Gray et al. LC 96-85243. 212p. (Orig.). 1996. pap. 10.95 (*0-9652829-1-0*) Creekwood Pr TN.

Writing Together: A Peer-Editing Approach to Composition. Richard R. Adler. 144p. 1990. per. 21.47 (*0-8403-5927-6*) Kendall-Hunt.

***Writing Together: How to Transform Your Writing in a Writing Group.** Dawn D. Haines et al. LC 96-54845. 224p. 1997. pap. 12.00 (*0-399-52338-3*, Perigee Bks) Berkley Pub.

Writing Toward Home: Tales & Lessons to Find Your Way. Georgia Heard. LC 95-11031. 146p. 1995. pap. 14.95 (*0-435-08124-1*, 08124) Heinemann.

Writing Towards Wisdom: The Writer As Shaman. Robert B. Sweet. LC 89-81927. 183p. (Orig.). 1990. pap. 9.95 (*0-923490-01-9*) Helios Hse.

Writing Trade: A Year in the Life. John Jerome. 272p. 1995. pap. 14.95 (*1-55821-424-0*) Lyons & Burford.

***Writing Travel Books & Articles.** Susan M. Boyce et al. 160p. (Orig.). 1997. pap. 14.95 (*1-55180-104-3*) Self-Counsel Pr.

***Writing Treatments That Sell: How to Create & Market Your Story Ideas to the Motion Picture Industry.** Kenneth Atchity. LC 97-1534. 1997. pap. text ed. 14.95 (*0-8050-4283-0*, Owl) H Holt & Co.

Writing Trends Across the Decade, 1974-1984. 84p. 1988. 12.50 (*0-317-67886-8*) Educ Testing Serv.

Writing Tricksters: Mythic Gambols in American Ethnic Fiction. Jeanne R. Smith. LC 96-20038. 1997. 45.00 (*0-520-20654-1*); pap. 15.95 (*0-520-20656-8*) U CA Pr.

Writing True Life Stories. Susan C. Feldhake. 1994. pap. 9.95 (*1-56924-999-7*) Marlowe & Co.

Writing Tutor, with Disk. Laurence G. Avery et al. 98p. (C). 1989. pap. text ed. 16.00 (*0-685-45455-X*); pap. text ed. 16.00 (*0-685-45456-8*) HarBrace.

Writing Tutor's Training Manual. Dianne E. Irwin & Linda L. Sherman. LC 82-61481. 125p. (Orig.). (C). 1985. pap. text ed. 10.95 (*0-88247-721-8*) R & E Pubs.

Writing under Pressure: The Quick Writing Process. Sanford Kaye. 208p. 1988. 19.95 (*0-19-505223-4*) OUP.

Writing under Pressure: The Quick Writing Process. Sanford Kaye. 208p. 1990. reprint ed. pap. 9.95 (*0-19-506661-8*) OUP.

Writing UNIX Device Drivers. George Pajari. 1991. pap. 39.95 (*0-201-52374-4*) Addison-Wesley.

Writing Unix Device Drivers In C. Philip M. Adams & Clovis L. Tondo. 400p. 1993. pap. 48.95 (*0-13-963869-5*) P-H.

Writing Up Qualitative Research. Harry F. Wolcott. (Qualitative Research Methods Ser.: Vol. 20). (Illus.). 100p. (C). 1990. text ed. 22.95 (*0-8039-3792-X*); pap. text ed. 9.95 (*0-8039-3793-8*) Sage.

Writing Up Research: Experimental Research Report Writing for Students of English. Robert Weissburg & Suzanne Buker. 208p. (C). 1990. pap. text ed. 21.90 (*0-13-970831-6*) P-H.

Writing User Documentation: A Practical Guide for Those Who Want to Be Read. Roderick Low et al. LC 93-25427. 1993. pap. text ed. 30.00 (*0-13-336835-1*) P-H Gen Ref & Trav.

Writing VAX-VMS Applications Using Pascal. Theo De Klerk. (VAX-VMS Ser.). (Illus.). 700p. 1991. 49.95 (*1-55558-067-X*, EY-F592E-DP, Digital DEC) Buttrwrth-Heinemann.

Writing Video Scripts with WordPerfect. Gene Bjerke. (Orig.). 1992. DOS disk, 3.5" 720K. 3.5 hd 5.00 (*0-9631505-2-9*); DOS disk, 5.25" 360K. 5.25 hd 5.00 (*0-9631505-1-0*) Petrel Pub.

Writing Video Scripts with WordPerfect. large type ed. Gene Bjerke. (Illus.). 96p. (Orig.). 1992. pap. 12.00 (*0-9631505-0-2*, Z52.5.W65.B4 19) Petrel Pub.

Writing Voyage: A Process Approach to Basic Writing. 4th ed. Thomas E. Tyner. 284p. 1994. pap. 27.25 (*0-534-21270-0*) Wadsworth Pub.

Writing Voyage: A Process Approach to Basic Writing. 5th ed. Thomas E. Tyner. (Developmental Study/Study Skills Ser.). (C). 1997. pap. text ed. 37.95 (*0-534-51748-X*) Wadsworth Pub.

Writing Voyage: An Integrated, Process Approach to Basic Writing. 3rd ed. Thomas E. Tyner. 310p. (C). 1991. pap. 25.95 (*0-534-14604-X*) Wadsworth Pub.

Writing VX-REXX Programs. Ronny Richardson. LC 94-20646. 1995. pap. text ed. 39.95 (*0-07-911911-5*) McGraw.

Writing War: Fiction, Gender, & Memory. Lynne Hanley. LC 90-49252. 168p. (Orig.). (C). 1991. pap. 14.95 (*0-87023-748-9*); lib. bdg. 25.00 (*0-87023-738-1*) U of Mass Pr.

Writing Warm-Ups. Lori Mammen. 80p. (gr. k-6). 1989. pap. text ed. 9.95 (*0-944459-07-2*) ECS Lrn Systs.

Writing Warm-Ups. Lori Mammen. 80p. (YA). (gr. 7-12). 1989. pap. text ed. 9.95 (*0-944459-08-0*) ECS Lrn Systs.

Writing Warm Ups: Seventy Activities for Prewriting. Tom & McKay. 126p. 1989. teacher ed. 19.95 (*0-13-971110-4*) Alemany Pr.

Writing Warm-ups Two K-6: Quick, Creative, & Challenging Writing Exercises. Lori Mammen. 80p. 1992. pap. text ed. 9.95 (*0-944459-45-5*) ECS Lrn Systs.

Writing Warm-ups Two 7-12: Quick, Creative, & Challenging Writing Exercises. Lori Mammen. 80p. 1992. pap. text ed. 9.95 (*0-944459-46-3*) ECS Lrn Systs.

Writing Warthog. Beverly Armstrong. 56p. (J). (gr. 4-6). 1995. 6.95 (*0-88160-243-4*, LW338) Learning Wks.

Writing Was Everything. Alfred Kazin. LC 95-5625. (The William E. Massey Sr. Lectures in the History of American Civilization: Vol. 1994). 152p. (C). 1995. 17.95 (*0-674-96237-0*) HUP.

Writing Well. John F. Dean. (J). (gr. 5-12). 1985. pap. 8.99 (*0-8224-7530-8*) Fearon Teach Aids.

Writing Well. 8th ed. Donald Hall & Sven P. Birkerts. LC 93-13752. (C). 1994. text ed. 29.50 (*0-673-46916-6*) Addson-Wesley Educ.

Writing Well. 8th ed. Donald Hall. 1996. pap. text ed. 29.95 (*0-8230-6532-4*) Watsn-Guptill.

***Writing Well.** 9th ed. Donald Hall & Sven Birkerts. LC 96-39857. (C). 1998. text ed. 27.81 (*0-321-01206-2*) Addison-Wesley.

Writing Well in the Real World: The Official Guide to Grammatik. Wayne Rash & Hugh Kenner. 1992. 40.00 (*0-679-74112-7*) Random.

Writing Western History: Essays on Major Western Historians. Ed. by Richard W. Etulain. LC 91-15290. 379p. (C). 1991. pap. 18.95 (*0-8263-1289-6*) U of NM Pr.

Writing Whirlwind: Grades 2-4. Linda Polon. (Illus.). 44p. (Orig.). 1986. pap. 6.95 (*0-673-18310-6*, GoodYrBooks) Addson-Wesley Educ.

Writing Windows Device Drivers. Daniel A. Norton. 448p. 1991. pap. 34.95 (*0-201-57795-X*) Addison-Wesley.

Writing Windows Device Drivers. 2nd ed. Daniel A. Norton. (C). 1996. pap. text ed. write for info. (*0-201-62486-9*) Addison-Wesley.

Writing Windows Virtual Device Drivers. David Thielen. 1994. pap. 39.95 (*0-201-62706-X*) Addison-Wesley.

Writing Windows VXDS & Device Drivers. 2nd ed. Karen Hazzah. 1997. pap. text ed. 49.95 incl. disk (*0-87930-438-3*) R & D Books.

Writing Windows 95 Shell Extensions. Karl Heubaum. (C). 1997. pap. text ed., pap. 34.95 incl. disk (*0-201-48840-X*) Addison-Wesley.

Writing Winning Business Proposals: Your Guide to Landing the Client, Making the Sale. Richard C. Freed. 1995. pap. text ed. 16.95 (*0-07-021925-7*) McGraw.

Writing Winning Proposals. Judith M. Gooch. 87p. 1987. 32.00 (*0-89964-249-7*, 28101) Coun Adv & Supp Ed.

Writing Wisely & Well. Marlene Martin & Maureen Girard. LC 92-37244. 1993. pap. text ed. write for info. (*0-07-023472-8*) McGraw.

Writing With: New Directions in Collaborative Teaching, Learning, & Research. Ed. by Sally B. Reagan et al. LC 93-15365. (SUNY Series, Feminist Theory in Education). 311p. 1994. text ed. 64.50 (*0-7914-1841-3*); pap. text ed. 21.95 (*0-7914-1842-1*) State U NY Pr.

Writing with a Byte: A Computer Guide for Freshman Composition. Marlene Forester & Barbara Williamson. 160p. (C). 1994. per. 26.19 (*0-8403-9415-2*) Kendall-Hunt.

***Writing with a Purpose, 11 Vols.** Joseph F. Trimmer. (C). 1995. teacher ed., text ed. 11.96 (*0-395-72324-8*) HM.

Writing with a Purpose. 6th ed. James M. McCrimmon. 1976. text ed. 10.95 (*0-685-42615-7*) HM.

***Writing with a Purpose, 11 Vols.** 11th ed. Joseph F. Trimmer. 576p. (C). 1994. text ed. 35.96 (*0-395-43237-5*) HM.

Writing with a Thesis. 5th ed. David Skwire. (C). 1990. teacher ed. write for info. (*0-03-031618-9*); text ed. 20.00 (*0-03-011503-5*) HB Coll Pubs.

***Writing with a Thesis.** 6th ed. Skwire. (C). 1994. pap. write for info. (*0-03-079101-4*) HB Coll Pubs.

Writing with a Thesis. 6th ed. David Skwire. (C). 1994. teacher ed., pap. text ed. 3.00 (*0-03-079102-2*) HB Coll Pubs.

Writing with a Thesis. 7th ed. David Skwire. (C). 1997. pap. text ed. 22.75 (*0-15-503740-4*) HB Coll Pubs.

Writing with a Voice: A Rhetoric & Handbook. 2nd ed. Diana Hacker & Betty Renshaw. (C). 1989. pap. text ed. 32.00 (*0-673-39670-3*) Addson-Wesley Educ.

Writing with Appleworks. Ellen J. Ljung. (EC - HS Communication/Engl Ser.). 1992. pap. 19.95 (*0-538-61212-6*) S-W Pub.

Writing with Authority. Steven D. Vivian. Ed. by Leslie Taggart & Dawn Youngblood. LC 89-7421. 300p. (Orig.). (C). 1990. pap. text ed. 18.75 (*0-03-025474-4*) HB Coll Pubs.

Writing with Authority: A Guide to the Research Process. Delija Valiukenas. 368p. (C). 1987. pap. text ed. write for info. (*0-07-555042-3*) McGraw.

***Writing with Computers.** Zimmerman & Palmquist. 1997. pap. text ed. 24.00 (*0-205-27487-0*) P-H.

Writing with Computers in the Early Grades. Ed. by James L. Hoot & Steven B. Silvern. 240p. (Orig.). (C). 1988. text ed. 34.00 (*0-8077-2920-5*); pap. text ed. 19.95 (*0-8077-2919-1*) Tchrs Coll.

***Writing with Confidence.** 4th ed. Meyers. (C). 1992. teacher ed., text ed. write for info. (*0-321-40633-8*) Addson-Wesley Educ.

W

An Asterisk (*) at the beginning of an entry indicates that the title is appearing in BIP for the first time.

Writing with Confidence. 4th ed. Alan Meyers. LC 91-26028. (C). 1991. text ed. 34.50 (0-673-46444-X) Addson-Wesley Educ.
Writing with Confidence. 5th ed. Meyers. LC 95-25067. (C). 1995. suppl. ed., teacher ed. write for info. (0-673-55897-5) Addson-Wesley Educ.
Writing with Confidence. 5th ed. Alan Meyers. LC 95-25067. (Illus.). 416p. (C). 1996. text ed. 34.50 (0-673-99497-X) Addson-Wesley Educ.
Writing with Confidence, Form B. 4th ed. Alan Meyers. (C). 1994. text ed. 39.50 (0-673-46801-1) Addson-Wesley Educ.
Writing with Confidence: A Composition Program for High School Juniors & Seniors. Jim Mika. (Illus.). 160p. 1993. pap. text ed. 11.95 (0-9639717-0-0) Jennifer Pubng.
Writing with Confidence: A Modern College Rhetoric. James W. Kirkland et al. LC 88-81519. 479p. (C). 1989. text ed. 35.96 (0-669-13675-1); Instr.'s guide. teacher ed. 2.66 (0-669-13678-6) HM College Div.
Writing with Light: A Simple Workshop in Basic Photography. Paul C. Czaja. LC 72-93261. 96p. (J). (gr. 6 up). 1973. 12.95 (0-85699-068-X) Chatham Pr.
*__Writing with Light: Meditations for Caregivers in Word & Image.__ Robert M. Eddy & Kathy W. Eddy. LC 96-51907. 128p. (Orig.). 1997. pap. 12.95 (0-8298-1166-4) Pilgrim OH.
Writing with Logic in Mind. Boyd. (C). 1994. pap. text ed. 10.50 (0-15-501909-0) HB Coll Pubs.
Writing with Microsoft Works on Mac. Grizinski. (EC - HS Communication/Engl Ser.). 1995. 68.95 (0-538-62670-4) S-W Pub.
Writing with Microsoft Works on the Macintosh. Ellen J. Ljung. (EC - HS Communication/Engl. Ser.). 1995. 20.95 (0-538-62669-0) S-W Pub.
*__Writing with Microsoft Works on the Macintosh.__ large type ed. Ellen J. Ljung. 300p. 74.50 (0-614-20560-3, L-85332-00 APHB) Am Printing Hse.
Writing with Passion: Life Stories, Multiple Genres. Tom Romano. LC 95-8647. 238p. 1995. pap. text ed. 22.50 (0-86709-362-5, 0362) Boynton Cook Pubs.
*__Writing with Pictures: How to Write & Illustrate Children's Books.__ Uri Shulevitz. 1997. pap. text ed. 29.95 (0-8230-5935-9) Watsn-Guptill.
Writing with Power: Techniques for Mastering the Writing Process. Peter Elbow. 356p. 1981. 25.00 (0-19-502912-7); pap. 11.95 (0-19-502913-5) OUP.
*__Writing with Precision: America's Classic Guide to Plain English.__ 7th expanded rev. ed. Jefferson D. Bates. 288p. 1997. pap. 13.95 (1-889051-25-X) Acrpls Bks CO.
Writing with Precision: How to Write So That You Cannot Possibly Be Misunderstood. 6th ed. Jefferson D. Bates. 1993. pap. 12.95 (0-87491-991-6) Acrpls Bks CO.
*__Writing with Purpose & Passion.__ Stalcup & Rovasio. 1997. pap. text ed. 25.33 (0-13-437609-9) P-H.
Writing with Reason: The Emergence of Authorship in Young Children. Ed. by Nigel Hall. (Illus.). 140p. (Orig.). (C). 1989. pap. text ed. 19.50 (0-435-08498-4, 08498) Heinemann.
Writing with Scripture: The Authority & Uses of the Hebrew Bible in the Torah of Formative Judaism. Jacob Neusner. (USF Studies in the History of Judaism). 188p. (Orig.). 1993. 49.95 (1-55540-886-9, 240085) Scholars Pr GA.
Writing with Style. Laraine Fergenson. 608p. (C). 1989. pap. text ed. 24.00 (0-03-009907-2) HB Coll Pubs.
*__Writing with Style.__ Sue K. Young. (J). 1997. pap. 12.95 (0-590-50977-2) Scholastic Inc.
Writing with Style: Conversations on the Art of Writing. John R. Trimble. (Illus.). 160p. (C). 1974. pap. text ed. 20.60 (0-13-970368-3) P-H.
Writing with Style: The News Story & the Feature. Peter Jacobi. LC 82-62576. (Communications Library). 111p. (Orig.). (C). 1982. pap. 19.95 (0-931368-12-X) Ragan Comm.
Writing with the Lights On: From Sentence to Paragraph. O'Harra & Kristbjorg E. O'Harra. 1995. pap. text ed. 33.60 (0-13-670100-0) P-H.
Writing with the Macintosh: Using Microsoft Word. Ann H. Duin & Kathleen S. Gorak. (Illus.). 368p. (C). 1991. pap. text ed. 25.00 (1-878748-25-4) Course Tech.
Writing with the Masters: From Interests & Abilities. Frank Schaffer Publications, Inc. Staff. (Middle School Bks.). (Illus.). 1996. wbk. ed. 10.95 (0-7647-0062-6, FS-10214) Schaffer Pubns.
Writing with WordPerfect 5.1 for MS-DOS Machines. Halio. LC 94-5830. (C). 1995. teacher ed., pap. write for info. (0-673-55413-9) Addson-Wesley Educ.
Writing with WordPerfect 5.1 for MS-DOS Machines. Marcia P. Halio. LC 94-5830. 208p. (C). 1995. text ed., pap. 19.95 incl. disk (0-673-99047-8) Addson-Wesley Educ.
Writing with Writers. Thomas E. Tyner. LC 94-12902. 276p. 1995. pap. 31.95 (0-534-23616-2) Wadsworth Pub.
Writing without Taboos: The New East German Literature. J. H. Reid. 268p. 1990. 19.95 (0-85496-020-1) Berg Pubs.
Writing without Teachers. Peter Elbow. LC 72-96608. 208p. 1975. pap. 8.95 (0-19-501679-3) OUP.
Writing Without the Muse: Fifty Beginning Exercises for the Creative Writer. Beth Joselow. LC 95-37783. (SLP Writer's Guides Ser.). 90p. (Orig.). 1995. pap. 8.00 (1-885266-12-X) Story Line.
Writing Without Words: Alternative Literacies in Mesoamerica & the Andes. Ed. by Elizabeth H. Boone & Walter D. Mignolo. LC 93-4531. (Illus.). 352p. 1994. text ed. 49.95 (0-8223-1377-4); pap. text ed. 18.95 (0-8223-1388-X) Duke.
*__Writing Without Worry.__ Alice P. Franklin. 108p. (Orig.). (C). 1997. pap. text ed. 19.95 (1-890870-00-5) Comn Opport.

Writing Wizardry: The Basics, Vol. I. Nancy B. Culberson. 144p. 1992. per. 18.84 (0-8403-8125-5) Kendall-Hunt.
Writing Wizardry, Vol. II: The Basics. Nancy B. Culberson. 144p. (C). 1993. per. 18.84 (0-8403-8597-8) Kendall-Hunt.
Writing Women: Contemporary Women Novelists. Olga Kenyon. 150p. (C). 51.50 (0-7453-0307-2, Pub. by Pluto Pr UK); pap. 16.95 (0-7453-0564-4, Pub. by Pluto Pr UK) LPC InBook.
Writing, Women, & Space: Women's Colonial & Postcolonial Geographies. Ed. by Alison Blunt & Gillian Rose. LC 94-11691. (Mappings Ser.). 195p. 1994. pap. text ed. 18.95 (0-89862-498-3, 2498); lib. bdg. 42.00 (0-89862-497-5, 2497) Guilford Pr.
Writing Women in Jacobean England. Barbara K. Lewalski. (Illus.). 431p. (C). 1993. text ed. 47.50 (0-674-96242-7) HUP.
Writing Women in Jacobean England. Barbara K. Lewalski. (Illus.). 431p. 1994. pap. text ed. 19.95 (0-674-96243-5, LEWWRX) HUP.
*__Writing Women in Late Imperial China.__ Ellen Widmer & Kang-I Sung Chang. LC 96-30597. 1997. write for info. (0-8047-2871-2) Stanford U Pr.
*__Writing Women in Late Imperial China.__ Ellen Widmer & Sun C. Kang-I. LC 96-30597. 1997. pap. write for info. (0-8047-2872-0) Stanford U Pr.
Writing Women in Late Medieval & Early Modern Spain: The Mothers of Saint Teresa of Avila. Ronald E. Surtz. LC 95-5353. (Middle Ages Ser.). 256p. 1995. text ed. 33.95 (0-8122-3292-5) U of Pa Pr.
*__Writing Women in Modern China: An Anthology of Literature by Early-Twentieth-Century Chinese Women.__ Amy D. Dooling & Kristina M. Torgeson. LC 97-19306. 1998. write for info. (0-231-10700-5); pap. write for info. (0-231-10701-3) Col U Pr.
Writing Women of New England, 1630-1900: An Anthology. Ed. by Arlen G. Westbrook & Perry D. Westbrook. LC 82-5459. 282p. 1982. 25.00 (0-8108-1544-3) Scarecrow.
*__Writing Women, Writing Power.__ Ed. by Greg Kucich & Keith Hanley. 1996. pap. text ed. 18.00 (2-88449-245-3) Gordon & Breach.
*__Writing Women's Communities: The Politics & Poetics of Contemporary Multi-Genre Anthologies.__ Cynthia G. Franklin. LC 97-9460. 278p. 1997. 34.95 (0-299-15600-1); pap. 18.95 (0-299-15604-4) U of Wis Pr.
Writing Women's History: International Perspectives. Ed. by Karen M. Offen et al. LC 90-49155. 596p. 1991. 37.50 (0-253-34160-4); pap. 18.95 (0-253-20651-0, MB-651) Ind U Pr.
Writing Women's Literary History. Margaret J. Ezell. 224p. 1993. text ed. 35.95 (0-8018-4432-0) Johns Hopkins.
Writing Women's Literary History. Margaret J. Ezell. 216p. 1996. reprint ed. pap. text ed. 14.95 (0-8018-5508-X) Johns Hopkins.
Writing Women's Lives. Voyager Company Staff. Date not set. write for info. (1-55940-713-1) Voyager NY.
Writing Women's Lives: An Anthology of Autobiographical Narratives by Twentieth-Century Women Writers. Ed. by Susan Cahill. LC 93-41136. 608p. (Orig.). 1994. pap. 15.00 (0-06-096998-9, PL) HarpC.
Writing Women's Lives: An Anthology of Autobiographical Narratives by Twentieth-Century Women Writers. Ed. by Susan Cahill. 608p. 1994. lib. bdg. 39.00 (0-8095-9145-6) Borgo Pr.
Writing Women's Worlds: Bedouin Stories. Lila Abu-Lughod. (C). 1993. pap. 12.00 (0-520-08304-0) U CA Pr.
Writing Word Processing Strategies: WordPerfect 6.0. Art Lyons & Vicki Lyons. LC 94-5829. 224p. 1994. pap. text ed. 19.20 (0-13-606062-5) P-H.
Writing Workout. Huizenga & Ruzic. 1990. pap. 21.95 (0-8384-3960-8) Heinle & Heinle.
Writing Works a Manager's Alphabet. Krystyna Weinstein. 176p. 1995. pap. 39.00 (0-85292-577-8, Pub. by IPM UK) St Mut.
Writing Works Catalogue: Retail Edition, Vol. 1. Ed. by Michael P. Jones. 198p. 1983. 6.00 (0-89904-095-0); pap. text ed. 5.00 (0-89904-094-2) Crumb Elbow Pub.
Writing Works Catalogue: Wholesale Edition Vol. 1. Ed. by Michael P. Jones. (Illus.). 202p. (J). 1984. pap. 5.00 (0-89904-059-4); 6.00 (0-89904-058-6) Crumb Elbow Pub.
*__Writing Workshop.__ Patricia D'Arcy. LC 95-90989. (Illus.). 72p. (Orig.). 1997. pap. 10.00 (1-56002-640-5, Univ Edtns) Aegina Pr.
Writing Workshop: A World of Difference. Lucy M. Calkins & Shelley Harwayne. 149p. 1987. pap. text ed. 23.50 (0-435-08450-X, 08450) Heinemann.
Writing Workshop: How to Teach Creative Writing, Vol. 1. Alan Ziegler. 175p. (Orig.). 1981. pap. 12.95 (0-915924-11-0) Tchrs & Writers Coll.
Writing Workshop: How to Teach Creative Writing, Vol. 2. Alan Ziegler. 274p. (Orig.). 1984. pap. 14.95 (0-915924-07-2) Tchrs & Writers Coll.
Writing Workshop: Morals of Aesop's Fables. T. Y. Mayer. (Writing Workshop, Human Condition Ser.: Vol. 1). 100p. 1996. teacher ed., spiral bd. 40.00 (1-889008-04-4) Projects.
Writing Workshop: Paragraph & Sentence Practice. Joyce Pagurek. 1984. pap. 21.95 (0-8384-2998-X, Newbury) Heinle & Heinle.
Writing Workshop Teacher's Survival Kit. Gary R. Muschla. 288p. 1993. pap. 28.95 (0-87628-972-3) Ctr Appl Res.
Writing Worlds: Discourse, Text & Metaphor in the Representation of Landscape. Trevor J. Barnes & James S. Duncan. LC 91-12898. 304p. (C). 1991. pap. 19.95 (0-415-06983-1, A6548) Routledge.

Writing Worlds: Discourse, Text & Metaphor in the Representation of Landscape. Trevor J. Barnes & James S. Duncan. LC 91-12898. 304p. (C). (gr. 13). 1991. text ed. 69.95 (0-415-05499-0, A6544) Routledge.
Writing Worth Reading: A Practical Guide. 2nd ed. Nancy H. Packer & John Timpane. LC 92-75239. 504p. (C). 1993. pap. text ed. 11.50 (0-312-09206-7, Bedford Bks) St Martin.
Writing, Writing. Robert Duncan. (Orig.). 1971. pap. 5.00 (0-932264-15-8) Trask Hse Bks.
*__Writing Wrongs: The Work of Wallace Shawn.__ W. D. King & Wallace Shawn. LC 96-2750. (American Subjects Ser.). 1997. 29.95 (1-56639-517-8) Temple U Pr.
Writing Yellow Pages for Students & Teachers. LC 87-83366. (Yellow Pages Ser.). 64p. (J). (gr. k-8). 1988. pap. text ed. 8.95 (0-86530-038-0) Incentive Pubns.
*__Writing Your A+ Scientific Technical Paper.__ Research & Education Association Staff. 112p. 1997. pap. 9.95 (0-87891-913-9) Res & Educ.
Writing Your Autobiography. Gareth W. Weldon & Barry Weinstock. (Illus.). 1995. pap. 9.95 (0-9648303-2-9) TR Pr.
Writing Your College Application Essay. rev. ed. Sarah M. McGinty. 131p. (Orig.). 1991. pap. 9.95 (0-87447-429-9) College Bd.
Writing Your First Play. Roger Hall. 160p. 1991. pap. 24.95 (0-240-80117-2, Focal) Buttrwrth-Heinemann.
Writing Your Heritage: A Sequence of Thinking, Reading & Writing Assignments. Debra Dixon. Ed. by Miriam Ylvisaker. (Illus.). 88p. (Orig.). 1993. pap. 8.00 (1-883920-08-6) Nat Writing Proj.
Writing Your Life: A Journey of Discovery. Patti Miller. 144p. 1995. pap. 11.95 (1-86373-641-7) IPG Chicago.
Writing Your Life: An Easy-to-Follow Guide to Writing an Autobiography. rev. ed. Mary Borg. (Illus.). 100p. 1989. pap. 15.95 (1-877673-07-2, WLA) Cottonwood Pr.
Writing Your Life: Autobiographical Writing Activities for Young People. Mary Borg. 46p. (YA). (gr. 5-12). 1989. pap. text ed. 14.95 (1-877673-09-9, WLT) Cottonwood Pr.
Writing Your Life: Putting Your Past on Paper. Lou W. Stanek. LC 96-19329. 192p. (Orig.). 1996. pap. 12.00 (0-380-78625-7) Avon.
Writing Your Own Worship Materials. G. Temp Sparkman. 1980. pap. 10.00 (0-8170-0857-8) Judson.
Writing Your Way. 2nd rev. ed. Peter Stillman. LC 94-28553. 173p. 1995. pap. text ed. 16.50 (0-86709-343-9, 0343) Boynton Cook Pubs.
*__Writing Your Way to Success: Finding Your Own Voice in Academic Publishing.__ Susan M. Drake & Glen A. Jones. (Faculty Development Ser.). 64p. (Orig.). 1997. pap. 7.95 (0-913507-63-6) New Forums.
Writing Your Way to Wholeness: Creative Exercises for Personal Growth. Terre Ouwehand. LC 94-24332. 205p. (Orig.). (C). 1995. pap. 17.95 (0-89390-312-4) Resource Pubns.
Writing Your Will. Holmes F. Crouch. Ed. by Irma J. Crouch. LC 92-73877. (Series 300 Tax Guides: Vol. 303). (Illus.). 224p. 1992. pap. text ed. 16.95 (0-944817-11-4) Allyear Tax.
*__Writing Your Will: A Contingency Plan Every Adult Must Have.__ 2nd rev. ed. Holmes F. Crouch. Ed. by Irma J. Crouch. (Three Hundred Tax Guides Ser.: Vol. 302). (Illus.). 224p. 1997. pap. 18.95 (0-944817-37-8, T/G 302) Allyear Tax.
Writing Your Winning Resume: Getting Your Resume Through the Corporate Personnel Office. Thomas R. Wims. 132p. (Orig.). 1990. pap. 14.95 (0-9628599-0-7) Roberts Pubns.
Writing Yourself Home: A Woman's Guided Journey of Self-Discovery. Kimberley Snow. 204p. 1991. reprint ed. lib. bdg. 31.00 (0-8095-5858-0) Borgo Pr.
Writing Yourself Home: A Woman's Guided Journey of Self Discovery. Kimberly Snow. (Illus.). 204p. 1992. reprint ed. pap. 10.95 (0-943233-32-1) Conari Press.
Writing 101. Claudia Sorsby. 1996. mass mkt. 4.99 (0-312-95975-3) St Martin.
Writings, 25 vols., Set. George Eliot. (BCL1-PR English Literature Ser.). 1992. reprint ed. lib. bdg. 2,250.00 (0-7812-7524-5) Rprt Serv.
Writings, 24 vols, Set. John Fiske. LC 70-168032. reprint ed. 1,080.00 (0-404-02410-6) AMS Pr.
Writings, 7 Vols, Set. James Monroe. Ed. by Stanislaus M. Hamilton. LC 69-18218. reprint ed. write for info. (0-404-04400-X) AMS Pr.
Writings, 16 vols, Set. Harriet Beecher Stowe. LC 76-182724. reprint ed. 1,224.00 (0-404-00220-X) AMS Pr.
Writings, 20 vols, Set. Henry David Thoreau. LC 80-25514. reprint ed. 1,530.00 (0-404-59580-4) AMS Pr.
Writings, 7 Vols, Set. John Greenleaf Whittier. Ed. by Horace E. Scudder. LC 69-15587. reprint ed. 595.00 (0-404-06950-9) AMS Pr.
Writings, Vol. 3. Junipero Serra. Ed. by Antonine Tibesar. 1955. 50.00 (0-614-05574-1) AAFH.
Writings, Vol. 4. Junipero Serra. Ed. by Antonine Tibesar. 1955. 50.00 (0-614-05575-X) AAFH.
Writings: Autobiography; A Summary View of the Rights of British America; Notes on the State of Virginia; Addresses, Messages, Letters. Thomas Jefferson. Ed. by Merrill D. Peterson. LC 83-19917. 1600p. 1984. 35.00 (0-940450-16-X) Library of America.
Writings: In Prose & Verse, 2 vols. Robert C. Sands. LC 72-5813. (Essay Index Reprint Ser.). 1977. reprint ed. Set. 53.95 (0-8369-7291-0) Ayer.
Writings: Incl. Silence Dogood; Poor Richard's Almanacks; The Autobiography; Essays; Letters. Benjamin Franklin. Ed. by J. A. Lemay. LC 87-3303. 1605p. 1987. 40.00 (0-940450-29-1) Library of America.

Writings: The Fount of Knowledge. John. LC 59-792. (Fathers of the Church Ser.: Vol. 37). 476p. 1981. reprint ed. pap. 135.70 (0-7837-9203-4, 2049953) Bks Demand.
Writings: The Suppression of the African Slave-Trade; The Souls of Black Folk; Dusk of Dawn; Essay; Articles from The Crisis. W. E. B. Du Bois. Ed. by Nathan I. Huggins. LC 86-10565. 1334p. 1987. 35.00 (0-940450-33-X) Library of America.
Writings: The Suppression of the African Slave-Trade; The Souls of Black Folk; Dusk of Dawn; Essays; Articles from the Crisis. W. E. B. Du Bois. Ed. by Nathan I. Huggins. LC 86-10565. (Library of America College Editions). 1334p. 1996. pap. 15.95 (1-883011-31-0) Library of America.
Writings see Works of M. P. Shiel
Writings - Interviews. Richard Serra. LC 93-46459. 286p. 1994. pap. 17.95 (0-226-74880-4) U Ch Pr.
Writings about Art. Carole G. Calo. 320p. (C). 1993. pap. text ed. 32.67 (0-13-761701-1) P-H.
Writings about Henry Cowell: An Annotated Bibliography. Martha L. Manion. LC 82-81925. (I.S.A.M. Monographs: No. 16). (Illus.). 368p. (Orig.). 1982. pap. 15.00 (0-914678-17-5) Inst Am Music.
Writings about John Cage. Ed. by Richard Kostelanetz. (C). 1996. pap. 26.95 (0-472-08391-0) U of Mich Pr.
Writings about Music. Steve Reich. LC 73-87481. (Nova Scotia Ser.). (Illus.). 82p. (C). 1975. text ed. 24.00 (0-8147-7358-3); pap. text ed. 12.00 (0-8147-7357-5) NYU Pr.
Writings & Drawings. James Thurber. Ed. by Garrison Keillor. LC 96-5853. (Library of America). (Illus.). 1020p. 1986. 35.00 (1-883011-22-1) Library of America.
Writings & Life of George Meredith. M. Gretton. LC 70-117580. (Studies in George Meredith: No. 21). 1970. reprint ed. lib. bdg. 49.95 (0-8383-1013-3) M S G Haskell Hse.
Writings & Speeches of Daniel Webster, 18 vols., Set. Daniel Webster. Ed. by J. W. McIntyre. LC 74-15126. (Illus.). reprint ed. 392.00 (0-404-11950-6) AMS Pr.
Writings & Speeches of Edmund Burke: Vol. IX: The Revolutionary War, 1794-1797, & Ireland. Edmund E. Burke. Ed. by Robert B. McDowell. 744p. 1992. 170.00 (0-19-821787-0) OUP.
Writings & Speeches of Edmund Burke: Vol. VI: India: The Launching of the Hastings Impeachment 1786-1788. Edmund E. Burke. Ed. by P. J. Marshall. 528p. 1991. 140.00 (0-19-821788-9) OUP.
Writings & Speeches of Edmund Burke, Vol. III: Party, Parliament, & the American Crisis 1774-1780. Edmund E. Burke. Ed. by Warren M. Elofson. 736p. (C). 1996. 138.00 (0-19-822414-1, 7708) OUP.
Writings & Speeches of Oliver Cromwell with an Introduction, Notes & a Sketch of His Life, Vol. IV: The Protectorate, 1655-1658. Ed. by Wilbur C. Abbott. (Illus.). 1102p. 1989. 180.00 (0-19-821774-9) OUP.
Writings by Re: Poems & Guided Writings to Inspire Each Day. 2nd rev. ed. Marie A. Van Duyne. Ed. by Kitty Overall. 416p. 1994. pap. 14.50 (1-881311-27-9) Plus Pubns CT.
Writings for a Liberation Psychology. Ignacio Martin-Baro. Ed. by Adrianne Aron & Shawn Corne. LC 94-20987. (Illus.). 256p. 1994. text ed. 32.00 (0-674-96246-X, MARWRI) HUP.
Writings for a Liberation Psychology. Ignacio Martin-Baro. Ed. by Adrianne Aron & Shawn Corne. (Illus.). 256p. 1996. pap. 16.95 (0-674-96247-8) HUP.
Writings from Ancient Israel: A Handbook of Historical & Religious Documents. Klaas A. Smelik. (Illus.). 206p. (Orig.). 1992. pap. 23.00 (0-664-25308-3) Westminster John Knox.
Writings from Japan. Lafcadio Hearn. (Nonfiction Ser.). 368p. 1985. pap. 8.95 (0-14-009532-2, Penguin Bks) Viking Penguin.
Writings from Japan: An Anthology. Lafcadio Hearn. Ed. & Intro. by Francis King. 368p. 1995. pap. 10.95 (0-14-043463-1, Penguin Classics) Viking Penguin.
Writings from Ox. Gregory Corso. Ed. by Michael Andre. (Illus.). 160p. (Orig.). 1981. pap. 9.95 (0-934450-10-2) Unmuzzled Ox.
Writings from the New Yorker: 1927-1976. E. B. White. LC 89-46564. 256p. 1991. reprint ed. pap. 13.00 (0-06-092123-4, PL) HarpC.
Writings from the Philokalia on Prayer of the Heart. E. Kadloubovsky. 420p. 1992. pap. 18.95 (0-571-16393-9) Faber & Faber.
Writings from the "Western Standard" George Q. Cannon. reprint ed. 49.50 (0-404-01379-1) AMS Pr.
Writings from the Workplace: Documents, Models, & Cases. Margot K. Soven. LC 94-32252. 1994. pap. text ed. 32.00 (0-205-15012-8) Allyn.
Writings in General Linguistics: On Sound Alternation (1881) & Outline of Linguistic Science (1883) Mikolaj Kruszewski. Ed. & Intro. by Konrad Koerner. LC 95-43683. (Amsterdam Classics in Linguistics, 1800-1925 Ser.: Vol. 11). xi, 188p. 1995. 77.00 (1-55619-315-7) Benjamins North Am.
Writings in General Linguistics: On Vocal Alternation (Kazan, 1881) & "Prinzipien der Sprachentwicklung (Leipzig 1884-90)" Mikolaj Kruszewski. (Amsterdam Classics in Linguistics Ser.: No. 11). xi, 188p. 1995. 77.00 (90-272-0977-4) Benjamins North Am.
Writings in Indian History, 1985-1990. Compiled by Jay Miller et al. LC 95-8776. (D'Arcy McNickle Center Bibliographies in American Indian History Ser.: Vol. 2). 232p. 1995. 27.95 (0-8061-2759-7) U of Okla Pr.
Writings in Jazz. 5th ed. Nathan Davis. 288p. (C). 1996. pap. text ed. 25.14 (0-7872-1895-2) Kendall-Hunt.
Writings in Prose & Verse of Hezekiah Salem, Late of New England. Philip M. Freneau. LC 75-15901. (Illus.). 88p. 1975. lib. bdg. 50.00 (0-8201-1156-2) Schol Facsimiles.

Writings-Kethubim: A New Translation of the Holy Scriptures According to the Traditional Hebrew Text. 624p. 19.95 (*0-8276-0202-2*) JPS Phila.

Writings 1902-1910: The Varieties of Religious Experience; Pragmatism; A Pluralistic Universe; The Meaning of Truth; Some Problems of Philosophy; Essays. William James. Ed. by Bruce Kuklick. 1379p. 1988. 37.50 (*0-940450-38-0*) Library of America.

***Writings of a Battle Fatigued Teacher.** Charles A. Crawford. (Orig.). 1997. pap. write for info. (*1-57553-479-7*) Watermrk Pr.

Writings of a Savage. Paul Gauguin. Ed. by Daniel Guerin. Tr. by Eleanor Levieux from FRE. LC 95-46759. 346p. (FRE.). 1996. reprint ed. pap. 14.95 (*0-306-80700-9*) Da Capo.

Writings of Benjamin Franklin, 10 Vols. Benjamin Franklin. Ed. by Albert H. Smyth et al. LC 68-24976. (American History & Americana Ser.: No. 47). 1969. reprint ed. lib. bdg. 350.00 (*0-8383-0194-0*) M S G Haskell Hse.

Writings of Bradford, Vols. 1 & 2. John Bradford. 1979. 56.99 (*0-85151-359-X*) Banner of Truth.

Writings of Braulio of Saragossa, Fructuosus of Braga. Iberian Fathers. Tr. by Claude W. Barlow. LC 70-80270. (Fathers of the Church Ser.: Vol. 63). 250p. 1969. 16.95 (*0-8132-0063-6*) Cath U Pr.

Writings of Brendan Behan. Colbert Kearney. LC 77-24780. 1977. text ed. 29.95 (*0-312-89442-2*) St Martin.

Writings of Bret Harte, 20 Vols, Set. Bret Harte. reprint ed. write for info. (*0-404-03170-6*) AMS Pr.

Writings of Carlos Fuentes: History, Culture, & Identity. Raymond L. Williams. LC 95-43526. (Texas Pan American Ser.). 208p. 1996. 24.95 (*0-292-79097-X*) U of Tex Pr.

Writings of Carrie Williams Clifford & Carrie L. M. Figgs. Gates. LC 96-38729. 1996. 25.00 (*0-7838-1435-6*, Hall Reference) Macmillan.

Writings of Cassius Marcellus Clay: Including Speeches & Addresses. Cassius M. Clay. Ed. by Horace Greeley. LC 70-82185. (Anti-Slavery Crusade in America Ser.). 1970. reprint ed. 26.95 (*0-405-00634-9*) Ayer.

Writings of Catherine Booth, 6 vols. Catherine Booth. 1101p. 1986. 25.95 (*0-685-17948-6*) Salv Army Suppl South.

Writings of Charles S. Peirce: A Chronological Edition: Vol. 1, 1857-1866. Charles S. Peirce. Ed. by Edward C. Moore et al. LC 79-1993. (Illus.). 738p. 1982. 57.50 (*0-253-37201-1*) Ind U Pr.

Writings of Charles S. Peirce: A Chronological Edition: Vol. 2, 1867-1871. Charles S. Peirce. Ed. by Christian J. Kloesel et al. LC 79-1993. (Illus.). 704p. 1984. 57.50 (*0-253-37202-X*) Ind U Pr.

Writings of Charles S. Peirce: A Chronological Edition: Vol. 3, 1872-1878. Charles S. Peirce. Ed. by Christian J. Kloesel et al. LC 79-1993. (Illus.). 672p. 1986. 57.50 (*0-253-37203-8*) Ind U Pr.

Writings of Charles S. Peirce: A Chronological Edition, Vol. 4: 1879-1884. Charles S. Peirce. LC 79-1993. 768p. 1989. 67.50 (*0-253-37204-6*) Ind U Pr.

Writings of Charles S. Peirce: A Chronological Edition, Vol. 5, 1884-1886. Charles S. Peirce. LC 79-1993. (Illus.). 592p. 1993. 75.00 (*0-253-37205-4*) Ind U Pr.

Writings of Christine de Pizan. Christine De Pizan. Tr. by Willard et al. 400p. (Orig.). 1994. 35.00 (*0-89255-180-1*); pap. 12.95 (*0-89255-188-7*) Persea Bks.

Writings of Colonel William Byrd. William Byrd. (Works of William Byrd). 1989. reprint ed. lib. bdg. 79.00 (*0-7812-2234-6*) Rprt Serv.

***Writings of D. Bonhoeffer.** (Great Devotional Classics Ser.). pap. 1.85 (*0-687-61424-4*) Abingdon.

Writings of Daniel Berrigan. Ross Labrie. (Illus.). 284p. (C). 1989. lib. bdg. 50.00 (*0-8191-7495-5*) U Pr of Amer.

Writings of Dirk Philips. Ed. by C. J. Dyck et al. Tr. by William E. Keeney et al. from DUT. LC 91-31658. (Classics of the Radical Reformation Ser.: Vol. 6). 672p. 1992. text ed. 44.99 (*0-8361-3111-8*) Herald Pr.

Writings of Edward Fitzgerald, 7 Vols. variorum ed. Edward Fitzgerald. LC 67-18645. 2068p. Set. 400.00 (*0-87753-015-7*) Phaeton.

Writings of Elizabeth Swift Brengle, 4 vols. 1990. Set. 19.95 (*0-86544-061-1*) Salv Army Suppl South.

Writings of Elliott Carter: An American Composer Looks at Modern Music. Elliott Carter. Ed. by Else Stone & Kurt Stone. LC 76-48539. 407p. reprint ed. pap. 116.60 (*0-7837-1761-X*, 2057299) Bks Demand.

***Writings of Evelyn Underhill.** (Great Devotional Classics Ser.). pap. 1.85 (*0-687-61439-2*) Abingdon.

Writings of Evelyn Waugh. Ian Littlewood. LC 82-18513. 256p. (C). 1983. text ed. 58.50 (*0-389-80350-2*, 07208) B&N Imports.

Writings of Fermin Francisco Lasuen, 2 vols., Set. Ed. by Finbar Kenneally. (Documentary Ser.). (Illus.). 1965. 50.00 (*0-88382-008-0*) AAFH.

Writings of Florence Scovel Shinn. Florence S. Shinn. 365p. (Orig.). (J). 1988. pap. 15.95 (*0-87516-610-5*) DeVorss.

***Writings of Francois Fenelon.** (Great Devotional Classics Ser.). pap. 1.85 (*0-687-61433-3*) Abingdon.

Writings of Gandhi. Ed. by Ronald Duncan. (C). 1993. text ed. 9.00 (*0-8364-2890-0*, Pub. by Rupa II) S Asia.

Writings of General John Forbes Relating to His Service in North America. John M. Forbes. LC 78-106091. (First American Frontier Ser.). 1971. reprint ed. 24.95 (*0-405-02849-0*) Ayer.

Writings of George Eliot with the Life by J. W. Cross, 25 vols. George Eliot. LC 74-114748. (Illus.). reprint ed. Set. 1,500.00 (*0-404-02280-4*) AMS Pr.

Writings of German Composers: Bach, Brahms, Mozart. Ed. by James Steakley & Jost Hermand. (German Library: Vol. 51). 304p. 1985. 29.50 (*0-8264-0292-5*); pap. text ed. 16.95 (*0-8264-0293-3*) Continuum.

Writings of Harriet Beecher Stowe, 16 vols. Harriet Beecher Stowe. (BCL1-PS American Literature Ser.). 1992. reprint ed. Set. lib. bdg. 1,440.00 (*0-7812-6869-9*) Rprt Serv.

Writings of Havelock Ellis, 12 vols, Ea. Havelock Ellis. 1975. lib. bdg. 50.00 (*0-8490-1338-0*) Gordon Pr.

Writings of Henry Cowell: A Descriptive Bibliography. Bruce Saylor. LC 77-81276. (I.S.A.M. Monographs: No. 7). 44p. 1977. pap. 10.00 (*0-914678-07-8*) Inst Am Music.

Writings of Henry D. Thoreau. Incl. Walden. Ed. by J. Lyndon Shanley. 404p. 1988. text ed. 65.00 (*0-691-06194-7*); Maine Woods. Ed. by Joseph J. Moldenhauer. 468p. 1972. text ed. 70.00 (*0-691-06224-2*); Maine Woods. Ed. by Joseph J. Moldenhauer. 468p. 1972. pap. text ed. 17.95 (*0-691-01404-3*); Reform Papers. Ed. by Wendell Glick. 436p. 1973. text ed. 55.00 (*0-691-06241-2*); Early Essays & Miscellanies. Ed. by Joseph J. Moldenhauer & Edwin Moser. 430p. 1975. text ed. 69.50 (*0-691-06286-2*); Vol. 1. Journal, 1837-1844. Ed. by John C. Broderick. 712p. 1981. text ed. 69.50 (*0-691-06361-3*); Week on the Concord & Merrimack Rivers. Ed. by Carl Hoyde. 624p. 1980. text ed. 69.50 (*0-691-06376-1*); write for info. (*0-318-55372-4*) Princeton U Pr.

Writings of Henry D. Thoreau: Cape Cod. Henry David Thoreau. Ed. by Joseph J. Moldenhauer. LC 93-15293. 452p. 1988. pap. text ed. 9.95 (*0-691-00076-X*) Princeton U Pr.

Writings of Henry D. Thoreau Journal, Vol. 4: 1851-1852. Ed. by Leonard N. Neufeldt & Nancy C. Simmons. (Illus.). 450p. 1992. text ed. 65.00 (*0-691-06535-7*) Princeton U Pr.

Writings of J. Frank Dobie: A Bibliography. Mary L. McVicker. LC 68-23421. 1968. 13.95 (*0-685-85505-8*) Mus Great Plains.

Writings of J. Frank Dobie: A Bibliography. deluxe limited ed. Mary L. McVicker. LC 68-23421. 1968. boxed 25.00 (*0-685-85504-X*) Mus Great Plains.

Writings of James M. Nack: The Deaf & Dumb Poet. James M. Nack. 1972. 59.95 (*0-8490-1339-9*) Gordon Pr.

Writings of James Monroe, Including a Collection of His Public & Private Papers & Correspondence, Now for the First Time Printed, 7 vols. James Monroe. (American Biography Ser.). 1991. reprint ed. Set. lib. bdg. 630.00 (*0-7812-8289-6*) Rprt Serv.

Writings of James Stephens: Variations on a Theme of Love. Patricia McFate. LC 78-13287. 1979. text ed. 29.95 (*0-312-89509-7*) St Martin.

***Writings of John Bunyon.** (Great Devotional Classics Ser.). pap. 1.85 (*0-687-61425-2*) Abingdon.

Writings of John Burroughs, 26 vols., Set. John Burroughs. 1993. reprint ed. lib. bdg. 2,054.00 (*0-7812-5141-9*) Rprt Serv.

***Writings of John Calvin.** (Great Devotional Classics Ser.). pap. 1.85 (*0-687-61426-0*) Abingdon.

Writings of John Calvin: An Introductory Guide. Wulfert De Greef. Tr. by Lyle D. Bierma from DUT. LC 93-42701. (Illus.). 256p. (C). 1994. reprint ed. pap. 19.99 (*0-8010-3021-8*) Baker Bks.

Writings of John Evelyn. John Evelyn. Ed. by Guy De la Bedoyere. (Illus.). 435p. (C). 1995. 71.00 (*0-85115-631-2*) Boydell & Brewer.

***Writings of John Knox.** (Great Devotional Classics Ser.). pap. 2.95 (*0-687-61435-X*) Abingdon.

Writings of John Lothrop Motley, 17 vols, Set. John L. Motley. Ed. by George W. Curtis. Incl. 1. Rise of the Dutch Republic. 67.50 (*0-404-04521-9*); 2. Rise of the Dutch Republic. 67.50 (*0-404-04522-7*); 3. Rise of the Dutch Republic. 67.50 (*0-404-04523-5*); 4. Rise of the Dutch Republic. 67.50 (*0-404-04524-3*); 5. Rise of the Dutch Republic. 67.50 (*0-404-04525-1*); 6. History of the United Netherlands. 67.50 (*0-404-04526-X*); 7. History of the United Netherlands. 67.50 (*0-404-04527-8*); 8. History of the United Netherlands. 67.50 (*0-404-04528-6*); 9. History of the United Netherlands. 67.50 (*0-404-04529-4*); 10. History of the United Netherlands. 67.50 (*0-404-04530-8*); 11. History of the United Netherlands. 67.50 (*0-404-04531-6*); 12. Life & Death of John of Barneveld, Advocate of Holland, with a View of the Primary Causes & Movements of the Thirty Years' War. 67.50 (*0-404-04532-4*); 13. Life & Death of John of Barneveld, Advocate of Holland, with a View of the Primary Causes & Movements of the Thirty Years' War. 67.50 (*0-404-04533-2*); 14. Life & Death of John of Barneveld, Advocate of Holland, with a View of the Primary Causes & Movements of the Thirty Years' War. 67.50 (*0-404-04534-0*); 15. Correspondence. 67.50 (*0-404-04535-9*); 16. Correspondence. 67.50 (*0-404-04536-7*); 17. Correspondence. 67.50 (*0-404-04537-5*); reprint ed. 552.50 (*0-685-00418-X*) AMS Pr.

Writings of John Quincy Adams, 7 vols., Set. John Q. Adams. Ed. by Worthington C. Ford. (History - United States Ser.). 1992. reprint ed. lib. bdg. 630.00 (*0-7812-6148-1*) Rprt Serv.

Writings of Jonathan Edwards: Theme, Motif, & Style. William J. Scheick. LC 75-18689. 192p. 1975. 29.95 (*0-89096-004-6*) Tex A&M Univ Pr.

Writings of Jonathan Swift. Jonathan Swift. Ed. by Robert A. Greenberg & William Piper. (Critical Editions Ser.). 500p. (C). 1973. pap. text ed. 17.95 (*0-393-09415-4*) Norton.

Writings of King Alfred. Frederick Harrison. (Beowulf & the Literature of the Anglo-Saxons Ser.: No. 2). 1970. reprint ed. pap. 39.95 (*0-8383-0042-1*) M S G Haskell Hse.

Writings of Koda Aya, a Japanese Literary Daughter. Alan M. Tansman. LC 92-33630. 224p. (C). 1993. text ed. 32.50 (*0-300-05724-5*) Yale U Pr.

Writings of Lafcadio Hearn, 16 vols. Lafcadio Hearn. (BCL1-PS American Literature Ser.). 1992. reprint ed. Set. lib. bdg. 1,440.00 (*0-7812-6736-6*) Rprt Serv.

Writings of Larry E. Axel (1946-1991) Ed. by Michael Shermis. LC 92-37851. (Studies in Liberal Religious Thought). 276p. 1993. text ed. 89.95 (*0-7734-9185-6*) E Mellen.

Writings of Leon Trotsky, 14 vols., Set. Leon Trotsky. 1979. reprint ed. pap. 375.00 (*0-87348-730-3*) Pathfinder NY.

Writings of Leon Trotsky: Supplement (1929-33) Leon Trotsky. Ed. by George Breitman. LC 73-80226. 1979. pap. 27.95 (*0-87348-563-7*); lib. bdg. 65.00 (*0-87348-562-9*) Pathfinder NY.

Writings of Leon Trotsky: Supplement (1934-40) Leon Trotsky. Ed. by George Breitman. LC 73-80226. 1979. pap. 31.95 (*0-87348-565-3*); lib. bdg. 75.00 (*0-87348-564-5*) Pathfinder NY.

Writings of Leon Trotsky, 1929. Leon Trotsky. Ed. by George Breitman & Sarah Lovell. Tr. by Iain Fraser et al. LC 73-88120. (Illus.). 460p. 1975. pap. 28.95 (*0-87348-459-2*); lib. bdg. 70.00 (*0-87348-458-4*) Pathfinder NY.

Writings of Leon Trotsky, 1930. Leon Trotsky. Ed. by George Breitman & Sarah Lovell. Tr. by Russell Block et al. from FRE. LC 73-88120. (Illus.). 443p. 1975. pap. 27.95 (*0-87348-413-4*); lib. bdg. 70.00 (*0-87348-412-6*) Pathfinder NY.

Writings of Leon Trotsky, 1930-31. Leon Trotsky. Ed. by George Breitman & Sarah Lovell. Tr. by George Saunders et al. LC 73-88120. 440p. 1973. reprint ed. pap. 27.95 (*0-87348-350-2*); reprint ed. lib. bdg. 65.00 (*0-87348-324-3*) Pathfinder NY.

Writings of Leon Trotsky, 1932. Leon Trotsky. Ed. by George Breitman & Sarah Lovell. Tr. by Iain Fraser et al. from BUL. LC 73-88120. (Illus.). 415p. 1973. reprint ed. lib. bdg. 65.00 (*0-87348-310-3*); reprint ed. pap. 26.95 (*0-87348-311-1*) Pathfinder NY.

Writings of Leon Trotsky, 1932-33. Leon Trotsky. Ed. by George Breitman & Sarah Lovell. Tr. by George Saunders et al. from FRE. LC 73-85709. (Illus.). 364p. 1972. reprint ed. pap. 25.95 (*0-87348-228-X*); reprint ed. lib. bdg. 65.00 (*0-87348-227-1*) Pathfinder NY.

Writings of Leon Trotsky, 1933-34. 2nd ed. Leon Trotsky. Ed. by George Breitman & Beverly Scott. Tr. by John G. Wright et al. from FRE. LC 73-80226. 379p. 1975. pap. 25.95 (*0-87348-418-5*); lib. bdg. 65.00 (*0-87348-572-6*) Pathfinder NY.

Writings of Leon Trotsky, 1934-35. 2nd ed. Leon Trotsky. Ed. by George Breitman & Beverly Scott. Tr. by John G. Wright et al. from RUS. LC 73-80226. (Illus.). 416p. (Orig.). 1974. pap. 26.95 (*0-87348-403-7*); lib. bdg. 65.00 (*0-87348-194-1*) Pathfinder NY.

Writings of Leon Trotsky, 1935-36. 2nd ed. Leon Trotsky. Ed. by Naomi Allen & George Breitman. LC 73-80226. (Illus.). 574p. 1977. pap. 31.95 (*0-87348-502-5*); lib. bdg. 75.00 (*0-87348-501-7*) Pathfinder NY.

Writings of Leon Trotsky, 1936-37. 2nd ed. Leon Trotsky. Ed. by Naomi Allen & George Breitman. LC 73-80226. (Illus.). 573p. 1978. pap. 31.95 (*0-87348-512-2*); lib. bdg. 75.00 (*0-87348-511-4*) Pathfinder NY.

Writings of Leon Trotsky, 1937-38. 2nd ed. Leon Trotsky. Ed. by Naomi Allen & George Breitman. LC 73-80226. (Writings of Leon Trotsky (1929-40)). (Illus.). 511p. 1976. pap. 29.95 (*0-87348-469-X*); lib. bdg. 70.00 (*0-87348-468-1*) Pathfinder NY.

Writings of Leon Trotsky, 1938-39. 2nd ed. Leon Trotsky. Ed. by Naomi Allen & George Breitman. LC 73-88120. (Illus.). 429p. 1974. pap. 27.95 (*0-87348-366-9*); lib. bdg. 65.00 (*0-87348-365-0*) Pathfinder NY.

Writings of Leon Trotsky, 1939-1940. 2nd ed. Leon Trotsky. Ed. by George Breitman & Naomi Allen. LC 73-80226. (Illus.). 465p. 1973. pap. 28.95 (*0-87348-313-8*); lib. bdg. 70.00 (*0-87348-312-X*) Pathfinder NY.

Writings of Mao Tse-Tung. Mao Tse-Tung. 24.95 (*0-8488-1209-3*) Amereon Ltd.

Writings of Mao Zedong, 1949-1976 Vol. 2: January 1956-December 1957, Vol, 2. Ed. by Michael Y. Kau & John K. Leung. LC 86-17910. 912p. (gr. 13). 1992. text ed. 140.00 (*0-87332-392-0*, East Gate Bk) M E Sharpe.

Writings of Mao Zedong, 1949-1976, Vol. 1: Sept. 1949-Dec. 1955, Vol. 1. Ed. by Michael Y. Kau & John K. Leung. LC 86-17910. 814p. (C). (gr. 13). 1986. text ed. 140.00 (*0-87332-391-2*, East Gate Bk) M E Sharpe.

Writings of Marcel Duchamp. Ed. by Michel Sanouillet & Elmer Peterson. (Quality Paperbacks Ser.). (Illus.). 208p. 1989. reprint ed. pap. text ed. 13.95 (*0-306-80341-0*) Da Capo.

Writings of Margaret Fuller. Sarah M. Ossoli. Ed. by Mason Wade. LC 72-122079. xi, 608p. 1973. reprint ed. lib. bdg. 49.50 (*0-678-03177-0*) Kelley.

Writings of Margaret Fuller. Sarah M. Ossoli. (BCL1-PS American Literature Ser.). 608p. 1993. reprint ed. lib. bdg. 129.00 (*0-7812-6996-2*) Rprt Serv.

Writings of Margaret of Oingt. Ed. by Renate Blumenfeld-Kosinski. (Focus Library of Medieval Women). 100p. (Orig.). (C). 1990. pap. 8.95 (*0-941051-08-0*, P26) Focus Pub-R Pullins.

***Writings of Margart of Oingt, Medieval Prioress & Mystic.** Renate Blumenfeld-Kosinski. (Library of Medieval Women). 96p. 1997. 23.00 (*0-85991-442-9*, DS Brewer) Boydell & Brewer.

Writings of Marie Corelli, 28 vols., Ea. Marie Corelli. 1976. lib. bdg. 34.95 (*0-318-52718-9*) Gordon Pr.

Writings of Mark Twain, Vol 11: Life on the Mississippi. Mark Twain, pseud. 1991. 69.00 (*0-403-02341-6*) Scholarly.

Writings of Mark Twain, Vol. 12: Adventures of Tom Sawyer. Mark Twain, pseud. 1991. 69.00 (*0-403-02342-4*) Scholarly.

Writings of Mark Twain, Vol. 13: Huckleberry Finn. Mark Twain, pseud. 1991. 59.00 (*0-403-02335-1*) Scholarly.

Writings of Mark Twain, Vol. 14: Pudd'nhead Wilson. Mark Twain, pseud. 1991. 59.00 (*0-403-02336-X*) Scholarly.

Writings of Mark Twain, Vol. 15: The Prince & the Pauper. Mark Twain, pseud. 1991. 59.00 (*0-403-02337-8*) Scholarly.

Writings of Mark Twain, Vol. 16: A Connecticut Yankee in King Arthur's Court. Mark Twain, pseud. 1991. 59.00 (*0-403-02338-6*) Scholarly.

Writings of Mark Twain, Vol. 20: Tom Sawyer Abroad. Mark Twain, pseud. 1991. 59.00 (*0-403-02343-2*) Scholarly.

Writings of Mark Twain, Vol. 24: The Thirty Thousand Bequest. Mark Twain, pseud. 1991. 59.00 (*0-403-02348-3*) Scholarly.

Writings of Mark Twain, Vol. 25: Christian Science. Mark Twain, pseud. 1991. 59.00 (*0-403-02349-1*) Scholarly.

Writings of Mark Twain, Vols. 1 & 2, Pts. 1 & 2: Innocents Abroad. Mark Twain, pseud. 1991. Set. 150.00 (*0-403-02376-9*) Scholarly.

Writings of Mark Twain, Vols. 1 & 2, Pts. 1 & 2: Innocents Abroad, 1. Mark Twain, pseud. 1991. write for info. (*0-403-02325-4*) Scholarly.

Writings of Mark Twain, Vols. 1 & 2, Pts. 1 & 2: Innocents Abroad, 2. Mark Twain, pseud. 1991. write for info. (*0-403-02326-2*) Scholarly.

Writings of Mark Twain, Vols. 17 & 18, Pts. 1 & 2: Joan of Arc. Mark Twain, pseud. 1991. Set. 145.00 (*0-403-02377-7*) Scholarly.

Writings of Mark Twain, Vols. 17 & 18, Pts. 1 & 2: Joan of Arc, 17. Mark Twain, pseud. 1991. write for info. (*0-403-02240-1*) Scholarly.

Writings of Mark Twain, Vols. 17 & 18, Pts. 1 & 2: Joan of Arc, 18. Mark Twain, pseud. 1991. write for info. (*0-403-02239-8*) Scholarly.

Writings of Mark Twain, Vols. 3 & 4, Pts. 1 & 2: The Gilded Age. Mark Twain, pseud. 1991. Set. 150.00 (*0-403-02378-5*) Scholarly.

Writings of Mark Twain, Vols. 3 & 4, Pts. 1 & 2: The Gilded Age, 3. Mark Twain, pseud. 1991. write for info. (*0-403-02327-0*) Scholarly.

Writings of Mark Twain, Vols. 3 & 4, Pts. 1 & 2: The Gilded Age, 4. Mark Twain, pseud. 1991. write for info. (*0-403-02328-9*) Scholarly.

Writings of Mark Twain, Vols. 5 & 6, Pts. 1 & 2: A Tramp Abroad. Mark Twain, pseud. 1991. Set. 69.00 (*0-403-02379-3*) Scholarly.

Writings of Mark Twain, Vols. 5 & 6, Pts. 1 & 2: A Tramp Abroad, 5. Mark Twain, pseud. 1991. write for info. (*0-403-02329-7*) Scholarly.

Writings of Mark Twain, Vols. 5 & 6, Pts. 1 & 2: A Tramp Abroad, 6. Mark Twain, pseud. 1991. write for info. (*0-403-02330-0*) Scholarly.

Writings of Mark Twain, Vols. 7 & 8, Pts. 1 & 2: Following the Equator. Mark Twain, pseud. 1991. Set. 150.00 (*0-403-02380-7*) Scholarly.

Writings of Mark Twain, Vols. 7 & 8, Pts. 1 & 2: Following the Equator, 7. Mark Twain, pseud. 1991. write for info. (*0-403-02331-9*) Scholarly.

Writings of Mark Twain, Vols. 7 & 8, Pts. 1 & 2: Following the Equator, 8. Mark Twain, pseud. 1991. write for info. (*0-403-02332-7*) Scholarly.

Writings of Mark Twain, Vols. 9 & 10, Pts. 1 & 2: Roughing It. Mark Twain, pseud. 1991. Set. 150.00 (*0-403-02381-5*) Scholarly.

Writings of Mark Twain, Vols. 9 & 10, Pts. 1 & 2: Roughing It, 9. Mark Twain, pseud. 1991. write for info. (*0-403-02333-5*) Scholarly.

Writings of Mark Twain, Vols. 9 & 10, Pts. 1 & 2: Roughing It, 10. Mark Twain, pseud. 1991. write for info. (*0-403-02334-3*) Scholarly.

Writings of Mark Twain, 1869-1909, 25 vols. Mark Twain, pseud. LC 79-7769. 1991. Set. 1,495.00 (*0-403-03736-0*) Scholarly.

Writings of Martin of Braga, Paschasius, Leander. Iberian Fathers. Tr. by Claude W. Barlow. LC 70-80270. (Fathers of the Church Ser.: Vol. 62). 261p. 1969. 16.95 (*0-8132-0062-8*) Cath U Pr.

Writings of Medieval Women: An Anthology. 2nd ed. Intro. by Marcelle Thiebaux. LC 93-36822. (Library of Medieval Literature: Vol. 100B). 568p. 1994. text ed. 45.00 (*0-8153-0409-9*); pap. text ed. 22.95 (*0-8153-1392-6*) Garland.

Writings of Melanie Klein, 4 vols. Melanie Klein. 1712p. (C). 1984. Set. 160.00 (*0-02-918460-6*, Free Press) Free Pr.

Writings of Paul Rolland: An Annotated Bibliography. Mark Joseph Eisele. 22p. 4.00 (*0-318-18119-3*) Am String Tchrs.

Writings of Pedro Albizu Campos. Pedro A. Campos. (Puerto Rico Ser.). 1979. lib. bdg. 69.95 (*0-8490-3016-1*) Gordon Pr.

Writings of Peter Abrahams. Kolawole Ogungbesan. LC 78-26133. 156p. (C). 1979. 17.50 (*0-8419-0480-4*, Africana) Holmes & Meier.

Writings of Ramon Betances, 9 vols. Ramon Betances. (Puerto Rico Ser.). 1979. Set. lib. bdg. 1,800.00 (*0-8490-3017-X*) Gordon Pr.

Writings of Robert Smithson: Essays with Illustrations. Ed. by Nancy Holt. LC 78-58536. (C). 1979. text ed. 40.00 (*0-8147-3394-8*); pap. text ed. 18.00 (*0-8147-3395-6*) NYU Pr.

***Writings of S. Kierkegaard.** (Great Devotional Classics Ser.). pap. 1.85 (*0-687-61434-1*) Abingdon.

W

Writings of Saint Augustine Vol. 1: Saint Augustine: the Happy Life by Ludwig Schopp. Augustine, Saint. LC 66-20314. (Fathers of the Church Ser.: Vol. 5). 454p. 1948. reprint ed. pap. 129.40 (*0-7837-9147-X*, 2049947) Bks Demand.

Writings of Saint Francis of Assisi. Frances D'Assisi. Tr. by Paschal Robinson. 1977. lib. bdg. 250.00 (*0-8490-2822-1*) Gordon Pr.

***Writings of St Francis of Assissi.** (Great Devotional Classics Ser.). pap. 1.85 (*0-687-61436-8*) Abingdon.

Writings of St. Patrick, with the Metrical Life of St. Patrick. Patrick & Fiacc. pap. 2.95 (*0-89981-109-4*) Eastern Orthodox.

Writings of St. Paul. St. Paul. Ed. by Wayne A. Meeks. (Critical Editions Ser.). (C). 1972. pap. text ed. 12.95 (*0-393-09979-2*) Norton.

Writings of Stephen B. Luce. Ed. by John D. Hayes & John B. Hattendorf. LC 76-51419. (Historical Monographs: No. 1). (Illus.). 262p. (C). 1975. reprint ed. pap. 10.00 (*0-9637973-4-4*) Naval War Coll.

Writings of the Late Elder John Leland, by Leland. Ed. by L. F. Greene. 1986. reprint ed. 35.00 (*0-317-47642-4*) Church History.

Writings of the Late Elder John Leland, Including Some Events of His Life. John Leland. Ed. by L. F. Greene. LC 73-83420. (Religion in America, Ser. 1). 1977. reprint ed. 60.95 (*0-405-00245-9*) Ayer.

Writings of the Mantira, Bk. I. George Goulding. 156p. (Orig.). 1991. pap. 10.95 (*0-9624831-1-7*) DeVorss.

Writings of the New Testament: An Interpretation. Luke T. Johnson. LC 85-16202. 640p. 1986. pap. 27.00 (*0-8006-1886-6*, 1-1886, Fortress Pr) Augsburg Fortress.

Writings of the Nicene & Post-Nicene Fathers, 28 vols. Incl. First Series. , 14 vols. 1988. 385.00 (*0-8028-8114-9*); Second Series. 385.00 (*0-8028-8129-7*); 1956. reprint ed. 900.00 (*0-8028-8130-0*) Eerdmans.

Writings of the Rabbis & Other Important Discoveries. Joshua M. Bennett. LC 89-92668. (Illus.). (gr. 8 up). 1990. text ed. 13.00 (*0-9625910-0-9*) Mornng Star Pub.

Writings of the Sanhedrin & Talmud. 1991. lib. bdg. 64.75 (*0-8490-4448-0*) Gordon Pr.

Writings of Theodore Roosevelt. Theodore Roosevelt. Ed. by William H. Harbaugh. LC 66-14828. 407p. 1967. 39. 50 (*0-8290-0221-9*) Irvington.

Writings of Thomas Bailey Aldrich, 9 Vols. Thomas B. Aldrich. reprint ed. Set. 373.50 (*0-404-00370-2*) AMS Pr.

***Writings of Thomas Coke.** (Great Devotional Classics Ser.). pap. 1.85 (*0-687-61432-5*) Abingdon.

Writings of Thomas Hooker: Spiritual Adventure in Two Worlds. Sargent Bush. LC 79-5404. 399p. 1980. reprint ed. pap. 113.80 (*0-608-01976-3*, 2062631) Bks Demand.

Writings of Thomas Paine: The Standard Edition, 4 vols, Set. Thomas Paine. Ed. by Moncure D. Conway. LC 78-181966. reprint ed. 175.00 (*0-404-04870-6*) AMS Pr.

Writings of Thomas Wentworth Higginson, 7 vols., Set. Thomas W. Higginson. (Notable American Authors Ser.). 1992. reprint ed. lib. bdg. 630.00 (*0-7812-3118-3*) Rprt Serv.

Writings of Walter Pater, 1860-1890. Helen H. Young. LC 68-1792. (Studies in Comparative Literature: No. 35). 1969. reprint ed. lib. bdg. 49.95 (*0-8383-0646-2*) M S G Haskell Hse.

Writings of William Carlos Williams: Publicity for the Self. Daniel Morris. 224p. 1995. text ed. 34.95 (*0-8262-1002-3*) U of Mo Pr.

Writings of William James: A Comprehensive Edition. William James. LC 77-89625. 912p. 1978. pap. text ed. 23.95 (*0-226-39188-4*, P742) U Ch Pr.

Writings of William Paterson: Of Dumfrieshire, & a Citizen of London, Founder of the Bank of England, & of the Darien Colony, 3 Vols, Set. 2nd ed. Ed. by Saxe Bannister. LC 68-54311. (Library of Money & Banking History). 1968. reprint ed. 150.00 (*0-678-00427-7*) Kelley.

***Writings of William Temple.** (Great Devotional Classics Ser.). pap. 1.85 (*0-687-61438-4*) Abingdon.

Writings of Wole Soyinka. 3rd ed. Eldred D. Jones. LC 87-25167. (Studies in African Literature). 242p. (Orig.). (C). 1987. pap. 17.50 (*0-435-08021-0*, 08021) Heinemann.

Writings on African Archives. John McIlwaine. 200p. 1996. 75.00 (*1-873836-66-X*) Bowker-Saur.

***Writings on Art & Literature.** Sigmund Freud. LC 96-51922. (Meridian: Crossing Aesthetics Ser.). 1997. write for info. (*0-8047-2972-7*); pap. write for info. (*0-8047-2973-5*) Stanford U Pr.

***Writings on Black Women of the Diaspora: History, Language & Identity.** Bracks. LC 97-25403. (Croscurrents in African American History Ser.). 1997. write for info. (*0-8153-2734-X*) Garland.

Writings on China. Gottfried W. Leibniz. Ed. by Daniel J. Cook & Henry Rosemont, Jr. 173p. 1994. 32.95 (*0-8126-9250-0*); pap. 17.95 (*0-8126-9251-9*) Open Court.

Writings on Cities. Henri LeFebvre. Tr. by Eleonore Kofman & Elizabeth Le Bas from FRE. 272p. 1995. 59. 95 (*0-631-19187-9*); pap. 24.95 (*0-631-19188-7*) Blackwell Pubs.

***Writings on Development.** Sukhamoy Chakravarty. Ed. by Mihir Rakshit. 320p. 1997. pap. text ed. 21.95 (*0-19-564093-4*) OUP.

Writings on Economics. David Hume. Ed. & Intro. by Eugene Rotwein. LC 72-3303. (Essay Index Reprint Ser.). 1977. reprint ed. 24.95 (*0-8369-2907-1*) Ayer.

Writings on Geometrical Loci. Pierre Fermat. (Illus.). 110p. 1988. lib. bdg. 22.00 (*0-318-35241-9*) Golden Hind Pr.

Writings on Glass: Thirty Years of Critical Essays. Andre Kostelanetz. LC 96-35215. 1997. 30.00 (*0-02-864657-6*) Schirmer Bks.

Writings on India, Vol. 30. John Stuart Mill. Ed. by John M. Robson et al. (Collected Works of John Stuart Mill). 340p. 1990. text ed. 90.00 (*0-8020-2717-2*) U of Toronto Pr.

Writings on Indian Constitution, 1861-1985. M. S. Rana. 548p. (C). 1987. 57.50 (*0-8364-2093-4*, Pub. by Usha II) S Asia.

***Writings on International Economics.** Jagdish Bhagwati. Ed. by V. N. Balasubramanyam. (Illus.). 450p. 1997. 45. 00 (*0-19-563985-5*) OUP.

Writings on Literature. N. S. Trubetzkoy. Tr. & Intro. by Anatoly Liberman. (Theory & History of Literature Ser.: Vol. 72). 192p. (C). 1990. pap. text ed. 14.95 (*0-8166-1793-7*) U of Minn Pr.

Writings on Logic & Metaphysics. F. H. Bradley. Ed. by James W. Allard & Guy Stock. LC 94-10327. 320p. 1995. 68.00 (*0-19-824445-2*); pap. 28.00 (*0-19-824438-X*) OUP.

Writings on Physics & Philosophy. K. V. Meyenn. LC 94-15098. 1996. 44.95 (*0-387-56859-X*) Spr-Verlag.

Writings on Psychoanalysis: Freud & Lacan. Louis Althusser. 208p. 1996. 29.50 (*0-231-10168-6*) Col U Pr.

Writings on Soviet Law & Soviet International Law: A Bibliography of Books & Articles Published Since 1917 in Languages Other than East European. Harvard University, Law School Library Staff. xii, 177p. 1966. 17.50 (*0-674-96250-8*) HUP.

***Writings on the Nile.** Joan Rees. (Illus.). 128p. 1995. pap. 19.95 (*0-948695-40-4*, Pub. by Rubicon Pr UK) David Brown.

Writings on the Wall: Peace at the Berlin Wall. Terry Tillman. Ed. by Marilyn Ferguson. Tr. by George Morgan from ENG. (Illus.). 152p. (Orig.). (C). 1990. pap. 19.95 (*0-9626551-0-4*) Twenty-Two Sevens.

Writings on Wright: Selected Comment on Frank Lloyd Wright. Ed. by H. Allen Brooks. (Illus.). 160p. 1983. pap. 14.00 (*0-262-52086-9*) MIT Pr.

Writings on Writing. Rudyard Kipling. Ed. by Sandra Kemp & Lisa Lewis. (Illus.). 234p. (C). 1996. text ed. 59.95 (*0-521-44527-2*) Cambridge U Pr.

Writings on Writing. May Sarton. Ed. by Constance Hunting. 55p. (C). 1980. pap. 6.95 (*0-913006-20-3*) Puckerbrush.

Writings on Writing: A Compendium of 1209 Quotations from Authors on Their Craft. Ed. by Thomas Brennan. LC 93-24477. 189p. 1994. lib. bdg. 28.95 (*0-89950-765-4*) McFarland & Co.

Writings, 1878-1899: Includes: Psychology: Briefer Course; The Will to Believe; Talks to Teachers; Essays. William James. Ed. by Gerald E. Myers. 1212p. 1992. 35.00 (*0-940450-72-0*) Library of America.

***Writings 1903-1932: Q. E. D.; Three Lives; Autobiography of Alice B. Toklas; Portraits.** Gertrude Stein. Ed. by Catherine Stimpson & Harriet Chessman. (Library of America Ser.: Vol. 99). 900p. 1998. 35.00 (*1-883011-40-X*) Library of America.

***Writings 1932-1946.** Gertrude Stein. Ed. by Catherine Stimpson & Harriet Chessman. 900p. 1998. 35.00 (*1-883011-41-8*) Library of America.

Written Also for Our Sake: Paul & the Art of Biblical Interpretation. James W. Aageson. LC 92-33996. 160p. (Orig.). 1993. pap. 11.00 (*0-664-25361-X*) Westminster John Knox.

Written & Illustrated by... David Melton. LC 85-50637. 1985. pap. 15.95 (*0-933849-00-1*) Landmark Edns.

Written & Illustrated by Children: Developing Children's Writing & Illustration Together. Johnson. LC 96-44623. (J). 1995. pap. text ed. 27.50 (*0-435-08883-1*) Heinemann.

Written & Interpersonal Communication. Roberson & Harvey Wallace. 392p. (C). 1996. pap. text ed. 29.40 (*0-13-335472-5*) P-H.

Written & Spoken Arabic: Based on Modern Standard Arabic. Don Y. Lee. (ARA & ENG.). (C). 1993. text ed. 57.50 (*0-939758-26-1*) Eastern Pr.

Written Arabic: An Approach to the Basic Structures. Alfred F. Beeston. 124p. (Orig.). (C). 1968. pap. text ed. 23.95 (*0-521-09559-X*) Cambridge U Pr.

Written by Herself, Vol. 2. Jill Ker Conway. 1996. pap. write for info. (*0-679-77597-8*) Random.

***Written by Herself, Vol. 3.** Jill Ker Conway. 1997. pap. write for info. (*0-679-78153-6*, Vin) Random.

Written by Herself: Autobiographies of American Women: an Anthology. Intro. by Jill Ker Conway. LC 92-50081. 656p. 1992. pap. 15.00 (*0-679-73633-6*, Vin) Random.

Written by Herself: Literary Production by African American Women, 1746-1892. Frances S. Foster. LC 92-23916. (Blacks in the Diaspora Ser.). 224p. 1993. 35. 00 (*0-253-32409-2*); pap. 13.95 (*0-253-20786-X*, MB-786) Ind U Pr.

Written by Herself Vol. II: Women's Memoirs from Four Continents. Jill Ker Conway. 1996. pap. 16.00 (*0-679-75109-2*, Vin) Random.

Written by the Wind: British Columbia Wilderness Adventures. Randy Stoltmann. (Illus.). 96p. (Orig.). 1993. pap. 9.99 (*1-55143-003-7*) Orca Bk Pubs.

Written Communication for Data Processing. Rhandi S. Smith. LC 76-44292. 207p. reprint ed. pap. 59.00 (*0-317-09930-2*, 2014904) Bks Demand.

Written Communication for Today's Manager. Barbara Jones. LC 80-15315. 1980. pap. 26.95 (*0-912016-87-6*) Lebhar Friedman.

Written Communication in Business: A Selective Bibliography. Mary Ann Bowman & Joan D. Stamas. 104p. (Orig.). 1980. pap. 6.90 (*0-931874-09-2*) Assn Busn Comm.

Written Communication in Family Medicine. Ed. by Robert B. Taylor & K. A. Munning. (Illus.). 180p. 1984. 90.00 (*0-387-90979-6*) Spr-Verlag.

Written Communication Skills. rev. ed. Wilbert Schaal. 114p. 1980. pap. 8.50 (*0-87771-022-8*) Grad School.

Written Communication Skills see Productive Supervisor: A Program of Practical Managerial Skills

Written Communications & the School Administrator. Audrey B. Joyce. 400p. 1990. text ed. 62.95 (*0-205-12578-6*, H25786) Allyn.

Written Composition: Process, Product, Program. Ed. by Charles R. Chew & Sheila A. Schlawin. 165p. 1983. pap. text ed. 7.00 (*0-930348-09-5*) NY St Eng Coun.

Written Composition Interests of Junior & Senior High School Pupils. John H. Coleman. LC 71-176662. (Columbia University. Teachers College. Contributions to Education Ser.: No. 494). reprint ed. 37.50 (*0-404-55494-6*) AMS Pr.

Written Constitution for the United Kingdom. Institute for Public Policy Research Staff. Ed. by Robert Blackburn. LC 92-39397. (Constitutional Reform Ser.). 192p. 1993. 70.00 (*0-7201-2154-X*, Mansell Pub) Cassell.

Written Constitution for the United Kingdom. Institute for Public Policy Research Staff. (Constitutional Reform Ser.). 304p. 1995. pap. 32.95 (*0-7201-2272-4*, Mansell Pub) Cassell.

Written Dialects n Spelling Reforms: History n Alternatives. Kenneth H. Ives. LC 78-54745. 112p. (C). 1979. pap. 5.00 (*0-89670-004-6*) Progresiv Pub.

Written English: An Introduction for Beginning Students of English As a Second Language. Robert Rainsbury. 1977. pap. text ed. 17.70 (*0-13-970673-9*) P-H.

Written English Paper, Elem. School, Jr. & Sr. H. S. Jack Rudman. (Teachers License Examination Ser.: T-61). 1994. pap. 27.95 (*0-8373-8061-8*) Nat Learn.

***Written Expression: The Principal's Survival Guide.** India Podsen. (School Leadership Library Ser.). 1997. write for info. (*1-883001-34-X*) Eye On Educ.

Written Expression Disorders. Noel Gregg. LC 95-1441. (Neuropsychology & Cognition Ser.: Vol. 10). 1995. lib. bdg. 99.00 (*0-7923-3355-1*) Kluwer Ac.

Written for Children: An Outline of English-Language Children's Literature. 6th ed. John R. Townsend. LC 95-47714. (Illus.). 399p. 1996. 37.50 (*0-8108-3117-1*) Scarecrow.

***Written for Our Learning.** F. E. Stallan. 1996. 29.99 (*0-946351-42-2*) Loizeaux.

Written Hazard Communication Program, Vol. 2. Forum for Scientific Excellence, Inc. Staff. (Practical Guide to Safety Compliance Standards for Medical Facilities Ser.). 100p. 1990. ring bd. 50.00 (*0-87489-651-7*) Med Econ.

***Written Hazard Communication Program for Schools & Colleges.** George R. Thompson. 105p. Date not set. pap. text ed. 29.95 (*0-397-53022-6*) Lppncott-Raven.

Written in Blood. Caroline Graham. 384p. 1996. mass mkt. 5.99 (*0-380-71297-0*) Avon.

***Written in Blood: A History of the 126th New York Regiment in the Civil War.** Wayne Mahood. (Illus.). 540p. 1997. 40.00 (*0-944413-33-1*, NB 133) Longstreet Hse.

Written in Blood: Detectives & Detection. Colin Wilson. 1991. mass mkt. 4.95 (*0-446-36120-8*) Warner Bks.

Written in Blood: The Criminal Mind & Method. Colin Wilson. 288p. 1992. reprint ed. mass mkt. 4.99 (*0-446-36163-1*) Warner Bks.

Written in Blood: The Story of the Haitian People, 1492-1995. Robert D. Heinl, Jr. & Nancy G. Heinl. LC 95-42547. (Illus.). (C). 1996. pap. text ed. 34.00 (*0-7618-0230-4*) U Pr of Amer.

Written in Blood: The Story of the Haitian People, 1492-1995. 2nd expanded rev. ed. Robert D. Heinl, Jr. & Nancy G. Heinl. LC 95-42547. (Illus.). 902p. (C). 1996. reprint ed. lib. bdg. 65.00 (*0-7618-0229-0*) U Pr of Amer.

Written in Blood: The Trail & the Hunt. Colin Wilson. 1991. mass mkt. 4.99 (*0-446-36162-3*) Warner Bks.

Written in Fire: A Lobo Black/Quinn Booker Mystery. William L. DeAndrea. 168p. 1995. 19.95 (*0-8027-3270-4*) Walker & Co.

Written in Memory: Portraits of the Holocaust. Jeffrey A. Wolin. LC 96-22439. 1997. 35.00 (*0-8118-1390-8*); pap. 19.95 (*0-8118-1366-5*) Chronicle Bks.

Written in Our Hearts: The Practice of Spiritual Transformation. Theodore J. Nottingham. (Illus.). 176p. (Orig.). 1993. pap. 14.95 (*0-9638181-0-4*) Inner Life.

Written in Red: Selected Poems. Intro. by Franklin Rosemont. (Poets of Revolt Ser.: No. 2). 56p. 1991. pap. 5.00 (*0-88286-121-2*); lib. bdg. 20.00 (*0-88286-146-8*) C H Kerr.

***Written in Stone.** Mary A. Downie & M. A. Thompson. (Illus.). 264p. 1993. pap. 19.95 (*1-55082-063-X*, Pub. by Quarry Pr CN) LPC InBook.

Written in Stone: Ethics for the Heart. Rubel Shelly. 228p. 1994. 12.99 (*1-878990-36-5*) Howard Pub LA.

Written in Stone: Ethics for the Heart. Rubel Shelly. 1994. audio 14.99 (*1-878990-42-X*) Howard Pub LA.

Written in Stone: Making "The Ten Commandments" Katherine Orrison. (Illus.). 206p. (Orig.). 1998. pap. 21. 95 (*1-879511-24-X*) Madison Bks UPA.

Written in Water. T. L. Parkinson. Date not set. pap. 20.00 (*0-525-93642-4*) NAL-Dutton.

Written in Water: The Life of Benjamin Harrison Eaton. Jane E. Norris & Lee G. Norris. LC 90-9497. (Illus.). 311p. (C). 1990. text ed. 29.95 (*0-8040-0934-1*) Swallow.

Written in Water, Written in Stone: Twenty Years of Poets on Poetry. Ed. by Martin Lammon. LC 96-43380. (Orig.). 1996. pap. 15.95 (*0-472-06634-X*); text ed. 39.50 (*0-472-09634-6*) U of Mich Pr.

Written in 1920. Elsie L. Benedict & Ralph P. Benedict. 310p. (Orig.). 1986. 14.95 (*0-915659-06-9*) Video Athlete.

Written Japanese: An Introduction. David E. Ashworth & Ikumi Hitosugi. 232p. (C). 1993. pap. text ed. 28.00 (*0-8248-1508-4*) UH Pr.

***Written Judgments, 3 vols., Vol. 1.** 2nd ed. E. Bernard Jordan. Ed. by Deborah Jones. 64p. (Orig.). 1989. reprint ed. pap. 10.00 (*0-939241-05-6*) Faith Print.

Written Language Assessment. J. Jeffrey Grill & Margaret M. Kirwin. Ed. by Rick Brownell. (Illus.). 111p. (Orig.). 1989. ring bd. 65.00 (*0-87879-640-1*); 12.00 (*0-87879-642-8*); lp 18.00 (*0-87879-641-X*) Acad Therapy.

Written Language Disorders. Ed. by R. Malatesha Joshi. (C). 1991. lib. bdg. 133.00 (*0-7923-0902-2*) Kluwer Ac.

Written Language Disorders: Theory into Practice. Laura L. Bailet & Louisa C. Moats. Ed. by Ann M. Bain et al. LC 89-13839. (Illus.). 209p. 1991. pap. text ed. 27.00 (*0-89079-417-0*, 1580) PRO-ED.

Written Language Instruction for Students with Disabilities. Tom E. Smith et al. 1995. pap. 14.95 (*0-89108-235-2*, 9403) Love Pub Co.

Written Language Revisited. Josef Vachek. LC 88-36907. xiv, 221p. (C). 1989. 71.00 (*90-272-2064-6*) Benjamins North Am.

Written Language Skills: Famous Places: Grades 4-8. 1988. pap. 5.95 (*0-89108-194-1*, 8823) Love Pub Co.

Written Language Skills: Holidays & Celebrations: Grades 4-8. 1988. pap. 5.95 (*0-89108-195-X*, 8824) Love Pub Co.

Written Language Skills: Sports: Grades 4-8. 1988. pap. 5.95 (*0-89108-193-3*, 8822) Love Pub Co.

Written Letters: Thirty-Three Alphabets for Calligraphers. 2nd rev. ed. Jacqueline Svaren. (Illus.). 80p. 1986. pap. 16.95 (*0-8008-8735-2*) Taplinger.

Written on a Body. Tr. by Carol Maier. 131p. 1989. pap. 10.95 (*0-930829-11-5*) Lumen Inc.

Written on a Body. Severo Sarduy. Tr. by Carol Maier from SPA. Orig. Title: Escrito sobre un Cuerpo. 150p. (Orig.). 1989. pap. 10.95 (*0-930829-04-2*) Lumen Inc.

Written on Our Hearts: Helping Children Understand, Memorize & Retain God's Word. Susan L. Lingo. 112p. 1996. pap. 14.99 (*0-310-20100-4*) Zondervan.

Written on Scrolls, Inscribed in Hearts. David Thomas. LC 88-83362. 75p. (Orig.). 1989. pap. 4.95 (*0-87029-220-X*, 20210-1) Abbey.

Written on the Body. Jeanette Winterson. 1994. pap. 11.00 (*0-679-74447-9*) Random.

***Written on the Heart: The Case for Natural Law.** J. Budziszewski. LC 96-29818. 240p. (Orig.). 1997. pap. 14.99 (*0-8308-1891-X*, 1891) InterVarsity.

Written on the Hills: The Making of the Akron Landscape. Frances McGovern. (Ohio History & Culture Ser.). (Illus.). 241p. 1996. 39.95 (*1-884836-21-6*); pap. 19.95 (*1-884836-22-4*) U Akron Pr.

Written on Water. Takashi Kojima. 1995. 19.95 (*0-8048-2040-6*) C E Tuttle.

Written Out of Television: A TV Lover's Guide to Cast Changes 1945-1994. Steven Lance. LC 95-47417. (Illus.). 505p. 1996. pap. 24.95 (*1-56833-071-5*) Madison Bks UPA.

Written Out of Television: The Complete Couch Potato's Guide to Cast Changes & Character Replacements, 1945-1994. Steven Lance. LC 95-47417. 1996. text ed. write for info. (*1-56833-070-7*) Madison Bks UPA.

Written Out of Television: The Encyclopedia of Cast Changes & Character Replacements, 1945-Present. Steven Lance. LC 94-15370. 528p. 1996. text ed. 89.50 (*0-8108-2902-9*) Scarecrow.

Written Paths to Healing: Education & Jungian Child Counseling. John Allan & Judi Bertoia. LC 92-7531. (Illus.). 260p. (Orig.). 1992. pap. 21.00 (*0-88214-350-6*) Spring Pubns.

Written Problems in Math: Grade 2. Fred Justus. (Math Ser.). 24p. 1980. student ed. 5.00 (*0-8209-0122-9*, A-32) ESP.

Written Problems in Math: Grade 4. Dale McMasters. (Math Ser.). 24p. 1981. student ed. 5.00 (*0-8209-0124-5*, A-34) ESP.

***Written Script.** Annalita Marsigli Alexander. LC 97-19718. 1997. write for info. (*0-87951-820-0*) Overlook Pr.

Written Standard Chinese, Vol 1. Huang & Hugh M. Stimson. (Standard Chinese Ser.). 272p. (CHI.). 1980. pap. text ed. 21.95 (*0-88710-129-1*); audio 63.95 (*0-88710-130-5*) Yale Far Eastern Pubns.

Written Standard Chinese, Vol. II. Huang & Hugh M. Stimson. (Standard Chinese Ser.). 264p. (CHI.). 1980. pap. text ed. 21.95 (*0-88710-131-3*); audio 53.95 (*0-88710-132-1*) Yale Far Eastern Pubns.

Written Standard Chinese, Vol. III. Parker P. Huang & Hugh M. Stimson. (Standard Chinese Ser.). 250p. (CHI.). 1986. pap. text ed. 17.95 (*0-88710-138-0*) Yale Far Eastern Pubns.

Written Standard Chinese, Vol. IV. Parker P. Huang & Hugh M. Stimson. (Standard Chinese Ser.). (Illus.). 238p. (CHI.). 1991. pap. text ed. 17.95 (*0-88710-158-5*) Yale Far Eastern Pubns.

Written Standard Chinese Workbook, Vol. 1. Lu V. Wong-Quincey. 200p. (CHI.). 1983. student ed. 14.95 (*0-88710-133-X*) Yale Far Eastern Pubns.

Written Standard Chinese Workbook, Vol. 2. Vivien Wong & Quincey Lu. (Standard Chinese Ser.). 172p. (C). 1983. student ed. 15.95 (*0-88710-134-8*) Yale Far Eastern Pubns.

Written Suburb: An American Site, an Ethnographic Dilemma. John D. Dorst. LC 89-37485. (Contemporary Ethnography Ser.). (Illus.). 232p. (C). 1989. text ed. 49. 95 (*0-8122-8160-8*); pap. text ed. 17.95 (*0-8122-1282-7*) U of Pa Pr.

***Written Suburb: An American Site, an Ethnographic Dilemma.** John D. Dorst. LC 88-37485. (Contemporary Ethnography Ser.). 232p. pap. 66.20 (*0-608-04820-8*, 2065477) Bks Demand.

An Asterisk (*) at the beginning of an entry indicates that the title is appearing in BIP for the first time.

***Written Voices, Spoken Signs: Tradition, Performance, & the Epic Text.** Egbert J. Bakker & Ahuvia Kahane. LC 96-46776. (Center for Hellenic Studies Colloquia Ser.). 1997. write for info. (0-674-96260-5) HUP.

Written Wars: American War Prose Through the Civil War. Joseph T. Cox. LC 95-32374. xviii, 282p. (C). 1996. lib. bdg. 39.50 (0-208-02344-5, Archon Bks) Shoe String.

Written with a Spoon: A Poet's Cookbook. Ed. by Nancy Fay & Judith Rafaela. 200p. 1995. pap. 18.00 (0-9644196-2-9) S Asher Pub.

Written with Lead: Legendary American Gunfights & Gunfighters. William Weir. LC 91-46338. (Illus.). xii, 300p. (C). 1992. lib. bdg. 32.50 (0-208-02319-4, Archon Bks) Shoe String.

Written Word in Sculpture: Twenty-Seven Monumental Works by David Margolis. Howard E. Wooden. LC 85-50230. (Illus.). 40p. 1985. pap. 5.00 (0-939324-19-9) Wichita Art Mus.

***Written Work: Langland, Labor, & Authorship.** Ed. by Steven Justice & Kathryn Kerby-Fulton. LC 97-2224. (Middle Ages Ser.). 320p. 1997. text ed. 45.00 (0-8122-3396-4) U of Pa Pr.

Written Work Papers for Volumes One, Two & Three. Martha Miner et al. 1993. wbk. ed. 5.00 (1-881986-17-9) Demibach Eds.

Written World. Ed. by R. Saljo. (Language & Communication Ser.: Vol. 23). (Illus.). 225p. 1988. 86.95 (0-387-18145-8) Spr-Verlag.

Written World: Youth & Literature. Ed. by Agnes Nieuwenhuizen. 349p. 1994. pap. 30.00 (1-875589-30-9) D W Thorpe.

Written Worlds: Reading & Writing Culture. 2nd ed. Compiled by Susan Miller. LC 92-18636. (C). 1993. text ed. 30.50 (0-06-500585-6) Addson-Wesley Educ.

Wrong Again Dan! Karachi to Krakatoa. Dan Raschen. 256p. 1984. 40.00 (0-7212-0638-7, Pub. by Regency Press UK) St Mut.

Wrong Box. Robert Louis Stevenson. Ed. by David Trotter. (Oxford Popular Fiction Ser.). 192p. 1995. pap. 8.95 (0-19-282426-0) OUP.

Wrong Box. large type ed. Robert Louis Stevenson. (Large-Print Ser.). 296p. 1992. reprint ed. lib. bdg. 22.00 (0-939495-32-5) North Bks.

Wrong Bride, Right Groom. Merline Lovelace. 1996. mass mkt. 3.50 (0-373-76037-X, 1-76037-0) Silhouette.

Wrong Case. James Crumley. 1986. pap. 11.00 (0-394-73558-7, Publishers Media) Random.

Wrong Face in the Mirror: An Autobiography of Race & Identity. Lolo Houbein. 1990. pap. 14.95 (0-7022-2248-8, Pub. by Univ Queensland Pr AT) Intl Spec Bk.

Wrong for All the Right Reasons: How White Liberals Have Been Undone by Race. Gordon Macinnes. 320p. (C). 1996. 21.95 (0-8147-5543-7) NYU Pr.

***Wrong for Each Other.** Norm Foster. LC 94-225166. 1997. pap. text ed. 11.95 (0-88754-522-X, Pub. by Playwrights CN Pr CN) Theatre Comm.

Wrong-Handed Man: Stories. Lawrence Millman. LC 87-27200. 112p. (Orig.). 1988. pap. 12.95 (0-8262-0674-3) U of Mo Pr.

Wrong Horse: An Odyssey Through the American Racing Scene. William Murray. LC 92-15250. 1992. pap. 20.00 (0-671-76774-7) S&S Trade.

Wrong Kind of Girl. Francine Pascal. (Sweet Valley High Ser.: No. 10). 144p. (J). (gr. 7 up). 1984. mass mkt. 3.99 (0-553-27668-9) Bantam.

Wrong Kind of Man. Rosemary Hammond. (Romance Ser.: No. 193). 1992. pap. 2.89 (0-373-03193-9, 1-03193-9) Harlequin Bks.

***Wrong Kind of Money.** Stephen Birmingham. 1997. 23.95 (0-614-27942-9); pap. 24.95 (0-525-94331-5) NAL-Dutton.

***Wrong Kind of Shirts: Outrageous Football Excuses, Whinges & Verbal Own Goals.** Compiled by Mark Reynolds. (Illus.). 112p. 1997. pap. 8.95 (1-85702-602-0, Pub. by Fourth Estate UK) Trafalgar.

Wrong Kind of Wife. Roberta Leigh & Sally Wentworth. (Presents Ser.). 1995. pap. 3.25 (0-373-11725-6, 1-11725-8) Harlequin Bks.

Wrong Kind of Wife. large type ed. Roberta Leigh. (Harlequin Romance Ser.). 283p. 1995. 20.95 (0-263-14213-2, Pub. by Mills & Boon UK) Thorndike Pr.

***Wrong Man.** Anderson. 1992. pap. text ed. write for info. (0-582-06071-0, Drumbeat) Longman.

Wrong Man. Kevin Davis. 360p. (Orig.). 1996. mass mkt. 5.99 (0-380-77815-7) Avon.

Wrong Man. Ann Major. (Men in America Ser.). 1994. mass mkt. 3.99 (0-373-45188-1, 1-45188-9) Harlequin Bks.

***Wrong Man.** Danny Morrison. 208p. 1997. pap. 12.95 (1-57098-102-7) R Rinehart.

***Wrong Man.** Kelsey Roberts. 1997. pap. 3.75 (0-373-22429-X, 1-22429-4) Harlequin Bks.

***Wrong Man...The Right Time.** Carole Halston. (Special Edition Ser.). 1997. mass mkt. 3.99 (0-373-24089-9, 1-24089-4) Silhouette.

Wrong Medicine: Doctors, Patients, & Futile Treatment. Lawrence J. Schneiderman & Nancy S. Jecker. 216p. 1995. 25.95 (0-8018-5036-3) Johns Hopkins.

Wrong Mirror. Emma Darcy. (Presents Ser.). 1991. pap. 2.79 (0-373-15154-3) Harlequin Bks.

Wrong Murder. Craig Rice. LC 90-80762. 312p. 1990. reprint ed. pap. 7.95 (1-55882-067-1) Intl Polygonics.

Wrong Number 2. R. L. Stine. Ed. by Patricia MacDonald. (Fear Street Ser.). 176p. (Orig.). (J). (gr. 7 up). 1995. mass mkt. 3.99 (0-671-78607-5) PB.

***Wrong Place Right Time.** Michael J. Macoun. 1996. text ed. 39.50 (1-86064-019-2) St Martin.

Wrong Place, Wrong Time: The Three Hundred Fifth Bomb Group & the 2nd Schweinfurt Raid - October 14, 1943. George C. Kuhl. LC 92-62388. (Illus.). 240p. 1993. 24.95 (0-88740-445-6) Schiffer.

Wrong Rite. Alisa Craig, pseud. 288p. 1993. mass mkt. 4.99 (0-380-71043-9) Avon.

Wrong Road. Vivian D. Gunderson. (J). (gr. k-8). 1964. pap. 3.25 (0-915374-15-3, 15-3) Rapids Christian.

***Wrong Side of the Alps.** Anthony Glavin. 54p. 1989. pap. 11.95 (1-85235-048-2) Dufour.

Wrong Side of the Bed. Wallace E. Keller. 1992. 14.95 (0-8478-1471-8) Rizzoli Intl.

Wrong Side of the Fence: A United States Army Air Corps POW in World War II. Eugene E. Halmos. LC 96-10220. (Illus.). 200p. 1996. 24.95 (1-57249-034-9) White Mane Pub.

Wrong Side of the Law. Franklin W. Dixon. (Hardy Boys Casefiles Ser.: No. 102). (YA). (gr. 6 up). 1995. mass mkt. 3.99 (0-671-88213-9, Archway) PB.

***Wrong Side of the Neighborhood Witch.** Kendall Haven. 117p. (Orig.). 1997. mass mkt. 4.99 (1-55237-053-4, Pub. by Comnwlth Pub CN) Partners Pubs Grp.

Wrong Side of the Pattern. Kristine Litchman. (YA). (gr. 7 up). 1997. pap. 6.99 (0-88092-381-4) Royal Fireworks.

Wrong Songs. James Tate. 1970. 20.00 (0-912604-02-6) Halty Ferguson.

Wrong Stories Dennis Cooper. Denise Cooper. LC 91-29524. 176p. 1993. pap. 11.00 (0-8021-3367-3, Grove) Grove-Atltic.

***Wrong Stuff.** John Moore. (Illus.). 216p. 1997. 19.95 (1-883809-10-X) Specialty Pr.

***Wrong Stuff: The Adventures & Mis-Adventures of an 8th Air Force Aviator.** Truman Smith. Ed. by Byron L. Kennedy, III. 360p. (Orig.). 1996. pap. 15.95 (0-941072-23-1) Southern Herit.

***Wrong Stuff: The Space Program's Nuclear Threat to Our Planet.** Karl Grossman. LC 97-11915. 225p. 1997. 22.95 (1-56751-125-2) Common Courage.

***Wrong Stuff: The Space Program's Nuclear Threat to Our Planet.** Karl Grossman. LC 97-11915. 1997. pap. write for info. (1-56751-124-4) Common Courage.

Wrong Time, Wrong Place. Lesley Choyce. (YA). (gr. 6 up). 1995. pap. 8.95 (0-88780-098-X); bds. 16.95 (0-88780-099-8) Formac Dist Ltd.

Wrong Track. Carolyn Keene. Ed. by Anne Greenberg. (Nancy Drew Files Ser.: No. 64). 160p. (Orig.). (YA). (gr. 6 up). pap. 3.99 (0-671-73068-1, Archway) PB.

***Wrong Trousers.** (Wallace & Gromit Ser.). 1997. 6.99 (1-55853-526-8) Rutledge Hill Pr.

Wrong Twin: (9 Months) Rebecca Winters. (Superromance Ser.). 1995. pap. 3.75 (0-373-70636-7, 1-70636-5) Harlequin Bks.

Wrong War: American Policy & the Dimensions of the Korean Conflict, 1950-1953. Rosemary Foot. LC 84-29305. (Cornell Studies in Security Affairs). 296p. 1985. 37.50 (0-8014-1800-3) Cornell U Pr.

***Wrong Way.** Sheryl Prenzlau. (B. Y. Times Kid Sisters Ser.: No. 11). 112p. (J). (gr. 4-7). Date not set. pap. 7.95 (1-56871-073-9) Feldheim.

Wrong-Way Comet & Other Mysteries of Our Solar System. Barry Evans. 192p. 1992. 22.95 (0-8306-2679-4); pap. 14.95 (0-8306-2670-0) McGraw-Hill Prof.

Wrong-Way Comet & Other Mysteries of the Solar System. Barry Evans. 1992. text ed. 22.95 (0-07-019753-9) McGraw.

Wrong Way Home: Uncovering the Patterns of Cult Behavior in American Society. Arthur J. Deikman. 208p. (C). 1994. pap. 12.95 (0-8070-2915-7) Beacon Pr.

Wrong Way Light Bulb. Leonard Spigelglass. 1969. pap. 5.25 (0-8222-1280-3) Dramatists Play.

Wrong-Way Rabbit. Teddy Slater. LC 92-14334. (Hello Reader! Ser.). (Illus.). 32p. (J). (gr. k-2). 1993. pap. 2.95 (0-590-45359-9) Scholastic Inc.

Wrong Way Renee. Fern C. Waskovich. 61p. (J). (gr. 4-6). 1994. pap. 5.00 (0-88092-114-5) Royal Fireworks.

Wrong Ways & Right Ways in the Study of Formative Judaism: Critical Methid & Literature, History & the History of Religion. Jacob Neusner. LC 88-4546. (Brown Judaic Studies). 275p. 1988. 39.95 (1-55540-228-3, 14-01-45) Scholars Pr GA.

Wrong Wife? Jule McBride. (American Romance Ser.). 1994. mass mkt. 3.50 (0-373-16546-3, 1-16546-3) Harlequin Bks.

***Wrong Wife.** Eileen Wilks. 1997. mass mkt. 3.50 (0-373-76065-5, 1-76065-1) Silhouette.

Wrong Winner: The Coming Debacle in the Electoral College. David W. Abbott & James P. Levine. LC 90-49220. 184p. 1991. text ed. 49.95 (0-275-93780-1, C3780, Praeger Pubs); pap. text ed. 15.95 (0-275-93871-9, B3871, Praeger Pubs) Greenwood.

Wrong Wrong Wrong. Jennifer Blowdryer. 20p. (Orig.). 1991. pap. 3.00 (0-929730-34-8) Zeitgeist Pr.

Wrongful Appropriation in Islamic Law. S. H. Amin. 224p. (C). 1983. 125.00 (0-946706-01-8, Pub. by Royston Ltd) St Mut.

Wrongful Death: A Medical Tragedy. Sandra M. Gilbert. (Illus.). 352p. 1995. 22.50 (0-393-03721-5) Norton.

Wrongful Death: A Memoir. Sandra M. Gilbert. LC 96-52868. 368p. 1997. pap. 13.00 (0-393-31516-9) Norton.

Wrongful Death: One Child's Fatal Encounter with Public Health & Private Greed. Leon Bing. LC 96-50338. 1997. 25.00 (0-679-44841-1) Random.

Wrongful Death in Ohio with Forms. John W. McCormac. 194p. 1982. 37.50 (0-87084-560-8) Anderson Pub Co.

Wrongful Discharge & Employment Practices Manual, 1994. Ed. by Richard J. Simmons. 641p. 1994. per. 69.00 (0-943178-12-6) Castle Pubns.

Wrongful Discharge & the Derogation of the At-Will Employment Doctrine. Andrew D. Hill. LC 86-83224. (Labor Relations & Public Policy Ser.). (Orig.). 1987. pap. 27.50 (0-89546-066-1) U PA Ctr Hum Res.

Wrongful Dismissal Handbook. John Mole. 216p. 1990. pap. 37.00 (0-409-88842-7) MICHIE.

Wrongful Dismissal in Quebec. Audet et al. 496p. 1990. pap. 83.00 (0-89073-730-4) MICHIE.

Wrongful Employment Termination Practice. 923p. 1987. 105.00 (0-88124-155-5, CP-30900) Cont Ed Bar-CA.

Wrongful Termination Claims: A Preventive Approach. Stuart H. Bompey et al. 765p. 1991. text ed. 40.00 (0-87224-014-2, H1-3000) PLI.

***Wrongful Termination Law: Cases & Materials.** Don D. Sessions. xiv, 375p. 1997. text ed. write for info. (0-9658449-0-0) Pretium Pr.

Wrongfully Terminated. Allison-Garrett. 40p. (Orig.). 1990. pap. text ed. 29.99 (1-878235-03-6) Taylor Pub MI.

Wrongly Dividing the Word of Truth. Henry A. Ironside. LC 89-36830. 1989. Pkg. of 5. pap. 14.95 (0-87213-563-2); pap. 2.99 (0-87213-392-3) Loizeaux.

***Wrongness, Wisdom, & Wilderness: Toward a Libertarian Theory of Ethics & the Environment.** Tal Scriven. LC 96-26396. (SUNY Series in Social & Political Thought). 352p. (C). 1997. pap. text ed. 20.95 (0-7914-3372-2) State U NY Pr.

***Wrongness, Wisdom, & Wilderness: Toward a Libertarian Theory of Ethics & the Environment.** Tal Scriven. LC 96-26396. (SUNY Series in Social & Political Thought). 352p. (C). 1997. text ed. 62.50 (0-7914-3371-4) State U NY Pr.

Wrongs & Remedies in the Twenty-First Century. Ed. by Peter Birks. 352p. 1996. 80.00 (0-19-826292-2) OUP.

Wrongs of Indian Womanhood. Marcus Fuller. 1984. reprint ed. 32.50 (0-8364-1160-9, Pub. by Inter-India Pubns) S Asia.

Wrongs of Tort. Conaghan & Mansell. (Law & Social Theory Ser.). (C). 51.50 (0-7453-0526-1, Pub. by Pluto Pr UK) LPC InBook.

Wrongs of Tort. Joanne Conaghan & Wade Mansell. (Law & Social Theory Ser.). (C). pap. 18.00 (0-7453-0527-X, Pub. by Pluto Pr UK) LPC InBook.

Wrongway Santa. Rae Oetting. LC 90-62546. (Illus.). 32p. (J). 1991. lib. bdg. 15.95 (0-87783-254-4) Oddo.

Wros-tonne & Other Stories of Science Fantasy. Mary A. Schuller. LC 87-90482. (Illus.). 134p. (Orig.). (J). (gr. 3-8). 1987. pap. 4.95 (0-9617889-0-9) Sweet Koala Pr.

Wrought Iron. Fritz Kuhn. Tr. by Charles B. Johnson. (Illus.). 120p. 1983. reprint ed. 42.95 (3-8030-4010-8) Larson Publng.

Wrought Iron Artistry. Otto Schmirler. Tr. by A. Muron. (Illus.). 168p. 1986. 54.95 (3-8030-5044-8) Larson Publng.

Wrought Iron in Architecture: An Illustrated Survey. Gerald K. Geerlings. (Antiques Ser.). 202p. 1984. reprint ed. pap. 12.95 (0-486-24535-7) Dover.

WRTH Equipment Buyers Guide 1995. Willem Bos & Jonathan Marks. (Illus.). 272p. 1995. pap. 24.95 (0-8230-5966-9, Billboard Bks) Watsn-Guptill.

WRTH Satellite Broadcasting Guide 1996. Bart Kuperus. 376p. 1996. pap. 24.95 (0-8230-5957-X, RAC Bks) Watsn-Guptill.

Wry Martinis. Christopher Buckley. LC 96-8336. (Illus.). 294p. 1997. 22.00 (0-679-45233-8) Random.

WSC '93: Winter Simulation Conference Proceedings. IEEE Computer Society & Systems, Man & Cybernetics Society Staff. Ed. by IEEE Staff. LC 87-654182. 1500p. 1993. pap. text ed. write for info. (0-7803-1380-1, 93CH3338-1); lib. bdg. write for info. (0-7803-1381-X, 93CH3338-1); fiche write for info. (0-7803-1382-8, 93CH3338-1) Inst Electrical.

WSFI Rule Book. Linda Bowlby et al. 20p. 1996. pap. 3.00 (1-884011-07-1) Wrld Sidesaddle.

WT: Australia. (Illus.). 128p. 1995. 12.98 (0-8317-9353-8) Smithmark.

WT: Brazil. (Illus.). 128p. 1995. 12.98 (0-8317-9354-6) Smithmark.

WT: Greece. Simonetta Crescimbene. (Illus.). 128p. 1995. 12.98 (0-8317-3922-3) Smithmark.

WT: India. (Illus.). 128p. 1995. 12.98 (0-8317-9359-7) Smithmark.

WT: South Africa. (Illus.). 128p. 1995. 12.98 (0-8317-9360-0) Smithmark.

WT: Thailand. Steve Van Beek. (Illus.). 128p. 1995. 12.98 (0-8317-9361-9) Smithmark.

WTEC Panel Report on European Nuclear Instrumentation & Controls. Ed. by James D. White & David D. Lanning. (WTEC Panel Reports). xix, 196p. 1991. pap. write for info. (1-883712-10-6, JTEC) Intl Tech Res.

WTO: Final Text of the GATT, Uruguay Round Agreements, Article-by-Article Analysis & Summary with a Fully Searchable Diskette. Ed. by Philip M. Raworth. (The Practitioner's Deskbook Ser.). 1995. pap. text ed. 69.95 incl. disk (0-379-21354-0) Oceana.

WTO 2000: Setting the Course for World Trade. Jeffrey J. Schott. (Policy Analyses in International Economics Ser.: Vol. 45). (Illus.). 64p. (Orig.). (C). 1996. pap. 11.95 (0-88132-231-8) Inst Intl Eco.

W:Tungsten. John K. Shannon. 1976. pap. 3.00 (0-87924-037-7) Membrane Pr.

Wu Guanzhong: A Contemporary Chinese Artist. Ed. by Lucy Lim. LC 89-60262. (Illus.). 184p. 1989. 60.00 (0-295-96992-X) U of Wash Pr.

Wu Guanzhong on Life & Art: Selected Works of Wu Guanzhong. R. S. Chen. 380p. 1992. pap. text ed. 13.00 (1-879771-00-4) Global Pub NJ.

Wu Han: Attacking the Present Through the Past. James R. Pusey. (East Asian Monographs: No. 33). 94p. 1969. pap. 11.00 (0-674-96275-3) HUP.

Wu Leichuan: A Confucian-Christian in Republican China. Chu Sin-Jan. LC 94-16415. (Asian Thought & Culture Ser.: Vol. 19). 232p. (C). 1995. text ed. 43.95 (0-8204-2531-1) P Lang Pubng.

Wu Liang Shrine: The Ideology of Early Chinese Pictorial Art. Wu Hung. (Illus.). 440p. 1989. 67.50 (0-8047-1529-7); pap. 24.95 (0-8047-2016-9) Stanford U Pr.

Wu Qiong Hong Yan Yan Chen Li. Wang Li. (CHI.). pap. 12.95 (7-5004-1701-2, Pub. by China Intl Bk CH) Distribks Inc.

Wu Style of Tai Chi Chuan. T. C. Lee. LC 81-50511. (Illus.). 120p. (Orig.). 1981. pap. 9.95 (0-86568-022-1, 211) Unique Pubns.

Wu Style Tai Chi Chuan: The Thirteen Golden Postures. Johnny K. Lee. (Illus.). 42p. (Orig.). 1992. pap. 15.00 (0-9635087-1-7) On-Line Pub.

Wu Style Tai Chi Practitioners of North America. On-Line Publishing Staff. (Illus.). 48p. (Orig.). 1993. pap. 9.95 (0-9635087-2-5) On-Line Pub.

Wu Sung Kills a Tiger see Supplementary Readers for Intermediate Chinese Reader

Wu Tingfang (1842-1922) Reform & Modernization in Modern Chinese History. Linda Pomerantz-Zhang. 320p. (Orig.). 1992. pap. 67.50 (962-209-287-X, Pub. by Hong Kong Univ Pr HK) Coronet Bks.

Wu Tse-t'ien & the Politics of Legitimation in T'ang China. R. W. Guisso. LC 78-4840. (Occasional Papers: Vol. 11). (Illus.). 335p. 1978. 12.00 (0-914584-11-1) WWUCEAS.

Wu Way: A Path to Natural Healing. Mark D. Mincolla. 52p. (Orig.). 1992. pap. 10.95 (0-9632811-0-0) Pennyroyal Pr.

Wu Wenying & the Art of Southern Song Ci Poetry. Grace S. Fong. 192p. 1987. text ed. 35.00 (0-691-06703-1) Princeton U Pr.

Wu Zuoren & Xiao Shufang: Selected Paintings. Robert Rorex. (Illus.). 15p. (Orig.). (C). 1983. pap. 2.00 (0-614-11346-6) Univ Miss-KC Art.

***Wubbulous Countdown.** Dr. Seuss. (Chunky Shape Bks.). (J). 1997. 3.99 (0-679-88750-4) Random Bks Yng Read.

***Wubbulous Gallery: Portraits to Color & Frame.** 1997. pap. 2.75 (0-679-88515-3) Random Bks Yng Read.

***Wubbulous Playhouse.** Dr. Seuss. (J). 1998. write for info. (0-679-88620-6) Random Bks Yng Read.

Wuerttemberg Emigration Index, Vol. II. Compiled by Trudy Schenk & Ruth Frolke. LC 85-52453. (Illus.). 248p. 1986. 19.95 (0-916489-15-9) Ancestry.

Wuerttemberg Emigration Index, Vol. III. Trudy Schenk & Ruth Froelke. LC 85-52453. (Illus.). 248p. 1987. 19.95 (0-916489-25-6, 395) Ancestry.

Wuerttemberg Emigration Index, Vol. IV. Trudy Schenk & Ruth Froelke. LC 85-52453. (Illus.). 248p. 1988. 19.95 (0-916489-26-4, 396) Ancestry.

Wuerttemberg Emigration Index, Vol. V. Trudy Schenk & Ruth Froelke. 248p. 1988. 19.95 (0-916489-34-5) Ancestry.

Wuerttemberg Emigration Index, Vol. VI. Trudy Schenk & Ruth Froelke. 496p. 1993. 29.95 (0-916489-36-1) Ancestry.

Wuerttemberg Emigration Index, Vol. I. Ed. by Ruth Froelke & Inge Bork. LC 85-52453. 240p. 1986. 19.95 (0-916489-08-6) Ancestry.

Wuggly Ump. Edward Gorey. LC 86-11273. (Illus.). (J). (ps up). 1986. 6.95 (0-915361-56-6, Watts) Hemed Bks.

Wulfeck's Virginia Marriages. A. Maxim & Coppage. (Second Ser.). 280p. 1990. 42.50 (0-317-02847-2) A M Coppage.

Wulff Construction: A Global Shape from Local Interaction. R. Dobrushin et al. LC 92-9200. (Translations of Mathematical Monographs: Vol. 104). 204p. 1992. 130.00 (0-8218-4563-2, MMONO/104) Am Math.

Wulfheim. Sax Rohmer. 1972. 12.50 (0-685-33438-4) Bookfinger.

***Wulfstan.** Arthur Napier. viii, 367p. 1967. write for info. (3-296-25100-6, Pub. by Weidmann GW) Lubrecht & Cramer.

Wulfstan's Canons of Edgar. Ed. by R. G. Fowler. (EETS Original Ser.: Vol. 266). 1972. 30.00 (0-19-722266-8, Pub. by EETS UK) Boydell & Brewer.

Wulfsyarn. Phillip Mann. 368p. 1993. mass mkt. 4.99 (0-380-71717-4, AvoNova) Avon.

Wump World. Bill Peet. LC 72-124999. (Illus.). (J). (gr. 3-5). 1974. 14.95 (0-395-19841-0) HM.

Wump World. Bill Peet. LC 72-124999. (Illus.). (J). (gr. 3-5). 1981. pap. 5.95 (0-395-31129-2) HM.

Wump World. Bill Peet. (Illus.). (J). 1991. 7.95 (0-395-58412-4) HM.

Wumples of Wigwump. Margaret C. Clarke. (Illus.). (J). (gr. k-3). Date not set. pap. write for info. (0-9614659-8-0) Cuchullain Pubns.

Wunderbare Neue Welt: German Books about the Americas in the John Carter Brown Library, 1493-1840, 2 vols., Vol. II: 1619-1763, 520p. Compiled by Ilse E. Kramer. write for info. (0-318-68993-6) J C Brown.

Wunderbaren Jahre. Prosa. Reiner Kunze. 128p. (GER.). 1996. pap. 11.75 (3-596-22074-2, Pub. by Fischer Taschbch Verlag GW) Intl Bk Import.

Wunderkind: The Reputation of Carson McCullers, 1940-1990. Judith G. James. (LCENG Ser.). xii, 230p. (C). 1995. 54.95 (1-879751-88-7) Camden Hse.

Wunderlich (Paul) Paintings, Gouaches & Drawings, 1957-78: Catalogue Raisonne. Jens C. Jensen. (Illus.). 228p. (GER.). 1979. 195.00 (1-55660-098-4) A Wofsy Fine Arts.

Wunderlich (Paul) Sculpture: Catalogue Raisonne. Heinz Spielmann. (Illus.). 316p. (GER.). 1988. 375.00 (1-55660-099-2) A Wofsy Fine Arts.

Wunderlich's Graphics, 1948-87. Thomas Gadeke. (Illus.). 256p. (GER.). 1987. pap. 95.00 (1-55660-203-0) A Wofsy Fine Arts.

W

Wunderlich's Salute: The Interrelationship of the German-American Bund, Camp Siegfried, Yaphank, Long Island, & the Young Siegfrieds & Their Relationship with American & Nazi Institutions. Marvin D. Miller. LC 82-62515. (Illus.). 336p. 1983. pap. 15.95 (0-9610466-0-0) Malamud-Rose.
Wunderwelt Film. H. W. Siska. 1976. lib. bdg. 105.95 (0-8490-2823-X) Gordon Pr.
Wundt Studies: A Centennial Collection. Ed. by Wolfgang G. Bringmann & Ryan D. Tweney. 350p. (C). 1980. pap. text ed. 28.00 (0-88937-001-X) Hogrefe & Huber Pubs.
Wunnissoo. William Allen. (Works of William Allen). 1989. reprint ed. lib. bdg. 79.00 (0-685-44734-0) Rprt Serv.
***Wunschbilder Werden wahr Gemacht: Aneignung von Urlaubswelt durch Fotosouvenirs am Beispiel Deutscher Italientouristen der 50er und 60er Jahre.** Birgit Mandel. 312p. (GER.). 1996. 57.95 (3-631-30095-6) P Lang Pubng.
Wunschloses Unglueck. Peter Handke. Ed. by Barbara Becker-Cantarino. LC 84-2746. (Suhrkamp/Insel Ser.). xiv, 130p. (Orig.). (ENG & GER.). (C). 1985. pap. 8.00 (3-518-02972-X, Pub. by Suhr Verlag GW) Intl Bk Import.
Wupatki & Walnut Canyon: New Perspectives on History, Prehistory & Rock Art. 2nd ed. Ed. by David G. Noble. LC 92-55034. (Illus.). 48p. (C). 1993. reprint ed. pap. 7.95 (0-941270-75-0) Ancient City Pr.
Wupatki National Monument. Susan Lamb. Ed. by Sandra Scott. LC 94-66873. (Illus.). 16p. 1995. pap. 3.95 (1-877856-47-9) SW Pks Mnmts.
Wurlitzer Service Instructions & Parts Catalog for Model 1015 Commercial Phonograph. rev. ed. Wurlitzer, Rudolph, Co. Staff. Ed. by Ricky J. Botts. (Illus.). 106p. 1984. reprint ed. pap. 20.00 (0-912789-02-6) Jukebox Coll New.
Wurts, Genealogical Record of the Wurts Family: Descendants of Rev. Johannes Conrad Wirz, Who Came to America from Zurich, Switzerland, in 1734; Also a Record of His Ancestry from the 13th Century. C. P. Wurts. (Descendants of Rev. Johannes Conrad Wirz, Who Came to America from Zurich, Switzerland, in 1734; Also a Record of His Ancestry from the 13th Century). (Illus.). 91p. 1994. reprint ed. pap. 18.00 (0-8328-4393-8); reprint ed. lib. bdg. 28.00 (0-8328-4392-X) Higginson Bk Co.
***Wurts Short Stories.** Janny Wurts. 1975. mass mkt. write for info. (0-06-105468-2, Harp PBks) HarpC.
Wurzelatlas Mitteleuropaeischer Gruenlandpflanzen, Vol 1: Monocotyledoneae. L. Kutschera & E. Lichtenegger. (Illus.). 516p. (GER.). 1982. lib. bdg. 160.00 (3-437-30359-7) Lubrecht & Cramer.
Wurzeln der Weisheit see Roots of Wisdom: The Oldest Proverbs of Israel & Other Peoples
Wustenadel. Foppe B. Klynstra. (Documenta Hippologica Ser.). (Illus.). 172p. 1978. write for info. (3-487-08173-3) G Olms Pubs.
Wuthering Heights. (Fiction Ser.). (YA). 1993. pap. text ed. 6.50 (0-582-09672-3, 79835) Longman.
Wuthering Heights. 1992. pap. 5.25 (0-19-422686-7) OUP.
Wuthering Heights. 1993. pap. 5.25 (0-19-585474-8) OUP.
Wuthering Heights. (Read-Along Ser.). 1994. 34.95 incl. audio (0-88432-973-9, S23926) Audio-Forum.
***Wuthering Heights.** (Classics Illustrated Study Guides Ser.). (Illus.). (Orig.). 1997. mass mkt. write for info. (1-57840-051-1) Acclaim Bks.
***Wuthering Heights.** Bronte. 1997. pap. 7.75 (0-03-051489-4) HR&W Schl Div.
***Wuthering Heights.** Bronte. 1991. pap. text ed. write for info. (0-17-556575-9) Addison-Wesley.
Wuthering Heights. Emily Bronte. (Classics Ser.). (YA). (gr. 9 up). 1963. mass mkt. 4.95 (0-8049-0011-6, CL-11) Airmont.
Wuthering Heights. Emily Bronte. 416p. 1991. 17.00 (0-679-40543-7, Everymans Lib) Knopf.
Wuthering Heights. Emily Bronte. 320p. (YA). (gr. 7-12). 1983. 3.95 (0-553-21258-3, Bantam Classics) Bantam.
Wuthering Heights. Emily Bronte. Ed. by Walter Kendrick. (Classics Ser.). 400p. (C). 1980. 19.95 (0-8464-1072-9) Beekman Pubs.
Wuthering Heights. Emily Bronte & Rick Geary. (Classics Illustrated Ser.). (Illus.). 52p. (YA). pap. 4.95 (1-57209-011-1) Classics Int Ent.
Wuthering Heights. Emily Bronte. LC 91-70970. (Literary Classics Ser.). 247p. 1991. 5.98 (1-56138-035-0) Courage Bks.
Wuthering Heights. Emily Bronte. Ed. by Victor S. Pritchett. LC 56-14017. (YA). (gr. 9 up). 1956. pap. 11.56 (0-395-05102-9, RivEd) HM.
Wuthering Heights. Emily Bronte. Ed. by Roy Blatchford. (Literature Ser.). 1993. pap. 5.95 (0-582-07782-6, TG7655) Longman.
Wuthering Heights. Emily Bronte. LC 93-4881. 1993. write for info. (0-451-52583-3, Sig Classics) NAL-Dutton.
Wuthering Heights. Emily Bronte. Ed. by Sally Peters. 352p. mass mkt. 4.99 (0-671-79022-6) PB.
***Wuthering Heights.** Emily Bronte. 1997. mass mkt. 5.99 (0-671-01480-3) PB.
Wuthering Heights. Emily Bronte. LC 25-26570. (Illus.). 400p. 12.95 (0-394-60458-X, Modern Lib) Random.
Wuthering Heights. Emily Bronte. 448p. 1994. 16.50 (0-679-60135-X, Modern Lib) Random.
Wuthering Heights. Emily Bronte. Ed. by Heather Glen. (English Texts Ser.). 400p. (C). 1988. pap. text ed. 12.50 (0-415-00667-8) Routledge.
Wuthering Heights. Emily Bronte. Ed. by Ross C. Murfin & Linda H. Peterson. LC 90-71625. (Case Studies in Contemporary Criticism). 480p. (C). 1991. pap. text ed. 7.50 (0-312-03547-0) St Martin.
Wuthering Heights. Emily Bronte. Ed. by Patsy Stoneman. LC 93-14830. (New Casebooks Ser.). 208p. 1993. text ed. 39.95 (0-312-09689-5) St Martin.
Wuthering Heights. Emily Bronte. 224p. (YA). 1989. pap. 2.99 (0-8125-0516-6) Tor Bks.
Wuthering Heights. Emily Bronte. pap. 2.95 (0-89375-706-3) Troll Communs.
Wuthering Heights. Emily Bronte. Ed. by David Daiches. (English Library). 382p. 1990. pap. 5.95 (0-14-043001-6, Penguin Classics) Viking Penguin.
Wuthering Heights. Emily Bronte. (Classics Ser.). 448p. (YA). (gr. 5 up). 1995. pap. 3.99 (0-14-036694-6) Puffin Bks.
Wuthering Heights. Emily Bronte. 400p. 1996. pap. 6.95 (0-14-043418-6) Viking Penguin.
Wuthering Heights. Emily Bronte. Ed. by Berg. LC 96-31198. 1996. 23.95 (0-8057-8051-3, Twayne) Scribnrs Ref.
Wuthering Heights. Emily Bronte. Ed. by Berg. LC 96-31198. 1996. pap. 13.95 (0-8057-8101-3, Twayne) Scribnrs Ref.
Wuthering Heights. Emily Bronte. 1996. pap. 11.95 (0-312-13826-1) St Martin.
***Wuthering Heights.** Emily Bronte. Ed. by Richard Hoyes. (Literature Ser.). 416p. (C). 1997. pap. text ed. 10.95 (0-521-58949-5) Cambridge U Pr.
***Wuthering Heights.** Emily Bronte. (Thornes Classic Novels Ser.). (Orig.). 1997. pap. 16.95 (0-7487-2978-X, Pub. by Stanley Thornes UK) Trans-Atl Phila.
***Wuthering Heights.** Holbrook. (C). 1992. text ed. 32.00 (0-8147-3482-0) NYU Pr.
Wuthering Heights. Graham Holderness. (Open Guides to Literature Ser.). 112p. 1985. 75.00 (0-335-15087-X, Open Univ Pr); pap. 22.00 (0-335-15073-X, Open Univ Pr) Taylor & Francis.
Wuthering Heights. Holt & Company Staff. (YA). 1989. student ed., pap. 10.00 (0-03-031643-X) HR&W Schl Div.
Wuthering Heights. Meyer. (Bedford Introduction to Literature Ser.). Date not set. pap. text ed. 37.80 (0-312-13894-6) St Martin.
Wuthering Heights. Wright. LC 81-15786. (Short Classics Ser.). (Illus.). 48p. (J). (gr. 4 up). 1982. 22.83 (0-8172-1682-0) Raintree Steck-V.
Wuthering Heights. abr. ed. Emily Bronte. Ed. by Naunerle Farr. (Now Age Illustrated III Ser.). (Illus.). (J). (gr. 4-12). 1977. pap. text ed. 2.95 (0-88301-272-3) Pendulum Pr.
Wuthering Heights. large type ed. Emily Bronte. (Clear Type Classics Ser.). 418p. 1992. 22.95 (1-85695-310-6, Pub. by ISIS UK) Transaction Pubs.
***Wuthering Heights.** large type ed. Emily Bronte. (Large Print Ser.). 566p. 1992. lib. bdg. 24.00 (0-939495-28-7) North Bks.
***Wuthering Heights.** large type ed. Emily Bronte. 551p. 1997. 23.95 (0-7089-8950-0) Ulverscroft.
Wuthering Heights. unabridged ed. Emily Bronte. LC 96-20636. (Thrift Editions Ser.). 272p. reprint ed. pap. text ed. 2.00 (0-486-29256-8) Dover.
***Wuthering Heights.** unabridged ed. Emily Bronte. 230p. 1997. reprint ed. pap. 14.95 (1-57002-048-5) Univ Publng Hse.
Wuthering Heights. 2nd ed. Emily Bronte. (The World's Classics Ser.). 408p. 1995. pap. 4.95 (0-19-282350-7) OUP.
Wuthering Heights. 3rd rev. ed. Emily Bronte. Ed. by William M. Sale, Jr. & Richard J. Dunn. (Critical Editions Ser.). (YA). (gr. 9-12). 1990. pap. text ed. 9.95 (0-393-95760-8) Norton.
Wuthering Heights. Emily Bronte. 320p. 1986. reprint ed. lib. bdg. 23.95 (0-89966-520-9) Buccaneer Bks.
Wuthering Heights. Emily Bronte. 320p. (YA). (gr. 10). 1959. reprint ed. pap. 4.95 (0-451-52338-5, Sig Classics) NAL-Dutton.
Wuthering Heights: A. Emily Bronte. (C). Date not set. pap. text ed. 3.00 (0-393-99772-3) Norton.
Wuthering Heights: A Study. U. C. Knoepflmacher. LC 93-39317. 151p. (C). 1994. reprint ed. pap. text ed. 14.95 (0-8214-1078-4) Ohio U Pr.
Wuthering Heights: And Poems. Emily Bronte. Ed. by Margaret Drabble. 432p. 1993. pap. 5.95 (0-460-87311-3, Everyman's Classic Lib) C E Tuttle.
Wuthering Heights: Student Activity Book. Marcia Sohl & Gerald Dackerman. (Now Age Illustrated Ser.). (Illus.). (gr. 4-12). 1976. student ed. 1.25 (0-88301-296-0) Pendulum Pr.
Wuthering Heights - Emily Bronte see Bloom's Notes
Wuthering Heights (Bronte) Carey. (Book Notes Ser.). (C). 1984. pap. 2.95 (0-8120-3448-1) Barron.
Wuthering Heights Literature Guide. Johanna Wrinkle. 96p. 1992. pap. text ed. 10.95 (0-944459-55-2) ECS Lrn Systs.
Wuthering Heights Notes. Janet C. James. 1979. pap. 4.50 (0-8220-1393-2) Cliffs.
***Wuthering Heights Readalong.** Emily Bronte. (Illustrated Classics Collection 3). 64p. 1994. pap. 14.95 incl. audio (0-7854-0745-6, 40476) Am Guidance.
Wuzzy Takes Off. Robin Lester & Helen Lester. LC 95-10694. (Gund Children's Library). (Illus.). (J). (ps up). 1995. 9.99 (1-56402-498-9) Candlewick Pr.
Wuzzy Takes Off. Robin Lester & Helen Lester. LC 95-10694. (Gund Children's Library). (Illus.). 32p. (J). (ps up). 1997. reprint ed. pap. 3.99 (0-7636-0097-0) Candlewick Pr.
Wuzzy the Witch. Margaret H. Matens. LC 93-77128. (Illus.). 42p. (J). (gr. k-5). 1993. 14.95 (1-882959-54-X) Foxglove TN.
***WV Golf GTI & Derivatives: Collector's Guide.** J. Blunsden. (Illus.). 128p. 1996. 19.98 (0-947981-63-2, Pub. by Motor Racing UK) Motorbooks Intl.
WVPS 1994 Contest Winners: Anthology 1994. Ed. by Melba Dungey. 76p. 1994. write for info. (0-9643888-0-4) West VA Poetry.
WVPS 1995 Contest Winners: West. Ed. by Melba Dungey. 88p. write for info. (0-9643888-1-2) West VA Poetry.
WW Fat Sorter. 1995. 3.00 (0-02-860032-0) Macmillan.
WW II: A Global Perspective. David Latyon. 208p. (C). 1995. per., pap. text ed. 30.19 (0-7872-0421-8) Kendall-Hunt.
WW II see Stones in Water
WW II from the Turret. Dwight K. Strickler. LC 89-92424. (Illus.). 130p. (Orig.). 1989. pap. 7.00 (0-9624681-0-X) D K Strickler.
WW II in Baltimore. Thomas Antonucci & Historical Briefs, Inc. Staff. Ed. by Michael Antonucci. 176p. 1993. pap. 14.95 (0-89677-051-6) Hist Briefs.
WW II in Brooklyn. Historical Briefs, Inc. Staff. Ed. by Thomas Antonucci & Michael Antonucci. 200p. 1993. pap. 14.95 (0-89677-047-8) Hist Briefs.
WW II Wrecks of Palau. Dan E. Bailey. LC 90-60053. (Illus.). 246p. 1991. 42.95 (0-911615-04-0) North Valley.
WW III No. 3: World in Flames. Ian Slater. 448p. 1991. mass mkt. 5.99 (0-449-14564-6, GM) Fawcett.
WW III No. 4: Arctic Front. Ian Slater. 1992. mass mkt. 5.99 (0-449-14756-8, GM) Fawcett.
WW III No. 5: Warshot. Ian Slater. (Orig.). 1992. mass mkt. 5.99 (0-449-14757-6, GM) Fawcett.
WW III No. 6: Asian Front. Ian Slater. (WW III Ser.). 1993. mass mkt. 5.99 (0-449-14854-8) Fawcett.
WW III No. 7: Force of Arms. Ian Slater. (WW III Ser.). 1994. mass mkt. 5.99 (0-449-14855-6, GM) Fawcett.
WW III No. 8: South China Sea. Ian Slater. (WW III Ser.). 1996. mass mkt. 5.99 (0-449-14932-3) Fawcett.
WWAP: Exams, 11 Vols. Joseph F. Trimmer. (C). Date not set. text ed. write for info. (0-395-47367-5) HM.
WWF Superstars. (World Wrestling Federation Poster Bks.). (Illus.). 8p. (J). 1992. pap. 4.95 (1-56288-199-X) Checkerboard.
WWF Tag Teams. (World Wrestling Federation Poster Bks.). (Illus.). 8p. (J). 1992. pap. 4.95 (1-56288-198-1) Checkerboard.
***WWII Airwar: The Men, the Machines, the Missions.** Cowles History Group, Inc. Staff. LC 96-47007. 300p. 1996. write for info. (0-86573-858-0) Cowles Creative.
WWII War Eagles: Global Air War in Original Color. Jeffrey L. Ethell & Warren M. Bodie. (Illus.). 224p. 1995. 39.95 (0-9629359-2-1) Widewing Pubns.
WWTMMA? (Who Was That Masked Man Anyway?) Kenneth F. Byers. 1700p. (Orig.). 1993. pap. 12.95 (0-9619040-4-6) Journeys Together.
WWTMMA? Who Was That Masked Man Anyway? Kenneth F. Byers. 140p. (Orig.). 1993. pap. 12.95 (0-685-55199-7) Journeys Together.
WWW: A Guide to the Best World Wide Web Graphics. Daniel Donnelly. (Illus.). 160p. 1997. write for info. incl. cd-rom (1-56496-335-7) Rockport Pubs.
***WWW: Shadow of the Chameleon.** (Orig.). 1997. pap. 10.95 (1-57532-042-8) Press-Tige Pub.
WWW Database Developer's Guide. 816p. 1996. 59.99 (1-57521-048-7, SamsNet Bks) Sams.
WWW Publishing Kit. Samsnet Publishing Staff. 1995. pap. 49.99 (1-57521-063-0, SamsNet Bks) Sams.
Wyandotte. Frank J. Irgang. LC 95-61852. 615p. 1996. 16.95 (1-55523-770-3) Winston-Derek.
Wyandotte, or the Hutted Knoll: A Tale. James Fenimore Cooper. Ed. by Thomas Philbrick & Marianne Philbrick. LC 81-1132. 434p. 1981. text ed. 59.50 (0-87395-414-9); pap. text ed. 19.95 (0-87395-469-6) State U NY Pr.
Wyandotte, or the Hutted Knoll: A Tale. James Fenimore Cooper. (Works of James Fenimore Cooper Ser.). 1990. reprint ed. lib. bdg. 79.00 (0-7812-2390-3) Rprt Serv.
Wyatt Earp. Matt Braun. 1994. mass mkt. 5.50 (0-312-95325-9, Thomas Dunne Bks) St Martin.
Wyatt Earp. Dan Gordon. 256p. 1994. mass mkt. 5.99 (0-446-60161-6) Warner Bks.
Wyatt Earp. Carl R. Green & William R. Sanford. LC 91-29855. (Outlaws & Lawmen of the Wild West Ser.). (Illus.). 48p. (J). (gr. 4-10). 1992. lib. bdg. 14.95 (0-89490-367-5) Enslow Pubs.
Wyatt Earp. Winter. (J). 1999. pap. 3.50 (0-7868-4030-7) Disney Pr.
Wyatt Earp. Winter. (J). 1999. lib. bdg. 12.89 (0-7868-5020-5) Disney Pr.
Wyatt Earp. large type ed. Matt Braun. (Niagara Large Print Ser.). 1995. 27.99 (0-7089-5800-1) Ulverscroft.
Wyatt Earp: Frontier Marshall. Stuart N. Lake. Ed. by Doug Grad. 416p. 1994. reprint ed. pap. 6.50 (0-671-88537-5) PB.
Wyatt Earp: Legends of the West. LC 97-3941. (J). (gr. 4-7). 1997. lib. bdg. 15.95 (0-7910-3852-1) Chelsea Hse.
Wyatt Earp: The Film & the Filmmakers. Lawrence Kasdan & Jake Kasdan. LC 94-6296. (Pictorial Moviebook Ser.). (Illus.). 176p. 1994. pap. 17.95 (1-55704-198-9) Newmarket.
Wyatt Earp: The Illustrated Life & Times. Bob B. Bell. (Old West Ser.). (Illus.). 128p. 1993. pap. 24.95 (0-9639549-1-1) Honkytonk Sue.
***Wyatt Earp: The Life Behind the Legend.** Casey Tefertiller. LC 97-2932. 400p. 1997. 30.00 (0-471-18967-7) Wiley.
Wyatt Earp Vol. 1: The Making of the Legend. Lee A. Silva. LC 95-75010. 448p. 1998. write for info. (1-882824-12-1) Graphic Pubs.
***Wyatt Earp Speaks! My Side of the O. K. Corral Shootout, Plus Interviews with Doc Holliday.** Wyatt Earp. (Illus.). 125p. (Orig.). 1997. pap. 11.95 (0-9654646-6-0) Fern Canyon.
Wyatt Earp's Tombstone Vendetta. Glenn G. Boyer. 368p. 1993. 29.95 (0-9631772-2-2) Talei Pubs.
Wyatt Earp's Tombstone Vendetta. large type ed. Compiled by Glenn G. Boyer. LC 94-739. (J). 1994. lib. bdg. 21.95 (0-8161-5959-9, GK Hall) Thorndike Pr.
Wyatt Earp's West: Images & Portraits. Jim Wilson. 1994. 39.95 (1-55704-197-7) Newmarket.
Wyatt Earp's West: Images & Words. Jim Wilson. (Illus.). 128p. 1994. 39.95 (1-55704-201-2) Newmarket.
***Wyatt, Surrey, & Early Tudor Poetry.** Elizabeth Heale. LC 97-15377. (Medieval & Renaissance Library). 1998. text ed. write for info. (0-582-09353-8); pap. text ed. write for info. (0-582-09352-X) Longman.
Wyatt the Whale. Dan Slottje. LC 94-9298. (Illus.). 24p. (J). (ps up). 1994. 14.95 (1-885108-03-6) Armstrong CT.
***Wyatt's Most Wanted Wife.** Sandra Steffen. 1997. pap. 3.25 (0-373-19241-X, 1-19241-8) Silhouette.
***Wycherly Woman.** Ross MacDonald. 1998. pap. write for info. (0-375-70144-3, Vin) Random.
Wychwood. large type ed. E. V. Thompson. 464p. 1993. 27.99 (0-7089-8715-X) Ulverscroft.
Wychwood: The Secret Cotswold Forest. Mollie Harris. (Illus.). 1991. 30.00 (0-86299-788-7, Pub. by Sutton Pubng UK) Bks Intl VA.
Wycinanki: Polish Paper Cuts. Leona W. Barthle. 120p. 1994. pap. write for info. (0-9641189-0-4) L W Barthle.
Wyclif & the Oxford Schools: The Relation of the "Summa de Ente" to Scholastic Debates at Oxford in the Later Fourteenth Century. John A. Robson. LC 61-16171. (Cambridge Studies in Medieval Life & Thought: Vol. 8). 282p. reprint ed. pap. 80.40 (0-317-08005-9, 2051448) Bks Demand.
Wyclif on Simony. Tr. by Terrence A. McVeigh from LAT. LC 92-9844. ix, 179p. 1992. 27.00 (0-8232-1349-8) Fordham.
***Wycliffe & How to Kill a Cat.** large type ed. W. J. Burley. (Magna Large Print Ser.). 303p. 1997. 27.50 (0-7505-1120-6) Thorndike Pr.
Wycliffe & Movements for Reform. Reginald L. Poole. LC 77-84729. reprint ed. 39.50 (0-404-16129-4) AMS Pr.
Wycliffe & the House of Death. W. J. Burley. 192p. 1995. 19.95 (0-312-14080-0) St Martin.
Wycliffe & the Lollards. J. C. Carrick. 1977. lib. bdg. 59.95 (0-8490-2824-8) Gordon Pr.
Wycliffe & the Pea Green Boat. W. Burley. 208p. 1993. mass mkt. 4.99 (0-552-12804-X) Bantam.
Wycliffe & the Quiet Virgin. W. J. Burley. 176p. 1988. mass mkt. 2.95 (0-380-70510-9) Avon.
***Wycliffe & the Three-Toed Pussy.** large type ed. W. J. Burley. (Magna Large Print Ser.). 320p. 1996. 25.99 (0-7505-0963-5, Pub. by Magna Print Bks UK) Ulverscroft.
Wycliffe & Winsor Blue. W. J. Barley. 1988. mass mkt. 2.95 (0-380-70633-4) Avon.
Wycliffe Bible Commentary. Ed. by Everett F. Harrison & Charles F. Pfeiffer. (C). 1980. text ed. 39.99 (0-8024-9695-4) Moody.
Wycliffe Bible Commentary: N. T. see Comentario Biblico Moody: Nuevo Testamento
Wycliffe in the Making: Memoirs of W. Cameron Townsend, 1920-1933. Hugh Steven. 360p. 1995. pap. 14.99 (0-87788-890-6) Shaw Pubs.
Wycliffe International Cookbook. Ed. by Gaylyn Whalin & Terry Whalin. (Illus.). 281p. (Orig.). 1989. pap. 9.95 (0-938978-11-X) Wycliffe Bible.
Wycliffe, Select English Writings. John D. Wycliffe. Ed. by Herbert E. Winn. LC 75-41303. reprint ed. 37.50 (0-404-14635-X) AMS Pr.
Wye Island. Boyd Gibbons. LC 87-61748. 227p. 1987. pap. 12.95 (0-915707-34-9) Resources Future.
Wye Island: Outsiders, Insiders & Resistance to Change. Boyd Gibbons. LC 76-47399. (Resources for the Future Ser.). (Illus.). 248p. 1977. 20.95 (0-8018-1936-9) Johns Hopkins.
Wye Oak: The History of a Great Tree. Dickson J. Preston. LC 72-12911. (Illus.). 144p. 1972. reprint ed. pap. 41.10 (0-608-02463-5, 2063107) Bks Demand.
Wye Valley & Forest of Dean Walks. (Ordnance Survey Pathfinder Guides Ser.). (Illus.). 80p. 1993. pap. 14.95 (0-7117-0549-6) Seven Hills Bk.
Wyeth's Oregon, or a Short History of a Long Journey, 1832.: Townsend's Narrative of a Journey Across the Rocky Mountains, 1834 see Early Western Travels, 1748-1846
Wyeth's Repository of Sacred Music, 1 & 2 pts., Pt. 1. John Wyeth. LC 64-18989. (Music Reprint Ser.). 148p. 1964. reprint ed. 25.00 (0-306-70903-1) Da Capo.
Wyeth's Repository of Sacred Music, 1 & 2 pts., Pt. 2. John Wyeth. LC 64-18989. (Music Reprint Ser.). 148p. 1964. reprint ed. 25.00 (0-686-85854-9) Da Capo.
Wykked Wyves & the Woes of Marriage: Misogamous Literature from Juvenal to Chaucer. Ed. by Katharina M. Wilson & Elizabeth M. Makowski. LC 88-29156. (SUNY Series in Medieval Studies). 206p. 1990. pap. text ed. 21.95 (0-7914-0063-8) State U NY Pr.
Wykked Wyves & the Woes of Marriage: Misogamous Literature from Juvenal to Chaucer. Ed. by Katharina M. Wilson & Elizabeth M. Makowski. LC 88-29156. (SUNY Series in Medieval Studies). 206p. 1990. text ed. 64.50 (0-7914-0062-X) State U NY Pr.
***Wyland, the Whaling Walls.** Wyland. Ed. by Angela Eaton. (Illus.). 198p. (Orig.). 1997. 39.95 (1-884840-13-2) Wyland Galleries.

***Wyland, the Whaling Walls. Wyland. Ed. by Angela Eaton. (Illus.). 198p. (Orig.). 1997. pap. 29.95 (1-884840-11-6) Wyland Galleries.**
Sold over 50,000 copies so far! Wyland, the world's finest ocean artist... this name to millions of people around the world has become synonymous with whales & man's efforts to save these magnificent creatures from extinction. This beautifully designed coffee table book features color plates chosen from over 300,000 slides, & the genesis of Wyland's stunning murals,

paintings, & sculpture. WYLAND, THE WHALING WALLS takes you with Wyland around the world as he completes 66 magnificent Whaling Walls. From his first wall in Laguna Beach, California, to Whaling Wall 33, "Planet Ocean" in Long Beach, California, acknowledged by the Guinness Book of World Records (May 4, 1992) as the largest mural in the world. Then topping that feat by barnstorming down the Eastern Seaboard of the United States, completing 17 walls, in 17 cities, in 17 weeks. Then the following year 13 walls, in 8 cities, in 8 weeks down the West Coast, from Alaska to Mexico City. This book is a must for marine art enthusiasts & anyone who appreciates the ocean & the life within it. All ages are captivated by Wyland's art & vision. ***Publisher Provided Annotation.***

Wylder's Hand. J. Sheridan Lefanu. LC 77-84059. 1978. reprint ed. pap. 8.95 (*0-486-23570-X*) Dover.

Wylder's Hand: A Novel, 3 Vols., Set. Joseph S. Le Fanu. Ed. by Devendra P. Varma. LC 76-5281. (Collected Works). 1977. reprint ed. 87.95 (*0-405-09246-6*) Ayer.

Wylder's Hand: A Novel, 3 Vols., Vol. 1. Joseph S. Le Fanu. Ed. by Devendra P. Varma. LC 76-5281. (Collected Works). 1977. reprint ed. 29.95 (*0-405-09247-4*) Ayer.

Wylder's Hand: A Novel, 3 Vols., Vol. 2. Joseph S. Le Fanu. Ed. by Devendra P. Varma. LC 76-5281. (Collected Works). 1977. reprint ed. 29.95 (*0-405-09248-2*) Ayer.

Wylder's Hand: A Novel, 3 Vols., Vol. 3. Joseph S. Le Fanu. Ed. by Devendra P. Varma. LC 76-5281. (Collected Works). 1977. reprint ed. 29.95 (*0-405-09249-0*) Ayer.

Wylie: Irish Conveyancing Law. J. C. Wylie & Justice Kenny. 1980. 120.00 (*0-903486-45-8*) MICHIE.

Wylie: Irish Land Law. 2nd ed. J. C. Wylie & Justice Kenny. 1986. 94.00 (*0-86205-217-3*) MICHIE.

Wylie: Taxation of Husband & Wife - the New Rules. P. Wylie. 1990. pap. 70.00 (*0-406-51090-3*) MICHIE.

Wylie & Churchill-Davidson's: A Practice of Anaesthesia. 6th ed. Ed. by Thomas E. J. Healy & Peter J. Cohen. 1464p. 1995. 150.00 (*0-340-55309-X*, Pub. by Ed Arnold UK) OUP.

Wylie's Atlas of Vascular Surgery, 6 vols., Set. Ronald J. Stoney & David J. Effeney. (Illus.). 1500p. text ed. 499.00 (*0-397-51145-0*) Lppncott-Raven.

Wylie's Atlas of Vascular Surgery: Disorders of the Extremities. rev. ed. Ronald J. Stoney & David J. Effeney. LC 92-13271. 240p. 1993. text ed. 99.50 (*0-397-51149-3*) Lppncott-Raven.

Wylies Atlas of Vascular Surgery: Thoracoabdominal Aorta & Its Branches. Ronald J. Stoney & David J. Effeney. LC 92-12526. 304p. 1992. text ed. 99.50 (*0-397-51148-5*) Lppncott-Raven.

Wylma's La Trouvaille Cookbook: The Simple Joy of Cajun Cooking. Wylma D. Dusenbery. (Illus.). 80p. 1993. reprint ed. spiral bd. 14.95 (*0-944064-05-1*) Paupieres Pub.

Wylundt's Book of Incense: A Magical Primer. Wylundt. 312p. (Orig.). 1996. pap. 14.95 (*0-87728-679-5*) Weiser.

Wyman Historic District. Diane Wilk. (Historic Denver Guides Ser.). (Illus.). 96p. 1995. pap. 8.95 (*0-914248-05-7*) Hist Denver.

Wyman Sisters Cookbook. Ed. by Laura F. Tesseneer. (Illus.). 105p. (Orig.). 1984. pap. 5.95 (*0-9613793-0-8*) L F Tesseneer.

Wyman's Gardening Encyclopedia: Updated Edition. 2nd ed. Donald Wyman. (Illus.). 1221p. 1987. 65.00 (*0-02-632070-3*) Macmillan.

Wynderley. large type ed. Mary Williams. 1996. 20.95 (*0-7862-0784-1*, Thorndike Lrg Prnt) Thorndike Pr.

Wyndham Legacy. Catherine Coulter. 400p. 1994. reprint ed. mass mkt. 6.99 (*0-515-11449-9*) Jove Pubns.

Wyndham Lewis. Roy Campbell. Ed. by Jeffrey Meyers. 80p. 1985. pap. 9.95 (*0-86980-412-X*, Pub. by Univ Natal Pr SA) Intl Spec Bk.

Wyndham Lewis: A Discursive Explosion. H. Porteus. 1972. 59.95 (*0-8490-1341-0*) Gordon Pr.

Wyndham Lewis: A Revaluation. Jeffrey Meyers. 1980. 44.95 (*0-7735-0516-4*, Pub. by McGill CN) U of Toronto Pr.

Wyndham Lewis: Art & War. Paul Edwards. (Illus.). 140p. (C). 1992. pap. 39.95 (*0-85331-611-2*, Pub. by Lund Humphries UK) Antique Collect.

Wyndham Lewis: Religion & Modernism. Daniel Schenker. LC 91-13775. (Judaic Studies). 248p. (C). 1992. text ed. 34.95 (*0-8173-0535-1*) U of Ala Pr.

Wyndham Lewis: The Artist: Holding the Mirror up to Politics. Tom Normand. (Illus.). 230p. (C). 1993. text ed. 85.00 (*0-521-41054-1*) Cambridge U Pr.

Wyndham Lewis: The Novelist. Timothy Materer. LC 75-29310. 189p. reprint ed. pap. 53.90 (*0-7837-3666-5*, 2043539) Bks Demand.

Wyndham Lewis & the Avant-Garde: The Politics of the Intellect. Toby A. Foshay. 192p. 1992. 44.95 (*0-7735-0916-X*, Pub. by McGill CN) U of Toronto Pr.

Wyndham Lewis & Western Man. David Ayers. LC 91-27229. 261p. 1992. text ed. 39.95 (*0-312-07166-3*) St Martin.

Wyndham Lewis the Artist. Wyndham Lewis. LC 74-173843. (English Literature Ser.: No. 33). 1971. reprint ed. lib. bdg. 75.00 (*0-8383-1348-5*) M S G Haskell Hse.

Wyndmere. Carol Muske. LC 84-19565. (Poetry Ser.). 59p. 1985. 19.95 (*0-8229-3503-1*); pap. 10.95 (*0-8229-5365-X*) U of Pittsburgh Pr.

***Wynema: A Child of the Forest.** S. Alice Callahan. Ed. & Intro. by A. LaVonne Ruoff. LC 96-28385. (Illus.). xlviii, 120p. 1997. pap. 9.95 (*0-8032-6378-3*, Bison Books); text ed. 20.00 (*0-8032-1460-X*) U of Nebr Pr.

Wynken, Blynken, & Nod. Illus. by Cathy Beylon. (My First Golden Board Bks.). 24p. (J). (ps). 1992. bds. 3.95 (*0-307-06141-8*, 6141, Golden Books) Western Pub.

Wynken, Blynken & Nod. Eugene Field. 24p. (J). 1989. pap. 2.95 (*0-590-42422-X*) Scholastic Inc.

Wynken Blynken & Nod. Eugene Field. (Illus.). (J). (gr. k-3). 1989. pap. 15.95 incl. audio (*0-87499-142-0*) Live Oak Media.

Wynken, Blynken, & Nod. Eugene Field. 1992. pap. 4.99 (*0-14-054794-0*) NAL-Dutton.

Wynken Blynken & Nod, 4 bks., Set. Eugene Field. (Illus.). (J). (gr. k-3). 1989. pap. 31.95 incl. audio (*0-87499-144-7*) Live Oak Media.

Wynken, Blynken, & Nod: A Poem. Eugene Field. LC 95-11692. (Illus.). 32p. (J). Date not set. lib. bdg. 15.88 (*1-55858-423-4*) North-South Bks NYC.

Wynken, Blynken, & Nod: A Poem. Eugene Field. LC 95-11692. (Illus.). 32p. (J). (ps-1). Date not set. 15.95 (*1-55858-422-6*) North-South Bks NYC.

Wynnefield & Limer. Robert Litman. 237p. 1983. pap. 4.95 (*0-918921-00-7*) Ivy League Pr.

Wynnere & Wastoure. Ed. by Stephanie Trigg. (Early English Text Society Original Ser.: Vol. 297). (Illus.). 128p. 1996. 27.00 (*0-19-722299-4*) Boydell & Brewer.

Wynnere & Wastoure: And, The Parliament of Thre Ages. Ed. by Warren Ginsberg. LC 92-31284. (Teams Middle English Text Ser.). 1992. pap. 7.00 (*1-879288-26-5*) Medieval Inst.

Wynnere & Wastoure: Middle English Poem. Ed. by Israel Gollancz. LC 73-178508. reprint ed. 24.50 (*0-404-56690-1*) AMS Pr.

Wynnewood: Bledsoe's Lick, Castalian Springs, Tennessee. Walter T. Durham. LC 94-79974. (Illus.). 104p. 1994. 8.95 (*0-9644297-1-3*) Sumner Cnty Hist.

Wynonna. 56p. 1992. otabind 12.95 (*0-7935-1716-8*, 00308146) H Leonard.

Wynonna, No. 133. 48p. 1993. pap. 6.95 (*0-7935-2510-1*, 00102286) H Leonard.

Wynonna: Tell Me Why, No. 380. 48p. 1994. pap. 7.95 (*0-7935-3204-3*, 00102304) H Leonard.

Wynonna - Tell My Why. (Piano-Vocal-Guitar Ser.). 56p. (Orig.). 1993. pap. 12.95 (*0-7935-2697-3*, HL00308196) H Leonard.

Wynonna & Naomi Judd. Skip Press. LC 94-28465. (Star Families Ser.). (Illus.). (J). (gr. 5 up). 1995. pap. 7.95 (*0-382-24943-7*, Crstwood Hse) Silver Burdett Pr.

Wynonna & Naomi Judd. Skip Press Staff. LC 94-28465. (Star Families Ser.). (Illus.). (J). (gr. 5). 1995. lib. bdg. 15.95 (*0-89686-882-6*, Crstwood Hse) Silver Burdett Pr.

Wynonna Judd. Rosemary Wallner. LC 91-73037. (Reaching for the Stars Ser.). 202p. (J). 1991. lib. bdg. 13.98 (*1-56239-056-2*) Abdo & Dghtrs.

Wynston Wyc Mystery: The Gift Horse Murders. Brian Johnston. 288p. 1992. mass mkt. 3.99 (*1-55817-652-7*, Pinnacle Kensgtn) Kensgtn Pub Corp.

***Wynton Marsalis.** Veronica F. Ellis. LC 96-47440. (Contemporary African Americans Ser.). (J). 1997. lib. bdg. 24.26 (*0-8172-3988-X*) Raintree Steck-V.

***Wynton Marsalis: Ballads.** Ed. by Gill Gallifurd & Aaron Stang. (Illus.). 60p. (Orig.). 1997. pap. text ed. 19.95 (*1-57623-966-7*, 0007B) Warner Brothers.

Wynton Marsalis: Gifted Trumpet Player. Craig Awmiller. (Picture-Story Biographies Ser.). (Illus.). 32p. (J). (gr. 2-4). 1996. lib. bdg. 17.50 (*0-516-04196-7*) Childrens.

Wynton Marsalis: Gifted Trumpet Player. Craig Awmiller. (Picture-Story Biographies Ser.). (Illus.). 32p. (J). (gr. 2-4). 1996. pap. 3.95 (*0-516-20070-4*) Childrens.

***Wynton Marsalis: Standards.** Ed. by Bill Gallifurd & Aaron Stang. (Illus.). 96p. (Orig.). 1997. pap. text ed. 19.95 (*1-57623-967-5*, 0008B) Warner Brothers.

Wyoming. Nathaniel Burt. Ed. by Barry Parr. (Discover America Ser.). (Illus.). 370p. 1992. 22.95 (*1-878867-03-2*) Fodors Travel.

Wyoming. Dennis B. Fradin & Judith B. Fradin. LC 93-39880. (From Sea to Shining Sea Ser.). (Illus.). 64p. (J). (gr. 3-5). 1994. lib. bdg. 24.00 (*0-516-03850-8*) Childrens.

Wyoming. Carlienne Frisch. LC 93-23098. (Hello U. S. A. Ser.). (Illus.). (J). (gr. 3-6). 1995. lib. bdg. 18.95 (*0-8225-2736-7*, Lerner Publctns) Lerner Group.

Wyoming. William Stafford. 14p. 1985. pap. 2.50 (*0-9604740-8-0*) Ampersand RI.

Wyoming. Kathleen Thompson. LC 87-16442. (Portrait of America Library). 48p. (YA). (gr. 3 up). 1996. lib. bdg. 22.83 (*0-8114-7397-X*) Raintree Steck-V.

Wyoming. Kathleen Thompson. LC 87-16442. (Portrait of America Library). 48p. (YA). (gr. 3 up). 1996. pap. 5.95 (*0-8114-7478-X*) Raintree Steck-V.

Wyoming! large type ed. Dana F. Ross. 1993. 50.95 (*0-7838-1107-1*, GK Hall) Thorndike Pr.

Wyoming. rev. ed. Ann Heinrichs. LC 91-544. (America the Beautiful Ser.). (Illus.). 144p. (J). (gr. 4 up). 1992. lib. bdg. 28.30 (*0-516-00496-4*) Childrens.

Wyoming. 2nd ed. Nathaniel Burt. (Compass American Guides Ser.). (Illus.). 1995. pap. 18.95 (*1-878867-50-4*) Fodors Travel.

Wyoming: A Guide to Its History, Highways, & People. Federal Writers' Project Staff. LC 80-23038. (Illus.). xl, 570p. 1981. text ed. 35.00 (*0-8032-1958-X*) U of Nebr Pr.

Wyoming: A Guide to Its History, Highways & People. Federal Writers' Project. 490p. 1941. reprint ed. 79.00 (*0-403-02199-5*) Somerset Pub.

Wyoming: A Guide to Its History, Highways & People. Federal Writers' Project Staff & Writers Program-WPA Staff. (American Guide Ser.). 1989. reprint ed. lib. bdg. 79.00 (*0-7812-1049-6*, 1049) Rprt Serv.

Wyoming: A Guide to Its History, Highways, & People. Compiled by Writers Program Staff. LC 80-23038. (Bison Book Ser.). 610p. reprint ed. pap. 173.90 (*0-7837-7044-8*, 2046855) Bks Demand.

Wyoming: A History. Taft A. Larson. LC 77-3592. (States & the Nation Ser.). (Illus.). 1984. pap. 10.95 (*0-393-30183-4*) Norton.

Wyoming: A Source Book. Roy A. Jordan & Brett DeBoer. 370p. 1996. pap. 29.95 (*0-87081-424-9*) Univ Pr Colo.

Wyoming: Courage in a Lonesome Land - Centennial Edition. Randy L. Adams & Craig Sodaro. Ed. by Don Lynch. LC 90-82123. (Illus.). 313p. (J). (gr. 4-6). 1990. Centennial Edition. text ed. 21.50 (*0-913205-12-5*) Grace Dangberg.

Wyoming: From Territory to Statehood. Lewis L. Gould. LC 68-27754. 298p. 1989. 24.50 (*0-9623333-0-1*) High Plns WY.

Wyoming: Land of Echoing Canyons. Beverly E. Brink. LC 85-80478. (Old West Region Ser.: Vol. 3). (Illus.). 180p. 1986. 21.95 (*0-918532-15-9*) Flying Diamond Bks.

Wyoming: Off the Beaten Path: A Guide to Unique Places. Richard Maturi. LC 96-11671. (Off the Beaten Path Ser.). (Illus.). 160p. (Orig.). 1996. pap. 10.95 (*1-56440-854-X*) Globe Pequot.

Wyoming: The State & It's Educational System. Harold L. Hodgkinson. 8p. 1989. 7.00 (*0-937846-70-8*) Inst Educ Lead.

Wyoming: Time & Again. Michael A. Amundson. LC 91-9412. 231p. (Orig.). 1991. pap. 24.95 (*0-87108-803-7*) Pruett.

Wyoming see Atlas of Historical County Boundaries

Wyoming Almanac. 3rd rev. ed. Phil Roberts et al. LC 94-66659. 460p. (Orig.). (YA). (gr. 9 up). 1994. pap. 11.95 (*0-914767-21-6*) Skyline West Pr.

***Wyoming Almanac.** 4th rev. ed. Phil Roberts et al. 496p. 1996. pap. 12.95 (*0-914767-24-0*) Skyline West Pr.

Wyoming & Other State Greats (Biographies) Carole Marsh. (Carole Marsh Wyoming Bks.). (Illus.). (J). 1994. pap. 19.95 (*0-7933-2313-4*); lib. bdg. 29.95 (*0-7933-2312-6*); disk 29.95 (*0-7933-2314-2*) Gallopade Pub Group.

Wyoming Angling Guide. 2nd ed. Chuck Fothergill & Bob Sterling. LC 85-82611. (Illus.). 250p. (Orig.). 1993. spiral bd. 27.95 (*0-9614704-5-3*) Stream Stalker.

Wyoming Atlas & Gazetteer. DeLorme Staff. (Illus.). 72p. (Orig.). 1993. pap. 16.95 (*0-89933-248-X*, 5553) DeLorme Map.

Wyoming Bandits, Bushwackers, Outlaws, Crooks, Devils, Ghosts, Desperadoes & Other Assorted & Sundry Characters! Carole Marsh. (Carole Marsh Wyoming Bks.). (Illus.). (J). 1994. pap. 19.95 (*0-7933-1249-3*); lib. bdg. 29.95 (*0-7933-1250-7*); disk 29.95 (*0-7933-1251-5*) Gallopade Pub Group.

Wyoming Biographies. Lawrence M. Woods. LC 91-70461. (Illus.). 224p. 1991. 24.50 (*0-9623333-7-9*) High Plns WY.

Wyoming Bookstore Book: A Surprising Guide to Our State's Bookstores & Their Specialties for Students, Teachers, Writers & Publishers. Carole Marsh. (Wyoming Bks.). (Illus.). 1994. pap. 19.95 (*0-7933-3006-8*); lib. bdg. 29.95 (*0-7933-3005-X*); disk 29.95 (*0-7933-3007-6*) Gallopade Pub Group.

Wyoming Business Directory, 1997. rev. ed. 400p. 1996. boxed 295.00 (*1-56105-790-8*) Am Busn Direct.

***Wyoming Business Directory 1997.** rev. ed. American Business Directories Staff. 416p. 1996. boxed 295.00 (*1-56105-873-4*) Am Busn Direct.

***Wyoming Business Directory 1998.** rev. ed. American Business Directories Staff. 416p. 1997. boxed 295.00 (*1-56105-960-9*) Am Busn Direct.

Wyoming Census Index, 1870: Mortality Schedule. (Illus.). lib. bdg. 30.00 (*0-89593-541-4*) Accelerated Index.

Wyoming Census Index, 1880: Mortality Schedule. (Illus.). lib. bdg. 30.00 (*0-89593-542-2*) Accelerated Index.

Wyoming Census Index, 1890: Union Veterans. Ronald V. Jackson. (Illus.). lib. bdg. 48.00 (*0-89593-807-3*) Accelerated Index.

Wyoming Classic Christmas Trivia: Stories, Recipes, Activities, Legends, Lore & More! Carole Marsh. (Carole Marsh Wyoming Bks.). (Illus.). (J). 1994. pap. 19.95 (*0-7933-1252-3*); lib. bdg. 29.95 (*0-7933-1253-1*); disk 29.95 (*0-7933-1254-X*) Gallopade Pub Group.

Wyoming Coastales. Carole Marsh. (Carole Marsh Wyoming Bks.). (Illus.). (J). 1994. pap. 19.95 (*0-7933-2307-X*); lib. bdg. 29.95 (*0-7933-2306-1*); disk 29.95 (*0-7933-2308-8*) Gallopade Pub Group.

Wyoming Coastales! Carole Marsh. (Wyoming Bks.). (J). 1994. lib. bdg. 29.95 (*0-7933-7315-8*) Gallopade Pub Group.

Wyoming-Colorado Railroad. 40p. 1992. pap. 9.95 (*0-9611662-3-1*) J V Pubns.

Wyoming Conspiracy. Jon Sharpe. (Canyon O'Grady Ser.: No. 21). 176p. (Orig.). 1992. pap. 3.50 (*0-451-17370-8*, Sig) NAL-Dutton.

Wyoming County, (West) Virginia Death Records: 1853-1890. Compiled by Norma P. Evans. LC 84-72968. (Illus.). iv, 67p. (Orig.). 1984. pap. text ed. 15.00 (*0-937418-11-0*) N P Evans.

Wyoming Court Rules Annotated. D. P. Harriman & Mitchie Company Staff. 973p. 1991. ring bd. 80.00 (*0-87215-487-4*) MICHIE.

Wyoming Court Rules Annotated. Michie Butterworth Editorial Staff & D. P. Harriman. 973p. 1991. spiral bd. 85.00 (*0-87473-733-8*) MICHIE.

***Wyoming Court Rules for the Civil Law Practitioner.** 200p. 1997. ring bd. 24.95 (*1-878117-03-3*) Lagumo Corp.

***Wyoming Court Rules for the Criminal Law Practitioner.** 350p. 1997. ring bd. 27.95 (*1-878117-01-7*) Lagumo Corp.

Wyoming Crime Perpsective 1996. Ed. by Kathleen O. Morgan et al. 24p. 1996. pap. 19.00 (*1-56692-549-5*) Morgan Quitno Corp.

***Wyoming Crime Perspective 1997.** Ed. by Kathleen O. Morgan & Scott E. Morgan. 24p. 1997. pap. 19.00 (*1-56692-799-4*) Morgan Quitno Corp.

Wyoming Criminal & Traffic Law Manual, 1993 Edition. 25.00 (*0-614-06005-2*) MICHIE.

Wyoming Criminal Law & Motor Vehicle Handbook. Ed. by Gould Editorial Staff. 490p. 1991. ring bd. 21.95 (*0-87526-368-2*) Gould.

Wyoming "Crinkum-Crankum" A Funny Word Book about Our State. Carole Marsh. (Wyoming Bks.). (Illus.). (J). (gr. 3-12). 1994. 29.95 (*0-7933-4961-3*); pap. 19.95 (*0-7933-4962-1*); disk 29.95 (*0-7933-4963-X*) Gallopade Pub Group.

Wyoming Dingbats! Bk. 1: A Fun Book of Games, Stories, Activities & More about Our State That's All in Code! for You to Decipher. Carole Marsh. (Wyoming Bks.). (Illus.). (J). (gr. 3-12). 1994. pap. 19.95 (*0-7933-3924-3*); lib. bdg. 29.95 (*0-7933-3923-5*); disk 29.95 (*0-7933-3925-1*) Gallopade Pub Group.

Wyoming Facts & Factivities. Carole Marsh. (Carole Marsh State Bks.). (Illus.). 1996. 29.95 (*0-614-11564-7*, C Marsh); teacher ed., pap. 19.95 (*0-7933-7947-4*, C Marsh) Gallopade Pub Group.

Wyoming Federal Census Index, 1860. Ronald V. Jackson. (Illus.). lib. bdg. 50.00 (*0-89593-805-7*) Accelerated Index.

Wyoming Federal Census Index, 1870. Ronald V. Jackson. LC 77-86059. (Illus.). 1979. lib. bdg. 55.00 (*0-89593-208-3*) Accelerated Index.

Wyoming Federal Census Index, 1880. Ronald V. Jackson. (Illus.). lib. bdg. 70.00 (*0-89593-806-5*) Accelerated Index.

Wyoming Federal Census Index, 1910. Ronald V. Jackson. (Illus.). 1986. lib. bdg. 160.00 (*0-89593-842-1*) Accelerated Index.

Wyoming Festival Fun for Kids! Includes Reproducible Activities for Kids! Carole Marsh. (Wyoming Bks.). (Illus.). (J). (gr. 3-12). 1994. pap. 19.95 (*0-7933-4077-2*); lib. bdg. 29.95 (*0-7933-4076-4*); disk 29.95 (*0-7933-4078-0*) Gallopade Pub Group.

Wyoming Fishing: The Most Complete Guide to... 2nd ed. (Illus.). 248p. 1994. pap. 13.95 (*0-941875-20-2*) Wolverine Distrib.

***Wyoming Government! The Cornerstone of Everyday Life in Our State!** Carole Marsh. (Carole Marsh Wyoming Bks.). (Illus.). (J). (gr. 3-12). 1996. pap. 19.95 (*0-7933-6332-2*); lib. bdg. 29.95 (*0-7933-6331-4*); disk 29.95 (*0-7933-6333-0*) Gallopade Pub Group.

Wyoming Gun Law. large type ed. Lee Floren. LC 92-43521. 1993. lib. bdg. 15.95 (*1-56054-640-9*) Thorndike Pr.

***Wyoming Handbook: Includes Yellowstone & Grand Teton National Parks.** 3rd ed. Don Pitcher. 581p. 1997. pap. text ed. 17.95 (*1-56691-085-4*) Moon Trvl Hdbks.

Wyoming Health Care Perspective 1996. Ed. by Kathleen O. Morgan et al. 24p. 1996. pap. 19.00 (*1-56692-649-1*) Morgan Quitno Corp.

***Wyoming Health Care Perspective 1997.** Ed. by Kathleen O. Morgan & Scott E. Morgan. 24p. 1997. pap. 19.00 (*1-56692-749-8*) Morgan Quitno Corp.

Wyoming Historical Markers at 55 MPH: A Guide to Historical Markers & Monuments on Wyoming Highways. Susan C. Carlson. Ed. by Loren Jost. (Illus.). 104p. (Orig.). (C). 1994. pap. 12.00 (*0-9630248-2-5*) Beartooth.

Wyoming Historical Tour Guide. rev. ed. D. Ray Wilson. LC 90-81821. (Illus.). 264p. 1990. 12.95 (*0-916445-28-3*) Crossroads Comm.

***Wyoming History! Surprising Secrets about Our State's Founding Mothers, Fathers & Kids!** Carole Marsh. (Carole Marsh Wyoming Bks.). (Illus.). (J). (gr. 3-12). 1996. pap. 19.95 (*0-7933-6179-6*); lib. bdg. 29.95 (*0-7933-6178-8*); disk 29.95 (*0-7933-6180-X*) Gallopade Pub Group.

Wyoming Hot Air Balloon Mystery. Carole Marsh. (Carole Marsh Wyoming Bks.). (Illus.). (J). (gr. 2-9). 1994. 29.95 (*0-7933-2768-7*); pap. 19.95 (*0-7933-2769-5*); disk 29.95 (*0-7933-2770-9*) Gallopade Pub Group.

Wyoming in Perspective 1996. Ed. by Kathleen O. Morgan et al. 26p. 1996. pap. 19.00 (*1-56692-599-1*) Morgan Quitno Corp.

***Wyoming in Perspective 1997.** Ed. by Kathleen O. Morgan & Scott E. Morgan. 26p. 1997. pap. 19.00 (*1-56692-699-8*) Morgan Quitno Corp.

Wyoming Indian Dictionary for Kids! Carole Marsh. (Carole Marsh State Bks.). (J). (gr. 2-9). 1996. 29.95 (*0-7933-7794-3*, C Marsh); pap. 19.95 (*0-7933-7795-1*, C Marsh) Gallopade Pub Group.

Wyoming Jeopardy! Answers & Questions about Our State! Carole Marsh. (Wyoming Bks.). (Illus.). (J). (gr. 3-12). 1994. pap. 19.95 (*0-7933-4230-9*); lib. bdg. 29.95 (*0-7933-4229-5*); disk 29.95 (*0-7933-4231-7*) Gallopade Pub Group.

Wyoming "Jography" A Fun Run Thru Our State! Carole Marsh. (Carole Marsh Wyoming Bks.). (Illus.). (J). (gr. 3-12). 1994. pap. 19.95 (*1-55609-296-2*); lib. bdg. 29.95 (*1-55609-295-4*); disk 29.95 (*1-55609-297-0*) Gallopade Pub Group.

Wyoming Journeys. Ed. by John Nesbitt. (Illus.). 32p. (Orig.). 1995. pap. 5.00 (*0-917557-04-2*) Wyo Writers.

Wyoming Kid's Cookbook: Recipes, How-To, History, Lore & More. Carole Marsh. (Carole Marsh Wyoming Bks.). (Illus.). (J). 1994. pap. 19.95 (*0-7933-1261-2*); lib. bdg. 29.95 (*0-7933-1262-0*); 29.95 (*0-7933-1263-9*) Gallopade Pub Group.

W

Wyoming Library Book: A Surprising Guide to the Unusual Special Collections in Libraries Across Our State for Students, Teachers, Writers & Publishers. Carole Marsh. (Wyoming Bks.). (Illus.). 1994. pap. 19.95 (0-7933-3156-0); lib. bdg. 29.95 (0-7933-3155-2); disk 29.95 (0-7933-3157-9) Gallopade Pub Group.

Wyoming Lynching of Cattle Kate, 1889. George W. Hufsmith. LC 92-35361. (Illus.). 368p. 1993. 22.95 (0-931271-14-2); pap. 13.95 (0-931271-16-9) Hi Plains Pr.

***Wyoming Manufacturers Register, 1997.** 2nd ed. Ed. by Kathleen Scott. 168p. 1997. pap. 45.00 (1-57541-046-X) Database Pub Co.

Wyoming Media Book: A Surprising Guide to the Amazing Print, Broadcast & Online Media of Our State for Students, Teachers, Writers & Publishers - Includes Reproducible Mailing Labels Plus Activities for Young People! Carole Marsh. (Wyoming Bks.). (Illus.). 1994. pap. 19.95 (0-7933-3312-1); lib. bdg. 29.95 (0-7933-3311-3); disk 29.95 (0-7933-3313-X) Gallopade Pub Group.

Wyoming Moods: Reminiscences of Wyoming by a Tenderfoot. Louise F. Underhill. (Illus.). 60p. (Orig.). 1981. pap. 5.00 (0-9616734-3-5) Underhill Ent.

Wyoming Mystery Van Takes Off! Book 1: Handicapped Wyoming Kids Sneak Off on a Big Adventure. Carole Marsh. (Wyoming Bks.). (Illus.). (J). (gr. 3-12). 1994. 29.95 (0-7933-5114-6); pap. 19.95 (0-7933-5115-4); disk 29.95 (0-7933-5116-2) Gallopade Pub Group.

Wyoming Place Names. rev. ed. Mae Urbanek. LC 87-5755. 238p. (Orig.). 1988. reprint ed. pap. 9.95 (0-87842-204-8) Mountain Pr.

Wyoming Promises: Poetry about Frontier Women. Peggy S. Curry et al. Ed. by Nancy Curtis. (Illus.). 24p. (Orig.). 1984. pap. 3.95 (0-931271-04-5) Hi Plains Pr.

Wyoming Quiz Bowl Crash Course! Carole Marsh. (Carole Marsh Wyoming Bks.). (Illus.). (J). 1994. pap. 19.95 (0-7933-2304-5); lib. bdg. 29.95 (0-7933-2303-7); disk 29.95 (0-7933-2305-3) Gallopade Pub Group.

***Wyoming Renegade.** Susan Amarillas. (Historical Ser.). 1997. 4.99 (0-373-28951-0, 1-28951-1) Harlequin Bks.

Wyoming Rollercoasters! Carole Marsh. (Wyoming Bks.). (Illus.). (YA). (gr. 3-12). 1994. pap. 19.95 (0-7933-5375-0); lib. bdg. 29.95 (0-7933-5374-2); disk 29.95 (0-7933-5376-9) Gallopade Pub Group.

Wyoming School Trivia: An Amazing & Fascinating Look at Our State's Teachers, Schools & Students! Carole Marsh. (Carole Marsh Wyoming Bks.). (Illus.). (J). 1994. pap. 19.95 (0-7933-1258-2); lib. bdg. 29.95 (0-7933-1259-0); disk 29.95 (0-7933-1260-4) Gallopade Pub Group.

Wyoming Showdown. large type ed. Lee Floren. (Linford Western Library). 1991. pap. 15.99 (0-7089-7093-1) Ulverscroft.

Wyoming Shrubland Ecology: A Chronologic Supplemented Multiple Source Annotated Bibliography. Herbert G. Fisser. Ed. by Debra Beck. (Agriculture Publications: SM-49). (Illus.). 661p. 1987. text ed. 32.50 (0-941570-04-5) U of Wyoming.

Wyoming Silly Basketball Sportsmysteries, Vol. 1. Carole Marsh. (Carole Marsh Wyoming Bks.). (Illus.). (J). 1994. pap. 19.95 (0-7933-1255-8); lib. bdg. 29.95 (0-7933-1256-6); disk 29.95 (0-7933-1257-4) Gallopade Pub Group.

Wyoming Silly Basketball Sportsmysteries, Vol. 2. Carole Marsh. (Carole Marsh Wyoming Bks.). (Illus.). (J). 1994. pap. 19.95 (0-7933-2316-9); lib. bdg. 29.95 (0-7933-2315-0); disk 29.95 (0-7933-2317-7) Gallopade Pub Group.

Wyoming Silly Football Sportsmysteries, Vol. 1. Carole Marsh. (Carole Marsh Wyoming Bks.). (Illus.). (J). 1994. pap. 19.95 (0-7933-2295-2); lib. bdg. 29.95 (0-7933-2294-4); disk 29.95 (0-7933-2296-0) Gallopade Pub Group.

Wyoming Silly Football Sportsmysteries, Vol. 2. Carole Marsh. (Carole Marsh Wyoming Bks.). (Illus.). (J). 1994. pap. 19.95 (0-7933-2298-7); lib. bdg. 29.95 (0-7933-2297-9); disk 29.95 (0-7933-2299-5) Gallopade Pub Group.

Wyoming Silly Trivia. Carole Marsh. (Carole Marsh Wyoming Bks.). (Illus.). (J). (gr. 3-12). 1994. pap. 19.95 (1-55609-293-8); lib. bdg. 29.95 (1-55609-292-X); disk 29.95 (1-55609-294-6) Gallopade Pub Group.

Wyoming State Constitution: A Reference Guide. Robert S. Keiter & Tim Newcomb. LC 92-14610. (Reference Guides to the State Constitutions of the United States Ser.: No. 7). 352p. 1992. text ed. 79.50 (0-313-27247-6, KWY, Greenwood Pr) Greenwood.

Wyoming Statutes, Annotated, 12 vols. with indexes & rules. 1979. write for info. (0-87215-139-5) MICHIE.

Wyoming Statutes Annotated. write for info. (0-614-06006-0) MICHIE.

Wyoming Territorial Sheriffs. Ann Gorzalka. LC 97-6456. (Illus.). (Orig.). 1997. write for info. (0-931271-39-8); pap. write for info. (0-931271-38-X) Hi Plains Pr.

Wyoming Territory. Jackie Merritt. (Historical Ser.: No. 714). 1992. mass mkt. 3.99 (0-373-28714-3, 1-28714-3) Harlequin Bks.

Wyoming Timeline: A Chronology of Wyoming History, Mystery, Trivia, Legend, Lore & More. Carole Marsh. (Carole Marsh Wyoming Bks.). (Illus.). (J). (gr. 3-12). 1996. pap. 19.95 (0-7933-6026-9); lib. bdg. 29.95 (0-7933-6025-0); disk 29.95 (0-7933-6027-7) Gallopade Pub Group.

Wyoming U. S. Marshal: A Fictional Novel about the Escapades of a U. S. Marshall in & about Laramie, Wyoming. Gary Twesten. 1984. write for info. (0-9602428-0-5) G Twesten.

Wyoming University: The First 100 Years. Deborah Hardy et al. Ed. by N. Roberts & D. Beck. (Illus.). 320p. 1986. lib. bdg. 19.95 (0-941570-01-0) U of Wyoming.

Wyoming, upon the Great Plains. David Sumner. (Illus.). 64p. (Orig.). 1993. pap. 10.95 (0-941875-21-0) Wolverine Distrib.

Wyoming Valley, PA: An American City. Edward F. Hanlon. 1984. 24.95 (0-89781-073-2) Am Historical Pr.

Wyoming Valley Trolleys: Street Railways of Wilkes-Barre, Nanticoke & Pittston, Pennsylvania. Harold E. Cox. (Illus.). 100p. (Orig.). 1988. pap. 15.00 (0-911940-45-6) Cox.

Wyoming, Vol. 1: A Photographic Celebration. (Illus.). 104p. (Orig.). 1990. pap. 14.95 (0-938314-78-5) Am Wrld Geog.

Wyoming Wedding. Barbara McMahon. (Romance Ser.). 1996. mass mkt. 3.25 (0-373-03428-8, 1-03428-9) Harlequin Bks.

***Wyoming Wedding.** large type ed. Barbara McMahon. (Hitched Ser.). 1996. mass mkt. 3.25 (0-373-15674-X) Harlequin Bks.

Wyoming Wench - Portland Pussycat. Dirk Fletcher. (Spur Double Edition Ser.). 400p. 1994. mass mkt., pap. text ed. 4.99 (0-8439-3699-1) Dorchester Pub Co.

***Wyoming Wife?** Shawna Delacorte. 1997. mass mkt. 3.50 (0-373-76110-4, 1-76110-5) Silhouette.

***Wyoming Wildlife Viewing Tour Guide.** Wyoming Game & Fish Department Staff. 216p. pap. 19.95 (1-889290-20-3) Wyo Game & Fish.

***Wyoming's Big Horn Basin to 1901: A Late Frontier.** Lawrence M. Woods & Milton L. Woods. LC 96-43310. (Western Lands & Waters Ser.: Vol. XVIII). 280p. 1997. 39.50 (0-87062-267-6) A H Clark.

Wyoming's (Most Devastating!) Disasters & (Most Calamitous!) Catastrophies! Carole Marsh. (Carole Marsh Wyoming Bks.). (Illus.). (J). 1994. pap. 19.95 (0-7933-1246-9); lib. bdg. 29.95 (0-7933-1247-7); disk 29.95 (0-7933-1248-5) Gallopade Pub Group.

Wyoming's Unsolved Mysteries (& Their "Solutions") Includes Scientific Information & Other Activities for Students. Carole Marsh. (Wyoming Bks.). (Illus.). (J). (gr. 3-12). 1994. pap. 19.95 (0-7933-5873-6); lib. bdg. 29.95 (0-7933-5872-8); disk 29.95 (0-7933-5874-4) Gallopade Pub Group.

Wyoming's Wind River Range. Joe Kelsey. LC 88-19824. (Wyoming Geographic Ser.: No. 2). (Illus.). 104p. (Orig.). 1988. pap. 15.95 (0-938314-54-8) Am Wrld Geog.

Wyrd Sisters. Terry Pratchett. 320p. 1990. pap. 5.99 (0-451-45012-4, ROC) NAL-Dutton.

Wyrldmaker. Terry Bisson. 176p. 1988. mass mkt. 2.95 (0-380-75359-6) Avon.

***Wyrm.** Mark Fabi. LC 96-50942. (Bantam Spectra Bk.). 1997. pap. 13.95 (0-553-37871-6) Bantam.

Wyrms. Orson Scott Card. 1992. mass mkt. 4.99 (0-8125-2136-6) Tor Bks.

Wyrms Footprints: Gloranthan Legends & Lore. Greg Stafford et al. Ed. by David Hall et al. (Gloranthan Fiction Ser.). (Illus.). 112p. (Orig.). 1995. pap. 15.95 (1-56882-043-7, 4501) Chaosium.

Wyrmship Technical Manual. David B. Pilurs. Ed. by Lenore Caruso & Tom Caruso. (Illus.). 144p. (YA). (gr. 7 up). 1994. 16.95 (0-9636551-3-2, 26640) Storm Pr.

Wysiwyg: A Survival Manual for the Straight White American Male. William L. Chapman. 300p. 1992. pap. 24.95 (1-880361-01-9) Premier Pubns.

Wysong Health Letter, Vol. 7. Wysong Institute Staff. (Illus.). 96p. 1995. 29.95 (0-918112-08-7) Inquiry Pr.

Wyst: Alastor 1716 see Alastor

Wystan & Chester: A Personal Memoir of W. H. Auden & Chester Kallman. Thekla Clark. LC 96-8842. (Illus.). 130p. 1996. 19.95 (0-231-10706-4); write for info. (0-231-10760-9) Col U Pr.

***Wystan & Chester: A Personal Memoir of W. H. Auden & Chester Kallman.** Thekla Clark. 1997. pap. text ed. 12.95 (0-231-10707-2) Col U Pr.

Wyster & Chester: A Personal Memoir of W. H. Auden & Chester Kallman. Thekla Clark. LC 96-8842. 1996. pap. write for info. (0-231-10761-7) Col U Pr.

Wythe County Marriages, Seventeen Ninety to Eighteen Fifty. John Vogt & T. William Kethley, Jr. (Virginia Historic Marriage Register Ser.). (Illus.). ix, 224p. (Orig.). 1985. pap. 13.00 (0-935931-21-X) Borgo Pr.

Wythe County Marriages, Seventeen Ninety to Eighteen Fifty. John Vogt & T. William Kethley, Jr. (Virginia Historic Marriage Register Ser.). ix, 224p. (Orig.). (C). 1985. reprint ed. lib. bdg. 35.00 (0-8095-8235-X) Borgo Pr.

Wythe County, Virginia: A Bicentennial History. Mary B. Kegley. LC 89-50689. (Illus.). 500p. 1989. lib. bdg. write for info. (0-9623387-0-2) Wythe County.

Wyvern: The Insider's Guide. Compiled by U. S. Games Systems Staff. (Illus.). 128p. 1995. pap. 12.95 (0-88079-773-8, BK146) US Games Syst.

Wyvern Deck/Book Set. Illus. by Peter Pracownik. 146p. 1995. pap. 25.00 (0-88079-781-9, WY99) US Games Syst.

Wyvern Mystery: A Novel, 3 Vols., Set. Joseph S. Le Fanu. Ed. by Devendra P. Varma. LC 76-5282. (Collected Works). 1977. reprint ed. 76.95 (0-405-09250-4) Ayer.

Wyvern Mystery: A Novel, 3 Vols., Vol. 1. Joseph S. Le Fanu. Ed. by Devendra P. Varma. LC 76-5282. (Collected Works). 1977. reprint ed. 25.95 (0-405-09251-2) Ayer.

Wyvern Mystery: A Novel, 3 Vols., Vol. 2. Joseph S. Le Fanu. Ed. by Devendra P. Varma. LC 76-5282. (Collected Works). 1977. reprint ed. 25.95 (0-405-09252-0) Ayer.

Wyvern Mystery: A Novel, 3 Vols., Vol. 3. Joseph S. Le Fanu. Ed. by Devendra P. Varma. LC 76-5282. (Collected Works). 1977. reprint ed. 25.95 (0-405-09253-9) Ayer.

***Wyvern's Dance.** J. Gregory Hickey, Jr. LC 96-90119. 208p. (Orig.). 1997. pap. 8.00 (1-56002-660-X, Univ Edtns) Aegina Pr.

Wyving & Thryving: The Making of the English Gementwoman 1550-1750. Helen Mead. (C). 1988. 45.00 (0-9515798-3-5, Pub. by H Copeman UK) St Mut.

Wyznania Niechrzescijanskie na Drugim Soborze Watykanskim. Jan Lichten. 24p. 1965. 2.50 (0-940962-46-2) Polish Inst Art & Sci.

W1FB's Antenna Notebook. 1987. pap. 10.00 (0-87259-261-8) Am Radio.

W1FB's Design Notebook. 1990. pap. 10.00 (0-87259-320-7) Am Radio.

W1FB's Help for New Hams. 1994. pap. 10.00 (0-87259-443-2) Am Radio.

W6SAI HF Antenna Handbook. William I. Orr. LC 96-84315. (Illus.). 172p. (Orig.). 1996. pap. 19.95 (0-943016-15-0) CQ Commns Inc.

X

X. Sue Coe & Francoise Mouly. LC 92-61377. (Illus.). 32p. 1993. 9.95 (1-56584-032-1) New Press NY.

X. Lara Vanian. 102p. 1996. reprint ed. pap. 9.98 (0-9645519-8-5) Ult Mind Pub.

Coping for Kids: A Complete Stress-Control Program for Students Ages 8-18. Gerald Herzfeld & Robin Powell. Orig. Title: x. 202p. (J). (gr. 3-12). 1985. student ed. 6.95 (0-317-43482-9) Ctr Appl Res.

X: Writings '79-'82. John Cage. LC 83-18275. (Illus.). 199p. 1986. pap. 17.95 (0-8195-6098-7, Wesleyan Univ Pr) U Pr of New Eng.

X... see Oeuvres

X.. see Oeuvres

x see Coping for Kids: A Complete Stress-Control Program for Students Ages 8-18

X- & Gamma-Ray Astronomy: Proceedings of the International Astronomical Union, Symposium, 55, Madrid, May 11-13, 1972. International Astronomical Union Staff. Ed. by H. Bradt & R. Giaconni. LC 72-92526. (Illus.). 323p. 1973. lib. bdg. 129.50 (90-277-0303-5) Kluwer Ac.

X- & Gamma-Ray Astronomy: Proceedings of the International Astronomical Union, Symposium, 55, Madrid, May 11-13, 1972. International Astronomical Union Staff. Ed. by H. Bradt & R. Giaconni. LC 72-92526. (Illus.). 323p. 1973. pap. text ed. 70.50 (90-277-0337-X) Kluwer Ac.

X & Motif Quick Reference Guide: X Window System 11.4 & Motif 1.1. 2nd ed. Randi J. Rost. (X & Motif Ser.). (Illus.). 328p. (Orig.). 1993. pap. 31.95 (1-55558-118-8, EY-P953E-DP, Digital DEC) Buttrwrth-Heinemann.

X-Bar Grammar: Attribution & Prediction in Dutch. F. C. Van Gestel. xii, 189p. 1986. pap. 34.65 (90-6765-251-2) Mouton.

X Basic Smartstart. 1994. 25.99 (1-56529-402-5) Que.

X-Com Apocalypse: The Official Strategy Guide. Dave Ellis. 352p. 1997. per. 19.99 (0-7615-0277-7) Prima Pub.

X-Com Strategies & Secrets. Neil Randall. LC 95-67376. 199p. 1995. 12.99 (0-7821-1671-X, Strategies & Secrets) Sybex.

X-Com Terror from the Deep the Official Strategy Guide. David Ellis. 1995. pap. 19.95 (0-7615-0074-X) Prima Pub.

X-Com UFO Defense: A Novel. Diane Duane. 1995. mass mkt. 5.99 (0-7615-0235-1) Prima Pub.

X-Com UFO Defense: Official Strategy Guide. David Ellis. 1994. pap. 19.95 (1-55958-764-4) Prima Pub.

X-Com 3. Brady Computer Books Staff. 1996. 19.99 (1-56686-535-2) Brady Pub.

***X-Cyclopedia.** James Hatfield & George D. Burt. 336p. 1997. pap. 15.00 (1-57566-233-7, Knsington) Kensgtn Pub Corp.

X Desktop Cookbook. Mike Burgard & Mike Moore. LC 92-18622. 1992. pap. text ed. 65.00 (0-13-978537-X) P-H Gen Ref & Trav.

X-Efficiency: Theory, Evidence & Applications. Rodger S. Frantz. 1988. lib. bdg. 76.50 (0-89838-242-4) Kluwer Ac.

***X-Efficiency: Theory, Evidence & Applications.** 2nd ed. Roger S. Frantz. LC 96-28940. (Topics in Regulatory Economics & Policy). 1996. text ed. write for info. (0-7923-9768-1) Kluwer Ac.

X Factor. large type ed. Domini Wiles. 400p. 1985. 25.99 (0-7089-1304-0) Ulverscroft.

X Factor: A Quest for Excellence. George Plimpton. 144p. 1994. 18.95 (0-393-03484-4) Norton.

X-Factor: A Quest for Excellence. George Plimpton. 172p. 1996. pap. 12.00 (0-393-31468-5, Norton Paperbks) Norton.

***X-Factor: David Duchovny.** Chris Nickson. 192p. 1996. mass mkt. 5.99 (0-380-78851-9) Avon.

X-Factor: Prisoner of Love. Jim Starlin. (Illus.). 48p. 1990. 4.95 (0-87135-695-3) Marvel Entmnt.

***X Factor: What It Is & How to Find It, the Relationship Between Inherited Heart Size & Racing Performance.** Marianna Haun. LC 96-41931. 1997. 30.00 (0-929346-46-7) R Meerdink Co Ltd.

***X-Factor Swing: And Other Secrets to Power & Distance.** Jim McLean & John Andrisani. LC 96-43829. (Illus.). 144p. 1997. 22.50 (0-06-270142-8, Harper Ref) HarpC.

***X Factory: Inside the American Hardcore Film Industry.** Anthony Petkovich. (Illus.). 196p. (Orig.). 1997. pap. 19.95 (0-9523288-7-9, Pub. by Headpress UK) AK Pr Dist.

***X-Files.** Charles Grant. 288p. mass mkt. 5.99 (0-06-105625-1, HarperPrism) HarpC.

X-Files. Stefan Petrucha et al. (YA). (gr. 10 up). 1996. 19.95 (1-883313-10-4) Topps Comics.

X-Files, No. 4. 1996. 22.00 (0-614-96772-4, HarperPrism) HarpC.

X-Files, No. 4. 1996. 22.00 (0-614-96942-5, HarperPrism) HarpC.

X-Files, 4 vols., Set. (X-Files Ser.). (YA). (gr. 5 up). 1996. boxed, pap. 15.80 (0-06-449629-5, Trophy) HarpC Child Bks.

***X-Files, Vol. II.** Stefan Petrucha et al. 180p. (YA). (gr. 10 up). 1997. pap. 19.95 (1-883313-23-6) Topps Comics.

***X-Files: Ruins.** Kevin J. Anderson. 1997. mass mkt. 5.99 (0-614-20511-5, Harp PBks) HarpC.

X-Files No. 3: Hunter. Grant. 1995. mass mkt. 4.99 (0-06-105416-X) HarpC.

***X-Files No. 4.** Kevin Anderson. 1998. pap. write for info. (0-06-105644-8, HarperPrism) HarpC.

***X-Files No. 5.** 288p. 1998. pap. 5.99 (0-06-105624-3, HarperPrism) HarpC.

X-Files Book of the Unexplained. Jane Goldman. 352p. 1996. 29.95 (0-06-105236-1, HarperPrism) HarpC.

X-Files Book of the Unexplained. Jane Goldman. 1997. mass mkt. 19.95 (0-06-105334-1, HarperPrism) HarpC.

***X-Files Book of the Unexplained, Vol. 2.** Jane Goldman. 352p. 1997. 29.95 (0-06-105280-9, HarperPrism) HarpC.

X-Files Collection. Topps Comics Staff. 1995. pap. 19.95 (1-883313-07-4) Topps Comics.

X-Files Confidential: The Unauthorized X-Philes Compendium. Ted Edwards. 1996. pap. text ed. 14.95 (0-316-21252-0) Little.

***X-Files Confidential: The Unauthorized X-Philes Compendium.** Ted Edwards. 1997. pap. text ed. 15.95 (0-316-21808-1) Little.

X-Files Declassified: The Unauthorized Guide. Frank Lovece. LC 95-26390. (Illus.). 288p. 1996. pap. 17.95 (0-8065-1745-X) Carol Pub Group.

***X-Files Lexicon: X-References from Anti-Waltons to Zunis.** N. E. Genge. LC 96-46336. 256p. (Orig.). 1997. pap. 12.00 (0-380-79023-8) Avon.

X-Files Postcard Book. Harper Prism Staff. 60p. 1996. pap. 8.99 (0-06-105527-1, HarperPrism) HarpC.

***X-Files Postcard Book: Unexplained Phenomena, Vol. 3.** Harperprism Staff. (X-Files Ser.). 1997. pap. text ed. 8.99 (0-06-105538-7, HarperPrism) HarpC.

X-Files Trivia. 1996. pap. 112.00 (1-57566-989-7) Kensgtn Pub Corp.

X.500 Directory Services: Technology & Deployment. Sara Radicati. 1994. text ed. 39.95 (1-85032-879-X) ITCP.

X in Paris. Michael Brodsky. 192p. (Orig.). 1988. 18.95 (0-941062-44-9) Begos & Rosenberg.

X in Paris. Michael Brodsky. LC 88-16034. 186p. (Orig.). 1988. pap. 9.95 (0-941423-13-1) FWEW.

X-Ing Warm. Ronald Bayes. 34p. (Orig.). 1968. pap. 2.00 (0-932264-06-9) Trask Hse Bks.

X-Linked Mental Retardation & Verbal Disability. Ed. by Daniel Bergsma. (March of Dimes Ser.: Vol. 10, No. 1). 11.50 (0-686-10022-0) March of Dimes.

***X Marks the Spot.** Catherine Chambers. LC 97-2396. (Hello Out There! Ser.). (J). 1997. write for info. (0-531-14471-2) Watts.

X Marks the Spot. Les Martin. (X-Files Ser.: No. 1). 128p. (YA). (gr. 5 up). 1995. pap. 3.95 (0-06-440613-X, Trophy) HarpC Child Bks.

X-mas Wish. Angela McAllister. Date not set. pap. write for info. (0-14-054430-5) NAL-Dutton.

X-Men. (Look & Find Ser.). (Illus.). 24p. (J). 1993. 7.98 (1-56173-703-8) Pubns Intl Ltd.

X-Men. Claremont et al. (Marvel Masterworks Ser.: Vol. 12). 183p. 1990. 34.95 (0-87135-628-7) Marvel Entmnt.

X-Men. Chris Claremont et al. (Illus.). 160p. 1995. pap. 15.95 (0-7851-0137-3) Marvel Entmnt.

X-Men. Clarmont et al. (Marvel Masterworks Ser.: Vol. 11). 169p. 1989. 29.95 (0-87135-597-3) Marvel Entmnt.

X-Men. Stan Lee & Jack Kirby. (Marvel Masterworks Ser.: Vol. 3). (Illus.). 232p. 1987. 34.95 (0-87135-308-3) Marvel Entmnt.

X-Men. Stan Lee & Jack Kirby. (Marvel Masterworks Ser.: Vol. 7). 232p. 1988. 34.95 (0-87135-482-9) Marvel Entmnt.

X-Men. Stan Lee. (Masterworks Ser.). 1994. pap. 34.95 (0-7851-0052-0) Marvel Entmnt.

X-Men, No. 3. Marvel Comics Staff. 1996. mass mkt. 3.99 (0-8125-4405-6) Tor Bks.

X-Men, No. 4. Marvel Comics Staff. 1996. mass mkt. 3.99 (0-8125-5540-6) Tor Bks.

X-Men: Annuals. Chris Claremont. 1996. pap. text ed. 19.95 (0-7851-0195-0) Marvel Entmnt.

X-Men: Children of the Atom. 96p. 1998. per., pap. 14.99 (0-7615-0784-1) Prima Pub.

X-Men: Dawn of the Age Apocalypse. Jeph Loeb. 1996. pap. 8.95 (0-7851-0180-2) Marvel Entmnt.

X-Men: Days of Future Past. Claremont et al. 48p. 1989. 5.95 (0-87135-582-5) Marvel Entmnt.

***X-Men: Empire's End.** Diane Duane. LC 97-24452. (X-Men Ser.). 352p. 1997. 22.95 (0-399-14334-3) Putnam Pub Group.

X-Men: Fatal Attractions. Fabian Nicieza. (X-Men Ser.). 256p. 1994. pap. 17.95 (0-7851-0065-2) Marvel Entmnt.

X-Men: From the Ashes. Walter Simonson et al. (Illus.). 226p. 1990. pap. 16.95 (0-87135-615-5) Marvel Entmnt.

X-Men: God Loves, Man Kills. Claremont & Anderson. 64p. 1982. 9.95 (0-939766-22-1) Marvel Entmnt.

X-Men: God Loves, Man Kills Bookshelf Edition. Chris Claremont. (X-Men Ser.). 64p. 1994. pap. 6.95 (0-7851-0039-3) Marvel Entmnt.

***X-Men: Inferno.** Chris Claremont. 1996. pap. text ed. 19.95 (0-7851-0222-1) Marvel Entmnt.

X-Men: Legion Quest. Fabian Nicieza. 1996. pap. 8.95 (0-7851-0179-9) Marvel Entmnt.

X-Men: Logan. Howard Mackie. 1996. pap. text ed. 5.95 (0-7851-0172-1) Marvel Entmnt.

XYZ

An Asterisk (*) at the beginning of an entry indicates that the title is appearing in BIP for the first time.

***X-Men: Mutant Empire Book 2, Sanctuary.** Christopher Golden. 1996. mass mkt. 5.99 (*1-57297-180-0*) Blvd Books.

***X-Men: Mutant Massacre.** Chris Claremount. 1996. pap. text ed. 24.95 (*0-7851-0224-8*) Marvel Entmnt.

X-Men: Mutations. Chris Claremont. 1996. pap. text ed. 16.95 (*0-7851-0197-7*) Marvel Entmnt.

X-Men: Repo Man. (Favorite Sound Story Bks.). (Illus.). 20p. (J). (ps). 1995. 9.95 (*0-307-70931-0*, Golden Pr) Western Pub.

X-Men: Savage Land. Claremont et al. 80p. 1988. pap. 9.95 (*0-87135-338-5*) Marvel Entmnt.

X-Men: Savage Land. Chris Claremont. (Spiderman Ser.). (Illus.). 1991. 9.95 (*0-87135-552-3*) Marvel Entmnt.

***X-Men: Smoke & Mirrors.** 1997. mass mkt. 5.99 (*1-57297-291-2*) Blvd Books.

X-Men: The Adventures of Cyclops & Phoenix. Scott Lobdell. 1996. pap. text ed. 12.95 (*0-7851-0171-3*) Marvel Entmnt.

X-Men: The Asgardian Wars. Smith et al. 228p. 1988. pap. 15.95 (*0-87135-434-9*) Marvel Entmnt.

X-Men: The Coming of Bishop. John Byrne. 96p. 1995. pap. 12.95 (*0-7851-0099-7*) Marvel Entmnt.

X-Men: The Dark Phoenix Saga. Chris Claremont et al. (Spiderman Ser.). (Illus.). 192p. 1984. pap. 15.95 (*0-939766-96-5*) Marvel Entmnt.

***X-Men: The Jewel of Cyttorak.** Dean W. Smith. 1997. mass mkt. write for info. (*1-57297-329-3*) Blvd Books.

X-Men: The Origin of Generation X. Larry Hama. 1996. pap. text ed. 24.95 (*0-7851-0196-9*) Marvel Entmnt.

X-Men: Twilight of the Age of Apocalypse. Scott Lobdell. 1996. pap. 8.95 (*0-7851-0181-0*) Marvel Entmnt.

X-Men: X-Cutioner's Song. Kelly Corvese & Bob Harras. (Illus.). 272p. 1994. pap. 24.95 (*0-7851-0025-3*) Marvel Entmnt.

X-Men: X-Tinction Agenda. Chris Claremont & Louise Simonson. (Illus.). 224p. 1992. pap. 24.95 (*0-87135-922-7*) Marvel Entmnt.

X-Men No. 1: Mutant Empire: Seige. Christopher Golden. 352p. 1996. mass mkt. 5.99 (*1-57297-114-2*) Blvd Books.

X-Men - Avengers: Bloodties. Fabian Nicieza et al. (Illus.). 128p. 1995. pap. 15.95 (*0-7851-0103-9*) Marvel Entmnt.

X-Men - Ghost Rider: Brood Trouble in the Big Easy. 64p. 1993. 6.95 (*0-87135-974-X*) Marvel Entmnt.

X-Men Adventures. 96p. 1993. 4.95 (*0-7851-0006-7*) Marvel Entmnt.

X-Men Adventures, Vol. 2. Ralph Macchio. 1994. pap. 4.95 (*0-7851-0028-8*) Marvel Entmnt.

X-Men Adventures, Vol. III. Ralph Macchio. 96p. 1994. pap. 5.95 (*0-7851-0044-X*) Marvel Entmnt.

X-Men Adventures, Vol. 4. Ralph Macchio. (Illus.). 96p. 1995. pap. 4.95 (*0-7851-0113-6*) Marvel Entmnt.

X-Men Cartoon Adaption Pryde of the X-Men. Danny Fingeroth. 64p. 1990. 10.95 (*0-87135-694-5*) Marvel Entmnt.

X-Men Cartoon Maker. Knowledge Adventure Staff. 1995. 16.00 (*1-56997-190-0*) Knowldge Adv.

X-Men, Enter the Phoenix. Chris Clarement. 1996. mass mkt., pap. 3.99 (*0-8125-4325-4*) Tor Bks.

X-Men Gallery of Heroes. (J). 1994. pap. 0.49 (*0-679-86924-7*) Random.

X-Men in the Savage Land. (J). 1994. 0.55 (*0-679-86926-3*) Random.

X-Men Index, No. 1. 48p. 1987. 2.95 (*0-87135-216-8*) Marvel Entmnt.

X-Men, Magneto's Master Plan: Magneto's Master Plan. Michael Gallagher. (Illus.). 24p. (YA). (gr. k up). text ed. 12.95 (*0-9627001-6-9*) Futech Educ Prods.

X-Men Postcard Book. Running Press Staff. 1995. pap. text ed. 8.95 (*1-56138-584-0*) Running Pr.

X-Men, Scourge of the Savage Land. Michael Gallagher. (Illus.). 24p. (YA). (gr. k up). text ed. 12.95 (*0-9627001-7-7*) Futech Educ Prods.

X-Men "Spotlight - Starjammers", Vol. 1. Kavanagh et al. 48p. 1990. 4.50 (*0-87135-658-9*) Marvel Entmnt.

X-Men "Spotlight - Starjammers", Vol. 2. Kavanagh et al. 48p. 1990. 4.50 (*0-87135-659-7*) Marvel Entmnt.

X-Men Survival Guide to the Mansion. 54p. 1993. 6.95 (*0-685-67222-0*) Marvel Entmnt.

X-Men Visionaries: The Art of Andy & Adam Kubert. Fabian Nicieza. 1996. pap. text ed. 8.95 (*0-7851-0182-9*) Marvel Entmnt.

X-Men Visonaries: The Neal Adams Collection. Roy Thomas. 1996. pap. 15.95 (*0-7851-0198-5*) Marvel Entmnt.

***X-Men vs. the Brood: Day of Wrath.** John Ostrander. 1997. pap. text ed. 16.95 (*0-7851-0558-1*) Marvel Entmnt.

***X-1999: Sonata.** Clamp. 1997. pap. text ed. 15.95 (*1-56931-227-3*, Viz Comics) Viz Commns Inc.

X-One: Experimental Fiction. Alvin Greenberg et al. Ed. by Harry Smith. LC 76-20256. 232p. 1976. pap. 7.50 (*0-912292-41-5*) Smith.

X-Open & Object Technology. X-Open Staff. (Illus.). 162p. (C). 1994. pap. text ed. 35.00 (*0-13-353434-0*) P-H.

X-Open Framework & Models. X-Open Staff. (Illus.). 100p. (C). 1994. pap. text ed. 35.00 (*0-13-353442-1*) P-H.

X-Open Software Directory. X-Open Staff. 1989. 29.95 (*0-13-972134-7*) P-H.

X-Open Transport (XTI) Version 2. X-Open Staff. (Illus.). 244p. (C). 1994. pap. text ed. 50.00 (*0-13-353459-6*) P-H.

X Peters-Macleod. Peters & Macleod. 1989. 179.50 (*0-89296-700-5*) Mysterious Pr.

X-Planes at Edwards. Steve Pace. (Enthusiast Color Ser.). (Illus.). 96p. 1995. pap. 12.95 (*0-87938-985-0*) Motorbooks Intl.

X-PLOR Version 3.1: A System for X-ray Crystallography & NMR. Axel T. Brunger. (Illus.). 405p. (C). 1993. text ed. 37.50 (*0-300-05402-5*) Yale U Pr.

X Programmer's Handbook, Vol. 9. Age Logic Staff. 800p. 1995. 29.95 (*1-56592-133-X*) OReilly & Assocs.

***X-Rated: The Paranormal Experiences of the Movie Star Greats.** Michael Munn. (Illus.). 204p. 1996. 24.95 (*1-86105-017-8*) Parkwest Pubns.

X-Rated Bible: An Irreverent Survey of Sex in the Scriptures. Ben E. Akerley. (Illus.). 428p. (Orig.). 1985. pap. 14.00 (*0-910309-19-1*, 5000) Am Atheist.

***X-Rated Cocktails & Other Amusements.** Harold Washington. 145p. 1996. pap. 14.95 (*0-9648379-6-X*) Hughes Co.

X-Rated Drinks. Hymie Lipshitz. 1991. pap. 6.90 (*0-9617655-0-X*) Foley Pub.

***X-Rated Gay Video Guide.** Sabin. 200p. 1997. pap. 12.95 (*1-889138-03-7*) Companion Press.

X-Rated Media Bloopers & Messups: A Choice Collection of Sexy Newsworthy Boners. Robert W. Pelton. LC 93-74665. 120p. (Orig.). 1994. pap. 10.00 (*0-918751-38-1*, 38) Delta Pr.

X-Rated Riddles. Matt Phillips. 1981. pap. 2.50 (*0-8431-0540-2*) Putnam Pub Group.

X-Rated Romance. Tina Sunshine. 142p. (YA). (gr. 7 up). 1982. mass mkt. 2.50 (*0-380-79905-7*, Flare) Avon.

X-Rated Romance No. 3: Operation: Sex. Jonathon J. Thompson, Jr. (Illus.). 60p. (C). 1992. 4.50 (*0-933479-18-2*) Thompson.

X-Rated Romance Classics. Jonathon J. Thompson, Jr. (Illus.). 60p. (C). 1992. write for info. (*0-933479-20-4*) Thompson.

X-Rated Romance, No. 1 - Sexercise. Jonathon J. Thompson, Jr. (Illus.). 175p. (C). 1987. 7.00 (*0-933479-14-X*) Thompson.

X-Rated Romance, No. 2 - Condom-Miniums. Jonathon J. Thompson, Jr. (Illus.). 70p. (C). 1992. 5.50 (*0-933479-16-6*) Thompson.

X-Rated Super Romances. Jonathon J. Thompson, Jr. (Illus.). 50p. (C). 1992. write for info. (*0-933479-00-X*) Thompson.

X-Rated Videotape Guide, Vol. 1. Robert H. Rimmer. 654p. 1993. pap. 19.95 (*0-87975-799-X*) Prometheus Bks.

X-Rated Videotape Guide, 3 vols., Vol. 1, 2 & 3. Robert H. Rimmer. 1993. Set. pap. 49.95 (*0-87975-835-X*) Prometheus Bks.

X-Rated Videotape Guide, Vol. 3. Robert H. Rimmer & Patrick Riley. LC 92-42911. (Illus.). 573p. (C). 1993. pap. 19.95 (*0-87975-818-X*) Prometheus Bks.

X-Rated Videotape Guide II: More Than 1200 New Reviews & Ratings. Robert H. Rimmer. (Illus.). 625p. 1991. pap. 19.95 (*0-87975-673-X*) Prometheus Bks.

X-Rated Videotape Guide IV. Robert H. Rimmer & Patrick Riley. (Illus.). 628p. 1994. pap. 19.95 (*0-87975-897-X*) Prometheus Bks.

X-Rated Videotape Guide V: Over 1000 Reviews of 1994 Adult Movies. Patrick Riley. LC 94-42854. (Illus.). 600p. 1995. pap. 21.95 (*0-87975-950-X*) Prometheus Bks.

X-Rated Videotape Guide VI. Patrick Riley. (Illus.). 600p. (Orig.). 1996. pap. 22.95 (*1-57392-102-5*) Prometheus Bks.

***X-Rated Videotape Star Index.** 2nd ed. Patrick Riley. 1997. pap. text ed. 22.95 (*1-57392-168-8*) Prometheus Bks.

X-Rated Videotape Star Index 1994. Patrick Riley. (Illus.). 526p. (Orig.). 1994. pap. 22.95 (*0-87975-916-X*) Prometheus Bks.

X-Ray. Ray Davies. 1999. pap. 19.95 (*0-525-93697-1*) NAL-Dutton.

X-Ray: The Unauthorized Autobiography. Ray Davies. LC 95-17328. 420p. 1995. 24.95 (*0-87951-611-9*) Overlook Pr.

X-Ray: The Unauthorized Autobiography. Ray Davies. 420p. 1996. pap. 15.95 (*0-87951-664-X*) Overlook Pr.

X-Ray Absorption: Principles, Applications, Techniques of EXAFS, SEXAFS & XANES. Ed. by D. C. Koningsberger & R. Prins. LC 86-28991. (Chemical Analysis Ser.). 673p. 1988. text ed. 199.00 (*0-471-87547-3*) Wiley.

X-Ray Absorption Fine Structure (XAFS) for Catalysts & Surfaces, Vol. 2. Yasuhiro Iwasawa. (Series on Synchrotron Radiation Techniques & Applications: Vol. 2). 350p. 1996. text ed. 86.00 (*981-02-2323-4*) World Scientific Pub.

X-Ray Absorption in Bulk & Surfaces: Proceedings of the International Workshop. K. B. Garg et al. 228p. 1994. text ed. 95.00 (*981-02-1159-7*) World Scientific Pub.

X-Ray Analysis & the Structure of Organic Chemistry. Jack D. Dunitz. LC 78-15588. (Illus.). 514p. (C). 1995. reprint ed. 70.00 (*3-906390-14-4*, VCH) Wiley.

X-Ray Anatomy of the Vascular System. G. Luzsa. 388p. (C). 1975. 75.00 (*963-05-0060-4*, Pub. by Akad Kiado HU) St Mut.

X-Ray & Atomic Inner-Shell Physics, 1982. Ed. by Bernd Crasemann. LC 82-74075. (AIP Conference Proceedings Ser.: No. 94). 802p. 1982. lib. bdg. 44.50 (*0-88318-193-2*) Am Inst Physics.

X-Ray & Electron-Diffraction Study of Langmuir-Blodgett Films, Vol. 114. L. A. Feigin et al. (Soviet Scientific Reviews Ser.: Vol. 11, Pt. 4). 100p. 1989. pap. text ed. 91.00 (*3-7186-4905-5*) Gordon & Breach.

X-Ray & Gamma-Ray Astronomy. Ed. by J. A. Bleeker & W. Hermsen. (Advances in Space Research Ser.: No. 10). (Illus.). 324p. 1989. pap. 95.00 (*0-08-040158-9*, Pergamon Pr) Elsevier.

X-Ray & Image Analysis in Electron Microscopy. John J. Friel. 112p. 1994. pap. text ed. 19.00 (*0-9641455-0-2*) Prncton Gamma-Tech.

X-Ray & Inner-Shell Processes. Ed. by T. Carlson et al. 900p. 1991. 99.00 (*0-88318-790-6*) Am Inst Physics.

***X-Ray & Inner Shell Processes, Vol. 389.** Ed. by Robert L. Johnson et al. (Illus.). 780p. 1997. 200.00 (*1-56396-563-1*) Am Inst Physics.

***X-Ray & Neutron Diffraction.** 1995. text ed. 129.00 (*3-540-50564-4*) Spr-Verlag.

X-Ray & Neutron Diffraction in Nonideal Crystals. Mikhail A. Krivoglaz. Ed. by V. G. Baryakhtar et al. (Illus.). 464p. 1995. 129.00 (*0-387-50564-4*) Spr-Verlag.

***X-Ray & Neutron Dynamical Diffraction, Theory & Applications: Proceedings of a NATO ASI Held in Erice, Italy, April 9-21, 1996.** Ed. by Andre Authier et al. (NATO ASI Series B: Vol. 357). 412p. 1997. 125.00 (*0-306-45501-3*) Plenum.

X-Ray & Neutron Structure Analysis in Materials Science. Ed. by J. Hasek. (Illus.). 418p. 1989. 115.00 (*0-306-43107-6*, Plenum Pr) Plenum.

X-Ray & Optical Emission Analysis of High-Temperature Alloys: A Symposium. American Society for Testing & Materials Staff. LC 65-18213. (American Society for Testing & Materials Special Technical Publication Ser.: No. 376). 52p. reprint ed. pap. 25.00 (*0-317-09803-9*, 2000851) Bks Demand.

X-Ray Assessment for Nurses. Patricia A. Dettenmeier. 275p. (C). (gr. 13). 1994. pap. text ed. 34.95 (*0-8016-7245-7*) Mosby Yr Bk.

X-Ray Astronomy. Riccardo Giacconi. 1981. lib. bdg. 100.50 (*90-277-1261-1*) Kluwer Ac.

X-Ray Astronomy. Ed. by Richard Giacconi & Giancarlo Setti. (NATO Advanced Study Institutes Series C, Mathematical & Physical Sciences: No. 60). 400p. 1980. lib. bdg. 104.50 (*90-277-1156-9*) Kluwer Ac.

X-Ray Astronomy: Selected Reprints. Ed. by Claude R. Canizares. (Reprint Bks.). 144p. (Orig.). 1986. pap. text ed. 26.00 (*0-917853-21-0*, RB44) Am Assn Physics.

X-Ray Astronomy: Ten Years from Einstein to AXAF. Ed. by Martin Elvis. 300p. (C). 1990. text ed. 74.95 (*0-521-38105-3*) Cambridge U Pr.

X-Ray Astronomy in the Exosat Era. Ed. by A. Peacock. 1985. lib. bdg. 253.50 (*90-277-2099-1*) Kluwer Ac.

X-Ray Astronomy, Including a Catalogue & Bibliography of Galactic X-Ray Sources: Proceedings of the 21st Plenary Meeting, Innsbruck, Austria, 1978. Ray Armstong. Ed. by W. A. Baity & L. E. Peterson. (Illus.). 1979. 76.00 (*0-08-023418-6*, Pergamon Pr) Elsevier.

X-Ray Atlas of the Royal Mummies. Ed. by James E. Harris & Edward F. Wente. LC 79-23704. (Illus.). 432p. 1980. lib. bdg. 90.00 (*0-226-31745-5*) U Ch Pr.

X-Ray Background. Ed. by X. Barcons & Andrew C. Fabian. (Illus.). 320p. (C). 1992. text ed. 69.95 (*0-521-41651-5*) Cambridge U Pr.

X-Ray Binaries. Ed. by Walter H. Lewin et al. (Astrophysics Ser.: Vol. 26). (Illus.). 640p. (C). 1995. text ed. 95.00 (*0-521-41684-1*) Cambridge U Pr.

X-Ray Binaries & Recycled Pulsars: Proceedings of the NATO Advanced Research Workshop on "X-Ray Binaries & the Formation of Binary & Millisecond Radio Pulsars," January 21-25, 1991. Edward P. Van Den Heuvel, pseud. LC 92-26378. 584p. (C). 1992. lib. bdg. 278.50 (*0-7923-1940-0*) Kluwer Ac.

***X-Ray Charge Densities & Chemical Bonding.** Philip Coppens. (International Union of Crystallography Texts on Crystallography: No. 4). (Illus.). 368p. (C). 1997. text ed. 85.00 (*0-19-509823-4*) OUP.

X-Ray Contrast Media: Overview, Use & Pharmaceutical Aspects. 2nd ed. Ed. by U. Speck. (Illus.). 40p. 1992. pap. 20.00 (*0-387-52909-8*) Spr-Verlag.

X-Ray Coordinator. Jack Rudman. (Career Examination Ser.: C-1536). 1994. pap. 34.95 (*0-8373-1536-0*) Nat Learn.

X-Ray Detection by Superconducting Tunnel Junctions: Proceedings of the International Workshop, Naples, Italy, 12-14 December 1990. Ed. by Antonio Barone et al. 350p. (C). 1991. text ed. 83.00 (*981-02-0649-6*) World Scientific Pub.

X-Ray Detectors in Astronomy. G. W. Fraser. (Cambridge Astrophysics Ser.: No. 15). (Illus.). 320p. (C). 1989. text ed. 80.00 (*0-521-32663-X*) Cambridge U Pr.

X-Ray Diagnosis see Manual on Radiation Protection in Hospitals & General Practice

X-Ray Diagnosis in Neonates. Gy. Koteles. 174p. (C). 1982. 60.00 (*963-05-3061-9*, Pub. by Akad Kiado HU) St Mut.

X-Ray Diagnosis of the Alimentary Tract in Infants & Children. Edward B. Singleton. LC 58-14433. 352p. reprint ed. pap. 100.40 (*0-317-19894-7*, 2011940) Bks Demand.

X-Ray Differential Diagnosis in Small Bowel Disease: A Practical Approach. J. L. Sellink. (Series in Radiology). (C). 1988. lib. bdg. 171.00 (*0-89838-351-X*) Kluwer Ac.

***X-Ray Diffraction.** B. E. Warren. pap. 10.95 (*0-486-66317-5*) Dover.

X-Ray Diffraction. Bertram E. Warren. LC 68-25928. (Addison-Wesley Metallurgy & Materials Ser.). (Illus.). 391p. reprint ed. pap. 111.50 (*0-317-58234-8*, 2056385) Bks Demand.

X-Ray Diffraction: In Crystals, Imperfect Crystals, & Amorphous Bodies. A. Guinier. (Illus.). 378p. 1994. reprint ed. pap. 11.95 (*0-486-68011-8*) Dover.

***X-Ray Diffraction & the Identification & Analysis of Clay Minerals.** 2nd ed. Duane M. Moore & Robert C. Reynolds, Jr. (Illus.). 400p. 1997. pap. text ed. 38.00 (*0-19-508713-5*) OUP.

X-Ray Diffraction at Elevated Temperatures: A Method for in Situ Process Analysis. D. D. Chung et al. LC 92-21803. 1993. 95.00 (*0-89573-745-0*, VCH) Wiley.

***X-Ray Diffraction at Elevated Temperatures: A Method for In Situ Process Analysis.** D. D. Chung. 1993. text ed. 99.95 (*0-471-18726-7*) Wiley.

X-Ray Diffraction by Disordered Lamellar Structures. V. A. Drits & C. Tchoubar. (Illus.). 450p. 1990. 214.95 (*0-387-51222-5*) Spr-Verlag.

X-Ray Diffraction of Ions in Aqueous Solutions: Hydration & Complex Formation. Ed. by Mauro Magini. 288p. 1988. 158.00 (*0-8493-6945-2*, QD561, CRC Reprint) Franklin.

X-Ray Diffraction Procedures. 2nd ed. Harold P. Klug & Leroy E. Alexander. (Illus.). 966p. 1974. text ed. 244.00 (*0-471-49369-4*, Wiley-Interscience) Wiley.

X-Ray Diffraction Studies on the Deformation & Fracture of Solids. Ed. by K. Tanaka et al. LC 92-42941. (Current Japanese Materials Research Ser.: Vol. 10). 1993. 198.25 (*1-85861-005-2*, Pub. by Elsevier Applied Sci UK) Elsevier.

X-Ray Diffraction Studies on the Deformation & Fracture of Solids. Ed. by K. Tanaka et al. (Current Japanese Materials Research Ser.: Vol. 10). 338p. 1993. text ed. 216.25 (*0-444-81690-9*) Elsevier.

X-Ray Diffraction Topography. B. K. Tanner. LC 75-45196. 1976. 86.00 (*0-08-019692-6*, Pub. by Pergamon Repr UK) Franklin.

X-Ray Emission from Clusters of Galaxies. C. Sarazin. (Cambridge Astrophysics Ser.: No. 11). (Illus.). 250p. 1988. text ed. 64.95 (*0-521-32957-4*) Cambridge U Pr.

X-Ray Emission Line & Absorption Wave Lengths & Two-Theta Tables - DS37-A. 306p. 1993. 54.00 (*0-8031-0825-7*, 05-037010-39) ASTM.

X-Ray Emission Wavelengths & Kev Tables for Nondiffractive Analysis. Gerald G. Johnson, Jr. & E. W. White. LC 71-121001. (ASTM Data Ser.: No. DS 46). 51p. reprint ed. pap. 25.00 (*0-7837-4415-3*, 2044159) Bks Demand.

X-Ray Examination of the Stomach: A Description of the Roentgenologic Anatomy, Physiology, & Pathology of the Esophagus & Duodenum. rev. ed. Frederic E. Templeton. LC 64-23426. 616p. reprint ed. pap. 175.60 (*0-317-42269-3*, 2025792) Bks Demand.

X-Ray Film Markets. (Market Research Reports: No. 324). 138p. 1993. 795.00 (*0-317-05029-X*) Theta Corp.

X-Ray Flourescence Spectrometry for Field Analysis of Marine Sediments. (Illus.). 122p. (Orig.). (C). 1994. pap. text ed. 50.00 (*0-7881-1266-X*) DIANE Pub.

X-Ray Fluorescence Spectrometry. Ron Jenkins. LC 88-10797. (Chemical Analysis Ser.). 175p. 1988. text ed. 99.95 (*0-471-83675-3*) Wiley.

X-Ray Fluorescent Scanning of the Thyroid. Ed. by M. H. Jonckheer & F. Deconinck. 1983. lib. bdg. 104.50 (*0-89838-561-X*) Kluwer Ac.

X-Ray for Love. Silvia Cinca. LC 91-90111. (Orig.). 1991. pap. 15.00 (*0-9619930-2-2*) Moonfall Pr VA.

X-Ray Imaging Equipment: An Introduction. Euclid Seeram. (Illus.). 610p. (C). 1985. 67.95 (*0-398-05078-3*) C C Thomas.

X-Ray Instrumentation for the Photon Factory. Ed. by S. Hosoya et al. 1986. lib. bdg. 210.50 (*90-277-2243-9*) Kluwer Ac.

X-Ray Interpretation for MRCP. 2nd ed. R. K. Hind. (Illus.). 200p. (Orig.). 1992. pap. text ed. 33.00 (*0-443-04551-8*) Churchill.

X-Ray Lasers. Raymond C. Elton. 287p. 1990. text ed. 95.00 (*0-12-238080-0*) Acad Pr.

X-Ray Lasers: 2nd International Colloquium, York 1990. Ed. by G. Tallents. (Institute of Physics Conference Ser.: Vol. 116). 400p. 1991. 164.00 (*0-85498-044-X*) IOP Pub.

X-Ray Lasers, 1992: Proceedings of the 3rd International Colloquium on X-Ray Lasers, Schliersee, Germany, May 18-22, 1992. Ed. by E. Fill. (Institute of Physics Conference Ser.: No. 125). (Illus.). 476p. 1992. 196.00 (*0-85498-415-1*) IOP Pub.

X-Ray Lasers, 1994: Fourth International Colloquium. Dave C. Eder. (Conference Proceedings Ser.: No. 332). (Illus.). 613p. 1995. 135.00 (*1-56396-375-2*) Am Inst Physics.

X-Ray Lithography in Japan. Ed. by James T. Clemens & Robert W. Hill. (JTEC Panel Reports). xii, 158p. 1991. pap. write for info. (*1-883712-14-9*, JTEC) Intl Tech Res.

X-Ray Machine Vision & Computed Tomography: A Survey on Technology & Markets, No. 10. Richard K. Miller & Terri C. Walker. LC 88-80488. 36p. 1988. pap. text ed. 200.00 (*1-55865-009-1*) Future Tech Surveys.

X-Ray Methods. Clive Whiston. Ed. by F. Elizabeth Prichard. LC 86-32605. (Analytical Chemistry by Open Learning Ser.). 426p. 1987. text ed. 64.95 (*0-471-91387-1*) Wiley.

X-Ray Methods in Corrosion & Interfacial Electrochemistry, Vol. 92-1: Proceedings. Ed. by A. J. Davenport & J. G. Gordon, II. LC 92-70073. 350p. 1992. 42.00 (*1-56677-000-9*) Electrochem Soc.

X-Ray Microanalysis in Biology: Experimental Techniques & Applications. Ed. by David C. Sigee et al. (Illus.). 350p. (C). 1993. text ed. 90.00 (*0-521-41530-6*) Cambridge U Pr.

X-Ray Microanalysis in Electron Microscopy for Biologists. A. John Morgan. (Royal Microscopical Society Microscopy Handbooks Ser.). (Illus.). 72p. 1986. pap. 12.95 (*0-19-856409-0*) OUP.

X-Ray Microanalysis in the Electron Microscope. J. A. Chandler. (Practical Methods in Electron Microscopy Ser.: Vol. 5, Pt. II). 548p. 1981. pap. 46.50 (*0-7204-0607-2*, North Holland) Elsevier.

X-Ray Microscopy. P. C. Cheng & G. Jan. (Illus.). 430p. 1987. 129.95 (*0-387-18148-2*) Spr-Verlag.

X-Ray Microscopy: Proceedings of the International Symposium in Gottingen, West Germany, September 14-16, 1983. Ed. by G. Schmahl & D. Rudolph. (Optical Sciences Ser.: Vol. 43). (Illus.). 350p. 1984. 63.95 (*0-387-13271-6*) Spr-Verlag.

***X-Ray Microscopy: Techniques & Applications.** 360p. 1997. text ed. 53.00 (*981-02-2458-3*) World Scientific Pub.

X-Ray Microscopy in Biology & Medicine. Ed. by K. Shinohara & K. Yada. 250p. 1990. 100.95 (*0-387-50702-7*) Spr-Verlag.

X-Ray Microscopy Three. Alan G. Michette. (Optical Sciences Ser.: Vol. 67). (Illus.). 419p. 1992. 113.95 (*0-387-53605-1*) Spr-Verlag.

X-Ray Microscopy Two. David A. Sayre. (Optical Sciences Ser.: Vol. 56). (Illus.). xiv, 454p. 1988. 97.95 (*0-387-19392-8*) Spr-Verlag.

X-Ray Optics: Applications to Solids. Ed. by H. J. Queisser. (Topics in Applied Physics Ser.: Vol. 22). (Illus.). 1977. 56.95 (*0-387-08462-2*) Spr-Verlag.

X-Ray Optics & Microanalysis, 1992: Proceedings of the 13th International Conference 31 August - 4 September, 1992, Manchester, U. K. Ed. by P. B. Kenway et al. (Institute of Physics Conference Ser.: No. 130). (Illus.). 680p. 1993. 278.00 (*0-7503-0255-0*) IOP Pub.

X-Ray Photoelectron Spectroscopy of Solid Surfaces. V. I. Nefedov. viii, 200p. 1987. lib. bdg. 137.50 (*90-6764-080-8*, Pub. by VSP NE) Coronet Bks.

X-Ray Physics for Radiologic Technologists. Richard H. Schmidt. LC 72-75592. (Illus.). 160p. 1973. 10.60 (*0-87527-131-6*) Green.

X-Ray Plasma Spectroscopy & the Properties of Multiply-Charged Ions. Ed. by I. I. Sobel'man. (Proceedings of the Lebedev Physics Institute Ser.: Vol. 179). 256p. 1988. text ed. 135.00 (*0-941743-23-3*) Nova Sci Pubs.

***X-Ray Radiation of Highly Charged Ions.** H. F. Beyer et al. LC 97-25461. (Springer Series on Atoms & Plasmas). 1997. write for info. (*3-540-63185-2*) Spr-Verlag.

X-Ray Scattering & Absorption by Magnetic Materials. Steven W. Lovesey & S. P. Collins. (Oxford Series on Synchrotron Radiation: No. 1). (Illus.). 392p. 1996. 125.00 (*0-19-851737-8*) OUP.

X-Ray Scattering of Synthetic Polymers. F. J. Balta-Calleja & C. G. Vonk. (Polymer Science Library: No. 8). 318p. 1989. 238.50 (*0-444-87385-6*) Elsevier.

X-Ray Science & Technology. Alan G. Michette. (Illus.). 376p. 1993. 70.00 (*0-7503-0233-X*) IOP Pub.

X-Ray Shielding. 1995. lib. bdg. 250.95 (*0-8490-6639-5*) Gordon Pr.

X-Ray Spectra & Chemical Binding. Alan Meisel et al. (Chemical Physics Ser.: Vol. 37). (Illus.). 465p. 1989. 157.95 (*0-387-13325-9*) Spr-Verlag.

X-Ray Spectrometry in Electron Beam Instruments. David B. Williams. 370p. 1995. 79.50 (*0-306-44858-0*, Plenum Pr) Plenum.

X-Ray Spectroscopy. B. K. Agarwal. (Optical Sciences Ser.: Vol. 15). (Illus.). 1979. 54.50 (*0-387-09268-4*) Spr-Verlag.

X-Ray Spectroscopy: An Introduction. 2nd ed. Arthur L. Schawlow. (Optical Sciences Ser.: Vol. 15). (Illus.). xv, 419p. 1991. 64.95 (*0-387-50719-1*) Spr-Verlag.

X-Ray Spectroscopy in Atomic & Solid State Physics. Ed. by J. Gomes Ferreira. (NATO ASI Series B, Physics: Vol. 187). (Illus.). 374p. 1988. 120.00 (*0-306-43029-0*, Plenum Pr) Plenum.

X-Ray Spectroscopy in Environmental Sciences. Vlado Valkovic. 336p. 1989. 256.00 (*0-8493-4749-1*, TD193) CRC Pr.

X-Ray Structure Determination. 2nd ed. George H. Stout & Lyle H. Jensen. LC 88-27931. 453p. 1989. text ed. 74.95 (*0-471-60711-8*) Wiley.

X-Ray Symposium 1981. Ed. by A. G. Philip. 76p. 1981. pap. 12.00 (*0-9607902-0-9*) L Davis Pr.

X-Ray Technician. Jack Rudman. (Career Examination Ser.: C-910). 1994. pap. 27.95 (*0-8373-0910-7*) Nat Learn.

X-Ray Technician I. Jack Rudman. (Career Examination Ser.: C-1840). 1994. pap. 27.95 (*0-8373-1840-8*) Nat Learn.

X-Ray Technician II. Jack Rudman. (Career Examination Ser.: C-1841). 1994. pap. 29.95 (*0-8373-1841-6*) Nat Learn.

X-Ray Technician III. Jack Rudman. (Career Examination Ser.: C-1842). 1994. pap. 29.95 (*0-8373-1842-4*) Nat Learn.

X-Ray Technologist. Ronald R. Smith. Ed. by Diane Parker. LC 92-50915. (Smith's Career Notes Ser.). 24p. 1993. pap. 2.50 (*1-56875-001-3*) R & E Pubs.

X-Ray Technologist Risk Management: Medico-Legal Risk Management. Ricardo A. Scott. 100p. (Orig.). 1994. write for info. (*1-883427-16-9*) Crnerstone GA.

X-Ray Universe. Wallace Tucker & Riccardo Giacconi. (Harvard Books on Astronomy). (Illus.). 196p. 1985. 25.00 (*0-674-96285-0*) HUP.

X-Ray Universe. Wallace Tucker & Riccardo Giacconi. (Illus.). 196p. 1987. pap. text ed. 9.95 (*0-674-96286-9*) HUP.

X-Rayed Without Consent: Computer Health Hazards. Bert Dumpe. Ed. by Stephen Kepple. 388p. (Orig.). 1989. 19.75 (*0-9622907-0-X*) Ergotec Assn.

X-Rays. Rob Morrison. LC 93-28983. (Voyages Ser.). (Illus.). (J). 1994. 4.25 (*0-383-03789-1*) SRA McGraw.

X-Rays. Mary A. Dodge. (Notable American Authors Ser.). 1992. reprint ed. lib. bdg. 75.00 (*0-7812-2664-3*) Rprt Serv.

X-Rays: Health Effects of Common Exams. John W. Gofman & Egan O'Connor. LC 84-23527. (Illus.). 456p. 1985. 25.00 (*0-87156-838-1*, H M Gousha) P-H Gen Ref & Trav.

X-Rays: The First Hundred Years. Alan G. Michette & S. Awka Pfauntsch. LC 96-27880. 1996. text ed. 69.95 (*0-471-96502-2*) Wiley.

X-Rays see Encyclopedia of Physics

X-Rays & Radium in the Treatment of Diseases of the Skin. Anthony C. Cipollaro & Paul M. Crossland. LC 66-23240. (Illus.). 830p. reprint ed. 180.00 (*0-8357-9425-3*, 2014533) Bks Demand.

***X-Rays Binaries.** Edward P. Van Den Heuvel, pseud. (Illus.). 676p. 1997. pap. text ed. 39.95 (*0-521-59934-2*) Cambridge U Pr.

X-Rays in Atomic & Nuclear Physics. 2nd ed. N. A. Dyson. (Illus.). 384p. (C). 1990. text ed. 119.95 (*0-521-26280-1*) Cambridge U Pr.

X-SAR Picture Book: Radar Scanning of the Earth. Wolfgang Noack. 1996. 59.00 (*3-540-59441-8*) Spr-Verlag.

X Series Recommendations: Standards for Data Communications. 2nd ed. Ulysses D. Black. LC 94-40177. 1995. text ed. 55.00 (*0-07-005593-9*) McGraw.

X Stands for Excellence: Based on the Seven Ups of Life Presentation. STP (Porter) Staff. 84p. 1996. per., pap. text ed. 12.95 (*0-7872-2358-1*) Kendall-Hunt.

X-Stat: Statistical Experiment Design, Data Analysis, & Non-Linear Optimization, Verson 2.0. John Murray. 200p. 1992. 650.00 incl. disk (*0-471-52444-1*) Wiley.

X Syntax: A Study of Phrase Structure. Ray S. Jackendoff. (Linguistic Inquiry Monographs). 249p. (C). 1980. pap. 16.95 (*0-262-60009-9*) MIT Pr.

X-Texts. Derek Pell. 158p. Date not set. 7.00 (*1-57027-005-8*) Autonomedia.

X Tool Kit: Intrinsics & Athena Widgets. J. McCormack et al. 300p. (Orig.). 1990. pap. 29.95 (*0-929306-04-X*) Silicon Pr.

X-Toolkit Cookbook. Paul E. Kimball. 752p. 1995. pap. text ed. 49.00 (*0-13-973132-6*) P-H.

***X-Treme Possibilities.** Paul Cornell et al. 256p. (Orig.). 1997. mass mkt. 5.95 (*0-7535-0019-1*, Pub. by Virgin Pub UK) London Bridge.

***X20: A Novel of (Not) Smoking.** Richard Beard. 320p. 1997. 22.95 (*1-55970-399-7*) Arcade Pub Inc.

X User Reference Guide. 130p. (Orig.). 1989. pap. 9.95 (*0-935739-12-2*) ASP.

X User Tools. Linda Mui & Valerie Quercia. Ed. by Tim O'Reilly. (Illus.). 856p. (Orig.). 1994. 49.95 incl. cd-rom (*1-56592-019-8*) OReilly & Assocs.

X Window Program Design & Development. Steven Mikes. 1991. pap. 26.95 (*0-201-55077-6*) Addison-Wesley.

X Window System: An Overview. Niall Mansfield. (C). 1993. pap. text ed. 28.95 (*0-201-56512-9*) Addison-Wesley.

X Window System: Core & Extension Protocols: X Version 11, Releases 6 & 6.1. Robert W. Scheifler & James Gettys. LC 96-49766. 1016p. 1997. pap. 69.95 (*1-55558-148-X*, Digital DEC) Buttrwrth-Heinemann.

X Window System: Core Libraries & Standards. Robert W. Scheifler & James Gettys. LC 96-17218. 795p. 1996. pap. 49.95 (*1-55558-154-4*, Digital DEC) Buttrwrth-Heinemann.

X Window System: Extension Libraries. Robert W. Scheifler & James Gettys. LC 96-49773. 819p. 1997. pap. 59.95 (*1-55558-146-3*, Digital DEC) Buttrwrth-Heinemann.

X Window System Administrator's Guide, Vol. 8. Linda Mui & Eric Pearce. Ed. by Tim O'Reilly. (X Window System Ser.). (Illus.). 372p. (Orig.). 1992. pap. text ed. 29.95 (*0-937175-83-8*) OReilly & Assocs.

X Window System Server. Elias Israel & Erik Fortune. (X & Motif Ser.). (Illus.). 534p. 1992. pap. 54.95 (*1-55558-096-3*, EY-L518E-DP, Digital DEC) Buttrwrth-Heinemann.

X Window System Toolkit. 2nd ed. Paul Asente et al. 1997. pap. 59.95 (*1-55558-119-6*, Digital DEC) Buttrwrth-Heinemann.

X Window System ToolKit: The Complete Programmer's Guide & Specification. Paul Asente & Ralph Swick. (X & Motif Ser.). (Illus.). 967p. (Orig.). 1990. pap. 57.95 (*1-55558-051-3*, EY-E757E-DP, Digital DEC) Buttrwrth-Heinemann.

X Window System User's Guide. Uday O. Pabrai & Hemant Shah. LC 93-39579. 236p. 1994. 49.00 (*0-89006-740-6*) Artech Hse.

X Window System User's Guide, Vol. 3: Standard Edition. 4th ed. Valerie Quercia & Tim O'Reilly. (X Window System Ser.). (Illus.). 866p. 1993. pap. 34.95 (*1-56592-014-7*) OReilly & Assocs.

X Window System User's Guide, Vol. 3M: Motif Edition. 2nd ed. Valerie Quercia & Tim O'Reilly. (X Window System Ser.). (Illus.). 956p. 1993. pap. 34.95 (*1-56592-015-5*) OReilly & Assocs.

X Windows. Johnson & Kevin Reichard. 1989. 24.95 (*1-55828-016-2*); 59.95 (*1-55828-035-9*) MIS Press.

X Windows Developer's Technical Reference. Steven Mikes. 800p. 1989. pap. 34.95 (*0-201-52370-1*) Addison-Wesley.

X Windows on the World: Developing Internationalized Software with X, Motif & CDE. Thomas McFarland. 416p. (C). 1996. pap. text ed. 37.00 (*0-13-359787-3*) P-H.

X Windows System. Theodosios Pavlidis. (Computer Science Ser.). 1998. pap. 35.95 (*0-534-94980-0*) PWS Pubs.

X Windows System Programming. 2nd ed. Nabajyoti Barkakati. 800p. 1994. pap. 39.99 incl. disk (*0-672-30542-9*) Sams.

X-Wing: The Official Strategy Guide. Rusel DeMaria. LC 93-22788. (Illus.). 432p. (Orig.). 1993. pap. 19.95 (*1-55958-375-4*) Prima Pub.

X-Wing Collector's CD-ROM: The Official Strategy Guide. Rusel Demaria. 1995. pap. text ed. 19.95 (*1-55958-785-7*) Prima Pub.

***X-Wing vs. TIE Fighter: The Official Strategy Guide.** Mark Walker. 304p. 1997. per., pap. 19.99 (*0-7615-0938-0*) Prima Pub.

X World Conference Proceedings, '94. (Illus.). 180p. 1994. pap. 29.00 (*1-884842-01-1*) SIGS Bks & Multimedia.

***X-Y-Z Alphabook.** Karen Sevaly. (Illus.). 128p. 1995. teacher ed., pap. 10.95 (*0-943263-32-8*, TF1812) Teachers Friend Pubns.

X, Y, Z Letters. Ed. by Herman Ames et al. (BCL History Ser.). 1899. 19.00 (*0-403-00035-1*) Scholarly.

X, Y, Z, Letters. Herman V. Ames et al. (History - United States Ser.). 36p. 1992. reprint ed. lib. bdg. 59.00 (*0-7812-6140-6*) Rprt Serv.

***X-Open SQL & RDA.** 2nd ed. Prentice Hall Staff. 1996. pap. text ed. 54.00 (*0-13-496415-2*) P-H.

X-15 Rocket Plane. Wilma Ross. LC 93-1844. (Those Daring Machines Ser.). (Illus.). 48p. (J). (gr. 5-6). 1994. lib. bdg. 13.95 (*0-89686-831-1*, Crstwood Hse) Silver Burdett Pr.

X-25 Made Easy. Nicolas M. Thorpe & Derek E. Ross. 400p. 1993. pap. text ed. 75.00 (*0-13-972183-5*) P-H.

Xaipe. e. e. Cummings. Ed. by George J. Firmage. 1979. 9.95 (*0-87140-633-0*); pap. 10.95 (*0-87140-121-5*) Liveright.

***Xaipe.** E. E. Cummings. Ed. by George J. Firmage. 80p. 1997. pap. 12.00 (*0-614-30687-6*) Liveright.

***Xaipe.** E. E. Cummings. Ed. by George J. Firmage. 80p. (C). 1997. pap. 12.00 (*0-87140-168-1*) Liveright.

Xala. Sembene Ousmane. Tr. by Clive Wake from FRE. LC 75-41811. (Illus.). 110p. 1983. pap. 8.95 (*1-55652-070-0*) L Hill Bks.

Xanadu. Ed. by Jane Yolen & Martin H. Greenberg. 1993. 19.95 (*0-312-85672-5*) Tor Bks.

Xanadu. Ed. by Jane Yolen. 256p. 1994. mass mkt. 4.99 (*0-8125-2082-3*) Tor Bks.

Xanadu, Vol. 2. Ed. by Jane Yolen. 288p. 1996. pap. 12.95 (*0-312-86199-0*) St Martin.

Xanadu: Thief of Hearts. Vicky Wyman. 160p. 1993. pap. 12.95 (*1-883847-03-6*) MU Press.

***Xanadu3.** Jane Yolen. 1996. pap. 15.95 (*0-312-86303-9*) St Martin.

Xanadu 2. Ed. by Jane Yolen. 288p. 1994. 19.95 (*0-312-85368-8*) Tor Bks.

Xanadu 2. Ed. by Jane Yolen & Martin H. Greenberg. 288p. 1995. 4.99 (*0-8125-2083-1*) Tor Bks.

Xanadu 2. Ed. by Jane Yolen. 1996. pap. write for info. (*0-614-08662-0*) Tor Bks.

Xanadu 3. Ed. by Jane Yolen. LC 94-31273. 320p. 1995. 21.95 (*0-312-85898-1*) Tor Bks.

Xanta Vele's Dream Numbers Winners Book. Donald M. Plank. Ed. by Edgar S. Boone. (Illus.). 81p. (Orig.). 1992. 3.95 (*1-881938-02-6*) Economy Pubns.

Xanth No. 14: Question Quest. Piers Anthony. 368p. (Orig.). 1991. mass mkt. 5.99 (*0-380-75948-9*) Avon.

Xanth No. 15: The Color of Her Panties. Piers Anthony. 352p. (Orig.). 1992. mass mkt. 5.99 (*0-380-75949-7*) Avon.

Xanthates & Related Compounds. S. Ramachandra Rao. LC 77-141626. 512p. reprint ed. pap. 146.00 (*0-685-16367-9*, 2027130) Bks Demand.

Xanthines & Cancer: An Experimental Study of Tumour Inhibition. W. J. Neish. 192p. (C). 1988. pap. 35.00 (*0-08-036399-7*, Pub. by Aberdeen U Pr) Macmillan.

Xanthippe, Wife of Socrates. Eileen E. Smith. Ed. by Leota Janzen. 394p. (Orig.). 1994. 23.00 (*0-9643972-0-X*) Janzen Press.

Xanthomonas. Ed. by J. G. Swings & E. L. Civerolo. LC 92-43468. 416p. (gr. 13). 1994. text ed. 147.95 (*0-412-43420-2*) Chapman & Hall.

***Xanthus: Travels of Discovery in Turkey.** Enid Slatter. (Illus.). 376p. 1994. 32.95 (*0-948695-30-7*, Pub. by Rubicon Pr UK); pap. 24.95 (*0-948695-31-5*, Pub. by Rubicon Pr UK) David Brown.

Xanti Schawinsky: Photographs. Xanti Schawinsky. (Illus.). 120p. 1989. pap. 30.00 (*3-7165-0667-2*, Pub. by Benteli Verlag SZ) Dist Art Pubs.

Xantus Janos Geografus Amerikaban. Leslie Konnyu. (Illus.). 121p. (HUN.). 1975. pap. 4.25 (*0-685-63881-2*) Hungarian Rev.

Xarque & Other Poems. Gayl Jones. LC 85-80141. 70p. 1985. per. 6.00 (*0-916418-60-X*) Lotus.

Xavier De Maistre. Charles M. Lombard. LC 76-58855. (Twayne's World Authors Ser.). 155p. (C). 1977. 17.95 (*0-8057-6284-1*) Irvington.

***Xavier University Version: Functioning in the Real World, a Precalculus Experience.** Sheldon & Gordon. Ed. by Karen Guardino. 238p. (C). 1997. pap. text ed. 15.95 (*0-201-85750-2*) Addison-Wesley.

Xavier Villaurrutia. Frank Dauster. (Twayne's World Authors Ser.). 1971. pap. text ed. 4.95 (*0-8290-1960-X*); lib. bdg. 17.95 (*0-686-82929-8*) Irvington.

XBASE Programming. Cary N. Prague. (Illus.). 944p. 1993. pap. 36.95 (*0-8306-4051-7*, 4188, Windcrest) TAB Bks.

XBase Programming for the True Beginner. Eugene Kaluzniacky & Vijay Kanabar. 192p. (C). 1995. pap. write for info. (*0-697-22873-8*) Bus & Educ Tech.

Xbase Programming for the True Beginner: An Introduction to the Xbase Language in the Context of dBase III Plus, IV, 5, FoxPro, & Clipper. Eugene Kaluzniacky & Vijay Kanabar. 240p. (C). 1996. 12.75 (*0-256-20432-2*) Irwin.

Xbo. Dominique Fourcade. Tr. by Robert Kocik from FRE. (Sun & Moon Classics/A Blue Guitar Bk.: No. 35). 88p. (Orig.). 1994. pap. 9.95 (*1-55713-067-1*) Sun & Moon CA.

***Xeclogue.** Lisa Robertson. 96p. 1993. 8.95 (*0-921331-20-7*, Pub. by Tsunami Edits CN) SPD-Small Pr Dist.

Xelucha & Others. M. P. Shiel. LC 74-18654. 1975. 6.50 (*0-87054-069-6*) Arkham.

***Xena: Warrior Princess: The Empty Throne.** Ru Emerson. 1996. mass mkt. 5.99 (*1-57297-200-9*) Blvd Books.

Xenakis. Nouritza Matossian. 1991. pap. 19.95 (*0-912483-35-0*) Pro-Am Music.

Xenia. Arkadii Dragomoshchenko. Tr. by Lyn Hejinian & Elena Balashova from RUS. (Sun & Moon Classics Ser.: No. 29). 176p. (Orig.). 1993. pap. 12.95 (*1-55713-107-4*) Sun & Moon CA.

Xenia: A Hoard of Lost Words. Compiled by Coleman Barks. 179p. 1994. pap. 7.50 (*0-9618916-9-6*) Maypop.

XENIX Commands & Cross Development Services: Programmer's Rapid Reference. Baird Peterson. 250p. 1992. pap. 34.95 (*0-442-00540-7*) Van Nos Reinhold.

Xenix System Services. Baird Peterson. 1992. pap. write for info. (*0-442-00541-5*) Van Nos Reinhold.

XENIX User's Handbook. Weber Systems, Inc. Staff. LC 84-23705. 310p. (C). 1984. pap. 24.95 (*0-938862-44-8*) Weber Systems.

Xenobiotic Conjugation Chemistry. Ed. by Gaylord D. Paulson et al. LC 85-32553. (ACS Symposium Ser.: No. 299). (Illus.). x, 358p. 1986. 54.95 (*0-8412-0957-X*) Am Chemical.

***Xenobiotic Conjugation Chemistry.** Ed. by Gaylord D. Paulson et al. LC 85-32553. (ACS Symposium Ser.: Vol. 299). 368p. 1986. reprint ed. pap. 104.90 (*0-608-03845-8*, 2064292) Bks Demand.

Xenobiotic Metabolism: In Vitro Studies. Ed. by Gaylord D. Paulson et al. LC 79-789. (Symposium Ser.: No. 97). 1979. 37.95 (*0-8412-0486-1*) Am Chemical.

***Xenobiotic Metabolism: Nutritional Effects.** Ed. by John W. Finley & Daniel E. Schwass. LC 85-6191. (ACS Symposium Ser.: Vol. 277). 392p. 1985. reprint ed. pap. 111.80 (*0-608-03908-X*, 2064355) Bks Demand.

Xenobiotic Metabolism & Disposition. Ed. by Ryuichi Kato. 600p. 1989. 145.00 (*0-85066-737-2*) Taylor & Francis.

Xenobiotic Metabolism & Disposition: The Design of Studies on Novel Compounds. Ed. by H. P. Illing. 224p. 1989. 220.00 (*0-8493-6163-X*, QP529) CRC Pr.

***Xenobiotic Metabolism, in Vitro Methods: A Symposium.** Ed. by Gaylord D. Paulson et al. LC 79-789. (ACS Symposium Ser.: Vol. 97). 336p. 1979. reprint ed. pap. 95.80 (*0-608-03093-7*, 2063545) Bks Demand.

Xenobiotics & Cancer: Implications for Chemical Carcinogenesis & Cancer Chemotherapy. Ed. by Lars Ernster et al. (Princess Takamatsu Symposia Ser.: No. 21). 410p. 1991. 145.00 (*0-7484-0037-0*, Pub. by Tay Francis Ltd UK) Taylor & Francis.

Xenobiotics & Food-Producing Animals: Metabolism & Residues. Ed. by David H. Hutson et al. LC 92-25718. (ACS Symposium Ser.: No. 503). (Illus.). 240p. 1992. 58.95 (*0-8412-2472-2*) Am Chemical.

Xenobiotics & Inflammation: Roles of Cytokines & Growth Factors. Ed. by Debra L. Laskin & Lawrence B. Schook. (Illus.). 361p. 1994. text ed. 99.00 (*0-12-628930-1*) Acad Pr.

Xenobiotics in Foods & Feeds. Ed. by John W. Finely & Daniel E. Schwass. LC 83-15685. (ACS Symposium Ser.: No. 234). 421p. 1983. lib. bdg. 54.95 (*0-8412-0809-3*) Am Chemical.

***Xenobiotics in Foods & Feeds.** Ed. by John W. Finley & Daniel E. Schwass. LC 83-15685. (ACS Symposium Ser.: Vol. 234). 430p. 1983. reprint ed. pap. 122.60 (*0-608-03083-X*, 2063536) Bks Demand.

Xenocide. Orson Scott Card. 416p. 1996. pap. 12.95 (*0-312-86187-7*) St Martin.

Xenocide. Orson Scott Card. 608p. 1992. mass mkt. 6.99 (*0-8125-0925-0*) Tor Bks.

Xenogenesis, 3 vols. in 1. Octavia E. Butler. (Illus.). 736p. 1989. 14.98 (*1-56865-033-7*, GuildAmerica) Dblday Direct.

***Xenograffiti: Essays on Fantastic Literature.** Robert Reginald. LC 96-35246. (Evans Studies in the Philosophy & Criticism of Literature: No. 33). 224p. 1996. 33.00 (*0-8095-0900-8*); pap. 23.00 (*0-8095-1900-3*) Borgo Pr.

Xenokrates. Richard Heinze. xi, 204p. 1965. reprint ed. write for info. (*3-487-05121-4*) G Olms Pubs.

Xenon, Vol. 2: Heavy Metal Warrior. Masaomi Kanzaki. Ed. by Seiji Horibuchi. Tr. by Satoru Fujii from JPN. (Illus.). 192p. 1992. pap. 14.95 (*0-929279-42-5*) Viz Commns Inc.

Xenon, Vol. 3: Heavy Metal Warrior. Masaomi Kanzaki. Ed. by Seiji Horibuchi. Tr. by Satoru Fujii from JPN. (Illus.). 194p. 1992. pap. 14.95 (*0-929279-43-3*) Viz Commns Inc.

Xenon, Vol. 4: Heavy Metal Warrior. Masaomi Kanzaki. Ed. by Seiji Horibuchi. Tr. by Satoru Fujii from JPN. (Illus.). 176p. (YA). 1992. pap. 14.95 (*0-929279-47-6*) Viz Commns Inc.

Xenophanes - Lessico Di Senofane. Ed. by Nino Marinone. (Alpha-Omega, Reihe A Ser.: Bd. XX). 117p. 1972. reprint ed. write for info. (*3-487-04216-9*) G Olms Pubs.

Xenophanes of Colophon: Fragments - A Text & Translation with a Commentary. Ed. by J. H. Lesher. (Phoenix Supplementary Volumes Ser.: No. XXX: Pre-Socratics). 380p. 1992. 45.00 (*0-8020-5990-2*) U of Toronto Pr.

Xenophile see Signe Ascendant

***Xenophobe's Guide to the Americans.** Anne Taute. (Xenophobe's Guides Ser.). 1995. pap. text ed. 5.95 (*1-85304-780-5*, Pub. by Ravette Bks UK) Assoc Pubs Grp.

***Xenophobe's Guide to the Aussies.** Ed. by Anne Taute. (Xenophobe's Guides Ser.). 64p. 1996. pap. 5.95 (*1-85304-126-2*, Pub. by Ravette Bks UK) Assoc Pubs Grp.

***Xenophobe's Guide to the Austrians.** Ed. by Anne Taute. (Xenophobe's Guides Ser.). 64p. 1996. pap. 5.95 (*1-85304-740-6*, Pub. by Ravette Bks UK) Assoc Pubs Grp.

***Xenophobe's Guide to the Belgians.** Ed. by Anne Taute. (Xenophobe's Guides Ser.). 64p. 1996. pap. 5.95 (*1-85304-570-5*, Pub. by Ravette Bks UK) Assoc Pubs Grp.

***Xenophobe's Guide to the Chinese.** Ed. by Anne Taute. (Xenophobe's Guides Ser.). 64p. 1996. pap. 5.95 (*1-85304-582-9*, Pub. by Ravette Bks UK) Assoc Pubs Grp.

An Asterisk (*) at the beginning of an entry indicates that the title is appearing in BIP for the first time.

***Xenophobe's Guide to the Dutch.** Ed. by Anne Taute. (Xenophobe's Guides Ser.). 64p. 1996. pap. 5.95 (*1-85304-559-4*, Pub. by Ravette Bks UK) Assoc Pubs Grp.

***Xenophobe's Guide to the English.** Ed. by Anne Taute. (Xenophobe's Guides Ser.). 64p. 1996. pap. 5.95 (*1-85304-563-2*, Pub. by Ravette Bks UK) Assoc Pubs Grp.

***Xenophobe's Guide to the French.** Ed. by Anne Taute. (Xenophobe's Guides Ser.). 64p. 1996. pap. 5.95 (*1-85304-558-6*, Pub. by Ravette Bks UK) Assoc Pubs Grp.

***Xenophobe's Guide to the Germans.** Ed. by Anne Taute. (Xenophobe's Guides Ser.). 64p. 1996. pap. 5.95 (*1-85304-561-6*, Pub. by Ravette Bks UK) Assoc Pubs Grp.

***Xenophobe's Guide to the Greeks.** Ed. by Anne Taute. (Xenophobe's Guides Ser.). 64p. 1996. pap. 5.95 (*1-85304-562-4*, Pub. by Ravette Bks UK) Assoc Pubs Grp.

***Xenophobe's Guide to the Icelanders.** Ed. by Anne Taute. (Xenophobe's Guides Ser.). 64p. 1996. pap. 5.95 (*1-85304-779-1*, Pub. by Ravette Bks UK) Assoc Pubs Grp.

***Xenophobe's Guide to the Italians.** Ed. by Anne Taute. (Xenophobe's Guides Ser.). 64p. 1996. pap. 5.95 (*1-85304-571-3*, Pub. by Ravette Bks UK) Assoc Pubs Grp.

***Xenophobe's Guide to the Japanese.** 64p. 1997. pap. text ed. 5.99 (*1-85304-574-8*, Pub. by Ravette Bks UK) Assoc Pubs Grp.

***Xenophobe's Guide to the Kiwis.** Anne Taute. 64p. 1996. pap. text ed. 5.95 (*1-85304-583-7*, Pub. by Ravette Bks UK) Assoc Pubs Grp.

***Xenophobe's Guide to the Poles.** Ed. by Anne Taute. (Xenophobe's Guides Ser.). 64p. 1996. pap. 5.95 (*1-85304-739-2*, Pub. by Ravette Bks UK) Assoc Pubs Grp.

***Xenophobe's Guide to the Russians.** Ed. by Anne Taute. (Xenophobe's Guides Ser.). 64p. 1996. pap. 5.95 (*1-85304-737-6*, Pub. by Ravette Bks UK) Assoc Pubs Grp.

***Xenophobe's Guide to the Spanish.** Ed. by Anne Taute. (Xenophobe's Guides Ser.). 64p. 1996. pap. 5.95 (*1-85304-560-8*, Pub. by Ravette Bks UK) Assoc Pubs Grp.

***Xenophobe's Guide to the Swedes.** Ed. by Anne Taute. (Xenophobe's Guides Ser.). 64p. 1996. pap. 5.95 (*1-85304-741-4*, Pub. by Ravette Bks UK) Assoc Pubs Grp.

***Xenophobe's Guide to the Swiss.** Ed. by Anne Taute. (Xenophobe's Guides Ser.). 64p. 1996. pap. 5.95 (*1-85304-569-1*, Pub. by Ravette Bks UK) Assoc Pubs Grp.

***Xenophobia: The Hatred & Fear of Strangers.** Nathaniel I. Korman. 16p. (Orig.). 1997. pap. 0.95 (*0-9654300-2-2*) Runamiro Bks.

Xenophobia in United Germany: Generations, Modernization, & Ideology. Meredith W. Watts. LC 96-28131. 1997. text ed. 49.95 (*0-312-16250-2*) St Martin.

Xenophon. J. K. Anderson. 216p. 1986. pap. 24.95 (*0-7156-1610-2*, Pub. by Duckworth UK) Focus Pub-R Pullins.

Xenophon: Apology. David Konstan. 1987. 5.00 (*0-929524-36-5*) Bryn Mawr Commentaries.

Xenophon: Fall of Athens. Ed. by T. Horn. (Bristol Greek Texts Ser.). (Illus.). 109p. (GRE.). 1978. reprint ed. pap. 15.95 (*0-906515-12-2*, Pub. by Brstl Class Pr UK) Focus Pub-R Pullins.

***Xenophon: Hellenika II.3.11-IV.2.8.** Xenophon. Ed. & Tr. by Peter Krentz from GRE. (Classical Texts Ser.). 224p. 1995. text ed. 49.95 (*0-85668-641-7*, Pub. by Aris & Phillips UK); pap. text ed. 24.95 (*0-85668-642-5*, Pub. by Aris & Phillips UK) David Brown.

***Xenophon: Index Socraticorum Xenophontis Operum.** Contrib. by Francisco M. Garcia & Alfredo R. Lopez. viii, 236p. (GER.). 1995. write for info. (*3-487-10018-5*) G Olms Pubs.

Xenophon: Oeconomicus VII-XIII. Ed. by R. Doty. (Bristol Greek Texts Ser.). 96p. (GRE.). 1994. pap. 15.95 (*1-85399-394-8*, Pub. by Brstl Class Pr UK) Focus Pub-R Pullins.

Xenophon: The Persian Expedition. Ed. by J. Antrich & S. Usher. (Bristol Greek Texts Ser.). (Illus.). 200p. (GRE.). 1978. pap. 17.95 (*0-906515-11-4*, Pub. by Brstl Class Pr UK) Focus Pub-R Pullins.

Xenophon & the History of His Times. John Dillery. LC 94-30021. 320p. (C). (gr. 13). 1995. text ed. 69.95 (*0-415-09139-X*, C0190) Routledge.

Xenophon of Ephesus: His Compositional Technique & the Birth of the Novel. James N. O'Sullivan. (Untersuchungen zur Antiken Literatur und Geschichte Ser.: Vol. 44). 227p. (C). 1994. lib. bdg. 107.70 (*3-11-014310-0*) De Gruyter.

Xenophon the Athenian: The Problem of the Individual & the Society of Polis. William E. Higgins. LC 77-2392. 183p. 1977. text ed. 29.50 (*0-87395-369-X*) State U NY Pr.

Xenophon's Anabasis, Bks. 1-4. Maurice W. Mather & Joseph W. Hewitt. LC 62-18051. (Illus.). 528p. 1976. pap. 24.95 (*0-8061-1347-2*) U of Okla Pr.

Xenophon's Cyropaedia: Style, Genre, & Literary Technique. Deborah L. Gera. LC 92-16534. (Oxford Classical Monographs). 368p. 1993. pap. 75.00 (*0-19-814477-6*, Old Oregon Bk Store) OUP.

Xenophon's Imperial Fiction: On "The Education of Cyrus" James Tatum. 328p. 1989. text ed. 45.00 (*0-691-06757-0*) Princeton U Pr.

Xenophon's Socratic Discourse: An Interpretation of the Oeconomicus, with a New Literal Translation of the Oeconomicus by Carnes Lord. Leo Strauss. LC 70-108162. 219p. reprint ed. pap. 62.50 (*0-685-20911-3*, 2032050) Bks Demand.

Xenophon's Sparta: An Introduction. Gerald Proietti. (Mnemosyne, Bibliotheca Classica Batava Ser.: Vol. 98). (Orig.). 1987. pap. 33.00 (*90-04-08338-3*) E J Brill.

Xenophons Staats-und Gesellschaftsideal und Seine Zeit. Erwin Scharr. 321p. 1975. reprint ed. write for info. (*3-487-05410-8*) G Olms Pubs.

Xenopus: The South African Clawed Frog. Elizabeth M. Deuchar. LC 73-18927. 256p. reprint ed. pap. 73.00 (*0-317-28860-1*, 2020972) Bks Demand.

***Xenotransplantation: Science, Ethics, & Public Policy.** Committee on Xenograft Transplantation Institute of Medicine. 136p. (Orig.). (C). 1996. pap. text ed. 29.00 (*0-309-05549-0*) Natl Acad Pr.

***Xenotransplantation: The Transplantation of Organs & Tissues Between Species.** 2nd ed. Ed. by D. Cooper & E. Kemp. LC 96-39074. (Illus.). 850p. 1997. 355.00 (*3-540-61777-9*) Spr-Verlag.

***Xeriscape Color Guide.** Ed. by Denver Water, American Staff & Water Works Assn. Staff. (Illus.). 64p. 1998. pap. 14.95 (*1-55591-391-1*) Fulcrum Pub.

Xeriscape Flower Gardener: A Waterwise Guide for the Rocky Mountain Region. Jim Knopf. LC 91-2955. (Illus.). 192p. (Orig.). 1991. pap. 16.95 (*1-55566-077-0*) Johnson Bks.

Xeriscape Gardening. Connie Ellefson et al. (Illus.). 320p. 1992. 30.00 (*0-02-614125-6*) Macmillan.

Xeriscape Plant Guide. Fulcrum Publishing Staff et al. (Illus.). 176p. 1996. 34.95 (*1-55591-322-9*) Fulcrum Pub.

Xeriscape Programs for Water Utilities. Ken Ball. 104p. 1990. pap. 47.00 (*0-89867-525-1*, 20253) Am Water Wks Assn.

Xeriscaping for Florida Homes. Monica M. Brandies. (Illus.). 184p. (Orig.). 1994. pap. 18.95 (*0-8200-0411-1*) Great Outdoors.

Xerophytes. M. Fahn & D. F. Cutler. (Encyclopedia of Plant Anatomy Ser.: No. 13-3). (Illus.). 176p. 1992. lib. bdg. 84.95 (*3-443-14019-X*) Lubrecht & Cramer.

Xerox: American Samurai - The Behind-the-Scenes Story of How a Corporate Giant Beat the Japanese at Their Own Game. Gary Jacobson & John Hillkirk. 320p. 1987. pap. 13.95 (*0-02-033830-9*) Macmillan.

Xerox Ventura Publisher: From the Screen to the Page. 2nd ed. Susan G. Stevens & John A. Barry. 500p. 1989. pap. 25.00 (*1-55623-211-X*) Irwin Prof Pubng.

Xerox Ventura Publisher Companion: Macintosh Edition. Craig Danuloff. 416p. 1992. 29.00 (*1-55623-496-1*) Irwin Prof Pubng.

Xerox Ventura Publisher Sourcebook. Paul S. Klose & Dean K. Fueroghne. 300p. 1989. pap. 27.00 (*1-55623-215-2*) Irwin Prof Pubng.

Xerox 860 Made Easy. Sondra Bleich. 1984. pap. 25.00 (*0-8359-8943-7*, Reston) P-H.

***XH-1 Therapy.** Lai-Yin Yan. (Illus.). 154p. 1997. pap. 17.00 (*0-614-30215-3*) Dorrance.

Xhosa. Russell Kaschula. LC 96-42271. (Heritage Library of African Peoples: Set 4). (Illus.). 64p. (YA). (gr. 7-12). 1996. lib. bdg. 15.95 (*0-8239-2013-5*, D2013-5) Rosen Group.

Xhosa-English Dictionary. J. McLaren. Ed. by W. G. Bennie & J. J. Jolobe. (ENG & XHO.). 27.50 (*0-87559-069-1*) Shalom.

XI AIRAPT: Selected Soviet Papers from the International High Pressure Conference, July 12-17, 1987, Kiev, U. S. S. R.: A Special Issue of the Journal High Pressure Research. Ed. by N. V. Novikov. ii, 106p. 1989. pap. text ed. 125.00 (*2-88124-727-X*) Gordon & Breach.

XI, XII & XIII Olympiads: Berlin 1936, St. Moritz 1948. George Constable. LC 96-10657. (Olympic Century Ser.: No. 11). 1996. write for info. (*1-888383-11-9*, Wrld Spt) Wld Sport Resch.

Xi'an. (Illus.). 128p. 1992. pap. 7.95 (*0-8442-9820-4*, Passport Bks) NTC Pub Grp.

***Xi'an: An Ancient Capital of China.** He Zhenghuang. (Illus.). 190p. 1990. 39.95 (*7-119-00665-7*, Pub. by Foreign Lang CH) China Bks.

Xi'an: China's Ancient Capital. 2nd ed. Simon Holledge. (Illus.). 152p. 1994. pap. 15.95 (*0-8442-9809-3*, Passport Bks) NTC Pub Grp.

Xiangshui to Mandal Transect North China. 1991. 95.00 (*0-87590-779-2*, GGT 2) Am Geophysical.

Xiao Xia. Xiao Xia. (Illus.). 172p. 1991. 80.00 (*2-903004-13-7*, Pub. by Galerie Isy Brachot FR) Dist Art Pubs.

***Xibala Murders: An Archeological Mystery.** Lyn Hamilton. 304p. 1997. mass mkt. 3.99 (*0-425-15722-9*, Prime Crime) Berkley Pub.

Xibalba Arcane. Jack Hirschman. LC 93-72345. 64p. (Orig.). (C). 1994. pap. 10.95 (*0-9632363-4-2*) Azul Edits.

Xicano Progeny: Investigative Agents, Executive Council, & Other Representatives from the Sovereign State of Aztlan. Armando Rascon. Ed. by Suzanne Lipsett. (Illus.). 56p. (Orig.). (SPA.). 1995. 10.00 (*1-880508-03-6*) Mexican Museum.

XIE Applications. Syd Logan. 1996. pap. text ed. 54.00 (*0-13-442914-1*) P-H.

XII Panegyrici Latini. Ed. by Roger A. Mynors. (Oxford Classical Texts Ser.). 312p. 1964. 45.00 (*0-19-814647-7*) OUP.

XIII Winters: Reflections on Rugby League. Ed. by Dave Hadfield. (Illus.). 191p. 1995. pap. 17.95 (*1-85158-743-8*, Pub. by Mnstream UK) Trafalgar.

***XIII Worlds: Pursuing Rugby League Around the Globe.** Ed. by Dave Hadfield. (Illus.). 192p. 1996. 34.95 (*1-85158-759-4*, Pub. by Mnstream UK) Trafalgar.

Xing Yi Nei Gang: Xi Yi Health Maintenance & Internal Strength Development. Tim Cartnell & Dan Miller. (Illus.). 224p. (Orig.). 1994. pap. 19.95 (*1-883175-04-6*) High View Pubns.

Xingu. adapted ed. Edith Warton. 1939. pap. 5.25 (*0-8222-1281-1*) Dramatists Play.

XionFlight. Patricia Weber. (Illus.). 320p. 1986. 15.00 (*0-317-57627-5*) Pacifica Editions.

Xipehuz & the Death of the Earth (les Xipehuz & la Mort De la Terre), 2 Vols. J. H. Rosynyaine. Ed. by R. Reginald & Douglas Melville. LC 77-84283. (Lost Race & Adult Fantasy Ser.). 1978. lib. bdg. 23.95 (*0-405-11020-0*) Ayer.

XIT Ranch of Texas, & Early Days of the Llano Estacado. J. Evetts Haley. 1993. reprint ed. lib. bdg. 75.00 (*0-7812-5933-9*) Rprt Serv.

XIT Ranch of Texas & the Early Days of the Llano Estacado. J. Evetts Haley. (Western Frontier Library: No. 34). (Illus.). 1977. reprint ed. pap. 13.95 (*0-8061-1428-2*) U of Okla Pr.

XIXe Siecle see Textes & Litterature

XIXes Journees Nationales de Neonatologie, 1989. Ed. by J. P. Relier. (Progres en Neonatologie Ser.: Vol. 9). (Illus.). 268p. 1989. pap. 106.50 (*3-8055-5060-X*) S Karger.

XL Classic Knits. Pat Hampton. (Illus.). 58p. 1985. pap. 12.95 (*0-9614397-2-6*) P K Hampton.

***XL-Loto.** Tony Kandiew. 140p. (Orig.). 1997. mass mkt. 4.99 (*1-55237-386-X*, Pub. by Comnwlth Pub CN) Partners Pubs Grp.

XLib - The C Language X Interface: User Commands & Library Interface. 300p. (Orig.). 1990. pap. text ed. 29.95 (*0-929306-03-1*) Silicon Pr.

XLIB by Example. Cui-Qing Yang & Mahir S. Ali. (Illus.). 400p. 1994. pap. text ed., pap. 49.95 incl. disk (*0-12-050210-0*, AP Prof) Acad Pr.

Xlib Programming Manual, Vol. 1: For R4-R5. 3rd ed. Adrian Nye. (X Window System Ser.). (Illus.). 824p. 1992. pap. 34.95 (*1-56592-002-3*) OReilly & Assocs.

Xlib Reference Manual, Vol. 2: For R4-R5. 3rd ed. Adrian Nye. (X Window System Ser.). 1138p. 1992. pap. 34.95 (*1-56592-006-6*) OReilly & Assocs.

Xli's Prayer. Donald L. Westbrook. 224p. 1993. pap. 10.50 (*0-9636033-0-2*) Bayberry MD.

Xman. Michael Brodsky. LC 87-7389. 540p. 1987. 21.95 (*0-941423-01-8*); pap. 11.95 (*0-941423-02-6*) FWEW.

Xmas At Home. McCall's Needlework & Crafts Editors. 1986. 22.95 (*0-02-609160-7*) Macmillan.

***Xmas Collection.** Jill Barnett. 1997. mass mkt. 6.99 (*0-451-40800-4*, Onyx) NAL-Dutton.

***Xmas Ghost.** Brenda Seabrooke. 1998. pap. 14.99 (*0-525-65248-5*) NAL-Dutton.

Xmas in Las Vegas. Jack Richardson. 1966. pap. 5.25 (*0-8222-1282-X*) Dramatists Play.

***Xmas Surprise.** Mouseworks Staff. 1997. 10.98 (*1-57082-627-7*) Mouse Works.

Xmas Sutra. Patrick Smith. (Moon Bks.: No. 35). (Illus.). 62p. (Orig.). 1976. pap. 5.00 (*0-942908-02-3*) Pancake Pr.

Xoana & the Origins of Greek Sculpture. Alice A. Donohue. LC 86-6511. (American Philological Association, American Classical Studies). 509p. 1988. pap. 16.95 (*1-55540-154-6*, 40-04-15) Scholars Pr GA.

Xod Korolem: (The King's Visit) Arkady Rovner. (Illus.). 164p. (Orig.). (RUS.). 1988. pap. 15.00 (*0-922792-00-3*) Gnosis Pr.

Xodus: An African-American Male Journey. Garth K. Fletcher. 1995. pap. 15.00 (*0-8006-2918-3*) Augsburg Fortress.

***Xoloitzcuintle: Selected Poems, October '86-April '91.** Piaf Azul. LC 94-60978. (SFX Poets Ser.: Vol. 1). (Illus.). 40p. (Orig.). 1996. 25.00 (*0-935865-06-3*); pap. 13.00 (*0-935865-05-5*); pap. 7.00 (*0-935865-07-1*) SFX Pr.

Xorander. Christine Brooke-Rose. 224p. 1988. mass mkt. 2.95 (*0-380-70407-2*) Avon.

***Xothic Legend Cycle: The Mythos Fiction of Lin Carter.** Lin Carter et al. (Call of Cthulhu Fiction Ser.). (Illus.). 1997. pap. 10.95 (*1-56882-078-X*, 6013) Chaosium.

XPD. Len Deighton. 1983. mass mkt. 5.95 (*0-345-31337-2*) Ballantine.

XploRe: An Interactive Statistical Computing Environment. W. H. Ardle et al. LC 94-41488. (Statistics & Computing Ser.). 1995. 54.95 (*0-387-94429-X*) Spr-Verlag.

X(PLORE) Version 4 for MS-DOS Compatible Computers 3.5. Meredith. 1993. text ed. 33.60 (*0-13-014226-3*) P-H.

Xplore Version 4.0 For Macintosh. Meredith. 1994. pap. text ed. 32.00 (*0-13-014200-X*) P-H.

XPress It! A Step-by-Step Guide to Quark Express 3.0. Linda J. Chanda. 352p. (C). 1992. spiral bd. 33.25 (*0-697-14003-2*) Bus & Educ Tech.

Xpress Transfer Protocol. W. Timothy Strayer et al. LC 92-5580. (Illus.). 272p. 1992. 41.95 (*0-201-56351-7*) Addison-Wesley.

XRF Analysis of Ceramics, Minerals & Allied Materials. Henry Bennett & Graham J. Oliver. LC 92-8092. 298p. 1992. text ed. 154.00 (*0-471-93457-7*) Wiley.

XRF & PIXE Applications in Life Science. Renata Moro & Roberto Cesareo. 348p. (C). 1990. text ed. 113.00 (*981-02-0079-X*) World Scientific Pub.

Xsel's Progress: The Continuing Journey of an Expert System. Enid Mumford & Bruce Macdonald. LC 88-27013. (Series in Information Systems). 241p. 1989. text ed. 80.00 (*0-471-92322-2*) Wiley.

XSess Living: CDZeene, Bk. 2-1. Ed. by Sean Perkin. (Illus.). 102p. (Orig.). 1994. pap. 12.50 incl. audio compact disk (*1-57787-000-X*) ComEnt Media.

XSess Living: CDZeene, Bk. 2-2. Ed. by Sean Perkin. (Illus.). 172p. (Orig.). 1995. pap. 12.50 incl. audio compact disk (*1-57787-001-8*) ComEnt Media.

XSess Living: CDZeene, Bk. 2-4. Ed. by Sean Perkin. (Illus.). 148p. (Orig.). 1995. pap. 12.50 incl. audio compact disk (*1-57787-002-6*) ComEnt Media.

XSess Living: CDZeene, Bk. 3-1. Ed. by Sean Perkin. (Illus.). 148p. (Orig.). 1995. pap. 12.50 incl. audio compact disk (*1-57787-003-4*) ComEnt Media.

XSess Living: CDZeene, Bk. 5. Ed. by Sean Perkin. (Illus.). 144p. (Orig.). 1996. pap. 12.50 incl. audio compact disk (*1-57787-004-2*) ComEnt Media.

XSess Living: CDZeene, Bk. 6. Ed. by Sean Perkin. (Illus.). 148p. (Orig.). 1996. pap. 12.50 incl. audio compact disk (*1-57787-005-0*) ComEnt Media.

XSess Living: CDZeene, Bk. 7. Ed. by Sean Perkin. (Illus.). 148p. (Orig.). 1996. pap. 12.50 incl. audio compact disk (*1-57787-006-9*) ComEnt Media.

XSess Living: CDZeene, Bk. 8. Ed. by Sean Perkin. (Illus.). 148p. (Orig.). 1996. pap. 12.50 incl. audio compact disk (*1-57787-007-7*) ComEnt Media.

XSess Living: CDZeene, Bk. 9. Ed. by Sean Perkin. (Illus.). 148p. (Orig.). 1997. pap. 12.50 incl. audio compact disk (*1-57787-008-5*) ComEnt Media.

XSess Living: CDZeene, Bk. 10. Ed. by Sean Perkin. (Illus.). 148p. (Orig.). 1997. pap. write for info. incl. audio compact disk (*1-57787-009-3*) ComEnt Media.

XSess Living: CDZeene, Bk. 11. Ed. by Sean Perkin. (Illus.). 148p. (Orig.). 1997. pap. 12.50 incl. audio compact disk (*1-57787-010-7*) ComEnt Media.

XSess Living: CDZeene, Bk. 12. Ed. by Sean Perkin. (Illus.). 148p. (Orig.). 1997. pap. 12.50 incl. audio compact disk (*1-57787-011-5*) ComEnt Media.

XSess Music: CDZeene, Bk. 1. Sean Perkin. (Illus.). 148p. (Orig.). 1996. pap. 15.95 incl. audio compact disk (*1-57787-050-6*) ComEnt Media.

XSess Music: CDZeene, Bk. 2. Sean Perkin. (Illus.). 144p. (Orig.). 1996. pap. 15.95 incl. audio compact disk (*1-57787-051-4*) ComEnt Media.

XSess Music: CDZeene, Bk. 3. Sean Perkin. (Illus.). 144p. (Orig.). 1996. pap. 15.95 incl. audio compact disk (*1-57787-052-2*) ComEnt Media.

XSess Music: CDZeene, Bk. 4. Sean Perkin. (Illus.). 144p. (Orig.). 1997. pap. 15.95 incl. audio compact disk (*1-57787-053-0*) ComEnt Media.

XSess Music: CDZeene, Bk. 5. Sean Perkin. (Illus.). 144p. (Orig.). 1997. pap. 15.95 incl. audio compact disk (*1-57787-054-9*) ComEnt Media.

XSess Music: CDZeene, Bk. 6. Sean Perkin. (Illus.). 144p. (Orig.). 1997. pap. 15.95 incl. audio compact disk (*1-57787-055-7*) ComEnt Media.

X=T: The Art of X-Ray Photography. Photos by Seiju Toda. LC 94-40107. (Illus.). 176p. 1995. 75.00 (*1-55595-080-9*) Hudson Hills.

XT-AT Handbook: For Engineers, Programmers, & Other Serious PC-XT & PC-AT Users. 5th ed. John P. Choisser & John O. Foster. 92p. (Orig.). 1995. pap. 9.95 (*0-929392-26-4*) Annabooks.

Xtal Set Society Newsletter, Vol. 1. Philip Anderson. 36p. 1992. pap. 9.95 (*1-887736-01-8*) Xtal Set Soc.

Xtal Set Society Newsletter, Vol. 2. Philip Anderson. 36p. 1993. pap. 9.95 (*1-887736-02-6*) Xtal Set Soc.

Xtal Set Society Newsletter, Vol. 4. Philip Anderson. 85p. 1994. pap. 9.95 (*1-887736-04-2*) Xtal Set Soc.

Xtal Set Society Newsletter, Vol. 5. Philip Anderson. 85p. 1995. pap. 9.95 (*1-887736-07-7*) Xtal Set Soc.

Xtras for System 7. Sharon Z. Aker. 1992. pap. write for info. (*0-201-60853-7*) Addison-Wesley.

***Xtravaganza! The Essential Sourcebook for Macromedia Xtras.** Chuck Henderson & Josh Silverstein. 800p. 1997. 44.95 (*0-201-68893-X*) Peachpit Pr.

Xu Bing: Language Lost. Jeffrey Keough et al. (Illus.). 28p. (Orig.). 1995. pap. write for info. (*0-614-13734-9*) MA Collge Art.

Xuanzang: A Buddhist Pilgrim on the Silk Road. Sally H. Wriggins. (Illus.). 288p. 1996. text ed. 32.50 (*0-8133-2801-2*) Westview.

***Xuanzang: A Dugghist Pilgrim on the Silk Road.** Sally H. Wriggins. 2p. (C). 1997. pap. text ed. 21.00 (*0-8133-3407-1*) Westview.

***Xul Reader: An Anthology of Argentine Poetry (1981-1996)** Ed. by Jorge S. Perednik & Ernesto L. Grosman. (Illus.). 167p. (Orig.). (ENG & SPA.). 1996. pap. 14.95 (*0-937804-67-3*) Segue NYC.

Xultun (Mayan) Tarot Deck: A Maya Tarot Deck. 2nd ed. Peter Balin. (Illus.). 78p. (Orig.). 1982. pap. 15.95 (*0-910261-00-8*) Lotus Light.

Xunzi: A Translation & Study of the Complete Works. John Knoblock. LC 87-33578. 480p. (C). 1994. 125.00 (*0-8047-2447-4*) Stanford U Pr.

Xunzi: A Translation & Study of the Complete Works, Vol. 1, Bks. 1-6. John Knoblock. LC 87-33578. 360p. 1988. 55.00 (*0-8047-1451-7*) Stanford U Pr.

Xunzi: A Translation & Study of the Complete Works, Vol. II, Bks. 7-16. John Knoblock. 400p. 1990. 55.00 (*0-8047-1771-0*) Stanford U Pr.

Xunzi Bk. 17-32: A Translation & Study of the Complete Works, Vol. lll. Ohn Knoblock. x, 433p. Date not set. 55.00 (*0-8047-2298-6*) Stanford U Pr.

Xuxa: The Mega Marketing of Gender, Race, & Modernity. Amelia S. Simpson. LC 93-18121. (Illus.). 256p. 1993. 44.95 (*1-56639-101-6*); pap. 16.95 (*1-56639-107-5*) Temple U Pr.

XV Bookes Entytuled Metamorphosis. Ovid. Tr. by Arthur Golding. LC 77-7418. (English Experience Ser.: No. 881). 1977. reprint ed. lib. bdg. 70.00 (*90-221-0881-3*) Walter J Johnson.

XVIe Siecle see Textes & Litterature

XVIIe Siecle see Textes & Litterature

XVIIes Journees Nationales de Neonatologie, 1987: Paris, Mai Ser. Ed. by J. P. Relier. (Progres en Neonatologie Ser.: Vol. 7). vi, 382p. 1987. pap. 128.00 (3-8055-4652-1) S Karger.

XVIII Century Spanish Villancicos of Juan Frances de Iribarren. Marta Sanchez. Ed. by Yvette E. Miller. LC 86-33800. (Explorations Ser.). 352p. 1988. pap. text ed. 16.95 (0-935480-26-9) Lat Am Lit Rev Pr.

XVIIIe Siecle see Textes & Litterature

XX & Belgian Avant-Gardism, 1868-1894. Jane Block. Ed. by Stephen Foster. LC 83-17981. (Studies in the Fine Arts: The Avant-Garde: No. 41). 202p. reprint ed. 57.30 (0-8357-1463-2, 2070448) Bks Demand.

***XX Girls.** Richard Kern. 1997. 40.00 (4-309-90161-1, Pub. by Kawadeshobo Shinsha JA) Bks Nippan.

XXe Siecle see Textes & Litterature

XXIes Journees Nationales de Neonatologie, 1990. Ed. by J. P. Relier. (Progres en Neonatologie Ser.: Vol. 10). (Illus.). vi, 312p. 1990. pap. 137.50 (3-8055-5249-1) S Karger.

XXIIes Journees Nationales De Neonatologie Paris, May 1992. Ed. by J. P. Relier. (Progres en Neonatologie Ser.: Vol. 12). (Illus.). vi, 326p. 1992. pap. 169.75 (3-8055-5636-5) S Karger.

XXIII Olympiad: Los Angeles 1984, Calgary 1988. LC 95-52574. (Olympic Century Ser.: Vol. 21). 1996. write for info. (1-888383-21-6) Wld Sport Resch.

XXIIIes Journees Nationales de Neonatologie, 1993, Paris, May 1993. (Progres en Neonatologie Ser.: Vol. 13). (Illus.). vi, 292p. 1993. pap. 169.75 (3-8055-5828-7) S Karger.

XXIVemes Journees Nationales de Neonatologie 1994, No. 14. Ed. by J. P. Relier. (Progres en Neonatologie Ser.: Vol. 14). (Illus.). iv, 256p. 1994. pap. 170.50 (3-8055-6015-X) S Karger.

XXVes Journees Nationales de Neonatologie 1995. Ed. by J. P. Relier. (Progres en Neonatologie Ser.: Vol. 15). (Illus.). vi, 332p. 1995. pap. 170.50 (3-8055-6208-X) S Karger.

***XXVIes Journees Nationales de Neonatologie Paris, Mai, 1996.** (Progres en Neonatologie Ser.: Vol. 16, 1996). (Illus.). vi, 298p. 1996. pap. 170.50 (3-8055-6355-8) S Karger.

***XXX Woman's Right to Porn.** McElroy. Date not set. pap. 12.95 (0-312-15245-0) St Martin.

***XXX Women.** Fontirez. (Eros Graphic Novel Ser.: No. 14). 120p. 1995. pap. 14.95 (1-56097-212-2) Fantagraph Bks.

***XXXOOO: Love & Kisses from Annie Sprinkle, Vol. 1.** Annie Sprinkle. Ed. by Katharine Gates. (Illus.). 60p. (Orig.). 1997. pap. 11.95 (1-889539-00-7) Heck Editions.

***XXXOOO: Love & Kisses from Annie Sprinkle, Vol. 2.** Annie Sprinkle. Ed. by Katharine Gates. (Illus.). 60p. (Orig.). 1997. pap. 11.95 (1-889539-01-5) Heck Editions.

XY: On Masculine Identity. Elisabeth Badinter. LC 94-41016. (European Perspectives Ser.). 224p. 1995. 27.95 (0-231-08434-X) Col U Pr.

***XY: On Masculine Identity.** Elisabeth Badinter. 1997. pap. 16.50 (0-614-27591-1) Col U Pr.

XY Equals Z. Kay Rosen. (Illus.). 40p. 1992. pap. text ed. 20.00 (1-881138-02-X) Tallgrass Pr.

XY Files: Poems on the Male Experience. Ed. by Nancy Fay & Judith Rafaela. LC 97-15225. (Illus.). 196p. (Orig.). 1996. pap. 18.00 (0-9644196-6-1) S Asher Pub.

Xylans & Xylanases: Proceedings of an International Symposium, Wageningen, The Netherlands, December 8-11, 1991. Ed. by J. Visser et al. LC 92-24427. (Progress in Biotechnology Ser.: No. 7). 576p. 1992. 260.50 (0-444-89477-2) Elsevier.

Xylem Structure & the Ascent of Sap. Zimmerman. (Wood Science Ser.). (Illus.). 160p. 1983. 57.00 (0-387-12268-0) Spr-Verlag.

***Xylene.** WHO Staff. (Environmental Health Criteria Ser.: No. 190). 147p. 1997. 30.00 (92-4-157190-X) World Health.

Xylo-Fun I, Vol. 1. Nancy Poffenberger. 24p. 1995. pap. 6.95 (0-938293-13-3) Fun Pub OH.

Xylophone Music from Ghana. Joseph Kobom & Trevor Wiggins. Ed. by Larry W. Smith. (Performance in World Music Ser.: No. 6). (Illus.). 64p. 12.95 (0-941677-30-3) White Cliffs Media.

Xylophone Music from Ghana. Trevor Wiggins & Joseph Kobom. 64p. 29.95 (0-941677-31-1) White Cliffs Media.

Xylophone Music from Ghana. Trevor Wiggins & Joseph Kobom. Ed. by Larry W. Smith. (Performance in World Music Ser.: No. 6). (Illus.). 64p. 1992. spiral bd. 22.95 (0-941677-36-2); audio 12.95 (0-941677-32-X); audio 12.95 (0-941677-71-0) White Cliffs Media.

Xylorama. 1985. 46.50 (0-8176-1709-4) Spr-Verlag.

XYZ: With Tablature. 1990. 19.95 (0-89524-561-2, 02507049) Cherry Lane.

XYZ Adventure in Alphabet Town. Janet McDonnell. LC 92-2985. (Read Around Alphabet Town Ser.). (Illus.). 32p. (J). (ps-2). 1992. lib. bdg. 17.50 (0-516-05424-4) Childrens.

XYZ Affair. William Stinchcombe. LC 80-544. (Contributions in American History Ser.: No. 89). (Illus.). 167p. 1980. text ed. 45.00 (0-313-22234-7, SXY/, Greenwood Pr) Greenwood.

XYZ & Other Stories. Leslie W. Hedley. 151p. (Orig.). 1985. pap. 8.95 (0-933515-07-3) Exile Pr.

XYZ of Psychoanalysis: Epilogue to a Great Beginning. Harold Feldman. LC 87-21749. 192p. 1991. text ed. 49.95 (0-275-93957-X, C3957, Praeger Pubs) Greenwood.

X1-9 Strada 128 Race World. Alfred S. Cosentino. 308p. 1992. 15.95 (0-929991-07-9) A S Cosentino Bks.

X1-9 Strada 128 Race World & Repair Manual. Alfred S. Cosentino. 572p. 1983. 27.95 (0-929991-08-7) A S Cosentino Bks.

X1-9 Strada 128 Race World & Repair Manual. 6th ed. Alfred S. Cosentino. 160p. 1984. 6.00 (0-929991-09-5) A S Cosentino Bks.

X/1999: Prelude. Clamp. 1996. pap. text ed. 15.95 (1-56931-138-2, Viz Comics) Viz Commns Inc.

***X2: A History of American Counterespionage.** Tim Naftali. 352p. Date not set. pap. write for info. (0-465-09282-9) Basic.

***X2: A History of American Counterespionage.** Tim Naftali. 352p. 1998. 25.00 (0-465-09281-0) Basic.

X.25 & Related Protocols. Ulysses D. Black. LC 91-6511. 304p. 1991. 60.00 (0-8186-8976-5, 1976) IEEE Comp Soc.

X.25 & Related Protocols. Harold C. Folts & Kathleen L. Dally. 250p. 1984. 38.50 (0-07-606872-2) McGraw.

X.400 Use of Extended Character Sets. Harald Alvestrand. 18p. (Orig.). (C). 1995. pap. text ed. 25.00 (0-7881-1954-0) DIANE Pub.

X.400(88) for the Academic & Research Community in Europe. 39p. (Orig.). (C). 1995. pap. text ed. 25.00 (0-7881-1938-9) DIANE Pub.

X.500 Standards for Directory Services. Sara Radicati. 1993. 34.00 (0-13-145913-9) P-H.

Y

Y A-t-Il un Docteur dans la Salle? Rene Fallet. (FRE.). 1984. pap. 13.95 (0-7859-2491-4, 2070375684) Fr & Eur.

***Y & Other Stories.** Charles Clerc. LC 96-71248. 216p. (Orig.). 1997. pap. 11.00 (1-889883-01-8) Provine Pr.

Y Aun Podria Ser Agua - It Could Still Be Water. Allan Fowler. LC 92-7402. (Spanish Rookie Read-About Science Ser.). (Illus.). 32p. (SPA.). (J). (ps-2). 1993. pap. 3.95 (0-516-56003-4); lib. bdg. 15.30 (0-516-36003-5) Childrens.

Y-Ba-Cu-O & Related Superconductors: Current Indian Work: A Special Issue of the Journal Phase Transitions, Section B. Ed. by B. A. Dasannacharya & V. K. Wadnawan. 146p. 1989. pap. 290.00 (0-685-47166-7) Gordon & Breach.

Y Basketball Coaches Manual. Ed. by Stephen C. Jefferies & Robert Levin. (Illus.). 40p. 1984. pap. text ed. 7.00 (0-931250-86-2, LYMC4668, YMCA USA) Human Kinetics.

Y Basketball Dribblers Manual: For 5th-6th Grade Players. Ed. by Robert Levin. (Illus.). 40p. (J). (gr. 5-6). 1984. pap. text ed. 5.00 (0-931250-84-6, LYMC4666, YMCA USA) Human Kinetics.

Y Basketball Passers Manual: For 3rd-4th Grade Players. Ed. by Robert Levin. (Illus.). 36p. (J). (gr. 3-4). 1984. pap. text ed. 5.00 (0-931250-83-8, LYMC4665, YMCA USA) Human Kinetics.

Y Basketball Shooters Manual. YMCA of the U. S. A. Staff. Ed. by Robert Levin. 44p. (J). (gr. 7-9). 1985. pap. text ed. 5.00 (0-931250-85-4, LYMC4667, YMCA USA) Human Kinetics.

Y. C. James Yen's Thought on Mass Education & Rural Reconstruction: China & Beyond. 1993. 6.00 (0-942717-46-5) Intl Inst Rural.

Y Chromosome. Leona Gom. 272p. (Orig.). 1993. pap. 14.95 (0-929005-16-3, Pub. by Second Story Pr CN) LPC InBook.

Y Cristo Me Liberto. Orellano Buitrago. (SPA.). 1992. 4.99 (1-56063-214-3, 497708) Editorial Unilit.

***Y Cristo Me Liberto - And Jesus Set Me Free.** Perez Orellano. (SPA.). 1991. write for info. (1-56063-121-X) Editorial Unilit.

Y Domingo, Siete. Robert Baden. Ed. by Judith Mathews. Tr. by Alma F. Ada. LC 89-37823. (Illus.). 40p. (SPA.). (J). (ps-3). 1990. lib. bdg. 14.95 (0-8075-9355-9) A Whitman.

Y. E. S. Shapedown Youth Evaluation Scale. 2nd rev. ed. Laurel M. Mellin. LC 86-71116. (Illus.). 269p. 1986. write for info. (0-935902-10-4) Balboa Pub.

Y Fidel Creo el Punto X. Reinol Gonzalez. (Illus.). 320p. (Orig.). (SPA.). 1987. pap. 10.00 (0-917049-13-6) Saeta.

Y-Fourteen Report: Digital Representation of Physical Object Shapes, No. 1. 1976. 4.00 (0-317-31366-5, N00007) ASME.

Y-Fourteen Report, No. 2: Guideline for Documenting of Computer Systems Used in Computer-Aided Preparation of Product Definition Data - User Instructions Book No. N00078. 1977. pap. text ed. 2.50 (0-685-81929-9) ASME.

Y Geiriadur Mawr: The Complete English Welsh - Welsh English Dictionary. H. Meurig Evans & W. O. Thomas. 367p. (WEL.). (C). 1989. 45.00 (0-85088-462-4, Pub. by Gomer Pr UK) St Mut.

Y Geiriadur Mawr: The Complete Welsh-English, English-Welsh Dictionary. H. Meurig & W. O. Thomas. Ed. by S. J. Williams. 859p. (ENG & WEL.). 1981. 75.00 (0-8288-4684-7, M-9434) Fr & Eur.

Y-Indian Guide Programs: Leader's Manual. YMCA of the U. S. A. Staff. 40p. 1984. pap. text ed. 10.00 (0-931250-78-1, 4657, YMCA USA) Human Kinetics.

***Y-Indian Guide Programs Leaders Manual.** 2nd ed. YMCA of the U. S. A. Staff. (Illus.). 120p. 1997. pap. text ed. write for info. (0-614-31001-6) Human Kinetics.

Y Jesus Sanaba a Todos. Gloria Copeland. Tr. by Copeland, Kenneth, Publications Staff. 43p. (Orig.). (SPA.). 1985. pap. 3.95 (0-88114-315-4) K Copeland Pubns.

Y las Naranjas Azules. Herge. (Illus.). 62p. (SPA.). (J). 19.95 (0-8288-5005-4) Fr & Eur.

Y Los Angeles Guardaron Silencio: La Ultima Semana de Jesus. Max Lucado. 264p. (SPA.). 1992. pap. 7.99 (1-56063-396-4, 498546) Editorial Unilit.

Y Los Castores Trabajadores: The Berenstain Bears. Stan Berenstain & Jan Berenstain. Tr. by DigiPro Staff from ENG. (Comes to Life Bks.). 16p. (SPA.). (J). (ps-2). 1994. write for info. (1-57234-007-X) YES Ent.

Y No Se lo Trago la Tierra. rev. ed. Tomas Rivera. 115p. (SPA.). (YA). (gr. 6-12). 1996. pap. 5.95 (1-55885-151-8, Pinata Bks) Arte Publico.

Y No Se lo Trago la Tierra. 3rd ed. Tomas Rivera. Tr. by Evangelina Vigil. LC 87-70275. 206p. (SPA.). 1995. pap. 10.95 (1-55885-083-X) Arte Publico.

***Y Que Si Jesus, No Hubiera Nacido?/What If Jesus Had Never Been Born?** James Kennedy. 1996. pap. 10.99 (0-89922-293-5) Edit Caribe.

Y Skippers: An Aquatics Program for Children Five & Under. YMCA of the U. S. A. Staff. LC 86-32399. (Illus.). 240p. 1987. spiral bd. 25.00 (0-87322-100-1, LYMC4740, YMCA USA) Human Kinetics.

Y Soccer Coaches Manual. Ed. by Steven D. Houseworth & Stephen C. Jefferies. (Illus.). 40p. (Orig.). 1985. pap. text ed. 7.00 (0-87322-027-7, LYMC4735, YMCA USA) Human Kinetics.

Y Soccer Jugglers Manual. Ed. by Steven D. Houseworth. 44p. 1985. pap. text ed. 5.00 (0-87322-029-3, LYMC4731, YMCA USA) Human Kinetics.

Y Soccer Kickers Manual. Ed. by Steven D. Houseworth. 48p. 1985. pap. text ed. 5.00 (0-87322-028-5, LYMC4730, YMCA USA) Human Kinetics.

Y Soccer Strikers Manual. Ed. by Steven D. Houseworth. 36p. 1985. pap. text ed. 5.00 (0-87322-030-7, LYMC4734, YMCA USA) Human Kinetics.

***Y Track.** G. M. Freeman. 1996. mass mkt. 5.99 (1-55197-043-0, Pub. by Comnwlth Pub CN) Partners Pubs Grp.

Y-Trail Programs Manual. Ed. by YMCA of the U. S. A. Staff. (Illus.). 56p. 1987. text ed. 8.75 (0-87322-117-6, 4894, YMCA USA) Human Kinetics.

Y Tu. Jarvis. 1986. 49.25 (0-03-057507-9) HB Schl Dept.

Y Tu. Jarvis. 1986. text ed. 22.75 (0-03-057513-3) HR&W Schl Div.

Y Tu? Jarvis. (SPA.). 1986. teacher ed., pap. text ed. 63.25 (0-03-057508-7); wbk. ed., pap. text ed. 13.00 (0-03-057509-5) HR&W Schl Div.

Y Tu? Listening Activities. Jarvis. (SPA.). 1989. suppl. ed., pap. text ed. 10.00 (0-03-016678-0); teacher ed., pap. text ed. 16.25 (0-03-022739-9) HR&W Schl Div.

Y Tu? Testing Progress. Jarvis. (SPA.). 1989. suppl. ed., teacher ed., pap. text ed. 19.75 (0-03-022738-0) HR&W Schl Div.

Y Tu? Writing Activities. Jarvis. (SPA.). 1989. suppl. ed., pap. text ed. 13.00 (0-03-016679-9); suppl. ed., teacher ed., pap. text ed. 20.00 (0-03-022742-9) HR&W Schl Div.

Y Tu, Donde Vives? Big Book. Ina Cumpiano. (Que Maravilla! Ser.). (Illus.). 24p. (Orig.). (SPA.). (J). (gr. 1-3). 1992. pap. text ed. 29.95 (1-56334-019-4) Hampton-Brown.

Y Tu, Donde Vives? Small Book. Ina Cumpiano. (Que Maravilla! Ser.). (Illus.). 24p. (Orig.). (SPA.). (J). (gr. 1-3). 1992. pap. text ed. 6.00 (1-56334-045-3) Hampton-Brown.

Y Tu Parte Primera. Jarvis. (SPA.). 1989. teacher ed., pap. text ed. 50.50 (0-03-021423-8) HR&W Schl Div.

Y Tu Parte Segunda. Jarvis. 1988. 31.75 (0-03-022802-6) HR&W Schl Div.

Y Tu Primera, 1989. Jarvis. 1989. 31.75 (0-03-021422-X) HB Schl Dept.

Y Tu Que Dices? 2nd ed. Gene S. Kupferschmid. LC 85-82128. 253p. (C). 1986. pap. text ed. 33.96 (0-669-08902-8) HM College Div.

Y Tu, Que Dices? 3rd ed. Gene S. Kupferschmid. 256p. (SPA.). (C). 1992. Text shrinkwrapped with free student cassette. 33.96 incl. audio (0-669-28283-9); pap. text ed. 33.96 (0-669-20491-9); Instr.'s manual. teacher ed. 2.66 (0-669-28281-2) HM College Div.

Y Tu Spanish 1: 1989. Jarvis. 1989. 49.25 (0-03-014938-X); teacher ed. 59.25 (0-03-014939-8) HB Schl Dept.

Y Twelve M: Solution of Large & Sparse Systems of Linear Algebraic Equations. Zahari Zlatev et al. (Lecture Notes in Computer Science Ser.: Vol. 121). 128p. 1981. 20.00 (0-387-10874-2) Spr-Verlag.

Y Veinte Golpes Por America. Ana R. Nunez. LC 90-82805. (Coleccion Espejo de Paciencia). 48p. (Orig.). (SPA.). 1991. pap. 9.00 (0-89729-571-4) Ediciones.

Ya Basta, Sofia. Louise Leblanc. (Illus.). 60p. (SPA.). (YA). (gr. 5 up). 1994. pap. 5.95 (958-07-0080-X) Firefly Bks Ltd.

Ya Comprendo. Castells. 1990. wbk. ed., pap. text ed. write for info. (0-13-976432-1) P-H.

Ya Comprendo! A Communicative Course in Spanish. Matilda O. De Castells. 544p. (Orig.). (ENG & SPA.). (C). 1990. text ed. write for info. (0-13-976424-0) P-H.

Ya Gotta Wanna. Warren M. Hoffman. (Illus.). 110p. (Orig.). 1981. pap. 4.95 (0-940916-00-2) Daybreak Pr.

Ya No Seas Codependiente. Melody Beattie. 312p. (SPA.). 1994. pap. 15.00 (968-39-0473-4) Hazelden.

Y'A Qu'un Woodstock. Charles M. Schulz. (Peanuts Ser.). (Illus.). (FRE.). (J). 1985. 9.95 (0-8288-4529-8) Fr & Eur.

Y'A Qu'un Woodstock. Charles M. Schulz. LC 81-85097. (Illus.). 1982. pap. 5.95 (0-03-061654-9, Owl) H Holt & Co.

Ya Se Ingles. (Passport's Pull-Tab Language Bks.). (Illus.). 10p. (ENG & SPA.). (J). 1994. 12.95 (0-8442-9186-2, Passport Bks) NTC Pub Grp.

Scorpion Shards #2. Neal Shusterman. (YA). 1996. 17.95 (0-312-85507-9) Tor Bks.

Ya Veras!, Level III. Gutierrez et al. 1992. text ed. 53.95 (0-8384-2194-6) Heinle & Heinle.

Ya Veras!, Level III. Gutierrez et al. 1992. pap. 15.95 (0-8384-2196-2) Heinle & Heinle.

Ya Veras: Lab Manual A (Units 1-3), Level 1. Gutierrez. (Secondary Spanish Ser.). 1995. lab manual ed., wbk. ed., pap. 9.95 (0-8384-5468-2) Heinle & Heinle.

Ya Veras: Level 2. Gutierrez. (Secondary Spanish Ser.). (C). 1994. teacher ed., text ed. 53.95 (0-8384-5076-8) Heinle & Heinle.

Ya Veras Level 1. Gutierrez. (Secondary Spanish Ser.). 1991. suppl. ed. 130.00 incl. trans. (0-8384-2038-9) Heinle & Heinle.

Ya Veras Level 1. Gutierrez. (Secondary Spanish Ser.). (SPA.). 1995. wbk. ed., pap. 18.95 (0-8384-5566-2) Heinle & Heinle.

Ya Veras Level 1. expanded rev. ed. Gutierrez. (Secondary Spanish Ser.). (SPA.). 1995. teacher ed., text ed. 56.95 (0-8384-4874-7) Heinle & Heinle.

Ya Veras Level 1. rev. ed. Gutierrez. (Secondary Spanish Ser.). (SPA.). 1995. suppl. ed., pap. 21.95 (0-8384-4859-3); suppl. ed., pap. 182.95 (0-8384-4871-2); text ed. 46.95 (0-8384-4855-0) Heinle & Heinle.

Ya Veras Level 1. rev. ed. Gutierrez. (Secondary Spanish Ser.). (SPA.). 1995. wbk. ed., pap. 15.95 (0-8384-4857-7); suppl. ed., wbk. ed., pap. 6.95 (0-8384-4872-0) Heinle & Heinle.

Ya Veras Level 1. rev. ed. Gutierrez. (Secondary Spanish Ser.). (SPA.). 1995. teacher ed., pap. 36.95 (0-8384-4856-9) Heinle & Heinle.

Ya Veras Level 1. 2nd ed. Gutierrez. (Secondary Spanish Ser.). (SPA.). 1997. teacher ed., pap. 38.95 (0-8384-6186-7); suppl. ed., pap. 196.95 (0-8384-6200-6); suppl. ed. 130.95 incl. 3.5 hd, 5.25 hd, 3.5 ld (0-8384-6185-9); suppl. ed. 130.95 incl. mac hd, mac ld (0-8384-6204-9) Heinle & Heinle.

Ya Veras Level 1. 2nd ed. Gutierrez. (Secondary Spanish Ser.). (SPA.). 1997. teacher ed., wbk. ed., pap. 17.95 (0-8384-6184-0) Heinle & Heinle.

Ya Veras Level 1. 2nd ed. Gutierrez. (Secondary Spanish Ser.). (SPA.). 1997. lab manual ed., wbk. ed., pap. 16.95 (0-8384-6183-2); teacher ed., pap. 58.95 (0-8384-6196-4); lab manual ed., suppl. ed. 360.95 incl. audio (0-8384-6188-3) Heinle & Heinle.

Ya Veras Level 1. 2nd ed. Gutierrez. (Secondary Spanish Ser.). (SPA.). 1997. suppl. ed. 32.95 incl. audio (0-8384-6197-2) Heinle & Heinle.

Ya Veras Level 1: Primer Nivel. 2nd ed. John R. Gutierrez et al. (Secondary Spanish Ser.). (SPA.). 1997. 49.95 (0-8384-6176-X) Heinle & Heinle.

Ya Veras Level 1: Text B. 2nd ed. Gutierrez. (Secondary Spanish Ser.). (SPA.). 1996. wbk. ed., pap. 4.95 (0-8384-6182-4); text ed. 36.95 (0-8384-6180-8) Heinle & Heinle.

Ya Veras Units 1-3: Student Book A (Units 1-3), Level 1. rev. ed. Gutierrez. (Secondary Spanish Ser.). 1995. text ed. 37.95 (0-8384-5467-4) Heinle & Heinle.

Ya Veras! Level I. Harry L. Rosser et al. 1991. text ed. 36.00 (0-8384-2010-9) Heinle & Heinle.

Ya Veras! Level I. Harry L. Rosser et al. 1991. pap. 15.95 (0-8384-2011-7) Heinle & Heinle.

Ya Veras Level 2. Gutierrez. (Secondary Spanish Ser.). (SPA.). 1991. text ed. 39.00 (0-8384-3917-9) Heinle & Heinle.

Ya Veras Level 2. Gutierrez. (Secondary Spanish Ser.). 1991. wbk. ed., pap. 6.95 (0-8384-2614-X) Heinle & Heinle.

Ya Veras Level 2. Gutierrez. (Secondary Spanish Ser.). 1991. suppl. ed. 130.00 incl. trans. (0-8384-2043-5) Heinle & Heinle.

Ya Veras! Level 2. Harry L. Rosser et al. 1991. pap. 13.95 (0-8384-2013-3) Heinle & Heinle.

Ya Veras Level 2. expanded rev. ed. Gutierrez. (Secondary Spanish Ser.). (SPA.). 1995. teacher ed., text ed. 57.95 (0-8384-4895-X) Heinle & Heinle.

Ya Veras Level 2. rev. ed. Gutierrez. (Secondary Spanish Ser.). (SPA.). 1995. suppl. ed., pap. 17.95 (0-8384-4889-5) Heinle & Heinle.

Ya Veras Level 2. rev. ed. Gutierrez. (Secondary Spanish Ser.). (SPA.). 1995. wbk. ed., pap. 6.95 (0-8384-4881-X); suppl. ed., pap. 218.95 (0-8384-4885-2) Heinle & Heinle.

Ya Veras Level 2. rev. ed. Gutierrez. (Secondary Spanish Ser.). (SPA.). 1995. wbk. ed., pap. 15.95 (0-8384-4880-1); text ed. 53.95 (0-8384-4878-X) Heinle & Heinle.

Ya Veras Level 2. rev. ed. Gutierrez. (Secondary Spanish Ser.). (SPA.). 1995. wbk. ed., pap. 18.95 (0-8384-5567-0) Heinle & Heinle.

Ya Veras Level 2. 2nd ed. Gutierrez. (Secondary Spanish Ser.). (SPA.). 1997. teacher ed., wbk. ed., pap. 14.95 (0-8384-6213-8); teacher ed., pap. 58.95 (0-8384-6214-6) Heinle & Heinle.

Ya Veras Level 2. 2nd ed. Gutierrez. (Secondary Spanish Ser.). (SPA.). 1997. lab manual ed., wbk. ed., pap. 16.95 (0-8384-6212-X); suppl. ed., pap. 218.95 (0-8384-6217-0) Heinle & Heinle.

Ya Veras Level 2: Segundo Nivel. 2nd ed. John R. Gutierrez & Harry L. Rosser. LC 95-45122. (Secondary Spanish Ser.). (SPA.). 1997. student ed., text ed. 50.95 (0-8384-6177-8) Heinle & Heinle.

Ya Veras Level 3. Gutierrez. (Secondary Spanish Ser.). 1991. suppl. ed., pap. 87.95 (0-8384-2382-5) Heinle & Heinle.

Ya Veras Level 3. Gutierrez. (Secondary Spanish Ser.). 1992. suppl. ed. 75.00 incl. trans. (0-8384-2381-7) Heinle & Heinle.

Ya Veras Level 3. annot. ed. Gutierrez. (Secondary Spanish Ser.). (SPA.). 1994. teacher ed., text ed. 54.95 (0-8384-5077-6) Heinle & Heinle.

Ya Veras Level 3. expanded rev. ed. Gutierrez. (Secondary Spanish Ser.). (SPA.). 1995. teacher ed., wbk. ed., text ed. 59.95 (0-8384-4913-1) Heinle & Heinle.

An Asterisk (*) at the beginning of an entry indicates that the title is appearing in BIP for the first time.

Ya Veras Level 3. rev. ed. Gutierrez. (Secondary Spanish Ser.). (SPA.). 1995. suppl. ed., wbk. ed., pap. 6.95 (*0-8384-4903-4*); lab manual ed., suppl. ed., wbk. ed. 321.95 incl. audio (*0-8384-4905-0*) Heinle & Heinle.

Ya Veras Level 3. rev. ed. Gutierrez. (Secondary Spanish Ser.). (SPA.). 1995. suppl. ed., wbk. ed., pap. 182.95 (*0-8384-4907-7*) Heinle & Heinle.

Ya Veras Level 3. rev. ed. Gutierrez. (Secondary Spanish Ser.). (SPA.). 1995. text ed. 49.95 (*0-8384-4900-X*) Heinle & Heinle.

Ya Veras Level 3. rev. ed. Gutierrez. (Secondary Spanish Ser.). (SPA.). 1995. lab manual ed., wbk. ed., pap. 15.95 (*0-8384-4902-6*) Heinle & Heinle.

Ya Veras Level 3. rev. ed. Gutierrez. (Secondary Spanish Ser.). (SPA.). 1995. wbk. ed., pap. 18.95 (*0-8384-5568-9*) Heinle & Heinle.

Ya Veras Level 3. 2nd ed. Gutierrez. (Secondary Spanish Ser.). (SPA.). 1997. lab manual ed., wbk. ed., pap. 16.95 (*0-8384-6236-7*); teacher ed., wbk. ed., pap. 17.95 (*0-8384-6237-5*); suppl. ed., pap. 32.95 (*0-8384-6238-3*); student ed., text ed. 52.95 (*0-8384-6178-6*) Heinle & Heinle.

Ya Veras Level 3. 2nd ed. Gutierrez. (Secondary Spanish Ser.). (SPA.). 1997. teacher ed., pap. 58.95 (*0-8384-6239-1*) Heinle & Heinle.

Ya Veras Level 3. 2nd ed. Gutierrez. (Secondary Spanish Ser.). (SPA.). 1997. suppl. ed. 69.95 incl. trans. (*0-8384-6242-1*) Heinle & Heinle.

Ya Wanna Make a Movie: An Anthology. Mike Hirsch. Ed. by Carol Hirsch. 100p. Date not set. pap. 29.95 (*1-888349-03-4*) Katydid.

Ya, Ya! Those Were the Days! Nostalgic Tales of the Past. Bob Becker. (Illus.). 197p. 1993. pap. 8.95 (*1-885548-01-X*) Boot Prints.

Yabba Dabba Dinosaur. A. Child. (Cityscapes Ser.). 23p. (J). (gr. k). 1992. pap. text ed. 23.00 (*1-56843-009-4*); pap. text ed. 4.50 (*1-56843-059-0*) BGR Pub.

YAC Libraries: A User's Guide. Ed. by David L. Nelson & Bernard H. Brownstein. LC 93-13780. (University of Wisconsin Biotechnology Center Biotechnical Resource Ser.). (Illus.). 240p. 1993. pap. text ed. 48.00 (*0-7167-7014-8*) OUP.

YAC Protocols. Ed. by David Markie. LC 95-20892. (Methods in Molecular Biology Ser.: No. 54). (Illus.). 384p. 1995. spiral bd. 69.50 (*0-89603-313-9*) Humana.

Yachas Harav V'hatalmid. (HEB.). 1.00 (*0-914131-75-3*, D901) Torah Umesorah.

Yacht Care. Hinckley. LC 97-15960. 1997. text ed. 39.95 (*0-07-028997-2*) McGraw.

Yacht Chef's Guide to Freelancing. Jacqueline T. Mei. LC 95-68752. 80p. (Orig.). 1995. pap. text ed. 15.00 (*0-9646837-0-9*) Clouseau Pubns.

Yacht Construction for Beginners: How to Loft & Construct a Carvel Plank Sailing Yacht. rev. ed. Russel A. Boykiw, II. LC 93-86260. 176p. (Orig.). 1994. pap. 23.00 (*0-9638646-2-9*) Ligeia Pubns.

***Yacht Designing & Planning.** Howard I. Chapelle. 1996. text ed. 35.00 (*0-07-011679-2*) McGraw.

Yacht Designing & Planning: For Yachtsmen, Students, & Amateurs. Howard I. Chapell. (Illus.). 375p. 1995. 35.00 (*0-393-03756-8*) Norton.

Yacht Designs Two. William Garden. (Illus.). xii, 196p. 1992. 39.95 (*0-913372-61-7*) Mystic Seaport.

Yacht Master Offshore & Ocean. P. Clissold. (C). 1987. 75.00 (*0-85174-261-0*, Pub. by Brwn Son Ferg) St Mut.

Yacht Owners Register, 1984. (Illus.). 1152p. 1984. 85.00 (*0-915953-00-5*) Yacht Owners.

Yacht Racing Protests & Appeals. Jack Feller. 7.95 (*0-393-60008-4*) Norton.

***Yacht Style: Design & Decor Ideas for Your Boat.** Daniel Spurr. (Illus.). 320p. 1997. pap. text ed. 39.95 (*0-07-060563-7*) McGraw.

Yacht Style: Design & Decor Ideas from the World's Finest Yachts. Daniel Spurr. 1991. text ed. 49.95 (*0-07-157982-6*) McGraw.

Yacht Style: Designs & Decor Ideas from the World's Finest Yachts. Daniel Spurr. (Illus.). 336p. 1990. text ed. 49.95 (*0-87742-261-3*) Intl Marine.

Yachting. Meyer. Date not set. pap. 12.50 (*0-312-89529-1*) St Martin.

Yachting: The History of a Passion. Robin Knox-Johnston. LC 90-71511. (Illus.). 168p. 1990. 39.95 (*0-688-09991-2*, Hearst Marine Bks) Morrow.

Yachting Cookbook. Elizabeth Wheeler. 1990. 30.00 (*0-517-56883-7*, Crown) Crown Pub Group.

Yachting Dictionary. A. Tetsmann. 192p. (ENG, EST & RUS.). 1980. 14.95 (*0-8288-0431-1*, M 15596) Fr & Eur.

Yachting Dictionary: English-German, German-English. Joachim Schult. 496p. (ENG & GER.). 1994. 49.95 (*0-7859-9992-2*) Fr & Eur.

Yachting Guide to Bermuda. Ed. by Jane Harris & Edward Harris. (Illus.). 164p. 1994. pap. 16.95 (*1-877838-10-1*) Bluewater Bks.

Yachting in America: A Bibliography. Gerald E. Morris & Llewellyn Howland, III. x, 398p. 1991. 49.95 (*0-913372-49-8*) Mystic Seaport.

Yachting Signal Book. James R. Collier. LC 84-45262. (Illus.). 128p. 1985. 17.50 (*0-87033-324-0*) Cornell Maritime.

Yachtman's Emergency Handbook. rev. ed. Neil Hollander & Harald Mertes. Ed. by John R. Whiting. LC 86-12070. (Illus.). 288p. 1986. 19.95 (*0-688-06610-0*, Hearst Marine Bks) Morrow.

Yachtman's Legal Guide to Co-Ownership. Paula Odin & Dexter Odin. 166p. 1981. 4.95 (*0-8286-0104-6*, 60765) J De Graff.

Yachtmaster: An Examination Handbook with Exercises. 2nd ed. Pat L. Price & Philip Ouvry. (Illus.). 288p. 1993. 29.95 (*0-7136-3772-2*) Sheridan.

Yachtmaster Exercises. 2nd ed. Pat L. Price & Philip Ouvry. (Illus.). 128p. 1993. pap. 23.50 (*0-7136-3810-9*, Pub. by Adlard Coles UK) Sheridan.

Yachts & Yachting. Vanderdecken. 1979. reprint ed. 60.00 (*0-85967-568-8*, Pub. by Scolar Pr UK) Ashgate Pub Co.

Yachts in a Hurry. S. Philip Moore. 160p. 1994. 40.00 (*0-393-03576-X*) Norton.

Yachtsman's Almanac, 1992. Ed. by Michael B. Balmforth. (C). 1989. 80.00 (*0-685-54759-0*, Pub. by Imray Laurie Norie & Wilson UK) St Mut.

Yachtsman's Eight Language Dictionary. B. Webb. 160p. (DAN, DUT, ENG, FRE, GER, ITA, POR & SPA.). 1983. pap. 29.95 (*0-8288-8030-1*) Fr & Eur.

Yachtsman's Emergency Handbook. Neil Hollander & Harald Mertes. LC 86-12070. (Illus.). 320p. 1980. 18.45 (*0-87851-803-7*) Hearst Bks.

Yachtsman's Fiji. Michael Calder. 249p. (C). 1989. 115.00 (*0-685-40363-7*, Pub. by Imray Laurie Norie & Wilson UK) St Mut.

Yachtsman's Guide to the Atlantic Coasts of Spain & Portugal. D. M. Sloma et al. 140p. 1983. 100.00 (*0-85288-087-1*, Pub. by Imray Laurie Norie & Wilson UK) St Mut.

Yachtsman's Guide to the Bahamas. rev. ed. Tropic Isle Publishers, Inc. Staff. Ed. by Meredith Fields. (1996 Edition Ser.: No. 46). (Illus.). 470p. 1995. spiral bd. 31.95 (*0-937379-18-2*) Tropic Isle Pub.

Yachtsman's Guide to the Virgin Islands. 12th rev. ed. (Illus.). 256p. 1995. spiral bd. 15.95 (*0-937379-17-4*) Tropic Isle Pub.

Yachtsman's Pilot to the West Coast of Scotland: Clyde to Colonsay. Martin Lawrence. (Illus.). 152p. (C). 1993. pap. 36.95 (*0-85288-132-0*, Pub. by Imray Laurie Norie & Wilson UK) Bluewater Bks.

Yachtsman's Pilot to the West Coast of Scotland: Crinan to Canna. Martin Lawrence. (Illus.). 164p. 1994. pap. 36.95 (*0-85288-250-5*, Pub. by Imray Laurie Norie & Wilson UK) Bluewater Bks.

Yachtsman's Pilot to the West Coast of Scotland: Crinan to Canna. Martin Lawrence. 170p. (C). 1987. 110.00 (*0-85288-107-X*, Pub. by Imray Laurie Norie & Wilson UK) St Mut.

Yachtsman's Pilots Vol. V: The Scilly Isles. Robin Brandon. 40p. 1983. 100.00 (*0-85288-090-1*, Pub. by Imray Laurie Norie & Wilson UK) St Mut.

***Yachtsman's Ten Language Dictionary.** Barbara Webb & Michael Manton. 1997. pap. text ed. 23.50 (*0-07-068758-7*) McGraw.

Yachtsman's Ten Language Dictionary. enl. rev. ed. Cruising Association Staff et al. (Illus.). 160p. 1995. pap. 23.50 (*0-924486-96-1*) Sheridan.

Yad B'Yad Bowl-A-Thon see Kadima Kesher Series

***Yad Vashem: Children's Holocaust Memorial, Jerusalem.** 2nd limited large type ed. Peter Balakian. (Press of Appletree Alley Poets Ser.). (Illus.). 8p. 1996. pap. 45.00 (*0-916375-26-9*) Press Alley.

Yad Vashem Studies, Vol. XIV. 412p. 1988. 24.95 (*0-944007-34-1*) Sure Seller.

Yad Vashem Studies, Vol. XVIII. 406p. 1988. 24.95 (*0-933503-19-9*) Sure Seller.

Yad Vashem Studies, Vols. XVIII & XIX. 1988. write for info. (*0-318-63947-5*) Sure Seller.

***Yaderny Materialy Skvoz' Tuskoe Steklo? Tekhnicheskie i Politicheskie Aspekty Utilizatsii Plutonia i Vysokoobogaschennogo Urana.** Arjun Makhijani & Annie Makhijani. (Illus.). 132p. (Orig.). (RUS.). 1996. pap. write for info. (*0-614-30149-1*) IEER.

***Yadkin County, NC.** F. Casstevens. (Images of America Ser.). pap. 16.99 (*0-7524-0522-5*, Arcdia) Chalford.

Yadkin County, North Carolina Marriage Bonds & Certificates, 1851-1868. Francis T. Ingmire. 52p. 1994. pap. 10.00 (*0-8095-8713-0*); lib. bdg. 29.00 (*0-8095-8375-5*) Borgo Pr.

Yadong to Golmud Transect Qinghai-Tibet Plateau, China. 1991. 95.00 (*0-87590-780-6*, GGT 3) Am Geophysical.

Yaffa, God's Prickly Pear. Yaffa McPherson. LC 92-97176. 208p. (Orig.). 1992. pap. 10.95 (*0-9634792-0-2*) Intimate Awe.

Yag Laser Bronchoscopy. Jean-Francois Dumon et al. LC 84-26310. 128p. 1985. text ed. 45.00 (*0-275-91311-2*, C1311, Praeger Pubs) Greenwood.

Yage Letters. William S. Burroughs & Allen Ginsberg. LC 63-12222. (Orig.). 1963. pap. 8.95 (*0-87286-004-3*) City Lights.

Yagi Antenna Design. Lawson. 1986. 15.00 (*0-87259-041-0*) Am Radio.

Yagna (The Eternal Energy) Frwd. by Panduranga R. Malyala. (Illus.). 36p. (Orig.). 1984. pap. text ed. 5.00 (*0-938924-23-0*) Sri Shirdi Sai.

***Yagruma Nights.** Rodolfo Labourdette. 295p. (Orig.). 1996. pap. 15.00 (*0-9653347-0-8*) Transpersonal.

***Yagua Days.** Cruz Martel. (Illus.). (J). (gr. 3). 1995. 7.92 (*0-395-73235-2*) HM.

***Yagua Days.** large type ed. Cruz Martel. (Illus.). 62p. (J). (gr. 3). 15.50 (*0-614-20630-8*, L-38177-00 APHB) Am Printing Hse.

Yagua Mythology: Epic Tendencies in a New World Mythology. Paul S. Powlison. Ed. by William R. Merrifield. LC 84-63152. (International Museum of Cultures Publications: No. 16). (Illus.). 132p. (Orig.). 1985. fiche 8.00 (*0-88312-254-5*) Summer Instit Ling.

Yahoo! Unplugged: Your Discovery Guide to the World Wide Web 1996 Edition. Jerry Yang. 1995. pap. 39.99 (*1-56884-715-7*) IDG Bks.

Yahoo! Wild Web Rides. Ken Badertscher. 1996. pap. 24.99 (*0-7645-7003-X*) IDG Bks.

Yahweh: Shepherd of the People: Pastoral Symbolism in the Old Testament. Elena Bosetti. 174p. 1993. 40.00 (*0-85439-441-9*, Pub. by St Paul Pubns UK) St Mut.

Yahweh & the Gods of Canaan: An Historical Analysis of Two Contrasting Faiths. William F. Albright. xiv, 294p. 1990. reprint ed. 29.50 (*0-931464-01-3*) Eisenbrauns.

Yahweh & the Sun: Biblical & Archaeological Evidence for Sun Worship in Ancient Israel. Glen Taylor. (Journal for the Study of the Old Testament Supplement Ser.: Vol. 111). 308p. 60.00 (*1-85075-272-9*, Pub. by Sheffield Acad UK) CUP Services.

Yahweh-Baal Confrontation & Other Studies in Biblical Literature & Archaeology: Essays in Honour of Emmett Willard Hamrick. Ed. by Julia M. O'Brien & Fred L. Horton, Jr. LC 95-1377. (Studies in Bible & Early Christianity: Vol. 35). (Illus.). 194p. 1995. text ed. 79.95 (*0-7734-2426-1*, Mellen Biblical Pr) E Mellen.

Yahweh Encounters: Bible Astronauts, Ark Radiations & Temple Electronics. Ann Madden. Ed. by Joanye P. Jones. (Illus.). 373p. (Orig.). 1995. pap. 13.95 (*0-9615111-2-5*) Sandbird Pub.

Yahweh Is a Warrior. Millard C. Lind. LC 80-16038. (Christian Peace Shelf Ser.). 248p. 1980. pap. 14.99 (*0-8361-1233-4*) Herald Pr.

Yahweh the Patriarch: Ancient Images of God & Feminist Theology. Erhard S. Gerstenberger. Tr. by Frederick J. Gaiser. LC 96-18044. 176p. 1996. pap. 16.00 (*0-8006-2843-8*, Fortress Pr) Augsburg Fortress.

Yahweh's Activity in History & Nature in the Book of Joel. Ronald Simkins. LC 91-31164. (Ancient Near Eastern Texts & Studies: Vol. 10). 336p. 1991. lib. bdg. 99.95 (*0-7734-9683-1*) E Mellen.

Yahweh's Wife: The Influence of Sex in the Development of Monotheism; a Study of Yahweh & the Goddess Asherah in the Old Testament. Arthur F. Ide. LC 91-36135. (Woman in History Ser.: Vol. 19). 113p. (Orig.). 1991. pap. 15.00 (*0-930383-23-0*) Monument Pr.

Yahwist's Landscape: Nature & Religion in Early Israel. Theodore Hiebert. LC 95-11578. 232p. 1996. 45.00 (*0-19-509205-8*) OUP.

***Yahya: The Forebearing Prophet.** Amina I. Ali. Ed. by J. C. Cinquino. (Prophets' Stories for Children from the Holy Qur'an Ser.: No. 19). (Illus.). 28p. (Orig.). (J). (gr. 4-6). 1996. write for info. (*1-881963-40-3*); pap. 2.50 (*1-881963-41-1*) Al-Saadawi Pubns.

Yaina Shel Torah Haggadah. Binyamin Adler. Tr. by Yaakov Lavon. 1993. 14.95 (*0-87306-642-1*) Feldheim.

***Yairy Tale.** Jillian Hunter. 1997. mass mkt. 5.99 (*0-671-00157-4*) PB.

Yajnavalkya Smriti: With the Commentary of Vijnanesvara, Called the Mitaksara, & Notes from the Gloss of Balambhatta. Yajnavalkya. Tr. by Srisa Chandra Vidyarnava. LC 73-3813. (Sacred Books of the Hindus: No. 21). reprint ed. 48.00 (*0-404-57821-7*) AMS Pr.

Yajnavalkya's Smriti: With the Commentary of Vijnanesvara, Called the Mitaksara, & the Gloss of Balambhatta. Yajnavalkya. Tr. by Srisa Chandra Vasu. LC 73-3787. (Sacred Books of the Hindus: No. 2). reprint ed. 19.50 (*0-404-57802-0*) AMS Pr.

Yajur Veda. Bibek Debroy. (Great Epics of India Ser.: Veda 2). (C). 1992. pap. 3.00 (*0-8364-2780-7*, Pub. by BR Pub II) S Asia.

Yajur Veda. Tr. by Devichand. 479p. 1992. 27.50 (*0-685-72923-0*, Pub. by Sarvadeshik Arya II) Nataraj Bks.

***Yajurveda.** Devi Chand. (C). 1994. 30.00 (*81-215-0294-2*, Pub. by Munshiram Manoharial II) S Asia.

Yajurveda (Summary) 5.00 (*0-938924-30-3*) Sri Shirdi Sai.

Yak Butter & Black Tea: A Journey into Forbidden China. Wade Brackenbury. 252p. 1997. 19.95 (*1-56512-148-1*) Algonquin Bks.

Yak Yak Yak: Mike Yaconelli's Guide to Jerk-Free Christianity. Mike Yaconelli & James Tweed. 160p. 1992. 7.99 (*0-551-02466-6*) HarpC.

Yaka. Pepetela. Tr. by Marga Heinemann. (African Writers Ser.). 307p. 1996. pap. 11.95 (*0-435-90962-2*) Heinemann.

***Yakama.** Edward R. Ricciuti. LC 97-5899. (Native American People Ser.). (Illus.). (J). 1997. write for info. (*0-86625-604-0*) Rourke Pubns.

Yakety-Yak: The Midnight Confessions & Revelation of Thirty-Seven Rock Stars & Legends. Scott Cohen. 192p. 1994. pap. 12.50 (*0-671-88092-6*, Fireside) S&S Trade.

Yakima see Indians of North America

Yakima, Palouse, Cayuse, Umatilla, Walla Walla, & Wanapum Indians: An Historical Bibliography. Clifford E. Trafzer. LC 91-41052. (Native American Bibliography Ser.: No. 16). 263p. 1992. 32.50 (*0-8108-2517-1*) Scarecrow.

Yakima River, WA. Steve Probasco. (River Journal Ser.: Vol. 2, No. 2). (Illus.). 48p. 1994. pap. 14.95 (*1-878175-75-0*) F Amato Pubns.

Yakko's World: Animaniacs. Ed. by Debbie Cavalier. 72p. (Orig.). (YA). 1995. pap. text ed. 9.95 (*0-89724-581-4*, PF9513) Warner Brothers.

***Yakov Ilich Frenkel: His Work, Life & Letters.** V. Frenkel. 323p. 1996. 159.50 (*3-7643-2741-3*) Birkhauser.

***Yakovlev Aircraft since 1924.** Bill Gunston & Yefim Gordon. (Putnam Aviation Ser.). (Illus.). 288p. 1997. 59.95 (*1-55750-978-6*) Naval Inst Pr.

Yaksas: Essays in the Water Cosmology. Ananda K. Coomaraswamy. Ed. by Paul Schroeder. (Illus.). 358p. (C). 1994. 38.00 (*0-19-563385-7*) OUP.

Yakshagana: A Dance Drama of India. Martha B. Ashton. 1977. 35.00 (*0-88386-972-1*) S Asia.

Yakshi from Didarganj. P. Lal. 42p. 1973. 8.00 (*0-88253-267-7*); 4.00 (*0-89253-518-0*) Ind-US Inc.

Yakubu Gowon: Faith in a United Nigeria. J. D. Clarke. (Illus.). 150p. 1986. 32.50 (*0-7146-3286-4*, Pub. by F Cass Pubs UK) Intl Spec Bk.

Yakusan: Straight to the Point of Enlightenment. Osho. Ed. by Anand Robin. (Zen Ser.). 224p. 1992. 14.95 (*3-89338-084-1*, Pub. by Rebel Hse GW) Osho America.

Yakutia Before Its Incorporation into the Russian State. Alekseui P. Okladnikov. LC 71-102976. (Arctic Institute of North America-Anthropology of the North; Translation from Russian Sources Ser.: No. 8). (Illus.). 541p. reprint ed. pap. 154.20 (*0-7837-1171-9*, 2041700) Bks Demand.

Yakuza: The Japanese Godfather. Steven Schlossstein. 320p. 1990. 19.95 (*0-9627060-1-9*) Stratford Bks.

Yakuza Diary: Doing Time in the Japanese Underworld. Christopher Seymour. 208p. 1996. 21.00 (*0-87113-604-X*, Atlntc Mnthly) Grove-Atltic.

Yakuza, Go Home! A Mark Shigata Mystery. large type ed. Anne Wingate. LC 93-11416. 335p. 1993. reprint ed. lib. bdg. 20.95 (*0-7862-0009-X*) Thorndike Pr.

Yakuza Perfume. Akahige Namban. 1992. mass mkt. 5.95 (*0-929654-85-4*, 119) Blue Moon Bks.

Yale Bowl & the Open Trolleys. John D. Somers. 56p. 1996. 16.00 (*0-8059-3985-7*) Dorrance.

***Yale Center for British Art at Twenty: A Living Tribute to Louis Kahn.** Duncan Robinson & Louis Kahn. LC 97-5923. 1997. pap. write for info. (*0-300-06972-3*) Yale U Pr.

Yale Classical Studies, Vol. 19. Ed. by Lawrence Richardson. 292p. reprint ed. pap. 83.30 (*0-8357-8388-X*, 2033871) Bks Demand.

Yale Clock Company, New Haven, Conn. 1981. pap. 4.50 (*0-930476-08-5*) Am Clock & Watch.

Yale Collects Yale: 1950-1993. Nicholas F. Weber. Ed. by Sasha N. Newman & Lesley K. Baier. (Illus.). 1993. pap. 25.00 (*0-89467-064-6*) Yale Art Gallery.

***Yale Companion to Jewish Writing & Thought in German Culture, 1096-1996.** Sander L. Gilman & Jack D. Zipes. LC 96-49583. 1997. write for info. (*0-300-06824-7*) Yale U Pr.

Yale Critics: Deconstruction in America. Ed. by Jonathan Arac et al. LC 83-1127. (Theory & History of Literature Ser.: No. 6). 260p. reprint ed. pap. 74.10 (*0-7837-2979-0*, 2057475) Bks Demand.

***Yale Daily News Tips from Top Students.** Yale Daily News Staff. 1997. 15.00 (*0-684-83757-9*) S&S Trade.

Yale Edition of Horace Walpole's Correspondence, Vol. 43. Horace Walpole. Ed. by Edwine M. Martz et al. LC 65-11182. 408p. 1983. text ed. 80.00 (*0-300-02711-7*) Yale U Pr.

Yale Edition of Horace Walpole's Correspondence, Vols. 44-48. Horace Walpole. Ed. by Warren H. Smith et al. LC 65-11182. 424p. 1983. text ed. 400.00 (*0-300-02718-4*) Yale U Pr.

Yale Edition of the Shorter Poems of Edmund Spenser. Edmund Spenser. Ed. by William A. Oram et al. 860p. (C). 1989. pap. 22.00 (*0-300-04245-0*); text ed. 65.00 (*0-300-04244-2*) Yale U Pr.

Yale French Studies: Corps Mystique, Corps Sacre, Textual Transfigurations of the Body Form, Vol. 86. Francoise Jaouen. 1994. pap. text ed. 17.00 (*0-300-06193-5*) Yale U Pr.

Yale French Studies, 84: Boundaries: Writing & Drawing. Ed. by Martine Reid. 1993. 17.00 (*0-300-05836-5*) Yale U Pr.

Yale French Studies, 85: Discourses of Jewish Identity in Twentieth-Century France. Alan Astro. 1994. pap. 17.00 (*0-300-06015-7*) Yale U Pr.

***Yale French Studies, 89.** Ed. by Michel Contat et al. pap. 17.00 (*0-300-06708-9*) Yale U Pr.

***Yale French Studies, 90: Same Sex/Different Text? Gay & Lesbian Writing in French.** Brigitte Mahuzier et al. 1996. pap. 17.00 (*0-300-06955-3*) Yale U Pr.

***Yale French Studies, 92: Exploring the Conversible World: Text & Sociability from the Classical Age to the Enlightenment.** Ed. by Elena Russo. pap. 18.00 (*0-300-07329-1*) Yale U Pr.

Yale Genealogy: And History of Wales (with Biographies) Rodney H. Yale. (Illus.). 597p. 1993. reprint ed. pap. 91.00 (*0-8328-3438-6*); reprint ed. lib. bdg. 101.00 (*0-8328-3437-8*) Higginson Bk Co.

Yale Gertrude Stein. Gertrude Stein. LC 80-5398. 480p. 1980. pap. 22.00 (*0-300-02609-9*) Yale U Pr.

***Yale Guide to Children's Nutrition.** William V. Tamborlane & Janet Z. Weiswasser. LC 96-44774. 1997. write for info. (*0-300-06965-0*) Yale U Pr.

***Yale Guide to Children's Nutrition.** Ed. by William V. Tamborlane. 1997. pap. 18.00 (*0-300-07169-8*) Yale U Pr.

Yale in the World War, 2 vols. George H. Nettleton. 1925. 300.00 (*0-685-40002-6*) Elliots Bks.

Yale Law Journal: 1891-1995/96, 105 vols., Set. Bound set. 6,227.50 (*0-8377-9188-X*) Rothman.

Yale Lectures on Preaching. Henry W. Beecher. 1976. reprint ed. 49.00 (*0-403-06546-1*, Regency) Scholarly.

Yale Lectures on Preaching. Henry W. Beecher. (Works of Henry Ward Beecher). vii, 359p. reprint ed. lib. bdg. 59.00 (*0-7812-0911-0*) Rprt Serv.

Yale Lock Company Advertising Catalog of 1912. (Illus.). 200p. 1989. pap. 25.00 (*0-87556-175-6*) Saifer.

Yale Manuscript. Matthew Arnold. 1988. text ed. 55.00 (*0-472-10105-6*) U of Mich Pr.

Yale North India Expedition. Ezra T. Cresson, Jr. et al. (Connecticut Academy of Arts & Sciences Ser., Trans.: Vol. 10, Articles 1-9). 1934. pap. 200.00 (*0-685-44365-5*) Elliots Bks.

Yale North India Expedition. Carl W. Verhoeff et al. (Connecticut Academy of Arts & Sciences Ser., Trans.: Vol. 10, Articles 10-18). 1936. pap. 200.00 (*0-685-44366-3*) Elliots Bks.

Yale North India Expedition. Roger P. Wodehouse. (Connecticut Academy of Arts & Sciences Ser., Trans.: Vol. 9, Articles 1-4). 1935. pap. 100.00 (*0-685-22861-4*) Elliots Bks.

Yale North India Expedition: Geological Studies in the Northwest Himalaya Between the Kashmir & Indus Valleys. Hellmut De Terra. (Connecticut Academy of Arts & Sciences Ser., Trans.: Vol. 8, Article 2). 1935. pap. 100.00 (*0-685-22865-7*) Elliots Bks.

Yale North India Expedition: Palaeolithic Human Industries in the Northwest Punjab & Kashmir & Their Geological Significance. Jacquetta Hawkes et al. (Connecticut Academy of Arts & Sciences Ser., Trans.: Vol. 8, Article 1). 1934. pap. 49.50 (*0-685-22864-9*) Elliots Bks.

Yale Papyri in the Beinecke Rare Book & Manuscript Library, Vol. 1. John F. Oates et al. LC 75-81535. (American Studies in Papyrology: No. 2). 320p. reprint ed. pap. 91.20 (*0-7837-5485-X*, 2045250) Bks Demand.

Yale Papyri in the Beinecke Rare Book & Manuscript Library II. Susan A. Stephens. (American Studies in Papyrology: No. 24). 192p. 1985. 70.00 (*0-89130-513-0*, 31 00 24) Scholars Pr GA.

Yale Psychological Studies see Experimental Study of Decision Types & Their Mental Correlates

Yale Psychological Studies, N.S., Vol 1, No. 1. Ed. by Charles H. Judd. Bd. with Theory of Psychological Dispositions. Charles A. Dubray. ; Visual Illusion of Motion During Eye Closure. Harvey Carr. (Psychology Monographs General & Applied: Vol. 7). 1974. reprint ed. Set pap. 55.00 (*0-8115-1406-4*) Periodicals Srv.

Yale Psychology Studies see Scientific Study of the College Student

Yale Psychology Studies N. S. see Psychological Experiences Connected with Different Parts of Speech

Yale Review: Old Series, May 1892-Feb. 1911, 19 Vols. & Index, Set. LC 71-85769. (Reprints of Economic Classics Ser.). 1969. reprint ed. 995.00 (*0-678-00532-X*) Kelley.

Yale Review Anthology. Yale Review Staff. Ed. by Wilbur L. Cross & Helen MacAfee. LC 72-128336. (Essay Index Reprint Ser.). 1977. 23.95 (*0-8369-2098-8*) Ayer.

Yale Review of Law & Social Action: 1970-1973, Set, Vols. 1-3. Bound set. 120.00 (*0-8377-9189-8*) Rothman.

Yale Science: The First Hundred Years, 1701-1801. Louis W. McKeehan. 1947. 59.50 (*0-614-00148-X*) Elliots Bks.

***Yale Strike Dossier, Vol. 14, No. 4.** Ed. by Cary Nelson. 270p. 1997. pap. 12.00 (*0-8223-6443-3*) Duke.

***Yale University: Tests & Procedures.** Barry L. Zaret. Date not set. write for info. (*0-688-12051-2*) Hearst Bks.

Yale University Art Gallery Selections. Alan Shestack. (Illus.). 112p. (Orig.). 1984. pap. 8.00 (*0-89467-027-1*) Yale Art Gallery.

Yale University Publications in Anthropology, Nos. 1-7. LC 78-118240. 145p. 1970. pap. 20.00 (*0-87536-518-3*) HRAFP.

Yale University Publications in Anthropology, Nos. 8-13. LC 70-118246. 163p. 1970. pap. 20.00 (*0-87536-520-5*) HRAFP.

Y'All Come Back, Now: Recipes & Memories. Ibbie Ledford. LC 93-6074. (Illus.). 224p. 1994. 15.95 (*1-56554-015-8*) Pelican.

***Yalobusha County, Mississippi Original Land Entries, Bks. 1 & 2, 1833-1853.** Chris B. Morgan. (Illus.). 198p. (Orig.). 1997. pap. 27.00 (*1-885480-14-8*) Pioneer Pubng.

***Yalobusha County, Mississippi Will Abstracts & Estate Records Index.** Betty C. Wiltshire. 190p. (Orig.). 1997. pap. 20.00 (*1-885480-16-4*) Pioneer Pubng.

***Yalom Reader: On Writing, Living & Practicing Psychotherapy.** Irvin Yalom. 256p. 1997. 22.00 (*0-465-03610-4*) Basic.

Yalta. Pierre De Senarclens. Tr. by Jasmer Singh from FRE. 224p. 1987. 39.95 (*0-88738-152-9*) Transaction Pubs.

Yalta-Responsibility & Response: January-March 1945. Floyd H. Rodine. 156p. 1974. pap. 8.50 (*0-87291-049-0*) Coronado Pr.

Yalu Flows: A Korean Childhood. Mirok Li. Ed. by Kyu-Hwa Chung. Tr. by H. A. Hammelmann & Gertraud Gutensohn from KOR. (Illus.). 204p. 1987. 14.50 (*0-930878-75-2*) Hollym Intl.

Yam Good Cookbook. rev. ed. Dauphen Johnson. 112p. 1997. pap. 14.95 (*0-89896-079-7*) Larksdale.

Yamagata: The Car Series. Ed. by Edward Leffingwell. (Illus.). 96p. (Orig.). 1993. pap. 25.95 (*1-882299-02-7*) Minic Art Gall.

Yamagata Aritomo in the Rise of Modern Japan, 1838-1922. Roger F. Hackett. LC 74-139719. (Harvard East Asian Ser.: No. 60). 394p. 1971. reprint ed. pap. 112.30 (*0-7837-4105-7*, 2057928) Bks Demand.

Yamaha. Mick Walker. (Color Library). (Illus.). 128p. 1993. pap. 15.95 (*1-85532-342-7*, Pub. by Osprey Pubng Ltd UK) Motorbooks Intl.

Yamaha: YTM-YFM200 & 225, 1983-1986. (Illus.). Date not set. reprint ed. pap. 25.95 (*0-89287-450-3*, M394) Clymer Pub.

Yamaha: 650cc Twins, 1970-82, Service, Repair, Performance. 8th ed. (Illus.). Date not set. reprint ed. pap. 25.95 (*0-89287-233-0*, M403) Clymer Pub.

Yamaha DT & MX 100-400, 1977-1983. 3rd ed. (Illus.). (Orig.). Date not set. reprint ed. pap. 25.95 (*0-89287-331-0*, M412) Intertec Pub.

Yamaha DX100 Working Musicians Guide. Lorenz M. Rychner. 67p. (C). 1987. pap. 14.95 (*0-939067-38-2*) Alexander Pub.

Yamaha DX21: Getting the Most out of Yours. Lorenz M. Rychner. Ed. by Peter L. Alexander. (Yamaha DX Support Ser.). (Illus.). 84p. (C). 1987. pap. text ed. 19.95 (*0-939067-02-1*) Alexander Pub.

Yamaha DX7 Patch Fake Book. Scott Frankfurt & Lorenz M. Rychner. Ed. by Peter L. Alexander. (Yamaha DX7 Support Ser.). (Illus.). 164p. (C). 1987. pap. text ed. 24.95 (*0-939067-75-7*) Alexander Pub.

Yamaha DX7IIFD, Vol. 1. Lorenz M. Rychner. 152p. (C). 1987. pap. 24.95 (*0-939067-36-6*) Alexander Pub.

***Yamaha FJ1100 & 1200, 1984-1993.** (Illus.). Date not set. reprint ed. pap. 25.95 (*0-89287-605-0*, M397) Intertec Pub.

***Yamaha FZR600, 1989-1993.** (Illus.). Date not set. reprint ed. pap. 25.95 (*0-89287-592-5*, M396) Intertec Pub.

Yamaha FZ700-750 & Fazer, 1985-1987. (Illus.). Date not set. reprint ed. pap. 25.95 (*0-89287-438-4*, M392) Clymer Pub.

Yamaha IT125-490, 1976-1986: Service Repair Performance. 4th ed. Ed Scott. (Illus.). (Orig.). Date not set. reprint ed. pap. 25.95 (*0-89287-330-2*, M414) Intertec Pub.

Yamaha MTIX. Beau Carr & Lorenz M. Rychner. Ed. by Peter L. Alexander. (Illus.). 72p. (C). 1987. pap. text ed. 17.95 (*0-939067-74-9*) Alexander Pub.

Yamaha QX5 Sequencing & Recording Handbook. Dan Walker. Ed. by Peter L. Alexander. (Illus.). 203p. (C). 1988. pap. text ed. 24.95 (*0-939067-35-8*) Alexander Pub.

Yamaha Racing Motorcycle: Factory & Production Road Racing Two-Strokes 1955-93. Colin Mackellar. (Illus.). 192p. 1995. 34.95 (*1-85223-920-4*, Pub. by Crowood UK) Motorbooks Intl.

Yamaha Stern Drives, 1989-1991. (Illus.). Date not set. reprint ed. pap. 34.95 (*0-89287-544-5*, B787) Intertec Pub.

Yamaha TX802. Lorenz M. Rychner. Ed. by Peter L. Alexander. (Illus.). 110p. (C). 1988. pap. text ed. 19.95 (*0-939067-23-4*) Alexander Pub.

Yamaha TX81Z. Lorenz M. Rychner. Ed. by Peter L. Alexander. (Illus.). 104p. (C). 1987. pap. text ed. 19.95 (*0-939067-22-6*) Alexander Pub.

Yamaha Water Vehicles, 1987-1992. 2nd ed. Clymer Publications Staff. (Illus.). 1994. reprint ed. pap. 34.95 (*0-89287-594-1*, W805) Intertec Pub.

***Yamaha Water Vehicles, 1993-1996.** (Illus.). (Orig.). 1997. pap. 34.95 (*0-89287-686-7*, W806) Intertec Pub.

Yamaha XJ550 & F5600, 1981-85: Service, Repair, Performance. Ron Wright. (Illus.). 260p. 1986. 25.95 (*0-89287-372-8*, M387) Clymer Pub.

***Yamaha XJ550, XJ600 & FJ600, 1981-1992.** 3rd ed. (Illus.). Date not set. reprint ed. pap. 25.95 (*0-89287-621-2*, M387) Intertec Pub.

Yamaha XS1100 Fours: 1978-1981 Service-Repair-Performance. 2nd ed. Ed Scott. (Illus.). (Orig.). Date not set. reprint ed. pap. 25.95 (*0-89287-309-4*, M411) Clymer Pub.

Yamaha XS750 & 850, 1977-1981. 3rd ed. (Illus.). Date not set. reprint ed. pap. 25.95 (*0-89287-243-8*, M404) Intertec Pub.

Yamaha XT/TT350: 1985-90 Manual. 5th ed. (Illus.). Date not set. reprint ed. pap. 25.95 (*0-89287-545-3*, M480) Clymer Pub.

Yamaha XT/TT600, 1983-1989. (Illus.). Date not set. reprint ed. pap. 25.95 (*0-89287-546-1*, M416) Clymer Pub.

Yamaha XT125-250: 1980-1984 Service Repair Performance. 2nd ed. (Illus.). 254p. (Orig.). Date not set. reprint ed. pap. 25.95 (*0-89287-387-6*, M417) Clymer Pub.

Yamaha XT500 & TT500, 1976-1981. 3rd ed. (Illus.). Date not set. reprint ed. pap. 25.95 (*0-89287-240-3*, M405) Clymer Pub.

***Yamaha XV535-1100 Virago, 1981-1996.** (Illus.). (Orig.). 1997. pap. 25.95 (*0-89287-692-1*, M395-8) Intertec Pub.

Yamaha XV700-1100: 1981-92 Manual. 1991. pap. 25.95 (*0-89287-584-4*, M395) Clymer Pub.

***Yamaha YFM350 Big Bear, 1987-1996.** (Illus.). (Orig.). 1997. pap. 25.95 (*0-89287-688-3*, M490) Intertec Pub.

***Yamaha YFM350 Warrior, 1987-1995.** LC 94-77639. (Illus.). (Orig.). 1995. pap. 25.95 (*0-89287-636-0*, M487) Intertec Pub.

***Yamaha YFZ350 Banshee, 1987-1995.** LC 94-77638. (Illus.). (Orig.). 1995. pap. 25.95 (*0-89287-630-1*, M486) Intertec Pub.

Yamaha YX600 Radian & FZ600, 1986-1990. Intertec Publishing Staff. (Illus.). Date not set. reprint ed. pap. 25.95 (*0-89287-577-1*, M388) Clymer Pub.

Yamaha YZ100-490 Monoshock, 1976-1984: Service, Repair, Performance. 5th ed. (Illus.). 293p. (Orig.). Date not set. reprint ed. pap. 25.95 (*0-89287-329-9*, M413) Intertec Pub.

***Yamaha YZ125-250, 1985-1987 YZ490, 1985-1990.** 2nd ed. (Illus.). Date not set. reprint ed. pap. 25.95 (*0-89287-609-3*, M390) Intertec Pub.

***Yamaha YZ125-250, 1988-1993 WR250Z, 1991-1993.** 5th ed. (Illus.). Date not set. reprint ed. pap. 25.95 (*0-89287-618-2*, M391) Intertec Pub.

Yamaha YZ125-490, 1985-1987. 1988. 25.95 (*0-89287-456-2*, M390) Clymer Pub.

Yamaha YZ50-80 Monoshock, 1978-1990: Service, Repair, Performance. 5th ed. Ed Scott. (Illus.). (Orig.). Date not set. reprint ed. pap. 25.95 (*0-89287-495-3*, M393) Intertec Pub.

Yamaha 1984-1989. (Illus.). Date not set. reprint ed. pap. 29.95 (*0-89287-503-8*, S826) Intertec Pub.

Yamaha 2-225hp 2-Stroke Outboards, 1984-1989. Clymer Publications Staff. (Illus.). Date not set. reprint ed. pap. 34.95 (*0-89287-498-8*, B783) Intertec Pub.

***Yamaha 2-250hp 2-Stroke Outboards, 1990-1995.** (Illus.). Date not set. reprint ed. pap. 34.95 (*0-89287-650-6*, B784) Intertec Pub.

Yamaha 250-400cc Piston-Port, 1968-1976: 250-400cc Piston Port Singles, 1968-76, Service, Repair, Performance. 4th ed. Clymer Publications Staff. (Illus.). Date not set. reprint ed. pap. 25.95 (*0-89287-276-4*, M415) Intertec Pub.

***Yamaha 650 Twins 1970-83.** 1996. 20.95 (*1-85010-921-4*) Motorbooks Intl.

Yamaha 80-175 Piston-Port, 1968-1976: 80-175cc Piston Port Singles, 1968-1976. 4th ed. Clymer Publications Staff. (Illus.). Date not set. reprint ed. pap. 25.95 (*0-89287-235-7*, M410) Intertec Pub.

***Yamalo-Nenets Autonomous Okrug: Economy, Industry, Government, Business.** 2nd rev. ed. Russian Information & Business Center, Inc. Staff. (Russian Regional Business Directories Ser.). (Illus.). 200p. 1997. pap. 99.00 (*0-614-30772-4*) Russ Info & Busn Ctr.

Yamamoto Mission. John T. Wible. (Illus.). 48p. (Orig.). 1988. pap. text ed. 5.00 (*0-934841-15-2*) Adm Nimitz Foun.

Yamamoto Returns: A True Story of Reincarnation. Dennis Dallison. (Illus.). 132p. 1985. pap. 8.00 (*0-932642-98-5*) Unarius Acad Sci.

Yamara. Barbara Manui & Chris Adams. (Illus.). 1994. pap. 9.95 (*1-55634-292-6*) S Jackson Games.

Yamashiro School of Swordsmiths. Kizu. 1991. pap. 4.95 (*0-910704-14-7*) Hawley.

Yamashita Precedent: War Crimes & Command Responsibility. Richard L. Lael. LC 82-17024. 177p. 1982. lib. bdg. 40.00 (*0-8420-2202-3*) Scholarly Res Inc.

Yamato: A Rage in Heaven, Part 2. Ken Kato. 1991. mass mkt. 4.50 (*0-446-36189-5*) Warner Bks.

Yamato: A Rage in Heaven, Pt. 1. Ken Kato. 1991. mass mkt. 4.50 (*0-446-36141-0*) Warner Bks.

Yamato II: The Way of the Warrior, Pt. 1. Ken Kato. 384p. (Orig.). 1992. mass mkt. 4.99 (*0-446-36180-1*, Aspect) Warner Bks.

Yamato II: The Way of the Warrior, Pt. 2. Ken Kato. 304p. (Orig.). 1992. mass mkt. 4.99 (*0-446-36265-4*, Aspect) Warner Bks.

Yamato School of Swordsmiths. Kizu. 1991. pap. 4.95 (*0-910704-15-5*) Hawley.

Yami Fishing Practices: Migratory Fish. Ying-Chan Hsu. (Taiwan Aborigine Monograph: No. 1). 1982. 70.00 (*0-89986-359-0*) Oriental Bk Store.

Yamilla. Mildred E. Riley. 1990. pap. 4.75 (*1-878634-01-1*) Odyssey Bks.

Yamin Nora'im-Laws of the Synagogue. write for info. (*0-318-56759-8*) USCJE.

***Yami's Origami: First Steps to a Thousand Paper Cranes. large type ed. Yoichi Yamauchi. (Illus.). 84p. (Orig.). (J). 1997. 16.95 (*1-890597-00-7*) Woodbridge Pub.**

YAMI'S ORIGAMI is a step-by-step approach to learning the basics of origami "paper-folding." Unlike many origami books where the drawings must be learned by frustrating trial & error, Yami carefully explains each symbol & folding step to get beginning folder off to a fast & painless start. Symbols & methods learned in Yami's book can be applied in almost any other origami book. So, a whole world of new & challenging origami is opened up by Yami's lessons. Yami re-discovered origami after the tragic loss of his son. Origami helped him "re-fold" his life along more positive lines. The lessons learned from origami practice can benefit anyone, he says. Yami starts the book with simple models, but quickly moves into more advanced projects. All are fascinating & capture the imagination. Yami's enthusiasm & love of origami teach more than just how to fold paper. He teaches that good work habits, a step-by-step approach, & a positive outlook go a long way to reaching success. These are lessons in folding origami & unfolding life. Yami shows that in carefully worked out, well-chosen stages, anyone can accomplish just about anything. Woodbridge Publishing, P.O. Box 18, Haworth, NJ 07641. 201-387-7038. ***Publisher Provided Annotation.***

Yamisevul: An Archaeological Treatment Plan & Testing Report for CA-RIV-269, Riverside County, California. fac. ed. Steven D. Shelley. (Statistical Research (Tucson, Arizona) Technical Ser.: No. 9). (Illus.). 186p. 1987. reprint ed. pap. text ed. 16.85 (*1-55567-569-7*) Coyote Press.

Yammering Away. Gregg Fedchak. (Illus.). 112p. 1985. pap. 9.95 (*0-935939-00-8*) Night Tree Pr.

Yamsi: A Year in the Life of a Wilderness Ranch. Dayton Hyde. LC 96-25463. (Northwest Reprints Ser.). (Illus.). 288p. 1996. reprint ed. pap. 15.95 (*0-87071-522-4*) Oreg St U Pr.

Yamunacarya's: Sri Stotra-ratna. Srila Yamunacarya. Tr. by Kusakratha Dasa. (Krsna Library: Vol. 10). 43p. (Orig.). (C). 1987. pap. 6.00 (*0-944833-09-8*) Krsna Inst.

Yamuna's Table. Yamuna Devi. 1995. pap. 13.95 (*0-452-27238-6*, Plume) NAL-Dutton.

Yan Can Cook Book. Martin Yan. LC 80-2987. (Illus.). 355p. 1982. pap. 14.95 (*0-385-17606-6*) Doubleday.

Yan-kit's Classic Chinese Cookbook. Yan-kit So. LC 93-34277. (Illus.). 240p. 1994. pap. 10.95 (*1-56458-545-X*) DK Pub Inc.

Yana Dictionary. Edward Sapir & Morris Swadesh. Ed. by Mary R. Haas. LC 60-63595. (University of California Publications in Social Welfare: No. 22). 279p. reprint ed. pap. 79.60 (*0-8357-6861-9*, 2035559) Bks Demand.

Yana Indians. T. T. Waterman. (University of California Publications in American Archaeology & Ethnology: Vol. 13: 2). 70p. (C). 1918. pap. text ed. 6.25 (*1-55567-210-8*) Coyote Press.

Yana Terms of Relationship. fac. ed. Edward Sapir. (University of California Publications in American Archaeology & Ethnology: Vol. 13: 4). 20p. (C). 1918. reprint ed. pap. text ed. 2.15 (*1-55567-211-6*) Coyote Press.

Yana Texts. fac. ed. Edward Sapir. (University of California Publications in American Archaeology & Ethnology: Vol. 9: 1). 235p. (C). 1910. reprint ed. pap. text ed. 21.20 (*1-55567-184-5*) Coyote Press.

Yanagita Kunio Guide to the Japanese Folk Tale. Ed. & Tr. by Fanny H. Mayer from JPN. LC 85-45291. (Illus.). 392p. (C). 1986. 31.50 (*0-253-36812-X*) Ind U Pr.

Yancy & Bear. Hazel Hutchins. (Illus.). 24p. (Orig.). (J). (ps). 1996. 15.95 (*1-55037-503-2*, Pub. by Annick CN); pap. 5.95 (*1-55037-502-4*, Pub. by Annick CN) Firefly Bks Ltd.

Yandicu: De Curandero a Evangelista. Jeanette Windle & Jan Clements. Tr. by Sylvette Greeding. 24p. (SPA.). (J). (gr. 2-7). 1992. pap. 2.50 (*0-9617490-3-2*) Gospel Missionary.

Yandicu: Ein Medizinmann Wird Evangelist. Jeanette Windle & Jan Clements. (Illus.). (GER.). (J). (gr. 2-7). 1998. pap. write for info. (*0-9617490-5-9*) Gospel Missionary.

Yandilli Trilogy. Rodney Hall. 512p. 1995. pap. 16.00 (*0-374-52439-4*, Noonday) FS&G.

Yang-Baxter Equation & Quantum Enveloping Algebras. Z. Q. Ma. 328p. 1993. text ed. 86.00 (*981-02-1383-2*) World Scientific Pub.

Yang Baxter Equation in Interpable Systems. Michio Jimbo. 728p. (C). 1990. text ed. 86.00 (*981-02-0120-6*); pap. text ed. 46.00 (*981-02-0121-4*) World Scientific Pub.

Yang-Baxter Equations, Conformal Invariance & Integrability in Statistical Mechanics & Field Theory. Michael Barber & Paul Pearce. 426p. 1990. text ed. 92.00 (*981-02-0067-6*) World Scientific Pub.

Yang-Baxter Equations in Paris: Proceedings of the Conference. J. M. Millard. 300p. 1993. text ed. 95.00 (*981-02-1343-3*) World Scientific Pub.

Yang-Bibliography see Biographical Dictionary of Republican China

Yang Kuei-Fei: The Most Artful. rev. ed. Shu-Chiung. (Beauties of Ancient China Ser.). 91p. 1981. reprint ed. pap. 8.95 (*9971-901-04-8*) Heian Intl.

Yang-Mills Fields & Extension Theory. Robert Pool. LC 86-28809. (Memoirs of the American Mathematical Society Ser.: No. 358). 63p. 1987. pap. 15.00 (*0-8218-2422-8*, MEMO/65/358C) Am Math.

Yang-Mills, Kaluza-Klein & the Einstein Program. Robert Hermann. (Interdisciplinary Mathematics Ser.: No. 19). 198p. 1978. 36.00 (*0-915692-25-2*, 9916500304) Math Sci Pr.

Yang-Mills Theories in Algebraic Non-Covariant Gauges. A. Bassetto et al. 240p. (C). 1991. text ed. 41.00 (*981-02-0578-3*) World Scientific Pub.

Yang Style Taijiquan. 1988. 14.95 (*0-8351-2041-4*) China Bks.

Yang Tai Chi Chuan. John Hine. pap. 28.95 (*0-7136-3576-2*, 92769, Pub. by A&C Black UK) Talman.

Yang the Third & Her Impossible Family. Lensey Namioka. LC 94-30110. (Illus.). (J). 1995. 15.95 (*0-316-59726-0*) Little.

***Yang the Third & Her Impossible Family.** Lensey Namioka. 144p. (J). (gr. 4-7). 1996. pap. 3.99 (*0-440-41231-5*, YB BDD) BDD Bks Young Read.

Yang the Youngest. Bonnie Ferraro. Ed. by J. Friedland & R. Kessler. (Novel-Ties Ser.). 1995. student ed., pap. text ed. 15.95 (*1-56982-289-1*) Lrn Links.

Yang the Youngest & His Terrible Ear. Lensey Namioka. 144p. (J). (gr. 4-7). 1994. pap. 3.99 (*0-440-40917-9*) Dell.

***Yang the Youngest & His Terrible Ear.** Lensey Namioka. (Illus.). (J). (gr. 4). 1995. 9.00 (*0-395-73239-5*) HM.

***Yang the Youngest & His Terrible Ear.** large type ed. Lensey Namioka. (Illus.). 164p. (J). (gr. 4). 41.00 (*0-614-20631-6*, L-38184-00 APHB) Am Printing Hse.

***Yang-ts'ai: The Foreign Colors: Rose Porcelians of the Ch'ing Dynasty.** H. A. Forbes. (Illus.). 62p. 1982. pap. 15.00 (*0-937650-03-X*, PEMP159) Peabody Essex Mus.

Yanga, the Miracle Village. V. Ben Kendrick. LC 83-11033. 167p. 1988. pap. 5.95 (*0-87227-095-5*, RBP5121) Reg Baptist.

***Yang's Jump Shifts - A Powerful Bidding Approach for Slams.** Cliff Yang. Orig. Title: The Super Forcing System. 172p. 1996. pap. 12.95 (*0-9655855-0-6*) ABridge Pub.

***Yangtze.** M. Pollard. LC 97-3539. (Great Rivers Ser.: Group 1). (Illus.). 48p. (J). (gr. 4-8). 1997. lib. bdg. 14.95 (*0-7614-0505-4*, Benchmark NY) Marshall Cavendish.

Yangtze. large type ed. Alan Fisher. 649p. 1989. 25.99 (*0-7089-1993-6*) Ulverscroft.

Yangtze Patrol: The U. S. Navy in China. Kemp Tolley. LC 73-146534. (Illus.). 354p. reprint ed. pap. 100.90 (*0-317-08245-0*, 2006316) Bks Demand.

***Yangtze River: The Wildest, Wickedest River on Earth.** Ed. by Madeleine Lynn. (Illus.). 304p. 1997. text ed. 29.95 (*0-19-586920-6*) OUP.

Yangtze River Collection: Later Chinese Jades. unabridged ed. Daphne L. Rosenzweig. (Illus.). 100p. (Orig.). 1993. pap. 40.00 (*0-9635570-0-9*) H Wall-Apelt.

Yangzi River. China Guides Editors. (China Guides Ser.). 192p. 1991. pap. 10.95 (*0-8442-9805-0*, Passport Bks) NTC Pub Grp.

Yangzi River. 3rd ed. Thomas Cook. (Illustrated Travel Guides from Thomas Cook Ser.). 1994. pap. 15.95 (*0-8442-9681-3*, Passport Bks) NTC Pub Grp.

Yani: The Brush of Innocence. Wai-Ching Ho et al. LC 88-34805. (Illus.). 143p. (Orig.). 1989. pap. 24.95 (*0-942614-14-3*) Nelson-Atkins.

XYZ

Yania Tierra. Aida C. Portalatin. Tr. & Intro. by M. J. Fenwick. LC 94-79182. 196p. (Orig.). 1995. pap. 12.95 (*0-9632363-9-3*) Azul Edits.

Yank: Irish Poems. Patrick Hammer, Jr. (Illus.). 50p. (Orig.). 1988. pap. 3.00 (*0-945085-07-9*) Sub Rosa.

Yank: The Story of World War II As Written by the Soldiers. Ed. by Yank, the Army Weekly Staff. (Brassey's WWII Commemorative Ser.). (Illus.). 264p. 1991. pap. 16.95 (*0-08-041067-7*) Brasseys Inc.

***Yank among Us.** Wanda Dionne. LC 96-29633. (J). 1997. pap. 12.95 (*1-57168-108-6*, Eakin Pr) Sunbelt Media.

Yank in the British YMCA. Fred L. Parrish. 183p. 1975. pap. text ed. 27.00 (*0-89126-009-9*) MA-AH Pub.

Yank in Yucatan: Adventures & Guide Through Eastern Mexico. Lois W. Schell & Rolfe F. Schell. LC 85-82462. (Illus.). 302p. 1986. pap. 9.95 (*0-87208-102-8*) Shoeless Pub.

Yankee. large type ed. Dana F. Ross. 1993. 21.95 (*1-56895-044-6*) Wheeler Pub.

Yankee Ace in the RAF: The World War I Letters of Captain Bogart Rogers. Ed. by John H. Morrow, Jr. & Earl Rogers. LC 87-46161. (Modern War Studies). (Illus.). 256p. 1996. 24.95 (*0-7006-0798-6*) U Pr of KS.

Yankee Among the Nullifiers: An Autobiography. Asa Greene. LC 72-104468. reprint ed. lib. bdg. 16.50 (*0-8398-0667-1*) Irvington.

Yankee Auctioneer. George Bean. (American Autobiography Ser.). 247p. 1995. reprint ed. lib. bdg. 79.00 (*0-7812-8452-X*) Rprt Serv.

Yankee Beacon of Buddhist Light: The Life of Colonel Henry S. Olcott. rev. ed. Howard Murphet. LC 88-40133. Orig. Title: Hammer on the Mountain. (Illus.). 350p. (Orig.). 1988. reprint ed. pap. 8.75 (*0-8356-0638-4*, Quest) Theos Pub Hse.

Yankee Belles in Dixie. Gilbert Morris. (Bonnets & Bugles Ser.: Vol. 2). (J). (gr. 5-9). 1995. pap. 5.99 (*0-8024-0912-1*) Moody.

Yankee Blitzkrieg: Wilson's Raid through Alabama & Georgia. James P. Jones. LC 74-15206. (Brown Thrasher Bks.). 270p. 1987. reprint ed. pap. 15.95 (*0-8203-0970-2*) U of Ga Pr.

Yankee Blues: Musical Culture & American Identity. MacDonald S. Moore. LC 83-49407. (Illus.). 223p. reprint ed. pap. 63.60 (*0-7837-3720-3*, 2057898) Bks Demand.

Yankee Botanist in the Carolinas, the Reverend Moses Ashley Curtis, D. D. (1808-1872) E. Berkeley & D. Smith Berkeley. (Illus.). 242p. 1986. pap. text ed. 65.00 (*3-443-50005-6*) Lubrecht & Cramer.

***Yankee Boy.** Ethel M. Comins. LC 88-18871. (Illus.). (J). 1988. 7.95 (*0-932334-97-0*) Empire St Bks.

Yankee Bride - Rebel Bride: Montclair Divided. Jane Peart. (Brides of Montclair Ser.: Vol. 5). 188p. 1990. pap. 8.99 (*0-310-66991-X*) Zondervan.

Yankee Cavalrymen: Through the Civil War with the Ninth Pennsylvania Calvary. John W. Rowell. LC 70-126939. 296p. 1971. reprint ed. pap. 84.40 (*0-608-00260-7*, 2016172) Bks Demand.

Yankee Cavalrymen: Through the Civil War with the Ninth Pennsylvania Cavalry. John W. Rowell. LC 70-126939. (Illus.). 280p. 1975. 32.95 (*0-87049-125-3*) U of Tenn Pr.

Yankee Christmas Featuring Vermont Celebrations: Feasts, Treats, Crafts, & Traditions of Wintertime New England. Sally R. Brady. (Illus.). 160p. 1993. 24.95 (*0-89909-358-2*, 80-152-9) Yankee Bks.

Yankee Church Supper Cookbook. Ed. by Clarissa M. Silitch. LC 80-612. 240p. 1980. pap. 12.95 (*0-911658-14-9*, 80-152-4) Yankee Bks.

***Yankee Cinderella.** Thomas B. Smith. 192p. (Orig.). 1996. pap. 12.95 (*0-924771-79-8*, Covered Brdge Pr) D C Press.

Yankee Cooking Conch & All Dem Other Sea Critters. Carlo DiNapoli. Ed. by R. Constantine. (Illus.). 250p. (Orig.). 1993. pap. 14.95 (*0-9627946-5-1*) Hawk FL.

Yankee Correspondence: Civil War Letters Between New England Soldiers & the Home Front. Ed. by Nina Silber & Mary B. Sievens. (Nation Divided Ser.). 205p. (C). 1996. 29.95 (*0-8139-1668-2*) U Pr of Va.

***Yankee Crosses the Wide Rio Grande.** (Illus.). vii, 197p. 1995. pap. 12.00 (*0-9652571-2-6*) T R Gagnon.

Yankee Dawg You Die. Philip K. Gotanda. 1991. pap. 5.25 (*0-8222-1283-8*) Dramatists Play.

Yankee Denim Dandies. Barbara Fehr. LC 74-79127. (Illus.). 96p. (J). (gr. 6 up). 1984. 15.00 (*0-87832-014-8*) Piper.

Yankee Destinies: The Lives of Ordinary Nineteenth-Century Bostonians. Peter R. Knights. LC 90-23936. (Illus.). xxviii, 281p. (C). 1991. 39.95 (*0-8078-1969-7*) U of NC Pr.

Yankee Dictionary. 2.95 (*0-936672-29-3*) Aerial Photo.

Yankee Diplomacy: U. S. Intervention in Argentina. Oscar E. Smith, Jr. LC 79-25196. (Arnold Foundation Studies: Vol. III, New Ser.). 196p. 1980. reprint ed. text ed. 65.00 (*0-313-22124-3*, SMYD, Greenwood Pr) Greenwood.

Yankee Doodle. Gary Chalk. LC 92-53482. (Illus.). 48p. (J). (gr. k-3). 1993. 14.95 (*1-56458-202-7*) DK Pub Inc.

Yankee Doodle. Jonathan Edward. LC 92-10776. 176p. 1993. 22.00 (*1-881119-63-7*); pap. 13.00 (*1-881119-79-3*) Pyncheon Hse.

Yankee Doodle. Illus. by Steven Kellogg. 40p. (J). (ps-3). 1996. pap. 5.99 (*0-689-80726-0*, Aladdin Paperbacks) S&S Childrens.

Yankee Doodle. Steven Kellogg. LC 80-17024. (Illus.). 40p. (J). (ps-3). 1996. 16.00 (*0-689-80158-0*, S&S Bks Young Read) S&S Childrens.

Yankee Doodle. Contrib. by Richard Schackburg & Ed Emberley. LC 93-28633. (J). 1994. pap. 5.95 (*0-671-88645-2*, Half Moon Paper) S&S Childrens.

Yankee Doodle. Coley B. Taylor. 10.00 (*0-8159-7400-0*) Devin.

Yankee Doodle: A Drama of the American Revolution. Coley B. Taylor. 172p. reprint ed. pap. 49.10 (*0-317-28245-X*, 2022705) Bks Demand.

Yankee Doodle: Musical. Aurand Harris. (J). (gr. 1-7). 1975. 5.00 (*0-87602-223-9*) Anchorage.

Yankee Doodle Boy. Joseph P. Martin. Ed. by George F. Scheer. (Illus.). (YA). (gr. 5 up). 1995. pap. 8.95 (*0-8234-1180-X*) Holiday.

Yankee Doodle Boy: A Young Soldier's Adventures in the American Revolution. Ed. by George F. Scheer. LC 94-34227. (Illus.). 192p. (YA). (gr. 7 up). 1995. 15.95 (*0-8234-1176-1*) Holiday.

Yankee Doodle Boy: A Young Soldier's Adventures in the American Revolution Told by Himself. Joseph P. Martin. (American Biography Ser.). 190p. 1991. reprint ed. lib. bdg. 59.00 (*0-7812-8273-X*) Rprt Serv.

Yankee Doodle Dandy. Ed. by Patrick McGilligan. LC 80-52293. (Warner Bros. Screenplay Ser.). (Illus.). 192p. (Orig.). 1981. 11.95 (*0-299-08470-1*); pap. 6.95 (*0-299-08474-4*) U of Wis Pr.

Yankee Doodle Days: Exploring the American Revolution. Lincoln Diamant. LC 96-17054. 179p. 1996. 25.00 (*0-935796-73-8*) Purple Mnt Pr.

Yankee Doodle-Doo: A Collection of Songs of the Early American Stage. Compiled by Grenville Vernon. LC 70-174847. (Illus.). 1972. reprint ed. 21.95 (*0-405-09040-4*, Pub. by Blom Pubns UK) Ayer.

Yankee Doodle Drumsticks. Patricia R. Giff. (Lincoln Lions Band Ser.: No. 2). (Illus.). 80p. (Orig.). (J). (gr. 1-4). 1992. pap. 3.25 (*0-440-40518-1*, YB BDD) BDD Bks Young Read.

***Yankee Dreamers & Doers: The Story of Connecticut Manufacturing.** 2nd ed. Ellsworth S. Grant. LC 96-84115. (Illus.). 358p. 1996. 29.95 (*1-881061-27-2*) Conn Hist Soc.

Yankee Drover: Being the Unpretending Life of Asa Sheldon, Farmer, Trader, & Working Man, 1788-1870. Asa Sheldon. LC 88-229. (Illus.). 214p. 1988. pap. 13.95 (*0-87451-439-8*) U Pr of New Eng.

Yankee Dryer & Drying: A TAPPI Press Anthology of Published Papers. Ed. by W. G. Corboy, Jr. 275p. (Orig.). 1993. pap. 103.00 (*0-89852-310-9*, 0101R217) TAPPI.

Yankee Dryers: Guidelines for Safety & Condition Assessment. Technical Association of the Pulp & Paper Industry Staff. Ed. by William G. Corboy, Jr. LC 92-3944. 84p. reprint ed. pap. 25.00 (*0-7837-2053-X*, 2042328) Bks Demand.

Yankee Duchess. J. Ramiorez. 304p. mass mkt. 4.50 (*0-06-108075-6*, Harp PBks) HarpC.

Yankee Dutchman: The Life of Franz Sigel. Stephen D. Engle. LC 92-30696. (Illus.). 416p. 1993. 40.00 (*1-55728-273-0*) U of Ark Pr.

Yankee Eloquence in the Middle West: The Ohio Lyceum, 1850-1870. Carl D. Mead. LC 77-5130. 1977. reprint ed. text ed. 65.00 (*0-8371-9323-0*, MEYE, Greenwood Pr) Greenwood.

Yankee Encyclopedia. 2nd ed. Mark Gallagher. Ed. by Russ K. Lake. LC 96-67358. (Illus.). 535p. (Orig.). 1996. 39.95 (*1-57167-011-4*) Sagamore Pub.

***Yankee Encyclopedia: Includes 1996 World Championship Season, Vol. 3.** Mark Gallagher. 1997. 39.95 (*1-57167-114-5*) Sagamore Pub.

Yankee Enterprise: The Rise of the American System of Manufactures. Ed. by Otto Mayr & Robert C. Post. LC 81-607315. (Illus.). 236p. (Orig.). (C). 1982. pap. text ed. 14.95 (*0-87474-631-0*, MAYEP) Smithsonian.

Yankee Family. James R. McGovern. LC 75-4470. 191p. 1978. pap. text ed. 24.95 (*0-87855-674-5*) Transaction Pubs.

Yankee Firehouse Cooking: Firefighter's Cookbook. Ronald E. Shaw. 100p. (Orig.). 1988. spiral bd. 6.99 (*0-9620647-0-X*) R E Shaw.

Yankee Generations: A History of the Case Family in America. Charles C. Case. LC 81-40638. (Illus.). 338p. (Orig.). 1982. 60.00 (*0-8191-1947-4*) U Pr of Amer.

Yankee Girls in Zulu Land. Louise V. Sheldon. 1977. text ed. 40.95 (*0-8369-9237-7*, 9091) Ayer.

Yankee Go Home. J. L. Granatstein. 320p. 1996. 22.00 (*0-00-255301-5*) Harper SF.

Yankee Hobo in the Orient: Why Japan Was Strong. John Patric. 1979. 25.00 (*0-685-96533-3*) Revisionist Pr.

Yankee Home Hints: From Stains in the Carpet to Squirrels in the Attic, More Than 1500 Ingenious Solutions for Everyday Household Problems. Yankee Magazine Editors & Earl Proulx. LC 92-46642. 1993. write for info. (*0-89909-365-5*) Yankee Bks.

Yankee Image: The Life & Times of Roger Lowell Putnam. William L. Putnam. LC 91-36425. (Illus.). 172p. 1991. 25.00 (*0-914659-55-3*) Phoenix Pub.

Yankee in a Red Neck Court! Garry De Young. 25.00 (*0-685-67809-1*) De Young Pr.

Yankee in Canada, with Anti-Slavery & Reform Papers. Henry David Thoreau. 1972. 250.00 (*0-87968-015-6*) Gordon Pr.

Yankee in Canada, with Anti-Slavery & Reform Papers. Henry David Thoreau. LC 69-14117. 286p. 1970. reprint ed. text ed. 59.75 (*0-8371-2044-6*, THYC, Greenwood Pr) Greenwood.

Yankee in Canada, with Anti-Slavery & Reform Papers. Henry David Thoreau. LC 68-25271. (Studies in Black History & Culture: No. 54). (C). 1969. reprint ed. lib. bdg. 39.95 (*0-8383-0248-3*) M S G Haskell Hse.

Yankee in Canada, with Anti-Slavery & Reform Papers. Henry David Thoreau. (BCL1 - History - Canada Ser.). 286p. 1991. reprint ed. lib. bdg. 79.00 (*0-7812-6369-7*) Rprt Serv.

Yankee Ingenuity. Brownstone & Franck. 1994. pap. 18.00 (*0-671-85037-7*) S&S Trade.

***Yankee Ingenuity.** Tyler. 1996. 25.00 (*0-8050-4426-4*) St Martin.

Yankee Inventor's Flying Ship. Rufus Porter. Ed. by Rhoda R. Gilman. LC 75-95571. (Illus.). vi, 51p. 1969. 7.25 (*0-87351-052-6*) Minn Hist.

Yankee Lawyer: The Autobiography of Ephram Tutt. Arthur Train. reprint ed. lib. bdg. 30.95 (*0-89190-586-3*, Rivercity Pr) Amereon Ltd.

Yankee Leviathan: The Origins of Central State Authority in America, 1859-1877. Richard F. Bensel. (Illus.). 354p. (C). 1991. text ed. 69.95 (*0-521-39136-9*); pap. text ed. 23.95 (*0-521-39817-7*) Cambridge U Pr.

Yankee Lyre: Musical Instruments by American Makers: An Exhibition of Instruments by 19th-Century American Makers with Supplementary Exhibits of Graphics, Books & Furniture. Nicholas Renouf. (Illus.). 62p. (Orig.). 1985. pap. 5.00 (*0-929530-04-7*) Yale U Coll Musical Instruments.

***Yankee Magazine Country.** Yankee Magazine Staff. Date not set. write for info. (*0-688-14176-5*) Morrow.

Yankee Magazine's Church & Potluck Dinners Cookbook. Ed. by Yankee Magazine Editors & Andrea Chesman. 320p. 1996. 25.00 (*0-679-43208-6*, Villard Bks) Random.

Yankee Magazine's Church Supper & Potluck Dinners Cookbook. Yankee Magazine Editors. 1996. 25.00 (*0-614-95795-8*, Villard Bks) Random.

Yankee Magazine's Make it Last: Over 1,000 Ingenious Ways to Extend the Life of Everything You Own. Earl Proulx. 1996. 27.95 (*0-87596-296-3*) Rodale Pr Inc.

Yankee Magazine's New England Innkeepers Cookbook. Ed. by Sandra J. Taylor & Yankee Magazine Editors. (Illus.). 320p. 1996. 25.00 (*0-679-43207-8*, Villard Bks) Random.

Yankee Magazine's Street Maps of Boston & Vicinity. 5th ed. Yankee Magazine Editors. (Illus.). 32p. (Orig.). 1991. pap. 7.95 (*0-89909-355-8*, 80-651-4) Yankee Bks.

Yankee Mariner & Sea Power: America's Challenge of Ocean Space. Center for Study of the American Experience Staff. Ed. by Joyce J. Bartell. 300p. 1982. 44.95 (*0-88474-105-2*) Transaction Pubs.

Yankee Merchants & the Making of the Urban West: The Rise & Fall of Antebellum St. Louis. Jeffrey S. Adler. (Interdisciplinary Perspectives on Modern History Ser.). 256p. (C). 1991. text ed. 54.95 (*0-521-41284-6*) Cambridge U Pr.

Yankee Musician in Europe No. 110: The 1837 Journals of Lowell Mason. Ed. by Michael Broyles. LC 89-20256. 214p. 1991. 50.00 (*0-8357-2002-0*) Univ Rochester Pr.

Yankee Named Blueberry. Jean-Michel Charlier. Tr. by Starwatcher Graphics Staff from FRE. (Young Blueberry Ser.). (Illus.). 56p. (Orig.). (YA). (gr. 12 up). 1990. pap. 7.95 (*0-87416-087-1*, Comcat Comics) Catalan Communs.

***Yankee Notions.** Anne Chislett. LC 93-243252. 1997. pap. text ed. 10.95 (*0-88754-497-5*, Pub. by Playwrights CN Pr CN) Theatre Comm.

Yankee of the Yards: The Biography of Gustavus Franklin Swift. L. F. Swift & A. Van Vlissingen. LC 78-112003. reprint ed. 42.50 (*0-404-06309-8*) AMS Pr.

Yankee on the Prairie: Howard R. Barnard, Pioneer Educator. Allan R. Miller. (Illus.). 216p. 1995. pap. 15.95 (*0-89745-184-8*) Sunflower U Pr.

Yankee Panky: Decline & Fall of New England. Peter Farrow. (Illus.). 64p. 1990. pap. 6.95 (*0-924771-24-0*, Covered Brdge Pr) D C Press.

Yankee Politics in Rural Vermont. Frank M. Bryan. LC 73-78913. 334p. reprint ed. pap. 95.20 (*0-7837-0372-4*, 2040692) Bks Demand.

Yankee Quaker Confederate General: The Curious Career of Bushrod Rust Johnson. Charles M. Cummings. (Illus.). 420p. 1993. reprint ed. 28.95 (*0-9626034-3-0*) Generals Bks.

Yankee Raid to East Tennessee - Christmas 1862: A True Civil War Story. 28p. 1989. 5.95 (*0-911666-38-9*) Fine Arts Pr.

Yankee Recipe 92. Yankee Books Staff. Date not set. 7.95 (*0-89909-233-0*) Yankee Bks.

Yankee Red: Nonorthodox Marxism in Liberal America. Robert A. Gorman. LC 88-25882. 192p. 1989. text ed. 49.95 (*0-275-92766-0*, C2766, Praeger Pubs) Greenwood.

Yankee Rock & Ice: A History of Climbing in the Northeastern United States. Laura Waterman & Guy Waterman. LC 92-26562. (Illus.). 352p. 1993. 19.95 (*0-8117-1633-3*) Stackpole.

Yankee Rogue. large type ed. Dana F. Ross. LC 94-8217. 1994. 22.95 (*1-56895-066-7*) Wheeler Pub.

Yankee Sailors in British Gaols: Prisoners of War at Forton & Mill, 1777-1783. Sheldon S. Cohen. LC 95-2448. 280p. 1996. 42.50 (*0-87413-564-8*) U Delaware Pr.

Yankee Saint: John Humphrey Noyes & the Oneida Community. Robert A. Parker. 322p. 1993. reprint ed. lib. bdg. 89.00 (*0-7812-5314-4*) Rprt Serv.

Yankee Saints & Southern Sinners. Bertram Wyatt-Brown. LC 85-8112. xi, 227p. 1985. pap. text ed. 13.95 (*0-8071-1607-6*) La State U Pr.

Yankee Salmon: The Atlantic Salmon of the Connecticut River. Charles H. Foster. 236p. 1991. pap. text ed. 17.45 (*0-9635001-0-4*) Environ Inst.

Yankee School-Teacher in Virginia. Lydia W. Baldwin. LC 70-37583. (Black Heritage Library Collection). 1977. reprint ed. 22.95 (*0-8369-8959-7*) Ayer.

Yankee Science in the Making. Dirk J. Struik. (Illus.). 220p. 1991. reprint ed. pap. 13.95 (*0-486-26927-2*) Dover.

Yankee Ships & Yankee Sailors: Tales of 1812. James Barnes. 1977. lib. bdg. 59.95 (*0-8490-2850-7*) Gordon Pr.

Yankee Ships in China Seas. Daniel M. Henderson. LC 76-128258. (Essay Index Reprint Ser.). 1977. 24.95 (*0-8369-1950-5*) Ayer.

Yankee Shoes: A Light Verse Saunter Through Our Second Hundred Years. Mollee Kruger. LC 75-21446. 100p. 1975. pap. 2.50 (*0-913184-03-9*) Maryben Bks.

***Yankee Shorts: 501 Of The Funniest One-Liners.** Glenn Liebman. LC 97-20726. 1997. write for info. (*0-8092-2983-8*) Contemp Bks.

Yankee Skippers to the Rescue. Felix Riesenberg. LC 78-93374. (Essay Index Reprint Ser.). 1977. 23.95 (*0-8369-1313-2*) Ayer.

Yankee Spy in Richmond: The Civil War Diary of "Crazy Bet" Van Lew. Ed. by David D. Ryan. (Illus.). 176p. 1996. 22.95 (*0-8117-0554-4*) Stackpole.

Yankee Stepfather: General O. O. Howard & the Freedmen. William S. McFeely. 1994. pap. 10.95 (*0-393-31178-3*) Norton.

Yankee Stonecutters. Albert T. Gardner. LC 68-58790. (Essay Index Reprint Ser.). 1977. 23.95 (*0-8369-0114-2*) Ayer.

Yankee Storekeeper. Ralph Gould. (American Autobiography Ser.). 195p. 1995. reprint ed. lib. bdg. 69.00 (*0-7812-8535-6*) Rprt Serv.

Yankee Stranger. Elswyth Thane. 1993. reprint ed. lib. bdg. 28.95 (*1-56849-229-4*) Buccaneer Bks.

Yankee Surgeon: Life & Times of Usher Parsons, 1788-1868. Seebert J. Goldowsky. (Illus.). 450p. 1988. 24.50 (*0-317-03260-7*) F A Countway.

Yankee Surgeon: The Life & Times of Usher Parsons. Seebert J. Goldowsky. 405p. 1988. 24.50 (*0-88135-088-5*) Watson Pub Intl.

Yankee Swap. Bonnie Bryant. (The Saddle Club Ser.: Vol. 50). 144p. (J). (gr. 3-7). 1996. pap. 3.99 (*0-553-48268-8*, Skylark BDD) BDD Bks Young Read.

Yankee, Swedish & Italian Acculturation & Economic Mobility in Jamestown, New York from 1860 to 1920. Paul A. Spengler. Ed. by Francesco Cordasco. LC 80-897. (American Ethnic Groups Ser.). 1981. lib. bdg. 42.95 (*0-405-13457-6*) Ayer.

Yankee Talk: A Dictionary of New England Expressions. Robert Hendrickson. (Facts on File Dictionary of American Regionalisms Ser.: Vol. 3). 1996. write for info. (*0-8160-2111-2*) Facts on File.

Yankee Talk: A Dictionary of New England Expressions. Robert Hendrickson. 1996. pap. text ed. 14.95 (*0-8160-3507-5*) Facts on File.

Yankee Team. Robert L. MacNaughton. 76p. 1996. reprint ed. pap. 11.50 (*0-923135-31-6*) Dalley Bk Service.

Yankee Theatre; the Image of America on the Stage. Francis Hodge. 1977. text ed. 22.95 (*0-8369-8198-7*, 8336) Ayer.

Yankee Town, Southern City: Race & Class Relations in Civil War Lynchburg. Steven E. Tripp. (American Social Experience Ser.: Vol. 36). 344p. (C). 1997. 45.00 (*0-8147-8205-1*) NYU Pr.

***Yankee Trivia Book.** Jay David. 1997. pap. 9.95 (*0-614-27667-5*) Morrow.

Yankee Warrior: The Story of a Civil War Hero from Maine. Robert L. Haskell. Ed. by V. Paul Reynolds et al. (Illus.). 230p. 1993. 21.95 (*0-9623890-1-3*) Bangor Pub Co.

Yankee Way to Simplify Your Life: Old-Fashioned Wisdom for a New-Fangled World. Jay Heinrichs & Yankee Magazine Editors. LC 96-11152. 304p. 1996. 20.00 (*0-688-14186-2*) Morrow.

Yankee West: Community Life on the Michigan Frontier. Susan E. Gray. LC 96-7269. 288p. (C). 1996. pap. text ed. 17.95 (*0-8078-4610-4*) U of NC Pr.

Yankee West: Community Life on the Michigan Frontier. Susan E. Gray. LC 96-7269. 288p. (C). (gr. 13). 1996. lib. bdg. 39.95 (*0-8078-2301-5*) U of NC Pr.

Yankee Whaler. Clifford W. Ashley. (Illus.). 304p. reprint ed. pap. 10.95 (*0-486-26854-3*) Dover.

Yankee Wife. Linda L. Miller. Ed. by Linda Marrow. 368p. (Orig.). 1993. mass mkt. 6.99 (*0-671-73755-4*, Pocket Star Bks) PB.

Yankee Wildlife. Hilbert R. Siegler. 336p. 1982. pap. 12.95 (*0-924771-35-6*, Covered Brdge Pr) D C Press.

Yankee Wisdom: New England Proverbs. Wolfgang Mieder. LC 89-61223. (Illus.). 72p. (Orig.). 1989. pap. text ed. 6.95 (*0-933050-73-9*) New Eng Pr VT.

Yankee Witches: Fifteen Short Stories of Horror & Humor. Ed. by Charles Waugh et al. (Illus.). 315p. (Orig.). 1992. pap. 12.95 (*0-912769-32-7*, 80-451-3) Yankee Bks.

Yankee Women: Gender Battles in the Civil War. Elizabeth D. Leonard. LC 93-48813. (Illus.). 1994. 23.00 (*0-393-03666-9*) Norton.

Yankee Women: Gender Battles in the Civil War. Elizabeth D. Leonard. (Illus.). 336p. 1995. pap. 12.95 (*0-393-31372-7*, Norton Paperbks) Norton.

Yankees. Phil Pepe. 240p. 1995. 39.95 (*0-87833-095-X*) Taylor Pub.

***Yankees.** Phil Pepe. (Illus.). 256p. (Orig.). 1997. pap. 24.95 (*0-87833-142-5*) Taylor Pub.

***Yankees: An Illustrated History.** Ed. by George Sullivan & John Powers. LC 97-6536. (Baseball in America Ser.). (Illus.). 400p. 1997. 34.95 (*1-56639-553-4*) Temple U Pr.

Yankees: Limited. Phil Pepe. 240p. 1995. 75.00 (*0-87833-096-8*) Taylor Pub.

Yankees & the City: Struggling over Urban Representation in Connecticut, 1880 to World War I. Terry A. Baney. LC 92-27523. (Modern American History: New Studies & Outstanding Dissertations). 288p. 1992. text ed. 20.00 (*0-8153-1098-6*) Garland.

Yankees at the Court. Susan M. Alsop. pap. 4.95 (*0-685-18039-5*) PB.

Yankee's Guide to Florida Gardening. Hank Bruce & Marlene Bruce. Ed. by Erv Lampert. (Illus.). 168p. (Orig.). 1995. pap. 11.95 (*0-932855-45-8*) Winner Enter.

Yankees in Canada. Ed. by James Doyle. 231p. (C). 1980. pap. text ed. 3.50 (*0-920802-28-1*, Pub. by ECW Press CN) Genl Dist Srvs.

Yankees in Santo Domingo: Data & Official Documents. Max H. Urena. (Santo Domingo Ser.). 1979. lib. bdg. 69. 95 (*0-8490-3018-8*) Gordon Pr.

Yankees in the Republic of Texas: Their Origin & Impact. Arthur C. Burnett. 1952. 7.50 (*0-685-05007-6*) A Jones.

Yankee's Lady. Kay McMahon. mass mkt. 3.95 (*0-317-43142-0*, Zebra Kensgtn) Kensgtn Pub Corp.

Yankees Reader. Ed. by Miro Weinberger & Dan Riley. (Illus.). 272p. 1991. pap. 10.95 (*0-395-58777-8*) HM.

Yanks & Some Rebs in Texas - Eighteen Ninety. Ed. by Kathryn H. Davis. LC 91-76908. 443p. 1991. pap. 45.00 (*0-911317-50-3*) Ericson Bks.

Yanks Meet Reds: Recollections of U. S. & Soviet Vets from the Linkup in World War II. Intro. by Mark C. Scott. (Illus.). 224p. 1988. pap. 9.95 (*0-88496-276-8*) Fountain Publications Oregon.

Yanks over Europe: American Flyers in World War II. Jerome Klinkowitz. 160p. 1996. 19.95 (*0-8131-1961-8*) U Pr of Ky.

Yanks, Rebels, Rats, & Rations: Scratching for Food in Civil War Prison Camps. Patricia B. Mitchell. 1993. pap. 4.00 (*0-925117-70-6*) Mitchells.

Yanktonai Sioux Water Colors: Cultural Remembrances of John Saul. Martin Brokenleg & Herbert T. Hoover. (Illus.). 66p. 1992. 15.95 (*0-931170-53-2*) Ctr Western Studies.

***Yanmar: I&T Shop Manual - Models YM135, YM135D, YM155, YM155D, YM195, YM195D, YM240, YM240D, YM330, YM330D.** (Illus.). Date not set. reprint ed. pap. 22.95 (*0-87288-443-0*, YM-1) Intertec Pub.

***Yann & the Whale.** Frissen. LC 97-16260. (Illus.). 32p. (J). (ps-3). 1997. 13.95 (*0-916291-71-5*) Kane-Miller Bk.

Yanni - In My Time. (Piano Solos Ser.). (Illus.). 64p. (Orig.). 1993. pap. 14.95 (*0-7935-2436-9*, HL00308187) H Leonard.

Yannis Manglis. Harry T. Hionides. LC 74-31009. (Twayne's World Authors Ser.). 162p. (C). 1975. 17.95 (*0-8057-2578-4*) Irvington.

Yannis Ritsos: Repetitions, Testimonies, Parentheses. Tr. by Edmund Keeley. (Modern Greek Studies). 246p. 1991. pap. 13.95 (*0-691-01908-8*); text ed. 45.00 (*0-691-06878-X*) Princeton U Pr.

Yannis Ritsos: Selected Poems 1938-1988. Yannis Ritsos. Ed. by Kimon Friar & Kostas Myrsiades. Tr. by Kostas Myrsiades. 1989. 30.00 (*0-918526-66-3*); pap. 15.00 (*0-918526-67-1*) BOA Edns.

Yanoama: The Narrative of a Young Girl Kidnapped by Amazonian Indians. Ettore Biocca. Ed. by Philip Turner. LC 96-42704. (Illus.). 368p. 1996. pap. 15.00 (*1-56836-108-4*, Kodansha Globe) Kodansha.

Yanomami: Masters of the Spirit World. Paul Henley. LC 94-40059. (Illus.). 64p. 1995. 9.95 (*0-8118-0807-6*) Chronicle Bks.

Yanomami: People of the Amazon. David M. Schwartz. LC 93-48616. (Vanishing Peoples Ser). (Illus.). 48p. (J). (gr. 3 up). 1995. 16.00 (*0-688-11157-2*) Lothrop.

Yanomami: People of the Amazon. David M. Schwartz. LC 93-48616. (Vanishing Peoples Ser). (Illus.). 48p. (YA). (gr. 3 up). 1995. lib. bdg. 15.93 (*0-688-11158-0*) Lothrop.

***Yanomami & Their Interpreters: Fierce People or Fierce Interpreters?** Frank A. Salamone. 148p. 1997. text ed. 36.50 (*0-7618-0654-7*) U Pr of Amer.

Yanomami Warfare: A Political History. R. Brian Ferguson. 450p. 1995. pap. text ed. 27.50 (*0-933452-41-1*) Schol Am Res.

Yanomamo: The Fierce People. 3rd ed. Napolean Chagnon. LC 83-313. 224p. (C). 1983. pap. text ed. 13.50 (*0-03-062328-6*) HB Coll Pubs.

Yanomamo: The Fierce People. 4th ed. Napoleon A. Chagnon. 145p. (C). 1992. pap. text ed. write for info. (*0-318-69118-3*) HB Coll Pubs.

Yanomamo: The Last Days of Eden. Napoleon A. Chagnon. LC 92-1630. 1992. pap. 17.00 (*0-15-699682-0*, Harvest Bks) HarBrace.

Yanomamo Film Study Guide. Timothy Asch et al. Ed. by Gary Seaman. (Illus.). 220p. (Orig.). (C). 1993. pap. 15. 00 (*1-878986-10-4*) Ethnographics Pr.

Yanomano: Case Studies in Cultural Anthropology. 5th ed. Napoleon A. Chagnon. 304p. (C). 1997. pap. text ed. 17. 50 (*0-15-505327-2*) HB Coll Pubs.

Yanqui Guajiro. Jock MacKelvie. LC 97-91638. 504p. 1997. 27.00 (*0-9656624-1-1*) Condor Pub. It is NOCHEBUENA - the "Good Night" - Christmas Eve in the People's Republic of Cuba, & atop a mesa high in the Sierra Maestra mountains, Pablo Montoya sits cross-legged before a rapt, spellbound audience of Guajiro (white, fiercely independent, Cuban peasant) families, spinning the fabric of legend: the tale of the YANQUI GUAJIRO - But what Pablo doesn't say, because such niceties dim, lost in the swirling mists of time, is that, when the story opens, EL JEFE, Jefferson Tanner, is a selfish, whining, unremitting, unregenerate, foursquare bastard. It is 1963, when Fate, with her current maddening aplomb, casts him ashore on Cuba's Oriente province where he must fight with all the strength & determination he can muster, not just for his freedom, but for his very existence. More than just a story of adventure, YANQUI GUAJIRO is a tale of epic, transcendent betrayal & the legendary ordeal of one man's tortured, soul-shattering re-birth... CONDOR PUBLISHING, 759 Camino Manzanas, Thousand Oaks, CA 91360, (805) 499-9018, FAX: (805) 499-0899. $27.00 plus $4.00 S&H.** ***Publisher Provided Annotation.

Yanqui Prince. Janice Kaiser. 1994. 3.50 (*0-373-70597-2*) Harlequin Bks.

Yantra: The Tantric Symbol of Cosmic Unity. Madhu Khanna. LC 79-3953. (Illus.). 176p. 1997. reprint ed. pap. 24.95 (*0-500-27234-4*) Thames Hudson.

Yantra Kosha. Sourindro M. Tagore. LC 74-24227. 1976. reprint ed. 52.50 (*0-404-12839-4*) AMS Pr.

Yao: The Chiikala Cha Wayao. Yohanna B. Abdallah. Tr. by M. Sanderson. 132p. 1973. 45.00 (*0-7146-2462-4*, BHA-02462, Pub. by F Cass Pubs UK) Intl Spec Bk.

Yao-English Dictionary. Sylvia J. Lombard. Ed. by Herbert C. Purnell, Jr. LC 76-29799. (Cornell University, Southeast Asia Program, Data Paper Ser.: No. 69). 392p. reprint ed. pap. 111.80 (*0-317-10129-3*, 2010474) Bks Demand.

Yap Regains Its Sovereignty: The Story of the First Yap State Constitutional Convention, Vol. I, Background & Preparations. Dave Bird. 275p. 1994. pap. 17.00 (*0-9642897-0-9*) Koolau Writ.

Yapese-English Dictionary. John T. Jensen. LC 76-47495. (Pali Language Texts Micronesia Ser.). 202p. reprint ed. pap. 57.60 (*0-317-55704-1*, 2029582) Bks Demand.

Yaquai Terror. Buck Gentry. (Scout Ser.: No. 11). (Orig.). 1983. mass mkt. 2.50 (*0-317-00700-9*, Zebra Kensgtn) Kensgtn Pub Corp.

Yaqui Deer Songs - Maso Bwikam: A Native American Poetry. Larry Evers & Felipe S. Molina. LC 86-19313. (Sun Tracks Ser.: No. 14). 239p. 1986. pap. 17.95 (*0-8165-0995-6*) U of Ariz Pr.

Yaqui Easter. Muriel T. Painter. LC 74-153706. 40p. 1971. pap. 8.50 (*0-8165-0168-8*) U of Ariz Pr.

Yaqui Life: The Personal Chronicle of a Yaqui Indian. Rosalio Moises et al. LC 76-56789. Orig. Title: The Tall Candle: the Personal Chronicle of a Yaqui Indian. (Illus.). lxviii, 261p. 1977. reprint ed. pap. 14.95 (*0-8032-8175-7*, Bison Books) U of Nebr Pr.

Yaqui Myths & Legends. Ruth W. Giddings. Ed. by Harry Behn. LC 60-63129. (Illus.). 184p. reprint ed. pap. 47.90 (*0-8357-8583-1*, 2034953) Bks Demand.

Yaqui Myths & Legends. Ruth W. Giddings. LC 60-63129. (Illus.). 180p. 1993. reprint ed. pap. 11.95 (*0-8165-0467-9*) U of Ariz Pr.

Yaqui Resistance & Survival: The Struggle for Land & Autonomy, 1821-1910. Evelyn Hu-DeHart. LC 83-40265. (Illus.). 400p. 1984. text ed. 27.50 (*0-299-09660-2*) U of Wis Pr.

Yaqui Women: Contemporary Life Histories. Jane H. Kelley. LC 77-14063. (Illus.). viii, 265p. 1978. reprint ed. pap. 9.95 (*0-8032-7774-1*, Bison Books) U of Nebr Pr.

Yaquina Lighthouses on the Oregon Coast. Dorothy Wall & Bert Webber. LC 93-26330. (Illus.). 128p. (Orig.). 1994. pap. 10.95 (*0-936738-07-3*) Webb Research.

***Yaquis: A Celebration.** Harris S. Choate. (Illus.). 112p. (Orig.). 1997. pap. 17.95 (*0-9639519-7-1*) Whitewing Pr.

***Yaquis: A Celebration.** limited ed. Harris S. Choate. (Illus.). 112p. (Orig.). 1997. 50.00 (*0-9639519-9-8*) Whitewing Pr.

***Yaquis: A Cultural History.** Edward H. Spicer. 406p. 1980. write for info. (*0-8165-1747-9*) U of Ariz Pr.

Yaquis: A Cultural History. Edward H. Spicer. LC 79-27660. (Illus.). 407p. reprint ed. pap. 116.00 (*0-7837-5055-2*, 2044733) Bks Demand.

Yarb & Cretine: or Rising from Bonds. George B. Swayze. LC 72-4644. (Black Heritage Library Collection). 1977. reprint ed. 37.95 (*0-8369-9128-1*) Ayer.

Yard & Garden Furnishings. Cy DeCosse Incorporated Staff. LC 96-24422. (Portable Workshop Ser.). 1996. 14. 95 (*0-86573-668-5*) Cowles Creative.

Yard & Garden Tractor Service Manual, Multi-Cylinder Models. 1991. 24.95 (*0-87288-469-4*, YGT 2-1) Intertec Pub.

Yard & Garden Tractor Service Manual, Single-Cylinder Models. Intertec Publishing Staff. 1992. 24.95 (*0-87288-468-6*, YGT1-1) Intertec Pub.

Yard-Long Prints, Bk. III. William D. Keagy et al. (Illus.). 144p. 1995. 19.95 (*0-9633922-3-9*) W D Keagy.

Yard of Poplin. Dick Poplin. (Illus.). 96p. (Orig.). 1991. pap. 9.95 (*0-9624100-3-9*) Bell Buckle.

Yard Sale. James Stevenson. LC 95-4445. 32p. (J). (gr. k up). 1996. 15.00 (*0-688-14126-9*); lib. bdg. 14.93 (*0-688-14127-7*) Greenwillow.

***Yard Sale: Level 3.** Catherine Peters. (Little Reader Ser.). 1997. pap. text ed. 2.50 (*0-395-88300-8*) HM.

Yard, Street, Park: The Design of Suburban Open Space. Cynthia L. Girling & Kenneth I. Helphand. 256p. 1994. text ed. 54.95 (*0-471-55600-9*) Wiley.

***Yard, Street, Park: The Design of Suburban Open Space.** Cynthia L. Girling & Kenneth I. Helphand. LC 93-49454. 1996. pap. text ed. 34.95 (*0-471-17844-6*) Wiley.

Yardbird Suite. Deborah M. Rothschild. LC 94-938. (Illus.). 72p. 1995. pap. text ed. 18.95 (*0-913697-19-2*) Williams Art.

Yardbird Suite: A Compendium of the Music & Life of Charlie Parker. Lawrence O. Koch. LC 83-73435. (Illus.). 336p. 1988. 40.95 (*0-87972-259-2*) Bowling Green Univ Popular Press.

***Yardbirds: The Ultimate Rave Up.** (Illus.). 160p. (Orig.). 1997. pap. 19.95 (*0-9648157-2-9*) Crossfire NY.

Yardstick. Russell Epprecht. (New York Quarter Ser.: Vol. II). 208p. (Orig.). 1984. pap. 8.95 (*0-912195-11-8*) Domesday Bks.

***Yardsticks: Children in the Classroom, Ages 4-14, a Resource for Parents & Teachers.** 2nd rev. ed. Chip Wood. (Illus.). 240p. 1997. pap. 14.95 (*0-9618636-4-1*) NE Found Child.

Yardsticks: Retarded Characters & Their Roles in Fiction. Patricia M. Puccinelli. LC 92-43532. (AUS IV: Vol. 155). 104p. (C). 1995. text ed. 32.95 (*0-8204-2001-8*) P Lang Pubng.

Yardsticks for Assessing Displacement & Neighborhood Change. 100p. 1982. 20.00 (*0-318-17710-2*, DG 82-902) Pub Tech Inc.

Yarmouth - Old Homes & Gathering Places: An Historical Inventory. rev. ed. Ed. by Priscilla Gregory. (Illus.). 148p. 1989. pap. 18.00 (*0-317-94059-7*) Yarmouth Historical.

Yarmouth, Nova Scotia Genealogies: Transcribed from the Yarmouth Herald. George S. Brown. Ed. by Martha Reamy & William Reamy. 956p. 1993. 60.00 (*0-8063-1372-2*, 705) Genealog Pub.

***Yarmouth Register, 1904 (Town History & Directory)** Mitchell & Remick. 112p. 1997. reprint ed. pap. 19.50 (*0-8328-5934-6*) Higginson Bk Co.

Yarmouth's Proud Packets: The Commodore Hull Didn't Sail So Dull. Haynes R. Mahoney. (Illus.). 46p. 1986. pap. 4.00 (*0-9625068-1-8*) Hist Soc Yarmouth.

Yarmuk 636 AD. David Nicolle. (Campaign Ser.). (Illus.). 96p. 1994. pap. 14.95 (*1-85532-414-8*, 9530, Pub. by Osprey UK) Stackpole.

Yarmukian Culture of the Neolithic Period. M. Stekelis. (Illus.). 120p. 1973. text ed. 25.00 (*965-223-575-X*, Pub. by Magnes Press IS) Eisenbrauns.

Yarn. Babette Katz. (Illus.). 48p. (Orig.). 1992. pap. 10.00 (*0-89822-073-4*) Visual Studies.

Yarn Preparation: A Handbook. John Iredale. (Small-Scale Textiles Ser.). 48p. (Orig.). 1992. pap. 13.50 (*1-85339-042-9*, Pub. by Intermed Tech UK) Women Ink.

Yarn Production & Properties. E. Dyson et al. 96p. 1974. 80.00 (*0-686-63811-5*) St Mut.

Yarn Production & Properties. W. Nutter. 110p. 1971. 95. 00 (*0-686-63812-3*) St Mut.

Yarn Revolution. P. W. Harrison. 162p. 1976. 60.00 (*0-686-63814-X*) St Mut.

***Yarn Texturizing Technology.** L. Hes & P. Ursiny. 1994. pap. 42.00 (*0-614-20951-X*, Pub. by Textile Inst UK) St Mut.

Yarns. Tristan Jones. 272p. 1990. pap. 14.95 (*0-924486-02-3*) Sheridan.

Yarns of a Cyprus Pilot. G. V. Clark. 192p. (C). 1989. text ed. 65.00 (*1-872795-08-0*, Pub. by Pentland Pr UK) St Mut.

***Yaroslavl Oblast: Economy, Industry, Government, Business.** 2nd rev. ed. Russian Information & Business Center, Inc. Staff. (Russian Regional Business Directories Ser.). (Illus.). 200p. 1997. pap. 99.00 (*1-57751-426-2*) Russ Info & Busn Ctr.

***Yarrow.** De Lint. LC 97-24803. 1997. pap. 12.95 (*0-312-86393-4*) St Martin.

***Yarrow: A New Tale of Enchantment & Wonder.** Charles De Lint. 245p. (Orig.). 1993. pap. 14.95 (*0-330-31112-3*, Pub. by Pan Books UK) Trans-Atl Phila.

Yarrow Field. Regina McBride. Ed. by Kathleen Iddings. LC 90-60171. (American Bk.). 91p. (Orig.). 1990. per. 10.00 (*0-931289-04-1*) San Diego Poet Pr.

Yas. Sterling N. Daniels, 2nd. (Illus.). 36p. (J). (gr. k-3). pap. text ed. 4.95 (*0-9628081-2-1*) Daw Enter.

Yasavarman of Kanauj: Study of Political History, Society & Cultural Life of Northern India. Shyam M. Mishra. 1978. 15.00 (*0-8364-0105-0*) S Asia.

***Yasgur's Homeopathic Dictionary & Holistic Health Reference.** 4th ed. Jay Yasgur. LC 97-60094. Orig. Title: A Dictionary of Homeopathic Medical Terminology. 325p. (Orig.). 1997. pap. text ed. 21.95 (*1-886149-04-6*) Van Hoy Pubs.

Yasir Arafat. Rebecca Stefoff. (World Leaders - Past & Present Ser.). (Illus.). 112p. (YA). (gr. 5 up). 1989. lib. bdg. 19.95 (*1-55546-826-8*) Chelsea Hse.

Yasir Arafat: A Life of War & Peace. Elizabeth Ferber. LC 94-48285. (Illus.). 144p. (YA). (gr. 7 up). 1995. lib. bdg. 17.90 (*1-56294-585-8*) Millbrook Pr.

Yasmin. large type ed. Lowing. 1995. 25.99 (*0-7089-3419-6*) Ulverscroft.

Yasser Arafat - A Biblical Character? An Urgent Call to the Nation of Israel & the Body of Christ. Marvin Byers. 280p. (Orig.). 1996. pap. write for info. (*0-9647871-3-X*, Hope of Israel) Hebron Minist.

Yasser Arafat - Un Personaje Biblico? Un Llamado Urgente a la Nacion de Israel y Al Cuerpo de Cristo. Marvin Byers. 280p. (Orig.). (ENG & SPA.). 1996. pap. write for info. (*0-9647871-4-8*, Hope of Israel) Hebron Minist.

***Yasser Arafat an Apocalyptic Character.** rev. ed. Marvin Byers. 288p. 1996. pap. 12.98 (*0-9647871-5-6*, Hope of Israel) Hebron Minist.

Yasserna al-Qur'an: Arabic Qaidah - Rhythmic Methods of Learning Qur'anic Arabic. 3rd rev. ed. Muhammad S. Haque. LC 85-63835. (Illus.). viii, 88p. 1995. per. 4.50 incl. audio (*0-933057-03-2*) Namuk Intl Inc.

Yassi Ada: Vol. I, A Seventh-Century Byzantine Shipwreck. George F. Bass et al. LC 81-40401. (Nautical Archaeology Ser.: No. 1). (Illus.). 368p. 1982. 89.50 (*0-89096-063-1*) Tex A&M Univ Pr.

***Yastiks: Cushion Covers & Storage Bags of Anatolia.** Brian Morehouse. Ed. by Bethany Mendenhall. (Illus.). 116p. 1996. 55.00 (*1-889066-01-7*, 01) Phila Eighth ICOC.

Yasuo Kuniyoshi: Artist As Photographer. Bruce Weber. (Illus.). 80p. 1983. pap. 10.00 (*0-614-01859-5*) Norton Gal Art.

Yates City Community Centennial, 1957. (Illus.). 159p. 1995. reprint ed. pap. 24.50 (*0-8328-5012-8*) Higginson Bk Co.

Yatindramatadipika. Srinivasadasa. Tr. by Swami Adidevananda. 256p. Bilingual ed. pap. 2.95 (*0-87481-428-6*, Pub. by Ramakrishna Math II) Vedanta Pr.

Yatra, No. 5. Ed. by Alok Bhalla. (C). 1995. pap. 17.50 (*81-7223-188-1*, Pub. by Indus Pub II) S Asia.

Yatra of a Sometime Maverick. Lewis L. Baldwin. (Illus.). 210p. 1989. write for info. (*0-318-64899-7*) Sea Hse Pubs.

Yatra 3. Ed. by Alok Bhalla et al. (C). 1994. pap. text ed. 12.50 (*81-7223-148-2*, Pub. by Indus Pub II) S Asia.

Yatra 4. Ed. by Alok Bhalla et al. (C). 1994. pap. text ed. 12.50 (*81-7223-160-1*, Pub. by Indus Pub II) S Asia.

Yats in Movieland. Michael Russo. LC 94-76900. 336p. (Orig.). 1995. pap. 14.95 (*1-878044-22-2*) Mayhaven Pub.

Yattering & Jack. Clive Barker. 1991. pap. 7.95 (*1-56060-127-2*) Eclipse Bks.

Yattering & Jack: A Graphic Novel. Clive Barker. (Illus.). pap. 9.99 (*1-56060-183-3*) Eclipse Bks.

Yavanajataka of Sphujidhvaja, 2 vols., Set. Tr. by David Pingree. (Harvard Oriental Ser.: No. 48). 1024p. 1978. 90.00 (*0-674-96373-3*) HUP.

***Yavapai County-Coconino County (Arizona) Street & Road Atlas, 1996.** Wide World of Maps, Inc. Staff. (Illus.). 63p. 1995. spiral bd. 12.95 (*1-887749-00-4*, Phoenix Map Svce) Wide World Maps.

Yavapai People of the Red Rocks: People of the Sun. Kate Ruland-Thorne. Ed. by Aliza Caillou. (Illus.). 102p. (Orig.). 1993. pap. 6.95 (*0-9628329-5-2*) Thorne Enterprises.

***Yavin & Bespin.** (Star Wars Galaxy Guides Ser.: No. 2). 15.00 (*0-87431-262-0*, 40119) West End Games.

Yawar Fiesta. Jose M. Arguedas. Tr. by Frances H. Barraclough from SPA. LC 84-19625. (Texas Pan American Ser.). 224p. 1985. 22.50 (*0-292-79601-3*); pap. 11.95 (*0-292-79602-1*) U of Tex Pr.

Yawn, et Al: A Key to Reserve Buoyancy for Human Flight. Millicent Linden. LC 78-64375. (Evolutionary New Material from Tension in Repose Ser.). (Illus.). 1978. 7.00 (*0-912628-06-5*) M Linden NY.

Yawn Maker. Elaine Weimann & Rita Friedman. (Read to Me Bks.). (Illus.). 30p. (J). (ps-1). 1986. lib. bdg. 12.50 (*0-89796-993-6*) New Dimens Educ.

Yawn-Maker Wanted. Rita Friedman & Elaine Weimann. (Fables from the Letter People Ser.). (Illus.). 30p. (J). (ps-1). 1989. lib. bdg. 12.95 (*0-89796-024-6*) New Dimens Educ.

Yawning Gap. Crescenciano Gonzaga. 146p. (Orig.). 1991. pap. 10.00 (*971-10-0452-6*, Pub. by New Day Pub PH) Cellar.

Yawoldo. Young K. Shin. Tr. by Song S. Kim. 144p. (Orig.). 1996. pap. 7.95 (*1-883928-16-8*) Longwood.

Yaxchilan: Antologia de Su Descubrimiento y Estudios. Ed. by Roberto Garcia & Daniel Juarez. 206p. 1992. pap. 9.00 (*968-6038-34-5*, IN002) UPLAAP.

Yaxchilan: The Design of a Maya Ceremonial City. Carolyn E. Tate. LC 91-3248. (Illus.). 320p. 1992. text ed. 40.00 (*0-292-77041-3*) U of Tex Pr.

***Yay!** Emily Rodda. LC 96-46251. (Illus.). 40p. (J). (gr. k up). 1997. 15.00 (*0-688-15255-4*) Greenwillow.

***Yay!** Emily Rodda. LC 96-46251. (Illus.). (J). Date not set. lib. bdg. write for info. (*0-688-15256-2*) Morrow.

Ya/Ya! Young New Orleans Artists & Their Storytelling Chairs (& How to Ya/Ya in Your Neighborhood) Claudia Barker. LC 96-31548. (Illus.). 152p. 1996. 34.95 (*0-8071-2092-8*) La State U Pr.

Yayoi Kusama: The 1950s & 1960s Paintings, Sculpture, Works on Paper. Alexandra Munroe. (Illus.). 40p. (Orig.). 1996. pap. 22.00 (*0-9608210-3-1*) Paula Cooper Gallery.

Yaz Baseball the Wall & Me. Carl Yastrzemski. 1991. mass mkt. 4.95 (*0-446-36103-8*) Warner Bks.

Yazoo: Law & Politics in the New Republic: The Case of Fletcher v. Peck. C. Peter Magrath. LC 66-19584. 259p. reprint ed. pap. 73.90 (*0-685-44067-2*, 2030026) Bks Demand.

Yazoo County, Mississippi, Eighteen Fifty Census & Marriages. Diane F. Roos. 140p. (Orig.). 1990. pap. 20. 00 (*1-55613-343-X*) Heritage Bk.

Yazoo County, Mississippi Pioneers. Betty C. Wiltshire. vi, 263p. (Orig.). 1993. pap. text ed. 21.00 (*1-55613-692-7*) Heritage Bk.

Yazoo River. Frank E. Smith. LC 88-1123. (Illus.). 362p. 1988. reprint ed. 40.00 (*0-87805-353-0*); reprint ed. pap. 16.95 (*0-87805-355-7*) U Pr of Miss.

YBH: Getting Serious about Faith. Vernon Grounds. LC 91-21255. 128p. 1991. pap. 8.99 (*0-929239-50-4*) Discovery Hse Pubs.

Ybor City Chronicles: A Memoir. Ferdie Pacheco. LC 94-822. (Illus.). 320p. 1994. 24.95 (*0-8130-1296-1*) U Press Fla.

Ye Are Gods. Annalee Skarin. 343p. 1973. reprint ed. pap. 6.95 (*0-87516-344-0*) DeVorss.

Ye Banks & Braes O' Bonnie Doon: Full Score. P. Grainger. 8p. 1986. pap. 7.50 (*0-7935-5100-5*, 50349800) H Leonard.

***Ye Booke of Monsters Vol. II: The Aniolowski Collection.** Scott D. Aniolowski. Ed. by Janice Sellers. (Call of Cthulhu Roleplaying Game System Ser.). (Illus.). 60p. (Orig.). 1996. pap. 11.95 (*1-56882-052-6*, 2358) Chaosium.

Ye Fathers. David Burkholder. 360p. 1996. 9.60 (*0-614-17639-5*, 2112) Rod & Staff.

Ye Followers of the Lamb. E. Ferguson. 20p. 1986. pap. 1.60 (*0-7935-5507-8*) H Leonard.

Ye Giglampz: A Weekly Illustrated Journal Devoted to Art, Literature & Satire. Jon C. Hughes. Ed. by Lafcadio Hearn & Henry Farny. (Illus.). 100p. 1973. 95.00 (*0-686-47721-9*) Crossroad Bks Public.

An Asterisk (*) at the beginning of an entry indicates that the title is appearing in BIP for the first time.

Ye Gods! Anne S. Baumgartner. 192p. 1984. 14.95 (*0-8184-0349-7*) Carol Pub Group.
Ye Gods. Helen Britt. (J). 1987. pap. text ed. 11.16 (*0-88334-196-4*, 76161) Longman.
Ye Historie of Ye Town of Greenwich, Co. of Fairfield & State of Conn., with Genealogical Notes on (Many) Families. Spencer P. Mead. (Illus.). 768p. 1995. reprint ed. lib. bdg. 77.50 (*0-8328-4605-8*) Higginson Bk Co.
Ye Historie of Ye Town of Greenwich, Connecticut. Spencer P. Mead. LC 92-60184. (Illus.). 862p. 1992. reprint ed. 49.50 (*0-89725-079-6*, 1348) Picton Pr.
Ye Hysterical Historie of Ye Norfolk Towne: With Master of Mirth. 2nd ed. Frank S. Wing & William G. Wing. Ed. by Calvert W. Tazewell. LC 90-81465. (Illus.). 76p. 1990. pap. 9.00 (*1-878515-24-1*) W S Dawson.
Ye Kingdom of Accawmacke, or the Eastern Shore of Virginia in the 17th Century. J. C. Wise. (Illus.). 416p. 1989. reprint ed. lib. bdg. 42.50 (*0-8328-0578-5*) Higginson Bk Co.
Ye Must Be Born Again. Chester Wilkins. 1979. pap. 2.99 (*0-685-70970-1*) Schmul Pub Co.
Ye Olde Coffey Grounds: The Coffey-Galloway Cemetery at Woodbury Common, Central Valley, New York. Marjorie Smeltzer-Stevenot. LC 93-85750. (Illus.). 68p. (Orig.). (C). 1994. pap. text ed. 10.95 (*0-9608634-5-1*) M Smeltzer-Stevenot.
Ye Olde Dream Book. Frater Zarathustra, pseud. LC 86-51388. 56p. (Orig.). (C). 1987. pap. 15.00 (*0-939856-69-7*) Tech Group.
Ye Olde Osborne Cemetery. M. Edward Burtt. (Illus.). 13p. (Orig.). 1995. pap. write for info. (*1-888913-18-5*) M E Burtt.
Ye Search the Scriptures. Watchman Nee. Tr. by Stephen Kaung. 173p. 1974. 8.00 (*0-935008-46-2*); pap. 5.00 (*0-935008-47-0*) Christian Fellow Pubs.
*__Ye Shall Be Witnesses.__ Date not set. pap. 1.20 (*0-8341-9290-X*) Lillenas.
Ye Shall Know the Truth. Daniel J. Armstrong, Sr. 48p. 1995. pap. 7.00 (*0-8059-3783-8*) Dorrance.
Ye Shall Receive Power: Devotional Readings from the Bible for 1996. E. G. White. 1995. 10.99 (*0-8280-0972-4*) Review & Herald.
Ye Shall Receive Power: The Amazing Miracle of Holy Spirit Baptism. Peter Popoff. Ed. by Don Tanner. LC 82-71629. (Illus.). 96p. 1982. pap. 2.00 (*0-938544-14-4*) Faith Messenger.
Ye Solace of Pilgrimes. John Capgrave. Ed. by C. A. Mills. LC 78-63453. (Crusades & Military Orders Ser.: Second Series). reprint ed. 52.50 (*0-404-16375-0*) AMS Pr.
Ye Yaille, Chere: Traditional Cajun Dance Music. Raymond E. Francois. 506p. 1995. reprint ed. 39.95 (*0-9625542-0-0*) Thndrstn Pr.
Yea! I'm an Orphan. Ruth M. Bowen. 1986. write for info. (*0-935087-12-5*) Wright Pub Co.
Yea Though I Walk. Carla Cadzow. Ed. by M. L. Jones. LC 94-76892. 171p. (Orig.). 1994. pap. 6.95 (*1-882270-17-7*) Old Rugged Cross.
Yea! Wildcats. John R. Tunis. 320p. (J). (gr. 3-7). 1989. pap. 4.00 (*0-15-299718-0*, Odyssey) HarBrace.
Yeager: An Autobiography. Chuck Yeager. Ed. by Leo Janos. 448p. 1986. mass mkt. 6.99 (*0-553-25674-2*) Bantam.
Yeager Meditation Tarot. Marty Yeager. 24p. 1982. pap. 15.00 (*0-88079-006-7*) US Games Syst.
Yeah but, Children Need... Karen L. Rancourt. 144p. 1978. 18.95 (*0-87073-959-X*) Schenkman Bks Inc.
Yeah, But How Would She Look Beside the Go-Kart Trophy. Nancy Jo Batman. LC 92-19199. (Illus.). 104p. (Orig.). 1992. pap. 9.99 (*0-8272-4403-7*) Chalice Pr.
Yeah, You Rite! An Adventure in Comedy & Courage. Jo A. Rosenfeld. (Illus.). 240p. (Orig.). 1995. pap. 11.95 (*0-9647266-0-2*) Medica-Spera.
Year. Suzanne Lange. LC 78-120787. (J). (gr. 8 up). 1970. 24.95 (*0-87599-173-4*) S G Phillips.
Year: A Celebration. Tom Tolnay. (Illus.). 32p. (Orig.). 1988. pap. 10.00 (*0-913559-05-9*) Birch Brook Pr.
Year after Childbirth. Sheila Kitzinger. 320p. 1996. pap. 13.00 (*0-684-82520-1*) S&S Trade.
Year after Childbirth: Surviving the First Year of Motherhood. Sheila Kitzinger. (Illus.). 288p. 1994. 25.00 (*0-684-19615-8*) S&S Trade.
Year after the Riots: American Responses to the Palestinian Crisis of 1929-30. Naomi W. Cohen. LC 87-32538. 212p. 1988. 29.95 (*0-8143-1914-9*) Wayne St U Pr.
Year Ahead: 1987. Naisbitt Group Staff & John Naisbitt. (Orig.). 1999. mass mkt. 6.95 (*0-446-38342-2*) Warner Bks.
Year America Discovered Texas: Centennial '36. Kenneth B. Ragsdale. LC 86-30041. (Centennial Series of the Association of Former Students: No. 23). (Illus.). 352p. 1987. 19.95 (*0-89096-299-5*) Tex A&M Univ Pr.
Year Amongst the Persians: Impressions As to the Life, Character, & Thought of the People of Persia. 3rd ed. Edward G. Browne. LC 83-45722. reprint ed. 61.50 (*0-404-20046-X*) AMS Pr.
Year & a Day. Marian Edwards. 400p. 1994. mass mkt. 4.50 (*0-8217-4601-4*, Zebra Kensgtn) Kensgtn Pub Corp.
Year & a Day. William Mayne. (J). (gr. 4-7). 1990. 19.25 (*0-8446-6431-6*) Peter Smith.
Year & Our Children: Planning the Family Activities for Christian Feasts & Seasons. 2nd ed. Mary R. Newland. 192p. 1995. pap. 11.95 (*1-885553-37-4*) Firefly Press.
Year Around: Poems for Children. Compiled by Alice I. Hazeltine & Smith Hazeltine. LC 72-11921. (Granger Index Reprint Ser.). (YA). (gr. 7 up). 1977. reprint ed. 18.95 (*0-8369-6403-9*) Ayer.
Year at Elk Meadow. Jackie Gilmore. 16p. (J). (ps-3). 1986. pap. 4.95 (*0-911797-24-6*) R Rinehart.
Year at Great Dixter. Christopher Lloyd. Date not set. pap. 12.95 (*0-14-046744-0*) Viking Penguin.
Year at Hartlebury: or The Election. Benjamin Disraeli & Sarah Disraeli. 221p. 1983. 24.95 (*0-8020-2439-4*) U of Toronto Pr.
Year at Monticello: 1795. Donald Jackson. LC 89-7847. (Illus.). 126p. 1989. 17.95 (*1-55591-050-5*) Fulcrum Pub.
Year at North Hill: Four Seasons in a Vermont Garden. Joe Eck & Wayne Winterrowd. 224p. 1996. pap. 19.95 (*0-8050-4614-3*) H Holt & Co.
Year at North Hill, Four Seasons in a Vermont Garden Vol. 1. Joe Eck. 1995. 35.00 (*0-316-20916-3*) Little.
Year at Thrush Green. Grace Read. 272p. 1996. 21.95 (*0-395-79570-2*) HM.
*__Year at Thrush Green.__ large type ed. Grace Read. LC 96-42155. (Core Ser.). 349p. 1996. 25.95 (*0-7838-1964-1*, Thorndike Lrg Prnt) Thorndike Pr.
Year at Yattabilla. large type ed. Amanda Doyle. 306p. 1980. 25.99 (*0-7089-0537-4*) Ulverscroft.
Year Before Death. Clive Seale & Ann Cartwright. 252p. 1994. 59.95 (*1-85628-604-5*, Pub. by Avebury Pub UK) Ashgate Pub Co.
Year Book. American Philosophical Society Staff. LC 39-2034. 1997. pap. 20.00 (*0-87169-991-5*, YRBK-1994) Am Philos.
Year Book. Alex Gildzen. 150p. (Orig.). 1975. pap. 3.00 (*0-913028-27-4*) North Atlantic.
Year Book Neurology & Neurosurgery, 1994. Bradley. 490p. (C). (gr. 13). 1994. text ed. 69.95 (*0-8151-2143-1*, Yr Bk Med Pubs) Mosby Yr Bk.
Year Book Neurology & Neurosurgery, 1995. Bradley. 490p. (C). (gr. 13). 1995. text ed. 69.95 (*0-8151-2144-X*, Yr Bk Med Pubs) Mosby Yr Bk.
Year Book Neurology & Neurosurgery, 1996. Bradley. 490p. (C). (gr. 13). 1996. text ed. 72.95 (*0-8151-2145-8*, Yr Bk Med Pubs) Mosby Yr Bk.
Year Book Obstetrics & Gynecology, 1994. Daniel R. Mishell. 525p. (C). (gr. 13). 1994. text ed. 72.95 (*0-8151-6016-X*, Yr Bk Med Pubs) Mosby Yr Bk.
Year Book Obstetrics & Gynecology, 1996. Daniel R. Mishell. 525p. (C). (gr. 13). 1996. text ed. 75.95 (*0-8151-6018-6*, Yr Bk Med Pubs) Mosby Yr Bk.
Year Book of Allergy & Clinical Immunology, 1994. Lanny J. Rosenwasser. 320p. (C). (gr. 13). 1994. text ed. 61.95 (*0-8151-7275-3*, Yr Bk Med Pubs) Mosby Yr Bk.
Year Book of Allergy & Clinical Immunology, 1995. 2nd ed. Lanny J. Rosenwasser. 320p. (C). (gr. 13). 1995. text ed. 64.95 (*0-8151-7276-1*, Yr Bk Med Pubs) Mosby Yr Bk.
Year Book of Allergy & Clinical Immunology, 1996. 3rd ed. Lanny J. Rosenwasser. 320p. (C). (gr. 13). 1996. text ed. 74.95 (*0-8151-7277-X*, Yr Bk Med Pubs) Mosby Yr Bk.
Year Book of Allergy & Clinical Immunology, 1998. 5th ed. Lanny J. Rosenwasser. 320p. (C). (gr. 13). 1998. text ed. 74.95 (*0-8151-7279-6*, Yr Bk Med Pubs) Mosby Yr Bk.
Year Book of Anesthesia, 1995. Miller. 400p. (C). (gr. 13). 1995. text ed. 72.95 (*0-8151-5987-0*, Yr Bk Med Pubs) Mosby Yr Bk.
Year Book of Anesthesia, 1996. Miller. 400p. (C). (gr. 13). 1996. text ed. 75.95 (*0-8151-5988-9*, Yr Bk Med Pubs) Mosby Yr Bk.
Year Book of Cardiology, 1992. Year Book of Cardiology Staff. Ed. by Robert C. Schlant. LC 78-647167. 455p. 1992. reprint ed. pap. 129.70 (*0-608-02417-1*, 2063059) Bks Demand.
Year Book of Cardiology, 1994. Robert C. Schlant. 375p. (C). (gr. 13). 1994. text ed. 74.95 (*0-8151-7521-3*, Yr Bk Med Pubs) Mosby Yr Bk.
Year Book of Cardiology, 1995. Robert C. Schlant. 375p. (C). (gr. 13). 1995. text ed. 74.95 (*0-8151-7522-1*, Yr Bk Med Pubs) Mosby Yr Bk.
Year Book of Cardiology, 1996. Robert C. Schlant. 375p. (C). (gr. 13). 1996. text ed. 76.95 (*0-8151-7524-8*, Yr Bk Med Pubs) Mosby Yr Bk.
Year Book of Chiropractic, 1995. Phillips & Adams. 352p. (gr. 13). 1995. text ed. 62.95 (*0-8151-6735-0*, Yr Bk Med Pubs) Mosby Yr Bk.
Year Book of Chiropractic, 1996. Phillips & Adams. 352p. (gr. 13). 1996. text ed. 69.95 (*0-8151-6736-9*, Yr Bk Med Pubs) Mosby Yr Bk.
*__Year Book of Chiropractic, 1996.__ Ed. by Dana J. Lawrence. LC 94-657513. (Illus.). 464p. 1996. reprint ed. pap. 132.30 (*0-608-04223-4*, 2064967) Bks Demand.
Year Book of Clinical Microbiology: 1991. Ed. by James W. Snyder. 400p. 1991. 163.00 (*0-8493-3310-5*, QA, CRC Reprint) Franklin.
Year Book of Clinical Microbiology, 1993. James W. Snyder. 272p. 1993. 102.00 (*0-8493-3313-X*, QA) CRC Pr.
Year Book of Critical Care Medicine, 1991. Year Book of Critical Care Medicine Staff. Ed. by Mark C. Rogers & Joseph E. Parrillo. LC 84-8032. 374p. 1991. reprint ed. pap. 106.60 (*0-608-02415-5*, 2063057) Bks Demand.
Year Book of Critical Care Medicine, 1993. Year Book of Critical Care Medicine Staff. Ed. by Mark C. Rogers & Joseph E. Parrillo. LC 84-8032. 426p. 1993. reprint ed. pap. 121.50 (*0-608-02458-9*, 2063102) Bks Demand.
Year Book of Critical Care Medicine, 1995. D. Rogers. 348p. (C). (gr. 13). 1995. text ed. 72.95 (*0-8151-7256-7*, Yr Bk Med Pubs) Mosby Yr Bk.
Year Book of Critical Care Medicine, 1996. D. Rogers. 348p. (C). (gr. 13). 1996. text ed. 72.95 (*0-8151-7257-5*, Yr Bk Med Pubs) Mosby Yr Bk.
Year Book of Daily Recreation & Information. William Hone. LC 89-71339. (Illus.). 1644p. 1998. reprint ed. lib. bdg. 60.00 (*1-55888-924-8*) Omnigraphics Inc.
Year Book of Dentistry, 1995. Lawrence Meskin. 450p. (C). (gr. 13). 1995. text ed. 66.95 (*0-8151-5878-5*, Yr Bk Med Pubs) Mosby Yr Bk.
Year Book of Dentistry, 1996. Lawrence Meskin. 450p. (C). (gr. 13). 1996. text ed. 72.95 (*0-8151-5879-3*, Yr Bk Med Pubs) Mosby Yr Bk.
Year Book of Dermatologic Surgery, 1992. Year Book of Dermatologic Surgery Staff. Ed. by Neil A. Swanson. LC 91-3627. 264p. 1992. reprint ed. pap. 75.30 (*0-608-02412-0*, 2063054) Bks Demand.
Year Book of Dermatologic Surgery, 1995. Swanson. 250p. (C). (gr. 13). 1995. text ed. 72.95 (*0-8151-8688-6*, Yr Bk Med Pubs) Mosby Yr Bk.
Year Book of Dermatologic Surgery, 1996. Swanson. 250p. (C). (gr. 13). 1996. text ed. 79.95 (*0-8151-8689-4*, Yr Bk Med Pubs) Mosby Yr Bk.
Year Book of Dermatology, 1994. Arthur J. Sober. 500p. (C). (gr. 13). 1994. text ed. 74.95 (*0-8151-7916-2*, Yr Bk Med Pubs) Mosby Yr Bk.
Year Book of Dermatology, 1995. Arthur J. Sober. 500p. (C). (gr. 13). 1995. text ed. 74.95 (*0-8151-7917-0*, Yr Bk Med Pubs) Mosby Yr Bk.
Year Book of Dermatology, 1996. Arthur J. Sober. 500p. (C). (gr. 13). 1996. text ed. 77.95 (*0-8151-7918-9*, Yr Bk Med Pubs) Mosby Yr Bk.
Year Book of Developmental Biology. Ed. by Joel M. Schindler. 224p. 1989. 146.00 (*0-8493-3300-8*, QH, CRC Reprint) Franklin.
Year Book of Diagnostic Radiology, 1995. Michael P. Federle. 570p. (C). (gr. 13). 1995. text ed. 68.95 (*0-8151-1140-1*, Yr Bk Med Pubs) Mosby Yr Bk.
*__Year Book of Diagnostic Radiology, 1995.__ Ed. by Michael P. Federle et al. (Illus.). 804p. 1995. reprint ed. pap. 180.00 (*0-608-04224-2*, 2064968) Bks Demand.
Year Book of Diagnostic Radiology, 1996. Michael P. Federle et al. 570p. (C). (gr. 13). 1996. text ed. 71.95 (*0-8151-1141-X*, Yr Bk Med Pubs) Mosby Yr Bk.
Year Book of Digestive Diseases, 1992. Year Book of Digestive Diseases Staff. Ed. by Norton J. Greenberger & Frank G. Moody. LC 85-641221. 476p. 1992. reprint ed. pap. 135.70 (*0-608-02410-4*, 2063052) Bks Demand.
Year Book of Digestive Diseases, 1993. Year Book of Digestive Diseases Staff. Ed. by Norton J. Greenberger & Frank G. Moody. LC 85-641221. 528p. 1993. reprint ed. pap. 150.50 (*0-608-02479-1*, 2063093) Bks Demand.
Year Book of Digestive Diseases, 1994. Greenberger. 450p. (C). (gr. 13). 1994. text ed. 72.95 (*0-8151-3891-1*, Yr Bk Med Pubs) Mosby Yr Bk.
Year Book of Digestive Diseases, 1995. Greenberger. 450p. (C). (gr. 13). 1995. text ed. 72.95 (*0-8151-3892-X*, Yr Bk Med Pubs) Mosby Yr Bk.
Year Book of Digestive Diseases, 1996. Greenberger. 450p. (C). (gr. 13). 1996. text ed. 77.95 (*0-8151-3893-8*, Yr Bk Med Pubs) Mosby Yr Bk.
Year Book of Drug Therapy, 1995. Louis Lasagna. 350p. (C). (gr. 13). 1995. text ed. 66.95 (*0-8151-5293-0*, Yr Bk Med Pubs) Mosby Yr Bk.
Year Book of Drug Therapy, 1996. Louis Lasagna. 350p. (C). (gr. 13). 1996. text ed. 79.95 (*0-8151-5294-9*, Yr Bk Med Pubs) Mosby Yr Bk.
Year Book of Emergency Medicine, 1992. Year Book of Emergency Medicine Staff. Ed. by David K. Wagner. LC 81-642219. 427p. 1992. reprint ed. pap. 121.70 (*0-608-02416-3*, 2063058) Bks Demand.
Year Book of Emergency Medicine, 1994. Wagner. 420p. (C). (gr. 13). 1994. text ed. 72.95 (*0-8151-9065-4*, Yr Bk Med Pubs) Mosby Yr Bk.
Year Book of Emergency Medicine, 1995. Wagner. 420p. (C). (gr. 13). 1995. text ed. 73.95 (*0-8151-9068-9*, Yr Bk Med Pubs) Mosby Yr Bk.
Year Book of Emergency Medicine, 1996. Wagner. 420p. (C). (gr. 13). 1996. text ed. 76.95 (*0-8151-9069-7*, Yr Bk Med Pubs) Mosby Yr Bk.
Year Book of Endocrinology, 1994. Bagdade. 370p. (C). (gr. 13). 1994. text ed. 72.95 (*0-8151-0442-1*, Yr Bk Med Pubs) Mosby Yr Bk.
Year Book of Endocrinology, 1995. Bagdade. 370p. (C). (gr. 13). 1995. text ed. 72.95 (*0-8151-0443-X*, Yr Bk Med Pubs) Mosby Yr Bk.
Year Book of Endocrinology, 1996. Bagdade. 370p. (C). (gr. 13). 1996. text ed. 75.95 (*0-8151-0444-8*, Yr Bk Med Pubs) Mosby Yr Bk.
Year Book of Family Practice, 1995. Berg. 550p. (C). (gr. 13). 1995. text ed. 59.95 (*0-8151-0753-6*, Yr Bk Med Pubs) Mosby Yr Bk.
Year Book of Family Practice, 1996. Berg. 550p. (C). (gr. 13). 1996. text ed. 64.95 (*0-8151-0754-4*, Yr Bk Med Pubs) Mosby Yr Bk.
Year Book of Famous Lyrics. Frederic L. Knowles. LC 70-109143. (Granger Index Reprint Ser.). 1977. 25.95 (*0-8369-6127-7*) Ayer.
Year Book of Geriatrics & Gerontology, 1995. Beck. 290p. (C). (gr. 13). 1995. text ed. 66.95 (*0-8151-0638-6*, Yr Bk Med Pubs) Mosby Yr Bk.
Year Book of Geriatrics & Gerontology, 1996. Beck. 290p. (C). (gr. 13). 1996. text ed. 66.95 (*0-8151-0639-4*, Yr Bk Med Pubs) Mosby Yr Bk.
Year Book of Hand Surgery, 1993. Year Book of Hand Surgery Staff. Ed. by Peter C. Amadio. LC 85-641951. 394p. 1993. reprint ed. pap. 112.30 (*0-608-02404-X*, 2063046) Bks Demand.
Year Book of Hand Surgery, 1995. Amadio. 350p. (C). (gr. 13). 1995. text ed. 72.95 (*0-8151-2647-6*, Yr Bk Med Pubs) Mosby Yr Bk.
Year Book of Hand Surgery, 1996. Amadio. 350p. (C). (gr. 13). 1996. text ed. 75.95 (*0-8151-2648-4*, Yr Bk Med Pubs) Mosby Yr Bk.
Year Book of Health Care Management, 1994. Heyssel. 250p. 1994. 64.95 (*0-8151-4297-8*, Yr Bk Med Pubs) Mosby Yr Bk.
Year Book of Health Care Management, 1995. Heyssel. 245p. 1995. 64.95 (*0-8151-4298-6*, Yr Bk Med Pubs) Mosby Yr Bk.
Year Book of Health Care Management, 1996. Heyssel. 245p. 1996. 64.95 (*0-8151-4299-4*, Yr Bk Med Pubs) Mosby Yr Bk.
Year Book of Hematology, 1995. Jerry L. Spivak. 456p. (C). (gr. 13). 1994. text ed. 74.95 (*0-8151-8128-0*, Yr Bk Med Pubs) Mosby Yr Bk.
Year Book of Hematology, 1996. Jerry L. Spivak. 456p. (C). (gr. 13). 1995. text ed. 77.95 (*0-8151-8129-9*, Yr Bk Med Pubs) Mosby Yr Bk.
Year Book of Infectious Diseases, 1994. Year Book of Infectious Diseases Staff. Ed. by Gerald T. Keusch & Sheldon M. Wolff. LC 86-659565. 416p. 1994. reprint ed. pap. 118.60 (*0-608-02407-4*, 2063049) Bks Demand.
Year Book of Infectious Diseases, 1995. Wolff. 400p. (C). (gr. 13). 1995. pap. text ed. 72.95 (*0-8151-9384-X*, Yr Bk Med Pubs) Mosby Yr Bk.
Year Book of Infectious Diseases, 1995. Year Book of Infectious Diseases Staff. Ed. by Gerald T. Keusch. LC 86-659565. 572p. 1995. reprint ed. pap. 163.10 (*0-608-02446-5*, 2063089) Bks Demand.
Year Book of Infectious Diseases, 1996. Wolff. 400p. (C). (gr. 13). 1995. text ed. 72.95 (*0-8151-9385-8*, Yr Bk Med Pubs) Mosby Yr Bk.
Year Book of Infertility, 1994. Daniel R. Mishell. 285p. (C). (gr. 13). 1994. text ed. 72.95 (*0-8151-6005-4*, Yr Bk Med Pubs) Mosby Yr Bk.
Year Book of Infertility, 1995. Daniel R. Mishell. 285p. (C). (gr. 13). 1995. text ed. 66.95 (*0-8151-6006-2*, Yr Bk Med Pubs) Mosby Yr Bk.
Year Book of Infertility, 1996. Daniel R. Mishell. 285p. (C). (gr. 13). 1996. text ed. 74.95 (*0-8151-6007-0*, Yr Bk Med Pubs) Mosby Yr Bk.
Year Book of Medicine, 1995. D. Rogers. 805p. (C). (gr. 13). 1995. text ed. 66.95 (*0-8151-7268-0*, Yr Bk Med Pubs) Mosby Yr Bk.
Year Book of Medicine, 1996. D. Rogers. 805p. (C). (gr. 13). 1996. text ed. 72.95 (*0-8151-7269-9*, Yr Bk Med Pubs) Mosby Yr Bk.
Year Book of Neonatal & Perinatal Medicine, 1995. Klaus. 350p. (C). (gr. 13). 1995. text ed. 72.95 (*0-8151-5230-2*, Yr Bk Med Pubs) Mosby Yr Bk.
Year Book of Neonatal & Perinatal Medicine, 1996. Klaus. 350p. (C). (gr. 13). 1996. text ed. 76.95 (*0-8151-5231-0*, Yr Bk Med Pubs) Mosby Yr Bk.
Year Book of Nephrology, 1995. Coe. 400p. (C). (gr. 13). 1995. text ed. 74.95 (*0-8151-1931-3*, Yr Bk Med Pubs) Mosby Yr Bk.
Year Book of Nephrology, 1996. Coe. 400p. (C). (gr. 13). 1996. text ed. 79.95 (*0-8151-1932-1*, Yr Bk Med Pubs) Mosby Yr Bk.
Year Book of Neurology & Neurosurgery, 1993. Year Book of Neurology & Neurosurgery Staff. Ed. by Walter G. Bradley & Robert M. Crowell. LC 79-8269. 480p. 1993. reprint ed. pap. 136.80 (*0-608-02411-2*, 2063053) Bks Demand.
Year Book of Neuroradiology, 1994. Year Book of Neuroradiology Staff. Ed. by Anne G. Osborn. LC 92-4593. 400p. 1994. reprint ed. pap. 114.00 (*0-608-02405-8*, 2063047) Bks Demand.
Year Book of Neuroradiology, 1995: Head & Neck Radiology. Osborn et al. 350p. (C). (gr. 13). 1995. text ed. 84.95 (*0-8151-6591-9*, Yr Bk Med Pubs) Mosby Yr Bk.
Year Book of Neuroradiology, 1996: Head & Neck Radiology. Osborn et al. 350p. (C). (gr. 13). 1996. text ed. 94.95 (*0-8151-6592-7*, Yr Bk Med Pubs) Mosby Yr Bk.
Year Book of Nuclear Medicine, 1995. Paul B. Hoffer. 380p. (C). (gr. 13). 1995. text ed. 74.95 (*0-8151-4513-6*, Yr Bk Med Pubs) Mosby Yr Bk.
Year Book of Obstetrics & Gynecology, 1995. Daniel R. Mishell. 525p. (C). (gr. 13). 1995. text ed. 72.95 (*0-8151-6017-8*, Yr Bk Med Pubs) Mosby Yr Bk.
Year Book of Occupational & Environmental Medicine, 1992. Year Book of Occupational & Environmental Medicine Staff. Ed. by Edward A. Emmett. LC 90-660238. 275p. 1992. reprint ed. pap. 78.40 (*0-608-02408-2*, 2063050) Bks Demand.
Year Book of Occupational Medicine & Environmental Health, 1995. Emmett. 234p. (C). (gr. 13). 1995. text ed. 69.95 (*0-8151-3087-2*, Yr Bk Med Pubs) Mosby Yr Bk.
Year Book of Occupational Medicine & Environmental Health, 1996. Emmett. 234p. (C). (gr. 13). 1996. text ed. 72.95 (*0-8151-3088-0*, Yr Bk Med Pubs) Mosby Yr Bk.
Year Book of Oncology Nursing, 1994. Christine Miaskowski et al. 320p. 1994. 39.95 (*0-8151-6140-9*, Yr Bk Med Pubs) Mosby Yr Bk.
Year Book of Oncology Nursing, 1995. Christine Miaskowski et al. 320p. 1995. 39.95 (*0-8151-6141-7*, Yr Bk Med Pubs) Mosby Yr Bk.
Year Book of Oncology Nursing, 1996. Christine Miaskowski et al. 320p. 1996. 39.95 (*0-8151-6142-5*, Yr Bk Med Pubs) Mosby Yr Bk.
Year Book of Oncology, 1995. Young. 390p. (C). (gr. 13). 1995. text ed. 74.95 (*0-8151-9757-8*, Yr Bk Med Pubs) Mosby Yr Bk.
Year Book of Oncology, 1996. Young. 390p. (C). (gr. 13). 1996. text ed. 84.95 (*0-8151-9758-6*, Yr Bk Med Pubs) Mosby Yr Bk.
Year Book of Ophthalmology, 1994. Peter R. Laibson. 253p. (C). (gr. 13). 1994. text ed. 75.95 (*0-8151-5270-1*, Yr Bk Med Pubs) Mosby Yr Bk.
Year Book of Ophthalmology, 1995. Peter R. Laibson. 253p. (C). (gr. 13). 1995. text ed. 75.95 (*0-8151-5271-X*, Yr Bk Med Pubs) Mosby Yr Bk.
Year Book of Ophthalmology, 1996. Peter R. Laibson. 253p. (C). (gr. 13). 1996. text ed. 78.95 (*0-8151-5272-8*, Yr Bk Med Pubs) Mosby Yr Bk.
Year Book of Orthopedics, 1994. Clement B. Sledge. 404p. (C). (gr. 13). 1994. text ed. 75.95 (*0-8151-7811-5*, Yr Bk Med Pubs) Mosby Yr Bk.

Year Book of Orthopedics, 1995. Clement B. Sledge. 404p. (C). (gr. 13). 1995. text ed. 78.95 (0-8151-7812-3, Yr Bk Med Pubs) Mosby Yr Bk.

Year Book of Orthopedics, 1996. Clement B. Sledge. 404p. (C). (gr. 13). 1996. text ed. 79.95 (0-8151-7813-1, Yr Bk Med Pubs) Mosby Yr Bk.

Year Book of Otolaryngology, 1995: Head & Neck Surgery. Holt & Papparella. 300p. (C). (gr. 13). 1995. text ed. 72.95 (0-8151-0539-8, Yr Bk Med Pubs) Mosby Yr Bk.

Year Book of Otolaryngology, 1996: Head & Neck. Holt & Papparella. 300p. (C). (gr. 13). 1996. text ed. 72.95 (0-8151-0540-1, Yr Bk Med Pubs) Mosby Yr Bk.

Year Book of Pain, 1994. Gerald F. Gebhart. 320p. (C). (gr. 13). 1994. text ed. 61.95 (0-8151-3401-0, Yr Bk Med Pubs) Mosby Yr Bk.

Year Book of Pain, 1995. 2nd ed. Gerald F. Gebhart. 320p. (C). (gr. 13). 1995. text ed. 61.95 (0-8151-3402-9, Yr Bk Med Pubs) Mosby Yr Bk.

Year Book of Pathology & Clinical Pathology, 1995. Erle Stanley Gardner. 380p. (C). (gr. 13). 1995. text ed. 73.95 (0-8151-1223-8, Yr Bk Med Pubs) Mosby Yr Bk.

Year Book of Pathology & Clinical Pathology, 1996. Erle Stanley Gardner. 380p. (C). (gr. 13). 1996. text ed. 76.95 (0-8151-1224-6, Yr Bk Med Pubs) Mosby Yr Bk.

Year Book of Pathology & Clinical Pathology, 1993. Year Book of Pathology & Clinical Pathology Staff. Ed. by William A. Gardner, Jr. LC 82-4567. 439p. 1993. reprint ed. pap. 125.20 (0-608-02418-X, 2063060) Bks Demand.

Year Book of Pediatrics, 1991. Year Book of Pediatrics Staff. Ed. by Frank A. Oski & James A. Stockman. LC 38-22. 546p. 1991. reprint ed. pap. 155.70 (0-608-02403-1, 2063045) Bks Demand.

Year Book of Pediatrics, 1993. Year Book of Pediatrics Staff. Ed. by James A. Stockman. LC 38-22. 594p. 1993. reprint ed. pap. 169.30 (0-608-02440-6, 2063083) Bks Demand.

Year Book of Pediatrics, 1994. James E. Stockman. 560p. (C). (gr. 13). 1994. text ed. 66.95 (0-8151-8527-8, Yr Bk Med Pubs) Mosby Yr Bk.

Year Book of Pediatrics, 1995. James E. Stockman. 560p. (C). (gr. 13). 1995. text ed. 66.95 (0-8151-8528-6, Yr Bk Med Pubs) Mosby Yr Bk.

Year Book of Pediatrics, 1996. James E. Stockman. 560p. (C). (gr. 13). 1996. text ed. 66.95 (0-8151-8529-4, Yr Bk Med Pubs) Mosby Yr Bk.

Year Book of Plastic & Reconstructive Surgery, 1995. Miller. 320p. (C). (gr. 13). 1995. text ed. 72.95 (0-8151-6042-9, Yr Bk Med Pubs) Mosby Yr Bk.

Year Book of Plastic & Reconstructive Surgery, 1996. Miller. 341p. (C). (gr. 13). 1996. text ed. 75.95 (0-8151-6043-7, Yr Bk Med Pubs) Mosby Yr Bk.

Year Book of Podiatric Medicine & Surgery, 1995. Kominsky. 355p. (gr. 13). 1995. text ed. 66.95 (0-8151-5177-2, Yr Bk Med Pubs) Mosby Yr Bk.

Year Book of Podiatric Medicine & Surgery, 1996. Kominsky. 355p. (gr. 13). 1996. text ed. 69.95 (0-8151-5178-0, Yr Bk Med Pubs) Mosby Yr Bk.

Year Book of Psychiatry & Applied Mental Health, 1995. Talbott. 530p. (C). (gr. 13). 1995. text ed. 69.95 (0-8151-8935-4, Yr Bk Med Pubs) Mosby Yr Bk.

Year Book of Psychiatry & Applied Mental Health, 1996. Talbott. 530p. (C). (gr. 13). 1996. text ed. 69.95 (0-8151-8936-2, Yr Bk Med Pubs) Mosby Yr Bk.

Year Book of Pulmonary Disease, 1992. Year Book of Pulmonary Disease Staff. LC 87-641197. 537p. 1992. reprint ed. pap. 153.10 (0-608-02399-X, 2063041) Bks Demand.

Year Book of Pulmonary Disease, 1994. Bone. 385p. (C). (gr. 13). 1994. text ed. 72.95 (0-8151-3876-8, Yr Bk Med Pubs) Mosby Yr Bk.

Year Book of Pulmonary Disease, 1995. Bone. 385p. (C). (gr. 13). 1995. text ed. 72.95 (0-8151-3877-6, Yr Bk Med Pubs) Mosby Yr Bk.

Year Book of Pulmonary Disease, 1996. Bone. 385p. (C). (gr. 13). 1996. text ed. 75.95 (0-8151-3878-4, Yr Bk Med Pubs) Mosby Yr Bk.

Year Book of Rheumatology, 1995. 2nd ed. Sergent. 425p. (C). (gr. 13). 1995. text ed. 79.95 (0-8151-7861-1, Yr Bk Med Pubs) Mosby Yr Bk.

Year Book of Rheumatology, 1996. 3rd ed. Sergent. 352p. (C). (gr. 13). 1996. text ed. 82.95 (0-8151-7862-X, Yr Bk Med Pubs) Mosby Yr Bk.

Year Book of Sports Medicine, 1991. Year Book of Sports Medicine Staff. Ed. by Roy J. Shephard. LC 80-642356. 517p. 1991. reprint ed. pap. 147.40 (0-608-02406-6, 2063048) Bks Demand.

Year Book of Surgery, 1994. Copeland. 400p. (C). (gr. 13). 1994. text ed. 66.95 (0-8151-7793-3, Yr Bk Med Pubs) Mosby Yr Bk.

Year Book of Surgery, 1995. Copeland. 400p. (C). (gr. 13). 1995. text ed. 67.95 (0-8151-7794-1, Yr Bk Med Pubs) Mosby Yr Bk.

Year Book of Surgery, 1996. Copeland. 400p. (C). (gr. 13). 1996. text ed. 70.95 (0-8151-7795-X, Yr Bk Med Pubs) Mosby Yr Bk.

Year Book of the Holland Society of New York 1906. Holland Society of New York Staff. 386p. 1995. reprint ed. pap. 25.00 (0-7884-0274-9) Heritage Bk.

Year Book of Thoracic & Cardiovascular Surgery, 1996. 3rd ed. Andrew S. Wechsler. 320p. (C). (gr. 13). 1996. text ed. 74.95 (0-8151-9170-7, Yr Bk Med Pubs) Mosby Yr Bk.

Year Book of Thoracic & Cardiovascular Surgery, 1998. 5th ed. Andrew S. Wechsler. 320p. (C). (gr. 13). 1998. text ed. 79.95 (0-8151-9172-3, Yr Bk Med Pubs) Mosby Yr Bk.

Year Book of Toxicology, 1989. Ed. by Irving Sunshine. 272p. 1989. 121.00 (0-8493-3301-6, RA, CRC Reprint) Franklin.

Year Book of Transplantation, 1995. Ascher et al. 376p. (C). (gr. 13). 1995. text ed. 80.95 (0-8151-0253-4, Yr Bk Med Pubs) Mosby Yr Bk.

Year Book of Ultrasound, 1995. Merritt. 328p. (C). (gr. 13). 1995. text ed. 85.95 (0-8151-6048-8, Yr Bk Med Pubs) Mosby Yr Bk.

Year Book of Ultrasound, 1996. Merritt. 350p. (C). (gr. 13). 1996. text ed. 95.00 (0-8151-6049-6, Yr Bk Med Pubs) Mosby Yr Bk.

Year Book of Urology, 1994. Jay Y. Gillenwater. 320p. (C). (gr. 13). 1994. text ed. 77.95 (0-8151-3482-7, Yr Bk Med Pubs) Mosby Yr Bk.

Year Book of Urology, 1995. Jay Y. Gillenwater. 315p. (C). (gr. 13). 1995. text ed. 78.95 (0-8151-3483-5, Yr Bk Med Pubs) Mosby Yr Bk.

Year Book of Urology, 1996. Jay Y. Gillenwater. 320p. (C). (gr. 13). 1996. text ed. 78.95 (0-8151-3484-3, Yr Bk Med Pubs) Mosby Yr Bk.

Year Book of Vascular Surgery, 1994. Porter. 400p. (C). (gr. 13). 1994. text ed. 72.95 (0-8151-0683-1, Yr Bk Med Pubs) Mosby Yr Bk.

Year Book of Vascular Surgery, 1996. Porter. 400p. (C). (gr. 13). 1996. text ed. 79.95 (0-8151-0685-8, Yr Bk Med Pubs) Mosby Yr Bk.

Year Books: Lectures Delivered in the University of London at the Request of the Faculty of Laws. William C. Bolland. xi, 84p. 1986. reprint ed. lib. bdg. 22.50 (0-8377-1937-2) Rothman.

Year Book's Medical Licensure Reviews: Clinical Sciences, Vol. 2. Ed. by Alfred J. Bollet. 408p. (C). (gr. 13). 1988. pap. text ed. 45.95 (0-8151-1022-7, BR02-1, Yr Bk Med Pubs) Mosby Yr Bk.

Year Books of the Reign of King Edward I, Years 20-35, 5 vols., 1. Ed. by Alfred J. Horwood. (Rolls Ser.: No. 31A). 1974. reprint ed. write for info. (0-8115-1060-3) Periodicals Srv.

Year Books of the Reign of King Edward I, Years 20-35, 5 vols., 2. Ed. by Alfred J. Horwood. (Rolls Ser.: No. 31A). 1974. reprint ed. write for info. (0-8115-1061-1) Periodicals Srv.

Year Books of the Reign of King Edward I, Years 20-35, 5 vols., 3. Ed. by Alfred J. Horwood. (Rolls Ser.: No. 31A). 1974. reprint ed. write for info. (0-8115-1062-X) Periodicals Srv.

Year Books of the Reign of King Edward I, Years 20-35, 5 vols., 4. Ed. by Alfred J. Horwood. (Rolls Ser.: No. 31A). 1974. reprint ed. write for info. (0-8115-1063-8) Periodicals Srv.

Year Books of the Reign of King Edward I, Years 20-35, 5 vols., 5. Ed. by Alfred J. Horwood. (Rolls Ser.: No. 31A). 1974. reprint ed. write for info. (0-8115-1064-6) Periodicals Srv.

Year Books of the Reign of King Edward I, Years 20-35, 5 vols., Set. Ed. by Alfred J. Horwood. (Rolls Ser.: No. 31A). 1974. reprint ed. 350.00 (0-8115-3574-6) Periodicals Srv.

Year Books of the Reign of King Edward III, Years 11-20, 15 vols., Set. Ed. by Alfred J. Horwood & Luke O. Pike. (Rolls Ser.: No. 31B). 1974. reprint ed. 1,050.00 (0-8115-3575-4) Periodicals Srv.

Year Books of the South Congregational Church Concord New Hampshire 1889-1890 & 1981-1982. Intro. by Charles D. Townsend. 1996. reprint ed. pap. 15.00 (1-878545-18-3) ACETO Bookmen.

Year by Year in the Rock Era. Herb Hendler. LC 87-2381. 375p. 1987. pap. text ed. 19.95 (0-275-92708-3, C2708, Praeger Pubs) Greenwood.

Year by Year in the Rock Era: Events & Conditions Shaping the Rock Generations That Reshaped America. Herb Hendler. LC 82-11722. (Illus.). xxv, 350p. 1983. text ed. 38.95 (0-313-23456-6, HRE/, Greenwood Pr) Greenwood.

***Year C: Worship Aids for the Revised Common Lectionary.** David Hostetter. (Prayers for the Seasons of God's People Ser.). 1997. pap. text ed. 14.95 (0-687-33601-5) Abingdon.

Year Christmas Almost Stopped. Francis J. Kreysa. (Illus.). 106p. (J). (gr. 4-7). 1982. pap. 3.00 (0-9611398-0-3) Kreysa.

Year End Tax Planning for Partnerships & S Corporations: 1992 Edition. Bruce K. Benesh et al. 250p. 1991. pap. 59.00 (1-878375-69-5) Panel Pubs.

Year-End Tax Strategies, 1992. 32p. 1992. pap. 5.00 (0-685-67065-1, 5498) Commerce.

***Year 501: The Conquest Continues.** Noam Chomsky. 331p. (Orig.). 48.99 (1-895431-63-8, Pub. by Black Rose Bks CN); pap. 19.99 (1-895431-62-X, Pub. by Black Rose Bks CN) Consort Bk Sales.

Year 501: The Conquest Continues. Noam Chomsky. 330p. (Orig.). 1992. 30.00 (0-89608-445-0); pap. 16.00 (0-89608-444-2) South End Pr.

***Year for Kiko.** Ferida Wolff. LC 96-42537. (Illus.). (J). 1997. 15.00 (0-395-77396-2) HM.

Year from a Reporter's Notebook. Richard H. Davis. LC 70-125691. (American Journalists Ser.). (Illus.). 1971. reprint ed. 25.95 (0-405-01668-9) Ayer.

Year from a Reporter's Notebook. Richard H. Davis. (American Biography Ser.). 305p. 1991. reprint ed. lib. bdg. 79.00 (0-7812-8102-4) Rprt Serv.

Year from Monday: New Lectures & Writings. John Cage. LC 67-24105. (Illus.). 179p. 1969. reprint ed. pap. 15.95 (0-8195-6002-2, Wesleyan Univ Pr) U Pr of New Eng.

Year Full of Poems. Ed. by Michael Harrison & Christopher Stuart-Clark. (Illus.). 142p. (J). (gr. 3 up). 1991. 22.00 (0-19-276097-1) OUP.

Year Full of Poems. Ed. by Michael Harrison & Christopher Stuart-Clark. (Illus.). 142p. (J). 1996. pap. 12.95 (0-19-276149-8) OUP.

***Year Full of Stories: 366 Days of Story & Rhyme.** Georgie Adams. LC 97-1407. (Illus.). (J). 1997. write for info. (0-385-32527-4) Doubleday.

Year-God. Gerrye Payne. Ed. by Tom Trusky. LC 91-71533. (Ahsahta Press Modern & Contemporary Poets of the West Ser.). 60p. (Orig.). 1992. pap. 6.95 (0-916272-51-6) Ahsahta Pr.

Year Growing Ancient. large type ed. Irene H. Steiner. 384p. 1982. 25.99 (0-7089-0891-8) Ulverscroft.

Year in a Coal-Mine. Joseph Husband. Ed. by Leon Stein. LC 77-70508. 1977. reprint ed. lib. bdg. 19.95 (0-405-10178-3) Ayer.

Year in a Yawl. 1995. reprint ed. 12.00 (0-944428-24-X) Cruising Guide.

Year in American Music, 1946-47 - 1947-48, 2 vols., Set. 1993. reprint ed. lib. bdg. 150.00 (0-7812-9704-4) Rprt Serv.

Year in Annapolis. Deborah Seylor. (Illus.). 24p. pap. 5.00 (0-942720-04-0) Fishergate.

Year in Baghdad. Joan C. Baez, Sr. & Albert V. Baez. LC 88-11721. (Illus.). 224p. (Orig.). 1988. pap. 9.95 (0-936784-38-5) J Daniel.

Year in Bloom: Gardening for All Seasons in the Pacific Northwest. Ann Lovejoy. LC 87-60480. (Illus.). 288p. 1987. pap. 11.95 (0-912365-11-0) Sasquatch Bks.

Year in Business: An Irreverant Look. Jeffrey L. Seglin & Robert M. Edwards. 100p. 1990. pap. 22.00 (1-55623-312-4) Irwin Prof Pubng.

Year in Complement. Ed. by J. M. Cruse. (Journal: Immunologic Research: Vol. 12, No. 3, 1993). (Illus.). 108p. 1993. pap. 35.00 (3-8055-5880-5) S Karger.

***Year in Faith.** Nora Gallagher. 1998. write for info. (0-679-45132-3) Knopf.

Year in Figure Skating. Smith. Date not set. 35.00 (0-7710-2754-0) St Martin.

***Year in Figure Skating.** Beverly Smith. 1997. 19.95 (0-7710-2755-9) St Martin.

Year in Flowers: A Daybook. Katy Gilmore. (Illus.). 128p. 1994. 19.95 (0-88240-460-1) Alaska Northwest.

Year in Freethought 1996. Ed. by Leslie Kilbride. (Freethought Calendars Ser.). 26p. 1995. pap. 10.00 (1-887392-02-5) Atl Freethought Soc.

Year in Immunology, Vol. 2, 1985-1986. Ed. by J. M. Cruse & R. E. Lewis, Jr. (Illus.). vi, 386p. 1986. 236.00 (3-8055-4342-5) S Karger.

Year in Immunology, 1982. Ed. by Lazar M. Schwartz. (Journal: Survey of Immunologic Research: Vol. 2, No. 3). (Illus.). 132p. 1983. pap. 57.75 (3-8055-3760-3) S Karger.

Year in Immunology, 1983. Ed. by J. M. Cruse & L. M. Schwartz. (Journal: Survey of Immunologic Research: Vol. 3, No. 2-3). (Illus.). 156p. 1984. pap. 64.00 (3-8055-3881-2) S Karger.

Year in Immunology, 1984-85. Ed. by J. M. Cruse & R. E. Lewis, Jr. (Illus.). vi, 234p. 1985. 126.50 (3-8055-4025-6) S Karger.

Year in Immunology, 1986-87. Ed. by J. M. Cruse & R. E. Lewis, Jr. (Year in Immunology Ser.: Vol. 3). (Illus.). 350p. 1988. 206.50 (3-8055-4616-5) S Karger.

Year in Immunology, 1988, Vol. 4 & 5. Ed. by J. M. Cruse & R. E. Lewis, Jr. (Illus.). xvi, 536p. 1989. 318.50 (3-8055-5044-8) S Karger.

Year in Immunology, 1988: Cellular, Molecular & Clinical Aspects. Ed. by J. M. Cruse & R. E. Lewis, Jr. (Year in Immunology Ser.: Vol. 4). (Illus.). vii, 312p. 1989. 204.00 (3-8055-4808-7) S Karger.

Year in Immunology 1988: Immunoregulatory Cytokines & Cell Growth. Ed. by J. M. Cruse & R. E. Lewis, Jr. (Year in Immunology Ser.: Vol. 5). (Illus.). viii, 224p. 1989. 158.50 (3-8055-4895-8) S Karger.

Year in Immunology, 1989-90: Molecules & Cells of Immunity. Ed. by J. M. Cruse & R. E. Lewis, Jr. (Illus.). vi, 284p. 1990. 258.50 (3-8055-5084-7) S Karger.

Year in Immunopathology. Ed. by J. M. Cruse & R. E. Lewis. (Journal: Pathology & Immunopathology Research: Vol. 5, No. 3-5, 1986). (Illus.). 248p. 1987. pap. 70.50 (3-8055-4576-2) S Karger.

Year in Ireland. Kevin Danaher. (Illus.). 276p. 1997. reprint ed. pap. 19.95 (0-937702-13-7) Irish Bks Media.

Year in Lapland: Guest of the Reindeer Herders. Hugh Beach. LC 92-30436. (Illus.). 280p. 1993. 24.95 (1-56098-230-6) Smithsonian.

Year in My Garden. Angela DeNevi. (Illus.). 185p. 1989. pap. 7.50 (0-930830-12-1) Great Basin.

Year in New York. Elisha Cooper. 1995. 20.00 (1-885492-24-3) City & Co.

Year in Nutritional Medicine: 1986. 2nd ed. Ed. by Jeffrey S. Bland. 1986. text ed. 39.95 (0-87983-383-1) Keats.

***Year in Pictures.** Barbara Carey. 80p. 1989. pap. 12.95 (0-919627-53-6, Pub. by Quarry Pr CN) LPC InBook.

***Year in Poetry.** Thomas Foster. 1997. pap. write for info. (0-517-88850-5, Crown) Crown Pub Group.

Year in Poetry: A Treasury of Classic & Modern Verses for Every Date on the Calendar. Ed. by Thomas E. Foster & Elizabeth C. Guthrie. LC 95-772. 512p. 1995. 25.00 (0-517-70008-5, Crown) Crown Pub Group.

Year in Provence. Peter Mayle. 1990. 23.00 (0-394-57230-0) Knopf.

Year in Provence. Peter Mayle. LC 90-50623. 224p. 1991. pap. 11.00 (0-679-73114-8, Vin) Random.

Year in Provence: Toujours Provence, 2 vols., Set. Peter Mayle. 1993. Boxed set. pap. 22.00 (0-679-74943-8) Knopf.

Year in Reference 1993. 93th ed. Ed. by Charles Toase. 488p. 1994. 130.00 (1-873477-15-5, Gale Res Intl) Gale.

Year in Reference 1994. 2nd ed. 1995. 120.00 (1-873477-26-0, 102298) Gale.

Year in San Fernando. Michael Anthony. (Caribbean Writers Ser.). 137p. (C). 1970. pap. 7.95 (0-435-98031-9, 98031) Heinemann.

Year in the City. Kathy Henderson. LC 95-45095. (Illus.). 32p. (J). 1996. 15.99 (1-56402-872-0) Candlewick Pr.

Year in the Country. 2nd ed. Ed. by Jean Van Dyke. LC 89-61836. 100p. 1989. 14.95 (0-89821-090-9, 5302) Reiman Pubns.

Year in the Country. 4th ed. Ed. by Linda Piepenbrink. LC 91-62330. 100p. 1991. 14.95 (0-89821-095-X, 6663) Reiman Pubns.

Year in the Desert. Auguste Nicaise. 125p. 1980. 19.95 (0-87770-237-3) Ye Galleon.

Year in the Life of a Factory. Maynard Seider. LC 83-50914. 152p. (Orig.). 1984. pap. 8.95 (0-917300-16-5) Singlejack Bks.

Year in the Life of a Rose. Rayford C. Reddell. 192p. 1996. 23.00 (0-517-70669-5, Harmony) Crown Pub Group.

Year in the Life of a Rose. Rayford C. Reddell. 1997. pap. write for info. (0-609-80013-2, Derrydale Bks) Random Hse Value.

Year in the Life of a Shinto Shrine. John K. Nelson. LC 95-23257. (Illus.). 288p. 1996. pap. 17.50 (0-295-97500-8); text ed. 35.00 (0-295-97499-0) U of Wash Pr.

Year in the Life of an Excellent Elementary School. Edward Wynne. LC 92-56466. 175p. 1992. pap. text ed. 29.95 (0-87762-963-3) Technomic.

Year in the Life of the Supreme Court. Paul Barrett et al. Ed. by Rodney A. Smolla. LC 95-4130. (Constitutional Conflicts Ser.). 312p. 1995. pap. text ed. 14.95 (0-8223-1665-X) Duke.

Year in the Life of the Supreme Court. Paul Barrett et al. Ed. by Rodney A. Smolla & Neal Devins. LC 95-4130. (Constitutional Conflicts Ser.). 312p. 1995. text ed. 39.95 (0-8223-1653-6) Duke.

Year in the Lives of the Damned: Reagan-Reaganism 1986. Stanley J. Marks. 1988. pap. 14.95 (0-685-17796-3) Bur Intl Aff.

Year in the Lives of the Damned! Reagan-Reaganism, 1986. Stanley J. Marks. 292p. (Orig.). 1988. pap. 14.95 (0-938780-18-2) Bur Intl Aff.

Year in the Maine Woods. Bernd Heinrich. LC 94-16534. (William Patrick Ser.). 1994. 22.00 (0-201-62252-1) Addison-Wesley.

Year in the Maine Woods. Bernd Heinrich. 272p. (YA). 1995. pap. 13.00 (0-201-48939-2) Addison-Wesley.

Year in Thoreau's Journal. Henry David Thoreau. Ed. & Intro. by H. Daniel Peck. 464p. 1993. pap. 12.95 (0-14-039085-5, Penguin Classics) Viking Penguin.

Year in Trade: Operation of the Trade Agreements Program, 46th Report. (Illus.). 171p. (Orig.). (C). 1995. pap. text ed. 35.00 (0-7881-2430-7) DIANE Pub.

Year in Trees: Superb Woody Plants for Four-Season Gardens. Kim E. Tripp & J. C. Raulston. (Illus.). 208p. 1995. 44.95 (0-88192-320-6) Timber.

***Year Is a Circle: A Celebration of Henry David Thoreau.** Victor C. Friesen. Date not set. pap. 24.95 (1-896219-03-9) Coun Oak Bks.

Year Left: An American Socialist Yearbook. Ed. by M. Davis et al. (Haymarket Ser.). 358p. 1985. text ed. 44.95 (0-86091-114-4, A1111, Pub. by Verso UK) Routledge Chapman & Hall.

Year Left II; Towards a Rainbow Socialism: Essays on Race, Ethnicity, Class & Gender. Ed. by Mike Davis et al. 300p. 1987. 50.00 (0-86091-171-3, A1112, Pub. by Verso UK) Routledge Chapman & Hall.

Year Left II; Towards a Rainbow Socialism: Essays on Race, Ethnicity, Class & Gender. Ed. by Mike Davis et al. 300p. (C). 1987. pap. text ed. 20.00 (0-86091-883-1, A1116, Pub. by Vrso UK) Norton.

Year Like a Fuse. Rakshat Puri. (Writers Workshop Redbird Ser.). 28p. 1978. 8.00 (0-86578-273-3); 4.00 (0-86578-274-1) Ind-US Inc.

Year Mom Won the Pennant. Matt Christopher. (Illus.). 160p. (J). (gr. 4 up). 1986. mass mkt. 3.95 (0-316-13988-2) Little.

***Year My Parents Ruined My Life.** Martha Freeman. 160p. (J). (gr. 5-9). 1997. 15.95 (0-8234-1324-1) Holiday.

***Year of Afghans.** Leisure Arts Staff. 144p. 1996. pap. text ed. 14.95 (1-57486-049-6) Oxmoor Hse.

***Year of Afghans, 2.** Leisure Arts Staff. 1997. pap. 14.95 (1-57486-045-3) Leisure AR.

Year of an Expatriate. James Hardwicke. LC 94-79055. 354p. (Orig.). 1994. pap. 6.95 (0-9635133-1-1) Add-Write.

Year of Back Issues of Credit Card Merchant Newsletter. 11th ed. Larry Schwartz & Pearl Sax. 100p. 1997. 99.00 (0-914801-06-6) Nat Assn Credit.

Year of Beasts. Ashley Wolff. LC 85-27419. (Illus.). 32p. (J). (ps-1). 1986. pap. 11.95 (0-525-44240-5) Dutton Child Bks.

***Year of Beer: 260 Seasonal Homebrew Recipes.** Ed. by Amahl Turczyn & Kim Adams. LC 97-13169. 300p. 1997. pap. 14.95 (0-937381-53-5) Brewers Pubns.

Year of Birth: A Month by Month Companion to Pregnancy, Birth & the First Three Months of Infancy. Robbie Snow & John Milder. (Illus.). 115p. (Orig.). 1991. pap. 14.95 (0-9623321-2-7) Crystal Press.

Year of Born. Yang Fang. 120p. 1995. pap. 5.00 (1-888065-00-1) New Wrld Poetry.

***Year of Celebrations: Hundreds of Ideas & Activities for Family Fun.** Dina Anastasio. (Illus.). 164p. (Orig.). 1997. pap. write for info. (0-614-29765-6) CTV Workshop.

***Year of Celebrations: Hundreds of Ideas & Activities for Family Fun.** Dina Anastasio. (Illus.). 160p. (Orig.). 1997. pap. 17.95 (1-884013-00-7) CTV Workshop.

Year of Chance. LC 89-92158. 1989. 18.95 (0-9624136-0-7) Songs Sottongs.

Year of Change. E. J. Kahn, Jr. 1999. pap. write for info. (0-14-011455-6, Viking) Viking Penguin.

XYZ

An Asterisk (*) at the beginning of an entry indicates that the title is appearing in BIP for the first time.

Year of Crisis, Year of Hope: Russian Jewry & the Pogroms of 1881-1882. Stephen M. Berk. LC 84-25216. (Contributions in Ethnic Studies: No. 11). xvi, 231p. 1985. text ed. 59.95 (*0-313-24609-2*, BPG/, Greenwood Pr) Greenwood.
Year of Cross-Stitch: Patterns for Every Season. Jodie Davis. LC 95-1794. 1995. 24.95 (*1-56799-217-X*, Friedman-Fairfax); pap. write for info. (*1-56799-213-7*, Friedman-Fairfax) M Friedman Pub Grp Inc.
Year of D-Day: The Nineteen Forty-Four Diary of Admiral Sir Bertram Ramsay, RN. Ed. by Robert W. Love, Jr. & John Major. (Illus.). 208p. 1994. 25.00 (*0-85958-622-7*, Pub. by Univ of Hull Pr UK) Paul & Co Pubs.
Year of Delicious Low-Fat Diet Desserts: 365 Quick & Easy Low-Calorie Recipes. Joan Bingham. LC 96-1567. (Illus.). 288p. (Orig.). 1997. pap. 14.95 (*0-940159-35-X*) Camino Bks.
Year of Doubt. Joyce Good. 272p. 1989. 8.35 (*0-317-01816-7*) Rod & Staff.
Year of Fire. Teddy Jam. LC 92-2882. (Illus.). 48p. (J). (gr. 1-5). 1993. text ed. 14.95 (*0-689-50566-3*, McElderry) S&S Childrens.
Year of Grace: A Spiritual Journal. Andrew M. Greeley. 1990. pap. 16.95 (*0-88347-262-7*) Res Christian Liv.
Year of Grace: Hymns for the Church Year. Carl P. Daw, Jr. LC 90-80709. 167p. (C). 1990. 11.95 (*0-916642-41-0*, 935) Hope Pub.
Year of Grace of the Lord. Ed. by Deborah Cowen. 254p. (Orig.). 1980. pap. 10.95 (*0-913836-68-0*) St Vladimirs.
Year of Grace with Mary. Rene Laurentin. 162p. 1989. pap. 22.00 (*0-86217-797-9*, Pub. by Veritas IE) St Mut.
Year of Grace with Mary: Rediscovering Her Presence. Rene Laurentin. 161p. (Orig.). 1987. pap. 10.95 (*0-86217-279-9*) Ignatius Pr.
Year of Hare Poems. 1988. 3.00 (*0-318-41322-1*) Man-Root.
Year of Health Hints. large type ed. Don R. Powell. 664p. 1992. lib. bdg. 13.95 (*1-56054-943-2*) Thorndike Pr.
Year of Health Hints: Three Hundred Sixty-Five Practical Ways to Feel Better & Live Longer. rev. ed. Don R. Powell. 374p. (C). 1997. reprint ed. 23.95 (*0-9635612-1-9*) Am Inst Prevent.
Year of Holidays: A Planning & Idea Book for Holiday Activities in Nursing Homes. Vicki L. Parsons. (Illus.). 177p. (Orig.). (C). 1993. pap. text ed. 14.50 (*1-877735-41-8*, 225) M&H Pub Co TX.
***Year of Images.** Christina Tischio. LC 96-90928. 90p. (Orig.). 1997. pap. 9.95 (*1-57502-383-0*, P01218) Morris Pubng.
Year of Impossible Goodbyes. Sook N. Choi. 176p. (J). (gr. 4-7). 1993. pap. 4.50 (*0-440-40759-1*) Dell.
Year of Impossible Goodbyes. Sook Nyul Choi. 176p. (J). (gr. 5 up). 1991. 15.95 (*0-395-57419-6*, Sandpiper) HM.
***Year of Lesser.** David Bergen. 216p. 1997. pap. 12.00 (*0-00-648107-8*) HarperColl Wrld.
Year of Living Dangerously. C. J. Koch. 304p. 1983. pap. 10.95 (*0-14-006535-0*, Penguin Bks) Viking Penguin.
Year of Living Perilously. Patrick Oliphant. (Illus.). 160p. 1992. pap. 6.95 (*0-8362-2056-0*) Andrews & McMeel.
***Year of Miracles: A Healing Journey from Cancer to Wholeness.** Susan W. Sternberg. LC 96-92246. (Illus.). 256p. (Orig.). 1996. pap. 13.95 (*0-9653755-0-1*, YOMP) Star Mtn Pr.
Year of Monsters. Dian C. Regan. (J). 1996. 15.95 (*0-8050-4676-3*) H Holt & Co.
Year of My Rebirth. 2nd ed. Jesse H. Stuart. LC 90-62357. 392p. (J). (gr. 7 up). 1991. 24.00 (*0-945084-17-X*) J Stuart Found.
Year of Mystery. Duncan Basil. 96p. 1994. pap. 35.00 (*0-85439-505-9*, Pub. by St Paul Pubns UK) St Mut.
Year of No More Corn. Helen Ketteman. LC 90-29092. (Illus.). 32p. (J). (ps-2). 1993. 15.95 (*0-531-05950-2*) Orchard Bks Watts.
Year of Our Birth. Sandra McPherson. LC 77-85295. (American Poetry Ser.: No. 15). 1979. pap. 6.95 (*0-912946-49-0*) Ecco Pr.
Year of Prayer: 365 Reflections for Spiritual Growth. LC 95-17188. 1995. kivar 10.99 (*0-8066-2757-3*) Augsburg Fortress.
Year of Progress in School-to-Career System Building: The Benchmark Communities Initiative. Martha I. Martinez et al. (Illus.). 70p. (Orig.). 1996. pap. 15.00 (*1-887410-83-X*) Jobs for Future.
Year of Progress in School-to-Career System Building: The Benchmark Communities Initiative - Executive Summary. Jobs for the Future Staff. (Illus.). 18p. (Orig.). 1996. pap. 5.00 (*1-887410-84-8*) Jobs for Future.
Year of Prophecy. 1989. write for info. (*0-614-16996-8*) Summit Univ.
***Year of Reading Proust: A Memoir in Real Time.** Phyllis Rose. 1997. 23.00 (*0-684-83984-9*) S&S Trade.
Year of Reckoning: El Salvador a Decade after the Assassination of Archbishop Romero. Americas Watch Staff. 200p. 1990. pap. 15.00 (*0-929692-50-0*, Am Watch) Hum Rts Watch.
***Year of Revolutions: Fanny Lewald's Recollections of 1848.** Ed. & Tr. by Hanna B. Lewis from GER. LC 96-43633. (Illus.). 200p. 1997. 42.00 (*1-57181-099-4*) Berghahn Bks.
Year of Roses. Stephen Scanniello. LC 96-6807. (Illus.). 224p. 1997. 25.00 (*0-8050-4409-4*) H Holt & Co.
Year of Sailing: 1996 Weekly Planner. Photos by Onne Van Der Wal. 110p. 1995. pap. 14.95 (*0-9646878-0-1*) Bushman Pub.
Year of Sailing Vol. 2: Photography by Onne Van Der Wal - 1997 Weekly Planner. Photos by Onne Van Der Wal. (Illus.). 108p. 1996. spiral bd. 14.95 (*0-9646878-1-X*, OVDB 97) Bushman Pub.
Year of Shapes: Reinforcing Shape Concepts with Hands-On Learning Activities. Margery A. Kranyik. (Creative Concept Ser.). (Illus.). 48p. 1990. pap. 6.95 (*1-878727-02-8*) First Teacher.
Year of Sharing. 1995. pap. 5.25 (*0-19-421674-8*) OUP.
Year of Silence. Madison Smartt Bell. 208p. 1989. pap. 12.95 (*0-14-011533-1*, Penguin Bks) Viking Penguin.
Year of Sorrows: The Great Famine of 1709 in Lyon. W. Gregory Monahan. LC 92-45193. 256p. 1993. 55.00 (*0-8142-0608-5*) Ohio St U Pr.
Year of Terror. L. Kay Pierce. LC 86-91612. 234p. 1987. 14.95 (*0-941321-00-2*) Hogue Pub.
Year of the Angler. rev. ed. Steve Raymond. (Illus.). 256p. 1995. pap. 12.95 (*1-57061-023-1*) Sasquatch Bks.
Year of the Angler & Year of the Trout, 2 vols., Set. Steve Raymond. 1995. boxed, pap. 25.00 (*1-57061-032-0*) Sasquatch Bks.
Year of the Black Pony. Walt Morey. (Walt Morey Adventure Library). 160p. (YA). (gr. 4-8). 1989. reprint ed. pap. 6.95 (*0-936085-14-2*) Blue Heron OR.
Year of the Buck: And Other Stories. Susan R. Harper. LC 91-46769. 112p. (Orig.). 1992. pap. 9.95 (*0-936784-96-2*) J Daniel.
***Year of the Buffalo: A Novel of Love & Minor League Baseball.** Marshall J. Cook. (Illus.). 160p. (Orig.). 1997. pap. 13.95 (*1-886028-22-2*) Savage Pr.
Year of the Bull. Oscar Parland. Ed. by Joan Tate. 198p. 9100. 29.00 (*0-7206-0807-4*, Pub. by P Owen Ltd UK) Dufour.
***Year of the Cat.** Fowler. 1997. 23.00 (*0-684-84448-6*) S&S Trade.
***Year of the Cat.** Prisco. LC 97-16520. 1997. 23.95 (*0-312-17123-4*) St Martin.
Year of the Cat: The Amulet. Zoe Daniels. 240p. (Orig.). (YA). 1995. pap. text ed. 3.99 (*0-425-14862-9*) Berkley Pub.
Year of the Cat: The Dream. Zoe Daniels. 240p. (Orig.). 1995. pap. text ed. 3.99 (*0-425-14768-1*) Berkley Pub.
Year of the Cat: The Hunt. Zoe Daniels. 256p. (Orig.). (YA). 1995. pap. text ed. 3.99 (*0-425-14778-9*) Berkley Pub.
Year of the 'Cats: A Look Back at Northern Michigan University's 1990-91 Championship Hockey Season. Jim LaJoie & Ron Plumb. 150p. 1991. pap. 9.95 (*0-9630901-0-0*) J LaJoie.
***Year of the Child.** Michael Lancy. 80p. 1983. pap. 5.00 (*1-890298-12-3*) Centerstage Pr.
Year of the Death of Ricardo Reis. Jose Saramago. 416p. 1991. 21.95 (*0-15-199735-7*) HarBrace.
Year of the Death of Ricardo Reis. Jose Saramago. 1992. pap. 12.95 (*0-15-699693-6*, Harvest Bks) HarBrace.
***Year of the Dragon.** Robert Daley. 528p. 1997. mass mkt. write for info. (*0-446-36572-6*) Warner Bks.
Year of the Dragon. large type ed. Basil Copper. (Linford Mystery Library). 1991. pap. 15.99 (*0-7089-7077-X*) Ulverscroft.
Year of the Duck. Israel Horovitz. 1988. pap. 5.25 (*0-8222-1284-6*) Dramatists Play.
Year of the Elephant: A Moroccan Woman's Journey Toward Independence. Lelia Abouzeid. Tr. by Barbara M. Parmenter from ARA. (Modern Middle Eastern Literature in Translation Ser.). 129p. (Orig.). 1989. pap. 9.95 (*0-292-79603-X*) U of Tex Pr.
Year of the Fires & Other Poems. Joyce Nower. LC 81-70725. 83p. 1983. pap. 4.75 (*0-9600856-2-9*) Ctr Womens Studies.
Year of the Flood. Eduardo Mendoza. Tr. by Nick Castor. 128p. 1997. pap. 10.00 (*1-86046-044-5*) HarperColl Wrld.
***Year of the Flood.** Eduardo Mendoza. 1997. pap. text ed. 10.00 (*1-86046-045-3*) Harvill Pr UK.
Year of the French. Thomas Flanagan. LC 78-23539. 528p. 1989. pap. 14.95 (*0-8050-1020-3*, Owl) H Holt & Co.
Year of the Frog. Martin M. Simecka. 256p. 1996. pap. 12.00 (*0-684-81367-X*) S&S Trade.
Year of the Frog. A Novel. Martin M. Simecka. Tr. by Peter Petro from SLO. LC 93-13353. 240p. 1993. 22.95 (*0-8071-1869-9*) La State U Pr.
Year of the Golden Ape. Colin Forbes. 255p. 1975. pap. 13.95 (*0-330-24627-5*, Pub. by Pan Books UK) Trans-Atl Phila.
Year of the Gorilla. George B. Schaller. (Illus.). 304p. 1988. pap. 16.95 (*0-226-73648-2*) U Ch Pr.
***Year of the Griz.** Kim Briggeman. (Saga of the Sierras Ser.). 1996. pap. text ed. 2.95 (*1-56037-101-3*) Am Wrld Geog.
Year of the Grizzly. Brock Thoene & Bodie Thoene. (Saga of the Sierras Ser.: Vol. 6). 192p. (Orig.). 1992. pap. 7.99 (*1-55661-167-6*) Bethany Hse.
Year of the Hare. Arto Paasilinna. Tr. by Herbert Lomas from FIN. 135p. 1995. 29.00 (*0-7206-0949-6*, Pub. by P Owen Ltd UK) Dufour.
Year of the Hare. Arto Paasilinna. Tr. by Herbert Lomas from FIN. 136p. 9600. pap. 17.95 (*0-7206-1017-6*, Pub. by P Owen Ltd UK) Dufour.
Year of the Hare: America in Vietnam, January 25, 1963-February 15, 1964. Francis X. Winters. LC 96-12163. (C). 1997. 29.95 (*0-8203-1874-4*) U of Ga Pr.
Year of the Heart: A Spirituality for Lovers. Daniel J. O'Leary. LC 89-9233. 224p. 1989. pap. 8.95 (*0-8091-3081-5*) Paulist Pr.
***Year of the Heavenly Dog.** LC 96-49692. 1997. 22.00 (*0-395-85012-6*) HM.
Year of the Heroic Guerrilla: World Revolution & Counterrevolution in 1968. Robert Daniels. (Illus.). 288p. 1996. pap. 15.95 (*0-674-96451-9*) HUP.
Year of the Horse: A Journey Through Russia & China. Douglas Fetherling. (Illus.). 208p. 1991. 19.95 (*0-7737-2495-8*) Genl Dist Srvs.
Year of the Horse, Poems of Prophesy & the Human Predicament. Ellis Ovesen. (Illus.). 63p. 1991. 4.50 (*0-8233-0472-8*) Tesseract SD.
***Year of the Horse: Vietnam: 1st Air Cavalry in the Highlands 1965-1967.** Kenneth D. Mertel. (Illus.). 384p. 1997. 35.00 (*0-7643-0138-1*) Schiffer.
Year of the Hunter. Czeslaw Milosz. Tr. by Madeline G. Levine. LC 93-49598. 1994. 27.50 (*0-374-29344-9*) FS&G.
Year of the Hunter. Czeslaw Milosz. Tr. by Madeline G. Levine. 294p. 12.00 (*0-374-52444-0*) FS&G.
Year of the Indians. Gerald N. Hill. (Illus.). 54p. (Orig.). (J). (gr. 4-7). 1985. pap. 4.95 (*0-912133-06-6*) Hilltop Pub Co.
Year of the Intern. Robin Cook. 224p. 1973. pap. 4.99 (*0-451-16555-1*, Sig) NAL-Dutton.
Year of the Intern. Robin Cook. LC 72-75414. 220p. 1993. reprint ed. lib. bdg. 25.95 (*0-89968-317-7*, Lghtyr Pr) Buccaneer Bks.
Year of the King: An Actor's Diary & Sketchbook. Antony Sher. LC 92-21034. (Illus.). 304p. 1992. reprint ed. pap. 17.95 (*0-87910-165-2*) Limelight Edns.
Year of the Leopard Song. Eric Campbell. 224p. (YA). (gr. 5 up). 1995. pap. 5.00 (*0-15-200873-X*) HarBrace.
Year of the Locust. David Nixon. 80p. (Orig.). 1980. pap. 7.99 (*0-8341-0675-2*) Beacon Hill.
Year of the Longley. Willis Johnson. LC 78-70046. (Illus.). 1978. pap. 4.75 (*0-941238-01-6*) Penobscot Bay.
Year of the Lord. Herbert O'Driscoll. LC 86-23835. 143p. (Orig.). 1987. pap. 8.95 (*0-8192-1400-0*) Morehouse Pub.
Year of the Lucy. Anne McCaffrey. 320p. 1987. pap. 3.95 (*0-8125-8565-8*) Tor Bks.
Year of the Oath. George R. Stewart. LC 77-150422. (Civil Liberties in American History Ser.). 1971. reprint ed. lib. bdg. 25.00 (*0-306-70103-0*) Da Capo.
Year of the Olive Oil. Charles North. 1989. 15.00 (*0-914610-67-8*); pap. 8.00 (*0-914610-66-X*) Hanging Loose.
Year of the Panda. Miriam Schlein. LC 89-71307. (Illus.). 96p. (J). (gr. 3-7). 1990. lib. bdg. 14.89 (*0-690-04866-1*, Crowell Jr Bks) HarpC Child Bks.
Year of the Panda. Miriam Schlein. LC 89-71307. (Trophy Bk.). (Illus.). 96p. (J). (gr. 2-5). 1992. pap. 3.95 (*0-06-440366-1*, Trophy) HarpC Child Bks.
Year of the Panda. large type ed. Miriam Schlein. 1995. 25.00 (*0-614-09620-0*, L-34778-00) Am Printing Hse.
Year of the Perfect Christmas Tree. Gloria M. Houston. LC 87-245515. (Illus.). 32p. (J). (ps-3). 1988. pap. 15.99 (*0-8037-0299-X*) Dial Bks Young.
Year of the Perfect Christmas Tree: An Appalachian Story. Gloria Houston. (Illus.). 32p. (J). 1996. pap. 4.99 (*0-14-055877-2*) Puffin Bks.
Year of the Perfect Christmas Tree: An Appalachian Story. Gloria M. Houston. LC 87-245515. (Illus.). 32p. (J). (ps-3). 1988. lib. bdg. 14.89 (*0-8037-0300-7*) Dial Bks Young.
***Year of the Persian Lamb.** Sherman Cohen. 60p. 1995. 6.95 (*0-9657286-0-9*) Sherman Cohen.
Year of the Rams. large type ed. Elizabeth Arthursson. 1991. 25.99 (*0-7089-2546-4*) Ulverscroft.
Year of the Ranch. Alice McLerran. LC 95-46308. (Illus.). 32p. (J). (ps-3). 1996. pap. 14.99 (*0-670-85131-0*, Viking) Viking Child Bks.
Year of the Ransom. Poul Anderson. 1988. 15.95 (*0-8027-6800-8*) Walker & Co.
Year of the Reader! Creative Activities to Promote Reading Excitement. Jan G. Philpot. Ed. by Jan Keeling. (Illus.). 96p. (Orig.). 1993. teacher ed. 9.95 (*0-86530-247-2*) Incentive Pubns.
Year of the Salamis, 480-479 B.C. The Greco-Persian Wars. Peter Green. LC 95-46654. (C). 1996. pap. write for info. (*0-520-20313-5*) U CA Pr.
***Year of the Sawdust Man.** A. Lafaye. LC 97-14501. (J). 1998. 16.00 (*0-689-81513-1*) S&S Childrens.
Year of the Scorpion. large type ed. Michael Hartland. 1994. 25.99 (*0-7089-3187-1*) Ulverscroft.
Year of the Seal. Victor B. Scheffer. 224p. 1991. pap. 14.95 (*1-55821-107-1*) Lyons & Burford.
Year of the Sevens. Geri K. Strigenz. LC 91-33190. (History's Children Ser.). (Illus.). 48p. (J). (gr. 4-5). 1992. pap. write for info. (*0-8114-6430-X*); lib. bdg. 21.36 (*0-8114-3505-9*) Raintree Steck-V.
Year of the Silence. Madge Reinhardt. LC 78-59573. 177p. 1978. pap. 6.50 (*0-917162-08-0*) Back Row Pr.
Year of the Sorrats, Vol. I. Steven W. Snider. (Mandrake Saga Ser.). (Illus.). 242p. (Orig.). 1994. pap. 8.00 (*0-9605980-3-0*) J T Richards.
Year of the Sorrats, Vol. 2. Steven W. Snider. (Mandrake Saga Ser.). (Illus.). 175p. (Orig.). 1994. pap. 8.00 (*0-9605980-2-2*) J T Richards.
Year of the Storms: The Destructive Kansas Weather of 1990. Howard Inglish et al. LC 90-84588. (Illus.). 128p. (Orig.). 1990. pap. 14.95 (*0-9627947-0-8*) Hearth KS.
Year of the Sword. Avner Gold. Ed. by Y. Y. Reinman. (Ruach Ami Ser.: No. 3). (Illus.). 112p. (J). (gr. 5 up). 1984. pap. 7.95 (*0-935063-02-1*) CIS Comm.
Year of the Tapeworm: A Novel. Chris Van Wyk. (Ravan Writers Ser.). 216p. (Orig.). 1996. pap. text ed. 14.95 (*0-86975-488-2*, Pub. by Ravan Pr ZA) Ohio U Pr.
***Year of the Tiger.** Jack Higgins. 1996. mass mkt. 6.99 (*0-425-15517-X*) Berkley Pub.
Year of the Trout. rev. ed. Steve Raymond. (Illus.). 288p. 1995. pap. 12.95 (*1-57061-022-3*) Sasquatch Bks.
Year of the Turtle. David M. Carroll. LC 96-17877. 192p. 1996. pap. 17.95 (*0-312-14772-4*) St Martin.
Year of the Virgins. Catherine Cookson. 1995. 22.00 (*0-671-89650-4*) S&S Trade.
Year of the Virgins. Catherine Cookson. 352p. 1994. mass mkt. 6.99 (*0-552-13247-0*) Bantam.
Year of the Virgins. large type ed. Catherine Cookson. LC 95-34857. 1995. 24.95 (*1-56895-247-3*, Compass) Wheeler Pub.
Year of the Whale. Victor B. Scheffer. LC 95-38425. 224p. 1996. pap. 14.95 (*1-55821-448-8*) Lyons & Burford.
Year of the Wild Boar. Helen Mears. LC 73-7457. 346p. 1973. reprint ed. text ed. 65.00 (*0-8371-6936-4*, MEWB, Greenwood Pr) Greenwood.
Year of the World. William B. Scott. LC 72-148299. reprint ed. 34.50 (*0-404-05649-0*) AMS Pr.
Year of the Zinc Penny. Rick Demarinis. Date not set. pap. 18.95 (*0-670-82575-1*) Viking Penguin.
***Year of Tuscan Cooking.** Five Brothers Staff. 1997. 24.95 (*1-56799-545-4*, Friedman-Fairfax) M Friedman Pub Grp Inc.
***Year of Waction.** Susanna Cuyler. 20.00 (*0-614-29347-2*) B Rugged.
Year of Wonder, 1968: Reflections on Travel. rev. ed. Pierson F. Melcher. LC 91-27393. 176p. (Orig.). 1991. pap. 6.95 (*0-9630071-0-6*) Windhover CO.
Year of Wreck. George C. Benham. LC 75-38639. (Black Heritage Library Collection). 1977. reprint ed. 28.95 (*0-8369-8997-X*) Ayer.
Year on a Monitor & the Destruction of Fort Sumter. Alvah F. Hunter. Ed. by William N. Still, Jr. LC 87-20971. (Studies in Maritime History). (Illus.). 203p. 1991. reprint ed. pap. 14.95 (*0-87249-761-5*) U of SC Pr.
Year on Monhegan Island. Photos & Text by Julia Dean. LC 93-24534. (Illus.). 48p. (J). (gr. 2-4). 1995. 14.95 (*0-395-66476-4*) Ticknor & Flds Bks Yng Read.
Year on My Street. Mary Quattebaum. 48p. (J). (gr. 2 up). 1996. 13.95 (*0-385-32170-8*) Doubleday.
Year on My Street. Mary Quattlebaum. 48p. (J). 1996. pap. 3.99 (*0-440-41106-8*) Dell.
Year on the Thames. Paul Felix & Bill Charlton. (Illus.). 192p. 1990. 34.00 (*0-86299-738-0*, Pub. by Sutton Pubng UK) Bks Intl VA.
Year One: An Intimate Look Inside Harvard Business School. Robert Reid. 336p. 1995. reprint ed. pap. 11.00 (*0-380-72559-2*) Avon.
Year One see Give Us This Day: Reflections for Each Day of the Liturgical Year
Year One of the Russian Revolution. Victor Serge. 1992. pap. 14.95 (*0-86316-150-2*) Writers & Readers.
Year 'Round Activities for Four-Year-Old Children. Anthony Coletta & Kathleen Coletta. LC 85-30934. 248p. 1986. pap. 19.95 (*0-87628-983-5*) Ctr Appl Res.
Year 'Round Activities for Three-Year-Old Children. Anthony Coletta & Kathleen Coletta. LC 85-26998. 244p. 1986. pap. 19.95 (*0-87628-982-7*) Ctr Appl Res.
Year 'Round Activities for Two-Year-Old Children. Anthony Coletta & Kathleen Coletta. LC 85-24264. 254p. 1986. pap. 19.95 (*0-87628-981-9*) Ctr Appl Res.
Year-Round Crafts for Kids. Barbara L. Dondiego. 1987. pap. text ed. 16.95 (*0-07-155774-1*) McGraw.
Year-Round Crafts for Kids. Barbara L. Dondiego. (Illus.). 256p. 1987. 19.95 (*0-8306-0904-0*); pap. 13.95 (*0-8306-2904-1*) McGraw-Hill Prof.
Year Round Creative Thinking Activities for the Primary Classroom. Margaret C. Riley & Donna L. Taylor. 272p. 1990. pap. 22.95 (*0-87628-985-5*) P-H.
Year-Round Developmental Activities for Pre-School Children. JoAnne C. Calvarese & Charon C. Sundman. 1990. pap. 27.95 (*0-87628-984-7*) Ctr Appl Res.
Year-Round Education: A Collection of Articles. Ed. by Robin Fogarty. LC 96-75270. (Illus.). 216p. (Orig.). 1996. pap. 22.95 (*1-57517-020-5*, 1388) IRI-SkyLght.
Year-Round Education: History, Philosophy, Future. Don Glines. LC 94-74904. (Trilogy Ser.). 280p. (Orig.). (C). 1995. text ed. 33.00 (*1-886666-04-0*) Educ Futures Proj.
Year-Round Education: History, Philosophy, Future see Educational Futures Trilogy
Year-Round Education, Year-Round Opportunities: A Study of Year-Round Education in California. California Department of Education Staff. 134p. 1987. pap. 6.75 (*0-8011-0686-9*) Calif Education.
Year Round Gas BBQ Cookbook. J. Bennett. 1993. pap. 12.50 (*0-394-22335-7*) Random.
***Year Round Holidays.** (Country Friends Ser.). (Illus.). 31p. pap. 6.95 (*1-888052-17-1*) Gooseberry Patch.
Year Round Low Fat Holiday Meals in Minutes. M. J. Smith. 1995. pap. 12.95 (*1-56561-074-1*) Chronimed.
Year-Round Programs for Young Players. Aileen Fisher. LC 85-8153. 334p. (Orig.). (J). (gr. 2-5). 1985. pap. 14.95 (*0-8238-0266-3*) Plays.
Year-Round Recruitment & Retention Plan. Marta Monetti-Souple. (How to Development Ser.). 53p. (Orig.). 1990. pap. 8.00 (*1-55833-047-X*) Natl Cath Educ.
Year-Round Wreaths: Creative Ideas for Every Season. Richard Kollath & Carol Spier. (Illus.). 144p. 1992. 21.95 (*0-8160-2601-7*) Facts on File.
Year-Round Wreaths: Creative Ideas for Every Season. Richard Kollath. LC 93-19590. (Illus.). 1993. reprint ed. pap. 12.95 (*0-395-64052-0*) HM.
Year Santa Got Sick. Bruce Babcock. (Illus.). 24p. (J). (gr. 1-3). 1996. pap. 7.00 (*0-8059-3784-6*) Dorrance.
Year Seven. Molleen Zanger. 240p. 1993. pap. 9.95 (*1-56280-034-5*) Naiad Pr.
Year That Santa Goofed & Other Short Stories. Auguste R. Black. (Illus.). 22p. (Orig.). (J). (gr. 1-5). 1990. pap. 2.95 (*0-9628010-2-X*) A R Black.
Year the Dragon Came. Sang Ye. Ed. by Linda Jaivin. 206p. 1996. pap. 18.95 (*0-7022-2731-5*, Pub. by Univ Queensland Pr AT) Intl Spec Bk.
Year the Dream Died: Revisiting 1968 in America. Jules Witcover. LC 96-42017. 560p. 1997. 25.00 (*0-446-51849-2*) Warner Bks.
Year the Horses Came. Mackey. LC 92-56119. pap. 10.00 (*0-06-250736-2*, PL) HarpC.

Year the Horses Came. Mary Mackey. 400p. 1995. mass mkt., pap. 5.99 (*0-451-18298-7*, Onyx) NAL-Dutton.

Year the Lights Came On: A Novel. Terry Kay. LC 88-7690. (Brown Thrasher Bks.). 312p. 1989. reprint ed. pap. 12.95 (*0-8203-1128-6*) U of Ga Pr.

Year the Wolves Came. Bebe F. Rice. 128p. (J). (gr. 3-7). 1994. pap. 14.99 (*0-525-45209-5*) Dutton Child Bks.

Year They Walked: Rosa Parks & the Montgomery Bus Boycott. Beatrice Siegel. LC 91-14078. (Illus.). 128p. (J). (gr. 4-7). 1992. text ed. 16.00 (*0-02-782631-7*, Four Winds Pr) S&S Childrens.

Year to Live. John Bowker. 1992. pap. text ed. 15.95 (*0-687-86700-2*); pap. text ed. 15.95 (*0-281-04558-5*) Abingdon.

***Year to Live.** Stephen Levine. 1998. pap. write for info. (*0-609-80194-5*, Crown) Crown Pub Group.

***Year to Live: How to Live This Year As If It Were Your Last.** Stephen Levine. LC 97-4072. 1997. 20.00 (*0-517-70879-5*, Harmony) Crown Pub Group.

Year Twelve: Students Expectations & Experiences. Margaret Batten. (C). 1992. 75.00 (*0-86431-044-7*, Pub. by Aust Council Educ Res AT) St Mut.

Year Two see Give Us This Day: Reflections for Each Day of the Liturgical Year

***Year 2000: Will Your Information Systems Survive.** Ed McPherson. 650p. 1997. 39.99 (*0-7897-0993-7*) Que.

Year Two Thousand & After. Torkom Saraydarian. LC 90-90139. 224p. 1991. pap. 10.95 (*0-929874-14-5*) TSG Pub Found.

***Year 2000 Problem Solver: A Five Step Disaster Prevention Plan.** Bryce Ragland. LC 96-47076. (Illus.). 300p. 1996. pap. text ed. 29.95 (*0-07-052517-X*) McGraw.

***Year 2000 Software Crisis: IBM Legacy Application Conversion.** Keith Jones. 1997. pap. text ed. 44.99 (*1-85032-903-6*) ITCP.

***Year with Butch & Spike.** Gail Gauthier. LC 97-13823. (J). 1998. write for info. (*0-399-23216-8*) Putnam Pub Group.

Year with Gayle, & Others. David Starkey. 27p. (Orig.). 1993. pap. 5.00 (*0-926935-78-X*) Runaway Spoon.

Year with Molly & Emmett. Marylin Hafner. LC 96-18426. (Illus.). 32p. (J). (gr. k-2). 1997. 15.99 (*1-56402-966-2*) Candlewick Pr.

Year with Swollen Appendices: The Diary of Brian Eno. Brian Eno. 416p. (Orig.). 1996. pap. 16.95 (*0-571-17995-9*) Faber & Faber.

Year with the Baha'is of India & Burma. Sidney Sprague. (Historical Reprint Ser.). (Illus.). 1986. 8.95 (*0-933770-57-X*) Kalimat.

***Year with the Bible, 1998.** Walter C. Sutton. 1997. pap. text ed. 6.00 (*0-664-29056-6*) Westminster John Knox.

***Year with the Saints.** Mark Water. LC 96-53169. (Illus.). 128p. 1997. 15.00 (*0-7648-0112-0*, Triumph Books) Liguori Pubns.

Year with the Saints. 2nd ed. Tr. by Order of Mercy, Mt. St. Joseph Seminary Staff. LC 88-50638. (Illus.). 364p. 1988. reprint ed. pap. 16.50 (*0-89555-339-2*) TAN Bks Pubs.

Year with the Three Mean Alligators - Oy! Joy Vaughan-Brown. Ed. by Eric H. Brown. (Illus.). 32p. (Orig.). (J). (gr. k-5). 1998. 12.95 (*1-889306-01-0*) Hilton A Vaughan.

Year with Two Winters. Martin Robbins. 74p. (Orig.). 1989. pap. 10.00 (*0-932662-85-4*) St Andrews NC.

***Year Without Christmas.** Created by Francine Pascal. (Sweet Valley Twins Super Edition Ser.: No. 10). 192p. (Orig.). (J). (gr. 3-7). 1997. pap. 3.99 (*0-553-48348-X*) BDD Bks Young Read.

Year without Michael. Susan B. Pfeffer. 176p. (YA). (gr. 7-12). 1988. mass mkt. 3.99 (*0-553-27373-6*, Starfire BDD) BDD Bks Young Read.

Year You Were Born, 1981. Jeanne Martinet. (J). (gr. 4-7). 1994. pap. 7.95 (*0-688-12875-0*, Tambourine Bks); lib. bdg. 14.93 (*0-688-12874-2*, Tambourine Bks) Morrow.

Year You Were Born, 1982. Jeanne Martinet. (J). (gr. 4-7). 1994. pap. 7.95 (*0-688-12877-7*, Tambourine Bks); lib. bdg. 14.93 (*0-688-12876-9*, Tambourine Bks) Morrow.

Year You Were Born, 1983. Jeanne Martinet. LC 91-31605. (Year You Were Born Ser.). (Illus.). 56p. (J). 1992. pap. 7.95 (*0-688-11077-0*, Tambourine Bks) Morrow.

Year You Were Born, 1984. Jeanne Martinet. LC 91-34577. (Year You Were Born Ser.). (Illus.). 56p. (J). 1992. pap. 7.95 (*0-688-11079-7*, Tambourine Bks) Morrow.

Year You Were Born, 1985. Jeanne Martinet. LC 91-37439. (Year You Were Born Ser.). (Illus.). 56p. (J). 1992. pap. 7.95 (*0-688-11081-9*, Tambourine Bks) Morrow.

Year You Were Born, 1986. Jeanne Martinet. (Illus.). 56p. (J). (gr. 2 up). 1993. pap. 7.95 (*0-688-11968-9*, Tambourine Bks) Morrow.

Year You Were Born, 1987. Jeanne Martinet. (Illus.). 56p. (J). (gr. 2 up). 1993. pap. 7.95 (*0-688-11970-0*, Tambourine Bks) Morrow.

Year You Were Born, 1988. Jeanne Martinet. (Illus.). 56p. (J). (gr. 1 up). 1995. pap. 7.95 (*0-688-13862-4*, Tambourine Bks); lib. bdg. 15.93 (*0-688-13861-6*, Tambourine Bks) Morrow.

Year You Were Born, 1989. Jeanne Martinet. 56p. (J). 1996. pap. 7.95 (*0-688-14386-5*, Tambourine Bks); lib. bdg. 14.93 (*0-688-14385-7*, Tambourine Bks) Morrow.

Year 1: A Time of Change. Ed. by Edward J. McFadden & Tom Piccirilli. 98p. (Orig.). 1996. pap. 9.99 (*0-9640168-4-2*) Pirate Writings.

***Year 2000.** Jennings & Hagan. 1997. pap. text ed. 40.00 (*0-13-646506-4*) P-H.

***Year 2000: Essays on the End.** Ed. by Charles B. Strozier & Michael Flynn. LC 97-4786. 430p. 1997. 65.00 (*0-8147-8030-X*) NYU Pr.

***Year 2000: Essays on the End.** Ed. by Charles B. Strozier & Michael Flynn. LC 97-4786. 430p. 1997. pap. 24.95 (*0-8147-8031-8*) NYU Pr.

***Year 2,000: Essays on the End.** Ed. by Charles B. Strozier & Michael Flynn. 1997. pap. 24.95 (*0-614-27586-5*) NYU Pr.

***Year 2000 Compliance.** Ed. by Pam Roth. (Management & Technology Ser.). (Illus.). 212p. (Orig.). 1997. pap. 39.95 (*1-57109-014-2*) Spiral Books.

***Year 2000 Compliance: A Guide to Successful Implementation.** Computer Technology Research Corp. Staff. (Illus.). (Orig.). Date not set. pap. write for info. (*1-56607-988-8*) Comput Tech Res.

***Year 2000 Computer Crisis: An Investor's Survival Guide.** Tony Keyes. 250p. 1997. pap. 29.95 (*0-9658939-0-1*) YZK Invest.

Year 2000 Computing Crisis: A Millennium Date Conversion Plan. Jerome T. Murray & Marilyn J. Murray. (Illus.). 320p. 1996. pap. 39.95 incl. cd-rom (*0-07-912945-5*) McGraw.

***Year 2000 Crisis: Developing a Successful Plan for Information Systems.** Computer Technology Research Corp. Staff. (Illus.). 200p. (Orig.). 1996. pap. 290.00 (*1-56607-978-0*) Comput Tech Res.

***Year 2000 Date Problem: Study & Resource Guide.** Larry W. Smith. (Illus.). 150p. 1997. 45.00 (*1-57914-020-3*) Campbell-Smith.

***Year 2000 Software Systems Crisis: Challenge of thr Century.** William Ulrich. 1997. pap. 39.95 (*0-13-655664-7*) P-H.

***Year 2000 Solutions: A Manager's Guide to the Impending Collapse of Every IT System.** S. S. Miller. LC 97-22860. 243p. 1997. 29.95 (*0-387-98278-7*) Spr-Verlag.

Yearbook. Peter Lerangis. 176p. (YA). (gr. 7-9). 1994. pap. 3.50 (*0-590-46678-X*) Scholastic Inc.

***Yearbook - Musical.** Darcy Rice. 113p. (YA). (gr. 9-12). 1996. pap. 5.50 (*0-87129-658-6*, Y03) Dramatic Pub.

***Yearbook Commercial Arbitration.** 1980. pap. text ed. 82.00 (*90-6544-537-4*) Kluwer Ac.

***Yearbook Commercial Arbitration.** 1990. lib. bdg. 82.00 (*90-6544-533-1*) Kluwer Ac.

Yearbook Commercial Arbitration, Vol. II. Ed. by P. Sanders. 294p. 1977. 64.00 (*90-268-0923-9*) Kluwer Law Tax Pubs.

Yearbook Commercial Arbitration, Vol. V. Ed. by P. Sanders. 350p. 1980. pap. 64.00 (*90-268-1152-7*) Kluwer Law Tax Pubs.

Yearbook Commercial Arbitration, Vol. VII. Ed. by P. Sanders. 465p. 1982. 72.00 (*90-6544-046-1*) Kluwer Law Tax Pubs.

Yearbook Commercial Arbitration, Vol. VIII. Ed. by P. Sanders. 432p. 1983. pap. 72.00 (*90-6544-118-2*) Kluwer Law Tax Pubs.

Yearbook Commercial Arbitration, Vol. 9. Ed. by P. Sanders. 1984. pap. 79.00 (*90-6544-171-9*) Kluwer Law Tax Pubs.

Yearbook Commercial Arbitration, 5 vols., Vols. I-V, 1976-1980. Ed. by P. Sanders. 432p. 1983. 75.00 (*0-685-07569-9*) Kluwer Law Tax Pubs.

Yearbook Commercial Arbitration 1978, Vol. III. Ed. by Albert J. Van den Berg. 334p. 1991. pap. 64.00 (*90-6544-535-8*) Kluwer Law Tax Pubs.

Yearbook Commercial Arbitration 1979, Vol. IV. Ed. by Albert J. Van den Berg. 420p. 1991. pap. 64.00 (*90-6544-536-6*) Kluwer Law Tax Pubs.

Yearbook Commercial Arbitration 1981, Vol. VI. Ed. by P. Sanders. 352p. 64.00 (*90-6544-003-8*) Kluwer Law Tax Pubs.

Yearbook Commercial Arbitration 1985, Vol. X. Ed. by Albert J. Van den Berg. 634p. 1991. pap. 87.00 (*90-6544-213-8*) Kluwer Law Tax Pubs.

Yearbook Commercial Arbitration 1986, Vol. XI. Ed. by Albert J. Van den Berg. 670p. 1991. pap. 107.00 (*90-6544-247-2*) Kluwer Law Tax Pubs.

Yearbook Commercial Arbitration 1987, Vol. XII. Ed. by Albert J. Van den Berg. 628p. 1991. pap. 116.00 (*90-6544-301-0*) Kluwer Law Tax Pubs.

Yearbook Commercial Arbitration 1988, Vol. XIII. Ed. by Albert J. Van den Berg. 770p. 1991. pap. 125.00 (*90-6544-359-2*) Kluwer Law Tax Pubs.

Yearbook Commercial Arbitration 1989, Vol. XIV. Ed. by Albert J. Van den Berg. 868p. 1991. pap. 123.00 (*90-6544-408-4*) Kluwer Law Tax Pubs.

Yearbook Commercial Arbitration 1990, Vol. XV. Ed. by Albert J. Van den Berg. 754p. 1991. pap. 163.00 (*90-6544-479-3*) Kluwer Law Tax Pubs.

Yearbook Commercial Arbitration 1991, Vol. XVI. Ed. by Albert J. Van den Berg. 768p. 1991. pap. 124.00 (*90-6544-552-8*) Kluwer Law Tax Pubs.

Yearbook for Traditional Music. Ed. by D. Christensen. Orig. Title: International Folk Music Council Journal. 230p. (ENG, FRE & GER.). 45.00 (*0-318-14547-2*) Intl Coun Trad.

Yearbook Health Care Management, 1992. Heyssel. 246p. 1992. 59.95 (*0-685-65031-6*, Yr Bk Med Pubs) Mosby Yr Bk.

***Yearbook Islamic Middle Eastern.** 1996. lib. bdg. 284.00 (*90-411-0883-1*) Kluwer Law Tax Pubs.

Yearbook Killer. Tom Philbin. (Orig.). 1981. pap. 1.95 (*0-449-14400-3*, GM) Fawcett.

***Yearbook Law & Amp - Legal Practice in East Asia, 1996, Vol. 2.** 1997. lib. bdg. 116.00 (*90-411-0359-7*) Kluwer Ac.

Yearbook Maritime Law, Vol. 1. Ed. by Ignacio Arroyo. 528p. 1986. 165.00 (*90-6544-254-5*) Kluwer Law Tax Pubs.

Yearbook Maritime Law, Vol. 2. Ed. by Ignacio Arroyo. 468p. 1987. 104.00 (*90-6544-311-8*) Kluwer Law Tax Pubs.

Yearbook Maritime Law, Vol. 3. Ed. by Ignacio Arroyo. 428p. 1988. 106.00 (*90-6544-361-4*) Kluwer Law Tax Pubs.

Yearbook Maritime Law, Vol. 4. Ed. by Ignacio Arroyo. 522p. 1990. 103.00 (*90-6544-464-5*) Kluwer Law Tax Pubs.

Yearbook Nineteen, 1983. Ed. by A. F. Finch. (Theilheimer's Synthetic Methods of Organic Chemistry Ser.: Vol. 37). xxiv, 576p. 1983. 427.25 (*3-8055-3600-3*) S Karger.

Yearbook of Agriculture, 1939: Food & Life; Part 1: Human Nutrition. U. S. Department of Agriculture Staff. LC 75-26321. (World Food Supply Ser.). (Illus.). 1976. reprint ed. 35.95 (*0-405-07797-1*) Ayer.

Yearbook of Agriculture, 1940: Farmers in a Changing World. U. S. Department of Agriculture Staff. LC 75-26320. (Illus.). 1976. reprint ed. 101.95 (*0-405-07796-3*) Ayer.

Yearbook of American & Canadian Churches 1994. Kenneth Bedell. 1994. pap. 29.95 (*0-687-46650-4*) Abingdon.

Yearbook of American & Canadian Churches 1995. Kenneth B. Bedell. (Orig.). 1995. pap. 29.95 (*0-687-00826-3*) Abingdon.

Yearbook of American & Canadian Churches, 1996. Kenneth B. Bedell. 312p. 1996. pap. 29.95 (*0-687-05589-X*) Abingdon.

***Yearbook of Architecture in the Netherlands, 1996-1997.** Ruud Brouwers. (Illus.). 176p. 1997. pap. 49.50 (*90-5662-040-1*) Dist Art Pubs.

Yearbook of Buddhist Wisdom. Norma Levine. (Illus.). 128p. 1996. 24.00 (*0-8356-0743-7*, Quest) Theos Pub Hse.

***Yearbook of Cell & Tissue Transplantation, 1996-1997.** Ed. by Robert P. Lanza & William L. Chick. 224p. 1996. lib. bdg. 167.50 (*0-7923-3844-8*) Kluwer Ac.

Yearbook of Comparative & General Literature, No. 32, 1983. National Council of Teachers of English, Comparative Literature Committee. 160p. pap. 45.60 (*0-317-30475-5*, 2024821) Bks Demand.

Yearbook of Comparative & General Literature Vol. 41: 1993. National Council of Teachers of English, Comparative Literature Committee. 245p. 1993. reprint ed. pap. 69.90 (*0-608-01625-X*, 2062210) Bks Demand.

Yearbook of Comparative & General Literature Vol. 42: 1994. National Council of Teachers of English, Comparative Literature Committee. 188p. 1994. reprint ed. pap. 53.60 (*0-608-01626-8*, 2062211) Bks Demand.

Yearbook of Comparative & General Literature, No. 31, 1982. National Council of Teachers of English, Comparative Literature Committee. 167p. reprint ed. pap. 47.60 (*0-317-29731-7*, 2022204) Bks Demand.

Yearbook of Comparative & General Literature, No. 33, 1984. National Council of Teachers of English, Comparative Literature Committee. 128p. pap. 36.50 (*0-685-15956-6*, 2026243) Bks Demand.

Yearbook of Developmental Biology. Ed. by Schindler. 336p. 1990. 187.00 (*0-8493-3304-0*, QH, CRC Reprint) Franklin.

Yearbook of Developmental Biology: 1991. Ed. by Joel M. Schindler. 1991. 181.00 (*0-8493-3308-3*, 3308FV, CRC Reprint) Franklin.

Yearbook of Drug Abuse, Vol. I. Ed. by Leon Brill & Ernest Harms. LC 70-174271. (Illus.). 386p. 1973. 52.00 (*0-87705-060-0*) Human Sci Pr.

Yearbook of Drug Therapy, 1990. Leo E. Hollister. 328p. 1990. 57.95 (*0-685-54085-5*, Yr Bk Med Pubs) Mosby Yr Bk.

Yearbook of Education Law 1994. Ed. by Stephen B. Thomas. LC 52-2403. 328p. 1994. 45.95 (*1-56534-063-9*) Ed Law Assn.

Yearbook of Education Law 1995. annuals Charles J. Russo. LC 52-2403. 391p. 1995. 45.95 (*1-56534-090-6*) Ed Law Assn.

***Yearbook of Education Law 1996.** Ed. by Charles J. Russo. LC 52-2403. Orig. Title: The Yearbook of School Law. 381p. 1996. text ed. 45.95 (*1-56534-092-2*) Ed Law Assn.

Yearbook of Education, Nineteen Fifty-Eight: The Secondary School Curriculum. Ed. by George Z. Bereday & Joseph A. Lauwerys. LC 73-38704. (Essay Index Reprint Ser.). 1977. reprint ed. 35.95 (*0-8369-2680-3*) Ayer.

Yearbook of Education, 1957: Education & Philosophy. Ed. by George Z. Bereday & Joseph A. Lauwerys. LC 73-38704. (Essay Index Reprint Ser.). 1977. reprint ed. 24.95 (*0-8369-2679-X*) Ayer.

Yearbook of Education, 1959: Higher Education. Ed. by George Z. Bereday & Joseph A. Lauwerys. LC 73-38704. (Essay Index Reprint Ser.). 1977. reprint ed. 31.95 (*0-8369-2681-1*) Ayer.

Yearbook of English Festivals. Dorothy G. Spicer. LC 93-8916. 298p. 1993. reprint ed. lib. bdg. 38.00 (*0-7808-0002-8*) Omnigraphics Inc.

Yearbook of European Law, Vol. 12. Ed. by Ami Barav & D. A. Wyatt. 864p. 1994. 175.00 (*0-19-825780-5*) OUP.

***Yearbook of European Law: 1995, 15.** Ed. by A. Barav & D. A. Wyatt. 800p. 1997. 215.00 (*0-19-825783-X*) OUP.

Yearbook of European Law Vol. 13: 1993. Ed. by Ami Barav & Derrick A. Wyatt. 800p. 1995. 155.00 (*0-19-825781-3*) OUP.

Yearbook of European Law Vol. 14: 1994, Vol. 14. Ed. by Ami Barav & Derrick A. Wyatt. 800p. 1996. 195.00 (*0-19-825782-1*) OUP.

Yearbook of European Law Vol. 8, 1988. Ami Barav. Ed. by Derrick A. Wyatt. 400p. 1990. 130.00 (*0-19-825263-3*) OUP.

Yearbook of European Law 1990, Vol. 10. Ed. by Ami Barav & Derrick A. Wyatt. 680p. 1992. 175.00 (*0-19-825705-8*) OUP.

***Yearbook of Experts, Authorities, & Spokespersons: An Encyclopedia of Sources.** 15th rev. ed. Ed. by Mitchell P. Davis. 888p. 1996. pap. 37.50 (*0-934333-27-0*) Broadcast Inter.

***Yearbook of Facts in Science & Art: Primary Source Material on the Postindustrial Revolution, 45 vols.** (C). 1996. text ed. 5,425.00 (*0-415-14761-1*) Routledge.

Yearbook of Fisheries Statistics: 1985, Vol. 61. 317p. 1987. text ed. 55.00 (*92-5-002506-8*, F3085, Pub. by FAO IT) Bernan Associates.

Yearbook of Fishery Statistics: Catches & Landings, Vol. 64. (Fisheries Reports: No. 32). 490p. 1989. pap. 55.00 (*92-5-002811-3*, F8113, Pub. by FAO IT) Bernan Associates.

***Yearbook of Fishery Statistics (FAO) Vol. 78: 1994 Catches & Landings.** (Illus.). 400p. 1996. pap. 55.00 (*92-5-003838-0*, F38380, Pub. by FAO IT) Bernan Associates.

***Yearbook of Fishery Statistics (FAO) Vol. 78: 1994 Catches & Landings.** FAO Staff. 400p. 1996. pap. 55.00 (*0-614-30308-7*, Pub. by FAO IT) Bernan Associates.

Yearbook of Fishery Statistics (FAO) 1992. Food & Agriculture Organization Staff. (Yearbook of Fishery Statistics (FAO) Ser.: Vol. 75). 400p. 1994. pap. 60.00 (*92-5-003526-8*, F35268, Pub. by FAO IT) Bernan Associates.

***Yearbook of Fishery Statistics (FAO), 1994 Vol. 79.** FAO Staff. (Illus.). 400p. 1996. pap. 46.00 (*92-5-003866-6*, F38666, Pub. by FAO IT) Bernan Associates.

Yearbook of Fishery Statistics, 1986: Fishery Commodities, Vol. 62. (Second Ser.: No. 4: Fisheries, No. 7: Statistics). (Illus.). 479p. (ENG, FRE & SPA.). 1988. pap. 55.00 (*92-5-002627-7*, F3226, Pub. by FAO IT) Bernan Associates.

Yearbook of Fishery Statistics, 1986: Fishery Commodities, Vol. 63. (Second Ser.: No. 4: Fisheries, No. 7: Statistics). (Illus.). 305p. (ENG, FRE & SPA.). 1998. pap. 55.00 (*92-5-002628-5*, F3225, Pub. by FAO IT) Bernan Associates.

Yearbook of Fishery Statistics, 1987, Vol. 65: Commodities. (Fisheries & Statistics Ser.: Nos. 33 & 86). (Illus.). 369p. (ENG, FRE & SPA.). 1989. pap. 55.00 (*92-5-002812-1*, F9121, Pub. by FAO IT) Bernan Associates.

***Yearbook of Fishery Statistics 1988 Vol. 66: Catches & Landings.** (Statistics Ser.: No. 92). 502p. 1990. 75.00 (*92-5-002937-3*, Pub. by FAO IT) Bernan Associates.

***Yearbook of Fishery Statistics 1988 Vol. 67: Commodities.** (Statistics Ser.: No. 93). 397p. 1990. 70.00 (*92-5-002938-1*, Pub. by FAO IT) Bernan Associates.

***Yearbook of Fishery Statistics 1989 Vol. 69: Commodities.** (Statistics Ser.: No. 101). 411p. 1991. 65.00 (*92-5-003045-2*, F0452, Pub. by FAO IT) Bernan Associates.

***Yearbook of Fishery Statistics 1990 Vol. 70: Catches & Landings.** (Statistics Ser.: No. 105). 655p. 1992. 60.00 (*92-5-003173-4*, F31734, Pub. by FAO IT) Bernan Associates.

Yearbook of Fishery Statistics, 1990, Vol. 71, No. 108: Fishery Commodities Stats. (Fisheries Reports: No. 39). 400p. 1992. pap. 55.00 (*92-5-003174-2*, F31742, Pub. by FAO IT) Bernan Associates.

***Yearbook of Fishery Statistics 1991 Vol. 72: Catches & Landings.** (Statistics Ser.: No. 111). 679p. 1993. 65.00 (*92-5-003328-1*, F33281, Pub. by FAO IT) Bernan Associates.

Yearbook of Fishery Statistics, 1991, Vol. 73: Commodities Stats. (Fisheries Reports: No. 113). 400p. 1993. pap. 60.00 (*92-5-003329-X*, F3329X, Pub. by FAO IT) Bernan Associates.

Yearbook of Fixed Income Investing 1995. Fixed Income Analysts Society, Inc. Staff & Martin S. Fridson. 512p. 1995. text ed. 75.00 (*0-7863-0544-4*) Irwin Prof Pubng.

Yearbook of Forest Products, 1975-1986. (Forestry & Statistics Ser.). (Illus.). 348p. (ENG, FRE & SPA.). 1988. 55.00 (*92-5-002635-8*, F3229, Pub. by FAO IT) Bernan Associates.

Yearbook of Forest Products, 1978-1989. 348p. (ps-3). 1991. pap. 45.00 (*92-5-003030-4*, F0304, Pub. by FAO IT) Bernan Associates.

Yearbook of Forest Products 1979-1990. 348p. 1992. pap. 50.00 (*92-5-003111-4*, F0114, Pub. by FAO IT) Bernan Associates.

Yearbook of Forest Products, 1980-1991. 372p. 1993. pap. 50.00 (*92-5-003261-7*, F32617, Pub. by FAO IT) Bernan Associates.

***Yearbook of Forest Products 1983-1994.** FAO Staff. 377p. 1997. pap. 40.00 (*92-5-003830-5*, F38305, Pub. by FAO IT) Bernan Associates.

***Yearbook of Forest Products, 1988.** (Statistics Ser.: No. 90). 348p. 1990. 45.00 (*92-5-002892-X*, F892X, Pub. by FAO IT) Bernan Associates.

***Yearbook of Forest Products 1992.** (Statistics Ser.: No. 116). 380p. 1994. 45.00 (*92-5-003480-6*, Pub. by FAO IT) Bernan Associates.

Yearbook of Hope & Inspiration. Celia Haddon. LC 90-60565. 160p. 1990. pap. 10.95 (*0-7181-3217-3*, M Joseph) Viking Penguin.

Yearbook of Human Rights, 1979. 330p. 39.00 (*92-1-154051-8*, E.85.XIV.7) UN.

Yearbook of India's Foreign Policy, 1985-1986, Vol. 4. Ed. by Satish Kumar. 300p. (C). 1988. text ed. 49.95 (*0-8039-9559-8*) Sage.

Yearbook of Intensive Care & Emergency Medicine, 1993. Ed. by J. L. Vincent. (Illus.). xviii, 691p. 1993. pap. 98.00 (*0-387-56463-2*) Spr-Verlag.

Yearbook of Intensive Care Medicine 1996. Ed. by J. L. Vincent. (Illus.). 800p. 1996. pap. 109.00 (*3-540-60552-5*) Spr-Verlag.

Yearbook of Interdisciplinary Studies in the Fine Arts, Vol. III, 12/91. Ed. by William E. Grim & Michael B. Harper. (Illus.). 632p. 1992. lib. bdg. 129.95 (*0-7734-9235-6*) E Mellen.

An Asterisk (*) at the beginning of an entry indicates that the title is appearing in BIP for the first time.

Yearbook of International Environmental Law, Vol. 3, 1992. Ed. by Gunther Handl. 864p. (C). 1993. lib. bdg. 238.00 (*1-85333-791-9*, Pub. by Graham & Trotman UK) Kluwer Ac.

Yearbook of International Environmental Law, Vol. 4. Ed. by Gunther Handl. 800p. 1995. 150.00 (*0-19-825895-X*) OUP.

Yearbook of International Environmental Law Vol. 5: 1994, Vol. 5. Ed. by Gunther Handl. 984p. 1996. text ed. 155. 00 (*0-19-825913-1*) OUP.

Yearbook of International Environmental Law, 1990, Vol. 1. Ed. by Gunther Handl. (C). 1991. lib. bdg. 208.00 (*1-85333-576-2*, Pub. by Graham & Trotman UK) Kluwer Ac.

***Yearbook of International Environmental Law 1995, Vol. 6.** Ed. by Gunther Handl. 1042p. 1997. text ed. 175.00 (*0-19-826276-0*) OUP.

Yearbook of International Organizations, 1989-90, Vol. 1. 1989. 300.00 (*3-598-22201-7*) Taylor & Francis.

Yearbook of International Organizations, 1989-90, Vol. 2. 1990. 300.00 (*0-685-31923-7*) Taylor & Francis.

Yearbook of International Organizations, 1989-90, Vol. 3. 1990. 300.00 (*0-685-31924-5*) Taylor & Francis.

Yearbook of International Organizations 1996/1997, 4 vols. Union of International Associations Staff. 1996. 1,155. 00 (*3-598-23351-5*) K G Saur.

Yearbook of International Organizations 1996/1997 Vol. 1: Organization Descriptions & Index. 33th ed. Union of International Associations Staff. 1700p. 1996. 437.50 (*3-598-23352-3*) K G Saur.

Yearbook of International Organizations 1996/1997 Vol. 2: International Organization Participation. 14th ed. Union of International Associations Staff. 1996. 385.00 (*3-598-23353-1*) K G Saur.

Yearbook of International Organizations 1996/1997 Vol. 3: Global Action Networks. 14th ed. Ed. by Union of International Associations Staff. 1500p. 1996. 385.00 (*3-598-23354-X*) K G Saur.

Yearbook of International Organizations 1996/1997 Vol. 4: International Organization Bibliography & Resources. Ed. by Union of International Associations Staff. 420p. 1996. 220.00 (*3-598-23355-8*) K G Saur.

***Yearbook of Islamic & Middle Eastern Law.** 1997. lib. bdg. 276.00 (*90-411-0257-4*) Kluwer Ac.

Yearbook of Labor Statistics, 1987. 47th ed. 910p. 1988. 98.00 (*92-2-006256-9*) Taylor & Francis.

Yearbook of Labor Statistics, 1989-1990. 1170p. 1990. 135. 50 (*92-2-006426-X*) Intl Labour Office.

Yearbook of Labor Statistics 1994: 53rd Issue & Sources of Methods: Labour Statistics, 2 vols. 53th ed. 1149p. 1995. 189.00 (*92-2-007347-1*) Intl Labour Office.

Yearbook of Labour Statistics, 1995 Vol. 2: 54th Issue & Sources & Methods - Labour Statistics: Employment, Wages & Hours of Work & Labour Cost (Establishment Surveys), 2 vols., Set. 54th ed. 1200p. 1996. 168.00 (*92-2-007350-1*) Intl Labour Office.

***Yearbook of Labour Statistics, 1996, 2 vols., Issue 55.** 1996. 189.00 (*92-2-007352-8*) Intl Labour Office.

Yearbook of Langland Studies, Vol. 1. Ed. by John A. Alford & M. Teresa Tavormina. 214p. 1987. 32.00 (*0-937191-05-1*) Colleagues Pr Inc.

Yearbook of Langland Studies, Vol. 2. Ed. by John A. Alford & M. Teresa Tavormina. ix, 214p. 1988. 32.00 (*0-937191-08-6*) Colleagues Pr Inc.

Yearbook of Langland Studies, Vol. 5. Ed. by John A. Alford & M. Teresa Tavormina. ix, 260p. 1991. 32.00 (*0-937191-43-4*) Colleagues Pr Inc.

Yearbook of Langland Studies, Vol. 7. Ed. by John A. Alford & M. Teresa Tavormina. 218p. 1993. 32.00 (*0-937191-56-6*) Colleagues Pr Inc.

Yearbook of Langland Studies, Vol. 8. Ed. by John A. Alford & James Simpson. 240p. 1995. 32.00 (*0-937191-57-4*) Colleagues Pr Inc.

***Yearbook of Langland Studies, Vol. 9.** Ed. by John A. Alford & M. Teresa Tavormina. 240p. 1996. 32.00 (*0-937191-62-0*) Colleagues Pr Inc.

Yearbook of Law & Medicine, 1992. Daniel J. Sullivan. 300p. 1991. 74.95 (*0-9631342-0-5*) Phys Law Rev.

Yearbook of Love & Wisdom. Celia Haddon. (Illus.). 160p. 1994. pap. 10.95 (*0-7181-3740-X*, M Joseph) Viking Penguin.

Yearbook of Media & Entertainment Law Vol. 1: 1995. Ed. by Eric Barendt et al. 500p. 1995. 225.00 (*0-19-825927-1*) OUP.

***Yearbook of Media & Entertainment Law, 1996, Vol. 2.** Ed. by Eric Barendt. 640p. 1997. 245.00 (*0-19-826277-9*) OUP.

Yearbook of Medical Informatics 93: Sharing Knowledge & Information. Jan H. Van Bemmel & Alexa T. McCray. 521p. 1995. pap. text ed. 143.50 (*0-471-04904-2*) Wiley.

Yearbook of Morphology. Ed. by Geert Booy & Jaap Van Marle. viii, 328p. (Orig.). (C). 1988. 98.50 (*90-6765-375-6*); pap. 73.10 (*90-6765-376-4*) Mouton.

Yearbook of Morphology, 1989. Geert Booij & Jaap Van Marle. 300p. 80.00 (*90-6765-444-2*); pap. 57.70 (*90-6765-445-0*) Mouton.

Yearbook of Morphology, 1990. Ed. by Geert Booij & Jaap Van Marle. vi, 241p. (Orig.). (C). 1991. pap. text ed. 53. 85 (*3-11-013374-1*) Mouton.

Yearbook of Morphology, 1991. Ed. by Geert Booij & Jaap Van Marle. (Yearbook of Morphology Ser.). 268p. (C). 1992. lib. bdg. 103.00 (*0-7923-1416-6*) Kluwer Ac.

Yearbook of Morphology, 1992. Ed. by Geert Booij. 300p. (C). 1993. lib. bdg. 157.50 (*0-7923-1937-0*) Kluwer Ac.

Yearbook of Morphology, 1993. Ed. by Geert Booij. 288p. (C). 1994. lib. bdg. 169.00 (*0-7923-2494-3*) Kluwer Ac.

Yearbook of Morphology, 1994. Ed. by Geert Booij. (Yearbook of Morphology Ser.). 320p. (C). 1995. lib. bdg. 199.00 (*0-7923-3244-X*) Kluwer Ac.

***Yearbook of Morphology 1996.** 1997. lib. bdg. 190.00 (*0-7923-4563-0*) Kluwer Ac.

Yearbook of Nephrology, 1991. Coe. 1991. write for info. (*0-8151-5015-6*, Yr Bk Med Pubs) Mosby Yr Bk.

Yearbook of Norwegian Art 1995-1996. Ed. by Olga Schmedling et al. 1995. 63.00 (*82-00-03946-3*) Scandnvan Univ Pr.

Yearbook of Nutritional Medicine, 1984-1985. Ed. by Jeffrey S. Bland. 336p. 1985. 39.95 (*0-87983-359-9*) Keats.

Yearbook of Pharmacology. Ed. by Mannfred A. Hollinger. 1990. 248.00 (*0-8493-3302-4*, RM, CRC Reprint) Franklin.

Yearbook of Pharmacology: 1992. Ed. by Mannfred A. Hollinger. LC 90-660185. 464p. 1992. 253.00 (*0-8493-3312-1*, RM, CRC Reprint) Franklin.

Yearbook of Pharmacology, 1991. Ed. by Mannfred A. Hollinger. 432p. 1991. 236.00 (*0-8493-3306-7*, RM, CRC Reprint) Franklin.

Yearbook of Psychoanalysis & Psychotherapy, Vol. 1-1985. Robert J. Langs. 432p. 1985. text ed. 49.95 (*0-931231-04-3*) Newconcept Pr.

Yearbook of Psychoanalysis & Psychotherapy, Vol. 2. Robert J. Langs. LC 86-641022. 356p. 1987. text ed. 45. 00 (*0-89876-141-7*) Gardner Pr.

Yearbook of Rehabilitation, 1990. Kaplan. 1990. 59.95 (*0-8151-5028-8*, Yr Bk Med Pubs) Mosby Yr Bk.

Yearbook of Renewable Energies, 1994. Ed. by Hermann Scheer et al. (Orig.). (C). 1993. pap. 45.00 (*1-873936-29-X*, Pub. by J & J Sci Pubs UK) Bks Intl VA.

Yearbook of Renewable Energies 1995/96. Ed. by Hermann Scheer & Maneka Gandhi. 286p. (Orig.). 1995. pap. text ed. 55.00 (*1-873936-41-9*, Pub. by J & J Sci Pubs UK) Bks Intl VA.

***Yearbook of Small Business Icons.** (Illus.). 100p. 1997. write for info. (*0-9656359-0-2*) ICON Pubns.

Yearbook of Soviet Foreign Relations, 1991. Ed. by Alex Pravda. 400p. 1991. text ed. 110.00 (*1-85043-242-2*, Pub. by I B Tauris UK) St Martin.

Yearbook of Substance Use & Abuse, Vol. II. Leon Brill & Charles Winick. LC 70-174271. 360p. 1980. 52.00 (*0-87705-487-8*) Human Sci Pr.

Yearbook of Substance Use & Abuse, Vol. III. Ed. by Leon Brill & Charles Winick. 351p. 1985. 52.00 (*0-89885-216-1*) Human Sci Pr.

Yearbook of the AAA, 1974: 1974. Panhuys. (Association of Attenders & Alumni of the Hague Academy of International Law Ser: No. 44). 1977. pap. text ed. 76.00 (*90-247-1945-3*) Kluwer Ac.

Yearbook of the Association of Pacific Coast Geographers, 1990, Vol. 52. Association of Pacific Coast Geographers. Ed. by Robin E. Datel & Dennis Dingemans. LC 37-13376. (Illus.). 256p. 1990. pap. 2.00 (*0-87071-286-1*) Oreg St U Pr.

Yearbook of the Association of Pacific Coast Geographers, 1991, Vol. 53. Association of Pacific Coast Geographers. Ed. by Robin E. Datel & Dennis Dingemans. LC 37-13376. (Illus.). 272p. 1991. pap. 2.00 (*0-87071-287-X*) Oreg St U Pr.

Yearbook of the Association of Pacific Coast Geographers, 1992, Vol. 54. Association of Pacific Coast Geographers. Ed. by Robin E. Datel & Dennis Dingemans. LC 37-13376. (Illus.). 192p. 1992. pap. 20. 00 (*0-87071-288-8*) Oreg St U Pr.

Yearbook of the Association of Pacific Coast Geographers, 1994 Vol. 55. Association of Pacific Coast Geographers. Ed. by Daniel Turbeville, 3rd. LC 37-13376. (Illus.). 197p. 1994. pap. 20.00 (*0-87071-289-6*) Oreg St U Pr.

Yearbook of the European Communities & Other European Organizations 1994. 1,141th ed. 528p. 1994. 275.00 (*2-8029-0114-1*, ED1141, Pub. by ED BE) Bernan Associates.

Yearbook of the European Convention on Human Rights. Ed. by Council of Europe Staff. (European Convention on Human Rights Ser.: No. 22). 688p. 1980. lib. bdg. 330.00 (*90-247-2383-3*) Kluwer Ac.

Yearbook of the European Convention on Human Rights. Ed. by Council of Europe Staff. (C). 1990. lib. bdg. 301. 50 (*0-7923-0207-9*) Kluwer Ac.

Yearbook of the European Convention on Human Rights. Ed. by Council of Europe Staff. (C). 1993. lib. bdg. 289. 00 (*0-7923-1787-4*) Kluwer Ac.

Yearbook of the European Convention on Human Rights, Vol. 21. Council of Europe Staff. 1979. lib. bdg. 330.00 (*90-247-2215-2*) Kluwer Ac.

***Yearbook of the European Convention on Human Rights, Vol. 36, 1993.** Ed. by Council of Europe Staff. 1076p. 1996. 385.00 (*90-411-0151-9*) MNP-G&T.

Yearbook of the European Convention on Human Rights: Annuaire De la Convention Europeenne Des Droit De l'Homme, 1990, Vol. 33. Ed. by Council of Europe Staff. 748p. (C). 1994. lib. bdg. 288.00 (*0-7923-2572-9*) Kluwer Ac.

Yearbook of the European Convention on Human Rights: Vol. 25, 1982. Ed. by Council of Europe Staff. 1986. lib. bdg. 331.00 (*90-247-3262-X*) Kluwer Ac.

Yearbook of the European Convention on Human Rights - Annuaire de la Convention Europeenne des Droit de l'Homme, Vol. 1: 1955-1956-1957 (Documents & - et Decisions) (European Commission of Human Rights) Ed. by Council of Europe - Conseil de l'Europe Staff. 276p. (C). 1959. lib. bdg. 223.50 (*0-7923-2571-0*) Kluwer Ac.

Yearbook of the European Convention on Human Rights - Annuaire de la Convention Europeenne des Droits de l'Homme, Vol. 30, 1987. Ed. by Council of Europe - Conseil de l'Europe Staff. 704p. (C). 1992. lib. bdg. 289. 00 (*0-7923-1575-8*) Kluwer Ac.

Yearbook of the European Convention on Human Rights, Vol. 28: 1985. Ed. by Council of Europe Staff. 656p. 1991. lib. bdg. 293.50 (*0-7923-0652-X*) Kluwer Ac.

Yearbook of the European Convention on Human Rights, Vol. 32: 1989. Ed. by Council of Europe Staff. 660p. (C). 1993. lib. bdg. 272.00 (*0-7923-2132-4*) Kluwer Ac.

Yearbook of the European Convention on Human Rights, 1986: Annuaire de la Convention Europeenne de l'Homme, Vol. 29. Ed. by Council of Europe Staff. 624p. (C). 1991. lib. bdg. 276.00 (*0-7923-1109-4*) Kluwer Ac.

***Yearbook of the European Convention on Human Rights/ Annuaire.** Date not set. text ed. 575.00 (*90-411-0217-5*) Kluwer Law Tax Pubs.

***Yearbook of the European Convention on Human Rights/ Annuaire de la Convention Europe.** 1997. text ed. 244. 00 (*90-411-0367-8*) Kluwer Ac.

***Yearbook of the European Convention on Human Rights/ Annuaire de la Convention Europeenne des Droits de l'Homme.** 1997. lib. bdg. 452.00 (*90-411-0346-5*) Kluwer Law Tax Pubs.

Yearbook of the Human Rights Committee, Vol. I. 577p. 1988. 65.00 (*92-1-154073-9*) UN.

Yearbook of the Human Rights Committee Vol. 1: 1985-1986 Edition. 523p. 1990. 60.00 (*92-1-154080-1*) UN.

Yearbook of the Human Rights Committee Vol. 1: 1987 Edition. 212p. 1992. 60.00 (*92-1-154089-5*) UN.

Yearbook of the Human Rights Committee Vol. 2: 1983-1984 Edition. 656p. 1989. 65.00 (*92-1-154077-1*) UN.

Yearbook of the Human Rights Committee Vol. 2: 1985-1986 Edition. 551p. 1991. 60.00 (*92-1-154086-0*) UN.

Yearbook of the Human Rights Committee Vol. 2: 1987 Edition. 350p. 1987. 60.00 (*92-1-154094-1*) UN.

Yearbook of the Human Rights Committee, 1977-1978, Vol. II. 232p. 1987. 35.00 (*92-1-154054-2*, E.85.XIV.10) UN.

Yearbook of the Human Rights Committee, 1979-1980, Vol. I. 1985. pap. 51.00 (*92-1-154057-7*, E.85.XIV.12) UN.

Yearbook of the Human Rights Committee, 1979-1980, Vol. II. 612p. 1980. 66.00 (*92-1-154059-3*, 86.XIV.2) UN.

Yearbook of the Human Rights Committee, 1981-1982, Vol. I. 405p. 54.00 (*92-1-154062-3*) UN.

Yearbook of the International Court of Justice No. 46: 1991-1992. 257p. Date not set. 22.00 (*92-1-170067-1*) UN.

Yearbook of the International Court of Justice No. 48: 1993-1994. 261p. Date not set. 22.00 (*92-1-170070-1*) UN.

Yearbook of the International Law Commission. 112p. Date not set. 30.00 (*92-1-133432-2*, E.92.V.10/PT.2) UN.

Yearbook of the International Law Commission Vol. 1: 1990 Edition. 389p. 1992. 50.00 (*92-1-133430-6*, E.92. V.9) UN.

Yearbook of the International Law Commission Vol. 1: 1991 Edition. 300p. 1993. 55.00 (*92-1-133445-4*, E.93. V.8.) UN.

Yearbook of the International Law Commission Vol. 1: 1992 Edition. 254p. 1994. 55.00 (*92-1-133458-6*) UN.

Yearbook of the International Law Commission Vol. 2, Pt. 1: 1990 Edition. 112p. 1992. 30.00 (*92-1-133431-4*, E. 92.V.10/PT.1) UN.

Yearbook of the International Law Commission Vol. 2, Pt. 1: 1991 Edition. Date not set. 35.00 (*92-1-133446-2*, E. 93.V.9/PT.1) UN.

Yearbook of the International Law Commission Vol. II, Pt. 1: 1992. 1994. 35.00 (*92-1-133459-4*) UN.

Yearbook of the International Law Commission Vol. II, Pt. 1: 1993. 1995. 35.00 (*92-1-133481-0*) UN.

Yearbook of the International Law Commission Vol. 2, Pt. 2: 1991 Edition. 136p. 1993. 38.00 (*92-1-133447-0*, E. 93.V.9/PT.2) UN.

Yearbook of the International Law Commission Vol. II, Pt. 2: 1992. 82p. 1994. 38.00 (*92-1-133460-8*) UN.

Yearbook of the International Law Commission Vol. II, Pt. 2: 1993. 1995. 38.00 (*92-1-133482-9*, E.95.V.4PT.2) UN.

Yearbook of the International Law Commission, 1985, Vol. II, Pt. 1. 222p. 1985. 35.00 (*92-1-133324-5*) UN.

Yearbook of the International Law Commission, 1986, 2 pts., Pt. 1. 169p. 1986. 19.00 (*92-1-133296-6*) UN.

Yearbook of the International Law Commission, 1986, 2 pts., Pt. 2. 68p. 1986. 9.00 (*92-1-133297-4*) UN.

Yearbook of the International Law Commission, 1986, Vol. I. 301p. 1986. 38.00 (*92-1-133295-8*) UN.

Yearbook of the International Law Commission, 1987, 2 pts., Pt. 2. 59p. 1987. 19.00 (*92-1-133311-3*) UN.

Yearbook of the International Law Commission, 1987, Vol. I. 280p. 1987. 45.00 (*92-1-133309-1*) UN.

Yearbook of the International Law Commission, 1987, 2 pts., Vol. II. 1987. write for info. (*0-318-68739-9*) UN.

Yearbook of the International Law Commission, 1987, 2 pts., Vol. 7. 59p. 1988. Pt. 1, 59p. 19.00 (*92-1-133310-5*) UN.

Yearbook of the International Law Commission, 1988, Vol. I. 351p. 1988. 45.00 (*92-1-133329-6*) UN.

Yearbook of the International Law Commission, 1988, Vol. II, Pt. 2. 115p. 1988. 30.00 (*92-1-133398-9*) UN.

Yearbook of the International Law Commission, 1993 Vol. 1: United Nations Meetings on the Yearbook of the International Law Commission, 45th, 1993, New York & Geneva. 195p. 1995. 55.00 (*92-1-133480-2*) UN.

***Yearbook of the International Law Commission, 1994: United Nations Meetings on the Yearbook of the International Law Commission, 46th, New York & Geneva, 1994.** 317p. 1996. pap. 55.00 (*92-1-133502-7*, JX3091) UN.

Yearbook of the Music World. Jahrbuch Der Musikwelt. 696p. 1993. reprint ed. lib. bdg. 109.00 (*0-7812-9559-9*) Rprt Serv.

Yearbook of the Royal College of Obstetricians & Gynaecologists 1994. John W. Studd. (Illus.). 340p. 1995. text ed. 48.00 (*0-902331-65-5*) Prthnon Pub.

Yearbook of the Royal College of Obstetricians & Gynaecologists 1995. John W. Studd. (Illus.). 308p. 1996. 55.00 (*0-902331-77-9*) Prthnon Pub.

Yearbook of the United Holy Church of America, Inc., 1994: Includes Minutes of Conventions, Convocations & Conferences, 1988-1993. Ed. by Chester W. Gregory, Sr. 260p. (Orig.). 1994. pap. 11.95 (*1-877971-13-8*) Mid Atl Reg Pr.

Yearbook of the United Nations, Vol. 30. 1153p. 1976. 42. 00 (*0-685-42740-4*, E.78.I.1) UN.

Yearbook of the United Nations, Vol. 32. 1978. 60.00 (*0-685-05114-5*, E.80.I.1) UN.

Yearbook of the United Nations, Vol. 33. 1450p. 1979. 72. 00 (*0-685-06497-2*, E.82.I.1) UN.

Yearbook of the United Nations, Vol. 34. 1450p. 1980. 72. 00 (*0-685-42741-2*, E.83.I.1) UN.

Yearbook of the United Nations, Vol. 35. 1623p. 1984. 75. 00 (*92-1-100038-6*, E.84.I.1) UN.

Yearbook of the United Nations, Vol. 36. 1716p. 1985. 75. 00 (*92-1-100295-8*, E.85.I.1) UN.

Yearbook of the United Nations: Special Edition. 50th anniversary ed. 443p. 1996. text ed. 95.00 (*0-7923-3112-5*) Taylor & Francis.

Yearbook of the United Nations: 1946-1977. Incl. Vol. 3. 1948-49. 1171p. reprint ed. 75.00 (*0-685-12891-1*, UN50/1/11); Vol. 4. 1950-1951. 1068p. reprint ed. 75. 00 (*0-685-12892-X*, UN51/1/24); Vol. 5. 1950-1951. 1030p. reprint ed. 50.00 (*0-685-12893-8*, UN52/1/30); reprint ed. write for info. (*0-318-60600-3*) UN.

Yearbook of the United Nations, 1983, Vol. 37. 1431p. 1986. 85.00 (*92-1-100312-1*, E.86.I.1) UN.

Yearbook of the United Nations, 1984, Vol. 38. 1409p. 1987. 90.00 (*92-1-100398-9*, E.87.I.1) UN.

Yearbook of the United Nations, 1985, Vol. 39. 1494p. 1990. 95.00 (*92-1-100403-9*, E.88.I.1) UN.

Yearbook of the United Nations, 1985, Vol. 39. Ed. by Department of Public Information United Nations Staff. (C). 1990. lib. bdg. 147.50 (*0-7923-0503-5*) Kluwer Ac.

Yearbook of the United Nations 1986, Vol. 40. Ed. by Department of Public Information, UN. 1333p. 1991. lib. bdg. 147.50 (*0-7923-1076-4*) Kluwer Ac.

Yearbook of the United Nations, 1987, Vol. 41. Ed. by United Nations, Department of Public Information Staff. 1322p. (C). 1992. lib. bdg. 137.00 (*0-7923-1613-4*) Kluwer Ac.

Yearbook of the United Nations, 1988 Vol. 42. Ed. by United Nations, Dept. of Public Information Staff. 1112p. (C). 1994. lib. bdg. 150.00 (*0-7923-2716-0*) Kluwer Ac.

Yearbook of the United Nations, 1991, Vol. 45. Ed. by Department of Public Information United Nations, Staff. 1124p. (C). 1992. lib. bdg. 137.00 (*0-7923-1970-2*) Kluwer Ac.

Yearbook of the United Nations, 1992, Vol. 46. Ed. by United Nations, Department of Public Information Staff. 1277p. (C). 1994. lib. bdg. 150.00 (*0-7923-2583-4*) Kluwer Ac.

***Yearbook of the United Nations 1995, Vol. 49.** 1997. text ed. 150.00 (*90-411-0376-7*) Kluwer Ac.

Yearbook of Tourism Statistics 1995, 2 vols., Set. 47th ed. WTO Staff. 1995. pap. 125.00 (*92-844-0122-4*, WTO0122, Pub. by Wrld Tourism Org SP) Bernan Associates.

Yearbook of Toxicology: 1990. Irving Sunshine. 360p. 1990. 200.00 (*0-8493-3305-9*, R, CRC Reprint) Franklin.

Yearbook of Toxicology, 1991. Irving Sunshine. 408p. 1991. 225.00 (*0-8493-3309-1*, R, CRC Reprint) Franklin.

Yearbook of Toxicology, 1992. Sunshine Staff. 448p. 1992. 79.00 (*0-8493-3311-3*) CRC Pr.

Yearbook of United Nations 199. 1995. lib. bdg. 150.00 (*0-7923-3077-3*) Kluwer Ac.

Yearbook of World Armaments & Disarmament 1986. Stockholm International Peace Research Institute Staff. (SIPRI Yearbook Ser.). (Illus.). 496p. 1986. 72.00 (*0-19-829100-0*) OUP.

Yearbook of World Armaments & Disarmaments, 1987. Stockholm International Peace Research Institute Staff. (SIPRI Yearbook Ser.). (Illus.). 536p. 1987. 75.00 (*0-19-829114-0*) OUP.

Yearbook of World Electronic Data 1994: Emerging Countries & World Summary, Vol. 3. 3rd ed. Kenneth F. Wilson. 188p. 1994. pap. 776.75 (*1-85617-202-3*, Pub. by Elsevier Applied Sci UK) Elsevier.

***Yearbook of World Electronics Data, 2 vols.** Ken Wilson. pap. 1,976.00 (*1-85617-256-2*) Elsevier.

Yearbook of World Electronics Data: Vol. 4: East Europe & World Summary 1994. K. Wilson. 160p. 1993. 840.00 (*1-85617-173-6*, Pub. by Elsevier Applied Sci UK) Elsevier.

***Yearbook of World Electronics Data Vol. 1: 1995.** Ken Wilson. 266p. 1994. 894.00 (*1-85617-247-3*, Pub. by Elsvr Adv Tech UK) Elsevier.

***Yearbook of World Electronics Data Vol. 2: 1995.** Ken Wilson. 260p. 1995. 1,332.75 (*1-85617-255-4*, Pub. by Elsvr Adv Tech UK) Elsevier.

***Yearbook of World Electronics Data 1994.** Kenneth F. Wilson. 256p. 1994. 1,302.00 (*1-85617-200-7*, Pub. by Elsvr Adv Tech UK) Elsevier.

Yearbook of World Electronics Data 1996, 4 vols., Set. Yearbook Staff. 1996. 3,350.00 (*1-85617-314-3*, Pergamon Pr) Elsevier.

Yearbook of World Electronics Data 1996: Emerging Countries, Vol. 3. Yearbook Staff. 1996. pap. 905.00 (*1-85617-307-0*, Pergamon Pr) Elsevier.

***Yearbook of World Electronics Data 1996- Vol. 1: West Europe.** Ken Wilson. 1995. 933.50 (*1-85617-284-8*, Pub. by Elsvr Adv Tech UK) Elsevier.

***Yearbook of World Electronics Date, 4 vols.** Andrew Fletcher. 1995. 3,128.50 (*1-85617-258-9*, Pub. by Elsvr Adv Tech UK) Elsevier.

XYZ

Yearbook on Government & Public Administration. Fritz W. Scharpf. 603p. 1990. 161.00 (3-7890-1788-4, Pub. by Nomos Verlags GW) Intl Bk Import.
Yearbook on Human Rights. 169p. 1984. 27.00 (92-1-154068-2) UN.
Yearbook on Human Rights: Lake Success, United Nations, 1947. LC 96-75537. 1996. reprint ed. 995.00 (1-57588-074-1, 309050) W S Hein.
Yearbook on Human Rights for 1980. 269p. 1988. 45.00 (92-1-154055-0, E.85.XIV.8) UN.
Yearbook on Human Rights for 1981. 294p. 35.00 (92-1-154070-4, E.88.XIV.5) UN.
Yearbook on Human Rights for 1982. 296p. 30.00 (92-1-154071-2, E.88.XIV.6) UN.
Yearbook on Human Rights for 1983. 281p. 35.00 (92-1-154072-0, E.88.XIV.7) UN.
Yearbook on Human Rights, 1985. 158p. 1988. 30.00 (92-1-154069-0, 88.XIV.4) UN.
Yearbook on Human Rights, 1986. 206p. 1991. 25.00 (92-1-154085-2) UN.
Yearbook on Human Rights, 1987. 172p. 1992. 25.00 (92-1-154087-9) UN.
Yearbook on Human Rights, 1988. 150p. 1988. 25.00 (92-1-154088-7) UN.
Yearbook on India's Foreign Policy 1984-1985. Ed. by Satish Kumar. 286p. (C). 1988. text ed. 49.95 (0-8039-9533-4) Sage.
Yearbook on India's Foreign Policy, 1987-1988. Ed. by Satish Kumar. (Yearbook on India's Foreign Policy Ser.: Vol. 5). 280p. (C). 1989. text ed. 49.95 (0-8039-9583-0) Sage.
Yearbook on India's Foreign Policy, 1989, Vol. 6. Satish Kumar. (Illus.). 238p. (C). 1989. text ed. 49.95 (0-8039-9634-9) Sage.
Yearbook on International Affairs. Ed. by Richard F. Staar. Incl. 1970. 1971. 25.00 (0-8179-6001-5); 1971. 833p. 1972. 25.00 (0-8179-6051-1); 1972. 700p. 1993. 25.00 (0-8179-6181-X); 1974. 648p. 1975. 25.00 (0-8179-6401-0); 1975. 678p. 1976. 25.00 (0-8179-6461-4); 1976. 686p. 1997. 25.00 (0-8179-6601-3); 1979. 484p. 1980. 35.00 (0-8179-7151-3); 1982. 576p. 1983. 39.95 (0-8179-7721-X); 1983. 534p. 1984. 44.95 (0-8179-7861-5); . LC 49-3353. 593p. 1986. 49.95 (0-8179-8271-X); 1974. 648p. 1975. 25.00 (0-8179-6401-0); (Publication Ser.). write for info. (0-318-59445-5) Hoover Inst Pr.
Yearbook on International Communist Affairs: Parties & Revolutionary Movements, 1989. Ed. by Richard F. Staar. 650p. (C). 1989. 54.95 (0-8179-8851-3) Hoover Inst Pr.
Yearbook on International Communist Affairs, 1984. Ed. by Richard F. Staar. 1984. 49.95 (0-8179-8031-8) Hoover Inst Pr.
Yearbook on International Communist Affairs, 1986. Ed. by Richard F. Staar. 608p. 1986. 49.95 (0-8179-8321-X) Hoover Inst Pr.
Yearbook on International Communist Affairs, 1987. Ed. by Richard F. Staar & Margit N. Grigory. 1987. 49.95 (0-8179-8651-0) Hoover Inst Pr.
Yearbook on International Communist Affairs, 1988: Parties & Revolutionary Movements. Ed. by Richard F. Staar. (P-380 Ser.). 640p. (C). 1988. text ed. 49.95 (0-8179-8801-7) Hoover Inst Pr.
Yearbook on International Communist Affairs, 1990: Parties & Revolutionary Movements. Ed. by Richard F. Staar. (P. Ser.: No. 394). 640p. (C). 1990. text ed. 59.95 (0-8179-8941-2) Hoover Inst Pr.
Yearbook on International Communist Affairs, 1991. Ed. by Richard F. Staar & Margit N. Grigory. 689p. 1991. 59.95 (0-8179-9161-1, P408) Hoover Inst Pr.
***Yearbook United Nations 1994.** 1564p. 1996. 250.00 (90-411-0172-1) Kluwer Law Tax Pubs.
Yearbook, 1956 see Theilheimer's Synthetic Methods of Organic Chemistry: Synthetische Methoden der Organischen Chemie
Yearbook, 1962 see Theilheimer's Synthetic Methods of Organic Chemistry: Synthetische Methoden der Organischen Chemie
Yearbook, 1963 see Theilheimer's Synthetic Methods of Organic Chemistry: Synthetische Methoden der Organischen Chemie
Yearbook, 1964 see Theilheimer's Synthetic Methods of Organic Chemistry: Synthetische Methoden der Organischen Chemie
Yearbook, 1965 see Theilheimer's Synthetic Methods of Organic Chemistry: Synthetische Methoden der Organischen Chemie
Yearbook, 1966 see Theilheimer's Synthetic Methods of Organic Chemistry: Synthetische Methoden der Organischen Chemie
Yearbook, 1971 see Theilheimer's Synthetic Methods of Organic Chemistry: Synthetische Methoden der Organischen Chemie
Yearbook, 1976 see Theilheimer's Synthetic Methods of Organic Chemistry: Synthetische Methoden der Organischen Chemie
Yearbook 1980 Mit deutschem Registerschluessel. Ed. by W. Theilheimer. (Synthetic Methods of Organic Chemistry Ser.: Vol. 34). xx, 524p. 1980. 390.50 (3-8055-0327-X) S Karger.
Yearbook, 1981. Ed. by W. Theilheimer. (Synthetic Methods of Organic Chemistry Ser.: Vol. 35). xviii, 838p. 1981. 558.50 (3-8055-1607-X) S Karger.
Yearbook, 1982. Ed. by A. F. Finch. (Theilheimer's Synthetic Methods of Organic Chemistry Ser.: Vol. 36). xxiv, 532p. 1982. 398.50 (3-8055-3446-9) S Karger.
Yearbook, 1984. Ed. by A. F. Finch. (Theilheimer's Synthetic Methods of Organic Chemistry Ser.: Vol. 38). (Illus.). xxiv, 624p. 1984. 462.50 (3-8055-3817-0) S Karger.
Yearbook, 1985. Ed. by A. F. Finch. (Theilheimer's Synthetic Methods of Organic Chemistry Ser.: Vol. 39). xxiv, 548p. 1985. 457.75 (3-8055-3987-8) S Karger.
Yearbook, 1986, with Reaction Titles & Cumulative Index of Vols. 36. Ed. by A. F. Finch. (Theilheimer's Synthetic Methods of Organic Chemistry Ser.: Vol. 40). xxiv, 1016p. 1986. ring bd. 712.00 (3-8055-4241-0) S Karger.
Yearbook, 1987. A. F. Finch. (Theilheimer's Synthetic Methods of Organic Chemistry Ser.: Vol. 41). xx, 520p. 1987. 472.00 (3-8055-4496-0) S Karger.
Yearbook, 1988. Ed. by A. F. Finch. (Theilheimer's Synthetic Methods of Organic Chemistry Ser.: Vol. 42). (Illus.). xx, 596p. 1988. 472.00 (3-8055-4698-X) S Karger.
Yearbook, 1989. Ed. by A. F. Finch. (Theilheimer's Synthetic Methods of Organic Chemistry Ser.: Vol. 43). xxii, 506p. 1989. 557.75 (3-8055-4896-6) S Karger.
Yearbook, 1990. Ed. by A. F. Finch. (Theilheimer's Synthetic Methods of Organic Chemistry Ser.: Vol. 44). xxiv, 544p. 1990. 674.00 (3-8055-5090-1) S Karger.
Yearbook, 1991: With Reaction Titles & Cumulative Index of Volumes, 41-45. Ed. by A. F. Finch. (Theilheimer's Synthetic Methods of Organic Chemistry Ser.: Vol. 45). (Illus.). xxiv, 816p. 1991. 953.25 (3-8055-5300-5) S Karger.
Yearbook 1992. Ed. by A. F. Finch. (Theilheimer's Synthetic Methods of Organic Chemistry Ser.: Vol. 46). xxii, 506p. 1992. 694.00 (3-8055-5509-1) S Karger.
Yearbook, 1993. Ed. by A. F. Finch. (Theilheimer's Synthetic Methods of Organic Chemistry Ser.: Vol. 47). xxiv, 532p. 1993. 756.75 (3-8055-5641-1) S Karger.
Yearbook, 1994. Ed. by A. F. Finch. (Theilheimer's Synthetic Methods of Organic Chemistry Ser.: Vol. 48). xxviii, 514p. 1994. 843.50 (3-8055-5863-5) S Karger.
Yearbook, 1994: International Tribunal for the Prosecution of Persons Responsible for Serious Violations of International Humanitarian Law Committed in the Territory of the Former Yugoslavia since 1991. 308p. 1994. 42.00 (92-1-156700-9) UN.
Yearbook 1995. Ed. by A. F. Finch. (Theilheimer's Synthetic Methods of Organic Chemistry Ser.: Vol. 49). (Illus.). xxviii, 496p. 1995. 848.25 (3-8055-6045-1) S Karger.
***Yearbook, 1995: International Tribunal for the Prosecution of Persons Responsible for Serious Violations of International Humanitarian Law Committed in the Territory of the Former Yugoslavia since 1991.** 362p. 1995. pap. text ed. 45.00 (92-1-156701-7) UN.
Yearbook 1996: With Cumulative Reaction Titles of Volumes 46-50. Ed. by A. F. Finch. (Theilheimer's Synthetic Methods of Organic Chemistry Ser.: Vol. 50). (Illus.). xxviii, 512p. 1996. 848.25 (3-8055-6231-4) S Karger.
***Yearbook 1997.** 1998. 140.00 (0-7876-2519-1, 00158184) Gale.
Yearbooks in Science Ser., 9 Vol., Set. (Illus.). 80p. (J). (gr. 5-8). 1995. lib. bdg. 152.80 (0-8050-4282-2) TFC Bks NY.
Yearbooks of the Association of Pacific Coast Geographers, 1935-1993, Vols. 1-53. Association of Pacific Coast Geographers. LC 37-13376. One Copy. pap. 2.00 (0-318-37527-3) Oreg St U Pr.
Yearbooks, 1957 see Theilheimer's Synthetic Methods of Organic Chemistry: Synthetische Methoden der Organischen Chemie
Yearbooks, 1967 see Theilheimer's Synthetic Methods of Organic Chemistry: Synthetische Methoden der Organischen Chemie
Yearbooks, 1968 see Theilheimer's Synthetic Methods of Organic Chemistry: Synthetische Methoden der Organischen Chemie
Yearbooks, 1969 see Theilheimer's Synthetic Methods of Organic Chemistry: Synthetische Methoden der Organischen Chemie
Yearbooks, 1970 see Theilheimer's Synthetic Methods of Organic Chemistry: Synthetische Methoden der Organischen Chemie
Yearbooks, 1972 see Theilheimer's Synthetic Methods of Organic Chemistry: Synthetische Methoden der Organischen Chemie
Yearbooks, 1973 see Theilheimer's Synthetic Methods of Organic Chemistry: Synthetische Methoden der Organischen Chemie
Yearbooks, 1974 see Theilheimer's Synthetic Methods of Organic Chemistry: Synthetische Methoden der Organischen Chemie
Yearbooks, 1975 see Theilheimer's Synthetic Methods of Organic Chemistry: Synthetische Methoden der Organischen Chemie
Yearbooks, 1977 see Theilheimer's Synthetic Methods of Organic Chemistry: Synthetische Methoden der Organischen Chemie
Yearbooks, 1978 see Theilheimer's Synthetic Methods of Organic Chemistry: Synthetische Methoden der Organischen Chemie
Yearful of Circle Times. Liz Wilmes & Dick Wilmes. 232p. (Orig.). 1989. pap. 16.95 (0-943452-10-4) Building Blocks.
Yearling. (Illus.). 040p. 1982. pap. 7.95 (0-88188-123-6, 00385215) H Leonard.
Yearling. Created by Harcourt Brace Staff. 1990. student ed., teacher ed., pap. 22.75 (0-15-348526-4) HR&W Schl Div.
Yearling. Created by Harcourt Brace Staff. 1990. student ed., pap. 10.00 (0-15-348520-5) HR&W Schl Div.
Yearling. Holt. 1989. student ed., pap. 10.00 (0-03-023442-5) HR&W Schl Div.
Yearling. Marjorie K. Rawlings. LC 85-40301. (Scribner's Illustrated Classics Ser.). (Illus.). 416p. (J). 1985. text ed. 25.00 (0-684-18461-3, C Scribner Sons Young) S&S Childrens.
Yearling. large type ed. Marjorie K. Rawlings. LC 94-15061. 559p. 1994. lib. bdg. 22.95 (0-8161-5992-0, GK Hall) Thorndike Pr.
Yearling. 2nd ed. Marjorie K. Rawlings. LC 86-20743. (Illus.). 448p. (YA). (gr. 5 up). 1988. reprint ed. pap. 5.95 (0-02-044931-3) Macmillan.
Yearling. Marjorie K. Rawlings. 250p. (YA). 1991. reprint ed. lib. bdg. 19.95 (0-89966-841-0) Buccaneer Bks.
Yearling - Study Guide. Rosemary Villanella. Ed. by Joyce Friedland & Rikki Kessler. (Novel-Ties Ser.). (YA). (gr. 7-11). 1993. pap. text ed. 15.95 (0-88122-061-2) Lrn Links.
Yearly All India Criminal Digest, 1988. Ed. by A. Awasthi & B. Bagga. (C). 1990. 210.00 (0-89771-191-2) St Mut.
Yearly Digest of Supreme Court Criminal Cases. Surendra Malik. 1988. 80.00 (0-317-54840-9) St Mut.
Yearly Programs, Units & Daily Lesson Plans: Physical Education for Elementary School Children: a Developmental Approach. 4th ed. Glenn Kirchner & Graham Fishburne. 256p. (C). 1995. spiral bd. write for info. (0-697-24154-8) Brown & Benchmark.
Yearly Supreme Court & Full Bench Cases Digest 1986. 1986. 150.00 (0-685-18898-1, Pub. by Capital Law Hse II) St Mut.
Yearning: Living Between How It Is & How It Ought to Be. M. Craig Barnes. LC 91-30416. 190p. (Orig.). 1992. pap. 9.99 (0-8308-1378-0, 1378) InterVarsity.
Yearning: Race, Gender, & Cultural Politics. Bell Hooks. 248p. (Orig.). (C). 1990. 30.00 (0-89608-386-1); pap. 15.00 (0-89608-385-3) South End Pr.
Yearning for the Holy Land: Hasidic Tales of Israel. Ed. by Yoel Rappel. Tr. by Shmuel Himmelstein. (Illus.). 176p. 1987. reprint ed. 11.95 (0-317-56162-6, Watts); reprint ed. pap. 9.95 (0-915361-86-8, Watts) Hemed Bks.
Yearning Heart. Joyce H. Frost. (Wellspring Romance Ser.). 185p. 1990. 5.95 (0-9614712-6-3) Wellspring Bks.
Yearning, Learning, Earning & Returning: a Community-Adult Teacher's Handbook. David W. Cochran. 32p. 1981. pap. text ed. 4.00 (0-939926-03-2) Fruition Pubns.
***Yearning Minds & Burning Hearts: Rediscovering the Spirituality of Jesus.** Glandion Carney & William Long. 256p. Date not set. pap. 14.99 (0-8010-5783-3) Baker Bks.
Yearning Soul. Moshe Einstadter. 1992. 13.95 (0-87306-614-6) Feldheim.
Yearning to Breathe Free. Richard A. Spiegel. 32p. (Orig.). (J). (gr. 4-9). 1984. pap. 2.00 (0-934830-33-9) Ten Penny.
Yearning to Breathe Free: Liberation Theologies in the U. S. Ed. by Mar Peter-Raoul et al. LC 90-46164. 1991. pap. 19.00 (0-88344-732-0) Orbis Bks.
Yearning to Know God's Will: A Workbook for Discerning God's Guidance for Your Life. Danny Morris. 144p. 1991. pap. 8.99 (0-310-75491-7) Zondervan.
Yearning to Understand: Why Our Quest to Live in Space Must Never End. Douglas Kirk. Ed. by Valerie Matthews. LC 86-60530. (Illus.). 166p. (Orig.). 1986. pap. 6.95 (0-934279-03-9) Morton Falls Pub.
Yearning Toward Wildness: Environmental Quotations from the Writings of Henry David Thoreau. Tim Homan. 192p. (Orig.). 1991. pap. 9.95 (1-56145-035-9) Peachtree Pubs.
Years. Cindy L. Johnson. 1994. pap. 5.25 (0-8222-1353-2) Dramatists Play.
Years. LaVyrle Spencer. 496p. 1986. mass mkt. 6.99 (0-515-08489-1) Jove Pubns.
Years. large type ed. LaVyrle Spencer. LC 93-44942. (General Ser.). 1994. pap. 18.95 (0-8161-5763-4, GK Hall) Thorndike Pr.
Years. Virginia Woolf. LC 37-27268. 435p. 1969. reprint ed. pap. 14.00 (0-15-699701-0, Harvest Bks) HarBrace.
Years: The Last Decade of Imperial Russia, 1906-1917. V. V. Shulgin. 1990. pap. 11.95 (0-87052-928-5) Hippocrene Bks.
Years after Fifty. Wingate M. Johnson. 17.95 (0-405-18502-2) Ayer.
Years Ago. Ruth Gordon. 1948. pap. 5.25 (0-8222-1285-4) Dramatists Play.
Years Ago: A Play. Ruth Gordon. (American Autobiography Ser.). 173p. 1995. reprint ed. lib. bdg. 69.00 (0-7812-8532-1) Rprt Serv.
Years Ago Now Medina County, Ohio Gazette 1854-1895. Sharon L. Kraynek. 129p. 1994. pap. text ed. 9.50 (1-55856-174-9) Closson Pr.
Years Ahead: Perils, Problems, & Promises. Ed. by Howard F. Didsbury, Jr. 1993. pap. 21.00 (0-930242-46-7) World Future.
Years As Catches. Robert Duncan. 1977. 3.00 (0-685-80007-5) Oyez.
Years at the Edge of Existence Vol. XV: War Memoirs 1939-1945. Frank Morgens. LC 96-15576. (Studies in the Shoah). (Illus.). 208p. (C). 1996. lib. bdg. 42.50 (0-7618-0332-7) U Pr of Amer.
Years at the Ending. Joseph Leftwich. LC 83-45131. 72p. 1984. 11.95 (0-8453-4767-5, Cornwall Bks) Assoc Univ Prs.
Years at the Spring. large type ed. Dilys Gater. (General Fiction Ser.). 480p. 1993. 25.99 (0-7089-2931-1) Ulverscroft.
***Years Best Fan & Horror.** 10th ed. Datlow. Date not set. 29.95 (0-312-15700-2) St Martin.
Year's Best Fantasy. Ed. by Ellen Datlow. 1989. pap. 13.95 (0-312-03007-X) St Martin.
Year's Best Fantasy. 3rd ed. Ed. by Ellen Datlow. 1990. pap. 14.95 (0-312-04450-X) St Martin.
Year's Best Fantasy: First Annual Collection. Ed. by Ellen Datlow & Terri Windling. 512p. 1988. pap. 12.95 (0-312-01852-5) St Martin.
Year's Best Fantasy & Horror. 4th ed. Ed. by Ellen Datlow. 1991. 27.95 (0-312-06005-X); pap. 15.95 (0-312-06007-6) St Martin.
Year's Best Fantasy & Horror. 7th ed. Ed. by Ellen Datlow & Terri Windling. 624p. 1994. pap. 16.95 (0-312-11102-9) St Martin.
Year's Best Fantasy & Horror. 9th ed. Ellen Datlow. 624p. 1996. 27.95 (0-312-14449-0); pap. 17.95 (0-312-14450-4) St Martin.
Year's Best Fantasy & Horror: Eighth Annual Collection. Ed. by Ellen Daltow & Terri Windling. 1995. pap. 16.95 (0-312-13219-0) St Martin.
Year's Best Fantasy & Horror: Eighth Annual Collection. Ed. by Ellen Datlow & Terri Windling. 624p. 1995. 27.95 (0-312-13220-4) St Martin.
Year's Best Fantasy & Horror: Fifth Annual Collection. Ed. by Ellen Datlow & Terri Windling. 624p. 1992. pap. 15.95 (0-312-07888-9) St Martin.
Year's Best Fantasy & Horror: Sixth Annual Collection. Ed. by Ellen Datlow & Terri Windling. 624p. (Orig.). 1993. pap. 16.95 (0-312-09422-1) St Martin.
***Years Best Fantasy & Horror: Tenth Annual Collection.** Ellen Datlow. 1997. pap. 17.95 (0-312-15701-0, Griffin) St Martin.
Year's Best Horror Stories: Twentieth Anniversary Edition. Ed. by Karl E. Wagner. 368p. (Orig.). 1992. mass mkt. 5.50 (0-88677-526-4) DAW Bks.
Year's Best Horror Stories 21. Ed. by Karl E. Wagner. 368p. (Orig.). 1993. mass mkt. 5.50 (0-88677-572-8) DAW Bks.
Year's Best Mystery & Suspense Stories 1983. Ed. by Edward D. Hoch. 264p. 1983. 13.95 (0-8027-0747-5); pap. 6.95 (0-8027-7235-8) Walker & Co.
Years Best Mystery & Suspense Stories, 1984. Ed. by Edward D. Hoch. 252p. 1984. 14.95 (0-8027-5597-6) Walker & Co.
Year's Best Mystery & Suspense Stories, 1985. Ed. by Edward D. Hoch. 256p. 1985. 15.95 (0-8027-5634-4); pap. 8.95 (0-8027-7286-2) Walker & Co.
Year's Best Mystery & Suspense Stories, 1986. Ed. by Edward D. Hoch. 228p. 1986. 16.95 (0-8027-0919-2); pap. 9.95 (0-8027-7292-7) Walker & Co.
Year's Best Mystery & Suspense Stories 1987. Ed. by Edward D. Hoch. 1987. 17.95 (0-8027-0983-4) Walker & Co.
Year's Best Mystery & Suspense Stories 1988. Ed. by Edward D. Hoch. 246p. 1988. 17.95 (0-8027-1050-6) Walker & Co.
Year's Best Mystery & Suspense Stories, 1989. Ed. by Edward D. Hoch. 246p. 1989. 18.95 (0-8027-1097-2) Walker & Co.
Year's Best Mystery & Suspense Stories, 1990. Ed. by Edward D. Hoch. 224p. 1990. 18.95 (0-8027-1139-1) Walker & Co.
Year's Best Mystery & Suspense Stories 1991. Ed. by Edward D. Hoch. 254p. 1991. 19.95 (0-8027-3200-3) Walker & Co.
Year's Best Mystery & Suspense Stories, 1992. Edward D. Hoch. 239p. 1992. 21.95 (0-8027-1240-1) Walker & Co.
Year's Best Mystery & Suspense Stories, 1993. Edward D. Hoch. 1993. 21.95 (0-8027-3238-0) Walker & Co.
Year's Best Mystery & Suspense Stories, 1994. Ed. by Edward D. Hoch. 256p. 1994. 21.95 (0-8027-3192-9) Walker & Co.
Year's Best Mystery & Suspense Stories, 1995. Ed. by Edward D. Hoch. 300p. 1995. 23.95 (0-8027-3266-6) Walker & Co.
***Years Best Science Fiction.** Dozois. 1997. 29.95 (0-312-15702-9) St Martin.
***Year's Best Science Fiction.** David Hartwell. 1997. mass mkt. 5.99 (0-06-105746-0) HarpC.
Year's Best Science Fiction. David G. Hartwell. 496p. 1996. mass mkt. 5.50 (0-06-105641-3, HarperPrism) HarpC.
Year's Best Science Fiction. 4th ed. Ed. by Gardner Dozois. 608p. 1987. pap. 11.95 (0-312-00710-8) St Martin.
Year's Best Science Fiction. 7th ed. E. Gardner Dozois. mass mkt. write for info. (0-312-92390-2) Tor Bks.
Year's Best Science Fiction. 11th ed. Ed. by Gardner Dozois. 624p. 1994. pap. 16.95 (0-312-11104-5) St Martin.
Year's Best Science Fiction. 12th ed. Gardner Dozois. 1995. 27.95 (0-312-13222-0) St Martin.
Year's Best Science Fiction. 12th ed. Gardner Dozois. 1995. pap. 16.95 (0-312-13221-2) St Martin.
***Years Best Science Fiction.** 14th ed. Dozois. 1997. pap. 17.95 (0-312-15703-7) St Martin.
Year's Best Science Fiction: Eighth Annual Collection. Ed. by Gardner Dozois. 1991. pap. 15.95 (0-312-06009-2) St Martin.
Year's Best Science Fiction: Fifth Annual Collection. Ed. by Gardner Dozois. 624p. 1988. pap. 15.95 (0-312-01854-1) St Martin.
Year's Best Science Fiction: Ninth Annual Collection. Ed. by Gardner Dozois. 624p. 1992. pap. 15.95 (0-312-07891-9) St Martin.
Year's Best Science Fiction: Seventh Annual Collection. Ed. by Gardner Dozois. 624p. (Orig.). 1990. pap. 14.95 (0-312-04452-6) St Martin.
Year's Best Science Fiction: Tenth Annual Collection. Ed. by Gardner Dozois. 624p. (Orig.). 1993. pap. 16.95 (0-312-09424-8) St Martin.
Year's Best Science Fiction: Thirteenth Annual Collection. 13th ed. Ed. by Gardner Dozois. 624p. 1996. pap. 17.95 (0-312-14452-0) St Martin.
***Year's Best SF 2.** Ed. by David G. Hartwell. (Orig.). 1997. mass mkt. 5.99 (0-614-27750-7, HarperPrism) HarpC.

An Asterisk (*) at the beginning of an entry indicates that the title is appearing in BIP for the first time.

Years Between. large type ed. Iris Bromige. (General Ser.). 304p. 1993. 25.99 (*0-7089-2837-4*) Ulverscroft.

Years from Now. Gary Glickman. LC 86-46320. (Illus.). 1987. 16.95 (*0-394-55513-9*) Knopf.

Years in Exile: The Liberal Democrats, 1950-1959. Arlene Lazarowitz. LC 88-25978. (Modern American History Ser.). 200p. 1988. 25.00 (*0-8240-4333-2*) Garland.

Years Like Brief Days. Fabian Dobles. Tr. by Joan Henry from SPA. 128p. 9600. 29.00 (*0-7206-0987-9*, Pub. by P Owen Ltd UK) Dufour.

Years of Attrition: 1940-1941. Richard Collier. 1995. pap. text ed. 15.95 (*0-7490-0236-0*, Pub. by A & B UK) London Brdge.

Years of Awakening. Mary Luyters. 1991. pap. 9.95 (*0-380-00734-7*) Avon.

Years of Big Spending in Alaska: How Good Is the Record? Gordon S. Harrison. (Occasional Papers: No. 20). (Illus.). 1989. pap. 2.00 (*0-88353-041-4*) U Alaska Inst Res.

***Years of Change.** Mike Soper. (Illus.). 500p. 1995. pap. 13. 95 (*0-85236-313-3*, Pub. by Farming Pr UK) Diamond Farm Bk.

Years of Change. large type ed. Alan White. 544p. 1985. 27. 99 (*0-7089-8251-4*) Ulverscroft.

Years of Change: Reading the Russian Press. 2nd ed. ACTR Staff & Simes. 292p. 1996. per., pap. text ed. 40. 00 (*0-7872-2202-X*) Kendall-Hunt.

***Years of Confusion: Stage II in the Series.** Mary M. Shideler. LC 96-72116. (Visions & Nightmares, Ends & Beginnings Ser.: Vol. 2). 360p. 1997. write for info. (*0-9649509-8-7*); pap. write for info. (*0-9649509-2-8*) Scribendi Pr.

Years of Decision: American Politics in the 1890's. rev. ed. R. Hal Williams. 219p. (C). 1993. reprint ed. pap. text ed. 10.95 (*0-88133-727-7*) Waveland Pr.

Years of Discord: American Politics & Society, 1961-1974. John M. Blum. (Illus.). 608p. 1991. 25.00 (*0-393-02969-7*) Norton.

Years of Discord: American Politics & Society 1961-1974. John M. Blum. 544p. 1992. pap. 16.95 (*0-393-30910-X*) Norton.

Years of Emigration, Vol. 1. Lavrov. (Russian Series on Social History). 1987. lib. bdg. 41.50 (*90-277-0384-1*) Kluwer Ac.

Years of Emigration, Vol. 2. Lavrov. (Russian Series on Social History). 1987. lib. bdg. 41.50 (*90-277-0443-0*) Kluwer Ac.

Years of Endeavour: Selected Speeches, 1969-1972. Indira Gandhi. 826p. reprint ed. 34.95 (*0-940500-97-3*, Pub. by Pubns Div II) Asia Bk Corp.

***Years of Estrangement.** Erich Leyens. 128p. 1996. pap. 12. 95 (*0-8101-1166-7*) Northwestern U Pr.

***Years of Estrangement.** Erich Leyens & Lotte Andor. Tr. by Brigitte Goldstein from GER. LC 96-33080. (Jewish Lives Ser.). 128p. 1996. 39.95 (*0-8101-1181-0*) Northwestern U Pr.

***Years of Estrangement: American Relations with The Soviet Union, 1933-1941.** Thomas R. Maddux. LC 79-26489. 248p. reprint ed. pap. 70.70 (*0-608-04458-X*, 2065202) Bks Demand.

Years of Experience. Georgiana Kirby. LC 79-134373. reprint ed. 47.50 (*0-404-08421-4*) AMS Pr.

Years of Fighting Exile: Collected Poems. Milton V. Williams. 85p. (C). 1986. pap. 10.00 (*0-948833-01-7*, Three Contnts) Lynne Rienner.

Years of Fulfillment see Indiana University: Midwestern Pioneer

***Years of Glory: The National Hockey League's Official Book of the Six-Team Era.** Dan Diamond. 1997. 29.95 (*0-9656949-2-5*) Total Sprts.

Years of Glory, 1942-1967: The National Hockey League's Official Book of the Six-Team Era. Ed. by Dan Diamond. (Illus.). 256p. 1994. 40.00 (*0-7710-2817-2*) McCland & Stewart.

Years of Grace. Margaret A. Barnes. 1991. lib. bdg. 21.95 (*1-56849-055-0*) Buccaneer Bks.

Years of Grace, Days of Glory: The Legacy of Germaine Laville. Peter A. Soderbergh. (Illus.). 186p. (Orig.). 1988. pap. write for info. (*0-9620557-0-0*) Amer Lgn Boyd-Ewing.

Years of Grief & Laughter: A Biography of Ammon Hennacy. Joan Thomas. pap. 9.95 (*0-89019-002-X*) Fortkamp.

Years of High Purpose: From Trusteeship to Nationhood. Mason Sears. LC 80-5161. (Illus.). 205p. 1980. text ed. 45.00 (*0-8191-1052-3*); pap. text ed. 19.00 (*0-8191-1053-1*) U Pr of Amer.

***Years of Hope.** Snow. Date not set. text ed. write for info. (*1-86064-147-4*, Pub. by I B Tauris UK) St Martin.

Years of Infamy: The Untold Story of America's Concentration Camps. Michi N. Weglyn. (Illus.). 352p. (C). 1995. pap. 16.95 (*0-295-97484-2*) U of Wash Pr.

Years of My Youth. William Dean Howells. LC 70-146859. (Select Bibliographies Reprint Ser.). 1977. reprint ed. 18. 95 (*0-8369-5626-5*) Ayer.

Years of My Youth. William Dean Howells. (Notable American Authors Ser.). 1992. reprint ed. lib. bdg. 75.00 (*0-7812-3284-8*) Rprt Serv.

Years of My Youth & Three Essays. William Dean Howells. LC 78-166119. (Selected Edition of W. D. Howells Ser.). 448p. 1975. 31.50 (*0-253-36850-2*) Ind U Pr.

Years of No Decision. Muhammad El Farra. 350p. 1987. 39.50 (*0-7103-0215-0*) Routledge Chapman & Hall.

Years of O'Casey, 1921-1926: A Documentary History. Robert T. Hogan & Richard Burnham. LC 90-50841. 440p. 1992. 55.00 (*0-87413-421-8*) U Delaware Pr.

Years of Our Friendship: Robert Lowell & Allen Tate. William Doreski. LC 89-49308. 264p. 1990. 35.00 (*0-87805-429-4*) U Pr of Miss.

Years of Passages. Reda Bensmaia. 1995. pap. 21.95 (*0-8166-2393-7*) U of Minn Pr.

Years of Poverty, Years of Plenty. Greg J. Duncan. 204p. text ed. 26.95 (*0-472-00702-5*) U of Mich Pr.

Years of Poverty, Years of Plenty: The Changing Economic Fortunes of American Workers & Families. Greg J. Duncan et al. LC 83-12923. (Illus.). 200p. (C). 1984. 24. 00 (*0-87944-285-9*); pap. 14.00 (*0-87944-298-0*) Inst Soc Res.

Years of Recovery: British Economic Policy, 1945-1951. Alec Cairncross. LC 85-18541. 544p. 1985. text ed. 59. 95 (*0-416-37920-6*, 9522) Routledge Chapman & Hall.

Years of Struggle: The Farm Diary of Elmer G. Powers, 1931-1936. rev. ed. Ed. by H. Roger Grant & L. Edward Purcell. LC 95-22954. (Illus.). 240p. 1995. pap. 15.00 (*0-87580-569-8*); lib. bdg. 28.00 (*0-87580-202-8*) N Ill U Pr.

Years of the Barbarians. Elspeth Davies. 210p. (C). 1989. text ed. 50.00 (*0-946270-49-X*, Pub. by Pentland Pr UK) St Mut.

Years of the City. Frederik Pohl. 336p. 1995. mass mkt. 5.99 (*0-671-87639-2*) Baen Bks.

Years of the Electric Ear. As told by Norman Corwin. LC 94-5101. 1994. 45.00 (*0-8108-2885-5*) Scarecrow.

***Years of the Fury.** large type ed. Frederick E. Smith. (Charnwood Large Print Ser.). 448p. 1997. 29.50 (*0-7089-8941-1*, Charnwood) Ulverscroft.

Years of the Locust. W. J. Gruffydd. Tr. by D. Myrddin Lloyd. 207p. (C). 1976. 25.00 (*0-85088-342-3*, Pub. by Gomer Pr UK) St Mut.

Years of Triumphs, Trials & Errors. Noah Bee. 208p. 1988. 13.95 (*0-8197-0555-1*) Bloch.

Years of Upheaval. Henry A. Kissinger. (Illus.). 1982. 29.95 (*0-316-28591-9*) Little.

Years of Victory 1944-1945. Richard Collier. (Illus.). 464p. 1995. pap. 14.95 (*0-7490-0251-4*, Pub. by A & B UK) London Brdge.

Years of Wrath, Days of Glory. 2nd ed. Yitshaq Ben-Ami. LC 83-60834. (Illus.). 620p. (C). 1983. reprint ed. 25.00 (*0-88400-096-6*) Shengold.

Year's Residence in America. Cobbett. (BCL1 - U. S. History Ser.). 275p. 1991. reprint ed. lib. bdg. 79.00 (*0-7812-6011-6*) Rprt Serv.

Years Rich & Fruitful: University of Montevallo 1896-1996. Mary F. Tipton. (Illus.). 160p. 1996. 34.95 (*0-9625875-0-8*) Univ Montevallo Pr.

Year's Scholarship in Science Fiction & Fantasy, 1972-1975. Marshall B. Tymn & Roger C. Schlobin. LC 78-21976. (Serif Series: Bibliographies & Checklists: No. 36). 238p. reprint ed. pap. 67.90 (*0-7837-1314-2*, 2041462) Bks Demand.

Year's Scholarship in Science Fiction, Fantasy, & Horror Literature, 1980. Ed. by Marshall B. Tymn. LC 83-169221. 118p. reprint ed. pap. 33.70 (*0-7837-1332-0*, 2041480) Bks Demand.

Year's Scholarship in Science Fiction, Fantasy, & Horror Literature, 1981. Ed. by Marshall B. Tymn. 111p. reprint ed. pap. 31.70 (*0-7837-1338-X*, 2041486) Bks Demand.

Year's Supply: "Take Heed, Prepare, Watch, & Be Ready" Barry G. Crockett & Lynette B. Crockett. LC 88-71201. (Illus.). 117p. 1988. pap. 13.95 (*0-915131-88-9*) Crockett Pub Co.

Years That Changed the World. Rob Lindsted et al. 92p. (Orig.). 1995. pap. 7.95 (*1-879366-92-4*) Hearthstone OK.

Years the Locust Has Eaten. Sherri Thomas. LC 91-65533. 212p. 1991. 10.95 (*1-55523-441-0*) Winston-Derek.

***Years the Locusts Have Eaten.** Marilyn Ryerson. (Illus.). 80p. (Orig.). 1997. pap. 18.95 (*0-9658025-0-7*) TRIAGE Inc.

Years the Locusts Stole: Vol. 1, The Ordeal, 1. Capstan Turner. 160p. 1984. 4.95 (*0-318-03353-4*) Sozo Pub Co.

Years, the Wind, & the Rain: A Biography of Dorothy M. Johnson. Steve Smith. LC 84-61543. (Illus.). 256p. 1984. 12.95 (*0-933126-50-6*) Pictorial Hist.

Years to Grow. Marta Yemm. LC 81-68369. (Illus.). 600p. (Orig.). (J). (ps). 1981. pap. 31.95 (*0-513-01724-0*) Denison.

Years-to-Share. Peggy H. Benjamin. (Illus.). 256p. 1990. pap. 12.50 (*0-9627634-0-3*) P Benjamin.

Years-to-Share. 2nd ed. Peggy H. Benjamin. (First, Second, Third Paperback Ser.). (Illus.). 256p. 1986. 17.50 (*0-9617063-0-9*) Service Pr.

Years-to-Share. 2nd ed. Peggy H. Benjamin. (First, Second, Third Paperback Ser.). (Illus.). 256p. 1986. reprint ed. pap. 12.95 (*0-685-38389-X*) Service Pr.

***Year's Turning.** Michael Viney. 232p. 9700. 24.95 (*0-85640-562-0*, Pub. by Blackstaff Pr IE) Dufour.

Year's Twenty-Five Finest Crime & Mystery Stories. Mystery Scene Magazine Editors. 320p. 1992. 21.00 (*0-88184-903-0*) Carroll & Graf.

Year's Twenty-Five Finest Crime & Mystery Stories. Ed. by Mystery Scene Magazine Editors. 352p. 1994. pap. 12.95 (*0-7867-0018-1*) Carroll & Graf.

Year's Twenty Five Finest Crime & Mystery Stories. 2nd ed. Mystery Scene Magazine Editors. 352p. 1993. 20.00 (*0-88184-999-5*) Carroll & Graf.

Year's Twenty-Five Finest Crime & Mystery Stories. 3rd ed. Ed. by Mystery Scene Magazine Editors. 352p. 1994. 20.00 (*0-7867-0141-2*) Carroll & Graf.

Years with Frank Lloyd Wright: Apprentice to Genius. Edgar Tafel. (Architecture Ser.). 288p. 1985. reprint ed. pap. 10.95 (*0-486-24801-1*) Dover.

Years with Ross. James Thurber. LC 83-45899. (Illus.). reprint ed. 30.00 (*0-404-20256-X*, PN4874) AMS Pr.

***Year's Work in Critical & Cultural Theory.** Ed. by Kate McGowan. 384p. (C). 1997. text ed. 89.95 (*0-631-20523-3*) Blackwell Pubs.

***Year's Work in Critical & Cultural Theory, Vol. 1.** Stephen Regan. 256p. Date not set. 59.95 (*0-631-18858-4*) Blackwell Pubs.

Year's Work in Critical & Cultural Theory, Vol.2. Ed. by Stephen Regan & Elaine Treharne. 368p. (C). 1996. 59. 95 (*0-631-18859-2*) Blackwell Pubs.

Year's Work in Critical & Cultural Theory: 1993, vol. 3. Ed. by Kate McGowan. (Year's Work in Critical & Cultural Theory Ser.). 504p. 1997. 69.95 (*0-631-18861-4*) Blackwell Pubs.

Year's Work in English Studies. Ed. by Peter Kitson & Elaine Treharne. 900p. Date not set. text ed. 140.00 (*0-631-20010-X*) Blackwell Pubs.

***Year's Work in English Studies, Vol. 75.** Ed. by Peter J. Kitson. 900p. 1997. 150.00 (*0-631-20460-1*) Blackwell Pubs.

Year's 25 Finest Crime & Mystery Stories. Ed. by Mystery Scene Magazine Editors. 352p. 1996. 24.00 (*0-7867-0361-X*) Carroll & Graf.

Year's 25 Finest Crime & Mystery Stories. 4th ed. Mystery Scene Magazine Editors. 398p. (YA). 1995. 24.00 (*0-7867-0251-6*) Carroll & Graf.

***Year's 25 Finest Crime & Mystery Stories.** annuals 6th ed. Ed. by Joan Hess et al. 400p. 1997. 24.00 (*0-7867-0495-0*) Carroll & Graf.

Yeas & Nays: Normal Decision-Making in the U. S. House of Representatives. Donald R. Matthews & James A. Stimson. LC 75-16124. (Wiley-Interscience Publications). (Illus.). 106p. reprint ed. pap. 30.30 (*0-317-09266-9*, 2012589) Bks Demand.

Yeast. Ed. by I. Campbell & J. H. Duffus. (Practical Approach Ser.). 308p. 1988. pap. 55.00 (*0-947946-79-9*, IRL Pr) OUP.

Yeast Biotechnology. Ed. by D. R. Berry et al. (Illus.). 512p. 1987. text ed. 125.00 (*0-04-574042-9*) Routledge Chapman & Hall.

Yeast Breads. 2nd rev. ed. Sue Gregg. (Illus.). 75p. 1993. spiral bd., pap. 7.00 (*1-878272-07-1*) Eating Better.

Yeast, Cakes & Pastries. George Greenstein. 1997. 25.00 (*0-02-861017-2*) Macmillan.

Yeast Cell Envelopes: Biochemistry, Biophysics, & Ultrastructure, Vol. I. Ed. by Wilfred N. Arnold. 144p. 1981. 83.00 (*0-8493-5965-1*, QK617, CRC Reprint) Franklin.

Yeast Cell Envelopes: Biochemistry, Biophysics, & Ultrastructure, Vol. II. Ed. by Wilfred N. Arnold. 192p. 1981. Vol. Ii, 192p. 107.00 (*0-8493-5966-X*, QK617, CRC Reprint) Franklin.

Yeast Connection. 3rd ed. William G. Crook. (Illus.). 438p. 1989. reprint ed. pap. 8.95 (*0-933478-11-9*) Prof Bks Future Health.

Yeast Connection: A Medical Breakthrough. William G. Crook. LC 83-62508. (Illus.). 304p. 1985. 15.95 (*0-933478-10-0*) Prof Bks Future Health.

Yeast Connection: A Medical Breakthrough. William G. Crook. 1986. pap. 14.00 (*0-394-74700-3*, Vin) Random.

Yeast Connection & the Woman. William G. Crook. (Illus.). 768p. (Orig.). (C). 1995. pap. 17.95 (*0-933478-22-4*) Prof Bks Future Health.

Yeast Connection Cook Book. William G. Crook & Marge H. Jones. (Illus.). 384p. 1989. 12.95 (*0-933478-16-X*) Prof Bks Future Health.

Yeast Connection Cookbook. William Crook. 1991. 18.95 (*0-933478-17-8*) Prof Bks Future Health.

***Yeast Connection Handbook.** William G. Crook. (Illus.). 260p. (Orig.). 1996. pap. write for info. (*0-933478-23-2*) Prof Bks Future Health.

Yeast Genetic Engineering. Philip J. Barr et al. (Biotechnology Ser.). 354p. 1989. 47.59 (*0-409-90117-2*) Buttrwrth-Heinemann.

Yeast Genetics. 1989. 53.95 (*0-387-18805-3*) Spr-Verlag.

Yeast Genetics: Fundamental & Applied Aspects. Ed. by J. F. Spencer et al. (Molecular Biology Ser.). (Illus.). 533p. 1983. 174.95 (*0-387-90793-9*) Spr-Verlag.

Yeast Molecular Biology-Recombinant DNA: Recent Advances. Ed. by Michael S. Esposito. LC 84-4096. (Illus.). 349p. 1984. 35.00 (*0-8155-0987-1*) Noyes.

Yeast Protocols. Ed. by Ivor H. Evans. (Methods in Molecular Biology Ser.: Vol. 53). (Illus.). 448p. 1996. spiral bd. 74.50 (*0-89603-319-8*) Humana.

Yeast Strain Selection. Panchal. (Bioprocess Technology Ser.: Vol. 8). 368p. 1990. 185.00 (*0-8247-8276-3*) Dekker.

***Yeast Stress Responses.** Stefan Hohmann & Willem H. Mager. LC 96-51840. (Molecular Biology Intelligence Unit Ser.). 217p. 1997. 89.95 (*1-57059-421-X*) R G Landes.

***Yeast Stress Responses.** Stefan Hohmann & Willem H. Mager. LC 96-51840. (Molecular Biology Intelligence Unit Ser.). 252p. 1997. 89.95 (*0-412-13251-6*) Chapman & Hall.

***Yeast Sugar Metabolism: Biochemistry, Genetics, Biotechnology, & Applications.** Ed. by Friedrich K. Zimmermann & K. D. Entian. LC 96-61823. 580p. 1997. text ed. 199.95 (*1-56676-466-1*) Technomic.

Yeast Syndrome. John P. Trowbridge & Morton. 448p. 1986. mass mkt. 6.99 (*0-553-27751-0*) Bantam.

***Yeast Two-Hybrid System.** P. L. Bartel & Stanley Fields. (Advances in Molecular Biology Ser.). (Illus.). 464p. 1997. pap. 45.00 (*0-19-510938-4*) OUP.

Yeasts. Ed. by B. E. Kirsop & C. P. Kurtzman. (Living Resources for Biotechnology Ser.). (Illus.). 256p. 1988. text ed. 36.95 (*0-521-35227-4*) Cambridge U Pr.

Yeasts, Vol. 5. 2nd ed. Ed. by A. H. Rose & J. S. Harrison. (Illus.). 660p. 1993. text ed. 99.00 (*0-12-596415-3*) Acad Pr.

***Yeasts: A Taxonomic Study.** 4th ed. C. P. Kurtzman & Jack W. Fell. LC 96-46920. 1997. write for info. (*0-444-81312-8*) Elsevier.

Yeasts: Biotechnology & Biocatalysis. Verachtert & DeMot. (Bioprocess Technology Ser.: Vol. 5). 536p. 1989. 225.00 (*0-8247-8142-2*) Dekker.

Yeasts: Characteristics & Identification. 2nd ed. J. A. Barnett et al. (Illus.). 1000p. (C). 1991. text ed. 260.00 (*0-521-35056-5*) Cambridge U Pr.

Yeasts: Edited Treatise, Vol. 1. 2nd ed. A. H. Rose & J. S. Harrison. 391p. 1987. text ed. 99.00 (*0-12-596411-0*) Acad Pr.

***Yeasts: Their Lives in Natural & Artificial Habitats.** John F. Spencer & Dorothy M. Spencer. LC 96-50359. 1997. write for info. (*3-540-56820-4*) Spr-Verlag.

Yeasts Vol. 6: Yeast Genetics, Vol. 6. 2nd ed. Alan E. Wheals. (Illus.). 708p. 1995. boxed 99.95 (*0-12-596416-1*) Acad Pr.

Yeasts & Yeast-Like Microorganisms in Medical Science: Proceedings of the Second International Specialized Symposium on Yeasts, Held 1972, Tokyo, Japan. International Specialized Symposium on Yeasts Staff. Ed. by Kazuo Iwata. LC 77-372105. 358p. 1976. reprint ed. pap. 102.10 (*0-608-01220-3*, 2061909) Bks Demand.

Yeasts & Yeast-Like Organisms. Anna Kockova-Kratochvilova. LC 89-8936. 528p. 1990. 120.00 (*3-527-26162-1*, VCH) Wiley.

Yeasts, Vol. 3: Metabolism & Physiology of Yeasts. 2nd ed. Ed. by A. H. Rose & J. S. Harrison. 635p. 1989. text ed. 99.00 (*0-12-596413-7*) Acad Pr.

Yeasts, Vol. 4: Yeast Organelles. 2nd ed. Ed. by A. H. Rose & J. S. Harrison. (Serial Publication Ser.). 765p. 1991. text ed. 99.00 (*0-12-596414-5*) Acad Pr.

Yeats. Douglas Archibald. (Irish Studies). 296p. 1986. pap. 16.95 (*0-8156-2391-7*) Syracuse U Pr.

Yeats. William Butler Yeats. Ed. & Intro. by G. J. Watson. 320p. 1996. pap. 12.95 (*0-14-018002-8*) Penguin.

Yeats. Harold Bloom. 512p. 1972. reprint ed. pap. 15.95 (*0-19-501603-3*) OUP.

Yeats: A Psychoanalytic Study. Brenda S. Webster. LC 73-80623. 256p. 1973. 37.50 (*0-8047-0846-0*) Stanford U Pr.

Yeats: An Annual of Critical & Textual Studies, Vol. 4. Ed. by Richard J. Finneran. LC 84-640978. (Studies in Modern Literature: Nos. 61 & 76). (Illus.). 247p. 1986. pap. 64.30 (*0-8357-7678-6*, 2070545) Bks Demand.

Yeats: An Annual of Critical & Textual Studies, Vol. 5. Ed. by Richard J. Finneran. LC 84-640978. (Studies in Modern Literature: Nos. 61 & 76). (Illus.). 286p. 1987. pap. 81.60 (*0-8357-7679-4*) Bks Demand.

Yeats: An Annual of Critical & Textual Studies, Vol. VI, 1986. Ed. by Richard J. Finneran. 250p. 1989. text ed. 49.50 (*0-472-10107-2*) U of Mich Pr.

Yeats: An Annual of Critical & Textual Studies, Vol. IX, 1991. Ed. by Richard J. Finneran. (Illus.). 300p. 1991. text ed. 49.50 (*0-472-10279-6*) U of Mich Pr.

Yeats: An Annual of Critical & Textual Studies, 1983, Vol. I. Ed. by Richard J. Finneran. (Illus.). 231p. 1983. 49. 95 (*0-8014-1635-3*) Cornell U Pr.

Yeats: An Annual of Critical & Textual Studies 1983 Edition, Vol. 1. Ed. by Richard J. Finneran. 231p. 1983. reprint ed. pap. 65.90 (*0-608-01691-8*, 2062347) Bks Demand.

Yeats: An Annual of Critical & Textual Studies 1985 Edition, Vol. 3. Ed. by Richard J. Finneran. 274p. 1985. reprint ed. pap. 78.10 (*0-608-01692-6*, 2062347) Bks Demand.

Yeats: An Annual of Critical & Textual Studies, 1993, Vol. XI. Ed. by Richard J. Finneran. 250p. 1994. text ed. 49. 50 (*0-472-10555-8*) U of Mich Pr.

***Yeats: An Annual of Critical & Textual Studies, 1995.** Ed. by Richard J. Finneran. (C). 1997. 49.50 (*0-472-10828-X*) U of Mich Pr.

Yeats: An Illustrated Biography. Frank Tuohy. (Illus.). 232p. 1991. 21.95 (*1-56131-020-4*) New Amsterdam Bks.

***Yeats: Coole Park & Ballylee.** Daniel A. Harris. LC 74-5185. 270p. 1974. reprint ed. pap. 77.00 (*0-608-03700-1*, 2064525) Bks Demand.

***Yeats: Portrait of an Artistic Family.** Hilary Pyle. (Illus.). 304p. 1997. 60.00 (*1-85894-040-0*, Pub. by Merrell Holberton Pubs UK) U of Wash Pr.

***Yeats: Selected Poetry.** William Butler Yeats. 1998. pap. 5.95 (*0-451-52658-9*, Sig Classics) NAL-Dutton.

Yeats: The Man & the Masks. rev. ed. Richard Ellmann. 1978. reprint ed. pap. 13.95 (*0-393-00859-2*) Norton.

Yeats: The Poet in Contemporary Ireland. J. W. Hone. 1972. lib. bdg. 59.95 (*0-8490-1342-9*) Gordon Pr.

Yeats: The Tower & the Winding Stair. Peter Faulkner. (Open Guides to Literature Ser.). 112p. 1987. 75.00 (*0-335-15256-2*, Open Univ Pr); pap. 22.00 (*0-335-15255-4*, Open Univ Pr) Taylor & Francis.

Yeats & Alchemy. William T. Gorski. LC 95-12789. (SUNY Series in Western Esoteric Traditions). 223p. 1996. text ed. 57.50 (*0-7914-2841-9*); pap. text ed. 18.95 (*0-7914-2842-7*) State U NY Pr.

Yeats & American Poetry: The Traditional of the Self. Terrence Diggory. LC 82-15070. 280p. 1983. text ed. 49.50 (*0-691-06558-6*) Princeton U Pr.

Yeats & Artistic Power. Phillip L. Marcus. 320p. (C). 1992. 45.00 (*0-8147-5471-6*) NYU Pr.

Yeats & English Renaissance Literature. Wayne K. Chapman. LC 90-22923. 256p. 1991. text ed. 45.00 (*0-312-06017-3*) St Martin.

Yeats & Magic: The Earlier Works. Mary C. Flannery. 1977. 30.00 (*0-901072-69-9*, Pub. by Colin Smythe Ltd UK) Dufour.

Yeats & Postmodernism. Ed. by Leonard D. Orr. (Irish Studies). 192p. 1990. text ed. 34.95 (*0-8156-2506-5*) Syracuse U Pr.

Yeats & the Beginning of the Irish Renaissance. 2nd ed. Phillip L. Marcus. LC 86-22969. (Irish Studies). 336p. 1987. reprint ed. pap. text ed. 16.95 (*0-8156-2398-4*) Syracuse U Pr.

Yeats & the Irish Literary Revival. Horatio S. Krans & William Butler. LC 68-637. 1970. reprint ed. text ed. 75.00 (0-8383-0691-8) M S G Haskell Hse.

Yeats & the Masks of Syntax: A Study in Connections. Joseph Adams. 190p. 1984. text ed. 39.50 (0-231-04818-1) Col U Pr.

Yeats & the Poetry of Death: Elegy, Self-Elegy & the Sublime. Jahan Ramazani. 240p. (C). 1990. text ed. 30.00 (0-300-04804-1) Yale U Pr.

Yeats & the Rhymers' Club: A Nineties' Perspective. Johann Gardner. (American University Studies: English Language & Literature: Ser. IV, Vol. 47). 249p. (C). 1989. text ed. 39.50 (0-8204-0769-0) P Lang Pubng.

Yeats & the Visual Arts. Elizabeth B. Loizeaux. (Illus.). 264p. (C). 1986. text ed. 40.00 (0-8135-1175-5) Rutgers U Pr.

***Yeats & Women.** 2nd ed. Toomey. LC 97-2178. 1997. text ed. 59.95 (0-312-17408-X); text ed. 19.95 (0-312-17409-8) St Martin.

***Yeats Annual, No. 11.** Gould. 1994. text ed. 59.95 (0-312-12184-9) St Martin.

Yeats at Songs & Choruses. David R. Clark. LC 81-16096. (Illus.). 308p. 1983. lib. bdg. 35.00 (0-87023-358-0) U of Mass Pr.

Yeats at Work. Ed. by Curtis B. Bradford. 192p. 1990. reprint ed. pap. 9.95 (0-88001-241-2) Ecco Pr.

***Yeat's Book of Fairy & Folk Tales of Ireland.** William Butler Yeats. 1996. 10.98 (0-7651-9703-0) Smithmark.

Yeat's Book of the Nineties: Poetry, Politics, & Rhetoric. Stephen W. Myers. LC 92-17894. (American University Studies: English Language & Literature: Ser. IV, Vol. 150). 186p. (C). 1993. text ed. 35.95 (0-8204-1957-5) P Lang Pubng.

Yeats Country. Sheelah Kirby. 96p. 8500. pap. 9.95 (0-85105-333-5, Pub. by Colin Smythe Ltd UK) Dufour.

Yeats, Folklore & Occultism: Contexts of the Early Work & Thought. Frank Kinahan. LC 87-32603. 256p. (C). (gr. 13). 1988. text ed. 59.95 (0-04-800062-0) Routledge Chapman & Hall.

***Yeat's Lady Gregory's Complete Irish Mythology.** William Butler Yeats. 1996. 10.98 (0-7651-9824-X) Smithmark.

***Yeats Reader.** William Butler Yeats. 1997. 30.00 (0-684-83188-0); 16.00 (0-684-83960-1) S&S Trade.

Yeats Sisters: A Biography of Susan & Elizabeth Yeats. Joan Hardwick. 256p. 1996. pap. 15.00 (0-04-440924-9) Harper SF.

***Yeats Sisters: A Biography of Susan & Elizabeth Yeats.** Joan Hardwick. (Illus.). 256p. 1996. 39.00 (0-8095-9227-4) Borgo Pr.

Yeats Sisters & the Cuala. Gifford Lewis. (Illus.). 222p. 1994. 37.50 (0-7165-2525-9, Pub. by Irish Acad Pr IE) Intl Spec Bk.

Yeats, Sligo & Irland. Ed. by Norman A. Jeffares. (Irish Literary Studies: Vol. # 6). 270p. 8000. 37.00 (0-86140-041-0) Dufour.

Yeats the European. Ed. by A. Norman Jeffares. 336p. (C). 1989. text ed. 64.50 (0-389-20875-2) B&N Imports.

Yeats the Initiate: Essays on Certain Themes in the Work of W. B. Yeats. Kathleen Rainer. (Illus.). 449p. (C). 1990. text ed. 83.00 (0-389-20951-1) B&N Imports.

Yeats the Initiate: Essays on Certain Themes in the Work of William Butler Yeats. Kathleen Raine. LC 86-6086. (Illus.). 456p. 1987. 30.00 (0-8076-1073-9) Braziller.

Yeats the Poet. Edward Larrissy. 224p. 1995. pap. 24.95 (0-13-320706-4) P-H.

Yeats, 1989, Vol. VII. Ed. by Richard J. Finneran. 274p. (C). 1990. reprint ed. text ed. 49.50 (0-472-10207-9) U of Mich Pr.

Yeats's Autobiography: Life As Symbolic Pattern. Joseph Ronsley. LC 68-15642. 184p. 1968. reprint ed. pap. 52.50 (0-7837-6088-4, 2059134) Bks Demand.

Yeats's Daimonic Renewal. Herbert J. Levine. LC 83-6989. (Studies in Modern Literature: No. 16). 179p. reprint ed. pap. 51.10 (0-8357-1427-6, 2070503) Bks Demand.

Yeats's Heroic Figures: Wilde, Parnell, Swift, Casement. Michael Steinman. LC 82-19157. 197p. (C). 1984. text ed. 64.50 (0-87395-698-2); pap. text ed. 21.95 (0-87395-699-0) State U NY Pr.

Yeats's Interactions with Tradition. Patrick J. Keane. LC 86-30883. 352p. 1987. text ed. 37.50 (0-8262-0645-X) U of Mo Pr.

Yeats's Myth of Self: The Autobiographical Prose. David G. Wright. 160p. 1987. 50.00 (0-389-20760-8, N8319) B&N Imports.

***Yeats's Nations: Gender, Class, & Irishness.** Marjorie Howes. 250p. (C). 1997. text ed. 54.95 (0-521-56362-3) Cambridge U Pr.

Yeats's Poetry & Poetics. Michael J. Sidnell. 292p. 1996. text ed. 49.95 (0-312-15969-2) St Martin.

Yeats's Political Identities: Selected Essays. Ed. by Jonathan Allison. LC 95-50287. (C). 1995. 47.50 (0-472-10445-4) U of Mich Pr.

Yeats's Vision & the Later Plays. Helen H. Vendler. LC 63-9565. reprint ed. 57.00 (0-8357-9186-6, 0216547) Bks Demand.

Yeats's "Vision" Papers Vol. 3: Sleep & Dream Notebooks, "Vision" Notebooks 1 & 2, Card File. William B. Yeats. Ed. by Margaret M. Harper et al. LC 91-75175. (Illus.). 458p. 1992. 55.00 (0-87745-353-5) U of Iowa Pr.

Yeats's Vision Papers, Vol. 1: The Automatic Script: 5 November 1917 to 18 June 1918. William B. Yeats. Ed. by George M. Harper et al. LC 91-75175. (Illus.). 579p. 1992. 55.00 (0-87745-351-9) U of Iowa Pr.

Yeats's Vision Papers, Vol. 2: The Automatic Script: 25 June 1918 to 29 March 1920. William B. Yeats. Ed. by George M. Harper et al. LC 91-75175. (Illus.). 610p. 1992. 55.00 (0-87745-352-7) U of Iowa Pr.

Yeats's Worlds: Ireland, England & the Poetic Imagination. David Pierce. LC 95-2457. (Illus.). 346p. 1995. 40.00 (0-300-06323-7) Yale U Pr.

Yebamoth, 3 vols. (ENG & HEB.). 45.00 (0-910218-64-1) Bennet Pub.

Yedidut. Chaya Weisfish. 214p. (HEB.). (YA). (gr. 9-12). 1991. student ed. write for info. (0-9630241-0-8) C Weisfish.

Yedidya & the Esrog Tree. 1982. pap. 2.95 (0-87306-235-3) Feldheim.

***Yee & the Wolves, Vol. 5.** John Vornholt. (Warriors of Virtue Ser.: No. 5). 112p. 1997. mass mkt. 3.99 (1-57297-287-4) Blvd Books.

Yefief One: A Narrative of Culture at the End of the Century. Lucile Adler et al. (Illus.). 176p. (Orig.). 1994. pap. 7.95 (1-884434-00-2) Images For Media.

Yefief 2: Health & Human Rights (A View along the Running Edge) R. Bart Kowech. (Illus.). 160p. (Orig.). 1995. pap. 7.95 (1-884434-01-0) Images For Media.

***Yefief 2: Health & Human Rights, a View Along the Running Edge.** abr. rev. ed. Nicole Brossard et al. (Yefief Asia Editions Ser.). (Illus.). 100p. (Orig.). 1998. pap. 8.95 (1-884434-02-9) Images For Media.

Yefief 3: The Force of Good. Duane Locke et al. Tr. by Noemi Alindogan-Medina. (Illus.). 179p. (Orig.). (C). 1996. pap. 10.95 (1-884434-03-7) Images For Media.

***Yefief 4: The Constitution of Mercy, Pt. I.** Ann Bacuya-Robbins et al. (Illus.). 150p. (Orig.). 1997. pap. 10.95 (1-884434-06-1) Images For Media.

***Yefief 5: The Constitution of Mercy, Pt. II.** Sheila Murphy et al. (Illus.). 150p. (Orig.). 1997. pap. 10.95 (1-884434-10-X) Images For Media.

Yeh Shen: A Cinderella Story from China. Al-Ling Louie. (Illus.). 32p. (J). (ps-2). 1982. 15.95 (0-399-20900-X, Philomel Bks) Putnam Pub Group.

Yeh-Shen: A Cinderella Story from China. Al-Ling Louie. (Illus.). 32p. (J). (ps-3). 1996. pap. 5.95 (0-698-11388-8, Paperstar) Putnam Pub Group.

Yehuda Amichai: A Life of Poetry, 1948-1994. Yehuda Amichai. Tr. by Benjamin Harshav & Barbara Harschav. 496p. 1995. lib. bdg. 39.00 (0-614-11654-6) Borgo Pr.

Yehuda Amichai: A Life of Poetry, 1948-1994. Yehuda Amichai. 496p. 1995. pap. 15.00 (0-06-092666-X, HarpT) HarpC.

***Yehudi Menuhin: Unfinished Journey.** expanded ed. Yehudi Menuhin. LC 97-9122. (Illus.). 552p. 1997. 29.95 (0-88064-179-7) Fromm Intl Pub.

Yehudis Prepares for Shabbos. 1982. pap. 1.95 (0-686-76280-0) Feldheim.

Yekl & the Imported Bridegroom & Other Stories of the New York Ghetto. Abraham Cahan. 1978. pap. 5.95 (0-486-22427-9) Dover.

Yekl & the Imported Bridegroom & Other Stories of the New York Ghetto. Abraham Cahan. 1990. 11.75 (0-8446-0048-2) Peter Smith.

***Yell County, Arkansas Newspaper Abstracts, 1875-1879.** Fay G. Sandy. 339p. (Orig.). 1997. pap. 39.00 (1-56546-109-6) Arkansas Res.

Yell Ruddy Murder. large type ed. Joseph Shallit. (Linford Mystery Library). 1991. pap. 15.99 (0-7089-7156-3) Ulverscroft.

Yella Pessl, First Lady of the Harpsichord: A Life of Fire & Conviction. Catherine Dower. LC 92-37521. (Studies in the History & Interpretation of Music: Vol. 21). (Illus.). 212p. 1993. text ed. 89.95 (0-88946-446-4) E Mellen.

Yellow. Karen Bryant-Mole. (Images Ser.). (J). 1996. pap. 4.95 (0-382-39619-7, Silver Pr NJ); lib. bdg. 10.95 (0-382-39583-2, Silver Pr NJ) Silver Burdett Pr.

Yellow. Anne Pitkin. (Orig.). 1989. 22.00 (0-934847-08-8); pap. 9.00 (0-934847-09-6) Arrowood Bks.

Yellow. Gabrielle Woolfitt. (J). (gr. k-3). 1992. lib. bdg. 17.50 (0-87614-707-4, Carolrhoda) Lerner Group.

Yellow: A Novel. Daniel Lynch. LC 92-17332. 211p. 1992. 19.95 (0-8027-1226-6) Walker & Co.

Yellow Admiral. Patrick O'Brian. 262p. 1996. 24.00 (0-393-04044-5) Norton.

***Yellow Admiral.** Patrick O'Brian. LC 97-9697. 1997. 26.95 (1-56895-430-1, Compass) Wheeler Pub.

***Yellow Admiral.** Patrick O'Brian. Date not set. pap. 12.95 (0-393-31704-8) Norton.

Yellow & Pink. William Steig. LC 84-80503. (Illus.). 32p. (J). (ps up). 1984. 12.00 (0-374-38670-6) FS&G.

Yellow & Pink. William Steig. LC 84-80503. (Sunburst Ser.). 32p. (J). (ps up). 1988. pap. 3.95 (0-374-48735-9) FS&G.

Yellow Arrow. Victor Pelevin. Tr. by Andrew Bromfield from RUS. LC 96-773. 96p. 1996. 17.95 (0-8112-1324-2) New Directions.

***Yellow Arrow.** Victor Pelevin. Tr. by Andrew Bromfield from RUS. 96p. 1997. pap. 8.95 (0-8112-1355-2, NDP845) New Directions.

Yellow Ball. Molly Bang. LC 92-40722. (Illus.). 32p. (J). (ps-1). 1993. pap. 4.50 (0-14-054828-9, Puffin) Puffin Bks.

Yellow Ball. Molly Bang. LC 90-46077. (Illus.). 24p. (J). (ps up). 1991. 16.00 (0-688-06314-4, Morrow Junior); lib. bdg. 15.93 (0-688-06315-2, Morrow Junior) Morrow.

Yellow Ball. 93th ed. 1993. pap. text ed. 9.00 (0-15-300314-6, HB Juv Bks) HarBrace.

Yellow Bell: A Brief Sketch of the History of Chinese Music. Mei-Po Chao. 1974. lib. bdg. 250.00 (0-87968-135-7) Krishna Pr.

Yellow Bird. Rick Boyer. (Boston Mysteries Ser.). 1995. mass mkt. 4.99 (0-8041-1036-0) Ivy Books.

***Yellow Bird.** Deanna Ritz. 192p. 1996. 16.00 (0-8059-3981-4) Dorrance.

Yellow Bird & Me. Joyce Hanen. LC 85-484. 128p. (J). (gr. 3-7). 1991. reprint ed. pap. 6.95 (0-395-55388-1, Clarion Bks) HM.

Yellow Blue Bus Means I Love You. Morse Hamilton. LC 93-19408. (YA). (gr. 7 up). 1994. 14.00 (0-688-12800-9) Greenwillow.

Yellow Blue Jay. Johanna Hurwitz. LC 85-25868. (Illus.). 128p. (J). (gr. 2-5). 1993. reprint ed. pap. 3.95 (0-688-12278-7, Morrow Junior) Morrow.

Yellow Boat. Margaret Hillert. (Illus.). (J). (ps-k). 1966. pap. 5.10 (0-8136-5533-1, TK2389); lib. bdg. 7.95 (0-8136-5033-X, TK2388) Modern Curr.

***Yellow Boat.** David Saar. (Orig.). (J). 1997. pap. 5.50 (0-87602-352-9) Anchorage.

Yellow Book, Set. reprint ed. 487.50 (0-404-19565-2) AMS Pr.

Yellow Book see Miquon Math Lab Series

Yellow Book of Lecan. Intro. by Robert Atkinson. LC 78-72657. (Celtic Language & Literature Ser.: Goidelic & Brythonic). reprint ed. 125.00 (0-404-17616-X) AMS Pr.

Yellow Brick Road: Steps Toward a New Way of Life. Ed. by David Steinberg & Ann Dilworth. (Illus.). 1974. pap. 8.95 (0-914906-01-1) Red Alder.

Yellow Claw. Sax Rohmer. 1976. lib. bdg. 13.95 (0-89968-142-5, Lghtyr Pr) Buccaneer Bks.

Yellow Claw. Sax Rohmer. 14.95 (0-8488-1463-0) Amereon Ltd.

Yellow Coat. Donatella Cardillo-Young. LC 94-61588. (Illus.). 44p. (J). (gr. k-3). 1995. per., pap. 5.95 (1-55523-729-0) Winston-Derek.

Yellow Cover, Bk. C. (Big Christmas Coloring & Activity Ser.). (Illus.). 160p. (Orig.). (J). (gr. k-2). 1994. pap. 4.95 (1-56144-512-6, Honey Bear Bks) Modern Pub NYC.

Yellow Day. Barbour. Date not set. write for info. (0-15-201525-6) HarBrace.

Yellow Dog Contract. Joel I. Seidman. LC 78-64146. (Johns Hopkins University. Studies in the Social Sciences. Thirtieth Ser. 1912: 4). reprint ed. 45.00 (0-404-61257-1) AMS Pr.

Yellow Dog Dreaming. Kenny Mann. (Illus.). 74p. 1996. pap. 15.00 (1-887478-06-X, WiseAcre) Red Sea NY.

***Yellow Dog Dreaming.** 2nd ed. Kenny Mann. (Illus.). 73p. 1995. reprint ed. 15.00 (0-9657999-0-5) rafIki Bks.

Yellow Dog Journal. Judith Minty. 75p. 1991. pap. 8.00 (0-938077-85-6) Parallax Pr.

Yellow Dog Party. Earl W. Emerson. (Northwest Mysteries Ser.). 1992. mass mkt. 5.99 (0-345-37716-8) Ballantine.

Yellow Dogaudio. F. Fontess et al. 1995. pap. 9.95 (0-7871-0362-4, Dove Bks) Dove Audio.

Yellow Doggy (Moving to the City) Connie E. Kelly. (Illus.). 8p. (J). (ps-3). 1995. pap. text ed. 2.95 (0-9641814-1-X) C E Kelly.

Yellow Dogs, Hushpuppies, & Bluetick Hounds: The Official Encyclopedia of Southern Culture Quiz Book. Compiled by Lisa N. Howorth. 140p. (C). 1996. pap. 9.95 (0-8078-4592-2) U of NC Pr.

Yellow Earth, Green Jade: Constants in Chinese Political Mores. Simon De Beaufort. (Harvard Studies in International Affairs: No. 41). 90p. 1984. reprint ed. pap. text ed. 13.50 (0-8191-4059-7) U Pr of Amer.

Yellow Emperor's Classic of Internal Medicine. Tr. by Ilza Veith. 1966. pap. 15.00 (0-520-02158-4) U CA Pr.

Yellow Emperor's Classic of Medicine: A New Translation of the Neijing Suwen with Commentary. Maoshing Ni. (Orig.). 1995. pap. 16.00 (1-57062-080-6) Shambhala Pubns.

Yellow Eyes. Date not set. pap. 1.75 (0-590-02429-9) Scholastic Inc.

Yellow Fairy Book. Ed. by Andrew Lang. (Illus.). 321p. (J). (gr. 4-6). pap. 6.95 (0-486-21674-8) Dover.

Yellow Fairy Book. Andrew Lang. (Illus.). (J). (gr. 2 up). 1990. 21.00 (0-8446-0758-4) Peter Smith.

Yellow Feather Mystery. Franklin W. Dixon. (Hardy Boys Ser.: Vol. 33). 180p. (J). (gr. 5-9). 1954. 5.95 (0-448-08933-5, G&D) Putnam Pub Group.

Yellow Feaver Booklet. Absalom Jones & Richard Allen. 1993. pap. 1.75 (0-915992-58-2) Eastern Acorn.

Yellow Fever & Public Health in the New South. John H. Ellis. LC 91-35692. (Illus.). 248p. 1992. text ed. 28.00 (0-8131-1781-X) U Pr of Ky.

Yellow Fever & the South. Margaret Humphreys. LC 91-41138. (Health & Medicine in American Society Ser.). 235p. (C). 1992. text ed. 45.00 (0-8135-1820-2) Rutgers U Pr.

***Yellow Fever, Black Goddess.** Wills. 1996. pap. write for info. (0-201-32818-6) Addison-Wesley.

Yellow Fever, Black Goddess: The Coevolution of People & Plagues. Christopher Wills. Ed. by Heather Mimnaugh. 224p. (C). 1996. 24.00 (0-201-44235-3) Addison-Wesley.

Yellow Fever in the North: The Methods of Early Epidemiology. William Coleman. LC 86-40456. (Wisconsin Publications in the History of Science & Medicine: No. 6). 224p. 1987. text ed. 49.50 (0-299-11110-5); pap. text ed. 17.50 (0-299-11114-8) U of Wis Pr.

Yellow Fever Studies: An Original Anthology. Ed. by Barbara G. Rosenkrantz. LC 76-40355. (Public Health in America Ser.). 1977. reprint ed. lib. bdg. 26.95 (0-405-09882-0) Ayer.

***Yellow-Fever Vaccinating Centres for International Travel.** 68p. 1985. pap. text ed. 11.00 (92-4-058011-5) World Health.

Yellow Fever Vaccinating Centres for International Travel: Situation As on 1 January 1991. 82p. 1991. pap. text ed. 14.00 (92-4-058012-3, 0150357) World Health.

Yellow Fish! Blue Fish! Stewart Cowley. LC 94-67216. (Tiny Magic Window Bks.). (Illus.). 14p. (J). (ps). 1994. 2.99 (0-89577-597-2) RD Assn.

Yellow Floor: Poems 1978-1983. Gil Ott. 76p. 1987. pap. 6.95 (0-940650-89-4) Sun & Moon CA.

Yellow Flowers. Andrew Wylie. 1972. pap. 4.95 (0-934450-04-8) Unmuzzled Ox.

Yellow Flowers in the Antipodean Room. Janet Frame. 256p. 1994. pap. 11.95 (0-8076-1340-1) Braziller.

***Yellow Flowers Petite Photo Album.** Illus. by Jenny Faw. (Petite Photo Albums Ser.). 15p. 1997. 4.95 (0-88088-653-6) Peter Pauper.

Yellow Fog. Les Daniels. (Illus.). 1986. 30.00 (0-937986-82-8) D M Grant.

Yellow Glove. Naomi S. Nye. LC 86-21534. 86p. 1986. pap. 8.00 (0-932576-42-7) Breitenbush Bks.

Yellow-Green Vaseline! A Guide to the Magic Glass. Jay L. Glickman. (Illus.). 128p. (Orig.). 1991. 27.95 (0-915410-77-X, 3073); pap. 19.95 (0-915410-76-1, 3072) Antique Pubns.

Yellow Heart. Pablo Neruda. Tr. by William O'Daly from SPA. LC 89-81834. 112p. (Orig.). 1990. 17.00 (1-55659-028-8); pap. 10.00 (1-55659-029-6) Copper Canyon.

Yellow Hippo. Alan Rogers. LC 90-9834. (Little Giants Ser.). (Illus.). 16p. (J). (ps-1). 1990. lib. bdg. 17.27 (0-8368-0405-8) Gareth Stevens Inc.

***Yellow Hippo.** Alan Rogers. (J). (ps-2). 1997. 7.95 (0-7166-4407-X); pap. 2.95 (0-7166-4403-7) World Bk.

Yellow Hordes Are Coming! or, Xenophobia Rampant: Several Possible Chapters in History. Ed. by Robert Reginald. (Classics of Fantastic Literature Ser.). lib. bdg. write for info. (0-89370-356-7) Borgo Pr.

Yellow House. Blake Morrison. LC 93-36274. (Illus.). 32p. (J). (ps up). 1994. pap. 4.99 (1-56402-385-0) Candlewick Pr.

Yellow House Mystery. Gertrude C. Warner. LC 53-13243. (Boxcar Children Mysteries Ser.: No. 3). (Illus.). 128p. (J). (gr. 2-7). 1953. pap. 3.95 (0-8075-9366-4); lib. bdg. 13.95 (0-8075-9365-6) A Whitman.

Yellow House on the Corner. Rita Dove. LC 80-65700. (Classic Contemporaries Ser.). 1980. pap. 12.95 (0-88748-092-6) Carnegie-Mellon.

***Yellow Inspiration.** Mark Blayock. 216p. 1997. 22.95 (0-9654440-2-3); pap. 13.50 (0-9654440-3-1) Ironwood Pr AZ.

Yellow Jacket: A Four Corners Anasazi Ceremonial Center. rev. ed. Frederick Lange et al. LC 86-82465. (Illus.). 72p. (Orig.). 1986. pap. 5.95 (1-55566-005-3) Johnson Bks.

Yellow Jackets: Four Corners for Keyboards Saxophone Bass Drums. 144p. 1988. per. 18.95 (0-7935-3634-0, 00675800) H Leonard.

***Yellow Jackets Handbook: Stories, Stats & Stuff about Georgia Tech Basketball.** Bill Ballew. (Illus.). 160p. (Orig.). 1996. pap. 9.95 (1-880652-67-6) Wichita Eagle.

Yellow Jersey. Ralph Hume. 256p. 1996. pap. 14.95 (1-55821-452-6, 14526) Lyons & Burford.

Yellow Kid. Richard F. Outcault. (Illus.). 1990. 49.95 (1-56060-059-4) Eclipse Bks.

Yellow Kid: A Centennial Celebration of the Kid Who Started the Comics. Richard F. Outcault. Ed. by Bill Blackbeard. 1995. 55.00 (0-87816-380-8) Kitchen Sink.

Yellow Kid: A Centennial Celebration of the Kid Who Started the Comics. Richard F. Outcault. Ed. by Bill Blackbeard. 304p. 1995. pap. 39.95 (0-87816-379-4) Kitchen Sink.

Yellow Kowhai. large type ed. Eva Burfield. 352p. 1987. 25.99 (0-7089-1708-9) Ulverscroft.

Yellow Lady: Australian Impressions of Asia. Alison Broinowski. (Illus.). 272p. 1994. reprint ed. pap. 26.00 (0-19-553452-2) OUP.

Yellow Leaves: Children of the Rolling Thunder. Than C. Nguyen. 76p. (Orig.). 1994. 10.00 (0-9631569-2-6) Backyard Pr.

Yellow Light: Poems. Garrett K. Hongo. LC 81-16050. (Wesleyan Poetry Program Ser.: Vol. 104). 78p. 1982. pap. 11.95 (0-8195-1104-8, Wesleyan Univ Pr) U Pr of New Eng.

Yellow Lion: The First Adventure in John's Colorful World. Margaret S. Campilonga. LC 95-69561. (John's Colorful World Ser.: Bk. 1). (Illus.). 32p. (J). (ps-3). 1995. lib. bdg. 13.95 (0-9646904-0-3) Chicken Soup.

Yellow, Mellow, Green, & Brown see Brown Cow, Green Grass, Yellow Mellow Sun

Yellow Men Sleep. Jeremy Lane. (Illus.). 1983. 15.00 (0-937986-99-2) D M Grant.

Yellow Moon. David J. Searls. 256p. (Orig.). 1994. mass mkt. 5.50 (0-446-36528-9) Warner Bks.

Yellow Napoleon: A Romance of West Africa. Arthur E. Southon. LC 72-4613. (Black Heritage Library Collection). 1977. reprint ed. 19.95 (0-8369-9127-3) Ayer.

Yellow Pages: A Catalogue of Intentions. Nicole Markotic. 168p. 1995. pap. 10.95 (0-88995-132-2, Pub. by Red Deer CN) Orca Bk Pubs.

Yellow Pages Advertising: How to Get the Greatest Return on Your Investment. Jeffrey Price. (Illus.). 115p. 1991. write for info. (0-945909-01-2) Idlewood Pub.

***Yellow Pages for Mobile Phones: Texas.** rev. ed. Susan D. Sams & Jerry B. Sams. (Illus.). 60p. 1997. pap. 3.50 (0-9652013-1-7) EZ Access.

Yellow Pages for Mobile Phones - Texas. Susan D. Sams & Jerry B. Sams. 48p. (Orig.). 1996. pap. 3.50 (0-9652013-0-9) EZ Access.

Yellow Pages Handbook of Objections & Responses. Jeffrey Price. (Illus.). 132p. (Orig.). 1988. pap. 13.95 (0-945909-00-4) Idlewood Pub.

***Yellow Pages Market Forecast.** 9th ed. 1997. 1,995.00 (0-614-25710-7) Simba Info.

Yellow Pages Market Forecast, 1995. Natalie Schwartz & Tim Maguire. (Illus.). 139p. 1995. 2,593.00 (0-88709-084-2) Simba Info Inc.

Yellow Pages Market Forecast, 1996. 8th ed. Natalie Schwartz & Tom Maguire. (Illus.). 170p. 1996. 1,995.00 (0-88709-112-1) Simba Info Inc.

***Yellow Pages Market Forecast, 1997.** Tom Maguire et al. 179p. Date not set. write for info. (0-88709-150-4) Simba Info Inc.

Yellow Pages of Golf: The Most Comprehensive & Largest Circulated Directory of Its Kind. 1995. pap. 14.95 (1-884315-05-4) Activity Dir.

An Asterisk (*) at the beginning of an entry indicates that the title is appearing in BIP for the first time.

Yellow Pages of Skiing: The Most Complete & User Friendly Ski Travel Planner Ever. 1995. pap. 14.95 (*1-884315-06-2*) Activity Dir.

Yellow Pages of Undergraduate Innovations: A Guide to Innovations in Higher Education. Ed. by Douglas A. Kleiber. 243p. 1974. pap. 19.95 (*0-87855-123-9*, Pub. by Change Mag) Transaction Pubs.

***Yellow Pages Sales & Marketing, 1996.** Tom Maguire. (Illus.). 183p. 1996. 2,495.00 (*0-88709-137-7*) Simba Info Inc.

Yellow Pages 2000: Forecast & Analysis. Carl Mercurio & Natalie Schwartz. Ed. by Chris Elwell. (Illus.). 324p. 1994. 4,995.00 (*0-88709-070-2*) Simba Info Inc.

Yellow Peril: Chinese Americans in American Fiction, 1850-1940. William F. Wu. (Illus.). 241p. 1982. 69.50 (*0-208-01915-4*) Elliots Bks.

Yellow Peril, Eighteen Ninety to Nineteen Twenty-Four, 2 Vols. Richard A. Thompson. Ed. by Roger Daniels. LC 78-54833. (Asian Experience in North America Ser.). 1979. lib. bdg. 42.95 (*0-405-11290-4*) Ayer.

Yellow Peril in Action: A Possible Chapter in History. Ed. by Robert Reginald. (Imaginary Wars & Battles Ser.: No. 2). pap. write for info. (*0-89370-456-3*) Borgo Pr.

Yellow Raft in Blue Water. Michael Dorris. 384p. 1988. reprint ed. pap. 12.99 (*0-446-38787-8*) Warner Bks.

Yellow Rain. Steven Spetz. 384p. (Orig.). 1989. mass mkt. 3.95 (*0-373-97100-1*) Harlequin Bks.

Yellow Rain: A Special Issue of the Journal Comments on Toxicology. Ed. by H. B. Schiefer. 62p. 1988. pap. text ed. 56.00 (*2-88124-416-5*) Gordon & Breach.

Yellow Rainmakers: Are Chemical Weapons Being Used in Southeast Asia? Grant Evans. 202p. 1983. pap. text ed. 12.95 (*0-86091-770-3*, Pub. by Verso UK) Routledge Chapman & Hall.

Yellow Ribbons. large type ed. Jane Edwards. 206p. 1993. reprint ed. pap. 13.95 (*1-56054-678-6*) Thorndike Pr.

Yellow Ribbons, Worried Hearts. Molly A. Minnick. (Illus.). 65p. (C). 1991. 20.00 (*1-878526-33-2*) Pineapple MI.

Yellow River Valley: A Geopolitical Appraisal. Joseph D. Lowe. LC 90-91744. (Illus.). vii, 46p. 1982. reprint ed. pap. 20.00 (*0-9605506-4-X*) Lowe Pub.

Yellow Room. 1996. pap. 5.50 (*0-8217-5537-4*) Kensgtn Pub Corp.

Yellow Room. Mary R. Rinehart. 352p. 1996. mass mkt. 5.50 (*1-57566-119-5*, Knsington) Kensgtn Pub Corp.

Yellow Room. 2nd ed. 1996. mass mkt. 5.95 (*1-56333-378-3*) Masquerade.

Yellow Room Conspiracy. Peter Dickinson. 256p. 1995. mass mkt. 5.99 (*0-446-40373-3*, Mysterious Paperbk) Warner Bks.

Yellow Room Conspiracy. large type ed. Peter Dickinson. LC 94-13806. (Cloak & Dagger Ser.). 395p. 1994. lib. bdg. 20.95 (*0-7862-0261-0*) Thorndike Pr.

Yellow Silk: Erotic Arts & Letters. Ed. by Lily Pond & Richard Russo. 320p. 1992. pap. 12.00 (*0-517-58736-X*, Harmony) Crown Pub Group.

Yellow Slicker: A Fable for Women. Pegi C. Pearson. (Illus.). 28p. 1995. 12.95 (*1-879198-16-9*) Knwldg Ideas & Trnds.

Yellow Sofa. Eca de Queiros. Tr. by John Vetch from POR. (New Directions Classic Ser.). 112p. (Orig.). 1996. pap. 10.95 (*0-8112-1339-0*, NDP833) New Directions.

Yellow Star. Simcha B. Unsdorfer. LC 61-6930. 1983. reprint ed. pap. 9.95 (*0-87306-337-6*) Feldheim.

Yellow Stars & Ice. Susan Stewart. LC 80-8587. (Contemporary Poets Ser.). 82p. 1981. pap. 9.95 (*0-691-01379-9*) Princeton U Pr.

Yellow Stocking: One Woman's Hotel in Peace & War. Lotte Eisenberg. 192p. 1995. 18.00 (*965-229-144-7*, Pub. by Gefen Pub Hse IS) Gefen Bks.

Yellow Street. Veza Canetti. Tr. by Ian Mitchell from GER. LC 90-22154. 144p. 1991. 18.95 (*0-8112-1159-2*); pap. 10.95 (*0-8112-1160-6*, NDP709) New Directions.

Yellow Student Activity Book. Debbie Strayer & Susan S. Simpson. (Learning Language Arts Through Literature Ser.). 196p. 1992. 16.00 (*1-880892-26-X*) Com Sense FL.

Yellow Submarine. John Lennon & Paul McCartney. (Piano-Vocal-Guitar Ser.). 6p. 1987. pap. 3.95 (*0-88188-959-8*, 00355727) H Leonard.

Yellow Submarine. John Lennon & Paul McCartney. (Sing-a-Song Storybooks Ser.). (Illus.). 24p. (J). 1993. 9.95 (*0-7935-1859-8*, 00183013) H Leonard.

Yellow Tractor. Beth Esh. (HighReach Learning Big Bks.). 8p. (J). (ps-k). 1994. pap. text ed. 10.95 (*1-57332-006-4*) HighReach Lrning.

***Yellow Transparents.** Joan Aleshire. LC 96-86553. 80p. 1997. pap. 12.95 (*1-884800-13-0*) Four Way Bks.

Yellow Wall-Paper. Charlotte Perkins Gilman. LC 73-5795. 64p. 1996. pap. 5.95 (*1-55861-158-4*) Feminist Pr.

Yellow Wallpaper. Charlotte Perkins Gilman. Ed. by Thomas L. Erskine & Connie L. Richards. LC 92-42099. 250p. (C). 1993. text ed. 30.00 (*0-8135-1993-4*); pap. text ed. 12.00 (*0-8135-1994-2*) Rutgers U Pr.

Yellow Wallpaper. Charlotte Perkins Gilman. LC 90-30492. 16p. 1990. reprint ed. pap. 2.00 (*0-914061-16-X*) Orchises Pr.

Yellow Wallpaper: The Wallpaper Replies. Charlotte Perkins Gilman & Charles Taylor. 80p. (C). 1994. pap. 9.95 (*0-941720-88-8*) Slough Pr TX.

Yellow Wallpaper: The Wallpaper Replies. Charlotte Perkins Gilman & Chuck Taylor. 70p. (C). 1994. pap. 9.95 (*0-941720-89-6*) Slough Pr TX.

***Yellow Wallpaper & Other Stories.** Charlotte P. Gilman. LC 97-20948. (Dover Thrift Editions Ser.). 1997. pap. write for info. (*0-486-29857-4*) Dover.

Yellow Wallpaper & Other Stories. Charlotte Perkins Gilman. Ed. & Intro. by Robert Shulman. (World's Classics Ser.). 384p. 1996. pap. 8.95 (*0-19-282449-X*) OUP.

Yellow Wallpaper & Other Writings. Charlotte Perkins Gilman. 272p. 1989. pap. 5.95 (*0-553-21375-X*) Bantam.

Yellow Wallpaper & Selected Stories of Charlotte Perkins Gilman. Charlotte Perkins Gilman. LC 93-20706. 1994. 36.50 (*0-87413-479-X*) U Delaware Pr.

Yellow Ware. rev. ed. Joan Leibowitz. LC 85-61524. (Illus.). 119p. (Orig.). 1993. pap. 19.95 (*0-88740-508-8*) Schiffer.

Yellow Ware Collecting, Bk. 2. Lisz McAllister. 1996. pap. text ed. 17.95 (*0-89145-741-0*) Collector Bks.

Yellow Wind. David Grossman. Tr. by Haim Watzman from HEB. 188p. 1988. 17.95 (*0-374-29345-7*) FS&G.

Yellow Wolf: His Own Story. Lucullus V. McWhorter. LC 85-16659. (Illus.). 324p. 1984. reprint ed. 19.95 (*0-87004-317-X*); reprint ed. pap. 16.95 (*0-87004-315-3*) Caxton.

Yellow Woman. Leslie M. Silko. LC 93-20141. (Woman Writers: Text & Contexts Ser.). 220p. (C). 1993. text ed. 35.00 (*0-8135-2004-5*); pap. text ed. 12.00 (*0-8135-2005-3*) Rutgers U Pr.

***Yellow Woman & A Beauty of the Spirit.** Leslie M. Silko. 1997. pap. 11.00 (*0-684-82707-7*, Touchstone Bks) S&S Trade.

Yellow Woman & a Beauty of the Spirit: Essays on Native American Life Today. Leslie M. Silko. (Illus.). 208p. 1996. 23.00 (*0-684-81153-7*) S&S Trade.

***Yellow Woman Reading Group Guide.** Leslie M. Silko. 1997. pap. write for info. (*0-684-00484-4*, Touchstone Bks) S&S Trade.

Yellowbuddy: The Runaway School Bus. Kathleen Neville. (J). (gr. 4-7). 1993. pap. 8.95 (*0-933905-22-X*) Claycomb Pr.

Yellowcake: The International Uranium Cartel. June Taylor & Michael Yokell. (Policy Studies). 1980. 88.00 (*0-08-022473-3*, Pergamon Pr) Elsevier.

***Yellowdog.** LC 96-45670. 1997. 29.95 (*0-8212-2343-7*) Little.

Yellowfin. Mark Brown. LC 91-36801. (Ben McMillen Hawaiian Mystery Ser.). 256p. 1992. 19.95 (*0-918024-93-5*) Ox Bow.

Yellowhair. limited ed. Charles G. Taylor & Jason Kane. (Custer Monograph: No. 6). 1979. reprint ed. 10.00 (*0-940696-08-8*) Monroe County Lib.

Yellowjackets. Edward S. Ross. LC 92-42934. (Nature Bks.). 32p. (J). (gr. 2-6). 1993. lib. bdg. 22.79 (*1-56766-017-7*) Childs World.

Yellowstone. Erwin A. Bauer. LC 92-38044. (Illus.). 128p. 1994. pap. 19.95 (*0-89658-248-5*) Voyageur Pr.

Yellowstone. Erwin A. Bauer. LC 92-38044. (Illus.). 128p. 1993. 29.95 (*0-89658-177-2*) Voyageur Pr.

Yellowstone. Marjorie Benson. LC 94-34461. (Wonders of the World Ser.). (J). 1995. lib. bdg. 25.68 (*0-8114-6365-6*) Raintree Steck-V.

Yellowstone. Jason Cooper. LC 95-13262. (Natural Wonders Ser.). (Illus.). (J). (gr. 2-6). 1995. write for info. (*1-57103-013-1*) Rourke Pr.

Yellowstone. Ed. by Jeff Nicholas. (Wish You Were Here Postcard Bks.). (Illus.). 32p. 1992. pap. 4.95 (*0-939365-05-7*) Sierra Pr CA.

Yellowstone. Richard S. Wheeler. (Skye's West Ser.). 1990. pap. 3.95 (*0-8125-0894-7*) Tor Bks.

Yellowstone: A Children's Guide. Judy Beach-Balthis. Ed. by Frank Balthis. (Children's Guides on the National Parks Ser.). (Illus.). 36p. (Orig.). (J). (gr. k-8). 1994. pap. 3.95 (*0-918355-01-X*) Firehole Pr.

Yellowstone: A Visitor's Companion. George Wuerthner. LC 91-29403. (Illus.). 240p. 1992. pap. 14.95 (*0-8117-3078-6*) Stackpole.

Yellowstone: A Wilderness Besieged. Richard A. Bartlett. LC 85-988. 437p. 1989. reprint ed. pap. 19.95 (*0-8165-1098-9*) U of Ariz Pr.

Yellowstone: National Park. National Parks & Conservation Association Staff & David Dunbar. LC 94-18570. (Stylebooks Ser.). (Illus.). 328p. 1996. pap. 11.95 (*1-55859-825-1*) Abbeville Pr.

Yellowstone: Selected Photographs, 1870-1960. Carl Schreier. LC 88-80159. (Illus.). 160p. (Orig.). 1989. 24.95 (*0-943972-12-4*); pap. 18.95 (*0-943972-11-6*) Homestead WY.

Yellowstone: The Cycle of the Seasons. George B. Robinson. Ed. by Nicky Leach. (Wish You Were Here Postcard Bks.). 96p. (Orig.). 1994. 24.95 (*0-939365-32-4*); pap. 14.95 (*0-939365-31-6*) Sierra Pr CA.

Yellowstone: The Story Behind the Scenery. Hugh Crandall. LC 76-57453. (Illus.). 48p. (Orig.). 1977. pap. 7.95 (*0-916122-21-2*) KC Pubns.

Yellowstone ABC. Cyd Martin. (Illus.). 20p. (J). 1992. pap. 5.95 (*1-879373-12-2*) R Rinehart.

***Yellowstone Album: A Photographic Celebration of the First National Park.** Compiled by Lee H. Whittlesey. (Illus.). 160p. 1997. 29.95 (*1-57098-148-5*); pap. 19.95 (*1-57098-147-7*) R Rinehart.

Yellowstone & Grand Teton: A Comprehensive Guide to Outdoor Activities. Matt Harding & Freddie Snalam. (Illus.). 288p. (Orig.). 1995. pap. 14.95 (*1-884294-01-4*) All Pts Pub.

Yellowstone & Grand Teton National Parks: An Activity Guide. Daniel Ginsberg. (Illus.). 32p. 1990. 2.95 (*0-911797-79-3*) R Rinehart.

Yellowstone & Grand Teton National Parks & the Middle Rocky Mountains. Ed. by Love. (IGC Field Trip Guidebooks Ser.). 104p. 1989. 21.00 (*0-87590-668-0*, T328) Am Geophysical.

***Yellowstone & the Biology of Time: Photographs Across a Century.** Mary Meagher & Doug Houston. (Illus.). 1998. 80.00 (*0-8061-2996-4*) U of Okla Pr.

Yellowstone & the Northern Rockies. rev. ed. Consumer Guide Staff. 1987. 0.99 (*0-517-28867-2*) Random Hse Value.

Yellowstone Bear Tales. Ed. by Paul D. Schullery. (Illus.). 224p. 1991. pap. 12.95 (*0-911797-98-X*) R Rinehart.

***Yellowstone Branch of the Union Pacific: Route of the Yellowstone Special.** Thornton Waite. (Illus.). 100p. 1997. pap. text ed. 19.95 (*0-9657729-0-X*) Brueggenjohann.

Yellowstone Command: Colonel Nelson A. Miles & the Great Sioux War, 1876-1877. Jerome A. Greene. LC 91-2269. (Illus.). xvi, 333p. 1991. pap. 13.95 (*0-8032-7046-1*, Bison Books) U of Nebr Pr.

Yellowstone Country: The Enduring Wonder. Seymour L. Fishbein. Ed. by Donald J. Crump. (Special Publications Series 24: No. 1). (Illus.). (YA). 1989. lib. bdg. 12.95 (*0-87044-718-1*) Natl Geog.

Yellowstone Country Fly Pattern. Tom Travis. (Illus.). 250p. (Orig.). 1997. pap. write for info. (*0-87108-873-8*) Pruett.

Yellowstone Explorers Guide. Carl Schreier. LC 82-84287. (Explorers Guide Ser.). (Illus.). 64p. (Orig.). 1996. reprint ed. pap. 12.95 (*0-943972-02-7*) Homestead WY.

***Yellowstone Explorers Guide.** Carl Schreier. LC 82-84287. (Explorers Guide Ser.). (Illus.). 64p. (Orig.). 1996. reprint ed. 24.95 (*0-943972-56-6*) Homestead WY.

Yellowstone Fires: Flames & Rebirth. Dorothy H. Patent. LC 89-24544. (Illus.). 40p. (J). (gr. 3-7). 1990. lib. bdg. 14.95 (*0-8234-0807-8*) Holiday.

Yellowstone Fishing Guide. Robert E. Charlton. (Illus.). 168p. (Orig.). pap. 17.95 (*0-614-06143-1*) Falcon Pr MT.

Yellowstone Fishing Guide. Robert E. Charlton. (Illus.). 51p. (Orig.). 1982. pap. 4.50 (*0-943390-00-1*) Tri-County.

Yellowstone Fishing Guide. 3rd ed. Robert E. Charlton. (Illus.). 168p. (Orig.). 1995. pap. 17.95 (*1-885719-00-0*) Lost River Pr.

***Yellowstone Fly-Fishing Guide.** Craig Mathews & Clayton Molinero. LC 97-6966. (Illus.). 150p. (Orig.). 1997. pap. 16.95 (*1-55821-545-X*) Lyons & Burford.

Yellowstone Grand Teton Roadguide. rev. ed. Jeremy C. Schmidt. (Illus.). 96p. (Orig.). 1995. reprint ed. pap. 4.95 (*1-881480-05-4*) Free Wheel Trvl.

Yellowstone in the Eagle's Eye. Intro. by Robert Barbee. 100p. (Orig.). (FRE, GER & JPN.). 1991. pap. 14.95 (*0-9627618-2-6*) Billings Gazette.

Yellowstone Is... Mike Logan. (Illus.). 94p. 1987. pap. 13.95 (*0-937959-20-0*) Falcon Pr MT.

Yellowstone Kelly. Peter Bowen. LC 86-27193. 260p. 1988. 27.50 (*0-915463-40-7*) Jameson Bks.

Yellowstone Kelly: The Memoirs of Luther S. Kelly. Luther S. Kelly. (American Biography Ser.). 268p. 1991. reprint ed. lib. bdg. 69.00 (*0-7812-8232-2*) Rprt Serv.

Yellowstone Kelly: The Memoirs of Luther S. Kelly. Luther S. Kelly. Ed. by Milo M. Quaife. LC 26-9001. (Illus.). xiv, 300p. 1973. reprint ed. pap. 10.95 (*0-8032-5784-8*, Bison Books) U of Nebr Pr.

***Yellowstone Mystery: On Top at Eagle Creek.** Karl R. Hemr. 115p. (Orig.). 1996. pap. 9.95 (*1-57502-288-5*, PO995) Morris Pubng.

Yellowstone National Park. Hiram M. Chittenden. LC 64-11334. (Illus.). 208p. 1973. pap. 11.95 (*0-8061-0937-8*) U of Okla Pr.

Yellowstone National Park. Deborah Kent. LC 93-37521. (Cornerstones of Freedom Ser.). (Illus.). 32p. (J). 1994. lib. bdg. 18.00 (*0-516-06678-1*) Childrens.

Yellowstone National Park. Deborah Kent. (Cornerstones of Freedom Ser.). (Illus.). 32p. (J). (gr. 3-6). 1994. pap. 4.95 (*0-516-46678-X*) Childrens.

Yellowstone National Park. Jenny Markert. (Vision Bks.). 32p. (J). (gr. 2-6). 1992. lib. bdg. 22.79 (*0-89565-859-3*) Childs World.

Yellowstone National Park. John Muir. (Illus.). 64p. 1978. pap. 5.50 (*0-89646-079-7*) Vistabooks.

Yellowstone National Park. David Petersen. LC 91-37292. (New True Bks.). (Illus.). 48p. (J). (gr. k-4). 1992. pap. 5.50 (*0-516-41148-9*); lib. bdg. 19.00 (*0-516-01148-0*) Childrens.

***Yellowstone National Park: A Postcard Book.** Illus. by Carl Schreier. 50p. (Orig.). 1997. pap. 8.95 (*0-943972-61-2*) Homestead WY.

***Yellowstone National Park: 125th Anniversary.** Michael Milstein. Ed. by Richard Wesnick. (Illus.). 112p. 1996. pap. 19.95 (*0-9627618-9-3*) Billings Gazette.

Yellowstone National Park - Mammoth, WY. rev. ed. Ed. by Trails Illustrated Staff. (Illus.). 1994. 6.99 (*0-925873-73-X*) Trails Illustrated.

Yellowstone National Park - Old Faithful, WY. rev. ed. Ed. by Trails Illustrated Staff. 1994. 6.99 (*0-925873-83-7*) Trails Illustrated.

Yellowstone National Park - Tower - Canyon, WY. rev. ed. Ed. by Trails Illustrated Staff. 1994. 6.99 (*0-925873-74-8*) Trails Illustrated.

***Yellowstone National Park - WY.** (Illus.). 1996. pap. 2.95 (*1-56695-025-2*) Trails Illustrated.

Yellowstone National Park - Yellowstone Lake, WY. rev. ed. Ed. by Trails Illustrated Staff. 1993. 6.99 (*0-925873-75-6*) Trails Illustrated.

***Yellowstone National Park, & the Mountain Regions of Idaho, Nevada, Colorado, & Utah.** 2nd deluxe ed. F. V. Hayden. (Illus.). 52p. Date not set. reprint ed. boxed 200.00 (*1-884101-02-X*) T Gilcrease Mus.

***Yellowstone National Park, & the Mountain Regions of Idaho, Nevada, Colorado, & Utah.** 2nd ed. F. V. Hayden. (Illus.). 52p. Date not set. reprint ed. pap. 24.95 (*1-884101-01-1*) T Gilcrease Mus.

Yellowstone National Park, WY. rev. ed. Ed. by Trails Illustrated Staff. (Illus.). 1994. Folded topographical map. 8.99 (*0-925873-01-2*) Trails Illustrated.

Yellowstone on Fire. rev. ed. Bob Ekey & Patricia Bellinghausen. 128p. pap. 14.95 (*0-9627618-7-7*) Billings Gazette.

Yellowstone Park. Frank Staub. LC 89-34371. (Let's Take a Trip Ser.). (Illus.). 32p. (J). (gr. 3-6). 1990. lib. bdg. 11.50 (*0-8167-1737-0*) Troll Communs.

Yellowstone Park Waters. Bruce Staples. (River Journal Ser.: Vol. 4, No. 1). (Illus.). 48p. 1995. pap. 15.95 (*1-57188-044-5*) F Amato Pubns.

Yellowstone Pioneers: The Story of Hamilton Stores & Yellowstone National Park. Gwen Petersen. Ed. by Linda S. Davis. LC 85-50965. (Illus.). 120p. 1989. pap. 9.95 (*0-917859-23-5*) Sunrise SBCA.

Yellowstone Place Names. Lee H. Whittlesey. LC 88-21610. (Illus.). 200p. (Orig.). (YA). (gr. 8 up). 1988. pap. 7.95 (*0-917298-15-2*) MT Hist Soc.

Yellowstone Place Names. unabridged ed. Lee H. Whittlesey. LC 88-21610. (Illus.). xiii, 179p. (Orig.). (YA). (gr. 8 up). 1988. fiche 8.95 (*0-917298-20-9*) MT Hist Soc.

Yellowstone Place Names: Mirror of History. Aubrey L. Haines. LC 96-4463. (Illus.). 216p. 1996. 32.50 (*0-87081-382-X*); pap. 17.50 (*0-87081-383-8*) Univ Pr Colo.

Yellowstone Primer: Land & Resource Management in the Greater Yellowstone Ecosystem. Ed. by John A. Baden & Donald E. Leal. LC 88-64201. (Illus.). 226p. (Orig.). 1990. 29.95 (*0-936488-23-9*); pap. 12.95 (*0-936488-24-7*) PRIPP.

Yellowstone Reflections: An Artist's Inspiration & Canoe Flyers Love Song. Roger Clawson. LC 91-67241. (Yellowstone Ser.: No. 1). (Illus.). 1991. 30.00 (*0-9631762-0-X*) Prose Works.

Yellowstone River & Its Angling. Dave Hughes. (Illus.). 96p. (Orig.). 1992. pap. 19.95 (*1-878175-22-X*) F Amato Pubns.

Yellowstone River Country of Montana & Wyoming. Tom N. Thayer. Ed. by Jean E. Thayer. (Montana Speaks Ser.: Vol. I). (Illus.). 116p. 1996. pap. text ed. 34.95 (*0-9652439-1-5*) Montana Speaks.

Yellowstone River Country of Montana & Wyoming. Tom N. Thayer. Ed. by Jean E Thayer & Chris Nelson. (Montana Ser.: Vol. I). (Illus.). 116p. 1996. boxed 44.95 (*0-9652439-0-7*) Montana Speaks.

Yellowstone Run - New Orleans Run. David Robbins. (Endworld Double Edition Ser.). 384p. 1993. mass mkt., pap. text ed. 4.50 (*0-8439-3418-2*) Dorchester Pub Co.

Yellowstone Savage: Life in Nature's Wonderland. Joyce B. Lohse. LC 87-34212. (Illus.). 144p. (Orig.). 1988. pap. 7.95 (*0-944915-00-0*) J D Charles.

Yellowstone Stage Holdups. Jack E. Haynes. LC 59-52123. (Illus.). 30p. (C). 1988. reprint ed. lib. bdg. 25.00 (*0-8095-6109-3*) Borgo Pr.

Yellowstone Story, Vol. 1. 2nd rev. ed. Aubrey L. Haines. (Illus.). 408p. 1996. pap. text ed. 19.95 (*0-87081-390-0*) Univ Pr Colo.

Yellowstone Story, Vol. 2. 2nd rev. ed. Aubrey L. Haines. (Illus.). 928p. 1996. pap. text ed. 19.95 (*0-87081-391-9*) Univ Pr Colo.

Yellowstone Teton Wit. William Gibson. (Illus.). 216p. 1986. 8.95 (*0-936023-03-1*, 34504) Interp Mktg Prods.

Yellowstone Trails, A Hiking Guide. 5th ed. Mark Marschall. LC 90-70639. (Illus.). 160p. 1995. 4.95 (*0-89288-197-6*) Yellowstone Assn.

Yellowstone Vegetation: Consequences of Environment & History in a Natural Setting. Donald Despain. 254p. 1991. pap. 14.95 (*0-911797-75-0*) R Rinehart.

Yellowstone Wildlife. Ed. by Jeff Nicholas. (Wish You Were Here Postcard Bks.). (Illus.). 32p. 1994. pap. 4.95 (*0-939365-34-0*) Sierra Pr CA.

Yellowstone Wildlife: A Watcher's Guide. Todd Wilkinson. (Illus.). 96p. 1992. pap. 9.95 (*1-55971-140-X*) NorthWord.

Yellowstone Winter Guide. Jeff Henry. (Illus.). 108p. 1992. pap. 11.95 (*0-911797-90-4*) R Rinehart.

Yellowstone Wolf: A Guide & Sourcebook. Ed. by Paul D. Schullery. (Illus.). 352p. 1996. 32.50 (*1-881019-13-6*) Mountain Pr.

Yellowstone Wolves: The First Year. Gary Ferguson. LC 96-84578. 178p. 1996. pap. 12.95 (*1-56044-500-9*) Falcon Pr MT.

***Yellowstone 88.** Matt Welter. 26p. (Orig.). 1996. pap. 6.50 (*1-886895-07-4*) Poetry Harbor.

Yellowstone's Cycle of Fire. Frank Staub. LC 92-29631. (J). (gr. 1-4). 1993. lib. bdg. 14.96 (*0-87614-778-3*, Carolrhoda) Lerner Group.

Yellowstone's Ski Pioneers: Peril & Heroism on the Winter Trail. Paul Schuller. (Illus.). 176p. (Orig.). 19.95 (*1-881019-11-X*) High Plns WY.

Yellowtail, Crow Medicine Man & Sun Dance Chief: An Autobiography. Thomas Yellowtail. LC 90-50702. (Illus.). 272p. 1994. pap. 11.95 (*0-8061-2602-7*) U of Okla Pr.

Yellowthroat. Penny Hayes. 240p. 1988. pap. 8.95 (*0-941483-10-X*) Naiad Pr.

***Yeltsin: A Political Portrait.** 4th ed. Valentin Fedorov. 1996. pap. write for info. (*0-9653218-8-6*) Imperial Publng.

Yemassee. William G. Simms. Ed. by Joseph V. Ridgely. (Masterworks of Literature Ser.). 1964. pap. 16.95 (*0-8084-0337-0*) NCUP.

Yemassee: A Romance of Carolina. William G. Simms. LC 93-24124. (Selected Fiction of William Gilmore Simms Ser.). 504p. 1993. 44.00 (*1-55728-302-8*) U of Ark Pr.

***Yemaya y Ochun: Kariocha, Iyalorichas y Olorichas.** Lydia Cabrera. LC 79-90203. (Coleccion del Chichereku). 370p. (Orig.). (SPA.). 1996. reprint ed. pap. 25.00 (*0-89729-761-X*) Ediciones.

Yemei Breshis. 464p. (HEB.). 1993. 35.00 (*0-8266-5335-9*) Kehot Pubn Soc.

Yemen. (Insight Guides Ser.). 1993. pap. 21.95 (*0-395-66272-9*) HM.

Yemen. Laurence Deonna. (Illus.). 201p. 1991. 32.00 (*0-89410-710-0*, Three Contnts); pap. 16.00 (*0-89410-711-9*, Three Contnts) Lynne Rienner.

Yemen. Peter Wald. (Illus.). 336p. 1996. pap. 24.95 (*1-873429-11-8*, Pub. by Pallas Athene UK) Boydell & Brewer.

Yemen: The Fluctuations of Unity. Joseph Kostiner. LC 97-5014. (CHP Ser.). 128p. (C). 1996. pap. 15.95 (*1-85567-349-5*, Pub. by Pntr Pubs UK); text ed. 39.95 (*1-85567-348-7*, Pub. by Pntr Pubs UK) Bks Intl VA.

Yemen: The Search for a Modern State. John E. Peterson. LC 81-48187. 224p. 1982. 25.00 (*0-8018-2784-1*) Johns Hopkins.

Yemen: Traditionalism vs. Modernity. Mohammed A. Zabarah. LC 81-20982. 176p. 1982. text ed. 49.95 (*0-275-90929-8*, C0929, Praeger Pubs) Greenwood.

Yemen: Travel Survival Kit. 3rd ed. Pertti Hamalainen. (Illus.). 256p. 1996. pap. 13.95 (*0-86442-319-5*) Lonely Planet.

Yemen - in Pictures. LC 93-3178. (YA). (gr. 5 up). 1993. lib. bdg. 19.95 (*0-8225-1911-9*, Lerner Publctns) Lerner Group.

Yemen & the U. S. A. A Super-Power & a Small-State Relationship, 1962-1992. Ahmed Nomen Al-Madhaqi. 224p. 1996. text ed. 59.50 (*1-85043-772-6*, Pub. by I B Tauris UK) St Martin.

Yemeni Arabic, Bk. 1. Hamdi A. Qafisheh. 482p. (ARA.). 1993. 22.95 (*0-86685-665-X*, LDL665X, Pub. by Librairie du Liban FR) Intl Bk Ctr.

Yemeni Arabic, Bk. 2. Hamdi A. Qafisheh. 482p. (ARA.). 24.95 (*0-86685-557-2*, LDL5572, Pub. by Librairie du Liban FR) Intl Bk Ctr.

***Yemeni Passage.** Derek Franck. (Illus.). 487p. 1997. 15.00 (*0-9656570-0-0*) Azimuth.

Yemenis in New York City: The Folklore of Ethnicity. 20.00 (*0-614-14848-0*) Balch Inst Ethnic Studies.

Yemenite Jewry: Origins, Culture, & Literature. Reuben Ahroni. LC 84-48649. (Jewish Literature & Culture Ser.). (Illus.). 237p. 1986. reprint ed. pap. 68.20 (*0-7837-3689-4*, 2057867) Bks Demand.

Yemenite Midrash. Tr. by Yitzhak T. Langermann. LC 96-22669. 400p. 1996. pap. 20.00 (*0-06-065391-4*) Harper SF.

Yemin Moshe: The Story of a Jerusalem Neighborhood. Eliezer D. Jaffe. LC 87-21819. 88p. 1988. text ed. 49.95 (*0-275-92690-7*, C2690, Praeger Pubs) Greenwood.

Yeminis in New York City: The Folklore of Ethnicity. Shalom Staub. LC 88-71299. (Illus.). 210p. 1989. 38.50 (*0-944190-05-7*) Balch IES Pr.

Yemoja - Olukun: Ifa & the Spirit of the Ocean. Fa'lokum Fatunmbi. 32p. 1993. pap. 4.95 (*0-942272-33-1*) Original Pubns.

Yen Appreciation & the International Economy. Dilip K. Das. 208p. (C). 1992. 55.00 (*0-8147-1852-3*) NYU Pr.

Yen-Dollar Agreement: Liberalizing Japanese Capital Markets. Jeffrey A. Frankel. LC 84-27842. (Policy Analyses in International Economics Ser.: No. 9). 76p. (Orig.). 1984. pap. 10.00 (*0-88132-035-8*) Inst Intl Eco.

Yen for Development: Japanese Foreign Aid & the Politics of Burdensharing. Ed. by Shafiqul Islam. 176p. 1991. pap. 18.95 (*0-87609-096-X*) Coun Foreign.

Yenan Way in Revolutionary China. Mark Selden. LC 79-152272. (East Asian Ser.: No. 62). 311p. 1972. pap. 12.95 (*0-674-96561-2*, HP40) HUP.

Yenching Journal of Chinese Studies: 1927-1949, 20 vols. Harvard-Yenching Institute, Staff. (CHI.). 700.00 (*0-89986-260-8*) Oriental Bk Store.

Yenching University & Sino-Western Relations, 1916-1952. Philip West. (East Asian Monographs: No. 85). 258p. 1976. 29.00 (*0-674-96569-8*) HUP.

Yendi. Steven Brust. 1987. mass mkt. 5.99 (*0-441-94460-4*) Ace Bks.

Yendo a Traves. Carlos Gonzalez. (SPA.). 1991. write for info. (*1-56491-000-8*) Imagine Pubs.

Yengema Cave Report. Carleton S. Coon et al. (University Museum Monographs: No. 31). (Illus.). 77p. 1968. pap. 15.00 (*0-934718-23-7*) U PA Mus Pubns.

Yenlo & the Mystic Brotherhood. Arline L. Richmond. 140p. 1996. pap. 16.95 (*1-56459-824-1*) Kessinger Pub.

Yenlo & the Mystic Brotherhood. Arline L. Richmond. reprint ed. spiral bd. 10.50 (*0-7873-0716-5*) Hlth Research.

Yens Yenson's Yingles. Ed. by Mique Heed. 48p. (Orig.). 1988. reprint ed. pap. 3.95 (*0-944996-02-7*) Carlsons.

***Yentl: Movie Selections.** Ed. by Carol Cuellar. 100p. (Orig.). (C). 1983. pap. text ed. 16.95 (*0-7692-0829-0*, TSF0049) Warner Brothers.

Yeoman Farmer & Westward Expansion of U. S. Cotton Production. James D. Foust. LC 75-2581. (Dissertations in American Economic History Ser.). (Illus.). 1975. 25.95 (*0-405-07201-5*) Ayer.

Yeoman in Tudor & Stuart England. Albert J. Schmidt. (Folger Guides to the Age of Shakespeare Ser.). 1961. 4.95 (*0-918016-20-7*) Folger Bks.

Yeoman of the Guard. (Vocal Score Ser.). 1986. pap. 18.95 (*0-88188-729-3*, 50337860) H Leonard.

Yeoman of the Guard: Vocal Score with Dialogue the Merryman & His Maid. Gilbert & Sullivan. 244p. 1986. per. 20.00 (*0-7935-5378-4*, 50337860) H Leonard.

Yeoman Service: Contemporary Cartoons of the Suffolk Yeomanry 1880-1910. W. B. Giles & G. D. Giles. (C). 1991. 135.00 (*0-946771-78-2*, Pub. by Spellmount UK) St Mut.

Yeoman Versus Cavalier: The Old Southwest's Fictional Road to Rebellion. Ritchie D. Watson, Jr. LC 93-14001. (Southern Literary Studies). xii, 208p. (C). 1993. text ed. 30.00 (*0-8071-1829-X*) La State U Pr.

***Yer-Vos-Vu-Ven: Interesting & Curious Facts from the Bible, Talmud & Midrash.** Nissan Mindel. Ed. by Gershon Kranzler & Uriel Zimmer. (Illus.). 78p. (YID.). 1964. 8.00 (*0-8266-0371-8*) Kehot Pubn Soc.

Yerbamente Suyo. 3rd ed. Penny C. Royal. 130p. 1987. pap. 7.95 (*0-9609226-3-6*) Sound Nutri.

Yerbas de la Gente: A Study of Hispano-American Medicinal Plants. Karen C. Ford. (Anthropological Papers: No. 60). 446p. reprint ed. pap. 127.20 (*0-7837-0550-6*, 2040884) Bks Demand.

Yerbury: A Photographic Collection, 1850-1991: Photographs by Four Generations of the Yerbury Family. Ed. by Malcolm Cant. 200p. (C). 1992. text ed. 120.00 (*0-85976-348-X*, Pub. by J Donald UK) St Mut.

Yerkes Observatory 1892-1950. Donald E. Osterbrock. LC 96-25450. 1996. 40.00 (*0-226-63945-2*) U Ch Pr.

Yerkes Observatory, 1892-1950: The Birth, Near Death, & Resurrection of a Scientific Research Institution. Donald E. Osterbrock. LC 96-25450. 1998. pap. 22.95 (*0-226-63946-0*) U Ch Pr.

Yerma. Federico Garcia Lorca. Ed. by Miguel Garcia Posada. (Nueva Austral Ser.: Vol. 80). (SPA.). pap. 12.95 (*84-239-1880-7*) Elliots Bks.

Yerma. Federico Garcia Lorca. 165p. (SPA.). 1989. 14.95 (*0-8288-7044-6*, S30169); 13.95 (*0-8288-7148-5*) Fr & Eur.

Yerma. 4th ed. Federico Garcia Lorca. 196p. (SPA.). 1990. pap. 13.95 (*0-7859-4978-X*) Fr & Eur.

Yerma: A Tragic Poem in Three Acts & Six Scenes. Federico Garcia Lorca. Ed. by Macpherson. (Hispanic Classics Ser.). 1987. 49.95 (*0-85668-337-X*, Pub. by Aris & Phillips UK); pap. 22.00 (*0-85668-338-8*, Pub. by Aris & Phillips UK) David Brown.

Yerma-Garcia Lorca Vol. 1. Robin Warner. 1994. text ed. 15.95 (*0-7190-4131-7*, Pub. by Manchester Univ Pr UK) St Martin.

Yersinia Enterocolitica. Ed. by Edward J. Bottone. 240p. 1981. 135.00 (*0-8493-5545-1*, QK201, CRC Reprint) Franklin.

Yersinia Enterocolitica: Proceedings of the International Symposium on Yersinia, 3rd, Montreal, September, 1977. International Symposium on Yersinia Staff. Ed. by Philip B. Carter et al. (Contributions to Microbiology & Immunology Ser.: Vol. 5). (Illus.). 1979. 124.00 (*3-8055-2927-9*) S Karger.

Yersiniosis: Present & Future. Ed. by G. Ravagnan & C. Chiesa. (Contributions to Microbiology & Immunology Ser.: Vol. 13). (Illus.). xii, 340p. 1995. 299.25 (*3-8055-6138-5*) S Karger.

***Yersiniosis: Report on a WHO Meeting.** (Euro Reports & Studies Ser.: No. 60). 31p. 1983. pap. text ed. 4.00 (*92-890-1226-9*) World Health.

Yertle the Turtle & Other Stories. Dr. Seuss. (Illus.). (J). (gr. k-3). 1966. 14.00 (*0-394-80087-7*); lib. bdg. 15.99 (*0-394-90087-1*) Random Bks Yng Read.

Yerushalmi Fragments from the Genizah, Vol. 1. Louis Ginzberg. (Text & Studies of the Jewish Theological Seminary of America: Vol. III). ix, 372p. 1970. reprint ed. 63.70 (*0-685-66468-6*, 05103036) G Olms Pubs.

Yerushalmi-the Talmud of the Land of Israel: An Introduction. Jacob Neusner. LC 91-19713. 208p. 1993. 30.00 (*0-87668-812-1*) Aronson.

Yes. Douglas Anderson. 111p. 1979. pap. 6.95 (*0-912549-08-4*) Bread & Butter.

Yes. Thomas Bernhard. Tr. by Ewald Osers from GER. LC 92-17921. (Phoenix Fiction Ser.). iv, 140p. 1992. pap. 10.95 (*0-226-04390-8*) U Ch Pr.

***Yes.** Josse Goffin. Date not set. lib. bdg. write for info. (*0-688-12376-7*) Lothrop.

Yes. Alexandra Hieb. (Illus.). 61p. 1993. pap. 12.50 (*0-9637568-0-X*) Daybreak ND.

Yes: A Dozen Linked Poems. Alexis K. Rotella & Florence Miller. 51p. 1994. pap. 13.00 (*0-916133-99-0*) Jade Mtn.

Yes: Irises. Ken Pobo. 32p. (Orig.). 1992. pap. 4.00 (*1-880286-08-4*) Singular Speech Pr.

***Yes - Complete Deluxe Edition.** Ed. by Carol Cuellar. 484p. (Orig.). (C). 1981. pap. text ed. 29.95 (*0-7692-0865-7*, VF0896) Warner Brothers.

***Yes - Talk.** Ed. by Carol Cuellar. 80p. (Orig.). (C). 1994. pap. text ed. 19.95 (*0-7692-0873-8*, VF2156) Warner Brothers.

***Yes - The Big Generator.** Ed. by Carol Cuellar. 92p. (Orig.). (C). 1988. pap. text ed. 12.95 (*0-7692-0863-0*, VF1444) Warner Brothers.

Yes, Americans, a Conspiracy Murdered JFK! Stanley J. Marks & Ethel M. Marks. LC 92-71289. (Illus.). 220p. (Orig.). 1992. pap. 14.50 (*0-685-59495-5*); pap. 16.95 (*0-938780-25-5*) Bur Intl Aff.

Yes & Know. (J). (gr. 3 up). 1991. pap. 2.47 (*1-56297-001-1*, YK-08); pap. 2.47 (*1-56297-003-8*, YK-14) Lee Pubns KY.

Yes & Know. (J). (gr. 4 up). 1991. pap. 2.47 (*1-56297-002-X*, YK-09) Lee Pubns KY.

Yes & Know Books. (J). (gr. 3 up). 1991. pap. 1.47 (*1-56297-000-3*, YK-15) Lee Pubns KY.

Yes & Know Line Up. (J). 1991. pap. 2.47 (*1-56297-074-7*, L-18) Lee Pubns KY.

Yes & Know More Line Up. (J). 1991. pap. 2.47 (*1-56297-075-5*, L-18) Lee Pubns KY.

Yes & No: The Intimate Folklore of Africa. Alta Jablow. LC 72-13867. 223p. 1973. reprint ed. text ed. 39.75 (*0-8371-6757-4*, JAYN, Greenwood Pr) Greenwood.

Yes Anxiety: Taming the Fear of Commitment in Relationships, Career, Spiritual Life, Daily Decisions. M. Blaine Smith. LC 95-30878. 192p. (Orig.). 1995. pap. 9.99 (*0-8308-1647-X*, 1647) InterVarsity.

Yes Book: An Answer to Life (a Manual of Christian Existentialism) Jose De Vinck. LC 77-190621. 200p. (C). 1972. 15.75 (*0-911726-12-8*, CODE YBC); pap. 12.75 (*0-911726-11-X*, CODE YBB) Alleluia Pr.

Yes, But: The Top Forty Killer Phrases & How You Can Fight Them. Charles C. Thompson & Lael Lyons. LC 93-39848. (Illus.). 96p. (Orig.). 1994. pap. 11.00 (*0-88730-660-8*) Harper Busn.

Yes, Comrade! Manuel Rui. Tr. by Ronald W. Sousa. LC 92-32341. (Emergent Literatures Ser.: Vol. 11). 176p. (C). 1993. 17.95 (*0-8166-1966-2*) U of Minn Pr.

Yes, Craft Shows Can Make You Money. Barbara Massie. 36p. 1992. pap. text ed. 6.50 (*1-884053-00-9*) Magnolia AR.

***Yes Dear.** Diana W. Jones. (J). Date not set. lib. bdg. write for info. (*0-688-11196-3*) Greenwillow.

Yes! English for Children: Book A. 2nd ed. Michael Walker. 1983. pap. text ed. 9.96 (*0-201-65601-9*); pap. text ed. 5.85 (*0-201-65602-7*) Addison-Wesley.

Yes! English for Children: Book B. 2nd ed. Michael Walker. 1983. pap. text ed. 10.13 (*0-201-65604-3*); wbk. ed., pap. text ed. 5.85 (*0-201-65605-1*) Addison-Wesley.

Yes! English for Children: Book C. 2nd ed. Michael Walker. 1983. pap. text ed. 10.45 (*0-201-65607-8*); wbk. ed., pap. text ed. 6.40 (*0-201-65608-6*) Addison-Wesley.

Yes! English for Children: Book D. 2nd ed. Michael Walker. 1983. wbk. ed., pap. text ed. 6.40 (*0-201-65612-4*) Addison-Wesley.

Yes! English for Children: Book E. 2nd ed. Michael Walker. 1983. pap. text ed. 10.45 (*0-201-65614-0*) Addison-Wesley.

Yes! English for Children: Book F. 2nd ed. Michael Walker. 1983. pap. text ed. 10.45 (*0-201-65617-5*); wbk. ed., pap. text ed. 6.40 (*0-201-65618-3*) Addison-Wesley.

Yes! English for Children Bk. D. 2nd ed. L. Mellgren. 1983. text ed. 10.49 (*0-201-05611-9*) Addison-Wesley.

Yes! English for Children Bk. E. 2nd ed. L. Mellgren. 1983. student ed., text ed. 6.58 (*0-201-05615-1*) Addison-Wesley.

Yes, Even You Can Be a Country Person. Wayne Allred. LC 95-91060. (Illus.). 124p. (Orig.). 1995. reprint ed. pap. 5.95 (*1-885027-04-4*) Willow T Bks.

Yes, Everything: New Poems. Robert Dana. LC 93-36543. 1994. 19.95 (*0-929968-37-9*); pap. 12.95 (*0-929968-36-0*) Another Chicago Pr.

Yes, God of the Gentiles, Too: The Missionary Message of the Old Testament. David Filbeck. (BGC Monograph). 230p. (Orig.). 1994. pap. 7.95 (*1-879089-14-9*) B Graham Ctr.

Yes, Helen, There were Dinosaurs. Lewis S. Brown. Ed. by Lena M. Brown. (Illus.). 152p. (Orig.). 1982. pap. 7.95 (*0-9608542-0-7*) L S Brown Pub.

Yes, Helen, There Were Dinosaurs. Lewis S. Brown. (Illus.). 143p. (Orig.). (J). (ps-12). 1982. pap. 7.95 (*0-9647505-0-3*, 82144370-AC-R90) L Brown Pubng.

***Yes I Can!** Heidi Bratton. LC 97-7465. (Walking with God Ser.). (J). 1997. write for info. (*0-8091-6639-9*) Paulist Pr.

Yes I Can. Marty Links & Marilyn Knight. (Illus.). (J). 1990. 4.95 (*0-685-57229-3*) Arts Pubns.

Yes, I Can: Action Projects to Resolve Equity Issues in Educational Computing. Ed. by Alice Fredman. 80p. 1990. 15.00 (*0-924667-71-0*) Intl Society Tech Educ.

Yes I Can: The Story of Sammy Davis, Jr. Sammy Davis, Jr. & Jane Boyar. 1990. pap. 9.95 (*0-374-52268-5*, Noonday) FS&G.

Yes I Can: Yes I Did. Marty Links. Ed. by Barbara Lins. (Illus.). 32p. (Orig.). (J). (ps). 1990. pap. write for info. (*1-878079-00-X*) Arts Pubns.

Yes, I Do Mind If You Smoke. Rhoda Nichter. LC 77-83110. 1978. 22.95 (*0-87949-114-0*) Ashley Bks.

Yes, I Love You. Little Golden Books Staff. (First Little Golden Bks). (Illus.). 24p. (J). (ps). 1995. bds. 1.19 (*0-307-10177-0*, Golden Books) Western Pub.

Yes, I Make Housecalls. H. J. Hirshfield. (Illus.). 90p. 1993. pap. 9.95 (*1-879260-14-X*) Evanston Pub.

Yes, I Remember. Jessie Ivey. 21p. pap. 2.00 (*0-686-97738-6*) Ivey Pubns.

Yes I Said Yes I Will. Judith McDaniel. 256p. (Orig.). 1996. pap. 10.95 (*1-56280-138-4*) Naiad Pr.

Yes, I Saw Gandhi. Annada S. Ray. 215p. 1994. 15.00 (*0-934676-78-X*) Greenlf Bks.

Yes, Inspector McLean. George Goodchild. 320p. 1995. 18.50 (*0-7451-8662-9*, Black Dagger) Chivers N Amer.

YES International Entomology Resource Guide: The Insect Study Sourcebook. 4th ed. Gary A. Dunn. (YES Special Publication Ser.: No. 1). 90p. 1992. pap. text ed. 8.95 (*1-884256-07-4*) Yng Entomol.

Yes Is Better Than No. Byrd Baylor. (Illus.). 242p. 1991. reprint ed. pap. 9.95 (*0-918080-53-3*) Treas Chest Bks.

Yes Is Forever. Daughters of St. Paul. LC 79-22266. (Encounter Ser.). (Illus.). 109p. 1982. 3.00 (*0-8198-8700-5*, EN0260); pap. 2.00 (*0-8198-8702-1*) Pauline Bks.

***Yes! It's in the Bible.** Henry R. Rust. 98p. 1995. pap. 8.45 (*1-877871-87-7*, 6465) Ed Ministries.

Yes, It's Made from My Dog's Fur: An Owner's Guide to Harvesting Your Pet's Coat & Spinning it into Yarn. Detta Juusola. Ed. by Jacqueline Reina. (Illus.). 8p. (Orig.). 1995. pap. 3.50 (*0-9639736-1-4*) Woofspun Pubng.

Yes James, Yes Joyce & Other Poems. Crag Hill. 31p. (C). 1994. pap. text ed. 6.00 (*0-9647342-0-6*) Loose Gravel Pr.

***Yes, Let's: New & Selected Poems.** Thomas M. Disch. LC 88-46116. (Johns Hopkins, Poetry & Fiction Ser.). 129p. 1989. reprint ed. pap. 36.80 (*0-608-03726-5*, 2064551) Bks Demand.

Yes! Life of a Blessed Josemaria for Young Readers. Michael Carceles & Elizabeth Torra. 110p. 1994. pap. 14.95 (*0-933932-68-5*) Scepter Pubs.

Yes, Lord, I Have Sinned but I Have Several Excellent Excuses. James W. Moore. LC 90-40832. 112p. 1991. pap. 8.95 (*0-687-46661-X*) Abingdon.

Yes, Lord, I'm Comin' Home! Country Music Stars Share Their Stories of Knowing God. Lesley Sussman. LC 96-24876. 256p. 1997. 19.95 (*0-385-48445-3*) Doubleday.

Yes Means No. Howard E. Rogers. 1950. pap. 5.25 (*0-8222-1286-2*) Dramatists Play.

Yes, Mrs. Williams: A Personal Record of My Mother. William C. Williams. 1959. 19.95 (*0-8392-1136-8*) Astor-Honor.

Yes, Mrs. Williams: A Personal Record of My Mother. 2nd ed. William C. Williams. LC 59-9887. 160p. (C). 1982. reprint ed. pap. 5.95 (*0-8112-0832-X*, NDP534) New Directions.

Yes, Mush: A Cockney Dictionary: The Cockney Language & Its World. Robert Barltrop. (Illus.). 240p. (C). 1995. pap. 17.50 (*0-485-12047-X*, Pub. by Athlone Pr UK) Humanities.

Yes, Mush: A Cockney Dictionary: The Cockney Language & Its World. Robert Barltrop. (Illus.). 240p. (C). 1995. text ed. 49.95 (*0-485-11253-1*, Pub. by Athlone Pr UK) Humanities.

Yes No. Francis Picabia. Tr. by Remy Hall from FRE. 57p. (Orig.). 1990. pap. 5.95 (*0-937815-41-1*) Hanuman Bks.

Yes No. Jan Pienkowski. (Illus.). 24p. (J). (ps). 1992. pap. 2.95 (*0-671-74520-4*, Litl Simon S&S) S&S Childrens.

Yes, No, Little Hippo. Jane B. Moncure. LC 87-21211. (Magic Castle Readers Ser.). (Illus.). 32p. (J). (ps-2). 1987. lib. bdg. 21.36 (*0-89565-411-3*) Childs World.

Yes, No, Maybe. Glen Brown. Ed. by Carol Spelius. 80p. (Orig.). 1995. pap. 9.95 (*0-941363-37-6*) Lake Shore Pub.

Yes, No, Maybe So? Dealing with Doubt. Jeff Munroe. (Life Wise Ser.). 35p. 1996. teacher ed. 7.35 (*1-56212-163-4*, 1210-4012) CRC Pubns.

***Yes, of Course, but No.** Karl Patten. (Press of Appletree alley Poets Ser.). (Illus.). 12p. 1997. 35.00 (*0-916375-32-3*) Press Alley.

Yes of the Heart. Rusty Edwards. Ed. by Jack Schrader. LC 92-75282. 64p. (Orig.). (C). 1993. pap. text ed. 6.95 (*0-916642-52-6*, 776) Hope Pub.

Yes or No. 1991. 20.00 (*0-671-69491-X*) S&S Trade.

Yes or No? Straight Answers to Tough Questions about Christianity. Peter Kreeft. LC 90-85102. 191p. (Orig.). 1991. pap. 10.95 (*0-89870-358-1*) Ignatius Pr.

Yes or No: The Guide to Better Decisions. Spencer Johnson. LC 91-57929. 112p. 1993. reprint ed. pap. 11.00 (*0-88730-631-4*) Harper Busn.

Yes Review Workbook, High School Entrance. Leonard Bennet et al. 1986. pap. 8.95 (*0-87738-026-0*) Youth Ed.

Yes Sir, That's My Baby! A Parent's Guide to Child Modeling. Katie A. Kramer. (Illus.). 48p. 1990. pap. text ed. 15.95 (*0-9630912-0-4*) Protege Models.

***Yes, There Is Joy in Jesus.** Melva J. Harris. 47p. (Orig.). 1996. pap. text ed. 10.00 (*0-614-29917-9*) M J Harris.

Yes, There Is Life after Aerospace: Career Transition from Military Defense - Aerospace to Commercial Civilian Life. Marie H. Reichelt. Ed. by Reece Franklin & Joanne Fischer. (Illus.). 132p. (Orig.). 1994. pap. 14.95 (*0-9639036-5-9*) ABP Assocs.

Yes, There Is Life after Bankruptcy: Step-by-Step Guide to Getting Your Life Back on Track. Paige McClinte. LC 94-65049. 320p. (Orig.). 1997. 29.95 (*1-884573-05-3*); pap. 19.95 (*1-884573-14-2*) S-By-S Pubns.

***Yes, They're All Ours: Six of One, Half a Dozen of the Other.** Rick Boyer & Marilyn Boyer. 185p. 1997. lib. bdg. 9.99 (*0-9645396-4-0*, Home School Pr) GCB.

Yes to a Global Ethic: Voices from Religion & Politics. Ed. by Hans Kung. 260p. 1996. pap. text ed. 16.95 (*0-8264-0907-5*) Continuum.

Yes to Career Success! For Women in Transition. Candace A. Hennekens. 110p. 1992. pap. 12.95 (*0-9630148-1-1*) Prowrit Srvs Pr.

***Yes, Tyler Jeannette's (Tyler's Mother) Writing Some More!! Jeannette's (Tyler R. Webb's, III), Tyler's Mother's Poetry.** Jeannette E. Sellers. 55p. 1997. text ed. 16.95 (*0-9653581-3-5*) Jeannettes Adven.

Yes, Virginia. Illus. by Suzanne Hausman. (J). 6.95 (*0-685-86235-6*) Pubns Devl Co.

Yes, Virginia... Peg Sutherland. (American Romance Ser.). 1993. mass mkt. 3.50 (*0-373-16514-5*, 1-16514-1) Harlequin Bks.

Yes, Virginia, There Is a Santa Claus. Francis P. Church. LC 92-12268. 32p. (J). 1992. 10.95 (*0-385-30854-X*) Delacorte.

***Yes, Virginia, There Is a Santa Claus.** Cyndy Szekeres & Francis P. Church. LC 96-48181. (J). 1997. write for info. (*0-590-69196-1*) Scholastic Inc.

Yes Virginie...There Is a Pet Heaven: Understanding Our Older Dogs & Cats. Corienne Jones. (Illus.). 144p. (Orig.). 1991. pap. 12.95 (*0-9631169-0-8*) Pebbles Pub.

Yes, We Came Home. Rachel Araten. 120p. 1995. pap. text ed. 9.95 (*965-229-141-2*, Pub. by Gefen Pub Hse IS) Gefen Bks.

Yes We Can! Black Achievement. Robert Lawson & Gene Murphy. 320p. 1995. boxed 49.95 (*0-7872-0575-3*) Kendall-Hunt.

***Yes We Can Love One Another! Catholics & Protestants Can Share a Common Faith.** Warren Angel. LC 96-94822. 143p. (Orig.). 1997. pap. 12.00 (*0-9654806-0-7*) Magnus Pr.

***Yes, We Have No Neutrons: An Eye-Opening Tour Through the Twists & Turns of Bad Science.** A. K. Dewdney. LC 96-35312. 1997. text ed. 22.95 (*0-471-10806-5*) Wiley.

Yes, We Love God's Word! Living Street Ministry Staff. 32p. 2.00 (*0-87083-603-X*, 17011001) Living Stream Ministry.

Yes, with Variations. Ken McLaren. 72p. (Orig.). 1983. pap. 6.00 (*0-939196-00-X*) Smith.

***Yes Yes Living in a No No World.** Neil Eskelin. 192p. 1997. pap. 10.99 (*1-888848-09-X*) Western Front.

Yes, You Can! Sam Deep & Lyle Sussman. LC 95-40695. 288p. 1996. pap. 13.00 (*0-201-47965-6*) Addison-Wesley.

***Yes You Can! A Guide for Parents with Disabilities.** Mark Nagler & Adam Nagler. 224p. 1997. pap. 13.95 (0-7737-5866-6, Pub. by Stoddart Pubng CN) Genl Dist Srvs.

Yes You Can! A Guide for Sexuality Education. Dorothy L. Williams. (Values & Choices Ser.). 182p. 1987. pap. text ed. 8.95 (1-57482-212-8) Search Inst.

Yes, You Can: A Guide to Empowerment Groups. Charlotte D. Kasl. (Orig.). 1995. pap. 14.00 (0-9644520-0-6) Castle Consult.

Yes, You Can! A Guide to Self-Care for Persons with Spinal Cord Injury. 2nd ed. Ed. by Marget C. Hammond et al. Tr. by Jorge Garcia. LC 89-62035. (Illus.). 174p. (ENG & SPA.). 1993. pap. 9.50 (0-929819-01-2) Paralyzed Vets.

Yes, You Can-- Achieve Financial Independence. James E. Stowers & Jack Jonathan. LC 94-19990. 304p. 1994. 24.95 (0-8362-8078-4) Andrews & McMeel.

Yes You Can! An Innovative Approach to Happiness. Raymond L. Lemke. Ed. by Lucie Wilcox. LC 88-61002. (Illus.). 192p. (Orig.). 1988. pap. 6.95 (0-929099-00-1) Omaha Pr Pub.

Yes, You Can: One Thousand One Hundred Five Empowering Ideas for Life, Work, & Happiness. Sam Deep & Lyle Sussman. 288p. 1993. pap. write for info. (0-9638019-3-7) Sem by Sam Deep.

Yes, You Can Achieve Financial Independence. James E. Stowers, Jr. & Jack Jonathan. (Illus.). 1992. text ed. 29.95 (0-9629788-0-9) Deer Pub Co.

Yes, You Can Beat City Hall. John J. Murray, Jr. 372p. 1994. 18.95 (0-89914-039-4) Third Party Pub.

Yes, You Can, Heather! The Story of Heather Whitestone, Miss America 1995. Daphne Gray. 242p. 1996. pap. 12.99 (0-310-20985-4) Zondervan.

Yes, You Can Kelli! Renee Kent. Ed. by Cindy McClain. 109p. (Orig.). (J). (gr. 1-6). 1991. pap. text ed. 3.50 (1-56309-012-0, New Hope AL) Womans Mission Union.

Yes! You Can Learn a Foreign Language. Marjory Brown-Azarowicz et al. 128p. 1993. pap. 4.95 (0-8442-9514-0, Natl Textbk) NTC Pub Grp.

Yes, You Can, Little Duck! Nicola Baxter. 14p. (J). 1996. pap. 14.95 (0-689-80781-3, Atheneum S&S) S&S Trade.

Yes You Can! Make Stunning Quilts from Simple Patterns. Judy Martin. (Illus.). 112p. (Orig.). 1992. pap. 6.95 (0-929589-02-5) Crosley-Griffith.

Yes, You Can, Moses! Sandy Brooks. (Happy Day Bks.). (Illus.). 24p. (J). (ps). 1995. pap. 1.99 (0-7847-0355-8, 04235) Standard Pub.

***Yes, You Can Moses!** Standard Publishing Staff. (Happy Day Coloring Bks.). 12p. (J). 1996. pap. 0.99 (0-7847-0434-1, 22204) Standard Pub.

Yes! You Can Own a Piece of the Block. George E. Hill. (Illus.). 91p. (Orig.). 1986. pap. 16.59 (0-9617555-0-4); audio 12.95 (0-9617555-1-2) Fawncrest Assocs.

Yes! You Can Own the Home You Want: You Can Own the Home You Want. Gary W. Eldred. LC 95-1371. 246p. 1995. pap. text ed. 15.95 (0-471-09978-3) Wiley.

Yes! You Can Own the Home You Want: You Can Own the Home You Want. Gary W. Eldred. LC 95-1371. 246p. 1995. text ed. 35.00 (0-471-09946-5) Wiley.

Yes! You Can Stop Smoking: Even If You Don't Want To. large type rev. ed. David C. Jones. Ed. by Derick D. Schermerhorn. 232p. 1995. pap. 11.95 (1-878400-02-9) Dolphin Pub.

Yes, You Can...Draw! Nancy Margulies. Ed. by Diana Rose. (Illus.). 75p. (Orig.). 1991. pap. text ed. 29.95 (0-905553-35-7, Pub. by Accel Lrn Sys UK) Acclrtd Learn.

Yes, You Have to Wipe Your Feet! White House Trivia. Carole Marsh. (Quantum Leap Ser.). (J). 1994. pap. text ed. 19.95 (0-7933-6872-3); lib. bdg. 29.95 (0-7933-6873-1); disk 29.95 (0-7933-6874-X) Gallopade Pub Group.

Yes...But. Ginni D. Snodgrass. Ed. by J. Douglas Watson. 64p. (Orig.). 1987. pap. 3.95 (0-9620410-0-9) GS Enterprise.

Yesh Lanu Llama, Level 1. Varda Cohen et al. (J). 1995. pap. 5.50 (0-87441-492-X); wbk. ed., pap. 3.95 (0-87441-503-9) Behrman.

Yesh Lanu Llama, Level 2. Varda Cohen et al. (J). 1995. pap. 5.50 (0-87441-569-1) Behrman.

Yeshiva University Haggada. Ed. by Steven F. Cohen & Kenneth Brander. 1985. 15.95 (0-88125-098-8) Ktav.

Yeshiva University of New York. Ed. by Jonathan Helfand. LC 89-16915. (Archives of the Holocaust Ser.: Vol. 18). 324p. 1991. text ed. 100.00 (0-8240-5576-4) Garland.

Yeshu Hannosri: For God So Loved the World. Joseph Costa. LC 93-80536. 353p. (Orig.). 1994. pap. 14.95 (1-883333-10-5) Better Lfe Bks.

Yeshua: A Guide to the Real Jesus & the Original Church. Ron Moseley. 224p. 1996. pap. 12.99 (1-884369-26-X, EBED Pubns) McDougal Pubng.

Yeshua: A Model for Moderns. Leonard Swidler. LC 88-61573. 140p. (Orig.). 1988. pap. 8.95 (1-55612-182-2) Sheed & Ward MO.

Yeshua: The Gospel of St. Thomas. Alan D. McNarie. 1993. 21.00 (0-916366-83-9) Pushcart Pr.

***Yeshua: The Name of Jesus Revealed in the Old Testament.** Yacov Rambsel. 173p. pap. 11.95 (0-921714-34-3, Pub. by Frontier Res CN) Spring Arbor Dist.

Yeshua Buddha. Jay G. Williams. LC 78-8789. (Orig.). 1978. pap. 5.95 (0-8356-0515-9, Quest) Theos Pub Hse.

Yesstories. Tim Morse. 192p. 1996. pap. 15.95 (0-312-14453-9) St Martin.

Yester Days I. Bill Adams. (Illus.). 220p. 1992. reprint ed. pap. text ed. 19.95 (0-9634793-0-X) Peoria Jrnl.

Yester Days II. Bill Adams. (Illus.). 211p. 1993. pap. text ed. 19.95 (0-9634793-1-8) Peoria Jrnl.

Yester Days III. Bill Adams. (Illus.). 209p. 1994. pap. text ed. 19.95 (0-9634793-2-6) Peoria Jrnl.

***Yesterday.** Betty S. Scardaville. 205p. (Orig.). 1997. mass mkt. 4.99 (1-55197-750-8, Pub. by Comnwlth Pub CN) Partners Pubs Grp.

Yesterday: A Memoir of a Russian Jewish Family. Miriam S. Zunser. (American Biography Ser.). 274p. 1991. reprint ed. lib. bdg. 69.00 (0-7812-8437-6) Rprt Serv.

***Yesterday: Photographs of the Beatles.** Robert Freeman. 1997. pap. text ed. 12.95 (1-56025-138-7) Thunders Mouth.

Yesterday: The Hampton, McCracken, Longwith, Mabry, & Wells Families. Diana L. Mellen. (Illus.). vi, 324p. (Orig.). 1991. pap. 26.00 (1-55613-505-X) Heritage Bk.

Yesterday - Today & Tomorrow. Douglas Beggs. (Orig.). 1995. pap. write for info. (1-57553-100-3) Watermrk Pr.

Yesterday & Forever. large type ed. Sandra Marton. 1993. reprint ed. lib. bdg. 19.95 (0-263-13198-X, Pub. by Mills & Boon UK) Thorndike Pr.

Yesterday & Today. Larbi Layachi. LC 85-3912. 189p. (Orig.). 1985. 14.00 (0-87685-632-6); pap. 8.50 (0-87685-631-8) Black Sparrow.

Yesterday & Today, signed ed. deluxe ed. Larbi Layachi. LC 85-3912. 189p. (Orig.). 1985. 25.00 (0-87685-633-4) Black Sparrow.

***Yesterday & Today at Luther Burbank Home & Gardens.** Dee Blackman. (Illus.). 36p. (Orig.). 1997. pap. write for info. (0-9637883-2-9) L Burbank Home.

Yesterday & Today in the U. S. A. Intermediate ESL Reader. 2nd ed. Anna H. Live. (Illus.). 288p. (C). 1988. pap. text ed. write for info. (0-318-62497-4) P-H.

Yesterday & Today in USA. 2nd ed. 277p. 1988. pap. text ed. 19.80 (0-13-971888-5) P-H.

Yesterday & Tomorrow. Erin Yorke. 384p. 1987. mass mkt. 3.95 (0-373-97034-X) Harlequin Bks.

Yesterday & Tomorrow: California Women Artists. Ed. by Sylvia Moore. LC 88-63871. (Regional Women Artists Ser.). (Illus.). 378p. (Orig.). 1989. pap. text ed. 15.95 (0-9602476-9-6) Midmarch Arts-WAN.

Yesterday at Kalaupapa - A Photographic History: A Saga of Pain & Joy. Emmett Cahill. (Illus.). 128p. 1991. pap. 18.95 (0-935180-82-6) Mutual Pub HI.

Yesterday: Book One of a Trilogy see Yesterday, Today, & Tomorrow

Yesterday Comes Tomorrow. Rebecca Flanders. 1992. mass mkt. 4.99 (0-373-83247-8, 247) Harlequin Bks.

Yesterday I Dreamed of Dreams. Molly A. Minnick. 25p. 1991. 1.00 (1-878526-10-3) Pineapple MI.

Yesterday I Lost a Sneaker (And Found the Great Goob Sick) David M. McPhail. LC 94-22862. (Illus.). (J). 1995. 13.95 (0-382-24906-2); pap. text ed. 5.95 (0-382-24907-0); lib. bdg. 15.95 (0-382-24905-4) Silver Burdett Pr.

Yesterday I Was Leaving. Tr. by Rich Ives from GER. (Orig.). 1986. pap. 7.00 (0-937669-25-3) Owl Creek Pr.

***Yesterday in Hodunk: Voices from the Michigan Countryside.** Jerry Morton. (Illus.). 96p. 1985. mass mkt. 4.95 (0-9655400-0-6) J Lee Pr.

Yesterday in Oregon: A Pictorial Scrapbook. Edwin D. Culp. LC 90-46636. (Illus.). 1990. pap. 12.95 (0-87004-329-3) Caxton.

Yesterday in Salem: A Collection of Nostalgic Articles. Dale E. Shaffer. (Illus.). 90p. (Orig.). 1986. pap. 4.25 (0-915060-23-X) D E Shaffer.

Yesterday in San Diego. Arthur Ribbel. LC 90-61926. (Illus.). (Orig.). 1990. pap. 8.95 (0-9627384-0-9) Rancho Pr CA.

Yesterday in Santa Fe. Marc Simmons. LC 87-6449. (Illus.). 96p. (Orig.). 1987. pap. 8.95 (0-86534-108-7) Sunstone Pr.

Yesterday in the Hills. Floyd C. Watkins & Charles H. Watkins. LC 82-2642. (Brown Thrasher Bks.). 200p. 1982. reprint ed. pap. 12.95 (0-8203-0623-1) U of Ga Pr.

Yesterday in the Texas Hill Country. Gilbert J. Jordan. LC 78-21774. (Illus.). 192p. 1995. pap. 11.95 (0-89096-657-5) Tex A&M Univ Pr.

Yesterday in Village Church & Churchyard. Donald Gregory. 104p. (C). 1989. 30.00 (0-86383-484-1, Pub. by Gomer Pr UK); pap. 20.00 (0-86383-461-2, Pub. by Gomer Pr UK) St Mut.

***Yesterday Is Gone.** Beverly Clark. 1997. pap. 10.95 (1-885478-12-7) Genesis Press.

Yesterday Is Today. Ruth E. Nelson. 160p. (Orig.). 1994. 8.00 (0-9643648-1-6) R E Nelson.

Yesterday Is Tommorrow & Today Can Be Either: Journeying Into Our Other Dimensions. Timothy J. Cortis & Cynthia L. Garavaglia. 112p. (Orig.). 1995. pap. 11.95 (0-9647399-0-9) Beacon Res Inst.

Yesterday Love. large type ed. Juliet Gray. LC 95-30273. (Nightingale Ser.). 177p. 1996. pap. 17.95 (0-7838-1449-6, GK Hall) Thorndike Pr.

Yesterday Once More. large type ed. (Linford Romance Library). 288p. 1994. pap. 15.99 (0-7089-7506-2, Linford) Ulverscroft.

Yesterday or Tomorrow? Questions of Vision in the Fiction of Robert A. Heinlein. Ed. by Robert Reginald & George E. Slusser. (Starmont Studies in Literary Criticism: No. 5). 160p. 1996. reprint ed. lib. bdg. 19.95 (0-89370-977-8) Borgo Pr.

Yesterday the Children Were Dancing. Gratien Galinas. Tr. by Maror Moore. 76p. reprint ed. pap. 12.95 (0-88784-529-0, Pub. by Hse of Anansi Pr CN) Genl Dist Srvs.

***Yesterday This Hadn't Happened Yet.** Philip W. Case. (Illus.). 175p. 1996. pap. 11.95 (0-9653983-0-7) Sloan Cnslting.

Yesterday to Color at Gunston Hall. Louise Turner. (Illus.). 15p. (Orig.). (J). 1990. pap. 3.95 (1-884085-05-9) Bd Regents.

Yesterday, Today & Forever. Edythe E. Bregnard. (Illus.). 96p. (Orig.). 1978. 6.50 (0-9616565-1-4, TX 641-587); pap. 3.50 (0-9616565-0-6) Pisces Pr AZ.

Yesterday, Today & Forever. Jeane Dixon. 394p. 1987. pap. 8.95 (0-8362-7941-7) Andrews & McMeel.

Yesterday, Today & Forever. Maria Von Trapp. LC 75-32010. 176p. 1975. pap. 4.50 (0-89221-035-4) New Leaf.

Yesterday, Today & Forever: Jesus Christ & the Holy Trinity in the Leading of the Seven Ecumenical Councils. Peter Toon. 224p. 1995. 19.95 (1-886412-06-5); pap. 15.95 (1-886412-05-7) Preserv Press.

***Yesterday, Today & Forever: The Continuing Relevance of the Old Testament.** Larry R. Helyer. 459p. (Orig.). 1996. pap. 19.95 (1-879215-31-4) Sheffield WI.

Yesterday, Today, & Tomomorrow. Leydel J. Willis. Incl. Yesterday: Book One of a Trilogy. 1976. 4.95 (0-685-02116-5); 1976. write for info. (0-318-52991-2) Harlo Pr.

Yesterday, Today, & Tomorrow. Etta J. Dorsey. LC 90-71975. 126p. (Orig.). 1991. pap. 8.00 (1-56002-035-0) Aegina Pr.

Yesterday, Today & Tomorrow: Book Three of a Trilogy. Leydel J. Willis. LC 80-65230. 1980. 8.95 (0-930416-06-6) Clodele.

Yesterday, Today, & Tomorrow: Exploring Contemporary Judaism from the Perspective of Jewish History. Mordechai Katz. LC 93-28277. 1993. 18.95 (0-87306-656-1) Feldheim.

***Yesterday, Today & Tomorrow: Meeting the Challenge of Our Multicultural America & Beyond.** Paul D. Christiansen & Michelle Young. LC 96-30359. 1996. 29.95 (1-880192-18-7) Caddo Gap Pr.

Yesterday, Today & Tomorrow: The Farmer Takes a Hand. rev. ed. Marquis W. Childs. LC 52-5629. 178p. 1980. reprint ed. pap. 2.25 (0-686-28113-6) Natl Rural.

Yesterday, Today, & Tomorrow: Yesterday, Book One of a Trilogy. Leydel J. Willis. 1976. 8.95 (0-8187-0021-1) Clodele.

Yesterday, Today, & Tomorrow, Bk. 2: Today. Leydel J. Willis. (J). (gr. 8-12). 1977. 4.95 (0-8187-0030-0) Harlo Press.

Yesterday, Today & Tomorrow (Today) Book Two of a Trilogy. Leydel J. Willis. 1978. 8.95 (0-930416-04-X) Clodele.

***Yesterday, Today, Tomorrow: A History of Pittston Farm.** Durward J. Ferland, Jr. (Illus.). 62p. (Orig.). 1996. pap. 6.95 (0-9646054-3-0) Moosehead Communs.

Yesterday Was Silent. Chudi Uwazurike. LC 94-65391. (Orig.). 1994. text ed. 29.95 (0-9635245-2-6); pap. text ed. 11.95 (0-9635245-3-4) Sungai Bks.

Yesterday Was Sunday. Marais Duncane. 180p. (Orig.). 1990. pap. 4.50 (0-939551-04-7) Trejos Lit Cnslt.

Yesterday We Saw Mermaids. Esther Friesner. 160p. 1993. mass mkt. 3.99 (0-8125-1345-2) Tor Bks.

***Yesterday Will Make You Cry.** Chester Himes. Date not set. 25.00 (0-393-04577-3) Norton.

Yesterdays. Harold S. Ladoo. 110p. (Orig.). 1974. pap. 4.95 (0-88784-329-8, Pub. by Hse of Anansi Pr CN) Genl Dist Srvs.

Yesterdays: A Collection of Short Stories, Nostalgic Photographs, & Related Programming Materials for Older Adults. Nancy Dezan. 106p. (Orig.). 1995. pap. 30.95 (1-879633-23-X, P211) Eldersong.

Yesterdays: Popular Song in America. Charles Hamm. (Illus.). 560p. 1983. reprint ed. pap. 16.95 (0-393-30062-5) Norton.

Yesterday's Addicts: American Society & Drug Abuse, 1865-1920. H. Wayne Morgan. LC 73-7421. 220p. 1974. pap. 13.95 (0-8061-1636-6) U of Okla Pr.

Yesterday's & Today's Island. Mary Miles. (Illus.). 200p. (Orig.). 1989. pap. write for info. (0-318-65208-0) Yesterdays Island.

Yesterday's Answers: Development & Decline of Schools for Young Offenders. Jim Hyland. 202p. 1994. 55.00 (1-871177-43-X, Pub. by Whiting & Birch UK) Paul & Co Pubs.

Yesterday's Atlanta. Franklin M. Garrett. LC 94-13434. (Illus.). 168p. 1994. reprint ed. pap. 14.95 (0-87797-247-8) Cherokee.

Yesterday's Authors of Books for Children: Facts & Pictures about Authors & Illustrators of Books for Young People, 2 vols., Vol. 1. Ed. by Anne Commire. (Yesterday's Authors of Books for Children Ser.). (Illus.). (YA). (gr. 7-12). 1994. 93.00 (0-8103-0073-7) Gale.

Yesterday's Authors of Books for Children: Facts & Pictures about Authors & Illustrators of Books for Young People, 2 vols., Vol. 2. Ed. by Anne Commire. (Yesterday's Authors of Books for Children Ser.). (Illus.). (YA). (gr. 7-12). 1993. 93.00 (0-8103-0090-7) Gale.

***Yesterday's Bride.** Alison Kelly. 1997. pap. 3.50 (0-373-11903-8, 1-11903-1) Harlequin Bks.

***Yesterday's Bride.** Charlotte Walker. (Intimate Moments Ser.). 1997. 3.99 (0-373-07768-8, 1-07768-4) Silhouette.

Yesterday's Burdens: A Novel. Robert M. Coates. LC 74-23583. (Lost American Fiction Ser.). 275p. 1975. 12.95 (0-8093-0717-0) S Ill U Pr.

Yesterday's Charm: Traditional or Contemporary Techniques for Creating a Masterpiece. Nancy Smith & Lynda S. Milligan. Ed. by Sharon Holmes. (Illus.). 20p. 1992. pap. 8.95 (0-9622477-8-2) Pssblts Denver.

Yesterday's Child. Levitin. LC 96-31649. (J). 1997. 17.00 (0-689-80810-0) S&S Childrens.

Yesterday's Children: The Antiques & History of Childcare. Sally Kevill-Davies. (Illus.). 316p. 1994. pap. 39.50 (1-85149-184-8) Antique Collect.

Yesterday's Daughter. Patricia Calvert. (YA). 1988. pap. 2.75 (0-380-70470-6, Flare) Avon.

Yesterday's Dawn. Theresa Scott. (Hunters of the Ice Age Ser.). 448p. (Orig.). 1994. mass mkt., pap. text ed. 4.99 (0-505-51920-8, Love Spell) Dorchester Pub Co.

Yesterday's Deterrent: Tirpitz & the Birth of the German Battle Fleet. Jonathan Steinberg. (Modern Revivals in History Ser.). 240p. 1993. 61.95 (0-7512-0076-X, Pub. by Gregg Revivals UK) Ashgate Pub Co.

Yesterday's Detroit. Frank Angelo. (Illus.). 160p. (C). 1988. reprint ed. pap. 14.95 (0-9615297-7-6) Four Pr.

Yesterday's Dream. Judy Baer. (Cedar River Daydreams Ser.: Vol. 9). 144p. (Orig.). (YA). (gr. 7-10). 1990. mass mkt. 4.99 (1-55661-142-0) Bethany Hse.

Yesterday's Echoes. large type ed. Penny Jordan. (Harlequin Ser.). 1993. lib. bdg. 19.95 (0-263-13539-X) Thorndike Pr.

Yesterday's Echoes (Presents Plus) Penny Jordan. 1995. mass mkt. 3.25 (0-373-11774-4) Harlequin Bks.

Yesterday's Enemies. William Haggard. 20.95 (0-88411-665-4) Amereon Ltd.

Yesterday's Faces: A Study in the Series Characters in the Early Pulp Magazines: Violent Lives, Vol. 6. Robert Sampson. 297p. (C). 1993. 39.95 (0-87972-614-8); pap. 18.95 (0-87972-615-6) Bowling Green Univ Popular Press.

Yesterday's Faces: A Study of Series Characters in the Early Pulp Magazine: Dangerous Horizons, Vol. 5. Robert Sampson. LC 82-73597. 165p. (C). 1991. 35.95 (0-87972-513-3); pap. 17.95 (0-87972-514-1) Bowling Green Univ Popular Press.

Yesterday's Faces: A Study of Series Characters in the Early Pulp Magazine: From the Dark Side, Vol. 3. Robert Sampson. LC 82-73597. (Illus.). 266p. 1897. 30.95 (0-87972-362-9); pap. 14.95 (0-87972-363-7) Bowling Green Univ Popular Press.

Yesterday's Faces: A Study of Series Characters in the Early Pulp Magazines: Glory Figures, Vol. 1. Robert Sampson. LC 82-73597. 1983. 21.95 (0-87972-217-7); pap. 11.95 (0-87972-218-5) Bowling Green Univ Popular Press.

Yesterday's Faces: A Study of Series Characters in the Early Pulp Magazines: Strange Days, Vol. 2. Robert Sampson. LC 82-73597. 1984. 25.95 (0-87972-262-2) Bowling Green Univ Popular Press.

Yesterday's Faces, a Study of Series Characters in the Early Pulp Magazines: The Solvers, Vol. 4. Robert Sampson. LC 82-73597. (Illus.). 320p. (C). 1987. 36.95 (0-87972-414-5); pap. 18.95 (0-87972-415-3) Bowling Green Univ Popular Press.

***Yesterday's Fires.** large type ed. Kate Kingston. (Magna Large Print Ser.). 319p. 1996. 25.99 (0-7505-1012-9, Pub. by Magna Print Bks UK) Ulverscroft.

Yesterday's Florida Keys. Stan Windhorn & Wright Langley. LC 74-76691. (Seemann's Historic Cities Ser.: No. 12). (Illus.). 128p. 1985. reprint ed. pap. 13.95 (0-911607-00-5) Langley Pr Inc.

***Yesterday's Friends.** Pamela Evans. LC 97-23510. 1997. write for info. (0-7862-1209-8) Thorndike Pr.

***Yesterday's Gold.** Bobby Hutchinson. 368p. (Orig.). 1997. mass mkt. 5.50 (0-8439-4311-4, Leisure Bks) Dorchester Pub Co.

Yesterday's Gower. J. Mansel Thomas. 234p. (C). 1982. pap. 20.00 (0-85088-747-X, Pub. by Gomer Pr UK) St Mut.

Yesterday's Heroes. Natalie J. Prior. (YA). 1995. pap. 11.95 (0-7022-2808-7, Pub. by Univ Queensland Pr AT) Intl Spec Bk.

Yesterday's Heroes: 433 Men of World War II Awarded the Medal of Honor 1941-1945. Kenneth N. Jordan, Sr. 614p. 1996. 35.00 (0-7643-0061-X) Schiffer.

Yesterday's Husband. large type ed. Angela Devine. (Harlequin Romance Ser.). 286p. 1995. 20.95 (0-263-14212-4, Pub. by Mills & Boon UK) Thorndike Pr.

Yesterday's Key West. Stan Windhorn & Wright Langley. LC 73-80596. (Seemann's Historic Cities Ser.). (Illus.). 144p. 1983. reprint ed. pap. 13.95 (0-911607-01-3) Langley Pr Inc.

Yesterday's Kitchen: Jewish Communities & Their Food Before 1939. Ed. by Gillian Burr & Marion Cohen. LC 93-30054. (Illus.). 225p. 1993. text ed. 19.50 (0-85303-264-5, Pub. by Vallentine Mitchell UK) Intl Spec Bk.

Yesterday's Lies. Lisa Jackson. (Western Lovers Ser.). 1995. mass mkt. 3.99 (0-373-88531-8, 1-88531-8) Harlequin Bks.

Yesterday's Lifestyle-Today's Survival: The Life of a Real Ozark Mountain Hillbilly. Dee-Dee McWilliams. (Illus.). 80p. (Orig.). 1983. pap. 7.95 (0-943962-01-3) Viewpoint Pr.

Yesterday's Love. large type ed. Grace Richmond. (Linford Romance Library). 1991. pap. 15.99 (0-7089-7052-4) Ulverscroft.

Yesterday's Love. large type ed. Nina Tinsley. (Linford Romance Library). 320p. 1993. pap. 15.99 (0-7089-7416-3, Linford) Ulverscroft.

Yesterday's Love Song. Jan McDaniel. 192p. 1994. 17.95 (0-8034-9044-5) Bouregy.

Yesterday's Men. George Turner. 224p. 1996. mass mkt. 5.99 (0-380-77886-6, AvoNova) Avon.

Yesterday's Milk Glass Today. 2nd ed. Regis F. Ferson & Mary F. Ferson. (Illus.). 188p. (Orig.). 1981. 45.00 (0-9614006-0-9) Ferson.

Yesterday's Motorcycles. Robert F. Karolevitz. LC 85-81540. (Illus.). 136p. 1986. text ed. 11.95 (0-940161-05-2); pap. text ed. 7.95 (0-940161-02-8) Dakota Homestead Pub.

Yesterday's News: A Novel of Suspense. Jeremiah Healy. Ed. by Jane Chelius. 256p. 1990. reprint ed. mass mkt. 5.50 (0-671-69584-3) PB.

Yesterday's Outlaw. Raye Morgan. (Desire Ser.). 1994. mass mkt. 2.99 (0-373-05836-5, 5-05836-7) Silhouette.

Yesterday's Papers: The Rolling Stones in Print, 1963-1984. Jessica MacPhail. (Rock & Roll Reference Ser.: No. 19). (Illus.). 236p. 1986. 39.50 (0-87650-209-5) Popular Culture.

***Yesterday's Passion.** Cheryl Biggs. 320p. 1996. mass mkt. 2.99 (0-06-108464-6) HarpC.

***Yesterday's People: A Parson's Search for the Answers to Life after Death.** J. Aelwyn Roberts. LC 97-16945. 1997. pap. 12.95 (1-86204-000-1) Element MA.

Yesterday's People: Life in Contemporary Appalachia. Jack E. Weller. LC 65-27012. 184p. 1965. pap. 11.95 (0-8131-0109-3) U Pr of Ky.

Yesterday's Polk County. Louise K. Frisbie. LC 75-44454. (Illus.). 1976. 8.95 (0-912458-64-X) Imperial Pub Co.

Yesterday's Promise. Teresa George. 400p. 1995. mass mkt. 4.99 (0-8217-0128-2, Zebra Kensgtn) Kensgtn Pub Corp.

***Yesterday's Rain.** Billi Caye. 46p. (Orig.). 1997. pap. 6.50 (1-57688-009-5, 80095) Branch & Vine.

Yesterday's Reveille: An Epic of the Seventh Cavalry. Robert Vaughan. 1996. mass mkt. 5.99 (0-312-95694-0) Tor Bks.

Yesterday's River: The Archaeology of Ten Thousand Years along the Tennessee-Tombigbee Waterway. David S. Brose. (Illus.). 160p. (YA). (gr. 10). 1990. pap. 9.75 (1-878600-00-1) Cleve Mus Nat Hist.

Yesterday's Roses. Heather Cullman. 384p. (Orig.). 1995. mass mkt., pap. 4.99 (0-451-40574-9, Topaz) NAL-Dutton.

Yesterday's Rulers: The Making of the British Colonial Service. Robert Heussler. LC 63-8326. (Illus.). 1963. 35.00 (0-8156-0029-1) Syracuse U Pr.

Yesterday's Schools Vol. 1: Public Elementary Education in Prince William County, Virginia 1869-1969. Lucy Phinney. (Illus.). 220p. 1993. 20.00 (0-9612862-9-6) R E F Typesetting Pub.

Yesterday's Science, Today's Technology Series, 6 Vol., Set. Robert Gardner. (Illus.). 96p. (J). (gr. 5-8). 1994. lib. bdg. 101.88 (0-8050-3463-3) TFC Bks NY.

Yesterday's Secrets. Tara T. Quinn. (Superromance Ser.). 1993. mass mkt. 3.50 (0-373-70567-0, 1-70567-2) Harlequin Bks.

Yesterday's Soldiers: European Military Professionalism in South America, 1890-1940. Frederick M. Nunn. LC 82-6961. xiv, 365p. 1983. text ed. 40.00 (0-8032-3305-1) U of Nebr Pr.

Yesterday's Sports, Today's Math. Don Fraser. Ed. by Joan Gideon. (Illus.). 94p. (Orig.). 1996. teacher ed., pap. 13.95 (1-57232-200-4, DS21492) Seymour Pubns.

Yesterday's Stories: Popular Women's Novels of the Twenties & Thirties. Patricia Raub. LC 94-4794. (Contributions in American Studies). 160p. 1994. text ed. 49.95 (0-313-29259-0, Greenwood Pr) Greenwood.

Yesterday's Structure: Bracing Today for Tomorrow. Lonnie Hovey. 1993. pap. 35.00 (1-879304-29-5) AIA DC.

Yesterday's Summer. Leydel J. Willis. 24p. 1984. pap. 5.00 (0-930416-09-0) Clodele.

***Yesterday's Tomorrow: Recovery Meditations for Hard Cases.** L. Barry. LC 97-15767. 1997. write for info. (1-56838-160-3) Hazelden.

Yesterday's Tomorrows. Margaret Lane. 336p. 1995. mass mkt. 4.50 (0-06-108353-4) HarpC.

Yesterday's Tomorrows: Past Visions of the American Future. Joseph J. Corn & Brian Horrigan. (Illus.). 176p. (C). 1996. reprint ed. pap. 24.95 (0-8018-5399-0) Johns Hopkins.

Yesterday's Tomorrows: The Golden Age of Science Fiction Movie Posters. Bruce L. Wright. LC 92-34613. 192p. 1993. 29.95 (0-87833-818-7); pap. 19.95 (0-87833-824-1) Taylor Pub.

***Yesterday's Toys.** Teruhisa Kitahara. 1997. 29.98 (1-884822-95-9) Blck Dog & Leventhal.

Yesterday's Toys & Games. Samuel J. Touchstone. (Illus.). 109p. 1995. pap. text ed. 6.95 (0-914917-18-8) Folk-Life.

Yesterdays Trails. Howard L. Norskog. 35p. (Orig.). 1994. pap. 6.00 (0-9625171-0-0) H L Norskog.

Yesterdays Trails: Cowboy Poetry. Howard L. Norskog. (DNA Ser.). 49p. (YA). (gr. 8 up). 1989. pap. 6.99 (0-685-30410-8) H L Norskog.

***Yesterday's Train: A Rail Odyssey Through Mexican History.** Terry Pindell. 1998. pap. text ed. 14.95 (0-8050-5598-3) H Holt & Co.

Yesterday's Train: A Railway Odessy Through Mexican History. Terry Pindell. 288p. 1997. 30.00 (0-8050-3791-8) H Holt & Co.

***Yesterday's Visions.** Mitchell Ricks. 5p. 1997. 9.95 (1-887750-45-2) Rutledge Bks.

Yesterday's Vows see Promesas del Pasado

***Yesterday's Ways, Tomorrow's Treasures: A Guide to Memory.** Nazarea et al. 50p. (C). 1997. spiral bd. 6.25 (0-7872-3895-3) Kendall-Hunt.

Yesterdays with Actors. Catherine M. Winslow. LC 72-1481. (Essay Index Reprint Ser.). 1977. reprint ed. 20.95 (0-8369-2879-2) Ayer.

Yesterdays with Authors. James T. Fields. (Illus.). 1970. reprint ed. 39.50 (0-404-00603-5) AMS Pr.

Yesterdays with Authors. James T. Fields. (Notable American Authors Ser.). 1992. reprint ed. lib. bdg. 75.00 (0-7812-2836-0) Rprt Serv.

Yesterdays with Authors. James T. Fields. (BCL1-PR English Literature Ser.). 419p. 1992. reprint ed. lib. bdg. 99.00 (0-7812-7051-0) Rprt Serv.

Yesterdays with Authors. James T. Fields. LC 75-108481. (Illus.). 1970. reprint ed. 14.00 (0-403-00209-5) Scholarly.

Yesterdays Yesteryears: The Lesney "Matchbox" Models. Robert Carter & Eddy Rubinstein. (Illus.). 128p. 1987. 39.95 (0-85429-578-X, F578, Pub. by G T Foulis Ltd) Haynes Pubns.

Yesterday's Youth. Leo Gamow. LC 88-71010. 618p. 1988. 21.95 (0-9624480-0-1) Dabarson Pr.

Yesterdaze Kures. Mat Bohannon. LC 91-67745. (Illus.). 64p. 1993. pap. 9.00 (1-56002-146-2, Univ Edtns) Aegina Pr.

Yesteryear. Dorothy Garlock. 384p. (Orig.). 1995. mass mkt. 5.99 (0-446-36371-5) Warner Bks.

***Yesteryear.** Ralph S. Stevens. LC 96-69083. 169p. 1997. 17.95 (1-57197-032-0) Pentland Pr.

Yesteryear. large type ed. Dorothy Garlock. (Americana Ser.). 542p. (Orig.). 1995. 22.95 (0-7862-0542-3) Thorndike Pr.

Yesteryear in Annapolis. Harold N. Burdett. LC 74-26773. (Illus.). 102p. 1974. reprint ed. pap. 29.10 (0-608-02455-4, 2063099) Bks Demand.

Yesteryear in Clark County, Ohio, 2 vols. in one. Ed. by Mary A. Skardon. (Annual Monograph). 76p. 1978. pap. 4.00 (0-686-29091-7) Clark County Hist Soc.

Yesteryears. Muriel R. Kulwin. 124p. 1992. pap. 20.00 (1-889080-01-2) Doublem Bks.

Yesteryears. Lee T. Rector. 117p. 1982. write for info. (0-318-58391-7) Rector Pub.

***Yesteryears: A Pictorial History of Stark County, Ohio.** Ruth H. Basner. LC 96-28363. 1996. write for info. (0-89865-973-6) Donning Co.

Yesteryear's Child: Golden Days & Summer Nights. Phoebe L. Westwood & Richard W. Rohrbacher. LC 93-77688. 176p. (YA). (gr. 10). 1993. pap. 11.95 (0-9623048-7-5) Heritage West.

Yesteryears of Green Oak, Eighteen Thirty to Nineteen Thirty. Green Oak Township Historical Society Staff. LC 81-2270. (Illus.). xii, 338p. 1981. 25.00 (0-936792-00-0) Green Oak Township.

Yesteryears of Hot Springs, North Carolina. Della H. Moore. (Illus.). 150p. (Orig.). 1995. lib. bdg. write for info. (0-9642625-1-7) D H Moore.

Yet. Cid Corman. 1974. pap. 6.00 (0-685-40886-8) Elizabeth Pr.

Yet. deluxe ed. Cid Corman. 1974. pap. 8.00 (0-685-40887-6) Elizabeth Pr.

Yet Another Introduction to Analysis. Victor W. Bryant. (Illus.). 256p. (C). 1990. text ed. 69.95 (0-521-38166-5); pap. text ed. 24.95 (0-521-38835-X) Cambridge U Pr.

Yet I Weep, Yet I Joy. Salvatore Cipparone. 4.95 (0-686-20578-2) Ivory Scroll.

Yet She Must Die. large type ed. Stella Phillips. (Linford Mystery Library). 352p. 1993. pap. 15.99 (0-7089-7343-4, Linford) Ulverscroft.

Yet Still We Rise: African American Art in Cleveland 1920-1970. Samuel W. Black et al. Ed. by Ursula Korneitchouk. (Illus.). 90p. (Orig.). (C). 1996. pap. text ed. write for info. (0-9639562-4-8) Clevelnd Art.

Yet with a Steady Beat: The African American Struggle for Recognition in the Episcopal Church. Harold T. Lewis. LC 95-46837. (Illus.). 264p. (Orig.). (C). 1995. pap. 20.00 (1-56338-130-3) TPI PA.

Yeti: The Abominable Snowman of the Silent Snows of the Himalayas. M. Majapuria. (C). 1993. 40.00 (0-7855-0223-8, Pub. by Ratna Pustak Bhandar) St Mut.

Yeti, Abominable Snowman of the Himalayas. Elaine Landau. LC 92-35147. (Mysteries of Science Ser.). (Illus.). 48p. (J). (gr. 3-6). 1993. lib. bdg. 15.40 (1-56294-349-9) Millbrook Pr.

Yettele's Feathers. Joan Rothenberg. LC 94-26623. (Illus.). 40p. (J). (ps-3). 1996. pap. 4.95 (0-7868-1149-8) Hyprn Child.

Yettele's Feathers. large type ed. Joan Rothenberg. LC 94-26623. (Illus.). 40p. (J). (ps-3). 1995. 14.95 (0-7868-0097-6); lib. bdg. 14.89 (0-7868-2081-0) Hyprn Child.

Yetzer: A Kabbalistic Psychology on Eroticism & Human Sexuality. Mordechai Rotenberg. LC 96-33126. 208p. 1997. pap. 30.00 (1-56821-898-2) Aronson.

Yeux Baissees. Tahar B. Jelloun. (FRE.). 1992. pap. 16.95 (0-7859-2726-3) Fr & Eur.

***Yeux d'Emeraude.** Denis Cote. (Novels in the Roman Jeunesse Ser.). 96p. (FRE.). (J). (gr. 4-7). 1996. pap. 7.95 (2-89021-165-7, Pub. by Les Editions CN) Firefly Bks Ltd.

Yeux Plus Gros Que le Ventre. Jim Davis. (Garfield Ser.). (FRE.). (J). 1985. 18.95 (0-8288-4590-5, F91520) Fr & Eur.

Yevgeny Onegin. rev. ed. Aleksandr Pushkin. Ed. by A. D. Briggs. Tr. by Oliver Elton. (Everyman Paperback Classics Ser.). 272p. (C). 1995. pap. 7.95 (0-460-87595-7, Everyman's Classic Lib) C E Tuttle.

Yevgeny Yevtushenko: Selected Poetry. Ed. by R. R. Milner-Gulland. 1963. 6.70 (0-08-009808-8, Pergamon Pr); pap. 5.15 (0-08-009807-X, Pergamon Pr) Elsevier.

***Yevreyskaya Autonomous Oblast: Economy, Industry, Government, Business.** 2nd rev. ed. Russian Information & Business Center, Inc. Staff. (Russian Regional Business Directories Ser.). (Illus.). 200p. 1997. pap. 99.00 (1-57751-432-7) Russ Info & Busn Ctr.

Yew Tree: A Thousand Whispers. Hal Hartzell, Jr. (Illus.). 320p. (Orig.). (C). 1991. pap. 19.95 (0-938493-14-0) Hulogosi Inc.

Yewka & the Two Pear Trees: A Family Story. Sophie O. Cox. (Illus.). 24p. (YA). (gr. 7-12). 1995. spiral bd. 15.00 (0-9641138-1-3) Beach Pebbles.

Yezidis: A Study in Survival. John S. Guest. (Illus.). 220p. 1986. 42.50 (0-7103-0115-4, 01154) Routledge Chapman & Hall.

Yezidis: The Devil Worshippers of the Middle East; Their Beliefs & Sacred Books. Alphonse Mingana. 1995. pap. 5.95 (1-55818-231-4, Sure Fire) Holmes Pub.

Yezidism-Its Background, Observances & Textual Tradition. Philip Kreyenbroek. LC 94-23547. (Texts & Studies in Religion: No. 62). 368p. 1995. text ed. 99.95 (0-7734-9004-3) E Mellen.

Yhantishor: A Fantasy Based in Truth. Daniel S. Johnson. LC 88-51542. (Illus.). 222p. (Orig.). 1989. pap. 12.95 (0-922848-07-6) Mystic Garden.

YHWH: Divine Language & Electricity. Jerry Ziegler. 161p. 1977. pap. 8.00 (0-940268-29-9) Metron Pubns.

***YHWH Is the Husband of His People: Analysis of a Biblical Metaphor with Special Reference to Translation.** Nelly Stienstra. 252p. 1993. pap. 35.75 (90-390-0103-0, Pub. by KOK Pharos NE) Eisenbrauns.

YHWH's Combat with the Sea: A Canaanite Tradition in the Religion of Ancient Israel. Carola Kloos. 243p. 1986. pap. 60.25 (90-04-08096-1) E J Brill.

Yi Jing. Tr. by Jing-Nuan Wu from CHI. 344p. (C). 1991. text ed. 32.00 (0-8248-1362-6) UH Pr.

Yi Shi Gui Ze Gai Lun-An Introduction to Parliamentary Procedures. Tian Xie. 70p. (CHI.). 1993. pap. 16.00 (0-9638798-0-4) Cresco.

Yiddish: A Survey & a Grammar. Salomo A. Birnbaum. LC 80-480492. (Illus.). 415p. reprint ed. pap. 118.30 (0-8357-6357-9, 2035711) Bks Demand.

Yiddish: An Introduction to the Language, Literature & Culture. Sheva Zucker. LC 94-3551. 1995. 19.95 (0-88125-500-9) Ktav.

Yiddish: Turning to Life. Joshua A. Fishman. LC 91-7243. xii, 522p. 1991. 124.00 (1-55619-111-1); pap. 37.95 (1-55619-450-1) Benjamins North Am.

Yiddish American Popular Songs from 1895-1950: A Catalog Based on the Lawrence Marwick Roster of Copyright Entries. Irene Heskes. LC 92-6519. 527p. 1992. 44.00 (0-16-036180-X) Lib Congress.

Yiddish-American Popular Songs, 1895 to 1950: A Chronological List with Annotations. 1993. lib. bdg. 299.95 (0-8490-8931-X) Gordon Pr.

Yiddish American Popular Songs, 1895-1950, 2 vols., Set. 1994. lib. bdg. 495.00 (0-8490-5720-5) Gordon Pr.

Yiddish & English: A Century of Yiddish in America. Sol Steinmetz. LC 84-16201. 185p. 1986. pap. 52.80 (0-7837-8408-2, 2059219) Bks Demand.

Yiddish Are Coming. Robyn Cohen & Robyn Rousso. LC 94-77583. (Illus.). 56p. 1994. pap. 8.95 (1-56352-169-5) Longstreet Pr Inc.

Yiddish As a Language of the People. Moshe Perlman. 17.85 (0-317-58555-X) P-H.

Yiddish Catalog & Authority File of the YIVO Library: YIVO Institute for Jewish Research, New York, 5 vols., Set. (Catalog Ser.). 3600p. 1990. 950.00 (0-8161-0493-X) G K Hall.

Yiddish Cuisine: A Gourmet's Approach to Jewish Cooking. Robert Sternberg. LC 93-14848. 368p. 1993. 39.95 (0-87668-156-9) Aronson.

Yiddish Cuisine: A Gourmet's Approach to Jewish Cooking. Robert Sternberg. LC 93-14848. 368p. 1995. pap. 30.00 (1-56821-709-9) Aronson.

Yiddish Dictionary Sourcebook. Herman Galvin. 1983. 29.50 (0-87068-715-8) Ktav.

Yiddish-English - English-Yiddish Practical Dictionary. 3rd rev. ed. David Gross. (Practical Dictionaries Ser.). 215p. (ENG & YID.). 1996. pap. 9.95 (0-7818-0439-6) Hippocrene Bks.

Yiddish-English Dictionary. 35.00 (0-87559-193-0) Shalom.

Yiddish-English-Hebrew Dictionary. 2nd enl. ed. Alexander Harkavy. xlv, 583p. (HEB & YID.). 1988. reprint ed. 30.00 (0-914512-49-8) Yivo Inst.

Yiddish-English-Hebrew Dictionary. Ed. by Alexander Harkavy. LC 86-31414. 624p. 1988. reprint ed. 35.00 (0-8052-4027-6) Schocken.

Yiddish Film. R. Gordon. 1977. lib. bdg. 59.95 (0-8490-2851-5) Gordon Pr.

Yiddish Folktales. Ed. by Beatrice S. Weinreich. Tr. by Leonard Wolf. LC 88-42594. (Fairy Tale & Folklore Library). (Illus.). 448p. 1990. pap. 18.00 (0-679-73097-4) Pantheon.

Yiddish Folktales. Ed. by Beatrice S. Weinreich. Tr. by Leonard Wolf. LC 88-42594. (Illus.). 413p. 1988. 21.95 (0-394-54618-0) Yivo Inst.

***Yiddish Folktales.** Beatrice S. Weinreich. 1997. pap. 18.00 (0-8052-1090-3) Schocken.

Yiddish in America: Social & Cultural Foundations. Milton Doroshkin. LC 72-78612. (Illus.). 281p. 1975. 38.50 (0-8386-7453-4) Fairleigh Dickinson.

Yiddish in America: Socio-Linguistic Description & Analysis. Joshua A. Fishman. LC 65-63395. (General Publications: Vol. 36). (Orig.). 1965. pap. text ed. 18.00 (0-87750-110-6) Res Inst Inner Asian Studies.

Yiddish Linguistics: A Classified Bilingual Index of Yiddish Serials & Collections, 1913-1958. David M. Bunis & Andrew Sunshine. LC 93-34051. 216p. 1994. reprint ed. text ed. 15.00 (0-8240-9758-0, H175) Garland.

Yiddish Literature, 10 Vols., No. I. Ed. by R. Grodon. 1986. lib. bdg. 975.95 (0-8490-3856-1) Gordon Pr.

Yiddish Literature, 10 Vols., No. II. Ed. by R. Gordon. 1986. lib. bdg. 975.00 (0-8490-3857-X) Gordon Pr.

Yiddish Literature, 10 Vols., No. III. Ed. by R. Gordon. 1986. lib. bdg. 950.95 (0-8490-3858-8) Gordon Pr.

Yiddish Literature, 10 Vols., No. IV. Ed. by R. Gordon. 1986. lib. bdg. 975.00 (0-8490-3859-6) Gordon Pr.

Yiddish Matthew. Tr. by Henry Einspruch. 85p. (YID.). 1964. pap. 3.95 (1-880226-03-0) M J Pubs.

Yiddish Melodies in Swing: A Century of Klezmer Music in America 1895-1995. Henry Sapoznik. 300p. 1998. 30.00 (0-02-864574-X, Hall Reference) Macmillan.

Yiddish Music: An Annotated Catalogue. 1991. lib. bdg. 79.95 (0-8490-5202-5) Gordon Pr.

Yiddish Parody: Twas the Last Night of Hanukkah. Daniel Bloom. (Illus.). 52p. 1988. pap. 5.95 (0-933503-93-8) Sure Seller.

Yiddish Press: An Americanizing Agency. Mordecai Soltes. LC 75-89237. (American Education: Its Men, Institutions, & Ideas. Series 1). 1977. reprint ed. 18.95 (0-405-01474-0) Ayer.

Yiddish Scientific Institute Historishe Shriftn. Ed. by Yiddish Scientific Institute, Warsaw Staff. 1977. lib. bdg. 132.95 (0-8490-2852-3) Gordon Pr.

Yiddish Song Favorites. 1994. 16.95 (0-8256-1419-8, AM92051) Omnibus NY.

Yiddish Tales. Ed. by Moses Rischin. Tr. by Helena Frank from YID. LC 74-29531. (Modern Jewish Experience Ser.). 1975. reprint ed. 52.95 (0-405-06755-0) Ayer.

Yiddish Teacher. rev. ed. Hyman E. Goldin. 144p. 1977. pap. 7.50 (0-88482-687-2) Hebrew Pub.

Yiddish Theater in America: David's Violin (1897) & Shloyme Gorgl (189-) Ed. by Mark Slobin. LC 93-46076. (Nineteenth-Century American Musical Theater Ser.: No. 11). (Illus.). 200p. 1994. text ed. 80.00 (0-8153-1381-0) Garland.

Yiddish Theatre & Jacob P. Adler. rev. ed. Lulla A. Rosenfeld. LC 86-29677. (Illus.). 408p. 1988. 11.95 (0-933503-26-1) Sure Seller.

Yiddish Trojan Women. Carole Braverman. 1996. pap. 5.25 (0-8222-1536-5) Dramatists Play.

Yiddish Wisdom - Yiddishe Chochma. Illus. by Kristina Swarner. LC 95-41292. 60p. (ENG & YID.). 1996. 9.95 (0-8118-1202-2) Chronicle Bks.

Yiddishe Kinder Alef. 3rd ed. Joseph Mlotek. 128p. 1985. pap. 5.00 (0-318-22116-0) Workmen's Circle.

Yiddishe Kinder Beyz. Joseph Mlotek & Matis Olitsky. 120p. 1975. pap. 5.00 (0-318-22117-9) Workmen's Circle.

Yiddishe Kinder Giml. S. Efron & Yudel Mark. 271p. 1985. pap. 6.00 (0-318-22118-7) Workmen's Circle.

***Yiddishe Kup Dictionary.** Ken Abel. 64p. (Orig.). 1997. pap. 4.95 (0-944214-13-4) ABELexpress.

***Yidish af Yidish: Grammatical Lexical, & Conversational Materials for the Second & Third Years of Study.** David Goldberg. (Language Ser.). (Illus.). 296p. 1996. 35.00 (0-300-06414-4) Yale U Pr.

***Yield & Nutritional Value of the Commercially More Important Fish Species.** 192p. 1989. 25.00 (92-5-102870-2, F8702, Pub. by FAO IT) Bernan Associates.

Yield & Reliability in Microwave Circuit & System Design. Michael D. Meehan & John Purviance. LC 92-27018. (Microwave Library). 243p. (C). 1992. text ed. 59.00 (0-89006-527-6) Artech Hse.

Yield & Variability Optimization of Integrated Circuits. J. C. Zhang & M. A. Styblinski. LC 94-44624. 256p. (C). 1995. lib. bdg. 107.50 (0-7923-9551-4) Kluwer Ac.

Yield Curve Analysis: The Fundamentals of Risk & Return. Livingston G. Douglas. 1988. 65.00 (0-13-972456-7) NY Inst Finance.

Yield Curve Estimation & Interpretation. Nicola Anderson et al. LC 95-43597. (Series in Financial Economics & Quantitative Analysis). 1996. text ed. 75.00 (0-471-96207-4) Wiley.

Yield Curves for Gilt-Edged Stocks: A New Model. Katerina Mastronikola. (Bank of England. Discussion Papers. Technical Ser.: No. 49). 40p. reprint ed. pap. 25.00 (0-7837-3208-2, 2043204) Bks Demand.

Yield Formation in the Main Field Crops. J. Petr et al. (Developments in Crop Science Ser.: No. 13). 336p. 1988. 160.00 (0-444-98954-4) Elsevier.

Yield Management: Applications to Air Transport & Other Service Industries. Sylvain Daudel et al. 150p. 1994. pap. 39.00 (2-908537-10-9, Pub. by Inst Air Transport FR) Bks Intl VA.

***Yield of Douglas Fir in Pacific NW.** McArdle. pap. 4.95 (0-88246-023-4) Oreg St U Bkstrs.

Yield on Insured Residential Mortgages. Anthony J. Curley & Jack M. Guttentag. (Explorations in Economic Research One Ser.: No. 1). 48p. 1974. reprint ed. 35.00 (0-685-61370-4) Natl Bur Econ Res.

Yielded Life: A Spiritual Journey. Sheila Buonaiuto. 168p. 1994. pap. 6.95 (1-884369-11-1, Serenity Bks) McDougal Pubng.

Yielding: Prayers for Those in Need of Hope. William J. O'Malley. LC 91-76677. 176p. (Orig.). 1992. pap. 7.95 (0-89243-422-8) Liguori Pubns.

Yielding Time. large type ed. Sally Shaw. (Linford Romance Library). 224p. 1987. pap. 8.95 (0-7089-6369-2, Linford) Ulverscroft.

Yielding to the Holy Spirit. Dennis Burke. 80p. 1993. mass mkt. 4.99 (0-89274-468-5, HH-468) Harrison Hse.

Yielding to the Power of God. Ann Shields. 46p. 1990. pap. 2.95 (0-940535-37-8, UP137) Franciscan U Pr.

Yields on Corporate Debt Directly Placed. Avery B. Cohan. (General Ser.: No. 84). 202p. 1967. reprint ed. 52.50 (0-87014-472-3) Natl Bur Econ Res.

YIG Resonators & Filters. fac. ed. Joseph Helszajn. LC 84-17308. (Illus.). 250p. 1985. reprint ed. pap. 71.30 (0-608-00959-8, 2061807) Bks Demand.

Yikes! In Seven Wild Adventures, Who Would You Be? Alison Lester. (Illus.). 32p. (J). (ps-3). 1995. 14.95 (0-395-71252-1) HM.

***Yikes: Your Body up Close.** Mike Janulewicz. (J). 1997. 15.00 (0-689-81520-4) S&S Childrens.

Yikes! It's Another Birthday! Fred Sahner. Ed. by Cliff Carle. 1996. pap. 5.95 (1-57644-004-4) CCC Pubns.

Yimas Language of New Guinea. William A. Foley. LC 91-17261. (Illus.). 512p. 1991. 59.50 (0-8047-1582-3) Stanford U Pr.

Yin: New Poems. Carolyn Kizer. 1984. pap. 10.00 (0-918526-45-0) BOA Edns.

Yin & Yang: Two Hands Clapping. John W. Garvy, Jr. Ed. by Jeremiah Liebermann. (Five Phase Energetics Ser.: No. 2). (Illus.). 1985. pap. 6.00 (0-943450-01-2) Wellbeing Bks.

***Yin & Yang of American Values: Reimagining Our National Character.** Eun Y. Kim. 208p. 1998. 20.00 (1-56836-206-4) Kodansha.

XYZ

Yin & Yang of Astrology. Elizabeth Greenwood. 144p. 1991. 17.00 (*0-86690-402-6*, G3203-014) Am Fed Astrologers.
Yin & Yang Patterns: Asian Art Motifs from Korea. Weatherhill Staff. 1994. 40.00 (*89-7059-004-8*, Pub. by Ahn Graphics KN) Weatherhill.
Yin & Yang the Inner Story. Bernice Kentner. (Illus.). 40p. 1988. spiral bd. 7.95 (*0-941522-04-0*) Ken Kra Pubs.

Yin & Yang Universes. James Carter. (Illus.). 256p. (Orig.). 1996. pap. 27.00 (*0-9636592-2-7*) Absolute Motion.
The ancient metaphysical principle of Yin & Yang is used in a new & imaginative way to probe & question the fundamental concepts of physics & cosmology. The Yin & Yang dichotomy is a very powerful conceptual tool that is able to reveal the many mysteries & paradoxes of physics. At each level of reality, from its ultimate beginning before the big bang to the study of human interactions this dynamic principle elucidates even the most difficult problems by conceptually dividing them into a dichotomy of their yin & yang components. Even the most perplexing issues of science such as the Uncertainty principle, the Equivalence principle, & the speed of light can be easily understood when viewed from their Yin & Yang aspects. Dark Matter, Quasars, Antimatter, The Big Bang, Black Holes, Wave-Particle Duality, Space Travel, & Gravity all fit precisely into this cosmic jigsaw puzzle of Existence. See how these ancient truths can teach even the old dogs some new tricks. Order from Absolute Motion, 29500 Green River Gorge Rd., Enumclaw, WA 98022, FAX 360-886-2454. ***Publisher Provided Annotation.***

Yin Chih Wen: The Tract of the Quiet Way. Yin Chih Wen. Tr. by Teitaro Suzuki & Paul Carus from CHI. LC 78-70142. reprint ed. 29.50 (*0-404-17415-9*) AMS Pr.
Yin Deficiency & Yin-Yang: Index of New Information & Research Guide. Helena R. Rathman. 150p. 1994. 44.50 (*0-7883-0106-3*); pap. 39.50 (*0-7883-0107-1*) ABBE Pubs Assn.
***Yin for Change: Awakening Imagination for More Life in Your Living.** Sonny Brewer. 134p. (Orig.). 1996. pap. 9.95 (*0-9643727-1-1*) Over the Transom.
Yin Jiaqi & China's Struggle for Democracy. Ed. by David Bachman & Dali L. Yang. Tr. by Dali L. Yang from CHI. LC 90-9051. (Chinese Studies on China). 240p. (C). (gr. 13). 1991. text ed. 67.95 (*0-87332-780-2*); pap. text ed. 30.95 (*0-87332-781-0*) M E Sharpe.
Yin-Sloth Jungles. Kevin Siembieda & Patrick Nowak. Ed. by James Osten et al. (Palladium RPG Ser.: Vol. 7). (Illus.). 160p. (Orig.). 1994. pap. 15.95 (*0-916211-81-9*, 459) Palladium Bks.
Yin-Yang Butterfly: Ancient Chinese Sexual Secrets for Western Lovers. Valentin Chu. 272p. 1994. pap. 15.95 (*0-87477-778-X*, Tarcher Putnam) Putnam Pub Group.
yIndices I-IV Continens see Gospel According to Mother Goose
Ying-Ling Does Mitzvot. Neva Goldstein-Alpern. (Judaica Board Bks.). (Illus.). 12p. (J). (ps-2). 1987. 4.95 (*0-910818-72-X*) Judaica Pr.
Yip Harburg Songbook. CPP Belwin Staff. 1994. pap. 16.95 (*0-89898-555-2*, P1024SMX) Warner Brothers.
***Yippee-Yay! A Book about Cowboys & Cowgirls.** Gail Gibbons. LC 97-6113. (Illus.). (J). 1998. write for info. (*0-316-30944-3*) Little.
Yir-Yoront Lexicon: Sketch & Dictionary of an Australian Language. Barry Alpher. LC 91-32572. (Trends in Linguistics, Documentation Ser.: No. 6). xii, 795p. (C). 1991. lib. bdg. 229.25 (*3-11-012682-6*) Mouton.
Yira Yira Tango for Advanced Dancers. (Ballroom Dance Ser.). 1986. lib. bdg. 75.00 (*0-8490-3297-0*) Gordon Pr.
Yira Yira Tango for Advanced Dancers. (Ballroom Dance Ser.). 1985. lib. bdg. 60.00 (*0-87700-751-9*) Revisionist Pr.
Yirrkala Community School - Case Study. Ed. by Deakin University Press Staff. (C). 1985. 24.00 (*0-7300-0316-7*, Pub. by Deakin Univ AT); 111.00 (*0-685-57278-1*, Pub. by Deakin Univ AT) St Mut.
Yishuv in the Shadow of the Holocaust: Zionist Politics & Rescue Aliya, 1933-1939. Abraham J. Edelheit. 347p. (C). 1996. text ed. 69.95 (*0-8133-3039-4*) Westview.
Yitzhak Rabin: Israel's Soldier Statesman. Michael G. Kort. (Illus.). 176p. (YA). (gr. 7 up). 1996. pap. 8.95 (*0-7613-0135-6*); lib. bdg. 17.90 (*0-7613-0100-3*) Millbrook Pr.
Yitzhak Rabin Remembered, 1922-1995. Dove Books Staff. 176p. 1996. pap. 29.95 (*0-7871-1117-1*, Dove Bks) Dove Audio.
Yitzhak Rabin 1922-1995. Dov B. Ben Meir. Ed. by Henry Nijk & Stephen Bagish. (Illus.). 191p. 1996. 24.95 (*0-9652606-0-7*) Syndicated Intl.
Yitzy & the G.O.L.E.M. Sholem Cohen. (Yitz Berg from Pittsburgh Ser.). 128p. (J). (gr. 4-8). 1992. pap. text ed. 6.95 (*0-922613-50-8*) Hachai Pubns.
Yivaraich Es Hanorim. Shlomo Cohen. 250p. (C). 1990. text ed. 15.00 (*0-9626586-0-X*) Sheldon Cohen.
Yivo. annuals Ed. by Deborah D. Moore. 536p. 1996. text ed. 69.95 (*0-8101-0933-6*) Northwestern U Pr.
YIVO Annual, Vol. 22. Ed. by Deborah D. Moore. 300p. 1994. 49.95 (*0-8101-1196-9*) Northwestern U Pr.
Yizkor Prayers, Memorial Service. large type ed. Ed. by Pearl N. Wadler. (ENG & HEB.). (*0-318-65996-4*) Jewish Braille Inst.
Ylides & Imines of Phosphorus. A. William Johnson et al. LC 92-39601. 624p. 1993. text ed. 98.00 (*0-471-52217-1*) Wiley.
Ylla's Cats. Ylla. 1990. 17.25 (*0-8446-6408-1*) Peter Smith.
Ylla's Cats: Eighty-Five Photographs. Ylla, pseud. 80p. 1988. reprint ed. pap. 5.95 (*0-486-25615-4*) Dover.
YMCA Community Development. 56p. (Orig.). 1991. text ed., spiral bd. 16.00 (*0-87322-344-6*, 5147, YMCA USA) Human Kinetics.
YMCA Exercise Instructor Manual. YMCA of the U. S. A. Staff. LC 94-45137. (Illus.). 216p. 1995. spiral bd. 26.00 (*0-87322-884-7*, Y5280, YMCA USA) Human Kinetics.
YMCA Family Time. YMCA of The U.S.A. Staff. (Illus.). 112p. 1996. spiral bd. 35.00 (*0-88011-586-6*, Y5310, YMCA USA) Human Kinetics.
YMCA Gymnastics. 3rd rev. ed. LC 90-46979. (Illus.). 58p. 1991. spiral bd. 25.00 (*0-87322-310-1*, 5107, YMCA USA) Human Kinetics.
YMCA Healthy Back Book. Patricia Sammann. LC 93-31736. 120p. 1994. pap. 11.95 (*0-87322-629-1*, PYMC0629) Human Kinetics.
YMCA Healthy Back Program Instructor's Guide. YMCA for USA Staff. (Illus.). 72p. 1994. spiral bd. 20.00 (*0-87322-717-4*, Y5267, YMCA USA) Human Kinetics.
YMCA Infant-Toddler Child Care. YMCA of the U. S. A. Staff. 160p. 1990. ring bd. 55.00 (*0-87322-280-6*, LYMC5057, YMCA USA) Human Kinetics.
YMCA Membership Retention: A Project of the Urban Group Marketing Task Force. YMCA of the U. S. A. Staff. 392p. 1988. ring bd. 64.00 (*0-87322-184-2*, 4958, YMCA USA) Human Kinetics.
YMCA Personnel & Salary Administration Plan. 3rd ed. Ed. by Earl Armstrong. LC 89-7550. 248p. 1989. ring bd. 64.00 (*0-87322-261-X*, 5043, YMCA USA) Human Kinetics.
YMCA Pool Operations Manual. 2nd ed. Ralph L. Johnson. LC 93-38999. 145p. 1993. pap. text ed. 21.00 (*0-87322-656-9*, Y5229, YMCA USA) Human Kinetics.
YMCA Prenatal Exercise Instructor Guide. YMCA of The U.S.A. Staff. LC 94-44689. (Illus.). 112p. 1995. ring bd. 34.00 (*0-87322-825-1*, Y5270, YMCA USA) Human Kinetics.
YMCA Preschool Age Child Care. 2nd ed. YMCA of The U.S.A. Staff. LC 95-2203. (Illus.). 248p. 1995. ring bd. 70.00 (*0-87322-891-X*, Y5273, YMCA USA) Human Kinetics.
YMCA Preschool Age Child Care Manual. 152p. 1987. ring bd. 51.00 (*0-87322-093-5*, 4882, YMCA USA) Human Kinetics.
YMCA Preschool Movement & Health Program. YMCA of the U. S. A. Staff et al. (Illus.). 160p. (Orig.). 1991. spiral bd. 47.00 (*0-87322-312-8*, 5093, YMCA USA) Human Kinetics.
YMCA Progressive Swimming Instructor's Guide. YMCA of the U. S. A. Staff. 120p. (Orig.). pap. text ed. 16.00 (*0-87322-057-9*, LYMC5162, YMCA USA) Human Kinetics.
YMCA Risk Management Program. YMCA of the U. S. A. Staff. 84p. 1983. pap. text ed. 13.50 (*0-88035-059-8*, 4571, YMCA USA) Human Kinetics.
YMCA School Age Child Care. 208p. 1982. ring bd. 62.00 (*0-88035-006-7*, 4468, YMCA USA) Human Kinetics.
YMCA School Age Child Care, Vol. II. 248p. 1992. ring bd. 64.00 (*0-87322-346-2*, 5134, YMCA USA) Human Kinetics.
***YMCA Splash.** (Illus.). 64p. (Orig.). 1997. pap. text ed. write for info. (*0-88011-742-7*, Y5328, YMCA USA) Human Kinetics.
***YMCA Triathlon Director's Manual.** Colleen Gibler & Young Men's Christian Association Staff. 72p. (Orig.). 1997. pap. text ed., spiral bd. write for info. (*0-88011-768-0*, YMCA USA) Human Kinetics.
YMCA Walk Reebok Instructor's Manual. YMCA of The U.S.A. Staff. (Illus.). 184p. 1996. spiral bd. 49.00 (*0-88011-543-2*, Y5281, YMCA USA) Human Kinetics.
YMCA Wellness Notebook. (Illus.). 1983. ring bd. 20.00 (*0-88035-043-1*, Y4514, YMCA USA) Human Kinetics.
YMCA Youth Fitness Program. Katherine T. Thomas et al. LC 90-30509. (Illus.). 616p. 1990. ring bd. 70.00 (*0-87322-292-X*, LYMC5059, YMCA USA) Human Kinetics.
YMCA Youth Fitness Test Manual. B. Don Franks. LC 89-33612. (Illus.). 72p. 1989. pap. text ed. 12.00 (*0-87322-263-6*, LFRA5048, YMCA USA) Human Kinetics.
YMCA Youth Sports Administrator's Manual. YMCA of the U. S. A. Staff. LC 89-28260. (Illus.). 152p. 1990. ring bd. 45.00 (*0-87322-279-2*, 5061, YMCA USA) Human Kinetics.
YMCA Youth Sports Director's Manual. 2nd ed. YMCA of The U.S.A. Staff. 192p. 1994. ring bd. 45.00 (*0-87322-790-5*, Y5264, YMCA USA) Human Kinetics.
YMINLA? (Why Am I in LA?) A PL8SPK Book. Daniel Nussbaum. LC 95-51768. (Illus.). 96p. 1996. pap. 11.00 (*0-06-258611-4*) Harper SF.
Ynamine: A Versatile Tool in Organic Synthesis. Ed. by Jacqueline Ficini. 38p. 1976. pap. 15.50 (*0-08-020466-X*, Pergamon Pr) Elsevier.
Ynez Johnston. Gerald Nordland. LC 95-80817. (Illus.). 120p. 1996. 40.00 (*0-9628514-9-3*) Grassfield Pr.
Yngling in Yamato. John Dalmas. (Orig.). 1994. mass mkt. 5.99 (*0-671-87634-1*) Baen Bks.
Yngwie Malmsteen: Eclipse. (Recorded Versions - Guitar Ser.). 118p. 1991. pap. 19.95 (*0-7935-0313-2*, 00660174) H Leonard.
Yntema: Family of Hessel P. Yntema, Frisian Immigrant to Michigan, 1847. Mary E. Yntema. 72p. 1994. reprint ed. pap. 15.00 (*0-8328-4250-8*); reprint ed. lib. bdg. 25.00 (*0-8328-4249-4*) Higginson Bk Co.
Yntema - Family of Hessel P. Yntema, Frisian Immigrant to Michigan, 1847. Mary E. Yntema. 72p. 1994. reprint ed. pap. 15.00 (*0-8328-4510-8*); reprint ed. lib. bdg. 25.00 (*0-8328-4509-4*) Higginson Bk Co.
Yo! Julia Alvarez. LC 96-24611. 322p. 1997. 18.95 (*1-56512-157-0*) Algonquin Bks.
***Yo.** Julia Alvarez. 1997. pap. 11.95 (*0-452-27918-6*, Plume) NAL-Dutton.
Yo - Pho's: Young Photographers. Bill Morong. Ed. by Judy Berk. (Illus.). 145p. 1989. 29.95 (*0-923486-00-3*) F-Stop Pubns.
Yo, Aesop! Rosenthal. (J). 1998. 16.00 (*0-689-80100-9*, S&S Bks Young Read) S&S Childrens.
***Yo Amo a la Iglesia.** rev. ed. Regular Baptist Press Staff. Ed. by Richard Meyer. (Adult Sunday School Ser.). 103p. (SPA.). 1994. 3.95 (*1-879892-26-X*) Editorial Bautista.
***Yo Baby It's Attitude! The New Bad Boyz of the NBA, Take the Jordan Test.** Roland Lazenby. Ed. by Susan Storey. LC 97-8587. 144p. (Orig.). 1997. pap. 14.95 (*1-886110-15-8*) Addax Pubng.
***Yo, Don Juan Manuel: Apologia de una Vida.** Reinaldo Ayerbe-Chaux. (Spanish Ser.: No. 91). xxii, 241p. 1993. 25.00 (*1-56954-003-9*) Hispanic Seminary.
Yo! Dudes! Dudettes! You Got a Call! David J. Rentfrow. 130p. (Orig.). 1995. pap. write for info. (*1-57502-069-6*) Morris Pubng.
Yo, el Mejor de Todos: Biografia No Autorizada del Che Guevara. Roberto L. Escalona. LC 94-70349. (Coleccion Cuba y Sus Jueces). (Orig.). (SPA.). 1994. pap. 18.00 (*0-89729-723-7*) Ediciones.
Yo, en Cristo Resucitado see I, in Christ Arisen
Yo, Grocer. B. Martin. (J). (gr. 4 up). 1996. 12.95 (*0-8050-0329-0*) H Holt & Co.
Yo He Visto Llorar a Dios. Carlos Jimenez. 254p. (SPA.). 5.99 (*1-56063-369-7*, 550120) Editorial Unilit.
Yo-Ho & Kim. Ruth Jaynes. 58p. (J). (gr. 1-6). 1965. 2.50 (*0-89986-386-8*) Oriental Bk Store.
Yo-Ho & Kim at Sea. Ruth Jaynes. 58p. (J). (gr. 1-6). 1965. 2.50 (*0-89986-387-6*) Oriental Bk Store.
Yo Ho! Yo Ho! Virginia Ferguson & Peter Durkin. LC 93-20018. (J). 1994. write for info. (*0-383-03729-8*) SRA McGraw.
Yo-Hungry Wolf! A Nursery Rap. David Vozar. (Illus.). 48p. (J). (ps-3). 1995. pap. 5.99 (*0-440-40953-5*) Dell.
Yo Igual Voy a Orar (Daniel) Marilyn Lashbrook. 32p. (SPA.). 1988. pap. 3.50 (*0-8254-1435-0*, Edit Portavoz) Kregel.
Yo, Juan de Pareja. Elizabeth B. De Trevino. Tr. by Enrique R. Trevino Borton from ENG. 192p. (SPA.). (YA). (gr. 12 up). 1994. 16.00 (*0-374-38699-4*) FS&G.
Yo, Juan de Pareja - I, Juan de Pareja. Elizabeth B. De Trevino. Tr. by Enrique T. Borton. 224p. (SPA.). (YA). (gr. 7 up). 1996. pap. 4.95 (*0-374-49292-1*, Mirasol) FS&G.
Yo-Leven. Roidon Co. Staff. (United States Ser.). (Illus.). 108p. (Orig.). 1990. pap. 7.00 (*1-879374-00-5*) Roidon.
Yo' Mama. Snap C. Pop. Ed. by Kid Rank. 128p. (Orig.). 1995. pap. 8.00 (*0-425-14861-0*, Berkley Trade) Berkley Pub.
***Yo' Mama's Disfunktional! Fighting the Culture Wars in Urban America.** Robin D. Kelley. LC 97-20067. 208p. 1997. 22.00 (*0-8070-0940-7*) Beacon Pr.
Yo Me Acuerdo: Diccionario de Nostalgias Cubanas. Jose Pardo-Llada. LC 93-72254. (Coleccion Diccionarios). (Illus.). 256p. (SPA.). 1993. pap. 19.00 (*0-89729-701-6*) Ediciones.
***Yo, Millard Fillmore! And All Those Other Presidents You Don't Know.** Will Cleveland & Mark Alvarez. LC 96-42098. (Illus.). 128p. (J). (gr. 5-9). 1997. 6.95 (*0-7613-0236-0*) Millbrook Pr.
***Yo, Millard Fillmore! And All Those Other Presidents You Don't Know.** Will Cleveland & Mark Alvarez. LC 96-42098. (Illus.). 112p. (YA). (gr. 5-9). 1997. lib. bdg. 15.90 (*0-7613-0253-0*) Millbrook Pr.
Yo! Millard Fillmore: And All Those Other Presidents You Never Heard Of. Will Cleveland & Mark Alvarez. (Fundamental Memory Book). (Illus.). 112p. (J). (gr. 5). 1992. pap. 7.95 (*0-9632778-0-4*) Goodwood Pr.
Yo, Millard Fillmore! And All Those Other Presidents You Never Heard Of. 2nd rev. ed. Will Cleveland & Mark Alvarez. (Goodwood Memory Book). (Illus.). 112p. (Orig.). (J). (gr. 5). 1993. reprint ed. pap. write for info. (*0-9632778-1-2*) Goodwood Pr.
Yo? Obedecer a Mi Marido? Elizabeth R. Handford. 128p. (SPA.). 1984. mass mkt. 4.50 (*0-8254-1302-8*, Edit Portavoz) Kregel.
***Yo Puedo Ayudar.** Bonnie Worth. (Naptime Tales Bks.). (Illus.). 18p. (SPA.). (J). (ps). 1996. write for info. (*0-614-19537-3*, P12425-10, Golden Books) Western Pub.
Yo Puedo Contar. Illus. by Stephanie Longfoot. (Juega y Aprende Ser.). 12p. (ENG & SPA.). (J). (ps). 1995. bds. 3.98 (*1-85854-332-0*) Brimax Bks.
***Yo Puedo Escoger el Camino Correcto.** Glorianne Muggli. Tr. by Annie Payne & Lorena Stevens. (Primary Theme Bks.). (Illus.). 100p. (Orig.). (SPA.). 1996. pap. 8.95 (*1-57665-023-5*) Muggli Graphics.
Yo Puedo Escribir. Y tu? Josie Stewart & Lynn Salem. Tr. by Mariana Robles from ENG. (Illus.). 8p. (Orig.). (SPA.). (J). (gr. k-1). 1995. pap. 3.50 (*1-880612-42-9*) Seedling Pubns.
***Yo Puedo Tomar Una Siesta.** Bonnie Worth. (Naptime Tales Bks.). (Illus.). 18p. (SPA.). (J). (ps). 1996. write for info. (*0-614-19536-5*, P12426-10, Golden Books) Western Pub.
Yo Quiero Ser un Misionero-I Want to Be a Missionary. Barbara Hibschman et al. (Missionary-That's Me! Ser.). (SPA.). (J). 1994. spiral bd. 4.99 (*0-87509-540-2*) Chr Pubns.
Yo, Sacramento! And All Those Other State Capitals You Don't Know. Will Cleveland. 1994. pap. 7.95 (*0-9632778-2-0*) Goodwood Pr.
***Yo, Sacramento! And All Those Other State Capitals You Don't Know.** Will Cleveland & Mark Alvarez. LC 96-42099. (Illus.). 128p. (YA). (gr. 5-9). 1997. lib. bdg. 15.90 (*0-7613-0252-2*) Millbrook Pr.
***Yo! Sacramento (& All Those Capitals You Don't Know)** Will Cleveland & Mark Alvarez. LC 96-42099. (Illus.). 128p. (YA). (gr. 5-9). 1997. 6.95 (*0-7613-0237-9*) Millbrook Pr.
Yo Se Que Estas Sufriendo. Lauren Strafford. 251p. (SPA.). 1989. pap. 7.99 (*1-56063-543-6*, 490209) Editorial Unilit.
Yo Solito. Mercer Mayer. (Spanish Language Look-Look Bks.). (Illus.). 24p. (SPA.). (J). 1994. 2.25 (*0-307-71938-3*, Golden Pr) Western Pub.
Yo Soy (I Am) Rita Milios. LC 87-5163. (Spanish Rookie Readers Ser.). 32p. (SPA.). (J). (ps-2). 1990. pap. 3.50 (*0-516-52081-4*) Childrens.
Yo Soy un Medico. Cynthia Benjamin. (Illus.). 24p. (J). (ps). 1994. 6.95 (*0-8120-6414-3*) Barron.
***Yo Soy Winnie Puh.** Walt Disney Staff. (Illus.). 22p. (SPA.). (J). (ps). 1996. write for info. (*0-614-19545-4*, P12456-10, Golden Books) Western Pub.
Yo Te Amo (I Love You) Alex. (SPA.). 4.99 (*0-685-74988-6*, 490250) Editorial Unilit.
Yo Tengo Papa? Do I Have a Daddy? Un Cuento Sobre Un Nino de Madre Soltera, A Story about a Single-Parent Child. Jeanne W. Lindsay. Tr. by Argentina Palacios from SPA. (Illus.). 48p. (Orig.). (SPA.). (J). (ps-3). 1994. 12.95 (*0-930934-83-0*) Morning Glory.
Yo Tengo Papa? Do I Have a Daddy? Un Cuento Sobre Un Nino de Madre Soltera, A Story about a Single-Parent Child. Jeanne W. Lindsay. Tr. by Argentina Palacios. (Illus.). 48p. (Orig.). (SPA.). (J). (ps-3). 1994. pap. 5.95 (*0-930934-82-2*) Morning Glory.
Yo Tengo un Gato. Tr. by Marissa Zamora-Pearson from ENG. (Illus.). (SPA.). (J). (ps-2). 1993. pap. text ed. 14.00 (*0-922053-29-4*) N Edge Res.
***Yo Tenia un Hipopotamo.** Hector Viveros Lee. LC 96-36897. (Illus.). 32p. (SPA.). (J). (ps-2). 1997. pap. 6.95 (*1-880000-52-0*) Lee & Low Bks.
***Yo Tenia un Hipopotamo.** Hector Viveros Lee. LC 96-36897. (Illus.). 32p. (SPA.). (J). (ps up). 1997. 15.95 (*1-880000-51-2*) Lee & Low Bks.
Yo Vengo de los Arabos. Esteban J. Palacios. LC 86-82605. (Coleccion Caniqui). 131p. (Orig.). 1987. pap. 9.95 (*0-89729-420-3*) Ediciones.
***Yo y Mi Casa.** Walter Wangerin. (SPA.). 1.50 (*0-8297-0955-X*) Life Pubs Intl.
Yo! Yes? Chris Raschka. LC 92-25644. (Illus.). 32p. (J). (ps-1). 1993. 15.95 (*0-531-05469-1*); lib. bdg. 16.99 (*0-531-08619-4*) Orchard Bks Watts.
***Yo-Yo.** (Mad Jack Bks.). (Illus.). (J). 1996. 10.95 (*0-7894-0755-8*) DK Pub Inc.
Yo-Yo-Company (The Beginning) 2nd rev. ed. Denise Bredfeldt. (Illus.). iii, 43p. 1993. wbk. ed. 30.00 (*0-9653067-0-4*) Bizlit.
Yo-Yo Diet Syndrome: How to Heal & Stabilize Your Appetite & Weight. 2nd rev. ed. Doreen L. Virtue. LC 96-46439. 250p. 1997. pap. 12.95 (*1-56170-352-4*, 836) Hay House.
Yo-Yo Relationships: How to Break the "I Need a Man" Habit & Find Stability. Doreen L. Virtue. LC 94-21345. 224p. 1994. pap. 12.95 (*0-925190-35-7*) Fairview Press.
***Yoba: Lessons from the Street & Other Places.** Malik Yoba & Howard Manly. (Illus.). 176p. (Orig.). 1996. pap. 12.00 (*0-385-48686-3*, Main St Bks) Doubleday.
Yobbo Nowt. John McGrath. 72p. (Orig.). 1981. pap. 6.95 (*0-904383-76-8*, NO. 4135) Routledge Chapman & Hall.
Yobo: A Novel of Korea. Whalen M. Wehry. LC 83-82585. 458p. 1984. 19.50 (*0-930878-38-8*) Hollym Intl.
Yochib: The River Cave. C. William Steele. LC 85-5894. (Illus.). 176p. (Orig.). 1985. 15.95 (*0-939748-09-6*); pap. 10.95 (*0-939748-10-X*) Cave Bks MO.
Yocundra in the Paradise of Nada. Zoe Valdes. LC 97-4005. 160p. 1997. lib. bdg. 21.95 (*1-55970-362-8*) Arcade Pub Inc.
Yod: Its Esoteric Meaning. Joan Kellogg. pap. 9.00 (*0-86690-369-0*, 3020-014) Am Fed Astrologers.
Yod, Your Special Life Purpose. Miss Dee. LC 83-70271. 72p. 1983. 11.00 (*0-86690-234-1*, D2287-014) Am Fed Astrologers.
Yodeling. Ralph F. Parkison. Ed. by Marion O. Withrow. (Illus.). 71p. (Orig.). (J). (gr. 2-8). 1988. pap. write for info. (*0-318-63998-X*) Little Wood Bks.
Yoder Outsiders. James D. Yoder. Ed. by Maynard Shelly. LC 88-82410. (Illus.). 185p. (Orig.). 1988. pap. 9.95 (*0-87303-133-4*) Faith & Life.
***Yoder, University of Alabama-Birmingham Custom Pub.** Yoder-Wise. (C). (gr. 13 up). 1996. 49.95 (*0-8151-2571-2*, 31310) Mosby Yr Bk.
Yoffie's International Trade & Competition: Cases & Notes. David B. Yoffie. 1990. 17.95 (*0-07-072277-3*) McGraw.
***Yog Phoo Ntawv Suav Xim Thab Thag Xim (Hmong)** Tr. by Yer J. Thao. (J). (gr. k-2). 1993. write for info. (*1-57842-110-1*) Delmas Creat.
Yoga. (101 Essential Tips Ser.). (Illus.). 72p. 1997. pap. 6.95 (*1-56458-991-9*) DK Pub Inc.
Yoga. J. F. C. Fuller. 180p. 1975. 13.50 (*0-911662-55-3*) Yoga.
Yoga. James Hewitt. (Teach Yourself Ser.). (Illus.). 209p. 1988. pap. 7.95 (*0-679-72118-5*) Random.
Yoga. Mary Stewart. (Headway Lifeguides Ser.). (Illus.). 128p. 1995. pap. 15.95 (*0-340-55948-9*, Pub. by Headway UK) Trafalgar.
Yoga: A Gem for Women. Geeta Iyengar. LC 90-43112. (Illus.). 424p. 1995. pap. 21.95 (*0-931454-20-4*) Timeless Bks.

Yoga: Disipline of Freedom. Comment by Barbara S. Miller. 160p. (C). 1996. 17.95 (0-520-20190-6) U CA Pr.

Yoga: Immortality & Freedom. Mircea Eliade. Tr. by W. R. Trask. (Bollingen Ser.: No. LVI). 560p. 1991. pap. text ed. 16.95 (0-691-01764-6) Princeton U Pr.

Yoga: Immortality & Freedom. Mircea Eliade. (Illus.). 560p. 1989. pap. 10.95 (0-14-019158-5, Penguin Bks) Viking Penguin.

Yoga: Index of New Information & Medical Research Bible. Lazaar O. Krolle. 150p. 1994. 44.50 (0-7883-0108-X); pap. 39.50 (0-7883-0109-8) ABBE Pubs Assn.

Yoga: Its Various Aspects. pap. 4.95 (0-87481-512-6, Pub. by Ramakrishna Math II) Vedanta Pr.

Yoga: Mastering the Secrets of Matter & the Universe. Alain Danielou. 192p. (Orig.). 1990. pap. 14.95 (0-89281-301-6) Inner Tradit.

Yoga: Meaning, Values & Practice. Phulgenda Sinha. 1973. pap. 2.50 (0-88253-259-6) Ind-US Inc.

Yoga: Moving into Stillness. Erich Schiffman. LC 96-41662. 1996. pap. 14.00 (0-671-53480-7) PB.

Yoga: Step by Step. Cheryl Isaacson. 1991. pap. 13.00 (0-7225-2422-6) Thorsons SF.

Yoga: The Art of Flexibility. Joseph A. Uphoff, Jr. LC 93-24906. 96p. 1993. pap. text ed. 6.00 (0-943123-23-2) Arjuna Lib Pr.

Yoga: The Hatha Yoga & the Raja Yoga. Annie Besant. 73p. 1974. reprint ed. spiral bd. 5.50 (0-7873-0104-3) Hlth Research.

***Yoga: The Spirit & Practice of Moving into Stillness.** Erich Schiffmann. 1996. pap. 12.00 (0-614-20760-6, PB Trade Paper) PB.

Yoga: The Spirit of Union. 3rd ed. Larry Caughlan. 112p. (C). 1996. per., pap. text ed. 16.41 (0-7872-2115-5) Kendall-Hunt.

Yoga: The Technique of Health & Happiness. I. Devi. 76p. 1992. 6.95 (0-318-37203-7) Asia Bk Corp.

Yoga: Yogic Suksma Vyayama. Dhirenda Brahmachari. (Illus.). 232p. 1975. 8.95 (0-88253-802-0) Ind-US Inc.

Yoga . . . The Art of Living: The Hunza-Yoga Way to Better Living. Renee Taylor. LC 78-75329. (Illus.). 224p. 1975. reprint ed. pap. 9.95 (0-87983-112-X) Keats.

Yoga - Practicing Postures: An Easy-to-use Workbook. Connie Weiss. (Illus.). 90p. 1991. student ed. 19.95 (0-9629676-0-2) Lurie Ln Pub.

Yoga & Depth Psychology. I. P. Sachdeva. 269p. 1978. 19.95 (0-317-12334-3, Pub. by Motilal Bnarsidass II) Asia Bk Corp.

Yoga & Depth Psychology. I. P. Sachdeva. 1979. 16.00 (0-8364-0454-8) S Asia.

Yoga & Health. Selvarajan Yesudian & Elisabeth Haich. (Unwin Paperbacks Ser.). (Illus.). 1988. pap. 8.95 (0-04-149033-9) Routledge Chapman & Hall.

Yoga & Indian Philosophy. Karel Werner. 1979. 12.50 (0-8364-0479-3) S Asia.

Yoga & Its Objects. Sri Aurobindo. 33p. 1984. pap. 1.50 (0-89071-314-6, Pub. by SAA II) Aurobindo Assn.

Yoga & Long Life. 5th ed. Yogi Gupta. LC 58-9502. (Illus.). 1983. 15.00 (0-911664-01-7) Yogi Gupta.

Yoga & Mysticism: An Introduction to Vedanta. Swami Prabhavananda. 53p. 1984. reprint ed. pap. 4.95 (0-87481-020-5) Vedanta Pr.

Yoga & Psychotherapy: The Evolution of Consciousness. Swami Rama et al. LC 76-356228. 332p. 1976. pap. 15.95 (0-89389-036-7) Himalayan Inst.

Yoga & Spiritual Life. rev. ed. Sri Chinmoy. LC 74-81309. 9p. 1974. pap. 8.95 (0-88497-040-X) Aum Pubns.

Yoga & the Hindu Tradition. Jean Varenne. (C). 1989. 17.50 (81-208-0532-1, Pub. by Motilal Banarsidass II) S Asia.

Yoga & the Hindu Tradition. Jean Varenne. Tr. by Derek Coltman from FRE. LC 75-19506. 264p. 1977. pap. text ed. 15.50 (0-226-85116-8, P744) U Ch Pr.

Yoga & Yogic Powers. Yogi Gupta. LC 63-14948. (Illus.). 1963. 20.00 (0-911664-02-5) Yogi Gupta.

***Yoga & You: Energizing & Relaxing Yoga for New & Experienced Teachers.** Esther Myers. LC 96-36916. (Illus.). 256p. 1997. pap. 17.00 (1-57062-320-1) Shambhala Pubns.

Yoga Aphorisms. William Q. Judge. 1972. 59.95 (0-8490-1343-7) Gordon Pr.

Yoga Aphorisms of Patanjali. Tr. & Pref. by William Q. Judge. xxi, 74p. 1930. reprint ed. 4.00 (0-938998-11-0) Theosophy.

Yoga As Philosophy & Religion. S. Dasgupta. 1974. lib. bdg. 300.00 (0-87968-104-7) Krishna Pr.

Yoga As Philosophy & Religion. Surendranath Dasgupta. 200p. 1978. 15.95 (0-318-37199-5) Asia Bk Corp.

Yoga As Philosophy & Religion. Surendranath Dasgupta. (C). 1995. reprint ed. 14.00 (81-208-0217-9, Pub. by Motilal Banarsidass II) S Asia.

Yoga at Work: 10-Minute Yoga Workouts for Busy People. Miriam Freedman & Janis Hanks. LC 96-13139. 160p. 1996. pap. 9.95 (1-85230-817-6) Element MA.

Yoga Back Book: The Gentle Yet Effective Way to Spinal Health. Stella Weller & W. Harry Gahrni. 1993. pap. 16.00 (0-7225-2785-3) Thorsons SF.

Yoga Book. Couch. (Runner's World Ser.). 1982. pap. 9.95 (0-02-499670-X, Macmillan Coll) P-H.

Yoga Book, No. 2. Couch. (Runner's World Ser.). 1983. pap. 9.95 (0-02-499680-7, Macmillan Coll) P-H.

***Yoga Book: A Practical Guide to Self-Realization.** Stephen Sturgess. LC 97-1808. 1997. pap. 15.95 (1-85230-972-5) Element MA.

Yoga Can Change Your Life. Swami Jyotinmayananda. (Illus.). 1975. pap. 9.95 (0-934664-14-5) Yoga Res Foun.

Yoga Cards: Create Your Own Yoga Program. Loretta McArthur & Tim Clark. (Illus.). 24p. 1995. pap. 14.95 (0-89087-740-8) Celestial Arts.

Yoga During Pregnancy. Vibeke Berg. 1983. 6.95 (0-671-45987-2, Fireside) S&S Trade.

Yoga During Pregnancy. Sandra Jordan. (Illus.). 132p. (Orig.). 1987. pap. 12.00 (0-9619374-0-8) Sun Moon Hl.

Yoga Essays for Self-Improvement. Jyotir Swami & Maya Nanda. LC 81-65248. 248p. 1981. pap. 6.99 (0-934664-39-0, 030) Yoga Res Foun.

Yoga Exercises for Every Body. Ruth Bender. 1975. spiral bd. 9.95 (0-917434-00-5) Ruben Pub.

Yoga Exercises for Health & Happiness. Swami Jyotinmayananda. (Illus.). 1973. pap. 9.95 (0-934664-15-3) Yoga Res Foun.

Yoga Exercises for More Flexible Bodies. Ruth Bender. 1977. spiral bd. 9.95 (0-917434-02-1) Ruben Pub.

Yoga Food Book: A Guide to Vegetarian Eating & Cooking. Larry M. Buxbaum. (Illus.). 115p. 1975. spiral bd. 4.00 (0-915594-01-3) Univ Great Brother.

Yoga for a New Age: A Modern Approach to Hatha Yoga. Bob Smith & Linda B. Smith. Ed. by Helen P. Smith. LC 86-90391. (Illus.). Mukerjip. 1986. reprint ed. pap. text ed. 13.95 (0-9616545-0-3) Smith Prod.

Yoga for Body, Breath, & Mind: A Guide to Personal Reintegration. rev. ed. A. G. Mohan. Ed. by Kathaleen Miller. LC 92-32175. (Illus.). 219p. 1995. pap. 16.95 (0-915801-51-5) Rudra Pr.

Yoga for Busy People: Increase Energy & Reduce Stress in Minutes a Day. Dawn Groves. LC 94-40501. (Illus.). 160p. (Orig.). 1995. pap. 10.95 (1-880032-47-3) New Wrld Lib.

Yoga for Cats. Talia Katasanda. 48p. 1995. per. 7.95 (0-920304-77-X, Pub. by Gynergy-Ragweed CN) LPC InBook.

Yoga for Cats. Traudl Reiner. 1990. pap. 6.95 (0-312-92438-0) St Martin.

Yoga for Children. E. R. Kumar. (C). 1994. pap. text ed. 8.50 (81-7223-101-6, Pub. by Indus Pub II) S Asia.

Yoga for Children. Mary Stewart & Kathy Phillips. (Illus.). 128p. (Orig.). 1993. pap. 14.00 (0-671-78712-8, Fireside) S&S Trade.

Yoga for Children. Stella Weller. (Illus.). 128p. (Orig.). 1996. pap. 16.00 (0-7225-3206-7) Thorsons SF.

Yoga for Common Ailments. R. Nagarathna et al. (Illus.). 96p. (Orig.). 1991. pap. 12.95 (0-671-70528-8, Fireside) S&S Trade.

Yoga for Every Athlete: Secrets of an Olympic Coach. Aladar Kogler. LC 95-13900. (Llewellyn's Health & Healing Ser.). (Illus.). 336p. 1995. pap. 16.95 (1-56718-387-5) Llewellyn Pubns.

Yoga for Health. Richard L. Hittleman. LC 82-90825. 256p. 1985. pap. 14.00 (0-345-32798-5) Ballantine.

Yoga for Health & Healing: From the Teachings of Yogi Bhajan, Ph.D. Ed. by Alice B. Clagett & Elandra K. Meredith. (Illus.). 144p. (Orig.). 1995. pap. 14.95 (0-940992-01-9) A B Clagett.

Yoga for People over Fifty: Exercise Without Exhaustion. Suza Norton. LC 76-18445. 1977. 15.95 (0-8159-7404-3) Devin.

Yoga for Pets. Jean Farrar. LC 89-83902. (Illus.). xi, 205p. (Orig.). 1989. pap. 9.95 (0-9623201-0-2) Finlayson Pubns.

Yoga for Physical Fitness. Richard L. Hittleman. 255p. 1994. 8.95 (0-318-37195-2) Asia Bk Corp.

Yoga for Pregnancy: Ninety-Two Safe, Gentle Stretches Appropriate for Pregnant Women & New Mothers. Sandra Jordan. (Illus.). 144p. 1988. pap. 13.95 (0-312-02322-7) St Martin.

***Yoga for Stress Relief.** 1998. pap. write for info. (0-679-77817-9) Random.

Yoga for the Fun of It! Hatha Yoga for Preschool Children. 4th ed. Suzanne L. Schreiber. (Illus.). 54p. (Orig.). (J). (ps). 1991. reprint ed. pap. 9.00 (0-9608320-0-9) Sugar Marbel Pr.

Yoga for the Modern Man. M. P. Pandit. 128p. 1988. text ed. 12.95 (81-207-0759-1, Pub. by Sterling Pubs II) Apt Bks.

Yoga for the Modern Man. M. P. Pandit. 115p. 1979. 4.00 (0-941524-13-2) Lotus Light.

***Yoga for the Special Child: A Therapeutic Approach for Infants & Children with Down Syndrome, Cerebral Palsy, Microcephaly, Learning Disabilities, & Attention Deficit Disorder.** Sonia Sumar. Tr. by Jeffrey Volk & Adriana Marusso from POR. (Illus.). 200p. (Orig.). 1997. pap. 19.95 (0-9658024-0-X) Special Yoga.

Yoga for the Young at Heart: Gentle Flow Yoga for Seniors. Susan W. Ward. (Illus.). 112p. (Orig.). 1994. lib. bdg. 35.00 (0-8095-4124-6) Borgo Pr.

Yoga for the Young at Heart: Gentle Flow Yoga for Seniors. Susan W. Ward. LC 93-42586. (Illus.). 112p. (Orig.). 1994. pap. 12.95 (0-88496-376-4) Capra Pr.

Yoga for the 21st Century. 2nd ed. Tamal K. Goswami. 211p. pap. write for info. (0-9643485-0-0) T K Goswami.

***Yoga for Wellness.** Gary Kraftsow. 1998. pap. 19.95 (0-14-025806-X) Viking Penguin.

Yoga for Women. Paddy O'Brien. (Illus.). 108p. pap. 14.00 (1-85538-426-4, Pub. by Aquarian Pr UK) Thorsons SF.

Yoga for You. I. Devi. 184p. 1991. 9.95 (0-318-37200-2) Asia Bk Corp.

Yoga for Your Life: A Practice Manual of Breath & Movement for Every Body. Margaret D. Pierce & Martin G. Pierce. (Illus.). 160p. (Orig.). 1996. pap. 20.00 (0-915801-60-4) Rudra Pr.

Yoga Guide. Swami Jyotirmayananda. (Illus.). 1972. pap. 6.99 (0-934664-16-1) Yoga Res Foun.

Yoga Hygiene Simplified. S. Yogendra. 155p. 1982. 8.95 (0-318-37196-0) Asia Bk Corp.

Yoga Illustrated Dictionary. H. Day. (Illus.). 186p. 1986. 8.95 (0-318-37201-0) Asia Bk Corp.

Yoga in Life. Swami Lalitananda. (Illus.). 1972. pap. 4.99 (0-934664-17-X) Yoga Res Foun.

Yoga in Practice. Swami Jyotirmayananda. (Illus.). 1974. pap. 1.99 (0-934664-18-8) Yoga Res Foun.

Yoga in Pregnancy. Vibeke Berg. 135p. 1983. 12.95 (0-940500-24-8, Pub. by D B Taraporwala II) Asia Bk Corp.

Yoga in Sri Aurobindo's Epic Savitri. M. P. Pandit. 236p. 1979. 10.95 (0-941524-15-9) Lotus Light.

Yoga Integral. Swami Jyotir Maya Nanda. (Illus.). 112p. (SPA.). 1984. pap. 4.99 (0-934664-51-X) Yoga Res Foun.

***Yoga Journal's Yoga Basics: The Essential Beginner's Guide to Yoga for a Lifetime of Health.** Mara Carrico. LC 97-11495. 1997. pap. 15.95 (0-8050-4571-6, Owl) H Holt & Co.

***Yoga Kundalini: Para el Cuerpo la Mente y mas Alla.** Ravi Singh. Tr. by Josefina Guerra. (Illus.). 224p. (SPA.). 1996. reprint ed. wbk. ed., pap. 17.95 (1-886942-10-2) White Lion Pr.

Yoga Lessons for Developing Spiritual Consciousness. A. P. Mukerji. 10.00 (0-911662-24-3) Yoga.

Yoga Made Easy: A Personal Yoga Program That Will Transform Your Daily Life. Howard Kent. LC 93-46469. 160p. 1994. pap. 14.95 (1-882606-12-4) Peoples Med Soc.

Yoga, Meditation & the Guru: Critical Reflections on the Australian Scenario. Purusottama Bilimoria. 79p. (C). 1989. 45.00 (0-685-57499-7, Pub. by Deakin Univ AT) St Mut.

***Yoga, Meditation & the Guru: Critical Reflections on the Australian Scenario.** Purusottama Bilimoria. (Illus.). 64p. 1997. pap. 14.95 (0-9587718-2-0, Pub. by Indra Pub AT) Intl Spec Bk.

Yoga Mind & Body. Swami Sivananda & Swami Vishnu de Vananda. LC 95-44387. 168p. 1996. 24.95 (0-7894-0447-8) DK Pub Inc.

Yoga Mystic Poems. 240p. 1975. pap. 5.95 (0-934664-40-4) Yoga Res Foun.

Yoga Mystic Songs for Meditation, 7 Vols. Swami Lalitananda. 1975. pap. 4.99 (0-934664-19-6) Yoga Res Foun.

Yoga Mystic Stories & Parables. Swami Jyotinmayananda. (Illus.). 1974. pap. 6.99 (0-934664-24-2) Yoga Res Foun.

Yoga of Christ: In the Gospel According to St. John. R. Ravindra. 1993. pap. 14.95 (1-85230-139-2) Element MA.

Yoga of Delight, Wonder, & Astonishment: A Translation of the Vijnana-bhairava with an Introduction & Notes by Jaideva Singh. Paul E. Muller-Ortega. Tr. by Jaideva Singh. (SUNY Series in Tantric Studies). 219p. 1991. pap. text ed. 14.95 (0-7914-1074-9) State U NY Pr.

Yoga of Delight, Wonder, & Astonishment: A Translation of the Vijnana-bhairava with an Introduction & Notes by Jaideva Singh. Jaideva Singh & Paul E. Muller-Ortega. (SUNY Series in Tantric Studies). 173p. 1991. text ed. 42.50 (0-7914-1073-0) State U NY Pr.

Yoga of Discipline. Swami Chidvilasananda. LC 96-19254. 264p. (Orig.). 1996. pap. 13.95 (0-911307-44-3) SYDA Found.

Yoga of Divine Love: A Commentary on Narada Bhakti Sutras. Swami Jyotir Maya Nanda. 1982. pap. 6.99 (0-934664-42-0) Yoga Res Foun.

Yoga of Divine Works. 2nd ed. Sri Aurobindo. (Life Companion Library). (Illus.). 270p. pap. 8.95 (0-89744-015-3) Auromere.

Yoga of Enlightenment: Book of Unenlightenment. Lee Lozowick. LC 80-85141. 250p. 1980. pap. 9.95 (0-934252-06-8) Hohm Pr.

Yoga of Enlightenment: Chapter Eighteen of the Bhagavad Gita. 176p. 1987. pap. 6.99 (0-934664-45-5) Yoga Res Foun.

Yoga of Herbs: (An Ayurvedic Guide to Herbal Medicine) David Frawley & Vasant Lad. LC 86-81365. (Illus.). 268p. (Orig.). 1992. reprint ed. pap. 12.95 (0-941524-24-8) Lotus Light.

Yoga of Knowledge: Talks at Centre, Vol. II. M. P. Pandit. LC 86-80692. 282p. (Orig.). 1986. pap. 7.95 (0-941524-23-X) Lotus Light.

Yoga of Light: Hatha-Yoga-Pradipika with a Commentary by Hans-Urlich Rieker. Hans-Urlich Rieker. 208p. 1990. pap. 12.95 (0-04-440600-2) Routledge Chapman & Hall.

Yoga of Light: The Classic Esoteric Handbook of Kundalini Yoga. Hans-Ulrich Rieker. Tr. by Elsy Becherer. LC 79-167868. (Illus.). 203p. 1974. pap. 14.95 (0-913922-07-2) Dawn Horse Pr.

Yoga of Love. M. P. Pandit. LC 81-86373. (Talks at Center Ser.: Vol. III). 112p. (Orig.). 1982. pap. 3.95 (0-941524-16-7) Lotus Light.

Yoga of Nutrition. 2nd ed. Omraam M. Aivanhov. LC 91-70254. (Izvor Collection: No. 204). 139p. 1991. pap. 6.95 (0-911857-10-9) Prosveta USA.

Yoga of Perfect Sight. 3rd ed. R. S. Agarwal. 1979. pap. 5.95 (0-89744-948-7) Auromere.

Yoga of Perfect Sight: With Letters of Sri Aurobindo. R. S. Agarwal. (Illus.). 223p. 1986. pap. 7.95 (81-7058-209-1) Aurobindo Assn.

Yoga of Perfection (Srimad Bhagavad Gita) Swami Jyotinmayananda. (Illus.). 1973. pap. 6.99 (0-934664-25-0) Yoga Res Foun.

Yoga of Power: Tantra, Shakti, & the Secret Way. Julius Evola. Tr. by Guido Stucco. 256p. (Orig.). 1993. pap. 16.95 (0-89281-368-7) Inner Tradit.

Yoga of Self-Perfection. M. P. Pandit. LC 83-81299. (Talks at Center Ser.: Vol. IV). 312p. (Orig.). 1983. pap. 7.95 (0-941524-20-5) Lotus Light.

Yoga of Sex-Sublimation, Truth & Non-Violence. Swami Jyotinmayananda. (Illus.). 1974. pap. 6.99 (0-934664-26-9) Yoga Res Foun.

Yoga of Six Limbs: An Introduction to the History of Sadanga Yoga. Gunter Gronbold. Tr. by Robert L. Hutwohl from GER. (Illus.). 88p. (Orig.). 1996. pap. text ed. 14.50 (0-9651315-0-5) Spirit of the Sun.

Yoga of the Guhyasamajanantra: A Buddhist Tantra Commentary. Alex Wayman. (C). 1991. reprint ed. 20.00 (81-208-0872-X, Pub. by Motilal Banarsidass II) S Asia.

Yoga of the Inward Path. Ronald P. Beesley. 1978. reprint ed. pap. 5.95 (0-87516-269-X) DeVorss.

Yoga of Vibration & Divine Pulsation: A Translation of the Spanda Karika with Ksemaraja's Commentary, the Spanda Nirnaya. Jaideva Singh. (SUNY Series in Tantric Studies). 210p. 1991. pap. text ed. 19.95 (0-7914-1180-X) State U NY Pr.

Yoga of Vibration & Divine Pulsation: A Translation of the Spanda Karika with Ksemaraja's Commentary, the Spanda Nirnaya. Jaideva Singh. (SUNY Series in Tantric Studies). 210p. 1991. text ed. 59.50 (0-7914-1179-6) State U NY Pr.

Yoga of Works: Talks at Centre I. M. P. Pandit. LC 85-50695. 192p. (C). 1985. pap. 7.95 (0-941524-21-3) Lotus Light.

Yoga of Yama. W. Gorn Old. 64p. 1970. reprint ed. spiral bd. 5.00 (0-7873-1169-3) Hlth Research.

Yoga on War & Peace. Pandit R. Tigunait. LC 91-14248. 142p. (Orig.). (C). 1991. pap. 12.95 (0-89389-125-8) Himalayan Inst.

Yoga over Fifty: The Way to Vitality, Health & Energy in Later Life. Mary Stewart. LC 93-41514. (Illus.). 128p. 1994. pap. 15.00 (0-671-88510-3, Fireside) S&S Trade.

Yoga Philosophy & Practice. Hari P. Shastri. 96p. 1996. pap. 8.50 (0-89540-200-9, SB-200) Sun Pub.

Yoga Philosophy of Patanjali: Containing His Yoga Aphorisms with Commentary by Vyasa & Annotations & Copious Hints on the Practice of Yoga. Swami A. Hariharananda. Tr. by P. N. Mukerji from SAN. LC 83-4944. 483p. (C). 1984. reprint ed. text ed. 39.50 (0-87395-728-8); reprint ed. pap. text ed. 14.95 (0-87395-729-6) State U NY Pr.

Yoga Postures for Higher Awareness. 2nd enl. ed. Sri Kriyananda. LC 89-189782. (Illus.). 160p. 1971. pap. 9.95 (0-916124-25-8, DW52) Crystal Clarity.

Yoga Practice. S. Sivananda. 66p. 1977. 5.95 (0-318-37202-9) Asia Bk Corp.

Yoga Psychology. Swami Abhedananda. pap. 8.95 (0-87481-614-9, Pub. by Rama Ved Math II) Vedanta Pr.

Yoga Psychology: A Practical Guide to Meditation. rev. ed. Swami Ajaya. LC 76-374539. 115p. 1976. pap. 12.95 (0-89389-052-9) Himalayan Inst.

Yoga Quotations from the Wisdom of Swami Jyotir Maya Nanda. Ed. by Swami Lalitananda. (Illus.). 1974. pap. 6.95 (0-934664-27-7) Yoga Res Foun.

Yoga, Sadhana & Samadhi. Pranab Bandyopadhyay. (C). 1987. 16.00 (0-8364-2132-9, KL Mukhopadhyay) S Asia.

Yoga Science of the Soul, Vol. 2. Rajneesh Osho Staff. 1984. pap. 4.95 (0-88050-678-4) Osho America.

Yoga Science of the Soul, Vol. 3. Rajneesh Osho Staff. 1984. pap. 4.95 (0-88050-679-2) Osho America.

Yoga Secrets of Psychic Powers. Swami Jyotir Maya Nanda. (Illus.). 1974. pap. 6.99 (0-934664-28-5) Yoga Res Foun.

Yoga Stories & Parables. Swami Jyotir Manda. (Illus.). 1976. pap. 6.99 (0-934664-41-2) Yoga Res Foun.

Yoga-Sutra of Patanjali. Georg Feuerstein. 192p. 1990. pap. 14.95 (0-89281-262-1) Inner Tradit.

Yoga Sutras of Patanjali. 36p. 1995. pap. 9.00 (0-923569-17-0, D-07) Maharishi U Mgmt Pr.

***Yoga-Sutras of Patanjali.** Sai B. Sathya. Date not set. pap. 1.50 (0-614-19101-7, BW-235) Sathya Sai Bk Ctr.

Yoga Sutras of Patanjali. rev. ed. Sri S. Satchidananda. LC 78-56636. 263p. 1984. pap. 14.95 (0-932040-38-1) Integral Yoga Pubns.

Yoga Sutras of Patanjali. 2nd ed. Archie J. Bahm. LC 92-39859. 160p. 1993. reprint ed. pap. 12.95 (0-87573-024-8) Jain Pub Co.

Yoga Sutras of Patanjali. 2nd rev. ed. Tr. by Charles Johnston from SAN. 116p. 1993. pap. 10.00 (0-914732-08-0) Bro Life Inc.

Yoga Sutras of Patanjali. Fernando Tola. Tr. by KD Pirthi Paul. (C). 1990. reprint ed. 17.50 (81-208-0258-6, Pub. by Motilal Banarsidass II) S Asia.

Yoga-Sutras of Patanjali with the Exposition of Vyasa: A Translation & Commentary, Vol. I. Pandit U. Arya et al. LC 85-7570. 493p. (C). 1986. pap. 16.95 (0-89389-092-8) Himalayan Inst.

Yoga System of Patanjali. James H. Woods. (C). 1989. 28.50 (81-208-0570-4) S Asia.

Yoga-System of Patanjali. Tr. by James H. Woods. 1992. reprint ed. 18.00 (81-208-0577-1, Pub. by Motilal Banarsidass II) S Asia.

Yoga-Systems of Patanjali: The Doctrine of the Concentration of the Mind. James Woods. 1973. lib. bdg. 300.00 (0-87968-083-0) Krishna Pr.

Yoga, Tantra & Meditation in Daily Life. rev. ed. Swami J. Saraswati. LC 95-15860. (Illus.). 189p. (Orig.). 1992. pap. 13.95 (0-87728-768-6) Weiser.

Yoga the College Way. Yvonne Banuet-Alvers. 216p. (C). 1996. boxed 23.69 (0-7872-2443-X) Kendall-Hunt.

Yoga the Iyengar Way. Mira Mehta. 1990. pap. 23.00 (0-679-72287-4) Knopf.

Yoga the Technique of Liberation. Virendra Shekhavat. 80p. 1980. 10.95 (0-317-07708-2, Pub. by Sterling II) Asia Bk Corp.

Yoga Transitions: Spelman Method Preparation for YOGA Series, 7 bks., Set. Marva Spelman. LC 90-70428. (Illus.). 260p. 1990. 29.95 (0-923145-06-0) Ten Star Pr.

Yoga Twenty-Eight Day Exercise Plan. Richard L. Hittleman. 320p. 1983. mass mkt. 6.99 (0-553-27748-0) Bantam.

Yoga Twenty-Eight Day Exercise Plan. Richard L. Hittleman. LC 74-87903. (Illus.). 224p. 1969. pap. 10.95 (0-911104-21-6, 194) Workman Pub.

An Asterisk (*) at the beginning of an entry indicates that the title is appearing in BIP for the first time.

Yoga Unveiled, Pt. 2. U. A. Asrani. (C). 1993. text ed. 22.00 (81-208-0946-7, Pub. by Motilal Banarsidass II) S Asia.
Yoga Vasistha, 3 vols. Incl. Vol. 1. . Joyotir M. Nanda. 1977. pap. 9.99 (0-934664-30-7); Vol. 2. . Jyotir M. Nanda. 288p. 1980. pap. 9.99 (0-934664-31-5); write for info. (0-934664-29-3) Yoga Res Foun.
Yoga Vasistha, Vol. 4. Incl. Vol. 1. . Joyotir M. Nanda. 1977. pap. 9.99 (0-934664-30-7); Vol. 2. . Jyotir M. Nanda. 288p. 1980. pap. 9.99 (0-934664-31-5); 320p. 1995. Set pap. 9.99 (0-934664-33-1) Yoga Res Foun.
***Yoga Vision: A Selection of Yoga Sutras.** Ed. & Tr. by Vijayendra Pratap from SAN. LC 95-68061. (Illus.). 80p. (Orig.). 1995. mass mkt. 6.90 (0-944731-01-5) Sky Fnd.
Yoga Week by Week. Selvarajan Yesudian. Tr. by D. Q. Stephenson. 1988. 12.95 (0-04-149051-7) Routledge Chapman & Hall.
Yoga Wisdom of the Upanishads: Kena..Mundaka..Prashna..Ishavasya. Jyotir M. Nanda. (Illus.). 1974. pap. 6.99 (0-934664-36-6) Yoga Res Foun.
Yoga, You, Your New Life. K. Japananda. (Illus.). 208p. spiral bd. 5.95 (0-9613099-0-3) Temple Kriya Yoga.
***Yoga, Youth, & Reincarnation.** Jess Stearn. LC 92-8770. 1992. pap. 12.95 (0-87604-288-4) ARE Pr.
Yoga, Youth & Reincarnation. rev. ed. Jess Stearn. 336p. 1965. write for info. (0-87554-563-7, B935) Valley Sun.
Yogacara Idealism. Ashok K. Chatterjee. (C). 1987. reprint ed. 12.75 (81-208-0315-9, Pub. by Motilal Banarsidass II) S Asia.
Yogacara School of Buddhism: A Bibliography. John Powers. LC 91-37139. (American Theological Library Association Monograph: No. 27). 267p. 1991. 32.00 (0-8108-2502-3) Scarecrow.
Yogacise: The No-Sweat' Exercise Programme for the 90s. Lyn Marshall. (Illus.). 95p. 1995. pap. 9.95 (0-563-36279-0, Pub. by BBC UK) Parkwest Pubns.
Yogananda Returns. Robert R. Leichtman. (From Heaven to Earth Ser.). 104p. (Orig.). 1981. pap. 3.50 (0-89804-066-3) Ariel GA.
Yoganomics: Pure Motion & the Law of Economic Erosion. Paul C. Du Houx. 144p. 1992. pap. 11.95 (1-882190-00-9) Polar Bear ME.
Yogarobic Wellness: The Esoteric Art & Science of Fitness, Health, & Longevity. S. A. Swami. 1994. write for info. (0-941553-03-5) Minibook Pub.
Yogavarttika of Vijnanabhiksu, Vol. 3: Vibhutipada. Tr. by T. S. Rukmani. 1988. 26.00 (81-215-0057-5, Pub. by Munshiram Manoharial II) S Asia.
Yogi: A Fascinating Biography of One of Baseball's Most Illustrious Hall-of-Famers. Gene Schoor. Date not set. write for info. (0-688-04416-6) Morrow.
Yogi: Portraits of Swami Vishnu-Devananda. Gopala Krishna. LC 95-4692. (Illus.). 150p. (Orig.). 1995. pap. 12.95 (0-936663-12-X) Yes Intl.
Yogi & the Bear: Story of Indo-Soviet Relations. S. Nihal Singh. LC 85-62583. 324p. (C). 1986. 29.00 (0-913215-12-0) Riverdale Co.
Yogi & the Mystic: Studies in Indian & Comparative Mysticism. Ed. by Karel Werner. (Durham Indological Ser.: No. 1). 1989. 42.00 (0-913215-35-X) Riverdale Co.
Yogi & the Mystic: Studies in Indian & Comparative Mysticism. Karel Werner. 208p. (C). 1993. pap. text ed. 20.00 (0-7007-0272-5, Pub. by Curzon Press UK) UH Pr.
Yogi Bear - Wild Winter: A Pop-Up Fun Book. Bedrock Staff. 1995. 6.98 (1-57036-250-5, Bedrock Press) Turner Pub GA.
Yogi Bear ABC Adventure. (Shaped Hanna Barbera Board Bks.). (Illus.). 12p. (J). (ps-6). Date not set. bds. write for info. (1-56987-436-0) Landoll.
Yogi Berra. Marty Appel. (Baseball Legends Ser.). (Illus.). 64p. (J). (gr. 3 up). 1992. lib. bdg. 15.95 (0-7910-1169-0) Chelsea Hse.
Yogi of Cockroach Court. Frank Waters. LC 72-91922. 277p. 1947. pap. 12.95 (0-8040-0613-X) Swallow.
Yogi Philosophy & Oriental Occultism: Correspondence Class Course, Lessons 1 Through VII. Yogi Ramacharaka. (Yogi Bks.). 139p. 1972. reprint ed. spiral bd. 6.50 (0-7873-0690-8) Hlth Research.
Yogic Cure for Common Diseases. enl. rev. ed. Phulgenda Sinha. (Orient Paperbacks Ser.). 204p. 1981. 9.50 (0-86578-227-X); pap. 4.95 (0-86578-076-5) Ind-US Inc.
Yogic Deeds of Bodhisattvas: Gyeltsap on Aryadeva's Four Hundred. Ed. & Tr. by Ruth Sonam from TIB. LC 93-23972. (Textual Studies & Translations in Indo-Tibetan Buddhism Ser.). 450p. 1994. 40.00 (1-55939-014-X); pap. 24.95 (1-55939-019-0) Snow Lion Pubns.
Yogic Management of Asthma & Diabetes. S. Saraswati. 1979. 11.95 (0-318-37197-9) Asia Bk Corp.
Yogic Perspective on the Twelve Steps. Yogi A. Desai. 22p. (Orig.). 1993. pap. 4.95 (0-940258-27-7) Kripalu Pubns.
Yogic Pranayama: Breathing for Long & Good Health. K. S. Joshi. (C). 1992. pap. 8.50 (81-222-0089-3, Pub. by Vision) S Asia.
Yogic Pranayama: Breathing for Long, Long Life. K. S. Joshi. 180p. 1983. pap. 9.00 (0-86578-222-9) Ind-US Inc.
Yogic Psalter. Henry Compton. 64p. 1984. 45.00 (0-7212-0679-4, Pub. by Regency Press UK) St Mut.
Yogic Treatments & Natural Remedies. Prabhat Rainjan Sarkar. 100p. (Orig.). 1989. text ed. 5.95 (0-88476-029-4) Ananda Marga.
Yogis & Mystics. Pranab Bandyopadhyay. (C). 1988. 32.50 (81-85094-13-6) S Asia.
Yogi's Big Jungle Adventure. (Fantastic Discoveries Ser.). 28p. (J). (ps-6). Date not set. text ed. 9.95 (1-56987-218-X) Landoll.
Yogo: The Great American Sapphire. rev. ed. Stephen M. Voynick. LC 87-25683. (Illus.). 219p. 1987. pap. 12.00 (0-87842-217-X) Mountain Pr.
Yogurt: All about It. D. Westhoff. 144p. 1980. 9.95 (0-8159-5025-X) Devin.
Yogurt Market. Ed. by Peter Allen. 100p. 1989. pap. 795.00 (0-941285-43-X) FIND-SVP.
Yogurt, Yoghurt, Yoghourt: An International Cookbook. Linda K. Fuller. LC 92-45045. 270p. 1994. pap. 14.95 (1-56022-034-1); lib. bdg. 39.95 (1-56022-033-3) Haworth Pr.
Yohan English-Japanese-English Dictionary. Fujihiko Kaneda. 526p. (ENG & JPN.). 1983. 49.95 (0-8288-1012-5, M1754) Fr & Eur.
***Yohannes IV of Ethiopia: A Political Biography.** Zewde Gabre-Sellassie. LC 97-11227. 1997. pap. 18.95 (1-56902-043-4) Red Sea Pr.
***Yohannes IV of Ethiopia: A Political Biography.** Gabre-Sellassie Zewde. LC 97-11227. 1997. write for info. (1-56902-042-6) Red Sea Pr.
***Yohimbe.** Ita Elkins. (The Woodland Health Ser.). 1997. pap. text ed. 3.95 (1-885670-70-2) Woodland UT.
Yohkoh (Solar-A) Mission. Ed. by Z. Svestka & Y. Uchida. (C). 1992. lib. bdg. 129.50 (0-7923-1532-4) Kluwer Ac.
Yoke of Christ: Martin Bucer & Christian Discipline. Amy Burnett. LC 93-47542. (Sixteenth Century Essays & Studies: Vol. 27). 1994. 40.00 (0-940474-28-X) Sixteenth Cent.
Yoke of Love: Prophetic Riddles in The Merchant of Venice. Avraham Oz. LC 93-31278. 264p. 1995. 39.50 (0-87413-490-0) U Delaware Pr.
***Yoke of Obedience.** Campbell. 10.35 (0-687-46660-1) Abingdon.
Yoke of the Thorah. Henry Harland. LC 75-104474. 320p. reprint ed. lib. bdg. 21.50 (0-8398-0759-7) Irvington.
Yoke of the Thorah. Henry Harland. 320p. 1986. reprint ed. pap. text ed. 8.95 (0-8290-1962-6) Irvington.
Yoke up with Jesus. Betty P. Peebles. 10p. (Orig.). 1989. pap. text ed. 4.00 (0-918925-27-4) Jericho Chr Trng.
Yoked with a Lamb, & Other Stories. Helen R. Martin. LC 76-152948. (Short Story Index Reprint Ser.). 1977. reprint ed. 21.95 (0-8369-3807-0) Ayer.
Yokibics...A Mindbody Workbook for Everyday Living. Gail Chiarella. Ed. by Leah Aron. (Illus.). 120p. 1992. Wkbk. student ed. 19.95 (0-9635563-1-2) Yokibics.
Yoking Science & Religion: The Life & Thought of Ralph Wendell Burhoe. David R. Breed. LC 91-67648. (Zygon Bks.: No. 2). (Illus.). 150p. (Orig.). 1992. pap. 12.95 (0-9618233-1-3) Zygon Jrnl of Rel.
Yoknapatawpha: The Land of William Faulkner. Alain Desvergnes. 1993. pap. text ed. 21.95 (2-86234-041-3, Pub. by Marval FR) Dist Art Pubs.
Yoknapatawpha Chronicle of Gavin Stevens. John K. Crane. LC 87-42809. 312p. 1988. 42.50 (0-941664-90-2) Susquehanna U Pr.
***Yoko.** Wells. Date not set. 14.95 (0-7868-0395-9); 14.89 (0-7868-2345-3) Hyperion.
Yoko Ono: The Bronze Age. 51p. 1989. pap. 15.00 (1-880337-06-1) Cranbrook Acad.
Yokohama: Prints from Nineteenth-Century Japan. Ann Yonemura. LC 90-9479. (Illus.). 224p. 1990. pap. 26.95 (0-87474-999-9) Smithsonian.
Yokohama, California. Toshio Mori & Lawson F. Inada. LC 84-21987. 176p. (Orig.). 1985. reprint ed. pap. 12.95 (0-295-96167-8) U of Wash Pr.
Yokomitsu Riichi, Modernist. Dennis Keene. LC 79-28532. (Modern Asian Literature Ser.). 1980. text ed. 47.50 (0-231-04938-2) Col U Pr.
Yokuts & Western Mono Ethnography I: Tulare Lake, Southern Valley, & Central Foothill Yokuts. fac. ed. A. H. Gayton. Ed. by Robert H. Lowie et al. (University of California Publications: No. 10:1). (Illus.). 140p. (C). 1948. reprint ed. pap. 13.70 (1-55567-034-2) Coyote Press.
Yokuts & Western Mono Ethnography II: Northern Foothill Yokuts & Western Mono. fac. ed. A. H. Gayton. Ed. by A. L. Kroeber et al. (University of California Publications: No. 10:2). (Illus.). 301p. (C). 1948. reprint ed. pap. 15.00 (1-55567-035-0) Coyote Press.
Yokuts & Western Mono Myths. fac. ed. A. H. Gayton & S. S. Newman. Ed. by Robert H. Lowie et al. (University of California Publications: No. 5:1). 115p. (C). 1940. reprint ed. pap. 10.30 (1-55567-081-4) Coyote Press.
Yokuts & Western Mono Potter-Making. fac. ed. A. H. Gayton. (University of California Publications in American Archaeology & Ethnology: Vol. 24: 3). 24p. (C). 1929. reprint ed. pap. text ed. 2.50 (1-55567-267-1) Coyote Press.
Yokuts Dialect Survey. fac. ed. A. L. Kroeber. Ed. by J. H. Rowe et al. (University of California Publications: No. 11:3). 83p. (C). 1963. reprint ed. pap. 7.50 (1-55567-126-8) Coyote Press.
Yokuts Language of South Central California. fac. ed. A. L. Kroeber. (University of California Publications in American Archaeology & Ethnology: Vol. 2: 5). 213p. (C). 1907. reprint ed. pap. text ed. 19.40 (1-55567-161-6) Coyote Press.
Yokuts-Mono Chiefs & Shamans. fac. ed. A. H. Gayton. (University of California Publications in American Archaeology & Ethnology: Vol. 24: 8). 62p. (C). 1930. reprint ed. pap. text ed. 5.55 (1-55567-271-X) Coyote Press.
Yokuts Texts. Ed. by Geoffrey Gamble. LC 93-39338. (Native American Texts Ser.: No. 1). ix, 108p. (Orig.). (C). 1994. pap. text ed. 14.95 (3-11-012955-8) Mouton.
Yolanda & the Strange Objects. Lezley Saar. LC 78-64740. (Illus.). 1978. pap. 6.95 (0-918408-10-5) Reed & Cannon.
Yolanda's Genius. Carol Fenner. 1997. 4.50 (0-689-81327-9) Mac Pub USA.
Yolanda's Genius. Carol Fenner. LC 94-46962. (J). 1995. 17.00 (0-689-80001-0, McElderry) S&S Childrens.
***Yolanda's Genius.** Carol Fenner. (J). (gr. 3-7). 1997. reprint ed. pap. 4.50 (0-614-29086-4, Aladdin Paperbacks) S&S Childrens.
Yolanda's Yellow School. Kelly A. Asbury. LC 96-21714. 1996. 7.95 (0-8050-4023-4) H Holt & Co.
Yolk. Josip Novakovich. LC 95-77951. 205p. (Orig.). 1995. pap. 12.95 (1-55597-229-2) Graywolf.
Yolngu & Their Land: A System of Land Tenure & the Fight for Its Recognition. Nancy M. Williams. LC 85-61474. (Illus.). xvi, 264p. 1986. 39.50 (0-8047-1306-5) Stanford U Pr.
***Yolonda's Genius.** Carol Fenner. 1997. audio 18.99 (0-553-47821-4) Bantam.
***Yolteotl: Eight Latino/Chicano/Hispanic Artists.** Jay A. Miskowiec et al. (Illus.). 16p. (Orig.). 1993. pap. 10.00 (1-889523-07-0) Tweed Mus.
Yom Kippur. Y. Ganz. (ArtScroll Youth Holiday Ser.). (YA). 1991. 8.99 (0-89906-977-0) Mesorah Pubns.
Yom Kippur. Norma Simon. (Festival Series of Picture Storybooks). (Illus.). (J). (ps). 1959. spiral bd. 4.50 (0-8381-0702-8) USCJE.
Yom Kippur. Philip Goodman. LC 72-151312. (Holiday Anthologies Ser.). (Illus.). 400p. 1992. reprint ed. pap. text ed. 15.95 (0-8276-0409-2) JPS Phila.
Yom Kippur: Its Significance, Laws & Prayers. Avie Gold. (ArtScroll Mesorah Ser.). 180p. 1989. 17.99 (0-89906-216-4); pap. 14.99 (0-89906-217-2) Mesorah Pubns.
Yom Kippur - A Family Service. Judith Z. Abrams. LC 90-4862. (Illus.). 22p. (Orig.). (J). (ps-4). 1990. pap. 3.95 (0-929371-17-8) Kar-Ben.
Yom Kippur - Ashkenaz: Zichron Yosef see Machzor
Yom Kippur Machzor: A New Translation with Instructions & Anthologized Commentary. Nosson Scherman. (ArtScroll Mesorah Ser.). 1989. 25.99 (0-89906-677-1) Mesorah Pubns.
Yom Kippur Murder. Lee Harris. (Holiday Mysteries Ser.). (Orig.). 1992. mass mkt. 5.50 (0-449-14763-0, GM) Fawcett.
Yom Kippur-Sefard: Zichron Zev see Machzor
Yom Kippur War: Israel & the Jewish People. Ed. by Moshe Davis. LC 74-10466. 381p. 1975. 13.95 (0-405-06192-7) Ayer.
Yom Tov Sheinikehilchaso: The Second Day of Yom Tov in Israel & Abroad. Yerachmiel D. Fried. Tr. by Moshe Dombey from HEB. 152p. 1990. 11.95 (0-944070-57-4) Targum Pr.
Yom Tov Shiurim. M. Miller. LC 94-6787. 1994. 16.95 (0-87306-673-1) Feldheim.
Yoma: Or, Yom Kippur, 2 vols. (ENG & HEB.). 30.00 (0-910218-57-9) Bennet Pub.
***Yomoria the Lawmaker: Stories of the Dene.** George Blondin. (Northwest Passage Ser.). (Illus.). 263p. 1997. pap. 17.95 (1-896300-20-0, Pub. by NeWest Pub CN) Genl Dist Srvs.
Yomtevdike Teg. Illus. by Tsirl Waletszky. (Songbook for the Holidays Ser.). 105p. pap. 6.00 (0-318-20363-4) Workmen's Circle.
Yon Ill Wind. Piers Anthony. LC 96-16216. 320p. 1996. 23.95 (0-312-86227-X) St Martin.
Yonah: Kanfei Yonah. Yaakov Y. Yehudi. 183p. (C). 1994. 12.00 (1-880880-05-9) Israeli Trad.
Yonah-Jonah. Meir Zlotowitz. (Art Scroll Tanach Ser.). 160p. 1978. 17.99 (0-89906-081-1); pap. 14.99 (0-89906-082-X) Mesorah Pubns.
Yonder. Tony Johnston. LC 86-11549. (Illus.). 32p. (J). (ps-3). 1988. pap. 12.95 (0-8037-0277-9); lib. bdg. 12.89 (0-8037-0278-7) Dial Bks Young.
Yonder. Tony Johnston. (J). 1992. pap. 5.99 (0-14-054731-2) NAL-Dutton.
Yonder. Tony Johnston. LC 86-11549. (Illus.). 32p. (J). (ps-3). 1991. pap. 4.95 (0-8037-0987-0, Puff Pied Piper) Puffin Bks.
Yonder: Life on the Far Side of Change. Jim W. Corder. LC 91-33931. 256p. 1992. 24.95 (0-8203-1419-6) U of Ga Pr.
Yonder Comes the Train. Lance Phillips. 1993. 24.98 (0-88365-715-5) Galahad Bks.
Yonder Hills: Shady Cove, Elk Creek, Persist, Trail, Etna. Barbara Morehouse Hegne. 128p. (Orig.). 1989. spiral bd. 13.95 (0-9623847-1-2) B Hegne.
***Yonder Man.** Hank Edwards. 288p. 1997. mass mkt. 4.99 (0-06-101162-2, Harp PBks) HarpC.
Yonder the Bridge: The Story of an Impossible Courtship. Eva Berck. Ed. by Robert C. Alberts. 496p. 1991. 19.95 (0-9629937-0-0); pap. 11.95 (0-9629937-1-9) Somerset PA.
Yonderin' To the Far Horizon. Ruth Grewe. 182p. 1992. pap. 16.95 (0-9634435-0-X) Farview Pr.
Yondering. rev. ed. Louis L'Amour. (Orig.). 1989. pap. 3.99 (0-553-28203-4) Random Hse Value.
Yoni. Howard I. Bogot. (Illus.). (J). (ps). 1982. pap. 4.00 (0-8074-0166-8, 101980) UAHC.
Yoni: Sacred Symbol of Female Creative Power. Rufus C. Camphausen. (Illus.). 144p. 1996. pap. 19.95 (0-89281-562-0) Inner Tradit.
Yoni Netanyahu: Commando at Entebbe. Deborah Speregen. (Young Biography Ser.). (Illus.). 128p. (J). (gr. 4 up). 1995. 14.95 (0-8276-0523-4) JPS Phila.
***Yoni Netanyahu: Commando at Entebbe.** Devra N. Spergen. (Illus.). 128p. (YA). (gr. 8 up). 1997. pap. 10.95 (0-8276-0642-7) JPS Phila.
***Yonie Wondernose.** Marguerite De Angeli. LC 97-18919. (Illus.). 48p. (J). (gr. k-3). 1997. pap. 10.99 (0-8361-9083-1) Herald Pr.
Yonitantra. Ed. by J. A. Schoterman. 1985. 11.00 (0-8364-1326-1, Pub. by Manohar II) S Asia.
Yonkers, Illustrated. Compiled by Yonkers Board of Trade Staff. (Illus.). 192p. 1995. reprint ed. lib. bdg. 32.50 (0-8328-4606-6) Higginson Bk Co.
Yonnondio. 160p. 1979. pap. 11.95 (0-385-29179-5, Delta) Dell.
Yonnondio. Tillie Olsen. 1984. 22.00 (0-8446-6089-2) Peter Smith.
Yoo Hoo: I'm over Here. Harriet P. McIntosh. (Illus.). 108p. (Orig.). 1996. pap. 9.95 (0-614-07235-2) Jokake Pr.
***Yoo Hoo! I'm over Here!** Harriet P. McIntosh. (Illus.). 108p. (Orig.). 1996. pap. write for info. (0-614-30154-8) Jokake Pr.
Yoo-Hoo Little Rabbit. J. P. Miller. LC 85-61529. (J). (ps). 1986. 4.99 (0-394-87884-1) Random Bks Yng Read.
Yoo Hoo, Moon! Mary Blocksma. (Illus.). 32p. (J). 1992. pap. 3.99 (0-553-35212-1) Bantam.
Yoo Hoo Prosperity: The Eddie Cantor Five-Year Plan. Eddie Cantor & David Freedman. LC 92-74295. (Illus.). 64p. 1992. reprint ed. pap. 8.00 (0-87034-107-3) Fraser Pub Co.
Yookoso! An Invitation to Contemporary Japanese. Yasu-Hiko Tohsaku. LC 93-7948. (ENG & JPN.). 1993. text ed. write for info. (0-07-072291-9) McGraw.
***Yookoso! An Invitation to Contemporary Japanese, Pt. A.** Yasu-Hiko Tohsaku. 1993. lab manual ed., wbk. ed., pap. text ed. write for info. (0-07-072293-5) McGraw.
Yookoso! Continuing with Contemporary Japanese. Yasu-Hiko Tohsaku. 1995. text ed. write for info. (0-07-072298-6) McGraw.
Yookoso! Continuing with Contemporary Japanese. Yasu-Hiko Tohsaku. 1995. lab manual ed., wbk. ed., pap. text ed. write for info. (0-07-072299-4) McGraw.
Yoomee & the Wonder Team. Ray Wilkins. (Illus.). 39p. (J). (gr. k-3). 1995. text ed. 14.95 (0-9648290-0-2) Red Carnation Trng Inst.
***Yoong Bae: Late Works.** Kumja P. Kim & Margaret Lee. Ed. by Michael Morrison. (Illus.). 24p. (Orig.). 1996. pap. 5.00 (0-939117-08-8) Asian Art Mus.
Yordan Yovkov. Edward Mozejko. 117p. 1984. pap. 14.95 (0-89357-117-2) Slavica.
Yorick & the Critics: Sterne's Reputation in England, 1760-1868. Alan B. Howes. LC 75-163005. (Yale Studies in English: No. 139). x, 186p. (C). 1971. reprint ed. lib. bdg. 32.50 (0-208-01129-3, Archon Bks) Shoe String.
Yorick's World: Science & the Knowing Subject. Peter Caws. LC 92-31834. (C). 1993. 45.00 (0-520-07919-1) U CA Pr.
York. Pevensey Pr. Staff. (C). 1987. text ed. 55.00 (0-907115-21-7, Pub. by Pevensey UK); pap. text ed. 40.00 (0-907115-22-5, Pub. by Pevensey UK) St Mut.
York, 2 vols., Set. Ed. by Alexandra F. Johnston & Margaret Rogerson. LC 78-14756. (Records of Early English Drama Ser.). 1979. 95.00 (0-8020-2304-5) U of Toronto Pr.
York: Being the Story of Mrs. Osgoods Will. Mark Dunster. 50p. (Orig.). 1981. pap. 4.00 (0-89642-082-5) Linden Pubs.
York: To the Setting of the Sun. Georg R. Sheets. 22.95 (0-89781-023-6) Am Historical Pr.
York & the Moors. (Ordnance Survey Landranger Guides Ser.). (Illus.). 144p. 1993. pap. 15.95 (0-7117-0567-4) Seven Hills Bk.
York-Antwerp Rules. N. G. Hudson. 287p. 1991. 100.00 (1-85044-294-0) LLP.
York As They Saw It From Alcuin to Lord Esher. David Palliser & Mary Palliser. (C). 1988. 60.00 (0-900657-45-6, Pub. by W Sessions UK) St Mut.
York Blitz Nineteen Forty-Two. Leo Kessler & Eric Taylor. (C). 1988. 24.00 (1-85072-009-6, Pub. by W Sessions UK) St Mut.
York Butchers Gild from AD Twelve Seventy-Two. Sessions, William Ltd., Staff. (C). 1990. 26.00 (0-900657-20-0, Pub. by W Sessions UK) St Mut.
York Company of Merchant Adventurers. David Palliser. (C). 1990. 30.00 (0-685-37378-9, Pub. by W Sessions UK) St Mut.
York County: Virginia Publick Claims. Janice L. Abercrombie & Richard Slatten. (Virginia Publick Claims Ser.). ix, 27p. 1992. pap. 5.00 (0-8095-8714-9) Borgo Pr.
York County: Virginia Publick Claims. Janice L. Abercrombie & Richard Slatten. (Virginia Publick Claims Ser.). ix, 27p. (C). 1992. reprint ed. lib. bdg. 25.00 (0-8095-8368-2) Borgo Pr.
York County Marriage Returns, 1771-1794. George W. Chamberlain. 14p. 1986. reprint ed. pap. 2.50 (0-935207-34-1) Danbury Hse Bks.
York County, Virginia, Orders, Wills, & Inventories, 1733-1734. T.L.C. Genealogy Staff. 117p. (Orig.). 1992. spiral bd., pap. 14.00 (1-57445-010-7) TLC Genealogy.
York County, Virginia Records, 1659-1662. Benjamin B. Weisiger, 3rd. 180p. 1989. pap. 15.00 (0-8095-8715-7); lib. bdg. 39.00 (0-8095-8264-3) Borgo Pr.
York County, Virginia Records, 1665-1672. Benjamin B. Weisiger, 3rd. 281p. 1987. pap. 20.00 (0-8095-8716-5); lib. bdg. 49.00 (0-8095-8263-5) Borgo Pr.
York County, Virginia Records, 1672-1676. Benjamin B. Weisiger, 3rd. 216p. 1991. pap. 22.00 (0-8095-8717-3); lib. bdg. 52.00 (0-8095-8265-1) Borgo Pr.
York County, Virginia Wills, Deeds, Orders, 1657-1659, Vol. 5. Lindsay O. Duvall. (Virginia Colonial Abstracts, Series II). 1978. reprint ed. 17.50 (0-89308-066-7) Southern Hist Pr.
York Ferry. Annie Dawid. LC 92-53146. 179p. (Orig.). (C). 1992. pap. text ed. 10.95 (0-943433-10-X) Cane Hill Pr.
***York Handbooks: Studying Shakespeare.** Stephen & Franks. 1984. pap. text ed. 9.50 (0-582-03572-4, Pub. by Longman UK) Longman.
York House Books 1461-1490, 2 vols., Set. Lorraine C. Attreed. (Illus.). (C). 1991. text ed. 150.00 (0-86299-936-7, Pub. by Sutton Pubng UK) Bks Intl VA.
York Legal Record, 108 vols., Set. 1979. 1,650.00 (1-57588-380-5, 501700) W S Hein.

York, Maine, Marriages, 1697-1760. Michael J. Denis. 25p. 1985. pap. 4.00 (*0-935207-15-5*) Danbury Hse Bks.

York Minster: The Great East Window. Ed. by Thomas French. (Corpus Vitraearum Medii Aevi: Great Britain Summary Catalogue 1 British Academy Ser.: No. 2). (Illus.). 190p. 1995. text ed. 95.00 (*0-19-726136-1*) OUP.

York Music: The Story of a City's Music from 1304-1896. James Merryweather. (C). 1988. 85.00 (*1-85072-034-7*, Pub. by W Sessions UK) St Mut.

York Mystery Play. Eileen White. (C). 1988. 35.00 (*0-900657-93-6*, Pub. by W Sessions UK); 50.00 (*1-85072-094-0*, Pub. by W Sessions UK) St Mut.

York Mystery Plays: A Selection in Modern Spelling. Ed. by Richard Beadle & Pamela King. (World's Classics Ser.). 420p. 1995. pap. 10.95 (*0-19-282437-6*) OUP.

***York Notes: Billy Lair.** Waterhouse. 1992. pap. text ed. write for info. (*0-582-03822-7*, Pub. by Longman UK) Longman.

***York Notes: Mansfield Park.** Austen. 1992. pap. text ed. write for info. (*0-582-03967-3*, Pub. by Longman UK) Longman.

***York Notes on Lee's Cider with Rosie.** Lee. 1992. pap. text ed. write for info. (*0-582-03365-9*) Addison-Wesley.

***York Notes on Miller's View from the Bridge.** Miller. 1992. pap. text ed. write for info. (*0-582-02091-3*) Addison-Wesley.

***York Pocket Guide.** Ian Sampson. (Illus.). 80p. (Orig.). 1997. pap. 8.95 (*1-900455-19-6*, Pub. by Colin Baxter Ltd UK) Voyageur Pr.

York Retreat: In the Light of the Quaker Way. Kathleen A. Stewart. (C). 1989. pap. 21.00 (*1-85072-089-4*, Pub. by W Sessions UK) St Mut.

York Silver, 1475-1858: Illustrated Catalogue of the William Lee Collection in York Minster. Sessions, William Ltd., Staff. (C). 1988. 40.00 (*0-900657-59-6*, Pub. by W Sessions UK) St Mut.

York, South Carolina, Newspapers Marriage & Death Notices 1823-1865. Brent H. Holcomb. LC 81-17743. 129p. 1989. 25.00 (*0-87152-353-1*) Reprint.

York, 1831-1981: The British Association One Hundred Fiftieth Anniversary. C. H. Feinstein. (C). 1988. 210.00 (*0-900657-55-3*, Pub. by W Sessions UK); pap. 90.00 (*0-900657-56-1*, Pub. by W Sessions UK) St Mut.

Yorke the Adventurer, & Other Stories. Louis Becke. LC 71-37535. (Short Story Index Reprint Ser.). 1977. reprint ed. 20.95 (*0-8369-4094-6*) Ayer.

Yorkie Doodle Dandy: The Other Woman Was a Real Dog. William A. Wynne. LC 96-90158. (Illus.). 188p. (Orig.). 1996. 15.95 (*0-9652254-0-2*) Wynnesome.

***Yorkie Doodle Dandy: The Other Woman Was a Real Dog.** William A. Wynne. LC 96-90158. (Illus.). 188p. (Orig.). 1996. pap. 15.95 (*0-9652254-5-3*) Wynnesome.

Yorkies Today. Anne Fisher. (Illus.). 160p. 1993. 24.95 (*0-948955-77-5*, Pub. by Ringpr Bks UK) Seven Hills Bk.

Yorkshire Anthology. James O. Halliwell. 404p. 1973. 49.95 (*0-8464-1440-6*) Beekman Pubs.

Yorkshire Car Tours. Ed. by Jarrold Publishing Staff. (Ordnance Survey Travelmaster Guides Ser.). (Illus.). 96p. (Orig.). 1995. pap. 15.95 (*0-7117-0826-6*, Pub. by Jarrold Pub UK) Seven Hills Bk.

Yorkshire Churches. Frank Bottomley. (Orig.). 1993. pap. 15.99 (*0-7509-0344-9*, Pub. by Sutton Pubng UK) Bks Intl VA.

Yorkshire Cricket Greats. John Callaghan. 180p. (C). 1989. text ed. 35.00 (*0-85976-325-0*, Pub. by J Donald UK) St Mut.

Yorkshire Dales. Mike Gerrard. (Passport's Regional Guides of Great Britain Ser.). (Illus.). 128p. 1996. pap. 12.95 (*0-8442-4884-3*, Passport Bks) NTC Pub Grp.

***Yorkshire Dales.** Insight Guides Staff. (Insight Compact Guides Ser.). 1997. pap. 7.95 (*0-395-82939-9*) HM.

***Yorkshire Dales.** Richard Mabey. (Illus.). 96p. 1997. 29.95 (*1-900455-09-9*, Pub. by Colin Baxter Ltd UK) Voyageur Pr.

Yorkshire Dales & York. (Ordnance Survey Landranger Guides Ser.). (Illus.). 144p. 1993. pap. 15.95 (*0-7117-0566-6*) Seven Hills Bk.

Yorkshire Dales Walks. (Ordnance Survey Pathfinder Guides Ser.). (Illus.). 80p. 1993. pap. 14.95 (*0-7117-0516-X*) Seven Hills Bk.

Yorkshire Families: Directory 1987. (C). 1987. 39.00 (*0-317-89898-1*, Pub. by Birmingham Midland Soc UK) St Mut.

Yorkshire, Fascicule 3. S. Rinaldo Tufi. (Corpus Signorum Imperii Romani, Great Britain: Vol. I). (Illus.). 1983. 19. 98 (*0-19-726019-5*) David Brown.

Yorkshire Gold. Kay Stephens. 512p. 1995. pap. 11.95 (*0-7472-4431-6*, Pub. by Headline UK) Trafalgar.

Yorkshire Gyspy Fairs, Customs & Caravans 1885-1985. Alan E. Jones. 125p. 1986. 45.00 (*0-907033-43-1*) St Mut.

Yorkshire Legends. 2nd ed. Compiled by Dalesman. (Illus.). 71p. (Orig.). 1976. pap. 4.50 (*0-686-64123-X*) Legacy Books.

Yorkshire Legends & Traditions. Thomas Parkinson. Ed. by Richard M. Dorson. LC 77-70615. (International Folklore Ser.). 1977. reprint ed. lib. bdg. 21.95 (*0-405-10117-1*) Ayer.

Yorkshire Moors & Dales. Pevensey Pr. Staff. (C). 1987. text ed. 60.00 (*0-907115-33-0*, Pub. by Pevensey UK); pap. text ed. 40.00 (*0-907115-34-9*, Pub. by Pevensey UK) St Mut.

Yorkshire Moors & Dales. Rob Talbot & Robin Whiteman. (Country Ser.). (Illus.). 160p. 1994. pap. 17.95 (*0-297-83040-6*) Trafalgar.

***Yorkshire of One Hundred Years Ago.** David Gerrard. (Illus.). 128p. 1997. text ed. 33.95 (*0-7509-1422-X*, Pub. by Sutton Pubng UK) Bks Intl VA.

***Yorkshire Rose.** large type ed. Margaret Pemberton. (Magna Large Print Ser.). 526p. 1997. 27.50 (*0-7505-0772-1*) Ulverscroft.

Yorkshire Smiles. Geoffrey Robinson. (C). 1989. text ed. 40.00 (*0-948929-26-X*) St Mut.

Yorkshire Sonnets. John Barry. (C). 1988. 30.00 (*0-904524-46-9*, Pub. by Rivelin Grapheme Pr) St Mut.

Yorkshire Stage, 1766-1803: A Calendar of Plays, Together with Cast Lists for Tate Wilkinson's Circuit of Theatres (Doncaster, Hull, Leeds, Pontefract, Wakefield, & York) & the Yorkshire Company's Engagements in Beverly, Halifax, Newcastle, Sheffield, & Edinburgh. Ed. by Linda Fitzsimmons & Arthur W. McDonald. LC 88-35569. 1103p. 1989. 87.50 (*0-8108-2187-7*) Scarecrow.

Yorkshire Terrier Champions, 1952-1980. Jan L. Pata. (Illus.). 214p. 1981. pap. 36.95 (*0-940808-08-0*) Camino E E & Bk.

Yorkshire Terrier Champions, 1981-1986. Camino E. E. & Bk. Co. Staff. (Illus.). 129p. 1987. pap. 28.95 (*0-940808-28-5*) Camino E E & Bk.

Yorkshire Terrier Champions, 1987-1993. Camino E. E. & Bk. Co. Staff. (Illus.). 105p. 1994. pap. 32.95 (*1-55893-034-5*) Camino E E & Bk.

***Yorkshire Terriers.** Stuart A. Kallen. LC 97-14828. (Dogs Ser.). (J). 1998. write for info. (*1-56239-577-7*) Abdo & Dghtrs.

Yorkshire Terriers. Osman Sameja. (Owner's Companion Ser.). (Illus.). 240p. 1992. 39.95 (*1-85223-529-2*, Pub. by Crowood Pr UK) Trafalgar.

Yorkshire Terriers, AKC Rank No. 11. Kerry Donnelly. (Illus.). 224p. 1996. pap. 9.95 (*0-7938-2386-2*, KW007S) TFH Pubns.

Yorkshire Terriers: Barron's Complete Pet Owner's Manual. Armin Kriechbaumer. 1996. pap. text ed. 6.95 (*0-8120-9750-5*) Barron.

Yorkshire Tragedy. LC 71-133776. (Tudor Facsimile Texts. Old English Plays Ser.: No. 125). reprint ed. 49.50 (*0-404-53425-2*) AMS Pr.

Yorkshire Wold Rangers. Angela Antrim. 120p. 1981. 40. 00 (*0-907033-06-7*) St Mut.

***Yorktown.** Blackbirch. 1997. 16.98 (*0-8050-5226-7*) H Holt & Co.

Yorktown Activity Book. Thomas Publications Staff. (Illus.). 40p. (Orig.). (J). (gr. k-4). 1996. pap. 2.50 (*0-939631-99-7*) Thomas Publications.

Yorktown Campaign & the Surrender of Cornwallis 1781. Henry P. Johnston. (Select Bibliographies Reprint Ser.). 1977. reprint ed. 23.95 (*0-8369-5846-2*) Ayer.

Yorktown Campaign & the Surrender of Cornwallis, 1781. Henry P. Johnston. LC 75-146149. (Era of the American Revolution Ser.). 1971. reprint ed. lib. bdg. 27.50 (*0-306-70142-1*) Da Capo.

Yorktown Campaign & the Surrender of Cornwallis, 1781. Henry P. Johnston. 206p. 1975. reprint ed. 23.95 (*0-87928-064-6*) Corner Hse.

Yorktown's Captive Fleet. John O. Sands. (Illus.). 267p. 1983. text ed. 35.00 (*0-917376-38-2*) U Pr of Va.

Yorro Yorro - Aboriginal Creation & the Renewal of Nature: The Art & Stories of the People of the Australian Kimberley. David Mowaljarlai & Jutta Malnic. (Illus.). 248p. (Orig.). 1993. pap. 19.95 (*0-89281-460-8*) Inner Tradit.

Yorston, Fortescue & Turner: Australian Commercial Law. 18th ed. Clive Turner. lxxi, 888p. 1990. 73.00 (*0-455-20924-3*, Pub. by Law Bk Co AT); pap. 49.00 (*0-455-20925-1*, Pub. by Law Bk Co AT) Gaunt.

Yorston, Fortescue & Turner: Australian Commercial Law. 20th rev. ed. Clive Turner. 1067p. 1995. pap. 57.00 (*0-455-21306-2*, Pub. by Law Bk Co AT) Gaunt.

Yoruba, 14 vols. Michael O. Anda. Ed. by George Bond & Gary V. Wyck. LC 95-15070. (Heritage Library of African Peoples). (Illus.). 64p. (YA). (gr. 7-12). 1996. lib. bdg. 15.95 (*0-8239-1988-9*) Rosen Group.

Yoruba: Nine Centuries of African Art & Thought. Henry J. Drewal & John Pemberton, III. (Illus.). 256p. 1990. 65. 00 (*0-8109-1794-7*) Abrams.

Yoruba: Nine Centuries of African Art & Thought. Henry J. Drewal et al. Ed. by Allen Wardwell. LC 89-22182. (Illus.). 1989. pap. 38.00 (*0-945802-04-8*) Museum African.

Yoruba Basic Course. Foreign Service Institute Staff. 381p. (C). 1963. pap. 295.00 (*0-88432-112-6*, AFYR01) Audio-Forum.

Yoruba Cultural Fashion. Taiyewo Ogunade. 85p. 1994. lib. bdg. write for info. (*1-881549-04-6*) Oluweri Pubns.

***Yoruba Dance: Semiotics, Movement & Yoruba Body Attitude in Communication.** Omofolabo S. Ajayi. LC 97-13295. 1997. pap. text ed. 16.95 (*0-86543-563-4*) Africa World.

***Yoruba Dance: The Semiotics of Movement & Yoruba Body Attitude.** Omofolabo S. Ajayi. LC 97-13295. 1997. write for info. (*0-86543-562-6*) Africa World.

Yoruba Drama in English: Interpretation & Production. J. B. Alston. LC 88-34185. (Studies in African Literature). 192p. 1989. lib. bdg. 79.95 (*0-88946-726-9*) E Mellen.

Yoruba-English, English-Yoruba Concise Dictionary. Olabiyi Yai. 375p. (Orig.). (ENG & YOR.). 1996. pap. 14.95 (*0-7818-0263-6*) Hippocrene Bks.

Yoruba Fables: Patakie of the Orush. Oba Ecun. (Illus.). 135p. (Orig.). (C). 1992. pap. 22.00 (*0-926603-09-4*) Obaecun Bks.

Yoruba Girl Dancing. Simi Bedford. 192p. 1994. pap. 10.95 (*0-14-023293-1*, Penguin Bks) Viking Penguin.

Yoruba Historiography. Ed. by Toyin Falola. LC 91-32517. (Illus.). 214p. (Orig.). 1991. pap. 24.00 (*0-942615-10-7*) U Wis African Stud.

Yoruba Legends. M. I. Ogumefu. LC 78-63217. (Folktale Ser.). 96p. 1985. reprint ed. 27.50 (*0-404-16153-7*) AMS Pr.

Yoruba of Southwestern Nigeria. William Bascom. (Illus.). 118p. 1984. reprint ed. pap. text ed. 9.50 (*0-88133-038-8*) Waveland Pr.

Yoruba of West Africa, 6, Set. Jamie Hetfield. LC 96-6993. (Celebrating the Peoples & Civilizations of Africa Ser.). (Illus.). 24p. (J). (gr. k-4). 1996. lib. bdg. 10.46 (*0-8239-2332-0*, PowerKids) Rosen Group.

Yoruba Poetry: An Anthology of Traditional Poems. Ulli Beier. LC 77-92244. 126p. reprint ed. pap. 36.00 (*0-317-26051-0*, 2024420) Bks Demand.

Yoruba Popular Theatre: Three Plays by the Oyin Adejobi Company. Ed. by Bayo Ogundijo. Tr. by Karin Barter. LC 94-29997. 1994. 35.00 (*0-918456-70-3*) African Studies Assn.

Yoruba Religion: Introduction to its Practice. Conrad E. Mauge. 112p. (Orig.). 1993. pap. text ed. 12.95 (*0-9637516-0-3*) Hse of Providence.

Yoruba Religious Worship, Traditional God Worship, Belief & Practice. Taiyewo Ogunade. LC 92-91208. 182p. 1995. lib. bdg. 19.95 (*1-881549-03-8*) Oluweri Pubns.

Yoruba Ritual: Performers, Play, Agency. Margaret T. Drewal. LC 91-8414. (African Systems of Thought Ser.). (Illus.). 276p. 1992. text ed. 35.00 (*0-253-31817-3*); pap. text ed. 15.95 (*0-253-20684-7*, MB-684) Ind U Pr.

Yoruba Sacred Kingship: A Power Like That of the Gods. John Pemberton, III & Funso S. Afolayan. LC 95-26789. 256p. 1996. text ed. 49.00 (*1-56098-631-X*) Smithsonian.

Yoruba-Speaking Peoples of South-Western Nigeria. Cyril D. Forde. LC 70-575491. (Ethnographic Survey of Africa: Western Africa Ser.: No. 4). 115p. reprint ed. pap. 32.80 (*0-8357-6953-4*, 2039012) Bks Demand.

Yoruba-Speaking Peoples of the Slave Coast of West Africa. Alfred B. Ellis. 1964. 25.00 (*0-910216-03-7*) Benin.

***Yoruba Trickster Tales.** Oyekan Owomoyela. LC 96-37321. 240p. 1997. pap. 15.00 (*0-8032-8611-2*, Bison Books); text ed. 40.00 (*0-8032-3563-1*) U of Nebr Pr.

Yoruba World of Good & Evil. Conrad E. Mauge. (Illus.). 180p. (Orig.). 1994. pap. 12.95 (*0-9637516-1-1*) Hse of Providence.

Yorubaland: The Flowering of Genius. Philip Koslow. (Kingdoms of Africa Ser.). (Illus.). 64p. (J). (gr. 3 up). 1995. lib. bdg. 17.95 (*0-7910-3131-4*) Chelsea Hse.

***Yorubaland: The Flowering of Genius.** Philip Koslow. (Kingdoms of Africa Ser.). (Illus.). 63p. (J). (gr. 3 up). 1995. pap. 8.95 (*0-7910-3132-2*) Chelsea Hse.

Yosef's Gift of Many Colors: An Easter Story. Cassandre Maxwell. LC 92-44189. 32p. (J). (ps-3). 1993. 14.99 (*0-8066-2627-5*, 9-2627) Augsburg Fortress.

Yosemite. (Album Ser.: No. 4). 1976. pap. 7.95 (*0-87130-054-0*) Eakins.

Yosemite. Ansel Adams. 1995. 18.95 (*0-614-15013-2*) Little.

Yosemite. Jenny Markert. (Vision Bks.). 32p. (J). (gr. 2-6). 1992. lib. bdg. 22.79 (*0-89565-857-7*); lib. bdg. 22.79 (*1-56766-033-9*) Childs World.

Yosemite. Gary McCarthy. 384p. 1995. mass mkt. 5.99 (*0-8217-0144-4*, Zebra Kensgtn) Kensgtn Pub Corp.

Yosemite. National Park Service Staff. LC 88-17932. (Handbook Ser.: No. 138). (Illus.). 144p. (Orig.). 1989. pap. 5.50 (*0-912627-37-9*) Natl Park Serv.

Yosemite. Andrea G. Stillman. LC 95-12010. (Illus.). 112p. 1995. pap. 18.95 (*0-8212-2196-5*) Bulfinch Pr.

Yosemite. 3rd ed. Ed. by Jeff Nicholas. (Wish You Were Here Postcard Bks.). (Illus.). 32p. 1992. pap. 4.95 (*0-939365-10-3*) Sierra Pr CA.

Yosemite. John Muir. 1992. reprint ed. lib. bdg. 75.00 (*0-7812-5068-4*) Rprt Serv.

Yosemite. John Muir. LC 87-23573. (John Muir Library). (Illus.). 288p. 1988. reprint ed. pap. 10.00 (*0-87156-782-2*) Sierra.

Yosemite. Galen A. Rowell. LC 88-34919. (Illus.). 224p. 1992. reprint ed. pap. 25.00 (*0-87156-587-0*) Sierra.

***Yosemite: A Guide to Yosemite National Park.** 1997. lib. bdg. 250.95 (*0-8490-8173-4*) Gordon Pr.

Yosemite: A Sweeping Epic Novel of the American Wilderness in the Bestselling Tradition of James Michener... Gary McCarthy. 476p. 1995. mass mkt. 5.99 (*0-7860-0144-5*, Pinncle Kensgtn) Kensgtn Pub Corp.

Yosemite: A Visitor's Companion. George Wuerthner. (Illus.). 240p. 1994. pap. 14.95 (*0-8117-2598-7*) Stackpole.

Yosemite: A Visitors Guide. (Illus.). 145p. (Orig.). (C). 1994. pap. 25.00 (*0-7881-1099-3*) DIANE Pub.

Yosemite: An American Treasure. Ed. by Donald J. Crump. LC 90-5655. (Special Publications Series 25: No. 1). (Illus.). (YA). 1990. 12.95 (*0-87044-789-0*) Natl Geog.

Yosemite: Cycle of the Seasons. rev. ed. Lynn Wilson et al. Ed. by Nicky Leach. (Wish You Were Here Postcard Bks.). 96p. 1993. 24.95 (*0-939365-30-8*); pap. 14.95 (*0-939365-29-4*) Sierra Pr CA.

Yosemite: Its Discovery, Its Wonders & Its People. Margaret Sanborn. (Illus.). 292p. 1989. reprint ed. pap. 9.95 (*0-939666-50-2*) Yosemite Assn.

Yosemite: The Embattled Wilderness. Alfred E. Runte. LC 89-35128. (Illus.). xii, 319p. 1990. pap. 14.95 (*0-8032-8941-3*, Bison Books) U of Nebr Pr.

Yosemite: The Story Behind the Scenery. 3rd rev. ed. William R. Jones. LC 88-81691. (Illus.). 48p. (Orig.). 1989. pap. 7.95 (*0-88714-024-6*) KC Pubns.

Yosemite: The Ultimate Park Print Book. Jim Wilson. Ed. by Jeff Nicholas. (Illus.). 28p. (Orig.). 1996. pap. 7.95 (*0-939365-51-0*) Sierra Pr CA.

Yosemite: Valley of Thunder. Ann Awinger. (Genesis Ser.). 1996. 37.50 (*0-614-96864-X*) Harper SF.

Yosemite - A Landscape of Life. Jay Mather & Dale Maharidge. Ed. by Terry Hennessy. LC 90-41607. (Illus.). 120p. (Orig.). 1990. pap. 14.95 (*0-939666-56-1*) Yosemite Assn.

Yosemite & Eastern Sierra in a Nutshell. Leslie D. Cole. (In a Nutshell Ser.). (Illus.). 1995. pap. 5.95 (*1-884497-04-7*) Nutshell TourMaps.

Yosemite & Its Innkeepers. Shirley Sargent. (Illus.). 1975. 10.00 (*0-685-29092-1*) Flying Spur Pr.

Yosemite & Sequoia: A Century of California National Parks. Ed. by Richard J. Orsi et al. LC 92-42370. 1993. 40.00 (*0-520-08160-9*); pap. 15.00 (*0-520-08161-7*) U CA Pr.

Yosemite & the High Sierra. Ansel Adams. Ed. by Andrea G. Stillman. LC 94-8522. (Illus.). 136p. 1994. 50.00 (*0-8212-2134-5*) Bulfinch Pr.

Yosemite As We Saw It - A Centennial Collection of Early Writings & Art. David Robertson & Henry Berrey. LC 89-28251. (Illus.). 104p. 1990. 34.95 (*0-939666-53-7*) Yosemite Assn.

Yosemite Climbs Big Walls. rev. ed. Don Reid. (Illus.). 216p. 1996. pap. 20.00 (*0-934641-54-4*) Chockstone Pr.

Yosemite Climbs Free Climbs: Free Climbs. Don Reid. (Illus.). 424p. (Orig.). 1994. pap. 25.00 (*0-934641-59-5*) Chockstone Pr.

Yosemite Fun Book: A Kid's Guide to Yosemite. Michael E. Ross. (Illus.). 48p. (J). (gr. 3-8). 1987. pap. 2.95 (*0-939666-45-6*) Yosemite Assn.

Yosemite Grant, 1864-1906: A Pictorial History. Hank Johnston. (Illus.). 288p. 1995. 29.95 (*0-939666-79-0*) Yosemite Assn.

Yosemite in Winter: An 1892 Account. James M. Carson. Ed. by William R. Jones. (Illus.). 64p. 1979. reprint ed. pap. 2.95 (*0-89646-053-3*) Vistabooks.

Yosemite Indians. Elizabeth Godfrey. (Illus.). 36p. 1977. reprint ed. pap. 2.95 (*0-939666-21-9*) Yosemite Assn.

Yosemite National Park. Photos by Jerry Pavia. (Tiny Folios Ser.). (Illus.). 320p. 1996. pap. 11.95 (*0-7892-0131-3*) Abbeville Pr.

Yosemite National Park. David Petersen. LC 92-39156. (New True Bks.). (Illus.). 48p. (J). (gr. k-4). 1993. lib. bdg. 19.00 (*0-516-01335-1*) Childrens.

Yosemite National Park. 3rd rev. ed. Jeffrey P. Schaffer. LC 89-22444. (Illus.). 280p. (Orig.). 1992. pap. 16.95 (*0-89997-107-5*) Wilderness Pr.

Yosemite National Park: A Postcard Folio Book. Ansel Adams. (Illus.). 1996. pap. text ed. 9.95 (*0-8212-2283-X*) Bulfinch Pr.

Yosemite National Park, CA. rev. ed. Ed. by Trails Illustrated Staff. (Illus.). 1994. Folded topographical map. 8.99 (*0-925873-06-3*) Trails Illustrated.

Yosemite Naturalist's Odyssey. William L. Neely. LC 94-77019. (Illus.). 300p. (Orig.). 1994. pap. 9.95 (*1-882803-08-6*) Jerseydale Ranch.

Yosemite Place Names. Peter Browning. LC 87-29793. (Illus.). 256p. (Orig.). (C). 1988. pap. 12.95 (*0-944220-00-2*) Great West Bks.

Yosemite Reflections. Ed. by Hank Johnston. (Illus.). 1997. 4.95 (*1-878345-06-0*) Flying Spur Pr.

Yosemite Road Guide. Richard P. Ditton et al. (Illus.). 84p. 1981. reprint ed. pap. 3.50 (*0-939666-24-3*) Yosemite Assn.

Yosemite Select. rev. ed. Don Reid. (Illus.). 130p. 1993. pap. 15.00 (*0-934641-41-2*) Chockstone Pr.

Yosemite Tomboy. 2nd ed. Shirley Sargent. Ed. by Peter Browning. LC 67-16835. (Illus.). 128p. (J). (gr. 4-8). 1994. pap. 9.95 (*0-9642244-0-2*) Ponderosa CA.

Yosemite Trails. Ginny Clark. 1980. pap. 12.95 (*0-931532-01-9*) West Trails Pubns.

Yosemite Trout Fishing. Hank Johnston. 1969. 2.50 (*0-685-28947-8*) Flying Spur Pr.

Yosemite Trout Fishing Guide. Steve Beck. (Illus.). 158p. 1996. pap. text ed. 14.95 (*1-57188-042-9*) F Amato Pubns.

Yosemite Valley: Secret Places & Magic Moments. Phil Arnot. (Illus.). 198p. (Orig.). 1992. pap. 9.95 (*0-933174-82-9*) Wide World-Tetra.

Yosemite Valley & the Mariposa Big Trees: A Preliminary Report, 1865. Frederick L. Olmstead. LC 93-22909. (Illus.). 1995. 85.00 (*0-939666-68-5*); pap. 6.95 (*0-939666-69-3*) Yosemite Assn.

Yosemite Wildflower Trails. Dana C. Morgenson. (Illus.). 88p. (Orig.). 1975. pap. 6.95 (*0-939666-27-8*) Yosemite Assn.

Yosemite Winters. Adams. 1995. 30.00 (*0-8212-2183-3*) Bulfinch Pr.

Yosemite Yarns-Stagecoach Stories. (YA). (gr. 7 up). pap. 2.00 (*0-915266-04-0*) Awani Pr.

Yosemite's High Sierra Camps. Shirley Sargent. (Illus.). 1977. 2.50 (*1-878345-14-1*) Flying Spur Pr.

Yosemite's Yesterdays. Hank Johnston. 1989. 6.95 (*0-685-28944-3*) Flying Spur Pr.

Yosemite's Yesterdays, Vol. II. Hank Johnston. 1991. 6.95 (*0-685-74774-3*) Flying Spur Pr.

***Yoshi Island 64 Players Guide.** Ed. by J. Douglas Arnold. (Gaming Mastery Ser.). 224p. (Orig.). 1997. pap. 12.95 (*1-884364-43-8*) Sandwich Islands.

Yoshi Untitled Picture Book # 2. Yoshi. (J). 1998. 17.00 (*0-689-80564-0*) S&S Childrens.

Yoshida Memoirs: The Story of Japan in Crisis. Shigeru Yoshida. LC 72-12336. 305p. 1973. reprint ed. text ed. 38.50 (*0-8371-6733-7*, YOYM, Greenwood Pr) Greenwood.

***Yoshihiko Ueda.** Toshihara Ito. (Illus.). 96p. 1997. 29.95 (*4-7713-2836-6*) Dist Art Pubs.

Yoshiko & the Foreigner. Mimi O. Little. 40p. (J). (ps up). 1996. 16.00 (*0-374-32448-4*) FS&G.

Yoshi's Island Strategy Guide. J. Douglas Arnold & Zach Meston. (Gaming Mastery Ser.). (Illus.). 240p. (Orig.). 1995. pap. 12.95 (*1-884364-21-7*) Sandwich Islands.

Yoshitoshi's Thirty-Six Ghosts. John Stevenson. LC 83-6735. (Illus.). 92p. 1992. pap. 29.95 (*0-295-97170-3*) U of Wash Pr.

An Asterisk (*) at the beginning of an entry indicates that the title is appearing in BIP for the first time.

Yoshitoshi's Women: The Woodblock-Print Series Fuzoku Sanjuniso. John Stevenson. (Illus.). 96p. 1995. 30.00 (*0-295-97431-1*) U of Wash Pr.

Yoshitoshi's 100 Aspects of the Moon. John Stevenson. (Illus.). 272p. 1996. write for info. (*0-614-15018-3*) Avery Pr CO.

Yoshitsune: A Fifteenth-Century Japanese Chronicle. Tr. by Helen C. McCullough. viii, 367p. 1966. 42.50 (*0-8047-0270-5*) Stanford U Pr.

Yoshitsune & the Thousand Cherry Trees: A Masterpiece of the Eighteenth-Century Japanese Puppet Theater. Tr. & Intro. by Stanleigh H. Jones. LC 92-46481. 1993. 37.50 (*0-231-08502-8*) Col U Pr.

Yoshitsune & the Thousand Cherry Trees: A Masterpiece of the Eighteenth-Century Japanese Puppet Theater. Izumo Takeda, Jr. Tr. by Stanleigh H. Jones, Jr. LC 92-46481. (Illus.). 286p. 1993. 37.50 (*0-231-08052-2*) Col U Pr.

*__Yoshiwara.__ S. Longstreet & E. Longstreet. 1996. pap. 20.95 (*0-8048-1599-2*) C E Tuttle.

Yoshiwara: The Glittering World of the Japanese Courtesan. Cecilia S. Seigle. LC 92-30544. (Illus.). 336p. 1993. text ed. 32.00 (*0-8248-1488-6*) UH Pr.

Yoshko the Dumbbell. Gershon Kranzler. (J). (gr. 4-9). pap. 6.95 (*0-87306-246-9*) Feldheim.

Yossef Mokir Shabbos: Hebrew-English. 1982. pap. 9.95 (*0-87306-189-6*) Feldheim.

Yossel Rakover Speaks to God: Holocaust Challenges to Religious Faith. Zvi Kolitz. LC 95-18831. 1995. 19.95 (*0-88125-526-2*) Ktav.

Yossel Zissel & the Wisdom of Chelm. Amy Schwartz. (Illus.). 32p. (J). (gr. k-4). 1986. 14.95 (*0-8276-0258-8*) JPS Phila.

Yossi & Laibel Hot on the Trail. Dina Rosenfeld. (Illus.). 32p. (J). (ps-1). 1991. 9.95 (*0-922613-47-8*); pap. 6.95 (*0-922613-48-6*) Hachai Pubns.

*__Yossi & Laibel on the Ball.__ Dina Rosenfeld. (Illus.). (J). 1997. write for info. (*0-922613-83-4*) Hachai Pubns.

Yossiph Shyryn. Santo Cali. Ed. by Nat Scammacca. 132p. (ENG & ITA.). 1980. 20.00 (*0-89304-563-2*); pap. 10.00 (*0-89304-564-0*) Cross-Cultrl NY.

*__You.__ Palencia. 1996. student ed., pap. text ed. write for info. (*0-17-557009-4*) Addison-Wesley.

You. Clare Trenkle. 152p. 1986. student ed. 5.50 (*0-88323-087-9*, 183); 1.25 (*0-685-04355-X*, 205); text ed. 6.50 (*0-88323-216-2*, 182) Pendergrass Pub.

You. Frances Wilshire. 1935. pap. 7.95 (*0-87516-319-X*) DeVorss.

You. G. S. Arundale. LC 73-4783. 156p. 1973. reprint ed. pap. 1.75 (*0-8356-0434-9*, Quest) Theos Pub Hse.

You: Become a Full Person. Edward A. Maziarz. (Illus.). 132p. (Orig.). 1983. pap. text ed. 6.95 (*0-9611274-0-6*) Shaman Bks.

You: Living, Learning, & Caring. Martha Strohecker & Deborah T. Tippett. 382p. 1997. 38.64 (*1-56637-307-7*) Goodheart.

*__You: Open the Door.__ Eloise Mellor. 1969. 5.00 (*0-87516-710-1*) DeVorss.

You: Some Possible Mechanics of Our Soul. Michael S. Wilber. LC 95-94807. (Illus.). 147p. (Orig.). (C). 1995. pap. 19.95 (*0-9648577-0-7*) MOE Elect Res.

You - the City. Fiona Templeton. LC 90-60189. (Roof Bks.). 150p. (Orig.). 1990. pap. 11.95 (*0-937804-38-X*) Segue NYC.

You, a Gift from God. Donna B. Jackson. 8p. 1994. pap. 3.50 (*1-880837-65-X*) Smyth & Helwys.

You Again. Peggy Nicholson. (Harlequin Superromance Ser.: No. 698). 1996. mass mkt. 3.99 (*0-373-70698-7*, 1-70698-5) Harlequin Bks.

You Ain't Heard Nothin' Yet! Compiled by John P. Fennell. 1989. pap. 7.95 (*0-8065-1150-8*, Citadel Pr) Carol Pub Group.

You Ain't Lived Til You Grow Old. Lenore Glassman & Yvette Jackson. (Illus.). 104p. (Orig.). 1980. pap. 4.95 (*0-918464-44-7*) LYCO Pub.

You Ain't Seen Nothing Yet. Rajneesh Osho Staff. Ed. by Ma P. Maneesha. LC 84-42614. (Initiation Talks Ser.). 304p. (Orig.). 1984. pap. 4.95 (*0-88050-687-3*) Osho America.

You Alone Are Dancing. Brenda Flanagan. LC 96-25848. (Orig.). 1995. 34.50 (*0-472-09627-3*); pap. 13.95 (*0-472-06627-7*) U of Mich Pr.

You Always Think of Home: A Portrait of Clay County, Alabama. Pamela Grundy. LC 90-43615. (Illus.). 304p. 1991. 29.95 (*0-8203-1304-1*) U of Ga Pr.

*__You & Co. The 70 Most Important Skills to: Stay Employed! Get Promoted! Get a Better Job!__ Dianna Booher. LC 97-9261. 192p. 1997. pap. text ed. 12.95 (*0-07-006648-5*) McGraw.

You & Contemporary Poetry. George Abbe. 1968. pap. 6.95 (*0-87233-010-9*) Bauhan.

*__You & Foreign Money.__ 1996. lib. bdg. 251.75 (*0-8490-6941-6*) Gordon Pr.

You & Foreign Money: The International Payments Process, Foreign Currency Units & Spending Money Abroad. 1992. lib. bdg. 250.00 (*0-8490-5584-9*) Gordon Pr.

You & God: Friends Forever - A Faith Book for Catholic Children. Francine M. O'Connor. LC 92-75082. (Illus.). 64p. (J). (gr. 1-4). 1993. pap. text ed. 3.95 (*0-89243-515-1*) Liguori Pubns.

You & God & Me Together: A Special Book for Parent & Teen. Jan Kempe. LC 91-39183. 160p. 1992. pap. 12.99 (*0-929239-55-5*) Discovery Hse Pubs.

You & God At Work: On the Job Training for Life. Frederick Sale, Jr. LC 91-25149. 160p. (Orig.). 1995. pap. 7.95 (*0-88243-414-4*) Gospel Pub.

You & God Together...Friends Forever. John Schmidt. 36p. (J). (ps-2). lib. bdg. 7.95 (*1-881907-12-0*) Two Bytes Pub.

You & HIV: A Day at a Time. Baker. (Illus.). 272p. (J). 1991. pap. text ed. 23.95 (*0-7216-3606-3*) Saunders.

You & I. Susanne Dubroff. LC 94-76455. 54p. 1994. pap. 8.95 (*0-9637040-0-1*) Kinsman Pr.

You & I & the World. Werner Aspenstrom. Ed. by Stanley H. Barkan. Tr. by Siv Cedering from ENG. (Cross-Cultural Review Chapbook Ser.: No. 5). 40p. 15.00 (*0-89304-878-X*, CCC130); pap. 5.00 (*0-89304-804-6*) Cross-Cultrl NY.

You & I Have Simply Got to Stop Meeting This Way. enl. ed. Richard J. Dunsing. LC 78-2516. 172p. reprint ed. pap. 49.10 (*0-317-58126-0*, 2029677) Bks Demand.

You & I in Business & Life: What Makes People Give Their Best. 4th rev. ed. N. H. Atthreya. 154p. 1987. pap. 9.95 (*0-942207-05-X*) Starsong CA.

You & I Together: The Meaning of Life. Daniel Shepard. LC 96-68766. (Illus.). 325p. (Orig.). 1996. 21.95 (*1-882792-24-6*); pap. 14.95 (*1-882792-23-8*) Proctor Pubns.

*__You & I...How Incredible!__ (Tender Hearts Collection). 32p. 1997. 9.99 (*1-881830-43-8*, DS18462) Garborgs.

You & Leukemia. Baker. 1988. pap. text ed. 25.00 (*0-7216-1495-7*) Saunders.

You & Marriage. Ed. by Helen M. Jordan. LC 70-177960. (Essay Index Reprint Ser.). 1977. reprint ed. 25.95 (*0-8369-2911-X*) Ayer.

*__You & Me.__ Caroline Grimshaw. LC 97-9316. (Follow Me Ser.). (J). 1997. write for info. (*0-7166-8802-6*); pap. write for info. (*0-7166-8803-4*) World Bk.

*__You & Me: Poems of Friendship.__ Illus. & Selected by Salley Mavor. LC 97-10062. 32p. (J). (ps-3). 1997. 16.95 (*0-531-30045-5*); lib. bdg. 17.99 (*0-531-33045-1*) Orchard Bks Watts.

You & Me: The Skills of Communicating & Relating to Others. Gerard Egan. LC 77-6475. (Illus.). 346p. (C). 1977. pap. 35.95 (*0-8185-0238-X*) Brooks-Cole.

You & Me - Me & You: A Kid's Own Life Story. Arlene L. Lousberg. (Illus.). 40p. (Orig.). (J). (gr. 3-9). 1990. pap. 9.95 (*0-9625397-1-6*) Memories In Print.

You & Me, Little Bear. Martin Waddell. LC 95-39342. (Illus.). 32p. (J). (ps-1). 1996. 15.99 (*1-56402-879-8*) Candlewick Pr.

*__You & Me, Little Bear.__ Martin Waddell. 1996. 16.95 (*1-85430-518-2*, Pub. by Magi Pubns UK); 16.95 (*1-85430-519-0*, Pub. by Magi Pubns UK); 16.95 (*1-85430-520-4*, Pub. by Magi Pubns UK); 16.95 (*1-85430-521-2*, Pub. by Magi Pubns UK); 16.95 (*1-85430-522-0*, Pub. by Magi Pubns UK); 16.95 (*1-85430-523-9*, Pub. by Magi Pubns UK) Talman.

*__You & Me, Lord.__ 1996. pap. 3.99 (*0-570-09626-X*, 20-2603) Concordia.

You & Me, Mom. Leydel J. Willis. 64p. 1991. 8.95 (*0-930416-10-4*) Clodele.

*__You & Money: Would It Be All Right with You If Life Got Easier?__ Maria Nemeth. (Illus.). viii, 348p. (Orig.). 1997. pap. 18.95 (*1-890507-50-4*) Vildehiya.

You & No Other. Cathy Maxwell. 375p. (Orig.). 1996. mass mkt. 5.99 (*0-380-78716-4*) Avon.

You & No Other. Jo-Ann Power. Ed. by Caroline Tolley. 352p. (Orig.). 1994. mass mkt. 5.50 (*0-671-89704-7*) PB.

You & PKU. Margaret Taylor & Virginia E. Schuett. (Illus.). 43p. (J). 1988. pap. text ed. 5.00 (*0-299-97065-5*) U of Wis Pr.

You & Public Opinion. Spiros Zodhiates. (1 Corinthians Commentary Ser.). (Illus.). 196p. 1977. pap. 5.99 (*0-89957-014-3*) AMG Pubs.

You & School: A Survival Guide for Adolescence. Gail C. Roberts & Lorraine Guttormson. Ed. by Rosemary Wallner. (Self-Help for Kids Ser.). 120p. (Orig.). (YA). (gr. 4-8). 1990. pap. 8.95 (*0-915793-25-3*) Free Spirit Pub.

You & Self-Esteem: It's the Key to Happiness & Success. Bettie B. Youngs. 160p. (YA). (gr. 5-12). 1992. pap. 16.95 (*0-915190-83-4*, JP-9083-4) Jalmar Pr.

You & Small Claims Court: 95 Questions & Answers. Jon R. Abele. (Illus.). 32p. 1994. pap. text ed. 1.80 (*0-88450-611-8*, 6118) Lawyers & Judges.

You & Stress: A Survival Guide for Adolescence. Gail C. Roberts & Lorraine Guttormson. Ed. by Rosemary Wallner. (Self-Help for Kids Ser.). 128p. (Orig.). (YA). (gr. 4-8). 1990. pap. 8.95 (*0-915793-26-1*) Free Spirit Pub.

You & the Law. write for info. (*0-944253-80-6*) Inst Dev Indian Law.

You & the Law. American Bar Association Staff. (Illus.). 608p. 1993. 19.98 (*0-88176-663-1*, 4004700) Pubns Intl Ltd.

*__You & the Law.__ Susan Singleton. (Daily Express Guides Ser.). 1994. pap. 12.95 (*0-7494-1133-3*) Kogan Page Ltd.

You & the Law. Visual Education Corporation Staff & Debra Goldentyer. LC 92-12063. 1993. text ed. 44.95 (*0-538-61467-6*) S-W Pub.

You & the Law. Visual Education Corporation Staff. (LA - Business Law Ser.). 1993. wbk. ed., pap. 13.95 (*0-538-61468-4*) S-W Pub.

You & the Law. 2nd ed. American Bar Association Staff. 1994. 35.00 (*0-8129-2361-8*) Random.

You & the Law! About Louisiana Law. Billie Woodard. 276p. 1993. 12.95 (*0-88415-093-3*) Gulf Pub.

You & the Law in New Jersey: A Resource Guide. Melville D. Miller, Jr. & Nancy Goldhill. 384p. 1988. text ed. 38.00 (*0-8135-1342-1*) Rutgers U Pr.

You & the Man in the Moon: The Almanac User's Complete Instruction Book. Taylor Reese & Jack R. Pyle. (Illus.). 150p. (Orig.). 1995. pap. 13.95 (*1-878086-44-8*) Down Home NC.

You & the Media: A "How-to" Publicity Handbook for Non-Profit Organizations. Sheila Solano. 58p. (Orig.). 1990. spiral bd. 12.95 (*0-940269-03-1*) OTR Pubns.

You & the New World Order: How You Can Influence the Alarming & Growing International & Domestic Problems. Richard Hobbs. LC 95-70416. 256p. (Orig.). 1995. pap. 19.95 (*0-9647788-6-6*) ColDoc Pubng.

You & the Night & the Music. James Cushing. 86p. 1991. pap. 10.00 (*0-9649240-2-1*) Cahuenga Pr.

You & the Night & the Music. James Cushing. 88p. 1991. pap. 10.00 (*0-685-56977-2*) SPD-Small Pr Dist.

You & the Other Guy: An Anatomy of Interpersonal Communication. Merle V. Zimmer. Ed. by Sandra C. Zimmer. (Illus.). 83p. (Orig.). (C). 1994. pap. 15.00 (*0-9641662-0-8*) M V Zimmer.

*__You & the Other Guy: An Anatomy of Interpersonal Communication.__ Ed. by Sandra C. Zimmer. (Illus.). 83p. (Orig.). 1994. teacher ed., pap. text ed. write for info. (*0-9641662-1-6*) M V Zimmer.

You & the Police! Boston T. Party. Ed. by Kenneth W. Royce. (Illus.). 128p. (Orig.). 1996. pap. 14.95 (*1-888766-01-8*) Javelin Pr.

You & the Utility Company. 3.50 (*0-944253-79-2*) Inst Dev Indian Law.

You & the World of Work. Fiona Armstrong et al. (Lifeworks Ser.). (Illus.). 1979. text ed. 13.96 (*0-07-002515-0*) McGraw.

You & Your Action Research Project. Jean Mcniff. 168p. (C). 1996. pap. 19.95 (*0-415-14475-2*) Routledge.

You & Your ADD Child. Paul Warren & Jody Capehart. 252p. 1995. pap. 12.99 (*0-7852-7895-8*, J Thoma Bks) Nelson.

*__You & Your Adolescent: A Parent's Guide for Ages 10-20.__ rev. ed. Laurence Steinberg & Le Ann. 432p. 1997. pap. 14.00 (*0-06-273461-X*, PL) HarpC.

You & Your Aging Parent: A Family Guide to Emotional, Physical, & Financial Problems. 3rd ed. Barbara Silverstone & Helen K. Hyman. LC 89-42559. 272p. 1990. pap. 16.00 (*0-679-72154-1*) Pantheon.

You & Your Aging Parent: The Practical Side of Love. Jill A. Boughton. 140p. (Orig.). 1994. pap. 7.95 (*0-937779-28-8*) Greenlawn Pr.

You & Your Aging Parents. William Coleman. LC 94-31604. 160p. (Orig.). 1994. pap. 9.99 (*0-929239-90-3*) Discovery Hse Pubs.

You & Your Aging Parents. Ed. by Allison Greene. 82p. 1995. pap. 8.95 (*1-57312-013-8*) Smyth & Helwys.

You & Your Aquarium. Dick Mills. 1986. pap. 17.00 (*0-394-72985-4*) Knopf.

*__You & Your Assets: A Practical Guide to Financial Management & Estate Planning.__ Martin R. Dunetz. LC 96-52480. 176p. 1997. text ed. 14.95 (*1-56833-091-X*) Madison Bks UPA.

You & Your Attitude. Los Angeles Unified School District Staff. (Project Get That Job Ser.). (Illus.). 48p. (Orig.). (YA). (gr. 7-12). 1990. student ed. 4.95 (*1-56119-087-X*); teacher ed. 1.95 (*1-56119-088-8*) Educ Pr MD.

You & Your Attitude, Set. Los Angeles Unified School District Staff. (Project Get That Job Ser.). (Illus.). 48p. (Orig.). (YA). (gr. 7-12). 1990. 44.95 (*1-56119-089-6*) Educ Pr MD.

You & Your Baby. Frederick Rutherford. (Orig.). 1971. pap. 4.50 (*0-451-14321-3*, AE2177, Sig) NAL-Dutton.

You & Your Bible: An Introduction to the Word. 90p. 1990. teacher ed., ring bd. 19.95 (*0-910566-29-1*) Evang Trg Assn.

You & Your Bible: An Introduction to the Word. rev. ed. 96p. 1990. pap. text ed. 8.95 (*0-910566-12-7*) Evang Trg Assn.

You & Your Bible-You & Your Life. Clarence Y. Fretz. (Christian Day School Ser.). (J). (gr. 8). 1968. teacher ed. 12.80 (*0-87813-903-6*); pap. 3.25 (*0-87813-902-8*) Christian Light.

You & Your Blood: A Few Answers to Your Questions. Norton D. Ritz. 1995. pap. 10.95 (*0-533-11326-1*) Vantage.

You & Your Body. (Starting Point Science Ser.). (Illus.). 120p. (J). (gr. 1 up). 1994. 17.95 (*0-7460-1858-4*, Usborne) EDC.

You & Your Body. Angela Royston. LC 94-16304. (One Hundred One Questions Ser.). (Illus.). 48p. (J). 1994. 9.95 (*0-8160-3217-3*) Facts on File.

You & Your Body, Bk. C. (J). Date not set. pap. 3.50 (*0-590-49778-2*) Scholastic Inc.

You & Your Body, Bk. C. Date not set. teacher ed., pap. 5.50 (*0-590-49779-0*) Scholastic Inc.

You & Your Body, Bk. D. (J). Date not set. pap. 3.50 (*0-590-49780-4*) Scholastic Inc.

You & Your Body, Bk. D. Date not set. teacher ed., pap. 5.50 (*0-590-49781-2*) Scholastic Inc.

You & Your Body, Bk. A. (J). Date not set. pap. 3.50 (*0-590-49774-X*) Scholastic Inc.

You & Your Body, Bk. A. Date not set. teacher ed. 5.50 (*0-590-49775-8*) Scholastic Inc.

You & Your Body, Bk. B. (J). Date not set. pap. 3.50 (*0-590-49776-6*) Scholastic Inc.

You & Your Body, Bk. B. Date not set. teacher ed., pap. 5.50 (*0-590-49777-4*) Scholastic Inc.

You & Your Body, Bk. E. (J). Date not set. pap. 3.50 (*0-590-49782-0*) Scholastic Inc.

You & Your Body, Bk. E. Date not set. teacher ed., pap. 5.50 (*0-590-49783-9*) Scholastic Inc.

You & Your Body, Bk. F. (J). Date not set. pap. 3.50 (*0-590-49784-7*) Scholastic Inc.

You & Your Body, Bk. F. Date not set. teacher ed., pap. 5.50 (*0-590-49785-5*) Scholastic Inc.

You & Your Cat. David Taylor. 1986. pap. 16.00 (*0-394-72984-6*) Knopf.

*__You & Your Child.__ (Illus.). 1997. write for info. (*1-886614-20-2*) Intl Masters Pub.

You & Your Child's Teacher: Reading Level 3-4. 1993. 6.95 (*0-88336-627-4*) New Readers.

You & Your Clients: A Guide to a More Successful Law Practice Through Behavior Management. 2nd ed. Stanley S. Clawar. LC 96-6865. (Illus.). 1996. write for info. (*1-57073-275-2*) Amer Bar Assn.

You & Your Clients: How to Improve Your Practice Through Behavior Management. 1988. 29.95 (*0-685-29699-7*, 515-0081-01) Amer Bar Assn.

You & Your Clients: Human Relations for Cosmetology. Leslie Edgerton. LC 90-27866. 224p. (C). 1991. pap. 19.95 (*1-56253-058-5*) Milady Pub.

You & Your Credit: Tools for Understanding & Repairing Your Own Credit. Darryl R. White. Ed. by Brian R. White & Renee E. Nichols. LC 92-91096. (Illus.). 520p. (Orig.). 1994. 39.95 (*0-9635199-7-2*); pap. 29.95 (*0-9635199-9-9*) Pyramid Pub.

You & Your Dad. Lou Alpert. LC 91-44412. (Illus.). 32p. (J). 1992. 12.95 (*1-879085-36-4*) Whsprng Coyote Pr.

*__You & Your Deaf Child: A Self-Help Guide for Parents of Deaf & Hard of Hearing Children.__ John W. Adams. LC 97-18820. 240p. 1997. 19.95 (*1-56368-060-2*) Gallaudet Univ Pr.

You & Your Dog. Fred C. Kelly. 1991. lib. bdg. 75.00 (*0-8490-5231-9*) Gordon Pr.

You & Your Dog. David Taylor. 1986. pap. 17.00 (*0-394-72983-8*) Knopf.

You & Your Emotions. Maxie C. Maultsby, Jr. (Illus.). 109p. 1990. reprint ed. pap. 7.95 (*0-932838-01-4*) Tangrm Bks.

You & Your Family. Ed. by John Robson. (Illus.). 30p. (Orig.). (J). (gr. 2-4). 1981. pap. 2.50 (*0-936098-30-9*) Intl Marriage.

You & Your Family: A Survival Guide for Adolescence. Gail C. Roberts & Lorraine Guttormson. Ed. by Pamela Espeland. (Self-Help for Kids Ser.). 112p. (Orig.). (YA). (gr. 4-8). 1990. pap. 8.95 (*0-915793-24-5*) Free Spirit Pub.

You & Your Grandchildren: Special Ways to Keep in Touch. Sunie Levin. (Illus.). 56p. 1991. pap. 7.95 (*0-8431-2873-9*) Grandparents Little Div.

You & Your Hand: A Textbook of Modern Hand Analysis. rev. ed. Beverly C. Jaegers. (Illus.). 176p. 1984. pap. text ed. 8.00 (*0-685-09893-1*) Aries Prod.

*__You & Your Handicap: The Arithmetic of Golf.__ Jonathon Cummings. 61p. 1997. pap. 8.00 (*0-8059-4062-6*) Dorrance.

You & Your Hearing-Impaired Child: A Self-Instructional Guide for Parents. John W. Adams. LC 88-29948. (Illus.). 150p. 1988. pap. text ed. 12.95 (*0-930323-40-8*, Clerc Bks) Gallaudet Univ Pr.

You & Your Home. Richard M. Chapman. 1984. pap. 50.00 (*0-7219-0990-6*, Pub. by Scientific UK) St Mut.

You & Your Hormones. Max D. Rubenstein. 1960. 15.95 (*0-8084-0387-7*) NCUP.

You & Your Lawyer. Nancy B. Stern et al. (Illus.). 20p. (Orig.). 1995. pap. 1.80 (*0-913875-19-8*) Lawyers & Judges.

You & Your Money: A Guide to Financial Self-Confidence for the Suddenly Single. Alan B. Ungar. Ed. by Cathy Ungar. (Illus.). 185p. 1989. pap. 14.95 (*0-9622434-0-X*) Calabasas Pr.

You & Your MP. N. L. Fyson & E. Deakins. (C). 1987. 30.00 (*0-85950-715-7*, Pub. by S Thornes Pubs UK) St Mut.

You & Your National Government. rev. ed. League of Women Voters Education Fund Staff. (Illus.). 32p. 1985. pap. 1.75 (*0-89959-027-6*, 273) LWVUS.

*__You & Your Neighbour in a Broken World.__ Ralston Nembhard. 68p. (Orig.). 1997. pap. 8.75 (*1-57502-516-7*, P01532) Morris Pubng.

You & Your Network: Getting the Most Out of Life. Fred Smith. 206p. 1991. reprint ed. pap. 4.95 (*0-937539-17-1*) Executive Bks.

You & Your Newborn Baby: A Guide to the First Months after Birth. Linda Todd. Ed. by Linda Ziedrich. LC 92-47389. (Illus.). 112p. 1993. 11.95 (*1-55832-055-5*); pap. 6.95 (*1-55832-054-7*) Harvard Common Pr.

*__You & Your Only Child: The Joys, Myths, & Challenges of Raising an Only Child.__ Patricia Nachman & Andrea Thompson. 256p. 1997. 22.00 (*0-06-017331-9*) HarpC.

You & Your Pastor: What Can You Expect? Marvin I. Judy. (Pocket Guide Ser.). 64p. (Orig.). 1992. pap. 5.95 (*0-687-46773-X*) Abingdon.

You & Your Pension. Ralph Nader & Kate Blackwell. 215p. 1973. pap. 1.65 (*0-686-36546-1*) Ctr Responsive Law.

You & Your Pet Bird. David Alderton. 1992. pap. 17.00 (*0-679-74061-9*) McKay.

You & Your Pony. Pepper M. Healey. 1978. pap. 6.00 (*0-87980-360-6*) Wilshire.

You & Your Pregnancy: The Most Commonly Asked Questions Before, During, & After. James P. Guerrieri & Gregory R. Moore. LC 95-49813. 1996. 9.95 (*0-915253-48-8*) Hlth Edu Lit.

You & Your Private I: Personality & the Written Self-Image. 3rd rev. ed. Jane N. Green. (Illus.). 320p. reprint ed. pap. 10.95 (*0-9624145-0-6*) Tyestring Prodns.

*__You & Your Puppy.__ Contrib. by Herbert Axelrod. (Cats & Dogs). (Illus.). (YA). (gr. 3 up). 1998. lib. bdg. 19.95 (*0-7910-4823-3*) Chelsea Hse.

You & Your Puppy: Training & Health Care for Puppy's First Year. Sarah Hodgson & James DeBitetto. LC 95-12044. (Illus.). 256p. 1995. pap. 19.95 (*0-87605-784-9*) Howell Bk.

You & Your Retarded Child: A Manual for Parents of Retarded Children. 2nd ed. Samuel A. Kirk et al. LC 67-20824. (Paperbounds Ser.: No. PB-2). (Orig.). 1968. pap. 4.95 (*0-87015-161-4*) Pacific Bks.

You & Your Small Wonder: Activities for Busy Parents & Babies, Book 1. Merle B. Karnes. LC 82-71049. (Illus.). 163p. (Orig.). 1982. pap. 15.95 (*0-913476-58-7*, 7911) Am Guidance.

You & Your Small Wonder: 18-36 Months, Bk. 2. Merle B. Karnes. 1984. pap. 6.95 (*0-394-72414-3*) Random.

You & Your Teen. Charles Bradshaw. (Family Ministry Ser.). (Illus.). 84p. 1985. pap. text ed. 19.95 (0-89191-950-3, 24695) Cook.

You & Your Thoughts - Chinese Edition. Earl D. Radmacher. Tr. by Thomas Tso & Tony Huang. 135p. (CHI.). 1981. pap. 4.00 (1-56582-093-2) Christ Renew Min.

***You & Your Used Automobile: Things You Should Know & Do Before & after You Purchase a Used Automobile.** Cleveland McCloud & Rudolph McCloud. 16p. 1997. pap. 7.00 (0-8059-4096-0) Dorrance.

You & Your Voice Are One: A Renegade Voice Teacher Speaks Out. Don Allton. Ed. by Mary K. Allton. (Illus.). 157p. (Orig.). 1991. pap. text ed. 14.95 (0-9625217-1-X) M E K A.

You & Your Wedding. rev. ed. Winifred Gray. 368p. (Orig.). 1986. mass mkt. 4.95 (0-553-27143-1) Bantam.

You & Your Will. Paul Ashley. 240p. 1985. pap. 3.95 (0-451-62569-2, Ment) NAL-Dutton.

You & Your World. Paul H. Dunn. 1977. 7.95 (0-88494-327-5) Bookcraft Inc.

You & Your 401(K) Julie Jason. 192p. 1996. pap. 10.00 (0-684-81401-3, Fireside) S&S Trade.

You Animal! Jerry Booth. LC 95-8457. (Illus.). 48p. (J). 1996. 15.00 (0-15-200696-6, Gulliver Bks) HarBrace.

You Are: A Word-Book to Help You Remember. Christine Tarantino. LC 96-90173. 52p. (Orig.). 1996. pap. 9.95 (1-887480-16-1) Wrds Lght Intl.

***You Are a Mathematician: A Wise & Witty Introduction to the Joy of Numbers.** David Wells. LC 96-53548. 1997. text ed. 24.95 (0-471-18077-7) Wiley.

You Are a Millionaire, No. 98. Jay Leibold. 128p. (J). 1990. pap. 3.50 (0-553-28351-0) Bantam.

You Are a Miracle: Waiting to Happen. Ken Houts. 210p. (Orig.). 1996. pap. 9.99 (1-56043-260-8) Destiny Image.

You Are a Miracle: Why You Are Who You Are. Forest E. Conder. (Illus.). 315p. (Orig.). 1989. pap. 7.95 (0-685-25987-0) F E Conder.

You Are a Money Brain. William C. Drollinger. LC 81-67503. 1981. write for info. (0-914244-07-8) Epic Pubns.

You Are a Person of Worth. Jefferson Breen. LC 86-91860. 1988. 12.00 (0-87212-202-6) Libra.

You Are a Rainbow. Ed. by Norah Hills. LC 79-13393. (Illus.). 125p. (Orig.). 1979. pap. 6.95 (0-916438-25-2) Dr Hills Technol.

You Are a Sacrament. Charles Gallagher. (Celebrate Love Ser.). 61p. (Orig.). 1992. pap. text ed. 3.95 (0-911905-45-6) Past & Mat Rene Ctr.

You Are a Special Person. Bob Bird. 16p. (Orig.). 1974. pap. 2.00 (0-934804-06-0) Happiness.

You Are a Star. C. Joy Belk. (Illus.). (Orig.). (C). 1991. pap. 6.95 (0-9620258-0-1) Babe Co.

You Are a Success! 61 Proven Strategies for Developing Success. Mary Robinson & Sandy Ryan. LC 90-85787. 195p. (Orig.). 1991. pap. 14.95 (0-9628496-4-2) Heart Pub Prodns.

You Are A Winner. Marjorie B. Sherratt. LC 85-91150. 71p. (Orig.). 1985. pap. 5.25 (0-9615778-0-0, 01) You Are Winner.

You Are All Sanpaku. Sakurazawa Nyoiti, pseud. 224p. 1980. pap. 5.95 (0-8065-0728-4, Citadel Pr) Carol Pub Group.

You Are Always in Our Hearts: A Book for Divorced Parents. Casey Self. 64p. 1996. spiral bd. 10.44 (0-7872-2028-0) Kendall-Hunt.

***You Are Always with Me.** 24p. (J). Date not set. write for info. (1-55513-623-0, Chariot Bks) Chariot Victor.

You Are Always Your Own Experience! 5th deluxe ed. Tom Johnson. 282p. 1989. 9.95 (0-941992-17-9) Los Arboles Pub.

You Are an Alien. Edward Packard. (Choose Your Own Adventure Ser.: No. 156). 128p. (J). (gr. 4-7). 1995. pap. 3.50 (0-553-56010-7) Bantam.

You Are An Enlightened Omnibeing: In Our Messianic Age. Milton Ward. 87p. 1991. pap. 15.00 (0-939835-06-1) Optimus Bks.

You Are Barbara Jordan: An In-Basket Exercise on Nursing Service Administration. (C). 1970. 7.50 (0-87914-015-1, 654630); teacher ed. 7.50 (0-87914-016-X, 654631) Hosp Res & Educ.

You Are Beautiful: A Practical Guide to Loving Yourself & Others. Nadya Giusi. Ed. by Mort Leavitt. (Illus.). (Orig.). 1989. pap. write for info. (0-318-65324-9) Carmel Prodns.

You Are Becoming a Galactic Human. Virginia Essene & Sheldon Nidle. LC 94-66226. (Illus.). 250p. (Orig.). 1994. pap. 11.95 (0-937147-08-7) SEE Pub Co.

You Are Born to Victory. John Glossinger & C. F. Diercksmeier, Jr. 115p. 1981. reprint ed. pap. 3.95 (0-87516-445-5) DeVorss.

You Are Going to Prison. Jim Hogshire. LC 94-78105. 192p. (Orig.). (C). 1994. pap. text ed. 14.95 (1-55950-119-7, 40083) Loompanics.

You Are Greater Than You Know. Lou Austin. 1955. 8.50 (0-934538-16-6) Partnership Foundation.

You Are Healed. Kenneth Copeland. 23p. 1979. pap. 1.00 (0-88114-733-8) K Copeland Pubns.

***You Are Here.** Nina Crews. Date not set. write for info. (0-688-15753-X); lib. bdg. write for info. (0-688-15754-8) Greenwillow.

You Are Here: A Guide to Evereday Maps, Plans, & Diagrams, Reading Level 4.5. 1993. 9.70 (0-88336-499-9) Peoples Pub Grp.

You Are Here, Dainty Dinosaur. (Illus.). (J). (ps-2). 1991. pap. 5.10 (0-8136-5714-8); lib. bdg. 7.95 (0-8136-5214-6) Modern Curr.

You Are Here Now. Ricco Fruscio. 51p. (Orig.). 1995. pap. 9.95 (0-9638502-4-5) Sunstar Pubng.

You Are in the Right Place: A Guide to Non-Sectarian Practical Spirituality. O. A. Ham. (Illus.). 173p. 1996. text ed. 19.95 (0-9646397-0-X) Whte Feather Pr.

You Are Invisible. Susan Saunders. (Choose Your Own Adventure Ser.: No. 38). 64p. (J). 1989. pap. 3.50 (0-553-15685-3) Bantam.

You Are Invisible. 2nd enl. ed. Raymond C. Barker. LC 73-1654. 160p. 1986. reprint ed. pap. 7.95 (0-87516-576-1) DeVorss.

You Are Invited: To Receive Love, Life & Joy As You Journey Through John. Ruth Thornhill. 156p. (Orig.). 1983. pap. 4.00 (1-880960-25-7) Script Memory Fl.

You Are Involved in a Fable. Barry Goodman. 64p. (Orig.). 1986. 9.95 (0-939395-04-5); pap. 5.95 (0-939395-05-3) Thorntree Pr.

You Are Loved! Donna B. Jackson. 8p. 1994. pap. 3.50 (1-880837-66-8) Smyth & Helwys.

You Are Loved. Ronald L. Johnson. Ed. by Jan Beatty. LC 95-69511. (Illus.). 196p. 1995. pap. write for info. (0-88100-087-6) Natl Writ Pr.

You Are Loved. Alma Kern. (Illus.). 136p. 1991. pap. 5.00 (0-9614955-1-0, 2060) Lutheran Womens.

You Are Mine: A View of the Spiritual Life. Myles Rearden. 142p. (Orig.). 1995. pap. 14.95 (1-85607-105-7, Pub. by Columba Pr IE) Twenty-Third.

You Are More Prosperous Than You Think: A Book of Activities That Will Enhance Your Life. Libby Rosenauer. (Aware Person Ser.). 96p. 1993. pap. 9.95 (1-881762-01-7) Aware Pr.

You Are More Than What You Weigh: Handbook: Improving Your Self-Esteem No Matter What Your Weight. Sharon Sward. LC 95-61855. 264p. (Orig.). 1995. wbk. ed. 16.95 (0-9648874-0-1) Wholesome Publng.

***You Are More Than What You Weigh: Improving Your Self Esteem No Matter What Your Weight.** 2nd rev. ed. Sharon Sward. Ed. by Pat Patterson. (Illus.). 235p. 1997. per., pap. 18.95 (0-9648874-2-8) Wholesome Publng.

You Are More Than Your Job: Making a Living vs. Making a Life. Earl Harrison. 216p. 1993. pap. 9.95 (0-925190-70-5) Fairview Press.

You Are Mountain. Mary Donahoe. 32p. 1984. 6.00 (0-911051-11-2) Plain View.

You Are My Darling Zita. Glenn Busch. (Visual Studies). (C). 1991. 39.95 (0-87722-791-8) Temple U Pr.

You Are My Friend. St. Paul Publications Staff. (C). 1990. text ed. 40.00 (0-85439-358-7, Pub. by St Paul Pubns UK) St Mut.

You Are My Friend: A Celebration of Friendship. Illus. by Susan Larson. LC 90-3028. 156p. (Orig.). 1991. pap. 9.95 (0-9622874-8-2) Halo Bks.

You Are My Friend, Because. Jeanne Davis. (Illus.). 1993. Gift boxed. boxed 8.95 (0-8378-5303-6) Gibson.

You Are My Friends. Ron Wormser et al. 40p. 1995. pap. 4.00 (0-934396-42-6) Churches Alive.

You Are My Hiding Place. rev. ed. Amy Carmichael. Ed. by David Hazard. (Rekindling the Inner Fire Ser.: Vol. 2). 128p. 1991. pap. 8.99 (1-55661-205-2) Bethany Hse.

You Are My Son, The Beloved. Living Street Ministry Staff. 32p. 2.00 (0-87083-742-7, 17013001) Living Stream Ministry.

***You Are My Stronghold: Psalm 91.** Evelyn Dittimus. 98p. (Orig.). 1997. pap. 9.95 (1-56550-030-X) Vis Bks Intl.

You Are My Sunshine: The Jimmie Davis Story. Gus Weill. LC 87-11898. (Illus.). 200p. 1987. reprint ed. pap. 11.95 (0-88289-660-1) Pelican.

You Are My Witnesses. Gordon J. Keddie. 1993. pap. 14.99 (0-85234-307-8, Pub. by Evangelical Pr) Presby & Reformed.

You Are My Witnesses. rev. ed. Giorgio Tourn et al. 350p. 1989. pap. 18.95 (88-7016-089-0) Friendship Pr.

You Are Not Alone. Bernard Mandelbaum. LC 88-43148. 96p. 1989. pap. 10.00 (0-88400-133-4) Shengold.

You Are Not Alone. 2nd abr. ed. Linda P. Rouse. 1993. pap. 12.95 (1-55691-089-4, 899x) Learning Pubns.

You Are Not Alone: A Guide for Battered Women. 2nd unabridged ed. Linda P. Rouse. 136p. 1994. pap. 12.95 (1-55691-088-6, 886) Learning Pubns.

You Are Not Alone: Compulsive Hairpulling: The Enemy Within. Cheryn Salazar. (Illus.). 262p. (Orig.). 1996. pap. 14.95 (0-9650670-0-9) Rophe Pr.

You Are Not Alone: Understanding & Dealing with Mental Illness. Clara C. Park & Leon N. Shapiro. 1979. 17.50 (0-316-69073-2) Little.

You Are Not Alone: Words of Experience & Hope for the Journey Through Depression. Julia Thorne & Larry Rothstein. LC 92-56255. 192p. (Orig.). 1993. pap. 12.50 (0-06-096977-6, PL) HarpC.

***You Are Not Alone: 15 People with Behcet's.** Joanne Zeis. i, 141p. (Orig.). 1997. pap. 30.00 (0-9658403-0-1) J Zeis.

You Are Not Far from the Kingdom of God: One Hundred Sayings of Jesus, Plus Their Hebrew Sources, That Reveal the Anti-Christianity of Anti-Semitism. Eugene M. Schwartz. LC 92-16764. 198p. 1992. 19.98 (0-963139-0-8) Sec Creat Pr.

***You Are Not I.** Millicent Dillon. LC 97-26220. 1998. write for info. (0-520-21104-9) U CA Pr.

You Are Not My Father (Laos) Reading Level 2. (Fitting In Ser.). 1993. 2.95 (0-88336-999-0); audio 6.95 (0-88336-774-2) New Readers.

You Are Not Stendhal: New & Selected Poems. Daniel Hughes. LC 91-35866. 158p. 1992. pap. 16.95 (0-8143-2387-1) Wayne St U Pr.

***You Are Not the Target.** Laura A. Huxley. 1995. pap. text ed. 9.95 (1-55552-009-X) Metamorphous Pr.

You Are Not Your Illness: Seven Principles for Meeting the Challenge of Illness. Hal Z. Bennett & Linda N. Topf. LC 94-39618. 1995. pap. 12.00 (0-684-80124-8, Fireside) S&S Trade.

***You Are Not Your Own: Becoming God's Steward.** Mike Armour. (Small Group Studies). 39p. 1996. pap. 4.99 (0-89900-701-5, T96-701-5) College Pr Pub.

You Are Number One! Beverly Amstutz. (Illus.). 30p. (J). (gr. k-9). 1986. pap. 2.50 (0-937836-08-7) Precious Res.

You Are on Indian Land: Alcatraz Island, 1969-1971. Ed. by Troy R. Johnson. LC 94-79442. (Native American Politics Ser.: 5). 160p. 1995. 25.00 (0-935626-42-5) U Cal AISC.

You Are on Indian Land: Alcatraz Island, 1969-1971. Ed. by Troy R. Johnson. LC 94-79442. (Native American Politics Ser.: 5). 160p. 1995. pap. text ed. 15.00 (0-935626-43-3) U Cal AISC.

You Are One in a Million! The Art of Asking Questions That Produce Results. Marianne Clyde. 144p. 1995. pap. write for info. (0-9649278-0-2) May Day Press.

You Are Precious. Alma Kern. (Illus.). 125p. (Orig.). 1995. pap. 5.00 (0-9614955-3-7, 2070) Lutheran Womens.

You Are Psychic! Peter A. Sanders, Jr. 288p. 1990. pap. 12.50 (0-449-90507-1, Columbine) Fawcett.

***You Are Respectfully Invited to My Execution.** Larry Brown. LC 97-2511. 1997. write for info. (0-931271-42-8); pap. write for info. (0-931271-41-X) Hi Plains Pr.

You Are Responsible! George King. LC 73-263274. 173p. 1961. 12.95 (0-937249-03-3) Aetherius Soc.

You Are Sentenced to Life. W. D. Chesney. 118p. 1970. reprint ed. spiral bd. 10.00 (0-7873-0168-X) Hlth Research.

You Are Smarter Than You Think! A Practical Guide to Academic Success Using Your Personal Learning Style. Renee Mollan-Masters. (Orig.). (C). 1992. audio 10.00 (0-9608622-2-6); vhs 30.00 (0-9608622-3-4) Reality Prods.

***You Are Smarter Than You Think! Learning Made Easier in Three Simple Steps.** 2nd rev. ed. Renee Mollan-Masters. LC 96-95469. (Illus.). 177p. 1997. pap. text ed. 19.95 (0-9608622-4-2) Reality Prods.

You Are Somebody Special. 2nd ed. Bill Cosby et al. Ed. by Charlie W. Shedd. (Skills for Living Ser.). 205p. (YA). (gr. 9-12). 1989. reprint ed. text ed. 10.95 (0-933419-50-3) Quest Intl.

You Are Special! (Wellinworld Tapes & Books for Children: 2-9). 36p. (J). (ps-4). 1985. 8.95 (0-88684-176-3); audio write for info. (0-318-59508-7) Listen USA.

You Are Special. Alma Kern. (Illus.). 144p. (Orig.). 1985. pap. 5.00 (0-9614955-0-2, 2050) Lutheran Womens.

***You Are Special.** Max Lucado. LC 97-5387. (Illus.). 32p. (J). (gr. k-3). 1997. 14.99 (0-89107-931-9) Crossway Bks.

You Are Special: A Child's Guide for Successful Living. Mary H. Johnson. Ed. by Robin M. Bennefield. (Illus.). 36p. (Orig.). (J). (gr. 4-7). 1993. student ed. write for info. (0-911849-02-5) Comptex Assocs Inc.

You Are Special: Words of Wisdom for All Ages from a Beloved Neighbor. Fred Rogers. 192p. 1995. pap. 8.95 (0-14-023514-0, Penguin Bks) Viking Penguin.

You Are Spider Man. Richie Chevat. (Spider-Man Ser.: No. 1). (YA). 1996. mass mkt. 3.99 (0-671-00319-4) PB.

You Are That! Satsang with Gangaji, Vol. I. Gangaji. LC 95-71521. 165p. (Orig.). 1995. pap. 12.00 (0-9632194-3-X) Satsang Fndtn.

You Are That! Satsang with Gangaji, Vol. II. Gangaji. LC 95-71521. 274p. (Orig.). 1996. pap. 15.00 (1-887984-00-3) Satsang Fndtn.

You Are the Adventure. J. Boone. 1980. pap. 8.00 (0-933062-20-6) R H Sommer.

You Are the Body of Christ: A Revealing Look at Who We Really Are in Christ. Lee A. Howard. (Illus.). 72p. (Orig.). 1995. pap. 5.95 (0-9647573-0-3) Beautiful Ft Pubng.

You Are the Christ? Nine One-Act Plays. Royce E. Makin. LC 93-12109. 152p. (Orig.). 1993. pap. 10.99 (0-8272-4404-5) Chalice Pr.

You Are the Corporate Executive. Nathan Aaseng. LC 96-4570. (Great Decisions Ser.). (Illus.). 160p. (YA). (gr. 5-12). 1997. lib. bdg. 16.95 (1-881508-35-8) Oliver Pr MN.

You Are the Editor: Sixty-One Editing Lessons That Improve Writing Skills. Eric Johnson. (Makemaster Bk.). (J). (gr. 5 up). 1981. pap. 13.99 (0-8224-7696-7) Fearon Teach Aids.

You Are the General. Nathan Aaseng. LC 93-11661. (Great Decisions Ser.). (Illus.). 160p. (YA). (gr. 5-12). 1994. lib. bdg. 16.95 (1-881508-11-0) Oliver Pr MN.

You Are the General II: 1800-1899. Nathan Aaseng. LC 94-46910. (Great Decisions Ser.). (Illus.). 160p. (YA). (gr. 5-12). 1995. lib. bdg. 16.95 (1-881508-25-0) Oliver Pr MN.

You Are the Juror. Nathan Aaseng. LC 96-53046. (Great Decisions Ser.). (Illus.). 160p. (J). (gr. 5-12). 1997. lib. bdg. 16.95 (1-881508-40-4) Oliver Pr MN.

You Are the Justice. Michel Lipman. 80p. 1993. pap. 12.00 (0-87879-982-6) High Noon Bks.

***You Are the Light.** 1988. 1.20 (0-8341-9014-1) Nazarene.

You Are the Light of the World. Don Rittenhouse & Jane Rittenhouse. (Illus.). 24p. (J). (ps-5). pap. 4.00 (0-9646494-0-3) Memor-Eyes.

You Are the Light of the World. Rickey Singleton. (Illus.). 64p. (Orig.). 1996. pap. 10.95 (1-887305-01-7) Exousia Pubns.

You Are the Message. Roger Ailes. 1996. pap. 12.95 (0-614-12578-2) Doubleday.

You Are the Message: Getting What You Want by Being Who You Are. Roger Ailes & Jon Kraushar. 240p. pap. 12.95 (0-385-26542-5, Currency) Doubleday.

You Are the Message: Secrets of the Master Communicators. Roger Ailes & Jon Kraushar. 1988. 12.00 (0-671-66224-4) S&S Trade.

You Are the Music: Discovering God's Plan for Your Life. Betty Saunders. LC 94-69881. (Illus.). 128p. (Orig.). 1995. pap. 12.95 (1-884570-15-1) Research Triangle.

You Are the One. Mary M. Jaeger & Kathleen Juline. 207p. 1988. pap. 12.95 (0-917849-08-6) Sci of Mind.

You Are the Power: A Guide to Personal Greatness. J. Kennedy Shultz. Ed. by Dan Olmos. LC 93-23932. 224p. (Orig.). 1993. pap. 12.95 (1-56170-074-6, 106) Hay House.

You Are the President. Nathan Aaseng. LC 93-5776. (Great Decisions Ser.). (Illus.). 160p. (YA). (gr. 5-12). 1994. lib. bdg. 16.95 (1-881508-10-2) Oliver Pr MN.

You Are the President II: 1800-1899. Nathan Aaseng. LC 93-46308. (Great Decisions Ser.). (Illus.). 160p. (YA). (gr. 5-12). 1994. lib. bdg. 16.95 (1-881508-15-3) Oliver Pr MN.

You Are the Product: Powerful Self-Marketing for Practicing Professionals. Lester W. Anderson & Shelley A. Lee. 215p. 1996. reprint ed. 29.95 (0-9634809-4-4) Financial Mktg.

You Are the Senator. Nathan Aaseng. LC 96-4569. (Great Decisions Ser.). (Illus.). 160p. (YA). (gr. 5-12). 1997. lib. bdg. 16.95 (1-881508-36-6) Oliver Pr MN.

You Are the Supreme Court Justice. Nathan Aaseng. LC 93-46307. (Great Decisions Ser.). (Illus.). 160p. (YA). (gr. 5-12). 1994. lib. bdg. 16.95 (1-881508-14-5) Oliver Pr MN.

***You Are the Weather: Photographs.** Roni Horn. 1997. 45.00 (3-931141-45-4) Dist Art Pubs.

You Are the World: Authentic Report of Talks & Discussions in American Universities. Jiddu Krishnamurti. LC 73-172504. 160p. 1989. reprint ed. pap. 10.00 (0-06-091611-7, PL) HarpC.

***You Are There Teleplays: The Critical Edition.** rev. ed. Abraham Polonsky. Ed. by Mark Schaubert & John Schultheiss. LC 97-67547. (Film As Literature Ser.). (Illus.). 328p. (C). 1997. text ed. 30.00 (0-9635823-2-1) Sadanlaur Pubns.

You Are Thinking of Teaching? Opportunities, Problems, Realities. Seymour B. Sarason. LC 93-10694. (Education-Higher Education Ser.). 156p. text ed. 26.95 (1-55542-569-0) Jossey-Bass.

You Are This Nation. Harold Norris. LC 75-27812. 160p. 1976. 7.50 (0-8187-0020-3) Harlo Press.

You Are Unique. June K. Burke. (Orig.). 1995. pap. 9.95 (0-929377-03-6) Burke-Srour Pubns Inc.

You Are Valuable. Billy J. Daugherty. 32p. 1991. pap. 0.50 (1-56267-017-4) Victory Ctr OK.

You Are Very Special: A Biblical Guide to Self-Worth. Verna Birkey. LC 77-23805. 168p. (gr. 10). 1987. pap. 7.99 (0-8007-5032-2) Revell.

***You Are Very Special: With a Suprise to Show How Special God Made You.** Su Box. (Illus.). 32p. (J). 1996. 12.95 (0-7459-3638-5) Lion USA.

You Are What You Are. (Illus.). (J). (ps-2). 1991. pap. 5.10 (0-8136-5581-1); lib. bdg. 7.95 (0-8136-5081-X) Modern Curr.

You Are What You Ate. Sherry A. Rogers. 225p. (Orig.). (C). 1988. pap. 9.95 (0-9618821-1-5) Prestige NY.

You Are What You Ate. rev. ed. Sherry A. Roger. 303p. 1995. pap. 12.95 (0-9618821-8-2) Prestige NY.

You Are What You Drink: The Authoritative Report on What Alcohol Does to Your Mind, Body & Longevity. Allan Luks & Joseph Barbato. 1989. pap. 7.95 (0-679-72364-1, Vin) Random.

You Are What You Drink: The Authoritative Report on What Alcohol Does to Your Mind, Body & Longevity. Allan Luks & Joseph Barbato. 1989. pap. 7.95 (0-318-41620-4, Villard Bks) Random.

You Are What You Eat. Melvin Berger. Ed. by Lisa Trumbauer. (Early Science Big Bks.). (Illus.). 16p. (J). (ps-2). 1994. pap. 14.95 (1-56784-014-0) Newbridge Comms.

You Are What You Eat. Victor H. Lindlahr. LC 80-19722. 128p. 1990. reprint ed. pap. 17.00 (0-89370-990-5); reprint ed. lib. bdg. 27.00 (0-89370-604-3) Borgo Pr.

You Are What You Eat Theme Pack. Melvin Berger. Ed. by Susan Evento. (Macmillan Early Science Big Bks.). (Illus.). (J). (ps-2). 1995. pap. write for info. (1-56784-146-5) Newbridge Comms.

You Are What You See. Elizabeth Lide. 1993. 25.00 (0-932526-47-0) Nexus Pr.

You Are What You Think, 2 vols., I. Doug Hooper. (C). 1980. pap. write for info. (0-9604702-0-4) D Hooper.

You Are What You Think, 2 vols., II. Doug Hooper. (C). 1980. pap. write for info. (0-9604702-1-2) D Hooper.

You Are What You Think: A Guide to Self-Realization. Charles H. Zastrow. 300p. 1993. pap. text ed. 19.95 (0-8304-1314-6) Nelson-Hall.

You Are What You Think: Make Your Thoughts Delicious. Betsy O. Thompson. LC 92-73096. (Illus.). (Orig.). 1993. pap. 10.95 (1-879023-07-5) Ascension Pub.

You Are What You Wear. William Thourlby. Ed. by Patricia Wood. (Illus.). 194p. 1990. 9.95 (0-945429-00-2) Forbes-Wittenburg & Brown.

***You Are What You Write.** Huntington Hartford. 400p. 1975. 30.00 (0-7206-0044-8, Pub. by P Owen Ltd UK) Dufour.

You Are Who You Hate: The Alchemy of Dissonance. Elide M. Solomont. 1995. pap. 10.95 (0-533-11568-X) Vantage.

You Are with Me: A Personal Story of God's Sustaining Grace. Kenneth T. Meredith. 79p. 1995. per., pap. 6.99 (0-8341-1551-4) Beacon Hill.

***You Are Wonderful.** 24p. (J). Date not set. write for info. (1-55513-621-4, Chariot Bks) Chariot Victor.

You Are Worth a Fortune. Arthur Milton. 1977. 6.95 (0-8065-0589-3, Citadel Pr) Carol Pub Group.

***You Are Your Car.** Dale W. Emme. (Illus.). 83p. (Orig.). 1983. pap. 11.95 (1-889529-00-1) Two Feathers.

You Are Your Child's First Teacher. Rahima Baldwin. LC 88-3983. (Illus.). 380p. 1995. 19.95 (0-89087-569-3); pap. 12.95 (0-89087-519-7) Celestial Arts.

You Are Your Father's Daughter. Earl R. Henslin. LC 94-20711. 1994. pap. 14.99 (0-8407-7722-1) Nelson.

You Are Your Instrument: The Definitive Musician's Guide to Practice & Performance. Julie L. Lieberman. (Illus.). 152p. 1991. pap. 20.00 (1-879730-20-0) Huiksi Music.

You Are Your Own Psysician: The Holistic Workbook. George F. Barth. (Illus.). 1993. pap. 14.95 (0-533-10462-9) Vantage.

You Asked? Over 300 Great Questions & Astounding Answers. Owl Magazine Editors. (Illus.). 160p. (Orig.). (J). (gr. 4 up). 1996. 24.95 (1-895688-58-2, Pub. by Owl Bks CN); pap. 14.95 (1-895688-59-0, Pub. by Owl Bks CN) Firefly Bks Ltd.

You Asked about Rheumatoid Arthritis: Reassuring Advice from a Distinguished Medical Team for All Who Suffer from North America's No. 1 Crippling Disease. Ed. by Harold S. Robinson. LC 81-17048. (Illus.). 128p. 1982. 9.95 (0-8253-0088-6) Beaufort Bks NY.

You Asked Us... About Canada. Walter Stefaniuk. 288p. 1996. pap. 9.95 (0-385-25578-0) Doubleday.

You Be Good & I'll Be Night: Jump-on-the-Bed-Poems. Eve Merriam. LC 87-24859. (Illus.). 40p. (J). (ps-2). 1988. 16.00 (0-688-06742-5, Morrow Junior) Morrow.

You Be Good & I'll Be Night: Jump-on-the-Bed Poems. Eve Merriam. LC 87-24859. 40p. (J). 1996. pap. 4.95 (0-688-13984-1, Mulberry) Morrow.

You Be Good Vet, Doc: Venture in Grenada. C. Ashby & Ann F. Ashby. LC 88-90725. (Illus.). 227p. (Orig.). 1988. pap. 11.95 (0-9621103-0-2) A F Ashby.

You Be Hoobee. H. Pleiman, Jr. (Illus.). 45p. (J). (gr. 1 up). 1994. 24.95 (0-9621755-1-X) Metahomin Pub.

You Be Hoobee. H. Pleiman, Jr. (Illus.). 45p. (J). (gr. 1 up). 1994. pap. 17.95 (0-9621755-2-8) Metahomin Pub.

You Be Me, I'll Be You. Pili Mandelbaum. (Illus.). 40p. (J). (ps-3). 1990. 13.95 (0-916291-27-8) Kane-Miller Bk.

You Be Me, I'll Be You. Pili Mandelbaum. (Illus.). 40p. (J). (ps-3). reprint ed. pap. 6.95 (0-916291-47-2) Kane-Miller Bk.

You Be the Author! Beginning Writers: Twenty Exciting Mini Books Kids Love to Write & Read. Jill F. Hauser. (Illus.). 64p. (J). (gr. k-3). 1994. 8.99 (0-86653-803-8, GA1495) Good Apple.

You Be the Author! Intermediate Writers: Sixteen Exciting Mini Books Kids Love to Write & Read. Jill F. Hauser. (Illus.). 64p. (J). (gr. 4-7). 1994. 8.99 (0-86653-804-6, GA1496) Good Apple.

You Be the Boxing Judge! Judging Professional Boxing for the TV Boxing Fan. Thomas A. Kaczmarek. (Illus.). 32p. 1996. pap. 9.95 (0-8059-3903-2) Dorrance.

You Be the Detective. Marvin Miller. 96p. (J). (gr. 4-6). 1991. pap. 2.50 (0-590-42731-8) Scholastic Inc.

You Be the Detective, No. II. Marvin Miller. 96p. (J). (gr. 4-6). 1992. pap. 2.50 (0-590-45690-3) Scholastic Inc.

You Be the Jury: Courtroom Four. Marvin Miller. 96p. (J). (gr. 7-9). 1992. 3.50 (0-590-45723-3, 066) Scholastic Inc.

You Be the Jury: Courtroom Three. Marvin Miller. 96p. (J). (gr. 7-9). 1992. pap. 3.50 (0-590-45724-1) Scholastic Inc.

You Be the Jury: Courtroom Two. Marvin Miller. 96p. (J). (gr. 7-9). 1992. pap. 2.50 (0-590-45727-6); pap. 3.50 (0-590-45725-X) Scholastic Inc.

You Be the Jury: Courtroom V. Marvin Miller. (J). 1996. pap. text ed. 3.50 (0-590-73910-7) Scholastic Inc.

You Be the Mother Follies. Claire Burch. ii, 142p. 1991. reprint ed. pap. 14.95 (0-916147-13-4) Regent Pr.

You Be the Witch. Jeri Kroll. (Illus.). 32p. (J). (gr. k-2). 1995. 12.95 (0-85091-564-3, Pub. by Lothian Pub AT) Seven Hills Bk.

You Belong: A Handbook for Church Members. rev. ed. Allen H. Marheine. LC 95-16991. 112p. 1995. pap. 4.95 (0-8298-1104-4) Pilgrim OH.

You Belong to Me. Eileen Goudge. Date not set. pap. 3.50 (0-14-036016-6, Viking) Viking Penguin.

You Belong to Me. Johanna Lindsey. 432p. (Orig.). 1994. mass mkt. 6.99 (0-380-76258-7) Avon.

You Belong to Me. large type ed. Johanna Lindsey. LC 95-15707. (Large Print Bks.). 1995. 25.95 (1-56895-213-9) Wheeler Pub.

You Belong to Me. large type ed. Kathleen Treves. 1989. 25.99 (0-7089-2112-4) Ulverscroft.

You Belong to Me & Other True Cases: Ann Rule's Crime Files, Vol. 2. Ann Rule. Ed. by Julie Rubenstein. (Illus.). 556p. (Orig.). 1994. pap. 6.99 (0-671-79354-3) PB.

***You Belong to My Heart.** Nan Ryan. 384p. mass mkt. write for info. (0-06-108437-9, Harp PBks) HarpC.

You Belong to My Heart. Nan Ryan. 384p. 1996. mass mkt. 5.99 (0-06-108416-6) HarpC.

You Belong to My Heart. large type ed. Nan Ryan. LC 96-14350. (Large Print Bks.). 1996. pap. 22.95 (1-56895-333-X) Wheeler Pub.

You Bet Your Life. Julie R. Deaver. LC 92-28211. (Charlotte Zolotow Bk.). 224p. (YA). (gr. 7 up). 1993. lib. bdg. 14.89 (0-06-021517-8) HarpC Child Bks.

***You Bet Your Life.** Christine T. Jorgensen. 1997. pap. 4.99 (0-373-26245-0, 1-26245-0, Wrldwide Lib) Harlequin Bks.

You Bet Your Life: A Stella Stargazer Mystery. Christine Jorgensen. 224p. 1995. 19.95 (0-8027-3265-8) Walker & Co.

You Better Believe It. Kenneth J. Roberts. LC 77-84944. (Illus.). 1977. pap. 6.95 (0-87973-750-6) Our Sunday Visitor.

You Book: A Treasury of Health & Healing. Earlyne C. Chaney. LC 90-84838. 328p. 1991. per. 16.95 (0-918936-23-3) Astara.

You Break It, You Buy It: And Three Dozen More Opportune Moments to Teach Family Values. Kass P. Dotterweich. LC 95-21247. (Teachable Moment Bks.). 128p. 1995. pap. 8.95 (0-89243-811-8) Liguori Pubns.

You Break It, You Buy It & Three Dozen More Opportune Moments to Teach Family Values. Kass P. Dotterweich. LC 94-77399. 64p. 1994. pap. 3.95 (0-89243-678-6) Liguori Pubns.

***You Brew Good Ale: A History of Home-Brewed Ales.** Ian P. Peaty. (Illus.). 224p. 1997. pap. 22.95 (0-7509-1592-7, Pub. by Sutton Pubng UK) Bks Intl VA.

You Bright & Risen Angels. William T. Vollmann. 640p. 1988. pap. 12.95 (0-14-011087-9, Penguin Bks) Viking Penguin.

You Bring Out the Music in Me: Music in Nursing Homes. Ed. by Beckie Karras. LC 87-22931. (Activities, Adaptation & Aging Ser.: Vol. 10, Nos. 1 & 2). (Illus.). 135p. 1996. 24.95 (0-86656-699-6) Haworth Pr.

You Bring Out the Music in Me: Music in Nursing Homes. Ed. by Beckie Karras. LC 87-22931. (Activities, Adaptation & Aging Ser.: Vol. 10, Nos. 1 & 2). 135p. 1996. reprint ed. pap. 14.95 (0-7890-6038-8) Haworth Pr.

***You Bring the Bagels I'll Bring the Gospel: Sharing the Messiah with Your Jewish Neighbor.** rev. ed. Barry A. Rubin. (Illus.). 256p. 1997. pap. 10.95 (1-880226-65-0) M J Pubs.

***You Bring the Confetti, God Brings the Joy.** Luci Swindoll. 1997. pap. 10.99 (0-8499-4000-1) Word Pub.

***You Call Me Louis, Not Mr. Horst.** Dorothy Madden. (Choreography & Dance Studies). 1997. text ed. 99.00 (3-7186-5877-1, Harwood Acad Pubs); pap. text ed. 33.00 (3-7186-5887-9, Harwood Acad Pubs) Gordon & Breach.

You Call That a Farm? Raising Leeches, Alligators, Weeds, & Other Unusual Things. Sam Epstein & Beryl Epstein. (Illus.). 64p. (J). (gr. 2-5). 1991. 13.95 (0-374-38705-2) FS&G.

You Call the Play: Baseball, Catcher in Command. Peter Strupp. (Sports Illustrated Ser.). 96p. (YA). 1994. pap. 3.50 (0-553-48161-4) Bantam.

You Call This Living? A Collection of East European Political Jokes. C. Banc & Alan Dundes. LC 90-39416. 184p. 1990. pap. 14.95 (0-8203-1283-5) U of Ga Pr.

***You Call, We Haul.** Tana Reiff. LC 94-76140. (Working for Myself Ser.). 80p. 1994. pap. 4.95 (0-7854-1114-3, 40830) Am Guidance.

***You Called? Vol. 1: Times When I Can't Yack on the Phone, & Why.** Ham Koba. (Illus.). 80p. (Orig.). (C). 1996. pap. 10.00 (0-9654925-0-8) T H K Bks.

You Came to Meet Someone Else. Carolyn Stoloff. LC 93-70301. 96p. (Orig.). 1993. pap. 9.95 (1-878580-38-8) Asylum Arts.

You Can! Frank B. Minirth & Mark Littleton. LC 94-27191. 1994. write for info. (0-8407-7749-3) Nelson Comm.

***You Can Afford College.** Kaplan Staff. 1997. pap. 24.95 incl. cd-rom (0-684-84171-1) S&S Trade.

You Can Afford College, 1997. Kaplan. Date not set. pap. 27.95 incl. disk (0-684-83387-5) S&S Trade.

You Can Afford College, 1997. Kaplan. 1996. pap. 20.00 (0-684-83388-3) S&S Trade.

You Can Afford the Wedding of Your Dreams. Kay M. Strom & Lisa Ringnalda. 220p. 1995. pap. 10.99 (0-89283-926-0, Vine Bks) Servant.

You Can Afford to Retire! The No-Nonsense Guide to Pre-Financial Planning. William W. Parrott & John L. Parrott. 1992. pap. 14.95 (0-13-980160-X, Busn) P-H.

You Can Always Trust a Spotted Horse. Stephen Bly. LC 92-46667. (Nathan T. Riggins Western Adventure Ser.). 128p. (Orig.). (J). (gr. 4-7). 1993. pap. 4.99 (0-89107-716-2) Crossway Bks.

You Can Always Win. Michele D. Anderson. 33p. 1994. 4.95 (0-9644222-0-4) Artistic Insights.

You Can Analyze Your Own Handwriting. Robert Holder. 1969. pap. 5.99 (0-451-16244-7, Sig) NAL-Dutton.

You Can & Should Sell Cars. Jack A. Bennett. (Illus.). 164p. (Orig.). 1989. pap. 14.95 (0-9625254-0-5) J B Pub WI.

You Can Be a Columnist: Writing & Selling Your Way to Prestige. Charlotte Digregorio. LC 90-71020. (Illus.). 232p. (Orig.). 1993. pap. 13.95 (0-9623318-1-3) Civetta Pr.

***You Can Be a Joyful Tither.** Fletcher C. Spruce. 1985. pap. 3.99 (0-8341-1087-3) Beacon Hill.

You Can Be a Musician & a Missionary, Too. Renee Kent. Ed. by Cindy McClain. (Illus.). 64p. (Orig.). (J). (gr. 4-6). 1988. pap. 3.95 (0-936625-37-6, PZ7.K419Y) Womans Mission Union.

You Can Be a National Champion. Doug Gelbert. LC 96-39450. (Illus.). 224p. (Orig.). 1996. pap. 12.95 (1-57028-105-X) Masters Pr IN.

You Can Be a Peak Performer: 10 Steps to Unlimited Success Which Anyone Can Take. Dan Sherman. 160p. (Orig.). 1996. pap. 14.95 (0-9651436-0-0) D Sherman & Assocs.

You Can Be a Philanthropist: Why Let Rich People Have All the Fun? David G. Clough. LC 95-92684. 95p. (Orig.). 1996. 12.95 (0-9649810-0-9) Planned Giv Spec.

You Can Be a Powerful Leader. rev. ed. Ivan W. Fitzwater. LC 78-55516. (Illus.). x, 174p. 1991. 12.00 (0-934955-22-0) Watercress Pr.

You Can Be a Powerful Leader. Ivan W. Fitzwater. LC 78-55516. (Illus.). 155p. 1984. reprint ed. pap. 11.00 (0-941420-04-3) Mandel Pubns.

***You Can Be a Soul Winner.** Alvin Jennings. 224p. (Orig.). 1988. pap. 5.95 (0-940999-37-4, C-2149) Star Bible.

You Can Be a Soul Winner, Here's How! Nate Krupp. LC 78-64961. 176p. 1978. reprint ed. pap. 5.95 (0-89221-050-8) New Leaf.

***You Can Be a Stock Market Genius: (Even If You're Not Too Smart) Uncover the Secret Hiding Places of Stock Market Profits.** Joel Greenblatt. LC 96-50310. 1997. 25.00 (0-684-83213-5) S&S Trade.

You Can Be a Successful Teacher of Adults. Adult Education Association Staff. Ed. by Phillip D. Langerman. LC 74-81224. 186p. 1974. pap. 6.50 (0-317-36197-X) A A A C E.

You Can Be a Winner in the Invisible War: The Power of Binding & Loosing. James D. Marocco. 96p. (Orig.). 1992. pap. 5.95 (1-881227-00-6) Bartimaeus.

You Can Be a Witnessing Christian. Beverly Burgess. (Christian Living Ser.). 56p. 1990. pap. 3.25 (0-8341-1375-9) Beacon Hill.

You Can Be a Woman Architect. Judith L. Cohen & Margot Siegel. (Illus.). 40p. (Orig.). (J). 1992. pap. 6.00 (1-880599-04-X) Cascade Pass.

You Can Be a Woman Astronomer. Andrea Ghez & Judith L. Conen. LC 95-35156. (Illus.). 40p. (J). (gr. 3-6). 1995. pap. 6.00 (1-880599-17-1) Cascade Pass.

You Can Be a Woman Cardiologist. Rita Redborg & Judith L. Cohen. LC 96-8865. (Illus.). 40p. (J). (gr. 3-6). 1996. pap. 6.00 (1-880599-18-X) Cascade Pass.

You Can Be a Woman Egyptologist. Betsy Bryan & Judith Cohen. LC 93-1267. (Illus.). 40p. (Orig.). (J). (gr. 3-6). 1993. pap. 6.00 (1-880599-10-4) Cascade Pass.

You Can Be a Woman Engineer. Judith L. Cohen. LC 95-35232. 40p. (Orig.). (J). (gr. 3-7). 1991. pap. 6.00 (1-880599-01-5); audio 4.00 (1-880599-02-3) Cascade Pass.

You Can Be a Woman Engineer. Judith L. Cohen. (Illus.). 40p. (Orig.). (J). (gr. 3-6). 1996. pap. 20.00 incl. cd-rom (1-880599-19-8) Cascade Pass.

You Can Be a Woman Marine Biologist. Florence McAlary & Judith L. Cohen. (Illus.). 40p. (Orig.). (J). (gr. 4-7). 1992. pap. 6.00 (1-880599-06-6) Cascade Pass.

***You Can Be a Woman Marine Biologist.** Florence McAlary & David A. Katz. 40p. (Orig.). (J). (gr. 3-6). 1997. pap. 19.95 incl. cd-rom (1-880599-21-X) Cascade Pass.

You Can Be a Woman Oceanographer. Sharon Franks & Judith Cohen. LC 94-14982. (Illus.). 40p. (J). (gr. 3-6). 1994. pap. 6.00 (1-880599-14-7) Cascade Pass.

You Can Be a Woman Paleontologist. Diane Gabriel & Judith Cohen. LC 93-21349. (Illus.). 40p. (J). (gr. 3-6). 1993. pap. 6.00 (1-880599-12-0) Cascade Pass.

You Can Be a Woman Zoologist. Judith L. Cohen & Valerie Thompson. LC 93-1092. (Illus.). 40p. (Orig.). (J). (gr. 3-7). 1992. pap. 6.00 (1-880599-08-2) Cascade Pass.

You Can Be Absolutely Irrefutably Supernaturally Healed by God Today. Walter E. Adams. 100p. (Orig.). 1987. pap. 4.95 (0-937408-39-5) GMI Pubns Inc.

You Can Be an Effective Board Member. Joseph D. Biscoe. (Christian Living Ser.). 40p. 1988. pap. 3.25 (0-8341-1233-7) Beacon Hill.

You Can Be an Information Writer. Duncan Long. LC 91-60974. 176p. (Orig.). 1991. pap. 16.95 (1-55950-066-2, 64112) Loompanics.

You Can Be Beautiful: With Beauty That Never Fades. 25th ed. Lottie B. Hobbs. 95p. 1959. reprint ed. pap. 5.95 (0-913838-01-2) Harvest TX.

You Can Be Beautiful: With Beauty That Never Fades. Lottie B. Hobbs. 95p. 1959. reprint ed. 7.95 (0-913838-02-0) Harvest TX.

You Can Be Driven Sane! Know Yourself to Heal Yourself - a Journal of Self Discovery. Justin Thomas. 1994. pap. 5.50 (1-56171-337-6, S P I Bks) Sure Seller.

You Can Be Fit! A Simple Guide to Understanding Fitness & Nutrition. Steven M. Horwitz. (Illus.). 77p. (Orig.). 1993. 10.95 (0-9631715-3-4) Fnd Chiro Educ Res.

You Can Be Free: An Easy-to-Read Handbook for Abused Women. Ginny NiCarthy & Sue Davidson. LC 88-36245. (New Leaf Ser.). 120p. (Orig.). 1989. pap. 8.95 (0-931188-68-7) Seal Pr WA.

***You Can Be Free: An Easy-to-Read Handbook for Abused Women.** Ginny NiCarthy & Sue Davidson. (New Leaf Ser.). 120p. 1997. pap. 10.95 (1-878067-06-0) Seal Pr WA.

You Can Be Free: Overcoming the Sinful Habits & Desires in Your Life. Jeffrey B. Krall. 40p. (Orig.). 1996. pap. 3.50 (1-57688-007-9, 007-9) Branch & Vine.

***You Can Be Happy.** Rose S. Bell. 150p. (Orig.). 1997. pap. text ed. 10.95 (0-9614788-5-3) Tivoli Pub.

***You Can Be Happy No Matter What: Five Principles Your Therapist Never Told You.** 2nd rev. ed. Richard Carlson. LC 97-15902. 192p. 1997. pap. 12.95 (1-57731-064-0) New Wrld Lib.

You Can Be Happy No Matter What: Four Principles Your Therapist Never Told You. Richard Carlson. LC 91-38494. 192p. 1992. pap. 11.95 (0-931432-91-X) New Wrld Lib.

You Can Be Healed. Billy J. Daugherty. 114p. (Orig.). 1991. pap. 6.99 (0-89274-876-1, HH876) Harrison Hse.

You Can Be Healed. Clara Palmer. 1937. 6.95 (0-87159-181-2) Unity Bks.

You Can Be President (or Anything Else) Bob Moore. LC 80-36832. 128p. 1980. 12.95 (0-88289-268-1) Pelican.

***You Can Be Rich & Free: Automatically with the Power of Your Own Mind.** Oscar Josef. LC 96-95435. (Illus.). 146p. (Orig.). 1997. pap. 12.50 (0-9655962-4-9) Action Pub CA.

***You Can Be Rich by Thursday: The Secrets of Making a Fortune in Multi-Level Marketing.** Tom Pinnock. 125p. (Orig.). 1997. pap. 12.00 (1-882467-14-0) Wildstone Media.

You Can Be Righteous. Carroll Thompson. 64p. (Orig.). 1991. pap. write for info. (1-879655-00-4) CTM Dallas.

***You Can Be Sanctified Wholly.** 1959. pap. 0.75 (0-8341-0436-9) Nazarene.

You Can Be Sanctified Wholly. Richard Neiderhiser. (Christian Living Ser.). 24p. 1988. pap. 3.25 (0-8341-1217-5) Beacon Hill.

You Can Be Set Free from Demonic Influence. Karl D. Strader. 32p. (Orig.). 1995. pap. 1.95 (0-939241-02-1) Faith Print.

You Can Be Successful: How to Achieve Your Goals in 10 Easy Steps. Eleanor Jacobs. 72p. 1991. pap. 10.95 (0-9632874-1-9) Jacobs Hse.

You Can Be Sure. large type ed. write for info. (0-318-68670-8, 8004) LBW.

You Can Be the Best: Most Requested Selections from the Author's Nationally Acclaimed Radio Series. Jim Davidson. LC 91-76202. 256p. 1991. pap. 9.95 (0-9630963-3-8) Cont Educ Srvs.

You Can Be the Best Chiropractor in Your Town: The Nuts & Bolts of Running a Successful Practice. Dave Barber. (Illus.). 224p. (Orig.). 1993. pap. 49.95 (0-9637594-0-X) Kick-Start Pr.

***You Can Be the Wife of a Happy Husband.** Darien B. Cooper. 156p. 1996. pap. text ed. 9.99 (1-56476-711-6) SP Pubns.

***You Can Be Your Own Sex Therapist.** Carole Altman. reprint ed. pap. 12.95 (0-9657527-9-8) Casper Pubng.

You Can Beat Depression: A Guide to Prevention & Recovery. 2nd rev. ed. John Preston. LC 96-20175. 176p. (Orig.). 1996. pap. 11.95 (1-886230-02-1) Impact Pubs CA.

You Can Become a Dynamic Intercessor. Mina Kohlhafer. 1993. student ed. 3.95 (0-87508-299-8) Chr Lit.

You Can Become the Person You Want to Be. Robert H. Schuller. 160p. 1986. mass mkt. 5.50 (0-515-08988-5) Jove Pubns.

You Can Bet on It! How to Get Maximum Value for Your Gambling Dollar. Larry Grossman. (Casino Games Ser.: Vol. 1). (Illus.). 200p. (Orig.). 1994. pap. 14.95 (0-9641272-4-5) Promot Cassettes.

You Can Bet on It! How to Get Maximum Value for Your Gambling Dollar. Larry Grossman. (Sports Betting Ser.: Vol. 2). (Illus.). 200p. (Orig.). 1994. pap. 14.95 (0-9641272-8-8) Promot Cassettes.

You Can Bet on It! How to Get Maximum Value for Your Gambling Dollar, 2 vols., Set. Larry Grossman. (Illus.). 400p. (Orig.). 1994. pap. 24.95 (0-9641272-2-9) Promot Cassettes.

You Can Bet the Ranch. Pat Wellman. 96p. (Orig.). 1986. pap. 6.99 (0-8341-1155-1) Beacon Hill.

You Can Break That Habit. Forrest E. Ladd. (Christian Living Ser.). 32p. 1988. pap. 3.25 (0-8341-0056-8) Beacon Hill.

You Can Build It! Council of American Building Officials Staff. pap. 4.50 (1-884590-31-4, 223S00) Intl Conf Bldg Off.

***You Can, but Will You?** Orison S. Marden. 338p. 1997. pap. 30.00 (0-89540-342-0) Sun Pub.

You Can Call Me Willy: A Story for Children about AIDS. Judith Stern et al. (Illus.). 80p. (J). (ps-3). 1996. pap. 16.95 (0-945354-61-4) Magination Pr.

You Can Call Me Willy: A Story for Children about AIDS. Joan C. Verniero. (Illus.). 32p. (J). (ps-3). 1994. pap. 8.95 (0-945354-60-6) Magination Pr.

***You Can Call Me Worm.** Dan Haas. LC 97-6466. (J). 1998. 15.00 (0-395-85783-X) HM.

You Can Carve Fantastic Jack-o-Lanterns. Rhonda M. Hart. Ed. by Kim Foster. LC 90-55042. (Illus.). 112p. (J). 1990. pap. 6.95 (0-88266-580-4) Storey Comm Inc.

***You Can Change How You Feel.** Gerald Kranzler. 6.95 (0-614-23913-3, B039) Inst Rational-Emotive.

You Can Change the World. Charles Gallagher. (Celebrate Love Ser.). 74p. (Orig.). 1990. pap. text ed. 3.95 (0-911905-31-6) Past & Mat Rene Ctr.

You Can Change the World, Vol. 1. Jill Johnstone & Daphne Spraggett. 128p. (J). (gr. 3-7). 1993. 16.99 (0-310-40041-4) Zondervan.

You Can Change the World Vol. 2: Learning to Pray for People Around the World. Daphne Spraggett & Jill Johnstone. 128p. (J). 1996. boxed 16.99 (0-310-20565-4) Zondervan.

***You Can Change Your Destiny.** John Osteen. Date not set. mass mkt. 2.25 (0-912631-17-1) J O Pubns.

You Can Change Your Life by Changing Your Mind. Beth S. Jarman. (Illus.). 1986. pap. 9.95 (0-9626605-0-7) Leadership Two Thousand.

You Can Choose Your Own Life: A Decision-Making Program for Students. Barbara K. Davis & Barry Sommer. 56p. 1992. teacher ed. 16.00 (0-89106-057-X) Consulting Psychol.

You Can Choose Your Own Life: Stories for Decision Making. Barbara K. Davis & Barry Sommer. 112p. (J). (gr. 6-8). 1992. student ed. 5.00 (0-89106-058-8) Consulting Psychol.

You Can Come Back. Robyn Runyan. 1996. pap. 12.95 (1-885487-22-3) Brownell & Carroll.

You Can Conquer Cancer: Prevention & Managememt. Ian Gawler. 260p. (Orig.). 1994. pap. 13.95 (0-85572-141-3, Pub. by Hill Content Pubng AT) Seven Hills Bk.

You Can Conquer Life's Conflicts. Dennis Burke. 128p. 1988. pap. 4.99 (0-89274-524-X, HH-524) Harrison Hse.

You Can Conquer Your Headaches. Frank R. Di Fiore. (Illus.). 66p. (Orig.). 1980. pap. 10.00 (0-932896-03-0) Westcliff Pubns.

***You Can Control Diabetes: A Personal Guide to Self Empowerment.** Abdul Ghani & Gary Scheiner. (Illus.). 344p. 1997. pap. 24.95 (0-9656880-0-3) Midtown Pub.

You Can Control Your Class. A. Gudmundsen et al. Ed. by Betty L. Kratoville. 88p. (Orig.). 1996. 10.00 (1-57128-017-0) Acad Therapy.

You Can Control Your Feelings! Twenty-Four Guides to Emotional Well-Being. Bill Borcherdt. LC 92-46866. 270p. (Orig.). 1993. pap. 21.70 (0-943158-73-7, YCCBP, Prof Resc Pr) Pro Resource.

You Can Cook Anything Chinese: Simpler & Surer by Eleven Cooking Methods. 5th ed. Yee Yo. 167p. 1993. pap. 12.95 (0-914929-91-7, Pub. by Hilt Pubng HK) ACCESS Pubs Network.

You Can Cook If You Can Read see Cooking for Absolute Beginners

***You Can Count on It: God's Design Through Numbers.** Eli Borden. (Orig.). 1988. pap. 8.95 (*0-940999-32-3*, C-2145) Star Bible.

You Can Count on Me. Charles M. Schulz. LC 96-17764. (Peanuts Wisdom Bks.). (Illus.). 32p. (Orig.). 1996. 4.95 (*0-00-225168-X*) Collins SF.

You Can Deal Me In. large type ed. William Newton. (Linford Mystery Library). 1991. pap. 15.99 (*0-7089-7079-6*) Ulverscroft.

***You Can Destroy the Gates of Hell.** Lester Sumrall. Date not set. mass mkt. 4.99 (*0-937580-68-6*) LeSEA Pub Co.

You Can Do Anything with Crepes. Virginia Pasley & Jane Green. write for info. (*0-671-20663-X*) S&S Trade.

You-Can-Do Bible Activity Sheets. Mary Currier. (Illus.). 96p. (Orig.). (J). (ps). 1990. pap. 10.99 (*0-8010-2552-4*) Baker Bks.

You Can Do Christian Puppets: A Beginner's Book of Puppet Craft & Playscripts. Bea Carlton & Anne Kircher. Ed. by Arthur L. Zapel. LC 89-3210. (Illus.). 176p. (Orig.). 1989. pap. text ed. 10.95 (*0-916260-58-5*, B196) Meriwether Pub.

You Can Do Great Lettering. Kim Gamble. 48p. (J). (gr. 3-7). 1996. pap. text ed. 6.95 (*1-86373-864-9*) IPG Chicago.

You Can Do It. Ed. by Bob Budler. LC 92-60702. (Illus.). 314p. 1994. pap. 10.95 (*0-937539-19-8*) Executive Bks.

***You Can Do It! A Guide to Christian Self-Publishing.** Athena Dean. 1996. pap. 7.99 (*1-883893-82-8*) WinePress Pub.

You Can Do It: A PR Skills Manual for Librarians. Krysta A. Tepper. LC 80-24217. xii, 232p. 1981. pap. 25.00 (*0-8108-1401-3*) Scarecrow.

***You Can Do It! A Study Guide for Adult Learners.** Harry Turner. 250p. (Orig.). 1997. pap. 14.95 (*1-56343-153-X*) Merritt Pub.

You Can Do It! How to Boost Your Child's Achievement in School. Michael E. Bernard. LC 96-48245. 416p. 1997. pap. 12.99 (*0-446-67193-2*) Warner Bks.

***You Can Do It! What Every Student (& Parent) Should Know about Success in School & Life.** Michael Bernard & Darko J. Hajzler. 16.95 (*0-614-23932-X*, B120) Inst Rational-Emotive.

You Can Do It - Just Try. William J. Bond. 120p. (Orig.). 1993. 12.95 (*0-918694-02-7*); pap. 5.95 (*0-918694-03-5*) Career Pub MA.

You Can Do It Books. 1994. lib. bdg. 52.95 (*0-8225-9999-6*) Lerner Group.

You Can Do It Guide to School Success. Rebecca Allen. 128p. (Orig.). (J). (gr. 5-8). 1989. pap. text ed. 2.25 (*0-87406-414-7*) Willowisp Pr.

You Can Do It, Lamb Chop: Featuring Aesop's the Tortoise & the Hare. Shari Lewis. Ed. by Robert A. Doyle. LC 93-46420. (Illus.). 32p. (J). (ps-5). 1994. 5.95 (*0-8094-7832-3*) Time-Life.

You Can Do It, Lamb Chop! With Puppet. Shari Lewis. (J). (ps-5). 1994. pap. 16.95 (*0-8094-7833-1*) Time-Life.

You Can Do It Together: A User Friendly Guide to Using the Microcomputer. Ed. by Kathleen Smith et al. LC 86-18440. 177p. 1986. spiral bd. 19.95 (*0-86656-430-6*) Haworth Pr.

***You Can Do it Too!!! How to Self-Publish Your Creativity.** large type ed. Lonzie Symonette. (Illus.). 17p. (C). 1996. lab manual ed. 11.95 (*0-9633078-0-0*) LMS Pubs.

You Can Do Something about Your Allergies. Nelson L. Novick. LC 93-832957. (Lisa Drew Book Ser.). 211p. 1994. 20.00 (*0-02-590785-9*) Macmillan.

You Can Do Something about Your Allergies. Nelson L. Novick. 256p. 1995. mass mkt. 5.99 (*0-553-57267-9*) Bantam.

You Can Do Thousands of Things with String. David Miller. 48p. (J). (gr. 3-7). 1996. pap. text ed. 6.95 (*1-86373-959-9*) IPG Chicago.

You Can Dough It! Paulette S. Jarvey. (Illus.). 96p. (Orig.). 1980. pap. 6.95 (*0-9605904-0-4*) Hot off Pr.

You Can Draw. Bruce Robertson. (Illus.). 192p. 1986. 22.95 (*0-13-972621-7*) P-H.

***You Can Draw a Kangaroo.** 50p. 3.95 (*0-644-22381-2*, Pub. by Aust Gov Pub AT) Aubrey Bks.

You Can Draw Animals. Consumer Guide Editors. (Illus.). 80p. 1989. 5.95 (*0-88176-601-1*) Pubns Intl Ltd.

You Can Draw Anything. Kim Gamble. (Orig.). (J). (gr. 3-7). 1996. pap. text ed. 6.95 (*1-86373-680-8*, Pub. by Allen & Unwin Aust Pty AT) IPG Chicago.

You Can Draw Buildings. (You Can Draw Ser.). (Illus.). 80p. (J). 1993. spiral bd. 5.95 (*1-56173-109-9*) Pubns Intl Ltd.

You Can Draw Cars, Planes, Boats & Other Vehicles. Consumer Guide Editors. (Illus.). 80p. 1989. 5.95 (*0-88176-605-4*) Pubns Intl Ltd.

You Can Draw Cartoons. (You Can Draw Ser.). (Illus.). 80p. (J). 1993. spiral bd. 5.95 (*1-56173-112-9*) Pubns Intl Ltd.

You Can Draw Dinosaurs & Other Prehistoric Animals. Consumer Guide Editors. (Illus.). 80p. 1989. 5.95 (*0-88176-604-6*) Pubns Intl Ltd.

You Can Draw Faces. (You Can Draw Ser.). (Illus.). 80p. (J). 1993. spiral bd. 5.95 (*1-56173-113-7*) Pubns Intl Ltd.

You Can Draw Fashions. (Illus.). 80p. (J). 1993. spiral bd. 5.95 (*1-56173-110-2*) Pubns Intl Ltd.

You Can Draw Flowers & Plants. (You Can Draw Ser.). (Illus.). 80p. (J). 1993. spiral bd. 5.95 (*1-56173-114-5*) Pubns Intl Ltd.

You Can Draw Funny Animals. Carrie A. Snyder. LC 81-69659. (Illus.). 32p. (J). (gr. 2-6). 1981. pap. 2.50 (*0-89375-409-9*); lib. bdg. 12.95 (*0-89375-689-X*) Troll Communs.

You Can Draw Landscapes. (You Can Draw Ser.). (Illus.). 80p. (J). 1993. spiral bd. 5.95 (*1-56173-111-0*) Pubns Intl Ltd.

You Can Draw People. Consumer Guide Editors. (Illus.). 80p. 1989. 5.95 (*0-88176-603-8*) Pubns Intl Ltd.

You Can Eliminate Stress from the IRS: Your Chance of Being Audited? At Least Once or Twice in Your Lifetime. Fulton N. Dobson. 112p. 1992. pap. 7.95 (*0-914984-40-3*) Starburst.

You Can Encourage Your High School Student to Read. Jamie Myers. 24p. 1989. pap. 2.00 (*0-87207-162-6*) Intl Reading.

You Can Enjoy Music. Helen L. Kaufmann. (New Reprints in Essay & General Literature Index Ser.). 1977. reprint ed. 26.95 (*0-518-10203-3*, 10203) Ayer.

You Can Excel in Times of Change. Shad Helmstetter. Ed. by Denise Silvestro. 272p. 1992. reprint ed. mass mkt. 5.99 (*0-671-74889-0*) PB.

You Can Feel Good Again: Common-Sense Therapy for Releasing Depression & Changing Your Life. Richard Carlson. 192p. 1994. pap. 10.95 (*0-452-27242-4*, Plume) NAL-Dutton.

You Can Fight Back: Learn How to Easily - Defend Yourself, Foresee Danger, Improve Your Self-Esteem, Feel Confident & Safe at All Times. Richard D. Feroce. (Illus.). 167p. (Orig.). 1995. pap. 9.95 (*1-56790-040-2*) Bkwrld Press.

You Can Fight for Your Life: Emotional Factors in the Treatment of Cancer. Lawrence LeShan. LC 76-30464. 216p. 1980. pap. 9.95 (*0-87131-494-0*) M Evans.

You Can Find a Way. Patrick F. Mahony. 1985. 20.00 (*0-941694-10-0*) Inst Study Man.

You Can Find Anyone! A Complete Guide on How to Locate Missing Persons. Eugene Ferraro. (Illus.). 142p. (Orig.). 1995. reprint ed. pap. 19.95 (*0-915216-75-2*) Marathon Intl Bk.

You Can Find Gold: With a Metal Detector. Charles Garrett et al. Ed. by Hal Dawson. LC 95-74805. (Illus.). 150p. 1996. pap. 9.95 (*0-915920-86-7*) Ram Pub.

You Can Find More Time for Yourself Every Day. Stephanie Culp. 208p. (Orig.). 1994. pap. 12.99 (*1-55870-358-6*, Betrwy Bks) F & W Pubns Inc.

***You Can Find Teachers.** Stewart. 8.90 (*0-687-04605-X*) Abingdon.

You Can Fly a Kite Activity Book. Margaret Greger. (Illus.). (Orig.). (J). (gr. k-6). 1996. pap. 14.00 incl. vhs (*1-887102-03-5*) Blackboard Ent.

You Can Forgive Yourself: If God Can Forgive You...You Can Forgive Yourself. Dennis Leonard. 1991. pap. 4.95 (*1-880809-00-1*) D Leonard Pubns.

You Can Get Anything You Want: But You Have to Do More Than Ask. Roger Dawson. 1985. 15.95 (*0-910019-34-7*) Lghthse Pub Gp.

***You Can Get Bitter Or.** Moore. pap. 16.30 (*0-687-46781-0*) Abingdon.

You Can Get into Medical School: Letters from Premeds. Sanford J. Brown. LC 85-61493. (Illus.). 144p. (Orig.). 1986. pap. 7.95 (*0-9615167-0-4*) Mendocino Found Health.

***You Can Get There from Here.** 109p. 1990. 9.99 (*0-8341-9555-0*) Lillenas.

You Can Get There from Here. Ed. by Andrea J. Enscoe. (YA). 1990. 9.99 (*0-685-68697-3*, MP-655) Lillenas.

You Can Get There from Here. Shirley MacLaine. 224p. 1976. mass mkt. 6.99 (*0-553-26173-8*) Bantam.

You Can Get There from Here. Shirley MacLaine. 249p. 1975. 17.95 (*0-393-07489-7*) Norton.

You Can Get There from Here: Life Lessons on Growth & Self Discovery for the Black Woman. D. Anne Browne. LC 95-77774. 204p. (Orig.). 1995. pap. 12.95 (*0-9638672-6-1*) Bryant & Dillon.

You Can Get There from Here: The Road to Downsizing in Higher Education. Barbara S. Butterfield & Susan Wolfe. 136p. 1994. 20.00 (*1-878240-38-2*) Coll & U Personnel.

You Can Get Well. Adelle Davis. 1975. pap. 2.95 (*0-87904-033-5*) Lust.

You Can Give First Aid: Reading Level 4.5. 1993. 4.80 (*0-88336-550-2*); teacher ed. 5.95 (*0-88336-551-0*) New Readers.

You Can Go Feet First. large type ed. William Newton. (Linford Mystery Library). 1991. pap. 15.99 (*0-7089-7067-2*) Ulverscroft.

You Can Go Home Again. Jirina Marton. (Illus.). 32p. (J). (gr. k-2). 1994. pap. 5.95 (*1-55037-990-9*, Pub. by Annick CN) Firefly Bks Ltd.

You Can Go Home Again. Jirina Marton. (Illus.). 32p. (J). (gr. k-2). 1994. lib. bdg. 15.95 (*1-55037-991-7*, Pub. by Annick CN) Firefly Bks Ltd.

You Can Go Home Again: Reconnecting with Your Family. Monica McGoldrick. LC 93-48812. 1994. 27.50 (*0-393-03494-1*) Norton.

***You Can Go Home Again: Reconnecting with Your Family.** Monica McGoldrick. (Illus.). 336p. 1997. pap. 15.95 (*0-393-31650-5*) Norton.

You Can Go Home Again: The Career Woman's Guide to Leaving the Work Force. Pamela A. Piljac. (Illus.). (Orig.). 1985. pap. 9.95 (*0-913339-03-2*) Bryce-Waterton Pubns.

You Can Go Home Again: The Focus on Family in the Works of Horton Foote. Rebecca L. Briley. LC 92-45641. (American University Studies: American Literature: Ser. XXIV, Vol. 45). 205p. (C). 1994. text ed. 43.95 (*0-8204-2004-2*) P Lang Pubng.

You Can Go Jump. (Illus.). (J). (ps-2). 1991. pap. 5.10 (*0-8136-5582-X*); lib. bdg. 7.95 (*0-8136-5082-8*) Modern Curr.

You Can Go Up. William W. Stringfellow & DeLoras I. Stringfellow. 144p. (Orig.). 1984. pap. 3.95 (*0-939286-03-3*) Concerned Pubns.

You Can Grow Cattleya Orchids. 2nd ed. Mary Noble. LC 90-92175. 100p. 1991. pap. 12.95 (*0-913928-07-0*) McQuerry Orchid.

You Can Grow in a Small Group. Ronald J. Lavin. 144p. 1976. pap. 6.00 (*0-89536-273-2*, 2500) CSS OH.

You Can Grow Orchids. 5th rev. ed. Mary Noble. LC 87-90685. (Illus.). 128p. 1995. reprint ed. pap. 12.95 (*0-913928-06-2*) McQuerry Orchid.

You Can Grow Phalaenopsis Orchids. 2nd rev. ed. Mary Noble. LC 90-92175. (Illus.). 102p. 1994. pap. 12.95 (*0-913928-08-9*) McQuerry Orchid.

You Can Grow Roses in Florida. Linus Olson. (Illus.). 80p. 1978. pap. 5.95 (*0-8200-0407-3*) Great Outdoors.

You Can Grow Tropical Fruit Trees. Robert H. Mohlenbrock. (Illus.). 80p. 1979. pap. 3.95 (*0-8200-0409-X*) Great Outdoors.

You Can Handle Them All. Robert L. DeBruyn & Jack L. Larson. LC 83-62445. 320p. (Orig.). 1984. text ed. 24.95 (*0-914607-04-9*) Master Tchr.

***You Can Have a Children's Choir.** 8.90 (*0-687-04603-3*) Abingdon.

***You Can Have a Church Library.** 8.90 (*0-687-04604-1*) Abingdon.

You Can Have a Family Where Everybody Wins: Christian Perspectives on Parent Effectiveness Training. Earl H. Gaulke. LC 75-23574. 93p. 1975. pap. 4.99 (*0-570-03723-9*, 12-2625) Concordia.

You Can Have a New Life: An Introduction to God & His Word. Don Humphrey. 1992. pap. 2.99 (*0-89225-417-3*) Gospel Advocate.

You Can Have Abundant Life. Jerry Savelle. (Mini-Bks.). 32p. 1992. pap. 0.99 (*0-89274-327-1*, HH-327) Harrison Hse.

You Can Have It All. Arnold M. Patent. LC 96-42942. 1997. pap. 12.00 (*0-671-00076-4*) PB.

You Can Have It All. rev. ed. Arnold M. Patent. LC 90-84993. 200p. 1991. pap. 11.00 (*0-9613663-4-6*) Celebration Pub.

You Can Have it All. 3rd rev. ed. Arnold M. Patent. LC 94-41441. (The/Business of Life Ser.). 210p. (C). 1995. 16.95 (*1-885223-05-6*) Beyond Words Pub.

You Can Have Lasting Joy. Nina B. Skeen. (Illus.). 336p. (Orig.). (YA). 1990. 17.95 (*0-9626994-0-3*); pap. 14.95 (*0-9626994-1-1*); audio 26.95 (*0-685-47240-X*) Joy Pubs.

You Can Have Lasting Joy. Nina B. Skeen. (Illus.). 336p. (Orig.). 1991. 17.95 (*0-685-39469-7*) Joy Pubs.

You Can Have What You Say. Kenneth E. Hagin. 1978. pap. 0.75 (*0-89276-054-0*) Hagin Ministries.

You Can Have What You Say: It Works It Really Works. Chris Long & Yolanda Long. 78p. (Orig.). 1995. pap. write for info. (*1-885591-85-3*) Morris Pubng.

You Can Have What You Want. Julia Hastings. 96p. 1994. pap. 9.00 (*0-425-15826-8*, Berkley Trade) Berkley Pub.

***You Can Have Your Permaculture & Eat It Too.** Robin Clayfield. Date not set. 34.95 (*0-646-28784-2*) Permaculture.

You Can Heal Your Life. Louise L. Hay. 230p. (Orig.). (SPA.). 1995. pap. 12.00 (*84-86344-65-4*, 128) Hay House.

You Can Heal Your Life. Louise L. Hay. LC 88-200391. 226p. (Orig.). 1987. reprint ed. pap. 12.00 (*0-937611-01-8*, 101) Hay House.

You Can Heal Your Life: Special 10th Anniversary Edition. Louise L. Hay. 1994. 16.95 (*1-56170-094-0*, 101H) Hay House.

You Can Hear the Darkness Stirring. Joan P. Kincaid. Ed. by Robert Bixby. 35p. 1993. pap. 6.00 (*1-882983-02-5*) March Street Pr.

***You Can Hear the Ice Talking: The Ways of People & Ice on Lake Champlain.** I. Sheldon Possen. (Illus.). 72p. 1995. pap. 10.00 (*0-614-26428-6*) Purple Mnt Pr.

You Can Help Me. large type ed. Maisie Birmingham. (Linford Mystery Library). 320p. 1987. pap. 15.99 (*0-7089-6358-7*, Linford) Ulverscroft.

You Can Help Pregnant & Parenting Teens Book 1. Jeanne W. Lindsay. LC 91-30316. (Teens Parenting Ser.). 96p. (Orig.). 1991. teacher ed., pap. 7.95 (*0-930934-67-9*) Morning Glory.

You Can Help Pregnant & Parenting Teens, Bk. 2: Curriculum Guide. Jeanne W. Lindsay. (Teens Parenting Ser.). 192p. (Orig.). 1993. teacher ed., pap. 24.95 (*0-930934-73-3*) Morning Glory.

You Can Help Someone Who's Grieving: A How-to Healing Handbook. Victoria Frigo & Diane Fisher. 128p. 1996. pap. 9.95 (*0-14-025907-4*) Viking Penguin.

You Can Help With Your Healing: A Guide for Recovering Wholeness in Body, Mind, & Spirit. rev. ed. Vernon J. Bittner. LC 92-34279. 160p. 1992. pap. 11.99 (*0-8066-2656-9*, 9-2656) Augsburg Fortress.

You Can Help Your Young Child with Writing. Marcia Baghban. 16p. 1989. pap. 2.00 (*0-87207-160-X*) Intl Reading.

You Can Help Yourself to Beauty. James M. Piwonka. 31p. 1994. reprint ed. spiral bd. 4.50 (*0-7873-1166-9*) Hlth Research.

***You Can Hurry Love: An Action Guide for Singles Tired of Waiting.** Richard Gosse. 230p. (Orig.). Date not set. pap. 12.95 (*0-934377-16-2*) Marin Pubns.

You Can Hype Anything: Creative Tactics & Advice for Anyone with a Product, Business or Talent to Promote. Raleigh Pinskey. LC 94-45497. 184p. 1995. pap. 10.95 (*0-8065-1630-5*, Citadel Pr) Carol Pub Group.

You Can If You Think You Can. Norman Vincent Peale. 320p. 1987. pap. 8.00 (*0-671-76591-4*, Fireside) S&S Trade.

You Can If You Think You Can. Norman Vincent Peale. 1988. audio 12.00 (*0-671-66072-1*) S&S Trade.

You Can Illustrate Jack & the Beanstalk. Summit Group Staff. (J). (gr. 4-7). 1993. pap. 5.95 (*1-56530-057-2*) Summit TX.

You Can Illustrate Johnny Appleseed. Summit Group Staff. (J). (gr. 4-7). 1993. pap. 5.95 (*1-56530-055-6*) Summit TX.

You Can Illustrate Paul Bunyan. Summit Group Staff. (J). (gr. 4-7). 1993. pap. 5.95 (*1-56530-056-4*) Summit TX.

You Can Illustrate Rumpelstiltskin. Summit Group Staff. (J). (gr. 4-7). 1993. pap. 5.95 (*1-56530-058-0*) Summit TX.

***You Can Improve Your Students' Writing Skills Immediately! A Revolutionary, No-Nonsense, Two-Brain Approach for Teaching Your Students How to Write Better & Enjoy It More.** David Melton. LC 97-19445. 1997. pap. write for info. (*0-933849-67-2*) Landmark Edns.

***You Can Increase Sunday School Attendance.** 8.90 (*0-687-04608-4*) Abingdon.

You Can Juggle. Peter Murray. LC 92-9504. (Umbrella Bks.). 32p. (J). (gr. 2-6). 1992. lib. bdg. 21.36 (*0-89565-966-2*) Childs World.

***You Can Jump Higher on the Moon & Other Amazing Facts about Space Exploration.** Kate Petty. (I Didn't Know That Ser.). (Illus.). 32p. (J). (gr. 1-3). 1997. 8.95 (*0-7613-0592-0*, Copper Beech Bks); lib. bdg. 14.90 (*0-7613-0564-5*, Copper Beech Bks) Millbrook Pr.

You Can Kick the Habit! Walter E. Kloss. (Better Living Ser.). 1976. pap. 0.75 (*0-8127-0128-3*) Review & Herald.

You Can Knock Out AIDS *see* **AIDS Fighters**

You Can Know God: Christian Spirituality for Daily Living. Marilyn Gustin. LC 92-74594. 224p. (Orig.). 1993. pap. text ed. 9.95 (*0-89243-479-1*) Liguori Pubns.

You Can Lead a Bible Discussion Group. Terry Powell. LC 96-34702. 180p. 1996. pap. 10.99 (*0-88070-884-0*, Multnomah Bks) Multnomah Pubs.

You Can Lead Roman Catholics to Christ. Wilson Ewin. 171p. reprint ed. pap. 5.50 (*0-317-00779-3*) Bible Baptist.

You Can Lead Singing: A Song Leader's Manual. Glenn Lehman. LC 95-6327. (Illus.). 96p. (Orig.). 1994. pap. 6.95 (*1-56148-117-3*) Good Bks PA.

You Can Learn to Relax. Samuel Gutwirth. 1976. pap. 5.00 (*0-87980-177-8*) Wilshire.

You Can Live Comfortably on Less in Mexico: Smart Retirees & Vacationers Tell You How. L. A. Wiesend. (Illus.). 128p. (Orig.). 1992. pap. 12.95 (*0-685-59576-5*) Total Rsch Pub.

You Can Live in Divine Health. Joyce Boisseau. 302p. 1993. pap. 6.95 (*0-914984-02-0*) Starburst.

You Can Look Younger at Any Age. Nelson L. Novick. LC 95-24962. 1996. 14.95 (*0-8050-3970-8*) H Holt & Co.

You Can Look Younger at Any Age: A Leading Dermatologist's Guide. Nelson L. Novick. 192p. 1996. pap. 14.95 (*0-8050-3971-6*, Owl) H Holt & Co.

You Can Lose Weight. Alan Dolit. 130p. 1980. 7.95 (*0-8290-1571-X*) Irvington.

You Can Make a Difference. Tony Campolo. (YA). 1995. pap. 9.99 (*0-8499-3635-7*) Word Pub.

You Can Make a Difference. Jack Graham. LC 92-12732. 1992. 8.99 (*0-8054-3010-5*, 4230-10) Broadman.

You Can Make a Difference: Changing Situations That Hurt Others. Betty Bock. Ed. by Judy Edwards. 116p. 1993. pap. text ed. 6.95 (*1-56309-060-0*) Womans Mission Union.

You Can Make a Difference: Help Protect the Earth. Judith Getis. 96p. (C). 1991. per. write for info. (*0-697-13923-9*) Wm C Brown Pubs.

You Can Make a Difference! Helping Others & Yourself Through Volunteering. Marlene Wilson. Ed. by Lisa K. Wilson. LC 90-70355. (Illus.). (Orig.). 1990. pap. 14.95 (*0-9603362-3-0*) Volunteer Mgmt.

You Can Make It Back: Coping with Serious Illness. Paul M. Levitt & Elissa S. Guralnick. LC 84-26049. 226p. reprint ed. pap. 64.50 (*0-7837-1362-2*, 2041510) Bks Demand.

***You Can Make It Happen.** Graham. LC 96-45457. 1997. 23.00 (*0-684-81448-X*) S&S Trade.

You Can Make It Selling Real Estate. Richard Steacy. 224p. 1988. 23.95 (*0-7737-2245-9*) Genl Dist Srvs.

You Can Make It Without a College Degree. Roberta Roesch. 1986. 8.95 (*0-13-976812-2*) S&S Trade.

You Can Make It! You Can Do It! 101 E-Z Holiday Craft-Tivities for Children. Ann Peaslee & Jullien Kille. (Illus.). 120p. (Orig.). (J). (gr. 3-6). 1991. pap. 14.50 (*0-89346-337-X*) Heian Intl.

***You Can Make Mobiles.** Tibor. (Illus.). 48p. (Orig.). (J). (gr. 2-6). 1997. pap. 6.95 (*1-86448-118-8*, Pub. by Allen & Unwin Aust Pty AT) IPG Chicago.

You Can Make Money from Your Arts & Crafts: The Arts & Crafts Marketing Book. rev. ed. Steve Long & Cindy Long. Ed. by Al Strickland. (Be Your Own Boss Ser.). (Illus.). 224p. 1988. pap. 17.95 (*0-937769-04-5*) Mark Inc CA.

You Can Make Money in MuSic: Everything a Musician Needs to Know to Become Steadily Employed as a Live Performer. Craig W. Colley. 88p. 1991. pap. 14.95 (*1-56516-000-2*) H Leonard.

You Can Make Paper Sculptures. David Miller. (Illus.). 48p. (Orig.). (J). (gr. 3-7). 1996. pap. 6.95 (*1-86373-863-0*, Pub. by Allen & Unwin Aust Pty AT) IPG Chicago.

You Can Make the Right Decision. George Rich. (New Life Ser.). 32p. 1992. student ed., pap. 1.95 (*0-87227-159-5*, RBP5199); teacher ed., pap. 1.95 (*0-87227-168-4*, RBP5198) Reg Baptist.

You Can Manage That Finishing Shop. Lawrence J. Durney. 216p. (C). 1984. text ed. 19.95 (*1-56990-012-4*) Hanser-Gardner.

You Can Master Jewelry Design & Creation: A Revolutionary Technique - Temporary Impression Molding - Which Enables Even Those Without Technical Skills to Design & Make Fine, Precious Metal & Gemstone Jewelry. Gerald L. Wykoff. (Illus.). 275p. 1989. text ed. 24.50 (*0-9607892-5-1*) Adamas Pubs.

An Asterisk (*) at the beginning of an entry indicates that the title is appearing in BIP for the first time.

You Can Name 100 Dinosaurs! And Other Prehistoric Animals. Randy Chewning. (Illus.). 14p. (J). (ps). 1994. bds. 8.95 (*0-590-47913-X*, Cartwheel) Scholastic Inc.

You Can Name 100 Trucks! Jim Becker. (Illus.). 14p. (J). (ps). 1994. bds. 8.95 (*0-590-46302-0*, Cartwheel) Scholastic Inc.

You Can Negotiate Anything. Herb Cohen. 256p. 1983. mass mkt. 6.50 (*0-553-28109-7*) Bantam.

You Can Negotiate Anything. Herb Cohen. 1980. 12.00 (*0-8184-0305-5*) Carol Pub Group.

You Can Negotiate Anything. Herb Cohen. 264p. (C). 1995. reprint ed. pap. 10.95 (*0-8065-0847-7*, Citadel Pr) Carol Pub Group.

You Can Never Go Home Again. Dyan Sheldon. (J). 1995. pap. 3.50 (*0-8167-3691-X*) Troll Communs.

You Can Only Be as Great as You Think You Can Be: You Are Only As Great As You Are. Cornell Thomas. LC 93-60239. 84p. 1993. pap. 7.95 (*1-55523-597-2*) Winston-Derek.

You Can Overcome. James McKeever. 350p. (C). text ed. 14.99 (*0-86694-091-X*); pap. text ed. 9.99 (*0-86694-092-8*) Omega Pubns OR.

***You Can Overcome Evil.** Carlton P. Gleason, Sr. 200p. Date not set. write for info. (*0-9653588-1-X*) Mocking Bird.

You Can Paint Anything in Oils or Acrylics. Sherry Nelson & Jackie Shaw. (Illus.). 32p. (Orig.). 1987. pap. 7.95 (*0-941284-38-7*) J Shaw Studio.

You Can Pass the GED. 2nd rev. ed. Jerry Bobrow. (Cliffs Test Preparation Ser.). (Illus.). 596p. 1995. pap. text ed. 11.95 (*0-8220-2077-7*) Cliffs.

***You Can Pick Me up at Peggy's Cove.** Brian Doyle. (J). (gr. 4-6). 1996. pap. 5.95 (*0-88899-231-9*, Pub. by Groundwood-Douglas & McIntyre CN) Firefly Bks Ltd.

***You Can Plan & Select Music.** 8.90 (*0-687-04606-8*) Abingdon.

You Can Play Harmonica. Amy Appleby & Peter Pickow. (Illus.). 64p. 1990. pap. 14.95 incl. audio (*0-8256-2576-9*, AM76191) Music Sales.

You Can Play Harmonica. Amy Appleby & Peter Pickow. (You Can...Ser.). (Illus.). 64p. (Orig.). pap. 17.95 incl. cd-rom (*0-8256-1517-8*, AM 932350) Omnibus NY.

You Can Play Hymns: A Basic Course in Piano Hymn-Playing. Donna R. Wangsgard. 149p. 1991. pap. 14.98 (*0-88290-373-X*) Horizon Utah.

You Can Play Piano. Amy Appleby. (You Can...Ser.). (Illus.). 92p. (Orig.). pap. 17.95 incl. cd-rom (*0-8256-1516-X*, AM 932349) Music Sales.

You Can Play the Ukulele. D. Ball. 40p. 1986. pap. 4.95 (*0-7935-3764-9*) H Leonard.

You Can Postpone Anything but Love: Expanding Our Potential As Parents. Randall C. Rolfe. 1990. pap. 9.95 (*0-446-39058-5*) Warner Bks.

***You Can Preach to the Kids Too! Designing Sermons for Adults & Children.** Carolyn C. Brown. 1997. pap. text ed. 13.95 (*0-687-06157-1*) Abingdon.

You Can Predict Your Future. Tom Brown. 192p. 1996. mass mkt. 4.99 (*0-88368-386-5*) Whitaker Hse.

***You Can Prevent Breast Cancer.** Harvey Diamond. (Illus.). 273p. (Orig.). 1995. pap. 12.95 (*1-57901-011-3*) Intl Promotions.

You Can Prevent Cancer. Ernest H. Rosenbaum. Ed. by Sheila Mahoney & Nancy Wiltsek. (Illus.). 29p. 1984. pap. 2.50 (*0-933161-00-X*) Better H Prog.

You Can Prevent or Correct Learning Disorders: The Complete Handbook of Children's Reading Disorders. Hilde Mosse. 732p. (C). 1989. reprint ed. pap. text ed. 34.95 (*0-8077-2983-3*) Tchrs Coll.

You Can Raise a Well-Mannered Child. June H. Moore. 192p. 1996. pap. 10.99 (*0-8054-6076-4*, 4260-76) Broadman.

You Can Reach Your Goals Through Creative Visualization. Donald Sandin. 215p. 1993. pap. text ed. write for info. (*0-9638517-0-5*) Sandin Creat.

***You Can Read Me Like a Book.** Maureen Lipman. 1997. 26.95 (*0-86051-979-1*, Robson-Parkwest) Parkwest Pubns.

You Can Read Music. Amy Appleby. (Illus.). 88p. 1990. pap. 14.95 incl. audio (*0-8256-2578-5*, AM76209) Music Sales.

You Can Receive Healing & Prosperity When You Don't Feel Worthy Enough: How to Get off Satan's Guilt Trip. Jay S. Snell. 160p. (Orig.). 1995. pap. text ed. 10.00 (*1-877744-01-8*) J Snell Evangelistic.

You Can Receive the Holy Ghost Today. Bob Buess. 1967. pap. 2.50 (*0-934244-14-6*) Sweeter Than Honey.

You Can Remember Your Past Lives. Robert C. Smith. Ed. by Charles T. Cayce. 282p. (Orig.). 1989. mass mkt. 5.99 (*0-446-34979-8*) Warner Bks.

You Can Repair Your Own Sewing Machine. Grover J. Tharp. (Illus.). 34p. 1977. reprint ed. pap. 4.00 (*0-9614713-0-1*) Sewing Machine Man.

You Can Reprogram Your Brain to Perfect Health: Unsolved Health Problems Solved. Devi S. Nambudripad. (Illus.). 140p. (Orig.). 1990. pap. 47.60 (*0-685-29804-3*) Singer Pub.

You Can Run a Capital Campaign. John W. Zehring. LC 89-36874. 48p. 1989. pap. 2.38 (*0-687-04625-4*) Abingdon.

***You Can Run But You Can't Hide: The Secret Diary of My Life with George Foreman.** Cynthia L. Foreman & Stuart White. 1997. pap. 17.95 (*0-7871-1045-0*, Dove Bks) Dove Audio.

***You Can Run but You Can't Hide: The Secret Diary of My Life with George Foreman.** Cynthia L. Foreman & Stuart White. 1997. pap. 17.95 (*0-7871-1227-5*, Dove Bks) Dove Audio.

You Can Save the Animals: Fifty Simple Things to Do Right Now. Michael W. Fox. 1991. pap. 3.95 (*0-312-92521-2*) St Martin.

You Can Say "No" to Drugs! Gretchen Super. (Drug-Free Kids Ser.). (Illus.). 48p. (J). (gr. k-3). 1991. lib. bdg. 14.98 (*0-8050-2628-2*) TFC Bks NY.

You Can Say No to Your Teenager: And Other Strategies for Effective Parenting in the 1990's. Jeanette Shalov. 1992. pap. 10.00 (*0-201-60826-X*) Addison-Wesley.

You Can Say That Again: An Anthology of Words Fitly Spoken. R. E. White. 1993. text ed. 4.99 (*0-310-96253-6*) Zondervan.

You Can Sell Anything by Telephone! Gary S. Goodman. 132p. 1984. pap. 9.00 (*0-671-76592-2*) P-H.

You Can Sing. Jerold B. Stone. (You Can...Ser.). (Illus.). 80p. (Orig.). pap. 17.95 incl. cd-rom (*0-8256-1515-1*, AM 932338) Omnibus NY.

You Can Sing Great - At Any Age: How to Sing Great. Rick Wiesend. Ed. by L. A. Peterson. (Illus.). 128p. (Orig.). 1989. pap. 16.95 (*1-878459-00-7*) Total Rsch Pub.

You Can Sound Like You Know What You're Saying: So People Will Take You Seriously. Garrett H. Gardner. 144p. (Orig.). 1996. pap. 14.95 (*0-9649852-0-9*) Attune Pubns.

You Can Start a Bible Study Group: Making Friends, Changing Lives. rev. ed. Gladys Hunt. (Fisherman Bible Studyguide Ser.). 96p. 1984. reprint ed. pap. 5.99 (*0-87788-974-0*) Shaw Pubs.

You Can Start Over. Billy J. Daugherty. 32p. (Orig.). 1991. pap. 0.50 (*1-56267-018-2*) Victory Ctr OK.

You Can Stay Alive: Wilderness Living & Emergency Survival. Larry Wells & Roger D. Giles. LC 81-80952. 7p. (Orig.). 1981. pap. 9.98 (*0-88290-181-8*, 4028) Horizon Utah.

You Can Still Change the World. 3.50 (*0-318-02218-4*) Chrstphrs NY.

You Can Stop Feeling Guilty see Tu Puedes Dejar de Sentirte Culpable

You Can Stop Longing: You're Not Alone & You Can Change. Linda Keller. LC 93-102461. 120p. (Orig.). 1990. 10.00 (*0-9625718-0-6*) Tindari Pr.

You Can Stop Smoking. Jacqueline Rogers. 288p. 1990. mass mkt. 5.50 (*0-671-70295-5*) PB.

You Can Stop Smoking. Jacqueline Rogers. 1995. mass mkt. 6.99 (*0-671-52303-1*) PB.

***You Can Stop the Cravings Now! Vol. 1: A Drug Free Biochemical Approach to Relapse Prevention.** Sandra Klippel & Kathryn Wolf. (Illus.). xii, 90p. (Orig.). 1996. pap. 15.00 (*0-9653813-0-7*) S Klippel.

You Can Succeed! Eric P. Jensen. LC 79-13489. (gr. 10-12). 1979. pap. 5.95 (*0-8120-2084-7*) Barron.

You Can Surf the Net! Your Guide to the World of the Internet. Marc Gascoigne. (Illus.). 128p. (J). 1996. pap. 3.99 (*0-14-038265-8*) Puffin Bks.

You Can Survive College - We Did! A Guide for Kids & Their Parents. Beverly P. Faaborg & Tony Faaborg. LC 92-71012. (Illus.). 160p. (Orig.). 1992. pap. 9.95 (*0-932796-45-1*) Ed Media Corp.

You Can Take Care of Yourself. Cowan. 1989. 60.00 (*0-295-96838-9*) U of Wash Pr.

You Can Take It with You. Burko et al. 144p. (C). 1988. pap. text ed. 11.50 (*0-13-972688-8*) P-H.

You Can Take It with You. Bo Mitchell. LC 89-33093. 144p. (Orig.). 1990. pap. 6.99 (*0-8054-5739-9*, 4257-39) Broadman.

You Can Talk to (Almost) Anyone about (Almost) Anything: A Speaking Guide for Business & Professional People. Elaine Cogan & Ben Padrow. LC 84-15531. (Illus.). 116p. (Orig.). 1984. pap. 7.95 (*0-87678-022-2*); lib. bdg. 14.95 (*0-87678-021-4*) PSU CE Pr.

***You Can Talk with Animals.** Myers. 1997. pap. write for info. (*0-8092-3149-2*) Contemp Bks.

You Can Talk with God! Edwin St. George. 72p. 1961. reprint ed. spiral bd. 10.50 (*0-7873-0814-5*) Hlth Research.

You Can Teach Hitting: A Systematic Approach for Parents, Coaches, & Players. Dusty Baker, Jr. et al. (Illus.). 256p. (Orig.). 1993. pap. 24.95 (*0-940279-73-8*) Masters Pr IN.

You Can Teach Old Type New Tricks. Phillip R. Baldus & Harold L. Baldus. (Illus.). 24p. 1985. pap. 10.00 (*0-933107-01-3*) Phils Photo.

You Can Teach Your Child Successfully: Grades 4-8. 2nd ed. Ruth Beechick. LC 88-200410. (Illus.). 488p. 1992. 19.00 (*0-940319-05-5*); pap. 14.00 (*0-940319-04-7*) Arrow Press.

A classic in homeschooling. Gives nitty-gritty help for each grade (4-8) & each subject on what to teach & how to teach it. Builds parent confidence by giving them the information they need in plain language, not "educationese." Teaching moms say they refer to this book repeatedly -- for ideas, for guidance, & for a dose of common sense when they need to get back on track. This has become one of the best known & most widely used books among homeschoolers. Reviewers give it high marks, it won a "Best Book of the Year" award, & readers write unsolicited letters of praise. Some examples: "I wish I had this three years ago when I began homeschooling." "...the most practical manual I've ever read on the subject." "...just what I've been looking for ever since I started." "The simplicity of it all! I don't think any homeschooler should be without it." The author has been both a professor of education & a teacher of children, & is well known for her work in curriculum development. Distributed by Education Services, 8825 Blue Mountain Drive, Golden, CO 80403. Leave orders or messages at 303-234-5245. FAX 303-642-1288. ***Publisher Provided Annotation.***

You Can Teach Your Dog to Eliminate on Command. M. L. Smith. (Illus.). 83p. (Orig.). 1984. pap. 7.95 (*0-9617649-0-2*) T P S Strategies.

You Can Teach Yourself about Music. L. Dean Bye. 1993. 9.95 (*0-87166-261-2*, 94300) Mel Bay.

You Can Teach Yourself Autoharp. Meg Peterson. 9.95 (*0-7866-0017-9*, 95024); audio 9.98 (*0-7866-0018-7*, 95024C) Mel Bay.

***You Can Teach Yourself Autoharp.** Meg Peterson. 18.95 incl. audio (*0-7866-1179-0*, 95024P); audio compact disk 15.98 (*0-7866-2029-3*, 95024CD) Mel Bay.

You Can Teach Yourself Banjo. Janet Davis. 1993. 9.95 (*1-56222-001-2*, 94429); audio 9.98 (*1-56222-002-0*, 94429C); audio 18.95 (*1-56222-515-4*, 94429P) Mel Bay.

***You Can Teach Yourself Banjo.** Janet Davis. 1993. 24.95 incl. audio compact disk (*0-7866-1030-1*, 94429CDP); audio compact disk 15.98 (*0-7866-0381-X*, 94429CD) Mel Bay.

You Can Teach Yourself Blues Guitar. Mike Christiansen. 1993. 9.95 (*1-56222-308-9*, 94699); audio 9.98 (*1-56222-329-1*, 94699C); audio 18.95 (*1-56222-516-2*, 94699P) Mel Bay.

***You Can Teach Yourself Blues Guitar.** Mike Christiansen. 1993. 24.95 incl. audio compact disk (*0-7866-1097-2*, 94699CDP); vhs 29.95 (*0-7866-1397-1*, 94699VX); audio compact disk 15.98 (*0-7866-0385-2*, 94699CD) Mel Bay.

You Can Teach Yourself Blues Harp. Phil Duncan. 1993. 9.95 (*1-56222-309-7*, 94698); audio 9.98 (*1-56222-330-5*, 94698C); audio 18.95 (*1-56222-517-0*, 94698P) Mel Bay.

***You Can Teach Yourself Blues Harp.** Phil Duncan. 1993. 24.95 incl. audio compact disk (*0-7866-1095-6*, 94698CDP); vhs 24.95 (*0-7866-0172-8*, 94698VX); audio compact disk 15.98 (*0-7866-0384-4*, 94698CD) Mel Bay.

You Can Teach Yourself Classic Guitar. William Bay. 9.95 (*0-7866-0015-2*, 95119); audio 9.98 (*0-7866-0016-0*, 95119C) Mel Bay.

***You Can Teach Yourself Classic Guitar.** William Bay. vhs 29.95 (*0-7866-0427-1*, 95119VX); audio compact disk 15.98 (*0-7866-0390-9*, 95119CD) Mel Bay.

You Can Teach Yourself Country Guitar. Dix Bruce. 1993. 9.95 (*1-56222-456-5*, 94818); audio 9.98 (*1-56222-457-3*, 94818C) Mel Bay.

***You Can Teach Yourself Country Guitar.** Dix Bruce. 1993. 38.95 incl. vhs (*0-7866-0614-2*, 94818VPX); 24.95 incl. audio compact disk (*0-7866-1121-9*, 94818CDP); 18.95 incl. audio (*0-7866-1122-7*, 94818P); vhs 29.95 (*0-7866-0613-4*, 94818VX); audio compact disk 15.98 (*0-7866-0387-9*, 94818CD) Mel Bay.

You Can Teach Yourself Dobro. Janet Davis. 9.95 (*0-7866-0801-3*, 95227); audio 9.98 (*0-7866-0802-1*, 95227C) Mel Bay.

***You Can Teach Yourself Dobro.** Janet Davis. audio compact disk 15.98 (*0-7866-1440-4*, 95227CD) Mel Bay.

You Can Teach Yourself Drums. James Morton. 1993. 9.95 (*1-56222-033-0*, 94495); audio 9.98 (*1-56222-034-9*, 94495C); audio 18.95 (*1-56222-518-9*, 94495P) Mel Bay.

***You Can Teach Yourself Drums.** James Morton. 1993. 24.95 incl. audio compact disk (*0-7866-1034-4*, 94495CDP); audio compact disk 15.98 (*0-7866-0383-6*, 94495CD) Mel Bay.

You Can Teach Yourself Dulcimer. Madeline MacNeil. 1993. 9.95 (*0-87166-266-3*, 94304); audio 9.98 (*0-87166-322-8*, 94304C); audio 18.95 (*0-87166-309-0*, 94304P) Mel Bay.

***You Can Teach Yourself Dulcimer.** Madeline MacNeil. 1993. 24.95 incl. audio compact disk (*0-7866-0987-7*, 94304CDP); vhs 29.95 (*0-7866-0617-7*, 94304VX); audio compact disk 15.98 (*0-7866-0376-3*, 94304CD) Mel Bay.

You Can Teach Yourself Electric Bass. Mike Hiland. 1993. 9.95 (*0-87166-776-2*, 94358); audio 9.98 (*0-87166-777-0*, 94358C); audio 18.95 (*1-56222-520-0*, 94358P) Mel Bay.

***You Can Teach Yourself Electric Bass.** Mike Hiland. 1993. 24.95 incl. audio compact disk (*0-7866-1009-3*, 94358CDP); audio compact disk 15.98 (*0-7866-0380-1*, 94358CD) Mel Bay.

You Can Teach Yourself Fiddling. Craig Duncan. 1993. 9.95 (*1-56222-003-9*, 94430); audio 9.98 (*1-56222-004-7*, 94430C); audio 18.95 (*1-56222-521-9*, 94430P) Mel Bay.

***You Can Teach Yourself Fiddling.** Craig Duncan. 1993. 24.95 incl. audio compact disk (*0-7866-1031-X*, 94430CDP); vhs 29.95 (*1-56222-316-X*, 94717VX); audio compact disk 15.98 (*0-7866-0382-8*, 94430CD) Mel Bay.

You Can Teach Yourself Flatpick Guitar. Steven Kaufman. 9.95 (*0-7866-0057-8*, 95190); audio 9.98 (*0-7866-0058-6*, 95190C) Mel Bay.

***You Can Teach Yourself Flatpick Guitar.** Steven Kaufman. vhs 29.95 (*0-7866-0460-3*, 95190VX); audio compact disk 15.98 (*0-7866-0392-5*, 95190CD) Mel Bay.

You Can Teach Yourself Folk Singing. Jerry Silverman. 9.95 (*1-56222-423-9*, 94718); audio 9.98 (*1-56222-689-4*, 94718C) Mel Bay.

***You Can Teach Yourself Folk Singing.** Jerry Silverman. 18.95 incl. audio (*0-7866-1103-0*, 94718P) Mel Bay.

You Can Teach Yourself Guitar. William Bay. 1993. 9.95 (*0-87166-262-0*, 94301); audio 9.98 (*0-87166-749-5*, 94301C); audio 18.95 (*0-87166-750-9*, 94301P) Mel Bay.

***You Can Teach Yourself Guitar.** William Bay. 1993. 24.95 incl. audio compact disk (*0-7866-0981-8*, 94301CDP); vhs 29.95 (*0-7866-0171-X*, 94301VX); audio compact disk 15.98 (*0-7866-0347-X*, 94301CD) Mel Bay.

***You Can Teach Yourself Guitar.** William Bay. 1996. cd-rom 49.95 (*0-7866-2457-4*, 94301CDR) Mel Bay.

You Can Teach Yourself Guitar by Ear. Mike Christiansen. 9.95 (*0-7866-0019-5*, 95121); audio 9.98 (*0-7866-0020-9*, 95121C) Mel Bay.

***You Can Teach Yourself Guitar by Ear.** Mike Christiansen. 19.95 incl. audio compact disk (*0-7866-2866-9*, 95121BCD); vhs 29.95 (*0-7866-1403-X*, 95121VX) Mel Bay.

You Can Teach Yourself Guitar Chords. William Bay. 9.95 (*0-7866-0055-1*, 95120) Mel Bay.

You Can Teach Yourself Harmonica. George Heaps-Nelson & Barbara Koehler. 1993. 9.95 (*0-87166-264-7*, 94303); audio 9.98 (*0-87166-320-1*, 94303C); audio 18.95 (*0-87166-307-4*, 94303P) Mel Bay.

***You Can Teach Yourself Harmonica.** George Heaps-Nelson & Barbara Koehler. 1993. 24.95 incl. audio compact disk (*0-7866-0985-0*, 94303CDP); vhs 24.95 (*0-7866-0426-3*, 94303VX); audio compact disk 15.98 (*0-7866-0375-5*, 94303CD) Mel Bay.

You Can Teach Yourself Jazz Guitar. John Griggs. 9.95 (*1-56222-998-2*, 95162); audio 9.98 (*0-7866-0059-4*, 95162C) Mel Bay.

***You Can Teach Yourself Jazz Guitar.** John Griggs. 18.95 incl. audio (*0-7866-1221-5*, 95162P) Mel Bay.

You Can Teach Yourself Mandolin. Dix Bruce. 1993. 9.95 (*1-56222-447-6*, 94331); audio 9.98 (*1-56222-171-X*, 94331C); audio 18.95 (*1-56222-524-3*, 94331P) Mel Bay.

***You Can Teach Yourself Mandolin.** Dix Bruce. 1993. 24.95 incl. audio compact disk (*0-7866-0990-7*, 94331CDP); vhs 29.95 (*0-7866-0615-0*, 94331VX); audio compact disk 15.98 (*0-7866-0378-X*, 94331CD) Mel Bay.

You Can Teach Yourself Piano. Matt Dennis. (SPA.). 11.95 (*1-56222-431-X*, 94302SP) Mel Bay.

You Can Teach Yourself Piano. Matt Dennis. 1993. 9.95 (*0-87166-263-9*, 94302); audio 9.98 (*0-87166-751-7*, 94302C); audio 18.95 (*0-87166-752-5*, 94302P) Mel Bay.

***You Can Teach Yourself Piano.** Matt Dennis. 1993. 24.95 incl. audio compact disk (*0-7866-0983-4*, 94302CDP); vhs 29.95 (*0-7866-0436-0*, 94302VX); audio compact disk 15.98 (*0-7866-0349-6*, 94302CD) Mel Bay.

You Can Teach Yourself Piano by Ear. Robin Jarman. 1993. 7.95 (*0-87166-265-5*, 94270); audio 9.98 (*0-87166-323-6*, 94270C); audio 16.95 (*0-87166-310-4*, 94270P) Mel Bay.

***You Can Teach Yourself Piano by Ear.** Robin Jarman. 1993. vhs 29.95 (*0-7866-0428-X*, 94270VX) Mel Bay.

You Can Teach Yourself Recorder. William Bay. 1993. 7.95 (*0-87166-742-8*, 94337); audio 9.98 (*0-87166-753-3*, 94337C); audio 16.95 (*0-87166-754-1*, 94337) Mel Bay.

***You Can Teach Yourself Recorder.** William Bay. 1993. 12.95 (*0-7866-0800-5*, 94337PIX); audio compact disk 15.98 (*0-7866-0379-8*, 94337CD) Mel Bay.

***You Can Teach Yourself Recorder.** David Reiner & Peter Anick. 1993. vhs 29.95 (*0-7866-2057-9*, 94337VX) Mel Bay.

You Can Teach Yourself Rock Guitar. William Bay & Mark Lonergan. 1993. 9.95 (*0-87166-267-1*, 94305); audio 9.98 (*0-87166-321-X*, 94305C); audio 18.95 (*0-87166-308-2*, 94305P) Mel Bay.

***You Can Teach Yourself Rock Guitar.** William Bay & Mark Lonergan. 1993. 24.95 incl. audio compact disk (*0-7866-0988-5*, 94305CDP); vhs 29.95 (*0-7866-2055-2*, 94305VX); audio compact disk 15.98 (*0-7866-0377-1*, 94305CD) Mel Bay.

You Can Teach Yourself Uke. William Bay. 1993. 9.95 (*1-56222-454-9*, 94809); audio 9.98 (*1-56222-455-7*, 94809C) Mel Bay.

***You Can Teach Yourself Uke.** William Bay. 1993. 24.95 incl. audio compact disk (*0-7866-1114-6*, 94809CDP); 18.95 incl. audio (*0-7866-1115-4*, 94809P); 38.95 incl. vhs (*0-7866-2491-4*, 94809VPX); vhs 29.95 (*0-7866-2056-0*, 94809VX); audio compact disk 15.98 (*0-7866-0386-0*, 94809CD) Mel Bay.

You Can Tell Your Kid Will Grow up to Be a Librarian When: Cartoons about the Profession. Richard Lee. LC 92-50309. (Illus.). 128p. 1992. pap. 20.95 (*0-89950-743-3*) McFarland & Co.

***You Can Tell You're a Yorker If...** W. Lee Woodmansee. (Illus.). 86p. (Orig.). 1996. 6.95 (*0-9655877-1-1*) Winemiller Pr.

You Can Too. Mary C. Crowley. LC 79-20131. 176p. (gr. 10). 1987. pap. 6.99 (*0-8007-5028-4*) Revell.

You Can Too: A Guide to Homestyle Cajun Cooking. 2nd ed. Jeanette McGurk. (Illus.). 170p. (C). 1989. reprint ed. pap. 9.95 (*0-9624251-0-9*) Cajun Pantry.

You Can Trade Stocks & Profit: Learn How to Buy Stocks & a System for Profit! Ron Stark. (Illus.). 110p. 1996. pap. 14.95 (*0-9650571-4-3*) Future Security.

You Can Train Your Cat. Paul Loeb. 1990. mass mkt. 5.50 (*0-671-73906-9*) PB.

You Can Trust God. Jerry Bridges. 1991. pap. 2.50 (*0-89109-571-3*) NavPress.

You Can Trust Your Bible. Neale Pryor. 1980. 4.95 (*0-89137-524-4*); student ed. 1.50 (*0-89137-568-6*) Quality Pubns.

You Can Type for Doctors at Home! rev. ed. Ruth De Menezes. 72p. 1993. pap. 16.00 (*0-941358-00-3*) Claremont CA.

***You Can Understand the Bible.** rev. ed. Fernon Retzer & Mike Speegle. (Illus.). 32p. 1996. pap. 5.95 (*1-57847-001-3*) MAGCOS-DA.

You Can Understand the Bible: A Study of the Science of Interpretation. Grayson H. Ensign. LC 90-82985. 512p. 1990. pap. 7.95 (*0-9613185-2-X*) Recovery Pubns.

You Can Understand the Old Testament: A Book-by-Book Guide for Catholics. Peter Kreeft. 180p. (Orig.). 1990. pap. 10.99 (*0-89283-689-X*, Charis) Servant.

You Can Win: No Losers in God's Family. Roger Campbell. LC 92-40958. 144p. 1993. pap. 8.99 (*0-8254-2323-6*) Kregel.

You Can Win at the Polls: A Finance Campaign Kit. 325.00 (*0-87545-034-2*) Natl Sch PR.

You Can Win with Love. Dale E. Galloway. 171p. 1976. pap. 5.95 (*1-885605-05-6*) Scott-Twnty-Twnty.

You Can Win Your Florida Election: A Step-by-Step Guide. Robert H. Mehaffey. 239p. 1992. 29.95 (*0-9634145-0-X*) R H Mehaffey & Assocs.

You Can with Beakman: Science Stuff You Can Do. Jok Church. LC 92-24979. (You Can Write with Beakman Bk.: Science Ser.). (Illus.). 156p. (Orig.). (J). 1992. pap. 8.95 (*0-8362-7004-5*) Andrews & McMeel.

You Can with Beakman & Jax: More Science Stuff You Can Do. Jok Church. (Illus.). 156p. 1994. pap. 8.95 (*0-8362-7008-8*) Andrews & McMeel.

You Can with Beakman & Jax: Way More Science Stuff You Can Do. Jok Church. (Illus.). 160p. (J). 1995. pap. 8.95 (*0-8362-7043-6*) Andrews & McMeel.

You Can Witness with Confidence. Rosalind Rinker. LC 91-72627. 72p. 1991. reprint ed. pap. 8.95 (*0-940232-44-8*) Seedsowers.

You Can Work Your Own Miracle. Napoleon Hill. 1986. mass mkt. 5.99 (*0-449-13066-5*) Fawcett.

***You Can Work Your Own Miracles.** Napoleon Hill. 1996. pap. 10.00 (*0-449-91177-2*) Fawcett.

You Can Write a Romance & Get It Published. rev. ed. Yvonne MacManus. 240p. (Orig.). 1996. pap. 14.95 (*0-9637498-1-1*) Toad Hall PA.

You Can Write a Song. Amy Appleby. (Illus.). 72p. 1990. pap. 14.95 incl. audio (*0-8256-2580-7*, AM76183) Music Sales.

You Can, You Can. Belk Clothilde. 12p. (Orig.). 1988. write for info. (*0-318-63034-6*) Babe Co.

***You Cannot Borrow Your Way Out of Debt.** Barbara R. Edwards. 63p. (Orig.). 1997. pap. 15.84 (*0-9657751-0-0*) Edway Pubns.

You Cannot Die: The Incredible Findings of a Century of Research on Death. Ian Currie. 1995. pap. 14.95 (*1-85230-615-7*) Element MA.

You Cannot Unsneeze a Sneeze & Other Tales from Liberia. Esther W. Dendel. (Illus.). 144p. 1995. pap. 14.95 (*0-87081-415-X*) Univ Pr Colo.

You Cannot Unsneeze a Sneeze & Other Tales from Liberia. Esther W. Dendel. (Illus.). 1995. 22.50 (*0-87081-414-1*) Univ Pr Colo.

***You Can't Afford the Luxury of a Negative Thought.** Peter McWilliams. 1997. 12.95 (*0-931580-57-9*) Prelude Press.

You Can't Afford the Luxury of a Negative Thought: A Book for People with Any Life-Threatening Illness - Including Life. Peter McWilliams. 1995. audio 24.95 (*0-931580-13-7*) Prelude Press.

You Can't Afford the Luxury of a Negative Thought: A Book for People with Any Life-Threatening Illness - Including Life. rev. ed. Peter McWilliams. 622p. 1995. pap. 5.95 (*0-931580-24-2*) Prelude Press.

You Can't Always Get What You Want. Winston Wu. 242p. (Orig.). 1996. pap. write for info. (*0-9649238-1-5*) Bolinas Pr.

You Can't Be a Smart Cookie if You Have a Crummy Attitude. John Maxwell. 160p. Date not set. pap. 5.99 (*1-56292-105-3*, HB-105) Honor Bks OK.

You Can't Be Neutral on a Moving Train: A Personal History of Our Times. Howard Zinn. 224p. (C). 1995. pap. 12.00 (*0-8070-7059-9*) Beacon Pr.

You Can't Be Too Careful. David Pryce-Jones. LC 92-50291. (Illus.). 80p. 1992. pap. 4.95 (*1-56305-156-7*, 3156) Workman Pub.

You Can't Beat God Givin' R. W. Schambach. 96p. 1994. pap. 5.99 (*0-89274-690-4*, HH-690) Harrison Hse.

You Can't Beat the Enemy While Raising His Flag see Strategic Outlook & Alliances

You Can't Book a Judge By Its Cover. Randy S. Johnson. LC 94-96157. 300p. 1994. 24.90 (*0-9642072-0-6*) Johnson Pubs.

You Can't Build a Chimney from the Top. Joseph W. Holley. (American Autobiography Ser.). 226p. 1995. reprint ed. lib. bdg. 79.00 (*0-7812-8558-5*) Rprt Serv.

You Can't Build a Chimney from the Top. Joseph W. Holley. Ed. by Russell W. Ramsey. LC 92-15736. 276p. 1992. reprint ed. pap. text ed. 29.50 (*0-8191-8483-7*) U Pr of Amer.

***You Can't Catch Me.** Charlottw L. Doyle. LC 96-42350. (Illus.). (J). 1997. write for info. (*0-694-01038-3*) HarpC.

You Can't Catch Me. Rosamond Smith. 304p. 1996. pap. 5.99 (*0-451-40682-6*, Onyx) NAL-Dutton.

You Can't Count on Dying. Natalie H. Cabot. Ed. by Leon Stein. LC 79-8662. (Growing Old Ser.). 1980. reprint ed. lib. bdg. 28.95 (*0-405-12779-0*) Ayer.

You Can't Curl Your Hair with Holy Rollers. Mike Nolan & Eve Sarrett. LC 93-2115. 1993. 7.99 (*0-8407-3444-1*) Nelson.

You Can't Do That. G. Seldes. LC 70-37287. (Civil Liberties in American History Ser.). 308p. 1972. reprint ed. lib. bdg. 37.50 (*0-306-70201-0*) Da Capo.

You Can't Do That! Beatles Bootlegs & Novelty Records, 1963-1980. Charles Reinhart. (Rock & Roll Reference Ser.: No. 5). (Illus.). 450p. 1989. reprint ed. 29.50 (*1-56075-009-X*) Popular Culture.

You Can't Do That, Governor! Wallace G. Wilkinson. (Illus.). 330p. Date not set. 24.00 (*0-9648058-0-4*) Wallaces Pub.

You Can't Eat Your Chicken Pox, Amber Brown. Paula Danziger. LC 93-37761. (Illus.). 80p. (J). (gr. 3 up). 1995. 13.95 (*0-399-22702-4*, Putnam) Putnam Pub Group.

You Can't Eat Your Chicken Pox, Amber Brown. Paula Danziger. (J). (gr. 2-5). 1996. pap. 3.50 (*0-590-50207-7*) Scholastic Inc.

You Can't Get Away from Your Shadow. Dolores B. Dace. (Illus.). 32p. (J). (ps-k). 1995. pap. 8.00 (*0-8059-3702-1*) Dorrance.

You Can't Get the Coons All up One Tree: True Life Story of John N. Jones. Ed. by Leona P. Carver. 244p. (Orig.). (C). 1980. pap. 7.95 (*0-686-36932-7*) Coltharp Pub.

You Can't Get There from Here. Pat Cook. 1993. pap. 5.25 (*0-87129-213-0*, Y19) Dramatic Pub.

You Can't Get There from Here. Hanlon. Date not set. 27.95 (*0-312-12909-2*) St Martin.

You Can't Get There from Here. Marion O. Hanna. 415p. 1996. 24.95 (*0-9650410-0-X*) Magnolia Hse.

You Can't Get There from Here. Hugh Hood. 202p. 1984. pap. 3.95 (*0-7736-7065-3*) Genl Dist Srvs.

You Can't Get There from Here. Earl Hamner, Jr. 1993. reprint ed. lib. bdg. 27.95 (*1-56849-023-2*) Buccaneer Bks.

You Can't Go Back, Exactly. Louis D. Brodsky. LC 89-50806. 57p. 1989. 18.95 (*1-877770-00-0*); pap. 19.95 incl. audio (*1-877770-02-7*); audio 12.95 (*1-877770-01-9*) Time Being Bks.

You Can't Go Home Again. Thomas Wolfe. 33.95 (*0-8488-0683-2*) Amereon Ltd.

You Can't Go Home Again. Thomas Wolfe. 390p. 1981. reprint ed. lib. bdg. 39.95 (*0-89966-294-3*) Buccaneer Bks.

You Can't Go Home Again. Thomas Wolfe. LC 88-45967. 848p. 1989. reprint ed. pap. 7.50 (*0-06-080986-8*, P 986, PL) HarpC.

You Can't Grow up Till You Go Back Home: A Safe Journey to See Your Parents As Human. William F. Nerin. LC 92-42915. (Illus.). 194p. 1995. reprint ed. 22.95 (*0-9646789-0-X*) Magic Mtn.

You Can't Hide on Leather Seats. limited ed. Laura Ryder. (Codex Booklet Ser.). (Illus.). 12p. 1993. pap. 10.00 (*1-884185-02-9*) O Zone.

You Can't Hit the Ball with the Bat on Your Shoulder: The Baseball Life & Times of Bobby Bragan. Bobby Bragan & Jeff Guinn. (Illus.). 360p. 1992. 19.95 (*1-56530-015-7*) Summit TX.

You Can't Hurry Love: (A Guide to Christian Dating) Timothy Scott. 10p. (Orig.). (YA). (gr. 10-12). 1989. pap. write for info. (*1-877784-05-2*) T Scott Pub.

You Can't Keep a Good Woman Down: Stories. Alice Walker. LC 80-8761. 180p. 1982. pap. 8.00 (*0-15-699778-9*, Harvest Bks) HarBrace.

***You Can't Kill Your Father Twice.** Robert Aronstein. 124p. (Orig.). 1997. mass mkt. 4.99 (*1-55237-332-0*, Pub. by Comnwlth Pub CN) Partners Pubs Grp.

You Can't Legislate Attitudes. Leon J. Leborgne. LC 94-96686. 68p. (Orig.). 1995. pap. text ed. 4.95 (*1-886707-00-6*) L & L Enter.

You Can't Live on Radishes: Some Funny Things Happened on the Way Back to the Land. Jerry Bledsoe. 175p. 1990. 6.95 (*0-9624255-4-0*) Down Home NC.

You Can't Lose. James A. Aderman. Ed. by William E. Fischer. (Bible Class Course for Young Adults Ser.). (Illus.). 36p. (Orig.). 1987. teacher ed., pap. 5.50 (*0-938272-28-4*, 22-2193); student ed. 3.50 (*0-938272-29-2*, 22-2192) WELS Board.

***You Can't Lose Trading Commodities.** 6th ed. Robert F. Wiest. 396p. 1996. 29.95 (*0-9651111-0-5*) Beacon Cos.

You Can't Make Me! A Behavior Management Handbook. Judith K. Schneider et al. (Competent Caregiver Ser.). (Illus.). 62p. (C). 1986. student ed. 8.95 (*0-944454-13-5*); pap. text ed. 8.95 (*0-944454-03-8*) CAPE Center.

***You-Can't-Make-Me Bride.** Leanne Banks. (Desire Ser.: No. 1082). 1997. mass mkt. 3.50 (*0-373-76082-5*, 1-76082-6) Silhouette.

You Can't Make Me Go to Church! The Church of Acts. Eddy Hall. (Generation Why Ser.: Vol. 1:4). 40p. (YA). (gr. 9-12). 1995. pap. 12.95 (*0-87303-260-8*) Faith & Life.

You Can't Manage What You Don't Measure: Control & Evaluation in Organisations. Ayre Globerson et al. (Avebury Business Library). 313p. 1991. text ed. 68.95 (*1-85628-163-9*, Pub. by Avebury Pub UK) Ashgate Pub Co.

***You Can't Never Get to Puckum: Folks & Tales from Delmarva.** Hal Roth. (Illus.). 192p. (Orig.). 1997. pap. 10.95 (*0-9647694-1-7*) Nanticoke Bks.

You Can't Plant Tomatoes in Central Park: The Urban Dropouts Guide to Rural Relocation. Frank Ruegg & Paul Bianchina. LC 90-53281. 303p. 1990. 18.95 (*0-88282-060-5*); pap. 13.95 (*0-88282-107-5*) New Horizon NJ.

You Can't Play the Game If You Don't Know the Rules: Career Opportunities in Sports Management. David M. Carter. LC 93-47435. 1994. pap. 14.95 (*1-57023-005-6*) Impact VA.

***You Can't Put No Boogie-Woogie.** Lewis Grizzard. 1997. pap. 11.00 (*0-345-41931-6*) Ballantine.

You Can't Put No Boogie-Woogie on the King of Rock & Roll. Lewis Grizzard. 1992. mass mkt. 5.99 (*0-345-37803-2*) Ballantine.

You Can't Put No Boogie Woogie on the King of Rock & Roll. Lewis Grizzard. 288p. 1991. 18.00 (*0-679-40704-9*, Villard Bks) Random.

You Can't Quit Until You Know What's Eating You: Overcoming Compulsive Eating. Donna Leblanc. 1990. pap. 7.95 (*1-55874-103-8*) Health Comm.

You Can't Run Forever. Valerie N. Koski. LC 92-56937. 213p. 1993. pap. 7.95 (*1-55523-580-8*) Winston-Derek.

***You Can't Say That to Me.** Suzzette Elgin. 1997. mass mkt. 5.99 (*0-614-27812-0*) Wiley.

You Can't Say That to Me: Stopping the Pain of Verbal Abuse: An Eight-Step Program. Suzette H. Elgin. LC 94-36128. 206p. 1995. text ed. 37.95 (*0-471-00395-6*); pap. text ed. 15.95 (*0-471-00399-9*) Wiley.

You Can't Say You Can't Play. Vivian G. Paley. (Illus.). 134p. 1992. text ed. 19.95 (*0-674-96589-2*) HUP.

You Can't Say You Can't Play. Vivian G. Paley. 144p. 1993. pap. text ed. 10.00 (*0-674-96590-6*) HUP.

You Can't Scare Me! R. L. Stine. (Goosebumps Ser.: No. 15). 160p. (J). (gr. 4-6). 1994. pap. 3.99 (*0-590-49450-3*) Scholastic Inc.

***You Can't Scare Me!, Vol. 14.** R. L. Stine. (Goosebumps TV Ser.). (J). 1997. pap. text ed. 3.99 (*0-590-30663-4*) Scholastic Inc.

You Can't Sell your Brother. Beth Brainard & Behr. 144p. 1992. pap. 11.95 (*0-440-50438-4*, Dell Trade Pbks) Dell.

***You Can't Shrink Your Way to Greatness: The Circle of Innovation.** Tom Peters. 1998. write for info. (*0-375-40157-1*) Random.

You Can't Smell a Flower with Your Ear! All about Your 5 Senses. Joanna Cole. LC 93-27264. (All Aboard Reading Ser.). (Illus.). (J). (gr. 1-3). 1994. pap. 3.95 (*0-448-40469-9*, G&D) Putnam Pub Group.

You Can't Spank a Kid in a Snowsuit & Other Lessons on Parenting. Bruce Howard. LC 94-6420. 144p. 1994. pap. 7.99 (*0-8423-1334-6*) Tyndale.

You Can't Spoil a Child with Love! Ila A. Bishop. 52p. 1994. pap. 6.95 (*0-9639089-0-1*) Hali Prods.

You Can't Steal Second with Your Foot on First: Choosing to Become Independent in a Job-Dependent World. Burke Hedges. Ed. by Steve Price. 150p. (Orig.). 1995. pap. 9.95 (*0-9632667-1-3*) Intl Netwk Train.

You Can't Take It with You. Moss Hart & George S. Kaufman. 1937. pap. 5.25 (*0-8222-1287-0*) Dramatists Play.

You Can't Teach a Kid to Ride a Bike at a Seminar: Using a Revolutionary New Selling System to Make Top Sales. David H. Sandler. 240p. 1996. pap. 23.95 (*0-525-94195-9*) NAL-Dutton.

You Can't Tell the Players. Barton R. Friedman. (Cleveland Poets Ser.: No. 21). 46p. (Orig.). 1979. pap. 3.50 (*0-914946-17-X*) Cleveland St Univ Poetry Ctr.

You Can't Trust the Male. Randy Noojin. 1991. pap. 3.00 (*0-87129-059-6*, Y18) Dramatic Pub.

You Can't Turn Back. Darwin Gross. 98p. (Orig.). 1985. pap. 4.95 (*0-931689-02-3*) D Gross.

You Can't Walk on Water If You Stay in the Boat: And More "Rondom Thoughts" Ron Birk. LC 93-91678. 112p. (Orig.). 1993. pap. 10.00 (*0-9629331-1-2*) Golden Goat.

You Can't Win. Jack Black. LC 92-17682. 1992. reprint ed. 18.95 (*0-944204-15-5*) Omniun.

You Can't Win, Charlie Brown. Charles M. Schulz. (Illus.). 1994. pap. 7.95 (*0-8050-3309-2*) H Holt & Co.

You Can't Work in the Dark! Understanding Automated Data Center Operations. George E. Kurtz. LC 91-111200. 220p. (Orig.). (C). 1990. pap. 42.95 (*0-9625751-2-7*) Strategic Tech Inst.

You Caught Me Dancing. Bernard Sabath. 54p. 1990. pap. 5.00 (*0-87129-005-7*, Y17) Dramatic Pub.

You Chi: The Healing Spirit. Donna Boone & Laura Boone. 80p. (Orig.). 1993. pap. 9.95 (*1-56664-048-2*) WorldComm.

You Come Too. Robert Frost. LC 59-12940. (Illus.). 96p. (J). (gr. 4-6). 1959. 14.95 (*0-8050-0299-5*, Bks Young Read) H Holt & Co.

You Come Too. Robert Frost. LC 59-12940. (Illus.). 96p. (J). (gr. 4-6). 1988. pap. 6.95 (*0-8050-0316-9*, Bks Young Read) H Holt & Co.

***You Come Too, Vol. 1.** R. Frost. Date not set. write for info. (*0-03-089530-8*) H Holt & Co.

***You Come When I Call You.** Clegg. 1995. pap. 5.50 (*0-671-67278-9*) PB.

You Come with Naked Hands: The Story of the San Francisco to Moscow March for Peace. Bradford Lyttle. LC 66-1279. (Illus.). 289p. 1966. 25.00 (*0-934676-08-9*) Greenlf Bks.

You Could Call It Murder. Lawrence Block. 240p. 1996. mass mkt. 4.95 (*0-7867-0342-3*) Carroll & Graf.

You Could Feel Good: A Self-Esteem Guide: Growing & Changing into Your True Self. Suzanne E. Harrill. 1990. audio 19.95 (*0-9625996-6-2*) Innerworks Pub.

You Could Feel Good: A Self-Esteem Guide: Growing & Changing into Your True Self. rev. ed. Suzanne E. Harrill. 144p. 1990. reprint ed. pap. 8.95 (*0-9625996-0-3*) Innerworks Pub.

You Could Feel Good Curriculum Guide. Suzanne E. Harrill. 90p. 1993. 19.95 (*1-883648-02-5*) Innerworks Pub.

You Could Go Home Again. deluxe limited ed. Howard Waldrop. (Illus.). 80p. 1993. boxed 198.00 (*0-941826-22-8*) Cheap St.

You Could Love Me. Phyllis Halldorson. (Special Edition Ser.: No. 734). 1992. mass mkt. 3.39 (*0-373-09734-4*, 5-09734-0) Harlequin Bks.

***You Could Say Hello.** Robert G. Simmons, Jr. 267p. (Orig.). 1998. mass mkt. 7.99 (*1-889501-50-6*, Appaloosa) Sovereign.

You Create Your Own Destiny. Lao Russell. Ed. by Emilia L. Lombardi. 20p. (Orig.). 1991. pap. text ed. 5.00 (*1-879605-34-1*) U Sci & Philos.

You Crown the Year with Your Goodness: Sermons Through the Liturgical Year. Hans U. Von Balthasar. Tr. by Graham Harrison from GER. LC 89-83743. 323p. (Orig.). 1989. pap. text ed. 16.95 (*0-89870-058-2*) Ignatius Pr.

You Decide: A Power of Attorney Handbook. Robert Norris. 80p. (Orig.). 1989. pap. 15.95 (*0-317-93747-2*) Peoples Birmingham.

You Decide: Using Living Wills & Other Advance Directives to Guide Your Treatment Choices. Evelyn J. Van Allen. LC 93-16867. 180p. 1993. per. 18.00 (*1-55623-936-X*) Irwin Prof Pubng.

You Deserve the Best. Pat Pearson. 180p. 1991. pap. 12.95 (*0-9629462-0-6*) Connemara Pub.

***You Deserve to Be Rich: Attracting Wealth & Success with Prosp.** Janice Campbell. LC 97-14093. 224p. 1997. per. 12.00 (*0-7615-1018-4*) Prima Pub.

You Developed It: Can Your Training Programs Survive the Reality Test? Edward W. Jones. 300p. 1995. pap. 24.95 (*0-87425-252-0*) HRD Press.

You Dirty Dog. Stephen Caitlin. LC 87-19182. (Giant First Start Reader Ser.). (Illus.). (J). (gr. k-2). 1988. lib. bdg. 12.95 (*0-8167-1103-8*) Troll Communs.

You Dirty Dog. Stephen Caitlin. LC 87-19182. (Giant First Start Reader Ser.). (Illus.). (J). (gr. k-2). 1996. pap. 3.95 (*0-8167-1104-6*) Troll Communs.

You Do Not Have to Die From Cancer: The Causes, Prevention & Other Facts about Cancer. Roger J. Harrison. 1991. 16.95 (*0-533-08968-9*) Vantage.

You Do Not Have to Wait. Tom Johnson. 64p. 1987. pap. 3.50 (*0-941992-11-X*) Los Arboles Pub.

You Don't Always Get What You Ask For: Using Direct Mail Tests to Raise More Money for Your Organization. Mal Warwick. 132p. 1992. pap. 19.95 (*0-9624891-1-5*) Strathmoor Pr.

You Don't Always Get What You Hope For. Rick Walton. LC 96-5218. (Illus.). (J). 1996. 14.95 (*0-87905-739-4*) Gibbs Smith Pub.

***You Don't Change a Company by Memo: The Simple Truths about Management Change.** Marti Smye. 1997. pap. text ed. 14.95 (*1-55209-123-6*) Firefly Bks Ltd.

You Don't Change a Company by Memo: The Simple Truths about Managing. Marti Smye & Anne McKague. 220p. 1994. 19.95 (*1-55013-616-X*, Pub. by Key Porter Bks CN) Firefly Bks Ltd.

You Don't Cry for Heroes. Frank D. Simons. 197p. (Orig.). (YA). (gr. 12 up). 1989. pap. 11.95 (*0-685-26939-6*) CFFC POWs MIAs.

You Don't Cry for Heroes. Frank D. Simons. (Orig.). 1990. pap. 11.95 (*0-9623659-0-4*) CFFC POWs MIAs.

You Don't Find Water on the Mountaintop: Discovering Nourishment in Life's Valleys. Wayne F. Monbleau. LC 95-38911. 192p. (Orig.). (YA). (gr. 10). 1996. pap. 8.99 (*0-8007-5581-2*) Revell.

You Don't Get a Carrot Unless You're a Bunny. Brian Mangas. (J). 1989. pap. 5.95 (*0-671-67201-0*, Litl Simon S&S) S&S Childrens.

You Don't Get a Carrot Unless You're a Bunny. Brian Mangas. LC 88-19763. (Illus.). 32p. (J). (ps). 1991. pap. 2.25 (*0-671-74200-0*, Litl Simon S&S) S&S Childrens.

You Don't Have to Be a Computer Genius to Land a Computer Job: How to Find a Career in the World's Fastest Growing Field. Jack L. Stone & Stephen S. Roberts. LC 83-17910. 252p. 1984. pap. write for info. (*0-672-52790-1*) Macmillan.

***You Don't Have to Be a Kid to Do Magic: Magic for Adults.** Paul Daniels & Barry Murray. LC 97-17778. 160p. 1997. pap. 19.95 (*1-56980-119-3*) Barricade Bks.

You Don't Have to Be a Poet to Put Your Love into Words. James D. Donovan. (Illus.). 138p. 1989. 14.95 (*0-9621051-0-4*, DV0) J D Donovan.

You Don't Have to Be Blind to See. Jim Stovall. 288p. 1996. 18.99 (*0-7852-7737-4*) Nelson.

***You Don't Have to Be Blind to See: Find & Fulfill Your Destiny Regardless of Your Circumstances.** Jim Stovall. 1996. audio 14.99 (*0-7852-7685-8*) Nelson.

***You Don't Have to Be Dumb to Be Stupid.** Bill Engvall. 1997. pap. 9.95 (*1-56352-389-2*) Longstreet Pr Inc.

You Don't Have to Be Dyslexic. Joan M. Smith. LC 91-60923. (Illus.). 205p. (Orig.). 1991. pap. 19.95 (*0-9628758-0-5*) Learning Time.

You Don't Have to Be Dyslexic. Joan M. Smith. 256p. (Orig.). 1996. pap. 19.95 (*0-9628758-1-3*) Learning Time.

You Don't Have to Be in Harlem: The Story of the Glasgow Apollo. Russell Leadbetter. (Illus.). 160p. 1996. 35.00 (*1-85158-746-2*, Pub. by Mnstream UK) Trafalgar.

You Don't Have to Be Neurotic to Be Insecure: Finding the Courage to Cope with Guilt... Reginald Stackhouse. 1994. 12.95 (*0-7737-5564-0*) Genl Dist Srvs.

You Don't Have to Be Next. Dr. Jochen Aumiller. 1980. pap. 5.95 (*0-8065-0683-0*, Citadel Pr) Carol Pub Group.

You Don't Have to Be Sick, 4 bks. in 1. Lady P. Cilento. 336p. 1984. reprint ed. pap. 3.50 (*0-87983-403-X*) Keats.

You Don't Have to Be Smart to Walk with God. Dale Sides. 96p. (Orig.). 1994. pap. 6.99 (*1-56043-830-4*) Destiny Image.

You Don't Have to Be Your Mother. Gayle Feldman. 1995. pap. 12.00 (*0-449-90993-X*) Fawcett.

You Don't Have to Be Your Mother: One Family's Story of Breast Cancer, Birth & Renewal. Gayle Feldman. LC 93-43778. 1994. 23.00 (*0-393-03640-5*) Norton.

You Don't Have to Count Your Birthdays Until... Martin A. Ragaway. (Laughter Library). (Illus.). 1979. pap. 2.50 (*0-8431-0534-8*) Putnam Pub Group.

You Don't Have to Die. John Mattera. 71p. 1991. pap. 5.00 (*0-87129-083-9*, Y16) Dramatic Pub.

You Don't Have to Die: Unraveling the AIDS Myth. Leon Chaitow. LC 94-72701. 1994. pap. 14.95 (*0-9636334-4-9*) Future Md Pub.

You Don't Have to Die from Cancer: Taking Active Charge. Abraham Khazam. 1996. pap. text ed. 14.95 (*0-85572-266-5*, Pub. by Hill Content Pubng AT) Seven Hills Bk.

***You Don't Have to Die to Win: Success & Succession for Family Businesses.** D. Wayne Rivers & Thomas H. Campbell. Date not set. pap. 17.95 (*0-9653193-1-8*) Fmly Busn.

You Don't Have to Feel Unwell: Nutrition, Lifestyle, Herbs & Homeopathy - A Home Guide. 2nd ed. Robin Needes. 336p. (Orig.). 1994. pap. 18.95 (*1-85860-009-X*, Pub. by Gateway Books UK) ACCESS Pubs Network.

You Don't Have to Go Home from Work Exhausted! Ann McGee-Cooper et al. 288p. 1992. pap. 12.95 (*0-553-37061-8*) Bantam.

An Asterisk (*) at the beginning of an entry indicates that the title is appearing in BIP for the first time.

You Don't Have to Go Home from Work Exhausted! The Energy Engineering Approach. Ann McGee-Cooper et al. Ed. by Alison Tartt. (Illus.). 376p. 1990. 29.95 (*0-9625617-0-3*) Bowen & Rogers Pub.

You Don't Have to Go Home from Work Exhausted! The Energy Engineering Approach. Ann McGee-Cooper et al. Ed. by Alison Tartt. (Illus.). 376p. 1990. pap. 19.95 (*0-9625617-1-1*) Bowen & Rogers Pub.

***You Don't Have to Hit Bottom: Facing Your Drinking Problem Before It Destroys Your Life.** P. Jerry. LC 97-8010. 1997. write for info. (*1-56246-140-0*) Johnsn Inst.

***You Don't Have to Hurt: Attention Deficit Disorder in Intimate Relationships.** Daniel G. Amen. 184p. (Orig.). 1997. pap. 29.95 (*1-886554-06-4*) MindWrks.

You Don't Have to If You Don't Want To. Ben Kinchlow. 224p. 1995. 16.99 (*0-7852-7875-3*, J Thoma Bks) Nelson.

***You Don't Have to Live with Arthritis.** Gwynne H. Davies. 96p. (Orig.). 1998. pap. 10.95 (*1-85398-108-7*, Pub. by Ashgrove UK) Words Distrib.

You Don't Have to Live with Cystitis. rev. ed. Larrian Gillespie. LC 96-22962. 304p. 1996. pap. 11.00 (*0-380-78779-2*) Avon.

You Don't Have to Live with Cystitis! How to Avoid It - What to Do about It. Larrian Gillespie. 304p. 1988. pap. 10.00 (*0-380-70486-2*) Avon.

You Don't Have to Pay Retail: Nashville's Guide to Discount Shopping. 2nd rev. ed. Paula G. Kirwan. 125p. 1994. pap. 7.95 (*0-9633294-1-3*) KAM Pub.

You Don't Have to Slay a Dragon. John M. Stuart & Marjorie L. Stuart. LC 75-14540. (Illus.). 313p. 1976. 8.95 (*0-915730-01-4*) Marburger.

You Don't Have to Suffer: A Complete Guide to Relieving Cancer Pain for Patients & Their Families. Susan S. Lang & Richard B. Patt. (Illus.). 384p. 1994. 30.00 (*0-19-508418-7*) OUP.

You Don't Have to Suffer: A Complete Guide to Relieving Cancer Pain for Patients & Their Families. Susan S. Lang & Richard B. Patt. (Illus.). 384p. 1995. pap. 10.95 (*0-19-508419-5*) OUP.

You Don't Have to Suffer: A Handbook for Moving Beyond Life's Crises. Judy Tatelbaum. LC 88-45528. 224p. 1990. reprint ed. pap. 12.00 (*0-06-091645-1*, PL) HarpC.

You Don't Have to Take It! A Woman's Guide to Confronting Emotional Abuse at Work. Ginny NiCarthy et al. LC 93-12873. (New Leaf Ser.). 397p. (Orig.). 1993. pap. 14.95 (*1-878067-35-4*) Seal Pr WA.

You Don't Know Beans about Bats. Jamie Gilson. LC 93-559. (J). 1994. 13.95 (*0-395-67063-2*, Clarion Bks) HM.

***You Don't Know Jack: The Irreverent Quiz Book, Based on the Irreverent Quiz Show Party Game.** Ed. by Jellyvision Staff. 192p. (Orig.). 1997. pap. 8.95 (*0-8362-3175-9*) Andrews & McMeel.

You Don't Know My God. Peter A. Duro & Carol J. Duro. LC 85-81388. 238p. (Orig.). 1985. pap. 5.95 (*0-9615955-0-7*) Emmanuel Christian.

You Don't Know What Love Is: Contemporary American Stories. Ed. by Ron Hansen. LC 87-15219. 312p. (Orig.). 1987. pap. 13.95 (*0-86538-060-0*) Ontario Rev NJ.

You Don't Live on My Street. Rebera E. Foston. 96p. 1991. pap. text ed. 12.00 (*0-9641709-0-6*) Foston Adolescent.

You Don't Look Like a Musician. Bud Freeman. LC 73-89352. 135p. 1974. 5.95 (*0-913642-05-3*) Balamp Pub.

***You Don't Look 35, Charlie Brown!** Charles M. Schulz. LC 97-18499. 1997. pap. write for info. (*0-8050-5650-5*) H Holt & Co.

You Don't Love Yourself. Nathalie Sarraute. Tr. by Barbara Wright. LC 90-44526. 216p. 1990. 17.95 (*0-8076-1254-5*) Braziller.

You Don't Miss Your Water: Poems. Cornelius Eady. LC 94-45810. 1995. pap. 12.00 (*0-8050-3668-7*) H Holt & Co.

You Don't Need a Hysterectomy: New & Effective Ways of Avoiding Major Surgery. Ivan K. Strausz. (Illus.). 320p. 1994. pap. 12.00 (*0-201-62697-7*) Addison-Wesley.

You Don't Need a Hysterectomy: New & Effective Ways of Avoiding Surgery. Ivan K. Strausz. (Illus.). 1993. 24.95 (*0-201-60827-8*) Addison-Wesley.

***You Don't Need Experience If You've Got Attitude.** Scott Adams. 1996. 6.95 (*0-8362-2196-6*) Andrews & McMeel.

You Don't Need Four Women to Play Shakespeare: Bias in Contemporary American Theater. Ida Prosky. LC 92-54091. (Illus.). 172p. 1992. lib. bdg. 27.50 (*0-89950-729-8*) McFarland & Co.

You Don't Need to Have a Repeat Cesarean. Nicki Royall. Ed. by Sherri Adelman. 204p. 1989. 8.95 (*0-8119-0184-X*) LIFETIME.

You Don't Need Words. Ruth B. Gross. (Illus.). 48p. (J). 1991. 14.95 (*0-590-43897-2*, Scholastic Hardcover) Scholastic Inc.

You Don't Outgrow It. Marnell L. Hayes. Ed. by Betty L. Kratoville. 240p. 1993. pap. 16.00 (*0-87879-967-2*, 967-2) Acad Therapy.

***You Don't Say! The Ten Worst Mistakes You Can Make in Speech & Writing.** Tom Parks. 112p. (Orig.). 1998. mass mkt. 5.99 (*0-446-60428-3*) Warner Bks.

You Don't See Me. Kathryn S. Miller. 22p. 1986. reprint ed. pap. 3.45 (*0-87129-022-7*, Y15) Dramatic Pub.

***You Don't Want to Die in Africa: Adventures in Underdeveloped Countries.** Rosemarie Grabski. 116p. (Orig.). 1997. pap. 12.95 (*1-57502-453-5*, PO1366) Morris Pubng.

You-Draw Book: Ming-Shu & Her Cat. Lois Danes. (Illus.). 56p. (J). (gr. k-3). 1995. text ed. 9.00 (*0-8059-3825-7*) Dorrance.

You Dropped It, You Pick It Up! Jim Paul. Ed. by Joe Planas. LC 83-82572. (Illus.). 222p. 1984. 14.95 (*0-9612822-0-7*) Green Rose.

You Either Know What's Going on in Your Marketplace or You Lose: How to Identify & Develop a Powerful Market Awareness Program. Business Development Systems, Inc. Staff. (Self-Improvement Business Ser.). 30p. 1993. pap. 8.95 (*1-884392-02-4*) Busn Develop.

You Find Yourself Believing in Things. Deborah Gilbert. (Cleveland Poets Ser.: No. 48). 64p. (Orig.). 1996. pap. 8.00 (*1-880834-27-8*) Cleveland St Univ Poetry Ctr.

You Forever. T. Lobsang Rampa. LC 90-40257. 288p. (Orig.). 1990. pap. 9.95 (*0-87728-717-1*) Weiser.

You-Forever. T. Lobsang Rampa. 224p. 1991. reprint ed. lib. bdg. 19.95 (*0-89966-775-9*) Buccaneer Bks.

You Forget Too. Rita Friedman & Elaine Weimann. (Fables from the Letter People Ser.). (Illus.). 30p. (J). (ps-1). 1989. lib. bdg. 12.50 (*0-89796-020-3*) New Dimens Educ.

You Gave Me These Rivers. Stephan Torre. (Orig.). 1989. pap. 6.00 (*0-912449-24-1*) Floating Island.

You Gentiles. Maurice Samuels. 1979. lib. bdg. 59.95 (*0-8490-3019-6*) Gordon Pr.

You Gentiles. Maurice Samuels. pap. 5.00 (*0-911038-08-6*, Noontide Pr) Legion Survival.

You Get So Alone at Times That It Just Makes Sense. Charles Bukowski. LC 86-13662. 318p. 1997. reprint ed. 25.00 (*0-87685-684-9*); reprint ed. pap. 14.00 (*0-87685-683-0*) Black Sparrow.

You Get Two for the Price of One! Ed Gamble. (Editorial Cartoonists Ser.). (Illus.). 160p. 1995. pap. 8.95 (*1-56554-128-6*) Pelican.

You Give Great Meeting, Sid. Garry B. Trudeau. 128p. 1983. pap. 5.00 (*0-03-061733-2*) H Holt & Co.

You Give Me New Life: A 40-Day Journey in the Company of the Early Disciples: Devotional Readings. Compiled by David Hazard. LC 95-42404. (Rekindling the Inner Fire Ser.: Vol. 9). 160p. 1995. pap. 8.99 (*1-55661-677-5*) Bethany Hse.

You Go Away. Dorothy Corey. LC 75-33015. (Self Starter Bks.). (Illus.). 32p. (J). (ps-1). 1976. lib. bdg. 11.95 (*0-8075-9441-5*) A Whitman.

You Go to My Head: Lovers & Legends. Bobby Hutchinson. (Temptation Ser.). 1993. mass mkt. 2.99 (*0-373-25557-8*, 1-25557-9) Harlequin Bks.

***You, God & Me.** Jose E. Radzinsky. (Illus.). 100p. 1996. 11.00 (*0-9653748-7-4*) Enigma Publng.

You, God & Your Sexuality. Dawson McAllister & Tim Altman. Ed. by Wayne Peterson. (Illus.). (J). (gr. 5-12). 1988. pap. 3.95 (*0-923417-01-X*) Shepherd Minst.

You Got It. Art Freifeld. (Illus.). 74p. (Orig.). 1988. student ed. 8.95 (*0-916177-33-5*) Am Eng Pubns.

You Got to Be Original, Man! The Music of Lester Young. Frank Buchmann-Moller. LC 89-11986. (Discographies Ser.: No. 33). 541p. 1990. text ed. 59.95 (*0-313-26514-3*, BLY/, Greenwood Pr) Greenwood.

You Got to Be Stupid to Sing Country Music: And Other Unusual Song Lyrics. Jim Terr. LC 88-91346. (Illus.). 96p. (Orig.). 1988. pap. 5.95 (*0-929830-00-8*) Blue Canyon Bks.

You Got to Burn to Shine. John Giorno. 160p. (Orig.). 1994. pap. 11.99 (*1-85242-321-8*, High Risk Bks) Serpents Tail.

***You Gotta Be the Book: Teaching Engaged & Reflective Reading with Adolescents.** Jeffrey D. Wilhelm. (Language & Literacy Ser.). 216p. (C). 1996. text ed. 40.00 (*0-8077-3567-1*); pap. text ed. 18.95 (*0-8077-3566-3*) Tchrs Coll.

You Gotta Believe! George Shinn & Jim N. Black. 250p. 1996. 19.99 (*0-8423-8584-3*) Tyndale.

You Gotta Believe! The Inspiring Life Story of a True American Hero. Drew T. Brown, III. (Illus.). 288p. 1992. pap. 10.00 (*0-380-71007-2*) Avon.

You Gotta Have Heart: Dallas Green's Rebuilding of the Cubs. Ned Colletti. LC 85-4405. (Illus.). 272p. 1985. 15.95 (*0-912083-11-5*) Diamond Communications.

You Gotta Have Wa: When Two Cultures Collide on a Baseball Diamond. Robert Whiting. LC 90-50150. (Vintage Departures Ser.). (Illus.). 368p. 1990. pap. 13.00 (*0-679-72947-X*, Vin) Random.

You Gotta Keep Dancin' Tim Hansel. LC 85-11298. 150p. 1986. pap. 9.99 (*1-55513-108-5*, 51086, LifeJourney) Chariot Victor.

You Gotta Play Hurt. Dan Jenkins. Ed. by Julie Rubenstein. 400p. 1993. reprint ed. mass mkt. 5.99 (*0-671-78461-7*, Pocket Star Bks) PB.

***You Gotta Try This!** Vicki Cobb. Date not set. write for info. (*0-688-15740-8*, Morrow Junior) Morrow.

You Gotta Wanna: A Physician's Autobiography. Jack G. Hendershot. LC 91-90994. (Illus.). 416p. 1993. 21.95 (*0-9629567-3-2*) Von Hayderschatte.

You, Had a Great Life. Dottie Baxter. Ed. by Jen Theobald. (Orig.). 1988. pap. 2.99 (*0-9621988-0-3*) D Baxter.

You Had to Be There. Cleta McQuerry. 90p. (Orig.). 1996. pap. 9.95 (*1-57502-131-5*) Morris Pubng.

***You Have a Brother Named Spike?** Charles M. Schulz. (Peanuts Ser.). (Illus.). 32p. (J). (ps-3). 1997. 3.25 (*0-694-00958-X*, Festival) HarpC Child Bks.

You Have a Friend, Dainty Dinosaur. (Illus.). (J). (ps-2). 1991. pap. 5.10 (*0-8136-5712-1*); lib. bdg. 7.95 (*0-8136-5212-X*) Modern Curr.

You Have a Pacemaker. rev. ed. Barbara J. Fletcher & Julia A. Purcell. Ed. by Nancy R. Hull. LC 81-23461. 32p. 1994. pap. text ed. 5.95 (*0-939838-12-5*) Pritchett & Hull.

You Have a Right to Be Free. Wayne E. Anderson. 40p. 1986. pap. 1.95 (*0-913748-08-0*) Orovan Bks.

***You Have Been Here Before.** Edith Fiore. 1997. pap. 12.00 (*0-345-42022-5*) Ballantine.

You Have Been Here Before: A Psychologist Looks at Past Lives. Edith Fiore. 256p. 1986. mass mkt. 5.99 (*0-345-33822-7*) Ballantine.

You Have Choices: Recovering from Anxiety, Panic & Phobia. William N. Penzer & Bonnie Goodman. Ed. by Myra Gross. Orig. Title: Overcoming Anxiety, Panic, Phobias Through a Support Group. (Illus.). 256p. (Orig.). 1991. pap. 11.95 (*0-9622658-1-0*) Esperance Pub.

***You Have More Than You Think.** Gardner. 1998. 24.00 (*0-684-84399-4*) S&S Trade.

You Have My Word on It. large type ed. Bob Miller. Ed. by Kathleen Allen. LC TXU 660-807. (Illus.). 85p. (Orig.). 1994. pap. 4.95 (*0-9634161-1-1*) Vanquish Pubns.

You Have No Country! Workers' Struggle Against War. Intro. by Franklin Rosemont. 80p. pap. 4.95 (*0-88286-058-5*) C H Kerr.

You Have No Courts with Any Sure Rule of Law: The Saga of the Supreme Judicial Court of Massachusetts. James B. Muldoon. (Illus.). 353p. (Orig.). 1992. pap. 16.95 (*0-9632270-0-9*) Lookout Hill.

You Have Not Many Fathers: Recovering the Generational Blessing. Mark Hanby & Craig L. Ervin. 256p. (Orig.). 1996. pap. 9.99 (*1-56043-166-0*) Destiny Image.

You Have Seen Our Faces: Stories about America. large type ed. Richard L. Allington et al. 1993. 39.50 (*0-614-09864-5*, L-78685-00) Am Printing Hse.

You Have Seen Their Faces. Erskine Caldwell & Margaret Bourke-White. Ed. by Dan C. McCurry & Richard E. Rubenstein. LC 74-30622. (American Farmers & the Rise of Agribusiness Ser.). (Illus.). 1975. reprint ed. 23.95 (*0-405-06769-0*) Ayer.

You Have Seen Their Faces. Erskine Caldwell & Margaret Bourke-White. LC 74-30622. (Brown Thrasher Bks.). (Illus.). 136p. 1995. reprint ed. 40.00 (*0-8203-1691-1*); reprint ed. pap. 19.95 (*0-8203-1692-X*) U of Ga Pr.

You Have Stept Out of Your Place: A History of Women & Religion in America. Susan H. Lindley. 384p. 1996. 35.00 (*0-664-22081-9*) Westminster John Knox.

***You Have the Right to Know about Drugs.** Sue Rusche & Paula Kemp. (You Have the Right to Know Ser.: No. 5). 114p. (J). (gr. 5). 1995. pap. write for info. (*1-880958-05-8*) Natl Fam Act.

You Have the Right to Know, Vol. 1: Cocaine. Sue Rusche & Paula Kemp. 140p. 1990. pap. write for info. (*1-880958-00-7*) Natl Fam Act.

You Have the Right to Know, Vol. 2: Alcohol. Sue Rusche & Paula Kemp. 175p. 1991. pap. write for info. (*1-880958-01-5*) Natl Fam Act.

You Have the Wrong Man: Stories. Maria Flook. 242p. 1996. 23.00 (*0-679-43184-5*) Pantheon.

***You Have to Go to School...You're the Teacher! 200 Tips to Make Your Job Easier & More Fun!!!** Renee Rosenblum-Lowden. LC 96-51288. 104p. 1997. 37.00 (*0-8039-6555-9*); pap. 17.00 (*0-8039-6556-7*) Sage.

You Have to Scream with Your Mouth Shut: Violence in the Home. Karina Colgan. 190p. 1996. pap. 16.95 (*1-86023-018-0*) Dufour.

***You Have to Serve Somebody.** Werner Trieschmann. 74p. 1997. pap. write for info. (*0-87129-775-2*, Y21) Dramatic Pub.

You Have Words of Eternal Life. Hans U. Von Balthasar. Tr. by Dennis D. Martin from GER. LC 90-85062. 275p. (Orig.). 1991. pap. 16.95 (*0-89870-308-5*) Ignatius Pr.

You Hear the Ice Talking: The Ways of People & Ice on Lake Champlain. I. Sheldon Posen. LC 86-29914. (Illus.). 70p. (Orig.). 1986. pap. 11.00 (*0-9617701-1-2*) C E F Lib Syst.

You Hold Me & I'll Hold You. Jo Carson. LC 91-16370. (Illus.). 32p. (J). (ps-2). 1992. 15.95 (*0-531-05895-6*); lib. bdg. 16.99 (*0-531-08495-7*) Orchard Bks Watts.

***You Hold Me & I'll Hold You.** Jo Carson. LC 91-16370. (Illus.). 32p. (J). (ps-2). 1997. pap. 6.95 (*0-531-07088-3*) Orchard Bks Watts.

You, I, & the Others. Paul Weiss. LC 79-13375. 428p. 1980. 29.95 (*0-8093-0923-8*) S Ill U Pr.

***You in Business: How to Build a Strong Business from the Inside Out.** Timothy A. Duff. LC 96-92916. 122p. 1997. pap. 15.95 (*0-7880-0922-2*, Express Pr) CSS OH.

You in History. Kathryn S. Smith. 1993. pap. 4.95 (*0-685-61096-9*) Intac.

You in Your Hand: Do It Yourself Palm Reading. Drora Shirai. (Illus.). 216p. (Orig.). 1995. pap. text ed. 15.95 (*965-229-137-4*, Pub. by Gefen Pub Hse IS) Gefen Bks.

You, Inc. 10 Simple Principles for Dramatically Improving the Value of the Most Important Company in Your Life - You! Burke Hedges. Ed. by Steve Price. 200p. (Orig.). 1996. pap. 12.95 (*0-9632667-3-X*) Intl Netwk Train.

You! Jonah! Thomas J. Carlisle. LC 68-20587. (Illus.). 64p. reprint ed. pap. 25.00 (*0-8357-9134-3*, 2012750) Bks Demand.

You Just Don't Duct Tape a Baby: True Tales & Sensible Suggestions from a Veteran Pediatrician. Norman Weinberger & Alison Pohn. 320p. 1997. 22.00 (*0-446-51965-0*) Warner Bks.

***You Just Don't Duct Tape a Baby! True Tales & Sensible Suggestions from a Veteran Pediatrician.** Norman Weinberger & Alison Pohn. 1998. mass mkt. write for info. (*0-446-60543-3*) Warner Bks.

You Just Don't Understand: Women & Men in Conversation. Deborah Tannen. 330p. 1991. pap. 12.50 (*0-345-37205-0*, Ballantine Trade) Ballantine.

You Just Fight for Your Life: The Story of Lester Young. Frank Buchmann-Moller. LC 89-3786. 298p. 1990. text ed. 35.00 (*0-275-93265-6*, C3265, Praeger Pubs) Greenwood.

You Just Glow! And Other Lies of Pregnancy, Childbirth, & Beyond. Lisa K. Weiss. (Illus.). 128p. 1994. pap. 8.00 (*0-671-86969-8*, Fireside) S&S Trade.

You Just Wait 'Til Sunday: How to Organize, Conduct & Maintain Your Own Family Council. Jason E. Hammer. LC 88-50768. (Illus.). 192p. 1989. pap. 9.95 (*0-9621075-1-4*) Baseline Pub.

You Kan Red This! Spelling & Punctuation for Whole Language Classrooms, K-6. Sandra Wilde. LC 91-23922. (Illus.). 208p. 1991. pap. text ed. 21.50 (*0-435-08595-6*, 08595) Heinemann.

You Keep Waiting for Geese. Viola Wendt. LC 75-29746. (Illus.). 1975. text ed. 6.75 (*0-916120-01-5*); pap. text ed. 3.95 (*0-916120-02-3*) Carroll Coll.

You Know: A Discourse-Functional Study. Jan-Ola Ostman. (Pragmatics & Beyond Ser.: II: 7). ix, 91p. (Orig.). 1981. pap. 29.00 (*90-272-2516-8*) Benjamins North Am.

You Know I Can't Hear You When the Water's Running: Four Plays. Robert Anderson. 1968. pap. 5.25 (*0-8222-1288-9*) Dramatists Play.

You Know I Wouldn't Say This... The Rise & Fall of Criticism. rev. ed. Jennifer James. LC 86-2303. (Illus.). 74p. (Orig.). 1984. reprint ed. pap. text ed. 9.95 (*0-915423-01-4*) Jennifer J.

You Know I Wouldn't Say This If I Didn't Love You: How to Defend Yourself Against Verbal Zaps & Zingers. Jennifer James. LC 89-48771. 144p. 1991. pap. 10.95 (*1-55704-049-4*) Newmarket.

You Know Me Al. Ring Lardner, Jr. 1987. 30.00 (*0-02-568440-X*) S&S Trade.

You Know Me Al. Ring Lardner. (Prairie State Bks.). 272p. 1992. pap. text ed. 10.95 (*0-252-06230-2*) U of Ill Pr.

You Know Me Al. unabridged ed. Ring Lardner, Jr. (Thrift Editions Ser.). 128p. 1995. pap. text ed. 1.00 (*0-486-28513-8*) Dover.

You Know Me Al. Ring Lardner, Jr. 218p. reprint ed. lib. bdg. 21.95 (*0-88411-584-4*) Amereon Ltd.

You Know Me Al. Ring Lardner, Jr. 1993. reprint ed. lib. bdg. 18.95 (*1-56849-207-3*) Buccaneer Bks.

You Know Me Al: A Busher's Letters. Ring Lardner, Jr. 224p. 1991. pap. 9.95 (*0-02-022342-0*) Macmillan.

You Know My Method: The Science of the Detective. J. Kenneth Van Dover. LC 93-72934. 262p. 1994. 42.95 (*0-87972-639-3*); pap. 16.95 (*0-87972-640-7*) Bowling Green Univ Popular Press.

You Know the Fair Rule. Bill Rogers. (C). 1990. 75.00 (*0-86431-068-4*, Pub. by Aust Council Educ Res AT) St Mut.

You Know Who. John Ciardi. LC 90-85903. (Illus.). 64p. (J). (gr. k up). 1991. reprint ed. 13.95 (*1-878093-34-7*, Wordsong) Boyds Mills Pr.

You Know You Don't Have a Life When... Ken Wickerham. 96p. 1996. mass mkt. 5.99 (*0-7860-0295-6*, Pinncle Kensgtn) Kensgtn Pub Corp.

***You Know You Have In-Laws from Hell When...** Allison Thorne & Rebecca Alfieri. (Illus.). 206p. (Orig.). 1997. pap. 6.95 (*0-9657878-0-X*) Blonde Bouffants.

You Know You'll Never Solo When... Wingover Productions Staff. LC 88-51947. (Illus.). 96p. (Orig.). 1989. pap. 6.95 (*0-9621843-0-6*) Wingover Prodns.

You Know You're a Catholic... A Self-Help Book for Gentiles & Other People... Keith Fraundorf. LC 96-92203. (Illus.). 96p. (Orig.). 1996. pap. 8.95 (*0-9651837-0-X*) Creative Niche.

***You Know You're a Mormon If...** Jim Brinkerhoff. (Illus.). 166p. (Orig.). 1996. pap. 12.95 (*0-9653327-0-5*) BF Publng.

You Know You're a Nebraskan. Roger Welsch & Paul Fell. (Illus.). 84p. 1989. pap. 5.95 (*0-934904-09-X*) J & L Lee.

You Know You're a New Parent When... Jeff Justice & Diane Pfeifer. LC 91-65001. (Illus.). 96p. (Orig.). 1991. pap. 5.95 (*0-9618306-5-4*) Strawberry GA.

You Know You're a Peace Officer's Wife When... Ann Coughlin et al. 56p. (Orig.). 1978. pap. 7.50 (*1-56325-016-0*, DH016) Davis Pub Law.

You Know You're a Scrooge When... Scott Matthews & Barbara Alpert. 96p. 1996. 5.99 (*0-7860-0323-5*, Pinncle Kensgtn) Kensgtn Pub Corp.

***You Know You're a Womanizing Slimeball When...** Jon Michaels. Ed. by Cliff Carle. (Illus.). 96p. (Orig.). 1997. pap. 5.95 (*1-57644-045-1*) CCC Pubns.

You Know You're a Workaholic When... Jeanne Hanson & Patricia Mark. LC 92-50935. (Illus.). 96p. 1993. pap. 5.95 (*1-56305-470-1*, 3470) Workman Pub.

You Know You're an Arizona Native, When. Don Dedera. (Illus.). 100p. (Orig.). 1993. pap. 9.95 (*0-9624499-2-X*) Prickly AZ.

You Know You're an Old Fart When: Recognizing the Tell-Tale Signs of Old Age. Dusty Rumsey. Ed. by Cliff Carle. 1993. pap. 4.95 (*0-918259-52-5*) CCC Pubns.

You Know You're Anonymous in Washington When... 1996. mass mkt. 3.99 (*0-312-96119-7*) St Martin.

You Know You're Drinking Too Much Coffee When... Aviv M. Ilan & David Han. 144p. 1996. pap. text ed. 5.95 (*1-55850-688-8*) Adams Media.

You Know You're Gay When... Those Unforgettable Moments That Make Us Who We Are. Joseph Cohen. LC 95-515. 112p. 1995. 9.95 (*0-8092-3320-7*) Contemp Bks.

You Know You're Getting Older When. Lois L. Kaufman & Evelyn L. Beilenson. (Personals Ser.). (Illus.). 80p. 1994. 6.99 (*0-88088-614-5*) Peter Pauper.

You Know You're Grown up When... Jeanne Hanson. LC 91-50383. (Illus.). 96p. (Orig.). 1991. pap. 4.95 (*1-56305-115-X*, 3115) Workman Pub.

You Know You're Middle-Aged When... G. Gaynor McTigue. 96p. 1994. mass mkt. 4.50 (*0-7860-0066-X*, Pinnacle Kensgtn) Kensgtn Pub Corp.

***You Know You're over 30.** Herbert Kavet. (Illus.). 64p. 1997. pap. 5.95 (*1-889647-22-5*) Boston Am.

***You Know You're over 40.** Herbert Kavet. (Illus.). 64p. 1997. pap. 5.95 (*1-889647-23-3*) Boston Am.

***You Know You're over 50.** Herbert Kavet. (Illus.). 64p. 1997. pap. 5.95 (*1-889647-24-1*) Boston Am.

You Know You're Pregnant When... Jeff Justice & Diane Pfeifer. Ed. by Diane Pfeifer. LC 94-68529. (Illus.). 96p. (Orig.). 1995. pap. 5.95 (*0-9618306-4-6*) Strawberry GA.

You Learn by Living. Eleanor Roosevelt. LC 83-6838. 224p. 1983. reprint ed. pap. 11.00 (0-664-24494-7, Westminster) Westminster John Knox.

You Learn to Type. Alan C. Lloyd & R. Krevolin. 1966. text ed. 26.52 (0-07-038160-7) McGraw.

You Light the Fire. Kristen Garrett. 176p. 1992. pap. 9.95 (0-9628938-5-4) Rising NY.

You Look Funny! Joy Kim. LC 86-30839. (Illus.). 32p. (J). (gr. k-2). 1997. pap. 2.50 (0-8167-0977-7) Troll Communs.

You Look Ridiculous Said the Rhinoceros to the Hippopotamus. Bernard Waber. (Illus.). (J). (gr. k-3). 1973. 17.95 (0-395-07156-9) HM.

You Look Ridiculous Said the Rhinoceros to the Hippopotamus. Bernard Waber. (Illus.). (J). (gr. k-3). 1979. pap. 5.95 (0-395-28007-9) HM.

You Make the Call: Baseball's Knotty Problems. Sporting News Editors. 1994. pap. 9.95 (0-88486-091-4, Bristol Park Bks) Arrowood Pr.

***You Make the Credit Call: Interactive Case Studies in Credit Management.** Basil P. Marroritis. Ed. by Teresa G. Donohue. 314p. (Orig.). 1996. pap. 34.50 (1-888505-00-1) NACM.

You May Already Be a Winner & Other Marginal Considerations. Jan C. Snow. LC 92-3869. (Illus.). 168p. (Orig.). 1992. pap. 9.00 (0-87338-467-9) Kent St U Pr.

You May Kiss the Bride: Choice, Engagement, Courtship, Marriage, Divorce, Remarriage, Polygamy...& the Christian. Okey Onuzo. Ed. by Anne Ndego. 209p. (Orig.). 1992. pap. text ed. 8.50 (1-880608-02-2) Life Link.

You May Plow Here: The Narrative of Sara Brooks. Ed. by Thordis Simonsen. 224p. 1992. pap. 8.95 (0-393-30866-9) Norton.

You, Me, & Gracie Makes Three. Dean Marney. (J). (gr. 6-8). 1989. pap. 2.50 (0-590-41637-5, Apple Paperbacks) Scholastic Inc.

You, Me & Technology. Piel. (Tech & Industrial Education Ser.). 1989. teacher ed., pap. 8.00 (0-8273-3406-0) Delmar.

You, Me, Sky. Knight. (J). 16.00 (0-689-80252-8, S&S Bks Young Read) S&S Childrens.

You Mean I Don't Have to Feel This Way? New Help for Depression, Anxiety, & Addiction. Colette Dowling. 384p. 1992. text ed. 19.95 (0-684-19257-8) S&S Trade.

You Mean I Don't Have to Feel This Way? New Help for Depression, Anxiety, & Addiction. Colette Dowling. LC 92-46657. 320p. 1993. reprint ed. pap. 13.95 (0-553-37169-X) Bantam.

You Mean I Have to Stand Up & Say Something? Joan Detz. LC 86-3611. (Illus.). 96p. (J). (gr. 5-9). 1986. lib. bdg. 13.95 (0-689-31221-0, Atheneum Bks Young) S&S Childrens.

You Mean I'm Not Lazy, Stupid, Crazy: Self-Help Book Adults Attention Disorder. Kate Kelly & Peggy Ramundo. (Illus.). 464p. 1996. pap. 14.00 (0-684-81531-1, Fireside) S&S Trade.

You Mean I'm Not Lazy, Stupid, or Crazy?! A Self-Help Book for Adults with Attention Deficit Disorder. Kate Kelly & Peggy Ramundo. (Illus.). 350p. 1993. 19.95 (1-882522-00-1) Tyrell & Jerem.

You Mean I'm Not Lazy, Stupid or Crazy?! A Self-Help Book for Adults with Attention Deficit Disorder. Kate Kelly & Peggy Ramundo. (Illus.). 448p. 1995. 23.00 (0-684-80116-7) S&S Trade.

You Mean to Say You Still Don't Know Who We Are? Ed. by Cellia Gluck & Yasushi Takeda. 112p. (Orig.). 1992. pap. 7.50 (4-89360-033-8, Pub. by Personally Oriented JA) Weatherhill.

You Meet Such Interesting People. Bess W. Scott. LC 88-30371. (Centennial Series of the Association of Former Students: No. 33). (Illus.). 208p. 1989. 18.95 (0-89096-404-1) Tex A&M Univ Pr.

***You Might As Well Laugh: Surviving the Joys of Parenthood.** Sandi K. Shelton. Ed. by Evonne Smit. LC 96-86486. 269p. 1997. 19.95 (0-9631246-3-3) Bancroft MD.

***You Might Be a Disciple If...** Ed. by David P. Polk. 56p. (Orig.). 1997. pap. 5.00 (0-8272-4406-1) Chalice Pr.

You Might Be a Preacher If... Stan Toler. 1996. pap. text ed. 7.95 (1-880089-46-7) Albury Pub.

***You Might Be a Preacher If...** Stan Toler. Date not set. pap. 5.99 (1-56292-276-9) Honor Bks OK.

You Might Be a Redneck If . . . Jeff Foxworthy. LC 89-80277. (Illus.). 80p. (Orig.). 1989. pap. 6.95 (0-929264-57-6) Longstreet Pr Inc.

You Might Be a Redneck If... A Laugh-a-Day for 1996. Jeff Foxworthy. 1995. pap. 8.95 (1-56352-209-8) Longstreet Pr Inc.

You Might Be a Redneck If... A Postcard Book. Jeff Foxworthy. 1995. pap. text ed. 8.95 (1-56352-253-5) Longstreet Pr Inc.

***You Might Be a Redneck If... Your Bicycle Has a Gun Rack.** Jeff Foxworthy. (Little Bks.). 1997. 4.95 (0-8362-3738-2) Andrews & McMeel.

You Might Be a Talk Show Addict If... Linda S. Amstutz. 112p. 1995. pap. 6.95 (0-9640362-8-2) Off Color Pr.

***You Might Be a Youth Worker If...** Jon Middendorf. (Illus.). 96p. (Orig.). 1997. pap. 8.99 (0-8341-1668-5) Beacon Hill.

You Might Consider Losing a Few Pounds If... Joe Hobby. 1996. pap. text ed. 7.95 (1-886049-11-4) Best Times Inc.

You Might Have Asked. Stuart J. Olyott. 1983. pap. 7.99 (0-85234-175-X, Pub. by Evangelical Pr) Presby & Reformed.

You Must Be Dreaming. Barbara Noel & Kathryn Watterson. LC 92-16265. 1992. 21.00 (0-671-74153-5) S&S Trade.

***You Must Be Joking.** Green. 9.95 (0-340-56784-8, Pub. by H & S UK) Trafalgar.

You Must Break Out Sometimes & Other Stories. Thomas O. Beachcroft. LC 75-113648. (Short Story Index Reprint Ser.). 1977. 20.95 (0-8369-3377-X) Ayer.

***You Must Inhale to Exhale: A Psychotherapeutic Book on Relational Shortcomings & How to Cope after Shock.** Rasul. 128p. (Orig.). 1996. pap. 12.95 (0-9656137-0-4) M Bey.

You Must Know Everything. Isaac Babel. Tr. by Max Hayward. 304p. 1984. pap. 8.95 (0-88184-027-0) Carroll & Graf.

You Must Not Let Them Con You! There's Too Much at Stake: On the Snares of Language & How to Avoid Getting Caught in Them. Irving D. Shapiro. 279p. (Orig.). 1993. pap. 29.95 (0-9642755-0-3) Mens Sana Fnd.

You Must Relax. Edmund Jacobson. 303p. 1991. pap. write for info. (1-880081-00-8) Natl Found Prog Relax.

You Must Remember This. Karen L. Evans & Pat Dade. LC 96-4242. (J). 1997. 13.95 (0-7868-0090-9) Hyprn Child.

You Must Remember This. Karen L. Evans & Pat Dade. LC 96-4242. (J). 1997. lib. bdg. 13.89 (0-7868-2075-6) Hyprn Child.

You Must Remember This. Clara Wimberly. (Intimate Moments Ser.). 1996. mass mkt. 3.99 (0-373-07718-1, 1-07718-9) Silhouette.

You Must Remember This 1955: Milestones, Memories, Trivia & Facts, News Events, Prominent Personalities & Sports Highlights of the Year. Compiled by Mary A. Pradt. 24p. 1995. write for info. (0-446-51919-7) Warner Bks.

You Must Remember This 1968: Milestones, Memories, Trivia & Facts, News Events, Prominent Personalities & Sports Highlights of the Year. Compiled by Mary A. Pradt. 24p. 1995. write for info. (0-446-51931-6) Warner Bks.

You Must Remember This 1975: Milestones, Memories, Trivia & Facts, News Events, Prominent Personalities & Sports Highlights of the Year. Compiled by Mary A. Pradt. 24p. 1995. write for info. (0-446-51937-5) Warner Bks.

You Must Tell Your Children. Karen J. Walsh et al. LC 79-84288. (Illus.). 64p. 1981. pap. 9.95 (0-935046-01-1); pap. 9.95 (0-935046-00-3); audio 14.95 (0-685-01044-9) Chateau Thierry.

You Need a Bath, Mustard. Paul Dowling. LC 92-72933. (Illus.). 32p. (J). (ps-k). 1993. 9.95 (1-56282-392-2) Hyprn Child.

You Need a Pay Raise, Damnit. Ronald C. Johnson. 120p. (Orig.). 1994. pap. text ed. 6.95 (1-884005-00-4) Max Imprint.

You Need Family Devotions. Lois B. Dunn. (Christian Living Ser.). 32p. 1990. pap. 3.25 (0-8341-1380-5) Beacon Hill.

You Need to Memorize Scripture. N. A. Woychuk. (Illus.). 173p. 1993. 5.99 (1-880960-01-X) Script Memory Fl.

***You Need...Dispensational Understanding.** unabridged ed. Kerry D. Anderholm. Ed. by Jerry Jensen. (Illus.). 100p. (Orig.). 1995. pap. 5.99 (0-9655407-9-0) True Light Pubns.

You Never Can Tell. Ellen Conford. (Illus.). 156p. (J). (gr. 7 up). 1984. 14.95 (0-316-15267-6) Little.

You Never Can Tell. George Bernard Shaw. Ed. by Daniel J. Leary. LC 79-56704. (Bernard Shaw Early Texts: Play Manuscripts in Facsimile). 330p. 1981. text ed. 20.00 (0-8240-4580-7) Garland.

You Never Can Tell. George Bernard Shaw. LC 91-51224. (Shaw Ser.). 92p. 1992. pap. 7.00 (0-88734-236-1) Players Pr.

You Never Know. Isabel Huggan. 224p. 1994. pap. 11.95 (0-14-014987-2, Penguin Bks) Viking Penguin.

You Never Know. Samsventi Tazwell & Syd Bradford. (Illus.). 105p. (Orig.). 1994. pap. 9.00 (1-879663-03-1) Audacious PA.

***You Never Know: A Legend of the Lamed-Vavniks.** Francine Drose. LC 97-24764. 1998. write for info. (0-688-15806-4) Greenwillow.

***You Never Know: A Legend of the Lamed-Vavniks.** Francine Drose. LC 97-24764. 1998. lib. bdg. write for info. (0-688-15807-2) Morrow.

You Never Miss the Water till... The Ogallalla Story. Morton N. Bittinger & Elizabeth B. Green. LC 80-50167. 1981. pap. 15.00 (0-918334-33-0) WRP.

You Never Sausage Love. Brian P. Cleary. LC 95-23530. (Illus.). 32p. (J). (gr. 3-6). 1996. lib. bdg. 13.13 (0-8225-2115-6) Lerner Group.

You New Jersey & the World. rev. ed. 320p. 1994. teacher ed., spiral bd. write for info. (0-89359-101-7) Afton Pub.

You New Jersey & the World. rev. ed. 256p. (J). (gr. 4). 1995. write for info. (0-89359-102-5) Afton Pub.

You Now Have Custody of You. Richard M. Cromie. 36p. (Orig.). 1987. pap. 3.00 (0-914733-10-9) Desert Min.

You Only Feel Wet When You're Out of the Water: Thoughts on Psychology & Competitive Swimming. Keith Bell. LC 91-3321. 140p. (Orig.). 1992. pap. 16.95 (0-945609-15-9) Keel Pubns.

You Only Get What You Settle For: A Collection of Poems. Stephen R. Boulhosa. LC 92-44219. 64p. 1993. pap. 12.95 (0-7734-2760-0, Mellen Poetry Pr) E Mellen.

You Only Live Once: Memories of Ian Fleming. Ivar Bryce. (Foreign Intelligence Book Ser.). 152p. 1975. reprint ed. text ed. 45.00 (0-313-26999-8, U6999, Greenwood Pr) Greenwood.

You Only Live Twice. Ian Fleming. pap. 9.95 (0-685-11630-1); pap. 9.95 (0-685-11631-X) Fr & Eur.

You Only Live Twice. Ian Fleming. pap. 2.95 (0-451-13708-6, AE2108, Sig) NAL-Dutton.

You Only Live Twice. Ian Fleming. (James Bond Ser.). 1995. 6.98 (1-56731-080-X, MJF Bks) Fine Comms.

You Ought to Write All That Down: A Guide to Organizing & Writing Genealogical Narrative. Paul Drake. (Illus.). 196p. (Orig.). 1996. pap. 32.50 (0-7884-0445-8, D612) Heritage Bk.

You Oughta Be Me: How to be a Lounge Singer & Live Like One. Bud E. Luv. (Illus.). 256p. (Orig.). 1993. pap. 10.95 (0-312-09947-9) St Martin.

You Owe Yourself a Drunk: An Ethnography of Urban Nomads. James P. Spradley. 314p. (C). 1988. reprint ed. pap. text ed. 23.00 (0-8191-6856-4) U Pr of Amer.

You Publish It: How to Start a Home Publishing Company for under One Hundred Dollars. Robert Cooper. Ed. by Peggy Cooper. (Illus.). 100p. (Orig.). 1994. pap. 24.95 (0-939121-05-0) Cooper Hse.

You Put up with Me, I'll Put up with You. Barbara Corcoran. 176p. (J). (gr. 3-7). 1989. pap. 2.50 (0-380-70558-3, Camelot) Avon.

You Read to Me, I'll Read to You. John Ciardi. LC 62-16296. (Trophy Nonfiction Bk). (Illus.). 64p. (J). (gr. k-4). 1987. reprint ed. pap. 6.95 (0-06-446060-6, Trophy) HarpC Child Bks.

You Really Got Me: An Illustrated World Discography of the Kinks, 1964-1993. Doug Hinman & Jason Brabazon. LC 94-216558. (Kinks Ser.: Pt. 1). (Illus.). 572p. 1994. pap. text ed. 45.00 (0-9641005-0-9) D E Hinman.

You Really Got Me: An Illustrated World Discography of the Kinks, 1964-1993. Doug Hinman & Jason Brabazon. (Kinks Ser.: Pt. 1). (Illus.). 572p. 1994. text ed. 65.00 (0-9641005-1-7) D E Hinman.

You Said a Mouthful. Ronald D. Fuchs. 160p. 1996. 14.95 (0-312-14773-2) St Martin.

You Said a Mouthful. Roger Karshner. 64p. (Orig.). 1991. pap. 7.95 (0-940669-15-3, D-25) Dramaline Pubns.

***You Said It.** Wong. Date not set. pap. text ed. write for info. (0-312-11974-7); pap. text ed. write for info. (0-312-11975-5) St Martin.

You Said, Why This Interest in Goddesses. Susan Lee & Susanaha Libana. (Fastbook 1985 Ser.). 20p. 1985. 6.00 (0-911051-17-1) Plain View.

You Say You Want a Revolution? Douglas R. Arnts. 50p. 1995. pap. text ed. 18.95 (0-9648923-0-8) Abailard Pub.

You Say You Want a Revolution: Rock Music in American Culture. Robert G. Pielke. LC 85-25940. 270p. 1986. pap. 21.95 (0-8304-1201-8) Nelson-Hall.

You Say You're from Where? An Entertaining & Informational Collection of Unique. J. Thomas, pseud. 1995. pap. 5.95 (0-9637794-3-5) Machia.

You See I Don't Forget, Selected Poems & Stories. Ernest Tedlock. Ed. by Gary Elder. LC 80-12807. 1980. pap. 4.95 (0-914974-22-X) Holmgangers.

You Send Me: From Gospel to Pop - The Life of Sam Cooke. Daniel Wolff et al. LC 94-3547. (Illus.). 352p. 1995. 23.00 (0-688-12403-8) Morrow.

You Send Me: The Life & Times of Sam Cooke. Daniel Wolff. 1996. pap. 15.00 (0-688-14620-1, Quill) Morrow.

You Set My Spirit Free: A 40-Day Journey in the Company of John of the Cross. David Hazard. (Rekindling the Inner Fire Ser.: Vol. 7). 176p. 1994. pap. 8.99 (1-55661-481-0) Bethany Hse.

You Shall Be As Gods: A Radical Interpretation of the Old Testament & Its Tradition. Erich Fromm. 192p. 1991. pap. 10.95 (0-8050-1605-8, Owl) H Holt & Co.

You Shall Be My People: 250th Synod Reformed Church in the U. S. Paul Treick et al. Ed. & Intro. by Robert E. Grossmann. (Illus.). 230p. 1996. write for info. (1-57579-014-9) Pine Hill Pr.

You Shall Be My Witnesses: How to Reach Your City for Christ. Larry Rosenbaum. LC 86-90426. 144p. (Orig.). 1986. pap. 5.00 (0-938573-00-4) SOS Minist Pr.

You Shall Have No Other Gods: Israelite Religion in the Light of Hebrew Inscriptions. Jeffrey H. Tigay. LC 86-20442. (Harvard Semitic Studies). 130p. 1987. 19.95 (1-55540-063-9, 04-04-31) Scholars Pr GA.

You Shall Not Abhor an Edomite for He Is Your Brother: Edom & Seir in History & Tradition. Ed. by Diane Edelman. LC 94-40041. (Archaeology & Biblical Studies: No. 3). xiv, 190p. 1995. reprint ed. pap. 24.95 (0-7885-0063-5) Scholars Pr GA.

***You Shall Not Abhor an Edomite for He Is Your Brother: Edom & Seir in History & Tradtion.** Diane V. Edelman. (SBL Archaeology & Biblical Studies). 204p. 1995. 39.95 (0-7885-0136-4, 061703) Scholars Pr GA.

You Shall Not Bear False Witness, Vol. 9. Daniel D'Aria. (Reflections on the Commandments Ser.). 64p. 1995. pap. 2.95 (0-8198-8806-0) Pauline Bks.

You Shall Not Commit Adultery, Nor Covet Your Neighbor's Wife, Vol. 7. Joseph Anfossi. (Reflections on the Commandments Ser.). 1995. pap. 2.95 (0-8198-8804-4) Pauline Bks.

You Shall Not Have Strange Gods Before Me, Vol. 2. Joseph Anfossi & John Villata. (Reflections on the Commandments Ser.). 1995. pap. 2.95 (0-8198-8801-X) Pauline Bks.

You Shall Not Kill, Vol. 6. Edward Menichelli & Lionel Crocetta. (Reflections on the Commandments Ser.). 64p. 1995. pap. 2.95 (0-8198-8803-6) Pauline Bks.

You Shall Not Steal: Community & Property in the Biblical Tradition. Robert Karl Gnuse. LC 85-4810. 176p. (Orig.). 1985. reprint ed. pap. 50.20 (0-7837-6412-X, 2046392) Bks Demand.

You Shall Not Steal, Nor Covet Your Neighbor's Goods, Vol. 8. Daniel D'Aria. (Reflections on the Commandments Ser.). 64p. 1995. pap. 2.95 (0-8198-8805-2) Pauline Bks.

You Shall Not Take the Lord's Name in Vain, Vol. 3. Paul Tammi. (Reflections on the Commandments Ser.). 48p. 1995. pap. 2.95 (0-8198-8802-8) Pauline Bks.

You Shall Not Test The Lord Your God! Living Street Ministry Staff. 32p. 2.00 (0-87083-784-2, 17016001) Living Stream Ministry.

You Shall Not Want: A Spiritual Journey Based on the Psalms. Richard W. Chilson. LC 95-80889. (Thirty Days with a Great Spiritual Teacher Ser.). 216p. (Orig.). 1996. pap. 6.95 (0-87793-571-8) Ave Maria.

You Shall Worship... rev. ed. B. E. Underwood. 1992. pap. 4.95 (0-911866-07-8) LifeSprings Res.

You Shall Worship: Study Guide. Shirley G. Spencer. 1992. pap. 4.95 (0-911866-11-6) LifeSprings Res.

You Should Be So Lucky. Charles Busch. 128p. 1995. 8.99 (1-56865-126-0, GuildAmerica) Dblday Direct.

You Should Brew Too! Clive La Pensee. 1992. pap. 35.00 (0-9515685-2-3, Pub. by Montag Pubns UK) St Mut.

You Should Have Been Here Yesterday: A Guide to Cultural Documentation in Maryland. Ed. by Elaine Eff et al. LC 95-40733. 1995. pap. 10.00 (1-878399-66-7, MD Hist Trust) Div Hist Cult Progs.

You Should Have Been Here Yesterday (Cartoons) John Troy. LC 94-36900. (Illus.). 144p. 1995. 20.00 (1-55821-360-0) Lyons & Burford.

"You Should Meet Them" Your Ancestors & Descendants. Elizabeth W. Davis. LC 83-71329. 1983. write for info. (0-9611384-0-8) E W H Davis.

You Should Not Get a Home Equity Line of Credit: Thirteen Reasons - the Answer Book. Larry Oxenham. (Answer Bk.: Vol. II). (Illus.). 40p. 1987. 4.75 (0-943813-01-8) Page One Pub.

You Shouldn't Have to Say Good-Bye. Patricia Hermes. 128p. (J). (gr. 3-7). 1984. pap. 3.25 (0-590-43174-9) Scholastic Inc.

You Sign. Terence P. O'Halloran. 100p. 1992. 75.00 (1-85609-038-8, Pub. by Witherby & Co UK) St Mut.

You Silly Goose. Ellen S. Walsh. (Illus.). 32p. (J). (ps-3). 1992. 14.00 (0-15-299865-9, HB Juv Bks) HarBrace.

You Silly Goose. Ellen S. Walsh. LC 91-6968. (Illus.). 32p. (J). (ps-3). 1996. pap. 6.00 (0-15-201012-2, Voyager Bks) HarBrace.

***You Smell: And Taste & Feel & See & Hear.** Mary Murphy. (Illus.). 32p. (J). (ps-k). 1997. 9.95 (0-7894-2471-1) DK Pub Inc.

You So Crazy. Martin Lawrence. (Illus.). 128p. 1994. pap. 7.95 (0-7868-8083-X) Hyperion.

***You Stand There.** D. Kleiler & R. Moses. 1997. pap. 16.00 (0-609-80036-1) Random Hse Value.

***You Still Ghetto.** Berry. Date not set. pap. write for info. (0-312-18236-8) St Martin.

You Take Jesus, I'll Take God. Samuel Levine. LC 80-82731. 134p. (Orig.). 1980. pap. 6.95 (0-9604754-1-9) Hamoroh Pr.

You Tarzan: Masculinity, Movies & Men. Ed. by Pat Kirkham & Janet Thumim. (Illus.). 221p. 1993. text ed. 15.95 (0-312-09998-3) St Martin.

You Tell Me: Connecting the Self, Nature & Humanity. Symbol Staff. (Illus.). 80p. 1992. 29.95 (0-9633323-0-9) The Symbol.

You Tell Me: Learning Basic Information. Mary J. Haugen. (Life Skills Educational Board Game Ser.: No. 2). 50p. 1991. teacher ed., text ed. 49.95 (1-884074-01-4) Program Concepts.

You the Consumer. Cheryl S. Johnson & Richard L. Johnson. (Living Skills Ser.). 110p. 1993. teacher ed. 8.95 (1-884245-22-6); pap. text ed. 7.95 (1-884245-21-8) Life Choices.

You the Graduate. rev. ed. Harold J. Drown. 1990. 2.38 (0-687-46854-X) Abingdon.

You the Healer: The World-Famous Silva Method on How to Heal Yourself & Others. Jose Silva & Robert B. Stone. Ed. by Gregory Armstrong & Suzanne Lipsett. LC 88-91462. 275p. 1989. pap. 12.00 (0-915811-37-5) H J Kramer Inc.

You the Healer: The World Famous Silva Method on How to Heal Yourself & Others. Jose Silva & Robert B. Stone. LC 91-45427. 263p. 1992. reprint ed. 29.98 (0-941683-17-6) Instant Improve.

You, the Jury. Anne C. Martens. 1965. pap. 3.00 (0-87129-249-1, Y12) Dramatic Pub.

***You the Jury: A Recovered Memory Case.** Mark E. Roseman et al. LC 96-48102. 288p. 1997. 27.95 (0-929765-54-0) Seven Locks Pr.

You the Man. Marvin Cohen. 320p. 1996. pap. 14.95 (0-942963-72-5) Distinctive Pub.

You the Mayor? The Education of a City Politician. Barbara Ackermann. LC 88-14643. 281p. 1989. text ed. 55.00 (0-86569-178-9, T178, Auburn Hse) Greenwood.

You, the Medium: Psychic Development Through Home Circles. Nancy North & Raymond Berube. 120p. (Orig.). 1995. pap. write for info. (0-9646600-1-6) Northray Pubns.

You the Singer. Barbara Harlow. 158p. 1985. pap. 18.95 (0-937276-06-5) Hinshaw Mus.

***You the Writer: Reading, Writing, Thinking.** Gabriele L. Rico & Hans Guth. (C). 1997. teacher ed., text ed. 11.96 (0-395-83836-3) HM.

You Too Can Be a Kahuna see Huna: A Beginner's Guide

You, Too, Can Be Forgiven. Myrle Morris. 208p. 1978. mass mkt. 4.99 (0-88368-082-3) Whitaker Hse.

You Too Can Be in TV Commercials. Georgette Baker. Ed. by Mark Doughty. (Illus.). 86p. (Orig.). 1988. pap. 7.95 (0-9623930-0-2) Cantemos.

You Too Can Be Prosperous. Robert A. Russell. 162p. 1975. reprint ed. pap. 6.95 (0-87516-205-3) DeVorss.

You, Too, Can be Successful! Simple Steps to Personal, Social & Spiritual Fulfillment, for All Ages. Marvin L. Smith. LC 89-82270. (Illus.). 118p. 1990. pap. 6.95 (0-9625115-1-X) Campbell Rd Pr.

You, Too, Can Canoe. John Foshee. LC 76-58244. 1977. 14.95 (0-87397-116-7, Strode Pubs) Circle Bk Service.

***You Too Can Do It!** Patricia T. Kienzle & Kathryn K. Simmons. (Illus.). 101p. 1996. 19.95 (1-890798-04-5) P T Kienzle.

An Asterisk (*) at the beginning of an entry indicates that the title is appearing in BIP for the first time.

You Too Can Find Anybody: A Reference Manual. rev. ed. Joseph J. Culligan. LC 91-91166. (Illus.). 370p. 1997. reprint ed. pap. 19.95 (0-9630621-0-7) FJA.

You Too Can Find Peace: Growing Through Life's Experiences. Madge Haines. LC 86-22107. 128p. reprint ed. pap. 36.50 (0-7837-6433-2, 2046431) Bks Demand.

You Too Can Have Fun in South Bend (& it's Neighbors) Jeffrey D. Roberts. 79p. 1994. pap. 5.00 (0-9649858-0-2) Having Fun.

You Too Can Heal. George King. LC 86-198689. (Illus.). 133p. 1976. pap. 12.95 (0-937249-09-2) Aetherius Soc.

You Too Can Heal: Energy Key of the Future. Colin R. Lambert. 220p. (Orig.). 1993. pap. text ed. 16.50 (0-908807-03-1) Ka Io Prods.

***You Too Can Know Jesus.** 24p. (J). 1997. pap. write for info. (0-7814-0938-1, Chariot Bks) Chariot Victor.

You Too Can Know Jesus. Chariot Family Staff. 1992. pap. text ed. 9.90 (0-7814-0920-9) Chariot Victor.

You Too Can Play Piano & Organ Without a Teacher, Vol. 1. Vladislav Celik. (Music Instructional Ser.). (Illus.). 96p. (Orig.). 1991. pap. text ed. 16.95 (0-9624062-1-X) Music Inst CA.

You Too Can Play Piano & Organ Without a Teacher, Vol. 2. Vladislav Celik. (Music Instructional Ser.). (Illus.). 92p. (Orig.). 1991. pap. text ed. 16.95 (0-9624062-0-1) Music Inst CA.

You Touched Me. D. H. Lawrence. (Creative's Classics Ser.). 48p. (J). (gr. 6 up). 1982. lib. bdg. 13.95 (0-87191-894-3) Creative Ed.

You Try It. Robert A. Russell. 1953. pap. 5.95 (0-87516-326-2) DeVorss.

You Unlimited. Norman Lunde. LC 65-23608. 1985. reprint ed. pap. 7.95 (0-87516-249-5) DeVorss.

You Want a What for a Pet? Betsy S. Siino. 224p. 1996. 19.95 (0-87605-485-8) Howell Bk.

***You Want It When?!** Jack Parker. 128p. 39.00 (0-614-25581-3, 00GM44678) Print Indus Am.

***You Want Me to Do What? When, Where & How to Draw the Line.** Nan DeMars. Ed. by Brad Thompson. LC 97-66113. 320p. (Orig.). 1997. pap. 19.95 (0-918351-04-9) Thompson Co Inc.

You Want Proof - I'll Give You Proof: Sidney Harris Laughs at Science. Sidney Harris. 160p. 1995. pap. text ed. write for info. (0-7167-2159-7) W H Freeman.

You Want to Build & Fly a What? Dick Starks. (Illus.). 262p. 1992. pap. 12.95 (0-932579-06-X) Butterfield Pr.

***You Want to Write a Book? Then Do It! A Self-Publishing Manual - Non-Traditional Method.** Gary A. Knox. Ed. by Kim McShane. (Orig.). 1997. pap. text ed. 24.95 (1-887212-10-8) AQC Resource.

***You Want Us to Do What? 75 Active Devotions for Youth Groups.** Mike Gillespie. 80p. 1996. teacher ed., per. 11.99 (0-570-04863-X, 12-3354) Concordia.

You Want Women to Vote, Lizzie Stanton? Jean Fritz. LC 94-30018. (Illus.). 88p. (J). (gr. 5-9). 1995. 15.95 (0-399-22786-5, Putnam) Putnam Pub Group.

You Wanted to Know . . . What a Waldorf School Is . . . & What It Is Not. Alan Howard. 1984. pap. 3.95 (0-916786-72-2, Saint George Pubns) R Steiner Col Pubns.

You Were Born Agin. Dick Sutphen. 253p. 1987. mass mkt. 6.99 (0-671-64846-2) PB.

You Were Born on a Rotten Day. Christopher Sergel. 1971. pap. 5.00 (0-87129-352-8, Y13) Dramatic Pub.

You Were Born on Your Very First Birthday. Linda Girard. Ed. by Kathy Tucker. LC 82-13700. (Albert Whitman Concept Bks.). (Illus.). 32p. (J). (ps-3). 1983. pap. 5.95 (0-8075-9456-3) A Whitman.

You Were Designed to Live for One Hundred & Forty Years. Arnold Perrin. 1979. pap. 1.00 (0-939736-06-3) Wings ME.

You Were Meant for Me. Elise Title. (Temptation Ser.). 1993. mass mkt. 2.99 (0-373-25555-1, 1-25555-3) Harlequin Bks.

You Who Know. Nicolas Freeling. 224p. 1995. mass mkt. 5.50 (0-446-40370-9, Mysterious Paperbk) Warner Bks.

You Who Know. large type ed. Nicolas Freeling. LC 94-38991. 1995. 21.95 (0-7838-1182-9, GK Hall) Thorndike Pr.

You Will Be King: Gallantry, Bk. 2: Age Three. rev. ed. Joan Abell. (Illus.). 50p. (J). (gr. 5-8). 1993. 28.00 (1-56611-025-4); pap. 28.00 (1-56611-449-7) Jones.

You Will Be Satisfied. Bob Tasca & Peter Caldwell. (Illus.). 208p. 1996. 23.00 (0-88730-798-1) Harper Busn.

***You Will Be Satisfied.** Bob Tasca. 1997. pap. 12.50 (0-88730-859-7) Harper Busn.

You Will Increase. Billy J. Daugherty. 29p. 1991. pap. 0.50 (1-56267-046-8) Victory Ctr OK.

You Will Learn to Love Me. Susan Chace. LC 93-40839. 1995. 18.00 (0-394-58384-1) Random.

You Will Live Again: Dramatic Case Histories of Reincarnation. Brad Steiger. LC 96-14988. (Illus.). 248p. (Orig.). 1996. pap. 12.95 (0-931892-29-5) B Dolphin Pub.

You Will Never Be the Same. Basilea M. Schlink. 192p. 1972. mass mkt. 5.99 (0-87123-661-3) Bethany Hse.

You Will Never Die Laughing. Arnold B. Poole. LC 91-62231. 78p. 1991. reprint ed. pap. 3.95 (0-9624008-5-8) Pulpit Rock.

You Will Plant Your Vineyards Once More. Georgia B. Houle. (Illus.). 60p. (Orig.). 1986. pap. 7.95 (0-940139-08-1) Consortium RI.

You Won't Believe It's Kosher. Yocheved Hirsch. (Illus.). 190p. (Orig.). 1994. pap. 18.00 (0-9637022-1-1) Gldn Sun Bks.

You Won't Believe This, But... Responding to Student Complaints & Excuses. Gary Colwell. 96p. (Orig.). (C). 1996. pap. text ed. 14.95 (1-55059-137-1, Pub. by Detselig CN) Temeron Bks.

You Won't Believe Your Eyes. National Geographic Society Staff. Ed. by Donald J. Crump. LC 86-7637. (Books for World Explorers Series 8: No. 3). (Illus.). 104p. (J). (gr. 3-8). 1994. 12.50 (0-87044-611-8) Natl Geog.

You Won't Believe Your Eyes. Milan Tytla & Nancy Crystal. (Illus.). 88p. (J). (gr. 2-8). 1992. pap. 9.95 (1-55037-218-1, Pub. by Annick CN) Firefly Bks Ltd.

You Won't Remember This. Michael D. Browne. (Poetry Ser.). 88p. (Orig.). 1992. pap. 11.95 (0-88748-135-3) Carnegie-Mellon.

***You Won't Think of Me at All.** Caroline Pitcher. (Illus.). 32p. (J). (ps-2). 1998. 14.95 (1-888444-29-0) Little Tiger.

You Won't Understand If You Have to Ask Why. Kenneth Quade. 16.95 (0-533-11343-1) Vantage.

You Would If You Loved Me. Nora Stirling. 176p. (gr. 7-10). 1976. pap. 2.50 (0-380-01631-1, Flare) Avon.

You Wouldn't Believe What My Grandchild Did... Lois Wyse. 1994. 15.00 (0-671-89293-2) S&S Trade.

You Wouldn't Believe What My Grandchild Did. Lois Wyse. 1995. pap. 9.00 (0-684-80404-2, Fireside) S&S Trade.

You Wouldn't Believe What My Grandchild Did... large type ed. Lois Wyse. LC 94-20365. 180p. 1994. lib. bdg. 19.95 (0-7862-0270-X) Thorndike Pr.

You Wouldn't Believe What My Grandchild Did... large type ed. Lois Wyse. LC 94-20365. (Illus.). 1995. lib. bdg. 13.95 (0-7862-0271-8) Thorndike Pr.

You Wrote My Life: Lyrical Themes in Country Music. Ed. by Melton McLaurin. (Cultural Perspectives on the American Society Ser.). 180p. 1992. text ed. 45.00 (2-88124-548-X); pap. text ed. 18.00 (2-88124-554-4) Gordon & Breach.

You You Don't Know: Covert Influences on Your Behavior. W. Webster Riggs, Jr. LC 96-48012. 332p. 1997. 26.95 (1-57392-116-5) Prometheus Bks.

You, Your Child, & Special Education: A Guide to Making the System Work. Barbara C. Cutler. LC 92-18844. 272p. (C). 1993. pap. text ed. 22.00 (1-55766-115-4, 1154) P H Brookes.

You, Your Family & the Law: A Legal Guide for Today's Families. Wesley J. Smith. (Orig.). 1993. pap. write for info. (0-910073-18-X) HALT DC.

You, Your Parent, & the Nursing Home. Nancy Fox. LC 86-83887. 175p. 1986. pap. 17.95 (0-87975-371-X) Prometheus Bks.

You, Yours & Crime Resistance: How You, Your Family, & Your Community Can Work to Reduce Crime. (FBI Ser.). 1986. lib. bdg. 150.00 (0-8490-3810-3) Gordon Pr.

You...& Being a Student: Motivational Study Activities. rev. ed. Feryl J. Bergin. (Illus.). 112p. (YA). (gr. 6-12). 1995. student ed., per. 8.95 (0-936955-01-5) Eminent Pubns.

You...& Being a Success: Motivational Speaking Communication Skills. Feryl J. Bergin. (Illus.). 112p. (Orig.). (YA). (gr. 6-12). 1994. student ed., per., pap. 8.95 (0-936955-04-X) Eminent Pubns.

You...& Being a Teenager: Motivational Activities for Teens. rev. ed. Feryl J. Bergin. (Illus.). 112p. (YA). (gr. 6-12). 1991. per., pap. 8.95 (0-936955-00-7) Eminent Pubns.

You...& Being a Winner: Motivational Writing Communication Skills. Feryl J. Bergin. (Illus.). 112p. (Orig.). (YA). (gr. 6-12). 1994. student ed., per., pap. 8.95 (0-936955-03-1) Eminent Pubns.

You...& Being a Worker: Motivational Work Activities. Feryl J. Bergin. 112p. (Orig.). (YA). (gr. 6-12). 1991. student ed., per., pap. 8.95 (0-936955-02-3) Eminent Pubns.

You...& Being an Achiever: Motivational Activities in Functional Writing. Feryl J. Bergin. (Illus.). 112p. (YA). (gr. 6-12). 1996. pap. text ed. 8.95 (0-936955-06-6) Eminent Pubns.

***You...& Being an Adventurer: Motivational Exercises in Creative Writing.** Feryl J. Bergin. (Illus.). 112p. (YA). (gr. 6-12). 1997. pap. 9.95 (0-936955-07-4) Craftsman.

You...& Being an Explorer: Motivational Self-Awareness Activities. Feryl J. Bergin. (Illus.). 112p. (Orig.). (YA). (gr. 6-12). 1991. student ed., per., pap. 8.95 (0-936955-05-8) Eminent Pubns.

You'd Better Believe It! Kenneth D. Barney. LC 75-22608. (Radiant Life Ser.). 125p. 1976. pap. 3.95 (0-88243-887-5, 02-0887); teacher ed., pap. 5.50 (0-88243-161-7, 32-0161) Gospel Pub.

You'd Better Believe It. Bill James. (Detective Colin Harpur Novel Ser.). 158p. pap. 4.95 (0-88150-197-2) Countryman.

You'd Better Come Quietly. Leonard Feeney. LC 79-105011. (Essay Index Reprint Ser.). 1977. 40.95 (0-8369-1569-0) Ayer.

***You'd Better Watch Out.** Scott Adams. (Little Bks.). (J). 1997. 4.95 (0-8362-3739-0) Andrews & McMeel.

You'd Betters: The Rules Writers Break That Keep Them from Getting Published - (And How to Stop!) Carole Marsh. (Lifewrite Ser.). 1994. 29.95 (1-55609-346-2); pap. 19.95 (1-55609-347-0); disk 29.95 (1-55609-600-3) Gallopade Pub Group.

You'd Betters: The Rules Writers Break That Keep Them from Getting Published - (And How to Stop!) Carole Marsh. (Lifewrite Ser.). 1997. ring bd. 39.95 (1-55609-348-9) Gallopade Pub Group.

You'd Never Know It from the Way I Talk: Lectures & Readings. Kenneth H. Brown. LC 90-83801. (Writers-in-Residence Ser.). 88p. 1990. pap. 7.00 (0-912592-29-X) Ashland Poetry.

Youghal & Other Irish Laces. Pat Earnshaw. (Illus.). 36p. 1988. 15.00 (0-9513891-0-6, Pub. by Gorse Pubns UK) Lacis Pubns.

Youghal Lace, the Craft & the Cream. Pat Earnshaw. (Illus.). 48p. 1990. 21.00 (0-9513891-2-2, Pub. by Gorse Pubns UK) Lacis Pubns.

Youghiogheny: Appalachian River. Tim Palmer. LC 84-2301. (Illus.). 350p. 1984. 35.00 (0-8229-3495-7); pap. 19.95 (0-8229-5361-7) U of Pittsburgh Pr.

Youghiogheny River Flip Map. Ron Rathnow. LC 86-12654. (Great American Rivers Flip Map Ser.). (Illus.). 36p. 1987. pap. text ed. 5.95 (0-89732-056-5) Menasha Ridge.

***You'll Be Late!** Ares Torres. (Illus.). 14p. (Orig.). (J). (gr. 2-3). 1995. pap. 3.95 (1-887578-03-X) SpanPr.

You'll Be Surprised What the Lord Can Do. Homer Larsen. Ed. by Connie G. Giles & Francis W. Heatherley. 144p. (Orig.). 1993. pap. 8.95 (0-929488-99-7) Balcony Pub Inc.

***You'll Catch Your Death.** Hugh Hood. 164p. 1992. pap. 12.95 (0-88984-144-6, Pub. by Porcupines Quill CN) Genl Dist Srvs.

You'll Die Next! Harry Whittington. 176p. 1992. pap. 3.95 (0-88184-835-2) Carroll & Graf.

***You'll Die Next!** Henry Whittington. 3.95 (0-7867-0835-2) Carroll & Graf.

You'll Die Today. Marjorie J. Grove. (Mystery Puzzler Ser.: No. 22). (Illus.). (Orig.). 1979. mass mkt. 1.95 (0-685-94562-6, Zebra Kensgtn) Kensgtn Pub Corp.

You'll Never Be Here Again. Mark Blackaby. 320p. 1995. pap. 10.95 (0-575-05897-8, Pub. by V Gollancz UK) Trafalgar.

You'll Never Believe What They Told Me: Trusting God Through Serious Illness. Emily Dockrey & Karen Dockrey. Ed. by LoraBeth Norton. LC 94-4729. (Kids Helping Kids Ser.). 48p. (J). (gr. 3-8). 1994. pap. 4.99 (0-7814-0111-9, Chariot Bks) Chariot Victor.

You'll Never Eat Lunch in This Town Again. Julia Phillips. 656p. 1992. pap. 6.99 (0-451-17072-5, Sig) NAL-Dutton.

You'll Never Get No for an Answer. Jack Carew. 224p. 1990. pap. 14.00 (0-671-73649-3) PB.

You'll Never Guess What We Did in Gym Today! Kenneth G. Tillman & Patricia R. Toner. LC 83-22071. 228p. 1984. 18.95 (0-13-977075-5, Busn) P-H.

***You'll Never Make Love in This Town Again.** 1996. mass mkt. 5.99 (0-7871-1118-X, Dove Bks) Dove Audio.

You'll Never Make Love in this Town Again. Robin & Liza. 256p. 1995. 16.95 (0-7871-0380-2, Dove Bks) Dove Audio.

You'll Never Make Love in This Town Again: The Flip Side to the Pretty Woman Story. Robin et al. 1995. pap. 22.95 (0-7871-0404-3) Dove Audio.

You'll Never Walk Alone: From Carousel. Rodgers & Oscar Hammerstein. 4p. 1987. 3.95 (0-7935-0736-7, 01120241) H Leonard.

You'll Pay for This...All of You! Bill Rechin et al. 1979. pap. 1.95 (0-449-14121-7, GM) Fawcett.

You'll See It When You Believe It. Wayne W. Dyer. 288p. 1990. reprint ed. mass mkt. 6.50 (0-380-70658-X) Avon.

You'll Soon Grow into Them, Titch. Pat Hutchins. LC 82-11755. (Illus.). 32p. (J). (gr. k-3). 1983. lib. bdg. 15.93 (0-688-01771-1) Greenwillow.

You'll Soon Grow into Them, Titch. Pat Hutchins. LC 82-11755. (Illus.). 32p. (J). (ps up). 1992. pap. 4.95 (0-688-11507-1, Mulberry) Morrow.

Youma: The Story of a West Indian Slave. Lafcadio Hearn. LC 74-80890. reprint ed. 45.00 (0-404-03208-7) AMS Pr.

Youma: The Story of a West Indian Slave. Lafcadio Hearn. (BCL1-PS American Literature Ser.). 193p. 1992. reprint ed. lib. bdg. 69.00 (0-7812-6737-4) Rprt Serv.

Youn Hee & Me. C. S. Adler. LC 94-31060. 192p. (J). (gr. 3-7). 1995. 11.00 (0-15-200073-9); pap. 5.00 (0-15-200376-2) HarBrace.

Young: Our Young Family in America. Edward H. Young. (Illus.). 315p. 1992. reprint ed. pap. 48.00 (0-8328-6588-5); reprint ed. lib. bdg. 58.00 (0-8328-2209-4) Higginson Bk Co.

Young: Robert John Young & Daisie Frances Denton; Ancestral Notes & Some Descendants. R. M. Young-Widdifield. (Illus.). 194p. 1991. reprint ed. pap. 31.00 (0-685-47723-1); reprint ed. lib. bdg. 41.00 (0-685-38995-2) Higginson Bk Co.

Young Abe Lincoln. Harness. (J). 1996. 16.00 (0-689-80184-X, S&S Bks Young Read) S&S Childrens.

Young Abe Lincoln: The Frontier Days, 1809-1837. Cheryl Harness. LC 95-43143. (Illus.). 32p. (J). (gr. 3-6). 1996. 15.95 (0-7922-2713-1) Natl Geog.

Young Abe Lincoln - His Teenage Years in Indiana. W. Fred Conway. (Illus.). 136p. (Orig.). 1992. pap. 9.95 (0-925165-09-3) Fire Buff Hse.

Young Abigail Adams. Francene Sabin. LC 91-17112. (Illus.). 48p. (J). (gr. 4-6). 1992. lib. bdg. 12.95 (0-8167-2503-9) Troll Communs.

Young Abigail Adams. Francene Sabin. LC 91-17112. (Illus.). 48p. (J). (gr. 4-6). 1996. pap. 3.95 (0-8167-2504-7) Troll Communs.

Young Abolitionists: Or, Conversations on Slavery. J. Elizabeth Jones. LC 75-138339. (Black Heritage Library Collection). 1977. 15.95 (0-8369-8731-4) Ayer.

Young Abraham Lincoln, Log-Cabin President. Andrew Woods. LC 91-26570. (Illus.). 32p. (J). (gr. k-2). 1992. pap. 3.50 (0-8167-2533-0) Troll Communs.

Young Acrobat. Horatio Alger, Jr. (Works of Horatio Alger Jr.). 1989. reprint ed. lib. bdg. 79.00 (0-7812-3622-3) Rprt Serv.

Young Actor's Workbook. Judith R. Seto. LC 83-49383. 360p. 1984. pap. 11.95 (0-8021-5082-9, Grove) Grove-Atltic.

Young Adam. rev. ed. Alexander Trocchi. 208p. (Orig.). 1991. mass mkt. 4.95 (1-878320-63-7) Masquerade.

***Young Adam.** Alexander Trocchi. 152p. 1996. reprint ed. pap. 14.95 (0-86241-624-8, Pub. by Rebel UK) AK Pr Dist.

Young Adolescent. Peter Blos. LC 73-125597. 1974. pap. 14.95 (0-02-904300-X, Free Press) Free Pr.

Young Adolescent Development & School Practices: Promoting Harmony. David B. Strahan. 48p. 1988. 8.00 (1-56090-037-7) Natl Middle Schl.

Young Adolf. Beryl Bainbridge. 208p. 1995. pap. 9.95 (0-7867-0258-3) Carroll & Graf.

Young Adult: Development After Adolescence. Gene Bocknek. LC 85-29202. 232p. 1986. pap. 19.95 (0-89876-129-8) Gardner Pr.

Young Adult & Intellectual Freedom: Proceedings of the University of Wisconsin, Madison Conference, Wisconsin, June 14-18, 1976. University of Wisconsin, Madison Conference Staff. Ed. by Mary L. Woodworth. 228p. 1977. pap. 5.00 (0-936442-05-0) U Wis Sch Lib.

***Young Adult Authors.** Jack D. Zipes. (Education Reference Ser.). 300p. Date not set. text ed. 40.00 (0-8153-0650-4) Garland.

Young Adult Book Review Index, 1987. 87th ed. Ed. by Barbara Beach. 1988. 103.00 (0-8103-4373-8) Gale.

Young Adult Catalog of the Boston Public Library. Boston Public Library Staff. 1994. 245.00 (0-7838-2283-9) G K Hall.

Young Adult Chronic Patient. Ed. by Bert Pepper & Hilary Ryglewicz. LC 81-48483. (New Directions for Mental Health Services Ser.: No. MHS 14). 1982. pap. 19.00 (0-87589-908-0) Jossey-Bass.

Young Adult Fiction by African American Writers, 1968-1993 + A Critical & Annotated Guide. Ed. by Deborah Kutenplon & Ellen Olmstead. LC 95-20051. (Illus.). 432p. 1995. text ed. 60.00 (0-8153-0873-6) Garland.

Young Adult Librarian's Knowledge of & Attitudes about Sex. Susan Steinfirst. LC 88-39488. (VOYA Occasional Papers). (Illus.). 61p. 1989. pap. 12.50 (0-8108-2185-0) Scarecrow.

Young Adult Literature: The Heart of the Middle School Curriculum. Lois Stover. LC 96-9687. (Orig.). 1996. pap. text ed. 19.50 (0-86709-376-5, 376) Boynton Cook Pubs.

Young Adult Literature & Nonprint Materials: Resources for Selection. Millicent Lenz & Mary Meachem. LC 94-13774. 1994. 37.50 (0-8108-2906-1) Scarecrow.

Young Adult Ministry. Terry Hershey. 274p. (Orig.). 1986. pap. 14.99 (0-931529-08-5) Group Pub.

Young Adult Piano Course, Bk. 1. John Brimhall. (Piano Course Ser.). 32p. (Orig.). 1985. pap. text ed. 4.95 (0-8494-1356-7, T561) Hansen Ed Mus.

Young Adult Piano Course, Bk. 2. John Brimhall. (Piano Course Ser.). 32p. (Orig.). 1984. pap. text ed. 4.95 (0-8494-1357-5, T562) Hansen Ed Mus.

Young Adult Program Idea Booklet. WLA, Youth Services Section Staff. 1991. 11.00 (0-614-04668-8) Wisc Lib Assn.

Young Adult Reader's Adviser, 2 vols., 1. 1702p. 1992. write for info. (0-8352-3069-4) Bowker.

Young Adult Reader's Adviser, 2 vols., 2. 1702p. 1992. write for info. (0-8352-3070-8) Bowker.

Young Adult Reader's Adviser, 2 vols., Set. 1702p. 1992. 79.95 (0-8352-3068-6) Bowker.

Young Adult Reading Activities Library, 6 bks. Berry & Morris. Incl. Biography & Autobiography. 1992. 16.95 (0-87628-190-0); Modern Realistic Fiction. 1992. pap. 101.70 (0-87628-993-6); Historical Fiction. 1992. 16.95 (0-87628-585-X); Science Fiction & Fantasy. 1992. 16.95 (0-87628-856-5); Mystery & Suspense. 1992. 16.95 (0-87628-603-1); Nonfiction. 1992. 16.95 (0-87628-612-0); 101.70 (0-87628-393-8) Ctr Appl Res.

Young Adult Services in the Small Library. Lesley S. Farmer. (Small Library Publications: No. 20). 12p. (Orig.). 1992. pap. text ed. 5.00 (0-8389-5749-8) ALA.

Young Adults. Daniel M. Pinkwater. (Illus.). 192p. (Orig.). 1991. mass mkt. 3.99 (0-8125-1519-6) Tor Bks.

Young Adults: A Call to Dialogue. L. June Montgomery. LC 79-92088. 1980. 12.00 (0-87212-112-7) Libra.

Young Adults: Self Perceptions & Life Contexts. Glen Evans & Millicent E. Poole. 326p. 1991. 75.00 (1-85000-938-4, Falmer Pr); pap. 31.00 (1-85000-939-2, Falmer Pr) Taylor & Francis.

Young Adults with Special Needs: Assessment, Law & Practice - Caught in the Act. John Friel. LC 95-5882. 140p. 1995. pap. 24.95 (1-85302-231-4) Taylor & Francis.

Young African American. Date not set. pap. 19.95 (0-525-45275-3) NAL-Dutton.

Young Again! Roy A. Alterwein. (Illus.). 308p. (Orig.). 1994. pap. 11.95 (0-9640992-0-9) Med Hlth Pub.

***Young Again! How to Reverse the Aging Process.** John Thomas. Ed. by Elizabeth Beryl. (Illus.). 384p. (Orig.). 1994. pap. 19.95 (1-884757-77-4) Plexus Pr.

Young Again! How to Reverse the Aging Process. 3rd rev. ed. John Thomas. Ed. by Elizabeth Beryl. (Illus.). 384p. (Orig.). 1995. pap. 19.95 (1-884757-76-6) Plexus Pr.

Young Alaskans. Emerson Hough. 1976. lib. bdg. 14.25 (0-89968-049-6, Lghtyr Pr) Buccaneer Bks.

Young Alaskans in the Rockies. Emerson Hough. 1976. lib. bdg. 15.25 (0-89968-050-X, Lghtyr Pr) Buccaneer Bks.

Young Albert Einstein. Laurence Santrey. LC 89-33940. (Illus.). 48p. (J). (gr. 4-6). 1990. pap. 3.95 (0-8167-1778-8); lib. bdg. 12.95 (0-8167-1777-X) Troll Communs.

Young Amelia Earhart: A Dream to Fly. Sarah Alcott. LC 91-24974. (Illus.). 32p. (J). (gr. k-2). 1992. pap. 3.50 (0-8167-2529-2) Troll Communs.

Young America. Fitz-Greene Halleck. (Notable American Authors Ser.). 1992. reprint ed. lib. bdg. 75.00 (0-7812-2993-6) Rprt Serv.

***Young America: A Folk Art History.** Lipman et al. (Illus.). 200p. 29.98 (0-8317-6231-4) Smithmark.

Young America: A Newspaper Published at Delafield Waukesha County, Wisconsin 1859-1860. Ed. by Nelson C. Hawks. 43p. 1984. pap. 5.00 (0-9613121-0-6) Hawks Inn Hist Soc.

***Young America: A Selection of Paintings from the Collection of the Penn. Academy of the Fine Arts.** Louise W. Lippincott & Richard J. Boyle. (Illus.). 80p. (Orig.). 1975. pap. 12.95 (*0-614-30568-3*) Penn Acad Art.

Young American Photography. Ed. by Gary Wolfson. LC 74-13172. (Illus.). 108p. 1976. pap. 9.95 (*0-912810-17-3*) Lustrum Pr.

Young American Writers. Ed. by Richard Kostelanetz. LC 67-28160. 1978. reprint ed. 30.00 (*0-932360-05-X*); reprint ed. pap. 15.00 (*0-932360-04-1*) Archae Edns.

***Young Americans: New American Art in the Saatchi Collection.** (Illus.). 111p. 1996. pap. 29.95 (*0-9527453-0-5*) D A Pub.

Young & Ardent Eye: The Story of Minnie Bullack McFarland. Minnie B. McFarland & Afton S. Olsen. 106p. (Orig.). pap. text ed. 25.00 (*0-9629578-6-0*) Intl Long WA.

Young & Dangerous. Gwyneth Boswell. 184p. 1996. 55.95 (*1-85972-191-5*, Pub. by Avebury Pub UK) Ashgate Pub Co.

Young & Evil. Charles H. Ford. 1996. reprint ed. pap. 12.95 (*1-56333-431-3*, R Kasak Bks) Masquerade.

Young & Evil: Homosexuality. Charles Ford & Parker Tyler. LC 75-12351. 1975. reprint ed. 22.95 (*0-405-07392-5*) Ayer.

Young & Fair. N. Richard Nash. 1948. pap. 5.25 (*0-8222-1289-7*) Dramatists Play.

Young & Homeless in Hollywood: Mapping Social Identities. Susan M. Ruddick. LC 94-21839. 256p. (C). (gr. 13). 1995. pap. 17.95 (*0-415-91031-5*, B3865, Routledge NY) Routledge.

Young & Old Serving Together: Meeting Community Needs Through Intergenerational Partnerships. Tess Scannell & Angela Roberts. 15.00 (*0-87868-566-9*) Child Welfare.

Young & Old Together. Carol Seefeldt & Barbara Warman. LC 90-61183. 88p. 1990. pap. 7.00 (*0-935989-34-X*, NAEYC #347) Natl Assn Child Ed.

Young & Rubicam Traveling Creative Workshop. Hanley Norins. 352p. 1989. 29.95 (*0-13-973116-4*) P-H.

Young & the Restless: Most Memorable Moments. Mary Cassata. (Illus.). 288p. 1996. 29.95 (*1-881649-87-3*) Genl Pub Grp.

Young Art & Old Hector. Neil Gunn. 255p. 1991. 21.95 (*0-8027-1177-4*) Walker & Co.

***Young Arthur.** Robert D. San Souci. LC 96-27248. (Illus.). (J). 1997. write for info. (*0-385-32268-2*, DD Bks Yng Read) BDD Bks Young Read.

Young Arthur Ashe: Brave Champion. Ed. by Robin Dexter. LC 95-10021. (First-Start Biography Ser.). (Illus.). 32p. (J). (gr. k-2). 1995. lib. bdg. 12.95 (*0-8167-3772-X*) Troll Communs.

Young Arthur Ashe: Brave Champion. Ed. by Robin Dexter. LC 95-10021. (First-Start Biography Ser.). (Illus.). 32p. (J). (ps-2). 1996. pap. 3.50 (*0-8167-3773-8*) Troll Communs.

Young Artist. Thomas Locker. (Illus.). 32p. (J). 1993. pap. 4.99 (*0-14-054923-4*, Puff Pied Piper) Puffin Bks.

Young Artists Painting Pack. (Illus.). (J). (gr. 3-6). 1992. pap. 7.95 (*1-56680-501-5*) Mad Hatter Pub.

Young Astronauts, No. 2. Rick North. (J). 1990. mass mkt. 2.95 (*0-8217-3173-4*, Zebra Kensgtn) Kensgtn Pub Corp.

Young Astronomer. S. Snowden. (Hobby Guides Ser.). (Illus.). 32p. (YA). (gr. 5-10). 1983. pap. 6.95 (*0-86020-651-3*); lib. bdg. 14.95 (*0-88110-028-5*) EDC.

Young at Art: (Twenty Drawing Lessons) Jane H. Stroschin. 100p. 1992. spiral bd. 9.00 (*1-883960-10-X*) Henry Quill.

Young at Eighty: The Prolific Public Life of Michael Young. Ed. by Dench et al. 256p. (Orig.). 1996. 35.00 (*1-85754-243-6*, Pub. by Carcanet Pr UK) Paul & Co Pubs.

Young at Heart: Computing for Seniors. Mary Furlong & Stefan B. Lipson. 320p. 1996. pap. text ed. 22.95 (*0-07-882178-9*) McGraw.

***Young at Heart: Johnny Kelley.** Fred Lewis. 208p. 1992. 16.95 (*0-915297-18-3*) Cedarwinds.

Young Athletes: Biological, Psychological, & Educational Perspectives. Ed. by Robert M. Malina. (Illus.). 312p. 1988. text ed. 40.00 (*0-87322-173-7*, BMAL0173) Human Kinetics.

Young Athletes: The Purple Heart - Sports Story for Athletes. (J). 1988. 32.00 (*0-614-14680-1*) Jones.

Young Athletes: The Purple Heart - Sports Story for Athletes. (J). (gr. 1-8). 1988. pap. 28.00 (*0-614-14681-X*) Jones.

Young Author's Do-It-Yourself Book: How to Write, Illustrate, & Produce Your Own Book. Donna Guthrie et al. LC 93-9736. (Illus.). 64p. (J). (gr. 2-4). 1994. lib. bdg. 16.40 (*1-56294-350-2*) Millbrook Pr.

Young Author's Do-It-Yourself Book: How to Write, Illustrate, & Produce Your Own Book. Donna Guthrie. 64p. (J). (gr. 2-4). 1994. pap. 7.95 (*1-56294-723-0*) Millbrook Pr.

Young Authors Guide to Publishers. rev. ed. (Illus.). 1995. pap. 8.95 (*1-884825-20-6*) Raspberry Pubns.

Young Ball Player's Guide to Safe Pitching: Ages Eight Thru Adult with Conditioning, Strengthening. William J. Maitland. (Illus.). 140p. (YA). (gr. 3 up). 1994. pap. 14.95 (*0-936759-14-3*) Maitland Enter.

Young Bank Messenger. Horatio Alger, Jr. (Works of Horatio Alger Jr.). 1989. reprint ed. lib. bdg. 79.00 (*0-7812-3623-1*) Rprt Serv.

Young Basketball Player. Chris Mullen. (Illus.). 48p. (J). 1995. 15.95 (*0-7894-0220-3*, 5-70633) DK Pub Inc.

Young Beginner, Vol. 1. Julianne Dent & Kathleen Bauer. 57p. (J). (gr. k-3). 1992. wbk. ed. 5.00 (*1-881986-00-4*) Demibach Eds.

Young Beginner, Vol. 1. Julianne Dent et al. 23p. (J). (gr. k-3). 1992. suppl. ed. 5.00 (*1-881986-04-7*) Demibach Eds.

Young Beginner, Vol. 2. Julianne Dent & Kathleen Bauer. 23p. (J). (gr. k-3). 1993. suppl. ed. 5.00 (*1-881986-05-5*) Demibach Eds.

Young Beginner, Vol. 2. Julianne Dent & Kathleen Bauer. 57p. (J). (gr. k-3). 1992. wbk. ed. 5.00 (*1-881986-01-2*) Demibach Eds.

Young Beginner, Vol. 3. Julianne Dent & Kathleen Bauer. 57p. (J). (gr. k-3). 1992. wbk. ed. 5.00 (*1-881986-02-0*) Demibach Eds.

Young Ben Franklin. Laurence Santrey. LC 81-23067. (Illus.). 48p. (J). (gr. 4-6). 1982. lib. bdg. 12.95 (*0-89375-768-3*) Troll Communs.

Young Ben Franklin. Laurence Santrey. LC 81-23067. (Illus.). 48p. (J). (gr. 4-6). 1996. pap. 3.95 (*0-89375-769-1*) Troll Communs.

Young Bess. large type ed. Margaret E. Irwin. (Shadows of the Crown Ser.). 1974. 25.99 (*0-85456-638-4*) Ulverscroft.

***Young, Black, & Determined: A Biography of Lorraine Hansberry.** Patricia C. McKissack. LC 97-2084. (Illus.). 160p. (YA). 1997. pap. 18.95 (*0-8234-1300-4*) Holiday.

Young, Black & Male in America: An Endangered Species. Ed. by Jewelle T. Gibbs. LC 87-19340. 410p. 1988. text ed. 55.00 (*0-86569-169-X*, Auburn Hse); pap. text ed. 19.95 (*0-86569-180-0*, Auburn Hse) Greenwood.

Young Black Beauty. Aurand Harris. (Orig.). (J). (gr. k-6). 1996. pap. 5.50 (*0-87602-338-3*) Anchorage.

Young Black Stallion. Walter Farley & Steven Farley. LC 89-42763. (Black Stallion Bks.). 192p. (J). (gr. 5-9). 1989. 10.95 (*0-394-84562-5*) Random Bks Yng Read.

Young Black Stallion. Walter Farley. pap. 2.99 (*0-517-11121-7*) Random Hse Value.

Young Bleys. Gordon R. Dickson. 448p. 1992. mass mkt. 5.99 (*0-8125-0947-1*) Tor Bks.

Young Blood. Ed. by Mike Baker. 352p. 1994. mass mkt. 4.50 (*0-8217-4498-4*, Zebra Kensgtn) Kensgtn Pub Corp.

Young Blood: Juvenile Justice & the Death Penalty. Ed. by Shirley Dicks. LC 95-6336. 295p. 1995. 25.95 (*0-87975-953-4*) Prometheus Bks.

Young Boatman of Pine Point. Horatio Alger, Jr. (Works of Horatio Alger Jr.). 1989. reprint ed. lib. bdg. 79.00 (*0-7812-3624-X*) Rprt Serv.

Young Book Agent. Horatio Alger, Jr. (Works of Horatio Alger Jr.). 1989. reprint ed. lib. bdg. 79.00 (*0-685-27530-2*) Rprt Serv.

Young Boswell. Chauncey B. Tinker. LC 71-131850. 1970. reprint ed. 13.00 (*0-403-00737-2*) Scholarly.

Young Boswell: Chapters on James Bosewell, the Biographer. Chauncey B. Tinker. (BCL1-PR English Literature Ser.). 266p. 1992. reprint ed. lib. bdg. 79.00 (*0-7812-7322-6*) Rprt Serv.

Young Brecht. Hanns O. Munsterer. (Illus.). 220p. 35.00 (*1-870352-73-4*, Pub. by Libris UK) Paul & Co Pubs.

Young Brer Rabbit: And other Trickster Tales of the Americas. Jacqueline S. Weiss. (Illus.). 72p. 1987. audio 8.95 (*0-88045-104-1*) Stemmer Hse.

Young Brer Rabbit: And other Trickster Tales of the Americas. Jacqueline S. Weiss. (Illus.). 72p. 1987. pap. 9.95 (*0-88045-138-6*); pap. 21.90 (*0-88045-105-X*) Stemmer Hse.

Young Brer Rabbit & Other Trickster Tales from the Americas. Jaqueline S. Weiss. (Illus.). 80p. (J). (gr. 3-7). 1985. 14.95 (*0-88045-037-1*) Stemmer Hse.

Young Britain. Euromonitor Staff. (C). 1989. 4,790.00 (*0-685-37357-6*, Pub. by Euromonitor Pubns UK) Gale.

***Young Britain.** Rutherford. 1997. pap. 19.50 (*0-85315-845-2*) NYU Pr.

Young, British & Black: A Monograph on the Work of Sankofa Film-Video Collective & Black Audio Film Collective. Coco Fusco. (Illus.). 64p. (Orig.). 1988. pap. 4.00 (*0-936739-15-0*) Hallwalls Inc.

Young Brothers Massacre. Paul W. Barrett & Mary H. Barrett. LC 87-19156. (Illus.). 160p. (Orig.). 1988. pap. 14.95 (*0-8262-0650-6*) U of Mo Pr.

Young Bussey, Young Stud: An All-American Legend. Ralph B. Cushman. 248p. 1993. 22.95 (*0-9637761-0-X*) Bigco Pr.

***Young Calvin.** Ganoczy. 49.95 (*0-567-09486-3*, Pub. by T & T Clark UK) Bks Intl VA.

Young Calvin in Paris: Or, the Scholar & the Cripple. William W. Blackburn. LC 83-45602. reprint ed. 40.00 (*0-404-19869-4*) AMS Pr.

Young Cam Jansen & the Dinosaur Game. David A. Adler. LC 95-46463. (Viking Easy-to-Read Ser.). (Illus.). 32p. (J). (gr. k-3). 1996. pap. 11.99 (*0-670-86399-8*, Viking) Viking Child Bks.

***Young Cam Jansen & the Lost Tooth.** David A. Adler. LC 96-47357. (Viking Easy-To-Read Ser.). (Illus.). (J). 1997. pap. 11.99 (*0-670-87354-3*) Viking Penguin.

Young Cam Jansen & the Missing Cookie. David A. Adler. LC 95-46462. (Viking Easy-to-Read Ser.). (Illus.). 32p. (J). (gr. k-3). 1996. pap. 11.99 (*0-670-86772-1*, Viking) Viking Child Bks.

Young Captain Jack. Horatio Alger, Jr. (Works of Horatio Alger Jr.). 1989. reprint ed. lib. bdg. 79.00 (*0-7812-3626-6*) Rprt Serv.

Young Carl Jung. Robert W. Brockway. LC 96-25223. (Illus.). 180p. 1996. pap. 17.95 (*1-888602-01-5*, 015) Chiron Pubns.

Young Cartoonist. Judy Tatchell & C. Evans. (Young Artist Ser.). 72p. (YA). (gr. 5 up). 1987. pap. 8.95 (*0-7460-0083-9*) EDC.

***Young Champions.** Peter Regan. Date not set. pap. 8.95 (*0-947962-92-1*) Dufour.

Young Charles Lamb, 1775-1802. Winifred F. Courtney. (Gotham Library). (Illus.). 412p. (C). 1983. reprint ed. pap. text ed. 16.00 (*0-8147-1388-2*) NYU Pr.

Young Chef's Nutrition Guide & Cookbook. Carolyn E. Moore et al. LC 89-18218. 224p. 1990. spiral bd. 13.95 (*0-8120-5789-9*) Barron.

Young Chemists & Great Discoveries. James Kendall. LC 76-76907. (Essay Index Reprint Ser.). 1977. 21.95 (*0-8369-0023-5*) Ayer.

Young Chidren: Growing & Learning Together. Elisabeth Nichols. (Orig.). 1990. pap. text ed. 3.95 (*0-935493-37-9*) Programs Educ.

Young Child: Development from Prebirth Through Age Eight. 2nd rev. ed. Janet K. Black & Margaret B. Puckett. LC 95-8646. 1995. pap. text ed. 46.00 (*0-02-310241-1*, Macmillan Coll) P-H.

Young Child: Learning with Understanding. Rosemary Althouse. LC 81-4600. (Illus.). 283p. 1981. reprint ed. pap. 80.70 (*0-7837-8944-0*, 2049655) Bks Demand.

Young Child: Reviews of Research, Vol. 3. Ed. by Catherine R. Cooper. LC 67-24993. 304p. (Orig.). 1982. pap. text ed. 5.00 (*0-912674-78-4*, NAEYC #206) Natl Assn Child Ed.

***Young Child & Music: Contemporary Principles in Child Development & Music Education: Proceedings of the Music in Early Childhood Conference, Brigham Young University, June 28-30, 1984, Provo, Utah.** Music in Early Childhood Conference Staff. Ed. by Jacquelyn Boswell. LC 85-226520. (Illus.). 128p. 1985. reprint ed. pap. 36.50 (*0-608-04214-5*, 2064955) Bks Demand.

Young Child As Person: Toward the Development of Healthy Conscience. Martha Snyder et al. LC 79-15779. 239p. 1980. 32.95 (*0-87705-466-5*); pap. 16.95 (*0-89885-226-9*) Human Sci Pr.

Young Child As Scientist: A Constructive Approach to Early Childhood Science Education. 2nd ed. Christine Chaille & Lory Britain. LC 96-20745. (C). 1997. text ed. 27.95 (*0-673-99091-5*) Longman.

Young Child at Play: Reviews of Research, Vol. 4. Ed. by Greta Fein & Mary Rivkin. LC 67-24993. 230p. 1986. pap. text ed. 8.00 (*0-935989-02-1*, NAEYC 320) Natl Assn Child Ed.

Young Child in the Home: A Survey of Three Thousand American Families. White House Conference on Child Health & Protection Staff. LC 71-169371. (Family in America Ser.). 446p. 1977. reprint ed. 33.95 (*0-405-03847-X*) Ayer.

Young Child, Old Spirit: A Preschool Chemical Dependency Curriculum. Phyllis W. Gough. 119p. 1990. student ed. 85.00 (*1-881949-01-X*) MN Ind Wom Res.

Young Child with Down Syndrome. Siegfried M. Pueschel. 371p. 1984. 45.95 (*0-89885-120-3*) Human Sci Pr.

Young Children: Active Learners in a Technological Age. Daniel D. Shade. LC 94-68838. (Illus.). 196p. (Orig.). 1994. pap. text ed. 7.00 (*0-935989-63-3*, 341) Natl Assn Child Ed.

Young Children: An Introduction to Early Childhood Education. Stephen B. Graves et al. LC 94-38891. 500p. (C). 1996. text ed. 49.25 (*0-314-04466-3*) West Pub.

Young Children & Computers. Charles Hohmann. LC 89-26703. (Illus.). 128p. (Orig.). 1990. pap. text ed. 15.95 (*0-931114-24-1*) High-Scope.

Young Children & Picture Books: Literature from Infancy to Six. Mary R. Jalongo. LC 88-62969. 119p. 1988. pap. 10.00 (*0-935989-17-X*, NAEYC #160) Natl Assn Child Ed.

Young Children & Social Policy. Ed. by William M. Bridgeland & Edward A. Duane. (Annals of the American Academy of Political & Social Science Ser.: Vol. 461). (Illus.). 224p. 1982. 26.00 (*0-8039-1831-3*); pap. 17.00 (*0-8039-1832-1*) Sage.

***Young Children & Spirituality.** Barbara K. Myers. LC 96-45442. (C). 1996. pap. 17.95 (*0-415-91655-0*, Routledge NY); text ed. 59.95 (*0-415-91654-2*, Routledge NY) Routledge.

Young Children & Their Drawings. Joseph DiLeo. 384p. 1996. pap. text ed. 29.95 (*0-87630-833-7*) Brunner-Mazel.

Young Children & Worship. Sonja M. Stewart & Jerome W. Berryman. LC 88-17766. 176p. 1988. pap. 23.00 (*0-664-25040-8*, Westminster) Westminster John Knox.

Young Children at Home & in School: 212 Educational Activities for Their Parents, Teachers, & Caregivers. Philip S. Morse & Lillian B. Brand. 1995. pap. 17.00 (*0-205-15420-4*) Allyn.

Young Children Continue to Reinvent Arithmetic, 2nd Grade: Implications of Piaget's Theory. Constance Kamii & Linda Joseph. (Early Childhood Education Ser.: No. 24). 224p. 1989. text ed. 30.00 (*0-8077-2958-2*); pap. text ed. 17.95 (*0-8077-2957-4*) Tchrs Coll.

Young Children Grow Up: Effects of the Perry Preschool Program on Youths Through Age 15. D. P. Weikart & Lawrence J. Schweinhart. LC 80-26061. (Monographs of the High/Scope Educational Research Foundation: No. 7). 110p. (Orig.). 1980. pap. 12.95 (*0-931114-08-X*) High-Scope.

Young Children in a Computerized Environment. Ed. by Mary Frank. LC 81-20028. (Journal of Children in Contemporary Society: Vol. 14, No. 1). 96p. 1981. text ed. 32.95 (*0-86656-108-0*) Haworth Pr.

Young Children in Action. Mary Hohmann et al. Ed. by Charles Silverman. LC 83-13030. (Illus.). 336p. (Orig.). 1979. pap. 29.95 (*0-931114-05-5*) High-Scope.

Young Children in China. Rita Liljestrom et al. 262p. 1984. 79.00 (*0-905028-30-9*, Pub. by Multilingual Matters UK); pap. 29.95 (*0-905028-29-5*, Pub. by Multilingual Matters UK) Taylor & Francis.

Young Children in Family Therapy. Joan J. Zilbach. LC 94-31261. 196p. 1995. pap. 25.00 (*1-56821-399-9*) Aronson.

Young Children in Poverty: An Annotated Bibliography of Books & Reports, 1995. Carole Oshinsky. 80p. (Orig.). 1995. pap. text ed. 12.00 (*0-926582-15-1*) NCCP.

Young Children Learning. Barbara Tizard & Martin Hughes. 288p. 1985. 26.50 (*0-674-96595-7*) HUP.

Young Children, Parents & Profesionals. Henry. 232p. (C). 1996. pap. 18.95 (*0-415-12832-3*); text ed. 65.00 (*0-415-12831-5*) Routledge.

Young Children Rap to Learn about Famous African-Americans. Chris Meissel. Ed. by Jan Keeling. (Illus.). 80p. (Orig.). (J). 1993. pap. text ed. 9.95 (*0-86530-265-0*) Incentive Pubns.

Young Children Reinvent Arithmetic: Implications of Piaget's Theory. Constance Kamii. (Early Childhood Education Ser.). 269p. (C). 1984. text ed. 30.00 (*0-8077-2759-8*); pap. text ed. 18.95 (*0-8077-2707-5*) Tchrs Coll.

Young Children Reinvent Arithmetic, Third Grade: Implications of Piaget's Theory. Constance Kamil & Sally Jones-Livingston. LC 93-43026. (Early Childhood Education Ser.). 240p. (C). 1994. text ed. 39.00 (*0-8077-3324-5*); pap. text ed. 17.95 (*0-8077-3323-7*) Tchrs Coll.

***Young Children Sing.** Date not set. write for info. (*0-88207-454-7*, Chariot Bks) Chariot Victor.

Young Children with Special Needs. 2nd ed. Fallen. 1990. text ed. 79.00 (*0-675-20400-3*, Merrill Coll) P-H.

***Young Children with Special Needs.** 3rd ed. Umansky & Stephen Hooper. LC 97-24506. (C). 1997. text ed. 56.00 (*0-13-612052-0*) P-H.

Young Children's Close Relationships: Beyond Attachment. Judy Dunn. (Individual Differences & Development Ser.: Vol. 4). (Illus.). 160p. (C). 1993. text ed. 45.00 (*0-8039-4490-X*); pap. text ed. 19.95 (*0-8039-4491-8*) Sage.

Young Children's Dyadic Pretend Play: A Communication Analysis of Plot Structure & Plot Generative Strategies. Ursula V. Schwartz. LC 91-6488. (Pragmatics & Beyond Ser.: Vol. 14). vi, 151p. 1991. 44.00 (*1-55619-280-0*) Benjamins North Am.

Young Children's Encyclopedia. Ed. by Howard L. Goodkind. (Illus.). 2560p. (J). (ps-3). 1988. 149.50 (*0-85229-478-6*) Ency Brit Inc.

Young Children's Knowledge about Thinking. Ed. by John H. Flavell et al. (Monographs of the Society for Research in Child Development, Serial No. 243: No. 243, Vol. 60, No. 1, 1995). 128p. 1995. pap. text ed. 15.00 (*0-226-25323-6*) U Ch Pr.

Young Children's Knowledge of Relational Terms. L. A. French & K. Nelson. (Language & Communication Ser.: Vol. 19). (Illus.). 160p. 1985. 92.95 (*0-387-96164-X*) Spr-Verlag.

***Young Children's Talent Education & Its Method.** Shinichi Suzuki. 72p. 1996. pap. text ed. 19.95 (*0-87487-770-9*) Summy-Birchard.

Young Children's Thinking: Studies of Some Aspects of Piaget's Theory. Millie C. Almy et al. LC 66-16091. (Illus.). 168p. reprint ed. pap. 47.90 (*0-317-10467-5*, 2013176) Bks Demand.

Young Children's Understanding of Pretense. Paul L. Harris & Robert D. Kavanaugh. (Monographs of the Society for Research in Child Development: No. 231, Vol. 58, No. 1). 116p. (C). 1993. pap. text ed. 15.00 (*0-226-31736-6*) U Ch Pr.

Young Child's Busy Book: Of Playing, Learning, Stories & Rhymes. Margaret Carter. LC 92-53094. (Illus.). 96p. (J). (ps). 1992. 14.95 (*1-85697-822-2*, Kingfisher LKC) LKC.

Young Christian. M. Henry. (J). 1995. 5.99 (*0-906731-56-9*, Pub. by Christian Focus UK) Spring Arbor Dist.

Young Christian Observes the Law. Albert H. Shuster et al. Ed. by William H. Cooper. LC 83-80868. (Illus.). 106p. (J). (gr. 4-8). 1983. pap. text ed. 6.27 (*0-914127-02-0*) Univ Class.

Young Christian's Puzzle Book: For Becoming a Grown-Up Christian. Linda Faulkner. (Illus.). 40p. (J). (gr. 5-7). 1992. pap. 3.50 (*0-88243-828-X*, 02-0828) Gospel Pub.

Young Christopher Columbus: Discoverer of the New Worlds. Eric Carpenter. LC 91-24975. (Illus.). 32p. (J). (gr. k-2). 1996. pap. 3.50 (*0-8167-2527-6*) Troll Communs.

Young Churchill. Celia Sandys. Date not set. pap. 14.95 (*0-452-27550-4*, Plume) NAL-Dutton.

Young Circus Rider. Horatio Alger, Jr. (Works of Horatio Alger Jr.). 1989. reprint ed. lib. bdg. 79.00 (*0-7812-3627-4*) Rprt Serv.

Young Citizen Observes the Law. Albert H. Shuster & Russell R. Miller. Ed. by William H. Cooper. LC 83-80867. (Illus.). 93p. (J). (gr. 4-8). 1983. teacher ed. 4.27 (*0-914127-59-4*); pap. text ed. 4.27 (*0-914127-03-9*) Univ Class.

***Young Citizens of World, Vol. 1.** Zevin. Date not set. pap. text ed. write for info. (*0-312-11214-9*) St Martin.

Young Clara Barton: Battlefield Nurse. Sarah Alcott. LC 95-8110. (First-Start Biography Ser.). (Illus.). 32p. (J). (gr. k-2). 1995. pap. text ed. 3.50 (*0-8167-3767-3*); lib. bdg. 12.95 (*0-8167-3766-5*) Troll Communs.

Young Claudia. large type ed. Rose Franken. 428p. 1982. 25.99 (*0-7089-0819-5*) Ulverscroft.

Young Claus: The Legend of the Boy Who Became Santa. J. Michael Sims. 112p. (J). (ps-3). 1995. 12.95 (*0-9645976-6-7*) Cygnet Trumpeter.

Young Colonel from Virginia. Jane Lipsomb. LC 92-64468. 64p. 1993. pap. 8.00 (*1-56002-199-3*, Univ Edtns) Aegina Pr.

Young Community Leaders of America. 2nd ed. Ed. by J. M. Evans. LC 68-5856. 500p. 1987. 47.50 (*0-934544-40-9*) Am Biog Inst.

Young Consumers. 2nd ed. Linda Riekes. Ed. by Sally M. Ackerly. (Law in Action Ser.). (Illus.). 124p. (J). (gr. 5-9). 1980. pap. text ed. 26.75 (*0-8299-1021-2*); teacher ed., pap. text ed. 26.75 (*0-8299-1022-0*) West Pub.

Young Cowboy. Will James. 1993. reprint ed. lib. bdg. 21.95 (*1-56849-173-5*) Buccaneer Bks.

Young Curmudgeon. large type ed. Leslie Lance. 352p. 1987. 25.99 (*0-7089-1686-4*) Ulverscroft.

Young Cushing in Oklahoma Territory. Laura L. Wells. LC 85-70034. (Illus.). 221p. 1985. reprint ed. 15.95 (*0-934188-15-7*) Evans Pubns.

An Asterisk (*) at the beginning of an entry indicates that the title is appearing in BIP for the first time.

Young Dancer. Darcy Bussell & Patricia Linton. LC 93-367901. (Illus.). 72p. (J). (gr. 2-6). 1994. 15.95 (1-56458-468-2) DK Pub Inc.

Young Darwin & His Cultural Circle. Edward Manier. (Studies in the History of Modern Science: No. 2). 254p. 1978. lib. bdg. 88.00 (90-277-0856-8, D Reidel) Kluwer Ac.

Young Davy Crockett: Frontier Pioneer. Eric Carpenter. LC 95-7598. (First-Start Biography Ser.). (Illus.). 32p. (J). (gr. k-2). 1995. pap. text ed. 3.50 (0-8167-3759-2); lib. bdg. 12.95 (0-8167-3758-4) Troll Communs.

Young Deaf Adults & the Transition from High School to Postsecondary Careers. Thomas E. Allen. (Illus.). 70p. (Orig.). (C). 1995. pap. text ed. 20.00 (0-7881-2362-9) DIANE Pub.

Young Detective. (First Activity Packs Ser.). 24p. (J). (ps-3). 1995. pap. 15.95 (1-56458-899-8) DK Pub Inc.

Young Detectives. Yaw A. Boateng. (Junior African Writers Ser.). (Illus.). (J). (gr. 5-6). 1992. pap. 4.99 (0-7910-2918-2) Chelsea Hse.

Young Diana: An Experiment of the Future (1918) Marie Corelli. 381p. 1996. pap. 24.95 (1-56459-917-5) Kessinger Pub.

Young Diana, an Experiment of the Future. Marie Corelli. 381p. 1972. reprint ed. spiral bd. 10.00 (0-7873-0210-4) Hlth Research.

Young Dick Whittington. Alan Broadhurst. (J). (gr. 1-7). 1964. 5.00 (0-87602-224-7) Anchorage.

Young Disraeli, 1804-1846. Jane Ridley. LC 94-25543. 1995. 35.00 (0-517-58643-6) Crown Pub Group.

Young Doctor Mason. large type ed. Alex Stuart. 416p. 1985. 25.99 (0-7089-1396-2) Ulverscroft.

Young Dogs in the Moonlight. Jeff Walker. LC 76-27962. (Illus.). 60p. 1977. pap. 6.00 (0-89924-006-2) Lynx Hse.

Young Dracula Graphic Novel. Gary Francis & David Mack. (Illus.). 160p. 1994. 18.95 (0-941613-47-X) Stabur Pr.

Young Dragons. Peter Albano. 352p. 1992. mass mkt. 4.99 (0-8217-3904-2, Zebra Kensgtn) Kensgtn Pub Corp.

Young Dreiser: A Critical Study. Yoshinobu Hakutani. LC 78-66797. 232p. 1980. 34.50 (0-8386-2268-2) Fairleigh Dickinson.

Young Duke, etc. see Works of Benjamin Disraeli

***Young Earth.** John D. Morris. 192p. 1996. pap. 14.95 (0-89051-174-8, YOUEAR) Master Bks.

Young Earth: An Introduction to Archean Geology. Euan G. Nisbet. 400p. 1987. text ed. 90.00 (0-04-550045-2); pap. text ed. 49.95 (0-04-550049-5) Routledge Chapman & Hall.

***Young Edward Gibbon, Gentleman of Letters.** Patricia B. Craddock. LC 81-13726. 399p. 1982. reprint ed. pap. 113.80 (0-608-03654-4, 2064480) Bks Demand.

Young Einstein: The Advent of Relativity. Lewis Pyenson. (Illus.). 272p. 1995. 65.00 (0-85274-779-9) IOP Pub.

Young Elder: From Ambrose of Milkova. Anthony Medvedev. 70p. 1974. pap. 3.00 (0-317-30442-9) Holy Trinity.

Young Eleanor Roosevelt. Francene Sabin. LC 89-33939. (Illus.). 48p. (J). (gr. 4-6). 1990. lib. bdg. 12.95 (0-8167-1779-6) Troll Communs.

Young Eleanor Roosevelt. Francene Sabin. LC 89-33939. (Illus.). 48p. (J). (gr. 4-6). 1996. pap. 3.95 (0-8167-1780-X) Troll Communs.

Young Elizabeth. Jennette Letton & Francis Letton. 1955. pap. 5.25 (0-8222-1290-0) Dramatists Play.

Young Elizabeth. Jennette F. Letton & Frances Letton. reprint ed. lib. bdg. 23.95 (0-89244-014-7, Queens House) Amereon Ltd.

Young Emma. W. H. Davies. 166p. 1991. 21.95 (1-85089-506-6, Pub. by ISIS UK) Transaction Pubs.

Young Emmanuel. large type ed. Naomi Jacob. 432p. 1985. 27.99 (0-7089-8242-5, Trail West Pubs) Ulverscroft.

Young Emperor: William the Second of Germany. Harold Frederic. (Collected Works of Harold Frederic). 1988. reprint ed. lib. bdg. 79.00 (0-7812-1186-7) Rprt Serv.

Young Emperor: William the Second of Germany see Collected Works of Harold Frederic

Young Engineer: An Annotated Bibliography 1890-1978. Ed. by L. Gillespie. 104p. 9.00 (0-318-12198-0, EC47) Accred Bd Eng & Tech.

Young Entrepreneur's Guide to Creating What Matters Most: Building Attitudes, Behaviors & an Action Plan for Success in Your Own Business. Mary S. Moore. LC 94-92392. 64p. (YA). (gr. 6-12). 1994. pap. text ed. 9.95 (1-885574-03-7) Courage Press.

Young Entrepreneur's Guide to Starting & Running a Business. Steve Mariotti & Tony Towle. 256p. 1996. pap. 15.00 (0-8129-2627-7, Times Bks) Random.

Young Eucalypt Report: Management Options for Australia's Regrowth Forests. C. M. Kerruish & W. H. Rawlins. (Illus.). 250p. 1991. pap. 50.00 (0-643-05103-1, Pub. by CSIRO AT) Aubrey Bks.

Young Event Horse: Buying, Breaking, Training, Competing. Clarissa Strachan. (Illus.). 200p. 1989. 22.95 (0-943955-21-1, Trafalgar Sq Pub) Trafalgar.

Young Explorer's Guide to Undersea Life. Pam Armstrong. LC 96-1051. (Illus.). 60p. (J). (gr. k-4). 1996. 16.95 (1-878244-10-8) Monterey Bay Aquarium.

Young Explorers Series. (J). 1994. 64.00 (0-679-87013-X) Random.

Young Families of the Mohawk Valley, 1710-1946. Clifford M. Young. (Illus.). 354p. 1994. reprint ed. pap. 55.00 (0-8328-4254-0); reprint ed. lib. bdg. 65.00 (0-8328-4253-2) Higginson Bk Co.

***Young Farmer Bill.** Lawrence McGee. (Illus.). 24p. (J). (gr. k-4). 1997. pap. 8.00 (0-8059-3943-1) Dorrance.

Young, Female & Black. Heidi S. Mirza. LC 91-30180. 224p. (Orig.). (C). 1992. pap. text ed. 17.95 (0-415-06705-7, A6792) Routledge.

Young, Female & Black. Heidi S. Mirza. LC 91-30180. 224p. (Orig.). (C). (gr. 13). 1992. text ed. 79.95 (0-415-06704-9, A6788) Routledge.

Young First Offenders: Their Criminal Careers. G. L. Webb. LC 78-72958. 1979. 9.95 (0-933012-03-9) Coker Pub.

Young Florist. Joseph Breck. LC 87-31444. (Illus.). 168p. 1988. reprint ed. 13.95 (0-940983-20-6) OPUS Pubns.

Young Flutist's Recital Book: 3 Centuries of Flute Music. L. Moyse. 48p. 1986. pap. 7.95 (0-7935-5103-X, 50336720) H Leonard.

Young Folks' Book of Mirth: A Collection of the Best Fun in Prose & Verse. LC 79-51961. (Granger Poetry Library). (J). (gr. 2-6). 1980. reprint ed. 25.00 (0-89609-197-X) Roth Pub Inc.

Young Folks' Book of Mirth: A Collection of the Best Fun in Prose & Verse. Compiled by Mary R. Thomas. LC 75-38604. (Granger Index Reprint Ser.). 1977. reprint ed. 20.95 (0-8369-6336-9) Ayer.

Young Folks' Entertainments: Comprising Many New & Novel Motion Songs, Charades, Pantomimes, Tableaux, Concert Recitations, Drills, etc., for Home - School Entertainment. Ed. by E. C. Rook & Lizzie J. Rook. LC 72-168787. (Granger Index Reprint Ser.). 1977. reprint ed. 17.95 (0-8369-6307-5) Ayer.

Young Folks' Hawaiian Time. Gene Pitchford. (Illus.). (J). (ps). 1965. pap. 3.00 (0-87505-275-4) Borden.

Young Folks' History of the United States. Thomas W. Higginson. (Notable American Authors Ser.). (J). 1992. reprint ed. lib. bdg. 90.00 (0-7812-3113-2) Rprt Serv.

Young Folks Recitations: Designed for Young People of Fourteen Years; Containing Selections in Prose & Poetry; Together with Some Short Dialogues & Tableaux. Compiled by J. W. Shoemaker. LC 73-2839. (Granger Index Reprint Ser.). (J). (gr. 8-10). 1977. reprint ed. 17.95 (0-8369-6413-6) Ayer.

***Young Forester.** Zane Grey. Date not set. lib. bdg. 21.95 (0-8488-1031-7) Amereon Ltd.

Young Frederick Douglass: Fight for Freedom. Laurence Santrey. LC 82-15993. (Illus.). 48p. (J). (gr. k-2). 1983. pap. 3.95 (0-89375-858-2) Troll Communs.

Young Frederick Douglass: Fight for Freedom. Laurence Santrey. LC 82-15993. (Illus.). 48p. (J). (gr. 4-6). 1983. lib. bdg. 12.95 (0-89375-857-4) Troll Communs.

Young Frederick Douglass: Freedom Fighter. Andrew Woods. LC 95-7631. (First-Start Biography Ser.). 32p. (J). (gr. k-2). 1995. lib. bdg. 12.95 (0-8167-3768-1) Troll Communs.

Young Frederick Douglass: Freedom Fighter. Andrew Woods. LC 95-7631. (First-Start Biography Ser.). (Illus.). 32p. (J). (gr. 1-4). 1996. pap. 3.50 (0-8167-3769-X) Troll Communs.

Young Frederick Douglass: The Maryland Years. Dickson J. Preston. LC 80-7992. (Maryland Paperback Bookshelf Ser.). 264p. (C). 1985. reprint ed. pap. 9.95 (0-8018-2739-6) Johns Hopkins.

Young Frederick Douglass: The Slave Who Learned to Read. Linda W. Girard. LC 93-28245. (Illus.). (J). 1994. lib. bdg. 14.95 (0-8075-9463-6) A Whitman.

Young Fu of the Upper Yangtze. Elizabeth F. Lewis. 288p. (J). (gr. k-6). 1990. mass mkt. 3.99 (0-440-49043-X, YB BDD) BDD Bks Young Read.

Young Fu of the Upper Yangtze. Elizabeth F. Lewis. LC 72-91654. (Illus.). 268p. (J). (gr. 4-6). 1973. 18.95 (0-8050-0549-8, Bks Young Read) H Holt & Co.

Young Gaia Atlas of Earthcare. Miles Litvinoff. LC 96-31417. (Illus.). 192p. (J). 1996. 24.95 (0-8160-3470-2) Facts on File.

Young, Gay, & Proud! 4th ed. Ed. by Don Romesburg. (Illus.). 120p. (YA). (gr. 7-12). 1995. pap. 5.95 (1-55583-279-2) Alyson Pubns.

Young Genius Book of Brain Teasers. Philip J. Carter & Ken A. Russell. (Illus.). 128p. (J). 1993. pap. 5.95 (0-7063-7102-X, Pub. by Ward Lock UK) Sterling.

Young George Washington: America's First President. Andrew Woods. LC 91-26405. (Illus.). 32p. (J). (gr. k-2). 1996. pap. 3.50 (0-8167-2541-1) Troll Communs.

Young George Washington: The Making of a Hero. John M. Rosenburg. LC 96-21665. (Illus.). 176p. (J). (gr. 4-6). 1997. lib. bdg. 16.90 (0-7613-0043-0) Millbrook Pr.

Young Germany: A History of the German Youth Movement. Walter Laqueur. 260p. 1984. 34.95 (0-88738-002-6); pap. 21.95 (0-87855-960-4) Transaction Pubs.

Young Ghosts. Daniel Cohen. LC 93-45924. (Illus.). 122p. (J). (gr. 4 up). 1994. pap. 13.99 (0-525-65154-3, Cobblehill Bks) Dutton Child Bks.

Young Ghosts. Daniel Cohen. (J). 1995. pap. 3.50 (0-590-62429-6) Scholastic Inc.

Young, Gifted & Black: Student-Teacher Relations in the Schooling of Black Youth. Mairtin Mac an Ghaill. 160p. 1988. pap. 29.00 (0-335-09507-0, Open Univ Pr) Taylor & Francis.

Young Gifted Children: Identification Programming & Socio-Psychological Issues. J. W. Murphy. 164p. 1991. pap. text ed. 201.00 (2-88124-788-1) Gordon & Breach.

Young Girls: A Portrait of Adolescence. Gisela Konopka. LC 84-19755. (Child & Youth Services Ser.: Vol. 6, Nos. 3 & 4). 176p. 1985. pap. text ed. 19.95 (0-918393-08-6) Harrington Pk.

Young Girls: A Portrait of Adolescence. Gisela Konopka. LC 83-22588. (Child & Youth Services Ser.: Vol. 6, Nos. 3 & 4). 176p. 1983. reprint ed. text ed. 32.95 (0-86656-281-8) Haworth Pr.

Young Girl's Diary. Sigmund Freud. 1972. 300.00 (0-87968-040-7) Gordon Pr.

Young Goat's Discovery. Arline W. Tinus. LC 93-38777. (Illus.). 32p. (J). (ps-3). 1994. 13.95 (1-878610-38-4) Red Crane Bks.

Young Goodman Brown. Nathaniel Hawthorne. (Short Stories Ser.). (J). (gr. 5 up). 1992. lib. bdg. 13.95 (0-88682-498-2) Creative Ed.

Young Goodman Brown & Other Short Stories. Nathaniel Hawthorne. (Thrift Editions Ser.). 128p. (Orig.). 1992. pap. 1.00 (0-486-27060-2) Dover.

Young Goodman Brown & Other Tales. Nathaniel Hawthorne. Ed. by Brian Harding. (World's Classics Ser.). 416p. 1988. pap. 7.95 (0-19-281746-9) OUP.

Young Guard! The Communist Youth League, Petrograd 1917-1920. Isabel A. Tirado. LC 87-28041. (Contributions to the Study of World History Ser.: No. 9). 288p. 1988. text ed. 55.00 (0-313-25922-4, TPE/, Greenwood Pr) Greenwood.

Young Guide to Famous Florida! Restaurants. Joyce L. Young. 1990. pap. 9.95 (0-942084-93-4) SeaSide Pub.

Young Guinevere. Robert D. San Souci. (Illus.). 32p. (J). 1996. pap. 5.99 (0-440-41291-9) Dell.

Young Guinevere. Robert D. San Souci. LC 91-12499. (Illus.). 32p. (J). (ps-3). 1993. 16.95 (0-385-41623-7) Doubleday.

Young Gun. Schiff Davis. 1989. mass mkt. 2.95 (0-8217-2846-6, Zebra Kensgtn) Kensgtn Pub Corp.

***Young Gunnies.** large type ed. John Blaze. (Linford Western Library). 272p. 1996. pap. 15.99 (0-7089-7946-7, Linford) Ulverscroft.

Young Gymnast. Joan Jackman. LC 94-36256. (Illus.). 48p. (J). (gr. 3-6). 1995. 15.95 (1-56458-677-4) DK Pub Inc.

Young Hamlet: Essays on Shakespeare's Tragedies. Barbara Everett. 240p. 1990. reprint ed. pap. 22.00 (0-19-812254-3) OUP.

Young Harriet Tubman: Freedom Fighter. Anne Benjamin. LC 91-26404. (Illus.). 32p. (J). (gr. k-2). 1997. pap. 3.50 (0-8167-2539-X) Troll Communs.

Young Hegelians. William J. Brazill. 305p. 1970. 79.50 (0-300-01275-6) Elliots Bks.

Young Hegelians: An Anthology. Ed. by Lawrence S. Stepelevich. LC 96-52981. (Paperback Library). 432p. (C). 1997. pap. 22.50 (0-391-04017-0) Humanities.

Young Heidegger: Rumor of the Hidden King. John Van Buren. LC 94-4292. (Studies in Continental Thought). 452p. 1994. 35.00 (0-253-36202-4) Ind U Pr.

Young Helen Keller: Woman of Courage. Anne Benjamin. LC 91-26406. (Illus.). 32p. (J). (gr. k-2). 1992. pap. 3.50 (0-8167-2531-4) Troll Communs.

***Young Henry Ford: A Picture History of the First Forty Years.** Sidney Olson. (Illus.). 204p. 1997. reprint ed. pap. text ed. 29.95 (0-8143-1224-1) Wayne St U Pr.

Young Henry James 1813-1876. Robert C. Le Clair. LC 77-153337. reprint ed. 39.50 (0-404-03897-2) AMS Pr.

Young Henry of Navarre. Heinrich Mann. Tr. by Eric Sutton from GER. LC 84-42673. 585p. 1986. reprint ed. Tusk. 25.00 (0-87951-981-9); reprint ed. Tusk. pap. 19.95 (0-87951-206-7) Overlook Pr.

Young Heroes. F. I. Rejab. (Illus.). 40p. (J). 1995. 9.95 (983-9808-28-1, Pub. by Delta Edits MY) Weatherhill.

Young Heroines. Nancy Polette. (Illus.). 48p. (Orig.). 1991. pap. 5.95 (0-913839-96-5) Pieces of Lrning.

Young Hickory. Helen McKenna. (J). (gr. 1-7). 1940. 5.00 (0-87602-225-5) Anchorage.

Young Hollywood. James Cameron-Wilson. LC 94-19583. 1995. 34.95 (1-56833-038-3) Madison Bks UPA.

***Young Hoods in Love.** Ho C. Anderson. 72p. 1995. pap. 9.95 (1-56097-192-4) Fantagraph Bks.

Young Horse: Breaking & Training. Jennie Loriston-Clarke. (Illus.). 192p. 1995. 29.95 (1-57076-023-3, Trafalgar Sq Pub) Trafalgar.

Young Horses. Herbert Rudofsky. (Breed Ser.). 1977. pap. 4.95 (0-88376-009-6) Dreenan Pr.

Young Howells & John Brown: Episodes in a Radical Education. Edwin H. Cady. LC 85-5013. 128p. 1985. 37.50 (0-8142-0388-4) Ohio St U Pr.

Young Husband or, Duties of Man in the Marriage Relation. William A. Alcott. LC 70-169368. (Family in America Ser.). (Illus.). 392p. 1976. reprint ed. 25.95 (0-405-03844-5) Ayer.

Young Hyperactive Child: Answers to Questions about Diagnosis, Prognosis & Treatment. Ed. by Jan Loney. LC 87-178. (Journal of Children in Contemporary Society: Vol. 19, Nos. 1-2). 178p. (Orig.). 1987. text ed. 49.95 (0-86656-670-8) Haworth Pr.

Young Ideas. 3.50 (0-318-02217-6) Chrstphrs NY.

Young Ideas. David J. Caspi. LC 96-90136. (Orig.). 1996. pap. 13.95 (0-533-11899-9) Vantage.

Young Imagination: Writing & Artwork by Children of New South Wales. Ed. by Susan Roy & Jeremy Steele. (Illus.). 96p. (Orig.). 1988. pap. 13.50 (0-909955-79-4, 00597) Heinemann.

Young in Illinois. Robert Wilson. LC 75-17572. (Illus.). 112p. (C). 1975. pap. 12.50 (0-913204-06-4) December Pr.

Young In-Line Skater. Chris Edwards. (Illus.). 40p. (J). 1996. 15.95 (0-7894-1124-5) DK Pub Inc.

Young in One Another's Arms. Jane Rule. 224p. 1984. reprint ed. pap. 9.95 (0-930044-53-3) Naiad Pr.

Young Indiana Jones & the Circle of Death, Bk. 3. William McCay. LC 89-43390. (Young Indiana Jones Ser.). 112p. (Orig.). (J). (gr. 3-7). 1990. lib. bdg. 6.99 (0-679-90578-2) Random Bks Yng Read.

Young Indiana Jones & the Curse of the Ruby Cross, Bk. 8. William McCay. LC 90-53242. (Young Indiana Jones Ser.). 128p. (Orig.). (J). (gr. 3-7). 1991. pap. 2.95 (0-679-81181-8) Random Bks Yng Read.

Young Indiana Jones & the Ghostly Riders, Bk. 7. William McCay. LC 90-53241. (Young Indiana Jones Ser.). 128p. (Orig.). (J). (gr. 3-7). 1991. pap. 3.50 (0-679-81180-X) Random Bks Yng Read.

Young Indiana Jones & the Gypsy Revenge, Bk. 6. Les Martin. LC 90-52818. (Young Indiana Jones Ser.). 128p. (Orig.). (J). (gr. 3-7). 1991. pap. 2.95 (0-679-81179-6) Random Bks Yng Read.

Young Indiana Jones & the Mask of the Madman. Megan Stine & H. William Stine. LC 95-8575. (Young Indiana Jones Chronicles Ser.). (J). 1995. 3.99 (0-679-87037-7, Bullseye Bks) Random Bks Yng Read.

Young Indiana Jones & the Plantation Treasure, Bk. 1. William McCay. LC 89-43388. (Young Indiana Jones Ser.). 112p. (Orig.). (J). (gr. 3-7). 1990. pap. 3.99 (0-679-80579-6) Random Bks Yng Read.

Young Indiana Jones & the Princess of Peril, Bk. 5. Les Martin. LC 90-52817. (Young Indiana Jones Ser.). 128p. (Orig.). (J). (gr. 3-7). 1991. pap. 2.95 (0-679-81178-8) Random Bks Yng Read.

Young Indiana Jones & the Secret City, Bk. 4. Les Martin. LC 89-43391. (Young Indiana Jones Ser.). 112p. (Orig.). (J). (gr. 3-7). 1990. lib. bdg. 6.99 (0-679-90580-4) Random Bks Yng Read.

Young Indiana Jones & the Secret City, Bk. 4. Les Martin. LC 89-43391. (Young Indiana Jones Ser.). 112p. (Orig.). (J). (gr. 3-7). 1990. pap. 2.95 (0-679-80580-X) Random Bks Yng Read.

Young Indiana Jones & the Tomb of Terror, Bk. 2. Les Martin. LC 89-43389. (Young Indiana Jones Ser.). 112p. (Orig.). (J). (gr. 3-7). 1990. pap. 3.99 (0-679-80581-8) Random Bks Yng Read.

Young Internationalists. Ed. by Thomas A. Hiatt & Mark F. Gerzon. LC 70-188981. (East-West Center Book Ser.). (Illus.). 274p. reprint ed. pap. 78.10 (0-7837-3979-6, 2043809) Bks Demand.

Young Inventors. Annie Beaugrand-Champagne & Suzanne Dubuc. 32p. 1994. spiral bd. 7.95 (2-7625-7677-6, Pub. by Edits Chouette CN) Orca Bk Pubs.

Young Ireland: A Fragment of Irish History, 1840-1850. Charles G. Duffy. LC 71-127257. (Europe 1815-1945 Ser.). 796p. 1973. reprint ed. lib. bdg. 79.50 (0-306-71119-2) Da Capo.

Young Jackie Robinson, Baseball Hero. Edward Farrell. LC 91-26480. (Illus.). 32p. (J). (gr. k-2). 1996. pap. 3.50 (0-8167-2537-3) Troll Communs.

Young James of Acadiana. James J. Bollich. (Illus.). 300p. 1994. 20.00 (0-9643275-0-3) J J Bollich.

***Young James to Jim.** unabridged ed. James T. Bollich & Celia F. Bollich. (Illus.). 275p. (Orig.). 1997. pap. 20.00 (0-9643275-1-1) J J Bollich.

Young Jedi Knights: Heirs of the Force. Kevin J. Anderson. (Star Wars Ser.). 1995. mass mkt. 4.99 (1-57297-066-9) Blvd Books.

Young Jefferson Davis, 1808-1846. William A. Shelton. 1981. 35.95 (0-405-14108-4) Ayer.

Young Jesus in the Temple. Alyce Bergey. (Arch Bks.). (Illus.). 24p. (J). (gr. k-4). 1986. pap. 1.99 (0-570-06203-9, 59-1426) Concordia.

Young Jethro see Valiant & the Damned

Young Jim Thorpe: All-American Athlete. Edward Farrell. LC 95-10022. (First-Start Biography Ser.). (Illus.). 32p. (J). (gr. k-2). 1995. pap. text ed. 3.50 (0-8167-3765-7); lib. bdg. 12.95 (0-8167-3764-9) Troll Communs.

***Young Joan.** Barbara Dana. LC 90-39494. 352p. (YA). (gr. 5 up). 1997. pap. 4.95 (0-06-440661-X, Trophy) HarpC Child Bks.

Young John Quincy. Cheryl Harness. LC 92-37266. (Illus.). 48p. (J). (gr. k-5). 1994. text ed. 15.95 (0-02-742644-0, Bradbury S&S) S&S Childrens.

Young John Tyler. Katherine T. Ellett. (Illus.). 1976. 4.75 (0-87517-016-1) Dietz.

Young Kangaroo. Margaret Wise Brown. 48p. (J). (ps). 1992. mass mkt. 3.99 (0-440-40670-6, YB BDD) BDD Bks Young Read.

Young Kangaroo. Margaret Wise Brown. LC 92-54866. (Illus.). 40p. (J). (gr. k-4). 1993. 14.95 (1-56282-409-0); lib. bdg. 14.89 (1-56282-410-4) Hyprn Child.

Young Kant: Between Mathematics & Epistemology, No. I. J. Fang. LC 94-92229. (Studies on the Integration of Humanities & Mathematical Knowledge). 295p. (Orig.). (C). 1995. pap. text ed. 19.50 (0-912490-19-5) PAIDEIA & PM.

Young Kennedys. Barbara Gibson. Date not set. pap. 23.00 (0-525-93657-2) NAL-Dutton.

***Young King Arthur.** Howard Pyle. Date not set. 14.95 (0-399-21723-1) Putnam Pub Group.

Young Krishna. Francis G. Hutchins. LC 80-66834. (Illus.). 132p. 1980. 29.50 (0-935100-01-6) Amarta Pr.

Young La Fontaine. Philip A. Wadsworth. LC 78-128943. (Northwestern Humanities Ser.: No. 29). 1970. reprint ed. 34.50 (0-404-50729-8) AMS Pr.

Young Lady of Property: Six Short Plays. Horton Foote. 1955. pap. 5.25 (0-8222-1291-9) Dramatists Play.

Young Lady's Accidence. Caleb Bingham. LC 81-5663. (American Linguistics Ser.). 1981. reprint ed. 50.00 (0-8201-1360-3) Schol Facsimiles.

Young Lady's Friend, by a Lady. Eliza W. Farrar. LC 74-3947. (Women in America Ser.). 452p. 1974. reprint ed. 35.95 (0-405-06093-9) Ayer.

***Young Lady's Pocket Library, or Parental Monitor: 1790 Edition.** Ed. by Marie M. Roberts. (For Her Own Good Ser.). 352p. 1996. reprint ed. pap. write for info. (1-85506-382-4) Bks Intl VA.

Young Lancelot. Robert D. San Souci. LC 95-21361. (Illus.). 32p. (J). 1996. 15.95 (0-385-32171-6) Doubleday.

Young Landlords. Walter D. Myers. (J). (gr. 6-10). 1992. 18.25 (0-8446-6569-X) Peter Smith.

Young Landlords. Walter D. Myers. (ALA Notable Bk.). 208p. (J). (gr. 5-9). 1989. pap. 4.99 (0-14-034244-3, Puffin) Puffin Bks.

***Young Larry.** Daniel Pinkwater. LC 96-41670. (Illus.). 32p. (J). (gr. k-3). 1997. lib. bdg. 14.95 (0-7614-5004-1) Marshall Cavendish.

Young Lawyer for New Deal. Thomas I. Emerson. 400p. (C). 1990. lib. bdg. 55.00 (0-8476-7626-9) Rowman.

Young Lawyer's Handbook - Legal Administration Office: What They Don't Teach You in Law School. Polly A. McGlew. 154p. (C). 1990. pap. text ed. 15.95 (*1-885477-06-6*) Fut Horizons.

***Young Lawyer's Jungle Book: A Survival Guide.** Thane J. Messinger. LC 95-83497. 174p. (Orig.). 1996. pap. 18.95 (*1-888960-01-9*) Fine Print Pr.

Young Learners. 1994. 12.95 (*0-19-437195-6*) OUP.

Young Learners & the Microcomputer. Daniel Chandler. 128p. 1984. pap. 27.00 (*0-335-10578-5*, Open Univ Pr) Taylor & Francis.

Young Leaves. Robert F. Mainone. (Haiku Series: Vol. 6). (Illus.). 44p. 1974. pap. 7.00 (*1-888693-06-1*) Wnderlnd MI.

Young Lieutenant. Martin H. Weik. LC 87-31922. 1989. 18.95 (*0-87949-275-9*) Ashley Bks.

Young Life of Mother Teresa of Calcutta. Claire J. Mohan. (Illus.). 64p. (Orig.). (J). (gr. 4-8). 1996. pap. 7.95 (*0-943135-25-7*); text ed. 14.95 (*0-943135-26-5*) Young Sparrow Pr.

Young Life of Pope John Paul II. Claire J. Mohan. (Illus.). 64p. (Orig.). (J). (gr. 3-5). 1995. pap. 7.95 (*0-943135-12-5*); text ed. 14.95 (*0-943135-11-7*) Young Sparrow Pr.

Young Lion Hunter. Zane Grey. 1976. 23.95 (*0-8488-1032-5*) Amereon Ltd.

Young Lions. Houghton Mifflin Company Staff. (Literature Experience 1993 Ser.). (J). (gr. 1). 1992. pap. 7.80 (*0-395-61762-6*) HM.

Young Lions. Barbara Lewis. (Illus.). 243p. (Orig.). 1993. pap. 9.95 (*0-87579-771-7*) Deseret Bk.

***Young Lions: Confederate Cadets at War.** James Conrad. LC 97-9907. (Illus.). 384p. 1997. 29.95 (*0-8117-1975-8*) Stackpole.

***Young Liszt.** Iwo Zaluski & Pamela Zaluski. (Illus.). 224p. 9600. 32.00 (*0-7206-1003-6*, Pub. by P Owen Ltd UK) Dufour.

Young Living. large type ed. Nanalee Clayton. 1994. 136.50 (*0-614-09812-2*, L-31472-00) Am Printing Hse.

Young Look. Eloise Franco. (Illus.). (J). (gr. 3-7). 1979. pap. 5.95 (*0-87516-294-0*) DeVorss.

Young Love & Other Infidelities. Stepas Zobarskas. 1971. 4.95 (*0-87141-035-4*) Manyland.

Young Lovell: A Romance. Ford M. Hueffer. LC 90-6160. 320p. reprint ed. lib. bdg. write for info. (*0-7734-9990-3*) E Mellen.

Young Lucretia & Other Stories by Mary E. Wilkins Freeman. Mary E. Wilkins Freeman. LC 79-106287. (Short Story Index Reprint Ser.). 1977. 20.95 (*0-8369-3324-9*) Ayer.

Young Lukacs. Lee Congdon. LC 82-11162. xiii, 235p. (C). 1983. 34.95 (*0-8078-1538-1*) U of NC Pr.

Young Luther. Robert H. Fife. LC 79-131040. 1970. reprint ed. 37.50 (*0-404-02385-1*) AMS Pr.

Young Man. Botho Strauss. Tr. by Roslyn Theobald. 276p. 1995. 24.95 (*0-8101-1338-4*, Hydra Bks) Northwestern U Pr.

Young Man & the Sea. Gilbert G. Coombs. LC 91-71742. 224p. 1993. pap. 14.95 (*0-942963-17-2*) Distinctive Pub.

Young Man, Be Strong. David Burkholder. 246p. 1988. 8.00 (*0-318-41782-0*) Rod & Staff.

Young Man from Atlanta. Horton Foote. 1995. pap. 5.25 (*0-8222-1483-0*) Dramatists Play.

Young Man from Atlanta. Horton Foote. 1995. pap. 19.95 (*0-525-94114-2*, Dutton) NAL-Dutton.

Young Man from Atlanta. Horton Foote. 128p. 1996. pap. 9.95 (*0-452-27633-0*, Plume) NAL-Dutton.

***Young Man from the Provinces.** Alan Helms. 272p. 1997. pap. 12.00 (*0-380-72900-8*) Avon.

Young Man from the Provinces: A Gay Life before Stonewall. Alan Helms. 208p. 1995. 22.95 (*0-571-19880-5*) Faber & Faber.

Young Man, I Think You're Dying. Joan Fleming. 200p. 1994. 18.50 (*0-7451-8625-4*, Black Dagger) Chivers N Amer.

Young Man in a Hurry & Other Short Stories. Robert W. Chambers. LC 71-103504. (Short Story Index Reprint Ser.). 1977. 21.95 (*0-8369-3246-3*) Ayer.

Young Man In God's Plan. Witness Lee. 37p. 1.50 (*0-87083-264-6*, 16009001) Living Stream Ministry.

Young Man Luther. Erik H. Erikson. (J). 1994. 21.00 (*0-8446-6744-7*) Peter Smith.

Young Man Luther: A Study in Psychoanalysis & History. Erik H. Erikson. LC 92-38851. (Austen Riggs Monograph Ser.: No. 4). 288p. 1993. pap. 9.95 (*0-393-31036-1*) Norton.

***Young Man Thoreau.** Richard Lebeaux. LC 76-44851. 272p. 1977. reprint ed. pap. 77.60 (*0-608-04440-7*, 2064972) Bks Demand.

***Young Man West.** Edwin Gibson. 150p. (Orig.). 1997. mass mkt. 10.95 (*1-57532-112-2*) Press-Tige Pub.

Young Man with a Horn. Baker. 20.95 (*0-8488-0877-0*, Queens House) Amereon Ltd.

Young Man with a Horn. Dorothy Baker. 1977. reprint ed. lib. bdg. 20.95 (*0-89244-025-2*, Queens House) Amereon Ltd.

Young Managers at the Crossroads: The Trishanku Complex. Pulin K. Garg & Indira J. Parikh. LC 92-43393. 176p. 1993. 32.00 (*0-8039-9109-6*) Sage.

Young Man's Darling. Lee Scofield. 352p. 1995. mass mkt. 4.50 (*0-06-108274-0*, Harp PBks) HarpC.

Young Man's Guide to Autos. 2nd ed. Jeff S. Bouquet. 100p. (Orig.). 1992. pap. 29.00 (*1-56216-111-3*); text ed. 59.00 (*1-56216-110-5*) Systems Co.

Young Man's Guide to Autos: Basics, Operation, Safety & Maintenance. Jeff S. Bouquet. (Illus.). 80p. (YA). 1991. 55.00 (*1-56216-017-6*); pap. 25.00 (*1-56216-018-4*) Systems Co.

***Young Man's Journey with Aids: The Story of Nick Trevor.** Luellen Reese. LC 97-21622. (Issues-Teen Ser.). 1997. 22.00 (*0-531-11366-3*) Watts.

***Young Marian's Adventures in Sherwood Forest.** Mooser. (J). 1997. pap. 4.50 (*0-671-57551-1*) S&S Childrens.

***Young Marian's Adventures in Sherwood Forest: A Girls to the Rescue Novel.** Stephen Mooser. LC 96-53114. (J). 1997. write for info. (*0-88166-277-1*) Meadowbrook.

Young Marilyn: Becoming the Legend. James Haspiel. (Illus.). 168p. 1995. 34.95 (*0-7868-6077-4*) Hyperion.

Young Mark Twain. Louis Sabin. LC 89-33982. (Illus.). 48p. (J). (gr. 4-6). 1990. lib. bdg. 12.95 (*0-8167-1783-4*) Troll Communs.

Young Mark Twain. Louis Sabin. LC 89-33982. (Illus.). 48p. (J). (gr. 4-6). 1997. pap. 3.95 (*0-8167-1784-2*) Troll Communs.

Young Marooners. Francis R. Goulding. 1973. reprint ed. lib. bdg. 59.95 (*0-8490-1344-5*) Gordon Pr.

Young Martial Artist. David Mitchell. (Illus.). 128p. (J). 1992. 25.00 (*0-87951-422-1*) Overlook Pr.

Young Martial Artist. David Mitchell. (Illus.). 128p. (J). 1995. pap. 17.95 (*0-87951-582-1*) Overlook Pr.

***Young Martial Arts Enthusiast.** David Mitchell. LC 96-38171. (Young Enthusiast Ser.). (Illus.). 64p. (J). 1997. 15.95 (*0-7894-1508-9*) DK Pub Inc.

Young Martin Luther King, Jr. I Have a Dream. Joanne Mattern. LC 91-26478. (Illus.). 32p. (J). (gr. k-2). 1992. pap. 3.50 (*0-8167-2545-4*) Troll Communs.

Young Martin's Promise. Walter D. Myers. LC 92-18070. (Stories of America Ser.). (Illus.). 32p. (J). (gr. 2-5). 1992. lib. bdg. 22.83 (*0-8114-7210-8*) Raintree Steck-V.

Young Men & Fire. Norman Maclean. LC 92-11890. (Illus.). 310p. 1992. 19.95 (*0-226-50061-6*) U Ch Pr.

Young Men & Fire. Norman Maclean. LC 92-11890. (Illus.). xiv, 320p. 1993. pap. 10.95 (*0-226-50062-4*) U Ch Pr.

Young Men & Fire. large type ed. Norman Maclean. LC 92-45046. (General Ser.). 1993. lib. bdg. 21.95 (*0-8161-5734-0*, GK Hall) Thorndike Pr.

Young Men & Military Service. Jerome Johnston & Jerald G. Bachman. LC 72-612412. (Youth in Transition Ser.: No. 5). (Illus.). 274p. reprint ed. pap. 78.10 (*0-7837-5372-1*, 2045136) Bks Demand.

Young Men & Military Service see Youth in Transition

***Young Men at War.** Noel Currer-Briggs. 240p. 1996. pap. 14.95 (*0-85449-236-4*, Pub. by Gay Mens Pr UK) LPC InBook.

Young Men in Prison: The Criminal Identity Explored Through the Rules of Behaviour. Michael Little. 174p. 1990. pap. text ed. 19.95 (*1-85521-093-2*, Pub. by Dartmth Pub UK) Ashgate Pub Co.

Young Men in the Street: Help-Seeking Behavior of Young Male Prostitutes. Cudore L. Snell. LC 92-41604. 152p. 1995. text ed. 39.95 (*0-275-93874-3*, C3874, Praeger Pubs) Greenwood.

Young Men Look at Military Service: A Preliminary Report. Jerome Johnston & Jerald C. Bachman. LC 79-633213. (University of Michigan. Survey Research Center, Monograph Ser.: No. 193). 127p. reprint ed. pap. 36.20 (*0-317-09335-5*, 2004633) Bks Demand.

Young Men's Gold. Daniel M. Epstein. LC 77-20739. 72p. 1978. pap. 13.95 (*0-87951-076-5*) Overlook Pr.

Young Merlin. Robert D. San Souci. (Illus.). 32p. (J). 1996. pap. 5.99 (*0-440-41159-9*) Dell.

***Young Miles.** Lois M. Bujold. LC 97-2168. 544p. 1997. 22.00 (*0-671-87787-9*); pap. 15.00 (*0-671-87782-8*) Baen Bks.

Young Mill-Wright & Miller's Guide. Oliver Evans. LC 72-5047. (Technology & Society Ser.). (Illus.). 438p. 1979. reprint ed. 35.95 (*0-405-04699-5*) Ayer.

Young Miner. Horatio Alger, Jr. (Works of Horatio Alger Jr.). 1989. reprint ed. lib. bdg. 79.00 (*0-7812-3628-2*) Rprt Serv.

Young Mistley. Henry S. Merriman. Ed. by Herbert Van Thal. 6600. 12.95 (*0-685-09212-7*); pap. 8.95 (*0-304-93090-3*) Dufour.

Young Moses, Crown Prince of Egypt. Asher Lehmann. Tr. by Gertrude Hirschler from GER. (Illus.). 150p. (YA). (gr. 9-12). 1987. 10.95 (*0-910818-64-9*); pap. 7.95 (*0-614-07635-8*) Judaica Pr.

Young Mothers? Ann Phoenix. 250p. 1991. pap. 29.95 (*0-7456-0854-X*) Blackwell Pubs.

Young Mountaineers. Mary N. Murfree. LC 70-98588. (Short Story Index Reprint Ser.). 1977. 20.95 (*0-8369-3162-9*) Ayer.

Young Mouse & Elephant: An East African Folktale. Pamela J. Farris. LC 94-48835. (Illus.). 32p. (J). (gr. k-3). 1996. 14.95 (*0-395-73977-2*) HM.

Young Mozart. Rachel Isadora. (J). 1997. pap. 14.99 (*0-670-87120-6*) Viking Penguin.

Young Mrs. Burton. Margaret Penn. 256p. 1981. pap. text ed. 19.95 (*0-521-28298-5*) Cambridge U Pr.

Young Mrs. Cavendish. K. K. Beck. 1987. 16.95 (*0-8027-0979-6*) Walker & Co.

***Young Mrs. Winthrop.** Bronson Howard. Ed. & Intro. by Walter J. Meserve. (On Stage, America! Ser.). 49p. 1996. spiral bd. 3.95 (*0-937657-30-1*) Feedbk Theabks & Prospero.

Young Musician. Horatio Alger, Jr. (Works of Horatio Alger Jr.). 1989. reprint ed. lib. bdg. 79.00 (*0-7812-3629-0*) Rprt Serv.

Young Musician's Series, 5 vols., Set. Melvin H. Epstein. LC 92-80357. (Illus.). (Orig.). (J). (gr. 4-9). 1992. Five vol. set. pap. text ed. 65.00 (*1-881136-00-0*) Word Hse.

Young Musician's Series, Vol. 1: The Basics of Music. Melvin H. Epstein. LC 92-80357. (Illus.). (Orig.). (J). (gr. 4-9). 1992. write for info. (*1-881136-01-9*) Word Hse.

Young Musician's Series, Vol. 2: Melody. Melvin H. Epstein. LC 92-80357. (Illus.). (Orig.). (J). (gr. 4-9). 1992. pap. text ed. 14.95 (*1-881136-02-7*) Word Hse.

Young Musician's Series, Vol. 3: Harmony. Melvin H. Epstein. LC 92-80357. (Illus.). (Orig.). (J). (gr. 4-9). 1992. pap. text ed. 14.94 (*1-881136-03-5*) Word Hse.

Young Musician's Series, Vol. 4: Time & Rhythm. Melvin H. Epstein. LC 92-80357. (Illus.). (Orig.). (J). (gr. 4-9). 1992. pap. text ed. 12.95 (*1-881136-04-3*) Word Hse.

Young Musician's Series, Vol. 5: Special Effects. Melvin H. Epstein. LC 92-80357. (Illus.). (Orig.). (J). (gr. 4-9). 1992. pap. text ed. 12.95 (*1-881136-05-1*) Word Hse.

Young Muslim's Guide to the Modern World. Seyyed H. Nasr. 270p. (J). 1994. pap. 14.95 (*1-56744-476-8*) Kazi Pubns.

***Young Muslim's Guide to the Modern World.** Seyyed H. Nasr. 270p. 1996. pap. 14.95 (*0-614-21614-1*, 3) Kazi Pubns.

***Young Muslim's Guide to the Modern World.** Seyyed H. Nasr. 270p. 1996. 29.95 (*0-614-21615-X*, 3) Kazi Pubns.

Young Muslim's Guide to the Modern World. Seyyed Hossein Nasr. 270p. (YA). 1993. text ed. 29.95 (*1-56744-495-4*); pap. text ed. 14.95 (*1-56744-478-4*) Kazi Pubns.

Young Naturalist. A. Mitchell. (Hobby Guides Ser.). (Illus.). 32p. (J). (gr. 5-10). 1984. pap. 6.95 (*0-86020-653-X*); lib. bdg. 14.95 (*0-88110-235-0*) EDC.

Young Naturalist's Guide to Florida. Peggy S. Lantz & Wendy A. Hale. LC 94-15485. (Illus.). 128p. 1994. pap. 16.95 (*1-56164-051-4*) Pineapple Pr.

Young Nietzsche: Becoming a Genius. Carl Pletsch. 261p. 1992. pap. 14.95 (*0-02-925042-0*, Free Press) Free Pr.

Young Nietzsche & the Wagnerian Experience. Frederick R. Love. LC 63-63585. (North Carolina. University. Studies in the Germanic Languages & Literatures: No. 39). reprint ed. 27.00 (*0-404-50939-8*) AMS Pr.

Young Nixon: An Oral Inquiry. Ed. by Renee K. Schulte. 1978. 13.95 (*0-930046-02-1*); pap. 7.95 (*0-930046-01-3*) CSUF Oral Hist.

Young Nurse Rayburn. large type ed. Arlene J. Fitzgerald. (Linford Romance Library). 288p. 1994. pap. 15.99 (*0-7089-7540-2*) Ulverscroft.

Young Offender. Donald J. West. 334p. 1967. 42.50 (*0-8236-7020-1*) Intl Univs Pr.

Young Offenders Act & Regulations: Consolidated 1993-94 Edition. 144p. 1993. pap. 25.00 (*0-409-91526-2*, CN) MICHIE.

Young Offenders Act Revolution: Changing the Face of Canadian Juvenile Justice. Ed. by Alan W. Leschied et al. 256p. 1991. 60.00 (*0-8020-2623-0*); pap. 24.95 (*0-8020-6714-X*) U of Toronto Pr.

Young Offenders & Alcohol Related Crime: A Practitioner's Guidebook. Mary McMurran. (Wiley Series in Offender Rehabilitation). 195p. 1993. text ed. 60.00 (*0-471-93925-0*) Wiley.

Young Offenders Law in Canada. Platt. 352p. 1990. 87.00 (*0-409-80990-X*) MICHIE.

***Young Ones.** large type ed. Mary J. Staples. (Magna Large Print Ser.). 363p. 1997. 27.50 (*0-7505-1099-4*) Thorndike Pr.

Young Orville & Wilbur Wright: First to Fly. Andrew Woods. LC 91-26479. (Illus.). 32p. (J). (gr. k-2). 1992. pap. 3.50 (*0-8167-2543-8*) Troll Communs.

***Young Oxford Book of Archaeology.** Norah Moloney. LC 97-16096. (Illus.). 160p. (J). 1997. lib. bdg. 27.00 (*0-19-521248-7*) OUP.

***Young Oxford Book of Archaeology.** Norah Moloney. LC 97-16096. (Illus.). 160p. (J). 1997. 25.00 (*0-19-910067-5*) OUP.

Young Oxford Book of Astronomy. Simon Mitton & Jacqueline Mitton. (Illus.). 160p. (YA). (gr. 7 up). 1995. 25.00 (*0-19-521169-3*) OUP.

Young Oxford Book of Ecology. Michael Scott. (Illus.). 160p. (YA). (gr. 7 up). 1995. 25.00 (*0-19-521167-7*) OUP.

***Young Oxford Book of Ghost Stories.** Ed. by Dennis Pepper. (Illus.). 320p. 1997. pap. 14.95 (*0-19-278145-6*) OUP.

***Young Oxford Book of the Human Being: The Body, the Mind & the Way We Live.** David Glover. (Illus.). 160p. (J). 1997. 25.00 (*0-19-521375-0*) OUP.

***Young Oxford Book of the Human Being: The Body, the Mind & the Way We Live.** David Glover. (Illus.). 160p. (J). 1997. lib. bdg. 27.00 (*0-19-521374-2*) OUP.

Young Oxford Book of the Prehistoric World. Tony Seddon & Jill Bailey. LC 95-7014. (Illus.). 160p. (J). (gr. 5-9). 1995. 25.00 (*0-19-521163-4*) OUP.

Young Oxford Companion to Governments of the World, 2 vols. Richard M. Pious. (Illus.). 512p. (YA). (gr. 7 up). 1998. lib. bdg. 120.00 (*0-19-508486-1*) OUP.

Young Oxford Companion to Maps & Mapmaking. Rebecca Stefoff. (Illus.). 304p. (YA). (gr. 5 up). 1995. lib. bdg. 40.00 (*0-19-508042-4*) OUP.

Young Oxford Companion to the Congress of the United States. Donald A. Richie. LC 93-6466. (Illus.). 368p. (YA). (gr. 7 up). 1993. 40.00 (*0-19-507777-6*) OUP.

Young Oxford Companion to the Presidency of the United States. Richard M. Pious. LC 93-19908. (Illus.). 368p. (YA). (gr. 7 up). 1994. Alk. paper. 40.00 (*0-19-507799-7*) OUP.

Young Oxford Companion to the Supreme Court of the United States. John J. Patrick. LC 93-6467. 368p. (J). (gr. 5 up). 1994. 40.00 (*0-19-507877-2*) OUP.

Young Oxford Companion to the U. S. Government, 3 vols., Set. Richard M. Pious et al. (Illus.). 912p. (J). 1995. lib. bdg. 120.00 (*0-19-509737-8*) OUP.

Young Oxford Guide to the Elements. Albert Stwertka. (Illus.). 240p. (YA). (gr. 7 up). 1996. 35.00 (*0-19-508083-1*) OUP.

Young Oxford History of African Americans, 11 vols. Incl. Strange New Land: African Americans 1617-1776. Peter Wood. Ed. by Robin D. G. Kelley & Earl Lewis. (Illus.). 128p. (YA). (gr. 6-12). 1996. lib. bdg. 21.00 (*0-19-508700-3*); First Passage: Blacks in the Americas, 1501-1617. Colin Palmer. (Illus.). 128p. (J). 1995. 18.95 (*0-19-509905-2*); First Passage: Blacks in the Americas, 1501-1617. Colin Palmer. (Illus.). 128p. (J). 1995. lib. bdg. 21.00 (*0-19-508699-6*); Let My People Go: African Americans 1804-1860. Deborah G. White. Ed. by Robin D. Kelley & Earl Lewis. (Illus.). 144p. (YA). (gr. 6-12). 1996. lib. bdg. 21.00 (*0-19-508769-0*); Break Those Chains at Last: African Americans 1860-1880. Noralee Frankel. Ed. by Robin D. Kelley & Earl Lewis. LC 95-1848. (Illus.). 144p. (YA). (gr. 8 up). 1996. lib. bdg. 21.00 (*0-19-508798-4*); From a Raw Deal to a New Deal?: African Americans 1929-1945. Joe Trotter. Ed. by Robin D. Kelley & Earl Lewis. (Illus.). 128p. (YA). (gr. 7 up). 1996. lib. bdg. 21.00 (*0-19-508771-2*); Into the Fire: African Americans since 1970. Robin D. Kelley. Ed. by Earl Lewis. (Illus.). 144p. (YA). (gr. 8 up). 1996. lib. bdg. 21.00 (*0-19-508701-1*); Revolutionary Citizens: African Americans 1776-1804. Daniel C. Littlefield. Ed. by Earl Lewis & Robin D. Kelley. LC 96-8470. (Illus.). 144p. (YA). (gr. 6-12). 1997. lib. bdg. 21.00 (*0-19-508715-1*); Barbara Bair: Though Justice Sleeps: African Americans 1880-1900. Barbara Bair & Robin D. Kelley. LC 96-8472. (Illus.). 144p. (YA). (gr. 6-12). 1997. lib. bdg. 21.00 (*0-19-509343-7*); Chance to Make Good: African Americans 1900-1929. James R. Grossman. Ed. by Earl Lewis & Robin D. Kelley. LC 96-8471. (Illus.). 160p. (YA). (gr. 6-12). 1997. lib. bdg. 21.00 (*0-19-508770-4*); We Changed the World: African Americans 1945-1970. Vincent Harding. Ed. by Earl Lewis & Robin D. Kelley. LC 96-52146. (Illus.). 192p. (YA). (gr. 6-12). 1997. lib. bdg. 21.00 (*0-19-508796-8*); Young Oxford History of African Americans: Biographical Supplement & Index. Robin D. Kelley. Ed. by Earl Lewis. LC 96-54619. (Illus.). 160p. (YA). (gr. 6-12). 1997. lib. bdg. 21.00 (*0-19-510258-4*); 1616p. (YA). 1997. 231.00 (*0-19-508502-7*) OUP.

Young Oxford History of African Americans, 5 vols. Ed. by Earl Lewis & Robin D. G. Kelly. (Illus.). (YA). (gr. 6-12). 1997. lib. bdg. 105.00 (*0-19-510381-5*) OUP.

Young Oxford History of African Americans, 6 Vol., Set. Ed. by Earl Lewis & Robin D. Kelley. (The Young Oxford History of African Americans Ser.). (Illus.). (YA). (gr. 6-12). 1996. lib. bdg. 126.00 (*0-19-510380-7*) OUP.

Young Oxford History of African Americans: Biographical Supplement & Index see Young Oxford History of African Americans

***Young Oxford History of Britain & Ireland.** Mike Corbishley et al. Ed. by Kenneth O. Morgan. LC 97-19451. (Illus.). 416p. (J). 1997. 39.95 (*0-19-910035-7*) OUP.

Young Oxford History of Women in the United States, 11 vols. Incl. Vol. 10. Road to Equality: American Women Since 1962. William Chafe. (Illus.). 144p. (J). 1994. lib. bdg. 22.00 (*0-19-508325-3*); Vol. 1. Tried & True: Native American Women Confronting Colonization. John Demos. (Illus.). 144p. (J). 1995. 22.00 (*0-19-508142-0*); Vol. 2. Colonial Mosaic: American Women, 1600-1760. Jane Kamensky. (Illus.). 144p. (J). 1995. lib. bdg. 22.00 (*0-19-508015-7*); Vol. 3. Limits of Independence: American Women, 1760-1800. Marylynn Salmon. LC 93-30330. (Illus.). 144p. (J). 1994. lib. bdg. 22.00 (*0-19-508125-0*); Vol. 4. Breaking New Ground: American Women, 1800-1848. Michael Goldberg. LC 93-33739. (Illus.). 144p. (J). 1994. lib. bdg. 22.00 (*0-19-508202-8*); Vol. 5. Unfinished Battle: American Women 1848-1865. Harriet Sigerman. (Illus.). 144p. (J). 1994. lib. bdg. 22.00 (*0-19-508110-2*); Vol. 6. Laborers for Liberty: American Women 1865-1890. Harriet Sigerman. (Illus.). 144p. (J). 1994. lib. bdg. 22.00 (*0-19-508046-7*); Vol. 7. New Paths to Power: American Women 1890-1920. Karen M. Smith. LC 93-33598. (Illus.). 144p. (J). 1994. lib. bdg. 22.00 (*0-19-508111-0*); Vol. 8. From Ballots to Breadlines: American Women, 1920-1940. Sarah Deutsch. LC 93-30664. 144p. (J). 1994. 22.00 (*0-19-508063-7*); Vol. 9. Young Oxford History of Women in the United States, Vol. 9: Pushing the Limits: American Women 1940-1961. Elaine T. May. (Illus.). 144p. (J). 1994. lib. bdg. 22.00 (*0-19-508084-X*); Vol. 11. Young Oxford History of Women in the United States Supplement & Index. Harriett Sigerman. Ed. by Nancy F. Cott. (Illus.). 144p. (J). 1995. lib. bdg. 20.00 (*0-19-508829-8*); 1995. 242.00 (*0-19-508830-1*) OUP.

Young Oxford History of Women in the United States, Vol. 9: Pushing the Limits: American Women 1940-1961 see Young Oxford History of Women in the United States

Young Oxford History of Women in the United States Supplement & Index see Young Oxford History of Women in the United States

Young Oxford Science Library, 3 vols. 1996. 81.00 (*0-19-521186-3*) OUP.

Young Painter: The Life & Paintings of Wang Yani - China's Extraordinary Young Artist. 80p. (J). 1991. 17.95 (*0-590-44906-0*, Scholastic Hardcover) Scholastic Inc.

***Young Painter: The Life & Paintings of Wang Yani, China's Extraordinary Young Artist.** Zheng Zhensun & Alice Low. (Illus.). (J). (gr. 6). 1995. 8.64 (*0-395-73268-9*) HM.

***Young Painter: The Life & Paintings of Wang Yani, China's Extraordinary Young Artist.** large type ed. Zheng Zhensun & Alice Low. (Illus.). 102p. (J). (gr. 6). 25.50 (*0-614-20632-4*, L-38203-00 APHB) Am Printing Hse.

XYZ

An Asterisk (*) at the beginning of an entry indicates that the title is appearing in BIP for the first time.

Young Patriot: The American Revolution As Experienced by One Boy. Jim Murphy. LC 93-38789. (Illus.). 49p. (J). (gr. 4 up). 1996. 16.00 (*0-395-60523-7*, Clarion Bks) HM.

Young Patriots: Six Brave Boys in the Civil War. Horatio Alger, Jr. (Gold Signature Ser.). (Illus.). 154p. 1987. 24.00 (*0-685-43920-8*) G K Westgard.

Young Pattullo. J. I. Stewart. 320p. 1976. 7.95 (*0-393-08367-5*) Norton.

Young Paul Robeson: On My Journey Now. Lloyd L. Brown. 1996. text ed. 24.00 (*0-8133-3178-1*) Westview.

Young Paul Robeson: On My Journey Now. Lloyd L. Brown. LC 96-24715. (C). 1997. pap. text ed. 15.95 (*0-8133-3177-3*) Westview.

Young Peacemakers' Project Book. Kathleen Fry-Miller & Judith Myers-Walls. 208p. (Orig.). 1988. pap. 14.95 (*0-87178-976-0*) Brethren.

Young People & ... You Know What: Eroding the New Paganism. William O'Malley. (Spirit Life Ser.). 40p. (Orig.). 1993. pap. 3.50 (*1-878718-13-4*) Resurrection.

***Young People & Alcohol, Drugs & Tobacco.** K. Anderson. (WHO Regional Publications, European Ser.: No. 66). 87p. 1995. pap. text ed. 20.00 (*92-890-1330-3*) World Health.

Young People & Death. Ed. by John D. Morgan. LC 90-28402. 224p. (Orig.). 1991. pap. 18.95 (*0-914783-49-1*) Charles.

***Young People & Physical Activity.** Neil Armstrong & Joanne Wellsman. (Illus.). 384p. 1996. 115.00 (*0-19-262660-4*); pap. 57.00 (*0-19-262659-0*) OUP.

***Young People & Social Change: Individualization & Risk in Late Modernity.** Andy Furlong & Fred Cartmel. LC 96-45149. (Sociology & Social Change Ser.). 1997. write for info. (*0-335-19465-6*, Open Univ Pr); pap. write for info. (*0-335-19464-8*, Open Univ Pr) Taylor & Francis.

Young People at Risk: Fightings AIDs in Northern Tanzania. Ed. by Knut-Inge Klepp et al. 242p. 1995. 36.00 (*82-00-22698-0*) Scandnvan Univ Pr.

Young People from Bosnia Talk about War. Harvey Fireside & Bryna J. Fireside. LC 96-11613. (Issues in Focus Ser.). 104p. (YA). (gr. 6 up). 1996. lib. bdg. 18.95 (*0-89490-730-1*) Enslow Pubs.

Young People, Health, & Family Life. Julia Brannen et al. LC 93-22709. 229p. 1994. pap. 27.50 (*0-335-19097-9*, Open Univ Pr) Taylor & Francis.

Young People in Post-Communist Russia & Eastern Europe. Ed. by Igor Ilynsky et al. (Illus.). 240p. 1995. text ed. 62.95 (*1-85521-672-8*, Pub. by Dartmth Pub UK) Ashgate Pub Co.

Young People Leaving Home. Patrick Ainley. 160p. 1991. text ed. 60.00 (*0-304-32443-4*); pap. text ed. 19.95 (*0-304-32446-9*) Cassell.

Young People of Leningrad: School & Work Options & Attitudes. Evelina Vasil'eva. LC 75-46109. reprint ed. pap. 52.30 (*0-317-41982-X*, 2026126) Bks Demand.

Young People Reading: Culture & Response. Charles Sarland. 176p. 1991. pap. 27.00 (*0-335-09879-7*, Open Univ Pr) Taylor & Francis.

Young People Speak: Surviving the Holocaust in Hungary. Andrew Handler & Susan V. Meschel. (Illus.). 144p. (YA). (gr. 9-12). 1993. lib. bdg. 22.70 (*0-531-11044-3*) Watts.

Young People with Cancer: A Handbook for Parents. (Illus.). 86p. (Orig.). (C). 1992. pap. text ed. 20.00 (*1-56806-101-3*) DIANE Pub.

Young People with Problems: A Guide to Bibliotherapy. Jean A. Pardeck & John T. Pardeck. LC 83-18601. xv, 176p. 1984. text ed. 47.95 (*0-313-23836-7*, PYP/, Greenwood Pr) Greenwood.

Young People's Atlas of the United States. James Harrison & Eleanor Van Zandt. LC 92-53116. 128p. (J). (gr. 3 up). 1996. 19.95 (*0-7534-5022-4*, Kingfisher LKC) LKC.

***Young People's Atlas of the World.** Jon Richards. (Illus.). 40p. (J). (gr. 3-6). 1997. 12.95 (*0-7613-0588-2*, Copper Beech Bks); lib. bdg. 16.90 (*0-7613-0563-7*, Copper Beech Bks) Millbrook Pr.

Young People's Book of Music. Keith Spence. (Illus.). 144p. (J). (gr. 5-9). 1995. pap. 14.95 (*1-56294-784-2*) Millbrook Pr.

Young People's Book of Music. Keith Spence. LC 94-36699. (Illus.). 144p. (J). (gr. 5-9). 1995. lib. bdg. 22.90 (*1-56294-605-6*) Millbrook Pr.

Young People's Dyirbal: An Example of Language Death from Australia. Annette Schmidt. (Cambridge Studies in Linguistics: Supplementary Volumes). 300p. 1985. 57.95 (*0-521-30510-1*) Cambridge U Pr.

***Young People's Encyclopedia of the United States.** William E. Shapiro. Date not set. pap. text ed. write for info. (*1-56294-514-9*) Marlowe & Co.

Young People's Encyclopedia of the United States, 10 vols., Set. Ed. by William E. Shapiro. LC 91-4141. (Illus.). 800p. (J). (gr. 4 up). lib. bdg. 149.00 (*1-56294-151-8*) Millbrook Pr.

Young People's Guide to Rock 'n' Roll. Jim Bessman. 250p. 1997. 18.00 (*0-02-864582-0*) Schirmer Bks.

Young People's Health: A Challenge for Society. (Technical Report Ser.: No. 731). 117p. 1986. pap. text ed. 14.40 (*92-4-120731-0*, 1100731) World Health.

Young People's Images of Science. Rosalind Driver et al. 160p. 1995. 75.00 (*0-335-19382-X*, Open Univ Pr); pap. 23.95 (*0-335-19381-1*, Open Univ Pr) Taylor & Francis.

***Young People's Involvement in Sport.** John M. Kremer et al. LC 97-1609. (Adolescence & Society Ser.). 304p. (C). 1997. pap. write for info. (*0-415-16650-0*); text ed. write for info. (*0-415-16649-7*) Routledge.

Young Peoples Job List. Bonnie Sose. 1985. pap. 5.99 (*0-9615279-0-0*) Character Builders.

Young People's Leisure & Lifestyles. Leo B. Hendry et al. LC 92-45832. (Adolescence & Society Ser.). 240p. (C). 1993. pap. 18.95 (*0-415-04350-6*, B2219, Routledge NY) Routledge.

Young People's Mass Book. Ed. by Tony Castle. (Illus.). 64p. (Orig.). 1989. pap. 3.95 (*0-8146-1844-8*) Liturgical Pr.

Young People's Nature Guide. Allen H. Benton & Richard L. Bunting. (Illus.). 177p. (J). (gr. 2-4). 1978. pap. text ed. 3.00 (*0-942788-05-2*); 6.00 (*0-942788-06-0*) Iris Visual.

Young People's Speaker: Designed for Young People of Twelve Years. Ed. by E. C. Rook & Lizzie J. Rook. LC 70-37019. (Granger Index Reprint Ser.). (YA). (gr. 7 up). 1977. reprint ed. 17.95 (*0-8369-6318-0*) Ayer.

Young People's Story of DuPage County. Jean Moore & Richard Crabb. (Illus.). 120p. 1981. 8.95 (*0-916445-03-8*) Crossroads Comm.

Young People's Training. Witness Lee. 212p. per. 8.00 (*0-87083-467-3*, 16010001) Living Stream Ministry.

Young People's Understanding of Society. Adrian F. Furnham & Barrie Stacey. (Adolescence & Society Ser.). 256p. (C). 1991. pap. text ed. 16.95 (*0-415-01709-2*, A5211) Routledge.

Young Person's First Book of Wealth. A. David Silver. (Illus.). 300p. (YA). (gr. 7-12). 1987. student ed. 15.95 (*0-945214-00-6*) Silver Prescrip Pr.

Young Person's Guide to Becoming a Writer. rev. ed. Janet E. Grant. LC 95-19541. 184p. (Orig.). (YA). (gr. 6 up). 1995. reprint ed. pap. 13.95 (*0-915793-90-3*) Free Spirit Pub.

Young Person's Guide to Military Service. rev. ed. Jeff Bradley. LC 86-33719. (Illus.). 207p. 1987. pap. 9.95 (*0-916782-83-2*) Harvard Common Pr.

Young Person's Guide to Music: A Listener's Guide, Incl. audio CD. Neil Ardley. LC 95-19595. (Illus.). 80p. (J). (gr. 4-9). 1995. 24.95 (*0-7894-0313-7*, 5-70667) DK Pub Inc.

Young Person's Guide to New Orleans Houses. Lloyd Vogt. LC 91-15213. (Illus.). 40p. (J). 1991. pap. 7.95 (*0-88289-829-9*) Pelican.

Young Person's Guide to Science: Ideas That Change the World. Roy A. Gallant. LC 92-12332. (Illus.). 256p. (J). (gr. 5 up). 1993. text ed. 16.95 (*0-02-735775-9*, Mac Bks Young Read) S&S Childrens.

***Young Person's Guide to the Ballet: With Music on CD from the Nutcracker, Swan Lake, & the Sleeping Beauty.** Anita Ganeri. LC 97-3806. (J). 1997. write for info. (*0-15-201184-6*) HarBrace.

***Young Person's Guide to the Opera.** Ariane C. Comstock. LC 96-78048. (Illus.). 288p. (YA). (gr. 5 up). 1997. 29.95 (*1-889923-13-3*, Monarch Books) Monarch Westlake Village.

Young Person's Guide to the Orchestra: Benjamin Britten's Composition on CD. Narrated by Anita Ganeri. 64p. (J). 1996. 25.00 incl. cd-rom (*0-15-201304-0*) HarBrace.

Young Person's Guide to the Twleve Steps. Stephen Roos. LC 92-21818. 128p. (YA). (gr. 7 up). 1992. 6.00 (*0-89486-851-9*, 5432A) Hazelden.

Young Person's History of Israel. 2nd ed. David Bamberger. Ed. by Nicholas D. Mandelkern. (Illus.). 150p. (Orig.). (J). (gr. 5-7). 1985. pap. 7.50 (*0-87441-393-1*) Behrman.

Young Person's History of Israel. 2nd ed. Priscilla Fishman et al. Ed. by Nicholas D. Mandelkern. (Illus.). 150p. (Orig.). (J). (gr. 5-7). 1985. wbk. ed., pap. 4.95 (*0-87441-429-6*) Behrman.

Young Person's History of Israel. 2nd rev. ed. Sara M. Schachter & Priscilla Fishman. (J). 1995. teacher ed., pap. 14.95 (*0-87441-444-X*) Behrman.

Young Person's OOH (Occupational Outlook Handbook) JIST Works, Inc. Staff. (Illus.). 262p. (J). (gr. 6-10). 1996. pap. 19.95 (*1-56370-201-0*, J2010) JIST Works.

Young Person's Philosophical Dictionary. Florence J. Goodman. 53p. (J). (gr. 5-12). 1978. pap. 10.00 (*0-917232-06-2*) Gee Tee Bee.

***Young Person's Picture Dictionary.** Scott. (J). 1990. pap. text ed. write for info. (*0-05-004375-7*) Addison-Wesley.

Young Phenomenon: Paperbacks in Our Schools. John Gillespie & Diana L. Spirt. LC 72-2653. (ALA Studies in Librarianship: No. 3). 152p. reprint ed. pap. 43.40 (*0-317-26350-1*, 2024228) Bks Demand.

Young Philip Sidney, Fifteen Seventy-Two to Fifteen Seventy-Seven. James M. Osborn. LC 77-151584. (Elizabethan Club Ser.: No. 5). 591p. reprint ed. pap. 168.50 (*0-317-29286-2*, 2022026) Bks Demand.

Young Pianist: An Approach for Teachers & Students. 2nd ed. Joan Last. (Illus.). 168p. 1985. pap. 17.95 (*0-19-322287-6*) OUP.

***Young Picasso.** Boardingham. 1997. 19.95 (*0-7893-0093-1*) Universe.

Young Pilot of the Belle Creole. Caroline L. Hentz. (Notable American Authors Ser.). 1992. reprint ed. lib. bdg. 90.00 (*0-7812-3086-1*) Rprt Serv.

Young Pioneers. Rose W. Lane. 1976. 17.95 (*0-8488-0557-7*) Amereon Ltd.

Young Pioneers on the Oregon Trail. Joy Stickney. (Illus.). 20p. (J). (gr. 4-6). 1992. pap. 4.50 (*1-884563-01-5*) Canyon Creat.

Young Pitcher. Zane Grey. 1976. 21.95 (*0-8488-1033-3*) Amereon Ltd.

Young Pitcher. Zane Grey. LC 91-23670. 256p. (YA). (gr. 7 up). 1992. reprint ed. pap. 4.95 (*0-688-11262-5*, Morrow Junior) Morrow.

Young Pocahontas: Indian Princess. Anne Benjamin. LC 91-32654. (Illus.). 32p. (J). (gr. k-2). 1996. pap. 3.50 (*0-8167-2535-7*) Troll Communs.

Young Pocahontas in the Indian World. Helen C. Rountree. (Illus.). 52p. (Orig.). (J). (gr. 4-6). 1995. pap. 8.95 (*0-9648727-0-6*) H C Rountree.

Young Poets of a New Bulgaria. Belin Tonchev. 112p. 9000. pap. 21.00 (*0-948259-71-X*, Pub. by Forest Bks UK) Dufour.

Young Poets of a New Poland: Anthology. Ed. & Tr. by Donald Pirie from POL. (Illus.). 280p. 1994. pap. 24.00 (*1-85610-010-3*, Pub. by Forest Bks UK) Dufour.

Young Poets of a New Romania. Ed. by Ion Stoica. Tr. by B. Walker from ROM. LC 90-71088. (Illus.). 160p. (Orig.). 9100. pap. 19.95 (*0-948259-89-2*, Pub. by Forest Bks UK) Dufour.

Young Poets of Germany: An Anthology. Ed. by Uwe-Michael Gutzschhahn. Tr. by Raymond Hargreaves. (Illus.). 164p. 1994. pap. 22.00 (*1-85610-032-4*, Pub. by Forest Bks UK) Dufour.

Young, Poor, & Pregnant: The Psychology of Teenage Motherhood. Judith S. Musick. 1995. 14.00 (*0-300-06195-1*) Yale U Pr.

Young Preacher's Guide to Success. Thomas Champness. 1993. reprint ed. pap. 8.99 (*0-88019-308-5*) Schmul Pub Co.

Young Producer's Video Book: How to Write, Shoot & Direct Your Own Videos. Nancy Bentley & Donna W. Guthrie. (Illus.). 64p. (J). (gr. 3-5). 1995. pap. 7.95 (*1-56294-688-9*) Millbrook Pr.

Young Producer's Video Book: How to Write, Shoot & Direct Your Own Videos. Nancy Bentley et al. LC 94-48300. (Illus.). 64p. (J). (gr. 3-5). 1995. lib. bdg. 16.40 (*1-56294-566-1*) Millbrook Pr.

***Young Professional's Guide to Personal Finance.** Liz Walkington. (Daily Telegraph Guides Ser.). 1996. pap. 15.95 (*0-7494-1961-X*) Kogan Page Ltd.

Young Prometheus. Haratey Khem. 76p. (Orig.). 1994. pap. write for info. (*1-885206-04-6*, Iliad Pr) Cader Pubng.

Young Puzzle Adventure. Karen Dolby. (Illus.). 96p. (J). (ps-1). 1996. pap. 11.95 (*0-7460-2290-5*, Usborne) EDC.

Young Queen Elizabeth. Francene Sabin. LC 89-33941. (Illus.). 48p. (J). (gr. 4-6). 1990. lib. bdg. 12.95 (*0-8167-1785-0*) Troll Communs.

Young Queen Elizabeth. Francene Sabin. LC 89-33941. (Illus.). 48p. (J). (gr. 4-6). 1997. pap. 3.95 (*0-8167-1786-9*) Troll Communs.

Young Rakes. Julie McDonald. Ed. by Anne B. Bergren & Melissa M. Joy. 140p. (Orig.). 1991. pap. 9.95 (*1-878326-01-5*) East Hall Pr.

Young Razzle. John R. Tunis. LC 49-9796. 192p. (J). (gr. 5 up). 1991. reprint ed. pap. 4.95 (*0-688-10153-4*) Morrow.

Young Reader's Bible Double Fun Pad. (Double Fun Pads Ser.: No. 1). 32p. (J). 1995. pap. 1.49 (*0-7847-0387-6*, 22107) Standard Pub.

Young Reader's Bible Double Fun Pad. (Double Fun Pads Ser.: No. 2). 32p. (J). 1995. pap. 1.49 (*0-7847-0388-4*, 22108) Standard Pub.

Young Reader's Book of Science. 1991. pap. 12.95 (*0-671-73239-0*) S&S Trade.

Young Reader's Christian Library. (Illus.). (J). 1992. boxed, pap. text ed. 9.97 (*1-55748-488-0*) Barbour & Co.

Young Readers Christian Library, 8 vols. Incl. Miriam. Kjersti H. Baez. (Illus.). 224p. (J). 1995. pap. text ed. 2.50 (*1-55748-350-7*); Esther. Susan M. Miller. 224p. (J). (gr. 3 up). 1992. pap. text ed. 2.50 (*1-55748-260-8*); Ruth. Kjersti H. Baez. (Illus.). 224p. (J). (gr. 3 up). per. 2.50 (*1-55748-173-3*); Elijah. Susan M. Miller. (Illus.). 224p. (J). (gr. 3 up). pap. text ed. 2.50 (*1-55748-189-X*); Joseph. Rex Williams. (Illus.). 224p. (J). (gr. 3 up). 1990. pap. text ed. 2.50 (*1-55748-116-4*); Jesus. Dan Larsen. (Illus.). 224p. (J). (gr. 4-8). 1989. pap. text ed. 2.50 (*1-55748-100-8*); Paul. Dan Larsen. (Illus.). 224p. (J). (gr. 3 up). pap. 2.50 (*1-55748-135-0*); Peter. Susan M. Miller. 224p. (J). 1994. pap. text ed. 2.50 (*1-55748-659-X*); write for info. (*1-55748-833-9*) Barbour & Co.

Young Reader's Companion. Ed. by Gordon Carruth. LC 93-6662. 681p. (J). (gr. 4 up). 1993. 49.95 (*0-8352-2765-0*) Bowker.

Young Reader's Companion to American History. Ed. by John A. Garraty. (Illus.). 300p. (J). 1994. 39.95 (*0-395-66920-0*) HM.

Young Reader's Encyclopedia of Jewish History. Ed. by Ilana Shamir & Shlomo Shavit. LC 87-10599. (YA). (gr. 7 up). 1987. pap. 17.95 (*0-670-81738-4*) Viking Child Bks.

Young Readers, New Readings. Ed. by Emrys Evans. (Illus.). 170p. (Orig.). 1992. pap. text ed. 18.95 (*0-85958-602-2*, Pub. by Univ of Hull Pr UK) Paul & Co Pubs.

Young Readers' Picturebook of Tar Heel Authors. 5th rev. ed. Richard Walser & Mary R. Peacock. (Illus.). vi, 74p. 1981. pap. 3.00 (*0-86526-184-9*) NC Archives.

Young Rebecca: Writings of Rebecca West, 1911-17. Intro. by Jane Marcus. LC 89-31300. 416p. 1989. pap. 6.95 (*0-253-23101-9*) Ind U Pr.

Young Recruit. Jean Day. LC 88-90722. (Roof Bks.). 75p. (Orig.). 1988. pap. 6.00 (*0-937804-30-4*) Segue NYC.

Young Reggie Jackson: Hall of Fame Champion. Andrew Woods. LC 95-10020. (First-Start Biography Ser.). (Illus.). 32p. (J). (gr. k-2). 1995. lib. bdg. 12.95 (*0-8167-3762-2*) Troll Communs.

Young Reggie Jackson: Hall of Fame Champion. Andrew Woods. LC 95-10020. (First Start Biography Ser.). (Illus.). 32p. (J). (gr. 1-4). 1996. pap. 3.50 (*0-8167-3763-0*) Troll Communs.

Young Revolutionary see Life of Friedrich Engels

Young Rider. Lucinda Green. LC 93-22103. (Illus.). 64p. (J). (gr. 3-6). 1993. 15.95 (*1-56458-320-1*) DK Pub Inc.

Young Rider's Book of Horses & Horsemanship. Isabelle Von Neumann-Cosel-Nebe. Ed. & Tr. by Felicitas Von Neumann-Cosel from GER. (Illus.). 208p. (J). (gr. 4 up). 1992. 24.95 (*0-939481-24-3*) Half Halt Pr.

Young Riders Guide to Riding a Horse. Lesley Ward. (J). 1996. 12.95 (*0-87605-928-0*) Mac Pub USA.

Young Robert Duncan: Portrait of the Poet as Homosexual in Society. Ekbert Faas. LC 83-15541. 400p. (Orig.). 1983. 20.00 (*0-87685-489-7*); pap. 15.00 (*0-87685-488-9*) Black Sparrow.

Young Rocky: A True Story of Attilio Rocky Castellani. Joseph Kinney & Adolph Caso. 1985. pap. 9.95 (*0-8283-1902-2*) Branden Pub Co.

Young Rosa Parks: A Civil Rights Heroine. Anne Benjamin. LC 95-7599. (Illus.). 32p. (J). (gr. k-2). 1995. lib. bdg. 12.95 (*0-8167-3774-6*) Troll Communs.

Young Rosa Parks: A Civil Rights Heroine. Anne Benjamin. LC 95-7599. (Illus.). 32p. (J). (gr. 1-4). 1997. pap. 3.50 (*0-8167-3775-4*) Troll Communs.

Young Run Away. Anthony Washington. (Illus.). (Orig.). (J). (gr. 3-6). 1984. pap. 2.98 (*0-9613078-2-X*) Detroit Black.

Young Runaways. K. M. Kapadia. 212p. 1971. 8.50 (*0-318-36941-9*) Asia Bk Corp.

Young Sailor: An Introduction to Sailing & the Sea. Basil Mosenthal. (Illus.). 48p. (YA). (gr. 8 up). 1993. 13.95 (*0-924486-61-9*) Sheridan.

Young Sailor & Other Poems. Luis Cernuda. Tr. & Intro. by Rick Lipinski. (Illus.). 128p. (Orig.). 1987. pap. 7.95 (*0-940567-01-6*); lib. bdg. 25.00 (*0-940567-00-8*) Gay Sunshine.

Young Salesman. Horatio Alger, Jr. (Works of Horatio Alger Jr.). 1989. reprint ed. lib. bdg. 79.00 (*0-7812-3630-4*) Rprt Serv.

***Young Savages.** Stewart. Date not set. write for info. (*0-312-86412-4*) St Martin.

***Young Scholars Pocket Calendar.** 3rd ed. Menachem M. Schneerson. 144p. (Orig.). 1973. reprint ed. pap. 5.00 (*0-8266-0302-5*) Kehot Pubn Soc.

Young Scientist, 6 Vols. (J). 1996. pap. 15.95 (*0-7894-0573-3*) DK Pub Inc.

Young Scientist Takes a Walk: Guide to Outdoor Observations see Outdoor Science Projects for Young People

Young Scientists: America's Future & the Winning of the Westinghouse. Joseph Berger. LC 92-25339. 243p. 1993. 21.95 (*0-201-63255-1*) Addison-Wesley.

Young Scientist's Guide to Successful Science Projects. Sandra Markle. LC 89-45290. (Illus.). 128p. (J). (gr. 3-7). 1990. lib. bdg. 12.93 (*0-688-07217-8*) Lothrop.

Young Sea Officer's Sheet Anchor, or, a Key to the Leading of Rigging, or to Practical Seamanship - With Appendix. 2nd ed. Darcy Lever. (Illus.). 124p. 1995. reprint ed. lib. bdg. 35.00 (*0-8328-4490-X*) Higginson Bk Co.

Young Server's Book of the Mass. Kenneth Guentert. LC 86-60894. 88p. (J). (gr. 6-8). 1987. pap. 4.95 (*0-89390-078-8*) Resource Pubns.

Young Shakespeare. Russell A. Fraser. 247p. 1992. pap. 16.00 (*0-231-06765-8*) Col U Pr.

***Young Sidney Hook: Marxist & Pragmatist.** Christopher Phelps. LC 97-23738. (Illus.). 280p. 1997. 35.00 (*0-8014-3328-2*) Cornell U Pr.

Young Sixes. Jim Grant. 40p. (Orig.). 1992. pap. text ed. 6.00 (*0-935493-91-3*) Programs Educ.

Young Skin for Life: Your Guide to Smoother, Clearer, More Beautiful Skin-at Any Age. Julie Davis & Prevention Magazine Editors. 304p. 1995. 26.95 (*0-87596-240-8*) Rodale Pr Inc.

Young Skin for Life: Your Guide to Smoother, Clearer, More Beautiful Skin At Any Age, Vol. 1. Prevention Magazine Editors & Julie Davis. 304p. 1995. pap. text ed. 14.95 (*0-87596-241-6*) Rodale Pr Inc.

***Young Snowboarder.** Bryan Iguchi. LC 97-11789. (Young Enthusiast Ser.). (J). 1997. write for info. (*0-7894-2062-7*) DK Pub Inc.

Young, Sober, & Free. Ed. by Shelly Marshall. 137p. 1978. 10.00 (*0-89486-055-0*, 1116A) Hazelden.

Young Soccer Player. Gary Lineker. LC 93-41145. (Illus.). 32p. (J). (gr. 2-6). 1994. 9.95 (*1-56458-592-1*) DK Pub Inc.

Young Soldier's Adventure in Vietnam with the 101st Airborne Division, 1968-1969: A Brief Scrapbook. Roger Borroel. (Illus.). 100p. (Orig.). (J). (ps-12). 1996. pap. 6.98 (*0-9624727-1-9*) LaVillita Pubns.

Young Squanto: The First Thanksgiving. Andrew Woods. LC 95-10030. (First-Start Biography Ser.). (Illus.). 32p. (J). (gr. k-2). 1995. pap. text ed. 3.50 (*0-8167-3761-4*); lib. bdg. 12.95 (*0-8167-3760-6*) Troll Communs.

Young Stamp Collector. Mike Frank. Ed. by Carol Benanti. 48p. (Orig.). (J). (gr. 3-7). 1991. pap. 2.95 (*1-880592-00-2*) Pace Prods.

Young Stamp-Collectors. Rosamond Praeger. (Illus.). 56p. 1985. 15.95 (*0-9508551-1-1*, Pub. by Portmoon Pr UK) R Clark.

Young Stars. Randi Reisfeld. Ed. by Lisa Clancy. 144p. (Orig.). 1992. pap. 3.50 (*0-671-76987-1*) PB.

Young-Stirs: The Pittsburgh Children's Cookbook. (Illus.). 200p. (Orig.). (J). (ps-12). 1985. pap. 7.95 (*0-9615457-0-4*) Genesis Inc.

Young Students Library, 6 bks. & 6 cass., Set. 39.95 incl. audio (*0-86545-168-0*) Spizzirri.

***Young Swimmer.** Jeff Rouse. LC 97-12474. (Young Enthusiast Ser.). (Illus.). 40p. (J). 1997. 15.95 (*0-7894-1533-X*) DK Pub Inc.

***Young Swiss Architects: A Documentaion by Carmen Humbel.** Carmen Humbel. 128p. 1996. pap. text ed. 45.00 (*3-7643-5548-4*) Birkhauser.

Young Tableaux: With Applications to Representation Theory & Geometry. William Fulton. (London Mathematical Society Student Texts Ser.: No. 35). 200p. (C). 1996. text ed. 59.95 (*0-521-56144-2*); student ed., pap. text ed. 19.95 (*0-521-56724-6*) Cambridge U Pr.

Young Tennis Player: A Young Enthusiast's Guide to Tennis. Arantxa S. Vicario. 48p. (J). (gr. 3-7). 1996. 15.95 (*0-7894-0473-7*) DK Pub Inc.

Young Think Program One: A Pre-School Thinking Skills Program. Sydney Tyler-Parker. (Young Think Program Ser.). 74p. (Orig.). (ps-1). 1982. pap. text ed. 15.00 (0-912781-01-7) Thomas Geale.

Young Think Program Two. Sydney Tyler-Parker. (Young Think Program Ser.). 90p. (Orig.). (J). (gr. k-1). 1988. pap. text ed. 25.00 (0-912781-13-0) Thomas Geale.

Young Think Reading. Sydney Tyler-Parker. 156p. (Orig.). 1990. pap. 35.00 (0-912781-16-5) Thomas Geale.

Young Thomas Edison: Great Inventor. Ed. by Claire Nemes. LC 95-8107. (First-Start Biography Ser.). (Illus.). 32p. (J). (gr. k-2). 1995. pap. text ed. 3.50 (0-8167-3777-0); lib. bdg. 12.95 (0-8167-3776-2) Troll Communs.

Young Thomas Jefferson. Francene Sabin. LC 85-1093. (Illus.). 48p. (J). (gr. 4-6). 1985. lib. bdg. 12.95 (0-8167-0561-5) Troll Communs.

Young Thomas Jefferson. Francene Sabin. LC 85-1093. (Illus.). 48p. (J). (gr. 4-6). 1996. pap. 3.95 (0-8167-0562-3) Troll Communs.

Young Thurgood Marshall: Fighter for Equality. Eric Carpenter. LC 95-10023. (First-Start Biography Ser.). (Illus.). 332p. (J). (gr. k-2). 1995. lib. bdg. 12.95 (0-8167-3770-3) Troll Communs.

Young Thurgood Marshall: Fighter for Equality. Eric Carpenter. LC 95-10023. (First-Start Biography Ser.). (Illus.). 32p. (J). (gr. 1-4). 1996. pap. 3.50 (0-8167-3771-1) Troll Communs.

Young Titan. F. Van Wyck Mason. 1976. reprint ed. lib. bdg. 34.95 (0-89190-355-0, Rivercity Pr) Amereon Ltd.

Young Tom. Forrest Reid. 173p. (Orig.). 1987. pap. 8.95 (0-85449-102-3, Pub. by Gay Mens Pr UK) LPC InBook.

Young Tom & the Retreat. large type ed. Forrest Reid. 525p. 1995. lib. bdg. 24.00 (0-939495-85-6) North Bks.

Young Tongues, No. I: A Poetic Exchange. Jabari Asim et al. 1992. pap. write for info. (0-9632456-0-0) First Civil.

***Young Too Are Heroic.** William L. Crow. (Illus.). 160p. 1997. 14.00 (0-8059-4197-5) Dorrance.

Young Track & Field Athlete: A Young Enthusiast's Guide to Track & Field Athletics. Colin Jackson. 32p. (J). (gr. 3-7). 1996. pap. 9.95 (0-7894-0474-5) DK Pub Inc.

Young Track & Field Athlete: A Young Enthusiast's Guide to Track & Field Athletics. Colin Jackson. 32p. (J). (gr. 3-7). 1996. 15.95 (0-7894-0855-4) DK Pub Inc.

Young Trailers. Joseph Altsheler. 1976. lib. bdg. 25.95 (0-89968-005-4, Lghtyr Pr) Buccaneer Bks.

Young Trailers. Joseph Altsheler. (Young Trailer Ser.). reprint ed. lib. bdg. 25.95 (0-89966-479-2) Buccaneer Bks.

***Young Troopers: Stories of Army Children on the Frontier.** Paige Ramsey-Palmer. LC 96-35089. (Illus.). 64p. (J). 1997. pap. 12.95 (1-877856-68-1) SW Pks Mnmts.

Young Turks. Stephen Seemayer. LC 81-68126. (Illus.). 160p. (Orig.). 1981. pap. 10.00 (0-937122-06-8) Astro Artz Eighteenth St.

Young Turks in Opposition. M. Sukru Hanioglu. 416p. 1995. 35.00 (0-19-509115-9) OUP.

Young Unicorns. Madeleine L'Engle. 224p. (YA). (gr. 8 up). 1989. mass mkt. 4.50 (0-440-99919-7, LLL BDD) BDD Bks Young Read.

Young Unicorns. Madeleine L'Engle. LC 68-13682. 256p. (J). (gr. 7 up). 1968. 16.95 (0-374-38778-8) FS&G.

Young Unwed Fathers: Changing Roles & Emerging Policies. Ed. by Robert I. Lerman & Theodora J. Ooms. LC 92-39617. 384p. 1993. 59.95 (1-56639-048-6) Temple U Pr.

Young Unwed Fathers: Changing Roles & Emerging Policies. Robert I. Lerman. (C). 1994. pap. text ed. 19.95 (1-56639-318-3) Temple U Pr.

Young Vegetarian's Companion. Jan Parr. 144p. (J). 1996. pap. 9.00 (0-531-15789-X) Watts.

Young Vegetarian's Companion. Jan Parr. LC 96-13303. 144p. (YA). (gr. 7-12). 1996. lib. bdg. 22.70 (0-531-11277-2) Watts.

Young Victims, Young Offenders. Ed. by Nathaniel J. Pallone. LC 94-31967. (Journal of Offender Rehabilitation). (Illus.). 252p. 1994. lib. bdg. 49.95 (1-56024-703-7) Haworth Pr.

Young Visitirs. Daisy Ashford. (Illus.). 105p. 1991. reprint ed. 15.00 (0-89733-365-9) Academy Chi Pubs.

Young Voices of the Adirondacks. Nadine B. McLaughlin. (Illus.). 100p. (Orig.). (J). 1994. pap. 10.95 (0-9643452-0-X) Graphics North.

Young Voltaire. Cleveland B. Chase. LC 79-160962. (Select Bibliographies Reprint Ser.). 1977. reprint ed. 24.95 (0-8369-5830-6) Ayer.

Young Volunteer: The Everday Experiences of a Soldier Boy in the Civil War. Joseph E. Crowell. (Illus.). 500p. 1996. reprint ed. pap. 24.95 (0-9638692-0-5) NOVA Pubns.

Young Voyageur: Trade & Treachery at Michilimackinac. rev. ed. Dirk Gringhuis. (Illus.). 202p. (J). (gr. 9 up). 1969. reprint ed. pap. 6.00 (0-911872-34-5) Mackinac St Hist Pks.

Young vs. Old: Generational Combat in the 21st Century. Susan A. MacManus. 288p. (C). 1995. pap. text ed. 23.00 (0-8133-1759-2) Westview.

Young West: A Sequel to Edward Bellamy's Celebrated Novel Looking Backward. Solomon Schindler. LC 70-154462. (Utopian Literature Ser.). 1976. reprint ed. 21.95 (0-405-03544-6) Ayer.

Young, White, & Miserable: Growing up Female in the Fifties. Wini Breines. LC 91-28608. 288p. 1994. pap. 15.00 (0-8070-7503-5) Beacon Pr.

Young Widow. Ferguson. 1981. 15.95 (0-405-13935-7) Ayer.

Young Wife, or Duties of Woman in the Marriage Relation. William A. Alcott. LC 73-169369. (Family in America Ser.). (Illus.). 382p. 1974. reprint ed. 25.95 (0-405-03845-3) Ayer.

***Young Wings.** Gertrude S. Ward. LC 96-91007. 1997. 18.95 (0-533-12245-7) Vantage.

***Young Winners' Way.** Mimi Noland & J. Noland. 1996. pap. 3.25 (0-89638-069-6) Hazelden.

Young Winston, 1874-1898: A Biography Using Stamps. Dalton Newfield. (Educational Ser.: No. 2). (Illus.). 16p. 1990. pap. 5.00 (0-943879-04-3) Intl Churchill Soc.

Young Witches. Barreiro & F. Solano Lopez. (Eros Graphic Novel Ser.: No. 3). 104p. 1992. pap. 12.95 (1-56097-202-5) Fantagraph Bks.

Young Wolf & Spirit Horse. Janice J. Shefelman. (J). 1997. pap. 3.99 (0-679-88207-3, Bullseye Bks) Random Bks Yng Read.

***Young Wolf & Spirit Horse.** Janice J. Shefelman. (J). 1997. lib. bdg. 11.99 (0-679-98207-8) Random.

Young Wolf's First Hunt. Janice J. Shefelman. (J). (gr. k-4). 1995. pap. 3.99 (0-679-86364-8) Random Bks Yng Read.

Young Wolf's First Hunt. Janice J. Shefelman. (J). (gr. k-4). 1995. lib. bdg. 11.99 (0-679-96364-2) Random.

Young Woman & Her Self-Esteem. Anita Canfield. 93p. (YA). (gr. 7-12). 1990. reprint ed. pap. 4.95 (0-87579-365-7) Deseret Bk.

Young Woman Citizen. Mary Austin. LC 18-21835. 1976. reprint ed. pap. 12.95 (0-685-01429-0) Designs Three.

Young Woman's Guide to Sex. Jacqueline Voss & Jay Gale. LC 86-4786. (Illus.). 256p. 1987. 16.95 (0-8050-0082-8) H Holt & Co.

***Young Women Activities.** Beth Lefgren & Jennifer Jackson. 1997. pap. 7.95 (1-57008-298-7) Bookcraft Inc.

Young Women Activities: Activities That Build Young Women, Activities That Build Young Women, Set Vols. 1 & 2. Cindy Parry. 1994. pap. 14.98 (0-88290-472-8) Horizon Utah.

Young Women Inspirational Activities: Activities That Inspire Young Women, Activities That Inspire Young Women, Set, Vols. 1 & 2. Cindy Parry. 1994. pap. 14.98 (0-88290-518-X) Horizon Utah.

Young Women Leadership Made Easy. Glenetske & Cortright. 1996. pap. 7.95 (1-55503-653-8, 01111523) Covenant Comms.

***Young Womens' Guide to Sports.** Billy Libby. Date not set. write for info. (0-688-05536-2); lib. bdg. write for info. (0-688-05537-0) Lothrop.

Young Women's Handbook: Beyond Surviving in the 90s. Institute for Women's Policy Research, The Young Women's Project Staff. 675p. (Orig.). (YA). (gr. 10 up). 1991. pap. 30.00 (1-878428-05-5) Inst Womens Policy Rsch.

Young Wordsworth. K. Johnston. 27.95 (0-06-019008-6, HarpT) HarpC.

***Young Wordsworth.** Kenneth Johnston. Date not set. write for info. (0-393-04607-9) Norton.

Young Writer. J. A. Christensen. LC 74-88375. (Illus.). xii, 364p. (Orig.). (YA). (gr. 8-12). 1970. text ed. 16.95 (0-87015-180-0) Pacific Bks.

Young Writer's Contest Manual: Competitions for Students Work. 2nd rev. ed. Penny Lent. LC 94-79466. (Young Writer's Ser.). 68p. (J). (gr. k up). 1994. per., pap. 7.95 (1-885371-05-5) Kldoscope Pr.

Young Writers in the Making: Sharing the Process with Parents. Alison Preece & Diane Cowden. LC 93-24636. 144p. (YA). 1993. pap. text ed. 18.50 (0-435-08778-9, 08778) Heinemann.

Young Writer's Manuscript Manual: A Guide on How to Send Writing for Publication. rev. ed. Penny Lent. LC 94-76618. (Young Writers Ser.). (Illus.). 84p. 1994. pap. 7.95 (1-885371-01-2) Kldoscope Pr.

Young Writer's Market Manual: Publications Seeking Student Work. 2nd rev. ed. Penny Lent. LC 94-76617. (Young Writers Ser.). 80p. 1994. pap. 7.95 (1-885371-02-0) Kldoscope Pr.

***Young Writer's Thesaurus.** Koutsoukis. 1991. pap. text ed. write for info. (0-582-87185-9, Pub. by Longman UK) Longman.

Young Years. June Pomerinke. LC 85-90524. (Illus.). 300p. (Orig.). 1986. pap. 8.50 (0-9616273-0-1) Young Pr Idaho.

***Young Youth Leader's Guide: Year 3, Bk. 2.** Smyth. (Intersection Ser.). 1995. mass mkt. 15.99 (1-57312-117-7) Smyth & Helwys.

***Young Youth Leader's Guide: Year 4, Bk. 1.** Smyth. (Intersection Ser.). 1995. pap. 16.99 (1-57312-100-2) Smyth & Helwys.

Youngblood. John O. Killens. LC 81-16156. (Brown Thrasher Bks.). 512p. 1982. reprint ed. pap. 14.95 (0-8203-0602-9) U of Ga Pr.

Youngblood Hawke. Herman Wouk. 800p. 1992. pap. 10.95 (0-316-95517-5) Little.

Youngblood of the Peace. Shirlee S. Matheson. (Illus.). 235p. (Orig.). 1991. pap. 14.95 (1-55059-033-2) Temeron Bks.

Youngblood on Mechanic's & Materialman's Liens in Texas. Eldon L. Youngblood. 400p. 1995. 495.00 incl. cd-rom (1-887181-25-3) Kirk Publ.

Younge Site: An Archaeological Record from Michigan. Emerson F. Greenman. (Occasional Contributions Ser.: No. 6). (Illus.). 1937. reprint ed. pap. 2.00 (0-932206-01-8) U Mich Mus Anthro.

***Younger.** H. A. Maxson. 210p. (Orig.). 1997. mass mkt. 4.99 (1-55197-565-3, Pub. by Comnwlth Pub CN) Partners Pubs Grp.

Younger American Poets. Jessie B. Rittenhouse. LC 68-16971. (Essay Index Reprint Ser.). 1977. 23.95 (0-8369-0826-0) Ayer.

***Younger at Last.** Steven Lamm & Gerald S. Couzens. LC 97-13557. 1997. 23.00 (0-684-83438-3) S&S Trade.

Younger Brother, Don Yod: A Tibetan Play, Being the Secret Biography from the Words of the Glorious Lama, the Holy Reverend Blo Bzang Ye Shes. Ye Shes Blo Bzang. Tr. by Robert B. Ekvall & Thubten J. Norbu. LC 74-19623. 158p. reprint ed. pap. 45.10 (0-317-10095-5, 2050129) Bks Demand.

Younger Brothers. Carl R. Green & William R. Sanford. LC 94-30109. (Outlaws & Lawmen of the Wild West Ser.). 48p. (J). (gr. 4-10). 1995. lib. bdg. 14.95 (0-89490-592-9) Enslow Pubs.

Younger Churchmen Look at the Church. Ed. by Ralph H. Read. LC 74-156708. (Essay Index Reprint Ser.). 1977. reprint ed. 23.95 (0-8369-2330-8) Ayer.

Younger Critics in North America. Ed. by Richard Kostelanetz. 205p. (Orig.). 1984. reprint ed. pap. text ed. 20.00 (0-932360-47-5) Archae Edns.

Younger Dryas. S. R. Troelstra et al. 236p. 50.00 (0-444-85806-7, North Holland) Elsevier.

Younger Earth. Alex Stella. LC 85-73469. 220p. 1985. 7.95 (0-9602044-3-1) Deinotation Seven.

Younger French Poets see Some Modern French Poets

Younger Generation. Rudolf Steiner. LC 67-29493. 179p. 1984. reprint ed. pap. 12.95 (0-910142-42-4) Anthroposophic.

Younger Irish Poets. Ed. by Gerald Dawe. 176p. 1982. pap. 12.95 (0-685-25870-X, Pub. by Blackstaff Pr IE) Dufour.

Younger Irish Poets. Ed. by Gerald Dawe. 176p. 1982. pap. 12.95 (0-85640-261-3) Dufour.

Younger Man Guns. Lewis B. Patten. 1986. pap. 2.75 (0-451-14266-7, Sig) NAL-Dutton.

Younger Men: How to Find Them, Date Them, Mate Them & Marry Them. Valerie Gibson. 1994. pap. 5.99 (1-56171-278-7, S P I Bks) Sure Seller.

Younger Men Are Better Than Retin A. Allia Zobel. Ed. by Cliff Carle. 1994. pap. 4.99 (0-918259-60-6) CCC Pubns.

***Younger Pitt: The Consuming Struggle.** John Ehrman. (Illus.). 914p. 1996. 75.00 (0-8047-2754-6) Stanford U Pr.

Younger Pitt: The Reluctant Transition. John Ehrman. LC 82-42859. (Illus.). 704p. 1983. 75.00 (0-8047-1184-4) Stanford U Pr.

Younger Pitt: The Years of Acclaim. John Ehrman. (Illus.). 726p. 1969. 75.00 (0-8047-1186-0) Stanford U Pr.

Younger Son, Vol. 1. Karl Shapiro. LC 88-6204. 304p. 1988. 19.95 (0-912697-86-5) Algonquin Bks.

Younger Than Springtime. Greg Williams. Date not set. pap. 22.95 (1-55611-506-7) D I Fine.

Younger Than Springtime. Greg Williams. LC 96-38224. 1997. pap. 22.95 (1-55611-511-3) D I Fine.

Younger Than Springtime: From South Pacific. Richard Rodgers & Oscar Hammerstein. 1981. 3.95 (0-7935-0735-9, 00305823) H Leonard.

Younger Than That Now: A Peace Corps Volunteer Remembers Morocco. Michael Moran. LC 94-96345. 143p. (Orig.). 1994. pap. 12.95 (0-9631597-8-X) Full Ct TX.

***Younger Voices, Stronger Choices: Promise Project's Guide to Forming Youth/Adult Partnerships.** Loring Leifer & Michael McLarney. (Illus.). 95p. (Orig.). 1997. pap. 14.95 (0-9658035-0-3) Kansas City Consensus.

Younger Women/Older Men. Beliza A. Furman. LC 95-15360. 256p. 1995. 22.00 (1-56980-040-5) Barricade Bks.

***Younger Writers Issue: W. T. Vollmann, S. Daitch, & D. F. Wallace.** (Review of Contemporary Fiction Ser.: Vol. 3, No. 2). 1993. pap. 8.00 (1-56478-123-2) Dalkey Arch.

Youngest. Margorie Thayer. 1982. 8.95 (0-396-08047-2) WC Stone PMA.

***Youngest Crew.** Paul Wagner. (Illus.). 227p. 1997. 29.95 (1-878117-13-0) Lagumo Corp.

Youngest Doll. Rosario Ferre. LC 90-33548. (Latin American Women Writers Ser.). xiv, 171p. 1991. pap. 10.95 (0-8032-6874-2, Bison Books); text ed. 33.50 (0-8032-1983-0) U of Nebr Pr.

Youngest Drover. Ronald G. Carter. 176p. 1995. 19.95 (0-9643672-1-1); pap. 14.95 (0-9643672-0-3) Harbour Bks.

Youngest Drover: One Man's True Story about Growing Up on a Real Cattle Drive. Ron Carter. 1995. write for info. (0-615-00306-0) Harbour Bks.

***Youngest Goalie.** Brian Mcfarlane. (Warwick Sports Young Adult Novels). 1997. pap. 8.95 (1-895629-95-0, Pub. by Warwick Pub CN) Firefly Bks Ltd.

Youngest Mothers: The Experience of Pregnancy & Motherhood Among Young Women of School Age. Gillian Schofield. 151p. 1994. 51.95 (1-85628-843-9, Pub. by Avebury Pub UK) Ashgate Pub Co.

***Youngest Parents.** Robert Coles. (Illus.). 192p. (YA). 1997. 27.50 (0-393-04082-8) Norton.

Youngest Pilgrim. J. G. Green. Ed. by Cathy Butler. 102p. (Orig.). 1991. pap. text ed. 5.95 (1-56309-001-5) Womans Mission Union.

Youngest Prophet: The Life of Jacinta Marto, Fatima Visionary. Christopher Rengers. LC 85-30789. 144p. (Orig.). 1986. pap. 5.95 (0-8189-0496-8) Alba.

Youngest Science: Notes of a Medicine Watcher. Lewis Thomas. 288p. 1995. pap. 11.95 (0-14-024327-5, Penguin Bks) Viking Penguin.

Youngest Sister. large type ed. Jan Tempest. 432p. 1988. 25.99 (0-7089-1794-1) Ulverscroft.

Youngest Voyageur. Duane R. Lund. 1985. pap. 7.95 (0-934860-41-6) Adventure Pubns.

***Younghusband: The Last Great Imperial Adventurer.** Patrick French. 440p. 1997. pap. 13.00 (0-00-637601-0) HarperColl Wrld.

Young's Analytical Concordance to the Bible. Robert Young. 1216p. 1984. 29.95 (0-917006-29-1) Hendrickson MA.

Young's Analytical Concordance to the Bible. Ed. by Robert Young. 1216p. 36.99 (0-529-06674-2, YC1) World Publng.

Young's Analytical Concordance to the Bible. rev. ed. Robert Young. LC 82-14203. 1220p. 1985. 39.99 (0-8407-4947-3) Nelson.

Young's Analytical Concordance to the Bible. rev. ed. Robert Young. LC 82-14203. 1216p. 1994. 34.99 (0-8407-4945-7) Nelson.

Young's Compact Bible Dictionary. Young. 578p. 1989. mass mkt. 7.99 (0-8423-8597-5) Tyndale.

Youngs' Psychology. Loy Young. 122p. (Orig.). 1993. pap. 9.95 (1-882888-38-3) Aquarius Hse.

Younguns of Mansfield. Thomas L. Tedrow. (Younguns Ser.: Bk. 1). (Illus.). 224p. (Orig.). (J). 1996. pap. 4.99 (0-8407-4132-4) Nelson.

Youniverse: Gestalt Therapy, Non-Western Religions & the Present Age. Jesse J. Thomas. LC 77-89164. (Illus.). (C). 1990. 12.95 (0-930626-01-X) Psych & Consul Assocs.

Youniverse: Gestalt Therapy, Non-Western Religions & the Present Age. 2nd ed. Jesse J. Thomas. LC 77-89164. (Illus.). (C). 1990. student ed., pap. 5.95 (0-930626-00-1) Psych & Consul Assocs.

***Your ABC Guide to the Environment.** 128p. 1991. pap. 8.95 (0-614-30373-7, H4) Terrene Inst.

Your ABC Guide to the Environment. JT&A, Inc. Staff. (ABC Guides). 128p. (Orig.). 1992. 12.95 (0-9631282-0-5) JT&A.

Your Aching Back: A Doctor's Guide to Relief. rev. ed. Augustus A. White. 336p. 1990. pap. 12.00 (0-671-71000-1) S&S Trade.

Your Advantage. Kahn. 1988. write for info. (0-318-63789-8) Viking Penguin.

***Your Adversary, the Devil.** J. Dwight Pentecost. LC 96-46395. 1997. pap. 10.99 (0-8254-3455-6) Kregel.

***Your Agency: Handle with Care.** Spencer J. Condie. 1996. 13.95 (1-57008-286-3) Bookcraft Inc.

***Your Aging Cat: How to Keep Your Cat Physically & Mentally Healthy into Old Age.** Kim C. Thornton & John Hamil. LC 96-34091. 1997. 24.95 (0-87605-085-2) Howell Bk.

Your Aging Parents. John Deedy. 192p. (Orig.). 1984. pap. 10.95 (0-88347-160-4) Res Christian Liv.

***Your Aging Parents: Reflections for Caregivers.** rev. ed. Earl A. Grollman & Sharon H. Grollman. LC 97-11597. Orig. Title: Caring for Your Aged Parents. 176p. 1997. pap. 10.00 (0-8070-2799-5) Beacon Pr.

***Your Aging Worker Dilemma.** Kathleen W. Stratton. 70p. 1996. spiral bd. 47.00 (0-925773-31-X) M Lee Smith.

Your Aladdin's Lamp. William H. Hornaday & Harlan Ware. 288p. 1979. pap. 10.95 (0-911336-75-3) Sci of Mind.

Your Amazing Body. Jeanne K. Hanson. (Illus.). 96p. (J). (gr. 3-7). 1995. pap. text ed. 8.95 (0-7167-6552-7, Sci Am Yng Rdrs) W H Freeman.

Your Amazing Brain. (Illus.). 16p. (J). (gr. 2 up). 1996. 12.99 (0-88705-930-9, Wshng Well Bks) Joshua Morris.

Your Amazing Senses: Thirty-Six Games, Puzzles & Tricks to Show How Your Senses Work. Ron Van Der Meer & Atie Van Der Meer. (Illus.). 12p. (J). (gr. 4-7). 1987. pap. 9.95 (0-689-71184-0, Mac Bks Young Read) S&S Childrens.

Your Amiable Uncle. Booth Tarkington. (American Autobiography Ser.). 192p. 1995. reprint ed. lib. bdg. 69.00 (0-7812-8650-6) Rprt Serv.

***Your & Mine.** Debbie Macomber. 1997. mass mkt. 3.99 (0-373-83355-5, 1-83355-7) Harlequin Bks.

Your Angels Guard My Steps: A 40-Day Journey in the Company of Bernard of Clairvaux. Bernard of Clairvaux. Ed. by David Hazard. (Rekindling the Inner Fire Ser.: Vol. 10). 160p. (Orig.). Date not set. pap. 8.99 (1-55661-723-2) Bethany Hse.

Your Animal Life Heritage. L. Bardsley. 79p. (C). 1989. pap. 40.00 (0-7223-2261-5, Pub. by A H S Ltd UK) St Mut.

Your Anxious Child: Raising a Healthy Child in a Frightening World. Mary A. Shaw. 160p. 1995. 14.95 (1-55972-318-1, Birch Ln Pr) Carol Pub Group.

***Your Anxious Child: Recognizing & Responding to Your Child's Needs & Fears.** Mary A. Shaw. 192p. 1997. pap. 12.95 (0-8065-1889-8, Citadel Pr) Carol Pub Group.

Your Apple II Needs You: Thirty Programming Projects for the Apple II. Frank Wattenberg. (Illus.). 352p. 1984. pap. text ed. 15.95 (0-13-977975-2) P-H.

Your Are in Charge: The IM Method Total Fitness for the Fit & Not So Fit. Ina Marx. 148p. (Orig.). 1990. pap. text ed. 19.95 (0-9626194-0-X) Esperanza Pubns.

***Your Asthma: Real Information You Can Use.** Randy Shields. LC 96-70814. 162p. (Orig.). 1996. mass mkt. 4.99 (1-888886-08-0) CEPI.

Your Attitude. 7th ed. Chapman. 1992. teacher ed., pap. text ed. 2.00 (0-02-321511-9, Macmillan Coll) P-H.

Your Attitude Counts. Rosemary T. Fruehling & Neild B. Oldham. 212p. (C). 1990. teacher ed. 8.00 (1-56118-072-6); student ed. 8.95 (1-56118-074-2); pap. text ed. 15.95 (1-56118-073-4) Paradigm MN.

Your Attitude Determines Your Attitude. Ed. by Mac Anderson. 77p. (Orig.). 1992. pap. 7.95 (1-880461-22-6) Celebrat Excell.

Your Attitude Is Showing: A Primer of Human Relations. 6th ed. Elwood N. Chapman. (Illus.). 203p. 1990. pap. write for info. (0-02-321504-6, Macmillan Coll) P-H.

Your Attitude Is Showing: A Primer of Human Relations - Self Paced Guide. 7th ed. Chapman. 1992. pap. text ed. 14.80 (0-02-321512-7, Macmillan Coll) P-H.

Your Attitude Is Showing: A Primer of Human Relationships. 8th ed. Elwood N. Chapman. LC 95-8749. (C). 1995. pap. text ed. 29.20 (0-13-442468-9) P-H.

Your Aura & Your Keynote. Julia S. Sears. 61p. 1975. reprint ed. spiral bd. 5.50 (0-7873-0757-2) Hlth Research.

XYZ

An Asterisk (*) at the beginning of an entry indicates that the title is appearing in BIP for the first time.

Your Autobiography: More Than Three Hundred Questions to Help You Write Your Personal History. Ray Mungo. 132p. (Orig.). 1994. pap. 8.95 (*0-02-029545-6*) Macmillan.

Your Available Power. Charles H. Spurgeon. 128p. 1996. mass mkt. 4.99 (*0-88368-266-4*) Whitaker Hse.

Your Baby: An Owner's Manual. Tom Carey. 1996. pap. text ed. 7.95 (*1-877590-83-5*) DE Pr IL.

***Your Baby: From Birth to 18 Months.** Nancy Stewart. LC 97-8170. (Illus.). 192p. (Orig.). 1997. pap. 15.95 (*1-55561-134-6*) Fisher Bks.

Your Baby . . . Gift of God. Elizabeth A. Hambrick-Stowe. (Looking up Ser.). (Orig.). 1985. pap. 1.95 (*0-8298-0549-4*) Pilgrim OH.

Your Baby & Child. enl. rev. ed. Penelope Leach. (Illus.). 1989. 29.95 (*0-394-57951-8*); pap. 19.95 (*0-679-72425-7*) Knopf.

***Your Baby & Child: From Birth to Age Five.** Penelope Leach. 1997. 35.00 (*0-375-40007-9*); pap. 20.00 (*0-375-70000-5*) Knopf.

***Your Baby & Your Work: Balancing Your Life.** Teresa Wilson. LC 97-22975. (National Childbirth Trust Guides). (Illus.). 192p. (Orig.). 1997. pap. 12.95 (*1-55561-126-5*) Fisher Bks.

Your Baby Book: Birth to Six Years. Robin Paterson. (Illus.). 120p. 1993. 32.00 (*0-9638231-0-8*) Pacific Eagle.

Your Baby Food Book. Demoss. 1984. pap. 8.95 (*0-02-499930-X*, Macmillan Coll) P-H.

Your Baby Needs Music. Barbara Cass-Beggs. (Illus.). 144p. 1980. pap. 5.95 (*0-312-89768-5*) St Martin.

***Your Baby or Mine?** Marie Ferrarella. (Bundles of Joy Ser.). 1997. mass mkt. 3.25 (*0-373-19216-9*, 1-19216-0) Silhouette.

Your Baby Talks to You. 2nd ed. Ruth Bowdin. (Illus.). 57p. 1993. teacher ed., pap. write for info. (*1-55997-168-1*) Websters Intl.

Your Baby Talks to You. 2nd rev. ed. Ruth Bowdin. (Illus.). 63p. 1993. pap. write for info. (*1-55997-167-3*) Websters Intl.

Your Baby, Your Way: Making Pregnancy Decisions & Birth Plans. Sheila Kitzinger. 1987. pap. 15.00 (*0-394-75249-X*) Pantheon.

Your Baby's Baptism: CSSR England. 16p. (Orig.). 1985. pap. 2.95 (*0-89243-445-7*) Liguori Pubns.

Your Baby's Baptism in the Orthodox Church. Anthony M. Coniaris. 1991. pap. 9.95 (*0-937032-83-2*) Light&Life Pub Co MN.

Your Baby's Development. Joan Miller. 128p. 1995. pap. 6.95 (*0-572-01657-3*, Pub. by Foulsham UK) Assoc Pubs Grp.

***Your Baby's First Year: Month by Month.** Alison MacKonochie. 1996. 12.98 (*0-8317-7486-X*) Smithmark.

***Your Baby's First Year: Seeing God's Purpose in Natural Development.** Ruth A. Parish. LC 96-50943. 1997. pap. 10.99 (*0-87788-560-5*) Shaw Pubs.

***Your Baby's First Year: Spiritual Reflections on Infant Development.** Ruth A. Parish. 1997. 11.99 (*0-614-27549-0*) Shaw Pubs.

Your Baby's Mind. rev. ed. S. H. Jacob. 288p. 1992. pap. 5.95 (*1-55850-137-1*) Adams Media.

Your Baby's Secret World: Four Phases for Effective Parenting (A Professional & Practical Guide) Larry V. Cheldelin. Ed. by J. Brown. (Illus.). (Orig.). 1983. pap. 9.50 (*0-8283-1850-6*) Branden Pub Co.

Your Backyard Herb Garden: A Gardener's Guide to Growing, Using & Enjoying Herbs. Miranda Smith. LC 96-23153. 1996. 27.95 (*0-87596-767-1*) Rodale Pr Inc.

Your Backyard Wildlife Garden: How to Attract & Identify Wildlife in Your Yard. Marcus H. Schneck. (Illus.). 160p. 1992. 24.95 (*0-87596-129-0*, 01-649-0) Rodale Pr Inc.

Your Backyard Wildlife Garden: How to Attract Birds, Butterflies, & Other Animals Every Month of the Year. Marcus H. Schneck. LC 95-25963. 160p. 1996. 26.95 (*0-87596-706-X*) Rodale Pr Inc.

Your Balancing Act: Discovering New Life Through Five Dimensions of Wellness. rev. ed. Carolyn Taylor. (Skill Builder Ser.). (Illus.). 208p. (Orig.). 1988. pap. 12.95 (*0-943920-75-2*) Metamorphous Pr.

***Your Bank Is Ripping You Off: How They're Doing It & How You Can Fight Back & Save a Fortune.** Edward F. Mrkvicka. LC 96-30824. 1997. pap. 12.95 (*0-312-15246-9*) St Martin.

Your Beginning with God. Ed. by Dwayne Norman. 31p. 1982. pap. 1.95 (*0-88144-063-9*) Christian Pub.

Your Behavior Is Showing: Over Forty Prescriptions for Understanding & Liking Yourself. Perry W. Buffington. 224p. 1988. pap. 9.95 (*0-929893-00-X*) Hillbrook Hse.

Your Best Foot Forward: Keys to Getting the Job You Want. Mary L. Hogenson. Ed. by Jane H. Combs. (Success Ser.). (Illus.). 34p. (Orig.). 1991. pap. text ed. 3.25 (*0-9625440-4-3*) Longmuir Jones Pub.

Your Best Foot Forward: Winning Strategies for the Job Interview. Maryann Miller. LC 93-44347. (Lifeskills Library). (Illus.). 48p. (YA). 1994. lib. bdg. 14.95 (*0-8239-1697-9*) Rosen Group.

Your Best Friend: The Privilege of Friendship with Christ. Lottie B. Hobbs. 136p. 1969. reprint ed. pap. 5.95 (*0-913838-11-X*) Harvest TX.

Your Best Friend, Kate. Pat Brisson. LC 88-6037. (Illus.). 40p. (J). (gr. k-3). 1989. text ed. 15.00 (*0-02-714350-3*, Bradbury S&S) S&S Childrens.

Your Best Interest: A Money Book for the Computer Age. Tom Weishaar. LC 85-81877. (Illus.). 172p. (Orig.). 1985. pap. 19.95 (*0-931137-00-4*) Infobooks.

Your Best Is Good Enough: Caring for Your Aging Parents. Vivian E. Greenberg. 301p. 18.95 (*0-669-21332-2*, Lexington) Jossey-Bass.

Your Best Money Moves Now. Money Magazine Editors. 224p. 1993. 19.95 (*0-8487-1157-2*) Oxmoor Hse.

Your Best Sport: How to Choose & Play It. Jonathan P. Niednagel. LC 92-60519. (Illus.). 385p. (Orig.). 1992. pap. 19.95 (*0-916309-01-0*) Laguna Pr.

***Your Best Year Yet.** David S. Kirkwood. 682p. 1996. 19.95 (*0-9629625-6-2*) Ethnos.

Your Better Self: A Guide to Self-Improvement Based on Chassidic Teachings. Chaim Dalfin. 158p. 1994. 14.95 (*1-56871-086-0*) Targum Pr.

Your Bible's Alive: How to Get Friendly with God's Book. (Custom Curriculum Ser.). (Illus.). (YA). (gr. 10-12). 1994. pap. 12.99 (*0-7814-5152-3*, 17277) Cook.

Your Blues Ain't Like Mine. Bebe Moore Campbell. 336p. 1993. pap. 12.00 (*0-345-38395-8*, One World) Ballantine.

Your Blues Ain't Like Mine. Bebe Moore Campbell. 1995. mass mkt. 6.99 (*0-345-40112-3*) Ballantine.

Your Blues Ain't Like Mine. Bebe Moore Campbell. 352p. 1992. 23.95 (*0-399-13746-7*, Putnam) Putnam Pub Group.

Your Blues Ain't Like Mine. large type ed. Bebe Moore Campbell. LC 95-8920. (Large Print Bks.). 1995. 24.95 (*1-56895-221-X*) Wheeler Pub.

Your Boat's Electrical System. rev. ed. Conrad Miller & E. S. Maloney. LC 88-11002. (Illus.). 512p. 1988. 23.00 (*0-688-08132-0*, Hearst Marine Bks) Morrow.

***Your Body.** LC 96-35293. (It's a Fact! Ser.). (J). 1997. lib. bdg. 14.95 (*0-88682-857-0*) Creative Ed.

Your Body. (Learners Ser.). 48p. (J). 3.50 (*0-7214-1703-5*, Ladybrd) Penguin.

Your Body. (Information Activity Ser.). 24p. (J). 3.50 (*0-7214-3441-X*, Ladybrd) Penguin.

Your Body. Linda Schwartz. (Science Mini Units Ser.). (Illus.). 48p. (J). (gr. 2-5). 1990. 6.95 (*0-88160-191-8*, LW 150) Learning Wks.

Your Body. Kathryn Senior. LC 93-40314. (X-Ray Picture Bks.). 48p. (J). 1994. lib. bdg. 22.70 (*0-531-14336-8*) Watts.

Your Body. Kathryn Senior. (X-Ray Picture Bks.). (Illus.). 48p. (J). (gr. 5-8). 1994. pap. 8.95 (*0-531-15717-2*) Watts.

Your Body: The Ultimate Lethal Weapon. Keith D. Yates. (Illus.). 104p. 1987. pap. 12.00 (*0-87364-438-7*) Paladin Pr.

Your Body: Treasures Inside. Donna K. Wells. LC 90-30632. (Discovery World Ser.). (Illus.). 32p. (J). (ps-2). 1990. lib. bdg. 21.36 (*0-89565-576-4*) Childs World.

Your Body, an Owner's Manual: (Positively Yoga) Eleanor M. Howard. Ed. by Lorraine Meier. (Illus.). 85p. 1990. write for info. (*0-9627077-0-8*) E M Howard.

Your Body Believes Every Word You Say: The Language of the Body - Mind Connection. Barbara H. Levine. LC 90-1169. 224p. (Orig.). 1991. pap. 13.95 (*0-944031-07-2*) Aslan Pub.

***Your Body Believes Every Word You Say: The Language of the Body & Mind Connection.** Barbara H. Levine. 1997. pap. text ed. 15.95 (*0-944031-74-9*) Aslan Pub.

***Your Body Belongs to You.** Cornelia Spelman. LC 97-1787. (Concept Bks.). (Illus.). 24p. (J). (ps-1). 1997. lib. bdg. 12.95 (*0-8075-9474-1*) A Whitman.

Your Body Can Talk: Learning to Listen to What Your Boby Knows & Needs Through Simple Muscle Testing. Susan L. Levy & Carol Lehr. LC 96-14124. (Illus.). 350p. (Orig.). 1996. pap. 19.95 (*0-934252-68-8*) Hohm Pr.

Your Body Doesn't Lie. John Diamond. 208p. 1989. mass mkt. 5.99 (*0-446-35847-9*) Warner Bks.

Your Body Intuitive Series, 4 vols. Catherine M. Darnell. Ed. by Stella Ghetie. Incl. Understanding Your Body's Architecture. (Illus.). (Orig.). 1995. pap. 4.95 (*0-9650325-0-7*); Understanding Your Body's Wiring. (Illus.). (Orig.). 1995. pap. 6.95 (*0-9650325-1-5*); Understanding Your Body's Vascular Container. (Illus.). 1995. pap. 6.95 (*0-9650325-2-3*); Understanding Your Body's Inner Workings. (Illus.). (Orig.). 1995. pap. 6.95 (*0-9650325-3-1*); 28.95 (*0-9650325-7-4*) Cottage Wrks.

Your Body Is Your Best Doctor. Melvin E. Page. Orig. Title: Health Versus Disease. 236p. 1991. reprint ed. pap. 5.95 (*0-87983-540-0*) Keats.

***Your Body Know Best.** Gittleman. 1997. mass mkt. 6.50 (*0-671-87591-4*) PB.

Your Body Knows Best: The Revolutionary Eating Plan That Helps You Achieve Your Optimal Weight & Energy Level for Life. Ann L. Gittleman et al. Ed. by Amelia Sheldon. LC 95-33222. 288p. 1996. 23.00 (*0-671-87592-2*, PB Hardcover) PB.

Your Body Never Lies. Carmen R. Berry. 218p. (Orig.). 1994. 21.95 (*1-879290-02-2*); pap. 12.95 (*1-879290-03-0*) PageMill Pr.

Your Body Remembers: A Conscious Choice to Live. Kandis Blakely. 96p. (Orig.). (C). 1994. pap. text ed. 12.95 (*1-886531-49-8*) K Blakely.

***Your Body Speaks: Having 'Pun' with Your Body.** Darlana Montague. (Illus.). 184p. (Orig.). 1998. pap. 11.95 (*1-889529-05-2*) Two Feathers.

Your Body Speaks Its Mind. Stanley Keleman. 188p. 1981. reprint ed. 10.95 (*0-934320-03-9*); reprint ed. pap. 10.95 (*0-934320-01-2*) Center Pr.

***Your Body Speaks Your Mind: How Your Thoughts & Emotions Create Your Health.** Debbie Shapiro. (Illus.). 256p. (Orig.). 1997. pap. 14.95 (*0-89594-893-1*) Crossing Pr.

Your Body, Yourself. rev. ed. Alison Bell & Lisa Rooney. (Illus.). 160p. (J). (gr. 4-8). 1996. pap. 8.95 (*1-56565-532-X*) Lowell Hse Juvenile.

Your Body, Yourself: A Guide to Your Changing Body. Alison Bell & Lisa Rooney. (Illus.). 128p. (YA). 1993. pap. 6.95 (*1-56565-045-X*) Lowell Hse.

***Your Body's Heroes & Villains.** P. Bauerle. (Microexplorers). 1997. 11.95 (*0-7641-5051-0*) Barron.

Your Body's Many Cries for Water: You Are Not Sick, You Are Thirsty! F. Batmanghelidj. (Illus.). 200p. 1995. pap. 14.95 (*0-9629942-3-5*) Global Hlth.

***Your Body's Many Cries for Water: You Are Not Sick, You Are Thirsty.** 2nd rev. ed. F. Batmanghelidj. (Illus.). 200p. 1997. 27.00 (*0-9629942-5-1*) Global Hlth.

Your Body's Response. Edgar Brown & Kaye Behrens. LC 82-90165. (Illus.). 192p. (Orig.). 1985. 22.95 (*0-9613697-1-X*); pap. 16.95 (*0-9613697-0-1*) Madison Ave Pub.

***Your Body's Wisdom: A Body Centered Approach to Transformation.** Renee Welfeld. LC 97-5371. 256p. (Orig.). 1997. pap. 15.00 (*1-57071-147-X*) Sourcebks.

Your Bones: An Inside Look at Skeletons. Peter Murray. LC 92-7460. (Umbrella Bks.). (Illus.). 32p. (J). (gr. 2-6). 1992. lib. bdg. 21.36 (*0-89565-968-9*) Childs World.

Your Book of Financial Planning. Ed. by Loren Dunton. 1983. 32.95 (*0-8359-9505-4*, Reston) P-H.

Your Book of Heraldry. Richard Slade. 7.95 (*0-685-91533-6*) Transatl Arts.

Your Book of Magic. Alexander Van Rensselaer. (J). (gr. 9 up). 1968. 7.95 (*0-571-06939-8*) Transatl Arts.

Your Book of Modelling. Richard Slade. (J). (gr. 4 up). 1968. 7.95 (*0-571-08387-0*) Transatl Arts.

Your Book of Money. David Jones. (J). (gr. 7 up). 1971. 7.95 (*0-571-09341-8*) Transatl Arts.

Your Book of Veteran & Edwardian Cars. John Coleman. (J). (gr. 7 up). 1972. 7.95 (*0-571-09375-2*) Transatl Arts.

Your Book of Vintage Cars. John Coleman. (Illus.). (J). (gr. 7 up). 1969. 7.95 (*0-571-08276-9*) Transatl Arts.

Your Book of Watching Wildlife. Michael Blackmore. (YA). (gr. 7 up). 1972. 7.95 (*0-571-08347-1*) Transatl Arts.

Your Boss Is Not Your Mother: Breaking Free from Emotional Politics to Achieve Independence & Success at Work. Brian Des Roches. 240p. 1996. pap. 11.00 (*0-380-71924-X*) Avon.

Your Bowels & Better Health. 1991. lib. bdg. 75.00 (*0-8490-5122-3*) Gordon Pr.

Your Brain: How You Got It & How It Works. Tabitha M. Powledge. LC 94-14273. (J). 1994. text ed. 14.95 (*0-684-19659-X*) S&S Trade.

Your Brain & Nervous System. Leslie J. LeMaster. LC 84-7635. (New True Bks.). (Illus.). 48p. (J). (gr. k-4). 1984. pap. 5.50 (*0-516-41931-5*); lib. bdg. 19.00 (*0-516-01931-7*) Childrens.

Your Brain & P. M. S. 1996. lib. bdg. 250.75 (*0-8490-5891-0*) Gordon Pr.

Your Brain & the Mind of Christ. William G. Rorick. LC 84-50081. 140p. 1984. 12.95 (*0-938232-43-6*) Winston-Derek.

Your Brain at Work: A New View of Personality & Behavior. Margaret A. Golton. 114p. (Orig.). 1983. pap. 7.95 (*0-685-07800-0*) Frank Pubns.

Your Brain Glossary for the Brain Decade: A Neurobrowser. Ken A. Sifr. LC 96-90126. (Orig.). 1996. pap. 11.95 (*0-533-11910-3*) Vantage.

Your Breast & You: What Every Woman Needs to Know about Breast Diseases, Breast Cancer & Cosmetic Breast Surgery Before She Has a Breast Problem. D. S. Halbert. Ed. by Delno Roberts. LC 84-72983. (Illus.). 238p. 1986. 14.95 (*0-931609-00-3*) Askon Pub.

Your Breast Cancer Treatment Handbook: A Patient's Guide to Understanding the Disease, Treatment Options, & Physical & Emotional Recovery from Breast Cancer. Judy C. Kneece. LC 94-31864. (Illus.). 203p. 1995. pap. 19.95 (*1-886665-01-X*) EduCare Pub.

***Your Bridge to a Better Future.** John C. Maxwell. 208p. 1997. 12.99 (*0-7852-7433-2*) Nelson.

Your Brother's Keeper: A Guide for Families Confronting Psychiatric Illness. James R. Morrison. LC 79-27810. 352p. 1981. 28.95 (*0-88229-563-2*) Nelson-Hall.

***Your Business: Making It Work for You.** Mike Shaw. (Small Business Ser.). 1996. pap. 24.95 (*0-7494-2061-8*) Kogan Page Ltd.

Your Business Almanack, Vol. 1: The ABCs of Business Management. Paul B. Fawthrop & Poor Richard. 62p. (Orig.). 1992. pap. 4.75 (*0-9631498-3-0*); pap. text ed. 6.75 (*0-9631498-4-9*) Firetowne.

Your Business-America's Best Tax Shelter. Irving L. Blackman. LC 84-102848. (Special Report Ser.: No. 1). 51p. 1987. pap. 25.00 (*0-916181-00-6*) Blackman Kallick Bartelstein.

Your Business Is Either Growing or Dying: How to Start & Properly Manage Your Business for Growth. (Self-Improvement Business Ser.). 28p. 1993. pap. text ed. 8.95 (*1-884392-00-8*) Busn Develop.

***Your Business Now: A Self Diagnostic Workbook.** 216p. 39.95 (*0-644-06988-0*, Pub. by Aust Gov Pub AT) Aubrey Bks.

Your Business Plan. 2nd ed. Dennis J. Sargent et al. (Oregon SBDC Network Workbooks Ser.). 87p. 1995. 20.00 (*1-878475-15-0*) Oregon Small Busn Dev Ctr.

Your Business Plan. 4th ed. Dennis J. Sargent et al. (Oregon SBDC Network Workbook Ser.). 86p. (C). 1994. student ed. 20.00 (*1-878475-05-3*) Oregon Small Busn Dev Ctr.

Your Business Plan: How to Create It, How to Use It. Leon Rogers & Brent Weidman. Ed. by Sharon Lamberton. LC 93-37571. (Illus.). 128p. (Orig.). 1993. pap. 22.00 (*0-86718-390-X*) Home Builder.

Your Business Records. 32p. 1982. 3.25 (*0-685-07421-8*, 97818-0) P-H.

Your Business, Your Son & You. Jack H. McQuaig. 192p. 1979. 10.00 (*0-686-62444-0*) B Klein Pubns.

Your Calf: A Kid's Guide to Raising & Showing Beef & Dairy Calves. Heather S. Thomas. LC 96-32097. (Illus.). 192p. (Orig.). (J). (gr. 4 up). Date not set. pap. 12.95 (*0-88266-947-8*) Storey Comm Inc.

Your California Business: Everything You Should Know to Start & Run a Business in California. John F. Hulpke. 560p. 1993. pap. 27.95 (*0-88415-052-6*) Gulf Pub.

Your Calling in God: A Release from the Cage of Mediocrity to the Path of Your Destiny. John Tetsola. Ed. by Perry M. Mallory. 150p. (Orig.). 1996. pap. 9.99 (*0-9634306-5-3*) End-Time Wave.

Your Car (Or Truck) & the Environment: An Environmental Guide for Owners & Drivers of Cars, Vans, Trucks & Other Motor Vehicles. (Illus.). 24p. (Orig.). 1996. pap. 15.00 (*0-7881-2916-3*) DIANE Pub.

Your Career: A Contemporary Approach to Self-Development. 368p. 1975. write for info. (*0-672-96833-9*); teacher ed. write for info. (*0-672-96869-X*) Macmillan.

Your Career: How to Make It Happen. 2nd ed. Julie G. Levitt. (C). 1990. pap. 28.95 (*0-538-70167-6*, CA42BB) S-W Pub.

Your Career: How to Make It Happen. 3rd ed. Julie G. Levitt. (CA - Career Development Ser.). 1996. pap. 28.95 (*0-538-71259-7*) S-W Pub.

Your Career: Thinking about Jobs & Careers. Susan Christophersen & J. Michael Farr. Ed. by Greg Croy. (Career & Life Skills Ser.). (Illus.). 58p. (YA). (gr. 9-12). 1991. pap. 5.95 (*0-942784-60-X*, YC) JIST Works.

Your Career Adventure. Miller. Date not set. text ed. 42.50 (*0-314-69753-5*) West Pub.

***Your Career Adventure.** 2nd ed. Miller. Date not set. write for info. (*0-314-22322-3*) Wadsworth Pub.

Your Career As a Medical Secretary Transcriber. Selma G. Berkeley & Barbara E. Jackson. LC 74-34233. (Wiley Biomedical-Health Publication Ser.). 208p. reprint ed. pap. 59.30 (*0-317-28655-2*, 2055088) Bks Demand.

Your Career Fast Track Starts in College: Develop Your Talents to Win in a Competitive World. Roger Cameron. 246p. (Orig.). 1992. pap. 19.95 (*0-9623216-3-X*) Odenwald Pr.

Your Career in Administrative Medical Services. Roberta C. Weiss. Ed. by Lisa Biello. LC 95-17451. (Illus.). 384p. 1996. text ed. 36.00 (*0-7216-6077-0*) Saunders.

Your Career in Administrative Services: Teacher's Resource Package. Roberta C. Weiss. Ed. by Lisa Biello. 128p. 1996. teacher ed., pap. text ed. 125.00 (*0-7216-6078-9*) Saunders.

Your Career in Cardiovascular Technology. Roberta C. Weiss. LC 95-17718. 1996. pap. text ed. 36.00 (*0-7216-6074-6*) Saunders.

Your Career in Cardiovascular Technology: Teacher's Resource Package. Roberta C. Weiss. Ed. by Lisa Biello. 128p. 1996. teacher ed., pap. text ed. 167.00 (*0-7216-6075-4*) Saunders.

Your Career in Changing Times. Lee Ellis & Larry Burkett. 1993. 18.99 (*0-8024-1667-5*) Moody.

Your Career in Coaching: Study Guide for EFA/NCAS Level 1 (G) Accreditation. Sue H. Brown & Sandra Pearson-Adams. 240p. 1995. spiral bd. 59.95 (*0-644-45215-3*, Pub. by AGPS Pr AT) Intl Spec Bk.

Your Career in Health Care. Beverly J. Rambo & Diane Watson. 1976. text ed. 30.95 (*0-07-051166-7*) McGraw.

Your Career in Health Care. Robert Wilson. LC 96-1229. 1996. 12.95 (*0-8120-9599-5*) Barron.

Your Career in Marketing. 2nd ed. John A. Beaumont et al. 1976. text ed. 25.32 (*0-07-004245-4*) McGraw.

Your Career in Nursing. 2nd ed. Lila Anastas. (Illus.). 240p. 1988. pap. 12.95 (*0-88737-396-8*, 14-2216) Natl League Nurse.

Your Career in Physical Medicine. Weiss. LC 97-10170. 1997. pap. text ed. 39.95 (*0-7216-6453-9*) Saunders.

Your Career in Physical Medicine: Teacher's Resource Package. Robert C. Weiss. Ed. by Lisa Beillo. 240p. 1997. teacher ed., text ed. 175.00 (*0-7216-6454-7*) Saunders.

Your Career in the Comics. Lee Nordling & Newspaper Features Council Staff. (Illus.). 304p. 1995. pap. 9.95 (*0-8362-0748-3*) Andrews & McMeel.

Your Career in the World of Work. Milton Berlye. LC 75-12236. 1975. pap. write for info. (*0-672-97534-3*) Macmillan.

Your Career, Travel, Tourism & Hospitality. 2nd ed. Stevens. (Food & Hospitality Ser.). 1988. text ed. 21.95 (*0-8273-3332-3*) Delmar.

Your Caribbean Souvenir Song Book. Irving Burgie. Ed. by Mark Phillips. (Illus.). (Orig.). 1990. pap. text ed. 12.95 (*0-89524-404-7*) Cherry Lane.

***Your Catholic Wedding: A Complete Plan-Book.** rev. ed. Chris Aridas. LC 97-565. 192p. 1997. pap. 8.95 (*0-8245-1675-3*) Crossroad NY.

Your Cat's First Year. Jane Burton & Kim Taylor. 1985. 12.95 (*0-671-60090-7*) S&S Trade.

Your Cat's Wild Cousins. Photos & Text by Hope Ryden. (Illus.). 48p. (J). (gr. 2-5). 1992. pap. 16.00 (*0-525-67354-7*, Lodestar Bks) Dutton Child Bks.

Your Character, Your Life! Classic Wit & Wisdom for the Year 2000. William M. Shaw, II. 96p. 1993. pap. text ed. 9.00 (*0-9637665-0-3*) Honor Mention.

Your Cheatin' Heart. Chet Flippo. 1993. mass mkt. 4.99 (*0-312-95103-5*) St Martin.

Your Check Is in the Mail. rev. ed. Bruce Goldman et al. 432p. 1984. mass mkt. 7.95 (*0-446-37926-3*) Warner Bks.

Your Chickens: A Kid's Guide to Raising & Showing. Gail Damerow. Ed. by Gwen Steege & Lorin Driggs. LC 92-54655. (Illus.). 144p. (Orig.). 1993. pap. 12.95 (*0-88266-823-4*, Garden Way Pub) Storey Comm Inc.

Your Child: A Medical Guide. Consumer Guide Editors & Ira J. Chasnoff. (Illus.). 576p. 1993. 9.98 (*0-88176-391-8*, 3200700) Pubns Intl Ltd.

Your Child & Cholesterol. Eugene Eisman. Ed. by Diane Eisman. 196p. 1990. 9.95 (*0-8119-0034-7*) LIFETIME.

Your Child & Epilepsy. Robert J. Gumnit. 243p. 1995. pap. 24.95 (*0-939957-76-0*) Demos Vermande.

Your Child & Health Care: A "Dollars & Sense" Guide for Families with Special Needs. Lynn R. Rosenfeld. 608p. 1994. pap. 29.00 (1-55766-154-5, 1545) P H Brookes.

Your Child & the Piano: More Joy in Music for Parent, Child & Teacher. Margaret Grant. 89p. 1980. pap. 5.95 (0-7736-1060-X) Genl Dist Srvs.

Your Child & Vitamin E. Wilfrid E. Shute. LC 79-88120. 1979. pap. 2.25 (0-87983-202-9) Keats.

Your Child & X-Rays: A Parent's Guide to Radiation, X-Rays & Other Imaging Procedures. Avice M. O'Connell & Norma L. Leone. LC 87-37854. (Illus.). 104p. (Orig.). 1989. pap. 8.95 (0-936635-05-3) Lion Pr & Vid.

Your Child at Play: Birth to One Year. Marilyn Segal. LC 85-325. (Your Child at Play Ser.). (Illus.). 288p. 1991. 21.95 (0-937858-50-1); pap. 14.95 (0-937858-51-X) Newmarket.

Your Child at Play: One to Two Years. Marilyn Segal & Don Adcock. LC 84-14318. (Your Child at Play Ser.). (Illus.). 224p. 1991. 16.95 (0-937858-52-8); pap. 14.95 (0-937858-53-6) Newmarket.

Your Child at Play: Three to Five Years. Marilyn Segal & Don Adcock. LC 86-60294. (Your Child at Play Ser.: Vol. 4). (Illus.). 224p. 1991. 16.95 (0-937858-72-2) Newmarket.

Your Child at Play: Three to Five Years. Marilyn Segal & Don Adcock. LC 86-60294. (Your Child at Play Ser.: Vol. 4). (Illus.). 224p. (J). (ps-k). 1991. pap. 14.95 (0-937858-73-0) Newmarket.

Your Child at Play: Two to Three Years. Marilyn Segal & Don Adcock. LC 84-12598. (Your Child at Play Ser.). (Illus.). 208p. 1991. 21.95 (0-937858-54-4); pap. 14.95 (0-937858-55-2) Newmarket.

Your Child Can Read Better: Handbook for Parents. Donna Hartmann & Arlyss Stump. LC 79-84490. (Orig.). 1980. pap. text ed. 17.95 (0-918452-19-8, 198) Learning Pubns.

***Your Child Doesn't Have to Die! How You Can Help Your Child Overcome Cancer Using Nutritional Therapy.** Usa C. Ragsdale. (Orig.). 1996. pap. 12.00 (0-9654714-0-3) Abundant Living.

Your Child from One to Six. Richard H. Granger. (Illus.). 92p. (C). 1995. pap. text ed. 15.00 (0-7881-2073-5) DIANE Pub.

Your Child from One to Ten. Peter Bowler. (C). 1990. 65.00 (0-86431-034-X, Pub. by Aust Council Educ Res AT) St Mut.

Your Child, God's Champion! Chuck Zimmer. (Illus.). 144p. (Orig.). (C). 1992. pap. 9.95 (0-9635208-0-6) Sunergos Minist.

Your Child Has a Handicap: A Practical Guide to Daily Care. Mark L. Batshaw. 1991. pap. 18.95 (0-316-08368-2) Little.

Your Child Has a Handicap: A Practical Guide to Daily Care. Mark L. Batshaw. 1993. 33.95 (0-316-08369-0) Little.

***Your Child in the Hospital.** Nancy Keene & Rachel Prentice. Ed. by Linda Lamb. (Orig.). pap. write for info. (1-56592-346-4) OReilly & Assocs.

***Your Child Is Smart.** Dawna Markova & Anne R. Powell. 1997. 6.98 (1-56731-196-2, MJF Bks) Fine Comms.

Your Child Is Smarter Than You Think. Wanda Draper. Ed. by Staci Elder. (Living & Working with Children Ser.). 272p. (Orig.). 1993. pap. 12.00 (0-939965-06-2) Macedon Prod.

Your Child Makes Sense: A Guidebook for Parents. Edith Buxbaum. 204p. (Orig.). 1961. pap. 24.95 (0-8236-8350-8, 027040) Intl Univs Pr.

Your Child, My Child. Jennifer Mikels. 1993. mass mkt. 3.39 (0-373-09807-3, 5-09807-4) Silhouette.

***Your Child Needs a Champion: Mastering the A.D.D. Challenge by Making the Right Choices.** Jane F. Miller. LC 97-93086. (Illus.). 224p. 1997. spiral bd., pap. 16.95 (0-9658190-0-0) J Miller Assocs.

Your Child with Arthritis: A Family Guide for Caregiving. Lori B. Tucker et al. LC 95-49212. (Health Book Ser.). (Illus.). 256p. (C). 1996. 25.95 (0-8018-5293-5) Johns Hopkins.

***Your Child, Your Family, & Autosomal Recessive Polycystic Kidney Disease.** 2nd rev. ed. Lisa Guay-Woodford et al. Ed. by Wendy Rueb & Deborah Hirsch. (Illus.). 40p. 1996. pap. 15.00 (0-614-30096-7) PKR Foundation.

Your Children Should Know: Teach Your Children the Strategies That Will Keep Them Safe from Assault & Crime. Flora Colao & Tamar Hosansky. LC 83-5981. (Illus.). 192p. 1983. write for info. (0-672-52777-4) Macmillan.

Your Child's Baptism. 16p. (Orig.). 1989. pap. 2.95 (0-8146-1883-9) Liturgical Pr.

Your Child's Birth: A Comprehensive Guide for Pregnancy, Birth, & Postpartum. Ed. by Sheila T. Woerth et al. (Avery's Childbirth Education Ser.). (Illus.). 96p. (Orig.). 1983. pap. 5.95 (0-89529-182-7) Avery Pub.

Your Child's Confirmation: Reflections for Parents on the Sacrament of Christian Identity. Carol Luebering. 32p. 1990. pap. text ed. 1.95 (0-86716-076-4) St Anthony Mess Pr.

Your Child's Emotional Health: Adolescence. Philadelphia Child Guidance Center Staff & Jack Maguire. 160p. 1995. 9.95 (0-02-860003-7) Macmillan.

Your Child's Emotional Health: The Early Years. Philadelphia Child Guidance Center Staff & Jack Maguire. LC 94-34151. 176p. 1995. 9.95 (0-02-860001-0) Macmillan.

Your Child's Emotional Health: The Middle Years. Philadelphia Child Guidance Center Staff & Jack Maguire. 160p. 1995. 9.95 (0-02-860002-9) Macmillan.

Your Child's Faith: Building a Foundation. Larry D. Stephens. 224p. 1996. pap. 10.99 (0-310-20203-5) Zondervan.

Your Child's First Communion. Redemptorist Pastoral Pubns. Staff. (Illus.). 16p. 1990. pap. 2.95 (0-89243-328-0) Liguori Pubns.

Your Child's First Communion: A Look at Your Dreams. Carol Luebering. 32p. (Orig.). 1984. pap. text ed. 1.95 (0-86716-035-7) St Anthony Mess Pr.

Your Child's First Confession: Preparing for the Sacrament of Reconciliation. Rosemary Gallagher. (Redemptorist Pastoral Publications). (Illus.). 16p. 1994. reprint ed. pap. 2.95 (0-89243-656-5) Liguori Pubns.

Your Child's First Journey: A Guide to Prepared Birth from Pregnancy to Parenthood. 2nd ed. Ginny Brinkley et al. LC 87-33657. 272p. 1988. pap. 10.95 (0-89529-372-2) Avery Pub.

Your Child's First School: A Handbook for Parents. Diana Townsend-Butterworth. 271p. (Orig.). 1992. 22.95 (0-8027-1169-3); pap. 14.95 (0-8027-7358-3) Walker & Co.

Your Child's Fitness: Practical Advice for Parents. Susan Kalish. LC 95-8976. (Illus.). 182p. (Orig.). 1995. pap. 14.95 (0-87322-540-6, PKAL0540) Human Kinetics.

Your Child's Food Allergies: Detecting & Treating Hyperactivity, Congestion, Irritability & Other Symptoms Caused by Common Food Allergies. Jane McNicol. LC 91-34661. 176p. 1992. pap. text ed. 9.95 (0-471-55801-X) Wiley.

Your Child's Growing Mind: A Guide to Learning & Brain Development from Birth to Adolescence. Jane M. Healy. LC 93-29178. 368p. 1994. pap. 12.95 (0-385-46930-6) Doubleday.

Your Child's Health: A Pediatric Guide for Parents. Barton D. Schmitt. LC 87-47687. 304p. (Orig.). 1991. pap. 17.95 (0-553-35339-X) Bantam.

***Your Child's Medical Journal.** Sharon Larson. 1998. pap. write for info. (0-609-80244-5) Crown Pub Group.

Your Child's Mind: The Complete Guide to Infant & Child Emotional Well-Being. Herman Roiphe & Anne Roiphe. 448p. 1986. pap. 10.95 (0-312-89784-7) St Martin.

***Your Child's Profession of Faith.** Dennis Gundersen. 64p. (Orig.). 1997. pap. 3.95 (1-879737-23-X) Calvary Press.

Your Child's Self-Esteem: The Key to His Life. Dorothy C. Briggs. LC 70-121948. 360p. 1975. pap. 11.95 (0-385-04020-2, Dolp) Doubleday.

Your Child's Speech & Language: Guidelines for Parents. Mary Brooks et al. 52p. 1978. pap. text ed. 13.00 (0-89079-039-6, 1070) PRO-ED.

Your Child's Symptoms. John Garwood & Amanda Bennett. 224p. (Orig.). 1995. pap. 11.00 (0-425-14734-7, Berkley Trade) Berkley Pub.

Your Child's Vision Is Important. Caroline Beverstock. 24p. 1990. 2.00 (0-87207-167-7) Intl Reading.

Your Chinese Horoscope 1997. Neil Somerville. 272p. 1996. pap. 10.00 (0-7225-3303-9) Harper SF.

***Your Chinese Horoscope 1998: What the Year of the Tiger Holds in Store for You.** Neil Somerville. 320p. 1997. pap. 10.00 (0-7225-3440-X) Thorsons SF.

Your Chinese Roots. Thomas Tsu-wee Tan. (Illus.). 264p. 1987. pap. 9.95 (0-89346-285-3) Heian Intl.

***Your Choice.** Mangelsdorf. 1996. pap. text ed. 0.45 (0-312-11154-1) St Martin.

Your Choice: Basic Writing Guide. Mangelsdorf. 1996. pap. text ed. 20.50 (0-312-11153-3) St Martin.

***Your Choice & Pocket Style.** 2nd ed. Mangelsdorf. 1997. pap. text ed. 25.65 (0-312-17141-2) St Martin.

Your Church: Basic Doctrines & Practices of the Church of the Nazarene. Robert Troutman. (Illus.). 32p. 1989. pap. 1.99 (0-8341-1299-X) Beacon Hill.

Your Church & Its Mission: A Congregational Self-Study Program. Michael B. Regele. 96p. (Orig.). 1989. 99.95 (0-317-93394-9) Percept Grp.

Your Church Bulletin Board: 3-D Ideas for All Seasons. Cindy L. Carr & George Rich. (Illus.). 64p. 1995. wbk. ed. 9.95 (0-87227-185-4, RBP5222) Reg Baptist.

Your Church Can Be - Family Friendly: How You Can Launch a Successful Family Ministry in Your Congregation. Steve Thomas. 1996. 10.99 (0-89900-746-5) College Pr Pub.

***Your Church Has Personality: Find Your Focus - Maximize Your Mission.** 2nd rev. ed. 140p. 1997. pap. 12.95 (0-912961-98-8) Ch Growth Ctr.

Your City. Edward L. Thorndike. LC 75-22842. (America in Two Centuries Ser.). 1976. reprint ed. 18.95 (0-405-07713-0) Ayer.

Your City's 1040: Federal Tax Reform & Municipalities. 110p. 1987. 15.00 (0-933729-17-0) Natl League Cities.

Your Code Name Is Jonah. large type ed. Edward Packard. (Choose Your Own Adventure Ser.). 114p. (J). (gr. 3-7). 1987. reprint ed. 8.95 (0-942545-15-X); reprint ed. lib. bdg. 9.95 (0-942545-20-6) Grey Castle.

Your College Application. rev. ed. Scott Gelband. 133p. 1991. pap. 9.95 (0-87447-428-0) College Bd.

Your College Experience: Activities Split. 3rd ed. John N. Gardner. (Freshman Orientation Ser.). 1997. suppl. ed., pap. 17.95 (0-534-51897-4) Wadsworth Pub.

Your College Experience: Reader Split. 3rd ed. John N. Gardner. LC 96-36691. (Freshman Orientation Ser.). 1997. suppl. ed., pap. 19.95 (0-534-51898-2) Wadsworth Pub.

Your College Experience: Strategies for Success. John N. Gardner et al. LC 95-30980. 388p. (C). 1992. pap. 24.95 (0-534-16140-5) Wadsworth Pub.

Your College Experience: Strategies for Success. 2nd ed. John N. Gardner & A. Jerome Jewler. LC 94-36748. 1995. pap. 28.95 (0-534-30960-7) Wadsworth Pub.

Your College Experience: Strategies for Success. 3rd ed. John N. Gardner & A. Jerome Jewler. (Freshman Orientation Ser.). (C). 1997. pap. text ed. 28.95 (0-534-51894-X) Wadsworth Pub.

Your College Experience: Strategies for Success, Concise Edition. A. Jerome Jewler & John N. Gardner. 240p. (C). 1993. pap. 18.75 (0-534-19962-3) Wadsworth Pub.

Your College Experience: Strategies for Success, Concise Edition. 2nd abr. ed. John N. Gardner & A. Jerome Jewler. LC 95-30980. (C). 1996. pap. 19.95 (0-534-26520-0) Wadsworth Pub.

***Your College Experience, Concise.** 3rd ed. John N. Gardner & A. Jerome Jewler. (Freshman Orientation Ser.). (C). (gr. 11 up). 1997. pap. text ed. 27.95 (0-534-53748-0) Wadsworth Pub.

Your Colon, Its Character, Care & Therapy. Stan Malstrom. (Tree of Knowledge Ser.: No. 3). 34p. pap. 3.95 (0-913923-36-2) Woodland UT.

***Your Commonsense Guide to Personal Financial Planning: Learn How to Budget, Protect & Save Your Money.** Charles Ross. 1997. pap. text ed. 6.50 (0-7852-7222-4) Nelson.

Your Companion to Twelve Step Recovery. Robert Odom. LC 94-10243. 192p. 1994. pap. 8.95 (1-56170-098-3, 161) Hay House.

***Your Company Safety & Heatlh Manual.** O. Dan Nwaelele. (Illus.). 450p. 1997. pap. text ed. 79.00 (0-86587-590-1) Gov Insts.

***Your Competent, Confident Child: Raising Your Baby the RIE Way.** Magda Gerber & Allan Johnson. LC 97-18840. 304p. (YA). 1998. pap. 15.95 (0-471-17883-7) Wiley.

Your Complete Guide to Buying, Selling, or Exporting Cars Profitably. Myrna Sison. (Illus.). 160p. (Orig.). 1996. spiral bd. 40.00 (1-883614-93-7) CA Kit Direct.

***Your Complete Guide to Financial Security: How to Invest & Prepare for Your Future Peace of Mind.** Larry Burkett. 1998. 12.99 (0-88486-170-8, Inspirational Pr) Arrowood Pr.

***Your Complete Guide to Money Happiness: How to Achieve Financial Success, Security & Peace of Mind.** Henry S. Brock. LC 96-77754. (Illus.). 576p. 1997. 24.95 (0-9653886-9-7) Legacy NV.

Your Complete Guide to Self-Protection Against Violent Criminals: Protect Yourself, Home & Family Against Robbers, Burglars, Rapists & Other Violent Criminals. Michael T. Petro, Jr. LC 95-92799. 293p. 1996. pap. 38.95 (0-9650411-1-5) Petro Pubns.

Your Complete Guide to Sexual Health. Elizabeth T. Ortiz. 1989. pap. 32.25 (0-13-679572-2) P-H.

Your Complete Guide to the Solar Eclipse of Jan. 4, 1992. Joe Rao & Ken Abel. (Illus.). 64p. (Orig.). 1991. pap. text ed. 4.95 (0-944214-00-2) ABELexpress.

Your Complete Guide to the Solar Eclipse of May 10, 1994. B. Ralph Chou & Ken Abel. 128p. 1994. pap. 6.95 (0-944214-04-5) ABELexpress.

Your Complete Medical Record. People's Medical Society Staff. 1993. pap. 12.95 (1-882606-00-0) Peoples Med Soc.

Your Complete Real Estate Game Plan & Playbook. Business Facts Press Editors. LC 91-73124. 130p. (Orig.). 1991. pap. 24.00 (0-9630224-0-7) Busn Facts.

Your Complete Study Guide on Salvation & the Holy Spirit. Avaneda D. Hobbs. (Illus.). 82p. (Orig.). 1991. 12.95 (1-878898-05-1) Christian Star.

Your Complete Wedding Planner. rev. ed. Marjabelle Y. Stewart. (Illus.). 224p. 1988. pap. 14.95 (0-312-02531-9) St Martin.

Your Comprehensive School Guidance & Counseling Program: A Handbook of Practical Activities. C. E. Van Zandt & J. B. Hayslip. LC 93-25770. 208p. (C). 1994. pap. text ed. 27.50 (0-8013-1147-0, 79621) Longman.

Your Computer Can Kill You. Fred Bamberger. 1984. ring bd. 74.95 (0-917194-15-2) Prog Studies.

Your Condo-Co-Op: Tips for Living Comfortably in a Small Space. Jean E. Laird. 1983. pap. write for info. (0-8289-0515-0) Viking Penguin.

***Your Confirmation.** Stott. 13.99 (0-340-63017-5, Pub. by H & S UK) Trafalgar.

***Your Confirmation.** Stott. 15.95 (0-340-52180-5, Pub. by H & S UK) Trafalgar.

Your Conflict Cookbook: A Teacher's Handbook for Helping Students Deal with Anger & Violence. Thomas Crum & Judith Warner. 80p. 1994. pap. text ed. 19.95 (1-877803-08-1) Aiki Works.

***Your Constitution.** Jerome Agel. LC 87-3694. (J). 1987. 9.95 (0-671-64458-0, Litl Simon S&S) S&S Childrens.

Your Country Is Desolate. Willard Bickers. (Orig.). 1996. pap. 7.95 (0-533-11611-2) Vantage.

Your Country 'Tis of Thee. Zulma Gonzalez-Parker. (Orig.). 1989. pap. write for info. (0-318-65770-8) Heartfelt Pr.

Your Creative Rights. Catherine Kirkman. 1998. pap. 12.95 (0-452-27689-6, Plume) NAL-Dutton.

Your Creative Self. 2nd ed. Tom Johnson. 1987. reprint ed. pap. 3.50 (0-941992-15-2) Los Arboles Pub.

***Your Creative Voice: Reaching & Teaching from Your Experience.** Ed. by Marjorie Reynolds. (Illus.). 212p. 1996. per., pap. 14.95 (0-9601302-0-9) Adventures Time.

Your Credit Your Car Your Choice. Elsie Allen. 48p. 1992. student ed. write for info. (1-882783-49-2) Auto-Know Cnslting.

Your Customers Must Come in Second Place to Your Employees If Your Objective Is Total Customer Satisfaction: How to Rate, Praise, Recognize, & Motivate Your Employees to Provide the Best Customer Service. Business Development Systems, Inc. Staff. (Self-Improvement Business Ser.). 27p. 1994. pap. text ed. 8.95 (1-884392-07-5) Busn Develop.

Your Dad Was Just Like You. Dolores Johnson. LC 92-6347. (Illus.). 32p. (J). (gr. k-3). 1993. text ed. 13.95 (0-02-747838-6, Mac Bks Young Read) S&S Childrens.

Your Daily Walk. (Walk Through the Bible Ser.). 464p. (Orig.). 1991. pap. 12.99 (0-310-53651-0) Zondervan.

***Your Daughter Is Crying.** John D. Kershaw. 289p. (Orig.). 1997. mass mkt. 4.99 (1-55197-727-3, Pub. by Comnwlth Pub CN) Partners Pubs Grp.

Your Daughters Shall Prophesy: Women in Ministry in the Church. Ed. by Valerie Rempel et al. 222p. (Orig.). (C). 1992. pap. 11.50 (0-921788-14-2) Kindred Prods.

Your Day & Night. Walter Russell. 23p. 1946. 1.50 (1-879605-09-0) U Sci & Philos.

Your Day in Court. rev. ed. Jon R. Abele & Joseph M. Sindell. 36p. 1994. pap. text ed. 1.80 (0-913875-04-X, 6112) Lawyers & Judges.

Your Days Are Numbered. 21th ed. Florence Campbell. 255p. 1980. reprint ed. pap. 9.95 (0-87516-422-6) DeVorss.

Your Days Are Numbered in Calendar Math. Helene Silverman & Sheila Siderman. 64p. (J). (gr. 2-6). 1980. pap. text ed. 9.50 (0-914040-84-7) Cuisenaire.

Your Death Is None of Your Business: Your Business Is Your Life & What You Are Going to Do With the Rest of It. Ken Standley. 158p. (Orig.). 1995. pap. 8.95 (0-9645373-2-X) Mywa Pubns.

Your Debt As the Bankers Gain. 1992. lib. bdg. 79.00 (0-8490-5427-3) Gordon Pr.

Your Decision. Neal Starkman. LC 88-71482. (Illus.). 118p. (Orig.). (YA). (gr. 9-12). 1988. pap. 13.00 (0-935529-10-1) Comprehen Health Educ.

Your Destiny: Your Life & Work Become One. rev. ed. Robert Natiuk. 96p. 1994. pap. 8.00 (1-884667-07-4) Gage Res & Develop.

Your Destiny in the Zodiac & Its Mastery. Louise B. Brownell. 1991. lib. bdg. 79.95 (0-8490-4935-0) Gordon Pr.

Your Destiny in the Zodiac & Its Mastery. Louise B. Brownell. 106p. 1972. reprint ed. spiral bd. 5.50 (0-7873-0125-6) Hlth Research.

Your Destiny in Thumb. R. G. Rao. (Illus.). 1991. write for info. (0-318-68201-X, Pub. by Ranjan Pubs II) S Asia.

Your Destiny in Your Name. Edna P. Walsh. 60p. 1971. reprint ed. spiral bd. 4.50 (0-7873-1077-8) Hlth Research.

***Your Detox System: Unleash Nature's Awesome Super-Healing Power.** S. J. Farley. 32p. (Orig.). 1997. pap. text ed. 6.95 (1-889623-04-0) Alternat Med Pub.

***Your Diabetes: Real Information You Can Use.** Randy Shields. LC 96-70815. 176p. (Orig.). 1996. mass mkt. 4.99 (1-888886-10-2) CEPI.

Your Diamond Dreams Cut Open My Arteries: Poems by Else Lasker-Schuler. Else Lasker-Schuler. LC 82-2656. (Germanic Languages & Literatures Ser.: No. 100). ix, 317p. 1983. 32.50 (0-8078-8100-7) U of NC Pr.

Your Diet Coach. Barbara DeBetz. 224p. (Orig.). 1990. pap. 10.95 (0-685-31174-0) P-H.

Your Dieting Daughter: Is She Dying for Attention? Carolyn Costin. LC 96-38423. 240p. 1996. pap. 19.95 (0-87630-836-1) Brunner-Mazel.

***Your Doctor Does Hypnosis.** Gary R. Elkins. LC 97-10739. (Illus.). (J). 1997. write for info. (1-886610-03-7) Am Soc Clin Hyp Pr.

Your Doctor Is Not In: Healthy Skepticism about National Health Care. Jane M. Orient. LC 93-38180. 1994. 23.00 (0-517-59011-5) Hacienda Pub.

YOUR DOCTOR IS NOT IN: HEALTHY SKEPTICISM ABOUT NATIONAL HEALTH CARE adds fresh energy to the debate over the quality & availability of medical care in America. Jane M. Orient, M.D., rejects the liberal approaches to the problem - as implemented in England, Canada, Germany, & in American "managed care" systems - & proposes a free market-based national medical policy. From her perspective, there is already too much government involvement in medicine, too much regulation, & too much insurance - which is actually prepayment in disguise. These are not the root causes of the accelerating rise in fees & costs, the neglect of patients, & stagnation in the science of medicine itself. Dr. Orient's solutions are bold, thoughtful & based on her extensive experience as a practicing internist, teacher & executive. She says we must return power to its rightful holder, the patients; create true (not "managed") competition; & restore the primacy of the physician- patient relationship. ***Publisher Provided Annotation.***

Your Doctor, My Doctor. Joan Drescher. 32p. (J). (gr. 1-3). 1987. 10.95 (0-8027-6668-4); lib. bdg. 11.85 (0-8027-6669-2) Walker & Co.

***Your Dog: A Guide to Solving Behaviour Problems.** John Cree. (Illus.). 160p. 1997. 35.00 (1-85223-954-9, Pub. by Crowood Pr UK) Trafalgar.

Your Dog & the Law. Godfrey Sandys-Winsch. 1984. 35.00 (0-7219-1010-6, Pub. by Scientific UK) St Mut.

Your Dog Plays Hockey? Charles M. Schulz. (Peanuts Ser.). (Illus.). 32p. (J). (ps-3). 1996. pap. 3.25 (0-694-00909-1, Festival) HarpC Child Bks.

***Your Dog's Life: Choosing, Training & Caring for Your Pet from Puppyhood to Old Age.** Deborah L. Gray. 1997. 24.00 (0-06-017391-2) HarpC.

Your Dog's Wild Cousins. Photos by Hope Ryden. LC 93-26855. (Illus.). 48p. (J). (gr. 2-5). 1994. pap. 16.99 (0-525-67482-9, Lodestar Bks) Dutton Child Bks.

An Asterisk (*) at the beginning of an entry indicates that the title is appearing in BIP for the first time.

Your Dolphin High-Performance Business Brain - An Operator's Manual: 21st Century Thinking Skills for Ambitious People under Challenge or under Fire. Dudley Lynch. (Illus.). 260p. 1993. pap. 25.00 (0-945822-04-9) Brain Technologies.

Your Dragon Coloring Book. Dora B. Johnson & Pat McGuire. (Illus.). (Orig.). 1987. pap. text ed. 5.95 (0-685-24335-4) Baldwin Ctr.

Your Dream Home: A Comprehensive Guide to Buying a House, Condo, or Co-op. Marguerite Smith. LC 96-43899. 256p. (Orig.). 1997. pap. 10.99 (0-446-67245-9) Warner Bks.

Your Dream of Recovery: Dream Interpretation & the Twelve Steps. Shelly Marshall. 220p. 1995. pap. 14.95 (0-87604-332-5, 405) ARE Pr.

Your Dream Relationship: Eleven Steps to Finding Unconditional Love. Alix Gavran & Ronald Gavran. LC 93-27333. 112p. (Orig.). 1993. pap. 10.00 (0-931892-75-9) B Dolphin Pub.

Your Dream Vacation Home. Mary S. Ludwig. 224p. 1991. pap. 14.95 (0-8306-8687-8, 3687, Liberty Hall Pr) TAB Bks.

Your Dreams & What They Mean. Nerys Dee. (Illus.). 1991. 4.99 (0-517-61543-6) Random Hse Value.

***Your Dreams & What They Mean.** 3rd ed. Clement Wood. 282p. 1997. reprint ed. pap. 14.95 (0-87877-239-1) Newcastle Pub.

Your Driving & the Law: A Crash Course in Traffic Tickets & Courts, Auto Accidents & Insurance, & Vehicle-Related Lawsuits. Carol Haas. 80p. 1991. 8.98 (0-88290-420-5) Horizon Utah.

Your Ears: Reactivating Them. Brown Landone. 28p. 1976. reprint ed. spiral bd. 6.50 (0-7873-0532-4) Hlth Research.

Your Easy Guide to Care, Training & Breeding of Common Green Iguanas. Dolly ELlerbrock. (Illus.). 44p. (Orig.). 1996. pap. 6.95 (0-944214-08-8) ABELexpress.

Your Educational Plan: A Simple Guide to Planning Your College Career. Norman C. Tognazzini. 12p. 1997. pap. 3.00 (1-57967-011-3, P0318) Energeia Pub.

Your Eight Year Old. Louise B. Ames et al. 160p. 1990. pap. 10.95 (0-440-50681-6) Dell.

Your Electronic Body: The Electronic Potentials of Food. Brown Landone. (Alternative Medicine Ser.). 1991. lib. bdg. 79.95 (0-8490-4300-X) Gordon Pr.

Your Electronic Body & Electronic Potentials of Food. Brown Landone. 249p. 1966. reprint ed. spiral bd. 22.50 (0-7873-1072-7) Hlth Research.

Your Emotions, Yourself: A Guide to Your Changing Emotions. Doreen L. Virtue. LC 96-35883. (Your Body, Yourself Ser.). (Illus.). 144p. (J). (gr. 4-8). 1996. pap. 9.95 (1-56565-534-6) Lowell Hse Juvenile.

Your Employee Assistance Program: Check It Out for Yourself. Paula King. 16p. (Orig.). 1980. 2.05 (0-89486-092-5, 1938B) Hazelden.

Your Employees Are Stealing You Blind. Robert C. New. 172p. 1994. pap. 12.95 (0-87425-966-5) HRD Press.

***Your Employment Rights.** Michael Malone. (Careers & Testing Ser.). 1992. pap. 12.95 (0-7494-0723-9) Kogan Page Ltd.

***Your Encounter with Life, Death, Immortality.** 6th unabridged ed. Ruth Norman. LC 89-90108. (Illus.). 71p. (Orig.). 1990. pap. 6.00 (0-932642-43-8) Unarius Acad Sci.

***Your English Bk. 1.** Ridout. Date not set. pap. text ed. write for info. (0-582-18784-2, Pub. by Longman UK); wbk. ed., pap. text ed. write for info. (0-582-18788-5, Pub. by Longman UK) Longman.

***Your English Bk. 4.** Ridout. Date not set. pap. text ed. write for info. (0-582-18787-7, Pub. by Longman UK); wbk. ed., pap. text ed. write for info. (0-582-18791-5, Pub. by Longman UK) Longman.

Your English Ancestry: A Guide for North Americans. Sherry Irvine. LC 93-8461. 168p. 1993. pap. 12.95 (0-916489-53-1) Ancestry.

Your Entrepreneurial Success Story: Participant Workbook. William H. Truesdell & Richard G. Stuart. 128p. 1991. student ed. 59.95 (1-880879-28-X); teacher ed. 20.00 (1-880879-26-3); 35.95 (1-880879-25-5); vhs 31.95 (1-880879-27-1) Garage Prods.

Your Environment & What You Can Do about It: A Citizen's Guide. Richard Saltonstall, Jr. LC 75-126112. 260p. 1970. 14.95 (0-8027-0320-8) Devin.

Your Erroneous Zones. Wayne W. Dyer. 1977. mass mkt. 4.95 (0-380-01669-9) Avon.

Your Erroneous Zones. Wayne W. Dyer. 320p. 1993. mass mkt. 5.99 (0-06-109148-0, Harp PBks) HarpC.

Your Erroneous Zones: Step-by-Step Advice for Escaping the Trap of Negative Thinking & Taking Control of Your Life. Wayne W. Dyer. LC 91-2718. 256p. 1991. reprint ed. pap. 11.00 (0-06-091976-0, PL) HarpC.

Your Executive Image: The Art of Self-Packaging for Men & Women. Victoria A. Seitz. 300p. 1992. pap. 10.95 (1-55850-139-8) Adams Media.

Your Executor Duties. Holmes F. Crouch. Ed. by Irma J. Crouch. LC 92-73878. (Series 300 Tax Guides: Vol. 304). (Illus.). 224p. 1992. pap. 16.95 (0-944817-12-2) Allyear Tax.

Your Eyelids Are Growing Heavy. Barbara Paul. LC 92-70413. 188p. 1992. reprint ed. pap. 5.95 (1-55882-126-0, Lib Crime Classics) Intl Polygonics.

Your Eyes. 3rd ed. Thomas H. Chalkley. LC 94-45400. (Illus.). 128p. (C). 1995. pap. text ed. 22.95 (0-398-05976-4) C C Thomas.

Your Eyes! A Comprehensive Look at the Understanding & Treatment of Vision Problems. rev. ed. Thomas L. D'Alonzo. LC 91-71193. (Illus.). 251p. (C). 1991. pap. 14.95 (0-9629063-5-2) Avanti.

Your Eyes: An Owner's Manual. James F. Collins. (Illus.). 224p. (Orig.). 1989. pap. write for info. (0-9621975-0-5) Infinity NY.

Your Eyes: Questions You Have...Answers You Need. Sandra Salmans. 1996. pap. 12.95 (1-882606-59-0) Peoples Med Soc.

Your Eyes - Rejuvenating Them. Brown Landone. 47p. reprint ed. spiral bd. 7.00 (0-7873-1074-3) Hlth Research.

Your Eyes Will Be Opened: A Study of the Greek (Ethiopic) Apocalypse of Peter. Dennis D. Buchholz. LC 86-27900. (Society of Biblical Literature Dissertation Ser.). 500p. 1987. 34.95 (1-55540-024-8, 06-01-97); pap. 22.95 (1-55540-025-6) Scholars Pr GA.

Your Fabulous Volunteers: A History of the Washington Emergency Squad & Emergency Services in Warren County. rev. ed. Richard E. Harpster. Ed. by Larry K. Smith. (Illus.). 365p. 1985. 14.95 (0-9604020-1-2) Wash Emerg Squad.

Your Face. Jack Winder. Ed. by Alton Jordan. (I Can Read Ser.). (Illus.). (J). (gr. k-3). 1984. 7.95 (0-89868-008-5, Read Res); pap. 3.95 (0-89868-041-7, Read Res) ARO Pub.

Your Face Never Lies: An Introduction to Oriental Diagnosis. Michio Kushi. (Macrobiotic Home Library). (Illus.). 96p. pap. 6.95 (0-89529-214-9) Avery Pub.

Your Faith: A Popular Presentation of Catholic Belief. rev. ed. Redemptorists of London Province Staff. LC 93-79048. 88p. (Orig.). 1993. pap. 7.95 (0-89243-617-4) Liguori Pubns.

Your Faith Account. Dana Holmes. 48p. (Orig.). 1983. pap. 0.95 (0-88144-019-1, CPS/019) Christian Pub.

Your Faith in God Will Work. Kenneth E. Hagin. 1991. pap. 0.75 (0-89276-274-8) Hagin Ministries.

Your Faith Is Growing! N. R. Day. 51p. (Orig.). 1981. pap. 6.95 (0-940754-10-X) Ed Ministries.

Your Faith Is Your Fortune. Neville. 1941. pap. 8.95 (0-87516-078-6) DeVorss.

Your Faith on Trial. Wallis C. Metts. 180p. (Orig.). 1979. pap. 5.49 (0-89084-112-8, 003707) Bob Jones Univ Pr.

Your Family. Kenn Gangle & Betty Gangle. 1995. pap. 11.99 (1-885305-29-X) Multnomah Pubs.

Your Family - Your Self: How to Analyze Your Family System to Understand Yourself. William L. Blevins. 185p. (Orig.). 1993. 24.95 (1-879237-54-7); pap. 12.95 (1-879237-53-9) New Harbinger.

Your Family Album Series, 2 Vols., Set. Gretchen Super. (Illus.). 56p. (J). (gr. k-3). 1994. lib. bdg. 31.96 (0-8050-3461-7) TFC Bks NY.

Your Family Finances: Record for Expense & Savings. rev. ed. Dorothy Simmons & Herbert B. Howell. 38p. 1949. pap. text ed. 2.50 (0-8138-1830-3) Iowa St U Pr.

Your Family, God's Way. Wayne A. Mack. 239p. 1991. pap. 8.99 (0-87552-358-7, Pub. by Evangelical Pr) Presby & Reformed.

Your Family Heritage: A Guide to Preserving Family History. Ronald D. Ross. LC 88-60501. 144p. 1988. 19.95 (0-9620144-0-0) R D Ross.

Your Family History: A Handbook for Research & Writing. David Kyvig & Myron A. Marty. LC 77-86030. 96p. (C). 1978. pap. text ed. write for info. (0-88295-774-0) Harlan Davidson.

Your Family in Focus: Appreciating What You Have Making It Even Better. Mitch Finley. LC 92-75250. 128p. (Orig.). 1993. pap. 6.95 (0-87793-493-2) Ave Maria.

***Your Family Is Your Fortune.** Richard D. Dobbins. 15p. (Orig.). 1989. pap. 1.00 (1-890329-09-6) Totally Alive.

Your Family, My Family. Joan Drescher. (Illus.). 32p. (J). (gr. 2-5). 1980. lib. bdg. 13.85 (0-8027-6383-9) Walker & Co.

***Your Family Time with God.** 336p. 1997. pap. write for info. (1-56476-701-9, Victor Bks) Chariot Victor.

Your Family Time with God: A Weekly Plan for Family Devotions. John Maxwell & Brad Lewis. 352p. 1995. 17.99 (0-7814-0240-9) Chariot Victor.

Your Family Tree. Garland E. Hopkins. 1949. pap. 2.50 (0-87517-035-8) Dietz.

Your Family Tree: Using Your PC. Jim Oldfield, Jr. (Illus.). 220p. (Orig.). 1997. pap. 25.95 incl. cd-rom (1-55755-310-6) Abacus MI.

Your Family Tree Connection. Chris M. Reading & Ross S. Meillon. Orig. Title: Relatively Speaking. (Illus.). 288p. (Orig.). 1988. reprint ed. pap. 9.95 (0-87983-483-8) Keats.

Your Family Will Love It: Quick & Healthy Weekday Meals for the Hard to Please. Prevention Magazine Health Book Editors. LC 94-23899. (Illus.). 368p. 1995. 27.95 (0-87596-256-4) Rodale Pr Inc.

***Your Family Will Love It! Cook Book: Quick & Healthy Weekday Meals for the Hard-to-Please.** Ed. by Prevention Magazine Health Books Food Editors. (Illus.). 432p. 1997. pap. 14.95 (0-87596-447-8) Rodale Pr Inc.

Your Family's Care Guide: A Compact Family Guide to Wellness, Signs, & Symptoms of Illness, Communicable Disease & Basic First Aid. Celeste Stuhring & Glen T. Stuhring. LC 95-40783. 1996. pap. 7.95 (0-933701-63-2) Westport Pubs.

Your Family's Financial Survival Guide: How to Organize Your Estate & Provide a Valuable Guide for Your Heirs. John L. Pennewell. 44p. (Orig.). 1995. pap. 8.95 (0-9647207-0-1) Lakeside FL.

Your Family's Rights under the New Fair Housing Law. Children's Defense Fund Staff. 26p. (Orig.). 1989. pap. 4.75 (0-938008-74-9) Childrens Defense.

Your Fantasies May Be Hazardous to Your Health. Ligia Dantes. 1995. pap. 10.95 (1-85230-687-4) Element MA.

***Your Farm Bureau.** 2nd ed. AFBF Staff. 272p. 1996. pap. text ed. 15.00 (0-7872-2880-X) Kendall-Hunt.

***Your Fat Can Make You Thin!** Calvin Ezrin & Robert E. Kowalski. Date not set. 25.00 (1-56565-651-2) Contemp Bks.

***Your Fat Is Not Your Fault: How to Overcome Your Body's Resistance to Permanent Weight Loss.** Carol N. Simontacchi & Margaret West. LC 96-53489. 1997. pap. write for info. (1-57683-003-9) Pinon Press.

***Your Fat Is Not Your Fault: How to Overcome Your Body's Resistance to Permanent Weight Lost.** Carol N. Simontacchi & Margaret West. 240p. 1998. 19.95 (0-87477-897-2, Tarcher Putnam) Putnam Pub Group.

Your Father. James L. Weil. 1973. pap. 8.00 (0-685-36873-4) Elizabeth Pr.

Your Father Loves You: Daily Insights for Knowing God. J. I. Packer. Ed. & Compiled by Jean Watson. LC 86-1770. 380p. 1986. 14.99 (0-87788-875-2) Shaw Pubs.

Your Father, Your Self: How Sons & Daughters Can Understand & Heal Relationships with Their Fathers. Barry H. Gordon. LC 96-24926. 1996. write for info. (1-55972-378-5, Birch Ln Pr) Carol Pub Group.

Your Favorite Hymns for Guitar, No. 1. Contrib. by Ernie Allee. 1964. 9.99 (0-8341-9294-2, MB-233) Lillenas.

Your Favorite Shorts: Memorable Selections by America's Storyteller. Robert C. Enderle. LC 90-82753. 140p. (Orig.). 1990. pap. write for info. (0-9618186-1-1) Enderle Pub Co.

***Your Feelings...Friend or Foe? Biblical Guidelines for Managing Your Emotions.** Richard D. Dobbins. (Illus.). (Orig.). 1993. pap. 12.50 (1-890329-02-9) Totally Alive.

***Your Feelings...Friend or Foe? Biblical Guidelines for Managing Your Emotions.** Richard D. Dobbins. 201p. (Orig.). 1994. pap. 10.00 (1-890329-03-7) Totally Alive.

Your Fertile Hours. Emily Faugno. LC 85-71462. 248p. 1986. 17.95 (0-86690-295-3, F2346-014) Am Fed Astrologers.

Your Fertility Signals: Using Them to Achieve or Avoid Pregnancy, Naturally. Merryl Winstein. LC 87-92011. (Illus.). 160p. (Orig.). 1996. pap. 12.95 (0-9619401-0-7) Smooth Stone Pr.

***Your Field of Dreams: Making Money on Your Land.** Wally Wirths. 1997. pap. text ed. 19.95 (1-887269-39-8) J Culler & Sons.

Your Film Acting Career: How to Break into the Movies & TV & Survive in Hollywood. 3rd rev. ed. M. K. Lewis & Rosemary R. Lewis. LC 92-74915. (Illus.). 320p. 1993. pap. 15.95 (0-929149-01-7) Gorham Hse.

Your Finances in Changing Times. Larry Burkett. (Christian Financial Concepts Ser.). 1982. pap. 9.99 (0-8024-2548-8) Moody.

Your Finances in Changing Times see Familia y Sus Finanzas

Your Financial Care Plan. H. L. Yates. LC 92-43233. (Illus.). 104p. 1993. 10.95 (0-944957-16-1) Rivercross Pub.

Your Financial Guide: Advice for Every Stage of Your Life. Ray Martin. 304p. 1996. 18.95 (0-02-861114-4) Macmillan.

Your First Aquarium. Sylvan Cohen. (Illus.). 32p. 1992. pap. 2.29 (0-86622-057-7, YF100) TFH Pubns.

Your First Book of Personal Computing. Joe Kraynak. 300p. 1995. 19.99 (1-56761-503-1, Alpha Ref) Macmillan Gen Ref.

Your First Business Plan. Joseph A. Covello & Brian J. Hazelgran. LC 92-41063. (Small Business Sourcebooks Ser.). (Illus.). 1993. 17.95 (0-942061-47-0) Sourcebks.

Your First Business Plan. 2nd ed. Joseph Covello & Brian J. Hazelgren. LC 95-1465. (Small Business Sourcebooks Ser.). 152p. 1993. pap. 9.95 (1-57071-044-9) Sourcebks.

Your First Business Plan: Learn the Critical Steps to Writing a Winning Business Plan. Joseph A. Covello & Brian J. Hazelgren. (Small Business Sourcebooks Ser.). 152p. 1993. pap. 8.95 (0-942061-44-6) Sourcebks.

***Your First Business Plan: Learn the Critical Steps to Writing a Winning Business Plan.** 3rd rev. ed. Joseph Covello & Brian Hazelgren. 152p. 1997. pap. 12.95 (1-57071-219-0) Sourcebks.

Your First C-C++ Program. Alan Neibauer. LC 93-87421. 367p. 1994. pap. 24.99 (0-7821-1414-8) Sybex.

Your First Canary. Sue-Rhee Pasca. (YF Ser.). (Illus.). 36p. (Orig.). (YA). 1991. pap. 2.29 (0-86622-059-3, YF-103) TFH Pubns.

Your First Car. George Fremon & Suzanne Fremon. LC 81-80572. (Illus.). 176p. 1981. pap. 5.95 (0-89709-024-1) Liberty Pub.

Your First Classic Car: Buying, Renovating & Driving. Patrick Smith. (Illus.). 192p. 1995. 42.95 (1-85260-410-7) Motorbooks Intl.

Your First Cockatiel. J. E. Lohr. (YF Ser.). (Illus.). 36p. (Orig.). (YA). 1991. pap. 2.29 (0-86622-060-7, YF-104) TFH Pubns.

Your First Computer. Alan Simpson. LC 93-86584. 380p. 1993. 19.99 (0-7821-1418-0) Sybex.

Your First Ferret. Adelle Porch. (Illus.). 34p. (Orig.). 1991. pap. 2.29 (0-86622-115-8, YF-105) TFH Pubns.

Your First Finch. George W. Noreen. (YF Ser.). (Illus.). 36p. (Orig.). (YA). 1991. pap. 2.29 (0-86622-062-3, YF-106) TFH Pubns.

Your First Garden Book. Marc T. Brown. (Illus.). (J). (gr. 1 up). 1981. 12.45i (0-316-11217-8); mass mkt. 6.95 (0-316-11215-1) Little.

Your First Gerbil. Leroy Mervan. (Illus.). 34p. (Orig.). 1991. pap. 2.29 (0-86622-063-1, YF-107) TFH Pubns.

Your First Goldfish. Mariana Gilbert. (YF Ser.). (Illus.). 36p. (Orig.). (YA). 1991. pap. 2.29 (0-86622-065-8, YF-108) TFH Pubns.

Your First Guinea Pig. Anja J. Steinkamp. (YF Ser.). (Illus.). 36p. (Orig.). (YA). 1991. pap. 2.29 (0-7938-0012-9, YF-109) TFH Pubns.

Your First Hamster. Peter Smith. (YF Ser.). (Illus.). 36p. (Orig.). (YA). 1991. pap. 2.29 (0-86622-067-4, YF-110) TFH Pubns.

***Your First Horse: How to Buy & Care for Your First Horse. Jacqueline Dwelle. LC 96-94983. (Illus.). 180p. (Orig.). 1997. pap. 17.95 (0-9655048-6-7) Hoofbeat Pubns.**

YOUR FIRST HORSE is a practical manual describing how to buy & care for a horse. Jacqueline discusses the factors involved in selecting a horse & notes the pitfalls to avoid. Topics include: where to look, what type of horse to buy, how to evaluate prospects, trial periods & pre-purchase exams. How to recognize good conformation is analyzed & clarified with diagrams & summary tables. Jacqueline shares her experience describing how to find & evaluate equestrian professionals (Veterinarians, Farriers, Boarding Stables & Equine Dentists). The second part of the book is devoted to horse care. Subjects include the care of stabled horses, pasture management, grooming techniques, choosing & buying feedstuffs, health maintenance, common ailments, lameness & hoof care. YOUR FIRST HORSE is an invaluable guide for current & future horse owners. The author writes knowledgeably from a horseman's viewpoint, thoroughly addressing horse buying. The horse care section is spiced with tips from professional stable managers, & is a detailed horse care manual. To order: Hoofbeat Publications, P.O. Box 2133-HM, Southern Pines, NC 28388. 910-695-1644. ***Publisher Provided Annotation.***

Your First Horse Book. Peter R. Winkelaar. LC 96-18326. (Illus.). 48p. (J). 1996. 14.95 (0-8069-9525-4) Sterling.

Your First Interview. 3rd ed. Ronald W. Fry. 192p. 1995. pap. 9.99 (1-56414-188-8) Career Pr Inc.

Your First Job. 2nd ed. Ronald W. Fry. 192p. (Orig.). 1995. pap. 9.99 (1-56414-189-6) Career Pr Inc.

***Your First Job.** 3rd ed. Vivian Donald. (Careers & Testing Ser.). 1997. pap. 14.95 (0-7494-2150-9) Kogan Page Ltd.

Your First Job Interview. Richard Duornek. 10p. 1991. pap. 3.50 (0-937652-55-5) Natl Art Ed.

Your First Kitten. Marie Dupont. (YF Ser.). (Illus.). 36p. (Orig.). (YA). 1991. pap. 2.29 (0-86622-061-5, YF-118) TFH Pubns.

Your First Lizard. Jerry G. Walls. 34p. (Orig.). (J). (gr. 1-6). 1991. pap. 2.29 (0-86622-068-2, YF-111) TFH Pubns.

Your First Lovebird. Michael Kelly. (Illus.). 34p. (Orig.). (J). 1991. pap. 2.29 (0-86622-069-0, YF-112) TFH Pubns.

Your First Mac. Tom Cuthbertson. LC 93-85349. 384p. 1993. pap. 19.99 (0-7821-1316-8) Sybex.

Your First Microprocessor: Organizing, Construction, Debugging. James W. Coffron. LC 83-62032. (Illus.). 352p. 1984. 17.95 (0-13-978446-2) P-H.

Your First Modem. 2nd ed. Sharon Crawford. LC 94-80051. 314p. 1995. 22.99 (0-7821-1683-3) Sybex.

Your First Mouse. Nick Mays. (Illus.). 32p. 1995. pap. text ed. 2.29 (0-7938-0179-6, YF120) TFH Pubns.

Your First Move. A. Sololsky. 296p. 1987. 6.95 (0-8285-2160-3) Firebird NY.

Your First Parakeet. J. E. Lohr. (YF Ser.). (Illus.). 36p. (Orig.). (YA). 1991. pap. 2.29 (0-86622-058-5, YF-102) TFH Pubns.

Your First Parakeet. J. E. Lohr. (YF Ser.). (Illus.). 36p. (YA). 1991. pap. 2.29 (0-7938-0015-3, YF-102) TFH Pubns.

Your First Puppy. Marcel Carpentier. (Illus.). 34p. (Orig.). (J). (gr. 1-6). 1991. pap. 2.29 (0-86622-064-X, YF-119) TFH Pubns.

***Your First Quilt Book: (Or It Should Be!)** Carol Doak. Ed. by Ursula Reikes. LC 97-20672. (Illus.). 230p. (Orig.). 1997. pap. 16.95 (1-56477-198-9, B312) That Patchwork.

Your First Rabbit. Louise Vernier. (YF Ser.). (Illus.). 36p. (Orig.). (YA). 1991. pap. 2.29 (0-86622-071-2, YF-114) TFH Pubns.

Your First Resume. 4th ed. Ronald W. Fry. 192p. 1995. pap. 9.99 (1-56414-187-X) Career Pr Inc.

Your First Snake. Ray Hunziker. (Illus.). 34p. (Orig.). (J). (gr. 1-6). 1991. pap. 2.29 (0-86622-072-0, YF-115) TFH Pubns.

Your First Step. Henri Sorensen. LC 95-44222. (Illus.). (J). (ps up). 1996. 15.00 (0-688-14667-8); lib. bdg. 14.93 (0-688-14668-6) Lothrop.

Your First Thirty Days: Building a Professional Image in a New Job. Elwood N. Chapman. Ed. by Michael G. Crisp & Tony Hicks. LC 89-81250. (Fifty-Minute Ser.). (Illus.). 64p. (Orig.). 1990. pap. 10.95 (1-56052-003-5) Crisp Pubns.

Your First Trip to Europe: Where, What & How, Vol. 1. Jordan Levenson. LC 84-82461. 110p. 1985. pap. 18.50 (0-914442-11-2) Levenson Pr.

Your First Tropical Fish. Herbert Axelrod. (Illus.). 32p. 1992. pap. 2.29 (0-86622-104-2, YF116) TFH Pubns.

Your First Year of Teaching & Beyond. 2nd ed. Ellen L. Kronowitz. LC 95-19385. 224p. (C). 1996. pap. text ed. 22.80 (0-8013-1558-1) Longman.

***Your First 30 Days: Getting Started in a New Job.** 2nd rev. ed. Elwood Chapman & Robert Maddux. (50 Minute Ser.). (Illus.). 120p. 1997. pap. 10.95 (1-56052-453-7) Crisp Pubns.

Your Five Senses. Ray Broekel. LC 84-7603. (New True Bks.). (Illus.). 48p. (J). (gr. k-4). 1984. pap. 5.50 (0-516-41932-3); lib. bdg. 19.00 (0-516-01932-5) Childrens.

Your Five Year Old. Louise B. Ames et al. 123p. 1981. pap. 10.95 (*0-440-50673-5*) Dell.

Your Five Year Old Owner's Manual. Jim Grant & Margot Azen. (Illus.). 8p. (Orig.). 1987. pap. 12.95 (*0-935493-07-7*, RRB 325) Programs Educ.

Your Flag. (Illus.). 64p. (J). (gr. 6-12). 1986. pap. 6.95 (*0-8395-3188-5*, 33188) BSA.

Your Florida Dooryard Citrus Guide. 2nd ed. Jim Ferguson. (Illus.). 64p. 1995. pap. 5.00 (*0-916287-12-2*, SP178) Univ Fla Food.

Your Florida Garden. abr. rev. ed. John V. Watkins & Herbert S. Wolfe. LC 68-23403. 368p. 1987. reprint ed. pap. 14.95 (*0-8130-0862-X*) U Press Fla.

Your Florida Landscape. (Illus.). 234p. 1995. pap. 9.00 (*0-916287-08-4*, SP135) Univ Fla Food.

Your Food. Norman Parkinson & Lisa Ackerley. (C). 1989. 30.00 (*0-86242-099-7*, Pub. by Age Concern Eng UK) St Mut.

Your Foot's on My Feet: And Other Tricky Nouns. Marvin Terban. LC 85-19561. (J). (gr. 2-5). 1986. pap. 6.95 (*0-89919-413-3*, Clarion Bks) HM.

Your Fortune in Real Estate Photography. G. W. Bates. 1996. pap. 19.95 (*0-9629759-7-4*) Batax Mus.

Your Fortune in the Microcomputer Business: Getting Started, Vol. I. Victor Wild. (Illus.). 304p. 1982. pap. 15.95 (*0-938444-04-2*) Wildfire Pub.

Your Fortune in the Microcomputer Business: Growth, Survival, Success, Vol. II. Victor Wild. (Illus.). 256p. 1982. pap. 15.95 (*0-938444-05-0*) Wildfire Pub.

Your Fortune in Your Name: Kabalistic Astrology. 6th ed. A. Sepharial. 96p. 1973. reprint ed. spiral bd. 5.50 (*0-7873-0768-8*) Hlth Research.

Your Four Great Emotions. David Seabury. 108p. 1969. pap. 5.95 (*0-911336-22-2*) Sci of Mind.

Your Four Point Plan for Life: How to Achieve a Balance Between the Physical, Emotional, Mental & Spiritual Aspects of Ourselves. Ursula Markham. (Illus.). 144p. 1993. pap. 12.95 (*1-85230-212-7*) Element MA.

Your Four Year Old. Louise B. Ames et al. 160p. 1989. pap. 10.95 (*0-440-50675-1*) Dell.

Your Four Year Old Owner's Manual. Jim Grant & Margot Azen. (Illus.). 16p. (Orig.). 1988. pap. 12.95 (*0-935493-17-4*, RRB404) Programs Educ.

Your FoxPro for Windows Consultant: From the Ground Up. Martin S. Matthews. (Illus.). 560p. (Orig.). 1993. pap. 39.95 (*1-55958-305-3*) Prima Pub.

Your Freedom to Be. deluxe ed. Jack H. Holland. LC 77-92780. 1977. pap. 4.50 (*0-87852-002-3*) Inst Human Growth.

Your French-Canadian Connection Guide, No. 1. Alfred J. Dahlquist. 32p. 1989. pap. 5.00 (*0-915709-00-7*) Pk Geneal Bk.

Your Friend the Holy Spirit. Morris L. Venden. (Anchor Ser.). 95p. (Orig.). 1987. pap. 6.99 (*0-8163-0682-6*) Pacific Pr Pub Assn.

Your Friends from Sesame Street. Sesame Street Staff. (Cloth Bks.). (Illus.). (J). (ps). 1979. pap. 3.50 (*0-394-84137-9*) Random Bks Yng Read.

Your Front Yard. John Burrow. 136p. 1994. per. 9.95 (*0-943629-12-8*) Swan Pub.

Your Future - Student Supplement: Plans & Choices. Daggett. (CA - Career Development Ser.). 1985. pap. 9.95 (*0-538-16351-8*) S-W Pub.

Your Future, an A-Z Index to Prophecy. Jack Van Impe. 145p. 1989. pap. 10.00 (*0-934803-68-4*) J Van Impe.

***Your Future As a Consumer.** Barker & Taylor. 1990. pap. text ed. write for info. (*0-582-66250-8*, Pub. by Longman UK) Longman.

Your Future As a Lawyer. Charles Z. Cohen. (Careers in Depth Ser.). (YA). (gr. 7-12). 1977. lib. bdg. 7.97 (*0-8239-0382-6*) Rosen Group.

Your Future Home. Architect's Small House Service Bureau Staff. (Illus.). 170p. 1992. reprint ed. pap. 19.95 (*1-55835-041-1*) AIA Press.

Your Future in Art. Design Schools Staff. (Illus.). 32p. (YA). (gr. 10-12). 1981. pap. text ed. 1.25 (*0-9607016-0-5*) Design Schools.

Your Future in Fashion. Design Schools Staff. (Illus.). 32p. (YA). (gr. 10-12). 1983. pap. text ed. 1.25 (*0-9607016-1-3*) Design Schools.

Your Future in Space: The U. S. Space Camp Training Program. Penelope McPhee & Raymond McPhee. LC 86-9003. (Illus.). 128p. (YA). (gr. 7 up). 1986. pap. 14.95 (*0-517-56418-1*) Crown Bks Yng Read.

Your Future Is Your Friend. Robert H. Schuller. 100p. 1991. 12.95 (*1-879989-01-8*) New Hope Pub.

Your Future Lives. Brad Steiger et al. (Illus.). 200p. (Orig.). 1988. pap. 14.95 (*0-914918-82-6*, Whitford Pr) Schiffer.

Your Future, Your Choice: Christian Character in a Changing Economy. Kerry J. Koller. LC 93-80409. 104p. 1994. pap. 5.95 (*0-937779-27-X*) Greenlawn Pr.

***Your Fyre Shall Burn No More: Iroquois Policy Toward New France.** Jose A. Brandao. LC 97-9846. (Illus.). 456p. 1997. text ed. 60.00 (*0-8032-1274-7*) U of Nebr Pr.

Your Garden Pond. (Colorguide Ser.). 1982. pap. 6.95 (*0-940842-13-0*) South Group.

Your Garden Pond. K. H. Weiser & Paul V. Loiselle. (Illus.). 142p. 14.95 (*3-923880-21-9*, 16052) Tetra Pr.

***Your Garden Shouldn't Make You Crazy! A Commonsense Guide to No-Pressure, Low-Maintnenace Gardening.** C. L. Fornari. LC 97-66085. (Illus.). 256p. 1997. pap. 16.95 (*0-940160-72-2*) Parnassus Imprints.

Your Genealogy: A Practical Guide. Larry D. Schenck. (Orig.). 1989. pap. 7.95 (*0-87595-191-0*) Oregon Hist.

***Your Geography Bk. A.** Boyle. (J). Date not set. pap. text ed. write for info. (*0-582-18799-0*, Pub. by Longman UK) Longman.

***Your Geography Bk. B.** Boyle. (J). Date not set. pap. text ed. write for info. (*0-582-18800-8*, Pub. by Longman UK) Longman.

Your Gifted Child: How to Recognize & Develop the Special Talents in Your Child from Birth to Age Seven. Joan F. Smutny et al. 224p. 1991. pap. 10.00 (*0-345-36830-4*, Ballantine Trade) Ballantine.

Your Gifted Child: How to Recognize & Develop the Special Talents in Your Child from Birth to Age Seven. Joan F. Smutny et al. LC 88-27411. 224p. reprint ed. pap. 63.90 (*0-7837-1361-4*, 2041509) Bks Demand.

Your Gift...Should You Decide to Accept: Communications from Aristotle. Jeanne Logan. 243p. (Orig.). 1987. pap. 10.00 (*0-9619742-0-6*) Harmony Haus.

Your Glory Reflected: Twenty Outstanding Christians of the Twentieth Century. Sheilah W. Ling. 288p. 1993. 19.95 (*0-85439-457-5*, Pub. by St Paul Pubns UK) St Mut.

Your Goats: A Kid's Guide to Raising & Showing. Gail Damerow. LC 92-54656. (Illus.). 144p. (Orig.). 1993. pap. 12.95 (*0-88266-825-0*, Garden Way Pub) Storey Comm Inc.

***Your God Is Too Small.** Phillips. 1997. pap. 5.00 (*0-684-84696-9*) S&S Trade.

Your God Is Too Small. 2nd ed. John B. Phillips. 124p. 1987. reprint ed. pap. 3.95 (*0-02-088510-5*) Macmillan.

Your Golden Angel. Christina Anello. (Charming Petites Ser.). (Illus.). 80p. 1996. 4.95 (*0-88088-800-8*) Peter Pauper.

Your Golden Key to Success: A Self Help Odyssey. Al G. Manning. LC 82-60767. (Illus.). 1982. 12.95 (*0-941698-04-1*); pap. 6.95 (*0-941698-05-X*) Pan Ishtar.

Your Good Health. William I. Bennett et al. (Illus.). 520p. 1989. pap. text ed. 14.95 (*0-674-96632-5*) HUP.

Your Good Health: A Whole Health Program to Live Healthier, Live Happier, & Live Longer. Bob Montgomery & Laurel Morris. 264p. (Orig.). 1995. pap. 14.95 (*0-85091-411-6*, Pub. by Lothian Pub AT) Seven Hills Bk.

Your Good Health: How to Stay Well, & What to Do When You're Not. Ed. by William I. Bennett & G. Timothy Johnson. LC 87-19671. (Illus.). 448p. 1987. text ed. 34.50 (*0-674-96631-7*) HUP.

Your Good Health Garden. Pauline James. LC 95-11904. (Illus.). 128p. 1996. pap. 9.95 (*0-88007-208-3*) Woodbridge Pr.

Your Good Health-Thank God. Yvon Morris. 51p. 1996. pap. 9.98 (*1-888139-01-3*) Y Morris Carib.

Your Good Thoughts Have Power. J. David King. (Illus.). 128p. (Orig.). 1987. pap. 5.00 (*0-9617359-0-2*) Friend Man Assn.

Your Government & You: Simplified American Government. John H. Hoek. (Illus.). 96p. 1994. teacher ed. 1.50 (*0-88323-125-5*, 213); pap. 5.50 (*0-88323-257-X*, 212) Pendergrass Pub.

Your Greater Self: The Inner Consciousness. William W. Atkinson. 94p. 1970. reprint ed. spiral bd. 5.50 (*0-7873-0062-4*) Hlth Research.

Your Greatest Power. J. Martin Kohe. 1977. 8.95 (*0-918448-01-8*) Success Unltd.

Your Green Scene: How to Care for Indoor Plants. large type ed. pap. 7.00 (*0-317-01862-0*) Cath Guild Blind.

Your Growing Child: From Babyhood Through Adolescence. Penelope Leach. 1986. pap. 19.95 (*0-394-71066-5*) Knopf.

Your Guardian Angels: Use the Power of Angelic Messengers to Enrich & Empower Your Life. Linda Georgian. 174p. 1994. pap. 11.00 (*0-671-88126-4*, Fireside) S&S Trade.

Your Guide to a Better Memory. Jack Maguire. 160p. (Orig.). 1995. mass mkt. 4.99 (*0-425-15100-X*) Berkley Pub.

Your Guide to a Successful Garage Sale. Kenneth C. Koffler. Ed. by Carlotta Henslee. (Illus.). 112p. (Orig.). 1992. pap. 8.95 (*0-9633042-0-8*) Hen-Ken Pub.

Your Guide to an Informed Mind: A New Approach to a Complete Education. Michael Freedman. (Illus.). (YA). (gr. 9-12). 1995. pap. 20.00 (*0-679-75366-4*, Villard Bks) Random.

Your Guide to an Informed Mind: What You Should Know at Each Grade Level. Liz Buffa. (Culturescope Ser.). (J). (gr. 1-6). 1995. pap. 18.00 (*0-679-75365-6*) Random.

Your Guide to Better Nutrition. 3rd ed. Sarah S. Strawn & Elizabeth C. Zimmer. 68p. (C). 1994. pap. text ed. 15.95 (*0-89892-122-8*) Contemp Pub Co of Raleigh.

Your Guide to Canadian Colleges: Select a Program, Choose a College, & Succeed When You Get There. Kevin Paul. (Reference Ser.). 256p. 1993. pap. 14.95 (*0-88908-291-X*) Self-Counsel Pr.

Your Guide to Child Care Savings. 2nd rev. ed. Liza Lidke. 94p. 1995. pap. 8.95 (*1-888523-00-X*) Lidke & Assocs.

Your Guide to Corporate Survival. Scott Choate. Ed. by Cliff Carle. (Illus.). 192p. (Orig.). 1990. pap. 4.95 (*0-918259-20-7*) CCC Pubns.

Your Guide to Cost Reduction Through Pneumatics Automation. Ed. by National Fluid Power Association Staff. (Illus.). 64p. (Orig.). (C). 1990. pap. 3.00 (*0-942220-23-4*) Natl Fluid Power.

Your Guide to Easy Model Railroad Wiring. Andy Sperandeo. (Illus.). 104p. (Orig.). 1990. reprint ed. pap. 12.95 (*0-89024-060-4*, 12093, Kalmbach Books) Kalmbach.

Your Guide to Effective Publications: A Handbook for Campus Publications Professionals. Kelvin J. Arden & William J. Whalen. 167p. 1991. pap. 24.00 (*0-89964-282-9*, 20022) Coun Adv & Supp Ed.

Your Guide to Federal Firearms Regulations. 1996. lib. bdg. 250.95 (*0-8490-6015-X*) Gordon Pr.

Your Guide to Financial Success! A Do-It-Yourself Guide to No-Load & Low-Load Mutual Funds. Dale D. Oliver. LC 92-60501. (Illus.). 160p. (Orig.). 1992. pap. 14.95 (*0-938041-09-6*) Arc Pr AR.

Your Guide to Finding the Right One & Being the Right One, Book 1. Delia Passi & Ted Biza. (Illus.). 70p. 1994. 8.95 (*0-9641081-0-0*); pap. 5.95 (*0-9641081-1-9*) Tedel Pubns.

***Your Guide to Florida Bedding Plants: Selection, Establishment & Maintenance.** Robert J. Black & Edward F. Gilman. LC 96-46935. (Illus.). 80p. (Orig.). 1996. pap. write for info. (*0-916287-17-3*, SP 185) Univ Fla Food.

Your Guide to Getting Fit. 3rd ed. Ivan Kusinitz & Morton Fine. LC 94-34354. 320p. (Orig.). (C). 1994. pap. text ed. 19.95 (*1-55934-380-X*, 1380); disk write for info. (*0-318-68370-9*) Mayfield Pub.

Your Guide to Getting Fit, Instructor's Manual. 3rd ed. Ivan Kusinitz & Morton Fine. LC 94-34354. (Orig.). 1994. teacher ed., pap. text ed. write for info. (*1-55934-381-8*, 1381) Mayfield Pub.

Your Guide to Good Nutrition. Fredrick J. Stare et al. 213p. 1991. pap. 17.95 (*0-87975-692-6*) Prometheus Bks.

Your Guide to Greatness. Earl Paulk. 64p. 1990. 3.50 (*0-917595-38-6*) Kingdom Pubs.

Your Guide to Healthy Houseplants. (Illus.). 64p. 1993. spiral bd. 5.98 (*1-56173-653-8*, 3604300) Pubns Intl Ltd.

Your Guide to Living Trusts & Other Trusts: How Trusts Can Help You Avoid Probate & Taxes. Kay A. Ostberg et al. (Orig.). 1994. write for info. (*0-910073-19-8*) HALT DC.

Your Guide to Medical Hypnosis. Lynn Phelps. LC 93-9545. (Focus on Health Ser.). (Illus.). 108p. (Orig.). 1993. pap. 7.95 (*0-944838-28-6*) Med Physics Pub.

Your Guide to Medical Schools & Residency Programs: The Information You Need to Know, You Should Know, You Must Know. Robert M. Maloney. Ed. by Richard A. DeVito. (Illus.). 250p. (Orig.). 1996. pap. 189.95 (*0-932834-25-6*) Prime Natl Pub.

Your Guide to Non-Prescription Drugs. American Pharmaceutical Association Staff. (Illus.). 500p. write for info. (*0-8290-1580-9*) Irvington.

Your Guide to Planning the Wedding Day. Carol Chapman. 160p. (Orig.). 1993. pap. 13.95 (*0-572-01874-6*, Pub. by W Foulsham UK) Trans-Atl Phila.

Your Guide to POSIX. 3rd ed. Hal Jespersen. 42p. 1993. pap. 10.00 (*0-936593-27-X*) UniForum.

Your Guide to Retiring to Mexico, Costa Rica & Beyond: Finding the Good Life on a Fixed Income. Shelley Emling. LC 96-4180. 238p. Date not set. pap. 11.95 (*0-89529-719-1*) Avery Pub.

Your Guide to Safe Astral Projection: A Handbook for Self-Growth Through Out-of-Body Experience. Charlotte A. Wolter. 55p. (Orig.). 1989. student ed., pap. 14.95 (*0-9624066-0-0*) Olympic Professional.

Your Guide to Safe Travel in the U. S. A. 225 Ways to Protect Yourself Against Crime. Richard W. Eaves. (Orig.). 1994. pap. text ed. write for info. (*0-9632355-5-9*) Guardian Pr.

Your Guide to Slide: The Slacker's Guide to College. Brady Lessard. (Illus.). 96p. (Orig.). 1995. pap. 6.95 (*0-9640713-1-2*) Fine Print.

Your Guide to Social Security Benefits, 1991-92. Leona G. Rubin & Alison I. Porter. (Illus.). 188p. 1991. 19.95 (*0-8160-2615-7*) Facts on File.

Your Guide to Standardized Herbal Products. Rebecca Flynn & Mark Roest. 104p. 1995. pap. text ed. 14.95 (*0-9644958-0-5*) One Wrld Press.

Your Guide to the Electronic Control of Fluid Power. Ed. by National Fluid Power Association Staff. (Illus.). 64p. (Orig.). 1992. pap. 5.00 (*0-942220-28-5*) Natl Fluid Power.

Your Guide to the Home Boutique Bonanza: How to Organize & Run a Successful Home Holiday Boutique. Barb Griffin. (Illus.). 16p. 1989. pap. 5.00 (*0-937679-05-4*) Sewing Sampler.

Your Guide to the ISO Commercial Lines Policies. 5th ed. Ed. by Standard Publishing Staff. 288p. pap. 64.50 (*0-923240-11-X*) Stndrd Publishing.

Your Guide to the Skies. Rick Shaffer. (Illus.). 176p. (Orig.). 1993. pap. 17.95 (*1-56565-047-6*) Lowell Hse.

***Your Guide to the Sky.** Rick Shaffer. Date not set. pap. 17.95 (*1-56565-652-0*) Contemp Bks.

Your Guide to Writing Research Papers. Ed. by Julie Hutchinson. 36p. (C). 1985. reprint ed. student ed., pap. text ed. 9.95 (*0-89892-059-0*) Contemp Pub Co of Raleigh.

***Your Guided Hunt: And What You Should Know. Randy Blackburn. (Illus.). 126p. (Orig.). 1996. pap. 14.95 (*0-9654123-0-X*) R Blackburn. This newly released book, self-published by the author is an in-depth look at the guided hunt from the guide's point of view. Real stories of the hunt, & "how-to's" blend well to prepare the hunter for his guided hunt anywhere in North America. The reader will learn how to book the hunt of his dreams, as well as what to expect during the hunt. This piece covers most big game hunting in all types of regions & conditions. A must read for the serious hunter, this book is 5 1/2 by 8 1/2 inches, soft glossy cover, ten chapters, 126 pages, & 21 photos. Randy Blackburn is a professional back country guide with sixteen years of experience guiding hunters to nine species of big game. He has won several awards in his field, including Guide of the Year for Cody Country Outfitters & Guides Association 1995. Randy has written numerous outdoor articles for various publications & was the outdoor columnist for THE CODY ENTERPRISES for six years in his hometown of Cody, Wyoming. YOUR GUIDED HUNT retails at $14.95/wholesale $8.97 to dealers. Contact Randy Blackburn, 84 South Fk. Rd., Cody, WY 82414.** *Publisher Provided Annotation.*

Your Guiding Lights. Wanda M. Vonderhaar. 180p. (Orig.). 1988. pap. 6.95 (*0-9620055-4-1*) Wizards Pr.

Your Guinea Pig: A Kid's Guide to Raising & Showing. Wanda L. Curran. LC 94-42164. 128p. (J). 1995. pap. 12.95 (*0-88266-889-7*, Garden Way Pub) Storey Comm Inc.

Your Gut Feelings. rev. ed. Henry D. Janowitz. (Illus.). 224p. 1994. 27.50 (*0-19-508935-9*); pap. 12.95 (*0-19-508936-7*) OUP.

Your Ham Antenna Companion. 1995. pap. 10.00 (*0-87259-511-0*) Am Radio.

Your Handbook for Healing. Craig Carter. 64p. 1981. pap. 7.95 (*0-911336-86-9*) Sci of Mind.

Your Handbook of Everyday Law. 5th rev. ed. George G. Coughlin, Jr. LC 93-25283. Orig. Title: Your Introduction to Law. 384p. 1993. pap. 15.00 (*0-06-273240-4*, Harper Ref) HarpC.

Your Hands Can Heal: Learn to Channel Healing Energy. Ric A. Weinman. 152p. 1992. pap. 10.95 (*0-14-019361-8*, Arkana) Viking Penguin.

Your Handwriting & What It Means. William L. French. (Self-Enrichment Ser.). (Illus.). 228p. 1976. pap. 9.95 (*0-87877-036-4*, G-36) Newcastle Pub.

Your Happiness Here & Hereafter. Irwinn F. Krimm. 1977. pap. 5.95 (*0-685-02046-0*) Happy Health.

Your Healing Hands: The Polarity Experience. Richard Gordon. LC 78-12527. (Illus.). 142p. (Orig.). 1984. reprint ed. pap. 16.95 (*0-914728-49-0*) Wingbow Pr.

Your Healing Is Today. 5th ed. Tom Johnson. 64p. 1986. reprint ed. pap. 4.95 (*0-941992-07-1*) Los Arboles Pub.

Your Healing Is Within You. Canon J. Glennon. LC 80-82616. 189p. 1980. pap. 7.95 (*0-88270-457-5*) Bridge-Logos.

Your Healing Mind. Reed C. Moskowitz. 304p. 1993. reprint ed. pap. 10.00 (*0-380-71470-1*) Avon.

Your Healing Power: A Comprehensive Guide to Channelling Your Healing Energies. Jack Angelo. 256p. 1996. pap. 14.95 (*0-7499-1326-6*, Pub. by Piatkus Bks UK) London Brdge.

***Your Healing Power: Awaken & Develop Your Ability to Heal Yourself & Others.** David Furlong. 1997. pap. text ed. 10.95 (*0-8065-1917-7*, Citadel Pr) Carol Pub Group.

Your Health. Dianne R. Hales. 525p. 1991. pap. text ed. 29.25 (*0-8053-2770-3*) Benjamin-Cummings.

***Your Health & Safety at Work: A Collection of Modules.** 1996. pap. 45.50 (*92-2-108014-5*) Intl Labour Office.

Your Health & Sanity in the Age of Treason. R. Swinburne Clymer. 396p. 1957. reprint ed. 10.00 (*0-916285-32-4*) Humanitarian.

Your Health & the Indoor Environment: A Complete Guide to Better Health Through Control of the Indoor Atmosphere. 2nd rev. ed. Randall E. Dunford. LC 90-92083. (Illus.). 272p. (Orig.). 1994. pap. 12.95 (*0-9628093-4-9*) NuDawn Pub.

Your Health & Your House. Nina Anderson & Albert Benoist. 1994. pap. 16.95 (*0-87983-630-X*) Keats.

***Your Health Habits Checkup.** Harold E. Buttram. 32p. 1968. pap. 2.00 (*0-916285-59-6*) Humanitarian.

Your Health in Retirement. J. A. Gray & Pat Blair. 80p. (C). 1990. 50.00 (*0-86242-082-2*, Pub. by Age Concern Eng UK) St Mut.

Your Health Made Simple: You Are the Key to Your Health, Happiness & Love. Kay Henrion. LC 93-70447. (Illus.). 192p. (Orig.). 1993. pap. 14.95 (*0-9636181-5-6*) Angelbear Pub.

Your Health, Your Choice: A New Holistic Approach to Disease Prevention & a Healthier You. M. T. Morter, Jr. 224p. 1990. 17.95 (*0-8119-0655-8*) LIFETIME.

Your Health, Your Choice: A New Holistic Approach to Disease Prevention & a Healthier You. rev. ed. M. T. Morter, Jr. 224p. 1995. pap. 14.95 (*0-8119-0667-1*) LIFETIME.

Your Health, Your Style: Strategies for Wellness. Lon H. Seiger & Jan Richter. 272p. (C). 1996. per. write for info. (*0-697-26231-6*) Brown & Benchmark.

Your Healthy Body. rev. ed. 1992. 12.95 (*0-942361-57-1*) MasterMedia Pub.

Your Healthy Cat: Homeopathic Medicines for Common Feline Ailments. H. G. Wolff. 131p. 1991. pap. 9.95 (*1-55643-113-9*) North Atlantic.

***Your Healthy Child's Medical Workbook: The Essential Organizer for Parents.** Dylan Landis. 176p. 1997. pap. 9.00 (*0-425-15982-5*, Berkley Trade) Berkley Pub.

Your Healthy Pet: A Practical Guide to Raising Happier, Healthier Dogs & Cats. Amy Marder. LC 93-27730. 224p. 1994. pap. 14.95 (*0-87596-185-1*) Rodale Pr Inc.

Your Healthy Pregnancy Workbook. Dylan Landis. 240p. (Orig.). 1995. pap. 12.00 (*0-425-14952-8*, Berkley Trade) Berkley Pub.

Your Heart. American. 1995. text ed. 27.95 (*0-13-443623-7*) P-H.

***Your Heart.** Thomson. 1996. pap. 2.95 (*0-85207-127-2*, Pub. by C W Daniel UK) Natl Bk Netwk.

Your Heart. James C. Thomson. Ed. by C. Leslie Thomson. 80p. 1974. pap. 6.95 (*0-8464-1058-3*) Beekman Pubs.

Your Heart: A Basic Book for Heart Patients. 2nd ed. James E. Crockett. (Illus.). 216p. 1989. pap. 12.00 (*0-685-44369-8*) Eucalyptus Pr.

Your Heart: In Sickness & in Health. James E. Crockett. (Illus.). 176p. (Orig.). 1984. pap. 10.00 (*0-9611980-0-1*) Eucalyptus Pr.

Your Heart: Questions You Have--Answers You Need. 4th ed. LC 95-49182. 224p. 1996. 13.95 (*1-882606-60-4*) Peoples Med Soc.

An Asterisk (*) at the beginning of an entry indicates that the title is appearing in BIP for the first time.

Your Heart & Blood. Leslie J. LeMaster. LC 84-7604. (New True Bks.). (Illus.). 48p. (J). (gr. k-4). 1984. pap. 5.50 (*0-516-41933-1*) Childrens.

Your Heart Will Fly Away. David Rigsbee. LC 92-80447. 80p. (Orig.). 1992. pap. 10.95 (*0-912292-97-0*) Smith.

***Your Heartburn: Real Information You Can Use.** Randy Shields. LC 96-70817. 118p. (Orig.). 1996. mass mkt. 4.99 (*1-888886-07-2*) CEPI.

Your Heart's Desire. Ken Keyes, Jr. LC 83-19924. 168p. 1983. pap. 6.95 (*0-915972-05-0*) Love Line Bks.

Your Heart's Desire: Instructions for Creating the Life You Really Want. Sonia Choquette. 1997. pap. 18.00 (*0-609-80011-6*, Chatham River Pr) Random Hse Value.

Your Help Is at Hand. Mary L. Kupferle. LC 89-50272. 146p. 1990. 8.95 (*0-87159-184-7*) Unity Bks.

Your Herbal Medicine Chest. David L. Hoffmann. 1989. pap. 2.50 (*0-87983-508-7*) Keats.

Your HF Digital Companion. 1995. pap. 10.00 (*0-87259-481-5*) Am Radio.

Your Hidden Assets: The Key to Getting Executive Jobs. Orrin G. Wood, Jr. LC 81-67116. 300p. 1981. text ed. 17.95 (*0-87094-266-2*) Irwin Prof Pubng.

Your Hidden Assets: The Key to Getting Executive Jobs. Orrin G. Wood, Jr. 287p. 1981. reprint ed. 20.00 (*0-9631178-0-7*) N D Pr.

Your Hidden Powers. Wickenburg. 222p. 1992. 16.00 (*0-86690-405-0*) Am Fed Astrologers.

***Your High Cholesterol: Real Information You Can Use.** Randy Shields & William Frishman. LC 96-70818. 132p. (Orig.). 1996. mass mkt. 4.99 (*1-888886-06-4*) CEPI.

Your History. J. A. Rogers. LC 89-61277. (Illus.). 100p. 1983. reprint ed. pap. 8.95 (*0-933121-04-0*, BC-10) Black Classic.

Your Hit Parade & American Top Ten Hits: A Week-by-Week Guide to the Nations Favorite Music, 1935-1994. Bruce Elrod. Ed. by Thomas Schultheiss. (Illus.). 672p. 1994. lib. bdg. 80.00 (*1-56075-037-5*) Popular Culture.

Your Home, a Lighthouse. rev. ed. Bob Jacks et al. LC 87-60179. 150p. 1987. reprint ed. pap. 9.00 (*0-89109-127-0*) NavPress.

Your Home Aquarium. Jorg Vierke. 1991. 35.95 (*0-86622-075-5*, TS-139) TFH Pubns.

Your Home Color Guide: Making Color Work. Virginia Carr. Ed. by Maria Catalfio. (Illus.). 206p. 1994. pap. 14.95 (*0-9640510-1-X*) Smart Home Moves.

Your Home Cooling Energy Guide. John T. Krigger. 64p. 1991. pap. text ed. 12.50 (*1-880120-04-6*) Saturn Rsce.

***Your Home for Health, Happiness & Fitness: Good Family Health Starts in the Home.** Bernard Jensen. (Dr. Jensen's Health Handbooks Ser.: Vol. 4). (Illus.). 152p. (Orig.). 1996. pap. text ed. 10.00 (*0-932615-29-5*) B Jensen.

***Your Home in Italy.** Dyson. Date not set. pap. text ed. write for info. (*0-85121-521-1*) Addison-Wesley.

Your Home in Retirement: An Owner's Guide. Age Concern England Staff. (C). 1989. 25.00 (*0-86242-095-4*, Pub. by Age Concern Eng UK) St Mut.

Your Home in the West. Rod Wooden. (Methuen New Theatrescripts Ser.). 82p. (Orig.). (C). 1991. pap. 9.95 (*0-413-65760-4*, Pub. by Methuen UK) Heinemann.

Your Home Inspection Guide. William L. Ventolo, Jr. (Illus.). 261p. (Orig.). 1995. pap. 15.95 (*0-7931-1336-9*, 1913-0802, Real Estate Ed) Dearborn Finan.

Your Home Is a Learning Place: Reading Level 3-4. Pamela Weinberg. LC 93-423. 1993. pap. 6.95 (*0-88336-641-X*) New Readers.

Your Home Is Your Sanctuary: A Mezuzah House-Warming Party. Ahammai Engelmayer & Charles Simon. (Illus.). 24p. (Orig.). 1994. student ed., pap. text ed. 7.75 (*0-935665-23-4*) Fed Jewish Mens Clubs.

Your Home Mortgage. Michael C. Thomsett. LC 91-37900. (ICFP Personal Wealth-Building Guides Ser.). 240p. 1992. pap. text ed. 10.95 (*0-471-54829-4*) Wiley.

Your Home Mortgage Answer Book: 100 Questions & the Answers You Need. Mary Callegari. 208p. (Orig.). 1995. pap. 14.95 (*0-7931-1298-2*, 1913-3001, Real Estate Ed) Dearborn Finan.

***Your Home Office.** 2nd ed. Peter Chatterton. (Daily Express Guides Ser.). 1995. pap. 12.95 (*0-7494-1642-4*) Kogan Page Ltd.

Your Home, Your Health & Well Being. David Rousseau et al. LC 87-7080. (Illus.). 320p. 1988. pap. 14.95 (*0-89815-223-2*) Ten Speed Pr.

Your Hope of Glory. Elizabeth S. Turner. Ed. by Michael Maday. LC 90-70728. 1996. reprint ed. 11.95 (*0-87159-187-1*, 67) Unity Bks.

***Your Hormoneous Life: Learn the Secrets of Progesterone.** Calvin Ross. (Illus.). 180p. (Orig.). 1996. pap. 12.95 (*1-57901-013-X*) Intl Promotions.

Your Horoscope Hidden Magic. abr. ed. Intro. by Luanna C. Blagrove. (Illus.). 225p. 1987. 24.95 (*0-939776-39-1*) Blagrove Pubns.

Your Horoscope Progressed. John A. Hanson. 10p. 1971. 5.00 (*0-86690-190-6*, H1175-014) Am Fed Astrologers.

Your Horse: A Step-by-Step Guide to Horse Ownership. Judy Chapple. LC 84-22280. (Illus.). 144p. (J). (gr. 8 up). 1984. pap. 14.95 (*0-88266-353-4*, Garden Way Pub) Storey Comm Inc.

Your Horse's Health. Tony Pavord. (Crowood Equestrian Guides Ser.). (Illus.). 96p. 1992. pap. 17.95 (*1-85223-532-2*, Pub. by Crowood Pr UK) Trafalgar.

***Your Horse's Mind.** Leonie Marshall. (Illus.). 160p. 1997. 35.00 (*1-85223-978-6*, Pub. by Crowood Pr UK) Trafalgar.

Your Hospital Care Guide: What You Need to Know & Questions to Ask. Sonya N. Washington. 160p. (Orig.). 1995. pap. 9.95 (*1-886583-05-6*) SeaStar Pub.

Your Hospital Care Guide Pt. 2: What You Need to Know in These Times of Health Care Changes. Sonya N. Washington. (InfoMed Book Ser.). 100p. 1998. pap. write for info. (*1-886583-06-4*) SeaStar Pub.

Your Hospital Stay...It'll Be Okay. James M. Sorg. (Illus.). 36p. (Orig.). (J). (ps-5). 1988. pap. 4.95 (*0-9622172-1-2*) D Miller Fndtn.

Your Hospitality Field Experience: A Student Workbook. Jack E. Miller & Karen E. Drummond. LC 95-12109. 304p. 1995. pap. text ed. 49.95 (*0-471-05327-9*) Wiley.

Your Hot Button. Ed. by Liz McGehee. LC 90-34193. (Illus.). 24p. (Orig.). (C). 1990. pap. 4.95 (*0-943574-71-4*, L602) That Patchwork.

Your Hour. M. Raymond. 216p. 1995. reprint ed. text ed. 19.95 (*0-912141-23-9*) Roman Cath Bks.

Your Housekeeper's Cookbook: Bilingual Recipes, Menus & More. fac. ed. Nancy S. Levicki. LC 85-5179. 151p. (ENG.). pap. 43.10 (*0-7837-7415-X*, 2047210) Bks Demand.

Your Husband, My Lover. Jennifer Rain, pseud. Ed. by Anne Frost. 350p. (Orig.). 1989. pap. text ed. 12.95 (*0-9614624-6-9*) Frost Pub.

Your Husband, Your Friend. Bob Barnes. 1993. pap. 8.99 (*0-89081-959-9*) Harvest Hse.

Your Hyperactive Child: A Parents Guide to Coping with Attention Deficit Disorder. Barbara D. Ingersoll. LC 87-36535. 240p. 1988. pap. 10.95 (*0-385-24070-8*) Doubleday.

***Your Hypertension: Real Information You Can Use.** Randy Shields & William Frishman. LC 96-70820. 132p. (Orig.). 1996. mass mkt. 4.99 (*1-888886-00-5*) CEPI.

Your Ideal Silhouette: Body Proportion Analysis. rev. ed. Gail Florin. (Illus.). 64p. 1992. 6.75 (*0-945247-01-X*) Meridian Educ.

***Your Ideal Silhouette Personal Shopping Guide.** Gail Florin. (Illus.). 73p. (Orig.). 1991. 7.85 (*1-56191-187-9*, 8035) Meridian Educ.

Your Ideal Silhouette Workbook. rev. ed. (Illus.). 40p. 1992. pap. 6.75 (*1-56191-195-X*, 8033) Meridian Educ.

Your IIGS Guide. Shelly Lisoskie & Pete Lisoskie. (Illus.). 308p. (Orig.). 1990. pap. 21.95 (*1-879141-01-9*) Busn Toolbox.

Your Illustrated Guide to Foreclosure Gold Mining: High Profit, Low Risk Real Estate for the 90's. Ted Thomas. LC 91-91008. (Illus.). 416p. (Orig.). 1991. pap. text ed. 29.95 (*0-9623701-7-7*) New Growth Fin.

***Your in Charge.** N. H. Laursen. 1997. pap. 12.00 (*0-449-45763-X*) Fawcett.

Your in Control: A Practical & Effective Way to Enhance Learning Using a Step-by-Step Guide to Self-Control. Lori W. Williford. 22p. 1995. 69.95 (*0-9645381-4-8*) Univrsl Skills.

Your Infallible Instinct. Milton Ward. LC 65-92058. 150p. 1981. pap. 15.00 (*0-939835-03-7*) Optimus Bks.

Your Infinite Power to Be Rich. Joseph Murphy. 1968. pap. text ed. 9.95 (*0-13-979591-X*, Reward) P-H.

Your Injury: A Common Sense Guide to Sports Injuries. Merrill A. Ritter & Marjorie J. Albohm. (Illus.). 188p. 1987. spiral bd. write for info. (*0-697-14824-6*) Brown & Benchmark.

Your Injury: A Common Sense Guide to Sports Injuries. Merrill A. Ritter & Marjorie J. Albohm. (Illus.). 192p. 1994. reprint ed. pap. 14.95 (*1-57028-011-8*) Masters Pr IN.

Your Inner Child of the Past. W. Hugh Missildine. 1991. pap. 5.99 (*0-671-74703-7*) S&S Trade.

Your Inner Enemy. Gregory L. Little & Kenneth D. Robinson. (Illus.). 105p. (Orig.). 1989. pap. 8.95 (*0-940829-00-2*) Eagle Wing Bks.

Your Inner Music: Creative Analysis & Music Memory. Gregory M. Rolla. LC 93-25463. 144p. (Orig.). 1993. pap. 3.95 (*0-933029-74-8*) Chiron Pubns.

Your Inner Path to Investment Success: Insights into the Psychology of Investing. Albert Mehrabian. 225p. 1991. text ed. 22.95 (*1-55738-210-7*) Irwin Prof Pubng.

***Your Inner Physician & You: Craniosacral Therapy & Somatoemotional Release.** 2nd rev. ed. John E. Upledger. LC 96-37576. 163p. 1997. pap. 12.95 (*1-55643-246-1*) North Atlantic.

Your Inner Physician & You: Craniosacral Therapy SomatoEmotional Release. John E. Upledger. (Illus.). 163p. (Orig.). 1991. pap. 12.95 (*1-55643-148-1*) North Atlantic.

Your Intelligent Computer Assistant: How You Can Profit from Artificial Intelligence - in Your Business, Home, & Investing. Jerry Felsen. 150p. (Orig.). 1985. pap. 34.00 (*0-916376-09-5*) CDS Pub.

Your Intelligent Heart: Notes to Women Who Work. Susan B. Wilson. LC 94-41741. 128p. 1995. 12.95 (*0-8144-0274-7*) AMACOM.

***Your Interrupted Journey of Evolution Through the Universes from the Beginning to Now & Beyond.** Margurite Marie. (Illus.). 137p. (Orig.). 1997. pap. write for info. (*0-9656394-0-1*) Margurite Marie.

***Your Intimacy Quotient: The Symptoms, Causes & Consequences of Intimacy Deprivation.** Fred Sowder. LC 96-96848. (Illus.). 160p. (Orig.). 1996. pap. 12.95 (*0-9653781-0-1*, E-010) Estes Pr.

Your Introduction to Law see **Your Handbook of Everyday Law**

Your Introduction to S Gauge. 72p. 1989. pap. 7.95 (*0-911581-19-7*) Heimburger Hse Pub.

Your Intuition Is Wrong! Marc T. Simon. (Illus.). 60p. 1996. pap. 9.00 (*0-8059-3834-6*) Dorrance.

Your Investing: A Dollar & Sense Guide to Personal Investing. rev. ed. George W. Trivoli. LC 92-96982. (Personal Finance Investing Ser.). (Illus.). 155p. (Orig.). (C). 1993. reprint ed. pap. text ed. 14.95 (*0-9632407-0-6*) Smart Ideas.
Seasoned investors, students & beginners alike learn to make better investment decisions from this readable, concise volume. Based on Dr. Trivoli's weekly column, YOUR INVESTING, distributed through THE NEW YORK TIMES regional wire service, this volume guides the reader through the complexities of today's investment environment. Dr. Trivoli's column is now syndicated by United Press International, (U.P.I.) Financial Features & appears in CompuServe & Bloomberg Business News. Dr. Trivoli shares his vast experience as a teacher/researcher in finance & investments, as well as his practical experience in advising & lecturing on personal investing. Beginning with the basics of personal investing, risk avoidance, maximizing returns & diversification techniques, the book covers a full range of securities, including stocks, bonds, options, futures & collectibles. Various investment strategies are outlined, including a detailed discussion of investment alternatives to bank C.D.s & money-market funds. Special topics covered involve investing for retirement & children's education. An entire chapter is devoted to mutual funds: selecting the best funds, monitoring performance, & deciding when to sell. Various investment timing techniques are discussed, including the Dow Theory & Contrarian View to investing. Finally, the relationship of money & the stock market is covered, along with predicting economic conditions. Copies may be ordered by sending either a check or money order for $14.95 for each copy to: Smart Ideas Publishing Co., P.O. Box 982, Jacksonville, AL 36265. Phone: (205) 435-6983, FAX (205) 435-1448. ***Publisher Provided Annotation.***

Your Invisible Power. Genevieve Behrend. 1921. pap. 6.95 (*0-87516-004-2*) DeVorss.

Your Invisible Power. Genevieve Behrend. 92p. 1975. reprint ed. spiral bd. 5.50 (*0-7873-0088-8*) Hlth Research.

Your Invisible Power: Working Principles & Concrete Examples in Applied Mental Science (1927) Genevieve Behrend. 92p. 1996. pap. 14.95 (*1-56459-889-6*) Kessinger Pub.

Your Isadora: The Love Story of Isadora Duncan & Gordon Craig Told Through Letters. Ed. by Francis Steegmuller. LC 74-5178. (Illus.). 399p. 1974. 25.00 (*0-87104-256-8*) NY Pub Lib.

Your Jewish Child. Morrison D. Bial. 1978. 5.00 (*0-8074-0012-2*, 101200) UAHC.

Your Jewish Lexicon. Edith Samuel et al. 192p. (Orig.). (HEB.). 1982. pap. 7.95 (*0-8074-0061-0*, 383805) UAHC.

Your Job, Your Future. Ed. by Carolyn Hettich. (Illus.). 144p. 1986. pap. text ed. 9.95 (*0-935920-27-7*, Ntl Pubs Blck) P-H.

Your Job, Your Future. 3rd ed. Hettich. 1986. pap. text ed. 15.40 (*0-13-973074-5*) P-H.

Your John: The Love Letters of Radclyffe Hall. Ed. & Intro. by Joanne Glasgow. 320p. (C). 1997. 24.95 (*0-8147-3092-2*) NYU Pr.

Your Journey. Susan Florence. (Illus.). 40p. 1990. 6.95 (*0-8378-1880-X*) Gibson.

***Your Journey to Jewels: The Map to Motivation.** (Illus.). 90p. (Orig.). 1997. pap. text ed. 7.95 (*0-9657368-0-6*) Majestic Rose.

Your Journey to Success: A Guide for Young Lithuanians. Raimonda Mikatavage. LC 95-77918. (Illus.). 192p. (Orig.). 1996. pap. 14.95 (*0-9647213-8-4*) Melodija Bks.

***Your Journey's Destiny.** Michael Rothman & Carolyn Rothman. LC 96-61624. 94p. 1996. pap. 12.95 (*0-9643126-7-0*) Woodburner Pr.

Your Joy Ride to Health. Bill Proxmire. LC 93-93538. 318p. 1994. 24.95 (*0-9637988-2-0*) B Proxmire.

Your KdF Car - Dein KdF-Wagen. Tr. by Inge Froebe from GER. (Illus.). 36p. (Orig.). 1993. reprint ed. pap. 10.00 (*0-910667-39-X*) USM.

***Your Key to Healthy Persian Cooking.** Mehrnaz Sajedi. 188p. 1996. pap. 19.95 (*0-614-21526-9*, 1340) Kazi Pubns.

Your Key to Healthy Persian Cooking. Mehrnaz Sajedi. 178p. 1993. otabind 19.95 (*0-9639411-1-9*) Nima Pubs.

Your Key to His Kingdom. James McKeever. 336p. (C). pap. text ed. 10.99 (*0-86694-124-X*) Omega Pubns OR.

***Your Key to His Kingdom.** James McKeever. 336p. (C). text ed. 14.99 (*0-86694-123-1*) Omega Pubns OR.

Your Key to the Practice. Linda Miles & Walter Hailey. Ed. by Kirpal Gordon. (Illus.). 96p. (Orig.). 1995. pap. text ed. 19.95 (*1-882306-06-6*) Planned Mktg.

Your Keys to a New Life: The Psychology of Weight Loss. Tamara. (Illus.). 160p. (Orig.). 1994. pap. 19.95 (*0-9640581-0-3*) Renewal Res.

***Your Kid Ought to Be in Pictures: A How-To Guide for Would-Be Child Actors & Their Parents.** Kelly F. Kidwell & Ruth Devorin. LC 97-10416. 160p. (Orig.). 1997. pap. 16.95 (*0-943728-90-8*) Lone Eagle Pub.

***Your Kids & Mind.** Tana Reiff. LC 94-76139. (Working for Myself Ser.). 80p. 1994. pap. 4.95 (*0-7854-1115-1*, 40829) Am Guidance.

Your Kids Are Grown: Moving on with & Without Them. Francine A. Toder. (Illus.). 278p. (C). 1994. 25.95 (*0-306-44761-4*, Plenum Insight) Plenum.

***Your Kids Have a Plan-- Do You?** Pat Holt & Lori Dodson. LC 96-1907. 1997. pap. 9.99 (*0-8423-4984-7*) Tyndale.

Your King Comes! Janice B. Wyatt. 1991. pap. 3.25 (*1-55673-406-9*, 9219) CSS OH.

Your Kitten's First Year. Don Harper. 1994. 12.98 (*0-7858-0163-4*) Bk Sales Inc.

Your Kitten's First Year. Shawn Messonnier. LC 96-48154. 144p. (Orig.). 1996. pap. 12.95 (*1-55622-527-X*, Seaside Pr) Wordware Pub.

Your Land, My Land: Children in the Process of Acculturation. Jacklyn B. Clayton. LC 95-37843. 139p. 1995. pap. text ed. 18.50 (*0-435-08852-1*, 08852) Heinemann.

Your Last Diet Plan. George R. Abraham & Katherine Abraham. (Illus.). 208p. (Orig.). 1983. boxed 9.95 (*0-915469-00-6*) Abraham Assocs Inc.

Your Last Goodbye. Salem Kirban. LC 70-87000. (Illus.). 1969. pap. 5.95 (*0-912582-06-5*) Kirban.

***Your Lawyer on a Short Leash: A Survivor's Guide to Dealing with Lawyers.** Avraham Azrieli. LC 96-42170. 1997. 16.95 (*1-57105-036-1*) Bridge St Bks.

Your Leadership Style. Rima Miller. 62p. 1987. pap. 17.95 (*1-56602-019-0*) Research Better.

Your Legacy from Thaddeus Stevens Republican of the First Time. Charles W. Boyd. 206p. 1987. pap. 15.00 (*0-318-23880-2*) Bomax Pubs.

Your Legal Guide to Consumer Credit. 48p. 1994. pap. 2.50 (*0-89707-356-8*, 235-0023-01) Amer Bar Assn.

Your Legal Guide to Marriage & Other Relationships. 79p. 1989. pap. 2.50 (*0-89707-436-X*, 235-0005-01) Amer Bar Assn.

Your Legal Rights. Elaine Landau. LC 94-42718. 128p. (YA). 1995. 13.95 (*0-8027-8359-7*); lib. bdg. 14.85 (*0-8027-8360-0*) Walker & Co.

Your Legal Rights on the Job. Workers Rights Project. 0.25 (*0-685-14955-2*) Natl Lawyers Guild.

Your Legal Will. Guy G. Gibson, Jr. 1988. 9.95 (*1-880037-24-6*) Info Plus CA.

Your Library. 2nd ed. William A. Katz. 242p. (C). 1984. pap. text ed. 22.75 (*0-03-063012-6*) HB Coll Pubs.

Your Library: A Friend. Isabel D. Prucha. Tr. by Hoang Chu Duy. (Illus.). 77p. (Orig.). (ENG & VIE.). 1986. pap. 10.95 (*0-937319-00-7*) Golden Palm Pr.

Your Life: His Glory. John Beaumont. 56p. (Orig.). 1986. pap. 3.50 (*0-914903-10-1*) Destiny Image.

Your Life: Why It Is the Way It Is & What You Can Do about It: An Exploration of the Universal Laws That Govern all of Us. Bruce McArthur. 273p. (Orig.). 1993. pap. 12.95 (*0-87604-300-7*, 375) ARE Pr.

Your Life & Love Beyond Death. David Hyatt. Ed. by George W. Fisk. LC 92-27748. 192p. (Orig.). 1992. pap. 11.95 (*0-9620507-3-3*) Cosmic Concepts Pr.

***Your Life As Story: Writing the New Autobiography.** Tristine Rainer. LC 96-41764. 368p. 1997. 24.95 (*0-87477-861-1*, Tarcher Putnam) Putnam Pub Group.

Your Life Depends On It!, 2 vol. set. Henry Wadsworth Longfellow. Ed. & Intro. by Tarea Molina. (Illus.). 1994. student ed. write for info. (*0-9642779-2-1*) T Molina Ent.

Your Life Depends on It: Four Easy Steps to Food Storage, Vol. 1. Tarea Molina. Ed. by Toni Lamb. (Illus.). 33p. (Orig.). 1993. student ed., pap. 7.99 (*0-9642779-6-4*) T Molina Ent.

Your Life Depends on It Vol. II: A Complete Emergency Workbook. Tarea Molina. Ed. by Toni Lamb. (Illus.). 70p. 1994. pap. 11.99 (*0-9642779-1-3*) T Molina Ent.

Your Life in Christ. W. Hal Brooks. 1972. 2.75 (*0-8054-2520-9*, 4225-20) Broadman.

Your Life in Christ. rev. ed. Ed. by Navigators Staff. (Design for Discipleship Ser.: Bk. 1). 31p. 1980. pap. 4.00 (*0-89109-036-3*) NavPress.

Your Life in the Palm of Your Hand, a Hand Analysis System of Self Discovery. Kathryn Harwig. 145p. pap. 12.95 (*0-9638822-0-1*) Spring Pr MN.

Your Life in Your Words: Your Story As Only You Can Write It. R. W. Delaney. 90p. 1995. pap. 19.95 (*0-9645363-0-7*) Flagship Pr.

Your Life Insurance Options. Alan Lavine. LC 92-14939. (ICFP Personal Wealth Building Guides Ser.). 240p. 1993. text ed. 55.00 (*0-471-54918-5*); pap. text ed. 12.95 (*0-471-54919-3*) Wiley.

Your Life Is a Gift: So Make the Most of It. Ken Keyes, Jr. LC 86-21385. Orig. Title: How to Make Your Life Work or Why Aren't You Happy?. (Illus.). 216p. (Orig.). 1987. pap. 6.95 (*0-915972-12-3*) Love Line Bks.

***Your Life Is in Your Chakras.** Rattana K. Khalsa, pseud. 199p. 1996. spiral bd. 25.00 (*1-888029-01-3*, Yoga Tech Pr) Heart Quest.

Your Life Is Worth Mine: Story Never Told Before of How Polish Nuns in World War II Saved Hundred. Ewa Kurek. LC 96-36226. 1996. 24.95 (*0-7818-0409-4*) Hippocrene Bks.

Your Life Is Your Message: Finding Harmony with Yourself, Others & the Earth. Eknath Easwaran. LC 95-46095. 128p. 1996. 14.95 (*0-7868-6220-3*) Hyperion.

***Your Life Is Your Message: Finding Harmony with Yourself, Others & the Earth.** Eknath Easwaran. 1997. pap. text ed. 9.75 (*0-7868-8266-2*) Hyperion.

Your Life Story: A Step-by-Step Workbook. John L. Myers & Karen K. Kroman. Ed. by Robert Gryder. (C). 1989. student ed. 19.50 (*0-929690-06-0*) Herit Pubs AZ.

Your Life Story: How to Write, Print, Publish & Sell It Yourself. Earlynne Webber. LC 84-4051. 164p. (Orig.). 1984. pap. 9.95 (*0-916121-00-3*) Echo Pub Co.

Your Life Story: Self-Discovery & Beyond. 181p. 1993. pap. 8.95 (*0-86716-177-9*) St Anthony Mess Pr.

Your Life Story by Someone Else. Ferd Eggan. (Illus.). 88p. (Orig.). 1989. pap. 10.00 (*0-924418-15-X*) Editorial El Coqui.

Your Life to Live. Romen Basu. 180p. 1972. 7.95 (*0-317-00321-6*, Pub. by Filma K L Mukhopadhyay II) R Basu.

Your Life Touched Mine. Perry Tanksley. 4.50 (*0-686-15449-5*) Allgood Bks.

XYZ

Your Life, Your Choices: The People, Stories, & Facts from Listen Magazine. Lincoln Steed. LC 96-24389. (J). 1996. write for info. (*0-8280-1249-0*) Review & Herald.

Your Limitless Inventing Machine. Win Wenger & Susan Wenger. (Psychegenic Library of Experiential Protocols). (Illus.). 150p. (C). 1981. pap. 20.00 (*0-931865-02-6*) Psychegenics.

Your Lion Guards the Threshold: Tools for the Psychological Challenges of Spiritual Change. Nancy Little. LC 96-9021. (Illus.). 168p. 1996. pap. 14.95 (*0-9647966-9-4*) Tara Pr.

Your Liver...Your Lifeline. Jack Tips. 150p. 1995. pap. 11.95 (*0-929167-06-6*) Apple-a-Day.

Your Living Trust & Estate Plan: How to Maximize Your Family's Assets & Protect Your Loved Ones. Harvey J. Platt. LC 95-75284. 256p. (Orig.). 1995. pap. 14.95 (*1-880559-25-0*) Allworth Pr.

Your Living Will: Why, When & How to Write One. Eileen P. Flynn. 1992. pap. 7.95 (*0-8065-1294-6*, Citadel Pr) Carol Pub Group.

Your Louisiana Legal Advisor. rev. ed. Stephen E. Covell & Covell K. Lauren. LC 85-733336. 297p. (Orig.). 1989. pap. 9.95 (*0-685-21019-7*) Charleston Pr.

***Your Love Life, Venus in Your Chart.** Maritha Pottenger. 36p. 1996. pap. 4.95 (*0-935127-40-2*) ACS Pubns.

***Your Lovedone Lives on Within You: A Beautiful & Inspiring Approach to Handling Unresolved Grief.** Alexandra Kennedy. 176p. 1997. pap. 12.00 (*0-425-15453-X*, Berkley Trade) Berkley Pub.

Your Loving Anna: Letters from the Ontario Frontier. Louis Tivy. LC 72-86392. (Illus.). 128p. reprint ed. pap. 36.50 (*0-317-09103-4*, 2016092) Bks Demand.

Your Loving Son "Ed" Letters from a World War II GI Boot Camp to the Battlefields of Europe. Fern Jennings. (Boot Camp to the Battlefields of Europe Ser.). (Illus.). 160p. (Orig.). 1994. pap. 7.00 (*0-9638762-0-1*) F Jennings.

Your Low-Tax Dream House: A New Approach to Slashing the Costs of Home Ownership. Steve Carlson. (Illus.). 304p. (Orig.). 1989. pap. 12.95 (*0-942679-07-5*); lib. bdg. 17.95 (*0-942679-06-7*) Upper Access.

Your Lucky Number: Understand Its Vibration & Impact on Your Personality & Relationships. S. J. Culbert. 96p. 1995. pap. 6.95 (*0-572-01398-1*, Pub. by Foulsham UK) Assoc Pubs Grp.

Your Lucky Number Forever. Anna Riva. 144p. (Orig.). 1993. pap. text ed. 4.95 (*0-943832-17-9*) Intl Imports.

***Your Magic Gargen: A Guide to the Discovery of Life Work - Look to the Child Within.** Joanna V. Dunn. (Illus.). 52p. (Orig.). 1997. pap. 14.95 (*0-9658120-0-6*) Sky Pub Co.

Your Magical Child. Maria K. Simms. 544p. (Orig.). 1996. pap. 16.00 (*0-935127-32-1*) ACS Pubns.

Your Magical Keyboard. Albert De Vito. LC 86-80117. (Illus.). 56p. (Orig.). 1986. pap. 8.95 (*0-934286-66-3*) Kenyon.

Your Manager Abroad: How Welcome? How Prepared? Alison R. Lanier. LC 75-26584. (AMA Management Briefing Ser.). 51p. reprint ed. pap. 25.00 (*0-317-09625-7*, 2050195) Bks Demand.

***Your Manifest Destiny.** Wayne Dyer. mass mkt. 6.99 (*0-06-109494-3*, Harp PBks) HarpC.

Your Many Faces. Virginia M. Satir. LC 78-54477. 128p. 1995. pap. 6.95 (*0-89087-120-5*) Celestial Arts.

***Your Marketing Plan.** 2nd ed. Chris Pryor. (Oregon SBDC Network Workbook Ser.). 79p. (C). 1996. wbk. ed. 20.00 (*1-878475-14-2*) Oregon Small Busn Dev Ctr.

***Your Marketing Program Audit: 100 Thought-Provoking, Self-Appraisal Questions Designed to Improve Your Marketing.** Hal Goetsoh. (Illus.). 102p. (Orig.). 1997. wbk. ed., pap. 24.95 (*0-9656965-0-2*) Busn Mktging.

Your Marriage Can Be Great. Ed. by Thomas B. Warren. 692p. 1978. pap. 9.00 (*0-934916-44-6*) Natl Christian Pr.

Your Marriage Is What You Make It! Kenneth Balster. 96p. 1994. 9.95 (*0-8059-3571-1*) Dorrance.

Your Maryland: A History. rev. ed. Vera F. Rollo. 414p. 1993. 22.50 (*0-917882-35-0*) MD Hist Pr.

Your Massachusetts Government. 10th ed. Donald Levitan & Elwyn Mariner. LC 84-13554. (Illus.). 272p. (Orig.). 1984. pap. text ed. 25.00 (*0-931684-07-2*) Gov Res Pubns.

Your Maximum Mind. Herbert Benson & William Proctor. 272p. 1989. mass mkt. 5.50 (*0-380-70664-4*) Avon.

Your Maximum Mind. Herbert Benson & William Proctor. 272p. 1987. 15.45 (*0-8129-1705-7*, Times Bks) Random.

Your Maze Adventure, No. 6. Richard Brightfield. 1986. 1.95 (*0-8125-6046-9*) Tor Bks.

Your Medical Rights: How to Become an Empowered Consumer. 2nd ed. Charles B. Inlander & Eugene I. Pavalon. LC 94-1578. 416p. 1994. pap. 14.95 (*1-882606-09-4*) Peoples Med Soc.

Your Medicare Handbook. 1984. text ed. 250.00 (*0-87700-541-9*) Revisionist Pr.

***Your Medicare Handbook, 1996.** rev. ed. Health & Human Services Dept. Staff & Health Care Financing Administration Staff. (Illus.). 30p. 1996. pap. 2.25 (*0-16-048594-0*, 017-060-00586-6) USGPO.

Your Memoirs: The Emerson Guide to Tape Recording Your Memoirs, a Do-It-Yourself Manual. rev. ed. Robert E. Treacy. (Illus.). 54p. 1989. pap. text ed. write for info. (*0-318-65559-4*) Emerson Archive.

Your Memoirs, the Emerson Guide to Tape Recording Your Memoirs: A Do-It-Yourself Manual. Robert E. Treacy. LC 88-82614. (Illus.). 54p. (Orig.). 1988. pap. text ed. write for info. (*0-9623954-3-9*) Emerson Archive.

***Your Memory: A User's Guide.** Alan D. Baddeley. 390p. 1996. pap. 14.95 (*1-85375-213-4*, Pub. by Prion UK) Trafalgar.

Your Memory: How It Works & How to Improve It. 2nd ed. Kenneth Higbee. 256p. 1996. pap. 12.95 (*1-56924-801-X*) Marlowe & Co.

***Your Menopause: Real Information You Can Use.** Randy Shields. LC 96-70813. 148p. (Orig.). 1996. mass mkt. 4.99 (*1-888886-04-8*) CEPI.

Your Mental Mythology: 100 Lies That Shatter Self-Esteem. Kenneth A. Beavers. LC 93-81043. 304p. 1995. pap. 11.95 (*1-883660-32-7*) Galloway Pr.

Your Mesmeric Forces & How to Develop Them. Frank H. Randall. 151p. 1971. reprint ed. spiral bd. 7.00 (*0-7873-0693-2*) Hlth Research.

Your Mexican Holiday. A. Brenner. 1976. lib. bdg. 59.95 (*0-8490-2853-1*) Gordon Pr.

Your Mind: Unlocking Your Hidden Powers. Henry Reed. Orig. Title: Edgar Cayce on Mysteries of the Mind. 288p. (Orig.). 1996. pap. 14.95 (*0-87604-365-1*, 480) ARE Pr.

Your Mind & How to Use It. William W. Atkinson. 224p. 1974. reprint ed. spiral bd. 10.50 (*0-7873-0050-0*) Hlth Research.

Your Mind & How to Use It (1911) William W. Atkinson. 224p. 1996. pap. 17.95 (*1-56459-749-0*) Kessinger Pub.

Your Mind & Your Health. Ellen G. White. 31p. 1964. pap. 0.99 (*0-8163-0083-6*, 24505-0) Pacific Pr Pub Assn.

Your Mind Can Drive You Crazy...Only If You Let It!, No. 1. 3rd ed. James A. Takacs. LC 79-87577. 202p. (Orig.). reprint ed. pap. 9.95 (*0-910673-00-4*) J A Takacs.

Your Mind Can Heal You. Frederick W. Bailes. LC 78-128864. 206p. 1975. reprint ed. pap. 8.95 (*0-87516-201-0*) DeVorss.

Your Mind Matters. John R. Stott. LC 72-94672. 64p. (Orig.). 1973. pap. 5.99 (*0-87784-441-0*, 441) InterVarsity.

Your Mind the Magician. Allen M. Rosenthal. LC 90-82481. (Illus.). 143p. (Orig.). 1991. pap. 10.95 (*0-87516-619-9*) DeVorss.

Your Ministry of Evangelism. LC 78-97811. 90p. 1991. teacher ed., ring bd. 19.95 (*0-910566-50-X*) Evang Trg Assn.

Your Ministry of Evangelism. Elmer L. Towns. LC 78-97811. 96p. 1991. pap. text ed. 8.95 (*0-910566-48-8*) Evang Trg Assn.

Your Miracle Source. Marilyn Hickey. 1982. pap. 4.95 (*0-89274-240-2*) M Hickey Min.

***Your Mission Should You Accept It... An Introduction for World Christians.** Stephen Gaukroger. LC 96-35034. 144p. (Orig.). 1997. pap. 9.99 (*0-8308-1366-7*, 1366) InterVarsity.

***Your Mission Should You Choose to Accept It.** large type ed. Katherine E. Anderson. (Illus.). 120p. (Orig.). 1997. spiral bd., pap. 19.95 (*1-57876-999-X*) Triple U Prods.

Your Mobile Companion. 1995. pap. 12.00 (*0-614-15798-6*) Am Radio.

Your Mobile Home: Energy & Repair for Manufactured Housing. 3rd rev. ed. John T. Krigger. Ed. by Paul Richards. (Illus.). 210p. (C). 1994. pap. 20.00 (*1-880120-05-4*) Saturn Rsce.

Your Money. George Fooshee. 240p. 1993. pap. 3.97 (*1-55748-458-9*) Barbour & Co.

***Your Money.** 2nd ed. Niki Chesworth. (Daily Express Guides Ser.). 1995. pap. 12.95 (*0-7494-1641-6*) Kogan Page Ltd.

Your Money: A Review of Money in the United States. 1994. lib. bdg. 250.95 (*0-8490-5785-X*) Gordon Pr.

Your Money: Frustration or Freedom? Howard Dayton. 160p. 1979. pap. 8.99 (*0-8423-8725-0*) Tyndale.

Your Money: It's a Family Affair. Joan M. Gruber. LC 96-15081. 144p. (Orig.). 1996. pap. 17.95 (*1-884363-09-1*) Odenwald Pr.

***Your Money & Life.** Aliber. 1996. lib. bdg. 38.00 (*0-226-01387-1*) U Ch Pr.

Your Money & Possessions: Making Them Count for Eternity. Randy Alcorn. 436p. 1989. pap. 10.99 (*0-8423-8731-5*) Tyndale.

Your Money & What to Do With It. Gilbert M. Tucker. 1960. 9.95 (*0-8159-7401-9*) Devin.

Your Money & You. Cheryl S. Johnson & Richard L. Johnson. (Living Skills Ser.). 78p. 1993. teacher ed. 8.95 (*1-884245-31-5*); pap. text ed. 7.95 (*1-884245-30-7*) Life Choices.

Your Money & Your Home: A Step-by-Step Guide to Financing or Refinancing Your Home. Sidney Lenz. (Orig.). 1992. pap. 12.95 (*1-882180-00-3*) Griffin CA.

Your Money & Your Life. large type ed. George Milner. (Linford Mystery Library). 352p. 1988. pap. 15.99 (*0-7089-6514-8*) Ulverscroft.

Your Money & Your Life: Five Keys to the Puzzle. Robert Z. Aliber. 250p. 1989. 19.95 (*1-55623-073-7*) Irwin Prof Pubng.

Your Money & Your Life: Planning Your Financial Future. 2nd ed. C. Colburn Hardy. LC 82-71317. 317p. reprint ed. pap. 90.40 (*0-317-27198-9*, 2023933) Bks Demand.

***Your Money Counts.** Dayton. 1997. pap. 9.99 (*0-8423-8592-4*) Tyndale.

Your Money Matters. Malcolm MacGregor & Stanley C. Baldwin. LC 76-56123. 176p. 1977. pap. 7.99 (*0-87123-662-1*) Bethany Hse.

Your Money or Your Life. Nora Stirling. LC 73-11808. 256p. 1974. 7.95 (*0-672-51891-0*, Bobbs) Macmillan.

Your Money or Your Life: Economy & Religion in the Middle Ages. Jacques Le Goff. Tr. by Patricia M. Ranum from FRE. LC 87-25248. 116p. 1988. 24.95 (*0-942299-14-0*); pap. 10.95 (*0-942299-15-9*) Zone Bks.

Your Money or Your Life: How to Save Thousands on Your Health-Care Insurance. Donald J. Korn. 256p. 1992. pap. 10.00 (*0-02-080441-5*) Macmillan.

Your Money or Your Life: Transforming Your Relationship with Money & Achieving Financial Independence. Joe Dominguez & Vicki Robin. 384p. 1993. reprint ed. pap. 11.95 (*0-14-016715-3*, Penguin Bks) Viking Penguin.

***Your Money or Your Life: Why We Must Abolish the Income Tax.** Sheldon Richman. 175p. (Orig.). 1997. write for info. (*0-9640447-8-1*) Future of Freedom.

***Your Money or Your Life: Why We Must Abolish the Income Tax.** Sheldon Richman. 175p. (Orig.). 1997. pap. write for info. (*0-9640447-9-X*) Future of Freedom.

Your Money's Worth in Food: How to Buy Food in a Recession Or Depression. 1992. lib. bdg. 69.00 (*0-8490-5505-9*) Gordon Pr.

Your Mother Was a Neanderthal. Jon Scieszka. (Illus.). 80p. (J). 1995. pap. 2.99 (*0-14-036372-6*) Puffin Bks.

Your Mother Was a Neanderthal. Jon Scieszka. (Illus.). 64p. (J). (gr. 2-6). 1993. pap. 11.99 (*0-670-84481-0*) Viking Child Bks.

Your Mother Wears Army Boots! A Treasure Trove of Insults, Slurs & Putdowns. Jordan L. Linfield & Joe Kay. 288p. (Orig.). 1992. pap. 9.00 (*0-380-76591-8*) Avon.

***Your Mother's Tongue: A Book of European Invective.** Stephen Burgen. 224p. 1997. 35.00 (*0-575-06131-6*, Pub. by V Gollancz UK) Trafalgar.

***Your Mother's Tongue: A Book of European Invective.** Stephen Burgen. 224p. 1997. pap. 15.95 (*0-575-40090-0*, Pub. by V Gollancz UK) Trafalgar.

Your Motive Factor. Olson & Hanratty. 24p. 1981. 6.00 (*0-86690-218-X*, O1361-014) Am Fed Astrologers.

Your Move. Bunting. LC 96-18603. 1997. write for info. (*0-15-200181-6*) HarBrace.

Your Move. A. J. Gillam. (Better Chess Ser.). 96p. (Orig.). 1994. pap. 6.00 (*0-945470-30-4*) Chess Ent.

Your Move: A New Approach to the Study of Movement & Dance. Ann H. Guest. 322p. 1983. teacher ed., pap. 23.00 (*0-677-06395-4*); text ed. 53.00 (*0-677-06350-4*); pap. text ed. 32.00 (*0-677-06365-2*); 12.00 (*0-677-22310-2*); audio 14.00 (*0-685-07960-0*) Gordon & Breach.

Your Move: Logic, Math & Word Puzzles for Enthusiasts. David L. Silverman. 1991. pap. 8.95 (*0-486-26731-8*) Dover.

Your Move, God. Francis Clare. LC 82-81212. 144p. 1982. pap. 6.95 (*0-89221-102-4*) New Leaf.

Your Move, J. P.! Lois Lowry. 128p. (J). (gr. 3-7). 1990. 14.95 (*0-395-53639-1*) HM.

Your Move, J. P. Lois Lowry. 128p. (J). (gr. 4-7). 1991. pap. 3.99 (*0-440-40497-5*) Dell.

Your Movie Guide to Mystery-Suspense Tapes & Discs. Ed. by Video Times Consumer Guide Editors. 1985. pap. 1.95 (*0-317-01003-4*, Sig) NAL-Dutton.

Your Musical Road to Success: Reference Book. Terri A. Senecal. Ed. by Kelly Johnson. 150p. (Orig.). 1989. pap. text ed. 19.95 (*0-926485-15-6*) Rosebudd Prodn.

Your Mythic Journey: Finding Meaning in Your Life Through Writing & Storytelling. rev. ed. Sam Keen & Anne Valley-Fox. Orig. Title: Telling Your Story. 160p. reprint ed. 11.95 (*0-87477-543-4*, Tarcher Putnam) Putnam Pub Group.

Your Name & Colors: Blueprints to Your Chemistry--The Rolliet Letter-Color Theory. D. G. Rolliet. (Illus.). (Orig.). 1988. pap. text ed. write for info. (*0-318-64366-9*) Spectra Pubns Hse.

Your Name & Colors: Secret Keys to Your Beauty, Personality & Success, the Rolliett Letter-Color Theory. D. G. Rolliet. Ed. by Michael Reanult & Jeannie Wolf. LC 89-91991. (Illus.). 192p. (Orig.). (YA). 1990. pap. 12.95 (*0-9621693-0-7*) Spectra Pubns Hse.

Your Name Here. Cris Mazza. LC 94-45779. 288p. (Orig.). 1995. pap. 12.95 (*1-56689-031-4*) Coffee Hse.

Your Name Is Hughes Hannibal Shanks: A Caregiver's Guide to Alzheimer's. Lela K. Shanks. LC 96-3691. (Agendas for Aging Ser.). xviii, 197p. 1996. 22.50 (*0-8032-4245-X*) U of Nebr Pr.

Your Name Is Renee: Ruth's Story As a Hidden Child. Stacy Cretzmeyer. LC 93-73504. (Illus.). 176p. (Orig.). 1994. pap. 11.95 (*1-879418-12-6*) Biddle Pub.

Your Name Shall Be Tanga. Calixthe Beyala. (African Writers Ser.). 144p. 1996. pap. 10.95 (*0-435-90950-9*) Heinemann.

Your Name Shall be Tanga. Calixthe Beyala. Tr. by Marjolijin De Jager. 1996. pap. 10.95 (*0-614-97781-9*) Heinemann.

Your Native Land, Your Life. Adrienne Rich. 128p. 1993. reprint ed. pap. 8.95 (*0-393-31082-5*) Norton.

Your Native Shade Trees. 1972. 0.15 (*0-686-20734-3*) SUNY Environ.

Your Natural Beauty Sampler. Linda Clark et al. LC 77-92810. 1978. pap. 1.95 (*0-87983-168-5*) Keats.

Your Natural Dog: A Guide to Behavior & Health Care. Angela Patmore & Tim Couzens. LC 93-17397. (Illus.). 128p. 1993. 18.95 (*0-88184-947-2*) Carroll & Graf.

Your Natural Gifts: How to Recognize Them & Develop Them for Success & Self-Fulfillment. 3rd ed. Margaret E. Broadley. LC 91-21721. 157p. 1991. pap. 7.95 (*0-939009-56-0*) EPM Pubns.

***Your Natural Health Makeover.** Aesoph. 1997. pap. 14.95 (*0-13-628645-3*) P-H.

Your Natural Home: A Complete Sourcebook & Design Manual for Creating a Healthy, Beautiful, & Environmentally Sensitive House. Janet Marinelli & Paul Bierman-Lytle. LC 94-46327. (Illus.). 272p. 1994. 45.00 (*0-316-09302-5*) Little.

Your Natural Home: A Complete Sourcebook & Design Manual for Creating a Healthy, Beautiful, & Environmentally Sensitive House. Janet Marinelli & Paul Bierman-Lytle. LC 94-46327. (Illus.). 272p. 1995. pap. 21.95 (*0-316-09303-3*) Little.

Your Natural Pregnancy: A Guide to Complementary Therapies. Anne Charlish. LC 95-83567. (Illus.). 160p. (Orig.). 1996. pap. 16.95 (*1-56975-059-9*) Ulysses Pr.

Your Needs Met. Jack Addington & Cornelia Addington. 156p. 1982. reprint ed. pap. 7.95 (*0-87516-490-0*) DeVorss.

***Your Neighbor As Yourself.** Brian A. Brown. 300p. (Orig.). 1997. pap. 19.95 (*0-940121-41-7*, P311) Cross Cultural Pubns.

***Your New Beginning.** Randy Clark. 35p. (Orig.). 1996. 1.00 (*0-9652425-0-1*) Randy Clark.

Your New Beginning: Step Two. Willie Malone. 64p. (Orig.). 1983. pap. 2.50 (*0-88144-008-6*) Christian Pub.

Your New Birth. Robert Halverstadt. 1982. pap. 0.75 (*0-88144-001-9*, CPS-001) Christian Pub.

Your New Business: A Personal Plan for Success. Charles Martin. Ed. by Philip Gerould. LC 92-54374. (Small Business & Entrepreneurship Ser.). 234p. (Orig.). 1993. pap. 15.95 (*1-56052-170-8*) Crisp Pubns.

Your New Fashion Image: Clare Spiegel's Reference Book on Fashion & Beauty for Real Life. Clare Spiegel. (Illus.). 84p. 1995. pap. text ed. 14.95 (*1-886960-00-3*) Your New Fashion.

Your New Garden Pond. Anmarie Barrie. (Illus.). 64p. 1991. pap. 6.95 (*0-86622-533-1*, TU-021) TFH Pubns.

Your New Home & How to Take Care of It. LC 95-33639. (Illus.). 64p. (Orig.). 1995. pap. 22.00 (*0-86718-412-4*) Home Builder.

Your New House: The Alert Consumer's Guide to Buying & Building a Quality Home. 2nd ed. Alan S. Fields. 304p. (Orig.). 1996. pap. 13.95 (*0-9626556-8-6*) Windsor Peak Pr.

Your New Lawyer: The Legal Employer's Complete Guide to Recruitment, Development & Management. LC 92-72418. 382p. 1992. pap. 84.95 (*0-89707-766-0*, 511-0312) Amer Bar Assn.

Your New Life. Ed. by R. M. Davis & P. D. Buford. 160p. reprint ed. pap. 5.99 (*1-56722-064-9*) Word Aflame.

***Your New Life: Steps to Strengthening Your New Relationship with Christ.** rev. ed. Bill Bright. 36p. 1.95 (*1-57229-054-4*) FamilyLife.

Your New Life in Christ. Luis Palau. LC 95-45413. (Orig.). 1996. pap. 8.99 (*0-89107-871-1*) Crossway Bks.

Your New Life in Christ: A Twelve-Week Self-Study on Basic Bible Doctrines. Michael H. Clarensau. LC 90-83497. 112p. 1991. student ed., pap. 6.95 (*0-88243-766-6*, 02-0766) Gospel Pub.

Your New Life in the United States. LORC Staff. 215p. (CAM, CHI, LAO, SPA & VIE.). 1984. pap. 5.00 (*0-685-16936-7*) Ctr Appl Ling.

Your New Potty. Joanna Cole. LC 88-39862. (Illus.). 40p. (J). (ps). 1989. lib. bdg. 10.88 (*0-688-06106-0*) Morrow.

Your New Potty. Joanna Cole. LC 88-39862. (Illus.). 40p. (J). (ps). 1989. pap. 5.95 (*0-688-08966-6*) Morrow.

***Your New Puppy.** Contrib. by Herbert Axelrod. (Cats & Dogs). (Illus.). (YA). (gr. 3 up). 1998. lib. bdg. 19.95 (*0-7910-4822-5*) Chelsea Hse.

Your New Restaurant: All the Necessary Ingredients for Success. Vincent Mischitelli. 190p. 1990. pap. 10.95 (*1-55850-857-0*) Adams Media.

Your New Retirement Nest Egg: A Consumer Guide to the New Reverse Mortgages. 2nd rev. ed. Ken Scholen. 342p. (Orig.). 1996. pap. 24.95 (*0-9630119-9-5*) NCHEC Pr.

"Reverse" mortgages turn every home into a new source of RETIREMENT INCOME, without having to sell or make monthly loan payments. This "ideal study book rates a ten"--(SF Examiner) & "guides homeowners through the reverse mortgage maze"--(Minneapolis Star Tribune). It's "an easily understood nuts & bolts guide"--(N.Y. Times) that's "clearly written"--(Library Journal). It compares all the newest varieties of REVERSE MORTGAGES: how much cash you can get, what it really costs, what to look out for. By "The LEADING AUTHORITY on reverse mortgages"--(L.A. Times). Practical STUDY GUIDE for retirees & pre-retirees. Also of interest to attorneys, accountants, financial planners, care managers, senior service providers & adult children of aging parents. A basic reference & directory, with 58 tables, locations, phone numbers. Includes Glossary, Bibliography, Index, Appendixes. Order from: Baker & Taylor, Brodart, The Bookmen, Blackwell, or directly from NCHEC Press, Suite 115, 7373 147th St., W., Apple Valley, MN 55124; Telephone 612-953-4474.

Publisher Provided Annotation.

***Your Newborn & You: A National Childbirth Trust Guide.** Anna McGrail. LC 94-10364. (Illus.). 254p. 1997. pap. 12.95 (*1-55561-125-7*) Fisher Bks.

Your Newborn Baby. 1999. 9.95 (*0-446-39010-0*) Warner Bks.

Your Next Baby. 1989. pap. 0.45 (*0-685-30738-7*) Centering Corp.

Your Next Fifty Years: A Completely New Way to Look at How, When & If You Should Retire. Victoria Collins. 240p. 1997. pap. 14.95 (*0-8050-4568-6*) H Holt & Co.

***Your Next Move.** Philip Pedley & Paul McEvoy. (Careers & Testing Ser.). 1994. pap. 14.95 (*0-7494-1265-8*) Kogan Page Ltd.

Your Next Pastorate: Starting the Search. Richard N. Bolles et al. LC 90-83135. 88p. (Orig.). 1990. pap. 8.95 (*1-56699-041-6*, AL122) Alban Inst.

Your Nine Year Old. Louise B. Ames et al. 176p. 1991. pap. 10.95 (*0-440-50676-X*) Dell.

Your Nineteen Eighty-Six Money Saving Tax Guide. Lasser, J. K., Tax Institute Staff. write for info. (*0-318-59611-3*) S&S Trade.

An Asterisk (*) at the beginning of an entry indicates that the title is appearing in BIP for the first time.

Your Numbers of Destiny. Urna Gray. 1996. mass mkt. 4.99 (*0-312-95701-7*) Tor Bks.

Your Number's Up: A Calculus Approach to Successful Math Study. C. A. Oxrieder. 1982. teacher ed. 1.50 (*0-201-05527-9*); text ed. write for info. (*0-201-05526-0*) Addison-Wesley.

***Your Number's Up! Money, Romance & Predictions Through Numerology.** Anne Oscard. Ed. by Lucene Graham & Chris Woodyard. LC 94-12045. (Illus.). 150p. (Orig.). 1997. pap. 9.95 (*0-9645166-2-4*) Hermit Pubns.

Your Nutrition Fiber. Ed Blonz. 1996. pap. 3.99 (*0-451-18487-4*, Sig) NAL-Dutton.

***Your Oasis on Flame Lake.** Lorna Landvik. 1997. 23.00 (*0-449-91278-7*) Fawcett.

Your Offshore Doctor: A Manual of Medical Self-Sufficiency at Sea. 2nd ed. Michael H. Beilan. (Illus.). 184p. 1996. pap. 17.50 (*1-57409-013-5*) Sheridan.

Your Old House: Fixtures & Fixups That Give New Life to Your Old House. Time-Life Books Editors. LC 96-19374. (Illus.). 256p. 1996. 24.95 (*0-7835-4829-X*) Time-Life.

Your Old Pal Al. Constance C. Greene. Date not set. pap. 3.99 (*0-14-036849-3*) Viking Penguin.

Your Older Cat: Loving Care for the Golden Years. Jane E. Leon. 1992. pap. 9.95 (*0-9625043-6-X*) Pecos Pr.

Your Older Dog: Loving Care for the Golden Years. Jane E. Leon. 1992. pap. 9.95 (*0-9625043-5-1*) Pecos Pr.

Your One Year Diet Diary: An Easy to Keep Daily Record of Your Successes. Diane Mentzer. Ed. by Elletro Productions Staff. 72p. (Orig.). 1992. pap. 6.95 (*0-88247-928-8*, 928) R & E Pubs.

Your One Year Old. Louise B. Ames et al. 178p. 1983. pap. 10.95 (*0-440-50672-7*) Dell.

Your Opinion, Please! How to Build the Best Questionnaires in the Field of Education. James Cox. LC 96-27821. (1-Off Ser.). (Illus.). 112p. 1996. 49.95 (*0-8039-6522-2*); pap. 21.95 (*0-8039-6523-0*) Corwin Pr.

Your Opportunities As a Dental Assistant. Margie Sherman. (Illus.). 8p. 1994. pap. 2.50 (*1-884241-03-4*, OS106) Energeia Pub.

Your Opportunities As a Diesel Mechanic. Shawn E. Strahan. (Illus.). 8p. 1994. pap. 2.50 (*1-884241-07-7*, OS111) Energeia Pub.

***Your Opportunities As a Home Health Aide.** Margie Sherman. (Illus.). 8p. (Orig.). 1995. pap. 2.50 (*1-884241-56-5*, OS129) Energeia Pub.

Your Opportunities As a Massage Therapist. Laurie Bean. (Illus.). 8p. 1994. pap. 2.50 (*1-884241-11-5*, OS115) Energeia Pub.

***Your Opportunities As a Paralegal.** (Illus.). 8p. (Orig.). 1997. pap. 2.50 (*1-884241-83-2*, OS125) Energeia Pub.

***Your Opportunities As a Physical Therapist.** (Illus.). 8p. (Orig.). 1997. pap. 2.50 (*1-884241-86-7*, OS130) Energeia Pub.

***Your Opportunities As a Professional Driver.** (Illus.). 8p. (Orig.). 1997. pap. 2.50 (*1-884241-87-5*, OS131) Energeia Pub.

Your Opportunities As a Secretary (Executive & Legal) Laurie Bean. (Illus.). 8p. 1994. pap. 2.50 (*1-884241-18-2*, OS122) Energeia Pub.

***Your Opportunities As an Emergency Medical Technician.** 8p. (Orig.). 1997. pap. 2.50 (*1-884241-85-9*, OS127) Energeia Pub.

Your Opportunities in Accounting. Terry L. Rich. (Illus.). 8p. 1994. pap. 2.50 (*1-884241-00-X*, OS100) Energeia Pub.

Your Opportunities in Agriculture. Victor D. Tognazzini. (Illus.). 8p. 1993. pap. 2.50 (*0-9626591-5-0*, OS101) Energeia Pub.

***Your Opportunities in an Environmental Career.** (Illus.). 8p. (Orig.). 1997. pap. 2.50 (*1-884241-84-0*, OS126) Energeia Pub.

Your Opportunities in Bookkeeping. Shawn E. Strahan. (Illus.). 8p. 1994. pap. 2.50 (*1-884241-31-X*, OS102) Energeia Pub.

Your Opportunities in Childcare. Suzanne Tognazzini. (Illus.). 8p. 1994. pap. 2.50 (*1-884241-01-8*, OS103) Energeia Pub.

Your Opportunities in Computer Programming. Douglas B. Cross. (Illus.). 8p. 1994. pap. 2.50 (*0-614-04321-2*) Energeia Pub.

Your Opportunities in Computers. John Tribbett. (Illus.). 8p. 1994. pap. 2.50 (*0-9626591-7-7*, OS105) Energeia Pub.

***Your Opportunities in Corrections.** (Illus.). 8p. (Orig.). 1997. pap. 2.50 (*1-884241-66-2*, OS124) Energeia Pub.

***Your Opportunities in Cosmetology (Making Others Beautiful)** Margie Sherman. (Illus.). 8p. (Orig.). 1995. pap. 2.50 (*1-884241-57-3*, OS128) Energeia Pub.

Your Opportunities in Drafting. Victor D. Tognazzini. (Illus.). 8p. 1994. pap. 2.50 (*1-884241-04-2*, OS107) Energeia Pub.

Your Opportunities in Electronics. Victor D. Tognazzini. 8p. 1994. pap. 2.50 (*1-884241-05-0*, OS108) Energeia Pub.

Your Opportunities in Food Service. Laurie Bean. (Illus.). 8p. (Orig.). 1994. pap. 2.50 (*1-884210-06-6*) Energeia Pub.

***Your Opportunities in Food Service.** Laurie Bean. (Illus.). 8p. (Orig.). 1995. pap. 2.50 (*1-884241-06-9*, OS110) Energeia Pub.

Your Opportunities in Law Enforcement. Victor D. Tognazzini. (Illus.). 8p. 1994. pap. 2.50 (*1-884241-08-5*, OS112) Energeia Pub.

Your Opportunities in Legal Support. Laurie Bean. (Illus.). 8p. 1994. pap. 2.50 (*1-884241-09-3*, OS113) Energeia Pub.

Your Opportunities in Medical Support. Margie Sherman. (Illus.). 8p. 1994. pap. 2.50 (*1-884241-10-7*, OS114) Energeia Pub.

Your Opportunities in Nursing. Margie Sherman. (Illus.). 8p. 1994. pap. 2.50 (*1-884241-12-3*, OS116) Energeia Pub.

Your Opportunities in Real Estate. Laurie Bean. (Illus.). 8p. 1994. pap. 2.50 (*1-884241-14-X*, OS118) Energeia Pub.

Your Opportunities in Recreation, Travel & Tourism. Laurie Bean. (Illus.). 8p. 1994. pap. 2.50 (*1-884241-15-8*, OS119) Energeia Pub.

Your Opportunities in Retail. Shawn E. Strahan. (Illus.). 8p. 1994. pap. 2.50 (*1-884241-16-6*, OS120) Energeia Pub.

Your Opportunities in Sales. Shawn E. Strahan. (Illus.). 8p. 1994. pap. 2.50 (*1-884241-17-4*, OS121) Energeia Pub.

Your Opportunities in the Fashion World. Susan K. Richie. (Illus.). 8p. 1993. pap. 2.50 (*0-9626591-8-5*, OS109) Energeia Pub.

Your Opportunities in the Printing Industry. Laurie Bean. (Illus.). 8p. 1994. pap. 2.50 (*1-884241-13-1*, OS117) Energeia Pub.

***Your Opportunities in the Trades.** Ramel Waltman. (Illus.). 8p. (Orig.). 1995. pap. 2.50 (*1-884241-19-0*, PS123) Energeia Pub.

Your Organic Garden with Jeff Cox. Jeff Cox & Rodale Press Garden Books Editors. LC 93-21061. (Illus.). 352p. 1994. pap. 16.95 (*0-87596-624-1*) Rodale Pr Inc.

Your Organization: What Is It For? Challenging Traditional Organizational Aims. John Argenti. LC 92-43398. 1993. 24.95 (*0-07-707799-7*) McGraw.

Your Original Personal Ad: The Complete Guide to Expressing Your Unique Sentiments to Find Your Dream Person. Charlotte Digregorio. LC 94-71932. 156p. 1995. pap. 13.95 (*0-9623318-2-1*) Civetta Pr.

***Your Osteoarthritis: Real Information You Can Use.** Randy Shields. LC 96-70821. 162p. (Orig.). 1996. mass mkt. 4.99 (*1-888886-03-X*) CEPI.

***Your Osteoporosis: Real Information You Can Use.** Randy Shields. 162p. (Orig.). 1996. mass mkt. 4.99 (*1-888886-13-7*) CEPI.

Your Outplacement Handbook: Redesigning Your Career. Fern Lebo. (Illus.). 200p. (Orig.). 1996. pap. 19.95 (*1-57444-029-2*) St Lucie Pr.

Your Own ABC. Marcie Baron. (Illus.). 14p. (J). (ps-2). 1996. 12.95 (*1-55037-497-4*, Pub. by Annick CN) Firefly Bks Ltd.

Your Own Business in Your Own Home! 1992. pap. 8.00 (*0-910553-33-5*) Ken-Bks.

Your Own Christmas Magic Show. Marvin Miller. 32p. (J). (gr. 4-6). 1993. pap. 6.95 (*0-590-47558-4*) Scholastic Inc.

Your Own Magic Puzzle Show. Marvin Miller. 1995. pap. 7.95 (*0-590-25994-6*) Scholastic Inc.

Your Own Mother. Sherry M. Tuck. 194p. (Orig.). 1996. pap. 12.95 (*1-57502-145-5*) Morris Pubng.

Your Own Path. Elise N. Morgan. (Meditation Ser.). 1928. pap. 6.95 (*0-87516-333-5*) DeVorss.

Your Own Perfect Medicine. Martha M. Christy. 221p. (Orig.). 1994. pap. 19.95 (*0-9632091-1-6*) FutureMed Inc.

Your Own Pigs You May Not Eat. Rubel & Rosman. (Australian National University Press Ser.). 1996. write for info. (*0-08-033012-6*, Pergamon Pr) Elsevier.

Your Own Shop: How to Open & Operate A Successful Retail Business. Ruth Jacobson. (Illus.). 224p. 1990. pap. 12.95 (*0-8306-3466-5*, 3466) McGraw-Hill Prof.

Your Own Shortcut Shorthand. Lauren R. Geringer. LC 79-55059. (Orig.). 1980. pap. 5.95 (*0-935020-06-3*) Gehry Pr.

Your Own Thing: Individual Art Projects for Primary Grades. Lynn Molyneux & Mike Bucur. (Illus.). 160p. (J). (gr. k-6). 1983. per. 9.95 (*0-685-29140-5*) Trellis Bks Inc.

Your Own Way in Music. Nancy Uscher. 1990. 18.95 (*0-312-05186-7*) St Martin.

Your Own Way in Music. Nancy Uscher. 320p. 1993. pap. 14.95 (*0-312-08342-4*) St Martin.

Your Own Worst Enemy: How to Overcome Career Self-Sabotage. Andrew J. DuBrin. 256p. 1993. pap. 14.95 (*0-8144-7861-1*) AMACOM.

Your Own Worst Enemy: Understanding the Paradox of Self-Defeating Behavior. Steven Berglas & Roy F. Baumeister. LC 92-53238. 208p. 1994. reprint ed. pap. 11.00 (*0-465-09341-8*) Basic.

Your Owner's Manual. Burt Hotchkiss. 138p. 1992. pap. 4.95 (*0-9635365-0-8*) B Hotchkiss.

Your Packet Companion. 1992. pap. 10.00 (*0-87259-395-9*) Am Radio.

Your Painting Companion. Paul Taggart. (Illus.). 128p. 1994. 29.95 (*0-09-177420-9*, Pub. by Ebury Pr UK) Trafalgar.

Your Painting Questions Answered from A to Z. Helen Van Wyk. Ed. by Herbert Rogoff. (Illus.). 198p. (Orig.). 1997. pap. 16.95 (*0-929552-04-0*) Art Instr Assocs.

Your Parents & You. Pat Springle et al. 350p. 1990. pap. 12.99 (*0-945276-13-3*) Rapha Pub.

Your Parents & You Small Group Leader's Guide. Robert S. McGee et al. 85p. 1990. pap. 5.00 (*0-945276-15-X*) Rapha Pub.

Your Parents' Financial Security. Barbara Weltman. LC 91-42268. 288p. 1992. pap. text ed. 10.95 (*0-471-54477-9*) Wiley.

Your Particular Grief. Wayne E. Oates. LC 81-3328. 114p. 1981. pap. 10.00 (*0-664-24376-2*, Westminster) Westminster John Knox.

Your Passport to Arabic. Charles Berlitz. Date not set. pap. 5.99 (*0-451-18165-4*, Sig) NAL-Dutton.

Your Passport to Making It Abroad. Mark Altschuler. pap. 2.95 (*0-8315-0133-2*) Speller.

Your Past Lives: A Reincarnation Handbook. Michael Talbot. 1989. mass mkt. 4.95 (*0-449-21679-9*, Crest) Fawcett.

Your Past Lives & the Healing Process: A Psychiatrist Looks at Reincarnation & Spiritual Healing. expanded ed. Adrian Finkelstein. 187p. 1996. 15.95 (*0-9647831-1-8*) Fifty Gates.

Your Pastor Is an Endangered Species. H. B. London & Neil B. Wiseman. LC 96-15082. 200p. 1996. 16.99 (*1-56476-585-7*) SP Pubns.

Your Pastor, Your Shepherd. James L. Beall. LC 77-77579. 208p. (Orig.). 1994. pap. 7.95 (*0-88270-216-5*) Bridge-Logos.

Your Path Direct to the Goal You Desire. Brown Landone. (Self-Help Ser.). 1991. lib. bdg. 75.00 (*0-8490-4292-5*) Gordon Pr.

Your Path Direct to the Goal You Desire. Brown Landone. 518p. 1968. reprint ed. spiral bd. 27.50 (*0-7873-0529-4*) Hlth Research.

***Your Path to Spiritual Starhood: Empowering Your Sacred Self.** Rusty Berkus. (Illus.). 64p. (Orig.). 1997. pap. write for info. (*1-889891-97-5*) Red Rose Pr.

Your Pennsylvania. Lucille Wallower. Ed. by Daphne B. Brebner & S. K. Stevens. (J). (gr. 4-6). 1959. 6.35 (*0-931992-07-9*) Penns Valley.

Your Pension: Things You Should Know about Your Pension Plan. 1991. lib. bdg. 79.95 (*0-8490-5143-6*) Gordon Pr.

***Your Pension & Your Spouse: The Joint & Survivor Dilemma.** 4th ed. R. George Martorana. 24p. 1996. pap. 8.50 (*0-89154-503-4*) Intl Found Employ.

Your Pension & Your Spouse: The Joint & Survivor Dilemma, Canadian Edition. R. George Martorana & Susan Rowland. (Illus.). 24p. (Orig.). 1991. pap. 7.95 (*0-89154-429-1*) Intl Found Employ.

Your Pension Guarantee. 1996. lib. bdg. 250.75 (*0-8490-6027-3*) Gordon Pr.

Your People, My People. Lena Romanoff. 1996. pap. text ed. 16.95 (*0-8276-0564-1*) JPS Phila.

Your Perfect Fit see What You Do Best: In the Body of Christ

Your Perfect Right: A Guide to Assertive Living. 7th rev. ed. Robert E. Alberti & Michael L. Emmons. LC 95-18417. 256p. 1995. 17.95 (*0-915166-11-9*); pap. 12.95 (*0-915166-12-7*) Impact Pubs CA.

***Your Perfect Wedding Planner.** Cathy Bouchard. LC 97-6194. 300p. 1997. 22.95 (*1-57071-168-2*, Casablanca) Sourcebks.

Your Personal Career Consultant: A Step-by-Step Guide to Finding a Successful & Satisfying Career. Michele Shapiro. Ed. by Gail Lehman. (ARCO Education & Guidance Ser.). 256p. (Orig.). (C). 1988. pap. 8.95 (*0-685-19369-1*, Arco) Macmillan Gen Ref.

Your Personal Computer Can Make You Rich in Stocks & Commodities. Curtis M. Arnold. LC 83-51498. (Illus.). 300p. 14.95 (*0-9613048-0-4*) M D Weiss Pub.

Your Personal Financial Fitness Program, 1995-1996. Elizabeth S. Lewin. 156p. 1995. pap. 13.95 (*0-8160-3146-0*) Facts on File.

***Your Personal Financial Fitness Program 1997-98.** rev. ed. Elizabeth S. Lewin. 60p. 1997. pap. 14.95 (*0-8160-3575-X*) Facts on File.

Your Personal Fitness Survey: A Guide to Your Current State of Health. David Gamon & Kathleen O'Brien. 192p. (Orig.). 1991. pap. 12.95 (*0-87877-158-1*) Newcastle Pub.

Your Personal Fitness Trainer. 1995. 39.95 (*1-56276-313-X*, Ziff-Davis Pr) Que.

Your Personal Fitness Trainer. David Bass. 1995. 29.95 (*0-7897-0771-3*) Que.

Your Personal Guide to Immunization Exemptions. Grace Girdwain. 36p. 1992. pap. 10.95 (*0-8059-3319-0*) Dorrance.

Your Personal Guide to Marketing a Nonprofit Organization. Robert S. Topor. 153p. 1988. 32.00 (*0-89964-254-3*, 24201) Coun Adv & Supp Ed.

Your Personal Guide to Pre-Retirement Planning. Pilot Staff. LC 83-13275. 43p. 1983. pap. 5.00 (*0-87576-106-2*) Pilot Bks.

***Your Personal Guide to Sales & Marketing Success.** 1993. ring bd. 295.00 incl. audio (*1-58034-004-0*) IML Pubns.

***Your Personal Horoscope for 1998.** Joseph Polansky. 416p. (Orig.). 1997. pap. 12.00 (*0-7225-3421-3*) Thorsons SF.

Your Personal Horoscope, 1995: Month-by-Month Forecast for Every Sign. Joseph Polansky. 1994. pap. 9.00 (*1-85538-376-4*, Pub. by Aquarian Pr UK) Thorsons SF.

Your Personal Horoscope, 1997: Month-by-Month Forecast for Every Sign. Joseph Polansky. 416p. 1996. pap. 12.00 (*0-7225-3236-9*) Harper SF.

Your Personal Medical Symptoms Diary. Lawrence Smith et al. Ed. by Chris Roerden. 128p. (Orig.). 1996. 9.95 (*0-9648452-0-2*) M&H Pr.

***Your Personal Net Guide: Your Complete Guide to the Internet & Online Services.** Michael Wolff. 1997. mass mkt. 7.99 (*0-440-22390-3*) Dell.

***Your Personal Net Sci-Fi.** Michael Wolff. (Your Personal Net Ser.). 336p. 1997. mass mkt. 6.99 (*0-440-22423-3*) Dell.

***Your Personal Net Sports.** Michael Wolff. (Your Personal Net Ser.). 304p. 1997. mass mkt. 6.99 (*0-440-22420-9*) Dell.

***Your Personal Net Study.** Michael Wolff. (Your Personal Net Ser.). 352p. 1997. mass mkt. 6.99 (*0-440-22429-2*) Dell.

Your Personal Nutritionist: Antioxidant Counter. Ed Blonz. 1996. mass mkt. 3.99 (*0-451-18488-2*, Sig) NAL-Dutton.

Your Personal Nutritionist: Calcium & Other Minerals Counter. Ed Blonz. 96p. 1996. mass mkt. 3.99 (*0-451-18880-2*) NAL-Dutton.

***Your Personal Nutritionist: Food Additives.** Ed Blonz. 1997. pap. 3.99 (*0-451-18881-0*, Sig) NAL-Dutton.

Your Personal Plumber. L. F. Greer. LC 79-54891. 1979. 24.95 (*0-686-26464-9*) Plumbing Pubns.

Your Personal Revival. James A. Stewart. pap. 0.79 (*1-56632-066-6*) Revival Lit.

Your Personal Smart Profile: A Qualitative Approach for Describing Yourself in Your Everyday Life. Lynda Miller. 134p. 1993. pap. 29.00 (*0-9636140-1-0*) Smart Alternat.

Your Personal Stress Profile & Activity Workbook. Jerrold S. Greenberg. 128p. (C). 1991. wbk. ed., per. write for info. (*0-697-14109-8*) Brown & Benchmark.

Your Personal Stress Profile & Activity Workbook. 2nd ed. Jerrold S. Greenberg. 128p. (C). 1995. per. write for info. (*0-697-22304-3*) Brown & Benchmark.

Your Personal Trainer's Secret Recipe Book: Quick & Easy Recipes from Two of America's Leading Fitness Trainers. Marla B. Footer & Ed Gaut. LC 95-60576. 140p. (Orig.). 1995. pap. text ed. 14.95 (*0-9640945-7-6*) Pierpoint-Martin.

Your Personal Vitamin Profile: A Medical Scientist Shows You How to Chart Your Individual Vitamin & Mineral Formala. Michael Colgan. LC 82-12560. 1982. pap. 10.00 (*0-688-01506-9*, Quill) Morrow.

Your Personality Analysis in Addition to Poetry. Silvia Silk. (Illus.). 27p. (Orig.). (J). (ps-3). 1979. pap. 5.50 (*0-938861-00-X*) Jasmine Texts.

Your Personality & the Spiritual Life. Reginald Johndon. LC 94-28319. Orig. Title: Celebrate, My Soul. 180p. 1995. pap. 9.99 (*1-56476-385-4*, 6-3385, Victor Bks) Chariot Victor.

Your Personality Tree. Florence Littauer. 237p. 1989. pap. 10.99 (*0-8499-3169-X*) Word Pub.

Your Personally Tailored Diet. Stephen Lehane. (Illus.). 1984. 15.95 (*0-13-980541-9*, Busn); pap. 5.95 (*0-13-980525-7*, Busn) P-H.

Your Pet Bear. (J). pap. 1.95 (*0-590-32434-9*) Scholastic Inc.

Your Pet Bear. Bobbie Hamsa. LC 79-24938. (Far-Fetched Pets Ser.). (Illus.). 32p. (J). (ps-3). 1994. lib. bdg. 16.90 (*0-516-04481-8*) Childrens.

Your Pet Beaver. Bobbie Hamsa. LC 79-23379. (Far-Fetched Pets Ser.). (Illus.). 32p. (J). (ps-3). 1994. lib. bdg. 16.90 (*0-516-04482-6*) Childrens.

***Your Pet Cat.** Elaine Landau. LC 97-15626. (True Books--Animals Ser.). 1997. 20.00 (*0-516-20381-9*) Childrens.

***Your Pet Dinosaur.** Hudson Talbott. (J). Date not set. pap. write for info. (*0-688-11339-7*, Beech Tree Bks) Morrow.

***Your Pet Dog.** Elaine Landau. LC 97-15627. (True Books--Animals Ser.). 1997. 20.00 (*0-516-20382-7*) Childrens.

Your Pet Elephant. Bobbie Hamsa. LC 79-26412. (Far-Fetched Pets Ser.). (Illus.). 32p. (J). (ps-3). 1994. lib. bdg. 16.90 (*0-516-04483-4*) Childrens.

***Your Pet Gerbil.** Elaine Landau. LC 97-17179. (True Books--Animals Ser.). 1997. 20.00 (*0-516-20384-3*) Childrens.

***Your Pet Hamster.** Elaine Landau. LC 97-15625. (True Books--Animals Ser.). 1997. 20.00 (*0-516-20383-5*) Childrens.

***Your Pet Iguana.** Elaine Landau. LC 97-17311. (True Books--Animals Ser.). 1997. 20.00 (*0-516-20387-8*) Childrens.

Your Pet Newt: How to Care for Him & a History Lesson. Michael Glasser. 24p. 1995. pap. 5.95 (*0-9648318-0-5*) Pet Newt.

Your Pet Penguin. Bobbie Hamsa. LC 80-15588. (Far-Fetched Pets Ser.). (Illus.). 32p. (J). (ps-3). 1994. lib. bdg. 16.90 (*0-516-04484-2*) Childrens.

***Your Pet Tropical Fish.** Elaine Landau. LC 97-17378. (True Books--Animals Ser.). 1997. 20.00 (*0-516-20386-X*) Childrens.

Your Phobia: Understanding Your Fears Through Contextual Therapy. Manuel D. Zane & Harry Milt. LC 84-12454. 283p. 1984. text ed. 19.95 (*0-88048-008-4*, 8008) Am Psychiatric.

Your Piano & Your Piano Technician. Virgil E. Smith. LC 80-82009. 56p. 1981. pap. 3.45 (*0-8497-5078-4*, WP71) Kjos.

Your Pilot's License. 4th ed. Joe Christy & Clay Johnson. (Illus.). 160p. 1988. pap. 13.95 (*0-8306-2477-5*, 2477P) McGraw-Hill Prof.

Your Pilot's License. 5th ed. Joe Christy. LC 93-44633. 1994. pap. text ed. 14.95 (*0-07-019281-2*) McGraw-Hill Prof.

Your Place at God's Table. Max Lucado. 32p. 1995. pap. 2.99 (*0-8499-5150-X*) Word Pub.

Your Place in the Cosmos, Vol. I: A Layman's Book of Astronomy & the Mythology of the Eighty-Eight Celestial Constellations & Registry. James E. Magee. (Illus.). 530p. (YA). 1985. text ed. 34.45 (*0-9614354-0-2*) Mosele & Assocs.

Your Place in the Cosmos, Vol. II: A Layman's Book of Astronomy & the Mythology of the Eighty-Eight Celestial Constellations & Registry. James E. Magee. (Illus.). 508p. (YA). 1988. text ed. 34.45 (*0-9614354-1-0*) Mosele & Assocs.

Your Place in the Cosmos, Vol. III: A Layman's Book of Astronomy & the Mythology of the Eighty-Eight Celestial Constellations & Registry. James E. Magee. (Illus.). 388p. (YA). 1992. text ed. 49.45 (*0-9614354-2-9*) Mosele & Assocs.

Your Planetary Personality: Everything You Need to Make Sense of Your Horoscope. Dennis Oakland. LC 91-47574. (Modern Astrology Library). 580p. 1992. pap. 24.95 (*0-87542-594-1*) Llewellyn Pubns.

Your Pony Book. Hermann Wiederhold. 1977. pap. 2.00 (*0-87980-331-2*) Wilshire.

Your Pony, Your Horse: A Kid's Guide to Care & Enjoyment. Cherry Hill. Ed. by Deborah Balmuth. LC 95-18319. (Illus.). 160p. (Orig.). (J). (gr. 4 up). 1995. pap. 12.95 (*0-88266-908-7*, 908-7, Storey Pub) Storey Comm Inc.

Your Power of Natural Knowing. Vernon Howard. 227p. 1995. pap. 8.95 (*0-911203-34-6*) New Life.

Your Power to Say No. Vernon Howard. 1981. pap. 1.50 (*0-911203-06-0*) New Life.

Your Prayerful Journal for Lent. Bridget M. Meehan. LC 93-79677. 180p. (Orig.). 1994. spiral bd. 13.95 (*0-89243-534-8*) Liguori Pubns.

***Your Preacher.** Charles Hodge. 90p. (Orig.). 1977. pap. 2.95 (*0-933672-39-X*, C-0972) Star Bible.

Your Prechool Child. (Parents' Guides Ser.). (Illus.). 96p. 1987. pap. 12.95 (*0-7460-0133-9*); lib. bdg. 20.95 (*0-88110-289-X*) EDC.

Your Pregnancy: Reassuring Answers to the Questions of Mothers-to-Be. Ronald M. Caplan & Betty Rothbart. LC 92-14145. 1992. pap. 5.95 (*0-688-10826-1*, Quill) Morrow.

Your Pregnancy after 30. Glade B. Curtis. LC 96-22165. (Your Pregnancy Ser.). (Illus.). 384p. (Orig.). 1996. pap. 12.95 (*1-55561-088-9*) Fisher Bks.

Your Pregnancy Month by Month: A Comprehensive Guide & Personal Diary from Conception to Birth. 4th rev. ed. Clark Gillespie. LC 91-58473. (Illus.). 320p. 1992. pap. 13.00 (*0-06-096533-9*, HarpT) HarpC.

Your Pregnancy Questions & Answers. Glade B. Curtis. LC 95-24480. (Your Pregnancy Ser.). (Illus.). 448p. 1995. pap. 12.95 (*1-55561-077-3*) Fisher Bks.

***Your Pregnancy Questions & Answers.** Glade B. Curtis. LC 95-24480. (Your Pregnancy Ser.). (Illus.). 448p. 1995. pap. 12.95 (*1-55561-150-8*) Fisher Bks.

Your Pregnancy Week-by-Week. expanded rev. ed. Glade B. Curtis. LC 94-30005. (Your Pregnancy Ser.). (Illus.). 432p. (Orig.). 1994. pap. 12.95 (*1-55561-068-4*) Fisher Bks.

***Your Pregnancy Week by Week.** 3rd ed. Glade B. Curtis. LC 97-22933. (Your Pregnancy Ser.). (Illus.). 400p. 1997. pap. 12.95 (*1-55561-143-5*) Fisher Bks.

***Your Pregnancy Week by Week: Everything You Need to Know to Feel Good About Yourself.** Alison MacKonochie. 1996. 12.98 (*0-8317-7221-2*) Smithmark.

Your Premature Baby: Everything You Need to Know about the Childbirth Treatment & Parenting of Premature Infants. Frank P. Manginello & Theresa F. DiGeronimo. LC 91-10572. 296p. 1991. pap. text ed. 15. 95 (*0-471-53587-7*) Wiley.

Your Prenatal Eclipse. Rose Lineman. pap. 9.00 (*0-86690-415-8*) Am Fed Astrologers.

Your Press-Away Pain Guide to Headache Relief. T. Louis Emmons. Ed. by Harmony Bentosino. (Illus.). 64p. (Orig.). 1994. pap. text ed. 4.95 (*0-9643151-8-1*) T L Emmons.

Your Privacy: Protecting It in a Nosy World. Edward F. Dolan. LC 94-14168. (YA). (gr. 6 up). 1995. pap. 14.99 (*0-525-65187-X*, Dutton) NAL-Dutton.

Your Problem Horse. Sallie Walrond. (Illus.). 160p. (Orig.). 1994. pap. 18.95 (*1-85310-422-1*, Pub. by Swan Hill UK) Voyageur Pr.

Your Prostate: What Every Man over Forty Needs to Know, Now! Chet Cunningham. LC 90-71251. (Illus.). 192p. (Orig.). 1994. pap. 12.95 (*0-9614924-6-5*) United Res CA.

Your Psyche, the Cigarette & the Pill: The Psychogenic Theory of Disease. Harold E. Simmons. 1969. pap. 10. 00 (*0-87312-003-5*) Gen Welfare Pubns.

Your Psychic Potential. M. J. Abadie. 320p. (Orig.). 1995. pap. 10.95 (*1-55850-475-3*) Adams Media.

***Your Psychic Powers: A Beginner's Guide.** Craig Hamilton-Parker. (Beginner's Ser.). 96p. 1997. pap. 11. 95 (*0-340-67417-2*, Pub. by Headway UK) Trafalgar.

Your Psychic Powers & How to Develop Them. Hereward Carrington. (Occult Ser.). 390p. 1975. pap. 12.95 (*0-87877-033-X*, P-33) Newcastle Pub.

Your Psychic Powers & How to Develop Them. Hereward Carrington. 358p. 1976. reprint ed. spiral bd. 13.50 (*0-7873-0157-4*) Hlth Research.

Your Psychic Powers & How to Develop Them (1920) Hereward Carrington. 358p. 1996. pap. 24.95 (*1-56459-939-6*) Kessinger Pub.

Your Public Best: The Complete Guide to Making Successful Public Appearances in the Meeting Room, on the Platform, & on TV. Lillian Brown. LC 89-30759. 240p. 1991. 19.95 (*1-55704-042-7*) Newmarket.

Your Public Best: The Complete Guide to Making Successful Public Appearances in the Meeting Room, on the Platform, & on TV. Lillian Brown. LC 89-30759. 240p. 1992. pap. 12.95 (*1-55704-079-6*) Newmarket.

Your Public Schools: What You Can Do to Help Them. Barbara J. Hansen & Philip E. Mackey. LC 93-24954. 240p. 1993. 19.95 (*0-945774-21-4*, LC225.3.H36) Catbird Pr.

***Your Puppy, Your Dog: A Kid's Guide to Raising a Happy, Healthy Dog.** Pat Storer. LC 97-5725. (Illus.). 160p. (Orig.). (J). (gr. 4-7). 1997. pap. 12.95 (*0-88266-959-1*) Storey Comm Inc.

Your Puppy's First Year. Don Harper. 1994. 12.98 (*0-7858-0162-6*) Bk Sales Inc.

Your Puppy's First Year. Shawn Messonnier. LC 94-48892. 144p. 1995. pap. 12.95 (*1-55622-386-2*, Seaside Pr) Wordware Pub.

Your Purebred Kitten. Michele Lowell. 1995. pap. 12.95 (*0-8050-3269-X*) H Holt & Co.

Your Purebred Puppy. Michele Lowell. 1990. 22.00 (*0-8050-1411-X*) H Holt & Co.

***Your Purpose in Life.** Carol Adrienne. Date not set. write for info. (*0-688-15512-X*) Morrow.

Your Pursuit of Profit. Christine Harvey & Bill Sykes. 208p. 1988. 16.50 (*1-86287-008-X*, Pub. by Federation Pr AU) Gaunt.

Your QRP Operating Companion. 1992. pap. 6.00 (*0-87259-376-2*) Am Radio.

Your Quest for God. Richard Bennett. 1996. 3.99 (*1-85792-216-6*, Pub. by Christian Focus UK) Spring Arbor Dist.

Your Questions God's Answers. Peter Kreeft. LC 93-80505. 121p. pap. 8.95 (*0-89870-488-X*) Ignatius Pr.

Your Rabbit: A Kid's Guide to Raising & Showing. Nancy Searle. Ed. by Gwen Steege. LC 91-57949. (Illus.). 160p. 1992. pap. 12.95 (*0-88266-767-X*) Storey Comm Inc.

Your Radiant Body Series of Booklets. rev. ed. Juanita O. Keith. 148p. Date not set. pap. text ed. write for info. (*0-9628351-3-7*) Archer Creat Pr.

Your Reactions Are Showing. J. A. Peterson. 1980. pap. 2.50 (*0-8474-0999-6*) Back to Bible.

Your Reading: An Annotated Booklist for Middle School & Junior High. Ed. by Barbara G. Samuels & G. Kylene Beers. (NCTE Bibliography Ser.). 381p. (Orig.). (J). (gr. 6-9). 1995. pap. 21.95 (*0-8141-5943-5*) NCTE.

Your Real Beauty. Cindy Christovale. 80p. (Orig.). 1983. pap. 2.95 (*0-88144-018-3*, CPS-018) Christian Pub.

Your Real Medicare Handbook. 2nd ed. Betsy Abramson & Margie Groom. (Illus.). 104p. 1989. pap. 8.00 (*0-932622-25-9*) Ctr Public Rep.

Your Reason & Blake's System. Allen Ginsberg. (Illus.). 52p. (Orig.). 1988. pap. 5.95 (*0-937815-23-3*) Hanuman Bks.

***Your Reincarnating Child.** Gilbert Childs. 1996. pap. text ed. 14.95 (*1-85584-037-5*) Anthroposophic.

Your Relationship to God. George Rich. (New Life Ser.). 32p. 1991. student ed., pap. 1.95 (*0-87227-156-0*, RBP5197); teacher ed., pap. 1.95 (*0-87227-167-6*, RBP5196) Reg Baptist.

Your Relationship to God: A Four Week Study to Help Teenagers Understand Their Relationship to God. Angelyn Rodriguez. Ed. by Gary Swyers. (Bible Basics Ser.). (Illus.). 32p. (YA). (gr. 6-12). 1991. pap. 8.95 (*0-89827-084-7*, BKS00) Wesleyan Pub Hse.

***Your Remarkable Anatomy: An Overview for Health Professionals, Students, & the General Public.** Don L. Fisher. (Illus.). 128p. 1997. pap. text ed. 25.00 (*1-889743-01-1*) R Dean Pr.

Your Renaissance Years. large type ed. Robert L. Veninga. 675p. 1992. lib. bdg. 15.95 (*1-56054-939-4*) Thorndike Pr.

Your Research. Blankenship. Date not set. pap. text ed. 24. 00 (*0-314-01531-0*) West Pub.

Your Research. Plutzer. Date not set. pap. text ed. 24.50 (*0-314-04043-9*) West Pub.

Your Research. 2nd ed. Blankenship. Date not set. pap. text ed. 24.50 (*0-314-08753-2*) West Pub.

***Your Research: Data Analysis for Introduction.** 2nd ed. Hinze. (C). 1993. pap. 20.00 (*0-314-01535-3*) West Pub.

Your Resource Guide to Environmental Organizations. Ed. by John Seredich. LC 90-91949. (Illus.). 514p. (Orig.). 1991. pap. 15.95 (*1-879072-00-9*) Smiling Dolphins Pr.

Your Resume: Key to a Better Job. 6th ed. Leonard Corwen. 192p. (Orig.). 1995. 10.95 (*0-02-860343-5*, Arco) Macmillan Gen Ref.

***Your Resume: Key to a Better Job.** 6th ed. Leonard Corwen. 200p. (Orig.). 1996. pap. 24.95 incl. 3.5 ld (*0-02-861315-5*, Arco) Macmillan Gen Ref.

***Your Retail Store: Owner's Manual A-Z.** Robert Wells. (Illus.). 175p. 1997. pap. write for info. (*0-9657040-0-9*) RST Pr.

***Your Retirement & How to Make the Most of It.** 2nd ed. Rosemary Brown. (Personal Finance Ser.). 1996. pap. 14.95 (*0-7494-2044-8*) Kogan Page Ltd.

Your Retirement Benefits. Peter E. Gaudio & Virginia S. Nicols. LC 91-37446. 272p. 1992. pap. text ed. 10.95 (*0-471-53966-X*) Wiley.

Your Retirement Money: How to Make It Last. Philip G. McCracken. 263p. (Orig.). 1992. pap. 17.95 (*0-9633349-0-5*) B&G Pub.

Your Revenge Is in the Mail. Keith Wade. LC 87-83526. 176p. (Orig.). 1988. pap. 12.95 (*0-915179-74-1*, 19146) Loompanics.

Your Right Action Number. Juno Jordan. LC 79-50006. 1978. pap. 8.95 (*0-87516-287-8*) DeVorss.

Your Right-Standing with God. Kenneth Copeland. 16p. 1983. pap. 1.00 (*0-88114-795-8*) K Copeland Pubns.

Your Right to Choose. Darwin Gross. 292p. (Orig.). 1986. pap. 4.95 (*0-931689-05-8*) D Gross.

Your Right to Fly. James E. Melton. LC 80-82961. (Illus.). 218p. 1979. pap. 8.95 (*0-9604752-0-6*) Global Pubns CA.

Your Right to Government Information. 2nd rev. ed. Christine M. Marwick. (ACLU Ser.). 284p. 1985. pap. 6.95 (*0-8093-9960-1*) S Ill U Pr.

Your Right to Know: The Call to Action. Patricia G. Schumann et al. (Illus.). 109p. (Orig.). 1993. pap. text ed. 20.00 (*0-8389-3428-5*) ALA.

Your Right to Privacy: A Basic Guide to Legal Rights in an Information Society. 2nd ed. Evan Hendricks et al. LC 89-21844. (American Civil Liberties Union Handbook Ser.). 184p. (C). 1990. pap. 8.95 (*0-8093-1632-3*) S Ill U Pr.

Your Right to Religious Liberty: A Basic Guide to Religious Rights. Barry Lynn et al. LC 94-13635. (ACLU Handbook Ser.). 128p. (C). 1995. pap. 8.95 (*0-8093-1967-5*) S Ill U Pr.

***Your Rightful Childhood: New & Selected Poems.** Paula Rankin. 120p. 1997. 20.95 (*0-88748-245-7*); pap. 11.95 (*0-88748-246-5*) Carnegie-Mellon.

Your Rights: The Liberty Guide. 5th rev. ed. Ed. by John Wadham. LC 94-1041. (C). 66.50 (*0-7453-0778-7*, Pub. by Pluto Pr UK) LPC InBook.

***Your Rights As a Consumer.** Ed. by Richard L. Strohm. LC 96-37518. (Layman's Law Guides Ser.). 128p. 1997. lib. bdg. 16.95 (*0-7910-4445-9*) Chelsea Hse.

Your Rights As a Consumer. 2nd ed. Marc R. Lieberman. (Layman's Law Guides Ser.). 128p. 1994. pap. 8.95 (*1-56414-083-0*) Career Pr Inc.

Your Rights As American Indians. 7.50 (*0-944253-74-1*) Inst Dev Indian Law.

Your Rights at Work. Bill Birtles & Patricia Hewitt. 1983. 35.00 (*0-946088-06-3*, Pub. by NCCL UK) St Mut.

***Your Rights in the Workplace.** Richard L. Strohm. LC 96-49389. 128p. 1997. lib. bdg. 16.95 (*0-7910-4442-4*) Chelsea Hse.

Your Rights in the Workplace. 2nd ed. Barbara K. Repa. 352p. 1995. pap. 15.95 (*0-87337-200-X*) Nolo Pr.

Your Rights in the Workplace. 2nd ed. Richard L. Strohm. (Layman's Law Guides Ser.). 128p. 1994. pap. 8.95 (*1-56414-087-3*) Career Pr Inc.

Your Rights in the Workplace: Everything Employees Need to Know. Henry H. Perritt, Jr. 250p. 1993. pap. 14.95 (*0-87224-049-5*) PLI.

Your Rights on the Job: A Practical Guide to Employment Laws in Massachusetts. Robert M. Schwartz. LC 82-84617. (Illus.). 250p. 1983. pap. 14.95 (*0-9611038-0-9*) Labor Guild Bost.

Your Rights on the Job: A Practical Guide to Employment Laws in Massachusetts. 3rd ed. Robert M. Schwartz. LC 92-23665. (Illus.). 1992. 25.95 (*0-9611038-2-5*) Labor Guild Bost.

Your Rights on the Job: A Practical Guide to Employment Laws in Massachusetts. Robert M. Schwartz. (Illus.). 288p. (C). 1987. reprint ed. pap. text ed. 19.95 (*0-9611038-1-7*) Labor Guild Bost.

Your Road Map to Lifelong Happiness: A Guide to the Life You Want. Ken Keyes, Jr. (Illus.). 300p. 1995. 19.95 (*0-915972-22-0*) Love Line Bks.

Your Rod & Your Staff. Sinai Adler. Tr. & Adapted by Tzvi Barish. 1995. 17.95 (*0-87306-736-3*) Feldheim.

Your Roles & Responsibilities As a Board Member. John Carver & Miriam M. Carver. LC 96-10045. (CarverGuide Series on Effective Board Governance: Vol. 2). 1996. pap. write for info. (*0-7879-0297-7*) Jossey-Bass.

Your Rugged Constitution. 3rd ed. Bruce Allyn & Esther B. Findlay. (Illus.). 296p. (C). 1969. 35.00 (*0-8047-0405-8*); pap. 11.95 (*0-8047-0407-4*) Stanford U Pr.

***Your RX for Success. Luella Gunter. Ed. by J. Gibb. 179p. (Orig.). 1996. pap. 14.95 (*0-9655691-0-1*) Lupresco. Zig Ziglar summarizes YOUR RX FOR SUCCESS as follows: "Luella Gunter has developed a game plan which is easy-to-read, simple-to-follow, & yet comprehensive in its coverage of some of the fundamentals we must follow if we want balanced success in all areas of life." Twenty-four chapters, YOUR RX FOR SUCCESS covers 96 subjects concerning business development, personal development & attitude development & is designed to be read one chapter at a time. Each subject has an action plan designed to turn potential into unlimited power! Audaciously honest, superbly written by an individual who has experienced outstanding success in business, direct sales & management. This book will benefit anyone in any business, at any age, in any walk of life to enjoy outstanding success & get more out of living. Lupresco, Inc., 5902 Torreon N.E., Albuquerque, NM 87109. 505-822-0706. Dealer & or bulk prices available.**

Publisher Provided Annotation.

Your Sacred Self. Wayne W. Dyer. 400p. 1996. mass mkt. 6.99 (*0-06-109475-7*) HarpC.

***Your School-Age Child.** Lawrence Kutner. 224p. 1997. pap. 11.00 (*0-380-71354-3*) Avon.

Your School-Age Child, Vol. 1. Lawrence Kutner. 224p. 1996. 20.00 (*0-688-10217-4*) Morrow.

Your School Report (TM) (Illus.). 51p. (J). (gr. 5-11). 1994. 19.95 (*1-884618-00-6*) Unique Information.

***Your Scottish Ancestry: A Guide for North Americans.** Sherry Irvine. LC 96-39342. 267p. 1996. pap. 17.95 (*0-916489-65-5*) Ancestry.

Your Second Child. Joan S. Weiss. 288p. 1981. pap. 11.00 (*0-671-25619-X*) Summit Bks.

***Your Second Mattress Will Last Forever: And Other Guarantees of Marriage & Parenting.** Bill Corbin. (Illus.). 144p. (Orig.). 1996. pap. 10.95 (*0-9634373-9-9*) Beckett-Highland.

Your Second Pregnancy: What to Expect This Time. Katie Tamony. LC 94-47662. 244p. (Orig.). 1995. pap. 11.95 (*1-55652-234-7*) Chicago Review.

Your Secret Angel. Suzanne S. Zenkel. (Deluxe Gift Editions Ser.). (Illus.). 56p. 1995. 8.99 (*0-88088-595-5*) Peter Pauper.

Your Secret Self: Illuminating the Mysteries of the Twelfth House. Tracy Marks. 264p. (Orig.). 1989. pap. 15.95 (*0-916360-43-1*) CRCS Pubns CA.

Your Secret Self: The Enneagram Personality Test. Alan Fensin & George Ryan. 240p. (Orig.). 1993. mass mkt. 4.99 (*0-380-76674-4*) Avon.

***Your Secret Sex Diary.** Anne Hooper. Date not set. 14.95 (*0-7894-1469-4*) DK Pub Inc.

Your Self As History: Family History & Its Effect on Your Personality: A Research Guide. Valentine R. Winsey. 114p. (Orig.). 1992. pap. text ed. 18.50 (*0-944473-11-3*) Pace Univ Pr.

Your Self As History: Family History & Its Effect on Your Personality: A Research Guide. Valentine R. Winsey. 114p. (Orig.). 1992. lib. bdg. 38.00 (*0-944473-10-5*) Pace Univ Pr.

Your Self As History: Tracing Your Past to Enrich Your Future. Valentine R. Winsey. 115p. 1996. pap. 10.95 (*1-56833-074-X*) Madison Bks UPA.

Your Seven Year Old. Louise B. Ames et al. 176p. 1987. pap. 10.95 (*0-440-50650-6*) Dell.

Your Seven Year Old Owner's Manual. Jim Grant & Margot Sale. (Illus.). 16p. (Orig.). 1988. pap. 12.95 (*0-935493-18-2*, RRB407) Programs Educ.

Your Sexual Health: What Every Teen Should Know about Sex. Jenny McCloskey. LC 92-35228. 336p. 1993. 15. 95 (*1-879904-08-X*) Halo Bks.

Your Sexual Self: Pathway to Authentic Intimacy. Fran Ferder & John Heagle. LC 91-77483. 176p. (Orig.). 1992. pap. 7.95 (*0-87793-479-7*) Ave Maria.

Your Sexuality: A Self Assessment. 2nd ed. Robert F. Valois & Sandra K. Kammermann. 1992. pap. text ed. write for info. (*0-07-066848-5*) McGraw.

***Your Sexuality: A Self Assessment.** 3rd ed. Robert F. Valois & Sandra K. Kammermann. 1996. pap. text ed. write for info. (*0-07-066853-1*) McGraw.

Your Sexuality Workbook. 3rd ed. Mary A. Watson. 248p. (C). 1996. per., pap. text ed. 33.54 (*0-7872-1824-3*) Kendall-Hunt.

***Your Shadow.** Robin Robertson. LC 97-16808. (Illus.). 198p. (Orig.). 1997. pap. 15.95 (*0-87604-391-0*, 489) ARE Pr.

Your Shadow Side - the Fourth Function: Achilles' Heel & Pearl of Great Price. Terence Duniho. 36p. 1991. pap. text ed. 5.95 (*1-878287-30-3*, BDAF) Type & Temperament.

Your Shape, Your Clothes & You: Secrets of a Successful Wardrobe. rev. ed. Darlene Miller. (Illus.). 80p. 1994. 14.95 (*0-9642936-0-9*) Clothes For You.

Your Sheep: A Kid's Guide to Raising & Showing. Paula Simmons & Darrell L. Salsbury. Ed. by Gwen Steege. LC 91-57947. (Illus.). 128p. (J). 1992. pap. 12.95 (*0-88266-769-6*, Garden Way Pub) Storey Comm Inc.

Your Show of Shows. Ted Sennett. (Quality Paperbacks Ser.). (Illus.). 180p. 1985. reprint ed. pap. 10.95 (*0-306-80235-X*) Da Capo.

Your Sight & Hearing. Merle A. Wilson. 135p. 1973. reprint ed. spiral bd. 11.50 (*0-7873-0975-3*) Hlth Research.

Your Signature Path: Gaining New Perspectives on Life & Work. Geoffrey M. Bellman. LC 96-31515. 250p. 1996. 24.95 (*1-57675-004-3*) Berrett-Koehler.

Your Sins Are Forgiven You: Rediscovering the Sacrament of Reconciliation. George A. Maloney. LC 93-43836. 142p. 1994. pap. 7.95 (*0-8189-0691-X*) Alba.

Your Six Year Old. Louise B. Ames et al. 132p. 1981. pap. 10.95 (*0-440-50674-3*) Dell.

Your Six Year Old Owner's Manual. Jim Grant & Margot Azen. (Illus.). 8p. (Orig.). 1987. pap. 12.95 (*0-935493-08-5*, RRB 326) Programs Educ.

***Your Sixth Sense: Activating Your Psychic Potential.** Belleruth Naparstek. LC 96-30248. 1997. 22.00 (*0-06-251359-1*); pap. 12.00 (*0-06-251360-5*) Harper SF.

Your Skeleton & Skin. Ray Broekel. LC 84-7746. (New True Bks.). (Illus.). 48p. (J). (gr. k-4). 1984. lib. bdg. 19. 00 (*0-516-01934-1*) Childrens.

Your Skin: An Owner's Guide. Joseph Bark. 284p. pap. 10. 95 (*0-13-199663-0*) P-H.

Your Skin & Mine. rev. ed. Paul Showers. LC 90-37429. (Trophy Let's-Read-&-Find-Out Bk.). (Illus.). 32p. (J). (gr. k-4). 1991. pap. 4.95 (*0-06-445102-X*, Trophy) HarpC Child Bks.

Your Skin & Mine. rev. ed. Paul Showers. LC 90-37430. (Let's-Read-&-Find-Out Science Bk.). (Illus.). 32p. (J). (gr. k-4). 1991. lib. bdg. 14.89 (*0-06-022523-8*) HarpC Child Bks.

Your Skin Is a Country. Nora Mitchell. LC 88-14632. 72p. (Orig.). (C). 1988. pap. 9.95 (*0-914086-83-9*) Alicejamesbooks.

Your Skin Is Showing. A. Bernard Ackerman. (Illus.). 32p. 1979. text ed. 12.00 (*0-8121-1212-1*) Williams & Wilkins.

Your Slice of the Melon: A Guide to Greater Job Success. 2nd ed. James E. Neal, Jr. LC 87-92044. 144p. (C). 1989. pap. 4.95 (*0-9609006-1-6*) Neal Pubns Inc.

Your Slip Is Showing: Indian Press Today. S. Nihal Singh. (C). 1992. 14.00 (*0-685-66243-8*, Pub. by UBS Pubs Dist II) S Asia.

Your Small Business Made Simple. Richard R. Gallagher. 160p. 1989. pap. 12.00 (*0-385-23742-1*) Doubleday.

***Your Solar Return: A Living Diary of Life Through the Annual Solar Revolutions.** Cynthia Bohannon & Ted George. LC 96-78499. 90p. 1997. pap. 13.00 (*0-932782-07-8*) Arthur Pubns.

Your Son, Calvin Coolidge. Ed. by Edward C. Lathem. 244p. 1968. pap. 7.50 (*0-914960-35-0*) Academy Bks.

Your Special Baby: Real Lamaze Prepared Childbirth. Stacy McCullough. (Illus.). 90p. 10.95 (*0-9643837-0-5*) Luckenbooth.

Your Spectacular Quest. Sweet Seminars Staff. 208p. 1994. per., pap. text ed. 15.95 (*0-8403-9574-4*) Kendall-Hunt.

Your Spicy Life: Guide to Herbing & Spicing Even the Simplest Foods. Fairfax Stephenson. LC 77-85847. 52p. 1977. spiral bd. 6.95 (*0-931490-01-4*) Gotuit Ent.

Your Spirit Guides Are Thoroughbreds: A Self Help Manual for Mule Headed People. Rachel L. Manning. LC 86-62341. 160p. (Orig.). 1988. pap. 7.95 (*0-941698-14-9*) Pan Ishtar.

Your Spiritual & Emotional Power see Su Poder Espiritual Y Emocional

Your Spiritual Child. Barbara Milicevic. (Illus.). 96p. 1984. pap. 7.00 (*0-87516-528-1*) DeVorss.

Your Spiritual Gifts Can Help Your Church Grow. C. Peter Wagner. Ed. by Virginia Woodard. LC 93-43253. 272p. 1994. 15.99 (*0-8307-1673-4*, 5112455) Regal.

***Your Spiritual Gifts Inventory.** Charles V. Bryant. 1997. pap. text ed. 19.95 (*0-8358-0819-X*) Upper Room Bks.

An Asterisk (*) at the beginning of an entry indicates that the title is appearing in BIP for the first time.

Your Spiritual Weapons. Terry Law. (Illus.). 48p. 1985. reprint ed. pap. 2.25 (*0-932081-00-2*) Victory Hse.

Your Spiritual Weapons & How to Use Them. Terry Law. (Orig.). 1983. pap. write for info. (*0-88144-028-0*, CPS028) Christian Pub.

*__Your Stained Glass Workshop.__ Gene Mayo. (Illus.). 26p. 1996. 8.95 (*0-936459-34-4*) Stained Glass.

Your Star Child: Birthing an Evolved Soul. Mary Mayhew. Ed. by Rodney Charles. LC 95-68465. (Illus.). 400p. (Orig.). 1995. pap. 16.95 (*0-9638502-2-9*) Sunstar Pubng.

Your Starchild: An Astrology Guide for You & Your Child. Haydn Paul. 320p. 1992. mass mkt. 4.99 (*0-380-76355-9*) Avon.

Your Stars At Work. Carole Golder. 1997. pap. 10.95 (*0-8050-5101-5*) H Holt & Co.

Your Starway to Love: Better Romance with Astrology. 2nd rev. ed. Maritha Pottenger. (Illus.). 352p. 1996. pap. 14.95 (*0-935127-44-5*) ACS Pubns.

Your State: Pennsylvania. Lucille Wallower. Ed. by Patricia L. Gump. (J). (gr. 3-4). 1984. pap. 4.90 (*0-931992-09-5*) Penns Valley.

Your Story: A Guided Interview Through Your Personal & Family History. Gift to the Future 200, Inc. Staff. (Illus.). 64p. 1992. 16.95 (*0-9634249-4-7*) Gift Future Two Thous.

Your Story - a Writing Guide for Genealogists. Carla J. Eardley. 110p. (Orig.). 1994. pap. text ed. 11.50 (*0-7884-0110-6*) Heritage Bk.

*__Your Story Matters: Introducing the Pleasures of Personal Writing.__ 3rd rev. ed. Susan Paul. Ed. by Glenda Schlahta. (Illus.). 160p. 1997. pap. 14.95 (*0-9650231-1-7*) Inner Edge.

Your Subconscious Power. Charles M. Simmons. 1975. pap. 7.00 (*0-87980-178-6*) Wilshire.

*__Your Success Story: How to Rewrite Your Brain's Own Programs to Design a Perfect Life.__ Ajit Damodaran. LC 96-90759. (Illus.). 262p. (Orig.). 1997. pap. 14.95 (*0-9655084-4-7*) VSDN Pub.

*__Your Successful Massage - Bodywork Practice: Professional Edition.__ rev. ed. Jefferson Saunders & Deborah Nucci. (Orig.). (C). 1997. write for info. (*1-877738-03-4*) Superior Pub WA.

*__Your Successful Massage/Bodywork Practice: Bodywork Practice.__ 3rd rev. ed. Jefferson C. Saunders & Deborah Nucci. 1995. pap. text ed. 39.50 (*1-877738-02-6*) Superior Pub WA.

Your Successful Real Estate Career. Kenneth W. Edwards. LC 92-23014. 192p. 1992. pap. 14.95 (*0-8144-7785-2*) AMACOM.

*__Your Successful Real Estate Career.__ 3rd ed. Kenneth W. Edwards. LC 96-51466. 224p. 1997. pap. 17.95 (*0-8144-7931-6*) AMACOM.

Your Sun Sign As a Spiritual Guide. 6th ed. Sri Kriyananda. LC 89-190047. 160p. 1974. pap. 9.95 (*0-916124-23-1*, CCP15) Crystal Clarity.

Your Sweatband's Too Tight When.... E. Jay Isaacs. LC 85-3985. (Illus.). 90p. 1986. pap. 5.95 (*0-937219-00-2*) Iron Horse Pr.

*__Your Talking Pet.__ Ann Walker. (Illus.). (Orig.). 1997. pap. 19.95 (*1-898307-87-3*, Pub. by Capall Bann Pubng UK) Holmes Pub.

*__Your Tax Questions Answered.__ Ed Slott. (Illus.). 168p. (Orig.). 1997. pap. 9.95 (*1-882663-11-X*) Plymouth MI.

Your Tax Return: How to Organize & Prepare It. Donald O. Ramsey. 140p. 1991. student ed. 15.95 (*0-9630667-0-6*) KISS Enter.

Your Taxpayer Rights: Minimal at Best: Use Them...or Lose Them. Holmes F. Crouch. Ed. by Irma J. Crouch. LC 96-84934. (Series 500 Tax Guides: Vol. 503). (Illus.). 224p. (Orig.). 1996. pap. 18.95 (*0-944817-32-7*, T/G 503) Allyear Tax.

Your Temperament Can Be Changed. Tim LaHaye. 60p. 1978. mass mkt. 2.99 (*0-8423-8750-1*) Tyndale.

Your Ten to Fourteen Year Old. Louise A. Bates et al. 368p. 1989. pap. 11.95 (*0-440-50678-6*) Dell.

Your Texas Business. 2nd ed. Richard Alderman & Tom Oldham. 220p. 1992. pap. 27.95 (*0-88415-024-0*) Gulf Pub.

Your Thoughts Can Change Your Life. Donald Curtis. 224p. 1996. pap. 10.99 (*0-446-67196-7*) Warner Bks.

Your Three Year Old. Louise B. Ames et al. 176p. 1980. pap. 10.95 (*0-440-50649-2*) Dell.

Your Three Year Old Owner's Manual. Jim Grant & Margot Azen. (Illus.). 16p. (Orig.). 1988. pap. 12.95 (*0-935493-16-6*, RRB 403) Programs Educ.

Your Thwarts in Pieces, Your Mooring Rope Cut: Poetry from Babylonia & Assyria. Erica Reiner. Ed. by Ladislav Matejka. (Michigan Studies in the Humanities: No. 5). (C). 1985. 10.00 (*0-936534-04-4*) Mich Studies Human.

*__Your Thyroid.__ Lawrence D. Wood. 1996. pap. 12.00 (*0-345-41006-8*) Ballantine.

Your Thyroid. rev. ed. Lawrence C. Wood et al. 1995. mass mkt. 5.99 (*0-345-39170-5*) Ballantine.

*__Your Ticket to a Better Ticket: A Fan's Guide for the Best Concert Experience.__ Steve Maples. Ed. by Erin Hand. (Illus.). 124p. 1996. pap. 14.95 (*0-9653448-2-7*) S Maples.

Your Time Is at Hand. Patricia D. Cota-Robles. (Illus.). 231p. (Orig.). 1992. pap. text ed. 16.00 (*0-9615287-2-9*) New Age Study Human.

Your Time Will Come: The Law of Age Discrimination & Mandatory Retirement. Lawrence M. Friedman. LC 84-60650. (Social Research Perspectives: Occasional Reports on Current Topics Ser.). 160p. 1985. text ed. 9.95 (*0-87154-295-1*) Russell Sage.

Your Tomorrows Can Be Different from Your Yesterdays. 2nd ed. H. Norman Wright. LC 92-38776. 240p. (gr. 10). 1995. pap. 9.99 (*0-8007-5550-2*) Revell.

*__Your Top Health Concerns.__ Andrew Weil. 1997. mass mkt. 2.99 (*0-8041-1677-6*) Ivy Books.

Your Total Body Health. B & A Neilbauer Staff. 1998. 24.95 (*0-7897-0769-1*) Mac Pub USA.

Your Total Health Handbook - Body - Soul - Spirit. 1993. 9.95 (*1-56441-024-2*) M Hickey Min.

*__Your Total Image: How to Communicate Success.__ Philippa Davies. 1996. pap. 14.95 (*0-7499-1641-9*, Pub. by Piatkus Bks UK) London Brdge.

Your Touch Can Heal: A Guide to Healing Touch & How to Use It. Malcolm Miner. 143p. 1992. pap. 6.95 (*0-9633796-0-7*) Faith Ridge.

Your Traffic Ticket Adventure. William D. Moffatt. 270p. 1992. pap. text ed. 23.95 (*0-9634069-0-6*) W D Moffatt.

Your Transfer Planner: Strategic Tools & Guerrilla Tactics. Carey E. Harbin. LC 94-11444. 227p. (C). 1995. pap. 16.95 (*0-534-24372-X*) Wadsworth Pub.

Your Trip Abroad. 1994. lib. bdg. 250.00 (*0-8490-6486-4*) Gordon Pr.

Your True Brother. Compiled by Shoghi Effendi & Robert Weinberg. (Illus.). 24p. (Orig.). (YA). (gr. 8-10). 1991. pap. 7.50 (*0-85398-324-0*) G Ronald Pub.

Your True Marcus: The Civil War Letters of a Jewish Colonel. Marcus M. Spiegel. Ed. by Frank L. Byrne & Jean P. Soman. LC 84-12266. (Illus.). 367p. reprint ed. pap. 104.60 (*0-7837-4067-0*, 2044017) Bks Demand.

Your Turn to Clean the Stair & Fugue. Rona Munro. 1996. pap. text ed. 14.95 (*1-85459-248-3*, Pub. by N Hern Bks UK) Theatre Comm.

Your Turn to Lead: Children's Group Activities. Sarah H. Healton. LC 93-12503. 1993. pap. text ed. 12.95 (*0-8306-4392-3*) McGraw-Hill Prof.

Your Turn to Lead! Children's Group Activities. Kay H. Whiteside & Sarah H. Healton. 1993. text ed. 12.95 (*0-07-027706-0*) McGraw.

Your Two Year Old. Louise B. Ames et al. 160p. 1980. pap. 10.95 (*0-440-50638-7*) Dell.

*__Your Ulcer: Real Information You Can Use.__ Randy Shields. LC 96-70824. 118p. (Orig.). 1996. mass mkt. 4.99 (*1-888886-11-0*) CEPI.

Your Ultimate Secret Power. James R. Ball. Ed. by Vicki Shannon. (Illus.). 24p. 1993. pap. 2.75 (*0-9633184-0-3*) Goals Inst.

Your Uncaring Child: Survival Manual for Parents of Difficult Children. Norman E. Hoffman. (Illus.). 153p. (Orig.). 1996. pap. 12.95 (*0-9652414-8-3*) V G Pr.

Your United Nations: The Official Guide Book. 89p. pap. 6.95 (*92-1-100405-5*) UN.

Your United Nations: The Official Guide Book. (General Information Publications). 89p. 1987. 11.95 (*92-1-100315-6*, E.87.I.10) UN.

Your United States. Arnold Bennett. LC 74-16408. (Collected Works of Arnold Bennett: Vol. 90). 1977. reprint ed. 22.95 (*0-518-19171-0*) Ayer.

Your Unseen Guide. Carolyn S. Halsted. 101p. 1992. pap. 9.00 (*0-89540-223-8*, SB-223) Sun Pub.

Your Ups & Downs. Philip B. Knoche. (Uplook Ser.). 32p. 1970. pap. 0.99 (*0-8163-0085-2*, 24535-7) Pacific Pr Pub Assn.

*__Your Utah State Experience: Strategies for Success.__ 3rd ed. Utah State University Staff. 240p. (C). 1997. spiral bd. 23.95 (*0-7872-3779-5*) Kendall-Hunt.

Your Valves: Channels to a Healthy Heart: For Valve Disease & Valve Surgery Patients. Susan D. Allen et al. (Illus.). 64p. 1991. pap. text ed. 3.25 (*0-916999-10-6*) HERC Inc.

Your VCR: Easy Step-by-Step Instructions to Operate, Maintain, & Repair. Consumer Guide Editors. 96p. 1996. pap. 7.99 (*0-451-82308-7*) NAL-Dutton.

Your VCR: How to Operate, Maintain, & Repair. Consumer Guide Editors. (Illus.). 64p. 1993. spiral bd. 5.98 (*1-56173-739-9*, 3615200) Pubns Intl Ltd.

Your VHF Companion. 1992. pap. 8.00 (*0-87259-387-8*) Am Radio.

*__Your Victorian Locality.__ (Sense of History Ser.). 1993. pap. text ed. write for info. (*0-582-09218-3*, Pub. by Longman UK) Longman.

Your View of God ... God's View of You: Inspirational Devotions for Women. Kathy C. Miller. 136p. 1992. pap. 8.99 (*0-8341-1431-3*) Beacon Hill.

Your Vision: All about Modern Eye Care. Warren D. Cross, Jr. & Lawrence Lynn. (Illus.). 192p. 1994. 19.95 (*1-57101-018-1*); pap. 13.95 (*1-57101-019-X*) MasterMedia Pub.

Your Vision Is Your Future. Casey Treat. 107p. 1987. pap. 4.95 (*0-88144-097-3*) Christian Pub.

Your Vital Statistics. Gyles Brandreth. 128p. 1986. pap. 8.95 (*0-8065-0980-5*) Carol Pub Group.

Your Vitality Quotient: The Clinically Proven Program That Can Reduce Your Body Age - & Increase Your Zest for Life. Richard Earle et al. 1990. pap. 14.95 (*0-446-39155-7*) Warner Bks.

Your Voice Nos. 1-12. Intro. by Ed Hubbard. 64p. 1994. pap. 7.50 (*1-57353-100-6*) Eschaton Prods.

Your Voice & Articulation. 3rd ed. Ethel C. Glenn et al. LC 92-10748. 288p. (C). 1992. pap. text ed. 47.00 (*0-13-953241-2*) P-H.

*__Your Voice & Articulation.__ 4th ed. Glenn. LC 97-10113. 1997. pap. text ed. 43.00 (*0-205-27302-5*) P-H.

Your Voice & How to Use It: The Classical Guide to Speaking with Confidence. Cicely Berry. 160p. 1995. pap. 10.95 (*0-86369-826-3*, Pub. by Virgin Pub UK) London Brdge.

Your Voice, God's Word: Reading the Bible in Church. William Sydnor. LC 88-9374. 60p. (Orig.). 1988. pap. 5.95 (*0-8192-1438-8*) Morehouse Pub.

Your Voice Like a Ram's Horn: Themes & Texts in Traditional Jewish Preaching. Marc Saperstein. (Monographs of the Hebrew Union College: Vol. 18). 1996. 49.95 (*0-87820-417-2*) Hebrew Union Coll Pr.

Your Water & Your Health. rev. ed. Allen E. Banik & Carlson Wade. (Illus.). 128p. 1990. pap. 4.95 (*0-87983-514-1*) Keats.

Your Way with God's Word: Discovering Your Distinctive Preaching Voice. David J. Schlafer. 144p. 1995. pap. 11.95 (*1-56101-118-5*) Cowley Pubns.

Your Weaknesses Are Your Strengths: Transformation of the Self Through Analysis of Personal Weaknesses. David Edman. LC 93-33156. (Illus.). 89p. 1994. pap. 12.95 (*0-8294-0777-4*) Loyola Pr.

Your Wealth Building Years: Financial Planning for 18 to 38 Year Olds. rev. ed. Adriane G. Berg. LC 90-5467. 272p. 1991. pap. 11.95 (*1-55704-116-4*) Newmarket.

Your Wealth-Building Years: Financial Planning for 18-38 Year-Olds. 3rd ed. Adriane G. Berg. LC 94-29154. 272p. 1995. pap. 12.95 (*1-55704-209-8*) Newmarket.

Your Wedding. Betty B. Peterson. 1982. pap. 3.00 (*0-89036-211-4*) Hawkes Pub Inc.

Your Wedding. Bibi Winfield & Annette Spence. 144p. 1987. pap. 9.95 (*0-671-63506-9*, Fireside) S&S Trade.

Your Wedding: A Guide to Getting Married in the Catholic Church. Redemptorist Pastoral Publication Staff. 26p. (Orig.). 1995. pap. 3.95 (*0-89243-803-7*) Liguori Pubns.

Your Wedding: A Planning Guide. Greg Friedman. 128p. 1991. pap. 5.95 (*0-86716-117-5*) St Anthony Mess Pr.

Your Wedding: Making It Perfect. Yetta F. Gruen. 384p. 1986. pap. 9.95 (*0-14-046755-6*, Penguin Bks) Viking Penguin.

Your Wedding Planner. Carol Chapman. 160p. (Orig.). 1993. pap. 11.95 (*0-572-01761-8*, Pub. by W Foulsham UK) Trans-Atl Phila.

Your Wedding Workbook. 6th ed. Natalia M. Belting & James R. Hine. (Illus.). 1993. pap. 12.95 (*0-8134-2953-6*) Interstate.

Your Wife Was Sexually Abused. John Courtright & Sid Rogers. 160p. 1994. pap. 10.99 (*0-310-44291-5*) Zondervan.

Your Will & What to Do about It. Samuel G. Kling. 1980. pap. 7.00 (*0-87980-216-2*) Wilshire.

Your Will Be Done. Mary O'Rourke. 240p. 1994. per., pap. text ed. 14.95 (*0-7872-0191-X*) Kendall-Hunt.

Your Will Be Done on Earth: Eco-Spirituality Activities for 12-15 Year-Olds. Christie L. Jenkins. LC 92-45777. (Illus.). 128p. 1993. 14.95 (*0-89390-254-3*) Resource Pubns.

*__Your Window Looking South.__ Samuel Adame. LC 96-90867. 1997. 21.95 (*0-533-12195-7*) Vantage.

Your Windows 95 Internet Surfboard. Allen L. Wyatt. 1995. pap. 24.99 (*1-56884-721-1*) IDG Bks.

Your Winning Edge: Your Complete Job Search Guide from Self-Assessment to Resumes to Interviews. (Illus.). 40p. (Orig.). (C). 1995. pap. text ed. 25.00 (*0-7881-1985-0*) DIANE Pub.

*__Your Wonderful Heart.__ Cecilia Avalos. (Illus.). 20p. (Orig.). (J). 1995. pap. 3.95 (*1-887578-06-4*) SpanPr.

Your Woodworking Shop. David H. Jacobs. 1994. pap. text ed. 14.95 (*0-07-032403-4*) McGraw.

*__Your Word & Your Work.__ Tim Gilligan. 33p. (Orig.). 1996. pap. 4.00 (*0-9654627-0-6*) Ocala Word.

Your Word in Me: Confessions for Teens. Beverly Tucker. 30p. 1985. pap. 0.99 (*0-89274-353-0*) Harrison Hse.

Your Word Is Fire: The Hasidic Masters on Contemplative Prayer. enl. ed. Ed. by Arthur Green & Barry W. Holtz. Tr. by Barry Holtz. LC 93-25865. 152p. (Orig.). 1993. reprint ed. pap. 14.95 (*1-879045-25-7*) Jewish Lights.

Your Word is Near: Contemporary Christian Prayers. Huub Oosterhuis. Tr. by N. David Smith. LC 68-20848. 164p. reprint ed. pap. 46.80 (*0-8357-4631-3*, 2037560) Bks Demand.

Your Word Is Your Wand. Florence S. Shinn. 7.95 (*0-685-05347-4*) Wehman.

Your Word Is Your Wand. Florence S. Shinn. 1978. reprint ed. pap. 5.95 (*0-87516-259-2*) DeVorss.

Your Words: Public & Private. 2nd ed. Anne Passel. LC 81-40773. (Illus.). 248p. 1982. pap. text ed. 22.00 (*0-8191-1867-2*) U Pr of Amer.

Your Words in Prayer in Time of Illness. Arnaldo Pangrazzi. 72p. (Orig.). 1982. pap. 1.95 (*0-8189-0417-8*) Alba.

Your Work Matters to God. Doug Sherman & William Hendricks. LC 87-62854. 288p. (Orig.). 1987. pap. 14.00 (*0-89109-372-9*) NavPress.

Your Work on the Pulpit Committee. Leonard E. Hill. LC 70-93916. 1970. pap. 3.99 (*0-8054-3502-6*, 4235-02) Broadman.

Your Working Life: A Guide to Getting & Holding a Job. Edwin L. Herr & Roberta Moore. LC 79-28360. Orig. Title: Career Education. (Illus.). 464p. 1980. text ed. 29.96 (*0-07-028342-7*) McGraw.

Your World & Mine. Halbert L. Dunn. 1970. 5.95 (*0-87948-001-7*) Beatty.

*__Your World Explained, 5.__ LC 97-11968. 1997. pap. 18.95 (*0-8050-4875-8*) St Martin.

*__Your World Explained, 6.__ 1997. pap. 18.95 (*0-8050-4876-6*) St Martin.

*__Your World Explained Series, 4 vols.__ Incl. Religions Explained: A Beginner's Guide to World Religions. Anita Ganeri & Marcus Braybrooke. LC 96-42996. (Illus.). 72p. (J). (gr. 4-8). 1997. lib. bdg. 18.95 (*0-8050-4874-X*); Prehistoric Life Explained: A Beginner's Guide to the World of Dinosaurs. Jinny Johnson. (Illus.). 72p. (J). (gr. 4-8). 1996. lib. bdg. 18.95 (*0-8050-4871-5*); Space Explained: A Beginner's Guide to the Universe. Robin Scagell. (Illus.). 72p. (J). (gr. 4-8). 1996. lib. bdg. 18.95 (*0-8050-4872-3*); Earth Explained: A Beginner's Guide to Our Planet. Barbara Taylor. LC 96-41139. (Illus.). 72p. (J). (gr. 4-8). 1997. lib. bdg. 18.95 (*0-8050-4873-1*); 60.64 (*0-8050-5384-0*) TFC Bks NY.

*__Your World Explained Series.__ Variono. (J). 1996. 37.90 (*0-8050-5017-5*) H Holt & Co.

Your World of Pets. Susan McGrath. Ed. by Donald J. Crump. LC 85-7288. (Books for World Explorers Series 6: No. 4). (Illus.). 104p. (J). (gr. 3-8). 1985. lib. bdg. 8.95 (*0-87044-522-7*) Natl Geog.

Your World of Pets. Susan McGrath & National Geographic Staff. Ed. by Donald J. Crump. LC 85-7288. (Books for World Explorers Series 6: No. 4). (Illus.). 104p. (J). (gr. 3-8). 1994. 12.50 (*0-87044-517-0*) Natl Geog.

Your Worldly Possessions: A Complete Guide to Preserving, Passing on & Inheriting Property. Theodore L. Kubicek. 1992. pap. text ed. 17.95 (*0-07-035835-4*) McGraw.

Your Youth Can Be Restored: The Truth about Aging. 2nd rev. ed. Evelyn Chiaverini & Rozella Roberts. Ed. by Bruce S. Holms. 318p. 1994. pap. text ed. 12.95 (*0-9633452-1-4*) Roxanne Unltd.

Your 401(K) Plan: How & Where to Invest. Mark L. Schwanbeck. LC 94-2847. 144p. 1994. per. 16.95 (*0-7863-0124-4*) Irwin Prof Pubng.

Yourcenar Collection: A Descriptive Catalogue. Robert R. Nunn & Edward J. Geary. (Illus.). 1984. pap. 6.00 (*0-916606-07-4*) Bowdoin Coll.

Yourdon Systems Method (YSM) Model-Driven Systems Development: Reference Manual Release 3.0. Yourdon Press Staff. LC 92-44387. (Yourdon Press Computing Ser.). (Illus.). 720p. (C). 1993. text ed. 62.00 (*0-13-045162-2*, Yourdon) P-H.

You're a Better Parent Than You Think: A Guide to Common-Sense Parenting. Raymond N. Guarendi. 240p. 1984. pap. 10.00 (*0-671-76595-7*, Fireside) S&S Trade.

You're a Better Student Than You Think: A Guide to Memory Improvement, Effective Study Skills & Motivation for Academic Success. Moses Adetumbi. LC 91-78006. (Orig.). (C). 1992. pap. 8.95 (*0-9632502-2-1*) Adex Bk.

*__You're a Community Helper.__ Karen Bryant-Mole. LC 97-20058. 1997. lib. bdg. write for info. (*1-57572-184-8*) Heinemann.

*__You're a Dirty Old Man.__ Jerry Cooper. 24p. (Orig.). 1996. pap. 3.95 (*1-889419-09-5*) J Cooper.

You're a Fabulous Fifty! Ed. by Lois L. Kaufman. (Gift Editions Ser.). (Illus.). 64p. 1996. 7.99 (*0-88088-594-7*) Peter Pauper.

You're a Genius - & I Can Prove It! Unlock Your Natural Ability to Achieve Excellence. Kimberly Kassner. Ed. by John Fremont & Cynthia Frank. (Illus.). 250p. (Orig.). 1995. pap. 19.95 (*0-9642818-3-X*) EmpowerMind.

You're a Genius, Blackboard Bear. Martha Alexander. LC 94-11060. (J). 1995. 12.95 (*1-56402-238-2*) Candlewick Pr.

*__You're a Genius, Blackboard Bear.__ Martha Alexander. LC 94-11060. (Illus.). 32p. (J). (ps-2). 1997. reprint ed. pap. 5.99 (*0-7636-0366-X*) Candlewick Pr.

You're a Good Man Charlie Brown. Clark Gesner. 120p. 1995. 40.00 (*0-7935-4970-1*, 00740596) H Leonard.

You're a Good Sport Charlie Brown. Charles M. Schulz. (J). Date not set. pap. 46.80 (*0-590-06079-1*) Scholastic Inc.

You're a Grand Old Flag. R. Eugene Jackson & Mark Rogers. 68p. (Orig.). 1992. pap. 4.50 (*0-88680-373-X*); 15.00 (*0-88680-374-8*) I E Clark.

*__You're a Grownup.__ Karen Bryant-Mole. LC 97-16971. (Pretend Ser.). (J). 1997. write for info. (*1-57572-185-6*) Rigby Interact Libr.

You're a Hero, Daley B.! Jon Blake. LC 91-58725. Orig. Title: Daley B.!. (Illus.). 32p. (J). (ps up). 1994. reprint ed. 13.95 (*1-56402-078-9*); reprint ed. pap. 4.99 (*1-56402-367-2*) Candlewick Pr.

You're a Little Kid with a Big Heart. Bernard Waber. (Illus.). (J). (gr. k-3). 1980. 14.95 (*0-395-29163-1*) HM.

*__You're a Sports Pro.__ Karen Bryant-Mole. LC 97-20057. (Pretend Ser.). (J). 1997. lib. bdg. write for info. (*1-57572-187-2*) Rigby Interact Libr.

*__You're a Star.__ Karen Bryant-Mole. LC 97-20059. (Pretend Ser.). (J). 1997. lib. bdg. write for info. (*1-57572-186-4*) Rigby Interact Libr.

You're a Stepparent...Now What? A Supportive Guide for Stepmothers & Stepfathers. Joseph Cerquone. LC 94-66761. 192p. 1994. pap. 12.95 (*0-88282-129-6*) New Horizon NJ.

You're a Very Special Person. Vivian B. Wood. (Illus.). 38p. (Orig.). (J). (gr. 1). 1988. pap. 5.95 (*0-9621567-0-1*) V B Wood.

You're Aboard Spaceship Earth. Patricia Lauber. LC 94-18704. (Let's-Read-&-Find-Out Science Bk., Stage 2). (Illus.). 32p. (J). (gr. k-4). 1996. 14.95 (*0-06-024407-0*); pap. 4.95 (*0-06-445159-3*, Trophy); lib. bdg. 14.89 (*0-06-024408-9*) HarpC Child Bks.

You're All Alone. Fritz Leiber. 245p. 1990. pap. 3.95 (*0-88184-679-1*) Carroll & Graf.

You're All Grown up, Vancouver. Margaret Evans. Ed. by Diane Brown. 96p. (Orig.). 1987. pap. 2.95 (*0-88839-996-0*) Hancock House.

*__You're All Wet!__ (Golden Look-Look Bks.). (Illus.). 24p. (J). (ps-3). 1996. write for info. (*0-614-19525-X*, 12933, Golden Books) Western Pub.

*__You're Always in My Heart.__ (Tender Hearts Collection). 32p. 1997. 9.99 (*1-881830-45-4*, DS18464) Garborgs.

You're an Orphan, Mollie Brown. Mary Penson. LC 92-23407. (Illus.). 122p. (J). (gr. 5-8). 1993. pap. 9.95 (*0-87565-111-9*) Tex Christian.

You're Beautiful: Quick Reference Self Help Program for All Situations. Al G. Manning & Rachel L. Manning. LC 87-62127. 1987. pap. 7.95 (*0-941698-16-5*) Pan Ishtar.

You're Dead, David Borelli. Susan M. Brown. 155p. (J). (gr. 4-8). 1995. 15.00 (*0-689-31959-2*, Atheneum Bks Young) S&S Childrens.

XYZ

An Asterisk (*) at the beginning of an entry indicates that the title is appearing in BIP for the first time.

*You're Divine, Valentine! Charles M. Schulz. (Festive Peanuts Bks.). (Illus.). 32p. 1997. 4.95 (0-00-649239-8) Collins SF.

You're Entitled! Patrick Mayo. Ed. by Thomas P. Browne. LC 89-80335. 144p. (Orig.). 1989. pap. 9.95 (0-926991-00-0) Linmar Assocs.

You're Fired. Byron A. Dickman. LC 76-73206. 1978. write for info. (0-932984-00-2) Gracelaine.

*You're Fired, Now What? Martin Elkhort. 1997. pap. 14.95 (0-02-861737-1) Macmillan.

*You're Great! 3 Steps to Self-Confidence. Julia Hastings. 144p. 1997. 19.95 (0-9520282-6-3, Pub. by Touchstone Pubns UK) ACCESS Pubs Network.

You're Grounded for Life: And 49 Other Crazy Things That Parents Say. Joey O'Connor. LC 94-31929. (Illus.). 192p. (Orig.). (YA). (gr. 8-11). 1995. pap. 7.99 (0-8007-5549-9) Revell.

You're Grounded Till You're Thirty! What Works & What Doesn't in Parenting Teens Today. Judith E. Craig. 1996. pap. 12.00 (0-688-13196-4) Hearst Bks.

You're Hired. 1991. teacher ed., pap. 7.40 (0-8092-4029-7) Contemp Bks.

You're Hired. McDonnell. 1995. pap. 12.00 (0-671-50053-8) S&S Trade.

You're Hired! Albert C. Van Roden & Thomas D. Bachhuber. LC 81-80571. (Illus.). 80p. 1981. pap. 3.95 (0-89709-025-X) Liberty Pub.

You're Hired! A Complete Guide for Conducting a Successful Job Search. 2nd ed. Asa Fisk. LC 92-61788. 147p. 1992. pap. 14.95 (0-9632926-2-5) Merechip.

You're Hired: Getting the Right Job, No. 2. 1991. pap. 9.86 (0-8092-4030-0) Contemp Bks.

You're Hired! Secrets to Successful Job Interviews. Sharon McDonnell. LC 95-40390. 224p. 1995. 12.95 (0-02-860347-8, Arco) Macmillan Gen Ref.

*You're Hired: The Nuts & Bolts of Job Hunting. Karli & Associates, Inc. Staff. 144p. 1996. per., pap. text ed. 18.00 (0-7872-3232-7) Kendall-Hunt.

You're Hired: Your Career Path, No. 1. 1991. pap. 9.86 (0-8092-4031-9) Contemp Bks.

You're in Business: Building Business English Skills. John T. French. (C). 1984. pap. text ed. 20.00 (0-201-11498-4) Addison-Wesley.

You're in Charge: A Guide to Becoming Your Own Therapist. Virginia M. Satir. LC 82-9104. 221p. 1985. reprint ed. pap. 11.00 (0-87516-552-4) DeVorss.

You're in Charge, but Who's in Control? Janet Hauter. 16p. 1994. pap. text ed. 49.00 (1-57323-032-4) Natl Inst Child Mgmt.

You're in Good Zodiac Company. Lois H. Sargent. 128p. 1972. 6.00 (0-86690-154-X, S1447-014) Am Fed Astrologers.

You're in Love, I Don't Wanna Cry & Other Top Hits: Easy Piano. (Easy Play Ser.). 1991. pap. 7.95 (0-7935-0892-4, 00222536) H Leonard.

You're in Your Mother's Arms: The Life & Legacy of Congressman Phil Burton. Judith Robinson. LC 94-92365. (Illus.). 700p. (Orig.). 1994. pap. 35.00 (0-9643382-0-3) M J Robinson.

You're Invited. St. Anthony of Padua Mother's Guild Staff. Ed. by Judy Hein & Eileen Rathgaber. (Cookbook Ser.). (Illus.). 261p. (Orig.). 1986. spiral bd. 10.00 (0-9616243-0-2) St Anthony Northport.

You're Invited to a Day at the Circus. Sunny Griffin. (Little Landoll Bunny Bunch Ser.). (Illus.). 32p. (J). (ps-3). Date not set. 1.25 (1-56987-081-0) Landoll.

You're Invited to a Storybook Tea Party. Storybook Heirlooms Staff. (Sticker Paperdolls Ser.). (Illus.). 14p. (J). (ps-6). 1994. 9.00 (0-9638614-1-7) Strybook Heirlooms.

You're Invited to Bruce Lansky's Poetry Party. Bruce Lansky. LC 95-51245. (Illus.). (J). 1996. write for info. (0-88166-245-3) Meadowbrook.

*You're Invited to Mary-Kate & Ashley's Christmas Party. Scholastic, Inc. Staff. (J). 1997. 12.95 (0-590-76958-8) Scholastic Inc.

*You're Invited to Mary-Kate & Ashley's Hawaiian Beach Party. (You're Invited to Mary-Kate & Ashley's Ser.). (J). (gr. 2-4). 1997. pap. 3.99 (0-614-29017-1) Scholastic Inc.

You're Invited to Mary-Kate & Ashley's Sleepover Party. Scholastic Staff. 48p. (J). (ps-3). 1996. pap. text ed. 12.95 (0-590-88007-1) Scholastic Inc.

You're It: How to Enjoy a Successful Life by Using a Creative Attitude. Kay Slesinger. 206p. 1992. 19.95 (0-9628690-0-7) K Slesinger Entrps.

*You're Just What I Need. Ruth Krauss. LC 96-48581. (Illus.). (J). 1998. write for info. (0-06-027514-6); lib. bdg. write for info. (0-06-027515-4) HarpC.

You're Killing Yourself When You Don't Have To: A Natural Hygiene Primer. Chet Day. 34p. 1994. pap. 8.50 (1-885194-01-3) Hlth & Beyond.

*You're Making a Scene. Playwrights Canada Press Staff. 1997. pap. text ed. 17.95 (0-88754-489-4, Pub. by Playwrights CN Pr CN) Theatre Comm.

*You're My Angel. Carl Finley. 144p. (Orig.). 1997. mass mkt. 4.99 (1-55197-774-5, Pub. by Comnwlth Pub CN) Partners Pubs Grp.

You're My Best Friend, Lord: Story Devotions for Girls. Lois W. Johnson. LC 76-3866. (Young Reader's Ser.). 112p. (Orig.). (J). (gr. 4-7). 1976. pap. 5.99 (0-8066-1541-9, 10-7490, Augsburg) Augsburg Fortress.

You're My Friend. Illus. by Ken Skalski. (Puzzle Place Board Bks.). 16p. (J). (ps). 1996. bds. 4.50 (0-448-41296-9, G&D) Putnam Pub Group.

You're My Friend Be Claus. Susan Pierce & Jean Schick-Jacobowitz. (Charming Petites Ser.). (Illus.). 64p. 1996. 4.95 (0-88088-803-2) Peter Pauper.

You're My Nikki. Phyllis R. Eisenberg. (Illus.). 32p. (J). (ps-3). 1995. pap. 5.99 (0-14-055463-7) Puffin Bks.

You're Never Alone. Marie Shropshire. LC 95-44475. 1996. pap. 8.99 (1-56507-426-2) Harvest Hse.

You're Never Alone: The Story of Thomas Merton. David R. Collins. LC 96-6880. (Weaver Bks.). 64p. (YA). (gr. 6-9). 1996. pap. 2.95 (0-8198-8708-0) Pauline Bks.

You're Never over the Hill. June E. Weikel. 112p. 1996. mass mkt. 4.99 (1-55197-000-7, Pub. by Comnwlth Pub CN) Partners Pubs Grp.

You're Never Too Old for Nuts & Berries. Garry B. Trudeau. LC 76-6751. 128p. 1976. pap. 3.95 (0-03-018216-6, Owl) H Holt & Co.

You're Never Too Old to Laugh. Paul B. Baron. (Orig.). pap. write for info. (0-936936-53-3) Ctr Busn Info.

*You're Never Too Old to Laugh. Larry Wilde. 160p. 1997. mass mkt. 4.99 (0-7860-0431-2, Pinncle Kensgtn) Kensgtn Pub Corp.

You're No Good to Me Dead: Behind Japanese Lines in the Philippines. Bobert Stahl. LC 95-11424. (Naval Institute Special Warfare Ser.). (Illus.). 184p. 1995. 28.95 (1-55750-793-7) Naval Inst Pr.

You're No Spring Chicken. Ed Fischer. (Illus.). 126p. (Orig.). 1995. pap. 6.95 (0-9615394-8-8) Skandisk.

You're Not a Kid Anymore. Jeff Foxworthy. LC 93-79656. 1993. pap. 6.95 (1-56352-102-4) Longstreet Pr Inc.

You're Not Alone. Ruth L. Frazier. 151p. (YA). 1995. pap. text ed. 10.95 (0-9649881-5-1) Frazier Bks.

*You're Not Alone, Vol. 1. Wong. Date not set. pap. text ed. write for info. (0-312-11973-9) St Martin.

You're Not Alone: A Planning Guide for Families. Liz McKinney. 63p. (Orig.). 1990. pap. 5.00 (1-877592-17-X) GSH&MC.

You're Not Alone: With the Personal Stories of 38 Amputees. John Sabolich. Ed. by Carol Sorrels & Linda Adlof. (Illus.). 358p. (Orig.). 1993. 14.95 (0-9637331-2-5) Sabolich Pros & Res.

You're Not Alone: With the Personal Stories of 38 Amputees. John Sabolich. Ed. by Carol Yandell & Linda Adlof. (Illus.). 358p. (Orig.). 1993. pap. 9.95 (0-9637331-1-7); lib. bdg. 6.50 (0-9637331-0-9) Sabolich Pros & Res.

You're Not Alone, Charlie Brown. Charles M. Schulz. (Illus.). 128p. (Orig.). 1992. mass mkt. 3.99 (0-449-22022-2) Fawcett.

You're Not Alone When You're Alone. Tucker Mitchell. LC 92-70981. (Illus.). 130p. (J). 1992. 12.95 (1-55523-522-0) Winston-Derek.

*You're Not As Good As You Think You Are: A Demotivational Guide. Chris Gudgeon. 1997. pap. text ed. 10.95 (1-55152-040-0, Pub. by Arsenal Pulp CN) LPC InBook.

*You're Not Forgotten. Marlyn M. Singer. LC 96-90423. (Orig.). 1997. pap. 8.95 (0-533-12042-X) Vantage.

You're Not Listening. Sharaf N. Rehman. 80p. (Orig.). (YA). pap. 7.95 (1-883120-06-3) Northern St U.

You're Not My Best Friend Anymore. Charlotte Pomerantz. LC 93-42595. (J). 1998. pap. 14.99 (0-8037-1559-5); pap. 14.89 (0-8037-1560-9) Dial Bks Young.

*You're Not Old until You're Ninety: Best to Be Prepared, However. Rebecca H. Latimer. LC 97-6720. 208p. 1997. pap. 11.00 (1-57733-009-9, Pelican Pond) B Dolphin Pub.

You're Not Overdrawn - Just Underdeposited. Beverlee Kelley. 1993. pap. 12.95 (1-882180-01-1) Griffin CA.

You're Not That Body. Bir K. Swami. (Illus.). 64p. (Orig.). pap. 2.00 (0-944969-01-1) ISKCON NC.

You're Not Too Old to Win at Tennis. Edward B. Gellert. LC 84-71251. (Illus.). 64p. (Orig.). 1984. pap. 6.95 (0-9613520-0-0) CIPRA.

*You're Not What I Expected: Learning to Love the Opposite Sex. Polly Young-Eisendrath. 416p. 1997. reprint ed. pap. 15.95 (0-88064-187-8) Fromm Intl Pub.

You're OK, It's Just a Bruise: A Doctor's Sideline Secrets about Pro Football's Most... Rob Huizenga. 1995. pap. 12.95 (0-312-13627-7) St Martin.

You're OK-The World's All Wrong. C. W. Dalton. Ed. by Sara Herschler & L. D. Garland. LC 84-70707. 542p. 1985. 17.95 (0-916969-00-2) Big Blue Bks.

You're OK, Your Cat's OK. Jill Caravan. 1992. 12.98 (1-55521-816-4) Bk Sales Inc.

You're OK, Your Dog's OK. Jill Caravan. 1992. 12.98 (1-55521-817-2) Bk Sales Inc.

*You're On. Galbraith. 1991. pap. text ed. write for info. (0-582-86991-9, Pub. by Longman UK) Longman.

You're On! A Speaker's Handbook Plus 1000 Jokes & Quips. Theodore W. Hatlen. 300p. 1993. pap. text ed. 12.50 (0-9635205-1-2) Dorcas Pr.

You're on... Teaching Assertiveness & Communication Skills. Honey Loring & Jeremy Birch. (Illus.). 85p. (Orig.). 1984. pap. 10.95 (0-9613102-0-0) StressPress.

You're on Air. Graham Andrews. 156p. (C). 1994. pap. 19.95 (0-86819-404-2) Aubrey Bks.

You're on the Air with Mike Miller. Mike Miller. LC 74-78647. (Illus.). 155p. (Orig.). 1975. pap. 3.95 (0-88435-001-0) Chateau Pub.

*You're One in a Million. R. W. Schambach. 44p. 1996. pap. 2.00 (1-888361-12-3) Power Publns.

You're Only Human Once. Grace Moore. Ed. by Andrew Farkas. LC 76-29958. (Opera Biographies Ser.). (Illus.). 1977. reprint ed. lib. bdg. 25.95 (0-405-09698-4) Ayer.

You're Only Old Once! Dr. Seuss. LC 85-20495. (Illus.). 48p. 1986. 18.00 (0-394-55190-7) Random.

*You're Our New Mascot, Chuck! Charles M. Schulz. (Peanuts Ser.). (Illus.). 32p. (J). (ps-3). 1997. 3.25 (0-694-00957-1, Festival) HarpC Child Bks.

*You're Out & Youre Ugly Too. Merill. Date not set. write for info. (0-312-18237-6) St Martin.

You're Out of Your Mind. Charles M. Schulz. (Illus.). 128p. 1993. pap. 7.95 (0-8050-2890-0) H Holt & Co.

You're over the Hill, Honey. Nina B. Lovel. 18p. 1991. 10.95 (0-685-71232-X) About You.

You're Pregnant! A Guide for the Longest Nine Months of Your Life. Kathryn Hammer. (Illus.). 192p. 1995. pap. 8.95 (0-8092-3472-6) Contemp Bks.

You're Pregnant & Your Dreams Are Driving You Crazy: How the Dream Worlds of Pregnancy Can Help You Bond with Your Baby. Eileen Stukane. 1997. pap. text ed. 12.95 (1-886449-19-8) Barrytown Ltd.

*You're Safe Now, Waterdog. Richard Edwards. (Illus.). 32p. (J). (ps-3). 1997. pap. 14.99 (0-670-87385-3, Viking) Viking Penguin.

*You're Sittin' on Boomey! The Best of Ludlow Porch. Ludlow Porch. 1997. 18.95 (1-56352-436-8) Longstreet Pr Inc.

You're Smokin' Now, Mr. Butts! A Doonesbury Book. Garry B. Trudeau. (Illus.). 96p. (Orig.). 1990. pap. 7.95 (0-8362-1814-0) Andrews & McMeel.

*You're So Beautiful. Fitzgerald. Date not set. pap. 11.95 (0-312-17069-6) St Martin.

You're So Beautiful: Stories. Eileen FitzGerald. LC 96-20054. 198p. 1996. 21.95 (0-312-14530-6) St Martin.

You're So Clever. Bronwen Scarffe. LC 92-34339. (Voyages Ser.). (Illus.). (J). 1993. 3.75 (0-383-03669-0) SRA McGraw.

You're So Fine, I'd Drink a Tub of Your Bathwater: Over 500 No-Fail Pick-Up Lines That Work on the Bus, in the Bar & in the Neighborhood Store. Stephan Dweck & Monteria Ivey. LC 96-20116. 256p. 1997. pap. 9.95 (0-7868-8202-6) Hyperion.

You're Somebody Special to God. Jerry Savelle. (Mini-Bks.). 32p. 1994. pap. 0.99 (0-89274-687-4, HH-687) Harrison Hse.

You're Someone Special. 2nd ed. Bruce S. Narramore. 174p. 1980. pap. 8.99 (0-310-30331-1, 11038P) Zondervan.

You're Special, Too. Alexandra Parsons. LC 96-16323. (Life Education Ser.). (J). 1997. lib. bdg. 17.50 (0-531-14422-4) Watts.

You're Still a Doctor, Doctor! large type ed. Robert Clifford. 224p. 1992. 25.99 (0-7089-2600-2) Ulverscroft.

You're the Apple of My Face. 2nd ed. Barry Rudner. 30p. (Orig.). (J). (gr. k-6). 1995. pap. 4.95 (0-9642206-0-1) Windword Pr.

You're the Apple of My Face, 20 bks., Set. 2nd ed. Barry Rudner. (Illus.). 30p. (Orig.). (J). (gr. k-6). 1995. pap. 49.60 (0-9642206-1-X) Windword Pr.

You're the Best! Illus. by Jenny Faw. (Charming Petites Ser.). 80p. 1994. 4.95 (0-88088-788-5) Peter Pauper.

You're the Best. 2nd rev. ed. Donna Martin. (Love 'n Hug Notes Ser.). (Illus.). 10p. (J). 1993. write for info. (1-879127-43-1) Lighten Up Enter.

You're the Best, Jesse Bear. Carlstrom. (J). 1998. 16.00 (0-689-80701-5) S&S Childrens.

You're the Boss. Edward J. Flynn. LC 82-24156. x, 244p. 1983. reprint ed. text ed. 59.75 (0-313-23627-5, FLYB, Greenwood Pr) Greenwood.

You're the Boss: A Guide to Managing People with Understanding & Effectiveness. Natasha Josefowitz. LC 84-15332. 272p. (Orig.). 1985. pap. 10.99 (0-446-37744-9) Warner Bks.

You're the Boss, Baby Duck. Amy Hest. LC 96-46640. (Illus.). 32p. (J). (ps up). 1997. 16.99 (1-56402-667-1) Candlewick Pr.

You're the Detective! Twenty-Four Solve-Them-Yourself Picture Mysteries. Lawrence Treat. LC 82-49346. (Illus.). 80p. (Orig.). (J). (gr. 3-6). 1983. pap. 7.95 (0-87923-478-4) Godine.

You're the Greatest Charlie Brown. (J). Date not set. pap. 29.25 (0-590-39523-8) Scholastic Inc.

You're the Greatest Charlie Brown. (J). Date not set. pap. 1.95 (0-590-72029-5) Scholastic Inc.

You're the Guest of Honor. Charles M. Schulz. (Illus.). 128p. 1993. pap. 6.95 (0-8050-2892-7) H Holt & Co.

You're the Judge! How to Understand Sports, Torts, & Courts. John M. Fotiades. Ed. by Marilyn Ross & Clyde McVicar. (Illus.). 1989. 24.95 (0-926565-00-1); pap. 19.95 (0-926565-01-X) Edgeworth & North.

You're the Jury: Solve Twelve Real-Life Court Cases along with the Juries Who Decided Them. Norbert Ehrenfreund & Lawrence Treat. (Illus.). 224p. 1992. pap. 9.95 (0-8050-1951-0, Owl) H Holt & Co.

You're the Professor What Next? Ideas & Resources for Preparing College Teachers. Ed. by Bettye A. Case. (Notes Ser.: Vol. 35). 362p. 1994. pap. 29.95 (0-88385-091-5, NTE-35) Math Assn.

You're the Scaredy-Cat. Mercer Mayer. (Illus.). 40p. (J). 1991. reprint ed. pap. 5.95 (1-879920-01-8) Rain Bird Prods.

You're the Top: Cole Porter in the 1930s. Robert Kimball et al. (Illus.). 112p. 1992. pap. 49.95 incl. cd-rom (0-87195-089-8); pap. 42.95 incl. audio (0-87195-088-X) Ind Hist Soc.

*You're the Tops Pops. Charles Schulz. (Peanuts Program Ser.). 1997. 7.95 (0-06-757447-5) HarpC.

You're the Tutor. National Commission on Resources for Youth. 66p. 1970. pap. 2.00 (0-912041-03-X) Natl Comm Res Youth.

You're Too Sweet. John P. Connelly. (J). (gr. 4-9). 1968. 9.95 (0-8392-1173-2) Astor-Honor.

You're under Arrest, I'm Not Kidding: The Trials & Tribulations of a Reluctant Cop. Don Parker. 243p. 1990. reprint ed. pap. 9.95 (0-9620073-1-5) Caroldon Bks.

You're Under Arrest, Ms. Wiz. Terence Blacker. (Arch Bks.). (Illus.). 64p. (J). (gr. 2-5). 1990. pap. 2.95 (0-8120-4499-1) Barron.

You're Weird, Sir! Charles M. Schulz. (Peanuts Classics Ser.). 128p. 1993. pap. 7.95 (0-8050-1868-9) H Holt & Co.

*You're Welcome! Harkess & Wherly. 1991. student ed., pap. text ed. write for info. (0-17-556246-6) Addison-Wesley.

You're What?! Anne Eames. (Desire Ser.). 1996. mass mkt. 3.50 (0-373-76025-6, 1-76025-5) Silhouette.

*You're What You Write. Hartford Huntington. Date not set. write for info. (0-688-04844-7) Morrow.

You're Working Too Hard to Make the Sale! More Than 100 Insider Tools to Sell Faster & Easier! William T. Brooks & Tom Travisano. LC 94-42726. 272p. 1995. text ed. 22.95 (0-7863-0395-6) Irwin Prof Pubng.

You're You, Charlie Brown. Charles M. Schulz. 1968. pap. 1.00 (0-03-073000-7, Owl) H Holt & Co.

Yourowquains, A Wyandot Indian Queen: The Story of Caty Sage. Bill Bland. Ed. by Rhonda Catron. (Illus.). 288p. 1992. 19.95 (0-9634133-0-9) Hist Pubns VA.

Yours Always: A Holocaust Love Story. Kitty Zilversmit. LC 95-46767. (Occasional Publications of the Department of Near Eastern Studies & the Program of Jewish Studies, Cornell University: Vol. 2). 1995. 25.00 (1-883053-21-8) CDL Pr.

Yours for a Day. Francine Pascal. (Sweet Valley Twins Ser.: No. 76). 144p. (J). (gr. 4-7). 1994. pap. 3.50 (0-553-48096-0) Bantam.

Yours for Health: The Life & Times of Herbert M. Shelton. Jean A. Oswald. (Illus.). 168p. (Orig.). 1989. pap. 9.95 (0-9620490-0-X) Franklin Bks.

Yours for the Asking: A Cornucopia of Free Information. Ed. by David Corn & Randi Vladimer. 102p. 1981. 5.00 (0-936758-02-3) Ctr Responsive Law.

Yours for the Asking (Usted Tambien Podra Disfrutar De Ella) Ana Diosdado. Ed. by Martha T. Halsey. Tr. by Patricia W. O'Connor from SPA. LC 94-72547. (Contemporary Spanish Plays Ser.: Vol. 7). x, 170p. 1995. pap. 6.00 (0-9631212-6-X) Estreno.

Yours for the Revolution: The Appeal to Reason, 1895-1922. John Graham. LC 89-35721. (Illus.). 344p. 1990. reprint ed. pap. 98.10 (0-7837-8879-7, 2049590) Bks Demand.

Yours for the Taking: Getting More of Your Share of Desert Gold! Ronald S. Wielgus. (Illus.). 128p. (Orig.). 1994. pap. 18.95 (0-9635601-1-5) R S Wielgus.

Yours for the Union! The Making of the South African Working Class. Baruch Hirson. LC 89-35870. (Illus.). 256p. (C). 1989. pap. 17.50 (0-86232-370-3, Pub. by Zed Bks Ltd UK); text ed. 55.00 (0-86232-369-X, Pub. by Zed Bks Ltd UK) Humanities.

Yours Forever. Robin J. Gunn. (Christy Miller Ser.: Vol. 3). 160p. (Orig.). (YA). (gr. 7-11). 1990. pap. 5.99 (0-929608-90-9) Focus Family.

Yours If You Ask. Susan P. Schutz. LC 78-56321. (Illus.). 1978. 16.95 (0-88396-028-1) Blue Mtn Pr CO.

Your's in Love: The Birmingham Civil War Letters. Zoe Von Ende Lappin. (Illus.). 258p. 1989. pap. 15.00 (0-940133-20-2) Kinseeker Pubns.

Yours in Struggle: Three Feminist Perspectives on Anti-Semitism & Racism. Elly Bulkin et al. LC 88-24411. 232p. 1984. pap. 11.95 (0-932379-53-2) Firebrand Bks.

*Yours Is a Precious Witness: Memoirs of Jews & Catholics in Wartime Italy. Margherita Marchione. LC 96-35039. (Stimulus Bks.). (Illus.). 1997. text ed. 14.95 (0-8091-0485-7) Paulist Pr.

Yours Is the Power. Florence Widutis. LC 57-9315. 1978. reprint ed. pap. 4.95 (0-87516-245-2) DeVorss.

Yours, Isaac Asimov: A Life in Letters. Stanley Asimov. 384p. 1996. pap. 12.95 (0-385-47624-8) Doubleday.

Yours, Mine & Ours. Jacqueline Diamond. (American Romance Ser.). 1996. mass mkt. 3.50 (0-373-16615-X, 1-16615-6) Harlequin Bks.

Yours, Mine & Ours: Equal Opportunities, an Unexpected Family, Gathering Place. Penny Jordan et al. 1997. mass mkt. 5.99 (0-373-20133-8, 1-20133-4) Harlequin Bks.

Yours, Mine, & Ours: How Families Change When Remarried Parents Have a Child Together. Anne C. Bernstein. 1990. pap. 10.95 (0-393-30668-2) Norton.

*Yours, Mine & We Decided Not to Have Ours. Cecelia Garceau. LC 97-60464. 128p. (Orig.). 1997. pap. 15.00 (1-57921-018-X) WinePress Pub.

Yours or Mine. Ezra H. Heywood. 1972. 59.95 (0-8490-1345-3) Gordon Pr.

Yours, Plum. P. G. Wodehouse. Ed. by Frances Donaldson. (Letters of P. G. Wodehouse in Translation Ser.). (Illus.). 257p. 1995. 22.95 (0-87008-130-6) JAS Heineman.

Yours Sincerely, Ann W. Shephard (Letters from a College Dean) Ed. by Ann Squires. 1978. pap. 6.00 (0-911518-48-7) Touchstone Oregon.

Yours 'til Banana Splits. Joanna Cole & Stephanie Calmenson. LC 94-10654. (Illus.). 64p. (J). (gr. 2 up). 1995. pap. 6.95 (0-688-14019-X) Morrow.

Yours 'Till Banana Splits: 201 Autograph Rhymes. Joanna Cole et al. LC 94-10654. (Illus.). 64p. (J). (gr. 2 up). 1995. 15.00 (0-688-13185-9, Morrow Junior); lib. bdg. 14.93 (0-688-13186-7, Morrow Junior) Morrow.

*Yours Till Niagara Falls, Abbey. Jane O'Connor. LC 79-19782. (Illus.). 128p. (Orig.). (J). (gr. 3-7). 1997. pap. 5.95 (0-698-11597-X, Paperstar) Putnam Pub Group.

Yours Till Niagara Falls, Abbey see Best-Selling Apples

Yours to Love: Words of Wisdom from Your New Baby. Marie Shropshire. LC 96-41229. (Illus.). 68p. (Orig.). 1996. pap. 9.95 (0-7880-0718-1) CSS OH.

*Yours to Love: Words of Wisdom from Your New Baby. Marie Shropshire. (Illus.). 1996. 19.95 (0-7880-0857-9) CSS OH.

Yours to Reason Why: Decision in Battle. William Seymour. (Quality Paperbacks Ser.). (Illus.). 368p. 1983. reprint ed. pap. 13.95 (0-306-80199-X) Da Capo.

Yours Truly. Sharon Harlow. 1994. mass mkt. 4.99 (0-7865-0001-8) Diamond.

Yours Truly, from Hell. Terrence L. Smith. 384p. 1987. 17.95 (0-317-53573-0) St Martin.

*Yours Truly Goldilocks. Alma F. Ada. LC 97-10696. (Illus.). (J). 1998. 17.00 (0-689-81608-1, Atheneum S&S) S&S Trade.

XYZ

An Asterisk (*) at the beginning of an entry indicates that the title is appearing in BIP for the first time.

Yours Truly, Harvey Donaldson. Harvey Donaldson. Ed. by Dave Wolfe. 271p. 1981. text ed. 19.50 (*0-935632-01-8*) Wolfe Pub Co.

Yours Truly, King Arthur: How Medieval People Wrote... & How You Can, Too. Marc Drogin. LC 79-66643. (Illus.). 95p. 1983. pap. 9.95 (*0-8008-8766-2*) Taplinger.

***Youth.** Eleanor C. Goldstein. (Social Issues Resources Ser.: Vol. 5). 1996. 19.00 (*0-89777-200-8*) Sirs Inc.

Youth. Garrison Keillor. 1995. pap. 11.00 (*1-56511-111-7*) Viking Penguin.

Youth. LC 75-133777. (Tudor Facsimile Texts. Old English Plays Ser.: No. 19). reprint ed. 49.50 (*0-404-53319-1*) AMS Pr.

Youth, Vol. 3, incl. 1986-1990 Suppls. Ed. by Eleanor C. Goldstein. (Social Issues Resources Ser.). 1991. Incl. 1986-1990 Supplements. 95.00 (*0-89777-086-2*) Sirs Inc.

Youth: A Narrative. Joseph Conrad. 1976. 19.95 (*0-8488-0464-3*) Amereon Ltd.

Youth: Change & Challenge - India. Dhurjati Mukherjee. 1977. 7.50 (*0-8364-0481-5*) S Asia.

Youth: Extracts from the Writings of Baha'u'llah, Abdu'l-Baha & Shoghi Effendi. Universal House of Justice Staff. 32p. 1995. pap. 3.95 (*0-909991-94-4*) Bahai.

Youth: Open the Door. Eloise Mellor. 1969. pap. 3.00 (*0-87516-114-6*) DeVorss.

Youth: Position & Oppositions. Shane Blackman. 288p. 1995. 59.95 (*1-85628-637-1*, Pub. by Avebury Pub UK) Ashgate Pub Co.

Youth: Problems & Approaches. Ed. by S. J. Shamsie. LC 72-79353. 398p. reprint ed. pap. 113.50 (*0-317-09751-2*, 2014579) Bks Demand.

Youth: Transition to Adulthood. James S. Coleman et al. LC 73-92757. viii, 202p. 1986. reprint ed. pap. text ed. 16.00 (*0-226-11343-4*, Midway Reprint) U Ch Pr.

Youth: Unemployment, Identity & Policy. C. H. Verhaar. LC 96-20427. 384p. 1997. 76.95 (*1-85972-216-4*, Pub. by Avebury Pub UK) Ashgate Pub Co.

Youth Vol. 4: (Incl. 1991-94 Supplements) Ed. by Eleanor C. Goldstein. (Social Issues Resources Ser.). 1995. 95.00 (*0-89777-168-0*) Sirs Inc.

Youth Aflame. Winkie Pratney. LC 82-74507. 448p. (Orig.). 1983. pap. 9.99 (*0-87123-659-1*) Bethany Hse.

Youth, AIDS, & Sexually Transmitted Diseases. Doreen A. Rosenthal et al. LC 96-11013. (Adolescence & Society Ser.). 192p. (C). 1996. pap. 16.95 (*0-415-10633-8*); text ed. 55.00 (*0-415-10632-X*) Routledge.

Youth, Alcohol, & Social Policy. Ed. by Howard T. Blane & M. E. Chafetz. LC 79-9094. (Illus.). 450p. 1979. 65.00 (*0-306-40253-X*, Plenum Pr) Plenum.

Youth & Adult: The Shared Journey Toward Wholeness. Robert Cardelle. LC 88-11699. 1989. pap. 19.95 (*0-89876-155-7*) Gardner Pr.

Youth & Age in American Literature: The Rhetoric of Old Men in the Mathers, Franklin, Adams, Cooper, Hawthorne, Melville, & James. Marco Portales. (American University Studies: American Literature: Ser. XXIV, Vol. 20). 169p. (C). 1990. text ed. 35.00 (*0-8204-1181-7*) P Lang Pubng.

Youth & Alcohol: A National Survey, Drinking Habits, Access, Attitudes, & Knowledge. (Illus.). 44p. (Orig.). (C). 1995. reprint ed. pap. text ed. 25.00 (*0-7881-2412-9*) DIANE Pub.

Youth & America's Future: A Special Report on Youth, Embodying Research Analysis & Recommendations, 2 vols., Set. Ed. by Margaret W. Young. 1825p. 1989. 95.00 (*1-55888-814-4*) Omnigraphics Inc.

Youth & Authority: Formative Experiences in England 1560-1640. Paul Griffiths. LC 95-40416. (Illus.). 472p. (C). 1996. 90.00 (*0-19-820475-2*) OUP.

Youth & Drugs. Francis H. Wise. (Illus.). (YA). (gr. 10 up). 4.95 (*0-8096-1781-1*) Wise Pub.

Youth & Drugs: Proceedings of the WHO Scientific Group, Geneva, 1971. WHO Staff. (Technical Report Ser.: No. 516). 1973. pap. text ed. 6.00 (*92-4-120516-4*, 1100516) World Health.

Youth & Drugs: Society's Mixed Messages. Ed. by Hank Resnik. 174p. (Orig.). (C). 1994. pap. text ed. 30.00 (*0-7881-0296-6*) DIANE Pub.

Youth & Drugs in the Community. Ed. by M. A. Gocek. 110p. 1989. 12.95 (*0-912526-48-3*) Lib Res.

Youth & Employment in Modern Britain. Ken Roberts. (Oxford Modern Britain Ser.). (Illus.). 144p. 1995. text ed. 49.95 (*0-19-827965-5*) OUP.

Youth & Exploitation: A Process Leading to Running Away, Violence, Substance Abuse & Suicide. Alan W. McEvoy & Edsel Erickson. 1990. pap. 12.95 (*1-55691-042-8*, 428) Learning Pubns.

Youth & HIV: It's up to You & Me: A Reference Guide for Service Providers. Mary Rathlev & Martha Riley. (YA). 1994. pap. 7.95 (*0-9634295-0-7*) Childs Hosp.

Youth & Inequality. Inge Bates & George Riseborough. LC 92-43088. 1993. pap. 32.50 (*0-335-15695-9*, Open Univ Pr) Taylor & Francis.

Youth & Leisure. Kenneth Roberts. (Leisure & Recreation Studies: No. 3). 240p. 1985. pap. text ed. 18.95 (*0-04-301204-3*) Routledge Chapman & Hall.

Youth & Life. Randolph Bourne. 1972. 59.95 (*0-8490-1346-1*) Gordon Pr.

Youth & Life. Randolph S. Bourne. LC 67-23184. (Essay Index Reprint Ser.). 1977. 23.95 (*0-8369-0229-7*) Ayer.

Youth & Other Stories. Mori Ogai. Ed. by J. Thomas Rimer. LC 93-38737. (SHAPS Library of Translations). 576p. 1994. text ed. 38.00 (*0-8248-1600-5*) UH Pr.

Youth & Revolution in the 1790s: Letters of William Pattisson, Thomas Amyot & Henry Crabb Robinson. Penelope Corfield & Chris Evans. (Illus.). 192p. 1996. 37.95 (*0-7509-1163-8*, Pub. by Sutton Pubng UK) Bks Intl VA.

Youth & Sex: Pleasure & Responsibility. 2nd ed. Gordon D. Jensen. LC 72-77121. (Illus.). 1979. 28.95 (*0-911012-99-0*) Nelson-Hall.

Youth & Sexuality. John T. Chirban & Dean Talagan. 52p. 1984. pap. 1.00 (*0-917653-10-6*) Holy Cross Orthodox.

Youth & Social Change. Ed. by Morton Levitt & Ben Rubenstein. LC 73-157414. 420p. reprint ed. pap. 119.70 (*0-317-52059-8*, 2027499) Bks Demand.

***Youth & Social Justice: Toward the Twenty-First Century.** Nanette J. Davis. 1997. pap. 19.95 (*0-8133-2501-3*) Westview.

***Youth & Social Justice: Toward the Twenty-First Century.** Nanette J. Davis Nanette. 1997. 59.00 (*0-8133-2500-5*) Westview.

Youth & Society: Educational Environment in India. Brij B. Khare. 1986. 18.00 (*0-317-53512-9*, Pub. by Firma KLM II) S Asia.

Youth & Students. Matthew A. Kraljic. 1996. lib. bdg. 60.00 (*0-87436-846-4*) ABC-CLIO.

Youth & the Condition of England: Images of Adolescent Conflict. John Davis. Ed. by Paul E. Rock & David Downes. LC 89-18550. (Conflict & Change in Britain - A New Audit Ser.). 240p. (C). 1990. pap. 25.00 (*0-485-80101-9*, Pub. by Athlone Pr UK); text ed. 50.00 (*0-485-80001-2*, Pub. by Athlone Pr UK) Humanities.

Youth & the End of the Tether. Joseph Conrad. 176p. 1976. pap. 3.95 (*0-14-004055-2*, Penguin Bks) Viking Penguin.

Youth & the Labor Market: Analyses from the National Longitudinal Survey. Ed. by Michael E. Borus. LC 84-2367. 295p. 1984. text ed. 24.00 (*0-88099-015-5*); pap. text ed. 14.00 (*0-88099-016-3*) W E Upjohn.

Youth & the Law. 79p. (Orig.). (C). 1995. pap. text ed. 20.00 (*0-7881-1890-0*) DIANE Pub.

Youth & Work: What We Know; What We Don't Know; What We Need to Know. Ivan Charner & Bryna S. Fraser. 82p. 1987. 10.00 (*0-86510-058-6*) Natl Inst Work.

Youth Apprenticeship American Style: A Strategy for Expanding School & Career Opportunities. 44p. 1990. pap. 10.00 (*1-887410-74-0*) Jobs for Future.

Youth As Learners. Leroy Kettinger. (Christian Education Ministries Ser.). 96p. 1983. pap. 3.95 (*0-89367-086-3*) Light & Life Comm.

***Youth at Risk.** Ed. by Bertha Cato et al. 140p. (Orig.). 1994. pap. text ed. 31.00 (*0-697-25752-5*, 300-10005) AAHPERD.

Youth at Risk: A Resource for Counselors, Teachers, & Parents. 2nd ed. Ed. by David Capuzzi & Douglas R. Gross. 416p. 1996. pap. 33.95 (*1-55620-151-6*, 72622) Am Coun Assn.

Youth at Work: An International Survey. Ed. by Beatrice G. Reubens. LC 83-8631. (Conservation of Human Resources Ser.: No. 22). 366p. (C). 1983. text ed. 76.50 (*0-86598-101-9*) Rowman.

Youth Automation. Leigou. LC 97-19070. (IFAC Postprint Ser.). 1997. pap. write for info. (*0-08-042369-8*, Pergamon Pr) Elsevier.

***Youth Baseball: A Coach's & Parents Guide.** Wendell Kim & Salley T. Rains. 1997. 15.00 (*1-57167-097-1*) Sagamore Pub.

Youth Baseball: A Complete Handbook. Ed. by Michael A. Clark et al. (Illus.). 528p. (Orig.). 1993. pap. 30.00 (*1-884125-01-8*) Cooper Pubng.

Youth Baseball: The Guide for Coaches & Parents. 2nd rev. ed. John P. McCarthy, Jr. LC 95-38878. (Coaching Kids Ser.). (Illus.). 176p. 1996. pap. 12.99 (*1-55870-398-5*, Betrwy Bks) F & W Pubns Inc.

Youth Baseball IV: Training & Conditioning. Ysi. 1992. text ed. write for info. (*0-697-19199-0*) Irwin Prof Pubng.

Youth Basketball: A Complete Handbook. Ed. by Karen Garchow & Amy Dickinson. LC 88-43254. (Illus.). 391p. 1992. reprint ed. pap. 30.00 (*1-884125-44-1*) Cooper Pubng.

Youth Basketball: Complete Handbook. Vern Seefeldt. 391p. (C). 1992. Section III, Individual Basketball Techniques. text ed. write for info. (*0-697-15187-5*); Section V, Methods for Effective Coaching. text ed. write for info. (*0-697-15189-1*); Section VI, Sports Medicine & Training. text ed. write for info. (*0-697-15190-5*) Brown & Benchmark.

Youth Basketball: Complete Handbook, Section I, Organizing for the Season. Vern Seefeldt. 391p. (C). 1992. write for info. (*0-697-15185-9*) Brown & Benchmark.

Youth Basketball: Complete Handbook, Section II, Rules of Play. Vern Seefeldt. 391p. (C). 1992. write for info. (*0-697-15186-7*) Brown & Benchmark.

Youth Basketball: The Guide for Coaches & Parents. John P. McCarthy, Jr. (Coaching Kids Ser.). (Illus.). 176p. 1996. pap. 12.99 (*1-55870-414-0*, Betrwy Bks) F & W Pubns Inc.

Youth Builder: A Resource for Relational Youth Ministry. Jim Burns. LC 87-81664. 240p. (Orig.). 1988. 16.99 (*0-89081-576-3*) Harvest Hse.

***Youth Charter: How Communities Can Work Together to Raise the Standards for All Our Children.** William Damon. LC 97-23786. 1997. 24.00 (*0-684-82995-9*) Free Pr.

Youth Corps Project Director. Jack Rudman. (Career Examination Ser.: C-2208). 1994. pap. 39.95 (*0-8373-2208-1*) Nat Learn.

Youth Corps Recruiter. Jack Rudman. (Career Examination Ser.: C-1537). 1994. pap. 29.95 (*0-8373-1537-9*) Nat Learn.

Youth Counselor. Jack Rudman. (Career Examination Ser.: C-2906). 1994. pap. 29.95 (*0-8373-2906-X*) Nat Learn.

Youth, Creators of the Future. Omraam M. Aivanhov. (Izvor Collection: No. 233). 194p. 1993. pap. 8.95 (*1-895978-01-7*) Prosveta USA.

Youth Crime & Juvenile Justice in California: A Report to the Legislature. Franklin E. Zimring et al. LC 83-9530. 164p. 1983. pap. 15.00 (*0-8330-0504-9*, R-3016-CSA) Rand Corp.

***Youth Crime & Police Work.** Lee. Date not set. text ed. 65.00 (*0-312-17762-3*) St Martin.

***Youth Crime Prevention: Proceedings of a Policy Forum.** Ed. by B. Halstead. 258p. 1991. pap. 25.00 (*0-642-15878-9*, Pub. by Aust Inst Criminology) Willow Tree NY.

Youth Crime-Violence & the Cause. Marcella Royal. LC 94-94495. (Illus.). 208p. (Orig.). 1994. pap. 12.95 (*0-9642111-0-6*) BARRONS WA.

Youth Culture: A Comparative Study in the Indon Context. V. D. Mishra. (C). 1993. 18.00 (*81-210-0311-3*, Pub. by Inter-India Pubns) S Asia.

Youth Culture in Late Modernity. Johan Fornas & Goran Bolin. 208p. 1995. 69.95 (*0-8039-8898-2*); pap. 21.95 (*0-8039-8899-0*) Sage.

Youth Cultures: A Cross Cultural Perspective. Ed. by Vered Amit-Talai & Helena Wulff. LC 94-46793. 224p. (C). 1995. pap. 17.95 (*0-415-10984-1*, C0042) Routledge.

Youth Development: Discovering the Profession. Sherril L. York & Debra J. Jordan. Ed. by Debra J. Jordan. 79p. (C). 1995. pap. text ed. 10.00 (*1-881516-03-2*) U of NI Inst Youth Lead.

Youth Development & Critical Education: The Promise of Democratic Action. Richard D. Lakes. LC 96-21038. (SUNY Series, Democracy & Education). (Illus.). 181p. (C). 1997. text ed. 49.50 (*0-7914-3349-8*); pap. text ed. 16.95 (*0-7914-3350-1*) State U NY Pr.

***Youth Development & Neighborhood Influences: Challenges & Opportunities.** National Research Council Staff. 40p. (Orig.). 1996. pap. text ed. 10.00 (*0-309-05649-7*, Joseph Henry Pr) Natl Acad Pr.

Youth Development in Congregations: An Exploration of the Potential & Barriers. Eugene C. Roehlkepartain. 96p. (Orig.). 1995. pap. 14.95 (*1-57482-123-7*) Search Inst.

Youth Development Professionals: Building Practice on Knowledge. Ed. by Robert F. Long & Cathy L. Martinez. (Youth Development Professionals Monographs: No. 3). 162p. (C). 1993. pap. text ed. 10.00 (*1-881516-02-4*) U of NI Inst Youth Lead.

Youth Development Professionals: Connecting Competencies & Curriculum. Ed. by Robert F. Long. (Youth Development Professionals Monographs: No. 1). 64p. (C). 1992. pap. text ed. 10.00 (*1-881516-00-8*) U of NI Inst Youth Lead.

Youth Development Programs. (YMCA Program Discovery Ser.: Vol. 1, No. 2). 88p. 1990. pap. text ed. 18.00 (*0-87322-296-2*, 5083, YMCA USA) Human Kinetics.

Youth Develpment Professionals: Common Ground for Professional Development. Ed. by Robert F. Long. (Youth Development Professionals Monographs: No. 2). 62p. (C). 1992. pap. text ed. 10.00 (*1-881516-01-6*) U of NI Inst Youth Lead.

Youth Division Counselor. Jack Rudman. (Career Examination Ser.: C-2107). 1994. pap. 29.95 (*0-8373-2107-7*) Nat Learn.

Youth Do You Dare! Colin D. Standish. 144p. (Orig.). 1988. pap. 4.95 (*0-923309-12-8*) Hartland Pubns.

***Youth Education & Services Directory.** Frances Konour. 148p. (Orig.). 1996. pap. 12.00 (*0-9655036-0-7*) YES Inc CO.

Youth Education & Unemployment Problems: An International Perspective. Margaret S. Gordon. LC 79-54989. (Education & Youth Employment in Contemporary Societies Ser.). 188p. reprint ed. pap. 53.60 (*0-317-55381-X*, 2029489) Bks Demand.

Youth Education Coordinator. Jack Rudman. (Career Examination Ser.: C-2534). 1994. pap. 34.95 (*0-8373-2534-X*) Nat Learn.

Youth Employment & Public Policy. Ed. by Bernard E. Anderson & Isabel V. Sawhill. LC 79-27022. 1980. 11.95 (*0-13-982413-8*) Am Assembly.

Youth Employment & Public Policy. American Assembly Staff. LC 79-27022. (Spectrum Bks.). 175p. reprint ed. pap. 49.90 (*0-685-16212-5*, 2056256) Bks Demand.

Youth Employment & Training in Developing Countries: An Annotated Bibliography. Oscar Corvalan-Vasquez. vii, 172p. (Orig.). 1984. pap. 15.75 (*92-2-103420-8*) Intl Labour Office.

Youth Employment in American Industry. Robert B. Hill & Regina Nixon. (Illus.). 156p. 1984. pap. 19.95 (*0-87855-986-8*) Transaction Pubs.

Youth Employment Program Specialist. Jack Rudman. (Career Examination Ser.: C-3538). 1994. pap. 34.95 (*0-8373-3538-8*) Nat Learn.

***Youth Environmental Service (YES) in Action: Program Summary.** Robert C. Cronin. (Illus.). 39p. (Orig.). 1996. pap. 20.00 (*0-7881-3720-4*) DIANE Pub.

***Youth Evangelism.** David R. Veerman. 216p. (J). 1996. pap. 9.99 (*1-56476-600-4*, Victor Bks) Chariot Victor.

Youth Exchanges: The Complete Guide to the Homestay Experience Abroad. John K. Hawks. LC 93-14178. 240p. 1994. 22.95 (*0-8160-2922-9*) Facts on File.

Youth Exchanges: The Complete Guide to the Homestay Experience Abroad. John K. Hawks. 240p. 1995. pap. 12.95 (*0-8160-2923-7*) Facts on File.

Youth Experiential Annual Resource 1. Steve Clapp et al. 122p. (Orig.). 1981. pap. 10.00 (*0-914527-42-8*) C-Four Res.

Youth, Family, & Citizenship. Gill Jones & Claire Wallace. LC 91-45491. 181p. 1992. pap. 29.00 (*0-335-09294-2*, Open Univ Pr) Taylor & Francis.

***Youth, Family & Citizenship.** Gill Jones & Claire Wallace. 192p. 1992. 42.50 (*0-335-09299-3*, Open Univ Pr) Taylor & Francis.

Youth Football: A Complete Handbook. Ed. by Jerry Cvengros. LC 88-43249. (Illus.). 296p. 1992. reprint ed. pap. 30.00 (*1-884125-45-X*) Cooper Pubng.

Youth Football: Complete Handbook. Vern Seefeldt. 312p. (C). 1992. pap. text ed. write for info. (*0-697-15191-3*) Brown & Benchmark.

Youth Football: Complete Handbook. Vern Seefeldt. 312p. (C). 1992. Section I, Skills & Strategies. text ed. write for info. (*0-697-15192-1*); Section III, Conditioning & Training. text ed. write for info. (*0-697-15194-8*) Brown & Benchmark.

Youth for Youth Staying Free. Pam Aubry. 20p. (J). (gr. 1-2). 1990. pap. 2.22 (*0-914127-50-0*) Univ Class.

Youth Fundraisers: Raising Money That Counts. Lynn Hinkle. (Essentials for Christian Youth Ser.). 1995. pap. 13.95 (*0-687-01010-1*) Abingdon.

Youth Gang Problem: A Community Approach. Irving A. Spergel. (Illus.). 352p. 1995. pap. 28.00 (*0-19-509203-1*) OUP.

Youth Gangs in American Society. Randall G. Sheldon et al. (Criminal Justice Ser.). (Illus.). 256p. (C). 1997. pap. text ed. 21.95 (*0-534-22134-3*) Wadsworth Pub.

Youth Goes Over. Robert Brasillach. 1972. 59.95 (*0-8490-1347-X*) Gordon Pr.

Youth Golf: For Parents & Players. Cliff Schrock. (Spalding Youth Ser.). (Illus.). 224p. (Orig.). 1994. pap. 12.95 (*0-940279-87-8*, Spalding Sports) Masters Pr IN.

Youth Group Supervisor. Jack Rudman. (Career Examination Ser.: C-1540). 1994. pap. 29.95 (*0-8373-1540-9*) Nat Learn.

Youth Group Worker. Jack Rudman. (Career Examination Ser.: C-1538). 1994. pap. 27.95 (*0-8373-1538-7*) Nat Learn.

Youth Group Worker Aide. Jack Rudman. (Career Examination Ser.: C-1539). 1994. pap. 23.95 (*0-8373-1539-5*) Nat Learn.

Youth Guidance Technician. Jack Rudman. (Career Examination Ser.: C-920). 1994. pap. 29.95 (*0-8373-0920-4*) Nat Learn.

Youth, Heart of Darkness & the End of the Tether. Joseph Conrad. 294p. 1992. pap. 7.95 (*0-460-87046-7*, Everyman's Classic Lib) C E Tuttle.

Youth-Heart of Darkness-the End of the Tether. Joseph Conrad. Ed. & Intro. by John Lyon. 384p. 1995. pap. 7.95 (*0-14-018513-5*, Penguin Classics) Viking Penguin.

Youth Helping Youth: A Handbook for Training Peer Facilitators. Robert D. Myrick & Tom Erney. Ed. by Don L. Sorenson. LC 78-70544. (Illus.). 224p. 1985. pap. text ed. 8.95 (*0-932796-02-8*) Ed Media Corp.

***Youth Helping Youth Succeed: A Peer Mentor Curriculum.** Julie Evans. (Illus.). 104p. (Orig.). (J). (gr. 6-10). 1997. wbk. ed., pap. text ed. 15.95 (*0-9647066-9-5*) Wellstone Pr.

Youth Hockey: Coaching & Playing. Gerald A. Walford & Gerald E. Walford. (Spalding Youth Ser.). (Illus.). 192p. (Orig.). 1994. pap. 12.95 (*0-940279-89-4*, Spalding Sports) Masters Pr IN.

Youth Homelessness: Courage & Hope. Helen Sykes. 176p. (Orig.). 1993. pap. 24.95 (*0-522-84572-X*, Pub. by Melbourne Univ Pr AT) Paul & Co Pubs.

Youth Identifying Measures for Strenthening Channels of Communication Between the United Nations & Youth & Youth Organizations. 46p. 1986. 8.00 (*92-1-130106-8*, E.85.IV.9) UN.

Youth, Identity, Power: The Chicano Movement. Carlos Munoz. (Haymarket Ser.). 320p. 1989. 50.00 (*0-86091-197-7*, Pub. by Verso UK) Routledge Chapman & Hall.

Youth, Identity, Power: The Chicano Movement. Carlos Munoz. (Haymarket Ser.). 320p. (C). 1989. pap. text ed. 19.00 (*0-86091-913-7*, Pub. by Vrso UK) Norton.

Youth in a Changing World: Cross-Cultural Perspectives on Adolescence. Ed. by Estelle Fuchs. (World Anthropology Ser.). (Illus.). xiv, 346p. 1976. 37.75 (*90-279-7779-8*) Mouton.

Youth in Agricultural Villages. Bruce L. Melvin & Elna N. Smith. LC 79-165603. (Research Monographs: Vol. 21). 1971. reprint ed. lib. bdg. 19.50 (*0-306-70353-X*) Da Capo.

Youth in Asia. Ed. by Association of Asian Social Science Research Councils Staff. 350p. 1988. text ed. 40.00 (*0-89891-027-7*, Pub. by New Stateman Pub II) Advent Bks Div.

Youth in Australia: Policy, Administration & Politics. Geoffrey Sherington et al. 432p. 1995. 69.95 (*0-7329-1921-5*); pap. 34.95 (*0-7329-1920-7*) Paul & Co Pubs.

Youth in Babylon: Confessions of a Trash-Film King. David Friedman. (Sexual Autobiographies Ser.). (Illus.). 355p. (C). 1990. 26.95 (*0-87975-608-X*) Prometheus Bks.

***Youth in Charge: How to Develop Youth Leadership.** Abingdon Press. (Skill Abilities for Youth Ministry Ser.). 1997. pap. text ed. 4.95 (*0-687-06200-4*) Abingdon.

Youth in Conflict. Miriam Van Waters. LC 70-120218. reprint ed. 41.50 (*0-404-06754-9*) AMS Pr.

Youth in Contemporary Society. Intro. by David Gottlieb. LC 72-84050. 384p. reprint ed. pap. 109.50 (*0-317-09700-8*, 2021908) Bks Demand.

Youth in Ernest. Henry Harbaugh. (Notable American Authors Ser.). 1992. reprint ed. lib. bdg. 90.00 (*0-7812-3013-6*) Rprt Serv.

Youth in Europe. Ed. by Alessandro Cavalli & Olivier Galland. LC 94-45076. (Social Change in Western Europe Ser.). 160p. 1995. 50.00 (*1-85567-305-3*, Pub. by Pntr Pubs UK); pap. 16.00 (*1-85567-306-1*, Pub. by Pntr Pubs UK) Bks Intl VA.

Youth in Low-Income Environments, Alcohol, Tobacco & Other Drugs: A Resource Guide. 1995. lib. bdg. 251.95 (*0-8490-6795-2*) Gordon Pr.

***Youth in Prison: We the People of Unit Four.** M. A. Bortner & Linda M. Williams. 256p. (C). 1997. text ed. 69.95 (*0-415-91438-8*, Routledge NY) Routledge.

***Youth in Prison: We the People of Unit Four.** Margaret Bortner & Linda Williams. 256p. 1997. pap. 17.95 (*0-415-91439-6*, Routledge NY) Routledge.

Youth in Protestant Churches: A Special Search Institute Report. Peter L. Benson & Eugene C. Roehlkepartain. 148p. 1993. pap. 14.95 (*1-57482-121-0*) Search Inst.

Youth in Revolt. Shmarya Levin. Tr. by Maurice Samuel. LC 74-27998. (Modern Jewish Experience Ser.). 1975. reprint ed. 26.95 (*0-405-06725-9*) Ayer.

Youth in Revolt: The Journals of Nick Twisp. C. D. Payne. 512p. 1996. pap. 14.95 (*0-385-48196-9*, Main St Bks) Doubleday.

Youth in Single Parent Families: Risk & Resiliency. Eugene C. Roehlkepartain. 23p. 1993. pap. 6.50 (*1-57482-319-1*) Search Inst.

***Youth in Society: Contemporary Theory, Policy & Practice.** Ed. by Jeremy Roche & Stanley Tucker. 304p. 1997. 75.00 (*0-7619-5372-8*); pap. 22.95 (*0-7619-5373-6*) Sage.

Youth in Sports Clubs: Towards a Youth-Friendly Approach. Paul De Knop et al. 200p. 1994. pap. 29.50 (*90-5487-071-0*, Pub. by VUB Univ Pr BE) Paul & Co Pubs.

Youth in the CCC. Kenneth Holland & Frank E. Hill. LC 74-1685. (Children & Youth Ser.: Vol. 27). 284p. 1974. reprint ed. 23.95 (*0-405-05962-0*) Ayer.

Youth in the Vanguard: Memoirs & Letters Collected by the First Baha'i Student at Berkeley & at Stanford University. Marion C. Yazdi. LC 82-6793. (Illus.). 267p. 1982. 5.00 (*0-87743-173-6*, 332-089) Bahai.

Youth in Transition. Jerald G. Bachman et al. Incl. Vol. 5. Young Men & Military Service. 260p. 1972. 12.00 (*0-87944-119-4*); Vol. 5. Young Men & Military Service. 260p. 1972. pap. 8.00 (*0-87944-118-6*); Vol. 6. Adolescence to Adulthood--Change & Stability in the Lives of Young Men. 350p. 1978. 18.00 (*0-87944-224-7*); write for info. (*0-318-53547-5*) Inst Soc Res.

Youth in Transition: The Sociology of Youth & Youth Policy. Ed. by Clarie Wallace & Malcolm Cross. (Explorations in Sociology Ser.: No. 37). 200p. 1990. 55.00 (*1-85000-797-7*, Falmer Pr); pap. 28.00 (*1-85000-798-5*, Falmer Pr) Taylor & Francis.

Youth in Two Worlds: United States & Denmark. Denise B. Kandel & Gerald S. Lesser. LC 70-186582. (Jossey-Bass Behavioral Science Ser.). 240p. reprint ed. 68.40 (*0-8357-9355-9*, 2013855) Bks Demand.

***Youth in Vienna, a Life in America: A Memoir.** Stephen. (Illus.). 216p. (Orig.). (C). 1996. pap. 12.95 (*0-9653917-0-1*) S Roberts CA.

Youth Indicators, Youth Trends in the Well-Being of American Youth. 1994. lib. bdg. 250.00 (*0-8490-8590-X*) Gordon Pr.

Youth Indicators, 1993: Trends in the Well-Being of American Youth. Thomas D. Snyder et al. (Illus.). 153p. (Orig.). (C). 1994. pap. text ed. 35.00 (*0-7881-0811-5*) DIANE Pub.

Youth Information Resources: An Annotated Guide for Parents, Professionals, Students, Researchers & Concerned Citizens. Ed. by Donna L. Richardson. LC 86-33492. (Bibliographies & Indexes in Sociology Ser.: No. 10). 371p. 1987. text ed. 75.00 (*0-313-25304-8*, WYI/) Greenwood.

Youth Involvement Programs to Decrease Violence: Monographs of Proceedings of the First & Second National Symposiums to Decrease Youth Violence. Ed. by Adele Somers. (Illus.). 165p. (Orig.). 1989. reprint ed. pap. 15.00 (*0-9615032-3-8*) World Relations Pr.

Youth, Its Education, Regimen & Hygiene. Granville S. Hall. LC 76-169383. (Family in America Ser.). 384p. 1972. reprint ed. 21.95 (*0-405-03861-5*) Ayer.

Youth Labor Market Problem: Its Nature, Causes, & Consequences. Ed. by Richard B. Freeman & David A. Wise. LC 81-11438. (National Bureau of Economic Research Conference Report Ser.). 608p. 1982. lib. bdg. 64.00 (*0-226-26161-1*) U Ch Pr.

Youth Labour Market in Britain: The Role of Intervention. Brian Deakin. (Cambridge Department of Applied Economics Occasional Papers: No. 62). (Illus.). 225p. (C). 1996. text ed. 54.95 (*0-521-55328-8*) Cambridge U Pr.

***Youth Leader's Guide: Year 2, Bk. 2.** Smyth. (Intersection Ser.). 1994. pap. text ed. 15.99 (*1-880837-51-X*) Smyth & Helwys.

Youth Leadership in Action. Fortier & Project Adventure Inc. Staff. 208p. 1994. per., pap. text ed. 12.00 (*0-7872-0107-3*) Kendall-Hunt.

Youth League Baseball. Skip Bertman. (Spalding Youth Ser.). (Illus.). 192p. 1993. reprint ed. pap. 12.95 (*0-940279-68-1*) Masters Pr IN.

Youth League Basketball. Joe Williams & Stan Wilson. (Spalding Youth Ser.). (Illus.). 128p. 1993. reprint ed. pap. 9.95 (*0-940279-70-3*) Masters Pr IN.

Youth League Football. Tom Flores & Bob O'Connor. (Spalding Youth Ser.). (Illus.). 192p. (Orig.). 1993. pap. 12.95 (*0-940279-69-X*) Masters Pr IN.

Youth League Soccer. (Spalding Youth Ser.). (Illus.). 192p. 1993. reprint ed. pap. 9.95 (*0-940279-67-3*) Masters Pr IN.

***Youth League Softball: The Complete Guide to Coaching.** Amateur Softball Association of America Staff. (Illus.). 128p. (Orig.). 1998. pap. 12.95 (*1-57028-155-6*) Masters Pr IN.

Youth Literature: An Interdisciplinary, Annotated Guide to North American Dissertation Research, 1930-1985. Stewart Lukenbill. LC 87-38077. 482p. 1988. text ed. 85.00 (*0-8240-8498-5*) Garland.

***Youth Longs to Know.** John Gardner. LC 97-11408. 224p. (Orig.). 1997. pap. 16.95 (*0-88010-445-7*, 2032) Anthroposophic.

Youth Ministries: Thinking Big With Small Groups. Carolyn C. Brown. LC 83-15891. (Griggs Educational Resources Ser.). 96p. 1984. pap. 10.95 (*0-687-47203-2*) Abingdon.

Youth Ministries Handbook. Barrie Smith & Ruth Smith. 120p. 1984. pap. text ed. 5.00 (*0-8309-0402-6*) Herald Hse.

Youth Ministries Ideas II. Lauren E. Say et al. (Orig.). (C). 1985. pap. 2.00 (*0-8309-0427-1*) Herald Hse.

Youth Ministries Ideas III. Dale Jones. 1986. pap. 2.00 (*0-8309-0470-0*) Herald Hse.

Youth Ministry. Jeffrey J. Kaster. (Ministry Ser.). 48p. 1989. pap. 1.95 (*0-8146-1786-7*) Liturgical Pr.

Youth Ministry. Lawrence O. Richards. 320p. 1990. pap. 19.99 (*0-310-32011-9*) Zondervan.

Youth Ministry Activity Book. Rose T. Stupak. LC 88-23991. 105p. (Orig.). (C). 1988. pap. 9.95 (*0-89390-127-X*) Resource Pubns.

***Youth Ministry & Evangelism.** Clement. 8.90 (*0-687-67050-0*) Abingdon.

Youth Ministry Clip Art. Dave Adamson & Steve Hunt. (Illus.). 126p. (Orig.). 1987. pap. 13.99 (*0-931529-26-3*) Group Pub.

***Youth Ministry Crash Course: Everything You Need to Know from Adolescence to Zits.** Rick Bundschuh & E. G. Von Trutzschler. LC 96-45054. 96p. 1997. pap. 8.99 (*0-310-21528-5*) Youth Spec.

Youth Ministry for the Volunteer. Mark Schaufler. 18p. 1993. student ed. 2.00 (*1-886904-02-2*) MST Minist.

Youth Ministry for the Volunteer. Mark Schaufler. 20p. 1995. teacher ed. 5.00 (*1-886904-03-0*) MST Minist.

Youth Ministry Handbook. Ed. by Edward A. Trimmer. LC 94-28848. (Essentials for Christian Youth Ser.). 176p. (Orig.). 1994. pap. 14.95 (*0-687-01034-9*) Abingdon.

Youth Ministry in Small Churches. Rick Chromey. 168p. (Orig.). 1989. pap. 12.99 (*0-931529-76-X*, Group Bks) Group Pub.

***Youth Ministry Sketchbook: 130 Practical Ideas for Ministry.** Terry K. Dittmer. 1995. 12.99 (*0-570-04827-3*, 12-3269) Concordia.

***Youth Ministry That Makes a Difference: 30 Keys to Strengthening Your Congregation's Youth Ministry.** Eugene C. Roehlkepartain & Margaret R. Hinchey. (Illus.). 64p. (Orig.). 1997. pap. 8.95 (*1-57482-160-1*) Search Inst.

Youth Ministry That Works: Practical Ideas for Working with Young People. George Boran. 160p. 1996. pap. 11.95 (*0-8091-3666-X*) Paulist Pr.

Youth Ministry...Finding Your Way: Catholic Youth Ministry, Youth Ministry Training. Sofia Berrones. (Illus.). 56p. (Orig.). 1987. pap. text ed. write for info. (*0-942417-00-3*) Mission Catechists.

Youth Movement in China. Tsi C. Wang. 1972. lib. bdg. 79.95 (*0-87968-565-4*) Krishna Pr.

Youth Movement in North East India. A. C. Sinha. (C). 1995. 27.50 (*81-241-0249-X*, Pub. by Har-Anand Pubns II) S Asia.

Youth Movement to Bruderhof: Letters & Diaries of Annemarie Arnold (Nee Wachter) Annemarie Arnold. Ed. by Hutterian Brethren Staff & Woodcrest Bruderhof. LC 85-12434. (Illus.). 248p. (Orig.). 1985. pap. 4.00 (*0-87486-183-7*) Plough.

Youth Movements of the World. Angel. 1991. 130.00 (*0-582-06271-3*) Longman.

Youth Movements of the World. Ed. by William D. Angel. 650p. 1991. 130.00 (*0-685-65376-5*) Gale.

Youth, Murder, Spectacle: The Cultural Politics of "Youth in Crisis" Charles R. Acland. LC 94-16491. (Cultural Studies). (C). 1994. pap. text ed. 21.50 (*0-8133-2287-1*) Westview.

Youth of Europe. Anthony J. Kerr. LC 64-25505. 1964. 10.00 (*0-8023-1068-0*) Dufour.

Youth of Frederick the Great. Ernest Lavisse. LC 71-172308. reprint ed. 45.00 (*0-404-03891-3*) AMS Pr.

Youth of Goethe. P. H. Brown. LC 77-133283. (Studies in German Literature: No. 13). 1970. reprint ed. lib. bdg. 54.95 (*0-8383-1182-2*) M S G Haskell Hse.

Youth of Haouch el Harimi, a Lebanese Village. Judith R. Williams. LC 68-23032. (Middle Eastern Monographs: No. 20). 152p. 1968. pap. 4.50 (*0-674-96675-9*) HUP.

Youth of the Apocalypse: And the Last True Rebellion. John Marler & Andrew Wermuth. (Illus.). 103p. (Orig.). (YA). 1995. pap. 7.00 (*0-938635-89-1*) St Herman Pr.

Youth of the 80s, Vol. 22. James G. Luna. 152p. (Orig.). 1994. pap. text ed. 10.95 (*0-9641606-0-9*) Easy Break.

Youth on Mission Vol. 1: Risk the Journey, Vol. 1. Karen Simons. Ed. by Becky Nelson. (Year's Worth of Plans for the Youth on Mission Leader Ser.). 114p. 1995. pap. 12.95 (*1-56309-160-7*) Womans Mission Union.

Youth or Experience? Manning the Modern Military. Martin Binkin & Irene Kyriakopoulos. LC 79-12633. (Studies in Defense Policy). 84p. 1979. pap. 8.95 (*0-8157-0969-2*) Brookings.

Youth-Parent Socialization Panel Study, 1965 & 1973, 2 vols., 1. M. Kent Jennings & Richard G. Niemi. LC 81-81765. 1981. write for info. (*0-89138-948-2*) ICPSR.

Youth-Parent Socialization Panel Study, 1965 & 1973, 2 vols., 2. M. Kent Jennings & Richard G. Niemi. LC 81-81765. 1981. write for info. (*0-89138-949-0*) ICPSR.

Youth-Parent Socialization Panel Study, 1965 & 1973, 2 vols., Set. M. Kent Jennings & Richard G. Niemi. LC 81-81765. 1981. write for info. (*0-89138-947-4*) ICPSR.

Youth Participation & Experiential Education: Theory, Research, & Programs. Ed. by Daniel Conrad & Diane Hedin. LC 81-20114. (Child & Youth Services Ser.: Vol. 4, Nos. 3 & 4). 156p. 1982. text ed. 49.95 (*0-917724-99-2*) Haworth Pr.

***Youth Participation in School & Public Libraries: It Works.** YALSA Staff. 126p. 1995. 25.00 (*0-8389-7798-7*) ALA.

Youth Policy. Gordon Blakely & Seymour M. House. LC 89-24183. (Spicers European Policy Reports). 192p. (C). 1990. pap. text ed. 150.00 (*0-415-03832-4*, A4382) Routledge.

Youth Policy in the 1990s: Way Forward. Ed. by John Coleman & Chris Warren-Adamson. LC 91-31694. 256p. (C). 1992. text ed. 89.95 (*0-415-05835-X*, Routledge NY) Routledge.

Youth Power for God. Benny B. Bristow. (YA). 1994. pap. 5.50 (*0-89137-831-6*) Quality Pubns.

***Youth! Praise Songbook: Singer's Edition.** 1992. 1.25 (*0-687-75928-5*) Abingdon.

Youth Preparation for Employment: A Policy Reference Document. 40p. 1995. pap. write for info. (*0-614-96300-1*) Coun Chief St Schl Offs.

Youth Programming Workbook. Robert G. Davidson. 40p. (Orig.). (YA). 1989. pap. 8.50 (*0-940754-67-3*) Ed Ministries.

Youth Programs: Promoting Quality Services. Christopher R. Edginton. 289p. 1994. 24.95 (*0-915611-97-X*) Sagamore Pub.

Youth Relationships Manual: A Group Approach with Adolescents for the Prevention of Woman Abuse & the Promotion of Healthy Relationships. David A. Wolfe. 248p. 1996. pap. 29.95 (*0-7619-0194-9*) Sage.

***Youth Retreats for All Occasions.** Kelly Stevens. 98p. 1996. pap. 12.95 (*1-57438-007-9*, 8350) Ed Ministries.

Youth, Schooling, & Work: Policy & Transition. Peter Watkins. 123p. (C). 1984. 60.00 (*0-7300-0114-8*, Pub. by Deakin Univ AT) St Mut.

Youth Service: A Guidebook for Developing & Operating Effective Programs. 70p. 1987. 10.00 (*0-318-37629-6*) Ind Sector.

Youth Services Coordinator. Jack Rudman. (Career Examination Ser.: C-2324). 1994. pap. 34.95 (*0-8373-2324-X*) Nat Learn.

Youth Services Librarians as Managers: A How-to Guide from Budgeting to Personnel. Ed. by Kathleen Staerkel et al. 171p. (Orig.). 1995. pap. 30.00 (*0-8389-3446-3*, 3446-6-2045) ALA.

Youth Services Specialist. Jack Rudman. (Career Examination Ser.: C-1641). 1994. reprint ed. pap. 27.95 (*0-8373-1641-3*) Nat Learn.

***Youth-Serving Organizations Directory.** 1979. 22.00 (*0-8103-0237-3*, 00009759, Gale Res Intl) Gale.

Youth-Serving Organizations Directory. 2nd ed. Ed. by Annie M. Brewer. 1185p. 1980. 85.00 (*0-8103-0238-1*) Gale.

Youth Soccer. Paul Harris. (Spalding Sports Library). (Illus.). 128p. (Orig.). 1992. pap. 9.95 (*0-940279-47-9*) Masters Pr IN.

Youth Soccer. Vern Seefeldt. 79p. (C). 1992. Section II, Methods of Effective Coaching. write for info. (*0-697-15202-2*); Section III, Rules of Play. write for info. (*0-697-15203-0*); Section IV, Individual Techniques for Soccer Field Players. write for info. (*0-697-15204-9*); Section V, Individual Techniques for Soccer Goal Keepers. write for info. (*0-697-15205-7*); Section VI, Basic Strategies of Soccer. write for info. (*0-697-15206-5*); Section VII, Sports Medicine & Training. write for info. (*0-697-15207-3*) Brown & Benchmark.

Youth Soccer, Section I, Organizing for the Season. Vern Seefeldt. 79p. (C). 1992. pap. text ed. write for info. (*0-697-15201-4*) Brown & Benchmark.

Youth Soccer: A Complete Handbook. Ed. by Youth Sports Institute Staff & Eugene Brown. LC 88-70145. (Illus.). 580p. 1992. reprint ed. pap. text ed. 30.00 (*1-884125-23-9*) Cooper Pubng.

Youth Soccer: Amateur Coach. Gerald O'Shea. 1986. 10.95 (*0-317-54063-7*) Viking Penguin.

***Youth Soccer Coaching: A Complete Guide to Building a Successful Team.** Tony Carr. 1997. pap. text ed. 21.95 (*0-7063-7578-5*, Pub. by Ward Lock UK) Sterling.

Youth Soccer Drills. James Garland. LC 96-8064. (Illus.). 216p. (Orig.). 1996. pap. 14.95 (*0-88011-528-9*, PGAR0528) Human Kinetics.

Youth, Socialization & Mental Health. Conference on Culture & Mental Health Research in Asia & the Pacific Staff. Ed. by William P. Lebra. LC 73-85581. (Mental Health Research in Asia & the Pacific Ser.: No. 3). 320p. reprint ed. pap. 91.20 (*0-7837-0995-1*, 2041301) Bks Demand.

Youth Softball: A Complete Handbook. Ed. by Jill Elliott & Martha Ewing. LC 88-43250. (Illus.). 442p. 1992. reprint ed. pap. 30.00 (*1-884125-46-8*) Cooper Pubng.

Youth Softball: Complete Handbook. Vern Seefeldt. 456p. (C). 1992. Section III, Skills & Strategies. write for info. (*0-697-16417-9*) Brown & Benchmark.

Youth Softball: Complete Handbook. Vern Seefeldt. 456p. (C). 1992. Section II, Rules of Play. text ed. write for info. (*0-697-16418-7*); Section IV, Methods of Effective Coaching. text ed. write for info. (*0-697-16420-9*); Section V, Sports Medicine & Training. text ed. write for info. (*0-697-16419-5*) Brown & Benchmark.

Youth Softball: Organizing for the Season, Section 1. Vern Seefeldt. 65p. (C). 1992. write for info. (*0-697-17468-9*) Brown & Benchmark.

Youth Specialties Clip Art Book, 2 vols., Vol. 2. Compiled by Wayne Rice. 131p. (Orig.). 1987. pap. 19.99 (*0-310-39791-X*, 10828P) Zondervan.

Youth Sport: A Social Approach. Ed. by William Duquest et al. (Illus.). 248p. 1994. pap. 29.95 (*90-70289-99-7*) Paul & Co Pubs.

Youth Sport Director Guide. Rainer Martens. LC 94-28875. 224p. (Orig.). 1994. ring bd. 49.00 (*0-87322-751-4*, ACEP0480) Human Kinetics.

Youth, Sports & Self Esteem: A Guide for Parents. Darrell J. Burnett. (Spalding Youth Ser.). (Illus.). 1993. pap. 12.95 (*0-940279-80-0*) Masters Pr IN.

***Youth Street Gangs: Breaking the Gangs Cycle in Urban America.** Vernon T. Harlan. 84p. 1997. 54.95 (*1-57292-073-4*); pap. 29.95 (*1-57292-072-6*) Austin & Winfield.

Youth Strength & Conditioning. Matt Bryzcki. (Spalding Youth Ser.). (Illus.). 160p. (Orig.). (J). (gr. 1-5). 1996. pap. 12.95 (*1-57028-041-X*, Spalding Sports) Masters Pr IN.

Youth Suicide. Michael Peck et al. (Death & Suicide Ser.: Vol. 6). 224p. 1987. pap. 29.95 (*0-8261-4481-0*) Springer Pub.

Youth Suicide: A Comprehensive Manual for Prevention & Intervention. Barbara B. Hicks. 131p. (Orig.). 1990. pap. 19.95 (*1-879639-10-6*) Natl Educ Serv.

Youth Suicide: Issues, Assessment, & Intervention. Ed. by Peter Cimbolic & David A. Jobes. 138p. (C). 1990. text ed. 31.95 (*0-398-05706-0*) C C Thomas.

Youth Suicide: Issues, Assessment, & Intervention. Ed. by Peter Cimbolic & David A. Jobes. 138p. 1990. pap. 17.95 (*0-398-06057-6*) C C Thomas.

Youth Suicide - What the Educator Should Know. Eleanor Guetzloe. 208p. 1989. pap. text ed. 8.00 (*0-86586-188-9*, P331) Coun Exc Child.

Youth Suicide Prevention: Lessons from Literature. Ed. by S. M. Deats & L. T. Lenker. (Illus.). 250p. 1989. 19.95 (*0-306-43198-X*, Plenum Insight) Plenum.

Youth Suicide Prevention Programs: A Resource Guide. 190p. (Orig.). (C). 1993. pap. text ed. 30.00 (*0-7881-0082-3*) DIANE Pub.

***Youth Teacher's Guide Vol. 1: Sinai Summitt.** Chris Hatchett. LC 95-69739. 76p. (Orig.). (YA). (gr. 9-12). 1996. teacher ed., pap. 15.95 (*0-8344-0248-3*, TGYSS) Sweet Pub.

Youth Tell Their Story: A Study of the Conditions & Attitudes of Young People in Maryland Between the Ages of 16 & 24. Howard M. Bell. LC 74-1665. (Children & Youth Ser.). 290p. 1974. reprint ed. 26.95 (*0-405-05946-9*) Ayer.

Youth Tennis: Coaching & Playing. Chuck Kriese. (Spalding Youth Ser.). (Illus.). 192p. (Orig.). 1994. pap. 12.95 (*0-940279-88-6*, Spalding Sports) Masters Pr IN.

***Youth, the Underclass & Social Exclusion.** Robert MacDonald. LC 97-1608. 248p. (C). 1997. pap. write for info. (*0-415-15830-3*); text ed. write for info. (*0-415-15829-X*) Routledge.

Youth Training & Employment: From New Deal to New Federalism. Paul Bullock. (Monograph & Research Ser.: No. 43). 359p. 1985. 15.00 (*0-89215-133-1*) U Cal LA Indus Rel.

Youth Transit & Social Research. Anderson & Anderson Blakers. (Australian National University Press Ser.). 1983. pap. text ed. 19.50 (*0-08-032988-8*, Pergamon Pr) Elsevier.

***Youth Transition Program Case Study Report.** Richard Horne & Susan Hubbard. (Cross Case Report & Case Studies). 50p. 1995. teacher ed., text ed. 20.00 (*0-614-24550-8*); teacher ed., pap. text ed. 10.00 (*0-614-24551-6*) Natl Inst Work.

Youth Tutoring Youth: A Manual for Trainers. 120p. 1970. pap. 5.00 (*0-912041-05-6*) Natl Comm Res Youth.

Youth Tutoring Youth: Supervisor's Manual. 64p. (Orig.). 1968. pap. 3.50 (*0-912041-00-5*) Natl Comm Res Youth.

Youth, Unemployment & Schooling. Ed. by Stephen Walker & Len Barton. 192p. 1986. 85.00 (*0-335-15228-7*, Open Univ Pr); pap. 32.00 (*0-335-15227-9*, Open Univ Pr) Taylor & Francis.

Youth Unemployment & Society. Ed. by Anne C. Petersen & Jeylan T. Mortimer. (Illus.). 586p. (C). 1994. text ed. 47.95 (*0-521-44473-X*) Cambridge U Pr.

Youth, University, & Canadian Society: Essays in the Social History of Higher Education. Ed. by Paul Axelrod & John G. Reid. 416p. (C). 1989. text ed. 55.00 (*0-7735-0685-3*, Pub. by McGill CN); pap. text ed. 24.95 (*0-7735-0709-4*, Pub. by McGill CN) U of Toronto Pr.

Youth Update Sourcebook - 1996. 1996. ring bd. 29.95 (*0-86716-274-0*) St Anthony Mess Pr.

Youth Violence. Ed. by Michael D. Biskup & Charles P. Cozic. LC 92-23592. (Current Controversies Ser.). 272p. (YA). (gr. 10 up). 1992. pap. text ed. 12.96 (*1-56510-016-6*); lib. bdg. 20.96 (*1-56510-017-4*) Greenhaven.

Youth Violence: An American Epidemic? JoAnn B. Guernsey. LC 95-40076. (Frontline Ser.). (J). 1996. lib. bdg. 18.95 (*0-8225-2627-1*, Lerner Publctns) Lerner Group.

Youth Volleyball: Championship Skills. Terry Liskevych & Don Patterson. (Illus.). (Orig.). 1995. pap. 12.95 (*1-57028-028-2*) Masters Pr IN.

Youth Walk: Sex, Parents, Popularity & 49 Other Topics on Teen Survival. 272p. 1991. pap. 12.99 (*0-310-54231-6*) Zondervan.

Youth with Disabilities. Ed. by David W. Kaplan. (Journal: Pediatrician: Vol. 18, No. 2, 1991). (Illus.). 76p. 1991. pap. 45.25 (*3-8055-5406-0*) S Karger.

Youth with Disabilities: Strategies for Interagency Transition Programs. Jane M. Everson. 166p. 1992. pap. 39.95 (*1-56372-012-3*) PRO-ED.

Youth with Disabilities for Interagency Transition Programs. Jane M. Everson. LC 94-40054. 1995. write for info. (*0-89079-654-8*) PRO-ED.

Youth Without Old Age & Life Without Death: A Romanian Fairy Tale. Ed. by Gabriel Stanescu. Tr. by Mac L. Ricketts from RUM. (Illus.). 26p. (ENG.). (J). (gr. 3 up). 1996. lib. bdg. 9.95 (*1-887304-00-2*) Criterion GA.

Youth Without Youth & Other Novellas. Mircea Eliade. Tr. by Mac L. Ricketts from RUM. 256p. 1988. 30.00 (*0-8142-0457-0*) Ohio St U Pr.

Youth Work & Working Class Youth Culture: Rules & Resistance in West Belfast. Norman Gillespie et al. LC 92-9361. 1992. 90.00 (*0-335-09481-3*, Open Univ Pr); pap. 32.00 (*0-335-09480-5*, Open Univ Pr) Taylor & Francis.
Youth Work Programs: Problems & Policies, Vol. 3. Lewis L. Lorwin. LC 74-1694. (Children & Youth Ser.). 212p. 1974. reprint ed. 23.95 (*0-405-05970-1*) Ayer.
***Youth Work, Youth Development & the Transition from Schooling to Employment in England: Impressions from a Study Mission.** Glenda Partee. 72p. 1996. pap. text ed. write for info. (*1-887031-56-1*) Am Youth Policy.
Youth Workers Artsource Vol. 2: Borders, Symbols, Holidays & Attention Grabbers. 96p. 1991. pap. 12.99 (*0-310-53851-3*) Zondervan.
Youth Worker's Clip Art Book. Tom Finley. (Illus.). 1984. teacher ed., pap. 15.99 (*0-8307-1014-0*) Gospel Lght.
Youth Workers' Handbook. Steve Clapp & Jerry O. Cook. 280p. 1981. pap. 11.00 (*0-914527-05-3*) C-Four Res.
Youth Workers' Handbook. rev. ed. Steve Clapp & Jerry O. Cook. 224p. 1992. reprint ed. pap. 16.95 (*0-87178-979-5*) Brethren.
***Youth Worker's Handbook to Family Ministry: Strategies & Practical Ideas for Reaching Your Students' Families.** Chap Clark. LC 97-13808. 1997. write for info. (*0-310-22025-4*) Zondervan.
Youthful High School Noncompleters: Enhancing Opportunities for Employment & Education. Larry G. Martin. 59p. 1987. 7.00 (*0-318-23415-7*, IN316) Ctr Educ Trng Employ.
Youthful Indiscretions. 192p. 1991. pap. 4.50 (*0-88184-778-X*) Carroll & Graf.
***Youthful Indiscretions.** 4.50 (*0-7867-0778-X*) Carroll & Graf.
Youthful Musings: A Book of Poetry. Jeffrey J. Ake. 68p. 1995. pap. 16.95 (*1-888249-00-5*) Intl Vision.
***Youthful Nuggets & Adult Gems.** 384p. 1996. pap. 11.99 (*0-9655357-0-3*) Vivian Butler.
Youthful Recreations. (Illus.). 1810. 1.50 (*0-911132-07-4*) Phila Free Lib.
Youthful Sex Offender: The Rational & Goals of Early Intervention of Treatment. Fay H. Knopp. 36p. 1985. reprint ed. pap. 7.00 (*1-884444-27-X*) Safer Soc.
Youthful Writings. Albert Camus. 1994. pap. 12.95 (*1-56924-968-7*) Marlowe & Co.
Youthjobs: Toward a Private-Public Partnership. David Bresnick. LC 84-3343. 160p. 1984. text ed. 45.00 (*0-89930-093-6*, BYJ/, Quorum Bks) Greenwood.
Youthjobs: Toward a Private-Public Partnership. David Bresnick. 151p. 1986. pap. text ed. 14.95 (*0-8290-1004-2-5*) Human Serv Pr.
Youths & Reggae: Foundation Legends Speak. Ricardo A. Scott. (Illus.). 110p. (Orig.). 1994. write for info. (*1-883427-13-4*) Crnerstone GA.
Youth's Battle for the Ballot: A History of Voting Age in America. Wendell W. Cultice. LC 91-26373. (Contributions in Political Science Ser.: No. 291). 288p. 1992. text ed. 55.00 (*0-313-27962-4*, CYB/, Greenwood Pr) Greenwood.
Youths' Guide to Job Hunting. Margaret Brownley. 28p. (Orig.). (YA). (gr. 8-12). 1988. pap. 3.95 (*0-945485-02-6*) Comm Intervention.
***Youths Living with HIV: Self-Evident Truths.** G. Cajetan Luna. LC 96-51906. 206p. (C). 1997. pap. 14.95 (*1-56023-904-2*); lib. bdg. 39.95 (*0-7890-0176-4*) Harrington Pk.
Youth's Noble Path see Tales of All Times
Youthwalk Again. Walk Thru the Bible Staff. (Youthwalk Ser.: No. 3). 272p. (YA). 1993. pap. 12.99 (*0-310-54601-X*) Zondervan.
You've Always Been Wrong. Rene Daumal. Tr. by Thomas Vosteen. LC 94-37337. (French Modernist Library). (Illus.). xxvii, 133p. (ENG & FRE.). 1995. text ed. 25.00 (*0-8032-1699-8*) U of Nebr Pr.
You've Built a Successful Business, Now What? Dickson C. Buxton. 1996. pap. text ed. 19.95 (*1-882180-62-3*) Griffin CA.
You've Come a Long Way, Charlie Brown. Charles M. Schulz. 1995. pap. 6.95 (*0-8050-3573-7*) H Holt & Co.
You've Come a Long Way, Snoopy: Selected Cartoons from "Thompson Is in Trouble", Vol. I. Charles M. Schulz. (Peanuts Ser.). (Illus.). 1983. mass mkt. 3.99 (*0-449-20358-1*, Crest) Fawcett.
You've Done It All, So What's Left but Making the Impossible Happen. Tracy Goss. write for info. (*0-614-16415-X*, Currency) Doubleday.
***You've Earned It, Don't Lose It.** Oman. 1996. 19.95 (*1-55704-285-3*, Newmkt Medall) Newmarket.
***You've Earned It, Don't Lose It.** Oman. 1997. 23.00 (*1-55704-322-1*); pap. 15.00 (*1-55704-316-7*) Newmarket.
You've Earned It, Don't Lose It: Mistakes You Can't Afford to Make When You Retire. Suze Orman. LC 94-27895. 208p. 1994. 22.00 (*1-55704-212-8*) Newmarket.
***You've Earned It, Don't Lose It: Mistakes You Can't Afford to Make When You Retire.** Suze Orman & Linda Mead. 1997. pap. write for info. (*1-55704-320-5*) Newmarket.
***You've Got a Friend: Thoughts to Celebrate the Joy of Friendship.** Dan Zadra. 1997. 12.95 (*1-888387-19-X*) Compendium Inc.
You've Got an Idea - Now What? Robert M. Sperry. Ed. by Heather Goulding. LC 92-233376. 120p. (Orig.). (C). 1992. pap. text ed. 14.95 (*0-9633785-0-3*) B&B Ent.
You've Got the Power: A Recovery Guide for Young People with Alcohol & Drug Problems. Edward M. Read & Dennis C. Daley. (Illus.). 98p. (Orig.). 1993. pap. 11.00 (*0-929310-87-X*, 349) Am Correctional.
You've Got to Be Believed. Bert Decker. 1992. pap. 15.95 (*1-55927-192-2*) St Martin.
You've Got to Be Believed to Be Heard. Bert Decker. (Illus.). 320p. 1993. pap. 13.95 (*0-312-09949-5*) St Martin.
You've Got to Be Choking! & General Trivia. Ray Comfort. (Illus.). 80p. (Orig.). 1990. pap. write for info. (*1-878859-00-5*) Living Wat CA.
You've Got to Be Kiddin'! Nell Brasher. 184p. 1981. pap. 8.95 (*1-881548-85-6*) Crane Hill AL.
***You've Got to Have a Sense of Humor to Have a Wedding.** Margaret G. Bigger. LC 96-86617. (Illus.). 128p. (Orig.). 1997. pap. 9.95 (*0-9640606-5-5*) A Borough Bks.
You've Got to Have Gold. large type ed. Eunice Buckley. 516p. 1977. 25.99 (*0-85456-527-2*) Ulverscroft.
You've Got to Read This: Contemporary American Writers Introduce Stories that Held Them in Awe. Ed. by Ron Hansen & Jim Shepard. LC 92-54841. 448p. (Orig.). 1994. pap. 16.00 (*0-06-098202-0*, PL) HarpC.
You've Got to Read This Book!! Answers to Those Questions That Have Been Bothering You for Years! 2nd ed. Heidi R. Monroe-Terrance. LC 95-95233. (Illus.). 80p. (Orig.). 1996. pap. 4.95 (*0-9646797-1-X*) H Monroe-Terrance.
You've Got to Ride the Subway. Madge Reinhardt. LC 76-4760. 278p. 1977. pap. 7.00 (*0-917162-02-1*) Back Row Pr.
You've Got What It Takes. Judy Hamlin. (Searching for Answers Ser.: No. 1). 64p. 1992. pap. 1.00 (*0-89693-095-5*, 6-1095) SP Pubns.
You've Gotta Hand It to God! Timothy M. Powell. LC 84-73557. (Radiant Life Ser.). 125p. 1985. pap. 3.95 (*0-88243-859-X*, 02-0859); teacher ed., pap. 5.50 (*0-88243-199-4*, 32-0199) Gospel Pub.
You've Only Got Three Seconds: How to Make the Right Impression in Your Business & Social Life. Camille Lavington. LC 96-24887. 288p. 1997. 22.95 (*0-385-48244-2*) Doubleday.
Yovgo's Stories. Caroline B. Vlasis & Charlie O. York. (Illus.). 14p. (Orig.). (J). (gr. k up). 1995. pap. 5.00 (*0-9648783-0-5*) You & Me SC.
Yovhannes Tclkurancci & the Mediaeval Armenian Lyric Tradition. James R. Russell. LC 85-22066. (Armenian Texts & Studies). 260p. 1987. 17.95 (*0-89130-929-2*, 21-02-07); pap. 13.95 (*0-89130-930-6*) Scholars Pr GA.
Yoxford Boys. Merle C. Olmsted. Ed. by Kenn Rust. LC 77-135044. (Orig.). 1971. pap. 7.95 (*0-8168-9766-2*, 29766, TAB-Aero) TAB Bks.
Yoyo. Jim Simmerman & Beth Richards. Ed. by William Trowbridge et al. (Missouri Chapbook Ser.). 36p. (Orig.). 1994. pap. 5.00 (*0-9616467-9-9*) GreenTower Pr.
YP Standard Operating Procedures 676 Class. 2nd ed. USNA (Taylor) Staff. 120p. 1996. ring bd. 22.00 (*0-8403-9420-9*) Kendall-Hunt.
Ypodigma Neustriae, a Thoma Walsingham see Chronica Monasterii S. Albani
Ypres 1914: An Official German Account by the General Staff. German General Staff. (Great War Ser.: No. 31). 160p. reprint ed. 34.95 (*0-89839-203-9*) Battery Pr.
Ypsilanti Perry Preschool Project: Preschool Years & Longitudinal Results Through Fourth Grade. David P. Weikart et al. LC 77-92916. (Monographs of the High/Scope Educational Research Foundation: No. 3). 142p. (Orig.). 1978. pap. 12.95 (*0-931114-02-0*) High-Scope.
Ypsilanti Preschool Curriculum Demonstration Project: Preschool Years & Longitudinal Results. D. P. Weikart et al. LC 77-92917. (Monographs of the High/Scope Educational Research Foundation: No. 4). 152p. 1978. pap. 12.95 (*0-931114-03-9*) High-Scope.
***Ypthree.** Playwrights Canada Press Staff. LC 95-152246. 1997. pap. text ed. 19.95 (*0-88754-475-4*, Pub. by Playwrights CN Pr CN) Theatre Comm.
Y's Way to a Healthy Back. Alexander Melleby. LC 82-14474. (Illus.). 192p. 1982. pap. 11.95 (*0-8329-0147-4*) New Win Pub.
Y's Way to Better Aerobics. Susan K. Wilmoth. LC 88-5590. (Illus.). 80p. 1988. pap. text ed. 7.00 (*0-87322-189-3*, LWIL4952, YMCA USA) Human Kinetics.
Y's Way to Better Aerobics Leader's Guide. Susan K. Wilmoth. LC 88-5587. (Illus.). 152p. 1988. pap. text ed. 17.00 (*0-87322-190-7*, 4951, YMCA USA) Human Kinetics.
Y's Way to Physical Fitness: The Complete Guide to Fitness Testing & Instruction. 3rd ed. Ed. by Lawrence A. Golding et al. LC 88-27719. (Illus.). 202p. 1989. text ed. 33.00 (*0-87322-214-8*, LGOL4998, YMCA USA) Human Kinetics.
Y's Way to Water Exercise Instructor's Guide. Joseph A. Krasevec. LC 88-30384. (Illus.). 148p. (Orig.). 1989. pap. text ed. 17.00 (*0-87322-221-0*, LYMC4927, YMCA USA) Human Kinetics.
Y's Way to Weight Management. Sandra K. Cotterman. 152p. (Orig.). 1985. pap. text ed. 15.00 (*0-87322-032-3*, LCOT4725, YMCA USA) Human Kinetics.
Ysabella de Trastamara - First Lady of the Renaissance: The Epic Reign of Queen Isabella of Spain. Elizabeth Long. Ed. by Auriole Douglas. 414p. 1992. 26.95 (*0-9631244-5-5*); pap. 16.95 (*0-9631244-6-3*) Alhamar Pub.
Ysaye: His Life, Work & Influence. Antoine Ysaye & Ra Ysaye. reprint ed. lib. bdg. 75.00 (*0-7812-0116-0*) Rprt Serv.
Ysaye: His Life, Work & Influence. Antoine Ysaye & Betram Ratcliffe. LC 70-181298. 1947. reprint ed. 59.00 (*0-403-01723-8*) Scholarly.
Ysaye: Violins. Antoine Ysaye. (Illus.). 218p. 1984. 37.50 (*0-87556-720-7*) Saifer.
Ysengrimus. Magister Nivardus. Tr. by F. J. Sypher & Eleanor Sypher from LAT. (Illus.). 280p. 1980. 95.00 (*0-317-00052-7*) F Sypher.
Ysengrimus. Ed. by Ernst Voigt. 470p. 1974. reprint ed. write for info. (*3-487-05284-9*) G Olms Pubs.
Y'shua: The Jewish Way to Say Jesus. Moishe Rosen. 128p. (Orig.). 1983. mass mkt., pap. 4.99 (*0-8024-9842-6*) Moody.
Ystoria Taliesin: The Story of Taliesin. Ed. by Patrick K. Ford. 175p. 1992. 25.00 (*0-7083-1092-3*) Bks Intl VA.
***Yu Study Bible.** 2nd ed. M. Leekung Yu. (Illus.). 2000p. (CHI.). 1985. reprint ed. 45.00 (*1-890610-03-8*) Hymnody & Bible.
Yuan Hung-tao & the Kung-an School. Chih-P'ing Chou. (Cambridge Studies in Chinese History, Literature & Institutions). 190p. 1988. text ed. 64.95 (*0-521-34207-4*) Cambridge U Pr.
Yuan Mei: Eighteenth Century Chinese Poet. Arthur Waley. 227p. 1956. 37.50 (*0-8047-0718-9*) Stanford U Pr.
Yuan Shih-k'ai. 2nd ed. Jerome Ch'en. LC 76-153815. xii, 258p. 1972. 39.50 (*0-8047-0789-8*) Stanford U Pr.
Yuba & Sutter Counties: Changes in Harmony, an Illustrated History. Marjorie Gordon. 1988. 25.95 (*0-89781-232-8*, 5254) Am Historical Pr.
Yuba Trails - a Selection of Historic Hiking Trails in the Yuba River Watershed. 2nd ed. Susan Lamela & Hank Meals. 200p. 1996. pap. text ed. 13.95 (*0-9640817-1-7*) S E Lamela.
Yucatan. L. Dame. 1976. lib. bdg. 59.95 (*0-8490-2854-X*) Gordon Pr.
Yucatan: A Guide to the Land of Maya Mysteries. 3rd ed. Antoinette May. (Illus.). 296p. (Orig.). 1993. pap. text ed. 10.95 (*0-933174-90-X*) Wide World-Tetra.
Yucatan, a World Apart. Ed. by Edward H. Moseley & Edward D. Terry. LC 79-26492. (Illus.). 347p. 1980. reprint ed. pap. 98.90 (*0-608-01677-2*, 2062333) Bks Demand.
Yucatan Before & After the Conquest. Diego De Landa. Ed. by William Gates. LC 77-91231. (Illus.). 1978. reprint ed. pap. 4.95 (*0-486-23622-6*) Dover.
Yucatan Cookbook: Recipes & Tales. Lyman Morton. (Illus.). 256p. 1996. pap. 24.95 (*1-878610-51-1*) Red Crane Bks.
Yucatan Peninsula. (Insight Pocket Guides Ser.). (Illus.). 94p. 1994. pap. 12.95 (*0-395-71061-8*) HM.
Yucatan Peninsula. Photos & Text by C. C. Lockwood. LC 88-27260. (Illus.). xiv, 160p. 1989. 34.95 (*0-8071-1524-X*) La State U Pr.
Yucatan Peninsula Handbook: The Gulf of Mexico to the Caribbean Sea. 5th ed. Chicki Mallan. LC 94-4898. 400p. 1994. pap. 15.95 (*1-56691-024-2*) Moon Trvl Hdbks.
Yucatan's Maya Peasantry & the Origins of the Caste War. Terry Rugeley. LC 95-42405. (Illus.). 272p. 1996. pap. 19.95 (*0-292-77078-2*); text ed. 40.00 (*0-292-77074-X*) U of Tex Pr.
Yuchi Tales. Gunter Wagner. LC 73-3549. (American Ethnological Society Publications: No. 13). reprint ed. 52.50 (*0-404-58163-3*) AMS Pr.
Yuck! A Big Book of Little Horrors. Robert Snedden. 32p. (J). (gr. k-5). 1996. 15.00 (*0-689-80676-0*, S&S Bks Young Read) S&S Childrens.
***Yucka Drucka Droni.** Eugenia Radunsky. LC 97-14750. 1998. write for info. (*0-590-09837-3*) Scholastic Inc.
Yuckers. Mel Gilden. (Fifth Grade Monsters Ser.: No. 8). 96p. (J). 1989. pap. 2.95 (*0-380-75787-7*, Camelot) Avon.
Yucky Jokes & Riddles. Jeffrey S. Nelson. (Illus.). 24p. (J). (gr. 3 up). 1991. pap. 1.95 (*1-56288-014-4*) Checkerboard.
Yucky Reptile Alphabet Book. Jerry Pallotta. LC 89-60425. (Jerry Pallotta Alphabet Bks.). (J). (ps-3). 1990. 14.95 (*0-88106-460-2*); pap. 6.95 (*0-88106-454-8*); lib. bdg. 15.88 (*0-88106-680-X*) Charlesbridge Pub.
Yugo de los Infieles. Evelina V. Flores. 116p. (SPA.). 1985. reprint ed. pap. 6.50 (*0-311-37008-X*) Casa Bautista.
Yugoslav-American Economic Relations since World War II. John R. Lampe et al. LC 90-38619. 262p. (C). 1990. text ed. 39.95 (*0-8223-1061-9*) Duke.
Yugoslav Auschwitz & the Vatican: The Croatian Massacre of the Serbs During WWII. Vladimir Dedijer. Tr. by Harvey Kendall. (Illus.). 444p. (C). 1992. 29.95 (*0-87975-752-3*) Prometheus Bks.
Yugoslav Communism & the Macedonian Question. Stephen E. Palmer, Jr. & Robert King. 247p. 1971. 69.50 (*0-208-00821-7*) Elliots Bks.
Yugoslav Community of Nations. Frits W. Hondius. 1968. pap. text ed. 70.80 (*3-10-800068-3*) Mouton.
Yugoslav Crisis in International Law. Ed. by Daniel Bethlehem et al. 800p. (C). 1993. pap. text ed. 150.00 (*1-85701-016-7*, Pub. by Grotius Pubns UK) St Mut.
Yugoslav Crisis in International Law: General Issues. Ed. by Daniel L. Bethlehem & Marc Weller. (International Documents Ser.: Vol. 5). 800p. (C). 1997. pap. text ed. 125.00 (*0-521-46304-1*) Cambridge U Pr.
Yugoslav Dance: An Introduction & List of Sources Available in United States Libraries. Elsie I. Dunin & Nancy L. Ruyter. LC 80-51688. 100p. 1981. per. 10.00 (*0-918660-12-2*) Ragusan Pr.
Yugoslav Drama. Mihailo Crnobrnja. 264p. 1994. pap. 16.95 (*0-7735-1213-6*, Pub. by McGill CN) U of Toronto Pr.
Yugoslav Drama. Mihailo Crnobrnja. 264p. 1994. 44.95 (*0-7735-1203-9*, Pub. by McGill CN) U of Toronto Pr.
***Yugoslav Dream.** 2nd ed. Mihailo Crnobrnja. 1996. pap. 16.95 (*0-7735-1429-5*, Pub. by McGill CN) U of Toronto Pr.
Yugoslav Economic System: The First Labor-Managed Economy. Branko Horvat. LC 75-46111. 296p. 1976. reprint ed. pap. 84.40 (*0-7837-9945-4*, 2060672) Bks Demand.
Yugoslav Economic System & Its Performance in the Nineteen Seventies. Laura D. Tyson. LC 80-24650. (Research Ser.: No. 44). x, 115p. 1980. pap. text ed. 5.95 (*0-87725-144-4*) U of Cal IAS.
Yugoslav Economists on Problems of a Socialist Economy. Ed. by Radmila Stojanovic. Tr. by Marko Pavicic. LC 64-21436. 175p. reprint ed. pap. 49.90 (*0-317-41935-8*, 2026139) Bks Demand.
Yugoslav Economy under Self-Management. Ljubo Sirc. LC 79-11374. 1979. text ed. 35.00 (*0-312-89832-0*) St Martin.
Yugoslav Folk Music, 4 vols., Set. Bela Bartok. Ed. by Benjamin Suchoff. LC 78-8188. 1981p. 1979. text ed. 395.00 (*0-87395-383-5*) State U NY Pr.
Yugoslav Folklore: An Annotated Bibliography of Contributions in English. Yvonne R. Lockwood. LC 75-38305. 1976. per. 10.00 (*0-88247-401-4*) Ragusan Pr.
Yugoslav General Linguistics. Ed. by Milorad Radovanovic. LC 88-7614. (Linguistic & Literary Studies in Eastern Europe: Vol. 26). viii, 381p. (C). 1989. 148.00 (*90-272-1531-6*) Benjamins North Am.
Yugoslav Linguistics in English: A Bibliography 1900-1980. Dragan D. Milivojevic & Vasa D. Mihailovich. 122p. (Orig.). 1990. pap. 18.95 (*0-89357-213-6*) Slavica.
Yugoslav Literary-Theoretical Thought, 2 vols., Set. Ed. by Petar Milosavljevic. Date not set. write for info. (*90-272-1544-8*) Benjamins North Am.
Yugoslav Literary-Theoretical Thought, 2 vols., Vol. 2: 1955-1985. Ed. by Petar Milosavljevic. 400p. 1992. write for info. (*90-272-1543-X*) Benjamins North Am.
Yugoslav Literary-Theoretical Thought, Vol. 1: 1500-1955. Ed. by Petar Milosavljevic. LC 90-1117. (Linguistic & Literary Studies in Eastern Europe: Vol. 32). xxi, 521p. 1990. 153.00 (*90-272-1538-3*) Benjamins North Am.
Yugoslav Migrations to America. Branko A. Colakovic. LC 73-76007. (Illus.). 1973. pap. 15.00 (*0-88247-209-7*) Ragusan Pr.
Yugoslav Travel Pack. (Hugo's Travel Packs Ser.). 128p. (Orig.). 1990. Includes audio cassette. pap. 14.95 incl. audio (*0-85285-144-8*) Hunter NJ.
Yugoslavia. (Panorama Bks.). (Illus.). (FRE.). 3.95 (*0-685-11632-8*) Fr & Eur.
Yugoslavia. Paul Blanchard. (Blue Guides Ser.). (Illus.). 1989. pap. 18.95 (*0-393-30485-X*) Norton.
Yugoslavia. Bruce McFarlane. (Marxist Regimes Ser.). 220p. 1988. text ed. 49.00 (*0-86187-452-8*); text ed. 17.50 (*0-86187-453-6*) St Martin.
Yugoslavia. annot. rev. ed. John J. Horton. (World Bibliographical Ser.: No. 1). 279p. 1990. reprint ed. lib. bdg. 71.00 (*1-85109-105-X*) ABC-CLIO.
Yugoslavia: A Comprehensive English-Language Bibliography. Compiled by Francine Friedman. LC 92-43079. 1993. 120.00 (*0-8420-2340-2*) Scholarly Res Inc.
Yugoslavia: A Fractured Federalism. Ed. by Dennison Rusinow. LC 88-14356. (Woodrow Wilson Center Perspectives Ser.). (Illus.). 198p. (Orig.). (C). 1988. pap. text ed. 14.25 (*0-943875-07-2*, Johns Hopkins); lib. bdg. 32.00 (*0-943875-08-0*, Johns Hopkins) W Wilson Ctr Pr.
Yugoslavia: Death of a Nation. Laura Silber & Allan Little. 306p. 1996. 29.95 (*1-57500-005-9*) TV Bks.
Yugoslavia: Death of a Nation. Laura Silber. LC 96-36086. 1997. pap. 12.95 (*0-14-026263-6*, Penguin Bks) Viking Penguin.
Yugoslavia: Mistreatment of Ethnic Albanians: A Case Study. Physicians for Human Rights Staff & Barend Cohen. 30p. 1991. pap. text ed. 3.00 (*1-879707-03-9*) Phy Human Rights.
Yugoslavia: Prisoners of Conscience. Amnesty International Staff. 95p. (Orig.). (SPA.). 1985. pap. 5.00 (*0-86210-084-4*, Pub. by Amnesty Intl Pubns UK) Amnesty Intl USA.
Yugoslavia: Self-Management Socialism & the Challenges of Development. Martin Schrenk et al. LC 79-84316. (World Bank Country Economic Report Ser.). 412p. reprint ed. pap. 117.50 (*0-7837-4272-X*, 2043964) Bks Demand.
Yugoslavia: The Failure of "Democratic" Communism. Yugoslav Emigres & Dissidents Staff. LC 87-24657. (Perspectives on Freedom Ser.: No. 9). 98p. (Orig.). (C). 1988. pap. text ed. 12.75 (*0-932088-17-1*); lib. bdg. 26.25 (*0-932088-18-X*) Freedom Hse.
Yugoslavia: The New Class in Crisis. Nenad D. Popovic. LC 68-26995. 256p. reprint ed. pap. 73.00 (*0-317-52022-9*, 2027416) Bks Demand.
***Yugoslavia - Peoples, States & Society: Guide to the Microfilm Collection.** Compiled by Christopher Coleman et al. LC 96-43395. ix, 191p. 1996. lib. bdg. 125.00 (*0-88354-228-5*) N Ross.
Yugoslavia After Tito. Andrew Borowiec. LC 77-83466. (Praeger Special Studies). 138p. 1977. text ed. 55.00 (*0-275-90255-2*, C0255, Praeger Pubs) Greenwood.
***Yugoslavia & After: A Study in Fragmentation, Despair & Rebirth.** D. Dyker. (C). 1997. pap. text ed. 22.50 (*0-582-24637-7*) Addison-Wesley.
***Yugoslavia & Its Destroyers: America's Last Ambassador Tells What Happened & Why.** Warren Zimmerman. (Illus.). 269p. 25.00 (*0-614-22234-6*) Random.
Yugoslavia Army Insignia & Decorations - 1918-1990. Marian Forlan & Henad Bjelos. (Illus.). 92p. (Orig.). 1991. pap. 10.00 (*0-929757-43-2*, Pub. by Militaria Hse CN) Regt QM.
Yugoslavia As History: Twice There Was a Country. John R. Lampe. (Illus.). 300p. (C). 1996. text ed. 59.95 (*0-521-46122-7*); pap. text ed. 19.95 (*0-521-46705-5*) Cambridge U Pr.
Yugoslavia Dismembered. Catherine Samary. Tr. by Peter Drucker. 224p. 1995. 30.00 (*0-85345-921-5*, CL9215); pap. 16.00 (*0-85345-922-3*, PB9223) Monthly Rev.
Yugoslavia, East Europe & the Fourth International: The Evolution of Pabloist Liquidation. Jan Norden. Ed. by Prometheus Research Library Staff. (Prometheus Research Ser.: No. 4). 70p. 1993. 6.00 (*0-9633828-2-9*) Spartacist Pub.
Yugoslavia in Our Time. Milos Acin-Kosta & S. K. Lindsay. 200p. 1991. pap. 20.00 (*0-931931-33-9*) Ravnogorski.

Yugoslavia in Our Time, Vol. 2: Dismembered. Milos Acin-Kosta. Ed. by S. K. Lindsay. 316p. 1992. pap. 20.00 (*0-931931-34-7*) Ravnogorski.

Yugoslavia in the Age of Democracy: Essays on Economic & Political Reform. Ed. by George Macesich. LC 91-34495. 250p. 1992. text ed. 49.95 (*0-275-94175-2*, C4175, Praeger Pubs) Greenwood.

Yugoslavia in Transition: Choices & Constraints. Ed. by John B. Allcock et al. 470p. 1992. 74.00 (*0-85496-609-9*) Berg Pubs.

Yugoslavia in Turmoil: After Self-Management. Ed. by James Simmie & Jose Dekleva. 224p. 1992. text ed. 59.00 (*0-86187-141-3*) St Martin.

Yugoslavia, the Former & Future: Reflections by Scholars from the Region. Ed. by Payam Akhavan & Robert Howse. (Integrating National Economies: Promise & Pitfalls Ser.). 180p. (C). 1995. pap. 14.95 (*0-8157-0253-1*) Brookings.

Yugoslavia, the Former & Future: Reflections by Scholars from the Region. Ed. by Payam Akhavan & Robert Howse. LC 95-7556. (Integrating National Economies: Promise & Pitfalls Ser.). 181p. (C). 1995. 34.95 (*0-8157-0254-X*) Brookings.

Yugoslavia Through Documents: From Its Creation to Its Dissolution. Ed. by Snezana Trifunovska. LC 93-46785. 1104p. (C). 1994. lib. bdg. 288.00 (*0-7923-2670-9*) Kluwer Ac.

Yugoslavia, Vol. 1: A Bibliography. Valentin Leskovsek. LC 77-374918. 192p. 1974. 10.00 (*0-686-28383-X*) Studia Slovenica.

Yugoslavia, Vol. 2: A Bibliography. Valentin Leskovsek. LC 77-374918. 168p. 1978. 10.00 (*0-686-28386-4*) Studia Slovenica.

Yugoslavia, Vol. 3: A Bibliography. Valentin Leskovsek. LC 77-374918. 120p. 1980. pap. 10.00 (*0-686-26712-5*) Studia Slovenica.

Yugoslavia, Vol. 4: A Bibliography. Valentin Leskovsek. LC 77-374918. 153p. 1982. 10.00 (*0-938616-15-3*) Studia Slovenica.

Yugoslavia, 1991-1992: Could Diplomacy Have Prevented a Tragedy? James E. Bjork & Allan E. Goodman. (Pew Case Studies in International Affairs). 50p. (C). 1992. pap. text ed. 3.50 (*1-56927-453-3*) Geo U Inst Dplmcy.

***Yugoslavian Translation of the Quran.** 920p. 1996. 49.00 (*0-614-21079-8*, 1341) Kazi Pubns.

Yugoslavia's Bloody Collapse: Causes, Course & Consequences. Christopher Bennett. 272p. (C). 1995. 35.00 (*0-8147-1234-7*) NYU Pr.

Yugoslavia's Bloody Collapse: Causes, Course & Consequences. Christopher Bennett. 272p. (C). 1997. pap. 16.95 (*0-8147-1288-6*) NYU Pr.

Yugoslavia's Disintegration & the Struggle for Truth. Alex N. Dragnich. 250p. 1996. 35.00 (*0-88033-333-2*) Col U Pr.

Yugoslavia's Military Industries. Marko Milivojevic. 1992. write for info. (*0-275-93769-0*, C3769, Praeger Pubs) Greenwood.

Yugoslavia's Security Dilemmas: Army Forces, National Defence & Foreign Policy. Ed. by Marko Milivojevic et al. LC 87-23081. 332p. 1988. 72.00 (*0-85496-149-6*) Berg Pubs.

Yugoslavs & Italians in San Pedro: Political Culture & Civic Involvement. Nicholas P. Lovrich. LC 77-75809. 173p. 1977. pap. 10.00 (*0-918660-01-7*) Ragusan Pr.

Yugoslavs in Nevada: Eighteen Fifty-Nine to Nineteen Hundred. Adam S. Eterovich. LC 72-85223. 1972. pap. 10.00 (*0-88247-189-9*) Ragusan Pr.

Yuit. Yvette Edmonds. 12p. 1996. pap. text ed. 5.95 (*0-929141-20-2*, Pub. by Napoleon Pubng CN) ACCESS Pubs Network.

Yuk It up with Urkel! C. M. Appleton. 64p. (J). (ps-3). 1992. pap. 2.95 (*0-590-45745-4*) Scholastic Inc.

Yukaghir & the Yukaghirized Tungus. Vladimir I. Iokhel'son. LC 73-3531. (Jesup North Pacific Expedition Publications: Vol. 9). reprint ed. 115.00 (*0-404-58109-9*) AMS Pr.

***Yukawa Couplings & the Origins of Mass.** Ed. by Pierre Ramand. (Series in Physics). 350p. (C). 1996. 42.00 (*1-57146-025-X*) Intl Pr Boston.

Yuki. Ken Crawford. LC 95-26202. 92p. (J). (gr. 4-7). 1996. pap. 7.99 (*0-8280-1052-8*) Review & Herald.

Yuki Basketry. fac. ed. Isabel T. Kelly. (University of California Publications in American Archaeology & Ethnology: Vol. 24: 9). (Illus.). 35p. (C). 1930. reprint ed. pap. text ed. 3.35 (*1-55567-272-8*) Coyote Press.

Yuki, Temple Dog: How a California Pound Dog Became Guardian of a Japanese Buddhist Temple. Yuki. (Illus.). 1986. 18.95 (*0-914910-37-X*) Buddhist Bks.

Yuki Vocabulary. Jesse O. Sawyer & Alice Schlichter. LC 83-3465. (University of California Publications in Entomology: No. 101). 322p. 1984. pap. 91.80 (*0-7837-8424-4*, 2049226) Bks Demand.

Yukinko see Girl from the Snow Country

***Yukon.** Harry Beckett. LC 97-20690. (Journey Across Canada Ser.). 1997. write for info. (*1-55916-208-2*) Rourke Bk Co.

Yukon. Lyn Hancock. LC 95-9626. (Hello Canada Ser.). (J). 1996. lib. bdg. 18.95 (*0-8225-2765-0*, Lerner Publctns) Lerner Group.

Yukon. Suzanne LeVert. (Let's Discover Canada Ser.). (Illus.). (J). (gr. 3 up). 1992. lib. bdg. 17.95 (*0-7910-1032-5*) Chelsea Hse.

***Yukon.** Pat Morrow. 1997. pap. text ed. 24.95 (*1-55209-108-2*) Firefly Bks Ltd.

Yukon. Anne Templeman-Kluit. (Discover Canada Ser.). (Illus.). 144p. (J). (gr. 4 up). 1994. lib. bdg. 29.30 (*0-516-06622-6*) Childrens.

Yukon: The Last Frontier. Melody Webb. LC 93-12536. (Illus.). xviii, 416p. 1993. pap. 15.95 (*0-8032-9745-9*, Bison Books) U of Nebr Pr.

Yukon Challenge. John Firth. 1990. pap. text ed. 10.95 (*0-919433-85-5*) Lone Pine.

Yukon Gold. large type ed. William D. Blankenship. 507p. 1980. 25.99 (*0-7089-0532-3*) Ulverscroft.

Yukon Gold: High Hopes & Dashed Dreams. James Preyde & Susan Preyde. 1995. pap. 12.95 (*0-88839-362-8*) Hancock House.

Yukon Ho! Bill Watterson. (Calvin & Hobbes Collection). (Illus.). 128p. (Orig.). 1989. pap. 9.95 (*0-8362-1835-3*) Andrews & McMeel.

Yukon Justice. Dana F. Ross. (Holts, an American Dynasty Ser.: No. 7). 368p. 1992. 5.99 (*0-553-29763-5*) Bantam.

Yukon Justice. large type ed. Dana F. Ross. LC 92-15296. (General Ser.). 1992. 18.95 (*0-8161-5488-0*) G K Hall.

***Yukon Justice.** large type ed. Dana F. Ross. LC 92-15296. (General Ser.). 1992. lib. bdg. 21.95 (*0-8161-5487-2*, GK Hall) Thorndike Pr.

Yukon Kid. James B. Hendryx. 1976. 24.95 (*0-88411-838-X*) Amereon Ltd.

Yukon Lady: A Tale of Loyalty & Courage. Hugh Maclean & Emma Smythe. (Illus.). 180p. 1985. pap. text ed. 11.95 (*0-88839-186-2*) Hancock House.

Yukon Massacre. Jon Sharpe. (Trailsman Ser.: No. 163). 176p. (Orig.). 1995. mass mkt. 3.99 (*0-451-18220-0*, Sig) NAL-Dutton.

***Yukon Memories: A Mounties Story.** Jack T. Watson. 1994. pap. 12.95 (*1-55110-052-5*, Pub. by Whitecap Bks CN) Gr Arts Ctr Pub.

Yukon Paradise. Edith R. Tjepkema. (Northwest Paradise Ser.: Vol. 3). 126p. (Orig.). (YA). (gr. 8-12). 1990. pap. 4.50 (*0-9620280-2-9*) Northland Pr.

Yukon Poems. Robert W. Service. LC 75-17021. (Wild & Woolly West Ser., No. 4). (Illus.). 36p. 1967. pap. 3.50 (*0-910584-04-4*) Filter.

***Yukon Poems of Robert W. Service.** rev. ed. Robert W. Service. (Illus.). 26p. 1997. reprint ed. pap. 3.95 (*0-86541-040-2*) Filter.

Yukon Queen. Gilbert Morris. (House of Winslow Ser.: Bk. 17). 288p. 1995. pap. 9.99 (*1-55661-393-8*) Bethany Hse.

Yukon River: An Adventure to the Gold Fields of the Klondike. Peter Lourie. LC 91-77600. (Illus.). 48p. (J). (gr. 3-7). 1992. lib. bdg. 15.95 (*1-878093-90-8*) Boyds Mills Pr.

Yukon River Steamboats: A Pictorial History. Stan B. Cohen. LC 82-81717. (Illus.). 128p. (Orig.). 1982. pap. text ed. 9.95 (*0-933126-19-0*) Pictorial Hist.

Yukon Riverboat Days. Joyce Yardley. 192p. (Orig.). (C). 1996. pap. 12.95 (*0-88839-386-5*) Hancock House.

Yukon Solo. Karal Dohnal. LC 83-70953. (Illus.). 240p. 1984. pap. 8.95 (*0-8323-0421-2*) Binford Mort.

Yukon Territory. Alaska Geographic Staff. Ed. by Penny Rennick. (Alaska Geographic Ser.: Vol. 25-2). (Illus.). 112p. (Orig.). 1998. pap. 21.95 (*1-56661-041-9*) Alaska Geog Soc.

Yukon Territory: The Narrative of W. H. Dall, Leader of the Expedition to Alaska in 1866-1868 & the Narrative of an Exploration Made in 1887 in the Yukon District by George M. Dawson. F. Mortimer Trimmer. LC 74-5885. reprint ed. 74.50 (*0-404-11694-9*) AMS Pr.

Yukoners: True Tales of the Yukon. Harry Gordon-Cooper. (Illus.). 144p. (Orig.). 1990. pap. 12.95 (*0-88839-232-X*) Hancock House.

Yukpa Cultivation System: A Study of Shifting Cultivation in Colombia & Venezuela. Kenneth Ruddle. LC 73-78557. (Ibero-Americana Ser.: No. 52). (Illus.). 234p. reprint ed. pap. 66.70 (*0-685-23797-4*, 2032896) Bks Demand.

Yul: The Man Who Would Be King. large type ed. Rock Brynner. LC 90-10935. 475p. 1990. reprint ed. lib. bdg. 18.95 (*1-56054-017-6*) Thorndike Pr.

Yul Brynner, Photographer. Ed. by Victoria Brynner. LC 95-47200. (Illus.). 210p. 1996. 39.95 (*0-8109-3144-3*) Abrams.

Yule & Christmas. Alexander Tille. 1977. lib. bdg. 59.95 (*0-8490-2855-8*) Gordon Pr.

***Yule of Witches, Vol. 2.** Jeff N. Foster. 13p. 1997. 7.50 (*0-9654720-3-5*) Dormant Press.

***Yule of Witches Working in the Nude.** Jeff N. Foster. 13p. 1995. 7.50 (*0-9654720-2-7*) Dormant Press.

Yuletide at Winterthur: Tastes & Visions of the Season. (Illus.). 1980. pap. 5.00 (*0-912724-09-9*) Winterthur.

Yuletide Breads. Ann Babcock. 26p. (Orig.). 1995. pap. 6.95 (*0-9627121-1-6*) A&G Babcock.

***Yuletide Bride.** Daniels. 1997. mass mkt. 3.99 (*0-373-07827-7*) Harlequin Bks.

Yuletide Bride. Mary Lyons. 1995. mass mkt. 3.25 (*0-373-11781-7*, 1-11781-1) Harlequin Bks.

***Yuletide Delights: With Antique Changing Pictures.** Piggytoes Press Staff. (Ernest Nister's Mini Christmas Books Ser.). 1997. 4.95 (*1-888443-32-4*, Piggytoes Pr) Intervisual Bks.

Yuletide Guitar Songbook. rev. ed. Ed. by Aaron Stang. 48p. (Orig.). (YA). 1995. pap. text ed. 8.95 (*0-89898-640-0*, F3347GTA) Warner Brothers.

Yuletide Lost. Mark Day. 1981. 5.20 (*0-89536-484-0*, 2506) CSS OH.

Yuletide Match. Margaret Westhaven. 224p. (Orig.). 1993. pap. 3.99 (*0-451-17740-1*, Sig) NAL-Dutton.

Yuletide Stories. Ed. by Benjamin Thorpe. LC 68-55557. (Bohn's Antiquarian Library). reprint ed. 42.50 (*0-404-50024-2*) AMS Pr.

Yuletide Treasures. Ed. by John P. Beilenson. (Keepsakes with CDs Ser.). 1995. 11.99 incl. audio compact disk (*0-88088-945-4*) Peter Pauper.

Yulkina Skazka - Yuly's Tale. Leonid Posudievsky. (Illus.). 50p. (Orig.). (RUS.). write for info. (*1-885563-03-5*) VIA Press MD.

Yum! Irresistible, Fun-to-Create, Reliable Recipes. John L. Leonard. LC 90-94321. (Illus.). 394p. 1995. text ed. 17.95 (*0-9646465-5-2*) Heron Hill Pr.

Yum! Yum! Illus. by Kate Gleeson. (Golden Cozy Bks.). 8p. (J). (ps). 1994. text ed. 4.94 (*0-307-13351-6*, Golden Books) Western Pub.

***Yum-Yum!** Mick Manning & Brita Granstrom. LC 97-10726. (J). 1997. write for info. (*0-531-14484-4*); pap. write for info. (*0-531-15322-3*) Watts.

Yum Yum. Sian Tucker. (J). 1994. 4.50 (*0-671-89114-6*, Litl Simon S&S) S&S Childrens.

***Yum Yum Gum.** Groves. 1991. pap. text ed. write for info. (*0-582-05904-6*, Pub. by Longman UK) Longman.

Yum, Yum, Yum. Andy Warhol. 1996. 10.95 (*0-8212-2133-7*) Bulfinch Pr.

Yuma. large type ed. Russell Smith. (Linford Western Library). 256p. 1985. pap. 15.99 (*0-7089-6192-4*) Ulverscroft.

***Yuma: Frontier Crossing of the Far Southwest.** Clifford E. Trafzer. 1980. pap. 7.95 (*0-86546-013-2*) Yuma Cnty Hist.

Yuma see Indians of North America

Yuma Crossing. fac. ed. Douglas D. Martin. LC 54-10446. (Illus.). 260p. 1995. pap. 9.95 (*0-9632228-1-3*) Yuma Cnty Hist.

Yuman & Yaqui Music. Frances Densmore. (Bureau of American Ethnology Bulletins Ser.). 216p. 1995. lib. bdg. 89.00 (*0-7812-4110-3*) Rprt Serv.

Yuman & Yaqui Music. Frances Densmore. LC 72-1884. (Music Ser.). (Illus.). 272p. 1972. reprint ed. lib. bdg. 27.50 (*0-306-70512-5*) Da Capo.

Yuman Tribes of the Gila River. Leslie Spier. LC 74-118641. (Illus.). 1970. reprint ed. lib. bdg. 53.50 (*0-8154-0333-X*) Cooper Sq.

Yuman Tribes of the Gila River. Leslie Spier. LC 77-92480. (Illus.). 1978. reprint ed. pap. 8.95 (*0-486-23611-0*) Dover.

Yuman Tribes of the Lower Colorado. fac. ed. A. L. Kroeber. (University of California Publications in American Archaeology & Ethnology: Vol. 16: 8). 10p. (C). 1920. reprint ed. pap. text ed. 1.20 (*1-55567-226-4*) Coyote Press.

Yumayk Yumayk: Long Ago. Villiana Hyde & Eric Elliot. LC 94-16392. 1995. 150.00 (*0-520-09791-2*) U CA Pr.

Yummers! James Marshall. LC 72-5400. (Illus.). 32p. (J). (gr. k-3). 1973. 14.95 (*0-395-14757-3*) HM.

Yummers! James Marshall. (Illus.). (J). (gr. 4-8). 1986. pap. 5.95 (*0-395-39590-9*, Sandpiper) HM.

Yummers Too: The Second Course. James Marshall. (Illus.). 32p. (J). (gr. k-3). 1990. pap. 5.95 (*0-395-53967-6*) HM.

***Yummy Treat.** 1997. pap. write for info. (*0-8289-1007-3*) Viking Penguin.

***Yun & the Sea Serpent, Vol. 1.** John Vornholt. (Warriors of Virtue Ser.: No. 1). 112p. 1997. mass mkt. 3.99 (*1-57297-283-1*) Blvd Books.

***Yunas Emre & His Mystical Poetry.** 3rd ed. Ed. by Talat Halman. LC 81-81923. 208p. (C). Date not set. pap. text ed. 16.95 (*1-878318-01-2*) IN Univ Turkish.

Yundong: Mass Campaigns in Chinese Communist Leadership. Gordon Bennett. LC 75-620060. (China Research Monographs: No. 12). 133p. 1976. pap. text ed. 2.25 (*0-912966-15-7*) IEAS.

Yung Wing: The First Chinese Student in the United States. Shao Yuen Carol. (Connecticut Educational History Ser.). 24p. 1987. pap. 2.50 (*0-685-09437-5*) I N Thut World Educ Ctr.

Yunini's Story of the Trail of Tears. Ada L. Barry. LC 74-7924. (Illus.). reprint ed. 49.50 (*0-404-11810-0*) AMS Pr.

Yunmi & Halmoni's Trip. Choi Sook Nyul. LC 96-22013. (J). 1997. 15.00 (*0-395-81180-5*) HM.

Yunnan. Paddy Booz. (Illus.). 208p. 1987. pap. 9.95 (*0-8442-9822-0*, Passport Bks) NTC Pub Grp.

Yunnan. 2nd ed. Thomas Cook. (Illustrated Travel Guides from Thomas Cook Ser.). 1995. pap. 16.95 (*0-8442-9664-3*, Passport Bks) NTC Pub Grp.

Yunnan Camellias of China. Ed. by Academia Sinica, Kunming Inst. of Botany Staff. (Illus.). 169p. 1986. text ed. 75.00 (*0-945345-10-0*, Pub. by Sci Pr CH) Lubrecht & Cramer.

Yunnan Province, China Business: A Trade, Business & Investment Encyclopedia with Major Companies Directory. Sherman Hayes et al. (Illus.). 300p. 1995. 99.00 (*0-9640857-0-4*) Busn Connect.

Yunnan School: A Renaissance in Chinese Painting. Joan L. Cohen. LC 87-83744. (Illus.). 160p. 1988. 75.00 (*0-9619771-0-8*) Fingerhut Group.

***Yunus: The Repentant.** Amina I. Ali. Ed. by J. C. Cinquino. (Prophets' Stories for Children from the Holy Qur'an Ser.: No. 17). (Illus.). 28p. (Orig.). (J). (gr. 4-6). 1996. write for info. (*1-881963-36-5*); pap. 2.50 (*1-881963-37-3*) Al-Saadawi Pubns.

Yunus Emre & His Mystical Poetry. 2nd ed. Yunus Emre. Ed. by Ilhan Basgoz. Tr. & Intro. by Talat S. Halman. (Turkish Studies Ser.: Vol. 2, No. 9). 199p. (C). 1981. text ed. 11.95 (*0-685-29319-X*) IN Univ Turkish.

Yupiaq Worldview: A Pathway to Ecology & Spirit. A. Oscar Kawagley. (Illus.). 165p. (Orig.). (C). 1995. pap. text ed. 10.50 (*0-88133-859-1*) Waveland Pr.

Yup'ik Eskimo Dictionary. Illus. by Cindy Davis. viii, 757p. (C). 1984. pap. 25.00 (*0-933769-21-0*) Alaska Native.

Yup'ik Eskimo Prosodic Systems: Descriptive & Comparative Studies. Michael Krauss et al. (Alaska Native Language Center Research Papers Ser.: No. 7). (Illus.). vi, 216p. 1985. pap. 15.00 (*0-933769-37-7*) Alaska Native.

Yup'ik Eskimo Word Chooser. Steven A. Jacobson & Anna Jacobson. 27p. (Orig.). 1996. pap. text ed. 2.00 (*1-55500-055-X*, CY14) Alaska Native.

Yup'ik Phrase & Conversation Lessons. Anna W. Jacobson. Ed. by Steven A. Jacobson. 62p. (Orig.). (ESK.). 1996. pap. 16.00 incl. audio (*1-55500-056-8*) Alaska Native.

Yuppies from Hell, No. 1. Barbara Slate. 48p. 1989. 2.95 (*0-87135-609-0*) Marvel Entmnt.

Yuppies from Hell, No. 3. Barbara Slate. 48p. 1992. 2.95 (*0-87135-893-X*) Marvel Entmnt.

Yuppies Invade My House at Dinnertime: A Tale of Brunch, Bombs, & Gentrification in an American City. Ed. by Joseph Barry & John Derevlany. LC 87-82140. (Illus.). 208p. (Orig.). 1987. pap. 7.95 (*0-944421-01-6*) Big River NJ.

Yuqui: Forest Nomads in a Changing World. Allyn M. Stearman. 192p. (C). 1989. text ed. 13.50 (*0-03-022702-X*) HB Coll Pubs.

Yurak Chrestomathy. Gyula Decsy. LC 65-63391. (Uralic & Altaic Ser.: Vol. 50). (Orig.). 1966. pap. text ed. 9.00 (*0-87750-004-5*) Res Inst Inner Asian Studies.

Yuraq Janka: A Guide to Cordilleras Blanca & Rosco. John F. Ricker. LC 77-82861. (Illus.). 180p. 1977. pap. 12.95 (*0-930410-05-X*) Amer Alpine Club.

Yuri Andropov. Solovyov. 1982. 15.95 (*0-02-612290-1*) Macmillan.

Yuri Kuper: Homage to the Box. Tr. by Regina Kozakova. 28p. (Orig.). 1992. pap. 20.00 (*0-9626731-1-0*) Yoshii Gallery.

Yuri Trifonov's The Moscow Cycle: A Critical Study. Colin Partridge. LC 89-12941. (Studies in Slavic Language & Literature: Vol. 3). 208p. 1990. lib. bdg. 89.95 (*0-88946-293-3*) E Mellen.

Yurok Affixes. fac. ed. T. T. Waterman. (University of California Publications in American Archaeology & Ethnology: Vol. 20: 18). 20p. (C). 1923. reprint ed. pap. text ed. 2.15 (*1-55567-254-X*) Coyote Press.

Yurok & Neighboring Kin Term Systems. fac. ed. A. L. Kroeber. (University of California Publications in American Archaeology & Ethnology: Vol. 35: 2). 10p. (C). 1934. reprint ed. pap. text ed. 1.20 (*1-55567-298-1*) Coyote Press.

Yurok Geography. fac. ed. T. T. Waterman. (University of California Publications in American Archaeology & Ethnology: Vol. 16: 5). 209p. (C). 1920. reprint ed. pap. text ed. 18.70 (*1-55567-225-6*) Coyote Press.

Yurok-Karok Basket Weavers. Lila M. O'Neale. LC 95-36643. (Classics in California Anthropology Ser.). 1995. write for info. (*0-936127-06-6*); pap. write for info. (*0-936127-04-X*) P A Hearst Mus.

Yurok-Karok Basket Weavers. fac. ed. Lila M. O'Neale. (University of California Publications in American Archaeology & Ethnology: Vol. 32: 1). (Illus.). 244p. (C). 1932. reprint ed. pap. text ed. 21.85 (*1-55567-287-6*) Coyote Press.

Yurok Marriages. fac. ed. T. T. Waterman & A. L. Kroeber. (University of California Publications in American Archaeology & Ethnology: Vol. 35: 1). 16p. (C). 1934. reprint ed. pap. text ed. 1.80 (*1-55567-297-3*) Coyote Press.

Yurok Myths. Alfred L. Kroeber. LC 75-3772. 460p. 1975. 42.50 (*0-520-02977-1*); pap. 13.00 (*0-520-03639-5*) U CA Pr.

Yurok Narratives. fac. ed. Robert Spott & A. L. Kroeber. (University of California Publications in American Archaeology & Ethnology: Vol. 35: 9). 117p. (C). 1942. reprint ed. pap. text ed. 10.65 (*1-55567-302-3*) Coyote Press.

Yurugu: An Afrocentric Critique of European Cultural Thought & Behavior. Marimba Ani. LC 91-71027. 1994. 59.95 (*0-86543-249-X*); pap. 18.95 (*0-86543-248-1*) Africa World.

Yurupari: Studies of an Amazonian Foundation Myth. Gerardo Reichel-Dolmatoff. LC 95-41259. (Religions of the World Ser.). 348p. 1996. 24.95 (*0-945454-08-2*) Harvard U Wrld Relig.

Yury Trifonov: A Critical Study. Nina Kolesnikoff. 1990. 32.95 (*0-87501-051-2*) Ardis Pubs.

Yusef: The Journey of the Frangi; a Crusade in the East. John R. Browne. Ed. by Moshe Davis. LC 77-70686. (America & the Holy Land Ser.). (Illus.). 1977. reprint ed. lib. bdg. 35.95 (*0-405-10232-1*) Ayer.

Yusef: or The Journey of the Frangi: A Crusade in the East. John R. Browne. (American Biography Ser.). 421p. 1991. reprint ed. lib. bdg. 89.00 (*0-7812-8045-1*) Rprt Serv.

Yushi & the Thunder Dragon. Chuck Hudson. 22p. (Orig.). (J). (gr. 2-9). 1993. pap. 3.50 (*1-57514-129-9*, 1141) Encore Perform Pub.

Yust for Fun. Eleonora Olson & Ethel Olson. (Illus.). 60p. 1979. reprint ed. pap. 2.50 (*0-9602914-1-5*) Eggs Pr.

***Yusuf: The Honest.** Amina I. Ali. Ed. by J. C. Cinquino. (Prophets' Stories for Children from the Holy Qur'an Ser.: No. 10). (Illus.). 28p. (Orig.). (J). (gr. 4-6). 1996. write for info. (*1-881963-22-5*); pap. 2.50 (*1-881963-23-3*) Al-Saadawi Pubns.

***Yusuf African Yearbook 1994.** 1995. lib. bdg. 178.00 (*0-7923-3284-9*) Kluwer Ac.

***Yusuf African Yearbook 1995.** 1996. 295.00 (*90-411-0268-X*) Kluwer Law Tax Pubs.

Yusuf & Zulaikha. Jami. Tr. by David L. Pendlebury. 185p. 1980. 22.00 (*0-900860-77-4*, Pub. by Octagon Pr UK) ISHK.

Yusuf Idris: Changing Visions. Dalya Cohen-Mor. (C). 1992. 39.95 (*1-880613-00-X*) Sheba Pr.

Yusuf Idris: The Piper Dies & Other Stories. Dalya Cohen-Mor. (C). 1992. pap. 15.95 (*1-880613-03-4*) Sheba Pr.

Yusuf Meherally: Quest for New Horizons. Madhu Dandavate. 1986. 19.00 (*0-86132-139-1*, Pub. by Popular Prakashan II) S Asia.

***YUUP's Adventure in the Dords.** Constance Hewes. (Illus.). 16p. (Orig.). (J). (ps-2). 1996. mass mkt. write for info. (*1-889969-01-X*) Zuka Pub.

Yuwipi: Vision & Experience in Oglala Ritual. William K. Powers. LC 81-10501. (Illus.). xiii, 113p. 1982. reprint ed. pap. 6.95 (*0-8032-8710-0*, Bison Books) U of Nebr Pr.

Yvain & Gawain, Sir Percyvell, The Anturs of Arthur. Intro. by Maldwyn Mills. 256p. 1992. pap. text ed. 10.95 (*0-460-87077-7*, Everyman's Classic Lib) C E Tuttle.

Yvain dans le Miroir: Une Poetique de la reflexion dans le "Chevalier au lion" de Chretien de Troyes. Joan T. Grimbert. LC 87-35322. (Purdue University Monographs in Romance Languages: Vol. 25). xii, 226p. (C). 1988. 65.00 (*1-55619-004-2*); pap. 19.95 (*1-55619-055-7*) Benjamins North Am.

Yvain (Le Chevalier au Lion) Chretien De Troyes. (French Texts Ser.). 288p. (Orig.). (FRE.). 1984. reprint ed. pap. text ed. 11.95 (*0-7190-0134-X*, Pub. by Manchester Univ Pr UK) St Martin.

Yvain: or The Knight with the Lion. Chretien de Troyes. Tr. by Ruth H. Cline from FRE. LC 73-85026. 222p. 1975. pap. 15.00 (*0-8203-0758-0*) U of Ga Pr.

Yvain, Ou le Chevalier Au Lion. Chretien De Troyes. Ed. by Jan A. Nelson. LC 68-22800. (Medieval French Literature Ser.). (Orig.). (C). 1968. pap. 6.95 (*0-89197-477-6*) Irvington.

Yvain, the Knight of the Lion. Chretien De Troyes. LC 86-23346. 224p. 1987. pap. 15.00 (*0-300-03838-0*) Yale U Pr.

***Yves Brunier: Landscape Architect.** Rem Koolhaas. (Illus.). 128p. 1996. pap. 56.00 (*3-7643-5436-4*) Birkhauser.

Yves de Vallone: The Making of an Espirit-Fort. James O'Higgins. 1982. lib. bdg. 93.00 (*90-247-2520-8*) Kluwer Ac.

***Yves Duteil - Ton Absence.** Ed. by Michael Lefferts. 84p. (Orig.). (C). 1997. pap. text ed. 25.95 (*0-7692-0837-1*, 01020684) Warner Brothers.

Yves Klein. Sidra Stich. (Illus.). 296p. 1995. 60.00 (*3-89322-657-5*) Dist Art Pubs.

Yves Klein: Fire at the Heart of the Void. Pierre Restany. Ed. by Klaus Ottmann. Tr. by Andrea Loselle from FRE. (Journal of Contemporary Art Editions). (Illus.). 160p. (Orig.). (C). 1992. pap. 19.95 (*0-9634713-0-9*) Jrnl Contemp.

Yves Klein Nineteen Twenty-Eight to Nineteen Sixty-Two: A Retrospective. Ed. by Institute for the Arts Staff. LC 81-86085. (Illus.). 1982. pap. 25.00 (*0-914412-27-2*) Inst for the Arts.

***Yves Klein Nineteen Twenty-Eight to Nineteen Sixty-Two: A Retrospective.** Ed. by Institute for the Arts Staff. (Illus.). 1982. 45.00 (*0-614-23211-2*) Inst for the Arts.

Yves Saint Laurent. Berge. 1997. 18.95 (*0-7893-0067-2*) Universe.

Yves Saint Laurent. Rawsthorn Alice. 320p. 1997. 27.50 (*0-385-47645-0*, N A Talese) Doubleday.

Yves Tanguy. James T. Soby. LC 75-169321. (Museum of Modern Art Publications in Reprint). 72p. 1979. reprint ed. 18.95 (*0-405-01579-8*) Ayer.

Yves Theriault, Master Storyteller. Gudrun M. Hesse. LC 92-28961. (American University Studies: Romance Languages & Literature: Ser. II, Vol. 145). 182p. (C). 1993. text ed. 39.95 (*0-8204-1322-4*) P Lang Pubng.

Yvette-a Novelette, & Ten Other Stories. Guy De Maupassant. Tr. by John Galsworthy. LC 70-150550. (Short Story Index Reprint Ser.). 1977. reprint ed. 18.95 (*0-8369-3847-X*) Ayer.

Yvon Delbos at the Quai D'Orsay: French Foreign Policy During the Popular Front, 1936-1938. John E. Dreifort. LC 72-85252. xiv, 274p. 1973. 29.95 (*0-7006-0094-9*) U Pr of KS.

Yvonne Goes to York. large type ed. Marion Chesney. LC 93-8878. (Travelling Matchmaker Ser.: Vol. 6). 1993. lib. bdg. 15.95 (*0-8161-5834-7*, GK Hall) Thorndike Pr.

Yvonne Jacquette: Tokyo Nightviews. LC 86-60688. (Illus.). 10p. (Orig.). 1986. pap. 5.00 (*0-916606-11-2*) Bowdoin Coll.

Yvonne Porcella: A Colorful Book. Yvonne Porcella. LC 85-90510. (Illus.). 120p. (Orig.). 1986. pap. 22.00 (*0-936589-00-0*) Porcella Studios.

***Yvonne's 10001 Nights.** Yvonne De Carlo & H. Arch. Date not set. write for info. (*0-688-04511-1*) Morrow.

Ywain: The Knight of the Lion. rev. ed. Chretien De Troyes. Tr. by Robert Ackerman et al. from FRE. 114p. (C). 1992. reprint ed. pap. text ed. 6.95 (*0-88133-716-1*) Waveland Pr.

Z

Z. Vassilis Vassilikos. Tr. by Marilyn Calman. LC 91-10184. 406p. 1991. pap. 10.95 (*0-941423-50-6*) FWEW.

Z: A Beginner's Guide. D. Rann. 1994. pap. 31.95 (*0-412-55660-X*, Blackie & Son-Chapman NY) Routledge Chapman & Hall.

***Z: A Dave Riley Novel.** Bob Mayer. LC 96-43054. (Dave Riley Adventures Ser.: Vol. 6). 288p. 1997. 21.95 (*0-89141-510-6*) Presidio Pr.

Z: An Introduction to Formal Methods. 2nd ed. Antoni Diller. LC 94-4943. 374p. 1994. pap. text ed. 72.00 (*0-471-93973-0*) Wiley.

Z Best of Windows Shareware. Richard Petersen. 1995. pap. text ed. 34.95 (*1-57001-004-8*) Pacif Pub Grp.

Z Camelopardalis Light Curves 1927-1995: AAVSO Monograph 6. Janet A. Mattei et al. (Illus.). 72p. 1996. pap. text ed. 10.00 (*1-878174-12-6*) Am Assn Var Star.

Z-Candide. Gordon. Date not set. pap. text ed. write for info. (*0-312-14854-2*) St Martin.

Z Car: A Legend in Its Own Time. Ben Millspauch. 1993. pap. 16.95 (*0-8306-4339-7*) McGraw-Hill Prof.

Z Car: A Legend in Its Own Time. Ben P. Millspaugh. (Illus.). 208p. 1990. 24.95 (*0-8306-3536-X*, 3536) McGraw-Hill Prof.

Z-Comparative World History Reading. Stearus. Date not set. pap. text ed. write for info. (*0-312-14855-0*) St Martin.

Z-Contours of Power. 2nd ed. Snow. Date not set. pap. text ed. write for info. (*0-312-14829-1*) St Martin.

Z-D Generation. Ed Sanders. 32p. 1981. pap. 3.50 (*0-930794-35-4*) Station Hill Pr.

Z Degree Physics: Cargese 1990. Ed. by M. Levy et al. (NATO ASI Series B, Physics: Vol. 261). (Illus.). 522p. 1991. 135.00 (*0-306-43934-4*, Plenum Pr) Plenum.

Z Eros. Alurista. LC 94-32330. (Orig.). 1995. pap. 9.00 (*0-927534-45-2*) Biling Rev-Pr.

***Z Files: A Ziggy Collection.** Tom Wilson. (Illus.). 128p. (Orig.). 1997. pap. 7.95 (*0-8362-3681-5*) Andrews & McMeel.

Z-5 - Secret Teachings of the Golden Dawn Bk. I: The Neophyte Ritual O Equals O. A. L. Soror. LC 90-26728. (Golden Dawn Ser.). (Illus.). 229p. (Orig.). 1991. pap. 12.95 (*0-87542-897-5*) Llewellyn Pubns.

Z-5 - Secret Teachings of the Golden Dawn Bk. II: The Zelator Ritual One Equals Ten. Pat Zalewski & Christine Zalewski. LC 90-26728. (Golden Dawn Ser.). (Illus.). 240p. 1992. pap. 12.95 (*0-87542-896-7*) Llewellyn Pubns.

Z for Software Engineers. Lesley Semmens & Allen. (Computers & Their Applications Ser.). 250p. 1992. text ed. 55.00 (*0-13-978230-3*, 260302) P-H.

Z for Zachariah. Robert C. O'Brien. LC 86-23228. 256p. (YA). (gr. 7 up). 1987. reprint ed. pap. 4.50 (*0-02-044650-0*) Macmillan.

Z-Im Poetry Intro. 2nd ed. Meyer. Date not set. pap. text ed. write for info. (*0-312-14836-4*) St Martin.

Z-Im Presence of Others. Andrea A. Lunsford. Date not set. pap. text ed. write for info. (*0-312-14831-3*) St Martin.

Z in Practice. Rosalind Barden et al. LC 94-30571. (BCS Practitioner Ser.). 407p. (C). 1995. pap. text ed. 48.00 (*0-13-124934-7*) P-H.

Z Is for Zebra. Beth Tubbs. (Illus.). 32p. (J). (ps). 1992. 9.95 (*0-9632993-3-6*) Storytime Pub.

Z Is for Zombie. Mel Gilden. (Fifth Grade Monsters Ser.: No. 5). 96p. (J). (gr. 3-7). 1988. pap. 2.75 (*0-380-75686-2*, Camelot) Avon.

Z Is for Zorglub. Andre Franquin. Tr. by Kim Thompson from FRE. (Spirou & Fantasio Ser.: No. 1). (Illus.). 64p. (Orig.). (J). (gr. 2-7). 1995. pap. 8.95 (*1-887911-51-0*) Fantsy Flight.

Z Notation: A Reference Manual. 2nd ed. Mike Spivey. 200p. 1992. pap. text ed. 43.00 (*0-13-978529-9*) P-H.

Z R Wins. Fitzhugh Green. Ed. by R. Reginald & Douglas Melville. LC 77-84232. (Lost Race & Adult Fantasy Ser.). 1978. reprint ed. lib. bdg. 26.95 (*0-405-10980-6*) Ayer.

Z-Town Trilogy. Achmat Dangor. 160p. (Orig.). 1989. pap. 19.95 (*0-86975-395-9*, Pub. by Ravan Pr ZA) Ohio U Pr.

Z Transform Theory & Applications. Robert Vich. (C). 1987. lib. bdg. 139.00 (*90-277-1917-9*) Kluwer Ac.

Z User Workshop: Proceedings of the Fourth Annual Z User Meeting, 15 December 1989, Oxford, U. K. Ed. by J. E. Nicholls & C. J. Van Rijsbergen. (Workshops in Computing Ser.). (Illus.). 288p. 1990. pap. 59.00 (*0-387-19627-7*) Spr-Verlag.

Z User Workshop: Proceedings of the Seventh Annual Z user Meeting, London, 14-15 December 1992. 7th ed. Ed. by J. P. Bowen & J. E. Edward. LC 93-3819. 1993. 85.95 (*0-387-19818-0*) Spr-Verlag.

Z User Workshop, Cambridge, 1994: Proceedings of the 8th Z User Meeting, Cambridge, 29-30 June 1994. Ed. by J. P. Bowen & J. A. Hall. LC 94-15509. (Workshops in Computing Ser.). 1994. 78.95 (*0-387-19884-9*) Spr-Verlag.

Z User Workshop Oxford 1990: Proceedings of the Annual Meeting, 5th, December 17-18, 1990, U. K. Ed. by J. E. Nicholls & C. J. Van Rijsbergen. (Workshops in Computing Ser.). ix, 387p. 1991. pap. 59.00 (*0-387-19672-2*) Spr-Verlag.

Z User Workshop, York 1991: Proceedings of the Sixth Annual Z User Meeting York, 16-17 December 1991. J. E. Nicholls. Ed. by C. J. Van Rijsbergen. (Workshops in Computing Ser.). (Illus.). viii, 403p. 1992. 69.00 (*0-387-19780-X*) Spr-Verlag.

Z Was Zapped: A Play in Twenty-Six Acts. Chris Van Allsburg. (Illus.). 56p. (J). (ps up). 1987. 17.95 (*0-395-44612-0*, Clarion Bks) HM.

Z-World of Ideas. 5th ed. Jacobus. Date not set. pap. text ed. write for info. (*0-312-14863-1*) St Martin.

Z-80 Microprocessor. 2nd ed. Gaonkar. 1992. text ed. 87.00 (*0-02-340484-1*, Macmillan Coll) P-H.

Z-80 Microprocessor Technology: Hardware, Software & Interfacing. James W. Bignell & Robert Donovan. 416p. 1986. text ed. 52.50 (*0-8273-2492-8*) Delmar.

Z-80 Microprocessor Technology: Hardware, Software & Interfacing. James W. Bignell & Robert Donovan. 416p. 1986. teacher ed. 16.00 (*0-8273-2493-6*) Delmar.

Z-80 Tutor, Applications Vol. III: Assembly Language for TRS-80 & Other Z-80 Computers. Christopher Fara. 37p. 1990. lab manual ed., student ed. 9.95 (*1-880099-07-1*) Microdex Bkshelf.

Z-80 Tutor, Introduction Vol. I: Assembly Language for TRS-80 & Other Z-80 Computers. Christopher Fara. 39p. 1990. lab manual ed., student ed. 9.95 (*1-880099-05-5*) Microdex Bkshelf.

Z-80 Tutor, Reference Vol. X: Assembly Language for TRS-80 & Other Z-80 Computers. Christopher Fara. 63p. 1990. lab manual ed., student ed. 12.95 (*1-880099-08-X*) Microdex Bkshelf.

Z-80 Tutor, Toolbox Vol. II: Assembly Language for TRS-80 & Other Z-80 Computers. Christopher Fara. 33p. 1990. student ed. 9.95 (*1-880099-06-3*) Microdex Bkshelf.

Za Grekhi Roditelei (For the Parents Sins) Povesti I Rasskazy (Novels & Stories) Larisa Morskaya. (Illus.). 224p. (C). 1991. pap. 14.00 (*0-911971-55-6*) Effect Pub.

Za Trideviat Zemel: Antologiia Emigrantskoi Prozy 1980s. Aksenov et al. LC 92-21114. 162p. (Orig.). (RUS.). 1992. pap. 12.00 (*1-55779-022-1*) Hermitage.

Za-Za's Baby Brother. Lucy Cousins. LC 94-47190. (Illus.). (J). (ps up). 1995. 16.95 (*1-56402-582-9*) Candlewick Pr.

***Za-Za's Baby Brother.** Lucy Cousins. LC 94-47190. (Illus.). 32p. (J). (ps-k). 1997. reprint ed. pap. 7.99 (*0-7636-0337-6*) Candlewick Pr.

Zab: Brevet Major Zabdiel Boylston Adams, 1829-1902, Physician. Charles N. Peabody. 255p. 1984. 17.50 (*0-8139-1066-8*) F A Countway.

Zabajaba Jungle. William Steig. LC 87-17690. (Michael di Capua Bks.). (Illus.). (J). (ps-4). 1987. 15.00 (*0-374-38790-7*) FS&G.

Zabajaba Jungle. William Steig. LC 87-17690. (Michael di Capua Bks.). (Illus.). (J). (ps-4). 1991. pap. 4.95 (*0-374-49594-7*) FS&G.

Zabavi Nasmeshlivoi Zvezdi. Mark Kogan. Ed. by Olga Chotianovsky. (Illus.). 129p. (Orig.). (YA). 1991. pap. text ed. 9.00 (*0-9624922-3-X*) Hazar NY.

Zabern Affair, 1913-1914. Richard W. Mackey. 268p. (C). 1991. lib. bdg. 44.50 (*0-8191-8408-X*) U Pr of Amer.

Zable's Fables: Erotic Fables. Jeffrey A. Zable. 50p. (Orig.). 1991. pap. text ed. 5.00 (*1-879594-15-3*) Androgyne Bks.

Zabriskie. Family: A Three Hundred One-Year History of the Descendants of Albrecht Zaborowskij, (c.1638-1711), of Bergen Co., NJ. G. O. Zabriskie. (Illus.). 1950p. 1992. reprint ed. pap. 215.00 (*0-8328-2591-3*); reprint ed. lib. bdg. 225.00 (*0-8328-2590-5*) Higginson Bk Co.

Zabut: Italian Poetry. Angelo Pendola. Ed. by Nat Scammacca. 40p. 1983. pap. 5.00 (*0-89304-565-9*) Cross-Cultrl NY.

Zac Dakota's Book of Creepy Critters. Lawrence R. Sims et al. (Illus.). 96p. (Orig.). (YA). 1996. pap. 11.95 (*1-889155-13-6*, ODS3101) Optimus Design.

Zacaras-el Profeta Esperanza. F. B. Meyer. Orig. Title: The Prophet of Hope - Zechariah. 128p. (SPA.). 1986. pap. 1.50 (*0-8297-0895-2*) Life Pubs Intl.

Zacchaeus. Lee Jenkins. (Building Faith & Literacy Ser.: Bk. 1). (Illus.). 32p. (Orig.). (J). (ps-3). 1993. pap. 6.95 (*1-883952-03-4*) Hse of Steno.

Zacchaeus: Luke 19:1-10. Ed. by Loyal A. Kolbrek. (Arch Bks.). (Illus.). 24p. (Orig.). (J). (gr. k-4). 1994. pap. 1.99 (*0-570-09037-7*, 59-1460) Concordia.

Zacchaeus' Cash Bag: Level Two. Lavaun Linde & Mary Quishenberry. (Bible Stories for Early Readers Ser.: Bk. 2). (Illus.). 32p. (Orig.). (J). (gr. 1). 1988. pap. text ed. 4.99 (*0-945107-06-4*) Bradshaw Pubs.

***Zacchaeus Has a Good Day.** Sharilyn S. Adair. 24p. (J). 1997. pap. 4.95 (*0-687-05876-7*) Abingdon.

Zacchaeus, the Little Man. Robin Currie. (Bible Buddies Ser.). (Illus.). 12p. (J). 1995. bds. 4.29 (*0-7814-0199-2*) Chariot Victor.

Zaccheus Meets Jesus. Diane M. Stortz. (Happy Day Ser.). (Illus.). 24p. (J). (ps-2). 1996. reprint ed. pap. 1.99 (*0-7847-0561-5*, 04251) Standard Pub.

***Zach Reads.** large type ed. Norma A. Callender. (Beginning Reader Comprehension Ser.: Vol. 1). (Illus.). 12p. (Orig.). (J). (ps-2). 1997. pap. 4.95 (*1-890274-01-1*) BATA Bks.

Zacharias Solution. G. Raymond Humphries. 120p. (Orig.). 1996. mass mkt. 4.99 (*1-55197-118-6*, Pub. by Comnwlth Pub CN) Partners Pubs Grp.

Zachary in Camping Out. Bertrand Gauthier. LC 93-15457. (Just Me & My Dad Ser.). (Illus.). (J). 1993. lib. bdg. 17.27 (*0-8368-1012-0*) Gareth Stevens Inc.

Zachary in I'm Zachary! Bertrand Gauthier. LC 93-1168. (Just Me & My Dad Ser.). (Illus.). (J). 1993. lib. bdg. 17.27 (*0-8368-1007-4*) Gareth Stevens Inc.

Zachary in the Championship. Bertrand Gauthier. LC 93-1169. (Just Me & My Dad Ser.). (Illus.). (J). 1993. lib. bdg. 17.27 (*0-8368-1008-2*) Gareth Stevens Inc.

Zachary in the Present. Bertrand Gauthier. LC 93-7719. (Just Me & My Dad Ser.). (Illus.). (J). 1993. lib. bdg. 17.27 (*0-8368-1010-4*) Gareth Stevens Inc.

Zachary in the Wawabongbong. Bertrand Gauthier. LC 93-15456. (Just Me & My Dad Ser.). (Illus.). (J). 1993. lib. bdg. 17.27 (*0-8368-1011-2*) Gareth Stevens Inc.

Zachary in the Winner. Bertrand Gauthier. LC 93-7718. (Just Me & My Dad Ser.). (Illus.). (J). 1993. lib. bdg. 17.27 (*0-8368-1009-0*) Gareth Stevens Inc.

Zachary of the Wings. David Manber. 88p. (YA). (gr. 9-12). 1993. lib. bdg. 10.95 (*1-879567-27-X*) Wonder Well.

Zachary Taylor. Zachary Kent. LC 87-35774. (Encyclopedia of Presidents Ser.). (Illus.). 100p. (J). (gr. 3 up). 1988. lib. bdg. 22.00 (*0-516-01352-1*) Childrens.

Zachary Taylor: Soldier, Planter, Statesman of the Old Southwest. K. Jack Bauer. LC 85-11028. (Southern Biography Ser.). (Illus.). 348p. (C). 1993. pap. 14.95 (*0-8071-1851-6*) La State U Pr.

Zachary Taylor: Soldier, Planter, Statesman of the Old Southwest. K. Jack Bauer. LC 94-71615. (Signature Ser.). (Illus.). 347p. 1994. reprint ed. 32.50 (*0-945707-08-8*) Amer Political.

Zachary Taylor: Twelfth President of the United States. David R. Collins. Ed. by Richard G. Young. LC 88-24539. (Presidents of the United States Ser.). (Illus.). (J). (gr. 5-9). 1989. lib. bdg. 17.26 (*0-944483-17-8*) Garrett Ed Corp.

Zachary's New Home: A Story for Foster & Adopted Children. Geraldine M. Blomquist & Paul B. Blomquist. LC 90-49114. (Illus.). 32p. (J). (ps-2). 1990. 11.95 (*0-945354-28-2*); pap. 8.95 (*0-945354-27-4*) Magination Pr.

Zachry: The Man & His Companies. Amado F. Cavazos. LC 92-83993. (Illus.). 525p. 1993. 30.00 (*0-9635379-0-3*) Metro Pr TX.

Zack Attacks. Diana Loski. Ed. by Wendy S. Kolsen. (Illus.). 108p. (Orig.). (J). (gr. 3-8). 1995. pap. 3.50 (*1-885101-10-4*) Writers Pr Srv.

Zack Attacks: Classroom Set, 40 bks., Set. Linda M. Sniffen. (Illus.). 108p. (Orig.). (J). (gr. 3-7). pap. 87.50 (*1-885101-48-1*) Writers Pr Srv.

Zack Attacks: Library Set, 5 bks., Set. Linda M. Sniffen. (Illus.). 108p. (Orig.). (J). (gr. 3-7). pap. 17.50 (*1-885101-47-3*) Writers Pr Srv.

Zack, Come Back! J.J. LC 94-90222. (Illus.). 64p. (Orig.). (J). 1995. pap. 8.00 (*1-56002-465-8*, Univ Edtns) Aegina Pr.

***Zack Files, Vol. 10.** Dan Greenburg. (Illus.). 64p. (J). (gr. 1-5). 1997. 11.99 (*0-448-41648-4*, G&D) Putnam Pub Group.

Zack's Alligator. Shirley Mozelle. LC 88-32069. (I Can Read Bk.). (Illus.). 64p. (J). (gr. k-3). 1989. lib. bdg. 14.89 (*0-06-024310-4*) HarpC Child Bks.

Zack's Alligator. Shirley Mozelle. LC 88-32067. (I Can Read Bk.). (Illus.). 64p. (J). (ps-2). 1995. pap. 3.75 (*0-06-444186-5*) HarpC Child Bks.

Zack's Alligator Goes to School. Shirley Mozelle. LC 92-29871. (I Can Read Bk.). (Illus.). 64p. (J). (gr. k-3). 1994. 14.00 (*0-06-022887-3*); lib. bdg. 13.89 (*0-06-022888-1*) HarpC Child Bks.

Zack's Story: Growing up with Same-Sex Parents. Keith E. Greenberg. (Illus.). (J). 1996. 19.95 (*0-8225-2581-X*, Lerner Publctns) Lerner Group.

Zacualpa: A Study of Ancient Quiche Artifacts. Samuel K. Lothrop. LC 77-11508. (Carnegie Institution of Washington. Publications: No. 472). 1977. reprint ed. 37.50 (*0-404-16269-X*) AMS Pr.

Zacualpa, El Quiche, Guatemala: An Ancient Provincial Center of the Highland Maya. Robert Wauchope. (Publications: No. 39). (Illus.). xvi, 308p. 1975. 30.00 (*0-939238-44-6*) Tulane MARI.

ZAD User's Manual. Christopher E. Strangio. (Illus.). 98p. (Orig.). (C). 1989. pap. text ed. 15.00 (*0-929955-05-6*) CAMI Research.

ZAD User's Manual for the FOX. Christopher E. Strangio. (Illus.). 143p. (Orig.). (C). 1989. pap. text ed. 18.00 (*0-929955-08-0*) CAMI Research.

Zaddick Christ: A Suite of Wood Engravings. Bernard A. Solomon. (Illus.). 84p. 1974. 16.95 (*0-87921-022-2*) Attic Pr.

Zaddik. David Rosenbaum. LC 92-50695. 448p. 1993. 19.95 (*0-89296-540-1*) Mysterious Pr.

Zaddik. David Rosenbaum. 464p. 1994. mass mkt. 5.99 (*0-446-40322-9*, Mysterious Paperbk) Warner Bks.

Zadig. Francois-Marie De Voltaire. (Classiques de la Civilisation Francaise Ser.). pap. 3.95 (*0-685-34065-1*) Fr & Eur.

Zadig avec Memnon. Francois-Marie De Voltaire. Ed. by Jacques Spica. 128p. 1977. 3.95 (*0-686-55762-X*) Fr & Eur.

Zadig et Autres Contes. unabridged ed. Voltaire. (FRE.). pap. 7.95 (*2-87714-122-5*, Pub. by Bookking Intl FR) Distribks Inc.

Zadig, L'Ingenu. Voltaire. Ed. & Tr. by John Butt from FRE. (Classics Ser.). 192p. 1978. pap. 8.95 (*0-14-044126-3*, Penguin Classics) Viking Penguin.

Zadig, Micromegas et Autres Contes Orientaux. Francois-Marie De Voltaire. Ed. by Grimal. (Bibliotheque de Cluny Ser.). (FRE.). 1990. pap. 13.95 (*0-7859-3229-1*, 2266033700) Fr & Eur.

Zadoc Pine & Other Stories. Henry C. Bunner. LC 70-94704. (Short Story Index Reprint Ser.). 1977. 20.95 (*0-8369-3086-X*) Ayer.

Zadok's Treasure. Margot Arnold. (Penny Spring & Sir Toby Glendower Mystery Ser.). 192p. reprint ed. pap. 6.50 (*0-88150-133-6*) Countryman.

***Zadruga.** large type ed. Margaret A. Pemberton. (Magna Large Print Ser.). 631p. 1996. 25.99 (*0-7505-0946-5*, Pub. by Magna Print Bks UK) Ulverscroft.

Zaehnsdorfs, 1842-1947: Craft Bookbinders. Frank Broomhead. 110p. 1986. 40.00 (*0-900002-74-3*, Pub. by Priv Lib Assn UK) Oak Knoll.

Zafloya: or the Moor: A Romance of the Fifteenth Century, 3 Vols., Set. Charlotte Dacre. LC 73-22763. (Gothic Novels Ser.). 802p. 1979. reprint ed. 94.95 (*0-405-06014-9*) Ayer.

Zagadka Tolstogo. Mark A. Aldanov. LC 79-91652. (Brown University Slavic Reprint Ser.: No. 7). 138p. reprint ed. pap. 39.40 (*0-317-28393-6*, 2022394) Bks Demand.

Zagat 1997 Miami-South Florida. Zagat Survey Staff. 1996. pap. text ed. 9.95 (*1-57006-039-8*) Zagat.

***Zagat 1998 America's Top Restaurants.** Zagat Survey Staff. 1997. pap. 12.95 (*1-57006-099-1*) Zagat.

***Zagat 1998 Boston Restaurant Survey.** Zagat Survey Staff. 1997. pap. 10.95 (*1-57006-100-9*) Zagat.

***Zagat 1998 Chicago Restaurant Survey Update.** Zagat Survey Staff. 1997. pap. 10.95 (*1-57006-101-7*) Zagat.

***Zagat 1998 Connecticut/South New York State Restaurant Survey.** Zagat Survey Staff. 1997. pap. 9.95 (*1-57006-091-6*) Zagat.

***Zagat 1998 London Restaurant Survey.** Zagat Survey Staff. 1997. pap. 11.95 (*1-57006-102-5*) Zagat.

***Zagat 1998 Long Island Restaurant Survey.** Zagat Survey Staff. 1997. pap. 9.95 (*1-57006-092-4*) Zagat.

***Zagat 1998 Los Angeles Marketplace Update.** Zagat Survey Staff. 1997. pap. 10.95 (*1-57006-089-4*) Zagat.

***Zagat 1998 Los Angeles/Southern California Restaurant Survey.** Zagat Survey Staff. 1997. pap. 10.95 (*1-57006-103-3*) Zagat.

***Zagat 1998 New Jersey Restaurant Survey.** Zagat Survey Staff. 1997. pap. 9.95 (*1-57006-093-2*) Zagat.

***Zagat 1998 New Orleans Restaurant Survey.** Zagat Survey Staff. 1998. pap. 9.95 (*1-57006-104-1*) Zagat.

***Zagat 1998 New York City Restaurant Survey.** Zagat Survey Staff. 1997. pap. 11.95 (*1-57006-105-X*) Zagat.

***Zagat 1998 Ohio Restaurant Survey.** Zagat Survey Staff. 1997. pap. 9.95 (*1-57006-118-1*) Zagat.

***Zagat 1998 Philadelphia Restaurant Survey Update.** Zagat Survey Staff. 1997. pap. 10.95 (*1-57006-106-8*) Zagat.

***Zagat 1998 Atlanta Restaurant Survey/Update.** Zagat Survey Staff. 1997. pap. 9.95 (*1-57006-117-3*) Zagat.

***Zagat 1998 San Diego Restaurant Survey Update.** Zagat Survey Staff. 1997. pap. 9.95 (*1-57006-119-X*) Zagat.

***Zagat 1998 Seattle/Portland Restaurant Survey Update.** Zagat Survey Staff. 1998. pap. 9.95 (*1-57006-108-4*) Zagat.

***Zagat 1998 Southwest Restaurant Survey.** Zagat Survey Staff. 1997. pap. 9.95 (*1-57006-120-3*) Zagat.

***Zagat 1998 Washington D. C./Baltimore Restaurant Survey Update.** Zagat Survey Staff. 1997. pap. 10.95 (*1-57006-109-2*) Zagat.

Zagat Nineteen Ninety-Seven see Zagat 1997 Long Island

Zagat 1997 America's Top Restaurants. Zagat Survey Staff. 1996. pap. text ed. 12.95 (*1-57006-035-5*) Zagat.

Zagat 1997 Boston. Zagat Survey Staff. 1996. pap. text ed. 10.95 (*1-57006-044-4*) Zagat.

Gulf Coast. Zagat Survey Staff. 1996. pap. text ed. 9.95 (*1-57006-045-2*) Zagat.

Zagat 1997 Chicago. Zagat Survey Staff. 1996. pap. text ed. 10.95 (*1-57006-046-0*) Zagat.

Zagat 1997 Connecticut-South New York State. Zagat Survey Staff. 1996. pap. text ed. 9.95 (*1-57006-038-X*) Zagat.

Zagat 1997 Houston-Galveston. Zagat Survey Staff. 1996. pap. text ed. 9.95 (*1-57006-030-4*) Zagat.

Zagat 1997 Kansas City. Zagat Survey Staff. 1996. pap. text ed. 9.95 (*1-57006-032-0*) Zagat.

Zagat 1997 Las Vegas. Zagat Survey Staff. 1996. pap. text ed. 9.95 (*1-57006-072-X*) Zagat.

Zagat 1997 London. Zagat Survey Staff. 1996. pap. text ed. 11.95 (*1-57006-079-7*) Zagat.

Zagat 1997 Los Angeles Marketplace. Zagat Survey Staff. 1996. pap. text ed. 10.95 (*1-57006-043-6*) Zagat.

South California. Zagat Survey Staff. 1996. pap. text ed. 10.95 (*1-57006-047-9*) Zagat.

Zagat 1997 Michigan. Zagat Survey Staff. 1996. pap. text ed. 9.95 (*1-57006-048-7*) Zagat.

Zagat 1997 New Jersey. Zagat Survey Staff. 1996. pap. text ed. 9.95 (*1-57006-037-1*) Zagat.

Zagat 1997 New York City. Zagat Survey Staff. 1996. pap. text ed. 11.95 (*1-57006-049-5*) Zagat.

***Zagat 1997/98 America's Best Meal Deals.** Zagat Survey Staff. 1997. pap. 12.95 (*1-57006-090-8*) Zagat.

Zagat 1997 Philadelphia. Zagat Survey Staff. 1996. pap. text ed. 10.95 (*1-57006-075-4*) Zagat.

Zagat 1997 San Francisco. Zagat Survey Staff. 1996. pap. text ed. 10.95 (*1-57006-077-0*) Zagat.

Zagat 1997 St Louis. Zagat Survey Staff. 1996. pap. text ed. 9.95 (*1-57006-033-9*) Zagat.

Zagat 1997 Washington, D. C.-Baltimore. Zagat Survey Staff. 1996. pap. text ed. 10.95 (*1-57006-040-1*) Zagat.

Zagat 1997 Minneapolis, St. Paul. Zagat Survey Staff. 1997. pap. text ed. 9.95 (*1-57006-029-0*) Zagat.

Zagat 1997 Dallas-Ft. Worth. Zagat Survey Staff. 1996. pap. text ed. 9.95 (*1-57006-031-2*) Zagat.

Zagat 1997 New York City Marketplace. Zagat Survey Staff. 1996. pap. text ed. 10.95 (*1-57006-042-8*) Zagat.

Zagat Survey: Carolinas - Virginia Restaurant Survey. Eugene H. Zagat & Nina S. Zagat. Date not set. pap. 9.95 (*0-614-07489-4*) Zagat.

Zagat Survey: Hawaii Restaurant Survey. Eugene H. Zagat, Jr. & Nina S. Zagat. 160p. 1995. pap. 9.95 (*1-57006-006-1*) Zagat.

Zagat Survey: Los Angeles Marketplace Survey. Eugene H. Zagat, Jr. & Nina S. Zagat. Ed. by Merrill Schindler et al. 272p. 1995. pap. 10.95 (*1-57006-024-X*) Zagat.

Zagat Survey: Miss Lea's Bible Stories for Children. 244p. (J). 1994. 14.95 (*1-57006-003-7*) Zagat.

Zagat Survey: New York City Marketplace Survey. Joan M. Lang et al. 200p. 1995. pap. 10.95 (*1-57006-009-6*) Zagat.

Zagat Survey: New York City Restaurant Survey. Eugene H. Zagat, Jr. & Nina S. Zagat. 220p. 1994. pap. 10.95 (*1-57006-008-8*) Zagat.

Zagat Survey: Washington D.C. - Baltimore Restaurant Survey. Eugene H. Zagat, Jr. & Nina S. Zagat. Ed. by Olga Boikess. 224p. 1995. pap. 9.95 (*1-57006-012-6*) Zagat.

***Zagat U. S. Hotels, Resorts & Spas.** 5th ed. Zagat Survey Staff. 1997. pap. 19.95 (*1-57006-081-9*) Zagat.

Zagat, 1993: Rocky Mountains. Zagat Survey Staff. 1993. pap. 9.95 (*0-943421-82-9*) Zagat.

Zagat 1996: Ohio. 1995. pap. text ed. 9.95 (*1-57006-053-3*) Zagat.

***Zagat 1997 Atlanta.** Zagat Survey Staff. 1997. pap. text ed. 9.95 (*1-57006-084-3*) Zagat.

***Zagat, 1997 Hawaii.** Zagat Survey Staff. 1997. pap. text ed. 9.95 (*1-57006-085-1*) Zagat.

Zagat 1997 Long Island. Zagat Survey Staff. Orig. Title: Zagat Nineteen Ninety-Seven. 1996. pap. text ed. 9.95 (*1-57006-036-3*) Zagat.

***Zagat 1997 New Orleans.** Zagat Survey Staff. 1997. pap. 9.95 (*1-57006-083-5*) Zagat.

***Zagat 1997 NYC Restaurant Map.** Zagat Survey Staff. 1997. pap. text ed. 5.95 (*1-57006-082-7*) Zagat.

Zagat 1997 Rocky Mountain. Zagat Servey Staff. 1997. pap. text ed. 9.95 (*1-57006-027-4*) Zagat.

Zagat 1997 Seattle: Portland Restaurant Survey. Zagat Survey Staff. 1996. pap. text ed. 9.95 (*1-57006-041-X*) Zagat.

Zagat 1997 Vancouver Restaurant Survey. Zagat Survey Staff. 1996. pap. text ed. 9.95 (*1-57006-078-9*) Zagat.

***Zagat 1998: Las Vegas.** Zagat Survey Staff. 1998. pap. text ed. 9.95 (*1-57006-114-9*) Zagat.

***Zagat 1998: San Francisco Bay Area.** Zagat Survey Staff. 1997. pap. text ed. 10.95 (*1-57006-107-6*) Zagat.

Zagato: Fiat 8VZ, Alfa Romeo 1900 SSZ. Michele Marchiano. (Illus.). 110p. 24.95 (*88-7672-008-1*, Pub. by Giorgio Nada Editore IT) Howell Pr VA.

Zagato: Seventy Years in the Fast Lane. Michele Marchiano. (Illus.). 176p. 55.00 (*88-7911-021-7*, Pub. by Giorgio Nada Editore IT) Howell Pr VA.

***Zaghawa from an Ecological Perspective.** Maire-Jose Tubiana & Joseph Tubiana. 140p. 1977. 46.00 (*90-6191-015-3*, Pub. by A A Balkema NE) Ashgate Pub Co.

Zagid Avec Memnon. Voltaire. 128p. (FRE.). 1985. pap. 10.95 (*0-7859-1267-3*, 2040160930) Fr & Eur.

Zagorsk Museum of History & Art: A Guide. Collet's Holdings, Ltd. Staff. (RUS.). 1983. 40.00 (*0-317-57311-X*) St Mut.

Zagreb Croatia. Ljelja Dobronic. 232p. 1985. 30.00 (*0-918660-85-8*) Ragusan Pr.

Zagreb, Croatia Solists, 1954-1984. Miroslav Poljanec. 104p. 1985. 10.00 (*0-918660-87-4*) Ragusan Pr.

Zagreb Croatian National Theatre. Nikola Batusic. 189p. 1985. 25.00 (*0-918660-84-X*) Ragusan Pr.

***Zagros & Nature Force.** Reza Esmaili. (Illus.). 73p. (J). (gr. 1). 1996. 10.00 (*0-9656185-0-1*); pap. 2.00 (*0-9656185-1-X*) Esmaili.

Zagros, Hindu Kush, Himalaya: Geodynamic Evolution. H. K. Gupta & F. M. Delany. (Geodynamics Ser.: Vol. 3). 323p. 1981. 36.00 (*0-87590-507-2*) Am Geophysical.

Zahiriten. Ihr Lehrsystem und Ihre Geschichte, Ein Beitrag Zur Geschichte der Muhammedanischen Theologie. Ignaz Goldziher. xiv, 232p. 1967. reprint ed. write for info. (*0-318-71513-9*) G Olms Pubs.

Zahl und Zeit: Grammatik der Numeralia und des Verbalsystems Im Spatbabylonischen. Michael P. Streck. xxix, 293p. (GER.). 1995. 100.00 (*90-72371-85-2*, Pub. by Styx NE) Eisenbrauns.

Zahlen. (Meyers Klien Kinderbibliothek). 24p. (GER.). (J). 1994. 13.25 (*3-411-08701-3*) Langenscheidt.

Zahn - Mund - Kiefer: Rezepte und Therapien. E. Lautenbach. (Illus.). vi, 1266p. 1990. 741.75 (*3-8055-5098-7*) S Karger.

Zahniser: The Zahnisers: a History of the Family in America. Kate M. Zahniser & Charles R. Zahniser. (Illus.). 218p. 1992. reprint ed. pap. 33.00 (*0-8328-2399-6*); reprint ed. lib. bdg. 43.00 (*0-8328-2398-8*) Higginson Bk Co.

Zai Jinsho Zhong. Chen Ran. (CHI.). pap. 9.95 (*7-80005-258-3*, Pub. by China Intl Bk CH) Distribks Inc.

Zaibatsu. Lewis Perdue. 400p. (Orig.). 1988. pap. 4.95 (*0-373-97085-4*) Harlequin Bks.

Zaibatsu: The Rise & Fall of Family Enterprise Groups in Japan. Hidemasa Morikawa. 283p. 1992. 52.50 (*0-86008-488-4*, Pub. by U of Tokyo JA) Col U Pr.

Zainab. M. H. Haikal. 216p. (C). 1989. 30.00 (*1-85077-215-0*, Pub. by Darf Pubs Ltd UK) St Mut.

Zaire. Christa Mang. (Bradt Country Guides Ser.). (Illus.). 224p. (Orig.). 1994. pap. 15.95 (*1-56440-557-5*, Pub. by Bradt Pubns UK) Globe Pequot.

Zaire. Joseph Sevigny. LC 95-22471. (Country Guide Series Report from the AACRAO-AID Project). 1995. 22.00 (*0-929851-63-3*) Am Assn Coll Registrars.

***Zaire.** U. S. Government Staff. (Country Studies). 1994. 22.00 (*0-614-30824-0*, UZAIRE) Claitors.

Zaire. Dawn B. Williams. (World Bibliographies Ser.: Vol. 176). 268p. 1995. lib. bdg. 77.00 (*1-85109-218-8*) ABC-CLIO.

***Zaire: Background Information & Statistical Data.** Philippe Beaugrand. (IMF Staff Country Report Ser.: Vol. 96/28). (Illus.). 108p. pap. 30.80 (*0-608-04852-6*, 2065511) Bks Demand.

Zaire: Reports of Torture & Killings Committed by the Armed Forces in Shaba Region. 1986. 3.00 (*0-86210-096-8*) Amnesty Intl USA.

Zaire: Repression as Policy. Lawyers Committee for Human Rights Staff. 230p. 1990. pap. text ed. 12.00 (*0-934143-35-8*) Lawyers Comm Human.

Zaire: The Political Economy of Underdevelopment. Guy Gran. LC 79-19512. (Praeger Special Studies). 352p. 1979. text ed. 55.00 (*0-275-90358-3*, C0358, Praeger Pubs) Greenwood.

Zaire Country Studies: Area Handbook. 4th ed. Tim L. Merrill. LC 94-25092. (Area Handbook DA Pam Ser.: 550-67). 1994. 22.00 (*0-8444-0795-X*) Lib Congress.

Zaire in Pictures. Ed. by Lerner Geography Department Staff. (Visual Geography Ser.). (Illus.). 64p. (YA). (gr. 5 up). 1992. lib. bdg. 19.95 (*0-8225-1899-6*, Lerner Publctns) Lerner Group.

Zais see Oeuvres Completes de Jean-Philippe Rameau

Zak. large type ed. Frances Thomas. 200p. (J). (gr. 5 up). 1988. 16.95 (*0-7451-0727-3*, Galaxy Child Lrg Print) Chivers N Amer.

***Zak: The One-of-a-Kind Dog.** Jane Lidz. (Illus.). (J). 1997. pap. 12.95 (*0-8109-3995-9*) Abrams.

Zak & Ben. (Illus.). (J). (ps-2). 1991. pap. 5.10 (*0-8136-5661-3*); lib. bdg. 7.95 (*0-8136-5161-1*) Modern Curr.

***Zakaria: The Warshipper.** Amina I. Ali. Ed. by J. C. Cinquino. (Prophets' Stories for Children from the Holy Qur'an Ser.: No. 18). (Illus.). 28p. (Orig.). (J). (gr. 4-6). 1996. write for info. (*1-881963-38-1*); pap. 2.50 (*1-881963-39-X*) Al-Saadawi Pubns.

Zakat. A. Kondrat'ev. 54p. (Orig.). (RUS.). 1990. 10.00 (*1-878445-56-1*) Antiquary CT.

Zakennayo: The Real Japanese You Were Never Taught in School. Philip J. Cunningham. (Illus.). 1995. pap. 8.95 (*0-452-27506-7*, Plume) NAL-Dutton.

Zakhor: Jewish History & Jewish Memory. Yosef H. Yerushalmi. (Samuel & Althea Stroum Lectures in Jewish Studies). 154p. 1996. pap. 12.95 (*0-295-97519-9*) U of Wash Pr.

***Zakhor: Jewish History & Jewish Memory.** Yosef H. Yerushalmi. 1995. pap. 18.95 (*0-295-97526-1*) U of Wash Pr.

Zakir Husain: Life & Times. B. Sheikh Ali. 525p. (C). 1992. 40.00 (*0-7069-5924-8*, Pub. by Vikas II) S Asia.

Zakir Hussain: A Photo Essay. Ed. by Dayanita Singh. 80p. (C). 1987. 165.00 (*81-7002-021-2*, Pub. by Himalayan Bks II) St Mut.

Zaki's Ramadhan Fast. Ann El-Moslimany. Ed. by Rafiah Khokhar. LC 94-71836. (Illus.). 32p. (J). (ps-6). 1995. 14.95 (*1-884187-08-0*) AMICA Pub Hse.

Zakliatie Sten: Skazochki i Stat'i. Fedor Sologub. 230p. (RUS.). (C). 1989. reprint ed. pap. 14.00 (*0-933884-71-0*) Berkeley Slavic.

Zakros: The Discovery of a Lost Palace of Ancient Crete. Nicholas Platon. 345p. 1985. reprint ed. pap. 98.00 (*90-256-0865-5*, Pub. by A M Hakkert NE) Benjamins North Am.

***Zak's Lunch.** Margie Palatini. LC 97-18799. 1998. write for info. (*0-395-81674-2*, Clarion Bks) HM.

Zalacain el Aventurero. Pio Baroja. Ed. by Ricardo Senabre. (Nueva Austral Ser.: No. 3). (SPA.). pap. 14.95 (*84-239-1803-3*) Elliots Bks.

Zalacain el Aventurero see Zalacain the Adventurer

***Zalacain the Adventurer.** Pio Baroja. Tr. by James P. Diendl from SPA. Orig. Title: Zalacain el Aventurero. 234p. 1997. pap. 16.95 (*1-882897-13-7*) Lost Coast.

Zalkin's Handbook of Thimbles & Sewing Implements. Estelle Zalkin. LC 88-50383. (Illus.). 288p. 1988. pap. 24.95 (*0-911594-14-0*, Wallace-Hmestead) Chilton.

Zalm & I. Bill Kay. 328p. 1993. pap. 22.95 (*0-88839-328-8*) Hancock House.

Zalm 23. Vladimir Uhri. 60p. (Orig.). (SLO.). 1996. pap. 3.00 (*1-56983-044-4*) New Creat WI.

Zalman's Menorah: Based on Old Jewish Folktale. Charles Wengrov. 1987. 10.95 (*0-87306-450-X*); pap. 7.95 (*0-87306-451-8*) Feldheim.

Zalmen or the Madness of God. Elie Wiesel. 1975. 6.95 (*0-394-49637-X*) Random.

Zamani Goes to Market. Muriel Feelings. LC 88-70729. (Young Reader's Ser.). (Illus.). 50p. 1989. reprint ed. 14.95 (*0-86543-094-2*); reprint ed. pap. 6.95 (*0-86543-095-0*) Africa World.

Zambesi Salient: Conflict in Southern Africa. Al J. Venter. 1975. 12.50 (*0-8159-7500-7*) Devin.

Zambezi Trails. U. G. De Woronin. LC 79-51772. (Illus.). 1987. 19.95 (*0-930422-17-1*) Dennis-Landman.

***Zambia.** LC 97-22298. (Cultures of the World Ser.: Group 15). (Illus.). 128p. (YA). (gr. 5 up). 1997. lib. bdg. 23.95 (*0-7614-0694-8*) Marshall Cavendish.

Zambia. Ed. by Anne M. Bliss & J. A. Rigg. (World Bibliographical Ser.: No. 51). 233p. 1985. lib. bdg. 60.00 (*0-903450-88-7*) ABC-CLIO.

Zambia. Holly A. O'Neill. LC 95-22477. (Country Guide Series Report from the AACRAO-AID Project). 1996. 22.00 (*0-929851-64-1*) Am Assn Coll Registrars.

Zambia. Richard Vaughan. (Illus.). 184p. 1992. lib. bdg. 74.50 (*0-9515209-0-3*) Rowman.

Zambia. rev. ed. Jason Laure. LC 89-34281. (Enchantment of the World Ser.). (Illus.). 128p. (J). (gr. 5-9). 1991. lib. bdg. 30.00 (*0-516-02716-6*) Childrens.

Zambia: Debt & Poverty. John Clark & Caroline Allison. 80p. (C). 1989. pap. 9.95 (*0-85598-115-6*, Pub. by Oxfam UK) Humanities.

Zambia: Security & Conflict, 1964-1973. Jan Pettman. LC 74-79129. 381p. (C). 1974. text ed. 32.50 (*0-312-89845-2*) St Martin.

Zambia: The Dawn of Freedom. K. K. Virmani. xviii, 223p. 1989. 18.00 (*81-85163-05-7*, Pub. by Kalinga Pubns) Nataraj Bks.

***Zambia Country Assistance Review: Turning an Economy Around.** Gladstone G. Bonnick. (Operations Evaluation Department Studies). (Illus.). 176p. 1997. 20.00 (*0-8213-3879-X*, 13879) World Bank.

Zambia in Maps. Ed. by D. H. Davies. LC 73-653626. (Graphic Perspectives in Developing Countries Ser.). 128p. (C). 1972. 37.95 (*0-8419-0081-7*, Africana) Holmes & Meier.

Zambia Is My Home. (My Home Country Ser.). (Illus.). 48p. (J). (gr. 2-8). 1992. lib. bdg. 19.93 (*0-8368-0906-8*) Gareth Stevens Inc.

Zambia Shall Be Free. Kenneth Kaunda. (African Writers Ser.). 202p. (C). 1962. pap. 8.95 (*0-435-90004-8*, 90004) Heinemann.

Zambian Crisis Behaviour: Confronting Rhodesia's Unilateral Declaration of Independence, 1965-1966. Douglas G. Anglin. 400p. 1994. 55.00 (*0-7735-1219-5*, Pub. by McGill CN) U of Toronto Pr.

Zami: A New Spelling of My Name. Audre Lorde. LC 82-15086. (Feminist Ser.). 256p. 1983. pap. 10.95 (*0-89594-122-8*) Crossing Pr.

***Zamocitas 95.** Compiled by Keith L. Andrews. 62p. (Orig.). (SPA.). 1995. pap. write for info. (*1-885995-28-8*) Escuela Agricola.

Zamora: A Regional Economy in Mexico see Studies in Middle American Economics

Zamorano Index to Bancroft's History of California, 2 vols., Set. Hubert H. Bancroft et al. LC 85-51515. 759p. 1985. 125.00 (*0-88474-147-8*) Dawsons.

Zamper: New Adventures. Gareth Roberts. (Dr. Who New Adventures Ser.). 1995. mass mkt. 5.95 (*0-426-20450-6*, Pub. by Virgin Pub UK) London Brdge.

Zamrznute Vatre. Milos Acin-Kosta. 212p. (SER.). 1967. 15.00 (*0-931931-07-X*) Ravnogorski.

Zamyatin: We (My) Ed. by A. Barratt. (Bristol Russian Texts Ser.). 166p. (RUS.). 1994. pap. 15.95 (*1-85399-378-6*, Pub. by Brstl Class Pr UK) Focus Pub-R Pullins.

Zamyatin's We: A Collection of Critical Essays. Gary Kern. 200p. 1987. 25.00 (*0-88233-804-8*); pap. 11.50 (*0-88233-832-3*) Ardis Pubs.

Zanalug: (A Simulation Exercise) Ali K. Galaydh & Celia S. Pangalis. (Pew Case Studies in International Affairs). 50p. (C). 1992. pap. text ed. 3.50 (*1-56927-112-7*) Geo U Inst Dplmcy.

Zand. Mark Dunster. 52p. (Orig.). 1994. pap. 6.00 (*0-89642-244-5*) Linden Pubs.

Zande Scheme: An Anthropological Case Study of Development in Africa. Conrad C. Reining. LC 65-24665. (Northwestern University African Studies Ser.: No. 17). 285p. reprint ed. pap. 81.30 (*0-317-29802-X*, 2016721) Bks Demand.

Zander. Barrie Rickards & Neville Fickling. (Angling Library). (Illus.). 214p. 1991. pap. 17.00 (*0-85115-298-8*) Boydell & Brewer.

Zander: Cases & Materials on the English Legal System. 7th ed. Michael Zander. 624p. 1996. 36.95 (*0-406-08176-X*) MICHIE.

Zandra. Norma L. Clark. 224p. (Orig.). 1980. pap. 1.75 (*0-449-50075-6*, Coventry) Fawcett.

Zandunga: Of Fieldwork & Friendship in Southern Mexico. Beverly Chinas. (Illus.). 178p. (Orig.). (C). 1993. pap. text ed. 10.50 (*0-88133-680-7*) Waveland Pr.

Zane Grey. Ann Ronald. LC 75-7010. (Western Writers Ser.: No. 17). (Illus.). 46p. (Orig.). 1975. pap. 4.95 (*0-88430-016-1*) Boise St U W Writ Ser.

Zane Grey: A Biography. Frank Gruber. 298p. reprint ed. lib. bdg. 22.95 (*0-89190-756-4*, Rivercity Pr) Amereon Ltd.

***Zane Grey: Romancing the West.** Stephen J. May. LC 97-353. (Illus.). 180p. (Orig.). 1997. pap. 14.95 (*0-8214-1182-9*); text ed. 29.95 (*0-8214-1181-0*) Ohio U Pr.

Zane Grey & the Movies. Ed Hulse. 1994. pap. 24.95 (*1-880756-10-2*) Riverwood Pr.

Zane Grey Annotated Book Checklist. G. M. Farley. reprint ed. pap. 17.95 (*0-89190-768-8*) Amereon Ltd.

Zane Grey Omnibus. Zane Grey. 433p. 1993. 34.95 (*1-56723-117-9*) Yestermorrow.

Zane Grey's Book of Camp & Trails. Zane Grey. 35.00 (*0-8488-0808-8*) Yestermorrow.

Zane Grey's Nevada Jim Lacy: Beyond the Mogollon Rim. Romer Z. Grey. 224p. (Orig.). 1988. mass mkt., pap. text ed. 2.75 (*0-8439-2666-X*) Dorchester Pub Co.

Zane Grey's Yacqui: Siege at Forlorn River. Romer Z. Grey. 288p. 1988. mass mkt., pap. text ed. 2.95 (*0-8439-2621-X*) Dorchester Pub Co.

***Zangy, the Watchdog.** Kelsey Rexroat. LC 96-27278. (Illus.). (J). 1997. write for info. (*1-56763-233-5*); pap. write for info. (*1-56763-234-3*) Ozark Pub.

Zanichelli Super-Mini Italian & English Dictionary. 328p. 1995. pap. 4.95 (*0-8442-8447-5*, Natl Textbk) NTC Pub Grp.

Zanichelli's New College Italian & English Dictionary. Guideppe Ragazzini & Adele Biagi. 1200p. (ENG & SPA.). 1994. 29.95 (*0-8442-8449-1*, Natl Textbk) NTC Pub Grp.

Zaniest Riddle Book in the World. Joseph Rosenbloom. LC 83-18102. (Illus.). 128p. (J). (gr. 3 up). 1985. pap. 4.95 (*0-8069-6252-6*) Sterling.

***Zanj Nan Miwa - Angels in the Mirror: Haitian Vodou Music & Culture & the People...** Elizabeth A. McAlister. 1996. 28.95 incl. cd-rom (*1-55961-387-4*, Ellipsis Arts) Relaxtn Co.

***Zankhana (Gujerati)** large type ed. Mohammad Mankad. (Charnwood Large Print Ser.). 1990. 27.99 (*0-7089-2268-6*, Charnwood) Ulverscroft.

Zanoni. Bart Lytton & Edward Bulwer. 398p. 1970. reprint ed. spiral bd. 17.50 (*0-7873-0573-1*) Hlth Research.

Zanoni: A Rosicrucian Tale, Vol. 4. Edward G. Bulwer-Lytton. LC 78-157505. 412p. 1971. lib. bdg. 18.95 (*0-89345-014-6*, Spir Sci Lib) Garber Comm.

Zanouba: A Novel. Out el Kouloub. Tr. & Intro. by Nayra Atiya. LC 96-21142. (Middle East Literature in Translation Ser.). 192p. 1996. 39.95 (*0-8156-2718-1*, ATZA); pap. 14.95 (*0-8156-0408-4*, ATZAP) Syracuse U Pr.

Zanshin: Meditation & the Mind in Modern Martial Arts. Vince Morris. LC 92-1758. (Illus.). 108p. (Orig.). 1992. pap. 7.95 (*0-87728-756-2*) Weiser.

Zanskar: The Hidden Kingdom. large type ed. Michel Peissel. 397p. 1981. 25.99 (*0-7089-0714-8*) Ulverscroft.

***Zanuck.** Dee Lee Enterprises Staff. Date not set. write for info. (*0-688-05685-7*) Hearst Bks.

Zany Animals ABC: A Changing Picture Book. Laura Galvin. (Illus.). 16p. (J). 1995. 12.99 (*0-88705-786-1*, Wshng Well Bks) Joshua Morris.

Zany Characters of the Ad World, Collector's Identification & Value Guide: 1995 Values. Mary J. Lamphier. 176p. 1995. pap. 16.95 (*0-89145-652-X*, 3979) Collector Bks.

Zany Knock Knocks. Ronny M. Cole. LC 92-43068. (Illus.). 96p. 1993. 14.95 (*0-8069-8588-7*) Sterling.

Zany Knock Knocks. Ronny M. Cole. LC 92-43068. (Illus.). 96p. (J). (gr. 2-7). 1993. pap. 4.95 (*0-8069-8589-5*) Sterling.

***Zany Mazes: Maze Funbook.** Illus. by John Hull. (Troubador Ser.). Orig. Title: MazeCraze 2. 32p. (J). (ps up). 1997. reprint ed. pap. 3.50 (*0-8431-8231-8*) Price Stern Sloan.

Zany Niagara: Funny Things People Say about Niagara Falls. Paul Gromosiak. 1992. pap. 4.95 (*1-879201-06-2*) Meyer Enter.

Zany Tales. Pat Ingoldsby. 1990. pap. 7.95 (*0-86278-151-5*) Dufour.

An Asterisk (*) at the beginning of an entry indicates that the title is appearing in BIP for the first time.

Zany Zoo. Max Knight. 110p. 1993. pap. 15.95 (0-916147-40-1) Regent Pr.

Zanzibar: Its History & Its People. William H. Ingrams. (Illus.). 527p. 1967. reprint ed. 55.00 (0-7146-1102-6, Pub. by F Cass Pubs UK) Intl Spec Bk.

Zanzibar, Its Society & Politics. John Middleton & Jane Campbell. LC 84-29046. (Illus.). 71p. 1985. reprint ed. text ed. 49.75 (0-313-24739-0, MIZA, Greenwood Pr) Greenwood.

Zanzibar: The Island Metropolis of Eastern Africa. F. B. Pearce. (Illus.). 431p. 1967. reprint ed. 47.50 (0-7146-1098-4, Pub. by F Cass Pubs UK) Intl Spec Bk.

Zanzibar in Contemporary Times. R. N. Lyne. 384p. 1987. 270.00 (1-85077-173-1, Pub. by Darf Pubs Ltd UK) St Mut.

Zanzibar, Its History & Its People. William H. Ingrams. LC 74-15053. (Illus.). reprint ed. 37.50 (0-404-12091-1) AMS Pr.

Zanzibar Revolution & Its Aftermath. Anthony Clayton. LC 81-3486. (Illus.). xvi, 166p. (C). 1981. 29.50 (0-208-01925-1, Archon Bks) Shoe String.

Zanzibar under Colonial Rule. Ed. by Abdul Sheriff & Ed Ferguson. LC 90-25407. (Eastern African Studies). (Illus.). 288p. (C). 1991. text ed. 34.95 (0-8214-0995-6); pap. text ed. 19.95 (0-8214-0996-4) Ohio U Pr.

Zanzibar Under the Foreign Office: 1890-1913. Lawrence W. Hollingsworth. LC 75-31770. (Illus.). 232p. 1975. reprint ed. text ed. 35.00 (0-8371-8447-9, HOZA, Greenwood Pr) Greenwood.

Zanzotto. Vivienne Hand. (Writers of Italy Ser.). 256p. (C). 1994. pap. 70.00 (0-7486-0411-1, Pub. by Edinburgh U Pr UK) Col U Pr.

Zap! How Your Computer Can Hurt You - & What You Can Do About It. Don Sellers. (Illus.). 160p. (Orig.). (C). 1994. pap. text ed. 12.95 (1-56609-021-0) Peachpit Pr.

Zap! Ray Gun Classics. Leslie Singer. (Illus.). 96p. 1991. pap. 12.95 (0-8118-0033-4) Chronicle Bks.

Zap! Electrical Circuits & Fields No. 2. Jerry Pine et al. LC 95-18694. (Physics Ser.). 128p. 1995. spiral bd. 28.75 (0-86720-482-6) Jones & Bartlett.

***Zap Gun.** Philip K. Dick. 3.95 (0-7867-0553-1) Carroll & Graf.

Zap Gun. Philip K. Dick. 1989. pap. 3.95 (0-88184-553-1) Carroll & Graf.

Zap! I'm a Mind Reader. Dan Greenberg. LC 96-7116. (Zack Files Ser.: No. 4). (Illus.). 64p. (J). (gr. 2-5). 1996. pap. 3.95 (0-448-41263-2, G&D) Putnam Pub Group.

Zap! I'm a Mind Reader. Dan Greenburg. LC 96-7116. (Zack Files Ser.: No. 4). (Illus.). 64p. (J). (gr. 2-5). 1996. lib. bdg. 11.99 (0-448-41292-6, G&D) Putnam Pub Group.

Zap It! A Microwave Cookbook Just for Kids. Tamar Peterseil. (J). (gr. 4-7). 1993. 12.95 (0-943706-13-0) Pitspopany.

Zap It! Microwave Recipes. Michelle N. Spencer. 160p. 1990. spiral bd. 5.95 (0-941016-75-7) Penfield.

***Zap Science: A Scientific Playground in a Book.** John Cassidy et al. (Illus.). 66p. (J). (gr. 2 up). 1997. spiral bd. 19.95 (1-57054-108-6) Klutz Pr.

Zap the Fat. John French. 160p. 1994. pap. 14.95 (1-55725-042-1) Paraclete MA.

Zap Zero - The Delivery Man. rev. ed. Diane Wilmer. (Quality Time Easy Readers Ser.). (Illus.). 32p. (J). (gr. k-2). 1990. reprint ed. lib. bdg. 11.95 (1-878363-11-5) Forest Hse.

Zapata. John Steinbeck. 352p. (Orig.). 1993. pap. 12.95 (0-14-017322-6, Penguin Bks) Viking Penguin.

Zapata: The Ideology of a Peasant Revolution. Robert P. Millon. LC 94-31757. 1995. pap. 7.50 (0-7178-0710-X) Intl Pubs Co.

Zapata & the Mexican Revolution. John Womack, Jr. LC 68-23947. 1970. pap. 15.00 (0-394-70853-9, V627, Vin) Random.

Zapata of Mexico. Peter E. Newell. (Orig.). 1980. pap. 5.50 (0-932366-08-2) Black Thorn Bks.

Zapata of Mexico. Peter E. Newell. 180p. (Orig.). 1996. 48.99 (1-55164-073-2, Pub. by Black Rose Bks CN); pap. 19.99 (1-55164-072-4, Pub. by Black Rose Bks CN) Consort Bk Sales.

Zapata's Revenge: Free Trade & the Farm Crisis in Mexico. Tom Barry. 250p. 1995. 35.00 (0-89608-500-7); pap. 16.00 (0-89608-499-X) South End Pr.

Zapatera Prodigiosa. Federico Garcia Lorca. Ed. by Joaquin Forradellas. (Nueva Austral Ser.: Vol. 126). (SPA.). pap. 11.95 (84-239-1926-9) Fr & Eur.

Zapatera Prodigiosa. 13th ed. Federico Garcia Lorca. 184p. (SPA.). 1990. pap. write for info. (0-7859-4976-3) Fr & Eur.

***Zapaticos de Rosa (The Pink Shoes)** Jose Marti. 1997. 11.95 (1-880507-33-1) Lectorum Pubns.

***Zapatista Encuentro: Documents from the Encounter for Humanity & Against Neoliberalism, La Realida, Mexico.** Zapatistas Staff. (Open Mediapamphlet Ser.: Vol. 5). 64p. (Orig.). 1997. pap. 4.95 (1-888363-58-4) Seven Stories.

Zapatistas! Documents of the New Mexican Revolution. Members of the Emiliano Zapata Liberation Movement. 360p. Date not set. 12.00 (1-57027-014-7) Autonomedia.

Zapatistas: Spreading Hope for Grassroots Change Starting from Chiapas. Marc Cooper et al. Ed. by Greg Ruggiero & Stuart Sahulka. (Open Magazine Pamphlet Ser.). 24p. (Orig.). 1994. 4.00 (1-884519-06-7) Open Media.

Zapatos Nuevos Del Herry. (Illus.). 24p. (SPA.). (J). (ps-3). 1993. pap. 3.50 (0-307-52061-7, Golden Pr) Western Pub.

Zapcrafts: Microwaves Are for Much More Than Cooking. Nancy Birnes. (Illus.). 256p. (Orig.). 1990. pap. 14.95 (0-89815-290-9) Ten Speed Pr.

Zapiski Palomnitsi. Alexandra Gavriilova. 175p. (Orig.). 1968. pap. 6.00 (0-317-30250-7) Holy Trinity.

Zapiski Sledovatelia (Notes of An Investigator) Fridrikh Neznansky. LC 89-61028. 342p. (Orig.). (RUS.). (C). 1990. pap. 16.00 (0-911971-44-0) Effect Pub.

Zapiski Sotsial Demokrate, 1906-1921. Petr Garvi & L. Haimson. (Russian Archive Ser.: No. 1). 400p. 1982. 42.00 (0-89250-300-9) Orient Res Partners.

Zapisnaia Knizhka Velimira Khlebnikova. 2nd rev. ed. Velimir Khlebnikov. Ed. by Aleksei Kruchenykh. 30p. (RUS.). 1995. pap. 8.00 (1-57201-019-3) Berkeley Slavic.

Zapotec Civilization: How Urban Society Evolved in Mexico's Oaxaca Valley. Joyce Marcus & Kent Flannery. LC 95-60561. (Illus.). 256p. 1996. 60.00 (0-500-05078-3) Thames Hudson.

Zapotec Elite Ethnohistory. Ronald M. Spores & John D. Monaghan. (Publications in Anthropology: No. 39). 160p. (Orig.). 1990. pap. 23.75 (0-935462-30-9) VUPA.

Zapotec Renaissance: Ethnic Politics & Cultural Revivalism in Southern Mexico. Howard Campbell. LC 93-46953. (Illus.). 347p. 1994. 27.00 (0-8263-1537-2) U of NM Pr.

Zapotec Stoneworkers: The Dynamics of Rural Simple Commodity Production in Modern Mexican Capitalism. Scott Cook. LC 81-40584. (Illus.). 454p. (Orig.). 1982. pap. text ed. 32.00 (0-8191-2420-6); lib. bdg. 67.00 (0-8191-2419-2) U Pr of Amer.

Zapotec Struggles: Histories, Politics, & Representations from Juchitan, Oaxaca. Ed. by Howard Campbell et al. Tr. by Nathaniel Tarn. LC 92-36113. (Series in Ethnographic Inquiry). (Illus.). 352p. 1993. text ed. 45.00 (1-56098-268-3); pap. text ed. 19.95 (1-56098-293-4) Smithsonian.

Zapotec Women. Lynn Stephen. LC 91-8904. (Sourcebooks in Anthropology: No. 16). (Illus.). 332p. 1991. pap. 16.95 (0-292-79065-1); text ed. 35.00 (0-292-79064-3) U of Tex Pr.

Zapp: Empowerment in Health Care. William C. Byham. 1993. pap. 11.00 (0-449-90885-2) Fawcett.

Zapp! The Human Lightning of Empowerment. William C. Byham. Ed. by Jeff Cox. 224p. (Orig.). (C). 1989. pap. 9.95 (0-9623483-1-7) Dev Dimensions.

Zapp! The Lightning of Empowerment. William C. Byham. 1991. 20.00 (0-517-58283-X, Harmony) Crown Pub Group.

Zapp! The Lightning of Empowerment. William C. Byham & Jeff Cox. 208p. 1992. pap. 11.00 (0-449-90705-8, Columbine) Fawcett.

Zapp! in Education. William C. Byham. 1992. pap. 11.00 (0-449-90796-1) Fawcett.

***Zapped: How to Profit from Electricity Deregulation.** Paul F. Levy. LC 97-60745. 160p. 1997. 75.00 (1-886284-06-7) Databks.

***Zapped: How to Profit from Electricity Deregulation.** Paul F. Levy. 160p. (Orig.). 1997. pap. 25.00 (1-886284-08-3, Tatnuck) Databks.

Zapped: Two Novellas: Asbestos: a Book for Lepers, How to Make Love to a Foot. Robert Peters. 135p. (Orig.). 1993. pap. 11.95 (1-879194-10-4) GLB Pubs.

Zappone Family History. James E. Maule. 153p. 1986. pap. 12.00 (0-9647362-1-7) JEMBk Pub.

Zappy Holidays: Super Edition. Diana G. Gallagher. (Secret World of Alex Mack Ser.: No. 10). (J). (gr. 3-5). 1996. mass mkt. 3.99 (0-671-00084-5) PB.

Zaprisky O Rossik: The Notes About Russia. 2nd ed. Marquis De Custine. Ed. by K. Kustanovich. 160p. (Orig.). (RUS.). 1995. pap. 15.00 (0-940294-07-9) Silver Age Pub.

Zapuphizo: Voice of the Nagas. Pieter Steyn. LC 95-7467. 1995. write for info. (0-7103-0506-0) Routledge Chapman & Hall.

Zaqaq al Madak: Madaq Alley. Naguib Mahfouz. 246p. (ARA.). pap. 8.95 (0-86685-163-1, LDL542, Pub. by Librairie du Liban FR) Intl Bk Ctr.

***Zara.** Meredith Steinbach. 277p. 1996. pap. 15.95 (0-8101-5059-X) TriQuarterly.

***Zara: The Roommate.** Wendy C. Staub. (Campus Life 101 Ser.: No. 2). 240p. 1997. mass mkt. 4.50 (0-425-16084-X) Berkley Pub.

Zarabanda: Beginning Spanish. 5th ed. David J. Curland. 512p. 1991. per. 34.59 (0-8403-6814-3) Kendall-Hunt.

***Zaras Hats.** Paul Meisel. 1998. pap. 14.99 (0-525-45465-9) NAL-Dutton.

Zarathushtra in the Gathas & in the Greek & Roman Classics. 2nd ed. Ed. by Wilhelm Geiger & Friedrich Windischmann. LC 74-21260. reprint ed. 51.50 (0-404-12810-6) AMS Pr.

Zarathushtra, Philo, the Achaemenids & Israel. Lawrence H. Mills. LC 74-21261. reprint ed. 49.50 (0-404-12815-7) AMS Pr.

Zarathustra, a God That Can Dance: Talks on Friedrich Nietzsche's Thus Spoke Zarathustra. Osho. Ed. by Prem Agama & Prabodh Nityo. (Zarathustra Ser.). 570p. 24.95 (3-89338-007-8, Pub. by Rebel Hse GW) Osho America.

Zarathustra, a God That Can Dance: Talks on Friedrich Nietzsche's Thus Spoke Zarathustra. Osho. Ed. by Prabodh Nityo & P. Agama. (Zarathustra Ser.). 570p. pap. write for info. (0-614-01947-8, Pub. by Rebel Hse GW) Osho America.

Zarathustra & the Ethical Ideal. Timely Meditations on Philosophy. Robert H. Cousineau. LC 91-21726. x, 224p. 1992. 76.00 (1-55619-114-6) Benjamins North Am.

***Zarathustra Speaking - Speaking of Zarathustra.** Adrian Del Caro. (GERM Ser.). Date not set. 55.00 (1-57113-134-5) Camden Hse.

Zarathustra the Laughing Prophet: Talks on Friedrich Nietzsche's Thus Spoke Zarathustra. Ma A. Shanti. (Zarathustra Ser.). 570p. 24.95 (3-89338-008-6, Pub. by Rebel Hse GW); pap. write for info. (0-614-01927-3, Pub. by Rebel Hse GW) Osho America.

***Zarathustra's Children: A Study of a Lost Generation.** Raymond Furness. (GERM Ser.). 250p. Date not set. 54.95 (1-57113-255-4) Camden Hse.

Zarathustra's Secret. Kohler. 1996. write for info. (0-201-40898-8) Addison-Wesley.

Zarathustra's Secret. Joachim Kohler. Date not set. write for info. (0-8050-4918-5) H Holt & Co.

***Zardozi: Glittering Gold Embroidery.** Charu S. Gupta. (C). 1996. 150.00 (81-7017-319-1, Pub. by Abhinav II) S Asia.

Zarela's Mexican Table. Martinez. 25.00 (0-06-016837-4, HarpT) HarpC.

Zaria's Fire: Engendered Moments in Manam Ethnography. Nancy C. Lutkehaus. LC 95-68695. (Illus.). 506p. 1995. boxed 65.00 (0-89089-800-6) Carolina Acad Pr.

Zariguerya y el Gran Creador de Fuego - Opossum & the Great Filmmaker: Una Leyenda Mexicana. Jan M. Mike. LC 92-36459. (J). (gr. 4-7). 1993. pap. 4.95 (0-8167-3073-3); lib. bdg. 13.95 (0-8167-3125-X) Troll Communs.

Zariski Surfaces & Differential Equations in Characteristic P <O. Blass & Lang. (Pure & Applied Mathematics Ser.: Vol. 106). 456p. 1987. 155.00 (0-8247-7637-2) Dekker.

***Zariskian Filtrations.** Li Huishi & F. Van Oystaeyen. LC 96-32738. (K-Monographs). 264p. (C). 1996. lib. bdg. 127.00 (0-7923-4184-8) Kluwer Ac.

Zarza Sique Ardiendo. Lloyd J. Ogilvie. Orig. Title: The Bush Is Still Burning. 336p. (SPA.). 1986. pap. 1.50 (0-8297-1094-9) Life Pubs Intl.

***Zastrozzi.** George Walker. LC 92-212209. 1997. pap. text ed. 10.95 (0-88754-471-1, Pub. by Playwrights CN Pr CN) Theatre Comm.

Zastrozzi, a Romance & St. Irvyns: Or, The Rosicrucian, 2 Vols., Set. Percy Bysshe Shelley. Ed. by Devendra P. Varma. LC 77-2046. (Gothic Novels III Ser.). 1977. reprint ed. lib. bdg. 27.95 (0-405-10144-9) Ayer.

Zatovarennaya Bochkotara - Randevu. 2nd ed. Vassily Aksyonov. Ed. by Gregory Poliak. (Illus.). 100p. (Orig.). (RUS.). reprint ed. pap. 7.50 (0-940294-02-8) Silver Age Pub.

Zatti! Peter Lappin. 77p. 1987. pap. 2.50 (0-89944-090-8) Salesiana Pubs.

***Zauber der Charakterpuppen: Ebenbilder der Kinder.** Sabine Reinelt. (Illus.). 96p. (GER.). (C). 1993. 34.00 (3-8170-1013-3, Pub. by Knstvrlag Weingrtn GW) Intl Bk Import.

***Zauber der Puppenwelt.** Sabine Reinelt. (Illus.). 128p. (GER.). (C). 1992. 67.00 (3-8170-1010-9, Pub. by Knstvrlag Weingrtn GW) Intl Bk Import.

Zauberberg. Roman. Thomas Mann. 1008p. (GER.). 1991. pap. 22.50 (3-596-29433-9, Pub. by Fischer Taschbch Verlag GW) Intl Bk Import.

Zaugg General Chemistry. Date not set. text ed. write for info. (0-314-05820-6) West Pub.

Zawistowski Collection: The Library & Papers of the Reverend Senior Jozef Lebiedzik Zawistowski of the Polish National Catholic Church, Vol. 1. Theodore L. Zawistowski. viii, 164p. (Orig.). (C). 1972. pap. text ed. 2.50 (0-9619137-0-3) T L Zawistowski.

Zawiyet El-Aryan: The Cemeteries Adjacent to the Layer Pyramid. Dows Dunham. (Illus.). 78p. 1978. pap. 30.00 (0-685-41460-4) Mus Fine Arts Boston.

Zaydeh Danced on Eldridge Street. Elsa O. Rael. LC 96-35045. (J). 1997. 16.00 (0-689-80451-2) S&S Childrens.

Zaydie's Special Esrogim. Aydel Lebovics. (Illus.). 28p. (J). 1991. reprint ed. 10.00 (0-8266-0357-2, Merkos L'Inyonei Chinuch) Kehot Pubn Soc.

***Zaza's Big Break.** McCully. (J). 1997. pap. write for info. (0-15-201569-8, HB Juv Bks) HarBrace.

Zazie dans le Metro. Raymond Queneau. (FRE.). 1972. pap. 10.95 (0-8288-3725-2, F120461) Fr & Eur.

Zazie dans le Metro. Raymond Queneau. (Folio Ser.: No. 108). (FRE.). 1972. pap. 6.95 (2-07-036103-9) Schoenhof.

Zazu's View: Disney's The Lion King. Justine Korman. (Illus.). 24p. (J). (ps-3). 1994. pap. text ed. 1.95 (0-307-10009-X, Golden Books) Western Pub.

ZByte High Tech Playing Cards. Harold A. Layer. (Illus.). 32p. 1992. boxed write for info. (1-882569-00-8) ZByte Play Card.

Zbyx: Tokens. Velande Taylor. LC 96-90204. (Illus.). 64p. (Orig.). 1997. pap. 15.00 (0-9649947-2-0) WrdCraft Bks.

Ze-Ami & His Theories of Noh Drama. Masaru Sekine. (Illus.). 200p. (C). 8500. 45.00 (0-86140-214-6, Pub. by Colin Smythe Ltd UK) Dufour.

Zea Mexican Diary: 7 September, 1926 - 7 September, 1986. Kamau Brathwaite. LC 92-56924. (Studies in American Autobiography). 112p. (C). 1993. 10.95 (0-299-13640-X) U of Wis Pr.

Zeal for Christian Education: Memoirs of B. J. Haan. B. J. Haan. (Orig.). 1992. pap. 10.95 (0-932914-24-1) Dordt Coll Pr.

Zeal of the Convert: The Life of Erskine Childers. Burke Wilkinson. LC 84-50878. 272p. 1985. reprint ed. 22.00 (0-933256-53-1) Second Chance.

Zealand. Rebecca Byrkit. (Illus.). 80p. 1995. 25.00 (0-933313-27-6); pap. 14.95 (0-933313-28-4) SUN Gemini Pr.

Zealand. deluxe limited ed. Rebecca Byrkit. (Illus.). 1995. 35.00 (0-933313-26-8) SUN Gemini Pr.

Zealotry & Academic Freedom: A Legal & Historical Perspective. Neil Hamilton. LC 95-819. 274p. 1995. 39.95 (1-56000-205-0) Transaction Pubs.

Zealots: Investigations into the Jewish Freedom Movement in the Period from Herod I until 70 A.D. Martin Hengel. Tr. by David Smith. 512p. (C). 1997. 69.95 (0-567-09372-7, Pub. by T & T Clark UK) Bks Intl VA.

***Zealots: Investigations into the Jewish Freedom Movement in the Period from Herod I until 70 A.D.** Martin Hengel. Tr. by David Smith. 512p. 1997. pap. 29.95 (0-567-29372-6, Pub. by T & T Clark UK) Bks Intl VA.

Zealots for Zion: Inside Israel's West Bank Settlement Movement. Robert I. Friedman. LC 93-37867. 265p. (C). 1994. reprint ed. pap. 14.95 (0-8135-2062-2) Rutgers U Pr.

Zealous Pilgrimage. A. Garrison. 136p. (C). 1989. text ed. 45.00 (0-946270-70-8, Pub. by Pentland Pr UK) St Mut.

Zeami's Style: The Noh Plays of Zeami Motokiyo. Thomas B. Hare. LC 85-17345. (Illus.). 336p. (Orig.). 1986. 49.50 (0-8047-1290-5) Stanford U Pr.

Zeami's Style: The Noh Plays of Zeami Motokiyo. Thomas B. Hare. 334p. (Orig.). 1996. pap. 17.95 (0-8047-2677-9) Stanford U Pr.

Zeami's Talks on Sarugaku: An Annotated Translation of the Sarugaku Dangi. Erika De Poorter. (Japonica Neerlandica Ser.: Vol. 2). 303p. (C). 1986. 60.00 (90-70265-30-3, Pub. by Gieben NE) Benjamins North Am.

Zeb, the Cow's on the Roof Again! And Other Tales of Early Texas Dwellings. Scott Arbuckle. LC 96-8489. (Illus.). 128p. (J). (gr. 4-8). 1996. 14.95 (1-57168-102-7, Eakin Pr) Sunbelt Media.

Zebahim, 2 vols. (ENG & HEB.). 36.00 (0-910218-79-X) Bennet Pub.

Zeballos, Its Gold Its People Yesterday & Today: An Historical Documentation. Warren Cullins & Laura Cullins. (Orig.). 1982. pap. 7.75 (0-9608386-0-0) Cullins.

Zebina's Kin, the Descendancy of a Puritan People. Lana D. Davis. 171p. (Orig.). 1995. pap. 27.00 (0-7884-0349-4) Heritage Bk.

Zebo & the Dirty Planet. Kim Fernandes & Pat Lacroix. (J). (ps-1). 1991. 14.95 (1-55037-183-5, Pub. by Annick CN); pap. 4.95 (1-55037-180-0, Pub. by Annick CN) Firefly Bks Ltd.

Zebra. (Flap up Joke Ser.). 10p. (J). 1996. pap. 5.95 (0-7871-1048-5, Dove Bks) Dove Audio.

Zebra. Mary Hoffman. LC 84-24793. (Animals in the Wild Ser.). (Illus.). 24p. (J). (gr. k-5). 1985. pap. 3.95 (0-8114-6895-X) Raintree Steck-V.

Zebra. Caroline Arnold. LC 87-1503. (Illus.). 48p. (J). (gr. 2-5). 1993. reprint ed. pap. 5.95 (0-688-12273-6, Morrow Junior) Morrow.

Zebra, Reading Level 3-4. Vouillemin. (World Animal Library). (Illus.). 28p. (J). (gr. 2-5). 1983. lib. bdg. 16.67 (0-86592-858-4); lib. bdg. 12.50 (0-685-58829-7) Rourke Corp.

Zebra among the Lions. Wanger. LC 97-2257. 1997. 25.00 (0-684-82970-3) S&S Trade.

Zebra & Other Stories. Chaim Potok. 1998. write for info. (0-679-85440-1); lib. bdg. write for info. (0-679-95440-6) Random.

Zebra Cards: An Aid to Obscure Diagnosis. John G. Sotos. 88p. 1989. pap. 23.00 (0-943126-13-4, ZEC89) Amer Coll Phys.

Zebra Finch: A Synthesis of Field & Laboratory Studies. Richard A. Zann. (Illus.). 352p. 1996. 105.00 (0-19-854079-5) OUP.

***Zebra Finch: An Owner's Guide to a Happy, Healthy Pet.** Matthew Vriends. (Illus.). 128p. 1997. 12.95 (0-87605-525-0) Howell Bk.

Zebra Finches. (Pet Care Ser.). 80p. (Orig.). 1985. pap. 6.95 (0-8120-3497-X) Barron.

Zebra Finches. K. J. Lawrence. (Colorguide Ser.). 1982. pap. 6.95 (0-940842-12-2) South Group.

Zebra Finches. Mervin F. Roberts. (Illus.). 1981. 9.95 (0-86622-762-8, KW-055) TFH Pubns.

***Zebra Mussel: Impacts & Control.** Charles R. O'Neill, Jr. Ed. by Susan E. Pohl. (Illus.). 60p. (Orig.). 1996. pap. 12.75 (1-57753-010-1, 104IB238) Corn Coop Ext.

Zebra Mussel (Dreissena Polymorpha) Ecology, Biological Monitoring & First Applications in Water Quality Management. Ed. by Dietrich Neumann et al. (Limnologie Aktuell Ser.: Vol. 4). 270p. 1992. pap. 80.00 (1-56081-349-0, Pub. by G Fischer Verlag GW) Lubrecht & Cramer.

Zebra Mussel Dreissena Polymorphia: Ecology, Biological Monitoring & First Applications in the Water Quality Management. Dietrich Neumann. Ed. by Henk A. Jenner. (Limnologie Aktuell Ser.: Vol. 4). (Illus.). 263p. 1992. pap. text ed. 89.60 (0-685-65636-5, Pub. by G Fischer Verlag GW) Lubrecht & Cramer.

Zebra Mussels: Biology, Impacts, & Control. Ed. by Thomas F. Nalepa & Don Schloesser. 832p. 1992. 79.95 (0-87371-696-5, L696) Lewis Pubs.

***Zebra Mussels & Aquatic Nuisance Species: Proceedings, International Zebra Mussel & Other Aquatic Nuisance Species Conference (6th, 1996, Dearborn, MI)** Ed. by Frank M. D'Itri. 638p. 1997. 85.00 (1-57504-036-0) Ann Arbor Chelsea.

***Zebra Riding Cowboy: A Folk Song from the Old West.** Angela S. Medearis. 1997. pap. text ed. 5.95 (0-8050-5302-6) H Holt & Co.

Zebra-Riding Cowboy: A Folk Song of the Old West. Illus. by Maria C. Brusca. LC 91-27941. 32p. (J). (ps-2). 1992. 14.95 (0-8050-1712-7, Bks Young Read) H Holt & Co.

***Zebra Storyteller: Collected Storied.** Spencer Holst. 1997. pap. text ed. 14.95 (1-886449-44-9) Barrytown Ltd.

Zebra Storyteller: Collected Stories. Spencer Holst. LC 93-4201. 1993. 28.95 (0-88268-143-5); 12.95 (0-88268-124-9) Station Hill Pr.

***Zebra-Striped Hearse.** Ross MacDonald. 1998. pap. write for info. (0-375-70145-1, Vin) Random.

Zebra-Striped Hearse see Archer in Jeopardy

Zebra Talk. Vanessa Vargo. LC 92-11028. (J). 1991. pap. 5.99 (0-85953-395-6, Pub. by Childs Play UK) Childs Play.

***Zebra Talk.** Vanessa Vargo. (ITA.). (J). 1991. pap. 5.99 (*0-85953-565-7*) Childs Play.

***Zebra Wall.** Kevin Henkes. Date not set. lib. bdg. 99.98 (*0-688-07569-X*) Greenwillow.

Zebra Wall. Kevin Henkes. LC 87-18454. 160p. (J). (gr. 3 up). 1988. 15.95 (*0-688-07568-1*) Greenwillow.

Zebra Wall. Kevin Henkes. (Illus.). 160p. (J). (gr. 3-7). 1989. pap. 4.99 (*0-14-032969-2*, Puffin) Puffin Bks.

Zebrage. Michel Leiris. (FRE.). 1992. pap. 17.95 (*0-7859-2828-6*) Fr & Eur.

Zebras. Emilie U. Lepthien. LC 94-10945. (New True Bks.). (Illus.). 48p. (J). (gr. k-4). 1994. pap. 5.50 (*0-516-41072-5*); lib. bdg. 19.00 (*0-516-01072-7*) Childrens.

Zebras. Jenny Markert. (Nature Bks.). 32p. (J). (gr. 2-6). 1992. lib. bdg. 22.79 (*0-89565-839-9*) Childs World.

Zebras. Lynn M. Stone. (African Animals Discovery Library). (Illus.). 24p. (J). (gr. k-5). 1990. lib. bdg. 11.94 (*0-86593-048-1*); lib. bdg. 8.95 (*0-685-36349-X*) Rourke Corp.

Zebras. Wildlife Education, Ltd. Staff. (Zoobooks Ser.). (Illus.). 24p. (J). 1992. 13.95 (*0-937934-91-7*); pap. 2.75 (*0-937934-57-7*) Wildlife Educ.

Zebras. Linda C. Wood. (Zoobooks Ser.). (J). 1991. lib. bdg. 14.95 (*0-88682-420-6*) Creative Ed.

Zebras: Or, Contour Lines. Carol Berge. LC 91-68421. 320p. (Orig.). 1991. pap. 20.00 (*0-916185-01-X*) Ctr Pr NM.

Zebra's Hiccups. David McKee. LC 92-14453. (J). 1993. pap. 14.00 (*0-671-79440-X*, S&S Bks Young Read) S&S Childrens.

Zebras, Horses, & Asses: An Action Plan for the Conservation of Wild Equids. Ed. by P. Duncan. (Illus.). 60p. (Orig.). 1992. pap. 10.00 (*2-8317-0056-6*, Pub. by IUCN SZ) Island Pr.

Zebre. rev. ed. Alexandre Jardin. 220p. (FRE.). 1990. pap. 11.95 (*0-7859-2595-3*, 2070382753) Fr & Eur.

Zebulon B. Vance & the "Scattered Nation" Ed. by Maurice A. Weinstein. LC 95-60697. (Illus.). 160p. 1995. 12.00 (*0-9646363-0-1*) Wildacres Pr.

Zebulon Butler: Hero of the Revolutionary Frontier. James R. Williamson & Linda A. Fossler. Ed. & Frwd. by John L. Butler, Jr. LC 94-29356. (Contributions in American History Ser.: No. 160). 184p. 1995. text ed. 52.95 (*0-313-29357-0*, Greenwood Pr) Greenwood.

Zebulon Pike: Explorer of the Southwest. William R. Sanford & Carl R. Green. LC 95-53939. (Legendary Heroes of the Wild West Ser.). 48p. (J). (gr. 4-10). 1996. lib. bdg. 14.95 (*0-89490-671-2*) Enslow Pubs.

Zebulon Pike & the Explorers of the American Southwest. Jared Stallones. Ed. by William H. Goetzmann. (World Explorers Ser.). (Illus.). 112p. (YA). (gr. 5 up). 1992. lib. bdg. 19.95 (*0-7910-1317-0*) Chelsea Hse.

Zebulon Pike's Arkansas Journal. Zebulon M. Pike. Ed. by Stephen H. Hart & Archer B. Hulbert. LC 72-138172. (Illus.). 200p. 1972. reprint ed. text ed. 38.50 (*0-8371-5629-7*, PIAJ, Greenwood Pr) Greenwood.

Zeby Polska...(Let Poland Be...) Aleksander Biedak. (Illus.). 60p. (Orig.). (POL.). 1986. 6.00 (*0-930401-06-9*) Artex Pub.

Zechariah. J. Carl Laney. (Everyman's Bible Commentary Ser.). (Orig.). (C). 1984. pap. 9.99 (*0-8024-0445-6*) Moody.

Zechariah & His Prophecies. Charles H. Wright. Ed. by Franz Delizsch. 694p. 1987. lib. bdg. 26.99 (*0-8254-5276-7*) Kregel.

Zechariah & Jewish Renewal: From Gloom to Glory. Fred P. Miller. 255p. 1992. pap. 15.95 (*1-883116-02-3*) Moellerhaus.

Zechariah Chafee, Jr. Donald L. Smith. (Illus.). 368p. 1986. 37.00 (*0-674-96685-6*) HUP.

Zechariah Nine-Fourteen: A New Translation with Introduction & Commentary. Carol L. Meyers & Eric M. Meyers. LC 92-34535. (Anchor Bible Ser.: Vol. 25C). 576p. 1993. 40.00 (*0-385-14483-0*, Anchor NY) Doubleday.

Zechariah 9-14 & Malachi: A Commentary. David L. Petersen. LC 94-43410. (Old Testament Library). 272p. 1995. 28.00 (*0-664-21298-0*) Westminster John Knox.

Zechstein Basin with Emphasis on Carbonate Sequences. Ed. by H. Fuechtbauer & T. M. Peryt. (Contributions to Sedimentology Monograph: No. 9). (Illus.). 328p. 1980. pap. text ed. 81.50 (*3-510-57009-X*) Lubrecht & Cramer.

Zechstein Facies in Europe. Ed. by T. M. Peryt. (Lecture Notes in Earth Sciences Ser.: Vol. 10). x, 272p. 1987. 62.95 (*0-387-17710-8*) Spr-Verlag.

Zeee. Elizabeth Enright. LC 92-29611. (Illus.). 48p. (J). (gr. 1-5). 1993. 16.00 (*0-15-299958-2*) HarBrace.

Zeek: A Cowboy's True Story of Rodeo Life in the 1950's. D. L. Travis. LC 93-84936. (Illus.). 165p. 1994. reprint ed. 12.95 (*0-9636936-1-1*) Stone-Hill Pub.

Zeek: A Cowboy's True Story of Rodeo Life in the 1950's. D. L. Travis. LC 93-84936. (Illus.). 165p. 1996. reprint ed. pap. 7.95 (*0-9636936-0-3*) Stone-Hill Pub.

Zeely. Virginia Hamilton. LC 67-10266. (Illus.). 128p. (J). (gr. 5-7). 1968. text ed. 16.00 (*0-02-742470-7*, Mac Bks Young Read) S&S Childrens.

Zeely. 2nd ed. Virginia Hamilton. LC 92-28769. (Illus.). 128p. (J). (gr. 3-7). 1993. reprint ed. pap. 3.95 (*0-689-71695-8*, Aladdin Paperbacks) S&S Childrens.

Zeely. 93th ed. 1993. pap. text ed. 13.25 (*0-15-300358-8*, HB Juv Bks) HarBrace.

***Zeely Zebra.** Barbara DeRubertis. LC 96-52644. (Illus.). 32p. (Orig.). (J). (ps-2). 1997. pap. 4.95 (*1-57565-023-1*); pap. 7.95 incl. audio (*1-57565-033-9*) Kane Pr.

Zeena. Elizabeth Cooke. LC 96-20059. 352p. 1996. 23.95 (*0-312-14775-9*) St Martin.

Ze'enah U-Re'enah: Book of Genesis by Jacob Ben Isaac Ashkenazi of Yanow. Ed. by Joseph P. Schultz. Tr. by Israel M. Hurwitz. LC 85-71074. xxiii, 448p. 1985. text ed. 24.50 (*0-685-49419-5*, Ctr Judaic Studies) Eisenbrauns.

***Zeenarchs.** (Shatterzone Ser.). 12.00 (*0-87431-235-3*, 21022) West End Games.

***Zefiro Torna or Scenes from the Life of George Maciunas (Fluxus)** Jonas Mekas. (Illus.). 28p. (Orig.). 1997. pap. 10.00 (*1-889873-00-4*, Arthse Bks) Arthouse.

***Zeguts.** Tom Connor & Jim Downey. 96p. 1997. pap. 9.00 (*1-57566-152-7*, Knsington) Kensgtn Pub Corp.

Zehn Kleine Zappelmaenner: Handbuch. R. Cros. 112p. (GER.). (J). 1991. pap. text ed. 20.75 (*3-12-675091-5*, Pub. by Klett Edition GW); audio 27.00 (*3-12-675092-3*, Pub. by Klett Edition GW) Intl Bk Import.

Zehn Kleine Zappelmaenner. Deutsch als Fremdsprache fuer Vor- und Grundschulkinder: Heft fuer Kinder. R. Cros. 40p. (GER.). (J). 1991. pap. text ed. 10.75 (*3-12-675090-7*, Pub. by Klett Edition GW) Intl Bk Import.

Zeichen und Bezeichnetes: Sprachphilosophische Untersuchungen zum Problem der Referenz. Edmund Runnggaldier. (Grundlagen der Kommunikation-Bibliotheksausgabe Ser.). xii, 363p. (GER.). 1985. 97.70 (*3-11-010107-6*) De Gruyter.

***Zeichen und Herrlichkeit: Die Christologische Relevanz der Semeiaquelle in Den Kanawundern Joh 2, 1-11 und John 4, 46-54.** Hermann Riedl. (Regensburger Studien Zur Theologie Ser.: Bd. 51). 362p. (GER.). 1997. 63.95 (*3-631-30451-X*) P Lang Pubng.

Zeis' Manual of Plastic Surgery. Eduard Zeis. Tr. by T. J. Patterson from GER. (Illus.). 256p. 1988. 57.50 (*0-19-261746-X*) OUP.

Zeisberger's Indian Dictionary: English, German, Iroquois - the Onandaga & Algonquin - the Delaware. David Zeisberger. LC 76-43905. 248p. (ENG, GER & IRO.). reprint ed. 49.50 (*0-404-15802-1*) AMS Pr.

***Zeit der Bewegung - Strukturdynamik und Transformationsprozesse: Beitraege Zur Theorie Sozialer Bewegungen und Zur Analyse Kollektiven Handelns.** Harald Bender. (Europaische Hochschulschriften Ser.: Reihe 22, Bd. 301). 274p. (GER.). 1997. 54.95 (*3-631-30053-0*) P Lang Pubng.

Zeit des Fasans see Time of the Pheasant

Zeit Des Jahwisten: Ein Beitrag zur Datierung Jahwistischer Vatertexte. Kare Berge. (Beiheft zur Zeitschrift fuer die Alttestamentliche Wissenschaft Ser.: Band). xi, 329p. (C). 1990. lib. bdg. 113.85 (*3-11-011892-0*) De Gruyter.

Zeit des Ressentiments, Zeit der Erloesung: Nietzsches Typologie Temporaler Interpretation und Ihre Aufhebung in der Zeit. Christian Koecke. (Monographien und Texte Zur Nietzsche-Forschung Ser.: Bd. 29). 2543p. (GER.). (C). 1994. lib. bdg. 98.50 (*3-11-014066-7*) De Gruyter.

Zeit und Ewigkeit: Studien zum Wortschatz der Geistlichen Texte des Alt-und Fruehmittelhochdeutschen. Harald Burger. LC 74-174177. (Studia Linguistica Germanica: Vol. 6). (C). 1972. 90.00 (*3-11-003995-8*) De Gruyter.

Zeit und Zeiterfahrung in der Deutschsprachigen Lyrik der Funfziger Jahre: Marie Luise Kaschnitz, Ingeborg Bachmann und Christine Lavant. Cordula Drossel-Brown. (Studies in Modern German Literature: Vol. 66). 18p. (GER.). (C). 1995. text ed. 45.95 (*0-8204-2388-2*) P Lang Pubng.

Zeit und Zeiterlebnis in den Werken Max Frischs: Bedeutung und Technische Darstellung. Erna M. Dahms. (Quellen und Forschungen zur Sprach und Kulturgeschichte der Germanischen Voelker Ser.). (C). 1976. 80.80 (*3-11-006679-3*) De Gruyter.

Zeit Von Den Leoniden see Time of the Leonids

Zeit, Zahl und Bild: Studien Zur Vergindung Von Philosophie und Wissenschaft Bei Abbo Von Fleury. Eva-Maria Engelen. (Philosophie und Wissenschaft - Transdisziplinaere Studien Ser.: No. 2). viii, 171p. 1993. pap. 32.35 (*3-11-013849-2*) De Gruyter.

***Zeit zur Abreise.** Jacob Adam. Ed. by J. Fehrs & M. Heitmann. (Haskala - Wissenschaftliche Abhandlungen Ser.: Vol. 5). 161p. (GER.). 1993. write for info. (*3-487-09772-9*) G Olms Pubs.

Zeitalter des Uebergangs see Geschichte der Literaturkritik 1750-1950

Zeitalter Iustinians, Band 2. Berthold Rubin. (Illus.). x, 315p. (C). 1995. lib. bdg. 152.30 (*3-11-003411-5*) De Gruyter.

Zeiten, Volker und Menschen, 7 Vols. Karl Hillebrad. LC 78-67356. (European Political Thought Ser.). (GER.). 1980. reprint ed. lib. bdg. 202.95 (*0-405-11701-9*) Ayer.

Zeiten, Volker und Menschen, 7 Vols., Vol. 1. Karl Hillebrad. LC 78-67356. (European Political Thought Ser.). (GER.). 1980. reprint ed. lib. bdg. 50.95 (*0-405-11702-7*) Ayer.

Zeiten, Volker und Menschen, 7 Vols., Vol. 2. Karl Hillebrad. LC 78-67356. (European Political Thought Ser.). (GER.). 1980. reprint ed. lib. bdg. 50.95 (*0-405-11703-5*) Ayer.

Zeiten, Volker und Menschen, 7 Vols., Vol. 3. Karl Hillebrad. LC 78-67356. (European Political Thought Ser.). (GER.). 1980. reprint ed. lib. bdg. 50.95 (*0-405-11704-3*) Ayer.

Zeiten, Volker und Menschen, 7 Vols., Vol. 4. Karl Hillebrad. LC 78-67356. (European Political Thought Ser.). (GER.). 1980. reprint ed. lib. bdg. 50.95 (*0-405-11705-1*) Ayer.

Zeitgeist. Paul Heapy. (C). 1989. 30.00 (*1-871058-01-5*, Pub. by Dragonheart Pr UK) St Mut.

Zeitgeist: A Novel. Todd Wiggins. LC 96-7309. 320p. 1996. 17.95 (*0-8050-4417-5*) H Holt & Co.

Zeitgeist in Babel: The Postmodernist Controversy. Ed. by Ingeborg Hoesterey. LC 89-46333. (Illus.). 288p. 1991. 37.50 (*0-253-32835-7*); pap. 13.95 (*0-253-20611-1*, MB-611) Ind U Pr.

Zeitgenossische Kunst der Indianer und Eskimos in Kanada. (Illus.). 641p. 1988. 80.00 (*3-89322-014-3*, Pub. by Edition Cantz GW) Dist Art Pubs.

Zeitgenossischen Drucke von Klopstocks Werken. Band 1 Bibliographie, Section Addenda, Bd. 3. (Werke und Briefe. Historisch-kritische Ausgabe (Hamburger Klopstock-Ausgabe)). 1981. 213.85 (*3-11-008119-9*) De Gruyter.

Zeitgenossischen Drucke von Klopstocks Werken. Band 2 Bibliographie, Section Addenda, Bd. 3. (Werke und Briefe. Historisch-kritische Ausgabe (Hamburger Klopstock-Ausgabe)). 1981. 213.85 (*3-11-008570-4*) De Gruyter.

Zeitgenossischen Drucke von Klopstocks Werken. Band 1 Bibliographie see Werke und Briefe. Historisch-kritische Ausgabe (Hamburger Klopstock-Ausgabe)

Zeitgenossischen Drucke von Klopstocks Werken. Band 2 Bibliographie see Werke und Briefe. Historisch-kritische Ausgabe (Hamburger Klopstock-Ausgabe)

Zeitmosaik: A Course in German Conversation Skill. G. Cumming. (C). 1978. student ed. 39.00 (*0-7175-0780-7*, Pub. by S Thornes Pubs UK); audio 75.00 (*0-7175-0854-4*, Pub. by S Thornes Pubs UK) St Mut.

***Zeitreise: Dresden 1954-1995.** Christian Borchert. (GER.). 1996. text ed. 47.00 (*90-5705-023-4*) Gordon & Breach.

Zeitroman: The Novel & Society in Germany, 1830-1900. Roger Hillman. LC 83-5461. (Australian & New Zealand Studies in German Language & Literature: Vol. 12). 186p. (C). 1983. pap. text ed. 19.45 (*0-8204-0010-6*) P Lang Pubng.

Zeitroman of the Late Weimar Republic, Vol. 77. Elke Matijevich. (Studies in Modern German Literature). 208p. (C). 1995. text ed. 45.95 (*0-8204-2751-9*) P Lang Pubng.

Zeitschridt Fur Hebraische Bibliographie, 21 vols. in 4, Set. Ed. by Moritz Steinschneider & Julius Benzian. 1972. reprint ed. 785.00 (*3-487-04266-5*) G Olms Pubs.

Zeitschrift Fur Bucherfreunde, 1897-1936: Gesamtregister, 3 vols. in 1. Ed. by Hans Ruppert & Conrad Hofer. vi, 665p. 1964. reprint ed. write for info. (*0-318-71881-2*) G Olms Pubs.

Zeitschrift fur die Geschichte der Juden in Deutschland, 5 vols., Set. Ed. by Ludwig Geiger. (GER.). write for info. (*0-318-70569-9*); write for info. (*0-318-70570-2*) G Olms Pubs.

Zeitschrift Fur Sport und Kultur Im Altertum, Bd. 1. Nikephoros. Ed. by Wolfgang Decker et al. 320p. 1988. write for info. (*3-615-00038-2*) G Olms Pubs.

Zeitschrift Fur Sport und Kultur Im Altertum, Bd. 2. Nikephoros. Ed. by Wolfgang Decker et al. 330p. 1989. write for info. (*3-615-00058-7*) G Olms Pubs.

Zeitschrift Fur Sport und Kultur Im Altertum, Bd. 3. Nikephoros. Ed. by Wolfgang Decker et al. 338p. 1990. write for info. (*3-615-00067-6*) G Olms Pubs.

Zeitschriften der Romantik. Johannes Bobeth. x, 431p. 1970. reprint ed. 115.00 (*0-318-71741-7*) G Olms Pubs.

Zeitschriften des Jungen Deutschland: Indices, 2 vols. Alfred Estermann. (Illus.). (GER.). 1975. 180.00 (*0-318-23475-0*) Periodicals Srv.

Zeitschriften des Jungen Deutschlands, 2 vols., Set. Heinrich H. Houben. 1970. reprint ed. write for info. (*0-318-71803-0*) G Olms Pubs.

Zeitschriften in Deutschen Bibliotheken. Staatsbibliothek zu Berlin. (Bibliothekspraxis 35 Ser.). 360p. 1995. 100.00 (*3-598-21166-X*) K G Saur.

Zeitschriften und Anthologien des Expressionismus in Osterreich, 2. 1995. 315.00 (*3-598-11222-X*) K G Saur.

Zeitscshrift fur Sport und Kultur Im Altertum, Band 4. Nikephoros. Ed. by Joachim Decker et al. 334p. (GER.). 1991. write for info. (*3-615-00077-3*) G Olms Pubs.

Zeitungswissenschaften in Koln. Hans-Georg Klose. 239p. (GER.). 1989. pap. text ed. 25.00 (*3-598-21302-6*) K G Saur.

***Zeitzeichen Streifzuge Von Bosch Bis Beckmann.** Wilhelm Fraenger. 1996. text ed. 47.00 (*90-5705-004-8*) Gordon & Breach.

***Zejeles para el Clavel.** Gladys Zaldivar. (SPA.). pap. write for info. (*0-89729-284-7*) Ediciones.

Zeke. Annette Broadrick. (Desire Ser.). 1993. mass mkt. 2.99 (*0-373-05793-8*, 5-05793-0) Silhouette.

***Zeke & Ned.** McMurtry. 1997. mass mkt. 7.50 (*0-671-89168-5*) PB.

***Zeke & Ned: A Novel.** Larry McMurtry & Diana Ossana. LC 97-1514. 1997. pap. 20.00 (*0-7838-8095-2*) G K Hall.

***Zeke & Ned: A Novel.** Larry McMurtry & Diana Ossana. LC 97-1514. 1997. 28.95 (*0-7838-8094-4*) G K Hall.

Zeke & Ned: A Novel. Larry McMurtry & Diana Ossana. LC 96-44906. 592p. 1997. 25.00 (*0-684-81152-9*) S&S Trade.

Zeke Berman: Photographs. Craig A. Subler. (Illus.). 12p. (Orig.). 1992. pap. 5.00 (*0-914489-10-0*) Univ Miss-KC Art.

Zeke Hatfield & a Ghost Named Rocky. John Barrett. (City Stories Ser.). (Illus.). (J). (gr. k-10). 1978. 1.99 (*0-686-22892-8*) Silver Dollar.

Zeke Pippin. William Steig. LC 94-76111. (Illus.). 32p. (J). (ps-3). 1994. 15.00 (*0-06-205076-1*); lib. bdg. 14.89 (*0-06-205077-X*) HarpC Child Bks.

***Zeke Pippin.** William Steig. LC 94-76111. (Picture Bks.). (Illus.). 32p. (J). (ps up). 1995. pap. 5.95 (*0-614-19175-0*, Trophy) HarpC Child Bks.

***Zeke Pippin.** William Steig. LC 94-76111. (Trophy Picture Book Ser.). (Illus.). 32p. (J). (ps up). 1997. pap. text ed. 5.95 (*0-06-205924-6*, Trophy) HarpC Child Bks.

Zeke Proctor: Cherokee Outlaw. Robert J. Conley. Ed. by Doug Grad. 192p. (Orig.). 1994. mass mkt. 4.99 (*0-671-77901-X*) PB.

***ZEKE Spectroscopy.** E. W. Schlag. LC 96-50385. (Illus.). 180p. (C). 1997. text ed. 44.95 (*0-521-58128-1*) Cambridge U Pr.

ZekeSpeak: Simple Truths in a Complex World. Zeke Daniels. LC 93-60375. 160p. (Orig.). 1993. pap. 5.95 (*0-934239-70-3*, One Wrld CA) Timely Visions.

***Zekmet, the Stone Carver.** Stolz. 1997. pap. write for info. (*0-15-201601-5*) HarBrace.

Zekmet the Stone Carver: A Tale of Ancient Egypt. Mary Stolz. LC 86-22931. (Illus.). 32p. (J). (gr. 2-5). 1988. 16.00 (*0-15-299961-2*) HarBrace.

***Zekmet, the Stone Carver: A Tale of Ancient Egypt.** Mary Stolz. (Illus.). (J). (gr. 6). 1995. 7.56 (*0-395-73266-2*) HM.

***Zekmet, the Stone Carver: A Tale of Ancient Egypt.** large type ed. Mary Stolz. (Illus.). 54p. 13.50 (*0-614-20633-2*, L-38212-00 APHB) Am Printing Hse.

Zekr. Ali Kianfar. (Illus.). 27p. (Orig.). 1985. pap. 4.00 (*0-918437-01-6*) Intl Sufism.

Zel. Donna Napoli. 196p. (YA). (gr. 6 up). 1996. pap. 15.99 (*0-525-45612-0*) NAL-Dutton.

***Zelazny Cover Art.** Roger Zelazny. Date not set. write for info. (*0-688-10950-0*) Morrow.

Zelda: Manuscript Edition. Sylvia Regan. 1969. pap. 13.00 (*0-8222-1292-7*) Dramatists Play.

Zelda-An Illustrated Life: The Private World of Zelda Fitzgerald. Ed. by Eleanor Lanahan. LC 95-38940. (Illus.). 128p. 1996. 24.95 (*0-8109-3983-5*) Abrams.

Zelda Complex: How to Avoid Toxic Relationships. John Baucom. LC 95-23635. 224p. 1996. (*0-925190-75-6*) Fairview Press.

Zelda Fitzgerald & the Failure of the American Dream for Women. Koula S. Hartnett. LC 90-48817. (American University Studies: American Literature: Ser. XXIV, Vol. 22). 275p. (C). 1990. text ed. 48.95 (*0-8204-1345-3*) P Lang Pubng.

Zelda Orangutan. Hanna Hale. (Illus.). 64p. (J). (gr. 4-6). 1994. Perfect bdg. per. 6.95 (*0-9638724-0-0*) Cando Pubng.

Zelda Strikes Again! Lynn Hall. 151p. (J). (gr. 3-7). 1988. 13.95 (*0-15-299966-3*) HarBrace.

Zelda 5 Official Strategy Guide. 1995. 9.99 (*1-56686-324-4*) Brady Pub.

***Zelda 64: Unauthorized Game Secrets.** Prima Development Staff. 96p. 1997. per., pap. 12.99 (*0-7615-0920-8*) Prima Pub.

Zelda's Cosmic Coloring Book. Zelda L. Gatuskin. (Illus.). 24p. (Orig.). (J). 1996. pap. 4.00 (*0-938513-21-4*) Amador Pubs.

Zelda's Secret. Pascal Lemaitre. LC 93-28448. (Illus.). (J). (ps-3). 1996. pap. 13.95 (*0-8167-3309-0*) BrdgeWater.

Zelda's Secret. Pascal Lemaitre. LC 93-28448. (Illus.). (J). (ps-3). 1997. pap. 3.95 (*0-8167-3310-4*, Troll Medallion) Troll Communs.

Zelda's Zombie Dance, No. 6. Gertrude Gruesome. (Monsterkids Ser.). 64p. (J). 1996. mass mkt. 3.50 (*0-06-106311-8*) HarpC.

Zelenoe Okno - Stikhi - Russian: The Green Window - Poems. Vadim Kreyd. LC 87-15536. 72p. (Orig.). (RUS.). 1987. 10.00 (*0-911971-22-X*) Effect Pub.

Zelf, the Christmas Elf. Nick Donahue. LC 94-27167. (Illus.). (J). 1994. 6.95 (*0-9641502-0-4*) Wildbasin Pubng.

Zelie Dans le Desert. Marcel Arland. 160p. (FRE.). 1974. pap. 10.95 (*0-7859-1774-8*, 2070365344) Fr & Eur.

Zella, Zack & Zodia. Bill Peet. 1986. 14.95 (*0-395-41069-X*) HM.

Zella, Zack & Zodiac. Bill Peet. (J). (gr. k-3). 1985. 12.95 (*0-317-40567-5*) HM.

Zella, Zack, & Zodiac. Bill Peet. (Illus.). 32p. (J). (gr. k-3). 1989. pap. 6.95 (*0-395-52207-2*) HM.

Zeller Free Dream - Zeller Sueno Libre. Ludwig Zeller et al. (Illus.). 108p. 1995. lib. bdg. 45.00 (*0-8095-4811-9*) Borgo Pr.

Zeller Free Dream - Zeller Sueno Libre. Ludwig Zeller et al. (Illus.). 108p. pap. 17.95 (*0-88962-497-6*) Mosaic.

Zelma, the Mystic: White Magic, versus Black. 3rd ed. Alwyn M. Thurber. 380p. 1971. reprint ed. spiral bd. 17.50 (*0-7873-0869-2*) Hlth Research.

Zemiros Shabbos. 1982. pap. 1.00 (*0-686-76284-3*); pap. 1.25 (*0-685-01638-2*); pap. 0.50 (*0-685-01639-0*) Feldheim.

Zemiroth - Sabbath Songs: Pocket Edition. Nosson Scherman. Ed. by Meir Zlotowitz. (ArtScroll Mesorah Ser.). 1979. 10.99 (*0-89906-235-0*); pap. 7.99 (*0-89906-236-9*) Mesorah Pubns.

Zemke's Stalag: The Final Days on World War II. Hubert Zemke. LC 90-10042. (Illus.). 164p. (C). 1991. 26.00 (*1-56098-018-4*) Smithsonian.

Zemke's Wolfpack: The Fifty-Sixth Fighter Group in World War II. William Hess. (Illus.). 192p. 1992. pap. 19.95 (*0-87938-622-3*) Motorbooks Intl.

Zemlja Imjeninnitsa. V. Nikiforoff-Volgin. 182p. 1960. reprint ed. pap. 6.00 (*0-317-30418-6*) Holy Trinity.

Zemlya za kholmom. Dora Shturman. 256p. (RUS.). 1983. pap. 7.00 (*0-938920-32-4*) Hermitage.

Zemnye Deti: Rasskazy. Fedor Sologub. 237p. (RUS.). (C). reprint ed. pap. text ed. 14.00 (*0-933884-79-6*) Berkeley Slavic.

Zempoala: El Estudio de una Ciudad Prehispanica. Jurgen K. Bruggemann et al. 400p. 1991. pap. 20.00 (*968-6487-88-3*, IN016) UPLAAP.

Zemstvo & the Emergence of Civil Society in Late Imperial Russia 1864-1917. Thomas E. Porter. LC 91-3067. (Distinguished Dissertations Ser.: Vol. 18). 324p. 1991. lib. bdg. 99.95 (*0-7734-9972-5*) E Mellen.

An Asterisk (*) at the beginning of an entry indicates that the title is appearing in BIP for the first time.

Zemstvo in Russia: An Experiment in Local Self-Government. Ed. by Terrence Emmons & Wayne S. Vucinich. LC 81-3897. 464p. 1982. text ed. 80.00 (*0-521-23416-6*) Cambridge U Pr.

Zen. Ariel Books Staff. (Illus.). 80p. 1995. 4.95 (*0-8362-3132-5*) Andrews & McMeel.

Zen: A Way of Life. Christmas Humphreys. LC 65-17332. 1971. mass mkt. 7.95 (*0-316-38160-8*) Little.

Zen: Direct Pointing to Reality. Anne Bancroft. (Art & Imagination Ser.). (Illus.). 1987. pap. 15.95 (*0-500-81018-4*) Thames Hudson.

Zen: Key to Your Undiscovered Happiness. C. N. Hu. 118p. (Orig.). (C). 1997. pap. 8.95 (*0-9620765-0-3*) Victory Press.

Zen: Merging of East and West. Roshi P. Kapleau. 330p. 9.95 (*0-385-26104-7*, Anchor NY) Doubleday.

Zen: Poems, Prayers, Sermons, Anecdotes, Interviews. Tr. by Lucien Stryk & Takashi Ikemoto from JPN. LC 81-50909. 210p. 1982. reprint ed. 18.95 (*0-8040-0377-7*) Swallow.

Zen: The Diamond Thunderbolt. Rajneesh Osho Staff. (Zen Ser.). (Illus.). 288p. 1988. 12.95 (*3-89338-043-4*, Pub. by Rebel Hse GW) Osho America.

Zen: The Mystery & the Poetry of the Beyond. Osho. Ed. by Krishna Prabhu. (Zen Ser.). 176p. 1992. 14.95 (*3-89338-082-5*, Pub. by Rebel Hse GW) Osho America.

Zen: The Quantum Leap from Mind to No-Mind. Rajneesh Osho Staff. Ed. by Anand Robin. (Zen Ser.). (Illus.). 288p. 1988. 12.95 (*3-89338-045-0*, Pub. by Rebel Hse GW) Osho America.

Zen: The Reason of Unreason; Eastern Wisdom. 64p. 1993. 9.95 (*0-8118-0403-8*) Chronicle Bks.

Zen: The Religion of the Samurai. Julius Evola. Ed. by J. D. Holmes. Tr. & Intro. by Guido Stucco. (Orig.). (ITA.). 1993. pap. 6.95 (*1-55818-329-9*, Oriental Classics) Holmes Pub.

Zen: The Solitary Bird, Cuckoo of the Forest. Rajneesh Osho Staff. Ed. by Ma D. Sarito. (Zen Ser.). (Illus.). 288p. 1988. 12.95 (*3-89338-044-2*, Pub. by Rebel Hse GW) Osho America.

Zen ABC. Jessie S. Zerne. LC 92-22940. (Illus.). 32p. (J). 1993. 14.95 (*0-8048-1806-1*) C E Tuttle.

Zen Action/Zen Person. Thomas P. Kasulis. LC 80-27858. 194p. 1987. pap. text ed. 10.00 (*0-8248-1023-6*) UH Pr.

Zen & American Thought. Van Meter Ames. LC 77-18523. 293p. 1978. reprint ed. text ed. 35.00 (*0-313-20066-1*, AMZA, Greenwood Pr) Greenwood.

Zen & Budo. Rotaishi S. Omori. Ed. by Brenda Wong. Tr. by Tenshin Tanouye from JPN. (Illus.). 23p. (Orig.). 1989. pap. 5.00 (*1-877982-02-4*) Daihonzan Chozen-ji.

Zen & Comparative Studies. Masao Abe. Ed. by Steven Heine. LC 96-7546. 224p. 1996. text ed. 28.00 (*0-8248-1831-8*); pap. text ed. 15.95 (*0-8248-1832-6*) UH Pr.

Zen & Creative Management. Albert Low. 256p. 1993. pap. 12.95 (*0-8048-1883-5*) C E Tuttle.

Zen & Hasidism: The Similarities Between Two Spiritual Disciplines. Compiled by Harold Heifetz. 1996. 25.00 (*0-88125-542-4*) Ktav.

Zen & Japanese Culture. D. T. Suzuki. (Princeton - Bollingen Series in World Mythology: Vol. 64). (Illus.). 502p. (C). 1993. pap. text ed. 17.95 (*0-691-01770-0*) Princeton U Pr.

***Zen & Japanese Culture.** D. T. Suzuki. (Illus.). 1996. 9.98 (*1-56731-124-5*, MJF Bks) Fine Comms.

Zen & Oriental Art. Hugo Munsterberg. (Illus.). 158p. 1993. pap. 12.95 (*0-8048-1902-5*) C E Tuttle.

Zen & Shinto: The Story of Japanese Philosophy. Chikao Fujisawa. LC 78-139133. 92p. 1971. reprint ed. text ed. 55.00 (*0-8371-5749-8*, FUZS, Greenwood Pr) Greenwood.

***Zen & the Art of Blues Harmonica.** David Harp. 1997. pap. 18.95 incl. cd-rom (*0-918321-74-3*) Musical Idiot.

Zen & the Art of Casino Gambling: An Insider's Guide to a Successful Gambling Experience. Miron Stabinsky & Jeremy Silman. 220p. 1996. pap. 14.95 (*0-945806-15-9*) Summit CA.

Zen & the Art of Changing Diapers. 2nd ed. Sarah Arsone. (Illus.). 63p. (Orig.). 1993. pap. text ed. 8.95 (*0-9632721-0-1*) S Arsone.

***Zen & the Art of Controlled Accident.** 18.95 (*1-56176-909-6*) Mystic Fire.

***Zen & the Art of Fatherhood.** Steven Lewis. 1997. pap. 11.95 (*0-452-27651-9*, Plume) NAL-Dutton.

Zen & the Art of Fatherhood: Lessons from a Master Dad. Steven Lewis. (Illus.). 208p. 1996. pap. 19.95 (*0-525-94147-9*, Dutton) NAL-Dutton.

Zen & the Art of Global Transformation: How to Hold Your Horses When Mother Earth Shifts Gears. Kevin J. Shay. (Illus.). 20p. (Orig.). 1994. pap. 3.95 (*1-881365-69-7*) Shay Pubns.

***Zen & the Art of Interactive Entertainment Design.** Eddie Dombrower. 1997. pap. text ed. 49.95 incl. cd-rom (*0-07-017497-0*) McGraw.

Zen & the Art of Internet. Brendan P. Kehoe & Mixon. LC 96-9693. (C). 1996. pap. text ed. 24.95 (*0-13-244674-X*) P-H.

Zen & the Art of Kicking Butts: The Ultimate Guide for Quitting Smoking Forever. Dennis G. Marthaler. 56p. (Orig.). 1995. pap. 8.95 (*0-9650994-0-7*) D G Marthaler.

Zen & the Art of Making a Living: A Practical Guide to Creative Career Design. rev. ed. Laurence G. Boldt. LC 93-17225. Orig. Title: Zen & the Art of Making a Living in the Post-Modern World. (Illus.). 672p. 1993. pap. 17.95 (*0-14-019469-X*, Penguin Bks) Viking Penguin.

Zen & the Art of Making a Living in the Post-Modern World see Zen & the Art of Making a Living: A Practical Guide to Creative Career Design

Zen & the Art of Motorcycle Maintenance. Robert Pirsig. 1996. 22.95 (*1-55927-378-X*) St Martin.

Zen & the Art of Motorcycle Maintenance: An Inquiry into Values. Robert M. Pirsig. 416p. 1984. pap. 7.50 (*0-553-27747-2*, Bantam Classics) Bantam.

Zen & the Art of Motorcycle Maintenance: An Inquiry into Values. Robert M. Pirsig. LC 73-12275. 1974. 22.95 (*0-688-00230-7*) Morrow.

Zen & the Art of Motorcycle Maintenance: An Inquiry into Values. Robert M. Pirsig. LC 73-12275. 1979. pap. 12.95 (*0-688-05230-4*) Morrow.

Zen & the Art of Pottery. Kenneth R. Beittel. (Illus.). 148p. 1989. 14.95 (*0-8348-0221-X*) Weatherhill.

Zen & the Art of Resedit. Derrick Schneider. 1995. pap. 30.00 incl. cd-rom (*1-56830-244-4*) Hayden.

Zen & the Art of Resource Editing. Berkeley Macintosh Users Group Staff. pap. 20.00 (*1-879791-00-5*) BMUG.

Zen & the Art of Screenwriting: Insights & Interviews. William Froug. 332p. 1996. pap. text ed. 20.95 (*1-879505-31-2*) Silman James Pr.

Zen & the Art of Street Fighting: True Battles of a Modern-Day Warrior. Jack Sabat. LC 96-23671. (Illus.). 500p. (Orig.). 1996. pap. 14.95 (*1-883319-45-5*) Frog Ltd CA.

Zen & the Art of the Internet. Brendan P. Kehoe. LC 92-18075. (Series in Innovative Technology). 128p. 1992. 22.00 (*0-13-010778-6*) P-H Gen Ref & Trav.

Zen & the Art of the Internet: A Beginner's Guide. 4th ed. Brendan P. Kehoe. LC 95-37456. 1995. 23.95 (*0-13-452914-6*) P-H Gen Ref & Trav.

Zen & the Art of the Internet: Parents & Educator's Guide. Brendan P. Kehoe. 1996. 23.95 (*0-614-14499-X*) P-H.

Zen & the Art of Writing. Manjushri J. Vitale. 90p. (Orig.). 1984. pap. 10.95 (*0-932896-07-3*) Westcliff Pubns.

***Zen & the Beat Way.** Alan Watts. 1997. pap. text ed. 12.95 (*0-8048-3117-3*) C E Tuttle.

Zen & the Bible. J. K. Kadowaki. 1988. pap. 12.95 (*0-14-019143-7*, Penguin Bks) Viking Penguin.

Zen & the Birds of Appetite. Thomas Merton. LC 68-25546. 1968. pap. 7.95 (*0-8112-0104-X*, NDP261) New Directions.

***Zen & the Brain.** James H. Austin. LC 97-24693. 1997. 35.00 (*0-262-01164-6*) MIT Pr.

Zen & the Psychology of Transformation: The Supreme Doctrine. rev. ed. Hubert Benoit. 264p. 1990. pap. 12.95 (*0-89281-272-9*) Inner Tradit.

Zen & the Way of the Sword: Arming the Samurai Psyche. Winston L. King. (Illus.). 288p. 1994. reprint ed. pap. 11.95 (*0-19-509261-9*) OUP.

Zen & the Way of the Sword: Arming the Warrior Psyche. Winston L. King. LC 92-24633. 288p. (C). 1993. 35.00 (*0-19-506810-6*) OUP.

Zen & the Ways. Trevor P. Leggett. LC 87-50165. (Illus.). 258p. 1987. pap. 12.95 (*0-8048-1524-0*) C E Tuttle.

Zen & Us. Karlfried G. Durckheim. Tr. by Vincent Nash from GER. 144p. 1987. pap. 8.95 (*0-525-48331-4*, Dutton) NAL-Dutton.

Zen & Western Thought. Masao Abe. Ed. & Intro. by William R. LaFleur. LC 83-24153. 332p. 1984. reprint ed. pap. text ed. 15.00 (*0-8248-1214-X*) UH Pr.

Zen & Zen Classics. Frederick Franck. 310p. (Orig.). 1992. pap. 11.95 (*0-89346-353-1*) Heian Intl.

Zen Antics: One Hundred Stories of Enlightenment. Ed. & Tr. by Thomas Cleary from JPN. LC 93-12213. 128p. (Orig.). 1993. pap. 10.00 (*0-87773-944-7*) Shambhala Pubns.

***Zen around the World: A 2,500-Year Journey from the Buddha to You.** C. Alexander Simpkins. LC 97-5564. 1997. pap. text ed. 21.95 (*0-8048-3082-7*) C E Tuttle.

Zen Art for Meditation. Stewart W. Holmes & Chimyo Horioka. LC 73-78279. (Illus.). 116p. 1978. pap. 9.95 (*0-8048-1255-1*) C E Tuttle.

Zen at Work. Les Kaye. 1997. pap. 14.00 (*0-517-88620-0*) Random Hse Value.

Zen Awakening & Society. Christopher Ives. LC 91-35863. 200p. (C). 1992. text ed. 27.00 (*0-8248-1452-5*); pap. text ed. 15.95 (*0-8248-1453-3*) UH Pr.

Zen Beyond All Words: A Western Zen Master's Instructions. Wolfgang Kopp. Tr. by Barbara Wittnberg-Hasenauer. (Tuttle Library of Enlightenment). 112p. (Orig.). 1996. pap. 12.95 (*0-8048-3086-X*) C E Tuttle.

Zen Buddhism. Christmas Humphreys. 1987. pap. 13.95 (*0-04-294130-X*) Routledge Chapman & Hall.

Zen Buddhism. Christmas Humphreys. 256p. 1988. pap. 13.95 (*0-04-294095-8*) Routledge Chapman & Hall.

Zen Buddhism: A Classified Bibliography of Western-Language Publications through 1990. James L. Gardner. LC 91-91037. 412p. 1991. 32.00 (*1-879222-02-7*, Wings Books); pap. 22.50 (*1-879222-03-5*, Wings Books) Random.

Zen Buddhism: A History: India & China. rev. ed. Heinrich Dumoulin. 386p. 1994. 20.00 (*0-02-897109-4*) P-H.

Zen Buddhism: An Analysis & Reflection. Lalan P. Singh & B. M. Sirsena. 192p. 1988. text ed. 25.00 (*0-938719-31-9*, Envoy Pr) Apt Bks.

Zen Buddhism: Selected Writings of D. T. Suzuki. Ed. by William Barrett. 320p. 1996. pap. 10.00 (*0-385-48349-X*, Image Bks) Doubleday.

Zen Buddhism: A History: Japan, Vol. 2. Heinrich Dumoulin. Tr. by Paul F. Knitter. (Illus.). 340p. 1989. 23.00 (*0-02-908240-4*, Free Press) Free Pr.

Zen Buddhism: A History: Japan, Vol. 2. 2nd ed. Heinrich Dumoulin. Tr. by Paul F. Knitter. (Illus.). 340p. 1989. 35.00 (*0-02-908250-1*, Free Press) Free Pr.

Zen Buddhism & Hasidism: A Comparative Study. Jacob Y. Teshima. 208p. (Orig.). (C). 1995. pap. text ed. 29.50 (*0-7618-0004-2*); lib. bdg. 48.00 (*0-7618-0003-4*) U Pr of Amer.

Zen Buddhism in the Twentieth Century. Heinrich Cumoulin. Tr. by Joseph S. O'Leary from GER. 192p. (Orig.). (C). 1992. pap. 14.95 (*0-8348-0247-3*) Weatherhill.

Zen Buddhist Encounters Quakerism. Teruyasu Tamura. LC 91-68487. 32p. (Orig.). 1992. pap. 3.00 (*0-87574-302-1*) Pendle Hill.

Zen Catholicism. Dom A. Graham. 240p. 1994. reprint ed. pap. 12.95 (*0-8245-1425-4*) Crossroad NY.

Zen Combat: The First, the Most Complete, & Still the Best. Jay Gluck. (Illus.). 240p. (Orig.). 1994. pap. 8.95 (*4-89360-038-9*, Pub. by Personally Oriented JA) Weatherhill.

Zen Comes West. Christmas Humphreys. 216p. (C). 1994. pap. text ed. 19.00 (*0-7007-0310-1*, Pub. by Curzon Press UK) UH Pr.

Zen Comics. Ioanna Salajan. LC 74-35679. 88p. 1974. pap. 6.95 (*0-8048-1120-2*) C E Tuttle.

Zen Comics, Vol. II. Ioanna Salajan. LC 82-50094. (Illus.). 88p. 1982. pap. 6.95 (*0-8048-1445-7*) C E Tuttle.

Zen Concrete & Etc. D. A. Levy et al. LC 91-70949. (Illus.). 245p. 1991. pap. 27.50 (*0-941160-04-1*) Ghost Pony Pr.

Zen Dance: Meditation in Movement. Sun O. Lee & Alan Heyman. (Illus.). 108p. 1985. 24.00 (*0-8048-1428-7*, Pub. by Seoul Intl Tourist KO) C E Tuttle.

Zen Dictionary. Ernest Wood. LC 72-77518. 166p. 1972. pap. 8.95 (*0-8048-1060-5*) C E Tuttle.

Zen Doctrine of No Mind. D. T. Suzuki. LC 92-47587. 189p. 1991. pap. 10.95 (*0-87728-182-3*) Weiser.

Zen Driving. K. T. Berger. 1988. pap. 9.00 (*0-345-35350-1*, Ballantine Trade) Ballantine.

Zen, Drugs & Mysticism. Robert C. Zaehner. LC 88-37081. 228p. (C). 1989. reprint ed. pap. text ed. 22.50 (*0-8191-7266-9*) U Pr of Amer.

Zen, Eastern Wisdom. James Bibo. LC 92-42257. (Eastern Wisdom Ser.). 192p. 1993. boxed 29.95 (*0-8118-0438-0*) Chronicle Bks.

Zen Enlightenment: Origins & Meaning. Heinrich Dumoulin. LC 78-27310. 188p. 1979. pap. 13.95 (*0-8348-0141-8*) Weatherhill.

***Zen Environment.** Marian Mountain. Date not set. pap. write for info. (*0-688-14957-X*, Quill) Morrow.

Zen Essence: The Science of Freedom. Thomas Cleary. LC 94-36157. (Pocket Classics Ser.). 1995. pap. 6.00 (*1-57062-097-0*) Shambhala Pubns.

Zen Eye: A Collection of Zen Talks by Sokei-an. Ed. by Mary Farkas. 208p. 1993. pap. 12.95 (*0-8348-0272-4*) Weatherhill.

Zen Flesh, Zen Bones: A Collection of Zen & Pre-Zen Writings. Ed. by Paul Reps. 192p. 1961. pap. 9.95 (*0-385-08130-8*, A233, Anchor NY) Doubleday.

Zen Flesh, Zen Bones: A Collection of Zen & Pre-Zen Writings. Ed. by Nyogen Senzaki. LC 94-13370. (Pocket Classics Ser.). 288p. 1994. pap. 6.00 (*1-57062-063-6*) Shambhala Pubns.

Zen Flesh, Zen Bones: A Collection of Zen & Pre-Zen Writings. Tr. by Nyogen Senzaki & Paul Reps. LC 57-10199. (Illus.). 212p. reprint ed. 16.95 (*0-8048-0644-6*) C E Tuttle.

Zen Flowers: Chabana for the Tea Ceremony. Henry Mittwer. 142p. 1992. 14.95 (*0-8048-1882-7*) C E Tuttle.

Zen for Beginners. Judith Blackstone & Zoran Josipovic. (Writers & Readers Documentary Comic Bks.). (Illus.). 176p. (Orig.). 1986. pap. 7.95 (*0-86316-116-2*) Writers & Readers.

***Zen for Cats.** Henry Beard. LC 97-19732. 1997. 10.00 (*0-375-50034-0*, Villard Bks) Random.

Zen for Cats. Alfred Birnbaum & Riku Kanmei. (Illus.). 96p. 1993. 12.95 (*0-8348-0292-9*); pap. 9.95 (*0-8348-0275-9*) Weatherhill.

Zen for Cats: Postcard Book. Alfred Birbaum & Riku Kammei. (Illus.). 48p. (Orig.). 1993. pap. 8.95 (*0-8348-0294-5*) Weatherhill.

Zen Forest: Sayings of the Masters. Soiku Shigematsu. (Illus.). 136p. 1992. reprint ed. pap. 7.95 (*0-8348-0259-7*, Inklings Edits) Weatherhill.

Zen Gardening: A Down-to-Earth Philosophy. Veronica Ray. 192p. 1996. pap. text ed. 10.00 (*0-425-15299-5*, Berkley Trade) Berkley Pub.

Zen Gardening Kit. D. Moore. (Illus.). 96p. 1992. 30.00 (*1-56138-148-9*) Running Pr.

Zen Golf. Jeff Wallach. 1998. pap. write for info. (*0-517-88720-7*) Random.

Zen Graffiti. Azuki. 97p. 1995. pap. 9.95 (*0-946672-24-5*, Pub. by Buddhist Pub UK) Assoc Pubs Grp.

Zen Guide: Where to Meditate in Japan. John Stevens & Martin Roth. (Illus.). 152p. 1985. pap. 9.95 (*0-8348-0202-3*) Weatherhill.

***Zen Guitar.** Philip T. Sudo. 1997. 20.00 (*0-684-83090-6*) S&S Trade.

Zen Haiku: Poems & Letters of Natsume Soseki. Tr. by Soiku Shigematsu from JPN. 128p. (Orig.). 1994. pap. 7.95 (*0-8348-0324-0*) Weatherhill.

***Zen Harvest.** Soiku Shigematsu. 1996. pap. 20.95 (*0-8348-0260-0*) Weatherhill.

Zen Harvest: Japanese Folk Zen Sayings (Haiku, Dodoitsu & Waka) Tr. by Soiku Shigematsu from JPN. LC 87-82594. 208p. 1988. pap. 12.95 (*0-86547-328-5*, North Pt Pr) FS&G.

Zen in America: Five Teachers & the Search for an American Buddhism. Helen Tworkov. (Illus.). 304p. 1994. pap. 15.00 (*1-56836-030-4*) Kodansha.

Zen in American Life & Letters. Ed. by Robert S. Ellwood. LC 87-51198. (Interplay Ser.: Vol. 6). 200p. (Orig.). 1987. 31.25 (*0-89003-261-0*); pap. 20.50 (*0-89003-260-2*) Undena Pubns.

Zen in English Literature & Oriental Classics. Reginald H. Blyth. (Illus.). 302p. 1942. reprint ed. pap. 27.95 (*0-9647040-1-3*) Book East.

Zen in Golf & Life. Peter G. Cranford. 76p. (Orig.). 1995. pap. text ed. 22.50 (*0-9605822-3-1*) Great Pyramid.

***Zen in Medieval Vietnam: A Study & Translation.** Cuong T. Nguyen. LC 97-15882. 1997. write for info. (*0-8248-1948-9*) UH Pr.

Zen in Motion: Lessons from a Master Archer on Breath, Posture, & the Path of Intuition. Neil Claremon. (Illus.). 144p. (Orig.). 1992. pap. 10.95 (*0-89281-361-X*) Inner Tradit.

Zen in the American Grain: Discovering the Teachings at Home. Kyogen Carlson. 1994. pap. 9.95 (*0-88268-158-3*) Station Hill Pr.

Zen in the Art of Archery. Eugene Herrigel. 1989. pap. 10.00 (*0-679-72297-1*, Vin) Random.

Zen in the Art of Child Maintenance. Michael Pastore & Larry Pastor. LC 92-82027. 120p. (Orig.). 1993. pap. 14.95 (*0-927379-28-7*, ZP 99) Zorba Pr.

Zen in the Art of Climbing Mountains. Neville Shulman. LC 91-67335. 128p. (Orig.). 1992. pap. 12.95 (*0-8048-1775-8*) C E Tuttle.

Zen in the Art of Close Encounters: Crazy Wisdom & UFO's. Ed. by Paul D. Pursglove. LC 94-80141. (Illus.). 333p. (Orig.). (C). 1995. pap. 14.50 (*0-9638691-0-8*) New Being Proj.

***Zen in the Art of Golf.** Joseph D. McLaughlin. LC 97-2824. 1997. write for info. (*0-89334-257-2*, Humanics Trade) Humanics Ltd.

Zen in the Art of Golf. rev. ed. Joseph McLaughlin. 80p. 1993. pap. 5.95 (*0-914720-09-0*) Pale Horse.

Zen in the Art of Helping. David Brandon. 128p. 1991. pap. 10.95 (*0-14-019188-7*, Arkana) Viking Penguin.

Zen in the Art of Rhetoric: An Inquiry into Coherence. Mark L. McPhail. LC 95-15882. (SUNY Series in Speech Communication). 220p. (C). 1995. text ed. 57.50 (*0-7914-2803-6*); pap. text ed. 18.95 (*0-7914-2804-4*) State U NY Pr.

Zen in the Art of Writing. Ray Bradbury. 176p. 1992. mass mkt. 5.99 (*0-553-29634-5*) Bantam.

Zen in the Art of Writing: Essays on Creativity. 3rd ed. Ray Bradbury. 1993. pap. 8.95 (*1-877741-09-4*) J Odell Editions.

Zen in the Markets: Confessions of a Zen Trader. Edward A. Toppel. 96p. (Orig.). 1992. pap. 12.95 (*1-878850-00-8*) Samurai Pr Ltd.

Zen in the Martial Arts. Joe Hyams. LC 78-62884. 144p. 8.95 (*0-87477-101-3*, Tarcher Putnam) Putnam Pub Group.

Zen in the Martial Arts. Kohl Susan. LC 78-62884. 1988. pap. 3.50 (*0-312-91037-1*) St Martin.

Zen Inklings: Some Stories, Fables, Parables & Sermons. Donald Richie. 128p. (C). 1992. reprint ed. pap. 9.95 (*0-8348-0230-9*) Weatherhill.

Zen Is Eternal Life. 3rd rev. ed. Roshi P. Jiyu-Kennett. (Illus.). 319p. 1987. pap. 12.95 (*0-930066-06-5*) Shasta Abbey.

Zen Keys. Thich Nhat Hanh. 208p. 1995. pap. 11.95 (*0-385-47561-6*) Doubleday.

Zen Koan. Isshu Miura & Ruth F. Sasaki. LC 65-19104. (Illus.). 156p. 1966. pap. 10.00 (*0-15-699981-1*, Harvest Bks) HarBrace.

Zen Koan: As a Means of Realizing Enlightenment. Intro. by Jan W. Van der Wetering. 208p. (Orig.). 1994. pap. 14.95 (*0-8048-3041-X*) C E Tuttle.

Zen Kobudo: Mysteries of Okinawan Weaponry & Te. Mark Bishop. 96p. 1995. pap. 12.95 (*0-8048-2027-9*) C E Tuttle.

Zen Leadership Team Management: The Human Side of Total Quality. Stephen Uzelac. 327p. (C). 1995. pap. 24.00 (*0-923231-24-2*) Mohican Pub.

Zen Lessons: The Art of Leadership. Tr. by Thomas Cleary from CHI. LC 88-18604. 144p. (Orig.). 1989. pap. 11.00 (*0-87773-446-1*) Shambhala Pubns.

Zen Lessons: The Art of Leadership. Tr. by Thomas Cleary from CHI. LC 92-56460. 248p. 1993. pap. 7.00 (*0-87773-893-9*, Sham Pocket Class) Shambhala Pubns.

Zen Letters: Teachings of Yuanwu. Ed. by J. C. Cleary & Thomas Cleary. Tr. by Thomas Cleary from CHI. LC 93-21937. (Illus.). 144p. 1994. pap. 10.00 (*0-87773-931-5*) Shambhala Pubns.

Zen Life: D. T. Suzuki Remembered. Ed. by Masao Abe. (Illus.). 288p. (Orig.). 1986. pap. 19.95 (*0-8348-0213-9*) Weatherhill.

Zen Life: Daily Life in a Zen Monastery. Koji Sato. Tr. by Ryojun Victoria. LC 79-185602. (Illus.). 194p. 1983. pap. 11.50 (*0-8348-1517-6*) Weatherhill.

***Zen Light: Unconventional Commentaries on the Denkoroku.** Stefano Barragato. LC 97-5244. 1997. pap. text ed. 14.95 (*0-8048-3106-8*) C E Tuttle.

Zen Macrobiotic Cooking. Michel Abehsera. 1976. mass mkt. 4.95 (*0-380-01483-1*) Avon.

Zen Macrobiotic Cooking. Michel Abehsera. 1971. reprint ed. pap. 9.95 (*0-8065-0893-0*, Citadel Pr) Carol Pub Group.

Zen Macrobiotics: The Art of Rejuvenation & Longevity. unabridged ed. George Ohsawa. Ed. by Carl Ferre. LC 95-69712. 208p. 1995. pap. 9.95 (*0-918860-54-7*) G Ohsawa.

Zen Manifesto: Freedom from Oneself. Osho. Ed. by Ma D. Sagar. (Zen Ser.). 1993. 18.95 (*3-89338-121-X*, Pub. by Rebel Hse GW) Osho America.

Zen Martial Arts. Joe Hyams. 144p. 1982. mass mkt. 5.99 (*0-553-27559-3*) Bantam.

Zen Master Eihei Dogen's Monastic Regulations. Eihei Dogen. Ed. & Tr. by Shohei ICHIMURA from CHI. (Institute's Ser.: No. 1). 405p. (C). 1993. 50.00 (*0-9643788-1-7*) NAmer Inst Zen.

Zen-Master Hakuin: Selected Writings. Hakuin. Tr. by Philip B. Yampolsky from JPN. LC 75-145390. (Records of Civilization: Sources & Studies: No. 86). 1985. pap. text ed. 18.50 (*0-231-06041-6*) Col U Pr.

Zen Master Keizan's Monastic Regulations. Keizan Jokin. Ed. & Tr. by Shohei ICHIMURA. (Institute's Ser.: No. 2). 455p. (C). 1994. 50.00 (*0-9643788-2-5*) NAmer Inst Zen.

***Zen Masters of Meditation in Images & Writings.** Helmut Brinker & Hiroshi Kanazawa. Tr. by Andreas Leisinger. (Illus.). 384p. 1996. text ed. 79.00 (*3-907070-62-3*) UH Pr.

Zen Meditation: A Broad View. rev. ed. Justin F. Stone. (Illus.). 160p. 1995. pap. 10.95 (*0-9620812-9-9*) Good Karma.

Zen Meditation see Serene Reflection Meditation

Zen Meditation & Psychotherapy. Tomio Hirai. (Orig.). 1986. pap. 18.00 (*0-87040-666-3*) Japan Pubns USA.

Zen Mind, Beginner's Mind. Shunryu Suzuki. Ed. by Trudy Dixon. LC 70-123326. 132p. 1970. 14.95 (*0-8348-0052-7*); pap. 7.95 (*0-8348-0079-9*) Weatherhill.

Zen Monastic Experience: Buddhist Practice in Contemporary Korea. Robert E. Buswell. 288p. (C). 1992. pap. text ed. 15.95 (*0-691-03477-X*) Princeton U Pr.

Zen Mover. Patrick Smith. (Illus.). 36p. (Orig.). 1977. pap. 5.00 (*0-942908-01-5*) Pancake Pr.

Zen Munchkins: Little Wisdoms. D. T. Munda. (Illus.). 104p. (Orig.). 1991. pap. 12.95 (*0-8048-1640-9*) C E Tuttle.

Zen of Bowel Movements: A Spiritual Approach to Constipation. Kathy A. Price. 184p. (Orig.). 1995. pap. 19.95 (*0-9642906-6-9*) Rock Rose Pubng.

Zen of Code Optimization. Michael Abrash. 449p. (Orig.). 1994. pap. 39.95 (*1-883577-03-9*) Coriolis Grp.

Zen of Cooking. Lucille Naimer. 224p. 1996. 23.95 (*0-87951-594-5*) Overlook Pr.

***Zen of Eating: Ancient Answers to Modern Weight Problems.** Ronna Kabatznick. LC 97-23778. 1998. write for info. (*0-399-52382-0*) Berkley Pub.

Zen of Graphics Programming. 2nd ed. Michael Abrash. 1996. pap. text ed. 44.99 incl. cd-rom (*1-883577-89-6*) Coriolis Grp.

Zen of Groups: A Handbook for People Meeting with a Purpose. Dale Hunter et al. LC 95-31932. 210p. 1995. pap. 17.95 (*1-55561-100-1*) Fisher Bks.

Zen of Hype: An Insider's Guide to the Publicity Game. Raleigh Pinskey. 208p. (Orig.). 1991. pap. 10.95 (*0-8065-1239-3*, Citadel Pr) Carol Pub Group.

Zen of Juggling. Dave Finnigan. LC 91-90251. 111p. (Orig.). 1993. pap. 9.95 (*0-9615521-5-8*, 185770) Jugglebug.

Zen of Programming. (Illus.). 128p. 1988. pap. text ed. 9.95 (*0-931137-09-8*) Infobooks.

Zen of Recovery. Mel Ash. LC 92-14154. 240p. (Orig.). 1993. 15.95 (*0-87477-706-2*, Tarcher Putnam) Putnam Pub Group.

Zen of Seeing. Frederick Franck. 1973. pap. 17.00 (*0-394-71968-9*, V968, Vin) Random.

Zen of the Bright Virtue. Manly P. Hall. pap. 10.50 (*0-89314-374-X*) Philos Res.

Zen of Windows 95 Programming. Lou Grinzo. 1995. pap. text ed. 39.99 (*1-883577-58-6*) Coriolis Grp.

Zen, Pen, & Sword: The Karate Experience. Randall G. Hassell. 170p. (Orig.). 1993. pap. 15.95 (*0-911921-13-3*) Focus Pubns MO.

Zen Philosophy, Zen Practice. Thich Thien-An. LC 75-20003. (Illus.). 192p. 1975. pap. 12.95 (*0-913546-33-X*) Dharma Pub.

Zen Physics: The Science of Death, the Logic of Reincarnation. David Darling. LC 95-51829. 1996. write for info. (*0-614-95860-1*) HarpC.

Zen Physics: The Science of Death, the Logic of Reincarnation. David Darling. LC 95-51829. 256p. 1996. 23.00 (*0-06-017352-1*) HarpC.

Zen Poems. 2nd ed. Teo Savory. (Illus.). 1976. pap. 9.00 (*0-87775-038-6*) Unicorn Pr.

Zen Poems of China & Japan: The Crane's Bill. Tr. by Lucien Stryk & Takashi Ikemoto from CHI. LC 87-7450. 208p. 1987. pap. 7.95 (*0-8021-3019-4*, Grove) Grove-Atltic.

Zen Poems of the Five Mountains. David Pollack. LC 84-13910. (American Academy of Religion, Studies in Religion). 166p. (C). 1985. pap. 16.95 (*0-89130-775-3*) Scholars Pr GA.

Zen Poetry. Lucien Stryk. 1988. pap. 10.95 (*0-14-058599-0*, Penguin Bks) Viking Penguin.

Zen Poetry: Let the Spring Breeze Enter. Tr. by Lucien Stryk & Takashi Ikemoto. 124p. 1995. pap. 11.00 (*0-8021-3407-6*, Grove) Grove-Atltic.

***Zen Poetry of Dogen: Verses from the Mountain of Eternal Peace.** Steve Heine. 1997. pap. text ed. 14.95 (*0-8048-3107-6*) C E Tuttle.

Zen, Poetry, the Art of Lucien Stryk. Ed. by Susan Porterfield. 360p. (C). 1993. text ed. 45.00 (*0-8040-0975-9*) Swallow.

***Zen Ranching & the Farming Game: A Touching Story of a Family & the Land They Loved & Fought For.** George Rohrbacher. LC 96-79210. (Illus.). 224p. 1997. pap. 14.95 (*1-885221-50-9*) BookPartners.

Zen Restaurants. (Architecture in Detail Ser.). (Illus.). 60p. 1993. pap. 29.95 (*0-7148-2746-0*, Pub. by Phaidon Press UK) Chronicle Bks.

Zen Romance: One Woman's Adventures in a Monastery. Deborah B. Boehm. Ed. by Elizabeth Floyd. 288p. 1996. 25.00 (*4-7700-2032-5*) Kodansha.

Zen Seeds: Reflections of a Female Priest. Shundo Aoyama. Tr. by Patricia D. Bennage. 168p. 1992. pap. 5.95 (*4-333-01478-6*, Pub. by Kosei Pub Co JA) C E Tuttle.

Zen Seeing, Zen Drawing: Meditation in Action. Frederick Franck. LC 92-32791. 192p. 1993. pap. 15.95 (*0-553-37146-0*) Bantam.

Zen Shaolin Karate: The Complete Practice, Philosophy & History. Nathan Johnson. (Illus.). 280p. 1993. pap. 21.95 (*0-8048-1918-1*) C E Tuttle.

Zen Shiatsu: How to Harmonize Yin & Yang for Better Health. Shizuto Masunaga & Wataru Ohashi. (Illus.). 176p. 1977. pap. 18.00 (*0-87040-394-X*) Japan Pubns USA.

***Zen Smoking.** Andy Stanfield. 213p. (Orig.). 1997. mass mkt. 4.99 (*1-55197-924-1*, Pub. by Comnwlth Pub CN) Partners Pubs Grp.

***Zen Soup: Tasty Morsels of Wisdom from Great Minds East & West.** Laurence G. Boldt. LC 97-5190. 1997. pap. 10.95 (*0-14-019560-2*) Viking Penguin.

Zen Speaks: Shouts of Nothingness. Tr. by Brian Bruya. (Illus.). 160p. 1996. pap. 10.95 (*0-385-47257-9*, Anchor NY) Doubleday.

Zen Spirit, Christian Spirit: The Place of Zen in Christian Life. Robert E. Kennedy. 128p. 1996. pap. text ed. 12.95 (*0-8264-0919-9*) Continuum.

Zen Spirit, Christian Spirit: The Place of Zen in Christian Life, Vol. 1. Robert E. Kennedy. 128p. 1995. 17.95 (*0-8264-0806-0*) Continuum.

Zen Teaching of Huang Po: On the Transmission of Mind. Tr. by John Blofeld. LC 93-36508. (Pocket Classics Ser.). 1994. pap. 6.00 (*0-87773-969-2*, Sham Pocket Class) Shambhala Pubns.

Zen Teaching of Zen Huang-Po on the Transmission of the Mind. John Blofeld. 136p. 1959. pap. 10.95 (*0-8021-5092-6*, Grove) Grove-Atltic.

Zen Teachings of Bodhidharma. bodhidharma. Tr. by Red Pine. LC 89-9229. (Bilingual Edition Ser.). 126p. 1989. pap. 11.00 (*0-86547-399-4*, North Pt Pr) FS&G.

Zen Teachings of Instantaneous Awakening. Hui Hai. Tr. by John Bloveld. 97p. 1995. pap. 14.95 (*0-946672-03-2*, Pub. by Buddhist Pub UK) Assoc Pubs Grp.

Zen Teachings of Jesus. Kenneth S. Leong. 202p. (Orig.). 1995. pap. 14.95 (*0-8245-1481-5*) Crossroad NY.

Zen Telegrams. Paul Reps. (Illus.). 92p. (Orig.). 1995. pap. 11.95 (*0-8048-2023-6*) C E Tuttle.

Zen, the Turn Towards Life. Hugh Woodworth. LC 68-28824. (Orig.). 1968. pap. 3.95 (*0-8283-1020-3*) Branden Pub Co.

Zen Therapy: Transcending the Sorrows of the Human Mind. David Brazier. LC 96-22591. 288p. 1996. text ed. 35.00 (*0-471-15563-2*) Wiley.

Zen to Go. Jon Winokur. (Illus.). 160p. 1990. pap. 9.95 (*0-452-26531-2*, Plume) NAL-Dutton.

Zen-Touch (tm) & the Art of Shiatsu: Fundamental Applications in Acupressure Massage. rev. ed. Seymour A. Koblin. (Illus.). 147p. reprint ed. pap. 15.95 (*0-9625000-2-X*) Soulstar Creations.

Zen: Tradition & Transition: A Sourcebook by Contemporary Zen Masters & Scholars. Ed. by Kenneth Kraft. LC 87-34594. 232p. 1989. pap. 10.95 (*0-8021-3162-X*, Grove) Grove-Atltic.

Zen Wave: Basho's Haiku & Zen. Robert Aitken. LC 78-13243. (Illus.). 192p. 1979. reprint ed. pap. 16.95 (*0-8348-0137-X*) Weatherhill.

Zen Way. Myokyo-Ni, pseud. 1995. pap. 12.95 (*0-8048-3076-2*) C E Tuttle.

Zen Way - Jesus Way. Tucker N. Callaway. 264p. 1993. pap. 12.95 (*0-8048-1885-1*) C E Tuttle.

Zen Way to Martial Arts: A Japanese Master Reveals the Secrets of the Samurai. Taisen Deshimaru. Tr. by Nancy Amphoux. (Illus.). 128p. 1992. pap. 11.95 (*0-14-019344-8*, Arkana) Viking Penguin.

***Zen Wisdom: Daily Teachings from the Zen Masters.** Timothy Freke. LC 97-19917. 1997. write for info. (*0-8069-9977-2*) Sterling.

Zen Wisdom: Knowing & Doing. Sheng-Yen Chang. LC 93-70852. 372p. 1993. pap. 15.00 (*0-9609854-6-8*) Dharma Drum Pubs.

Zen Without Zen Masters. Camden Benares. LC 85-70387. (Illus.). 128p. 1993. pap. 9.95 (*1-56184-073-4*) New Falcon Pubns.

Zen Word, Zen Calligraphy. Eido T. Shimano. (Illus.). 144p. 1995. pap. 13.00 (*1-57062-127-6*) Shambhala Pubns.

***Zen Works of Stonehouse: Poems & Talks of a Fourteenth - Century Chinese Hermit.** Stonehouse. Tr. & Intro. by Red Pine, pseud. LC 97-25577. (Illus.). 192p. (Orig.). 1997. pap. 14.95 (*1-56279-101-X*) Mercury Hse Inc.

Zen Yoga. P. J. Saher. (C). 1991. reprint ed. 21.00 (*81-208-0809-6*, Pub. by Motilal Banarsidass II) S Asia.

Zena Sutherland Lectures, 1983-1992. Ed. by Betsy Hearne. LC 92-29781. 240p. 1993. 18.95 (*0-395-64504-2*, Clarion Bks); pap. 9.95 (*0-395-64987-0*, Clarion Bks) HM.

Zend-Avesta, 3 vols, Set. James Darmesteter & L. H. Mills. 1974. lib. bdg. 900.00 (*0-87968-509-3*) Krishna Pr.

Zend-Avesta: Selections. Tr. by James Darmesteter. 1984. pap. 7.95 (*0-916411-41-9*, Near Eastern) Holmes Pub.

Zend-Avesta of Zarathustra. Edmond B. Szekely. (Illus.). 100p. 1973. pap. 5.95 (*0-89564-058-9*) IBS Intl.

Zend-Avesta, Ouvrage de Zoroastre. A. H. Anquetil-Duperron. LC 78-60878. (Myth & Romanticism Ser.). 1904p. 1984. text ed. 25.00 (*0-8240-3550-X*) Garland.

Zendege - Ye - Tofani: Sayeed Hassan Taghizadeh's Diary. Hassan T. Sayeed. 416p. (PER.). 1990. reprint ed. 35.00 (*0-9627664-0-2*); reprint ed. pap. 20.00 (*0-9627664-1-0*) A Afshar.

Zendegi-E Haj Seyed Mahmoud Ladjevardi. 2nd ed. Manouchehr Farhang. LC 90-70392. (Illus.). 125p. (PER.). 1990. reprint ed. text ed. 6.95 (*0-9626288-0-8*) Tahereh Fndtn.

Zener & Avalanche Diodes. C. D. Todd. LC 77-120709. 282p. reprint ed. pap. 80.40 (*0-8357-9379-6*, 2011966) Bks Demand.

Zenia, the Vestal: The Problem of Vibrations. Margaret B. Peeke. 355p. 1965. reprint ed. spiral bd. 17.50 (*0-7873-0665-7*) Hlth Research.

***Zenith of Desire.** Gerry G. Pearlberg. Date not set. 5.99 (*0-517-18027-8*) Random Hse Value.

Zenith of Desire: Contemporary Lesbian Poems About Sex. Ed. by Gerry G. Pearlberg. LC 95-34131. 1996. 12.00 (*0-517-70281-9*) Crown Pub Group.

***Zenith Radio: The Early Years, 1919-1935.** Harold N. Cones & John Bryant. LC 97-24669. 1997. pap. write for info. (*0-7643-0367-8*) Schiffer.

Zenith Trans-Oceanic: The Royalty of Radios. John Bryant & Harold Cones. LC 94-46624. (Illus.). 124p. (Orig.). 1995. pap. 24.95 (*0-88740-708-0*) Schiffer.

Zenj, Buganda: East Africa. Kenny Mann. LC 96-10618. (African Kingdoms of the Past Ser.). (J). 1996. pap. 7.95 (*0-382-39658-8*, Dillon Silver Burdett) Silver Burdett Pr.

Zenj, Buganda: East Africa. Kenny Mann. (African Kingdoms of the Past Ser.). 1996. 15.95 (*0-87518-660-2*, Dillon Silver Burdett) Silver Burdett Pr.

Zenkoji & Its Icon: A Study in Medieval Japanese Religious Art. Donald F. McCallum. LC 93-41543. 352p. 1994. text ed. 42.50 (*0-691-03203-3*) Princeton U Pr.

Zenlightenment! Insights into the Art of Living Miraculously. Michael Pastore. Tr. by Hokku Umeboshi. LC 89-50097. (Illus.). 104p. (Orig.). 1989. pap. 125.00 (*0-927379-00-7*) Zorba Pr.

Zenlux: Architecture & Electronics. Duncan Brown. (Illus.). 64p. (Orig.). 1997. pap. 15.00 (*0-930829-39-5*) Lumen Inc.

Zeno & the Discovery of Incommensurables in Greek Mathematics. Ed. by H. G. Zeuthen & Johann A. Hasse. LC 75-13270. (History of Ideas in Ancient Greece Ser.). (FRE & GER.). 1976. 13.95 (*0-405-07311-9*) Ayer.

Zenobia. Nick Dear. 96p. (Orig.). 1995. pap. 9.95 (*0-571-17676-3*) Faber & Faber.

Zenobia. Gellu Naum. 220p. 1995. pap. 14.95 (*0-8101-1255-8*) Northwestern U Pr.

Zenobia. Gellu Naum. Tr. by James Brook & Sasha Vlad from RUM. LC 95-10848. (Writings from an Unbound Europe). 220p. 1995. text ed. 39.95 (*0-8101-1254-X*) Northwestern U Pr.

Zenobia: Empress of the East. Glenn Barnett. 360p. 1994. pap. 15.00 (*0-9629405-1-8*) Wide Awake Pr.

Zenon: Girl of the 21st Century. Sadler. (J). 1996. 15.00 (*0-671-86671-0*, S&S Bks Young Read) S&S Childrens.

Zenon: Girl of the 21st Century. Marilyn Sadler. LC 95-14553. (Illus.). (J). (gr. k-4). 1996. 14.00 (*0-689-80514-4*, S&S Bks Young Read) S&S Childrens.

Zenon von Kition: Positionen und Probleme. Andreas Graeser. 1975. 106.95 (*3-11-004673-5*) De Gruyter.

Zeno's Paradise. Terry Bristol. (C). 1998. write for info. (*0-201-48961-9*) Addison-Wesley.

Zeno's Paradoxes. Zeno. Ed. by Wesley C. Salmon. LC 70-103935. 1970. pap. 4.90 (*0-672-60365-9*, LLA148, Bobbs) Macmillan.

Zenryu & Other Works, 1974. Alan Pizzarelli. (Xtras Ser.: No. 2). (Illus.). 36p. (Orig.). 1975. pap. 2.00 (*0-89120-001-0*) From Here.

Zensho: American Philosophy & Intermediate Warrior Training Manual. Jerry L. Aiello. 325p. (Orig.). 1994. pap. text ed. 29.95 (*1-883702-06-2*) Aiello Grp.

Zentraedi. Kevin Siembieba. Ed. by Alex Marciniszyn. (Robotech RPG Ser.: Bk. 3). (Illus.). 48p. (Orig.). (YA). (gr. 8 up). 1987. pap. 7.95 (*0-916211-22-3*, 552) Palladium Bks.

Zentraedi Rebellion. Jack McKinney. (Robotech, Lost Generation Ser.: No. 19). 224p. (Orig.). 1994. mass mkt. 5.99 (*0-345-38774-0*, Del Rey Discovery) Ballantine.

Zentrale Stelle der Landesjustizverwaltungen, Ludwigsburg. Ed. by Henry Friedlander & Sybil Milton. LC 89-16915. (Archives of the Holocaust Ser.: Vol. 22). 560p. 1993. text ed. 129.00 (*0-8240-5580-2*) Garland.

Zenzele: A Letter for My Daughter. J. Nozipo Maraire. 208p. 1996. 20.00 (*0-517-70242-8*) Crown Pub Group.

***Zenzele: A Letter for My Daughter.** J. Nozipo Maraire. 208p. 1997. pap. 9.95 (*0-385-31822-7*, Delta) Dell.

***Zeo Beginning.** Scott Peterson. (Power Rangers Zeo Ser.: No. 1). 24p. (J). (gr. k-3). 1996. 3.25 (*0-694-00988-1*, Festival) HarpC Child Bks.

Zeolite Catalysts: Principles & Applications. Subhash Bhatia. 320p. 1989. 242.00 (*0-8493-5628-8*, TP245, CRC Reprint) Franklin.

Zeolite-Catalyzed Nucleophilic Aromatic Substitution Reactions. M. H. Burgers. 208p. 1995. pap. 57.50 (*90-407-1078-3*, Pub. by Delft U Pr NE) Coronet Bks.

Zeolite Chemistry & Catalysis. Ed. by Jule A. Rabo. LC 76-17864. (ACS Monograph: No. 171). 1976. 87.95 (*0-8412-0276-1*) Am Chemical.

Zeolite Chemistry & Catalysis: Proc. of an Internat. Symp. Prague, Sept. 8-13, 1991. Ed. by P. A. Jacobs et al. (Studies in Surface Science & Catalysis: Vol. 69). 514p. 1991. 274.25 (*0-444-88245-6*) Elsevier.

Zeolite, Clay, & Heteropoly Acid in Organic Reactions. Yusuke Izumi et al. LC 92-30118. 168p. 1993. 855.00 (*3-527-29011-7*, VCH) Wiley.

Zeolite Molecular Sieves: Structure, Chemistry & Use. Donald W. Breck. LC 83-26809. 784p. 1984. reprint ed. lib. bdg. 98.50 (*0-89874-648-5*) Krieger.

Zeolite Science 1994: Recent Progress & Discussions: Supplementary Materials to the 10th International Zeolite Conference, Garmisch-Partenkirchen, Germany, July 17-22, 1994. Ed. by H. G. Karge & J. Weitkamp. LC 95-20477. (Studies in Surface Science & Catalysis: Vol.98). 530p. 1995. 311.25 (*0-444-82308-5*) Elsevier.

Zeolite Synthesis. Ed. by Mario L. Occelli & Harry E. Robson. LC 89-6884. (Symposium Ser.: No. 398). (Illus.). xi, 653p. 1989. 139.95 (*0-8412-1632-0*) Am Chemical.

***Zeolite Synthesis.** Ed. by Mario L. Occelli & Harry E. Robson. LC 89-6884. (ACS Symposium Ser.: No. 398). (Illus.). 663p. 1989. reprint ed. pap. 180.00 (*0-608-03146-1*, 2063599) Bks Demand.

Zeolites. Business Communications Co., Inc. Staff. 95p. 1990. 1,950.00 (*0-89336-770-2*, C-118) BCC.

Zeolites: A Refined Tool for Designing Catalytic Sites: Proceedings of the International Zeolite Symposium, Quebec, Canada, 15-20 October 1995. Ed. by L. Bonneviot & S. Kaliaguine. (Studies in Surface Science & Catalysis: Vol. 97). 584p. 1995. text ed. 278.50 (*0-444-82130-9*) Elsevier.

Zeolites: Facts, Figures, Future, 2 vols. Ed. by P. A. Jacobs & R. A. Van Santen. (Studies in Surface Science & Catalysis: No. 49). 1500p. 1989. 489.50 (*0-444-87466-6*) Elsevier.

Zeolites: Markets & Opportunities. 122p. 1993. 2,450.00 (*0-89336-970-5*, C-118R) BCC.

Zeolites: Proceedings: Science & Technology, NATO Advanced Study Institute on Zeolites, Portugal, 1983. NATO Advanced Study Institute Staff & F. Ramoa Ribeiro. 1984. lib. bdg. 239.50 (*90-247-2935-1*) Kluwer Ac.

Zeolites & Microporous Crystals: Proceedings of the International Symposium on Zeolites & Microporous Crystals, Nagoya, August 22-25, 1993. Ed. by T. Hattori & Taro Yashima. (Studies in Surface Science & Catalysis: Vol. 83). 538p. 1994. 328.25 (*0-444-98657-X*) Elsevier.

Zeolites & Related Microporous Materials: State of the Art 1994 International Zeolite Conference. J. Weitkamp et al. LC 94-3430. (Studies in Surface Science & Catalysis: Vol. 84). 2402p. 1994. 586.00 (*0-444-81847-2*) Elsevier.

Zeolites as Catalysts, Sorbents & Detergent Builders: Applications & Innovations. Ed. by H. G. Karge & J. Weikamp. 872p. 1989. 268.25 (*0-444-87383-X*) Elsevier.

Zeolitic Diagenesis of Tuffs in Miocene Lacustrine Rocks Near Harney Lake, Harney County, Oregon. Richard A. Sheppard. 1995. write for info. (*0-615-00125-4*) US Geol Survey.

Zeph. Helen H. Jackson. (Notable American Authors Ser.). 1992. reprint ed. lib. bdg. 75.00 (*0-7812-3358-5*) Rprt Serv.

Zeph: A Posthumous Story. Helen M. Jackson. LC 75-164569. (American Fiction Reprint Ser.). 1977. reprint ed. 28.95 (*0-8369-7046-2*) Ayer.

Zephaniah: A New Translation with Introduction & Commentary. Adele Berlin. LC 93-37736. (Anchor Bible Ser.: Vol. 25A). 192p. 1994. 29.00 (*0-385-26631-6*) Doubleday.

Zephaniah's Oracles Against the Nations: A Synchronic & Diachronic Study of Zephaniah 2:1-3:8. Daniel H. Ryou. LC 95-1102. (Biblical Interpretation Ser.: Vol. 13). 1995. 112.50 (*90-04-10311-2*) E J Brill.

Zephyr: Tracking a Dream Across America. Henry Kisor. (Illus.). 352p. 1995. pap. 12.95 (*1-55850-477-X*) Adams Media.

Zephyr & Boreas: Winds of Change in The Fiction of Ursula K. Le Guin. Ed. by R. Reginald & George E. Slusser. 160p. 1996. lib. bdg. write for info. (*0-89370-976-X*) Borgo Pr.

Zephyr Products: The Story of an Inmate-staffed Business. Herbert G. Callison. (Illus.). 68p. (Orig.). 1989. pap. text ed. 14.50 (*0-929310-17-9*, 402) Am Correctional.

Zephyr the Zebra. Sarita Mangum. (Illus.). 26p. (Orig.). (J). (gr. k-5). 1995. pap. text ed. 6.00 (*0-9649870-0-7*) Purpose Pub.

Zephyrs of Najd: The Poetics of Nostalgia in the Classical Arabic Nasib. Jaroslav Stetkevych. LC 93-14631. 338p. 1993. pap. text ed. 21.00 (*0-226-77336-1*); lib. bdg. 52.00 (*0-226-77335-3*) U Ch Pr.

Zeppelin in Combat: A History of the German Naval Airship Division, 1912-1918. Douglas Robinson. LC 93-84500. (Illus.). 410p. 1994. 49.95 (*0-88740-510-X*) Schiffer.

Zerebrale Bewegungsstoerungen. Ed. by E. Koeng. (Paediatrische Fortbildungskurse fuer die Praxis Ser.: Vol. 53). (Illus.). viii, 200p. 1981. pap. 65.75 (*3-8055-3413-2*) S Karger.

Zerebrale Bewegungsstoerungen beim Kind. Ed. by E. G. Koenig. (Paediatrische Fortbildungskurse fuer die Praxis Ser.: Vol. 40). (Illus.). 212p. 1974. 39.25 (*3-8055-1781-5*) S Karger.

Zerebrale Gefassreaktionen in der Fetalen Asphyxie. M. Kirschbaum. (Illus.). viii, 114p. 1996. pap. 85.25 (*3-8055-6351-5*) S Karger.

Zerebrale Mikrozirkulation. Ed. by F. Hammersen & K. Messmer. (Illus.). x, 112p. 1990. pap. 71.50 (*3-8055-5208-4*) S Karger.

Zernie: Z Is for Zernie. Avonelle Kelsey. (Downhome Style Mystery Ser.). 200p. (Orig.). 6.95 (*1-885351-06-2*) Cheval Intl.

Zero. Will Bennett. Ed. by Maureen Owen. LC 83-539. 1984. pap. 4.00 (*0-916382-31-1*) Telephone Bks.

Zero. C. Radhakrishnan. (Indian Novels Ser.: Vol. 1). 110p. 1974. 4.95 (*0-88253-462-9*) Ind-US Inc.

Zero. Eric Van Lustbader. 1989. mass mkt. 6.99 (*0-449-21449-4*, Crest) Fawcett.

Zero: A Review of Literature & Art, Nos. 1-7. Ed. by Albert Benveniste & Themistocles Hoetis. (Avant Garde Magazines Ser.). 1974. reprint ed. 28.95 (*0-405-01753-7*) Ayer.

Zero: Its Role & Prospects in Indian Thought. Anil K. Sarkar. 207p. reprint ed. pap. 59.00 (*0-7837-5201-6*, AU00439) Bks Demand.

Zero: Japan's Legendary WWII Fighter. Robert C. Mikesh. (Illus.). 128p. 1994. pap. 19.95 (*0-87938-915-X*) Motorbooks Intl.

Zero: The Air War in the Pacific in World War II, from the Japanese Viewpoint. Masatake Okumiya et al. LC 79-20670. 1979. reprint ed. 25.00 (*0-89201-082-7*) Zenger Pub.

Zero Acceptance Number Sampling Plans. 4th ed. Nicholas L. Squeglia. LC 93-46817. (Illus.). 34p. 1994. 22.00 (*0-87389-305-0*, H0862) ASQC Qual Pr.

An Asterisk (*) at the beginning of an entry indicates that the title is appearing in BIP for the first time.

***Zero & Ones.** Sadie Plant. LC 97-10916. 1997. 23.95 (*0-385-48260-4*) Doubleday.

Zero at the Bone. Michael Cadnum. 202p. (YA). (gr. 7 up). 1996. pap. 15.99 (*0-670-86725-X*) Viking Child Bks.

Zero at the Bone. Bryce Marshall & Paul Williams. Ed. by Paul McCarthy. 328p. (Orig.). 1991. mass mkt. 5.50 (*0-671-68511-2*, Pocket Star Bks) PB.

Zero at the Bone. Mary W. Walker. (Mystery Ser.). 1993. mass mkt. 3.99 (*0-373-26122-5*, 1-26122-1) Harlequin Bks.

***Zero At the Bone.** Mary W. Walker. 336p. 1997. mass mkt. 5.99 (*0-553-57505-8*) Bantam.

Zero at the Bone. large type ed. Mary W. Walker. (Niagara Large Print Ser.). 409p. 1996. 27.99 (*0-7089-5830-3*) Ulverscroft.

Zero-Base Budgeting: A Decision Package Manual. L. Allan Austin & Logan M. Cheek. LC 79-12657. 217p. reprint ed. pap. 61.90 (*0-317-20402-5*, 2023505) Bks Demand.

Zero-Base Budgeting Comes of Age: What It Is & What It Takes to Make It Work. Logan M. Cheek. LC 77-4362. 328p. reprint ed. pap. 93.50 (*0-317-26733-7*, 2023526) Bks Demand.

Zero Base Budgeting in State. Worthley. 1995. 25.95 (*0-03-049121-5*) HR&W Schl Div.

Zero-Base Budgeting in State & Local Government: Current Experiences & Cases. Ed. by John A. Worthley & William G. Ludwin. LC 79-10162. 190p. 1979. text ed. 45.00 (*0-275-90439-3*, C0439, Praeger Pubs) Greenwood.

***Zero-Base Hospital: Survival & Success in America's Evolving Healthcare System.** Matthew M. Person, III. LC 96-36383. 248p. 1997. 42.00 (*1-56793-049-2*) Health Admin Pr.

Zero-Base Pricing: Achieving World-Class Competitiveness Through Reduced All-in-Costs. David K. Burt. 1990. text ed. 50.00 (*1-55738-132-1*) Irwin Prof Pubng.

Zero-Budget Marketing. Ira S. Kalb. (Illus.). 250p. 1996. 49.95 (*0-924050-05-5*) K & A Pr.

***Zero Cash Success Techniques Kit.** 9th ed. Tyler G. Hicks. 876p. 1998. pap. 99.50 (*1-56150-205-7*) Intl Wealth.

Zero Cash Success Techniques Kit, Set. 8th ed. Tyler G. Hicks. 876p. 1996. pap. 99.50 incl. audio (*1-56150-155-7*) Intl Wealth.

Zero-Cost Marketing. Ed. by Paul Mladjenovic. 85p. 1996. pap. 30.00 (*0-915344-58-0*) Todd Pubns.

Zero Coupon. Paul Erdman. 352p. (C). 1994. pap. 5.99 (*0-8125-2145-5*) Forge NYC.

Zero Coupon Bonds: Bond Stripping. Alban De Clermont-Tonnerre & Michel Andre-Levy. 150p. 1995. 85.00 (*1-873446-31-4*, Pub. by IFR Pub UK) Am Educ Systs.

***Zero Dances: A Biography.** Arthur Sainer. (Illus.). 400p. 1997. 30.00 (*0-87910-096-6*) Limelight Edns.

Zero Defect Marketing: The Secrets of Selling High Tech Services. Lee A. Friedman & David H. Rothman. 250p. 1987. text ed. 40.00 (*1-55623-001-X*) Irwin Prof Pubng.

Zero-Dimensional Commutative Rings: Proceedings of the 1994 John H. Barrett Memorial Lectures & Conference on Commutative Ring Theory. Ed. by David F. Anderson & David E. Dobbs. LC 95-9891. (Lecture Notes in Pure & Applied Mathematics Ser.: Vol. 171). 400p. 1995. 145.00 (*0-8247-9605-5*) Dekker.

Zero-Dimensional Schemes: Proceedings of the International Conference held in Ravello, Italy, June 8-13, 1992. Ed. by Ferruccio Orecchia & Luca Chiantini. LC 94-20654. vii, 339p. (C). 1994. lib. bdg. 99.95 (*3-11-013934-0*) De Gruyter.

Zero Discharge & Virtual Elimination in the Great Lakes: A Collection of Viewpoints from Prominent Great Lakes Specialists. Ed. by Walter J. Hoagman. 55p. (Orig.). 1993. pap. 1.50 (*1-885756-04-6*, MICHU-SG93-702) MI Sea Grant.

Zero Downtime Hydraulics. John J. Pippenger. (Global Series in Fluid Power). (Illus.). 85p. (C). 1989. text ed. 24.95 (*0-929276-00-0*) Amalgam Pub Co.

Zero Downtime Pneumatics. John J. Pippenger & Z. J. Lansky. (Global Series in Fluid Power). (Illus.). 256p. 1994. 48.00 (*0-929276-03-5*) Amalgam Pub Co.

Zero Emission Vehicle Technical Support Document Pt. B. California Air Resources Board Staff. (Electric Vehicle Information Ser.: Vol. 3). 215p. 1995. pap. Not sold separately (*0-615-00422-9*) Bus Tech Bks.

Zero-Emission Vehicle Technology Assessment (Aug. 1995) Booz-Allen & Hamilton, Inc. Staff. (Electric Vehicle Information Ser.: Vol. 19). (Illus.). 105p. 1996. pap. 75.00 (*0-89934-277-9*, BT046); lib. bdg. 125.00 (*0-89934-278-7*, BT946) Bus Tech Bks.

***Zero Fallacy & Other Essays in Neoclassical Metaphysics.** Charles Hartshorne. Ed. by Mohammad Valady. LC 97-112. 256p. 1997. 38.95 (*0-8126-9323-X*); pap. 18.95 (*0-8126-9324-8*) Open Court.

Zero Fighter. Akira Yoshimura. Tr. by Retsu Kaiho & Michael Gregson. LC 95-19744. 224p. 1996. text ed. 19.95 (*0-275-95355-6*, Praeger Pubs) Greenwood.

Zero Gravity. Gloria Skurzynski. LC 93-46735. 32p. (J). 1994. text ed. 15.00 (*0-02-782925-1*, Mac Bks Young Read) S&S Childrens.

***Zero Hour.** Tony Abbott. (Time Surfers Ser.: No. 6). 96p. (J). 1997. mass mkt. 3.50 (*0-553-48463-X*, Skylark BDD) BDD Bks Young Read.

Zero Hour. Joseph Finder. LC 95-25865. 432p. 1996. 25.00 (*0-688-14450-0*) Morrow.

***Zero Hour.** Joseph Finder. 1997. mass mkt. 6.99 (*0-380-72665-3*) Avon.

Zero Hour. Kristjana Gunnars. 128p. 1991. pap. 8.95 (*0-88995-064-4*, Pub. by Red Deer CN) Orca Bk Pubs.

Zero Hour. Patrick F. Rogers. (Omega Ser.). 1993. mass mkt. 3.50 (*0-373-63208-8*, 1-63208-2) Harlequin Bks.

Zero Hour. large type ed. Joseph Finder. 630p. 1996. lib. bdg. 25.95 (*0-7838-1825-4*, GK Hall) Thorndike Pr.

Zero Hour: A Summons to the Free. Stephen Vincent Benet et al. LC 71-156734. (Essay Index Reprint Ser.). 1977. reprint ed. 20.95 (*0-8369-2341-3*) Ayer.

Zero Hour: Crisis in Time. DC Comics Staff. Ed. by Bob Kahan. (Illus.). 160p. 1994. pap. 9.95 (*1-56389-184-0*) DC Comics.

Zero Hour: Glasnost & Soviet Film in Transition. Andrew Horton & Michael Brashinsky. (Illus.). 344p. 1992. pap. text ed. 18.95 (*0-691-01920-7*) Princeton U Pr.

***Zero Hour: Program 5.** Rod Serling. 1997. pap. 16.95 (*1-56511-193-1*) D I Fine.

Zero Hour & Other Documentary Poems. Ernesto Cardenal. Ed. by Donald D. Walsh. Tr. by Paul W. Borgeson et al. from SPA. LC 80-36817. 1980. pap. 6.95 (*0-8112-0767-6*, NDP502) New Directions.

Zero, Hurricane & P-38: Legends of the Air 4. Australian Aviation Editors. (Legends of the Air Ser.: No. 4). (Illus.). 200p. 1996. pap. 22.95 (*1-875671-24-2*, Pub. by Aerospace Pubns AT) Motorbooks Intl.

Zero Inventories. Robert A. Hall & American Products & Inventory Control Society. LC 83-71736. 250p. 1983. text ed. 47.50 (*0-87094-461-4*) Irwin Prof Pubng.

Zero Inventories Seminar Proceedings: September 1983. Ed. by American Production & Inventory Control Society Staff. LC 83-72511. 82p. 1983. pap. 5.00 (*0-935406-32-8*, 40632) Am Prod & Inventory.

Zero Lot Line Housing. David Jensen. LC 81-40469. (Illus.). 150p. 1981. pap. 42.95 (*0-87420-600-6*, B10) Urban Land.

***Zero Minus Ten.** Raymond Benson. 288p. 1997. 22.95 (*0-399-14257-6*, Putnam) Putnam Pub Group.

***Zero Philadelphia.** James Douglas. 608p. 1997. 22.95 (*1-56924-749-8*) Marlowe & Co.

Zero-Phonon Lines & Spectral Hole Burning in Spectroscopy & Photochemistry. Ed. by O. Sild & K. Haller. (Illus.). 180p. 1988. 53.95 (*0-387-19214-X*) Spr-Verlag.

***Zero-Point Field.** Haisch. Date not set. 27.50 (*0-8050-5448-0*); pap. 14.95 (*0-8050-5449-9*) H Holt & Co.

***Zero Point 4: Light Registers London.** Peter Cook & Christine Hawley. (Illus.). 96p. (Orig.). 1997. pap. write for info. (*1-889629-03-0*) Form Zero.

Zero Pollution for Industry: Waste Minimization Through Industrial Complexes. Nelson L. Nemerow. LC 95-10072. 240p. 1995. text ed. 59.95 (*0-471-12164-9*) Wiley.

Zero Population Growth: Implications. Ed. by Joseph J. Spengler. (Illus.). 1975. pap. text ed. 5.00 (*0-89055-113-8*) Carolina Pop Ctr.

Zero Population Growth--For Whom? Differential Fertility & Minority Group Survival. Ed. by Milton Himmelfarb & Victor Baras. LC 77-87966. (Contributions in Sociology Ser.: No. 30). (Illus.). 213p. 1978. text ed. 55.00 (*0-313-20041-6*, AJC/, Greenwood Pr) Greenwood.

Zero Positive. Harry Kondoleon. 1989. pap. 5.25 (*0-8222-1293-5*) Dramatists Play.

Zero Proof: Two Hundred Nonalcoholic Drinks from America's Most Famous Bars & Restaurants. Pamela Stovall & Richard Lalich. 192p. 1994. pap. 10.95 (*0-312-11479-6*) St Martin.

Zero Quality Control: Source Inspection & the Poka-Yoke System. Shigeo Shingo. Tr. by Andrew P. Dillon from JPN. LC 85-63497. (Illus.). 328p. 1986. 75.00 (*0-915299-07-0*) Prod Press.

Zero-Range Potentials & Their Applications in Atomic Physics. Yu. N. Demkov & V. N. Ostrovskii. Ed. by P. G. Burke. Tr. by S. M. Ermolaev from RUS. (Physics of Atoms & Molecules Ser.). (Illus.). 274p. 1988. 95.00 (*0-306-42779-6*, Plenum Pr) Plenum.

***Zero-Resistance Selling.** Maxwell Maltz. 1997. 19.95 (*0-13-609074-5*) P-H.

Zero Seven Fifty-Five: Pearl Harbor Heroes: Heroism of 250 Men & Women 7 December 1941. Don Ross & Helen Ross. 200p. 1988. pap. 11.95 (*0-930942-15-9*) Rokalu Pr.

Zero Sum Game. A. C. Aaron. 224p. (Orig.). 1996. mass mkt. 4.99 (*1-55197-057-0*, Pub. by Comnwlth Pub CN) Partners Pubs Grp.

Zero Sum Mind. Stephen Gregg. 12p. 1991. pap. 3.00 (*0-87129-112-6*, Z11) Dramatic Pub.

Zero-Sum Society. Lester C. Thurow. 230p. 1981. pap. 12.95 (*0-14-005807-9*, Penguin Bks) Viking Penguin.

Zero Syntax: Experiences & Cascades. David Pesetsky. (Current Studies in Linguistics: No. 27). 250p. 1994. 39.95 (*0-262-16145-1*) MIT Pr.

Zero Syntax: Experiences & Cascades. David Pesetsky. (Current Studies in Linguistics: No. 27). (Illus.). 376p. 1996. pap. 20.00 (*0-262-66100-4*) MIT Pr.

Zero Tax Portfolio Manual. 2nd ed. Vernon K. Jacobs. 1991. pap. 49.50 (*0-9628172-1-X*) Res Pr KS.

Zero Three Bravo: Solo across America in a small plane. Mariana Gosnell. LC 92-28713. 384p. 1994. pap. 13.00 (*0-671-89208-8*, Touchstone Bks) S&S Trade.

Zero Time. Jack Anderson. 512p. 1993. mass mkt. 4.99 (*0-8217-4087-3*, Zebra Kensgtn) Kensgtn Pub Corp.

Zero to Einstein in 60. B. K. Hixson. 175p. 1993. pap. text ed. 19.99 (*1-57156-000-9*) Wild Goose UT.

***Zero to Hero.** Golden Books Staff. (Hercules Ser.). (Illus.). 1997. pap. text ed. 2.99 (*0-307-05136-6*, Golden Books) Western Pub.

Zero to Hero in Income Tax. R. N. Lakhotia. (C). 1990. 65.00 (*0-89771-267-6*) St Mut.

Zero to Lazy Eight. Alexander Humez et al. 288p. 1994. pap. 11.00 (*0-671-74281-7*, Touchstone Bks) S&S Trade.

Zero to Lazy Eight: The Romance of Numbers. Alexander Humez et al. (Illus.). 288p. 1993. 21.00 (*0-671-74282-5*) S&S Trade.

***Zero to Ninety-Nine.** Janine Blinko & Noel Graham. 96p. (J). (gr. k-3). pap. 17.50 (*1-871098-02-5*, Pub. by Claire Pubns UK) Parkwest Pubns.

***Zero Tolerance.** Pendleton. (Executioner Ser.: No. 229). 1998. mass mkt. 3.75 (*0-373-64229-6*) Harlequin Bks.

Zero Tolerance. Thomas Richards. LC 96-15656. 288p. 1997. 23.00 (*0-374-29662-6*) FS&G.

Zero Tolerance: A Virgil Proctor Mystery. J. D. Knight. 336p. 1995. mass mkt. 4.99 (*0-440-21864-0*) Dell.

***Zero Tolerance: An Employer's Guide to Preventing Sexual Harassment & Healing the Workplace.** Tony Cornish & Bureau of National Affairs Communications Staff. LC 97-11665. 1997. 29.00 (*1-55871-354-9*) BNAC.

Zero-Variable Theories & the Psychology of the Explainer. R. A. Wicklund. 160p. 1990. 80.95 (*0-387-97165-3*) Spr-Verlag.

Zero Vector: Time Travel Technology. Steven Gibbs. (Illus.). 115p. 1994. 20.00 (*1-57179-010-1*) Intern Guild ASRS.

Zero Word Going Ape Series, 6 bks., Set. Bob Reese. (Illus.). (J). 1983. 59.70 (*0-89868-139-1*); pap. 23.70 (*0-89868-138-3*) ARO Pub.

Zero 3 Bravo: Solo Across America. Mariana Gosnell. 25.00 (*0-614-13196-0*, 21-37673) EAA Aviation.

***Zeroes into Heroes.** 60p. 1990. 5.25 (*0-8341-9515-1*) Lillenas.

Zeroglyphics. enl. rev. ed. Adriano Spatola. Tr. by Guilia Niccolai & Paul Vangelisti. 1977. pap. 4.00 (*0-88031-045-6*) Invisible-Red Hill.

Zeros of Bernoulli, Generalized Bernoulli, & Euler Polynomials. Karl Dilcher. LC 88-6356. (Memoirs Ser.: No. 73/386). 94p. 1988. pap. 18.00 (*0-8218-2449-X*, MEMO/73/386) Am Math.

Zeros of Sections of Power Series. A. Edrei et al. (Lecture Notes in Mathematics Ser.: Vol. 1002). 115p. 1983. 29.95 (*0-387-12318-0*) Spr-Verlag.

Zero's Slider. Matt Christopher. LC 93-21177. (J). 1994. 13.95 (*0-316-14270-0*) Little.

Zero's Slider. Matt Christopher. (Illus.). 64p. (J). (gr. 2-4). 1996. pap. 3.95 (*0-316-14129-1*) Little.

Zerstreut in alle Winde see Scattered to All the Winds: 1685-1720, Migrations of the Dauphine French Hugeunots into Italy, Switzerland, & Germany

Zertanzten Schuhe see Twelve Dancing Princesses: A Fairy Tale by Jacob & Wilhelm Grimm

Zerubbabel: R&SM, No. 49. 200p. 1970. 14.50 (*0-88053-276-9*) Macoy Pub.

Zerubu & Other Angels I Have Met. Lewis F. Shaffer. 213p. (Orig.). 1988. pap. write for info. (*0-929389-02-6*) Son Shine Ministries.

Zespedes in East Florida, Seventeen Eighty-Four to Seventeen Ninety. Helen H. Tanner. 254p. 1989. pap. 18.95 (*0-8130-0958-8*) U Press Fla.

Zest for Life: The Story of Mary Bagot Stack. Prunella Stack. 182p. 8800. 28.00 (*0-7206-0697-7*, Pub. by P Owen Ltd UK) Dufour.

Zest Is Best: Poems. Harvey Jackins. 1973. 7.00 (*0-911214-06-2*); pap. 5.00 (*0-911214-24-0*) Rational Isl.

Zeta Art: With Artems. Artist Joseph. 1995. 8.95 (*0-533-11354-7*) Vantage.

Zeta-Function of Riemann. Edward C. Titchmarsh. (Cambridge Tracts in Mathematics & Mathematical Physics: No. 26). 1964. reprint ed. 8.95 (*0-02-853600-2*) Hafner.

Zeta Functions in Geometry. Ed. by N. Kurokawa & T. Sunada. (Advanced Studies in Pure Mathematics: Vol. 21). 450p. 1993. 80.00 (*4-314-10078-8*, ASPM/21C, Pub. by Kinokuniya JA) Am Math.

Zeta Regularization Techiques with Applications. E. Elicalde et al. 336p. 1994. text ed. 74.00 (*981-02-1441-3*) World Scientific Pub.

***ZetaTalk.** Nancy Lieder. LC 96-95997. (Illus.). 345p. (Orig.). 1996. pap. 25.00 (*0-9653455-0-5*) Saquo Design.

Zetetic Skepticism. Stewart Umphrey. LC 89-78464. 350p. 1990. 37.50 (*0-89341-585-5*, Longwood Academic) Hollowbrook.

Zettel. Ludwig Wittgenstein. Ed. by G. E. Anscombe & George H. Von Wright. 1967. pap. 12.00 (*0-520-01635-1*) U CA Pr.

Zettels Traum: Faksimile-Wiedergabe des 1334 Blaetter Umfassenden Original-Typoskripts mit Randglossen und Handskizzen des Autors. Arno B. Schmidt. 1352p. (GER.). 1986. 707.50 (*3-10-070607-2*, Pub. by S Fischer GW) Intl Bk Import.

***Zeuge Als Uberlieferungstrager Personaler Offenbarung: Zur Korrelation von Offenbarungsgehalt und Vermittlungsgestalt Im Kontext der Entafteten Moderne.** Ansgar Wolff. (Europaische Hochschulschriften Ser.: Reihe 23, Bd. 590). 291p. (GER.). 1997. 54.95 (*3-631-30467-6*) P Lang Pubng.

Zeuge im Attischen Recht & die Griechische Asylie, 2 Vols. Ernst Leisi & Eilhard Schlesinger. Ed. by Gregory Vlastos. LC 78-14608. (Morals & Law in Ancient Greece Ser.). 1979. reprint ed. lib. bdg. 23.95 (*0-405-11584-9*) Ayer.

Zeugnis & Zeichen see Summons & Sign

Zeugnisse Bildlicher Darstellung der Nachkommenschaft Heinrichs I. Nora Gadeke. (Arbeitem zur Fruehmittelalterforschung Ser.: No. 22). xii, 301p. (GER.). 1992. lib. bdg. 136.95 (*3-11-013241-9*, 106-92) De Gruyter.

Zeuner Kandidatenaufstell Bund. 1970. pap. text ed. 64.50 (*90-247-0506-1*, Pub. by M Nijhoff NE) Kluwer Ac.

Zeus: A Study of Ancient Religion, 2 vols. Arthur B. Cook. Incl. Vol. 2. Zeus, God of the Dark Sky: Thunder & Lightning. , 2 pts. reprint ed. 55.00 (*0-614-24501-X*); write for info. (*0-8196-0156-X*) Biblo.

Zeus Bk. 1: Apollo. A. D. King. 1995. pap. 12.50 (*0-533-11166-8*) Vantage.

Zeus & Co. David L. Jones. 288p. (Orig.). 1993. mass mkt. 4.99 (*0-380-76963-8*, AvoNova) Avon.

Zeus & Roxanne. Patricia Hermes. (J). (gr. 3-7). 1997. mass mkt. 3.99 (*0-671-00370-4*) PB.

Zeus, God of the Dark Sky: Thunder & Lightning see Zeus: A Study of Ancient Religion

Zeus Has Two Urns. Charles E. Jarvis. LC 76-377748. (Illus.). (Orig.). (C). 1976. pap. 4.95 (*0-915940-01-9*) Ithaca Pr MA.

Zeus Juice. LC 92-82569. 192p. 1993. pap. 4.95 (*1-56002-203-5*, Univ Edtns) Aegina Pr.

ZEV (Zero Emissions Vehicle) Book. Odyssey Group Staff. (Illus.). 30p. (J). 1995. pap. text ed. 4.00 (*1-57074-248-0*) Greyden Pr.

Zeven Stemmen Spreken see Seven Voices Speak

Zez Confrey: Piano Solos Ragtime. Ronny S. Schiff. 1985. pap. 28.95 (*0-910957-03-7*, 11712) Warner Brothers.

***Zfn Pranks & The Kind Heart Sutras.** Randy Fingland. 48p. 1996. pap. 4.95 (*0-9647373-3-7*) Marimbo Commun.

Zheleznaia Zhenshchina. Nina Berberova. LC 80-54020. 400p. (Orig.). (RUS.). 1981. 30.00 (*0-89830-131-9*) Russica Pubs.

Zheltyi d iavol see Gold: The Yellow Devil

Zhemchuzhina - A Pearl: A Book of Poems. Jan E. Probstein. Ed. by Natalia Kazakova. LC 94-94446. 104p. (RUS.). 1994. pap. text ed. 8.00 (*1-882725-09-3*) Arch-Arcada.

Zhen Mo. Sheng Liang. 200p. (Orig.). (CHI.). 1995. pap. text ed. 20.00 (*0-9642790-1-0*) Sayinga.

Zhenschiny-Missionerki - Women-Missionary. Vera Kuschnir. Ed. by Vera Michka & Nikolas Michka. 415p. (RUS.). 1994. pap. write for info. (*1-885024-06-1*) Slavic Christian.

Zhenskie Rasskazy: Women's Stories. Ruth Zernova. LC 81-6677. 160p. (RUS.). 1981. pap. 7.50 (*0-938920-04-9*) Hermitage.

Zhirinovsky! Vladimir Kartsev. LC 95-960. (Illus.). 198p. 1995. 24.95 (*0-231-10210-0*) Col U Pr.

Zhirinovsky: Russian Fascism & the Making of Dictator. Vladimir Solovyov & Elena Klepikova. Tr. by Catherine A. Fitzpatrick. 272p. 1995. 24.00 (*0-201-40948-8*) Addison-Wesley.

Zhitie Prepodobnago Antonija Velikago. Saint Athanasius. 47p. reprint ed. pap. 2.00 (*0-317-29181-5*) Holy Trinity.

Zhitie Prepodobnago Evfrosina Pskovskogo: Pervonachal'naia Redaktsiia. Ed. by N. Serebrianskii. (Monuments of Early Russian Literature Ser.: Vol. 3). 118p. (CHU.). 1982. reprint ed. pap. 8.00 (*0-933884-21-4*) Berkeley Slavic.

Zhitie Prepodobnogo Filippa Irapskago. Intro. by Vasily O. Kliuchevsky. (Momuments of Early Russian Literature Ser.: Vol. 6). xliv, 77p. (RUS.). (C). 1993. reprint ed. pap. 12.00 (*0-933884-91-5*) Berkeley Slavic.

Zhitiia Sviatykh Po Drevnerusskim Spiskam. Ed. by Aleksei I. Sobolevskii. (Early Slavic Literatures: Studies, Texts, & Seminar Materials: Vol. 4). 68p. (CHU & RUS.). (C). 1989. reprint ed. pap. text ed. 8.00 (*0-933884-64-8*) Berkeley Slavic.

Zhitija Russkikh Svatikh, v 2 tom, 2 vols., 1. Mother Thais. LC 82-81204. pap. 10.00 (*0-88465-012-X*) Holy Trinity.

Zhitija Russkikh Svatikh, v 2 tom, 2 vols., 2. Mother Thais. LC 82-81204. pap. 13.00 (*0-88465-020-0*) Holy Trinity.

Zhitija Svjatikh v 12 tomov, 12 vols. Saint Dimitri Rostov. 10000p. reprint ed. 360.00 (*0-317-29175-0*) Holy Trinity.

Zhivago Poems. Barbara Everest. LC 88-71121. (Illus.). 96p. (Orig.). 1989. pap. 8.95 (*0-916383-66-0*) Aegina Pr.

***Zhiwei Tu.** Shirl Smithson. (Illus.). 201p. (CHI & ENG.). 1996. 300.00 (*0-9637547-5-0*) Arbor Hill Pr.

Zhizn' Berdiaeva: Rossiia. Aleksandr Vadimov. (Modern Russian Literature & Culture, Studies & Texts: Vol. 29). (Illus.). 287p. (Orig.). (RUS.). (C). 1993. pap. 20.00 (*0-933884-84-2*) Berkeley Slavic.

Zhizn' I Smert Mikhaila Bulgakova. Anatoly Shvarts. LC 88-32030. (Russian Ser.). (Illus.). 215p. (Orig.). 1989. pap. 12.00 (*1-55779-007-8*) Hermitage.

***"Zhizn" I Zhitie Voino-Iasenetskogo - The Life & Religious Journey of Voino-Iasenetsky.** rev. ed. Mark A. Popovsky. (Illus.). 542p. (RUS.). 1996. pap. 25.00 (*1-55779-086-8*) Hermitage.

Zhizn' Valaamskago Monakha Germana (Aljaskinskago)-Amerikanskago Missionjera. 24p. reprint ed. pap. 1.00 (*0-317-29192-0*) Holy Trinity.

Zhizneopisanie i Tvorenije Blazhennejshago Antonia, Mitropolita Kievskago i Galitzkago, v 17 tomakh, 17 vols. Ed. by Archbishop Nikon Rklitsky. 6000p. 1971. pap. 200.00 (*0-317-29015-0*) Holy Trinity.

***Zhizneopisaniye Mgnovenia.** Mikhail Armalinsky. 90p. (Orig.). (RUS.). 1997. pap. 8.00 (*0-916201-21-X*) M I P Co.

Zhizn'i Sud'ba "Solomona Mikhoelsa" (The Life & the Fate of Solomon Mikhoels) Documents, Speaches, Letters of Solomon Mikhoels. Mikhail Goldenberg. LC 95-60253. (Illus.). 112p. (Orig.). (RUS.). 1995. pap. 8.00 (*1-885563-02-7*) VIA Press MD.

Zho-Chaka. Paul Kidd. Ed. by Janice Sellers. (Albedo Role Playing Game Ser.). (Illus.). 48p. (Orig.). 1994. pap. text ed. 10.00 (*1-883240-12-3*) Chessex.

Zhou Enlai: A Profile. Percy J. Fang & Lucy F. Pang. (Illus.). 240p. 1995. lib. bdg. 39.00 (*0-8095-4868-2*) Borgo Pr.

Zhou Enlai: A Profile. Percy J. Fang & Lucy G. Pang. (Illus.). 240p. pap. 14.95 (*0-8351-1712-X*) China Bks.

Zhou Enlai: Chinese Foreign Policy. Shao. LC 96-36088. 1996. text ed. 49.95 (*0-312-15892-0*) St Martin.

Zhou Enlai: The Early Years. Chae-Jin Lee. LC 93-33525. xiv, 241p. 1994. 35.00 (*0-8047-2302-8*) Stanford U Pr.

Zhou Enlai: The Early Years. Chae-Jin Lee. xiv, 241p. 1996. pap. 13.95 (*0-8047-2700-7*) Stanford U Pr.

Zhou Enlai & Deng Xiaping in the Chinese Leadership Succession Crisis. David W. Chang. LC 83-16863. 410p. (Orig.). (C). 1984. pap. text ed. 31.00 (*0-8191-3587-9*) U Pr of Amer.

Zhou Yi: A New Translation with Commentary of the Book of Changes. Richard Rutt. (Durham East Asia Ser.). 320p. (C). 1996. text ed. 65.00 (*0-7007-0467-1*, Pub. by Curzon Press UK) UH Pr.

Zhu Yuanzhang & Early Ming Legislation: The Reordering of Chinese Society Following the Era of Mongol Rule. Edward L. Farmer. (Sinica Leidensia Ser.: No. 34). 300p. 1995. 79.50 (*90-04-10391-0*) E J Brill.

***Zhuan Falun, 2 vols.** 2nd ed. Li Hongzhi. Tr. & Photos by Xiulian Dafa. (Illus.). viii, 352p. 1996. reprint ed. pap. 22.50 (*0-9656225-0-9*) Winancy Intl.

Zhuangzi Speaks: The Music of Nature. Tr. by Brian Bruya. 160p. 1992. pap. 14.95 (*0-691-00882-5*) Princeton U Pr.

***Zhuangzi Speaks II: More Music of Nature.** Ts Ai Chih-Chung et al. LC 96-40071. 1997. write for info. (*0-385-48742-8*, Anchor NY) Doubleday.

Zhukov. rev. ed. Oto P. Chaney. LC 95-26307. (Illus.). 560p. 1996. 39.95 (*0-8061-2807-0*) U of Okla Pr.

Zhukov: The Rise & Fall of a Great Captain. William J. Spahr. LC 92-42332. 304p. 1995. pap. 14.95 (*0-89141-551-3*) Presidio Pr.

Zia. Scott O'Dell. 192p. (J). (gr. 4-7). 1995. pap. 4.50 (*0-440-41001-0*) Dell.

Zia. Scott O'Dell. 144p. (J). 1995. mass mkt. 4.50 (*0-440-21956-6*) Dell.

Zia. Scott O'Dell. LC 75-44156. (Illus.). 224p. (J). (gr. 4-8). 1976. 16.00 (*0-395-24393-9*) HM.

***Zia Episode in Bangladesh Politics.** Ed. by Habib Zafarullah. (C). 1996. 28.00 (*81-7003-191-5*, Pub. by S Asia Pubs II) S Asia.

Zia's Pakistan. R. G. Sawhney. 200p. 1985. 19.95 (*0-318-37283-5*) Asia Bk Corp.

Zibaldone: A Selection by Giacomo Leopardi. Giacomo Leopardi. Ed. & Intro. by Martha King. LC 91-43276. (Studies in Italian Culture: Literature in History: Vol. 8). 209p. (C). 1993. text ed. 46.95 (*0-8204-1723-8*) P Lang Pubng.

Zibber Bibber. Kathleen Gibson. LC 96-92053. (Illus.). 32p. (Orig.). (J). (ps-3). 1996. pap. 12.50 incl. audio (*1-888862-00-9*, RR6200) Rainbow Rdrs.

Zibo: The Last Great Zen Master of China. Jonathan C. Cleary. LC 88-83532. 171p. (Orig.). reprint ed. pap. 48.80 (*0-7837-5210-5*, 2044941) Bks Demand.

***Zic-Zac & the Crocodile.** Susan Bassler-Pickford. LC 96-92540. (Illus.). 32p. (Orig.). (J). (gr. k-6). 1996. pap. 4.50 (*1-889664-04-9*) SBP.

***Zichron E Livnei Yisroel: Memoirs of Rabbi Israel Jacobson 1907-39.** Shalom D. Levin. (Illus.). 302p. (HEB.). 1996. 25.00 (*0-8266-5338-3*) Kehot Pubn Soc.

Zickzack, Level 1. Goodman-Stephens et al. Date not set. pap. 18.95 (*0-17-439300-8*) Heinle & Heinle.

Zickzack, Level 2. Goodman-Stephens et al. Date not set. pap. 18.95 (*0-17-439311-3*) Heinle & Heinle.

Zickzack, Level 3. Goodman-Stephens et al. Date not set. pap. 18.95 (*0-17-439320-2*) Heinle & Heinle.

ZickZack: Level One, Bk. 1A. Goodman & Stephens. (College German Ser.). Date not set. student ed., pap. 15.95 (*0-17-439573-6*) Heinle & Heinle.

ZickZack: Level One, Bk. 1B. Goodman & Stephens. (College German Ser.). Date not set. student ed., pap. 15.95 (*0-17-439574-4*) Heinle & Heinle.

Zickzack: Level 1. Goodman. (Illus.). (ENG & GER.). (C). Date not set. Repromasters. 102.95 (*0-17-439302-4*) Heinle & Heinle.

Zickzack: Level 1. Goodman. (Illus.). (ENG & GER.). (C). 1993. Tchr's manual. teacher ed., pap. 24.95 (*0-17-439301-6*) Heinle & Heinle.

Zickzack: Level 1, No. 1. Goodman. (Illus.). (ENG & GER.). (C). Date not set. Cassette 1. audio 26.95 (*0-17-439304-0*) Heinle & Heinle.

Zickzack: Level 1, No. 2. Goodman. (Illus.). (ENG & GER.). (C). 1993. Cassette 2. audio 26.95 (*0-17-439305-9*) Heinle & Heinle.

Zickzack: Level 1, No. 3. Goodman. (Illus.). (ENG & GER.). (C). Date not set. Cassette 3. audio 26.95 (*0-17-439306-7*) Heinle & Heinle.

Zickzack: Level 2. Goodman. (Illus.). (C). 1993. Tchr's manual. teacher ed., pap. 24.95 (*0-17-439310-5*); Repromasters. 102.95 (*0-17-439312-1*) Heinle & Heinle.

Zickzack: Level 2, No. 1. Goodman. (Illus.). (C). 1993. Cassette 1. audio 26.95 (*0-17-439314-8*) Heinle & Heinle.

Zickzack: Level 2, No. 2. Goodman. (Illus.). (C). 1993. Cassette 2. audio 26.95 (*0-17-439315-6*) Heinle & Heinle.

Zickzack: Level 2, No. 3. Goodman. (Illus.). (C). 1993. Cassette 3. audio 26.95 (*0-17-439316-4*) Heinle & Heinle.

Zickzack: Level 2, No. 4. Goodman. (Illus.). (C). 1993. Cassette 4. audio 26.95 (*0-17-439317-2*) Heinle & Heinle.

Zickzack: Level 3. Goodman. (Illus.). (ENG & GER.). (C). 1993. Tchr's manual. teacher ed., pap. 24.95 (*0-17-439319-9*); Repromasters. 102.95 (*0-17-439321-0*) Heinle & Heinle.

Zickzack: Level 3, No. 1. Goodman. (Illus.). (ENG & GER.). (C). 1993. Cassette 1. audio 26.95 (*0-17-439322-9*) Heinle & Heinle.

Zickzack: Level 3, No. 2. Goodman. (Illus.). (ENG & GER.). (C). 1993. Cassette 2. audio 26.95 (*0-17-439323-7*) Heinle & Heinle.

Zickzack: Level 3, No. 3. Goodman. (Illus.). (ENG & GER.). (C). Date not set. Cassette 3. audio 26.95 (*0-17-439324-5*) Heinle & Heinle.

Zickzack: Level 3, No. 4. Goodman. (Illus.). (ENG & GER.). (C). 1993. Cassette 4. audio 26.95 (*0-17-439325-3*) Heinle & Heinle.

ZickZack: Stage 1. 2nd ed. Goodman. (College German Ser.). 1995. student ed., pap. 18.95 (*0-17-439785-2*) Heinle & Heinle.

ZickZack: Stage 1. 2nd ed. Goodman. (College German Ser.). 1995. teacher ed., pap. 24.95 (*0-17-439786-0*) Heinle & Heinle.

ZickZack: Stage 2. 2nd ed. Goodman. (College German Ser.). 1995. student ed., pap. 18.95 (*0-17-439796-8*) Heinle & Heinle.

ZickZack: Stage 2. 2nd ed. Goodman. (College German Ser.). 1995. teacher ed., pap. 24.95 (*0-17-439797-6*) Heinle & Heinle.

ZickZack: Stage 3. 2nd ed. Goodman. (College German Ser.). 1995. teacher ed., pap. 24.95 (*0-17-439881-6*) Heinle & Heinle.

Zickzack: Stage 3. 2nd ed. Goodman. (College German Ser.). 1995. student ed., pap. 23.95 (*0-17-439880-8*) Wadsworth Pub.

Zickzack: Stage 3 Copymasters. 2nd ed. Goodman. (College German Ser.). 1995. pap. 102.95 (*0-17-439882-4*) Wadsworth Pub.

Zickzack Teachers Pack: Stage 1. Goodman. (Illus.). 1993. pap. 312.95 (*0-17-439308-3*) Heinle & Heinle.

Zickzack Teachers Pack: Stage 3. Goodman. (Illus.). (C). 1993. pap. 249.95 (*0-17-439326-1*) Heinle & Heinle.

Zickzack 1A: Assessment Pack. Goodman. (Illus.). (ENG & GER.). (C). 1900. Tchr's manual. teacher ed., pap. 18.95 (*0-17-439247-8*) Heinle & Heinle.

Zickzack 1A: Assessment Pack. Goodman. (Illus.). (ENG & GER.). (C). 1993. pap. 143.95 (*0-17-439245-1*) Heinle & Heinle.

Zickzack 1A: Assessment Pack. Goodman. (Illus.). (ENG & GER.). (C). 1994. Repromasters. 99.95 (*0-17-439248-6*); Cassette. audio 30.95 (*0-17-439249-4*) Heinle & Heinle.

Zickzack 1B: Assessment Pack. Goodman. (Illus.). (C). Date not set. pap. 143.95 (*0-17-439246-X*); Tchr's manual. teacher ed., pap. 15.95 (*0-17-439250-8*); Repromasters. pap. 99.95 (*0-17-439251-6*); Cassette. audio 30.95 (*0-17-439252-4*) Heinle & Heinle.

Zickzack 2: Assessment Pack. Goodman. (Illus.). (C). Date not set. pap. 147.95 (*0-17-439547-7*); Tchr's manual. teacher ed., pap. 27.95 (*0-17-439548-5*); Repromasters. pap. 82.95 (*0-17-439549-3*) Heinle & Heinle.

Zickzack 2: Assessment Pack. Goodman. (Illus.). (C). 1993. Cassette. audio 34.95 (*0-17-439550-7*) Heinle & Heinle.

Zidovudine in Therapeutic Uses: Index of New Information. Alton D. Livermore. 150p. 1994. 44.50 (*0-7883-0104-7*); pap. 39.50 (*0-7883-0105-5*) ABBE Pubs Assn.

Ziegler Catalysts: Recent Scientific Innovations & Technological Improvements. Ed. by G. Fink et al. 400p. 1995. 146.95 (*0-387-58225-8*) Spr-Verlag.

Ziegler Family Record: Complete Records of the Ziegler Family from Our Ancestor, Philip Ziegler, Born in Bern, Switzerland, in 1734, to 7th & 8th Generations. J. Ziegler & D. Ziegler. 118p. 1994. reprint ed. pap. 21.00 (*0-8328-4252-4*); reprint ed. pap. 21.00 (*0-8328-4536-1*); reprint ed. lib. bdg. 31.00 (*0-8328-4251-6*); reprint ed. lib. bdg. 31.00 (*0-8328-4535-3*) Higginson Bk Co.

Zielsprache Deutsch: Deutsch. Ellen Feld. Ed. by Von N. Feld. (C). 1981. text ed. write for info. (*0-13-087495-7*) P-H.

Zig Zag. Noel Hynd. 512p. 1994. mass mkt. 4.99 (*0-8217-4557-3*, Zebra Kensgtn) Kensgtn Pub Corp.

Zig-Zag. Richard Thornley. LC 88-70373. 172p. 1988. pap. 13.95 (*0-932274-45-5*) Cadmus Eds.

Zig-Zag-&-Swirl: Alfred W. Lawson's Quest for Greatness. Lyell D. Henry, Jr. LC 90-49730. (Illus.). 356p. 1991. 32.95 (*0-87745-312-8*) U of Iowa Pr.

Zig Zag Journeys. Hezekiah Butterworth. (Works of Hezekiah Butterworth). 1989. reprint ed. lib. bdg. 79.00 (*0-7812-2230-3*) Rprt Serv.

***Zig Zag Technology.** Johnsey. 1992. pap. text ed. write for info. (*0-582-08549-7*, Pub. by Longman UK) Longman.

Zig Ziglar's Favorite Quotations. Zig Ziglar. Ed. by Mac Anderson. 77p. (Orig.). 1990. pap. 7.50 (*1-880461-12-9*) Celebrat Excell.

Zig Ziglar's Favorite Quotations see Great Quotes from Zig Ziglar

***Zig Ziglar's Little Instruction Book: Inspiration & Wisdom from America's Top Motivator.** Zig Ziglar. 1997. pap. text ed. 6.99 (*1-56292-364-1*) Honor Bks OK.

Zig Ziglar's Secrets of Closing the Sale. Zig Ziglar. 416p. 1985. pap. 12.95 (*0-425-08102-8*, Berkley Trade) Berkley Pub.

Zigarren des Pharaos. Herge. (Illus.). 62p. (GER.). (J). pap. 19.95 (*0-8288-5006-2*) Fr & Eur.

Ziggle Dance at the Zoo. Bevan Kllair. LC 79-91133. (Kreative Kapers for Kids Ser.). (J). (ps-6). 1979. pap. 3.00 (*0-935712-01-1*) B A Scott.

Ziggy & Friends. Tom Wilson. LC 81-72006. (Illus.). 128p. 1982. pap. text ed. 3.95 (*0-8362-1136-7*) Andrews & McMeel.

Ziggy & the Black Dinosaurs. Sharon M. Draper. (Black Dinosaurs Ser.). (Illus.). 96p. (J). (gr. 3 up). 1994. 14.00 (*0-940975-47-5*); pap. 6.00 (*0-940975-48-3*) Just Us Bks.

***Ziggy & the Black Dinosaurs.** Sharon M. Draper. (Shadow of Caesar's Creek Ser.). 1997. 15.95 (*0-940975-78-5*); pap. text ed. 6.00 (*0-940975-76-9*) Just Us Bks.

Ziggy Cookbook: Great Food from Mom's Diner. Robin Benzle. LC 93-60839. (Illus.). 254p. (Orig.). 1993. pap. 16.00 (*0-9629398-2-X*) VanTine Pub.

Ziggy Faces Life. Tom Wilson. LC 81-65136. (Illus.). 104p. 1981. pap. 4.95 (*0-8362-1167-7*) Andrews & McMeel.

Ziggy in the Fast Lane. Tom Wilson. (Illus.). 256p. (Orig.). 1987. pap. 4.95 (*0-8362-2089-7*) Andrews & McMeel.

Ziggy on the Outside Looking In. Tom Wilson. (Illus.). 104p. (Orig.). 1990. pap. 5.95 (*0-8362-1811-6*) Andrews & McMeel.

***Ziggy Stardust: David Bowie.** Patriess. 1998. 18.00 (*0-02-864771-8*) S&S Trade.

Ziggy the Zombie from Zumbrota. Grandpa Blair. 14p. (YA). (gr. 10 up). 1991. pap. 5.75 (*0-930366-62-X*) Northcountry Pub.

Ziggy Treasury. Tom Wilson. LC 77-10302. (Illus.). 160p. 1977. pap. 8.95 (*0-8362-0738-6*) Andrews & McMeel.

Ziggy...A Rumor in His Own Time. Tom Wilson. 104p. 1992. pap. 6.95 (*0-8362-1887-6*) Andrews & McMeel.

***Ziggyisms: Notable Quotes of Wisdom for Everyday Living.** Tom Wilson. (Illus.). 374p. (Orig.). 1997. pap. write for info. (*0-8362-3682-3*) Andrews & McMeel.

Ziggy's Big Little Book. Tom Wilson. (Illus.). 256p. 1983. pap. 3.95 (*0-8362-1990-2*) Andrews & McMeel.

Ziggy's Christmas Book Level 1. Lani Smith. (Illus.). 32p. (Orig.). (J). 1991. pap. 5.95 (*0-89328-112-3*, KM148) Lorenz Corp.

Ziggy's Christmas Book Level 2. Lani Smith. (Illus.). 32p. (Orig.). (J). 1991. pap. 5.95 (*0-89328-113-1*, KM149) Lorenz Corp.

Ziggy's Follies. Tom Wilson. (Illus.). 104p. 1988. pap. 5.95 (*0-8362-1827-2*) Andrews & McMeel.

***Ziggy's Little Wish Book for Your Birthday.** Tom Wilson. (Little Bks.). (J). 1997. 4.95 (*0-8362-3680-7*) Andrews & McMeel.

Ziggy's Place. Tom Wilson. (Illus.). 256p. pap. 4.95 (*0-8362-7961-1*) Andrews & McMeel.

Ziggy's Play Today Guitar Method. Heritage Music Press Staff. (Illus.). 32p. 1991. pap. 4.95 (*0-89328-114-X*, PP328) Lorenz Corp.

Ziggy's School of Hard Knocks. Tom Wilson. (Illus.). 104p. (Orig.). 1989. pap. 5.95 (*0-8362-1839-6*) Andrews & McMeel.

Ziggy's Star Performances. Tom Wilson. (Illus.). 128p. (Orig.). 1989. pap. 8.95 (*0-8362-1859-0*) Andrews & McMeel.

Ziggy's Ups & Downs. Tom Wilson. (Illus.). 256p. 1986. pap. 4.95 (*0-8362-2078-1*) Andrews & McMeel.

***Ziggy's Wish Book for Someone Special.** Tom Wilson. (Little Bks.). (J). 1997. 4.95 (*0-8362-3679-3*) Andrews & McMeel.

Ziglar on Selling: The Ultimate Handbook for the Complete Sales Professional. Zig Ziglar. 320p. 1991. 19.99 (*0-8407-9131-3*) Nelson.

Ziglar on Selling: The Ultimate Handbook for the Complete Sales Professional. Zig Ziglar. 384p. 1993. pap. 12.00 (*0-345-37887-3*, Ballantine Trade) Ballantine.

Zigzag. Noel Hynd. 416p. 1992. 20.00 (*0-8217-3485-7*, Zebra Kensgtn) Kensgtn Pub Corp.

Zigzag Canyon. Ron Feldman & M. McPherson. LC 93-38633. 288p. (Orig.). 1994. pap. 14.95 (*0-86534-212-1*) Sunstone Pr.

***Zigzag Kid.** David Grossman & Betsi Rozenberg. LC 96-49824. 1997. write for info. (*0-374-29692-8*) FS&G.

Zikir Sumim: Assyriological Studies Presented to F. R. Kraus on the Occasion of His Seventieth Birthday. Ed. by G. Van Driel. vi, 509p. 1982. text ed. 168.00 (*90-6258-126-9*, Pub. by Netherlands Inst NE) Eisenbrauns.

Zikrullah Khadem: The Itinerant Hand of the Cause of God: With Love. Javidukht Khadem. (Champion Builder Bks.). (Illus.). 365p. 1990. pap. 8.00 (*0-87743-225-2*) Bahai.

Zikrullah Khadem: The Itinerant Hand of the Cause of God: With Love. Javidukht Khadem. (Champion Builder Bks.). (Illus.). 365p. 1990. 11.00 (*0-87743-224-4*) Bahai.

Zilla Sasparilla & the Mud Baby. Judith Gorog. LC 95-16163. (Illus.). 32p. (J). (gr. 1-4). 1996. 14.99 (*1-56402-295-1*) Candlewick Pr.

ZIM: The Autobiography of Eugene Zimmerman. Eugene Zimmerman. Ed. by Walter S. Brasch. LC 85-63420. (Illus.). 144p. 1988. 40.00 (*0-941664-23-6*) Susquehanna.

***Zimbabwe.** LC 97-18122. (Major World Nations Ser.). (Illus.). 120p. (YA). (gr. 5 up). 1997. lib. bdg. 19.95 (*0-7910-4753-9*) Chelsea Hse.

Zimbabwe. Colin Stoneman & Lionel Cliffe. (Marxist Regimes Ser.). 220p. 1989. text ed. 49.00 (*0-86187-454-4*); text ed. 17.50 (*0-86187-455-2*) St Martin.

Zimbabwe. Paul Tingay. (Passport's Regional Guides of Africa Ser.). (Illus.). 192p. 1996. pap. 19.95 (*0-8442-8961-2*, Passport Bks) NTC Pub Grp.

***Zimbabwe.** Paul Tingay. (Globetrotter Travel Guide Ser.). 1995. pap. 9.95 (*1-85368-366-3*) St Mut.

Zimbabwe. Richard Vaughan. (Illus.). 216p. 1992. lib. bdg. 74.50 (*0-9515209-1-1*) Rowman.

Zimbabwe. rev. ed. Potts Deborah. (World Bibliographical Ser.). 1994. lib. bdg. 82.50 (*1-85109-195-5*) ABC-CLIO.

Zimbabwe. rev. ed. Jason Laure. LC 87-35426. (Enchantment of the World Ser.). (Illus.). 128p. (J). (gr. 5-9). 1994. lib. bdg. 30.00 (*0-516-02704-2*) Childrens.

Zimbabwe: A Land Divided. Robin Palmer & Isobel Birch. (Country Profiles Ser.). (Illus.). 64p. (C). 1992. pap. 9.95 (*0-85598-178-4*, Pub. by Oxfam UK) Humanities.

Zimbabwe: A Treasure of Africa. Al Stark. LC 85-6944. (Discovering Our Heritage Ser.). (Illus.). 160p. (YA). (gr. 5 up). 1986. text ed. 14.95 (*0-87518-308-5*, Dillon Silver Burdett) Silver Burdett Pr.

***Zimbabwe: Recent Economic Developments.** Jurgen T. Reitmaier. (IMF Staff Country Report Ser.: Vol. 96/33). 96p. pap. 27.40 (*0-608-04857-7*, 2065516) Bks Demand.

Zimbabwe: The Beautiful Land. Gerald Cubitt. (Illus.). 80p. 1992. 14.95 (*1-56757-008-9*) Appleton Comms.

Zimbabwe see Cultures of the World - Group 6

Zimbabwe - Monomotapa Culture in Southeast Asia. Heinrich A. Wieschoff. LC 76-44801. reprint ed. 45.00 (*0-404-15981-8*) AMS Pr.

Zimbabwe, a Break with the Past: Human Rights & Political Unity. Africa Watch Staff. 114p. 1989. pap. 9.00 (*0-685-41312-8*, Africa Watch) Hum Rts Watch.

Zimbabwe & Botswana: A No Frills Guide. 2nd ed. David Else. (Bradt Country Guides Ser.). (Illus.). 82p. 1995. pap. 10.95 (*1-56440-566-4*, Pub. by Bradt Pubns UK) Globe Pequot.

***Zimbabwe & Malawi Handbook with Botswana, Mozambique & Zambia.** Sebastian Ballard. 1997. 19.95 (*0-8442-4912-2*) NTC Pub Grp.

Zimbabwe Atlas. Globe Pequot Press Staff. 1996. pap. text ed. 12.95 (*1-85368-518-6*) Globe Pequot.

***Zimbabwe, Botswana & Namibia.** Rupert Isaacson. (Cadogan Guides). 1997. pap. 21.95 (*1-86011-057-6*, Pub. by Cadogan Books UK) Macmillan.

Zimbabwe, Botswana & Namibia: Travel Survival Kit. 2nd ed. Myra L. Shackley. (Illus.). 800p. 1995. pap. 19.95 (*0-86442-313-6*) Lonely Planet.

Zimbabwe Controversy: A Case of Colonial Historiography. David Chanaiwa. (Foreign & Comparative Studies Program, Eastern Africa Ser.: No. 8). 142p. 1973. pap. 3.00 (*0-915984-05-9*) Syracuse U Foreign Comp.

Zimbabwe Dance: Rhythmic Forces, Ancestral Voices - An Aesthetic Analysis. Kariamu Welsh-Asante. LC 97-13294. 1997. pap. 16.95 (*0-86543-493-X*) Africa World.

***Zimbabwe Dance: Rhythmic Forces, Ancestral Voices, an Aesthetic Analysis.** Kariamu Welsh-Asante. LC 97-13294. 1997. write for info. (*0-86543-492-1*) Africa World.

Zimbabwe in Pictures. Department of Geography, Lerner Publications. (Visual Geography Ser.). (Illus.). 64p. (YA). (gr. 5 up). 1988. lib. bdg. 19.95 (*0-8225-1825-2*, Lerner Publctns) Lerner Group.

Zimbabwe Independence Movements: Select Documents. Ed. by Christopher Nyangoni & Gideon Nyandoro. LC 79-51834. 456p. 1979. text ed. 46.00 (*0-06-495222-3*, N6621) B&N Imports.

Zimbabwean Collectibles. Isabell P. Matsikidze. LC 90-60134. 72p. (Orig.). 1990. pap. 6.95 (*0-943512-34-4*) Linwood Pub.

Zimbabwe's Guerrilla War: Peasant Voices. Norma Kriger. (African Studies: No. 70). (Illus.). 304p. (C). 1991. 69.95 (*0-521-39254-3*) Cambridge U Pr.

Zimbawe, Botswana & Namibia Travel Atlas. Contrib. by Deanna Swaney. (Illus.). 60p. 1996. pap. 9.95 (*0-86442-274-1*) Lonely Planet.

Zimmer frei. Ulrike Cohen & Karl-Heinz Osterloh. Incl. Zimmer Frei. (GER.). 89p. text ed. 15.95 (*3-468-49420-3*); Zimmer Frei. (GER.). 57p. wbk. ed. 10.50 (*3-468-49421-1*); Zimmer Frei. (GER.). 32p. teacher ed. 7.95 (*3-468-49422-X*); Zimmer Frei. (GER.). audio 21.00 (*3-468-84440-9*); write for info. (*0-318-56964-7*) Langenscheidt.

Zimmer Frei see Zimmer frei

Zimmer Gunsul Frasca: Building Community. Ed. by Mildred F. Schmertz. (Illus.). 208p. 1995. 39.99 (*1-56496-197-4*) Rockport Pubs.

Zimmer in der Luft: Liebe, Exil, Ruckkehr & Wortervertrauen, Hilde Domins Lyrischer Entwicklungsweg & Interpretationszugange. Elfe Vallaster. LC 93-14222. (Exil Studien: Vol. 2). 266p. (GER.). (C). 1994. text ed. 49.95 (*0-8204-2225-8*) P Lang Pubng.

Zimmerman Site: A Report of Excavations at the Grand Village of Kaskaskia, LaSalle County, Illinois. Kenneth G. Orr et al. Ed. by James A. Brown. (Reports of Investigations Ser.: No. 9). (Illus.). 86p. 1974. pap. 2.10 (*0-89792-021-X*) Ill St Museum.

Zimmerman Site: Further Excavations at the Grand Village of Kaskaskia. Margaret K. Brown. (Reports of Investigations Ser.: No. 32). (Illus.). 124p. 1975. pap. 3.00 (*0-89792-058-9*) Ill St Museum.

Zimmermann Telegram. Barbara W. Tuchman. 1985. pap. 11.00 (*0-345-32425-0*, Ballantine Trade) Ballantine.

Zimmermann Telegram. Barbara W. Tuchman. 1994. pap. 11.00 (*0-02-054820-6*) Macmillan.

Zimmermann Telegram of January Sixteenth, Nineteen-Hundred Seventeen, & Its Cryptographic Background. William F. Friedman & Charles J. Mendelsohn. 65p. 1994. pap. 12.80 (*0-89412-239-8*) Aegean Park Pr.

Zimmerman's Complete Guide to Nonprescription Drugs. 2nd ed. David R. Zimmerman. 900p. 1992. 45.00 (*0-8103-8874-X*, 101518) Gale.

Zimmerman's Complete Guide to Nonprescription Drugs. 2nd ed. David R. Zimmerman. 850p. 1992. 19.95 (*0-8103-9421-9*, 089160) Visible Ink Pr.

Zimzum. Gordon Lish. LC 93-3360. 1993. 18.00 (*0-679-42685-X*) Pantheon.

Zin! Zin! Zin! A Violin. Lloyd Moss. LC 93-37902. (Illus.). (J). (gr. k-5). 1995. 16.00 (*0-671-88239-2*, S&S Bks Young Read) S&S Childrens.

Zina Garrison. A. P. Porter. (Sports Achievers Ser.). 56p. (J). (gr. 4-9). 1991. lib. bdg. 13.50 (*0-8225-0499-5*, Lerner Publctns) Lerner Group.

Zina Garrison: Ace. A. P. Porter. (Illus.). 64p. (J). (gr. 4-9). 1992. pap. 4.95 (*0-8225-9596-6*, Lerner Publctns) Lerner Group.

Zinacantecos of Mexico: A Modern Mayan Way of Life. 2nd ed. Evan Vogt. 200p. (C). 1990. pap. text ed. 13.50 (*0-03-033344-X*) HB Coll Pubs.

Zinc. (Metals & Minerals Ser.). 1993. lib. bdg. 250.95 (*0-8490-8960-3*) Gordon Pr.

Zinc: Clinical & Biochemical Significance. Stephen C. Cunnane. 224p. 1988. 126.00 (*0-8493-6735-2*, QP535, CRC Reprint) Franklin.

Zinc & Eating Disorders. Alexander G. Schauss. 1993. pap. 2.50 (*0-87983-507-9*) Keats.

Zinc & Its Role in Biology & Nutrition, Vol. 15. Sigel. (Metal Ions in Biological Systems Ser.: Vol. 15). 520p. 1983. 195.00 (*0-8247-7462-0*) Dekker.

An Asterisk (*) at the beginning of an entry indicates that the title is appearing in BIP for the first time.

Zinc & Other Micro-Nutrients. Carl C. Pfeiffer. LC 77-91321. (Illus.). 1978. pap. 3.50 (*0-87983-169-3*) Keats.

Zinc-Based Steel Coating Systems: Metallurgy & Performance. Minerals, Metals & Materials Society Staff. Ed. by George Krauss & David K. Matlock. LC 90-62420. (Illus.). 414p. 1990. reprint ed. pap. 118.00 (*0-608-01697-7*, 2062352) Bks Demand.

Zinc Chemicals: Applications. Harvey E. Brown. Ed. by Dodd S. Carr. 275p. (Orig.). 1989. pap. 10.00 (*0-932893-04-X*) Intl Lead Zinc.

Zinc Enzymes. Ed. by Thomas G. Spiro. 370p. 1991. reprint ed. 94.50 (*0-89464-331-2*) Krieger.

Zinc-Finger Proteins in Oncogenesis: DNA-Binding & Gene Regulation. Ed. by Mels Sluyser et al. LC 93-1623. (Annals Ser.: Vol. 684). 258p. 1993. write for info. (*0-89766-783-2*); pap. 60.00 (*0-89766-784-0*) NY Acad Sci.

Zinc Handbook: Properties, Processing & Use in Design. Frank Porter. (Mechanical Engineering Ser.: Vol. 73). 648p. 1991. 210.00 (*0-8247-8340-9*) Dekker.

***Zinc in Human Biology.** Ed. by C. F. Mills. (Illus.). 388p. 1989. 75.00 (*3-540-19529-7*, 195297) Spr-Verlag.

Zinc in Human Nutrition. A. Prasad. LC 79-15272. 96p. 1979. 61.00 (*0-8493-0145-9*, CRC Reprint) Franklin.

Zinc in Soils & Plants: Proceedings of the International Symposium Held at the University of Western Australia, Perth, Western Australia, 27-28 September, 1993. Ed. by A. D. Robson. LC 93-40339. (Developments in Plants & Soil Sciences Ser.: Vol. 55). 220p. (C). 1994. lib. bdg. 98.50 (*0-7923-2631-8*) Kluwer Ac.

Zinc Metalloproteases in Health & Disease. N. M. Hooper. 350p. 1996. 120.00 (*0-7484-0442-2*) Taylor & Francis.

***Zinc Oxide Thin Films: Fabrication, Properties, & Applications.** Engineering Index Staff. 85.00 (*0-614-18498-3*, 135P37) Info Gatekeepers.

***Zinc Plates.** Trajko Stojanovic. 100p. 1997. pap. write for info. (*0-9657106-0-2*) Zona Incerta.

Zinc Plating. FMJ Intl. Publ. Ltd. Staff. (C). 1989. 325.00 (*0-685-36803-3*, Pub. by Fuel Metallurgical Jrnl UK) St Mut.

Zinc Plating. H. Geduld. 372p. 1991. 295.00 (*0-904477-10-X*, Pub. by FMJ Intl UK) St Mut.

Zinc, the Science & Technology of the Metal, Its Alloys & Compounds. Champion H. Mathewson. LC 74-105708. 733p. reprint ed. pap. 180.00 (*0-317-10316-4*, 2015238) Bks Demand.

Zinc-65 see Toxicology of Radioactive Substances

***Zincali: An Account of the Gypsies in Spain.** George Borrow. Ed. by Gutenberg Project Staff. (European History Ser.: Vol. 14). 166p. 1997. 8.95 (*1-58057-016-X*, ZNCL001B) Digital Antiq.

Zine: How I Spent Six Years of My Life in the Underground & Finally Found Myself, I Think. Pagan Kennedy. LC 95-21097. 1995. pap. 15.95 (*0-312-13628-5*, Griffin) St Martin.

Zines! Incendiary Interviews with Independent Publishers, Vol. 1. Vale Vale. (Illus.). 184p. (Orig.). (C). 1996. pap. 18.99 (*0-9650469-0-7*) V Search.

***Zines! Incendiary Interviews with Independent Publishers, Vol. 2.** Vale Vale. (Illus.). 148p. (Orig.). 1997. pap. 14.99 (*0-9650469-2-3*) V Search.

Zinfandel Cookbook: Food to Go with California's Heritage Wine. Janeth J. Nix & Margaret A. Smith. Ed. by Barbara J. Braasch. (Illus.). 112p. (Orig.). 1994. pap. 14.95 (*0-9642901-0-3*) Toyon Hill Pr.

Zing-a-Long. Morton Cooper. (Illus.). 96p. (Orig.). 1989. pap. 3.95 (*1-877953-03-2*) Voice & Speech.

Zingara Fortune Teller. Gypsy Queen. 183p. 1997. pap. 15.00 (*0-89540-248-3*, SB-248) Sun Pub.

***Zingerman's Guide to Good Vinegar: An Introduction to Understanding, Eating, & Enjoying Vinegar.** Ari Weinzweig. Ed. by Corby Kummer. (Guides to Good Eating Ser.). (Illus.). 96p. (Orig.). (C). 1996. pap. write for info. (*0-9648956-1-7*) Zingermans.

Zingers: Twenty Five Poems. George Flynn. 32p. 1978. 6.00 (*0-686-00335-7*) G Flynn.

Zingers & Swingers. Mary V. March & Carroll A. Rindhart. (Illus.). 88p. (YA). 1994. pap. text ed. 10.95 (*0-910957-58-4*, BMR05109) Warner Brothers.

Zingers for Everybody. Morton Cooper. (Illus.). 96p. (Orig.). 1989. pap. 3.95 (*1-877953-00-8*) Voice & Speech.

Zingers for First to Third Graders: 12 Real-Life Character Builders. David Lynn & Kathy Lynn. 64p. (J). (gr. 1-3). 1993. pap. 8.99 (*0-310-37221-6*) Zondervan.

***Zingers for Life-Enrichment.** Jeannie Esposito. (Illus.). 50p. (Orig.). 1996. pap. 5.00 (*1-890681-00-8*) Hypmovation Prodns.

***Zingers for Management, Vol. 3.** Jeannie Esposito. (Illus.). 50p. (Orig.). 1996. pap. 5.00 (*1-890681-02-4*) Hypmovation Prodns.

***Zingers for Sales, Vol. 2.** Jeannie Esposito. (Illus.). 50p. (Orig.). 1996. pap. 5.00 (*1-890681-01-6*) Hypmovation Prodns.

***Zingers for the Information Highway, Vol. 4.** Jeannie Esposito. (Illus.). 50p. (Orig.). 1997. pap. 5.00 (*1-890681-03-2*) Hypmovation Prodns.

Zink. 1969. 385.00 (*0-387-93240-2*) Spr-Verlag.

Zink the Zebra: A Special Tale. Kelly Weil. LC 96-26693. (Illus.). 24p. (J). (ps up). 1996. lib. bdg. 18.60 (*0-8368-1626-9*) Gareth Stevens Inc.

Zinman's Rapid Writing EZ ABC Shorthand: Advanced Text. 8th rev. ed. M. E. Zinman. 40p. 1989. pap. text ed. 5.00 (*0-911672-50-8*) Zinmans.

Zinman's Rapid Writing EZ ABC Shorthand: Basic Book. M. E. Zinman. 122p. 1995. pap. text ed. 7.50 (*0-911672-53-2*) Zinmans.

Zinman's Rapid Writing EZ ABC Shorthand: Teacher's Guide & Key. rev. ed. Sara W. Zinman. 22p. 1989. teacher ed., pap. text ed. 0.50 (*0-911672-52-4*) Zinmans.

Zinman's Rapid Writing EZ ABC Shorthand: Workbook. rev. ed. M. E. Zinman. 72p. 1982. student ed., wbk. ed., pap. text ed. 5.00 (*0-911672-51-6*) Zinmans.

Zinn & the Art of Mountain Bike Maintenance. Lennard Zinn. (Illus.). 324p. 1996. pap. 16.95 (*1-884737-15-3*) VeloPress.

Zinngeschrei see Mensch und Zeit: An Anthology of German Radio Plays

***Zinnia.** Jayne Castle. 1997. mass mkt. 6.50 (*0-671-56901-5*) PB.

Zinnia & Dot. Lisa C. Ernst. 1995. pap. 4.99 (*0-14-054199-3*) Puffin Bks.

Zinnia & Dot. Lisa C. Ernst. (Illus.). 32p. (J). (ps-3). 1992. pap. 14.99 (*0-670-83091-7*) Viking Child Bks.

Zinnias Grow on Either Side of the River. Al Allen. 320p. 1995. 19.95 (*0-943099-17-X*) M&M Pr.

Zinsser Microbiology. 2nd ed. Wolfgang K. Joklik. (Illus.). 1294p. (C). 1992. text ed. 75.00 (*0-8385-9983-4*, A9983-6) Appleton & Lange.

Zinzendorf: Nine Public Lectures on Important Subjects in Religion. Ed. by George W. Forell. LC 74-93784. 170p. (C). 1973. text ed. 25.00 (*0-87745-036-6*) U of Iowa Pr.

Zion. rev. ed. Ed. by Jeff Nicholas. (Wish You Were Here Postcard Bks.). 32p. 1994. pap. 4.95 (*0-939365-33-2*) Sierra Pr CA.

***Zion: A Light in the Darkness.** Alexander B. Morrison. LC 97-11004. 1997. write for info. (*1-57345-260-2*) Deseret Bk.

Zion: A Visual Interpretation. Nicky Leach. Ed. by Rose Houck. (Wish You Were Here Postcard Bks.). 64p. (Orig.). 1994. pap. 9.95 (*0-939365-36-7*) Sierra Pr CA.

***Zion: The Story Behind the Scenery.** rev. ed. A. J. Eardley & James W. Schaack. LC 91-62368. (Illus.). 48p. 1991. pap. 7.95 (*0-88714-029-7*) KC Pubns.

Zion Album: A Nostalgic History of Zion Canyon. J. L. Crawford. LC 85-51614. (Illus.). 87p. 1986. pap. text ed. 6.95 (*0-915630-21-4*) Zion.

Zion & State: Nation, Class & the Shaping of Modern Israel. Mitchell Cohen. 336p. 1992. text ed. 49.50 (*0-231-07940-0*); pap. text ed. 17.00 (*0-231-07941-9*) Col U Pr.

Zion Before Zionism: Eighteen Thirty-Eight to Eighteen Eighty. Arnold B. Blumberg. LC 85-17287. (Illus.). 240p. 1985. text ed. 39.95 (*0-8156-2336-4*) Syracuse U Pr.

Zion Chronicles, 5 vols. Bodie Thoene. 1988. Boxed. boxed 54.99 (*1-55661-754-2*) Bethany Hse.

Zion City, Illinois: Twentieth-Century Utopia. Philip L. Cook. LC 95-33571. (Utopianism & Communitarianism Ser.). (Illus.). (C). 1996. pap. 14.95 (*0-8156-0349-5*, COZCP) Syracuse U Pr.

Zion City, Illinois: Twentieth-Century Utopia. Philip L. Cook. LC 95-33571. (Utopianism & Communitarianism Ser.). (Illus.). 260p. (C). 1996. text ed. 34.95 (*0-8156-2621-5*, COZC) Syracuse U Pr.

Zion Connection: Destroying the Myths, Forging an Alliance. Elwood McQuaid. LC 95-43853. 240p. 1996. pap. 9.99 (*1-56507-449-1*) Harvest Hse.

Zion Covenant, 3 bks., Bks. 1-3. Bodie Thoene. 1994. Set. 35.99 (*1-55661-779-8*) Bethany Hse.

Zion Covenant, 3 bks., Bks. 4-6. Bodie Thoene. 1993. Set. 36.99 (*1-55661-780-1*) Bethany Hse.

Zion Covenent, 6 bks., Bks. 1-6. Bodie Thoene. 1991. Set. pap. 72.99 (*1-55661-760-7*) Bethany Hse.

Zion in Jewish Literature. Ed. by Abraham S. Halkin. (Brown Classics in Judaica Ser.). 148p. (C). 1988. reprint ed. pap. text ed. 18.00 (*0-8191-6790-8*) U Pr of Amer.

Zion in the Courts: A Legal History of the Church of Jesus Christ of Latter-Day Saints, 1830-1900. Edwin B. Firmage & R. Collin Mangrum. LC 87-30171. 448p. 1988. text ed. 27.50 (*0-252-01498-7*) U of Ill Pr.

***Zion in the Valley Vol. I: The Jewish Community of St. Louis, 1807-1907.** Walter Ehrlich. LC 96-49340. (Illus.). 464p. 1997. 35.95 (*0-8262-1098-8*) U of Mo Pr.

Zion Liberated: The Life & Times of Max Seligman. Giveon Cornfield. Ed. by Joseph Simon. (Illus.). 288p. (C). 1991. 27.50 (*0-934710-22-8*) J Simon.

Zion National Park. David Petersen. LC 92-35048. (New True Bk.). (Illus.). 48p. (J). (gr. k-4). 1993. pap. 5.50 (*0-516-41336-8*); lib. bdg. 19.00 (*0-516-01336-X*) Childrens.

Zion National Park: An Illustrated History. J. C. Cranford. (Illus.). 48p. 1989. pap. 6.95 (*0-917859-26-X*) Sunrise SBCA.

Zion National Park: Towers of Stone. John L. Crawford. Ed. by Angela Tripp & Carey Vandrame. Tr. by Scott Belliston. (Illus.). 55p. (Orig.). (ENG & GER.). 1995. pap. 10.95 (*0-915630-38-9*) Zion.

Zion National Park: Towers of Stone. 2nd rev. ed. John L. Crawford. Ed. by Carey Vandrame & Angela Tripp. (Illus.). 55p. (Orig.). 1988. pap. 9.50 (*0-915630-33-8*) Zion.

Zion National Park, UT. rev. ed. Ed. by Trails Illustrated Staff. (Illus.). 1995. Folded topographical map. 8.99 (*0-925873-14-4*) Trails Illustrated.

Zion Presents: Jesus Christ & Him Crucified? (Orig.). Date not set. pap. write for info. (*1-885858-16-7*) KILN Bks.

Zion, the Growing Symbol. Ed. by David Premoe. 1980. pap. 8.50 (*0-8309-0301-1*) Herald Hse.

***Zion Traditions & the Aims of Jesus.** Kim H. Tan. (Society for New Testament Studies Monographs: No. 91). 292p. (C). 1997. text ed. 59.95 (*0-521-58006-4*) Cambridge U Pr.

Zionism. Stanislawski. 1997. 24.95 (*0-8057-7811-X*, Twayne); 15.95 (*0-8057-7812-8*, Twayne) Scribnrs Ref.

Zionism: A Basic Reader. Ed. by Mordechai Chertoff. 1976. 1.00 (*0-685-82601-5*) Herzl Pr.

Zionism: The Crucial Phase. David Vital. (Illus.). 408p. 1987. 85.00 (*0-19-821932-6*) OUP.

Zionism: The Formative Years. David Vital. (Illus.). 532p. 1982. reprint ed. 75.00 (*0-19-827443-2*) OUP.

Zionism: The Limits of Moral Discourse in Israeli Hebrew Fiction. Yerach Gover. LC 94-2527. 1994. text ed. 44.95 (*0-8166-2412-7*); pap. text ed. 19.95 (*0-8166-2413-5*) U of Minn Pr.

Zionism: The Myth & the Reality. Ismail Zayed. 1984. pap. 2.50 (*0-89259-013-0*) Am Trust Pubns.

Zionism: The Saga of a National Liberation Movement. Jacob Tsur. LC 76-24801. 112p. 1977. pap. text ed. 21.95 (*0-87855-631-1*) Transaction Pubs.

Zionism & Arabism in Palestine & Israel. Ed. by Elie Kedourie & Sylvia G. Haim. 266p. 1982. text ed. 45.00 (*0-7146-3169-8*, Pub. by F Cass Pubs UK) Intl Spec Bk.

Zionism & Faith-Healing in Rhodesia: Aspects of African Independent Churches. M. L. Daneel. Tr. by February, V. A., Communications Staff from DUT. (Illus.). 1970. pap. 29.25 (*90-279-6278-2*) Mouton.

Zionism & History: The Rise of a New Jewish Consciousness. Shumel Almog. Tr. by Ina R. Friedman from HEB. 350p. 1987. text ed. 39.95 (*0-312-89885-1*) St Martin.

Zionism & Racism. Abdeen Jabara. (Occasional Papers: No. 3). 14p. (Orig.). (C). 1976. pap. 1.50 (*0-937694-42-8*) Assn Arab-Amer U Grads.

Zionism & Technocracy: The Engineering of Jewish Settlement in Palestine, 1870-1918. Derek J. Penslar. LC 90-25043. (Modern Jewish Experience Ser.). (Illus.). 224p. 1991. 10.95 (*0-253-34290-2*) Ind U Pr.

Zionism & Territory: The Socio-Territorial Dimensions of Zionist Politics. Baruch Kimmerling. LC 83-102. (Research Ser.: No. 51). (Illus.). xii, 288p. 1983. pap. text ed. 13.95 (*0-87725-151-7*) U of Cal IAS.

***Zionism & the Arabs: An American Jewish Dilemma, 1898-1948.** Rafael Medoff. LC 96-47482. 200p. 1997. text ed. 55.00 (*0-275-95824-8*, Praeger Pubs) Greenwood.

Zionism & the Arabs 1882-1948: A Study of Ideology. Yosef Gorny. Tr. by Chaya Galai. 350p. 1987. 79.00 (*0-19-822721-3*) OUP.

Zionism & the Problem of Palestinian Human Rights. James J. Zogby. (Information Papers: No. 20). 44p. (Orig.). (C). 1976. pap. 2.00 (*0-937694-36-3*) Assn Arab-Amer U Grads.

Zionism As an Issue in Interwar Politics. Aaron Klieman. LC 90-44346. (American Zionism Ser.: Vol. 6). 160p. 1991. reprint ed. text ed. 20.00 (*0-8240-7354-1*) Garland.

Zionism at the Close of the Twentieth Century: A Dilemma. Zeev Ben-Sira. LC 93-1285. 132p. 1993. text ed. 69.95 (*0-7734-9291-7*) E Mellen.

Zionism-Conceptual Bases in the Prayerbook-Kit. pap. 2.00 (*0-686-96092-0*) USCJE.

Zionism in Poland: The Formative Years, 1915-1926. Ezra Mendelsohn. LC 81-10301. 384p. 1981. reprint ed. pap. 110.30 (*0-7837-3324-0*, 2057729) Bks Demand.

Zionism in the Age of Dictators: A Reappraisal. Lenni Brenner. 277p. 1986. pap. 13.00 (*1-55652-077-8*) L Hill Bks.

Zionism in Transition. Ed. by Moshe Davis. LC 80-67905. 1980. lib. bdg. 23.95 (*0-405-13825-3*) Ayer.

Zionism in Transition. Ed. by Moshe Davis. 1980. pap. 8.00 (*0-930832-61-2*) Herzl Pr.

***Zionism, Israel & the Arabs: Notes on the Historical Background of the Middle East Tragedy.** Hal Draper. viii, 235p. 1997. pap. 15.95 (*0-916695-09-3*) Ctr Social Hist.

Zionism, the Superpowers, & the P. L. O. Henry Paolucci. LC 82-15728. 80p. 1982. pap. 9.95 (*0-918680-18-2*, GHGP 708) Bagehot Council.

Zionism Today: A Symposium. Intro. by Stuart E. Eizenstat. LC 86-70642. 72p. (Orig.). 1986. pap. 5.00 (*0-87495-079-1*) Am Jewish Comm.

Zionism Within Early American Fundamentalism, 1878-1918: A Convergence of Two Traditions. David A. Rausch. LC 79-66371. (Texts & Studies in Religion: Vol. 4). viii, 386p. 1980. lib. bdg. 99.95 (*0-88946-875-3*) E Mellen.

Zionist Career of Louis Lipsky, 1900-1921. Deborah E. Lipstadt. 1981. 38.95 (*0-405-14086-X*) Ayer.

Zionist Christian Church in South Africa: A Case-Study in Oral Theology. Piet Naude. LC 94-39459. 164p. 1995. text ed. 79.95 (*0-7734-9147-3*) E Mellen.

Zionist Connection II. Alfred M. Lilienthal. 904p. 1986. pap. 29.00 (*0-949667-33-1*, Pub. by Veritas Pub AT) Legion Survival.

Zionist Culture & West European Jewry Before the First World War. Michael Berkowitz. (Illus.). 288p. (C). 1993. text ed. 59.95 (*0-521-42072-5*) Cambridge U Pr.

Zionist Culture & West European Jewry Before the First World War. Michael Berkowitz. LC 96-33936. 1996. reprint ed. pap. 16.95 (*0-8078-4605-8*) U of NC Pr.

Zionist Idea: A Historical Analysis & Reader. Ed. by Arthur Hertzberg. LC 70-97312. 638p. 1971. reprint ed. text ed. 35.00 (*0-8371-2565-0*, HEZI, Greenwood Pr) Greenwood.

***Zionist Idea: An Historical Analysis & Reader.** Arthur Hertzberg. LC 96-49372. 656p. 1997. reprint ed. pap. 24.95 (*0-8276-0622-2*) JPS Phila.

Zionist Ideology. Gideon Shimoni. LC 94-35265. (Tauber Institute Ser.: Vol. 21). 522p. 1995. 59.95 (*0-87451-703-6*) U Pr of New Eng.

***Zionist Ideology.** Gideon Shimoni. LC 94-35265. (Tauber Institute for the Study of European Jewry Ser.: Vol. 21). (Illus.). 522p. 1995. pap. text ed. 25.00 (*0-87451-833-4*) U Pr of New Eng.

Zionist Plan for the Middle East. Tr. by Oded Yinon & Israel Shahak. (Special Reports: No. 1). 26p. (Orig.). 1982. pap. text ed. 2.00 (*0-937694-56-8*) Assn Arab-Amer U Grads.

Zionist Relations with Nazi Germany. Faris Glubb. LC 79-90569. 6.00 (*0-911026-11-8*) New World Press NY.

Zionist Revisionism from Jabotinsky to Shamir. 1991. lib. bdg. 65.95 (*0-8490-4423-5*) Gordon Pr.

Zionist Stand. Zeev B. Begin. 1993. pap. 17.50 (*0-7146-4089-1*, Pub. by F Cass Pubs UK) Intl Spec Bk.

Zion's Call: Christian Contributions to the Origins & Development of Israel. Lawrence J. Epstein. LC 84-15184. 176p. (Orig.). 1984. pap. text ed. 20.00 (*0-8191-4186-0*) U Pr of Amer.

Zion's Camp. Rick Everett. LC 94-36030. (Illus.). 96p. (Orig.). 1994. pap. 8.95 (*1-56085-064-7*) Signature Bks.

Zion's Evangelical German Lutheran Church of Girardville, Schuylkill Co., Pa. Compiled by Schuylkill Roots Staff. 74p. 1989. pap. text ed. 8.50 (*1-55856-017-3*) Closson Pr.

Zion's Glad Morning. Willard A. Ramsey. (Illus.). 320p. (Orig.). 1990. 15.95 (*0-9625220-0-7*); pap. 9.95 (*0-9625220-1-5*) Millennium Three Pubs.

***Zip.** Bruce Brooks. LC 97-2049. (Wolfbay Wings Ser.: No. 2). 144p. (J). 1997. pap. 4.50 (*0-06-440598-2*, Trophy) HarpC Child Bks.

***Zip.** Bruce Brooks. (The Wolfbay Wings Ser.: Vol. 2). (J). 1997. 13.89 (*0-06-027350-X*) HarpC Child Bks.

Zip-a-Zap Zing see Phonics Is My Way Series

Zip Bible. Itsok Kespret. 1996. 24.95 incl. cd-rom (*1-55755-305-X*) Abacus MI.

***Zip Code.** Marie Brenner. Date not set. write for info. (*0-688-04779-3*) Morrow.

Zip Code Area Profiles 1994. Melvin I. Krasner et al. LC 94-34634. 358p. 1994. pap. 100.00 (*1-881277-20-8*) United Hosp Fund.

***Zip Code Data Atlas 1997.** Universal Staff. 1996. pap. text ed. 29.95 (*0-7625-0252-5*) Universal Map Enterprises Inc.

***Zip Code Finder, 1997.** Rand McNally Staff. 1996. pap. text ed. 7.95 (*0-528-81516-4*) Rand McNally.

Zip Code Mapbook of Metropolitan Areas. 2nd ed. CACI Marketing Systems Staff. 360p. 1992. 195.00 (*0-918417-12-0*, 101845) CACI Mktg Systs.

Zip Codes. Rita Friedman & Elaine Weimann. (Fables from the Letter People Ser.). (Illus.). 30p. (J). (ps-1). 1989. lib. bdg. 12.95 (*0-89796-025-4*) New Dimens Educ.

***Zip! Pop! Hop! And Other Fun Words to Say.** (First Little Golden Bks.). (Illus.). 24p. (J). (ps). 1996. write for info. (*0-614-19518-7*, 10155-30, Golden Books) Western Pub.

Zip Six: A Novel. Jack Gantos. LC 96-7436. 281p. 1996. 21.95 (*1-882593-15-4*) Bridge Wrks.

***Zip Zip: Mastering Your Nugget Detector.** rev. ed. Larry Sallee. (Illus.). 155p. 1996. spiral bd. 14.95 (*0-9654584-0-7*) Venture West.

***Zip Zip: The Advanced Course.** Larry Sallee. (Illus.). 1997. spiral bd., pap. 11.95 (*0-9654584-1-5*) Venture West.

***Zip-Zippity-Doo! I Love You!** Beth Tubbs. (Illus.). 30p. (Orig.). (J). (ps-3). 1995. spiral bd., pap. 9.95 (*0-9632993-6-0*) Storytime Pub.

***Zip/Area Code Directory: 1997 Edition.** rev. ed. LC 79-15214. 48p. 1997. pap. 7.95 (*0-87576-199-2*) Pilot Bks.

Ziping Method of Fate Calculation: As Seen from the Theory of Li, Qi & Shu. Ho Peng Yoke. (C). 1988. pap. text ed. 30.00 (*962-209-192-X*, Pub. by Hong Kong U Pr HK) St Mut.

Zipper! An Exploration in Novelty. 256p. 1994. 23.00 (*0-393-03599-9*) Norton.

Zipper: An Exploration in Novelty. Robert Friedel. (Illus.). 304p. 1996. pap. 13.00 (*0-393-31365-4*) Norton.

***Zipper, the Kid with ADHD.** Caroline Janover. (Illus.). 112p. (J). (gr. 3-6). 1997. pap. 11.95 (*0-933149-95-6*) Woodbine House.

Zipping for Beginners. Abacus Dev. Group Staff. 1996. 14.95 incl. disk (*1-55755-306-8*) Abacus MI.

Zipping, Zapping, Zooming Bats. Ann Earle. LC 93-11052. (Let's Read-&-Find-Out Science Bk., Stage 2). (Illus.). 32p. (J). (gr. k-4). 1995. 14.95 (*0-06-023479-2*) HarpC Child Bks.

Zipping, Zapping, Zooming Bats. Ann Earle. LC 93-11052. (Let's Read-&-Find-Out Science Bk., Stage 2). (Illus.). 32p. (J). (gr. 4 up). 1995. lib. bdg. 14.89 (*0-06-023480-6*) HarpC Child Bks.

Zipping, Zapping, Zooming Bats. Ann Earle. LC 93-11052. (Let's-Read-&-Find-Out Science Ser.). (Illus.). 32p. (J). (gr. k-4). 1995. pap. 4.95 (*0-06-445133-X*, Trophy) HarpC Child Bks.

Zipping Zippers Save the Zoo. Elaine Weimann & Rita Friedman. (Read to Me Bks.). (Illus.). 30p. (J). (ps-1). 1986. lib. bdg. 12.50 (*0-89796-991-X*) New Dimens Educ.

***Zippo: The Great American Lighter.** David Poore. LC 96-51118. (Illus.). 196p. 1997. 39.95 (*0-7643-0203-5*) Schiffer.

Zippy: Nation of Pinheads. Bill Griffith. 1982. pap. 5.95 (*0-915904-71-3*) And-Or Bks.

Zippy Nation of Pinheads. Bill Griffith. 96p. 1987. 5.95 (*0-86719-365-4*) Last Gasp.

Zippy Pindemonium. Bill Griffith. 1986. pap. 7.95 (*0-86719-348-4*) Last Gasp.

Zippy Pointed Behavior. Bill Griffith. 96p. 1983. 7.95 (*0-86719-315-8*) Last Gasp.

Zippy Postcard Book. Bill Griffith. 1992. 11.95 (*0-86719-386-7*) Last Gasp.

Zippy Stories. Bill Griffith. 120p. 1983. 14.95 (*0-86719-325-5*) Last Gasp.

Zippy the Ant Loses Her Way. LC 93-85481. (Baby Bug Bks.). (Illus.). 20p. (J). (ps-1). 1994. 3.99 (*0-89577-569-7*) RD Assn.

Zippy Zebra, Vol. IV. Katherine Oana. Ed. by Tate Baird. LC 88-51853. (Fables for Today Ser.). (Illus.). 16p. (Orig.). (J). (ps). 1989. pap. 5.52 (*0-914127-11-X*) Univ Class.

***Zippy's House of Fun.** limited ed. Bill Griffith. 112p. 1995. 39.95 (*1-56097-162-2*) Fantagraph Bks.

Zips, Pipes, & Pens. David L. Truby. (Illus.). 1600p. 1993. pap. 15.00 (*0-87364-702-5*) Paladin Pr.

Zircon Affair, No. PF1. Peter Thornton. 1987. pap. 20.00 (*0-946081-19-0*, Pub. by NCCL UK) St Mut.

***Zirconia.** Mitchell Market Reports Staff. 250p. 1993. 1, 090.25 (*1-85617-181-7*, Pub. by Elsvr Adv Tech UK) Elsevier.

Zirconium: International Strategic Minerals Inventory Summary Report. (Illus.). 52p. (Orig.). (C). 1994. pap. text ed. 30.00 (*1-56806-172-2*) DIANE Pub.

Zirconium & Hafnium. (Metals & Minerals Ser.). 1993. lib. bdg. 250.95 (*0-8490-8970-0*) Gordon Pr.

***Zirconium in Emission Control.** 1997. write for info. (*0-7680-0022-X*) Soc Auto Engineers.

Zirconium in Nuclear Applications - STP 551. 526p. 1974. 44.50 (*0-8031-0757-9*, 04-551000-35) ASTM.

Zirconium in the Nuclear Industry: Eighth International Symposium. Ed. by Leo F. Van Swam & Craig M. Eucken. LC 89-34780. (Special Technical Publication Ser.: No. STP 1023). (Illus.). 785p. 1989. text ed. 135.00 (*0-8031-1199-1*, 04-010230-04) ASTM.

***Zirconium in the Nuclear Industry: Eleventh International Symposium, No. 1295.** Ed. by C. Ross Bradley & George P. Sabol. (STP Ser.). (Illus.). 925p. 1996. text ed. 195.00 (*0-8031-2406-6*, 04-012950-04) ASTM.

Zirconium in the Nuclear Industry: Fourth Conference - STP 681. Ed. by J. H. Schemel & J. P. Papazoglou. 637p. 1979. 52.50 (*0-8031-0601-7*, 04-681000-35) ASTM.

Zirconium in the Nuclear Industry: Ninth International Symposium. Ed. by C. M. Eucken & A. M. Garde. (Special Technical Publication Ser.: No. 1132). (Illus.). 800p. 1991. text ed. 177.00 (*0-8031-1463-X*, 1050-7558) ASTM.

Zirconium in the Nuclear Industry: Seventh International Symposium. Ed. by Ronald B. Adamson & Leo F. Van Swam. LC 87-14537. (Special Technical Publication Ser.: No. 939). (Illus.). 815p. 1987. text ed. 110.00 (*0-8031-0935-0*, 04-939000-35) ASTM.

Zirconium in the Nuclear Industry: Tenth International Symposium, STP 1245. Ed. by Anand M. Garde & E. Ross Bradley. (Special Technical Publication Ser.). (Illus.). 800p. 1994. text ed. 145.00 (*0-8031-2011-7*, 04-012450-04) ASTM.

Zirconium in the Nuclear Industry: Third Conference - STP 633. Ed. by A. L. Lowe & G. W. Perry. 690p. 1977. 55. 50 (*0-8031-0756-0*, 04-633000-35) ASTM.

Zirconium in the Nuclear Industry - STP 824. D. Franklin & R. B. Adamson. LC 83-71644. 850p. 1984. text ed. 84.00 (*0-8031-0270-4*) ASTM.

Zirconium in the Nuclear Industry, Fifth Conference - STP 754. Ed. by D. Franklin. 498p. 1981. 52.00 (*0-8031-0754-4*, 04-754000-35) ASTM.

Zirconium Production, Processing, Harding & Storage. (Forty Ser.). 1987. pap. 16.75 (*0-685-58153-5*, 482-87) Natl Fire Prot.

Zirkus. (Meyers Klien Kinderbibliothek). 24p. (GER.). (J). 1994. 14.75 (*3-411-08651-3*) Langenscheidt.

Zirun Affair. Peter Thornton. (C). 1988. 45.00 (*0-685-33952-1*, Pub. by NCCL UK) St Mut.

Ziska. Marie Corelli. 88p. 1985. reprint ed. spiral bd. 12.50 (*0-7873-0219-8*) Hlth Research.

Zitate und Ausspruche, 12 vols., Vol. 12. (Duden Ser.). 832p. (GER.). 1996. 33.50 (*3-411-04121-8*) Langenscheidt.

Zivilrechtliche Haftung im Strassenverkehr: Grosskommentar zu 7-20 Strassenverkehrsgeseth und zum Haftpflichtgesetz unter Beruecksichtigung des Delikts, Vertrags und Versicherungsrechts Sowie des Schadensregresses. Reinhard Greger. (Grosskommentare der Praxis Ser.). xvi, 560p. (GER.). 1984. 229.25 (*3-11-008651-4*) De Gruyter.

Zivotopis Fra Dominika Mandica. Bazilije Pandzic. Ed. by Ziral Staff & Vinko D. Lasic. (Sabrana Djela Dr. O. Dominika Mandica, Sv. 12 Ser.). (Illus.). 236p. 1994. 25. 00 (*1-880829-04-5*) Z I R A L.

Zizanie. Rene De Goscinny & M. Uderzo. (Illus.). (FRE.). (J). 1990. 19.95 (*0-8288-4912-9*) Fr & Eur.

Zizz Cleans Up. Tom Allen & Patsy Allen. (Illus.). 32p. (J). (ps). 1993. 15.95 (*0-460-88102-7*, Pub. by J M Dent & Sons UK) Trafalgar.

Zlata's Diary: A Child's Life in Sarajevo. Zlata Filipovic. (Illus.). 220p. (YA). 1999. pap. 4.99 (*0-14-037583-X*) Puffin Bks.

Zlata's Diary: A Child's Life in Sarajevo. Zlata Filipovic. (Illus.). 220p. 1995. pap. 7.95 (*0-14-024205-8*, Penguin Bks) Viking Penguin.

Zlateh the Goat & Other Stories. Isaac B. Singer. LC 66-8114. (Illus.). (J). (gr. 1-6). 1966. 16.00 (*0-06-025698-2*) HarpC Child Bks.

Zlateh the Goat & Other Stories. Isaac B. Singer. Tr. by Elizabeth Shub. LC 66-8114. (Trophy Bk.). (Illus.). 96p. (J). (gr. 3-7). 1984. pap. 5.95 (*0-06-440147-2*, Trophy) HarpC Child Bks.

Zlateh the Goat & Other Stories. Isaac B. Singer. 1966. 15. 89 (*0-06-025699-0*) HarpC.

Zmile Treatment - How to Avoid Gum Surgery & Dentures. Vasilios Gardiakos. (Illus.). 150p. (Orig.). 1994. pap. 12. 95 (*0-9646271-0-8*, Enosis Pr) Albrite FL.

Zmluva. Vladimir Uhri. 36p. (Orig.). (SLO.). 1995. pap. 1.75 (*1-56983-045-2*) New Creat WI.

Znamenia Viery. 3rd ed. Vladimir Uhri. 32p. (SLO.). 1996. pap. 3.00 (*1-56983-046-0*) New Creat WI.

Zoar: Or the Evidence of Psychical Research Concerning Survival. W. H. Salter. LC 75-7399. (Perspectives in Psychical Research Ser.). 1975. reprint ed. 20.95 (*0-405-07048-9*) Ayer.

Zoar & Her Sisters: The Bible, Homosexuality & Jesus Christ. Arthur F. Ide. LC 91-14232. 1991. pap. 15.00 (*0-926899-02-3*) Minuteman Pr.

Zochor Veshomor. Sinai Malovitzki. (Bible in Yiddish Ser.). (Illus.). 200p. (YID.). (C). 1987. reprint ed. pap. text ed. 16.00 (*0-944704-67-0*) Sinai Heritage.

***Zod Wallop.** William B. Spencer. (Illus.). 1997. reprint ed. mass mkt. 5.99 (*1-56504-870-9*) White Wolf.

Zodiac. Robert Graysmith. 384p. 1987. mass mkt. 6.99 (*0-425-09808-7*) Berkley Pub.

Zodiac. deluxe limited ed. James Dickey. 1976. boxed 500. 00 (*0-89723-018-3*) Bruccoli.

***Zodiac.** large type ed. Richard Dilys. (Ulverscroft Large Print Ser.). 224p. 1996. 25.99 (*0-7089-3646-6*) Ulverscroft.

***Zodiac: A Historical Survey.** Robert Powell. 31p. 1996. pap. 4.95 (*0-917086-69-4*) ACS Pubns.

Zodiac: A Life Epitome. Walter H. Sampson. LC 75-25826. 1980. 22.00 (*0-88231-019-4*) ASI Pubs Inc.

Zodiac: A Monthly Periodical Devoted to Science, Literature & the Arts. (Illus.). 312p. 1980. reprint ed. 19.95 (*0-937438-00-6*) Am Pine Barrens.

Zodiac: An Analysis of Symbolic Degrees. Eric Schroeder. 216p. (Orig.). 1982. pap. 16.95 (*0-9609850-2-6*) Rob Briggs.

Zodiac: Exploring Human Qualities & Characteristics. 2nd rev. ed. Mary R. Moore. LC 84-17977. (Vocabureader Workbook Ser.: No. 1). (Illus.). 112p. 1994. pap. text ed. 10.50 (*0-86647-080-8*) Pro Lingua.

Zodiac: The Eco-Thriller. Neal Stephenson. 320p. 1995. mass mkt. 5.99 (*0-553-57386-1*, Spectra) Bantam.

Zodiac, a Life Epitome. Walter H. Sampson. 1972. 59.95 (*0-8490-1348-8*) Gordon Pr.

Zodiac & the Salts of Salvation. George W. Carey & Inez E. Perry. LC 77-166412. 352p. 1989. pap. 16.95 (*0-87728-708-2*) Weiser.

Zodiac & the Soul. C. E. Carter. 1972. 59.95 (*0-8490-1349-6*) Gordon Pr.

Zodiac Arrest. Rochelle Ratner. (Orig.). 1995. pap. text ed. 6.00 (*1-56439-047-0*) Ridgeway.

Zodiac Charted Designs for Cross-Stitch Needlepoint & Other Techniques. Ed. by Lindberg Press Staff. 48p. 1985. pap. 3.50 (*0-486-24932-8*) Dover.

Zodiac Conspiracy. Doug Shuler. Ed. by Rob Bell. (Champions Ser.). (Illus.). 56p. (Orig.). (C). 1989. pap. 11.00 (*1-55806-082-0*, 406) Hero Games.

Zodiac Degrees. Peter J. Weber. (Illus.). 128p. (Orig.). (YA). 1989. 14.95 (*0-940649-06-3*); pap. 9.95 (*0-940649-05-5*) Parnell Pub.

Zodiac Experience: Initiation Through the 12 Signs. Patricia Crowther. LC 91-35179. (Illus.). 240p. (Orig.). 1992. pap. 10.95 (*0-87728-739-2*) Weiser.

Zodiac Family. Julia Parker. 1989. 18.95 (*0-87951-374-8*) Overlook Pr.

Zodiac Family: How Astrology Can Help You Understand & Raise Your Child. Julia Parker. (Illus.). 1992. pap. 10. 95 (*0-87951-378-0*) Overlook Pr.

***Zodiac Fantastic.** Martin H. Greenberg. 1997. mass mkt. 5.99 (*0-88677-751-8*) DAW Bks.

Zodiac Image Handbook: The Mutable Signs - Virgo, Sagittarius, Pisces, Gemini. Helene Koppejan & Willem Koppejan. (Illus.). 432p. 1993. pap. 24.00 (*1-85230-198-8*) Element MA.

Zodiac, Key to Man & to the Universe, Vol. 220. 2nd ed. Omraam M. Aivanhov. (Izvor Collection: Vol. 220). 176p. 1989. pap. 7.95 (*2-85566-369-5*) Prosveta USA.

***Zodiac Killer, Vol. 1.** Crowley. 1997. mass mkt. write for info. (*0-312-96339-4*) St Martin.

***Zodiac Pack: A Visual Approach to Astrology.** Judy Hall. (Illus.). 320p. 1997. boxed 34.95 (*1-899171-85-1*, Pub. by Findhorn Pr UK) Words Distrib.

***Zodiac 17: Rome in Jubilee Year.** Abitare Segesta. 1997. 35.00 (*0-8230-5975-8*) Watsn-Guptill.

Zodiac Symbology. Faith Javane. LC 91-65239. (Illus.). 144p. (Orig.). 1991. pap. 14.95 (*0-924608-11-0*, Whitford Pr) Schiffer.

Zodiac Twelve. Segesta Editrice Arbitare Staff. (Illus.). 272p. 1995. pap. text ed. 29.00 (*0-8230-6235-X*) Watsn-Guptill.

Zodiac 1. Segesta Editrice Arbitare Staff. (Illus.). 272p. 1995. pap. 29.00 (*0-8230-6400-X*) Watsn-Guptill.

Zodiac 10. Segesta Editrice Abitare Staff. (Illus.). 272p. 1995. pap. 29.00 (*0-8230-6411-5*) Watsn-Guptill.

***Zodiac 11.** Compiled by Editrice Abitare Segesta Staff. (Illus.). 272p. pap. 29.00 (*0-8230-6412-3*) Watsn-Guptill.

Zodiac 13. Ed. by Abitare Segesta Staff. (Illus.). 272p. 1995. pap. 29.00 (*0-8230-6413-1*, Whitney Lib) Watsn-Guptill.

Zodiac 14. Ed. by Abitare Segesta Staff. (Illus.). 272p. 1995. pap. 29.00 (*0-8230-6477-8*, Whitney Lib) Watsn-Guptill.

Zodiac 15. Abitare Segesta. 1996. pap. text ed. 31.00 (*0-8230-6513-8*) Watsn-Guptill.

Zodiac 16. Segesta Editrice Abitare Staff. 1996. pap. text ed. 31.00 incl. disk (*0-8230-6554-5*) Watsn-Guptill.

Zodiac 2. Segesta Editrice Arbitare Staff. (Illus.). 272p. 1995. pap. 29.00 (*0-8230-6401-8*) Watsn-Guptill.

Zodiac 4. Segesta Editrice Arbitare Staff. (Illus.). 272p. 1995. pap. 29.00 (*0-8230-6403-4*) Watsn-Guptill.

Zodiac 5. Segesta Editrice Arbitare Staff. (Illus.). 1995. pap. 29.00 (*0-8230-6404-2*) Watsn-Guptill.

Zodiac 7. Segesta Editrice Arbitare Staff. (Illus.). 272p. 1995. pap. 29.00 (*0-8230-6406-9*) Watsn-Guptill.

Zodiac 8. Segesta Editrice Arbitare Staff. (Illus.). 272p. 1995. pap. 29.00 (*0-8230-6408-5*) Watsn-Guptill.

Zodiac 9. Segesta Editrice Arbitare Staff. (Illus.). 272p. 1995. pap. 29.00 (*0-8230-6409-3*) Watsn-Guptill.

Zodiacal Archetypes in Celtic Myths. Helen O'Clery. Ed. by Al H. Morrison. (Illus.). 48p. (Orig.). 1993. pap. 11. 00 (*0-9626761-2-8*) Al H Morrison.

Zodiacal Symbology & Its Power. Isidore Kozminsky. 192p. 10.00 (*0-86690-122-1*, K1270-014) Am Fed Astrologers.

Zodiake of Life. Marcellus Palingenius. Tr. by Barnabe Googe. LC 48-275. 1977. reprint ed. 60.00 (*0-8201-1214-3*) Schol Facsimiles.

Zodicat Speaks: Discover Your Cat's Astrological Signature. Zodicat. LC 96-3410. 1996. pap. 12.95 (*0-670-86858-2*, Viking) Viking Penguin.

Zoe: The God-Kind of Life. Kenneth E. Hagin. 1981. pap. 3.95 (*0-89276-402-3*) Hagin Ministries.

Zoe & Columbo. Susan Shreve. (Illus.). 96p. (J). (gr. 3-4). 1995. 15.00 (*0-688-13552-8*, Tambourine Bks) Morrow.

Zoe & the Best Man (Wedding Belles) Carole Buck. (Desire Ser.). 1996. mass mkt. 3.50 (*0-373-05989-2*, 1-05989-8) Silhouette.

Zoe McCully: Park Ranger. Jennifer Bryant. (Working Moms: A Portrait of Their Lives Ser.). (Illus.). 40p. (J). (gr. 2-4). 1991. lib. bdg. 15.98 (*0-941477-54-1*) TFC Bks NY.

Zoe Rising. Pam Conrad. LC 95-42663. 144p. (J). (gr. 4 up). 1996. 13.95 (*0-06-027217-1*); lib. bdg. 13.89 (*0-06-027218-X*) HarpC Child Bks.

***Zoe Rising.** Pam Conrad. LC 95-42663. (Trophy Book Ser.). (Illus.). 144p. (J). (gr. 4 up). 1997. pap. 4.50 (*0-06-440687-3*, Trophy) HarpC Child Bks.

Zoe's Cats. Zoe Stokes. LC 81-53055. (Illus.). 1982. 14.95 (*0-500-01273-3*) Thames Hudson.

***Zoe's Flower.** Beverly Kline. (J). 1998. 3.99 (*0-679-88900-0*) Random Bks Yng Read.

Zoe's Gift. Sheila Hayes. LC 93-42621. 144p. (J). 1994. pap. 14.99 (*0-525-67484-5*, Lodestar Bks) Dutton Child Bks.

Zoe's Gift. Leslie B. Hedley. (Orig.). 1995. pap. 12.95 (*0-87579-880-2*) Deseret Bk.

Zoe's Sheep. Rose Bursik. (Illus.). 32p. (J). 1996. pap. 5.95 (*0-8050-4642-9*) H Holt & Co.

***Zoe's Webs.** Thomas West & Judy Lambert. (FRE.). (J). pap. 6.99 (*0-590-73572-1*) Scholastic Inc.

Zoetrope Book. 2nd ed. Roger Kukes. LC 85-80709. (Illus.). 144p. 1989. reprint ed. pap. 14.95 (*0-9622330-0-5*) Klassrm Kinetics.

Zoey Fools Around. Katherine Applegate. 272p. 1994. mass mkt. 3.99 (*0-06-106202-2*, Harp PBks) HarpC.

Zofingia Lectures: The Collected Works of C. G. Jung. Carl G. Jung. Ed. by William McGuire. Tr. by Jan van Heurck. LC 83-42592. (Bollingen Ser.: Vol. XX). (Illus.). 160p. 1985. text ed. 29.95 (*0-691-09899-9*) Princeton U Pr.

***Zofloya: Or, the Moor.** Charlotte Dacre. Ed. & Intro. by Kim I. Michasiw. (The World's Classics Ser.). 320p. 1997. pap. 11.95 (*0-19-283239-5*) OUP.

Zohar, 5 vols., t. Tr. by Maurice Simon & Paul Levertoff. 1934. 100.00 (*0-900689-39-0*) Bloch.

Zohar: Bereshith. 4th rev. ed. Nurho De Manhar. LC 75-160173. (Secret Doctrine Reference Ser.). 432p. 1995. 25.00 (*0-913510-65-3*) Wizards.

Zohar: Hebrew Text, 10 vols. Shimon Bar Yohai. 1981. write for info. (*0-943688-68-X*) Res Ctr Kabbalah.

Zohar: Hebrew Text, 24 vols. Shimon Bar Yohai. 1992. Set. 345.00 (*0-943688-67-1*) Res Ctr Kabbalah.

Zohar: Parashat Pinhas, Vol. II. Tr. by Philip S. Berg from ARC. 256p. 1987. 12.95 (*0-943688-52-3*); pap. 12.95 (*0-943688-53-1*) Res Ctr Kabbalah.

Zohar: Parashat Pinhas, Vol. III. Tr. by Philip S. Berg. 256p. 1988. 12.95 (*0-943688-54-X*); pap. 12.95 (*0-943688-55-8*) Res Ctr Kabbalah.

Zohar: Parshat Pinhas, Vol. I. Tr. by Philip S. Berg. 288p. 1986. 13.95 (*0-943688-50-7*); pap. 13.95 (*0-943688-51-5*) Res Ctr Kabbalah.

Zohar: Parshat Pinhas I. Philip S. Berg. 15p. (SPA.). 1992. pap. 12.95 (*0-924457-78-3*) Res Ctr Kabbalah.

Zohar: Parshat Pinhas II. Philip S. Berg. 15p. (SPA.). 1993. pap. 12.95 (*0-924457-80-5*) Res Ctr Kabbalah.

Zohar: Parshat Pinhas III. Philip S. Berg. 256p. (SPA.). 1993. pap. 12.95 (*0-924457-82-1*) Res Ctr Kabbalah.

Zohar: The Book of Splendor; Basic Readings from the Kabbalah. Gershom G. Scholem. 1995. pap. 12.00 (*0-8052-1034-2*) Schocken.

Zohar-English Only, 5 vols. Set. 95.00 (*0-910218-91-9*) Bennet Pub.

Zohar, The Book of Enlightment. Daniel C. Matt. (Classics of Western Spirituality Ser.). 320p. 1982. pap. 19.95 (*0-8091-2387-8*) Paulist Pr.

Zohrab: An Introduction. Ed. & Tr. by Ara Baliozian. 79p. 1985. pap. 3.95 (*0-920553-00-1*) Natl Assn Arm.

Zoia! Memoir of Zoia Horn, Battler for the People's Right to Know. Zoia Horn. LC 94-44505. (Illus.). 334p. 1995. lib. bdg. 25.00 (*0-7864-0071-4*) McFarland & Co.

Zola. Emile Zola. Ed. by Marc Bernard. Tr. by Jean M. Leblon. LC 77-10959. (Illus.). 189p. 1977. reprint ed. text ed. 49.75 (*0-8371-9820-8*, BEZO, Greenwood Pr) Greenwood.

Zola: "L'Assommoir" David Baguley. (Landmarks of World Literature Ser.). (Illus.). 144p. (C). 1992. text ed. 36.95 (*0-521-38426-5*) Cambridge U Pr.

Zola: A Life. Frederick Brown. LC 94-33758. (Illus.). 888p. 1995. 37.50 (*0-374-29742-8*) FS&G.

Zola: A Life. Frederick Brown. 888p. 1996. reprint ed. pap. 24.95 (*0-8018-5463-6*) Johns Hopkins.

Zola: La Bete Humaine - Texte et Explications, Colloque du Centenaire. Geoff Woollen. 240p. 1993. 59.00 (*0-85261-279-6*, Pub. by Univ of Glasgow UK) St Mut.

Zola: Therese Raquin. Ed. by B. Nelson. (Bristol French Texts Ser.). 188p. (FRE.). 1993. pap. 19.95 (*1-85399-287-9*, Pub. by Brstl Class Pr UK) Focus Pub-R Pullins.

Zola & the Craft of Fiction. Ed. by Robert Lethbridge & Terry Keefe. 240p. 1990. text ed. 49.00 (*0-7185-1312-6*) St Martin.

Zola & the Craft of FIction. Ed. by Robert Lethbridge & Terry Keefe. 188p. 1993. pap. 14.95 (*1-85567-166-2*) St Martin.

Zola & the Dreyfus Case. Lee M. Friedman. 1972. 250.00 (*0-87968-029-6*) Gordon Pr.

Zola & the Dreyfus Case. Lee M. Friedman. (World History Ser.: No. 48). (Illus.). 1970. reprint ed. lib. bdg. 75.00 (*0-8383-0092-8*) M S G Haskell Hse.

Zola Dictionary. J. G. Patterson. 1972. 75.00 (*0-8490-1350-X*) Gordon Pr.

Zola Dictionary: The Characters of the Rougon-Macquart Novels of Emile Zola. J. G. Patterson. xi, 232p. 1973. reprint ed. 42.90 (*3-487-04854-X*) G Olms Pubs.

Zola et les Genres. David Baguley. 208p. 1993. 60.00 (*0-85261-278-8*, Pub. by Univ of Glasgow UK) St Mut.

Zoland Books Poetry Post Card Collection. Roland F. Pease, Jr. LC 88-51097. 20p. (Orig.). 1989. pap. 5.95 (*0-944072-04-6*) Zoland Bks.

Zolar's Astrological Tarot. Zolar Staff. 32p. 1983. pap. 12. 00 (*0-88079-016-4*) US Games Syst.

Zolar's Book of Dreams, Numbers & Lucky Days. Zolar Staff. 272p. 1989. pap. 11.00 (*0-671-76599-X*, Fireside) S&S Trade.

Zolar's Book of Reincarnation: How to Discover Your Past Lives. Zolar Staff. (Illus.). 218p. 1996. pap. 12.00 (*0-684-80969-9*, Fireside) S&S Trade.

Zolar's Encyclopedia & Dictionary of Dreams. Zolar Staff. 420p. 1989. pap. 12.00 (*0-671-76600-7*, Fireside) S&S Trade.

Zolar's It's All in the Stars. Zolar Staff. 350p. (Orig.). 1993. pap. 12.00 (*0-671-76782-8*, Fireside) S&S Trade.

Zolar's Magick of Color. Zolar Staff. 224p. 1994. pap. 11.00 (*0-671-76854-9*, Fireside) S&S Trade.

Zolar's Starmates. Zolar Staff. 464p. 1988. pap. 12.00 (*0-671-76603-1*, Fireside) S&S Trade.

Zola's Crowds. Naomi Schor. LC 78-1564. 240p. reprint ed. pap. 68.40 (*0-317-42338-X*, 2025869) Bks Demand.

Zola's Son Excellence Eugene Rougon. Richard B. Grant. LC 60-6649. 154p. reprint ed. pap. 43.90 (*0-317-26760-4*, 2023392) Bks Demand.

Zoli's Legacy, Pt. 1: Inheritance. Dawn L. Watkins. Ed. by Carolyn Cooper. (Light Line Ser.). (Illus.). 190p. (Orig.). (YA). (gr. 7-12). 1991. pap. 6.49 (*0-89084-596-4*, 055699) Bob Jones Univ Pr.

Zoli's Legacy, Pt. 2: Bequest. Dawn L. Watkins. Ed. by Carolyn Cooper. (Light Line Ser.). 142p. (Orig.). (YA). (gr. 7-12). 1991. pap. 6.49 (*0-89084-597-2*, 055707) Bob Jones Univ Pr.

***Zollie Tree.** rev. ed. Raymond E. Myers. (Filson Club Publications, Second Ser.: No. 2). (Illus.). 200p. 1997. reprint ed. 29.95 (*0-9601072-6-6*) Filson Club.

Zollikonor Seminars. Martin Heidegger. (Phenomenology & Existential Philosophy Studies). 42.95 (*0-8101-1102-0*); pap. 17.95 (*0-8101-1126-8*) Northwestern U Pr.

Zollverein. 2nd ed. W. O. Henderson. 375p. 1968. reprint ed. 37.50 (*0-7146-1322-3*, Pub. by F Cass Pubs UK) Intl Spec Bk.

Zoltan Kodaly, a Hungarian Musician. Percy M. Young. LC 75-45268. (Illus.). 231p. 1976. reprint ed. text ed. 41. 50 (*0-8371-8650-1*, YOZK, Greenwood Pr) Greenwood.

Zoltan Szabo Watercolor Techniques. Zoltan Szabo. (Illus.). 96p. (Orig.). 1994. pap. 16.99 (*0-89134-516-7*, North Lght Bks) F & W Pubns Inc.

Zoltan Szabo's 70 Favorite Watercolor Techniques. Zoltan Szabo. LC 95-1151. (Illus.). 144p. 1995. 28.99 (*0-89134-573-6*, North Lght Bks) F & W Pubns Inc.

Zoltan the Magnificent. Bob Graham. (Illus.). 32p. (J). (gr. k-3). 1995. 12.95 (*0-85091-648-8*, Pub. by Lothian Pub AT) Seven Hills Bk.

Zombie. Joyce Carol Oates. LC 95-8090. 181p. 1995. pap. 19.95 (*0-525-94045-6*, Dutton) NAL-Dutton.

Zombie. Joyce Carol Oates. 1996. pap. 16.95 (*0-14-086216-1*) Viking Penguin.

Zombie. Joyce Carol Oates. 192p. 1996. pap. 10.95 (*0-452-27500-8*, Dutton-W Abrahams Bk) NAL-Dutton.

Zombie Jamboree. Robert B. Merken. LC 86-745. Date not set. pap. write for info. (*0-688-01949-8*, Quill) Morrow.

Zombie Mystery Paintings: The Art Of... Robert Williams. 1991. pap. 24.95 (*0-86719-381-6*) Last Gasp.

Zombie Queen. Don Whittington. (Orig.). (J). 1996. pap. 3.50 (*0-380-78411-4*, Camelot) Avon.

***Zombie Saturday Night.** Terry M. West. (Confessions of a Teenage Vampire Ser.). (Illus.). (J). (gr. 4-7). 1997. mass mkt. 4.99 (*0-590-10467-5*) Scholastic Inc.

Zombie Surf Commandos from Mars. Tony Abbott. (Weird Zone Ser.: No. 1). (J). (gr. 2-5). 1996. pap. 2.99 (*0-590-67433-1*) Scholastic Inc.

Zombies Don't Do Windows. Erica Farber & J. R. Sansevere. LC 95-6799. (Creepy Critters Ser.). (Illus.). 80p. (J). (gr. 1-5). 1996. pap. 3.99 (*0-679-87361-9*, Bullseye Bks) Random Bks Yng Read.

Zombies Don't Play Soccer: The Adventures of the Bailey School Kids. Debbie Dadey. 96p. (J). 1995. pap. 2.99 (*0-590-22636-3*) Scholastic Inc.

***Zombies from the Beyond.** James Valcq. 1997. pap. 5.25 (*0-8222-1611-6*) Dramatists Play.

Zombies of the Gene Pool. Sharyn McCrumb. 1993. mass mkt. 5.99 (*0-345-37914-4*) Ballantine.

Zombies of the Gene Pool: A Jay Omega Mystery. Sharyn McCrumb. 192p. 1992. 18.00 (*0-671-70526-1*) S&S Trade.

Zombification: Stories from NPR. Andrei Codrescu. 1995. pap. 12.00 (*0-312-11933-X*) St Martin.

Zomo the Rabbit: A Trickster Tale from West Africa. Gerald McDermott. LC 91-14558. (Illus.). 32p. (J). (ps-3). 1992. 22.00 (*0-15-299967-1*, HB Juv Bks) HarBrace.

Zomo the Rabbit: A Trickster Tale from West Africa. Gerald McDermott. (Illus.). 32p. (J). (ps-3). 1996. pap. 22.00 (0-15-201011-4) HarBrace.

Zomo the Rabbit: A Trickster Tale from West Africa. Gerald McDermott. LC 91-14558. (Illus.). 32p. (J). (ps-3). 1996. pap. 5.00 (0-15-201010-6, Voyager Bks) HarBrace.

Zon. Gregory K. Morris. 367p. (Orig.). 1995. pap. text ed. 14.99 (0-9648617-0-4) ThreeTG Pr.

Zon the Dreamer: The Adventure of the Homeless One. Shukree Tilghman & Eleanor H. Tilghman. 100p. (J). (gr. 5-9). 1996. pap. 6.95 (1-888095-00-8) T E S T.

Zona Gale - Her Life & Writings: A Resource Guide. Jocelyn Riley. 114p. 1995. 20.00 (1-877933-08-2) Her Own Words.

Zona Home: Essential Designs for Living. Louis Sagar. LC 96-6195. 224p. 1996. 50.00 (0-06-270169-X) HarpC.

Zona Libre. Samuel E. Bell & James M. Smallwood. (Southwestern Studies: No. 69). 100p. 1982. pap. 5.00 (0-87404-129-5) Tex Western.

***Zonal Defending: The Flat Back Four... & All That Stuff.** Jack Detchon. Ed. by Bob Dunn. (Illus.). (Orig.). 1996. pap. 9.95 (1-896466-11-7) T Waiters.

Zonal Liver Cell Heterogeneity. Ed. by K. Jungermann. (Journal: Enzyme: Vol. 46, Nos. 1-3, 1992). (Illus.). 168p. 1992. pap. 46.25 (3-8055-5718-3) S Karger.

Zonal Polynomials. Akimichi Takemura. LC 84-47886. (IMS Lecture Notes - Monograph Ser.: Vol. 4). vi, 104p. 1984. pap. 15.00 (0-940600-05-6) Inst Math.

***Zonal Stratigraphy & Foraminifera of the Tethyan Jurassic, East Mediterranean.** K. Kuznetsova et al. 1996. text ed. 140.00 (2-88449-003-5) Gordon & Breach.

Zonas Arqueologicas: Tabasco. Isabel Fernandez et al. 110p. 1988. pap. 9.00 (968-6068-24-4, IN018) UPLAAP.

Zonas Arqueologicas: Yucatan. Adriana Velaquez et al. 129p. 1988. pap. 9.00 (968-6068-09-0, IN017) UPLAAP.

Zond. Mark Dunster. 45p. (Orig.). (J). 1989. pap. 5.00 (0-89642-168-6) Linden Pubs.

Zondervan Church & Nonprofit Organization Tax & Financial Guide. Daniel D. Busby. 208p. 1995. pap. 11. 99 (0-310-49701-9) Zondervan.

Zondervan Church & Nonprofit Organization Tax & Financial Guide, 1994. Donald D. Busby. 176p. 1993. pap. 11.99 (0-310-61641-7) Zondervan.

Zondervan Church & Nonprofit Organization Tax & Financial Guide, 1997. Daniel D. Busby. (Illus.). 208p. 1996. pap. 11.99 (0-310-21058-5) Zondervan.

Zondervan Classic Reference Library, 4 bks. 1994. pap. 31. 99 (0-310-48438-3) Zondervan.

Zondervan Compact Bible Dictionary. Ed. by T. Alton Bryant. 640p. 1972. pap. 8.99 (0-310-22082-3, 6726P) Zondervan.

***Zondervan Compact Bible Dictionary.** Ed. by T. Alton Bryant. 640p. 1993. 14.99 (0-310-48981-4) Zondervan.

Zondervan Compact Bible Dictionary. Ed. by T. Alton Bryant. 640p. 1993. reprint ed. 14.99 (0-310-40180-1) Zondervan.

Zondervan Family Cookbook. Patricia Gundry. 416p. 1993. 19.95 (1-882169-01-8) Suitcase Bks.

Zondervan Minister's Tax & Financial Guide, 1994. Daniel D. Busby. 144p. 1993. pap. 14.99 (0-310-61651-4) Zondervan.

Zondervan Minister's Tax & Financial Guide, 1996. Daniel D. Busby. 176p. 1995. pap. 14.99 (0-310-49711-6) Zondervan.

Zondervan Minister's Tax & Financial Guide, 1997. Daniel D. Busby. (Illus.). 176p. 1996. pap. 14.99 (0-310-21060-7) Zondervan.

***Zondervan NIV Bible Commentary, 2 vols.** Incl. Vol. 1. Old Testament. Kenneth Barker & John R. Kohlenberger, III. 1500p. 1994. 35.99 (0-310-57850-7); Vol. 2. New Testament. Kenneth L. Baker & John R. Kohlenberger, III. 1250p. 1994. 32.99 (0-310-57840-X); 59.99 (0-310-57858-2) Zondervan.

***Zondervan Pastor's Annual: An Idea & Resource Book.** T. T. Crabtree. 448p. 1997. pap. 15.99 (0-310-21398-3) Zondervan.

Zondervan Pastor's Annual, 1997: An Idea & Resource Book. annuals T. T. Crabtree. 416p. 1996. 15.99 (0-310-20963-3) Zondervan.

***Zondervan Pictorial Bible Dictionary.** Ed. by J. D. Douglas & Merrill Tenney. (Illus.). 1993. 24.99 (0-310-40138-0) Zondervan.

Zondervan Pictorial Bible Dictionary. Merrill C. Tenney. (Illus.). 1988. 24.99 (0-310-23560-X, 6745) Zondervan.

Zondervan Pictorial Encyclopedia of the Bible, 5 vols. Ed. by Merrill C. Tenney. (Illus.). 1975. 159.99 (0-310-33188-9, 6700) Zondervan.

Zone: A Dietary Road Map. Barry Sears. 336p. 1996. mass mkt. 5.99 (0-06-101000-6) HarpC.

Zone: A Dietary Road Map. Barry Sears. 304p. 1997. pap. 12.00 (0-06-098706-5) HarpC.

Zone: A Dietary Road Map to Lose Weight Permanently, Reset Your Genetic Code, Prevent Disease & Achieve Maximun Physical Performance. Barry Sears & Bill Lawren. 288p. 1995. 25.00 (0-06-039150-2, ReganBooks) HarpC.

***Zone: A Dietary Roadmap.** Barry Sears. 304p. 1997. pap. 72.00 (0-06-098804-5, ReganBooks) HarpC.

Zone Chiro (Simplified) F. T. Bailey. 48p. 1969. reprint ed. spiral bd. 6.00 (0-7873-0063-2) Hlth Research.

Zone du Jour. Dan Raphael. 28p. (Orig.). 1981. pap. 5.50 (0-937013-00-5) Potes Poets.

***Zone Free of Weapons of Mass Destruction in the Middle East.** Jan Prawitz et al. 134p. 1996. pap. 25.00 (92-9045-114-9) UN.

Zone Garden: A Surefire Guide to Gardening in Zones 3, 4, 5. Charlotte Frieze. LC 96-46057. 1997. pap. 22.95 (0-684-82465-5, Fireside) S&S Trade.

Zone Garden: A Surefire Guide to Gardening in Zones 5, 6, 7. Charlotte Frieze. LC 96-46057. 1997. pap. 22.95 (0-684-82560-0, Fireside) S&S Trade.

Zone Garden: A Surefire Guide to Gardening in Zones 8, 9, 10. Charlotte Frieze. LC 96-46057. 1997. pap. 22.95 (0-684-82561-9, Fireside) S&S Trade.

Zone Journals. Charles Wright. 1989. pap. 8.95 (0-374-52112-3, Noonday) FS&G.

***Zone Meals in Minutes.** Graybow. 1998. pap. 12.00 (0-684-84877-5) S&S Trade.

Zone, No. 2: Blind Fire. James Rouch. 1985. mass mkt. 2.50 (0-8217-1588-7, Zebra Kensgtn) Kensgtn Pub Corp.

Zone No. 3 English. (Illus.). (Orig.). (J). (gr. 4-5). 1993. pap. text ed. 6.50 (0-9627574-1-1) L M Dechochran.

Zone of Emergence: A Case Study of an Older Suburb. George S. Sternlieb & W. Patrick Beaton. LC 78-186710. 220p. 1972. 29.95 (0-87855-035-6) Transaction Pubs.

Zone of Engagement. Perry Anderson. 400p. (C). 1992. pap. text ed. 22.00 (0-86091-595-6, Pub. by Vrso UK) Norton.

***Zone Offenses for Men's & Women's Basketball.** Harry L. Harkins & Jerry Krause. 1997. 15.00 (1-57167-139-0) Sagamore Pub.

Zone Policeman 88: A Close Range Study of the Panama Canal & Its Workers. Harry A. Franck. LC 71-111713. (American Imperialism: Viewpoints of United States Foreign Policy, 1898-1941 Ser.). 1970. reprint ed. 23.95 (0-405-02019-8) Ayer.

Zone Reflex Plus Translation Diet: Hydro-Therapy & Swedish Massage. Joe S. Riley & W. E. Daglish. 78p. 1961. reprint ed. spiral bd. 16.00 (0-7873-1124-3) Hlth Research.

Zone Soldiers. Daniel Ransom. 1996. pap. 5.99 (0-88677-737-2) DAW Bks.

Zone System Craftbook: A Comprehensive Guide to the Zone System of Exposure & Development. John C. Woods. 176p. (C). 1992. per. write for info. (0-697-13190-4) Brown & Benchmark.

Zone System for 35mm Photographers. Carson Graves. (Illus.). 112p. (C). 1982. pap. 29.95 (0-240-51773-3, Focal) Buttrwrth-Heinemann.

Zone System for 35mm Photographers: A Basic Guide to Exposure Control. 2nd ed. Carson Graves. LC 96-17703. (Illus.). 144p. 1996. pap. 29.95 (0-240-80203-9, Focal) Buttrwrth-Heinemann.

Zone Systemizer. Richard D. Zakia & John Dowdell, III. LC 73-87272. 63p. 1973. pap. 33.00 (0-87100-040-7) Morgan.

Zone Therapy. Anika Bergson. 1989. mass mkt. 3.95 (1-55817-208-4, Pinncle Kensgtn) Kensgtn Pub Corp.

Zone Therapy. Harry B. Bressler. 173p. 1971. reprint ed. spiral bd. 12.00 (0-7873-1221-5) Hlth Research.

Zone Therapy. William H. Fitzgerald et al. 982p. 1994. reprint ed. spiral bd. 35.00 (0-7873-1167-7) Hlth Research.

Zone Therapy: Regeneration through Nerve Pressure. Benedict Lust. (Illus.). 1980. pap. 3.95 (0-87904-038-6) Lust.

Zone Therapy: Using Foot Massage. 3rd ed. Astrid I. Goosmann-Legger. (Illus.). 128p. pap. 14.95 (0-8464-4315-5) Beekman Pubs.

Zone Therapy Is Scientific: Subjectively & Objectively. W. D. Chesney. 9p. 1969. reprint ed. spiral bd. 6.50 (0-7873-0169-8) Hlth Research.

Zone Therapy Using Foot Massage. Astrid Goosemann-Legger. 112p. 1986. pap. 11.95 (0-85207-170-1, Pub. by C W Daniel UK) Natl Bk Netwk.

Zone Training. Edwards. 1995. pap. write for info. (0-8092-3397-5) Contemp Bks.

Zone VI Workshop. Fred Picker. (Illus.). 128p. 1978. 13.95 (0-8174-0574-7, Amphoto) Watsn-Guptill.

Zones of Contention: Essays on Art, Institutions, Gender, & Anxiety. Carol Becker. LC 95-32373. (SUNY Series, Interruptions). (Illus.). 268p. (C). 1996. pap. 17.95 (0-7914-2938-5); text ed. 54.50 (0-7914-2937-7) State U NY Pr.

***Zones of Life, 2 vols.** Alan C. Walter. Ed. by Beverly Miles. (Illus.). 258p. 1994. ring bd. 197.00 (1-57569-034-9) Wisdom Pubng.

Zones of the Spirit. Amlin Gray. 1984. pap. 5.25 (0-8222-1294-3) Dramatists Play.

Zones of the Spirit. August Strindberg. LC 73-21632. (Studies in Scandinavian Life & Literature: No. 18). 1974. lib. bdg. 75.00 (0-8383-1758-8) M S G Haskell Hse.

***Zones of Thought Sequel, No. 2.** Vinge. Date not set. write for info. (0-312-85683-0) St Martin.

***Zoni English System, No. 1.** Zoilo C. Nieto & Pat Ossa. Ed. by Keith W. Hansen. (Illus.). 148p. 1996. pap. text ed. 15.00 (0-9658015-0-0) Zoni Language.

Zoning: The Laws, Administration, & Court Decisions During the First Twenty-Five Years. Edward M. Bassett. LC 73-11916. (Metropolitan America Ser.). 280p. 1974. reprint ed. 19.95 (0-405-05385-1) Ayer.

Zoning & Land Use Controls, 10 vols., Set. Patrick J. Rohan. 1977. ring bd. write for info. (0-8205-1845-X) Bender.

Zoning & Planning Deskbook. Douglas W. Kmiec. LC 85-16833. (Real Property - Zoning Ser.). 1986. ring bd. 145. 00 (0-87632-479-0) Clark Boardman Callaghan.

***Zoning & Planning Law Handbook, 1996.** Alan M. Forrest. (Real Property - Zoning Ser.). 1996. write for info. (0-8366-1033-4) Clark Boardman Callaghan.

Zoning & Property Rights: A Theory & Hong Kong Case Studies. Lawrence L. Wai-chung. (Illus.). 192p. (Orig.). 1996. pap. 34.00 (962-209-405-8, Pub. by Hong Kong Univ Pr HK) Coronet Bks.

Zoning & Subdivision Law in Virginia: A Handbook. 1980. 4.00 (0-317-69892-3) U VA Ctr Pub Serv.

Zoning & the American Dream: Promises Still to Keep. Ed. by Charles M. Haar & Jerold S. Kayden. LC 88-71466. 386p. 1989. lib. bdg. 45.00 (0-918286-57-3) Planners Pr.

Zoning Board Manual. Frederick H. Bair, Jr. LC 84-60300. 132p. 1984. pap. 23.95 (0-918286-32-8) Planners Pr.

Zoning Board of Adjustment in North Carolina. rev. ed. Michael B. Brough & Philip P. Green, Jr. 128p. (C). 1984. pap. text ed. 9.50 (1-56011-150-X, 84.21) Institute Government.

***Zoning Board of Appeals Practice in New York.** Robert J. Flynn, Jr. 200p. 1996. 50.00 (0-614-26709-9, 4240) NYS Bar.

Zoning Game Revisited. Richard F. Babcock & Charles L. Siemon. LC 90-13471. 304p. 1985. pap. 14.50 (1-55844-116-6) Lincoln Inst Land.

Zoning Inspector. Jack Rudman. (Career Examination Ser.: C-2340). 1994. pap. 29.95 (0-8373-2340-1) Nat Learn.

Zoning Inspector II. Jack Rudman. (Career Examination Ser.: C-3079). 1994. pap. 34.95 (0-8373-3079-3) Nat Learn.

Zoning Law & Practice, 4 vols., Set. 4th ed. E. C. Yokley. 1981. 300.00 (0-87215-207-3) MICHIE.

Zoning Law & Practice, 8 vols., Set Incl. 1991 Cum. Suppl. 4th ed. E. C. Yokley. 1991. Set, incl. 1991 cum. suppl. suppl. ed. 95.00 (0-87473-790-7) MICHIE.

Zoning, Rent Control, & Affordable Housing. William Tucker. 72p. 1991. pap. 3.00 (0-932790-78-X) Cato Inst.

Zonitid Snails from Pacific Islands, 4 pts. in 3 vols., Pt. 1. H. B. Baker. (BMB Ser.). 1974. reprint ed. 25.00 (0-527-02266-7) Periodicals Srv.

Zonitid Snails from Pacific Islands, 4 pts. in 3 vols., Pt. 2. H. B. Baker. (BMB Ser.). 1974. reprint ed. 25.00 (0-527-02273-X) Periodicals Srv.

Zonitid Snails from Pacific Islands, 4 pts. in 3 vols., Pt. 3. H. B. Baker. (BMB Ser.). 1974. reprint ed. 25.00 (0-527-02274-8) Periodicals Srv.

Zonkey, the Donkey. Virginia Athey. (Illus.). 20p. (J). (ps-2). 1993. pap. 6.50 (0-922510-10-5) Lucky Bks.

Zonpower from Cyberspace. Frank R. Wallace. 352p. 1993. pap. 89.95 (0-911752-71-4) Neo-Tech Pub.

Zonpower Protection Kit, 2 vols. Wallace & Savage. (Illus.). 750p. 1991. pap. 100.00 (0-911752-65-X) Neo-Tech Pub.

Zoo. (Hidden Pictures Coloring Bks.). (Illus.). 48p. (Orig.). (J). (gr. k-4). 1987. pap. 3.95 (0-8431-1879-2) Price Stern Sloan.

Zoo. (Chubby Shape Bks.). (Illus.). 8p. (Orig.). (J). (ps). 1984. pap. 2.95 (0-671-49716-2, Litl Simon S&S) S&S Childrens.

Zoo. Gail Gibbons. LC 87-582. (Illus.). 32p. (J). (ps-3). 1987. lib. bdg. 14.89 (0-690-04633-2, Crowell Jr Bks) HarpC Child Bks.

Zoo. Gail Gibbons. (Illus.). (J). (gr. k-4). 1991. pap. 15.95 incl. audio (0-87499-210-9) Live Oak Media.

Zoo. Gail Gibbons. (Illus.). (J). (gr. k-4). 1991. 22.95 incl. audio (0-87499-211-7) Live Oak Media.

Zoo. Britta Jaschinski. (Illus.). 160p. 1996. 19.95 (0-7148-3472-6, Pub. by Phaidon Press UK) Chronicle Bks.

Zoo. Stuart A. Kallen. (Field Trips Ser.). (J). 1997. lib. bdg. 13.95 (1-56239-712-5) Abdo & Dghtrs.

Zoo. Gail Gibbons. LC 87-582. (Trophy Nonfiction Bk.). (Illus.). 32p. (J). (ps-3). 1991. reprint ed. pap. 4.95 (0-06-446096-7, Trophy) HarpC Child Bks.

Zoo, 4 bks., Set. Gail Gibbons. (Illus.). (J). (gr. k-4). 1991. pap. 33.95 incl. audio (0-87499-212-5) Live Oak Media.

Zoo: Avec: Le Fer et la Velours, Le Silence de la Mer, Vol. 1. Jean Vercors. 197p. (FRE.). 1978. pap. 24.95 (0-686-55146-X, 271860090X) Fr & Eur.

Zoo: First Readers. Jacqueline Harding. (Series 929). (Illus.). 28p. (J). (ps). 1992. 3.50 (0-7214-1490-7, Ladybrd) Penguin.

Zoo: Great Big Zoo Theme. Jean Warren. Ed. by Gayle Bittinger. LC 90-71743. (Great Big Theme Ser.). (Illus.). 48p. (Orig.). 1991. pap. 6.95 (0-911019-41-3, WPH 1403) Warren Pub Hse.

***Zoo: Ology.** Jerry Cooper. 24p. (Orig.). 1996. pap. 3.95 (1-889419-07-9) J Cooper.

Zoo: The Modern Ark. Jake Page. (Illus.). 192p. 1990. 35. 00 (0-8160-2345-X) Facts on File.

Zoo see Take Along Stories

Zoo Alphabet Book. Diane Hill. LC 94-96509. (Illus.). 54p. (J). (gr. k-5). 1995. lib. bdg. 19.95 (0-9643816-3-X); spiral bd. 15.95 (0-9643816-0-5) Hill Assocs.

***Zoo Alphabet Book & Activity Guide Set.** Diane Hill. LC 94-96509. (Illus.). 84p. 1997. pap. 19.95 (0-9643816-5-6) Hill Assocs.

Zoo Alphabet Book Kit. Diane Hill. LC 94-96509. (Illus.). 56p. (J). (gr. k-5). 1995. pap. 15.95 (0-9643816-1-3) Hill Assocs.

***Zoo Alphabet Book Kit & Activity Guide Set.** Diane Hill. LC 94-96509. (Illus.). 86p. 1997. pap. 19.95 (0-9643816-6-4) Hill Assocs.

Zoo Alphabet Book Kit Supplement, Filler Pages. Diane Hill. (Illus.). 2p. (J). (gr. k-5). 1995. pap. 1.00 (0-9643816-2-1) Hill Assocs.

Zoo & Cathedral. Nancy Johnson. 82p. (Orig.). 1996. pap. 12.00 (1-877727-58-X) White Pine.

Zoo & Wild Animal Medicine. 2nd ed. Murray E. Fowler. (Illus.). 1127p. 1986. text ed. 145.00 (0-7216-1013-7) Saunders.

Zoo & Wild Animal Medicine. 3rd ed. Murray E. Fowler. (Illus.). 864p. 1993. text ed. 105.00 (0-7216-3667-5) Saunders.

Zoo & Wild Animal Medicine: Current. 4th ed. Fowler. 1998. text ed. write for info. (0-7216-8664-8) HarBrace.

Zoo Animal Sticker Atlas. Carol Bloch. (Illus.). 32p. (J). (gr. k-6). 1993. reprint ed. pap. 3.95 (1-879424-18-5) Nickel Pr.

Zoo Animals. LC 90-48751. (Eye Openers Ser.). (Illus.). 24p. (J). (ps-k). 1991. bds. 7.95 (0-689-71406-8, Aladdin Paperbacks) S&S Childrens.

***Zoo Animals.** (Spotters Ser.). (Illus.). 32p. (J). 1997. pap. 4.95 (0-7894-1678-6) DK Pub Inc.

Zoo Animals. Byron Barton. (Illus.). 12p. (J). (ps). 1996. bds. 3.95 (0-694-00620-3, Festival) HarpC Child Bks.

Zoo Animals. Sandy Cortright. 80p. (J). (ps). 1990. pap. 6.95 (0-8120-4436-3) Barron.

Zoo Animals. Annie Ingle. LC 91-66561. (Chunky Bks.). (Illus.). 28p. (J). (ps). 1992. 3.99 (0-679-83070-7) Random Bks Yng Read.

Zoo Animals. Kaye Quinn. (Facts 'n' Fun Bks.). (Illus.). 80p. (Orig.). (J). (gr. k-4). 1991. pap. 2.95 (0-8431-2720-1) Price Stern Sloan.

Zoo Animals. Ingo Rieger. (Mini Fact Finders Ser.). 64p. 1991. pap. 4.95 (0-8120-4449-5) Barron.

Zoo Animals. Eileen Spinelli. (Childrens' Nature Library). (Illus.). 64p. (J). (gr. k-4). 1992. lib. bdg. 14.95 (1-878363-91-3, HTS Bks) Forest Hse.

Zoo Animals. Kim M. Thompson & Karen M. Hilderbrand. (Early Childhood Ser.). (Illus.). 24p. (J). (ps-2). 1995. pap. 9.98 incl. audio (1-882331-85-0, Twin417) Twin Sisters.

Zoo Animals. Zokeisha. (Chubby Board Bks.). (Illus.). 16p. (J). (ps). 1982. bds. 3.50 (0-671-44895-1, Litl Simon S&S) S&S Childrens.

Zoo Animals: A Smithsonian Guide. Michael H. Robinson & David Challinor. LC 94-48288. (Illus.). 256p. (J). 1995. 24.95 (0-02-860406-7); 18.00 (0-02-860407-5) Macmillan.

Zoo Animals: Alphabet Dot to Dot: Educational Activity-Coloring Book. Peter M. Spizzirri. Ed. by Linda Spizzirri. (Illus.). 32p. (J). (gr. k-3). 1992. pap. 1.25 (0-86545-208-3) Spizzirri.

Zoo Animals - Superdoodles. Beverly Armstrong. LC 93-80431. 32p. (J). (gr. 1-6). 1994. 4.95 (0-88160-230-2, LW325) Learning Wks.

Zoo Animals Action Ser, No. 1. Malcolm Whyte. (Action Sets Ser.). (Illus.). 24p. (Orig.). (J). (gr. 1 up). 1990. pap. 5.95 (0-8431-2741-4, Troubador) Price Stern Sloan.

Zoo Animals Hat Patterns & Activities. Patt Newbold & Anne Diebel. (Illus.). 46p. (J). (ps-4). 1996. pap. text ed. 8.95 (1-56422-990-4) Start Reading.

Zoo at Night. Martha Robinson. LC 94-12773. (Illus.). (J). 1995. text ed. 16.00 (0-689-50608-2, McElderry) S&S Childrens.

Zoo Babies see Books for Young Explorers

Zoo Book. Linda Koebner. 224p. (YA). 1994. 29.95 (0-312-85322-X) Forge NYC.

***Zoo Book.** Linda Koebner. 1997. pap. 19.95 (0-312-86271-7) St Martin.

Zoo Book. Jan Pfloog. (Golden Super Shape Bks.). (Illus.). 24p. (J). (ps-3). 1989. pap. 1.95 (0-307-58118-7, 10060, Golden Books) Western Pub.

***Zoo Book.** Linda Koebner. 1997. reprint ed. pap. 19.95 (0-614-29126-7) Tor Bks.

Zoo Book: A Guide to America's Best. Allen W. Nyhuis. LC 93-46925. (Illus.). 288p. (Orig.). 1994. pap. 14.95 (0-917120-13-2) Carousel Pr.

***Zoo Carousel Book.** Thunder Bay Press Staff. 1994. 10.95 (1-870956-79-6) Thunder Bay CA.

Zoo City: Reflections on the Decline & Fall of New York. 1992. lib. bdg. 75.00 (0-8490-5440-0) Gordon Pr.

Zoo Clues: Making the Most of Your Visit to the Zoo. Sheldon L. Gerstenfeld. (Illus.). 120p. (J). (gr. 2 up). 1993. pap. 4.99 (0-14-032813-0, Puffin) Puffin Bks.

***Zoo Crew.** Photos by Tom Arma. (Illus.). 14p. (J). (ps). 1997. bds. 5.95 (0-448-41142-3, G&D) Putnam Pub Group.

Zoo Crew. Daniel Donovan. (Illus.). 36p. 1989. pap. 8.95 (0-935133-30-5) CKE Pubns.

Zoo des Mots: Dictionnaire des Expressions Anamalieres: French-English-Spanish-German-Italian. Sylvie Girard. 192p. (FRE, GER & SPA.). 1989. pap. 26.95 (0-7859-8586-7, 0-245500960) Fr & Eur.

Zoo Doings. Alan Benjamin. (J). 1994. 3.95 (0-671-86599-4, Litl Simon S&S) S&S Childrens.

Zoo Doings: Animal Poems. Jack Prelutsky. LC 82-11996. (Illus.). 80p. (J). (gr. 1-3). 1983. 15.00 (0-688-01782-7); lib. bdg. 14.93 (0-688-01784-3) Greenwillow.

Zoo Dreams. Cor Hazelaar. LC 96-19438. 1997. write for info. (0-374-39730-9) FS&G.

Zoo Faces. Andrews & McMeel Staff. (Cuddly Cloth Bks.). 1996. 12.95 (0-8362-1492-7) Andrews & McMeel.

Zoo for Mister Muster. Arnold Lobel. LC 62-7313. (Illus.). 32p. (J). (ps-3). 1962. lib. bdg. 13.89 (0-06-023991-3) HarpC Child Bks.

Zoo Friends. LC 90-80289. (Animal Photo Bks.). (Illus.). 24p. (J). (ps-2). 1991. pap. 1.95 (1-56288-077-2) Checkerboard.

***Zoo Garden.** Chris Hastings. (J). 1997. 19.95 (1-56352-393-0) Longstreet Pr Inc.

Zoo-hire Family Cookbook for Todd & Jamey, Made with Love, by Mom & the Cats. Janet L. Rider-Zerhire. 344p. Date not set. pap. 22.95 (0-9649010-0-5) Zoo-Hire.

Zoo in My Luggage. Gerald Durrell. 192p. 1976. pap. 7.95 (0-14-002084-5, Penguin Bks) Viking Penguin.

Zoo in Willy's Bed. Kate S. Gorman. (Illus.). 16p. (Orig.). (J). (gr. k-1). 1994. pap. 3.50 (1-880612-31-3) Seedling Pubns.

Zoo Is Blue: And Should Be Read. Jim Dixon. (Personalized Children's Book Ser.). (Illus.). 36p. (J). (gr. k-2). 1991. 12.95 (1-880453-01-0) J Hefty Pub.

Zoo-Looking. Mem Fox. LC 95-14171. (Illus.). (J). 1995. pap. write for info. (1-57255-011-2) Mondo Pubng.

Zoo-Looking. Mem Fox. LC 95-14171. (Illus.). 32p. (J). (ps-2). 1995. 14.95 (1-57255-010-4); write for info. (1-57255-012-0) Mondo Pubng.

Zoo Man: Inside the Zoo Revolution. Terry L. Maple & Erika Archibald. LC 91-61926. (Illus.). 224p. 1993. 19.95 (1-56352-016-8) Longstreet Pr Inc.

Zoo Manuscript. John Bennett. 1968. 5.00 (0-686-20739-4) Sydon.

Zoo Maze: Educational Activity-Coloring Book. Peter M. Spizzirri. Ed. by Linda Spizzirri. (Illus.). 32p. (J). (gr. k-3). 1992. pap. 1.25 (0-86545-204-0) Spizzirri.

Zoo Miracles: Creatures of Courage. Georgeanne Irvine. (Zoo World Ser.). (J). 1997. write for info. (0-689-80560-8) S&S Childrens.

Zoo Numbers. Alan Benjamin. (J). 1994. 3.95 (0-671-86601-X, Litl Simon S&S) S&S Childrens.

Zoo-Phonics en Espanol - Manual de Instruccion para Maestros. 2nd rev. ed. Georgene Bradshaw et al. (Illus.). 60p. (ENG & SPA.). 1994. reprint ed. teacher ed., pap. text ed. 16.95 (1-886441-17-0) Zoo-phonics.

Zoo-Phonics Level B Reader: (a-b-c) Georgene Bradshaw & Charlene A. Wrighton. (Readers Ser.). (Illus.). 48p. (J). (gr. 1). 1987. pap. text ed. 6.95 (0-9617342-2-1) Zoo-phonics.

Zoo-phonics Nature Notes. Charlene A. Wrighton et al. (Illus.). 23p. (Orig.). (J). (ps-3). 1991. pap. text ed. 16.95 (0-9617342-7-2) Zoo-phonics.

Zoo-Phonics Reader: Level A. Georgene E. Bradshaw & Charlene A. Wrighton. (Readers Ser.). (Illus.). 32p. (J). (ps-1). 1986. pap. text ed. 6.95 (0-9617342-1-3) Zoo-phonics.

Zoo-Phonics Reader: Level B (d-e-f) Georgene E. Bradshaw & Charlene A. Wrighton. (Readers Ser.). (Illus.). 48p. (J). (gr. 1). 1987. pap. text ed. 6.95 (0-9617342-3-X) Zoo-phonics.

Zoo-Phonics Reader: Level C (g-h-i) Georgene E. Bradshaw & Charlene A. Wrighton. (Readers Ser.). (Illus.). 48p. (J). (gr. 1). 1988. pap. text ed. 6.95 (0-9617342-4-8) Zoo-phonics.

Zoo Poems. Ed. by Jennifer W. Bosveld. (Orig.). 1988. pap. 10.00 (0-317-66652-5) Pudding Hse Pubns.

***Zoo Savers.** Dick Corman. LC 96-71658. 248p. (Orig.). 1996. mass mkt. 9.95 (0-9655749-0-3) Dume Pub.

Zoo Story & The Sandbox: Two Short Plays. Edward Albee. 1961. pap. 5.25 (0-8222-1295-1) Dramatists Play.

Zoo Superstars. Irvine. (J). 1995. 15.00 (0-671-87190-0, S&S Bks Young Read) S&S Childrens.

Zoo Wheel of Knowledge. Henri Cole. LC 89-45307. 1989. pap. 13.00 (0-679-72594-6) Knopf.

Zoo Worker. Judith B. Stamper. LC 88-10046. (What's It Like to Be a...Ser.). (Illus.). 32p. (J). (gr. k-3). 1997. pap. 3.95 (0-8167-1441-X) Troll Communs.

***Zoo Zipping.** Cyndi H. Deiters. 40p. (Orig.). (J). (gr. 1-3). 1997. pap. 8.99 (1-55197-951-9, Pub. by Comnwlth Pub CN) Partners Pubs Grp.

ZooAllergy: A Fun Story about Allergy & Asthma Triggers. Kim Gosselin. Ed. by Barbara Mitchell. (Illus.). 32p. (Orig.). (J). (gr. k-6). 1996. pap. 9.95 (0-9639449-4-0) JayJo Bks.

Zooarchaeology of Six Prehistoric Sites in the Sierra Blance Region, New Mexico. Jonathan C. Driver. (Technical Reports: No. 17). (Illus.). 103p. (Orig.). 1985. pap. 5.00 (0-915703-07-6) U Mich Mus Anthro.

Zoobooks Thematic Curriculum: Animal Babies. Maria Fitz-Patrick. 4p. 1996. pap. 2.50 (1-888153-06-7) Wildlife Educ.

***Zoobooks Thematic Curriculum: Animal Wonders.** Maria Hagedorn. (Illus.). 4p. 1998. teacher ed., pap. 2.50 (1-888153-26-1) Wildlife Educ.

Zoobooks Thematic Curriculum: Apes. Maria Fitz-Patrick. 4p. 1996. pap. 2.50 (1-888153-13-X) Wildlife Educ.

Zoobooks Thematic Curriculum: Bears. Maria Fitz-Patrick. 4p. 1996. pap. 2.50 (1-888153-07-5) Wildlife Educ.

Zoobooks Thematic Curriculum: Big Cats. Maria Fitz-Patrick. 4p. 1996. pap. 2.50 (1-888153-12-1) Wildlife Educ.

***Zoobooks Thematic Curriculum: Eagles.** Maria Hagedorn. (Illus.). 4p. 1997. teacher ed., pap. 2.50 (1-888153-25-3) Wildlife Educ.

Zoobooks Thematic Curriculum: Endangered Animals. Maria Fitz-Patrick. 4p. 1996. pap. 2.50 (1-888153-11-3) Wildlife Educ.

Zoobooks Thematic Curriculum: Giraffes. Maria Fitz-Patrick. 4p. 1996. pap. 2.50 (1-888153-09-1) Wildlife Educ.

***Zoobooks Thematic Curriculum: Koalas & Other Marsupials.** Maria Hagedorn. (Illus.). 4p. (Orig.). 1997. teacher ed., pap. 2.50 (1-888153-24-5) Wildlife Educ.

***Zoobooks Thematic Curriculum: Little Cats.** Maria Hagedorn. (Illus.). 4p. 1998. teacher ed., pap. 2.50 (1-888153-28-8) Wildlife Educ.

Zoobooks Thematic Curriculum: Owls. Maria Fitz-Patrick. 4p. 1997. pap. 2.50 (1-888153-16-4) Wildlife Educ.

***Zoobooks Thematic Curriculum: Penguins.** Maria Hagedorn. (Illus.). 4p. 1998. teacher ed., pap. 2.50 (1-888153-29-6) Wildlife Educ.

***Zoobooks Thematic Curriculum: Polar Bears.** Maria Hagedorn. (Illus.). 4p. (Orig.). 1997. teacher ed., pap. 2.50 (1-888153-18-0) Wildlife Educ.

Zoobooks Thematic Curriculum: Seals & Sea Lions. Maria Fitz-Patrick. 4p. 1997. pap. 2.50 (1-888153-15-6) Wildlife Educ.

***Zoobooks Thematic Curriculum: Sharks.** Maria Hagedorn. (Illus.). 4p. 1998. teacher ed., pap. 2.50 (1-888153-27-X) Wildlife Educ.

***Zoobooks Thematic Curriculum: Skunks & Their Relatives.** Maria Hagedorn. (Illus.). 4p. 1997. reprint ed. teacher ed., pap. 2.50 (1-888153-20-2) Wildlife Educ.

Zoobooks Thematic Curriculum: Snakes. Maria Fitz-Patrick. 4p. 1997. pap. 2.50 (1-888153-14-8) Wildlife Educ.

***Zoobooks Thematic Curriculum: Spiders.** Maria Hagedorn. (Illus.). 4p. 1997. teacher ed., pap. 2.50 (1-888153-21-0) Wildlife Educ.

***Zoobooks Thematic Curriculum: The Deer Family.** Maria Hagedorn. (Illus.). 4p. (Orig.). 1997. teacher ed., pap. 2.50 (1-888153-19-9) Wildlife Educ.

Zoobooks Thematic Curriculum: Tigers. Maria Fitz-Patrick. 4p. 1997. pap. 2.50 (1-888153-17-2) Wildlife Educ.

***Zoobooks Thematic Curriculum: Turtles.** Maria Hagedorn. (Illus.). 4p. (Orig.). 1997. teacher ed., pap. 2.50 (1-888153-23-7) Wildlife Educ.

Zoobooks Thematic Curriculum: Whales. Maria Fitz-Patrick. 4p. 1996. pap. 2.50 (1-888153-10-5) Wildlife Educ.

***Zoobooks Thematic Curriculum: Wild Dogs.** Maria Hagedorn. (Illus.). 4p. 1997. teacher ed., pap. 2.50 (1-888153-22-9) Wildlife Educ.

Zoobooks Thematic Curriculum: Wild Horses. Maria Fitz-Patrick. 4p. 1996. pap. 2.50 (1-888153-08-3) Wildlife Educ.

Zoodles. Bernard Most. (Illus.). 32p. (J). (PS-3). 1992. 14.00 (0-15-299969-8, HB Juv Bks) HarBrace.

Zoodles. Bernard Most. LC 91-33490. (Illus.). 32p. (J). (ps-3). 1994. pap. 20.00 (0-15-200071-2, HB Juv Bks) HarBrace.

Zooful of Animals. William Cole. LC 91-21885. (Illus.). 96p. (J). 1996. pap. 8.95 (0-395-77873-5, Sandpiper) HM.

Zooful of Animals. Illus. by Lynn Munsinger. 96p. (J). (ps-8). 1992. 17.95 (0-395-52278-1) HM.

Zoogeography. Philip J. Darlington, Jr. LC 79-26913. 690p. 1980. reprint ed. lib. bdg. 63.50 (0-89874-109-2) Krieger.

Zoogeography. Ed. by Carl L. Hubbs. LC 73-17826. (Natural Sciences in America Ser.). (Illus.). 524p. 1974. reprint ed. 39.95 (0-405-05744-X) Ayer.

Zoogeography in the Caribbean: The 1975 Leidy Medal Symposium. Ed. by Frank B. Gill. (Special Publication: No. 13). (Illus.). 128p. 1978. pap. 5.00 (0-910006-40-7) Acad Nat Sci Phila.

Zoogeography of Caribbean Insects. Ed. by James K. Liebherr. LC 87-47868. (Illus.). 304p. 1988. 47.50 (0-8014-2143-8) Cornell U Pr.

Zoogeography of Israel: The Distribution & Abundance at a Zoogeographical Crossroad. Ed. by Y. Yom-Tov & E. Tchernov. (Monographiae Biologicae). (C). 1988. lib. bdg. 314.50 (90-6193-650-0) Kluwer Ac.

Zoogeomorphology: Animals As Geomorphic Agents. David R. Butler. (Illus.). 225p. (C). 1995. text ed. 52.95 (0-521-43343-6) Cambridge U Pr.

Zookeepers. Amy Moses. LC 96-6141. (Career Bks.). 32p. (J). (gr. k-4). 1996. lib. bdg. 21.36 (1-56766-303-6) Childs World.

Zookeepers. William Russell. LC 93-42482. (Careers Ser.). (J). 1994. write for info. (1-57103-055-7) Rourke Pr.

Zookeeper's Bad Day. Pawnee Elementary School Third Graders. (Wee Write Bks.: No. 5). (Illus.). 25p. (J). (ps-3). 1995. pap. 8.95 (1-884987-19-2) WeWrite.

***Zookeeper's Sleepers.** Bungalo Books Staff. 1997. pap. text ed. 5.95 (0-921285-58-2, Pub. by Bungalo Bks CN) Firefly Bks Ltd.

***Zookeeper's Sleepers.** Frank B. Edwards. 1997. 16.95 (0-921285-55-8, Pub. by Bungalo Bks CN); pap. text ed. 5.95 (0-921285-54-X, Pub. by Bungalo Bks CN) Firefly Bks Ltd.

Zoolexicon. Garst. 1995. 39.95 (0-02-542805-5) Mac Pub USA.

***Zoological Catalogue of Australia Vol. 10: Hymenoptera: Apoidea.** J. C. Cardale. 406p. 1993. 59.95 (0-644-29080-3, Pub. by CSIRO AT) Aubrey Bks.

***Zoological Catalogue of Australia Vol. 12: Porifera.** J. N. Hooper & F. Wiedenmayer. 624p. 1994. 69.95 (0-643-05686-6, Pub. by CSIRO AT) Aubrey Bks.

***Zoological Catalogue of Australia Vol. 26: Psocoptera, Phthiraptera, Thysanoptera.** 418p. 79.95 (0-643-05888-5, Pub. by CSIRO AT) Aubrey Bks.

Zoological Exploration of Southern Africa 1650-1790. L. C. Rookmaaker. (Illus.). 392p. (C). 1989. text ed. 130.00 (90-6191-867-7, Pub. by A A Balkema NE) Ashgate Pub Co.

Zoological Mythology. A. Gubernatis. 1972. 69.95 (0-8490-1351-8) Gordon Pr.

Zoological Mythology or the Legends of Amimals, 2 Vols. Angelo De Gubernatis. Ed. by Kees W. Bolle. LC 77-79129. (Mythology Ser.). 1978. reprint ed. lib. bdg. 75.95 (0-405-10540-1) Ayer.

Zoological Philosophy: An Exposition with Regard to the Natural History of Animals. Jean B. Lamarck. Tr. by Hugh Elliot. LC 82-45842. reprint ed. 57.50 (0-404-19353-6) AMS Pr.

Zoological Record Search Guide. rev. ed. 600p. 1992. ring bd. 60.00 (0-916246-25-6) BIOSIS.

Zoological Record Search Guide. rev. ed. 550p. 1995. otabind 75.00 (0-916246-29-9) BIOSIS.

***Zoological Record Search Guide.** rev. ed. 750p. 1997. 85.00 (0-916246-33-7) BIOSIS.

Zoologico. (Illus.). 24p. (SPA.). (J). (ps-3). 1993. pap. 1.95 (0-307-70060-7, Golden Books) Western Pub.

Zoologico en la Cama de Jose. Kate Gorman. Tr. by Mariana Robles from ENG. (Illus.). 16p. (Orig.). (SPA.). (J). (gr. k-1). pap. 3.50 (1-880612-39-9) Seedling Pubns.

Zoologie: Generalites, Protozoaires, Metazoaires I, Vol. 1. Pierre P. Grasse & Andree Tetry. (Methodique Ser.). 1268p. 41.50 (0-686-56434-0) Fr & Eur.

Zoologie: Metazoaires, Vol. 2. Pierre P. Grasse & Andree Tetry. (Methodique Ser.). 1056p. 39.95 (0-686-56435-9) Fr & Eur.

Zoologie: Metazoaires, Vol. 3. Andree Tetry. (Methodique Ser.). 1336p. 48.95 (0-686-56436-7) Fr & Eur.

Zoologie: Tetrapodes, Vol. 4. Andree Tetry. (Methodique Ser.). 1664p. 69.95 (0-686-56437-5) Fr & Eur.

Zoologie, Vol. 1: Generalites, Protozoaires, Metazoaires I. Pierre P. Grasse & Andree Tetry. 1268p. (FRE.). 1953. 115.00 (0-7859-4548-2) Fr & Eur.

Zoologie, Vol. 2: Metazoaires. Pierre P. Grasse & Andree Tetry. 1056p. (FRE.). 1963. 115.00 (0-7859-4549-0) Fr & Eur.

Zoologie, Vol. 3: Metazoaires. Andree Tetry. 1336p. (FRE.). 1973. 130.00 (0-7859-4553-9) Fr & Eur.

Zoologisches Woerterbuch Palearktische Tiere. Michael Klemm. 854p. (GER, LAT & RUS.). 1973. 125.00 (0-8288-6349-0, M-7692) Fr & Eur.

Zoologist. Kim M. Thompson & Karen M. Hilderbrand. (I'd Like to Be a(n) Ser.). (Illus.). 24p. (J). (ps-4). 1996. student ed. 9.98 incl. audio (1-57583-020-5, TWIN 425) Twin Sisters.

Zoology. Mimi Bres. LC 93-1659. (Applied Science Review Ser.). (Illus.). 192p. 1993. pap. 12.95 (0-87434-571-5) Springhouse Pub.

Zoology. Dorit. (C). 1991. suppl. ed., teacher ed., pap. text ed. 34.00 (0-03-030508-X) HB Coll Pubs.

Zoology. Robert Dorit et al. 1136p. (C). 1991. text ed. 61.25 (0-03-030504-7) SCP.

Zoology. Stephen A. Miller & John P. Harley. 60p. (C). 1991. write for info. (0-697-14072-5); write for info. (0-697-09928-8) Wm C Brown Pubs.

Zoology. Stephen A. Miller & John P. Harley. (C). 1995. student ed. write for info. (0-697-25689-8) Wm C Brown Pubs.

Zoology. Larry Mitchell. (Illus.). 912p. (C). 1988. teacher ed. 19.95 (0-8053-2566-2); text ed. 56.95 (0-8053-2562-X); student ed., spiral bd. 31.25 (0-8053-2563-8) Benjamin-Cummings.

Zoology. 2nd ed. Stephen A. Miller & John P. Harley. 744p. (C). 1993. per. write for info. (0-697-13704-X) Wm C Brown Pubs.

Zoology. 2nd ed. Stephen A. Miller & John P. Harley. 744p. (C). 1993. text ed. write for info. (0-697-16952-9); Study guide. student ed., spiral bd. write for info. (0-697-13706-6) Wm C Brown Pubs.

Zoology. 2nd ed. Stephen A. Miller & John P. Harley. (C). 1994. student ed., ring bd. write for info. (0-697-24628-0) Wm C Brown Pubs.

***Zoology.** 3rd ed. Stephen A. Miller & John P. Harley. 776p. (C). 1997. pap. text ed. write for info. (0-07-114983-X) Wm C Brown Pubs.

Zoology. 3rd ed. Stephen A. Miller & John P. Harley. 752p. (C). 1995. per. 80.47 (0-697-24373-7) Wm C Brown Pubs.

Zoology. 3rd ed. Stephen A. Miller & John P. Harley. 752p. (C). 1995. text ed. 80.47 (0-697-24374-5) Wm C Brown Pubs.

Zoology. 3rd ed. Stephen A. Miller. 148p. (C). 1995. lab manual ed., spiral bd. write for info. (0-697-31405-7) Wm C Brown Pubs.

***Zoology.** 4th ed. Harley Miller. 1998. pap. text ed. 45.00 (0-697-34555-6); student ed., pap. text ed. 13.00 (0-697-34558-0) McGraw.

***Zoology.** 4th ed. Harley Miller. 1998. text ed. 52.00 (0-697-34556-4) McGraw.

Zoology, 1. 2nd ed. Stephen A. Miller & John P. Harley. 744p. (C). 1993. per. write for info. (0-697-16953-7) Wm C Brown Pubs.

Zoology, 3. 2nd ed. Stephen A. Miller & John P. Harley. 744p. (C). 1993. pap. text ed. write for info. (0-697-16955-3) Wm C Brown Pubs.

Zoology, 4. 2nd ed. Stephen A. Miller & John P. Harley. 744p. (C). 1993. per. write for info. (0-697-20486-3) Wm C Brown Pubs.

Zoology: A Course Manual. rev. ed. Anthony V. DeFina. (Illus.). 333p. 1991. reprint ed. teacher ed. 25.00 (0-916209-09-1) Owlet Pubns.

Zoology: A Course Manual. rev. ed. Anthony V. DeFina. (Illus.). 333p. (YA). (gr. 11 up). 1991. reprint ed. student ed., pap. 20.00 (0-916209-01-6) Owlet Pubns.

Zoology: An Introduction to the Study of Animals. Richard A. Boolootian. (Illus.). (C). 1979. teacher ed. write for info. (0-318-54253-6); student ed. write for info. (0-318-54254-4); student ed. write for info. (0-318-54255-2) Macmillan.

***Zoology: Custom University of New Brunswick.** Harris. (C). 1997. pap. text ed. write for info. (0-201-30464-3) Addison-Wesley.

Zoology: Forty-Nine Science Fair Projects. H. Steven Dashefsky. (J). (gr. 4-7). 1994. pap. text ed. 11.95 (0-07-015683-2) McGraw.

Zoology: High School Science Fair Experiments. H. Steve Dashefsky. LC 94-29631. 1994. pap. text ed. 12.95 (0-07-015687-5) McGraw-Hill Prof.

Zoology: High School Science Fair Experiments. H. Steven Dashefsky. LC 94-29631. 1995. text ed. 21.95 (0-07-015686-7) McGraw-Hill Prof.

Zoology: Schaum's Outline Series Theory & Problems. Nancy M. Jessop. 1988. pap. text ed. 13.95 (0-07-032551-0) McGraw.

Zoology: The Animal Kingdom. Stephen A. Miller & John P. Harley. 400p. (C). 1995. per. write for info. (0-697-29036-0) Wm C Brown Pubs.

***Zoology: The Animal Kingdom.** Stephen A. Miller & John P. Harley. 400p. (C). 1997. per. write for info. (0-07-114982-1) Wm C Brown Pubs.

Zoology Coloring Book. Lawrence M. Elson. (Illus.). 240p. 1982. pap. 15.00 (0-06-460301-6, CO301, Harper Ref) HarpC.

Zoology I: Mammals. Magnus Degerbol. LC 74-20244. (Thule Expedition, 5th, 1921-1924 Ser.: Vol. 2, Pts. 4-5). (Illus.). 1976. reprint ed. 72.50 (0-404-58309-1) AMS Pr.

***Zoology II.** Thule Expedition Staff. LC 76-19379. (Thule Expedition, 5th, 1921-1924 Ser.: Vol. 2, No. 6-9). 1937. reprint ed. 62.50 (0-404-58310-5) AMS Pr.

Zoology Illustrated. Gerald G. Farr. (Illus.). 130p. 1979. pap. text ed. 19.95 (0-89641-056-0) American Pr.

Zoology in Court. Ed. by Daniel Lunney. 100p. (C). 1992. text ed. 120.00 (0-9599951-7-X, Pub. by Surrey Beatty & Sons AT) St Mut.

Zoology Laboratory Notebook. Robert McMahon. 528p. (C). 1995. ring bd. 40.89 (0-7872-1545-7) Kendall-Hunt.

***Zoology Laboratory Workbook.** Marlin O. Cherry & Billy J. Hart. 266p. (C). 1997. spiral bd. 30.95 (0-7872-3245-9) Kendall-Hunt.

Zoology, the Animal Kingdom: A Complete Course in 1000 Questions & Answers. adapted ed. Nancy M. Jessop. LC 94-4560. Orig. Title: Schaum's Outline of Theory & Problems of Zoology. 1994. pap. text ed. 14.95 (0-07-032569-3) McGraw.

Zoolutions: A Mathematical Expedition with Topics for Grades 4 Through 8. Vaunda M. Nelson & Anne S. Burgender. (School Library Media Ser.: Vol. 6). 120p. (J). (gr. 4-8). 1996. pap. 24.50 (0-8108-3075-2) Scarecrow.

Zoom. Simon Armitage. LC 89-82482. 80p. (Orig.). 9000. pap. 14.95 (1-85224-078-4, Pub. by Bloodaxe Bks UK) Dufour.

Zoom. Istvan Banyai. (Illus.). 64p. (J). 1995. pap. 13.99 (0-670-85804-8, Viking) Viking Penguin.

Zoom. Istvan Banyai. 1998. pap. 4.99 (0-14-055774-1) Viking Penguin.

Zoom. Charles Fishman. 48p. (Orig.). 1990. pap. text ed. 7.00 (1-880286-01-7) Singular Speech Pr.

Zoom. Hironori Yasuda. (Super Special Background Patterns (SPATS) Ser.: No. 15). (Illus.). 208p. 1993. pap. 29.95 (4-87708-106-2, Pub. by KDC Co Ltd JA) Bks Nippan.

ZOOM! The Complete Paper Airplane Kit. Margaret A. Hartelius. LC 90-84671. (Illus.). 32p. (J). (ps-3). 1991. pap. 7.95 (0-448-40138-X, G&D) Putnam Pub Group.

Zoom, Car, Zoom. Suzy McPartland. (Pee Wee Pops Ser.). (Illus.). 12p. (J). (ps). 1994. bds. 4.95 (0-689-71750-4, Aladdin Paperbacks) S&S Childrens.

***Zoom City.** Thatcher Hurd. LC 96-49437. (J). 1998. write for info. (0-694-01057-X) HarpC.

***Zoom Fire Engine!** Iain Smyth. LC 96-35985. (J). 1997. 12.00 (0-517-70956-2) Crown Pub Group.

***Zoom Leneses II.** Ed. by Ellis I. Betensky et al. 22p. 1997. pap. 59.00 (0-8194-2551-6) SPIE.

Zoom Lens Photography. Raymond Bial. (Illus.). 112p. 1996. pap. 15.95 (0-936262-45-1) Amherst Media.

***Zoom! Zoom! I'm off to the Moon.** Dan Yaccarino. LC 96-52705. (J). 1997. 15.95 (0-590-95610-8) Scholastic Inc.

Zoomba in Toyland. Monica Mody. Ed. by Margie Larsen. LC 95-75422. (Illus.). 24p. (J). (ps-3). 1995. 5.95 (1-57064-045-9) Lyrick Pub.

Zoomba in Toyland. Monica Mody. Ed. by Margie Larsen. LC 95-75422. (Barney Book & Tape Ser.). (Illus.). 24p. (J). (ps-3). 1996. pap. 6.95 incl. audio (1-57064-095-5) Lyrick Pub.

***Zoomorphic Penannular Brooches.** H. Kilbride-Jones. (Illus.). 154p. 1980. 19.98 (0-85431-226-9, Pub. by Soc Antiquaries UK) David Brown.

Zoomrimes: Poems About Things That Go. Sylvia Cassedy. LC 90-1463. (Illus.). 64p. (J). (gr. 3-7). 1993. lib. bdg. 14.89 (0-06-022633-1) HarpC Child Bks.

Zoonomia, or the Laws of Organic Life, 2 Vols. Erasmus Darwin. LC 79-147964. reprint ed. Set. write for info. (0-404-08215-7) AMS Pr.

Zoonoses: Recognition, Control, & Prevention. Martin E. Hugh-Jones et al. (Illus.). 384p. 1995. text ed. 49.95 (0-8138-1821-4) Iowa St U Pr.

Zoonoses: Report of the FAO-WHO Expert Committee on Zoonoses, 3rd, Geneva, 1966. FAO-WHO Expert Committee on Zoonoses. (Technical Report Ser.: No. 378). 127p. (ENG, FRE, RUS & SPA.). 1967. pap. text ed. 7.00 (92-4-120378-1, 1100378) World Health.

***Zoonoses & Communicable Diseases Common to Man & Animals.** 2nd ed. (Paho Scientific Publication Ser.: No. 503). 983p. 1987. text ed. 60.00 (92-75-11503-6) World Health.

Zoonoses & Medicine: Subject, Reference & Research Guide. Susan C. Sondez. LC 87-47632. 160p. 1987. 44.50 (0-88164-566-4); pap. 39.50 (0-88164-567-2) ABBE Pubs Assn.

***Zooplankton: Sensory Ecology & Physiology.** Ed. by P. H. Lenz et al. 1997. text ed. 150.00 (90-5699-022-5) Gordon & Breach.

Zooplankton der Binnengewaesser Pt. 2: Freilebende Copepoda - Freeliving Stages of Freshwater Parasitic Copepoda. Frederick Kiefer & G. Fryer. (Binnengewaesser Ser.: Vol. 26). (Illus.). 380p. (ENG & GER.). 1978. lib. bdg. 59.40 (3-510-40036-4, Pub. by Schweizerbartsche GW) Lubrecht & Cramer.

Zooplankton of the Great Lakes: A Guide to the Identification & Ecology of the Common Crustacean Species. Mary D. Balcer et al. LC 83-27426. (Illus.). 256p. 1984. spiral bd. 35.00 (0-299-09820-6) U of Wis Pr.

Zoorific -- A Typewriting Simulation. 2nd ed. Clayton. (TA - Typing/Keyboarding Ser.). 1987. pap. 13.95 (0-538-11820-2) S-W Pub.

Zoos. Jason Cooper. LC 92-12555. (J). 1992. 12.67 (0-86593-212-3); 9.50 (0-685-59388-6) Rourke Corp.

Zoos. Karen Jacobson. LC 82-9545. (New True Bks.). (Illus.). 48p. (J). (gr. k-4). 1982. pap. 5.50 (0-516-41664-2) Childrens.

Zoos. Diane Yancey. LC 94-8546. (Lucent Overview Ser.). (Illus.). 112p. (J). (gr. 5-8). 1995. lib. bdg. 17.96 (1-56006-163-4) Lucent Bks.

Zoos: Identifying Propaganda Techniques. Terry O'Neill. LC 90-3247. (Opposing Viewpoints Juniors Ser.). (Illus.). 36p. (J). (gr. 3-6). 1990. pap. text ed. 12.96 (0-89908-600-4) Greenhaven.

XYZ

An Asterisk (*) at the beginning of an entry indicates that the title is appearing in BIP for the first time.

Zoos & Animal Rights: The Ethics of Keeping Animals. Stephen S. Bostock. LC 92-35167. 232p. (C). (gr. 13). 1993. pap. 16.95 (*0-415-05058-8*, B2230, Routledge NY); text ed. 69.95 (*0-415-05057-X*, B2226, Routledge NY) Routledge.

Zoos & Aquariums in the Americas: Directory, 1992-93. 60.00 (*0-686-16897-6*) Am Assoc Z Pk.

Zoo's Who: Babies. Irvine. (J). 1994. lib. bdg. 3.95 (*0-671-86602-8*, Litl Simon S&S) S&S Childrens.

Zoo's Who: Colors. Irvine. (J). 1994. lib. bdg. 3.95 (*0-671-86600-1*, Litl Simon S&S) S&S Childrens.

Zoos Without Cages. Judith E Rinard. LC 79-3243. (Books for World Explorers Series 2: No. 3). (Illus.). 104p. (J). (gr. 3-8). 1981. 8.95 (*0-87044-335-6*); lib. bdg. 12.50 (*0-87044-340-2*) Natl Geog.

Zoosporic Fungi in Teaching & Research. Ed. by Melvin S. Fuller & Alan Jaworski. (Palfrey Contributions in Botany Ser.: No. 3). (Illus.). 310p. (Orig.). (C). 1987. pap. text ed. 35.00 (*0-935460-02-0*) SE Pub Corp.

Zoosporic Fungi of India. R. Dayal & Usha Kiran. (C). 1988. 44.00 (*81-210-0228-1*, Pub. by Inter-India Pubns) S Asia.

Zoot Suit & Other Plays. Luis Valdez. LC 91-421789. 214p. (Orig.). 1992. pap. 13.00 (*1-55885-048-1*) Arte Publico.

Zoot-Suit Murders. Thomas Sanchez. LC 90-55670. 224p. 1991. pap. 12.00 (*0-679-73396-5*, Vin) Random.

Zoot Suit Riot: Mini-Play. (Mexican American Ser.). (J). (gr. 5 up). 1975. 5.00 (*0-89550-306-9*) Stevens & Shea.

Zoot-Suit Riots: The Psychology of Symbolic Annihilation. Mauricio Mazon. (Mexican American Monographs: No. 8). (Illus.). 179p. 1984. reprint ed. pap. 9.95 (*0-292-79803-2*) U of Tex Pr.

Zootoxins & Animal Envenomation. Fowler. 272p. 1992. 99.95 (*0-8493-6791-3*, SF757) CRC Pr.

Zootsuits & Second-Hand Dresses: An Anthology of Fashion & Music. Ed. by Angela McRobbie. 288p. (C). 1989. pap. 18.95 (*0-04-445237-3*) Routledge Chapman & Hall.

Zopiclone: A Third Generation of Hypnotics. Ed. by A. Schlosberg et al. (Journal: Pharmacology: Vol. 27, Suppl. 2). (Illus.). iv, 252p. 1984. pap. 59.25 (*3-8055-3788-3*) S Karger.

Zora. Mark Dunster. 19p. (Orig.). 1985. pap. 4.00 (*0-89642-128-7*) Linden Pubs.

Zora Hurston & the Chinaberry Tree. William Miller. LC 94-1291. (Illus.). 32p. (J). (gr. 1 up). 1994. 14.95 (*1-880000-14-8*) Lee & Low Bks.

Zora Hurston & the Chinaberry Tree. William Miller. LC 94-1291. (Illus.). 32p. (J). (ps up). 1996. pap. 5.95 (*1-880000-33-4*) Lee & Low Bks.

Zora in Florida. Ed. by Steve Glassman & Kathryn L. Seidel. 256p. 1991. pap. text ed. 19.95 (*0-8130-1061-6*); lib. bdg. 39.95 (*0-8130-1050-0*) U Press Fla.

Zora Neale Hurston: A Literary Biography. Robert E. Hemenway. LC 77-9605. (Illus.). 397p. 1980. 12.50 (*0-252-00807-3*) U of Ill Pr.

Zora Neale Hurston: A Storyteller's Life. enl. ed. Janelle Yates. (Unsung Americans Ser.). (Illus.). 98p. (J). (gr. 4-10). 1993. pap. 9.95 (*0-9623380-1-X*) Ward Hill Pr.

Zora Neale Hurston: A Storyteller's Life. enl. ed. Janelle Yates. LC 91-65559. (Unsung Americans Ser.). (Illus.). 98p. (J). (gr. 4-10). 1993. lib. bdg. 14.95 (*0-9623380-3-6*) Ward Hill Pr.

Zora Neale Hurston: Author. Paul Witcover. Ed. by Nathan I. Huggins. (Black Americans of Achievement Ser.). (Illus.). 112p. (YA). (gr. 5 up). 1991. lib. bdg. 19.95 (*0-7910-1129-1*) Chelsea Hse.

***Zora Neale Hurston: Author.** Paul Witcover. Ed. by Nathan I. Huggins. (Black Americans of Achievement Ser.). (Illus.). (YA). (gr. 5 up). 1992. pap. 8.95 (*0-7910-1154-2*) Chelsea Hse.

Zora Neale Hurston: Author. Paul Witcover. (Black American Ser.). (Illus.). 192p. (YA). 1994. mass mkt. 3.95 (*0-87067-782-9*, Melrose Sq) Holloway.

Zora Neale Hurston: Critical Perspectives Past & Present. Henry Louis Gates, Jr. & K. A. Appiah. LC 92-45759. (Literary Ser.). 330p. 1993. 24.95 (*1-56743-015-5*); pap. 14.95 (*1-56743-028-7*) Amistad Pr.

Zora Neale Hurston: Southern Storyteller. Della A. Yannuzzi. LC 95-36363. (African-American Biographies Ser.). 104p. (YA). (gr. 6 up). 1996. lib. bdg. 18.95 (*0-89490-685-2*) Enslow Pubs.

Zora Neale Hurston: Storyteller of the South. Roz Calvert. (Junior Black Americans of Achievement Ser.). (Illus.). 80p. (J). (gr. 3-6). 1993. lib. bdg. 15.95 (*0-7910-1766-4*) Chelsea Hse.

Zora Neale Hurston: Writer & Storyteller. Patricia McKissack & Fredrick McKissack. LC 92-2588. (Great African Americans Ser.). (Illus.). 32p. (J). (gr. 1-4). 1992. lib. bdg. 12.95 (*0-89490-316-0*) Enslow Pubs.

Zora Neale Hurston see Modern Critical Views Series

Zora Neale Hurston, Eulalie Spence, Marita Bonner, & Others: The Prize Plays & Other One-Acts Published in Periodicals. Gates. (African American Women Writers, 1910-1940 Ser.). 216p. 1996. 25.00 (*0-7838-1436-4*, Hall Reference) Macmillan.

Zora Neale Hurston Forum. Ed. by Ruthe T. Sheffey. 60p. (Orig.). 1986. pap. 18.00 (*0-9610324-8-0*) Morgan State.

***Zora Neale Hurston's Their Eyes Were Watching God.** Harold Bloom. (Bloom's Notes Ser.). (YA). 1997. text ed. 16.95 (*0-7910-4520-X*) Chelsea Hse.

Zora Neale Hurston's Their Eyes Were Watching God see Modern Critical Interpretations

Zorach Explains Sculpture: What It Means & How It Is Made. William Zorach. LC 95-36242. (Illus.). 312p. Date not set. reprint ed. pap. 12.95 (*0-486-29048-4*) Dover.

***Zorah's Magic Carpet.** large type ed. Stefan Czernecki. (Illus.). 32p. (J). (gr. k-4). 1995. 14.95 (*1-895340-06-3*, Pub. by Hyperion Pr Ltd CN) Sterling.

Zorah's Margic Carpet. Stefan Czernecki. LC 94-24529. 32p. (J). (gr. k-4). 1996. 14.95 (*0-7868-0081-X*); lib. bdg. 14.89 (*0-7868-2066-7*) Hyprn Child.

Zora's House. Romonia G. O'Bannon. (J). 1994. 7.95 (*0-533-11056-4*) Vantage.

Zorastrians of Iran: Conversion, Assimilation, or Persistence. Amighi J. Kestenberg. LC 89-45374. (Studies in Anthropology: No. 3). 1989. 69.50 (*0-404-62603-3*) AMS Pr.

Zorba. Kander & Ebb. 40p. 1983. pap. 8.95 (*0-7935-3298-1*, 00361935) H Leonard.

Zorba the Buddha Rajneesh Cookbook. Zorba the Buddha Rajneesh Restaurants Staff. LC 84-61260. 240p. (Orig.). 1984. pap. 4.95 (*0-918963-00-1*) Osho America.

Zorba the Greek. Nikos Kazantzakis. 314p. 1971. pap. 11.00 (*0-671-21132-3*, Touchstone Bks) S&S Trade.

Zorba the Greek. Nikos Kazantzakis. 1996. pap. 11.00 (*0-684-82554-6*) S&S Trade.

Zorba the Greek. Nikos Kazantzakis. 1993. reprint ed. lib. bdg. 26.95 (*1-56849-178-6*) Buccaneer Bks.

***Zorba the Hutt's Revenge.** Paul Davids & Hollace Davids. LC 97-21969. (Star Wars Ser.). (J). 1997. lib. bdg. write for info. (*0-8368-1991-8*) Gareth Stevens Inc.

Zorina Ballerina. Enzo Giannini. LC 91-21970. (Illus.). 40p. (J). (ps-1). 1993. pap. 14.00 (*0-671-74776-2*, S&S Bks Young Read) S&S Childrens.

Zork. George A. Effinger. (INFOCOM Ser.: No. 5). 320p. 1990. mass mkt. 4.50 (*0-380-75388-X*) Avon.

Zork: Nemesis the Official Strategy Guide. Bradygames Staff. 300p. 1996. 19.99 (*1-56686-413-5*) Brady Pub.

***Zork Inquisitor: The Official Strategy Guide.** Prima Publishing Staff. 240p. 1997. per. 19.99 (*0-7615-1230-6*) Prima Pub.

Zork Nemesis. Rick Barba. 160p. 1996. per., pap. 14.99 (*0-7615-0711-6*) Prima Pub.

Zorn's Engraved Work, Set, Vols. 1 & 2. Karl Asplund. (Illus.). 666p. 1990. reprint ed. Set. 295.00 (*1-55660-034-8*) A Wofsy Fine Arts.

Zoroaster. Francis M. Crawford. LC 06-30882. 1885. 11.00 (*0-403-00100-5*) Scholarly.

Zoroaster. Francis M. Crawford. LC 74-126704. (BCL Ser. I). reprint ed. 34.50 (*0-404-01836-X*) AMS Pr.

Zoroaster. Francis M. Crawford. (Works of Francis Marion Crawford Ser.). 1990. reprint ed. lib. bdg. 79.00 (*0-7812-2528-0*) Rprt Serv.

Zoroaster: Life & Work of the Forerunner in Persia. (Forerunner Book: Vol. 3). 32p. (Orig.). Date not set. pap. 14.00 (*1-57461-012-0*) Grail Found Pr.

Zoroaster: Prophet of Ancient Iran. Abraham V. Jackson. LC 98-2277. (Columbia University. Indo-Iranian Ser.: No. 14). reprint ed. 32.50 (*0-404-50484-1*) AMS Pr.

Zoroaster: The Prophet of Ancient Iran. 1976. lib. bdg. 75.00 (*0-8490-2856-6*) Gordon Pr.

Zoroastre (Version of 1756) Jean-Philippe Rameau. Ed. by Charles Poisot & Arthur Pougin. (Chefs-d'oeuvre classiques de l'opera francaise Ser.: Vol. 36). (Illus.). 338p. (FRE.). 1970. reprint ed. pap. 35.00 (*0-8450-1136-7*) Broude.

Zoroastrian Civilization: From the Earliest Times to the Downfall of the Last Zoroastrian Empire, 651 A.D. Maneckji N. Dhalla. LC 74-21258. reprint ed. 45.00 (*0-404-12808-4*) AMS Pr.

Zoroastrian Civilization from the Earliest Times to the Downfall of the Last Zoroastrian Empire, 651 A.D. M. N. Dhalla. 1976. lib. bdg. 59.95 (*0-8490-2857-4*) Gordon Pr.

Zoroastrian Doctrine of a Future Life from Death to the Individual Judgment. 2nd ed. Jal D. Pavry. LC 79-10518. reprint ed. 32.50 (*0-404-50481-7*) AMS Pr.

Zoroastrian Faith: Tradition & Modern Research. Solomon A. Nigosian. 168p. 1993. 44.95 (*0-7735-1133-4*, Pub. by McGill CN); pap. 17.95 (*0-7735-1144-X*, Pub. by McGill CN) U of Toronto Pr.

Zoroastrian Studies: Iranian Religion & Various Monographs. Abraham V. Jackson. LC 28-29344. (Columbia University. Indo-Iranian Ser.: No. 12). reprint ed. 27.50 (*0-404-50482-5*) AMS Pr.

Zoroastrian Theology. M. N. Dhalla. 1972. lib. bdg. 250.00 (*0-87968-516-6*) Krishna Pr.

Zoroastrian Theology from the Earliest Times to the Present Day. Maneckji N. Dhalla. LC 70-131038. reprint ed. 42.50 (*0-404-02123-9*) AMS Pr.

Zoroastrian Tradition. Mehr Farhang. (Roots of Wisdom Bks.). 144p. 1988. pap. 12.95 (*0-916349-58-6*) Amity Hse Inc.

Zoroastrianism. Cyrus R. Pangborn. 178p. 1982. text ed. 25.00 (*0-89891-006-4*) Advent Bks Div.

Zoroastrianism: Its Antiquity & Constant Vigour. Mary Boyce. (Columbia Lectures on Iranian Studies: No. 7). 204p. 1992. pap. text ed. 16.95 (*0-939214-90-3*); lib. bdg. 25.00 (*0-939214-89-X*) Mazda Pubs.

Zoroastrianism & Judaism. George W. Carter. LC 70-112489. 1970. reprint ed. 32.50 (*0-404-01396-1*) AMS Pr.

Zoroastrianism in Armenia. James R. Russell. LC 87-18147. (Harvard Iranian Ser.: No. 5). (Illus.). 584p. (Orig.). 1988. pap. 39.95 (*0-674-96850-6*) HUP.

Zoroastrians. Mary Boyce. Ed. by John Hinnells. (Library of Religious Beliefs & Practices). 260p. (C). 1986. pap. text ed. 17.95 (*0-7102-0156-7*, RKP) Routledge.

Zoroastrians in Britain: The Ratanbai Katrak Lectures, University of Oxford 1985. John R. Hinnells. 352p. 1996. 75.00 (*0-19-826193-4*) OUP.

Zorostrian Religion & Customs. E. S. Bharucha. 210p. 1993. 11.95 (*0-318-36786-6*) Asia Bk Corp.

Zorra Negra. Betsy C. Byars. (SPA.). 1996. pap. text ed. 9.75 (*84-320-6173-5*) Lectorum Pubns.

Zorrillos (Skunks) L. Stone. (Spanish Language Books, Set 2: Animales Norteamericanos (North American Animals)). (J). 1991. 8.95 (*0-86592-799-5*) Rourke Enter.

Zorro. Janice Boland. Tr. by Raquel Torres. (Books for Young Learners). (Illus.). 8p. (Orig.). (SPA.). (J). (gr. k-2). 1996. pap. 5.00 (*1-57274-037-X*) R Owen Pubs.

Zorro. Mark Dunster. 17p. (Orig.). 1995. pap. 4.00 (*0-89642-262-3*) Linden Pubs.

***Zorro.** Luceno. 1998. mass mkt. 5.99 (*0-671-51989-1*) PB.

***Zorro.** Olivier Sechan. (SPA.). 1996. pap. text ed. 12.95 (*84-372-2191-9*) Santillana.

Zorro & Quwi: Tales of a Trickster Guinea Pig. Rebecca Hickox. LC 95-53304. (Illus.). 32p. (J). 1997. 14.95 (*0-385-32122-8*, DD Bks Yng Read) BDD Bks Young Read.

Zorro en la Escuels, Level 3. Edward Marshall. Tr. by Maria A. Fiol. (Easy-to-Read Ser.). Orig. Title: Fox at School. (Illus.). 56p. (SPA.). (J). (gr. 1-4). 1996. pap. 3.50 (*0-14-037980-0*, Puffin) Puffin Bks.

Zorro in Old California. Nedaud & Marcello. (Illus.). 1990. 10.95 (*0-913035-13-0*); pap. 6.95 (*0-913035-12-2*) Eclipse Bks.

***Zorro Unmasked: The Official History.** Sandra Curtis. (Illus.). 320p. 1998. pap. 14.95 (*0-7868-8285-9*) Hyperion.

Zorro, Vol. 1: The Complete Classic Adventures. Toth. (Illus.). 1990. pap. 9.95 (*0-913035-41-6*) Eclipse Bks.

Zorro, Vol. 2: The Complete Classic Adventures. Toth. (Illus.). 1990. pap. 9.95 (*0-913035-51-3*) Eclipse Bks.

Zorro y Sus Amigos: Fox & His Friends. Edward Marshall. Tr. by Maria A. Fiol. (Illus.). 56p. (SPA.). (J). 1996. pap. 3.50 (*0-14-038020-5*) Puffin Bks.

ZOS-KIA: An Introductory Essay on the Art & Sorcery of Austin Osman Spare. Gavin Semple. (Illus.). (Orig.). 1995. pap. 32.95 (*1-55818-342-6*) Holmes Pub.

***Zos Speaks! Encounters with Austin Osman Spare.** Grant et al. (Illus.). 1997. write for info. (*0-9531016-0-6*, Pub. by Fulgar UK) Holmes Pub.

Zoshchenko: Stories of the 1920s. Ed. by A. B. Murphy. 78p. (RUS.). 1991. reprint ed. pap. 14.95 (*0-631-14398-X*, Pub. by Blckwell Pubs UK) Focus Pub-R Pullins.

Zosimi Comitis Exadvocati Fisci Historia Nova. Zosimus. liv, 306p. 1963. reprint ed. write for info. (*3-487-05208-3*) G Olms Pubs.

***Zot!, Bk. 1.** Scott McCloud. 288p. 1996. 45.00 (*0-87816-492-8*) Kitchen Sink.

Zot!, Bk. 1. Scott McCloud. Ed. by Catherine Garnier. (Illus.). 288p. 1996. pap. 24.95 (*0-87816-427-8*) Kitchen Sink.

***Zot!, Bk. 1.** deluxe ed. Scott McCloud. 288p. 1996. 55.00 (*0-87816-525-8*) Kitchen Sink.

***Zot!, Vol. 2.** Scott McCloud. 1997. pap. text ed. 19.95 (*0-87816-428-6*) Kitchen Sink.

Zot: Book 1. McCloud. (Illus.). 1990. 29.95 (*0-913035-03-3*); pap. 14.95 (*0-913035-04-1*) Eclipse Bks.

Zouaves: The First & the Bravest. Michael J. McAfee. (Illus.). 124p. (C). 1994. pap. text ed. 12.95 (*0-939631-80-6*) Thomas Publications.

Zouaves of the American Civil War. Robin Smith. (Illus.). 64p. 1996. pap. 12.95 (*1-85532-571-3*, Pub. by Osprey UK) Stackpole.

Zouk: World Music in the West Indies. Jocelyne Guilbault et al. LC 92-27432. (Chicago Studies in Ethnomusicology). 312p. 1993. pap. text ed. 24.95 (*0-226-31042-6*); lib. bdg. 55.00 (*0-226-31041-8*) U Ch Pr.

Zoup Soup. Michele Palmer. LC 78-66342. (Illus.). (J). (ps-1). 1978. pap. 1.95 (*0-932306-00-4*) Rocking Horse.

ZOV - Poems: Tretia Kniga Stikhov. Michail Jupp. LC 87-61133. (Illus.). 224p. (RUS.). 1988. 30.00 (*0-911971-36-X*) Effect Pub.

Zoya. Danielle Steel. 456p. 1988. 19.95 (*0-385-29649-5*) Delacorte.

Zoya. deluxe limited ed. Danielle Steel. 448p. 1988. 100.00 (*0-385-29679-7*) Delacorte.

Zoya. Danielle Steel. 512p. 1989. reprint ed. mass mkt. 6.50 (*0-440-20385-6*) Dell.

Zoyka's Apartment. Mikhail Bulgakov. Tr. by Nicholas Saunders & Frank Dwyer. (Great Translations for Actors Ser.). 128p. 1996. pap. 11.95 (*1-880399-93-8*) Smith & Kraus.

ZR Rifle: The Plot to Kill Kennedy & Castro Cuba Opens Secret Files. 2nd rev. ed. Claudia Furiati. Tr. by Maxine Shaw. (Illus.). 184p. 1994. pap. 14.95 (*1-875284-85-0*, 93268) Ocean Pr NY.

Z's Gift. Neal Starkman. LC 88-71483. (Illus.). 52p. (Orig.). (J). (gr. 4-6). 1988. pap. 8.00 (*0-935529-08-X*) Comprehen Health Educ.

Zthorg - God's Computer. Harry McKinzie. 170p. (Orig.). pap. 20.00 (*0-86626-017-X*) McKinzie Pub.

Zu den aeltesten Beruehrungen zwischen Roemern und Germanen: Die Franken see Romania Germanica: Sprach-und Siedlungsgeschichte der Germanen auf dem Boden des alten Roemerreiches

***Zu Gast Auf den Kanarischen Inseln: Eine Kulinarische Reise.** Renate Kissel. (Illus.). 156p. (GER.). (C). 1995. 40.00 (*3-8170-0016-2*, Pub. by Knstvrlag Weingrtn GW) Intl Bk Import.

***Zu Gast in der Bretagne: Eine Kulinarische Reise.** Renate Kissel. (Illus.). 156p. (GER.). (C). 1993. 40.00 (*3-8170-0015-4*, Pub. by Knstvrlag Weingrtn GW) Intl Bk Import.

***Zu Gast in Griechenland: Die Specialitaten der griechischen Kuche.** Elisabeth Kitsakis & Tassos Kitsakis. (Illus.). 131p. (GER.). (C). 1986. 40.00 (*3-8170-0006-5*, Pub. by Knstvrlag Weingrtn GW) Intl Bk Import.

***Zu Gast in Israel: Eine Kulinarische Reise.** 3rd ed. Jutta Radel. (Illus.). 198p. (GER.). (C). 1994. 40.00 (*3-8170-0004-9*, Pub. by Knstvrlag Weingrtn GW) Intl Bk Import.

***Zu Gast in Portugal: Eine Kulinarische Reise im Garten Europas.** Maria Von Treskow. (Illus.). 144p. (GER.). (C). 1989. 40.00 (*3-8170-0012-X*) Intl Bk Import.

***Zu Gast in Russland: Eine Kulinarische Reise.** Wjatscheslaw M. Kowalew & Nikolaj P. Mogilni. (Illus.). 192p. (GER.). (C). 1988. 40.00 (*3-8170-0010-3*, Pub. by Knstvrlag Weingrtn GW) Intl Bk Import.

Zu Geschichte der Vereinigten Staaten von Amerika. 2nd rev. ed. Zu-Wernigerode Stolberg. (Sammlung Goeschen Ser.: Vol. 7005). 268p. (C). 1973. pap. 12.95 (*3-11-004364-5*) De Gruyter.

***Zubble-Wump.** Dr. Seuss. (Chunky Shape Bks.). (J). 1997. 3.99 (*0-679-88747-4*) Random Bks Yng Read.

Zubrick's Rock: Intrigue & Lunacy in Monte Carlo. Robert Eringer. 224p. 1995. 19.95 (*1-882605-21-7*) Natl Pr Bks.

Zucchini. Barbara Dana. 160p. (J). 1984. mass mkt. 3.99 (*0-553-15608-X*) Bantam.

Zucchini. Barbara Dana. LC 80-8448. (Charlotte Zolotow Bk.). (Illus.). 128p. (J). (gr. 3-6). 1982. lib. bdg. 14.89 (*0-06-021395-7*) HarpC Child Bks.

Zucchini & All That Squash. 2nd ed. Rachel Bard & Caroline Kellogg. LC 84-52215. 104p. (Orig.). 1990. pap. 7.95 (*0-9603666-6-0*) R & M Pr WA.

Zucchini & Other Stories. Jon Longhi. (Illus.). 20p. 1990. 3.00 (*0-916397-07-6*) Manic D Pr.

Zucchini at It's Best: 200 Delicious Ways to Use Zucchini. Paula R. Nolan. (Illus.). 90p. (Orig.). 1995. pap. 9.95 (*0-9647464-0-9*) P Nolan.

Zucchini Cookbook. Ed. by Donald Kubik. LC 92-90505. 230p. 1992. spiral bd. 14.95 (*0-9634191-0-2*) DKE Pubns.

Zucchini Cookery. Virg Lemley & Jo Lemley. 56p. 1976. pap. 5.99 (*0-931798-02-7*) Wilderness Hse.

***Zucchini Out West.** Barbara Dana. LC 96-28976. (Illus.). 160p. (J). (gr. 3-5). 1997. 14.95 (*0-06-024897-1*); lib. bdg. 14.89 (*0-06-024898-X*) HarpC Child Bks.

Zucchini Patch. Kathey L. Sherves & Bonnie Millhollin. Ed. by Ruth Blackett. (Illus.). 108p. (C). 1980. spiral bd. 5.95 (*0-940158-00-0*) Zucchini Patch.

***Zucchini, Pumpkins, & Squash.** Kathleen D. Stang. LC 96-38865. 1998. 9.95 (*0-8118-1389-4*) Chronicle Bks.

Zucchini Sampler. Jan Siegrist. (Illus.). 48p. (Orig.). 1986. pap. 3.95 (*0-933050-41-0*) New Eng Pr VT.

Zucchini Warriors. Gordon Korman. 208p. (J). 1991. pap. 4.50 (*0-590-44174-4*, Apple Paperbacks) Scholastic Inc.

Zuckerman Bound. 480p. 1986. mass mkt. 5.95 (*0-449-21090-1*, Crest) Fawcett.

Zuckerman Bound: A Trilogy & Epilogue. Philip Roth. LC 84-23265. 784p. 1985. 22.50 (*0-374-29943-9*) FS&G.

Zuckerman Unbound. Philip Roth. LC 95-6783. 1995. pap. 11.00 (*0-679-74899-7*, Vin) Random.

Zuercher Kunsthaus-ein Museumsbau Von Moser. Jehle. (Institut fuer Geschichte und Theorie der Architecture Ser.: Vol. 22). 158p. 1980. pap. text ed. 35.00 (*0-8176-1242-4*) Birkhauser.

Zuetoo Masqke Stories for Reading Programs. A. Doyle. (Illus.). 28p. (J). (gr. 1-7). 1996. ring bd. 24.95 (*1-56820-157-5*) Story Time.

Zug. (Hawkins Scribble Bks.). (Illus.). 16p. (J). 1996. 6.95 (*0-7894-1168-7*) DK Pub Inc.

Zug the Bug. (Hawkins Reading Ser.). (J). write for info. (*0-7894-0155-X*, 5-70601) DK Pub Inc.

Zugand von Juden zum Preubischen Justizdienst 1812-1918. 1995. 130.00 (*3-598-23225-X*) K G Saur.

***Zugmann/Schindler.** Ed. by William Mohline. (Illus.). 1996. 25.00 (*1-889629-00-6*) Form Zero.

***Zuihitsu: Poetic Journal & Jottings.** John Fairfax. (Illus.). 76p. 1996. 30.00 (*0-930126-51-3*) Typographeum.

Zukofsky's "A" An Introduction. Barry Ahearn. LC 81-13000. 254p. 1983. 35.00 (*0-520-04378-2*); pap. 12.00 (*0-520-04965-9*) U CA Pr.

Zukov At the Oder: The Decisive Battle for Berlin. Tony Le Tissier. LC 95-10099. 344p. 1996. text ed. 65.00 (*0-275-95230-4*, Praeger Pubs) Greenwood.

Zukunft Des Alterns und Gesellschaftliche Entwicklung. Juergen Mittelstrass. Ed. by Paul B. Baltes. (Akademie der Wissenschaften zu Berlin, Forschungsbericht Ser.: No. 5). xvi, 814p. (GER.). (C). 1992. pap. text ed. 113.85 (*3-11-013248-6*) De Gruyter.

Zuleika Dobson. Max Beerbohm. 22.95 (*0-8488-0914-9*) Amereon Ltd.

***Zulfikar Ali Bhutto & Pakistan.** Rafi Raza. 330p. 1996. 45.00 (*0-19-577697-6*) OUP.

Zulfiqar Ali Bhutto of Pakistan: The Last Days. Kausar Niazi. (Illus.). 244p. (C). 1992. text ed. 27.50 (*0-685-56704-4*, Pub. by Vikas II) S Asia.

Zulu. Russell Kaschula & Zolani Ngwane. LC 96-42293. (Heritage Library of African Peoples: Set 4). (Illus.). 64p. (YA). (gr. 7-12). 1997. lib. bdg. 15.95 (*0-8239-2014-3*, D2014-3) Rosen Group.

***Zulu Aftermath.** J. D. Omer-Cooper. Date not set. pap. text ed. write for info. (*0-582-64531-X*, Pub. by Longman UK) Longman.

Zulu & the Zayda: Manuscript Edition. Howard DaSilva et al. 1966. pap. 13.00 (*0-8222-1296-X*) Dramatists Play.

Zulu-English - English-Zulu Compact Dictionary. 5th ed. Dent. 150p. (ENG & ZUL.). 1990. pap. 9.50 (*0-7960-0265-7*, Pub. by Shuter & Shooter) IBD Ltd.

Zulu-English - English-Zulu Dictionary. 39.50 (*0-87557-096-8*) Saphrograph.

Zulu-English - English-Zulu Scholar's Dictionary. 2nd ed. C. L. Nyembezi. 519p. 1988. pap. 21.25 (*0-7960-0111-1*) IBD Ltd.

Zulu-English, English-Zulu Dictionary. Dent. 150p. (ENG & ZUL.). 1990. pap. 9.95 (*0-7859-7484-9*) Fr & Eur.

Zulu-English, English-Zulu Dictionary. G. R. Dent & C. L. Nyembezi. 519p. (ENG & ZUL.). 1994. pap. 29.50 (*0-7818-0255-5*) Hippocrene Bks.

Zulu-English, English-Zulu Dictionary. 2nd ed. C. L. Nyembezi. 519p. (ENG & ZUL.). 1988. pap. 19.95 (*0-7859-7523-3*) Fr & Eur.

Zulu Fireside Tales. Phyllis Savory. (Illus.). 1993. pap. 9.95 (*0-8065-1380-2*, Citadel Pr) Carol Pub Group.

Zulu Heart: A Novel. Shirley G. DuBois. LC 73-92801. 1973. 20.00 (*0-89388-132-5*) Okpaku Communications.

Zulu King Speaks: Statements Made by Cetshwayo Kampande on the History & Customs of His People. Colin D. Webb. (Illus.). 160p. 1987. text ed. 17.95 (*0-86980-576-2*, Pub. by Univ Natal Pr SA) Intl Spec Bk.

Zulu Medicinal Plants: An Inventory. Compiled by Anne Hutchings et al. 450p. 1996. pap. 133.00 (*0-86980-893-1*, Pub. by Univ Natal Pr SA) Intl Spec Bk.

Zulu Medicinal Plants: An Inventory. Compiled by Anne Hutchings et al. 450p. 1996. 159.30 (*0-86980-923-7*, Pub. by Univ Natal Pr SA) Intl Spec Bk.

Zulu of Southern Africa. Christine Cornell. LC 96-18271. (Celebrating the Peoples & Civilizations of Africa). (Illus.). (J). (gr. k-4). 1996. lib. bdg. 10.46 (*0-8239-2333-9*, PowerKids) Rosen Group.

Zulu People As They Were Before the White Man Came. Alfred T. Bryant. LC 75-100282. 769p. 1970. reprint ed. text ed. 35.00 (*0-8371-2933-8*, Greenwood Pr) Greenwood.

Zulu Principle. Jim Slater. 223p. Date not set. 40.00 (*0-614-13337-8*, Pub. by Euromoney UK) Am Educ Systs.

Zulu Proverbs. rev. ed. C. L. Nyembezi. 1963. 19.00 (*0-7960-0230-4*) IBD Ltd.

Zulu Proverbs. rev. ed. C. L. Nyembezi. (ENG & ZUL.). 1963. pap. 18.95 (*0-7859-7522-5*) Fr & Eur.

Zulu Rebellion 1906. rev. ed. Roberts Staff. (C). 1989. 90. 00 (*1-873058-00-4*, Pub. by Roberts UK) St Mut.

Zulu Song Book (1911) J. L. Dube. Ed. & Tr. by David Rycroft. (Colin Webb Natal & Zululand Ser.: No. 7). 104p. 1996. reprint ed. pap. 24.00 (*0-86980-910-5*, Pub. by Univ Natal Pr SA) Intl Spec Bk.

Zulu Thought-Patterns & Symbolism. Axel-Ivar Berglund. LC 89-11039. (Illus.). 402p. 1989. 39.95 (*0-253-31175-6*); pap. 9.95 (*0-253-21205-7*) Ind U Pr.

Zulu Time. West. LC 97-20293. 1997. 24.00 (*0-684-80032-2*) S&S Trade.

Zulu War. David Clammer. LC 89-576. (Battle Standards Ser.). (Illus.). 224p. (C). 1989. lib. bdg. 27.00 (*0-8095-7525-6*) Borgo Pr.

Zulu War. Angus McBride. (Men-at-Arms Ser.: No. 57). (Illus.). 48p. pap. 11.95 (*0-85045-256-2*, 9009, Pub. by Osprey UK) Stackpole.

Zulu War 1879: Twilight of a Warrior Nation. Ian Knight. (Campaign Ser.: No. 14). (Illus.). 96p. pap. 14.95 (*1-85532-165-3*, 9513, Pub. by Osprey UK) Stackpole.

Zulu 1816-1906. Ian Knight. (Warrior Ser.). (Illus.). 64p. 1995. pap. 12.95 (*1-85532-474-1*, Pub. by Osprey UK) Stackpole.

Zulus. Percival Everett. 248p. 1990. 22.00 (*0-932966-97-7*) Permanent Pr.

Zulus. Ian Knight. (Elite Ser.: No. 21). (Illus.). 64p. pap. 12. 95 (*0-85045-864-1*, 9421, Pub. by Osprey UK) Stackpole.

Zulus. Robert Nicholson. (Journey into Civilization Ser.). (Illus.). 32p. (J). (gr. 3-7). 1994. lib. bdg. 15.95 (*0-7910-2710-4*) Chelsea Hse.

Zulus. Robert Nicholson. (Journey into Civilization Ser.). (Illus.). 32p. (J). (gr. 3-7). 1994. pap. 7.95 (*0-7910-2734-1*) Chelsea Hse.

Zulus & the British Frontiers. Thomas J. Lucas. LC 73-78579. 371p. 1969. reprint ed. text ed. 38.50 (*0-8371-1413-6*, LUZ&, Greenwood Pr) Greenwood.

Zum Arabischen Pferd. Lukomski-Borowiak-Dunkelberg. (Documenta Hippologica Ser.). (Illus.). 78p. 1979. reprint ed. write for info. (*3-487-08192-X*) G Olms Pubs.

***Zum Begriff des Bosen Bei Augustinus und Kant: Der Wandel von der Ontologischen Zur Autonomen Perspektive.** Herbert Rommel. (Europaische Hochschulschriften Ser.: Reihe 20, Bd. 521). 335p. (GER.). 1997. 57.95 (*3-631-30888-4*) P Lang Pubng.

Zum Mineralstoffhaushalt Einiger Chenopodiaceae bei Hohen Boruns Salzangeboten: Freilandstudiens in den Suedwestlichen U. S. A. und Kulturversuche mit Atriplex Halimus L. und Hortensis L. U. Letschert. (Dissertationes Botanicae Ser.: Vol. 96). (Illus.). 244p. (GER.). 1986. pap. 64.00 (*3-443-64008-7*) Lubrecht & Cramer.

Zum Phologischen Werk J. A. Schmellers und Seiner Wissenschaftlichen Rezeption: Eine Studie zur Wissenschaftsgeschichte der Germanistik. Franz X. Scheuerer. (Studia Linguistica Germanica: Bd. 37). xii, 255p. (GER.). (C). 1995. lib. bdg. 123.10 (*3-11-014650-9*) De Gruyter.

Zum Problem der Begabung und Intelligenz. Hans Werder. (Psychologische Praxis Ser.: Vol. 55). vi, 194p. 1980. pap. 22.50 (*3-8055-1123-X*) S Karger.

Zum Problem des Pollenfluges in den Hochalpen, Vol. 90. Maren Jochimsen. (Dissertationes Botanicae Ser.). (Illus.). 252p. (GER.). 1986. pap. 72.00 (*3-443-64003-6*) Lubrecht & Cramer.

ZUM '95: The Z Formal Specification Notation: 9th International Conference of Z Users, Limerick, Ireland, September 7-9, 1995, Proceedings, Vol. XI. Ed. by Jonathan P. Bowen et al. LC 95-38127. (Lecture Notes in Computer Science Ser.: Vol. 967). 571p. 1995. 87.00 (*3-540-60271-2*) Spr-Verlag.

Zumarraga & His Family: Letters to Vizcaya 1536-1548. Ed. by Richard E. Greenleaf. Tr. by Neal Kaveny. (Documentary Ser.). 1979. 30.00 (*0-88382-013-7*) AAFH.

Zumikon Residence: Gwathmey Siegel. Charles Gwathmey & Robert Siegel. Ed. by Brad Collins. (One House Ser.). (Illus.). 72p. 1996. pap. 19.95 (*1-885254-28-8*) Monacelli Pr.

Zumpin, More Poems for Two Children. John M. Shaw. 1969. 5.00 (*0-9607778-9-X*) Friends Fla St.

Zumwalt's Fort: An Archaeological Study of Frontier Process in Missouri. Gregory A. Waselkov & Robert T. Bray. (Missouri Archaeologist Ser.: Vol. 40). (Illus.). 129p. (Orig.). 1979. pap. 5.00 (*0-943414-57-1*) MO Arch Soc.

Zund & Other Stories. Christoph Meckel. Tr. by Carol Bedwell from GER. LC 90-37947. (Studies in German Language & Literature: Vol. 2). (Illus.). 120p. 1991. lib. bdg. 59.95 (*0-88946-580-0*) E Mellen.

Zuni: A Village of Silversmiths. James Ostler et al. LC 95-70836. 143p. 1996. 45.00 (*0-912535-11-3*); pap. 29.95 (*0-912535-08-3*) Zuni Ashiwi.

Zuni: Selected Writings of Frank Hamilton Cushing. Frank H. Cushing. Ed. & Intro. by Jesse Green. LC 78-14295. (Illus.). xiv, 449p. 1979. pap. 12.95 (*0-8032-7007-0*, Bison Books) U of Nebr Pr.

Zuni & El Morro: Past & Present. 2nd ed. Ed. by David G. Noble & Richard B. Woodbury. LC 92-55033. (Illus.). 40p. (C). 1993. reprint ed. pap. 7.95 (*0-941270-77-7*) Ancient City Pr.

Zuni & the Courts: A Struggle for Sovereign Land Rights. Ed. by E. Richard Hart. LC 94-44026. (Development of Western Resources Ser.). (Illus.). 416p. 1995. 40.00 (*0-7006-0705-6*) U Pr of KS.

Zuni Artist Looks at Frank Hamilton Cushing. Phil Hughte. 125p. 1996. pap. text ed. 24.95 (*0-9641401-0-1*) U of NM Pr.

Zuni Atlas. T. J. Ferguson. LC 85-40474. (Civilization of the American Indian Ser.: Vol. 172). (Illus.). 154p. 1990. pap. 19.95 (*0-8061-2287-0*) U of Okla Pr.

Zuni Breadstuff. Frank H. Cushing. LC 74-7948. reprint ed. 62.50 (*0-404-11835-6*) AMS Pr.

Zuni Ceremonialism: Three Studies. Ruth L. Bunzel. LC 96-10861. 409p. (C). 1992. pap. 20.95 (*0-8263-1376-0*) U of NM Pr.

Zuni Daily Life. John M. Roberts. Bd. with Zuni Kin Terms. LC 67-2866. 145p. LC 67-2866. (Monographs). 174p. 1965. reprint ed. Set pap. 15.00 (*0-87536-810-7*) HRAFP.

Zuni Fetish Carvings. Harold Finkelstein. (Illus.). 32p. 1994. pap. 6.95 (*0-9641042-0-2*) S W Connection.

Zuni Fetishes. Frank H. Cushing. LC 66-23329. (Illus.). 52p. 1966. pap. 3.00 (*0-916122-03-4*) KC Pubns.

Zuni Fetishes: Using Native American Objects for Meditation, Reflection & Insight. Hal Z. Bennett. LC 92-53210. 186p. 1993. pap. 18.00 (*0-06-250069-4*) Harper SF.

Zuni Fetishism. Ruth Kirk. LC 88-19350. (Illus.). 72p. 1988. reprint ed. pap. 4.75 (*0-936755-06-7*) Avanyu Pub.

Zuni Folk Tales. Frank H. Cushing. 1977. lib. bdg. 59.95 (*0-8490-2858-2*) Gordon Pr.

Zuni Folk Tales. Frank H. Cushing. LC 74-7949. reprint ed. 62.50 (*0-404-11836-4*) AMS Pr.

Zuni Folk Tales. Frank H. Cushing. LC 85-28960. 474p. 1986. reprint ed. pap. 17.95 (*0-8165-0986-7*) U of Ariz Pr.

Zuni Indians & Their Uses of Plants. Matilda C. Stevenson. (Illus.). 80p. 1994. reprint ed. pap. text ed. 7.95 (*0-486-27869-7*) Dover.

Zuni Jewelry. Theda Bassman & Michael Bassman. LC 92-60622. (Illus.). 64p. 1992. pap. 12.95 (*0-88740-413-8*) Schiffer.

Zuni Katcinas: 47th Annual Report, B. A. E. Ruth L. Bunzel. LC 72-13917. (Beautiful Rio Grande Classics Ser.). (Illus.). 358p. 1984. reprint ed. lib. bdg. 40.00 (*0-87380-099-0*) Rio Grande.

Zuni Kin & Clan. Alfred L. Kroeber. LC 76-43765. (AMNH. Anthropological Papers: Vol. 18, Pt. 2). 1984. reprint ed. 49.50 (*0-404-15618-5*) AMS Pr.

Zuni Kin Terms see Zuni Daily Life

Zuni Man-Woman. Will Roscoe. LC 90-21397. (Illus.). 328p. 1992. pap. 14.95 (*0-8263-1370-1*) U of NM Pr.

Zuni Mythology, 2 Vols. Ruth Benedict. LC 75-82366. (Columbia Univ. Contributions to Anthropology Ser.: No. 21). 1969. reprint ed. Set. 70.00 (*0-404-50571-6*) AMS Pr.

Zuni Pottery. Marian Rodee & James Ostler. LC 87-60505. (Illus.). 92p. 1987. pap. 9.95 (*0-88740-100-7*) Schiffer.

Zuni-Southwest see Indians of North America

Zuni Texts. Ruth L. Bunzel. LC 73-3551. (American Ethnological Society Publications: No. 15). reprint ed. 42.50 (*0-404-58165-X*) AMS Pr.

Zuniga: An Album of His Sculpture. Carlos F. Echeverria. (Illus.). 150.00 (*0-686-30118-8*) Landmark NY.

***Zunik Dans Je Suis Zunik.** Bertrand Gauthier. (Zunik Ser.). (Illus.). 24p. (FRE.). (J). (ps up). 1996. pap. 4.95 (*2-89021-046-4*, Pub. by Les Editions CN) Firefly Bks Ltd.

***Zunik Dans la Pleine Lune.** Bertrand Gauthier. (Zunik Ser.). (Illus.). 24p. (FRE.). (J). (ps up). 1996. pap. 4.95 (*2-89021-102-9*, Pub. by Les Editions CN) Firefly Bks Ltd.

***Zunik Dans la Surprise.** Bertrand Gauthier. (Zunik Ser.). (Illus.). 24p. (FRE.). (J). (ps up). 1996. pap. 4.95 (*2-89021-069-3*, Pub. by Les Editions CN) Firefly Bks Ltd.

***Zunik Dans le Championnat.** Bertrand Gauthier. (Zunik Ser.). (Illus.). 24p. (FRE.). (J). (ps up). 1996. pap. 4.95 (*2-89021-058-8*, Pub. by Les Editions CN) Firefly Bks Ltd.

***Zunik Dans le Chouchou.** Betrand Gauthier. (Zunik Ser.). (Illus.). 24p. (FRE.). (J). (ps up). 1996. pap. 4.95 (*2-89021-068-5*, Pub. by Les Editions CN) Firefly Bks Ltd.

***Zunik Dans le Dragon.** Bertrand Gauthier. (Zunik Ser.). (Illus.). 24p. (FRE.). (J). (ps up). 1996. pap. 4.95 (*2-89021-153-3*, Pub. by Les Editions CN) Firefly Bks Ltd.

***Zunik Dans le Spectacle.** Bertrand Gauthier. (Zunik Ser.). (Illus.). 24p. (FRE.). (J). (ps up). 1996. pap. 4.95 (*2-89021-152-5*, Pub. by Les Editions CN) Firefly Bks Ltd.

***Zunik Dans le Wawazonzon.** Bertrand Gauthier. (Zunik Ser.). (Illus.). 24p. (FRE.). (J). (ps up). 1996. pap. 4.95 (*2-89021-101-0*, Pub. by Les Editions CN) Firefly Bks Ltd.

***Zunik le Rendez-vous.** Bertrand Gauthier. (Zunik Ser.). (Illus.). 24p. (FRE.). (J). (ps up). 1996. pap. 4.95 (*2-89021-216-5*, Pub. by Les Editions CN) Firefly Bks Ltd.

Zunis. Katherine M. Doherty & Craig A. Doherty. LC 93-18372. (First Bks.). 64p. (J). 1993. lib. bdg. 21.00 (*0-531-20157-0*) Watts.

Zunis. Katherine M. Doherty & Craig A. Coherty. (First Bks.). (Illus.). 64p. (J). (gr. 5-8). 1994. pap. 6.95 (*0-531-15704-0*) Watts.

***Zunis.** Alice Flanagan. LC 97-6712. (True Book Ser.). (J). 1998. write for info. (*0-516-20630-3*) Childrens.

Zunis of Cibola. Charles G. Crampton. LC 77-72586. (Illus.). 216p. reprint ed. pap. 61.60 (*0-8357-7080-X*, 2033360) Bks Demand.

***Zuordnung von Zinseinnahmen zu den Einzelnen Einkunften.** Annette Stuhldreier. xxxviii, 124p. (GER.). 1996. pap. 35.95 (*3-631-30843-4*) P Lang Pubng.

Zuppa! A Seventeen-Region Tour of the Soups of Italy, with 144 Inviting Recipes. G. Franco Romagnoli. 288p. 1996. 25.00 (*0-8050-3833-7*) H Holt & Co.

Zuppa! Italian Soups. Margaret Romagnoli & G. Franco Romagnoli. 1997. 13.50 (*0-8050-3834-5*) H Holt & Co.

Zuppa! Soups from the Italian Countryside. Anne Bianchi. LC 96-19067. (Cooking with Ecco Ser.). (Illus.). 2524p. 1996. 25.00 (*0-88001-513-6*) Ecco Pr.

***Zuppe Risotti Polenta! Italian Soup, Rice, & Polenta Dishes.** Time-Life Books Staff. LC 97-1242. (Pane & Vino Ser.). (Illus.). 128p. 1997. write for info. (*0-7835-4943-1*) Time-Life.

Zur Analyse, Begutachtung und Entwicklung von Lehrwerken Deutsch als Fremdsprache. Ed. by Bernd Kast & Gerd Neuner. 240p. (GER.). 1994. 31.50 (*3-468-49445-9*) Langenscheidt.

Zur Biologie des Phytopathogenen Pilzes: Gerlachia nivalis (Erreger des Schneeschimmels) Molekularbiologische Untersuchungen an verschiedenen Feldisolaten. Gabriele Leipoldt. (Bibliotheca Mycologica Ser.: Vol. 109). (Illus.). 164p. (GER.). (C). 1987. pap. text ed. 56. 95 (*3-443-59010-1*) Lubrecht & Cramer.

Zur Biologie und Systematik der Flechtengattungen Heppia und Peltula im suedlichen Afrika. B. Budel. (Bibliotheca Lichenologica Ser.: Vol. 23). (Illus.). 150p. (GER.). 1987. 80.00 (*3-443-58002-5*) Lubrecht & Cramer.

Zur Chemie Durch Halogene, Stickstoff Oder Sauerstoff Substituierter Organischer Schwefelverbindungen, Vol. 6. Alexander Senning et al. (Sulfer Reports: Vol. 6, No. 4). 120p. (GER.). 1986. pap. text ed. 91.00 (*3-7186-0365-9*) Gordon & Breach.

Zur Chemotaxonomie Mariner Rhodophyceen am Beispiel einer Leucin-Decarboxylase. B. Aufermann. (Bibliotheca Phycologica Ser.: No. 43). (Illus.). 1978. pap. text ed. 30.00 (*3-7682-1206-8*) Lubrecht & Cramer.

Zur Chronologie Mittelhellenistischer Muenzserien 220-160 vor Chr. Christof Boehringer. (Antike Muenzen und Geschnittene Steine Ser.: Vol. 5). (Illus.). 240p. (C). 1972. 136.95 (*3-11-001763-6*) De Gruyter.

***Zur Deregulierung des Europaischen Erdgasmarktes, Vol. XI.** Peter Rugge. (Europaische Hochschulschriften: Reihe 5: Bd. 1747). (Illus.). 291p. (GER.). 1995. pap. 57. 95 (*3-631-48481-X*) P Lang Pubng.

Zur Deutschen Literatur und Philosophie: Ausgewahlte Aufsatze. Hermann Boeschenstein. Ed. by Rodney Symington. (Kanadische Studien zur deutschen Sprache und Literatur: Vol. 35). 318p. 1986. text ed. 34.00 (*0-8204-0383-0*) P Lang Pubng.

Zur Dialektik von Exposition und Darstellung: Ansaetze zu einer Kritik der Arbeiten Martin Heideggers, Theodor W. Adornos & Jacques Derrida. Sabine Wilke. (Stanford German Studies: Vol. 24). 234p. (C). 1988. text ed. 36.00 (*0-8204-0766-6*) P Lang Pubng.

Zur Diskussion. 3rd ed. Sevin. 1987. pap. 39.95 (*0-8384-3604-8*) Heinle & Heinle.

***Zur Effektivitat der Forderung von Direktinvestitionen in Entwicklungslandern: Wirkungspotentiale von Investitionsanreizen der DEG.** Ralph Muhleck. (Illus.). 229p. (GER.). 1996. 44.95 (*3-631-30869-8*) P Lang Pubng.

Zur Eisenzeitlichen Bewaffnung und Kampfesweise Auf der Iberischen Halbinsel: Text & Documentation, 2 vols., Set. Peter F. Stary. (Madrider Forschungen Ser.: No. 18). (Illus.). (GER.). 1993. lib. bdg. 430.80 (*3-11-012799-7*) De Gruyter.

Zur Energieabhaengigkeit Von Photoelektronensatelliten. Burkhard Langer. LC 92-37269. (Studies of Vacuum Ultraviolet & X-Ray Processes: No. 2). 1992. 45.00 (*0-404-69952-9*) AMS Pr.

Zur Entwicklung der Perfektumschreibung im Deutschen. A. J. Zieglschmid. (LD Ser.: No. 6). 1974. reprint ed. pap. 25.00 (*0-527-00752-8*) Periodicals Srv.

Zur Fletchtenflora der Inneralpinen Trockentaeler unter Besonderer Beruecksichtinhung des Vinschgaus. A. Buschardt. (Bibliotheca Lichenologica Ser.: Vol. 10). 1979. lib. bdg. 80.00 (*3-7682-1226-2*) Lubrecht & Cramer.

Zur Frage der Gesetze und Andere Schriften aus dem Nachlass. Franz Kafka. 208p. (GER.). 1994. pap. 11.75 (*3-596-12447-6*, Pub. by Fischer Taschbch Verlag GW) Intl Bk Import.

Zur Genese des Selbstbewusstseins: Eine Studie ueber den Beitrag des phaenomenologischen Denkens zur Frage der Entwicklung des Selbstbewusstseins. Ursula Rohr-Dietschi. LC 72-81567. (Phaenomenologisch-Psychologische Forschungen Ser.: Vol. 14). 197p. (C). 1975. 79.25 (*3-11-004048-4*) De Gruyter.

Zur Geschichte der Deutschen Sprache. Wilhelm Scherer. LC 95-44072. (Amsterdam Classics in Linguistics Ser.: Vol. 16). lxii, 246p. (GER.). 1995. lib. bdg. 97.00 (*1-55619-770-5*) Benjamins North Am.

Zur Geschichte der Gymnischen Agone an Griechischen Festen. Theophil Klee. 136p. 1980. pap. 20.00 (*0-89005-336-7*) Ares.

Zur Geschichte der Lateinischen Schulpoesie Des 12. und 13. Jahrhunderts. Kuno Francke. 107p. 1968. reprint ed. write for info. (*0-318-71259-8*) G Olms Pubs.

Zur Geschichte Des Nietzsche-Archivs: Chronik, Studien und Dokumente. David M. Hoffmann. (Supplementa Nietzscheana Ser.: Vol. 2). (Illus.). xxiv, 843p. (GER.). (C). 1991. lib. bdg. 252.35 (*3-11-013014-9*) De Gruyter.

Zur Geschichte Lateinischer Eigennamen. Wilhelm Schulze. 650p. 1991. write for info. (*3-615-00061-7*) G Olms Pubs.

Zur Geschichte und Literatur. Leopold Zunz. viii, 607p. 1976. reprint ed. write for info. (*3-487-05946-0*) G Olms Pubs.

Zur Geschichtsschreibung des Chronisten: Literarisch-Historiographische Abweichungen der Chronik von Ihren Paralleltexten in den Samuel- & Koenigsbuechern. Isaac Kalimi. (Beihefte zur Zeitschrift fuer die Alttestamentliche Wissenschaft Ser.: Bd. 226). ix, 400p. (GER.). (C). 1995. lib. bdg. 144.60 (*3-11-014237-6*) De Gruyter.

***Zur Gesellschaftlichen Stellung der Kunst Zwischen Natur und Technik: Kritische Gesellschaftstheorie Zwischen Massenkultur und Kunsteliten.** Dieter R. Knoell. (Philosophische Texte und Studien: Vol. 38.1). viii, 290p. (GER.). 1993. write for info. (*3-487-09781-8*) G Olms Pubs.

***Zur Gesellschaftlichen Stellung der Kunst Zwischen Natur und Technik: Neopositivistische Kunsttheorie Zwischen Elitekunst und Massenproduktion.** Dieter R. Knoell. (Philosophische Texte und Studien: Vol. 38.2). viii, 236p. (GER.). 1994. write for info. (*3-487-09782-6*) G Olms Pubs.

***Zur Gestaltung Judischer Figuren In der Deutschsprachigen Literature Nach 1945.** Christiane Schmelzkopf. (Germanistische Texte und Studien: Bd. 16). xii, 277p. (GER.). 1983. write for info. (*3-487-07385-4*) G Olms Pubs.

***Zur Gleichnistechnik des Apollonios von Rhodos.** Christiane Reitz. (Studien Zur Klassischen Philologie Ser.: Bd. 99). vii, 170p. (GER.). 1996. 42.95 (*3-631-30751-9*) P Lang Pubng.

Zur Griechischen und Romischen Munzkunde. Friedrich Imhoof-Blumer. 324p. 1977. reprint ed. write for info. (*3-487-06407-3*) G Olms Pubs.

Zur Grundlegung Christlicher Ethik Theologische Konzeptionen der Gegenwart im Lichte des Analogie-Problems. Kotaro Okayama. (Theologische Bibliothek Toepelmann Ser.: Vol. 30). (C). 1977. 75.40 (*3-11-005812-X*) De Gruyter.

Zur Grundlegung der Sprachwissenschaft. Ernst Otto. vi, 39p. reprint ed. write for info. (*0-318-71464-7*) G Olms Pubs.

Zur Handschriftenkunde, 2 vols. in 1. Friedrich A. Ebert. xiii, 417p. 1976. reprint ed. write for info. (*3-487-05830-8*) G Olms Pubs.

Zur Handschriftenkunde, 2 vols. in 1, Bd. I, Die Bildung des Bibliothekars. Friedrich A. Ebert. xiii, 417p. 1976. reprint ed. Bd. I: Die Bildung des Bibliothekars. write for info. (*0-318-70739-X*) G Olms Pubs.

Zur Handschriftenkunde, 2 vols. in 1, Bd. II, Bibliothecae Guelferbytanae Codices Graeci. Friedrich A. Ebert. xiii, 417p. 1976. reprint ed. Bd. II: Bibliothecae Guelferbytanae Codices Graeci et Latini Classici. write for info. (*0-318-70740-3*) G Olms Pubs.

Zur Heliandmetrik: Das Verhaeltnis Von Rhythmus und Satzgewicht Im Altsaechsischen. Ingeborg Hinderschiedt. (German Language & Literature Monographs: No. 8). vi, 143p. 1979. 35.00 (*90-272-4001-9*) Benjamins North Am.

Zur Inflorezenzmorphologie der Malvales. Clemens Bayer. (Dissertationes Botanicae Ser.: Vol. 212). (Illus.). 285p. (GER.). 1994. pap. 90.00 (*3-443-64124-5*, Pub. by Cramer-Borntraeger GW) Lubrecht & Cramer.

Zur Kenntnis der Flechtenflora am Hohen Meissner und in Seinem Vorland (Hessen) unter Besonderer Beruecksichtigung Chemischer Merkmale. Heidi Kuemmerling. (Bibliotheca Lichenologica Ser.: Vol. 41). (Illus.). 315p. (GER.). 1991. pap. text ed. 79.20 (*3-443-58020-3*, Pub. by Cramer-Borntraeger GW) Lubrecht & Cramer.

Zur Lehre vom Inhalt und Gegenstand der Vorstellungen: Eine Psychologische Untersuchung. Kasimir Twardowski. (Philosophia Resources Library). 144p. (GER.). 1983. reprint ed. 46.00 (*3-88405-017-6*) Philosophia Pr.

Zur Logik Empirischer Theorien. Ed. by Wolfgang Balzer & Michael Heidelberger. Tr. by Michael Heidelberger from ENG. 331p. 1983. 66.95 (*3-11-008236-5*); pap. 32. 35 (*3-11-009711-7*) De Gruyter.

***Zur Messung der Dienstleistungsqualitat: Eine Theoretische und Empirische Studie zur Methodenentwicklung unter Besonderer Berucksichtigung des Ereignisorientierten Ansatzes.** Thomas Bezold. (Europaische Hochschulschriften: Reihe 5: Bd. 1932). (Illus.). 288p. (GER.). 1996. pap. 54.95 (*3-631-30364-5*) P Lang Pubng.

XYZ

Zur Modernen Deutung der Aristotelischen Logik, Bd. I: Uber den Folgerungsbegriff in der Aristotelischen Logik. Albert Menne & Niels Offenberger. 220p. (GER.). 1982. write for info. (3-487-07265-3) G Olms Pubs.

Zur Modernen Deutung der Aristotelischen Logik, Bd. II: Formale und Nicht-Formale Logik Bei Aristoteles. Albert Menne & Niels Offenberger. 262p. (GER.). 1985. write for info. (3-487-07266-1) G Olms Pubs.

Zur Modernen Deutung der Aristotelischen Logik, Bd. III: Modallogik und Mehrwertigkeit. Albert Menne & Niels Offenberger. 322p. (GER.). 1988. write for info. (3-487-07267-X) G Olms Pubs.

Zur Modernen Deutung der Aristotelischen Logik, Bd. IV: Niels Offenberger, Zur Vorgeschichte der Mehrwertigen Logik in der Antike. Niels Offenberger. viii, 172p. (GER.). 1990. write for info. (3-487-09350-2) G Olms Pubs.

Zur Modernen Deutung der Aristotelischen Logik, Bd. V: Jan Lukasiewicz, Uber Den Statz Des Widerspruchs Bei Aristoteles. Albert Menne. write for info. (0-318-71267-9) G Olms Pubs.

***Zur Narrativitat des Theologischen: Prolegomena Zu Einer Narrativen Texttheorie in Soteriologischer Hinsicht.** Knut Wenzel. (Regensburger Studien Zur Theologie Ser.: Bd. 52). 396p. (GER.). 1997. 63.95 (3-631-30229-0) P Lang Pubng.

Zur Oekologie der Mykorrhiza Pilze. R. Agerer. (Bibliotheca Mycologica Ser.: vol. 97). (Illus.). 160p. 1985. pap. text ed. 48.00 (3-7682-1423-0) Lubrecht & Cramer.

Zur Oekologie der Porlinge, II: Entwicklungsmorphologie der Fruchtkoerper und ihre Beeinflussung durch Klimatische und Andere Faktoren. Ingo Nuss. (Bibliotheca Mycologica Ser.: Vol. 105). (Illus.). 456p. (GER.). 1986. pap. text ed. 112.00 (3-443-59006-3) Lubrecht & Cramer.

Zur Okologie der Andinen Paramoregion. H. Sturm. (Biogeographica Ser.: No. 14). 1978. lib. bdg. 70.50 (90-6193-215-7) Kluwer Ac.

Zur Phaenologie des aequatorialen Regenwaldes im Ost-Zaire (Kivu) nebst Planzenliste und Klimadaten. F. Dieterlen. (Dissertationes Botanicae Ser.: No. 47). (Illus.). 1979. pap. 18.00 (3-7682-1215-7) Lubrecht & Cramer.

Zur Phanomenologie der Intersubjektivitat: Texte aus dem Nachlass, Dritter Teil, 1929-1935. Edmund Husserl. Tr. by I. Kern. (Husserliana Collected Works: Vol. 15). 811p. (GER.). 1973. lib. bdg. 198.00 (90-247-5030-X, Pub. by M Nijhoff NE) Kluwer Ac.

Zur Phanomenologie der Intersubjektivitat: Texte aus dem Nachlass, Erster Teil, 1905-1920. Edmund Husserl. Tr. by I. Kern. (Husserliana Collected Works: Vol. 13). 595p. (GER.). 1973. lib. bdg. 158.50 (90-247-5028-8, Pub. by M Nijhoff NE) Kluwer Ac.

Zur Phanomenologie der Intersubjektivitat: Texte aus dem Nachlass, Zweiter Teil, 1921-1928. Edmund Husserl. Tr. by I. Kern. (Husserliana Collected Works: Vol. 14). 659p. (GER.). 1973. lib. bdg. 171.00 (90-247-5029-6, Pub. by M Nijhoff NE) Kluwer Ac.

Zur Phanomenologie des Inneren Zeitbewustseins: (1893-1917) Edmund Husserl. (Husserliana Collected Sorks: No. 10). 526p. 1969. lib. bdg. 129.50 (90-247-0227-5, Pub. by M Nijhoff NE) Kluwer Ac.

Zur Philosophie Des Zeichens. Ed. by Tilman Borsche & Werner Stegmaier. xiii, 231p. (GER.). (C). 1992. lib. bdg. 75.40 (3-11-013638-4) De Gruyter.

Zur Rezeption des Deutschen Rechts in Korea. Ed. by Manfred Rehbinder & Ju-Chan Sonn. 111p. (GER.). 1990. pap. 27.00 (3-7890-1968-2, Pub. by Nomos Verlags GW) Intl Bk Import.

Zur Sozio-Genese des chronischen Alkoholismus. P. Wuethrich. (Sozialmedizinische und Paedagogische Jugendkunde Ser.: Band 10). (Illus.). 200p. 1974. 32.00 (3-8055-1695-9) S Karger.

Zur Spaet - und Postglazialen Vegetations - Geschichte Des Oberpfaelzer Waldes. Maria Knipping. (Dissertationes Botanicae Ser.: Vol. 140). (Illus.). 216p. (GER.). 1989. pap. text ed. 87.00 (3-443-64054-0) Lubrecht & Cramer.

Zur Sprache der Bekkennenden Kirche, 1934-43: Eine Soziolinguistische Untersuchung. Elke K. Fischer. LC 92-30535. (Berkeley Insights in Linguistics & Semiotics Ser.: Vol. 10). 213p. (GER.). (C). 1993. text ed. 48.95 (0-8204-1939-7) P Lang Pubng.

Zur Sprache und Literatur der Mandaer: Mit Beitraegen von Kurt Rudolph & Eric Segelberg. Rudolf Macuch. (C). 1976. 192.30 (3-11-004838-8) De Gruyter.

Zur Theorie der Vergleichenden Literaturwissenschaft. Ed. by Horst Ruediger et al. 87p. (C). 1971. 15.40 (3-11-003622-3) De Gruyter.

Zurbaran. Jonathan Brown. 1991. 22.95 (0-8109-3962-2) Abrams.

Zurich: The 1820's to the 1870's - A Study in Modernization. Frederick S. Allen. (Illus.). 146p. (Orig.). (C). 1986. pap. text ed. 19.50 (0-8191-5512-8) U Pr of Amer.

Zurich International Chess Tournament, Nineteen Fifty-Three. David Bronstein. Tr. by Jim Marfia from RUS. LC 78-74881. (Illus.). 1979. pap. 9.95 (0-486-23800-8) Dover.

Zurich Unfolds. Stephan C. VanDam & P. G. Pellett. (VanDam's the World Unfolds Ser.). 1985. pap. 6.95 (0-931141-09-5) VanDam Inc.

Zurich, 1995: Open Questions in Analytical Psychology. Mary A. Mattoon. 36p. 1996. pap. text ed. 29.80 (3-85630-556-4, Pub. by Daimon Pubs SZ) Continuum.

***Zurich 1995: Open Questions in Analytical Psychology.** Ed. by Mary A. Mattoon. 36p. 1996. 39.80 (3-85630-555-6, Pub. by Daimon Pubs SZ) Continuum.

Zuricher Novellen. unabridged ed. Keller. (World Classic Literature Ser.). (GER.). pap. 7.95 (3-89507-043-2, Pub. by Bookking Intl FR) Distribks Inc.

Zuro! A Tale of Alien Avengers. William A. Simms. Ed. by Nora Wright. LC 96-60062. 350p. 1996. pap. 14.95 (0-9650970-0-5, Z100) Waverly Hse.

Zuruan Mosaic: Collected Short Stories. Jerry W. Hardin. 95p. 1992. 8.95 (1-882446-29-1); pap. 5.95 (1-882446-30-5) I p e Alliance.

Zuruan Mosaic - O Mosaico De Zuruan: Bi-Lingual Edition. Jerry W. Hardin & Camilo De Andrade. 190p. 1992. 12.95 (1-882446-27-5); pap. 10.95 (1-882446-28-3) I p e Alliance.

Zurueck zu Freuds Texten: Stumme Dokumente Sprechen Machen. Ilse Gruebrich-Simitis. 399p. (GER.). 1993. 36.00 (3-10-028606-5, Pub. by S Fischer GW) Intl Bk Import.

Zurvan: A Zoroastrian Dilemma. Robert C. Zaehner. 1973. reprint ed. 32.00 (0-8196-0280-9) Biblo.

Zury, the Meanest Man in Spring County. Joseph Kirkland. (Collected Works of Joseph Kirkland). 1988. reprint ed. lib. bdg. 79.00 (0-7812-1317-7) Rprt Serv.

Zury, the Meanest Man in Spring County see Collected Works of Joseph Kirkland

***Zusammenhange Zwischen Energieversorgung und der Individuellen Mobilitat der Bevolkerung in der Bundesrepublik Deutschland (alte Lander), Vol. XXIV.** Franz X. Scharinger. (Studien zur Haushaltsokonomie: Bd. 12). 406p. (GER.). 1997. pap. 63.95 (3-631-31157-5) P Lang Pubng.

Zusetsu Chugoku no Keizai see China's New Political Economy: The Giant Awakes

***Zushe's Find: A Story about the Rebbe Reb Zushe.** Sterna Citron. LC 96-78004. (Children's Ser.). (Illus.). 24p. (J). (gr. k-2). 1996. 12.95 (1-889727-17-2) Kerem Pubng.

Zut, & Other Parisians. Guy W. Carryl. LC 76-81266. (Short Story Index Reprint Ser.). 1977. 20.95 (0-8369-3018-5) Ayer.

Zuverlassige Nachrichten von Den Vornehmsten Schriftstellern Vom Anfang der Welt Bis 1500, 4 vols., Set. Georg C. Hamberger. xlvi, 3458p. 1970. reprint ed. write for info. (0-318-70756-X) G Olms Pubs.

Zuverlassige Nachrichten Von Den Vornehmsten Schriftstellern Vom Anfang der Welt Bis 1500, 4 vols., Set. Georg C. Hamberger. 1970. reprint ed. write for info. (0-318-71913-4) G Olms Pubs.

***Zuwanderung & Sozialstaat: Fiskalische Effekte der Zuwanderung - Ihre Messung & Interpretation.** Dita Vogel. (Illus.). 220p. (GER.). 1996. 42.95 (3-631-30414-5) P Lang Pubng.

***Zuzu Bailey's It's A Wonderful Life Cookbook: Recipes, Anecdotes, & Trivia Quizzes Inspired by America's Favorite Music.** Karolyn Grimes & Franklin Dohanyos. 176p. 1996. 18.95 (1-55972-382-3, Birch Ln Pr) Carol Pub Group.

ZVI. Elwood McQuaid. LC 78-56149. 1978. pap. 4.95 (0-915540-23-1) Frnds Israel.

Zvi & the Next Generation. Elwood McQuaid. LC 88-80875. 1988. pap. 5.95 (0-915540-43-6) Frnds Israel.

***Zvi Hecker: The Heinz-Galinski-School in Berlin.** Ed. by Kristin Feireiss. (Illus.). 160p. 1996. 65.00 (3-8030-2503-6, 620641, Pub. by Ernst Wasmuth GW) Dist Art Pubs.

Zvi Ribak: A Jewish Artist. Menachem Michaelson. Ed. by Murray Grant. LC 91-52500. (Illus.). 162p. 1991. 80.00 (0-88734-615-4) Players Pr.

Zwang und Schizophrenie. H. Feer. (Bibliotheca Psychiatrica Ser.: No. 150). 108p. 1973. 36.00 (3-8055-1546-4) S Karger.

Zwanzigste Jahrhundert see Geschichte der Deutschen Poetik

Zwei Griechische Apologeten (Aristides von Athen und Anthenagoras) Johannes Geffcken. xliii, 333p. 1907. write for info. (0-318-70922-8) G Olms Pubs.

Zwei Griechische Apologeten (Aristides von Athen und Athenagoras) Johannes Geffcken. xliii, 333p. (GER.). 1970. reprint ed. write for info. (0-318-70603-2) G Olms Pubs.

Zwei Hundert-Jahr-Feier der I. Universitaets-Frauenklinik Wien: Universitaets-Frauenklinik Wien. Ed. by E. Gitsch. (Journal: Gynaekologische Rundschau: Vol. 29, Suppl. 3, 1989). (Illus.). iv, 60p. 1990. pap. 20.00 (3-8055-5107-X) S Karger.

***Zwei Schauspiele, Die Zwerge, Vol. 1.2.** Ed. by Wolfgang Mohrig. (Literatur der Romantik Ser.). (GER.). 1994. write for info. (3-487-09914-4) G Olms Pubs.

***Zweideutigkeit des Ursprunglichen Bei Martin Heidegger: aus Dem Spanischen Ubersetzt von Dieter Wiggert.** Jose L. Molinuevo. 211p. (GER.). 1996. 42.95 (3-631-30197-9) P Lang Pubng.

Zweifelhaftes im Corpus Aristotelicum - Studien zu einigen Dubia. Ed. by Paul Moraux et al. 401p. (GER.). 1983. 176.95 (3-11-008980-7) De Gruyter.

***Zweireichelehre Martin Luthers Im Dialog Mit der Befreiungstheologie Leonardo Boffs: Ein Okumenischer Beitrag Zum Verhaltnis von Christlichem Glauben und Gesellschaftlicher Verantwortung.** Silfredo B. Dalferth. (Europaische Hochschulschriften Ser.: Reihe 23, Bd. 586). 341p. (GER.). 1996. 57.95 (3-631-30908-2) P Lang Pubng.

Zweisprachiges Woerterbuch fuer Angenaeherte Operationelle Analyse Semantischer Entsprechungen Mittels EDV. G. Guckler. 300p. (GER & ITA.). 1975. pap. 75.00 (0-8288-5971-X, M7693) Fr & Eur.

***Zweisprachigkeit und Schulerfolg.** Klaus-Borge Boeckmann. (Arbeiten zur Sprachanalyse Ser.: Bd. 26). (Illus.). 208p. (GER.). 1997. 42.95 (3-631-31059-5) P Lang Pubng.

***Zweisprachigkeitserziehung in Gemischtsprachigen Familien: Eine Analyse der Erfolgsbedingenden Merkmale.** Susanne Mahlstedt. 233p. (GER.). 1996. 44.95 (3-631-30762-4) P Lang Pubng.

Zwickau in Transition, 1500-1547: The Reformation as an Agent of Change. Susan C. Karant-Nunn. LC 86-31267. 312p. 1987. 52.00 (0-8142-0421-X) Ohio St U Pr.

Zwingli: An Introduction to His Thought. W. P. Stephens. 192p. 1994. reprint ed. pap. 19.95 (0-19-826363-5) OUP.

Zwingli & Bullinger. Ed. by Geoffrey W. Bromiley. LC 53-1533. (Library of Christian Classics). 360p. 1979. pap. 25.00 (0-664-24159-X, Westminster) Westminster John Knox.

Zwingli & the Arts. Charles Garside, Jr. LC 81-4277. (Music Ser.). xiv, 190p. 1981. reprint ed. lib. bdg. 29.50 (0-306-76018-5) Da Capo.

Zwingli Bibliography. Compiled by H. Wayne Pipkin. LC 73-153549. (Bibliographia Tripotamopolitana Ser.: No. 7). 1972. 7.00 (0-931222-06-0) Pitts Theolog.

Zwingli or the Rise of the Reformation in Switzerland. R. Christoffel. 1977. lib. bdg. 59.95 (0-8490-2859-0) Gordon Pr.

***Zwischen Allwissenheitslehre und Verzweiflung.** Karl W. Wilhelm. (Studien und Materialien Zur Geschichte der Philosophie: Bd. 36). 184p. (GER.). 1994. write for info. (3-487-09857-1) G Olms Pubs.

Zwischen Bild und Text: Goethes Werdegang zum Klassizismus. Jutta Van Selm. (American University Studies: Germanic Languages & Literature: Ser. I, Vol. 48). 205p. 1986. text ed. 33.70 (0-8204-0325-3) P Lang Pubng.

***Zwischen Gestern und Morgen: Schrifstellerinnen der DDR aus Amerikanischer Sicht.** Ute Brandes. (GER.). 1992. 44.80 (3-86032-013-0) P Lang Pubng.

Zwischen Hadit und Theologie: Studien Zum Entstehen Praedestinatianischer Ueberlieferung. Josef Von Ess. LC 73-91809. (Studien zur Sprache, Geschichte und Kultur des Islamischen Orients: Vol. 7). (GER.). (C). 1974. 134.65 (3-11-004290-8) De Gruyter.

Zwischen Krieg und Frieden. William F. Sollmann. (C). 1948. pap. 3.00 (0-87574-045-6) Pendle Hill.

Zwischen Renaissance und Barocki: Das Zeitalter von Bruegel und Bellange. Albertina Vienna. 9.75 (0-685-43162-2, 19326) Ayer.

Zwischenreich des Dialogs. Waldenfels. (Phaenomenologica Ser.: No. 41). 442p. 1971. lib. bdg. 88.50 (90-247-5072-5, Pub. by M Nijhoff NE) Kluwer Ac.

***Zwliangrong Nagas: A Study of Tribal Christianity.** Ramkhun Pamei. 1996. 21.00 (81-85565-68-6, Pub. by Uppal Pub Hse II) S Asia.

Zwo Kurtzweilige - Lustige - und Lacherliche Historien. Niclas Ulenhart. 398p. reprint ed. write for info. (0-318-71642-9) G Olms Pubs.

Zwoelf Kantaten und Arien fuer Zwei Soprane und Bass mit Continuo und Instrumenten, Vol. 5. Ed. by Gottlieb Harms & Hilmar Trede. (Dietrich Buxtehudes Werke). 1978. pap. 80.00 (0-89371-015-6) Broude.

Zwolfte Lebensjahr see On the Threshold of Adolescence: The Struggle for Independence in the Twelfth Year

Zworykin: Pioneer of Television. Albert Abramson. LC 94-7464. 384p. 1994. text ed. 36.95 (0-252-02104-5) U of Ill Pr.

ZX Programmer's Companion. John Grant & Catherine Grant. LC 83-23967. 255p. reprint ed. pap. 72.70 (0-685-16185-4, 2027262) Bks Demand.

ZX-81 Timex: Programming in BASIC & Machine Language. Ekkehard Floegel. 139p. 9.95 (3-921682-98-3) Blue Cat.

ZX-81 TS-1000: Programming for Young Programmers. L. Hurley. (Illus.). 96p. (J). (gr. 9-p). 1983. pap. text ed. 9.95 (0-07-031449-7, BYTE Bks) McGraw.

Zyeux-Bleus. Jerome Charyn. 253p. (FRE.). 1989. pap. 10.95 (0-7859-2111-7, 2070381137) Fr & Eur.

Zygmunt Krasinski, Romantic Universalist: An International Tribute. Ed. by Waclaw Lednicki. 227p. 1964. 6.00 (0-940962-47-0) Polish Inst Art & Sci.

Zygmunt Zawirski: His Life & Work with Selected Writings on Time, Logic & the Methodology of Science. Ed. by Irena Szumilewicz-Lachman et al. LC 93-38214. (Boston Studies in the Philosophy of Science: Vol. 157). 1994. lib. bdg. 158.50 (0-7923-2566-4, Pub. by Klwr Acad Pubs NE) Kluwer Ac.

Zygnemacees Africaines. L. Gauthier-Lievre. 1965. 80.00 (3-7682-5420-8) Lubrecht & Cramer.

Zymonas: Index of New Information & Medical Research Bible. Della M. Stewart. 150p. 1994. 44.50 (0-7883-0140-3); pap. 39.50 (0-7883-0141-1) ABBE Pubs Assn.

Zyrian Folklore Texts. Karoly Redei. (Bibliotheca Uralica: No. 3). 652p. (C). 1978. 171.00 (963-05-1506-7, Pub. by Akad Kiado HU) St Mut.

Zyzyskqa's War & Other Stories. Peter W. Lay. 69p. (Orig.). 1992. pap. 7.50 (971-10-0491-7, Pub. by New Day Pub PH) Cellar.

***ZZ Top - Recycler.** Ed. by Carol Cuellar. 56p. (Orig.). (C). 1995. pap. text ed. 16.95 (0-7692-0877-0, VF1684) Warner Brothers.

***ZZ Top - Rhythmeen (Guitar) Rhythmeen.** Ed. by Carol Cuellar. (Illus.). 92p. (Orig.). (C). 1997. pap. text ed. 21.95 (1-57623-514-9, 0056B) Warner Brothers.

***ZZ Top Complete.** Ed. by Carol Cuellar. 180p. (Orig.). (C). 1990. pap. text ed. 24.95 (0-7692-0827-4, VF1642) Warner Brothers.

***ZZ Top Greatest Hits.** Ed. by Carol Cuellar. 84p. (Orig.). (C). 1992. pap. text ed. 18.95 (0-89724-014-6, VF1826) Warner Brothers.

ZZ Top Greatest Hits for Guitar. ZZ Top. 220p. (Orig.). (YA). 1993. pap. text ed. 24.95 (0-89898-638-9, P078GTX) Warner Brothers.

Zzaap! Taming ESD, RFI, & EMI. Bruce, M., Corporation Staff. 236p. 1990. text ed. 51.00 (0-12-189930-6) Acad Pr.

ZZYZX - History of an Oasis: San Bernardino County, California. Anne Q. Duffield-Stoll. (Illus.). 71p. (Orig.). 1995. pap. 9.00 (0-937048-49-6) Santa Susana.

***Zzyzx Encounters.** Thomson & Evans. LC 97-91456. 280p. 1997. lib. bdg. 12.95 (0-614-29888-1) San Diego Pub Co.

ZZYZX Encounters: A Political Novel. Thomas Thomson & Christopher Evans. 180p. 1997. lib. bdg. 19.95 (0-912495-17-0) San Diego Pub Co.

Zzzng! Zzzng! Zzzng! A Yoruba Tale. Illus. by Greg Henry. (J). 1997. lib. bdg. write for info. (0-531-08873-1) Orchard Bks Watts.

Zzzng! Zzzng! Zzzng! A Yoruba Tale. Illus. by Greg Henry. (J). 1997. write for info. (0-531-09523-1) Orchard Bks Watts.

ZZZZ. James Schuyler et al. Ed. by Kenward Elmslie. (Illus.). 96p. (Orig.). 1976. pap. 5.00 (0-915990-03-2) Z Pr.

ZZZZZ, Vol. 5. John Ashbery et al. Ed. by Kenward Elmslie. (Illus.). 1977. pap. 5.00 (0-915990-08-3) Z Pr.

ZZZZZZ. Kenneth Koch et al. Ed. by Kenward Elmslie. (Illus.). 1978. pap. 5.00 (0-915990-11-3) Z Pr.

Z39.53 - 1994 Codes for the Representation of Languages for Information Interchange. National Information Standards Organization Staff. LC 94-36086. (National Information Standards Ser.). 12p. 1995. 35.00 (1-880124-10-6) NISO.

Z80 Applications. Coffron. 1983. pap. 13.95 (0-89599-094-6) Smithsonian Bks.

Z80 Instruction Set & Programming Guide. Christopher E. Strangio. (Illus.). 355p. (Orig.). (C). 1986. pap. text ed. 25.00 (0-929955-02-1) CAMI Research.

Z80 Programming Video Course Guide. 2nd ed. Christopher E. Strangio. (Illus.). 482p. 1986. pap. text ed. 45.00 (0-614-13910-4) CAMI Research.

Z80 User's Manual. Joseph J. Carr. (Illus.). 352p. 1980. pap. 28.95 (0-8359-9516-X, Reston) P-H.

XYZ